A Final Report
to the People

Volume III

The Bicentennial of the United States of America

Prepared and Submitted to the
Congress of the United States
by the
American Revolution
Bicentennial Administration

Library of Congress Catalog Card
Number: 77-71949

American Revolution Bicentennial
Administration • The Bicentennial of the
United States of America:
A Final Report to the People
Washington, D.C.
June 30, 1977
American Revolution Bicentennial
Administration

For sale by the Superintendent of Documents
U.S. Government Printing Office
Washington, D.C. 20402
Stock Number 052-008-00028-0
ISBN 0-9601232-3-7 (Volume III)
ISBN 0-9601232-6-1 (Set)

Foreword

This five volume report has been prepared for the Congress and the American people as required by Public Law 93-179.

With the filing of this report, the American Revolution Bicentennial Administration (ARBA) is terminated.

The five volumes contain the following information:

—Volumes III (this volume), IV and V: a 56 section listing of Bicentennial activities in all the states, territories, the District of Columbia, the Commonwealth of Puerto Rico and foreign countries.

The sections are arranged alphabetically, and each begins with a brief descriptive overview. Following this, the projects and events are listed by city. These activity summaries are based on information reported to the ARBA and contained in the automated Bicentennial Information Network (BINET) system.

—Volume I: a narrative account from nine perspectives, with color photographs, of America's Bicentennial celebration as it occurred.

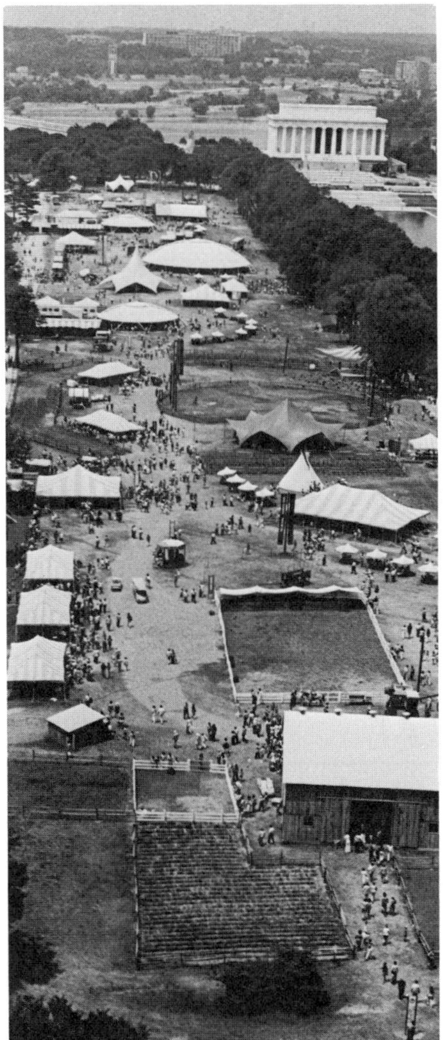

—Volume II: an appendix to Volume I which provides detailed lists and brief descriptions of officially endorsed projects; names of persons who served with various national, state and local Bicentennial groups; ARBA staff members; all the officially recognized Bicentennial Communities; tables detailing grant monies; details of federal agency participation; private sector involvement; lists of public information materials produced; and other such information. It includes a limited number of black and white photographs.

These five volumes contain only those events and projects which were reported to, or otherwise came to the attention of, the ARBC or the ARBA. There were undoubtedly thousands more.

Jean McKee

ARBA Acting Administrator

Contents

Tracking the Bicentennial/vii
Need for BINET
Gathering the Information
Weekly Update
Final BINET Tally

The BINET Bicentennial/ix
Names, Numbers and Narratives
Summaries of Activities

Bicentennial Activities
Alabama/2
Alaska/20
American Samoa/28
Arizona/32
Arkansas/52
California/72
Colorado/136
Connecticut/198
Delaware/222
District of Columbia/230
Florida/260
Georgia/306
Guam/340
Hawaii/344
Idaho/352
Illinois/358
Indiana/410
Iowa/436

Appendix
ARBA Reference Materials/A–1
Repositories of Reference
Materials/A–1
BINET Abbreviations/A–2
BINET Input Forms/A–3

Tracking the Bicentennial

Tracking and disseminating information on Bicentennial activities was a primary function of both the American Revolution Bicentennial Commission (ARBC) and the American Revolution Bicentennial Administration (ARBA). To accomplish these functions, the Bicentennial Information Network—BINET—was established in 1973 under the ARBC. BINET evolved into a system for gathering, cataloguing and publishing details on the activities comprising America's Bicentennial celebration.

The bulk of Volumes III, IV and V of this report contain summaries of the projects and events catalogued in the files of BINET during its nearly four years of operations.

Need for BINET

From the beginning, America's Bicentennial commemoration promised to be enormously diverse. Thousands of activities were to take place at local, state, regional, national and international levels, appealing to people throughout the world and touching on a multitude of themes.

Under the ARBC and the ARBA, guidelines and programs were developed to assist the country in planning and carrying out its Bicentennial celebration. Examples discussed in earlier volumes were the three themes—*Heritage '76, Festival USA* and *Horizons '76*—and the *Bicentennial Communities Program.*

To keep track of and coordinate the many Bicentennial efforts, ARBC staff devised various classifications for describing activities. In addition to the three themes, there were 44 subject areas, 31 methods of presentation and 18 segments of the population to which special emphasis might be given. Geographic scope could range from local to international. Events could take place on any one or more of the 672 days between March 1975 and December 31, 1976.

It soon became obvious that billions of combinations were possible and that a computer would be required to keep track of plans and programs and to monitor the overall balance of activities. BINET was the answer.

The development and operation of BINET was facilitated by a nationwide computer/communications facility available to the ARBC and the ARBA. Under a service contract arranged by the General Services Administration for all federal government agencies, Computer Sciences Corporation provided teleprocessing services to support BINET's computer processing and remote terminal communications requirements.

Gathering the Information

The chronology of BINET's development and the methods used to disseminate Bicentennial information are described in Volume II, Chapter 7, of this report. Described here are the sources of the data and the process of gathering, editing and cataloguing information.

Using the criteria and classifications they had developed, ARBC staff designed forms for gathering details on Bicentennial projects and events for input to BINET. They were to be filled out by project sponsors. The ARBC staff tested the forms initially by completing them for several hundred projects and events, using data from program plans and descriptions previously sent to the ARBC. In May 1973, these forms became the initial data base. Following the formal public introduction of BINET in July 1973, the forms (see the Appendix, p. A-3, for copies) were distributed widely to Bicentennial program planners, primarily through the state Bicentennial organizations and ARBC regional offices.

Completed BINET forms were returned to the ARBC/ARBA by every conceivable source, among them a Bicentennial totem pole carver in Alaska, a 14 year old Wisconsin lad who was editing a Bicentennial newspaper, and officials from thousands of local Bicentennial committees. After the forms were reviewed and edited by the ARBC, the information was transferred to punched cards which were fed into BINET.

Weekly Update

Each week the BINET file was updated with information obtained from the forms submitted on new or modified projects and events. Some updates involved only minor editorial changes. However, many involved substantial additions of new material or extensive changes. In those cases, a copy of the information, as it was filed in BINET, was prepared by the computer and distributed to the sponsor for confirmation. Copies were also sent to state Bicentennial organizations and ARBC/ARBA regional offices.

By the beginning of 1975, the volume of entries outgrew the capacity of ARBA's Master Calendar Services staff, who were responsible for operating the BINET system, and outside contractors were employed. From January 1975 through December 1976, the bulk of the editing and punched card preparation was performed by One America, Inc., a small minority-owned business in Washington, D.C.

As the Bicentennial interest and activity peaked during the first six months of 1976, the volume of new entries and corrections sometimes exceeded 2,500 per week. BINET was barely able to keep pace. By January 1977, nearly 200,000 corrections had been processed by the Master Calendar Services staff and contractors, while the record for each project or event had been updated an average of three times. Over the nearly four year period of BINET's operations, 122,000 copies of new or updated records were mailed out for confirmation.

Another contract was entered into in connection with a major ARBA effort to obtain details on Bicentennial events. From March through May 1975, Billboard Publications, Inc. conducted a series of solicitations to obtain details on events from program planners and sponsors.

Final BINET Tally

The last BINET update was carried out on January 28, 1977 and yielded a final total of 66,484 Bicentennial projects and events. From this final update, magnetic tapes were prepared containing summaries of those activities. At the U.S. Government Printing Office, the tapes were transformed by a computer-driven electronic photocomposition process into the typeset pages comprising the bulk of these three volumes.

Bicentennial project and event totals for states and other entities are shown in the accompanying table.

Project and Event Totals, by State and Other Entities

Location	*Number of Projects*	*Number of Events*	*Total Activities*
Alabama	317	427	744
Alaska	115	84	199
American Samoa	14	6	20
Arizona	373	418	791
Arkansas	343	379	722
California	1,023	1,919	2,942
Colorado	1,155	1,755	2,910
Connecticut	417	647	1,064
Delaware	149	116	265
District of Columbia	640	615	1,255
Florida	816	1,279	2,095
Georgia	777	739	1,516
Guam	23	6	29
Hawaii	97	103	200
Idaho	67	85	152
Illinois	876	1,522	2,398
Indiana	463	661	1,124
Iowa	1,922	1,808	3,730
Kansas	508	658	1,166
Kentucky	123	244	367
Louisiana	447	411	858
Maine	316	320	636
Maryland	469	623	1,092
Massachusetts	579	842	1,421
Michigan	611	893	1,504
Minnesota	633	1,225	1,858
Mississippi	307	337	644
Missouri	642	1,013	1,655
Montana	819	371	1,190
Nebraska	866	1,062	1,928
Nevada	182	228	410
New Hampshire	300	194	494
New Jersey	513	856	1,369
New Mexico	243	174	417
New York	1,349	1,800	3,149
North Carolina	340	619	959
North Dakota	782	339	1,121
Ohio	895	1,194	2,089
Oklahoma	401	810	1,211
Oregon	323	408	731
Pennsylvania	771	2,341	3,112
Puerto Rico	74	129	203
Rhode Island	160	176	336
South Carolina	195	344	539
South Dakota	355	451	806
Tennessee	774	1,724	2,498
Texas	1,339	2,640	3,979
Utah	118	126	244
Vermont	218	549	767
Virgin Islands	33	11	44
Virginia	316	918	1,234
Washington	551	635	1,186
West Virginia	121	190	311
Wisconsin	384	619	1,003
Wyoming	632	511	1,143
Other countries	213	441	654
Totals	27,489	38,995	66,484

The BINET Bicentennial

Volumes III, IV and V consist of 56 sections, one for each of the 50 states, the District of Columbia, the Commonwealth of Puerto Rico and the territories of Guam, American Samoa and the Virgin Islands, with a final section for other countries.

Names, Numbers, Narratives

Each section begins with two pages of introductory material. First is the name of the official Bicentennial organization of the state or comparable entity, with a brief statement on when and how it was created and its Bicentennial theme, where such existed. A reproduction of the symbol or logotype most commonly associated with the Bicentennial in the state or area is also presented.

Next are various statistics. The numbers of officially recognized Communities, Campuses and Military Installations are presented first. (The total may differ from those in the narratives. This is due to the ARBA's counting joint city-county applications as one, whereas a state may have counted them separately. Further, some states continued their own recognition program after the ARBA's was concluded.) The numbers of projects and events filed with BINET appear next. (The number derived from BINET usually is less than the actual number of activities in a given state or area. A single BINET entry may incorporate a number of relatively small local activities, as many lists of events received by the ARBA were too long for each event to be recorded individually. Nor were details submitted to BINET on every event taking place: some states, communities and foreign countries sent the ARBA just a sampling of their activities, and themselves maintained and published more complete and detailed compilations of Bicentennial activities.)

The final statistic is a population figure, which conveys an idea of the number of people served by Bicentennial programming. The figures, based on U.S. Bureau of the Census *Current Population Reports,* Series P–25, are estimates as of July 1, 1976 for the states and the District of Columbia and July 1, 1973 for Puerto Rico and the territories.

Following the statistics are the names and addresses of the official Bicentennial archives for the state or comparable entity.

The list of members of the official Bicentennial organization, which appears next, was supplied by each state or entity during the winter of 1976–77. Where the organization was still active at that time, it provided no final date after a member's name [i.e., J. Smith (1975–)]. The organization may since have concluded its activities. Some, however, are continuing their operations, in a few instances until 1989.

The final segment of the introductory material to each section is a narrative, written by the official Bicentennial organization and summarizing its state's or area's Bicentennial activities.

The photographs accompanying the sections came from the states or other localities, ARBA files and individuals. Credits appear in Volume I of this report.

Summaries of Activities

Each of the 56 sections concludes with BINET summaries of activities. Within each section they are organized by city, except for the section on other countries, which is organized by country and then by city. Under each city, projects are sorted alphabetically by title, while separate events are sorted by date.

The ARBA defined an event as something happening at a specific time and place with participants and an audience. Activities without these characteristics were termed projects. Restoration of a building is a project; its dedication ceremony is an event. Publication of a book is a project without an associated event; a fireworks display is an opposite example.

The 66,484 summaries in these volumes include 2,146 projects which involved the planning of one or more events.

Each summary provides a brief description of the activity, its geographic scope and the name, organization and address of the sponsor. The original BINET reference number is also given, and a special notation is made under those projects supported by ARBA grants or officially recognized by the ARBA. Where sponsors provided specific information on locations of events, it is also included.

The sample summaries below show the organization and content of each entry.

To conserve space and improve readability, not all information available in the BINET records was included in the activity summaries. For example, such items as subject classification, method of presentation and group emphasis were omitted, as were sponsor telephone numbers. The theme area of projects has not been included. Likewise, information on reservations, admission and tour arrangements has not been included for events. This additional information is available, however, in the BINET master file (see the Appendix, p. A–1).

Elements of Activity Summaries

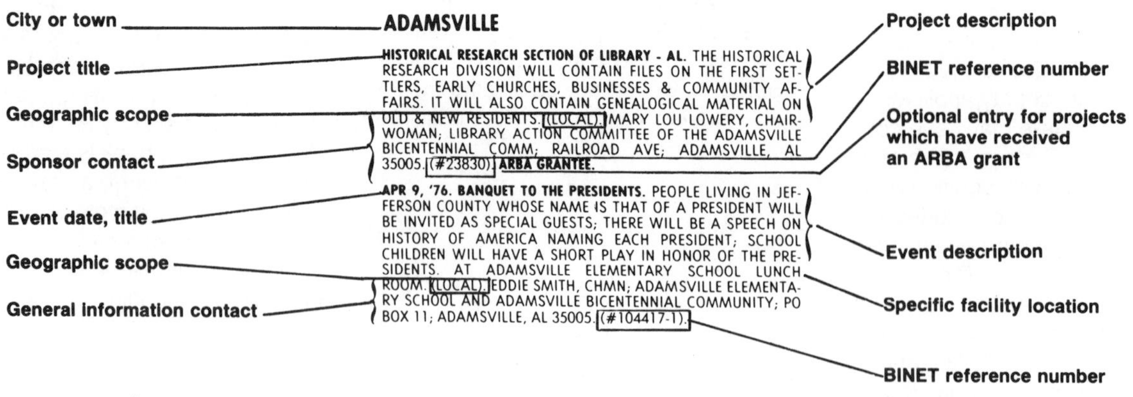

Bicentennial Activities:

Alabama

Iowa

AMERICAN REVOLUTION BICENTENNIAL 1776-1976 ™

ALABAMA
BICENTENNIAL
COMMISSION

Alabama

Alabama Bicentennial Commission

Commissioned by Executive Order Number 28 on December 29, 1971

Theme: How Ya Comin', Alabama?

ARBA Statistics

Officially Recognized
Communities—163
Colleges/Universities—22
Military Installations—4
BINET Projects—317
Events—427
1976 Population—3,665,000

Bicentennial Archives

Department of Archives and History
624 Washington Avenue
Montgomery, Alabama 36104

Membership

Seventy-six distinguished citizens and leaders of the state.

Governor George C. Wallace, *chairman* (1971-)
Robert M. Bowick, *executive director* (1971-75)
Jack W. Wallace, Jr., *executive director* (1975-76)
Dr. Ralph Adams, *president,* Troy State University
Mabel Amos, *secretary of state,* State Capitol
Honorable Melba Till Allen, *state auditor*
(Mrs.) Sidney Van Antwerp
Honorable Agnes Baggett, *state treasurer*
Doug Benton, *director,* State Bureau of Publicity and Information
Dick Biddle, WOWL
Dige Bishop
John Bloomer, *Birmingham News*
Cyril Brennan
Eugene Brock, Urban Consultant, Inc.
Johnny Brooks, Ray-Brooks Machinery Co., Inc.
Ben Brown, *executive vice-president,* South Central Bell Telephone Co.
Dr. LeRoy Brown, *superintendent of education*
Bob Bryan, *The Cullman Times*
J. C. Bull
Ned Butler
Dick Camp, WYAM
Dr. John A. Carrol, Troy State University
Honorable James S. Clark
Honorable Bobby Tom Crowe
Dick Darby, WALA-TV
Martin Darity, ARASERV Alabama State Park Resorts
Honorable Tom Drake
Dr. John Dunbar, School of Medicine, University of Alabama at Birmingham
Mildred Eaton
Nat Faulk, *The Dothan Eagle*
Joe Farley, *president,* Alabama Power Company
W. Warner Floyd, *executive director,* Historical Commission
Ida Goza
Gillis Griffin
Jesse H. Griffin
Hazel Hancock
Honorable Gene Hardin
General Taylor Hardin, *commissioner,* Department of Mental Health
Jimmy Hatcher, Town & Gown Theatre
Jimmy Hayes, Alabama Farm Bureau
Dorsey Haynes, George C. Wallace State Community College
Hal Hodgens, WBUL
Milo Howard, Jr., *director,* State Department of Archives and History
Dr. Paul R. Hubbert, Alabama Education Association
(Mrs.) Elmore Inscoe
Earl Johnson, WBHP Radio
(Mrs.) W. H. Link
Honorable Obie J. Littleton
Norman Lumpkin, WSFA-TV
Honorable Sage Lyons
Honorable Richard Malone
(Mrs.) James K. McKenzie
Dr. Malcolm C. McMillan, *chairman,* History Department, Auburn University
Dr. David Mathews, *president,* University of Alabama
Jimmie Morris, Mobile Chamber of Commerce
Jack Nason, Conservation Department
J. C. Niehuss, Vanity Fair Mills
Honorable L. W. Noonan
Dr. Harry Philpott, *president,* Auburn University
Richard Pizitz, Pizitz Department Store
Honorable Bill Roberts
(Mrs.) Bobbie Ross
George Rush
Frank Sanford, Jr., *president,* Liberty National Life Insurance Co.
Bob Scott
Barrett Shelton, Sr., *Decatur Daily*
Dr. Lathan N. Sibert, *president,* James H. Faulkner State Junior College
(Mrs.) James Sizemore, *assistant to the president,* Samford University
Richard Stone, *assistant director,* State Finance Department
Dr. Charles G. Summersell, *chairman,* History Department, University of Alabama
Dr. Richard Thigpen, *executive vice-president,* University of Alabama
C. C. Torbert
Dr. Rex A. Turner, *president,* Alabama Christian College
Gerald Walker
Jack Warner, *president,* Gulf States Paper Company
John Watkins, *executive director,* Alabama League of Municipalities
Dr. Levi Watkins, *president,* Alabama State University
M. J. Zakrzewski, State Council on the Arts and Humanities

Alabama

The Bicentennial celebration in Alabama evoked an enthusiastic response over five years, building up to a crescendo of celebrations around the weekend of July 4, 1976. Hundreds of programs in hundreds of communities were planned and executed over these years. Nearly everyone in the state, from first graders seeing *How Ya Comin', Alabama?* to their grandparents enjoying an old-fashioned barbecue on the Fourth of July, had a part in it.

Early in Alabama's planning, it was decided that the state should have a few statewide programs, but the main emphasis would be to encourage as broad involvement as possible by individuals and communities. There were 187 officially recognized Bicentennial communities, towns, cities, colleges, military installations and organizations. The University of Alabama was the nation's first university to be recognized as a Bicentennial Campus.

Federal funds in the form of matching grants were awarded to 101 Bicentennial Communities for projects of lasting value, reflecting the three Bicentennial themes of *Heritage '76, Festival USA* and *Horizons '76.* ARBA grants totaled over $350,000 in these programs. Where a small town such as Scottsboro (population 9,300) in Jackson County received $2,500 toward erecting a bust of the county's namesake, Andrew Jackson, the metropolis of Birmingham (350,000) received a like amount for its ambitious program.

How Ya Comin', Alabama?, an award-winning 25 minute multimedia presentation, was the first of Alabama's statewide projects. It was followed by others large and small, from a Bicentennial license tag to a quarterly *Bicentennial Gazette,* reprints of several Alabama histories, a *Bicentennial Trail* of 200 historic sites throughout the state, a statewide *Battle of the Bands* to pick Alabama's most representative bands and a *Bicentennial Belle Pageant,* to name a few. Active support and, in some cases, grants were given to programs of significance to the whole state, such as a film on the history of education in Alabama, restoration of the pre-Civil War iron foundry at Tannehill State Park, erection of a museum at historic Fort Toulouse and a summer reading program on Alabama historical subjects for 50,000 school children in the state.

National and regional programs were also welcomed in Alabama. The Tennessee Valley Bicentennial South inaugurated its tour of eight states of the southeast in January 1976. The Bicentennial Wagon Train Pilgrimage drew enthusiastic crowds which rode along with it, camped out and staged a professional show in 28 communities. It was on its way to join one of five wagon trains from all over the United States, to meet at Valley Forge on July 4th. Equally large crowds turned out for the Armed Forces Caravan in 11 cities, Armed Forces Band concerts and the Freedom Train.

The Bicentennial celebration has left its distinct mark in Alabama. It is a permanent mark, whether "bricks and mortar" or lasting impressions in the minds of young school children. Perhaps more important, though, are the renewed awareness of a rich heritage and the will to unite it with today's work and creative designs for an even fuller tomorrow.

ADAMSVILLE

BANDSTAND AT BALL PARK - ADAMSVILLE, AL. BANDSTAND WILL GIVE RESIDENTS A PLACE FOR ENTERTAINMENT IN A NATURAL SURROUNDING WITH MEMORIALS TO EARLY SETTLERS AND OTHERS. (LOCAL). LELAND C ADAMS, JR, CHAIRMAN; BANDSTAND ACTION COMMITTEE, ADAMSVILLE BICENTENNIAL COMMITTEE; 4808 PARK AVE; ADAMSVILLE, AL 35005. (#26567). **ARBA GRANTEE.**

HISTORICAL RESEARCH SECTION OF LIBRARY - AL. THE HISTORICAL RESEARCH DIVISION WILL CONTAIN FILES ON THE FIRST SETTLERS, EARLY CHURCHES, BUSINESSES & COMMUNITY AFFAIRS. IT WILL ALSO CONTAIN GENEALOGICAL MATERIAL ON OLD & NEW RESIDENTS. (LOCAL). MARY LOU LOWERY, CHAIRWOMAN; LIBRARY ACTION COMMITTEE OF THE ADAMSVILLE BICENTENNIAL COMM; RAILROAD AVE; ADAMSVILLE, AL 35005. (#23830). **ARBA GRANTEE.**

APR 9, '76. BANQUET TO THE PRESIDENTS. PEOPLE LIVING IN JEFFERSON COUNTY WHOSE NAME IS THAT OF A PRESIDENT WILL BE INVITED AS SPECIAL GUESTS; THERE WILL BE A SPEECH ON HISTORY OF AMERICA NAMING EACH PRESIDENT; SCHOOL CHILDREN WILL HAVE A SHORT PLAY IN HONOR OF THE PRESIDENTS. AT ADAMSVILLE ELEMENTARY SCHOOL LUNCH ROOM. (LOCAL). EDDIE SMITH, CHMN; ADAMSVILLE ELEMENTARY SCHOOL AND ADAMSVILLE BICENTENNIAL COMMUNITY; PO BOX 11; ADAMSVILLE, AL 35005. (#104417-1).

ALEXANDER CY

ORAL HISTORY & ARCHIVES PROGRAM, ALEXANDER CY, AL. INITIATE A NUMBER OF INDIVIDUAL ORAL HISTORY PROJECTS IN THE COMMUNITY, AT THE CAMPUS AND AT THE CORRECTIONAL CENTER EXTENSION. (LOCAL). ROBERT SCHREMSER, CHAIRPERSON; ALEXANDER CITY JUNIOR COLLEGE; PO BOX 699; ALEXANDER CY, AL 35010. (#14468).

OCT 1, '75 - MAY 1, '76. BICENTENNIAL MINI-GRANT PROGRAM (COMPETITIONS, EXHIBITS, AWARDS). PLANS FOR TWO PERIODS FOR COMPETITIONS & EXHIBITS; THE FIRST, NOVEMBER 1975 AND THE SECOND DURING FEBRUARY AND MARCH; THE SPRING EVENT WILL INCLUDE COMBINED ARTS EXHIBIT AND JUDGING OF GROUP PRESENTATIONS AND INDIVIDUAL PROJECTS. AT CAMPUS OF ALEXANDER CITY STATE JR COLLEGE. (LOCAL). BOB SCHREMSER, CHMN; ALEXANDER CITY STATE JUNIOR COLLEGE; ALEXANDER CY, AL 35010. (#100803-1).

ANDALUSIA

JAN 29 - 30, '76. UNITED STATES ARMED FORCES BICENTENNIAL CARAVAN. CARAVAN IS COMPOSED OF EXHIBIT VANS FOR EACH MILITARY SERVICE. PROJECT THEME IS 'HISTORY OF THE ARMED FORCES AND THEIR CONTRIBUTIONS TO THE NATION'. (LOCAL). MS CAROLINE CAVANAUGH; ANDALUSIA CHAMBER OF COMMERCE; PO BOX 667; ANDALUSIA, AL 36420. (#1775-388).

FEB 7, '76. BIRMINGHAM SYMPHONY ORCHESTRA IN CONCERT. LIVE PERFORMANCE AT ANDULUSIA HIGH SCHOOL AUDITORIUM. (LOCAL). TONI F SIKES, EXEC SEC; LBW COMMUNITY ARTS COUNCIL; PO BOX 759; ANDULUSIA, AL 36420. (#100721-1).

ANNISTON

ANNISTON STAR'S 'BICENTENNIAL SALUTE' - NBMRP. SPONSORED FREE 'BICENTENNIAL SALUTE' CONCERT BY THE 14TH ARMY BAND. PLANNING A SPECIAL EDITION ON JULY 4, 1976. ---. (LOCAL). PHILLIP A SANGUINETTI, PRESIDENT; THE ANNISTON STAR; 216 W 10TH STREET; ANNISTON, AL 36201. (#26068).

AUG 16, '75. ANNISTON CIVITAN CLUB HORSE SHOW. COMPETITION AT CIRCLE 'C' SADDLE CLUB ARENA. (LOCAL). JOHN W NORTON, COORD; CIVITAN CLUB OF ANNISTON ALABAMA; PO BOX 519; ANNISTON, AL 36201. (#200001-1).

JULY 16 - AUG 21, '76. ALABAMA SHAKESPEARE FESTIVAL '76. PLAYS BY SHAKESPEARE & MOLIERE FEATURED DURING A BICENTENNIAL CELEBRATION. AT ALABAMA SHAKESPEARE FESTIVAL THEATRE, 12TH & WOODSTOCK STREETS. (ST-WIDE). JOSEPHINE E AYERS; ALABAMA SHAKESPEARE FESTIVAL; PO BOX 141; ANNISTON, AL 36201. (#103416-456).

ARAB

BEAUTIFICATION PROJECT IN ARAB, ALABAMA. BEAUTIFICATION PROGRAM TO INCLUDE LITTER DAY & FACELIFTING OF DOWNTOWN AREA. (LOCAL). J MAURICE PERSALL, SUPT OF EDUCATION; ARAB BICENT COMMITTEE; PO DRAWER O; ARAB, AL 35016. (#10433).

HISTORICAL MUSEUM IN ARAB, ALABAMA. HISTORICAL SOCIETY TO RESTORE AUTHENTIC LOG CABIN TO BE USED AS A HISTORICAL MUSEUM. (LOCAL). J MAURICE PERSALL, SUPT OF EDUCATION; ARAB BICENT COMMITTEE; PO DRAWER O; ARAB, AL 35016. (#10434).

HISTORICAL MUSICAL PRESENTATION IN ARAB, AL. MUSICAL PRESENTATION OF MIDNIGHT RIDE OF PAUL REVERE, PERFORMED BY PERFORMING ARTS REPERTOIRE THEATRE, A NY BASED THEATRICAL GROUP. (LOCAL). J MAURICE PERSALL, SUPT OF EDUCATION; ARAB BICENT COMMITTEE; PO DRAWER O; ARAB, AL 35016. (#10435).

MAY 9, '76. SPEECH AT FORT TOULOUSE. WARNER FLOYD, EXEC DIRECTOR OF THE ALABAMA HISTORICAL COMMISSION IS GUEST SPEAKER ON THE FORT TOULOUSE BICENTENNIAL PROJECT. AT ELECTRIC CO AUDITORIUM. (LOCAL). DR MAURICE PERSALL; ARAB BICENTENNIAL COMMITTEE; ARAB, AL 35016. (#103416-268).

ASHFORD

MINI-PARK - ASHFORD, AL. SMALL PARK BUILT WITH 3-SIDED MARBLE SHAFT, DEDICATED TO FOUNDING FATHERS & TO THE PRESENT GENERATION. ALSO DEDICATED TO MEN & WOMEN WHO SERVED IN THE ARMED FORCES AND TO FUTURE GENERATIONS. (LOCAL). W W WELLS, CHAIRMAN; ASHFORD BICENTENNIAL COMMITTEE; PO BOX 407; ASHFORD, AL 36312. (#28592).

MAY 19 - 20, '76. ARTS & CRAFTS FAIR. FAIR AT OLD DEPOT. (LOCAL). W W WELLS, CHAIRMAN; ASHFORD BICENTENNIAL COMMITTEE; PO BOX 407; ASHFORD, AL 36312. (#200001-56).

ATHENS

OCT 1 - 2, '76. 10TH ANNUAL TENNESSEE VALLEY OLD-TIME FIDDLERS CONVENTION. EVENT IS ALWAYS FIRST WEEKEND IN OCT, 1977 DATES; 30 SEPT-1 OCT. AT ATHENS STATE COLLEGE. (NAT'L). BILL HARRISON, COORD; TENNESSEE VALLEY OLD-TIME FIDDLERS ASSOC; ROUTE 4, BOX 634; MADISON, AL 35758. (#103416-595).

ATMORE

APR 9, '76. AMERICAN MUSIC PROGRAM. CREATIVE MUSIC COMMITTEE OF ALABAMA CONSORTIUM FOR DEVELOPMENT OF HIGHER EDUCATION, JEANNE E SHAFFER, CHMN, DOING AN AMERICAN MUSIC PROGRAM IN ATMORE. (ST-WIDE). DR JEANNE SHAFFER; JUDSON COLLEGE ACDHE/ALABAMA CONSORTIUM FOR THE DEV OF HIGHER EDUCA; MARION, AL 36756. (#10234-3).

ATTALLA

SEPT 15 - 20, '75. ETOWAH COUNTY FAIR. EXHIBIT AT ETOWAH COUNTY FAIR GROUNDS. (LOCAL). VERLUS HOLLIDA, PRESIDENT; AMERICAN LEGION; PO BOX 561; ATTALLA, AL 35954. (#100701-1).

AUBURN

SOUTHERN HUMANITIES REVIEW, AUBURN, AL. PUBLICATION DEALING WITH BICENTENNIAL ISSUES. (LOCAL). DAVID K JEFFREY, BUSINESS MANAGER; SOUTHERN HUMANITIES REVIEW; 9090 HALEY CENTER, AUBURN UNIV; AUBURN, AL 36830. (#23549). **ARBA GRANTEE.**

DEC 13 - 14, '76. UNITED STATES ARMED FORCES BICENTENNIAL CARAVAN. CARAVAN IS COMPOSED OF EXHIBIT VANS FOR EACH MILITARY SERVICE. PROJECT THEME IS 'HISTORY OF THE ARMED FORCES & THEIR CONTRIBUTIONS TO THE NATION'. (LOCAL). MRS BETTY GREER; UNITED STATES ARMED FORCES BICENTENNIAL CARAVAN; PO BOX 1776; AUBURN, AL 36830. (#1775-786).

BAY MINETTE

BICENTENNIAL PAGEANT - BAY MINETTE, AL. THE BALDWIN COUNTY BICENTENNIAL CELEBRATION WILL BE HELD AT THE ROBERTSDALE FOOTBALL STADIUM. (LOCAL). A B HONKINS, CHAIRMAN; BALDWIN COUNTY BICENTENNIAL COMMISSION; 111 HOYLEE AVE; BAY MINETTE, AL 36507. (#27355). **ARBA GRANTEE.**

DEC 16, '75. THEATRICAL PRESENTATION. LIVE PERFORMANCE AT LATHEM N SIBERT GYMNASIUM. (LOCAL). STAN CRUSE, COORD; FAULKNER STATE JUNIOR COLLEGE; BAY MINETTE, AL 36507. (#200001-9).

JAN 14, '76. SENIOR CITIZENS MUSICAL GROUP. LIVE PERFORMANCE AT LATHEM N SIBERT GYMNASIUM. (LOCAL). KATHY HUDSON, COORD; FAULKNER STATE JUNIOR COLLEGE; BAY MINETTE, AL 36507. (#200001-7).

JAN 19 - MAR 15, '76. BALDWIN COUNTY HISTORY COURSE. SEMINAR AT FAULKNER CAMPUS. (LOCAL). MARY GRICE, COORD; FAULKNER STATE JUNIOR COLLEGE; BAY MINETTE, AL 36507. (#200001-8).

JAN '76. EDUCATION FOR THE 1970'S. SEMINAR AT LATHEM N SIBERT GYMNASIUM. (LOCAL). KATHY HUDSON, COORD; FAULKNER STATE JUNIOR COLLEGE; BAY MINETTE, AL 36507. (#200001-6).

FEB 12, '76. MUSICAL PRESENTATION. LIVE PERFORMANCE AT LATHEM N SIBERT GYMNASIUM. (LOCAL). KATHY HUDSON, COORD; FAULKNER STATE JUNIOR COLLEGE; BAY MINETTE, AL 36507. (#200001-3).

FEB 12, '76. PIONEER DAY. FESTIVAL AT FAULKNER CAMPUS. (LOCAL). KATHY HUDSON, COORD; FAULKNER STATE JUNIOR COLLEGE; BAY MINETTE, AL 36507. (#200001-5).

MAR '76. POLITICAL ISSUES FOR THE 1970'S. SEMINAR AT LATHEM N SIBERT GYMNASIUM. (LOCAL). KATHY HUDSON, COORD; FAULKNER STATE JUNIOR COLLEGE; BAY MINETTE, AL 36507. (#200001-4).

APR 6, '76. MORAL ISSUES FOR THE 1970'S. SEMINAR AT LATHEM N SIBERT GYMNASIUM. (LOCAL). KATHY HUDSON, COORD; FAULKNER STATE JUNIOR COLLEGE; BAY MINETTE, AL 36507. (#200001-2).

APR - MAY '76. FILM FESTIVAL. EXHIBIT AT REX THEATRE. (LOCAL). DR ED BROWN; FAULKNER STATE JUNIOR COLLEGE; BAY MINETTE, AL 36507. (#106522-2).

JUNE 22 - 26, '76. BICENTENNIAL PAGEANT. LIVE PERFORMANCE AT ROBERTSDALE FOOTBALL STADIUM. (LOCAL). A B HONKINS, CHAIRMAN; BALDWIN COUNTY BICENTENNIAL COMMISSION; 111 HOYLEE AVE; BAY MINETTE, AL 36507. (#27355-1).

BERRY

IRON GATES FOR CITY CEMETERY IN BERRY, ALABAMA. ERECT 3 SETS OF IRON GATES FOR ENTRANCES TO CITY CEMETERY. (LOCAL). MS SHERRY S GREY, CHAIRMAN; BERRY BICENTENNIAL COMMISSION; PO BOX 292; BERRY, AL 35546. (#33721).

RESTORE OLD TOWN WELL - BERRY, AL. RESTORATION OF OLD TOWN WELL LOCATED IN THE CENTER OF TOWN AND BEAUTIFICATION OF SURROUNDING GROUNDS. (LOCAL). SHERRY GREY, CHAIRPERSON; BERRY BICENTENNIAL COMMISSION; PO BOX 292; BERRY, AL 35546. (#28593).

SALE OF AMERICAN FLAGS IN BERRY, ALABAMA. SELL AMERICAN FLAGS & ENCOURAGEMENT PROGRAM TO DISPLAY THEM AT HOMES AND BUSINESS ESTABLISHMENTS. (LOCAL). MS SHERRY S GREY, CHAIRMAN; BERRY BICENTENNIAL COMMISSION; PO BOX 292; BERRY, AL 35546. (#33720).

JUNE 26, '76. STREET FAIR. FESTIVAL AT BERRY SQUARE. (LOCAL). SHERRY GREY, CHAIRMAN; BERRY BICENTENNIAL COMMISSION; PO BOX 292; BERRY, AL 35546. (#200001-57).

BESSEMER

BICENTENNIAL BELLS IN BESSEMER, AL. TIME CHIMES & CARILLON TO SOUND OUT ON THE HOUR W/ PATRIOTIC MUSIC. (LOCAL). E J KEAN, CHAIRMAN; BESSEMER BICENTENNIAL COMMISSION; 1621 ARLINGTON AVE; BESSEMER, AL 35020. (#29897).

SEPT 11, '75. BICENTENNIAL SING-ALONG & MOVIE 'HOW YOU COMING ALABAMA?'. LIVE PERFORMANCE AT DAVIS SCHOOL AUDITORIUM. (LOCAL). E J KEAN, CHMN; BESSEMER BICENTENNIAL COMMISSION; 1621 ARLINGTON AVE; BESSEMER, AL 35020. (#200001-81).

APR 10 - 11, '76. ARTS & CRAFTS BICENTENNIAL EVENT. QUILTING, CHINA PAINTING, OIL & WATERCOLOR PAINTING, BAND CONCERT & CRAFTSMEN AT WORK. AT ROOSEVELT PARK, HWY 150. (LOCAL). E J KEAN, CHMN; BESSEMER BICENTENNIAL COMMISSION; 1621 ARLINGTON AVE; BESSEMER, AL 35020. (#200001-86).

JUNE 14, '76. FLAG DAY USA. EXHIBIT, CEREMONY AT PUBLIC LIBRARY, 19TH ST & 4TH AVE. (LOCAL). E J KEAN, CHMN; BESSEMER BICENTENNIAL COMMISSION; 1621 ARLINGTON AVE; BESSEMER, AL 35020. (#200001-83).

JUNE 20, '76. BICENTENNIAL KICK OFF. CEREMONY. (LOCAL). E J KEAN, CHMN; BESSEMER BICENTENNIAL COMMISSION; 1621 ARLINGTON AVE; BESSEMER, AL 35020. (#200001-85).

JULY 4, '76. INDEPENDENCE DAY FESTIVAL. FESTIVAL AT ROOSEVELT PARK, HWY 50. (LOCAL). E J KEAN, CHMN; BESSEMER BICENTENNIAL COMMISSION; 1621 ARLINGTON AVE; BESSEMER, AL 35020. (#200001-84).

SEPT 27 - 28, '76. U S ARMY FIELD & SOLDIERS CHORUS CONCERT. LIVE PERFORMANCE. (LOCAL). E J KEAN, CHMN; BESSEMER BICENTENNIAL COMMISSION; 1621 ARLINGTON AVE; BESSEMER, AL 35020. (#200001-82).

BIRMINGHAM

ALL CAMPUS CLEANUP PROJ OF SAMFORD UNIV IN ALABAMA. STUDENTS WILL STAGE A WEEK LONG CLEAN-UP CAMPAIGN. (LOCAL). DEAN MARGARET SIZEMORE, CHAIRMAN; SAMFORD UNIV BICENTENNIAL COMMITTEE; 800 LAKESHORE DR; BIRMINGHAM, AL 35209. (#6629). **(??).**

ART FESTIVAL IN BIRMINGHAM, ALABAMA. ART EXHIBITS, THEATRE EVENTS, BALLET PERFORMANCES, FILM FESTIVAL, ETC WILL BE FEATURED AT AN ART FESTIVAL. (LOCAL). DR VIRGINIA HAMILTON, CHAIRPERSON; UNIV OF ALABAMA IN BIRMINGHAM BICENT COMMITTEE; 338 ULLMAN; BIRMINGHAM, AL 35294. (#8244).

ARTS CENTER AT SAMFORD UNIV, BIRMINGHAM, ALABAMA. WEEK LONG FESTIVAL AND CEREMONIES TO BE HELD FOR THE DEDICATION OF THE NEW CENTER FOR THE PERFORMING ARTS. (LOCAL). MARGARET SIZEMORE, DEAN; SAMFORD UNIV BICENTENNIAL COMMUNITY; 800 LAKESHORE DR; BIRMINGHAM, AL 35209. (#6635).

BICENTENNIAL DISPLAYS - BIRMINGHAM, AL. TRAVELING DISPLAYS DEPICTING THE HISTORY OF JEFFERSON COUNTY AND THE LIFE OF THOMAS JEFFERSON; ALSO, A BRIEF HISTORY WILL BE WRITTEN ABOUT THE COUNTY. (LOCAL). JAMES H WALKER, DIRECTOR; HALL OF HISTORY MUSEUM; 1830 4TH AVE N; BESSEMER, AL 35020. (#20240). **ARBA GRANTEE.**

BICENTENNIAL MINI-GARDENS AT UNIV OF ALABAMA. PERMANENT MINI-GARDENS TO CELEBRATE THE BICENTENNIAL WILL BE CONSTRUCTED ON THE BIRMINGHAM CAMPUS. (ST-WIDE). DR VIRGINIA HAMILTON, CHAIRPERSON; UNIV OF ALABAMA IN BIRMINGHAM BICENTENNIAL COMMITTEE; 338 ULLMAN; BIRMINGHAM, AL 35294. (#12191). **ARBA GRANTEE.**

'BIRMINGHAM COLLECTS' - AL. EXHIBIT AND CATALOGUE EXAMPLES OF AMERICAN ART SINCE 1776 THAT IS IN PRIVATE, PUBLIC, CORPORATE AND INSTITUTIONAL COLLECTIONS IN THE METROPOLITAN BIRMINGHAM AREA. (LOCAL). GAYLE

BIRMINGHAM — CONTINUED

SPRATLING, PROJECTS CHAIRMAN; BIRMINGHAM BICENTENNIAL COMMITTEE; 406 CITY HALL; BIRMINGHAM, AL 35203. (#26741). **ARBA GRANTEE.**

BOOK ACQUISITION - BIRMINGHAM, AL. BOOKS ON THE AMERICAN REVOLUTION WILL BE PURCHASED. (LOCAL). ANN HAMILTON, ASSOC LIBRARIAN; BIRMINGHAM SOUTHERN COLLEGE; 800 8TH AVE W; BIRMINGHAM, AL 35204. (#25108).

CHORAL COMPOSITION - BIRMINGHAM, AL. AN ORIGINAL CHORAL COMPOSITION HAS BEEN COMMISSIONED; IT WILL HAVE A BICENTENNIAL THEME. (LOCAL). HUGH THOMAS, PROJ CHAIRMAN; MUSIC DEPT, BIRMINGHAM SOUTHERN COLLEGE; 800 8TH AVE W; BIRMINGHAM, AL 35204. (#25107).

HISTORICAL ARBORETUM - BIRMINGHAM, AL. A HISTORICAL ARBORETUM WILL BE DEVELOPED ON THE CAMPUS OF BIRMINGHAM SOUTHERN COLLEGE. (LOCAL). SAMUEL N STAYER, ASSOC PROF OF HISTORY; BIRMINGHAM SOUTHERN COLLEGE; 800 8TH AVE W; BIRMINGHAM, AL 35204. (#25105).

JEFFERSON STATE NEWS BICENTENNIAL EDITION - AL. PUBLICATION OF SPECIAL EDITIONS OF THE JEFFERSON STATE NEWS MAGAZINE WHICH WILL INCLUDE FEATURE BICENTENNIAL ARTICLES AND COVER DESIGNS. (LOCAL). JERRY HAMMOND, EDITOR JEFFERSON STATE NEWS; JEFFERSON STATE JUNIOR COLLEGE; 2601 CARSON RD; BIRMINGHAM, AL 35215. (#17026).

METHODISM IN ALABAMA ARCHIVES - BIRMINGHAM, AL. THE RESEARCH PROJECT WAS DEVELOPED WITH THE COOPERATION OF THE NORTH ALABAMA CONFERENCE, UNITED METHODIST CHURCH. (LOCAL). KEENER BARNES, PROJ DIRECTOR; BIRMINGHAM SOUTHERN COLLEGE; 800 8TH AVE W; BIRMINGHAM, AL 35204. (#25106).

MUSEUM & RESEARCH ROOM FOR OAK HILL CHAPEL - AL. CREATION OF A ROOM IN THE BASEMENT OF OAK HILL HISTORIC CHAPEL FOR CONVENIENT STORAGE OF HISTORICAL & GENEALOGICAL RECORDS FOR A SMALL MUSEUM. (LOCAL). GAYLE SPRATLING, CHAIRMAN; BIRMINGHAM BICENTENNIAL COMMITTEE; 406 CITY HALL; BIRMINGHAM, AL 35203. (#27279). **ARBA GRANTEE.**

MUSICAL '1776', BIRMINGHAM, AL. PATRIOTIC MUSICAL PRODUCTION. (REGN'L). DEAN MARGARET SIZEMORE, COORDINATOR; SAMFORD UNIVERSITY BICENTENNIAL COMMUNITY; 800 LAKESHORE DR; BIRMINGHAM, AL 35209. (#21118). **ARBA GRANTEE.**

NON-TRADITIONAL STUDIES: BIRMINGHAM, ALABAMA. ESTABLISHMENT OF CENTER FOR USE OF INNOVATIVE EDUCATIONAL METHODS, SUCH AS COMPUTER-ASSISTED INSTRUCTION, TUTORIAL COURSES USING VISUAL MEDIA, ETC. (LOCAL). DR VIRGINIA HAMILTON, CHAIRPERSON; UNIV OF ALABAMA IN BIRMINGHAM BICENT COMMITTEE; 338 ULLMAN; BIRMINGHAM, AL 35294. (#8248). **(??).**

ORAL HISTORY COLLECTION IN BIRMINGHAM, ALABAMA. ESTABLISHMENT OF ORAL HISTORY COLLECTION CENTERING ON LIVES OF PLAIN ALABAMIANS WILL TAKE PLACE. (ST-WIDE). DR VIRGINIA HAMILTON, CHAIRPERSON; UNIV OF ALABAMA IN BIRMINGHAM BICENT COMMITTEE; 338 ULLMAN; BIRMINGHAM, AL 35294. (#8245).

'TO BELIEVE IN AMERICA', BIRMINGHAM, AL. MUSICAL SEGMENT OF THE 'HEAR & NOW' SINGERS ACT, TO BE PERFORMED ACROSS AMERICA. (REGN'L). DEAN MARGARET SIZEMORE, COORDINATOR; SAMFORD UNIVERSITY BICENTENNIAL COJMUNITY; 800 LAKESHORE DR; BIRMINGHAM, AL 35209. (#21119). **ARBA GRANTEE.**

TOWN AND GOWN THEATRE MUSEUM IN BIRMINGHAM, AL. TO OUTFIT EXISTING THEATRE WITH DISPLAYS, MEMORIABILIA AND ALSO FOR ACQUISITION OF MUSEUM PIECES WITH THE UNIVERSITY OF ALABAMA. (REGN'L). JAMES HATCHER, DIRECTOR; UNIVERSITY OF ALABAMA TOWN AND GOWN THEATRE; 1116 S 26TH ST; BIRMINGHAM, AL 35205. (#33306). **ARBA GRANTEE.**

JAN 1, '74 - JAN 1, '77. DISPLAY OF MATERIAL CONCERNING BICENTENNIAL IN SAMFORD LIBRARY. DISPLAYS OF THE COLONIAL CULTURAL MILIEU, REVOLUTIONARY HEROES, RELIGIOUS GROUPS OF THE TIMES & THE PHILADELPHIA CENTENNIAL. (LOCAL). DEAN MARGARET SIZEMORE; SAMFORD UNIV BICENTENNIAL COMMITTEE; 800 LAKESHORE DR; BIRMINGHAM, AL 35209. (#6628-501).

SEPT 24, '74 - APR 1, '76. A COURSE ON AMERICAN DECORATIVE ARTS. 200 YEARS OF AMERICAN DECORATIVE ARTS, ALABAMA. A COMMUNITY COURSE ON AMERICAN ANTIQUES AND THE DECORATIVE ARTS WITH SLIDES, LECTURES & ANTIQUES. (ST-WIDE). DEAN MARGARET SIZEMORE; SAMFORD UNIV BICENTENNIAL COMMUNITY; 800 LAKESHORE DR; BIRMINGHAM, AL 35209. (#6627-501).

JAN 2 - FEB 3, '75. 'REBELS & PATRIOTS OF 1776' HISTORY SEMINAR. SEMINAR. (LOCAL). DEAN MARGARET SIZEMORE; SAMFORD UNIV BICENTENNIAL COMMITTEE; 800 LAKESHORE DR; BIRMINGHAM, AL 35209. (#6620-501).

MAR 10 - OCT 25, '75. SLIDE PRESENTATION ON AMERICAN ARTS. COLLECTION OF SLIDES ON AMERICAN ARTS MADE AND COMPILED BY SAMFORD'S ART DEPARTMENT. (LOCAL). DEAN MARGARET SIZEMORE; SAMFORD UNIV BICENTENNIAL COMMUNITY; 800 LAKESHORE DR; BIRMINGHAM, AL 35209. (#6626-501).

APR 1, '75. HOMECOMING CONCERT OF AMERICAN MUSIC. HOMECOMING CONCERT OF AMERICAN MUSIC, SAMFORD UNIV. THE HEAR AND NOW SINGERS WILL BE PERFORMING FOR HOMECOMING AT SAMFORD UNIVERSITY IN BIRMINGHAM, ALABAMA. (LOCAL). DEAN MARGARET SIZEMORE; SAMFORD UNIV BICENTENNIAL COMMITTEE; 800 LAKESHORE DR; BIRMINGHAM, AL 35209. (#6640-501).

APR 1 - 10, '75. OAK TREES PLANTING & LANDSCAPING WEEK. OPENING. (LOCAL). DEAN MARGARET SIZEMORE; SAMFORD UNIV BICENTENNIAL COMMITTEE; 800 LAKESHORE DR; BIRMINGHAM, AL 35209. (#6622-501).

APR 1 - 20, '75. EVENING OF AMERICAN POP CONCERT. MUSIC CONCERT BY PHI MU ALPHA & DELTA OMICRON. (LOCAL). DEAN MARGARET SIZEMORE; SAMFORD UNIV BICENTENNIAL COMMUNITY; 800 LAKESHORE DR; BIRMINGHAM, AL 35209. (#6639-501).

SEPT 1, '75 - JUNE 30, '76. JEFFERSON STATE JUNIOR COLLEGE BICENTENNIAL EXHIBITION. EXHIBIT. (LOCAL). DAVE CAMPBELL, PROJ DIR; JEFFERSON STATE JUNIOR COLLEGE BICENTENNIAL COMMITTEE; 2601 CARSON RD; BIRMINGHAM, AL 35215. (#103099-2).

SEPT 13, '75. COUNTY FAIR IN SEPTEMBER 1975. TOURS CONDUCTED YEAR ROUND. AT ARLINGTON ANTEBELLUM HOME AND GARDENS. (LOCAL). CATHERINE M LACKMOND; ARLINGTON HISTORICAL ASSOCIATION; 331 COTTON AVE, SW; BIRMINGHAM, AL 35211. (#100481-1).

SEPT 19 - 21, '75. SEMINAR ON CERAMICS. SEMINAR AT SAMFORD UNIV STUDENT CENTER. (LOCAL). DEAN MARGARET SIZEMORE; SAMFORD UNIV BICENTENNIAL MODEL COMMUNITY; 800 LAKESHORE DR, SAMFORD UNIV; BIRMINGHAM, AL 35209. (#100482-1).

OCT 1 - 7, '75. THE PRODUCTION OF THE PLAY '1776'. LIVE PERFORMANCE, FESTIVAL. (LOCAL). DEAN MARGARET SIZEMORE; SAMFORD UNIV BICENTENNIAL COMMITTEE; 800 LAKESHORE DR; BIRMINGHAM, AL 35209. (#6624-501).

OCT 1 - 30, '75. AMERICAN DRAMA. FESTIVAL. (LOCAL). MARGARET SIZEMORE, DEAN; SAMFORD UNIV BICENTENNIAL COMMUNITY; 800 LAKESHORE DR; BIRMINGHAM, AL 35209. (#6635-504).

OCT 1 - 30, '75. EXHIBITION OF AMERICAN ART. FESTIVAL. (LOCAL). MARGARET SIZEMORE, DEAN; SAMFORD UNIV BICENTENNIAL COMMUNITY; 800 LAKESHORE DR; BIRMINGHAM, AL 35209. (#6635-503).

OCT 1 - 30, '75. SYMPOSIUM OF ARTS IN AMERICA DURING THE FINAL 1/4 OF 20TH CENTURY. FESTIVAL. (LOCAL). MARGARET SIZEMORE, DEAN; SAMFORD UNIV BICENTENNIAL COMMUNITY; 800 LAKESHORE DR; BIRMINGHAM, AL 35209. (#6635-502).

OCT 1 - NOV 2, '75. 'THE FOUNDING OF AMERICA' ESSAY CONTEST. COMPETITION. (LOCAL). DEAN MARGARET SIZEMORE; SAMFORD UNIV BICENTENNIAL COMMITTEE; 800 LAKESHORE DR; BIRMINGHAM, AL 35209. (#6625-501).

OCT 3 - 14, '75. HISTORICAL BOOK DISPLAY. DISPLAY OF BOOKS DEALING WITH HISTORICAL & BIOGRAPHICAL MATERIAL RELEVANT TO THE BICENTENNIAL. AT GEORGE ALLEN LIBRARY, JEFFERSON STATE JUNIOR COLLEGE. (LOCAL). JOHN KLUTTZ, CHMN; GEORGE ALLEN LIBRARY AND LEARNING RESOURCE CENTER; 2601 CARSON RD; BIRMINGHAM, AL 35215. (#200001-11).

OCT 6, '75. CONCERT OF AMERICAN CHORAL MUSIC. FESTIVAL. (LOCAL). MARGARET SIZEMORE, DEAN; SAMFORD UNIV BICENTENNIAL COMMUNITY; 800 LAKESHORE DR; BIRMINGHAM, AL 35209. (#6635-501).

OCT 15, '75 - MAY 15, '76. 'I BELIEVE IN AMERICA' - HEAR AND NOW SINGERS OF SAMFORD UNIV. 'I BELIEVE IN AMERICA' IS A MUSICAL WORK DEALING WITH THE 4 BASIC FREEDOMS EACH AMERICAN HAS: FREEDOM FROM FEAR, FREEDOM OF WORSHIP, FREEDOM FROM WANT & FREEDOM OF SPEECH; IT LOOKS AT THE PAST, PRESENT & FUTURE OF AMERICA AND GIVES A POSITIVE APPROACH TO AMERICA. (LOCAL). BOB BURROUGHS, DIRECTOR; SAMFORD UNIV; BOX 2275 SAMFORD UNIV; BIRMINGHAM, AL 35209. (#100728-1).

OCT 16, '75 - APR 25, '76. SYMPHONY CONCERT SERIES. CONCERTS INCLUDE YOUTH CONCERTS, ADULT EVENING PERFORMANCES; WILL ALSO FEATURE PREMIERE OF BICENTENNIAL WORKS. AT CIVIC CENTER CONCERT HALL. (ST-WIDE). GORDON G ANDREWS; BIRMINGHAM SYMPHONY ASSOC; 2133 7TH AVE,NORTH; BIRMINGHAM, AL 35203. (#100997-1).

OCT 24, '75. OPEN HOUSE RECEPTION DINNER CARMICHAEL ROOM REYNOLDS LIBRARY. FESTIVAL AT LISTER HILL LIBRARY OF THE HEALTH SCIENCES. (LOCAL). ROBERT P GLAZE, PHD; CADUCEUS, CENTURY AND ARGUS CLUBS; UNIVERSITY STATION; BIRMINGHAM, AL 35294. (#200001-13).

OCT 31 - NOV 1, '75. WAYNE BATES LECTURE WORKSHOP - CERAMIC TILE & ARCHITECTURE LECTURE. SEMINAR AT BIRMINGHAM MUSEUM OF ART. (LOCAL). JOSEPHINE EDMUNDSON, SEC; BIRMINGHAM ART ASSOCIATION; 2000 8TH AVE N; BIRMINGHAM, AL 35203. (#103379-3).

NOV 1, '75. TV EXTRAVAGANZA SALUTING ARMED FORCES. RADIO/TV. (ST-WIDE). DEAN MARGARET SIZEMORE; SAMFORD UNIV BICENTENNIAL COMMUNITY; 800 LAKESHORE DR; BIRMINGHAM, AL 35209. (#6636-501).

NOV 6 - 9, '75. MODEL U S SENATE. GUEST SPEAKERS-SEN TUNNEY & DR REDDICK. AT CAMPUS FACILITIES. (ST-WIDE). IRVIN PENFIELD, COORD; BIRMINGHAM SOUTHERN COLLEGE; 800 8TH AVE, W; BIRMINGHAM, AL 35204. (#200001-10).

NOV 11, '75. LECTURE BY COMMANDER LLOYD M BUCHER. THE COMMANDER OF THE USS PUEBLO WILL LECTURE ON AMERICA AND THE COMMUNIST WORLD. AT FITZGERALD STUDENT CENTER. (LOCAL). DOUG PATTERSON, PROJ DIR; CONCERT LECTURE SERIES, JEFFERSON STATE JUNIOR COLLEGE; 2601 CARSON RD; BIRMINGHAM, AL 35215. (#103099-9).

NOV 11, '75. VETERANS DAY PARADE. PARADE. (LOCAL). JOHN KLUTTZ, CHAIRMAN; JEFFERSON STATE JUNIOR COLLEGE BICENTENNIAL COMMITTEE; 2601 CARSON RD; BIRMINGHAM, AL 35215. (#103099-1).

NOV 23 - DEC 15, '75. JURIED CRAFTS EXHIBITION. EXHIBIT, AWARD AT 1818 FIRST AVE N. (REGN'L). TERE YOW, ASST DIRECTOR; GREATER BIRMINGHAM ARTS ALLIANCE; PO BOX 3325; BIRMINGHAM, AL 35205. (#102279-1).

DEC 15, '75 - DEC 15, '76. JEFFERSON BICENTENNIAL DISPLAYS. PORTABLE DISPLAYS ON THE HISTORY OF THE COUNTY AND THE LIFE OF THOMAS JEFFERSON. (LOCAL). JAMES H WALKER, CHAIRMAN; JEFFERSON COUNTY BICENTENNIAL COMMITTEE; PO BOX 202; BESSEMER, AL 35020. (#20240-1).

DEC 21 - 25, '75. BIRMINGHAM ART ASSOCIATION NON-JURY SHOW. AWARD, COMPETITION, EXHIBIT AT BIRMINGHAM MUSEUM OF ART. (LOCAL). JOSEPHINE EDMUNDSON, SEC; BIRMINGHAM ART ASSOC; 2000 8TH AVE N; BIRMINGHAM, AL 35203. (#103379-2).

JAN 1 - DEC 31, '76. ART EXHIBITS AT UNIV OF ALABAMA. FESTIVAL, EXHIBIT, LIVE PERFORMANCE. (LOCAL). DR VIRGINIA HAMILTON; UNIV OF ALABAMA IN BIRMINGHAM BICENT COMMITTEE; 338 ULLMAN; BIRMINGHAM, AL 35294. (#8244-501).

JAN 1 - DEC 31, '76. BALLET PERFORMANCES AT UNIV OF ALABAMA. FESTIVAL, EXHIBIT, LIVE PERFORMANCE. (LOCAL). DR VIRGINIA HAMILTON; UNIV OF ALABAMA IN BIRMINGHAM BICENT COMMITTEE; 338 ULLMAN; BIRMINGHAM, AL 35294. (#8244-503).

JAN 1 - DEC 31, '76. FILM FESTIVAL AT UNIV OF ALABAMA. FESTIVAL, EXHIBIT, LIVE PERFORMANCE. (LOCAL). DR VIRGINIA HAMILTON; UNIV OF ALABAMA IN BIRMINGHAM BICENT COMMITTEE; 338 ULLMAN; BIRMINGHAM, AL 35294. (#8244-504).

JAN 1 - DEC 31, '76. MEDICAL TOURS, EXHIBITS, LECTURES & DEMONSTRATIONS. MEDICAL HISTORY EVENTS IN BIRMINGHAM, ALABAMA. TOURS OF MEDICAL LIBRARY, HEALTH SCIENCE MUSEUM, HISTORICAL LIBRARY, DISPLAYS OF FIRST EDITIONS, MEDICAL HISTORY LECTURES, HISTORICAL COLLECTIONS LECTURES & TECHNOLOGY DEMONSTRATIONS ARE PLANNED. (LOCAL). DR VIRGINIA HAMILTON; UNIV OF ALABAMA IN BIRMINGHAM BICENT COMMITTEE; 338 ULLMAN; BIRMINGHAM, AL 35294. (#8247-501).

JAN 1 - DEC 31, '76. THEATRE EVENTS AT UNIV OF ALABAMA. FESTIVAL, EXHIBIT, LIVE PERFORMANCE. (LOCAL). DR VIRGINIA HAMILTON; UNIV OF ALABAMA IN BIRMINGHAM BICENT COMMITTEE; 338 ULLMAN; BIRMINGHAM, AL 35294. (#8244-502).

JAN 16 - 18, '76. UNITED STATES ARMED FORCES BICENTENNIAL CARAVAN. CARAVAN IS COMPOSED OF EXHIBIT VANS FOR EACH MILITARY SERVICE. PROJECT THEME IS 'HISTORY OF THE ARMED FORCES AND THEIR CONTRIBUTIONS TO THE NATION'. (LOCAL). DR CAROLYN SATTERFIELD; BIRMINGHAM BICENTENNIAL COMMITTEE; SAMFORD UNIV, PO BOX 2216; BIRMINGHAM, AL 35209. (#1775-382).

JAN 29, '76. CHARACTERIZATION OF GEORGE WASHINGTON BY HOWARD MANN. MR HOWARD MANN WILL PRESENT GEORGE WASHINGTON IN A HUMEROUS, HISTORIC PROGRAM. AT FITZGERALD STUDENT CENTER. (LOCAL). DOUG PATTERSON, PROJ DIR; CONCERT LECTURE SERIES, JEFFERSON STATE JUNIOR COLLEGE; 2601 CARSON RD; BIRMINGHAM, AL 35215. (#103099-7).

FEB 1 - 15, '76. TV PRODUCTION SALUTING AMERICAN FREEDOM. THE TESTAMENT OF FREEDOM - STAMFORD UNIV PROJECT. TV PRODUCTION BY MEN'S MUSIC FRATERNITY. (LOCAL). DEAN MARGARET SIZEMORE; SAMFORD UNIV BICENTENNIAL COMMUNITY; 800 LAKESHORE DR; BIRMINGHAM, AL 35209. (#6637-501).

FEB 1 - MAR 23, '76. CONCERT CHOIR BICENTENNIAL CONCERT TOUR. LIVE PERFORMANCE, TOUR AT SERIES OF CHURCHES AND AUDITORIUMS. (REGN'L). HUGH THOMAS, COORD; BIRMINGHAM SOUTHERN COLLEGE, MUSIC DEPT; BIRMINGHAM SOUTHERN COLLEGE; BIRMINGHAM, AL 35204. (#200001-12).

FEB 16, '76. AMERICAN ROOTS, BICENTENNIAL DINNER THEATRE. THIS IS A COMICAL, SATIRICAL PLAY ON THE AMERICAN HERITAGE. AT FITZGERALD STUDENT CENTER. (LOCAL). DOUG PATTERSON, PROJ DIR; CONCERT LECTURE SERIES, JEFFERSON STATE JUNIOR COLLEGE; 2601 CARSON RD; BIRMINGHAM, AL 35215. (#103099-4).

FEB 19, '76. 'THE ORIGINAL THIRTEEN STATES' BY ANDRE DE LA VARRE. THERE WILL BE A DOCUMENTARY FILM AND LECTURE ABOUT THE ORIGINAL 13 STATES. AT FITZGERALD STUDENT CENTER. (LOCAL). JOHN KLUTTZ, BICENT CHMN; STUDENT GOVERNMENT ASSOC, JEFFERSON STATE JUNIOR COLLEGE; 2601 CARSON RD; BIRMINGHAM, AL 35215. (#103099-5).

FEB 19, '76 - MAR 20, '77. SMITHSONIAN BLACK HISTORY EXHIBIT. EXHIBIT ON CONTRIBUTIONS OF BLACK AMERICANS TO THE NATION. (LOCAL). SAMUEL N STAYER, PROF; BIRMINGHAM SOUTHERN COLLEGE; 800 8TH AVE W; BIRMINGHAM, AL 35204. (#107922-1).

FEB 26 - 28, '76. HUGO L BLACK SYMPOSIUM ON AMERICAN HISTORY. ANNUAL SYMPOSIUM HONORING JUSTICE BLACK & CONCENTRATING EACH YEAR ON SOME ASPECT OF HISTORY AND THE PROGRESS OF MANKIND. AT ENGINEERING AUDITORIUM, U A B, 8TH AVE S, NEXT TO KAHLOR PLAZA HOTEL. (NAT'L). PHILIP EDGAR, PROJ DIR; UNIV OF ALABAMA BICENTENNIAL COMMITTEE; HISTORY DEPT, UNIV STATION; BIRMINGHAM, AL 35294. (#8595-1).

MAR 1 - 15, '76. AN AMERICAN ORATORIO BY UNIVERSITY CHORALE. HORA NOVISSIAN, AMERICAN ORATORIO AT SAMFORD UNIV. AN AMERICAN ORATORIO PRESENTED BY UNIVERSITY CHORALE. (LOCAL). DEAN MARGARET SIZEMORE; SAMFORD UNIV BICENTENNIAL COMMUNITY; 800 LAKESHORE DR; BIRMINGHAM, AL 35209. (#6638-501).

MAR 19 - 28, '76. FESTIVAL OF ARTS. HOURS ARE DIFFERENT FOR EACH EVENT; PAID ADMISSION AND RESERVATIONS REQUIRED FOR SOME EVENTS. A TEN DAY FESTIVAL WITH PERFORMANCES EACH DAY. WILL BE A SALUTE TO THE ARTS OF GREECE &

BIRMINGHAM — CONTINUED

AMERICA'S BICENTENNIAL. AT SUITE 1004, WOODWARD BLDG. (REGN'L). MRS GREGORY DESPINAKIS; BIRMINGHAM FESTIVAL OF ARTS; SUITE 1004, WOODWARD BLDG; BIRMINGHAM, AL 35203. (#102279-2).

MAR 21 - NOV 21, '76. JAPANESE TEA CEREMONY. MARCH, APRIL, MAY, SEPT, OCT AND NOV - 3RD SUNDAY. AT JAPANESE TEA HOUSE - JAPANESE GARDENS. (LOCAL). DEBBIE ESTES, PROJ SEC; BIRMINGHAM BOTANICAL GARDENS; 2612 LANE PARK RD; BIRMINGHAM, AL 35223. (#100714-1).

MAR 28 - APR ??, '76. JURIED ART EXHIBITION. EXHIBIT, AWARD AT 1818 FIRST AVE N. (REGN'L). TERE YOW, ASST DIRECTOR; GREATER BIRMINGHAM ARTS ALLIANCE; PO BOX 3325; BIRMINGHAM, AL 35205. (#102279-3).

APR 1, '76. OUTDOOR COSTUMED CELEBRATION. WILLIAMSBURG IN ALABAMA - BICENT CELEBRATION. ALL DAY OUTDOOR CELEBRATION BY ENTIRE CAMPUS, ALL STUDENTS WEARING REVOLUTIONARY ATTIRE, PLAYING GAMES OF THAT PERIOD. (LOCAL). DEAN MARGARET SIZEMORE; SAMFORD UNIV BICENTENNIAL COMMITTEE; 800 LAKESHORE DR; BIRMINGHAM, AL 35209. (#6623-501).

APR 1 - 3, '76. ALL CAMPUS SWIM MEET. SWIMMING MEET AT SAMFORD UNIV, BIRMINGHAM, ALABAMA. ALL CAMPUS SWIMMING MEET AT SAMFORD UNIV. (LOCAL). DEAN MARGARET SIZEMORE; SAMFORD UNIV BICENTENNIAL COMMITTEE; 800 LAKESHORE DR; BIRMINGHAM, AL 35209. (#6621-501).

APR 1 - OCT 31, '76. TOUR OF SAMFORD PLANETARIUM WITH LECTURE. 'TOUR OF THE HEAVENS' PROJ OF SAMFORD UNIV, AL. A GUIDED TOUR AND LECTURE IN SAMFORD'S PLANETARIUM. (LOCAL). DEAN MARGARET SIZEMORE; SAMFORD UNIV BICENTENNIAL COMMUNITY; 800 LAKESHORE DR; BIRMINGHAM, AL 35209. (#6634-501).

APR 2 - 8, '76. ALL CAMPUS TRACK AND FIELD COMPETITION. TRACK AND FIELD COMPETITION AT SAMFORD UNIV, AL. ALL CAMPUSTRACK AND FIELD COMPETITION FOR SPRING AT SAMFORD UNIV IN BIRMINGHAM. (LOCAL). DEAN MARGARET SIZEMORE; SAMFORD UNIV BICENTENNIAL COMMITTEE; 800 LAKESHORE DR; BIRMINGHAM, AL 35209. (#6642-501).

APR 7 - MAY 1, '76. ANNUAL EASTER DISPLAY, FEATURING TRADITIONAL EASTER LILLIES. FESTIVAL AT CONSERVATORY, PARKING AVAILABLE. (LOCAL). DEBBIE ESTES, PROJ SEC; BIRMINGHAM BOTANICAL GARDENS; 2612 LANE PARK RD; BIRMINGHAM, AL 35223. (#100715-1).

APR 20, '76. THE BOSTON TEA PARTY, BICENTENNIAL DINNER THEATRE. THIS IS A MUSICAL COMEDY DEPICTING THE BIRTH OF OUR NATION. AT FITZGERALD STUDENT CENTER. (LOCAL). DOUG PATTERSON, PROJ DIR; CONCERT LECTURE SERIES, JEFFERSON STATE JUNIOR COLLEGE; 2601 CARSON RD; BIRMINGHAM, AL 35215. (#103099-3).

APR 21 - MAY 4, '76. '1776', A BROADWAY MUSICAL. LIVE PERFORMANCE AT SAMFORD FINE ARTS THEATER. (LOCAL). ERIC OLSON, PROJ DIRECTOR; SAMFORD UNIVERSITY THEATER; SPEECH & DRAMATIC ARTS DEPT; BIRMINGHAM, AL 35209. (#100566-1).

APR 25 - MAY 16, '76. BIRMINGHAM SYMPHONY ASSOCIATION DECORATOR SHOWHOUSE. MT VERNON STYLE HOME REFURBISHED INCLUDES GARDEN AND GIFT SHOP. SUNDAY HOURS: 1-5 PM. AT 2917 FAIRWAY DRIVE. (LOCAL). DEBRA SMITH, PROJ DIR; BIRMINGHAM SYMPHONY ASSOC; 2133 7TH AVE N; BIRMINGHAM, AL 35203. (#103416-231).

APR 30 - MAY 16, '76. BICENTENNIAL STUDENT ART EXHIBIT. EXHIBIT AT FITZGERALD STUDENT CENTER. (LOCAL). JOHN KLUTTZ, BICENT CHMN; FINE ARTS DEPARTMENT, JEFFERSON STATE JUNIOR COLLEGE; 2601 CARSON RD; BIRMINGHAM, AL 35215. (#103099-8).

MAY 1, '76. CONCERT ON AMERICAN MUSIC BY ENTIRE MUSIC SCHOOL. CONCERT OF AMERICAN MUSIC AT SAMFORD UNIV, ALABAMA. CONCERT FEATURING THE ENTIRE MUSIC SCHOOL OF SAMFORD UNIVERSITY IN BIRMINGHAM, ALABAMA. (LOCAL). DEAN MARGARET SIZEMORE; SAMFORD UNIV BICENTENNIAL COMMITTEE; 800 LAKESHORE DR; BIRMINGHAM, AL 35209. (#6641-501).

MAY 2 - JUNE 5, '76. BIRMINGHAM ART ASSOCIATION JURY SHOW. AWARD, COMPETITION, EXHIBIT AT BIRMINGHAM MUSEUM OF ART. (LOCAL). JOSEPHINE EDMUNDSON, SEC; BIRMINGHAM ART ASSOC; 2000 8TH AVE N; BIRMINGHAM, AL 35203. (#103379-1).

MAY 18 - 20, '76. FASHION PRESENTED BY DRAMA DEPARTMENT. THIS EARLY AMERICAN PLAY IS IN RECOGNITION OF THE LITERARY CONTRIBUTIONS OF OUR COUNTRY. AT FITZGERALD STUDENT CENTER. (LOCAL). DAVID ELDER, PROJ COORD; DRAMA DEPARTMENT, JEFFERSON STATE JUNIOR COLLEGE; 2601 CARSON RD; BIRMINGHAM, AL 35215. (#103099-6).

MAY 27 - 30, '76. AMERICAN FREEDOM TRAIN DISPLAY DAYS AT BIRMINGHAM. THE AMERICAN FREEDOM TRAIN WILL INCLUDE 10 EXHIBIT CARS AND 2 SHOWCASE CARS DEPICTING DIFFERENT PHASES OF THE AMERICAN EXPERIENCE. ITS ARRIVAL WILL SERVE AS A CATALYST FOR LOCAL BICENTENNIAL CELEBRATIONS BY PEOPLE THROUGHOUT THIS NATION. (ST-WIDE). SY FREEDMAN, DIR OF P/R; THE AMERICAN FREEDOM TRAIN FOUNDATION, INC.; 5205 LEESBURG PKE, SUITE 800; BAILEY'S XRDS, VA 22041. (#1776-55).

JUNE 13 - 28, '76. ALUMNI TOURS OF HISTORIC SITES OF SEVERAL STATES. AMERICA'S BIRTHPLACE TOUR, SAMFORD UNIV PROJ. TOURS FOR SANFORD UNIV ALUMNI FROM PHILA, VALLEY FORGE, WILLIAMSBURG, WASHINGTON & CITIES OF THE EAST COAST. HISTORICAL SITES OF THE AREA WILL BE VIEWED WITH RENEWED INTEREST. (REGN'L). DEAN MARGARET SIZEMORE; SAMFORD UNIV BICENTENNIAL COMMITTEE; 800 LAKESHORE DR; BIRMINGHAM, AL 35209. (#6643-501).

JUNE 15, '76. MUSICAL NUMBERS SALUTING THE BICENTENNIAL AT SAMFORD UNIV. AMERICA SINGS PROJ OF SAMFORD UNIV IN ALABAMA. THE SORORITIES AND FRATERNITIES OF SAMFORD UNIV WILL PRESENT A MUSICAL W/SINGING AND DANCING ON THE THEME OF AMERICAN CULTURE. (LOCAL). DEAN MARGARET D SIZEMORE; SAMFORD UNIV BICENTENNIAL COMMITTEE; 800 LAKESHORE DR; BIRMINGHAM, AL 35209. (#6630-501).

JULY 4, '76. RELIGION WORSHIP SERVICE CIRCA 1776. WORSHIP SERVICE INCLUDED DIALOGUE BETWEEN MINISTER WHO TOOK ROLE OF DR JOHN WITHERSPOON ADDRESSING 1776 PRESBYTERIAN CONGREGATION IN PRINCETON NJ AND LAYPERSON AS CAPT WM MATHIS, CONTINENTAL SOLDIER; SERVICE MUSIC OF 1776. AT FIRST PRESBYTERIAN CHURCH SANCTUARY. (LOCAL). MRS SIDNEY TEAGUE, CHMN; FIRST PRESBYTERIAN CHURCH; 2100 FOURTH AVE N; BIRMINGHAM, AL 35203. (#200001-88).

JULY 9, '76. CORY BAND FROM WALES VISITS BIRMINGHAM. THIS 38-PIECE BAND, FOUNDED IN 1884, HAS REPRESENTED WALES IN NUMEROUS NATIONAL CONTESTS & IN 1974 WON THE TITLE 'CHAMPION BAND OF GREAT BRITAIN.'. (INT'L). MS EDITH HALL; LYRA ENTERTAINMENT, INC; 16 W 61ST ST; NEW YORK, NY 10023. (#109009-8).

SEPT 18 - NOV 1, '76. 'THE HISTORY OF JACOB' - 16 CENTURY FLEMISH TAPESTRIES. EXHIBIT AT BIRMINGHAM MUSEUM OF ART. (INT'L). CULTURAL ATTACHE; BELIGIAN EMBASSY & ROYAL MUSEUM OF ART & HISTORY; 3330 GARFIELD ST; WASHINGTON, DC 20008. (#31903-2).

OCT 7 - 16, '76. ALABAMA STATE FAIR. FAIR AT FAIRGROUNDS. (REGN'L). OFFA S NICHOLS, COORD; ALABAMA STATE FAIR AUTHORITY; PO BOX 3800B; BIRMINGHAM, AL 35208. (#106095-28).

NOV 27, '76 - JAN 2, '77. 'TREASURES OF LONDON' EXHIBITION. 500 YEARS OF BRITISH SILVER ARE REPRESENTED IN THIS EXHIBITION OF 46 ANTIQUE OBJECTS, 46 MODERN PIECES, & 100 PIECES OF MODERN JEWELRY. AT BIRMINGHAM MUSEUM OF ART. (INT'L). EILEEN HARAKAL, COORD; SMITHSONIAN INSTITUTION TRAVELING EXHIBITION SERVICE; 1000 JEFFERSON DR, SW; WASHINGTON, DC 20560. (#26660-1).

BIRMINGTON

OCT 25, '75. 10TH ANNUAL FALL FESTIVAL. THIS IS THE 10TH ANNUAL FESTIVAL; THE THEME WILL BE EARLY AMERICAN ANCESTORS; EMPHASIS WILL BE ON WHEREABOUTS OF ANCESTORS IN REVOLUTIONARY BATTLES; THIS WILL BE PINPOINTED ON MAP OF 13 ORIGINAL STATES. AT BIRMINGHAM PUBLIC LIBRARY, 2020-7 AVE N. (LOCAL). TOM O CALDWELL, CHMN; THE BIRMINGHAM GENEOLOGICAL SOCIETY, INC; PO BOX 2432; BIRMINGHAM, AL 35201. (#102237-1).

BLOUNTSVILLE

PICNIC SHELTER & HISTORY OF BLOUNTSVILLE, AL. 20' X 40' PICNIC SHELTER WILL BE CONSTRUCTED & LANDSCAPED AND A HISTORY OF BLOUNTSVILLE WILL BE WRITTEN. (LOCAL). MRS W R SUTTON, CHAIRMAN; BLOUNTSVILLE BICENTENNIAL COMMITTEE; PO BOX B; BLOUNTSVILLE, AL 35031. (#21334). **ARBA GRANTEE.**

BREWTON

OCT 15, '76. BICENTENNIAL FASHION SHOW. LIVE PERFORMANCE AT JUNIOR COLLEGE AUDITORIUM. (LOCAL). MRS FRED MITCHELL, CHMN; CIVIC LEAGUE; BREWTON, AL 36426. (#200001-59).

BRIDGEPORT

BICENTENNIAL MINI-PARK AT SOULARD SQUARE, AL. A CENTRALLY LOCATED MINI-PARK TO INCLUDE A PLAZA, PARK BENCHES. TREES, GRASS, SHRUBS AND LIGHTING. (LOCAL). DORIS N JANNEY, CHAIRPERSON; BRIDGEPORT BICENTENNIAL COMMISSION; PO BOX 283; BRIDGEPORT, AL 35740. (#20222). **ARBA GRANTEE.**

JULY 20, '75. NATL PK SVC '...A LITTLE LOOK AROUND' VISITS RUSSELL CAVE NM. THIS SHORT PROGRAM FEATURES ACTORS PORTRAYING FAMOUS AMERICANS OF THE PAST WHO'VE RETURNED TO SEE AMERICA'S GROWTH. (REGN'L). SUPERINTENDENT; NATIONAL PARK SERVICE - RUSSELL CAVE NATIONAL MONUMENT; ROUTE 1, BOX 175; BRIDGEPORT, AL 35740. (#5653-219).

MAY 3, '76. 'THE SMOKY MOUNTAIN QUEEN' ARRIVES IN BRIDGEPORT. THE 'SMOKY MOUNTAIN QUEEN' IS A BOAT SIMILAR TO THOSE USED BY PIONEERS; IT WILL CARRY CARGO TYPICAL OF THAT ERA. (LOCAL). JOHN B WATERS, JR, DIR; SEVIER COUNTY BICENTENNIAL COMMITTEE; PROFESSIONAL BLDG; SEVIERVILLE, TN 37862. (#102425-9).

MAY 16, '76. RUSSELL CAVE NM'S PGM ON THE AREA'S DEVELOPMENT FROM LAND GRANTS. DEMONSTRATIONS OF HUNTING & FOOD PREPARATION METHODS BY INDIANS, BEFORE THE COMMON ERA WILL BE SHOWN TO VISITORS,. (REGN'L). RUSSELL CAVE NM; NATIONAL PARK SERVICE; ROUTE 1-BOX 175; BRIDGEPORT, AL 35740. (#6728-219).

BRUNDIDGE

PUBLIC LIBRARY LANDSCAPING PROJECT - BRUNDIDGE, AL. BEAUTIFICATION AND LANDSCAPING OF BRUNDIDGE PUBLIC LIBRARY GROUNDS. (LOCAL). MRS J F REEVES, CHAIRMAN; BRUNDIDGE BICENTENNIAL STEERING COMMITTEE; PO BOX 3; BRUNDIDGE, AL 36010. (#27019). **ARBA GRANTEE.**

BUTLER

BICENTENNIAL BOOKLET, CHOCTAW COUNTY, AL. BOOKLET COMPOSED OF ESSAYS, DRAWINGS AND PHOTOGRAPHS PERTAINING TO THE HISTORY OF CHOCTAW COUNTY. (LOCAL). MRS JAMES DANSBY EVANS, CO-CHAIRMAN; BICENTENNIAL COMMISSION OF CHOCTAW COUNTY; 318 FARLEY LN; BUTLER, AL 36904. (#24064). **ARBA GRANTEE.**

CALERA

FREEDOM GARDEN - CALERA, AL. ROCK GARDEN CONSTRUCTED ON SCHOOL CAMPUS. (LOCAL). LAMONT FRANKLIN, CHAIRMAN; ADVANCED BIOLOGY CLASS, CALERA HIGH SCHOOL; HWY 31; CALERA, AL 35040. (#29184).

JULY 4, '76. COMMUNITY RELIGIOUS SERVICE. EACH CHURCH IN COMMUNITY WAS INVITED TO PARTICIPATE. COMMUNITY ADULT & CHILDRENS' CHOIRS PERFORMED. MINISTERS FROM EACH PARTICIPATING CHURCH HAD A PART IN THE SERVICE. AT CALERA HIGH SCHOOL GYM, 15TH STREET. (LOCAL). LON EULER, CHAIRMAN; CALERA BICENTENNIAL ACTION COMMISSION; 20TH AVENUE; CALERA, AL 35040. (#200001-42).

CAMDEN

SPECIAL COLLECTIONS & GENEALOGY DIVISION, AL. PURCHASE OF COPYING MACHINE, MICROFILM READER, FILES, PAPER SUPPLIES, CENSUS ROLLS, GENEALOGICAL REFERENCE BOOKS AND MATERIALS; REMODELING OF EXISTING SPACE FOR INSTALLATION OF MACHINES AND FILES. (LOCAL). DOT MCMILLON, CHAIRMAN; CAMDEN AREA BICENTENNIAL COMMITTEE; BOX 572; CAMDEN, AL 36726. (#23732). **ARBA GRANTEE.**

CARBON HILL

FEB 14, '76. BICENTENNIAL PARADE. CARBON HILL PTA IN COOPERATION WITH JASPER BICENTENNIAL COMMITTEE WILL HAVE A BICENTENNIAL PARADE. STUDENTS AND TOWNSPEOPLE WILL DRESS IN REVOLUTIONARY PERIOD CLOTHING. AT DOWNTOWN CARBON HILL. (LOCAL). JIMMIE SUE PAGE, DIRECTOR; CARBON HILL PTA/JASPER '76 ACTION COMMITTEE; PO BOX 252; CARBON HILL, AL 35549. (#104033-2).

FEB 16, '76. BICENTENNIAL CARNIVAL. CARBON HILL PTA IN COOPERATION WITH JASPER '76 ACTION COMMITTEE WILL PUT ON A CARNIVAL WITH BICENTENNIAL THEME. AT NATIONAL GUARD ARMORY. (LOCAL). JIMMIE SUE PAGE, DIRECTOR; CARBON HILL PTA/JASPER '76 ACTION COMMITTEE; PO BOX 252; CARBON HILL, AL 35549. (#104033-1).

CARRVILLE

ARCHIBALD PATTERSON LOG CABIN - AL. THE ARCHIBALD PATTERSON LOG CABIN WILL BE PURCHASED. (LOCAL). CLAIRE B CALDWELL, CHAIRPERSON; SOUTH TALLAPOOSA CO BICENTENNIAL COMMITTEE; BOX 457; E TALLASSEE, AL 36023. (#26113). **ARBA GRANTEE.**

CEDAR BLUFF

HISTORY OF CEDAR BLUFF, AL. COMPREHENSIVE, DOCUMENTED, ILLUSTRATED HISTORY OF CEDAR BLUFF BY COL ROBERT N MANN WAS PUBLISHED. (LOCAL). MRS JAMES H CAMP, CHAIRMAN; CEDAR BLUFF BICENTENNIAL COMMISSION; RT 1, BOX 61; CEDAR BLUFF, AL 35959. (#31977).

OCT 30, '75. STREET DANCE. LIVE PERFORMANCE AT PARKING LOT OF THE CEDAR BLUFF BANK. (LOCAL). MRS JAMES H CAMP, CHMN; CEDAR BLUFF BICENTENNIAL COMMISSION; CEDAR BLUFF, AL 35959. (#200001-74).

MAR 27 - 28, '76. BICENTENNIAL WAGON TRAIN STOPS IN CEDAR BLUFF. CEREMONY, LIVE PERFORMANCE AT LAKESHORE INN, HWY 68. (LOCAL). MRS JAMES H CAMP, CHMN; PRATVILLE BICENTENNIAL COMMISSION; CEDAR BLUFF, AL 35959. (#200001-76).

JUNE 18, '76. JUDGING FOR CEDAR BLUFF'S REPRESENTATIVE IN AL BICENT BELLE PAGEANT. COMPETITION, AWARD AT TOWN & GOWN THEATRE, UNIV OF ALABAMA, BIRMINGHAM, AL. (ST-WIDE). KATHY SUMMERS; PRATVILLE BICENTENNIAL COMMISSION; CEDAR BLUFF, AL 35959. (#200001-75).

JULY 10, '76. 1976 ARTS & CRAFTS FESTIVAL. EXHIBIT AT CEDAR BLUFF SCHOOL AUDITORIUM. (LOCAL). MRS JAMES H CAMP, CHMN; CEDAR BLUFF BICENTENNIAL COMMISSION; CEDAR BLUFF, AL 35959. (#200001-73).

CENTRE

ENLARGING AUTHENTIC LOG CABIN, CENTRE, AL. KITCHEN AND RESTROOM FACILITIES ADDED TO MAKE THIS BUILDING INTO A USEABLE MEETING PLACE. (LOCAL). JOSEPHINE NOLEN, COORDINATOR; PRATT CENTRE BUSINESS PROFESSIONAL WOMEN'S CLUB; 181 W MAIN ST; CENTRE, AL 35960. (#21825). **ARBA GRANTEE.**

CENTRE—CONTINUED

HISTORY OF CENTRE, AL. THE HISTORY OF CENTRE WILL BE RESEARCHED, WRITTEN AND PUBLISHED. (LOCAL). ANN JORDON, CHAIRMAN; CENTRE BICENTENNIAL COMMISSION; 181 W MAIN ST; CENTRE, AL 35960. (#21826). **ARBA GRANTEE.**

PRATT MEMORIAL PARK, CENTRE, AL. ONE ACRE OF LAND WILL BE ESTABLISHED AS MEMORIAL PARK FOR JOHN PRATT, INVENTOR OF TYPEWRITER. LANDSCAPING WILL BE DONE AND AN INFORMATION CENTER SET UP. (LOCAL). ANN JORDON, CHAIRMAN; PRATT CENTRE BUSINESS WOMENS CLUB; 181 W MAIN ST; CENTRE, AL 35960. (#21827). **ARBA GRANTEE.**

RESTORATION OF CORNWALL FURNANCE - CENTRE, AL. RESTORATION OF CORNWALL FURNACE AND THE WRITING OF THE HISTORY OF CHEROKEE COUNTY. (LOCAL). ESTELLE SMITH, CHAIRPERSON; CHEROKEE BICENTENNIAL COMMITTEE; CLORIS FARM; CENTRE, AL 35960. (#20898). **ARBA GRANTEE.**

DEC 17, '75. 'MIDNIGHT RIDE OF PAUL REVERE' - A HISTORICAL MUSICAL REVIEW. LIVE PERFORMANCE AT CHEROKEE COUNTY HIGH SCHOOL. (LOCAL). MARTHA JO JORDAN, COORD; CHEROKEE COUNTY ARTS COUNCIL; N RIVER ST; CENTRE, AL 35960. (#103640-1).

CENTREVILLE

BEAUTIFICATION OF CENTREVILLE, ALABAMA. TREES & SHRUBS TO BE PLANTED IN DOWNTOWN AREA; PRIZE AWARDED FOR MOST IMPROVEMENT IN AN INDIVIDUAL HOME. (LOCAL). GUINN KENNEDY, CHAIRMAN; CENTREVILLE BICENT COMMISSION; 476 WALNUT ST, PO BOX 98; CENTREVILLE, AL 35042. (#10432). **ARBA GRANTEE.**

CITY PARK AND MUSEUM IN CENTREVILLE, AL. LAND ON CAHAPA RIVER WILL BE BOUGHT BY CITY AND CONVERTED INTO A PARK AND RECREATIONAL AREA. ACCOMODATIONS FOR BOAT LAUNCHING, FISHING AND HIKING WILL BE MADE; SMALL MUSEUM ALSO TO BE CONSTRUCTED. (LOCAL). GUINN F KENNEDY, CHAIRMAN; CENTREVILLE BICENT COMMISSION; 496 WALNUT ST, PO BOX 98; CENTREVILLE, AL 35042. (#10705).

CLEAN-UP & PAINTING CAMPAIGN IN CENTREVILLE, AL. THE PROJECT INVOLVES A CAMPAIGN TO CLEAN-UP BUSINESS AND RESIDENTIAL AREAS OF THE CITY, THEN PAINT THEM; CLEAN-UP IS TO BE CONDUCTED BY HIGH SCHOOL CLUBS AND STUDENT COUNCILS. (LOCAL). GUINN KENNEDY, CHAIRMAN; CENTREVILLE BICENT COMMISSION; 476 WALNUT ST, PO BOX 98; CENTREVILLE, AL 35042. (#10431).

SEPT 15 - 20, '75. ART CONTEST; BEST DISPLAY OF NATION'S HISTORY. DISPLAYS INCLUDE ART ENTRIES, PRE-1900 SCHOOL TEXTS, CITY MAPS & RELICS. AT ALABAMA NATIONAL GUARD ARMORY. (LOCAL). MRS GUINN KENNEDY, CHMN; CENTREVILLE BICENTENNIAL COMMISSION; PO BOX 98; CENTREVILLE, AL 35042. (#10705-3).

DEC 12, '75. CHRISTMAS THROUGH THE YEARS PARADE. HISTORICAL CHRISTMAS FLOATS WILL BE BUILT BY HIGH SCHOOL STUDENTS; BANDS FROM LOCAL SCHOOLS WILL ALSO PARTICIPATE IN PARADE; TOUR OF ANTEBELLUM HOMES WILL FOLLOW. AT WALNUT ST & COURT SQUARE. (LOCAL). MRS GUINN KENNEDY, CHMN; CENTREVILLE BICENTENNIAL COMMISSION; PO BOX 98; CENTREVILLE, AL 35042. (#10705-1).

DEC 12 - 13, '75. TOUR OF ANTE-BELLUM HOMES. HOMES INCLUDE AN 1837 STAGECOACH INN & A RELOCATED LOG INN. OTHER SITES ARE A BIBB COUNTY COURTHOUSE & 1859 PRESBYTERIAN CHURCH. AT HOMES IN CENTREVILLE. (LOCAL). MRS J M KENNEDY, CHMN; CENTREVILLE BICENTENNIAL COMMISSION; PO BOX 98; CENTREVILLE, AL 35042. (#10705-2).

CLANTON

CHILTON COUNTY CLEAN AND GREEN PROGRAM, AL. A COUNTY WIDE SOLID WASTE COLLECTION AND LANDFILL PROGRAM. (LOCAL). MILTON DIEFENDERFER, DIRECTOR; CHILTON COUNTY CLEAN AND GREEN PROGRAM; PO BOX 87; CLANTON, AL 35045. (#20037).

OCT 5, '75. CHILTON COUNTY GOSPEL SINGING CONVENTION. LIVE PERFORMANCE AT CHILTON COUNTY COURTHOUSE. (LOCAL). WILLIAM HEAPS, PRESIDENT; CHILTON COUNTY GOSPEL SINGERS; BOX 67; CLANTON, AL 35045. (#100938-1).

CLAYTON

BEAUTIFICATION OF PARKS, CLAYTON, AL. PROJECT INCLUDES PLANTING TREES AND SHRUBS AND ERECTING FLAG POLE. (LOCAL). CHARLES L WESTON, CHAIRMAN; CLAYTON BICENTENNIAL PROJ; PO BOX 128; CLAYTON, AL 36016. (#22379).

MAY 1 - 2, '76. CLAYTON HISTORICAL TOUR. A TOUR OF HISTORIC HOMES IN CLAYTON ALABAMA. (LOCAL). SHARON MARTIN, COORD; CLAYTON HISTORICAL TOUR; PO BOX 423; CLAYTON, AL 36016. (#103416-267).

CLEBURNE

RAILWAY DEPOT - CLEBURNE, AL. RESTORE TO ORIGINAL APPEARANCE FOR USE AS CIVIC CENTER, ARTS & CRAFT EXHIBIT, MUSEUM & COMMUNITY ENTERTAINMENT; ADDING KITCHEN AND REST ROOMS & DISPLAY FIXTURES. (LOCAL). CLARA ROACH, PRESIDENT; CLEBURNE ARTS AND CRAFTS LEAGUE; EVANS BRIDGE RD; HEFLIN, AL 36264. (#20904). **ARBA GRANTEE.**

COLUMBIA

APR 11, '76. OPENING OF 1862 JAIL RESTORATION & EXHIBIT. 1862 JAIL HAS BEEN RESTORED AND WILL BE USED AS A MUSEUM; ITEMS ON DISPLAY ARE BEING DONATED BY AREA RESIDENTS AND ARE OF HISTORIC INTEREST TO THIS AREA. (LOCAL). SANDRA GRAY; COLUMBIA BICENTENNIAL COMM; PO BOX 369; COLUMBIA, AL 36319. (#11388-1).

APR 12, '76. PROGRAM OF PATRIOTIC MUSIC SUNG BY COMBINED CHURCH CHOIRS. LIVE PERFORMANCE AT HOUSTON COUNTY HIGH SCHOOL FOOTBALL FIELD. (LOCAL). SANDRA GRAY, CHAIRPERSON; COLUMBIA BICENTENNIAL COMMITTEE; PO BOX 369; COLUMBIA, AL 36319. (#100864-1).

APR 12, '76 - CONTINUING . RESTORED JAIL, LOG CABIN & FARM MACHINERY EXHIBIT. THE OLD JAIL WAS BUILT IN 1860; IT HAS BEEN RESTORED AND IS BEING USED AS A MUSEUM. ALSO INCLUDED IN THE PROJECT IS A LOG CABIN LOCATED BEHIND THE JAIL WITH A DISPLAY OF HISTORIC FARM MACHINERY. AT OLD 1860 JAIL, ONE BLOCK SOUTH OF HIGHWAY 52, LOCATED BEHIND LIBRARY. (LOCAL). SANDRA GRAY, CO-CHMN; COLUMBIA BICENTENNIAL COMMITTEE; PO BOX 369; COLUMBIA, AL 36319. (#100863-1).

APR 17, '76. PARADE & BAR B QUE WITH SPECIAL PERFORMANCE OF LIONETTES DRILL TEAM. FESTIVAL, LIVE PERFORMANCE AT HIGHWAY 52. (LOCAL). SANDRA GRAY, CHAIRPERSON; COLUMBIA BICENTENNIAL COMMITTEE; PO BOX 369; COLUMBIA, AL 36319. (#100865-1).

COMER BRIDGE

MAY 4, '76. 'THE SMOKY MOUNTAIN QUEEN' ARRIVES IN COMER BRIDGE. THE 'SMOKY MOUNTAIN QUEEN' IS A BOAT SIMILAR TO THOSE USED BY PIONEERS; IT WILL CARRY CARGO TYPICAL OF THAT ERA. (LOCAL). JOHN B WATERS, JR, DIR; SEVIER COUNTY BICENTENNIAL COMMITTEE; PROFESSIONAL BLDG; SEVIERVILLE, TN 37862. (#102425-10).

CROMWELL

PUSHMATAHA TRAIL, CROMWELL, AL. 5 BICENTENNIAL MARKERS PLACED ALONG THE TRAIL CHIEF PUSHMATAHA USED TO GET FROM HIS CAMP TO THE TOMBIGBEE RIVER. (LOCAL). MRS J T ALLEN, SR, PROJ DIRECTOR; CHOCTAW COUNTY BICENTENNIAL COMMISSION; CROMWELL, AL 36906. (#23795). **ARBA GRANTEE.**

CULLMAN

COVERED BRIDGE & MINI PARK IN CULLMAN CO, ALABAMA. PROJECT TO COMPLETELY RESTORE BRIDGE AND DEVELOPE A PARK THAT WILL INCLUDE TABLES, RESTROOM FACILITIES, INFORMATION CENTER, ROCKWATER MILL, SMALL DAM SITE AND A LOG CABIN CARETAKERS RESIDENCE. (LOCAL). MRS PAT GARDINER, CHAIRWOMAN; THE BICENTENNIAL COMMITTEE OF CULLMAN COUNTY; PO BOX 698; CULLMAN, AL 35055. (#5347).

FURNISHINGS FOR OLDEST HOUSE IN CULLMAN, AL. FURNISH HOUSE IN ITS ORIGINAL PRIMITIVE MANNER SO IT CAN BE USED AND ENJOYED BY FUTURE GENERATIONS. (LOCAL). PEGGY S SMITH, EXEC DIRECTOR; CULLMAN COMMUNITY DEVELOPMENT AGENCY; PO BOX 1009; CULLMAN, AL 35055. (#25904). **ARBA GRANTEE.**

MINI-PARK IN CULLMAN CITY, ALABAMA. IN ADDITION TO A COMPLETELY RESTORED BRIDGE, THE PARK WILL HAVE ITEMS SUCH AS AN INFORMATION CNTR, LOG CABIN REPLICAS & ROCK WATER MILL. (LOCAL). STANLEY T JOHNSON, CHAIRMAN; THE BICENTENNIAL COMMITTEE OF CULLMAN CITY; 714 3RD AVE SE; CULLMAN, AL 35055. (#3577).

DEC 7, '75. MISS LIBERTY PAGEANT, WINNER WILL BE FROM SCHOOLS' DAR REPS. OPENING. (LOCAL). MRS PAT GARDINER; THE BICENTENNIAL COMMITTEE OF CULLMAN COUNTY; PO BOX 698; CULLMAN, AL 35055. (#5347-501).

SEPT 20 - 25, '76. CULLMAN COUNTY FAIR. FAIR AT CULLMAN COUNTY FAIRGROUNDS. (ST-WIDE). DILLARD JOHNSON, MANAGER; CULLMAN LIONS CLUB; PO BOX 562; CULLMAN, AL 35055. (#106505-1).

DADEVILLE

HISTORY PROJECT IN DADEVILLE, AL. HISTORIC POSTCARDS AND A HISTORY OF TALLAPOOSA COUNTY WILL BE PRINTED. (LOCAL). JERRY ALLEN, CHAIRMAN; TALLAPOOSA COUNTY BICENTENNIAL COMMITTEE; PO BOX 699; ALEXANDER CTY, AL 35010. (#18101).

DAPHNE

DAPHNE BICENTENNIAL PROJECTS, AL. YEAR-ROUND MEETING, ACTIVITIES & PROJECTS, INCLUDING: THE PURCHASE OF 5 HISTORICAL MARKERS. (LOCAL). MARY GUARISCO, SECRETARY; BICENTENNIAL COMMITTEE OF DAPHNE; DAPHNE, AL 36526. (#29510).

AUG '76. DAPHNE BICENTENNIAL DAYS. FESTIVAL. (LOCAL). MISS MARY GUARISCO, CHMN; CITY OF DAPHNE; DAPHNE, AL 36526. (#200001-53).

DAUPHIN IS

JULY 16 - 18, '76. ALABAMA DEEP SEA FISHING. COMPETITION AT DAUPHIN ISLAND. (REGN'L). ROBERT MCKEAN, PRESIDENT; MOBILE JAYCEES; 1209 GOVERNMENT ST; MOBILE, AL 36602. (#100671-1).

DAVISTON

JUNE 1 - AUG 30, '76. EVENING BICENT SLIDE PRESENTATION AT HORSESHOE BEND NMP. PARK PERSONNEL PRESENT SPECIAL, WEEKLY BICENTENNIAL PROGRAM AT WIND CREEK STATE PARK; PROGRAMS DEAL WITH PLACES AND EVENTS ASSOCIATED WITH THE REVOLUTION AND THE MOVE FOR INDEPENDENCE. AT WIND CREEK STATE PARK. (REGN'L). HORSESHOE BEND NMP; NATIONAL PARK SERVICE; RT 1-BOX 63; DAVISTON, AL 36256. (#6730-108).

DECATUR

APPALACHIAN FOLK HERITAGE, DECATUR, AL. EDUCATIONAL OUTREACH PGM TO PROVIDE EXAMPLES OF REGIONAL ETHNIC AND HERITAGE FORMS FOR RESEARCH AND PRESERVATION. ESTABLISH CENTER TO STORE APPALACHIAN FOLK ARTS. (REGN'L). LOREN KOSLOWSKY, DIRECTOR FOLK ARTS PROGRAM; JOHN C CALHOUN STATE COMMUNITY COLLEGE; PO BOX 2216; DECATUR, AL 35611. (#17027).

BICENTENNIAL COMMITTEE ON RESTORATION - AL. RESTORE THE BANK BUILDING BUILT 1835 TO HOUSE DECATUR BRANCH OF THE STATE BANK OF ALABAMA, CHARTERED 1832. (LOCAL). ED PRICE, CHAIRPERSON; SESQUICENTENNIAL BICENTENNIAL COMMISSION; 750 DANVILLE RD SW; DECATUR, AL 35601. (#26033). **ARBA GRANTEE.**

ENVIRONMENTAL EDUCATION WORKSHOP. SEMINAR. (LOCAL). TERRY BYNUM, INSTRUCTOR; JOHN C CALHOUN STATE COMMUNITY COLLEGE; PO BOX 2216; DECATUR, AL 35611. (#103099-10). **(??).**

TOURISM PROMOTION - DECATUR, AL. PROMOTE VISITS TO THE HISTORICAL AND CULTURAL ATTRACTIONS OF THE SOUTHERN APPALACHIAN REGION. (ST-WIDE). MS BETTY HUTCHENS, COORDINATOR COMMUNITY SERVICES; JOHN C CALHOUN STATE COMMUNITY COLLEGE; PO BOX 2216; DECATUR, AL 35611. (#17028).

MAY 17 - SEPT 2, '75. 1975 AQUATIC CENTER OPENING AT POINT MALLARD PARK. OPENING AT AQUATIC CENTER, FREE PARKING. (REGN'L). FRANK SHEPHERD, PROJ CHMN; CITY OF DECATUR, POINT MALLARD PARK AUTHORITY; MALLARD DR, SE; DECATUR, AL 35601. (#100627-1).

APR 9 - 11, '76. 5TH ANNUAL ANTIQUE SHOW AND SALE. EXHIBIT AT AQUADOME 5TH AVE & 8TH ST. (LOCAL). MRS O B TYLER, DIRECTOR; DECATUR WOMANS' CLUB; 1710 IRIS ST SW; DECATUR, AL 35601. (#102919-1).

MAY 6, '76. 'THE SMOKY MOUNTAIN QUEEN' ARRIVES IN DECATUR. THE 'SMOKY MOUNTAIN QUEEN' IS A BOAT SIMILAR TO THOSE USED BY PIONEERS; IT WILL CARRY CARGO TYPICAL OF THAT ERA. (LOCAL). JOHN B WATERS, JR, DIR; SEVIER COUNTY BICENTENNIAL COMMITTEE; PROFESSIONAL BLDG; SEVIERVILLE, TN 37862. (#102425-12).

MAY 8, '76. SALE OF GRAPHIC ART FROM FERDINAND ROTEN GALLERIES, INC. FESTIVAL AT WHEELER BASIN REGIONAL LIBRARY, 504 CHERRY ST, NE. (LOCAL). PAUL HARGROVE, PROJ DIR; FRIENDS OF WHEELER BASIN REGIONAL LIBRARY; 2003 WOODMONT, SE; DECATUR, AL 35601. (#100628-1).

JULY 4, '76. SPIRIT OF AMERICA FESTIVAL. ACTIVITIES AT POINT MALLARD PARK COMPRISE ONE OF THE SOUTH'S LARGEST JULY 4TH CELEBRATIONS. AT POINT MALLARD PARK. (ST-WIDE). FRANK J SHEPHERD, COORD; POINT MALLARD PARK; 3101 8TH ST, SE; DECATUR, AL 35601. (#103416-429).

JULY 8, '76 - CONTINUING . OPENING OF RESTORED STATE BANK. STATE BANK BUILT 1832, ON NATIONAL REGISTER. AT 1832 BANK BUILDING. (LOCAL). ED PRICE, CHAIRMAN; 150-200 COMMITTEE; 750 DANVILLE RD, SW; DECATUR, AL 35601. (#100850-2).

AUG 10 - 14, '76. AAU MEN & WOMENS OUTDOOR DIVING CHAMPIONSHIPS. COMPETITION AT AQUATIC CENTER, POINT MALLARD PARK. (NAT'L). FRANK SHEPHERD, CHMN; POINT MALLARD & SOUTHEASTERN AAU DIVING ASSOC; POINT MALLARD DR, SE; DECATUR, AL 35601. (#100670-1).

DEC 8, '76. BICENTENNIAL RESTORATION & SESQUICENTENNIAL PARADE. PARADE AT BANK STREET. (LOCAL). ED PRICE, CHAIRMAN; 150-200 COMMITTEE; 750 DANVILLE RD SW; DECATUR, AL 35601. (#100850-1).

DEMOPOLIS

JAN 1, '76 - CONTINUING . BLUFF HALL, AN ANTEBELLUM HOUSE. 1832 ANTEBELLUM HOME WITH EARLY 19TH CENTURY FURNISHINGS & EXHIBITS. AT BLUFF HALL, 407 N COMMISSIONERS AVE. (LOCAL). MRS DAVID TURNER, DIR; MARENGO COUNTY HISTORICAL SOCIETY; 406 S MAIN ST; DEMOPOLIS, AL 36732. (#100478-1).

SEPT 25 - OCT 3, '76. BICENTENNIAL BLACK BELT PILGRIMAGE. FAIR AT NEWBERN, GREENSBORO, EUTAW, DEMOPOLIS, LIVINGSTON, MARION, GAINSVLE. (ST-WIDE). MRS DAVID TURNER, COORD; BLACK BELT PILGRIMAGE ASSOCIATION; PO BOX 236; DEMOPOLIS, AL 36732. (#103416-606).

DOTHAN

DOTHAN, AL, BICENTENNIAL VETERANS MEMORIAL. DEVELOP ONE ACRE OF LAND LANDSCAPED WITH FLOWERS, SHRUBS, LIGHTS AND FLAGPOLE WITH A VETERANS MEMORIAL. (LOCAL). DAVID E LUMNUS, CHAIRMAN; DOTHAN BICENTENNIAL COMMITTEE; CITY HALL; DOTHAN, AL 36301. (#25667). **ARBA GRANTEE.**

OCT 20 - 25, '75. NATIONAL PEANUT FESTIVAL AND FAIR. AWARD, EXHIBIT, FAIR, PARADE AT HOUSTON COUNTY FARM CENTER, ROSS CLARK CIRCLE, RT 9. (ST-WIDE). JOHN POWELL, EXEC DIR; NATIONAL PEANUT FESTIVAL ASSOC, INC; 300 N FOSTER, PO BOX 976; DOTHAN, AL 36301. (#101996-1).

OCT 18 - 23, '76. NATIONAL PEANUT FESTIVAL. CEREMONY, EXHIBIT, FESTIVAL, LIVE PERFORMANCE AT HOUSTON COUNTY FARM CENTER, 1699 ROSS CLARK CIRCLE SW. (REGN'L). JOHN T POWELL, EXEC DIR; NATIONAL PEANUT FESTIVAL ASSOCIATION, INC; PO BOX 976; DOTHAN, AL 36301. (#106801-1).

EAST BREWTON

BEAUTIFICATION OF FORT CRAWFORD PARK, E BREWTON,AL. BEAUTIFY CITY PARK WITH THE SETTING OUT OF PINES AND AZALEAS. THE PARK IS A HISTORICAL SITE WELL TO BE REMEMBERED. (LOCAL). HON MALCOLM EDWARDS, MAYOR; CITY OF EAST BREWTON; PO BOX 2010; EAST BREWTON, AL 36426. (#25724). **ARBA GRANTEE.**

EAST BREWTON FIRE DEPT, AL. THE FIRE DEPARTMENT BUILDING WILL BE RENOVATED. (LOCAL). HON MALCOLM EDWARDS, MAYOR; CITY OF EAST BREWTON; PO BOX 2010; EAST BREWTON, AL 36426. (#25763). **ARBA GRANTEE.**

ECLECTIC

MINI-PARK - ECLECTIC, AL. THE PARK IS CEMENTED WITH SHRUBS AND A FLAGPOLE. (LOCAL). MARY TAUNTON, CHAIRMAN; ECLECTIC WOMEN'S CLUB; BOX 192; ECLECTIC, AL 36024. (#29179).

ELKMONT

JAN 20, '76. HORIZONS '76 DEDICATION CEREMONY WITH FLAGS, BAND & GUEST SPEAKER. CEREMONY AT ELKMONT HIGH SCHOOL AUDITORIUM. (LOCAL). LEW WRIGHT, COORD; ELKMONT BICENTENNIAL ASSOCIATION; PO BOX 154; ELKMONT, AL 35620. (#200001-14).

JULY 4, '76. FESTIVAL USA. PARADE, ATHLETIC, PAGEANT, CEREMONY, DEDICATION. (LOCAL). LEW WRIGHT, CHAIRPERSON; ELKMONT BICENTENNIAL ASSOC; BOX 154; ELKMONT, AL 35620. (#107344-1).

ENTERPRISE

AMERICAN ISSUES FORUM - ENTERPRISE, AL. THE ENTERPRISE DAILY LEDGER WILL CARRY SERIES OF WEEKLY ARTICLES ON AMERICAN ISSUES. (LOCAL). ROY SHOFFNER, CHAIRMAN; ENTERPRISE BICENTENNIAL COMMISSION; 406 DOSTER ST; ENTERPRISE, AL 36330. (#17404).

ANTIQUE CAR SHOW - ENTERPRISE, AL. A DISPLAY OF OLD CARS ON SIDEWALKS OF THE CITY AND IN SHOPPING AREAS. (LOCAL). ROY SHOFFNER, CHAIRMAN OF HERITAGE COMMITTEE; ENTERPRISE BICENTENNIAL COMMISSION; 406 DOSTER ST; ENTERPRISE, AL 36330. (#17407).

ART CONTESTS IN ELEMENTARY SCHOOLS; ENTERPRISE, AL. STUDENTS IN GRADES THREE TO SIX WILL PARTICIPATE IN AN ART CONTESTS WITH A 1776 THEME. (LOCAL). ROY SHOFFNER, CHAIRMAN OF HERITAGE COMMITTEE; ENTERPRISE BICENTENNIAL COMMISSION; 406 DOSTER ST; ENTERPRISE, AL 36330. (#17406).

BLOODMOBILE DRIVE - ENTERPRISE, AL. PROMOTION OF THE QUARTERLY BLOODMOBILE; ENCOURAGING LOCAL CIVIC CLUBS TO PARTICIPATE. (LOCAL). JAMES E BARNES, CHAIRMAN; ENTERPRISE KIWANIS CLUB; PO BOX 639; ENTERPRISE, AL 36330. (#17402).

CANCER TESTS - ENTERPRISE, AL. THE COFFEE COUNTY CANCER UNIT WILL CONDUCT A CANCER CLINIC FOR WOMEN IN COOPERATION WITH LOCAL BICENTENNIAL COMMISSION. (LOCAL). PAUL DYKES, CHAIRMAN; COFFEE COUNTY CANCER UNIT; C/O FIRST FEDERAL SAVINGS & LOAN; ENTERPRISE, AL 36330. (#17403).

CARAVAN OF EXHIBITS - ENTERPRISE, AL. AN EXHIBITION OF LOCAL MEMORABILIA, ARTS AND CRAFTS TO TRAVEL THE LOCAL AREA. (LOCAL). ROY SHOFFNER, CHAIRMAN OF HERITAGE COMMITTEE; ENTERPRISE BICENTENNIAL COMMISSION; 406 DOSTER ST; ENTERPRISE, AL 36330. (#17410).

HERITAGE MUSEUM AND LIBRARY, ENTERPRISE, AL. HISTORIC DEPOT CONVERTED FOR USE AS A RAILROAD AND AGRICULTURAL MUSEUM AND HISTORICAL-GENEALOGICAL LIBRARY. (LOCAL). RAY SHOFFNER, HERITAGE CHAIRMAN; ENTERPRISE BICENTENNIAL COMMISSION; 406 DOSTER ST; ENTERPRISE, AL 36330. (#22288). **ARBA GRANTEE.**

MOVIE CLASSICS - ENTERPRISE, AL. ONE MOVIE CLASSIC EACH MONTH, JANUARY THROUGH JUNE AT LOCAL THEATRE. (LOCAL). ROY SHOFFNER, CHAIRMAN OF HERITAGE COMMITTEE; ENTERPRISE BICENTENNIAL COMMISSION; 406 DOSTER ST; ENTERPRISE, AL 36330. (#17408).

OLD COIN SHOW - ENTERPRISE, AL. A SHOW OF OLD COIN, CONFEDERATE MONEY AND OTHER PAPER MONEY COLLECTED BY MANY IN AREA. (LOCAL). ROY SHOFFNER, CHAIRMAN OF HERITAGE COMMITTEE; ENTERPRISE BICENTENNIAL COMMISSION; 406 DOSTER ST; ENTERPRISE, AL 36330. (#17409).

PAPER RECYCLING PROGRAM - ENTERPRISE, AL. COLLECTED PAPER, MAGAZINES AND BOOKS FOR CLEANUP PROGRAM AND RECYCLING. (LOCAL). B DOUGLAS BRADLEY, CHAIRMAN; ENTERPRISE BICENTENNIAL COMMITTEE; PO BOX 1976; ENTERPRISE, AL 36330. (#17400).

PATRIOTIC ESSAY CONTEST IN JUNIOR HIGHS - AL. PATRIOTIC ESSAYS TO BE WRITTEN ON 1776 SUBJECT BY STUDENTS OF CITY'S JUNIOR HIGH SCHOOLS. (LOCAL). ROY SHOFFNER, CHAIRMAN OF HERITAGE COMMITTEE; ENTERPRISE BICENTENNIAL COMMISSION; 406 DOSTER ST; ENTERPRISE, AL 36330. (#17405).

PATRIOTIC SKETCHES - ENTERPRISE, AL. THE SKETCHES WILL BE WRITTEN AND PRODUCED BY SPEECH CLASSES AND GIVEN ON REQUEST TO CLUBS AND SCHOOLS. THE SKETCHES HAVE A REVOLUTIONARY PERIOD THEME. (LOCAL). ROY SHOFFNER, CHAIRMAN-HERITAGE COMMITTEE; ENTERPRISE BICENTENNIAL COMMISSION; 406 DOSTER ST; ENTERPRISE, AL 36330. (#16944).

RELIGIOUS TRAIL, ENTERPRISE, AL. CHURCHES OF THE CITY WILL CARRY OUT HERITAGE THEME WITH EMPHASIS ON THE REVOLUTIONARY ERA. (LOCAL). ROY SHOFFNER, CHAIRMAN HERITAGE COMMITTEE; ENTERPRISE BICENTENNIAL COMMISSION; 406 DOSTER ST; ENTERPRISE, AL 36330. (#16940).

TRASH CAN PROJECT - ENTERPRISE, AL. CONVERTING 30 GAL DRUMS INTO TRASH CANS; NATIONAL AND LOCAL EMBLEM TO BE PAINTED ON THEM. (LOCAL). WAYNE DAVIS, CHAIRMAN; BOY SCOUT TROOP; 206 GEORGE WALLACE DR; ENTERPRISE, AL 36330. (#17401).

OCT 10, '75. HALF TIME SHOW. LIVE PERFORMANCE AT ENTERPRISE HIGH SCHOOL STADIUM. (LOCAL). BARTON STARR, CHAIRMAN; ENTERPRISE BICENTENNIAL COMMISSION; PO BOX 1776; ENTERPRISE, AL 36330. (#200001-15).

NOV 1, '75 - MAY '76. PATRIOTIC SKETCHES OF REVOLUTIONARY ERA FIGURES. ENTERPRISE HIGH SCHOOL STUDENTS RESEARCHED, WROTE, & PRODUCED THESE SKETCHES TO BE PERFORMED FOR COMMUNITY GROUPS. AT WHEREVER CLUBS MEET. (LOCAL). ROY SHOFFNER, CHMN; ENTERPRISE BICENTENNIAL COMMISSION; 406 DOSTER ST; ENTERPRISE, AL 36330. (#103312-3).

APR 6, '76. HERITAGE FAIR. HIGH SCHOOL STUDENTS TO CONDUCT HERITAGE FAIR WITH WIDE VARIETY OF EXHIBITS ON U S HERITAGE. AT ENTERPRISE HIGH SCHOOL. (LOCAL). ROY SHOFFNER, CHAIRMAN; ENTERPRISE BICENTENNIAL COMMISSION; 406 DOSTER ST; ENTERPRISE, AL 36330. (#103068-19).

APR 10, '76. ANTIQUE CAR SHOW. EXHIBIT. (LOCAL). ROY SHOFFNER, CHAIRMAN; ENTERPRISE BICENTENNIAL COMMITTEE; 406 DOSTER ST; ENTERPRISE, AL 36330. (#103068-26).

APR 18, '76. RELIGIOUS TRAIL DEDICATION. CEREMONY, EXHIBIT AT LOCAL AREA CHURCHES. (LOCAL). ROY SHOFFNER, CHMN; ENTERPRISE BICENTENNIAL COMMISSION; 406 DOSTER ST; ENTERPRISE, AL 36330. (#103312-5).

JULY 1 - 3, '76. ENTERPRISE HISTORICAL PAGEANT, FROM THE REVOLUTION TO PRESENT. LIVE PERFORMANCE AT ENTERPRISE HIGH SCHOOL STADIUM AT WATTS ST. (LOCAL). ROY SHOFFNER, CHMN; ENTERPRISE BICENTENNIAL COMMISSION; 406 DOSTER ST; ENTERPRISE, AL 36330. (#103312-1).

JULY 1 - 3, '76. HERITAGE ART SHOW. EXHIBIT AT ESJC GYM. (LOCAL). ROY SHOFFNER, CHMN; ENTERPRISE BICENTENNIAL COMMISSION; 406 DOSTER ST; ENTERPRISE, AL 36330. (#103312-4).

ETHELSVILLE

JULY 3, '76. OLD-FASHIONED DAY. FESTIVAL AT FOREST COMMUNITY CENTER. (LOCAL). JANICE TILLEY, CHAIRMAN; FOREST COMMUNITY CLUB; ROUTE 1; ETHELSVILLE, AL 35461. (#200001-48).

EUFAULA

SETH-LORE IDENTIFICATION HERITAGE '76 - AL. SEVENTY-EIGHT ANTEBELLUM HOMES, SOME OF WHICH ARE LISTED ON THE NATIONAL REGISTER OF HISTORIC PLACES, WILL BE IDENTIFIED WITH PLAQUES. A WALKING TOUR & A PARK ARE BEING PLANNED. (LOCAL). RICHARD LILES, PROJECT COORDINATOR; EUFAULA '76 ACTION COMMITTEE; PO BOX 1776; EUFAULA, AL 36027. (#22047). **ARBA GRANTEE.**

APR 1 - 4, '76. ELEVENTH ANNUAL EUFAULA PILGRIMAGE. TOUR. (LOCAL). MRS LYLE WILSON, CHMN; EUFAULA HERITAGE ASSOC; SHORTER MANSION EUFAULA AVE; EUFAULA, AL 36027. (#100568-1).

MAY 28 - 30, '76. ALABAMA FRESHWATER FISHING RODEO. COMPETITION, EXHIBIT AT CHEWALLA MARINA, LAKE EUFAULA. (REGN'L). JEAMS D BRADLEY, EXEC DIR; EUFAULA CHAMBER OF COMMERCE; EUFAULA, AL 36027. (#100732-1).

AUG 27 - 29, '76. EUFAULA LAKE FESTIVAL. EVENTS WILL INCLUDE BOAT RACES, SQUARE DANCING, ARTS & CRAFTS AND MUSIC. AT OLD CREEK TOWN PARK. (ST-WIDE). JAMES D BRADLEY, EXEC DIR; EUFAULA CHAMBER OF COMMERCE; EUFAULA, AL 36027. (#101408-1).

EUTAW

HISTORIC GREENE COUNTY COLORING BOOK - EUTAW, AL. HISTORIC SITES & PLACES IN GREENE COUNTY DEPICTED IN COLORING BOOK FOR CHILDREN. (LOCAL). CAROLYN CAGLE, CHAIRMAN; GREENE COUNTY BICENTENNIAL COMMITTEE; PO BOX 107; EUTAW, AL 35462. (#27356). **ARBA GRANTEE.**

HORIZONS '76 BICENTENNIAL PARK, EUTAW, AL. COMMUNITY PARK FOR CITY & COUNTY RESIDENTS. (LOCAL). CAROLYN CAGLE, CHAIRMAN; GREENE COUNTY BICENTENNIAL COMMITTEE; PO BOX 107; EUTAW, AL 35462. (#27368). **ARBA GRANTEE.**

EVERGREEN

APR 24 - MAY 1, '76. BICENTENNIAL CELEBRATION. SPEECHES BY CONGRESSMAN DICKINSON, BAND CONCERT, ARTS & CRAFTS & FOUNTAINS WILL BE PARTS OF THIS ACTIVITY. AT DOWNTOWN & AIRPORT. (LOCAL). SALTER OVIDA, CHAIRMAN; CONECUN CO BICENTENNIAL COMMISSION; 206 WILLIAMS AVE; EVERGREEN, AL 36401. (#200001-50).

FAIRFIELD

APR 7, '73 - DEC 4, '76. TRADE DAY, A FESTIVE ARTS & CRAFTS EXHIBITION. THE FAIR IS HELD THE FIRST SATURDAY OF EACH MONTH. AT PARK PLAZA, GARY AVE. (LOCAL). GRACE LANN, PROJ MGR; CITY OF FAIRFIELD; PO BOX 437; FAIRFIELD, AL 35064. (#100623-1).

FAIRHOPE

MAR 14 - 21, '76. 24TH ANNUAL ARTS & CRAFTS WEEK. WEEK-LONG FESTIVAL WILL INCLUDE AREA ARTISTS-CRAFTSMEN REPRESENTING VARIETY OF SKILLS; THE DISPLAYS, SALES AND SPECIAL EVENTS WILL BE HELD ALL WEEK LONG. (ST-WIDE). SUE BOONE, SECRETARY; EASTERN SHORE CHAMBER OF COMMERCE; PO BOX 507; FAIRHOPE, AL 36532. (#100964-1).

FLOMATON

COMMUNITY PARK ADDITIONS AND IMPROVEMENTS, AL. CONSTRUCTION OF PERMANENT BRUSH ARBOR, CONSTRUCTION OF ADDITIONAL TENNIS COURTS, PURCHASE OF PLAYGROUND EQUIPMENT, RESTORATION OF OLDEST DWELLING IN COMMUNITY ON PARK GROUNDS. (LOCAL). EUGENE PETTIS, CO-CHAIRPERSON; TRI-CITY BICENTENNIAL COMMITTEE; 501 POPLAR ST; FLOMATON, AL 36441. (#21133).

ORAL HISTORY RESEARCH & LOCAL THEATER, AL. RESEARCH THROUGH ORAL HISTORY TECHNIQUES INTO HISTORY OF FLOMATON; ALSO, THE ORGANIZATION OF A DRAMATICS GROUP FOR COMMUNITY ENRICHMENT. (LOCAL). EUGENE PETTIS, CO-CHAIRPERSON; TRI-CITY BICENTENNIAL COMMITTEE; 501 POPLAR ST; FLOMATON, AL 36441. (#21132).

JULY 3 - 4, '76. COMMUNITY-WIDE 4TH OF JULY CELEBRATION. TIME ON SUNDAY IS 11:00 AM TO 1:00 PM FESTIVAL ACTIVITIES ON SAT AND SUN INCL FORMAL PGM, MUSIC, TOURNAMENTS, ARTS & CRAFTS, COSTUME & BEARD CONTESTS, CONCERTS, PARADE, LITTLE THEATER PGM, DEDICATION OF WAR MEMORIAL. AT LIONS COMMUNITY PARK, MCCURDY ST, ONE BLOCK FROM DOWNTOWN AREA. (LOCAL). EUGENE PETTIS, CHAIRMAN; TRI-CITY BICENTENNIAL COMMITTEE; 501 POPLAR ST; FLOMATON, AL 36441. (#105153-1).

JULY 4, '76. DEDICATION OF MILITARY MONUMENT. CEREMONY TO DEDICATE MONUMENT TO SIDNEY MANNING OF FLOMATON; ALABAMA'S MOST DECORATED SOLDIER, WORLD WAR I MEDAL OF HONOR RECIPIENT; MONUMENT WILL INCLUDE INSCRIPTION OF DEDICATION TO ALL VETERANS. (LOCAL). EUGENE PETTIS, CHMN; TRI-CITY BICENTENNIAL COMMITTEE; 501 POPLAR ST; FLOMATON, AL 36441. (#21134-1).

FLORENCE

BICENTENNIAL COLUMN - FLORENCE, AL. SPECIAL COLUMN IN REGULAR EDITIONS OF STUDENT NEWSPAPER WILL BE PRINTED IN 1975-1976. (LOCAL). MRS DORIS KELSO, DIRECTOR UNIV PUBLICATIONS; UNIV OF NORTH ALABAMA; FLORENCE, AL 35630. (#13620).

BICENTENNIAL EDITION OF 'FLOR-ALA' - FLORENCE, AL. IN HONOR OF THE BICENTENNIAL, A SPECIAL EDITION OF THE STUDENT NEWSPAPER WILL BE PRINTED IN THE SPRING OF 1976. (LOCAL). MRS DORIS KELSO, DIRECTOR UNIV PUBLICATIONS; UNIV OF NORTH ALABAMA; FLORENCE, AL 35630. (#13619).

BICENTENNIAL EDITION OF UNA SUN - FLORENCE, AL. SPECIAL ATTENTION TO BICENTENNIAL IN SPRING ISSUE OF THE ALUMNI MAGAZINE. (REGN'L). MRS DORIS KELSO, DIRECTOR UNIV PUBLICATIONS; UNIV OF NORTH ALABAMA; FLORENCE, AL 35630. (#13621).

BICENTENNIAL GARDEN IN FLORENCE, AL. GARDEN SPOT DESIGNED AND MAINTAINED AS PERMANENT REMINDER OF BICENTENNIAL CELEBRATION. (LOCAL). DAVID BROWN, DIRECTOR OF ALUMNI AFFAIRS; UNIV OF NORTH ALABAMA; FLORENCE, AL 35630. (#13191).

BICENTENNIAL READINGS - FLORENCE, AL. SPECIAL READINGS ON AMERICAN HERITAGE WILL BECOME A COURSE REQUIREMENT. (LOCAL). DR WILLIAM FOSTER, CHAIRMAN; ENGLISH DEPT, UNIV OF NORTH ALABAMA; FLORENCE, AL 35630. (#13622).

FLORENCE — CONTINUED

BICENTENNIAL TOUR - UNIVERSITY OF NORTH ALABAMA. SPRING 1976 TOUR BY SOME STUDENTS AND FACULTY TO WILLIAMSBURG, JAMESTOWN, PHILADELPHIA, ETC. (LOCAL). DR FRANK MCARTHUR, DEAN, ARTS AND SCIENCES; UNIV OF NORTH ALABAMA; FLORENCE, AL 35630. (#13192).

BICENTENNIAL VETERANS MEMORIAL - FLORENCE, AL. COMPLETION OF MEMORIAL TO WAR VETERANS. (LOCAL). MRS G H MANESS, CHAIRMAN; FLORENCE BICENTENNIAL COMMISSION; UNIV OF NORTH ALABAMA; FLORENCE, AL 35210. (#10681). **ARBA GRANTEE.**

BICENTENNIAL YEARBOOK IN FLORENCE, AL. UNIV OF NORTH ALABAMA YEARBOOK WILL BE DIDICATED TO BICENTENNIAL THEMES. (LOCAL). MRS DORIS KELSO, DIRECTOR UNIV PUBLICATIONS; UNIV OF NORTH ALABAMA; FLORENCE, AL 35630. (#13627).

ESSAY CONTEST IN FLORENCE, AL. PRIZES WILL BE AWARDED TO STUDENTS WITH THE BEST HISTORICAL ESSAYS. (LOCAL). DR MILTON BAUGHN, CHAIRMAN; HISTORY DEPT, UNIV OF NORTH ALABAMA; FLORENCE, AL 35630. (#13626).

FILM SERIES - FLORENCE, AL. FILMS ON AMERICAN HERITAGE WILL BE SHOWN TO STUDENTS AND PUBLIC. (LOCAL). DR MILTON BAUGHN, CHAIRMAN; HISTORY DEPT, UNIV OF NORTH ALABAMA; FLORENCE, AL 35630. (#13624).

HISTORIC MARKERS IN FLORENCE, ALABAMA. ERECTION & DEDICATION OF MARKERS AT SITE OF THE HOME OF SUPREME COURT JUSTICE MCKINLEY AND FLORENCE WAGON WORKS. (LOCAL). MRS G H MANESS, CHAIRMAN; FLORENCE BICENTENNIAL COMMISSION; BOX 5206, UNA; FLORENCE, AL 35630. (#5844).

TREE PLANTING IN FLORENCE, ALABAMA. SCHOOLS GARDEN CLUBS WILL SPONSOR A PROJECT TO STUDY APPROPRIATE TREES. TVA ADVISES ON CORRECT PROCEDURE. (LOCAL). MRS G H MANESS, CHAIRMAN; FLORENCE BICENTENNIAL COMMISSION; BOX 5206, UNA; FLORENCE, AL 35630. (#5843).

'1776', MUSICAL PROJECT OF FLORENCE, ALABAMA. '1776'. IT WILL BE PERFORMED EXCLUSIVELY BY LOCAL TALENT. (LOCAL). MRS G H MANESS, CHAIRMAN; FLORENCE BICENTENNIAL COMMISSION; BOX 5206, UNA; FLORENCE, AL 35630. (#5848).

SEPT '75 - MAY '76. AMERICAN ISSUES FORUM. FORUM MEETS LAST MONDAY OF EACH MONTH. AT RM 121, VISUAL ARTS BLDG. (LOCAL). WILDER WATTS, COORD; HISTORY/POLITICAL SCIENCE DEPARTMENTS, UNIV OF NORTH ALABAMA; UNIV OF N ALABAMA; FLORENCE, AL 35630. (#105702-1).

JAN 7 - 8, '76. UNITED STATES ARMED FORCES BICENTENNIAL CARAVAN. CARAVAN IS COMPOSED OF EXHIBIT VANS FOR EACH MILITARY SERVICE. PROJJECT THEME IS 'HISTORY OF THE ARMED FORCES AND THEIR CONTRIBUTION TO THE NATION'. AT K-MART STORE PARKING AREA, 1520 FLORENCE BLVD, FLORENCE. (LOCAL). MAURINE MANESS, CHMN; FLORENCE '76 ACTION COMMISSION; UNIV OF NORTH ALA; FLORENCE, AL 35630. (#1775-379).

FEB 11 - 12, '76. THE WHITE ROOTS OF PEACE: AMERICAN INDIAN HISTORY AND CULTURE. CEREMONY, EXHIBIT. (LOCAL). ROBERT GUILLOT, PRESIDENT; CONVAOCATIONS COMMITTEE, UNIV OF NORTH ALABAMA; FLORENCE, AL 35630. (#200001-21).

FEB 18, '76. BICENTENNIAL PRAYER LUNCHEON. CEREMONY, FESTIVAL AT UNA SUITE, STUDENT UNION BLDG. (LOCAL). ROBERT GUILLOT, PRESIDENT; UNIV OF NORTH ALABAMA; FLORENCE, AL 35630. (#200001-22).

FEB 22, '76. BAND CONCERT. LIVE PERFORMANCE AT NORTON AUDITORIUM, UNA CAMPUS, NORTH PINE ST. (LOCAL). DR JAMES SIMPSON; DEPARTMENT OF MUSIC, UNIVERSITY OF NORTH ALABAMA; FLORENCE, AL 35630. (#200001-20).

FEB 23 - 28, '76. ART CONTEST & EXHIBITION. ART WORKS WILL PROJECT AMERICAN THEMES INTO THE FUTURE. AT COLLIER LIBRARY, STUDENT UNION BLDG & ART GALLERIES. (LOCAL). MORT SMITH; UNIV OF NORTH ALABAMA; FLORENCE, AL 35630. (#13618-1).

FEB 24, '76. CARL SANDBURG'S AMERICA. DRAMATIZATION OF SELECTIONS FROM WORKS OF CARL SANDBURG WILL BE PRESENTED IN AREA SCHOOLS. AT NORTON AUDITORIUM. (LOCAL). ROBERT HOLDER; UNIV OF NORTH ALABAMA; FLORENCE, AL 35630. (#13625-1).

FEB 24, '76. SPEECH ON AMERICAN HERITAGE BY MARGARET WALKER ALEXANDER. SEMINAR AT NORTON AUDITORIUM, UNA CAMPUS, NORTH PINE ST. (LOCAL). DR KENNETH JOHNSON; HISTORY DEPARTMENT, UNIVERSITY OF NORTH ALABAMA; FLORENCE, AL 35630. (#200001-17).

FEB 25, '76. COLONIAL FAIR: ARTS, CRAFTS, MUSIC & GAMES. EXHIBIT, LIVE PERFORMANCE, FAIR AT KILBY SCHOOL, UNA CAMPUS, NORTH PINE ST. (LOCAL). JOHN FINLEY, COORD; KILBY SCHOOL, UNIVERSITY OF NORTH ALABAMA; FLORENCE, AL 35630. (#200001-19).

FEB 25, '76. TWO HUNDRED YEARS IN REVIEW: MILITARY RETREAT CEREMONY. CEREMONY AT IN FRONT OF BIBB GRAVES HALL, UNA CAMPUS. (LOCAL). LTC RONALD MEEKS; RESERVE OFFICERS TRAINING CORPS, UNIVERSITY OF NORTH ALABAMA; FLORENCE, AL 35630. (#200001-16).

FEB 27, '76. FOSTER BROTHERS AND FRIENDS-BLUEGRASS MUSIC FESTIVAL. LIVE PERFORMANCE AT NORTON AUDITORIUM, UNA CAMPUS, NORTH PINE ST. (LOCAL). DR WILLIAM FOSTER; UNA AMERICAN REVOLUTION BICENTENNIAL COMMITTEE; FLORENCE, AL 35630. (#200001-18).

APR 29, '76. ORAL INTERPRETATION PROGRAM. THEATRE PRESENTATION OF LITERATURE OF THE REVOL PERIOD. TERPRETATION CLASS. AT NORTON AUDITORIUM. (LOCAL). MRS EMILY RICHESON; DEPT OF DRAMATIC ARTS & SPEECH, UNIV OF NORTH ALABAMA; FLORENCE, AL 35630. (#13623-1).

FOLEY

JUNE 5 - 6, '76. ANNUAL ARTS & CRAFTS SHOW. EXHIBIT, FESTIVAL AT FOLEY PARK & MAGNOLIA HOTEL. (LOCAL). ELIZABETH SANDERS, CHMN; PERFORMING ARTS ASSOCIATION; PO BOX 295; FOLEY, AL 36535. (#103297-1).

FORT DEPOSIT

JAN 12, '76. SPECIAL BICENTENNIAL CONCERT BY THE MAC FRAMPTON TRIUMVIRATE. AN OUTSTANDING MUSICAL TRIO, FEATURING MAC FRAMAPTON ON PIANO. (LOCAL). HENRY F CRENSHAW, COORD; FORT DEPOSIT ARTS COUNCIL; BOX 280; FORT DEPOSIT, AL 36032. (#103416-31).

APR 10 - 11, '76. 5TH ANNUAL CALICO FORT ARTS AND CRAFTS FAIR. OVER 200 EXHIBITS OF ARTS AND CRAFTS. (LOCAL). MRS HENRY F CRENSHAW, DIR; FORT DEPOSIT ARTS COUNCIL; BOX 280; FORT DEPOSIT, AL 36032. (#103416-230).

FORT PAYNE

FORT PAYNE OPERA HOUSE - AL. THE FORT PAYNE OPERA HOUSE WILL BE RENOVATED AND MURALS WILL BE PAINTED. (LOCAL). DEAN FRITZ, CHAIRMAN; FT PAYNE BICENTENNIAL COMMITTEE; RT 7, SCENIC DR; FT PAYNE, AL 35967. (#27686). **ARBA GRANTEE.**

SEPT 7, '75. MANITOU ARTS AND CRAFTS SHOW. EXHIBIT AT MANITOU CAVE GROUNDS, ONE MILE OFF I-59. (LOCAL). MRS L H FERGUSON, CHWMN; MARJORIES GIFTS & ANTIQUES; 603 GAULT AVE N; FORT PAYNE, AL 35967. (#100718-1).

MAY 15 - 16, '76. PILGRIMAGE TOUR OF HISTORIC PLACES. MUSIC FROM A RESTORED THEATRE PIPE ORGAN HIGHLIGHTS THE ACTIVITIES AT FORT PAYNE ALABAMA. AT FORT PAYNE OPERA HOUSE. (LOCAL). MRS CHARLES ISBELL, COORD; LANDMARKS OF DEKALB COUNTY; ROUTE 2; VALLEY HEAD, AL 35989. (#103416-270).

FT MCCLELLAN

MUSEUM CONSTRUCTION - FT MCCLELLAN, AL. THE EDITH NOURSE ROGERS MUSEUM IS BEING CONSTRUCTED FOR THE WOMEN'S ARMY CORPS. (LOCAL). MAJOR FRANCES GREEN, DIRECTOR; WAC FOUNDATION; PO BOX 5339; FT MCCLELLAN, AL 36201. (#25093).

MAY 14, '76 - MAY 14, '77. WOMEN'S ARMY CORPS MUSEUM. EXHIBITION OF WOMEN'S UNIFORMS & COSTUMES OVER THE YEARS; MEMORABILIA OF 1ST LADY GENERAL, BRIG GEN HOISINGTON; ASIAN DOLLS; PHOTOGRAPHIC EXHIBITS OF WAC HISTORICAL EVENTS. AT WAC MUSEUM. (REGN'L). MAJOR FRANCES GREEN, USA; WAC FOUNDATION, WAC CENTER & SCHOOL; PO BOX 5339; FT MCCLELLAN, AL 36201. (#107873-1).

FT MITCHELL

LOG CABIN RESTORATION PROJECT, FT MITCHELL, AL. A LOG CABIN BUILT BY ALABAMA'S FIRST CONGRESSMAN WILL BE MOVED & RESTORED ON THE SITE OF HIS ORIGINAL HOME AT HISTORIC FT MITCHELL PARK. (LOCAL). MRS LENORA C SMITH, CHAIRMAN; RUSSELL COUNTY BICENTENNIAL COMMITTEE; PO BOX 1776; PHENIX CITY, AL 36867. (#23547). **ARBA GRANTEE.**

FT RUCKER

JUNE 12, '76. CEREMONY SHOWING HISTORY OF U S & STATE FLAGS. LIVE PERFORMANCE, CEREMONY AT AVIATION CENTER PARADE FIELD. (LOCAL). HERBERT C STRICKLAND; U S ARMY AVIATION CENTER; FT RUCKER, AL 36362. (#200001-87).

GADSDEN

APR 1 - MAY 15, '75. HAPPY BIRTHDAY AMERICA CONTEST. COMPETITION. (LOCAL). MARY TEAT, SECRETARY; HORIZON COMMITTEE, SPIRIT OF '76 BICENTENNIAL; PO BOX 267; GADSDEN, AL 35902. (#200001-23).

APR 14, '75. THE DEDICATION OF THE NICHOLS LIBRARY. CEREMONY AT NICHOLS MEMORIAL LIBRARY, CABOT AVE. (LOCAL). JOE BARNES, COORDINATOR; HISTORICAL SOCIETY; ROUTE 11; GADSDEN, AL 35903. (#200001-24).

JUNE 14 - 15, '75. CHEROKEE INDIAN FESTIVAL. FESTIVAL, EXHIBIT AT NOCCALULA PARK. (LOCAL). NAN CALLAN, COORDINATOR; SPIRIT OF '76 BICENTENNIAL COMMISSION; 118 S 8TH ST; GADSDEN, AL 35901. (#200001-25).

AUG 2, '75. 'THIS IS MY COUNTRY' - PAGEANT. LIVE PERFORMANCE AT WALLACE HALL, GADSDEN STATE JUNIOR COLLEGE. (LOCAL). GLENDA BYARS, DIRECTOR; SPIRIT OF '76 BICENTENNIAL COMMISSION; GADSDEN, AL 35904. (#200001-26).

AUG 30 - 31, '75. FOLK FESTIVAL. FOLK SINGING & DANCING, LIVE EXHIBIT OF PIONEER DAYS. AT NOCCALULA PARK. (REGN'L). NAN CALLAN, COORD; SPIRIT OF '76 BICENTENNIAL COMMISSION; 118 S 8TH ST; GADSDEN, AL 35901. (#200001-27).

SEPT 20, '75. SACRED HARP SINGING. LIVE PERFORMANCE AT KIWANIS PAVILION - NOCCALULA PARK. (REGN'L). LOUIS WALL, COORD; SPIRIT OF '76 BICENTENNIAL COMMISSION; PO BOX 267; GADSDEN, AL 35902. (#200001-28).

NOV 22, '75. PATRIOTS' DAY BANQUET. FESTIVAL AT DOWNTOWN MOTOR INN BALL ROOM. (LOCAL). JOE BARNES, COORD; HERITAGE COMMITTEE & GADSDEN BICENTENNIAL COMMISSION; BROAD ST; GADSDEN, AL 35902. (#200001-29).

DEC 1, '75. A PROGRAM OF FILMS. EXHIBIT AT WALLACE HALL, GADSDEN STATE JR COLLEGE. (LOCAL). MARY TEAT, SECRETARY; SPIRIT OF '76 BICENTENNIAL COMMISSION; PO BOX 267; GADSDEN, AL 35902. (#200001-30).

JAN 13 - 15, '76. UNITED STATES ARMED FORCES BICENTENNIAL CARAVAN. CARAVAN IS COMPOSED OF EXHIBIT VANS FOR EACH MILITARY SERVICE. PROJECT THEME IS 'HISTORY OF THE ARMED FORCES AND THEIR CONTRIBUTIONS TO THE NATION'. (LOCAL). MS MARY TEAT, CHMN; SPIRIT OF '76 BICENTENNIAL COMMITTEE; PO BOX 267; GADSDEN, AL 35902. (#1775-381).

FEB 12, '76. OUR AMERICAN HERITAGE. LIVE PERFORMANCE AT WALLACE HALL - GADSDEN STATE JR COLLEGE. (LOCAL). JOE SMITH, PROJ DIR; GOODYEAR TIRE & RUBBER COMPANY; 464 GOODYEAR AVE; GADSDEN, AL 35903. (#104292-3).

MAR 4 - 6, '76. LONG MAY IT WAVE. LIVE PERFORMANCE AT WALLACE HALL - GADSDEN STATE JR COLLEGE. (LOCAL). JOHN AYCOCK, DIRECTOR; GADSDEN METRO CHAMBER OF COMMERCE; PO BOX 185; GADSDEN, AL 35902. (#104292-5).

APR 15, '76. HISTORICAL PARADE. PARADE AT BROAD ST. (LOCAL). DR WILLENE PERKINS, DIR; SPIRIT OF '76 BICENTENNIAL COMMISSION; 3704 MICHAEL ANN AVE; GADSDEN, AL 35904. (#104292-4).

JUNE 27, '76. VETERANS MEMORIAL - HALL OF HEROES. CEREMONY AT NICHOLS MEMORIAL LIBRARY - CABOT AVE. (LOCAL). JOE BARNES, DIRECTOR; HISTORICAL SOCIETY & GENEALOGICAL SOCIETY; CENTRAL BANK - BROAD ST; GADSDEN, AL 35901. (#104292-2).

JULY 1 - 3, '76. 'LET FREEDOM RING' - BICENTENNIAL SPECTACULAR W/FIREWORKS. FESTIVAL AT HIGH SCHOOL STADIUM. (LOCAL). HUGH W ELLIS, CHMN; GADSDEN BICENTENNIAL COMMISSION; PO BOX 267; GADSDEN, AL 35902. (#27228-1).

JULY 4, '76. LIGHT AND SOUND PAGEANT. LIVE PERFORMANCE. (LOCAL). DR WILLENE PERKINS, DIR; FESTIVAL COMMITTEE - SPIRIT OF '76 BICENTENNIAL COMMISSION; 3704 MICHAEL ANN AVE; GADSDEN, AL 35904. (#104292-1).

GAYLESVILLE

BICENTENNIAL BELLE. COMPETITION. (LOCAL). DEBORAH TUCKER, CHMN; TOWN OF GAYLESVILLE BICENTENNIAL COMMITTEE; GAYLESVILLE, AL 35973. (#200001-52).

PARK DEVELOPMENT - GAYLESVILLE, AL. PICNIC TABLES AT TRIANGLE OF INTERSECTION. ROCK GARDEN AND FLOWERS PLANTED. REMAINING BUILDING OF OLD GAYLESVILLE ACADEMY RENOVATED. (LOCAL). HON KATHRYN BLACK, MAYOR; TOWN OF GAYLESVILLE; GAYLESVILLE, AL 35973. (#28594).

GILBERTOWN

FIRST OILWELL SITE, GILBERTOWN, AL. MARKING AND BEAUTIFYING THE SITE OF THE 1ST OIL WELL IN ALABAMA AT GILBERTOWN. (ST-WIDE). J TRICE EDGAR, COORDINATOR; BICENTENNIAL COMMISSION OF CHOCTAW COUNTY; GILBERTOWN, AL 36908. (#24065). **ARBA GRANTEE.**

GORDO

CPR DEMONSTRATION - GORDO, AL. A DEMONSTRATION OF EMERGENCY CARDIO-PULMONARY RESUSCITATION WILL BE GIVEN TO THE COMMUNITY. (LOCAL). B E SMITHERMAN, PRESIDENT; FAIRVIEW BICENTENNIAL COMMUNITY CLUB; RT 5, BOX 293; GORDO, AL 35466. (#29324).

'FAIRVIEW, A TALENTED COMMUNITY'. DIFFERENT AGE GROUPS WILL DEMONSTRATE THEIR TALENTS IN A COMPETITION. TROPHIES WILL BE AWARDED FOR TOP TWO CONTESTANTS IN BOTH GROUPS. (LOCAL). BARRY E SMITHERMAN, CHMN; FAIRVIEW BICENTENNIAL COMMITTEE; RT 5, BOX 293; GORDA, AL 35466. (#200001-45).

GREENVILLE

BEAUTIFICATION OF CITY AREAS - GREENVILLE, AL. BEAUTIFY & RESTORE PARKS, PIONEER CEMETERY & BELLS IN CHURCHES. BEAUTIFY BAPTIST HILL & METHODIST HILL AREAS. ALSO ORAL HISTORY PROGRAMS BY STUDENTS. (LOCAL). ROBERT S KIMBROUGH, HORIZONS COMMITTEE CHAIRMAN; GREENVILLE BICENTENNIAL COMMISSION; 110 CEDAR ST, PO BOX 147; GREENVILLE, AL 36037. (#13779). **ARBA GRANTEE.**

IDENTIFYING BARTRAM TRAIL IN GREENVILLE, AL. MARKING & IDENTIFYING BARTRAM TRAIL THROUGH GREENVILLE AREA AND TO OTHER PARTS OF BUTLER COUNTY, PLACE COMMEMORATE MARKERS AT THE BEGINNING & END OF TRAIL AND MAKE HIKING TRAIL ON ROUTE. (LOCAL). MRS W Z MIDDLETON, CHAIRPERSON, HERITAGE COMMITTEE; GREENVILLE BICENTENNIAL COMMISSION; 110 CEDAR ST, PO BOX 147; GREENVILLE, AL 36037. (#13780). **ARBA GRANTEE.**

JULY 4TH CELEBRATION FOR 1976 - GREENVILLE, AL. CELEBRATION OF OLD FASHIONED PATRIOTISM. (LOCAL). MRS A E GAMBLE, CHAIRPERSON; GREENVILLE BICENTENNIAL COMMISSION FESTIVAL COMMITTEE; 401 COLLEGE ST; GREENVILLE, AL 36037. (#20801). **ARBA GRANTEE.**

GREENVILLE — CONTINUED

AN OLD FASHIONED FAIR - GREENVILLE, AL. AN OLD FASHIONED FAIR WITH FOLK ARTS, EXHIBITS, AN EXPOSITION, FOOD AND ENTERTAINMENT. (LOCAL). MRS A E GAMBLE, JR, CHAIRPERSON; GREENVILLE BICENTENNIAL COMMISSION FESTIVAL COMMITTEE; 401 COLLEGE ST; GREENVILLE, AL 36037. (#20800). **ARBA GRANTEE.**

REMODELING OF RAILROAD STATION, AL. REPAIRING OF RAILROAD DEPOT TO BE USED AS A MUSEUM FOR THE PRESERVATION OF LOCAL AND STATE MEMORABILIA. (LOCAL). MS W Z MIDDLETON, CHAIRPERSON; GREENVILLE BICENTENNIAL COMMISSION, HERITAGE COMMITTEE; PO BOX 158; GREENVILLE, AL 36037. (#23730). **ARBA GRANTEE.**

SHERLING LAKE AREA BEAUTIFICATION, GREENVILLE, AL. WILD PLANTS THAT HAVE BEEN IDENTIFIED BY NATURALIST WILLIAM BARTRAM AND VARIETIES OF CAMELLIA & AZALEAS WILL BE PLANTED ALONG A NATURE TRAIL. (LOCAL). ROBERT S KIMBROUGH, CHAIRMAN HORIZONS COMMITTEE; GREENVILLE BICENTENNIAL COMMISSION; 110 CEDAR ST, PO BOX 147; GREENVILLE, AL 36037. (#13781).

SEPT 13 - 18, '75. OLD FASHIONED FAIR. FAIR, RADIO/TV AT CITY OF GREENVILLE PARKING LOT HERBERT STREET ENTRANCE. (LOCAL). MRS A E GAMBLE JR, CHMN; GREENVILLE BICENTENNIAL COMMISSION FESTIVAL COMMITTEE; 401 COLLEGE ST; GREENVILLE, AL 36037. (#20800-1).

JULY 3 - 4, '76. JULY 4, 1976 CELEBRATION. FESTIVAL, PARADE AT PARADE ON COMMERCE STREET ON JULY 3, 1975; BATTLE ENACTMENT STADIUM. (LOCAL). MRS A E GAMBLE, CHMN; GREENVILLE BICENTENNIAL COMMISSION FESTIVAL COMMITTEE; 401 COLLEGE ST; GREENVILLE, AL 36037. (#20801-1).

JULY 3 - 5, '76. AMERICAN PAGEANTRY FESTIVAL. FESTIVITIES WILL INCLUDE: PARADES, BELL RINGING, GAMES, FIREWORKS, STREET BALL, PATRIOTIC ORATIONS, COSTUMED PAGEANT AND BATTLE REENACTMENTS, CHURCH CELEBRATION. ENACTMENTS, CHURCH CELEBRATION. (LOCAL). CECIL MOODY; GREENVILLE BICENTENNIAL COMMISSION; GREENVILLE HIGH SCHOOL; GREENVILLE, AL 36037. (#101430-1).

JULY 4, '77. RAILROAD STATION MUSEUM OPENS. RESTORED RAILROAD DEPOT TO BE USED AS MUSEUM TO HOUSE EXHIBIT OF LOCAL AND STATE MEMORABILIA. (LOCAL). MS W Z MIDDLETON, CHMN; GREENVILLE BICENTENNIAL COMMISSION, HERITAGE COMMITTEE; PO BOX 158; GREENVILLE, AL 36037. (#23730-1).

GROVE HILL

ARTS & CRAFTS FAIR PROJ, GROVE HILL, AL. ESTABLISHING OF ARTS & CRAFTS FAIR IN HONOR OF THE BICENTENNIAL. (LOCAL). FRED W KILGORE JR, DIRECTOR; TOWN OF GROVE HILL & PLANNING COMMISSION; PO BOX 896; GROVE HILL, AL 36451. (#21668). **ARBA GRANTEE.**

PARK DEVELOPMENT - GROVE HILL, AL. RESTROOMS WILL BE CONSTRUCTED IN THE PUBLIC PARK. (LOCAL). FRED W KILGORE, JR, CHAIRMAN; PUBLIC PARK CONVENIENCE CENTER; PO BOX 896; GROVE HILL, AL 36451. (#21667). **ARBA GRANTEE.**

APR 23, '76. 'BATTLE OF MAUVILLA' BOY SCOUT PAGEANT. A PAGEANT ABOUT A BATTLE THAT TOOK PLACE NEAR THIS SITE IN 1574, AS TOLD THROUGH THE WRITINGS OF FOUR TRAVELERS WITH HERNANDO DE SOTO. AT MAUBILA SCOUT RESERVATION. (LOCAL). LEO CONRAD, CONCLAVE ADVR; WOA CHOLENA LODGE, ORDER OF THE ARROW, BOY SCOUTS OF AMERICA; 2587 GOVERNMENT BLVD; MOBILE, AL 36606. (#105785-1).

MAY 1, '76. ARTS & CRAFTS. FAIR AT CITY PARK. (LOCAL). FRED W KILGORE JR, DIR; TOWN OF GROVE HILL & PLANNING COMMISSION; PO BOX 896; GROVE HILL, AL 36451. (#21668-1).

GULF SHORES

BICENTENNIAL BEAUTIFICATION - GULF SHORES, AL. TREES WILL BE PLANTED; A CITY BICENTENNIAL FLAG WILL BE FLOWN AND BICENTENNIAL BELLE CLUBS WILL BE FORMED. (LOCAL). LIZ DU MONT, CHAIRPERSON; GULF SHORES WOMAN'S CLUB; ROUTE BOX 100D; GULF SHORES, AL 36542. (#21800).

OCT 2 - 5, '75. 5TH ANNUAL ALABAMA SHRIMP FESTIVAL. FESTIVAL AT PUBLIC BEACH AREA. (LOCAL). WALTER J MERNIK, PROJ DIR; GULF SHORES TOURIST ASSOC; PO BOX 457; GULF SHORES, AL 36542. (#100716-1).

APR 7, '76. BALDWIN TEA PARTY. TEA PARTY TO RAISE FUNDS FOR BALDWIN COUNTY BICENTENNIAL COMMISSION PAGEANT AND GULF SHORES AREA BICENT COMMITTEE COMMEMORATIVE PROJECT. (LOCAL). LIZ DU MONT, CHPSN; GULF SHORES WOMEN'S CLUB; STAR RT BOX 100D; GULF SHORES, AL 36542. (#21800-1).

APR 23 - 25, '76. ANNUAL ALABAMA INVITATIONAL ANTIQUE AUTO SHOW AND SPRING FESTIVAL. THE AUTO SHOW INCLUDES SALES OF AUTO PARTS AND A PARADE. (LOCAL). THOMAS T MCDONALD, DIR; GULF SHORES TOURIST ASSOC; GULF SHORES, AL 36542. (#103416-226).

OCT 8 - 10, '76. 6TH ANNUAL ALABAMA SHRIMP FESTIVAL. FESTIVAL AT PLEASURE ISLE. (ST-WIDE). TOMMIE WERNETH, COORD; GULF SHORES TOURIST ASSOC; PO DRAWER 457; GULF SHORES, AL 35452. (#103416-632).

GUNTERSVILLE

BICENTENNIAL PROJECTS - GUNTERSVILLE, ALABAMA. BRONZE MARKER OF JOHN GUNTER, CREATED HERITAGE PARK, RESTORED 1838 LOG CABIN & MOVED TO PARK, BRONZE BUST OF JOHN WYETH AT CITY HALL, MEMORIAL FOR REVOL WAR, CONFED & UNION VETERANS FOR COURTHOUSE, ETC. (LOCAL). FRANK MCLAUGHLIN, CHAIRMAN; GUNTERSVILLE BICENTENNIAL COMMITTEE; 341 GUNTER; GUNTERSVILLE, AL 35976. (#29925).

'CULBERT CABIN' PROJECT OF GUNTERSVILLE, AL. THE 'CULBERT CABIN', ERECTED ABOUT 1830, HAS BEEN ACQUIRED BY DONATION OF THE CULBERTS' AND MOVED TO HERITAGE PARK. IT IS NOW BEING RESTORED TO ITS ORIGINAL CONDITION. (LOCAL). FRANK MCLAUGHLIN, CHMN; GUNTERSVILLE BICENTENNIAL COMMITTEE; 341 GUNTER AVE; GUNTERSVILLE, AL 35976. (#22099).

EDUCATION EXHIBITS PROJ OF GUNTERSVILLE, ALABAMA. MULTIPLE EXHIBITS IN THE COURTHOUSE SQUARE ON ART, MUSIC, DRAMA, HANDMADE ITEMS, CRAFTS & HISTORY. (LOCAL). FRANK MCLAUGHLIN, CHAIRMAN; GUNTERSVILLE BICENTENNIAL COMMITTE; 341 GUNTER; GUNTERSVILLE, AL 35976. (#4776).

HERITAGE PARK MUSEUM - GUNTERSVILLE, AL. PROJECT TO CREATE A MUSEUM IN HERITAGE PARK FOR SAFEGUARDING AND SHOWING OF HISTORIC OBJECTS AND DOCUMENTS. (LOCAL). FRANK MCLAUGHLIN, CHAIRMAN; GUNTERSVILLE BICENTENNIAL COMMITTEE; 341 GUNTER AVE; GUNTERSVILLE, AL 35976. (#4773).

HERITAGE '76 - GUNTERSVILLE, AL. LOCAL HISTORICAL FIGURES WILL BE RECOGNIZED THROUGH PLAQUES & BUSTS. (LOCAL). FRANK MCLAUGHLIN, CHAIRMAN; GUNTERSVILLE BICENTENNIAL COMMITTEE; 341 GUNTER AVE; GUNTERSVILLE, AL 35976. (#25055). **ARBA GRANTEE.**

MEMORIAL MARKERS & PLAQUES - GUNTERSVILLE, AL. MEMORIAL MARKERS, PLAQUES & A BRONZE BUST PLACED IN AND AROUND GUNTERSVILLE TO REMIND HER CITIZENS OF: JOHN GUNTER, DR WYETH, THE CONFEDERATE HERITAGE, AND ANDREW JACKSON. (LOCAL). FRANK MCLAUGHLIN, CHAIRMAN; GUNTERSVILLE BICENTENNIAL COMMITTEE; 341 GUNTER AVE; GUNTERSVILLE, AL 35976. (#22273).

PUBLICITY CAMPAIGN FOR BICENT-GUNTERSVILLE, ALA. SALE OF BICENTENNIAL CALENDARS & STICKERS. OFFICIAL TOWN BICENTENNIAL STATIONERY WITH OFFICIAL LOGO. (LOCAL). FRANK MCLAUGHLIN, CHAIRMAN; GUNTERSVILLE BICENTENNIAL COMMITTEE; 341 GUNTERSVILLE; GUNTERSVILLE, AL 35976. (#4149).

SPIRIT OF 76 MUSIC DRAMA - GUNTERSVILLE, ALABAMA. SPIRIT OF 76 -WHOLE BACK STAGE LOCAL TALENT, FOLK DANCING & CHORAL GROUPS. TO BE GIVEN IN THE COURTHOUSE SQUARE. (LOCAL). FRANK MCLAUGHLIN, CHAIRMAN; GUNTERSVILLE BICENTENNIAL COMMITTEE; 341 GUNTER; GUNTERSVILLE, AL 35976. (#4775).

JAN 3, '76. SING AMERICA - TRIBUTE TO 200 YEARS OF AMERICAN MUSIC. LIVE PERFORMANCE. (LOCAL). ELAINE BOGGS, PROJ DIR; BICENTENNIAL COMMITTEE AND WHOLE BACKSTAGE; 301 BLOUNT ST; GUNTERSVILLE, AL 35976. (#103416-29).

JUNE 28 - JULY 4, '76. BICENTENNIAL WEEK. STREET DANCES, FIREWORKS DISPLAY, PARADE, BAND CONCERT AND TOWN BARBEQUE. DURING WEEK, THE PLAY 'SPIRIT OF 1776' WILL BE PRESENTED BY GUNTERSVILLE WHOLE BACKSTAGE GROUP. 3 SHOWINGS PLANNED AT GUNTERSVILLE HIGH AUDITORIUM. (LOCAL). FRANK MCLAUGHLIN; GUNTERSVILLE BICENTENNIAL COMMITTEE; 341 GUNTER AVE; GUNTERSVILLE, AL 35976. (#3911-501).

HARTFORD

BEAUTIFICATION OF CITY SQUARE, HARTFORD, AL. ADD NECESSARY SHRUBS AND PLANTS TO COMPLETE LANDSCAPING OF CITY SQUARE. RECONDITION AND REFURBISH WATER FOUNTAIN AND SURROUNDING AREA. RELOCATE LIGHTING SYSTEM. ADD PARK BENCHES. (LOCAL). JAMES S RADFORD, CHAIRPERSON; HARTFORD BICENTENNIAL COMMITTEE; 304 CAROL ST; HARTFORD, AL 36344. (#21824). **ARBA GRANTEE.**

BICENTENNIAL RECREATION PARK, HARTFORD, AL. CONSTRUCT CONCESSION STAND AND REST ROOMS; UPGRADE LIGHTING ON PLAYING FIELDS; ADD BLEACHERS TO ACCOMODATE SPECTATORS; AND CONSTRUCT HARD SURFACE TENNIS COURT AREA. (LOCAL). JAMES S RADFORD, CHAIRPERSON; HARTFORD BICENTENNIAL COMMITTEE; 304 CAROL ST; HARTFORD, AL 36344. (#21887). **ARBA GRANTEE.**

CITY LIBRARY ADDITION, HARTFORD, AL. UPDATE AND ADD BOOKS ON HISTORY OF AREA TO CITY LIBRARY. (LOCAL). JAMES S RADFORD, CHAIRMAN; HARTFORD BICENTENNIAL COMMITTEE; 304 CAROL ST; HARTFORD, AL 36344. (#21669).

HEADLAND

BICENTENNIAL RECREATION PARK FOR HEADLANDS, AL. 14 ACRES OF LAND WITH 3 SOFTBALL FIELDS, 4 TENNIS COURTS, PLAYGROUND MULTIPURPOSE COURT, CONCESSIONS, RESTROOMS, FENCED AND LIGHTED, ALSO PICNIC AREAS & RECONSTRUCTED LOG CABIN. (LOCAL). SANDRA PARSONS; WIREGRASS 76 ACTION COMMISSION?; HEADLAND; AL, AL 36345. (#2621).

MUSEUM OF OLD LOG HOUSE IN HEADLAND, ALABAMA. MOVE OLD LOG HOUSE TO NEW CITY PARK. TO HOUSE BITS OF AMERICAN HISTORY. ALSO PLANT LIBERTY TREES. (LOCAL). BART FORD, CHAIRMAN; WIREGRASS '76 BICENTENNIAL COMMISSION; PO BOX 36; HEADLAND, AL 36345. (#2622). **(??).**

HEMBRICK HOL

MAY 5, '76. 'THE SMOKY MOUNTAIN QUEEN' ARRIVES IN HEMBRICK HOLLOW. THE 'SMOKY MOUNTAIN QUEEN' IS A BOAT SIMILAR TO THOSE USED BY PIONEERS; IT WILL CARRY CARGO TYPICAL OF THAT ERA. (LOCAL). JOHN B WATERS, JR, DIR; SEVIER COUNTY BICENTENNIAL COMMITTEE; PROFESSIONAL BLDG; SEVIERVILLE, TN 37862. (#102425-11).

HOBSON CITY

FILM DOCUMENTARY - HOBSON CITY, AL. A FILM DOCUMENTARY ON HOBSON CITY TO CREATE A SENSE OF PRIDE IN LOCAL CITIZENS; EMPHASIZES IMPORTANCE OF HOBSON CITY AS A PART OF THE AMERICAN CULTURE. (LOCAL). ELBERT JENKINS, CHAIRMAN; HOBSON CITY BICENTENNIAL COMMITTEE; 21 PARK AVE; HOBSON CITY, AL 36201. (#20685).

HOBSON CITY CEMETERY RESTORATION PROJECT - AL. THE HOBSON CITY CEMETERY, A BLACK BURIAL GROUND, IS BEING RESTORED. GRAVE SITES WILL BE CLEANED AND THE GROUNDS WILL BE LANDSCAPED. A CEREMONY WILL BE HELD UPON COMPLETION OF THIS PROJECT. (LOCAL). ELBERT JENKINS, CHAIRMAN; HOBSON CITY BICENTENNIAL COMMITTEE; 21 PARK AVE; HOBSON CITY, AL 36201. (#21670). **ARBA GRANTEE.**

HOBSON, ALABAMA TO BUILD MINI-PARKS. AT LEAST 2 MINI-PARKS TO BE BUILT FOR COMMUNITY USE. (LOCAL). ELBERT JENKINS, CITY PLANNER; HOBSON CITY BICENT COMMITTEE; 21 PARK AVE; HOBSON, AL 36201. (#9383).

RESTORATION OF VETERANS, HOBSON, AL. HOBSON CITY ERECT MONUMENT ENTRANCE. (LOCAL). ELBERT JENKINS, PROJ CHMN; TOWN OF HOBSON CITY BICENTENNIAL COMMITTEE; 21 PARK AVE; ANNISTON, AL 36201. (#21671). **ARBA GRANTEE.**

TREE PLANTING CEREMONY IN HOBSON, ALABAMA. THREE TREES TO BE PLANTED IN MEMORY OF 75 YEARS EXISTENCE OF HOBSON CITY; EACH TREE REPRESENTS 25 YRS IN HONOR OF HOBSON CITY BEING DECLARED A NATIONAL BICENTENNIAL COMMUNITY. (LOCAL). ELBERT JENKINS, CITY PLANNER; HOBSON BICENT COMMITTEE; 21 PARK AVE; HOBSON, AL 36201. (#9382).

NOV 6, '75. LECTURE & BENEFIT PERFORMANCE BY JAMES BROWN. LIVE PERFORMANCE. (LOCAL). ELBERT JENKINS, COORD; HOBSON CITY BICENTENNIAL COMMITTEE; 21 PARK AVE; HOBSON CITY, AL 36201. (#200001-41).

FEB 24, '76. HANK AARON DAY. HANK AARON VISITED THE SCHOOLS & SPOKE TO STUDENTS ABOUT THE U S & THE IMPORTANCE OF CONTINUING THEIR EDUCATION. (LOCAL). ELBERT JENKINS, COORD; COMMUNITY BICENTENNIAL ORGANIZATIONS; 21 PARK AVE; HOBSON CITY, AL 36201. (#200001-39).

APR 18, '76. MEMORIAL CEREMONY TO BLACK VETERANS AT EASTER SUNRISE SERVICE. MEMORIAL PLAQUES WILL BE PLACED ON THE GRAVES OF BLACK VETERANS OF ALL WARS. AT HOBSON CITY CEMETERY (SOUTHEASTERN SECTION OF THE CITY). (LOCAL). ELBERT JENKINS, CHMN; HOBSON CITY BICENTENNIAL COMMITTEE; 21 PARK AVE; HOBSON CITY, AL 36201. (#21670-1).

HOMEWOOD

PARK RESTORATION - HOMEWOOD, AL. THE HOMEWOOD PARK WILL BE RESTORED TO ITS ORIGINAL CONDITION. (LOCAL). DR GEORGE FRENCH, CHAIRMAN; HOMEWOOD BICENTENNIAL COMMISSION; PO BOX 6066; HOMEWOOD, AL 35209. (#29113).

HUNTSVILLE

BICENTENNIAL SCHOLARSHIP - HUNTSVILLE, AL. AWARDED TO JUNIOR STUDENT IN AMERICAN STUDIES. (LOCAL). CHARLES HIGGINS, ASST TO EXTERNAL AFFAIRS PRES; UNIV OF ALABAMA IN HUNTSVILLE BICENTENNIAL COMMISSION; PO BOX 1247; HUNTSVILLE, AL 35807. (#16026).

BICENTENNIAL SYMBOL FLAGS. BICENTENNIAL FLAG; BICENTENNIAL LICENSE NO 76-19-0594. (NAT'L). EDD CANTRELL, PROJ DIRECTOR; CHICAGO FLAG AND DECORATING COMPANY; 2410 HOLMES AVE; HUNTSVILLE, AL 35805. (#17828).

CAMPUS BEAUTIFICATION - UNIV OF ALABAMA. TREES WILL BE PLANTED AND A PLAQUE & FLAG POLE WILL BE ADDED ON THE CAMPUS. (LOCAL). CHARLES HIGGINS, ASST TO EXTERNAL AFFAIRS PRES; UNIV OF ALABAMA IN HUNTSVILLE BICENTENNIAL COMMISSION; PO BOX 1247; HUNTSVILLE, AL 35807. (#16030). **ARBA GRANTEE.**

ESTABLISHMENT OF SLIDE LIBRARY, HUNTSVILLE, AL. SLIDES ON AMERICAN ART AND HISTORY. (LOCAL). PHILIP BOUCHER, CHAIRMAN; UNIV OF ALABAMA IN HUNTSVILLE BICENTENNIAL COMMISSION; PO BOX 1247; HUNTSVILLE, AL 35807. (#16028).

GALILEO GALILEI, ORATORIO IN HUNTSVILLE, ALABAMA. MUSICAL COMPOSITION FOR MIXED CHORUS, ORCHESTRA AND SEVEN SOLOISTS, SIXTY MINUES DURATION, BASED ON THE LIFE OF GALILEI, FOR THE INAUGURAL CONCERT OF THE VON BRAUN CIVIC CENTER. (NAT'L). DR MARX PALES, CONDUCTOR; HUNTSVILLE SYMPHONY ORCHESTRA; 1015 TASCOSA DR SE; HUNTSVILLE, AL 35802. (#6601).

HUNTSVILLE RECONSTRUCTS - HUNTSVILLE, AL. AN EXHIBIT DEPICTING THE HISTORY, ART AND CULTURE OF HUNTSVILLE. (LOCAL). THOMAS A BOWLES, III, DIRECTOR; HUNTSVILLE MUSEUM OF ART; 700 MONROE ST; HUNTSVILLE, AL 35801. (#20500). **ARBA GRANTEE.**

HUNTSVILLE — CONTINUED

HUNTSVILLE, AL, 4TH OF JULY CELEBRATION. THE 4TH OF JULY FESTIVAL AND PARADE WILL BE HELD AT MILTON FRANK STADIUM. (LOCAL). STEVEN B ALEXANDER, CHAIRMAN; HUNTSVILLE-MADISON CO BICENTENNIAL COMMISSION; 320 PAWNEE TRAIL SE; HUNTSVILLE, AL 35803. (#27284). **ARBA GRANTEE.**

MEDICAL SCHOOL DISPLAY - UNIV OF ALABAMA. PAST AND PRESENT MEDICAL LITERATURE AND TECHNOLOGY. (LOCAL). PHILIP BOUCHER, CHAIRMAN; UNIV OF ALABAMA IN HUNTSVILLE BICENTENNIAL COMMISSION; PO BOX 1247; HUNTSVILLE, AL 35807. (#16031).

PEOPLE BEAUTIFICATION PROJ, HUNTSVILLE, AL. WEIGH-IN PROGRAM TO RAISE CONSCIOUSNESS ON THE NEED TO CONSERVE RESOURCES. (LOCAL). CHARLES HIGGINS, ASST TO EXTERNAL AFFAIRS PRES; UNIV OF ALABAMA IN HUNTSVILLE BICENTENNIAL COMMISSION; PO BOX 1247; HUNTSVILLE, AL 35807. (#16025).

PUBLIC POLICY AND QUALITY OF LIFE, INTERDISCIPLINARY. CONFERENCE AT HUMANITIES BUILDING AUDITORIUM. (LOCAL). WILLIAM MUNSON, PROJ CHMN; UNIV OF ALABAMA IN HUNTSVILLE BICENTENNIAL COMMISSION; PO BOX 1047; HUNTSVILLE, AL 35807. (#102678-3).

PUBLICATION OF UNIV OF ALABAMA HIST, HUNTSVILLE. DEVELOPMENT OF THIS UNIVERSITY WILL BE CHRONICLED AND PUBLISHED. (LOCAL). PHILIP BOUCHER, CHAIRMAN; UNIV OF ALABAMA IN HUNTSVILLE BICENTENNIAL COMMISSION; PO BOX 1247; HUNTSVILLE, AL 35807. (#16027).

RESTORATION OF GOTHIC STEAMBOAT HOUSE, AL. THE RESTORED GOTHIC STEAMBOAT HOUSE, WHICH RESEMBLES A MISSISSIPPI STEAM WHEELER WILL BE USED AS HEADQUARTERS FOR WOMEN'S CLUB. THE BUILDING IS LISTED IN THE NATIONAL REGISTER OF HISTORICAL SITES. (LOCAL). MRS LOXIE DOUD, CHAIRMAN, SPECIAL PROJECTS; MADISON COUNTY FEDERATION OF WOMEN'S CLUBS, INC; RT 4, YANCY RD; MADISON, AL 35758. (#19543). **ARBA GRANTEE.**

SCRAPBOOK PROJECT - UNIV OF ALABAMA, HUNTSVILLE. A SCRAPBOOK WILL BE MADE OF THE UNIVERSITY BICENT ACTIVITIES. (LOCAL). CHARLES HIGGINS, ASST TO EXTERNAL AFFAIRS PRES; UNIV OF ALABAMA IN HUNTSVILLE BICENTENNIAL COMMISSION; PO BOX 1247; HUNTSVILLE, AL 35807. (#16029).

WNDA-FM PGMS ON RELIGION'S INFLUENCE IN US -NBMRP. HALF-HOUR MONTHLY SERIES DEALING W/ RELIGIOUS INFLUENCE IN AMERICAN LIFE, DISTRIBUTION OF BICENT PRAYER REMINDER CARDS, RUNS 'AMERICA IS' SERIES 4 TIMES DAILY, SUPPORTS & REPORTS ON LOCAL BICENT PROJ. (LOCAL). MIKE WILSON, BICENTENNIAL COORDINATOR; WNDA-FM RADIO; 2407 9TH AVE; HUNTSVILLE, AL 35805. (#23259).

MAR 15 - 16, '75. PREMIERE PERFORMANCES OF THE ORATORIO BASED ON THE LIFE OF GALILEO. MUSICAL COMPOSITION FOR MIXED CHORUS, ORCHESTRA AND SEVEN SOLOISTS, SIXTY MINUES DURATION, BASED ON THE LIFE OF GALILEO GALIEI, FOR THE INAUGURAL CONCERT OF THE VON BRAUN CIVIC CENTER. (REGN'L). DR MARX PALES, CONDUCTOR; HUNTSVILLE SYMPHONY ORCHESTRA; 1015 TASCOSA DR SE; HUNTSVILLE, AL 35802. (#6601-501).

SEPT 1, '75. 1975 NORTHEAST ALABAMA STATE FAIR. FAIR OPEN MONDAY & SATURDAY FROM 1:00 PM TO MIDNIGHT AND TUESDAY THROUGH FRIDAY 4:00 PM TO MIDNIGHT. AT NE ALABAMA STATE FAIRGROUNDS, 3 MLE W OF HUNTSVILLE ON STATE HWY 72. (LOCAL). ALAN FORNEY, PROJ DIR; HUNTSVILLE JAYCEES; PO BOX 3127; HUNTSVILLE, AL 35810. (#100782-1).

OCT 1, '75 - DEC 31, '76. DISPLAY OF AMERICANA. EXHIBIT AT UNIVERSITY LIBRARY. (LOCAL). CHARLES HIGGINS, PROJ DIR; UNIV OF ALABAMA IN HUNTSVILLE BICENTENNIAL COMMISSION; PO BOX 1247; HUNTSVILLE, AL 35807. (#102678-14).

NOV 15, '75. AMERICANA I, CONCERT BY HUNTSVILLE COMMUNITY CHORUS. PROGRAM WILL FEATURE EARLY AMERICAN MUSIC WITH WORKS BY AARON COPLAND & RANDALL THOMPSON. ALSO INCLUDED ARE STAGED SCENES FROM THE BROADWAY MUSICAL 'OKLAHOMA'. AT VON BRAUN CIVIC CENTER CONCERT HALL. (LOCAL). CHARLES M BISHOP, CHMN; HUNTSVILLE COMMUNITY CHORUS; 1102 BESSEMER RD NW; HUNTSVILLE, AL 35805. (#103318-3).

DEC 5, '75. MESSIAH - CONCERT BY HUNTSVILLE COMMUNITY CHORUS. PEOPLE FROM CHOIRS AND CHORUSES THROUGHOUT THE COMMUNITY WILL JOIN THE HCC FOR THIS PRESENTATION OF HANDEL'S CHORAL MASTERPIECE. AT VON BRAUN CIVIC CENTER CONCERT HALL. (LOCAL). CHARLES M BISHOP, CHMN; HUNTSVILLE COMMUNITY CHORUS; 1102 BESSEMER RD NW; HUNTSVILLE, AL 35805. (#103318-2).

DEC 5 - 6, '75. 25TH ANNIVERSARY BICENTENNIAL BALL. FESTIVAL AT VON BRAUN CIVIC CENTER EXHIBIT HALL. (LOCAL). D ROYCE BOYER, PROJ CHMN; UNIV OF ALABAMA IN HUNTSVILLE BICENTENNIAL COMMISSION; PO BOX 1247; HUNTSVILLE, AL 35807. (#102678-1).

JAN 1 - DEC 31, '76. NASA TOUR OF MARSHALL SPACE FLIGHT CENTER. DAILY TOURS OF SOLAR HOUSE, SPACE SHUTTLE, ENGINE TEST FIRING AREAS AND SKYLAB SPACE STATION MOCKUP. AT ALABAMA SPACE AND ROCKET CENTER. (REGN'L). EDWARD O BUCKBEE, DIR; ALABAMA SPACE AND ROCKET CENTER; TRANQUILITY BASE; HUNTSVILLE, AL 35807. (#103416-200).

JAN 1, '76 - JAN 1, '77. LUNAR-ODYSSEY SPACE FLIGHT SIMULATOR. SIMULATED MOON FLIGHTS ALLOW PASSENGERS TO FEEL 2 G'S OF GRAVITATIONAL PRESSURE DURING LIFTOFF AND FLIGHT. HOURS ARE 9-5 FROM SEPT-MAY; 9-6 JUNE THROUGH AUGUST. AT 15 MI OFF I-65 ON ALA HWY 20 IN HUNTSVILLE, AL. (REGN'L). EDWARD O BUCKBEE, DIR; ALABAMA SPACE AND ROCKET CENTER; TRANQUILITY BASE; HUNTSVILLE, AL 35807. (#103564-1).

JAN 5, '76. TOWN MEETING. CONFERENCE AT STUDENT UNION BLDG. (LOCAL). CHARLES HIGGINS, PROJ DIR; UNIV OF ALABAMA IN HUNTSVILLE BICENTENNIAL COMMISSION; PO BOX 1247; HUNTSVILLE, AL 35807. (#102678-15).

JAN 9 - 11, '76. UNITED STATES ARMED FORCES BICENTENNIAL CARAVAN. CARAVAN IS COMPOSED OF EXHIBIT VANS FOR EACH MILITARY SERVICE. PROJECT THEME IS 'HISTORY OF THE ARMED FORCES AND THEIR CONTRIBUTIONS TO THE NATION'. (LOCAL). EDWARD O BUCKBEE, CHMN; US ARMED FORCES BICENTENNIAL EXHIBIT VANS PROJECT; ALABAMA SPACE AND ROCKET CENTER; HUNTSVILLE, AL 35807. (#1775-380).

JAN 31 - FEB 29, '76. HUNTSVILLE RECONSTRUCTS. EXHIBIT AT VON BRAUN CIVIC CENTER, 700 MONROE ST. (LOCAL). THOMAS A BOWLES, III, DIR; HUNTSVILLE MUSEUM OF ART; 700 MONROE ST; HUNTSVILLE, AL 35801. (#20500-1).

JAN '76. ERIC HAWKINS DANCE COMPANY. LIVE PERFORMANCE AT RECITAL HALL, HUMANITIES BLDG. (LOCAL). D ROYCE BOYER, PROJ COORD; UNIV OF ALABAMA IN HUNTSVILLE BICENTENNIAL COMMISSION; PO BOX 1247; HUNTSVILLE, AL 35807. (#102678-13).

FEB 6 - 8, '76. MISS ALABAMA UNIVERSE CONTEST. COMPETITION, LIVE PERFORMANCE AT SHERATON HOTEL HUNTSVILLE ALABAMA. (ST-WIDE). BILLIE MCLARTY, DIRECTOR; MISS UNIVERSE INC; 180 WALLACE RD, APT J-11; NASHVILLE, TN 37211. (#101198-1).

FEB 12 - 13, '76. BLACK HISTORY WEEK. CONFERENCE AT HUMANITIES BUILDING; AUDIO-VISUAL ROOM. (LOCAL). PHILIP BOUCHER, PROJ DIR; UNIV OF ALABAMA IN HUNTSVILLE BICENTENNIAL COMMISSION; PO BOX 1247; HUNTSVILLE, AL 35807. (#102678-10).

FEB 14 - 15, '76. AMERICANA II - CONCERT BY HUNTSVILLE COMMUNITY CHORUS. TWO MAJOR AMERICAN WORKS OF CLASSICAL CHORAL MUSIC, PROGRAM WILL FEATURE THE NEWLY INSTALLED 3 MANUAL ORGAN AT HISTORIC FIRST PRESBYTERIAN CHURCH. AT VON BRAUN CIVIC CENTER CONCERT HALL. (LOCAL). CHARLES M BISHOP, CHMN; HUNTSVILLE COMMUNITY CHORUS; 1102 BESSEMER RD NW; HUNTSVILLE, AL 35805. (#103318-4).

APR 24, '76. UAH FILM SERIES. FESTIVAL AT STUDENT UNION BUILDING. (LOCAL). RANDY PAUL, PROJ CHAIRMAN; UNIV OF ALABAMA IN HUNTSVILLE BICENTENNIAL COMMISSION; PO 1247, SGA; HUNTSVILLE, AL 35807. (#102678-11).

APR 26, '76. DRAMATIC READINGS OF REVOLUTIONARY ERA AUTHORS. LIVE PERFORMANCE AT RECITAL HALL, HUMANITIES BLDG. (LOCAL). PHILIP BOUCHER, PROJ DIR; UNIV OF ALABAMA IN HUNTSVILLE BICENTENNIAL COMMISSION; PO BOX 1247; HUNTSVILLE, AL 35807. (#102678-12).

APR 30 - MAY 2, '76. AMERICANA III - 'CAROUSEL', BY HUNTSVILLE COMMUNITY CHORUS. ROGERS AND HAMMERSTEIN'S POPULAR PLAY 'CAROUSEL' WILL BE PERFORMED BY LOCAL TALENTED SINGERS, DANCERS & ACTORS. THIS IS A COLORFUL PLAY DEPICTING AN AMUSEMENT PARK IN NEW ENGLAND DURING THE YEARS 1873-1888. AT VON BRAUN CIVIC CENTER CONCERT HALL. (LOCAL). CHARLES M BISHOP, CHMN; HUNTSVILLE COMMUNITY CHORUS; 1102 BESSEMER RD NW; HUNTSVILLE, AL 35805. (#103318-1).

MAY 20 - 21, '76. SEMINAR ON FOREIGN RELATIONS. SEMINAR AT HUNTSVILLE HILTON BALLROOM, FREEDOM PLAZA & VON BRAUN CIVIC CTR. (LOCAL). PHILIP BOUCHER, PROJ DIR; UNIV OF ALABAMA IN HUNTSVILLE BICENTENNIAL COMMISSION; PO BOX 1247; HUNTSVILLE, AL 35807. (#102678-2).

MAY 31 - JUNE 2, '76. AMERICAN FREEDOM TRAIN DISPLAY DAYS AT HUNTSVILLE. THE AMERICAN FREEDOM TRAIN INCLUDES 10 EXHIBIT CARS & 2 SHOW CASE CARS DEPICTING DIFFERENT PHASES OF THE AMERICAN EXPERIENCE. ITS ARRIVAL WILL SERVE AS A CATALYST FOR LOCAL BICENTENNIAL CELEBRATIONS BY PEOPLE THROUGHOUT THIS NATION. (ST-WIDE). SY FREEDMAN, DIR OF P/R; THE AMERICAN FREEDOM TRAIN FOUNDATION; 5205 LEESBURG PIKE, SUITE 800; BAILEY'S XRDS, VA 22041. (#1776-94).

JULY 4, '76. HUNTSVILLE 4TH OF JULY CELEBRATION. WILL INCLUDE 4TH OF JULY FESTIVAL & A PARADE. AT MILTON FRANK STADIUM. (LOCAL). STEVEN B ALEXANDER, CHMN; HUNTSVILLE-MADISON CO BICENTENNIAL COMMISSION; 320 PAWNEE TRAIL SE; HUNTSVILLE, AL 35803. (#27284-1).

AUG 28 - 29, '76. HUNTSVILLE HISTORY FOCUS - EXHIBIT & TOUR. BEST FRIEND OF CHARLESTON TRAIN, SOUTHERN RAILROAD EXHIBIT CAR & LOCAL HISTORY EXHIBIT. AT HUNTSVILLE DEPOT, 330 CHURCH ST NW. (LOCAL). HUGH J.DUDLEY, COORD; HUNTSVILLE DEPOT BOARD; 901 COLE DR, SE; HUNTSVILLE, AL 35802. (#106645-1).

JAN '77 - CONTINUING . PLANNING AMERICA'S GREAT CITIES, AN EXHIBITION. EXHIBIT, RADIO/TV AT ALABAMA SPACE & ROCKET CENTER. (REGN'L). MS LEE KIMCHE; ASSOC OF SCIENCE & TECHNOLOGY; 2100 PENNSYLVANIA AVE, NW; WASHINGTON, DC 20037. (#8615-6).

JACKSON

HISTORIC HOME RESTORATION - JACKSON, AL. A HISTORIC HOME IN THE AREA WILL BE RESTORED AND PRESERVED. (LOCAL). MRS W W ANDREWS, CHAIRMAN; JACKSON BICENTENNIAL COMMITTEE; 2230 KATHERINE ST; JACKSON, AL 36545. (#29182).

JULY 4, '76. ARTS & CRAFTS, ESSAY CONTEST, 4TH OF JULY FESTIVITIES. FESTIVAL. (LOCAL). MRS W W ANDREWS, CHMN; JACKSON BICENTENNIAL COMMITTEE; 2230 KATHERINE ST; JACKSON, AL 36545. (#200001-43).

JACKSONVILLE

BICENTENNIAL NEWSPAPER SERIES, JACKSONVILLE, AL. A SERIES OF ARTICLES ON THE AMERICAN REVOLUTION WILL BE WRITTEN BY MEMBERS OF THE HISTORY. (LOCAL). WORDEN WEAVER, PROJ COORDINATOR; HISTORY DEPT, JACKSONVILLE STATE UNIV; PELHAM RD; JACKSONVILLE, AL 36265. (#14445).

BICENTENNIAL SCHOLARSHIP - JACKSONVILLE, AL. A SCHOLARSHIP WILL BE GIVEN TO A DESERVING STUDENT BASED ON PATRIOTISM. (LOCAL). LARRY SMITH, CHAIRMAN; JACKSONVILLE STATE UNIV; PELHAM RD; JACKSONVILLE, AL 36265. (#14443).

GRAVE MARKER - JACKSONVILLE, AL. A MARKER WILL BE ERECTED AT THE GRAVE OF A REVOLUTIONARY WAR SOLDIER. (LOCAL). WORDEN WEAVER, PROJ DIRECTOR; HISTORY DEPT, JACKSONVILLE STATE UNIV; PELHAM RD; JACKSONVILLE, AL 36265. (#14444).

HISTORICAL MOVIES - JACKSONVILLE, AL. HISTORICAL MOVIES WILL BE SHOWN IN HONOR OF THE BICENTENNIAL. (LOCAL). JULIA SNEAD, COORDINATOR; ALUMNI AFFAIRS, JACKSONVILLE STATE UNIV; PELHAM RD; JACKSONVILLE, AL 36265. (#14442).

PATRIOTIC SPEECHES - JACKSONVILLE, AL. SPEECHES WILL BE DELIVERED AT CLUBS AND SCHOOLS BY FACULTY & STAFF. (LOCAL). WORDEN WEAVER, PROJ DIRECTOR; HISTORY DEPT, JACKSONVILLE STATE UNIV; PELHAM RD; JACKSONVILLE, AL 36265. (#14439).

STAGE BAND PERFORMANCES IN JACKSONVILLE, AL. STAGE BAND PERFORMING FOR CIVIC GROUPS, SCHOOLS, ETC COMPRISES THIS PROJECT. (ST-WIDE). WORDEN WEAVER, CHRM; JACKSONVILLE STATE UNIV; BOX 131, CAMPUS MAIL CTR; JACKSONVILLE, AL 36265. (#10362).

FEB 20 - 22, '75. CONFERENCE ON AMERICAN GOVERNMENT, AL. THIS ANNUAL CONFERENCE OF SELECT HIGH SCHOOL STUDENTS ON AMERICAN GOVERNMENT WILL BE CENTERED AROUND THE BICENTENNIAL. (ST-WIDE). SINDO MAYOR, COORDINATOR; STUDENT GOVERNMENT ASSOC, JACKSONVILLE STATE UNIV; PELHAM RD; JACKSONVILLE, AL 36265. (#14441-1).

SEPT 13, '75 - NOV 30, '76. MUSIC, GENERAL AND PATRIOTIC. THE MARCHING SOUTHERNERS WILL DO A NUMBER OF FLAG PRESENTATIONNS IN THEIR HALFTIME SHOWS AND WILL USE MUSIC DERIVED FROM THE EARLYY COLONIAL PERIOD. AT JACKSONVILLE STATE UNIV, MASON HALL & PAUL SNOW STADIUM. (LOCAL). DAVID WALTERS; JACKSONVILLE STATE UNIV; PELHAM RD; JACKSONVILLE, AL 36265. (#14440-1).

MAY '76. ARTS AND CRAFTS FAIR. EXHIBIT OF ARTS & CRAFTS DEPICTING OUR HISTORY AND HERITAGE. (LOCAL). LEE MANNERS, PROJ DIR; JACKSONVILLE STATE UNIV; PELHAM RD; JACKSONVILLE, AL 36265. (#101834-1).

JASPER

ALABAMA REPS FOR BICENT WAGON TRAIN - JASPER, AL. SINCE ALABAMA IS NOT SENDING A REPRESENTATIVE WITH THE WAGON TRAIN, JASPER IS SENDING 2 REPRESENTATIVES TO GO WITH THE TRAIN TO VALLEY FORGE AS REPRESENTATIVES. (LOCAL). JACK BOWMAN, CO-CHAIRMAN; JASPER '76 ACTION COMMITTEE; PO DRAWER E; CORDOVA, AL 35550. (#24138).

AUTOMOBILE TAG SALE - PROJ OF JASPER, AL. SALE OF JASPER BICENTENNIAL TAGS TO PROMOTE BICENTENNIAL. (LOCAL). JACK BOWMAN, CO-CHAIRMAN; JASPER '76 ACTION COMMITTEE; PO DRAWER E; CORDOVA, AL 35501. (#16041).

BICENTENNIAL FIREPLUGS & METERS - JASPER, AL. DOWNTOWN PARKING METERS & WASTE CANS WILL BE PAINTED RED, WHITE & BLUE; FIREPLUGS WILL BE PAINTED TO COMMEMORATE SERGEANT JASPER, THE REVOLUTIONARY WAR HERO FOR WHOM JASPER IS NAMED. (LOCAL). JACK BOWMAN, CHAIRMAN; JASPAR '76 ACTION COMMITTEE; PO BOX 1250; JASPER, AL 35501. (#15761).

BICENTENNIAL LOG CABIN RESTORATION PROJECT, AL. A 150 YEAR OLD LOG CABIN WILL BE MOVED FROM ITS ORIGINAL SITE TO THE WALKER COLLEGE CAMPUS & RESTORED BY COLLEGE STUDENTS. (LOCAL). BROWNLEE FIVEASH; WALKER COLLEGE '76 PATRIOTIC COMMITTEE; WALKER COLLEGE; JASPER, AL 35501. (#18329). **ARBA GRANTEE.**

COMMUNITY FLAG DISPLAY IN JASPER, AL. ALL HOUSEHOLDS IN WALKER COUNTY WILL BE ENCOURAGED TO PURCHASE AND DISPLAY THE AMERICAN FLAG. (LOCAL). JEFFREY L BANKS, COORDINATOR; WALKER COLLEGE '76 PATRIOTS COMMITTEE; GAMBLE AVE; JASPER, AL 35501. (#14473).

DAR-SPONSORED CITY FLAG CONTEST FOR LOCAL SCHOOL CHILDREN. COMPETITION. (LOCAL). MRS C SHERER, DIRECTOR; DAUGHTERS OF AMERICAN REVOLUTION; PINECREST; JASPER, AL 35501. (#103077-1). **(??).**

HISTORIC DRAMA IN JASPER, AL. A PAGEANT ABOUT THE REVOLUTIONARY WAR PERIOD WILL BE PRESENTED. (LOCAL). JIM COOK, CHAIRMAN; WALKER COLLEGE '76 PATRIOTS COMMITTEE; GAMBLE AVE; JASPER, AL 35501. (#14471).

HISTORICAL & ANTHROPOLOGICAL TRIPS, JASPER, AL. CLASS VISITS TO SHILOH BATTLEFIELD & RUSSELL CAVE, A NATIONAL PARK. (LOCAL). ERNEST PEAK, PRESIDENT ANTHROPOLOGY CLUB; WALKER COLLEGE '76 PATRIOTS COMMITTEE; GAMBLE AVE; JASPER, AL 35501. (#14470).

JASPER — CONTINUED

JASPER BICENTENNIAL PARK, AL. ESTABLISHMENT OF A PARK WITH A LIBERTY TREE, WALKWAYS & BENCHES. (LOCAL). CLARENCE FARLEY, CHAIRMAN; JASPER '76 ACTION COMMITTEE; PO BOX 1250; JASPER, AL 35501. (#24896). **ARBA GRANTEE.**

JASPER-WALKER COUNTY BICENTENNIAL TRAIL - AL. SITES OF HISTORIC INTEREST IN WALKER COUNTY ALABAMA WILL BE MARKED. A MAP SHOWING LOCATION OF SITES WITH BRIEF DESCRIPTION OF EACH WILL BE DISTRIBUTED. (LOCAL). PHILIP D JONES, PRESIDENT; WALKER COUNTY HERITAGE ASSOC; 803 DOGWOOD TRAIL; JASPER, AL 35501. (#18784).

MINI-PARK ON WALKER COLLEGE CAMPUS, JASPER, AL. LOG STRUCTURES ON WALKER COLLEGE WILL BE RECONSTRUCTED. (LOCAL). BROWNLEY FIVEASH, COORDINATOR; WALKER COLLEGE '76 PATRIOTS COMMITTEE; GAMBLE AVE; JASPER, AL 35501. (#14469).

REVOLUTIONARY SOLDIERS GRAVESITES - JASPER, AL. WALKER COUNTY HERITAGE ASSOC HAS LOCATED AND PLACED MARKERS ON THE GRAVESITES OF THREE REVOLUTIONARY WAR SOLDIERS. (ST-WIDE). PHILIP D JONES, PRESIDENT; WALKER COUNTY HERITAGE ASSOC & JASPER '76 ACTION COMMITTEE; JASPER, AL 35501. (#16983).

TREE PLANTING PROJECT IN JASPER, AL. TREES WILL BE PLANTED ON WALKER CAMPUS. (LOCAL). DARRON EAST, COORDINATOR; WALKER COLLEGE '76 PATRIOTS COMMITTEE; GAMBLE AVE; JASPER, AL 35501. (#14472).

WALKER COUNTY FLAG CONTEST. REPLICAS OF FLAGS ARE TO BE PRODUCED IN NEEDLEPOINT, CREWEL, EMBROIDERY, CROCHET OR PAINTING OF OLE GLORY OR FLAG CARRIED BY SERGEANT JASPER FOR PRIZES. (LOCAL). PHILIP D JONES, CHMN; WALKER COUNTY HERITAGE ASSOCIATION; PO BOX 1628; JASPER, AL 35501. (#102284-1). **(??).**

SEPT 18 - DEC 11, '75. DISPLAY OF INDIAN ARTIFACTS. EXHIBIT. (LOCAL). JUNE DEAVORS, PROJ DIR; WALKER COLLEGE '76 PATRIOTS COMMITTEE; GAMBLE AVE; JASPER, AL 35501. (#101838-2).

OCT 12, '75. DEDICATION OF GRAVESITES OF KNOWN REVOLUTIONARY WAR SOLDIERS. CEREMONY. (LOCAL). PHILIP D JONES, COORD; WALKER COUNTY HERITAGE ASSOC & JASPER '76 ACTION COMMITTEE; JASPER, AL 35501. (#200001-32).

JAN 17, '76. MUSICAL CONCERT. A 2-HOUR PROGRAM PERFORMED BY THE WALKER COLLEGE SINGERS CONSISTING OF PATRIOTIC MUSIC. AT WALKER COLLEGE GYM. (LOCAL). BOB MOORE, PROJ DIRECTOR; WALKER COLLEGE '76 PATRIOTS COMMITTEE; GAMBLE AVE; JASPER, AL 35501. (#101838-1).

FEB 28, '76. BOY SCOUT BICENTENNIAL SHOW. THE BOY SCOUTS OF AMERICA IN WALKER COUNTY ARE PUTTING ON A SHOW WITH THE THREE BICENTENNIAL THEMES. THERE WILL BE AWARDS FOR THE BEST EXHIBITS. AT PARKLAND SHOPPING CENTER, HWY 78 BYPASS. (LOCAL). LUTHER CAUGHORN, EXEC DIR; BOY SCOUTS OF AMERICA IN WALKER COUNTY; MARION HGTS; JASPER, AL 35501. (#102565-1).

JUNE 26, '76. ART IN THE PARK. MANY ART FORMS AND VARIOUS CRAFTS SUCH AS: POTTERY MAKING, GLASS BLOWING, CHAIR CANING AND QUILTING WILL BE EXHIBITED. AT GAMBLE AVENUE PARK, WALKER COLLEGE. (LOCAL). JANE WIEDERECHT, DIRECTOR; WALKER COUNTY VISUAL ARTS ASSOCIATION; ROUTE 2; NAUVOO, AL 35578. (#102283-2).

JULY 10, '76. CORY BAND FROM WALES VISITS JASPER, ALABAMA. THIS 38-PIECE BAND, FOUNDED IN 1884, HAS REPRESENTED WALES IN NUMEROUS NATIONAL CONTESTS & IN 1974 WON THE TITLE 'CHAMPION BAND OF GREAT BRITAIN.'. (INT'L). MS EDITH HALL; LYRA ENTERTAINMENT, INC; 16 W 61ST ST; NEW YORK, NY 10023. (#109009-9).

LANETT

CEMETERY RESTORATION, LANETTE, AL. RESTORATION OF REESE CEMETERY, OLDEST PIONEER BURIAL GROUND IN THE AREA. (REGN'L). ED BABB, PROJ DIRECTOR; BOY SCOUTS OF AMERICA; 802 3RD AVE W; WEST POINT, GA 31833. (#25388).

APR 22 - 24, '76. HI-FEVER FOLLIES. LIVE PERFORMANCE. (LOCAL). MRS ANN MURPHY, COORD; GEORGE H LANIER HOSPITAL AUXILIARY; FOREST LANE; WESTPOINT, GA 31833. (#200001-34).

JUNE 5, '76. GOD & COUNTRY SPECTACULAR W/JERRY CLOWER & THE HAPPY GOODMAN FAMILY. FESTIVAL AT LANETT STADIUM. (REGN'L). BILL GILBERT, COORDINATOR; VALLEY BICENTENNIAL COMMITTEE; BROAD ST; LANETT, AL 36863. (#108034-3).

OCT 2, '76. FESTIVAL OF BANDS WITH ALL AREA HIGH SCHOOL BANDS. FESTIVAL, LIVE PERFORMANCE. (REGN'L). BILL GILBERT, COORDINATOR; VALLEY BICENTENNIAL COMMITTEE; BROAD ST; LANETT, AL 36863. (#108034-2).

NOV 25, '76. THANKSGIVING DAY SERVICE FEATURING DR NOAH LANGDALE, SPEAKER. EMPHASIS WILL BE ON THE BICENTENNIAL. (LOCAL). AL THORNTON, COORDINATOR; VALLEY MINISTERIAL ASSOC; PO BOX 150; WEST POINT, GA 31833. (#108034-1).

LANGDALE

APR 7 - 10, '76. BICENTENNIAL BELLE CONTEST. COMPETITION. (LOCAL). DR JOANNE JORDAN; SOUTHERN UNION JR COLLEGE; LANGDALE BY-PASS; LANGDALE, AL 36864. (#108250-1).

LEEDS

MARKER HONORING CONGRESSIONAL MEDAL RECIPIENTS. ESTABLISH PERMANENT MARKER OF NATIVE LIMESTONE WITH BRONZE PLAQUE MADE BY LOCAL INDUSTRY HONORING CONGRESSIONAL MEDAL OF HONOR RECIPIENTS FROM LEEDS, ALABAMA. DISPLAY OF MEMORABILIA AT LIBRARY. (LOCAL). PRESTON MCLAUGHLIN, CHAIRMAN; LEEDS BICENTENNIAL COMMISSION; CITY HALL; LEEDS, AL 35094. (#2578). **ARBA GRANTEE.**

JULY 1, '74. DEDICATION CEREMONY UNVEILING MONUMENT FOR MEDAL OF HONOR HOLDERS. MARKER HONORING CONGRESSIONAL MEDAL RECIPIENTS. ESTABLISH PERMANENT MARKER OF NATIVE LIMESTONE WITH BRONZE PLAQUE MADE BY LOCAL INDUSTRY HONORING CONGRESSIONAL MEDAL OF HONOR RECIPIENTS FROM LEEDS, ALABAMA. (LOCAL). PRESTON MCLAUGHLIN; LEEDS BICENTENNIAL COMMISSION; CITY HALL; LEEDS, AL 35094. (#2578-901).

JULY 1, '75 - JULY 1, '76. EXHIBIT AT LIBRARY OF HISTORICAL MEMORABILIA OF MEDAL RECIPIENTS. OPENING, CEREMONY, EXHIBIT. (LOCAL). PRESTON MCLAUGHLIN; LEEDS BICENTENNIAL COMMISSION; CITY HALL; LEEDS, AL 35094. (#2578-502).

LEESBURG

COMMUNITY DEVELOPMENT OF PARK - LEESBURG, AL. A 20 ACRE PARK WITH FACILITIES FOR SPORTS TO APPEAL TO ALL AGES WILL BE DEVELOPED. (LOCAL). HON B C LOKEY, MAYOR; LEESBURG TOWN COUNCIL; LEESBURG, AL 35983. (#30945).

MAR 26 - 27, '76. NATIONAL WAGON TRAIN VISITS LEESBURG, AL. FESTIVAL AT LEESBURG COMMUNITY HOUSE. (LOCAL). MARY HALE; LEESBURG BICENTENNIAL COMMITTEE; R 1, BOX 151; LEESBURG, AL 35983. (#200001-77).

LINDEN

CHICKASAW STATE PARK IMPROVEMENTS, LINDEN, AL. IMPROVEMENTS WILL INCLUDE RELOCATING OLD PAVILLION, ERECT FLAG POLE, BUILD PARK ENTRANCE SIGN, REVAMP ALL TRAILS AND CONSTRUCT PICNIC TABLES. (LOCAL). MRS NICK DIXON, PROJ DIRECTOR; CITY OF LINDEN; RT 1 BOX 138-D; LINDEN, AL 36748. (#19086). **ARBA GRANTEE.**

OCT 9, '76. CHICKASAW ARTS & CRAFTS SHOW. EXHIBIT AT CHICKASAW STATE PARK, 4 MILES N OF LINDEN ON HWY 43. (LOCAL). MRS JOSEPHINE HALL; LINDEN BUSINESS & PROFESSIONAL WOMEN'S CLUB; HIGHLAND; LINDEN, AL 36748. (#200001-72).

LIPSCOMB

AVE OF FLAGS & DOGWOOD TRAIL, LIPSCOMB, AL. AN AVENUE OF FLAGS ALONG DOGWOOD TRAIL IN MEMORY THOSE WHO FOUGHT IN THE AMERICAN REVOLUTION, WORLD WARS I & II & THE KOREAN & VIETNAM CONFLICTS. (LOCAL). MRS PETER ZUKOW, CHAIRPERSON; LIPSCOMB BICENTENNIAL COMMITTEE; 512 AVE H; LIPSCOMB, AL 35020. (#25577). **ARBA GRANTEE.**

RESTORATION OF CITY PARK MONUMENT, LIPSCOMB, AL. FESTIVAL, CELEBRATION, COMMEMORATION & DEDICATION OF PARK & MONUMENT TO YOUTH OF CITY OF LIPSCOMB. (LOCAL). MRS PETER ZUKOW, CHAIRPERSON; LIPSCOMB BICENTENNIAL COMMITTEE; 512 AVE H; LIPSCOMB, AL 35020. (#25576). **ARBA GRANTEE.**

LIVINGSTON

THE COLLECTED WORKS OF RUBY PICKENS TARTT, AL. PUBLICATION OF ONE-VOLUME ARTICLES WRITTEN BY NOTED WEST ALABAMA FOLKLORIST. (ST-WIDE). DR NEIL SNIDER, HEAD LIBRARIAN; LIVINGSTON UNIV BICENTENNIAL COMMITTEE; LIVINGSTON UNIV; LIVINGSTON, AL 35470. (#17006).

THE HISTORY OF LIVINGSTON UNIVERSITY, AL. ONE-VOLUME HISTORY OF LIVINGSTON UNIVERSITY FROM ITS ACADEMY DAYS, THROUGH ITS NORMAL SCHOOL PERIOD AND ITS STATE TEACHER COLLEGE DAYS TO THE PRESENT DAY UNIVERSITY. (ST-WIDE). NATHANIEL REED, PROVOST; LIVINGSTON UNIV BICENTENNIAL COMMITTEE; LIVINGSTON UNIV; LIVINGSTON, AL 35470. (#17007).

LIVINGSTON HISTORICAL PAGEANT & FOLK MUSIC FESTIVAL. LIVE PERFORMANCE AT AUDITORIUM, LIVINGSTON UNIV. (LOCAL). DR NEIL SNIDER, CHAIRMAN; LIVINGSTON BICENTENNIAL COMMITTEE/LIVINGSTON UNIV; LIVINGSTON, AL 35470. (#20762-1).

LIVINGSTON, AL, BICENTENNIAL PROJECT. PUBLICATION OF HISTORICAL PAMPHLETS; PLANTING OF WILD FLOWER GARDENS AND NATURE TRAIL; COLLECTION OF LOCAL FOLK MUSIC AND HISTORICAL CELEBRATIONS. (LOCAL). DR NEIL SNIDER, CHAIRMAN; LIVINGSTON BICENTENNIAL COMMITTEE/ LIVINGSTON UNIV; LIVINGSTON, AL 35470. (#20762). **ARBA GRANTEE.**

SUMTER COUNTY RURAL DEVELOPMENT COMMITTEE, AL. IMPROVEMENT OF THE TOTAL RESOURCES OF A DEPRESSED RURAL COUNTY. THE COMMITTEE HAS DEVELOPED NEW PROGRAMS IN AGRICULTURE, HEALTH, EDUCATION AND RESPONDED OVER THE LONG HAUL. (LOCAL). B B WILLIAMSON, CHAIRMAN; ALABAMA-SUMTER COUNTY COOPERATIVE EXTENSION SERVICE; FEDERAL BLDG; LIVINGSTON, AL 35470. (#20046).

UNIVERSITY ARCHIVAL PROGRAM, LIVINGSTON, AL. DEVELOP, MAINTAIN AND EXPAND THE ARCHIVES AND RECORDS OF THE UNIVERSITY; CATALOG EXISTING RECORDS; ACQUIRE PAPERS AND RECORDS OF FORMER STUDENTS, FACULTY AND ADMINISTRATORS. (ST-WIDE). DR NEIL SNIDER, HEAD LIBRARIAN; LIVINGSTON UNIV BICENTENNIAL COMMITTEE; LIVINGSTON UNIV; LIVINGSTON, AL 35470. (#17008).

UNIVERSITY FOLKLORE COLLECTION, LIVINGSTON, AL. CATALOG AND EXPAND RUBY PICKENS TARTT COLLECTION OF WEST ALABAMA FOLKLORE MATERIALS; ADD OTHER FOLKLORE MANUSCRIPTS. (ST-WIDE). DR NEIL SNIDER, HEAD LIBRARIAN; LIVINGSTON UNIV BICENTENNIAL COMMITTEE; LIVINGSTON UNIV; LIVINGSTON, AL 35470. (#17009).

SEPT 15, '75 - MAY 31, '76. CONCERT AND PLAY SERIES. SERIES TO INCLUDE CHRISTMAS CHOIR PROGRAM; LU STAGE BAND PROGRAM, HONOR BAND FESTIVAL AND ONE STAGE PRODUCTION. AT BIBB GRAVES AUDITORIUM. (LOCAL). DR DENNIS KUDLAWIEL, DIR; LIVINGSTON UNIV BICENTENNIAL COMMITTEE; LIVINGSTON, AL 35470. (#103096-3).

SEPT 15, '75 - MAY 31, '76. LIVINGSTON UNIV BICENTENNIAL FORUM. SEMINAR AT WALLACE HALL AUDITORIUM. (LOCAL). DR JAMES P PATE, DIR; LIVINGSTON UNIV BICENTENNIAL COMMITTEE; LIVINGSTON, AL 35470. (#103096-1).

SEPT 15, '75 - MAY 31, '76. UNIV LECTURE SERIES. SEMINAR AT WALLACE HALL AUDITORIUM. (LOCAL). NATHANIEL REED, PROVOST; LIVINGSTON UNIV BICENTENNIAL COMMITTEE; LIVINGSTON, AL 35470. (#103096-4).

APR 25 - 28, '76. STUDENT-FACULTY ART SHOW. EXHIBIT AT FOUST HALL. (LOCAL). MRS ANNETTE MITCHELL, DIR; LIVINGSTON UNIV BICENTENNIAL COMMITTEE; LIVINGSTON, AL 35470. (#103096-2).

JULY 4, '76. FOURTH OF JULY CELEBRATION. FESTIVAL AT LIVINGSTON UNIV. (LOCAL). DR NEIL SNIDER, CHAIRMAN; LIVINGSTON BICENTENNIAL COMMITTEE/LIVINGSTON UNIV; LIVINGSTON, AL 35470. (#20762-3).

SEPT 27 - OCT 1, '76. LIVINGSTON HISTORICAL BUILDING & HOME PILGRIMAGE. TOUR. (LOCAL). DR NEIL SNIDER, CHAIRMAN; LIVINGSTON BICENTENNIAL COMMITTEE/LIVINGSTON UNIV; LIVINGSTON, AL 35470. (#20762-2).

LOWNDESBORO

MAR 26 - 28, '76. TOUR OF OLD HOMES AND COUNTRY STORE. TOUR WILL INCLUDE AN ANTIQUE AND COUNTRY CRAFTS SHOW. (LOCAL). DORABEL WOODRUFF, PRES; LOWNDESBORO HERITAGE SOCIETY; BOX 23; LOWNDESBORO, AL 36752. (#100785-1).

LUVERNE

BICENTENNIAL PARK, LUVERNE, AL. IMPROVE CITY PARK TO INCLUDE CONSTRUCTION OF BANDSTAND AND LANDSCAPING. (LOCAL). JOHN MILLS, CHAIRMAN; LUVERNE BICENTENNIAL COMMITTEE; 106 WOODFORD AVE; LUVERNE, AL 36049. (#23747). **ARBA GRANTEE.**

MADISON

MADISON BICENTENNIAL STREET FAIR - AL. ACTIVITIES INCLUDED ARE: MUSIC & DANCING COMMON TO THE AREA; DISPLAY OF LOCAL HERITAGE; TOURS OF ARCHITECTURAL HIGHLIGHTS; AND FOLK CRAFTS DEMONSTRATION. (LOCAL). THOMAS BOWLES, DIRECTOR; HUNTSVILLE MUSEUM ART; 700 MONROE ST, VON BRAUN CENTER; HUNTSVILLE, AL 35801. (#25723). **ARBA GRANTEE.**

OCT 17, '76. MADISON BICENTENNIAL STREET FAIR. INCLUDES: MUSIC & DANCING COMMON TO THE AREA; DISPLAY OF LOCAL HERITAGE; TOURS OF ARCHITECTURAL HIGHLIGHTS; AND FOLK CRAFTS DEMONSTRATION; ART COMPETITION. AT MAIN STREET, MADISON, AL. (LOCAL). THOMAS BOWLES, DIR; HUNTSVILLE MUSEUM OF ART; 700 MONROE ST, VON BRAUN CENTER; HUNTSVILLE, AL 35801. (#25723-1).

MAPLESVILLE

RESTORATION OF SOUTH DEPOT - MAPLESVILLE, AL. REMODEL ROOMS OF DEPOT WITH KITCHEN AND RESTROOMS FOR USE AS A COMMUNITY CIVIC CENTER WITH SPECIAL EMPHASIS ON SENIOR CITIZEN'S 'MEALS ON WHEELS' FOOD PROGRAM. (LOCAL). MRS BLANCHE M DENNIS, CHAIRPERSON; MAPLESVILLE BICENTENNIAL COMMISSION; PO BOX 51; MAPLESVILLE, AL 36750. (#29323).

APR 9, '76. COMMUNITY CENTER FLAGPOLE DEDICATION AND PARADE. CEREMONY, PARADE AT SOUTHERN DEPOT. (LOCAL). MRS BLANCHE M DENNIS; MAPLESVILLE BICENTENNIAL COMMISSION; PO BOX 51; MAPLESVILLE, AL 36750. (#200001-44).

MARION

ALABAMA WOMEN'S HALL OF FAME, IN MARION. PROGRAM EMPHASIZING ROLE OF WOMEN IN AMERICAN HISTORY, CULTURE, SOCIAL SERVICE & ARTS - TWO PROMINENT DECEASED WOMEN ARE ADDED TO THE HALL OF FAME EACH YEAR. (REGN'L). JONATHAN LINDSEY, LIBRARIAN; ALABAMA WOMEN'S HALL OF FAME AT JUDSON COLLEGE; MARION, AL 36756. (#10233).

BICENTENNIAL COLLECTION FROM MARION, ALABAMA. COLLECTION WILL INCLUDE: 200 BOOKS, TITLES SOLICITED FROM OUTSTANDING AMERICAN WOMEN; BOOKS PURCHASED BY COL-

MARION — CONTINUED

LEGE & AFFIXED WITH BOOKPLATE. (ST-WIDE). JONATHAN LINDSEY, LIBRARIAN; JUDSON COLLEGE, BOWLING LIBRARY; MARION, AL 36756. (#10232).

JAN 7, '76. FILM: 'THE EMERGING WOMAN' PART OF PROGRAM ON THE AMERICAN WOMAN. OPEN TO THE PUBLIC. PROGRAM, 'THE AMERICAN WOMAN: PAST, PRESENT, FUTURE', ALSO INVOLVES AN HONORS CONVOCATION ON APRIL 9 & J-DAY ON APRIL 10. AT CAVERN, JUDSON COLLEGE. (LOCAL). JONATHAN A LINDSEY; JUDSON COLLEGE; MARION, AL 36756. (#10231-1).

FEB 16, '76. 'ALL AMERICAN RECITAL' PRESENTED BY MUSIC FACULTY OF JUDSON COLLEGE. SCHEDULED FOR FEBRUARY 16: 'A PROGRAM OF AMERICAN ORGAN MUSIC', WITH ORGANIST JOHN G MARBERRY IN RAMSEY CHAPEL. PRESENTED BY JEANNE E SHAFFER, SOPRANO OF THE MUSIC FACULTY OF JUDSON COLLEGE. AT ALUMNAE AUDITORIUM. (REGN'L). DR JEANNE SHAFFER; JUDSON COLLEGE; MARION, AL 36756. (#10234-1).

MAR 31 - APR 4, '76. MARION INSTITUTE ART SHOW. GALLERY SHOW HOURS OPEN DO NOT INCLUDE 11:30-1:00 OR 4:30 TO 7:30; SATURDAY APRIL 3 HOURS ARE 9:00-12:00 & 1:00-4:00; SUNDAY APRIL 4 HOURS OPEN ARE 2:00-5:00. AT BAER MEMORIAL LIBRARY. (LOCAL). WOODY S MOORE, PGM MGR; MARION INSTITUTE; MARION, AL 36756. (#103795-1).

APR 10, '76. THESE FABULOUS 200 YEARS. LIVE PERFORMANCE AT BACK CAMPUS. (LOCAL). CHARLENE MOOTY, CO-CHMN; JUDSON COLLEGE; JUDSON COLLEGE; MARION, AL 36756. (#103392-1).

APR 14 - 16, '76. 'THE MAN WHO CAME TO DINNER'. LIVE PERFORMANCE AT ARTS BUILDING. (LOCAL). FRANK C MARSHALL, DIR; MARION MILITARY INST ARTS FESTIVAL; MARION, AL 36756. (#200001-35).

APR 22, '76. ALABAMA MILITARY HALL OF HONOR. SELECTION OF FOUR MEMBERS EACH YEAR, TWO HISTORICAL, TWO CURRENT BY COMMITTEE FROM OPEN NOMINATIONS. AT MARION MILITARY INST CHAPEL. (LOCAL). JAMES A JACKSON, COORD; MARION MILITARY INSTITUTE; MARION, AL 36756. (#200001-38).

JUNE 1, '76. MUSIC FACULTY RECITAL. ENTIRE MUSIC FACULTY INVOLVED. AT ALUMNI AUDITORIUM. (LOCAL). DR JEANNE SHAFFER; JUDSON COLLEGE; MARION, AL 36756. (#10234-2).

NOV 13, '76. AMERICAN BAND MUSIC REVIEW. LIVE PERFORMANCE AT DAVID ROBINSON STADIUM. (LOCAL). DON PATMON, CHAIRMAN; MARION MILITARY INSTITUTE; MARION, AL 36756. (#107451-1).

MAXWELL AFB

OPERATION PIONEER, MAXWELL AFB, AL. RECORDED INTERVIEWS OF AVIATION PIONEERS BY CIVIL AIR PATROL CADETS NATIONWIDE. (NAT'L). WILLIAM T CAPERS, DIRECTOR OF INFORMATION; CIVIL AIR PATROL; HQ CAP-USAF/OI; MAXWELL AFB, AL 36112. (#23251).

MCCALLA

BICENTENNIAL INTERPRETATION OF TANNEHILL - AL. PUBLICATION TO BE DISTRIBUTED BY THE PARK. (ST-WIDE). JAMES R BENNETT, CHAIRMAN; TANNEHILL HISTORICAL STATE PARK; RT 1, BOX 124; MCCALLA, AL 35111. (#28545). **ARBA GRANTEE.**

TANNEHILL IRONWORKS RESTORATION, MCCALLA, AL. RESTORATION OF TANNEHILL FURNACE NO 1; BUILT IN 1859; THIS CIVIL WAR IRONMAKER WAS OF STRATEGIC IMPORTANCE TO ALABAMA AND THE SOUTH; THE FURNACE WILL BE RETURNED TO OPERATING CONDITION. (LOCAL). JAMES R BENNETT, CHAIRMAN; TANEHILL FURNACE AND FOUNDRY COMMISSION; RTE 1, BOX 124; MCCALLA, AL 35111. (#14325). **ARBA GRANTEE.**

MCKENZIE

BICENTENNIAL PARK, MCKENZIE, AL. PRESERVATION & RESTORATION OF LOCAL NATURAL AREA. (LOCAL). BILLY MATTHEWS, CHAIRMAN; MCKENZIE BICENTENNIAL COMMITTEE; MCKENZIE, AL 36456. (#32358).

STREET DANCE & FESTIVAL USA. FESTIVAL, PARADE. (LOCAL). BILLY MATTHEWS, CHMN; MCKENZIE BICENTENNIAL COMMISSION; RT ONE; MCKENZIE, AL 36456. (#200001-79).

MCSHAN

COMMUNITY CULTURE. COMMUNITY CLUB AND CHURCH ACTIVITIES CENTERD AROUND THE BICENTENNIAL THEME. AT COMMUNITY CLUB HOUSE. (LOCAL). MRS JAMES L LANCASTER; COMMUNITY IMPROVEMENT CLUB; RT 1, BOX 425; ETHELSVILLE, AL 35461. (#200001-66).

HISTORICAL MARKER, MCSHAN, AL. THE COMMUNITY IMPROVEMENT CLUB HAS APPLIED FOR A MARKER AT MT MORIAN CHURCH, THE OLDEST FREE WILL BAPTIST CHURCH IN ALABAMA. (LOCAL). MRS JAMES L LANCASTER, CHAIRMAN; MCSHANE BICENTENNIAL COMMITTEE & COMMUNITY IMPROVEMENT CLUB; MCSHAN, AL 35471. (#29766).

MILLBROOK

APR 24, '75 - APR 25, '76. 10TH ANNUAL SEVENTEEN SPRINGS ARTS & CRAFTS HOBBY FAIR. EXHIBIT, FESTIVAL AT CAMP GRANDVIEW, SEVENTEEN SPRINGS. (LOCAL). JO LEAVELL, DIRECTOR; MONTGOMERY YWCO; PO BOX 134; MONTGOMERY, AL 36101. (#100939-1).

MOBILE

BICENTENNIAL LOGO ON COAST GUARD AIRCRAFT - AL. COAST GUARD AIRCRAFT FROM THIS COMMAND WERE MARKED WITH THE SPIRIT OF '76 LOGO, AND THEY THEN VISITED AREAS AS DISTANT AS THE SOUTH POLE. (LOCAL). LTJG WILLIAM M HAYES, PUBLIC AFFAIRS OFFICER; U S COAST GUARD AVIATION TRAINING CENTER; BATES FIELD; MOBILE, AL 36608. (#28596).

BICENTENNIAL PAPER CAMPUS PROGRAM, MOBILE, AL. BICENTENNIAL PAPER CAMPUS PROGRAM. 18 LECTURES ON THE BICENTENNIAL, SPONSORED BY SPRING HILL COLLEGE AND PRINTED WEEKLY IN THE WEST MOBILE SUBURBAN RECORD. (LOCAL). PATRICK F GUYTON, CHAIRPERSON; SPRING HILL COLLEGE BICENTENNIAL COMMITTEE; SPRING HILL COLLEGE; MOBILE, AL 36608. (#22500).

BICENTENNIAL PRESENCE AT THE REVOLUTION, AL. CONTINUING EDUCATION COURSE ON THE AMERICAN REVOLUTION WILL BE HELD AT SPRING HILL COLLEGE. (LOCAL). PATRICK F GUYTON, CHAIRPERSON; SPRING HILL COLLEGE BICENTENNIAL COMMITTEE; SPRING HILL COLLEGE; MOBILE, AL 36608. (#22499).

CONSTRUCTION OF FLAG PLAZA IN MOBILE, AL. MOBILE COLLEGE WILL CONSTRUCT A BICENTENNIAL COMMEMORATIVE FLAG PLAZA ON CAMPUS FROM DESIGNS SUBMITTED IN STATEWIDE COMPETITION, THE PLAZA TO BE DEDICATED IN APRIL '76 AT AN AMERICANA CONCERT. (ST-WIDE). THOMAS G HART, CHAIRMAN; MOBILE COLLEGE; PO BOX 13220; MOBILE, AL 36613. (#14419).

MOBILE CITY OF HISTORIC CHURCHES - TV SERIES, AL. 7 THIRTY-MINUTE TELEVISION PROGRAMS PREPARED AND AIRED DURING THE '75-'76 SCHOOL YEAR ON HISTORY & DISTINCTIVE TRADITIONS OF MOBILE'S 7 OLDEST CHURCHES. (LOCAL). THOMAS G HART, PROJ DIRECTOR; MOBILE COLLEGE; PO BOX 13220; MOBILE, AL 36613. (#14418).

PRESERVATION OF ORIGINAL DOCUMENTS, MOBILE, AL. STUDENT-FACULTY RESEARCH TEAMS WILL SORT, CATALOGUE AND PREPARE FOR POSSIBLE PUBLICATION ORIGINAL HISTORICAL DOCUMENTS GIVEN TO MOBILE COLLEGE LIBRARY, ESPECIALLY LETTERS WRITTEN DURING CIVIL WAR. (LOCAL). THOMAS G HART, CHAIRMAN; MOBILE COLLEGE; PO BOX 13220; MOBILE, AL 36613. (#14420).

RESTORATION OF YENNI HALL, MOBILE, AL. RENOVATION AND RESTORATION OF YENNI HALL INTO A HUMANITIES CENTER. (LOCAL). PATRICK F GUYTON, CHAIRPERSON; SPRING HILL COLLEGE BICENTENNIAL COMMITTEE; SPRING HILL; MOBILE, AL 36608. (#22501).

SPIRIT OF AMERICA LECTURE/PERFORMANCE SERIES, AL. THE UNIVERSITY OF SOUTH ALABAMA WILL SPONSOR A SPIRIT OF AMERICA LECTURE/PERFORMANCE SERIES FROM FEBRUARY THROUGH JULY, 1976. (LOCAL). MELTON MCLAURIN, PROGRAM DIRECTOR; UNIV OF SOUTH ALABAMA BICENTENNIAL COMMITTEE; MOBILE, AL 36688. (#24288). **ARBA GRANTEE.**

SPIRIT OF MOBILE MARCHING 200 AND FLAG CORP - AL. A 200 MEMBER MARCHING BAND AND 50 GIRL AMERICAN FLAG CORP FORMED TO BE A 'UNIQUE AND VISIBLE SYMBOL OF MOBILE ALABAMA'S COMMEMORATION OF AMERICA'S BICENTENNIAL.'. (ST-WIDE). JAMES N MORRIS, CHAIRMAN; MOBILE BICENTENNIAL COMMUNITY COMMITTEE; PO BOX 1771; MOBILE, AL 36601. (#20825). **ARBA GRANTEE.**

STUDENT GOVERNMENT SPEAKERS PROGRAM. SEMINAR. (LOCAL). PATRICK F GUYTON, DIR; SPRING HILL COLLEGE STUDENT GOVERNMENT; MOBILE, AL 36608. (#106126-1).

AUG 25 - OCT 31, '75. DESIGN COMPETITION FOR BICENTENNIAL FLAG PLAZA. DESIGN COMPETITION OPEN TO ALL ALABAMA RESIDENTS. AT MOBILE COLLEGE CAMPUS. (ST-WIDE). THOMAS G HART, PROJ DIR; MOBILE COLLEGE; PO BOX 13220; MOBILE, AL 36602. (#101829-1).

SEPT 1, '75 - MAY 29, '76. DECISIONS '75-'76 - AMERICAN ISSUES FORUM. SEMINAR. (LOCAL). PATRICK F GUYTON, DIR; SPRING HILL COLLEGE; MOBILE, AL 36608. (#106126-3).

SEPT 27 - 28, '75. MOBILE'S 11TH ANNUAL OUTDOOR ART & CRAFTS FAIR, 1975. FAIR WILL INCLUDE LIVE MUSICAL ENTERTAINMENT, FOOD, GAMES FOR CHILDREN AND POTTERY & PAINTING DEMONSTRATIONS; FAIR CLOSES SUNDAY, SEPT 28 AT 5 PM; ARTISTS REGISTER AND PAY FEE OF $25 PER SPACE. AT FINE ARTS MUSEUM, LANGAN (MUNICIPAL) PARK. (LOCAL). MRS MARTINA ROSER, COORD; MOBILE ART ASSOC, INC AND ART PATRONS LEAGUE OF MOBILE; PO BOX 8404, FINE ARTS MUSEUM; MOBILE, AL 36608. (#101095-1).

OCT 9, '75 - MAR 18, '76. NEW ORLEANS SYMPHONY ORCHESTRA. LIVE PERFORMANCE AT MOBILE MUNICIPAL THEATRE, CHURCH ST. (LOCAL). THOMAS A GREEN, MANAGER; GREATER MOBILE CONCERTS INC, PO BOX 16366 MOBILE, AL; RM 903, 203 CARONDELET ST; NEW ORLEANS, LA 70130. (#100717-1).

DEC 6 - 7, '75. CANDLELIGHT CHRISTMAS AT OAKLEIGH. CEREMONY AT OAKLEIGH HOUSE. (LOCAL). MS PATSY LOWE, PROJ DIR; HISTORIC MOBILE PRESERVATION SOCIETY; 350 OAKLEIGH PL; MOBILE, AL 36604. (#100975-1).

JAN 1 - 31, '76. CAMELLIA FLOWER SHOW. BICENTENNIAL WILL BE COMMEORATED THROUGHOUT THE YEAR BY FLORAL DISPLAYS DEPICTING EVENTS OF U S HISTORY. (LOCAL). JOHN M BROWN, COORDINATOR; BELLINGRAPH GARDENS; ROUTE 1, BOX 60; THEODORE, AL 36582. (#103416-33).

JAN 11, '76. AZALEA TRAIL QUEEN CORONATION. THE CORONATION WILL BE HELD PRIOR TO THE SENIOR BOWL FOOTBALL GAME. THE QUEEN WILL BE CHOSEN FROM OVER 50 LOCAL HIGH SCHOOL SENIORS. (LOCAL). CARL WILLIAMS, PROJ CHMN; JUNIOR CHAMBER OF COMMERCE; 1209 GOVERNMENT ST; MOBILE, AL 36604. (#103416-30).

JAN 11, '76. 27TH ANNUAL SENIOR BOWL ALL-STAR FOOTBALL GAME. ALL-STAR FOOTBALL GAME FEATURING OUTSTANDING SENIOR PLAYERS FROM THROUGHOUT THE UNITED STATES; NATIONALLY TELEVISED, 12:30 PM (CST); THERE WILL BE A BICENTENNIAL PRE-AIR AND HALF-TIME SHOW. AT LADD MEMORIAL STADIUM. (NAT'L). REA SCHUESSLER, PROJ MGR; MOBILE ARTS & SPORTS ASSOC; PO BOX 2527; MOBILE, AL 36622. (#100662-1).

JAN 13 - 14, '76. TRACK & FIELD SENIOR BOWL TRACK MEET 1976. OPENING AT MOBILE MUNICIPAL AUDITORIUM. (REGN'L). JOHN I WOOD, JR; TRACK AND FIELD ASSOCIATION OF MOBILE, INC; PO BOX 1748; MOBILE, AL 36601. (#100479-1).

JAN 17, '76. YOUNG PATRIOT'S CHILDREN'S HOUR. LIVE PERFORMANCE. (LOCAL). LEE MCCOY, PROJ DIRECTOR; OLD MONTEREY HOUSE & MUSEUM; 1552 MONTEREY PLACE; MOBILE, AL 36604. (#103416-32).

JAN 31 - FEB 1, '76. UNITED STATES ARMED FORCES BICENTENNIAL CARAVAN. CARAVAN IS COMPOSED OF EXHIBIT VANS FOR EACH MILITARY SERVICE. PROJECT THEME IS 'HISTORY OF THE ARMED FORCES AND THEIR CONTRIBUTIONS TO THE NATION'. (LOCAL). JIMMY MORRIS, CHMN; MOBILE BICENTENNIAL COMMISSION; ROOM 501, CHAMBER OF COMMERCE; MOBILE, AL 36608. (#1775-389).

MAR 7 - APR 1, '76. AZALEA TRAIL FESTIVAL. OBSERVANCE OF BLOSSOMING OF MOBILE AZALEAS. THIS 35-MILE FLORAL EXTRAVAGANZA HAS MADE MOBILE KNOWN AS ONE OF AMERICA'S MOST BEAUTIFUL CITIES. INCLUDES SAILBOAT RACE, SQUARE DANCE FESTIVAL, BIKE RIDES, AND BLOOMING AZALEAS. (REGN'L). CARL WILLIAMS, DIRECTOR; MOBILE AZALEA TRAILS, INC & MOBILE JAYCEES; PO BOX 2621; MOBILE, AL 36601. (#103416-112).

MAR 18, '76 - DEC 31, '77. 'BELGIUM & THE UNITED STATES - A BRIEF LOOK AT A LONG FRIENDSHIP'. EXHIBIT. (INT'L). CULTURAL ATTACHE; EMBASSY OF BELGIUM; 3330 GARFIELD ST; WASHINGTON, DC 20008. (#32961-1).

MAR 24 - 26, '76. AMERICAN OPERA 'SUSANNAH' BY CARLISLE FLOYD. EDUCATIONAL PROGRAMS IN SCHOOLS ON OPERA. AT MOBILE MUNICIPAL THEATER. (LOCAL). MRS T K JACKSON, COORD; MOBILE OPERA GUILD; PO BOX 8366; MOBILE, AL 36608. (#100700-1).

APR 17 - 18, '76. BICENTENNIAL ARMED FORCES DAY AIR SHOW. LIVE PERFORMANCE AT MOBILE AEROSPACE INDUSTRIAL COMPLEX. (LOCAL). LTJG W M HAYES, COORD; MOBILE JAYCEES; 1209 GOVERNMENT ST; MOBILE, AL 36601. (#200001-49).

APR 18 - 24, '76. AMERICAN HIGH SCHOOL JAZZ FESTIVAL. FESTIVAL, LIVE PERFORMANCE AT MOBILE MUNICIPAL THEATER. (REGN'L). J C MCALEER, PRESIDENT; MOBILE JAZZ FESTIVAL; PO BOX 1098; MOBILE, AL 36601. (#101820-1).

APR '76. CONCERT OF AMERICAN MUSIC, FLAG PLAZA DEDICATION CEREMONIES. CONCERT OF AMERICAN CLASSICAL AND POPULAR MUSIC WITH FULL CHOIR AND ORCHESTRA COMMEMORATING DEDICATION OF BICENTENNIAL FLAG PLAZA CONSTRUCTED IN MAIN QUADRANGLE OF THE MOBILE COLLEGE CAMPUS. AT MOBILE COLLEGE CAMPUS MAIN QUADRANGLE. (LOCAL). THOMAS G HART, CHAIRMAN; MOBILE COLLEGE ADMINISTRATION MUSIC DEPARTMENT; PO BOX 13220; MOBILE, AL 36613. (#101829-2).

MAY 6 - 10, '76. AMERICA'S JUNIOR MISS PAGEANT. THE OUTSTANDING HIGH SCHOOL SENIOR GIRL OF THE YEAR IS CHOSEN FROM AMONG COMPETITORS FROM THE 50 STATES, ON BASIS OF SCHOLASTIC ACHIEVEMENT, PHYSICAL WELL-BEING, POISE, APPEARANCE, CREATIVE AND PERFORMING ARTS, CONCERN AND ABILITY IN HUMAN RELATIONS. AT MOBILE, MUNICIPAL AUDITORIUM. (NAT'L). ROBERT W HOST, DIR; AMERICA'S JUNIOR MISS PAGEANT; PO BOX 457; MOBILE, AL 36601. (#103416-269).

MAY 11 - 13, '76. AMERICAN FREEDOM TRAIN DISPLAY DAYS AT MOBILE. THE AMERICAN FREEDOM TRAIN INCLUDES 10 EXHIBIT CARS & 2 SHOW CASE CARS DEPICTING DIFFERENT PHASES OF THE AMERICAN EXPERIENCE. ITS ARRIVAL WILL SERVE AS A CATALYST FOR LOCAL BICENTENNIAL CELEBRATIONS BY PEOPLE THROUGHOUT THIS NATION. (ST-WIDE). SY FREEDMAN, DIR OF P/R; THE AMERICAN FREEDOM TRAIN FOUNDATION; 5205 LEESBURG PIKE, SUITE 800; BAILEY'S XRDS, VA 22041. (#1776-91).

MAY 27 - JUNE 5, '76. '1776', A MUSICAL DRAMA. LIVE PERFORMANCE AT JOE JEFFERSON PLAYHOUSE, 11 S CARLEN ST. (LOCAL). SARAH JO ROUSH, SEC; THE JOE JEFFERSON PLAYERS; 216 C DE SALES AVE; MOBILE, AL 36607. (#102254-1).

JULY 1 - 31, '76. BICENTENNIAL ART EXHIBIT. COMPETITION, EXHIBIT AT FINE ARTS MUSEUM, LANGAN (MUNICIPAL) PARK. (LOCAL). MRS JOHN BALTUSNIK, CHMN; MOBILE ART ASSOC, INC; PO BOX 8521; MOBILE, AL 36608. (#101094-1).

JULY 4, '76. 'BATTLE OF MAUVILLA' BOY SCOUT PAGEANT. A PAGEANT ABOUT A BATTLE THAT TOOK PLACE NEAR THIS SITE IN 1574, AS TOLD THROUGH THE WRITINGS OF FOUR TRAVELERS WITH HERNANDO DE SOTO. AT FORT CONDE. (LOCAL). LEO CONRAD, CONCLAVE ADVR; WOA CHALENA LODGE, ORDER OF THE ARROW, BOY SCOUTS OF AMERICA; 2587 GOVERNMENT BLVD; MOBILE, AL 36606. (#105786-1).

MOBILE — CONTINUED

JULY 4, '76. DEDICATION OF RESTORED FORT CONDE. 140-MEMBER FRENCH DELEGATION TO PARTICIPATE IN DEDICATION OF FORT, WHOSE HISTORY SPANS THE ENTIRE AGE OF EXPLORATION, COLONIZATION & DEVELOPMENT OF THE 13 COLONIES. (INT'L). C DEWEY CROWDER, COORD; MOBILE SISTER CITIES FEDERATION; 253 ST ANTHONY ST; MOBILE, AL 36603. (#109007-1).

AUG 25 - 28, '76. SISTER CITIES INTERNATIONAL CONFERENCE. CELEBRATES 20TH ANNIVERSARY OF SCI. AT ADMIRAL SEMMES HOTEL. (REGN'L). TOM GITTENS, VICE PRES; SISTER CITIES INTERNATIONAL; 1612 K ST, NW; WASHINGTON, DC 20006. (#200001-68).

SEPT 7 - DEC 31, '76. SPRING HILL COLLEGE HISTORY DISPLAY. EXHIBIT AT THOMAS BAYNE LIBRARY & STUDENT CENTER. (LOCAL). PATRICK F GUYTON, DIR; SPRING HILL COLLEGE; MOBILE, AL 36608. (#106126-2).

SEPT 25 - 26, '76. 12TH ANNUAL OUTDOOR ARTS & CRAFTS FAIR. FAIR AT THE FINE ARTS MUSEUM OF THE SOUTH-LANGAN PARK. (LOCAL). MRS MARY O'NEILL VICTOR; THE FINE ARTS MUSEUM OF THE SOUTH-LANGAN PARK; MOBILE, AL 36608. (#103416-546).

DEC 11, '76 - JAN 9, '77. 'PITSEOLAK: A RETROSPECTIVE' EXHIBITION. THIS EXHIBITION OF 100 DRAWINGS BY ONE OF CANADA'S LEADING ESKIMO GRAPHIC ARTISTS DEPICTS THE LEGENDS AND THE SPIRIT WORLD OF ESKIMO TRADITIONS. AT THE FINE ARTS MUSEUM OF THE SOUTH. (INT'L). EILEEN HARAKAL, COORD; SMITHSONIAN INSTITUTION TRAVELING EXHIBITION SERVICE; 1000 JEFFERSON DR, SW; WASHINGTON, DC 20560. (#26655-1).

MAR 26 - MAY 1, '77. PERSIAN LOCKS EXHIBITION. THIS EXHIBITION CONTAINS 400 LOCKS DATING FROM EARLY ISLAMIC PERIOD TO EARLY 20TH CENTURY. IN VARIOUS METALS & NUMEROUS ANIMAL SHAPES, THEY REPRESENT OBJECTS FOR PROTECTION AND ITEMS OF RELIGIOUS SIGNIFICANCE. AT FINE ARTS MUSEUM OF THE SOUTH. (INT'L). EILEEN HARAKAL, COORD; SMITHSONIAN INSTITUTION TRAVELING EXHIBITION SERVICE; 1000 JEFFERSON DR, SW; WASHINGTON, DC 20560. (#26662-3).

MONROEVILLE

BEAUTIFICATION PROGRAMS - MONROEVILLE, AL. PLANT LIBERTY TREES AND CONSTRUCT 'BICENTENNIAL LAKE AREA' ON CAMPUS. (LOCAL). BOBBY B DEES, DIRECTOR; PATRICK HENRY STATE JUNIOR COLLEGE; MONROEVILLE, AL 36460. (#25465).

BICENTENNIAL SCHOLARSHIPS '76 - MONROEVILLE, AL. GIVE 15 SCHOLARSHIPS DURING MAY, 1976 TO BE USED IN THE FALL TO ATTEND PATRICK HENRY COLLEGE. (LOCAL). BOBBY B DEES, DIRECTOR; PATRICK HENRY STATE JUNIOR COLLEGE; MONROEVILLE, AL 36460. (#25464).

'CULTURALISM' - EXHIBIT. A DISPLAY OF A VARIETY OF HANDICRAFTS, WEARING APPAREL AND HISTORICAL NEWSPAPERS. (LOCAL). BOBBY B DEES, DIR; PATRICK HENRY STATE JUNIOR COLLEGE; MONROEVILLE, AL 36460. (#108062-2).

SEPT 26, '76. DANCE FESTIVAL. FESTIVAL AT ROLAND COOPER HALL. (LOCAL). BOBBY BARKSDALE DEES, DIR; PATRICK HENRY STATE JUNIOR COLLEGE; MONROEVILLE, AL 36460. (#108062-3).

OCT 16, '76. BICENTENNIAL PARADE. PARADE AT DOWNTOWN MONROEVILLE. (LOCAL). BOBBY BARKSDALE DEES, DIR; PATRICK HENRY STATE JUNIOR COLLEGE; MONROEVILLE, AL 36460. (#108062-1).

MONTEVALLO

COOPERATIVE PROJECT WITH PUBLIC SCHOOLS - AL. A COOPERATIVE PROJECT DESIGNED TO STIMULATE BICENTENNIAL ACTIVITIES IN PUBLIC SCHOOLS WHERE UNIV STUDENTS SERVE THEIR APPRENTICESHIPS. (LOCAL). CHARLES GORMLEY, ASSOC PROFESSOR; COLLEGE OF EDUCATION, UNIV OF MONTEVALLO; MONTEVALLO, AL 35115. (#13616).

LIBERTY TREE PLANTINGS - MONTEVALLO, AL. 1500 TREES WILL BE PLANTED BY SCHOOL STUDENTS. EACH STUDENT WILL GET ONE TREE. SCHOOLS WILL TEACH THE HISTORICAL NATURE OF LIBERTY TREES. (LOCAL). J DANNY COOPER, CHAIRPERSON; MONTEVALLO BICENTENNIAL COMMISSION; PO BOX 1776; MONTEVALLO, AL 35115. (#19473).

SCHOOL TEXTBOOKS & EQUIPMENT IN EARLIER TIMES - AL. EXHIBITS OF HISTORICAL EDUCATIONAL TEXTBOOKS AND EQUIPMENT BY THE COLLEGE OF EDUCATION. (LOCAL). CHARLES GORMLEY, ASSOC PROFESSOR; COLLEGE OF EDUCATION, UNIV OF MONTEVALLO; MONTEVALLO, AL 35115. (#13614).

SPIRIT OF '76 PARK PROJECT - MONTEVALLO, AL. RENOVATION OF DEPOT TO MAKE IT A COMMUNITY CENTER. (LOCAL). ERIC STIPE, PROJECT DIRECTOR; MONTEVALLO BICENTENNIAL COMMISSION; PO BOX 1776; MINTEVALLO, AL 35115. (#30055). **ARBA GRANTEE.**

UNIV OF MONTEVALLO LIBRARY COLLECTION - AL. A COLLECTION OF GREAT WORKS DEALING WITH AMERICAN HISTORY, LITERATURE, EDUCATION, BUSINESS AND MUSIC. (LOCAL). DAVID T MORGAN, CHAIRMAN; UNIV OF MONTEVALLO BICENTENNIAL COMMITTEE; MONTEVALLO, AL 35115. (#27354). **ARBA GRANTEE.**

SEPT 8 - 23, '75. PAINTING EXHIBITION, STUDENT WORK. EXHIBIT AT BLOCH HALL, U OF M CAMPUS. (LOCAL). JOHN B LOTT, DIRECTOR; UNIV OF MONTEVALLO BICENTENNIAL COMMITTEE & ART DEPT; ENGLISH DEPT, COMER HALL; MONTEVALLO, AL 35115. (#101153-1).

SEPT 16 - 18, '75. YARBROUGH AND COWAN DUO PIANISTS CONCERT, AMERICAN MUSIC. LIVE PERFORMANCE. (LOCAL). JOHN B LOTT, DIRECTOR; UNIV OF MONTEVALLO BICENTENNIAL COMMITTEE & MUSIC DEPT; ENGLISH DEPT, COMER HALL; MONTEVALLO, AL 35115. (#101156-1).

OCT 14, '75 - APR 15, '76. CONCERT & LECTURE SERIES BASED ON AMERICAN THEMES. 10/14: 'WHO KILLED JFK?', 11/4: LECTURER: KRAFFT EHRICKE, 2/17:PANTOMINE: LOTTIE GOSLAR, 4/7: BIRMINGHAM SYMPHONY 4/15: NATIONAL SHAKESPEARE CO: 'THE TEMPEST'. AT PALMER HALL AUDITORIUM, UNIV OF MONTEVALLO CAMPUS. (LOCAL). JOHN STEWART, CHAIRMAN; CONCERT & LECTURE SERIES COMMITTEE, UNIV OF MONTEVALLO; MONTEVALLO, AL 35115. (#13603-1).

OCT 20 - NOV 1, '75. SCULPTURE EXHIBITION, STUDENT WORK. EXHIBIT AT BLOCH HALL, U OF M CAMPUS. (LOCAL). JOHN B LOTT, DIRECTOR; UNIV OF MONTEVALLO BICENTENNIAL COMMITTEE & ART DEPT; ENGLISH DEPT, COMER HALL; MONTEVALLO, AL 35115. (#101154-1).

OCT 29 - NOV 13, '75. PRINT EXHIBITION BY DAVID BERNARD. EXHIBIT AT BLOCH HALL, U OF M CAMPUS. (LOCAL). JOHN B LOTT, DIRECTOR; UNIV OF MONTEVALLO BICENTENNIAL COMMITTEE & UNIV ART DEPT; ENGLISH DEPT, COMER HALL; MONTEVALLO, AL 35115. (#101157-1).

OCT 30, '75. UNIVERSITY OF MONTEVALLO JAZZ ENSEMBLE. LIVE PERFORMANCE. (LOCAL). JOHN B LOTT, DIRECTOR; UNIV OF MONTEVALLO BICENTENNIAL COMMITTEE & UNIV ART DEPT; ENGLISH DEPT, COMER HALL, U OF M; MONTEVALLO, AL 35115. (#101158-1).

NOV 10, '75. CHAMBER MUSIC SERIES CONCERT, AMERICAN MUSIC, STUDENT GROUP. LIVE PERFORMANCE. (LOCAL). JOHN B LOTT, DIRECTOR; UNIV OF MONTEVALLO BICENTENNIAL COMMITTEE & MUSIC DEPT; ENGLISH DEPT, COMER HALL; MONTEVALLO, AL 35115. (#101155-1).

NOV 19, '75. THEATRE PRODUCTION OF 'UNCLE TOM'S CABIN' BY UNIV OF MONTEVALLO. LIVE PERFORMANCE. (LOCAL). JOHN B LOTT, DIRECTOR; UNIV OF MONTEVALLO BICENTENNIAL COMMITTEE; SPEECH & THEATRE DEPT; ENGLISH DEPT, COMER HALL; MONTEVALLO, AL 35115. (#101159-1).

JAN 10, '76. MISS BICENTENNIAL CONTEST. MISS BICENTENNIAL WILL REIGN AT ALL OFFICIAL LOCAL BICENTENNIAL EVENTS AND WILL REPRESENT THE CITY THROUGHOUT 1976. (LOCAL). MRS CONNIE ADAMS; MONTEVALLO BICENTENNIAL COMMISSION; 488 PINEVIEW; MONTEVALLO, AL 35115. (#104449-3).

JAN 12 - 24, '76. PAINTING EXHIBITION, FACULTY WORK. EXHIBIT AT BLOCH HALL, U OF M CAMPUS. (LOCAL). JOHN B LOTT, DIRECTOR; UNIV OF MONTEVALLO BICENTENNIAL COMMITTEE & UNIV ART DEPT; ENGLISH DEPT, COMER HALL; MONTEVALLO, AL 35115. (#101161-1).

FEB 25, '76. UNIVERSITY OF MONTEVALLO CONCERT BAND. CONCERT OF AMERICAN SELECTIONS. (LOCAL). JOHN B LOTT, DIRECTOR; UNIV OF MONTEVALLO BICENTENNIAL COMMITTEE & UNIV MUSIC DEPT; ENGLISH DEPT, COMER HALL; MONTEVALLO, AL 35115. (#101160-1).

MAR 24 - 25, '76. CHILDREN'S THEATRE, AMERICAN PLAY PRODUCTION. LIVE PERFORMANCE AT PALMER HALL, U OF M CAMPUS. (LOCAL). JOHN B LOTT, DIRECTOR; UNIV OF MONTEVALLO BICENTENNIAL COMMITTEE; SPEECH & THEATRE DEPT; ENGLISH DEPT, COMER HALL, U OF M; MONTEVALLO, AL 35115. (#101166-1).

MAR 29, '76. THEATRE PRODUCTION OF 'ALL THE WAY HOME'. LIVE PERFORMANCE. (LOCAL). JOHN B LOTT, DIRECTOR; UNIV OF MONTEVALLO BICENTENNIAL COMMITTEE; SPEECH & THEATRE DEPT; ENGLISH DEPT, COMER HALL, U OF M; MONTEVALLO, AL 35115. (#101165-1).

APR 7, '76. U OF M CHAMBER CHOIR CONCERT, STUDENT CHOIR, AMERICAN SELECTIONS. LIVE PERFORMANCE AT NEW MUSIC BUILDING, U OF M CAMPUS. (LOCAL). JOHN B LOTT, DIRECTOR; UNIV OF MONTEVALLO BICENTENNIAL COMMITTEE & MUSIC DEPT; ENGLISH DEPT, COMER HALL, U OF M; MONTEVALLO, AL 35115. (#101164-1).

APR 12, '76. UNIV OF MONTEVALLO CAMPUS COMPOSERS CONCERT. ORIGINAL WORKS OF STUDENTS & FACULTY. AT NEW MUSIC BUILDING, U OF M CAMPUS. (LOCAL). JOHN B LOTT, DIRECTOR; UNIV OF MONTEVALLO BICENTENNIAL COMMITTEE & UNIV MUSIC DEPT; ENGLISH DEPT, COMER HALL; MONTEVALLO, AL 35115. (#101163-1).

APR 19, '76. RE-ENACTMENT OF PAUL REVERE RIDE. ALL LOCAL CITIZENS WHO RIDE HORSES & WANT TO, WILL DRESS LIKE PAUL REVERE. THEY WILL RIDE THROUGH THE CITY STREETS WITH LANTERNS IN HAND TO WARN THAT THE BRITISH ARE COMING. SCHOOL PROGRAMS WILL HELP EDUCATE PUBLIC IN ADVANCE & ASK PUBLIC TO PLACE LANTERNS IN WINDOWS. AT EVERY ST AVE & RD. (LOCAL). J DANNY COOPER; MONTEVALLO BICENTENNIAL COMMISSION; BOX 1776; MONTEVALLO, AL 35115. (#104449-2).

APR 19 - 24, '76. 'AMERICAN WAYS & VALUES: 1776-1976' LECTURE SERIES. LECTURES GIVEN TO UNIVERSITY COMMUNITY AND TOWNSPEOPLE - TO BE HELD DURING BICENTENNIAL WEEK (APRIL 19-23, 1976). AT UNIV OF MONTEVALLO CAMPUS. (LOCAL). DAVID T MORGAN, CHAIRMAN; SOCIAL SCIENCE DEPT, UNIV OF MONTEVALLO; MONTEVALLO, AL 35115. (#13611-1).

APR 19 - 24, '76. EXHIBITS, HISTORICAL & AMERICANA. COLLECTION OF HISTORICAL EXHIBITS & EXHIBITS OF AMERICANA. AT CARMICHAEL LIBRARY, UNIV OF MONTEVALLO. (LOCAL). MARY FRANCES TIPTON; CARMICHAEL LIBRARY, UNIV OF MONTEVALLO; MONTEVALLO, AL 35115. (#13613-1).

APR 21, '76. SPEECHES: AMERICAN POLITICAL TRADITION. LECTURES BY PROMINENT POLITICAL FIGURE DURING BICENTENNIAL WEEK, APRIL 19-23, 1976, ON SOME ASPECT OF THE AMERICAN POLITICAL TRADITION; INCLUDED WILL BE SOCIAL ACTIVITIES. AT PALMER HALL AUDITORIUM. (LOCAL). DAVID T MORGAN, CHAIRMAN; SOCIAL SCIENCE DEPT, UNIV OF MONTEVALLO; MONTEVALLO, AL 35115. (#13612-1).

APR 22, '76. THE AMERICAN WOMAN; FASHIONS, HISTORICAL CLOTHING; HOUSEHOLD EXHIB. EXHIBITS OF CLOTHING AND HOUSEHOLD GOODS FROM VARIOUS STAGES OF THE NATION'S DEVELOPMENT WILL BE DISPLAYED BY THE DEPT OF HOME ECONOMICS THROUGHOUT THE YEAR. FILMSTRIP ON 200 YRS OF FASHIONS SHOWN AT INTERVALS THROUGHOUT THE DAY. AT BLOCH HALL, 2ND FLOOR & ROOM 111.. (LOCAL). REBECCA LYON, CHAIRMAN; HOME ECONOMICS DEPT, UNIV OF MONTEVALLO; BLOCH HALL; MONTEVALLO, AL 35115. (#13615-1).

APR 26 - 30, '76. MUSICAL THEATRE OF SELECTED WORKS. LIVE PERFORMANCE AT PALMER HALL, U OF M CAMPUS. (LOCAL). JOHN B LOTT, DIRECTOR; UNIV OF MONTEVALLO BICENTENNIAL COMMITTEE & UNIV MUSIC DEPT; ENGLISH DEPT, COMER HALL; MONTEVALLO, AL 35115. (#101162-1).

MONTGOMERY

ALABAMA BICENTENNIAL BELLE PAGEANT, MONTGOMERY. A PAGEANT TO SELECT THE OFFICIAL STATE BICENTENNIAL HOSTESS. (ST-WIDE). JACK W WALLACE, JR, COORDINATOR; ALABAMA BICENTENNIAL COMMISSION; 321 N HULL; MONTGOMERY, AL 36104. (#26599). **ARBA GRANTEE.**

ALABAMA LIVING HISTORY. SHORT MULTI-MEDIA PRESENTATION OF ALABAMA HISTORY TO BE CARRIED BY VAN STATEWIDE TO COMMUNITIES & SCHOOLS. ALSO PUBLICATION OF HISTORY BOOKLET & GUIDE. (ST-WIDE). ROBERT M BOWICK, EXEC DIRECTOR; ALABAMA ARBC; 138 ADAMS ST; MONTGOMERY, AL 36104. (#821). **ARBA GRANTEE.**

BARTRAM TRAIL CONFERENCE - MONTGOMERY, AL. MONTGOMERY, AL, WILL HOST THE SOUTHEASTERN BARTRAM CONFERENCE. (REGN'L). MARTHA MCINNIS, EXEC DIRECTOR; ALABAMA ENVIRONMENTAL QUALITY ASSN-ENVIROSOUTH; PO BOX 11000; MONTGOMERY, AL 36111. (#19276). **ARBA GRANTEE.**

BARTRAM TRAIL HISTORIC MARKERS - MONTGOMERY, AL. COMMEMORATION OF THE PATH OF THE GREAT BOTANIST, WILLIAM BARTRAM. MARKERS WILL BE PLACED FROM PHENIX CITY TO MONTGOMERY TO MOBILE BAY. (LOCAL). W WARNER FLOYD, DIRECTOR; ALABAMA HISTORICAL COMMISSION; 725 MONROE ST; MONTGOMERY, AL 36130. (#27859). **ARBA GRANTEE.**

BICENTENNIAL TRAIL AND COMMUNITY PARKS, AL. A TRAIL CONSISTING OF TOP HISTORIC & SCENIC SITES IN STATE. 30 INCH DIAMETER SIGNS MARK EACH SITE. A PAMPHLET IS TO BE DISTRIBUTED DESCRIBING LOCATIONS, ACCESSABILITY AND SIGNIFICANCE. (ST-WIDE). ROBERT M BOSWICK, EXEC DIRECTOR; ALABAMA BICENTENNIAL COMMISSION; 321 N HALL ST; MONTGOMERY, AL 36104. (#13697). **ARBA GRANTEE.**

FIFE & DRUM CORPS - MONTGOMERY, AL. A 24-MEMBER UNIT AVAILABLE TO PLAY AT BICENTENNIAL FUNCTIONS. (LOCAL). MARY JO WIMSATT, DIRECTOR; MONTGOMERY BICENTENNIAL COMMITTEE; 1735 HIGHLAND AVE; MONTGOMERY, AL 36106. (#22285). **ARBA GRANTEE.**

FILM ON CAPITOL COMPLEX & STATE GOVERNMENT. A 16MM FILM ON THE CAPITOL COMPLEX AND THE WORKINGS OF THE STATE GOVERNMENT. (ST-WIDE). W RAYMOND JONES, CHIEF SPECIALIST; ALABAMA STATE DEPT OF EDUCATION; 346 STATE OFFICE BLDG; MONTGOMERY, AL 36104. (#23631). **ARBA GRANTEE.**

FRAME CABIN, MONTGOMERY, AL. A FRAME CABIN WILL BE MOVED AND RESTORED FOR USE AS A MUSEUM. (LOCAL). JOHN F VAUGHN, DIRECTOR; LANDMARKS FOUNDATION OF MONTGOMERY, INC; 220 N HULL ST; MONTGOMERY, AL 36104. (#23731). **ARBA GRANTEE.**

HEART OF HEART OF DIXIE TOUR, 5 STATE CAPITALS. HISTORIC SITES IN 5 STATE CAPITALS FROM DESOTO 1540; BIENVILLE 1714, FRENCH FORT TOULOUSE, GREEK INFLUENCE AT JASMINE GARDENS & PARTHENON REPLICA, JACKSON, BOONE; TUSCALOOSA, NASHVILLE, FRANKFORT, MONTGOMRY. (REGN'L). THOMAS J MCMAHON, DIRECTOR OF MARKETING; AMCON HOLIDAY INNS DIVISION; 2731 NONCONNAH BLVD; MEMPHIS, TN 38130. (#1839). **ARBA GRANTEE.**

'HOW YOU COMING ALABAMA' - MONTGOMERY, AL. A 16MM FILM WILL BE MADE ON A LIVING HISTORY PROJECT; IT WILL HAVE A 45RPM RECORDING OF ITS SOUNDTRACK. (ST-WIDE). ROBERT M BOWICK, EXEC DIRECTOR; ALABAMA BICENTENNIAL COMMISSION; 321 N HALL ST; MONTGOMERY, AL 36104. (#13445). **ARBA GRANTEE.**

JASMINE HILL AMPHITHEATRE - MONTGOMERY, AL. FACILITY WILL BE USED FOR MUSICAL AND STAGE PRESENTATIONS ON A REGULAR BASIS. (LOCAL). JIM INSCOE, CHAIRMAN; JASMINE HILL ARTS COUNCIL; 2437 LEONIDAS DR; MONTGOMERY, AL 36106. (#26005). **ARBA GRANTEE.**

LOG CABIN MUSEUM, MONTGOMERY, AL. THE LOG CABIN IS BEING MOVED TO THE ORDEMAN-SHAW MUSEUM. (LOCAL). JOHN F VAUGHN, DIRECTOR; LANDMARKS FOUNDATION OF MONTGOMERY, INC; 220 N HULL ST; MONTGOMERY, AL 36104. (#23729). **ARBA GRANTEE.**

MANUAL ON HOW TO WRITE A LOCAL HISTORY - AL. PREPARE, PUBLISH AND DISTRIBUTE A MANUAL ON HOW TO PREPARE A LOCAL HISTORY; IT WILL BE USED TO STIMULATE THE PREPARATION OF COUNTY HISTORIES. (ST-WIDE). W WARNER FLOYD, EXEC DIRECTOR; ALABAMA HISTORICAL COMMISSION; 725 MONROE ST; MONTGOMERY, AL 36130. (#23630). **ARBA GRANTEE.**

MONTGOMERY — CONTINUED

MONTGOMERY, AL, JULY 4TH CELEBRATION. 4TH OF JULY CELEBRATION WITH PARADE, TOUR, CEREMONY, DISPLAYS, FIREWORKS AND CRAFTS SHOW. (LOCAL). MARY J WIMSATT, DIRECTOR; MONTGOMERY BICENTENNIAL COMMITTEE; 1735 HIGHLAND AVE; MONTGOMERY, AL 36106. (#27283). **ARBA GRANTEE.**

SUMMER READING PROGRAM - MONTGOMERY, AL. THE ALABAMA PUBLIC LIBRARY SERVICE IS SPONSORING A SUMMER READING PROGRAM ON AMERICAN HISTORY. (ST-WIDE). SUE SMITH, CHAIRMAN; ALABAMA PUBLIC LIBRARY SERVICE; 155 ADMINISTRATIVE BLDG; MONTGOMERY, AL 36104. (#27207). **ARBA GRANTEE.**

WILLIAM BARTRAM ARBORETUM, MONTGOMERY, AL. PLANT LIFE FROM THE REVOLUTIONARY WAR PERIOD TO THE PRESENT AND INTO THE FUTURE WILL BE PORTRAYED. (LOCAL). W WARNER FLOYD, EXEC DIRECTOR; ALABAMA HISTORICAL COMMISSION; 725 MONROE ST; MONTGOMERY, AL 36130. (#27696). **ARBA GRANTEE.**

16 MM FILM ON THE HISTORY OF EDUCATION IN AL. THE ALABAMA STATE DEPT OF EDUCATION WILL PRODUCE A 16MM FILM ON THE HISTORY OF EDUCATION IN ALABAMA. (ST-WIDE). W RAYMOND JONES, CHIEF SPECIALIST; ALABAMA STATE DEPT OF EDUCATION; 346 STATE OFFICE BLDG; MONTGOMERY, AL 36130. (#23629). **ARBA GRANTEE.**

'76 ACTION PROJECT OF ALABAMA. PROGRAMS TO IMPROVE & DEVELOP VARIOUS COMMUNITY FACILITIES WILL BE DEVISED BY STATE GOVERNMENT OFFICIALS, PRIVATE ORGANIZATIONS & THE STATE'S 450 MAYORS. (ST-WIDE). ROBERT BOWICK, EXEC DIRECTOR; ALABAMA ARBC; 321 N HULL ST; MONTGOMERY, AL 36104. (#323).

MAR 1 - APR 1, '75. FLAG RAISING & EXHIBIT, LECTURES, PARADES, FLAG BALLET & DEBATES. INTERPRETIVE EXHIBITION OF ORIGINAL & HISTORIC FLAGS TRACING HISTORICAL & ARTISTIC MOTIFS OF USA FLAGS FROM COLONIZATION TO THE PRESENT & INTO THE FUTURE. THIS EXHIBIT HAS TOURED FOUR OTHER REGIONS OF THE NATION. (REGN'L). CHARLES E BRANNON; TUMBLING WATERS MUSEUM OF FLAGS; 2080 MYRTLEWOOD DR; MONTGOMERY, AL 36111. (#5642-501).

JUNE 1 - NOV 1, '75. ALABAMA FARM BUREAU WOMEN'S BICENTENNIAL CONTEST. CONTEST TO DEVELOP PROGRAM SUITABLE FOR RADIO, TV OR DRAMA PRESENTATION ON HISTORY OF AMERICA & ALABAMA FROM INDIAN TIMES TO 1976. MAY BE PRODUCED BY ANY AGE GROUP & MUST BE SPONSORED BY LOCAL FARM BUREAU WOMEN'S COUNTY GROUP, WHICH WILL JUDGE LOCAL CONTESTS. (ST-WIDE). MILLA D BOSCHUNG, DIR; WOMEN'S DIVISION, ALABAMA FARM BUREAU FEDERATION; PO BOX 11000; MONTGOMERY, AL 36111. (#100942-1).

NOV 3 - 4, '75. BARTRAM TRAIL CONFERENCE. CONFERENCE AT GOVERNOR'S HOUSE MOTEL. (REGN'L). MARTHA MCINNIS, EXEC DIR; ALABAMA ENVIRONMENTAL QUALITY ASSOCIATION-ENVIROSOUTH; PO BOX 11000; MONTGOMERY, AL 36111. (#19276-1).

DEC 19, '75. BLUE & GRAY FOOTBALL GAME, 1975. GAME WILL BE TELEVISED NATIONALLY. PLAYERS ARE FROM MAJOR UNIVERSITIES FROM ALL OVER THE U. S. AT CRAMTON BOWL, MADISON AVE. (NAT'L). ALLYN MCKEEN, GEN MANAGER; MONTGOMERY LIONS CLUB; PO BOX 11001; MONTGOMERY, AL 36111. (#100727-1).

JAN 22 - 24, '76. ALABAMA JUNIOR MISS PAGEANT 1976. LIVE PERFORMANCE, COMPETITION AT ROBERT E LEE HIGH SCHOOL AUDITORIUM, 225 ANN ST. (ST-WIDE). CHARLES B SAVAGE, PRES; ALABAMA JUNIOR MISS PAGEANT, INC; PO BOX 4117; MONTGOMERY, AL 36102. (#100784-1).

JAN 24 - 25, '76. UNITED STATES ARMED FORCES BICENTENNIAL CARAVAN. CARAVAN IS COMPOSED OF EXHIBIT VANS FOR EACH MILITARY SERVICE. PROJECT THEME IS 'HISTORY OF THE ARMED FORCES AND THEIR CONTRIBUTIONS TO THE NATION'. (LOCAL). MAJ CECIL G BRENDLE, DIR; MONTGOMERY BICENTENNIAL COMMITTEE; PO BOX 2584; MONTGOMERY, AL 36105. (#1775-385).

FEB 13, '76. THE TODAY SHOW FEATURES THE STATE OF ALABAMA. A CONTINUING WEEKLY SERIES OF PROGRAMS COMMEMORATING EACH STATE. ALABAMA WAS ADMITTED INTO THE UNION IN DECEMBER, 1819. (NAT'L). STUART SCHULBERG, EX PROD; NATIONAL BROADCASTING CO; 30 ROCKEFELLER PLAZA; NEW YORK, NY 10020. (#7981-12).

MAR 10 - 13, '76. WORLD CHAMPIONSHIP RODEO 1976. COMPETITION AT GARRETT COLISEUM, 1555 FEDERAL DR HWY 231 N, AMPLE PARKING. (REGN'L). E HAM WILSON, PROJ DIR; SOUTHEASTERN LIVESTOCK EXPOSITION INC & AL CATTEMEN'S ASSOC; 600 ADAMS AVE; MONTGOMERY, AL 36104. (#100719-1).

MAR 27, '76. YANKEE DOODLE FAIR. FAIR AT OAK PARK, 1010 FOREST AVE. (LOCAL). A BARRETT, SPB ADVISOR; S CENTRAL AL GIRL SCOUT COUNCIL & MONTGOMERY PARKS & RECREATION DEPT; 10 W PATTON AVE; MONTGOMERY, AL 36105. (#104025-1).

APR 23 - 25, '76. GEORGE LINDSEY CELEBRITY WEEKEND AND GOLF TOURNAMENT. COMPETITION, FESTIVAL AT GARRETT COLISEUM AND ARROWHEAD COUNTRY CLUB. (REGN'L). E TAYLOR SEALE, CHAIRMAN; ALABAMA SPECIAL OLYMPICS INC; PO BOX 1443; MONTGOMERY, AL 36102. (#103416-233).

JUNE 16 - 18, '76. BICENTENNIAL BELLE PAGEANT TO CHOOSE STATE BICENTENNIAL HOSTESS. COMPETITION, CEREMONY AT ROBERT E LEE HIGH SCHOOL AUDITORIUM. (ST-WIDE). JACK W WALLACE, JR; ALABAMA BICENTENNIAL COMMISSION; 321 N HULL; MONTGOMERY, AL 36104. (#26599-1).

JULY 2 - 5, '76. FOURTH OF JULY CELEBRATION. PARADE, TOURS, CEREMONIES, DISPLAYS, CRAFT SHOW & FIREWORKS DISPLAY. (LOCAL). MARY JO WIMSATT, DIRECTOR; MONTGOMERY BICENTENNIAL COMMITTEE; 1735 HIGHLAND AVE; MONTGOMERY, AL 36106. (#27283-1).

SEPT 25 - 26, '76. RUMMAGE ROUNDUP '76. FESTIVAL AT GARRETT COLISEUM, FEDERAL DR. (LOCAL). SUSAN HAIGLER, CHMN; JUNIOR LEAGUE OF MONTGOMERY; OLD FORT RD; FT DEPOSIT, AL 36032. (#101351-1).

OCT 18 - 23, '76. SOUTH ALABAMA STATE FAIR. FAIR AT GARRETT COLISEUM FEDERAL DRIVE MONTGOMERY, ALABAMA. (REGN'L). WILLIAM R LYNN, V-PRES; SOUTH ALABAMA STATE FAIR ASSOCIATION, INC; PERRY HILL OFFICE PARK, BOX 3304; MONTGOMERY, AL 36109. (#106095-34).

NOV 6, '76. ARTS & CRAFTS & FLEA MARKET. INCLUDES TIME CAPSULE CEREMONY & COSTUME CONTEST FOR 2076. PROCEEDS GO TOWARDS RESTORATION OF MARKS HOUSE, BUILT AROUND 1825. AT MARKS HOUSE, 1 MILE S PIKE RD, 10 MILES SE OF MONTGOMERY. (LOCAL). JULIA B NORRIS, PUBLICITY; PIKE RD CIVIC CLUB; 6850 VAUGHAN RD; MONTGOMERY, AL 36116. (#200001-67).

MOULTON

BEAUTIFICATION OF SCHOOL ENTRANCES - MOULTON, AL. SIGNS, SHRUBS & FLOWERS WILL BEAUTIFY SCHOOL ENTRANCES. (LOCAL). CECIL V LAUDERDALE, CHAIRMAN; LAWRENCE COUNTY BICENTENNIAL COMMITTEE; 202 W COURT ST; MOULTON, AL 35650. (#25687). **ARBA GRANTEE.**

BEAUTIFICATION PROJ - MOULTON, AL. HIGHWAY INTERSECTIONS WILL BE BEAUTIFIED WITH WELCOME SIGNS AND SHRUBBERY. (LOCAL). CECIL V LAUDERDALE, CHAIRMAN; LAWRENCE COUNTY BICENTENNIAL COMMITTEE; 202 W COURT ST; MOULTON, AL 35650. (#25686). **ARBA GRANTEE.**

LOG MCMILLIAN SCHOOLHOUSE - MOULTON, AL. RELOCATE AND REPAIR OLD SCHOOLHOUSE FOR MUSEUM. (LOCAL). CECIL V LAUDERDALE, CHAIRMAN; LAWRENCE CO BICENTENNIAL COMMITTEE; 202 W COURT ST; MOULTON, AL 35650. (#25905). **ARBA GRANTEE.**

MOUNDVILLE

APR 18, '76. THE ROAD TO CALVARY, ANNUAL EASTER PAGEANT. PAGEANT PRESENTED EASTER MORNING BEFORE DAWN ENDS AT SUNRISE. AT 3 INDIAN MOUNDS, MOUND STATE PARK, OPEN ARENA FOR SPECTATORS. (LOCAL). MRS CLYDE R SHIPLEY; MOUNDVILLE METHODIST CHURCH; PO BOX 36; MOUNDVILLE, AL 35474. (#100720-1).

MAY 7 - 8, '76. THE MOUND BUILDERS - A HERITAGE PAGEANT. CAST OF 65, DIRECTED BY MISS JAN WILSON. AT MOUND STATE PARK. (LOCAL). MRS ED THORNTON, COORD; MOUNDVILLE BICENTENNIAL COMMISSION & HALE CO COUNCIL FOR THE ARTS; PO BOX 50; CYPRESS, AL 35454. (#106248-1).

NORTHPORT

AMERICAN FLAGS ON MCFARLAND BOULEVARD, AL. AMERICAN FLAGS WILL BE FLYING ON MCFARLAND BOULEVARD THROUGH THE BICENTENNIAL YEAR. (LOCAL). MARVIN HARPER, CHAIRPERSON; NORTHPORT BICENTENNIAL COMMISSION; PO BOX 306; NORTHPORT, AL 35476. (#23833). **ARBA GRANTEE.**

MILITARY UNIFORM DISPLAY - NORTHPORT, AL. RESEARCH DATA ON AUTHENTIC MILITARY UNIFORM COLLECTION ON HAND AND ACQUIRE MANEQUINS TO DISPLAY UNIFORMS. (LOCAL). MARVIN L HARPER, CHAIRPERSON; NORTHPORT BICENTENNIAL COMMISSION; PO BOX 306; NORTHPORT, AL 35476. (#23832). **ARBA GRANTEE.**

NORTHPORT BEAUTIFICATION PROJ - NORTHPORT, AL. PLANTINGS AND CLEANUP ON MCFARLAND BOULEVARD, MAIN AVENUE AND ENTRANCE TO PARKS. (LOCAL). MARVIN L HARPER, CHAIRPERSON; NORTHPORT BICENTENNIAL COMMISSION; PO BOX 306; NORTHPORT, AL 35476. (#23831). **ARBA GRANTEE.**

RURAL MUSEUM - NORTHPORT, AL. ACQUIRE STRUCTURE AND INITIATE A RURAL MUSEUM CONTAINING ITEMS REPRESENTING YESTERYEAR OF TUSCALOOSA COUNTY. (LOCAL). MARVIN L HARPER, CHAIRPERSON; NORTHPORT BICENTENNIAL COMMISSION; PO BOX 306; NORTHPORT, AL 35476. (#23834). **ARBA GRANTEE.**

SEPT 5, '75. STREET DANCE WITH ROCK BAND AND COUNTRY BAND. FESTIVAL, LIVE PERFORMANCE AT MAIN ST. (LOCAL). AL KNIGHT, PROJ DIRECTOR; NORTHPORT CHAMBER OF COMMERCE; PO BOX 127; NORTHPORT, AL 35476. (#101263-1).

SEPT 6 - 7, '75. KENTUCK CRAFT FAIR. CRAFTS, GRAPHIC ARTS, PAINTINGS AND PHOTOGRAPHY WILL BE DEMONSTRATED AND SOLD. AT KENTUCK PARK ON WARRIOR RIVER, 3 BLOCKS FROM DOWNTOWN NORTHPORT. (ST-WIDE). AL KNIGHT, CHAIRMAN; KENTUCK FAIR COMMITTEE; PO BOX 127; NORTHPORT, AL 35476. (#101262-1).

ONEONTA

BEAUTIFICATION OF PALISADES PARK - ONEONTA, AL. PLANTING OF TREES, SHRUBS & LANDSCAPING OF A HOP COUNTY PARK FOR A BLOUNT COUNTY BICENTENNIAL PARK; IT WILL BE USED FOR OUTDOOR CLASSES AND FAMILY PICNIC AREAS. (LOCAL). AMILEA PORTER, PRESIDENT; VARIOSA CLUB AFWC; 308 5TH AVE E; ONEONTA, AL 35121. (#22286). **ARBA GRANTEE.**

FURNISHING LOG CABIN WITH PRIMITIVE FURNITURE, AL. MURPHREE LOG CABIN HAS BEEN RESTORED AND MOVED TO PALISADES PARK. IT IS 150 YEARS OLD AND ONE OF THE FIRST BUILT IN THE COUNTY. IT WILL BE FURNISHED WITH PRIMITIVE FURNITURE FOR THE BICENTENNIAL. (ST-WIDE). AMILEA PORTER, SECRETARY/TREASURER; BLOUNT COUNTY BICENTENNIAL COMMITTEE; 308 5 AVE, E; ONEONTA, AL 35121. (#23733). **ARBA GRANTEE.**

OPELIKA

MAR - MAY '76. OPELIKA JAYCEE'S DOGWOOD & AZALEA TRAIL. A 15-MINUTE DRIVE BY AUTO DOWN THE FLOWER TRAIL WHILE FLOWERS ARE IN FULL BLOOM. (LOCAL). JOHN C BEDSOLE JR, PRES; OPELIKA JAYCEES; 1300 PINEDALE DR; OPELIKA, AL 36801. (#100663-1).

OPP

PUBLICATION, OPP, AL. THE PUBLICATION WILL BE ON THE HISTORY OF COVINGTON COUNTY. (LOCAL). DOUGLAS SCHOFIELD, CHAIRMAN; OPP BICENTENNIAL COMMISSION; PO BOX 613; OPP, AL 36467. (#23734). **ARBA GRANTEE.**

ORANGE BEACH

JUNE 18 - 20, '76. ALABAMA'S PLEASURE ISLAND DEEP DEA FISHING TOURNAMENT. COMPETITION AT TERRY COVE MARINA. (REGN'L). ASHLEY CHAMBERS, JR, CHMN; FOLEY GULF SHORES JAYCEES; RT 3 BOX 600; FOLEY, AL 36535. (#102828-2).

ORRVILLE

DOWNTOWN RESTORATION, ORRVILLE, AL. RESTORATION OF CENTRAL BUSINESS DISTRICT TO 19TH CENTURY MOTIF. (LOCAL). STAN FRASIER, CHAIRMAN; ORRVILLE BICENTENNIAL COMMISSION; ORRVILLE, AL 36767. (#22372). **ARBA GRANTEE.**

STREET SIGNS, ORRVILLE, AL. PLACEMENT OF 19TH CENTURY-STYLE STREET SIGNS AT ALL INTERSECTIONS. (LOCAL). STAN FRASIER, CHAIRMAN; ORRVILLE BICENTENNIAL COMMISSION; ORRVILLE, AL 36767. (#22371). **ARBA GRANTEE.**

OZARK

MONUMENT AS MEMORIAL TO GENERAL SAM DALE, AL. PERMANENT MARKER HONORING THE COUNTY NAME-SAKE. (LOCAL). VAL L MCGEE, CHAIRMAN; DALE COUNTY BICENTENNIAL COMMISSION; PO BOX 86; OZARK, AL 36360. (#25578). **ARBA GRANTEE.**

PARRISH

JULY 3, '76. FOLK FAIR '76. FEATURES COLONIAL CRAFTS, FOLK & BLUEGRASS MUSIC, HOME COOKING, FUN AND GAMES, AS WELL AS ARTISTS FROM ACROSS ALABAMA & MISSISSIPPI. AT IN AND AROUND PARRISH HIGH GYMNASIUM-MAIN ST. (LOCAL). MARK B WILSON, CHMN; PARRISH BICENTENNIAL EXECUATIVE COMMITTEE; DRAWER J; PARRISH, AL 35580. (#102461-1).

PELL CITY

COOSA ARTS AND CRAFTS FAIR, PELL CITY, AL. FAIR & EXHIBITS FEATURING COMBINED ARTS & CRAFTS. (LOCAL). MARY MAYS, PROJ COORDINATOR; PELL CITY BICENTENNIAL COMMISSION; 2108 3RD AVE N; PELL CITY, AL 35125. (#24736). **ARBA GRANTEE.**

CROPWELL HISTORIC MARKER - PELL CITY, AL. IN A SMALL TRIANGULAR PLOT CONTAINING NATIVE BOULDERS, BRONZE PLAQUES WILL BE PLACED ON EACH BOULDER GIVING THE HISTORY OF CROPWELL FROM THE TIME OF THE INDIANS UP TO 1964. (LOCAL). MARY MAYS, CHAIRMAN; PELL CITY BICENTENNIAL COMMITTEE; 1905 FIRST AVE N; PELL CITY, AL 35125. (#24111). **ARBA GRANTEE.**

OCT 25, '75. COOSA ARTS AND CRAFTS FAIR. FAIR AT PELL CITY NATIONAL GUARD ARMORY. (LOCAL). MARY MAYS, CHMN; PELL CITY BICENTENNIAL COMMISSION; 2108 3RD AVE N; PELL CITY, AL 35125. (#24736-1).

PHENIX CITY

FT MITCHELL HISTORIC PARK - PHENIX CITY, ALABAMA. HISTORIC & RECREATIONAL DEVELOPMENT OF PARK SO IT WILL HAVE NATURE TRAILS & 2 CEMETERIES. A PARTIAL RESTORATION OF FT, AN INDIAN AGENCY, & EXPANSION OF CREEK INDIAN RESEARCH LIBRARY ARE ALSO INCLUDED. (ST-WIDE). MRS JOSEPH W SMITH, CHAIRMAN; RUSSELL COUNTY BICENTENNIAL COMMITTEE; 3301 14TH AVE; PHENIX CITY, AL 36867. (#4213). **(??).**

PHOENIX STATUE IN PHENIX CITY, AL. A STATUE OF THE LEGENDARY PHOENIX BIRD WILL BE ERECTED IN A PROMINENT LOCATION TO SYMBOLIZE THE HERITAGE OF PHENIX CITY. (LOCAL). MRS LENORA C SMITH, CHAIRMAN; PHENIX '76; 3301 14TH AVE; PHENIX CITY, AL 36867. (#21079). **ARBA GRANTEE.**

JULY 4, '76. DEDICATION OF PHOENIX STATUE. CEREMONY. (LOCAL). MRS LENORA SMITH, CHMN; PHENIX '76; 3301 14TH AVE; PHENIX CITY, AL 36867. (#21079-1).

PIEDMONT

PARADE HONORING VETERANS - PIEDMONT, AL. THE BICENTENNIAL COMMITTEE WILL SPONSOR A PARADE HONORING VETERANS; THE MAYOR & LOCAL STUDENTS WILL MAKE A SPEECH. (LOCAL). DR JOHN R KIRKPATRICK, CHAIRMAN; PIEDMONT BICENTENNIAL COMMITTEE; BOX 232; PIEDMONT, AL 36272. (#23390). **ARBA GRANTEE.**

PIEDMONT ROOM, PIEDMONT, AL. BUILDING A PIEDMONT ROOM IN THE LOCAL CITY LIBRARY. ALSO PRODUCING HISTORY OF PIEDMONT ALONG WITH THE ACQUISITION OF RELICS, ANTIQUES, ETC, FOR THE PIEDMONT ROOM. (LOCAL). DR JOHN R KIRKPATRICK, CHAIRMAN; PIEDMONT BICENTENNIAL COMMITTEE; BOX 232; PIEDMONT, AL 36272. (#21569). **ARBA GRANTEE.**

JUNE 4, '76. OPENING OF PIEDMONT ROOM. OPENING, EXHIBIT AT PIEDMONT LIBRARY, MAIN ST. (LOCAL). DR JOHN R KIRKPATRICK; BICENTENNIAL COMMITTEE; BOX 232; PIEDMONT, AL 36272. (#105435-1).

JUNE 4, '76. SPEECHES ON THE BICENTENNIAL. COMPETITION, FESTIVAL AT DOWNTOWN PIEDMONT. (LOCAL). DR JOHN R KIRKPATRICK; PIEDMONT BICENTENNIAL COMMITTEE; BOX 232; PIEDMONT, AL 36272. (#105434-1).

JULY 4, '76. PARADE HONORING VETERANS. PARADE. (LOCAL). DR JOHN R KIRKPATRICK; PIEDMONT BICENTENNIAL COMMITTEE; BOX 232; PIEDMONT, AL 36272. (#23390-1).

PINE HILL

COMMUNITY CULTURE IN PINE HILL, AL. BOOK CEREMONY, CRAFTS, MUSIC; & RESEARCH FILM FESTIVAL. (LOCAL). RUTH SLAUGHTER, DIRECTOR; TOWN OF PINE HILL; PINE HILL, AL 36769. (#31166).

'THE HISTORY OF PINE HILL' - ALABAMA. A 100-PAGE BOOK ON THE HISTORY OF THE PINE HILL AREA. (LOCAL). MRS RUTH SLAUGHTER, CHAIRMAN; PINE HILL BICENTENNIAL COMMITTEE; PO BOX 308; PINE HILL, AL 36769. (#33501).

OCT 28, '75 - JULY 4, '76. AMERICAN ISSUES RADIO FORUM. MUSEUM OF LOCAL CULTURE, WRITTEN HISTORY OF TOWN, CRAFTS, EXHIBITS, ATHLETIC CONTESTS, BURIAL OF TIME CAPSULE, SCHOOL ART, POETRY AND ESSAY CONTESTS. (LOCAL). RUTH SLAUGHTER, CHMN; TOWN OF PINE HILL; PINE HILL, AL 36769. (#200001-80).

JULY 3 - 4, '76. A SALUTE TO FREEDOM - BICENTENNIAL CELEBRATION. JULY 3: MUSEUM OPENING; BARBEQUE; 'RIGHT TO ASSEMBLE' PROGRAM; MUSIC AMERICANA; BICYCLE RACES; COMMUNITY SING; CITIZEN'S SUPPER; & FIREWORKS. JULY 4: CHURCH CARILLON; COMBINED CHURCH SERVICES; NATIONAL BELL RINGING & TIME CAPSULE BURIAL. (LOCAL). MRS RITH SLAUGHTER, CHMN; PINE HILL BICENTENNIAL COMMITTEE; PO BOX 308; PINE HILL, AL 36769. (#200001-90).

PLEASANT GRV

JULY 4, '76. FOURTH OF JULY CELEBRATION. PARADE, BOY SCOUT REVIEW, MAGIC SHOW, ART DISPLAY, SCHOOL AND COMMUNITY PHOTOS, SKILL GAMES, BAND CONCERT, BARBECUE/ICE CREAM BOOTH, DISPLAY OF CERAMICS AND PLANTS WERE INCLUDED IN THIS EVENT. AT PLEASANT GROVE ATHLETIC COMPLEX, FOURTH ST. (LOCAL). ETHEL S GLAZE, CHAIRMAN; PLEASANT GROVE BICENTENNIAL COMMITTEE; 901 ELEVENTH TERRACE; PLEASANT GRV, AL 35127. (#200001-54).

JULY 5, '76. DEDICATION OF SCULPTURE IN PLEASANT GROVE PARK. THIS SCULPTURE WAS DONE BY A LOCAL MAN, BRAD MORTON, ATTENDING UNIVERSITY OF ALABAMA. IT IS MADE OF LOCAL MATERIALS FROM THE STEEL MILLS, FAIRFIELD, AL. AT CITY PARK, PARK RD. (LOCAL). ETHEL S GLAZE, CHAIRMAN; CITY OF PLEASANT GROVE; 901 ELEVENTH TERRACE; PLEASANT GRV, AL 35127. (#200001-55).

PRATTVILLE

ALABAMA BICENTENNIAL BATTLE OF THE BANDS. A VARIETY OF BANDS PARTICIPATE IN THE COMPETITION. (ST-WIDE). RICHARD D GARRETT, CHAIRMAN; PRATTVILLE BICENTENNIAL COMMITTEE; PO BOX 1776; PRATTVILLE, AL 36067. (#25614). **ARBA GRANTEE.**

JULY 4TH BICENTENNIAL CELEBRATION - PRATTVILLE, AL. THE PRATTVILLE BICENTENNIAL COMMITTEE IS SPONSORING A 4TH OF JULY CELEBRATION. (LOCAL). RICHARD GARRETT, CHAIRMAN; PRATTVILLE BICENTENNIAL COMMITTEE; PO BOX 1776; PRATTVILLE, AL 36037. (#27282). **ARBA GRANTEE.**

PRATT MEMORIAL BICENTENNIAL CIVIC COMPLEX, AL. EXISTING CITY PARK & COMMUNITY CENTER RENOVATED & LOCAL NATIONAL GUARD ARMORY CONVERTED INTO A BICENTENNIAL CIVIC AREA CONSISTING OF PARK, LAKE, COMMUNITY CENTER AND CIVIC CENTER. (LOCAL). RICHARD D GARRETT, CHAIRMAN; PRATTVILLE AMERICAN REVOLUTION BICENTENNIAL COMMISSION; PO BOX 1776; PRATTVILLE, AL 36067. (#21333). **ARBA GRANTEE.**

SEPT 1, '75. LABOR DAY BARBECUE 1975. FESTIVAL INCLUDES CRAFTS, BARBECUE, GAMES AND BEAUTY CONTEST. AT PRATT PARK. (LOCAL). GAYLE MYERS, PROJ DIR; PRATTVILLE SERVICE LEAGUE; RT 2, BOX 34; PRATTVILLE, AL 36067. (#101004-1).

SEPT 22 - 28, '75. AUTAUGA COUNTY FAIR. COMPETITION, FESTIVAL AT PRATT PARK. (ST-WIDE). MICKEY T MAYS, PRESIDENT; AUTAUGA COUNTY FAIR ASSOC; PO BOX 566; PRATTVILLE, AL 36067. (#100729-1).

MAY 8, '76. ALABAMA BICENTENNIAL BATTLE OF THE BANDS. COMPETITION, LIVE PERFORMANCE AT LION'S STADIUM. (ST-WIDE). RICHARD D GARRETT, CHMN; PRATTVILLE BICENTENNIAL COMMITTEE; PO BOX 1776; PRATTVILLE, AL 36067. (#25614-1).

JULY 4, '76. JULY 4TH BICENTENNIAL CELEBRATION. FESTIVAL AT PRATT PARK. (LOCAL). RICHARD GARRETT, CHAIRMAN; PRATTVILLE BICENTENNIAL COMMITTEE; PO BOX 1776; PRATTVILLE, AL 36067. (#27282-1).

REFORM

MINI-PARK, REFORM, AL. DEVELOPMENT OF A MINI-PARK IN REFORM, AL. (LOCAL). FRANCES DAVIS, CHAIRPERSON; REFORM BICENTENNIAL; PO BOX 566; REFORM, AL 35481. (#24898). **ARBA GRANTEE.**

ROANOKE

BEAUTIFICATION PROJECT - ROANOKE, AL. FLOWERS AND SHRUBS WILL BE PLANTED AT THE RAILROAD SITE ON THE ALABAMA TRAIL. (LOCAL). JOHN B TATE, CHAIRPERSON; ROANOKE BICENTENNIAL COMMISSION & ROANOKE LIONS CLUB; 14 VAUGHN ST; ROANOKE, AL 36274. (#29183).

JUNE 27 - JULY 4, '76. PIONEER WEEK. FESTIVAL, PARADE. (LOCAL). JOHN B TATE, CHAIRMAN; ROANOKE BICENTENNIAL COMMISSION; 14 VAUGHN ST; ROANOKE, AL 36274. (#200001-78).

ROBERTSDALE

OCT 20 - 25, '75. 25TH ANNUAL BALDWIN COUNTY FAIR. FAIR AT ROBERTSDALE COLISEUM. (LOCAL). GEORGE THAMES, CHAIRMAN; BALDWIN COUNTY CATTLE AND FAIR ASSOC, INC; PO DRAWER 680; ROBERTSDALE, AL 36567. (#101294-1).

ROCKFORD

JAIL RESTORATION, AL. RESTORATION 1842 JAIL. (LOCAL). JOHN A SMITH, CHAIRMAN; COOSA COUNTY BICENTENNIAL COMMITTEE; NIXBURG, AL 36085. (#24735). **ARBA GRANTEE.**

RUSSELLVILLE

NOV 28, '75. 200 YEARS OF PROGRESS PARADE AND FESTIVAL. THIS EVENT IS PLANNED TO BE ONE OF THE LARGEST SMALL TOWN PARADES EVER HELD WITH NATIONALLY KNOWN ENTERTAINMENT AND CELEBRITIES. AT DOWNTOWN RUSSELLVILLE. (LOCAL). PERCY W PUGH; RUSSELLVILLE BICENTENNIAL ACTION COMMISSION; BOX 968; RUSSELLVILLE, AL 35653. (#103272-1).

SCOTTSBORO

CONSTRUCTION OF STATUE - SCOTTSBORO, AL. GEN ANDREW JACKSON'S STATUE TO BE CONSTRUCTED ON JACKSON COUNTY COURTHOUSE YARD. (LOCAL). CARLUS PAGE, CHAIRPERSON; JACKSON COUNTY & SCOTTSBORO BICENTENNIAL COMMITTEES; 301 BYNUM; SCOTTSBORO, AL 35768. (#23947).

HERITAGE '76, SCOTTSBORO, AL. A BUST OF GENERAL ANDREW JACKSON WILL BE DONE IN RECOGNITION OF HIS CONTRIBUTIONS TO THIS COUNTY. (LOCAL). WALTER HAMMER, CHAIRMAN; JACKSON COUNTY BICENTENNIAL COMMITTEE; PO BOX 52; SCOTTSBORO, AL 35768. (#25089). **ARBA GRANTEE.**

SLIDES OF HISTORICAL MATERIAL FOR THE LIBRARY, AL. THE SCOTTSBORO PUBLIC LIBRARY WILL PUT TOGETHER A SERIES OF SLIDES (AND PROJECTORS) TO PORTRAY THE HISTORICAL HERITAGE OF OUR COMMUNITY. (LOCAL). CARLUS PAGE, CHMN; SCOTTSBORO BICENTENNIAL COMMITTEE & FORTNIGHTLY BOOK CLUB; 301 BYNUM; SCOTTSBORO, AL 35768. (#21212). **ARBA GRANTEE.**

FEB 10, '76. TENNESSEE VALLEY BICENTENNIAL EXHIBIT. EXHIBIT AT BROAD ST & CHARLOTTE AVE. (LOCAL). CARLUS PAGE, CHAIRPERSON; SCOTTSBORO & JACKSON COUNTY BICENTENNIAL COMMITTEES; 301 BYNUM AVE; SCOTTSBORO, AL 35768. (#103481-1).

JULY 1 - AUG 31, '76. CRAFTS & ANTIQUE SHOW. OCCURS ON THE FIRST SUNDAY & MONDAY OF EVERY MONTH. (LOCAL). ANN WARNE, SECRETARY; CHAMBER OF COMMERCE; 916 S BROAD ST; SCOTTSBORO, AL 35768. (#100480-1).

SEALE

SEPT 6, '76. OLD COURTHOUSE COUNTRY FAIR, LIVE ENTERTAINMENT & CHILDREN'S EVENTS. BANDS, SINGERS, SQUARE DANCERS, PIT BARBECUE, HOT DOGS, HOME BAKED GOODS, ANTIQUES, FLEA MARKET, FARM PRODUCE, PLANTS, DEMONSTRATIONS, HISTORIC DISPLAYS, ANTIQUE TRAIN REPLICA, 'BEST FRIEND OF CHARLESTON', FREE RIDES, PROCEEDS BENEFIT OLD COURTHOUSE RESTORATION FUND. AT COURTHOUSE GROUNDS, HWY 431. (LOCAL). MRS C J DUDLEY, COORD; OLD RUSSELL COUNTY COURTHOUSE ASSOC; RT 2, BOX 92; SEALE, AL 36875. (#106648-1).

SELMA

BICENTENNIAL SUNDAYS IN SELMA, AL. THE MINISTERS WILL DESIGNATE CERTAIN SUNDAYS TO PREACH ON OUR FREEDOMS AND THE RESPONSIBILITIES THAT GO WITH SUCH, ALONG WITH THE IMPORTANCE OF TRUSTING IN GOD. (LOCAL). CHAPLAIN GEORGE C NORSWORTHY, PRES; DALLAS COUNTY MINISTERIAL ASSOCIATION; 970 RANDOLPH CIRLCLE; SELMA, AL 36701. (#13782).

CEMETERY RESTORATION, SELMA, AL. IN LIVE OAK CEMETERY ARE BURIED WILLIAM RUFUS KING, JOHN T MORGAN, NATHANIEL DAWSON, U S COMMISSIONER OF EDUCATION, EDMUND WINSTON PETTUS, U S CONGRESSMAN & ELODIE B TODD, LINCOLN'S SISTER-IN-LAW. (LOCAL). MRS CHARLES HOHENBERG, COMMITTEE CHAIRMAN; SELMA-DALLAS COUNTY HISTORIC PRESERVATION SOCIETY; FEDERAL BLDG, ALABAMA AVE; SELMA, AL 36701. (#13785).

DALLAS COUNTY MONUMENTS, AL. MONUMENTS WILL BE CLEANED, RECORDED AND LANDSCAPED. (LOCAL). MRS ALSTON KEITH, COMMITTEE CHAIRMAN; SELMA-DALLAS COUNTY HISTORIC PRESERVATION SOCIETY; FEDERAL BLDG, ALABAMA AVE; SELMA, AL 36701. (#13796).

EARLY MEMORIES OF SELMA CITIZENS, AL. CITIZENS OF ALL AGES WILL BE INTERVIEWED AND MATERIAL FILED FOR FUTURE USE. (LOCAL). THOMAS WILLIS, CHAIRMAN; SELMA BICENTENNIAL COMMISSION; 719 TREMONT ST; SELMA, AL 36701. (#13791).

FLAG FLYING IN SELMA, AL. IN ADDITION TO FLYING THE U S FLAGS ON LEGAL HOLIDAYS, CITIZENS WILL FLY THEIR FLAGS EVERY MONDAY. (LOCAL). MRS HENRY VAUGHAN, EXEC DIRECTOR; SELMA BICENTENNIAL COMMISSION; 719 TREMONT ST; SELMA, AL 36701. (#13783).

GAS STREET LIGHTS IN HISTORIC DISTRICT, SELMA, AL. ONE OF ALABAMA'S 4 HISTORIC COMMERICAL DISTRICTS, LOCATED IN SELMA, WILL BE RESTORED AND GAS STREET LIGHTS WILL BE INSTALLED. (LOCAL). HON JOE T SMITHERN, MAYOR; CITY OF SELMA; CITY HALL; SELMA, AL 36701. (#13787).

GRIST MILL RESTORATION, SELMA, AL. ONE OF THE 8 PRE-CIVIL WAR GRIST MILLS IN ALABAMA WILL BE RESTORED. (LOCAL). MRS JOHN CALLAWAY, PRESIDENT; SELMA-DALLAS COUNTY HISTORIC PRESERVATION SOCIETY; FEDERAL BLDG, ALABAMA AVE; SELMA, AL 36701. (#13784).

HISTORIC DEVELOPMENT COMMISSION - SELMA, AL. COMMISSION APPOINTED BY CITY & COUNTY GOVERNMENTS TO SET UP HISTORIC GUIDELINES & ACT AS CONSULTANTS FOR HISTORIC RESTORATION. (LOCAL). DONALD MILLS, JR, CHAIRMAN; SELMA-DALLAS HISTORIC DEVELOPMENT COMMISSION; 312 DALLAS AVE; SELMA, AL 36701. (#13794).

HISTORIC SURVEY IN SELMA, AL. AN ARCHITECTURAL SURVEY IS BEING MADE OF ALL THE BUILDINGS IN SELMA TO DETERMINE THEIR IMPORTANCE TO THE COMMUNITY; THE FINDINGS WILL BE PUBLISHED IN BOOK FORM. (LOCAL). MRS JOHN CALLAWAY, PRESIDENT; SELMA-DALLAS COUNTY HISTORIC PRESERVATION SOCIETY; FEDERAL BLDG, ALABAMA AVE; SELMA, AL 36701. (#13793).

JUNIOR BICENTENNIAL COMMISSIONS SELMA, AL. JUNIOR BICENTENNIAL COMMISSIONS WILL BE ORGANIZED IN ALL OF SELMA'S SCHOOLS, SO THAT YOUNG PEOPLE CAN PLAN THEIR OWN BICENTENNIAL ACTIVITIES. (LOCAL). MRS HENRY VAUGHAN, EXEC DIRECTOR; SELMA BICENTENNIAL COMMISSION; 719 TREMONT ST; SELMA, AL 36701. (#13790).

PARK PAVILLION IN SELMA, AL. PAVILLION IN LOCAL PARK WILL BE RECONSTRUCTED. (LOCAL). HON JOE T SMITHERMAN, MAYOR; CITY OF SELMA; CITY HALL; SELMA, AL 36701. (#13795).

PLANTING TREES - SELMA, AL. COMMISSION FORMED TO STUDY SELMA AREA & DETERMINE NEEDS FOR TREE PROGRAM & TO START PLANTING AT PROPER TIME. EACH OF SELMA'S 17 SCHOOLS WILL PLANT TREES TO COMMEMORATE SIGNERS OF DECL OF INDEP. (LOCAL). MRS CHARLES BREEDING, COMMITTEE CHAIRMAN; SELMA BICENTENNIAL COMMISSION; 719 TREMONT ST; SELMA, AL 36701. (#13792). **ARBA GRANTEE.**

PRESERVATION OF BLACK SPIRITUALS. A CHORAL GROUP WILL COLLECT AND PERFORM SPIRITUALS OF BYGONE DAYS. (LOCAL). JAMES PERKINS, CHAIRMAN; SELMA BICENTENNIAL COMMISSION; 719 TREMONT ST; SELMA, AL 36701. (#13788).

RESTORATION OF JOHN TYLER MORGAN HOME, SELMA, AL. THE HOME OF JOHN TYLER MORGAN, ONE OF THE USA'S GREATEST SENATORS, KNOWN AS THE FATHER OF THE PANAMA CANAL, WILL BE RESTORED. (REGN'L). MRS JOHN CALLAWAY, PRESIDENT; SELMA-DALLAS COUNTY HISTORIC PRESERVATION SOCIETY; FEDERAL BLDG, ALABAMA AVE; SELMA, AL 36701. (#13786).

STUDY CLUB PROGRAMS, SELMA, AL. ALL LITERARY, MUSIC & ART STUDY CLUBS IN SELMA WILL USE THEMES RELATED TO THE COLONIAL PERIOD, AS THEIR COURSE OF STUDY FOR 1975-76. (LOCAL). MRS HENRY VAUGHAN, EXEC DIRECTOR; SELMA BICENTENNIAL COMMISSION; 719 TREMONT ST; SELMA, AL 36701. (#13789).

JUNE 1 - AUG 21, '75. 'LET'S GO ALABAMA', CARNEGIE LIBRARY STORY HOUR. LIVE PERFORMANCE AT SELMA AVE. (LOCAL). MRS PAT BLALOCK, CHMN; CARNEGIE LIBRARY; CARNEGIE LIBRARY; SELMA, AL 36701. (#100911-1).

AUG 30, '75. RAFT RACE FROM EDMUND PETTUS BRIDGE ON ALABAMA RIVER TO KINGS BEND. EVENT OPEN TO PUBLIC, ANYTHING THAT FLOATS, WHICH IS NOT CLASSIFIED AS A BOAT, IS ELIGIBLE; DISTANCE IS 15 KNOTS, PRIZES GIVEN & PARTICIPANTS ARE ENTERTAINED WITH A PARTY AT END OF RACE. AT RACE STARTS AT EDMUND PETTUS BRIDGE. (LOCAL). GEORGE SINGLETON, CHMN; SELMA JAYCEES; PO BOX 1888; SELMA, AL 36701. (#100910-1).

NOV 22, '75. OLD FASHIONED RIVERFRONT MARKET FESTIVAL. THE ANNUAL XMAS PARADE MARKS OPENING OF MARKET FESTIVAL; ART EXHIBITERS MUST PAY FOR SPACE TO EXHIBIT;

SELMA—CONTINUED

A BALL WILL WRAP UP ACTIVITIES. AT HISTORIC RIVERFRONT DISTRICT. (LOCAL). JIM ARMOUR, PROJ CHMN; SELMA-DALLAS COUNTY HISTORIC PRESERVATION SOCIETY; MEDICAL CENTER HOSPITAL; SELMA, AL 36701. (#100912-1).

JAN 22 - 23, '76. UNITED STATES ARMED FORCES BICENTENNIAL CARAVAN. CARAVAN IS COMPOSED OF EXHIBIT VANS FOR EACH MILITARY SERVICE. PROJECT THEME IS 'HISTORY OF THE ARMED FORCES AND THEIR CONTRIBUTIONS TO THE NATION'. FRIDAY HOURS: 10AM - 8PM. (LOCAL). MRS HENRY VAUGHN, CHMN; SELMA BICENTENNIAL COMMITTEE; 719 TREMONT ST; SELMA, AL 36701. (#1775-384).

JAN 23 - 24, '76. 200 GRAND YEARS - FOLLIES WITH SINGING AND DANCING. FESTIVAL, LIVE PERFORMANCE. (LOCAL). ANITA SIMS, CHMN; SELMA CHARITY LEAGUE; 2105 DELANIC DR; SELMA, AL 36701. (#103416-34).

FEB 11, '76. OPENAIR MARKET FOR YESTERYEAR. FESTIVITIES WILL INCLUDE A HOUSE & GARDEN PLANT SALE, HOME-COOKED SOUP LUNCHEON; ODDS & ENDS SALE. AT STURDIVANT HALL GARDEN, 713 MABRY ST. (LOCAL). MRS M P AMES, CHMN; STURDIVANT MUSEUM ASSOC; 2008 ELKDALE; SELMA, AL 36701. (#102236-1).

MAR 19 - 21, '76. TOUR OF HISTORIC HOMES. TWELVE OF SELMA'S HISTORIC OLD HOMES WILL BE OPEN TO THE PUBLIC IN MARCH. (LOCAL). MRS HENRY VAUGHAN, CHMN; SELMA DALLAS COUNTY HISTORIC PRESERVATION SOCIETY; 719 TREMONT ST; SELMA, AL 36701. (#101237-1).

SEPT 3, '76. THE CRAIG AIR FORCE BASE - SELMA CELEBRATION. FESTIVAL AT CRAIG AIR FORCE BASE. (LOCAL). MRS HENRY VAUGHAN, CHMN; SELMA BICENTENNIAL COMMISSION; 719 TREMONT ST; SELMA, AL 35701. (#101238-1).

SHAWMUT

JUNE 5, '76. COUNTRY FAIR. ENTERTAINMENT, EXHIBITS, BOOTHS & SINGING & DANCING CONTESTS. AT SHAWMUT CIRCLE. (ST-WIDE). JACK KEITH, PRESIDENT; FIRST NATIONAL BANK; 10TH ST; WEST POINT, GA 31833. (#108035-1).

SHEFFIELD

REHABILITATION OF OLD STEAM ENGINE - AL. 1920 STEAM ENGINE TO BE RESTORED AND PUT ON PERMANENT EXHIBIT AT THE MUSEUM. WHEN OPERATIONAL, THE ENGINE AND PASSENGER CARS WILL BE USED IN 1976. (LOCAL). HAROLD DAMSGARD, CHAIRMAN; SHEFFIELD/COLBERT COUNTY BICENTENNIAL COMMITTEE; 203 RIVERMONT DR; SHEFFIELD, AL 35660. (#25922). **ARBA GRANTEE.**

SEPT 11 - 12, '76. STEAM ENGINE EXHIBIT. 1920 STEAM ENGINE WILL BE RESTORED AND PUT ON PERMANENT EXHIBIT AT THE MUSEUM. THE MUSEUM BLDG CONTAINS MANY OLD RAILROAD ITEMS ON PERMANENT DISPLAY. (ST-WIDE). HAROLD DAMSGARD, CHMN; SHEFFIELD/COLBERT COUNTY BICENTENNIAL COMMITTEE; 203 RIVERMONT DR; SHEFFIELD, AL 35660. (#25922-1).

SLOCOMB

HORIZONS '76 - SLOCOMB, AL. DEVELOPMENT OF A RECREATION AREA TO IMPROVE THE ENVIRONMENT AND ACTIVITIES OF SENIOR CITIZENS BY PROVIDING SHELTERS, OUTDOOR FURNITURE AND LANDSCAPING OF GROUNDS. (LOCAL). JAMES F HATCHER, DIRECTOR; SLOCOMB BICENTENNIAL PROJECT; BOX 71; SLOCOMB, AL 36375. (#25703). **ARBA GRANTEE.**

SPANISH FORT

RAISING OF FLAG POLE - SPANISH FORT, AL. A 40 FOOT FLAG POLE WILL BE RAISED ON U S HWY 90 98 31. IT WILL FLY A U S FLAG PLUS FLAGS FROM 21 STATES. (LOCAL). GEORGE FULLER, JR, COORDINATOR; SPANISH FORT BICENTENNIAL COMMITTEE; 126 PATRICIAN DR; SPANISH FORT, AL 36527. (#28597).

JAN 1, '76. COMMUNITY DAY. EXHIBIT, FESTIVAL. (LOCAL). GEORGE FULLER, JR, CHMN; SPANISH FORT BICENTENNIAL COMMISSION; 126 PATRICIAN DR; SPANISH FORT, AL 36527. (#200001-58).

SPRINGVILLE

'ALMOST ANYTHING GOES' - THREE GROUPS IN COMPETITION FOR GAME EVENTS. COMPETITION AT SPRINGVILLE HIGH SCHOOL STADIUM. (LOCAL). MARGARET WINDHAM, CHMN; SPRINGVILLE HERITAGE COMMITTEE; PO BOX B; SPRINGVILLE, AL 35146. (#200001-51).

RESTORATION OF OLD GRIST MILL - AL. GRIST MILL TO BE RESTORED FOR USE AS MUSEUM. (LOCAL). HAZEL F BROWNLEE, COORDINATOR; HIS AND HER GARDEN CLUB; PO DRAWER F; SPRINGVILLE, AL 35146. (#28595).

STEELE

STEELE, AL, RECREATION CENTER. MEMORIAL MONUMENT ERECTED AND RECREATION CENTER WILL BE FURNISHED. (LOCAL). VIVIAN B QUALLS, CHAIRMAN; STEELE BICENTENNIAL COMMITTEE; PO BOX 426; STEELE, AL 35987. (#22289). **ARBA GRANTEE.**

JULY 1 - AUG 3, '75. FLAT TOP SUMMIT. THE WORLD'S BEST FLAT TOP GUITAR MEN GATHER HERE TO PLAY WITH AND TO JUDGE THE PROGRESS OF THE TALENTED YOUNG BOYS FORM THE HILLS AND COVES OF THE LOWER APPALACHIANS. AT OUTDOOR THEATRE, TAKE ASHVILLE EXIT OFF I-59; PLENTY FREE PARKING. (LOCAL). WARREN MUSGROVE, DIRECTOR; LOWER HYATT GAP COMMUNITY CENTER AT HORSE PENS 40; RT 1, BOX 379; STEELE, AL 35987. (#100731-1).

OCT 4 - 5, '75. FOLK FESTIVAL. THE FESTIVAL, LOCATED 40 MILES FROM BIRMINGHAM, WILL FEATURE A NATIONAL HOLLERING CONTEST, NATIONAL SLING-SHOT CONTEST, NATIONAL FRENCH HARP CONTEST, QUILTS, BLACKSMITHING, FOLK FOODS, CRAFTS AND FOLK GAMES. AT OUTDOOR THEATRE, TAKE ASHVILLE EXIT OFF I-59; PLENTY FREE PARKING. (LOCAL). WARREN MUSGROVE, DIRECTOR; LOWER HYATT GAP COMMUNITY CENTER AT HORSE PENS 40; RT 1, BOX 379; STEELE, AL 35987. (#100730-1).

STEVENSON

ECOLOGY PROJECTS IN STEVENSON, AL. THE PROJECT WILL INCLUDE THE RESTORATION OF A LOG CABIN, DEVELOPMENT OF HERITAGE AND NATURE TRAILS, PUBLISHING OF A BOOKLET ON LOCAL HISTORY, PLANTING LIBERTY TREES AND ESTABLISHING AN ECOLOGY DUMP. (LOCAL). MRS E G HENNINGER, PROGRAM DIRECTOR; CITY OF STEVENSON; 206 W MAIN ST; STEVENSON, AL 35772. (#18317).

FLAG POLE & LANDSCAPING - STEVENSON, AL. ERECT A 40 FT METAL FLAG POLE AT STEVENSON COMMUNITY PARK, LANDSCAPED WITH SHRUBS & FLOWERS. (LOCAL). MRS E G HENEGAR, COORDINATOR; STEVENSON BICENTENNIAL COMMITTEE; 305 COLLEGE ST; STEVENSON, AL 35772. (#27064).

HERITAGE TRAIL - STEVENSON, AL. ESTABLISH TRAIL; ACQUIRE & RESTORE RR DEPOT; PLANT 'LIBERTY TREES'; PUBLISH BOOKLET ON COMMUNITY'S HISTORY & INDIAN HISTORY; ESTABLISH AN ECOLOGY DUMP. (LOCAL). MRS E G HENEGAR, COORDINATOR; STEVENSON BICENTENNIAL COMMITTEE; 305 COLLEGE ST; STEVENSON, AL 35772. (#27062).

MOVE & RESTORE OLD LOG CABIN - STEVENSON, AL. MOVE OLD LOG CABIN FROM PRESENT SITE TO COMMUNITY PARK AND RESTORE IT TO A USABLE STATE. (LOCAL). MRS E G HENEGAR, COORDINATOR; STEVENSON BICENTENNIAL COMMITTEE; 305 COLLEGE ST; STEVENSON, AL 35772. (#27063).

NATURE TRAIL - STEVENSON, AL. ESTABLISH NATURE TRAIL THROUGH WOODED AREA OF STEVENSON COMMUNITY PARK, LABELING PLANTS, WILD FLOWERS AND TREES. (LOCAL). MRS E G HENEGAR, COORDINATOR; STEVENSON BICENTENNIAL COMMITTEE; 305 COLLEGE ST; STEVENSON, AL 35772. (#27065).

STEVENSON BICENTENNIAL PROJECT - AL. RESTORATION OF LOG CABIN, HERITAGE AND NATURE TRAILS, FESTIVAL DAYS. HISTORICAL MUSIC, PAGEANT, PUBLISHING BOOKLET OF LOCAL HISTORY & PLANTING LIBERTY TREES. (LOCAL). MRS E G HENNINGER, PROGRAM DIRECTOR; CITY OF STEVENSON; 206 W MAIN ST; STEVENSON, AL 35772. (#23829). **ARBA GRANTEE.**

OCT 6 - 11, '75. BICENTENNIAL FESTIVAL DAYS. FESTIVAL AT STEVENSON COMMUNITY PARK. (LOCAL). MRS E G HENEGAR, CHMN; STEVENSON BICENTENNIAL COMMITTEE; 305 COLLEGE ST; STEVENSON, AL 35772. (#200001-70).

OCT 10, '75. HIGH SCHOOL BICENTENNIAL BAND CONCERT. CONCERT FEATURES HISTORICAL MUSIC, BARBER SHOP QUARTETS, CHORAL GROUPS, ETC. (LOCAL). MRS E G HENEGAR, CHMN; STEVENSON BICENTENNIAL COMMITTEE; 305 COLLEGE ST; STEVENSON, AL 35772. (#200001-69).

FEB 6, '76. BICENTENNIAL PAGEANT WITH 19TH CENTURY COSTUMES, VEHICLES & MUSIC. LIVE PERFORMANCE. (LOCAL). MRS E G HENEGAR, CHMN; STEVENSON BICENTENNIAL COMMITTEE; 305 COLLEGE ST; STEVENSON, AL 35772. (#18114-1).

JULY 4, '76. BICENTENNIAL CHURCH SERVICES. CEREMONY AT STEVENSON CITY PARK. (LOCAL). MRS E G HENEGAR, CHMN; STEVENSON BICENTENNIAL COMMITTEE; 305 COLLEGE ST; STEVENSON, AL 35772. (#18114-2).

STOCKTON

APR 2 - 4, '76. LIVE OAKS RIVERFRONT MARKET & COUNTY FAIR. OVERNIGHT CAMPING & MOTOR HOME FACILITIES AVAILABLE; MARKET AND FAIR HELD ON 67 PRIVATELY OWNED WOODED GROUNDS; FIDDLERS CONTEST, SQUARE DANCE; BLUE GRASS GOSPEL SINGING; FOOD & DRINKS TO BE SOLD ON GROUNDS; A FAMILY AFFAIR WITH GAMES & ENJOYMENT FOR ALL. AT LIVE OAK LODGE. (ST-WIDE). LYNN HASTIE JONES, MGR; LIVE OAKS COUNTRY CRAFTS; PO BOX 69; STOCKTON, AL 36579. (#101747-1).

SULLIGENT

MUSEUM/LIBRARY, AL. A MUSEUM/LIBRARY WILL BE ESTABLISHED IN TEH CIVIL WAR MANSION. (LOCAL). DWIGHT T GENTRY, CHAIRMAN; SULLIGENT BICENTENNIAL COMMITTEE; PO BOX 557; SULLIGENT, AL 35586. (#24734). **ARBA GRANTEE.**

SYLACAUGA

BICENTENNIAL NOTEPAPER, SYLACAUGA, AL. LOCAL ARTISTS' PEN AND INK DRAWINGS OF LOCAL LANDMARKS. (LOCAL). MRS JEAN CAMP, COORDINATOR; SYLACAUGA BICENTENNIAL COMMITTEE; 206 S ELM; SYLACAUGA, AL 35150. (#28988).

BICENTENNIAL SPEAKERS' COMMITTEE, SYLACAUGA, AL. SPEAKERS ON VARIOUS ASPECTS OF NATIONAL AND LOCAL HISTORY ARE AVAILABLE TO LOCAL SCHOOLS AND ORGANIZATIONS FOR PROGRAMS. (LOCAL). MRS PAUL BROWN, COORDINATOR; SYLACAUGA BICENTENNIAL COMMITTEE; 210 S ELM; SYLACAUGA, AL 35150. (#28985).

MINI PARKS, SYLACAUGA, AL. SYLACAUGA BEAUTIFICATION COUNCIL PLANTED RED, WHITE AND BLUE FLOWERS THROUGHOUT CITY. (LOCAL). CHAIRMAN; SYLACAUGA BEAUTIFICATION COUNCIL; SYLACAUGA, AL 35150. (#28983).

ORAL HISTORY PROJECT, SYLACAUGA, AL. SELECTED HIGH SCHOOL STUDENTS INTERVIEW OLDER CITIZENS AND RECORDED THEIR RECOLLECTIONS OF LOCAL AND NATIONAL EVENTS ON TAPES TO BE KEPT IN THE LOCAL LIBRARY. (LOCAL). MRS CRADDOCK HUFF, COORDINATOR; SYLACAUGA BICENTENNIAL COMMITTEE; SYLACAUGA, AL 35150. (#28986).

PLANTING OF LIBERTY TREES AT SCHOOLS-SYLACAUGA, AL. LIBERTY TREES WERE PLANTED AT LOCAL SCHOOLS. (LOCAL). LEON ARCHER, CHAIRMAN; MEN'S GARDEN CLUB; 705 SOUTH NORTON AVENUE; SYLACAUGA, AL 35150. (#28982).

SPONSORING OF VIETNAMESE FAMILY, SYLACAUGA, AL. SPONSOR PROVIDED HOME, TRANSPORTATION, EDUCATION & OTHER NECESSITIES FOR FAMILY OF SEVEN. (LOCAL). GEORGE PERKINS, DIRECTOR, RED CROSS; AMERICAN NATIONAL RED CROSS; 200 WEST SPRING ST; SYLACAUGA, AL 35150. (#28984).

SYLACAUGA MUSEUM, AL. PURCHASE OF SEVERAL DISPLAY CASES FOR NEW MUSEUM. (LOCAL). PENNY MOORE, COORDINATOR; SYLACAUGA BICENTENNIAL COMMITTEE; 711 W FT WILLIAM; SYLACAUGA, AL 35150. (#28987).

NOV 20, '75. COMMUNITY THANKSGIVING SERVICE. CEREMONY AT FIRST UNITED METHODIST CHURCH. (LOCAL). CONNIE WRIGHT, CHAIRMAN; SYLACAUGA MINISTERIAL ASSOCIATION; 2422 LAKE TERRACE RD; SYLACAUGA, AL 35150. (#200001-62).

NOV 25, '75. CHILDREN'S BICENTENNIAL PARADE. PARADE. (LOCAL). CONNIE WRIGHT, CHAIRMAN; NEWCOMERS' CLUB; 2422 LAKE TERRACE RD; SYLACAUGA, AL 35150. (#200001-63).

JAN 28, '76. TVA BICENTENNIAL CARAVAN. EXHIBIT, TOUR AT OGLETREE PLAZA SHOPPING CENTER. (LOCAL). CONNIE WRIGHT, CHAIRMAN; SYLACAUGA BANK; 2422 LAKE TERRACE RD; SYLACAUGA, AL 35150. (#200001-60).

MAR 18, '76. WAGON TRAIN. EXHIBIT, PARADE AT NOBLE PARK. (LOCAL). CONNIE WRIGHT, CHAIRMAN; SYLACAUGA SADDLE CLUB; 2422 LAKE TERRACE RD; SYLACAUGA, AL 35150. (#200001-64).

APR 2, '76. BICENTENNIAL COMMUNITY CONCERT. LIVE PERFORMANCE AT SYLACAUGA HIGH SCHOOL AUDITORIUM. (LOCAL). PENNY MOORE, CHAIRMAN; COUNCIL ON ARTS AND HUMANITIES; 711 W FT WILLIAMS; SYLACAUGA, AL 35150. (#200001-61).

JULY 4, '76. JULY FOURTH CELEBRATION. FESTIVAL, PARADE. (LOCAL). JOHN CONKLE, CHAIRMAN; SYLACAUGA BICENTENNIAL COMMITTEE; PO BOX 104; SYLACAUGA, AL 35150. (#200001-65).

DEC 4 - 5, '76. CHRISTMAS TOUR OF HOMES. TOUR. (LOCAL). MRS JAMES K GREEN, COORD; SYLACAUGA BICENTENNIAL COMMITTEE AND SYLACAUGA GARDEN CLUBS; 109 MAPLE RD; SYLACAUGA, AL 35150. (#109416-1).

TALLADEGA

CONSTRUCT A GAZEBO - TALLADEGA, AL. CONSTRUCT GAZEBO TO SERVE AS STAGE FOR MUSICAL EVENTS & CELEBRATIONS; INSCRIPTION ON GAZEBO WILL BE 'LET FREEDOM RING.'. (LOCAL). JAMES E SPRATLIN, CHAIRMAN; TALLEDEGA BICENTENNIAL COMMITTEE; PO DRAWER A; TALLADEGA, AL 35160. (#25906). **ARBA GRANTEE.**

APR 28 - MAY 2, '76. WINSTON 500 NASCAR WINSTON CUP GRAND NATIONAL STOCK CAR RACE. COMPETITION AT INTERSTATE #20-40 MILES E B'HAM AL, 100 MILES W OF ATLANTA, GA. (NAT'L). DON NAMAN, GEN MANAGER; ALABAMA INTERNATIONAL MOTOR SPEEDWAY; PO BOX 777; TALLADEGA, AL 35160. (#100722-1).

JULY 1 - 31, '76. 8TH ANNUAL MISS TALLADEGA 500 BEAUTY PAGEANT. CEREMONY, COMPETITION AT HARWELL AUDITORIUM. (ST-WIDE). LARRY ALLEN, PROJ MGR; TALLADEGA JAYCEES; PO BOX 777; TALLADEGA, AL 35160. (#100626-1).

AUG 4 - 8, '76. TALLADEGA 500 NASCAR WINSTON CUP GRAND NATIONAL STOCK CAR RACE. COMPETITION AT INTERSTATE #20 - 40 MILES E BIRMINGHAM, AL 100 MI W ATLANTA, GA. (NAT'L). DON NAMAN, GEN MANAGER; ALABAMA INTERNATIONAL MOTOR SPEEDWAY; PO BOX 777; TALLADEGA, AL 35160. (#100723-1).

TALLASSEE

MINI-PARK, TALLASSEE, AL. DEVELOPMENT OF A MINI-PARK WHICH WILL INCLUDE PRE-CIVIL WAR BELL WHICH WAS ONCE TOWN CLOCK, ROCK WHICH MARKED COUNCIL OAK SITE MEETING PLACE OF CREEK NATION DIGNITARES, AZALEAS & GROUND MAP OF AL. (LOCAL). BETTIE JEAN WATSON, COORDINATOR; TALLASSEE BICENTENNIAL COMMITTEE; PO BOX 548; TALLASSEE, AL 36078. (#24897). **ARBA GRANTEE.**

TALLASSEE MUSEUM, AL. A NEW MUSEUM DEDICATED TO THE PRESERVATION OF LOCAL HISTORY & CULTURE. (LOCAL). BETTIE JEAN WATSON, COORDINATOR; TALLASSEE BICENTENNIAL COMMITTEE; TALLASSEE, AL 36078. (#24899). **ARBA GRANTEE.**

THEODORE

FEB 1 - 29, '76. FLOWER SHOW. MASS BLOOMING OF CAMELLIAS, TULIPS, DAFFODILS. AZALEA BLOOMING SEASON BEGINS AROUND THE MIDDLE OF FEBRAUARY THROUGH MARCH. THE BICENTENNIAL WILL BE COMMEMORATED THE YEAR BY FLORAL DISPLAYS DEPICTING EVENTS OF OUR HISTORY. AT 20 MILES SOUTH OF MOBILE, AL, ON INTERSTATE-10. (REGN'L). JOHN M BROWN, DIRECTOR; BELLINGRATH GARDENS; ROUTE 1, BOX 60; THEODORE, AL 36582. (#103416-111).

JUNE 1 - 30, '76. SUMMER FLOWER SHOW. LANDSCAPED ARRANGEMENTS OF FLOWERING PLANTS DELIGHT THOUSANDS OF VISITORS TO THE 'CHARM SPOT OF THE DEEP SOUTH'. OPEN 7AM TO DUSK. THE BELLINGRATH HOME OPENS AT 8:30 AM UNTIL 5 PM WITH THE LAST TOUR BEGINNING AT 4:15 PM EACH DAY. AT 20 MILES SOUTH OF MOBILE. (LOCAL). JOHN N BROWN, GEN MGR; BELLINGRATH GARDENS; ROUTE #1, PO BOX 60; THEODORE, AL 36582. (#103416-357).

THOMASVILLE

THOMASVILLE BICENTENNIAL PROJECTS, AL. ROSES WILL BE PLANTED ALONG HWY THROUGHOUT CITY, A HUT, PROMOTING FESTIVALS & HISTORICAL EVENTS WILL BE SET UP. (LOCAL). AMOS LEDBETTER, CHAIRMAN; THOMASVILLE BICENTENNIAL COMMITTEE; HIGHLAND AVE; THOMASVILLE, AL 36784. (#23509).

TOWN CREEK

DEVELOPMENT OF PARK - TOWN CREEK, AL. TREES WILL BE PLANTED, A BASEBALL PARK AND OTHER FACILITIES ARE BEING BUILT. (LOCAL). J R KNOUFF, PRESIDENT; TOWN CREEK BICENTENNIAL CLUB; TOWN CREEK, AL 35672. (#29181).

HISTORY OF TOWN CREEK, AL. A HISTORY OF TOWN CREEK IS BEING WRITTEN. (LOCAL). J R KNOUFF, PRESIDENT; TOWN CREEK LIONS CLUB; BOX 96; TOWN CREEK, AL 35672. (#29180).

TROY

ART COMPETITION IN TROY, AL. IN HONOR OF BICENTENNIAL, TSU STUDENTS WILL COMPETE IN AN ART SHOW; BEST ART WORKS ON THE AMERICAN REVOLUTION WILL BE PERMANENTLY DISPLAYED ON CAMPUS. (LOCAL). MILTON MCPHERSON, PROJ DIRECTOR; TROY STATE UNIV AMERICAN REVOLUTION BICENTENNIAL COMMITTEE; TROY, AL 36081. (#14402).

BICENTENNIAL BEAUTIFICATION PROJECT, TROY, AL. A 2 ACRE FLOWER GARDEN WILL BE PLANTED. (LOCAL). NELL WHITTLE, CHAIRMAN; CITY OF TROY BICENTENNIAL COMMITTEE; 300 ELM ST; TROY, AL 36081. (#25725). **ARBA GRANTEE.**

BICENTENNIAL COMMEMORATIVE PARK IN TROY, AL. FACULTY, STAFF AND STUDENT VOLUNTEERS WILL CONSTRUCT COBBLED WALKS, PLANT FLOWERS, CONSTRUCT A GAZEBO AND DO BASIC LANDSCAPING IN AREA IMMEDIATELY IN FRONT OF BIBB GRAVES HALL. (LOCAL). MILTON MCPHERSON, PROJ DIRECTOR; TROY STATE UNIV AMERICAN REVOLUTION BICENTENNIAL COMMITTEE; TROY, AL 36081. (#14405).

BICENTENNIAL NATURE TRAIL, TROY, AL. A COMMEMORATIVE NATURE TRAIL WILL BE CONSTRUCTED ON A WOODED & REMOTE AREA OF THE CAMPUS TO COMMEMORATE WILLIAM BARTRAM'S TRAVELS AND REVOLUTIONARY ERA ALABAMA. (LOCAL). MILTON MCPHERSON, PROJ DIRECTOR; TROY STATE UNIV AMERICAN REVOLUTION BICENTENNIAL COMMITTEE; TROY, AL 36081. (#14404).

BICENTENNIAL SLIDES IN TROY, AL. 350 35MM SLIDES, COVERING VARIOUS ASPECTS OF THE REVOLUTION, WILL BE PREPARED AND MADE AVAILABLE TO LOCAL PUBLIC SCHOOL HISTORY TEACHERS. (LOCAL). MILTON MCPHERSON, PROJ DIRECTOR; TROY STATE UNIV AMERICAN REVOLUTION BICENTENNIAL COMMITTEE; TROY, AL 36081. (#14403).

BICENTENNIAL TELEVISION SERIES, TROY, AL. PROJECT IS A SERIES OF ILLUSTRATED PROGRAMS OF THE AMERICAN REVOLUTION TO BE PRESENTED ON EDUCATIONAL TELEVISION BY THE TROY STATE UNIV ARBC. (LOCAL). MILTON MCPHERSON, PROJ DIRECTOR; TROY STATE UNIV AMERICAN REVOLUTION BICENTENNIAL COMMITTEE; TROY, AL 36081. (#14406).

ESSAY CONTEST IN TROY, AL. AN ESSAY CONTEST, WITH THE THEME BEING ALABAMA INDIANS, IS BEING SPONSORED FOR TSU STUDENTS. (LOCAL). MILTON MCPHERSON, PROJ DIRECTOR; TROY STATE UNIV AMERICAN REVOLUTION BICENTENNIAL COMMISSION; TROY, AL 36081. (#14407).

HISTORIC DEBATES & SPEECHES, TROY AL. STUDENTS OF TROY STATE UNIV WILL PARTICIPATE IN COMPETITION TO RECREATE FAMOUS DEBATES AND SPEECHES OF THE REVOLUTIONARY ERA; WINNERS IN VARIOUS CATEGORIES WILL RECEIVE AWARDS. (LOCAL). MILTON MCPHERSON, PROJ CHAIRMAN; TROY STATE UNIV AMERICAN REVOLUTION BICENTENNIAL COMMITTEE; TROY, AL 36081. (#14397).

INDIAN HERITAGE ART FESTIVAL, TROY, AL. TSU STUDENTS WILL PARTICIPATE IN AN ART FESTIVAL THAT COVERS ALABAMA'S INDIAN HERITAGE DURING REVOLUTIONARY ERA; THE BEST ART WORKS WILL BE PERMANENTLY DISPLAYED ON CAMPUS. (LOCAL). MILTON MCPHERSON, CHAIRPERSON; TROY STATE UNIV AMERICAN REVOLUTIONARY BICENTENNIAL COMMITTEE; TROY, AL 36081. (#14400).

RADIO NEWS BROADCASTS IN TROY, AL. THE TROY STATE UNIV ARBC WILL PREPARE FOR TROY RADIO STATIONS DURING 1975-76 'SPOT' NEWS ANNOUNCEMENTS FOR CORRESPONDING DATES DURING 1775-1776. (LOCAL). MILTON MCPHERSON, CHAIRPERSON; TROY STATE UNIV AMERICAN REVOLUTION BICENTENNIAL COMMITTEE; TROY, AL 36081. (#14398).

WEEKLY COLUMN FOR 'TRIPOLITAN', TROY, AL. ARTICLES COVERING EVENTS BETWEEN 1775 AND 1776 WILL BE CARRIED IN THE TSU STUDENT NEWSPAPER DURING THE ACADEMIC YEAR 1975-1976. (LOCAL). MILTON M MCPHERSON, CHAIRPERSON; TROY STATE UNIV AMERICAN REVOLUTIONARY BICENTENNIAL COMMITTEE; TROY, AL 36081. (#14399).

SEPT '75 - APR '76. ART AND PHOTOGRAPHY EXHIBIT. THE EXHIBIT WILL BE COMPOSED OF ART WORK & PHOTOGRAPHY ON REVOLUTIONARY ERA EVENTS AND PERSONALITIES. (LOCAL). MILTON MCPHERSON, CHMN; TROY STATE UNIV BICENTENNIAL COMMITTEE; TROY STATE UNIV; TROY, AL 36081. (#101833-3).

OCT 29, '75. BICENTENNIAL QUIZ COMPETITION. ALL LOCAL PTO'S AND CIVIC CLUBS WILL BE INVITED TO PARTICIPATE IN A 'COLLEGE BOWL' TYPE QUIZ ON THE AMERICAN REVOLUTION. EVENTUAL WINNERS IN EACH CATEGORY WILL BE RECOGNIZED. (LOCAL). MILTON MCPHERSON, CHMN; TROY STATE UNIV BICENTENNIAL COMMITTEE; TROY STATE UNIV; TROY, AL 36081. (#101833-4).

JAN 28, '76. UNITED STATES ARMED FORCES BICENTENNIAL CARAVAN. CARAVAN IS COMPOSED OF EXHIBIT VANS FOR EACH MILITARY SERVICE. PROJECT THEME IS 'HISTORY OF THE ARMED FORCES AND THEIR CONTRIBUTIONS TO THE NATION'. (LOCAL). MRS BETTY WAGONER, CHMN; U S ARMED FORCES BICENTENNIAL EXHIBIT VANS PROJECT; 111 FIRST AVE; TROY, AL 36081. (#1775-387).

FEB 19 - 20, '76. 'INHERIT THE WIND' - PERFORMANCE. LIVE PERFORMANCE AT KILBY AUDITORIUM. (LOCAL). DR DAVID DYE, CHAIRMAN; TROY STATE UNIV BICENTENNIAL COMMITTEE; DRAMA DEPT, TROY STATE UNIV; TROY, AL 36081. (#101833-2).

JULY 4, '76. MUSIC OF THE AMERICAN REVOLUTION ERA - CONCERT. LIVE PERFORMANCE AT SMITH HALL. (LOCAL). DR JOHN M LONG, CHAIRMAN; TROY STATE UNIV BICENTENNIAL COMMITTEE; ARTS & SCIENCES DEPT, TSU; TROY, AL 36081. (#101833-1).

TUSCALOOSA

CHILDREN'S NATURAL SCIENCE MUSEUM: TUSCALOOSA, AL. PROJECT WILL ESTABLISH A CHILDREN'S MUSEUM. (LOCAL). GREGG FREE, BICENTENNIAL COORDINATOR; TUSCALOOSA BICENTENNIAL EXECUTIVE COMMITTEE; BOX 1776; TUSCALOOSA, AL 35401. (#13810).

ECHOLA SCHOOL BUILDING RESTORATION, AL. RESTORATION AND DEVELOPMENT OF ECHOLA SCHOOL BUILDING BUILT IN 1921 FOR USE AS A COMMUNITY BUILDING FOR COMMUNITY MEETINGS, SOCIAL AND RECREATIONAL GATHERINGS. (LOCAL). LEWIS E MCCRAY, CHAIRMAN; TUSCALOOSA COUNTY BICENTENNIAL COMMISSION; PO DRAWER 28; TUSCALOOSA, AL 35401. (#23016). **ARBA GRANTEE.**

GUILD-VERNER HOUSE RESTORATION IN TUSCALOOSA, AL. RESTORATION OF TOWN'S OLDEST BRICK HOUSE AS HEADQUARTERS FOR AN ARTS & HUMANITIES COUNCIL WITH ART GALLERY, THEATER, DANCE PRACTICE SPACE & JUNIOR LEAGUE OFFICE, AUDITORIUM & MEETING ROOMS. (LOCAL). TOM BOOZER, DIRECTOR; TUSCALOOSA ARTS & HUMANITIES COUNCIL; BOX 1117; TUSCALOOSA, AL 35401. (#13809).

LIBRARY PROJECT IN TUSCALOOSA, ALABAMA. NEW COUNTY LIBRARY AND PRESERVATION OF PRESENT STRUCTURE AS CHAMBER OF COMMERCE HEADQUARTERS. (LOCAL). GREGG FREE, BICENTENNIAL COORDINATOR; BICENTENNIAL EXECUTIVE BOARD OF TUSCALOOSA; BOX 1776; TUSCALOOSA, AL 35401. (#13811).

POST OFFICE RESTORATION IN TUSCALOOSA, ALABAMA. THE BROWNVILLE POST OFFICE WILL BE MOVED TO THE PARK & RESTORED AS A MUSEUM OF POSTAL SERVICE. (LOCAL). MARVIN HARPER, CHAIRMAN; NORTHPORT BICENTENNIAL COMMITTEE; PO BOX 306; NORTHPORT, AL 35401. (#13814).

PUBLISHED HISTORIES OF TUSCALOOSA, ALABAMA. HISTORIES OF TUSCALOOSA COUNTY WILL BE PUBLISHED IN VARIOUS SUBJECT AREAS, SUCH AS MEDICINE, LAW, RELIGION, RACIAL GROUPS & TECHNOLOGY (EG, DEVELOPMENT OF THE COTTON GIN). (ST-WIDE). GREGG FREE, BICENTENNIAL COORDINATOR; BICENTENNIAL EXECUTIVE BOARD OF TUSCALOOSA; BOX 1776; TUSCALOOSA, AL 35401. (#13812).

RESTORATION OF WASHINGTON MOODY HOUSE, AL. PRESERVATION & RESTORATION OF 1820'S HOUSE LISTED ON THE NATIONAL REGISTER. (LOCAL). CHRISTIE RUDNICK, COORDINATOR; BICENTENNIAL EXECUTIVE BOARD; PO BOX 1776; TUSCALOOSA, AL 35401. (#20849). **ARBA GRANTEE.**

TUSCALOOSA COUNTY RURAL MUSEUM IN ALABAMA. THE RURAL MUSEUM WILL DOCUMENT THE SOUTHERN FARM EXPERIENCE BY DISPLAYS OF TOOLS, MACHINERY & HOME ITEMS USED BY THE PEOPLE OF THE AREA. (ST-WIDE). MARVIN HARPER, CHAIRMAN; NORTHPORT BICENTENNIAL COMMITTEE; PO BOX 306; NORTHPORT, AL 35401. (#13813).

MAR 6, '75. ARTS CENTER OPENING. CEREMONY, OPENING AT GUILD-VERNER HOME, 19TH & UNIVERSITY BLVD. (LOCAL). TOM BOOZER, DIRECTOR; ARTS & HUMANITIES COUNCIL OF TUSCALOOSA; BOX 1117; TUSCALOOSA, AL 35401. (#200001-36).

SEPT 22 - 27, '75. WEST ALABAMA FAIR. FAIR, COMPETITION AT JAYCEE PARK, 1 BLOCK OFF UNIV BLVD AT ALBERTA CITY. (REGN'L). NAT JONES, PRESIDENT; TUSCALOOSA JUNIOR CHAMBER OF COMMERCE; 410 WOODLAND HILLS; TUSCALOOSA, AL 35401. (#101265-1).

DEC 19 - 24, '75. OPENING OF NEW ART COUNCIL HEADQUARTERS. IN HONOR OF THE OPENING OF THE GUILD VERNER HOUSE AS THE ART COUNCIL HEADQUARTERS, THERE WILL BE A CELEBRATION AND RECEPTION. AT GUILD VERNER HOUSE, UNIV BLVD. (LOCAL). TOM BOOZER, CHAIRMAN; TUSCALOOSA ARTS & HUMANITIES COUNCIL; PO BOX 1117; TUSCALOOSA, AL 35401. (#101260-1).

JAN 20 - 21, '76. UNITED STATES ARMED FORCES BICENTENNIAL CARAVAN. CARAVAN IS COMPOSED OF EXHIBIT VANS FOR EACH MILITARY SERVICE. PROJECT THEME IS 'HISTORY OF THE ARMED FORCES AND THEIR CONTRIBUTIONS TO THE NATION'. (LOCAL). GREGORY B FREE, CHMN; TUSCALOOSA BICENTENNIAL COMMITTEE; PO BOX 1776; TUSCALOOSA, AL 35401. (#1775-383).

FEB 19 - 21, '76. AN EVENING OF DANCE: PERFORMANCE BY STUDENTS OF MODERN DANCE. LIVE PERFORMANCE AT UNIVERSITY THEATER. (LOCAL). LOU WALL, DIRECTOR; UNIV OF ALABAMA; BOX 1967; UNIVERSITY, AL 35486. (#101191-1).

APR 2 - 17, '76. PRIDE IN AMERICA - BICENTENNIAL EVENTS. EVENTS WILL INCLUDE TOUR OF HOMES, ANTIQUE SHOW, FOLK FESTIVAL AND PARADE. (ST-WIDE). MRS JO HARRIS, PRESIDENT; TUSCALOOSA COUNTY PRESERVATION SOCIETY; PO BOX 1665; TUSCALOOSA, AL 35401. (#101264-1).

APR 3 - 11, '76. HERITAGE WEEK. ACTIVITIES INCL FESTIVAL ALL WEEK WITH ANTIQUE CAR SHOW, ENTERTAINMENT, OPEN HOUSE; QUILT EXHIBIT; HERITAGE ARTS TOUR; PILGRIMAGE; ANTIQUE SHOW/SALE. AT CAPITOL PARK. (LOCAL). JIM BENNIGHT, COORD; TUSCALOOSA COUNTY PRESERVATION SOCIETY; PO BOX 1302; TUSCALOOSA, AL 35401. (#103416-259).

MAY '76. BAND CONCERT. J C PENNY BICENTENNIAL MUSIC WILL BE PLAYED AT THE BAND CONCERT BY COMBINED BANDS OF THE COUNTY. (LOCAL). MARVIN HARPER, CHMN; NORTHPORT BICENTENNIAL COMMITTEE; PO BOX 306; NORTHPORT, AL 35476. (#101256-1).

JUNE 19 - 21, '76. TUSCALOOSA JUNIOR WELFARE CHARITY HORSESHOW. COMPETITION AT TUSCALOOSA RIDING CLUB, 1/2 BLOCK OFF OF HARGROVE. (ST-WIDE). MRS GUY MOMAN, PRESIDENT; TUSCALOOSA JUNIOR LEAGUE; PO BOX 1776; TUSCALOOSA, AL 35401. (#101261-1).

JULY 4, '76. FOURTH OF JULY FESTIVAL. CONTINUOUS ENTERTAINMENT, GAMES, BARBEQUE, PAGEANT OF FLAGS, FIREWORKS. AT J OVIATT PARK. (LOCAL). CHRISTIE RUDNICK, COORD; TUSCALOOSA BICENTENNIAL COMMISSION & TUSCALOOSA COUNTY BICENTENNIAL; PO BOX 1776; TUSCALOOSA, AL 35401. (#105061-2).

SEPT 27 - OCT 2, '76. WEST ALABAMA STATE FAIR. FAIR AT TUSCALOOSA JAYCEE WEST ALABAMA FAIR GROUNDS. (REGN'L). R EARL MITCHELL; CITY OF TUSCALOOSA; PO DRAWER L; TUSCALOOSA, AL 35401. (#106300-1).

TUSKEGEE

'AMERICA: 200 YEARS SINCE' - FESTIVAL & PARADE-AL. THE MACON COUNTY BICENTENNIAL COMMITTEE IS SPONSORING A 3 DAY FESTIVAL WITH BALLS, PAGEANTS AND A PARADE. (LOCAL). RONALD WILLIAMS, CHAIRMAN; MACON COUNTY BICENTENNIAL COMMITTEE; CITY HALL; TUSKEGEE, AL 36083. (#27357). **ARBA GRANTEE.**

JAN 27, '76. UNITED STATES ARMED FORCES BICENTENNIAL CARAVAN. CARAVAN IS COMPOSED OF EXHIBIT VANS FOR EACH MILITARY SERVICE. PROJECT THEME IS 'HISTORY OF THE ARMED FORCES AND THEIR CONTRIBUTIONS TO THE NATION'. (LOCAL). MRS ELAINE THOMAS, CHMN; MACON COUNTY '76 ACTION COMMITTEE; TUSKEGEE INSTITUTE; TUSKEGEE, AL 36088. (#1775-386).

MAY 9 - 16, '76. ARTS AND CRAFTS FESTIVAL 1976. FESTIVAL AT DOWNTOWN SQUARE. (LOCAL). ALLAN G JUNIER, CHMN; BEAUX ARTS GUILD; 2111 ETHEL DR; TUSKEGEE, AL 36088. (#100804-1).

JULY 3 - 5, '76. 'AMERICA: 200 YEARS SINCE' - FESTIVAL & PARADE. A THREE DAY FESTIVAL WITH BALLS, PAGEANTS & A PARADE. (LOCAL). RONALD WILLIAMS, CHAIRMAN; MACON COUNTY BICENTENNIAL COMMITTEE; CITY HALL; TUSKEGEE, AL 36083. (#27357-1).

UNION SPRINGS

JAN 16 - 23, '76. NATIONAL OPEN SHOOTING DOG CHAMPIONSHIP. COMPETITION AT SEDGEFIELDS PLANTATION. (NAT'L). VERLE FARROW, PROJ DIR; NATIONAL OPEN SHOOTING DOG CHAMPIONSHIP ASSOC; 13205 JOHNNY MOORE LANE; CLIFTON, VA 22024. (#100724-1).

FEB 22 - MAR 1, '76. NATIONAL SHOOTING DOG CHAMPIONSHIP. COMPETITION AT SEDGEFIELDS PLANTATION. (NAT'L). FRED WILSON, PROJ DIR; NATIONAL SHOOTING DOG CHAMPIONSHIP ASSOC; 300 S ROONEY ST; UNION SPRINGS, AL 36089. (#100725-1).

MAR 15 - 22, '76. THE DIXIE CLASSICS, DOG COMPETITION & FIELD TRIALS. FIELD TRIAL COMPETITION WILL BE HELD IN OPEN STAKES, PUPPY, DERBY & ALL-AGE. AT SEDGEFIELDS PLANTATION. (REGN'L). TERRELL DIXON, SECRETARY; THE DIXIE FIELD TRIAL CLUB; RFD 2; MIDWAY, AL 36053. (#100726-1).

UNIVERSITY

BICENTENNIAL REPRINT SERIES, UNIV OF ALABAMA. THE PROJECT INVOLVES REPRINTING FOUR OUT-OF-PRINT BOOKS OF HISTORICAL AND ACADEMIC SIGNIFICANCE. (LOCAL). ROBERT MCKENZIE, PROFESSOR; UNIV OF ALABAMA; UNIVERSITY, AL 35486. (#9570). **ARBA GRANTEE.**

AUG 13 - SEPT 11, '77. 'EDVARD MUNCH, THE MAJOR GRAPHICS' EXHIBIT. AN EXHIBITION FROM THE MUNCH MUSEUM IN OSLO BY ONE OF THE GREATEST FIGURES IN MODERN PRINTMAKING. AT UNIVERSITY OF ALABAMA. (INT'L). EILEEN HARAKAL, COORD; SMITHSONIAN INSTITUTION TRAVELING EXHIBITION SERVICE; 1000 JEFFERSON DR, SW; WASHINGTON, DC 20560. (#26704-13).

WADLEY

BICENTENNIAL GARDEN COMMITTEE - WADLEY, AL. OBJECTIVES OF COMMITTEE ARE THE PLANTING OF NATIVE FLOWERS AND SHRUBS IN SELECTED AREAS OF THE SOUTHERN UNION COLLEGE CAMPUS. THE PROJECT WILL INVOLVE STUDENTS AND WILL RELATE TO THE ENVIRONMENT. (LOCAL). RALPH R JONES, JR, CHAIRMAN; SOUTHERN UNION STATE JUNIOR COLLEGE; WADLEY, AL 36276. (#19029).

GUEST SPEAKERS - WADLEY, AL. SPEAKERS TO BE SCHEDULED TO VISIT CAMPUS AND COMMUNITY TO SPEAK ON BICENTENNIAL SUBJECTS. (LOCAL). ROBERT ADAMS, CHAIRMAN; SOUTHERN UNION BICENTENNIAL COMMITTEE; WADLEY, AL 36276. (#19031).

PRESERVATION OF LOG CABIN, WADLEY, AL. LOG CABIN TO BE RESTORED AND FURNISHED FOR USE AS A MUSEUM. (LOCAL). MARGARET SMITH, CHAIRMAN; SOUTHERN UNION BICENTENNIAL COMMITTEE; WADLEY, AL 36276. (#19032).

VISITS TO HISTORICAL PLACES, WADLEY, AL. VISITS TO LOCAL & NATIONAL HISTORICAL SITES ARE BEING PLANNED; AMONG THESE IS A TRIP TO WILLIAMSBURG. (LOCAL). WALTER FARR, CHAIRMAN; SOUTHERN UNION BICENTENNIAL COMMITTEE; WADLEY, AL 36276. (#19033).

THE 200 COMMITTEE - WADLEY, AL. A COMMITTEE HAS BEEN APPOINTED TO PROMOTE BICENTENNIAL ACTIVITIES, PREPARE MAILING LIST, PROVIDE A WELCOMING COMMITTEE AND COORDINATE BICENT ACTIVITIES WITH THE GENERAL COMMUNITY. (LOCAL). PAT SALATTO, JR, CHAIRMAN; SOUTHERN UNION BICENTENNIAL COMMITTEE; ROBERTS ST; WADLEY, AL 36276. (#19030).

MAY 21, '75. BALD ROCK GALA. FESTIVAL, CEREMONY. (LOCAL). LOUISE COX, CHMN; SOUTHERN UNION BICENTENNIAL; WADLEY, AL 36276. (#200001-37).

JAN 19 - 23, '76. AMERICAN REVOLUTION WEEK/HERITAGE WEEK. 1 WK OF FALL QUARTER RESERVED FOR TEACHING OF AMER REVOL & ITS RELATIONSHIP TO VARIOUS SUBJECTS. ALSO ARTS & CRAFTS DISPLAY WITH ONE DAY WHEN PERIOD COSTUMES WILL BE WORN; ESSAY CONTEST & RADIO PROGRAM. AT ADMINISTRATION BLDG. (LOCAL). HUEY BARRETT; PHI THETA KAPPA; SOUTHERN UNION COLLEGE; WADLEY, AL 36276. (#104122-4).

APR 7, '76. BICENTENNIAL COUNTRY FAIR AND COSTUME BALL. BOOTHS, CONCESSIONS, TEA ROOMS, ARTS & CRAFTS, COSTUME CONTEST, VIRGINIA REET & COSTUME BALL. AT COLLEGE PARKING LOT FOR SUDENTS BY MULTIPURPOSE. (LOCAL). ANN HARMON; SOUTHERN UNION BICENTENNIAL COMMITTEE; RT 9 BOX 543; OXFORD, AL 36201. (#104122-3).

APR 10, '76. COUNTRY FAIR AND BICENTENNIAL COSTUME BALL. FAIR, FESTIVAL. (LOCAL). DR RAY JONES, PRES; SOUTHERN UNION JR COLLEGE, WADLEY CAMPUS; SOUTHERN UNION ST JR COLL; WADLEY, AL 36276. (#200001-33).

WEST BLOCTON

MONUMENT TO WAR VETERANS - WEST BLOCTON, AL. A MONUMENT TO WAR VETERANS WILL BE ERECTED IN THE TOWN SQUARE. (LOCAL). LYDA M KEYES, COORDINATOR; WEST BLOCTON BICENTENNIAL GROUP; BOX 56; WEST BLOCTON, AL 35184. (#32153).

WETUMPKA

CALABOOSE RESTORATION - WETUMPKA, AL. RESTORE CALABOOSE, THE OLDEST KNOWN STRUCTURE ON EAST BANK OF THE COOSA RIVER. TO BE OPENED TO THE PUBLIC AS A MINI-MUSEUM TO DISPLAY ASPECTS OF EARLY WETUMPKA LIFE. (LOCAL). WILLIAM L LANCASTER, CHAIRMAN; ELMORE COUNTY BICENTENNIAL COMMITTEE; 608 TALLASSEE ST; WETUMPKA, AL 36092. (#27281). **ARBA GRANTEE.**

FT TOULOUSE DISPLAY IN WETUMPKA, AL. RECREATION OF STRUCTURE INSIDE FORT TO DISPLAY ARTIFACTS AND TO SHOW FORT-LIFE IN 18TH CENTURY; THE FORT IS THE SITE WHERE ANDREW JACKSON ACCEPTED CREEK SURRENDER IN 1814. (LOCAL). JOHN H BROOKS, PRESIDENT; FORT TOULOUSE FOUNDATION; PO BOX 231; MONTGOMERY, AL 36101. (#10719). **ARBA GRANTEE.**

OCT 4, '75. RUMBLING WATERS ARTS AND CRAFTS SHOW. EXHIBIT, FESTIVAL, LIVE PERFORMANCE AT WETUMPKA COMMUNITY HOUSE AND PARK. (LOCAL). GAIL BASS, PROJ DIRECTOR; RUMBLING WATERS ARTS CLUB; PO BOX 456; WETUMPKA, AL 36092. (#100567-1).

WILSON POINT

MAY 7, '76. 'THE SMOKEY MOUNTAIN QUEEN' ARRIVES IN WILSON POINT. THE 'SMOKY MOUNTAIN QUEEN' IS A BOAT SIMILAR TO THOSE USED BY PIONEERS; IT WILL CARRY CARGO TYPICAL OF THAT ERA. (LOCAL). JOHN B WATERS, JR, DIR; SEVIER COUNTY BICENTENNIAL COMMITTEE; PROFESSIONAL BLDG; SEVIERVILLE, TN 37862. (#102425-13).

WILSONVILLE

TOWN CLEANUP AND BEAUTIFICATION - WILSONVILLE, NY. FLAGPOLES ERECTED; CEMETERY CLEANED; FLOWER-BEDS PLANTED; TREES AND SHRUBS PLANTED THROUGHOUT TOWN; FIREPLUGS PAINTED. (LOCAL). MRS M L JONES, CHAIRMAN; WILSONVILLE BICENTENNIAL COMMITTEE; PO BOX 133; WILSONVILLE, AL 35186. (#29271).

JUNE 12 - JULY 6, '76. DISPLAY DAYS: ARTS & CRAFTS & PICTURES. EXHIBIT AT TOWN HALL. (LOCAL). MRS M L JONES, CHAIRMAN; FINE ARTS CLUB; PO BOX 133; WILSONVILLE, AL 35186. (#200001-46).

JULY 6, '76. BICENTENNIAL FESTIVAL. FESTIVAL AT HELMS PARK. (LOCAL). MRS M L JONES, CHAIRMAN; WILSONVILLE CIVITAN CLUB; PO BOX 133; WILSONVILLE, AL 35186. (#200001-47).

YORK

CITY OF YORK ENTIRE CONSTRUCT PROJECT - AL. PROJECT WILL INCLUDE CONSTRUCTION OF 4 CEMETERY ENTRACES, PARKS AND CABOOSE. (LOCAL). HAZEL TIDMORE, CHAIRMAN; YORK BICENTENNIAL COMMITTEE; PO DRAWER B; YORK, AL 36925. (#21890).

Alaska

Theme: The Great Land

Alaska American Revolution Bicentennial Commission

Established by an act of the Alaska State Legislature, effective May 2, 1972

ARBA Statistics

Officially Recognized
- Communities—30
- Colleges/Universities—3
- Military Installations—7

BINET Projects—115
- Events—84

1976 Population—382,000

Bicentennial Archives

State Archives and Records Center
141 Willoughby Avenue
Juneau, Alaska
(Mail: Pouch C, Juneau, Alaska 99811)

Membership

Rita Hendrickson, *chairman* (February 11, 1975-December 31, 1976), *secretary* (March 1, 1973-February 10, 1975)
Charles H. Parr, *chairman* (March 1, 1973-January 19, 1975)
Beatrice (Langnes) Graves, *executive director* (June 15, 1974-December 31, 1976)
Ed A. Tomco, *executive director* (July 1, 1973-June 14, 1974)
Sandra Kavanaugh (May 25, 1973-February 10, 1975), *secretary* (February 11, 1975-December 31, 1976)
Richard Engen, *ex officio* (August 1, 1974-December 31, 1976)
Michael Kennedy, *ex officio* (March 1, 1973-July 1, 1974)
Richard Montague, *ex officio* (February 1, 1975-December 31, 1976)
Guy Russo, *ex officio* (March 1, 1973-February 1, 1975)
Rose Arvidson (July 1, 1975-December 31, 1976)
Poldine Carlo (July 1, 1975-December 31, 1976)
John Gibbons (March 1, 1973-December 31, 1976)
Rae Hoopes (March 1, 1973-December 31, 1976)
Brenda Itta (March 1, 1973-April 1, 1973)
Nathan Jackson (March 1, 1973-November 10, 1974)
Roy Madsen (March 1, 1973-April 1, 1973)
Lydia Schuerch (May 25, 1973-December 31, 1976)

Alaska

Alaska filled its cornucopia of Bicentennial activities with fruit as diverse as the state's population and geography. As part of a living history village on the Alaska State Fairgrounds, historic buildings constructed during the settlement of the Matanuska Colony in the 1930's were renovated. A comprehensive oral history program involving those Matanuska settlers still living has added color and depth to this major restoration effort.

In addition, Resolution Park was established in honor of Captain James Cook, who gave his name to Alaska's Cook Inlet. Its main feature is a statue of Cook, which was donated by British Petroleum-Alaska.

Over 40 additional parks and playgrounds were developed around the state and are evidence of the widespread Bicentennial enthusiasm and effort. One, Anglanivik Park, is the first park in the community of Bethel. Appropriately, "Anglanivik" is a term in Yupik—an Eskimo language—meaning "a place to have fun."

The tourism industry in Alaska will benefit for years from numerous museums and tourist information centers created as a result of the Bicentennial. Fifteen communities constructed or expanded museums to preserve indigenous history and culture. From the northernmost town in Alaska, Shishmaref, to the southernmost tip at Metlakatla, residents volunteered much time and effort to see those museums through to completion.

Of special significance is the Last Chance Museum in Juneau. Original equipment used to mine gold when Juneau was first established was located, cleaned, inventoried and put on display. Much of it was actually put to use to complete the project.

Perhaps one of the most spectacular Bicentennial projects was carried out in Anchorage—*The Pageant of Alaskan Civilization,* a series of 20 panels done in bas relief. Each four foot by eight foot panel depicts a segment of Alaska's history, beginning with Peter the Great and ending with the Trans-Alaska Pipeline. The mural was sponsored by Alaska Mutual Savings Bank and hangs in its lobby.

Publications that originated during the Bicentennial era include histories of nursing and education in Alaska. The Future Homemakers of America, Alaska Chapter, recorded on tape and in writing the stories, reflections and opinions of many of Alaska's pioneer and homesteading citizens. *Beginning and Intermediate Tlingit* helps make the study of that language more easily accessible to those young members of the Alaska community who are searching for their native identity, almost lost in the development of the new state.

Other projects throughout the state included traveling exhibits and photographic displays, identification of historic sites, marking of the historic Iditarod Trail, festivals, special concerts and dance programs, Mt. McKinley expeditions, presentations of historical dramas, flag ceremonies and arts and crafts contests.

As evidenced by the widespread participation of Alaskans, the spirit of the Bicentennial abounded, and it will not be forgotten in the years to come in the "Great Land."

ADAK

ADAK BICENTENNIAL PARK - AK. PARK SURROUNDING MUSEUM; ONE OF ONLY TWO PARKS ON THIS ALEUTIAN ISLAND. SIXTY-FIVE FOOT RADIAL IN CENTER OF PARK WITH AMERICAN, BICENTENNIAL, ALASKAN FLAGS & 50 PLAQUES FOR EACH STATE. (LOCAL). LCDR GERALD JACOBSON, CHAIRMAN; ADAK BICENTENNIAL COMMISSION; BOX 48, FPO SEATTLE; SEATTLE, WA 98791. (#27417). **ARBA GRANTEE.**

ADAK BICENTENNIAL MUSEUM - AK. STRUCTURE TO HOUSE ARTIFACTS OF ADAK'S CULTURAL HERITAGE. INCLUDED WILL BE ALEUTIAN ARTIFACTS, NATURAL FLORA & FAUNA, WILDLIFE & ECOLOGICAL TRANGRESSION & PROGRESSION. (LOCAL). LCDR GERALD JACOBSON, CHAIRMAN; ADAK BICENTENNIAL COMMISSION; BOX 48, FPO SEATTLE; SEATTLE, WA 98791. (#27418). **ARBA GRANTEE.**

ADAK COAST GUARD AUXILIARY BOAT BASIN & PARK - AK. A FACILITY TO ACCOMMODATE LEISURE BOATS, AS WELL AS PARK AREA WITH RECREATION FACILITIES. (LOCAL). LCDR GERALD JACOBSON, CHAIRMAN; ADAK BICENTENNIAL COMMISSION; BOX 48, FPO SEATTLE; SEATTLE, WA 98791. (#27416). **ARBA GRANTEE.**

USCGC IRONWOOD CLOTHES COLLECTION - ADAK, AK. COLLECTED AND DISTRIBUTED CLOTHES AND TOYS TO NEEDY ALASKAN NATIVES. (LOCAL). COORDINATOR; U S COAST GUARD CUTTER IRONWOOD; FPO; SEATTLE, WA 98799. (#28591).

JULY 3 - 4, '76. ADAK 4TH OF JULY CELEBRATION. PARADE, FIREWORKS, SPORTS, PICNIC, DANCING AND TALENT SHOW. (LOCAL). LCDR GERALD JACOBSON; ADAK BICENTENNIAL COMMITTEE; BOX 48, ADAK NAVAL STATION; ADAK, AK 98791. (#108364-11).

ANCHORAGE

ALASKA PRESS WOMEN'S ORAL HISTORY SERIES - NBMRP. SERIES OF ARTICLES FROM ORAL HISTORIES OF PERSONS WHO'VE LIVED IN ALASKA FOR 30 OR MORE YRS. ARTICLES GIVEN TO LIBRARIES THROUGHOUT THE STATE; HOPE TO GET SERIES PUBLISHED IN BOOK FORM. (ST-WIDE). PHYLLIS CARLSON, BICENTENNIAL COORDINATOR; ALASKA PRESS WOMEN; BOX 141; ANCHORAGE, AK 99150. (#24418).

AMERICAN HERITAGE QUILTS IN ANCHORAGE, AK. PATTERN INCLUDES: 50 STARS, AN APPLIQUE FOR EACH STATE, EMBROIDERED NAMES OF THE SIGNERS OF THE DECLARATION OF INDEPENDENCE, REPLICA OF THE BETSY ROSS FLAG, & SEAL OF THE USA(EAGLE). (LOCAL). KAREN REED, DESIGNER; 139 N FLOWER ST; ANCHORAGE, AK 99504. (#9620).

AMERICAN HERITAGE - 200 YEARS OF STITCHERY, ALASKA. THIS PROJECT INVOLVES A STITCHERY CONTEST INCLUDING THE FOLLOWING: EMBROIDERY, APPLIQUE, WEAVING, KNITTING, RUG MAKING, CROCHET, CREWEL AND NEEDLEPOINT. (LOCAL). RUTH SILCOCK, CHAIRMAN; ANCHORAGE WOMEN'S CLUB; 2586 DISCOVERY CT; ANCHORAGE, AK 99503. (#9773).

BANNER ART COMPETITION - ANCHORAGE, AK. OF BANNERS ENTERED IN COMPETITION, 8 WERE EXECUTED IN FELT BY HOME EC DEPT; BANNERS WERE EXHIBITED DURING UAA BICENTENNIAL ARTS FAIR AND WILL HANG IN THE CONSORTIUM LIBRARY. (LOCAL). MARY HALE, CHAIRMAN; UNIV OF ALASKA, ANCHORAGE; 2533 PROVIDENCE; ANCHORAGE, AK 99504. (#32093).

BAS RELIEF SCULPTURE IN ANCHORAGE, ALASKA. 20 PANELS OF BAS RELIEF SCULPTURE TO EXTEND ACROSS FACIA OF BALCONY IN LOBBY OF ALASKA MUTUAL SAVINGS BANK WILL PORTRAY EVENTS & OUTSTANDING PERSONALITIES IN ALASKAN HISTORY. (LOCAL). HERB HILSCHER, HISTORIAN; ALASKA MUTUAL SAVINGS BANK; 601 W 5TH AVE; ANCHORAGE, AK 99501. (#8802).

BEAUTIFY ANCHORAGE MEMORIAL PARK, ALASKA. THE PROJECT INVOLVES REFURBISHING AND BEAUTIFYING ANCHORAGE MEMORIAL PARK AND THE DOWNTOWN CEMETERY. (LOCAL). MRS ARCHIE CUPPLES, CHAIRMAN; ANCHORAGE GARDEN CLUB; 744 E THIRD AVE; ANCHORAGE, AK 99501. (#9777).

BEGINNING TLINGIT & INTERMEDIATE TLINGIT - AK. PUBLICATION OF TEXTBOOKS TO ASSIST IN RETAINING THE TLINGIT INDIAN CULTURE IN ALASKA. (ST-WIDE). NORA DAUENHAUER, PRESIDENT; TLINGIT READERS, INC; 40 DAUENHAUER, BOX 25 AMU; ANCHORAGE, AK 99504. (#23772). **ARBA GRANTEE.**

BICENTENNIAL ART SCULPTURE AND CLOCK IN AK. DEDICATION OF ART SCULPTURE DEPICTING THE ALASKAN WOMAN, BOTH PIONEER AND MODERN-DAY TO BE PLACED IN NEW 6TH AVE PLAZA. A CLOCK WILL ALSO BE GIVEN. (LOCAL). MRS GORDON GREEN, CHAIRMAN; SOROPTIMIST INTERNATIONAL OF ANCHORAGE; 817 7TH AVE; ANCHORAGE, AK 99501. (#30019).

BICENTENNIAL PEDESTRIAN PLAZA IN ANCHORAGE, AK. PLAZA ON CORNER OF 6TH & G; TREES, FLOWERS, BENCHES, ART SCULPTURE ON ALASKAN WOMAN. (LOCAL). BOB ROBERTSON, DIRECTOR; URBAN BEAUTIFICATION COMMISSION & PARKS & RECREATION DEPT; POUCH 6-650; ARCHORAGE, AK 99502. (#30018).

BICENTENNIAL 'WELCOME TO ANCHORAGE' SIGNS - AK. 2 RED, WHITE & BLUE SIGNS WITH ANCHORAGE BICENTENNIAL LOGO USED TO WELCOME VISITORS AND REMIND RESIDENTS OF THE BICENTENNIAL TWO SIGNS, ONE AT THE NORTH ENTRANCE, THE OTHER AT THE SOUTH. (LOCAL). LCDR FHAYES I GORDON, COORDINATOR; NAVAL SECURITY GROUP ACTIVITY, ANCHORAGE; ELMENDORF AFB; ANCHORAGE, AK 99506. (#30022).

CITY HALL RESTORATION IN ANCHORAGE, AK. RESTORATION OF CITY HALL, GROUND FLOOR, TO ORIGINAL 1936 APPEARANCE, ORIGINAL LIGHT FIXTURES, SOCKETS, RED QUARRY TILE FLOORS, HIGH CEILING. (LOCAL). MARK HINSHAW, COORDINATOR; ANCHORAGE HISTORICAL LANDMARKS PRESERVATION COMMITTEE; POUCH 6-650; ANCHORAGE, AK 99502. (#30021).

COMMUNITY CULTURAL COMPLEX IN ANCHORAGE, ALASKA. IN HONOR OF THE BICENTENNIAL, A FACILITY TO HOUSE THE PERFORMING ARTS IN THE ANCHORAGE AREA WILL BE BUILT. (LOCAL). BETZI WOODMAN, CHAIRMAN; ANCHORAGE BICENT COMMISSION; TRANSAMERICA TITLE BLDG, 705 W 6; ANCHORAGE, AK 99501. (#9778).

EXPANDED LIBRARY SERVICES IN ANCHORAGE, ALASKA. SERVICES WILL INCLUDE: MICROFILM OF HISTORIC PRINTED MATERIAL NOT CURRENTLY ACCESSIBLE; CIRCULATING ART COLLECTION; & A PROGRAM OF LECTURES & FILMS TO BE TAKEN INTO THE COMMUNITY. (LOCAL). DOROTHY SHAVER, Z J LOUSSAC LIBRARY; GREATER ANCHORAGE AREA BOROUGH LIBRARY BOARD; 427 F STREET; ANCHORAGE, AK 99507. (#8794). **ARBA GRANTEE.**

FAR NORTH BICENTENNIAL PARK IN ANCHORAGE, ALASKA. THIS PROJECT INVOLVES THE DEVELOPMENT OF A RECREATIONAL PARK AND RESERVE ON 5000 ACRES OF LAND. (LOCAL). DORIE CLARK, DIRECTOR OF PARKS & RECREATION; ANCHORAGE BICENT COMMISSION; 705 W 6TH; ANCHORAGE, AK 99501. (#9774).

HISTORICAL/ARCHITECTURAL SURVEY OF ANCHORAGE, AK. TO RECORD IN PICTURES ORIGINAL OWNERS, PRESENT OWNERS AND USE, PLUS UNIQUE FEATURES OF EARLIEST BUILDINGS IN ORIGINAL DOWNTOWN AREA, WHETHER THAT BUILDING IS NOW STANDING OR NOT; 1ST PHASE, 2 YEARS. (LOCAL). VIRGIL E KNIGHT, CHAIRMAN; COOK INLET HISTORICAL SOCIETY; 1522 COFFEY LANE; ANCHORAGE, AK 99501. (#30024).

IDITAROD MAIL TRAIL RESTORATION, ANCHORAGE, AK. RESTORATION OF 25 MILES OF HISTORIC IDITAROD MAIL TRAIL BY GIRL SCOUT TROOP 83; THIS TRAIL WAS USED DURING ALASKA'S GOLD RUSH; HISTORIC SITES WILL BE MARKED & TRAIL WILL BE CLEARED FOR HIKING. (LOCAL). MRS TERRY DITTMAN, PROJ DIRECTOR; SUSITNA GIRL SCOUT COUNCIL & SENIOR TROOP #83; 2550 SPENARD RD; ANCHORAGE, AK 99503. (#13706). **ARBA GRANTEE.**

KIWANIS FISH CREEK PARK - ANCHORAGE, AK. DEVELOPMENT OVER 3-5 YEAR SPAN, OF A 17 ACRE PARK THAT WILL INCLUDE BIKE PATH, NATURE TRAIL, PICNIC AND FREE PLAY AREAS, SHELTERS, BARBEQUE AREAS, TENNIS COURTS AND OTHER ACTIVITY AREAS. (LOCAL). ROBERT J OPALINSKI, PROJECT CHAIRMAN; KIWANIS CLUB OF ANCHORAGE; 840 K ST, SUITE 203; ANCHORAGE, AK 99501. (#30023).

'LITTLE DRUM, DISTANT DRUM' - ANCHORAGE, AK. MUSICAL PUBLICATION TO BE DISTRIBUTED TO ALL ALASKAN ELEMENTARY SCHOOL TEACHERS. (ST-WIDE). FRANCES VADLA, CHMN OF EDITORIAL COMMITTEE; AK MUSIC EDUCATORS/DEPT OF EDUCATION; 4600 DEBARR RD (ADM BLDG); ANCHORAGE, AK 99504. (#22859). **ARBA GRANTEE.**

PERFORMING ARTS SPACE DESIGN CONFERENCE, ALASKA. MEETING ON DESIGN NECESSITIES AND DESIGN CRITERION FOR PERFORMING ARTS SPACES FOR ALASKA. (ST-WIDE). ROY H HELMS, EXEC DIRECTOR; ALASKA STATE COUNCIL ON THE ARTS; 360 K ST SUITE 240; ANCHORAGE, AK 99501. (#3056).

QUILT - SYMBOLS OF AMERICA - ANCHORAGE, AK. QUILT MADE BY SECOND GRADE CLASS AT WILLIWAW SCHOOL; EACH CHILD MADE A SQUARE DEPICTING A SUBJECT WHICH THEY FELT BELONGS TO AMERICA. (LOCAL). MARY JANE WINN, TEACHER; WILLIWAW ELEMENTARY SCHOOL; 1417 KARLUK; ANCHORAGE, AK 99501. (#30026).

REPLICA OF COLONIAL ROOM IN ANCHORAGE, AK. REPLICA OF A COLONIAL CLASSROOM TO BE USED ALTERNATINGLY BY ALL CLASSROOMS. DEMONSTRATIONS BY PARENTS ON COLONIAL CRAFTS; CANDLEMAKING, WEAVING, QUILT MAKING, SOAP MAKING. (LOCAL). MRS CARYL LEWIS, KINDERGARTEN TEACHER; AURORA ELEMENTARY SCHOOL; ELMENDORF AFB; ANCHORAGE, AK 99506. (#30020).

RESOLUTION PARK IN ANCHORAGE, AK. PARK OVERLOOKS COOK INLET & ALASKA RANGE. FACILITIES INCLUDE WOOD PLATFORMS, RAMP, BRONZE STATUE OF JAMES COOK. DEDICATED DECEMBER 19, 1976. (LOCAL). GWYNNETH WILSON, COORDINATOR; ANCHORAGE BICENTENNIAL COMMISSION; 6234 TANAINA DR; ANCHORAGE, AK 99502. (#30025).

SYMPOSIUM ON NATIVE ARTS & CRAFTS. THE PROJECT INVOLVES A SYMPOSIUM ON THE HISTORY & FUTURE OF NATIVE ARTS & CRAFTS. (REGN'L). EVERETT KENT, EXEC DIRECTOR; ALASKA NATIVE ARTS & CRAFTS FOUNDATION; 4190 W AIRCRAFT DR; ANCHORAGE, AK 99503. (#10997). **ARBA RECOGNIZED.**

A TIME CAPSULE IN ANCHORAGE, ALASKA. THE PROJECT INVOLVES A 4 X 4 CAPSULE IN CONCRETE BASE ADORNED WITH ALASKAN GEMS & MINERALS; CAPSULE TO BE FILLED WITH VARIETY OF ARTICLES ILLUSTRATING LIFE & CULTURE OF ANCHORAGE IN 1976. (LOCAL). MS ORO STEWART, CHAIRMAN; CHUGACH GEM & MINERAL SOCIETY; PO BOX 4-4027; ANCHORAGE, AK 99509. (#9775).

TV SHOWS ON HISTORY AND CULTURE OF ALASKA. PRODUCTION OF 10 1/2 HOUR TV SHOWS ON HISTORY AND CULTURE OF ALASKA FROM PRIOR TO COMING OF WHITE MAN THROUGH SECOND WORLD WAR, WHICH WILL BE AVAILABLE TO ALL SCHOOLS & TOURISM DEPARTMENTS. (ST-WIDE). LARRY BECK, MANAGER; ALASKA BICENTENNIAL REVIEW; 3727 SPENARD RD; ANCHORAGE, AK 99503. (#8213). **ARBA GRANTEE.**

UAA BICENTENNIAL BROCHURES - ANCHORAGE, AK. TWO BROCHURES PUBLISHED TO ANNOUNCE BICENTENNIAL PROJECTS AND COURSES OFFERED AT UAA. (LOCAL). MARY HALE, CHAIRMAN; UNIV OF ALASKA, ANCHORAGE; 2533 PROVIDENCE; ANCHORAGE, AK 99504. (#32094).

WALKING ART GUIDE OF DOWNTOWN ANCHORAGE, AK. PAMPHLET GIVING WALKING GUIDE TO ALL ART SITES IN ANCHORAGE, SUCH AS ANCHORAGE HISTORICA AND FINE ARTS MUSEUM, ART SCULPTURES, ART WORKS IN STATE AND LOCAL GOVERNMENT BUILDINGS. GUIDE MAINLY FOR TOURISTS. (LOCAL). CAROL DERFNER, EXEC DIRECTOR; ANCHORAGE ARTS COUNCIL; 419 W 7TH; ARCHORAGE, AK 99501. (#30017).

YUPIQ LITERATURE PROJECT IN ANCHORAGE. 130-PAGE BI-LINGUAL BOOK OF POETRY AND PICTURES PORTRAYING THE FOUR SEASONS IN THE LIFE OF THE YUPIQ PEOPLE. THE BOOK OF 50 POEMS IN YUPIQ AND ENGLISH WILL BE PUBLISHED IN MAY OF 1976. (LOCAL). ROY HELMS, EXEC DIRECTOR; ALASKA STATE COUNCIL ON THE ARTS; 360 K ST, RM 240; ANCHORAGE, AK 99501. (#12149).

OCT 21 - NOV 21, '74. PERF ARTS DESIGN NECESSITIES & CRITERION MEETINGS. PERFORMING ARTS SPACE DESIGN CONFERENCE, ALASKA. MEETING ON DESIGN NECESSITIES AND DESIGN CRITERION FOR PERFORMING ARTS SPACES FOR ALASKA. (ST-WIDE). ROY H HELMS, EXEC DIR; ALASKA STATE COUNCIL ON THE ARTS; 360 K ST SUITE 240; ANCHORAGE, AK 99501. (#3056-901).

OCT 23 - 24, '74. DESIGN MEETING. PERFORMING ARTS SPACE DESIGN CONFERENCE, ALASKA. MEETING ON DESIGN NECESSITIES AND DESIGN CRITERION FOR PERFORMING ARTS SPACES FOR ALASKA. (ST-WIDE). ROY H HELMS, EXEC DIR; ALASKA STATE COUNCIL ON THE ARTS; 360 K ST SUITE 240; ANCHORAGE, AK 99501. (#3056-903).

NOV 20 - 21, '74. CRITERION MEETING. PERFORMING ARTS SPACE DESIGN CONFERENCE, ALASKA. MEETING ON DESIGN NECESSITIES AND DESIGN CRITERION FOR PERFORMING ARTS SPACES FOR ALASKA. (ST-WIDE). ROY H HELMS, EXEC DIR; ALASKA STATE COUNCIL ON THE ARTS; 360 K ST SUITE 240; ANCHORAGE, AK 99501. (#3056-905).

APR 1 - 3, '75. ROUND TABLE DISCUSSION REGARDING NATIONAL ARCHIVES BICENT RESOURCES. PROJECT TO ASSIST ALASKAN COMMUNITIES IN UTILIZING NATIONAL ARCHIVES RESOURCES TO CELEBRATE THE BICENTENNIAL. THE ROUND TABLES WILL ALSO ACT AS LISTENING POSTS FOR FUTURE ASSISTANCE IN 1976 AND BEYOND. (ST-WIDE). PHILLIP E LOTHYAN, CHIEF; NATIONAL ARCHIVES AND RECORDS SERVICE, GSA; 6125 SAND POINT WAY, NE; SEATTLE, WA 98115. (#5623-501).

JULY 4, '75. EXHIBITION & JUDGING OF STITCHERY CONTEST. COMPETITION, EXHIBIT. (LOCAL). RUTH SILCOCK, CHAIRMAN; ANCHORAGE WOMEN'S CLUB; 2586 DISCOVERY CT; ANCHORAGE, AK 99503. (#9773-1).

JULY 25 - 27, '75. OPEN AIRE PLEASURE FAIRE. ARTS & CRAFTS SALES, DEMONSTRATIONS, ETHNIC FOOD, DRAMA PRESENTATION, BARBERSHOP QUARTETS, JUGGLERS. AT CAMPBELL PARK, LOCATED ON LAKE OTIS PKWY, SOUTH OF TUDOR ROAD. (LOCAL). LARRY HOLMAN, CHMN; GAAB & ANCHORAGE ARTS COUNCIL; PARKS & RECREATION, POUCH 6-650; ANCHORAGE, AK 99502. (#200002-11).

SEPT 19, '75 - MAY 3, '76. AMERICA: A FILM ODYSSEY (BICENTENNIAL FILM SERIES). EXHIBIT. (LOCAL). MARY HALE; UNIVERSITY OF ALASKA (ANCHORAGE) BICENTENNIAL COMMITTEE; 2533 PROVIDENCE AVE; ANCHORAGE, AK 99504. (#200002-17).

JAN 27, '76. 'SAVING THE OLD HOMESTEAD' - A MELODRAMA. MELODRAMA ABOUT FAMILY ABOUT TO HAVE THEIR MORTGAGE FORECLOSED BY EVIL VILLAIN WHO IS AFTER THEIR SUPPOSEDLY WORTHLESS OIL STOCKS. DEAR WILLIAM & LAWYER TRUE SAVE THE DAY. AT 701 E 72ND AVE. (LOCAL). MARGUERITE GRAU, CHMN; CAROL O'BRIAN, TEACHER, TAKU ELEMENTARY SCHOOL; 701 E 72ND AVE; ANCHORAGE, AK 99502. (#200002-2).

JAN 30, '76. COLONIAL DAY. TEACHERS, SECRETARIES, STUDENTS, & PRINCIPAL DRESS IN COLONIAL GARB. STUDENTS PARTICIPATE IN PLAYS, STUDY THE DECLARATION OF INDEPENDENCE, WEAVING, TASTING BAKED BREAD, CANDLE MAKING, STITCHERY, FOLK SINGING, COSTUME CONTEST WITH AWARD TO BEST COSTUME. (LOCAL). ANN BAKER, CHMN; RABBIT CREEK ELEMENTARY SCHOOL; PO BOX 2213; ANCHORAGE, AK 99510. (#200002-9).

FEB 13 - 22, '76. ANCHORAGE FUR RENDEZVOUS - A FESTIVAL. EVENTS INCLUDE WORLD CHAMPIONSHIP SLED DOG RACES, CHEECHAKO & SOURDOUGH BALL, WORLD CROSS COUNTRY SNOWMOBILE RACE, MONTE CARLO NITE, ICE RACING CHAMPIONSHIPS, FOLK & SQUARE DANCE FESTIVAL, ESKIMO BLANKET TOSS, RONDY DANCE FESTIVAL, CURLING AND MUCH MORE. (ST-WIDE). FARREL VAIL, CHMN; GREATER ANCHORAGE, INC; BOX 773; ANCHORAGE, AK 99510. (#103649-2).

FEB 17 - MAY 13, '76. 'THE ADAMS CHRONICLES' - TELEVISED EDUCATIONAL SERIES. A BROADCAST COURSE DETAILING FOUR GENERATIONS OF ADAMS FROM 1750 1900, OFFERED BY AMU FOR CREDIT OR AUDIT, IN COOPERATION WITH KAKM TELEVISION. (LOCAL). KAREN L LEW, CHMN; ALASKA METHODIST UNIVERSITY AND KAKM-TV; 3120 W 79TH AVE; ANCHORAGE, AK 99502. (#200002-4).

MAR 2, '76. BICENTENNIAL PAGEANT. MARCH, PLEDGE OF ALLEGIANCE, POEMS ABOUT GEORGE WASHINGTON AND ABE LINCOLN, SONGS, MISS AMERICA, PARENTS TAKING PART. AT SAND LAKE ELEMENTARY SCHOOL, 7500 JEWEL LAKE ROAD. (LOCAL). MRS JANE URSEL, CHMN; SAND LAKE ELEMENTARY SCHOOL KINDERGARTEN, MRS JANE URSEL, TEACHER; 7500 JEWEL LAKE RD; ANCHORAGE, AK 99502. (#200002-7).

MAR 5, '76. PLUM FULL OF HERITAGE. 'WIDE GAME' OR 'ROUND ROBIN' FORM. PARTICIPANTS EQUALLY DIVIDED BETWEEN FIVE STATIONS, TWENTY MINUTES AT EACH STATION. CANDLE DIPPING, GROUP SINGING, SEWING, CORNHUSK CRAFTS, SQUARE DANCING. THREE SESSIONS, EACH TWO HOURS LONG. AT NATIONAL GUARD ARMORY. (LOCAL). JANET S REINBOLD, CHMN; SUSITNA GIRL SCOUT COUNCIL; 2615 SECLUSION DR; ANCHORAGE, AK 99504. (#200002-5).

ANCHORAGE — CONTINUED

MAR 17 - 19, '76. SALUTE TO AMERICA, ICE SHOW. ICE REVIEW WITH BICENTENNIAL THEME. NUMBERS INCLUDE: 'THE FIRST AMERICANS', SQUARE DANCE ROUTINE, THREE RING CIRCUS, CAMPAIGN PICNIC DIXIELAND JAZZ NUMBER, COMEDY ROUTINE, OUTER SPACES NUMBER, FINALE: STATUE OF LIBERTY & AMERICAN FLAG. RED, WHITE AND BLUE PAINTED ICE. AT ANCHORAGE SPORTS ARENA, 100 W FIREWEED LANE. (LOCAL). KARIN REESE, CHMN; ANCHORAGE FIGURE SKATING CLUB; 1569 WINTERGREEN; ANCHORAGE, AK 99504. (#200002-3).

MAR 26 - 28, '76. ANCHORAGE COMMUNITY CHORUS PRESENTS 'GERSHWIN PLUS'. LIVE PERFORMANCE. (LOCAL). MARY HALE; UNIVERSITY OF ALASKA (ANCHORAGE) BICENTENNIAL COMMITTEE; 2533 PROVIDENCE AVE; ANCHORAGE, AK 99504. (#200002-16).

APR 25, '76. THE BIG BICENTENNIAL BIRTHDAY BASH. SKITS, SONGS, DANCES, CRAFTS, NATIVE PERSON REPRESENTING CERTAIN AREAS OF THE COUNTRY-COLONIES, SOUTHWEST, ETC. BRING FOOD FROM THAT PART OF COUNTRY THAT EACH TROOP IS RESPONSIBLE FOR. EACH GIRL CAN TASTE 4 FOODS, BRING RECIPES, COSTUMES WORN. AT CLARK JR HIGH SCHOOL AUDITORIUM. (LOCAL). MRS DAVID G ALEXANDER; CADETTE GIRL SCOUTS, SUSITNA GIRL SCOUT COUNCIL; 7-310-B J ST; ELMENDORF AFB, AK 99506. (#200002-6).

JUNE 11, '76. CULTURAL ARTS FESTIVAL. TO CELEBRATE THE AMERICAN FAMILY OVER THE PAST 200 YEARS, HIGHLIGHTING THE YEARS 1776, 1826, 1876, 1926, 1976. DISPLAYS, EXHIBITS, SKITS, CRAFT DEMONSTRATIONS, SALUTE TO GREAT AMERICANS, TWO 1 & 1/2 HOUR SHOWS FEATURING 'ROADSHOW' PRODUCTIONS. AT LATTER DAY SAINTS STAKE CENTER, 2501 MAPLEWOOD. (LOCAL). CYNTHIA RIEBEN, CHMN; ANCHORAGE ALASKA STAKE, CHURCH OF JESUS CHRIST OF LATTER DAY SAINTS; 5707 SAMOA DR; ANCHORAGE, AK 99507. (#200002-8).

JUNE 12 - 24, '76. ALASKA FESTIVAL OF MUSIC. A 21 YEAR OLD FESTIVAL OFFERS PERFORMANCES AND WORKSHOPS BY TOP ARTISTS, EACH YEAR EXPANDING ITS SCOPE OF ART FORMS PRESENTED. AT SYDNEY LAURENCE AUDITORIUM, WEST HIGH SCHOOL AUDITORIUM. (ST-WIDE). BETSY RALEIGH, EXEC DIR; ALASKA FESTIVAL OF MUSIC; PO BOX 325; ANCHORAGE, AK 99510. (#103416-258).

JUNE 14, '76. NATIONAL FLAG PAGEANT. THE HISTORY OF THE FLAG PORTRAYED IN NARRATIVE AND SONG WITH CHILDREN CARRYING FLAGS AND MARCHING TO BAND MUSIC. A PERFORMING TOUR UNIT OF THE SAINT PETERSBURG FESTIVAL OF STATES. AT WEST HIGH AUDITORIUM. (LOCAL). FARREL VAIL, CHMN; GREATER ANCHORAGE, INC; BOX 773; ANCHORAGE, AK 99510. (#103649-1).

JULY 1 - 5, '76. USS ANCHORAGE VISIT TO ANCHORAGE. USS ANCHORAGE WILL VISIT ITS NAMESAKE FOR FIVE DAYS BEFORE MANEUVERING ON MONTAGUE ISLAND. SHIP WILL HOST AN OPEN HOUSE. TOURS OF ANCHORAGE AREA WILL BE CONDUCTED FOR MEN ABORAD. LOCAL RESIDENTS HOST MEN IN THEIR HOMES, WELCOME TO ANCHORAGE FESTIVITIES. AT ANCHORAGE DOCK. (LOCAL). ROGER GRAVES, CHAIRMAN; ANCHORAGE SEA SERVICES COMMITTEE; ARMED SERVICES YMCA, 609 F ST; ANCHORAGE, AK 99501. (#108363-2).

JULY 2, '76. BICENTENNIAL HEADDRESS BALL. BICENTENNIAL DRESS, AWARDS TO BEST COUPLE, MOST HUMOROUS, CAKE WITH 200 CANDLES, DRAWING FOR FUR STOLE. AT CAPT COOK HOTEL, 5TH & K. (LOCAL). KAY LINTON, CHMN; THE ALASKA SCHOLARSHIP PROGRAM, INC; 1430 W 23RD; ANCHORAGE, AK 99503. (#200002-10).

JULY 3 - 5, '76. ANCHORAGE JULY 4 CELEBRATION. THE JULY 4 ACTIVITIES INCLUDE PARADE, ICE SHOWS, STARRING ARTISTS SALE, ETHNIC FOOD, BAND CONCERTS, CANNON SALUTES, FIREWORKS, SPECIAL ECUMENICAL WORSHIP, U S NAVY SHIP TOURS. AT MULCAHY STADIUM. (LOCAL). BETTE TRUMP, CHAIRMAN; ANCHORAGE BICENTENNIAL COMMISSION; BOX 400; ANCHORAGE, AK 99510. (#108363-1).

SEPT 11, '76. UAA BICENTENNIAL ARTS FAIR & PURCHASE AWARD. FAIR, CEREMONY, EXHIBIT, LIVE PERFORMANCE AT UAA CAMPUS. (LOCAL). MARY HALE; BICENTENNIAL COMMITTEE OF THE UNIV OF ALASKA AT ANCHORAGE; 2533 PROVIDENCE AVE; ANCHORAGE, AK 99504. (#200002-18).

SEPT 18, '76 - APR 23, '77. 'HOORAY FOR HOLLYWOOD USA' - A BICENTENNIAL FILM SERIES. LIVE PERFORMANCE. (LOCAL). MARY HALE, CHMN; UAA BICENTENNIAL COMMITTEE, UNIVERSITY OF ALASKA, ANCHORAGE; 2533 PROVIDENCE; ANCHORAGE, AK 99504. (#200002-19).

OCT 19 - DEC 1, '76. FINNISH ICONS EXHIBITION. THIS EXHIBITION OF ICONS REPRESENTS THE SACRED FIGURES & EVENTS IN EASTERN ORTHODOX CHRISTIANITY. THE ICONS ARE FROM MONASTERIES AND PARISHES OF KARELIA IN EASTERN FINLAND. AT MUSEUM OF FINE ARTS. (INT'L). EILEEN HARAKAL, COORD; SMITHSONIAN INSTITUTION TRAVELING EXHIBITION SERVICE; 1000 JEFFERSON DR, SW; WASHINGTON, DC 20560. (#26657-1).

JUNE 25 - JULY 24, '77. 'PITSEOLAK: A RETROSPECTIVE' EXHIBITION. THIS EXHIBITION OF 100 DRAWINGS BY ONE OF CANADA'S LEADING ESKIMO GRAPHIC ARTISTS DEPICTS THE LEGENDS AND THE SPIRIT WORLD OF ESKIMO TRADITIONS. AT ANCHORAGE MUSEUM OF FINE ARTS. (INT'L). EILEEN HARAKAL, COORD; SMITHSONIAN INSTITUTION TRAVELING EXHIBITION SERVICE; 1000 JEFFERSON DR, SW; WASHINGTON, DC 20560. (#26655-2).

ANGOON

TRIBAL & COMMUNITY HOUSE RENOVATIN - ANGOON, AK. TO RENOVATE AND RESTORE FOURTEEN EXISTING TRIBAL AND COMMUNITY BUILDIGS. (ST-WIDE). LYDIA M GEORGE, PLANNER; TLINGIT-HAIDA ANGON CHAPTER; BOX 132; ANGOON, AK 99820. (#22858). **ARBA GRANTEE.**

COLLEGE

NATURE TRAIL IN COLLEGE, AK. CREATION OF A NATURE TRAIL AND DEVELOPMENT OF ASSOCIATED EDUCATIONAL DISPLAYS. (LOCAL). RICHARD BISHOP, PRESIDENT; TANANA-YUKON CHAPTER OF THE ALASKA CONSERVATION SOCIETY; BOX 80071; COLLEGE, AK 99701. (#13109). **ARBA GRANTEE.**

PLAYGROUND BEAUTIFICATION, AK. IMPROVEMENT OF LAND FOR PARK IN COLLEGE, ALASKA. (LOCAL). MRS MARION BRAND, PRESIDENT; COLLEGE COMMUNITY WOMEN'S CLUB; PO BOX 80363; COLLEGE, AK 99701. (#24731). **ARBA GRANTEE.**

CORDOVA

'HISTORY OF CORDOVA', FILM - CORDOVA, AK. A FILM DEPICTING THE HISTORY OF CORDOVA. (ST-WIDE). BARBARA BEEDLE, CHAIRPERSON; CORDOVA BICENTENNIAL COMMISSION; BOX 819; CORDOVA, AK 99574. (#13008).

MUSEUM EXPANSION, CORDOVA, AK. THE CORDOVA CENTENNIAL MUSEUM WILL BE EXPANDED. (LOCAL). BARBARA BEEDLE, CHAIRWOMAN; CORDOVA BICENTENNIAL COMMISSION; BOX 819; CORDOVA, AK 99574. (#13006).

NERVANA PARK IN CORDOVA, AK. RESTORATION OF HISTORICAL PARK IN CORDOVA. (LOCAL). BARBARA BEEDLE, CHAIRWOMAN; CORDOVA BICENTENNIAL COMMISSION; BOX 819; CORDOVA, AK 99574. (#13007).

FEB 6 - 8, '76. CORDOVA ICEWORM BICENTENNIAL FESTIVAL. FESTIVAL INCLUDES PARADE, ARTS & CRAFTS SHOW, NATIVE POTLACH (DINER), SKIING EVENTS, ICEWORM WIGGLES (DANCE), SEAFOOD BANQUET AND AIRPLANE & CANNERY TOURS. (LOCAL). ROSE ARVIDSON, ADVISOR; CORDOVA CHAMBER OF COMMERCE & CORDOVA BICENTENNIAL COMMISSION; BOX 99; CORDOVA, AK 99574. (#100884-1).

CRAIG

CRAIG PLAYGROUND - AK. CREATE A CHILDREN'S PLAYGROUND USING RECYCLEABLE MATERIALS AND INVOLVING THE ENTIRE COMMUNITY IN THE BUILDING PROCESS. (LOCAL). GLORIA-JEAN ASKE, CHAIRMAN; CITY OF CRAIG BICENTENNIAL COMMITTEE; BOX 12; CRAIG, AK 99921. (#27242). **ARBA GRANTEE.**

JULY 3 - 4, '76. CRAIG 4TH OF JULY CELEBRATION. JULY 4 QUEEN CONTEST; BOAT RACES; PARADE AND FLAG RAISING; FISHING DERBY; 7-MILE RACE FROM KLAWOCK TO CRAIG; QUEEN'S BALL; FIREWORKS; RUSSIAN AND INDIAN DANCING; PERFORMANCE OF PLAY 'FISH PIRATES DAUGHTER'; MOVIE 'THE NEW LAND' & FLEA MARKET. (LOCAL). GLORIA ASKE, CHAIRMAN; CRAIG 4TH OF JULY COMMITTEE; BOX 12; CRAIG, AK 99921. (#108364-20).

EAGLE

ROALD AMUNDSEN MEMORIAL - EAGLE, ALASKA. MEMORIAL TO ROALD AMUNDSEN, EXPLORER, FIRST TO CONQUER NORTHWEST PASSAGE, THEN TRAVELLED 400 MILES OVERLAND TO EAGLE, WHERE HE DISPATCHED A TELEGRAM OF HIS ACHIEVEMENT. (LOCAL). ELVA SCOTT, TREASURER; EAGLE HISTORICAL SOCIETY; EAGLE, AK 99735. (#27215). **ARBA GRANTEE.**

JULY 3 - 4, '76. EAGLE 4TH OF JULY CELEBRATION. CARNIVAL, SPORTS, CONTESTS, DANCING AND FIREWORKS. (LOCAL). ESTHER MERLY, CHAIRMAN; EAGLE BICENTENNIAL COMMISSION; BOX 46; EAGLE, AK 99738. (#108364-12).

EAGLE RIVER

HERITAGE PARK INFORMATION/TOURIST CENTER - AK. NEW FACILITY TO HOUSE TOURIST INFORMATION CENTER. (LOCAL). MARY A WITMAN, CHAIRMAN; CHUGIAK-EAGLE RIVER BICENTENNIAL COMMISSION; STAR ROUTE BOX 232; EAGLE RIVER, AK 99577. (#27623). **ARBA GRANTEE.**

JULY 3 - 4, '76. CHUGIAK-EAGLE RIVER JULY 4TH CELEBRATION. FOURTH OF JULY ACTIVITIES WILL INCLUDE PARADE, WINNING FLOATS TO RECEIVE TROPHIES; CARNIVAL TO INCLUDE BOOTHS SPONSORED BY LOCAL ORGANIZATIONS, COMPETITIVE GAMES & SPORTS; DEDICATION OF SIGN FOR EKLUTNA INDIAN VILLAGE; TIME CAPSULE WILL BE BURIED AT SCHOOL. AT MAIN STREET. (LOCAL). MARY WITMAN, COORD; CHUGIAK-EAGLE RIVER BICENTENNIAL COMMISSION; BOX 232; EAGLE RIVER, AK 99577. (#108364-22).

FAIRBANKS

ALASKAN ATHABASCANS-STORY OF A LAND & ITS PEOPLE. 2 TRAVELING PHOTOGRAPHIC EXHIBITIONS COMMEMORATING THE 1ST MEETING OF ATHABASCANS & U S GOVERNMENT OFFICIALS ON JULY 4, 1915. (ST-WIDE). MELVIN CHARLIE, PRESIDENT; TANANA CHIEFS CONFERENCE, INC; DOYON BLDG, 1ST & HALL STS; FAIRBANKS, AK 99701. (#22576). **ARBA GRANTEE.**

BICENTENNIAL ART CONTEST. COMPETITION AT LOCAL ELEMENTARY SCHOOLS. (LOCAL). VELMA MUNSON, PROJ DIR; ALASKA ASSOC FOR THE ARTS; BOX 2786; FAIRBANKS, AK 99701. (#102371-5). **(??).**

FAIRBANKS BICENTENNIAL PARK - AK. NEW PARK AREA IN DOWNTOWN FAIRBANKS FEATURING FOUNTAIN SCULPTURE. (LOCAL). HELEN WALKER, CHAIRMAN; FAIRBANKS BICENTENNIAL COMMISSION; BOX 688; FAIRBANKS, AK 99707. (#27415). **ARBA GRANTEE.**

FAIRBANKS HISTORICAL BUILDING IDENTIFICATION, AK. IDENTIFY AND MARK HISTORIC BUILDINGS OF FAIRBANKS TO PREVENT INADVERTENT DESTRUCTION AND TO PROMOTE THE RICH HERITAGE OF FAIRBANKS FOR TOURISTS AND CITIZENS ALIKE. (LOCAL). EDWIN RHOADS, PRESIDENT; TANANA YUKON HISTORICAL SOCIETY; BOX 1794; FAIRBANKS, AK 99707. (#27258). **ARBA GRANTEE.**

FELIX PEDRO MEMORIAL TRAIL IN FAIRBANKS, AK. A CLASS OF SEVENTH GRADERS WILL RESEARCH, RECORD, AND RESTORE THE TRAIL FOLLOWED BY THE PIONEER WHO DISCOVERED GOLD IN THE AREA AND THUS FOUNDED THE CITY. (LOCAL). MRS AFTON BLANC, PROJ DIRECTOR; MAIN JUNIOR HIGH SCHOOL; BOX 10123; FAIRBANKS, AK 99701. (#15208).

FESTIVAL 1976 SUMMER PERFORMING ARTS EVENTS - AK. PRESENT A FESTIVAL OF THE ARTS FEATURING PERFORMANCES OF DRAMA, LIGHT OPERA, MUSIC, MODERN DANCE & FOLK DANCE BY LOCAL ARTISTS TO SHARE AMERICA'S HERITAGE IN THE PERFORMING ARTS. (LOCAL). MRS FLORENCE CAMERON, PRESIDENT; ALASKA ASSOCIATION FOR THE ARTS; BOX 2786; FAIRBANKS, AK 99707. (#27243). **ARBA GRANTEE.**

HERITAGE SITE FOR ENVIRONMENTAL PURPOSES IN AK. STATE WITHDRAWAL OF FEDERAL LANDS FOR ENVIRONMENTAL PURPOSES. (LOCAL). MRS AFTAN BLANC, CHAIRMAN; FAIRBANKS NORTH STAR BOROUGH SCHOOL DISTRICT; BOX 1250; FAIRBANKS, AK 99707. (#33338).

HISTORY OF EDUCATION IN ALASKA. COMPILATION OF HISTORICAL BACKGROUND, HAPPENINGS, DEVELOPMENTS AND EXPERIENCES IN EDUCATION IN ALASKA. (ST-WIDE). ALICE S WILSON, PRESIDENT; ALASKA STATE RETIRED TEACHERS ASSOCIATION; 526 EIGHTH AVE; FAIRBANKS, AK 99701. (#33340).

HISTORY OF NURSING IN ALASKA. COLLECTION OF RECORDS ON ALASKAN NURSES FOR ARCHIVAL PRESENTATION. (LOCAL). DORIS SOUTHALL, DIRECTOR; ALASKA NURSES ASSOCIATION; BOX 677; FAIRBANKS, AK 99707. (#33341).

JUNK CAR CLEAN-UP IN FAIRBANKS, AK. COLLECTING CRUSHING AND REMOVING JUNKED AUTOS FROM THE FAIRBANKS NORTH STAR BOROUGH. (LOCAL). HORACE E LEWIS, CODE ENFORCEMENT OFFICER; FAIRBANKS NORTH STAR BOROUGH; BOX 1267, 510 2ND AVE; FAIRBANKS, AK 99701. (#15207).

LIVING HISTORY NEWSPAPER PROJECT OF ALASKA. PUBLICATION OF A WEEKLY NEWSPAPER FROM JANUARY 1, 1976 TO DECEMBER 31, 1976 CARRYING STORIES OF THE CORRESPONDING WEEK IN 1776 BY UNIVERSITY OF ALASKA DEPARTMENT OF JOURNALISM. (ST-WIDE). JIMMY BEDFORD, HEAD, JOURNALISM DEPT; UNIV OF ALASKA; DEPT OF JOURNALISM; FAIRBANKS, AK 99701. (#521). **(??). ARBA GRANTEE.**

NATURE TRAIL, FAIRBANKS, AK. A NATURE TRAIL WILL BE DEVELOPED & ASSOCIATED MATERIALS WILL BE DISPLAYED. (LOCAL). RICHARD BISHOP, CHAIRMAN; TANANA-YUKON CHAPTER, ALASKA CONSERVATION SOCIETY; BOX 80071; COLLEGE, AK 99701. (#15206).

NOYES SLOUGH CLEAN-UP IN FAIRBANKS, AK. ORGANIZATION OF CLEAN-UP ON LOCAL WATERWAY TO DEVELOP IT AS A BOROUGH RECREATION AREA. (LOCAL). HELEN WALKER, CHAIRMAN; FNSB BICENTENNIAL COMMISSION; BOX 688; FAIRBANKS, AK 99707. (#33342).

OUR HERITAGE IN ART, FAIRBANKS, AK. COLLECTION AND PURCHASE OF LAST FOUR REMAINING ROCKWELL KENT ALASKAN PAINTINGS FOR A PERMANENT BICENTENNIAL EXHIBIT. (ST-WIDE). JUDGE ARTHUR ROBSON, CHAIRMAN; COUNCIL OF LIBRARY SUPPORTERS; 901 FIRST AVE; FAIRBANKS, AK 99701. (#13372). **ARBA GRANTEE.**

PLAYGROUND IMPROVEMENT PROJECT, FAIRBANKS, AK. IMPROVEMENT AND BEAUTIFICATION OF PLAYGROUND BY PURCHASE AND INSTALLATION OF WEATHER CONTROL SHELTER. (LOCAL). MARION BRAND, PROJ DIRECTOR; COLLEGE WOMEN'S CLUB; BOX P; COLLEGE, AK 99701. (#15209).

'REVOLUTION - THEN & NOW' PRODUCTIVITY PROJ OF AK. DISCOVERS THE STORY OF BUILDING ON THE HERITAGE OF THE PAST TO PRODUCE A LUSH GREEN REVOLUTION OF PRODUCTIVITY. (LOCAL). MRS JANET BAIRD, MANAGER; TANANA VALLEY STATE FAIR ASSOC; BOX 188; FAIRBANKS, AK 99701. (#1101). **ARBA GRANTEE.**

REVOLUTION-THEN AND NOW (AGRICULTURE MUSEUM) IN AK. MUSEUM CONTAINING IMPLEMENTS UTENSILS EQUIPMENT HISTORICAL DOCUMENTS & PICTURES THAT PRESERVE THE BEGINNING OF AGRICULTURE IN ALASKA. (ST-WIDE). JANET BAIRD, MANAGER; TANANA VALLEY STATE FAIR ASSOC; BOX 188; FAIRBANKS, AK 99707. (#846).

SALCHA TRAIL IN FAIRBANKS, AK. CONSTRUCTION OF 5 KILOMETER SKIING & RUNNING TRAIL & STUDY AREA FOR TRADITION, RECREATION, AWARENESS, INVOLVEMENT & LEARNING. (LOCAL). DARRELL COE, HEAD TEACHER; FAIRBANKS NORTH STAR BOROUGH SCHOOL DISTRICT; BOX 1250; FAIRBANKS, AK 99707. (#33339).

SALE OF LINCOLN PORTRAITS, FAIRBANKS, AK. SALE OF PRINTS OF AN ORIGINAL OIL PAINTING OF LINCOLN BY A LOCAL ARTIST; PROCEEDS WILL GO TOWARD OTHER BICENTENNIAL PROJECTS. (LOCAL). ROSE MARY JOHNSON, CHAIRMAN; BUSINESS AND PROFESSIONAL WOMEN'S CLUB OF FAIRBANKS; BOX 1041; FAIRBANKS, AK 99701. (#15204).

FAIRBANKS — CONTINUED

TIME CAPSULE, FAIRBANKS, AK. A CAPSULE CONTAINING INFORMATIONAL & CULTURAL ITEMS OF THE PRESENT WILL BE PRESERVED IN A TIME CAPSULE TO BE OPENED IN 25 YEARS. (LOCAL). HELEN WALKER, CHAIRPERSON; FNSB BICENTENNIAL COMMISSION; BOX 688; FAIRBANKS, AK 99701. (#15205).

TREE PLANTING PROJECT IN FAIRBANKS, AK. IN HONOR OF THE BICENTENNIAL, TREES WILL BE PLANTED IN FAIRBANKS. (LOCAL). PAULINE FISHBACK, REGENT; DAUGHTERS OF THE AMERICAN REVOLUTION-ALASKA CHAPTER; CHENA HOT SPRINGS RD; FAIRBANKS, AK 99701. (#15203).

WICKERSHAM HOUSE RESTORATION IN FAIRBANKS, ALASKA. RESTORATION OF ORIGINAL HOME OF AN ALASKAN PIONEER JUDGE AND ONE OF THE FOUNDERS OF FAIRBANKS, JAMES WICKERSHAM. (ST-WIDE). CLYDE TRENT, DIRECTOR ALASKALAND; CITY OF FAIRBANKS; 410 CUSHMAN ST; FAIRBANKS, AK 99701. (#8722). **ARBA GRANTEE.**

YOUNG ALASKANS - TOURING PERFORMING GROUP. PERFORMING 60-MEMBER GROUP OF YOUNG MUSICIANS TO TOUR ALASKA FOR THE BICENTENNIAL COMMEMORATION. (ST-WIDE). JANET BAIRD, MANAGER; TANANA VALLEY STATE FAIR ASSOC; BOX 188; FAIRBANKS, AK 99707. (#850).

'1776 GAZETTE' IN FAIRBANKS, AK. PUBLICATION OF WEEKLY NEWSPAPER, JANUARY 1 - DECEMBER 31, 1976, WHICH WILL CARRY NEWS OF CORRESPONDING WEEK IN 1776. (LOCAL). JIMMY BEDFORD, CHAIRMAN; DEPT OF JOURNALISM, UNIV OF ALASKA; FAIRBANKS, AK 99701. (#12361). **ARBA GRANTEE.**

APR 14 - MAY 2, '75. BICENTENNIAL SLOGAN CONTEST. STUDENTS WERE ENCOURAGED TO WRITE AND SUBMIT A SLOGAN FOR USE AS THE THEME FOR LOCAL BICENTENNIAL ACTIVITIES; THE CONTEST WINNER BEING GIVEN A $50 SAVINGS BOND. (LOCAL). HELEN WALKER, CHAIRMAN; FAIRBANKS NORTHSTAR BOROUGH BICENTENNIAL COMMISSION; BOX 688; FAIRBANKS, AK 99701. (#200002-1).

MAY 1 - DEC 31, '75. BICENTENNIAL FLAGS DISPLAY PROJECT. WITH FINANCIAL HELP FROM THE FAIRBANKS KIWANIS, 48 FLAGS WERE SECURED AND PLACED ON PUBLIC DISPLAY. (LOCAL). HELEN WALKER, CHAIRMAN; FAIRBANKS NORTH STAR BOROUGH BICENTENNIAL COMMISSION; BOX 688; FAIRBANKS, AK 99701. (#102371-4).

MAR 27, '76. BICENTENNIAL POPS CONCERT. LIVE PERFORMANCE AT ALASKALAND CIVIC CENTER. (LOCAL). GORDON WRIGHT, PROJ COORD; UNIV OF FAIRBANKS SYMPHONY AND ALASKA ASSOC FOR THE ARTS; BOX 80051; COLLEGE, AK 99701. (#102371-1).

APR 21, '76. US AIR FORCE BAND & SINGING SERGEANTS CONCERT. LIVE PERFORMANCE AT HERING AUDITORIUM, AIRPORT ROAD. (LOCAL). CAPTAIN KEITH GILLETTE; US AIR FORCE; EIELSON AFB INFORMATION OFFICER; FAIRBANKS, AK 99702. (#200002-14).

JUNE 12, '76. SWEET ADELINES BICENTENNIAL CONCERT. LIVE PERFORMANCE AT ALASKALAND CIVIC CENTER THEATER. (LOCAL). CATHERINE MCKECHNIE; SWEET ADELINES; BOX 1203; FAIRBANKS, AK 99701. (#102371-3).

JUNE 21 - AUG 31, '76. FESTIVAL 1976 SUMMER PERFORMING ARTS EVENTS. A FESTIVAL OF THE ARTS FEATURING PERFORMANCES OF DRAMA, LIGHT OPERA, MUSIC, MODERN DANCE & FOLK DANCE BY LOCAL ARTISTS TO SHARE AMERICA'S HERITAGE IN THE PERFORMING ARTS. (LOCAL). MRS FLORENCE CAMERON; ALASKA ASSOCIATION FOR THE ARTS; BOX 2786; FAIRBANKS, AK 99707. (#27243-1).

JULY 24, '76. GOLDEN DAYS PARADE. PARADE AT FIRST AVE, FAIRBANKS. (LOCAL). ROBERT MORTON, COORD; CHAMBER OF COMMERCE; 603 BENTLEY DR; FAIRBANKS, AK 99701. (#200002-15).

AUG 10, '76. ALASKA ATHABASCANS-EXHIBIT OF A LAND & ITS PEOPLES. EXHIBIT, TOUR. (ST-WIDE). MELVIN CHARLIE, PRESIDENT; TANANA CHIEFS CONFERENCE, INC; DOYON BLDG, 1ST & HALL STS; FAIRBANKS, AK 99701. (#22576-1).

AUG 11 - 16, '76. 1976 ALASKA STATE FAIR, THEME-REVOLUTION: THEN AND NOW. COMMUNITY AGRICULTURAL FAIR EVENT FEATURING YOUNG ALASKANS PROJECT# 000850; AGRICULTURAL MUSEUM PROJECT#000846; SPECIAL COMPETITIVE EXHIBIT DIVISION FOR BICENTENNIAL CALLED REVOLUTION THEN AND NOW, GENERAL EXHIBITS; VARIETY ENTERTAINMENT; CONTESTS: ETC. AT TANANA VALLEY FAIRGROUNDS 2 MILE COLLEGE ROAD. (REGN'L). JANET BAIRD, MANAGER; TANANA VALLEY STATE FAIR ASSOCIATION; PO BOX 188; FAIRBANKS, AK 99701. (#846-1).

FORT YUKON

FORT YUKON ATHABASCAN ARTS AND CRAFTS MUSEUM - AK. TRADITIONAL ATHABASCAN ARTS AND CRAFTS WILL BE TAUGHT AND DISPLAYED IN THIS NORTHERN ALASKA VILLAGE. (LOCAL). NANCY JAMES, COORDINATOR; GWITCHA GWITCHIN GINKYE CORP; BOX 134; FORT YUKON, AK 99740. (#27627). **ARBA GRANTEE.**

GAMBELL

JULY 4, '76. GAMBELL 4TH OF JULY CELEBRATION: PARADE, GAMES, RACES & DANCING. COMPETITION, FESTIVAL, PARADE. (LOCAL). DIRECTOR; GAMBELL 4TH OF JULY COMMITTEE; PO BOX 111; GAMBELL, AK 99742. (#108364-24).

HAINES

MUSEUM VISITORS INFORMATION CENTER - HAINES, AK. CONSTRUCTION OF MUSEUM AND VISITOR CENTER FOR DISPLAY OF NATIVE TLINGIT CULTURE AND TO PROVIDE FACILITY FOR EVER-INCREASING TOURIST POPULATION. (LOCAL). MRS MAYRELD PARKER, PRESIDENT; HAINES WOMEN'S CLUB; PO BOX 205; HAINES, AK 99827. (#16982). **ARBA GRANTEE.**

HOMER

HOMER FIRE BUILDING AND MEETING HALL, AK. THE PROVISION OF A MEETING & TRAINING ROOM, 2 NEW BAYS, OFFICE AND STORAGE SPACE AND A NEW RESTROOM TO COMPLEMENT. (LOCAL). CHARLES RYAN, CHAIRMAN; HOMER BICENTENNIAL COMMISSION; PO BOX 755; HOMER, AK 99603. (#27267). **ARBA GRANTEE.**

HOMER MUSEUM LIBRARY AND RESEARCH CENTER OF ALASKA. CONSTRUCTION OF LIBRARY AND RESEARCH CENTER WHICH ARE ADDITIONS TO THE HOMER ALASKA CENTENNIAL MUSEUM. (ST-WIDE). CARL G WILLIAMS, PRESIDENT; HOMER SOCIETY OF NATURAL HISTORY, INC; POST OFFICE BOX 682; HOMER, AK 99603. (#1033). **ARBA GRANTEE.**

HOONAH

HOONAH, ALASKA, NATIVE BROTHERHOOD COMMUNITY HALL. HOONAH, A SOUTHEAST ALASKA COMMUNITY, WILL HAVE A COMMUNITY CENTER STYLED AFTER THE HISTORIC CLAN HOUSES USED BY TLINGIT PEOPLE. (LOCAL). JAMES JACK, CHAIRMAN; HOONAH BICENTENNIAL COMMISSION; BOX 141; HOONAH, AK 99829. (#27360). **ARBA GRANTEE.**

JUNEAU

ALASKA MULTI-MEDIA EDUCATION PROGRAM. DISTRIBUTION OF AMERICAN REVOLUTION AND ALASKA HISTORY LEARNING KITS FOR JUNIOR AND SENIOR HIGH SCHOOL STUDENTS THROUGHOUT ALASKA. (ST-WIDE). DAN MONROE, EDUCATION MEDIA COORDINATOR; ALASKA STATE MUSEUM; POUCH FM; JUNEAU, AK 99801. (#847). **ARBA GRANTEE.**

CARVING AND ERECTING TOTEM POLES - JUNEAU, AK. IMPROVE THE AUKE TRIBE COUNCIL BUILDING BY THE ADDITIN OF CORNER TOTEM POLES, HOUSE FRONT PANELS & INTERIOR INDIAN DESIGNS IN THE TLINGIT MOTIF. (LOCAL). JAMES AUSTIN, JR DIRECTOR; AUKE TRIBAL COUNCIL; 623 W 10TH ST; JUNEAU, AK 99801. (#22857). **ARBA GRANTEE.**

JUNEAU MINING MUSEUM & OPERA HOUSE. RESTORATION OF HISTORICAL SITES. DEMONSTRATION OF TOTEMIC ART AND REPLACEMENT OF EXISTING STRUCTURES. ESTABLISHMENT OF MINING MUSEUM TO EXHIBIT MINING REMNANTS. (ST-WIDE). M B WINEGAR, CITY MANAGER; CITY & BOROUGH OF JUNEAU; 155 S SEWARD; JUNEAU, AK 99801. (#1034). **ARBA GRANTEE.**

JUNEAU 'SAVE THE ORGAN', AK. RESTORATION OF 1926 KIMBALL THEATER PIPE ORGAN FOR THE PLEASURE AND EDUCATION OF RESIDENTS AND VISITORS OF JUNEAU. (LOCAL). CONNIE BOOCHER, CHAIRMAN; GREATER JUNEAU ARTS AND HUMANITIES, INC; BOX 562; JUNEAU, AK 99802. (#27257). **ARBA GRANTEE.**

OCT 21 - 22, '74. DESIGN MEETING. PERFORMING ARTS SPACE DESIGN CONFERENCE, ALASKA. MEETING ON DESIGN NECESSITIES AND DESIGN CRITERION FOR PERFORMING ARTS SPACES FOR ALASKA. (ST-WIDE). ROY H HELMS, EXEC DIR; ALASKA STATE COUNCIL ON THE ARTS; 360 K ST SUITE 240; ANCHORAGE, AK 99501. (#3056-902).

NOV 18 - 19, '74. CRITERION MEETING. PERFORMING ARTS SPACE DESIGN CONFERENCE, ALASKA. MEETING ON DESIGN NECESSITIES AND DESIGN CRITERION FOR PERFORMING ARTS SPACES FOR ALASKA. (ST-WIDE). ROY H HELMS, EXEC DIR; ALASKA STATE COUNCIL ON THE ARTS; 360 K ST SUITE 240; ANCHORAGE, AK 99501. (#3056-904).

JULY 1 - 5, '76. USS JUNEAU VISIT TO JUNEAU, ALASKA. JUNEAU RESIDENTS WILL BE INVITED TO TOUR SHIP; A WELCOMING CEREMONY WILL INCLUDE MUSIC, INDIAN DANCES; COMMANDING OFFICER WILL RECEIVE STATE & BICENTENNIAL FLAGS; MEN ABOARD WILL BE HOSTED AT RECEPTION; DANCES, PICNIC; TOURS OF JUNEAU AREA & COMPETITIVE SPORTS. (LOCAL). CAROL DUNCAN, CHAIRMAN; JUNEAU BICENTENNIAL COMMISSION; BOX 4316; JUNEAU, AK 99801. (#108364-14).

KAKE

JULY 3 - 4, '76. KAKE 4TH OF JULY CELEBRATION. PARADE, FIREWORKS, PICNIC, DANCING, TALENT SHOW, FISHING DERBY AND SPORTS. (LOCAL). DIRECTOR; KAKE FOURTH OF JULY COMMITTEE; PO BOX 500; KAKE, AK 99830. (#108364-13).

KATMAI NM

JUNE 1 - SEPT 6, '76. CONSTRUCTION OF BIDARKA (ESKIMO SKIN BOAT). ALL FEATURES OF BUILDING A SKIN BOAT. AT BROOKS CAMP. (REGN'L). SUPERINTENDENT, KATMAI NM; NATIONAL PARK SERVICE; BOX 7; KING SALMON, AK 99613. (#6727-235).

JUNE 1 - SEPT 6, '76. PROGRAMS ON SPIRIT SKILLS & CRAFTS OF ESKIMO RESIDENTS. BASKET WEAVING, SKIN SEWING, BEAD WORK & SKIN BOAT BUILDING. AT BROOKS CAMP. (REGN'L). SUPERINTENDENT, KATMAI NM; NATIONAL PARK SERVICE; BOX 7; KING SALMON, AK 99613. (#6727-236).

KETCHIKAN

KETCHIKAN BICENTENNIAL ISLAND VIEW MANOR - AK. CREATION OF AN OUTDOOR PARK ADJACENT TO THE CITY'S EXISTING HOSPITAL AND CONVALESCENT HOME FOR THE RECREATION & ENJOYMENT OF KETCHIKAN'S LONG-TERM RESIDENTS AND INVALIDS. (LOCAL). ED ZASTROW, CHAIRMAN; KETCHIKAN BICENTENNIAL COMMITTEE; 3530 DENALI; KETCHIKAN, AK 99901. (#27278). **ARBA GRANTEE.**

KETCHIKAN MINER'S MUSEUM - AK. RECREATE AN AUTHENTIC STAMP MILL INSIDE A 1920-STYLE MINING STRUCTURE TO BE ERECTED TO SHOW ORIGINAL MINING TOOLS, TECHNIQUES AND PROCESSES. (LOCAL). KELLY ADAMS, CHAIRMAN; ALASKA MINERS ASSOCIATION-KETCHIKAN BRANCH; BOX A28; WARD COVE, AK 99928. (#28550). **ARBA GRANTEE.**

KETCHIKAN RADIO REPEATER - AK. FAWN MOUNTAIN, JUST OUT OF KETCHIKAN, WILL BE EQUIPPED WITH FACILITY UPGRADING COMMUNICATIONS IN SOUTHEASTERN ALASKA. (LOCAL). ED ZASTROW,CHAIRMAN; KETCHIKAN BICENTENNIAL COMMISSION; 3530 DENALI; KETCHIKAN, AK 99901. (#27359). **ARBA GRANTEE.**

PICTORIAL HISTORY OF SALMON & HALIBUT INDUSTRY, AK. HISTORY OF SALMON & HALIBUT INDUSTRY USING PICTURES THAT DATE BACK TO 1907. THESE PICTURES DEPICT CONSTRUCTION OF FLOATING FISH TRAP & SALMON CANNERIES IN KETCHIKAN. (ST-WIDE). VIRGINIA MCGILLVRAY, MUSEUM DIRECTOR; TONGASS HISTORICAL SOCIETY, INC; PO BOX 674; KETCHIKAN, AK 99901. (#18292).

JULY 3 - 4, '76. KETCHIKAN 4TH OF JULY CELEBRATION. FIREWORKS, BOAT RACES, FISHGN DERBY AND ARTS & CRAFTS DISPLAY. (LOCAL). W J YERWOLF, CHAIRMAN; KETCHIKAN BICENTENNIAL COMMISSION; 344 FRONT ST; KETCHIKAN, AK 99901. (#108364-8).

JULY 6 - 8, '76. BICENTENNIAL OPEN HOUSE USCGC RESOLUTE. EXHIBIT, CEREMONY, TOUR AT KETICHICAN COMMUNITY PIER. (LOCAL). ENS JAMES WESELCOUCH; U S COAST GUARD CUTTER RESOLUTE; USCGC RESOLUTE; ALAMEDA, CA 94501. (#200002-13).

KLAWOCK

JULY 3 - 4, '76. KLAWOCK 4TH OF JULY CELEBRATION. PARADE AND FLAG RAISING; FOOT RACES; BOAT RACES; CULMINATION OF 7MILE RACE FROM CRAIG; FISHING DERBY; PIE-EATING CONTEST; GREASED POLE CONTEST; PICNIC. (LOCAL). DIRECTOR; KLAWOCK FOURTH OF JULY COMMITTEE; BOX 113; KLAWOCK, AK 99925. (#108364-19).

KODIAK

KODIAK HERITAGE MUSEUM AND ARCHIVE CENTER - AK. THE CONSTRUCTION OF A MUSEUM AND ARCHIVE CENTER FOR THE STUDY AND EXPOSITION OF KODIAK'S HISTORY BEFORE AND AFTER THE RUSSIAN SETTLEMENT. (LOCAL). NORMA L HOLT, PROJ DIRECTOR; KODIAK ISLAND BOROUGH; BOX 1246; KODIAK, AK 99615. (#17689).

KODIAK VILLAGE PARK - AK. DEVELOPMENT OF HISTORIC ALEUT SITE ADJACENT TO RUSSIAN BUILDING TO EXEMPLIFY DIFFERENCES IN THEIR CULTURAL HERITAGES. A BARABARO, SKIFF & FISH RACK ILLUSTRATE THE HUNTING-EXPLORATION ASPECT OF ALEUT LIFE. (LOCAL). LUCY MCIVER, PRESIDENT; KODIAK AND ALEUTIAN ISLAND HISTORICAL SOCIETY; BOX 61; KODIAK, AK 99615. (#27358). **ARBA GRANTEE.**

OUTDOOR DRAMA 'CRY OF THE WILD RAM' - KODIAK, AK. REENACTMENT OF THE SETTLEMENT OF A RUSSIAN COLONY FOR FUR TRADING PURPOSES. (ST-WIDE). GILBERT A JARVELA, CHAIRMAN; KODIAK BARANOF PRODUCTIONS, INC; BOX 1792; KODIAK, AK 99615. (#13371). **ARBA GRANTEE.**

JUNE 9 - 13, '76. KODIAK CRAB FESTIVAL. FIVE FULL DAYS ACTIVITIES WITH SPECIAL BICENTENNIAL EMPHASIS. INCLUDING PARADE, 'PAT ROBERTS IN CONCERT', MILLIKEN SHOW, FESTIVAL FUN NIGHTS, BOAT RACES, EXHIBITIONS - CRAFTS; CHET OGDEN MEMORIAL 50-MILE FOOT RACE, WORLD CHAMPIONSHIP SEAL SKINNING CONTEST. (LOCAL). HAZEL HOGA, DIR; CHAMBER OF COMMERCE; BOX 1246; KODIAK, AK 90615. (#105831-1).

JULY 3 - 4, '76. KODIAK 4TH OF JULY CELEBRATION. CELEBRATION WILL INCLUDE PARADE; BALLGAMES; SPECIAL TOURS OF THE ERSKINE HOUSE, ALASKA'S MEETING HOUSE; COAST GUARD PARTICIPATION, CHILDREN'S ACTIVITIES AND SPECIAL SPIRIT OF '76 CEREMONY. (LOCAL). ALLEN J TAYLOR, CHAIRMAN; KODIAK 4TH OF JULY COMMITTEE; BOX 1776; KODIAK, AK 99615. (#108364-18).

JULY 30 - AUG 14, '76. OUTDOOR DRAMA 'CRY OF THE WILD RAM'. REENACTMENT OF THE SETTLEMENT OF A RUSSIAN COLONY FOR FUR TRADING PURPOSES. AT AMPHITHEATRE, MONASHKA BAY. (ST-WIDE). GILBERT A JARVELA; KODIAK BARANOF PRODUCTIONS, INC; BOX 1792; KODIAK, AK 99615. (#13371-1).

KOTZEBUE

INUPIAT PAITOT '76, KOTZEBUE, AK. COLLECT AND SHOW THE HISTORY OF THE INUPIAT ESKIMOS AND DEVELOP A LEARNING CENTER FOR THE BENEFIT OF ALL THE ESKIMO PEOPLE. (LOCAL).

KOTZEBUE — CONTINUED

DENNIS TIEPELMAN, PRESIDENT; MAUNELUK ASSOC; BOX 256; KOTZEBUE, AK 99752. (#27259). **ARBA GRANTEE.**

JULY 3 - 4, '76. KOTZEBUE 4TH OF JULY CELEBRATION. COMPETITIVE SPORTS, TALENT SHOW, DANCING, FIREWORKS AND SPECIAL ACTIVITIES FOR CHILDREN. (LOCAL). CHARLES M HUSS, CHAIRMAN; KOTZEBUE 4TH OF JULY COMMITTEE; PO BOX 46; KOTZEBUE, AK 99752. (#108364-3).

MCGRATH

JULY 4, '76. MCGRATH 4TH OF JULY CELEBRATION. CELEBRATION WILL FEAUTRE PARADE, DANCING, PICNIC AND BOOTHS. (LOCAL). EDNA E CRAVEN, COORD; MCGRATH 4TH OF JULY COMMITTEE; BOX 57; MCGRATH, AK 99627. (#108364-21).

MCKINLEY PARK

JUNE 1 - SEPT 7, '76. LIVING HISTORY DEMONSTRATION AT TOKLAT RANGER STATION. TO DEPICT LIFE OF EARLY PARK RANGER INCLUDING FOOD PREPARATION CABIN USE, CACHE, KENNELS & AIR CONDITIONING OF EARLY PARK PATROLS. AT TOKLAT RANGER STATION, MILE 53 ON MCKINLEY PARK ROAD. (REGN'L). SUPERINTENDENT; NATIONAL PARK SERVICE; MOUNT MCKINLEY NATIONAL PARK; MCKINLEY PARK, AK 99755. (#6727-237).

JUNE 11 - JULY 11, '76. NATIONAL PARK SERVICE BICENTENNIAL CLIMB OF MT MCKINLEY. OVER JULY 4, 1976, NATIONAL PARK SERVICE CLIMBING TEAM WILL ATTEMPT TO ASCEND MT MCKINLEY IN ORDER TO CONTACT THE NUMEROUS BICENTENNIAL CLIMBING GROUPS WHICH ARE ATTEMPTING TO SUMMIT ON JULY 4, 1976. AT MT MCKINLEY. (NAT'L). SUPERINTENDENT; NATIONAL PARK SERVICE; MOUNT MCKINLEY NATIONAL PARK; MCKINLEY PARK, AK 99755. (#6725-60).

METLAKATLA

TSIMSHEAN CULTURAL CENTER IN METLAKATLA, ALASKA. CONSTRUCTION OF CULTURAL CENTER, A LONG HOUSE, FOR RETENTION OF TSIMSHEAN INDIAN CULTURE. (LOCAL). HON SOLOMON GUTHRIE, MAYOR; METLAKATLA INDIAN COMMUNITY; BOX 8; METLAKATLA, AK 99926. (#22860). **ARBA GRANTEE.**

JULY 3 - 4, '76. METLAKATLA 4TH OF JULY CELEBRATION. FIREWORKS, CARNIVAL, SPORTS AND CONTESTS. (LOCAL). BONNIE SCUDERO, CHAIRMAN; METLAKATLA 4TH OF JULY COMMITTEE; BOX 458; METLAKATLA, AK 99926. (#108364-5).

MT MCKINLEY

BICENTENNIAL DENALI EXPEDITION: MT MCKINLEY, AK. 12 SEATTLE/KING COUNTY MOUNTAIN CLIMBERS TO CLIMB MT MCKINLEY IN JULY, 1976, BY WAY OF A NEW ROUTE AND TRANSMIT A MESSAGE OF CONGRATULATIONS. (NAT'L). DICK MITCHELL, EXPEDITION LEADER; DENALI EXPEDITION; 602 S 210TH; SEATTLE, WA 98148. (#19304).

TRAVERSE OF MT MCKINLEY, ALASKA. AN ATTEMPT WILL BE MADE TO TRAVERSE MT MCKINLEY WITH ASCENTS OF BOTH THE NORTH AND SOUTH SUMMITS; AN ASCENT OF MT FORAKER WILL THEN BE MADE. (NAT'L). EDE KRAMER, PROJ DIRECTOR; MT MCKINLEY EXPEDITION; PO BOX 821; FT COLLINS, CO 80522. (#18509).

JUNE 1 - JULY 31, '76. MT MCKINLEY BICENTENNIAL EXPEDITION. FOUR WOMEN AND EIGHT MEN CLIMB THE 20,320 FOOT PEAK FOR 60 DAYS. THE PROJECT ENTAILS A MOUNTAINEERING EXPEDITION TO CLIMB MT MCKINLEY AND MAKE A FILM ABOUT MOUNTAIN CLIMBING TECHNIQUES AND SAFETY BICENT & U S FLAGS TO BE PUT ON SUMMIT, JULY 4, 1976. (NAT'L). HOWARD ANGELL; NW 255 ANTHONY #6; PULLMAN, WA 99163. (#9410-501).

NAKNEK

BRISTOL BAY HISTORICAL MUSEUM, AK. GATHERING AND DISPLAY OF ARTIFACTS FROM BRISTOL BAY REGION OF ALASKA. (LOCAL). DOROTHY C HILL, PRESIDENT; BRISTOL BAY HISTORICAL SOCIETY; BOX 92; NAKNEK, AK 99633. (#22284). **ARBA GRANTEE.**

MAY 15, '76. BRISTOL BAY HISTORICAL MUSEUM EXHIBIT. GATHERING AND DISPLAY OF ARTIFACTS FROM THE BRISTOL BAY REGION OF ALASKA. (LOCAL). ANITA L ERICKSON, PRES; BRISTOL BAY HISTORICAL SOCIETY; BOX 136; NAKNEK, AK 99633. (#22284-1).

NENANA

BICENTENNIAL COMMUNITY CENTER - NENANA, AK. REHABILITATION OF THE NENANA COMMUNITY CENTER FOR FUTURE USE. (LOCAL). BRUCE R PENOSKE, CHAIRMAN; NENANA BICENTENNIAL COMMITTEE; PO BOX 48; NENANA, AK 99760. (#29400).

NENANA BICENTENNIAL COMMUNITY CENTER - AK. TO CREATE A COMMUNITY CENTER FOR THE CITY OF NENANA FOR THE USE OF THE ENTIRE COMMUNITY & FOR ANY & ALL EVENTS OF INTEREST TO THE COMMUNITY. (LOCAL). BRUCE R PENOSKE, CHAIRMAN; NENANA BICENTENNIAL COMMISSION; PO BOX 48; NENANA, AK 99760. (#32889). **ARBA GRANTEE.**

NOME

IDITAROD TRAIL HISTORIC MARKERS, NOME, AK. TRIPOD MARKERS, FOUR TO A MILE, WILL MARK THAT PORTION OF THE TRAIL WHICH RUNS FROM KALTAG TO UNALAKLEET AS FAR AS OLD WOMAN CABIN. (LOCAL). HOWARD FARLEY, PRESIDENT; NOME KENNEL CLUB; BOX 3; NOME, AK 99672. (#27230). **ARBA GRANTEE.**

NOME BICENTENNIAL PLAZA PROJ OF ALASKA. DESIGNATION AND DEVELOPMENT OF CITY AREA AS PARK, TO INCLUDE NEW FLAG POLE, PARK BENCHES, TOURIST INFORMATION CABIN, MARKER TO IDENTIFY IDITAROD TRAIL RACE FINISH LINE & WINTER SKATING RINK. (LOCAL). F G BREEDEN, CITY MANAGER; CITY OF NOME; BOX 281; NOME, AK 99762. (#8212). **ARBA GRANTEE.**

NORTH POLE

JULY 4, '76. NORTH POLE 4TH OF JULY CELEBRATION. PARADE, GAMES, PUBLIC PARK DEDICATION AND MUCH MORE. FROM NOON UNTIL DARK. AT PUBLIC PARK - NORTH POLE, AK. (LOCAL). CARLETTA LEWIS, MAYOR; NORTH POLE JAYCEES; PO BOX 5109; NORTH POLE, AK 99705. (#108364-1).

PALMER

ALASKA-YUKON RAILROAD MUSEUM. RELOCATION OF HISTORIC RAILROAD CARS FOR USE AS A MUSEUM. (LOCAL). ARYLN HANSON, CHAIRMAN; PALMER BICENTENNIAL COMMITTEE; PO BOX 739; PALMER, AK 99645. (#22861). **ARBA GRANTEE.**

MATANUSKA MEMORIES-RECORDS RECOVERY & RETRIEVAL. RECORDING FOR PRESERVATION ALL RECORDS OF IMPORTANCE TO MATANUSKA VALLEY PEOPLE IN GENERAL RELATED TO LETTERS, PICTURES & DOCUMENTS WITH A SPECIAL MACHINE FOR EASY STORAGE REFERENCE. (LOCAL). JOHN HALE, PRESIDENT; ALASKA STATE FAIR HISTORICAL, EDUCATIONAL & ARTS FOUNDATION, INC; PO BOX 1414; PALMER, AK 99645. (#27078). **ARBA GRANTEE.**

MATANUSKA VALLEY COLONY BARN RESTORATION, AK. RELOCATION AND RESTORATION OF BARN BUILT DURING THE SETTLEMENT OF THE MATANUSKA VALLEY. THE RESTORED BARN IS PART OF A TOTAL RESTORED FARM. (LOCAL). JOHN H HALE, PRESIDENT; ALASKA STATE FAIR HISTORICAL, EDUCATIONAL & ARTS FOUNDATION, INC; PO BOX 1414; PALMER, AK 99645. (#22575). **ARBA GRANTEE.**

MATANUSKA VALLEY ORAL HISTORY, PALMER, AK. RECORDING OF THE VIEWS, OPINIONS AND OBSERVATIONS OF ORIGINAL COLONISTS WHO ARE STILL LIVING, ON THE PAST, PRESENT AND FUTURE OF THE COLONY. (LOCAL). JOHN HALE, PRESIDENT; AK STATE FAIR, HISTORICAL, EDUCATIONAL & ARTS FOUNDATION, INC; PO BOX 1414; PALMER, AK 99645. (#27256). **ARBA GRANTEE.**

MUSEUM OF LOCAL CULTURE IN PALMER, ALASKA. MUSEUM DISPLAYING ITEMS OF HISTORICAL SIGNIFICANCE INCLUDING, NATIVE ABORIGINAL CULTURE, GOLD PROSPECTING, GOLD MINING, & AGRICULTURE. (LOCAL). EVERETT PEDERSEN, CHAIRMAN; PALMER BICENTENNIAL COMMISSION; BOX 583; PALMER, AK 99645. (#2735).

OPERATION FLAG STAFF - PALMER, AK. ENABLE ALASKANS AND TOURISTS TO RELIVE THE SPIRIT OF THE EARLY MATANUSKA VALLEY COLONISTS WITH THE FLYING OF THE AMERICAN FLAG AND THE PLAYING OF APPROPRIATE MUSIC FOR ACCOMPANIMENT. (LOCAL). JOHN HALE, PRESIDENT; ALASKA STATE FAIR HISTORICAL, EDUCATIONAL & ARTS FOUNDATION, INC; PO BOX 1414; PALMER, AK 99645. (#27079). **ARBA GRANTEE.**

RESTORATION OF HISTORIC CHURCH, PALMER, AK. RESTORATION OF FIRST CHURCH BUILT IN MATANUSKA VALLEY TO BE PART OF LIVING HISTORY DISPLAY. (LOCAL). JOHN H HALE, MANAGER; ALASKA STATE FAIR, INC; PO BOX 1128; PALMER, AK 99645. (#21664). **ARBA GRANTEE.**

JUNE 1 - 30, '76. MIDSUMMER FESTIVAL FOR BICENTENNIAL COMMEMORATION. OPENING, EXHIBIT. (LOCAL). MR CURTIS, CTY MGR; PALMER BICENTENNIAL COMMISSION; BOX 583; PALMER, AK 99645. (#2735-501).

JULY 3 - 5, '76. ALASKA BICENTENNIAL AIR SHOW. PICNIC, INDOOR EXHIBITS, OUTDOOR EXPERIMENTS, NEW AIRCRAFT DISPLAYS. AIR SHOW WILL INCLUDE SEVERAL ACROBATIC PERFORMANCES, HANG GLIDER, HELICOPTER, SOARING GLIDER AND HOT AIR BALLOON DEMONSTRATIONS, SKY DIVING AND UNUSUAL AIRCRAFT FLY-BYS. AT PALMER STATE FAIRGROUNDS. (LOCAL). CLARISSA QUINLAN, CHMN; NINETY-NINES ALASKA CHAPTER; 3640 W DIMOND BLVD; ANCHORAGE, AK 99502. (#108364-16).

AUG 27 - SEPT 6, '76. AGRICULTURAL AND INDUSTRIAL FAIR. FAIR AT MILE FORTY GLENN HIGHWAY. (ST-WIDE). MARSHA MELTON, CHAIRMAN; ALASKA STATE FAIR, INC; PO BOX 1128; PALMER, AK 99645. (#106299-1).

PELICAN

JULY 3 - 4, '76. PELICAN 4TH OF JULY CELEBRATION. COMMUNITY DANCE ON JULY 3 AND 4; PARADE; ATHLETIC EVENTS; PICNIC; LIVE BAND; FISHING CONTEST. (LOCAL). JO PADDOCK, CHAIRMAN; PELICAN FOURTH OF JULY CELEBRATION; BOX 757; PELICAN, AK 99832. (#108364-15).

PETERSBURG

HERITAGE OF THE SEA, PETERSBURG, AK. EXTENSION OF MUSEUM IN PETERSBURG TO HOUSE SPECIAL SEA DISPLAYS THAT ARE UNIQUE TO THE PETERSBURG'S FISHING INDUSTRY. (LOCAL). RAYMOND R SLACK, CHAIRMAN; PETERSBURG BICENTENNIAL COMMISSION; PO BOX 329; PETERSBURG, AK 99833. (#12536). **ARBA GRANTEE.**

PORT LIONS

JULY 3 - 4, '76. PORT LIONS 4TH OF JULY CELEBRATION. TALENT SHOW, DANCING, OLD-FASHIONED SPORTS, CONTESTS AND FIREWORKS. (LOCAL). DIRECTOR; PORT LIONS 4TH OF JULY COMMITTEE; PO BOX 278; PORT LIONS, AK 99550. (#108364-6).

PORTAGE CREEK

BICENTENNIAL TOUR FOR ALASKAN BILINGUAL RESIDENTS. ALASKAN FAMILIES WILL TRAVEL THROUGHOUT THE UNITED STATES TO OBSERVE AND PARTICIPATE IN BICENTENNIAL ACTIVITIES. (NAT'L). BEE PAUL, CHAIRMAN; ALASKA UNORGANIZED BOROUGH SCHOOL DISTRICT; PORTAGE CREEK VIA DILLINGMAN; PORTAGE CREEK, AK 99576. (#16724).

SELDOVIA

JULY 4, '76. SELDOVIA 4TH OF JULY CELEBRATION. IN THIS SMALL FISHING VILLAGE, A PARADE WILL BE HELD; ALSO INCLUDED: COMMUNITY PICNIC, GAMES, TALENT SHOW, CARNIVAL. (LOCAL). JUDI JOHNSON, PROJ DIR; SELDOVIA 4TH OF JULY COMMITTEE; PO BOX 87; SELDOVIA, AK 99633. (#108364-23).

SEWARD

ALASKA FLAG MEMORIAL. FREE-STANDING CONCRETE MONUMENT OF THE ALASKA FLAG. (ST-WIDE). JAMES R FILIP, CITY MANAGER; CITY OF SEWARD; BOX 337; SEWARD, AK 99664. (#848). **ARBA GRANTEE.**

HORIZON HALL, SEWARD, ALASKA. COMMUNITY CULTURAL CIVIC CENTER FOR USE BY ALL CITIZENS. (LOCAL). MS LEE MCANERNEY CHAIRMAN; SEWARD CHAMBER OF COMMERCE; 234 4TH AVE; SEWARD, AK 99664. (#2683).

SEWARD FIRST LAKE PARK - AK. A TWO-ACRE WOODED AREA WILL BE DEVELOPED INTO ORGANIZED PLAYGROUND AND SWIMMING FACILITY. FISH WILL BE STOCKED. WINTERTIME USE WILL BE SKIING AND SLEDDING. (LOCAL). LARRY STRALEY, CHAIRMAN; SEWARD BICENTENNIAL COMMISSION; BOX 615; SEWARD, AK 99664. (#27625). **ARBA GRANTEE.**

JULY 4, '75. FOURTH OF JULY MT MARATHON RACE AND PARADE. COMPETITION, PARADE AT FOURTH AVENUE DOWNTOWN SEWARD. (LOCAL). JAMES R FILIP; SEWARD JAYCEES AND SEWARD CHAMBER OF COMMERCE; P O BOX 337; SEWARD, AK 99664. (#50150-1).

JULY 4, '76. 4TH OF JULY CELEBRATION, MARATHON MOUNTAIN RACE. FESTIVAL, COMPETITION. (LOCAL). MS LEE MCANERNEY CHAIRMAN; SEWARD CHAMBER OF COMMERCE; 234 4TH AVE; SEWARD, AK 99664. (#2683-901).

AUG 14 - 22, '76. SEWARD SILVER SALMON DERBY. COMPETITION. (LOCAL). MS LEE MCANERNEY CHAIRMAN; SEWARD CHAMBER OF COMMERCE; 234 4TH AVE; SEWARD, AK 99664. (#2683-902).

SITKA

REGIONAL FINE ARTS CAMP OF ALASKA. SUMMER CAMP ON SHELDON JACKSON COLLEGE CAMPUS FOR JUNIOR AND SENIOR HIGHSCHOOL STUDENTS FOR INSTRUCTION IN INSTRUMENTAL AND CHORAL MUSIC DRAMA DANCE AND VISUAL ARTS. (ST-WIDE). MRS JAN CRADDICK, EXECUTIVE DIRECTOR; SOUTHEAST ALASKA REGIONAL ARTS COUNCIL; BOX 2133; SITKA, AK 99835. (#1035). **ARBA GRANTEE.**

TLINGIT LIFE IN SITKA, ALASKA IN 1776. EXHIBIT OF TLINGIT LIFE IN SITKA IN 1776, WITH FULL SIZE AND SMALL DIORAMAS. TO OPEN IN FALL 1975. (LOCAL). ESTHER BILLMAN, CURATOR; SHELDON JACKSON MUSEUM; PO BOX 479; SITKA, AK 99835. (#2327).

FEB 1 - OCT 31, '76. TLINGIT LIFE IN SITKA IN 1776. EXHIBIT OF TLINGIT LIFE IN SITKA IN 1776, WITH FULL SIZE & SMALL DIORAMAS. AT SHELDON JACKSON MUSEUM ON SHELDON JACKSON COLLEGE CAMPUS. (LOCAL). ESTHER BILLMAN, CURATOR; SHELDON JACKSON MUSEUM; PO BOX 479; SITKA, AK 99835. (#2327-2).

JULY 1 - 5, '76. SITKA 4TH OF JULY CELEBRATION. THE USS MOBILE WILL BE IN PORT; RECEPTION, DANCES, GAMES. PARADE ON JULY 4; CEREMONY TO PRESENT STATE & BICENTENNIAL FLAGS TO COMMANDING OFFICER OF THE SHIP; TOURS OF AREA FOR MEN ABOARD. (LOCAL). IVAN E REZEK, COORD; SITKA 4TH OF JULY COMMITTEE; PO BOX 351; SITKA, AK 99835. (#108364-25).

JULY 2 - 4, '76. ALL-ALASKA LOGGING CHAMPIONSHIP. THE TRADITIONS OF THE OLD-TIME LOGGING CAMPS ARE REVIVED IN A MYRIAD OF COMPETITIONS. AT BARANOF ELEMENTARY SCHOOL GROUNDS & CENTENNIAL BUILDING. (ST-WIDE). JIM DAVIS, CHAIRMAN; SITKA CHAMBER OF COMMERCE; PO BOX 638; SITKA, AK 99835. (#103416-409).

SITKA—CONTINUED

JULY 3 - 5, '76. BICENTENNIAL OPEN HOUSE USCGC RESOLUTE. RESOLUTE'S BICENTENNIAL OPEN HOUSE PROVIDED THE RESIDENTS OF SITKA ALASKA WITH AN OPPORTUNITY TO TOUR A COAST GUARD CUTTER AND TO VISIT WITH MEMBERS OF THE CREW. RESOLUTE'S WHISTLE AND BELLS WERE SOUNDED AT 2PM EDT TO HONOR THE NATIONS BICENTENNIAL ON JULY 4, 1976. AT CHEVRON FUEL PIER. (LOCAL). ENS JAMES WESELCOUCH; U S COAST GUARD CUTTER RESOLUTE; USCGC RESOLUTE; ALAMEDA, CA 94501. (#200002-12).

OCT 16 - 18, '76. ALASKA DAY FESTIVAL. FESTIVAL AT CASTLE HILL. (ST-WIDE). ALICE A HARRIGAN, COORD; ALASKA DAY FESTIVAL, INC; SITKA, AK 99835. (#103416-614).

SKAGWAY

ARTIC BROTHERHOOD HALL - SKAGWAY, ALASKA. PROVISION FOR COMMUNITY MEETING HALL DECORATED IN TURN OF THE CENTURY MOTIF. (LOCAL). IRENE HENRICKSON, CHAIRMAN; SKAGWAY BICENTENNIAL COMMISSION; BOX 234; SKAGWAY, AK 99840. (#33403). **ARBA GRANTEE.**

MOLLIE WALSH PARK, SKAGWAY, AK. ESTABLISHMENT OF A PARK IN SKAGWAY, TO HONOR MOLLIE WALSH, A COLORFUL AND IMPORTANT PERSON IN SKAGWAY'S HISTORY. (LOCAL). MRS EDITH LEE, PROJ COORDINATOR; SKAGWAY BICENTENNIAL COMMITTEE; BOX 415; SKAGWAY, AK 99840. (#22567). **ARBA GRANTEE.**

JULY 1 - 5, '76. SKAGWAY JULY 4TH CELEBRATION. THE CANADIAN DESTROYER HMCS KOOTENAY WILL BE IN PORT; EVENING DANCES AT THE AMERICAN LEGION HALL; DANCE AT ELKS CLUB JULY 3; CHURCH WORSHIP; PARADE-SPECIAL GUESTS ARE MIDNIGHT SUNS BAGPIPE BAND FROM WHITEHORSE, YT; MARCHING BAND FROM VANCOUVER, BC; CARNIVAL. AT MAIN STREET. (LOCAL). IRENE HENRICKSON, CHMN; SKAGWAY BICENTENNIAL COMMISSION; BOX 234; SKAGWAY, AK 99840. (#108364-17).

SOLODOTNA

TEACHERS' TRAINING PROJECT IN SOLDONTA, AK. PROJECT IS A 6 WEEK TRAINING PROGRAM FOR TEACHERS THROUGHOUT THE UNITED STATES, TO ASSIST THEM IN THEIR CLASSROOM CURRICULUM. (NAT'L). PAUL A FISCHER, DIRECTOR; YOUR AMERICA FOUNDATION, INC; PO BOX 784; SOLODOTNA, AK 99669. (#13934). **ARBA GRANTEE.**

JULY 1 - AUG 7, '76. TEACHERS' TRAINING PROJECT. PROJECT IS A 6 WEEK TRAINING PROGRAM FOR TEACHERS THROUGHOUT THE UNITED STATES, TO ASSIST THEM IN THEIR CLASSROOM CURRICULUM. (ST-WIDE). PAUL A FISCHER, DIRECTOR; YOUR AMERICA FOUNDATION, INC; PO BOX 784; SOLODOTNA, AK 99669. (#13934-1).

TALKEETNA

JUNE 15 - JULY 12, '76. MT MCKINLEY EXPEDITION COMMEMORATE HIST AMER MOUNTAINEER ACHIEVEMENT. COMMEMORATION WILL REFLECT THE ACHIEVEMENTS OF AMERICAN MOUNTAINEERS IN THE AREAS OF CONSERVATION, SCIENCE, RECREATION & SAFETY. (NAT'L). EDWARD S GULEKE, LIASON; MT MCKINLEY BICENTENNIAL EXPEDITION MOUNTAINEERS; 916 N EDGEWOOD; ARLINGTON, VA 22201. (#6546-501).

TENAKEE SPG

JULY 3 - 4, '76. TENAKEE SPRINGS 4TH OF JULY CELEBRATION. PARADE, GAMES, PICNIC, DANCING, CARNIVAL AND FIREWORKS. (LOCAL). ROSALIE BEATON, CHAIRMAN; TENAKEE SPRINGS FOURTH OF JULY COMMITTEE; BOX 52; TENAKEE SPG, AK 99841. (#108364-7).

UNALASKA

MUSEUM FOR UNALASKA, AK. CREATION OF A FACILITY TO HOUSE ARTIFACTS OF ALEUT VILLAGE AND SURROUNDING ALEUTIAN ISLANDS POPULATION. (ST-WIDE). VERA SKAFLESTAD, DIRECTOR; ALEUT LEAGUE; 833 GAMBELL ST; ANCHORAGE, AK 99501. (#33400). **ARBA GRANTEE.**

JULY 3 - 4, '76. UNALASKA 4TH OF JULY CELEBRATION. BOAT RACES, ARTS & CRAFTS DISPLAYS, CONTESTS, PICNIC, GAMES AND FIREWORKS. (LOCAL). DIRECTOR; UNALASKA FOURTH OF JULY COMMITTEE; PO BOX 89; UNALASKA, AK 99685. (#108364-10).

WAINWRIGHT

JULY 3 - 4, '76. WAINWRIGHT 4TH OF JULY CELEBRATION. GAMES, PICNIC, ARTS & CRAFTS, FIREWORKS, SPORTS & MUCH MORE. (LOCAL). DIRECTOR; WAINWRIGHT FOURTH OF JULY COMMITTEE; WAINWRIGHT, AK 99782. (#108364-2).

WASILLA

HISTORIC PHOTO & JOURNALISM DISPLAY & PROGRAM, AK. COMPILE PRE-PUBLISHED INFORMATION ON THE HISTORY OF THE WASILLAKNIK-WILLOW CREEK AREA OF ALASKA IN A MANUSCRIPT, SLIDE SHOW SCRAPBOOK DISPLAY FOR THE INFORMATION AND USE OF THE PUBLIC. (LOCAL). JUNE SCHEELE, PRESIDENT; CITY OF WASILLA HISTORICAL SOCIETY; PO BOX 330; WASILLA, AK 99687. (#27260). **ARBA GRANTEE.**

IDITAROD TRAIL MARKERS-PONTILLA LK-RHON RIVER, AK. MARK THE IDITAROD RACING TRAIL FOR THE SAFETY OF THE RACERS AND TO PROMOTE INTEREST IN THE HISTORICAL ASPECTS OF THE TRAIL AND THE RACE. (LOCAL). DAVE OLSEN, PRESIDENT; AURORA DOG MUSHERS CLUB; PO BOX 395; WASILLA, AK 99687. (#27245). **ARBA GRANTEE.**

IDITAROD TRL MARKERS-KNIK-RAINY/PTARMIGAN PASS, AK. ESTABLISH TRAIL MARKERS ALONG THE IDITAROD RACE TRAIL FOR THE SAFETY OF THE RACERS AND TO SPARK INTEREST IN THE HISTORICAL ASPECTS OF THE TRAIL. (LOCAL). DAVE OLSEN, PRESIDENT; AURORA DOG MUSHERS CLUB; PO BOX 395; WASILLA, AK 99687. (#27244). **ARBA GRANTEE.**

WASILLA TOWNSITE PARK - WASILLA, AK. ONE-ACRE PARK IN DOWNTOWN WASILLA, LOCATED IN A POPULAR RECREATION RESORT SETTING. (LOCAL). DOROTHY PAGE, CHAIRMAN; WASILLA BICENTENNIAL COMMISSION; BOX 430; WASILLA, AK 99687. (#27624). **ARBA GRANTEE.**

WHITTIER

COMMUNITY DESIGN PLAN FOR WHITTIER, ALASKA. RESEARCH AND STUDY OF DESIGN GUIDELINES FOR THE FUTURE DEVELOPMENT OF THE CITY OF WHITTIER. TO BE COMPLETED IN MARCH, 1975. (LOCAL). MARK L HINSHAW, DIRECTOR; 4801 MILLS DR #3; ANCHORAGE, AK 99504. (#2254). **(??).**

ENCOURAGEMENT OF LOCAL TALENTS AND ARTS OF ALASKA. PRESENTATION OF LOCAL ARTS IN WHITTIER, ALASKA. INCLUDES: OIL PAINTINGS, DRAWINGS, WOOD ITEMS, WRITINGS, COLLECTIONS, PHOTOS, FILM, SLIDES & PLAY. (LOCAL). KAY SHEPHERD, DIRECTOR; WHITTIER HISTORICAL AND FINE ARTS MUSEUM INC; BOX 728; WHITTIER, AK 99502. (#5106).

WRANGELL

WRANGELL MUSEUM - WRANGELL, AK. REFURBISH THE WRANGELL MUSEUM FOR YEAR-ROUND SERVICE AND SAFETY OF EXHIBITS WITH THE ADDITION OF AN ARTS AND CRAFTS PROGRAM, DARK ROOMS AND RADIO STATION FOR COMMUNITY USE. (LOCAL). MS HENRIETTA COLLINS, PRESIDENT; WRANGELL BICENTENNIAL COMMISSION; BOX 191; WRANGELL, AK 99929. (#27893). **ARBA GRANTEE.**

JULY 3 - 4, '76. WRANGELL 4TH OF JULY CELEBRATION. PARADE, GAMES, DANCING, TALENT SHOW, CONTEST, CARNIVAL AND SPECIAL ACTIVITIES FOR CHILDREN. (LOCAL). HENRIETTA COLLINS, CHMN; WRANGELL 4TH OF JULY COMMITTEE; BOX 733; WRANGELL, AK 99929. (#108364-4).

YAKUTAT

YAKUTAT, ALASKA, BICENTENNIAL SHELTER. CONSTRUCTION OF A 24' X 120' RIDGED FRAME, OPEN SIDED SHELTER TO PROTECT 70-YEAR-OLD YAKUTAT AND SOUTHERN RAILWAY CARS. (LOCAL). HON LARRY POWELL, MAYOR; CITY OF YAKUTAT; BOX 6; YAKUTAT, AK 99689. (#27216). **ARBA GRANTEE.**

JULY 3 - 4, '76. YAKUTAT 4TH JULY CELEBRATION. FIREWORKS, BOAT RACES, ARTS AND CRAFTS DISPLAYS, CARNIVAL AND TALENT. (LOCAL). RAY E MAPES, CHAIRMAN; YAKUTAT FOURTH OF JULY COMMITTEE; BOX 1; YAKUTAT, AK 99689. (#108364-9).

THE ALASKA DAILY EMPIRE
WOMAN SUFFRAGE PASSES
ALASKA
BALLOT BOX

JUNEAU
HARRIS

Territory of American Samoa

American Samoa Bicentennial Commission

Commissioned May 9, 1972

AMERICAN SAMOA
BICENTENNIAL
COMMISSION

ARBA Statistics

BINET Projects—14
Events—6
1973 Population—28,300

Bicentennial Archives

National Archives Depository
San Bruno, California 94066

Membership

The commission consisted of 11 members appointed by the governor.

Palauni (Brownie) Tuiasosopo, *chairman*
High Talking Chief Paopao Meko
High Talking Chief Sala Samiu
High Chief Te'o Gus Annesley
Reverend Peni Vai
Atafua Maina
Sanele Tuiteleleapaga
Jane Uhrle
District Governor Letuli Toloa
Senator Satele Mosegi
Senator Tagaloa M. Tuiolosega
Representative Tuiafono Matau
John Murray
Neal Corbett

American Samoa

The diverse Bicentennial activities in the Territory of American Samoa were a microcosm of the programs occurring in the 50 states. All ambitious undertakings, the activities are of interest and benefit to all citizens.

In honoring the past, a documentary film, *The Life Style of Samoa,* recorded the Samoan culture and customs as lived by Samoans today. It preserves and depicts present governmental and private development actions and traditional ceremonies of the territory. There was also a comprehensive educational program designed to acquaint Samoan children with essential elements of the American Revolution.

A *Flag Day Arts Festival* took place in Pago Pago, as well as a three day observance of the 200th anniversary which included competitions, parades, games and exhibitions. A school *Bicentennial Day,* sponsored by the American Samoa Arts Council and the Department of Education, encompassed students throughout the area. Additionally, the governor's office sponsored a *Youth Bicentennial Festival.*

American Samoa abounded with construction and improvement programs. The one and a half mile airport access road was beautified and renamed Saolotoga (Freedom) Drive. There was a general overhaul of the island's auditorium. This project will improve support for cultural performing arts of the Samoan people. The present stadium was improved, and the first recreation center on the island was also created with facilities for basketball, volleyball and tennis.

A replica of an ancient oceangoing canoe 40 feet in length was constructed and has become a floating museum, while an extension to the Museum of American Samoa will enable expansion of exhibits dealing with the natural and written history of Samoa. And, at Onesosopo, situated at the eastern portion of the bay area, a public park was developed.

A center was developed to train those involved in early childhood education throughout American Samoa. At the Government House, a project was underway to collect, identify and cultivate indigenous edible, ceremonial, medicinal and ornamental plants in the Botanical Garden. They will be for public exhibit, research and education.

American Samoans made invaluable contributions to the Bicentennial of the United States, and our country is more complete because of their participation.

ONESOSOPO

AMER-SAMOA BICENTENNIAL PARK - ONESOSOPO. PUBLIC PARK AT ONESOSOPO SITUATED AT EASTERN PORTION OF BAY AREA. (LOCAL). GOVERNOR'S OFFICE; AMERICAN SAMOA; PAGO PAGO, SM 96977. (#18350).

PAGO PAGO

ALIA - PAGO PAGO, SM. CONSTRUCTION OF ANCIENT OCEAN-GOING CANOE 40 FEET IN LENGTH. WILL BE USED AS FLOATING MUSEUM FOLLOWING DEDICATION ON JULY 4, 1976. (ST-WIDE). P M TUIASOSOPO, CHAIRMAN; AMERICAN SAMOA BICENTENNIAL COMMITTEE; GOVERNMENT HOUSE; PAGO PAGO, SM 96799. (#26563). **ARBA GRANTEE.**

AMER-SAMOAN DEMONSTRATION DAYS - PAGO PAGO. COMPREHENSIVE EDUCATIONAL PROGRAM DESIGNED TO ACQUAINT SAMOAN CHILDREN WITH ESSENTIAL ELEMENTS OF AMER REVOLUTION. (ST-WIDE). P M TUIASOSOPO, CHAIRMAN; AMERICAN SAMOA BICENTENNIAL COMMITTEE; GOVERNMENT HOUSE; PAGO PAGO, SM 96799. (#26564). **ARBA GRANTEE.**

ART GALLERY ADDITION TO MUSEUM OF AMERICAN SAMOA. ADDITION TO MUSEUM WILL HOUSE ART WORKS, EXTEND AUDIO-VISUAL CENTER. (ST-WIDE). MRS JOHN M HAYDON, CHAIRMAN; AMERICAN SAMOA BICENTENNIAL COMMISSION; C/O GOVERNMENT HOUSE; PAGO PAGO, SM 96920. (#786). **ARBA GRANTEE.**

BICENTENNIAL CONSTRUCTION PROJECT - PAGO PAGO, SM. NATIVE CONSTRUCTION PROJECT TO PROVIDE PERMANENT FACILITY FOR PUBLIC USE IN DOWNTOWN AREA. (LOCAL). PALAUNI M TUIASOSOP, CHAIRMAN; AMERICAN SAMOA BICENTENNIAL COMMISSION; GOVERNOR'S OFFICE; PAGO PAGO, SM 96977. (#27077). **ARBA GRANTEE.**

BICENTENNIAL DRIVE - PAGO PAGO, SM. ONE AND ONE HALF MILE AIRPORT ACCESS ROAD WILL BE BEAUTIFIED AND RENAMED SAOLOTOGA (FREEDOM) DRIVE. (ST-WIDE). P M TUIASOSOPO, CHAIRMAN; AMERICAN SAMOA BICENTENNIAL COMMITTEE; GOVERNMENT HOUSE; PAGO PAGO, SM 96799. (#26565). **ARBA GRANTEE.**

CULTURAL HERITAGE FILM: THE LIFE STYLE OF SAMOA. RECORD IN FILM DOCUMENTARY FORM THE SAMOAN CULTURE & CUSTOMS AS LIVED BY SAMOANS TODAY. TO PRESERVE & PRESENT GOVT & PRIVATE DEVELOPMENT ACTIONS & TRADITIONAL CEREMONIES. (ST-WIDE). PAULAUNI M TVIASOPO, CHAIRMAN; AMERICAN SAMOA BICENTENNIAL COMMISSION; GOVT OF AMERICAN SAMOA; PAGO PAGO, SM 96799. (#7913). **ARBA GRANTEE.**

EARLY CHILDHOOD EDUCATION TEACHER TRAINING CENTER. DEVELOPMENT OF TRAINING CENTER TO TRAIN THOSE INVOLVED IN EARLY CHILDHOOD EDUCATION THROUGHOUT AMERICAN SAMOA. ISLAND. (ST-WIDE). MRS JOHN HAYDON, CHAIRMAN; AMERICAN SAMOA BICENTENNIAL COMMISSION; GOVERNMENT HOUSE; PAGO PAGO, SM 96799. (#307).

FALE LAUMEL IMPROVEMENT PROJECT - PAGO PAGO, SM. A GENERAL OVERHAUL OF THE ISLAND'S AUDITORIUM; THIS PROJECT WILL IMPROVE SUPPORT FOR CULTURAL PERFORMING ARTS OF THE SAMOAN PEOPLE. (ST-WIDE). PALAONI TUIASOSOPO, CHAIRMAN; AMERICAN SAMOA BICENTENNIAL COMMISSION; GOVERNMENT HOUSE; PAGO PAGO, SM 96799. (#27212). **ARBA GRANTEE.**

MUSEUM ART GALLERY EXTENSION PROJECT - SAMOA. THE NEW ART GALLERY EXTENSION WILL ENABLE EXPANSION OF EXHIBITS DEALING WITH THE NATURAL AND WRITTEN HISTORY OF SAMOA. (ST-WIDE). PALAUNI TUIASOSOPO, CHAIRMAN; AMERICAN SAMOA BICENTENNIAL COMMISSION; GOVERNMENT HOUSE; PAGO PAGO, SM 96799. (#27214). **ARBA GRANTEE.**

PAGO PAGO RECREATION CENTER, AMERICAN SAMOA. PROJECT WILL INVOLVE CREATION OF FIRST RECREATION CENTER ON THE ISLAND. THERE WILL BE FACILITIES FOR BASKETBALL, VOLLEYBALL & TENNIS. (ST-WIDE). P M TUIASOSOPO, CHAIRMAN; AMERICAN SAMOAN BICENTENNIAL COMMITTEE; GOVT HOUSE; PAGO PAGO, SM 96799. (#26407). **ARBA GRANTEE.**

PAGO PAGO STADIUM IMPROVEMENT PROJECTS - SAMOA. IMPROVE PRESENT STADIUM WITH INSTALLATION OF PROPER DRAINAGE AND REFINISHING OF SURFACE AREA. (LOCAL). PALAUNI TUIASOSOPO, CHAIRMAN; AMERICAN SAMOA BICENTENNIAL COMMISSION; GOVERNMENT HOUSE; PAGO PAGO, SM 96799. (#27213). **ARBA GRANTEE.**

TUTOASI (INDEPENDENCE) WEEK - PAGO PAGO, SM. THREE DAY AMERICAN-SAMOAN OBSERVANCE OF 299TH ANNIVERSARY. COMPETITIONS, PARADES, GAMES, AND EXHIBITIONS. (ST-WIDE). P M TUIASOSOPO, CHAIRMAN; AMER-SAMOAN BICENTENNIAL COMMISSION; GOVT HOUSE; PAGO PAGO, SM 96799. (#26749). **ARBA GRANTEE.**

DEC 20 - 25, '75. BICENTENNIAL CHRISTMAS CONCERT. LIVE PERFORMANCE AT LEE AUDITORIUM. (LOCAL). PALAUNI M TUIASOSOPO, DIR; AMERICAN SAMOA ARTS COUNCIL; PAGO PAGO, SM 96799. (#103765-4).

MAY 15 - 18, '76. FLAG DAY ARTS FESTIVAL. LIVE PERFORMANCE, FESTIVAL. (LOCAL). PALAUNI M TUIASOSOPO, DIR; AMERICAN SAMOA ARTS COUNCIL; PAGO PAGO, SM 96799. (#103765-3).

JUNE 12, '76. SCHOOL BICENTENNIAL DAY. FESTIVAL, LIVE PERFORMANCE. (LOCAL). PALAUNI M TUIASOSOPO, DIR; AMERICAN SAMOA ARTS COUNCIL AND DEPARTMENT OF EDUCATION; PAGO PAGO, SM 96799. (#103765-1).

JULY 4, '76. FLOATING MUSEUM DEDICATION. CEREMONY, EXHIBIT. (LOCAL). P M TUIASOSOPO, CHAIRMAN; AMERICAN-SAMOAN BICENTENNIAL COMMITTEE; GOVERNMENT HOUSE; PAGO PAGO, SM 96799. (#26563-1).

JULY 4 - 6, '76. TUTOASI (INDEPENDENCE) WEEK. FESTIVAL. (LOCAL). P M TUIASOSOPO, CHAIRMAN; AMER-SAMOAN BICENTENNIAL COMMISSION; GOVT HOUSE; PAGO PAGO, SM 96799. (#26749-1).

DEC '76. YOUTH BICENTENNIAL FESTIVAL. LIVE PERFORMANCE. (LOCAL). PALAUNI M TUIASOSOPO, DIR; GOVERNOR'S OFFICE; PAGO PAGO, SM 96799. (#103765-2).

TAFUNA

TAFUNA RECREATION CENTER - AMERICAN SAMOA. CREATION OF RECREATION CENTER IN RURAL WESTERN DISTRICT. FACILITY IS MULTI-PURPOSE PARK WITH TWO TENNIS COURTS. (ST-WIDE). BROWNIE TUIASOSOPO, CHAIRMAN; AMERICAN SAMOA BICENTENNIAL COMMITTEE; OFFICE OF THE GOVERNOR; PAGO PAGO, SM 96977. (#26915). **ARBA GRANTEE.**

RICAN REVOLUTION BICENTENNIAL
1976

Arizona

Arizona Bicentennial Commission

Established by executive order June 9, 1972; established as an agency by a statute of the State Legislature, May 7, 1974

Theme: Arizona — Spirited Pioneer in America's Heritage

AMERICAN REVOLUTION BICENTENNIAL 1776-1976

ARIZONA BICENTENNIAL COMMISSION

ARBA Statistics

Officially Recognized
Communities—45
Colleges/Universities—5
Military Installations—4
BINET Projects—373
Events—418
1976 Population—2,270,000

Bicentennial Archives

Arizona State Library
Archives and Public Records Division
State Capitol, Third Floor
Phoenix, Arizona 85007

Arizona State Historical Society
949 East Second Street
Tucson, Arizona 85719

Membership

The commission consisted of 21 members: 15 appointed by the governor; three by the speaker of the House of Representatives from the House membership; and three by the president of the Senate from the Senate membership. Members serve at the pleasure of those appointing them.

Felix L. Goodwin, *chairman* (1976-77)
Dr. John R. Carney, *chairman* (1975-76)
John Henley Eversole, *chairman* (1972-74)
Yjinio Aguirre (1972-74)
Sidney Brinckerhoff (1972-77)
Senator Lucy Davidson (1975-77)
Larry Dugan (1972-74)
John Elias (1974-77)
Mabel Ellis (1975-77)
John V. Fels (1972-77)
John Flood (1975-77)
Felix L. Goodwin (1972-76)
Rosemarie Gwynn (1972-74)
Representative Benjamin Hanley (1974-77)
Senator Douglas S. Holsclaw (1974-77)
Senator Arthur J. Hubbard (1974-77)
Louis E. Laflin (1972-74)
Maxine Marshall (1975-77)
Fermin Martinez (1975-77)
Eric Maxwell (1972-74)
Mildred F. May (1972-74)
Father Kieran McCarty, O.F.M. (1972-77)
Harry Montgomery (1975-77)
Audrey Nations (1975-77)
Representative Thomas B. Richey (1974-76)
Representative Elizabeth Rockwell (1974-77)
Elizabeth Ruffner (1972-74)
Larry Salmon (1975-77)
Claire Seota (1972-74)
J. Lester Shaffer (1972-74)
Senator Bess Stinson (1974-77)
Senator Stan Turley (1974-77)
Maurice M. Giss, *executive director* (1972-77)

Arizona

Arizona's commemoration of our nation's Bicentennial could be characterized as a wave of broad involvement and enthusiasm. Communities, ranging in population from Phoenix with 1.2 million to Tombstone with 1,200, inspired large measures of citizen participation. Within these communities, the diverse age and cultural groups found relevant means to express their uniqueness as part of the great mosaic which makes up Arizona and the other 49 states. Over 1,000 events and projects which were on the Bicentennial agenda in Arizona were staged and sponsored by local volunteer Bicentennial committees, service clubs, Indian tribes, communities, high schools and state and federal agencies. Every individual in the state of Arizona was in some way touched by the Bicentennial, whether by a neighborhood celebration, or the *American Freedom Train,* or a school pageant. The primary movers

behind each project and event were volunteer citizens. Government agencies, though highly supportive, did not direct or plan Arizona's Bicentennial commemoration. This, of course, was exactly the way it had to be, and the way the country was created—through citizen participation and voluntary action.

Bicentennial activities followed many themes. Among Arizonans, there was a great deal of interest in the preservation and restoration of early Indian dwellings, Spanish missions and *presidios,* "Old West" towns, pioneer homes, cemeteries and community landmarks. Some representative examples include: The Rosson House, Phoenix; Schiefflin Historic District, Tombstone; Bashford House, Prescott; the *presidio* in Tubac; and Pioneer Arizona Living History Museum in Phoenix.

Native American groups were actively engaged in Bicentennial projects. The Hopi tribe is restoring the historic Walpi Village, which has been continuously inhabited for over 400 years. The Navajo Indian Nation, in October of 1974, broke and blessed ground for a new Navajo Heritage Center. Work is now underway to complete the center, along with a southwestern desert zoo. Phoenix urban Indians are developing a child care center designed to prepare Indian children for entrance into public schools and are also working on a model alcoholism rehabilitation center.

Arizona communities staged a variety of festivals, celebrations and dance and concert performances which highlighted the colorful history of the southwest. Notable events included: *The Tucson Festival,* Tucson; *Old Time Music Festivals,* Payson; *Brewery Gulch Days,* Bisbee; *Folk Arts Fair,* Prescott; *All-American Playwrights Festival,* Phoenix; and *Lake Havasu City's London Bridge Days.*

During the last four years, there were many outstanding national and regional Bicentennial programs which tied Arizona to the rest of the nation and to our neighbor Mexico. The reenactment of the 1775–76 Juan Bautista de Anza Expedition was one of the high points of the Bicentennial in Arizona. It involved trail riding groups, historians and school children from California, Arizona and Sonora, Mexico in an authentic and colorful reenactment of de Anza's trek from Horcasitas, Mexico to San Francisco, California. All along the trek, thousands of citizens attended local festivities, which honored the early Spanish explorers and the Spanish heritage of the southwest.

Other national and regional programs which caught the interest of Arizonans were the Commemoration of the 1776 Dominguez-Escalante Expedition; stops by the *American Freedom Train* in Yuma, Tempe and Tucson; the Wagon Train Pilgrimage across Arizona; and the Armed Services Bicentennial Caravan, which visited virtually every Arizona community.

The climax of Bicentennial activities was July 4, 1976. Every city and town celebrated. In Flagstaff, thousands watched the All-Indian Pow Wow; Prescott held a weekend *Frontier Days Rodeo and Parade.* Fountain Hills staged a tremendous fireworks display, and Eloy held a community dance in an airplane hangar. Every adult and child had the opportunity to share in a memorable 200th birthday commemoration.

The Bicentennial is more than just a memory in Arizona. The accomplishments of volunteer committees and civic groups remain. For those looking to the future, there are community action plans created at 10 different town meetings and the report on the status of senior citizens, "The Elderly Arizonan." There are the community gardens and tree-planting projects in Scottsdale, Nogales and Bisbee; there are the newly constructed parks in Duncan and Wickenburg. There are films on southwest history produced by the University of Arizona—*Paths in the Wilderness;* the Arizona and Nevada Bicentennial commissions' *Steamboats on the Colorado;* and the Maricopa County Community College District's *Days Remembered.* There are restored community landmarks and over 50 recently published books and pamphlets which depict various aspects of Arizona—its history and culture. All records of the Arizona Bicentennial Commission, memorabilia, etc. will be deposited with the State Department of Library and Archives and with the Arizona State Historical Society.

A fitting conclusion to Bicentennial activity occurred December 7, 1976 with the dedication of the *U.S.S. Arizona* Anchor Memorial. The memorial was constructed on the grounds of the Arizona State Capitol and financed by donations from thousands of Arizonans. The memorial will be a lasting tribute to those men who gave their lives for freedom at Pearl Harbor, and to all who have made service to country their first priority.

AJO

AJO, AZ, HISTORICAL SOCIETY PROJECT. THE HISTORICAL SOCIETY WILL RESTORE THE OLD MISSION FOR USE AS A MUSEUM. (LOCAL). MRS RUTH RASMUSSEN, PRESIDENT; AJO HISTORICAL SOCIETY; 401 ROCALLA AVE; AJO, AZ 85321. (#25534).

APACHE JCT

JULY 4, '76. BICENTENNIAL 4TH OF JULY CELEBRATION. FESTIVAL AT APACHE JUNCTION HIGH SCHOOL. (LOCAL). RUBY M FANSBERG; APACHE CHAMBER OF COMMERCE; PO BOX 101; APACHE JCT, AZ 85220. (#107670-1).

BENSON

HISTORICAL 94 YEAR OLD BENSON, AZ, RAILROAD DEPOT. THE SOUTHERN PACIFIC RAILROAD DEPOT BUILDING, WHICH IS NO LONGER IN USE, WILL BE PRESERVED AS A PERMANENT HISTORICAL LANDMARK AND THEN BE USED AS AN AREA MUSEUM. (LOCAL). MAX JONES, PROJ DIRECTOR; SAN PEDRO VALLEY HISTORICAL SOCIETY; BENSON, AZ 85602. (#14769). **ARBA GRANTEE.**

BISBEE

BISBEE BICENTENNIAL COOKBOOK, AZ. PUBLICATION OF UNUSUAL AND ETHNIC FOOD RECIPES IN A UNIQUE AND WELL ILLUSTRATED BOOK. (LOCAL). MRS ROBERT F O'NEAL, EDITOR; BISBEE WOMEN'S CLUB; PO BOX 1743; BISBEE, AZ 85603. (#24036).

BREWERY GULCH DAYS IN BISBEE, AZ. LABOR DAY WEEKEND FESTIVAL FEATURING HISTORIC PAGEANT, TOUR OF HISTORIC HOMES, SERBIAN FOLK FESTIVAL, SPORTS COMPETITIONS AND RECREATION. (LOCAL). MRS JAMES F MCNULTY, CHAIRMAN; BISBEE BICENTENNIAL COMMITTEE; BOX 4395; BISBEE, AZ 85603. (#13005).

CULTURE & HISTORY OF COCHISE COUNTY, AZ. 125 STUDENTS FROM ELEMENTARY AND SECONDARY SCHOOLS ARE GOING TO BECOME AWARE OF THE RICH CULTURAL HERITAGE OF THIS HISTORIC PART OF ARIZONA; RESULT WILL BE A COMMUNITY WIDE ORAL HISTORY PROJECT. (LOCAL). MICHAEL B BECKMAN, PROJ DIRECTOR; BISBEE BICENTENNIAL COMMITTEE; PO BOX DRAWER G; BISBEE, AZ 85603. (#14763). **ARBA GRANTEE.**

FIESTAS PATRIAS DE BISBEE, ARIZONA. A PARADE, DANCES, FOOD & EXHIBITS WITH MEXICAN-AMERICAN FLAVOR ON SEPTEMBER 15 & 16, 1976. (LOCAL). HARRY F CANTRELL, COORDINATOR; BUSHMASTERS CLUB OF BISBEE; 28 MAIN ST; BISBEE, AZ 85603. (#27371). **ARBA GRANTEE.**

GOOD EARTH SEED & BULB BANK - BISBEE, AZ. THIS IS AN EXCHANGE SERVICE TO PROVIDE TRANSFER OF GARDENERS' SURPLUS TO ANYONE DESIRING TO BEGIN OR IMPROVE THEIR GARDENS OR LANDSCAPE. (LOCAL). LARISON LOCKHART, DIRECTOR; GOOD EARTH SEED AND BULB BANK; 33 MOON CANYON, PO BOX X; BISBEE, AZ 85603. (#25446).

L C SHATTUCK MEMORIAL ARCHIVAL LIBRARY - AZ. THE L C SHATTUCK MEMORIAL ARCHIVAL LIBRARY WILL CONTAIN BOOKS & DOCUMENTS ON THE AREA'S HISTORY, GEOLOGY AND MINING DEVELOPMENTS. THE LIBRARY WILL ALSO CONTAIN AN EXTENSIVE ORAL HISTORY COLLECTION. (LOCAL). BARBARA HOOPER; SHATTUCK MEMORIAL ARCHIVAL LIBRARY; PO BOX 451; BISBEE, AZ 85603. (#14762). **ARBA GRANTEE.**

MAIN ST - BISBEE, AZ. PILOT PROGRAM TO REVITALIZE & RETAIN HISTORIC ATMOSPHERE OF THIS NATIONAL HISTORIC LANDMARK. (LOCAL). HARRY F CANTRELL, PROJ CHAIRMAN; BISBEE COMMUNITY BICENTENNIAL COMMITTEE; 28 MAIN PO BOX 1428; BISBEE, AZ 85603. (#25449).

PAINT THE TOWN BEAUTIFUL - BISBEE, AZ. CITIZENS OF THE COMMUNITY WILL WORK TO RESTORE, REPAIR & PAINT THE HISTORIC MINING TOWN. (LOCAL). CARMEN L GRAHAM, CHAIRMAN; BISBEE BICENTENNIAL COMMISSION; 907 TOMBSTONE CANYON; BISBEE, AZ 85603. (#25447).

RESTORATION PROJECT IN BISBEE, AZ. TOWNS PEOPLE IN BISBEE HAVE DECIDED TO TRANSFORM THE OLD GENERAL OF. FICE BUILDING INTO A CIVIC CENTER & MINING MUSEUM. (LOCAL). JACQUIE MCNULTY, CHAIRMAN; BISBEE BICENTENNIAL COMMITTEE; PO BOX 4395; BISBEE, AZ 85603. (#14752).

SURVEY HISTORICAL STRUCTURES IN BISBEE, ARIZONA. IDENTIFICATION & MARKING OF STRUCTURES OF HISTORICAL SIGNIFICANCE IN BISBEE. (LOCAL). MRS JAMES F MCNULTY, CHAIRMAN; BISBEE BICENT COMMITTEE; PO BOX 87; BISBEE, AZ 85603. (#8072).

TOUR OF HOMES IN BISBEE, AZ. THE CITY OF BISBEE WILL OFFER TOURS AND A TOUR GUIDE FOR VISITORS INTERESTED IN THE HISTORY & HOMES OF THIS OLD-WEST MINING TOWN. (LOCAL). MRS DIANE BRESINA, PROJ DIRECTOR; BISBEE BICENTENNIAL COMMITTEE; PO BOX 4395; BISBEE, AZ 85603. (#14945). **ARBA GRANTEE.**

TRAFFIC CIRCLE REVITALIZATION - BISBEE, AZ. BEAUTIFICATION OF THE ACCESS INTERCHANGE TO BISBEE, U S 80, 92 AND BISBEE RD. (LOCAL). VIOLET MORGAN, PROJ CHAIRMAN; GOOD EARTH SEED AND BULB BANK; 5 MOON CANYON, PO BOX 1862; BISBEE, AZ 85603. (#25448).

AUG 30, '75. PAGEANT OF PEOPLE AND PLACES IN BISBEE HISTORY. ORIGIN AND DEVELOPMENT OF AN URBAN COPPER MINING TOWN, 1877-1914 THROUGH NARRATIVE AND ACTS. AT WARREN BALL PARK, SOUTH VISTA. (LOCAL). MRS JOHN STICHT, PROJ DIR; BISBEE BICENTENNIAL COMMUNITY COMMITTEE; 512 DOUGLAS; BISBEE, AZ 85603. (#100887-1).

AUG 31, '75. 'NIGHT IN BELGRADE' - A SERBIAN FESTIVAL. NOCH EN BEOGRAD RELIVES AN EVENING IN A BELGRADE CABARET WITH KOLOS, TAMBOURITZA ORCHESTRA AND SERBIAN FOOD. AT ST STEPHEN NEMANJA HALL, 216 PARK AVE. (LOCAL). DUSHAN VLAHOVICH, CHMN; BISBEE BICENTENNIAL COMMITTEE; BOX 4307; BISBEE, AZ 85603. (#100885-1).

SEPT 5 - 7, '75. PAGEANT OF PEOPLE AND PLACES IN BISBEE HISTORY. LIVE PERFORMANCE. (LOCAL). MRS JAMES MCNULTY; BISBEE BICENT COMMISSION; PO BOX 87; BISBEE, AZ 85603. (#100143-1).

SEPT 5 - 7, '75. SERBIAN LABOR DAY FESTIVAL. PARADE, FOODS, ARTS, DANCE. AT CITYWIDE. (LOCAL). MR SAM PLAYER; CITY OF BISBEE; P O BOX 7; BISBEE, AZ 85603. (#50381-1).

NOV 1, '75 - DEC 31, '76. BISBEE HOMES IN HISTORY - TOURS. TOUR. (LOCAL). DIANE BRESINA, CHAIRMAN; BISBEE BICENTENNIAL COMMITTEE; PO BOX 4395; BISBEE, AZ 85603. (#14945-1).

FEB 1 - DEC 10, '76. QUEEN MINE TOUR & EXHIBITS. TOUR OF UNDERGROUND COPPER MINE OF GREAT HISTORIC VALUE TO BISBEE WITH HISTORIC EXHIBITS RELATED TO COPPER MINING TECHNIQUES SINCE 1880. AT QUEEN MINE TUNNEL. (LOCAL). HON CHARLES EADS, MAYOR; CITY OF BISBEE; PO BOX 7; BISBEE, AZ 85603. (#105882-1).

FEB 28, '76. UNITED STATES ARMED FORCES BICENTENNIAL CARAVAN. CARAVAN IS COMPOSED OF EXHIBIT VANS FOR EACH MILITARY SERVICE. PROJECT THEME IS 'HISTORY OF THE ARMED FORCES AND THEIR CONTRIBUTIONS TO THE NATION'. (LOCAL). MAURICE GISS, EXEC DIR; US ARMED FORCES EXHIBIT VANS PROJECT; 1807 N CENTRAL AVE, SUITE 108; PHOENIX, AZ 85004. (#1775-326).

MAR 13 - 14, '76. VUELTA DE BISBEE - AMATEUR BICYCLE RACING. A 60-MILE ROAD RACE AT 12:30 PM SATURDAY; TIME TRIALS AT 8 AM SUNDAY; CRITERIUM AT 1:30 PM SUNDAY; ALSO, BANDS, CAVALRY GROUP, ARTS & CRAFTS SHOW AND EQUIPMENT DISPLAYS. AT SAT & SUN AM - DOWNTOWN; SUN PM - VISTA PARK. (LOCAL). DOUGLAS SYSON, DIRECTOR; TUCSON WHEELMEN; 112 NACO RD; BISBEE, AZ 85603. (#105729-1).

JULY 4, '76. FOURTH OF JULY IN A MINING CAMP. CELEBRATION INCLUDES: A PARADE, SPORTS, SWIMMING, ROCK-DRILLING CONTEST, SOAP BOX DRBY AND RODEO. (LOCAL). MRS EDIE VALENCIA; BISBEE CHAMBER OF COMMERCE; DRAWER BA; BISBEE, AZ 85603. (#102500-7).

SEPT 3 - 5, '76. BREWERY GULCH DAYS. AN ANNUAL THREE DAY HISTORICAL CELEBRATION, THE FESTIVITIES INCLUDE A PARADE, HISTORICAL PAGEANT, AN OLD TIME MELODRAMA & ANTIQUE SHOW & SALE, NIGHT IN BELGRADE, HISTORICAL REENACTMENTS. (LOCAL). LENETTA HARRIS, COORD; BISKER RESTORATION ASSN & HISTORICAL SOCIETY, INC; PO BOX 271; BISBEE, AZ 85603. (#102500-4).

SEPT 15 - 16, '76. FIESTAS PATRIAS DE BISBEE. PARADE, DANCES, FOOD & EXHIBIT. AT BUSHMASTERS CLUB BLDG. (LOCAL). HARRY F CANTRELL, COORD; BUSHMASTERS CLUB OF BISBEE; 28 MAIN ST; BISBEE, AZ 85603. (#108082-1).

BUCKEYE

LAND OF OUR FATHERS COMMUNITY PAGEANT - AZ. A HISTORICAL PAGEANT SPONSORED BY THE BUCKEYE BICENTENNIAL COMMITTEE. (LOCAL). MRS LOLA JOHNSON, CHAIRMAN; BUCKEYE BICENTENNIAL COMMITTEE; STAR ROUTE, BOX 105; PALO VERDE, AZ 85326. (#20686). **ARBA GRANTEE.**

APR 23 - 24, '76. LAND OF OUR FATHERS COMMUNITY PAGEANT. LIVE PERFORMANCE AT BUCKEYE UNION HIGH SCHOOL. (LOCAL). MRS LOLA JOHNSON, CHMN; BUCKEYE BICENTENNIAL COMMITTEE; STAR ROUTE, BOX 105; PALO VERDE, AZ 85326. (#20686-1).

BULLHEAD CITY

COLLECTION OF 51 STATE FLAGS IN BULLHEAD, AZ. CITIZENS ARE PLACING ON PERMANENT DISPLAY IN THE LOCAL HIGH SCHOOL AUDITORIUM A COLLECTION OF 51 STATE FLAGS. PHOTOGRAPHS OF EACH STATE CAPITOL, AND EARLY AMERICAN HISTORIC FLAGS. (LOCAL). MOHAVE VALLEY BICENTENNIAL COMM; MOHAVE COUNTY BICENTENNIAL COMMISSION; PO BOX 1883; BULLHEAD, AZ 86430. (#14761).

1976 BICENTENNIAL PLANTER LANDMARK - AZ. THIS MONUMENT IS A PLANTER CENTER SECTION FOR 3-DIMENSIONAL PADDLEWHEEL STEAMBOAT; COMPATIBLE PLANTINGS WITH AUTOMATIC WATERING AND LIGHTS; BRONZE PLAQUE WITH LOCAL HISTORICAL INFORMATION. (LOCAL). MRS LARRY MERCER, CHAIRMAN; CHAMBER MAIDS; BOX 186; BULLHEAD CITY, AZ 86430. (#14959).

JULY 4 - 5, '75. DEDICATION OF THE RESTORATION OF THE HARDYVILLE CEMETERY. HISTORIC HARDYVILLE CEMETERY OVERLOOKING THE COLORADO RIVER WILL BE IMPROVED FOR THE BICENTENNIAL. AT HARDYVILLE PIONEER CEMETERY. (LOCAL). ROMAN MALACH; MOHAVE VALLEY BICENTENNIAL COMMISSION; PO BOX 1883; BULLHEAD CITY, AZ 86430. (#4899-1).

JULY 4, '76. DEDICATION OF HISTORICAL PLANTER. CEREMONY AT BULLHEAD COMMUNITY PARK. (LOCAL). VADA MERCER; CHAMBER MAIDS; PO BOX 186; BULLHEAD CITY, AZ 86430. (#107669-1).

CALABASAS

OCT 15 - 16, '75. DE ANZA EXPEDITION REENACTMENT, CELEBRATION & MASS AT CALAGASA RUINS. RE-ENACTMENT OF THE 1775 EXPEDITION FROM TUBAC, AZ, TO CALIFORNIA, ENDING WITH THE ESTABLISHMENT OF PRESIDIO AT SAN FRANCISCO. AT CITYWIDE. (REGN'L). MAURICE GISS; ARIZONA BICENTENNIAL COMMISSION; 1807 N CENTRAL #108; PHOENIX, AZ 85004. (#605-1).

CAMP VERDE

RESTORATION OF CLEAR CREEK CHURCH - CAMP VERDE, AZ. OLD CHURCH USED BY EARLY SETTLERS WILL BE RESTORED. (LOCAL). JIM KILBY, PRESIDENT; CAMP VERDE HISTORICAL SOCIETY; BOX 1184; CAMP VERDE, AZ 86322. (#16147). **ARBA GRANTEE.**

APR 17 - SEPT 19, '76. INDIAN CRAFT DEMONSTRATIONS. REFLECTING THE CULTURAL HERITAGE OF THE VERDE VALLEY THERE WILL BE DEMONSTRATIONS OF NATIVE ARTS COMMON TO THE YAVAPAI-APACHE TRIBES WHO INHABITED THE AREA 200 YEARS AGO. PRORAM PRESENTED ON WEEKENDS, MEMORIAL DAY, JULY 4, AND LABOR DAY. AT PARK VISITOR CENTER. (REGN'L). MONTEZUMA CASTLE NM; NATIONAL PARK SERVICE; PO BOX 219; CAMP VERDE, AZ 86322. (#6729-180).

CASA GRANDE

BICENTENNIAL ART ROOM, CASA GRANDE, AZ. CASA GRANDE IS MAKING A ROOM AVAILABLE FOR DISPLAYS OF ART IN ITS RECENTLY CONSTRUCTED LIBRARY. (LOCAL). RAY PRETTYMAN, COORDINATOR; CASA GRANDE LIBRARY; 930 E FLORENCE BLVD; CASA GRANDE, AZ 85222. (#14263). **ARBA GRANTEE.**

BOOK: EARTH SCIENCES, CASA GRANDE, AZ. PUBLICATION OF BOOK ON EARTH SCIENCES. (LOCAL). GLORIA VALDEZ, CHAIRMAN; WOMEN'S AUXILIARY - AMERICAN INSTITUTE MINING, METALURGICAL ENG; 1231 E CORDOVA; CASA GRANDE, AZ 85222. (#21972).

CASA GRANDE, AZ, BICENTENNIAL COMMUNITY CENTER. DEVELOPMENT OF 160 ACRES OF CITY LAND FOR COMMUNITY CENTER. AN ALL INDIAN VILLAGE WILL PRESERVE HERITAGE, EXHIBITION HALL, RODEO GROUNDS AND A PUBLIC PARK WILL BE USED YEAR AROUND. (LOCAL). DAVID WHITE, PRESIDENT; O'ODHAM TASH CINDIAN DAYS INC; CASA GRANDE, AZ 85222. (#16932).

CITY OF CASA GRANDE ROSE GARDEN, AZ. A ROSE GARDEN AS A COMMEMORATIVE EXHIBIT IN CITY PARK. (LOCAL). DAVE WHITE, DIRECTOR; CITY DEPARTMENT OF PARKS & RECREATION; 300 E 4TH ST; CASA GRANDE, AZ 85222. (#16931).

GRAFFITTI FOR BICENTENNIAL - CASA GRANDE, ARIZONA. STUDENTS IN ONE TEACHER'S AMERICAN HISTORY CLASSES HAVE PAINTED A LARGE WALL IN THEIR CLASSROOM WITH A MULTICOLORED PATTERN OF INTERESTING ANGLES, EACH WITH AN ASPECT OF AMERICAN HISTORY OR CULTURE. (LOCAL). PATRICK MCCLELLAN, PROJ DIRECTOR; CASA GRANDE UNION HIGH SCHOOL; 420 E FLORENCE BLVD; CASA GRANDE, AZ 85222. (#9215).

A PUBLISHED HISTORY OF THE CASA GRANDE VALLEY - AZ. LOCAL HISTORICAL SOCIETY & STUDENTS FROM CENTRAL ARIZONA COLLEGE WILL INTERVIEW OLD-TIME RESIDENTS, RESEARCH HISTORICAL MATERIALS ON THE AREA AND PRODUCE AN HISTORICAL PUBLICATION. (LOCAL). KAY BENEDICT, CHAIRMAN; CASA GRANDE BICENTENNIAL-CENTENNIAL COMMITTEE; 912 N PICACHO DR; CASA GRANDE, AZ 85222. (#2366). **ARBA GRANTEE.**

VOTER REGISTRATION PROJECT IN CASA GRANDE, AZ. THE WOMEN'S CLUB OF CASA GRANDE WILL HAVE A VOTER REGISTRATION PROJECT IN 1975-1976; THE PURPOSE IS TO GET EVERY ELIGIBLE ADULT REGISTERED AND VOTING IN 1976. (LOCAL). LOUISE HENNESS, PROJ CHAIRMAN; WOMEN'S CLUB OF CASA GRANDE; PO BOX 246; CASA GRANDE, AZ 85222. (#14256).

OCT 1, '75 - DEC 31, '76. MINERALS DISPLAY. EXHIBIT AT CASA GRANDE PUBLIC LIBRARY; 405 E 6TH ST, CASA GRANDE, AZ. (LOCAL). GLORIA VALDEZ, CHMN; WOMEN'S AUXILIARY - AMER INSTITUTE MINING, METALURGICAL ENGINEERING; 1231 E CORDOVA; CASA GRANDE, AZ 85222. (#21972-1).

NOV 1 - 2, '75. DE ANZA EXPEDITION REENACTMENT, CELEBRATION, RODEO, AT CASA GRANDE. RE-ENACTMENT OF THE 1775 EXPEDITION FROM TUBAC, AZ, TO CALIFORNIA, ENDING WITH THE ESTABLISHMENT OF PRESIDIO AT SAN FRANCISCO. AT CITYWIDE. (ST-WIDE). MAURICE GISS; ARIZONA BICENTENNIAL COMMISSION; 1807 N CENTRAL #108; PHOENIX, AZ 85004. (#605-6).

FEB 13 - 16, '76. 9TH O'ODHAM TASH-CASA GRANDE ALL INDIAN POW-WOW. TRIBES FROM ACROSS AMERICA COMPETE IN ALL-INDIAN RODEO, EXHIBIT CRAFTS AND PERFORM CEREMONIAL RITES; PARADES WILL BEGIN AT 10 AM AND THE RODEO WILL BEGIN AT 1:30 PM ON SATURDAY AND SUNDAY. AT CASA GRANDE RODEO GROUNDS. (REGN'L). JOANNA BOWSER, PROJ DIR; O'ODHAM TASH INDIAN POWWOW ASS'N; 1015 E FLORENCE BLVD; CASA GRANDE, AZ 85222. (#104483-1).

MAR 10 - 11, '76. UNITED STATES ARMED FORCES BICENTENNIAL CARAVAN. CARAVAN IS COMPOSED OF EXHIBIT VANS FOR EACH MILITARY SERVICE. PROJECT THEME IS 'HISTORY OF THE ARMED FORCES AND THEIR CONTRIBUTIONS TO THE NATION'. (LOCAL). JOANNE KELLY, CHMN; US ARMED FORCES EXHIBIT VANS PROJECT; 1214 E CORDOVA ST; CASA GRANDE, AZ 85222. (#1775-331).

CAVE CREEK

DEC '75. CAREFREE CHRISTMAS PAGEANT. NONDENOMINATIONAL PAGEANT WITH LIVE ANIMALS AND PERFORMERS. AT AM-

CAVE CREEK — CONTINUED

PHITHEATER ON SIDE OF BLACK MOUNTAIN. (LOCAL). MS GREGORY PAUL; TOWN OF CAVE CREEK; PO BOX 1849; CAVE CREEK, AZ 85331. (#102500-6).

CHINLE

MAY 19, '76. NATL PK SVC '...A LITTLE LOOK AROUND' VISITS CANYON DE CHELLY NM. THIS SHORT PROGRAM FEATURES ACTORS PORTRAYING FAMOUS AMERICANS OF THE PAST WHO'VE RETURNED TO SEE AMERICA'S GROWTH. (REGN'L). CANYON DE CHELLY NM; NATIONAL PARK SERVICE; P.O. BOX 588; CHINLE, AZ 86503. (#5653-60).

CHLORIDE

CERBAT CERAMICS - CHLORIDE, AZ. A MOCK CORPORATION FORMED BY 4TH, 5TH & 6TH GRADE PUPILS; THEY GET CLAY FROM THE LOCAL MINE, MAKE POTS AND WINDCHIMES & SELL THEM; PROFITS GO TO CHILDREN AND STOCKHOLDERS. (LOCAL). MRS CAROLYN STEWART, TEACHER; CHLORIDE SCHOOL; BOX 7; CHLORIDE, AZ 86431. (#25536).

DOUBLE BED QUILT, CHLORIDE, AZ. CHLORIDE ELEMENTARY SCHOOL CHILDREN BROUGHT IN FABRIC SQUARES TO BE USED FOR A QUILT THAT THEY WILL COMPLETE AS A CLASS PROJECT. (LOCAL). CAROLYN STEWART, TEACHER; CHLORIDE ELEMENTARY SCHOOL; BOX 7; CHLORIDE, AZ 86431. (#26046).

TIME CAPSULE - CHLORIDE, AZ. PLACEMENT OF AN OBELISK MONUMENT CONTAINING A CAPSULE WITH CULTURAL MATERIALS SUCH AS CHILDREN'S SCHOOL WORK, CATALOGS OF CURRENT STYLES AND GOODS AVAILABLE - THINGS OF INTEREST TO CHILDREN. (LOCAL). EDWARD E JARES, HEAD TEACHER; CHLORIDE SCHOOL; PO BOX 7; CHLORIDE, AZ 86431. (#25450).

JUNE 27, '76. MINERS DAY PARADE & ALL-DAY BICENTENNIAL CELEBRATION. AWARD, FESTIVAL, PARADE. (LOCAL). RUTH WHITE, CHMN; CHLORIDE CHAMBER OF COMMERCE & VOLUNTEER FIRE DEPT; PO BOX 67; CHLORIDE, AZ 86431. (#108447-1).

CLARKSDALE

MONTEZUEMA CASTLE INDIAN CULTURAL CENTER IN AZ. THE YAVAPI-APACHE INDIAN TRIBE IS DEVELOPING A CULTURAL & RECREATIONAL CENTER AT THE SITE OF THE ANCIENT MONTEZUMA CASTLE CLIFF DWELLINGS. (ST-WIDE). AARON RUSSELL, CHAIRMAN; YAVAPAI-APACHE INDIAN COMMUNITY; PO BOX 236; CLARKSDALE, AZ 85004. (#329). **ARBA GRANTEE.**

MAY 15 - SEPT 19, '76. INDIAN CRAFT DEMONSTRATIONS AT TUZIGOOT NM. REFLECTING THE CULTURAL HERITAGE OF THE VERDE VALLEY, THERE WILL BE DEMONSTRATIONS OF NATIVE ARTS COMMON TO THE YAVAPAI-APACHE TRIBES WHO INHABITED THE AREA 200 YEARS AGO. PROGRAM PRESENTED ON WEEKENDS, MEMORIAL DAY, JULY 4, AND LABOR DAY. AT PARK VISITOR CENTER. (REGN'L). TUZIGOOT NM; NATIONAL PARK SERVICE; PO BOX 68; CLARKDALE, AZ 86324. (#6727-222).

CLIFTON

GREENLEE COUNTY HISTORICAL MUSEUM - CLIFTON, AZ. RENOVATION OF A DOWNTOWN BUILDING FOR USE AS A MUSEUM. (LOCAL). THORA POLLOCK, CHAIRMAN; GREENLEE COUNTY HISTORICAL SOCIETY; BOX 767; CLIFTON, AZ 85533. (#26931). **ARBA GRANTEE.**

COOLIDGE

BATTLE OF PICACHO PASS, COOLIDGE, AZ. A SOUND MOTION PICTURE OF CIVIL WAR IN AZ. (LOCAL). VERN HARDEN, CHAIRMAN; CENTRAL ARIZONA COLLEGE; WOODRUFF AT OVERFIELD; COOLIDGE, AZ 85228. (#31619).

BICENTENNIAL ROSE & FLAG GARDEN - COOLIDGE, AZ. USED NEW ARIZONA BICENTENNIAL ROSE TO PLANT GARDEN AROUND FLAG STAGE WHERE 5 FLAGS OVER ARIZONA ARE FLOWN. (ST-WIDE). DR DALE GIBSON, CHAIRMAN; CENTRAL ARIZONA COLLEGE; WOODRUFF & OVERFIELD STS; COOLIDGE, AZ 85222. (#31617).

HISTORICAL RESEARCH AND METHODS - PINAL COUNTY, AZ. A PINAL COUNTY PROJECT FOR TEACHERS AND HISTORY BUFFS - A CLASS IN RESEARCH, INTERPRETATION AND PREPARATION OF HISTORY MATERIAL FOR PUBLICATION OR CURRICULUM AIDS IN THE SCHOOLS. (LOCAL). MRS DOROTHY POWELL, COORDINATOR; CENTRAL ARIZONA COLLEGE; OVERFIELD RD; COOLIDGE, AZ 85228. (#9216).

PINAL COUNTY HISTORICAL FILM SERIES, ARIZONA. SERIES OF SHORT FILMS DEPICTING HISTORY OF THE AREA. ONE FILM WILL FOCUS ON ARIZIONA'S ONLY CIVIL WAR BATTLE AT PICACHO PEAK. (LOCAL). VERNON HARDEN, DRAMA DIRECTOR; CENTRAL ARIZONA COLLEGE; SIGNAL PEAK CAMPUS; COOLIDGE, AZ 85228. (#4897). **ARBA GRANTEE.**

FEB 18 - 25, '76. AUDIO CHAIRS EXHIBIT ON NATIVE AMERICANS, BLACKS AND WOMEN IN 1776. IN SPECIAL LISTENING CHAIRS VISITORS WILL HEAR THREE DIFFERENT TAPE RECORDINGS WHICH DESCRIBE THE ROLES OF WOMEN, BLACKS, AND NATIVE AMERICANS DURING THE REVOLUTIONRARY PERIOD. AT PARK VISITOR CENTER. (REGN'L). CASA GRANDE RUINS NM; NATIONAL PARK SERVICE; PO BOX 518; COOLIDGE, AZ 85228. (#5581-13).

MAR 26 - 27, '76. TEXAS OPERA THEATER PRESENTS 'EL CAPITAN'. HILARIOUS OPERETTA MASTERPIECE BY AMERICAN 'MARCH KING' JOHN PHILIP SOUSA. (LOCAL). CAM WILLIAMS, MARKET REP; CENTRAL ARIZONA COLLEGE & TEXAS OPERA THEATER; 615 LOUISIANA; HOUSTON, TX 77002. (#106007-1).

MAY 12, '76. NATL PK SVC '...A LITTLE LOOK AROUND' VISITS CASA GRANDE NM. THIS SHORT PROGRAM FEATURES ACTORS PORTRAYING FAMOUS AMERICANS OF THE PAST WHO'VE RETURNED TO SEE AMERICA'S GROWTH. (REGN'L). CASA GRANDE NATL MON; NATIONAL PARK SERVICE; P.O. BOX 518; COOLIDGE, AZ 85228. (#5653-54).

OCT 31, '76. REENACTMENT OF DEANZA EXPEDITION OF 1775 FROM MEXICO TO MONTEREY. REENACTMENT OF PART OF THE 1775 EXPEDITION FROM TUBAC, AZ, TO CALIFORNIA ENDING WITH THE ESTABLISHMENT OF SAN FRANCISCO. TAGE & THE ROLE THE NATIONAL PARK SYSTEM HAS PLAYED. AT COMPOUND 'A' CASA GRANDE RUINS NATIONAL MONUMENT PARK. (REGN'L). SUPT, CASA GRANDE; NATIONAL PARK SERVICE; P.O. BOX 518; COOLIDGE, AZ 85228. (#6729-541).

CORDES JCT

ARCOSANTI. PROTOTYPE TOWN UNDER CONSTRUCTION 70 MILES N OF PHOENIX, ARIZ, OFFERS MODEL FOR ALTERNATIVE STYLE OF URBAN LIFE IN HARMONY WITH NATURE-DURING 76, TOURS FOR VISITORS, EXHIBITION/MTG CTRS, PERFORMANCE. (ST-WIDE). PAOLO SOLERI, FOUNDER; COSANTI FOUNDATION; 6433 DOUBLETREE RD; SCOTTSDALE, AZ 85253. (#709). **ARBA RECOGNIZED.**

SEPT 22, '75. ARCOSANTI AUTUMN EQUINOX CELEBRATION 1975. ARCOSANTI AUTUMN EQUINOX '76 CELEBRATION IS A CONTINUANCE OF BICENTENNIAL EVENTS ON DAYS OF NATURAL OCCURRENCES; TO INCLUDE A TOOUR SLIDE SHOW, REFRESHMENTS AND PERFORMERS OF NATIONALLY KNOWN TALENT. AT ARCOSANTI CONSTRUCTION SITE, OFF HGWY 17. (ST-WIDE). SUE BLOKER, COORDINATOR; COSANTI FOUNDATION AND AFFILIATED ARCOSANTI EVENTS PROGRAM; 6433 DOUBLE TREE; SCOTTSDALE, AZ 85253. (#709-1).

NOV 7 - 9, '75. ARCOSANTI OFFICIAL BICENTENNIAL CELEBRATION FESTIVAL. WEEKEND LONG FESTIVAL WITH GUESTS & PERFORMERS FROM ALL OVER THE U S STARTING AT 1:00 PM FRI, OCT 29 UNTIL MIDNIGHT SUNDAY. AT ARCOSANTI CONSTRUCTION SITE, OFF HGWY 17. (ST-WIDE). SUE BLOKER, COORDINATOR; COSANTI FOUNDATION AND AFFILIATED ARCOSANTI EVENTS PROGRAM; 6433 DOUBLE TREE; SCOTTSDALE, AZ 85253. (#709-2).

MAR 17 - NOV 30, '76. ARCOSANTI CONSTRUCTION SITE TOURS & SLIDE PRESENTATIONS. ARCOSANTI PROJECT IS AN EXPERIMENT IN BUILDING AN INNOVATIVE URBAN ENVIRONMENT IN HARMONY WITH THE NATURAL LANDSCAPE THAT CONSERVES ENERGY RESOURCES. THE WORK IS BEING DONE BY VOLUNTEERS UNDER THE DIRECTION OF ARCHITECT PAOLO SOLERI. AT ARCOSANTI CONSTRUCTION SITE, OFF HGWY 17. (ST-WIDE). SUE BLOKER, COORDINATOR; COSANTI FOUNDATION AND AFFILIATED ARCOSANTI EVENTS PROGRAM; 6433 DOUBLE TREE; SCOTTSDALE, AZ 85253. (#709-3).

MAR 21, '76. ARCOSANTI VERNAL EQUINOX '76 CELEBRATION. THE ARCOSANTI VERNAL EQUINOX SPRING '76 CELEBRATION OPENS THE ARCOSANTI CONSTRUCTION SITE TO THE PUBLIC FOR THE 1ST TIME IN 1976. THE DAY BEGINS WITH A TOUR OF THE SITE, A SLIDE SHOW, REFRESHMENTS AND IN THE EVENING A PERFORMANCE IN THE UNIQUE AMPHITHEATRE. AT ARCOSANTI CONSTRUCTION SITE, OFF HGWY 17. (ST-WIDE). SUE BLOKER, COORDINATOR; COSANTI FOUNDATION AND AFFILIATED ARCOSANTI EVENTS PROGRAM; 6433 DOUBLE TREE; SCOTTSDALE, AZ 85253. (#709-4).

JUNE 22, '76. ARCOSANTI SUMMER SOLSTICE '76 CELEBRATION. ARCOSANTI SUMMER SOLSTICE '76 CELEBRATION WILL CELEBRATE THE LONGEST DAY OF THE BICENTENNIAL YEAR. EVENTS WILL INCLUDE A VISUAL ARTS EXHIBITION, A MUSICAL, A THEATRICAL PERFORMANCE IN AN AMPHITHEATER AND TOURS OF THE SITE. AT ARCOSANTI CONSTRUCTION SITE, OFF HGWY 17. (ST-WIDE). SUE BLOKER, COORDINATOR; COSANTI FOUNDATION AND AFFILIATED ARCOSANTI EVENTS PROGRAM; 6433 DOUBLE TREE; SCOTTSDALE, AZ 85253. (#709-5).

SEPT 22, '76. ARCOSANTI FALL EQUINOX '76 CELEBRATION. ARCOSANTI AUTUMN EQUINOX '76 CELEBRATION IS A CONTINUATION OF BICENTENNIAL EVENTS ON DAYS OF NATURAL OCCURRENCES. TO INCLUDE A TOUR, SLIDE SHOW, REFRESHMENTS & PERFORMERS OF NATIONALLY KNOWN TALENT. AT ARCOSANTI SITE OFF HIGHWAY 17 AT CORDES JUNCTION. (ST-WIDE). SUE BLOKER, EVENTS DIR; ARCOSANTI FOUNDATION & ARCOSANTI EVENTS PROGRAM; 6433 DOUBLETREE; SCOTTSDALE, AZ 85253. (#709-7).

OCT 29 - 31, '76. ARCOSANTI BICENTENNIAL FESTIVAL. RESERVATIONS ARE AVAILABLE. AT ARCOSANTI SITE OFF HIGHWAY 17 AT CORDES JUNCTION. (ST-WIDE). SUE BLOKER, EVENTS DIR; ARCOSANTI FOUNDATION & ARCOSANTI EVENTS PROGRAM; 6433 DOUBLETREE; SCOTTSDALE, AZ 85253. (#709-6).

CORONADO

CAMP JOHN A RUCKER HISTORIC SITE IN ARIZONA. HISTORIC MARKER ESTABLISHING CAMP JOHN A RUCKER IN THE CHIRICAHUA MOUNTAINS OF SOUTHEASTERN ARIZONA AS AN HISTORIC SITE. (ST-WIDE). MRS WILLIAM L CHAPEL, COORDINATOR; ARIZ SOCIETY DAUGHTERS OF THE AMERICAN REVOLUTION; 320 LEISURE WORLD; MESA, AZ 85206. (#607).

DOLAN SPG

PANORAMA OF PATRIOTIC SYMBOLS, DOLAN SPRINGS, AZ. DISPLAY OF FIVE SYMBOLS: THE LIBERTY BELL, 1776 THIRTEEN STAR FLAG, AMERICAN EAGLE, 1976 FIFTY STAR FLAG & BICENTENNIAL SYMBOL. DISPLAY IS MADE OF ROCK SET IN CEMENT & PAINTED ON A HILL AT THE SCHOOL. (LOCAL). DEAUN A JOHNSON, COORDINATOR; MT TIPTON SCHOOL; BOX 248; DOLAN SPG, AZ 86441. (#26044).

DOUGLAS

CHILDREN, YOUTH & ALCOHOLISM, DOUGLAS, AZ. DEVELOPMENT OF MOBILE INSTRUCTION UNIT THAT WILL VISIT HIGH SCHOOLS THROUGHOUT COCHISE COUNTY FOR THE PURPOSE OF ACQUAINTING STUDENTS WITH DRUG & ALCOHOL ABUSE. (LOCAL). RICK HYDE, COORDINATOR; DOUGLAS LOCAL ALCOHOLIC RECEPTION CENTER; 363 8TH ST; DOUGLAS, AZ 85607. (#25477). **ARBA GRANTEE.**

'DOUGLAS, AZ, USA' - HISTORY. EXTENSIVE HISTORY OF THE CITY OF DOUGLAS PRIOR TO INCEPTION, UP TO AND INCLUDING THE PRESENT; HISTORY WILL COVER CITY AND LOCAL AREA. WILL BE COMPLETED THROUGH ORAL & DOCUMENTATIVE HISTORY. (LOCAL). JEANNE L GRAHAM, PRESIDENT; CONCHISE COUNTY HISTORICAL & ARCHAEOLOGICAL SOCIETY; PO BOX 477; DOUGLAS, AZ 85607. (#20973). **ARBA GRANTEE.**

FUND RAISING PROJECT FOR CLASS TRIP, DOUGLAS, AZ. 4TH GRADE CLASS CARLSON SCHOOL DOUGLAS, AZ, IS RAISING FUNDS TO CHARTER A BUS AND MAKE CROSS-COUNTRY TRIP TO PLACES OF HISTORICAL INTEREST SUCH AS WASHINGTON, DC, PHILADELPHIA & NEW YORK. (LOCAL). GEORGIA FAIRBANKS, TEACHER; BICENTENNIAL KIDS; 920 19TH ST; DOUGLAS, AZ 85607. (#25817).

8TH STREET PARK SWIMMING POOL - DOUGLAS, AZ. A SWIMMING POOL WITH A SMALL CHILDREN'S WADING POOL AND FACILITIES NECESSARY FOR OPERATION AND CONVENIENCE OF THE PUBLIC. (LOCAL). DAVE MARTIN, ASST DIRECTOR; CITY OF DOUGLAS; 425 10TH ST; DOUGLAS, AZ 85607. (#14962).

FEB 25 - 26, '76. UNITED STATES ARMED FORCES BICENTENNIAL CARAVAN. CARAVAN IS COMPOSED OF EXHIBIT VANS FOR EACH MILITARY SERVICE. PROJECT THEME IS 'HISTORY OF THE ARMED FORCES AND THEIR CONTRIBUTIONS TO THE NATION'. (LOCAL). FRANK MANGIN, CHMN; US ARMED FORCES EXHIBIT VANS PROJECT; PO DRAWER F; DOUGLAS, AZ 85607. (#1775-325).

APR 25, '76. CORONADO NMEM INTERNATIONAL HISTORICAL PAGEANT ON HISPANIC HERITAGE. CELEBRATION OF HISPANIC - MEXICAN - INDIAN HERITAGE & FRIENDSHIP BETWEEN MEXICO AND U S THROUGH DANCE, MUSIC, CRAFT, FOOD AND CEREMONY PAPAGO, APACHE, YAQUI CULTURAL GROUPS COMBINE WITH MARIACHI, BALLET FOLKLORICO AND HISTORICAL DRAMA GROUPS FOR A CULTURAL HAPPENING. AT CORONADO NATIONAL MEMORIAL PICNIC AREA. (REGN'L). CORONADO NMEM; NATIONAL PARK SERVICE; RURAL ROUTE #1, BOX 126; HEREFORD, AZ 85615. (#6728-258).

MAY 15, '76. NATL PK SVC '...A LITTLE LOOK AROUND' VISITS CORONADO NMEM. THIS SHORT PROGRAM FEATURES ACTORS PORTRAYING FAMOUS AMERICANS OF THE PAST WHO'VE RETURNED TO SEE AMERICA'S GROWTH. (REGN'L). CORONADO NATL MEM; NATIONAL PARK SERVICE; RURAL ROUTE 1, BOX 126; HEREFORD, AZ 85615. (#5653-57).

DEC 12 - 18, '76. STUDENT ARTISTS EXHIBIT AT CORONADO NMEM. THIS ART EXHIBIT CONSISTS OF 18 ORIGINAL PAINTINGS SELECTED FROM ENTRIES IN A NATIONWIDE STUDENT ART CONTEST. EACH PAINTING IS IDENTIFIED WITH PERSONS, PLACES, OR EVENTS OF THE AMER REVOLUTION. AT LITTLE ART GALLERY, 300 ELEVENTH ST. (REGN'L). DOUGLAS ART ASSOCIATION; NATIONAL PARK SERVICE, CHIRICAHUA NM AND LITTLE ART GALLERY; BOX 256; DOUGLAS, AZ 85607. (#1474-8).

DRAGOON

OCT 20 - DEC 20, '75. THE LAST CATTLE DRIVE. 1000 HEAD OF CATTLE TO BE DRIVEN OVER 350 MILES ON OLD CATTLE TRAILS FROM WILLCOX, AZ TO TUCSON, AZ. NET PROCEEDS TO GO TO MUSCULAR DYSTROPHY ASSOCIATION FROM CATTLE AUCTION TO BE HELD IN TUCSON IN IN LATE NOVEMBER. PUBLIC IS INVITED TO PARTICIPATE. (ST-WIDE). LESLIE DANIELS, PROJ DIR; TRIANGLE T GUEST RANCH; 4801 E 27TH ST; TUCSON, AZ 85711. (#17807-1).

DUNCAN

COMMUNITY CENTER IN DUNCAN, AZ. DUNCAN PURCHASED A HISTORIC BUILDING TO USE AS A MEETING PLACE FOR LOCAL ORGANIZATIONS AND DISPLAY AREAS FROM TOWN'S PAST; THE BUILDING WILL BE A SYMBOL OF THE COMMUNITY. (LOCAL). MRS JUNE E LARKEY, PROJ DIRECTOR; CITY OF DUNCAN; PO BOX 102; DUNCAN, AZ 85534. (#14268). **ARBA GRANTEE.**

DUNCAN BICENTENNIAL PARK IN DUNCAN, AZ. DUNCAN IS REBUILDING A PARK, WHICH WAS COVERED BY MUD DURING A 1972 FLOOD; THE TOWN PLANS TO NAME THE PARK 'BICENTENNIAL PARK' AND WILL HAVE IT TOTALLY COMPLETED BY 1976. (LOCAL). JUNE LACKEY, PROJ DIRECTOR; DUNCAN BICENTENNIAL PARK; PO BOX 102; DUNCAN, AZ 85534. (#14265). **ARBA GRANTEE.**

DUNCAN PIONEER FAMILY HISTORY - AZ. DUNCAN BICENTENNIAL COMMISSION IS GOING TO RECORD THE ONE HUNDRED YEAR

DUNCAN—CONTINUED

HISTORY OF THE DUNCAN VALLEY. ORAL INTERVIEWS WILL BE A PART OF THE PROGRAM, WITH DONATION OF HISTORICAL ITEMS TO LOCAL MUSEUM. (LOCAL). JUNE LACKEY, PROJ DIRECTOR; DUNCAN PIONEER FAMILY HISTORY; PO BOX 102; DUNCAN, AZ 85534. (#14765).

DUNCAN VALLEY CEMETERY RESTORATION, AZ. DUNCAN IS GOING TO RESTORE ITS FIRST PIONEER CEMETERY. CITIZENS WILL CLEAN STONES & PLANT BUSHES & TREES. (LOCAL). JUNE LACKEY, CHAIRMAN; DUNCAN BICENTENNIAL COMMITTEE; PO BOX 102; DUNCAN, AZ 85534. (#14753).

EAGAR

ROUND VALLEY, PAST & FUTURE - EAGAR, AZ. A MEMORIAL BUILDING WILL BE USED TO DISPLAY AND RECOGNIZE HISTORY OF ROUND VALLEY; THE BUILDING WILL BE MOVED TO A SITE NEAR SPRINGERVILLE CITY PARK. (LOCAL). ATELLA HAWS, PROJ CHAIRMAN; EAGAR TOWN; PO BOX 173; EAGAR, AZ 85925. (#14257).

ELOY

FREEDOM HALL COMMUNITY CENTER, ELOY, AZ. A COMMUNITY CENTER IS BEING BUILT IN A LOW INCOME NEIGHBORHOOD; THE CENTER IS THE ONLY MEETING FACILITY IN ELOY; 1ST STEP TOWARD INVOLVING CULTURAL GROUPS IN PLANNING COMMUNITY RECREATION. (LOCAL). OWEN C HAWSE, PROJ DIRECTOR; CITY OF ELOY; 420 E 3RD ST; ELOY, AZ 85231. (#14269).

OPERATION: FIRE HYDRANTS, ELOY, AZ. ELOY IS PAINTING 50 FIRE HYDRANTS SO THAT THEY RESEMBLE 'MINUTEMEN AND REDCOATS.' THE PROJECT IS A COOPERATIVE COMMUNITY EFFORT OF FAMILIES, SCHOOLS AND BUSINESSES. (LOCAL). BETH DEVEREUX, PROJ COORDINATOR; CITY OF ELOY; 104 W LA SIESTA DR; ELOY, AZ 85231. (#15469).

MAR 9, '76. UNITED STATES ARMED FORCES BICENTENNIAL CARAVAN. CARAVAN IS COMPOSED OF EXHIBIT VANS FOR EACH MILITARY SERVICE. PROJECT THEME IS 'HISTORY OF THE ARMED FORCES AND THEIR CONTRIBUTIONS TO THE NATION'. (LOCAL). OREN HAWSE, CHMN; US ARMED FORCES EXHIBIT VANS PROJECT; 420 E 3RD ST; ELOY, AZ 85231. (#1775-330).

JULY 3 - 5, '76. ELOY JULY 4TH COMMUNITY CELEBRATION. FESTIVAL AT CITY HALL PARK AND COMPLEX, AIRPORT, & HIGH SCHOOL ATHLETIC FIELD. (LOCAL). OREN C HAWSE; ELOY JULY 4TH COMMITTEE & ELOY BICENTENNIAL COMMITTEE; 420 E 3RD ST; ELOY, AZ 85231. (#107664-1).

FLAGSTAFF

AIR QUALITY MONITORING NETWORK - FLAGSTAFF, AZ. AN AIR QUALITY MONITORING NETWORK WILL BE SET UP FOR ASSESSMENT OF FLAGSTAFF'S AIR QUALITY. (LOCAL). WILLIAM C MALM, ASST PROFESSOR; NORTHERN ARIZONA STATE UNIV; 3128 N PATTERSON; FLAGSTAFF, AZ 86001. (#14965).

AMERICAN MUSICAL HERITAGE CONCERT TOURS IN ARIZONA. FREE CONCERTS THROUGHOUT AZ FEATURING WORKS BY AMERICAN COMPOSERS WITH SPECIAL EMPHASIS ON INDIAN & MEXICAN AMERICAN COMPOSERS. (ST-WIDE). THOMAS KIRSHBAUM, CONDUCTOR; FLAGSTAFF SYMPHONY ORCHESTRA; PO BOX 122; FLAGSTAFF, AZ 86001. (#642). **ARBA GRANTEE.**

ARIZONA 1776-1976- MOBILE HISTORY EXHIBITION. 37 PANELS WITH FILMS & VIDEO TAPES DEPICTING 3 SPANISH PARTIES CROSSING ARIZONA IN 1776, THEIR INFLUENCE ON COLONIZATION OF THE SOUTHWESTERN USA & TRADITIONS CONTINUING TODAY, INDIAN-ANGLO-HISPANIC. (ST-WIDE). E B DANSON, DIRECTOR; MUSEUM OF NORTHERN ARIZONA; PO BOX 1389; FLAGSTAFF, AZ 86001. (#776). **ARBA GRANTEE.**

BLACK AWARENESS CLASS, FLAGSTAFF, AZ. TRACING BLACK CULTURE FROM PAST TO PRESENT THROUGH LITERATURE. (LOCAL). THEODORE L JOHNSON, INSTRUCTOR; NAACP & FLAGSTAFF PUBLIC SCHOOL; 2 E SILVER SPRUCE; FLAGSTAFF, AZ 86001. (#20970).

BOOKLET & REPAIRS ON THE GENERAL CROOK TRAIL IN AZ. THE GENERAL CROOK TRAIL IS BEING REPAIRED & MARKED. A BOOKLET HAS BEEN PREPARED TO EXPLAIN THE HISTORICAL SIGNIFICANCE OF THIS IMPORTANT COMMUNICATIONS ROUTE THAT WENT FROM MCNARY TO PRESCOTT. (ST-WIDE). DR ELDON BOWMAN, PROJ DIRECTOR; GRAND CANYON COUNCIL, BOY SCOUTS OF AMERICA; PO BOX 8; FLAGSTAFF, AZ 86001. (#14946). **ARBA GRANTEE.**

BUFFALO SOLDIERS MUSEUM AND MONUMENT, AZ. ESTABLISH MUSEUM TO DEPICT BLACK CONTRIBUTION TO ARMED FORCES FROM 17TH CENTURY TO PRESENT; ERECT MONUMENT TO BLACK SOLDIERS THAT SERVE D IN SW U S IN 19TH AND 20TH CENTURY KNOWN AS THE BUFFALO SOLDIERS. (REGN'L). L DAVID NEALEY, PRESIDENT; BUFFALO SOLDIERS HISTORICAL SOCIETY; 3923 N GENEVA CIRCLE; FLAGSTAFF, AZ 86001. (#20972).

COURSE OFFERINGS FOR BICENTENNIAL CELEBRATION - AZ. AN INVITATION TO RECONSIDER THE AGE OF THE DECLARATION OF INDEPENDENCE; COURSES AND LECTURES ON THE HISTORY AND MEANING OF THE AMERICAN REVOLUTION. (LOCAL). W H LYON, CHAIRMAN; NORTHERN ARIZONA UNIV; BOX 6023; FLAGSTAFF, AZ 86001. (#17816).

CULTURAL PLURALISM IN FLAGSTAFF, AZ. PROJECT WILL SPONSOR PUBLIC FORUMS ON BILINGUAL MULTI-CULTURAL EDUCATION. (LOCAL). JEAN M TURNER, PROJ DIRECTOR; NORTHERN ARIZONA UNIV; BOX 5774; FLAGSTAFF, AZ 86001. (#24034).

EXHIBIT FOR THE GENERAL GEORGE CROOK TRAIL - AZ. A PHOTOGRAPHIC AND AUDIO DOCUMENTATION OF RECONSTRUCTION OF 100-YEAR OLD MILITARY ROAD ON THE MOGOLLOW RIM OF NORTHERN ARIZONA. (LOCAL). RAY NEWTON, PUBLIC RELATIONS; GRAND CANYON COUNCIL, BOY SCOUTS OF AMERICA; 3445 N KING; FLAGSTAFF, AZ 86001. (#24811). **ARBA GRANTEE.**

FLAGSTAFF COOPERATIVE INDEXING PROJECT OF ARIZONA. INDEXING OF THE FLAGSTAFF NEWSPAPER FROM 1883-1933 SO THAT A RECORD OF THE HISTORY OF THIS PERIOD WILL BE PERMANENTLY AVAILABLE TO ALL CITIZENS. (ST-WIDE). HAZEL ROBINSON, LIBRARIAN; NORTHERN ARIZONA UNIV & FLAGSTAFF-CONCONINO PUB LIBRARY; 11 W CHERRY AVE; FLAGSTAFF, AZ 86001. (#463). **ARBA GRANTEE.**

INDIAN MYTHS & LEGENDS - FLAGSTAFF, AZ. THE 9TH GRADE CULTURAL ENGLISH CLASS, COMPOSED OF NATIVE AMERICAN STUDENTS, PREPARED ORIGINAL & RETOLD INDIAN MYTHS. (LOCAL). MRS M J LINDSAY, TEACHER; EAST FLAG JUNIOR HIGH SCULTURAL ENGLISH CLASS; 2250 CEDAR; FLAGSTAFF, AZ 86001. (#25094). **ARBA GRANTEE.**

NUESTRA CULTURA - FLAGSTAFF, AZ. A PILOT PROGRAM DESIGNED TO EXPOSE FLAGSTAFF ELEMENTARY STUDENTS TO THE CULTURES THAT ARE LOCATED IN NORTHERN ARIZONA. (LOCAL). GUY BENSUSAN, COORDINATOR; NORTHERN ARIZONA UNIV; PO BOX 6031; FLAGSTAFF, AZ 86001. (#25907). **ARBA GRANTEE.**

PROGRAMS FOR SENIOR CITIZENS - FLAGSTAFF, AZ. FEATURED PROGRAM INCLUDE OUR CONSTITUTION, HISTORICAL BACKGROUND AND SAFETY & PERSONAL PROTECTION. (LOCAL). CHARLOTTE L HELSEL, COORDINATOR; KAPPA DELTA PI-PONDEROSA ALUMNI CHAPTER; 401 W SILVER SPRUCE; FLAGSTAFF, AZ 86001. (#25095).

PROJECT 76 BY '76 FLAGSTAFF, AZ. LEAGUE OF WOMEN VOTERS IS COOPERATING WITH THE COUNTY RECORDER'S OFFICE IN TRYING TO REGISTER 3/4 OF THE ELIGIBLE VOTERS BY THE 1976 GENERAL EELECTION. (LOCAL). MARY J MINOR, PRESIDENT; LEAGUE OF WOMEN VOTERS OF FLAGSTAFF; PO BOX 1691; FLAGSTAFF, AZ 86001. (#19263).

RAICES Y RITMOS/ROOTS & RHYTHMS - FLAGSTAFF, AZ. BILINGUAL RADIO SERIES OF 52 ONE-HOUR 1976 SUNDAY BROADCASTS PRESENTING THE GROWTH & VARIETY OF LATIN AMERICAN MUSIC (FOLK, POPULAR, RELIGIOUS & CONCERT). BROADCAST ON KCLS, 600 KC, SUNDAY, 7-8PM. (LOCAL). GUY BENSUSAN, PROGRAM DIRECTOR; LATIN AMERICAN HUMANITIES PROGRAM; NAU BOX 6031; FLAGSTAFF, AZ 86001. (#14963). **ARBA GRANTEE.**

SECURITY RENOVATION OF THE MUSEUM OF NORTH ARIZONA. INSTALLATION OF SPECIAL SECURITY DEVICES FOR PROTECTION OF EXHIBITS AND COLLECTIONS COVERING THE COLORADO PLATEAU AREA; NEW LOCKS, OUTDOOR LIGHTING, ALARM & EMERGENCY COMMUNICATIONS SYSTEMS -NEA GRANT. (ST-WIDE). ROXINE PHILLIPPI, BUSINESS OFFICER; NORTHERN ARIZONA SOCIETY OF SCIENCE AND ART, INC; PO BOX 1389, N FORT VALLEY RD; FLAGSTAFF, AZ 86001. (#2187).

SPANISH LANGUAGE SLIDE PRESENTATION ON VOTING - AZ. SLIDE PRESENTATION ON VOTING RIGHTS AND PROCEDURES IN SPANISH FOR MEXICAN-AMERICAN CITIZENS. (LOCAL). DOYEN SALSIG, PROJ DIRECTOR; NORTHERN ARIZONA COUNCIL OF GOVERNMENTS; 428 E BIRCH; FLAGSTAFF, AZ 86001. (#15243). **ARBA GRANTEE.**

'THEY CAME TO THE MOUNTAIN', FLAGSTAFF, AZ. THE STORY OF FLAGSTAFF'S BEGINNINGS TO BE PUBLISHED IN BOOK FORM. (ST-WIDE). DOWLING CAMPBELL, CHAIRMAN; FLAGSTAFF BICENTENNIAL-CENTENNIAL COMMISSION; PO BOX 1208; FLAGSTAFF, AZ 86001. (#26047).

THORPE PARK SCIENCE AREA IN FLAGSTAFF, AZ. A POND AND ITS SURROUNDINGS WILL BE USED FOR PLANNING, DESIGNING AND OPERATING AN ONGOING NATURAL AREA WITH AN EMPHASIS ON GUIDING INTERESTED PEOPLE IN ITS TOTAL OPERATION. (LOCAL). JIM R DAVID, PROJ DIRECTOR; BIOLOGY DEPT, FLAGSTAFF JUNIOR HIGH SCHOOL; 755 N BONITO; FLAGSTAFF, AZ 86001. (#14964). **ARBA GRANTEE.**

SEPT 4 - 5, '75. NATL PK SVC 'PEOPLE OF 1776' (PILOT) VISITS FLAGSTAFF. TRAVELING TROUPE WILL BRING VARIOUS ASPECTS OF COLONIAL LIFE (MILITARY LIFE, MUSIC, CRAFTS) TO VISITORS TO THIS NATIONAL PARK SERVICE AREA. (REGN'L). SWR BICENT COORDINATOR; NATIONAL PARK SERVICE; SANTA FE, NM 87501. (#1469-205).

SEPT 28, '75 - DEC 31, '76. ARIZONA 1776-1976 DAY. 37 PANELS WITH FILMS & VIDEO TAPES DEPICTING 3 SPANISH PARTIES CROSSING ARIZONA IN 1776, THEIR INFLUENCE ON COLONIZATION OF THE SOUTHWESTERN USA & TRADITIONS CONTINUING TODAY, INDIAN-ANGLO-HISPANIC. AT UNKNOWN. (ST-WIDE). E B DANSON DIRECTOR; MUSEUM OF NORTHERN ARIZONA & HEARD MUSEUM & AZ HISTORICAL SOCIETY; PO BOX 1389; FLAGSTAFF, AZ 86001. (#776-1).

SEPT 28, '75 - DEC 31, '76. DISCUSSIONS & FILMS OF SPANISH INFLUENCE ON SOUTHWEST COLONIZATION. 37 PANELS W/FILMS & VIDEO TAPES DEPICTING 3 SPANISH PARTIES CROSSING ARIZONA IN 1776, THEIR INFLUENCE ON COLONIZATION OF SOUTHWESTERN U S & CONDITIONS CONTINUING TODAY. INCLUDES INDIANS, ANGLO & SPANISH. WILL TRAVEL THROUGHOUT THE STATE. (LOCAL). DR E B DANSON; MUSEUM OF NORTHERN ARIZONA; PO BOX 1389; FLAGSTAFF, AZ 86001. (#100135-1).

JAN 4 - DEC 26, '76. 'RAICES Y RITMOS'/'ROOTS & RYTHMS: LATIN AMERICAN MUSIC RADIO SERIES. BILINGUAL RADIO SERIES (SPANISH & ENGLISH) ON MUSIC OF LATIN AMERICA (FOLK, POPULAR, RELIGIOUS & CONCERT). PURPOSE: TO PRESENT & EXPLAIN FINE MUSIC, TO PROVIDE LANGUAGE PRACTICE & PROMOTE BILINGUAL EDUCATION. AT KCLS RADIO, KAXR-FM RADIO. (LOCAL). GUY BENSUSAN, CHAIRMAN; FLAGSTAFF SYMPHONY; NAU BOX 6031; FLAGSTAFF, AZ 86001. (#14964-1).

JAN - DEC '76. AMERICAN MUSICAL HERITAGE CONCERT TOURS IN ARIZONA. FREE CONCERTS THROUGHOUT AZ FEATURING WORKS BY AMERICAN COMPOSERS WITH SPECIAL EMPHASIS ON INDIAN & MEXICAN AMERICAN COMPOSERS. (ST-WIDE). THOMAS KIRSHBAUM; FLAGSTAFF SYMPHONY ORCHESTRA; P O BOX 122; FLAGSTAFF, AZ 86001. (#642-1).

MAR 22 - 23, '76. UNITED STATES ARMED FORCES BICENTENNIAL CARAVAN. CARAVAN IS COMPOSED OF EXHIBIT VANS FOR EACH MILITARY SERVICE. PROJECT THEME IS 'HISTORY OF THE ARMED FORCES AND THEIR CONTRIBUTIONS TO THE NATION'. (LOCAL). MAURICE GISS, EXEC DIR; US ARMED FORCES EXHIBIT VANS PROJECT; 1807 N CENTRAL AVE, SUITE 108; PHOENIX, AZ 85004. (#1775-337).

MAR 30 - MAY 30, '76. PUBLIC FORUMS. THIS PROJECT WILL PRESENT A SERIES OF PUBLIC FORUMS DEALING WITH BILINGUAL MULTICULTURAL EDUCATION. (LOCAL). JEAN TURNER, PROJ DIR; NAU, FLAGSTAFF PUBLIC SCHOOLS & ASSOC OF EDUCATION OF YOUNG CHILDREN; BOX 5774 NAU; FLAGSTAFF, AZ 86001. (#107257-1).

MAY 14, '76. MUSICALE AMERICANA: AMERICAN MUSIC FROM 1890 TO PRESENT. NARRATION OF EVENTS AFFECTING OUR COUNTRY & ITS MUSIC. AT FLAGSTAFF HIGH AUDITORIUM, 601 N KENDRICK. (LOCAL). DONNA SAPP, COORD; FT VALLEY MAVERICKS 4-H CLUB; PO BOX 1544; FLAGSTAFF, AZ 86001. (#108256-1).

JUNE 6 - AUG 21, '76. FLAGSTAFF SUMMER FESTIVAL PRESENTS, ARIZONA: KALEIDISCOPE OF CULTURE. THIS PROGRAM WILL ALSO BE PERFORMED AT GRAND CANYON NATIONAL PARK SOUTH RIM. THE FESTIVAL ALSO OFFERS PROGRAMS OF ART, INDIAN ARTS & CRAFTS, BALLET, THEATRE, JAZZ, CHAMBER & SYMPHONY ORCHESTRA & POPS, COUNTRY & WESTERN AND FILM CLASSIC FESTIVAL - 76 JUNE 6 THRU AUG 21. AT FLAGSTAFF SUMMER FESTIVAL, INC. (LOCAL). C W CRAIG, MANAGING DIR; FLAGSTAFF SUMMER FESTIVAL,INC; PO BOX 1607; FLAGSTAFF, AZ 86001. (#4895-1).

JUNE 9 - 12, '76. HISTORY AND CULTURAL HERITAGE OF AMERICAN SOUTHWEST--SYMPOSIUM. GENERAL SUBJECTS OF SEMINARS AVAILABLE BUT DEFINITE TIME-DATES NOT SET. EVENTS TO RUN DAILY, ALL DAY. AT SOUTH CAMPUS. (ST-WIDE). DR ANDREW WALLACE; NORTHERN ARIZONA UNIV; BOX 5739, NORTHERN ARIZ UNIV; FLAGSTAFF, AZ 86001. (#547-1).

JUNE 9 - 12, '76. SOUTHWEST BICENTENNIAL CELEBRATION. SEMINAR. (ST-WIDE). DOWLING CAMPBELL; NORTHERN ARIZONA UNIVERSITY; 494 PHILOMENCE; FLAGSTAFF, AZ 86001. (#107660-1).

JUNE 12, '76. FLAGSTAFF BICENTENNIAL MASS. COMMEMORATIVE MASS & PROGRAM CELEBRATING 200TH ANNIVERSARY OF FRAY FRANCISCO GARCES, FIRST WHITE MAN TO DESCEND INTO GRAND CANYON CELEBRATED BY BISHOP OF PHOENIX AND REPRESENTATIVES FROM ALL OF ARIZONA. AT CROMER STADIUM, 1801 N IZABEL. (LOCAL). DR PAUL STASKEY, CHMN; FLAGSTAFF KNIGHTS OF COLUMBUS; 3515 E RANIER LOOP; FLAGSTAFF, AZ 86001. (#200004-16).

JUNE 25 - JULY 5, '76. 1776 BICENTENNIAL 1976 POW WOW. THE POW WOW FEATURES A PARADE, DANCES, BAZAAR AND A RODEO. IT WILL ALSO BE HELD FROM FRIDAY, JULY 2 - MONDAY, JULY 5. (LOCAL). WILLIAM E MEISNER, CHMN; FLAGSTAFF CHAMBER OF COMMERCE; 101 SANTA FE AVE; FLAGSTAFF, AZ 86001. (#103416-215).

JULY 3, '76. MEMORIES: BICENT BALLET, STEPHEN FOSTER MUSIC, ORIG CHOREOGRAPHY. BALLET FEATURED ON FULL BALLET PROGRAM, 11 TOUR PERFORMANCES IN STATE. FLAGSTAFF SUMMER FESTIVAL PERF DURING BICENTENNIAL POW-WOW. AT ARDREY AUDITORIUM, CREATIVE ARTS CENTER, NORTHERN ARIZONA UNIVERSITY. (ST-WIDE). TIMONA PITTMAN, EXEC DIR; ARIZONA BALLET THEATRE, INC; 4528 N 7TH ST; PHOENIX, AZ 85014. (#107255-7).

JULY 18, '76. FLAGSTAFF HERITAGE FASHION SHOW. LIVE PERFORMANCE AT FLAGSTAFF ART CENTER. (LOCAL). VIRGINIA DUSENBURY, COORD; FLAGSTAFF ART CENTER; NORTH FOOT VALLEY RD; FLAGSTAFF, AZ 86001. (#104657-2).

JULY 18 - 30, '76. ROBERT A TAFT INSTITUTE OF GOVERNMENT SEMINAR, TWO WEEK-SEMINAR. SEMINAR. (ST-WIDE). DR R O DAVIES, DIRECTOR; ROBERT A TAFT INSTITUTE OF GOVERNMENT SEMINAR; NORTHERN ARIZONA UNIV; FLAGSTAFF, AZ 86001. (#107254-1).

JULY 22 - 24, '76. FLAGSTAFF ART CENTER FESTIVAL. EXHIBIT, FESTIVAL AT FLAGSTAFF ART CENTER, NORTH FOOT VALLEY RD, BEHIND PIONEER MUSEUM. (ST-WIDE). ELSIE MAEHRINGER, COORD; FLAGSTAFF ART CENTER; 318 N AGASSIZ; FLAGSTAFF, AZ 86001. (#104657-1).

AUG 6 - 8, '76. MOUNTAINEER 28TH ANNUAL SQUARE & ROUND DANCE FESTIVAL. FRIDAY 8-11 PM, MULTIPLE CALLERS AND LIVE MUSIC; SAT, 9-11 AM, 'DONUT DANCE', 1-3 PM SQUARE DANCE WORKSHOP, 3-4:30 PM ROUND DANCE WORKSHOP, 4-7 PM BARBEQUE DINNER, 8 PM GRAND MARCH, 8-11 PM SQUARE DANCE; SUNDAY 9-11:30 AM 'DONUT DANCE'. AT AUG 6-7: EAST FLAGSTAFF JR HIGH SCHOOL; 8/8: NAU ELEMENTARY SCHOOL. (REGN'L). BARBARA HENDERSON, SEC; MOUNTAINEER SQUARE DANCE CLUB; 4390 N MOUNTAIN MEADOW DR; FLAGSTAFF, AZ 86001. (#108014-1).

SEPT 12, '76. 'AMERICA, THIRTEEN TO FIFTY', HISTORICAL SKIT AND DINNER. THE SKIT IS A COMEDY. THE DINNER IS A POT LUCK SUPPER WITH AN AUCTION OF HANDMADE ITEMS AND A SING ALONG OF PATRIOTIC SONGS. AT SOUTH CAMPUS BALLROOM. (LOCAL). ANN MONTGOMERY, CO-CHMN; NORTHERN ARIZONA UNIV FACULTY WIVES; 2012 N CRESCENT; FLAGSTAFF, AZ 86001. (#103065-3).

FLORENCE

FLORENCE FARMING MUSEUM - AZ. MUSEUM WILL HOUSE DISPLAYS OF EARLY AMERICAN FARMING & RANCHING IMPLEMENTS. (LOCAL). ALICE SJOBERG, COORDINATOR; PINAL COUNTY HISTORICAL SOCIETY; BOX 185; CASA GRANDE, AZ 85222. (#27022). **ARBA GRANTEE.**

OUTDOOR FARMING & MINING EQUIPMENT DISPLAY AREA-AZ. A FENCED AREA WILL BE BUILT BEHIND THE PRESENT MUSEUM TO DISPLAY EARLY FARMING AND MINING MACHINERY USED IN PINAL COUNTY. (LOCAL). ALICE SJOBERG, BICENTENNIAL COMMITTEE CHAIRMAN; PINAL COUNTY HISTORICAL SOCIETY, INC; PO BOX 851, 2201 S MAIN ST; FLORENCE, AZ 85232. (#26040).

4TH OF JULY CELEBRATION, FLORENCE, AZ. 2-DAY CELEBRATION TO INCLUDE PARADE, BARBECUE AND FIREWORKS. (LOCAL). PETE VILLA VERDE, COORDINATOR; CITY OF FLORENCE; BOX 10008; FLORENCE, AZ 85232. (#26598). **ARBA GRANTEE.**

MAR 12, '76. UNITED STATES ARMED FORCES BICENTENNIAL CARAVAN. CARAVAN IS COMPOSED OF EXHIBIT VANS FOR EACH MILITARY SERVICE. PROJECT THEME IS 'HISTORY OF THE ARMED FORCES AND THEIR CONTRIBUTIONS TO THE NATION'. (LOCAL). PETER VILLA VERDE, CHMN; US ARMED FORCES EXHIBIT VANS PROJECT; PO BOX 1008; FLORENCE, AZ 85232. (#1775-332).

JULY 3 - 4, '76. FLORENCE FOUTH OF JULY CELEBRATION - PARADE, BAR-B-Q, FIREWORKS. FESTIVAL, PARADE, EXHIBIT. (LOCAL). PETE VILLA VERDE, COORD; CITY OF FLORENCE; BOX 10008; FLORENCE, AZ 85232. (#26598-1).

FOUNTAIN HLS

JULY 2 - 4, '76. FOURTH OF JULY CELEBRATION. EXHIBIT, FESTIVAL, PARADE, LIVE PERFORMANCE AT FOUNTAIN HILLS PARK. (LOCAL). KAY KINDER, PROJ DIRECTOR; BICENTENNIAL FOURTH OF JULY CELEBRATION DIRECTORS; 170340 E CALLE DEL ORO; SCOTTSDALE, AZ 85268. (#105128-1).

FREDONIA

BEAUTIFICATION PROJECT IN FREDONIA, AZ. CURBS AND GUTTERS WILL BE BUILT ALONG THE TOWN'S MAIN STREET AND A TOWN SQUARE WILL BE CONSTRUCTED. (LOCAL). ALLEN M JUDD, PROJ MANAGER; FREDONIA TOWN AND STATE DEPARTMENT OF TRANSPORTATION; PO BOX 234; FREDONIA, AZ 86022. (#14259).

RESTORATION OF OLD MERCANTILE, FREDONIA, AZ. CITIZENS OF FREDONIA ARE RESTORING THE OLD HISTORIC JENSEN & BROOKSBY MERCANTILE. IT WILL PROVIDE SPACE TO DISPLAY THE MANY LOCAL HISTORIC ARTIFACTS THAT MAKE THIS COMMUNITY'S HISTORY SO EXCITING. (LOCAL). ALLEN M JUDD, CHAIRMAN; FREDONIA BICENTENNIAL COMMITTEE; PO BOX 234; FREDONIA, AZ 86022. (#14758). **ARBA GRANTEE.**

FT HUACHUCA

FT HUACHUCA, AZ, BICENTENNIAL CELEBRATION. FT HUACHUCA ARMY POST WILL STAGE EXTENSIVE PROGRAM OF BICENTENNIAL ACTIVITIES INCLUDING HISTORICAL PAGAENTS, REUNIONS OF REGIMENTS, AND PUBLICATION OF THE HISTORY OF THE FORT. (ST-WIDE). CORNELIUS SMITH, ASST TO THE COMMANDER; HEADQUARTERS FT HUACHUCA ARIZONA; FT HUACHUCA, AZ 85613. (#734).

JUNE 10 - 14, '75. 200TH ANNIVERSARY OF THE US ARMY-CELEBRATION, PAGEANTS, REUNIONS. FT HUACHUCA ARMY POST WILL STAGE EXTENSIVE PROGRAM OF BICENTENNIAL ACTIVITIES INCLUDING HISTORICAL PAGAENTS, REUNIONS OF REGIMENTS, AND PUBLICATION OF THE HISTORY OF THE FORT. (ST-WIDE). CORNELIUS SMITH; FT. HUACHUCA ARMY POST; HEADQUARTERS; FT. HUACHUCA, AZ 85613. (#734-1).

FT MCDOWELL

OCT 15, '76. CULTURE AND HISTORY OF YAVAPAI INDIANS IN ARIZONA. EXHIBIT DEPICTING MODERN AND ANCIENT HISTORY AND CULTURE OF YAVAPAI INDIANS IN ARIZONA. AT FT MCDOWELL, YAVAPAI RESERVATION, AZ. (LOCAL). DR SIGRID KHERA, COORD; ARIZONA STATE UNIV; DEPT OF ANTHRO, AZ ST UNIV; TEMPE, AZ 85281. (#27020-1).

GILA BEND

GILA BEND SOUTHERN PACIFIC RAILROAD DEPOT, AZ. FIRST RAILROAD COMPLETED INTO GILA BEND IN 1879. THE DEPOT BUILT SHORTLY AFTERWARDS NOW STANDS AS THE OLDEST OPERATING DEPOT IN SOUTH WESTERN AZ, STRUCTURE IS TO BE RESTORED AS A HISTORIC LANDMARK. (LOCAL). HOWARD HADLEY, PRESIDENT; BERNARD GILLESPIE HISTORICAL SOCIETY OF GILA BEND; PO BOX 766; GILA BEND, AZ 85337. (#24038). **ARBA GRANTEE.**

GLEN CANYON

JUNE 1 - SEPT 1, '75. DEMONSTRATIONS OF NAVAJO LIFE AT GLEN CANYON NRA. ALSO IN 1976. VISITORS CAN WATCH DEMONSTRATIONS OF VARIOUS ASPECTS OF NAVAJO LIFE--CONSTRUCTION & USE OF A HOGAN, COOKING, WEAVING, BASKET & POTTERY MAKING. (REGN'L). SUPT GLEN CANYON NRA; NATIONAL PARK SERVICE; P.O. BOX 1507; PAGE, AZ 86040. (#6727-36).

MAY 18, '76. NATL PK SVC '...A LITTLE LOOK AROUND' VISITS GLEN CANYON NRA. THIS SHORT PROGRAM FEATURES ACTORS PORTRAYING FAMOUS AMERICANS OF THE PAST WHO'VE RETURNED TO SEE AMERICA'S GROWTH. (REGN'L). GLEN CANYON N R A; NATIONAL PARK SERVICE; P.O. BOX 1507; PAGE, AZ 86040. (#5653-59).

JUNE 1 - SEPT 1, '76. DEMONSTRATIONS OF NAVAJO LIFE AT GLEN CANYON NRA. VISITORS CAN WATCH DEMONSTRATIONS OF VARIOUS ASPECTS OF NAVAJO LIFE INCLUDING CONSTRUCTION & USE OF A HOGAN, COOKING, WEAVING, BASKET & POTTERY MAKING. (REGN'L). GLEN CANYON NATL REC AREA; NATIONAL PARK SERVICE; P.O. BOX 1507; PAGE, AZ 86040. (#6727-536).

JULY 23, '76. NATL PK SVC 'PEOPLE OF 1776' PLAYS AT GLEN CANYON NRA. TRAVELING TROUPE WILL BRING VARIOUS ASPECTS OF COLONIAL LIFE (MILITARY LIFE, MUSIC, CRAFTS) TO VISITORS TO THIS NATIONAL PARK SERVICE AREA. (REGN'L). GLEN CANYON NATL REC AREA; NATIONAL PARK SERVICE; P.O. BOX 1507; PAGE, AZ 86040. (#1469-10).

GLENDALE

OCT 4 - 19, '75. GLENDALE BICENTENNIAL FESTIVAL OF THE ARTS. FESTIVAL, LIVE PERFORMANCE AT CITYWIDE. (LOCAL). CAROLYN MAYBERRY; GLENDALE BICENTENNIAL COMMITTEE; 4029 W SAN MIGUEL; GLENDALE, AZ 85019. (#50704-1).

NOV 8 - 9, '75. THUNDERBIRD INVITATIONAL BALLOON RACE. HOT AIR BALLOONS WILL RACE TO BENEFIT THE SCHOLARSHIP FUND OF AGSIM; AWARDS WILL BE MADE AT PILOTS BRUNCH - MALCOLM FORBES, PUBLISHER OF 'FORBES' MAGAZINE WILL BE THE GUEST SPEAKER; THE ENTIRE PROJECT PUT ON BY VOLUNTEERS WITH AID OF SCHOOL ADMINISTRATORS & STUDENTS. AT THUNDERBIRD CAMPUS OF AGSIM, 59 AVE & GREENWOOD RD, GLENDALE. (LOCAL). DORIS PAINE, CHAIRMAN; FRIENDS OF THUNDERBIRD; 6112 E MOCKINGBIRD LANE; PARADISE VLY, AZ 85253. (#17821-1).

DEC 6 - 7, '76. UNITED STATES ARMED FORCES BICENTENNIAL CARAVAN. CARAVAN IS COMPOSED OF EXHIBIT VANS FOR EACH MILITARY SERVICE. PROJECT THEME IS 'HISTORY OF THE ARMED FORCES & THEIR CONTRIBUTIONS TO THE NATION'. (LOCAL). LINDA PEDERSON; UNITED STATES ARMED FORCES BICENTENNIAL CARAVAN; PO 1556, CITY OF GLENDALE; GLENDALE, AZ 85301. (#1775-852).

GLOBE

PRESERVATION OF SECOND GILA COUNTY COURTHOUSE - AZ. PRESERVATION OF EXTERIOR OF HISTORIC COURTHOUSE BUILT IN 1888 IN THE OLD MINING COMMUNITY OF GLOBE. (ST-WIDE). MRS W E BISHOP, CHAIRMAN; GLOBE BICENTENNIAL COMMITTEE; 211 5 3RD ST; GLOBE, AZ 85501. (#4604). **ARBA GRANTEE.**

TWO BITS, ARIZONA - OLD WEST TOWN. LOCAL CITIZENS IN GLOBE AREA ARE CONSTRUCTING AN OLD STYLE WESTERN TOWN WITH AUTHENTIC BUILDING MATERIALS. (LOCAL). GUY ANDERSON, CHAIRMAN; GLOBE-MIAMI VIGILANTES; PO BOX 171; GLOBE, AZ 85501. (#5396). **ARBA GRANTEE.**

JAN 1, '76 - DEC 31, '77. BICENT AUDIO-VISUAL PROGRAMS AT TONTO NM. FILMS ON SEVERAL BICENTENNIAL TOPICS AS WELL AS OTHER FILMS ON AREAS OF OUR NATIONAL PARK SYSTEM ARE AVAILABLE FOR SHOWING TO LOCAL GROUPS. (REGN'L). TONTO NM; NATIONAL PARK SERVIE; ROOSEVELT, AZ 85545. (#6730-127).

FEB 20 - 21, '76. UNITED STATES ARMED FORCES BICENTENNIAL CARAVAN. CARAVAN IS COMPOSED OF EXHIBIT VANS FOR EACH MILITARY SERVICE. PROJECT THEME IS 'HISTORY OF THE ARMED FORCES AND THEIR CONTRIBUTIONS TO THE NATION'. (LOCAL). MRS MARIAN BISHOP, CHMN; US ARMED FORCES EXHIBIT VANS PROJECT; 211 S 3RD ST; GLOBE, AZ 85501. (#1775-322).

MAY 13 - 14, '76. NATL PK SVC '...A LITTLE LOOK AROUND' VISITS TONTO NATL MON. THIS SHORT PROGRAM FEATURES ACTORS PORTRAYING FAMOUS AMERICANS OF THE PAST WHO'VE RETURNED TO SEE AMERICA'S GROWTH. (REGN'L). TONTO NATL MON; NATIONAL PARK SERVICE; P.O. BOX 707; ROOSEVELT, AZ 85545. (#5653-55).

JULY 4, '76. JULY 4TH CELEBRATION. FESTIVAL AT GILA COUNTY COURTHOUSE. (LOCAL). DONNA ANDERSON; GILA CENTENNIALS, INC; PO BOX 2539; GLOBE, AZ 85501. (#107667-1).

JULY 18 - 24, '76. ARTISTS-IN-THE-PARKS EXHIBIT VISITS TONTO NM. THIS ART EXHIBIT CONSISTS OF 21 ORIGINAL PAINTINGS, EACH OF WHICH IS IDENTIFIED WITH PERSONS, PLACES, OR EVENTS OF THE AMER REVOLUTION. (REGN'L). TONTO NM; NATIONAL PARK SERVICE; ROOSEVELT, AZ 85545. (#1474-20).

SEPT 10 - 19, '76. GILA'S CENTENNIAL FESTIVAL. COUNTY FAIR 9/16-18; PARADE 9/11; RODEO 9/17-19; PAGEANT 9/15-19; CENTENNIAL BALL 9/11; APACHE INDIAN DAY 9/18. AT FAIR GROUNDS TRAILER FACILITIES AT INDUSTRIAL PARK. (LOCAL). MARIAN BISHOP; GILA CENTENNIALS INC; 211 SOUTH THIRD ST; GLOBE, AZ 85501. (#4604-1).

NOV 28 - DEC 4, '76. STUDENT ARTISTS EXHIBIT VISITS TONTO NM. ART EXHIBIT CONSISTS OF 18 ORIGINAL PAINTINGS SELECTED FROM ENTRIES IN A NATIONWIDE STUDENT ART CONTEST; EACH PAINTING IS IDENTIFIED WITH PERSONS, PLACES OR EVENTS OF THE AMERICAN REVOLUTIN. AT ART BARN, HIGHWAY 60, CLAYPOOL AZ. (REGN'L). TONTO NM; NATIONAL PARK SERVICE; ROOSEVELT, AZ 85545. (#1474-19).

GRAND CANYON

MAR 3, '76. 'UP WITH PEOPLE' YOUNG PEOPLE SINGING AND DANCING. UP WITH PEOPLE IS A NON-PROFIT, EDUCATIONAL PROGRAM BASED ON THE BELIEF THAT THE WORLD'S GREATEST RESOURCE IS ITS YOUNG PEOPLE; THE LIVELY PERFORMANCE OF AN INTERNATIONAL CAST HAS AN AMERICAN BICENTENNIAL THEME. AT GRAND CANYON HIGH SCHOOL, GRAND CANYON NATIONAL PARK. (REGN'L). GRAND CANYON NP; NATIONAL PARK SERVICE; PO BOX 506; GRAND CANYON, AZ 86023. (#6728-259).

JULY 5 - 15, '76. ARTISTS-IN-THE-PARK BICENT EXHIBIT AT GRAND CANYON NP. EXHIBIT CONTAINS 21 ORIGINAL PAINTING ON PERSON, PLACES OR EVENTS OF THE AMERICAN REVOLUTION, COMMISSIONED THROUGH THE ARTISTS-IN-THEPARKS PROGRAM; BROCHURES EXPLAINING THE ORIGIN OF THE ART, ARTISTS, AND AREAS REPRESENTED WILL BE AVAILABLE TO THE VISITORS. AT SOUTH RIM VISITOR CENTER, GRAND CANYON NATIONAL PARK. (REGN'L). GRAND CANYON NP; NATIONAL PARK SERVICE; PO BOX 129; GRAND CANYON, AZ 86023. (#1474-9).

NOV 15 - 25, '76. ARTISTS-IN-THE-PARKS BICENT EXHIBIT AT GRAND CANYON NP. EXHIBIT CONTAINS 21 ORIGINAL PAINTING ON PERSONS, PLACES OR EVENTS OF THE AMERICAN REVOLUTION, COMMISSIONED THROUGH THE ARTISTS-IN-THEPARKS PROGRAM; BROCHURES EXPLAINING THE ORIGIN OF THE ART, ARTISTS, AND AREAS REPRESENTED WILL BE AVAILABLE TO THE VISITORS. AT SOUTH RIM VISITOR CENTER, GRAND CANYON NATIONAL PARK. (REGN'L). GRAND CANYON NP; NATIONAL PARK SERVICE; PO BOX 129; GRAND CANYON, AZ 86023. (#1474-10).

GUADALUPE

RENEWAL AND DEVELOPMENT OF GUADALUPE, ARIZONA. RENEWAL & DEVELOPMENT OF GUADALUPE TO ELIMINATE SUBSTANDARD HOUSING, CREATE LOCAL INDUSTRY, & BUILD A LOCAL MARKET & CULTURAL CENTER & RECEIVING ARBA GRANT FOR DEVELOPMENT OF HISTORICAL MURALS. (ST-WIDE). LAURO GARCIA, JR, EXEC DIRECTOR; GUADALUPE ORGANIZATION; 8810 S 56TH ST; GUADALUPE, AZ 85283. (#305). **ARBA GRANTEE.**

HEBER

SEPT 11, '76. COUNTY FAIR. FAIR. (ST-WIDE). JOCIE TEUNEY; TOWN OF HEBER; TAYLOR, AZ 85939. (#107654-1).

HEREFORD

CORONADO INTERNATIONAL HISTORIC PAGEANT - ARIZONA. ANNUAL HISTORIC PAGEANT THAT COMMEMORATES THE EXPEDITION OF FRANCISCO CORONADO INTO THE SOUTHWEST. PAGEANT WILL FEATURE FOLK DANCERS FROM MEXICO & ARIZONA ALSO MEXICAN & INDIAN ARTS. (INT'L). LAUREL W DALE, PROJ COORDINATOR; NATIONAL PARK SERVICE; RURAL RT 1, BOX 126; HEREFORD, AZ 85615. (#8057).

AUG 20, '75. NATL PK SVC '...A LITTLE LOOK AROUND' VISITS CORONADO NM. THIS SHORT PROGRAM FEATURES ACTORS PORTRAYING FAMOUS AMERICANS OF THE PAST WHO'VE RETURNED TO SEE AMERICA'S GROWTH. (REGN'L). SUPERINTENDENT; NATIONAL PARK SERVICE - CORONADO NATIONAL MEMORIAL; RURAL ROUTE 1, BOX 126; HEREFORD, AZ 85615. (#5653-203).

APR 25, '76. CORONADO INTERNATIONAL-HISTORICAL PAGEANT. ACTIVITIES INCLUDE PRESENTATIONS BY 11 DIFFERENT DANCE GROUPS; A PLAY 'THE GHOSTS OF CORONADO'S ENTRADA'; CEREMONIES & SPEECHES; CRAFT DEMONSTRATIONS; AND MOCK PAPAGO, APACHE & MEXICAN CAMPS ON DISPLAY. (INT'L). SUPT, CORONADO NMEM; NATIONAL PARK SERVICE & TOURISM DEPT OF SONORA; RR 1 BOX 126; HEREFORD, AZ 85615. (#8057-1).

SEPT 26, '76. CORONADO BORDERLANDS SYMPOSIUM. INCL PRESENTATIONS BY SCHOLARS FROM MEXICO & THE US; MEXICAN BARBEQUE AVAILABLE; PERFORMANCE BY BALLET FOLKLORICO DE TUCSON DE PIMA COLLEGE; CAMPFIRE DISCUSSION. (INT'L). SUPT CORONADO NMEM; NATIONAL PARK SERVICE; RR 1 BOX 126; HEREFORD, AZ 85615. (#200004-32).

HOLBROOK

BICENTENNIAL PIONEER SERIES - HOLBROOK, AZ. EARLY PIONEER CITIZENS OF THE HOLBROOK AREA WILL BE INTERVIEWED DURING THE BICENTENNIAL ERA BY A SENIOR CITIZENS ORGANIZATION. INTERVIEWS WILL BE CARRIED ON LOCAL RADIO AND IN LOCAL NEWSPAPERS. (LOCAL). MARLENE SOUNDERS, CHAIRMAN; HOLBROOK BICENTENNIAL COMMITTEE; PO BOX 776; HOLBROOK, AZ 86025. (#14771).

HOLBROOK - CLEANEST CITY ON '66 BY '76 - AZ. AN EFFORT TO CLEANUP AND KEEP HOLBROOK THE CLEANEST CITY ALONG U S HIGHWAY 66. BUSINESSES AND HOMES REPAIRED; BLOCK COMMITTEES ARE CLEANING UP STREETS. (LOCAL). MS FRANCES GREER, PROJ DIRECTOR; CHAMBER OF COMMERCE; NAVAJO BLVD; HOLBROOK, AZ 86025. (#14264).

PAINTED DESERT BICENTENNIAL CENTER - HOLBROOK, AZ. CULTURAL DISPLAY CENTER AT PETRIFIED FOREST NATIONAL PARK THAT CONTAINS TOURIST INFO ON BICENTENNIAL PROJECTS IN THE SW & ALSO HAS DISPLAYS ON EARLY PIONEER TRAVEL ROUTES & MODES OF TRANSPORTATION. (LOCAL). JON

HOLBROOK — CONTINUED

ERICKSON, PROJ DIRECTOR; PETRIFIED FOREST NATIONAL PARK; HOLBROOK, AZ 86025. (#14958).

NOV 28, '75. HOLBROOK PETRIFIED FOREST CHAMBERS 10TH ANNUAL CHRISTMAS PARADE. PARADE. (LOCAL). DAVID J DICKERSON, V-PRES; HOLBROOK PETRIFIED FOREST CHAMBER OF COMMERCE; 217 ANITA DR; HOLBROOK, AZ 86025. (#200004-15).

DEC 2 - 6, '75. 'JOHN BROWN'S BODY' THEATRICAL PRESENTATION. LIVE PERFORMANCE AT WINSLOW HIGH SCHOOL, LOS STAKE CENTER, AUDITORIUM. (LOCAL). WILLIAM A BAHRT; NORTHLAND PIONEER COLLEGE; 203 W HOPI; HOLBROOK, AZ 86025. (#104249-3).

JAN 27 - 31, '76. HASHKNIFE PONY EXPRESS MAIL RIDE. SWEARING IN OF POSTAL CARRIERS TO TAKE PLACE ON JANUARY 25TH AT HOLBROOK, AZ POST OFFICE; NAVAJO COUNTY HASHKNIFE POSSE WILL PICK UP U S MAIL AT 9 POST OFFICES IN AZ; MAIL WILL BE CARRIED 200 MILES BY HORSEBACK TO SCOTTSDALE POST OFFICE TO RE-ENACT THE PONY EXPRESS. AT NAVAJO COUNTY SHERIFF OFFICE. (ST-WIDE). MARLIN GILLESPIE, COORD; NAVAJO COUNTY SHERIFF POSSE; NAVAJO COUNTY SHERIFF'S OFFICE; HOLBROOK, AZ 86025. (#104379-6).

MAR 26, '76. UNITED STATES ARMED FORCES BICENTENNIAL CARAVAN. CARAVAN IS COMPOSED OF EXHIBIT VANS FOR EACH MILITARY SERVICE. PROJECT THEME IS 'HISTORY OF THE ARMED FORCES AND THEIR CONTRIBUTIONS TO THE NATION'. (LOCAL). MAURICE GISS, EXEC DIR; US ARMED FORCES EXHIBIT VANS PROJECT; 1807 N CENTRAL AVE, SUITE 108; PHOENIX, AZ 85004. (#1775-339).

JULY 8, '76. BIKE-A-THON. COMPETITION. (ST-WIDE). MARLENE SAUNDERS; HOLBROOK ELKS; POBOX 776; HOLBROOK, AZ 86025. (#107666-1).

JULY 22 - 23, '76. TITLE OF LIBERTY - LIVE PERFORMANCE WITH RELIGIOUS THEME. LIVE PERFORMANCE. (LOCAL). MARLENE SAUNDERS, COORD; LATTER DAY SAINTS CHURCH; PO BOX 776; HOLBROOK, AZ 86025. (#108078-1).

JEROME

COMMISSION ENTERPRISES - ARIZONA RESTORATION PROJ. A GROUP OF CRAFTSMEN WILL MAKE FURNITURE AND ACCESSORIES FOR HOMES THAT WILL BE RESTORED IN THE OLD GHOST TOWN OF JEROME. THEY WILL ALSO SELL HANDCRAFTED PRODUCTS TO GENERATE FUNDS FOR RESTORATION. (LOCAL). RICHARD MOLL, CHAIRMAN; JEROME CENTENNIAL & RESTORATION COMMISSION; BOX 928; JEROME, AZ 86331. (#4896). **ARBA GRANTEE.**

JEROME HISTORICAL MAP & ACTIVITY GUIDE, AZ. JEROME WILL PRINT A GUIDE FOR VISITORS WITH INFORMATION ON THE LOCATION AND HERITAGE OF THE PIONEER TOWN. (LOCAL). RICHARD MOLL, CHAIRMAN; JEROME BICENTENNIAL COMMITTEE; PO BOX 1976; JEROME, AZ 86331. (#14750).

RESTORATION OF HOTEL JEROME, AZ. THIS HISTORIC HOTEL BUILT IN THE EARLY 20'S WILL BE RESTORED FOR USE AS A HISTORICAL DISPLAY AREA & WILL ALSO BE THE SITE OF ARTS & CRAFTS DISPLAY & THE ANNUAL BALL. (LOCAL). RICHARD MOLL, PROJ DIRECTOR; CITY OF JEROME; BOX 928; JEROME, AZ 86331. (#14954).

SOCIETY HILL MANSION RESTORATION OF JEROME, AZ. RESTORATION OF FIFTEEN TURN-OF-THE-CENTURY VICTORIAN MANSIONS THAT ONCE HOUSED MINING COMPANY EXECUTIVES. MANSIONS WILL BECOME MUSEUMS & GUIDED TOURS WILL BE AVAILABLE TO VISITING PUBLIC. (LOCAL). RICHARD A MOLL, PRESIDENT; JEROME CENTENNIAL & RESTORATION COMMISSION; COMPANY HILL - PO BOX 1976; JEROME, AZ 86331. (#1331).

MAY 3 - 4, '75. JEROME CENTENNIAL FESTIVAL: - ARTS, CRAFTS, HISTORIC DISPLAYS. ANNUAL FESTIVAL WHICH THIS YEAR WILL KICK-OFF JEROME'S CENTENNIAL-BICENTENNIAL CELEBRATION. (LOCAL). RICHARD MOLL, CHMN; JEROME CENTENNIAL COMMISSION; BOX 928; JEROME, AZ 86331. (#6888-1).

JUNE 21 - 22, '75. JEROME VICTORIAN BALL - TO RAISE FUNDS FOR RESTORATION. CEREMONY AT JEROME CENTENNIAL & RESTORATION COMMISSION. (LOCAL). RICHARD MOLL; ARIZ BICENT COMMISSION; PO BOX 1976; JEROME, AZ 86331. (#1331-1).

KINGMAN

CAMP BEALE SPRINGS - PROJ OF KINGMAN, AZ. RESTORATION OF THE ADOBE BUILDINGS, CORRALS AND SPRINGS AT THIS HISTORIC CAVALRY CAMP NEAR KINGMAN. (LOCAL). HARRY HUGHES, PROJ DIRECTOR; CITY OF KINGMAN; 310 N 4TH ST; KINGMAN, AZ 86401. (#14956).

LITTLE RED SCHOOL HOUSE - PROJ OF KINGMAN, AZ. RESTORATION OF THE LITTLE RED SCHOOL HOUSE TO ITS ORIGINAL STATE. THIS EARLY LANDMARK WILL BE USED AS A LIBRARY & CULTURAL CENTER. (LOCAL). BETTY GROUNDS, PROJ DIRECTOR; CITY OF KINGMAN; 310 N 4TH ST; KINGMAN, AZ 86401. (#14955).

THE LITTLEST AMERICANS - CHORAL GROUP IN ARIZONA. THE LITTLEST AMERICANS IS AN ON-GOING PATRIOTIC GROUP THAT HOPES TO REVIVE PATRIOTISM IN AMERICA IN FUTURE YEARS. (LOCAL). HELEN BLACK, PRESIDENT; LITTLEST AMERICANS; BOX 230; KINGMAN, AZ 86401. (#4892). **ARBA GRANTEE.**

MOHAVE COUNTY HISTORICAL MARKERS - KINGMAN, AZ. THREE PERMANENT MARKERS ARE BEING ERECTED ALONG HIGHWAY 93 NORTH OF KINGMAN. THE MARKERS WILL NOTE THE SITE OF TWO ABANDONED MINING COMMUNITIES AND THE STILL EXISTING MINING TOWN OF CHLORIDE. (LOCAL). ROMAN MALACH, CHAIRMAN; MOHAVE COUNTY BICENTENNIAL COMMISSION; 3024 SNAVELY; KINGMAN, AZ 86401. (#16143).

MOHAVE COUNTY - SKETCHES OF EARLY DAYS. WRITTEN HISTORY OF MOHAVE COUNTY ARIZONA. (LOCAL). ROMAN MALACH, MOHAVE COUNTY HISTORIAN; MOHAVE COUNTY HISTORICAL SOCIETY; 3024 SNAVELY AVE; KINGMAN, AZ 86401. (#1805).

MOHAVE COUNTY, AZ, HISTORICAL SERIES OF BOOKS. SERIES OF HISTORICAL BOOKS RELATING TO THE DEVELOPMENT OF MOHAVE COUNTY. (LOCAL). ROMAN MALACH, CHAIRMAN; MOHAVE COUNTY BICENT COMMISSION; PO BOX 390; KINGMAN, AZ 86401. (#9227). **ARBA GRANTEE.**

MOHAVE CO, AZ, BICENT GIRLS' BASKETBALL TEAM TOUR. GIRLS' BASKETBALL TEAM FROM NORTHWEST ARIZONA TO TOUR POLAND DURING SUMMER OF 1976. (INT'L). ALAN RINGS, EXEC VICE PRESIDENT; KINGMAN AREA CHAMBER OF COMMERCE; PO BOX 1150; KINGMAN, AZ 86401. (#25818).

MOHAVE MUSEUM OF HISTORY & ARTS, ARIZONA. NEW ADDITION TO THE MOHAVE MUSEUM IN KINGMAN WILL INCLUDE DISPLAY AREAS, GIFT SHOP & STORAGE SPACE. (LOCAL). DORIS LIGHTWINE, DIRECTOR; MOHAVE PIONEERS HISTORICAL SOCIETY; BOX 1229; KINGMAN, AZ 86401. (#4908). **ARBA GRANTEE.**

PALO CHRISTI NATURE TRAIL, KINGMAN, AZ. OUTDOOR EDUCATION AREA FOR ENTIRE COMMUNITY. SECTIONS ON GEOLOGY, FAUNA, FLORA, AND INDIAN CULTURES OF STATE. SELF-GUIDED OR STUDENT GUIDED TOURS, FREE OF CHARGE. (LOCAL). SHARON HACKLEY, PROJ COORDINATOR; PALO CHRISTI SCHOOL; 500 MAPLE ST; KINGMAN, AZ 86401. (#25819).

PALO CHRISTI TIME CAPSULE, KINGMAN, AZ. TIME CAPSULE TO CONTAIN INFORMATION ABOUT PRESENT AND PAST EVENTS AND LIFE IN KINGMAN TO BE OPENED IN 2076. (LOCAL). JAMES LEONARD, PRINCIPAL; PALO CHRISTI ELEMENTARY SCHOOL; 500 MAPLE ST; KINGMAN, AZ 86401. (#26045).

RENOVATION OF THE BONNELLI HOUSE - KINGMAN, AZ. THIS HISTORIC HOME BUILT IN THE 1880'S IS BEING REMODELED & WILL BECOME A MUSEUM. (LOCAL). BETTY GROUNDS, PROJ DIRECTOR; CITY OF KINGMAN; 310 N 4TH ST; KINGMAN, AZ 86401. (#14953).

MAR '75. MOHAVE COUNTY ART & ESSAY CONTEST. SCHOOL CHILDREN IN MOHAVE COUNTY WILL PARTICIPATE IN A BICENTENNIAL ART & ESSAY CONTEST. SUBJECTS WILL BE RELATED TO LOCAL HISTORY. (LOCAL). ROMAN MALACH, CHAIRMAN; MOHAVE COUNTY BICENTENNIAL COMMITTEE; 3024 SNAVELY; KINGMAN, AZ 86401. (#4898-1).

FEB 9, '76. UNITED STATES ARMED FORCES BICENTENNIAL CARAVAN. CARAVAN IS COMPOSED OF EXHIBIT VANS FOR EACH MILITARY SERVICE. PROJECT THEME IS 'HISTORY OF THE ARMED FORCES AND THEIR CONTRIBUTIONS TO THE NATION'. (LOCAL). HARRY HUGHES, CHMN; US ARMED FORCES EXHIBIT VANS PROJECT; 2011 SUNSET BLVD; KINGMAN, AZ 86401. (#1775-318).

JUNE 24 - 27, '76. ARIZONA AMERICAN LEGION CONVENTION. CONFERENCE AT 3RD & OAK STS. (ST-WIDE). JOE WHALEN, COMMANDER; KINGMAN AMERICAN LEGION POST #14; 4175 HIGHWAY 68; KINGMAN, AZ 86401. (#103855-1).

OCT 7, '76. ANDY DEVINE BIRTHDAY CELEBRATION. EXHIBIT AT NEW WING. (LOCAL). DORIS LIGHTWINE; MOHAVE PIONEERS HISTORICAL SOCIETY; 400 W BEALE ST; KINGMAN, AZ 86401. (#107657-1).

APR 11 - 15, '77. NATURE TRAIL WEEK. TOURS, PROGRAMS, OUTDOOR EDUCATIONAL ACTIVITIES TO BE CONDUCTED. (LOCAL). SHARON HACKLEY, COORD; PALO CHRISTI SCHOOL; 500 MAPLE ST; KINGMAN, AZ 86401. (#25819-1).

LAKE HAVASU

AVENUE OF FLAGS, LAKE HAVASU, AZ. 106 AMERICAN FLAGS FLY ALONG THE MAIN BOULEVARD TO THE FAMOUS LONDON BRIDGE. (LOCAL). BARBARA HALE, COORDINATOR; SOROPTIMIST CLUB; PO BOX 707; LAKE HAVASU, AZ 86403. (#26995). **ARBA GRANTEE.**

BICENTENNIAL FLAG PROJECT - AZ. LARGE BICENTENNIAL FLAG RAISED OVER LONDON BRIDGE. (LOCAL). ART DION, CHAIRMAN; LK HAVASU CITY BICENTENNIAL COMMITTEE; PO BOX 707; LK HAVASU CY, AZ 86403. (#31769).

BICENTENNIAL SCRAPBOOK - AZ. COMPOSED OF ARTICLES PERTAINING TO ALL BICENTENNIAL ACTIVITIES IN LAKE HAVASU CITY. BOOK TO BE DONATED TO L H C HISTORICAL SOCIETY TO BE PRESERVED WITH OTHER HISTORICAL RECORDS OF COMMUNITY. (LOCAL). JUANITA PRINCE, COORINATOR; LAKE HAVASU CITY BICENTENNIAL COMMITTEE; 1992 MCCULLOCH BLVD; LK HAVASU CY, AZ 86403. (#31763).

CHARLES HEALD FLAGPOLE - AZ. TRIBUTE TO CHARLES HEALD WHO HAS GIVEN HIS TIME TOWARD THE CREATION OF A CIVIC CENTER FOR LAKE HAVASU CITY. (LOCAL). CARL EDENLOFER, COORDINATOR; YOUTH BICENTENNIAL COMMITTEE; PO BOX 999; LK HAVASU CY, AZ 86403. (#31765).

HAVASU, AZ, BICENTENNIAL DOLLAR. A COPPER COIN COMMEMORATING THE LONDON BRIDGE IN ARIZONA AND THE AMERICAN BICENTENNIAL WILL BE USED AS A TRADE DOLLAR AND COLLECTOR'S ITEM. (LOCAL). ARTHUR TUBERMAN, PROJ DIRECTOR; LONDON BRIDGE ROTARY CLUB; BOX 549; LAKE HAVASU, AZ 86403. (#19265).

LAKE HAVASU CITY CENTER, AZ. FACILITIES FOR COMMUNITY ADMINISTRATION, CULTURAL ACTIVITIES, CONVENTIONS TO AID THE CITY'S ECONOMY. PROVIDE A PLACE FOR MEETINGS. CREATE A LASTING ATTRACTION FOR VISITORS. (LOCAL). ROGER JOHNSON, COORDINATOR; BICENTENNIAL COMMITTEE; PO BOX 707; LK HAVASU CT, AZ 86403. (#31764).

LAKE HAVASU CITY HISTORICAL PARK - AZ. AN INVENTORY OF 'WORTH PRESERVING BUILDINGS' WILL BE MADE, SELECTION OF 2 DOZEN BUILDINGS. THOSE SELECTED WILL BE MOVED TO SITE OF PARK. (LOCAL). ROGER JOHNSON, COORDINATOR; BICENTENNIAL COMMITTEE; PO BOX 707; LK HAVASU CY, AZ 86403. (#31766).

LAKE HAVASU HIGH SCHOOL TOUR OF PHOENIX. ONE OR MORE MEMBERS OF EACH BRAHCH OF GOVERNMENT, PLUS LOBBYISTS, WILL TAKE TO THE YOUTH GROUP ON APRIL 8, 1976. THERE WILL ALSO BE AN APRIL 7TH TOUR OF ARIZONA STATE UNIV & THE ARIZONA REPUBLIC. (LOCAL). PAT HOLT, CHAIRMAN; REPUBLICAN WOMEN OF LAKE HAVASU CITY; 1645 MESQUITE RD, PO BOX 999; LAKE HAVASU, AZ 86403. (#26671). **ARBA GRANTEE.**

LAKE HAVASU HISTORICAL SOCIETY - AZ. COLLECTING HISTORICAL MATERIAL, DOCUMENTS & OTHER MEMORABILIA OF HAVASU CITY. (LOCAL). ROGER JOHNSON, CHAIRMAN; BICENTENNIAL COMMITTEE; PO BOX 707; LK HAVASU CY, AZ 86403. (#31770).

LK HAVASU CITY YOUTH BICENTENNIAL COMMITTEE - AZ. A BICENTENNIAL COMMITTEE IS BEING SET UP FOR YOUTH, WITH THE SAME FORMAT AS THE SENIOR COMMITTEE. (LOCAL). JERRY HOLT, COORDINATOR; BICENTENNIAL COMMITTEE; 1645 MESQUITE; LK HAVASU CY, AZ 86403. (#31768).

UNDERWATER EXPLORATION OF HISTORIC SITES - AZ. AN EXTENSIVE RESEARCH TO LEARN ABOUT TWO HISTORIC SITES WHICH IN THE 1860'S PLAYED A ROLE IN THE DEVELOPMENT OF MOHAVE COUNTY. (LOCAL). ART DION, COORDINATOR; BICENTENNIAL COMMITTEE; PO BOX M07; LK HAVASU CY, AZ 86403. (#31767).

OCT 3 - 12, '75. BICENTENNIAL LONDON BRIDGE DAYS. COMBINE ENGLISH ASPECT OF THE BICENTENNIAL ERA WITH CULTURES THAT EXISTED IN ARIZONA & SOUTHWEST FROM 1750 TO 1850 AD, NAMELY INDIAN MEXICAN SPANISH FRONIERSMEN. AT WHOLE TOWN. (LOCAL). MILLARD DRANDT, COORD; CHAMBER OF COMMERCE; PO BOX 707; LAKE HAVASU, AZ 86403. (#200004-23).

JAN 19, '76. FILM ON HISTORY OF UNCLE SAM. FILM NARRATED BY E G MARSHALL, PHOTOGRAPHED IN TOWNS & COUNTRYSIDE WHERE REAL UNCLE SAM LIVED & DIED. AT CHURCHES & SCHOOLS. (LOCAL). THOMAS BARNHART JR, COORD; LAKE HAVASU CITY BOARD OF REALTORS; PO BOX 999; LAKE HAVASU, AZ 86403. (#200004-24).

FEB 7 - 8, '76. UNITED STATES ARMED FORCES BICENTENNIAL CARAVAN. CARAVAN IS COMPOSED OF EXHIBIT VANS FOR EACH MILITARY SERVICE. PROJECT THEME IS 'HISTORY OF THE ARMED FORCES AND THEIR CONTRIBUTIONS TO THE NATION'. (LOCAL). ART DION, CHMN; US ARMED FORCES EXHIBIT VANS PROJECT; 2010 MCCULLOCH BLVD; LAKE HAVASU C, AZ 86403. (#1775-317).

FEB 28, '76. ESSAY ON AMERICANISM. ANY STUDENT ELIGIBLE TO WRITE ESSAY, THEN READ TO ENGLISH CLASS ON AMERICANISM & HOW IT RELATES TO THE CONSTITUTION & DAILY LIFE. CLASS FINALISTS WILL BE 2 SENIORS, 1 JUNIOR, 1 SOPHOMORE & 1 FRESHMAN FROM FINALISTS. WINNERS RECEIVE $500 1ST PRIZE, $250 2ND & $125 3RD. AT LAKE HAVASU CITY HIGH SCHOOL, 2675 PALOVERDE, AMPLE FREE PARKING. (LOCAL). JERRY HOLT, COORDINATOR; BICENTENNIAL COMMITTEE; 1645 MESQUITE; LAKE HAVASU, AZ 86403. (#200004-22).

MAY 1, '76. LOYALTY DAY. SPEAKERS: ROMAN MALACH, MISS VICKI HOLT'S ESSAY ON AMERICANISM, JERRY HOLT ON LOYALTY DAY. ENTERTAINMENT: LAKE HAVASU BAND OF KNIGHTS, VFW COLOR GUARD FLAG CEREMONIES. AT UNDER LONDON BRIDGE PARKING AT ENGLISH VILLAGE. (LOCAL). EDWARD N KELLEY, CMDR; AMERICAN LEGION POST 81; 2180 LAKE DR; LAKE HAVASU, AZ 86403. (#107251-1).

JULY 3 - 4, '76. LAKE HAVASU CITY 4TH OF JULY CELEBRATION. DEDICATION OF AVENUE OF FLAGS, SPECIAL MATINEE, CINEMA ICE CREAM SOCIAL, BAND CONCERT, GIANT BIRTHDAY CAKE, MASS WORSHIP SERVICE, PANCAKE BREAKFAST, PARADE, COMMUNITY PICNIC WITH GAMES, BOAT PARADE & FIREWORKS. AT WHOLE TOWN. (LOCAL). PAT HOLT, CHAIRMAN; BICENTENNIAL COMMITTEE; 1645 MESQUITE; LAKE HAVASU, AZ 86403. (#200004-27).

JULY 4, '76. FIRST ANNUAL COMMUNITY FIREWORKS DISPLAY. LIVE PERFORMANCE, EXHIBIT AT AZ STATE BEACH & AZ STATE PARKS. (LOCAL). TERRY W SMITH, CHAIRMAN; LAKE HAVASU CITY JAYCEES; 3316 KIOWA; LAKE HAVASU, AZ 86403. (#200004-26).

AUG 1 - NOV 2, '76. '76 IN '76' - VOTER REGISTRATION DRIVE. EFFORT TO PUSH GREATER VOTER TURNOUT FOR PRIMARY & GENERAL ELECTION. AT WHOLE TOWN. (LOCAL). JOE SOLDWEDEL, COORD; LAKE HAVASU CITY HERALD; 296 CRYSTAL PLAZA; LAKE HAVASU, AZ 86403. (#200004-29).

SEPT 24 - 26, '76. LAKE HAVASU CB'ERS ANNUAL JAMBOREE. FESTIVAL AT NAUTICAL INN, 17 MI OFF OF I-40. (ST-WIDE). MARY ELLEN MONTGOMERY; LAKE HAVASU CB CLUB; PO BOX 582; LAKE HAVASU, AZ 86403. (#105728-1).

OCT 1 - 10, '76. LONDON BRIDGE DAYS. COMPETITION, FESTIVAL, PARADE AT LONDON BRIDGE. (LOCAL). JERRY FONAROW, COORD; LAKE HAVASU CITY CHAMBER OF COMMERCE; 8899 BEVERLY BLVD; LOS ANGELES, CA 90048. (#103416-638).

OCT 4 - 5, '76. LONDON BRIDGE COSTUME CONTEST. COSTUME STYLE SHOWS FOR CONVENTIONS, TOURS & LOCAL CLUBS ALL DURING THE YEAR, PLUS THE BIG CONTEST ONCE A YEAR. AT LONDON BRIDGE, AMPLE FREE PARKING. (LOCAL). ELROSE DUSSAULT; WESTERN WELCOME COMMUNITY CLUB; 2115 MCCULLOCH BLVD; LAKE HAVASU, AZ 86403. (#200004-28).

LAKE HAVASU — CONTINUED

OCT 5, '76. BICENTENNIAL QUEEN CONTEST. THE ONLY REQUIREMENT: 60 YEARS OF AGE. AT LONDON BRIDGE. (ST-WIDE). RICK KNEIDING, COORD; LAKE HAVASU CITY JAYCEES; 166 ACACIA LN; LAKE HAVASU, AZ 86403. (#200004-30).

JAN '77. COUNCIL OF CITIES. 3 DAY MEETING WILL SEEK WAYS TO PROMOTE TOURISM, INDUSTRIAL DEVELOPMENT & IMPROVE COOPERATION BETWEEN COMMUNITIES. AT LAKE HAVASU HIGH SCHOOL AUDITORIUM, MOHAVE COMMUNITY COLLEGE. (REGN'L). PATRICIA CREASON, CHMN; LAKE HAVASU CITY CHAMBER OF COMMERCE; PO BOX 707; LAKE HAVASU, AZ 86403. (#109502-1).

LITCHFIELD PK

LITCHFIELD PARK, AZ, BICENTENNIAL CELEBRATION. TWO DAY BICENTENNIAL CELEBRATION, INCLUDING FESTIVAL & PARADE ON JULY 3 & 4, 1976. (LOCAL). THOMAS E ROHRER, CHAIRMAN; LITCHFIELD PARK BICENTENNIAL COMMITTEE; BOX 1402; LITCHFIELD PK, AZ 85340. (#27375). **ARBA GRANTEE.**

JULY 3 - 4, '76. LITCHFIELD PARK BICENTENNIAL CELEBRATION. FESTIVAL, PARADE. (LOCAL). THOMAS E ROHRER, CHAIRMAN; LITCHFIELD PARK BICENTENNIAL COMMITTEE; BOX 1402; LITCHFIELD PK, AZ 85340. (#108182-1).

LUKE AFB

58 TACTICAL FIGHTER TRAINING WING, LUKE AFB, AZ. 5 USA FIGHTER AIRCRAFT PLACED ON STATIC DISPLAY; CONSTRUCTED BICENTENNIAL USING 11776 USED TIRES; BASE BEAUTIFICATION USING RED, WHITE AND BLUE PAINT SCHEMES; BEGAN WORK TOWARD OPENING FRANK LUKE MUSEUM. (NAT'L). CAPT MICHAEL E HEEMAN, CHIEF-INFORMATION DIVISION; 58TH TACTICAL FIGHTER TRAINING WING; LUKE AFB, AZ 85309. (#31025).

APR 30 - MAY 2, '76. ANNUAL CONVENTION OF ARIZONA MILITARY RESERVE OFFICERS. 7:00 PM FRI-RALLY; REG, 8:00 AM AT OFFICERS CLUB; WELCOME BY COL KIMES, BASE COMMANDER; LUNCH, SPEECH & TOUR F-15 STAT DISPLAY BY GEN HAEFFNER, WING CMDR; 6:30 PRESS RECPT; BANQUET & SPEECH, BICENT SKIT BY LTC DAVIS AND DANCE IN EVENING. AT OFFICERS OPEN MESS. (ST-WIDE). COL CHARLES MCKINNIS, DIR; DEPT OF ARIZONA RESERVE OFFICER ASSN OF THE UNITED STATES; 15825 110TH AVE; SUN CITY, AZ 85351. (#107253-1).

NOV 6, '76. LUKE DAY OPEN HOUSE. EXHIBIT, LIVE PERFORMANCE. (LOCAL). CAPT MIKE HEENAN; 58TH TACTICAL FIGHTER TRAINING WING; LUKE AFB, AZ 85309. (#200004-31).

MAMMOTH

MAMMOTH, AZ, BICENTENNIAL-CENTENNIAL CELEBRATION. 4 DAY CELEBRATION WITH: PARADE, FIREWORKS, ENTERTAINMENT, DANCING, QUEEN CORONATION, BBQ, GAMES & FOOD BOOTHS. (LOCAL). JOAQUIN F MARQUEZ, CHAIRMAN; TOWN OF MAMMOTH BICENTENNIAL COMMITTEE; PO BOX 606; MAMMOTH, AZ 85618. (#26597). **ARBA GRANTEE.**

MAY 28 - 31, '76. BICENTENNIAL-CENTENNIAL CELEBRATION. PARADE, FIREWORKS, ENTERTAINMENT, DANCING, QUEEN CORONATION, BBQ, GAMES & FOOD BOOTHS. (LOCAL). JOAQUIN F MARQUEZ, CHMN; TOWN OF MAMMOTH BICENTENNIAL COMMITTEE; PO BOX 606; MAMMOTH, AZ 85618. (#26597-1).

MAY 31, '76. DEDICATION OF SWIMMING POOL. CEREMONY, COMPETITION AT 5TH ST WEST OF HWY 77, SAN PEDRO VALLEY PARK. (LOCAL). ISABEL BALLARD, SECRETARY; TOWN OF MAMMOTH BICENTENNIAL COMMITTEE; PO BOX 606; MAMMOTH, AZ 85618. (#108246-1).

MEADVIEW

ASSEMBLING PICTURES - PROJ OF MEADVIEW, AZ. PICTURES OF LOCAL HOMES, RESIDENTS AND BUSINESSES WILL BE ASSEMBLED TO BE INSERTED IN BOUND VOLUMES OF THE MEADVIEW MONITOR. (LOCAL). HENRY WILSON, CHAIRMAN; MEADVIEW CIVIC ASSOC; BOX 2480, MEADVIEW RTE; DOLAN SPRINGS, AZ 86441. (#17812).

COMPILATION OF MEADVIEW, AZ, HISTORY. ALL ISSUES OF THE MEADVIEW MONITOR WILL BE ASSEMBLED INTO TWO BOUND VOLUMES. (LOCAL). HENRY WILSON, CHAIRMAN; MEADVIEW CIVIC ASSOC; BOX 2480, MEADVIEW RTE; DOLAN SPRINGS, AZ 86441. (#17811). **ARBA GRANTEE.**

GARDEN OF NATIVE PLANTS - PROJ OF MEADVIEW, AZ. PERMANENT GARDEN AT THE CIVIC CENTER WITH NATIVE CACTI, SCHRUBS AND TREES. (LOCAL). HENRY WILSON, CHAIRMAN; MEADVIEW CIVIC ASSOC; BOX 2480, MEADVIEW RTE; DOLAN SPRINGS, AZ 86441. (#17810).

JUNE 1 - JULY 4, '76. MEADVIEW HISTORICAL FESTIVAL. THE FESTIVAL WILL EXHIBIT OLD COPIES OF THE MEADVIEW MONITOR, PICTURES OF THE RESIDENTS AND THEIR HOMES, LOCAL SHRUBS AND TREES, AND HISTORICAL LANDMARKS. THERE WILL BE AWARDS GIVEN. AT MEADVIEW CIVIC CENTER. (LOCAL). HENRY W WILSON, DIRECTOR; MEADVIEW CIVIC ASSOCIATION; BOX 2480, MEADVIEW RD; DOLAN SPRINGS, AZ 86441. (#103065-1).

JULY 3, '76. ARTS & CRAFTS SHOW & SALE. EXHIBIT, FESTIVAL AT MEADVIEW CIVIC CENTER. (LOCAL). HENRY W WILSON; MEADVIEW CIVIC ASSOC; BOX 2480, MEADVIEW RT; DOLAN SPRINGS, AZ 86441. (#108446-2).

JULY 3, '76. DEDICATION CEREMONY FOR HISTORICAL MONUMENT, 'LOST BASIN'. THE MONUMENT TO BE DEDICATED IS 'LOST BASIN'. (LOCAL). HENRY W WILSON, CHMN; MEADVIEW CIVIC ASSOCIATION; BOX 2480, MEADVIEW RTE; DOLAN SPRINGS, AZ 86441. (#103065-2).

MESA

HISTORY OF THE MESA PUBLIC SCHOOLS, AZ. STUDENTS WILL COLLECT, WRITE & ILLUSTRATE THE HISTORY OF THE MESA PUBLIC SCHOOLS. (LOCAL). JEANNETTE S ROGERS, TEACHER; MESA PUBLIC SCHOOLS; 549 N STAPLEY; MESA, AZ 85203. (#20216). **ARBA GRANTEE.**

IDENTIFYING MESA'S EARLY BUILDINGS, MESA, AZ. HISTORIC MARKERS WILL DESIGNATE EARLY AND HISTORIC STRUCTURES IN MESA. (LOCAL). MIKE LEE, PROJ DIRECTOR; CITY OF MESA; PO BOX 1466; MESA, AZ 85201. (#20695). **ARBA GRANTEE.**

JOHN P HALE BRANDING IRON COLLECTION, MESA, AZ. PURCHASE OF JOHN P HALE BRANDING IRON COLLECTION, WHICH INCLUDES OVER 400 IRONS. TO BE ON DISPLAY AT LOCAL MUSEUM. (LOCAL). MELVIN FROST, CHAIRMAN; MESA HISTORICAL & ARCHEOLOGICAL SOCIETY; 253 N FRAER DR; MESA, AZ 85203. (#20215).

FEB 28, '76. DEDICATION AND OFFICIAL OPENING OF MESA'S FIRST SCHOOLHOUSE. CEREMONY, OPENING, TOUR AT 54 N MACDONALD. (LOCAL). ELEANOR TESELLE, DIR; MESA PUBLIC SCHOOLS; 14 W 2ND AVE; MESA, AZ 85202. (#19260-1).

FEB 29, '76 - CONTINUING . MESA'S FIRST SCHOOLHOUSE - TOUR & EXHIBIT. EXHIBIT, TOUR AT 54 N MACDONALD. (LOCAL). ELEANOR TESELLE, DIR; MESA PUBLIC SCHOOLS; 14 W 2ND AVE; MESA, AZ 85202. (#19260-2).

JUNE 12, '76. FLAG DEMONSTRATION. EXHIBIT, FESTIVAL, CEREMONY. (LOCAL). MICHAEL R LEE; MESA BICENTENNIAL COMMITTEE; PO BOX 1466; MESA, AZ 85201. (#107663-1).

JULY 4, '76. FIREWORKS DISPLAY. FESTIVAL AT MESA COMMUNITY COLLEGE STADIUM. (LOCAL). MICHAEL R LEE; MESA BICENTENNIAL COMMITTEE; PO BOX 1466; MESA, AZ 85201. (#107663-2).

JULY 15 - 24, '76. 'HELLO DOLLY' - PERFORMANCE. LIVE PERFORMANCE. (LOCAL). MICHAEL R LEE; MESA BICENTENNIAL COMMITTEE; PO BOX 1466; MESA, AZ 85201. (#107663-3).

NOV 11, '76. VETERAN'S DAY PARADE. PARADE AT MAIN STREET. (LOCAL). MICHAEL R LEE; MESA BICENTENNIAL COMMITTEE; PO BOX 1466; MESA, AZ 85201. (#107663-4).

MOCCASIN

JAN 1, '75 - DEC 31, '76. LIFE ON A PIONEER MORMON SETTLEMENT RELIVED AT PIPE SPRINGS NM. ADMISSION FEE TO THE PARK. THIS AREA WAS BUILT BY MORMON PIONEERS. AS PART OF ITS INTERPRETIVE PGM, VISITORS CAN WATCH COSTUMED PEOPLE DEMONSTRATE LIFE AS PRACTICED BY THE MORMON SETTLERS--QUILTING, RUGMAKING, GARDENING, & OTHER DOMESTIC AND FARM ARTS AND CRAFTS. (REGN'L). PIPE SPRINGS NATL MON; NATIONAL PARK SERVICE; MOCCASIN, AZ 86022. (#6727-37).

SEPT 9 - 13, '75. PIPE SPRING NM OPEN HOUSE AND WAGON TREK TO ST. GEORGE, UTAH. OPEN HOUSE CELEBRATION AT PIPE SPRING NATL MON INCLUDING OLD-TIME DANCE ORCHESTRA AND PAIUTE INDIAN DANCERS, FOLLOWED BY DEPARTURE OF WAGON TREK ACROSS DESERT TO ST. GEORGE FOR PARTICIPATION IN DIXIE DAY PARADE. TREK ENACTS HISTORIC 1870'S SUPPLY TRAIN. AT PIPE SPRING NM VISITOR CENTER & ST. GEORGE, UTAH. (REGN'L). SUPT, PIPE SPRING NM; NATIONAL PARK SERVICE; MOCCASIN, AZ 86022. (#6728-107).

SEPT 6 - 9, '76. PIPE SPRING NM OPEN HOUSE AND WAGON TREK TO ST. GEORGE, UTAH. OPEN HOUSE CELEBRATION AT PIPE SPRING NATL MON INCLUDING OLD-TIME DANCE ORCHESTRA AND PAIUTE INDIAN DANCERS, FOLLOWED BY DEPARTURE OF WAGON TREK ACROSS DESERT TO ST. GEORGE FOR PARTICIPATION IN DIXIE DAY PARADE. TREK REENACTS HISTORIC 1870'S SUPPLY TRAIN. AT MONUMENT'S VISITOR CENTER. (REGN'L). PIPE SPRING NATL MON; NATIONAL PARK SERVICE; MOCCASIN, AZ 86022. (#6728-607).

MT LEMMON

JULY 3 - 5, '76. ARTS & CRAFTS SHOW VILLAGE JULY 4 CELEBRATION. SUMMER RESORT AREA, SCENIC DRIVE TO VILLAGE, 34 MI FROM TUCSON, COUNTRY MUSIC, FOOD, DANCE, EXHIBITS, GAMES, GUIDED NATURE WALKS, OPEN TO PUBLIC. AT VILLAGE MAIN ST. (LOCAL). REGINA D RHIND; MT LEMMON WOMAN'S CLUB; 3232 E FLOWER AVE; TUCSON, AZ 85716. (#4553-1).

NOGALES

'ANZA - WHO'S HE?' - BOOK PROJECT OF NOGALES, AZ. A BOOK ON JAUN BAUTISTA DE ANZA, A SPANISH EXPLORER IN COLORADO, WILL BE PUBLISHED FOR HIGH SCHOOL STUDENTS. (LOCAL). DORIS SEIBOLD, CHAIRMAN; NOGALES UNIFIED SCHOOL DISTRICT 1, ENGLISH DEPT; 402 MARTINEZ ST; NOGALES, AZ 85621. (#15241). **ARBA GRANTEE.**

AVENUE OF TREES - NOGALES, AZ. PLANTING OF TREES AND SHRUBS ALONG WITH ARTISTIC LANDSCAPING; TREES IN PLANTERS WILL BE PLACED IN CEMENT AREAS. (LOCAL). VIVIAN ALLEN, CHAIRMAN; PIMERIA ALTA GARDEN CLUB & CHAMBER OF COMMERCE; NOGALES, AZ 85621. (#25535). **ARBA GRANTEE.**

OCT 14 - 15, '75. DE ANZA EXPEDITION REENACTMENT, CELEBRATION, CEREMONY. RE-ENACTMENT OF THE 1775 EXPEDITION FROM TUBAC, AZ, TO CALIFORNIA, ENDING WITH THE ESTABLISHMENT OF PRESIDIO AT SAN FRANCISCO. (ST-WIDE). MAURICE GISS; ARIZONA BICENTENNIAL COMMISSION; 1807 N CENTRAL #108; PHOENIX, AZ 85004. (#605-9).

FEB 21, '76. 'DINNER WITH GEORGE WASHINGTON'. A DINNER (BENEFIT) FEATURING MENU OF WASHINGTON ERA AS WELL AS BAROQUE MUSIC BY COSTUMED PERFORMERS. MARTHA & GEORGE IN COSTUME WILL GREET GUESTS. DINING ROOM HELP WILL BE IN COSTUME. ALSO PATRIOTIC SING-A-LONG. AT SACRED HEART SHERIDAN CENTER. (LOCAL). MRS RAYMOND F HOFF, PRES; SANTA CRUZ COUNTY COUNCIL SOUTHERN ARIZONA YOUNG AUDIENCES, INC; 1003 MEADOW HILLS DR; NOGALES, AZ 85621. (#106009-1).

MAR 3 - 4, '76. UNITED STATES ARMED FORCES BICENTENNIAL CARAVAN. CARAVAN IS COMPOSED OF EXHIBIT VANS FOR EACH MILITARY SERVICE. PROJECT THEME IS 'HISTORY OF THE ARMED FORCES AND THEIR CONTRIBUTIONS TO THE NATION'. (LOCAL). DAVID SYMONS, CHMN; US ARMED FORCES EXHIBIT VANS PROJECT; 1410 TARGET RANGE RD; NOGALES, AZ 85621. (#1775-328).

APR 1 - 5, '76. MORMON CULTURE - RELIGIOUS FREEDOM IN THE U S - PAGEANT. THE PAGEANT WILL PRESENT THE HISTORY OF THE CHURCH IN AMERICA. AT GRANT'S PARKING LOT. (REGN'L). VARD G HARRIS, CHAIRMAN; CHURCH OF JESUS CHRIST OF LATTER DAY SAINTS PAGEANT COMMITTEE; 2416 TUCSON HWY; NOGALES, AZ 85621. (#17804-1).

JUNE 28 - JULY 4, '76. RELIGIOUS FOUNDATIONS SEMINAR. SEMINAR. (LOCAL). BILL WOODRUFF, COORD; RELIGIOUS FOUNDATIONS; PO BOX 578; NOGALES, AZ 85681. (#108080-1).

OATMAN

OATMAN HISTORICAL MARKER PROJECT OF ARIZONA. HISTORICAL MARKER WILL BE ERECTED AT A PROMINENT PLACE WITHIN THE OLD MINING TOWN OF OATMAN. (LOCAL). HAZEL BOLTON, CHAIRMAN; OATMAN BICENTENNIAL COMMITTEE; BOX 36; OATMAN, AZ 86433. (#4900).

OATMAN MUSEUM - TOWN HALL PROJECT - ARIZONA. AN OLD SCHOOLHOUSE WILL BE REMODELED & CONVERTED INTO A MUSEUM AND TOWN HALL. (LOCAL). HAZEL BOLTON, CHAIRMAN; OATMAN BICENTENNIAL COMMITTEE; BOX 36; OATMAN, AZ 86433. (#4901). **(??).**

AUG 1, '75. LABOR DAY BICENTENNIAL CELEBRATION. FESTIVAL AT MAIN STREET. (LOCAL). HAZEL BOLTON; OATMAN BICENTENNIAL COMMITTEE; BOX 36; OATMAN, AZ 86433. (#50543-1).

ORAIBI

ROAD & STONE QUARRY SITE IMPROVEMENT IN AZ. TO ESTABLISH A PERMANENT STONE QUARRY SITE TO MEET ALL THE CONTINOUS IMPROVEMENTS OF THE TRIBE. (LOCAL). DR ABBOTT SEKAQUAPTEWA, CHAIRMAN; HOPI TRIBE; PO BOX 123; ORAIBI, AZ 86039. (#22854). **ARBA GRANTEE.**

PAGE

CITY PARK AMPHITHEATER, PAGE, AZ. BUILD AMPHITHEATER IN PROPOSED TOWN PARK. (LOCAL). WILLIAM WARNER, CHMN AMPHITHEATER COMMITTEE; ROTARY CLUB OF PAGE; PO BOX 283; PAGE, AZ 86040. (#21974).

ORAL HISTORY ARCHIVES - PAGE, AZ. AN ORAL HISTORY ARCHIVES WILL BE PLACED IN THE TOWN LIBRARY. (LOCAL). FRED M WARNER, CHAIRMAN; PAGE BICENTENNIAL BOARD; 360 ELM ST, PO BOX 2252; PAGE, AZ 86040. (#21920). **ARBA GRANTEE.**

SCHOOLHOUSE LEGACY - PAGE, AZ. PAINTING OF THE ORIGINAL SCHOOL BUILDING FOR THE LIBRARY. (LOCAL). FRED M WARNER, CHAIRMAN; PAGE BICENTENNIAL BOARD; 360 ELM ST, PO BOX 2252; PAGE, AZ 86040. (#21919).

JULY 4, '76. PAGE BICENTENNIAL FIREWORKS PRODUCTION. FESTIVAL AT PAGE AIRPORT. (LOCAL). HARRY EGGERT, COORD; PAGE-LAKE POWELL BOATING CLUB, INC; PO BOX 2368; PAGE, AZ 86040. (#105730-1).

PARADISE VLY

BICENTENNIAL NEEDLEWORK SHOW - PHOENIX, ARIZONA. NEEDLEWORK COMPETITION & EXHIBIT TO BE HELD IN MARCH, 1976. ENTRIES WILL COME FROM THE SOUTHWEST & WILL USE THEME 'SOUTHWEST HERITAGE--PAST, PRESENT, & FUTURE'. (REGN'L). MRS BETSY ROMINGER, PRESIDENT; PHOENIX NEEDLEWORK GUILD; 7520 N LAKESIDE LANE; SCOTTSDALE, AZ 85253. (#2368). **ARBA GRANTEE.**

LARKSPUR SCHOOL 'PERSONAL DECLARATIONS', AZ. STUDENTS AT LARKSPUR ELEMENTARY SCHOOL WILL BE INVITED TO SIGN THEIR OWN 'PERSONAL DECLARATION' RELATING TO GOOD QUALITIES OF CHARACTER DURING THE 1975-76 SCHOOL YEAR. (LOCAL). JOHN M ZANNIS, PRINCIPAL; LARKSPUR ELEMENTARY SCHOOL; 2450 E LARKSPUR; PHOENIX, AZ 85032. (#14261).

PARKER

PARKER ARTS AND CRAFTS FESTIVAL - AZ. THE FESTIVAL WILL BE HELD FROM DECEMBER 2-5, 1976 AT THE PARKER FAIRGROUNDS. (LOCAL). MEREL POLLARD, COORDINATOR;

PARKER—CONTINUED

COLORADO RIVER AREA BICENTENNIAL COMMISSION; PO BOX 25; PARKER, AZ 85344. (#27026). **ARBA GRANTEE.**

PARKER FESTIVAL USA. SCHOOLS IN PARKER ARE UNDERTAKING A FINE ARTS FESTIVAL FOR ALL AGES. (LOCAL). JANICE BRATT, COORD; PUBLIC SCHOOL SYSTEM OF PARKER; PO BOX 607; PARKER, AZ 85344. (#102500-5). **(??).**

SAVE THE JAIL FOR A MUSEUM - PROJ OF PARKER, AZ. PARKER IS RESTORING THE FIRST COUNTY BUILDING BUILT IN NORTHERN YUMA COUNTY IN 1914. THE HISTORIC BRICK BUILDING IS CENTRALLY LOCATED AND WILL BE UTILIZED TO DISPLAY EARLY ARTIFACTS. (LOCAL). JAN BRATT, CHAIRMAN; PARKER BICENTENNIAL COMMITTEE; PO BOX 607; PARKER, AZ 85344. (#14770). **ARBA GRANTEE.**

DEC 2 - 5, '76. PARKER ARTS & CRAFTS FESTIVAL. EXHIBIT, FESTIVAL AT PARKER FAIRGROUNDS. (LOCAL). MEREL POLLARD, COORD; COLORADO RIVER AREA BICENTENNIAL COMMISSION; PO BOX 25; PARKER, AZ 85344. (#27026-1).

PATAGONIA

PATAGONIA LIBRARY HERITAGE DISPLAY, AZ. A DISPLAY OF HISTORICAL BOOKS & ITEMS WITH EMPHASIS ON MATERIALS OF LOCAL & EDUCATIONAL INTEREST. (LOCAL). REV DENNIS VOLPER, PROJECT DIRECTOR; PATAGONIA PUBLIC LIBRARY; PO BOX 315; PATAGONIA, AZ 85624. (#17818). **ARBA GRANTEE.**

JULY 3, '76. UPPER SANTA CRUZ COUNTY BICENTENNIAL CELEBRATION. FESTIVAL. (LOCAL). DORIS SIEBOLD; UPPER SANTA CRUZ BICENTENNIAL COMMITTEE; PO BOX 625; PATAGONIA, AZ 85621. (#107665-1).

PAYSON

RUMSEY PARK BICENTENNIAL PROJECT, AZ. RECREATION AREA TO ACCOMODATE ALL AGES AND ETHNIC GROUPS WHO VISIT PAYSON. (LOCAL). JOHN BENNETT, CHAIRMAN; PAYSON BICENTENNIAL COMMITTEE AND TOWN OF PAYSON; 303 N BEELINE HWY, PO BOX 1250; PAYSON, AZ 85541. (#25311).

MAY 17 - 18, '75. OLD-TIME GOSPEL MUSIC FESTIVAL. SERIES OF OLD TIME MUSIC FESTIVALS INCLUDING A COUNTRY MUSIC FESTIVAL, A FIDDLERS CONTEST & A SPRING COUNTY GOSPEL FESTIVAL. AT PAYSON RODEO ARENA. (LOCAL). VERTIELEE FLOYD; PAYSON CHAMBER OF COMMERCE; DRAWER A; PAYSON, AZ 85541. (#4893-2).

SEPT 27 - 28, '75. ARIZONA OLD-TIME FIDDLERS' CONTEST & FESTIVAL. OLD TIME MUSIC FESTIVALS IN PAYSON, ARIZONA. SERIES OF OLD TIME MUSIC FESTIVALS INCLUDING A COUNTRY MUSIC FESTIVAL, A FIDDLERS CONTEST & A SPRING COUNTY GOSPEL FESTIVAL. (ST-WIDE). VERTIELEE FLOYD, CHAIRMAN; PAYSON CHAMBER OF COMMERCE; DRAWER A; PAYSON, AZ 85541. (#4893-503).

MAY 22 - 23, '76. ARIZONA OLD TIME GOSPEL MUSIC FESTIVAL. LIVE PERFORMANCE AT PAYSON RODEO ARENA. (ST-WIDE). VERTIELEE FLOYD, DIR; PAYSON CHAMBER OF COMMERCE; DRAWER A; PAYSON, AZ 85541. (#4893-3).

JUNE 26 - 27, '76. ARIZONA OLD TIME COUNTRY MUSIC FESTIVAL. FESTIVAL, LIVE PERFORMANCE AT PAYSON RODEO ARENA. (ST-WIDE). VERTIELEE FLOYD, DIR; PAYSON CHAMBER OF COMMERCE; DRAWER A; PAYSON, AZ 85541. (#4893-4).

SEPT 25 - 26, '76. ARIZONA'S OLD TIME FIDDLERS' CONTEST & FESTIVAL. FESTIVAL, LIVE PERFORMANCE AT PAYSON RODEO ARENA. (ST-WIDE). VERTIELEE FLOYD, DIR; PAYSON CHAMBER OF COMMERCE; DRAWER A; PAYSON, AZ 85541. (#4893-5).

PEARCE

'LAST FRONTIER', HISTORY BOOK - PEARCE, AZ. THE BOOK HAS TALES OF THE EARLY DAYS IN AMERICA'S LAST FRONTIER; SULPHUR SPRINGS VALLEY IS THE SCENE OF THE LAST INDIAN STRONGHOLD. (LOCAL). MRS BEN MAYO, CHAIRMAN; SULPHUR SPRINGS VALLEY BICENTENNIAL COMMITTEE; PO BOX 272; PEARCE, AZ 85625. (#24812).

APR 30 - MAY 2, '76. LAST FRONTIER BICENTENNIAL. BICENTENNIAL MUSEUM, GEOLOGY EXHIBIT, ART SHOW, CHILDREN'S EXHIBIT, FRONTIER HOME, HISTORY IN WHEELS, HISTORICAL PAGEANT, BANDS, SINGING GROUPS, SQUARE DANCE, BARBEQUE, GOLF TOURNAMENT, CONTEST, PONY EXPRESS. AT ARIZONA SUNSITES COMMUNITY CENTER & EXHIBIT GROUNDS. (LOCAL). MRS BEN MAYO, COORD; SULPHUR SPRINGS VALLEY BICENTENNIAL COMMITTEE; PO BOX 272; PEARCE, AZ 85625. (#200004-14).

PET. FOREST

JAN 1 - DEC 31, '76. BICENTENNIAL TRAVEL CENTER AT PETRIFIED FOREST NP. TRAVEL CENTER PROVIDES TRAVELERS WITH INFORMATION ON BICENTENNIAL EVENTS & SCENIC POINTS OF INTEREST IN UTAH, CALIF, ARIZONA, NEVADA, COLO, NEW MEXICO; INCLUDES SW CULTURAL CENTER DISPLAYING ARCHEOLOGICAL AND ETHNOLOGICAL ARTIFACTS, AUDITORIUM, AND LOUNGE. AT PAINTED DESERT INN. (REGN'L). PETRIFIED FOREST NP; NATIONAL PARK SERVICE; PET FOREST, AZ 86025. (#6728-84).

PHOENIX

AMERICAS 2 - CONCERT, PHOENIX, AZ. A CONCERT OF WORKS BY MEXICAN PERFORMERS. (LOCAL). ELIZABETH SHAW, COORDINATOR; PHOENIX FINE ARTS ASSOC; PO BOX 3726; TUCSON, AZ 85722. (#25622). **ARBA GRANTEE.**

ANGEL DRILL TEAM OF ARIZONA. OFFICIAL REPS SELECTED AS BEST PRECISION MARCHING UNIT IN AZ COMPOSED OF YOUNG LADIES FROM PARADISE VALLEY H S WILL PERFORM AT NUMEROUS CENTENNIAL EVENTS. WILL TOUR THE EAST FROM 6/6/76 TO 6/25/76. (ST-WIDE). KEITH W KAYLER, COMMANDER; PARADISE VALLEY HIGH SCHOOL; 3950 E BELL RD; PHOENIX, AZ 85032. (#4549). **ARBA GRANTEE.**

ARIZONA A-V MATERIALS - PHOENIX, AZ. LIST OF AUDIO-VISUAL MATERIALS ON ARIZONA FOR LOCAL SCHOOL LIBRARIES. (ST-WIDE). MARY CHONCOFF, DIRECTOR; ARIZONA DEPT OF EDUCATION, LIBRARY DIVISION; 1535 W JEFF; PHOENIX, AZ 85007. (#17815).

ARIZONA BICENTENNIAL RESOURCE MANUAL 1776-1976. THE MANUAL CONTAINS A COLLECTION OF SUGGESTED CLASSROOM ACTIVITIES FOR TEACHERS OF GRADES K THROUGH 12. THE 3 NATIONAL BICENTENNIAL THEMES ARE ENCOMPASSED IN THE MANUAL. (ST-WIDE). MIKE STEINBERG, CHMN; ARIZONA STATE DEPARTMENT OF EDUCATION; 1535 W JEFFERSON; PHOENIX, AZ 85007. (#17819).

ARIZONA BICENTENNIAL COURIERS - PHOENIX. TWO ARIZONA HIGH SCHOOL STUDENTS WILL BE REPRESENTING AMERICA FOR THREE MONTHS IN FOREIGN COUNTRIES. THEY WILL BE STAYING WITH LOCAL FAMILIES. (INT'L). MAURICE M GISS, CHAIRMAN; ARIZONA BICENTENNIAL COMMISSION; PHOENIX, AZ 85004. (#27021). **ARBA GRANTEE.**

ARIZONA ENVIRONMENTAL LIVING PROJECT. IMAGINATIVE PROGRAM FOR CHILDREN - AN ACTUAL LIVING OVER-NIGHT EXPERIENCE AT CULTURAL, HISTORIC OR PREHISTORIC SITES IN ARIZONA. (ST-WIDE). THOMAS E WHITE, INTERPRETIVE SPECIALIST; NATIONAL PARK SERVICE; 1115 N 1ST ST; PHOENIX, AZ 85004. (#713).

ARIZONA HERITAGE COOKBOOK. COOKBOOK THAT INCLUDES OUTSTANDING INDIAN, MEXICAN, & EARLY PIONEER RECIPES. ARIZONA GIRL SCOUTS WILL COMPILE THE RECIPES. (ST-WIDE). MRS WALLACE GREEN, COOKBOOK EDITOR; ARIZONA CACTUS-PINE GIRL SCOUTS COUNCIL; 1515 E OSBORN; PHOENIX, AZ 85014. (#4912).

ARIZONA LIVING THROUGH THE CENTURIES HISTORY BOOKS. ARIZONA VOCATIONAL CLUBS WILL RESEARCH & PRINT A HISTORICAL COLLECTION OF EARLY AZ FOLKLORE FOODS, & HOMEMAKER'S CRAFTS. (ST-WIDE). MRS CLIO REINWALD, HOME ECONOMICS SECTION; ARIZONA STATE DEPT OF EDUCATION; 1535 W JEFFERSON; PHOENIX, AZ 85059. (#4605). **ARBA GRANTEE.**

ARIZONA MOTHERS OF ACHIEVEMENT - PHOENIX. BOOK ON LIVES OF FAMOUS ARIZONA MOTHERS. (ST-WIDE). ELEANOR DAVIES, COORDINATOR; ARIZONA MOTHERS ASSOC; 242 E MCLELLAN BLVD; PHOENIX, AZ 85012. (#27033). **ARBA GRANTEE.**

ARIZONA NATIONAL GUARD MILITARY MUSEUM. A MUSEUM WILL BE BUILT NEAR THE ARIZONA NATIONAL GUARD HEADQUARTERS IN PHOENIX. THE MUSEUM WILL PRESERVE THE REMAINING TANGIBLE EVIDENCE OF OUR PAST AND OBJECTS SIGNIFICANT IN AMERICAN HISTORY AND CULTURE. (ST-WIDE). JOHN L JOHNSON, PROJ DIRECTOR; ARIZONA NATIONAL GUARD MUSEUM; 5636 E MCDOWELL RD; PHOENIX, AZ 85008. (#14759).

THE ARIZONA REPUBLIC'S FUND-RAISING DRIVE - NBMRP. SPONSORING BUILDING OF MEMORIAL TO USS ARIZONA, SUNK AT PEARL HARBOR. PAPER RAN CONTEST FOR DESIGN, THEN RAN FUND-RAISING DRIVE. (LOCAL). WALTER SVFT, JR, COMMUNITY RELATIONS MANAGER; THE ARIZONA REPUBLIC; 120 E VAN BUREN ST; PHOENIX, AZ 85001. (#28306).

ARIZONA SPECIAL OLYMPICS, PHOENIX. ANNUAL 2 DAY EVENT FOR HANDICAPPED INDIVIDUALS, FEATURING A VARIETY OF COMPETITIVE SPORTS, ALLOWING ALL PARTICIPANTS TO SHARE IN THE SPIRIT OF FUN & COMPETITION. (ST-WIDE). JOHN ANDREWS, DIRECTOR; ARIZONA SPECIAL OLYMPICS; PO BOX 1676; COOLIDGE, AZ 85228. (#25478). **ARBA GRANTEE.**

ARIZONA TOWN MEETINGS - PHOENIX, AZ. SERIES OF LOCAL GATHERINGS THROUGHOUT THE STATE; CITIZENS WILL BE INVOLVED IN DISCERNING COMMUNITY PROBLEMS & CREATING SOLUTIONS FOR THE FUTURE. (ST-WIDE). MARK POOLE, DIRECTOR; INSTITUTE OF CULTURAL AFFAIRS; 2206 W MONROE; PHOENIX, AZ 85009. (#20568). **ARBA GRANTEE.**

ARIZONA'S HERITAGE BLESSED BY GOD. CHILDREN FROM SEVERAL PHOENIX AREA CHURCHES WILL PUT ON A PAGEANT THAT WILL DRAMATICALLY & MUSICALLY PORTRAY THE ROLE OF CHRISTIANITY IN THE DEVELOPMENT OF ARIZONA. (ST-WIDE). MRS CLARICE LICHTENBERG, CHAIRMAN; ARIZONAS HERITAGE BLESSED BY GOD PROJECT; 13018 NORTH 32 AVE; PHOENIX, AZ 85029. (#4551). **ARBA GRANTEE.**

ARIZONA'S HIDDEN HEROINES, PAST & PRESENT. ESSAY & PHOTO CONTEST. STATE WIDE CELEBRATION FOCUSED ON WOMEN WHO CONTRIBUTED TO THE DEVELOPMENT OF ARIZONA. (ST-WIDE). MRS PETER LENDRUM, EXEC DIRECTOR; ARIZONA CACTUS-PINE GIRL SCOUTS COUNCIL; 1515 E OSBORN; PHOENIX, AZ 85014. (#4911).

AZ STATE EMPLOYEES CREDIT UNION BICENT CELEBRATION. THE ARIZONA STATE EMPLOYEES CREDIT UNION WILL SPONSOR THE FOLLOWING EVENTS IN HONOR OF THE BICENTENNIAL: OLD-FASHIONED AMERICAN DINNER MEETING, TUCSON BLDG DEDICATION CEREMONY & FELLOWSHIP BANQUET. (ST-WIDE). R C ROBERTSON, PRESIDENT; ARIZONA STATE EMPLOYEES CREDIT UNION; 1812 W MONROE ST; PHOENIX, AZ 85007. (#20884).

BICEN FORUM OF PHOENIX NEWSPAPERS INC - NBMRP. FORUM IS DESIGNED TO PROVOKE THOUGHT ON PART OF THE COMMUNITY & TO GIVE IT OPPORTUNITY TO CONSIDER PRESENT & FUTURE VIRTUES & PROBLEMS OF THE COUNTRY. TO BE PUBLISHED THROUGH JULY 4, 1976. (LOCAL). WILLIAM R SHOVER, COMMUNITY & CORPORATE SERVICES; PHOENIX NEWSPAPERS, INC; 120 E VAN BUREN; PHOENIX, AZ 85004. (#25878).

BICENTENNIAL BALLET TOUR OF ARIZONA BALLET THEATRE. THERE WILL BE 11 PERFORMANCES STATEWIDE, FEATURING ORIGINAL CHOREOGRAPHY BASED ON STEPHEN FOSTER MUSIC. (ST-WIDE). TIMONA PITTMAN, EXEC DIRECTOR; ARIZONA BALLET THEATRE, INC; 4528 N 7TH ST; PHOENIX, AZ 85014. (#27374). **ARBA GRANTEE.**

BICENTENNIAL JUBILEE - GIRL SCOUTS IN PHOENIX, AZ. ARIZONA GIRL SCOUTS PAY TRIBUTE TO TRADITIONS OF AMERICA ON MAY 15, 1976. (ST-WIDE). KEN MCCLURE, COORDINATOR; ARIZONA STATE OFFICE OF TOURISM; 1645 W JEFFERSON ST, ROOM 417; PHOENIX, AZ 85007. (#26672). **ARBA GRANTEE.**

BICENTENNIAL OPERA HOUSE PROJECT, PHOENIX, AZ. RECONSTRUCTION OF OPERA HOUSE FOR PUBLIC USE FOR DRAMA, MUSIC AND FILMS. (ST-WIDE). JOANN GRAHAM, MUSEUM DIRECTOR; PIONEER ARIZONA FOUNDATION; PO BOX 11242; PHOENIX, AZ 85019. (#7982). **ARBA GRANTEE.**

BLACK HERITAGE IN ARIZONA. WORKSHOPS FOR BLACK YOUTH IN PHOENIX. THEY WILL PRODUCE BLACK HISTORICAL DRAMA SKITS, HISTORICAL PUBLICATIONS & ART-PHOTO EXHIBITS. (LOCAL). RICHARD HARRIS, COORDINATOR; PHOENIX URBAN LEAGUE; 4732 S CENTRAL; PHOENIX, AZ 85041. (#2367). **ARBA GRANTEE.**

BLACK THEATRE TROUP - PHOENIX, AZ. A STATE-WIDE TOUR BY BLACK THEATRICAL & DANCE GROUP; PERFORMANCES WILL FOCUS ON BLACK HERITAGE AND WILL BE BASED ON ALEX HALEY'S NOVEL 'ROOTS'. (ST-WIDE). MRS HELEN MASON, PROJ DIRECTOR; BLACK THEATRE TROUP; 335 E ALVARADO RD; PHOENIX, AZ 85004. (#20693). **ARBA GRANTEE.**

BUFFALO SOLDIER RE-ACTIVATION PROJ OF PHOENIX, AZ. AS AN ARIZONA HISTORICAL ATTRACTION, THE 15 MOUNTED ACTOR/STUNTMEN WILL PERFORM DRILLS, STREET DRAMA & OTHER FORMS OF ENTERTAINMENT, DEPICTING THE LIFESTYLE OF THE 9TH & 10TH U S CAVALRY OF THE 1870'S. (LOCAL). SPENCER HOWARD, PRESIDENT; YOUNG BUFFALO TRADITION, INC; 1830 E WEIR ST; PHOENIX, AZ 85040. (#28185).

BUST OF LA FAYETTE FOR PHOENIX, AZ. BRONZE COPY OF HOUDON BUST OF LA FAYETT; GIFT OF COMITE FRANCAISE TO PHOENIX, AZ. (INT'L). L'AMBASSADEUR HERVE ALPHAND, PRESIDENT; COMITE FRANCAISE DU BICENTENAIRE DE L'INDEPENDENCE DES USA; 9, AVE FRANKLIN D ROOSEVELT; PARIS/FRANCE. (#21345).

CAPITOL AREA RENEWAL PROJECT OF PHOENIX, AZ. COMMUNITY RENEWAL PROJECT FOCUSED IN AN INNER CITY AREA OF PHOENIX. LOCAL CITIZENS WILL BE INVOLVED IN PLANNING & IMPLEMENTATION OF A COMPREHENSIVE NETWORK OF COMMUNITY SERVICES. (LOCAL). JAMES BELL, DIRECTOR; INSTITUTE OF CULTURAL AFFAIRS; 2206 W MONROE; PHOENIX, AZ 85009. (#1801).

CNTR FOR PRESERVATION OF SOUTHWESTERN CULTURES -AZ. CENTER IN DOWNTOWN PHOENIX CONTAINING MULTI-ETHNIC EDUCATIONAL FACILITIES, MUSEUM, SHOPS, ART EXHIBITS & PERFORMING AREAS. (ST-WIDE). PAUL H POZEN, DIR ARTS & HUMANITIES; MARICOPA COUNTY COMMUNITY COLLEGE DISTRICT; 903 N 2ND ST; PHOENIX, AZ 85004. (#1335). **(??).**

COMMEMORATIVE BICENTENNIAL BELT BUCKLE - AZ. ASPOT JAYCEES HAVE PRODUCED A BELT BUCKLE DESIGNED IN RED, WHITE & BLUE WITH JAYCEE MEMBERSHIP PIN CENTERED AND ON THE BACK THE CHAPTER INSIGNIA. (LOCAL). HOWARD PORTER, PROJ DIRECTOR; ARIZONA JAYCEES; 4301 S 7TH AVE; PHOENIX, AZ 85041. (#21916). **ARBA GRANTEE.**

'DAWNING OF THE THIRD CENTURY' CELEBRATION-PHOENIX. ALL PARKS CELEBRATION TO BE HELD ON FOURTH OF JULY, 1976. (LOCAL). MRS PAUL SINGER, COORDINATOR; PHOENIX BICENTENNIAL COMMISSION; 21 BILTMORE ESTATES; PHOENIX, AZ 85014. (#26013). **ARBA GRANTEE.**

DAYS REMEMBERED-ARIZONA PIONEERS TELL THEIR STORY. A 16 MM FILM OF INTERVIEWS WITH ELDER ARIZONA CITIZENS. (LOCAL). LARRY SALMON, COORDINATOR; MARICOPA COUNTY COMMUNITY COLLEGE DISTRICT; 903 N 2ND ST; PHOENIX, AZ 85004. (#25479). **ARBA GRANTEE.**

DEER VALLEY JAYCEE GHOST RIDERS, AZ. A MOUNTED RIDING GROUP AUTHENTICALLY REPRESENTING & DEPICTING CHARACTERS FROM ARIZONA'S HISTORY, SUCH AS BAT MASTERSON, WYATT EARP, AND OTHERS. AVAILABLE FOR PARADES. (ST-WIDE). JAMES COLBERT, CHAIRMAN; DEER VALLEY JAYCEE GHOST RIDERS; 2601 W WINDROSE DR; PHOENIX, AZ 85029. (#24043).

DESERT NATURE CENTER AND ITS TRAILS OF ARIZONA. EDUCATIONAL CENTER TO BE BUILT AT DESERT BOTANICAL GARDENS, PHOENIX. INCLUDES EXHIBIT AREA, INTERPRETIVE NATURE TRAILS & DAILY EDUCATION PROGRAMS FOR PUBLIC. (ST-WIDE). W H EARLE, DIRECTOR; AZ CACTUS & NATIVE FLORA SOCIETY; PO BOX 5415; PHOENIX, AZ 85010. (#712). **(??).**

DESERT TRILOGY: ARCHIVE OF THE SW, PROJ OF ARIZONA. A SERIES OF VIDEO TAPED CURRICULA & MASS MEDIA PROGRAMS FOCUSED ON THE PRE-COLUMBIAN SOUTHWEST & MEXICAN AMERICAN HERITAGE INCLUDING TAPED INTERVIEWS WITH PERSONS WHO LIVED IN THE AZ TERRITORIAL ERA. (ST-WIDE). DR JOHN L PRINCE, PRESIDENT; MARICOPA COUNTY COMMUNITY COLLEGE; 903 N 2ND ST; PHOENIX, AZ 85004. (#4910).

DEVELOPMENT OF METRO PHOENIX, AZ, OPTIONS. STUDY OF ALTERNATIVE TRANSPORTATION & URBAN GROWTH MODELS FOR

PHOENIX — CONTINUED

THE PHOENIX METRO AREA. MODELS WILL BE EXPLAINED TO PUBLIC VIA TV & NEWS. (LOCAL). JAMES W ELMORE, PROFESSOR; COLLEGE OF ARCHITECTURE; ARIZONA STATE UNIV; TEMPE, AZ 85281. (#1333). **ARBA GRANTEE.**

THE ELDERLY ARIZONAN - PHOENIX, AZ. FINAL REPORT OF THE GOVERNOR'S TASK FORCE ON RETIREMENT AND AGING. (ST-WIDE). HARRY HOLLAND, CHAIRMAN; GOVERNOR'S TASK FORCE ON RETIREMENT & AGING; 543 E MCDOWELL RD; PHOENIX, AZ 85004. (#23223). **ARBA GRANTEE.**

FREEDOM SHRINES - PHOENIX, AZ. THE EXCHANGE CLUB OF PHOENIX IS PLACING IN SKY HARBOR AIRPORT AND IN THE ARIZONA STATE CAPITOL ROTUNDA, A FREEDOM SHRINE. IT WILL DISPLAY APPROXIMATELY 24 DOCUMENTS DEALING WITH THE FOUNDING OF THE US. (ST-WIDE). ERIC MAXWELL, PROJ DIRECTOR; EXCHANGE CLUB OF PHOENIX; 1704 E PENNY DR; TEMPE, AZ 85282. (#14751).

GET OUT TO VOTE IN ARIZONA. ARIZONA NEWSPAPERS ASSOC IS SPONSORING A STATEWIDE VOTER AWARENESS GET OUT THE VOTE DRIVE. PROJECT AIMS AT MAKING ELIGIBLE VOTERS AWARE OF ISSUES AND CANDIDATES URGING THEM TO VOTE. (ST-WIDE). MR JOHN H EVERSOLE, CHAIRMAN; ARIZONA BICENTENNIAL COMMISSION; 1807 N CENTRAL AVE; PHOENIX, AZ 85004. (#14267).

GOALS FOR ARIZONA PROGRAM. MODEL PROGRAM TO BE USED IN ANY ARIZONA COMMUNITY FOR EXAMINING PROBLEMS, INVITING COMMUNITY PARTICIPATION IN PROBLEM SOLVING, AND ESTABLISHING LONG TERM GOALS. (ST-WIDE). DICK MALLERY, DIRECTOR; GOALS FOR ARIZONA, INC; SECURITY BUILDING; PHOENIX, AZ 85004. (#568). **(??).**

GUNS OF THE PIONEERS PROJECT OF ARIZONA. PROGRAM THAT WILL ACQUAINT PUBLIC WITH HISTORIC FIREARMS. THE POWDERHORN CLAN WILL HAVE SERIES OF TURKEY SHOOTS, MUZZLE LOADING RIFLE COMPETITIONS & SHOOTING DEMONSTRATIONS. (LOCAL). DALE SHADLE, PRESIDENT; POWDERHORN CLAN; 8122 N 41ST AVE; PHOENIX, AZ 85021. (#4608).

HAZEL COOL MEMORIAL MUSIC LIBRARY IN ARIZONA. FREE LENDING LIBRARY OF MUSIC WHICH WILL CONTAIN THE LATE HAZEL COOL'S LIFELONG COLLECTION OF INSTRUMENTAL & VOCAL SHEET MUSIC. SELECTIONS RANGE FROM CLASSICAL THROUGH BLUES, JAZZ & POPULAR. (LOCAL). HAL SUNDAY, PRESIDENT; PHOENIX FEDERATION OF MUSICIANS; 1202 E OAK; PHOENIX, AZ 85004. (#4891). **ARBA GRANTEE.**

'HELIOGRAPHS & HETERODYNES', EARLY COMMUNICATIONS. CITIZEN BAND RADIO ENTHUSIASTS ARE SETTING UP A WIRELESS COMMUNICATION SYSTEM SIMILAR TO THE SYSTEM USED BY THE ARMY IN THE LATE 19TH CENTURY. THE SYSTEM CAN BE USED FOR EMERGENCIES. (ST-WIDE). JAY BENNETT, PROJ DIRECTOR; SUPERSTITION REACT TEAM; 1401 E MULBERRY; PHOENIX, AZ 85014. (#14948). **ARBA GRANTEE.**

HERITAGE 76-FESTIVAL USA-HORIZONS 76 - ARIZONA. COMPREHENSIVE BICENTENNIAL PROGRAM THAT WILL INCLUDE THE STAGING OF BICENTENNIAL DANCES THROUGHOUT THE STATE & THE SPONSORSHIP OF FREE PUBLIC CONCERTS PERFORMED BY LOCAL MUSIC & DANCE GROUPS. (ST-WIDE). MRS SAM J HALDIMAN, PRESIDENT; ARIZONA FEDERATION OF WOMEN'S CLUBS; 83 W CAMBRIDGE; PHOENIX, AZ 85003. (#2370).

INDIAN ALCOHOLIC REHABILITATION DEMONSTRATION - AZ. REHABILITATION PROGRAM FOR INDIAN ALCOHOLICS LIVING IN PHOENIX URBAN AREA. PROGRAM WILL BE ADMINISTERED BY INDIANS & WILL USE A RESIDENTIAL COUNSELING CENTER. (LOCAL). JOSEPH W HAYES, PRESIDENT; INDIAN ALCOHOLIC REHABILITATION INC; 2141 W HEATHERBRAE APT 14; PHOENIX, AZ 85015. (#2362). **ARBA GRANTEE.**

INSTRUCTIONAL PGMS ON PARLIAMENTARY PROCEDURE -AZ. PROGRAMS WILL BE PROVIDED THROUGHOUT THE STATE OF ARIZONA ON PARLIAMENTARY PROCEDURE. (ST-WIDE). MRS HERMAN W KUNTZ, CHAIRMAN; ARIZONA STATE ASSOC OF PARLIAMENTARIANS; 2050 W DUNLAP, A-214; PHOENIX, AZ 85021. (#385).

INTEGRATED STATE AND LOCAL CELEBRATIONS - AZ. VARIETY OF STATE CELEBRATIONS WITH THEME 'ARIZONA'S PIONEER SPIRIT IN NEW NURSING FRONTIERS.'. (ST-WIDE). RUTH ANN ZORNOW, CHAIRMAN; ARIZONA NURSES ASSOCIATION; 4525 N 12TH ST; PHOENIX, AZ 85014. (#17813).

KEE N' BAH CHILD DEVELOPMENT CENTER, INC, AZ. FIELD TRIPS AND EQUIPMENT TO PROVIDE MORE LEARNING EXPERIENCES FOR INDIAN PRE-SCHOOL CHILDREN. (LOCAL). LIZ ABIETA, PRESIDENT BOARD OF DIRECTORS; KEE N' BAH CHILD DEVELOPMENT CENTER INC; 803 E CAMELBACK RD; PHOENIX, AZ 85014. (#23220). **ARBA GRANTEE.**

KMCR-FM BICENTENNIAL PROGRAMMING, PHOENIX. MARICOPA COUNTY COMMUNITY COLLEGE DISTRICT EDUCATIONAL RADIO STATION, PLANS A VARIETY OF PROGRAMS WHICH INCLUDES A WEEKLY HOUR PROGRAM ON ALL 50 STATES. (LOCAL). BILL SHOVER, PROJ DIRECTOR; PHOENIX REPUBLIC AND GAZETTE; 120 E VAN BUREN; PHOENIX, AZ 85004. (#14270).

KOOL RADIO-TV BICENTENNIAL PROMOTION - NBMRP. FOR PAST 20 YEARS HAS FLAG IDENTIFICATION AT STATION BREAKS & FOR PAST 3 HAS HAD BICENTENNIAL LOGO. HAS CARRIED LARGE AMOUNTS OF ARBA PRODUCED MATERIAL. ALSO HAS RED, WHITE & BLUE HELICOPTER. (LOCAL). MISS MARGARET INJASOULIAN; KOOL RADIO-TELEVISION, INC; 511 W ADAMS ST; PHOENIX, AZ 85003. (#25886).

LIVING HISTORY MUSEUM OF PIONEER ARIZONA. EXHIBITS PERTAINING TO THE LIFESTYLE, HISTORY, TOOLS, CRAFTS, TRADITIONS AND CUSTOMS OF PIONEER GROUPS IN ARIZONA WILL BE FEATURED AT THE MUSEUM. (ST-WIDE). JO ANN GRAHAM, DIRECTOR; PIONEER ARIZONA FOUNDATION; PO BOX 11242; PHOENIX, AZ 85019. (#608). **ARBA GRANTEE.**

MADRID SCHOOL SPECIAL PROGRAM IN PHOENIX, AZ. CHILDREN WILL PRESENT PROGRAMS, SKITS, PLAYS AND EVENTS OF AN HISTORICAL NATURE. (LOCAL). JOHN E COOPER, PRINCIPAL; MADRID ELEMENTARY SCHOOL; 3736 W OSBORN RD; PHOENIX, AZ 85019. (#14947). **ARBA GRANTEE.**

MARICOPA COUNTY, ARIZONA FILM PROJECT. PUBLIC INFORMATION FILM FOR DISTRIBUTION DURING THE BICENTENNIAL ERA. THE FILM WILL EXPLAIN FUNCTION OF COUNTY GOVERNMENT AND ITS AFFECT ON THE LIVES OF CITIZENS. (LOCAL). CLYDE MURRAY, PUBLIC INFORMATION OFFICER; MARICOPA COUNTY; 111 S 3RD AVE; PHOENIX, AZ 85003. (#5394). **(??).**

'NOW '76--THEN '76' PAGEANT OF PHOENIX, AZ. HISTORICAL PAGEANT THAT WILL HIGHLIGHT THE HISTORICAL DEVELOPMENT OF AMERICA. IT WILL FEATURE MUSIC, DANCE, FLAGS & COSTUMES FROM VARIOUS ERAS, & MILITARY UNITS IN HISTORICAL DRESS. (LOCAL). HUBERT J LAWRENCE, PRINCIPAL; PALO VERDE/ROAD RUNNER COMMUNITY SCHOOL; 7702 N 39TH AVE; PHOENIX, AZ 85021. (#2369). **ARBA GRANTEE.**

OLD PHOTOGRAPHS FOR PHOENIX CIVIC PLAZA - AZ. PHOTOS OF EARLY PHOENIX ARE BEING BLOWN UP AND WILL BE PLACED ON THE WALLS OF THE PHOENIX CIVIC PLAZA. (LOCAL). BILL SHOVER, CHAIRMAN; PHOENIX BICENTENNIAL COMMITTEE; 120 E VAN BUREN; PHOENIX, AZ 85004. (#20692). **ARBA GRANTEE.**

OPERATION BLOCKWATCH PROJECT OF PHOENIX, ARIZONA. PILOT PROJECT TO FIGHT NEIGHBORHOOD CRIME. CITIZENS WILL LEARN HOW TO PROTECT THEIR HOMES & TO LOOK OUT FOR THEIR NEIGHBOR'S HOMES. (LOCAL). ED POWELL, EX DIR; PHOENIX BOARD OF REALTORS; 2544 N 7TH ST; PHOENIX, AZ 85006. (#4886).

'OUR HERITAGE - OUR FUTURE' - PHOENIX, AZ. THE GIRL SCOUTS ARE PLANNING TOURS OF HISTORIC AREAS IN THE EAST; MEDIA EVENTS WITH HISTORIC THEMES, FILM & SLIDE SHOWS, A BICENT NEWS LETTER & CEREMONIES THAT WILL MAKE SCOUTS AWARE OF OUR HERITAGE. (LOCAL). FERN A DABILL, SCOUT LEADER; GIRL SCOUT TROOP 588; 4210 N 56TH AVE; PHOENIX, AZ 85031. (#17820).

'OVERTOURS' - PHOENIX, AZ. COMMUNITY TOURS FOR VISITING CONVENTION GROUPS. (LOCAL). MRS SHERWIN BLOCK, DIRECTOR; PHOENIX SYMPHONY GUILD; 6328 N 7TH ST; PHOENIX, AZ 85014. (#20259).

PACT FAMILY CONCERT - PHOENIX, AZ. THE CONCERT WILL BE HELD AT PHOENIX CONCERT HALL. (LOCAL). CHRISTIN MCGINNLEY, COORDINATOR; PACT; 1202 E OAK ST; PHOENIX, AZ 85006. (#25790). **ARBA GRANTEE.**

PAN AMERICAN CENTER - PHOENIX, AZ. A NEW CULTURAL CENTER WILL BE CONSTRUCTED IN SOUTH PHOENIX FOR SPANISH LANGUAGE CLASSES, MEXICAN EXPORTS DISTRIBUTING AND INTERNATIONAL DIPLOMACY. (LOCAL). JULIA ZOZAYA, COORDINATOR; MEXICAN CHAMBER OF COMMERCE OF PHOENIX; PO BOX 4323; PHOENIX, AZ 85030. (#27208). **ARBA GRANTEE.**

PEOPLES POPS - 4TH OF JULY CONCERT, PHOENIX, AZ. SPECIAL REVUE & CONCERT TO BE HELD AT PHOENIX CONCERT HALL. (LOCAL). TERESA PEREZ, COORDINATOR; PHOENIX PARKS & RECREATION DEPT; 2700 N 15TH AVE; PHOENIX, AZ 85007. (#25788). **ARBA GRANTEE.**

PHOENIX JAZZ FESTIVAL. FIRST ANNUAL PHOENIX JAZZ FESTIVAL FEATURING AMERICA'S GREATEST JAZZ ARTISTS. (LOCAL). STAN RUBINSKY, CHAIRMAN; PHOENIX JAZZ FESTIVAL COMMITTEE; HOTEL WESTWARD HO; PHOENIX, AZ 85004. (#6878).

PHOENIX LITTLE THEATRE ALL-AMERICAN FESTIVAL. PRESENTATION OF A SERIES OF PLAYS WRITTEN BY FAMOUS AMERICAN PLAYWRIGHTS. (LOCAL). TOM MATTHEWS, MANAGER; PHOENIX LITTLE THEATER; 25 E CORONADO; PHOENIX, AZ 85004. (#6886).

PHOENIX RISING, A HIST OF MODERN PHOENICIANS, AZ. PUBLICATION OF A STUDY ON THE MODERN SOCIAL HISTORY OF 20TH CENTURY PHOENIX. AUTHOR: DR WESLEY JOHNSON. (LOCAL). PRESIDENT; PHOENIX HISTORICAL SOCIETY; 1242 N CENTRAL; PHOENIX, AZ 85004. (#4909). **ARBA GRANTEE.**

PIONEER CEMETERY IN PHOENIX, ARIZONA. RESTORATION OF A PIONEER & MILITARY CEMETERY, CREATION OF AN HISTORICAL PARK LOCATED NEAR STATE CAPITOL. (ST-WIDE). WEBB ELLIS, CHAIRMAN; PHOENIX CHAMBER OF COMMERCE; 805 N 2ND ST; PHOENIX, AZ 85004. (#5391).

POETRY ANTHOLOGY IN ARIZONA. HARDCOVER, CLOTHBOUND ANTHOLOGY BY POETS LIVING IN ARIZONA. THE BOOK WILL BE ILLUSTRATED. (ST-WIDE). GENEVIEVE SARGEANT, SECRETARY; GRAND CANYON STATE POETS; PO BOX 1026; TEMPE, AZ 85281. (#10783).

POPS AMERICANA CONCERTS PROJECT OF ARIZONA. CONCERT SERIES MADE UP OF PATRIOTIC,BAND AND SYMPHONY MARCHES ALONG WITH MORE SERIOUS MUSIC COMPOSED BY AMERICANS WITH THEMES AMERICANA. (ST-WIDE). KASSON CROOKER, GENERAL MANAGER; PHOENIX SYMPHONY ASSOCIATION; 6238 N. 7TH ST.; PHOENIX, AZ 85014. (#465).

'PRIDE OF ARIZONA' - PHOENIX, AZ. 'PRIDE OF ARIZONA' IS A MULTI-MEDIA DANCE, DRAMA AND STAGE PERFORMANCE. (LOCAL). MAURICE GISS, CHAIRMAN; ARIZONA BICENTENNIAL COMMITTEE; 1807 N CENTRAL #108; PHOENIX, AZ 85004. (#22621). **ARBA GRANTEE.**

'PROCLAIM LIBERTY' - PHOENIX, AZ. MULTI-MEDIA PRODUCTION COMPARING ISRAEL'S FIGHT FOR INDEPENDENCE TO THE U S STRUGGLE FOR INDEPENDENCE. (LOCAL). TED KORT, CHAIRMAN; PHOENIX JEWISH FEDERATION; 1718 W MARYLAND; PHOENIX, AZ 85015. (#20976). **ARBA GRANTEE.**

PROJECT-ONE FOR THE TRAIL, PHOENIX, AZ. A PROJECT TO COORDINATE VOLUNTEER WORKERS & MANAGEMENT AGENCIES FOR THE PURPOSE OF CLEAN-UP AND REPAIR OF NON-MOTORIZED STATE TRAILS. (ST-WIDE). CHUCK HERON, CHMN, FIELD OPERATIONS SUBCOMMITTEE; ARIZONA HIKING & EQUESTRIAN TRAILS COMMITTEE, AZ STATE PARKS; 1688 W ADAMS; PHOENIX, AZ 85701. (#26135).

REAL SOUTHWEST: A MULTI-MEDIA HISTORY. COLLECTION OF AUDIO-VISUAL MATERIALS FOR PUBLIC USE THAT WILL ENCOMPASS SOUTHWEST CULTURE & HISTORY. (LOCAL). IRENE STEVENS, PROJ DIRECTOR; CITY OF PHOENIX LIBRARY DEPARTMENT; 12 E MCDOWELL RD; PHOENIX, AZ 85004. (#14949).

RIO SALADO-THE UNIQUE ALTERNATIVE. DEVELOPMENT OF THE DRY SALT RIVER BED WITHIN PHOENIX METRO AREA TO TRANSFORM AREA INTO SERIES OF LAKES OPEN SPACE & PARK LANDS AREAS AND INTEGRATED PEDESTRIAN & EQUESTRIAN TRAIL SYSTEMS. (LOCAL). DAN DEVERS, EXECUTIVE DIRECTOR; VALLEY FORWARD ASSOCIATION; 1114 W MCDOWELL, STE 3; PHOENIX, AZ 85007. (#1802).

ROSSON HOUSE RESTORATION IN PHOENIX. THE ARIZONA BICENTENNIAL COMMISSION HAS SELECTED THE HISTORIC ROSSON HOUSE TO BE ARIZONA'S MEETINGHOUSE. THE ROSSON HOUSE IS IN DOWNTOWN PHOENIX AND WILL BE RESTORED WITH FUNDS FROM MEETINGHOUSE BILL. (ST-WIDE). CARL CRAIG, COMMUNITY SERVICES REP; CITY OF PHOENIX; 251 W WASHINGTON; PHOENIX, AZ 85003. (#2373).

SHERIFF'S VOCATIONAL REHAB PROGRAM AT PIONEER. INMATES OF COUNTY JAIL UNDER VOC. ED. INSTRUCTORS RESTORE & RECONSTRUCT HISTORIC EXHIBITS AT A BICENTENNIAL PROJECT PIONEER ARIZONA IN PROCESS OF RECONSTRUCTING 2-STORY 1877 OPERA HOUSE. (ST-WIDE). JO ANN S GRAHAM, SEC-TREASURER; PIONEER ARIZONA FOUNDATION, INC; PO BOX 11242 I-17 AT PIONEER EXI; PHOENIX, AZ 85061. (#7807).

SOUTH PHOENIX FESTIVAL OF THANKSGIVING. ANNUAL WEEK LONG FESTIVAL HELD IN NOVEMBER - EACH DAY OF THE FESTIVAL IS DEVOTED TO A PARTICULAR PART OF THE COMMUNITY - OLD TIMERS DAY, PARADE DAY, SCHOOL DAY FAIR DAY, FAITH DAY ETC. (LOCAL). RON JOHNSON, CHAIRMAN; SOUTH PHOENIX FESTIVAL COMMITTEE; 39 E JACKSON; PHOENIX, AZ 85004. (#4552). **ARBA GRANTEE.**

SPIRIT OF '76 - MIRACLE OF AMERICA - PHOENIX, AZ. SCHOOL CONTEST TO ENCOURAGE APPRECIATION OF ART, LITERATURE AND MUSIC FOR OUR COUNTRY'S 200TH BIRTHDAY. (ST-WIDE). MARY ANN CROMPTON, CHAIRMAN; ARIZONA STATE PTA; 2721 N 7TH AVE; PHOENIX, AZ 85007. (#19266).

STEAMBOATS ON THE COLORADO - FILM OF ARIZONA. DOCUMENTARY FILM DESCRIBING THE HISTORY OF THE EARLY STEAMBOATS ON THE COLORADO RIVER, FROM 1851-1906. (REGN'L). MAURICE GISS, PROJ COORDINATOR; ARIZONA BICENT COMMISSION; 1807 N CENTRAL; PHOENIX, AZ 85004. (#9229). **ARBA GRANTEE.**

STRUMMING AMIGOS TOUR -MEXICAN MUSICAL TROUPE OF A. TOURING MUSICAL TROUPE FOR THE BICENTENNIAL. (ST-WIDE). ROBERT A DIAZ, DIRECTOR; STRUMMING AMIGOS; RT 1, BOX 717; LAVEEN, AZ 85339. (#27325). **ARBA GRANTEE.**

SUN CIRCLE TRAIL IN PHOENIX, ARIZONA. TRAIL SYSTEM THAT WILL CIRCLE THE PHOENIX AREA WILL BE COMPLETED BY 1976. IT WILL FOLLOW OLD INDIAN TRAILS THROUGH SCENIC DESERT TERRAIN. (ST-WIDE). HOWARD GILMORE, SUPERINTENDENT; MARICOPA COUNTY PARKS & RECREATION DEPARTMENT; 4701 E WASHINGTON; PHOENIX, AZ 85034. (#5392).

SUNNYSLOPE FIREWORKS DISPLAY & PICNIC - AZ. THE FIREWORKS DISPLAY AND PICNIC WILL BE HELD ON THE 4TH OF JULY AT NORTH MOUNTAIN PARK. (LOCAL). JAMES DUNN, CHAIRMAN; SUNNYSLOPE CITIZENS COUNCIL; 831 E PURDUE; PHOENIX, AZ 85020. (#26932). **ARBA GRANTEE.**

TAPED TV CONCERT OF SPANISH-AMERICAN HERITAGE. PHOENIX SYMPHONY WILL TAPE CONCERT HIGHLIGHTING SPANISH-AMERICAN HERITAGE FOR DISTRIBUTION OVER THE PUBLIC BROADCASTING SYSTEM. (INT'L). KASSON CROOKER, GENERAL MANAGER; PHOENIX SYMPHONY ASSOCIATION; 6328 N 7TH ST; PHOENIX, AZ 85014. (#468).

TUBAC PRESIDIO SOUTHWESTERN HERITAGE PROJECT OF AZ. PROJECT INVOLVES MANY ELEMENTS ACQUISITION OF SITE, HISTORICAL RESEARCH PUBLICATION, MUSEUM & VISITOR FACILITIES BUFFER ZONE, ARCHAEOLOGICAL EXCAVATION, MOTION PICTURE SLIDES FOR TV, SCHOOLS, ETC. (ST-WIDE). WALLACE VEGORS, ASSISTANT DIRECTOR; ARIZONA STATE PARKS BOARD; 1688 W. ADAMS; PHOENIX, AZ 85007. (#922). **ARBA GRANTEE.**

UNION OF THE 50 STATES PROJ OF PHOENIX, ARIZONA. STUDENTS AT BOURGADE CATHOLIC HIGH SCHOOL HAVE DECORATED THE SCHOOL WITH THE STATE FLAGS & SEALS OF THE 50 STATES. THE SCHOOL WILL ALSO HOLD SPECIAL BICENTENNIAL CEREMONIES & ASSEMBLIES. (LOCAL). FR TIMOTHY TEPSIC, COORDINATOR; BOURGADE CATHOLIC HIGH SCHOOL; 4602 N 31ST AVE; PHOENIX, AZ 85017. (#5399). **ARBA GRANTEE.**

USA'S, A PERFORMING GROUP OF PHOENIX, AZ. USA'S IS A SONG & DANCE GROUP CELEBRATING THE BICENTENNIAL. (ST-WIDE). MRS MARSHA BEGAN, PRODUCER; USA'S; 3432 W PARADISE DR; PHOENIX, AZ 85029. (#20471).

USS ARIZONA ANCHOR MEMORIAL - PHOENIX, AZ. THE ANCHOR FROM THE USS ARIZONA IS BEING PLACED IN A MEMORIAL ON THE GROUNDS OF THE ARIZONA STATE CAPITOL. (LOCAL). DR JOHN CARNEY, CHAIRMAN; USS ARIZONA MEMORIAL COMMITTEE; 1807 N CENTRAL, #108; PHOENIX, AZ 85004. (#31771).

'WE, THE PEOPLE' - PHOENIX, AZ. CAMPFIRE GIRLS IN TUCSON & PHOENIX WILL PARTICIPATE IN A NATIONAL PROJECT; IT WILL INCLUDE LEADERSHIP DEVELOPMENT WORKSHOPS, ENVIRON-

PHOENIX — CONTINUED

MENTAL EDUCATION, LOCAL PROJECTS & A SERIES OF BICENTENNIAL FORUMS. (LOCAL). JANET SANDERSON, DIRECTOR; MARICOPA COUNCIL CAMP FIRE GIRLS, INC; 1515 E OSBORN RD; PHOENIX, AZ 85014. (#14254).

WOMEN OF 76 - PHOENIX, ARIZONA. WEEKLY NEWSPAPER ARTICLES ON WOMEN WHO HAVE MADE IMPORTANT CONTRIBUTIONS TO THE GROWTH OF AMERICA. APPEARING NOVEMBER 1974 THROUGH JANUARY 1976 IN THE PHOENIX REPUBLIC & GAZETTE. (ST-WIDE). JEANNE WILLIAMS, WOMEN'S EDITOR; PHOENIX REPUBLIC & GAZETTE; 120 E VAN BUREN; PHOENIX, AZ 85004. (#2364).

THE WORLD'S LARGEST LOGO IN PHOENIX, ARIZONA. A BICENTENNIAL SYMBOL, THE WORLD'S LARGEST PAINTING, IS BEING DONE ATOP THE ARIZONA COLISEUM IN PHOENIX. PASSENGERS ON PLANES TO & FROM PHOENIX WILL SEE THE RED, WHITE & BLUE STAR BELOW THEM. (REGN'L). MAURICE GISS, EXEC DIRECTOR; ARIZONA BICENTENNIAL COMMISSION; 1807 N CENTRAL #108; PHOENIX, AZ 85004. (#2372).

YOUTH LEADERSHIP CHALLENGE - PHOENIX, AZ. A YEAR-LONG PROGRAM FOR MEMBERS OF THE PHOENIX BOY'S CLUB; ACTIVITIES INCLUDE A YOUTH CONGRESS, SPECIAL LECTURES, BIKE HIKES AND NEIGHBORHOOD FESTIVALS. (LOCAL). LARRY CIULLA, PROJ DIRECTOR; BOY'S CLUBS OF PHOENIX; 2218 W MISSOURI; PHOENIX, AZ 85015. (#20694). **ARBA GRANTEE.**

'200 YEARS OF BECOMING' - PROJ OF PHOENIX, AZ. 'FREE TO BE WHO WE ARE......200 YEARS OF BECOMING" IS A UNIQUE SUMMER CHURCH SCHOOL FOR ELEMENTARY AGED CHILDREN. CLASSROOMS ARE DESIGNED TO REPRESENT RURAL LIFE IN THE 1770'S. (LOCAL). ROBIN KREIDER, PROJ DIRECTOR; SHADOW ROCK CONGREGATIONAL CHURCH; 13644 N 19TH AVE; PHOENIX, AZ 85008. (#14764).

25TH ANNUAL MEETING - PHOENIX, AZ. AMERICAN BICENTENNIAL THEME: 'A PRACTICAL DEMONSTRATION OF THE DEMOCRATIC PROCESS - THE CREDIT UNION IS SOCIO-ECONOMIC DEMOCRACY IN ACTION'. (ST-WIDE). R C ROBERTSON, PRESIDENT; ARIZONA STATE EMPLOYEES CREDIT UNION; 1812 W MONROE ST; PHOENIX, AZ 85007. (#23661).

MAY 9 - 25, '74. PERFORMANCE OF '1776' HISTORICAL MUSICAL. '1776' - A UNIQUE MUSICAL OF PHOENIX, AZ PERFORMANCE OF THE HISTORICAL MUSICAL '1776' BY LITTLE THEATER GROUP. (LOCAL). MRS INA PRICE, PRESIDENT; PHOENIX LITTLE THEATRE; 25 E CORONADO RD; PHOENIX, AZ 85004. (#1808-901).

SEPT 18 - 21, '74. NATIONAL SISTER CITY CONFERENCE CONVENES. SISTER CITIES PROJECT. A PRIVATE NONPROFIT NATIONAL ORGANIZATION COORDINATING 420 US CITIES & THEIR AFFILIATED SISTER CITIES IN 61 OTHER COUNTRIES. PROGRAM AIMS TO ENCOURAGE INVOLVEMENT OF WORLD COMMUNITY IN BICENTENNIAL. (INT'L). THOMAS GITTINS, EXEC V/P; THE TOWN AFFILIATION ASSOCIATION, INC; 1625 K ST, NW; WASHINGTON, DC 20006. (#187-904).

SEPT 18 - 21, '74. 1974 GEORGE V ALLEN NATIONAL ESSAY CONTEST-STUDENT COMPETITION. SISTER CITIES PROJECT. A PRIVATE NONPROFIT NATIONAL ORGANIZATION COORDINATING 420 US CITIES & THEIR AFFILIATED SISTER CITIES IN 61 OTHER COUNTRIES. PROGRAM AIMS TO ENCOURAGE INVOLVEMENT OF WORLD COMMUNITY IN BICENTENNIAL. (INT'L). THOMAS GITTINS, EXEC V/P; THE TOWN AFFILIATION ASSOCIATION, INC; 1625 K ST, NW; WASHINGTON, DC 20006. (#187-905).

NOV 3, '74 - JULY 4, '76. UNION OF THE 50 STATES. EXHIBIT AT HIGH SCHOOL. (LOCAL). FATHER T TIMOTHY TEPSIC; BOURGADE CATHOLIC HIGH SCHOOL, 4602-N 31ST AVE, PHOENIX ARIZ 85017; 4602 N 31ST AVENUE; PHOENIX, AZ 85017. (#50113-1).

JAN 2, '75 - JAN 10, '76. 'THE SUBJECT WAS ROSES' - FRANK GILROY - ALL-AMERICAN PLAYWRIGHTS. PRESENTATION OF A SERIES OF PLAYS WRITTEN BY FAMOUS AMERICAN PLAYWRIGHTS. AT PHOENIX LITTLE THEATER 25 E CORONADO. (LOCAL). TOM MATTHEWS; PHOENIX LITTLE THEATER; 25 E. CORONADO; PHOENIX, AZ 85004. (#6886-8).

FEB 5 - 14, '75. 'VERONICA'S ROOM'-IRA LEVIN - ALL-AMERICAN PLAYWRIGHT FESTIVAL. LIVE PERFORMANCE AT PHOENIX LITTLE THEATER 25 E CORONADO. (LOCAL). TOM MATTHEWS; PHOENIX LITTLE THEATER; 25 E. CORONADO; PHOENIX, AZ 85004. (#6886-10).

APR 19 - 20, '75. ARIZONA STATE MUZZLE LOADING RIFLE CHAMPIONSHIPS. COMPETITION AT BLACK CANYON RIFLE RANGE. (ST-WIDE). DALE SHADLE; POWDERHORN CLAN; 8122 N 41ST AVE; PHOENIX, AZ 85021. (#4608-1).

APR 19 - 20, '75. PHOENIX HERITAGE DAYS IN THE PARK. AN ALL-CITY CELEBRATION, INCLUDING DISPLAYS, DANCERS, FOOD BOOTHS, BANDS & CRAFTSMEN. AT ENCANTO PARK. (LOCAL). SHIRLEY SINGER, DIR; PHOENIX BICENTENNIAL COMMITTEE; 21 BILTMORE ESTATES; PHOENIX, AZ 85016. (#6879-1).

APR 25 - 27, '75. PHOENIX JAZZ FESTIVAL. LIVE PERFORMANCE AT PHOENIX SYMPHONY HALL. (LOCAL). STAN RUGINSKY; PHOENIX JAZZ COMMITTEE; C/O KXTC WESTWARD HO HOTEL; PHOENIX, AZ 85004. (#6878-1).

MAY 15 - 16, '75. STATEWIDE PAGEANT & CELEBRATION IN THE ARIZONA VETERANS COLOSSEUM. FESTIVAL, COMPETITION. (ST-WIDE). MRS PETER LENDRUM; ARIZONA CACTUS-PINE GIRL SCOUTS COUNCIL; 1515 E OSBORN; PHOENIX, AZ 85014. (#4911-501).

JUNE 19 - JULY 5, '75. 'PLAY IT AGAIN, SAM' BY WOODY ALLEN - ALL-AMERICA FESTIVAL. PRESENTATION OF A SERIES OF PLAYS WRITTEN BY FAMOUS AMERICAN PLAYWRIGHTS. AT PHOENIX LITTLE THEATER 25 E CORONADO. (LOCAL). TOM MATTHEWS; PHOENIX LITTLE THEATER; 25 E CORONADO; PHOENIX, AZ 85004. (#6886-1).

JULY 1 - 6, '75. RINGLING BROS, BARNUM & BAILEY BICENTENNIAL SHOW. PROGRAM TO SALUTE THE BICENTENNIAL & GREAT MOMENTS OF OUR HISTORY, USING TRADITIONAL CIRCUS FORMAT, WITH PATRIOTIC & HISTORIC THEMES IN A VARIETY OF WAYS, BOTH INSIDE & OUTSIDE THE SHOW. AT ARIZONA VETERAN'S MEMORIAL COLLESEUM. (ST-WIDE). LEE SOLTERS; RINGLING BROS. BARNUM & BAILEY; 62 W 45TH ST; NEW YORK, NY 10036. (#1770-2).

JULY 17 - AUG 2, '75. 'THE SEVEN-YEAR ITCH' - GEORGE AXELROD - ALL-AMERICA FESTIVAL. PRESENTATION OF A SERIES OF PLAYS WRITTEN BY FAMOUS AMERICAN PLAYWRIGHTS. AT PHOENIX LITTLE THEATER 25 E CORONADO. (LOCAL). TOM MATTHEWS; PHOENIX LITTLE THEATER; 25 E. CORONADO; PHOENIX, AZ 85004. (#6886-2).

SEPT 4 - 13, '75. 'AMERICAN PRIMITIVE' - JOHN & ABIGAIL ADAMS - ALL-AMERICAN FESTIVAL. PRESENTATION OF A SERIES OF PLAYS WRITTEN BY FAMOUS AMERICAN PLAYWRIGHTS. AT PHOENIX LITTLE THEATER 25 E CORONADO. (LOCAL). TOM MATTHEWS; PHOENIX LITTLE THEATER; 25 E. CORONADO; PHOENIX, AZ 85004. (#6886-3).

SEPT 17, '75. EQUIPMENT EXPO '75. ST JOSEPH'S HOSPITAL WILL SPONSOR AN ANNUAL ONE DAY EXPOSITION OF MEDICAL EQUIPMENT AND SUPPLIES FROM COMMERCIAL EXHIBITORS AND DEPARTMENTS OF THE HOSPITAL. (LOCAL). BILL SHOVER, CHAIRMAN; PHOENIX BICENTENNIAL COMMITTEE & PHOENIX REPUBLIC AND GAZETTE; 120 E VAN BUREN; PHOENIX, AZ 85004. (#14253-1).

SEPT 17, '75 - JUNE 1, '77. PLAYS, SKITS & CEREMONIES OF HISTORICAL EVENTS. LIVE PERFORMANCE AT SCHOOL CAFETORIUM. (LOCAL). JOHN E COOPER, PRINCIPAL; MADRID SCHOOL PARENT - TEACHERS ASSOCIATION; 3736 W OSBORO RD; PHOENIX, AZ 85019. (#14947-1).

SEPT 18 - OCT 4, '75. 'BAREFOOT IN THE PARK'-NEIL SIMON - ALL-AMERICAN FESTIVAL. PRESENTATION OF A SERIES OF PLAYS WRITTEN BY FAMOUS AMERICAN PLAYWRIGHTS. AT PHOENIX LITTLE THEATER 25 E CORONADO. (LOCAL). TOM MATTHEWS; PHOENIX LITTLE THEATER; 25 E. CORONADO; PHOENIX, AZ 85004. (#6886-4).

OCT 5, '75 - JULY 4, '76. BLACK HERITAGE IN ARIZONA. BLACK WRITERS WORKSHOPS, TO START 10-5-75, WILL PRODUCE BI-MONTHLY PUBLICATIONS OF ART & PHOTOGRAPHY, AVAILABLE TO THE PUBLIC. FOLLOWUP EVENTS DURING BLACK HERITAGE WEEK, 4TH OF JULY & JUNE 19 FREEDOM CELEBRATION (1976) WILL INCLUDE EXHIBITS, ORIGINAL READINGS & SKITS. (LOCAL). RICHARD E HARRIS; PHOENIX URBAN LEAGUE; 4732 S CENTRAL AVE; PHOENIX, AZ 85040. (#102958-1).

OCT 16 - NOV 1, '75. 'PROMISES, PROMISES' - NEIL SIMON - ALL-AMERICAN PLAYWRIGHT FESTIVAL. PRESENTATION OF A SERIES OF PLAYS WRITTEN BY FAMOUS AMERICAN PLAYWRIGHTS. AT PHOENIX LITTLE THEATER 25 E CORONADO. (LOCAL). TOM MATTHEWS; PHOENIX LITTLE THEATER; 25 E. CORONADO; PHOENIX, AZ 85004. (#6886-5).

OCT 19 - 20, '75. ST JOSEPH'S CATHOLIC CHURCH - FESTIVAL '75. FESTIVAL AT ST JOSEPHS. (LOCAL). MAUREEN MURPHY; ST. JOSEPH'S CATHOLIC CHURCH; 40TH ST & DESERT COVE; PHOENIX, AZ 85028. (#50705-1).

OCT 24 - NOV 11, '75. ARIZONA STATE FAIR - FESTIVAL USA. FESTIVAL AT ARIZONA COLISEUM. (REGN'L). TOM CLARK; ARIZONA COLISEUM & FAIR BOARD; 1826 W MCDOWELL; PHOENIX, AZ 85007. (#50703-1).

OCT 31 - NOV 1, '75. ARIZONA EDUCATION FAIR. EDUCATION EXPOSITION FEATURING DISPLAYS OF EXEMPLARY PRACTICES IN TODAY'S EDUCATION - DURING THE BICENTENNIAL THE FAIR WILL FOCUS ON THE THEME 'AMERICA'S GREATEST FREEDOM: EDUCATION'. AT PHOENIX CIVIC PLAZA, 225 E ADAMS, PHOENIX, AZ. (ST-WIDE). LYMAN JACKSON; ARIZONA DEPT ED AND OTHER EDUCATION GROUPS,; 1535 W JEFFERSON; PHOENIX, AZ 85007. (#4602-1).

NOV 6 - 15, '75. 'DELICATE BALANCE' - EDWARD ALBEE - ALL-AMERICAN PLAYWRIGHT FESTIVAL. PRESENTATION OF A SERIES OF PLAYS WRITTEN BY FAMOUS AMERICAN PLAYWRIGHTS. AT PHOENIX LITTLE THEATER 25 E CORONADO. (LOCAL). TOM MATTHEWS; PHOENIX LITTLE THEATER; 25 E. CORONADO; PHOENIX, AZ 85004. (#6886-6).

NOV 15 - 23, '75. SOUTH PHOENIX FESTIVAL OF THANKSGIVING. EACH DAY OF FESTIVAL IS DEVOTED TO A PARTICULAR PART OF COMMUNITY THAT IS SHARED WITH ALL SEGMENTS IN HOPES OF PROMOTING BETTER COMMUNITY RELATIONS. (LOCAL). PHOENIX OIC; SOUTH PHOENIX FESTIVAL OF THANKSGIVING COMMITTEE; 39 E. JACKSON ST; PHOENIX, AZ 85004. (#4552-1).

NOV 18 - DEC 14, '75. DEVELOPMENT OF METRO PHOENIX,AZ,OPTIONS EXHIBIT. STUDY OF ALTERNATIVE TRANSPORTATION & URBAN GROWTH MODELS FOR THE PHOENIX METRO AREA. MODELS WILL BE EXPLAINED TO PUBLIC VIA TV & NEWS ALSO: MODEL PROJECT, RESEARCH, NEWSPAPER/NEWSLETTER. AT PHOENIX ART MUSEUM. (LOCAL). JAMES W ELMORE, PROFESSOR; COLLEGE OF ARCHITECTURE; ARIZONA STATE UNIV; TEMPE, AZ 85281. (#1333-1).

NOV 20 - DEC 6, '75. 'LIFE WITH FATHER' -HOWARD LINDSAY ALL-AMERICAN PLAYWRIGHT FESTIVAL. PRESENTATION OF A SERIES OF PLAYS WRITTEN BY FAMOUS AMERICAN PLAYWRIGHTS. AT PHOENIX LITTLE THEATER 25 E CORONADO. (LOCAL). TOM MATTHEWS; PHOENIX LITTLE THEATER; 25 E. CORONADO; PHOENIX, AZ 85004. (#6886-7).

NOV 22, '75. HISTORICAL PAGEANT PERFORMED BY CHILDREN. ARIZONA'S HERITAGE BLESSED BY GOD. CHILDREN FROM SEVERAL PHOENIX AREA CHURCHES WILL PUT ON A PAGEANT THAT WILL DRAMATICALLY & MUSICALLY PORTRAY THE ROLE OF CHRISTIANITY IN THE DEVELOPMENT OF ARIZONA. (ST-WIDE). MRS CLARICE LICHTENBERG; ARIZONAS HERITAGE BLESSED BY GOD PROJECT; 13018 NORTH 32 AVE; PHOENIX, AZ 85029. (#4551-501).

NOV 27 - 30, '75. OLD-FASHIONED HARVEST FESTIVAL AT PIONEER, AZ. LIVING HISTORY MUSEUM. CLOSED CHRISTMAS DAY. AT 12 MILES NORTH OF PHOENIX INTERSTATE 17,PIONEER RD EXIT. (ST-WIDE). JO ANN GRAHAM; PIONEER ARIZONA FOUNDATION; PO BOX 11242; PHOENIX, AZ 85061. (#608-1).

DEC 6 - 8, '75. YESTERYEAR-CHRISTMAS PAGEANT. ANNUAL TREE LIGHTING FESTIVAL IN STYLE OF PIONEER TIMES. INCLUDES ART EXHIBITS, PUPPET SHOWS, CHOIRS. AT PHOENIX CIVIC CENTER. (LOCAL). MRS. LOUIS MCCLENNAN; PHOENIX ART MUSEUM LEAGUE; 1625 N. CENTRAL AVE.; PHOENIX, AZ 85004. (#50707-1).

DEC 26, '75. FIESTA BOWL PARADE. PARADE AT CENTRAL AVENUE-PHOENIX. (ST-WIDE). JOHN REED; FIESTA BOWL; 3410 E VAN BUREN; PHOENIX, AZ 85008. (#50706-2).

DEC 29, '75 - JAN 4, '76. PIONEER CATTLEMEN & HORSEMEN SHOW. SPECIAL RECOGNITION OF PIONEER CATTLEMEN & HORSEMEN. EXHIBITS OF PIONEER LIVING. AT FAIRGROUNDS & COLISEUM W MCDOWELL RD & GRAND AVE. (LOCAL). NELSON STEVENSON, CHMN; ARIZONA NATIONAL LIVESTOCK SHOW ASSN & ARIZONA COLISEUM BOARD; PO BOX 13548; PHOENIX, AZ 85002. (#14966-1).

DEC 31, '75 - CONTINUING . CHILDREN'S THEATRE SALUTES BICENTENNIAL WITH 4 PLAYS. INCLUDING 'HUCKLEBERRY FINN' AND 'RIP VAN WINKLE.'. (LOCAL). J T GREENE, PRESIDENT; CHILDREN'S THEATRE; 4502 N CENTRAL AVE, SUITE 412; PHOENIX, AZ 85012. (#104249-2).

JAN 1 - MAR 26, '76. THE JEWISH AMERICAN EXPERIENCE, SERIES OF 8 LECTURES. 6 LECTURES IN MESA, ARIZONA; 1 LECTURE IN PHOENIX, AZ; 1 LECTURE IN SCOTTSDALE, AZ. AT TEMPLE BETH SHALOM; TEMPLE BETH ISRAEL; TEMPLE SOLEL. (LOCAL). JOAN FRAZER, CHMN; ARIZONA BICENTENNIAL COMMISSION & THE PHOENIX JEWISH FEDERATION; 1718 W MARYLAND; PHOENIX, AZ 85015. (#105129-1).

JAN 2 - 31, '76. AMERICAN ART 1900-1932 FROM WHITNEY ART MUSEUM. MAJOR LOAN EXHIBITION FROM COLLECTION OF WHITNEY MUSEUM OF AMERICAN ART. AT 1625 N CENTRAL. (ST-WIDE). BOB FRANKEL, CHAIRMAN; PHOENIX ART MUSEUM; 1625 N CENTRAL; PHOENIX, AZ 85004. (#15465-1).

JAN 15 - 31, '76. 'WHO WAS THAT LADY I SAW YOU WITH' - NORMAN KRASNA - ALL AMER PLAYS. PRESENTATION OF A SERIES OF PLAYS WRITTEN BY FAMOUS AMERICAN PLAYWRIGHTS. AT PHOENIX LITTLE THEATER 25 E CORONADO. (LOCAL). TOM MATTHEWS; PHOENIX LITTLE THEATER; 25 E. CORONADO; PHOENIX, AZ 85004. (#6886-9).

JAN 16 - 18, '76. ARIZONA LIONS TO MEXICO BICENTENNIAL FIESTA. INTERNATIONAL RELATIONSHIP WITH LIONS OF ARIZAONA & GUAYMAS SONORA CELEBRATE 200 YEARS OF USA & DEDICATE SITE FOR CHILDREN'S CAMP IN SAN CARLOS FOR UNDERPRIVELEDGED CHILDREN. AT LA POSADA DE SAN CARLOS, SAN CARLOS SENORA, MEXICO. (INT'L). WILLIAM R COHEN, DIR; ARIZONA LIONS CLUBS-DISTRICT 21; 38 W BETHANY HOME RD; PHOENIX, AZ 85013. (#17802-2).

JAN 16 - 25, '76. BICENTENNIAL AUDIO CHAIRS. IN SPECIAL LISTENING CHAIRS VISITORS HEAR THREE DIFFERENT TAPE RECORDINGS WHICH DESCRIBE THE ROLES OF WOMEN, BLACKS AND NATIVE AMERICANS DURING THE REVOLUTIONARY PERIOD. MUSEUM OPEN MONDAY THROUGH SATURDAY 10 AM TO 5 PM AND SUNDAY 12 PM TO 5 PM. AT HEARD MUSEUM, 22 EAST MONTE VISTA RD. (LOCAL). DIRECTOR; NATIONAL PARK SERVICE; 1115 N FIRST ST; PHOENIX, AZ 85004. (#200004-13).

FEB 1 - 7, '76. SELECTION OF ARIZONA'S IDEAL SENIOR GIRL, ARIZONA'S JUNIOR MISS-1976. SELECTION OF ARIZONA'S JUNIOR MISS CLIMAXES A WEEK OF ACTIVITIES WHICH INCLUDES EXAMINATIONS OF FINANCE, COMMUNICATIONS, THE ENERGY SITUATION, GOVERNMENT AND LAW, AND TECHNOLOGY. AT WEST HIGH SCHOOL AUDITORIUM, 19TH AVE & W THOMAS ROAD. (ST-WIDE). RICK MAZOLA, VICE PRES; ARIZONA JUNIOR MISS FOUNDATION, INC; 8686 N CENTRAL AVE, SUITE 206; PHOENIX, AZ 85020. (#17806-1).

FEB 1 - 29, '76. 1976 POETRY CONTEST. COMPETITION. (ST-WIDE). MRS BARBARA L'ECUYER; ARIZONA DEPT OF EDUCATION; 1535 W JEFFERSON; PHOENIX, AZ 85007. (#200004-11).

FEB 3, '76. AUTOGRAPHING PARTY BY GRAND CANYON STATE POETS. BOOKS WILL BE SOLD TO COMPENSATE FOR COMPLIMENTARY DISTRIBUTION. AT PUBLIC & SCHOOL LIBRARIES THROUGHOUT THE STATE. (LOCAL). BESS S NIXON, SECRETARY; GRAND CANYON STATE POETS; 5635 N 16TH ST; PHOENIX, AZ 85016. (#16145-1).

FEB 9 - JUNE 8, '76. 'WHAT PRICE - LIFE, LIBERTY, DEATH?', EDUCATION FORUM & TV SERIES. THIS FORUM INTENDS TO EXAMINE HOW RELIGIOUS VALUES INTERACT WITH MORAL, MEDICAL AND LEGAL DECISIONS. AT BETH EL CONGREGATION - 1118 W GLENDALE; PARKING AVAILABLE. (LOCAL). SR CHRISTINE ATHANS, BVM; NORTH PHOENIX CORPORATE MINISTRY; 555 W GLENDALE; PHOENIX, AZ 85021. (#105731-6).

FEB 13 - 15, '76. UNITED STATES ARMED FORCES BICENTENNIAL CARAVAN. CARAVAN IS COMPOSED OF EXHIBIT VANS FOR EACH MILITARY SERVICE. PROJECT THEME IS 'HISTORY OF THE ARMED FORCES AND THEIR CONTRIBUTIONS TO THE NATION'. (LOCAL). BILL SHOVER, CHMN; US ARMED FORCES EXHIBIT VANS PROJECT; PO BOX 1950; PHOENIX, AZ 85001. (#1775-320).

FEB 14, '76. 'PRIDE OF ARIZONA' - A MULTI-MEDIA DANCE, DRAMA & STAGE PERFORMANCE. LIVE PERFORMANCE AT PHOENIX CIVIC PLAZA. (LOCAL). MAURICE GISS, CHAIRMAN; ARIZONA BICENTENNIAL COMMISSION; 1807 N CENTRAL #108; PHOENIX, AZ 85004. (#22621-1).

PHOENIX — CONTINUED

FEB 18 - 21, '76. INTERNATIONAL CONFERENCE ON INTEGRATED CANCER MANAGEMENT. ALSO SPONSORED BY THE AMERICAN CANCER SOCIETY, ARIZONA DIVISION. CONFERENCE WILL INCLUDE FORMAL PRESENTATIONS & PANEL DISCUSSIONS. AT GOOD SAMARITAN HOSPITAL,ADAMS HOTEL - PHOENIX. (INT'L). DR R H THOENY; GOOD SAMARITAN HOSPITAL; P O BOX 2989; PHOENIX, AZ 85062. (#8909-1).

FEB 18 - 22, '76. AID TO ZOO NATIONAL HORSE SHOW. COMPETITION, LIVE PERFORMANCE. (ST-WIDE). CAROL DENNIS, CHAIRMAN; AID TO ZOO NATIONAL HORSE SHOW; PO BOX 16021; PHOENIX, AZ 85011. (#200004-12).

FEB 19 - MAR 6, '76. 'GAZEBO' - ALEX COPPEL - ALL-AMERICAN PLAYWRIGHT FESTIVAL. PRESENTATION OF A SERIES OF PLAYS WRITTEN BY FAMOUS AMERICAN PLAYWRIGHTS. AT PHOENIX LITTLE THEATER 25 E CORONADO. (LOCAL). TOM MATTHEWS; PHOENIX LITTLE THEATER; 25 E. CORONADO; PHOENIX, AZ 85004. (#6886-11).

FEB 25 - 28, '76. SMITHSONIAN NEEDLEWORK EXHIBIT. THEME: 'OUR SOUTHWEST HERITAGE - PAST, PRESENT, FUTURE'. AT PHOENIX ART MUSEUM, 1625 N CENTRAL. (LOCAL). MRS BETSY ROMINGER, PRES; PHOENIX NEEDLEWORK GUILD; 7520 N LAKESIDE LANE; SCOTTSDALE, AZ 85253. (#2368-1).

MAR 1 - 5, '76. 'RODEO OF RODEOS' WESTERN WEEK ACTIVITIES. FESTIVAL. (LOCAL). TOM SHAFFER, CHAIRMAN; PHOENIX JAYCEES; 4133 N 7TH ST; PHOENIX, AZ 85016. (#200004-9).

MAR 1 - JULY 4, '76. COVERED WAGON TOUR OF ARIZONA. 12 COVERED WAGONS WILL TOUR THE STATE OF ARIZONA FOR 4 MONTHS, COVERING 1500 MILES, CAMPING OUT & COOKING ON CAMPFIRES; BIG STREET DANCE IN EACH CITY WITH LIVE, WESTERN BAND. AT ALL SAFEWAY STORES ACROSS STATE OF ARIZONA. (ST-WIDE). COL BUD ADAIR, COORD; DESERT TROOP SEARCH & RESCUE SQUAD; PO BOX 1055; PEORIA, AZ 85345. (#105296-1).

MAR 6, '76. MUSICAL PROGRAM & EXHIBITS. COCKTAIL HOUR TO HONOR MEXICAN AMERICANS WITH MARIACHI BAND, INDIAN CULTURE AND WOMENS FASHIONS FROM THE 1800'S TO THE PRESENT; DINNER WILL FEATURE 1 HOUR BICENTENNIAL PRESENTATION BY THE 'UP WITH PEOPLE' SINGING GROUP. AT ADAMS HOTEL, CENTRAL AVE AND ADAMS. (LOCAL). BEVERLY SCANLON, CHAIRMAN; KAPPA KAPPA GAMMA ALUMNAE; 13602 N 2ND PL; PHOENIX, AZ 85022. (#20971-1).

MAR 6, '76. RODEO OF RODEOS - STREET DANCE. FESTIVAL, LIVE PERFORMANCE AT SEARS RHODES SHOPPING CENTER, 20TH ST & CAMELBACK RD. (LOCAL). TOM SHAFFER, COORD; PHOENIX JAYCEES; 4133 N 7TH ST; PHOENIX, AZ 85016. (#200004-19).

MAR 7 - 8, '76. PONY EXPRESS RIDE - PRESCOTT TO PHOENIX. LIVE PERFORMANCE. (LOCAL). TOM SHAFFER, CHAIRMAN; PHOENIX JAYCEES; 4133 N 7TH ST; PHOENIX, AZ 85016. (#200004-10).

MAR 10 - 14, '76. RODEO OF RODEOS. 3RD LARGEST INDOOR RODEO IN THE WORLD. AT ARIZONA VETERANS MEMORIAL COLISEUM, STATE FAIRGROUNDS. (LOCAL). TOM SHAFFER, COORD; PHOENIX JAYCEES; 4133 N 7TH ST; PHOENIX, AZ 85016. (#200004-20).

MAR 10 - 14, '76. 48TH ANNUAL RODEO OF RODEOS. COWBOYS FROM AROUND THE COUNTRY COMPETE FOR TOP PRIZES. AT ARIZONA MEMORIAL COLISEUM. (NAT'L). BILL VOLLRATH, GEN CHMN; PHOENIX JAYCEES; 4133 N 7TH ST; PHOENIX, AZ 85014. (#103416-211).

MAR 11 - 20, '76. 'SPOONRIVER ANTHOLOGY' - EDGAR LEE MASTERS - ALL-AMERICAN FESTIVAL. PRESENTATION OF A SERIES OF PLAYS WRITTEN BY FAMOUS AMERICAN PLAYWRIGHTS. AT PHOENIX LITTLE THEATER 25 E CORONADO. (LOCAL). TOM MATTHEWS; PHOENIX LITTLE THEATER; 25 E. CORONADO; PHOENIX, AZ 85004. (#6886-12).

MAR 12, '76. WORLD'S LONGEST HORSE DRAWN PARADE. PARADE. (LOCAL). TOM SHAFFER, CHAIRMAN; PHOENIX JAYCEES; 4133 N 7TH ST; PHOENIX, AZ 85016. (#200004-8).

MAR 28 - 30, '76. RUNNING FOR GOD & COUNTRY - HIGH SCHOOL TRACK COMPETITION. COMPETITION, FESTIVAL AT ATHLETIC FIELD & AUDITORIUM. (LOCAL). REV HAROLD BUCKNER; PHOENIX CHRISTIAN HIGH SCHOOL; 1751 W INDIAN SCHOOL; PHOENIX, AZ 85015. (#100097-1).

MAR 31 - APR 4, '76. MARICOPA COUNTY FAIR 1976, AN OLD-FASHIONED COUNTY FAIR. FESTIVAL AT STATE FAIRGROUNDS. (LOCAL). PHIL ARDEN, GEN MGR; MARICOPA COUNTY FAIR, INC; 4701 E WASHINGTON; PHOENIX, AZ 85034. (#105731-1).

APR 3 - 4, '76. RELIGION IN AMERICA - PAGEANT & EXPOSITION PRESENTED BY ALL FAITHS. EXHIBIT, LIVE PERFORMANCE AT PHOENIX SYMPHONY HALL & MALL AREA. (LOCAL). VICTOR SMITH, PROJ DIR; INTERFAITH COMMITTEE FOR THE BICENT; 4455 E LINCOLN DR; PARADISE VLY, AZ 85253. (#100093-1).

APR 7 - 8, '76. YOUTH TOUR OF ARIZONA CAPITOL. ONE OR MORE MEMBERS OF EACH BRANCH OF GOVERNMENT, PLUS LOBBYISTS, WILL TALK TO YOUTH GROUP; THERE WILL ALSO BE AN APRIL 7TH TOUR OF ARIZONA STATE UNIVERSITY AND THE ARIZONA REPUBLIC. AT STATE CAPITOL. (LOCAL). PAT HOLT, CHMN; REPUBLICAN WOMEN OF LAKE HAVASU CITY; 1645 MESQUITE, PO BOX 999; LAKE HAVASU, AZ 86403. (#105731-2).

APR 9 - 10, '76. ARIZONA HOME ECONOMICS ASSOC ANNUAL MEETING. PURPOSE IS TO ENCOURAGE MEMBERS TO REFLECT ON THE PAST, GAIN NEW SKILLS FOR THE FUTURE; THERE WILL BE 4 DISCOVERY SESSIONS AND A KEYNOTE SPEAKER ON ARIZONA'S WATER AND ENERGY SITUATION. AT HYATT REGENCY, 123 N 2ND ST. (ST-WIDE). KAREN CHRISTENSEN, COORD; ARIZONA HOME ECONOMICS ASSOCIATION; 4851 E WASHINGTON; PHOENIX, AZ 85034. (#105887-1).

APR 15 - 24, '76. 'MOON FOR THE MISBEGOTTEN' - EUGENE O'NEILL - ALL-AMERICAN FESTIVAL. PRESENTATION OF A SERIES OF PLAYS WRITTEN BY FAMOUS AMERICAN PLAYWRIGHTS. AT PHOENIX LITTLE THEATER 25 E CORONADO. (LOCAL). TOM MATTHEWS; PHOENIX LITTLE THEATER; 25 E. CORONADO; PHOENIX, AZ 85004. (#6886-13).

APR 17 - 18, '76. HISTORICAL PAGEANT ON ARIZONA'S HERITAGE & HISTORY. MASQUE OF THE YELLOW MOON - ARIZ HISTORY PAGEANT. A LONG-TIME PHOENIX PAGEANT WILL BE REVIVED FOR THE BICENTENNIAL. PAGEANT IS A HISTORICAL TRIBUTE TO ARIZONA'S INDIANS, MEXICAN AMERICANS & PIONEERS. (LOCAL). GERALD DEGROW; PHOENIX UNION HIGH SCHOOL SYSTEM; 2526 W OSBORN RD; PHOENIX, AZ 85017. (#4550-501).

APR 23 - 25, '76. PHOENIX JAZZ FESTIVAL. FIRST ANNUAL PHOENIX JAZZ FESTIVAL FEATURING AMERICA'S GREATEST JAZZ ARTISTS. AT PHOENIX SYMPHONY HALL. (LOCAL). STAN RUBINSKY; PHOENIX JAZZ COMMITTEE; C/O KXTC, WESTWARD HO HOTEL; PHOENIX, AZ 85004. (#6878-2).

APR 25, '76. POPS CONCERT - AMERICAN JEWISH COMPOSERS. LIVE PERFORMANCE AT PLAZA - SYMPHONY HALL. (LOCAL). JOAN FRAZER, CHAIRMAN; PHOENIX JEWISH FEDERATION; 5241 E CALLE VENTURA; PHOENIX, AZ 85018. (#20976-1).

MAY 1, '76. UNIV OF ARIZONA IN CONCERT: MUSIC OF THE SOUTHWEST & THE NATION. LIVE PERFORMANCE AT PHOENIX CIVIC CENTER AUDITORIUM. (ST-WIDE). DR ROBERT WERNER, COORD; ARIZONA ALUMNI ASSOC; UNIV OF ARIZONA; TUCSON, AZ 85721. (#104467-2).

MAY 1 - 2, '76. ARIZONA SPECIAL OLYMPICS. ANNUAL 2-DAY EVENT FOR HANDICAPPED INDIVIDUALS, FEATURING A VARIETY OF COMPETITIVE SPORTS, ALLOWING ALL PARTICIPANTS TO SHARE IN THE SPIRIT & FUN OF COMPETITION. AT ARIZONA STATE UNIVERSITY, TEMPE, ARIZONA. (ST-WIDE). JOHN ANDREWS, DIRECTOR; ARIZONA SPECIAL OLYMPICS; PO BOX 1676; COOLIDGE, AZ 85228. (#25478-1).

MAY 8, '76. SUNBURST FARMS BICENTENNIAL PARADE. PARADE ROUTE STARTS AT 41ST AND COUNTRY GABLES, PROCEEDING WEST ON COUNTRY GABLES TO 47TH AVE, NORTH TO GREENWAY ROAD AND ENDING AT GREENWAY ROAD AND 41ST AVE; REFRESHMENTS AVAILABLE AT GREENWAY HIGH SCHOOL PARKING LOT. AT GREENWAY HIGH SCHOOL, GREENWAY RD AND 41ST AVE. (LOCAL). MRS DARLENE BRISTOL, CHMN; SUNBURST FARMS HOMEOWNERS ASSOC; 4641 W TIERRA BUENA LANE; GLENDALE, AZ 85306. (#104379-5).

MAY 13 - JUNE 5, '76. '1776' - SHERMAN EDWARDS, PETER STONE - ALL-AMERICAN PLAYWRIGHT FEST. PRESENTATION OF A SERIES OF PLAYS WRITTEN BY FAMOUS AMERICAN PLAYWRIGHTS. AT PHOENIX LITTLE THEATER 25 E CORONADO. (LOCAL). TOM MATTHEWS; PHOENIX LITTLE THEATER; 25 E. CORONADO; PHOENIX, AZ 85004. (#6886-14).

MAY 15, '76. BICENTENNIAL JUBILEE - FESTIVAL OF THE GIRL SCOUTS. ARIZONA GIRL SCOUTS PAY TRIBUTE TO TRADITIONS OF COLONIAL AMERICA. AT TEMPE STADIUM. (ST-WIDE). KEN MCCLURE, COORD; ARIZONA STATE OFFICE OF TOURISM; 1645 W JEFFERSON ST, ROOM 417; PHOENIX, AZ 85007. (#103416-308).

MAY 23, '76. AMERICA'S 2 - CONCERT OF WORKS BY MEXICAN COMPOSERS. LIVE PERFORMANCE AT PHOENIX ART MUSEUM. (LOCAL). ELIZABETH SHAW, COORD; PHOENIX FINE ARTS ASSOC; PO BOX 3726; TUCSON, AZ 85722. (#25622-1).

MAY 23, '76. HISTORICAL PAGEANT & FIREWORKS DISPLAY. HISTORICAL PAGEANT THAT WILL HIGHLIGHT THE HISTORICAL DEVELOPMENT OF THE UNITED STATES & ARIZONA. DAILY PERFORMANCES ALSO AT 2:00PM. FOR ENTERTAINMENT GAMES DISPLAYS ETC. PLAY 'CASTLE KEEPER' PRESENTED AT SPRINGFIELD HS ON 'G' ST. AT GLENDALE COMMUNITY COLLEGE. (LOCAL). HUBERT J LAWRENCE, PRIN.; VARIOUS CIVIC ORGANIZATIONS COUNTYWIDE.; 7702 N 39TH AVE.; PHOENIX, AZ 85021. (#2369-1).

MAY 23, '76. THEN '76 - NOW '76, SCHOOL PAGEANT. THERE WILL BE TWO 90-MINUTE SHOWS, ONE AT 2PM, AND ONE AT 8 PM. (LOCAL). H J LAWRENCE, CHMN; PALO VERDE/ROADRUNNER COMMUNITY SCHOOL; 7502 N 39TH AVE; PHOENIX, AZ 85021. (#100453-1).

MAY 30, '76. PACT FAMILY CONCERT. LIVE PERFORMANCE AT PHOENIX CONCERT HALL. (LOCAL). CHRISTIN MCGINNLEY; PACT; 1202 E OAK ST; PHOENIX, AZ 85006. (#25790-1).

JUNE 6 - JULY 4, '76. PLAZA SUNDAYS. LIVE PERFORMANCE AT CIVIC PLAZA. (LOCAL). PACT; PERFORMING ARTS COMBINED TALENT; 1202 E OAK ST; PHOENIX, AZ 85006. (#107661-2).

JUNE 13, '76. FIRST MARINE DIVISION ASSOC 2ND ANNUAL MASSING OF THE COLORS. PRESENTATION OF ALL 50 STATE FLAGS AND ALL NATIONAL FLAGS WITH A MARINE DRESSED IN COMBAT UNIFORM OF THAT DAY, ALL VETERAN, MILITARY AND CIVIC ORGANIZATIONS WILL PARTICIPATE. AT LOV GRUBB CHEVOLET, 27TH AVE & CAMELBACK RD. (LOCAL). FRANK BRAUN, SECRETARY; FIRST MARINE DIVISION ASSOC - PHOENIX CHAPTER; 2011 W OSBORN RD; PHOENIX, AZ 85015. (#17805-1).

JUNE 13, '76. SECOND ANNUAL BREAKFAST AND FLAG DAY. SEMINAR AT LOU GRUBB CHEVROLET. (LOCAL). FRANK BRAUN; 1ST MARINE DIVISION ASSOCIATION; POBOX 2547; PHOENIX, AZ 85004. (#107661-1).

JUNE 19, '76. EDUCATIONAL PARADE & CELEBRATION HONORING BLACK HISTORY IN ARIZONA. HISTORIC MATERIAL WILL BE BROUGHT TO LIFE IN IA SERIES OF LIVE PERFORMANCES; THE BUFFALO SOLDIERS MUSEUM EXHIBITS AND LOCAL PERFORMING GROUPS ARE FEATURED. A PARADE THROUGH THE GREATER DOWNTOWN PHOENIX AREA WILL START THE DAY LONG ACTIVITIES. AT PIONEER ARIZONA BLACK CANYON FREEWAY TO PIONEER EXIT. (ST-WIDE). SPENCER HOWARD, PRES; YOUNG BUFFALO TRADITION, INC; 1830 E WEIR ST; PHOENIX, AZ 85040. (#105731-3).

JULY 4, '76. 'DAWNING OF THE THIRD CENTURY' - ALL PARKS CELEBRATION. FESTIVAL. (LOCAL). MRS PAUL SINGER, COORD; PHOENIX BICENTENNIAL COMMISSION; 21 BILTMORE ESTATES; PHOENIX, AZ 85014. (#26013-1).

JULY 4, '76. PEOPLES POPS 4TH OF JULY CONCERT - SPECIAL REVUE & CONCERT. PRESENTED BY PHOENIX PARKS & RECREATION DEPT IN COOPERATION WITH THE PHOENIX GAZETTE AND THE ARIZONA BICENTENNIAL COMMISSION. AT PHOENIX CONCERT HALL AND AT PHOENIX SYMPHONY HALL AT 7 PM.. (LOCAL). TERESA PEREZ; PHOENIX PARKS & RECREATION DEPT; 2700 N 15TH AVE; PHOENIX, AZ 85007. (#25788-1).

JULY 4, '76. SUNNYSLOPE FIREWORKS DISPLAY & PICNIC. EXHIBIT, FESTIVAL AT NORTH MOUNTAIN PARK. (LOCAL). JAMES DUNN, CHMN; SUNNYSLOPE CITIZENS COUNCIL; 831 E PURDUE; PHOENIX, AZ 85020. (#26932-1).

JULY 5, '76. DRUMS ACROSS AMERICA. EVENT WILL FEATURE 6 CHAMPIONSHIP DRUM & BUGLE CORPS FROM ENID, OK; REVERE, MA; ANAHEIM, CA; GREAT BEND, KS; MADISON, WI; THE 1975 INTL CHAMPIONS & KITCHENER, ONTARIO, CANADA. AT PHOENIX MUNICIPAL STADIUM. (INT'L). MARVIN FREEMAN, COORD; KTAR-TV & WRANGLERS DRUM & BUGLE CORPS; 1101 N CENTRAL; PHOENIX, AZ 85001. (#108314-1).

JULY 26 - 30, '76. NATL FINNISH AMERICAN BICENTENNIAL MEETING AND FESTIVAL. BICENT FESTIVALS WILL BE HELD IN FINNISH-AMERICAN CENTERS LOCATED IN SEVERAL CITIES DURING 1976. (REGN'L). RALPH J JALKANEN, PRES; SUOMI COLLEGE; QUINCY ST; HANCOCK, MI 49930. (#8628-11).

JULY 26 - AUG 6, '76. CARL HAVERLIN/BROADCAST MUSIC, INC, ARCHIVES BICENTENNIAL EXHIBIT. OFFERS A VERSATILE PICTURE OF HISTORY, REGIONAL LIFE & MUSIC FOR OVER 200 YEARS. CONTAINS PRESIDENTIAL LETTERS, LETTERS OF FAMOUS AMERICANS, OLD BOOKS, MANUSCRIPTS, HISTORY OF 'THE STAR SPANGLED BANNER' & COMPOSER AUTOGRAPHS, PLUS SHEET MUSIC OF THE PAST. AT PHOENIX CIVIC PLAZA, 200 W MONROE. (ST-WIDE). MRS ROBERT O HIRSCH, DIR; ARIZONA YOUNG AUDIENCES; 1202 E OAK ST; PHOENIX, AZ 85006. (#20784-2).

AUG 20 - SEPT 1, '76. STRUMMING AMIGO TOUR - MEXICAN MUSICAL TROUPE. LIVE PERFORMANCE, TOUR. (ST-WIDE). ROBERT A DIAZ, DIRECTOR; STRUMMING AMIGOS; RT 1, BOX 717; LAVEEN, AZ 85339. (#108183-1).

OCT 3 - DEC 24, '76. BRITISH 64TH REGIMENT OF FOOT, AZ DETACHMENT. THE 64TH REGIMENT RE-CREATES THE FAMOUS BRITISH 'REDCOATS' WITH HISTORICALLY ACCURATE UNIFORMS, FLAGS, CANNON, FLINTLOCK MUSKETS AND BAYONETS FOR DEMONSTRATIONS OF DRILL AND FIRING OR RE-ENACTMENTS OF HISTORIC BATTLES. (INT'L). GEORGE H DUCKWORTH, JR; BRITISH 64TH REGIMENT OF FOOT, AZ DETACHMENT; 917 W GLENDALE AVE, APT 16; PHOENIX, AZ 85021. (#104379-1).

OCT 22 - NOV 7, '76. ARIZONA STATE FAIR. FAIR AT ARIZONA STATE FAIRGROUNDS, 1826 W MCDOWELL RD. (REGN'L). THOMAS E CLARK, DIRECTOR; STATE OF ARIZONA; PO BOX 6715; PHOENIX, AZ 85005. (#106298-1).

NOV 13 - 21, '76. THANKSGIVING FESTIVAL AND CELEBRATION. FESTIVAL, EXHIBIT. (LOCAL). RON JOHNSON, CHAIRMAN; SOUTH PHOENIX FESTIVAL COMMITTEE; 39 E JACKSON; PHOENIX, AZ 85004. (#4552-2).

NOV 27, '76. MEMORIES: BICENT BALLET, STEPHEN FOSTER MUSIC, ORIGINAL CHOREOGRAPHY. BICENTENNIAL BALLET FEATURED ON FULL BALLET PROGRAM 27 MEMBERS OF BALLET COMPANY AND SOLOISTS. AT SYMPHONY HALL, CIVIC CENTER. (ST-WIDE). TIMONA PITTMAN, EXEC DIR; ARIZONA BALLET THEATRE, INC; 4528N 7TH ST; PHOENIX, AZ 85014. (#107255-1).

DEC 5, '76 - JAN 16, '77. THE AMERICAN INDIAN & THE AMERICAN FLAG EXHIBIT. AN EXHIBITION OF 200 EXAMPLES OF NATIVE AMERICAN ARTWORK, PRACTICAL, CEREMONIAL & AESTHETIC, FROM THE EARLIEST CRAFTSMEN TO CONTEMPORARY ARTISTS. EACH ITEM CARRIES THE AMERICAN FLAG OR OTHER PATRIOTIC MOTIFS. AT THE HEARD MUSEUM. (LOCAL). EVELYN N LEE, DIRECTOR; FLINT INSTITUTE OF ARTS; 1120 E KEARSLEY ST; FLINT, MI 48503. (#2190-5).

PINE

OCT 23, '76. 'AMERICA, WE LOVE YOU'. MUSICAL CONCERNING AMERICA'S INDEPENDENCE, TRADITIONS AND PATRIOTISM. AT PINE ELEMENTARY SCHOOL. (LOCAL). MARY LOU MYERS, TEACHERS; PINE ELEMENTARY SCHOOL; PO BOX 328; PINE, AZ 85544. (#109104-1).

PRESCOTT

BASHFORD HOUSE PRESERVATION IN PRESCOTT, AZ. RELOCATION & RESTORATION OF THE BASHFORD HOUSE IN PRESCOTT AZ. THIS 2 STORY VICTORIAN MANSION WAS BUILT IN 1878 & WAS THE HOME OF A PROMINENT LOCAL BUSINESSMAN & TERRITORIAL OFFICIAL. (LOCAL). KENNETH KIMSEY, DIRECTOR; SHARLOTT HALL MUSEUM; 415 W GURLEY; PRESCOTT, AZ 85281. (#1328). **ARBA GRANTEE.**

CARNEGIE LIBRARY RESTORATION IN PRESCOTT, ARIZONA. RESTORATION OF THE FIRST CARNEGIE LIBRARY TO BE BUILT IN ARIZONA. THE LIBRARY, LOCATED IN PRESCOTT, WILL HOUSE THE CITY ARCHIVES ON THE SECOND FLOOR. (LOCAL). PAUL AX, LIBRARY DIRECTOR; CITY OF PRESCOTT PUBLIC LIBRARY; 125 E GURLEY ST; PRESCOTT, AZ 86301. (#4913).

PRESCOTT — CONTINUED

COLONIAL FLAG - PROJ OF PRESCOTT, AZ. A HAND SEWN 6FT X 10FT FLAG WITH 13 STARS IN THE STYLE OF THE FLAG DURING THE AMERICAN REVOLUTION. (LOCAL). MARY E SEIDEL, CHAIRMAN; THE MONDAY CLUB; 1113 SMOKI AVE; PRESCOTT, AZ 86301. (#17808).

COMMUNITY NATURE CENTER - PRESCOTT, AZ. ENVIRONMENTAL STUDY AREA NEAR PRESCOTT; INCLUDES POND, TRAILS, & LIVING HISTORY AREA. (LOCAL). HENRY DAHLBERG, PROJ DIRECTOR; PRESCOTT PUBLIC SCHOOLS; PO BOX 1231; PRESCOTT, AZ 86301. (#20696). **ARBA GRANTEE.**

FLAG POLE - PROJ OF PRESCOTT, AZ. A NEW FLAG POLE WILL BE CONSTRUCTED AT THE NEW PUBLIC LIBRARY; THE AMERICAN FLAG AND THE ARIZONA FLAG WILL BE FLOWN. (LOCAL). MARY E SEIDEL, PRESIDENT; THE MONDAY CLUB; 1113 SMOKI AVE; PRESCOTT, AZ 86301. (#17809).

FOLK ARTS FAIR - PRESCOTT, ARIZONA. ANNUAL FOLK ARTS FAIR ON THE GROUNDS OF THE SHARLOTT HALL MUSEUM. FEATURES CRAFTS DEMONSTRATIONS. (LOCAL). KEN KIMSEY, DIRECTOR; SHARLOTT HALL MUSEUM; PO BOX 61; PRESCOTT, AZ 86301. (#6889).

GRANITE CREEK PARK DEVELOPMENT IN PRESCOTT, AZ. CITY OF PRESCOTT IS DEVELOPING A 5 MILE LONG GREENBELT ALONG THE GRANITE CREEK WHICH RUNS THROUGH THE CENTER OF PRESCOTT. (LOCAL). A C WILLIAMS, DIRECTOR; CITY OF PRESCOTT, PARKS AND RECREATION DEPT; PO BOX 2059; PRESCOTT, AZ 86301. (#4555).

HISTORY OF PRESCOTT AND VICINITY - PRESCOTT, AZ. COLLECTION OF PRIMARY HISTORIC MATERIALS OF PRESCOTT AND VICINITY. (LOCAL). EDDIE BROOKS SR, CHAIRMAN; PRESCOTT BICENTENNIAL COMMITTEE; PO BOX 1513; PRESCOTT, AZ 86301. (#14961).

MUSICALE AMERICANA - PRESCOTT, AZ. CONCERT OF AMERICAN MUSIC TO BE HELD ON JULY 30, 1976. (LOCAL). DONNA SAPP, COORDINATOR; FT VALLEY MAVERICKS 4-H CLUBS; PO BOX 1544; FLAGSTAFF, AZ 86001. (#27023). **ARBA GRANTEE.**

PLAYGROUND MAP OF U S - PRESCOTT, AZ. 55 X 32 FOOT COLORFUL MAP PAINTED ON CEMENT PLAYGROUND DEPICTING 48 STATES, THEIR CAPITALS, MAJOR RIVERS AND LAKES, PROJECTED ON EXACT SCALE, WILL BE PAINTED ON PLAYGROUND. (LOCAL). FRANCIS WILDMAN, DESIGNER; SACRED HEART SCHOOL; 131 N SUMMIT AVE; PRESCOTT, AZ 86301. (#26041).

SENIOR CITIZENS CENTER BUILDING PROJECT - AZ. CONSTRUCT A BUILDING AND FURNISH FACILITIES FOR A SENIOR CITIZENS CENTER TO PROVIDE EDUCATIONAL, CHARITABLE, SOCIAL AND RECREATIONAL ACTIVITIES FOR ALL SENIOR CITIZENS OF THE COMMUNITY. (LOCAL). LLOYD L ROE, CHAIRMAN; ADULT CENTER CLUB OF PRESCOTT, INC; PO BOX 573; PRESCOTT, AZ 86301. (#21917).

VOICES OF ARIZONA - ORAL HISTORY. TAPE-RECORDED INTERVIEWS WITH THIRTY LONG-TIME RESIDENTS OF ARIZONA CONCERNING EARLY TWENTIETH CENTURY HISTORY IN YAVAPAI COUNTY. INTERVIEWS VARY FROM 45 MINUTES TO 2 HOURS. TYPESCRIPTS PLANNED. (ST-WIDE). VIRGINIA E RICE, SOCIAL SCIENCE LIBRARIAN; UNIVERSITY OF ARIZONA LIBRARY; TUCSON, AZ 85721. (#16930).

YAVAPAI PRESERVATION FOUNDATION-PRESCOTT, AZ. RESIDENTS IN PRESCOTT HAVE ORGANIZED A PRESERVATION FOUNDATION WHICH WILL SURVEY HISTORICAL LANDMARKS & STRUCTURES IN THE COUNTY, & THEN WILL BEGIN A SYSTEMATIC PROGRAM OF PRESERVATION & MARKING. (LOCAL). ELIZABETH RUFFNER, PRES; YAVAPAI HERITAGE FOUNDATION; PO BOX 61; PRESCOTT, AZ 86301. (#2371).

YAVAPAI-PRESCOTT INDIAN TRIBE COMPREHENSIVE PLAN. COMMUNITY DEVELOPMENT ON SMALL INDIAN RESERVATION. (LOCAL). PATRICIA MCGEE, PRESIDENT; YAVAPAI-PRESCOTT INDIAN TRIBE; YAVAPAI INDIAN RESERVATION; PRESCOTT, AZ 86301. (#20109).

MAY 17 - 18, '75. FOLK ARTS FAIR. SATURDAY (17TH) 10:00 AM - 05:00 PM SUNDAY (18TH), 01:00PM-05:00PM ANNUAL FOLK ARTS FAIR ON THE GROUNDS OF THE SHARLOTT HALL MUSEUM. FEATURES CRAFTS DEMONSTRATIONS. AT 415 W GURLEY STREET. (ST-WIDE). KENNETH KIMSEY; SHARLOT HALL HISTORICAL SOCIETY; 415 W GURLEY STREET; PRESCOTT, AZ 86301. (#50776-1).

MAR 19 - 20, '76. UNITED STATES ARMED FORCES BICENTENNIAL CARAVAN. CARAVAN IS COMPOSED OF EXHIBIT VANS FOR EACH MILITARY SERVICE. PROJECT THEME IS 'HISTORY OF THE ARMED FORCES AND THEIR CONTRIBUTIONS TO THE NATION'. (LOCAL). JIM MUSGROVE, CHMN; US ARMED FORCES EXHIBIT VANS PROJECT; POB 591; PRESCOTT, AZ 86301. (#1775-335).

APR 3 - 25, '76. ARIZONA 1776-1976. THE FOUR MAJOR MUSEUM FACILITIES OF ARIZONA COOPERATE IN A TRAVELING EXHIBIT ILLUSTRATING 200 YEARS OF ARIZONA HISTORY. (ST-WIDE). ELIZABETH DOBRINSKI; MUSEUM OF NORTHERN ARIZONA; RT #4, PO BOX 720; FLAGSTAFF, AZ 86001. (#103416-273).

MAY 22, '76. MEMORIES: BICENT BALLET, STEPHEN FOSTER MUSIC, ORIGINAL CHOREOGRAPHY. BICENTENNIAL BALLET FEATURED ON FULL BALLET PROGRAM, 11 PERFORMANCES STATEWIDE, 27 BALLET COMPANY MEMBERS & GUEST SOLOISTS. AT HENDRIX AUDITORIUM, 300 SOUTH GRANITE, OFF MONTEZUMA. (ST-WIDE). TIMONA PITTMAN, EXEC DIR; ARIZONA BALLET THEATRE, INC; 4528 N 7TH ST; PHOENIX, AZ 85014. (#107255-3).

JUNE 30 - JULY 5, '76. COMMUNITY FINE ARTS - LIVE PERFORMANCE. ANNUAL MELODRAM HONORING 'FRONTIER DAYS' CELEBRATION. AT FINE ARTS CENTER, 208 N MARINA. (LOCAL). MRS J B BURHANS, COORD; PRESCOTT FINE ARTS ASSOC; 1143 MOHAWK TRAIL; PRESCOTT, AZ 86301. (#108910-1).

JULY 3 - 5, '76. PRESCOTT FRONTIER DAYS AND RODEO. FESTIVAL. (LOCAL). LEO SCOTT, PRESIDENT; PRESCOTT JAYCEES; PO BOX 1296; PRESCOTT, AZ 86301. (#102500-3).

JULY 30, '76. MUSICALE AMERICANA - CONCERT. LIVE PERFORMANCE. (LOCAL). DONNA SAPP, COORD; FT VALLEY MAVERICKS 4-H CLUBS; PO BOX 1544; FLAGSTAFF, AZ 86001. (#27023-1).

SEPT 23 - 26, '76. YAVAPAI COUNTY FAIR. MISS YAVAPAI PAGEANT AND THE ANNUAL HORSE SHOW ARE SOME OF THE SCHEDULED EVENTS. AT YAVAPAI COUNTY FAIRGROUNDS. (ST-WIDE). FAYE RUSSELL, EXEC SEC; YAVAPAI COUNTY FAIR ASSOCIATION; PO BOX 346; PRESCOTT, AZ 86301. (#106095-1).

SACATON

COMMUNITY FAIRGROUNDS - SACATON, AZ. TO INVENTORY AND DEVELOP TRIBAL MATERIAL RESOURCES FOR THE USE AND BENEFIT OF THE INDIAN PEOPLE; FAIRGROUNDS, PARKS & RECREATIONAL AREAS WILL BE DEVELOPED. (LOCAL). ALEXANDER LEWIS, SR GOVERNOR; GILA RIVER INDIAN COMMUNITY; PO BOX 97; SACATON, AZ 85247. (#22855). **ARBA GRANTEE.**

FESTIVAL COMMEMORATING DE ANZA EXPEDITION IN AZ. ONE DAY CELEBRATION AT GILA RIVER INDIAN RESERVATION COMMEMORATTION 2ND DE ANZA EXPEDITION TO SAN FRANXCISO EVENTS INCLU; JACK POT ROPING INDIAN DANCES, FREE BARBEQUE AND INDIAN ARTISANS. (ST-WIDE). CHRISTINE BROWN, CHAIRMAN; GILA RIVER ARTS & CRAFTS, INC; PO BOX 457; SACATON, AZ 85247. (#11003). **ARBA RECOGNIZED. ARBA GRANTEE.**

NOV 1 - 2, '75. FESTIVAL COMMEMORATING DE ANZA EXPEDITION. CELEBRATION INCLUDES CULTURAL INDIAN DANCES; FREE BARBEQUE; INDIAN FOOD BOOTHS; JACKPOT ROPING; NATIVE ARTISANS DEMONSTRATING POTTERYMAKING, BASKET-WEAVING & PAINTING; AND A PUBLIC DANCE. AT MUL-CHU-THA RECREATION FAIRGROUNDS. (ST-WIDE). CHRISTINE BROWN, CHAIRMAN; GILA RIVER ARTS & CRAFTS INC, AND GILA RIVER INDIAN COMMUNITY; PO BOX 338; SACATON, AZ 85247. (#11003-1).

SAFFORD

APR 25 - MAY 5, '74. CENTENNIAL CELEBRATION OF SAFFORD, ARIZONA. CENTENNIAL CELEBRATION FEATURING RODEOS, FESTIVALS AND HISTORICAL EXHIBITS. (ST-WIDE). ROBERT E. LEE, CHAIRMAN; SAFFORD CENTENNIAL COMMITTEE; 1100 THATCHER BLVD; SAFFORD, AZ 85546. (#467-901).

FEB 22 - 23, '76. UNITED STATES ARMED FORCES BICENTENNIAL CARAVAN. CARAVAN IS COMPOSED OF EXHIBIT VANS FOR EACH MILITARY SERVICE. PROJECT THEME IS 'HISTORY OF THE ARMED FORCES AND THEIR CONTRIBUTIONS TO THE NATION'. (LOCAL). JOHN MICKELSON, CHMN; US ARMED FORCES EXHIBIT VANS PROJECT; BOX 707; SAFFORD, AZ 85546. (#1775-323).

JULY 4, '76. AMERICAN LEGION BICENTENNIAL PARADE. PARADE. (LOCAL). JOHN MICKELSON; SAFFORD-GRAHAM COUNTY BICENTENNIAL COMMITTEE; PO BOX 707; SAFFORD, AZ 85546. (#107651-1).

SCOTTSDALE

ACT THEATRE RESIDENCY IN SCOTTSDALE, AZ. THE RESIDENCY WILL GO TOWARD THE DEVELOPMENT OF A STATE THEATRE IN ARIZONA. (ST-WIDE). SANDY ROSENTHAL, PRODUCING DIRECTOR; ARIZONA CIVIC THEATRE; 2719 E BROADWAY; TUCSON, AZ 85716. (#16146).

FREEDOM SEEKERS '76 - SCOTTSDALE, AZ. STUDENTS WILL TRAVEL THROUGH 26 STATES AS PART OF AN EDUCATIONAL COURSE. (REGN'L). MIKE TODD, GUIDE; FREEDOM SEEKERS '76; 7221 N 34TH AVE; PHOENIX, AZ 85021. (#24810).

HIGHLIGHTS OF ARIZONA - SCOTTSDALE. MULTI-MEDIA DANCE/DRAMA PAGEANT HIGHLIGHTING THE VARIOUS HISTORIC CULTURES IN ARIZONA WILL TOUR THE STATE IN 1976. (LOCAL). MARY MIZELL, COORDINATOR; ARIZONA BICENTENNIAL COMMITTEE; 4102 E BERYL LN; PHOENIX, AZ 85018. (#22695). **ARBA GRANTEE.**

PRIDE IN AMERICA - SCOTTSDALE, ARIZONA. SCOTTSDALE & AZ CHAPTERS OF JAYCEES ARE UNDERTAKING MODEL PROJECT FOR THE US JAYCEES THAT WILL PROMOTE PRIDE IN AMERICA THRU COMMUNITY SERVICE ACTIVITIES, ADVERTISING IN THE MEDIA, & EDUCATION MATERIAL. (LOCAL). DAN HEIRSHBERG, DIRECTOR; SCOTTSDALE JAYCEES; PO BOX 292; SCOTTSDALE, AZ 85252. (#2361). **(??).**

A REPOSITORY FOR HISTORICAL MEMORABILIA - AZ. SCOTTSDALE AND PARADISE VALLEY ARE GOING TO RENOVATE A CITY OWNED BUILDING AS A REPOSITORY FOR ARTIFACTS AND INTERVIEWS THAT ARE NOW BEING COLLECTED LOCALLY. (LOCAL). EILEEN RASSMUSSEN, CHAIRMAN; SCOTTSDALE BICENTENNIAL COMMITTEE; PO BOX 2054; SCOTTSDALE, AZ 85252. (#14772).

SCOTTSDALE THEATER FOR CHILDREN PUPPET SHOW - AZ. THE PUPPET SHOWS WILL BE HELD ON SATURDAYS FROM SEPTEMBER TO NOVEMBER. (LOCAL). DAVID SCHUMBACH, COORDINATOR; SCOTTSDALE THEATER FOR CHILDREN; BOX 543; SCOTTSDALE, AZ 85252. (#27025). **ARBA GRANTEE.**

SENIOR CITIZENS DOWNTOWN NEIGHBORHOOD CENTER - AZ. CONSTRUCTION OF DOWNTOWN CENTER FOR RECREATIONAL & SOCIAL ACTIVITIES FOR SENIOR CITIZENS. (LOCAL). JOHN HOLMES, PROJ DIRECTOR; CITY OF SCOTTSDALE; CIVIC PLAZA DR; SCOTTSDALE, AZ 85253. (#20691). **ARBA GRANTEE.**

'TWO SUNS ARCOLOGY'. TRAVELING EXHIBIT ON SOLAR ENERGY UTILIZATION & ECOLOGICALLY SOUND MANAGEMENT PRACTISES IN ENERGY & RESOURCE DEVELOPMENT. EXHIBIT OPEN IN ROCHESTER, NY, MAY 1976. (NAT'L). KAREN SUE BLACKER, PROJECT DIRECTOR; COSANTI FOUNDATION; 6433 DOUBLETREE RD; SCOTTSDALE, AZ 85253. (#7952). **ARBA RECOGNIZED. ARBA GRANTEE.**

YOUTH REPRESENTATIVES: SCOTTSDALE/PARADISE VALLEY. STUDENTS FROM SCOTTSDALE HIGH SCHOOLS WILL SERVE AS HOSTS/HOSTESSES AT LOCAL BICENTENNIAL ACTIVITIES. REPRESENTATIVES WILL BE CHOSEN ON THE BASIS OF THEIR UNDERSTANDING & INTEREST IN THE BICENTENNIAL. (LOCAL). ROBERTA UNTERBERGER, PRESIDENT; SCOTTSDALE/PARADISE VALLEY BICENTENNIAL COMMISSION; PO BOX 2054; SCOTTSDALE, AZ 85252. (#1806). **ARBA GRANTEE.**

1ST-HAND HISTORY OF SCOTTSDALE/PARADISE VALLEY, AZ. LOCAL HIGH SCHOOL STUDENTS CONDUCT RESEARCH INTERVIEWS WITH LONGTIME AREA RESIDENTS & GATHER PICTORIAL INFO. ILLUSTRATED HISTORY WILL BE PUBLISHED IN 1976. (LOCAL). DR WILLIAM PHILLIPS, HERITAGE CHAIRMAN; SCOTTSDALE/PARADISE VALLEY BICENTENNIAL COMMISSION; 8222 E LEWIS; SCOTTSDALE, AZ 85257. (#1807). **(??). ARBA GRANTEE.**

'200 TREES FOR 200 YEARS' IN SCOTTSDALE, AZ. INDIVIDUALS AND ORGANIZATIONS ARE BEING ASKED TO DONATE TREES PLANTING; PARK DEPT IS COORDINATING LAYOUT OF LOCATIONS AND TYPES OF TREES TO BE PLANTED. (LOCAL). EILEEN RASSMUSSEN, COORDINATOR; PARK DEPT; PO BOX 2054; SCOTTSDALE, AZ 85252. (#14258).

JULY 4 - 5, '75. SCOTTSDALE JAYCEES - BICENTENNIAL CELEBRATION. FAIR, FESTIVAL. (LOCAL). DAN HEIRSHBERG; SCOTTSDALE JAYCEES; PO BOX 292; SCOTTSDALE, AZ 85252. (#50379-1).

NOV 16 - 17, '75. SCOTTSDALE FESTIVAL OF NATIONS. FESTIVAL, EXHIBIT, LIVE PERFORMANCE AT ELDORADO PARK. (LOCAL). ROBERTA UNTERBERGER; SCOTTSDALE BICENTENNIAL COMMISSION; 8222 E LEWIS; SCOTTSDALE, AZ 85257. (#50787-1).

JAN 17 - FEB 15, '76. 'USA '76: THE FIRST TWO HUNDRED YEARS'. THIS A TRAVELING EXHIBIT WHICH WILL TOUR SEVERAL CITIES DURING THE BICENTENNIAL ERA. THE EXHIBIT EXPLORES THE CULTURAL & SCIENTIFIC HERITAGE OF THE USA. AT SCOTTSDALE CENTER FOR THE ARTS, 3839 CIVIC CENTER PLAZA. (LOCAL). JACK MASEY, PROJ DIR; AMERICAN REVOLUTION BICENTENNIAL ADMINISTRATION; 2401 E ST NW; WASHINGTON, DC 20276. (#5661-1).

JAN 18 - APR 27, '76. DEVELOPMENT OF A STATE THEATRE FOR ARIZONA. 3 PLAYS BEING PRESENTED INCLUDE: 'RASHOMON' BY FAY & MICHAEL KANIN (COMEDY); 'SOMETHING'S AFOOT' BY JIM MCDONALD & ROBERT GERLACH (MUSICAL); AND 'THE DEVIL'S DISCIPLE' BY GEORGE BERNARD SHAW (COMEDY). AT SCOTTSDALE CENTER FOR THE ARTS; 3839 CIVIC CTR PLAZA. (ST-WIDE). SANDY ROSENTHAL, CHMN; ARIZONA CIVIC THEATRE; 2719 E BROADWAY; TUCSON, AZ 85716. (#16146-1).

JAN 29 - FEB 1, '76. PARADA DEL SOL. FOUR DAYS OF RCA CHAMPIONSHIP RODEO WITH A BICENTENNIAL THEME. THREE HOUR BICENTENNIAL PARADE, ALL HORSE-DRAWN ON JAN 31. (REGN'L). SHEP SCHINDLER, DIRECTOR; SCOTTSDALE CHAMBER OF COMMERCE; PO BOX 129; SCOTTSDALE, AZ 85252. (#103560-1).

FEB 28, '76. MEMORIES: BICENTENNIAL BALLET AND STEPHEN FOSTER MUSIC. LIVE PERFORMANCE AT SCOTTSDALE CENTER FOR THE ARTS, CIVIC CENTER. (LOCAL). TIMONA PITTMAN, EXEC DIR; ARIZONA BALLET THEATRE, INC; 4528 N 7TH ST; PHOENIX, AZ 85014. (#200004-7).

MAR 13 - 14, '76. UNITED STATES ARMED FORCES BICENTENNIAL CARAVAN. CARAVAN IS COMPOSED OF EXHIBIT VANS FOR EACH MILITARY SERVICE. PROJECT THEME IS 'HISTORY OF THE ARMED FORCES AND THEIR CONTRIBUTIONS TO THE NATION'. (LOCAL). ROBERTA UNTERBERGER, CHMN; US ARMED FORCES EXHIBIT VANS PROJECT; 8222 E LEWIS; SCOTTSDALE, AZ 85257. (#1775-334).

MAR 23, '76. TEXAS OPERA THEATER PRESENTS 'EL CAPITAN'. HILARIOUS OPERETTA MASTERPIECE BY AMERICA'S 'MARCH KING' JOHN PHILIP SOUSA. (LOCAL). CAM WILLIAMS, COORD; SCOTTSDALE CENTER FOR THE PERFORMING ARTS; 615 LOUISIANA; HOUSTON, TX 77002. (#200004-17).

MAR 24, '76. TEXAS OPERA THEATER PRESENTS 'THE BARBER OF SEVILLE'. ROLLICKING COMIC OPERA BY ROSSINI PERFORMED IN ENGLISH WITH CHAMBER ORCHESTRA. (REGN'L). CAM WILLIAMS, COORD; SCOTTSDALE CENTER FOR THE PERFORMING ARTS; 615 LOUISIANA; HOUSTON, TX 77002. (#200004-18).

APR 4, '76. HIGHLIGHTS OF ARIZONA. HIGHLIGHTS WILL INCLUDE: REGIONAL FOLK-LIFE, PIONEER PILGRIMAGE, HISPANIC-AMERICAN TRADITION AND THE LEGEND OF CAMELBACK MOUNTAIN. INSPIRATIONAL FORCES OF THE SOUTHWEST; INDIAN CHANTS, DANCES; HISPANIC-AMER INFLUENCE SPEARHEADING INTO THE DRAMA OF TODAY. AT SCOTTSDALE PERFORMING ARTS CENTER, SCOTTSDALE CIVIC PLAZA. (LOCAL). PAULA NELSON, COORD.; SCOTTSDALE BICENT COMM & ARIZONA YOUNG AUDIENCES; 4813 N 75TH WAY; SCOTTSDALE, AZ 85251. (#102753-1).

MAY 8, '76. MEMORIES: BICENT BALLET, STEPHEN FOSTER MUSIC, ORIG CHOREOGRAPHY. LIVE PERFORMANCE AT SCOTTSDALE CENTER FOR THE ARTS, CIVIC CENTER. (ST-WIDE). TIMONA PITTMAN, EXEC DIR; ARIZONA BALLET THEATRE, INC; 4528 NORTH 7TH ST; PHOENIX, AZ 85014. (#107255-5).

MAY 25 - 29, '76. NJCAA MEN'S CHAMPIONSHIP TENNIS TOURNAMENT. COMPETITION. (LOCAL). LARRY PHILPOT, COORD; SCOTTSDALE COMMUNITY COLLEGE; SCOTTSDALE, AZ 85282. (#28033-10).

JULY 4, '76. BICENTENNIAL BIRTHDAY PARTY. FESTIVAL. (LOCAL). ADAIR JACKMAN, CHMN; SCOTTSDALE BICENTENNIAL COM-

SCOTTSDALE — CONTINUED

MISSION, INC; PO BOX 2054; SCOTTSDALE, AZ 85252. (#102311-1).

SEPT 1 - NOV 24, '76. SCOTTSDALE THEATRE FOR CHILDREN PUPPET PRODUCTION. LIVE PERFORMANCE AT SCOTTSDALE CENTER FOR THE ARTS. (LOCAL). DAVID SCHUMBACH, COORD; SCOTTSDALE THEATRE FOR CHILDREN; BOX 543; SCOTTSDALE, AZ 85252. (#27025-1).

OCT 9 - NOV 14, '76. EXHIBITION OF YUGOSLAV NAIVE ART - SITES. EXHIBIT ILLUSTRATES CURRENT DIRECTION & EVOLUTION OF NAIVE YUGOSLAV ART. INCLUDES ART BY VECENAJ, RABUZIN, SKURJENI, KOVACIC & LACKOVIC. WOOD SCULPTURES, PAINTINGS; MAPS, FILMS; TAPES ON TRADITIONAL YUGOSLAV FOLK MUSIC. AT SCOTTSDALE ARTS CENTER. (INT'L). JOHN ARMSTRONG, CHAIRMAN; SCOTTSDALE ARTS CENTER; 3839 CIVIC CENTER PLAZA; SCOTTSDALE, AZ 85251. (#106774-1).

SEDONA

MAR 21, '76. UNITED STATES ARMED FORCES BICENTENNIAL CARAVAN. CARAVAN IS COMPOSED OF EXHIBIT VANS FOR EACH MILITARY SERVICE. PROJECT THEME IS 'HISTORY OF THE ARMED FORCES AND THEIR CONTRIBUTIONS TO THE NATION'. (LOCAL). HOWARD HAWK, CHMN; US ARMED FORCES EXHIBIT VANS PROJECT; POB 247; SEDONA, AZ 86336. (#1775-336).

SELLS

SAN XAVIER BICENTENNIAL PLAZA - SELLS, AZ. CONSTRUCTION OF A CULTURAL, RECREATIONAL AND COMMERCIAL PLAZA ON THE PAPAGO INDIAN RESERVATION. (LOCAL). CECIL WILLIAMS, CHAIRMAN; PAPAGO TRIBE OF ARIZONA; PO BOX 837; SELLS, AZ 85634. (#23415). **ARBA GRANTEE.**

SHOW LOW

SHOW LOW PRARIE DOG PARK - AZ. A PARK IS BEING BUILT IN A SCENIC AREA OF SHOWLOW WITHIN WHICH RESIDES A PERMANENT COLONY OF PRAIRIE DOGS. (LOCAL). GIB FROST, CHAIRMAN; SHOWLOW CHAMBER OF COMMERCE; 222 E DEUCE OF CLUBS; SHOWLOW, AZ 85901. (#27424). **ARBA GRANTEE.**

MAR 28, '76. UNITED STATES ARMED FORCES BICENTENNIAL CARAVAN. CARAVAN IS COMPOSED OF EXHIBIT VANS FOR EACH MILITARY SERVICE. PROJECT THEME IS 'HISTORY OF THE ARMED FORCES AND THEIR CONTRIBUTIONS TO THE NATION'. (LOCAL). MAURICE GISS, EXEC DIR; US ARMED FORCES EXHIBIT VANS PROJECT; 1807 N CENTRAL AVE, SUITE 108; PHOENIX, AZ 85004. (#1775-341).

JULY 3, '76. BICENTENNIAL BARBEQUE. FESTIVAL AT RODEO GROUNDS, DEUCE OF CLUBS ST. (LOCAL). MERWYN FISH, DIRECTOR; LDS CHURCH; LINDEN, AZ 85901. (#104707-3).

JULY 3, '76. BICENTENNIAL FIREWORKS CELEBRATION. FESTIVAL AT RODEO GROUNDS, DEUCE OF CLUBS ST. (LOCAL). S GIBBONS FROST; SHOW LOW CHAMBER OF COMMERCE; SHOW LO, AZ 85901. (#104707-1).

JULY 3, '76. COLORFUL WESTERN AMERICANA PARADE. PARADE AT MAIN STREET, SHOW LOW, AZ. (LOCAL). GIB FROST, COORD; SHOW LOW BICENTENNIAL COMM; CHAMBER OF COMMERCE; 222 E DEUCE OF CLUBS; SHOW LOW, AZ 85901. (#104379-4).

JULY 3, '76. 4TH OF JULY PARADE. PARADE AT DEUCE OF CLUBS ST. (LOCAL). S GIBBONS FROST; SHOW LOW CHAMBER OF COMMERCE; SHOW LOW, AZ 85901. (#104707-2).

JULY 3 - 5, '76. SHOW LOW'S RODEO. COMPETITION, LIVE PERFORMANCE AT RODEO GROUNDS, DEUCE OF CLUBS ST. (LOCAL). MERWYN FISH, DIRECTOR; LDS CHURCH; LINDEN, AZ 85901. (#104707-4).

DEC 9, '76. UNITED STATES ARMED FORCES BICENTENNIAL CARAVAN. CARAVAN IS COMPOSED OF EXHIBIT VANS FOR EACH MILITARY SERVICE. PROJECT THEME IS 'HISTORY OF THE ARMED FORCES & THEIR CONTRIBUTIONS TO THE NATION'. (LOCAL). LE BARON JONES; UNITED STATES ARMED FORCES BICENTENNIAL CARAVAN; SHOW LOW, AZ 85901. (#1775-854).

SIERRA VISTA

MUSIC, MUSIC, MUSIC. AN ORIGINAL MUSICAL TO BE PERFORMED IN SOUTHEASTERN ARIZONA COMMUNITIES, TRACES AMERICAN MUSIC THROUGH TIME. (LOCAL). EDNA M COBURN; CITY OF SIERRA VISTA; PO BOX 1924; SIERRA VISTA, AZ 85635. (#102500-1). **(??).**

OUR ART HERITAGE, SIERRA VISTA, AZ. EXHIBITS OF HISTORICAL ARTS, CRAFTS & GRAPHICS DONATED BY LOCAL CITIZENS. (LOCAL). VERNON ROSAMOND, CHAIRMAN; HUACHUCHA ART ASSOC; SIERRA VISTA, AZ 85635. (#26993). **ARBA GRANTEE.**

SIERRA VISTA MINI PARK, AZ. A ROTARY CLUB IN SIERRA VISTA IS SPONSORING THE CREATION OF A MINI PARK IN THE CENTER OF THE CITY. THE PARK WILL BE PLANTED WITH ITALIAN CYPRESS, PFITZERS AND GRASS. (LOCAL). EDNA M COBURN, COORDINATOR; ROTARY CLUB; PO BOX 1924; SIERRA VISTA, AZ 85635. (#14260).

SOAP BOX IN THE PARK - SIERRA VISTA, AZ. CITIZENS ARE EXCERCISING ONE OF AMERICA'S BASIC FREEDOMS -- FREEDOM OF SPEECH. IN 1975 AND 76 A REGULAR ON-GOING SPEAKERS' FORUM WILL BE HELD IN THE CITY PARK. CITIZENS WILL BE ABLE TO EXPRESS VIEWS. (LOCAL). EVELYN ZOLL, COORDINATOR; CITY OF SIERRA VISTA; PO BOX 1849; SIERRA VISTA, AZ 85635. (#15468).

'1776' - SIERRA VISTA, AZ. THE SIERRA MUSICAL THEATRE WILL PERFORM THE PLAY '1776'. (LOCAL). DAVID MEEKER, DIRECTOR; COCHISE COLLEGE; 99 CARGIL NE; SIERRA VISTA, AZ 85635. (#26036). **ARBA GRANTEE.**

FEB 29 - MAR 1, '76. UNITED STATES ARMED FORCES BICENTENNIAL CARAVAN. CARAVAN IS COMPOSED OF EXHIBIT VANS FOR EACH MILITARY SERVICE. PROJECT THEME IS 'HISTORY OF THE ARMED FORCES AND THEIR CONTRIBUTIONS TO THE NATION'. (LOCAL). CHARLES YELL, CHMN; US ARMED FORCES EXHIBIT VANS PROJECT; PO BOX 1624; SIERRA VISTA, AZ 85635. (#1775-327).

JULY 2 - 29, '76. BUENA MUSICAL THEATRE PERFORMANCE OF '1776'. LIVE PERFORMANCE AT BUENA HIGH SCHOOL AUDITORIUM. (LOCAL). DAVID MEEKER, DIRECTOR; COCHISE COLLEGE; 99 CARGIL NE; SIERRA VISTA, AZ 85635. (#26036-1).

JULY 4, '76. 9TH ANNUAL JULY 4TH BICENTENNIAL FIREWORKS. THE DAYS EVENTS WILL INCLUDE ACTIVITIES FOR ALL AGES/ HORSE RACES BIKE RODEO/FIELD EVENTS/SOFTBALL GAMES/ BEARD CONTEST/SKYDIVING/A WEDDING/FIDDLERS CONCERT/ SWIM MEET/1776 FASHION SHOW. AT SIERRA VISTA CITY PARK AND HIGH SCHOOL STADIUM. (LOCAL). SCOTT C GRAINGER, CHMN; SIERRA VISTA ROTARY CLUB; POB 1344; SIERRA VISTA, AZ 85635. (#106457-1).

SNOWFLAKE

JUNE 5, '76. MEMORIES: BICENT BALLET, STEPHEN FOSTER MUSIC, ORIG CHOREOGRAPHY. BICENTENNIAL BALLET FEATURED ON FULL BALLET PROGRAM, 11 PERFORMANCES STATEWIDE. 27 BALLET COMPANY MEMBERS AND GUEST SOLOISTS. AT LOBO AUDITORIUM. (ST-WIDE). TIMONA PITTMAN, EXEC DIR; ARIZONA BALLET THEATRE, INC; 4528 N 7TH ST; PHOENIX, AZ 85014. (#107255-2).

JULY 1 - 31, '76. PIONEER DAY ANNUAL CELEBRATION. FESTIVAL. (LOCAL). BESS ERICKSON; SNOWFLAKE UNIFIED SCHOOL DIST; PO BOX 1100; SNOWFLAKE, AZ 85937. (#107652-2).

JULY 2 - 3, '76. AMERICAN LEGACIES - GREAT MOMENTS TO REMEMBER. FESTIVAL, LIVE PERFORMANCE AT TAYLOR PARK. (ST-WIDE). LENN SHUMWAY; LDS CHURCH - TAYLOR ARIZONA WARDS; TAYLOR, AZ 85939. (#107652-3).

SPRINGERVILLE

ROUND VALLEY SENIOR CITIZENS CENTER, AZ. A BUILDING IS BEING PURCHASED & MOVED TO SPRINGERVILLE. THE A-FRAME STRUCTURE WILL BECOME A SENIOR CITIZENS CENTER, TO BE COMPLETED BY AUGUST, 1976. (LOCAL). MAURICE M GISS, EXEC DIRECTOR; AMERICAN REVOLUTION BICENTENNIAL COMMISSION OF ARIZONA; 1807 N CENTRAL, SUITE 108; PHOENIX, AZ 85004. (#25654). **ARBA GRANTEE.**

JUNE 12, '76. OLD-FASHIONED COUNTRY FAIR. FAIR. (ST-WIDE). BEVERLY MARTIN, CHAIRMAN; SPRINGER/EAGAR BICENTENNIAL COMMITTEE; PO BOX 283; EAGAR, AZ 85925. (#200004-6).

ST JOHNS

OLD APACHE COUNTY JAIL - ST JOHNS, AZ. RESTORATION AND MOVING TO NEW LOCATION OF HISTORIC JAIL. (LOCAL). DELBERT LAMPSON, COORDINATOR; APACHE COUNTY HISTORICAL SOCIETY; ST JOHNS, AZ 85936. (#27024). **ARBA GRANTEE.**

ORAL HISTORY - ST JOHNS, AZ. ORAL HISTORY OF ST JOHN'S WILL BE RECORDED IN INTERVIEWS WITH ELDERLY CITIZENS. (LOCAL). DELBERT D LAMBSON, CHAIRMAN; ST JOHN'S BICENTENNIAL COMMITTEE; BOX 81; ST JOHN'S, AZ 85936. (#24037).

JUNE 24 - 27, '76. SAN JUAN DAY FESTIVAL. PARADE, BARBECUE, 2 DANCES, SOFTBALL, BASEBALL & MUSICAL PERFORMANCES. AT E MAIN ST. (LOCAL). FR O'KEEFE, DIRECTOR; ST JOHNS CATHOLIC CHURCH; ST JOHNS, AZ 85936. (#108081-1).

ST MICHAELS

ST MICHAELS HISTORICAL MUSEUM OF ARIZONA. HISTORIC FRANCISCAN MISSION ON NAVAJO RESERVATION NEEDS RESTORATION. DURING BICENT THE FRANCISCAN FATHERS ARE UNDERTAKING RESTORATION OF OLD TRADING POST & CONSTRUCTION OF LIBRARY & RESOURCE CENTER. (ST-WIDE). FRAN PAWLOWSKI, DIRECTOR; ST MICHAELS MISSION; ST MICHAELS, AZ 86511. (#1803). **ARBA GRANTEE.**

SUN CITY

MAR 17 - 18, '76. UNITED STATES ARMED FORCES BICENTENNIAL CARAVAN. CARAVAN IS COMPOSED OF EXHIBIT VANS FOR EACH MILITARY SERVICE. PROJECT THEME IS 'HISTORY OF THE ARMED FORCES AND THEIR CONTRIBUTIONS TO THE NATION'. (LOCAL). DON TUFFS, CHMN; US ARMED FORCES EXHIBIT VANS PROJECT; POB 555; SUN CITY, AZ 85351. (#1775-333).

JUNE 20, '76. FATHER'S DAY ROOT BEER BUST. FAIR AT SUN CITY SUN BOWL, 107TH AND CLAIR DRIVE. (LOCAL). JERRY SVENDSEN; DEL E WEBB DEVELOPMENT CO &; PO BOX 555; SUN CITY, AZ 85351. (#107656-1).

JULY 4, '76. FIREWORKS SHOW. FESTIVAL AT SUN CITY STADIUM, 111TH & GRAND, SUN CITY AZ 85351. (LOCAL). JERRY SVENDSEN; SUN CITY BICENTENNIAL COMMITTEE; PO BOX 555; SUN CITY, AZ 85351. (#107656-2).

TAYLOR

JULY 3, '76. PATRIOTIC PROGRAM. SEMINAR. (LOCAL). JOCIE TEUNEY; TOWN OF TAYLOR; TAYLOR, AZ 85939. (#107653-1).

JULY 23 - 24, '76. PIONEER DAYS. FAIR. (LOCAL). JOCIE TEUNEY; TOWN OF TAYLOR; TAYLOR, AZ 85939. (#107653-2).

TEMPE

ARIZONA STATE UNIVERSITY HISTORICAL SYMPOSIA. TWO PUBLIC CONFERENCES IN 1974 & 1975 ON THE THEMES OF 2 CENTURIES OF HISPANIC CONTRIBUTIONS TO ARIZONA AND THE SOUTHWEST AND ARIZONA SINCE STATEHOOD. 1975 CONFERENCE SCHEDULED FOR FEBRUARY. (REGN'L). W E ADAMS, CHAIRMAN; ARIZONA STATE UNIV; ARIZONA STATE UNIV; TEMPE, AZ 85281. (#593). **ARBA GRANTEE.**

COLONIAL CRAFTS - PROJ OF TEMPE, AZ. THE TEMPE HERITAGE COMMITTEE WILL MAKE AVAILABLE TO THE COMMUNITY DEMONSTRATIONS AND WORKSHOPS WITH 'ON HAND' EXPERIENCES OF THE COLONIAL CRAFTS. DEMONSTRATIONS WILL BE ON A REGULAR BASIS. (LOCAL). LOIS PORTER, PROJ DIRECTOR; TEMPE HERITAGE COMMITTEE; ROUTE 4, BOX 1135; APACHE JUNC, AZ 85220. (#14757).

COMMUNITY VISUAL ARTS CENTER, TEMPE, AZ. THE CENTER WILL PROVIDE SPACE & EQUIPMENT FOR ARTISTS IN THE AREA. (LOCAL). DOROTHY WACHTA, COORDINATOR; TEMPE ART LEAGUE; 316 W LAGUNA; TEMPE, AZ 85282. (#26596). **ARBA GRANTEE.**

COMPILED GUIDE TO DOCUMENTS IN ARIZONA HISTORY. GOAL IS TO LOCATE, DESCRIBE AND PUBLISH A GENERAL DIRECTORY TO PRIMARY COCUMENTS IN ARIZONA HISTORY. CONSULATION WITH LOCAL HIST-ORICAL GROUPS WILL BE EMPHASIZED. (LOCAL). DR CHARLES C COLLEY, HEAD OF SPECIAL COLLECTIONS; HAYDEN LIBRARY, ARIZONA STATE UNIVERSITY; TEMPE, AZ 85281. (#21378). **ARBA GRANTEE.**

FLAGS FOR KIWANIS PARK - TEMPE, AZ. TEMPE AMERICAN LEGION POST #2 IS ERECTING A MONUMENT AND FLAG AT KIWANIS PARK TO COMMEMORATE THE EFFORTS OF LOCAL VETERANS. (LOCAL). DONALD B PERRY, COORDINATOR; AMERICAN LEGION POST #2; BOX A; TEMPE, AZ 85281. (#27211). **ARBA GRANTEE.**

HISTORIC SITE MARKERS - PROJ OF TEMPE, AZ. HISTORIC SITES AND STRUCTURES IN TEMPE WILL BE MARKED WITH OFFICIAL ARIZONA HISTORICAL SOCIETY MARKERS. RESEARCH WILL BE DONE ON EACH SITE AND THEM A TEXT WILL BE WRITTEN. (LOCAL). FRANK HANNA JR, CHAIRMAN; ARIZONA HISTORICAL SOCIETY; 1272 E DEL RIO; TEMPE, AZ 85281. (#14755). **ARBA GRANTEE.**

THE HISTORY OF THE TEMPE FIRE DEPARTMENT - AZ. THE TEMPE HERITAGE COMMITTEE WILL RECORD THE HISTORY OF THE TEMPE FIRE DEPT BY INTERVIEWING 1ST VOLUNTEER FIREMEN IN THE COMMUNITY. THEY WILL MAKE TAPES & LOCATE PHOTOS OF OLD EQUIPMENT & LOCATIONS. (LOCAL). MRS RALPH BLANTON, CHAIRMAN; TEMPE HERITAGE COMMITTEE; 1860 E CONCORDO; TEMPE, AZ 85282. (#14756).

AN ORAL HISTORY PROGRAM - PIONEER HISTORY - AZ. TEMPE IS MAKING AN EFFORT TO INTERVIEW EARLY PIONEER FAMILIES. LOCAL STUDENTS ARE DOING THE INTERVIEWS AND RESEARCH. FINAL RESEARCH WILL BE PUBLISHED AND MADE AVAILABLE TO GENERAL PUBLIC. (LOCAL). EVERETT CUMMINS, CHAIRMAN; TEMPE BICENTENNIAL COMMITTEE; 106 BROADWAY LANE; TEMPE, AZ 85281. (#14773). **ARBA GRANTEE.**

PROJECT 1776 - SCHOOL PROJECT OF TEMPE, AZ. A BICENTENNIAL PROGRAM FOR 5TH GRADERS IN EARLY AMERICAN CULTURE. YOUNG PEOPLE IN AN EDUCATIONAL SETTING WILL EXPERIENCE THE CRAFTS, SKILLS, IMPLEMENTS & LIFESTYLE OF THE 1700'S. (ST-WIDE). JULIE CURTIS, PROJECT DIRECTOR; TEMPE SCHOOL DISTRICT #3; 3205 S RURAL RD; TEMPE, AZ 85282. (#4603). **ARBA GRANTEE.**

RE-DISCOVERING THE AMERICAN CINEMA - TEMPE, AZ. SERIES OF FILMS PRODUCED BY FAMOUS AMERICAN DIRECTORS, INCLUDING DEMILLE, GRIFFITH & FORD TO BE SHOWN. (LOCAL). JERRY KEERAN, CHAIRMAN; CULTURAL AFFAIRS BD/ASSOC OF STUDENTS; MEMORIAL UNION, AZ STATE UNIV; TEMPE, AZ 85281. (#9501).

TEMPE, AZ, 'YESTERYEAR' FASHION SHOW. MODEL AUTHENTIC PERIOD CLOTHING OF YESTERYEAR AT FASHION SHOW ON JAN 17, 1976 AT THE FIESTA INN. ACTIVITY WILL OFFICIALLY WELCOME THE FREEDOM TRAIN TO TEMPE. (LOCAL). PEGGY BURTON, DIRECTOR; TEMPE HISTORICAL MUSEUM; 3500 S RURAL RD; TEMPE, AZ 85282. (#21343). **ARBA GRANTEE.**

WORKSHOP IN SOUTHWEST AREA LINGUISTICS, ARIZONA. WORKSHOP DESIGNED TO ASSIST EDUCATIONAL INSTITUTIONS IN THE SOUTHWEST TO GAIN A GREATER UNDERSTANDING IN THE PROBLEMS & ADVANTAGES OF BILINGUALISM & BICULTURALISM. (REGN'L). DR GINA HARVEY, DIRECTOR; NORTHERN ARIZONA UNIV; BOX 6032; FLAGSTAFF, AZ 86001. (#714).

FEB 1 - 28, '74. CONFERENCE, ARIZ STATE UNIV - 2 CENTURIES OF HISPANIC CONTRIBUTIONS. ARIZONA STATE UNIVERSITY HISTORICAL SYMPOSIA. TWO PUBLIC CONFERENCES IN 1974 & 1975 ON THE THEMES OF 2 CENTURIES OF HISPANIC CONTRIBUTIONS TO ARIZONA AND THE SOUTHWEST AND ARIZONA SINCE STATEHOOD. 1975 CONFERENCE SCHEDULED FOR FEBRUARY. (REGN'L). W E ADAMS, CHAIRMAN; ARIZONA STATE UNIV; ARIZONA STATE UNIV; TEMPE, AZ 85281. (#593-901).

FEB 26 - 27, '75. CONFERENCE ON 'TWO CENTURIES OF HISPANIC CONTRIBUTIONS IN AZ'. ARIZONA STATE UNIVERSITY HISTORICAL SYMPOSIA. TWO PUBLIC CONFERENCES IN 1974 & 1975 ON THE THEMES OF 2 CENTURIES OF HISPANIC CONTRIBUTIONS TO

TEMPE—CONTINUED

ARIZONA AND THE SOUTHWEST AND ARIZONA SINCE STATEHOOD. 1975 CONFERENCE SCHEDULED FOR FEBRUARY. (REGN'L). W E ADAMS, CHAIRMAN; ARIZONA STATE UNIV; ARIZONA STATE UNIV; TEMPE, AZ 85281. (#593-902).

AUG 24, '75 - MAY 2, '76. FESTIVAL OF FILMS BY FAMOUS AMERICAN DIRECTORS. FESTIVAL AT STUDENT MEMORIAL UNION. (LOCAL). JERRY HEERAN, PROJ MGR; CULTURAL AFFAIRS BOARD - ARIZONA STATE UNIV; ASSOC STUDENTS OF AZ STATE UNIV; TEMPE, AZ 85281. (#100144-1).

SEPT 18, '75 - MAY 8, '76. 1975-76 THEATRE SEASON WITH AMERICAN PLAYS. LIVE PERFORMANCE AT LYCEUM THEATRE, ASU CAMPUS ON FORREST ST MALL. (LOCAL). NANCY TALLMAN, MANAGER; THEATRE DEPT, ARIZONA STATE UNIV; ARIZONA STATE UNIV; TEMPE, AZ 85281. (#17824-1).

NOV 13 - 15, '75. MALL BOOTH CONTEST. COMPETITION, EXHIBIT AT CAMPUS. (LOCAL). KEITH LEOFFLER, CO-CHMN; ARIZONA STATE UNIV; 184 PV WEST; ASU; TEMPE, AZ 85281. (#103065-8).

NOV 13 - 15, '75. UNIVERSITY BANNER CONTEST. COMPETITION, EXHIBIT AT CAMPUS. (LOCAL). KEITH LEOFFLER, CO-CHMN; ARIZONA STATE UNIV; 184 PV WEST; ASU; TEMPE, AZ 85281. (#103065-9).

NOV 14 - 15, '75. UNIVERSITY HOMECOMING DANCE. LIVE PERFORMANCE AT MEMORIAL UNION. (LOCAL). KEITH LEOFFLER, CO-CHMN; ARIZONA STATE UNIV; 184 PV WEST; ASU; TEMPE, AZ 85281. (#103065-10).

NOV 15, '75. ARIZONA STATE UNIVERSITY CAMPUS TOURS. THE TOUR IS BEING SPONSORED BY THE ASSOCIATED STUDENTS. AT CAMPUS. (LOCAL). KEITH LEOFFLER, CO-CHMN; ARIZONA STATE UNIV; 184 PV WEST; ASU; TEMPE, AZ 85281. (#103065-7).

NOV 22 - 23, '75. ARTS, CRAFTS & ANTIQUES - BANQUET, NATIONAL SPEAKERS - BREAKFAST. EXHIBITS OF ARIZONA INDUSTRY & CULTURE 11/22/75 1:00 PM TO 4:30 PM; BANQUET WITH U S REP JOHN J RHODES, EX-GOVERNOR J HOWARD PYLE AND DR W J LOPIANO, TEMPE MAYOR, 11/22/75 6:30 PM MEMBERS ONLY; BREAKFAST 11/23/75 OPEN TO PUBLIC WITH CHARGE. AT KNIGHTS OF PYTHIAS CASTLE HALL - W 7TH ST AT ASH. (NAT'L). ADDIE L DANNER, CHMN; GRAND TEMPLE PYTHIAN SISTERS - GRAND LODGE KNIGHTS OF PYTHIAS; 1350 W 14TH ST; TEMPE, AZ 85281. (#17803-1).

DEC 27, '75. FIESTA BOWL FOOTBALL GAME. ANNUAL MAJOR COLLEGE FOOTBALL GAME & FESTIVAL OF SPORTING EVENTS, BANQUETS, BALL & PARADE. AT SUN DEVIL STADIUM. (NAT'L). JOHN REED; FIESTA BOWL COMMITTEE; 3410 E VAN BUREN; PHOENIX, AZ 85008. (#50706-1).

JAN 17, '76. 'YESTERYEAR' FASHION SHOW. MODEL AUTHENTIC PERIOD CLOTHING OF YESTERYEAR WILL OFFICIALLY WELCOME THE 'FREEDOM TRAIN' TO TEMPE. AT FIESTA INN. (LOCAL). PEGGY BURTON, DIR; TEMPE HISTORICAL SOCIETY; 3500 S RURAL RD; TEMPE, AZ 85282. (#21343-1).

JAN 24 - 28, '76. AMERICAN FREEDOM TRAIN DISPLAY DAYS AT TEMPE, ARIZONA. THE AMERICAN FREEDOM TRAIN WILL INCLUDE 10 EXHIBIT CARS & 2 SHOWCASE CARS DEPICTING DIFFERENT PHASES OF THE AMERICAN EXPERIENCE. ITS ARRIVAL WILL SERVE AS A CATALYST FOR LOCAL BICENTENNIAL CELEBRATIONS BY PEOPLE THROUGHOUT THIS NATION. (ST-WIDE). SY FREEDMAN, DIR OF P/R; THE AMERICAN FREEDOM TRAIN FOUNDATION; 5205 LEESBURG PIKE, SUITE 800; BAILEY'S XRDS, VA 22041. (#1776-148).

FEB 16 - 18, '76. UNITED STATES ARMED FORCES BICENTENNIAL CARAVAN. CARAVAN IS COMPOSED OF EXHIBIT VANS FOR EACH MILITARY SERVICE. PROJECT THEME IS 'HISTORY OF THE ARMED FORCES AND THEIR CONTRIBUTIONS TO THE NATION'. (LOCAL). BILL PEDERSON, CHMN; US ARMED FORCES EXHIBIT VANS PROJECT; BOX 5002; TEMPE, AZ 85281. (#1775-321).

FEB 18, '76. 'THE BRITISH ARE COMING!' - BRITISH MILITARY BAND PERFORMANCE. TOUR OF MAJOR U S CITIES BY BRITISH MILITARY UNITS AS REPRESENTATIVE OF UNITS INVOLVED IN REVOLUTIONARY WAR CAMPAIGN. AT SUN DEVIL GYMNASIUM. (INT'L). CHARLES K JONES, PRES; COLUMBIA ARTISTS FESTIVALS CORP; 165 W 57TH ST; NEW YORK, NY 10019. (#6532-21).

APR 28, '76. NETHERLANDS CHAMBER ORCHESTRA VISITS ARIZONA STATE UNIV. LIVE PERFORMANCE. (INT'L). WILLIAM SIMONSZ, COORD; NETHERLANDS GOVERNMENT; NETHERLANDS EMBASSY-4200 LINNEAN; WASHINGTON, DC 20008. (#109013-10).

JUNE 12 - 14, '76. PYTHIAN GRAND SESSION. CONFERENCE. (ST-WIDE). ADDIE LOU DANNER; BUTT TEMPLE; 1350 W 14TH ST; TEMPE, AZ 85281. (#107655-3).

JUNE 14, '76. FLAG DAY. PARADE. (LOCAL). ART LIVINGSTON; TEMPE BICENTENNIAL COMMITTEE; 215 W 7TH ST; TEMPE, AZ 85282. (#107655-1).

JUNE 24 - 27, '76. THE BLACK WOMAN AND THE BICENTENNIAL, CONFERENCE. CONFERENCE AT MEMORIAL UNION. (LOCAL). PAT WASHINGTON, PROJ DIR; ARIZONA STATE UNIVERSITY; FARMER EDUCATION BUILDING; TEMPE, AZ 85281. (#16144-1).

JULY 4, '76. 4TH OF JULY CELEBRATION. FAIR, FESTIVAL. (LOCAL). ART LIVINGSTON; TEMPE BICENTENNIAL COMMISSION; 215 W 7TH ST; TEMPE, AZ 85282. (#107655-2).

SEPT 27 - OCT 8, '76. CARL HAVERLIN/BROADCAST MUSIC, INC, ARCHIVES BICENTENNIAL EXHIBIT. OFFERS A VERSATILE PICTURE OF HISTORY, REGIONAL LIFE & MUSIC FOR OVER 200 YEARS. CONTAINS PRESIDENTIAL LETTERS, LETTERS OF FAMOUS AMERICANS, OLD BOOKS, MANUSCRIPTS, HISTORY OF 'THE STAR SPANGLED BANNER' & COMPOSER AUTOGRAPHS, PLUS SHEET MUSIC OF THE PAST. AT MUSIC LIBRARY, ARIZONA STATE UNIV. (ST-WIDE). ARLYS L MCDONALD, DIR; ARIZONA STATE UNIV LIBRARY; TEMPE, AZ 85281. (#20784-3).

OCT 22 - 23, '76. LATIN AMERICAN STUDIES CONFERENCE - REVOLUTION IN THE AMERICAS. CONFERENCE. (INT'L). LEWIS TAMBS, PROJ MGR; CENTER FOR LATIN-AMERICAN STUDIES - ARIZONA STATE UNIV; ARIZONA STATE UNIV; TEMPE, AZ 85281. (#100092-1).

TOLLESON

MARINE CORPS JR ROTC DRILL TEAMS - TOLLESON, AZ. MARINE CORPS JR ROTC BOYS AND GIRLS PRECISION DRILL TEAMS; EACH TEAM COMPOSED OF TWENTY UNIFORMED CADETS CAPABLE OF MARCHING IN PARADES OR PRESENTING EXCITING EXHIBITION DRILL MANEUVERS. (ST-WIDE). PATRICK A CAMPBELL, MARINE INSTRUCTOR; TOLLESON UNION HIGH SCHOOL MARINE CORPS JR ROTC DRILL TEAMS; 9419 W VAN BUREN ST; TOLLESON, AZ 85353. (#17814).

MAY 3, '76. BICENTENNIAL LOYALTY DAY PRESENTATION. MILITARY INSPECTION OF CADETS & FORMAL PASS IN REVIEW, FLAG PAGEANT PRESENTATION, DRUM AND BUGLE CORPS EXHIBITION, DRILL BY BOYS AND GIRLS AND FIELD EVENTS WILL BE FEATURED IN THE PRESENTATION. AT TOLLESON UNION HS STADIUM. (LOCAL). PATRICK A CAMPBELL, COORD; MARINE CORPS JR ROTC UNIT; 9419 W VAN BUREN ST; TOLLESON, AZ 85353. (#17814-1).

TOMBSTONE

BICENTENNIAL FESTIVAL OF THE ARTS - TOMBSTONE, AZ. A THREE DAY FESTIVAL, ILLUSTRATING THE VARIOUS ART FORMS OF THE SOUTHWEST REGION. (ST-WIDE). TIM SHAUGHNESSY, FESTIVAL DIRECTOR; TOMBSTONE SCHOOL DISTRICT; BOX 68; TOMBSTONE, AZ 85638. (#20594). **ARBA GRANTEE.**

COMMEMORATION OF WESTERN PIONEER PLAYGROUND - AZ. WESTERN STYLE PLAYGROUND EQUIPMENT CONSTRUCTED OF CEDAR LOGS AND GALVANIZED HARDWARES. THIS EQUIPMENT CONSISTS OF FOUR INDIVIDUAL RELATED COMPONENTS, EACH A PLAY SYSTEM IN ITSELF. (LOCAL). JUDY ANN HOFFMAN, TREASURER; TAXPAYERS AND PARENTS ASSOC; PO BOX 601; TOMBSTONE, AZ 85638. (#21918). **ARBA GRANTEE.**

STABILIZATION & RESTORATION IN TOMBSTONE, AZ. STABILIZATION AND RESTORATION OF THE SCHIEFFELIN HISTORIC DISTRICT IN TOMBSTONE,AZ. IMPLEMENTATION OF COMPLETED PLAN TO INCLUDE RESTORING THE OLDER STRUCTURES AND EXPANSION OF NEEDED SUPPORT SYSTEMS. (ST-WIDE). THEDA MEDIGOVICH, PRESIDENT; TOMBSTONE RESTORATION COMMISSION, INC; BOX 606; TOMBSTONE, AZ 85638. (#464). **ARBA GRANTEE.**

OCT 24 - 26, '75. HELLDORADO HISTORICAL REENACTMENTS. 1880S PARADE, REENACTMENTS HISTORICAL EVENTS, CARNIVAL HELD 3 DAYS EACH YEAR IN OCTOBER SHOOT-OUT AT O.K. CORRAL BY 'WILD BUNCH' FIRST & THIRD SUNDAY EVERY MONTH-ADULTS 1.00 1880S COSTUMES & WESTERN WEAR WORN BY RESIDENTS. STREET REENACTMENTS FREE BY VIGILANTES. AT ALLEN STREET IN CENTER OF CITY. (ST-WIDE). THEDA MEDIGOVICH; TOMBSTONE RESTORATION COMMISSION & HELLDORADO INCORPORATED; PO BOX 567; TOMBSTONE, AZ 85638. (#50248-1).

FEB 20 - 22, '76. BICENTENNIAL FESTIVAL OF THE ARTS. FESTIVAL AT MAIN STREET OF TOMBSTONE. (ST-WIDE). TIM SHAUGHNESSY; TOMBSTONE SCHOOL DISTRICT; BOX 68; TOMBSTONE, AZ 85638. (#20594-1).

JUNE 18 - 20, '76. 4TH ANNUAL CONVENTION OF OLD BASTARDS. CONFERENCE. (LOCAL). EDWARD D HURLEY, COORD; INTERNATIONAL ORDER OF OLD BASTARDS; TOMBSTONE, AZ 85638. (#200004-5).

JULY 4, '76. 4TH OF JULY PROGRAM. FAIR. (LOCAL). EDWARD D HURLEY, SR; CITY OF TOMBSTONE; TOMBSTONE, AZ 85638. (#107668-1).

TSAILE

ARCHERY CHAMPIONSHIPS - TSAILE, AZ. THE FIRST INDIAN ARCHERY CHAMPIONSHIPS OF THE AMERICAS HELD AT THE GYMNASIUM & FIELD AREA OF NAVAJO COMMUNITY COLLEGE. (REGN'L). EVAN OSWALD, PROJ DIRECTOR; NAVAJO COMMUNITY COLLEGE; TSAILE, AZ 86556. (#25789). **ARBA GRANTEE.**

INDIAN JEWELRY FOR THE BICENTENNIAL. INDIAN SILVER, TURQUOISE & CORAL JEWELRY OF THE OFFICIAL BICENTENNIAL SYMBOL, ARBA LICENSE NO 76-19-0610. (NAT'L). ARTHUR LOMAX, PROJ DIRECTOR; BICENTENNIAL INDIAN ENTERPRISES; NAVAJO COMMUNITY COLLEGE; TSAILE, AZ 86556. (#22150).

NAVAJO COMMUNITY COLLEGE OUTDOOR THEATRE, AZ. THE BICENTENNIAL PRODUCTION WILL INCLUDE SEGMENTS OF NAVAJO HISTORY, TRADITION, CULTURE AND CONTEMPORARY LIFE TO BE PEFORMED ON AND OFF THE RESERVATION. (LOCAL). RANDALL ACKLEY, CHAIRMAN; NAVAJO BICENTENNIAL COMMISSION; WINDON ROCK, AZ 86515. (#32812).

MAY 28 - 31, '76. FIRST INDIAN ARCHERY CHAMPIONSHIPS OF THE AMERICAS. COMPETITION AT GYMNASIUM & FIELD AREA. (REGN'L). EVAN OSWALD; NAVAJO COMMUNITY COLLEGE; TSAILE, AZ 86556. (#25789-1).

TUBA CITY

APR 25 - MAY 7, '76. BAND PERFORMANCES, PARADES, CONCERTS. PARADE AT SHENANDOAH APPLE BLOSSOM FESTIVAL. (LOCAL). CHARLES W CARTER, CHMN; TUBA CITY PUBLIC SCHOOLS; PO BOX 67; TUBA CITY, AZ 86045. (#106012-2).

TUBAC

HISTORY OF TUBAC, ARIZONA. BOOKLET TELLING THE STORY OF ARIZONA'S FIRST EUROPEAN SETTLEMENT. TUBAC WAS THE SCENE OF THE RECENT MEETING OF PRESIDENT FORD AND MEXICAN PRESIDENT ECHEVERRIA. (ST-WIDE). DR ELIZABETH BROWNELL; TUBAC HISTORICAL SOCIETY; TUBAC, AZ 85640. (#4903). **ARBA GRANTEE.**

JUAN BAUTISTA DE ANZA EXPEDITION RE-ENACTMENT. RE-ENACTMENT OF THE 1775 EXPEDITION FROM TUBAC, AZ, TO CALIFORNIA, ENDING WITH THE ESTABLISHMENT OF PRESIDIO AT SAN FRANCISCO. (REGN'L). SIDNEY BRINCKERHOFF, PRESIDENT; ARIZONA HISTORICAL SOCIETY; 949 E 2ND ST; TUCSON, AZ 85638. (#605). **ARBA GRANTEE.**

TUBAC, ARIZONA, PRESERVATION PROJECT. PROJECT INVOLVES MANY ELEMENTS. ACQUISITION OF SITE, HISTORICAL RESEARCH PUBLICATION, MUSEUM & VISITOR FACILITIES BUFFER ZONE,ARCHAEOLOGICAL EXCAVATION, MOTION PICTURE & SLIDES FOR TV, SCHOOLS, ETC. (ST-WIDE). WALLACE VIGORS, ASST DIRECTOR; ARIZONA STATE PARKS; 1688 W ADAMS; PHOENIX, AZ 85007. (#606). **ARBA GRANTEE.**

OCT 22 - 23, '75. DE ANZA EXPEDITION REENACTMENT, OPENING CEREMONY, FESTIVAL AT TUBAC. RE-ENACTMENT OF THE 1775 EXPEDITION FROM TUBAC, AZ, TO CALIFORNIA, ENDING WITH THE ESTABLISHMENT OF PRESIDIO AT SAN FRANCISCO. AT CITYWIDE. (ST-WIDE). MAURICE GISS; ARIZONA BICENTENNIAL COMMISSION; 1807 N CENTRAL #108; PHOENIX, AZ 85004. (#605-3).

TUCSON

AIRCRAFT AQUISITION FOR PIMA COUNTY AIR MUSEUM, AZ. THE MARINE CORPS LEAGUE - TUCSON DETACHMENT - IS RESTORING A WORLD WAR II FIGHTER PLANE. THE AIRCRAFT WILL BE DONATED TO THE PIMA COUNTY AIR MUSEUM. (LOCAL). JOHN CARON, PROJ DIRECTOR; MARINE CORPS LEAGUE; TUCSON INN PO BOX 5666; TUCSON, AZ 85703. (#14767).

ALLIANCE TO REBUILD HISTORY-PIMA CO AIR MUSEUM, AZ. MILITARY & CIVILIAN GROUPS WILL ADOPT AN AIRCRAFT TO RESTORE FOR THE AIR MUSEUM. (LOCAL). CAPT JAN F DALBY, BICENTENNIAL COMMITTEE CHMN; DAVIS-MONTHAN AIR FORCE BASE; 803CSG/OI DM AFB; TUCSON, AZ 85707. (#20214).

ALL-AMERICA BICENTENNIAL ROSE GARDEN IN TUCSON, AZ. SPECIAL ROSE GARDEN IS PLANTED IN RANDOLPH PARK IN TUCSON. GARDEN CONTAINS THE ALL-AMERICAN ROSE SELECTIONS SINCE 1940 & CONTINUING NEW ROSES. (LOCAL). DR LEE BURKHART, PRESIDENT; ROSE SOCIETY OF TUCSON; DEPT OF HORTICULTURE, UNIV OF AZ; TUCSON, AZ 85721. (#4554).

ALL-ARIZONA BICENTENNIAL BAND - TUSCON, AZ. TOP ARIZONA MUSICIANS COMPRISE A SPECIAL ALL-STATE BAND WHICH WILL PERFORM THROUGHOUT ARIZONA AND IN PHILADELPHIA. (ST-WIDE). JACK LEE, DIRECTOR; UNIV OF ARIZONA, DEPT OF MUSIC; TUCSON, AZ 85721. (#20567). **ARBA GRANTEE.**

AMERICAN CUP '76 - TUCSON, AZ. THE AMERICAN CUP '76 GYMNASTICS MEET WILL BE HELD IN TUCSON. (NAT'L). FRANK BARE, COORDINATOR; U S GYMNASTIC FEDERATION; 1225 N 10TH AVE; TUCSON, AZ 85705. (#27943).

ART OF FUTURE PLANNING, TUCSON, AZ. A HIGH SCHOOL CLASS PROJECT INVOLVING COMMUNITY LEADERS' PERCEPTIONS OF THE FUTURE. STUDENTS, THEN WROTE SCENARIOS AND FUTURE HISTORIES. (LOCAL). LARRY WURST, CHAIRMAN; AMPHITHEATER SCHOOLS; 325 N YAVAPAI; TUCSON, AZ 85704. (#16220).

BICENT CELEBRATION BY ROMAN CATHOLIC CHURCH OF AZ. THE DIOCESES IN PHOENIX & TUCSON WILL MARK SITES OF EARLY BEGININGS OF CHRISTIANITY IN ARIZONA. THE CHURCH WILL CELEBRATE SPECIAL PONTIFICAL MASSES IN 1976 AT THE HISTORIC CHURCHES. (ST-WIDE). FR FRANCIS FOX, ARCHIVIST; ROMAN CATHOLIC CHURCH OF ARIZONA, TUCSON DIOCESE; PO BOX 31; TUCSON, AZ 85702. (#5397).

CABEZA DE VACA DRAMATIZATION IN ARIZONA. MULTI-MEDIA DANCE DRAMATIZATION DEPICTING THE HISTORY, ROMANCE AND DRAMA OF THE EXPEDITION OF EARLY SPANISH EXPLORER, CABEZA DE VACA. (LOCAL). MARY LITA HEWITT, COORDINATOR; AMPHITHEATER HIGH SCHOOL; 6242 CAMINO ESQUINA; TUCSON, AZ 85718. (#4890). **ARBA GRANTEE.**

CATALINA HS BICENT COMMEMORATION IN TUCSON, ARIZ. CLUB WILL DEVELOP A RENEWED PATRIOTISM & PROVIDE A COMPLETE EDUCATIONAL BICENT CURRICULUM FOR ALL INTERESTED STUDENTS AND FACULTY. (LOCAL). BENJAMIN F DAVIS, AMER HISTORY TEACHER; CATALINA HIGH SCHOOL; 3645 E PIMA ST; TUCSON, AZ 85716. (#4906).

CHILDREN'S ENSEMBLE CONCERTS IN ARIZONA. OVER 200 TUCSON CHILDREN WILL PERFORM IN A PRESENTATION OF AMERICAN MUSIC FROM REVOLUTIONARY DAYS TO THE PRESENT. (LOCAL). ALICE STOLLER SCOTT, PRESIDENT; TUCSON MUSIC TEACHERS ASSOC; 515 ETON DR; TUCSON, AZ 85734. (#4888). **ARBA GRANTEE.**

COMMUNITY RESOURCE CENTER IN TUCSON, AZ. PROJECT IS A COMMUNITY CONTACT CENTER WHICH SERVES AS A CLEARINGHOUSE OF INFORMATION ON COMMUNITY PROJECTS WHICH ARE IN NEED OF VOLUNTEERS. (LOCAL). TOM ANDERSON, DIRECTOR; FUTURACT; 2632 N MARTIN AVE; TUCSON, AZ 85719. (#14266).

TUCSON — CONTINUED

'EL TIRADITO' DANCE TROUPE OF TUCSON, AZ. A DANCE DRAMA OF A LOCAL LEGEND USING DANCE, DIALOGUE, SINGING, LIVE MUSIC & DRAMATIZATION: A FULL LENGTH THEATER PRODUCTION WILL BE PERFORMED THROUGHOUT 1976. (ST-WIDE). EILEEN FULLER, DIRECTOR; CITY DANCE THEATER; 900 S ALVERNON; TUCSON, AZ 85716. (#26542). **ARBA GRANTEE.**

EPA SYMPOSIUM PAPERS PUBLICATION - TUCSON, AZ. PUBLICATION OF PAPERS PRESENTED AT THE U S EPA SYMPOSIUM SERIES ON HAZARDOUS WASTES. (LOCAL). WALLACE H FULLER, DIRECTOR; UNIV OF ARIZONA DEPT OF SOILS, WATER & ENGINEERING; TUCSON, AZ 85721. (#20974).

EXHIBITION OF MEXICAN FOLK ART & COSTUMES, ARIZONA. EXHIBITION PRESENTED AT THE ARIZONA HISTORICAL SOCIETY NEW BUILDING DURING THE TUCSON FESTIVAL. (LOCAL). JARVIS HARRIMAN, EXEC DIRECTOR; TUCSON FESTIVAL SOCIETY; 8 W PASEO REDONDO; TUCSON, AZ 85705. (#4889). **ARBA GRANTEE.**

FOLK MUSIC FESTIVAL, TUCSON MEET YOURSELF. FOLK FESTIVAL FEATURING FOLK BANDS, SOLO MUSICIANS, DANCE GROUPS, FOOD DEMONSTRATIONS, COSTUME & CRAFT EXHIBITS. (LOCAL). MARY SOWLS, CHAIRMAN; CULTURAL EXCHANGE COUNCIL; 2128 E 5TH; TUCSON, AZ 85719. (#5401). **ARBA GRANTEE.**

FOLKLORE AMERICANA. MUSICAL BASED ON THE FOLKLORE, LEGENDS, MUSIC, SONGS AND DANCES OF VARIOUS REGIONS OF OUR COUNTRY. (LOCAL). HERBERT ERICKSON; TUCSON BICENTENNIAL COMMITTEE; 455 S IRVING AVE; TUCSON, AZ 85711. (#102500-8).

FOUNDERS MEMORIAL FOUNTAIN-UNIV OF ARIZONA. PROJECT WAS CELEBRATED WITH GROUND-BREAKING CEREMONIES & THE COMPLETED PROJECT WHICH NOW ADORNS THE MALL IN FRONT OF THE NEW LIBRARY WILL BE DEDICATED IN JANUARY 1977 WHEN THE NEW LIBRARY IS DEDICATED. (ST-WIDE). MARVIN D JOHNSON, VICE PRES UNIV RELATIONS; UNIV OF ARIZONA; TUCSON, AZ 85721. (#1332). **ARBA GRANTEE.**

'FRANTIC FACTS & INFECTIOUS IDEAS', TUCSON, AZ. A 30 MINUTE PLAY FEATURING AUDIENCE PARTICIPATION TO BE PERFORMED FOR YOUNG AUDIENCES THROUGHOUT THE STATE. PLAY DEMONSTRATES THAT WE CAN MAKE OUR WORLD A BETTER PLACE TO LIVE WITH PRESENT KNOWLEDGE. (ST-WIDE). JOAN BRINCKERHOFF, COORDINATOR; INVISIBLE THEATER; PO BOX 12; TUCSON, AZ 85702. (#21833). **ARBA GRANTEE.**

GREEN SURVIVAL, TUCSON, AZ. TUCSON CITIZENS ARE ENCOURAGED TO DO SOMETHING TO ENHANCE THE APPEARANCE OF THE COMMUNITY; FROM PLANTING TREES TO POTTING FLOWERS. (LOCAL). WILLIAM C HARLOW, PRESIDENT; ARIZONA NURSERYMEN'S ASSOC; 1644 N JEFFERSON AVE; TUCSON, AZ 85712. (#25310). **ARBA GRANTEE.**

'GROW Y'ER OWN' - TUCSON, AZ. CITIZENS ARE BEING ENCOURAGED TO GROW NEIGHBORHOOD AND PRIVATE VEGETABLE GARDENS; EXPERIENCED ADVICE AND MECHANICAL SUPPORT WILL BE PROVIDED. (LOCAL). MRS ALENE SMITH, CHAIRMAN; TUCSON BICENTENNIAL COMMITTEE; PO BOX 5547; TUCSON, AZ 85703. (#14262).

HERITAGE COOKBOOK, TUCSON, AZ. HERITAGE COOKBOOK CONTAINING VARIOUS HISTORICAL RECIPES. (LOCAL). ZELLA M MOON, PROJ DIRECTOR; COOPERATIVE EXTENSION OF PIMA COUNTY - HOMEMAKERS' STUDY GROUP; 131 W CONGRESS ST; TUCSON, AZ 85701. (#17822).

HISTORY OF AMERICAN REVOLUTION EXHIBIT. EXHIBIT INCLUDES REPLICAS OF VARIOUS ITEMS IMPORTANT IN ESTABLISHING THE AMERICAN REPULIC; COLONEL JOHN BROCKIE CONTRIBUTED GIFTS TO THE EXHIBIT. (LOCAL). HUGH BELDEN, DIRECTOR; TUCSON CHAPTER, SONS OF THE AMERICAN REVOLUTION; TUCSON, AZ 85711. (#102752-1).

HISTORY OF THE AMPHITHEATRE SCHOOL DISTRICT - AZ. THE SCHOOL DISTRICT IN TUCSON IS GOING TO PUBLISH A HISTORY OF THE DEVELOPMENT OF SCHOOLS IN THIS SUBURBAN SCHOOL DISTRICT. LOCAL COMMITTEE HAS AMASSED A WEALTH OF MATERIAL PERTAINING TO THEIR HISTORY. (LOCAL). DR THOMAS NEEL, SUPERINTENDENT; TUCSON SCHOOL SYSTEM; AMPHITHEATER SCHOOL; TUCSON, AZ 85703. (#14754).

HORTICULTURE IN ARID REGIONS - TUCSON, AZ. AN ENCYCLOPEDIA OF PRACTICAL INFORMATION ON THE GROWTH & CARE OF DESERT AND SUB-TROPICAL PLANT LIFE. THE TEXT CONTAINS OVER 300 PLANT BIOGRAPHIES, HISTORIES, DESIGN APPLICATIONS AND CROSS LISTINGS. (NAT'L). MS MARY ROSE DUFFIELD AND WARREN D JONES, AUTHORS; UNIV OF ARIZONA; 4125 N CAMINO ENCERRADO; TUCSON, AZ 85718. (#19262).

JUNIOR LEAGUE NEWSPAPER SUPPLEMENT - TUCSON, AZ. NEWSPAPER SUPPLEMENT THAT WILL BE DISTRIBUTED DURING TUCSON'S 200TH BIRTHDAY CELEBRATION & THAT WILL FOCUS ON THE DEVELOPMENT OF TUCSON, ITS PEOPLE & ITS HERITAGE. (LOCAL). MRS E J SAYRE, CHAIRMAN; JUNIOR LEAGUE; 4420 E PRESIDIO PL; TUCSON, AZ 85718. (#14951).

KEEPERS OF THE AMERICAN SPIRIT IN TUCSON, AZ. THE VETERANS OF FOREIGN WARS, POST 549, ARE CONDUCTING AN INTENSIVE, YEAR LONG EDUCATIONAL PROGRAM TO EDUCATE BOTH YOUNG PEOPLE AND ADULT ABOUT THE INVOLVEMENT OF AMERICAN, ARIZONAN FIGHTING MEN. (LOCAL). DON KISHBAUGH - COMMANDER; TUCSON VFW POST #549; 1884 S CRAYCROFT; TUCSON, AZ 85711. (#14768).

KINO COMMUNITY HOSPITAL, TUCSON, AZ. A $24,000,000 HOSPITAL UNDER CONSTRUCTION SINCE SEPT '74 OPENING DEC '76 TO REPLACE OLD COUNTY HOSPITAL. COMMUNITY DEDICATION ON OCT 24, 1976. (LOCAL). KRISTA A NEIS, DIRECTOR OF DEVELOPMENT; KINO COMMUNITY HOSPITAL; 2900 S 6 AVE; TUCSON, AZ 85713. (#23221).

KIVA HISTORICAL THEATER - PROJ OF TUCSON, AZ. A BILINGUAL PUPPET THEATER FOR CHILDREN WITH HISTORICAL FOLKLORE AND LEGEND SUBJECTS FROM INDIAN, MEXICAN-AMERICAN AND ANGLO CULTURES. (LOCAL). SIDNEY B BRINKERHOFF, DIRECTOR; ARIZONA HISTORICAL SOCIETY; 949 E 2ND ST; TUCSON, AZ 85719. (#14960). **ARBA GRANTEE.**

LA CASA CORDOVA: A MEXICAN MUSEUM - TUCSON, AZ. A NEW ADDITION TO TUCSON MUSEUM OF ART COMPLEX; WILL HIGHLIGHT THE LIFESTYLES OF THE MEXICAN PEOPLE OF TUCSON; MEXICAN CRAFTS AND ANTIQUES WILL BE SOLD AT THE MUSEUM. (LOCAL). MRS D J LYONS, DIRECTOR; TUCSON MUSEUM OF ART; 6146 SAN CRISTOBAL; TUCSON, AZ 85718. (#14952).

THE LEGACY OF FATHER KINO, PROJ OF TUCSON, ARIZONA. 30 MINUTE FILM ON THE LIFE OF THE 18TH CENTURY MISSIONARY, FATHER KINO. KINO FOUNDED SEVERAL IMPORTANT MISSIONS IN THE SOUTHWEST. (REGN'L). DAVID DUVAL, FILM PRODUCER; UNIVERSITY OF ARIZONA; RADIO-TV-FILM BUREAU; TUCSON, AZ 85721. (#4902). **ARBA GRANTEE.**

LITERATURE OF THE EARLY REPUBLIC 1775-1825 - ARIZ. A SERIES OF LECTURES ON AMERICAN WRITERS, LITERATURE & CULTURE TO BE BROADCAST OVER THE UNIV OF ARIZONA RADIO STATION FROM SEPT 1975 TO OCT 1977. (ST-WIDE). J H MCELROY, ASSOC PROFESSOR; DEPT OF ENGLISH; UNIV OF ARIZONA; TUCSON, AZ 85721. (#2365).

MANZO MEDIA PROJECT IN TUCSON, ARIZONA. LOCAL COMMUNITY ACTION PROGRAM WILL TRAIN 18 MANZO AREA YOUNG PEOPLE IN VIDEO PRODUCTION TECHNIQUES & WILL PRODUCE AN EDITED VIDEOTAPE ORAL HISTORY CELEBRATING MEXICAN-AMERICAN HERITAGE OF SOUTHWEST. (ST-WIDE). ROBERT L HORN, EXEC DIRECTOR; COMMITTEE FOR ECONOMIC OPPORTUNITY; 2555 N STONE; TUCSON, AZ 85705. (#4905). **(??). ARBA GRANTEE.**

MICROFILMING HISTORIC ARIZONA NEWSPAPERS, TUCSON. MICROFILM KEY HISTORIC NEWSPAPERS PUBLISHED IN ARIZONA BETWEEN 1882 AND 1930. (ST-WIDE). MARY DALE PALSSON, PUBLIC SERVICES LIBRARIAN; UNIVERSITY OF ARIZONA LIBRARY; TUCSON, AZ 85721. (#21975). **ARBA GRANTEE.**

MOUNT LEMMON CLEANUP NEAR TUCSON, AZ. HOMEOWNERS ON MT. LEMMON NEAR TUCSON ARE GOING TO CLEAN UP, OPERATE & BEAUTIFY THIS SCENIC AREA FOR THE BICENTENNIAL. (LOCAL). REGIONA RHIND, PRESIDENT; MT LEMMON WOMEN'S CLUB; 3222 E FLOWER; TUCSON, AZ 85716. (#4553).

MUG-A-PLUG, TUCSON, AZ. PAINTING OF FIRE HYDRANTS DEPICTING HISTORICAL FIGURES WHO FORMED ARIZONA'S HISTORY. (LOCAL). JOHN BONNER, MANAGER, CITY COMMUNITY RELATIONS OFF; TUCSON WOMEN'S CLUB; 6245 E BELLEVUE AVE; TUCSON, AZ 85712. (#24035).

NEW WEST TRAILS: PEOPLE'S YELLOW PAGES FOR TUCSON. ANNUAL CATALOG OF ALTERNATIVE SERVICES AND EXCHANGES FOUND IN THE TUCSON AREA; FEATURES INDIVIDUALS, COOPERATIVES & SURVIVAL SERVICES OPEN TO BARTER OR EXCHANGE & SERVICES OR PRODUCTS UNIQUE TO TUCSON. (LOCAL). JOYCE ENNIS, COORDINATOR; NEW WEST TRAILS COLLECTIVE / CENTER FOR SOCIAL CHANGE; 745 E 5TH ST; TUCSON, AZ 85719. (#15244).

OLD PUEBLO - PROJ OF TUCSON, AZ. THE ARIZONA DAILY STAR IN TUCSON IS FEATURING A SUNDAY HISTORIC COMIC SECTION IN 1975. THE COMICSTRIP WILL TRACE THE EARLY HISTORY OF THE SOUTHWEST. (ST-WIDE). WILLIAM WALTERS, PROJ DIRECTOR; ARIZONA DAILY STAR; PO BOX 26807; TUCSON, AZ 85726. (#14957).

OLD WOODY VIEWS BICENT ISSUE & WOODEN NICKEL, AZ. 15 PAGE BOOKLET FILLED WITH ARTICLES AND STORIES OF HISTORY ON WOODEN MONEY AS IT RELATES TO BICENTENNIAL. ALSO, A WOODEN NICKEL WILL BE ISSUED IN HONOR OF BICENTENNIAL. (REGN'L). JON PEPPER, EDITOR-PUBLISHER; AMERICAN WOODEN MONEY GUILD; PO BOX 3445; TUCSON, AZ 85715. (#26042).

OPERATION PATRIOTISM PROJ OF ARIZONA. DISSEMINATION OF MATERIALS & SCHOOL PROGRAMS THAT EXPLAIN THE PROPER USE & HISTORY OF THE AMERICAN FLAG BY THE ARIZONA AIR NATL GUARD. (ST-WIDE). TSG RAY R BAIN, JR, COORDINATOR; ARIZONA AIR NATIONAL GUARD; PO BOX 11037; TUCSON, AZ 85734. (#5398).

OUR SPANISH HERITAGE PROJECT OF ARIZONA. TRAVELING EXHIBIT DESIGNED TO PORTRAY THE IMPACT OF SPANISH EXPLORATION AND LIFE STYLE OF SPANISH SETTLEMENTS IN ARIZONA. (ST-WIDE). SIDNEY B BRINCKERHOFF, DIRECTOR; ARIZONA HISTORICAL SOCIETY; 949 E 2ND ST; TUCSON, AZ 85719. (#543).

PERIHELION - MODERN DANCE PROJECT OF ARIZONA. PERFORMING COMPANY OF MODERN DANCERS AND MUSICIANS WHO CELEBRATE THE AMERICAN ENVIRONMENT. (ST-WIDE). VERITY HAYNES, DIRECTOR; PERIHELION; 4330 N VIA SINVOSA; TUCSON, AZ 85705. (#1060). **ARBA GRANTEE.**

PITT HOUSE MEMORIAL MARKER IN TUCSON, ARIZONA. MARKER & MONUMENT IN DOWNTOWN TUCSON MARKING TUCSON'S FIRST SPANISH PRESIDIO & MARKING SITE OF A HOHOKAM INDIAN DWELLING (700-900 AD). (LOCAL). MRS EMERY C JOHNSON, CHAIRMAN; TUCSON HERITAGE FOUNDATION; 13 W PASEO REDONDO; TUCSON, AZ 85703. (#4904). **ARBA GRANTEE.**

PLACITA KINO, TUCSON, AZ. HISTORICAL GARDEN WILL COMMEMORATE PADRE KINO & THE POSITIVE CONTRIBUTIONS OF ALL TUCSON HOSPITALS TO THE QUALITY OF HEALTH CARE. TO BE LOCATED IN FRONT OF KINO COMMUNITY HOSPITAL. (LOCAL). KRISTA A NEIS, DIRECTOR OF DEVELOPMENT; KINO COMMUNITY HOSPITAL; 2900 S 6 AVE; TUCSON, AZ 85713. (#23222).

PRESERVATION OF NITRATE FILM, ARIZ HISTORICAL SOC. WE WILL DUPLICATE MORE THAN 10000 VALUABLE NITRATE NEGATIVES USING A TECHNIQUE MADE POSSIBLE BY A NEW FILM. PHOTOS WILL BE AVAILABLE TO RESEARCHERS & EXPERIENCE WILL HELP US PRESERVE ALL PHOTO DOCUMENTS. (ST-WIDE). SIDNEY B BRINCKERHOFF, DIRECTOR; ARIZONA HISTORICAL SOCIETY; 949 E SECOND ST; TUCSON, AZ 85719. (#2363). **ARBA GRANTEE.**

PROJECT ELECTRA - AIRPLANE PROJECT OF ARIZONA. RESTORATION OF LOCKHEED ELECTRA 10 WHICH IS A SISTERSHIP TO THE ONE FLOWN BY AMELIA ERHARDT. WILL BE LOCATED AT PIMA COUNTY AIR MUSEUM. (ST-WIDE). NANCY ENGEBRETSON, DIRECTOR; TUCSON CHAPTER OF THE 99'S, INC; 1448 E 1ST ST; TUCSON, AZ 85719. (#1750).

PUBLICATION OF THE TOMBSTONE EPITAPH - AZ. UNIVERSITY OF ARIZONA DEPARTMENT OF JOURNALISM STUDENTS HAVE NOW TAKEN OVER PUBLICATION OF THE TOMBSTONE EPITAPH WITH INTENTIONS TO PUBLISH THE HISTORIC PAPER ON A BIWEEKLY BASIS. (LOCAL). GEORGE RIDGE, PROJ DIRECTOR; DEPARTMENT OF JOURNALISM, UNIV OF ARIZONA; UNIV OF ARIZONA; TUCSON, AZ 85721. (#14766).

QUESTER'S BICENT PROJECTS IN TUCSON, AZ. SERVE AS 'INFORMATION' PEOPLE IN PERIOD COSTUMES; SHOW PRIVATE ANTIQUE COLLECTIONS & FURNISH SPEAKERS; RUN BICENT BOOTHS DISTRIBUTING LITERATURE; SPONSOR ANTIQUE DISPLAY IN LIBRARY. (ST-WIDE). MRS EVELYNNE MILLIGAN, PRESIDENT; BUSCADORES CHAPTER OF QUESTER'S INC #352; 95 W WINDSOR ST; TUCSON, AZ 85705. (#548). **ARBA GRANTEE.**

RECORD OF PIONEER CEMETERIES IN ARIZONA. PUBLICATION OF PAMPHLETS ON THE HISTORIC PIONEER CEMETERIES; TO INCLUDE PHOTOGRAPHS & WRITTEN DOCUMENTARY RECORDS. (ST-WIDE). MRS THOMAS P SALYER, PRESIDENT; ARIZONA STATE GENEALOGICAL SOCIETY, INC; PO BOX 6027; TUCSON, AZ 85733. (#550). **ARBA GRANTEE.**

'RECREATION OF CONTINENTAL DRAGOONS UNIT' OF ARIZ.. WILL PROVIDE A FULLY TRAINED & EQUIPPED 7 TO 10 MAN CONTINGENT OF CONTINENTAL DRAGOONS CIRCA 1778, WHICH WILL BE AVAILABLE FOR PUBLIC PERFORMANCES & RELATED BICENTENNIAL ACTIVITIES. (ST-WIDE). BRUCE H. SMITH,PRESIDENT; 5TH CALVALRY MEMORIAL REGIMENT; 186 N. MEYER AVENUE; TUCSON, AZ 85701. (#921). **(??). ARBA GRANTEE.**

RESTORATION OF SENTINEL PEAK - TUCSON, AZ. RESTORATION OF OLD RECREATION AREA ON SENTINEL PEAK, WITHIN THE CITY OF TUCSON. (LOCAL). TOM PETERSON, CHAIRMAN; TUCSON HISTORICAL COMMITTEE; PO BOX 5547; TUCSON, AZ 85703. (#21338). **ARBA GRANTEE.**

SALPOINTE CHS CAMPUS BEAUTIFICATION PROJECT, AZ. SHOWCASE PROJECT INVOLVES DESERT LANDSCAPING, PAVING PARKING LOT & RECREATION AREA, PROJECT WAS DESIGNED & IMPLEMENTED BY STUDENTS, PUBLIC PARTICIPATION INVITED. (LOCAL). PATRICK G PECORARO, PROJ DIRECTOR; SALPOINTE CATHOLIC HIGH SCHOOL; 1505 E HAMPTON ST; TUSCON, AZ 85719. (#26048).

SAN XAVIER BICENTENNIAL PLAZA - TUCSON, AZ. CULTURAL, RECREATIONAL & COMMERCIAL FACILITY NEAR HISTORIC SAN XAVIER MISSION. (REGN'L). CECIL WILLIAMS, TRIBAL CHAIRMAN; PAPAGO TRIBAL COUNCIL; BOX 837; SELLS, AZ 85634. (#24113).

SCULPTURE WORKSHOP FOR BARRIO CHILDREN - TUCSON. THE WORKSHOP WILL INVOLVE BILINGUAL TEACHING OF A VARIETY OF TECHNIQUES INCLUDING METAL CASTING, WELDING, CERAMICS, PLASTER AND CLAY. FIELD TRIPS WILL ALSO BE PART OF THE COURSE. (LOCAL). TOM WIPER, DIRECTOR OF EDUCATION; TUCSON MUSEUM OF ART SCHOOL; 179 N MAIN ST; TUCSON, AZ 85705. (#19516). **ARBA GRANTEE.**

SOUNDS & VISIONS IN TUCSON. MUSIC & DANCE CHAMBER CONCERTS FEATURING WORKS OF 20TH CENTURY MEXICAN COMPOSERS AND WORKS OF AMERICAN MASTERS. (ST-WIDE). MRS ELLSWORTH SHAW, PROJECT DIRECTOR; TUCSON CULTURAL EXCHANGE COUNCIL; PO BOX 3398; TUCSON, AZ 85719. (#2374).

SPANISH ARIZONA'S CONTRIBUTION TO THE REVOLUTION. PUBLICATION OF DOCUMENTS REGARDING THE CONTRIBUTIONS OF EARLY TUCSON RESIDENTS TO THE AMERICAN REVOLUTIONARY WAR EFFORT. (NAT'L). FR KIERAN, OFM; ARIZONA HISTORICAL SOCIETY; 940 E 2ND ST; TUCSON, AZ 85719. (#545). **ARBA GRANTEE.**

SPECIAL BICENTENNIAL MUSEUM EXHIBIT, TUCSON, AZ. MUSEUM DISPLAYING MAIL AND STAMPS OF THE SPANISH & MEXICAN ERA IN ARIZONA; MUSEUM FOR THE BICENT WILL HAVE AN EXHIBIT ENTITLED 'OLD GLORY AND THE 50 STATES'. (LOCAL). WM L ALEXANDER, DIRECTOR; WESTERN POSTAL HISTORY MUSEUM; 949 E 2ND ST; TUCSON, AZ 85717. (#10162).

TUCSON BOYS CHORUS, BICENTENNIAL TOURS PROJ OF AZ. SERIES OF CONCERTS WITH A PATRIOTIC EMPHASIS THROUGHOUT ARIZONA AND THE SOUTHWEST. (REGN'L). CHUCK KARTH, DIRECTOR; TUCSON, ARIZONA BOYS CHORUS; PO BOX 12034; TUCSON, AZ 85732. (#8059).

TUCSON HISTORY COLORING BOOK, AZ. THE BOOK WILL BE A CHRONOLOGICAL HISTORY OF TUCSON WITH BOLD LINE DRAWINGS AND A RESEARCHED TEXT. THE BOOK WILL BE DIRECTED TOWARD PRIMARY CHILDREN AND PUBLISHED IN TIME FOR TUCSON'S 200TH BIRTHDAY. (LOCAL). MRS H DUANE BOCK, PROJ MANAGER; PUEBLO JUNIOR WOMENS CLUB; 6141 E CALLE SILVOSA; TUCSON, AZ 85711. (#14749).

TUCSON MOUNTAIN MEN TREK TO PHILADELPHIA. TUSCON MOUNTAIN MEN WILL APPEAR IN TRADITIONAL PIONEER COSTUME AT PARADES AND CELEBRATION ALONG THE COURSE OF THEIR TRIP FROM TUCSON TO PHILADELPHIA IN 1976. (NAT'L). RALPH W BAKER, TRAIL BOSS; TUCSON MOUNTAIN MEN; ROUTE 9, BOX 479E; TUCSON, AZ 85704. (#544). **ARBA GRANTEE.**

TUCSON — CONTINUED

TUCSON MUSEUM OF ART - ARIZONA. CONSTRUCTION OF NEW ART & CULTURAL COMPLEX IN HISTORIC SECTION OF TUCSON. (ST-WIDE). ADINA WINGATE, P R COORDINATOR; TUCSON MUSEUM OF ART; 235 WEST ALAMEDA; TUCSON, AZ 85701. (#5393).

TUCSON VETERAN'S HOSPITAL CARILLION, AZ. THE MORGAN MCDERMOTT POST OF THE AMERICAN LEGION IS INSTALLING A CARILLION AT THE TUCSON VA HOSPITAL. (LOCAL). LEONARD MCCULLOCH, COMMANDER; MORGAN MCDERMOTT POST #7, AMERICAN LEGION; 300 N MAIN ST; TUCSON, AZ 85705. (#25769). **ARBA GRANTEE.**

TUCSON, ARIZONA, MULTI-CULTURAL FESTIVAL. GALA CIVIC CELEBRATION THAT WILL REFLECT SOUTHERN ARIZONA'S MULTI-CULTURAL HERITAGE THROUGH A VARIETY OF FESTIVE ACTIVITIES. (ST-WIDE). C J HARRIMAN JR, EXEC DIRECTOR; TUCSON FESTIVAL SOCIETY INC; 8 W PASEO REDONDO; TUCSON, AZ 85705. (#1330). **ARBA GRANTEE.**

TUCSON, AZ, RESIDENCY OF FREE STREET THEATRE. THE FREE STREET THEATRE WILL USE MANY LOCAL PERFORMING GROUPS IN PUBLIC PLACES. (LOCAL). RON GITECK, COORDINATOR; CITY OF TUCSON, DEPT OF HUMAN & COMMUNITY DEVELOPMENT; PO BOX 27210; TUCSON, AZ 85726. (#24564).

TUMAMOC ENVIRONMENTAL STUDY AREA - TUCSON, AZ. CREATION OF AN ENVIRONMENTAL STUDY AREA ON TUMAMOC HILL IN TUCSON. THE AREA, WHICH IS A UNSPOILED SECTION OF DESERT, WILL BE OBSERVED, & STUDIED BY TEACHERS & STUDENTS. (LOCAL). DR A R KASSANDER, VICE PRESIDENT RESEARCH; UNIV OF ARIZONA; ADMINISTRATION ROOM 603; TUCSON, AZ 85721. (#4556). **ARBA GRANTEE.**

TUSCON VISION QUEST WAGON TRAIN PRESERVATION, AZ. TROUBLED YOUTH FROM RESIDENTIAL TREATMENT PROGRAM, VISION QUEST, WILL RIDE WITH WAGON TRAIN. TRIP IS SEEN AS MEANINGFUL THERAPEUTIC TRIP FOR THE YOUTH. (ST-WIDE). R LEDGER BURTON, COORDINATOR; VISION QUEST; PO BOX 12906; TUCSON, AZ 85732. (#27370). **ARBA GRANTEE.**

US-MEXICO INSTITUTE OF THE FUTURE. A FORUM FOR CITIZENS OF MEXICO & THE U.S. TO EXCHANGE CULTURAL & INDUSTRIAL IDEAS & PLANS IN AREAS BOTH SHARE IN COMMON. (INT'L). MRS RUBEN ACOSTA, PROJECT DIRECTOR; CULTURAL EXCHANGE COUNCIL; 85 SIERRA DR; TUCSON, AZ 85719. (#330). **(??). ARBA GRANTEE.**

VISUAL PRESENTATION OF TUCSON'S HERITAGE. SLIDE PRESENTATION OF THE DEVELOPMENT OF TUCSON FROM PIONEER TIMES TO THE PRESENT. (LOCAL). LEE FULLER, CHAIRMAN; TUCSON BICENTENNIAL SLIDE SHOW COMMITTEE; 1171 E SENECA; TUCSON, AZ 85719. (#610).

VOICES OF ARIZONA, TUCSON. TRANSCRIPTIONS IN FORM OF PUBLICATION CONTAIN TAPED INTERVIEWS WITH EARLY ARIZONA PIONEERS. (ST-WIDE). MRS VIRGINIA RICE, COORD; SOCIAL SCIENCE REFERENCE LIBRARY; UNIV OF ARIZONA LIBRARY; TUCSON, AZ 85721. (#21321). **ARBA GRANTEE.**

WALKING TOUR OF TUCSON'S HISTORY, AZ. SELF GUIDING TOUR OF HISTORICAL SITES IN DOWNTOWN TUCSON, INCLUDES TOUR GUIDE. (LOCAL). MRS NORMA NIBLETT, CHAIRMAN; TUCSON AAUW; 7510 E 32ND; TUCSON, AZ 85710. (#26994). **ARBA GRANTEE.**

WATER IN A CHANGING WORLD FILM PROJ OF ARIZONA. FILM WILL DEPICT HISTORICAL CONTRIBUTION WATER HAS GIVEN TO THE DEVELOPMENT OF USA AND THE NEED TO CONSERVE WATER FOR THE FUTURE. (NAT'L). THOMASINE R HILL, PROJECT COORDINATOR; DEPT OF HYDROLOGY, UNIV OF ARIZONA; TUCSON, AZ 85721. (#3865). **(??).**

WE, THE PEOPLE - TUCSON, AZ. THE TUCSON CHAPTER OF CAMP FIRE GIRLS IS CREATING A MOBILE ART EXHIBIT FOR THE BICENTENNIAL HIGHLIGHTING AMERICAN AND SOUTHWEST HISTORY. (LOCAL). JOANNE CURTIS, PROJ CHAIRMAN; CAMP FIRE GIRLS; 629 N SWAN RD, SUITE A; TUCSON, AZ 85711. (#20689). **ARBA GRANTEE.**

'WINNING THE WEST WITH PICK & PAN' EXHIBIT -TUCSON. TRAVELING EXHIBITION OF GOLD RUSHES & PROSPECTING IN AMERICAN WEST WITH FULL SCALE, AUTHENTIC EQUIPMENT & DEMONSTRATIONS OF PROSPECTING WITH TALKS & DANCES. ROCKS, MINERALS & GOLD NUGGETS ON DISPLAY. (ST-WIDE). JOHN WATTS, CURATOR; THE MUSEUM OF SCIENCE & INDUSTRY/ARIZONA HISTORICAL SOCIETY; 810 E HENDRICK DR; TUCSON, AZ 85719. (#27326). **ARBA GRANTEE.**

5TH CALVARY MEMORIAL REGIMENT TROOP A OF ARIZONA. WILL PROVIDE A FULLY TRAINED & EQUIPPED 7 TO 10 MAN CONTINGENT OF REPRESENTATIVE OF THE STYLE OF BAYLOR'S 3RD CONTINENTAL DRAGOONS OF PERFORMANCES AND RELATED BICENTENNIAL ACTIVITIES. (ST-WIDE). BRUCE H SMITH, PRESIDENT; 5TH CALVARY MEMORIAL REGIMENT, TROOP A; 186 N MEYER AVE; TUCSON, AZ 85701. (#549). **(??). ARBA GRANTEE.**

APR 27 - 29, '73. LEGENDS OF SUPERSTITION MOUNTAIN - A BALLET ABOUT ARIZONA. A FULL-LENGTH BALLET PORTRAYING THE COLORFUL HISTORY OF THE SOUTHWEST. MUSIC BY BRANSON SMITH, CHOREOGRAPHY BY RICHARD FRANCE, BASED ON 'LEGENDS' FROM DEGRAZIA AND HIS MOUNTAIN THE SUPERSTITION BY TED DEGRAZIA. PREMIERE PRESENTATION APR 27, 28, 29, 1973. (ST-WIDE). LORRAINE M NELSON; TUCSON CIVIC BALLET; 3501 N MOUNTAIN; TUCSON, AZ 85719. (#1329-1).

MAR 26 - 28, '74. PERFORMANCE OF THE BALLET, IN TUCSON, ON SOUTHWESTERN CULTURE. LEGENDS OF SUPERSTITION MOUNTAINS - BALLET OF ARIZ. ORIGINAL BALLET PERFORMED BY TUCSON CIVIC BALLET. PORTRAYS COLORFUL HISTORY OF SOUTHWEST. MOOD OF BALLET INFLUENCED BY RENOWNED WESTERN ARTIST, TED DEGRAZIA. (ST-WIDE). BRANSON SMITH, COMPOSER; TUCSON CIVIC BALLET; PO BOX 6374; TUCSON, AZ 85733. (#1329-901).

AUG 17 - 24, '74. CITYWIDE CELEBRATION OF TUCSON'S 199TH BIRTHDAY. TUCSON'S 199TH BIRTHDAY CELEBRATION. COMMEMORATION OF TUCSON'S 199TH BIRTHDAY FEATURING PARADES, HISTORIC DISPLAYS, DANCES, OPEN AIR CONCERTS, FIREWORKS, RIDES, ETC. DISPLAYS AND SPECIAL SALES BY TRADE BUREAU MERCHANTS. (ST-WIDE). PATRICK PECORARO, CHMN; TUCSON BICENTENNIAL COMMITTEE; PO BOX 5547; TUCSON, AZ 85719. (#1804-901).

FEB 13 - 15, '75. BICENTENNIAL INTERPRETIVE WORKSHOP -AMER ASSOC STATE & LOCAL HISTORY. WORKSHOPS AND CONSULTING SERVICES FOR BICENTENNIAL. TWO-DAY REGIONAL PROGRAM FOR VOLUNTEERS, TRUSTEES, AND PROFESSIONAL STAFF OF HISTORICAL SOCIETIES DEALING WITH THE MEANING OF THE REVOLUTION TODAY AND HOW TO CONVEY THAT MEANING TO THE PUBLIC THEY SERVE. (NAT'L). PAMELA JOHNSON, ASSISTANT; AMERICAN ASSOCIATION FOR STATE AND LOCAL HISTORY; 1315 8TH AVE S; NASHVILLE, TN 37203. (#4329-902).

APR 11 - SEPT 1, '75. EXHIBITION OF MEXICAN FOLK ART & COSTUMES. EXHIBITION PRESENTED AT THE ARIZONA HISTORICAL SOCIETY NEW BUILDING DURING THE TUCSON FESTIVAL. AT ARIZONA HISTORICAL SOCIETY. (LOCAL). JARVIS HARRIMAN; TUCSON FESTIVAL SOCIETY; 8 W PASEO REDONDO; TUCSON, AZ 85705. (#4889-1).

MAY 15 - 16, '75. PIMA COLLEGE GRADUATION & BICENT COLLEGE RECOGNITION CEREMONY. CEREMONY. (LOCAL). MAURICE GISS; 1807 N CENTRAL #108; PHOENIX, AZ 85004. (#50294-1).

MAY 17 - 18, '75. SILVER & TURQUOISE BALL - FINALE OF THE TUCSON FESTIVAL SEASON. GALA CIVIC CELEBRATION THAT WILL REFLECT SOUTHERN ARIZONA'S MULTI-CULTURAL HERITAGE THROUGH A VARIETY OF FESTIVE ACTIVITIES. AT ARIZONA INN. (LOCAL). JARVIS HARRIMAN; TUCSON FESTIVAL SOCIETY; 8 W PASEO REDONDO; TUCSON, AZ 85705. (#1330-1).

JUNE 1 - 2, '75. ALL-AMERICA ROSE DAY-PRESENTATION OF ALL-AM. ROSE FESTIVAL WINNERS. CEREMONY AT RANDOLPH PARK. (LOCAL). DR. LEE BURKHART; ROSE SOCIETY OF TUCSON; DEPT OF HORTICULTURE UNIV. OF AZ; TUCSON, AZ 85721. (#4554-1).

JUNE 25 - 29, '75. RINGLING BROS. BARNUM & BAILEY BICENTENNIAL CIRCUS SHOW. PROGRAM TO SALUTE THE BICENTENNIAL & GREAT MOMENTS OF OUR HISTORY, USING TRADITIONAL CIRCUS FORMAT, WITH PATRIOTIC & HISTORIC THEMES IN A VARIETY OF WAYS, BOTH INSIDE & OUTSIDE THE SHOW. AT TUCSON COMMUNITY CENTER. (LOCAL). LEE SOLTERS; RINGLING BROS. BARNUM & BAILEY; 62 W 45TH ST.; NEW YORK, NY 10036. (#1770-1).

AUG 12, '75 - JUNE 10, '76. CHILDREN'S THEATRE EDUCATION WORKSHOP. THE CHILDRENS' WORKSHOP OFFERS THE OPPORTUNITY TO EXPLORE A CREATIVE ENVIRONMENT. AT SCHOOL AUDITORIUMS THROUGHOUT THE STATE. (LOCAL). JOAN BRINCKERHOFF, CHMN; INVISIBLE THEATRE; 4560 CERCO DEL CORAZON; TUCSON, AZ 85718. (#15245-1).

AUG 20, '75. GALA COSTUME BALL WITH BICENTENNIAL DIGNITARIES AT EL PRESIDIO PARK. CEREMONY AT EL PRESIDIO PARK. (LOCAL). PATRICK PECORARO; TUCSON BICENT COMMITTEE; 1505 E HAMPTON ST; TUCSON, AZ 85719. (#100145-2).

AUG 20, '75. WESTERN POSTAL HISTORY PHILATELIC EXHIBITION - 'TUPEX '75'. EXHIBIT AT WESTERN POSTAL HISTORY MUSEUM. (LOCAL). BILL ALEXANDER, PROJ DIR; ARIZONA HISTORICAL SOCIETY; 949 E 2ND ST; TUCSON, AZ 85719. (#8914-1).

AUG 23, '75. GALA COSTUME BALL WITH BICENTENNIAL DIGNITARIES. FESTIVAL AT ELDORADO COUNTRY CLUB. (LOCAL). PATRICK PECORARO; TUCSON BICENT COMMITTEE; 1505 E HAMPTON ST; TUCSON, AZ 85719. (#100145-3).

AUG 23, '75. TUCSON'S BICENTENNIAL BIRTHDAY PARADE. PARADE. (LOCAL). PATRICK PECORARO; TUCSON BICENT COMMITTEE; 1505 E HAMPTON ST; TUCSON, AZ 85719. (#100145-4).

AUG 24, '75. SENTINAL PEAK'S GALA COSTUME BALL WITH BICENTENNIAL DIGNITARIES. FESTIVAL AT SENTINEL PEAK. (LOCAL). PATRICK PECORARO; TUCSON BICENT COMMITTEE; 1505 E HAMPTON ST; TUCSON, AZ 85719. (#100145-6).

AUG 24, '75. SPECIAL TUCSON BICENTENNIAL CELEBRATED PONTIFICAL MASS. CEREMONY AT ST AUGUSTINE'S CATHEDRAL 192 S STONE AVE, PARKING AVAILABLE. (LOCAL). REV. F. J. FOX, SJ; DIOCESE OF TUCSON; CHANCERY OFFICE BOX 31; TUCSON, AZ 85702. (#50795-1).

SEPT 8 - 12, '75. BICENTENNIAL PROGRAM COMMUNITY SCHOOL WORKSHOP. STUDENTS & TEACHERS OF ALL DEPARTMENTS WITHIN A SCHOOL WILL DEVELOP A COORDINATED BICENTENNIAL PROGRAM. A 2-DAY WORKSHOP PROGRAM TO DEVELOP A PROGRAM FOR THE PARTICIPANTS OWN SCHOOL WILL END THE WEEK. AT CLASSROOMS AND AUDITORIUM OF HIGH SCHOOL. (LOCAL). BENJAMIN F DAVIS, LIAISON; CATALINA HIGH SCHOOL AND TUCSON PUBLIC SCHOOL BICENTENNIAL COMMITTEE; 3645 E PIMA; TUCSON, AZ 85716. (#100304-1).

OCT 3 - 5, '75. 'TUCSON MEET YOURSELF & FRIENDS' - FESTIVAL. A REGIONAL FESTIVAL OF SOUTHWESTERN & LOCAL TUCSON ETHNIC AND TRADITIONAL MUSIC, DANCE, CRAFTS AND FOOD. AT EL PRESIDIO PARK. (LOCAL). NAOMI RHODES, COORDINATOR; CULTURAL EXCHANGE COUNCIL OF UNA NOCHE PLATEADA; 314 SOUTH CONVENT AVE.; TUCSON, AZ 85701. (#101195-1).

OCT 25 - 27, '75. DE ANZA EXPEDITION REENACTMENT, CELEBRATION, EXHIBITS-TUCSON. RE-ENACTMENT OF THE 1775 EXPEDITION FROM TUBAC, AZ, TO CALIFORNIA, ENDING WITH THE ESTABLISHMENT OF PRESIDIO AT SAN FRANCISCO. AT CITYWIDE. (ST-WIDE). MAURICE GISS; ARIZONA BICENTENNIAL COMMISSION; 1807 N CENTRAL #108; PHOENIX, AZ 85004. (#605-4).

OCT 31 - NOV 2, '75. PERIHELION, ENVIRONMENTAL DANCE CO.. COMPANY OF MODERN DANCERS & MUSICIANS WHO CELEBRATE THE AMERICAN ENVIRONMENT. (ST-WIDE). VERITY SHORR; PERIHELION; 4330 N. VIA SINUOSA; TUCSON, AZ 85705. (#1060-1).

NOV 1, '75 - FEB 28, '76. 'WHAT IS RIGHT WITH AMERICA', AN ESSAY CONTEST. THE CONTEST IS PART OF 'OPERATION PATRIOTISM'. THE WINNER 'WHAT IS RIGHT WITH AMERICA' WILL RECEIVE A ONE YEAR SCHOLARSHIP TO PIMA COMMUNITY COLLEGE. HIGH SCHOOL SENIORS FROM PIMA COUNTY ARE ELIGIBLE. SCHOLARSHIP WILL BE AWARDED IN MAY '76. AT TUCSON INTERNATIONAL AIRPORT. (LOCAL). TSG RAY R BAIN, JR, CHMN; 162FTG AZ AIR NATL GUARD, CHAPTER 43, NCOA GRADUATE ASSOC; PO BOX 11037; TUCSON, AZ 85734. (#5398-1).

DEC 3, '75. BICENTENNIAL CELEBRATION & FEAST DAY MASS. THIS YEAR THE SAN XAVIER FESTIVAL IS BEING COMBINED WITH THE TUCSON BICENTENNIAL CELEBRATION. AT MISSION SAN XAVIER DEL BAC, RT 11, MISSION RD. (LOCAL). REV F J FOX, SJ; SAN XAVIER COUNCIL-DIOCESE OF TUCSON; PO BOX 31; TUCSON, AZ 85702. (#200004-1).

JAN 1 - DEC 31, '76. 'WINNING THE WEST WITH PICK & PAN' EXHIBIT. TRAVELING EXHIBITION OF GOLD RUSHES & PROSPECTING IN AMERICAN WEST WITH FULL SCALE, AUTHENTIC EQUIPMENT; DEMONSTRATIONS OF PROSPECTING WITH TALKS AND DANCES. ROCKS, MINERALS AND GOLD NUGGETS ON DISPLAY. AT SCHOOL YARD OR AUDITORIUM. (LOCAL). JOHN WATTS, CURATOR; THE MUSEUM OF SCIENCE & INDUSTRY/ARIZONA HISTORICAL SOCIETY; 810 E HENDRICK DR; TUCSON, AZ 85719. (#105727-1).

JAN 3 - FEB 28, '76. MUSICAL PRODUCTION OF THE PLAY '1776'. PRODUCTION OF THE BROADWAY MUSICAL '1776' STAGED IN TRAIL DUST TOWN. (LOCAL). TOME J COLLINS, MANAGER; PLAYBOX COMMUNITY THEATRE; PO BOX 12098; TUCSON, AZ 85732. (#4887-501).

JAN 23 - 25, '76. ARIPEX '76, PHILATELIC EXHIBITION- THEME: DAYS OF ANZA. U S POST OFFICE WITH SPECIAL PICTORAL CANCELLATION, OPEN DAILY, SOUVENIR ENVELOPES HONORING ANZA EXPEDITION FOR SALE AT EXHIBIT; SET OF 3 WITH PICTORAL CANCEL WILL COST $2.00; BANQUET SATURDAY AT 7:00 PM FEATURES TALK BY SIDNEY BRINCKERHOFF. AT RAMADA INN; 404 N FREEWAY. (LOCAL). REV JAMES L SMITH, CHMN; ARIZONA FEDERATION OF STAMP CLUBS; 4054 N PARK AVE; TUCSON, AZ 85719. (#104379-7).

JAN 29 - FEB 1, '76. AMERICAN FREEDOM TRAIN DISPLAY DAYS AT TUCSON. THE AMERICAN FREEDOM TRAIN WILL INCLUDE 10 EXHIBIT CARS & 2 SHOWCASE CARS DEPICTING DIFFERENT PHASES OF THE AMERICAN EXPERIENCE. ITS ARRIVAL WILL SERVE AS A CATALYST FOR LOCAL BICENTENNIAL CELEBRATIONS BY PEOPLE THROUGHOUT THIS NATION. (ST-WIDE). SY FREEDMAN, DIR OF P/R; THE AMERICAN FREEDOM TRAIN FOUNDATION; 5205 LEESBURG PIKE, SUITE 800; BAILEY'S XRDS, VA 22041. (#1776-149).

FEB 2 - 4, '76. HAZARDOUS WASTE RESEARCH SYMPOSIUM. SYMPOSIUM FOR EXCHANGE OF RECENT RESEARCH INFORMATION ON LAND DISPOSAL OF MUNICIPAL AND HAZARDOUS WASTES; ALSO PUBLICATION OF PAPERS PRESENTED IN THE US EPA SYMPOSIUM SERIES. AT BRANIFF PLACE HOTEL. (LOCAL). DR WALLACE H FULLER, DIR; UNIV OF TUSCON & US ENVIRONMENTAL PROTECTION AGENCY; TUCSON, AZ 85721. (#104531-1).

FEB 2 - 6, '76. CABEZA DE VACA DRAMATIZATION. MULTI-MEDIA DANCE DRAMATIZATION DEPICTING THE HISTORY, ROMANCE AND DRAMA OF THE EXPEDITION OF EARLY SPANISH EXPLORER, CABEZA DE VACA. AT AMPHITHEATER LITTLE THEATER. (ST-WIDE). MARY HEWLETT, CHMN; AMPHITHEATER PRINCIPALS ASSOCIATION; 6242 CAMINO ESQUINA; TUCSON, AZ 85718. (#4890-1).

FEB 2 - 12, '76. BICENTENNIAL AUDIO CHAIRS. IN SPECIAL LISTENING CHAIRS VISITORS WILL HEAR 3 DIFFERENT TAPE RECORDINGS ON THE ROLES OF WOMEN, BLACKS, AND NATIVE AMERICANS DURING THE REVOLUTION. MONDAY THROUGH SATURDAY 10 AM TO 5 PM AND SUNDAY 2 PM TO 5 PM. AT ARIZONA STATE MUSEUM ON UNIVERSITY OF ARIZONA CAMPUS. (REGN'L). SUPERINTENDENT; NATIONAL PARK SERVICE, SAGUARO NATIONAL MONUMENT; PO BOX 17210; TUCSON, AZ 85731. (#5581-18).

FEB 12 - 14, '76. '1776' - MUSICAL PRODUCTION. THE PRODUCTION WILL TRAVEL THROUGHOUT ARIZONA AFTER FEBRUARY 15. AT TUCSON COMMUNITY CENTER, MUSIC HALL PARKING. (ST-WIDE). TOM COLLINS, V-PRESIDENT; SOUTHERN ARIZONA LIGHT OPERA COMPANY; 2018 CALLE DE VIDA; TUCSON, AZ 85715. (#101042-1).

FEB 12 - 21, '76. 'AN EVENING WITH LINCOLN'. THERE WILL BE A DINNER BREAK FROM 7:30 TO 9:30, BETWEEN PLAYS. AT UNIV THEATER, SPEEDWAY AND OLIVE RD. (LOCAL). PETER MARRONEY, PROFESSOR; UNIV OF AZ, DEPT OF DRAMA, COLLEGE OF FINE ARTS; UNIVERSITY OF AZ; TUCSON, AZ 85721. (#104531-3).

FEB 13 - JULY 5, '76. VISION QUEST/TUCSON WAGON TRAIN TO VALLEY FORGE. TROUBLED YOUTH FROM THE RESIDENTIAL TREATMENT PROGRAM, VISIONQUEST, WILL RIDE WITH THE WAGON TRAIN. TRIP IS SEEN AS A MEANINGFUL, THERAPEUDIC TRIP FOR THE YOUTH. (REGN'L). R LEDGER BURTON, COORD; VISIONQUEST; PO BOX 12906; TUCSON, AZ 85732. (#108013-1).

FEB 14 - JUNE 1, '76. KIVA HISTORICAL THEATER. LIVE PERFORMANCE. (LOCAL). SIDNEY BRINKERHOFF, DIR; ARIZONA HISTORICAL SOCIETY; 949 E 2ND; TUCSON, AZ 85719. (#14960-1).

TUCSON — CONTINUED

FEB 17, '76. 'THE BRITISH ARE COMING!' - BRITISH MILITARY BAND PERFORMANCE. TOUR OF MAJOR U S CITIES BY BRITISH MILITARY UNITS AS REPRESENTATIVE OF UNITS INVOLVED IN REVOLUTIONARY WAR CAMPAIGN. AT MCKALE CENTER AUDITORIUM. (INT'L). CHARLES K JONES, PRES; COLUMBIA ARTISTS FESTIVAL CORP; 165 W 57TH ST; NEW YORK, NY 10019. (#6532-20).

FEB 21, '76. BICENTENNIAL YOUTH DEBATES. SELECTIONAL TOURNAMENT FOR HIGH SCHOOLS AND COLLEGES. AT TUCSON CAMPUS. (LOCAL). TIMOTHY BROWNING, COORD; UNIV OF ARIZONA; TUCSON, AZ 85721. (#104467-5).

FEB 26 - 29, '76. LA FIESTA DE LOS VAQUEROS - THE TUCSON RODEO. COWBOYS, CLOWNS & RIDING EVENTS. AN UNFORGETTABLE EXPERIENCE FOR ALL AGES; RODEO IS A CONSTANTLY COMPELLING SPORT, THE LAST LIVING CHAPTER OF THE OLD WEST. AT 4801 S 6TH AVE. (ST-WIDE). BILL A WEST, CHAIRMAN; TUCSON CHAMBER OF COMMERCE RODEO COMMITTEE; 420 W CONGRESS, PO BOX 991; TUCSON, AZ 85702. (#200004-2).

MAR 1 - 7, '76. THEATER PRODUCTION OF 'BALLAD OF BABY DOE'. THERE WILL BE SPECIAL STUDENT PRICES FOR ADMISSION AND ONE FREE PERFORMANCE FOR AREA SCHOOLS. THE PRODUCTION WILL PROBABLY TOUR TO PHOENIX AND OTHER CITIES. AT TUCSON COMMUNITY CENTER LITTLE THEATRE. (LOCAL). SUSAN JACKSON, PROJ DIR; TUCSON GILBERT AND SULLIVAN THEATRE, INC; 2112 E PRINCE; TUCSON, AZ 85719. (#103065-4).

MAR 1 - JUNE 15, '76. 'FRANTIC FACTS & INFECTIOUS IDEAS', THEATRE PRESENTATION. A 30 MINUTE PLAY FEATURING AUDIENCE PARTICIPATION TO BE PERFORMED FOR YOUNG AUDIENCES THROUGHOUT THE STATE. AT AUDITORIUMS, OUTSIDE, LARGE ROOMS AND/OR THEATRES. (ST-WIDE). JOAN BRINCKERHOFF, COORD; ARIZONA BICENTENNIAL COMMISSION; PO BOX 12; TUCSON, AZ 85702. (#21833-1).

MAR 5 - 7, '76. UNITED STATES ARMED FORCES BICENTENNIAL CARAVAN. CARAVAN IS COMPOSED OF EXHIBIT VANS FOR EACH MILITARY SERVICE. PROJECT THEME IS 'HISTORY OF THE ARMED FORCES AND THEIR CONTRIBUTIONS TO THE NATION'. (LOCAL). MRS ALENE SMITH, CHMN; US ARMED FORCES EXHIBIT VANS PROJECT; PO BOX 5547; TUCSON, AZ 85703. (#1775-329).

MAR 7 - 13, '76. NATIONAL NUTRITION WEEK: IMPROVING NUTRITION FOR THE NATION. FAIR, EXHIBIT. (ST-WIDE). MARY M ANDREWS, COORD; ARIZONA DIETETIC ASSOC; 830 S LANGLEY AVE, APT 203; TUCSON, AZ 85710. (#200004-4).

MAR 10 - 12, '76. AMERICAN BANDMASTERS' BICENT CONCERT-JOINT ARMED FORCES BAND. LIVE PERFORMANCE AT 3/10 & 3/12: COMMUNITY CNTR MUSIC HALL; 3/11: UNIV AUDITORIUM. (LOCAL). JACK LEE; UNIV OF ARIZONA MUSIC DEPT; MUSIC DEPT, UNIV OF ARIZONA; TUSCON, AZ 85721. (#100094-1).

MAR 12 - 14, '76. AEROSPACE & ARIZONA DAYS 1976. THE 3-DAY EVENT WILL BE DEDICATED TO THE CONTRIBUTIONS OF THE AIR FORCE IN ARIZONA, HIGHLIGHTED BY AN APPRECIATION LUNCHEON & A 2-DAY OPEN HOUSE AT DAVIS MONTHAN AFB; THE OPEN HOUSE WILL FEATURE FLYING DEMONSTRATIONS & STATIC DISPLAYS. AT BRANIFF PLACE HOTEL - LUNCHEON. (LOCAL). CHARLES T NIBLETT, PRES; TUCSON CHAPTER AIR FORCE ASSOC; 7510 E 32ND ST; TUCSON, AZ 85710. (#105888-1).

MAR 21, '76. AMERICAN MUSIC-COLONIAL DAYS THRU PRESENT DAY-PIANO ENSEMBLE. TEN-PIANO ENSEMBLE PRESENTING THE EVOLUTION OF AMERICAN MUSIC. AT MUSIC HALL TUCSON COMMUNITY CENTER. (LOCAL). JANICE MCCURNIN; TUCSON MUSIC TEACHERS ASSOCIATION; 4256 E. WHITTIER; TUCSON, AZ 85711. (#50561-1).

MAR 21, '76. CHILDREN'S ENSEMBLE PRESENTS PATRIOTIC PAGEANT. CHILDREN'S ENSEMBLE CONCERTS IN ARIZONA. OVER 200 TUCSON CHILDREN WILL PERFORM IN A PRESENTATION OF AMERICAN MUSIC FROM REVOLUTIONARY DAYS TO THE PRESENT. (LOCAL). ALICE STOLLER SCOTT; TUCSON MUSIC TEACHERS ASSOC; 515 ETON DR; TUCSON, AZ 85734. (#4888-501).

MAR 28, '76. THE MAGNIFICENT THIRTY SEVEN. LIVE PERFORMANCE AT TUCSON COMMUNITY CENTER MUSIC HALL, 260 S CHURCH AVE. (LOCAL). MRS A GOORWITCH, CHMN; OPERA GUILD OF SOUTHERN ARIZONA AND OPERA DAMES; 8 PASEO REDONDO; TUCSON, AZ 85705. (#106011-1).

MAR 28, '76. UNIVERSITY OF ARIZONA BICENTENNIAL CONCERT - SYMPHONIC CHOIR. LIVE PERFORMANCE AT UNIVERSITY AUDITORIUM. (LOCAL). DOUGLAS PRITCHARD, CHMN; UNIV OF ARIZONA SCHOOL OF MUSIC; TUCSON, AZ 85721. (#102310-1).

MAR 28 - APR 11, '76. BICENTENNIAL SUNDAY CONCERTS. 3 SUCCESSIVE SUNDAY CONCERTS HONORING THE BICENTENNIAL: 3/28, 4/14 & 4/11/76. AT UNIVERSITY MAIN AUDITORIUM. (LOCAL). DR ROBERT WERNER, COORD; UNIV OF ARIZONA; TUCSON, AZ 85721. (#104467-6).

MAR 29 - APR 4, '76. 'THE CRUCIBLE'. LIVE PERFORMANCE AT UNIVERSITY THEATRE, SPEEDWAY AND OLIVE RD. (LOCAL). PETER MARRONEY, PROFESSOR; UNIV OF ARIZONA DEPT OF DRAMA, COLLEGE OF FINE ARTS; TUCSON, AZ 85721. (#104531-2).

APR 4, '76. UNIVERSITY OF ARIZONA BICENTENNIAL CONCERT - UNIVERSITY ORCHESTRA. LIVE PERFORMANCE AT UNIVERSITY AUDITORIUM. (LOCAL). HENRY JOHNSON, CHMN; UNIV OF ARIZONA SCHOOL OF MUSIC; TUCSON, AZ 85721. (#102310-2).

APR 7 - 9, '76. 1976 INSTITUTE OF ELECTRICAL & ELECTRONICS ENGINEERS (IEEE). 12 SESSIONS, 50 PAPERS; THEME IS ENERGY FOR THE FUTURE. FEATURED LUNCHEON AND BANQUET SPEAKERS WILL BE DR LLOYD B CRAINE, DR HARRISON H SCHMITT (ASST ADMINISTRATOR FOR NASA'S ENERGY PROGRAMS), AND DR ROBERT M HANDY, DIR OF ARIZ SOLAR ENERGY RESEARCH COMM. AT BRANIFF PLACE HOTEL. (NAT'L). FRED FINNEY, COORD; INST OF ELECTRICAL & ELECTRONIC ENGR, TUCSON & FT HUACHUCA SECT; 220 W 6TH ST; TUCSON, AZ 85701. (#104467-1).

APR 11, '76. UNIVERSITY OF ARIZONA BICENTENNIAL CONCERT BAND. LIVE PERFORMANCE AT UNIVERSITY AUDITORIUM. (LOCAL). JACK LEE, DIRECTOR; UNIV OF ARIZONA SCHOOL OF MUSIC; TUCSON, AZ 85721. (#102310-3).

APR 19 - 25, '76. 'THE PURSUIT OF HAPPINESS'. LIVE PERFORMANCE AT UNIV THEATRE, SPEEDWAY AND OLIVE RD. (LOCAL). PETER MARRONEY, PROFESSOR; UNIV OF AZ, DEPT OF DRAMA, COLLEGE OF FINE ARTS; UNIV OF AZ; TUCSON, AZ 85721. (#104531-4).

APR 23 - MAY 15, '76. TUCSON FESTIVAL ANNUAL COMMUNITY CELE OF MULTICULTURAL HERITAGE. GALA CIVIC CELEBRATION THAT WILL REFLECT SOUTHERN ARIZONA'S MULTI-CULTURAL HERITAGE THROUGH A VARIETY OF FESTIVE ACTIVITIES. AT CITYWIDE. (ST-WIDE). JARVIS HARRIMAN, EXEC DIR; TUCSON FESTIVAL SOCIETY INC; 8 WEST PASEO REDONDO; TUCSON, AZ 85705. (#1330-2).

APR 27, '76. NETHERLANDS CHAMBER ORCHESTRA VISITS UNIVERSITY OF ARIZONA. LIVE PERFORMANCE. (INT'L). WILLIAM SIMONSZ, COORD; NETHERLANDS GOVERNMENT; NETHERLANDS EMBASSY-4200 LINNEAN; WASHINGTON, DC 20008. (#109013-9).

MAY 11 - DEC 31, '76. GIFT TO ARIZONA DAY, RESTORED TERRITORIAL GOV'S HOME, BUILT 1850'S. EXHIBIT IS OF RESTORED LAST EXTANT TERRITORIAL GOVERNOR'S HOME IN TUCSON; TERRITORIAL GOV'T MUSEUM; USED FOR CULTURAL EVENTS; FOR OFFICIAL STATE AND CITY RECEPTIONS ALSO. FURNISHED IN PERIOD ANTIQUES THROUGHOUT. AT JOHN FREMONT HOUSE, CASA DEL GOBERNADOR, 151 S GRANADA AVE. (ST-WIDE). MRS EMERY C JOHNSON, PRES; TUCSON HERITAGE FOUNDATION & ARIZONA HISTORICAL SOCIETY; 10 PASEO REDONO; TUCSON, AZ 85705. (#107256-1).

MAY 27, '76. MEMORIES: BICENT BALLET, STEPHEN FOSTER MUSIC, ORIG CHOREOGRAPHY. BICENTENNIAL BALLET FEATURED ON FULL BALLET PROGRAM 11 PERFORMANCES STATEWIDE; 27 COMPANY MEMBERS AND GUEST SOLOISTS, TAPED MUSIC. AT MUSIC HALL, COMMUNITY CENTER. (ST-WIDE). TIMONA PITTMAN, EXEC DIR; ARIZONA BALLET THEATRE INC; 4528 NORTH 7TH ST; PHOENIX, AZ 85014. (#107255-6).

JUNE 1 - 30, '76. PUBLIC ROSE GARDEN. EXHIBIT. (LOCAL). NORMA NIBLETT; ROSE SOCIETY OF TUCSON; PO BOX 5547; TUCSON, AZ 85703. (#107650-1).

JUNE 1 - AUG 13, '76. 1776 AMERICA DISCOVERED BY YOUTH 1976 - TUCSON, ARIZONA. INVOLVES A TRIP TO NEW YORK AND WASHINGTON, INCLUDING TOURS AND BUILDINGS. (LOCAL). CAROLYN BALL; TUCSON BICENTENNIAL CLUB, SUNNYSIDE DIVISION; 125 E INEZ ST; TUCSON, AZ 85706. (#107816-1).

JUNE 8 - AUG 10, '76. THE SEVENTH ANNUAL SUMMER FILM FESTIVAL SERIES. 10 WEEKLY FILM SHOWINGS ON AMERICAN THEMES. AT MODERN LANGUAGES AUDITORIUM. (LOCAL). C E EDDLEBLUTE, CHAIRMAN; UNIVERSITY OF ARIZONA; TUCSON, AZ 85721. (#104467-7).

JULY 4, '76. CARILLION MUSIC. LIVE PERFORMANCE AT VA HOSPITAL, S 6TH AVE; S ON 6TH AVE TO AJO WAY. (LOCAL). MORGAN MCDERMOTT, COORD; AMERICAN LEGION & AMERICAN LEGION AUXILIARY; 300 N MAIN ST; TUCSON, AZ 85705. (#105888-2).

JULY 19 - 22, '76. ARIZONA 4-H BICENTENNIAL PROGRAM. TWO-YEAR 4-H AWARENESS PROGRAM FOR THE BICENTENNIAL, PROVIDING A TEACHING/LEARNING OPPORTUNITY FOR 4-H MEMBERS & LEADERS. THIS EVENT CULMINATES THE BICENTENNIAL PROGRAMS FOR ALL 4-H CLUBS & GROUPS IN AZ. 'MUSICALE AMERICANA' IS PRODUCTION BY FT VALLEY MAVERICKS CLUB. (ST-WIDE). PAUL DRAKE, ASST LEADER; UNIVERSITY OF ARIZONA STATE 4-H OFFICE; AGRICULTURE 319; TUCSON, AZ 85721. (#105732-1).

AUG 15, '76. DEDICATION OF HISTORICAL GARDEN. COMMUNITY DEDICATION OF HISTORICAL GARDEN WILL COMMEMORATE PADRE KINO AND TUCSONANS' COMMITTMENT TO HEALTH CARE. TO BE LOCATED IN FRONT OF KINO COMMUNITY HOSPITAL. AT FRONT OF KINO COMMUNITY HOSPITAL. (LOCAL). KRISTA A NEIS, DIR; KINO COMMUNITY HOSPITAL; 2900 S 6TH AVE; TUCSON, AZ 85713. (#23222-1).

OCT 4 - 6, '76. FOLK MUSIC FESTIVAL: TUCSON MEET YOURSELF. FESTIVAL AT EL PRESIDIA PARK. (LOCAL). MRS MARY SOWLS; CULTURAL EXCHANGE COUNCIL OF UNA NOCHE PLATEADA BD, INC; 2128 E FIFTH; TUCSON, AZ 85716. (#50320-2).

OCT 31 - NOV 14, '76. ARIZONA'S HERITAGE IN WATERCOLOR. ARTIST'S RECEPTION SUNDAY OCTOBER 31, 1976: 2-4 PM. AT DE GRAZIA GALLERY IN THE SUN, 6300 N SWAN RD. (ST-WIDE). DOROTHY LITTLETON, COORD; SOUTHERN ARIZONA WATERCOLOR GUILD; 7363 SKYLINE DR; TUCSON, AZ 85718. (#108912-1).

NOV 11, '76. VETERAN'S DAY PARADE. PARADE THEME: AMERICA'S CALLING - PLEDGE ALLEGIANCE TO FREEDOM; SALUTING THE MEN AND WOMEN OF OUR NATION WHO HAVE GIVEN SO MUCH THAT OUR NATION MIGHT REMAIN THE FREE NATION THAT IT IS. AT MAIN ST. (LOCAL). SOLENG TOM, DIRECTOR; AMERICAN LEGION MORGAN MCDERMOTT POST 7; 300 N MAIN AVE; TUCSON, AZ 85705. (#104249-5).

APR 13, '77. UNIVERSITY LIBRARY DEDICATION CEREMONY. CEREMONY AT NEW MAIN LIBRARY. (LOCAL). W DAVID LAIRD; UNIV OF ARIZONA; UNIV LIBRARY; TUCSON, AZ 85703. (#14255-1).

TUMACACORI

OCT 21 - 22, '75. DE ANZA EXPEDITION REENACTMENT, CELEBRATION-TUMACAORI NATL MONUMENT. RE-ENACTMENT OF THE 1775 EXPEDITION FROM TUBAC, AZ, TO CALIFORNIA, ENDING WITH THE ESTABLISHMENT OF PRESIDIO AT SAN FRANCISCO. AT CITYWIDE. (ST-WIDE). MAURICE GISS; ARIZONA BICENTENNIAL COMMISSION; 1807 N CENTRAL; PHOENIX, AZ 85004. (#605-2).

MAR 15 - JUNE 30, '76. TUMACACORI NM'S OFFSITE BICENT PROGRAM. PROGRAM OF COMPARATIVE HISTORY OF THE SOUTHWEST AND THE EASTERN SEABOARD 200 YEARS AGO. AVAILABLE FOR PRESENTATION TO LOCAL SCHOOLS AND ORGANIZATIONS BY ARRANGEMENT WITH PARK STAFF. (LOCAL). TUMACACORI NM; NATIONAL PARK SERVICE; PO BOX 67; TUMACACORI, AZ 85640. (#6729-159).

MAY 16, '76. NATL PK SVC '...A LITTLE LOOK AROUND' VISITS TUMACACORI NM. THIS SHORT PROGRAM FEATURES ACTORS PORTRAYING FAMOUS AMERICANS OF THE PAST WHO'VE RETURNED TO SEE AMERICA'S GROWTH. (REGN'L). TUMACACORI NATL MON; NATIONAL PARK SERVICE; P.O. BOX 67; TUMACACORI, AZ 85640. (#5653-58).

DEC 5, '76. DECEMBER FIESTA AT TUMACACORI NM. THIS FIESTA FEATURES MEXICAN AND INDIAN DOMESTIC ARTS AND CRAFTS ALONG WITH FOLK AND ETHNIC ACTIVITIES. AT TO THE NORTH OF AND ADJACENT TO THE MONUMENT GROUNDS. (REGN'L). TUMACACORI NATL MON; NATIONAL PARK SERVICE & ARIZONA COMM ON ARTS & HUMANITIES; P.O. BOX 67; TUMACACORI, AZ 85640. (#6728-69).

DEC 22, '76 - JAN 22, '77. STUDENT ARTISTS EXHIBIT VISITS TUMACACORI NM. ART EXHIBIT OF 18 ORIGINAL PAINTINGS BY STUDENT ARTISTS ON PERSONS, PLACES, OR EVENTS OF THE AMERICAN REVOLUTION. IN ADDITION TO THE REGULAR HOURS OF EXHIBITION, THE EXHIBIT WILL BE OPEN ON CHRISTMAS EVE FROM 6 PM TO 9 PM. AT PARK VISITOR CENTER. (REGN'L). TUMACACORI NM; NATIONAL PARK SERVICE; PO BOX 67; TUMACACORI, AZ 85640. (#1474-18).

VALENTINE

TRUXTON COUNTY HISTORICAL BOOKLET, AZ. A BOOKLET W/ REFLECTIONS OF 100 YEARS OF HISTORY OF TRUXTON COUNTY. (LOCAL). PAULINE COLCORD, CHAIRMAN; VALENTINE-TRUXTON BICENTENNIAL COMMITTEE; STAR ROUTE BOX 21; PEACH SPG, AZ 86434. (#26043).

WHITE RIVER

REHABILITATION OF ORIGINAL FORT APACHE BARRACKS-AZ. RESTORATION OF FORT AND BARRACKS TO THEIR ORIGINAL CONDITION. (LOCAL). RONNIE LUPE, CHAIRMAN; WHITE MOUNTAIN APACHE TRIBE; PO BOX 1158; WHITE RIVER, AZ 85941. (#23413). **ARBA GRANTEE.**

WICKENBURG

MCGUIRE PARK PROJECT - WICKENBURG, AZ. TREES WILL BE PLANTED AND RECREATION EQUIPMENT INSTALLED IN MAGUIRE PARK. (LOCAL). AL DUFF, RECREATION DIRECTOR; WICKENBURG PARK BOARD; TOWN OF WICKENBURG; WICKENBURG, AZ 85358. (#23054). **ARBA GRANTEE.**

SADDLEBAG MAGAZINE, WICKENBURG, AZ. STUDENT PRODUCED COMMUNITY MAGAZINE FEATURING BICENTENNIAL-RELATED PROJECTS, ACTIVITIES; LOCAL HISTORICAL PICTURES AND ART; SCENIC PHOTOGRAPHY; REPRESENTATIVE PERSONALITY SKETCHES. (LOCAL). BETTE VOTE, SADDLEBAG ADVISER; WICKENBURG HIGH SCHOOL; BOX 1418; WICKENBURG, AZ 85358. (#15466).

WESTERN MUSEUM AND ART GALLERY - WICKENBURG, AZ. DIORAMAS, STREET SCENES AND PERIOD ROOMS OF EARLY WICKENBURG; ALSO, ARTIFACTS, MINERAL AND MINING DISPLAYS IN ART GALLERY AND EXHIBIT ROOMS. (LOCAL). HARRY T NEEDHAM, EXEC VICE PRESIDENT; MARICOPA COUNTY HISTORICAL SOCIETY; FRONTIER ST, PO BOX 1446; WICKENBURG, AZ 85358. (#15242). **ARBA GRANTEE.**

200 TREES FOR 200 YEARS, WICKENBURG, AZ. 200 SHADE TREE SEEDLINGS GIVEN FOR REFORESTATION, BEAUTIFICATION & CONSERVATION. TREES WERE BOUGHT BY THE RAINBOW GIRLS AND GIVEN TO LOCAL AREA RESIDENTS TO PLANT ON THEIR PROPERTY. (LOCAL). MRS LIZ VAN BRUNT, MOTHER ADVISOR; WISHING WELL ASSEMBLY NUMBER 12, ORDER OF RAINBOW FOR GIRLS; ROSE LANE, PO BOX 989; WICKENBURG, AZ 85358. (#25312).

DEC 21, '75. FORMAL OPENING OF REBUILT MUSEUM. 3RD ANNIVERSARY OF FIRE WHICH RAZED OLD MUSEUM; DEDICATION SERVICES & GALA CEREMONY. AT WESTERN MUSEUM, FRONTIER ST. (LOCAL). HARRY T NEEDHAM, CHAIRMAN; MARICOPA COUNTY HISTORICAL SOCIETY; FRONTIER ST, BOX 1446; WICKENBURG, AZ 85358. (#15242-1).

FEB 6 - 8, '76. GOLD RUSH DAYS. WESTERN FESTIVITIES AND EVENTS TO CELEBRATE THE BICENTENNIAL. & ALSO THE FIRST ARIZONA INTERNATIONAL CHICKEN FLYING CONTEST. (LOCAL). DANA BURDEN; CHAMBER OF COMMERCE; P.O. DRAWER CC; WICKENBURG, AZ 85358. (#102500-2).

FEB 11, '76. UNITED STATES ARMED FORCES BICENTENNIAL CARAVAN. CARAVAN IS COMPOSED OF EXHIBIT VANS FOR EACH MILITARY SERVICE. PROJECT THEME IS 'HISTORY OF THE ARMED FORCES AND THEIR CONTRIBUTIONS TO THE NATION'. (LOCAL). MRS MARY JONES, CHMN; US ARMED FORCES EX-

WICKENBURG — CONTINUED

HIBIT VANS PROJECT; PO BOX 1123; WICKENBURG, AZ 85358. (#1775-319).

APR 11, '76. AIR FORCE BICENTENNIAL EXHIBIT. LIVE PERFORMANCE AT COMMUNITY CENTER AUDITORIUM. (LOCAL). MARY M JONES, CHAIRMAN; THE FRIENDS OF MUSIC OF WICKENBURG; OCOTILLO RD, PO BOX 1123; WICKENBURG, AZ 85358. (#106312-1).

JUNE 14, '76. FLAG DAY. PARADE. (LOCAL). MARY JONES; WICKENBURG ELKS & WICKENBURG BICENT COMM; BOX 1123; WICKENBURG, AZ 85358. (#107659-1).

JUNE 27 - JULY 4, '76. LOCAL CITIZENS ERECT PARK STRUCTURES & OPEN PARK. DURING THE WEEK OF JULY 4 1976 CITIZENS OF WICKENBURG WILLALL HELP ERECT PARK & PLAYGROUND STRUCTURES AT A PARK SITE PREPARED BY THE CITY. WILL BE 'THE PEOPLE'S PARK' (MCQUIRE PARK). AT MACQUIRE PARK. (LOCAL). ALAN DUFF, DIR; WICKENBURG PARKS & RECREATION DEPARTMENT; P O BOX 1259; WICKENBURG, AZ 85358. (#1747-1).

JULY 4 - 5, '76. MCGUIRE PARK DEDICATION. CEREMONY, FESTIVAL. (LOCAL). AL DUFF, REC DIRECTOR; TOWN OF WICKENBURG; BOX 1269; WICKENBURG, AZ 85358. (#23054-1).

WIKIEUP

BIG SANDY COMMUNITY PARK, WIKIEUP, AZ. A NEW COMMUNITY PARK WILL SERVE AS A PLAYGROUND & PICNIC AREA. (LOCAL). JIM CORNWALL, CHAIRMAN; BIG SANDY BICENTENNIAL COMMITTEE; BOX 38; WIKIEUP, AZ 85360. (#17817). **ARBA GRANTEE.**

WILLCOX

RESTORATION OF THE OLD COMMERCIAL HOTEL, AZ. RESTORATION OF EARLY TERRITORIAL HOTEL FOR USE AS A WESTERN MUSEUM. (LOCAL). MARY LEIGHTON, CHAIRMAN; SULPHUR SPRINGS HISTORICAL SOCIETY; 137 E MALEY; WILLCOX, AZ 85643. (#22307). **ARBA GRANTEE.**

FEB 24, '76. UNITED STATES ARMED FORCES BICENTENNIAL CARAVAN. CARAVAN IS COMPOSED OF EXHIBIT VANS FOR EACH MILITARY SERVICE. PROJECT THEME IS 'HISTORY OF THE ARMED FORCES AND THEIR CONTRIBUTIONS TO THE NATION'. (LOCAL). WALT FOSTER, CHMN; US ARMED FORCES EXHIBIT VANS PROJECT; 155 NORTH HASKELL; WILLCOX, AZ 85643. (#1775-324).

JULY 25 - 31, '76. ARTISTS-IN-THE-PARKS BICENT EXHIBIT AT CHIRICAHUA NM. THIS ART EXHIBIT CONSISTS OF 21 ORIGINAL PAINTINGS, EACH OF WHICH IS IDENTIFIED WITH PERSONS, PLACES, OR EVENTS OF THE AMERICAN REVOLUTION. AT COCHISE VISITOR CENTER, INTERSTATE 10 AND FORT GRANT RD. (REGN'L). CHIRICAHUA NM; NATIONAL PARK SERVICE; 1100 CIRCLE R ROAD; WILLCOX, AZ 85643. (#1474-7).

WINDOW ROCK

MULTI-TRIBAL COMMUNICATIONS SYSTEM. ESTABLISHMENT OF A NETWORK WHICH WILL INCLUDE RADIO, TELEVISION, BOOK PUBLICATIONS, PHOTOGRAPHY, FILM PRODUCTIONS, NEWS RELEASES, WIRE SERVICE & PERFORMING ARTS. (REGN'L). VIRGIL WYACO, II, EXEC PLANNER; NAVAJO FILM & MEDIA COMMISSION; PO BOX 308 THE NAVAJO NATION; WINDOW ROCK, AZ 86515. (#6887).

NAVAJO BICENT HERITAGE CENTER AT WINDOW ROCK, AR. DESIGN & CONSTRUCTION OF A NAVAJO HERITAGE CENTER TO HOUSE INDIAN ARTIFACTS. CONSTRUCTION OF TRADE CENTER DESIGNED TO SERVE AS A MERCHANDISE MART FOR DISPLAY OF ARTS & CRAFTS. (ST-WIDE). PETER MACDONALD, CHAIRMAN; THE NAVAJO NATION; WINDOW ROCK, AZ 86515. (#8627). **ARBA GRANTEE.**

NAVAJO EXPO '76 IN ARIZONA. NAVAJO NATION (LARGEST IN COUNTRY) WILL STAGE A YEAR LONG EXPOSITION IN 1976 OF NORTH AMERICAN INDIAN HERITAGE, ARTS, DANCE, & CRAFTS. TO DEVELOP EDUCATIONAL PROGRAM, MORE JOBS AND IMPROVE THE ECONOMY. (REGN'L). MARSHALL TOME, CHAIRMAN; EXPO 76 COMMISSION; PO BOX 310; WINDOW ROCK, AZ 86515. (#327).

NAVAJO FAIRGROUNDS IN WINDOW ROCK, AZ. FAIRGROUND FUNCTIONS AS MEETING PLACE FOR VISITING TRIBES AND AMERICAN PEOPLE; WILL PROVIDE SPACE FOR ATHLETICS, DANCES, DISPLAYS, AWARDS, RODEOS, TRIBAL FAIRS & OTHER SOCIAL EVENTS. (LOCAL). PETER MACDONALD, PROJ COORDINATOR; NAVAJO TRIBE OF INDIANS; WINDOW ROCK, AZ 86515. (#10722).

NAVAJO TRADEMART IN WINDOW ROCK, AZ. CONSTRUCTION OF BUILDINGS TO ALLOW NAVAJO TO ENGAGE IN COMMERCIAL ARTS & CRAFTS. (ST-WIDE). PETER MACDONALD, PROJ CHAIRMAN; NAVAJO TRIBE OF INDIANS; WINDOW ROCK, AZ 86515. (#10716).

NAVAJO ZOO PARK PROJECT- AZ. THE CENTER WILL INCLUDE ARTIFACTS, A ZOO, A PARK, HISTORICAL EXHIBITS AND A LIBRARY. (LOCAL). MARTIN LINK, PROJ DIRECTOR; NAVAJO TRIBE OF INDIANS; WINDOW ROCK, AZ 86515. (#9081). **ARBA RECOGNIZED. ARBA GRANTEE.**

MAR 27, '76. UNITED STATES ARMED FORCES BICENTENNIAL CARAVAN. CARAVAN IS COMPOSED OF EXHIBIT VANS FOR EACH MILITARY SERVICE. PROJECT THEME IS 'HISTORY OF THE ARMED FORCES AND THEIR CONTRIBUTIONS TO THE NATION'. (LOCAL). MAURICE GISS, EXEC DIR; US ARMED FORCES EXHIBIT VANS PROJECT; 1807 N CENTRAL AVE, SUITE 108; PHOENIX, AZ 85004. (#1775-340).

JUNE 25 - 27, '76. NAVAJO NATIONAL BICENTENNIAL DAYS AND RODEO. FESTIVAL. (LOCAL). CHET MCCROURY, COORD; CITY OF WINDOW ROCK; PO BOX 310; WINDOW ROCK, AZ 85615. (#108079-1).

WINSLOW

FIREFIGHTERS' HALL OF FAME MUSEUM, WINSLOW, AZ. A TRIBUTE TO FIREFIGHTERS WHOSE TASK IT IS TO PROTECT THE COMMUNITY AND ITS NATURAL RESOURCES. (LOCAL). VADA CARLSON RODRIQUEZ, HERITAGE COMMITTEE CHMN; NAVAJO COUNTY HISTORICAL SOCIETY; 123 W 4TH ST; WINSLOW, AZ 86047. (#15464).

WINSLOW BICENTENNIAL SQUARE DANCE FESTIVAL, AZ. ANNUAL SQUARE DANCE FESTIVAL WILL HAVE PARTICIPANTS FROM ALL WESTERN STATES. (LOCAL). JOHN STEELE, PRESIDENT; WINSLOW SQUARE DANCE CLUB; 415 W HILLVIEW; WINSLOW, AZ 86047. (#21158). **ARBA GRANTEE.**

NOV 15, '75. WINSLOW BICENTENNIAL CHRISTMAS PARADE. PARADE AT DOWNTOWN WINSLOW. (LOCAL). WALTER GREER, CHMN; WINSLOW CHAMBER OF COMMERCE; PO BOX 220; WINSLOW, AZ 86047. (#102309-1).

MAR 25, '76. UNITED STATES ARMED FORCES BICENTENNIAL CARAVAN. CARAVAN IS COMPOSED OF EXHIBIT VANS FOR EACH MILITARY SERVICE. PROJECT THEME IS 'HISTORY OF THE ARMED FORCES AND THEIR CONTRIBUTIONS TO THE NATION'. (LOCAL). MAURICE GISS, EXEC DIR; US ARMED FORCES EXHIBIT VANS PROJECT; 1807 N CENTRAL AVE, SUITE 108; PHOENIX, AZ 85004. (#1775-338).

MAY 1, '76. LEE'S FERRY TO WINSLOW HORSEBACK RIDE. RIDE TO COMMEMORATE THE ARRIVAL OF THE FIRST MORMANS IN NORTHERN AZ AND WINSLOW, AZ. AT NORTHERN AZ. (ST-WIDE). C W HARDY, JR, DIR; L D S CHURCH; 310 E HILLVIEW; WINSLOW, AZ 86047. (#104379-2).

JUNE 19, '76. WINSLOW BICENTENNIAL SQUARE DANCE FESTIVAL. ANNUAL SQUARE DANCE FESTIVAL PARTICIPANTS FROM ALL WESTERN STATES. (ST-WIDE). LLOYD RIDDLE, PRESIDENT; WINSLOW SQUARE DANCE CLUB; BOX U; WINSLOW, AZ 86047. (#102428-1).

JULY 4, '76. BICENTENNIAL 4TH OF JULY FIREWORKS DISPLAY. FESTIVAL AT WINSLOW HIGH SCHOOL FOOTBALL FIELD & STADIUM. (LOCAL). GLEN HOWTH, COORD; AMERICAN LEGION POST 15; WINSLOW, AZ 86047. (#107252-1).

JULY 4, '76. OLD TIMERS JUBILEE. ALL DAY CELEBRATION COMBINING FAMILY FESTIVAL WITH OLD TIMERS' JUBILEE DINNER. AT CITY PARK, E MAPLE ST. (LOCAL). ALICE GRAHAM, COORD; WINSLOW WOMEN'S CLUB AND WINSLOW BICENTENNIAL COMMISSION; 1009 APACHE; WINSLOW, AZ 86047. (#104379-9).

JULY 31 - AUG 22, '76. I-40 ART EXPO. ARTS EXHIBIT WITH PERFORMING ARTS ENTERTAINMENT. CONSERVATIVE ART COMPETITION. AT WINSLOW CIVIC CENTER, AIRPORT RD, WINSLOW, ARIZONA. (REGN'L). DON AYRES, PRES; WINSLOW ARTS ASSOC; 617 W 4TH ST; WINSLOW, AZ 86047. (#104379-8).

YUMA

BICENTENNIAL CELEBRATION LANDSCAPING PROJECT IN AZ. DEVELOP FORMER CITY DUMP INTO YUMA CROSSING PARK; CONVERSION & REMODELING OF THE OLD RAILROAD DEPOT INTO A COMMUNITY ART CENTER; REFURBISHING AND LANDSCAPING TERRITORIAL MALL. (LOCAL). HON ERSEL C BYRD, MAYOR; CITY OF YUMA; 180 FIRST ST; YUMA, AZ 85364. (#22856). **ARBA GRANTEE.**

CAMINO DEL DIABLO TRAIL INVITATIONAL TOURS - AZ. TOURS IN 4-WHEEL DRIVE VEHICLES OF TRAILS USED BY EARLY INDIANS & SPANISH EXPLORERS IN SOUTHWESTERN ARIZONA. (LOCAL). MONTE DODSON, REFUGE MANAGER; U S FISH & WILDLIFE SERVICE; PO BOX 1032; YUMA, AZ 85364. (#14950).

DEPOT RENOVATION IN YUMA, ARIZONA. RENOVATION OF HISTORIC YUMA SOUTHERN PACIFIC RAILROAD DEPOT. DEPOT WILL BECOME A MULTI-MEDIA, MULTI-CULTURAL CENTER. (LOCAL). LAUREL MEINIG, EXEC DIRECTOR; YUMA FINE ARTS ASSOCIATION; PO BOX 1471; 281 GILA ST; YUMA, AZ 85364. (#4606). **ARBA GRANTEE.**

LIFE ON THE AMERICAN NILE PROJECT OF ARIZONA. COMPILATION & PUBLICATION OF HISTORICAL MATERIALS TO DEPICT FRONTIER AND TERRITORIAL LIFE ALONG THE COLORADO RIVER. (REGN'L). ROSALIE CROWE, EDITOR; YUMA COUNTY HISTORICAL SOCIETY; 240 MADISON AVE; YUMA, AZ 85364. (#546). **(??). ARBA GRANTEE.**

RESTORATION OF OLD CUSTOM HOUSE IN YUMA, AZ. CONTINUING PROGRAM OF RESTORATION AT THE OLD CUSTOMS HOUSE WHICH IS OVERLOOKING THE COLORADO RIVER IN YUMA, ARIZONA. (LOCAL). MRS A PHILLIP KERCKHOFF, CUSTOMS HOUSE HISTORIAN; ASSISTANCE LEAGUE OF YUMA; PO BOX 4057; YUMA, AZ 85364. (#1749).

SIGNIFICANT WOMEN OF YUMA, AZ. INFORMATION COMPILED ABOUT SIGNIFICANT HISTORICAL WOMEN OF ALL ETHNIC GROUPS IN THE YUMA AREA, ARRANGED WITH PHOTO OF MODEL IN PERIOD OR ETHNIC COSTUMES. (LOCAL). MARION ELLIOTT, CHARLENE MALONER - CO-CHRMN; ZONTA (INTERNATIONAL) OF YUMA; 2888 VISTA LANE; YUMA, AZ 85364. (#15467).

YUMA ART CENTER, AZ. RESTORE AND CONVERT SOUTHERN PACIFIC RAILWAY DEPOT INTO AN ART CENTER. (ST-WIDE). LAUREL MEINIG, DIRECTOR; YUMA FINE ARTS ASSOC; PO BOX 1471; YUMA, AZ 85364. (#25470).

YUMA RIVER, ARIZONA, GREEN BELT AREA. TO REDEVELOP THE YUMA RIVER CROSSING AS A PASSIVE AREA FOR HISTORICAL & RECREATIONAL INTERESTS TO BE ENJOYED BY ALL PEOPLE. (ST-WIDE). JOE ATMAR, CHAIRMAN; YUMA CITY-COUNTY BICENTENNIAL COMMISSION; 285 MAIN ST, PO BOX 5540; YUMA, AZ 85364. (#2820). **(??).**

AUG 23 - 24, '74. OPENING CEREMONIES, DINNER MEETING WITH SPEAKERS ON HISTORY OF AREA. CEREMONY. (ST-WIDE). ROBERT E YOUNT, VICE PRES; COUNCIL ON ABANDONED MILITARY POSTS-USA; 6811 6TH ST; SCOTTSDALE, AZ 85251. (#735-901).

MAY 2 - 6, '75. FATHER GARCES FESTIVAL OF THE ARTS - MUSIC, DANCE & THATRICAL EVENTS. ANNUAL CULTURAL FESTIVAL CELEBRATING THE LIFE OF THE EARLY SPANISH MISSIONARY, FATHER GARCES. (LOCAL). DON ENGLER, V/PRES; YUMA FINE ARTS ASSOC.; PO BOX 1471; YUMA, AZ 85364. (#6885-1).

NOV 28 - 30, '75. DE ANZA REENACTMENT--CELEBRATION, FAIR, EXHIBITS, BALL. RE-ENACTMENT OF THE 1775 EXPEDITION FROM TUBAC, AZ, TO CALIFORNIA, ENDING WITH THE ESTABLISHMENT OF PRESIDIO AT SAN FRANCISCO. AT CITYWIDE. (ST-WIDE). MAURICE GISS; ARIZONA BICENTENNIAL COMMISSION; 1807 N CENTRAL #108; PHOENIX, AZ 85004. (#605-7).

NOV 29, '75. BOOK REVIEW: SIGNIFICANT WOMEN OF YUMA. DRAMATIZATION OF BOOK COMPILED ABOUT OUTSTANDING HISTORICAL WOMEN, REPRESENTING ALL ETHNIC GROUPS OF YUMA AREA. PERFORMANCE WILL BE AVAILABLE TO GROUPS AND CLUBS UPON REQUEST. THE COMPLETED BOOK WILL BE GIVEN TO THE YUMA HISTORICAL SOCIETY & ARIZONA HIST SOCIETY. AT CENTURY HOUSE GARDENS OF YUMA COUNTY HISTORICAL SOC, 240 S MADISON. (LOCAL). M. ELLIOTT & C. MALONEY; ZONTA (INTERNATIONAL) CLUB OF YUMA; 2888 VISTA LA; YUMA, AZ 85364. (#15467-1).

JAN 22 - 23, '76. AMERICAN FREEDOM TRAIN DISPLAY DAYS AT YUMA. THE AMERICAN FREEDOM TRAIN WILL INCLUDE 10 EXHIBIT CARS AND 2 SHOW CASE CARS DEPICTING DIFFERENT PHASES OF THE AMERICAN EXPERIENCE. ITS ARRIVAL WILL SERVE AS A CATALYST FOR LOCAL BICENTENNIAL CELEBRATIONS BY PEOPLE THROUGHOUT THIS NATION. (ST-WIDE). DON MALLICOAT, EDIT SVCS; THE AMERICAN FREEDOM TRAIN, INC.; 5205 LEESBURGE PKE, SUITE 800; BAILEY'S XRDS, VA 22041. (#1776-40).

FEB 5 - 6, '76. UNITED STATES ARMED FORCES BICENTENNIAL CARAVAN. CARAVAN IS COMPOSED OF EXHIBIT VANS FOR EACH MILITARY SERVICE. PROJECT THEME IS 'HISTORY OF THE ARMED FORCES AND THEIR CONTRIBUTIONS TO THE NATION'. (LOCAL). JOE ATMAR, CHMN; US ARMED FORCES EXHIBIT VANS PROJECT; PO BOX 1130; YUMA, AZ 85364. (#1775-316).

MAY 14, '76. MEMORIES: BICENT BALLET, STEPHEN FOSTER MUSIC, ORIG CHOREOGRAPHY. BICENTENNIAL BALLET FEATURED ON FULL BALLET PROGRAM; TOURING 11 CITIES IN STATE: SCOTTSDALE, YUMA, PRESCOTT, TUCSON, SNOWFLAKE, FLAGSTAFF & PHOENIX, AZ; 27 BALLET COMPANY MEMBERS AND GUEST SOLOISTS; MUSIC WILL BE TAPED. AT ELIZ POST SCHOOL AUDITORIUM, 400 W 5TH ST. (ST-WIDE). TIMONA PITTMAN, EXEC DIR; ARIZONA BALLET THEATRE, INC; 4528 N 7TH ST; PHOENIX, AZ 85014. (#107255-4).

JULY 1, '76. TERRITORIAL PRISON CENTENNIAL. FESTIVAL. (LOCAL). JOE ATMAR; YUMA BICENTENNIAL COMMISSION; 1057 W PALMCROFT RD; YUMA, AZ 85364. (#107662-1).

JULY 3, '76. INNERTUBE RACE AND FLOATDOWN ON THE COLORADO. COMPETITION. (LOCAL). JOE ATMAR; YUMA BICENTENNIAL COMMISSION; 1057 W PALCROFT DR; YUMA, AZ 85364. (#107662-2).

76
LIBERTY
THE GREAT SEAL OF NEW YORK
ADMINISTRATION CENTER
E PLURIBUS UNUM
ANNUIT COEPTIS
NOVUS ORDO SECLORUM
THE GREAT SEAL OF THE STATE OF TENNESSEE
XVI
AGRICULTURE
COMMERCE
1796

Arkansas

Bicentennial Celebration Committee

Appointed by the governor in compliance with House Concurrent Resolutions 88 (1971) and 15 (1973)

ARBA Statistics

Officially Recognized
- Communities—238
- Colleges/Universities—12
- Military Installations—3

BINET Projects—343
- Events—379

1976 Population—2,109,000

Bicentennial Archives

Department of Parks and Tourism
Arkansas History Commission
300 West Markham
Little Rock, Arkansas 72201

Membership

Joe Basore (1976-77)
(Mrs.) Bernard Brazil (1974-76)
(Mrs.) Silas Carroll, Jr. (1973-74)
James S. Chase (1971-77)
(Mrs.) Elijah Coleman (1975-77)
Paul H. Dixon, Jr. (1974-75)
(Mrs.) Thomas F. Dodson (1971-75)
John L. Ferguson (1971-75)
J. B. Gardner (1971-75)
Galbraith Gould (1975-76)
Richard L. Gower (1971)
James E. Hyatt, Jr. (1971-77)
Earle W. Johnson (1971-77)
Perrin Jones (1971-72)
(Mrs.) James A. Marmouget (1976-77)
Joe Purcell (1975-77)
W. T. Robinson (1972-77)
(Mrs.) George Rose Smith (1971-77)
Charles Trammel (1971-75)
(Mrs.) Robert M. Twyford (1975-77)
J. S. Upton (1973-74)
Jim W. Williams (1975-77)

Arkansas

The *Arkansas American Revolution Bicentennial Celebration Program* was initiated with the passage of House Concurrent Resolution 88 by the General Assembly of 1971. Sponsored by Representative William F. Foster, Sr. of Lonoke County, the resolution requested that the governor appoint a Bicentennial Celebration Committee of nine members "to make plans for Arkansas' participation in the Bicentennial celebration of the formation of the United States."

The Bicentennial Celebration Committee was appointed by Governor Dale L. Bumpers. The General Assembly of 1973 expanded the membership of the committee from nine to 11 by the addition of the State Regent of the Daughters of the American Revolution and the State President of the Sons of the American Revolution (House Concurrent Resolution 15 of 1973).

Dr. John L. Ferguson, state historian, served as chairman of the Bicentennial Celebration Committee from 1971 until 1975, when he was replaced by Lieutenant Governor Joe Purcell. Mrs. Glennis Parker was employed as the first director of the *Bicentennial Celebration Program* in 1972. She resigned in 1975 and was succeeded by Mrs. Ruth Tate.

Headquarters of the Bicentennial program was the First State Capitol, Arkansas' old state house which was built in 1836. At its peak in 1975-76, the Bicentennial staff included five persons: director, program coordinator, grants administrator, information officer and a secretary.

The Arkansas program saw the designation of 266 official Bicentennial Communities in each of the state's 75 counties. Matching grants for Bicentennial projects numbered 264, with a total of $560,000 disbursed. In addition, one county received a Title X grant of $767,000 for a Bicentennial park.

Efforts in Arkansas were directed primarily toward local and community involvement, and the program was remarkably successful in small towns and rural areas. Mrs. Elaine Walker, a volunteer, organized a statewide Youth Rally at the State Capitol March 19, 1976 and led in the establishment of numerous Bicentennial Communities in northwestern Arkansas. A permanent Bicentennial memorial, housing a replica of the Liberty Bell, is under construction on the State Capitol grounds. A statewide cleanup or antilitter campaign is in progress as a development of the *Horizons* theme.

Projects at the local level have been as numerous and as diverse as the composition of the committees which planned them. All segments of the population—youth, minorities, the elderly and others—have been actively involved. The three themes of *Heritage, Festival* and *Horizons* have been amply represented and developed in projects all over Arkansas. Among the many highlights of the celebration were the founding of the Arkansas County Agricultural Museum in Stuttgart; Johnny Cash Day at Rison, March 20, 1976; the passage of the *Bicentennial Wagon Train Pilgrimage* across Arkansas in March 1976; and the commemoration of the Colbert Incident at Arkansas Post National Memorial, July 4, 1976.

ALICIA

JUNE 19, '76. CONTESTS FOR DIFFERENT AGE GROUPS. TYPES OF CONTESTS: EGG-THROWING; BUBBLEGUM BLOWING; HORSESHOES, HULA-HOOP; WHISTLING; APPLEDUNKING; SACK RACE; LOGSAWING. THE WINNER IN EACH CONTEST WAS GIVEN A RIBBON. AT GROUNDS OF THE METHODIST CHURCH. (LOCAL). SHELIA BULLARD, CHAIRMAN; ALICIA CITY COUNCIL; BOX 28; ALICIA, AR 72410. (#200005-36).

ARKADELPHIA

FEB 10, '76. AMERICA 200. DRAMATIC AND MUSICAL INTERPRETATION OF THE NATION'S 200 YEAR HISTORY TO BE PRESENTED IN 5 CITIES IN ARKANSAS. AT MITCHELL HALL AUDITORIUM. (LOCAL). MAC B SISSON, CHAIRMAN; OUACHITA BAPTIST UNIV; 10 CONCORD CIR; ARKADELPHIA, AR 71923. (#104548-9).

APR 25, '76. CLARK COUNTY PATRIOTIC-RELIGIOUS BICENTENNIAL CELBRATION. BAND & CHOIR PERFORMANCES & FLAG CEREMONY. AT HAYGOOD STADIUM - HENDERSON STATE UNIV. (LOCAL). MAC SISSON, PUBLICITY; CLARK COUNTY BICENTENNIAL COMMISSION & ROSS FOUNDATION; 10 CONCORD CIR; ARKADELPHIA, AR 71923. (#106803-2).

APR 26, '76. PANEL DISCUSSION ON DECLARATION OF INDEPENDENCE, ITS IMPACT TODAY. IMPACT OF DECLARATION OF INDEPENDENCE AS RELATED TO PRESENT DAY PROBLEMS. (LOCAL). MAC SISSON, PUBLICITY; CLARK COUNTY BICENTENNIAL COMMISSION; 10 CONCORD CIR; ARKADELPHIA, AR 71923. (#106803-1).

MAY 6, '76. PIONEER FARM & HOME SHOW. EXHIBIT, FESTIVAL AT CLARK COUNTY FAIRGROUNDS. (LOCAL). MAC SISSON, PUBLICITY; CLARK COUNTY BICENTENNIAL COMMISSION & CLARK CO EXTENSION HOMEMAKERS; 10 CONCORD CIR; ARKADELPHIA, AR 71923. (#106803-5).

MAY 20 - 22, '76. NATIONAL ASSOCIATION OF INTERCOLLEGIATE ATHLETICS OUTDOOR TRACK MEET. COMPETITION AT HAYGOOD STADIUM - HENDERSON STATE UNIV. (REGN'L). MAC SISSON, PUBLICITY; CLARK COUNTY BICENTENNIAL COMMISSION & NAIA; 10 CONÇORD CIR; ARKADELPHIA, AR 71923. (#106803-3).

JULY 3, '76. CLARK COUNTY BICENTENNIAL FOLK FESTIVAL. SQUARE DANCING, JIG & FIDDLING CONTEST, GAMES & EXHIBITS. AT CLARK COUNTY COURT HOUSE. (LOCAL). MAC SISSON, PUBLICITY; CLARK COUNTY BICENTENNIAL COMMISSION; 10 CONCORD CIR; ARKADELPHIA, AR 71923. (#106803-4).

NOV 10 - 12, '76. 'HISTORY OF CLARK COUNTY' - ORIGINAL PLAY. PLAY RESEARCHED & WRITTEN BY DANIEL STEIN, FINANCED BY GRANT FROM THE ROSS FOUNDATION. (LOCAL). MAC SISSON, PUBLICITY; CLARK COUNTY BICENTENNIAL COMMISSION; 10 CONCORD CIR; ARKADELPHIA, AR 71923. (#106803-6).

ARKANSAS CITY

COMMEMORATIVE MARKERS IN DESHA COUNTY, ARKANSAS. EIGHT COMMEMORATIVE MARKERS DEPICTING HISTORICAL PERSONS AND EVENTS IMPORTANT THROUGHOUT THE HISTORY OF THE AREA WILL BE PROVIDED BY THE DESHA COUNTY HISTORICAL SOCIETY TO STIMULATE INTEREST IN LOCAL HIST. (LOCAL). C C STUART, PRESIDENT; DESHA COUNTY HISTORICAL SOCIETY; DESHA COUNTY COURTHOUSE; ARKANSAS CITY, AR 71630. (#1031). **ARBA GRANTEE.**

JULY 24, '75. OTRABANDA COMPANY'S THIRD ANNUAL MISSISSIPPI RIVER TOUR. LIVE PERFORMANCE, PARADE AT COUNTY COURTHOUSE LAWN. (LOCAL). CULLEN GANNAWAY; TOWN OF ARKANSAS CITY; P. O. BOX 357; ARKANSAS CITY, AR 71630. (#50550-14).

ARKANSAS POST

APR 12 - JULY 1, '75. ARKANSAS COUNTY BOY SCOUT RALLY. AA STATE HWY 1 SOUTH OF DEWITT THEN STATE HWY 169 EAST. AT ARK POST NATIONAL MEMORIAL PARK. (LOCAL). MRS JEAN POLLARD; ARKANSAS COUNTY BICENTENNIAL; 808 WEST 18; STUTTGART, AR 72160. (#50053-3).

ATKINS

ATKINS CENTENNIAL BOOK - ARKANSAS. A HISTORY OF ATKINS AND SURROUNDING AREA IS BEING WRITTEN IN HONOR OF THE CITY'S CENTENNIAL IN 1976 AND THE BICENTENNIAL. THE BOOK WILL CONTAIN PICTURES, BIOGRAPHIES AND RESULTS OF RESEARCH. (LOCAL). DALLAS L SWAIN, CITY CLERK; CITY OF ATKINS; ATKINS, AR 72823. (#8221). **ARBA GRANTEE.**

ATKINS, ARKANSAS PUBLIC LIBRARY. A NEW PUBLIC LIBRARY WILL BE COMPLETED AND DEDICATED BY 1976. ONE ROOM WILL HOUSE ALL HISTORIC MATERIAL FROM THE CENTENNIAL & BICENTENNIAL. FILMED PROGRAM ON HISTORY OF NATION WILL BE AVAILABLE. (LOCAL). ROY J TAYLOR, CHAIRMAN; ATKINS CENTENNIAL BICENTENNIAL COMMITTEE; 703 E CENTRAL ST; ATKINS, AR 72823. (#3080).

COMMEMORATIVE MARKER, ATKINS, AR. A COMMEMORATIVE MARKER WILL BE ERECTED IN THE TOWN OF ATKINS. (LOCAL). DALLAS SWAIN, CITY CLERK; CITY OF ATKINS BICENTENNIAL COMMITTEE; CITY HALL; ATKINS, AR 72823. (#17615). **ARBA GRANTEE.**

GALLA CREEK WATERSHED PROJECT OF ATKINS, ARKANSAS. IMPROVEMENTS IN THE GALLA CREEK AREA FOR THE BICENTENNIAL. (LOCAL). HON STEVEN KENT, MAYOR; CITY OF ATKINS; ATKINS, AR 72823. (#3769). **(??).**

PUBLICATION OF HISTORY OF ATKINS, ARK, AREA. HISTORY OF THE ATKINS TRADE AREA, INCLUDING BLACK HISTORY, AND ALL OTHER ETHNIC GROUPS. (LOCAL). ROY J TAYLOR, CHAIRMAN; ATKINS CENTENNIAL BICENTENNIAL COMMISSION; 103 E CENTRAL; ATKINS, AR 72823. (#3772).

SENIOR CITIZENS HOUSING PROJ OF ATKINS, ARKANSAS. PROPER HOUSING FOR SENIOR CITIZENS IS ONE OF THE BICENTENNIAL GOALS. (LOCAL). HON STEVEN KENT, MAYOR; CITY OF ATKINS; ATKINS, AR 72823. (#3771). **(??).**

SHRUB PLANTING PROJECT OF ATKINS, ARKANSAS. PLANTING SHRUBS ON THE MAIN STREET. (LOCAL). MRS LEONA WEAVER, PRESIDENT; HEAVE HO GARDEN CLUB; ATKINS, AR 72823. (#3768).

OCT 23, '74. PRESENTATION OF BICENTENNIAL FLAG. CEREMONY. (ST-WIDE). ROY J TAYLOR, CHAIRMAN; ATKINS CENTENNIAL BICENTENNIAL COMMISSION; 103 E CENTRAL; ATKINS, AR 72823. (#3773-901).

JUNE 1, '75 - JULY 4, '76. FLAG DISPLAY EXHIBIT OF ATKINS, AR. DISPLAY OF SIX FLAGS REPRESENTING GOVTS OF THE AREA-FRENCH, SPANISH, CHEROKEE, US, ARK, & CONFEDERATE, PLUS THE BICENTENNIAL FLAG. FEATURING 7 FLAGS OF 6 DIFFERENT NATIONS AND A CONFEDERATE FLAG. AT HWY US 64 IN ATKINS. (ST-WIDE). ROY J TAYLOR, CHMN; ATKINS CENTENNIAL BICENTENNIAL COMMISSION; 103 E CENTRAL; ATKINS, AR 72823. (#3773-1).

OCT 11, '75. BICENTENNIAL PARADE. PARADE. (LOCAL). ROY J TAYLOR, DIRECTOR; CITY OF ATKINS; 103 CENTRAL; ATKINS, AR 72823. (#200005-14).

FEB 14, '76. BICENTENNIAL BALL. FESTIVAL AT MCLAIN PARK GYM. (LOCAL). ROY J TAYLOR, CHMN; ATKINS BICENTENNIAL COMMITTEE; 103 E CENTRAL; ATKINS, AR 72823. (#105110-3).

MAR 15 - 16, '76. PILGRIMAGE WAGON TRAIN ARRIVAL & ENTERTAINMENT. CEREMONY, FESTIVAL AT RODEO ARENA, HWY 105 N. (LOCAL). ROY J TAYLOR, CHMN; JAYCEES SECTION OF BICENTENNIAL COMMITTEE; 103 E CENTRAL; ATKINS, AR 72823. (#105110-6).

JULY 4, '76. ATKINS PIONEER CITIZENS PICNIC -ARKANSAS. A JULY 4 PICNIC WILL HONOR ATKINS CITIZENS 80 YRS OR OLDER. RESERVED SEATS PROVIDED AT ALL CENTENNIAL-BICENTENNIAL PGMS. INTERVIEWS ARE BEING TAPED TO PRESEVE LOCAL HISTORY THROUGH PIONEER CITIZENS. AT LATE ATKINS, HWY 105 S. (LOCAL). ROY TAYLOR, CHAIRMAN; ATKINS CENTENNIAL BICENTENNIAL COMMITTEE; 103 E CENTRAL; ATKINS, AR 72823. (#3084-1).

SEPT 9 - 12, '76. CENTENNIAL-BICENTENNIAL CELEBRATION WEEK. FESTIVAL, CEREMONY AT LAKE ATKINS. (LOCAL). ROY J TAYLOR, CHAIRMAN; ATKINS CENTENNIAL BICENTENNIAL COMMITTEE; 703 E CENTRAL ST; ATKINS, AR 72823. (#3079-1).

SEPT 11, '76. EXHIBIT OF PIONEER CLOTHES. LIVE PERFORMANCE, EXHIBIT. (LOCAL). DALLAS SWAIN, CITY CLERK; CITY OF ATKINS BICENTENNIAL COMMITTEE; CITY HALL; ATKINS, AR 72823. (#17615-1).

OCT 10 - 11, '76. BICENTENNIAL RODEO. COMPETITION, LIVE PERFORMANCE AT RODEO ARENA, HWY 105 N. (LOCAL). ROY J TAYLOR, CHMN; ATKINS RIDING CLUB; 103 E CENTRAL; ATKINS, AR 72823. (#105110-2).

OCT 10 - 12, '76. ANTIQUE; ARTS & CRAFTS SHOW. EXHIBIT AT MCLAIN PARK GYM. (LOCAL). ROY J TAYLOR, CHMN; ATKINS BICENTENNIAL COMMITTEE; 103 E CENTRAL; ATKINS, AR 72823. (#105110-5).

OCT 12, '76. HISTORIC HOMES OPEN HOUSE. TOUR. (LOCAL). ROY J TAYLOR, CHMN; ATKINS BICENTENNIAL COMMITTEE; 103 CENTRAL; ATKINS, AR 72823. (#105110-1).

AUGUSTA

HISTORY OF SCHOOLS IN WOODRUFF COUNTY, AR. RETIRED TEACHERS ARE COMPILING INFORMATION, PICTURES, STORIES AND HISTORY OF ALL SCHOOLS IN WOODRUFF COUNTU. (LOCAL). MRS ARTIS WARNER BERRY, PROJ CHAIRMAN; RETIRED TEACHERS OF WOODRUFF COUNTY; 308 LOCUST; AUGUSTA, AR 72006. (#18457).

RESTORATION OF FIRST CHURCH BUILDING - AUGUSTA, AR. OLDEST CHURCH IN WOODRUFF COUNTY WAS GIVEN TO THE COMMUNITY BY THOMAS HOUGH IN 1850; IT NOW STANDS AS JACKSON CHAPPELL COLORED METHODIST CHURCH. (LOCAL). JULIOUS WILLIAMS, PASTOR; COLORED METHODIST EPISCOPAL CONGREGATION; 600 CONNER & S 6TH ST; AUGUSTA, AR 72006. (#18454).

APR 29, '76. PATRIOTIC SPRING MUSICAL. AUGUSTA ELEMENTARY SCHOOL MUSICALS ARE ALWAYS VERY SHOWY. WELL ATTENDED. AT 905 N 4TH OR 1011 MAIN ST. (LOCAL). PHYLLIS STALLINGS, DIR; AUGUSTA ELEMENTARY SCHOOL; 905 N 4TH; AUGUSTA, AR 72006. (#103799-8).

AUG '76. SPECIAL PROGRAM FOR YOUNG PEOPLE. THIRTY EIGHT CHURCHES WILL PARTICIPATE IN PATRIOTIC CELEBRATIONS, DINNERS AND ENTERTAINMENT. AT NORTH 2ND ST. (LOCAL). WILLIE HARRIS, DIR; ST JOHN MISSIONARY BAPTIST CHURCH; 504 N 6TH; AUGUSTA, AR 72101. (#103799-2).

BARLING

DEC 21 - 22, '75. BICENTENNIAL TOWBOAT SGT FLOYD VISIT. EXHIBIT AT LOCK & DAM 13. (REGN'L). ROBERT M GARNER, CHAIRMAN; CRAWFORD COUNTY BICENTENNIAL COMMISSION; PO BOX 486; VAN BUREN, AR 72956. (#200005-70).

BASSETT

BASSETT, AR BICENTENNIAL PROJECT. FLAGPOLE ERECTION, ENGRAVED PLAQUE WITH NAMES OF BICENTENNIAL YEAR OFFICIALS. (LOCAL). HON CALVIN WILLIAMS, MAYOR; TOWN COUNCIL; BOX 54; BASSETT, AR 72313. (#28589).

MAY 7, '76. DEDICATION CEREMONIES. CEREMONY. (LOCAL). HON CALVIN WILLIAMS, MYR; TOWN OF BASSETT; BOX 54; BASSETT, AR 72313. (#109329-1).

BATESVILLE

ARKANSAS COLLEGE HERITAGE PROGRAM IN BATESVILLE. PRESERVATION OF A LOCAL HEWN LOG STRUCTURE WILL BE UNDERTAKEN BY THE COLLEGE. AN EXHIBIT OF LOCALLY MADE FURNITURE PRIOR TO 1876 WILL BE ASSEMBLED. (LOCAL). DANIEL W FAGG, CHAIRMAN; ARKANSAS COLLEGE BICENT STEERING COMMITTEE; PO BOX 2317; BATESVILLE, AR 72501. (#10160).

ARKANSAS COLLEGE FESTIVAL PROGRAM, BATESVILLE, AR. A SPECIAL FESTIVAL PROGRAM FEATURED BY THE COLLEGE WILL INCLUDE A CHOIR TOUR, 4TH OF JULY CELEBRATION, COMMENCEMENT OF THE 1976 CLASS AND FENT NOLAND FESTIVAL. (LOCAL). DANIEL W FAGG, CHAIRMAN; ARKANSAS COLLEGE BICENT STEERING COMMITTEE; PO BOX 2317; BATESVILLE, AR 72501. (#10166).

BATESVILLE, ARKANSAS, HISTORY SEMINARS. A SERIES OF CURRICULUM SEMINARS WILL BE OFFERED BY ARKANSAS COLLEGE DURING 1975-1976; FAMILY HISTORIES AND HISTORIC DOCUMENTS WILL BE AMONG THOSE TOPICS EXAMINED. (LOCAL). DANIEL W FAGG, JR, CHAIRMAN; ARKANSAS COLLEGE BICENT STEERING COMMITTEE; PO BOX 2317; BATESVILLE, AR 72501. (#10159).

BICENTENNIAL MEMORIAL HERITAGE HOUSE, AR. ESTABLISHMENT OF A HERITAGE HOUSE, LOG SWELLING WHICH WILL BE UTILIZED BY THE COLLEGE AS A FORMAL AND INFORMAL LEARNING CENTER. (LOCAL). DANIEL FOGG, CHAIRMAN; ARKANSAS COLLEGE BICENTENNIAL COMMITTEE; ARKANSAS COLLEGE; BATESVILLE, AR 72501. (#24732). **ARBA GRANTEE.**

ENVIRONMENTAL IMPROVEMENT PROJ IN BATESVILLE, AR. IN HONOR OF THE BICENT, A MEMORIAL TREE & AN ARBORETUM ARE BEING PLANNED. COLLEGE INVOLVEMENT IN BEAUTIFYING LOCAL PUBLIC AREAS IS BEING EMPHASIZED. (LOCAL). DANIEL W FAGG, JR, CHAIRMAN; ARKANSAS COLLEGE STEERING COMMITTEE; PO BOX 2317; BATESVILLE, AR 72501. (#8911).

FENT NOLAND DOCUMENTARY AND FESTIVAL - AR. A FOLK FESTIVAL AND DOCUMENTARY ON THE LIFE OF FENTON NOLAND WHO IS ASSOCIATED WITH THE MOST IMPORTANT POLITICAL EVENTS IN EARLY ARKANSAS HISTORY. (LOCAL). TERRELL TEBBETTS, DIRECTOR OF HUMANITIES; ARKANSAS COLLEGE; BATESVILLE, AR 72501. (#17588). **ARBA GRANTEE.**

PUBLIC EDUCATION: PROMISE & REALITY - ARKANSAS. AN INQUIRY INTO THE BASIC GOALS OF FREE UNIVERSAL PUBLIC EDUCATION AND AN ASSESSMENT OF THE PRESENT STATE OF PROGRESS, WILL BE SPONSORED BY ARKANSAS COLLEGE. (LOCAL). DANIEL W FAGG, JR, CHAIRMAN; ARKANSAS COLLEGE BICENT STEERING COMMITTEE; PO BOX 2317; BATESVILLE, AR 72501. (#10158).

STUDENT HORIZONS PROJECT IN BATESVILLE, ARKANSAS. STUDENTS OF ARKANSAS COLLEGE WILL RAISE MONEY FOR WORLD FAMINE RELIEF; THE MONEY WILL BE CHANNELED THROUGH THE INTERNATIONAL HEIFER PROJECT. (ST-WIDE). DANIELL W FAGG, JR, CHAIRMAN; ARKANSAS COLLEGE BICENT STEERING COMMITTEE; PO BOX 2317; BATESVILLE, AR 72501. (#8914).

BAY

APR 17, '76. BAY BICENTENNIAL CELEBRATION-HERITAGE '76. STREET DANCE, PARADE, ARTS & CRAFTS, GAMES, PRIZES, AWARDS, DISPLAYS, PERFORMANCES, SPEECHES, ETC. AT MAIN ST. (LOCAL). SANDI GRIFFIN; BAY BICENTENNIAL COMMITTEE; PO BOX 51; BAY, AR 72411. (#200005-85).

BEARDEN

HISTORY BOOK OF BEARDEN, AR. THE BICENTENNIAL COMMISSION AND LOCAL HOME DEMONSTRATION CLUB ARE COMPILING A BRIEF HISTORY OF THE COMMUNITY WITH LOTS OF OLD PHOTOS OF PAST EVENTS AND SCENES. (LOCAL). MRS IRENE JOHNSON, CHAIRMAN; BICENTENNIAL COMMISSION OF BEARDEN; BEARDEN, AR 71720. (#29726).

NOV 13, '76. ARTS & CRAFTS FAIR. FAIR, EXHIBIT AT LIONS CLUB BLDG. (LOCAL). IRENE JOHNSON; BICENTENNIAL COMMISSION & FREED EXTENSION HOMEMAKERS CLUB; PO BOX 224; BEARDEN, AR 71720. (#200005-97).

BELLA VISTA

BI-MONTHLY HISTORICAL BULLETIN BOARDS - AR. SHORT STORIES ABOUT HISTORICAL EVENTS OF THE BELLA VISTA AREA WILL BE POSTED ON BULLETIN BOARDS IN THE LOCAL BUILDINGS. (LOCAL). ELIZABETH BUCKLEY, DIRECTOR; CONCORDIA BICENTENNIAL COMMITTEE; BELLA VISTA, AR 72712. (#16299).

BELLA VISTA — CONTINUED

COUNTY ART SHOW IN BELLA VISTA, ARKANSAS. 3 ART SHOW CONTESTS WILL BE HELD FOR BENTON COUNTY YOUTH. ENTRIES MUST BE PATRIOTIC IN THEME & NATURE. AWARDS WILL BE GIVEN TO BEST WORK IN ELEMENTARY, JUNIOR HIGH & HIGH SCHOOL CATEGORIES. (LOCAL). DR E M COOPER, SR, CHAIRMAN; CONCORDIA BICENT COMMITTEE; CONCORDIA COMMUNITY; BELLA VISTA, AR 72712. (#8279).

LITERARY CONTEST IN BELLA VISTA, ARKANSAS. A LITERARY CONTEST WILL BE HELD FOR THE YOUTH OF BENTON COUNTY. THE CONTEST WILL FEATURE POETRY AND ESSAYS. (LOCAL). DR E M COOPER, SR, CHAIRMAN; CONCORDIA BICENT COMMITTEE; CONCORDIA COMMUNITY; BELLA VISTA, AR 72712. (#8278).

MUSIC FESTIVAL IN BELLA VISTA, ARKANSAS. A MUSIC FESTIVAL WILL BE HELD IN JUNE 75-76 IN THE SUMMER HOUSE OF THE CITY. MUSICIANS FROM THE AREA WILL BE INVITED TO ENTERTAIN WITH THE CLIMAX, A BARBEQUE SUPPER, TO BE HELD IN THE EVENING. (LOCAL). DR E M COOPER, SR, CHAIRMAN; CONCORDIA BICENT COMMITTEE; CONCORDIA COMMUNITY; BELLA VISTA, AR 72712. (#8281).

SEMINAR PROJECT IN BELLA VISTA, ARKANSAS. A SEMINAR WILL BE HELD AT CONCORDIA FOR THE PURPOSE OF STUDYING HOW A LIFE-CARE CENTER CAN BEST MEET THE NEEDS OF A MATURE LEISURED WOMAN IN 1975 AND THE FUTURE. PAPERS PRESENTED WILL BE PRINTED. ALSO: BOOK/GUIDE/OTHER PUBLICATION. (LOCAL). DR E M COOPER; CONCORDIA BICENT COMMITTEE; CONCORDIA COMMUNITY; BELLA VISTA, AR 72712. (#8276-1).

STATE FLOWERS BANNER, BELLA VISTA, AR. A BANNER COMPOSED OF 50 BLOCKS EMBROIDERED WITH STATE FLOWERS, ARRANGED IN THE ORDER OF THEIR STATE'S ADMISSION TO THE UNION WILL BE MADE BY THE STAFF OF CONCORDIA AND PRESENTED TO CONCORDIA. (LOCAL). ELIZABETH BUCKLEY, SOCIAL DIRECTOR; CONCORDIA BICENTENNIAL COMMITTEE; CONCORDIA OF BELLA VISTA; BELLA VISTA, AR 72712. (#18166).

'200 GIFTS' - BELLA VISTA, ARKANSAS. A PROJECT TO CELEBRATE THE BICENTENNIAL BY GIVING VARIOUS GIFTS TO COMMUNITY - GIFTS MAY BE ARTICLES NEEDED BY SCHOOLS, PARKS OR PUBLIC BUILDINGS SUCH AS LIBRARIES. A BIRTHDAY PARTY WILL HONOR THE DONORS. (LOCAL). DR E M COOPER, SR, CHAIRMAN; CONCORDIA BICENT COMMITTEE; CONCORDIA COMMUNITY; BELLA VISTA, AR 72712. (#8280).

SEPT 18, '75 - SEPT 18, '76. TOURS OF LOCAL HISTORICAL SITES. SHORT TOURS TO STATE PARKS, MEMORIALS & OTHER PLACES OF HISTORICAL INTEREST. OPEN ONLY TO CONCORDIA RESIDENTS & THEIR GUESTS. AT CONCORDIA CENTRAL ACTIVITIES. (LOCAL). ELIZABETH BUCKLEY, CHMN; CONCORDIA BICENTENNIAL COMMITTEE & ACTIVITIES COMMITTEE; CONCORDIA OF BELLA VISTA; BELLA VISTA, AR 72712. (#102722-1).

JAN 6 - JUNE 29, '76. SEE AMERICA THROUGH FILM. WILL PRESENT SHORT FILMS ABOUT EACH STATE IN THE UNION IN THE ORDER OF THEIR ADMISSION TO THE UNION; TWO STATES WILL BE COVERED EACH TUESDAY NIGHT FROM JANUARY 6 TO JUNE 29; SERIES WILL END WITH A FILM ABOUT THE UNITED STATES AS A NATION. AT CONCORDIA CENTRAL ACTIVITIES BUILDING. (LOCAL). ELIZABETH BUCKLEY, DIR; CONCORDIA BICENTENNIAL COMMITTEE; CONCORDIA OF BELLA VISTA; BELLA VISTA, AR 72712. (#8276-2).

JUNE 25, '76. BICENTENNIAL THEME DANCE. A DANCE WITH A BICENTENNIAL THEME; HOSTESSES IN BICENTENNIAL COSTUME. OPEN ONLY TO RESIDENTS AND GUESTS OF CONCORDIA. AT CONCORDIA CENTRAL ACTIVITIES BLDG. (LOCAL). ELIZABETH BUCKLEY, DIR; CONCORDIA BICENTENNIAL COMMITTEE, CONCORDIA ACTIVITIES COMMITTEE; CONCORDIA OF BELLA VISTA; BELLA VISTA, AR 72712. (#102866-1).

BENTON

BICENTENNIAL WEEK CELEBRATION - SALINE COUNTY, AR. A SPECIAL WEEK OF EVENTS SCHEDULED FOR THE CITIZENS OF SALINE CO FOR THE JULY 1976 CELEBRATION. THIS INCLUDES ART SHOWS, PICNICS, FIREWORKS, PAGEANTS AND BAND CONCERTS. (LOCAL). MRS PAUL HOGUE, CHAIRMAN; BICENTENNIAL FESTIVAL COMMITTEE & CHAMBER OF COMMERCE; BENTON, AR 72015. (#17587). **ARBA GRANTEE.**

SALINE COUNTY BICENT PROJECTS -AR. PROJECTS INCLUDE A PROGRAM TO PLACE MICROFILM RECORDS OF LOCAL NEWSPAPERS, CEMETERY RECORDS AND IMPORTANT DOCUMENTS IN A HISTORICAL LIBRARY. SALINE CO WILL ALSO HAVE A COMMUNITY FAIR. (LOCAL). HON JOE PURCELL, LT GOVERNOR; SALINE COUNTY BICENTENNIAL COMMITTEE; BENTON, AR 72015. (#17608). **ARBA GRANTEE.**

SALINE COUNTY HISTORICAL MARKERS PROJECT, AR. THE SALINE COUNTY BICENTENNIAL COMMITTEE HAS SELECTED 11 SITES OF HISTORICAL SIGNIFICANCE AND WILL PLACE MARKERS AT EACH, DESIGNATING IT AS SUCH. (LOCAL). HON JOE PURCELL, LT GOVERNOR; SALINE COUNTY BICENTENNIAL CELEBRATION COMMITTEE; BENTON, AR 72015. (#17614). **ARBA GRANTEE.**

JULY 4 - 10, '76. SALINE COUNTY BICENTENNIAL WEEK CELEBRATION. FESTIVAL. (LOCAL). MRS PAUL HOGUE, CHAIRMAN; SALINE COUNTY BICENTENNIAL COMMISSION & CHAMBER OF COMMERCE; BENTON, AR 72015. (#17587-1).

BENTONVILLE

'CHEROKEE TRAIL OF TEARS' - BOOK. A GUIDE TO THE ROUTE SOME OF THE CHEROKEE TRAVELED AS THEY NEARED CHEROKEE NATION IN 1838 AFTER THEY WERE DRIVEN FROM GEORGIA. (REGN'L). MRS MELVIN SMITH, SEC-TREASURE; BENTON COUNTY HISTORICAL SOCIETY; 109 N MADISON; SILOAM SPG, AR 72761. (#13049).

CITY OF BENTONVILLE ARKANSAS LIBRARY-MUSEUM PROJ. CITIZEN OF BENTONVILLE ARK WILL CELEBRATE THE BICENTENNIAL WITH THE EXPANSION OF THE LIBRARY-MUSEUM COMPLEX, CITY PARK & BUS SERVICE FOR ELDERLY & HANDICAPPED PERSONS. (LOCAL). CHUCK DAVIS, CHAIRMAN; BENTONVILLE BICENTENNIAL COMMITTEE; 122 SOUTH MAIN; BENTONVILLE, AR 72712. (#3935).

SEPT 19, '75. BENTON COUNTY FAIR PARADE WITH BICENTENNIAL THEME. FAIR, PARADE AT BENTONVILLE. (LOCAL). CHUCK DAVIS, PROJ DIR; BENTON COUNTY BICENTENNIAL COMMITTEE; CHAMBER OF COMMERCE; BENTONVILLE, AR 72712. (#100734-1).

BERRYVILLE

CARROLL COUNTY PARK AND COUNTY MUSEUM, AR. ESTABLISH A COUNTY MUSEUM FOR CARROLL COUNTY & MAKE IMPROVEMENTS ON THE SAUNDERS MUZZLELOADING GUN SHOOT RANGE PARK. (LOCAL). ARTHUR CARTER, COUNTY JUDGE; CARROLL COUNTY BICENTENNIAL COMMITTEE; PO BOX 1776; BERRYVILLE, AR 72616. (#18500). **ARBA GRANTEE.**

COURTHOUSE RESTORATION IN CARROLL COUNTY, ARK. RESTORATION OF THE 1880 COURTHOUSE HAS BEEN COMPLETED TO A LARGE EXTENT & AN HISTORIC MUSEUM HAS BEEN CREATED ON THE THIRD FLOOR. THERE WILL BE A RESEARCH LIBRARY IN CONNECTION WITH THE MUSEUM. (LOCAL). R G GATES, CHAIRMAN; CARROLL COUNTY BICENTENNIAL COMMITTEE; RT 4, BOX 81; BERRYVILLE, AR 72616. (#4862).

RESTORATION OF MASONIC LODGE & COURTHOUSE IN AR. PROJECT TO RESTORE CARROLL COUNTY'S MASONIC HALL LODGE & ORIGINAL CHARTER. ALSO RESTORE 1880 COURTHOUSE AT BERRYVILLE, CREATING COUNTY MUSEUM IN 3RD FLOOR COURTROOM. (LOCAL). R G GATES, CHAIRMAN; CARROLL COUNTY BICENTENNIAL COMMITTEE; RT 4, BOX 81; BERRYVILLE, AR 72616. (#4863). **(??).**

SEPT 22 - 28, '75. CARROLL COUNTY BICENTENNIAL HERITAGE DAYS CELEBRATION. RE-ENACTMENT OF ALEXANDER 1857 WAGON TRAIN, PIONEER SKILLS, FOLK ENTERTAINMENT & A BEAUTY PAGEANT FOR WOMEN 60 YEARS AND OLDER. AT CARROLL COUNTY FAIRGROUNDS. (LOCAL). FREDDIE NIXON, BICENT DIR; CARROLL COUNTY BICENTENNIAL COMMITTEE; PO BOX 1776; BERRYVILLE, AR 72616. (#101885-1).

SEPT 27 - 28, '75. SAUNDER'S MEMORIAL MUZZLE LOADING GUN SHOOT. LIVE PERFORMANCE AT LUTHER OWENS GUN RANGE & PARK. (LOCAL). LUTHER OWENS, CHAIRMAN; CHAMBER OF COMMERCE & CARROLL COUNTY BICENTENNIAL COMMITTEE; 406 N SPRINGFIELD; BERRYVILLE, AR 72616. (#101884-1).

BIGELOW

HISTORICAL BOOK ON PERRY COUNTY: BIGELOW, AR. EACH COMMUNITY IN PERRY COUNTY RESEARCHED AND WROTE A HISTORY. (LOCAL). MRS LOUIS G CARRARO, CHAIRMAN; BICENTENNIAL COMMITTEE OF PERRY COUNTY; PERRYVILLE, AR 72126. (#29559).

MAY 23, '76. LITTLE ITALY COMMUNITY CELEBRATION. AWARD, FESTIVAL AT COMMUNITY HALL, ST FRANCIS CHURCH. (LOCAL). MRS LOUIS G CARRARO, SR; PERRY COUNTY BICENTENNIAL COMMITTEE; RT 1, BOX 194; BIGELOW, AR 72016. (#200005-37).

BISCOE

JUNE 19, '76. BISCOE BICENTENNIAL DAY. PARADE WITH FLOATS, CROWNING OF JR BISCOE BICENT KING & QUEEN, SPEAKER, SONGS, RACES, TOBACCO SPITTING CONTEST, BINGO, CAKE WALK, GENERAL STORE WITH CRAFTS & CANNED GOODS. PROCEEDS FOR TOWN BALL FIELD. AT BISCOE COMMUNITY BLDG. (LOCAL). MRS HENRY HAMPTON, JR; TOWN OF BISCOE; RT 1, BOX 74; DE VALLS BLF, AR 72041. (#200005-33).

BLACK ROCK

JUNE 30 - JULY 4, '76. HISTORICAL PAGEANT, BICENTENNIAL PARADE & PROGRAM. EXHIBIT, PARADE, LIVE PERFORMANCE AT AMPHITHEATRE 3 MILES NORTHWEST OF POWHATAN. (LOCAL). MRS BOBBY FLIPPO, CHMN; LAWRENCE COUNTY BICENTENNIAL COMMITTEE; POWHATAN, AR 72458. (#200005-34).

JULY 2, '76. LAWRENCE COUNTY BICENTENNIAL PAGEANT. LIVE PERFORMANCE AT LAWRENCE COUNTY AMPHITHEATER. (LOCAL). MARTA JONES, CHMN; LAWRENCE COUNTY BICENTENNIAL COMMITTEE; BOX 48; MINTURN, AR 72445. (#200005-17).

BLYTHEVILLE

LIBRARY MARKER & LANDSCAPING AT BLYTHEVILLE, AR. A HISTORICAL MARKER DEPICTING EARLY BLYTHEVILLE CULTURE PLUS LANDFOR A PARK AREA WHICH ADJOINS LIBRARY. (LOCAL). JANE BROWN, CHAIRMAN; BLYTHEVILLE BICENTENNIAL COMMISSION; 1013 WARD LA; BLYTHEVILLE, AR 72315. (#30973).

MAR 4 - 8, '76. 'UP WITH PEOPLE' MUSICAL PRESENTATION. LIVE PERFORMANCE AT BLYTHEVILLE HIGH SCHOOL AUDITORIUM. (LOCAL). JANE BROWN; BLYTHEVILLE BICENTENNIAL COMMISSION, INC; 1013 WARD LANE; BLYTHEVILLE, AR 72315. (#200005-100).

MAY 7 - 9, '76. COUNTY FAIR & TEAM SHOW. THIS IS A FAIR WITH A BAZAAR, GAMES, BEARD CONTEST, PARADE, AND A TAKE OFF ON 'ALMOST ANYTHING GOES'. (LOCAL). JANE BROWN, CHAIRMAN; BLYTHEVILLE BICENTENNIAL COMMITTEE, INC; 1013 WARD LN; BLYTHEVILLE, AR 72315. (#200005-80).

MAY 8, '76. 'JUST ABOUT ANYTHING CAN HAPPEN'. AN 'ALMOST ANYTHING GOES' TYPE OF EVENT WITH COMPETING TEAMS FROM BLYTHEVILLE AFB, BLYTHEVILLE AND GOSNELL. IT WAS FEATURED ATTRACTION DURING THE BLYTHEVILLE BICENTENNIAL COMMUNITY FAIR. AT WALKER PARK. (LOCAL). LT COL DENNIS R SEE; BLYTHEVILLE AFB AND BLYTHEVILLE BICENTENNIAL COMMISSION; 1626B S 6TH ST; BLYTHEVL AFB, AR 72315. (#200005-127).

MAY 22, '76. BASE-COMMUNITY COUNCIL FISH FRY. FESTIVAL AT WALKER PARK. (LOCAL). LT COL DENNIS R SEE; BASE-COMMUNITY COUNCIL; 1626B S 6TH ST; BLYTHEVL AFB, AR 72315. (#200005-125).

JUNE 18 - 24, '76. 8TH AF BAND CONCERTS. PERFORMANCES GIVEN AT BLYTHEVILLE AFB; BLYTHEVILLE, AR; MEMPHIS, TN; MILLINGTON NAS, TN; GERMANTOWN, TN; AND NEW ALBANY, MS. AT VARIOUS LOCATIONS IN AREA COMMUNITIES. (LOCAL). LT COL DENNIS R SEE; 97TH BOMB WING AND MEMPHIS AIR FORCE ASSOC; 1626B S 6TH ST; BLYTHEVL AFB, AR 72315. (#200005-124).

JULY 4, '76. 4TH OF JULY FIREWORKS. EXHIBIT AT EAST JUNIOR HIGH SCHOOL, E MOULTRIE DR. (LOCAL). LT COL DENNIS R SEE; BLYTHEVILLE AFB AND BLYTHEVILLE BICENTENNIAL COMMISSION; 1626B S 6TH ST; BLYTHEVL AFB, AR 72315. (#200005-122).

BLYTHEVL AFB

BASE BEAUTIFICATION, BLYTHEVILLE AFB, AR. OVER 1200 TREES, BUSHES AND SHRUBS WERE PLANTED THROUGHOUT THE BASE AS PART OF THE BICENTENNIAL BEAUTIFICATION PROGRAM. (LOCAL). LT COL DENNIS R SEE, DEPUTY BASE COMMANDER; 97TH COMBAT SUPPORT GROUP; 1626B SO 6TH ST; BLYTHEVL AFB, AR 72315. (#29711).

BASE BICENTENNIAL DECORATION, BLYTHEVILLE AFB, AR. BASE FACILITIES AND STRUCTURES HAVE BEEN DECORATED IN A BICENTENNIAL MOTIF. DESIGNS OF RED, WHITE AND BLUE AND OF REVOLUTIONARY WAR PERIOD CUT-OUTS ARE PROMINENTLY DISPLAYED ON MANY BUILDINGS. (LOCAL). LT COL DENNIS R SEE, DEPUTY BASE COMMANDER; 97TH COMBAT SUPPORT GROUP; 1626B SO 6TH ST; BLYTHEVL AFB, AR 72315. (#29716).

BICENTENNIAL BUMPER DECALS - BLYTHEVILLE AFB, AR. FUNDS FROM SALE OF DECALS USED TO HELP FINANCE THE 4TH OF JULY FIREWORKS DISPLAY. (LOCAL). LT COL DENNIS R SEE, DEPUTY BASE COMMANDER; 97TH COMBAT SUPPORT GROUP; 1626B SO 6TH ST; BLYTHEVL AFB, AR 72315. (#29714).

LIBRARY BICENTENNIAL READING PROGRAM, AR. BASE LIBRARY OFFERS SPECIAL SELECTION OF READING MATERIAL AND DISPLAYS EACH WEEK. (LOCAL). LT COL DENNIS R SEE, DEPUTY BASE COMMANDER; 97TH COMBAT SUPPORT GROUP; 1626B SO 6TH ST; BLYTHEVL AFB, AR 72315. (#29713).

ORIGINAL 13 COLONY FLAG DISPLAY, BLYTHEVL AFB, AR. FLAGS ARE DISPLAYED AT SPECIAL CEREMONIES AND OCCASIONS ON THE BASE AND IN THE LOCAL COMMUNITY. (LOCAL). LT COL DENNIS R SEE, DEPUTY BASE COMMANDER; 97TH COMBAT SUPPORT GROUP; 1626B SO 6TH ST; BLYTHEVL AFB, AR 72315. (#29715).

SPEAKERS BUREAU, BLYTHEVILLE AFB, AR. THROUGH THE WING OFFICE OF INFORMATION, MANY BASE PERSONNEL SPEAK TO A VARIETY OF BUSINESS, SOCIAL AND PROFESSIONAL GROUPS IN THE COMMUNITY. A BICENTENNIAL BRIEFING IS A FEATURED SUBJECT. (LOCAL). LT COL DENNIS R SEE, DEPUTY BASE COMMANDER; 97TH COMBAT SUPPORT GROUP; 1626B SO 6TH ST; BLYTHEVL AFB, AR 72315. (#29712).

FEB 28 - 29, '76. HANGAR DANCE. PROCEEDS OF TICKET SALES FOR FIREWORKS DISPLAY. MUSIC PROVIDED BY THE GROUP 'SUMMER WINE'. AT HANGAR 107, BLYTHEVILLE AFB. (LOCAL). LT COL DENNIS R SEE; BLYTHEVILLE AFB BICENTENNIAL COMMITTEE; 1626B S 6TH ST; BLYTHEVL AFB, AR 72315. (#200005-76).

APR 4, '76. BICENTENNIAL DOG SHOW. BRIEFINGS ON HISTORY OF DIFFERENT BREEDS, DOGS IN AMERICAN HISTORY AND DOG HEROS. OBEDIENCE DEMONSTRATION AND MILITARY WORKING DOG DEMONSTRATION. AT HANGAR 107, BLYTHEVILLE AFB. (LOCAL). LT COL DENNIS R SEE; BLYTHEVILLE AFB BICENTENNIAL COMMITTEE AND ARK-MO KENNEL CLUB; 1626B S 6TH ST; BLYTHEVL AFB, AR 72315. (#200005-75).

MAY 1, '76. HANGAR DANCE. PROCEEDS OF TICKET SALES FOR FIREWORKS DISPLAY. MUSIC PROVIDED BY THE GROUP 'SILVER STRINGS'. AT HANGAR 107, BLYTHEVILLE AFB AR. (LOCAL). LT COL DENNIS R SEE; BLYTHEVILLE AFB BICENTENNIAL COMMITTEE; 1626B S 6TH ST; BLYTHEVL AFB, AR 72315. (#200005-128).

MAY 15, '76. ARMED FORCES DAY OPEN HOUSE. PERFORMANCES BY 8AF BAND, STATIC AIRCRAFT, AND DISPLAY BOOTHS. AT HANGAR 107 ON FLIGHT LINE AT BLYTHEVILLE AFB. (LOCAL). LT COL DENNIS R SEE; BLYTHEVILLE AFB; 1626B S 6TH ST; BLYTHEVL AFB, AR 72315. (#200005-126).

JUNE 19, '76. BICENTENNIAL DINNER AND DANCE. ENTERTAINMENT PROVIDED BY THE 8TH AIR FORCE BAND. AT OFFICERS CLUB. (LOCAL). LT COL DENNIS R SEE; BASE-COMMUNITY COUNCIL AND AIR FORCE ASSOC; 1626B S 6TH ST; BLYTHEVL AFB, AR 72315. (#200005-123).

BLYTHEVL AFB — CONTINUED

JUNE 24, '76 - CONTINUING . 8TH AIR FORCE BAND CONCERT. LIVE PERFORMANCE AT BLYTHEVILLE HIGH SCHOOL AUDITORIUM. (LOCAL). JANE BROWN; BLYTHEVILLE BICENTENNIAL COMMISSION INC; 1013 WARD LANE; BLYTHEVILLE, AR 72315. (#200005-99).

JULY 4, '76. JULY 4TH FIREWORKS DISPLAY. PAID FOR BY BLYTHEVILLE AIR FORCE BASE AS A GIFT TO THE CITY. AT SCHOOL PLAYGROUND. (LOCAL). JANE BROWN; BLYTHEVILLE BICENTENNIAL COMMISSION; 1013 WARD LANE; BLYTHEVILLE, AR 72315. (#200005-98).

BRADLEY

GRAVESITE RESTORATION - BRADLEY, AR. RESTORATION OF GRAVESITE OF FIRST GOVERNOR OF ARKANSAS. (LOCAL). MRS ODELL CLARY, COORDINATOR; BRADLEY ROSE GARDEN CLUB; RT 1, BOX 200D; BRADLEY, AR 71826. (#25921). **ARBA GRANTEE.**

NOV 1, '75. BICENTENNIAL FESTIVAL. ACTIVITIES FOR THE BICENTENNIAL CELEBRATION IN MEMORY OF THE FIRST GOVERNOR OF ARKANSAS, JAMES SEVIER CONWAY. AT AUDITORIUM. (LOCAL). MRS ODELL CLARY, CHAIRMAN; BRADLEY ROSE GARDEN CLUB; RT 1, BOX 200D; BRADLEY, AR 71826. (#200005-13).

BRINKLEY

MAR 8, '76. USA CORPS OF ENGINEERS MOBILE VAN VISITS BRINKLEY, AR. A MULTI-MEDIA SHOW DEPICTING THE 200 YEAR HISTORY OF THE CORPS OF ENGINEERS & ITS ROLE IN THE EVOLUTION OF OUR NATION. AT NATIONAL GUARD ARMORY. (LOCAL). KENT CARMAIN, CHMN; USA CORPS OF ENGINEERS; US ARMY CORPS OF ENGINEERS; MEMPHIS, TN 38103. (#31165-5).

MAY 7 - 9, '76. ARTS, CRAFTS & HOBBY SHOW. EXHIBIT AT 237 W CYPRESS. (LOCAL). MRS EARNEST LOENER; BRINKLEY ARB; DIAL CIRCLE; BRINKLEY, AR 72021. (#200005-78).

CABOT

JUNE 18 - 19, '76. NORTH LONOKE COUNTY BICENTENNIAL PICNIC. FESTIVAL AT HWY 67, 2 MILES NORTH OF CABOT. (LOCAL). HOWELL THOMPSON, CHMN; NORTH LONOKE COUNTY BICENTENNIAL COMMITTEE; ROUTE 2; CABOT, AR 72023. (#200005-23).

CAMDEN

JULY 4 - 6, '74. ANNUAL 3-DAY PIONEER CELEBRATION. PIONEER DAYS CELEBRATION - OUCHITA COUNTY, ARK. CELEBRATION OF THE SESQUICENTENNIAL OF THE FOUNDING OF CAMDEN.OUACHITA CO AREA EVENTS, CEREMONIES AND CRAFTS ARE PLANNED TO CREATE AN AWARENESS OF THE RICH HERITAGE OF THIS AREA. (LOCAL). CY CARNEY, ASST CITY MGR; CITY OF CAMDEN/OUACHITA COUNTY; CITY HALL; ARKANSAS, AR 71701. (#1702-901).

MAR 5, '76. UNITED STATES ARMED FORCES BICENTENNIAL CARAVAN. CARAVAN IS COMPOSED OF EXHIBIT VANS FOR EACH MILITARY SERVICE. PROJECT THEME IS 'HISTORY OF THE ARMED FORCES AND THEIR CONTRIBUTIONS TO THE NATION'. (LOCAL). JOSEPH COAN, CHMN; CAMDEN BICENTENNIAL COMMITTEE; 714 GRAHAM ST; CAMDEN, AR 71701. (#1775-403).

CARAWAY

PLAYGROUND EQUIPMENT - CARAWAY, AR. PLAYGROUND EQUIPMENT WILL BE ADDED TO THE CITY PARK. (LOCAL). HON RAY EMISON, MAYOR; CITY OF CARAWAY; CITY HALL; CARAWAY, AR 72419. (#26798). **ARBA GRANTEE.**

CASSCOE

SEPT 7, '76. HUNTER'S CHAPEL HOMECOMING. CEREMONY AT HUNTER'S CHAPEL METHODIST CHURCH. (LOCAL). JUDGE DALE SHELTON; ARKANSAS COUNTY BICENTENNIAL COMMITTEE; COURT HOUSE; DE WITT, AR 72042. (#102408-1).

CAVE SPRINGS

CAVE SPRINGS COMMUNITY IMPROVEMENT - AR. THE CITY PLANS TO MAKE SOME IMPROVEMENTS ON THEIR COMMUNITY BUILDING IN WHICH THEY HOLD BOTH PUBLIC AND ORGANIZATION FUNCTIONS. (LOCAL). HON ED CURTIS, MAYOR; CITY OF CAVE SPRINGS; CITY HALL; CAVE SPRINGS, AR 72718. (#26882). **ARBA GRANTEE.**

CEDARVILLE

MAY 1, '76. CEDARVILLE BICENTENNIAL FAIR & JUBILEE. FAIR AT CEDARVILLE SCHOOL GROUNDS & DOWNTOWN CEDARVILLE. (LOCAL). ROBERT N GARNER, CHAIRMAN; CRAWFORD COUNTY BICENTENNIAL COMMISSION; PO BOX 486; VAN BUREN, AR 72956. (#200005-66).

CHEROKEE VLG

JULY 3 - 4, '76. BICENTENNIAL CELEBRATION. TWO DAYS OF CELEBRATION WITH CONGRESSMEN & STATE OFFICIALS INCLUDE LARGE PARADE WITH FLOAT & PRIZES & BOAT PARADE. THERE WILL ALSO BE DANCES BOTH SQUARE & ROUND - PICNICS & CARNIVAL, GOLF & TENNIS, A CATFISH COOKOUT, BAND CONCERT, FIREWORKS & A RODEO. AT OMAHA CTR, LAKES & CHEROKEE VILLAGE SHOPPING MALL. (LOCAL). RICHARD W ABELE, CHPRSN; PROPERTY OWNERS ASSOC & CHEROKEE VILLAGE BICENTENNIAL COMMITTEE; BOX 540; CHEROKEE VLG, AR 72525. (#200005-19).

CLARENDON

NOV 9, '76. USA CORPS OF ENGINEERS FLOATING MUSEUM VISITS CLARENDON, AR. EXHIBIT. (LOCAL). KENT CARMAIN, CHMN; USA CORPS OF ENGINEERS; US ARMY CORPS OF ENGINEERS; MEMPHIS, TN 38103. (#30730-4).

CLARKSVILLE

CLARKSVILLE - JOHNSON CO, ARK BICENT CELEBRATION. CITIZENS OF JOHNSON CO WILL CELEBRATE OUR 200TH ANNIVERSARY ESTABLISHING A COUNTY MUSEUM. A MUSIC FESTIVAL THE ANNUAL PEACH FESTIVAL, AND A COMMEMORATIVE COIN WILL BE DEDICATED TO THE BICENTENNIAL. (LOCAL). WILLIE KIMBRELL, CHAIRMAN; CLARKSVILLE BICENTENNIAL COMMISSION; JOHNSON CO CHAMBER OF COMMERCE; CLARKSVILLE, AR 72830. (#4053).

STUDENTS PRESENT BICENTENNIAL PROGRAMS. STUDENTS WILL PRESENT A PROGRAM SHOWING A HISTORICAL LOOK AT AMERICA THROUGH MUSIC. PICNICS AND CELEBRATIONS WILL ALSO BE HELD. (LOCAL). NORA HAMPTON, CHMN; PHI BETA LAMBDA BICENTENNIAL COMMITTEE; COLLEGE STATION; CLARKSVILLE, AR 72830. (#107299-1). **(??).**

JUNE 21 - 22, '75. ARTS & CRAFTS FAIR. ARTS AND CRAFTS FAIR TO BE OPENED ON SAME DATE AS OFFICIAL CEREMONY FOR FLAG PRESENTATION FOR DESIGNATION AS BICENT. COMMUNITY AND WILL BE FOLLOWED BY A WEEK LONG CELEBRATION OF THE JOHNSON COUNTY PEACH FESTIVAL.22 JUNE HOURS 1:00 - 5:00 PM. AT JOHNSON COUNTY FAIR BUILDING. (LOCAL). JO ANN HOWELL; CLARKSVILLE BICENTENNIAL COMMISSION; JOHNSON COUNTY COURT HOUSE; CLARKSVILLE, AR 72830. (#4053-1).

AUG 10, '75. MUSIC & CHORAL FESTIVAL. AN ANNUAL FESTIVAL TO RECOGNIZE THE CULTURAL AND AESTHETIC VALUE OF INSTRUMENT AND CHORAL ACTIVITIES. (LOCAL). DR CHARLES DAWSON, CHMN; COLLEGE OF THE OZARKS, MUSIC DEPT; CLARKSVILLE, AR 72830. (#8729-1).

JUNE 1 - 30, '76. ARTS & CRAFTS FAIR. ESTABLISH AN ANNUAL ARTS AND CRAFTS FAIR TO RECOGNIZE AND GENERATE INTEREST IN BASIC ARTS AND CRAFTS NATIVE TO JOHNSON COUNTY AND THE OZARKS REGION. AT JOHNSON COUNTY FAIR BLDG. (LOCAL). MISS JO ANNE HOWELL; JOHNSON COUNTY EXTENSION OFFICE; COUNTY COURTHOUSE; CLARKSVILLE, AR 72830. (#8730-1).

CLINTON

SEPT 25, '75. VANBUREN COUNTY BICENTENNIAL FLAG PRESENTATION. CEREMONY AND CELEBRATION FORMER LT GOV MAURICE BRITT PRESENTED BICENTENNIAL FLAGS TO ALL BICENTENNIAL COMMUNITIES LOCATED IN VANBUREN COUNTY. AT MAIN STREET AND TOWN SQUARE. (LOCAL). JEAN MEACHAM; VANBUREN COUNTY AR BICENTENNIAL COMMITTEE; RTE 2 BOX 782; FAIRFIELD BAY, AR 72088. (#200005-103).

CLOVER BEND

TOUR OF RURAL PLANTATION HOME ON BLACK RIVER. RURAL HOME OF MR & MRS LANGE PHILLIPS WHICH IS IN THE NATL REGISTER OF HISTORIC PLACES, FORMERLY BELONGED TO ALICE FRENCH, A WRITER OF THE 1800'S. OPEN TO THE PUBLIC DURING THE FALL '76. (LOCAL). NOEL W BAKER, CHMN; CLOVER LEAF BICENTENNIAL GROUP; RT 1; CLOVER BEND, AR 72410. (#200005-120).

COLLEGE CITY

OVERALL BICENTENNIAL ACTIVITIES, COLLEGE CY, AR. PLANS CALL FOR THE CONSTRUCTION OF A HISTORICAL LIBRARY, MONUMENT, 4TH OF JULY CELEBRATION AND CONSTRUCTION OF A BALL FIELD. (ST-WIDE). B H JOHNSON, COORDINATOR; CITY OF COLLEGE CITY; BOX 39; COLLEGE CITY, AR 72476. (#22301). **ARBA GRANTEE.**

JULY 4, '76. 4TH OF JULY CELEBRATION. FESTIVAL. (LOCAL). B H JOHNSON, COORDINATOR; CITY OF COLLEGE CITY; BOX 39; COLLEGE CITY, AR 72476. (#22301-1).

CONCORDIA

NATURE TRAIL PROJECT IN CONCORDIA, ARKANSAS. A NATURE TRAIL WILL BE DEVELOPED ALONG SUGAR CREEK BY THE CITIZENS OF CONCORDIA. THE TRAIL WILL INCLUDE BENCHES SINCE MOST RESIDENTS ARE OF RETIREMENT AGE. THE TRAIL WILL BE OF LASTING BENEFIT. (LOCAL). DR E M COOPER, SR, CHAIRMAN; CONCORDIA BICENT COMMITTEE; CONCORDIA COMMUNITY; BELLA VISTA, AR 72712. (#8277).

CONWAY

CHORAL CONCERTS IN CONWAY, ARKANSAS. UNIVERSITY OF CENTRAL ARKANSAS CHORUS WILL TOUR THE STATE TO PRESENT A PROGRAM OF ORIGINAL PATRIOTIC MUSIC LED BY DR DON L COLLINS. (ST-WIDE). DON L COLLINS, DIRECTOR OF THE UCA CHORAL; UNIV CENTRAL ARKANSAS MUSIC DEPT/UCA ARBC COMMITTEE; BOX 964/UCA; CONWAY, AR 72032. (#16101).

COURSE: THE AMERICAN IDENTITY - CONWAY, ARKANSAS. COLLEGE CREDIT STUDY, INTERDISCIPLINARY, EXPLORING THE MEANING OF AMERICA; AN ACADEMIC TOWN MEETING ON THE SOURCES AND DEVELOPMENT OF THE AMERICAN SPIRIT. (ADULTS MAY ENROLL FOR NON-CREDIT). (LOCAL). RICHARD HUDSON, COORDINATOR; UCA ARB CELEBRATION COMMITTEE; 1818 BRUCE ST; CONWAY, AR 72032. (#16100).

FAULKNER COUNTY, ARK, BICENT COMMEMORATION. FAULKNER COUNTY CITIZENS WILL HONOR OUR BICENTENNIAL WITH THE DEVELOPMENT OF RECREATIONAL & HISTORICAL ATTRACTIONS. THREE COLLEGES IN THE AREA WILL PROVIDE PROGRAMS FOR STUDENTS & FAULKNER CO. CITIZENS. (LOCAL). CLETIS BARLOW, BICENTENNIAL CHAIRMAN; FAULKNER CO BICENTENNIAL COMMITTEE; #11 DEERWOOD; CONWAY, AR 72032. (#4052). **ARBA GRANTEE.**

FILMS ON THE AMERICAN HERITAGE - CONWAY, ARKANSAS. A 3-SEMESTER PROGRAM: 1ST SEMESTER FOCUSES ON THE REVOLUTIONARY LIFE & TIME; 2ND ON THE DEVELOPMENT OF 19TH CENTURY AMERICA; AND THE 3RD ON CURRENT CHALLENGES. (LOCAL). WADDY W MOORE, CHAIRMAN; UNIV OF CENTRAL ARKANSAS ARBC COMMITTEE; BOX 933/UCA; CONWAY, AR 72032. (#16103).

FORUM IN CONWAY, ARKANSAS. BRING SPEAKERS TO THE CAMPUS TO INSPIRE, TO DISCUSS THE AMERICAN HERITAGE AND SOME CONTEMPORARY PROBLEMS AND CONCERNS. (LOCAL). WADDY W MOORE, CHAIRMAN; UNIV OF CENTRAL ARKANSAS ARBC COMMITTEE; BOX 933/UCA; CONWAY, AR 72032. (#16102).

MOVIE SERIES - UNIV OF CENTRAL ARKANSAS. A SERIES OF MOTION PICTURES THAT REFLECT THE DEVELOPMENT OF THE MOVIE AS AN ART FORM AND DEPICTS THE AMERICAN HERITAGE; THE SERIES IS SPONSORED BY HISTORY & DRAMA DEPARTMENTS AND STUDENT SENATE. (LOCAL). DR WADDY MOORE, CHAIRMAN; UNIV OF CENTRAL ARKANSAS BICENT COMMITTEE; PO BOX 933; CONWAY, AR 72032. (#8920).

UCA MURAL: ARKANSAS, THE WONDER STATE. A MURAL WILL BE PAINTED AND PLACED ON DISPLAY IN THE MAIN AIRPORT CORRIDOR AT ADAMS FIELD IN LITTLE ROCK. NATURAL & UNIQUE SCENES WILL BE PORTRAYED IN THE MURAL. (LOCAL). WADDY W MOORE, CHAIRMAN; UCA BICENTENNIAL CELEBRATION COMMITTEE; BOX 933; CONWAY, AR 72032. (#17617). **ARBA GRANTEE.**

UNIV OF CENTRAL ARKANSAS CHORAL TOUR. PREPARATION & PRESENTATION OF A CONCERT OF AUTHENTIC AMERICAN MUSIC TO GO ON TOUR THROUGHOUT THE STATE. (ST-WIDE). WADDY W MOORE, CHAIRMAN; UNIV OF CENTRAL ARKANSAS REVOLUTIONARY COMMITTEE; CONWAY, AR 72032. (#17613). **ARBA GRANTEE.**

SEPT 11, '75 - MAY 30, '77. FILM SERIES, '1776'. SHOWINGS WILL BE AT 1:40 PM AND 7:00 PM. AT IDA WALDRAN AUDITORIUM UCA CAMPUS. (LOCAL). WADDY W MOORE, CHAIRMAN; UNIV OF CENTRAL ARKANSAS AMERICAN REVOLUTION BICENTENNIAL COMM; BOX 933 UCA; CONWAY, AR 72032. (#102772-1).

OCT 13 - 22, '75. BICENTENNIAL YOUTH DEBATES. THE SPEECH DEPT OF THE UNIVERSITY WILL SPONSOR A SPECIAL DEBATE REENACTING HISTORIC DEBATES FROM THE PAST & DEBATING CURRENT ISSUES. AT CAMPUS. (LOCAL). DR WAYNE EASLEY; UNIV OF CENTRAL ARKANSAS BICENTENNIAL COMMITTEE; PO BOX 933; CONWAY, AR 72032. (#8924-1).

OCT 16, '75. FILM SERIES, DRUMS ALONG THE MOHAWK. SHOWINGS WILL BE AT 1:40 PM AND 7:00 PM. AT IDA WALDRAN AUDITORIUM UCA CAMPUS. (LOCAL). WADDY W MOORE, CHAIRMAN; UNIV OF CENTRAL ARKANSAS AMERICAN REVOLUTION BICENTENNIAL COMM; BOX 933 UCA; CONWAY, AR 72032. (#102772-2).

OCT 26 - NOV 2, '75. CHORAL TOUR AND CONCERT. LIVE PERFORMANCE AT RECITAL HALL, SNOW FINE ARTS CENTER. (LOCAL). DON L COLLINS, PROJ DIR; UNIV OF CENTRAL ARKANSAS MUSIC DEPT & BICENTENNIAL COMMITTEE; BOX 964, UCA; CONWAY, AR 72032. (#16101-1).

NOV 13, '75. FILM SERIES, D W GRIFFITH'S 'AMERICA' AND TOCQUEVILLE'S 'AMERICA'. SHOWINGS WILL BE AT 1:40 PM AND 7:00 PM. AT IDA WALDRAN AUDITORIUM UCA CAMPUS. (LOCAL). WADDY W MOORE, CHAIRMAN; UNIV OF CENTRAL ARKANSAS AMERICAN REVOLUTION BICENTENNIAL COMM; BOX 933 UCA; CONWAY, AR 72032. (#102772-3).

NOV 19, '75. FORUM: ALEX HALEY, BLACK HERITAGE: A SAGA. SEMINAR AT RECITAL HALL, SNOW FINE ARTS BLDG. (LOCAL). WADDY W MOORE, CHAIRMAN; UNIV OF CENTRAL ARKANSAS BICENTENNIAL COMMITTEE; BOX 933, UCA; CONWAY, AR 72032. (#16102-1).

JAN 5 - MAY 7, '76. COURSE: 'THE AMERICAN IDENTITY'. SEMINAR AT HUMAN DEVELOPMENT CENTER ON UCA CAMPUS. (LOCAL). RICHARD HUDSON, PROJ DIR; UNIVERSITY OF CENTRAL ARKANSAS & UCA BICENTENNIAL COMMITTEE; 1818 BRUCE ST; CONWAY, AR 72032. (#16101-2).

FEB 17, '76. 'LET'S SET THE RECORD STRAIGHT, AN EVENING WITH GEORGE WASHINGTON'. A FORUM DIRECTED BY JAN LEIGHTON. AT IDA WALDRAN AUDITORIUM. (LOCAL). WADDY W MOORE, CHAIRMAN; UNIV OF CENTRAL ARKANSAS BICENTENNIAL COMMITTEE; BOX 933, UCA; CONWAY, AR 72032. (#16102-2).

CONWAY — CONTINUED

MAR 19, '76. FORUM: THE UNITED STATES NAVY BAND. 2 PERFORMANCES: 2:30 PM & 8:00 PM. AT FARRIS CENTER, UCA CAMPUS. (LOCAL). WADDY W MOORE, CHAIRMAN; UNIV OF CENTRAL ARKANSAS BICENTENNIAL COMMITTEE; BOX 933, UCA; CONWAY, AR 72032. (#16102-3).

CORNING

CORNING LIBRARY & HISTORICAL MUSEUM BUILDING, AR. CONSTRUCTION & EQUIPPING OF A LIBRARY-HISTORICAL MUSEUM. (LOCAL). MRS LOUISE SCOTT, CO-CHAIRPERSON; CORNING BICENTENNIAL COMMITTEE; BOX 188; CORNING, AR 72422. (#23551). **ARBA GRANTEE.**

COTTON PLANT

JAN 1 - DEC 30, '76. DISPLAYS OF SOME PHASE OF AMERICAN LIFE. BOOKS, POSTERS, PICTURES, ARTS & CRAFTS AND HISTORICAL MEMOIRS. AT LIBRARY BUILDING MAIN STREET. (LOCAL). MRS KEITH DUNBAR, COORD; COTTON PLANT LIBRARY; MAIN STREET; COTTON PLANT, AR 72036. (#103799-4).

FEB 16, '76. 'OUR FIVE MINUTES'. WILL HAVE FIVE MINUTES OF EACH MONTLY MEETING FOR A BICENTENNIAL NOTE. AT COTTON PLANT CLUB HOUSE. (LOCAL). MRS P O WILLIAMSON, PRES; HYPSION CLUB; COTTON PLANT, AR 72036. (#103799-3).

DANVILLE

COMMUNITY IMPROVEMENT PROJECT - DANVILLE, AR. PLANTING TREES, PAINTING FIRE HYDRANTS, PLACING PICNIC BENCHES IN THE CITY PARK. A BRONZE PLAQUE HONORING SERVICEMEN WILL BE PLACED ON THE COUNTY COURTHOUSE LAWN. (LOCAL). HON JOHN ED CHAMBERS, III, MAYOR; CITY OF DANVILLE; CITY HALL; DANVILLE, AR 72833. (#26934). **ARBA GRANTEE.**

DE WITT

ARKANSAS COUNTY BICENTENNIAL OBSERVANCE. OBSERVANCE INCLUDES CRAFT DISPLAYS, RECREATIONAL & HISTORICAL ACTIVITIES AND BAND & CHORUS CONCERTS. (LOCAL). DALE SHELTON, COUNTY JUDGE; ARKANSAS COUNTY; ARKANSAS COUNTY COURTHOUSE; DEWITT, AR 72042. (#26799). **ARBA GRANTEE.**

GRAND PRAIRIE HISTORICAL RECORDS BOOK, AR. PUBLISH BOOK OF EARLY ARKANSAS COUNTY RECORDS; EARLY FRENCH RECORDS WILL BE RESEARCHED AND TRANSLATED INTO ENGLISH. (ST-WIDE). MRS J S POLLARD, CHAIRMAN; ARKANSAS COUNTY BICENTENNIAL COMMUNITY; 808 W 18TH ST; STUTTGART, AR 72160. (#15407).

AUG 30 - SEPT 4, '76. ARKANSAS CO LIVESTOCK SHOW & FAIR. FAIR, QUEEN CONTEST, PARADE & RIDE. (ST-WIDE). MRS J S POLLARD, CHAIRMAN; ARKANSAS COUNTY BICENTENNIAL COMMITTEE; 808 W 18TH ST; STUTTGART, AR 72160. (#102501-2).

DELIGHT

DELIGHT BICENTENNIAL FESTIVAL, AR. A FESTIVAL IS PLANNED THAT WILL INCLUDE ARTS AND CRAFTS BOOTHS, ANTIQUE DISPLAYS, DEMONSTRATIONS OF OLD TIME EQUIPMENT AND VARIOUS CONTESTS FOR THE PARTICIPANTS. (LOCAL). HON CLIB MAY, MAYOR; CITY OF DELIGHT; CITY HALL; DELIGHT, AR 71940. (#26797). **ARBA GRANTEE.**

DEC '75. DELIGHT BICENTENNIAL FESTIVAL. FESTIVAL WILL INCLUDE ARTS & CRAFTS BOOTHS, ANTIQUE DISPLAYS, DEMONSTRATIONS OF OLD TIME EQUIPMENT AND VARIOUS CONTESTS FOR THE PARTICIPANTS. (LOCAL). HON CLIB MAY, MAYOR; CITY HALL; DELIGHT, AR 71940. (#26799-1).

DEQUEEN

DEQUEEN BICENTENNIAL CELEBRATIONS, AR. SEVIER COUNTY HAS PLANNED BICENTENNIAL ACTIVITIES THROUGH DECEMBER 1976; ACTIVITIES INCLUDE ART FESTIVAL, QUILTING & FIDDLERS CONTEST, PARADE & OTHERS. (LOCAL). B A MAULDIN, COUNTY JUDGE; SEVIER COUNTY; SEVIER COUNTY COURTHOUSE; DEQUEEN, AR 71832. (#27072). **ARBA GRANTEE.**

DERMOTT

DERMOTT'S SESQUICENTENNIAL CELEBRATION - ARKANSAS. 1976 WILL BE DERMOTT'S SESQUICENTENNIAL YEAR. A JOINT CELEBRATION IS PLANNED STARTING OCT 25, 1974. THE CELEBRATION WILL INCLUDE THE ENTIRE POPULATION AND INVOLVE OUTLYING COMMUNITIES. (LOCAL). JOHN HAMMOCK, CHAIRMAN; DERMOTT BICENTENNIAL COMMITTEE; 502 S PECAN; DERMOTT, AR 71638. (#2349).

MCDERMOTT CEMETERY RESTORATION - DERMOTT, ARKANSAS. THE FOUNDER OF DERMOTT, DR CHARLES MCDERMOTT, IS BURIED IN A FAMILY CEMETERY. CIVIC ORGANIZATIONS WILL RESTORE THE AREA AND CONSTRUCT A HOUSE FOR MEMORABOILIA. (LOCAL). JOHN HAMMOCK, CHAIRMAN; DERMOTT BICENTENNIAL COMMITTEE; 502 S PECAN; DERMOTT, AR 71638. (#2348).

TOUR OF HISTORIC HAMMOCK HOME - DERMOTT, ARK. CAPT HAMMOCK'S HOME WILL BE ON DISPLAY. HISTORICAL OBJECTS OF ART, & ITEMS OF INTEREST FROM ALL OVER THE WORLD WILL BE EXHIBITED. TOURS WILL BE CONDUCTED BY DAR & SAR REPRESENTATIVES. (LOCAL). JOHN HAMMOCK, CHAIRMAN; DERMOTT BICENTENNIAL COMMITTEE; 502 S PECAN; DERMOTT, AR 71638. (#2350).

OCT 25, '74. BICENTENNIAL PARADE, BARBECUE, HISTORIC TOURS & CRAFTS DISPLAY. A PAST TO REMEMBER A FUTURE TO MOLD PROJ OF ARK. A COMMEMORATION EMBRACING THE THEME OF THE BICENTENNIAL TO BE HELD IN DERMOTT. (LOCAL). MRS FRED PARIS, CHAIRMAN; CHAMBER OF COMMERCE; 117 E PEPDICORD; DERMOTT, AR 71638. (#2626-901).

OCT 25, '74. FLAG PRESENTATION AND PATRIOTIC SPEECHES. A PAST TO REMEMBER A FUTURE TO MOLD PROJ OF ARK. A COMMEMORATION EMBRACING THE THEME OF THE BICENTENNIAL TO BE HELD IN DERMOTT. (LOCAL). MRS FRED PARIS, CHAIRMAN; CHAMBER OF COMMERCE; 117 E PEPDICORD; DERMOTT, AR 71638. (#2626-902).

DES ARC

NOV 6 - 7, '76. USA CORPS OF ENGINEERS FLOATING MUSEUM VISITS DES ARC, AR. EXHIBIT. (LOCAL). KENT CARMAIN, CHMN; USA CORPS OF ENGINEERS; US ARMY CORPS OF ENGINEERS; MEMPHIS, TN 38103. (#30730-2).

DEVALLS BLUFF

PANSY PARK - DE VALLS BLUFF, AR. THE CITIZENS OF DEVALLS BLUFF HAVE A COMMUNITY PARK WHICH HAS BEEN NEGLECTED AND COVERED UP WITH WEEDS. THE CITY PLANS TO CLEAN UP THE PARK AND PURCHASE SOME PLAYGROUND EQUIPMENT. (LOCAL). HON GEORGE E ROBERTS, MAYOR; CITY OF DE VALLS BLUFF; CITY HALL; DE VALLS BLF, AR 72041. (#26800). **ARBA GRANTEE.**

NOV 8, '76. USA CORPS OF ENGINEERS FLOATING MUSEUM VISITS DEVALLS BLUFF, AR. EXHIBIT. (LOCAL). KENT CARMAIN, CHMN; USA CORPS OF ENGINEERS; US ARMY CORPS OF ENGINEERS; MEMPHIS, TN 38103. (#30730-3).

DIAZ

CITY OF DIAZ DRAINAGE PROJECT - ARKANSAS. CONSTRUCTION HAS BEGUN ON ADEQUATE DRAINAGE FOR THIS COMMUNITY. (LOCAL). HON BLUNT HOHN, MAYOR; CITY OF DIAZ; CITY HALL; DIAZ, AR 72043. (#7774).

DIXIE

SHRINE AND STATIONS OF CROSS - DIXIE, AR. THE SHRINE AND STATIONS OF CROSS WILL BE BUILT AND MAINTAINED BY YOUTH GROUPS. (LOCAL). MABEL RITTER, 4-H LEADER; ST BONIFACE, 4-H CLUB; RT 1 BOX 22; BIGELOW, AR 72016. (#23433).

JUNE 1 - 30, '76. DEDICATION OF SHRINE AND STATIONS OF CROSS. OPEN HOUSE OF ST BONIFACE CHURCH, BUILT IN 1906, AND ONE AT THE OLDEST CHURCHES IN USE IN STATE TODAY. AT HIGHWAY 60, 12 MILES WEST OF CONWAY, 10 MILES EAST OF PERRYVILLE. (LOCAL). MABEL RITTER, CHMN; ST BONIFACE 4-H CLUB; RT 1, BOX 22; BIGELOW, AR 72016. (#106583-1).

DUMAS

OUR RIVER HERITAGE - PROJECTS IN DUMAS, ARKANSAS. PAGEANT TO REFLECT POINTS IN HISTORY, PRESENTATION OF A DOCUMENTARY ON BLACK SPIRITUAL MUSIC & CONSTRUCTION OF A MUSEUM TO HOUSE ALL OF THE RIVER HISTORICAL ARTIFACTS. (LOCAL). JIM WILLIAMS, SECRETARY/TREASURER; CENTRAL DAY CARE CORPORATION; PO BOX DRAWER B; DUMAS, AR 71639. (#7884).

OUR RIVER HERITAGE FESTIVAL. PAGEANT WILL INCLUDE AN ARTS & CRAFTS FESTIVAL, OTRABAND PLAYERS AND A PLANNED DOCUMENTARY ON BLACK SPIRITUAL MUSIC. (LOCAL). HON BILLY FREE, MAYOR; DUMAS BICENTENNIAL CELEBRATION; CITY HALL; DUMAS, AR 71639. (#17590-1). **(??).**

NOV 19, '76. DELTA ARTS AND CRAFT FAIR & BICENTENNIAL CELEBRATION. FAIR AT CROWN MOBILE HOME BUILDING, HIGHWAY 65. (LOCAL). MRS BILL CANADA, CO-CHMN; WOMENS' SERVICE LEAGUE; 141 MOHAWK; DUMAS, AR 71639. (#100163-1).

DYER

MAY 15, '76. DYER BICENTENNIAL HOMECOMING & BURIAL OF TIME CAPSULE. CEREMONY, CONFERENCE, FESTIVAL, PARADE AT DYER CHURCHES, CITY HALL & MAIN ST. (LOCAL). ROBERT M GARNER, CHAIRMAN; CRAWFORD COUNTY BICENTENNIAL COMMISSION; PO BOX 486; VAN BUREN, AR 72956. (#200005-71).

DYESS

TOWN CIRCLE IMPROVEMENT - DYESS, AR. THE TOWN CIRCLE IN DYESS WILL BE RE-LANDSCAPED. (LOCAL). MRS LEO ALLEN, CHAIRMAN; DYESS BICENTENNIAL COMMITTEE; DYESS, AR 72330. (#29164).

JUNE 13, '76. FLAG DEDICATION. CEREMONY, LIVE PERFORMANCE, RADIO/TV. (LOCAL). MRS LEO ALLEN, CHAIRMAN; DYESS BICENTENNIAL COMMITTEE; DYESS, AR 72330. (#200005-27).

JULY 4, '76. JULY 4TH PICNIC. FESTIVAL. (LOCAL). MRS LEO ALLEN, CHAIRMAN; DYESS BICENTENNIAL COMMITTEE; DYESS, AR 72330. (#200005-117).

EARLE

BICENTENNIAL CELEBRATION, EARLE, AR. THE CITY OF EARLE WILL START OFFBY RAISING ITS BICENTENNIAL FLAG AT CITY HALL, A PARADE WILL FOLLOW. FLOAT, HOGCALLING & BEARDGROWING CONTESTS WILL BE HELD. (LOCAL). HON JAMES H KING, MAYOR; CITY OF EARLE; CITY HALL; EARLE, AR 72331. (#26722). **ARBA GRANTEE.**

JAN 31 - DEC 1, '76. EARLE MUSIC CLUB PRODUCTION. LIVE PERFORMANCE. (LOCAL). MRS G D JAY III, CHAIRMAN; CRITTENDEN COUNTY BICENTENNIAL COMMITTEE; 420 ROOSEVELT; WEST MEMPHIS, AR 72301. (#3440-504).

APR 17, '76. BICENTENNIAL CELEBRATION. THE CITY OF EARLE WILL START OFFBY RAISING ITS BICENTENNIAL FLAG AT CITY HALL, A PARADE WILL FOLLOW. FLOAT, HOGCALLING & BEARD GROWING CONTESTS WILL BE HELD. (LOCAL). HON JAMES H KING, MAYOR; CITY OF EARLE; CITY HALL; EARLE, AR 72331. (#26722-1).

EL DORADO

BICENTENNIAL OILWELL EQUIPMENT MUSEUM, AR. ESTABLISH MUSEUM TO PRESERVE OLD RECORDS & EQUIPMENT USED IN 1921 AT THE TIME THAT OIL WAS DISCOVERED IN UNION COUNTY. (ST-WIDE). MRS H C MCKINNEY, JR, CHAIRMAN; DESK AND DERICK CLUB & UNION COUNTY BICENTENNIAL COMMISSION; UNION COUNTY COURT HOUSE; EL DORADO, AR 71730. (#21588).

ELAINE

ELAINE LIBRARY, AR. A NEW PUBLIC LIBRARY HAS BEEN BUILT. (LOCAL). MRS MILAN WILKES, LIBRARIAN; ELAINE PUBLIC LIBRARY; ELAINE, AR 72333. (#28966).

MAY 9, '76. HORSE SHOW. COMPETITION, LIVE PERFORMANCE. (LOCAL). B H LUCY, CHMN; RICHARD B LUCY POST 238, AMERICAN LEGION; ELAINE, AR 72333. (#200005-15).

EUREKA SPGS

FALL FESTIVAL IN EUREKA SPRINGS, ARKANSAS. BLUEGRASS MUSIC, ARTS & CRAFTS FESTIVAL. (LOCAL). R G GATES, CHAIRMAN; CITY OF EUREKA SPRINGS; RT 4 BERRYVILLE; EUREKA SPG, AR 72632. (#4865).

TOURIST MAP & PICNIC AREA, EUREKA SPRINGS, AR. CERAMIC TILED BILLBOARD OF CONTOUR MAP OF NORTHWEST AR, ELECTRICALLY SHOWING AVAILABLE ACCOMODATIONS FOR TOURISTS; COOK-IT-YOURSELF PICNIC STOP, CORNER OF ONYX CAVE RD AND U S 62. (ST-WIDE). MURIEL H SCHMIDT, PRESIDENT; DESTINY OF AMERICA FOUNDATION, INC; RT 1, BOX 330; EUREKA SPGS, AR 72632. (#21215).

TWO HUNDRED YEARS OF BUTTON DESIGNS, ARKANSAS. BUTTONS FROM MILITARY AND CIVILIAN DRESS WILL BE DISPLAYED IN A LOCAL MUSEUM. THE EXHIBIT WILL FEATURE BUTTONS FROM PRE-REVOLUTIONARY DAYS THROUGH THE PRESENT. (LOCAL). MURIEL H SCHMIDT, DIRECTOR; DESTINY OF AMERICA FOUNDATION; RT 1, BOX 330; EUREKA SPG, AR 72632. (#8916).

OCT 22 - 25, '75. FALL FESTIVAL. EXHIBIT, FESTIVAL, PARADE AT CITY AUDITORIUM, BASIN PARK, SPRING ST. (LOCAL). FREDDIE NIXON, BICENT DIR; CHAMBER OF COMMERCE & CARROLL COUNTY BICENTENNIAL COMMITTEE; EUREKA SPG, AR 72632. (#101883-1).

MAR 1, '76 - DEC 31, '77. 'GAY 90' BUSTLE AND DOLL MUSEUM EXHIBIT. ONE ROOM LINED WITH GLASS DISPLAY CASES & SHELVES TO SHOW ANTIQUE COLLECTION OF FANS, BUTTONS, PATTERNS, FABRICS, FEATHERS MILLINERY DOLLS AND OVER 15 HISTORICALLY DESIGNED COSTUMES OF THE LAST CENTURY; LECTURE AND GUIDE IS AVAILABLE BY APPOINTMENT ONLY. AT MUSEUM BUILDING, ONYX CAVE PARK. (LOCAL). MURIEL H SCHMIDT, PRES; DESTINY OF AMERICA, INC; RT 1, BOX 330, ONYX CAVE RD; EUREKA SPG, AR 72632. (#21214-1).

OCT 27 - 30, '76. 27TH ANNUAL OZARK FOLK FESTIVAL. FESTIVAL. (LOCAL). J W EMMONS, CHMN; EUREKA SPRINGS CHAMBER OF COMMERCE; 5 N MAIN; EUREKA SPG, AR 72632. (#103416-647).

FAIRFIELD BAY

BEAUTIFICATION OF FAIRFIELD BAY & ENVIRONS, AR. PRESERVATION OF PLANTS, ANIMALS & TERRAIN THAT ARE NATIVE TO THE AREA & IMPROVE THESE FEATURES THROUGH SELECTIVE STUDY, PLANNING AND PROPOGATION. ACCOMPLISHED THROUGH CITIZEN PARTICIPATION. (LOCAL). KENNETH SHARP, PRESIDENT; FAIRFIELD BAY COMMUNITY CLUB; PO BOX 3008; FAIRFIELD BAY, AR 72088. (#32537).

BICENTENNIAL SCHOOL FESTIVAL IN FAIRFIELD BAY, AR. POSTER CONTEST, SCHOOL AWARDS, CEREMONY, EXHIBITS, AND OTHER SIMILAR ACTIVITIES TO INVOLVE SCHOOL CHILDREN IN THE BICENTENNIAL. PARENTS & TEACHERS INVOLVED. (LOCAL).

FAIRFIELD BAY — CONTINUED

MRS MARGARET HILTON, COORDINATOR; FAIRFIELD BICENTENNIAL COMMITTEE; FAIRFIELD BAY, AR 72088. (#33689).

FAIRFIELD BAY CULTURAL AND HISTORIC CENTER. THE COMMUNITY OF FAIRFIELD BAY HAVE RESTORED A 100 YEAR OLD LOG CABIN THAT HOUSES THEIR ARTS AND CRAFTS CENTER WHERE EXHIBITS OF LITERARY, HISTORIC, ARTISTIC AND CULTURAL ITEMS ARE HELD. (LOCAL). HERMAN HOLLIS, PRESIDENT; FAIRFIELD BAY LIONS CLUB; PO BOX 3008; FAIRFIELD BAY, AR 72153. (#30253). **ARBA GRANTEE.**

FAIRFIELD BAY HISTORY, AR. THE HISTORY OF LAND & BEGINNING OF FAIRFIELD BAY AS A NEW RETIREMENT COMMUNITY. (LOCAL). MRS DICK MEACHAM, CHAIRMAN; FAIRFIELD BAY BICENTENNIAL COMMITTEE; FAIRFIELD BAY, AR 72088. (#32535).

FAIRFIELD BAY LIBRARY BICENT READING CENTER, AR. USING BOOKS AND PUBLICATIONS SELECTED FROM THE PROGRAM OF THE AMERICAN ISSUES FORUM THE READING CENTER HAS A FOCAL POINT WITH THE UNITED STATES FLAG AND ETCHED SCENES OF COLONIAL AMERICA. (LOCAL). MRS MEREDITH WALKER, CHAIRMAN; FAIRFIELD BAY LIBRARY, FAULKNER-VANBUREN CO REGIONAL LIBRARY; FAIRFIELD BAY, AR 72088. (#32536).

INDIAN ROCK HOUSE, FAIRFIELD BAY, AR. RESTORATION OF GROUNDS SURROUNDING THE CAVE (HOUSE). IMPROVEMENT OF AREAS LEADING TO CAVE. (ST-WIDE). CLAY GRING, V PRESIDENT; FAIRFIELD COMMUNITIES LAND COMPANY; FAIRFIELD BAY, AR 72088. (#32539).

PAINTING OF FIRE HYDRANTS, FAIRFIELD BAY, AR. THE BOY SCOUTS OF FAIRFIELD BAY PAINTED THE FIRE HYDRANTS TO REPRESENT COLONIAL CHARACTERS. POLL WAS TAKEN OF BEST ONE-WINNER RECEIVED A NEW $2 BILL STAMPED WITH JULY 4, 1976 POSTAL MARK. (LOCAL). DON NOFSINGER, SCOUTMASTER; FAIRFIELD BAY BOY SCOUTS; FAIRFIELD BAY, AR 72088. (#32538).

PERMANENT MUSEUM FOR FAIRFIELD BAY, AR. PACKAGED LOG HOUSE ERECTED BY RESIDENTS OF FAIRFIELD BAY TO BE USED AS A MUSEUM HOUSING ARTIFACTS & PROVIDING DISPLAY SPACE FOR COLLECTIONS. (LOCAL). MRS A R MEACHAM CHAIRMAN, FAIRFIELD BAY BICENT COM; FAIRFIELD BAY BICENTENNIAL COMMITTEE; ROUTE 2 BOX 782; FAIRFIELD BAY, AR 72088. (#32534).

JUNE 22, '75. PATRIOTIC PROGRAM. COLLEGE PRESIDENT AS SPEAKER; BOY AND GIRL SCOUTS PERFORMED FLAG CEREMONY. THIS WAS THE 'KICK-OFF' BICENTENNIAL PROGRAM OF THE FAIRFIELD BAY COMMUNITY. AT CIVIC CENTER. (LOCAL). CARTER JOHNSON; FAIRFIELD BAY LIONS CLUB; 365-11 CHELSEA GLADE; FAIRFIELD BAY, AR 72088. (#200005-107).

NOV 23, '75. SPECIAL CHURCH SERVICES. MINISTERS OF EACH CHURCH CONDUCTED COMMEMORATIVE SERVICES ACCORDING TO THEIR INDIVIDUAL WISHES. (LOCAL). JEAN MEACHAM; FAIRFIELD BAY BICENTENNIAL COMMITTEE; ROUTE 2, BOX 782; FAIRFIELD BAY, AR 72088. (#200005-102).

DEC 16, '75 - JAN 2, '76. CHRISTMAS IN FAIRFIELD BAY. LIVE PERFORMANCE, CEREMONY AT ROTUNDA AT INFORMATION CENTER. (LOCAL). MRS KATHLEEN W WATERS; FAIRFIELD BAY COMMUNITIES LAND COMPANY; ROUTE 2, BOX 711; FAIRFIELD BAY, AR 72088. (#200005-105).

FEB 15, '76. BICENTENNIAL FASHION SHOW. 200 YEARS OF LADIES FASHION. AT CIVIC CENTER. (LOCAL). BARBARA HEWITT; FAIRFIELD BAY; PO BOX 3021; FAIRFIELD BAY, AR 72088. (#200005-83).

MAR 19, '76. WAGON TRAIN PILGRIMAGE - FAIRFIELD BAY TO LITTLE ROCK ARKANSAS. ONLY COMMUNITY FROM OUT OF STATE TO MAKE THE TRIP TO LITTLE ROCK TO CELEBRATE THE CROSSING OF THE WAGON TRAIN. SPECIAL CONTINENTAL TRAILWAYS BUS WAS USED FOR TRANSPORTATION. FAIRFIELD BAY SCROLLS PRESENTED TO WAGON MASTER AT BARTON ARENA. AT RENDEVOUS AT BARTON ARENA, LITTLE ROCK, AR. (LOCAL). JEAN MEACHAM; FAIRFIELD BAY BICENTENNIAL COMMITTEE; ROUTE 2 BOX 782; FAIRFIELD BAY, AR 72088. (#200005-101).

APR 1 - MAY 30, '76. BICENTENNIAL CHORAL CONCERT. BICENTENNIAL CHORAL CONCERT GIVEN ON THREE OCCASIONS EACH FOR PRINCIPALLY DIFFERENT AUDIENCES. CONCERT CONTENT ARRANGED SPECIFICALLY FOR BICENTENNIAL CELEBRATION. AT CIVIC CENTER AND RACQUET CLUB FAIRFIELD BAY PARKING NEARBY. (LOCAL). MRS MEREDITH WALKER; FAIRFIELD BY COMMUNITY CLUB ADULT MIXED CHORUS; RTE 2 BOX 448; FAIRFIELD BAY, AR 72088. (#200005-109).

APR 16 - 25, '76. ARTS & CRAFTS. CRAFT ITEMS ON EXHIBIT & FOR SALE. AT INFORMATION CENTER FAIRFIELD BAY. (LOCAL). BILL L WATKINS; FAIRFIELD BAY ARTS CRAFTS & HOBBIES ASSN; PO BOX 66; FAIRFIELD BAY, AR 72088. (#200005-81).

APR 16 - 25, '76. SPRING FESTIVAL. FLEA MARKET; OZARK FOLK MUSIC; FLOWER & PLANT DISPLAY FLOTILLA AND BLESSING OF BOATS; EASTER EGG HUNT; SQUARE DANCING; TENNIS TOURNAMENT; LITTLE THEATRE, COMMUNITY PICNIC. AT ROTUNDA AT INFORMATION CENTER. (LOCAL). MRS GERALDINE PELTON; FAIRFIELD COMMUNITY LAND COMPANY; P O BOX 3345; FAIRFIELD BAY, AR 72088. (#200005-110).

APR 23, '76. STATE RECOGNITION OF FAIRFIELD BAY. LT GOV JOE PURCELL WAS SPECIAL GUEST. LT GOV PURCELL PRESENTED BICENTENNIAL FLAG TO THE COMMUNITY. LOG CABIN MUSEUM PLANS WERE UNVEILED TO AUDIENCE. AT CIVIC CENTER. (LOCAL). JEAN MEACHAM; FAIRFIELD BAY BICENTENNIAL COMMITTEE; ROUTE 2 BOX 782; FAIRFIELD BAY, AR 72088. (#200005-106).

MAY 18 - AUG 28, '76. FAIRFIELD BAY SALUTE TO STATES. EXHIBIT AT ROTUNDA, INFORMATION CENTER. (LOCAL). MRS KATHLEEN W WATERS; FAIRFIELD COMMUNITIES LAND COMPANY; ROUTE 2, BOX 711; FAIRFIELD BAY, AR 72088. (#200005-114).

JUNE 14, '76 - CONTINUING . OLD FASHIONED ICE CREAM SOCIALS BENEFITING OLD MUSEUM. STRING MUSIC PROVIDED DURING SOCIALS BY RESIDENTS. DRESS - MANY COLONIAL COSTUMES, VISITORS ON BAY PROPERTY WERE NUMEROUS. AT ON LAWN IN VICINITY OF NEW MUSEUM AND INFORMATION CENTER. (LOCAL). JEAN MEACHAM; FAIRFIELD BAY BICENTENNIAL COMMITTEE; ROUTE 2 BOX 782; FAIRFIELD BAY, AR 72088. (#200005-115).

JULY 4, '76. DEDICATION OF LOG CABIN MUSEUM. RIBBON CUTTING CEREMONY; BOY SCOUT COLOR PRESENTATION; BELL RINGING IN CONJUNCTION WITH NATIONAL OBSERVANCE; ADDRESSES BY DIGNITARIES OF THE COMMUNITY. AT LOG CABIN MUSEUM IN VICINIY OF INFORMATION CENTER. (LOCAL). JEAN MEACHAM; FAIRFIELD BAY BICENTENNIAL COMMITTEE; RT 2 BOX 782; FAIRFIELD BAY, AR 72088. (#200005-104).

JULY 15 - AUG 7, '76. DISFARMER PRINT EXHIBIT. EXHIBIT AT INFORMATION CENTER. (LOCAL). CARL D HOIT; FAIRFIELD COMMUNITIES LAND CO; ARKANSAS ARTS CENTER; LITTLE ROCK, AR 72203. (#200005-113).

AUG 6 - 15, '76. FAIRFIELD BAY WATER FESTIVAL. FESTIVAL AT AR. (LOCAL). BARBARA HEWITT; FAIRFIELD BAY; PO BOX 3021; FAIRFIELD BAY, AR 72088. (#200005-84).

AUG 13 - 15, '76. ARTS & CRAFTS SHOW. CRAFT ITEMS ON EXHIBIT & FOR SALE. AT INFORMATION CENTER FAIRFIELD BAY. (LOCAL). BILL L WATKINS; FAIRFIELD BAY ARTS CRAFTS & HOBBIES ASSN; PO BOX 66; FAIRFIELD BAY, AR 72088. (#200005-82).

SEPT 1 - 7, '76. ARTMOBILE. EXHIBIT AT INFORMATION CENTER PARKING LOT. (LOCAL). CARL D HOIT; FAIRFIELD COMMUNITIES LAND CO.; ARKANSAS ARTS CENTER; LITTLE ROCK, AR 72203. (#200005-112).

SEPT 4 - 6, '76. BENEFIT ART EXHIBIT. PAINTINGS DEE DOUBLEDAY PERCENT OF PROCEEDS TO LOG MUSEUM. AT INFORMATION CENTER. (LOCAL). MRS LEWIS DOUBLEDAY; FAIRFIELD BAY LOG CABIN MUSEUM; RT 2 BOX 513; FAIRFIELD BAY, AR 72088. (#200005-111).

SEPT 10, '76 - CONTINUING . OLD FASHIONED ICE CREAM SOCIALS BENEFITING OLD MUSEUM. STRING MUSIC PROVIDED DURING SOCIALS BY RESIDENTS. DRESS - MANY COLONIAL COSTUMES, VISITORS ON BAY PROPERTY WERE NUEROUS. AT ON LAWN IN VICINITY OF NEW MUSEUM AND INFORMATION CENTER. (LOCAL). JEAN MEACHAM; FAIRFIELD BAY BICENTENNIAL COMMITTEE; ROUTE 2 BOX 782; FAIRFIELD BAY, AR 72088. (#200005-116).

MAR 18 - 19, '77. TABRIZ AUCTION. SURROUNDING COMMUNITIES WILL BE ASKED TO PARTICIPATE. DONATIONS OF MATERIALS, TIME, AND SERVICES WILL BE AUCTIONED. PROCEEDS GO TOWARDS OLD MUSEUM. AT CIVIC CENTER IN MOBILE HOME AREA. (LOCAL). MARIA HALEY; FAIRFIELD BAY BICENTENNIAL COMMITTEE; FAIRFIELD LAND CO REBSAMEN RD; LITTLE ROCK, AR 72201. (#200005-108).

FARMINGTON

FARMINGTON, ARKANSAS, BICENTENNIAL PARK. THE CITY IS DEVELOPING THEIR 1ST PARK ON 08 ACRES COMPLETE WITH PICNIC FACILITIES, BALL PARKS, PLAYGROUND EQUIPMENT, PAVILLION AND RESTROOMS, DRINKING FOUNTAINS, ETC, HOSTING ANNUAL FESTIVITIES. (LOCAL). HON BOBBY CARLISLE, MAYOR; CITY OF FARMINGTON; 241 RHEAS MILL RD; FARMINGTON, AR 72730. (#3524). **ARBA GRANTEE.**

FARMINGTON, ARK, HAWTHORN SCHOOL RESTORATION. RESTORE THE 1ST AREA SCHOOL ESTABLISHED IN 1848. (LOCAL). HON BOBBY CARLISLE, MAYOR; CITY OF FARMINGTON; 241 RHEAS MILL RD; FARMINGTON, AR 72730. (#3522). **(??).**

RESTORATION OF STONE HOUSE IN FARMINGTON, ARKANSAS. THE STONE HOUSE BUILT IN 1845 WILL BE RESTORED BY 1976. MUCH OF FAYETTEVILLES HISTORY REVOLVES AROUND THIS HOME, WHICH WAS DEDICATED TO STATE PARKS DEPT BY EDWARD D STONE, AN ANCESTOR & RENOWNED ARCHITECT. (LOCAL). ROBERT S MCKINNEY, CHAIRMAN; FAYETTEVILLE-WASHINGTON COUNTY BICENTENNIAL COMMITTEE; 200 W CENTRAL ST; FAYETTEVILLE, AR 72701. (#3098). **(??).**

JULY 1 - 5, '75. BICENTENNIAL FESTIVAL. FESTIVAL AT FARMINGTON BICENTENNIAL PARK. (LOCAL). HON BOBBY CARLISLE, MAYOR; CITY OF FARMINGTON; 241 RHEAS MILL RD; FARMINGTON, AR 72730. (#3524-1).

JULY 4, '75. FOURTH OF JULY FESTIVAL. STARTING JULY 4, '75 WITH COMPLETION OF BICENT PARK, ANNUAL WEEK LONG FESTIVAL IS SCHEDULED. ACTIVITIES WILL INCLUDE GAMES, ATHLETIC CONTESTS, ARTS & CRAFTS, FAMILY REUNIONS, DAY-LONG PICNICS, ETC. THERE WILL BE A PICNIC, MUSIC & A MOCK BLUE & GRAY BATTLE. AT NORTH OF FARMINGTON GRADE SCHOOL GROUNDS. (LOCAL). MAYOR BOBBY CARLISLE; FARMINGTON BICENTENNIAL COMMITTEE; PO BOX C; FARMINGTON, AR 72730. (#3085-1).

FAYETTEVILLE

ADOPT-A-GRANDPARENT PROJECT OF FAYETTEVILLE, ARK. CITY YOUTHS WILL ADOPT AN ELDERLY PERSON AS 'GRANDPARENT' PROVIDING ATTENTION & COMPANIONSHIP TO THOSE WITHOUT FAMILY. THE PROGRAM WILL BE SPONSORED BY THE FAYETTEVILLE SCHOOL SYSTEMS. (LOCAL). ROBERT MCKINNEY, CHAIRMAN; FAYETTEVILLE-WASHINGTON COUNTY BICENTENNIAL COMMITTEE; 200 W CENTRAL ST; FAYETTEVILLE, AR 72701. (#3095). **(??).**

ARKANSAS AMER HISTORY HIGH SCHOOL ESSAY CONTEST. AN ESSAY CONTEST FOR ALL ARKANSAS HIGH SCHOOL STUDENTS. PAPERS ON SOME ASPECT OF LOCAL, STATE OR AMERICAN HISTORY. WILL BE JUDGED & PRIZES AWARDED. (ST-WIDE). DR W DAVID BAIRD, PROJECT DIRECTOR; UNIV OF ARKANSAS, DEPT OF HISTORY; BA BLDG, ROOM 108, CAMPUS DR; FAYETTEVILLE, AR 72701. (#503). **ARBA GRANTEE.**

ARKANSAS ARCHIVES OF PUBLIC COMMUNICATION. THE SPEECH DEPT OF THE UNIV OF AR AT FAYETTEVILLE IS BUILDING A COLLECTION OF IMPORTANT PUBLIC COMMUNICATIONS BY CITIZENS OF ARKANSAS WHICH WILL BE PRESERVED AND MADE AVAILABLE FOR STUDY & RESEARCH. (ST-WIDE). DR M BLAIR HART, PROJ COORDINATOR; UNIV OF ARKANSAS AMER REVOL BICENT COMMITTEE; COMMUNICATIONS CNTR, RM 430; FAYETTEVILLE, AR 72701. (#8927).

ARKANSAS HISTORIC ARCHITECTURE PUBLICATIONS. PUBLICATION OF ILLUSTRATIONS AND INFORMATION ABOUT 19TH CENTURY ARCHITECTURE IN ARKANSAS; POSSIBILITY OF CATEGORICAL BREAKDOWN OF INFORMATION OR DIVISION BY GEOGRAPHICAL REGION. (ST-WIDE). CYRUS A SUTHERLAND, PROFESSOR; UNIV OF ARKANSAS; DEPARTMENT OF ARCHITECTURE; FAYETTEVILLE, AR 72701. (#529). **ARBA GRANTEE.**

FAYETTEVILLE BICENTENNIAL PROGRAMS, AR. THE OVERALL BICENTENNIAL PROGRAM FOR FAYETTEVILLE INCLUDES A TREE PLANTING, A GENERAL AWARENESS CAMPAIGN AND A FILM PROJECT. (LOCAL). DONALD GRIMES, CITY MANAGER; CITY OF FAYETTEVILLE; PO DRAWER F; FAYETTEVILLE, AR 72701. (#22577). **ARBA GRANTEE.**

MUSICAL MELTING POT, FACES OF AMER MUSIC, ARKANSAS. A 104-HOUR SERIES OF RADIO PROGRAMS ILLUSTRATING VARIOUS CULTURAL & ETHNIC HERITAGES WHICH HAVE CONTRIBUTED TO THE DEVELOPMENT OF AMERICAN MUSIC. PLANNED AS UNITS TO BE MADE AVAILABLE TO OTHER STATIONS. (LOCAL). DR M BLAIR HART, CHAIRMAN; UNIV OF ARKANSAS AMER REVOL BICENT COMMITTEE; COMMUNICATION CENTER - RM 417; FAYETTEVILLE, AR 72701. (#8918).

MUSICAL PRODUCTION-FAYETTEVILLE, ARKANSAS. DANCE ORGANIZATIONS OF THIS AREA WILL PRODUCE MUSICAL INTERPRETATIONS OF CUSTOMS OF PAST & PRESENT. THE GALA EVENTS WILL BE ASSISTED BY THE 'SUMMER THEATRE PROJECT' & HELD IN THE FAYETTEVILLE AREA. (LOCAL). ROBERT MCKINNEY, CHAIRMAN; FAYETTEVILLE-WASHINGTON COUNTY BICENTENNIAL COMMITTEE; 200 W CENTRAL ST; FAYETTEVILLE, AR 72701. (#3094).

OUR FEDERAL CONSTITUTION SERIES, UNIV OF ARKANSAS. TWO PUBLIC LECTURES BY DISTINGUISHED NATIONAL AUTHORITIES ON OUR CONSTITUTIONAL HISTORY & DEVELOPMENT. (ST-WIDE). DR JAMES S CHASE; DEPT OF HISTORY; UNIV OF ARKANSAS; FAYETTEVILLE, AR 72701. (#501). **ARBA GRANTEE.**

RELIGIOUS CHOIR PRESENTATIONS - FAYETTEVILLE, AR. THE MINISTERIAL ALLIANCE OF FAYETTEVILLE WILL CONDUCT RELIGIOUS CHOIR PRESENTATIONS FROM ALL CHURCHES TO RECOGNIZE THE FOUNDING OF AMERICA FOR THE PURPOSE OF RELIGIOUS FREEDOM. (LOCAL). ROBERT MCKINNEY, CHAIRMAN; FAYETTEVILLE-WASHINGTON COUNTY BICENTENNIAL COMMITTEE; 200 W CENTRAL ST; FAYETTEVILLE, AR 72701. (#3097).

UNIV OF ARKANSAS STUDENT UNION '76 PROGRAMS. THE STUDENT UNION IS PLANNING THREE PROGRAMS; A FILM SERIES, AN ART GALLERY & AN EXHIBIT OF EARLY AMERICAN FURNITURE. (LOCAL). DR M BLAIR HART, CHAIRMAN; UNIV OF ARKANSAS ARBC; PO BOX 600; FAYETTEVILLE, AR 72701. (#8928).

UNIV OF ARKANSAS LIBRARY TO UPDATE COUNTY RECORDS. THE DAVID MULLINS LIBRARY WILL INDEX & BRING THE COUNTY RECORDS UP TO DATE. THEY WILL MAKE AVAILABLE SIGNIFICANT BIBLIOGRAPHIES THAT HAVE NOT BEEN REPRODUCED. (ST-WIDE). DR M BLAIR HART, CHAIRMAN; UNIV OF ARKANSAS ARBC; COMMUNICATION CENTER, RM 417; FAYETTEVILLE, AR 72701. (#8929).

UNIV OF ARKANSAS SPONSORS MALL BEAUTIFICATION PROJ. THIS IS A JOINT PROJECT OF STUDENTS AND FACULTY TO MAKE THE AREA BETWEEN THE STUDENT UNION AND THE LIBRARY A PLACE OF BEAUTY & SIGNIFICANCE BY PLANTING THE AREA WITH FLORA THAT IS NATIVE TO ARKANSAS. (LOCAL). DR M BLAIR HART, CHAIRMAN; UNIV OF ARKANSAS, ARBC; COMMUNICATIONS CENTER, RM 417; FAYETTEVILLE, AR 72701. (#8930).

UNIV OF ARKANSAS HOSTS HISTORY OF REVOL IN SONG. THE HISTORY & MUSIC DEPTS WILL PRESENT A PROGRAM OF SONGS OF THE REVOLUTION SET AGAINST THE HISTORICAL SITUATION THAT INSPIRED THE SONGS. (LOCAL). DR M BLAIR HART, CHAIRMAN; UNIV OF ARKANSAS ARBC; COMMUNICATION CENTER, RM 417; FAYETTEVILLE, AR 72701. (#8931).

JAN 1, '74 - DEC 31, '76. 'OUR FEDERAL CONSTITUTION' LECTURE SERIES OF UNIV OF ARKANSAS. TWO PUBLIC LECTURES BY DISTINGUISHED NATIONAL AUTHORITIES ON OUR CONSTITUTIONAL HISTORY & DEVELOPMENT. AT UNIV OF ARKANSAS CAMPUS AT FAYETTEVILLE. (ST-WIDE). CHARLES N CARNES; UNIV OF ARKANSAS, SCHOOL OF LAW DEPT OF HISTORY POLITICAL SCIENCE; MAPLE & GARLAND STS; FAYETTEVILLE, AR 72701. (#501-1).

MAR 23 - 25, '76. UNITED STATES ARMED FORCES BICENTENNIAL CARAVAN. CARAVAN IS COMPOSED OF EXHIBIT VANS FOR EACH MILITARY SERVICE. PROJECT THEME IS 'HISTORY OF THE ARMED FORCES AND THEIR CONTRIBUTIONS TO THE NATION'. (LOCAL). BOB MCKINNEY, CHMN; US ARMED FORCES BICENTENNIAL EXHIBIT VANS PROJECT; 200 W CENTER; FAYETTEVILLE, AR 72701. (#1775-410).

FAYETTEVILLE — CONTINUED

JUNE 6 - JULY 30, '76. SUMMER PROGRAM EACH YEAR THROUGH 1976 FOR OFF-CAMPUS THEATER. A DRAMA SERIES TO ENCOURAGE, DEVELOP AND PRESENT ORIGINAL DRAMA IN COMMUNITIES THROUGHOUT THE STATE. (ST-WIDE). CHARLES HARRILL; UNIV ARK BICENT COMM; UNIV OF ARK, SPEECH & DRAMATIC ARTS DEPT; UNIV OF ARKANSAS; FAYETTEVILLE, AR 72701. (#1706-1).

SEPT 6 - 17, '76. CARL HAVERLIN/BROADCAST MUSIC, INC, ARCHIVES BICENTENNIAL EXHIBIT. OFFERS A VERSATILE PICTURE OF HISTORY, REGIONAL LIFE & MUSIC FOR OVER 200 YEARS. CONTAINS PRESIDENTIAL LETTERS, LETTERS OF FAMOUS AMERICANS, OLD BOOKS, MANUSCRIPTS, HISTORY OF 'THE STAR SPANGLED BANNER' & COMPOSER AUTOGRAPHS, PLUS SHEET MUSIC OF THE PAST. AT UNIVERSITY LIBRARY, UNIV OF ARKANSAS AT FAYETTEVILLE. (ST-WIDE). SAMUEL A SIZER, CURATOR; UNIV OF ARKANSAS AT FAYETTEVILLE; FAYETTEVILLE, AR 72701. (#20784-4).

FORDYCE

BICENTENNIAL PARK - FORDYCE, AR. DALLAS COUNTY CITIZENS PLAN TO BUILD A PARK WHICH WILL BE SITUATED ON THE SITE OF THE OLD COUNTY COURTHOUSE WHICH STOOD THERE FROM 1845 UNTIL 1908. (LOCAL). TROY BRADLEY, COUNTY JUDGE; DALLAS COUNTY; DALLAS COUNTY COURTHOUSE; FORDYCE, AR 71742. (#27074). **ARBA GRANTEE.**

FORREST CITY

MAR 9, '76. USA CORPS OF ENGINEERS MOBILE VAN VISITS FORREST CITY, AR. A MULTI-MEDIA SHOW DEPICTING THE 200 YEAR HISTORY OF THE CORPS OF ENGINEERS & ITS ROLE IN THE EVOLUTION OF OUR NATION. AT GYMNASIUM OF THE FORREST CITY HIGH SCHOOL COMPLEX. (LOCAL). KENT CARMAIN, CHMN; USA CORPS OF ENGINEERS; US ARMY CORPS OF ENGINEERS; MEMPHIS, TN 38103. (#31165-6).

JUNE 27, '76. VILLAGE CREEK STATE PARK DEDICATION & BICENTENNIAL CELEBRATION. STATE'S LARGEST PARK IS DEDICATED WITH HUGE PATRIOTIC CELEBRATION. AT VILLAGE CREEK STATE PARK. (LOCAL). WILLIAM E HENDERSON, DIR; ARKANSAS DEPT OF PARKS & TOURISM; 149 STATE CAPITOL; LITTLE ROCK, AR 72201. (#103416-452).

FORT SMITH

BICENTENNIAL GENEALOGICAL LIBRARY, FORT SMITH, AR. ESTABLISHMENT OF GENEALOGICAL LIBRARY IN THE EXISTING LIBRARY. (LOCAL). MRS THELMA J WRAY, LIBRARIAN; FORT SMITH PUBLIC LIBRARY; 61 S 8TH ST; FORT SMITH, AR 72901. (#18249). **ARBA GRANTEE.**

A BICENTENNIAL SALUTE TO YOUTH - FORT SMITH, AR. A MUSICAL PRODUCTION SALUTING THE YOUTH OF THE COMMUNITY. (LOCAL). JOE BEARDSLEY, DIRECTOR; HYLAND DISTRICT 2 OF ARKANSAS CREDIT UNION LEAGUE; S JENNY LIND RD; FORT SMITH, AR 72901. (#19063). **ARBA GRANTEE.**

DEMONSTRATIONS OF HERITAGE HANDICRAFTS, AR. DEMONSTRATIONS OF OBSOLETE PIONEER CRAFTS TO ENCOURAGE INTEREST IN PRESERVATION OF THESE CRAFTS. (LOCAL). MRS JOHN WOODS, VICE PRESIDENT; OLD COMMISSARY MUSEUM ASSOCIATION; 111 ROGERS AVE; FORT SMITH, AR 72901. (#21211). **ARBA GRANTEE.**

FILM ON BELLE STARR - FORT SMITH, AR. FILM WILL BE MADE ON BELLE STARR, FAMOUS OUTLAW IN FORT SMITH. (ST-WIDE). DIRECTOR; OFFICE OF ARKANSAS STATE ARTS & HUMANITIES; 300 W MARKHAM; LITTLE ROCK, AR 72901. (#26729).

FORT SMITH BICENTENNIAL PROJECTS, AR. FORT SMITH CHAMBER OF COMMERCE WILL PREPARE A NUMBER OF PROJECTS FOR THE 1976 COMMUNITY FAIR. (LOCAL). PAUL LATTURE, COORDINATOR; FORT SMITH CHAMBER OF COMMERCE; 613 GARRISON AVE; FORT SMITH, AR 72901. (#24895).

FORT SMITH HERITAGE FOUNDATION PROJECTS - ARKANSAS. COMPLETION AND DESIGNATION OF AREA PRESERVATION PROJECTS; SPONSOR PRESERVATION WEEK IN BELLE GROVE DISTRICT. PUBLICATION OF A LOCAL HISTORY & OPENING OF INDIAN MOUND TO TOURISTS. (LOCAL). JIM WILLIAMS, CHAIRMAN; FORT SMITH BICENTENNIAL COMMITTEE; 2518 S FRESNO; FORT SMITH, AR 72901. (#2353). **(??).**

A LOOK TO THE FUTURE OF AMERICA - FORT SMITH, AR. THE FORT SMITH PUBLIC LIBRARY HAS PURCHASED BOOKS & SLIDE PRESENTATIONS DIRECTLY RELATED TO THE ENVIRONMENT, ENERGY, FREE ENTERPRISE SYSTEM & CONSERVATION TO BE PRESENTED TO THE LIBRARY. (LOCAL). MRS THELMA WRAY, LIBRARIAN; FORT SMITH PUBLIC LIBRARY; FORT SMITH, AR 72901. (#27075). **ARBA GRANTEE.**

MARKERS ON HISTORIC BUILDINGS - FORT SMITH, AR. PERMANENT MARKERS RECOGNIZING THOSE GROUPS WHO HAVE RESTORED HOMES OR BUILDINGS IN THE HISTORIC BELLE GROVE DISTRICT. (LOCAL). MRS RALPH J SPEER, VICE-PRESIDENT; FORT SMITH HERITAGE FOUNDATION; UNITED SAVINGS BLDG; FORT SMITH, AR 72901. (#24110). **ARBA GRANTEE.**

MARKING HISTORICAL SITES - FORT SMITH, AR. 35 HISTORICAL LOCATIONS WILL BE MARKED IN A 6 COUNTY AREA. (ST-WIDE). RICHARD B SUGG, SECRETARY-TREASURER; BONANZA LAND INC; 613 GARRISON AVE; FORT SMITH, AR 72901. (#18498). **ARBA GRANTEE.**

MEMORIAL BATTLE MARKERS, FORT SMITH, AR. HISTORICAL MARKERS WILL BE PLACED IN HONOR OF 2 BATTLES WHICH TOOK PLACE NEAR FORT SMITH. (LOCAL). MRS BUFORD J POE, PRESIDENT; UNITED DAUGHTERS OF THE CONFEDERACY; 2404 S U ST; FORT SMITH, AR 72901. (#19363). **ARBA GRANTEE.**

OUR OLD GLORY - FORT SMITH, AR. A DAY OF RECOGNITION FOR THE RESIDENTS OF EACH NURSING HOME BY THE RAISING OF THE AMERICAN AND BICENTENNIAL FLAGS. (LOCAL). MRS J EARLE WHITE, PRESIDENT; PROJECT COMPASSION, INC; PO BOX 3489; FORT SMITH, AR 72901. (#21204). **ARBA GRANTEE.**

PATRIOTIC MUSICAL - FORT SMITH, AR. A PATRIOTIC MUSICAL IS BEING PLANNED FOR THE BICENT CELEBRATION. (LOCAL). WALTER C MINNICAR; FORT SMITH SYMPHONY ASSOC; 6800 SO 'W'; FORT SMITH, AR 72901. (#21350). **ARBA GRANTEE.**

SOUTHWEST TIMES RECORD BICENTENNIAL COVERAGE-NBMRP. 12 MONTH SERIES 'OF, BY AND FOR THE PEOPLE' DEMONSTRATING BASIC AMERICAN HUMAN VALUES, PLUS ON-GOING COLUMNS & FEATURES ON LOCAL HISTORY & OPINION, RELIGION, PLUS LOCAL, STATE & NATL ACTIVITIES. (LOCAL). JACK MOSELY, EDITOR; SOUTHWEST TIMES RECORD; PO BOX 1359; FORT SMITH, AR 72901. (#32946).

APR 28 - MAY 4, '75. JUDGE PARKER CENTENNIAL CELEBRATION. COMMEMORATION CEREMONY AT JUDGE PARKER'S GRAVESITE IN U.S. NATIONAL CEMETERY-HISTORICAL REENACTMENT OF TRIAL IN ORIGINAL COURTROOM AND A MOCK-HANGING ON RECONSTRUCTED GALLOWS WILL BE PERFORMED SEVERAL TIME S FROM 7-9PM MAY 2 1975 HISTORIC TOUR ON MAY 3-4 1975. AT JUDGE PARKER'S COURTROOM AND GALLOWS AT SOUTH THIRD AND ROGERS AVE. (ST-WIDE). JOHN V. ROBINSON; BELLE FORT SMITH ASSOCIATION; P.O. BOX 1412; FORT SMITH, AR 72901. (#4854-1).

MAY 3 - 4, '75. BELLE FORT SMITH TOUR-HISTORIC HOMES, SITES AND BUILDINGS. SECOND ANNUAL TOUR FEATURES SIX HOMES AND ONE CHURCH WITH SOME THAT HAVE RECENTLY BEEN RESTORED-OTHERS IN PROCESS. COSTUMED HOSTS AND HOSTESSES, TRAINED VOLUNTEER GUIDES, SPECIAL EXHIBITS AND ANTIQUE AUTO MOBILES INCLUDED. AT BEGINS AT HISTORIC IMMACULATE CONCEPTION CHURCH ON GARRISON AVENUE. (LOCAL). JOHN V. ROBINSON; BELLE FORT SMITH ASSOCIATION; P. O. BOX 1412; FORT SMITH, AR 72901. (#4855-1).

AUG 23, '75. NATL PK SVC 'PEOPLE OF 1776' (PILOT) VISITS FORT SMITH NHS. TRAVELING TROUPE WILL BRING VARIOUS ASPECTS OF COLONIAL LIFE (MILITARY LIFE, MUSIC, CRAFTS) TO VISITORS TO THIS NATIONAL PARK SERVICE AREA. (REGN'L). SUPERINTENDENT; NATIONAL PARK SERVICE - FORT SMITH NATIONAL HISTORIC SITE; PO BOX 1406; FORT SMITH, AR 72901. (#1469-210).

MAR 20 - 21, '76. UNITED STATES ARMED FORCES BICENTENNIAL CARAVAN. CARAVAN IS COMPOSED OF EXHIBIT VANS FOR EACH MILITARY SERVICE. PROJECT THEME IS 'HISTORY OF THE ARMED FORCES AND THEIR CONTRIBUTIONS TO THE NATION'. (LOCAL). JIM WILLIAMS, CHMN; US ARMED FORCES BICENTENNIAL EXHIBIT VANS PROJECT; 2518 FRESNO; FORT SMITH, AR 72901. (#1775-409).

APR 1 - 30, '76. FT SMITH AFFILIATION OF THE ARTS-CONCERTS & ART EXHIBITS CITYWIDE. A TWELVE MEMBER ORGANIZATION WILL PRESENT PROGRAMS IN 1976 FOR THE BICENTENNIAL PROGRAMS WILL INCLUDE THEATRE, ART SHOWS, MUSICAL PERFORMANCES, HISTORICAL PAGEANTS AND MUSEUM EXHIBITS. SYMPHONY CONCERTS ART EXHIBITS THROUGHOUT THE CITY. AT CITYWIDE. (LOCAL). JIM WILLIAMS, CHAIRMAN; FORT SMITH BICENTENNIAL COMMITTEE; 2518 S FRESNO; FORT SMITH, AR 72901. (#2352-1).

APR 1 - NOV 1, '76. NATURE TOURS THROUGH FORT SMITH NATURE AREA. NATURE AREA OF FORT SMITH, ARKANSAS. ESTABLISH AS A LITTLE WILDLIFE PLACE & USE AS NATURE CNTR WITH PROPER SIGNS & FENCING, PLANT BERRY & FRUIT TREES, MAKE TRAILS & CONDUCT TOURS. EDUCATE PEOPLE ON NATURAL HISTORY. (LOCAL). CAROL SUE WOOTEN; FORT SMITH AUDUBON SOCIETY; 2600 RIVIERA CIRCLE; FORT SMITH, AR 72901. (#3428-501).

APR 24 - 25, '76. 1976 BELLE FORT SMITH TOUR - FEATURING THE CITY'S HISTORIC DISTRICT. THIS 3RD ANNUAL TOUR WILL FEATURE THE 22 SQUARE BLOCK BELLE GROVE HISTORIC DISTRICT, THAT IS LISTED ON THE NATIONAL REGISTER AND CONTAINS THE LARGEST CONCENTRATION OF 19TH CENTURY HOUSES IN THE CITY, MANY OF WHICH HAVE BEEN, ARE BEING OR WILL BE RESTORED. AT BELLE GROVE HISTORIC DISTRICT - THREE BLOCKS NORTH OF GARRISON AVE. (LOCAL). JOHN V ROBINSON, PROJ DIR; BELLE FORT SMITH ASSOC; P O BOX 1412; FORT SMITH, AR 72901. (#100609-1).

MAY 1, '76. A BICENTENNIAL SALUTE TO YOUTH. LIVE PERFORMANCE AT FORT SMITH FAIRGROUNDS. (LOCAL). JOE BEARDSLEY, DIRECTOR; HYLAND DISTRICT 2 OF ARKANSAS CREDIT UNION LEAGUE; S JENNY LIND RD; FORT SMITH, AR 72901. (#19063-1).

MAY 15 - 16, '76. BICENTENNIAL FAIR. FAIR AT FORT SMITH EXHIBIT HALL. (ST-WIDE). DOROTHY RUCKER; FORT SMITH VOLUNTARY ACTION CENTER; PO BOX 3572; FORT SMITH, AR 72901. (#18669-1).

JUNE 18 - 19, '76. PATRIOTIC MUSICAL '1776'. LIVE PERFORMANCE AT FORT SMITH AUDITORIUM. (LOCAL). WALTER C MINNICAR; FORT SMITH SYMPHONY ASSOC; 6800 SO 'W'; FORT SMITH, AR 72901. (#21350-1).

JULY 13 - 14, '76. NATL PK SVC 'PEOPLE OF 1776' PLAYS AT FT SMITH NHS. TRAVELING TROUPE WILL BRING VARIOUS ASPECTS OF COLONIAL LIFE (MILITARY LIFE, MUSIC, CRAFTS) TO VISITORS TO THIS NATIONAL PARK SERVICE AREA. (REGN'L). FT SMITH N H S; NATIONAL PARK SERVICE; P.O. BOX 1406; FT SMITH, AR 72901. (#1469-8).

GENTRY

GENTRY BICENTENNIAL PROGRAMS, AR. THE CITY PLANS TO BUILD A BRICK PLANTER AROUND THE CITY FLAGPOLE WITH A PLAQUE INSCRIBED WITH THE LOGO AND INFORMATION ON GENTRY'S OFFICIAL DESIGNATION. BOOKS WILL BE BOUGHT & PLACED IN CITY LIBRARY. (LOCAL). HON LARRY DAGGS, MAYOR; CITY OF GENTRY; CITY HALL; GENTRY, AR 72734. (#26818). **ARBA GRANTEE.**

GILLETT

ECOLOGY MOVEMENT IN GILLETT, ARKANSAS. FURNISH TREES AND LABOR FOR ANYONE AT ANY LOCATION IN ARKANSAS SO THAT THEY MAY PARTICIPATE IN THIS BICENTENNIAL PROJECT. (LOCAL). MRS JEAN POLLARD, CHAIRMAN; ARKANSAS COUNTY BICENTENNIAL COMMITTEE; 808 W 18TH ST; STUTTGART, AR 72160. (#3882).

EXPANSION OF ARKANSAS COUNTY MUSEUM. NEW EXHIBITS & EXPANSION OF OLD DISPLAYS IN COUNTY MUSEUM INCL INSTALLATION OF ADEQUATE LIGHTING IN EXHIBIT AREA. (LOCAL). THELMA MATTMILLER, CURATOR; ARKANSAS COUNTY MUSEUM; STATE HIGHWAY 1; GILLETT, AR 72055. (#3875). **ARBA GRANTEE.**

GILLETT, ARKANSAS, BEAUTIFICATION PROJECT. COMMUNITY INVOLVEMENT PROG TO ENCOURAGE PRIDE IN LAWNS, HOMES & PUBLIC PROPERTY. (LOCAL). MRS JEAN POLLARD, CHAIRMAN; ARKANSAS COUNTY BICENTENNIAL COMMITTEE; 808 W 18TH; STUTTGART, AR 72160. (#3881).

GILLETT, AR, REVOLUTIONARY BATTLE COMMEMORATIVE. REPLICA OF FT SAN CARLOS, SITE OF COLBERT BATTLE, APRIL 1783; ONLY REVOLUTIONARY WAR INVOLVEMENT IN THE ARKANSAS AREA; AUDIO-VISUAL AIDS IN STRUCTURE LOCATED IN NATIONAL PARK. (LOCAL). MRS V S POLLARD, CHAIRMAN; ARKANSAS COUNTY BICENTENNIAL COMMITTEE; 808 W 18; STUTTGART, AR 72160. (#15237).

PUBLICATION OF HISTORIC DOCUMENTS IN ARKANSAS. TRANSLATION & PUBLICATION OF ABSTRACTS OF RECORDS OF FRENCH RULE & CATHOLIC MISSIONARY ACTIVITY IN ARKANSAS DURING THE 1700'S & 1800'S. 300 COPIES WILL BE AVAILABLE. (REGN'L). D L HUGGINS, PROJ DIRECTOR; GRAND PRAIRIE HISTORICAL SOCIETY OF ARKANSAS COUNTY; ARKANSAS COUNTY MUSEUM; GILLETT, AR 72055. (#11963). **ARBA GRANTEE.**

OCT 12, '75. EXPANSION OF ARKANSAS COUNTY MUSEUM - OPENING. NEW EXHIBITS & EXPANSION OF OLD DISPLAYS IN COUNTY MUSEUM INCL INSTALLATION OF ADEQUATE LIGHTING IN EXHIBIT AREA. AT NEAR ARK. POST MEMORIAL NEAR GILLETT. (LOCAL). MRS JEAN POLLARD, CHMN; ARKANSAS COUNTY BICENTENNIAL COMMISSION; 808 W 18TH STREET; STUTTGART, AR 72160. (#3875-1).

JAN 9, '76. 1976 RACOON SUPPER. LIVE PERFORMANCE AT GILLETT HIGH SCHOOL. (ST-WIDE). CLEON COLLIER, CO-CHMN; ARKANSAS COUNTY BICENTENNIAL COMMISSION; BOX 216; GILLETT, AR 72055. (#103389-1).

JUNE 10, '76. NATL PK SVC '...A LITTLE LOOK AROUND' VISITS ARKANSAS POST NM. THIS SHORT PROGRAM FEATURES ACTORS PORTRAYING FAMOUS AMERICANS OF THE PAST WHO'VE RETURNED TO SEE AMERICA'S PROGRESS. (REGN'L). ARKANSAS POST N MEM; NATIONAL PARK SERVICE; ROUTE 1, BOX 16; GILLETT, AR 72055. (#5653-74).

JULY 4, '76. ARKANSAS COUNTY BICENTENNIAL OBSERVANCE. FRENCH SPANISH & AM INDIANS WILL BE INVITED TO PARTICIPATE IN CEREMONY BECAUSE OF THEIR TIE TO THE HISTORY OF THIS AREA & RECOGNITION OF THEIR PART IN REVOLUTIONARY BATTLE FOUGHT AT THIS SITE. GOLF TOURNEY STARTS IN JUNE, MAJOR OBSERVANCE, JULY 4, 1976. AT ARKANSAS NATIONAL MEMORIAL PARK. (LOCAL). MRS J S POLLARD, CHMN; ARKANSAS COUNTY BICENTENNIAL COMMITTEE; 808 W 18TH; STUTTGART, AR 72160. (#102408-2).

JULY 4, '76. REVOLUTIONARY BATTLE COMMEMORATIVE DEDICATION. CEREMONY AT ARKANSAS POST NATIONAL MEMORIAL, HWY 1 S, FREE PARKING. (LOCAL). MRS J S POLLARD, CHMN; ARKANSAS COUNTY BICENTENNIAL COMMITTEE; 808 W 18TH; STUTTGART, AR 72160. (#102441-2).

GLENWOOD

GLENWOOD BICENTENNIAL CELEBRATION, AR. THE TOWN IS CONSTRUCTING A HISTORICAL MARKER AND EXHIBIT COMMEMORATING THE CREATION OF THE TOWN. THEY WILL CONSTRUCT A FLOAT FOR THE COUNTY FAIR AND A WELCOME SIGN AT ENTRANCE TO TOWN. (LOCAL). HON J HARDY SPRADLIN, MAYOR; CITY OF GLENWOOD; CITY HALL; GLENWOOD, AR 71943. (#26802). **ARBA GRANTEE.**

GRADY

NEW FLAG & POLE FOR SCHOOL IN GRADY, AR. ERECTED FLAGPOLE AT ELEMENTARY SCHOOL; STATE REPRESENTATIVE PRESENTED FLAG & LOCAL TELEVISION COVERED EVENT. (LOCAL). KAY M LEMORE, PRESIDENT; DELTA CHI SORORITY; GRADY, AR 71644. (#31164).

GRAVETTE

BICENT LIBRARY - MUSEUM IN GRAVETTE, ARKANSAS. A LIBRARY-MUSEUM COMPLEX WILL BE ESTABLISHED IN THE CIVIC

GRAVETTE — CONTINUED

CENTER OF GRAVETTE IN HONOR OF THE BICENTENNIAL; ITEMS OF SIGNIFICANCE FROM THE AREA WILL BE ON DISPLAY. (LOCAL). ROBERT D EVANS, CHAIRMAN; GRAVETTE BICENT COMMITTEE; PO BOX 117; GRAVETTE, AR 72736. (#8905).

GRAVETTE BICENTENNIAL PROJECTS -AR. PROJECTS INCLUDE THE ESTABLISHMENT OF A LIBRARY AND MUSEUM FOR THE CITY AND THE RENOVATION OF A GAZEBO FOR A COMMUNITY FACILITY. (LOCAL). HON ROBERT M WOODS, MAYOR; GRAVETTE BICENTENNIAL COMMITTEE; CITY HALL; GRAVETTE, AR 72736. (#17607). **ARBA GRANTEE.**

RENOVATION OF 'OLD TOWN PARK', GRAVETTE, ARKANSAS. A CLEAN-UP AND RENOVATION OF OLD TOWN PARK IS PLANNED. THE PARK WAS THE SITE OF NEBO, A COMMUNITY THAT PRECEDED GRAVETTE. THE PARK IS PRESENTLY UNUSABLE. (LOCAL). ROBERT D EVANS, CHAIRMAN; GRAVETTE BICENT COMMITTEE; PO BOX 117; GRAVETTE, AR 72736. (#10129).

AUG 14, '76. ANNIVERSARY CELEBRATION. A CELEBRATION TO COMMEMORATE THE FOUNDING OF GRAVETTE IS PLANNED BY HER CITIZENS. THE FESTIVITIES WILL INCLUDE A PARADE, A BAR-B-QUE, ENTERTAINMENT AND PAGEANT. AT KINDLEY MEMORIAL PARK. (LOCAL). ROBERT D EVANS, DIR; GRAVETTE BICENTENNIAL COMMITTEE; PO BOX 117; GRAVETTE, AR 72736. (#8902-1).

GREGORY

HISTORICAL LAND MARKERS - GREGORY, AR. 4 PERMANENT MARKERS TO IDENTIFY COMMUNITIES OF HISTORICAL INTEREST; ORGANIZATIONS & INDIVIDUALS ARE INVITED TO JOIN THE HISTORICAL SOCIETY IN FINDING LOCATIONS, BUYING AND PLACING THE MARKERS. (LOCAL). MRS JOHN B KITTRELL, PRESIDENT; WOODRUFF COUNTY HISTORICAL SOCIETY; GREGORY, AR 72059. (#18455).

HAMBURG

SEPT 10 - 13, '75. ASHLEY COUNTY FAIR & MISS ASHLEY COUNTY PAGEANT. COMPETITION, FAIR, LIVE PERFORMANCE AT FAIR GROUNDS & FAIR AUDITORIUM. (LOCAL). GORDON HARTRICK, COORD; ASHLEY COUNTRY FAIR ASSOC; S CHERRY; HAMBURG, AR 71646. (#200005-9).

OCT 23 - 26, '75. ASHLEY COUNTY ARTS AND CRAFTS FAIR. EXHIBIT, FAIR AT FAIRGROUNDS BUILDINGS. (LOCAL). MRS T J MALLOY, COORD; ASHLEY COUNTY EXTENSION SERVICES; CROSSETT, AR 71635. (#200005-10).

NOV 12, '75. FLAG RAISING CEREMONY. CEREMONY AT SQUARE IN HAMBURG. (LOCAL). HON W HIGGINBOTHAM, JUDGE; ASHLEY COUNTY BICENTENNIAL COMMITTEE; S MAIN; HAMBURG, AR 71646. (#200005-8).

NOV 27, '75. SQUARE DANCING FESTIVAL. FESTIVAL, LIVE PERFORMANCE AT CITY SQUARE. (LOCAL). MRS JACKIE TUMLISON, CHMN; HAMBURG SQUARE DANCING CLUB; HAMBURG, AR 71646. (#200005-11).

APR 29, '76. SUPER DAY OF CELEBRATION. GOVERNOR TO BE PRESENT, ALSO MISS ARKANSAS, REPRESENTATIVES, SENATORS, FREE BOX LUNCHES, DRINKS FOR PICNIC, BOXES USING RED, WHITE & BLUE BALLONS, FLAGS, IMPRINTED BUTTONS, ARMED FORCES, SCOUTS & NATIONAL GUARD PRESENT. AT FOOTBALL STADIUM. (LOCAL). JUDGE W T HIGGINBOTHAM; ASHLEY COUNTY AMERICAN REVOLUTION BICENTENNIAL COMMITTEE; ASHLEY COUNTY COURTHOUSE; HAMBURG, AR 71646. (#103671-1).

HAMPTON

CALHOUN COUNTY MONUMENT TO DECEASED VETERANS - AR. A MONUMENT TO HONOR THOSE MEN OF CALHOUN COUNTY WHO GAVE THEIR LIVES IN SERVICE TO THEIR COUNTRY. (LOCAL). MARION O'MARY, COUNTY JUDGE; CALHOUN COUNTY BICENTENNIAL COMMITTEE; BOX 566; HAMPTON, AR 71744. (#25786). **ARBA GRANTEE.**

HARRISBURG

BICENTENNIAL MINI-PARK, HARRISBURG, AR. DEVELOPMENT OF AN EMPTY LOT ON COURT SQUARE INTO A BEAUTIFUL, SMALL PARK AREA FINANCED BY PRIVATE DONATIONS AND A BICENTENNIAL GRANT. (LOCAL). MRS ARNOLD COOPER, CHAIRMAN; HARRISBURG BICENTENNIAL COMMISSION; 1 DOGWOOD LANE; HARRISBURG, AR 72432. (#23940).

MAY 1, '76. BICENTENNIAL FESTIVAL. DISPLAYS, CRAFT BOOTHS, CAKE WALKS, TORTOISE RACE, CONCESSION STANDS, FISH FRY, DEDICATION CEREMONY FOR HARRISBURG BICENTENNIAL MINI-PARK AND STREET DANCE. AT COURT SQUARE. (LOCAL). MRS ARNOLD COOPER, CHMN; HARRISBURG BICENTENNIAL COMMISSION; 1 DOGWOOD LANE; HARRISBURG, AR 72432. (#107111-1).

HARRISON

BOONE COUNTY BICENTENNIAL PHOTO ARCHIVES - AR. THE ESTABLISHMENT OF A LOCAL PHOTO ARCHIVES IN THE REGIONAL LIBRARY TO PRESERVE HISTORIC PHOTOGRAPHS AND PROMOTE INTEREST IN HISTORY AND THE BICENTENNIAL. (LOCAL). ROGER V LOGAN, JR, CHAIRMAN; BOONE CO BICENTENNIAL COMMITTEE; PO BOX 58; HARRISON, AR 72601. (#17609). **ARBA GRANTEE.**

HARTFORD

BICENTENNIAL FLOWER BEDS - HARTFORD, AR. FLOWER BEDS IN THE SHAPE OF THE BICENTENNIAL LOGO WERE PLANTED AT BOTH ENTRANCES TO THE TOWN. (LOCAL). HON NORMA MICHAEL, MAYOR; HARTFORD BICENTENNIAL COMMITTEE; BOX 69; HARTFORD, AR 72938. (#31292).

DEC 8 - 9, '76. ARTS & CRAFTS FAIR. FAIR AT W J HAMILTON MEMORIAL MUSEUM. (LOCAL). HON NORMA MICHAEL, MAYOR; HARTFORD BICENTENNIAL COMMITTEE; BOX 69; HARTFORD, AR 72938. (#109496-1).

HAVANA

COMMUNITY IMPROVEMENTS - HAVANA, AR. PLACING A FLAG POLE IN FRONT OF A BUILDING WHICH THE VFW IS RENOVATING FOR THE YOUNG PEOPLE OF THE COMMUNITY. TREES WILL BE PLANTED IN THE PARK AND ON THE SIDES OF THE HIGHWAY. (LOCAL). HON EUGENE BURROWS, MAYOR; CITY OF HAVANA; CITY HALL; HAVANA, AR 72842. (#26803). **ARBA GRANTEE.**

HEBER SPRINGS

OZARK FRONTIER TRAIL FESTIVAL & CRAFTS SHOW, AR. SHOW WILL FEATURE CRAFTS REFLECTING LOCAL CULTURE. (LOCAL). DEAN MASON, COORDINATOR; ORGANIZATIONS UNITER; 103 N 4TH ST; HEBER SPRINGS, AR 72543. (#21210). **ARBA GRANTEE.**

OCT 10 - 12, '75. OZARK FRONTIER TRAIL FESTIVAL & CRAFT SHOW. EXHIBIT, FESTIVAL AT COUNTY FAIRGROUNDS. (LOCAL). DEAN MASON, COORD; ORGANIZATIONS UNITER; 103 N 4TH ST; HEBER SPRINGS, AR 72543. (#21210-1).

HELENA

BICENTENNIAL CONCERTS FOR PHILLIPS COUNTY, ARK. A SERIES OF 5 ORGAN CONCERTS WILL BE PRESENTED TO THE PUBLIC FOR 3 YEARS AS A BICENTENNIAL CONTRIBUTION BY LILY PETER. CONCERTS WILL BE GIVEN BY AN EMINENT ORGANIST AND WILL BE FREE TO THE PUBLIC. (LOCAL). LILY PETER & CAROLYN CUNNINGHAM, CO-CHAIRMEN; PHILLIPS CO BICENTENNIAL COMMITTEE; RT 1; MARVELL, AR 72366. (#2357).

COMMUNITY BEAUTIFICATION AND EDUCATION, AR. OVERALL PROJECT OF BEAUTIFICATION IN HELENA-WEST HELENA. (LOCAL). DR JOHN EASLEY, PRESIDENT; PHILLIPS COUNTY COMMUNITY COLLEGE; 326 CHERRY ST; HELENA, AR 72342. (#18668).

FIRST FOURTH OF JULY CELEBRATION IN AMERICA - ARK. THE RECORDING OF THE FIRST JULY 4 CELEBRATION COMPOSED BY JOHN F. PETER OF THE MORAVIAN CHURCH WILL BE MADE AVAILABLE BY LILY PETER OF MARVELL, ARKANSAS, IN MEMORY OF HER ANCESTOR. (ST-WIDE). LILY PETER, CO-CHAIRMAN; PHILLIPS CO BICENTENNIAL COMMITTEE; RT 1; MARVELL, AR 72366. (#2356). **(??).**

HENDRIX COLLEGE CHOIR CONCERT IN ARKANSAS. A SPECIAL PERFORMANCE BY THE HENDRIX COLLEGE CHOIR, DEC 1 IN HELENA, ARK. IT'S THE FIRST IN A SERIES OF 5 CONCERTS. THE 'CANDLELIGHT SERVICE' IS SPONSORED BY LILLY PETER OF MARVELL, ARKANSAS. (LOCAL). LILY PETER, CO-CHAIRMAN; PHILLIPS COUNTY BICENTENNIAL ORGANIZATION; ROUTE 1; MARVELL, AR 72366. (#3082).

MEXICAN CARNIVAL - HELENA, ARKANSAS. THE MEXICAN CARNIVAL FROM COLUMBIA ARTISTS WILL PERFORM IN HELENA. MEXICAN ART, MUSIC, SONG & DANCE WILLBE PRESENTED RELATING TO THE SPANISH HERITAGE OF THE SOUTHWEST. (LOCAL). LILY PETER, CO-CHAIRMAN; PHILLIPS CO BICENTENNIAL COMMITTEE; RT 1; MARVELL, AR 72366. (#2358).

OLD ALMER STORE RESTORATION IN ARKANSAS. RESTORATION OF OLD ALMER STORE; ONE OF THE OLDEST BUILDINGS IN THE HELENA AREA TO BE USED AS A COMMUNITY ARTS AND CRAFTS COOPERATIVE;. (ST-WIDE). JOHN M CONWAY, PRESIDENT; PHILLIPS COUNTY FOUNDATION FOR HISTORIC PRESERVATION; PO BOX 367; HELENA, AR 72342. (#530). **ARBA GRANTEE.**

JULY '73. JOLLIET-MARQUETTE TRICENTENNIAL CELEBRATION - ARK. RE-CREATION OF THE JOLLIET-MARQUETTE VOYAGE TO CELEBRATE THE 300TH ANNIVERSARY OF THE EXPLORATION OF THE MISSISSIPPI RIVER. (LOCAL). CAROLYN CUNNINGHAM; JOLLIET-MARQUETTE COMMITTEE; 138 N 3RD ST; W HELENA, AR 72390. (#2354-1).

JULY 9 - 14, '74. SERENDIPITY WEEK - AN ANNUAL WEEK OF FESTIVITIES. FESTIVALS, PLAYS, CONCERTS, BALLS, TOURS, ARTS & CRAFTS SHOWS IN HONOR OF THE BICENTENNIAL & THE CIVIL WAR BATTLE OF HELENA. WILL BE HELD IN 1974, 1975 & 1976. (LOCAL). HUNTER BELL, CHAIRMAN; SERENDIPITY COMMITTEE; 14 OAK FOREST CIRCLE; HELENA, AR 72342. (#1705-901).

APR 18, '75. MILWAUKEE SYMPHONY BICENTENNIAL CONCERT. THE SECOND OF 5 BICENTENNIAL CONCERTS IN HELENA, THE PROGRAM WILL FEATURE SELECTIONS BY AMERICAN COMPOSERS. (LOCAL). LILY PETER, CO-CHAIRMAN; PHILLIPS COUNTY BICENTENNIAL ORGANIZATION; RT 1; MARVELL, AR 72366. (#3083-501).

JULY 16, '75. OTRABANDA COMPANY'S THIRD ANNUAL MISSISSIPPI RIVER TOUR. LIVE PERFORMANCE, PARADE AT CITY PARK, NORTH END OF CHERRY ST.. (LOCAL). CHARLES FITE, DIRECTOR; CHAMBER OF COMMERCE; P.O. BOX 447; HELENA, AR 72342. (#50550-11).

APR 24 - 25, '76. HELENA PILGRIMAGE. TOUR AT CITYWIDE. (LOCAL). MRS LJ PATRICK BELL; PHILLIPS COUNTY FOUNDATION FOR HISTORIC PRESERVATION INC.; WAVERLY WOODS; HELENA, AR 72342. (#50816-1).

SEPT 23, '76. AMERICAN WIND SYMPHONY'S FLOATING ARTS CENTER VISITS HELENA. EMBARKING UPON A BICENTENNIAL CULTURAL TOUR, THE WIND SYMPHONY WILL VISIT 76 CITIES BRINGING MUSIC, DANCE, SYMPOSIA & CHILDREN'S THEATER TO THE WATERWAYS OF AMERICA DURING ITS 6 MONTH TOUR. AT MISSISSIPPI RIVERFRONT ON MAIN STREET. (ST-WIDE). RAYMOND KUMMER, CHAIRMAN; AMERICAN WIND SYMPHONY & PHILLIPS CO. BICENT COMM; 306 CHERRY ST; HELENA, AR 72342. (#2800-41).

MAR 5 - 8, '77. LA SALLE EXPEDITION II, A HISTORIC RE-ENACTMENT. THIS IS AN AUTHENTIC RE-ENACTMENT OF THE 1681 LASALLE EXPEDITION FROM MONTREAL, CANADA TO NEW ORLEANS, LA WHICH WILL BEGIN TOURING ON AUGUST 11, 1976 AND END ON APRIL 9, 1977. (LOCAL). REID H LEWIS, DIRECTOR; LA SALLE EXPEDITION II; 135 S LA SALLE ST, RM 411; CHICAGO, IL 60690. (#102805-60).

HINDSVILLE

OCT 15 - 17, '76. 23RD ANNUAL OZARK ARTS AND CRAFTS FAIR. EXHIBIT, FESTIVAL AT WAR EAGLE MILLS FARM. (REGN'L). BLANCHE H ELLIOTT, COORD; OZARKS ART & CRAFTS FAIR ASSOC. INC.; ROUTE 1; HINDSVILLE, AR 72738. (#103416-637).

HOLIDAY ISL

JULY 3 - 5, '76. 4TH OF JULY CELEBRATION. FIREWORKS, WATER SHOW, AND NATIVE CRAFTS DEMONSTRATIONS. AT TABLE ROCK LAKE. (LOCAL). JIM QUIGGLE, CHAIRMAN; CARROLL COUNTY BICENTENNIAL COMMITTEE; HOLIDAY ISL, AR 72632. (#101882-1).

HORATIO

HISTORICAL MARKER PROJECT IN HORATIO, AR. HISTORICAL MARKERS WILL BE ERECTED IN HORATIO. (LOCAL). LUISE P THOMPSON, DIRECTOR; SEVIER COUNTY HISTORICAL SOCIETY; HORATIO, AR 71842. (#29883).

ORGANIZE HISTORICAL SOCIETY IN HORATIO, AR. ORGANIZE SEVIER CO HISTORICAL SOCIETY & HELP COMPILE LOCAL HISTORY FOR PRESERVATION OF PAST. (LOCAL). HENRY C MORRIS, PRESIDENT; SEVIER COUNTY HISTORICAL SOCIETY; 118 W STILWELL; DE QUEEN, AR 71832. (#29882).

PAINT FIREPLUGS WITH BICENT THEME - HORATIO, AR. LOCAL SCHOOL STUDENTS INVOLVED IN PAINTING FIREPLUGS FOR COMMUNITY IMPROVEMENT. (LOCAL). PAT ADCOCK, SPONSOR; HORATIO HIGH SCHOOL STUDENT COUNCIL; HORATIO, AR 71842. (#29880).

PLANT LIBERTY TREE IN HORATIO, AR. CENTENNIAL GARDEN CLUB DEDICATES MAGNOLIA TREE IN CITY PARK AS CLUB BICENT LIBERTY TREE. (LOCAL). MRS MILDRED BROWN; CENTENNIAL GARDEN CLUB; HORATIO, AR 71842. (#29881).

APR 9, '76. BICENTENNIAL FLAG CEREMONY. COMMUNITY PARTICIPATION WITH LT GOV OF AR. AT HORATIO CITY PARK. (LOCAL). LUISE P THOMPSON; HORATIO BICENTENNIAL COMMISSION; ROUTE 1; HORATIO, AR 71842. (#200005-91).

JULY 2 - 3, '76. ARTS & CRAFTS SHOW WITH LOCAL PROFESSIONAL ARTISTS FEATURED. EXHIBIT AT HORATIO HS. (LOCAL). LUISE P THOMPSON; HORATIO BICENTENNIAL COMMISSION; ROUTE 1; HORATIO, AR 71842. (#200005-90).

JULY 4, '76. OLD TIMEY PICNIC FOURTH OF JULY. LIVE PERFORMANCE AT CITY PARK. (LOCAL). LUISE P THOMPSON; HORATIO BICENTENNIAL COMMISSION; ROUTE ONE; HORATIO, AR 71842. (#200005-89).

OCT 26 - 27, '76. EXHIBIT OF OLD THINGS. EXHIBIT AT LIBRARY. (LOCAL). JOHNIE MEREDITH; HORATIO HS HISTORY DEPT; HORATIO, AR 71842. (#200005-88).

HOT SPRINGS

HOME AND GARDEN SHOW, HOT SPRINGS, AR. EXHIBIT OF CRAFTS AND LOCAL CULTURE. (LOCAL). CAROLYN HOLIMAN, COORDINATOR; HOT SPRINGS COUNCIL OF GARDEN CLUBS; 304 YORKSHIRE DR; HOT SPRINGS, AR 71901. (#23671). **ARBA GRANTEE.**

HOT SPRINGS BICENTENNIAL PARK IN ARKANSAS. CONSTRUCTION OF 2 PARK FACILITIES, INCLUDING LANDSCAPING ROADS, TRAILS AND PICNIC AREAS. (LOCAL). HON PAUL SHUFFIELD, JUDGE; HOT SPRINGS COUNTY; COURT HOUSE; MALVERN, AR 72104. (#22853). **ARBA GRANTEE.**

'76 HERITAGE HOUSE REPLICA - HOT SPRINGS, AR. PRODUCE AN AUTHENTIC REPLICA OF COLONIAL HOUSE IN MINIATURE FORM. (LOCAL). MRS CHARLOTTE B BROWN, CHAIRMAN; WOMENS COUNCIL OF 13; 203 DEANWOOD; HOT SPRINGS, AR 71901. (#18681). **ARBA GRANTEE.**

MAR 12 - 14, '76. UNITED STATES ARMED FORCES BICENTENNIAL CARAVAN. CARAVAN IS COMPOSED OF EXHIBIT VANS FOR EACH MILITARY SERVICE. PROJECT THEME IS 'HISTORY OF THE ARMED FORCES AND THEIR CONTRIBUTIONS TO THE NATION'. (LOCAL). MORT COX, CHMN; US ARMED FORCES BICENTENNIAL EXHIBIT VANS PROJECT; PO BOX 5640; HOT SPRINGS, AR 71901. (#1775-407).

HOT SPRINGS — CONTINUED

JUNE 8 - 9, '76. 'AMERICA THE BEAUTIFUL' BICENTENNIAL FLOWER SHOW. EXHIBIT AT CONVENTION AUDITORIUM. (LOCAL). GEORGE ISENHOWER, CHMN; HOT SPRINGS CHAMBER OF COMMERCE; PO BOX 1500; HOT SPRINGS, AR 71901. (#103416-359).

JUNE 11, '76. NATL PK SVC '...A LITTLE LOOK AROUND' VISITS HOT SPRINGS N P. THIS SHORT PROGRAM FEATURES ACTORS PORTRAYING FAMOUS AMERICANS OF THE PAST WHO'VE RETURNED TO SEE AMERICA'S PROGRESS. (REGN'L). HOT SPRINGS NATL PK; NATIONAL PARK SERVICE; P.O. BOX 1219; HOT SPRINGS, AR 71901. (#5653-75).

JUNE 12 - 13, '76. HOME AND GARDEN SHOW. EXHIBIT AT CONVENTION AUDITORIUM MAIN ROOM. (LOCAL). CAROLYN HOLIMAN; HOT SPRINGS COUNCIL OF GARDEN CLUBS; 304 YORKSHIRE DR; HOT SPRINGS, AR 71901. (#23671-1).

JUNE 28 - AUG 28, '76. 'HERNANDO DESOTO, CONQUISTADOR', OUTDOOR DRAMA. A NEW AMPHITHEATRE ACCOMODATES THE PREMIER SEASON OF THIS OFFICIALLY RECOGNIZED BICENTENNIAL DRAMA ON THE EXPEDITION OF 16TH CENTURY CONQUISTADOR, HERNANDO DESOTO. AT MID-AMERICA AMPHITHEATRE, US HWY 270. (REGN'L). JOHN E BLIZZARD; HOT SPRINGS NATIONAL PARK FOUNDATION FOR PERFORMING ARTS; PO BOX 1259; HOT SPRINGS, AR 71901. (#925-1).

OCT 1 - 3, '76. 8TH ANNUAL HOT SPRINGS ARTS & CRAFTS FAIR. FAIR AT GARLAND COUNTY FAIRGROUNDS. (LOCAL). JOYCE GRAVES, COORD; GARLAND COUNTY EXTENSION HOMEMAKERS COUNCIL; 1413 BLULLBAYOU RD; HOT SPRINGS, AR 71901. (#103416-547).

HOUSTON

HOUSTON BICENTENNIAL PARK IMPROVEMENT - AR. THE CITY OF HOUSTON PLANS TO CONSTRUCT RESTROOM FACILITIES IN THEIR CITY PARK. (LOCAL). HON B B WOOLF, MAYOR; CITY OF HOUSTON; PO BOX 217; HOUSTON, AR 72070. (#26936). **ARBA GRANTEE.**

HOXIE

COMMUNITY BEAUTIFICATION PROJECT - HOXIE, AR. EFFORT BY LOCAL YOUTH AND PUBLIC SCHOOL INSTRUCTORS TO PLANT 200 PINE SEEDLINGS AND 100 RED MAPLE TREE SEEDLINGS TO BEAUTIFY THE HOXIE AREA IN YEARS TO COME. (LOCAL). JOHN WEIR, CHAIRMAN; HOXIE BICENTGENNIAL COMMITTEE; HOXIE, AR 72433. (#29783).

HUNTER

CHURCH HISTORY - HUNTER, AR. EACH LOCAL CHURCH IS COMPILING HISTORY WHICH WILL BE INCORPORATED INTO ONE PUBLICATION. (LOCAL). MILDRED BURFORD, CO-CHAIRPERSON; HUNTER BICENTENNIAL COMMITTEE; HUNTER, AR 72074. (#23902).

JULY 3, '76. OLD-FASHIONED PICNIC. FESTIVAL. (LOCAL). SUE GREENE, CHAIRPERSON; HUNTER BICENTENNIAL COMMITTEE; HUNTER, AR 72074. (#107116-1).

JACKSONVILLE

AMPHITHEATRE PROJECT-JACKSONVILLE, AR. CITY OF JACKSONVILLE WILL CONSTRUCT AN AMPHITHEATRE WHICH WOULD BE A COMPLETE COMMUNITY FACILITY AND WOULD BE AVAILABLE TO ALL CIVIC GROUPS. (LOCAL). JAMES T CANFIELD, CHAIRMAN; JACKSONVILLE BICENTENNIAL COMMITTEE; 109 S 2ND ST; JACKSONVILLE, AR 72076. (#19059). **ARBA GRANTEE.**

HISTORICAL MARKERS PROJECT OF JACKSONVILLE, AR. THREE HISTORICAL MARKERS ARE BEING PLACED, INCLUDING ONE AT ENTRANCE OF BAYOU METO CEMETERY, A MEMPHIS MILITARY ROAD MARKER, & A SOUTHWEST TRAIL MARKER NEAR MAIN GATE OF LITTLE ROCK AIR FORCE BASE. (LOCAL). MICHAEL D HAGGE, GRANT COORDINATOR; CITY OF JACKSONVILLE; 109 S 2ND ST; JACKSONVILLE, AR 72076. (#28301).

MURRELL TAYLOR COMMEMORATION PROJECT IN ARK. CONSISTS OF A SUNDIAL AND A ROCK GARDEN LOCATED ON THE ELEMENTARY SCHOOL GROUNDS & PLACED THERE IN HONOR OF MISS MURRELL TAYLOR, PRINCIPAL OF THE SCHOOL, WHO DEDICATED HER LIFE TO JACKSONVILLE YOUTH. (LOCAL). HON JAMES G REID, MAYOR; CITY OF JACKSONVILLE; 109 S 2ND ST; JACKSONVILLE, AR 72076. (#26923). **ARBA GRANTEE.**

MAY 1, '76. LITTLE ROCK AIR FORCE BASE BICENTENNIAL OPEN HOUSE. MANY AIR FORCE AIRCRAFT ON DISPLAY; RETIREE CENTER; DEMONSTRATION BY AIR FORCE THUNDERBIRDS, ARMY GOLDEN NIGHTS, ARK AIR NATIONAL GUARD, ARMY NATIONAL GUARD, SECURITY POLICE WORKING DOGS; 308 MISSILE MAINT SQ DISPLAY AND RECRUITING DISPLAYS. AT LITTLE ROCK AIR FORCE BASE. (LOCAL). COL HAL DETRICK; LITTLE ROCK AIR FORCE BASE, MILITARY AIRLIFT WING; JACKSONVILLE, AR 72116. (#200005-77).

JASPER

NEWTON COUNTY BICENTENNIAL COOKBOOK, AR. THE WOMEN OF NEWTON COUNTY ARE COLLECTING THE OLD-TIME RECIPES THAT HAVE BEEN HANDED DOWN THROUGH GENERATIONS IN THEIR COUNTY. THEY PLAN TO EDIT THIS COLLECTION AND HAVE IT PRINTED AND BINDED. (LOCAL). COUNTY JUDGE; NEWTON COUNTY; JASPER, AR 72641. (#26816). **ARBA GRANTEE.**

JONESBORO

BICENTENNIAL EXHIBIT: SONS OF LIBERTY, AR. AN EXHIBIT OF REVOLUTIONARY WAR ARTIFACTS TO BE USED IN DEMONSTRATIONS AT SCHOOLS AND AT PUBLIC EVENTS. (LOCAL). DR EUGENE B WHITTLAKE, DIRECTOR; ARKANSAS STATE UNIV MUSEUM; DRAWER HH; JONESBORO, AR 72467. (#21209). **ARBA GRANTEE.**

HATTIE CARAWAY MEMORIAL, 1ST WOMAN IN SENATE, AR. A MEMORIAL IS BEING ERECTED IN HONOR OF HATTIE CARAWAY W/A PLAQUE LISTING HER CONTRIBUTION TO THE NATION'S HISTORY. SHE WAS APPOINTED TEMPORARY SUCESSOR TO HER HUSBAND, U S SEN THADDEUS H CARAWAY. (LOCAL). HON NEIL STALLINGS, MAYOR; CITY OF JONESBORO; JONESBORO, AR 72401. (#26720). **ARBA GRANTEE.**

PUBLICATION OF A BOOKLET - JONESBORO, AR. PUBLICATION OF A BOOKLET THAT WILL DESCRIBE ARKANSAS GOVERNMENT AS IT HAS DEVELOPED THROUGH ARKANSAS'S HISTORY. (LOCAL). BARBARA WEINSTOCK, PRESIDENT; LEAGUE OF WOMEN VOTERS OF ARKANSAS; 208 WILKINS; JONESBORO, AR 72401. (#23728). **ARBA GRANTEE.**

STATUE OF LIBERTY REPLICA, JONESBORO, AR. A REPLICA OF THE STATUE OF LIBERTY TO BE USED FOR ALL BICENTENNIAL ACTIVITIES IN THE AREA. (LOCAL). DR C L CRUMP, POST SURGEON; AMERICAN LEGION POST 21; 517 E WASHINGTON; JONESBORO, AR 72401. (#23508). **ARBA GRANTEE.**

DEC 1, '75 - CONTINUING . BICENTENNIAL EXHIBIT: SONS OF LIBERTY. A 3-PART DISPLAY: DOCUMENTS & NEWSPAPERS, MILITARY UNIFORMS, AND HOUSEHOLD TENSILS, CENTENNIAL OBJECTS, COMMEMORATIVE ITEMS & DOMESTIC OBJECTS. AT ENTRANCE HALL, MUSEUM, BASEMENT, D B ELLIS LIBRARY BLDG, CAMPUS. (REGN'L). DR EUGENE B WITTLAKE; ARKANSAS STATE UNIV MUSEUM - ASU CAMPUS; DRAWER HH; JONESBORO, AR 72467. (#21209-1).

MAR 10 - 11, '76. USA CORPS OF ENGINEERS MOBILE VAN VISITS JONESBORO, AR. A MULTI-MEDIA SHOW DEPICTING THE 200 YEAR HISTORY OF THE CORPS OF ENGINEERS & ITS ROLE IN THE EVOLUTION OF OUR NATION. AT JONESBORO NATIONAL GUARD ARMORY. (LOCAL). KENT CARMAIN, CHMN; USA CORPS OF ENGINEERS; US ARMY CORPS OF ENGINEERS; MEMPHIS, TN 38103. (#31165-7).

KINGSLAND

KINGSLAND PARK BEAUTIFICATION PROJECT - AR. CITY PARK WILL BE BEAUTIFIED. TWO LOGO SIGNS WILL BE HUNG, ANNOUNCING KINGSLAND'S OFFICIAL STATUS AS A BICENTENNIAL COMMUNITY. (LOCAL). HON LEONARD GRANDERSON, MAYOR; CITY OF KINGSLAND; CITY HALL; KINGSLAND, AR 71652. (#26933). **ARBA GRANTEE.**

LEAD HILL

HISTORICAL MARKER & PARK DEVELOPMENT - AR. A HISTORICAL MARKER AND FLAGPOLE WILL BE ERECTED TO COMMEMORATE AREA VETERANS; A MUSIC PAVILION AND BARBEQUE PIT WILL BE BUILT IN THE PARK. (LOCAL). GLADYS ZOBUS, PRESIDENT; LEAD HILL AREA CHAMBER OF COMMERCE; LEAD HILL, AR 72644. (#32073).

JULY 2 - 3, '76. LEAD HILL AREA FOURTH OF JULY CELEBRATION & PARK DEDICATION. ACTIVITIES INCLUDED A PARADE, CEREMONIES, AWARD, BAND CONCERT. AT LEAD HILL CITY PARK. (LOCAL). GLADYS ZOBUS, PRES; LEAD HILL AREA CHAMBER OF COMMERCE; LEAD HILL, AR 72644. (#200005-118).

LITTLE FLOCK

PARK BEAUTIFICATION - LITTLE FLOCK, AR. PLANS TO IMPROVE THE CITY PARK HAVE BEEN MADE INCLUDING THE PLANTING OF TREES & FLOWERS; HISTORICAL MARKER TO BE PLACED IN LITTLE FLOCK CHURCHYARD - ARMED TROOPS STATIONED THERE DURING THE CIVIL WAR. (LOCAL). HON J C MCLEOD, JR, MAYOR; CITY OF LITTLE FLOCK; ROUTE 2, BOX 70; ROGERS, AR 72756. (#26804). **ARBA GRANTEE.**

LITTLE ROCK

AFRO-AMERICAN HERITAGE THROUGH ORAL HISTORY, AR. THE ARKANSAS BRANCH OF THE ASSOCIATION FOR THE STUDY OF AFRO-AMERICAN LIFE AND HISTORY, PROPOSES TO BRING TO ARKANSAS AN OUTSTANDING HISTORIAN AS A GUEST LECTURER. (ST-WIDE). LARRY LEWIS, PRESIDENT; SOCIETY FOR THE STUDY OF AFRO-AMERICAN LIFE AND HISTORY; PO BOX 6103; LITTLE ROCK, AR 72206. (#21332). **ARBA GRANTEE.**

ARKANSAS ALLIANCE FOR THE ERADICATION OF VD. A STATE-WIDE EDUCATIONAL PROGRAM TO ERADICATE VENERAL DISEASE IS BEING SPONSORED BY THE ARKANSAS DEPARTMENT OF HEALTH & OTHER RELATED ORGANIZATIONS. (ST-WIDE). STEVE MCANALLY, COORDINATOR; ARKANSAS DEPT OF HEALTH; 4815 W MARKHAM; LITTLE ROCK, AR 72205. (#10133).

ARKANSAS BICENTENNIAL STATE MUSIC PROGRAM. THE ARKANSAS ORCHESTRA SOCIETY WILL PERFORM MUSIC OF AMERICAN COMPOSERS THROUGHOUT THE STATE IN AREAS WHICH HAVE NOT BEEN EXPOSED TO SYMPHONIC MUSIC. (ST-WIDE). KURT KLIPPSTATTER, MUSIC DIRECTOR; ARKANSAS ORCHESTRA SOCIETY; ROBINSON AUDITORIUM; LITTLE ROCK, AR 72201. (#18670). **ARBA GRANTEE.**

ARKANSAS BRANCH OF ASALH - DISPLAY. CREATE AND CIRCULATE THROUGHOUT THE STATE A PICTORIAL DISPLAY RELATING TO BLACKS IN ARKANSAS' SOCIETY. (ST-WIDE). DR DAN LITTLEFIELD, DIRECTOR; ARKANSAS BRNCH OF ASSC FOR THE STUDY OF AFRO-AMER LIFE & HISTORY; PO BOX 1603; LITTLE ROCK, AR 72206. (#21329). **ARBA GRANTEE.**

THE ARKANSAS ENTERPRISES FOR THE BLIND, INC. REHABILITATION CENTER FOR THE BLIND AND VISUALLY IMPAIRED. (LOCAL). JIM DAVIS, INFORMATION SPECIALIST; ARKANSAS ENTERPRISES FOR THE BLIND, INC; 2811 FAIR PARK BLVD; LITTLE ROCK, AR 72204. (#20033).

'ARKANSAS JUSTICE, THE FIRST 200 YEARS', A FILM. A 50 MINUTE TELEVISION FILM WILL BE UPDATED AND CONVERTED TO 16MM COLOR FILM, WHICH WILL BE MADE AVAILABLE TO SCHOOLS AND CIVIC CLUBS AS A FILMED ACCOUNT OF ARKANSAS HISTORY. (ST-WIDE). COL C E RANSICK, EXEC SECRETARY; ARKANSAS BAR FOUNDATION; 400 W MARKHAM; LITTLE ROCK, AR 72201. (#8219). **ARBA GRANTEE.**

ARMED FORCES VANS PROJECT OF ARKANSAS. FOUR VANS WILL TOUR THE STATE FOR ONE MONTH. EACH VAN WILL HAVE AN EXHIBIT RELATING TO THE BRANCHES OF THE ARMED FORCES ARMY, NAVY, MARINE, AND AIR FORCE. TO BE IN ARKANSAS ONE MONTH IN 30 CITIES. (ST-WIDE). CAPT JOHN FITCH, PROJECT OFFICER; DEPT OF DEFENSE; WRIGHT-PATTERSON AIR FORCE BASE; DAYTON, OH 45433. (#4318).

'AS WE DID IT' - LITTLE ROCK, AR. A PUBLICATION IN WHICH RETIRED TEACHERS IN ARKANSAS WILL COLLECT & COMPILE TEACHING EXPERIENCES WHICH WILL BE PRESERVED AS A CONTRIBUTION OF RETIRED TEACHERS TO THE STATE. (LOCAL). DOLPH CAMP, CHAIRPERSON; ARKANSAS RETIRED TEACHERS ASSOC; 7501 W MARKHAM; LITTLE ROCK, AR 72205. (#19061). **ARBA GRANTEE.**

BICENTENNIAL ART CONTEST IN LITTLE ROCK, AR. A BICENT ART CONTEST; FEATURING POETRY, PAINTING, PHOTOGRAPHY AND SCULPTURE WILL BE SPONSORED BY THE ART DEPARTMENT OF UNIVERSITY OF ARKANSAS, LITTLE ROCK. (LOCAL). DR CHARLES BOLTON, PROJ COORDINATOR; UNIV OF ARKANSAS, LITTLE ROCK, ARBC; 33RD & UNIVERSITY AVE; LITTLE ROCK, AR 72204. (#10131).

BICENTENNIAL FESTIVAL OF MUSIC - LITTLE ROCK, AR. A MUSIC FESTIVAL WILL BE HELD TO COMMEMORATE THE BICENTENNIAL. (LOCAL). MRS JOHN FORTENBERRY, DIRECTOR; ARKANSAS FEDERATION OF MUSIC CLUBS, INC; 201 AUBURN DR; LITTLE ROCK, AR 72205. (#18671). **ARBA GRANTEE.**

A BICENTENNIAL MUSICAL - LITTLE ROCK, AR. PRESENTATION OF AN ORIGINAL CHILDREN'S MUSICAL WITH A HISTORICAL, EDUCATIONAL AND INSPIRATIONAL CONTENT. (LOCAL). RAND HOPKINS, DIRECTOR CHILDRENS THEATRE; ARKANSAS ARTS CENTER; MACARTHUR PARK; LITTLE ROCK, AR 72201. (#19360). **ARBA GRANTEE.**

BICENTENNIAL PLAZA, LITTLE ROCK, AR. THE CITY OF LITTLE ROCK-BICENTENNIAL COMMITTEE PLANS A BICENTENNIAL PLAZA WITH A MEMORIAL DEDICATED TO ALL ARKANSANS WHO HAVE GIVEN THEIR LIVES IN SERVICE TO THEIR COUNTRY. (LOCAL). CARLETON MCMULLIN, CITY MANAGER; CITY OF LITTLE ROCK; MARKHAM AND BROADWAY; LITTLE ROCK, AR 72202. (#23590). **ARBA GRANTEE.**

BLACK ARKANSAS NEWSPAPERS, SURVEY, LITTLE ROCK, AR. A CHECKLIST OF APPROXIMATELY 150 NEWSPAPERS PUBLISHED IN ARKANSAS BY BLACKS BETWEEN 1869 AND THE PRESENT. (ST-WIDE). AMANDA SAAR, CIRCULATION INFORMATION LIBRARIAN; UNIV OF ARKANSAS MEDICAL CENTER; 4301 W MARKHAM; LITTLE ROCK, AR 72201. (#17612). **ARBA GRANTEE.**

BLACK FILM SERIES IN LITTLE ROCK, ARKANSAS. A SALUTE TO BLACK ARTISTS IN THE FILM INDUSTRY WITH A BLACK FILM FESTIVAL. A FILM CRITIC, EDITOR AND AUTHOR WILL CONDUCT SESSIONS AT THE FESTIVAL. (LOCAL). TOWNSEND WOLFE, DIRECTOR; ARKANSAS ARTS CENTER; MACARTHUR PARK; LITTLE ROCK, AR 72203. (#9736). **ARBA GRANTEE.**

CHILD CARE '76 PROJECT OF ARKANSAS. DEVELOP A PUBLIC AWARENESS OF THE NEED FOR SERVICES FOR YOUNG CHILDREN IN ARK. PROGRAMS TO STRENGTHEN FAMILIES, ASSESS NEEDS OF LOCAL COMMUNITIES, & FOCUS ATTENTION ON YOUNG CHILDREN IN THE STATE. (ST-WIDE). SARA MURPHY, COORDINATOR; OFFICE OF EARLY CHILDHOOD PLANNING; 12TH & MARSHALL ST; LITTLE ROCK, AR 72202. (#4088).

CONTEMPORARY ISSUES IN LITTLE ROCK, ARKANSAS. A BICENT COURSE FOCUSING ON CONTEMPORARY ISSUES IN LITTLE ROCK WILL BE OFFERED; CITIZEN PARTICIPATION IS ENCOURAGED. (LOCAL). DR CHARLES BOLTON, PROJ COORDINATOR; UNIV OF ARKANSAS - LITTLE ROCK, ARBC; 33RD & UNIVERSITY; LITTLE ROCK, AR 72205. (#10157).

DISFARMER OF HEBER SPRINGS - LITTLE ROCK, AR. AN EXHIBIT OF THE WORK OF MIKE DISFARMER, AN ARKANSAS PHOTOGRAPHER WHO WORKED IN RURAL AREAS. A PUBLICATION WILL BE PRINTED TO PRESERVE THE WORKS. (LOCAL). TOWNSEND WOLFE, EXEC DIRECTOR; ARKANSAS ARTS CENTER; MACARTHUR PARK; LITTLE ROCK, AR 72203. (#18680). **ARBA GRANTEE.**

EVERY CHILD BY '74 -IMMUNIZATION PROJ OF ARKANSAS. A DRIVE BY THE STATE OF ARKANSAS TO IMMUNIZE EVERY CHILD IN THE STATE AGAINST ALL PREVENTABLE COMMUNICABLE DISEASES. (ST-WIDE). GLENNIS PARKER, EXEC DIRECTOR; ARKANSAS BICENTENNIAL CELEBRATION COMMITTEE; 300 W MARKHAM ST; LITTLE ROCK, AR 72201. (#183). **ARBA GRANTEE.**

EVERY CHILD IN '76/'77. PURPOSE IS TO IMMUNIZE EVERY CHILD AGAINST ALL PREVENTABLE COMMUNICABLE DISEASES WITH SPECIAL EMPHASIS ON PRESCHOOL CHILD. THIS ON-GOING EFFORT ENCOURAGES VOLUNTEER PARTICIPATION. (NAT'L). MRS NELL BALKMAN, DIRECTOR, CONTINUING EDUCATION; ARKAN-

LITTLE ROCK — CONTINUED

SAS LEAGUE FOR NURSING; 1815 W 12TH ST; LITTLE ROCK, AR 72202. (#7893). **ARBA RECOGNIZED.**

HISTORY IN BLACKNESS, LITTLE ROCK, AR. VISUAL DEPICTION OF CONTRIBUTIONS OF BLACK PEOPLE TO THE HISTORICAL DEVELOPMENT OF PULASKI COUNTY, ARKANSAS. (LOCAL). DR E UPSHUR, PRESIDENT; BLACK FEMALE ACTION, INC; 1205 W 28TH ST; LITTLE ROCK, AR 72206. (#23727). **ARBA GRANTEE.**

THE LEGEND OF PETIT JEAN - LITTLE ROCK, AR. LITTLE ROCK BALLET OF THE ARTS CENTER WILL OFFER THE HISTORY OF ARKANSAS DEPICTED THROUGH DANCE. (LOCAL). TOWNSEND WOLFE, EXEC DIRECTOR; ARKANSAS ARTS CENTER; MACARTHUR PARK; LITTLE ROCK, AR 72203. (#18679). **ARBA GRANTEE.**

LITERATURE OF HISTORIC ARKANSAS - MAP. THE MAP 'LITERATURE OF HISTORIC ARKANSAS' WILL BE A PRESERVATION OF ARKANSAS HERITAGE. THE MODEL OF THE MAP WILL ILLUSTRATE TIMES AND PLACES WITH ILLUSTRATED QUOTES ABOUT ARKANSAS LITERATURE. (ST-WIDE). MARGARETTE MARTIN, COORDINATOR; ARKANSAS COUNCIL OF TEACHERS; 1512 BOSLEY; LITTLE ROCK, AR 72207. (#23507). **ARBA GRANTEE.**

LITTLE ROCK RESTORATION IN ARKANSAS. RESTORATION BY RIVERFRONT DEVELOPMENT CORPORATION OF LA PETITE ROCK AREA ALONG THE RIVERFRONT, THE POINT BEING SIGNIFICANT BECAUSE BERNARD DE LA HARPE LANDED THERE ON A DISCOVERY VOYAGE. (LOCAL). GEORGE MILLAR, EXEC DIRECTOR; RIVERFRONT DEVELOPMENT CORPORATION; 500 CONTINENTAL BLDG; LITTLE ROCK, AR 72201. (#527). **ARBA GRANTEE.**

MIGRANT STUDENT RECORD TRANSFER SYSTEM, AR. AUTOMATED TELEPROCESSING NETWORK THAT COVERS THE USA AND PUERTO RICO AND EXISTS AS A CENTRAL RECORDS DEPOSITORY IN TRANSFERING RECORDS FROM SCHOOL TO SCHOOL FOR FARM AND FISHING MIGRANT CHILDREN. (NAT'L). WINFORD MILLER, ADMINISTRATOR; MIGRANT STUDENT RECORD TRANSFER SYSTEM; 5TH AND WOODLANE; LITTLE ROCK, AR 72203. (#20072).

PAINTING OF FIRE HYDRANTS-BICENTENNIAL THEMES - AR. PAINTING OF FIRE HYDRANTS ON BASE, RED, WHITE & BLUE. (LOCAL). COLONEL DOUGLAS C BELL, PROJ COORDINATOR; 314 TACTICAL AIRLIFT WING; LITTLE RK AFB, AR 72076. (#31485).

PERSPECTIVES ON THE AMER REVOLUTION - LECTURES, AR. A SERIES OF PUBLIC LECTURES DELIVERED BY WELL-KNOWN HISTORIANS ON THE SUBJECT OF THE AMERICAN REVOLUTION AT THE UNIVERSITY OF ARKANSAS AT LITTLE ROCK. (LOCAL). DR SIDNEY CHARLES BOLTON, PROF OF HISTORY; UNIV OF ARKANSAS AT LITTLE ROCK; 33RD AND UNIVERSITY; LITTLE ROCK, AR 72204. (#8211). **ARBA GRANTEE.**

QUAWPAW QUARTER BICENTENNIAL TOUR, LITTLE ROCK, AR. BICENTENNIAL TOURS WILL BE SPONSORED BY QUAWPAW QUARTER ASSOC. (LOCAL). THOMAS E WILKES, DIR; QUAWPAW QUARTER ASSOC; PO BOX 1104; LITTLE ROCK, AR 72203. (#19085). **ARBA GRANTEE.**

RESTORATION OF THE ARKANSAS BATTLE FLAG COLLECTION. THE BATTLE FLAG COLLECTION CONSISTS OF TWENTY-EIGHT FLAGS CARRIED BY ARKANSAS SOLDIERS IN THE THREE WARS IN WHICH THE STATE PARTICIPATED DURING THE 19TH CENTURY. PLANS ARE TO RESTORE FLAGS. (LOCAL). ANNE BARTLEY, DIRECTOR; ARKANSAS COMMEMORATIVE COMMISSION; 300 W MARKHAM; LITTLE ROCK, AR 72201. (#26874). **ARBA GRANTEE.**

'SECOND FOURTH' -DRAMATIZATION, HOT SPRINGS, ARK. CONTINUING CELEBRATION OF THE ARB. WILL CULMINATE IN 76 WITH THE PRE MIERE PERFORMANCE OF A GREAT HISTORICAL MUSICAL DRAMA BASED ON HISTORY & HERITAGE OF THE AREA. 73-1ST-4TH, 74-2ND-4TH, 75-3RD-4TH, 76. (ST-WIDE). MRS GLENNIS PARKER, EXEC DIRECTOR; ARKANSAS BICENTENNIAL CELEBRATION COMMITTEE; 300 W MARKHAM ST; LITTLE ROCK, AR 72201. (#925). **ARBA GRANTEE.**

TOURING AMERICAN THEATRE, ARKANSAS ARTS CENTER. THE ARKANSAS ARTS CENTER WILL SPONSOR A PLAY WRITING CONTEST, THE WINNING PLAY WILL BE PERFORMED IN HIGH SCHOOLS THROUGHOUT THE STATE. (ST-WIDE). TOWNSEND WOLFE, DIRECTOR; ARKANSAS ARTS CENTER; MACARTHUR PARK; LITTLE ROCK, AR 72203. (#9739). **ARBA GRANTEE.**

U S ARMY BICENTENNIAL TIME CAPSULE, ARKANSAS. LITTLE ROCK DISTRICT, CORPS OF ENGINEERS WILL DESIGN & MAKE A TIME CAPSULE TO BE PLACED ON FEDERAL LAND IN LITTLE ROCK. MESSAGES FROM SCHOOL CHILDREN, THE GOVERNOR & CONGRESSIONAL DELEGATES ENCLOSED. (ST-WIDE). LTC CHARLES E DOWNS; LITTLE ROCK DISTRICT, CORPS OF ENGINEERS; BOX 867; LITTLE ROCK, AR 72203. (#6485).

UNIV OF ARKANSAS MEDICAL CENTER, LITTLE ROCK, AR. THE PROJECT IS AN OVER-ALL BICENTENNIAL PROGRAM FOR BOTH STUDENTS AND PATIENTS. IT COMBINES THE FUTURE OF MEDICINE AND THE HISTORY OF THE MEDICAL CENTER. (LOCAL). DR JAMES DUSENBERRY, DEAN OF PHARMACY SCHOOL; UNIV OF ARKANSAS MEDICAL CENTER; 4301 W MARKHAM ST; LITTLE ROCK, AR 72201. (#11664).

1931 BOOK: 'MUSIC OF GEORGE WASHINGTON'S TIME', AR. REPRINTING IN LITTLE ROCK OF THE 34 PAGE BOOK OF HISTORICAL AND MUSICAL DATA, WHICH WAS ORIGINALLY PRINTED IN 1931 FOR THE BICENTENNIAL OF THE BIRTH OF GEORGE WASHINGTON. (LOCAL). MRS MAYNARD HALL, BICENTENNIAL CHAIRMAN; ARKANSAS SOCIETY, DAUGHTERS OF THE AMERICAN COLONISTS; 2025 TOPF RD; N LITTLE ROCK, AR 72116. (#8199). **ARBA GRANTEE.**

JUNE 21 - 22, '74. STAMP EXHIBIT WITH THEME OF COUNT PULASKI. ARKPEX 74 STAMP EXHIBITION OF LITTLE ROCK, ARK. A DISPLAY OF STAMPS FROM ALL OVER THE WORLD, WITH COMPETITION AWARDS OF MEDALS AND RIBBONS. THE THEME IS BASED ON COUNT PULASKI. (ST-WIDE). BRUCE I ROBERTS, CHAIRMAN; ARKANSAS PHILATELIC ASSOCIATION; BOX 2874; LITTLE ROCK, AR 72203. (#1704-901).

JUNE 14, '75. PLACEMENT OF A TIME CAPSULE ON FEDERAL LAND IN LITTLE ROCK. LITTLE ROCK DISTRICT, CORPS OF ENGINEERS WILL DESIGN & MAKE A TIME CAPSULE TO BE PLACED ON FEDERAL LAND IN LITTLE ROCK. MESSAGES FROM SCHOOL CHILDREN, THE GOVERNOR & CONGRESSIONAL DELEGATES ENCLOSED. (ST-WIDE). LTC CHARLES E DOWNS; LITTLE ROCK DISTRICT, CORPS OF ENGINEERS; BOX 867; LITTLE ROCK, AR 72203. (#6485-501).

JUNE 27 - 29, '75. ARKPEX 74 STAMP EXHIBITION. THERE WILL BE A 250 FRAME PHILATELIC EXHIBIT, WORTH OVER $20,000. THE THEME OF THE EXHIBITION IS 'BATTLE OF LEXINGTON CONCORD.' THERE WILL BE COMPETITION FOR VARIOUS CATEGORIES&MEDALS & RIBBONS AWARDED. THERE WILL BE A POSTAL HIST. SYMPOSIUM, STAMP AUCTION. AT THE MALL 300 SOUTH UNIVERSITY AVE, LITTLE ROCK ARK.. (ST-WIDE). BRUCE I ROBERTS, CHMN; ARKANSAS PHILATELIC ASSOCIATION; BOX 2874; LITTLE ROCK, AR 72203. (#1704-1).

OCT 27, '75. 'THE BARBER OF SEVILLE', PRESENTED BY TEXAS OPERA THEATER. CLASSIC COMIC OPERA BY ROSSINI, PERFORMED IN ENGLISH BY A COMPANY OF PROFESSIONAL YOUNG AMERICAN ARTISTS. AT UNIVERSITY THEATER. (LOCAL). BLANCHE THEBOM, COORD; LECTURES AND SPECIAL EVENTS COMMITTEE - UNIV OF ARKANSAS; LITTLE ROCK, AR 72204. (#200005-7).

JAN 16, '76. THE TODAY SHOW FEATURES THE STATE OF ARKANSAS. A CONTINUING WEEKLY SERIES OF PROGRAMS COMMEMORATING EACH STATE. ARKANSAS WAS ADMITTED INTO THE UNION IN JUNE, 1836. (NAT'L). STUART SCHULBERG, EX PROD; NATIONAL BROADCASTING CO; 30 ROCKEFELLER PLAZA; NEW YORK, NY 10020. (#7981-8).

FEB 1 - 29, '76. BLACK FILM SERIES. A SALUTE TO BLACK ARTISTS IN THE FILM INDUSTRY WITH A BLACK FILM FESTIVAL. A FILM CRITIC, EDITOR & AUTHOR WILL CONDUCT SESSIONS AT THE FESTIVAL. WILL BE HELD FEB 1, 8, 15, 22, 23 & 29. (LOCAL). TOWNSEND WOLFE, DIRECTOR; ARKANSAS ARTS CENTER; MACARTHUR PARK; LITTLE ROCK, AR 72203. (#9736-1).

FEB 21, '76. AMERICA 200. LIVE PERFORMANCE AT ARKANSAS ARTS CENTER; MACARTHUR PARK. (LOCAL). MAC B SISSON, CHAIRMAN; OUACHITA BAPTIST UNIV; BOX 761; ARKADELPHIA, AR 71923. (#104862-3).

FEB 22, '76. BICENTENNIAL BALL IN 1976. THE LONOKE CENTURY LEAGUE IS PLANNING A BICENTENNIAL BALL WITH THE THEME 'SPIRIT OF '76'. AT CAMELOT INN. (LOCAL). MRS L C MCCRARY, COORD; LONOKE CENTURY LEAGUE; LONOKE CENTURY LEAGUE; LONOKE, AR 72086. (#7692-1).

MAR 16 - 18, '76. UNITED STATES ARMED FORCES BICENTENNIAL CARAVAN. CARAVAN IS COMPOSED OF EXHIBIT VANS FOR EACH MILITARY SERVICE. PROJECT THEME IS 'HISTORY OF THE ARMED FORCES AND THEIR CONTRIBUTIONS TO THE NATION'. (LOCAL). MRS RUTH TATE, CHMN; US ARMED FORCES BICENTENNIAL EXHIBIT VANS PROJECT; 300 W MARKHAM; LITTLE ROCK, AR 72201. (#1775-408).

MAR 17 - 20, '76. THE LEGEND OF PETIT JEAN. LITTLE ROCK BALLET OF THE ARTS CENTER WILL OFFER THE HISTORY OF ARKANSAS DEPICTED THROUGH DANCE. (LOCAL). TOWNSEND WOLFE, EXEC DIR; ARKANSAS ART CENTER; MACARTHUR PARK; LITTLE ROCK, AR 72203. (#18679-1).

APR 3 - 5, '76. BICENTENNIAL FESTIVAL OF MUSIC. LIVE PERFORMANCE AT CAMELOT INN. (ST-WIDE). MRS JOHN FORTENBERRY, DIR; ARKANSAS FEDERATION OF MUSIC CLUBS, INC; 201 AUBURN DR; LITTLE ROCK, AR 72205. (#18671-1).

APR 19 - MAY 2, '76. QUAWPAW QUARTER BICENTENNIAL TOUR. TOUR AT VILLA MARRE 1323 SCOTT ST. (ST-WIDE). THOMAS E WILKES, DIRECTOR; QUAWPAW QUARTER ASSOC; PO BOX 1104; LITTLE ROCK, AR 72203. (#19085-1).

MAY 1 - JUNE 30, '76. CRAFTS WORKSHOP. SEMINAR AT MACARTHUR PARK. (LOCAL). TOWNSENT WOLFE, DIRECTOR; THE ARKANSAS ARTS CENTER; MACARTHUR PARK; LITTLE ROCK, AR 72203. (#25281-1).

SEPT 12 - 30, '76. HISTORY IN BLACKNESS - EXHIBIT. EXHIBIT DEPICTING CONTRIBUTIONS OF BLACK PEOPLE TO THE HISTORICAL DEVELOPMENT OF PULASKI COUNTY, AR. (LOCAL). DR E UPSHUR, PRESIDENT; BLACK FEMALE ACTION, INC; 1205 W 28TH ST; LITTLE ROCK, AR 72206. (#23727-1).

SEPT 17 - 19, '76. CRAFTS WORKSHOP. CLASSES IN CRAFT MAKING, USING A KILN. (LOCAL). TOWNSEND WOLFE, EXEC DIR; ARKANSAS ART CENTER; MACARTHUR PK; LITTLE ROCK, AR 72203. (#107958-1).

OCT 1 - 10, '76. ARKANSAS STATE FAIR & LIVESTOCK SHOW. FAIR AT ARKANSAS STATE FAIRGROUNDS, WEST ROOSEVELT RD, LITTLE ROCK, ARK. (REGN'L). JOHN R HOLMES, GEN MGR; ARKANSAS STATE FAIR AND LIVESTOCK SHOW; PO BOX 907, 2600 HOWARD; LITTLE ROCK, AR 72205. (#106095-27).

JAN 6 - FEB 5, '78. 'EDVARD MUNCH, THE MAJOR GRAPHICS' EXHIBIT. AN EXHIBITION FROM THE MUNCH MUSEUM IN OSLO BY ONE OF THE GREATEST FIGURES IN MODERN PRINTMAKING. AT ARKANSAS ART CENTER. (INT'L). EILEEN HARAKAL, COORD; SMITHSONIAN INSTITUTION TRAVELING EXHIBITION SERVICE; 1000 JEFFERSON DR, SW; WASHINGTON, DC 20560. (#26704-12).

LONDON

BICENTENNIAL MEMORIAL, LONDON, AR. A MONUMENT WILL BE PLACED IN THE LONDON CEMETERY TO HONOR THE KNOWN AND UNKNOWN PIONEERS WHO HELPED ESTABLISH THE COMMUNITY. A PARADE WITH FLOATS, BANDS, SADDLE CLUBS & COLOR GUARD WILL TAKE PLACE. (LOCAL). HON THURMAN WHORTON, MAYOR; CITY OF LONDON; CITY HALL; LONDON, AR 72847. (#26724). **ARBA GRANTEE.**

LONOKE

BAND CONCERTS IN LONOKE, ARKANSAS. THE HIGH SCHOOL BAND WILL PRESENT A BICENTENNIAL SERIES OF CONCERTS DURING 1975 AND 1976. (LOCAL). BILL PHELPS, DIRECTOR; LONOKE HIGH SCHOOL BAND; LONOKE, AR 72086. (#7690).

BOOK FAIR IN LONOKE, ARKANSAS. THE LONOKE MIDDLE SCHOOL WILL HAVE A BOOK FAIR TO EMPHASIZE HISTORICAL PATRIOTIC BOOKS FOR THE SCHOOL LIBRARY. (LOCAL). MRS L C MCCRARY, JR, COORDINATOR; LONOKE MIDDLE SCHOOL; LONOKE, AR 72086. (#7691).

HISTORICAL AND PATRIOTIC BOOKS: LONOKE, ARKANSAS. THE LONOKE BOOK CLUB WILL PURCHASE HISTORICAL AND PATRIOTIC BOOKS TO BE PLACED ON A PERMANENT SHELF AT THE LONOKE COUNTY LIBRARY. (LOCAL). MRS L C MCCRARY, JR, COORDINATOR; LONOKE COUNTY LIBRARY; LONOKE, AR 72086. (#7693).

LONOKE CITY BEAUTIFICATION PROJECT IN ARKANSAS. THE CHAMBER OF COMMERCE WILL SPONSOR THE PLANTING OF SHRUBBERY AND THE BEAUTIFICATION OF PARKS AND PUBLIC BUILDINGS. ONE LOCAL FIRM, JACUZZI BROTHERS, IS BEAUTIFYING THE AREA NEAR THEIR PLANT. (LOCAL). MRS L C MCCRARY, JR, COORDINATOR; LONOKE CHAMBER OF COMMERCE; LONOKE, AR 72086. (#7687).

LONOKE CITY PARKS PROJECT IN ARKANSAS. DEVELOP BICENTENNIAL PARK WITH PLAYGROUNDS, PICNIC TABLES, BASEBALL DIAMONDS AND PAVILION. TO BE READY BY 1976. IN ADDITION, EXISTING PARKS WILL BE MAINTAINED AND IMPROVED. (LOCAL). HON ERIC SCHENEBECK, MAYOR; CITY OF LONOKE; CITY HALL; LONOKE, AR 72086. (#7694).

SPIRIT OF '76: LONOKE, AR, BICENT CELEBRATION. THE LONOKE BICENTENNIAL COMMITTEE PLANS A YEAR LONG CELEBRATION INCLUDING FAIRS, PARK PROJECTS AND PROJECTS FOR SCHOOLS. (LOCAL). MRS L C MCCRARY JR, CHAIRMAN; LONOKE BICENTENNIAL COMMITTEE; 118 S CENTER; LONOKE, AR 72086. (#17589). **ARBA GRANTEE.**

SEPT 18 - 20, '75. LONOKE COUNTY FAIR, PARADE AND RODEO. FAIR, COMPETITION, PARADE AT FAIRGROUNDS AND ARENA. (LOCAL). MRS L C MCCRARY, JR; LONOKE COUNTY FAIR BOARD; 406 JEFFERSON; LONOKE, AR 72086. (#200005-6).

NOV 8, '75. CHURCH BAZAAR. FESTIVAL AT CHURCH BLDG. (LOCAL). MS CALVIN RICE; METHODIST CHURCH; 806 S CENTER; LONOKE, AR 72086. (#102989-1).

NOV 18, '75. EXHIBIT OF ANTIQUE DOLL COLLECTION. EXHIBIT. (LOCAL). MRS DAN LAWSON, CHMN; BICENTENNIAL HERITAGE COMMITTEE; RT 1; LONOKE, AR 72086. (#200005-56).

FEB 19, '76. 'THE SONG OF THE CHIPPEWA' - BICENTENNIAL MUSICAL. WILL EMPHASIZE HISTORICAL PATRIOTIC MUSIC THROUGH THE YEARS. AT LONOKE HIGH SCHOOL AUDITORIUM. (LOCAL). MRS L C MCCRARY, COORD; LONOKE BICENTENNIAL COMMITTEE; LONOKE, AR 72086. (#103778-2).

MAR 12, '76. STUDENT FLAG PRESENTATION. CEREMONY AT LONOKE HIGH SCHOOL GROUNDS. (LOCAL). MRS DON LAWSON, CHMN; BICENTENNIAL HERITAGE COMMITTEE; RT 1; LONOKE, AR 72086. (#200005-60).

MAR 17, '76. CREPE MYRTLE TREE PLANTING. 120 CREPE MYRTLE TREES WERE PLANTED AT THE ENTRANCE TO LONOKE. (LOCAL). LOUIE HALFORD, CHMN; BICENTENNIAL HORIZON COMMITTEE; 206 LINCOLN; LONOKE, AR 72086. (#200005-57).

APR 8, '76. BICENTENNIAL BANQUET. 1975 AND 1976 BANQUETS IN LONOKE, ARKANSAS. CHAMBER OF COMMERCE BANQUETS WILL BE DEDICATED TO BICENTENNIAL IN 1975 AND 1976; THEIR THEME WILL BE 'HAPPY BIRTHDAY AMERICA, ARKANSAS AND LONOKE'. AT LONOKE HIGH SCHOOL CAFETERIA. (LOCAL). MRS L C MCCRARY; CHAMBER OF COMMERCE; CHAMBER OF COMMERCE; LONOKE, AR 72086. (#7688-501).

MAY 23, '76. DEDICATION OF THOMAS SLOAN BOYD HOUSE. ADDED TO THE NATIONAL REGISTER OF HISTORIC PLACES. (LOCAL). MRS DON LAWSON; BICENTENNIAL HERITAGE COMMITTEE; RT 1; LONOKE, AR 72086. (#200005-58).

JUNE 27, '76. 'I LOVE AMERICA' - RELIGIOUS & PATRIOTIC CANTATA. LIVE PERFORMANCE, CEREMONY AT IN CHURCHES. (LOCAL). MRS L C MCRARY III, CHMN; BICENTENNIAL FESTIVAL COMMITTEE; 107 MELTON; LONOKE, AR 72086. (#200005-59).

JULY 4, '76. OLD-TIME PICNIC IN 1976. JAYCEES & JAYCETTES WILL SPONSOR A BICENTENNIAL PICNIC IN 1976, WITH CONTESTS, RACES, BOOTHS & CONCESSIONS. IN ADDITION, THE LOCAL KIWANIS WILL SPONSOR LITTLE LEAGUE BASEBALL. LIONS CLUB STREET DECORATIONS, FLAGS & BANNERS. (LOCAL). MRS L C MCCRARY, JR; LONOKE JAYCEES & JAYCETTES; LONOKE JAYCEES; LONOKE, AR 72086. (#7689-1).

LOWELL

BIENTENNIAL PROJECTS - LOWELL, AR. RESTORATION OF A LANDMARK INTO A MUSEUM; HOMECOMING FESTIVAL; AND PLANTING OF RED BUD & DOGWOOD TREES IN A MINI-PARK. (LOCAL).

LOWELL — CONTINUED

ELZA TUCKER, CO-CHAIRMAN; CITY OF LOWELL; 102 LINCOLN ST; LOWELL, AR 72745. (#33434).

LYNN

LYNN PARK, AR. THE CITY OF LYNN PLANS TO PURCHASE PLAYGROUND EQUIPMENTS AND PLACE A WATER FOUNTAIN IN THEIR CITY PARK. (LOCAL). HON RAYMOND PENN, MAYOR; CITY OF LYNN; CITY HALL; LYNN, AR 72440. (#27073). **ARBA GRANTEE.**

MAGNOLIA

BICENTENNIAL FESTIVAL FOR COLUMBIA COUNTY - AR. FOUR-MONTH CELEBRATION WITH LOCAL CONCERTS BY BANDS & LOCAL TALENT; PAGEANTS ARE PLANNED, CLIMAXING WITH 2-DAY FESTIVAL JULY 3-4, '76. (LOCAL). ARCHIE MONROE, CHAIRMAN; COLUMBIA COUNTY BICENTENNIAL COMMISSION; PO BOX 866; MAGNOLIA, AR 71753. (#17564). **ARBA GRANTEE.**

FESTIVAL '76: AMERICA'S HERITAGE IN MUSIC - AR. A SERIES OF CONCERTS BY SOUTHERN STATE CHOIR & DRAMA DEPT TO CREATE AWARENESS AND CELEBRATE THE BICENTENNIAL. (LOCAL). DONALD A HAFFNER, VICE PRESIDENT; SOUTHERN STATE COLLEGE BICENTENNIAL COMMITTEE; MAGNOLIA, AR 71753. (#17562). **ARBA GRANTEE.**

HISTORY OF COLUMBIA COUNTY & SOUTHWEST, ARKANSAS. A COLLECTION OF DOCUMENTS, PHOTOGRAPHS AND MEMORABILIA DOCUMENTING THE HISTORY OF THE AREA. THESE WILL BE CATALOGUED AND HOUSED IN A PERMANENT COLLECTION ROOM. (LOCAL). DONALD A HEAFNER, VICE PRES FOR STUDENT AFFAIRS; SOUTHERN STATE COLLEGE; MAGNOLIA, AR 71753. (#8210). **ARBA GRANTEE.**

NOV 18, '75 - APR 20, '76. FESTIVAL '76: AMERICAS HERITAGE IN MUSIC. A SERIES OF CONCERTS BY SOUTHERN STATE CHOIR & DRAMA DEPT TO CREATE AWARENESS AND CELEBRATE THE BICENTENNIAL. AT SOUTHERN STATE COLLEGE CAMPUS. (LOCAL). DONALD A HAEFFNER, DIR; SOUTHERN STATE COLLEGE BICENT COMM AND MUSIC DEPARTMENT; MAGNOLIA, AR 71753. (#17562-1).

JAN 25 - JULY 4, '76. BICENTENNIAL FESTIVAL. A 4-MONTH CELEBRATION WITH LOCAL CONCERTS BY BANDS AND LOCAL TALENT; PAGEANTS ARE PLANNED DURING THIS PERIOD. (LOCAL). ARCHIE MONROE, CHMN; COLUMBIA COUNTY BICENTENNIAL COMMITTEE; PO BOX 866; MAGNOLIA, AR 71753. (#17564-1).

FEB 25 - 28, '76. SOUTHERN STATE COLLEGE DRAMATIC PRODUCTIONS. THE THEATER DEPARTMENT WILL PERFORM THE PLAY '1776'. AT HARTON THEATRE. (LOCAL). DONALD A HAEFNER; SOUTHERN STATE COLLEGE BICENTENNIAL COMMITTEE; MAGNOLIA, AR 71753. (#6489-1).

APR 22, '76. 'WAR REQUIEM' - A MUSICAL. THE COLLEGE MUSIC DEPARTMENT WILL PRESENT A MUSICAL ON THE BICENTENNIAL THEME. AT DOLPH CAMP RECITAL HALL. (LOCAL). DONALD A HAEFNER; SOUTHERN STATE COLLEGE BICENTENNIAL COMMITTEE; MAGNOLIA, AR 71753. (#6491-1).

MALVERN

CITY OF MALVERN, ARK, CENTENNIAL COMMEMORATION. DURING 1976 MALVERN WILL OBSERVE ITS CENTENNIAL AS AN INCORPORATED COMMUNITY IN ARKANSAS. THE CELEBRATION WILL INCLUDE PAGEANTS, THE DEVELOPMENT OF A PARK, HISTORICAL MARKER & SPECIAL 1976 CELEBRATION. (LOCAL). MAYOR WAYNE SELPH CHAIRMAN; MALVERN-HOT SPRING CO BICENTENNIAL COMMISSION; 1304 MCHENRY; MALVERN, AR 72104. (#3932).

FEB 21, '75. ANNUAL BANQUET, EXHIBITS, SWISHER COUNTY HISTORICAL SKITS. FESTIVAL, PARADE, LIVE PERFORMANCE, TOUR. (LOCAL). MAYOR WAYNE SELPH CHAIRMA; MALVERN-HOT SPRING CO BICENTENNIAL COMMISSION; 1304 MCHENRY; MALVERN, AR 72104. (#3932-901).

MAMMOTH SPG

MAMMOTH SPRING MUSEUM, AR. THE BAGGAGE ROOM OF OLD FRISCO DEPOT, WHICH HAS BEEN MADE A STATE PARK, WILL BE MADE INTO A MUSEUM CONTAINING ITEMS PERTAINING TO THE HISTORY OF MAMMOTH SPRINGS. (LOCAL). HON ARNO LASSITER, MAYOR; CITY OF MAMMOTH SPRING; CITY HALL; MAMMOTH SPG, AR 72554. (#26817). **ARBA GRANTEE.**

MAY 2, '76. LOYALTY DAY PARADE & CONTEST. A BIKE DECORATING CONTEST WILL BE SPONSORED BY THE 4-H CLUB. AT MAIN ST. (LOCAL). MRS G S PACE, JR, CHMN; VETERANS OF FOREIGN WARS AUXILIARY & 4-H CLUB; 650 BETHEL; MAMMOTH SPG, AR 72554. (#106496-3).

AUG 8, '76. BICENTENNIAL FLOWER AND ANTIQUE SHOW. EXHIBIT AT MAMMOTH SPG DEPOT MUSEUM. (LOCAL). MRS G S PACE, JR, CHMN; GARDEN CLUB; 650 BETHEL; MAMMOTH SPG, AR 72554. (#106496-4).

MARIANNA

FUN FOR THE FUTURE-PARK PROJ IN MARIANNA, AR. DEVELOPMENT AND MAINTAINENCE OF MILLER PARK. (LOCAL). JOHN OYNER, PROJ DIRECTOR; LEE COUNTY BICENTENNIAL COMMITTEE; MARIANNA, AR 72360. (#20375).

SCHOOL DAYS IN MARIANNA, AR. RESTORATION OF A ONE ROOM SCHOOLHOUSE. (LOCAL). MRS THOS H GIST, CHAIRMAN; LEE COUNTY ARTS ASSOC; ROUTE 3 BOX 261; MARIANNA, AR 72360. (#20374).

FEB 22, '76. BICENTENNIAL FLAG PRESENTATION AT ARKANSAS SYMPHONY CHAMBER CONCERT. FLAG PRESENTED BY LT GOV JOE PURCELL PRECEDING CONCERT; OPEN HOUSE TEA FOR ORCHESTRA AND GUESTS FOLLOWED. AT LEE HIGH SCHOOL AUDITORIUM. (LOCAL). MRS T H GIST, CHMN; MARIANNA BICENTENNIAL COMMITTEE & LEE COUNTY ARTS ASSOC; RT 3 BOX 261; MARIANNA, AR 72360. (#104786-1).

JUNE 12, '76. FLAG DAY OF FUN. PARADE, FAIR, QUILT EXHIBIT AND FIREWORKS IN MARIANNA. AT CITY PARK & STREETS IN TOWN; FIREWORKS AT MILLER PARK. (LOCAL). MRS T H GIST, CHAIRMAN; LEE COUNTY-MARIANNA BICENTENNIAL COMMUNITY; RT 3, BOX 261; MARIANNA, AR 72360. (#106488-1).

MARKED TREE

BICENTENNIAL CELEBRATION, MARKED TREE, AR. A COMMUNITY CELEBRATION IS PLANNED. THERE WILL BE ARTS AND CRAFTS BOOTHS, AN ANTIQUE AIRPLANE EXHIBIT, AN ANTIQUE CAR EXHIBIT AND A PARADE, CANOE RACE, BURIAL OF TIME CAPSULE. (LOCAL). HON WYLIE G KEY, MAYOR; CITY OF MARKED TREE; MARKED TREE, AR 72365. (#26723). **ARBA GRANTEE.**

JULY 2 - 3, '76. BICENTENNIAL CELEBRATION. A COMMUNITY CELEBRATION PLANNED. THERE WILL BE AN ARTS & CRAFTS BOOTH, AN ANTIQUE AIRPLANE EXHIBIT, AN ANTIQUE CAR EXHIBIT & A PARADE, A CANOE RACE, TIME CAPSULE. AT PIGGLY WIGGLY BUILDING. (LOCAL). HON WYLIE G KEY, MAYOR; CITY OF MARKED TREE; MARKED TREE, AR 72365. (#26723-1).

MARVELL

BICENTENNIAL BEAUTIFICATION CELEBRATION. THE TOWN IS WORKING ON LANDSCAPING TWO SMALL AREAS AT THE WEST AND EAST ENTRANCES INTO MARVELL. A FLAGPOLE WILL BE PLACED IN DOWNTOWN MARVELL & BICENTENNIAL DECORATED TRASH BARRELS PLACED IN CITY. (LOCAL). HON ROY KEMMER, MAYOR; CITY OF MARVELL; CITY HALL; MARVELL, AR 72366. (#26811). **ARBA GRANTEE.**

MAYFLOWER

MEMORIAL PARK - MAYFLOWER, AR. A CITY PARK FOR MAYFLOWER TO BE DEVELOPED AND DEDICATED TO ALL FROM THE MAYFLOWER AREA WHO SERVED OR LOST THEIR LIFE IN THE WARS. (LOCAL). HON MARY GANDY, MAYOR; CITY OF MAYFLOWER; RT 1, BOX 166; MAYFLOWER, AR 72106. (#26810). **ARBA GRANTEE.**

MAYSVILLE

HISTORICAL MARKERS PROJECT OF MAYSVILLE, AR. MARKERS WILL BE PLACED ON CIVIL WAR AND OTHER HISTORIC SITES. (LOCAL). BAILEY A STEELE, BENTON COUNTY JUDGE; MAYSVILLE BETTERMENT ASSOCIATION; PO BOX 2; MAYSVILLE, AR 72747. (#15575). **ARBA GRANTEE.**

MAYSVILLE, AR, HISTORY PROJECT. A BROCHURE WILL BE PRINTED AND FACILITIES IDENTIFIED FOR THIS PROJECT. (LOCAL). TOMMY HALEY, CHAIRMAN; MAYSVILLE BICENTENNIAL CELEBRATION COMMITTEE; PO BOX 2; MAYSVILLE, AR 72747. (#15576).

RESTORATION PROJECT IN MAYSVILLE, AR. PRESERVATION & RESTORATION OF OLD CEMETERY. (LOCAL). TOMMY HALEY, CHAIRMAN; MAYSVILLE BICENTENNIAL CELEBRATION COMMITTEE; PO BOX 2; MAYSVILLE, AR 72747. (#15574).

MC CRORY

HISTORY OF THE MCCRORY METHODIST CHURCH - AR. INCLUDED IN THE HISTORY WILL BE FAKES CHAPEL, DEVIEW, PATTERSON, CHAPPELL GROVE AND MCCRORY METHODIST CHURCH. (LOCAL). MRS EUGENE WRIGHT, PROJ DIRECTOR; UNITED METHODIST WOMEN; BOX 231; MCCRORY, AR 72101. (#18456).

A HISTORY OF THE METHODISTS AROUND MCCRORY, AR. THE METHODIST CHURCH WAS THE FIRST CHURCH ORGANIZED IN MCCRORY. THE CHURCH HISTORY REVEALS MUCH ABOUT THE HISTORY OF THE TOWN. (LOCAL). VICTOR GREEN, MINISTER; MCCRORY UNITED METHODIST CHURCH; 219 N EDMONDS; MCCRORY, AR 72101. (#27060). **ARBA GRANTEE.**

OCT 23, '75. 'USA-YEARS OF HER LIFE' - BICENTENNIAL FLOWER SHOW. EXHIBIT AT MCCRORY UNITED METHODIST CHURCH, FELLOWSHIP HALL. (LOCAL). MRS L V BURKETT, JR, CHMN; MCCRORY GARDEN CLUB; BOX 42; MCCRORY, AR 73101. (#200005-4).

NOV 11, '75. FLAG RAISING CEREMONY OF BICENTENNIAL FLAG. CEREMONY AT MUNICIPAL BUILDING (FRONT LAWN). (LOCAL). MRS GENE WRIGHT, CHMN; CITY COUNCIL & MAYOR OF MCCRORY; 903 N JOHNSON; MCCRORY, AR 72101. (#200005-5).

APR 12, '76. MUSICAL 1776-1976. LIVE PERFORMANCE AT MCCRORY HIGH SCHOOL AUDITORIUM, 405 N JACKSON. (LOCAL). MRS SHEILA SANDERS, DIR; MCCRORY HIGH SCHOOL CHORAL CHOIR; MCCRORY HIGH SCHOOL; MCCRORY, AR 72101. (#103799-9).

MINERAL SPGS

BEAUTIFICATION PROJECT IN MINERAL SPRINGS, AR. TREES & SHRUBBERY PLANTED IN NEW MINI-PARK; PURCHASED & PLANTED BY SOCIALITES CLUB. (LOCAL). HELEN SMITH, TREASURER; SOCIALITES EXTENSION HOMEMAKERS CLUB; BOX 1; MINERAL SPG, AR 71851. (#29885).

BICENT HISTORICAL PROGRAM - MINERAL SPG, AR. MUSICAL SONGS AND SKITS W/BICENT MOTIFS WERE PRESENTED AT MONTHLY PTA MEETINGS. (LOCAL). KAY ERWIN, CHAIRMAN; MINERAL SPRINGS PARENT/TEACHER ASSOC; RT 2, BOX 138; LOCKESBURG, AR 71846. (#33691).

BICENTENNIAL QUILT IN MINERAL SPRINGS, AR. ARTS & CRAFTS BICENTENNIAL QUILT PIECED AND QUILTED BY SENIOR CITIZEN'S SUNSHINE CLUB. (LOCAL). SANDY SYKES, DIRECTOR; SENIOR CITIZEN'S SUNSHINE CLUB; PO BOX 378, LEWIS ST; MINERAL SPG, AR 71851. (#29887).

COMMUNITY QUILT IN MINERAL SPRINGS, AR. QUILT TO BEAR NAMES OF PRESENT LOCAL RESIDENTS; PREPARED BY FHA & PLACED IN HOWARD CO MUSEUM IN WASHVILLE, AR. (LOCAL). DARYL S MCJUNKINS, SPONSOR; FUTURE HOMEMAKERS OF AMERICA; MINERAL SPG, AR 71851. (#29886).

ECOLOGY TOUR & CLEAN-UP IN MINERAL SPRINGS, AR. LEARNING EXPERIENCE FOR 5TH GRADERS, TOUR OF CITY PARK & CLEAN-UP OF EXISTING PARK WITH ECOLOGICAL THEME. (LOCAL). MARY TOLLESON, CHAIRMAN; MINERAL SPRINGS ELEMENTARY SCHOOL; CITY PARK; MINERAL SPG, AR 71851. (#33690).

RELIGIOUS SONG SERVICE IN MINERAL SPRINGS, AR. THE MINERAL SPRINGS CHURCH OF CHRIST SPONSORED A RELIGIOUS SONG SERVICE. (LOCAL). GLYNA RUTH LILLARD, CHAIRPERSON; MINERAL SPRINGS CHURCH OF CHRIST; BOX 1; MINERAL SPG, AR 71851. (#33673).

TREE PLANTING IN MINERAL SPRINGS, AR. BICENT TULIP TREE PLANTED IN CITY PARK. (LOCAL). GLYNNA RUTH LILLARD, VICE-PRESIDENT; SOCIALITES EXTENSION HOMEMAKERS CLUB; BOX 206; MINERAL SPG, AR 71851. (#29884).

MAR 8, '76. 'A NATION YET TO BE'-MOVIE & STUDY GROUP. MOVIE COVERING 200 YEARS OF METHODISM IN US. AT METHODIST CHURCH BLDG/HGWY 27 & 355 JCT. (LOCAL). ERNESTINE WEISSCHADEL; UNITED METHODIST WOMEN; PO BOX 362; MINERAL SPGS, AR 71851. (#200005-96).

APR 4, '76. RELIGION, BELL DEDICATION. CEREMONY AT HGWY 27 & 355 JCT AT MINERAL SPRINGS. (LOCAL). ROBERT WOODY, MINISTER; MINERAL SPGS METHODIST CHURCH; MINERAL SPGS, AR 71851. (#200005-86).

APR 29, '76. 'I HEAR AMERICA SINGING' - MUSICAL. PATRIOTIC SONGS & SKITS EMPHASIS ON AMERICA'S MUSICAL & HISTORICAL PAST & PRESENT. SPECIAL GUEST, JIMMY 'RED' JONES, AUDITOR, PRESENTED BICENTENNIAL FLAG TO CITY ACCEPTED BY MAYOR CHARLES SMITH. AT MINERAL SPRINGS OLD GYM. (LOCAL). MARJORIE COPELAND; MINERAL SPRINGS HS CHORUS & MUSIC DEPT; PO BOX 86; MINERAL SPGS, AR 71851. (#200005-87).

MAY 2, '76. OLD TIME SERMON AT CENTRAL BAPTIST CHURCH. CEREMONY AT CENTRAL BAPTIST CHURCH. (LOCAL). T WAYNE PRICE, MINISTER; CENTRAL BAPTIST CHURCH; PO BOX 68; MINERAL SPGS, AR 71851. (#200005-95).

JUNE 5, '76. 'WE THE PEOPLE' BICENTENNIAL CELEBRATION. AMONG THE DAY'S ACTIVITIES: MINI-PARADE, FILM, SINGING, PRIZES, SOFTBALL GAMES. AT MAIN ST. (LOCAL). GLYNA RUTH LILLARD; MINERAL SPRINGS BICENTENNIAL COMMITTEE; PO BOX 206; MINERAL SPGS, AR 71851. (#200005-94).

JUNE 5 - JULY 5, '76. 'AGRICULTURE TOOLS OF THE PAST'. EXHIBIT AT LOBBY OF PIKE CO BRANCH BANK. (LOCAL). CLYDE BELL; LIONS CLUB; PO BOX 158; MINERAL SPGS, AR 71851. (#200005-93).

JULY 3, '76. FIREWORKS DISPLAY. LIVE PERFORMANCE AT NEW MINI-PARK SITE LOCATED ON MAIN ST. (LOCAL). DARWIN JONES, FFA SPONSOR; FUTURE FARMERS OF AMERICA; MINERAL SPGS, AR 71851. (#200005-92).

MINTURN

PARADE & FLOATS. PARADE. (LOCAL). MARTA JONES, CHAIRM; CITY OF MINTURN BICENTENNIAL COMMITTEE; GENERAL DELIVERY; MINTURN, AR 72445. (#200005-16).

MONTICELLO

DREW COUNTY MUSEUM ADDITION, MONTICELLO, ARKANSAS. ADDITION TO EXISTING MUSEUM TO HOUSE PAPERS, BOOKS, MAGAZINES, OLD DOCUMENTS AND HISTORICAL ITEMS. (LOCAL). BOB MARSH, CHAIRMAN; DREW COUNTY BICENTENNIAL COMMITTEE; 110 E SHELTON; MONTICELLO, AR 71655. (#7686). **ARBA GRANTEE.**

ROUGH AND READY BICENTENNIAL PAGEANT IN ARKANSAS. THE PRODUCTION OF AN ORIGINAL MUSICAL DRAMA, TO BE WRITTEN, PRODUCED AND PERFORMED BY DREW COUNTY CITIZENS. (LOCAL). BOB MARSH, BICENT CHAIRMAN; DREW COUNTY CHAMBER OF COMMERCE; BOX 473; MONTICELLO, AR 71655. (#9737). **ARBA GRANTEE.**

APR 15 - 16, '76. ROUGH & READY PAGEANT. AN ORIGINAL DRAMA, A HISTORY OF DREW COUNTY FROM 1772 TO THE PRESENT WITH MEMBERS OF THE LOCAL COMMUNITY & THE UNIVERSITY. AT FINE ARTS AUDITORIUM, UNIV OF ARKANSAS AT MONTICELLO CAMPUS. (LOCAL). JACKIE DEHON, CHMN; DREW COUNTY BICENTENNIAL COMMITTEE & CHAMBER OF COMMERCE; 103 N MAIN; MONTICELLO, AR 71655. (#9737-1).

MONTICELLO — CONTINUED

JULY 3, '76. BURIAL OF TIME CAPSULE CONTAINING DOCUMENTS & MEMORABILIA. DREW COUNTY TIME CAPSULE, MONTICELLO, ARKANSAS. A TIME CAPSULE WILL BE BURIED ON JULY 3, 1976 ON GROUNDS AT DREW COUNTY MUSEUM. IT WILL CONTAIN DOCUMENTS AND MEMORABILIA. THERE WILL BE A MARKER ABOVE THE CAPSULE. (LOCAL). BOB MARSH, CHAIRMAN; DREW COUNTY BICENTENNIAL COMMITTEE; 110 E SHELTON; MONTICELLO, AR 71655. (#7697-501).

JULY 4, '76. ROUGH AND READY PAGEANT - ORIGINAL MUSICAL DRAMA. ROUGH AND READY BICENTENNIAL PAGEANT IN ARKANSAS. THE PRODUCTION OF AN ORIGINAL MUSICAL DRAMA, TO BE WRITTEN, PRODUCED AND PERFORMED BY DREW COUNTY CITIZENS. AT UNIV OF ARKANSAS AT MONTICELLO; FINE ARTS CENTER. (LOCAL). BOB MARSH; DREW COUNTY CHAMBER OF COMMERCE; BOX 473; MONTICELLO, AR 71655. (#9737-501).

MORRILTON

POINT REMOVE BOUNDARY LINE TRAIL OF TEARS, AR. POINT REMOVE BOUNDARY LINE TRAIL OF TEARS WAS THE SOUTHERN POINT OF THE BOUNDARY LINE FOR THE CHEROKEE NATION WEST. THE PROJECT WILL RETRACE, MARK & DEDICATE NATURAL AREAS TO THE TRAIL OF TEARS. (LOCAL). JAMES W KELLEY, ASSISTANT; 4-H CLUBS OF CONWAY COUNTY; CONWAY COUNTY COURTHOUSE; MORRILTON, AR 72110. (#20965). **ARBA GRANTEE.**

MORTON

MAR 15 - 20, '76. BICENTENNIAL LIFE OR LIBERTY CAMPAIGN. THIS IS A CELEBRATION OF ALL SOUTHERN BAPTIST CHURCHES IN ARKANSAS. AT ONE BLOCK OFF HWY 64, MORTON, ARK. (LOCAL). MRS PAUL GAINES, DIR; MORTON SOUTHERN BAPTIST CHURCH; RFD 2; MCCRORY, AR 72101. (#103799-7).

MOUNTAIN VIEW

OZARK FOLK CENTER, MOUNTAIN VIEW, AR. ARKANSAS STATE PARKS PROJECT FOR PRESERVATION AND PERPETUATION OF OZARK FOLK HERITAGE: CABIN CRAFTS, MUSIC, DANCE & LORE, THROUGH DEMONSTRATION, ENTERTAINMENT, SEMINARS & PUBLIC PARTICIPATION. (LOCAL). SUSAN MCMURRY, ADMINISTRATIVE ASSISTANT; OZARK FOLK CENTER; ARKANSAS HWY 9-5-14; MOUNTAIN VIEW, AR 72560. (#20030).

RECREATIONAL OPPORTUNITIES FOR TOMORROW - AR. THE CITIZENS OF STONE COUNTY THINK THAT A RECREATIONAL DEVELOPMENT LOCATED AT THE COUNTY SEAT WOULD BE A NEW AND APPRECIATED ASSET TO THEIR COUNTY. (LOCAL). HON EARL STOREY, JUDGE; STONE COUNTY; STONE COUNTY COURTHOUSE; MT VIEW, AR 72560. (#27076). **ARBA GRANTEE.**

APR 9 - 25, '76. 14TH ANNUAL ARKANSAS FOLK FESTIVAL. DATES OF FOLK FESTIVAL AT FOLK CENTER ARE: APRIL 9-11; APRIL 15-18; AND APRIL 23-25. REFLECTIONS OF ARKANSAS 'HILL COUNTRY' HERITAGE. AT OZARK FOLK CENTER, MOUNTAIN VIEW. (REGN'L). SUSAN MCMURRY; OZARK FOLK CENTER; ARKANSAS HWY 9-5-14; MOUNTAIN VIEW, AR 72560. (#20030-1).

MAY 1 - OCT 31, '76. 1976 SEASON AT OZARK FOLK CENTER. FAMILY HARVEST FESTIVAL AT FOLK CENTER OCT 11-31, 1976. AT OZARK FOLK CENTER, MOUNTAIN VIEW. (LOCAL). SUSAN MCMURRY; OZARK FOLK CENTER; ARKANSAS HWY 9-5-14; MOUNTAIN VIEW, AR 72560. (#20030-2).

OCT 11 - 31, '76. OZARK FOLK CENTER FAMILY FESTIVAL. FESTIVAL AT OZARK FOLK CENTER. (LOCAL). DIRECTOR; OZARK FOLK CENTER; MOUNTAIN VIEW, AR 72506. (#103416-634).

MOUNTAINBURG

APR 24, '76. ARTS & CRAFTS FAIR. FAIR, LIVE PERFORMANCE AT MOUNTAINBURG HIGH SCHOOL. (LOCAL). ROBERT M GARNER, CHAIRMAN; CRAWFORD COUNTY BICENTENNIAL COMMISSION; PO BOX 486; VAN BUREN, AR 72956. (#200005-73).

MAY 30, '76. ALL-CHURCH HYMN SING - PART OF BICENTENNIAL EVANGELISTIC CRUSADE. CEREMONY, LIVE PERFORMANCE AT FIRST BAPTIST CHURCH. (LOCAL). ROBERT M GARNER, CHAIRMAN; CRAWFORD COUNTY BICENTENNIAL COMMISSION; PO BOX 486; VAN BUREN, AR 72956. (#200005-72).

MULBERRY

JUNE 11 - 12, '76. MULBERRY BICENTENNIAL FETE. FESTIVAL, PARADE, EXHIBIT, CEREMONY, LIVE PERFORMANCE AT KIRKSEY PARK & FAIRGROUND, MULBERRY MAIN ST. (LOCAL). ROBERT M GARNER, CHAIRMAN; CRAWFORD COUNTY BICENTENNIAL COMMISSION; PO BOX 486; VAN BUREN, AR 72956. (#200005-67).

MURFREESBORO

PIKE COUNTY MUSEUM, MURFREESBORO, AR. PIKE COUNTY CITIZENS HAVE BEGUN WORK ON A COUNTY MUSEUM WHICH WILL BE COMPOSED OF AN OLD LOG CABIN WHICH THEY ACQUIRED AND AN ADDITIONAL BUILDING WHICH WILL BE BUILT ON THE SAME SITE. (LOCAL). HON A D MAY, COUNTY JUDGE; PIKE COUNTY; PO BOX 239; MURFREESBORO, AR 71958. (#27736). **ARBA GRANTEE.**

N LITTLE ROCK

BICENTENNIAL FESTIVAL, N LITTLE ROCK, AR. PROJECT WILL INCLUDE THE OBSERVANCE OF THE BIRTHDAY OF GIRL SCOUTS; A SPECIAL CEREMONY ON JULY 4, 1976 MARKING HISTORICAL STRUCTURES WITHIN THE HISTORIC QUAPAW QUARTER. (LOCAL). MRS JOHN PRATT, PRESIDENT; QUACHITA GIRL SCOUT COUNCIL; 615 W 29TH ST; N LITTLE ROCK, AR 72114. (#20963). **ARBA GRANTEE.**

RESTORATION OF E O MANEES HOME, AR. THE JUNIOR SERVICE LEAGUE PROPOSES TO COMPLETE THE RESTORATION OF THIS STRUCTURE TO PRESERVE ITS HERITAGE AND EXPAND ITS USEFULNESS TO THE CITIZENS AND THE CITY. (LOCAL). MRS PAUL DEAN, COORDINATOR; N LITTLE ROCK JUNIOR SERVICE LEAGUE; 216 W 4TH ST; N LITTLE ROCK, AR 72115. (#24733). **ARBA GRANTEE.**

APR 13 - 16, '76. AMERICAN FREEDOM TRAIN DISPLAY DAYS AT NORTH LITTLE ROCK. THE AMERICAN FREEDOM TRAIN WILL INCLUDE 10 EXHIBIT CARS AND 2 SHOWCASE CARS DEPICTING DIFFERENT PHASES OF THE AMERICAN EXPERIENCE. ITS ARRIVAL WILL SERVE AS A CATALYST FOR LOCAL BICENTENNIAL CELEBRATIONS BY PEOPLE THROUGHOUT THIS NATION. (ST-WIDE). SY FREEDMAN, DIR OF P/R; THE AMERICAN FREEDOM TRAIN FOUNDATION, INC; 5205 LEESBURG PKE, SUITE 800; BAILEY'S XRDS, VA 22041. (#1776-152).

JULY 4, '76. BICENTENNIAL FESTIVAL. SPECIAL CEREMONY ON JULY 4, 1976, MARKING HISTORICAL STRUCTURES WITHIN THE HISTORIC QUAPAW QUARTER; EXHIBIT OF CRAFTS. (LOCAL). MRS JOHN PRATT, PRES; QUACHITA GIRL SCOUT COUNCIL; 615 W 29TH ST; N LITTLE ROCK, AR 72114. (#20963-1).

NASHVILLE

PAINT HOWARD COUNTY MUSEUM - AR. THIS MUSEUM CONTAINS DISPLAYS OF HISTORICAL DOCUMENTS AND ITEMS PRIMARILY OF HOWARD COUNTY AND IS OPEN FREE TO THE PUBLIC. THE EXTERIOR OF THE BUILDING IS IN NEED OF REPAIR & WILL BE PAINTED. (LOCAL). HON O'NEAL DAVIDSON, JUDGE; HOWARD COUNTY; HOWARD COUNTY COURTHOUSE; NASHVILLE, AR 71852. (#27858). **ARBA GRANTEE.**

JULY 2 - 4, '76. FREEDOM RINGS IN NASHVILLE. HISTORICAL PLAY, NAME ENTERTAINER, FIREWORKS, DOWNTOWN DAY, BOOTHS ON MAIN ST, STUDENT ART SHOW/ESSAY CONTEST, RESTORATION OF VICTORIAN GOTHIC CHURCH INTO COUNTY MUSEUM, CHURCH DAY, GOSPEL SINGING & DINNER ON THE GROUND. (LOCAL). GLEN POWER, CHAIRPERSON; NASHVILLE BICENTENNIAL COMMITTEE; 1110 N 10TH ST; NASHVILLE, AR 71852. (#107346-1).

NATURAL DAM

JULY 4 - 5, '75. ARTS & CRAFTS FAIR. JUNIOR RODEO. HORSE QUADRILLE. NON-PROFESSIONAL FOLK MUSIC. AT HY 59 NORTH OF VAN BUREN. (LOCAL). ROBERT M GARNER; CRAWFORD COUNTY BICENTENNIAL COMMITTEE; PO BOX 486; VAN BUREN, AR 72956. (#50216-1).

OCT 2 - 3, '76. NATURAL DAM ARTS & CRAFTS FAIR. FAIR, LIVE PERFORMANCE AT NATURAL DAM COMMUNITY CENTER, HWY 59, N OF VAN BUREN. (LOCAL). NONA LOU HAILEY, COORD; CRAWFORD COUNTY BICENTENNIAL COMMISSION; STAR ROUTE; NATURAL DAM, AR 72948. (#200005-64).

NEWPORT

CONFEDERATE SOLDIER MONUMENT IN NEWPORT, ARKANSAS. THE CONFEDERATE MONUMENT WAS MOVED TO THE STATE PARK IN 1974. A WALKWAY OF BRICK IS BEING BUILT FROM THE COUNTY COURTHOUSE MUSEUM TO THE MONUMENT. (LOCAL). MILDRED MINOR GREGORY, PROJ COORDINATOR; JACKSON COUNTY HISTORICAL SOCIETY; NEWPORT, AR 72112. (#7773).

FIRE PROTECTION PROGRAM FOR JACKSON COUNTY, ARK. THE FIRE PROTECTION & PREVENTION PROGRAM FOR JACKSON COUNTY HAS BEEN SUBMITTED & IS AWAITING FUNDING. (LOCAL). HON JOE COE, JUDGE; WHITE RIVER DEVELOPMENT & PLANNING COMMISSION; COURT HOUSE, 3RD ST; NEWPORT, AR 72112. (#7717). **(??).**

JACKSON COUNTY HISTORICAL MARKER PROGRAM OF AR. PLACEMENT OF HISTORIC MARKERS TO IDENTIFY TWO LOCATIONS IN JACKSON COUNTY, ARKANSAS. ONE WILL BE A COUNTY SEAT MARKER AND THE OTHER A MEMORIAL TO THE REVOLUTIONARY WAR VETERANS WHO LIVED IN THE COUNTY. (LOCAL). WILLIAM H HEARD, PROJ COORDINATOR; JACKSON COUNTY HISTORICAL SOCIETY; 214 VINE; NEWPORT, AR 72112. (#8217). **ARBA GRANTEE.**

'MARY WOODS II' PADDLE WHEELER - NEWPORT, ARK. THE 'MARY WOODS II' OPENED TO THE PUBLIC ON MAY 5, 1976. INSIDE DEPICTS REPLICA OF OLD RIVER PASSENGER STEAMBOAT. OVER 7,000 PERSONS VIEWED HER IN 3 MONTHS. (LOCAL). MILDRED MINOR GREGORY, PROJ COORDINATOR; JACKSON COUNTY HISTORICAL SOCIETY; NEWPORT, AR 72112. (#30258).

MICROFILM LIBRARY PROJECT IN NEWPORT, ARKANSAS. THE JACKSON COUNTY HISTORICAL SOCIETY HAS DONATED A MICROFILM VIEWER TO THE BILLINGSLEY MEMORIAL LIBRARY. BUSINESSES AND INDIVIDUALS ARE DONATING THE MICROFILM. (LOCAL). RUBY HERRING, LIBRARIAN; W A BILLINGSLEY MEMORIAL LIBRARY; NEWPORT, AR 72112. (#7772).

NEWPORT PARK DEVELOPMENT PROGRAM - ARKANSAS. PLANS CALL FOR NEW PARKS & COMPLETE RECREATION PROGRAMS WITH NEW EQUIPMENT. A SWIMMING POOL IS ALSO INCLUDED. (LOCAL). TERRY LODGE, DIRECTOR; NEWPORT PARKS & RECREATION ASSOC; PO BOX 128; NEWPORT, AR 72112. (#7771). **(??).**

AUG 14 - 16, '75. NEWPORT CENTENNIAL 1975 - 3 DAY CELEBRATION. THREE DAYS OF ALL TYPES EVENTS- CEREMONIES, PARADES, TEA, RITUALS, BALL, MERCHANTS PARTICIPATION, ARTS & CRAFTS, ART SHOW. ETC. AT DOWNTOWN NEWPORT STAGE ETC.. (LOCAL). MILDRED MINOR GREGORY; NEWPORT CENTENNIAL COMMITTEE & CITY OF NEWPORT, ARK; 324 WALNUT ST; NEWPORT, AR 72112. (#50098-1).

MAR 30, '76. UNITED STATES ARMED FORCES BICENTENNIAL CARAVAN. CARAVAN IS COMPOSED OF EXHIBIT VANS FOR EACH MILITARY SERVICE. PROJECT THEME IS 'HISTORY OF THE ARMED FORCES AND THEIR CONTRIBUTIONS TO THE NATION'. (LOCAL). MRS MILDRED M GREGORY; US ARMED FORCES BICENTENNIAL EXHIBIT VANS PROJECT; 324 WALNUT ST; NEWPORT, AR 72112. (#1775-412).

NIMROD

JUNE 6, '76. OLD-FASHIONED HOMECOMING PICNIC. HORSEBACK TRAIL RIDE TO DELIVER SCROLLS TO WAGON TRAIN AT CO SEAT; MARKER FOR TREES PLANTED BY HORIZONS COMMITTEE; HERITAGE COMMITTEE COMPILED & WROTE HISTORY OF NIMROD. AT NIMROD COMMUNITY BLDG. (LOCAL). HERBY BRANSCUM, CHAIRMAN; NIMROD BICENTENNIAL COMMITTEE & PERRY COUNTY BICENTENNIAL COMMITTEE; PERRYVILLE, AR 72126. (#200005-31).

NORFORK

WOLF HOUSE MEMORIAL MUSEUM, NORFOLK, AR. FURNISHING & ADMINISTRATION OF THE WOLF HOUSE, SECOND OLDEST LOG STRUCTURE WEST OF THE MISSISSIPPI. (LOCAL). MARY A MESSICK, MEMORIAL CHAIRMAN; BAXTER COUNTY BICENTENNIAL COMMITTEE & WOLF HOUSE MEMORIAL CO; RT 1 BOX 110; GASSVILLE, AR 72635. (#31101).

JULY 3, '76. HISTORICAL PAGEANT, COUNTY WIDE CAST. HISTORY OF NORTHERN ARKANSAS FROM 1810-1863. (LOCAL). REX BAYLESS; BAXTER COUNTY BICENTENNIAL COMMITTEE; COTTER, AR 72626. (#200005-79).

JULY 3, '76. WOLF HOUSE BICENTENNIAL PAGEANT. ACTIVITIES INCLUDED A BARBEQUE AND PAGEANT HELD ON THE GROUNDS OF THE HISTORIC WOLF HOUSE. (LOCAL). ROBERT BOUNDS, CHMN; WOLF HOUSE MEMORIAL COMMITTEE; NORFORK, AR 72658. (#200005-119).

NORPHLET

JULY 4, '76. NEW FLAG POLE AT CITY HALL - DEDICATION CEREMONY. CEREMONY AT CITY HALL. (LOCAL). COY HENLEY, CHAIRMAN; NORPHLET BICENTENNIAL COMMITTEE; BOX 123; NORPHLET, AR 71759. (#200005-28).

OSCEOLA

VIOLET CEMETERY RESTORATION IN OSCEOLA, ARKANSAS. A PROJECT TO BEAUTIFY CEMETERY WHERE MANY EARLY SETTLERS ARE BURIED. PROVISIONS TO BE MADE FOR FUTURE MAINTENANCE. (LOCAL). RAY BAUM, CHAIRMAN; OSCEOLA BICENTENNIAL COMMITTEE; 705 W HALE; OSCEOLA, AR 72370. (#4858).

JULY 9, '75. OTRABANDA COMPANY'S THIRD ANNUAL MISSISSIPPI RIVER TOUR. LIVE PERFORMANCE, PARADE AT EAST ELEMENTARY SCHOOL GROUNDS; E. KEISER AND CHESTNUT STS.. (LOCAL). KEN KLINE, DIRECTOR; CHAMBER OF COMMERCE; 108 N. WALNUT ST.; OSCEOLA, AR 72370. (#50550-9).

OZARK

SEPT 17 - 18, '76. OLD-FASHIONED SQUARE GATHERING. CITY & COUNTY CIVIC GROUPS UNITED IN COURTHOUSE SQUARE FESTIVAL WITH MANY KINDS OF ENTERTAINMENT, INCLUDING A ROCKING CONTEST. AT ALL AROUND COURTHOUSE SQUARE. (LOCAL). DON SMITH, COORDINATOR; OZARK JAYCEES & JAYCETTES; 817 N 3RD; OZARK, AR 72949. (#200005-21).

OZONE

JULY 31 - AUG 1, '76. OLD FASHIONED DAYS FESTIVAL. OLD FIDDLERS' CONTEST & SQUARE DANCE; GREASED PIG CHASE; HORSESHOE TOSS, CANNED GOODS, COSTUMES, QUILTS & BOOTHS, WATERMELON BUST, HAND WEAVING, CARVING & OTHER CRAFTS; SOFTBALL, ICE CREAM SOCIAL, SACK RACE, ANTIQUES, 3 LEGGED RACE, SPELLING BEE, PAINTING & PHOTO SHOW. AT OZONE OLD SCHOOLHOUSE, HWY 21, NORTH OF CLARKSVILLE. (LOCAL). DONNA COPELAND, PROJ CHMN; OZONE JUNIOR GRANGE #21; GENERAL DELIVERY; OZONE, AR 72854. (#21577-1).

O'KEAN

JUNE 10 - 19, '76. COMMUNITY FESTIVAL. SQUARE DANCE, PIE SUPPER, BEAUTY PAGEANT, BINGO PARTY, HAYRIDE, PARADE, BARBEQUE LUNCHEON, GAMES & FIREWORKS. AT TOWN HALL. (LOCAL). BERNICE HOLDER, COORD; O'KEAN BICENTENNIAL COMMITTEE & TOWN COUNCIL; BOX 8; O'KEAN, AR 72449. (#200005-24).

PARAGOULD

BICENTENNIAL CONCERT SERIES - PARAGOULD, AR. A SERIES OF FOUR CONCERTS WHICH WILL BRING AMERICAN MUSIC & SHOW TO PARAGOULD. CONCERTS INCLUDE DIXIELAND, BLUEGRASS AND SYMPHONIC MUSIC. (LOCAL). FRANK PINEDA, BICENTENNIAL CHMN; GREENE COUNTY BICENTENNIAL COMMITTEE; 635 W KINGSHIGHWAY; PARAGOULD, AR 72450. (#17586). **ARBA GRANTEE.**

FOOTBALL GAME WITH BICENT HALF-TIME SHOW IN AR. AMERICAN MUSIC WILL BE PRESENTED DURING THE HALF-TIME OF THE GREENE COUNTY TECH - PARAGOULD HIGH SCHOOL FOOTBALL GAME TO BE HELD IN PARAGOULD IN 1976. (LOCAL). FRANK PINEDA, PROJECT COORDINATOR; GREENE COUNTY GOVERNMENT; 635 W KINGSHIGHWAY; PARAGOULD, AR 72450. (#7627).

MARMADUKE FOURTH OF JULY PICNIC IN PARAGOULD, AR. THE MARMADUKE PICNIC WILL BE HELD ON JULY 4, 1976. ACTIVITIES WILL INCLUDE A HISTORY PAGEANT AND A SPELLING CONTEST. (LOCAL). FRANK PINEDA, PROJECT COORDINATOR; GREENE COUNTY GOVERNMENT; 635 W KINGSHIGHWAY; PARAGOULD, AR 72450. (#7629).

PRESENT MUSICAL PLAY, '1776', IN PARAGOULD, AR. THE PLAY WILL BE PRESENTED IN 1976. (LOCAL). FRANK PINEDA, PROJECT COORDINATOR; GREENE COUNTY GOVERNMENT; 635 W KINGSHIGHWAY; PARAGOULD, AR 72450. (#7628).

RESTORE AMPHITHEATER IN ARKANSAS STATE PARK. THE AMPHITHEATER IN CROWLEY'S RIDGE STATE PARK WILL BE RENOVATED. THE STAGE WILL HAVE THE NECESSARY WIRING. (LOCAL). FRANK PINEDA, PROJECT COORDINATOR; GREENE COUNTY GOVERNMENT; 635 W KINGSHIGHWAY; PARAGOULD, AR 72450. (#7625).

SQUARE DANCE CLUBS PROJECT IN PARAGOULD, ARKANSAS. A SKIT WITH A REVOLUTIONARY PERIOD THEME WILL BE PRESENTED AT THE REGIONAL MEETING OF SQUARE DANCE CLUBS. (LOCAL). FRANK PINEDA, CHAIRMAN; GREENE COUNTY BICENT COMMITTEE; 635 W KINGSHIGHWAY; PARAGOULD, AR 72450. (#7696).

APR 18 - 19, '75. RE-ENACTMENT OF PAUL REVERE'S RIDE. THIS IS THE INITIAL BICENTENNIAL EVENT FOR THE AREA. (LOCAL). FRANK PINEDA, CHAIRMAN; GREENE COUNTY BICENT COMMITTEE; 635 W KINGSHIGHWAY; PARAGOULD, AR 72450. (#7695-501).

OCT 6, '75 - APR 25, '76. BICENTENNIAL CONCERT SERIES. A SERIES OF FOUR CONCERTS WHICH WILL BRING AMERICAN MUSIC TO PARAGOULD. CONCERTS INCLUDE DIXIELAND, BLUEGRASS AND SYMPHONIC MUSIC. CONCERT 1: 10/06/75; CONCERT 2: 11/11/75; CONCERT 3: 2/09/76; CONCERT 4: 4/25/76; ALL CONCERTS AT 8PM EXCEPT #4 AT 4PM. AT GREENE COUNTY COMMUNITY CENTER. (LOCAL). FRANK PINEDA, CHMN; GREENE COUNTY BICENTENNIAL COMMITTEE; 635 W KINGSHIGHWAY; PARAGOULD, AR 72450. (#17586-1).

MAR 12, '76. USA CORPS OF ENGINEERS MOBILE BICENT VAN VISITS PARAGOULD, AR. A MULTI-MEDIA SHOW DEPICTING THE 200 YEAR HISTORY OF THE CORPS OF ENGINEERS & ITS ROLE IN THE EVOLUTION OF OUR NATION. AT COMMUNITY CENTER. (LOCAL). KENT CARMAIN, CHMN; USA CORPS OF ENGINEERS; US ARMY CORPS OF ENGINEERS; MEMPHIS, TN 38103. (#31165-8).

PARKIN

BICENTENNIAL PARK PROJECT IN PARKIN, ARKANSAS. TEN ACRES WILL BE DEVELOPED AS A CITY PARK ONE MILE NORTH OF PARKIN ON BANKS OF TYRONZA & ST FRANCIS RIVERS. HISTORY CLASS AT HIGH SCHOOL TO ERECT MARKER TO 1927 FLOOD. BIKE & HIKING TRAILS DEVELOPED. (LOCAL). HON S SLABAUGH, JR, MAYOR; CITY OF PARKIN; BOX 498; PARKIN, AR 72373. (#4859). **ARBA GRANTEE.**

FLOOD OF 1927 MARKER IN PARKIN, ARKANSAS. HIGH SCHOOL STUDENTS ARE RAISING MONEY TO PLACE A MARKER WHICH WILL COMMEMORATE THE GREAT FLOOD OF 1927. (LOCAL). MRS ALMA H JOHNSON, CHAIRMAN; PARKIN HIGH SCHOOL HISTORY CLUB; PARKIN CITY, AR 72337. (#4860). (??). **ARBA GRANTEE.**

PARKIN, ARK, BICENTENNIAL CELEBRATION. JOINT CELEBRATION WITH OUTLYING COMMUNITIES IN OCTOBER 1975. WILL INVOLVE ENTIRE POPULATION. (LOCAL). MRS ALMA H JOHNSON, CHAIRPERSON; PARKIN BICENTENNIAL COMMITTEE; BOX 216; PARKIN, AR 72373. (#6423).

THE ZIRKLE MUSEUM - PARKIN, AR. THE LOG CABIN WAS BUILT IN 1861. IT HAS SINCE BEEN MOVED AND REBUILT TO HOUSE ANTIQUE TOOLS AND MACHINERY. (LOCAL). ROBERT ZIRKLE, OWNER-OPERATOR; ZIRKLE MUSEUM; PO BOX 404, EAST SMITHDALE; PARKIN, AR 72373. (#23335).

OCT 11, '75. ART EXHIBITION. EXHIBIT AT PARKIN CO-OP. (LOCAL). ALMA H JOHNSON, CHMN; PARKIN COMMUNITY BICENTENNIAL; 306 SPARROW ST, BOX 216; PARKIN, AR 72373. (#102489-4).

OCT 11, '75. RE-ENACTMENT OF THE ARRIVAL OF DESOTO AND THE SPANISH. LIVE PERFORMANCE. (LOCAL). JESSIE MCDERMOTT, CO-CHMN; PARKIN COMMUNITY BICENTENNIAL COMMISSION; 111 E PARK AVE; PARKIN, AR 72373. (#102490-1).

OCT 11, '75. SQUARE DANCING ON MAIN STREET & BICENTENNIAL PARADE. FESTIVAL, PARADE AT MAIN ST. (LOCAL). ALMA H JOHNSON, CHMN; PARKIN COMMUNITY BICENTENNIAL; 306 SPARROW ST, BOX 216; PARKIN, AR 72373. (#102489-2).

OCT 11 - 12, '75. PARKINS BICENTENNIAL CELEBRATION: PARADE AND CHURCH SERVICE. CELEBRATION INCLUDES A PARADE, SQUARE DANCING, CHURCH SERVICE, A BEARD GROWING CONTEST, A TOUR OF HISTORIC HOMES, FESTIVAL ROYALTY, & INSTALLMENT OF A MARKER TO COMMEMORATE THE FLOOD OF 1912. (LOCAL). MRS ALMA H JOHNSON; PARKIN BICENTENNIAL COMMITTEE; BOX 216; PARKIN, AR 72373. (#6423-501).

OCT 11 - 12, '75. 'RIP VAN WINKLE' PRESENTED BY THE UNIVERSITY OF ARKANSAS. THIS IS PART OF PARKIN'S BICENTENNIAL CELEBRATION. MATINEE AT 2:00, EVENING SHOW AT 7:00. AT PARKIN HIGH SCHOOL. (LOCAL). ALMA H JOHNSON, PARKIN BICENTENNIAL COMMITTEE; BOX 216; PARKIN, AR 72373. (#6423-502).

OCT 12, '75. BICENTENNIAL CEREMONY. CEREMONY AT BELL STADIUM. (LOCAL). ALMA H JOHNSON, CHMN; PARKIN COMMUNITY BICENTENNIAL; 306 SPARROW ST, BOX 216; PARKIN, AR 72373. (#102489-3).

APR 30 - MAY 2, '76. TOUR OF ZIRKLE MUSEUM. TOUR. (LOCAL). ALMA H JOHNSON, CHMN; PARKIN COMMUNITY; BOX 216; PARKIN, AR 72373. (#104319-1).

MAY 1, '76. TOUR OF HISTORIC HOMES. TOUR. (LOCAL). MRS JESSIE MCDERMOTT; PARKIN GARDEN CLUB; E PARK AVE; PARKIN, AR 72373. (#106688-1).

MAY 1 - 2, '76. FLEA MARKET. FESTIVAL. (LOCAL). MRS ALLEN CARDEN, COORD; GARDEN CLUB; PARKIN, AR 72373. (#200005-3).

MAY 9, '76. HONOR BANQUET. AWARD, CEREMONY. (LOCAL). ALMA JOHNSON, CHMN; PARKIN COMMUNITY; 309 SPARROW AVE; PARKIN, AR 72373. (#200005-2).

MAY 27 - 29, '76. TENNIS TOURNAMENT. COMPETITION AT PARKIN; JESSIE MCDERMOTT COURT. (LOCAL). ALMA H JOHNSON, CHMN; PARKIN COMMUNITY; BOX 216; PARKIN, AR 72373. (#104319-4).

JULY 3, '76. JULY 3RD CELEBRATION. AT 1:30PM, CARNIVAL & BOAT FAIR ON THE ST FRANCIS RIVER. LT GOV WILL SPEAK AT 3PM. RECEPTION TO FOLLOW. BARBEQUE, STREET DANCE 8PM-12AM, DEDICATION OF MARKER ON 'INDIAN MOUND', DED OF MEMORIAL ON OLD HIGH SCHOOL CAMPUS; ALSO, GOSPEL-SINGING 8-10 PM. (LOCAL). ALMA H JOHNSON, CHMN; PARKIN COMMUNITY; BOX 216; PARKIN, AR 72373. (#104319-3).

OCT 16 - 17, '76. CORNERSTONE DEDICATION. THIS MARKER IS A CORNER STONE THAT WAS ABOUT TO BE DESTROYED. WE TOOK IT, MOUNTED IT ON THE SITE WHERE THE FIRST HIGH SCHOOL STOOD TO PRESERVE HISTORY. THIS PROJECT WAS DONE BY THE BEAUTY OPERATORS OF THE TOWN. AT CORNER OF METHODIST CHURCH ON OLD HIGH SCHOOL GROUNDS. (LOCAL). MRS ALMA H JOHNSON, CHMN; PARKIN BEAUTY SHOPS; BOX 216; PARKIN, AR 72373. (#200005-39).

OCT 17, '76. PARKIN BICENTENNIAL PARK DEDICATION. FESTIVAL AT PARK IS 1 MILE NORTH OF PARKIN ON ST FRANCIS AND TYRONZA RIVERS. (LOCAL). MRS ALMA H JOHNSON, CHMN; BICENTENNIAL COMMITTEE OF PARKIN; BOX 216; PARKIN, AR 72373. (#200005-38).

OCT 17, '76. QUARTET'S BICENTENNIAL PRESENTATION. LIVE PERFORMANCE AT VICTORY QUARTET HIGH SCHOOL AUDITORIUM. (LOCAL). TOMMY WOOD, COORD; LIONS CLUB; PARKIN, AR 72373. (#200005-41).

OCT 17, '76. TOUR OF INDIAN MOUND MONUMENT. INDIAN MOUNT MONUMENT IS BELIEVED TO BE THE POINT REACHED BY DESOTO & HIS MEN. AT INDIAN MOUND MONUMENT. (ST-WIDE). MRS ALMA H JOHNSON, CHMN; HISTORY CLUB OF PARKIN HIGH SCHOOL; BOX 216; PARKIN, AR 72373. (#200005-40).

PATTERSON

SEPT 17 - 21, '75. WOODRUFF COUNTY FAIR AND LIVESTOCK SHOW. ALL PROJECTS, BOOTH, ENTERTAINMENT, DECORATIONS AND ACTIVITIES WILL HAVE BICENTENNIAL. AT HALFWAY BETWEEN MCCRORY & PATTERSON ON OLD HWY 64. (LOCAL). BOB ELAM, DIRECTOR; WOODRUFF COUNTY FAIR ASSOCIATION; PATTERSON, AR 72123. (#103799-1).

MAY '76. SENIOR CITIZENS FAIR. A GATHERING OF ALL SENIOR CITIZENS IN WOODRUFF CO & SOME AJOINING COUNTIES. AT WOODRUFF COUNTY FAIRGROUNDS HY 64W OF MCCRORY. (LOCAL). MRS SCOTT FOWLER, DIR; WOODRUFF COUNTY SENIOR CITIZENS; HOWELL, AR 72071. (#103799-5).

PEA RIDGE

COMPILE PICTORIAL HISTORY OF PEA RIDGE, ARKANSAS. PHOTOGRAPHS AND PRINTS REFLECTING THE HISTORY OF THE COMMUNITY WILL BE COLLECTED AND DISPLAYED. (LOCAL). JOYCE HALE, PROJECT COORDINATOR; CITY OF PEA RIDGE; RT 1, BOX 53C; PEA RIDGE, AR 72751. (#7636).

'PEA RIDGE' DAY PARK IN PEA RIDGE, ARKANSAS. LAND WILL BE DEVELOPED AS A CITY PARK TO BE NAMED IN HONOR OF CLYDE 'PEA RIDGE' DAY, FORMER BASEBALL PLAYER AND NATIVE SON. FACILITIES INCLUDE BALL FIELDS, PICNIC AREAS AND PLAYGROUND EQUIPMENT. (LOCAL). JOYCE HALE, BICENTENNIAL CHAIRMAN; CITY OF PEA RIDGE; CITY HALL; PEA RIDGE, AR 72751. (#8215). **ARBA GRANTEE.**

PUBLIC SCHOOLS' BICENT PROGRAM IN PEA RIDGE, AR. BICENT ACTIVITIES OF LOCAL PRIMARY & SECONDARY SCHOOLS TO INCLUDE FOLK DANCES, ASSEMBLIES, ART & ESSAY CONTESTS AND A PATRIOTIC MUSIC CONCERT. ACTIVITIES TO HAVE AMERICAN HERITAGE THEME. (LOCAL). JOYCE HALE, PROJ COORDINATOR; CITY OF PEA RIDGE; RT 1, BOX 53C; PEA RIDGE, AR 72751. (#7635).

RELIGIOUS FREEDOM POSTERS ON DISPLAY IN ARKANSAS. A SERIES OF POSTERS ON FREEDOM OF RELIGION TO BE DISPLAYED IN CITY OF PEA RIDGE. (LOCAL). JOYCE HALE, PROJECT COORDINATOR; CITY OF PEA RIDGE; RT 1, BOX 53C; PEA RIDGE, AR 72751. (#7637).

RENAME EXTENSION HOMEMAKER'S BLDG IN PEA RIDGE, AR. THE BUILDING WILL BE RENAMED AS THE 'HOMEMAKER'S TOWN HALL'. IT WILL BE USED FOR VARIOUS COMMUNITY PURPOSES. (LOCAL). JOYCE HALE; EXTENSION HOMEMAKERS CLUB OF PEA RIDGE; RT 1, BOX 53C; PEA RIDGE, AR 72751. (#7631-1).

RESTORATION PROJECT IN PEA RIDGE, ARKANSAS. REPAIR, RECONDITIONING AND DECORATION OF THE HOMEMAKERS TOWN HALL WILL BE UNDERTAKEN IN A RESTORATION EFFORT. (LOCAL). JOYCE HALE, COORDINATOR; EXTENSION HOMEMAKERS' CLUB OF PEA RIDGE; RT 1, BOX 53C; PEA RIDGE, AR 72751. (#7640).

SALE OF AMERICAN FLAGS IN PEA RIDGE, AR. SALE AND DISTRIBUTION OF AMERICAN FLAGS FOR DISPLAY BY BUSINESSES AND RESIDENTS. (LOCAL). JOYCE HALE, PROJECT COORDINATOR; CITY OF PEA RIDGE; RT 1, BOX 53C; PEA RIDGE, AR 72751. (#7633).

JULY 4, '75. COMMUNITY FAIR & PARADE. FAIR, PARADE. (LOCAL). JOYCE HALE; CITY OF PEA RIDGE; RT 1, BOX 53C; PEA RIDGE, AR 72751. (#7634-501).

JULY '75. DEDICATE HOMEMAKER'S TOWN HALL IN PEA RIDGE, AR. DEDICATION CEREMONIES FOR THE BUILDING WILL INCLUDE AN OPEN HOUSE. (LOCAL). JOYCE HALE; EXTENSION HOMEMAKERS CLUB OF PEA RIDGE; RT 1, BOX 53C; PEA RIDGE, AR 72751. (#7632-1).

JUNE 12, '76. NATL PK SVC '...A LITTLE LOOK AROUND' VISITS PEA RIDGE NMP. THIS SHORT PROGRAM FEATURES ACTORS PORTRAYING FAMOUS AMERICANS OF THE PAST WHO'VE RETURNED TO SEE AMERICA'S PROGRESS. (REGN'L). PEA RIDGE N M P; NATIONAL PARK SERVICE; PEA RIDGE, AR 72751. (#5653-76).

JULY 7 - 10, '76. COMMUNITY FAIR & PARADE. FAIR ACTIVITIES WILL TAKE PLACE JULY 7-10 WITH THE FINAL DAY FEATURING A PARADE AND THE 2ND ANNUAL HOMECOMING BARBEQUE. PROCEEDS FROM THE BARBEQUE WILL GO TO CITY PARK DEVELOPMENT, A BICENTENNIAL HORIZONS PROJECT. (LOCAL). JOYCE HALE; CITY OF PEA RIDGE; RT 1, BOX 53C; PEA RIDGE, AR 72751. (#7634-502).

OCT 9, '76. RE-ENACTMENT OF THE BLUE & GRAY AT PEA RIDGE NMP. A RE-DEDICATION OF THE MONUMENTS TO THREE CONFEDERATE GENERALS & THE MEN WHO DIED AT PEA RIDGE DURING THE WAR. USING ORIGINAL DANCE AND SOME OF THE FIRST SPEECHES. PROGRAM IN HONOR OF THE BLUE & GRAY COMING BACK TOGETHER IN PEACE. AT PEA RIDGE NATIONAL MILITARY PARK. (ST-WIDE). J DICKSON BLACK, CHMN; BENTON COUNTY ARBC; 124 W 2ND; BENTONVILLE, AR 72712. (#103487-1).

OCT '76. DEDICATION OF PARK. OPENING, CEREMONY. (LOCAL). JOYCE HALE; CITY OF PEA RIDGE; CITY HALL; PEA RIDGE, AR 72751. (#8215-501).

PERRYVILLE

HISTORICAL MEMORIAL - PERRYVILLE, AR. THE CITY OF PERRYVILLE PLANS TO ERECT A HISTORICAL MARKER AT THE RISON HOUSE, THE OLDEST HOUSE STILL STANDING AND OCCUPIED AT THE SITE OF OLD PERRYVILLE. (LOCAL). HON CHARLES A REEDER, MAYOR; CITY OF PERRYVILLE; CITY HALL; PERRYVILLE, AR 72126. (#26815). **ARBA GRANTEE.**

HISTORY BOOK AND RESTORATION IN PERRYVILLE, AR. COMPILING DATA ON COMMUNITY DEVELOPMENT AND RESIDENTS; RESTORATION AND PRESERVATION OF COMMUNITY BUILDING. (LOCAL). JOHNNIE BAILEY, CHAIRMAN; UNION VALLEY BICENTENNIAL ORGANIZATION; UNION VALLEY; PERRYVILLE, AR 72126. (#29286).

JULY 4, '76. JULY FOURTH CELEBRATION. CEREMONY, FESTIVAL, PARADE AT UNION VALLEY COMMUNITY BLDG. (LOCAL). JOHNNIE BAILEY, CHMN; UNION VALLEY BICENTENNIAL ORGANIZATION; BOX 97; PERRYVILLE, AR 72126. (#200005-25).

PINE BLUFF

BEAUTIFICATION PROGRAM IN PINE BLUFF, ARKANSAS. 'CLEANAIR '76' LANDSCAPING OF PUBLIC PROPERTY, NEW HOUSING CODES AND DEVELOPMENT OF SMALL PARKS WITH SCULPTURE, HISTORICAL MARKERS AND GLASSED EXHIBITS WILL BE UNDERTAKEN BY & IN JEFFERSON COUNTY. (LOCAL). C FRANK WILLIAMSON, CHAIRMAN; JEFFERSON COUNTY BICENT COMMITTEE; PO BOX 1776; PINE BLUFF, AR 71601. (#8270).

BICENTENNIAL FESTIVAL IN PINE BLUFF, ARKANSAS. DEDICATION OF THE PINE BLUFF CONVENTION CENTER ON VETERANS DAY, FLAG PRESENTATION CEREMONIES, CITIZENSHIP AWARDS & CRAFTS FESTIVALS WILL BE FEATURED FOR THE BICENTENNIAL IN JEFFERSON COUNTY. (LOCAL). C FRANK WILLIAMSON, CHAIRMAN; JEFFERSON COUNTY BICENT COMMITTEE; PO BOX 1776; PINE BLUFF, AR 71601. (#8271).

BLUES MUSIC IN THE ARKANSAS DELTA REGION. MUSICAL PRESENTATION OF THE UNIV OF ARKANSAS. (ST-WIDE). DR GRACE WILEY, PROJ DIRECTOR; UNIVERSITY OF ARKANSAS, PINE BLUFF; N CEDAR ST; PINE BLUFF, AR 71601. (#18667). **ARBA GRANTEE.**

DEXTER HARDING HOME, PINE BLUFF, ARKANSAS. RESTORATION OF THIS 1840 BUILDING TO SERVE AS A CITY MUSEUM; THE BUILDING TO BE LOCATED ON US HIGHWAY 65 BYPASS ON

PINE BLUFF — CONTINUED

PINE STREET, IDEAL LOCATION FOR VISITOR INFORMATION CENTER. (LOCAL). WILLIAM S HERCHER, CHAIRMAN; JEFFERSON COUNTY HISTORY COMMISSION; 610 W 20TH AVE; PINE BLUFF, AR 71601. (#528). **ARBA GRANTEE.**

HAWAII SUMMER PROGRAM - PINE BLUFF, ARKANSAS. THE STUDENTS WILL STUDY THE OCEANS AND VOLCANOES UNDER THE PROGRAM'S THEME, 'THIS GREAT LAND OF OURS'. THIS PROGRAM IS DEDICATED TO THE BICENTENNIAL IN STUDYING VARIOUS GEOGRAPHICAL AREAS OF AMERICA. (LOCAL). C FRANK WILLIAMSON, CHAIRMAN; BICENTENNIAL COMMITTEE; PO BOX 1776; PINE BLUFF, AR 71601. (#8272).

HISTORICAL RADIO SERIES IN PINE BLUFF, ARKANSAS. A MONTHLY SERIES ABOUT ARKANSAS HISTORY WILL BE AIRED ON A LOCAL RADIO STATION AND WILL BE PREPARED BY HISTORY DEPARTMENT PERSONNEL OF THE UNIVERSITY OF ARKANSAS AT PINE BLUFF. (LOCAL). C FRANK WILLIAMSON, CHAIRMAN; JEFFERSON COUNTY BICENT COMMITTEE; PO BOX 1776; PINE BLUFF, AR 71601. (#8274).

JEFFERSON COUNTY MARKERS: PINE BLUFF, ARKANSAS. HISTORICAL MARKERS WILL BE PLACED THROUGHOUT THE COUNTY THROUGH THE JEFFERSON COUNTY HISTORY COMMISSION. (LOCAL). PHILIP A KLOPFENSTEIN, GRANTS TRUSTEE; JEFFERSON COUNTY HISTORICAL COMMISSION; PO BOX 7009; PINE BLUFF, AR 71601. (#8275). **ARBA GRANTEE.**

PUBLISH 'WOMEN OF THE DELTA', PINE BLUFF, AR. GATHERING & PUBLICATION OF INFORMATION ABOUT THE WOMEN OF THE DELTATHEIR HISTORY & LIVES, THEIR HOPES, THEIR MUSIC & SONG & OTHER INTERESTING FACTS ABOUT THESE WOMEN. (ST-WIDE). CAROLYN ANN GETTLER, PRESIDENT; CITY OF PINE BLUFF; 1816 CHERRY ST; PINE BLUFF, AR 71601. (#23505). **ARBA GRANTEE.**

THE ROLE OF AM&N COLLEGE: AN ORAL HISTORY - AR. THE PURPOSE OF THE PROJECT IS TO DESCRIBE THE ROLE OF AM&N COLLEGE IN TRAINING BLACK LEADERS AND TO SHOW THE CONTRIBUTIONS OF AM&N GRADUATES TO THE DEVELOPMENT OF THE COMMUNITY AS A WHOLE. (LOCAL). MARTIN E MANTELL, ASST PROFESSOR; UNIV OF ARKANSAS AT PINE BLUFF; PINE BLUFF, AR 71601. (#20982). **ARBA GRANTEE.**

UNIVERSITY OF ARKANSAS' ENTERTAINMENT: PINE BLUFF. ALL HALF-TIME PROGRAMS, MUSICAL PERFORMANCES AND EXHIBITS PRODUCED BY THE BAND/CHORAL GROUP & HISTORY DEPARTMENT WILL BE DEDICATED TO BICENTENNIAL THEMES IN 1976. (LOCAL). C FRANK WILLIAMSON, CHAIRMAN; JEFFERSON COUNTY BICENT COMMITTEE; PO BOX 1776; PINE BLUFF, AR 71601. (#8268).

DEC 1, '75 - JUNE 1, '76. BLUES MUSIC IN THE ARKANSAS DELTA REGION. LIVE PERFORMANCE AT UNIVERSITY OF ARKANSAS, PINE BLUFF. (ST-WIDE). DR GRACE WILEY; UNIVERSITY OF ARKANSAS, PINE BLUFF; N CEDAR ST; PINE BLUFF, AR 71601. (#18667-1).

FEB 18, '76. AMERICA 200. LIVE PERFORMANCE AT FIRST BAPTIST CHURCH. (LOCAL). MAC B SISSON, CHAIRMAN; OUACHITA BAPTIST UNIV; BOX 761; ARKADELPHIA, AR 71923. (#104862-2).

MAR 10 - 11, '76. UNITED STATES ARMED FORCES BICENTENNIAL CARAVAN. CARAVAN IS COMPOSED OF EXHIBIT VANS FOR EACH MILITARY SERVICE. PROJECT THEME IS 'HISTORY OF THE ARMED FORCES AND THEIR CONTRIBUTIONS TO THE NATION'. (LOCAL). PHILLIP A KLOPFESTIEN; US ARMED FORCES BICENTENNIAL EXHIBIT VANS PROJECT; SOUTHWEST AK ARTS & SCIENCE CNTR; PINE BLUFF, AR 71601. (#1775-406).

PLUMERVILLE

JULY 3 - 5, '76. PLUMERVILLE BICENTENNIAL CELEBRATION. A GENERAL CELEBRATION WITH LOCAL PEOPLE PARTICIPATING IN A FESTIVAL TYPE ATMOSPHERE: PARADE, MELODRAMA, HISTORIC DISPLAY, TIME CAPSULE, RODEO, FIREWORKS, ARTS & CRAFTS, CONCESSIONS. AT CITY HALL. (LOCAL). BENNY HUIE, CHAIRMAN; PLUMERVILLE BICENTENNIAL COMMITTEE; BOX 176; PLUMERVILLE, AR 72127. (#200005-22).

POCAHONTAS

DEDICATION OF RESTORED COURTHOUSE. RESTORATION OF OLD RANDOLPH COUNTY COURTHOUSE IN POCAHONTAS, AR IS LISTED ON NATIONAL REGISTER OF HISTORIC PLACES. (LOCAL). CLIFF BROWN, COUNTY JUDGE; COUNTY OF RANDOLPH; POCAHONTAS, AR 72455. (#11107-501). **(??).**

RESTORATION OF OLD RANDOLPH COUNTY COURTHOUSE - AR. OLD RANDOLPH COUNTY COURTHOUSE IN POCAHONTAS IS LISTED ON NATIONAL REGISTER OF HISTORIC PLACES. THE GOAL IS TO RESTORE THE BUILDING BY LABOR DAY, 1976 AND DEDICATE TO THE BICENTENNIAL. (LOCAL). CLIFF BROWN, COUNTY JUDGE; COUNTY OF RANDOLPH; POCAHONTAS, AR 72455. (#11107). **ARBA GRANTEE.**

MAY 6 - 7, '76. POCAHONTAS HIGH SCHOOL BICENTENNIAL MUSICAL & FLAG PRESENTATION. A CAST OF APPROX 250 STUDENTS WILL PRESENT A BICENTENNIAL MUSICAL PAGEANT ON MAY 5TH. THE OFFICIAL FLAG PRESENTATION WILL BE MADE DURING THE LAST NIGHT'S PERFORMANCE. AT POCAHONTAS HIGH SCHOOL. (LOCAL). JOHN JACKSON, CHAIRMAN; POCAHONTAS BICENTENNIAL COMMITTEE; PO BOX 467; POCAHONTAS, AR 72455. (#200005-63).

POWHATAN

POWHATAN COURTHOUSE HISTORICAL LIBRARY & MUSEUM-AR. FILING OF HISTORICAL RECORDS DATING BACK TO 1812. COLLECTING MUSEUM ARTIFACTS. BEAUTIFICATION OF COURTHOUSE GROUNDS. (LOCAL). MRS BOBBY FLIPPO, CHAIRMAN; POWHATAN COURTHOUSE RESTORATION COMMITTEE; POWHATAN, AR 72458. (#28590).

PRAIRIE GROVE

BOB KIDD BICENTENNIAL PARK - PRAIRIE GROVE, AR. PICNIC AREA, RECREATION AREA, PLAYGROUNDS, FLAGPOLE & ENTRANCEWAY WILL BE INCLUDED IN THE PARK. (LOCAL). LARRY P DAVIS, CHAIRMAN; PRAIRIE GROVE BICENTENNIAL COMMITTEE; 112 S NEAL; PRAIRIE GROVE, AR 72753. (#29157).

JULY 4, '76. FOURTH OF JULY CELEBRATION. 4TH OF JULY ACTIVITIES TO BE AN ANNUAL EVENT AT BOB KIDD PARK, WITH PLANS FOR EXPANDED DEVELOPMENT OF PARK AREA BEING IMPLEMENTED. AT 2 MILES WEST OF PRAIRIE GROVE ON HWY 62. (LOCAL). LARRY P DAVIS, CHAIRMAN; CITY OF PRAIRIE GROVE BICENTENNIAL COMMITTEE; 115 E BUCHANAN; PRAIRIE GROVE, AR 72753. (#200005-20).

RISON

CLEVELAND COUNTY SENIOR CITIZENS PROGRAM-ARKANSAS. SENIOR CITIZENS TO REMAIN A VITAL PART OF THE COMMUNITY BY SHARING THEIR KNOWLEDGE, TALENTS, AND SPECIALITIES WITH THE STUDENTS. ALSO JOIN THE VOLUNTEERS ACTION GROUP. (LOCAL). MRS JAMES L MOORE, JR, BICENTENNIAL CHAIRPERSON; CLEVELAND COUNTY ARKANSAS BICENTENNIAL COMMITTEE; RISON, AR 71665. (#2805).

CLEVELAND COUNTY, ARKANSAS, BICENT PARK PROJECT. ESTABLISH A PARK IN EACH TOWN & COMMUNITY IN THE COUNTY. UPGRADE & BEAUTIFY THOSE PARKS EXISTING AT PRESENT. (LOCAL). MRS JAMES L MOORE, JR, CHAIRPERSON; CLEVELAND COUNTY BICENTENNIAL COMMITTEE; RISON, AR 71665. (#2825).

MINI-MUSEUM IN CLEVELAND COUNTY, ARKANSAS. FOUR LARGE DISPLAY CASES WILL BE PURCHASED TO HOUSE HISTORICAL ITEMS AND TO DISPLAY CRAFT ITEMS PRODUCED BY LOCAL RESIDENTS. THESE WILL BE IN THE COUNTY COURTHOUSE UNTIL A MUSEUM IS BUILT. (LOCAL). MRS JAMES L MOORE, PROJ COORDINATOR; CLEVELAND COUNTY; COUNTY COURTHOUSE; RISON, AR 71665. (#8216). **ARBA GRANTEE.**

PIONEER CRAFT FESTIVAL - RISON, ARKANSAS. PIONEER CRAFT FESTIVAL IS HELD TO PRESERVE CRAFTS AND SHOW THEIR RELEVANCE TO OUR PRESENT DAY LIFE. THE FESTIVAL TAKES PLACE THE 3RD WEEKEND OF MARCH. PROCEEDS WILL ENDOW A MUSEUM BUILDING FUND. (LOCAL). MRS JAMES L MOORE, CHAIRMAN BICENT EVENTS; CLEVELAND CO HISTORICAL SOCIETY; RISON, AR 71665. (#2345). **ARBA GRANTEE.**

OCT 1, '74. SENIOR CITIZENS LECTURE TO STUDENTS ABOUT THEIR SPECIALTIES. CLEVELAND COUNTY SENIOR CITIZENS PROGRAM-ARKANSAS. SENIOR CITIZENS TO REMAIN A VITAL PART OF THE COMMUNITY BY SHARING THEIR KNOWLEDGE, TALENTS, AND SPECIALITIES WITH THE STUDENTS. ALSO JOIN THE VOLUNTEERS ACTION GROUP. (LOCAL). MRS JAMES L MOORE, JR; CLEVELAND COUNTY ARKANSAS BICENTENNIAL COMMITTEE; RISON, AR 71665. (#2805-901).

MAR 15 - 16, '75. PIONEER CRAFT FESTIVAL. PIONEER CRAFT FESTIVAL - RISON, ARKANSAS. PIONEER CRAFT FESTIVAL IS HELD TO PRESERVE CRAFTS AND SHOW THEIR RELEVANCE TO OUR PRESENT DAY LIFE. THE FESTIVAL TAKES PLACE THE 3RD WEEKEND OF MARCH. PROCEEDS WILL ENDOW A MUSEUM BUILDING FUND. (LOCAL). MRS JAMES L MOORE, CHMN; CLEVELAND CO HISTORICAL SOCIETY; RISON, AR 71665. (#2345-901).

MAR 9, '76. UNITED STATES ARMED FORCES BICENTENNIAL CARAVAN. CARAVAN IS COMPOSED OF EXHIBIT VANS FOR EACH MILITARY SERVICE. PROJECT THEME IS 'HISTORY OF THE ARMED FORCES AND THEIR CONTRIBUTIONS TO THE NATION'. (LOCAL). MRS JAMES L MOORE JR, DIR; US ARMED FORCES BICENTENNIAL EXHIBIT VANS PROJECT; 715 MAIN ST; RISON, AR 71665. (#1775-405).

MAR 19 - 20, '76. CLEVELAND COUNTY HISTORICAL PAGEANT. WILL DEPICT THE HISTORY OF THE COUNTY FROM INDIAN TIMES TO THE PRESENT. NATIVE SONS JOHNNY CASH & BEAR BRYANT HAVE BEEN INVITED TO PARTICIPATE. AT RISON HIGH SCHOOL GYMNASIUM. (LOCAL). MRS PAM ROBINSON; CLEVELAND COUNTY BICENTENNIAL COMMITTEE; RISON HIGH SCHOOL; RISON, AR 71665. (#2346-1).

MAR 19 - 21, '76. PIONEER CRAFT FESTIVAL. JOHNNY CASH WILL BE THE PARADE MARSHAL AT THE 10:30AM PARADE, SAT MARCH 20, 1976. HE WILL ARRIVE IN RISON ON A SPECIAL 'COTTON BELT' TRAIN PULLED BY THEIR BICENT ENGINE. PARADE BEGINS WHEN TRAIN ARRIVES AT 10:30AM. AT CLEVELAND COUNTY FAIRGROUNDS RISON AR. (LOCAL). MRS JAMES L MOORE JR; CLEVELAND COUNTY HISTORICAL SOCIETY; RISON, AR 71665. (#2345-1).

MAY 8, '76. BICENTENNIAL HOMES TOUR - A DISPLAY OF THE COMMUNITY'S CULTURE. TOUR AT FOUR RISON HOMES. (LOCAL). MRS JAMES MOORE, CHMN; CLEVELAND COUNTY BICENTENNIAL COMMITTEE; RISON, AR 71665. (#16485-1).

JUNE 5, '76. NATIONAL CUTTING HORSE ASSOCIATION BICENTENNIAL SHOW. COUNTY BICENTENNIAL COMMITTEE IS SPONSORING THE 5000 DOLLAR ADDED CUTTING HORSE SHOW TO RAISE FUNDS FOR A MUSEUM AND PIONEER VILLAGE RESTORATION. AT CLEVELAND COUNTY FAIRGROUNDS. (REGN'L). MRS JAMES MOORE, JR, CHMN; CLEVELAND COUNTY BICENTENNIAL COMMITTEE; RISON, AR 71665. (#102702-1).

ROGERS

ART GUILD SHOWS IN ROGERS, ARKANSAS. ANNUAL SHOWING OF ART WORKS BY LOCAL AND REGIONAL ARTISTS. ALSO, TWO BENEFIT SHOWS ARE PRODUCED WITH PROCEEDS GOING TO BENEFIT PROGRAMS FOR YOUTH. (LOCAL). HUBERT MORRIS, CHAIRMAN; ROGERS ART GUILD; 1911 S 15TH ST; ROGERS, AR 72756. (#7641).

CITY PARK IMPROVEMENT, ROGERS, ARKANSAS. IMPROVEMENT AND EXPANSION OF FACILITIES AT ROGERS CITY PARK AT LAKE ATALANTA WILL BE UNDERTAKEN FOR USE BY THE GENERAL PUBLIC. (LOCAL). HUBERT MORRIS, COORDINATOR; CITY PARKS COMMISSION; 1911 S 15TH ST; ROGERS, AR 72756. (#7643).

CONSTRUCTION OF AMPHITHEATRE - ROGERS, AR. CONSTRUCTION OF AN AMPHITHEATRE FOR THE CITY OF ROGERS; THE STRUCTURE WILL BE IN A NATURAL SETTING AND WILL BE UTILIZED BY A BROAD BASIS. (LOCAL). HAROLD E JONES, PROJ COORDINATOR; PARKS & RECREATION DEPT; 212 W ELM; ROGERS, AR 72756. (#18496). **ARBA GRANTEE.**

DAISY INTERNATIONAL AIR GUN MUSEUM IN ROGERS, AR. DISPLAYS OF AIR GUNS FROM ANTIQUE TO MODERN WILL BE OPEN TO THE PUBLIC IN A PRIVATELY OWNED MUSEUM. (ST-WIDE). JOHN R POWERS JR; DAISY DIVISION, VICTOR COMPTOMETER CORP; ROGERS, AR 72756. (#6487).

GENEOLOGICAL CEMETERY RECORDS, ROGERS, AR. PROJECT ENTAILS RECORDING THE NAMES ON ALL TOMBSTONES IN BENTON COUNTY IN A BOOK. (LOCAL). MRS MELVIN SMITH, PROJ CHAIRPERSON; NORTHWESTERN ARKANSAS GENEALOGICAL SOCIETY; BOX 362; ROGERS, AR 72763. (#12517).

HERITAGE ART MURAL OF ROGERS, AR. 50 OUTSTANDING HISTORICAL FEATURES OF ROGERS & ENVIRONS WILL BE EXECUTED IN ART STUDIES, ASSEMBLED INTO A MURAL & SENT ON A 5 MONTH TOUR OF THE AREA AND THEN RETURN TO ROGERS AS A MOMENTO. (LOCAL). ALBERT W GASS, PRESIDENT; ROGERS ART GUILD; 701 PUTNAM RD; ROGERS, AR 72756. (#18248). **ARBA GRANTEE.**

ROGERS HISTORICAL MUSEUM, AR. AN HISTORICAL MUSEUM WILL BE ESTABLISHED IN ROGERS, AZ WHICH INCLUDES A COLLECTION OF ARTIFACTS AND MEMORABILIA, HISTORICAL & CULTURAL RELICS. PARTIALLY FUNDED WITH VOLUNTARY CITY TAX. (ST-WIDE). MRS VERA KEY, PROJ DIR; ROGERS MUSEUM COMMISSION; 114 S 1ST ST; ROGERS, AR 72756. (#18252). **ARBA GRANTEE.**

OCT 17 - 19, '75. WAR EAGLE ARTS & CRAFTS FESTIVAL. ANNUAL EVENT FEATURING ARTS & CRAFTS WHICH MAY HAVE BECOME UNCOMMON THRU DISUSE. FESTIVAL WILL HAVE A BICENTENNIAL THEME. (LOCAL). HUBERT MORRIS, CHAIRMAN; WAR EAGLE ARTS AND CRAFTS FESTIVAL; ROGERS, AR 72756. (#6486-501).

NOV 8, '75. 'SOUTHLAND ECHOES OF '76', A MUSICAL SHOW. SHOW WILL FEATURE GUEST BARBERSHOP QUARTET, THE GOOD TIMES FROM TULSA, OK. AT ROGERS HIGH SCHOOL AUDITORIUM. (LOCAL). MRS LOUISE WILSON, SEC; SWEET ADELINES, INC; 1513 W MAGNOLIA ST; ROGERS, AR 72756. (#103001-1).

ROWHER

JAPANESE RELOCATION CEMETERY & MONUMENT - ARKANSAS. THE JAPANESE RELOCATION CEMETERY & MONUMENT COMEMORATES THE HEROISM OF THE 442 BATTALION OF JAPANESE-AMERICANS IN WORLD WAR II. DESHA CO CITIZENS WILL MAINTAIN THE CEMETERY AS PART OF THEIR LOCAL HERITAGE. (LOCAL). MRS BONNIE ZOOK, CHAIRMAN; DESHA CO BICENTENNIAL COMMITTEE; DESHA COUNTY COURTHOUSE; ARKANSAS CITY, AR 71630. (#2347).

RUSSELLVILLE

DISSENT IN THE AMERICAN EXPERIENCE - AR. A BICENTENNIAL COURSE WILL BE PRESENTED FOR REGULAR AND CONTINUING EDUCATION STUDENTS, FOCUSING ON VARIOUS ASPECCTS OF DISSENT IN THE AMERICAN EXPERIENCE. TAUGHT BY MEMBERS AND GUEST SPEAKERS. (LOCAL). TRAVIS M ADAMS, COORDINATOR; ARKANSAS POLYTECHNIC COLLEGE; RUSSELLVILLE, AR 72801. (#24928).

PLAQUE FOR OLD POST ROAD PARK - RUSSELLVILLE, AR. A PLAQUE WILL BE PLACED WITH A SUITABLE HISTORICAL NARRATIVE TO NAME OLD POST ROAD PARK; IT WILL DRAW ATTENTION TO THE HISTORY OF THE AREA. (LOCAL). JUDGE ERMIL GRANT, PROJ DIRECTOR; POPE COUNTY; COUNTY COURTHOUSE; RUSSELLVILLE, AR 72801. (#18499). **ARBA GRANTEE.**

MAR 13, '76. WAGON TRAIN ARRIVAL, PARADE & PROGRAM. POPE COUNTY BICENTENNIAL COMMITTEE COORDINATED SEVERAL EVENTS WHICH TOOK PLACE ON THE DAY THE WAGON TRAIN ARRIVED IN RUSSELLVILLE. DINNER WAS PROVIDED FOR THE WAGON TRAIN CREW, WITH A PARADE & BICENTENNIAL PROGRAM HELD AT ARKANSAS TECH COLISEUM. (LOCAL). MRS A J CRABAUGH, CHMN; POPE COUNTY BICENTENNIAL COMMITTEE; RT 5, BOX 6; RUSSELLVILLE, AR 72801. (#200005-61).

SEPT 20, '76. PRESENTATION OF HAND FORGED KNIVES TO PRESIDENT FORD. JIMMY LYLE, AN ARKANSAS KNIFE MAKER, PRESENTED PRESIDENT FORD WITH A SET OF HAND FORGED, IVORY HANDLED KNIVES, A BOWIE KNIFE AND AN ARKANSAS TOOTHPICK. (LOCAL). MRS A J CRABAUGH, CHMN; POPE COUN-

RUSSELLVILLE — CONTINUED

TY BICENTENNIAL COMMITTEE; RT 5, BOX 6; RUSSELLVILLE, AR 72801. (#200005-62).

SEARCY

HISTORY OF SEARCY PAGEANT & FESTIVAL - AR. WRITING AND PRINTING OF THE HISTORY OF SEARCY. ALSO A PAGEANT WHICH WILL BE A VIVID ACCOUNT IN LIVE DRAMA THAT WILL SERVE TO INSPIRE GREATER DEDICATION TO THE IDEALS OF OUR NATION. (LOCAL). LESLIE CARMICHAEL, MAYOR; SEARCY BICENTENNIAL CELEBRATION COMMITTEE; 300 W ARCH AVE; SEARCY, AR 72143. (#17606). **ARBA GRANTEE.**

SEPT 18, '75. HARDING COLLEGE AMERICAN STUDIES LECTURE--DR JACK EVANS. DR EVANS IS PRESIDENT OF SOUTHWESTERN CHRISTIAN COLLEGE. (LOCAL). DR B R COX, SPONSOR; HARDING COLLEGE; SEARCY, AR 72143. (#29187-1).

SEPT 22, '75. HARDING COLLEGE AMERICAN STUDIES LECTURE--MR BOB BLEIBURG. MR BLEIBURG IS EDITOR OF BANNON'S NATIONAL BUSINESS AND FINANCE WORLD. (LOCAL). DR B R COX, SPONSOR; HARDING COLLEGE; SEARCY, AR 72143. (#29187-2).

OCT 2, '75. HARDING COLLEGE AMERICAN STUDIES LECTURE--MR ROBERT PIERPOINT. MR PIERPOINT IS CBS'S WHITE HOUSE CORRESPONDENT. (LOCAL). DR B R COX, SPONSOR; HARDING COLLEGE; SEARCY, AR 72143. (#29187-3).

NOV 3, '75. HARDING COLLEGE AMERICAN STUDIES LECTURE--MR BOB ANDERSON. MR ANDERSON IS WITH THE FOUNDATION FOR ECONOMIC EDUCATION. (LOCAL). DR B R COX, SPONSOR; HARDING COLLEGE; SEARCY, AR 72143. (#29187-4).

JAN 19, '76. HARDING COLLEGE AMERICAN STUDIES LECTURE--MR RALPH DE TOLEDANO. MR DE TOLEDANO IS A NATIONAL SYNDICATED COLUMNIST. (LOCAL). DR B R COX, SPONSOR; HARDING COLLEGE; SEARCY, AR 72143. (#29187-6).

JAN 23 - 24, '76. HARDING COLLEGE AMERICAN STUDIES LECTURE--MR FRANK GABLE. MR GABLE WILL LEAD THE 2-DAY MANAGEMENT SEMINAR. (LOCAL). DR B R COX, SPONSOR; HARDING COLLEGE; SEARCY, AR 72143. (#29187-7).

FEB 2, '76. HARDING COLLEGE AMERICAN STUDIES LECTURE--DR WALTER JUDD. DR JUDD IS AN INTERNATIONALLY RECOGNIZED EXPERT ON RUSSIA & CHINA. (LOCAL). DR B R COX, SPONSOR; HARDING COLLEGE; SEARCY, AR 72143. (#29187-8).

FEB 26, '76. HARDING COLLEGE AMERICAN STUDIES LECTURE--MR Z D BONNER. MR BONNER IS PRESIDENT OF GULF OIL COMPANY. (LOCAL). DR B R COX, SPONSOR; HARDING COLLEGE; SEARCY, AR 72143. (#29187-10).

FEB '76. HARDING COLLEGE AMERICAN STUDIES LECTURE--MR PHILLIP GRAMM. MR GRAMM IS A PROFESSOR OF ECONOMICS AT TEXAS A&M. (LOCAL). DR B R COX, SPONSOR; HARDING COLLEGE; SEARCY, AR 72143. (#29187-9).

APR 1, '76. HARDING COLLEGE AMERICAN STUDIES LECTURE--GEN W WESTMORELAND. GENERAL WESTMORELAND IS RETIRED FROM THE US ARMY. (LOCAL). DR B R COX, SPONSOR; HARDING COLLEGE; SEARCY, AR 72143. (#29187-11).

DEC 4, '76. HARDING COLLEGE AMERICAN STUDIES LECTURE--DR GEORGE BENSON. DR BENSON IS PRESIDENT OF THE NATIONAL EDUCATION PROGRAM. (LOCAL). DR B R COX, SPONSOR; HARDING COLLEGE; SEARCY, AR 72143. (#29187-5).

SEDGWICK

REMODELING SEDGWICK CITY HALL, AR. REPAIRS NEED TO BE MADE TO THE CITY HALL - A PLAQUE DUPLICATING THE PLEDGE OF REDEDICATION AND ONE COMMEMORATING THE BICENTENNIAL YEAR WILL BE PLACED IN CITY HALL. (LOCAL). HON HOWARD VANCE, MAYOR; CITY OF SEDGWICK; CITY HALL; SEDGWICK, AR 72465. (#26814). **ARBA GRANTEE.**

SHERWOOD

APR 19 - 25, '76. SHERWOOD WEEK CELEBRATION. THIS ENTIRE WEEK WILL BE FILLED WITH ACTIVITIES THAT WILL BRING ALL THE CITIZENS OUT TO CELEBRATE THE BICENTENNIAL AND SHERWOOD'S ZETH BIRTHDAY. AT SHERWOOD PARK, SHERWOOD & DELMONT AVES, RECREATION CENTER. (LOCAL). GINGER BAILEY; SHERWOOD BICENTENNIAL COMMISSION; PO BOX 6112; SHERWOOD, AR 72116. (#103638-2).

SILOAM SPG

BURIAL OF TIME CAPSULE - AR. CAPSULE TO BE OPENED BY TRICENTENNIAL COMMITTEE. TIME CAPSULE INCLUDES BUSINESS, INDUSTRY, CITY, SCHOOL, CHURCHES, LOCAL AUTHORS, ARTISTS, HISTORY OF CITY, PICTURES, COINS, STAMPS & BICENT FLAG. (LOCAL). LORRAINE MOSS, CHAIRMAN; HORIZONS COMMITTEE; N BROADWAY; SILOAM SPG, AR 72761. (#31759).

CHRISTIAN AMER HERITAGE WEEK IN SILOAM SPRINGS, AR. CHRISTIAN AMERICAN HERITAGE WEEK WILL BE HELD IN OCTOBER 1975. THE PROJECT WILL INVOLVE A SPECIAL LECTURE SERIES ON CHRISTIAN AMERICAN HERITAGE. (LOCAL). DR JOHN V TERRY, CHAIRMAN; JOHN BROWN UNIV BICENT COMMITTEE; PO BOX 600; SILOAM SPG, AR 72761. (#8925).

ERECTION OF HISTORICAL MARKERS - AR. NINE HISTORICAL MARKERS OF NATIVE STONE AND GRANITE & ONE OF BRONZE, ERECTED AT VARIOUS SITES. (LOCAL). LORRAINE MOSS, CHAIRMAN; HORIZONS COMMITTEE; N BROADWAY; SILOAM SPG, AR 72761. (#31761).

'HICO, A HERITAGE' - SILOAM SPRINGS HISTORY, AR. A HISTORY OF THE COMMUNITY OF SILOAM SPRINGS INCLUDING INFORMATION ON ITS PEOPLE, EVENTS & CHURCHES. (LOCAL). MS MAGGIE SMITH, COORDINATOR; SILOAM SPRINGS CHAMBER OF COMMERCE & BICENTENNIAL COMMITTEE; PO BOX 476; SILOAM SPG, AR 72761. (#23584). **ARBA GRANTEE.**

JOHN BROWN UNIVERSITY BICENTENNIAL HOMECOMING. A SPECIAL HOMECOMING WILL BE HELD FOR THE ALUMNI OF JBU IN APRIL, 1976. MUSICAL PRESENTATIONS, ART SHOWS & FORMAL DEDICATION OF THE SIMON SAGER CABIN ARE SCHEDULED. (LOCAL). DR JOHN TERRY, CHAIRMAN; JOHN BROWN UNIV BICENT COMMITTEE; PO BOX 600; SILOAM SPG, AR 72761. (#8926-1).

PLANTING OF TREES & SHRUBS - AR. PLANTING OF TREES AND SHRUBS IN SILOAM SPRINGS, AR. (LOCAL). LORRAINE MOSS, CHAIRMAN; PRIMAVERA GARDEN CLUB; N BROADWAY; SILOAM SPG, AR 72761. (#31760).

RESTORATION OF SIMON SAGER CABIN, ARKANSAS. HISTORIC CABIN ON CAMPUS OF JOHN BROWN UNIV. WILL BE RESTORED, MARKED, & PROPERLY FURNISHED IN KEEPING WITH ITS ROLE IN THE HISTORY OF BENTON COUNTY. (LOCAL). JOHN V TERRY, DIRECTOR OF DEVELOPMENT; JOHN BROWN UNIVERSITY; PO BOX 600; SILOAM SPG, AR 72761. (#502). **ARBA GRANTEE.**

SILOAM SPRINGS GOSPEL SING - AR. A GOSPEL MUSIC PERFORMANCE WILL BE GIVEN. (LOCAL). JAMES L SHEETS, EXEC VICE-PRESIDENT; SILOAM SPRINGS CHAMBER OF COMMERCE; PO BOX 476; SILOAM SPG, AR 72761. (#14631).

DEC 6, '75. ANNUAL CHAMBER BANQUET MEETING. FESTIVAL. (LOCAL). JAMES L SHEETS, V-PRES; SILOAM SPRINGS CHAMBER OF COMMERCE; PO BOX 476; SILOAM SPG, AR 72761. (#14599-1).

APR 19 - 26, '76. SIMON SAGER CABIN DEDICATION, MUSIC FESTIVAL. HISTORIC CABIN ON CAMPUS OF JOHN BROWN UNIV. WILL BE RESTORED, MARKED, & PROPERLY FURNISHED IN KEEPING WITH ITS ROLE IN THE HISTORY OF BENTON COUNTY. AT MAIN CAMPUS. (LOCAL). DR JOHN V TERRY; JOHN BROWN UNIVERSITY; JOHN BROWN UNIVERSITY; SILOAMSPRINGS, AR 72761. (#502-1).

APR 25 - 27, '76. ARTS AND CRAFTS FESTIVAL. FESTIVAL WILL BE HELD BOTH OUTSIDE AND INSIDE ALONG THE BANKS OF SAGER CREEK; LOCAL AS WELL AS AREA ARTISTS & CRAFTSMEN EXHIBIT & SELL THEIR WARES. AT SILOAM SPRINGS COMMUNITY BUILDING & CITY PARK. (LOCAL). JAMES L SHEETS, CHMN; SILOAM SPRINGS CHAMBER OF COMMERCE; PO BOX 476; SILOAM SPG, AR 72761. (#101927-1).

JUNE 17 - 19, '76. RODEO AND PARADE. FESTIVAL, PARADE, LIVE PERFORMANCE AT ARENA, HIGHWAY 204. (LOCAL). SHARON HART, SECRETARY; SILOAM SPRINGS RIDING CLUB; PO BOX 476; SILOAM SPG, AR 72761. (#101928-1).

JUNE 26, '76. INNER TUBE RACES. COMPETITION AT SAGER CREEK. (LOCAL). JAMES L SHEETS, VICE PRES; SILOAM SPRINGS CHAMBER OF COMMERCE; PO BOX 476; SILOAM SPG, AR 72761. (#14598-1).

JULY 10, '76. OZARK BIKEATHON. COMPETITION. (LOCAL). JAMES L SHEETS, VICE PRES; SILOAM SPRINGS CHAMBER OF COMMERCE; PO BOX 476; SILOAM SPG, AR 72761. (#14597-1).

SLOVAK

AUG 5, '77. SLOVAK BICENTENNIAL COMMUNITY CELEBRATION & PICNIC. FESTIVAL AT CHURCH GROUNDS. (LOCAL). REV JAMES P REYNOLDS; STS CYRIL & METHODIUS CATHOLIC PARISH; RT 1, BOX 117; STUTTGART, AR 72160. (#109360-1).

SPRINGDALE

HISTORICAL GOODWILL TOUR OF SPRINGDALE, ARKANSAS. 135 PERSONS FROM THE CITY OF SPRINGDALE WILL TAKE A WEEK TOUR OF THE MOST HISTORIC AREAS OF OUR NATION INCLUDING WASHINGTON, DC, PHILA, PA, WILLIAMSBURG, VA, ETC, TO HONOR THE BICENTENNIAL. (LOCAL). LEE ZACHARY, EXEC VICE PRESIDENT; SPRINGDALE CHAMBER OF COMMERCE; 704 W EMMA; SPRINGDALE, AR 72764. (#3285).

OVERALL BICENTENNIAL PROGRAM FOR SPRINGDALE, AR. ACTIVITIES IN OVERALL BICENTENNIAL PROGRAM INCLUDE AN ARTS & CRAFTS FAIR, A MUSICAL PRODUCTION & A TENT TO BE USED BY CIVIC, SOCIAL, CHURCH-RELATED, INDUSTRIAL INSTITUTIONAL & COMMUNITY ORGANIZATIONS. (LOCAL). LEE ZACHARY, PROJ COORDINATOR; CHAMBER OF COMMERCE; BOX 166; SPRINGDALE, AR 72764. (#8220). **ARBA GRANTEE.**

SPRINGDALE BICENTENNIAL PROGRAM FILM, AR. A 30 MINUTE FILM WILL BE MADE THROUGHOUT THE SPRINGDALE BICENTENNIAL TOUR OF CITIES INCLUDING: OLD SALEM, WILLIAMSBURG, WASHINGTON, PHILADELPHIA & DAYTON. (LOCAL). LEE ZACHARY, CHAIRMAN; SPRINGDALE CHAMBER OF COMMERCE; PO BOX 166; SPRINGDALE, AR 72764. (#18250). **ARBA GRANTEE.**

SPRINGDALE, AR, BICENTENNIAL PARK. CITY OF SPRINGDALE PLANS TO CONSTRUCT BICENTENNIAL PARK ON STREAM RUNNING THROUGH MAIN PART OF TOWN. STREAM HAS A HISTORICAL SIGNIFICANCE SINCE IT IS ON THE ORIGINAL TRAIL OF EARLY SETTLERS & INDIANS. (LOCAL). HON ROY C RITTER, MAYOR; CITY OF SPRINGDALE; ADMIN BLDG, SPRING ST; SPRINGDALE, AR 72764. (#26813). **ARBA GRANTEE.**

MAY 2 - 3, '75. NORTHWEST ARKANSAS POULTRY FESTIVAL. THERE WILL BE A CHICK-N-QUE; A PARADE, A CHICKEN COOK-OFF & A FESTIVAL, ALONG WITH ACTIVITIES REGARDING THE CITY'S HISTORY & TO CELEBRATE NORTHWEST ARKANSAS' ROLE IN THE POULTRY INDUSTRY. AT BULLDOG STADIUM. (LOCAL). LEE ZACHARY; NORTHWEST ARK POULTRY FESTIVAL COMMITTEE; 700 W EMMA; SPRINGDALE, AR 72764. (#3282-1).

MAR 26 - 27, '76. UNITED STATES ARMED FORCES BICENTENNIAL CARAVAN. CARAVAN IS COMPOSED OF EXHIBIT VANS FOR EACH MILITARY SERVICE. PROJECT THEME IS 'HISTORY OF THE ARMED FORCES AND THEIR CONTRIBUTIONS TO THE NATION'. (LOCAL). LEE ZACHARY, CHMN; SPRINGDALE CHAMBER OF COMMERCE; 700 EMMA AVE; SPRINGDALE, AR 72764. (#1775-411).

JULY 1 - 4, '76. AUSTRALIAN RODEO RIDERS ENTER RODEO OF THE OZARKS. TAKING PART IN SPRINGDALE RODEO. (INT'L). JOHN MAUNDER, DIRECTOR; AUSTRALIAN GOVERNMENT; AUSTRALIAN CG, 636 FIFTH AVE; NEW YORK, NY 10020. (#108021-16).

JULY 1 - 4, '76. RODEO OF THE OZARKS. RODEO OF THE OZARKS IN SPRINGDALE, ARKANSAS. THE TRADITIONAL RODEO HELD JULY 1,2,3,&4 WILL COMMEMORATE THE BICENTENNIAL BY FEATURING ADDED EVENTS JUST BEFORE AND DURING THE RODEO RELATING TO HISTORY, AND FESTIVITIES WITH FIREWORK DISPLAYS. (LOCAL). SHORTY PARSONS, PRESIDENT; SPRINGDALE BENEVOLENT ASSOC; 702 W EMMA; SPRINGDALE, AR 72764. (#3284-501).

ST CHARLES

ST CHARLES, ARK, TIMBER PRESERVATION PROGRAM. CONSERVATION OF TIMBER IN WHITE RIVER REFUGE AND PRESERVATION OF TOWNSITE GIANT OAKS. (LOCAL). MRS JEAN POLLARD, CHAIRMAN; ARKANSAS COUNTY BICENTENNIAL COMMITTEE; 808 W 18TH ST; STUTTGART, AR 72160. (#3876).

ST CHARLES, ARK, BEAUTIFICATION PROJECT. STREET RE-PAVEMENT, CLEANUP OF VACANT LOTS & THE DEMOLITION OF UNSOUND STRUCTURES ARE SOME THE ASPECTS OF THE CITY'S BICENTENNIAL PROGRAM. (LOCAL). MRS JEAN POLLARD, CHAIRMAN; ARKANSAS COUNTY BICENTENNIAL COMMITTEE; 808 W 18TH ST; STUTTGART, AR 72160. (#3877).

ST CHARLES, ARK, WATER & SEWER SYSTEM PROJ. A COMPLETE WATER & SEWER SYSTEM WILL BE INSTALLED FOR THE CITY OF ST CHARLES. (LOCAL). MRS JEAN POLLARD, CHAIRMAN; ARKANSAS COUNTY BICENTENNIAL COMMITTEE; 808 W 18TH; STUTTGART, AR 72160. (#3878). **(??).**

NOV 11, '76. USA CORPS OF ENGINEERS FLOATING MUSEUM VISITS ST CHARLES, AR. EXHIBIT. (LOCAL). KENT CARMAIN, CHMN; USA CORPS OF ENGINEERS; US ARMY CORPS OF ENGINEERS; MEMPHIS, TN 38103. (#30730-5).

ST PAUL

ROBBIE STEPHENS PARK, CITY OF ST PAUL. A CITY PARK WILL BE ESTABLISHED FOR THE CITIZENS OF ST PAUL. (LOCAL). HON ALVA STEPHENS, MAYOR; CITY OF ST PAUL BICENTENNIAL COMMITTEE; CITY HALL; ST PAUL, AR 72760. (#17616). **ARBA GRANTEE.**

STAR CITY

SEPT 14 - 18, '75. LINCOLN COUNTY FAIR STATIONARY PARADE. PARADE. (LOCAL). FRANCES HARPER, CHMN; LINCOLN COUNTY FAIR ASSOCIATION; BOX 279; STAR CITY, AR 77667. (#200005-32).

STATE UNIV

THE MEANING OF THE DECLARATION OF INDEPENDENCE, AR. A HISTORICAL SEMINAR HELD IN OCTOBER-NOVEMBER, 1975. (LOCAL). JEFFREY D WALLIN, PROJ DIRECTOR; ASU POLITICAL SCIENCE DEPT SGA; DRAWER NN; STATE UNIV, AR 72467. (#19060). **ARBA GRANTEE.**

JAN 28, '76. THE MEANING OF THE DECLARATION OF INDEPENDENCE. SEMINAR AT ARKANSAS STATE UNIVERSITY, ROUG CENTER BALLROOM. (LOCAL). JEFFREY D WALLIN; ASU POLITICAL SCIENCE DEPT, SGA, FACULTY ASSN; DRAWER NN; STATE UNIV, AR 72467. (#19060-1).

STEPHENS

JULY 3 - 13, '76. TOWN FESTIVAL. ARTS & CRAFTS DISPLAY; PET PARADE & BICENT AMER PARADE; BEARD CONTEST; LADIES DRESS CONTEST; OLD-FASHIONED GAMES; LOCAL CHURCH HISTORY BOOK TO BE PUT IN LIBRARY; BABY-JUDGING CONTEST & MERCHANT WINDOW DISPLAYS. AT BRUSH ARBOR, 200 RUBY ST, ST PARKING. (LOCAL). MARGIE L WAGNON, COORD; CITY OF STEPHENS & CHAMBER OF COMMERCE; BOX 337; STEPHENS, AR 71764. (#200005-26).

STUTTGART

ARKANSAS COUNTY, ARK, AGRICULTURAL MUSEUM. DEVELOP MUSEUM COMPLEX WITH ADDITIONAL EXHIBITS, AN EARLY PRAIRIE HOMESTEAD, A ONE ROOM SCHOOL, SMALL CHURCH, A SORGHUM MILL, & A COUNTRY STORE. (LOCAL). MRS BILLY J BURKETT, CURATOR; ARKANSAS COUNTY AGRICULTURAL MUSEUM; 921 E 4TH ST; STUTTGART, AR 72160. (#2360). **ARBA GRANTEE.**

STUTTGART — CONTINUED

BICENTENNIAL COLUMN IN STUTTGART, AR. NEWSPAPER COLUMN PUBLISHED MONTHLY CONCERNING BICENTENNIAL EVENTS AND HISTORIC FACTS OF THE COUNTY. (LOCAL). MRS J S POLLARD, CHAIRMAN; ARKANSAS COUNTY BICENTENNIAL COMMUNITY; 808 W 18TH ST; STUTTGART, AR 72160. (#15409).

GRAND PRAIRIE PRESERVATION PROJ-STUTTGART, ARK. CREATION OF PRESERVE ENCOMPASSING AT LEAST ONE REMNANT OF VIRGIN PRAIRIE. (LOCAL). MRS JEAN POLLARD, CHAIRMAN; ARKANSAS COUNTY BICENTENNIAL COMMITTEE; 808 W 18TH ST; STUTTGART, AR 72160. (#3880).

LIVING FOUNDATION - PROJ OF STUTTGART, AR. BEAUTIFICATION OF STUTTGART PUBLIC LIBRARY GROUNDS AND CONTINUED MAINTENANCE. (LOCAL). MRS ALLAN THOMAS, CHAIRMAN; ARKANSAS COUNTY BICENT COMMITTEE; 808 W 18TH ST; STUTTGART, AR 76120. (#9896).

STUTTGART, ARK, PUBLIC LIBRARY MICROFILM PROJ. INCREASE PATRON PARTICIPATION IN BUILDING MICROFILM HOLDINGS. (LOCAL). MRS JEAN POLLARD, CHAIRMAN; ARKANSAS COUNTY BICENTENNIAL COMMITTEE; 808 W 18TH; STUTTGART, AR 72160. (#3879).

SEPT 13 - 15, '74. ART FESTIVAL OF GRAND PRAIRIE, ARK HERITAGE THEME. GRAND PRAIRIE, ARKANSAS, FESTIVAL OF THE ARTS. AREA ARTS FESTIVAL WHICH WILL INCLUDE PAINTINGS, CRAFTS, PERFORMING ARTISTS, FESTIVAL TOURS, CREATIVE WRITING, & CHILDREN'S CATEGORIES. THEME OF HERITAGE IN 74, FESTIVAL IN 75, & HORIZONS IN 76. (LOCAL). MRS J S POLLARD, CHAIRMAN; GRAND PRAIRIE FESTIVAL OF ARTS; 808 W 18TH ST; STUTTGART, AR 72160. (#1703-901).

APR 4 - 6, '75. ANTIQUE SHOW AND SALE. REFRESHMENTS AVAILABLE OPEN ONE TO SIX PM SUNDAY. AT GRAND PRAIRIE WAR MEMORIAL AUDITORIUM 600 WEST 20. (LOCAL). MRS JEAN POLLARD; ARKANSAS COUNTY BICENTENNIAL; 808 WEST 18; STUTTGART, AR 72160. (#50053-2).

APR 25, '75. ARKANSAS COUNTY BICENTENNIAL TRACK MEET. TROPHY AWARDED TO OVERALL COUNTY TEAM. AT STUTTGART HIGH SCHOOL TRACK, BUERKLE STREET, EXTENSION BEHIND SCHOOL. (LOCAL). MRS JEAN POLLARD; ARKANSAS COUNTY BICENTENNIAL; 808 WEST 18; STUTTGART, AR 72160. (#50053-1).

SEPT 18 - 21, '75. GRAND PRAIRIE FESTIVAL OF ARTS. SUNDAY CLOTHESLINE SHOW OF ARTS NOON TIL 5PM ADMISSION FREE TO ALL BUT PREMIERE TOUR LISTS FOR ONE MAN SHOWS AROUND TOWN. AT GRAND PRAIRIE WAR MEMORIAL AUDITORIUM 600 WEST 20. (ST-WIDE). MRS JEAN POLLARD; ARKANSAS COUNTY BICENTENNIAL COMMUNITY; 808 WEST 18; STUTTGART, AR 72160. (#1703-1).

SEPT 19, '75. ARKANSAS COUNTY AGRICULTURAL MUSEUM CASE DEDICATION. DEDICATION OF NEW DISPLAY CASE ENTITLED FRAGILE TREASURES OF THE AGRICULTURAL IMPLEMENTS, PRODUCTS. AT 4TH AND PARK AVE. (LOCAL). JEAN POLLARD, CHAIRMAN; ARKANSAS CO BICENTENNIAL COMMITTEE; 808 W 18TH ST; STUTTGART, AR 72160. (#2360-1).

NOV 18, '75. QUEEN MALLARD CONTEST. COMPETITION AT GRAND PRAIRIE WAR MEMORIAL AUDITORIUM, 600 W 20-PARKING AROUND AREA. (LOCAL). MRS CHAS E SMITH; ARK COUNTY BICENTENNIAL COMMUNITY; 2005 BEUMER; STUTTGART, AR 72160. (#102975-3).

NOV 18 - 22, '75. 40TH ANNUAL CHAMPIONSHIP DUCK CALLING CONTEST, CHARLIE RICH, M C. A BICENTENNIAL THEME WILL PREVAIL OVER THE 5 DAYS OF CELEBRATION INCLUDING VARIOUS ACTIVITIES. AT MEMORIAL AUDITORIUM ON FRI, MAIN STREET STAGE ON SAT. (LOCAL). MRS J S POLLARD, CHAIRMAN; ARKANSAS COUNTY BICENTENNIAL COMMITTEE; 808 W 18TH ST; STUTTGART, AR 72160. (#102501-1).

NOV 21, '75. ALL-AMERICAN CONCERT BY CONCERT CHOIR AND RICELANDERS. LIVE PERFORMANCE AT STUTTGART JUNIOR HIGH AUDITORIUM - (PARKING AVAILABLE). (LOCAL). JIM SPARKS, PROJ DIR; ARKANSAS COUNTY BICENTENNIAL COMMUNITY; STUTTGART HIGH SCHOOL; STUTTGART, AR 72160. (#102894-1).

NOV 21, '75. DUCK CALLING CONTEST SPORTSMAN'S PARTY. FESTIVAL AT GRAND PRAIRIE WAR MEMORIAL, AUDITORIUM ADJACENT PARKING. (LOCAL). DR REX HANCOCK; ARK COUNTY BICENTENNIAL COMMUNITY; 515 S MAIN; STUTTGART, AR 72160. (#102975-5).

NOV 21 - 22, '75. WATERFOWL FESTIVAL. ON SAT THE HOURS WILL BE FROM 9:00 AM TO 5:00 PM. AT GRAND PRAIRIE WAR MEMORIAL AUDITORIUM, ADJACENT PARKING. (LOCAL). DR JIM BISBEE; ARK COUNTY BICENTENNIAL COMMUNITY; 1900 SO BUERKLE; STUTTGART, AR 72160. (#102975-6).

NOV 22, '75. WORLD CHAMPION DUCK CALLING CONTEST-CHARLIE RICH EMCEE. COMPETITION AT MAIN STREET WILL BE BLOCKED OFF FOR CONTEST AND CARNIVAL. (REGN'L). GARNER ALLEN; ARK COUNTY BICENTENNIAL COMMUNITY; THE DAILY LEADER NEWSPAPER; STUTTGART, AR 72160. (#102975-4).

DEC 13 - 17, '75. S H S CONCERT CHOIR PRESENTS 'OKLAHOMA'. LIVE PERFORMANCE AT STUTTGART JUNIOR HIGH AUDITORIUM - (PARKING AVAILABLE). (LOCAL). JIM SPARKS, PROJ DIR; ARKANSAS COUNTY BICENTENNIAL COMMUNITY; STUTTGART HIGH SCHOOL; STUTTGART, AR 72160. (#102895-1).

JAN 31, '76. STUTTGART FOUNDER'S DAY BICENTENNIAL OBSERVANCE. A BICENTENNIAL FLAG WILL BE PRESENTED TO CITY PROCLAMATION BY MAYOR; BICENTENNIAL CERTIFICATES WILL BE PRESENTED TO FOUNDER'S RELATIVES; CRAFTS & ACTIVITIES FROM THE PAST RELIVED AND PERMANENT COMMEMORATIVE WILL BE DEDICATED. AT GRAND PRARIE WAR MEMORIAL AUDITORIUM. (LOCAL). MRS JEAN POLLARD, CHMN; ARKANSAS COUNTY BICENTENNIAL COMMITTEE; 808 W 18TH; STUTTGART, AR 72160. (#102299-1).

FEB 29, '76. CLASS OF '45 BICENTENNIAL PROJECT. CEREMONY AT STUTTGART HIGH SCHOOL. (LOCAL). MRS HAROLD GOETZ; ARK COUNTY BICENTENNIAL COMMUNITY; 1712 STRAIT PL; STUTTGART, AR 72160. (#102975-1).

APR 2 - 4, '76. ANTIQUE SHOW & SALE IN STUTTGART, ARKANSAS. TREASURES OF THE PAST DISPLAYED FOR VIEWING OR BUYING IN RE-CREATED ATMOSPHERE OF THE PAST, DESIGNED TO ENCOURAGE REMEMBRANCE AND PRESERVATION OF PART OF OUR HERITAGE. ALSO: NEWSPAPER/NEWSLETTER. AT GRAND PRAIRIE WAR MEMORIAL AUDITORIUM, 600 W 20TH. (LOCAL). MRS JEAN POLLARD; ARKANSAS COUNTY BICENT COMMITTEE; 808 W 18TH; STUTTGART, AR 72160. (#6327-1).

APR 24, '76. 'LET'S SING AMERICA' BY THE RICELANDERS. LIVE PERFORMANCE AT STUTTGART JUNIOR HIGH AUDITORIUM - (PARKING AVAILABLE). (LOCAL). JIM SPARKS, PROJ DIR; ARKANSAS COUNTY BICENTENNIAL COMMUNITY; STUTTGART HIGH SCHOOL; STUTTGART, AR 72160. (#102892-1).

APR 24 - 25, '76. GRAND PRAIRIE GRAND PRIX. COMPETITION AT STUTTGART, AIRPORT, HGWY 11. (REGN'L). ED CARLE, SUPERVISOR; ARK COUNTY BICENTENNIAL COMMUNITY; 302 S MAIN; STUTTGART, AR 72160. (#102975-2).

APR 30, '76. ARKANSAS COUNTY BICENTENNIAL TRACK MEET. YOUTH EFFORT TO SHOW PHYSICAL READINESS TODAY AS WAS SHOWN BY THE YOUTH 200 YEARS AGO. AT HIGH SCHOOL TRACK, SO BUERKLE ST EXT. (LOCAL). MRS JEAN POLGARD; ARKANSAS COUNTY BICENTENNIAL; 808 W 18TH; STUTTGART, AR 72160. (#7376-1).

MAY 28, '76. 'SALUTE TO AMERICA', DANCE RECITAL. LIVE PERFORMANCE AT GRAND PRAIRIE WAR MEMORIAL AUDITORIUM. (LOCAL). MRS LEE THORELL, DIRECTOR; ARKANSAS COUNTY BICENTENNIAL COMMUNITY; 1904 S PRAIRIE; STUTTGART, AR 72160. (#103076-1).

SEPT 17 - 19, '76. ART FESTIVAL OF GRAND PRAIRIE, ARK HORIZONS THEME. AREA ARTS FESTIVAL WHICH WILL INCLUDE PAINTINGS, CRAFTS, PERFORMING ARTISTS, FESTIVAL TOURS, CREATIVE WRITING, & CHILDREN'S CATEGORIES. THEME OF HERITAGE IN 74, FESTIVAL IN 75, & HORIZONS IN 76. AT WAR MEMORIAL AUDITORIUM. (LOCAL). MRS J S POLLARD, CHMN; GRAND PRAIRIE FESTIVAL OF ARTS; 808 W 18TH STREET; STUTTGART, AR 72160. (#1703-3).

SULPHUR SPG

BEAUTIFICATION PROJ IN SULPHUR SPRINGS, ARKANSAS. PROJ INCLUDES THE RESTORATION OF THE PAVILLIONS HOUSING THE MINERAL SPRINGS, RESTORATION OF THE BANDSTAND AND BEAUTIFICATION OF A CITY PARK. A GALA FESTIVAL IS PLANNED IN 1976. (LOCAL). MRS BOBBY KENNARD, PROJ COORDINATOR; SULPHUR SPRINGS BICENT COMMITTEE; RT 1; SULPHUR SPG, AR 72768. (#10150).

HISTORY OF SULPHUR SPRINGS, ARKANSAS. THE HISTORY OF SULPHUR SPRINGS WILL BE WRITTEN & COPIES WILL BE DISTRIBUTED IN DESIGNATED AREAS THROUGHOUT THE CITY. (LOCAL). MRS BOBBY KENNARD, PROJ COORDINATOR; SULPHUR SPRINGS BICENT COMMITTEE; RT 1; SULPHUR SPG, AR 72768. (#10151).

PARK DEVELOPMENT - SULPHUR SPRINGS, AR. 4 REINFORCED CONCRETE PICNIC TABLES WILL BE PUT IN THE CITY PARK. (LOCAL). HON JOHN M HUTCHINSON, MAYOR; CITY OF SULPHUR SPRINGS; CITY HALL; SULPHUR SPG, AR 72768. (#26812). **ARBA GRANTEE.**

TEXARKANA

PERMANENT EXHIBIT ON CADDO CULTURES IN TEXARKANA. PERMANENT EXHIBIT AT THE TEXARKANA HISTORICAL MUSEUM DEPICTING THE RED RIVER ENVIRONMENT AND ITS INFLUENCE ON THE CADDO INDIANS, TO INCLUDE INFORMATION ON RELATIONS WITH THE FRENCH SETTLERS. (LOCAL). MRS KATY KAVER, CURATOR; TEXARKANA HISTORICAL MUSEUM; PO BOX 2343; TEXARKANA, AR 75501. (#508). **ARBA GRANTEE.**

TRAVELING EXHIBIT ON CULTURAL HERITAGE - TEXARKANA. TEXARKANA HISTORICAL SOC & MUSEUM WILL SPONSOR A TRAVELING EXHIBIT TO CREATE GREATER AWARENESS OF THE HISTORICAL AND CULTURAL DEVELOPMENT OF THE AREA AMONG ALL ITS CITIZENS. (ST-WIDE). MRS KATY CAVER, CURATOR; TEXARKANA HISTORICAL SOCIETY & MUSEUM; PO BOX 2343; TEXARKANA, AR 75501. (#8214). **ARBA GRANTEE.**

JAN 1, '74 - DEC 31, '77. CADDO CULTURES IN THE TEXARKANA AREA; EXHIBIT AT TEXARKANA MUSEUM. PERMANENT EXHIBIT AT THE TEXARKANA HISTORICAL MUSEUM DEPICTING THE RED RIVER ENVIRONMENT AND ITS INFLUENCE ON THE CADDO INDIANS, TO INCLUDE INFORMATION ON RELATIONS WITH THE FRENCH SETTLERS. AT 219 STATE LINE AVE. (REGN'L). MRS KATY KAVER; TEXARKANA HISTORICAL MUSEUM; PO BOX 2343; TEXARKANA, AR 75501. (#508-1).

MAR 3 - 4, '76. UNITED STATES ARMED FORCES BICENTENNIAL CARAVAN. CARAVAN IS COMPOSED OF EXHIBIT VANS FOR EACH MILITARY SERVICE. PROJECT THEME IS 'HISTORY OF THE ARMED FORCES AND THEIR CONTRIBUTIONS TO THE NATION'. (LOCAL). NICK DEMOPULOS, CHMN; TEXARKANA BICENTENNIAL COMMITTEE; PO BOX 2343; TEXARKANA, AR 75501. (#1775-402).

THORNTON

LIBRARY CONSTRUCTION, THORNTON, AR. THE CITY OF THORNTON IS CONSTRUCTING A LIBRARY AS A HORIZONS PROJECT FOR THE COMMUNITY. (LOCAL). HON JAMES W O'DELL, MAYOR; CITY OF THORNTON; CITY HALL; THORNTON, AR 71766. (#26957). **ARBA GRANTEE.**

TOLLVILLE

MAY 1 - 2, '76. HOMECOMING. AWARD, CEREMONY, FESTIVAL AT RT 1. (LOCAL). MRS ADOLPH SICKEL, CHMN; ST PETERS EPISCOPAL CHURCH; RT 1; DEVALLS BLUFF, AR 72041. (#200005-29).

TONTITOWN

HERITAGE -BEAUTIFICATION OF TONTITOWN - AR. A HERITAGE-BEAUTIFICATION PROJECT WHICH WILL INCLUDE A HISTORICAL MARKER, LANDSCAPING OF CITY HALL AND COLLECTION OF HISTORICAL RECORDS. (LOCAL). DOROTHY MARSANI, CHAIRMAN; TONTITOWN BICENTENNIAL COMMISSION; RT 4; SPRINGDALE, AR 72770. (#17610). **ARBA GRANTEE.**

HISTORICAL MARKER - TONTITOWN, AR. THE MARKER WILL HAVE THE FOUNDING DATE AND BICENTENNIAL DATE; THE ORIGINAL SCHOOL BELL WILL BE MOUNTED ON THE TOP. (LOCAL). DOROTHY MORSANI, CO-CHAIRMAN; SPRINGDALE BICENTENNIAL COMMITTEE; RT 4; SPRINGDALE, AR 72764. (#19124).

LANDSCAPING OF NEW CITY HALL - TONTITOWN, AR. THE NEW CITY HALL WILL BE LANDSCAPED IN HONOR OF THE BICENTENNIAL. (LOCAL). DOROTHY MORSANI, CO-CHAIRMAN; SPRINGDALE BICENTENNIAL COMMITTEE; RT 4; SPRINGDALE, AR 72764. (#19125).

AUG 19 - 21, '76. 77TH ANNUAL GRAPE FESTIVAL. FESTIVAL AT PARISH GROUNDS. (REGN'L). DOROTHY MORSANI, DIR; ST JOSEPH'S CATHOLIC CHURCH; RT 4; SPRINGDALE, AR 72764. (#104188-1).

TRUMANN

TRUMANN, ARKANSAS LIBRARY-MUSEUM COMPLEX. A LIBRARY-MUSEUM COMPLEX WILL BE DEDICATED AS A BICENTENNIAL PROJECT IN TRUMANN. THE LIBRARY- MUSEUM WILL BE BUILT WITH CITY FUNDS AND COMPLETED IN 1976. (LOCAL). DARLENE LAGRONE, CO-CHAIRMAN; TRUMANN BICENTENNIAL COMMITTEE; PO BOX 100; TRUMANN, AR 72472. (#3091). **ARBA GRANTEE.**

JUNE 27 - JULY 4, '76. FOURTH OF JULY BICENTENNIAL CELEBRATION WEEK - PARADES, COSTUME BALL. TRUMANN, ARKANSAS FOURTH OF JULY CELEBRATION. A WEEK OF CELEBRATION IS PLANNED IN TRUMANN DURING JULY 4,1976. ACTIVITIES WILL INCLUDE PARADES, COSTUME BALL, PICNICS, FIRE WORKS DISPLAY AND ARTS-CRAFTS SHOW. (LOCAL). DARLENE LAGRONE; TRUMANN BICENTENNIAL COMMITTEE; PO BOX 100; TRUMANN, AR 72472. (#3090-501).

TUCSON

JUNE 16 - 20, '76. CONFERENCE ON YOUTH NEEDS AND YOUTH EXHIBITION. CONFERENCE, EXHIBIT AT RAMADA INN, 404 NORTH FREEWAY. (REGN'L). STUART RADO, EXEC DIR; NATIONAL NETWORK OF YOUTH ADVISORY BOARDS; PO BOX 402036, OCEAN VIEW BRANCH; MIAMI BEACH, FL 33140. (#1536-1).

UMPIRE

LOG CABIN - UMPIRE, AL. A LOG CABIN IS BEING BUILT ON AN OLD LOG CABIN SITE. (LOCAL). DONALD MANNING, SUPERINTENDENT; UMPIRE BICENTENNIAL ORGANIZATION; UMPIRE, AR 71971. (#29158).

MAY 14, '76. BICENTENNIAL DAY. FESTIVAL AT AUDITORIUM. (LOCAL). DONALD MANNING, SUPT; UMPIRE PUBLIC SCHOOLS; UMPIRE, AR 71971. (#200005-18).

UNIONTOWN

JUNE 27, '76. UNIONTOWN MASONIC LODGE BICENTENNIAL CELEBRATION. CEREMONY, FESTIVAL AT UNIONTOWN LODGE, 395 F & AM. (LOCAL). ROBERT M GARNER, CHAIRMAN; CRAWFORD COUNTY BICENTENNIAL COMMISSION; PO BOX 486; VAN BUREN, AR 72956. (#200005-74).

VAN BUREN

CITY OF VAN BUREN DOWNTOWN RESTORATION IN ARKANSAS. EMPHASIS WILL BE ON PARKING FACILITIES & IMPROVED STREETS. HISTORIC DISTRICT COMMISSION WILL TRY TO INFLUENCE PROPERTY OWNERS TO RESTORE BUILDINGS TO THEIR ORIGINAL FACADE. (LOCAL). DR LOUIS H PEER, CHAIRMAN; COMMUNITY DEVELOPEMENT COMMISSION; 511 MAIN ST; VAN BUREN, AR 72956. (#6476).

CRAWFORD COUNTY, ARK, BICENTENNIAL COMMUNITY PARK. A MEMORIAL PARK, HERITAGE TOUR & PRESERVATION PROJECT WILL BE UNDERTAKEN BY CRAWFORD COUNTY. A HISTORICAL MARKERS PROGRAM & SCHOOL PARTICIPATION WILL BE SPONSORED BY THE LOCAL HISTORY CLUB. (LOCAL). ROBERT M GARNER, CHAIRMAN; CRAWFORD CO BICENTENNIAL COMMITTEE; PO BOX 486; VAN BUREN, AR 72956. (#4790).

CRAWFORD COUNTY, ARKANSAS, ORAL LIBRARY. PROJECT TO ESTABLISH AN ORAL TAPE LIBRARY TO RECORD FAMILY HISTORY & ANECDOTES ABOUT HISTORICAL SITES IN CRAWFORD

VAN BUREN — CONTINUED

COUNTY. (ST-WIDE). ROBERT N GARNER, PRESIDENT; CRAWFORD COUNTY HISTORICAL SOCIETY; PO BOX 486; VAN BUREN, AR 72956. (#6474).

FRISCO DEPOT ACQUISITION AND RESTORATION - AR. THE COMMUNITY PLANS TO RESTORE THE OLD FRISCO DEPOT TO ITS ORIGINAL APPEARANCE AND USE IT FOR A MUSEUM. (LOCAL). HON ALLAN R TOOTHAKER, MAYOR; CITY OF VAN BUREN; CITY HALL; VAN BUREN, AR 72956. (#27857). **ARBA GRANTEE.**

A HISTORICAL SALUTE TO CRAWFORD COUNTY, BOOK, AR. BRIEF GENERAL HISTORY OF CRAWFORD COUNTY W/A DETAILED HISTORY OF 16 TOWNS & COMMUNITIES IN THE COUNTY. (LOCAL). ROBERT M GARNER, CHAIRMAN; CRAWFORD COUNTY BICEN COMMISSION; PO BOX 486; VAN BUREN, AR 72956. (#31785).

MEMORIAL GARDEN PARK IN VAN BUREN, ARKANSAS. THE PARK WILL BE DEDICATED TO THE VETERANS OF CRAWFORD COUNTY WHO FOUGHT IN WWI, WWII, KOREA & VIET NAM. THERE WILL BE SEPARATE PLAQUES FOR EACH WAR, BENCHES, LANDSCAPING & A FLAG POLE. (LOCAL). SUSAN GUTHRIE, EXEC DIRECTOR; VAN BUREN URBAN RENEWAL AGENCY; 12 S 6TH ST; VAN BUREN, AR 72956. (#6475).

TIME CAPSULE, VAN BUREN, AR. TIME CAPSULE TO BE BURIED ON CRAWFORD COUNTY COURTHOUSE GROUNDS. CAPSULE TO BE OPENED JULY 4 2076 BY TRICENTENNIAL COMMITTEE. WILL CONTAIN COMMEMORATIVE ITEMS FROM OUR BICENTENNIAL EFFORTS. (LOCAL). ROBERT M GARNER, COORDINATOR; CRAWFORD COUNTY BICENTENNIAL COMMISSION; PO BOX 486; VAN BUREN, AR 72956. (#31782).

MAY 1, '75. DEDICATION OF MEMORIAL GARDEN PARK. OPENING. (LOCAL). SUSAN GUTHRIE; VAN BUREN URBAN RENEWAL AGENCY; 12 S 6TH ST; VAN BUREN, AR 72956. (#6475-501).

APR 28, '76. BICENTENNIAL FLAG PRESENTATION. AN EFFORT TO BRING THE BICENTENNIAL TO THE AGED & INFIRMED WHO WOULD BE LEFT OUT OF THE BICENTENNIAL CELEBRATION. AT CATE NURSING HOME, HWY 282. (LOCAL). ROBERT M GARNER, CHAIRMAN; CRAWFORD COUNTY BICENTENNIAL COMMISSION; PO BOX 486; VAN BUREN, AR 72956. (#200005-68).

MAY 1 - JUNE 30, '76. EXTENSION HOMEMAKERS COUNCIL BICENTENNIAL OBSERVANCE. EXHIBIT, CONFERENCE, COMPETITION, AWARD AT 10 EHC CLUBS IN COUNTY & EHC COUNTY COUNCIL. (LOCAL). DORIS GARNER, COORD; CRAWFORD COUNTY BICENTENNIAL COMMISSION; C/O COUNTY EXTENSION OFFICE; VAN BUREN, AR 72956. (#200005-65).

JULY 4, '76. CRAWFORD COUNTY BICENTENNIAL CELEBRATION. FESTIVAL, CEREMONY, COMPETITION, EXHIBIT, LIVE PERFORMANCE AT COUNTY COURTHOUSE & MAIN ST OF VAN BUREN. (LOCAL). ROBERT M GARNER, CHAIRMAN; CRAWFORD COUNTY BICENTENNIAL COMMISSION; PO BOX 486; VAN BUREN, AR 72956. (#200005-69).

WALNUT RIDGE

POWHATAN COURTHOUSE HISTORIC MEMORIAL LIBRARY, AR. THE POWHATAN LIBRARY WILL SERVE AS A REPOSITORY FOR EARLY RECORDS & MATERIALS OF THE AREA. THESE MATERIALS WILL BE MADE AVAILABLE TO THE PUBLIC ON A REGULAR BASIS. (LOCAL). JOHN ALLEN, PROJ DIRECTOR; LAWRENCE CO DEVELOPMENT COUNCIL; WALNUT RIDGE, AR 72476. (#11108). **ARBA GRANTEE.**

WARREN

DEVELOPING BRADLEY COUNTY, ARK, HISTORIC ARCHIVES. SECURE EARLY RECORDS, DOCUMENTS, MICRO-FILM, PHOTOS, TAPE RECORDERS, ESSAYS & WRITTEN HISTORIES OF PEOPLE, PLACES & THINGS IN THE COUNTY AS OF 1800. (LOCAL). ROBERT L GATEWOOD, CHAIRMAN; BRADLEY COUNTY ARBA; 305 S MAIN ST, PO BOX 751; WARREN, AR 71671. (#6267).

NEW LIBRARY FOR BRADLEY COUNTY, ARKANSAS. SECURE A NEW & LARGER BLDG AND INCREASE NUMBER OF BOOKS, DOCUMENTS & EXHIBITS TO FOSTER RESEARCH, READING & APPRECIATION OF GRAPHIC ARTS. (LOCAL). ROBERT L GATEWOOD, CHAIRMAN; BRADLEY COUNTY ARBA; 305 S MAIN ST, PO BOX 751; WARREN, AR 71671. (#6266).

WARREN BICENTENNIAL PROJECTS, AR. ESTABLISHMENT OF A MINI-MUSEUM, TOURS OF HOMES, ERECTION OF HISTORICAL MARKERS, PAGEANTS, PARADES & SCHOOL INVOLVEMENT IN BICENTENNIAL ACTIVITIES. (LOCAL). ROBERT L GATEWOOD, CHAIRMAN; WARREN BICENTENNIAL CELEBRATION COMMITTEE; 305 S MAIN ST; WARREN, AR 71671. (#17611). **ARBA GRANTEE.**

JAN 18 - DEC 31, '75. COLLECTION OF BIBLE RECORDS THRU HOME DEMOCRATIC CLUBS. EXHIBIT. (LOCAL). ROBERT L GATEWOOD; BRADLEY COUNTY ARBA; 305 S MAIN ST, PO BOX 751; WARREN, AR 71671. (#6267-504).

JAN 18, '75 - JAN 1, '77. DISPLAY OF ANTIQUES, EARLY FARM OR CITY ARTIFACTS. CONSTRUCTION OF LIBRARY IN BRADLEY COUNTY, ARKANSAS. SECURE A NEW & LARGER BLDG AND INCREASE NUMBER OF BOOKS, DOCUMENTS & EXHIBITS TO FOSTER RESEARCH, READING & APPRECIATION OF GRAPHIC ARTS. DONATIONS ACCEPTED. (LOCAL). ROBERT L GATEWOOD; BRADLEY COUNTY ARBA; 305 S MAIN ST, PO BOX 751; WARREN, AR 71671. (#6266-503).

MAR 1 - 31, '75. ESSAY CONTESTS IN THREE SENIOR HIGH SCHOOLS OF COUNTY. COMPETITION. (LOCAL). ROBERT L GATEWOOD; BRADLEY COUNTY ARBA; 305 S MAIN ST, PO BOX 751; WARREN, AR 71671. (#6267-501).

JULY 1 - AUG 31, '75. SUMMER LOCAL EXHIBIT WARREN PHOTOS 1900-1930 ERA. CONSTRUCTION OF LIBRARY IN BRADLEY COUNTY, ARKANSAS. SECURE A NEW & LARGER BLDG AND INCREASE NUMBER OF BOOKS, DOCUMENTS & EXHIBITS TO FOSTER RESEARCH, READING & APPRECIATION OF GRAPHIC ARTS. ADMISSION FREE, BUT DONATIONS ARE ACCEPTED. (LOCAL). ROBERT L GATEWOOD; BRADLEY COUNTY ARBA; 305 S MAIN ST, PO BOX 751; WARREN, AR 71671. (#6266-501).

NOV 1 - 30, '75. ESSAY CONTEST MIDDLE SCHOOL OF THE COUNTY 1776 ERA EMPHASIS. COMPETITION. (LOCAL). ROBERT L GATEWOOD; BRADLEY COUNTY ARBA; 305 S MAIN ST, PO BOX 751; WARREN, AR 71671. (#6267-502).

DEC 1 - 31, '75. ESSAY CONTEST JUNIOR HIGH LEVEL LOCAL HISTORY IN THREE JR HIGHS. COMPETITION. (LOCAL). ROBERT L GATEWOOD; BRADLEY COUNTY ARBA; 305 S MAIN ST, PO BOX 751; WARREN, AR 71671. (#6267-503).

JAN 1 - DEC 31, '76. COLLECTION OF CEMETERY RECORDS THRU LOCAL HOME DEMONSTRATION CLUBS. PLANS CALL FOR HOME DEMONSTRATOR'S CLUBS IN OCTOBER 75 TO SURVEY 30 CEMETERIES IN BRADLEY CO FOR NAMES,DATES OF BIRTH & DEATH OF PERSONS INTERRED IN VARIOUS LOCAL CEMETERIES. AS OF 1800. (LOCAL). ROBERT L GATEWOOD; BRADLEY COUNTY ARBA; 305 S MAIN ST, PO BOX 751; WARREN, AR 71671. (#6267-505).

MAR 6 - 7, '76. UNITED STATES ARMED FORCES BICENTENNIAL CARAVAN. CARAVAN IS COMPOSED OF EXHIBIT VANS FOR EACH MILITARY SERVICE. PROJECT THEME IS 'HISTORY OF THE ARMED FORCES AND THEIR CONTRIBUTIONS TO THE NATION'. (LOCAL). ROBERT GATEWOOD, CHMN; US ARMED FORCES BICENTENNIAL EXHIBIT VANS PROJECT; PO BOX 751; WARREN, AR 71671. (#1775-404).

MAY 1 - 31, '76. HISTORICAL DOCUMENTS OF WARREN AREA EXHIBIT. CONSTRUCTION OF LIBRARY IN BRADLEY COUNTY, ARKANSAS SECURE A NEW & LARGER BLDG AND INCREASE NUMBER OF BOOKS, DOCUMENTS & EXHIBITS TO FOSTER RESEARCH, READING & APPRECIATION OF GRAPHIC ARTS. FREE ADMISSION, BUT DONATIONS ACCEPTED. (LOCAL). ROBERT L GATEWOOD; BRADLEY COUNTY ARBA; 305 S MAIN ST, PO BOX 751; WARREN, AR 71671. (#6266-502).

JUNE 8 - 15, '76. BRADLEY COUNTY ANNUAL FESTIVAL. THE ANNUAL TOMATO FESTIVAL WILL BE DEDICATED TO THE BICENTENNIAL IN 1975, JUNE 7-14, 1976, JUNE 8-15. RESTORATION PROJECTS PAGEANTS, MARKER PROGRAM & A BICENT BALL ARE PLANNED BY CITIZENS FEATURING A PARADE AND LUNCHEON MADE EXCLUSIVELY OF TOMATOES. AT QUEENS CONTEST, HIGH SCHOOL GYM; LUNCHEON, FIRST METHODIST CHURCH. (ST-WIDE). ROBERT L GATEWOOD, CHMN; BRADLEY CHAMBER OF COMMERCE/WARREN BICENTENNIAL COMMITTEE; PO BOX 751; WARREN, AR 71671. (#3933-1).

JUNE 11 - 12, '76. BICENTENNIAL PINK TOMATO FESTIVAL. BRADLEY COUNTY CELEBRATES THE TOMATO CROP AND THE BICENTENNIAL. AT NATIONAL GUARD ARMORY. (LOCAL). ROBERT GATEWOOD, CHAIRMAN; WARREN BICENTENNIAL COMMITTEE; 305 S MAIN ST, PO BOX 751; WARREN, AR 71671. (#103416-360).

WASHINGTON

RESTORATION OF THE CARRUTH HOUSE - AR. THE CARRUTH HOUSE, LOCATED IN THE WASHINGTON HISTORIC DISTRICT, WILL BE RESTORED TO ITS ORIGINAL STATE BY THE PIONEER WASHINGTON RESTORATION FOUNDATION. (ST-WIDE). JAMES H PILKINGTON, PRESIDENT; PIONEER WASHINGTON RESTORATION FOUNDATION; PO BOX 583; HOPE, AR 71801. (#27856). **ARBA GRANTEE.**

WAYTON

AMERICAN HISTORY SLIDES - WAYTON, AR. SLIDES ON AMERICAN HISTORY WILL BE MADE. (LOCAL). COLUMBUS VAUGHN, CHAIRMAN; UNITED BAPTIST CHURCH; WAYTON, AR 72684. (#29128).

WEST MEMPHIS

CIVIC CNTR & AUDITORIUM PROJ OF WEST MEMPHIS, ARK. BEAUTIFICATION OF OUR CENTRALLY LOCATED & NEWLY CONSTRUCTED CENTER & AUDITORIUM WITH TREES, FLOWER BEDS, WATER FOUNTAINS & BENCHES. (LOCAL). MRS THOMAS J SIMS, CHAIRMAN; WEST MEMPHIS - CRITTENDEN COUNTY BICENTENNIAL COMMISSION; 401 GIBSON; WEST MEMPHIS, AR 72301. (#3435). **ARBA GRANTEE.**

CRITTENDEN COUNTY CULTURAL-AGRICULTURAL MUSEUM, AR. AN AGRICULTURAL-CULTURAL MUSEUM WILL BE ESTABLISHED DURING THE BICENTENNIAL BY THE CITIZENS OF CRITTENDEN CO. THE MUSEUM WILL FEATURE EXHIBITS INDIGENOUS TO THE AREA. COMPLETION IS EXPECTED BY 1976. (LOCAL). MRS THOMAS J SIMS, CHAIRMAN; CRITTENDEN COUNTY BICENTENNIAL COMMISSION; 401 GIBSON ST; WEST MEMPHIS, AR 72301. (#3092).

FORMATION OF COUNTY HISTORICAL SOCIETY IN ARKANSAS. TO FORM AN ORGANIZATION INTERESTED IN THE HISTORY OF CRITTENDEN COUNTY. ORG WILL EVENTUALLY TAKE OVER OPERATION OF THE LIBRARY. (LOCAL). GEORGE W HUMAN, DIRECTOR; CITY OF FT WORTH PLANNING DEPT; 420 ROOSEVELT; WEST MEMPHIS, AR 72301. (#3439). **(??).**

IMPROVING THE ESPERANZA TRAIL, W MEMPHIS, AR. ESTABLISH TRAIL MARKERS AND VISITOR'S INFORMATION CENTER. (ST-WIDE). A JAN THOMAS, JR, PROJ COORDINATOR; W MEMPHIS-CRITTENDEN CO BICENTENNIAL COMMITTEE; 420 0330)=ELT; W MEMPHIS, AR 72301. (#10711). **ARBA GRANTEE.**

NEW MATERIALS FOR MUSEUM IN ARKANSAS. MATERIALS WILL BE PROVIDED FOR NEW EXHIBIT DISPLAY CASES IN THE AGRICULTURAL AND HISTORICAL MUSEUM IN WEST MEMPHIS. (LOCAL). MRS THOMAS J SIMS, CHAIRMAN; CRITTENDEN COUNTY BICENTENNIAL COMMISSION; 401 GIBSON ST; WEST MEMPHIS, AR 72301. (#9738). **ARBA GRANTEE.**

WEST MEMPHIS BICENTENNIAL PLAZA PROJ, AR. PROJECT INCLUDES THE BEAUTIFICATION OF THE WEST MEMPHIS BICENTENNIAL PLAZA. (LOCAL). RUTH G TATE, PROJ DIRECTOR; ARKANSAS AMERICAN REVOLUTION BICENTENNIAL COMMITTEE; 300 W MARKET; LITTLE ROCK, AR 72201. (#18605). **ARBA GRANTEE.**

1976 CALENDAR OF EVENTS - CRITTENDEN COUNTY, ARK. MANY ORGANIZATIONS IN OUR COUNTY ARE PLANNING CELEBRATIONS AND FUND RAISING ACTIVITIES DURING OUR BICENTENNIAL YEAR. THESE WILL BE RECORDED & DISTRIBUTED. (LOCAL). MRS THOMAS J SIMS, CHAIRMAN; CRITTENDEN COUNTY BICENTENNIAL COMMISSION; 401 GIBSON ST; WEST MEMPHIS, AR 72301. (#3440).

NOV 16, '75. CRITTENDEN COUNTY ART EXHIBIT. EXHIBIT AT 626 E BROADWAY/MAIN BRANCH OF BANK OF WEST MEMPHIS. (LOCAL). MRS THOMAS J SIMS, CHRWMN; CRITTENDEN COUNTY BICENTENNIAL COMMISSION; 401 GIBSON ST; WEST MEMPHIS, AR 72301. (#103093-1).

DEC 7, '75. HERITAGE HOME TOUR. TOUR AT HOMES LOCATED IN CITY, MAP AVAILABLE. (LOCAL). MRS THOMAS J SIMS, CHRWMN; CRITTENDEN COUNTY BICENTENNIAL COMMISSION; 401 GIBSON ST; WEST MEMPHIS, AR 72301. (#103089-1).

FEB 6, '76. COSTUME BALL. FESTIVAL AT SOUTHLAND GREYHOUND TRACK. (LOCAL). MRS DON BELL, DIRECTOR; WEST MEMPHIS ARKANSAS JUNIOR AUXILIARY; 902 W BARTON; WEST MEMPHIS, AR 72301. (#103287-1).

MAR 31, '76. BICENTENNIAL WAGON TRAIN. EXHIBIT AT HOLIDAY PLAZA MALL. (LOCAL). TRUDIE EDMONDSON, COORD; WEST MEMPHIS BICENTENNIAL COMMISSION; 1015 CHERRY LA; WEST MEMPHIS, AR 72301. (#105759-1).

MAR 31, '76. UNITED STATES ARMED FORCES BICENTENNIAL CARAVAN. CARAVAN IS COMPOSED OF EXHIBIT VANS FOR EACH MILITARY SERVICE. PROJECT THEME IS 'HISTORY OF THE ARMED FORCES AND THEIR CONTRIBUTIONS TO THE NATION'. (LOCAL). MRS GILBERT D JAY III; US ARMED FORCES BICENTENNIAL EXHIBIT VANS PROJECT; 420 ROOSEVELT; WEST MEMPHIS, AR 72301. (#1775-413).

MAY 1 - DEC 31, '76. LITTLE THEATER PRODUCTION OF PLAY '1776'. 1976 CALENDAR OF EVENTS - CRITTENDEN COUNTY, ARK. MANY ORGANIZATIONS IN OUR COUNTY ARE PLANNING CELEBRATIONS AND FUND RAISING ACTIVITIES DURING OUR BICENTENNIAL YEAR. THESE WILL BE RECORDED & DISTRIBUTED. (LOCAL). MRS THOMAS J SIMS, CHRWMN; CRITTENDEN COUNTY BICENTENNIAL COMMITTEE; 401 GIBSON ST; WEST MEMPHIS, AR 72301. (#3440-502).

JULY 3, '76. GRAND OPENING OF NEW MUSEUM IN ARKANSAS. MATERIALS WILL BE PROVIDED FOR NEW EXHIBIT DISPLAY CASES IN THE AGRICULTURAL AND CULTURAL MUSEUM IN WEST MEMPHIS. (LOCAL). MRS THOMAS J SIMS, CHRM; CRITTENDON COUNTY HISTORICAL SOCIETY; 401 GIBSON ST; WEST MEMPHIS, AR 72301. (#9738-1).

SEPT 1 - 30, '76. JAYCETTES SPONSORED FLEA MARKET. 1976 CALENDAR OF EVENTS - CRITTENDEN COUNTY, ARK. MANY ORGANIZATIONS IN OUR COUNTY ARE PLANNING CELEBRATIONS AND FUND RAISING ACTIVITIES DURING OUR BICENTENNIAL YEAR. THESE WILL BE RECORDED & DISTRIBUTED. (LOCAL). MRS THOMAS J SIMS, CHRWMN; CRITTENDEN COUNTY BICENTENNIAL COMMITTEE; 401 GIBSON ST; WEST MEMPHIS, AR 72301. (#3440-503).

NOV 19, '76. QUOTE BICENTENNIAL MUSICAL. LIVE PERFORMANCE. (LOCAL). MRS THOMAS J SIMS, COORD; QUOTA CLUB OF WEST MEMPHIS; WEST MEMPHIS, AR 72301. (#106692-1).

WINSLOW

FLAGPOLE AND SCHOOL SCRAPBOOK - WINSLOW, AR. SCRAPBOOK WAS PREPARED BY THE STUDENT COUNCIL. FLAGPOLE WAS ERECTED AT THE SCHOOL. (LOCAL). VELMA DUNCAN, CHAIRPERSON; WINSLOW CITY COUNCIL; RT 2, BOX 22; WINSLOW, AR 72959. (#28588).

MAY 29 - 31, '76. COMMUNITY FESTIVAL. FESTIVAL AT WINSLOW SCHOOL CAFETERIA. (LOCAL). VELMA DUNCAN, CHMN; WINSLOW CITY COUNCIL; RT 2, BOX 22; WINSLOW, AR 72959. (#200005-30).

WINTHROP

HISTORICAL QUILT, WINTHROP, AR. HISTORY OF AMERICA DEPICTED IN QUILT ON EXHIBIT. (LOCAL). VETA A SARP, PRESIDENT; EXTENSION HOMEMAKERS CLUB; 202 HIGH ST; WINTHROP, AR 71866. (#28709).

MAY 2, '76. HISTORICAL MUSEUM. EXHIBIT. (LOCAL). VETA A SHARP, CHAIRMAN; EXTENISON HOMEMAKER CLUB; 202 HIGH ST; WINTHROP, AR 71866. (#200005-35).

WRIGHTSVILLE

EQUIPPING OF WRIGHTSVILLE LOG CABIN, AR. THE ECONOMIC OPPORTUNITY AGENCY AREA 4-B WILL SPONSOR THE FURNISHING & EQUIPPING OF THE WRIGHTSVILLE LOG CABIN BICENTENNIAL PROJECT; THE PROJECT WILL INVOLVE ALL SEGMENTS OF THE

WRIGHTSVILLE — CONTINUED

POPULATION OF THE AREA. (LOCAL). LUMAS KENDRICK, AREA DIRECTOR; ECONOMIC OPPORTUNITY AGENCY, AREA 4-B; PO BOX 187; WRIGHTSVILLE, AR 72183. (#20964). **ARBA GRANTEE.**

WYNNE

MAR 19, '76. AN EVENING OF MUSIC: A BICENTENNIAL EVENT. TRACES HIGHLIGHTS OF AMERICAN MUSIC FROM OUR COUNTRY'S BEGINNINGS TO THE PRESENT. INCLUDES FOLK, SPIRITUALS, CLASSICAL, AND POP. AT PROGRESS BUILDING. (LOCAL). ANDERA BETNAR, COORD; WYNNE MUSIC CLUB; 309 CRABB LN; WYNNE, AR 72396. (#200005-1).

MAY 7 - 8, '76. ARTS AND CRAFTS EXHIBITS. EXHIBIT AT PROGRESS CLUB, PARKING LOT. (ST-WIDE). WILLIAM R KITTRELL, DIR; WYNNE BICENTENNIAL COMMITTEE; 511 E POPLAR; WYNNE, AR 72396. (#106315-1).

YELLVILLE

TURKEY TROT, YELLVILLE, AR. IN ADDITION TO THE TURKEY TROT THERE WILL ALSO BE A CARNIVAL, A PARADE, A TALENT CONTEST, DANCE CONTEST, MISS DRUMSTICKS CONTEST, A TURKEY DINNER, AN OLD TIME FIDDLERS CONTEST & A BEAUTY PAGEANT. (LOCAL). HON JAMES C PEARSON, MAYOR; CITY OF YELLVILLE; CITY HALL; YELLVILLE, AR 72687. (#26721). **ARBA GRANTEE.**

OCT 22 - 23, '76. TURKEY TROT. ALSO ASSOCIATED WITH TURKEY TROT IS A CARNIVAL, PARADE, TALENT CONTEST, DANCE CONTEST, MISS DRUMSTICKS CONTEST, TURKEY DINNER, OLD TIME FIDDLERS CONTEST AND BEAUTY CONTEST. (LOCAL). HON JAMES PEARSON, MAYOR; CITY OF YELLVILLE; CITY HALL; YELLVILLE, AR 72687. (#26721-1).

Home Made
Lye Soap
Face Soap
30¢
a Bar

California

American Revolution Bicentennial Commission of California

Established by the State Legislature in August 1967 (Senate Bill 1327, Chapter 1425)

Theme: Gold Rush

Slogan: From a Golden Past to a Golden Future

ARBA Statistics

Officially Recognized
Communities—363
Colleges/Universities—69
Military Installations—91
BINET Projects—1,023
Events—1,919
1976 Population—21,520,000

Bicentennial Archives

California State Archives
Office of the Secretary of State
Room 200, 1020 "O" Street
Sacramento, California 95814

Membership

Twenty members appointed on a nonpartisan basis—10 by the governor, five by the speaker of the Assembly and five by the Senate Rules Committee.

Charles J. Conrad (1968-), *chairman* (1968-72)
Richard F. Pourade, *chairman* (1972-75)
Dr. Donald M. Dozer, *vice-chairman* (1968-75), *acting chairman* (1975-)
Gretchen Thomas, *secretary* (1968-)
Arnold E. Nielsen, *treasurer* (1974-)
Robert F. Beaver, *treasurer* (1968-71)
John A. Davis, (1968-74), *treasurer* (1971-74), deceased
Verna M. Hall (1968-)
(Mrs.) Anthony Kennedy (1968-)
Abraham Kofman (1968-)
Eleanor Lyon (1968-)
John McCarty (1968-)
Colonel William L. Shaw (1968-)
Dr. R. Coke Wood (1970-)
Colonel Paul Leos (1972-)
Dr. Samuel A. Reese (1972-)
Elsa Sandstrom (1972-)
Senator James E. Whetmore (1968-76)
Assemblyman Newton R. Russell (1973-75)
Edmund C. Sajor (1974-)
Sam Kalman (1975-)
Phillip Album (1975-)
Chester L. Washington (1974-)
Senator Jack Schrade (1976)
(Mrs.) Lee Whitebrook (1968-75)
Donald I. Segerstrom (1971-73), deceased
Sally B. Altick (1968-73)
Assemblyman Leo J. Ryan (1968-72)

Staff

Albert C. Johnson, *executive director* (1972-76)
June M. Tuton, *acting director* (1977-)

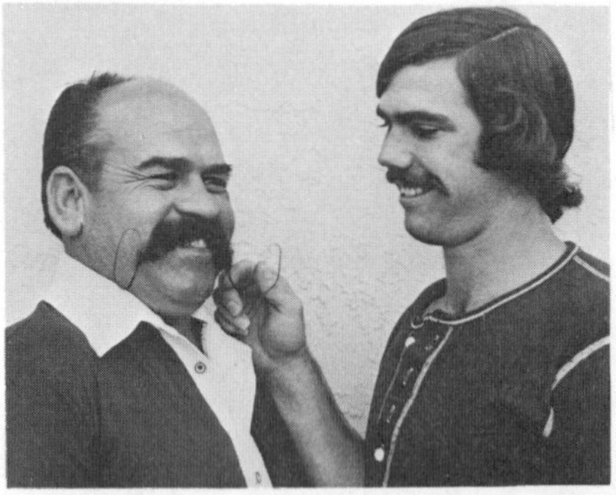

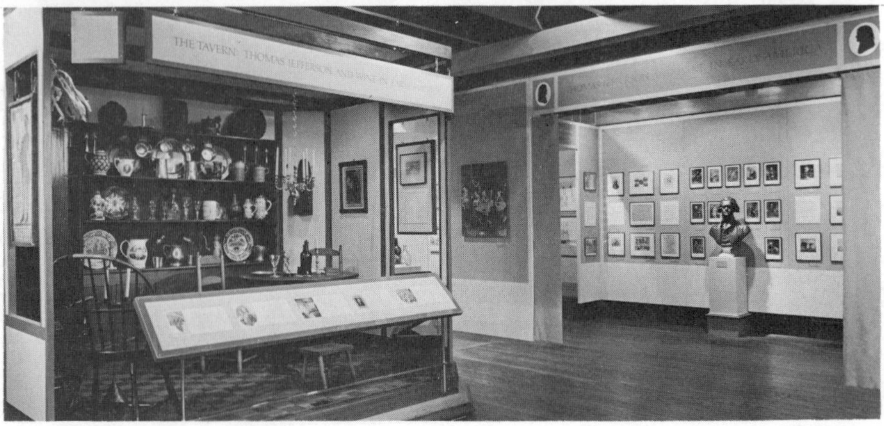

California

California's Bicentennial commission was faced with a problem unique among all the state Bicentennial commissions during the four years leading up to the Bicentennial celebration: the 1967 legislation which established the commission stipulated that it "must operate without the appropriation of state funds."

Thus, financing Bicentennial activities became the primary challenge for the commission.

According to the enabling legislation, expenditures of the commission were to be financed from donations, gifts and grants from private or public sources.

It was not quite that easy.

For one thing, legislators back in 1967 did not foresee the oil embargo, double-digit inflation and the ensuing recession.

Those factors made donations hard to raise.

Fortunately for Californians who wanted meaningful programs, the American Revolution Bicentennial Administration was supplied with matching grant monies for distribution to the states, which funded most of the state commission programs in California.

Industry also contributed some monies or personnel to commission efforts. Some funds came from sales of state medallions, but these did not measure up to expectations.

Thus, faced with a small budget and expensive tasks, the commission took the most practical course it could: it went to the people and enlisted grassroots support.

Before it could do so, the American Revolution Bicentennial Commission of California first had to draft a pamphlet of purposes and procedures so that local committees and other citizens could see how the state commission functioned and how local Bicentennial committees could be officially appointed. This task was accomplished early in 1973. Both the pamphlet and instructions for appointing the local Bicentennial committees were circulated throughout the state.

The people of California responded quickly, and soon local committees were planning Bicentennial programs. By May 1976, California had 361 officially designated Bicentennial Communities, ranking it 10th in the nation. By July 4, 1976, 95 percent of all Californians lived in cities or counties which had Bicentennial committees implementing patriotic activities and projects commemorating the nation's birth. And California led the nation in two fields: it was first in Bicentennial Colleges and Universities and first in Bicentennial Military Installations.

Meanwhile, the ARBCC has been able to adopt and bring to fruition over 200 official Bicentennial projects. It would take too long to detail all of them here. But some should be mentioned because of the impact they have already had or will continue to have on the state as a whole.

These include:

- *The California-Colonial History Time Line,* which synchronizes events on both coasts from 1769–1783;
- An interpretive brochure on the origin of mission music, and related mission music projects;
- Programs planned for students which depict California's musical and literary heritage;
- Historical restorations throughout the state;
- Statues and historical markers;
- An historic bicycle route developed and posted by the ARBCC and CALTRANS along the Pacific Coast;
- Guided tours through the Mother Lode country, developed by the ARBCC and the Department of Parks and Recreation;
- The Allensworth Film Project, depicting the only California community to be founded, financed and governed by Blacks;
- The Annual Afro-American History Week, which dramatizes historical contributions of Black Americans toward the development of California;
- Two Indian cultural centers, one on each side of the Sierra Nevada, serving the Miwok and Paiute-Shoshone tribes;
- A sound-slide show describing the reenactment of the de Anza expedition;
- Projects designed to help either handicapped or underprivileged children in California; and
- State and local tree-planting programs.

Four years ago, California's Bicentennial commission adopted the motto: *From a Golden Past to a Golden Future.*

One hundred years from now, when future Californians open the Commission Time Capsule and review what was done in 1976, they will see that today's Californians worked hard to make that transition a reality.

AGOURA

APR 24 - MAY 30, '76. RENAISSANCE PLEASURE FAIRE. AMERICA'S CULTURAL FOUNDATIONS ARE EXPLORED THROUGH A RE-CREATION OF ELIZABETHAN ENGLAND. AT OLD PARAMOUNT RANCH. (REGN'L). PHIL PALADINO, PRES; THEME EVENTS LTD; 627 COMMERCIAL ST; SAN FRANCISCO, CA 94111. (#103416-274).

ALAMEDA

AMERICA IN PATCH QUILT, ALAMEDA, CA. A 6'X12' QUILT WITH SYMBOLS ON SCENES OF US HISTORY. (LOCAL). A N KOSHIYAMA, VICE PRINCIPAL; WILL C WOOD MIDDLE SCHOOL; 420 GRAND AVE; ALAMEDA, CA 94501. (#20718).

AMERICA 1775-1975, ALAMEDA, CA. PROJECT IS TO HELP STUDENTS & PARENTS APPRECIATE AMERICAN HERITAGE & TO ALLOW STUDENTS TO CREATIVELY SELECT THE MEDIA OF REPRESENTATION; BUILDING WALL MURALS. (LOCAL). ALBERT KOSHIYAMA, VICE PRINCIPAL; WILL C WOOD MIDDLE SCHOOL; 420 GRAND AVE; ALAMEDA, CA 94501. (#20720).

BICENTENNIAL CLASSROOM PROGRAM - MUSIC, POETRY & DANCE. LIVE PERFORMANCE. (LOCAL). A N KOSHIYAMA, COORD; WILL C WOOD MIDDLE SCHOOL; 420 GRAND ST; ALAMEDA, CA 94501. (#104994-1).

BICENTENNIAL COMMUNITY GARDEN IN ALAMEDA, CA. GARDEN PLOTS PROVIDED FOR GROWING VEGETABLES; LAND ALSO TO BE USED FOR PERMANENT FLORAL DISPLAY; ENCOURAGE PEOPLE TO RETURN TO ROOT OF OUR HERITAGE, THE EARTH. (LOCAL). WILLETA O'DELL, CHAIRMAN; ALAMEDA BICENTENNIAL COMMITTEE; 2019 SHORELINE DR; ALAMEDA, CA 94501. (#11398).

DESIGNATION AS BICENTENNIAL COMMAND - CA. U S COAST GUARD TRAINING CENTER, ALAMEDA, DESIGNATED FOR HISTORICAL PURPOSES. (REGN'L). AF REEVES, PUBLIC AFFAIRS OFFICER; U S COAST GUARD TRAINING CENTER; GOVERNMENT ISLAND; ALAMEDA, CA 94501. (#29025).

EMBLEM DESIGN CONTEST - ALAMEDA, CA. STUDENTS DEVELOP LOGO FOR USE AS SCHOOL DESIGN FOR BICENTENNIAL PUBLICATIONS & LETTERHEAD. (LOCAL). A N KOSHIYAMA, VICE PRINCIPAL; WILL C WOOD MIDDLE SCHOOL; 420 GRAND AVE; ALAMEDA, CA 94501. (#20717).

ORAL HISTORY OF ALAMEDA, CALIFORNIA. UNIQUE HISTORY OF THIS ISLAND CITY WILL BE RECORDED ON AUDIO & VIDEO TAPE, THROUGH INTERVIEWS WITH LONG-TIME RESIDENTS; TAPES TO GO TO SCHOOLS & LIBRARIES. (LOCAL). PAULINE HENDERSON, PROJ COORDINATOR; ALAMEDA BICENTENNIAL COMMITTEE; 2437 SANTA CLARA AVE; ALAMEDA, CA 94501. (#11399).

SCHOOL ESSAY CONTEST, ALAMEDA, CA. ESSAYS INTENDED TO PROMOTE THE INTEREST IN THE ROLE OF WOMEN IN OUR AMERICAN HISTORY. (LOCAL). A N KOSHIYAMA, VICE PRINCIPAL; WILL C WOOD MIDDLE SCHOOL; 420 GRAND AVE; ALAMEDA, CA 94501. (#20719).

VOTINGEST CITY IN USA: 1976 GOAL PROJECT. A PROGRAM TO INITIATE NATIONAL COMPETITION BETWEEN CITIES TO RAISE THE NUMBER OF VOTING CITIZENS BY NOV 5, 1976, TO PROMOTE VOTING AS A KEY TO DEMOCRACY & THE IDEA OF A BIRTHDAY GIFT TO AMERICA. (ST-WIDE). RUTH DROSSEL, BICENT CHRMN; PARENT-TEACHER ASSOCIATION; 615 ROCK ISLE; ALAMEDA, CA 94501. (#5369).

JAN 27, '75 - DEC 30, '76. 1ST VOTER REGISTRATION DRIVE - AMERICA'S VOTINGEST CITY IN '76. ANNOUNCEMENTS OF AMERICA'S VOTINGEST CITY IN '76 AWARD DEC 30, 1976. A PROGRAM TO INITIATE NATIONAL COMPETITION BETWEEN CITIES TO RAISE THE NUMBER OF VOTING CITIZENS BY NOV 5, 1976, TO PROMOTE VOTING AS A KEY TO DEMOCRACY & THE IDEA OF A BIRTHDAY GIFT TO AMERICA. AT 265 TOTAL CITIES HAVE JOINED COMPETITION. (NAT'L). RUTH MCIVER DROSSEL; ALAMEDA COUNCIL PTA, JAYCEES, LEAGUE OF WOMEN VOTERS & OTHERS; 615 ROCK ISLE; ALAMEDA, CA 94501. (#5369-501).

FEB 1, '75. REGISTRATION OF FIRST TIME VOTERS-CITY HALL-LOCAL, STATE OFFICIALS. VOTINGEST CITY IN USA: 1976 GOAL PROJECT. A PROGRAM TO INITIATE NATIONAL COMPETITION BETWEEN CITIES TO RAISE THE NUMBER OF VOTING CITIZENS BY NOV 5, 1976, TO PROMOTE VOTING AS A KEY TO DEMOCRACY & THE IDEA OF A BIRTHDAY GIFT TO AMERICA. (ST-WIDE). RUTH DROSSEL, BICENT CHRM; PARENT-TEACHER ASSOCIATION; 615 ROCK ISLE; ALAMEDA, CA 94501. (#5369-902).

MAY 22, '76. BICENTENNIAL YOUTH PARADE. PARADE AT SHORELINE DRIVE, ALAMEDA, CA. (LOCAL). JOAN FRAYHER, CHAIRMAN; ALAMEDA GIRL SCOUT ASSOC; 880 WALNUT ST; ALAMEDA, CA 94501. (#100666-1).

ALBANY

ALBANY BICENTENNIAL BOOK & BUSINESS DIRECTORY - CA. PROJECT WILL PROVIDE CITIZENS & BUSINESS PEOPLE OF ALBANY WITH A COMMEMORATIVE HISTORICAL REVIEW OF ALBANY. (LOCAL). HAROLD G DENHAM, CHAIRMAN; ALBANY BICENTENNIAL COMMITTEE; 1108 SOLANO AVE; ALBANY, CA 94706. (#11630).

ALLENSWORTH

ALLENSWORTH, CA, FILM PROJECT. 16MM COLOR SOUND FILM INTERPRETING HISTORIC & CULTURAL SIGNIFICANCE OF ALLENSWORTH, THE ONLY TOWN IN CALIFORNIA FOUNDED, FINANCED AND GOVERNED BY BLACKS. (LOCAL). NORMAN L WILSON, PROJ DIRECTOR; CALIFORNIA DEPARTMENT OF PARKS & RECREATION; 1416 9TH ST; SACRAMENTO, CA 95814. (#15593). **ARBA GRANTEE.**

ALMADEN AFS

MAY 15 - 16, '76. ARMED FORCES DAY OPEN HOUSE. EXHIBIT, TOUR. (LOCAL). MSGT JOHN FULLER; 682 RADAR SQUADRON; BOX 454; ALMADEN AFS, CA 95042. (#200006-15).

ALPINE

SEPT 11 - 12, '76. VIEJAS DAYS, PARADE & HORSE SHOW - ALPINE, CALIFORNIA. ALL MEDIA ARTS & CRAFTS, EMPHASIS ON PRIMITIVE & HISTORICAL INC PHOTOS, A PHOTO BOOTH, FOOD & DRINK STANDS, MUSIC, ETC. AT ALPINE WOMEN'S CLUB, ALPINE BLVD, ALPINE. (LOCAL). BEATRICE LAFORCE; ALPINE BICENTENNIAL COMMITTEE & ALPINE CHAMBER OF COMMERCE; 787 S GRADE RD; ALPINE, CA 92001. (#107778-1).

ANAHEIM

'ABRAHAM LINCOLN ON STAMPS' - ANAHEIM, CA. THIS EXHIBIT CONSISTS OF STAMPS HONORING PRESIDENT ABRAHAM LINCOLN. (LOCAL). HARRY G BOYD, CURATOR; MUSEUM OF POSTAL HISTORY; PO BOX 3642; ANAHEIM, CA 92803. (#28532).

'ANAHEIM, GRAPES TO GREATNESS', CALIFORNIA. MANUSCRIPT; THE STORY ON THE FOUNDING OF ANAHEIM FOR CHILDREN. A PICTURE HISTORY BOOK. (LOCAL). MARGARET ZAPALA, DIRECTOR; ANAHEIM BICENTENNIAL COMMISSION; 2534 STRONG PLACE; ANAHEIM, CA 92806. (#19398).

ANTIQUE POSTCARD EXHIBIT - ANAHEIM, CA. A COLLECTION OF ANTIQUE POSTCARDS CIRCA 1900; EXAMPLES OF CHRISTMAS, THANKSGIVING AND PICTURE POSTCARDS. EXHIBIT WILL ALSO INCLUDE 2 RARE CARDS DEPICTING THE LIBERTY BELL AND INDEPENDENCE HALL. (LOCAL). HARRY G BOYD, CURATOR; MUSEUM OF POSTAL HISTORY; PO BOX 3642; ANAHEIM, CA 92807. (#28531).

BICENTENNIAL RUBBISH TRUCK, ANAHEIM, CA. REFUGE TRUCKS WILL BE PAINTED IN BICENTENNIAL MOTIF TO INSTILL PRIDE IN THE COUNTRY & CITY. (LOCAL). BILL TAORMINA, CHAIRMAN; ANAHEIM DISPOSAL, INC; 512 E VERMONT; ANAHEIM, CA 92805. (#19827).

BICENTENNIAL STITCHERY PROJECT, CA. INDIVIDUAL BICENTENNIAL STITCHERY-A TANGIBLE OBJECT TO KEEP FOR REMEMBRANCE OF OUR BICENTNENNIAL YEAR. (LOCAL). SALLY BANE, TEACHER; SUNKIST ELEMENTARY SCHOOL; 500 N SUNKIST; ANAHEIM, CA 92807. (#23339).

DISNEY STAMP EXHIBIT - ANAHEIM, CA. EXHIBIT INCLUDES STAMPS, AUTOGRAPHED COVERS AND PICTURES HONORING WALT DISNEY AND HIS CARTOON CHARACTERS. (LOCAL). HARRY G BOYD, CURATOR; MUSEUM OF POSTAL HISTORY; PO BOX 3642; ANAHEIM, CA 92803. (#28527).

'ERRORS, FREAKS & ODDITIES' - ANAHEIM, CA. AN EXHIBIT OF MINOR ERRORS OR MISTAKES ON U S STAMPS. (LOCAL). HARRY G BOYD, CURATOR; MUSEUM OF POSTAL HISTORY; PO BOX 3642; ANAHEIM, CA 92803. (#28529).

EXHIBIT OF EARLY CALIFORNIA MAIL - ANAHEIM, CA. EXHIBIT INCLUDES MAPS, PICTURES, ENVELOPES AND DESCRIPTIVE WRITINGS ABOUT CALIFORNIA POSTAL HISTORY. (LOCAL). HARRY G BOYD, CURATOR; MUSEUM OF POSTAL HISTORY; PO BOX 3642; ANAHEIM, CA 92803. (#28526).

'GEORGE WASHINGTON ON STAMPS' - ANAHEIM, CA. AN EXHIBIT OF GEORGE WASHINGTON STAMPS, COVERS, MAPS AND REPRODUCTIONS OF PAINTINGS. (LOCAL). HARRY G BOYD, CURATOR; MUSEUM OF POSTAL HISTORY; PO BOX 3642; ANAHEIM, CA 92803. (#28524).

'HEROES OF THE REVOLUTION' - ANAHEIM, CA. AN EXHIBIT OF STAMPS HONORING THOSE PEOPLE WHO PARTICIPATED IN THE AMERICAN REVOLUTION. (LOCAL). HARRY G BOYD, CURATOR; MUSEUM OF POSTAL HISTORY; PO BOX 3642; ANAHEIM, CA 92803. (#28530).

HISTORICAL CHARACTER TROUPE - ANAHEIM, CA. 11 INDIVIDUALS DRESS IN PERIOD COSTUME, STUDY THEIR CHARACTERS AND PRESENT THEMSELVES TO PUBLIC AS 'LIVE' REPRESENTATION OF ACHIEVEMENT, SIGNIFICANCE & GREATNESS OF AMERICA'S PAST. (LOCAL). MARK M HERRON, PROJ DIRECTOR; ANAHEIM PARKS, RECREATION & THE ARTS DEPT; 630 N ANAHEIM BLVD; ANAHEIM, CA 92805. (#24923).

MOSAIC ON AMERICAN HERITAGE, ANAHEIM, CA. THE MOSAIC MEASURES 3 FT BY 54 FT. IT STARTS WITH INDIANS AND ENDS WITH THE BICENTENNIAL EMBLEM. BY THE CHILDREN OF THE JAMES M GUINN SCHOOL. (LOCAL). JACQUE KELLY, PRESIDENT; JAMES M GUINN PTA; 1051 S SUNKIST; ANAHEIM, CA 92806. (#23340).

ONE MILLION MILE BICENTENNIAL BIKE-A-THON - CA. A CROSS COUNTY BICYCLE ADVENTURE TOUR OF 42 DAYS FROM ANAHEIM TO PHILADELPHIA. THE TOUR IS DESIGNED SO THAT PARTICIPANTS CAN SEE THE COUNTRY, MEET ITS PEOPLE, PROMOTE ECOLOGY & BICYCLING. (REGN'L). DANA J MORRISON, CHAIRMAN; BICYCLE THE AMERICAS CLUB; 10002 BURGUNDY PL; ANAHEIM, CA 92804. (#16823).

ORIGINAL ANAHEIM LANDMARK PAINTINGS, CA. PROJECT PURPOSE: PRESERVE & PERPETUATE THE HISTORY OF ANAHEIM IN PAINTINGS; DESCRIPTIVE BOOKLET OF PAINTINGS & HISTORY GIVEN AS SOUVENIR. (LOCAL). EILEEN ANTHONY, PRESIDENT; WOMEN'S DIVISION, ANAHEIM CHAMBER OF COMMERCE; 130 S LEMON ST; ANAHEIM, CA 92805. (#22111).

PATRIOTIC FIREPLUGS IN ANAHEIM, CA. REVOLUTIONARY FIGURES WILL BE PAINTED ON CITY FIREPLUGS. (LOCAL). WILLIAM F MARSHALL, CO-CHAIRMAN; KIWANIS CLUB OF GREATER ANAHEIM; 2565 E PARK LANE C; ANAHEIM, CA 92806. (#19399).

PIONEER ANAHEIM PROJECT - ANAHEIM, CA. RELOCATION AND RESTORATION OF THE PIONEER ANAHEIM HOME. (LOCAL). ANDREW L DENEAU, COORDINATOR; ANAHEIM HERITAGE COMMITTEE; 225 N CLAUDINA ST; ANAHEIM, CA 92805. (#28533).

'PRESIDENTS ON STAMPS' - ANAHEIM, CA. EXHIBIT OF STAMPS HONORING ALL OF AMERICAS PRESIDENTS. (LOCAL). HARRY G BOYD, CURATOR; MUSEUM OF POSTAL HISTORY; PO BOX 3642; ANAHEIM, CA 92803. (#28528).

QUILT PROJECT OF ANAHEIM, CA. QUILT: 'HISTORICAL & POLITICAL HERITAGE OF ORANGE COUNTY'. (LOCAL). MRS KERMIT HATFIELD, DIR; ORANGE COUNTY FEDERATED REPUBLICAN WOMEN; 327 N PHILADELPHIA; ANAHEIM, CA 92805. (#28176).

'WHAT'S COOKING AT CONNELLY?' - BOOK, ANAHEIM, CA. COOKBOOK EMPHASIS ON FAMILY RECIPES FROM PARENTS, FACULTY, FRIENDS & OTHERS. (LOCAL). VI FURFARO, PROJECT CHAIRMAN; CORNELIA CONNELLY SCHOOL MOTHERS AUXILIARY; 2323 W BROADWAY; ANAHEIM, CA 92804. (#19828).

'WHEN A STAMP IS NOT A STAMP' - ANAHEIM, CA. AN EXHIBIT OF LABELS AND SEALS FOR CHARITABLE, ECOLOGICAL AND RELIGIOUS PURPOSES; INCLUDES MANY FULL SHEETS OF OLDER SEALS. (LOCAL). HARRY G BOYD, CURATOR; MUSEUM OF POSTAL HISTORY; PO BOX 3642; ANAHEIM, CA 92803. (#28525).

25TH NATIONAL SQUARE DANCE CONVENTION. EMPHASIS ON SQUARE DANCING AS UNIQUE AMERICAN ART FORM. TRAIL DANCES WILL BE HELD PRIOR TO CONVENTION. STRONG INTERNATIONAL PARTICIPATION & EXTENSIVE MEDIA COVERAGE PLANNED. (NAT'L). G KEN PARKER, GENERAL CHAIRMAN; CALIFORNIA SQUARE DANCE COUNCIL; 426 PHILLIPS WAY; VISTA, CA 92083. (#122). **ARBA RECOGNIZED.**

MAY 30 - JUNE 1, '75. CARROUSEL OF ANAHEIM - EXHIBITION OF TALENTS, ARTS & CRAFTS. AUHS DISTRICT JAZZ FESTIVAL & ANAHEIM ELEMENTARY MUSIC FESTIVAL 100,000 SQ FT OF CULTURAL ARTS-CONTINUOUS EXHIBITS & PERFORMANCES. AT ANAHEIM CONVENTION CENTER 800 W KATELLA, ANAHEIM FREE PARKING. (LOCAL). ANAHEIM CHAMBER COMMERCE; WOMEN'S DIVISION - ANAHEIM CHAMBER OF COMMERCE; 130 S LEMON ST; ANAHEIM, CA 92805. (#50253-1).

JUNE 15 - SEPT 9, '75. SUMMER READING PROGRAM FOR CHILDREN PRESCHOOL THROUGH EIGHTH GRADE. SEMINAR, AWARD, EXHIBIT. (LOCAL). RUTH JACOBSEN, PGM MGR; PARKS, RECREATION & THE FINE ARTS DEPT; 222 E CHATRES; ANAHEIM, CA 92805. (#101081-1).

JULY 25, '75 - DEC 30, '76. WELCOME WORLD - FOREIGN HOST PROGRAM. TOUR AT ANAHEIM CONVENTION CENTER, 800 W KATELLA. (LOCAL). SYLVIA BULA, COORDINATOR; ANAHEIM DIPLOMETTES; 1730 W LA PALMA 'A'; ANAHEIM, CA 92801. (#102081-3).

AUG 15 - 24, '75. 21ST ANNUAL SOUTHLAND HOME & GARDEN. EXHIBIT, TOUR AT ANAHEIM CONVENTION CENTER. (LOCAL). WALLY BOYKO, GEN MGR; GEORGE COLOURIS PRODUCTIONS; 1782 W LINCOLN, SUITE J; ANAHEIM, CA 92801. (#101080-1).

AUG 23, '75. ALL STATES PICNIC - ORANGE COUNTY SENIOR CITIZENS. FESTIVAL AT LA PALMA PARK, CORNER OF HARBOR & LA PALMA; STREET PARKING. (LOCAL). RUTH JACOBSEN, CHMN; ANAHEIM SENIOR CITIZENS CLUB/PARKS, RECREATION & THE ARTS DEPT; 222 E CHARTRES; ANAHEIM, CA 92805. (#101082-1).

SEPT 1, '75 - APR 15, '76. OAK CANYON NATURE CENTER. EXHIBIT, TOUR AT SE OF ANAHEIM HILLS GOLF COURSE, OFF ANAHEIM HILLS RD. (LOCAL). AVON B CARLSON, PRES; ANAHEIM ROTARY CLUB; 4033 MAPLE TREE DR; ANAHEIM, CA 92807. (#200006-12).

OCT 22, '75. BICENTENNIAL BAND & DRILL TEAM SPECTACULAR. OPENING, PARADE, LIVE PERFORMANCE AT ANAHEIM STADIUM, 2000 SOUTH STATE COLLEGE BLVD. (LOCAL). JACK BROWN, PROJ MGR; ANAHEIM UNION HIGH SCHOOL DISTRICT; 501 CRESCENT WAY; ANAHEIM, CA 92801. (#102081-1).

OCT 24 - 26, '75. 52ND ANNUAL ANAHEIM HALLOWEEN FESTIVAL & PARADE. CHILDREN'S WINDOW PAINTING CONTEST; 2 BREAKFASTS (ONE IN COSTUME); BUSINESS FIRM CONTESTS; YOUTH COUNCIL'S FUN CARNIVAL; YOUTH PARADE; PRE-PARADE SHOW; ARTS & CRAFTS SHOW, COSTUME BALL, TEEN DANCE, FAMILY FUN DAY, TRICK OR TREAT, FIREWORKS DISPLAY. AT BREAKFAST AT PEARSON PARK, PARADE STARTS IN GLOVER STADIUM. (LOCAL). STEWART LINK, PRESIDENT; ANAHEIM CHAMBER OF COMMERCE & THE CITY OF ANAHEIM; 130 S LEMON ST; ANAHEIN, CA 92805. (#101083-1).

NOV 6, '75. WEST STREET WALK THRU HISTORY. TOUR AT 414 N WEST ST. (LOCAL). SARAH FAY PEARSON, CHMN; MOTHER COLONY ADVISORY BOARD; 685 N HELENA ST; ANAHEIM, CA 92805. (#200006-13).

NOV 11, '75. LUNCHEON EXHIBITS & ENTERTAINMENT. EXHIBIT, FESTIVAL, LIVE PERFORMANCE AT EBELL CLUB OF ANAHEIM, 244 N HELENA ST. (LOCAL). EDITH HOLSINGER, CHAIRMAN; EBELL CLUB OF ANAHEIM; 2044 GREENLEAF; SANTA ANA, CA 92706. (#200006-14).

NOV 11, '75 - MAR 1, '76. BICENTENNIAL STUDENT ART CONTEST. 2-DIMENSION ARTWORKS, DRAWINGS, PAINTINGS, COLLAGES AND STITCHERY DEPICTING THE REVOLUTIONARY PERIOD. (LOCAL). PATSY RAY, CHAIRMAN; ANAHEIM BICENTENNIAL COMMITTEE; 130 S LEMON ST; ANAHEIM, CA 92805. (#104289-1).

ANAHEIM — CONTINUED

DEC 2 - 4, '75. HOLIDAY IN MUSIC FEATURING A REVOLUTIONARY CHRISTMAS 1776. LIVE PERFORMANCE AT ANAHEIM CONVENTION CENTER. (LOCAL). JACK BROWN, EXEC DIRECTOR; ANAHEIM UNION HIGH SCHOOL DISTRICT; 501 CRESCENT WAY; ANAHEIM, CA 92801. (#200006-11).

JAN 2 - MAR 1, '76. BICENTENNIAL PHOTOGRAPHY CONTEST. PHOTO-JOURNALISM DOCUMENTING TODAY'S LIFESTYLES. (LOCAL). PATSY RAY, CHAIRMAN; ANAHEIM BICENTENNIAL COMMITTEE; 130 S LEMON ST; ANAHEIM, CA 92805. (#104289-2).

JAN 9 - 11, '76. ORCOEXPO, '76 STAMP SHOW. 200 FRAMES OF EXHIBITS, 38 STAMP DEALERS, U S AND FOREIGN POST OFFICES, BICENTENNIAL PHILATELIC SOUVENIRS, CLUBS AND MEETINGS, STAMP AUCTION, FREE 'ASK THE EXPERT' BOOTH. AT DISNEYLAND HOTEL EXHIBIT HALL, 1150 W CERRITOS AVE. (REGN'L). ALAN I FRIEDMAN; ORCOEXPO; P O BOX 5084; ORANGE, CA 92667. (#102081-2).

JAN 9 - 13, '76. AMERICAN FREEDOM TRAIN DISPLAY DAYS AT ANAHEIM. THE AMERICAN FREEDOM TRAIN WILL INCLUDE 10 EXHIBIT CARS & 2 SHOWCASE CARS DEPICTING DIFFERENT PHASES OF THE AMERICAN EXPERIENCE. ITS ARRIVAL WILL SERVE AS A CATALYST FOR LOCAL BICENTENNIAL CELEBRATIONS BY PEOPLE THROUGHOUT THIS NATION. (ST-WIDE). SY FREEDMAN, DIR OF P/R; THE AMERICAN FREEDOM TRAIN FOUNDATION; 5205 LEESBURG PIKE, SUITE 800; BAILEY'S XRDS, VA 22041. (#1776-146).

JAN 30, '76. 'PLANTING THE RED, WHITE AND BLUE'. ECOLOGY STUDENT COUNCIL DRESSED IN PERIOD COSTUMES WILL PLANT RED, WHITE AND BLUE FLOWERS; ALSO, PRESENTATION OF RED, WHITE AND BLUE TRASH CANS. AT COLONY PARK, LINCOLN AVE AT CLEMENTINE ST. (LOCAL). EVELYN BEVINS, DIRECTOR; JOHN MARSHALL ELEMENTARY SCHOOL; 322 N PINE ST; ANAHEIM, CA 92805. (#104289-8).

JAN 31, '76. INTERNATIONAL RUGBY - USA VS AUSTRALIA. COMPETITION AT GLOVER STADIUM. (INT'L). LARRY SIERK, EXEC V-PRES; ANAHEIM BICENTENNIAL COMMITTEE; 130 S LEMON ST; ANAHEIM, CA 92805. (#104565-2).

FEB 1 - JULY 4, '76. READER'S THEATRE ENSEMBLE. READER'S THEATRE BRINGS DIDACTIC DRAMA IN A SIMPLE, UNTROUBLED WAY TO THE PUBLIC. (LOCAL). MARK HERRON, CHAIRMAN; ANAHEIM PARKS & RECREATION DEPT; 630 N ANAHEIM BLVD; ANAHEIM, CA 92805. (#105911-3).

FEB 3, '76. SPIRIT OF '76 BRUNCH. FESTIVAL AT ASSISTANCE LEAGUE SERVICE CENTER. (LOCAL). MRS L A SIERK, CHAIRMAN; AUXILIA 'D ARTS OF ASSISTANCE LEAGUE OF ANAHEIM; 2094 S JUNE PLACE; ANAHEIM, CA 92804. (#200006-178).

FEB 7, '76. BICENTENNIAL FAIRE. FAIR AT HIGH SCHOOL AUDITORIUM. (LOCAL). MADELINE PARKER, DIR; CONNELLY HIGH SCHOOL; 2323 W BROADWAY; ANAHEIM, CA 92805. (#104565-1).

FEB 22, '76. 'THE BRITISH ARE COMING!' - BRITISH MILITARY BAND PERFORMANCE. TOUR OF MAJOR U S CITIES BY BRITISH MILITARY UNITS AS REPRESENTATIVE OF UNITS INVOLVED IN REVOLUTIONARY WAR CAMPAIGN. (INT'L). CHARLES K JONES, PRES; COLUMBIA ARTISTS FESTIVALS CORP; 165 W 57TH ST; NEW YORK, NY 10019. (#6532-24).

MAR 5, '76. ARBOR DAY CELEBRATION. ECOLOGY STUDENT COUNCIL DRESSED IN PERIOD COSTUMES WILL PLANT SOME TREES AND RED, WHITE AND BLUE FLOWERS WITH ENTIRE SCHOOL ATTENDING; PARENTS & GUESTS INVITED; THE BROOKHURST JUNIOR HIGH SCHOOL BAND WILL PLAY SELECTIONS. AT JOHN MARSHALL PARK, LA PALMA AVE AT COLUMBINE ST. (LOCAL). EVELYN BEVINS, CHMN; JOHN MARSHALL ELEMENTARY SCHOOL; 322 N PINE ST; ANAHEIM, CA 92805. (#104289-7).

APR 3, '76. 'THE AMERICAN WORKSHOP', CONFERENCE FOR HIGH SCHOOL STUDENTS. DESIGNED TO EMPHASIZE THE POSITIVE ASPECTS OF AMERICAN SOCIETY THRU EXPOSURE TO COMMITTED INDIVIDUALS IN FREE ENTERPRISE, LEGISLATION & THE MEDIA. AT DISNEYLAND HOTEL. (LOCAL). WILLIAM E MCLAUGHLIN, DIR; VOICES IN VITAL AMERICA; 10966 LE CONTE; LOS ANGELES, CA 90024. (#23092-1).

APR 29 - MAY 2, '76. CARROUSEL OF ANAHEIM CULTURAL ARTS SHOW. AUHS DISTRICT JAZZ FESTIVAL & ANAHEIM ELEMENTARY MUSIC FESTIVAL 100,000 SQ FT OR DULTURAL ARTS. CONTINUOUS EXHIBITS & PERFORMANCES. AT ANAHEIM CONVENTION CENTER, 800 W KATELLA. (LOCAL). DARLENE WEST, SECRETARY; WOMEN'S DIVISION ANAHEIM CHAMBER OF COMMERCE; 130 S LEMON ST; ANAHEIM, CA 92805. (#104289-5).

APR 29 - OCT 31, '76. BICENTENNIAL POSTAL EXHIBIT. EXHIBIT OF STAMPS AMERICANA AND THE WORLD'S LARGEST COLLECTION OF AUTOGRAPHED FIRST DAY COVERS. APR 29-30; MAY 1ST, JUNE 1 - JULY 6TH, AUG 2ND - AUG 30TH, OCT 1ST - 31ST. (LOCAL). HARRY G BOYD, CURATOR; MUSEUM OF POSTAL HISTORY; PO BOX 3642; ANAHEIM, CA 92803. (#105911-2).

APR 30 - MAY 3, '76. 'MARATHON RELAY - 200 YEARS, 200 MILES IN 72 HOURS'. COMPETITION AT KATELLA HIGH SCHOOL. (LOCAL). KEN HOLLAND, TREASURER; KATELLA ATHLETIC BOOSTER CLUB; ANAHEIM, CA 91802. (#200006-10).

MAY 1, '76. SHAKE HANDS WITH AMERICA: 'AN EVENING WITH RAY BOLGER'. LIVE PERFORMANCE AT ANAHEIM HIGH SCHOOL AUDITORIUM, 811 W LINCOLN AVE. (LOCAL). KATHLEEN B BROWN, CHMN; ANAHEIM BICENTENNIAL CELEBRATION COMMITTEE; 130 S LEMON ST; ANAHEIM, CA 92805. (#200006-398).

MAY 2 - 29, '76. CINCO DE MAYO FIESTA. FESTIVAL AT LA PALMA PARK. (LOCAL). JOEL GUERENA, CHAIRMAN; FREMONT PARENT ADVISORY COMMITTEE, TITLE I; 1334 S CLAREMONT; ANAHEIM, CA 92805. (#105911-1).

MAY 7 - 24, '76. CALIFORNIALAND MUSIC FESTIVAL. FESTIVAL, LIVE PERFORMANCE AT FREMONT JR HIGH SCHOOL AUDITORIUM. (LOCAL). SHARON GRAY; INTERNATIONAL FESTIVALS, INC; 202 E MICHIGAN AVE; KALAMAZOO, MI 49006. (#107233-5).

MAY 22, '76. SHAKE HANDS WITH AMERICA: 'THE YOUNG AMERICANS'. LIVE PERFORMANCE AT ANAHEIM HIGH SCHOOL AUDITORIUM, 811 W LINCOLN AVE. (LOCAL). KATHLEEN B BROWN, CHMN; ANAHEIM BICENTENNIAL CELEBRATION COMMITTEE; 130 S LEMON ST; ANAHEIM, CA 92805. (#200006-399).

MAY 23, '76. ANAHEIM PIONEER PICNIC. PICNIC WILL HONOR OLD AND NEW PIONEERS OF ANAHEIM. THERE WILL BE A BIRTHDAY CAKE FOR THE COUNTRY AND GERMAN & MEXICAN FOLK DANCING AND MUSIC. THERE WILL ALSO BE COSTUMES, PRIZES, BALLOONS, FREE COFFEE AND A MEMORABILIA DISPLAY. AT PEARSON PARK, HARBOR BLVD & SYCAMORE. (LOCAL). EILEEN D ANTHONY, PRES; WOMEN'S DIVISION OF ANAHEIM CHAMBER OF COMMERCE; 1345 AMBERWICH LN; ANAHEIM, CA 92804. (#108475-1).

MAY 30, '76. PIONEERS AND PATRIOTS MEMORIAL DAY SERVICE. CEREMONY AT ANAHEIM CEMETERY, 1400 E SYCAMORE. (LOCAL). MRS SARAH PEARSON; MOTHER COLONY HOUSEHOLD INC; 685 N HELENA ST; ANAHEIM, CA 92805. (#107976-2).

JUNE 11 - 12, '76. WINDOW PAINTING CONTEST FOR DOWNTOWN ANAHEIM. COMPETITION AT BEHIND THE ANAHEIM BULLETIN OFFICE AT LINCOLN & LEMON. (LOCAL). SANDRA KEMPF, PRES; ANAHEIM JAYCETTES; 1148 S CHANTILLY; ANAHEIM, CA 92806. (#104289-6).

JUNE 18 - 27, '76. SHAKE HANDS WITH AMERICA 'MUSIC MAN' FEATURING PERNEL ROBERTS. LIVE PERFORMANCE AT ANAHEIM HIGH SCHOOL AUDITORIUM, 811 W LINCOLN AVE. (LOCAL). KATHLEEN B BROWN, CHMN; ANAHEIM BICENTENNIAL CELEBRATION COMMITTEE; 130 S LEMON ST; ANAHEIM, CA 92805. (#200006-400).

JUNE 24 - 26, '76. 25TH NATIONAL SQUARE DANCE CONVENTION. EXHIBITIONS, PAGEANT, STYLE SHOW, EDUCATIONAL PANELS, FOLK DANCING, CONTRAS, SPECIAL FLAG PRESENTATION. AT ANAHEIM CONVENTION CENTER, KATELLA BLVD; AMPLE PAARKING. (NAT'L). G KEN PARKER; CALIFORNIA SQUARE DANCE COUNCIL; 426 PHILLIPS WAY; VISTA, CA 92083. (#122-1).

JULY 3 - 4, '76. TWO-DAY SQUARE DANCE JAMBOREE. TWO-DAY SQUARE DANCE JAMBOREE AND TRAIL-OUT DANCE FOLLOWING NATIONAL SQUARE DANCE CONVENTION HELD IN ANAHEIM, CALIFORNIA. (REGN'L). GREGG ANDERSON, PROJ MGR; COLORADO SPRINGS SQUARE DANCE CALLERS ASSOC; 1331 SUNSET RD; COLORADO SPG, CO 80909. (#8889-1).

JULY 4, '76. OLD-FASHIONED INDEPENDENCE DAY FIREWORKS SPECTACULAR AND PAGEANT. APPROVED BY ANAHEIM BICENTENNIAL COMMITTEE APRIL 15, 1975. AT ANAHEIM STADIUM, 2000 S STATE COLLEGE BLVD. (LOCAL). TOMMY WALKER, DIRECTOR; TOMMY WALKER PRODUCTIONS; SUITE 6, DISNEYLAND HOTEL PLAZA; ANAHEIM, CA 92802. (#100402-1).

JULY 4, '76. SPIRIT OF '76 SHOW. BETWEEN-THE-GAMES SHOW - A PAGEANTRY OF MUSIC AND DANCE WILL DEPICT THE SPIRIT OF THE AMERICAN REVOLUTION, THE FREEDOM AND DIGNITY OF MAN. AT ANAHEIM STADIUM. (REGN'L). GEORGE M WILLIAMS; NICHIREN SHOSHU ACADEMY; PO BOX 1427; SANTA MONICA, CA 90406. (#108208-1).

JULY 11 - 14, '76. 'AMERICA SKATES', SKATING SHOW AND ICE FAMILY. LIVE PERFORMANCE AT GLACIER FALLS ICE ARENA, 211 W KATELLA, 2 BLOCKS EAST OF HARBOR BLVD. (LOCAL). LARRY J FRANCOIS, COORD; GLACIER FALLS FIGURE SKATING CLUB; 332 DEVONSHIRE; BREA, CA 92631. (#109001-1).

JULY 23 - 25, '76. MODEL A SPIRIT OF '76 - NATL MODEL A RESTORERS' CLUB MEET. 1903-1976 ERA CAR SHOW, JULY 23: 6-12 PM; JULY 24: 1-10 PM. OPEN TO PUBLIC; OPEN TO THOSE WHO REGISTER ON JULY 23: LUAU-ERA FASHION SHOW; JULY 24: AWARDS BANQUET & DANCE. ALSO GYMKAHNA, TOURS & PARADES. AT ANAHEIM CONVENTION CENTER. (LOCAL). GORDON GRABAU, CHAIRMAN; MODEL A RESTORERS' CLUB; 14403 PERILLA AVE; PARAMOUNT, CA 90723. (#103283-1).

AUG 1 - 4, '76. YMCA'S 52ND INTERNATIONAL CONVENTION. CEREMONY, CONFERENCE, FESTIVAL AT DISNEYLAND HOTEL, 1150 W CERRITOS AVE. (INT'L). CLARE S GRAHAM, CHMN; INTERNATIONAL ASSOC OF Y'S MEN'S CLUBS; 1149 NORBY LN; FULLERTON, CA 92633. (#106222-1).

AUG 28, '76. PICNIC FOR ORANGE COUNTY SENIOR CITIZENS. BRING YOUR OWN PICNIC LUNCH, COMPLIMENTARY BEVERAGES WILL BE PROVIDED. AT LA PALMA PARK, CORNER OF HARBOR & LA PALMA. (LOCAL). RUTH JACOBSEN, COORD; ANAHEIM SENIOR CITIZENS CLUB; 222 E CHARTRES ST; ANAHEIM, CA 92805. (#107976-1).

SEPT 12, '76. SAINT BONIFACE PARISH FIESTA PATRIA - 'HERITAGE DAY'. FESTIVAL. (LOCAL). JOHN N RODENBOUR, CHMN; SAINT BONIFACE PARISH; 604 N CLEMENTINE ST; ANAHEIM, CA 92805. (#200006-327).

SEPT 17 - DEC 1, '76. MUSICAL PRESENTATION - 'I LOVE AMERICA'. CHOIR IS TAKING THE TRIBUTE TO THE UNITED STATES AROUND THE LOCAL AREA. (LOCAL). GARY A KUPP, COORDINATOR; ANAHEIM FRIENDS CHURCH; 13651 E FOXLEY DR, #1C; WHITTIER, CA 90605. (#108185-1).

SEPT 19, '76. 50TH ANNIVERSARY FIESTA, SACRED HEART MISSION AND INDEPENDENCIA. CEREMONY, FESTIVAL AT 10862 HARCOURT, PARKING AREA OF SACRED HEART MISSION. (LOCAL). GLORIA V LOPEZ, CHMN; ST JUSTIN MARTYR CHURCH & ANAHEIM INDEPENDENCIA COMMUNITY CENTER; 10874 GARZA AVE; ANAHEIM, CA 92804. (#200006-326).

OCT 25 - 31, '76. 53RD ANNUAL ANAHEIM HALLOWEEN FESTIVAL AND PARADES. FESTIVAL, PARADE AT CARNIVAL & ART FAIR AT PEARSON PARK; PARADE AT LA PALMA PARK. (LOCAL). STEWART LINK, COORD; ANAHEIM CHAMBER OF COMMERCE & THE CITY OF ANAHEIM; 130 S LEMON; ANAHEIM, CA 92805. (#109343-1).

APR 15 - 16, '77. CITIZEN ADVOCACY DAY AT DISNEYLAND. TOUR AT DISNEYLAND. (LOCAL). LINDA PALMER, COORD; LOS ANGELES CITY COUNCIL FOR THE HANDICAPPED RECREATION COMMITTEE; 1313 HARBOR BLVD; ANAHEIM, CA 92803. (#109457-1).

ANDERSON

OCT 18, '75. UNITED STATES ARMED FORCES BICENTENNIAL CARAVAN. THE CARAVAN IS COMPOSED OF EXHIBIT VANS FOR EACH BRANCH OF THE MILITARY SERVICE. THE THEME OF THE EXHIBITION IS 'HISTORY OF THE ARMED FORCES AND THEIR CONTRIBUTION TO THE NATION'. (LOCAL). MICKIE JACKEZ, CHAIRMAN; U S ARMED FORCES BICENTENNIAL EXHIBIT VANS PROJECT; 3476 SHASTA DRIVE; ANDERSON, CA 96007. (#1775-280).

ANGELS CAMP

MAY 20 - 23, '76. CALAVERAS COUNTY FAIR AND JUMPING FROG JUBILEE. FROGS COMPETE IN WORLD-FAMOUS JUMPING CONTEST. (LOCAL). SHARON SCOTT, PRES; CALAVERAS COUNTY FAIR AND JUMPING FROG JUBILEE; PO BOX 96; ANGELS CAMP, CA 95222. (#103416-335).

ANTIOCH

MAR 29 - APR 4, '76. DE ANZA DAYS. FESTIVAL, LIVE PERFORMANCE AT CONTRA COSTA FAIRGROUNDS, W 10TH ST. (LOCAL). EVA D LOZANO, CHAIRMAN; ANTIOCH BICENTENNIAL COMMITTEE; 45 W 16TH ST; ANTIOCH, CA 94509. (#105457-3).

MAY 21 - 22, '76. RED, WHITE & BLUE SPRING FAIR - HAPPY BIRTHDAY AMERICA. FAIR AT CONTRA COSTA FAIRGROUNDS, W 10TH ST. (LOCAL). EVA D LOZANO, CHMN; ANTIOCH BICENTENNIAL COMMITTEE/ANTIOCH SCHOOL DIST/PTA; 45 W 16TH ST; ANTIOCH, CA 94509. (#105457-4).

JULY 4, '76. 4TH OF JULY CELEBRATION. FESTIVAL AT CONTRA COSTA FAIRGROUNDS. (LOCAL). EVA D LOZANO, CHAIRMAN; ANTIOCH BICENTENNIAL COMMITTEE & CHAMBER OF COMMERCE; 45 W 16TH ST; ANTIOCH, CA 94509. (#105457-2).

AUG 20 - 21, '76. BICENTENNIAL PERFORMANCE. LIVE PERFORMANCE AT G ST. (LOCAL). HERB E ALLEN, DIRECTOR; ANTIOCH BICENTENNIAL COMMITTEE; 1133 KLENGLE; ANTIOCH, CA 94509. (#105457-1).

ARCADIA

'BADMAN'S ROOST' - A FILM ABOUT BODIE, CALIFORNIA. A VISUAL JOURNEY THROUGH THE GHOST TOWN OF BODIE, CALIFORNIA AS IT EXISTS TODAY. THE FILM USES SOUND EFFECTS AND INDUCED MOVEMENT TO SUGGEST THE PAST. (ST-WIDE). MICHAEL REGAN, PRODUCER; CINE ASSOCIATES; 1119 W HUNTINGTON DR; ARCADIA, CA 91006. (#9072).

APR 4 - 5, '76. UNITED STATES ARMED FORCES BICENTENNIAL CARAVAN. CARAVAN IS COMPOSED OF EXHIBIT VANS FOR EACH MILITARY SERVICE. PROJECT THEME IS ' HISTORY OF THE ARMED FORCES & THEIR CONTRIBUTIONS TO THE NATION'. AT PARKING LOT, SANTA ANITA FASHION PARK, BALDWIN AVE SIDE. (LOCAL). HAL ROACH, DIRECTOR; U S ARMED FORCES BICENTENNIAL CARAVAN; 1310 SAN CARLOS RD; ARCADIA, CA 91006. (#1775-547).

ARCATA

JULY 16, '76. UNITED STATES ARMED FORCES BICENTENNIAL CARAVAN. CARAVAN IS COMPOSED OF EXHIBIT VANS FOR EACH MILITARY SERVICE. PROJECT THEME IS 'HISTORY OF THE ARMED FORCES & THEIR CONTRIBUTIONS TO THE NATION.'. (LOCAL). CURTIS SIATS, CHMN; UNITED STATES ARMED FORCES BICENTENNIAL CARAVAN; 1468 HILFIKER; ARCATA, CA 95521. (#1775-690).

ARMONA

KINGS COUNTY CEMETERIES INDEX, ARMONA, CA. REGISTRATION & INDEXING OF PERSONS BURIED IN KINGS CO CEMETERIES. LIST TO BE LOADED TO EDP COMPUTERS & SORTED IN VARIOUS GROUPS FOR COMPUTER LISTINGS. (LOCAL). ROBERT L ATHLEY, CHAIRMAN; ARMONA BICENTENNIAL COMMITTEE; 13937 PIMO ST, PO BOX 865; ARMONA, CA 93202. (#28872).

THE 1876 ARMONA CENTENNIAL 1976 BOOK, CA. ONE HUNDRED YEARS OF HISTORY OF THE ARMONA AREA IN WORDS & PICTURES. (LOCAL). ROBERT L ATHEY, CHAIRMAN; ARMONA BICENTENNIAL COMMITTEE; 13937 PIMO ST, PO BOX 865; ARMONA, CA 93202. (#28871).

MAY 8, '76. BICENTENNIAL FIREWORKS SHOW. COMIC BASEBALL GAME BETWEEN ARMONA VOLUNTEER FIREMEN AND THE ARMONA LIONS CLUB FOLLOWED BY ONE HOUR OF FIREWORKS. AT LITTLE LEAGUE BALLPARK. (LOCAL). DOYLE DAVIS, CHAIRMAN; ARMONA VOLUNTEER FIRE DEPARTMENT; 13970 HOOD AVE; ARMONA, CA 93202. (#200006-354).

MAY 9, '76. BICENTENNIAL MOTHER'S DAY PARADE & COMMUNITY BAR-B-QUE. PATRIOTIC PARADE IN HONOR OF THE SELECTED

ARMONA — CONTINUED

MOTHER OF THE YEAR, FOLLOWED BY COMMUNITY ANNUAL BAR-BtQUE. AT ARMONA PARK. (LOCAL). HOMER M STRONG, CHAIRMAN; ARMONA LIONS CLUB; 14448 14TH AVE; HANFORD, CA 93230. (#200006-355).

DEC 31, '76. TIME CAPSULE BURIAL CEREMONY. THE TIME CAPSULE WILL CONTAIN THE COMMITTEE BICENTENNIAL FLAG, THE BENNINGTON FLAG, THE 50 STAR FLAG AND THE OFFICIAL BICENTENNIAL FLAG; IT WILL ALSO CONTAIN THE BOOK 'ARMONA CENTENNIAL 1876-1976', NEWSPAPERS & TELEPHONE DIRECTORY; IT WILL BE OPENED IN 2076. AT THE ATHLEY HUNDRED YEAR HOUSE, 13937 PIMO ST. (LOCAL). ROBERT L ATHEY, CHMN; ARMONA BICENTENNIAL COMMITTEE; 13937 PIMO ST, PO BOX 865; ARMONA, CA 93202. (#109406-1).

ARROYO GRANDE

MAY 20 - 28, '76. BICENTENNIAL FESTIVAL OF THE ARTS. FESTIVAL. (LOCAL). DICK BLANKENBURG; ARROYO GRANDE BICENT COMMITTEE; PO BOX 146; ARROYO GRANDE, CA 93420. (#200006-415).

JULY 3, '76. JULY 3RD IN ARROYO GRANDE. ACTIVITIES INCLUDED BARBEQUE, CHILDREN'S PARADE, GAMES, CONTESTS, ENTERTAINMENT. AT ENCINAS BONITAS PARK. (LOCAL). DICK BLANKENBURG; ARROYO GRANDE BICENTENNIAL COMMITTEE; PO BOX 146; ARROYO GRANDE, CA 93420. (#200006-499).

NOV 27, '76. GROUND BREAKING SOUTH COUNTY CIVIC CENTER. CEREMONY AT SOUTH COUNTY CIVIC CENTER, BRISCO RD. (LOCAL). HOWARD D MANKINS, COORD; COUNTY BOARD OF SUPERVISORS OF SAN LUIS OBISPO; RM 220 COURTHOUSE ANNEX; SAN LUIS OBIS, CA 93401. (#200006-493).

DEC 18, '76. GROUND BREAKING BIDDLE PARK. CEREMONY AT RURAL ARROYO GRANDE, SOUTH OF LOPEZ LAKE. (LOCAL). HOWARD D MANKINS, COORD; SAN LUIS OBISPO COUNTY BOARD OF SUPERVISORS; RM 220 COURTHOUSE ANNEX; SAN LUIS OBIS, CA 93401. (#200006-495).

ATASCADERO

ATASCADERO SOLAR HOUSE, CA. AT PRESIDENTIAL SUGGESTION AN INVENTOR COLLABORATED WITH FED ERALLY FUNDED UNIV TEAM TO VERIFY IMMEDIATE & ECONOMIC USE OF SOLAR HEATING/NIGHT COOLING FOR POLLUTION-FREE LOW- AIR CONDITIONING. (NAT'L). HAROLD ROBERT HAY, PROJECT MANAGER; SKYTHERM PROCESSES AND ENGINEERING; 2424 WILSHIRE BLVD; LOS ANGELES, CA 90057. (#20057).

MAY 26, '76. UNITED STATES ARMED FORCES BICENTENNIAL CARAVAN. CARAVAN IS COMPOSED OF EXHIBIT VANS FOR EACH MILITARY SERVICE. PROJECT THEME IS ' HISTORY OF THE ARMED FORCES & THEIR CONTRIBUTIONS TO THE NATION'. (LOCAL). MRS RUTH WILLIS, CHMN; U S ARMED FORCES BICENTENNIAL CARAVAN; 6085 EL CAMINO REAL; ATASCADERO, CA 93422. (#1775-575).

ATWATER

NOV 8, '75. UNITED STATES ARMED FORCES BICENTENNIAL CARAVAN. THE CARAVAN IS COMPOSED OF EXHIBIT VANS FOR EACH BRANCH OF THE MILITARY SERVICE. THE THEME OF THE EXHIBITION IS 'HISTORY OF THE ARMED FORCES AND THEIR CONTRIBUTION TO THE NATION'. (LOCAL). CHUCK GRIFFIN, CHAIRMAN; U S ARMED FORCES BICENTENNIAL EXHIBIT VANS PROJECT; 302 E BELLVUE ST; ATWATER, CA 95301. (#1775-293).

AUBURN

HISTORICAL MUSEUM PROJECT OF AUBURN, CALIFORNIA. HISTORICAL MUSEUM OF 9000 SQ FT TO BE BUILT & DEDICATED IN 1976. (LOCAL). WENDELL ROBIE, CHAIRMAN; AUBURN BICENTENNIAL COMMITTEE; BOX 1228; AUBURN, CA 95603. (#2975).

JULY 4, '75. 1975 FOURTH OF JULY CELEBRATION. FESTIVAL AT AUBURN DISTRICT FAIR GROUNDS. (LOCAL). ROD STANTON, COORD; COMBINED SERVICE CLUBS; 826 LINCOLN WAY; AUBURN, CA 95603. (#200006-8).

JULY 11, '75. BICENTENNIAL BRUNCH WITH FASHION SHOW. FESTIVAL AT HOME EC BLDG, AUBURN DISTRICT FAIR. (LOCAL). MRS RUNYAN, COORD; AUBURN CHRISTIAN WOMEN'S CLUB; 2260 SUNNY OAK DR; AUBURN, CA 95603. (#200006-9).

OCT 30, '75. UNITED STATES ARMED FORCES BICENTENNIAL CARAVAN. THE CARAVAN IS COMPOSED OF EXHIBIT VANS FOR EACH BRANCH OF THE MILITARY SERVICE. THE THEME OF THE EXHIBITION IS 'HISTORY OF THE ARMED FORCES AND THEIR CONTRIBUTION TO THE NATION'. (LOCAL). BERNARD HARTUNG, DIRECTOR; U S ARMED FORCES BICENTENNIAL EXHIBIT VANS PROJECT; 1101 HIGH ST; AUBURN, CA 95603. (#1775-287).

SEPT 11 - 14, '76. AUBURN DISTRICT FAIR. FAIR. (LOCAL). JAY M WOODS, DIRECTOR; AUBURN DISTRICT FAIR; 1273 HIGH ST; AUBURN, CA 95603. (#100759-1).

AVALON

AVALON BICENTENNIAL COMMUNITY CHORUS - CA. ESTABLISHMENT OF A COMMUNITY PATRIOTIC CHORAL GROUP FOR PERFORMANCES IN THE COMMUNITY. (LOCAL). MARGARET FELKLEY, CO-DIRECTOR; AVALON BICENTENNIAL COMMITTEE; 316 DESCANSO; AVALON, CA 90704. (#14641).

OCT 12, '75. COMMUNITY FISH FRY. COMMUNITY WIDE PICNIC FOR EVERYBODY FOLLOWED BY SINGING AND STREET DANCING. AT AVALON WATERFRONT. (LOCAL). WAYNE STOUT, DIRECTOR; LIONS CLUB; 334 CATALINA; AVALON, CA 90704. (#101938-1).

NOV 11, '75. CEREMONIAL AMERICAN FLAG (OLD) DISPOSITION. PATRIOTIC BURNING OF OLD FLAGS, CEREMONY ACCOMPANIED BY BICENTENNIAL CHORUS & U S MARINES SPECIAL PATRIOTIC AMERICAN FLAGS EXERCISE. AT CASINO MOLE. (LOCAL). RAYMOND A RYDELL,; AMERICAN LEGION; 108 VIEUDELOU; AVALON, CA 90704. (#101937-1).

AVILA BEACH

100 YEAR OLD NARROW GAUGE RAILROAD BRIDGE - CA. BRIDGE WILL BE RESTORED AND USED AS A BICYCLE PATH AND WALKWAY. A PARK WILL BE BUILT AT EACH END. (LOCAL). DICK MCDANIEL, CHAIRMAN; AVILA BEACH CENTENNIAL '76; 536 FRONT; AVILA BEACH, CA 93424. (#26605).

AZUSA

AZUSA TIME LINE - AZUSA, CA. BOOKLET ON THE HISTORY OF AZUSA TO BE SUPPLEMENTED BY TAPED INTERVIEWS OF OLD-TIMERS; BOOKLET AVAILABLE TO EVERYONE, TAPES AND SLIDES ON LOAN FROM LIBRARY. (LOCAL). MRS JOY RUBIO, TIME LINE CHAIRMAN; AZUSA BICENTENNIAL COMMITTEE; 213 E FOOTHILL BLVD; AZUSA, CA 91702. (#19134).

BICENTENNIAL COMMEMORATIVE MEDALLION FOR AZUSA, CA. SILVER MEDALLION DESIGNED AND MINTED IN AZUSA FOR AREA CITIZENS. (LOCAL). RICHARD ZISER, MEDALLION CHAIRMAN; AZUSA BICENTENNIAL COMMITTEE; 213 E FOOTHILL BLVD; AZUSA, CA 91702. (#19135).

POPPY PLANTING MONTH-NOVEMBER, AZUSA, CA. STATE FLOWER, THE CA POPPY WILL BE PLANTED ON ALL AVAILABLE LAND IN TOWN INCLUDING CIVIC CENTER AND PARKS; TIMING PLANNED SO FLOWERS WILL BLOOM SPRING THROUGH SUMMER 1976 AND EACH YEAR THEREAFTER. (LOCAL). MRS KAREN NOLTING, YOUTH CHAI*RMAN; AZUSA BICENTENNIAL COMMITTEE; 213 E FOOTHILL BLVD; AZUSA, CA 91702. (#19138).

MAY 1, '75 - CONTINUING . MEMORABILIA ART EXHIBIT. EXHIBIT AT COLLEGE ART GALLERY. (LOCAL). ROSS L HANDY, VICE PRES; CITRUS COLLEGE; 18824 E FOOTHILL BLVD; AZUSA, CA 91702. (#15400-1).

FEB 22, '76. ALL AMERICAN DAY. FESTIVAL, PARADE AT DOWNTOWN AZUSA AND MEMORIAL PARK. (LOCAL). MRS ARLENE SAMS, COORD; AZUSA BICENTENNIAL COMMITTEE; 213 E FOOTHILL BLVD; AZUSA, CA 91702. (#104181-2).

MAR 21, '76. AIRMEN OF NOTE, U S AIR FORCE ZAZZ ENSEMBLE CONCERT. LIVE PERFORMANCE AT CITRUS COLLEGE AUDITORIUM 18824 E FOOTHILL. (LOCAL). ROSS HANDY, VICE PRES; CITRUS COLLEGE; 18824 E FOOTHILL BLVD; AZUSA, CA 91702. (#200006-419).

MAR 21, '76. BEN FRANKLIN KITE FLYING AND GREAT AMERICAN APPLE PIE FESTIVAL. AWARDS WILL BE GIVEN FOR SEVERAL CATEGORIES OF KITES, COSTUMES AND AGES OF PARTICIPANTS; GREAT AMERICAN APPLE PIE WILL BE SUPPLIED BY A LOCAL MERCHANT TO SUSTAIN PARTICIPANTS DURING COMPETITION. AT NORTHSIDE PARK, ELEVENTH STREET. (LOCAL). PAULINE ASMUS, CHMN; AZUSA BICENTENNIAL COMMITTEE; 213 E FOOTHILL BLVD; AZUSA, CA 91702. (#104181-1).

JUNE 25 - 27, '76. SALUTE TO AMERICA, MUSICAL & DANCE. LIVE PERFORMANCE AT AUDITORIUM, 18824 E FOOTHILL BLVD. (LOCAL). ROSS HANDY, VICE PRES; CITRUS COLLEGE; 18824 E FOOTHILL BLVD; AZUSA, CA 91702. (#200006-418).

JUNE 27 - AUG 29, '76. AMERICAN MEMORABILIA ART DISPLAY. EXHIBIT OF EARLY TOOLS, PHOTOGRAPHS, DISHES, ORANGE CRATE LABELS, AND ITEMS OF LOCAL CITRUS GROVE ERA. MANY ITEMS FURNISHED BY AREA RESIDENTS. AT ART GALLERY, 18824 E FOOTHILL. (LOCAL). ROSS HANDY, VICE PRES; CITRUS COLLEGE; 18824 E FOOTHILL BLVD; AZUSA, CA 91702. (#200006-420).

JULY 4, '76. BICENTENNIAL SUNDAY. CEREMONY AT CIVIC CENTER. (LOCAL). MRS PAULINE ASMUS, CHMN; AZUSA BICENTENNIAL COMMITTEE; 213 E FOOTHILL BLVD; AZUSA, CA 91702. (#104181-3).

JUNE 3 - 5, '77. SALUTE TO AMERICA-MUSICAL & DANCE. STAGE MUSICAL PRODUCTION BY CITRUS COLLEGE SINGERS WITH ORCHESTRA, COSTUMES & DANCES CELEBRATING OUR COUNTRY. AT AUDITORIUM 18824 E FOOTHILL BLVD. (LOCAL). ROSS HANDY; CITRUS COLLEGE; 18824 E FOOTHILL BLVD; AZUSA, CA 91702. (#200006-456).

BAKERSFIELD

BAKERSFIELD COLLEGE BICENTENNIAL PROGRAM - CA. INCLUDES HISTORICAL LECTURE SERIES, AN ECOLOGY FILM SERIES, A CONCERT SERIES, 3 CONCERTS ON THE DEVELOPMENT OF JAZZ, SHOWINGS OF OLD MOVIES & MONTHLY 1/2 HOUR TV INTERVIEW/DISCUSSION PROGRAMS. (LOCAL). ROBERT L CLARK, CHAIRMAN; BAKERSFIELD COLLEGE BICENTENNIAL COMMITTEE; 1801 PANORAMA DR; BAKERSFIELD, CA 93305. (#28604).

KBAK-TV'S KERN COUNTY BICENT MINUTES -NBMRP. THESE MINUTES, PRODUCED SINCE 10/27/75, ARE AIRED 5 TIMES DAILY ON KBAK; TAPES PROVIDED TO 2 ADDITIONAL STATIONS & AUDIOS OF THE TAPES ARE PROVIDED TO 12 KERN COUNTY RADIO STATIONS, CASSETTES TO SCHOOLS. (LOCAL). DAVID MOORE, BICENT COORDINATOR; KBAK-TV STATION; 2210 CHESTER AVE; BAKERSFIELD, CA 93301. (#25303).

KERN COUNTY PIONEER VILLAGE JUNIOR MUSEUM IN CALIF. BUILDING OF JUNIOR MUSEUM AND PIONEER VILLAGE. (LOCAL). RICHARD C BAILEY, MUSEUM DIRECTOR; KERN COUNTY MUSEUM DEVELOPMENT COMMITTEE; 3801 CHESTER AVE; BAKERSFIELD, CA 93301. (#5119).

PINCKNEY RESIDENCE RESTORATION IN KERN COUNTY, CA. RESTORATION OF 18TH CENTURY HOME OF PIONEER BLACK SETTLER. (LOCAL). RICHARD BAILEY, MUSEUM DIRECTOR; KERN COUNTY MUSEUM ALLIANCE; 3801 CHESTER AVE; BAKERSFIELD, CA 93301. (#5118).

JUNE 15, '75. HISTORIC ROSE GARDEN DEDICATION AT PIONEER VILLAGE. OPENING, EXHIBIT. (LOCAL). RICHARD C BAILEY; KERN COUNTY MUSEUM ALLIANCE; 380 CHESTER AVE; BAKERSFIELD, CA 93301. (#5117-501).

FEB 10, '76. NETHERLANDS WIND ENSEMBLE. LIVE PERFORMANCE. (INT'L). DIRECTOR; ROYAL NETHERLANDS EMBASSY; 4200 LINNEAN ST, NW; WASHINGTON, DC 20008. (#200006-175).

MAY 1, '76. BICENTENNIAL FESTIVAL '76. ALL DAY EVENT COMBINED WITH HEALTH FAIR & ASB SPRING FAIRE. AT COLLEGE CAMPUS. (LOCAL). ROBERT L CLARK, CHAIRMAN; BAKERSFIELD COLLEGE BICENTENNIAL COMMITTEE; 1801 PANORAMA DR; BAKERSFIELD, CA 93305. (#109331-1).

BANNING

NOV 28, '76. UNITED STATES ARMED FORCES BICENTENNIAL CARAVAN. CARAVAN IS COMPOSED OF EXHIBIT VANS FOR EACH MILITARY SERVICE. PROJECT THEME IS 'HISTORY OF THE ARMED FORCES & THEIR CONTRIBUTIONS TO THE NATION'. (LOCAL). BOB WILKERSON; UNITED STATES ARMED FORCES BICENTENNIAL CARAVAN; 54 E HAYES; BANNING, CA 92220. (#1775-848).

BARSTOW

HISTORY OF MOJAVE DESERT, BARSTOW, CA. 200 YEAR HISTORICAL HERITAGE WRITTEN BY THOSE WHO LIVED IT. ARCHIVED DOCUMENTS, FAMILY PAPERS, PHOTOS USED THROUGHOUT. BOOK IS HARD COVER & HAS 280 PAGES. (LOCAL). MRS G L MOON, CHMN, PUBLICATION COMMITTEE; MOJAVE RIVER VALLEY MUSEUM ASSOC; BOX 1282; BARSTOW, CA 92311. (#28432).

PRESERVATION OF HARVEY HOUSE, BARSTOW, CA. THE HARVEY HOUSE WAS BUILT IN 1911 IN AN ARCHITECTURAL STYLE UNIQUE TO THE AREA. THE PROJECT INCLUDES ITS PRESERVATION & USE. THE HOUSE IS THE LAST OF ITS KIND IN THE AREA. (LOCAL). MICHAEL BELLOMY, ENGINEERING AIDE; AMERICAN REVOLUTION BICENTENNIAL COMMISSION; 220 E MOUNTAIN VIEW AVE; BARSTOW, CA 92311. (#18817).

DEC 1 - 2, '75. UNITED STATES ARMED FORCES BICENTENNIAL CARAVAN. THE CARAVAN IS COMPOSED OF EXHIBIT VANS FOR EACH BRANCH OF THE MILITARY SERVICE. THE THEME OF THE EXHIBITION IS 'HISTORY OF THE ARMED FORCES AND THEIR CONTRIBUTION TO THE NATION'. (LOCAL). GEORGE GOLDSMITH, CHMN; U S ARMED FORCES BICENTENNIAL EXHIBIT VANS PROJECT; 220 E MOUNTAIN VIEW; BARSTOW, CA 92311. (#1775-296).

BAUTISTA CTY

MISSION SAN JUAN BAUTISTA RESTORATION PROJECT, CA. COMMEMORATING 178TH ANNIVERSARY OF FOUNDING OF MISSION SAN JUAN BAUTISTA BY THE FRANCISCAN PADRES. EARLY MASS, PARADE THRU THE HISTORIC STREETS,CHICKEN BARBECUE ON MISSION GROUNDS, MUSIC, & RCA RODEO. (LOCAL). LEONARD A CAETANO, PRESIDENT; FIESTA RODEO DE SAN JUAN BAUTISTA INC; SECOND & MARIPOSA, P O BOX C; BAUTISTA CTY, CA 95045. (#4216).

BEALE AFB

AMERICAN ISSUES READING & STUDY PROGRAM, CA. STRUCTURED READING & STUDY PROGRAM TIME PHASED WITH MONTHLY AND WEEKLY THEMES OF AMERICAN ISSUES FORUM. (LOCAL). MAJOR WALTER M RYLAND, COORDINATOR; BEALE AIR FORCE BASE; BEALE AIR FORCE LIBRARY; BEALE AFB, CA 95903. (#20876).

BEALE AFB COLOR GUARD - CA. COLOR GUARD AVAILABLE FOR MEETINGS AND CEREMONIES FOR WHICH FORMAL POSTING OF COLORS IS APPROPRIATE. (LOCAL). MAJOR WALTER RYLAND, COORDINATOR; BEALE AIR FORCE BASE; 17 BOMBARDMENT WING/OI; BEALE AFB, CA 95903. (#19476).

BICENTENNIAL BEALETONES - BEALE AFB, CA. 14 VOICE CHORAL GROUP OF OFFICER'S WIVES CLUB HAS A PROGRAM OF BEST LOVED AMERICAN MUSIC SUITABLE FOR BICENTENNIAL PROGRAMS OF ALL TYPES. AVAILABLE FOR BICENTENNIAL EVENTS; ADVANCE 3 WEEKS NOTICE. (LOCAL). MAJOR WALTER M RYLAND, COORDINATOR; BEALE AIR FORCE BASE OFFICER'S WIVES CLUB; 17BMW/OI; BEALE AFB, CA 95903. (#21263).

BICENTENNIAL SPEAKERS BUREAU - BEALE AFB, CA. BUREAU OF SPEAKERS AVAILABLE TO ADDRESS MEETINGS OF GROUPS HAVING BICENTENNIAL PROGRAMS. (LOCAL). MAJOR WALTER M RYLAND, COORDINATOR; BEALE AFB - YUBA COUNTY BICENTENNIAL COMMITTEE; 17TH BONBARDMENT WING/OI; BEALE AFB, CA 95903. (#19475).

BEALE AFB — CONTINUED

SEPT 18, '75. U S AIR FORCE BIRTHDAY BALL. FESTIVAL AT HILLTOP NONCOMMISSIONED OFFICERS MESS, BEALE AFB, CA. (LOCAL). MAJOR WALTER RYLAND; BEALE AIR FORCE BASE; 17TH BMW/OI; BEALE AFB, CA 95903. (#104881-4).

OCT 4, '75. INTERNATIONAL FAIR DAY - FOLK DANCE, MUSIC & ART FESTIVAL. FAIR AT JETSTAR RECREATION CENTER, BEALE AFB. (LOCAL). DR LEWIS J FERRARI, CHMN; BEALE AIR FORCE BASE, YUBA COUNTY BICENTENNIAL COMMITTEE; 2205 COVILLAUD; MARYSVILLE, CA 95901. (#200006-7).

FEB 1 - 29, '76. BEALE AFB HISTORY MONTH. EXHIBIT, FESTIVAL. (LOCAL). MAJOR WALTER M RYLAND; BEALE AFB; 17 BMW/01; BEALE AFB, CA 95903. (#200006-176).

MAY 7, '76. HORIZONS '76 OPEN HOUSE-AIR SHOW-DISPLAY OF AIRCRAFT AND EQUIPMENT. INFORMATION AND AUDIOVISUAL DISPLAYS. AT BEALE AIR FORCE BASE. (LOCAL). MAJOR WALTER N RYLAND; BEALE AIR FORCE BASE; BEALE AIR FORCE BASE; BEALE AFB, CA 95903. (#105080-1).

SEPT 18, '76. U S AIR FORCE BIRTHDAY BALL. TICKETS WILL BE AVAILABLE AT MARYSVILLE CHAMBER OF COMMERCE. AT HILLTOP NONCOMMISSIONED OFFICERS OPEN MESS. (LOCAL). DR LEWIS FERRARI, CHMN; YUBA COUNTY BICENTENNIAL COMMITTEE; 2205 COVILLAUD; MARYSVILLE, CA 95901. (#200006-329).

BEAUMONT

JUNE 26 - JULY 4, '76. SPORTSARAMA. COMPETITION, FESTIVAL. (LOCAL). ARCHIE SONNTAG, CHAIRMAN; BICENTENNIAL COMMISSION OF BEAUMONT; 1444 MICHIGAN AVE; BEAUMONT, CA 92223. (#200006-396).

BELL GARDENS

BELL GARDENS BICENTENNIAL MEDALLION, CA. LOCALLY DESIGNED MEDALLION IS BEING SOLD TO FUND BICENT PROJECTS. (LOCAL). GARY MILLIMAN, DEPUTY CITY MANAGER; BELL GARDENS BICENTENNIAL COMMISSION; 7100 S GARFIELD AVE; BELL GARDENS, CA 90201. (#21631).

THE BICENTENNIAL: COLOR IT GREEN, BELL GARDENS, CA. DISTRIBUTION OF 200 TREES TO LOCAL RESIDENTS. (LOCAL). GARY MILLIMAN, DEPUTY CITY MANAGER; BELL GARDENS BICENTENNIAL COMMISSION; 7100 S GARFIELD AVE; BELL GARDENS, CA 90201. (#21632).

JULY 4, '76. OLD-FASHIONED PICNIC AND FIREWORKS DISPLAY ON THE 4TH OF JULY. FESTIVAL AT JOHN ANSON FORD PARK, 7840 PARK LANE. (LOCAL). GARY D MILLIMAN, CHAIRMAN; BELL GARDENS BICENTENNIAL COMMISSION; 7100 S GARFIELD AVE; BELL GARDENS, CA 90201. (#105498-1).

BELLFLOWER

HERITAGE SQUARE PARK, BELLFLOWER, CA. SPRR TICKET OFFICE RESTORATION TO FACILITATE DISPLAY OF BELLFLOWER'S HISTORICAL DOCUMENTS & DEVELOPMENT OF PARK AROUND 3 ONE HUNDRED YEAR OLD PEPPER TREES. (LOCAL). KEN CLEVELAND, CHAIRMAN; BELLFLOWER BICENTENNIAL COMMITTEE; 9838 E BELMONT ST; BELLFLOWER, CA 90706. (#29547).

BELMONT

COMMEMORATIVE STATUE IN BELMONT, CA. STATUE OF FATHER PALOU AND SGT RIVERA WHO VISITED BELMONT AREA IN 1769 WITH DON GASPAR PORTOLA WHILE LOOKING FOR THE SAN FRANCISCO BAY. (LOCAL). RUSSEL A ESTEP, CO-CHAIRMAN; BELMONT BICENTENNIAL COMMITTEE & CITY OF BELMONT; 1469 EL CAMINO REAL; BELMONT, CA 94002. (#13078).

LIBERTY TREES, BELMONT, CA. REDWOOD TREES PLANTED ON CAMPUS, IN COMMEMORATION OF BICENTENNIAL YEAR. (LOCAL). SISTER MARY LAZAGUE, COORDINATOR; COLLEGE OF NOTRE DAME BICENTENNIAL COMMITTEE; 1500 RALSTON AVE; BELMONT, CA 94002. (#28615).

SEPT 1, '75 - MAY 8, '76. DRAMA PRESENTATION ON WILLIAM C RALSTON. LIVE PERFORMANCE AT CARRIAGE HOUSE THEATER, 1500 RALSTON AVE. (LOCAL). SISTER MARY LAXAGUE; COLLEGE OF NOTRE DAME BELMONT; 1500 RALSTON AVE; BELMONT, CA 94002. (#200006-372).

OCT 5, '76. UNITED STATES ARMED FORCES BICENTENNIAL CARAVAN. CARAVAN IS COMPOSED OF EXHIBIT VANS FOR EACH MILITARY SERVICE. PROJECT THEME IS 'HISTORY OF THE ARMED FORCES & THEIR CONTRIBUTIONS TO THE NATION'. (LOCAL). JAMES MCLAUGHLIN; UNITED STATES ARMED FORCES BICENTENNIAL CARAVAN; 1365 5TH AVE; BELMONT, CA 94002. (#1775-820).

BENICIA

HISTORICAL RESTORATION OF BENICIA, CALIF. PLANS FOR RESTORATION OF FISCHER-HANLON HOME, AND FOR HISTORICAL MUSEUMS IN THE BENICIA ARSENAL FORT & THE FORMER HOME OF STEPHEN VINCENT BENET'S FATHER. (LOCAL). RUSS BLANCHARD, CHAIRMAN; BENICIA BICENTENNIAL COMMISSION; CITY HALL 250 EAST L ST; BENICIA, CA 94510. (#2284).

LIBERTY TREE PLANTING AND PLAQUES - BENICIA, CA. TREES WERE PLANTED AND PLAQUES PRESENTED TO ALL SEVEN SCHOOLS IN BENICIA. (LOCAL). RUSS BLANCHARD, CHAIRMAN; BENICIA BICENTENNIAL COMMITTEE & ROTARY CLUB; 494 WEST I ST; BENICIA, CA 94510. (#26439).

SCHOLARSHIPS FOR HISTORY STUDIES - BENICIA, CALIF. SCHOLARSHIP FUND TO BE ESTABLISHED FOR STUDIES CONCENTRATED IN HISTORY. (LOCAL). RUSS BLANCHARD, CHAIRMAN; BENICIA BICENTENNIAL COMMISSION; 250 E L ST; BENICIA, CA 94510. (#3236). **(??).**

SEPT 20, '75. BENICIA BICENTENNIAL BAY AREA BOAT CRUISE. WILL INCLUDE INSTRUMENTALISTS FOR MUSICAL BACKGROUND TOURISTS TO BE DRESSED IN APPROPRIATE COSTUMES. AT STARTING POINT: FISHERMAN'S WHARF SAN FRANCISCO CALIF. (LOCAL). RUSS BLANCHARD; BENICIA KIWANIS CLUB; 494 WEST 1 STREET; BENICIA, CA 94510. (#50680-1).

JUNE 1, '76. UNITED STATES ARMED FORCES BICENTENNIAL CARAVAN. CARAVAN IS COMPOSED OF EXHIBIT VANS FOR EACH MILITARY SERVICE. PROJECT THEME IS 'HISTORY OF THE ARMED FORCES AND THEIR CONTIBUTIONS TO THE NATION. AT WEST K ST BETWEEN FIRST AND WEST 2ND. (LOCAL). RUSS BLANCHARD, COORD; U S ARMED FORCES BICENTENNIAL CARAVAN; 494 W I ST; BENICIA, CA 94510. (#1775-720).

JULY 3, '76. TORCHLIGHT PARADE. PARADE AT UP FIRST STREET 3 MILES. (LOCAL). RUSS BLANCHARD, CHAIRMAN; BENICIA BICENTENNIAL COMMISSION; 494 WEST I ST; BENICIA, CA 94510. (#108887-7).

JULY 4, '76. CA HISTORICAL RESOURCES COMMISSION PLAQUE - 1850 MASONIC TEMPLE. CEREMONY AT CITY PARK. (LOCAL). RUSS BLANCHARD, CHAIRMAN; BENICIA BICENTENNIAL COMMISSION; 494 WEST I ST; BENICIA, CA 94510. (#108887-5).

JULY 4, '76. CA HISTORICAL RESOURCES COMMISSION PLAQUE - 1847 ARMY ARSENAL. CEREMONY, AWARD AT CITY PARK. (LOCAL). RUSS BLANCHARD; BENICIA BICENTENNIAL COMMISSION; 494 WEST I ST; BENICIA, CA 94510. (#108887-6).

JULY 4, '76. COLONIAL ARTS AND CRAFTS FAIR. THIRD YEAR OF BICENTENNIAL CELEBRATION INCLUDING COLONIAL SUBJECTS, HAND CRAFTS: SOAP MAKING, CANDLE MAKING, LEATHER CRAFT, FORGING QUILTING, ETC. AT CITY PARK. (LOCAL). RUSS BLANCHARD, CHAIRMAN; BENICIA BICENTENNIAL COMMISSION; 494 WEST I ST; BENICIA, CA 94510. (#108887-8).

JULY 4, '76. 'LET FREEDOM RING'. JOINING ALL NATION IN BELL RINGING FOR TWO MINUTES AT ELEVEN O'CLOCK HERE PDST W/ALL CHURCHES. LARGE CIRCLE IN CITY PARK TO JOIN WITH 150 HAND BELLS OF ALL SIZES. (LOCAL). RUSS BLANCHARD, CHAIRMAN; BENICIA BICENTENNIAL COMMISSION; 494 WEST I ST; BENICIA, CA 94510. (#108887-2).

JULY 4, '76. OLD FASHIONED GAZEBO DEDICATION. AUTHENTIC REPRODUCTION OF OCTAGONAL GAZEBO IN CITY PARK WILL BE DEDICATED. AT CITY PARK. (LOCAL). RUSS BLANCHARD, CHMN; BENICIA BICENTENNIAL COMMISSION; 494 WEST I ST; BENICIA, CA 94510. (#108887-9).

JULY 4, '76. OLD-FASHIONED PICNIC. THIRD YEAR OF THIS BICENTENNIAL EVENT GROWING EACH TIME AS MORE GAMES, MUSICAL TALENT, ETHNIC DANCE EXHIBITIONS, PUPPET THEATER WITH HISTORICAL SCENES, BELL RINGING AND CLOWNS. (LOCAL). RUSS BLANCHARD, CHAIRMAN; BENICIA BICENTENNIAL COMMISSION; 494 WEST I ST; BENICIA, CA 94510. (#108887-1).

JULY 4, '76. ST PAUL'S SQUARE DEDICATION. DEDICATION OF NEWLY BUILT SQUARE ON MAIN STREET IN FRONT OF ST PAUL'S EPISCOPAL CHURCH, FIRST EPISCOPAL CATHEDRAL IN NORTHERN CALIFORNIA BUILT IN 1876. AT ST PAUL'S EPISCOPAL CHURCH. (LOCAL). RUSS BLANCHARD, CHAIRMAN; BENICIA BICENTENNIAL COMMISSION; 494 WEST I ST; BENICIA, CA 94510. (#108887-4).

JULY 24, '76. HISTORICAL COSTUME GRAND BALL. GRAND BALL TO BE HELD IN NATIONAL GUARD ARMORY TO CELEBRATE ALL THE BICENTENNIAL PROJECTS OVER LAST THREE YEARS. AT NATIONAL GUARD ARMORY. (LOCAL). RUSS BLANCHARD, CHAIRMAN; BENICIA BICENTENNIAL COMMISSION; 494 WEST I ST; BENICIA, CA 94510. (#108887-3).

BERKELEY

AMERICA IN REVIEW: BERKELEY, CALIFORNIA. A REVUE ON THEMES & INCIDENTS FROM AMERICAN HISTORY WILL BE CREATED, PRODUCED AND ACTED OUT BY FACULTY, STAFF & ALUMNI. (LOCAL). PROF TRAVIS BOGARD; UNIV OF CALIFORNIA AT BERKELEY; BERKELEY, CA 94720. (#10518).

ART CONSERVATION PROJ OF UNIV OF CALIF, BERKELEY. CONSERVATION TREATMENT ON THE COLLECTION OF THE UNIVERSITY ART MUSEUM, UNIV OF CALIFORNIA, BERKELEY. (ST-WIDE). LAWRENCE DINNEAN, CURATOR/CONSERVATION; UNIVERSITY ART MUSEUM; 2626 BANCROFT WAY; BERKELEY, CA 94720. (#3099). **(??).**

BERKELEY BLACK MAIN STREET STUDY AND DESIGN. THROUGH USER PARTICIPATION TO DEVELOP DESIGN OPTIONS FOR THE LOWER SACRAMENTO ST IN BERKELEY CAL., EMPHASIZING ON THE RECOGNITION, PRESERVATION & ENHANCEMENT OF IDENTITY OF BLACK COMMUNITY STRIP. (LOCAL). PAUL TI-FU WANG, URBAN DESIGNER; 1830 ARCH ST; BERKELEY, CA 94709. (#4207). **(??).**

'BLACK CULTURE AND BLACK CONSCIOUSNESS' BOOK. WILL ANALYZE CHANGING ATTITUDES AND WORLD VIEW OF BLACK AMERICANS FROM EMANCIPATION TO WORLD WAR II AS EXPRESSED IN THEIR FOLK TRADITION, BY LAWRENCE LEVINE, UNDER PHI BETA KAPPA GRANT. (NAT'L). KENNETH M GREENE, SECRETARY; PHI BETA KAPPA; 1811 Q ST, NW; WASHINGTON, DC 20009. (#229). **ARBA GRANTEE.**

BOOK ON ENLIGHTENMENT IN AMERICA, BERKELEY, CA. DEALS WITH EUROPEAN THOUGHT IN AMERICA, EMPHASIS ON RELIGION FIRST, THEN POLITICS, INCLUDES BRIEF TREATMENT OF AMERICAN AND FRENCH REVOLUTIONS. (NAT'L). HENRY F MAY, PROFESSOR OF HISTORY; UNIV OF CALIF, BERKELEY; BERKELEY, CA 94720. (#5387).

BROCHURE ON POLISH CONTRIBUTIONS TO CALIFORNIA. 'THE POLISH CONTRIBUTION TO THE DEVELOPMENT OF CALIFORNIA', BY DR WITOLD SWORAKOWSKI, CURATOR EMERITUS OF THE POLISH COLLECTION OF THE HOOVER INSTITUTE, WILL BE PUBLISHED BY END OF BICENTENNIAL YEAR. (ST-WIDE). JOHN SWITALSKI, PROJECT CHAIRMAN; NORTHERN CALIFORNIA DIVISION, POLISH AMERICAN CONGRESS; 1098 AMITO AVE; BERKELEY, CA 94705. (#26988).

FAMOUS LEUTZE PAINTING TO TOUR CALIFORNIA. A TOUR OF THE PRINCIPLE CITIES OF CALIFORNIA BY THE FAMOUS LEUTZE PAINTING: 'GEORGE WASHINGTON RALLYING THE TROOPS AT THE BATTLE OF MONMOUTH', WHICH IS OWNED BY THE UNIV OF CALIFORNIA AT BERKELEY. (ST-WIDE). PROFESSOR GARFF B WILSON, PROJ DIRECTOR; UNIV OF CALIFORNIA; BERKELEY, CA 94720. (#10516).

'THE GREAT MINU', BOOK PROJ OF BERKELEY, CA. THE PURPOSE OF PROJECT IS TO FAMILIARIZE AMERICANS WITH THE HERITAGE OF BLACK AMERICANS BY PUBLICATION OF THIS WEST AFRICAN FOLKTALE WHICH ILLUSTRATES AND EXPLAINS SOME BLACK CULTURAL PATTERNS. (NAT'L). BETH P WILSON, AUTHOR; 945 SANTA BARBARA RD; BERKELEY, CA 94707. (#11624).

INDIAN ART OF THE AMERICAS IN BERKELEY, CA. THE PROJECT INVOLVES AN EXHIBIT OF PAINTINGS AND SCULPTURE BY NATIVE AMERICANS OF NORTH AND SOUTH AMERICA. (LOCAL). JOY FENBERG, CHAIRMAN; UNIV OF CALIFORNIA ART MUSEUM; BERKELEY, CA 94720. (#10513-1).

'LIVING SPACES' FILM PROJ OF CALIFORNIA. FILM ON US URBAN DEVELOPMENT, WILL EXAMINE THE SOCIAL & CONCEPTUAL CHANGES AS THEY AFFECTED THE GROWTH OF THREE REPRESENTATIVE WESTERN NEIGHBORHOODS. (NAT'L). PROF VICTOR ROSENBERG, DIRECTOR; CALIFORNIA HISTORICAL SOCIETY; 1545 SCENIC AVE; BERKELEY, CA 94708. (#217).

'MARTIN LUTHER KING, JR', A BOOK - BERKELEY, CA. TO MAKE AMERICANS MORE AWARE OF THE CONTRIBUTION OF THIS LEADER OF MEN AND MOVE THEM A LITTLE CLOSER TO BROTHERHOOD. (NAT'L). BETH P WILSON, AUTHOR; 945 SANTA BARBARA RD; BERKELEY, CA 94707. (#11625).

'MUHAMMAD ALI', A BOOK PROJ OF BERKELEY, CA. A BOOK TO HELP PEOPLE UNDERSTAND MUHAMMAD ALI, A CONTROVERSIAL WORLD CHAMPION IN THE FIELD OF SPORTS. (NAT'L). BETH P WILSON, AUTHOR; 945 SANTA BARBARA RD; BERKELEY, CA 94707. (#11626).

'SAGE SMOKE', A BOOK PROJ OF BERKELEY, CA. A BOOK DESIGNED TO ACQUAINT CHILDREN WITH INDIAN FOLKLORE AND THE RICH HERITAGE OF ORAL LITERATURE AMONG THE AMERICAN INDIANS. (NAT'L). ELEANOR B HEADY, AUTHOR; 1864 CAPISTRANO AVE; BERKELEY, CA 94707. (#11627).

'TALES OF THE NIMIPOO', BOOK PROJ OF BERKELEY, CA. 'TALES OF THE NIMIPOO' IS A JUVENILE BOOK OF INDIAN FOLKTALES. (NAT'L). ELEANOR B HEADY, AUTHOR; 1864 CAPISTRANO AVE; BERKELEY, CA 94707. (#11628).

UNIV OF CALIFORNIA BAND BICENTENNIAL TOUR. THE PROJECT INVOLVES A NATIONAL TOUR BY THE UNIV OF CALIFORNIA MARCHING BAND; THEY WILL PRESENT THE HERITAGE OF AMER BAND MUSIC. MUSICAL REVUE CELEBRATING OUR NATION'S BICENTENNIAL. (NAT'L). DAVID N PEARSON, EXEC DIRECTOR; UNIV OF CALIFORNIA BAND '76 TOUR; ALUMNI HOUSE; BERKELEY, CA 94720. (#10515). **ARBA RECOGNIZED.**

UNIV OF CALIFORNIA AFRO-AMER ART/SLIDE COLLECTION. THE COLLECTION OF 4300 SLIDE-PHOTOGRAPHS OF AFRO-AMERICAN ART REPRESENT PAINTINGS, SCULPTURES & MURALS FROM 1700-1970. (ST-WIDE). AUGUST MANZA, MANAGER; UNIV OF CALIFORNIA ANTHROPOLOGY & HISTORY DEPARTMENT; M11 WHEELER HALL; BERKELEY, CA 94720. (#10848). **ARBA RECOGNIZED. ARBA GRANTEE.**

'WHO WAS MALCOLM X?', BERKELEY, CA. TO ACQUAINT AMERICANS WITH THE LIFE OF ONE OF THE MOST DEDICATED BLACK LEADERS. (NAT'L). BETH P WILSON, AUTHOR; 945 SANTA BARBARA RD; BERKELEY, CA 94707. (#20721).

JAN 13 - FEB 22, '76. AMERICAN PRESIDENCY, POLITICAL CARTOONS, 1776-1976. EXHIBITION & CATALOG OF POLITICAL CARTOONS DEPICTING NATURE, ROLE & SCOPE OF PRESIDENCY; ANALYZING CHANGE IN PRESIDENCY & PUBLIC ATTITUDES TO IT; COMPARING RELATIONSHIPS BETWEEN IT, COURTS, & CONGRESS. RESERVATIONS ADVISED FOR GROUPS. AT 2525 BANCROFT WAY. (REGN'L). BONNIE J EARLS; UNIVERSITY ART MUSEUM BERKELEY; 2525 BANCROFT WAY; BERKELEY, CA 94720. (#1715-1).

APR 1, '76. AMERICAN ACHIEVEMENT IN ARTS & SCIENCES - LECTURES. SERIES OF 15 LECTURES BY CAMPUS AUTHORITIES DESCRIBING 200 YEARS OF ACHIEVEMENT IN THE ARTS AND SCIENCES. AT ON CAMPUS UNIV OF CALIF, BERKELEY. (LOCAL). PROF GARFF B WILSON; UNIV OF CALIFORNIA; 326 SPOUL HALL; BERKELEY, CA 94220. (#11800-1).

APR 1 - 4, '76. UNIV OF CALIFORNIA-BERKELEY SALUTES THE BICENTENNIAL. 4-DAY CELEBRATION, INCLUDING A GENERAL CAMPUS OPEN HOUSE, A FESTIVAL OF MUSIC, DRAMA & FILMS, SPECIAL LECTURES & A GIANT CONVOCATION. (ST-WIDE). PROF GARFF B WILSON; UNIV OF CALIFORNIA, BERKELEY; BERKELEY, CA 94720. (#7909-1).

MAY 7, '76. NETHERLANDS CHAMBER ORCHESTRA VISITS UNIV OF CALIFORNIA - BERKELEY. LIVE PERFORMANCE. (INT'L). WILLIAM SIMONSZ, COORD; NETHERLANDS GOVERNMENT; NETHER-

BERKELEY — CONTINUED

LANDS EMBASSY-4200 LINNEAN; WASHINGTON, DC 20008. (#109013-17).

MAY 14 - 15, '76. 'SPIRIT OF AMERICA', A BICENTENNIAL MUSIC REVUE BY THE UNIV OF CA. PREMIERE PERFORMANCE OF 'SPIRIT OF AMERICA', A COLLEGIATE MUSICAL REVUE CELEBRATING OUR NATION'S BICENTENNIAL. WILL BE PERFORMED IN 25 CITIES ACROSS THE USA AS PART OF AN ARBA OFFICIALLY RECOGNIZED SIX-WEEK TOUR. DONATIONS: (415)642-6634 WELCOMED. AT HARMON GYMNASIUM UIV OF CALIFORNIA. (LOCAL). ALAN WEAVER, P/R; UNIV OF CALIFORNIA MARCHING BAND; 57 STUDENT CENTER - CAL BAND; BERKELEY, CA 94720. (#10515-2).

MAY '76. FINNISH ARCHITECTURAL EXHIBIT. EXHIBIT AT UNIV OF CALIFORNIA. (INT'L). JAAKKO BERGQUIST; FINNISH-AMERICAN BICENTENNIAL COMMITTEE; 1900 24TH ST, NW; WASHINGTON, DC 20008. (#109040-2).

JULY 31, '76. UNIVERSITY OF CALIFORNIA MARCHING BAND PRESENTS 'SPIRIT OF AMERICA'. THIS IS PART OF A 6-WEEK PERFORMANCE TOUR OF THE U S; 'SPIRIT OF AMERICA' IS A COLLEGIATE MUSICAL REVIEW CELEBRATING OUR NATION'S BICENTENNIAL; WILL INCLUDE FOLK MUSIC, MARCHING, VAUDEVILLE, ROCK, DIXIELAND, JAZZ, BARBERSHOP & SOLOS. AT ZELLERBACH AUDITORIUM, BERKELEY CAMPUS. (ST-WIDE). DAVID N PEARSON, CHMN; CAL BAND TOUR COUNCIL; CAL BAND ALUMNI HOUSE; BERKELEY, CA 94720. (#10515-25).

BEVERLY HILLS

JAN 1 - DEC 31, '76. BICENTENNIAL FLAG CEREMONY. FLAG IS HONORED AT 8 AM & 5 PM EACH DAY. HOTEL GUESTS ARE ASKED TO JOIN IN THE CEREMONY. AT ALL HILTON HOTELS IN THE U S.. (LOCAL). JACQUES C COSSE, DIR; HILTON HOTELS CORP; 9880 WILSHIRE BLVD; BEVERLY HILLS, CA 90210. (#106448-1).

BIG BEAR LAKE

JUNE 13, '76. FLAG DAY CEREMONY - HISTORICAL VIGNETTES. HONOR TO FLAG AND COUNTRY; 20 LIVING VIGNETTES OF NATIONAL AND LOCAL HISTORY. (LOCAL). E F DOBROWOLSKI, COORD; ELKS LODGE 1787; BIG BEAR LAKE, CA 92315. (#105426-1).

JULY 3 - 4, '76. PICNIC AND PARADE. VIGNETTES OF HISTORY, ETHNIC GROUP SONGS AND DANCES, FIREWORKS. AT BIG BEAR LAKE MEADOW PARK, BIG BEAR CITY PARK. (LOCAL). HERBERT R SNELL, COORD; BIG BEAR VALLEY BICENTENNIAL COMMITTEE; 1520 E BIG BEAR BLVD; BIG BEAR CITY, CA 92314. (#105426-5).

AUG 1 - 8, '76. OLD MINERS DAYS: BIG BEAR VALLEY, THE WEST AND THE NATION. PARADE, ENTERTAINMENT, FLOATS, FLAG CEREMONY, PONY EXPRESS, DANCES, CONTESTS, SHOOTING, THEATRICAL PERFORMANCE, WHISKERINO & MULE DRIVING. AT BIG BEAR LAKE. (LOCAL). JIM MALONEY, COORD; OLD MINERS ASSOC; PO BOX 71; FAWNSKIN, CA 92333. (#105426-7).

SEPT 25 - OCT 4, '76. OKTOBERFEST. FESTIVAL AT GOLDMINE SKI AREA TENTS, BOOTHS, FREE PARKING ON GROUNDS. (LOCAL). HANS R BANDOWS, COORD; BIG BEAR CHAMBER OF COMMERCE; PO BOX 34; BIG BEAR LAKE, CA 92315. (#105426-3).

BIG PINE

INYO COUNTY PUPILS' HISTORIES - CA. PUPILS IN COUNTY SCHOOLS WILL WRITE HISTORIES OF THE COUNTY. (LOCAL). TOM MCGUIGAN, CHAIRMAN; BIG PINE CIVIC CLUB; 120 PINE RD; BIG PINE, CA 93513. (#14356).

BISHOP

INDIAN CULTURAL CENTER, OWENS VALLEY, CA. A CULTURAL VISITORS' COMPLEX PRESERVING INDIAN HERITAGE AND PROVIDING WORK FOR MANY FINE ARTISTS & CRAFTSMEN. (ST-WIDE). DIANE TOVELL, OWENS VALLEY BOARD OF TRUSTEES; OWENS VALLEY PAIUTE-SHOSHONE BAND OF INDIANS; PO BOX 273; BISHOP, CA 93514. (#15116). **ARBA GRANTEE.**

MAY 29 - 31, '76. MULE DAYS CELEBRATION. MULES FROM ACROSS THE WEST COMPETE FOR TITLE OF WORLD CHAMPION MULE. AT THROUGHOUT BISHOP. (LOCAL). MARSHA OSWALT; BISHOP CHAMBER OF COMMERCE; 690 N MAIN; BISHOP, CA 93514. (#103416-340).

OCT 29, '76. UNITED STATES ARMED FORCES BICENTENNIAL CARAVAN. CARAVAN IS COMPOSED OF EXHIBIT VANS FOR EACH MILITARY SERVICE. PROJECT THEME IS 'HISTORY OF THE ARMED FORCES & THEIR CONTRIBUTIONS TO THE NATION'. (LOCAL). HENRY RAUB; UNITED STATES ARMED FORCES BICENTENNIAL CARAVAN; C/O INYO CO BICENT COMMITTEE; INDEPENDENCE, CA 93526. (#1775-833).

BLUE LAKE

'PROJECT ABORIGINE' THEATER PROJ IN CALIFORNIA. DEVELOPMENT OF TWO PART THEATRE PIECE EXPLORING INDIAN COMIC CHARACTERS IN A COMMEDIA DELL'ARTE FORMAT. (ST-WIDE). JANE MAZZONE-CLEMENTI, EXEC DIRECTOR; DELL'ARTE, INC; BOX 816 FIRST & H STS; BLUE LAKE, CA 95501. (#5354).

BLYTHE

DEC 4, '76. UNITED STATES ARMED FORCES BICENTENNIAL CARAVAN. CARAVAN IS COMPOSED OF EXHIBIT VANS FOR EACH MILITARY SERVICE. PROJECT THEME IS 'HISTORY OF THE ARMED FORCES & THEIR CONTRIBUTIONS TO THE NATION'. (LOCAL). HOWARD RUTAN; UNITED STATES ARMED FORCES BICENTENNIAL CARAVAN; 187 N 7TH ST; BLYTHE, CA 92225. (#1775-851).

BOREAL RIDGE

FEB 15 - 17, '75. SNOWSHOE THOMPSON/ROY MIKKELSON NORDIC COMPETITIONS. COMPETITION, AWARD, CEREMONY, TOUR. (NAT'L). CHUCK MORSE, EXEC ADMIN; US SKI ASSOC & FAR WEST SKI ASSOC; 1313 W 8TH ST; LOS ANGELES, CA 90017. (#2438-901).

FEB 14 - 16, '76. SNOWSHOE THOMPSON/ROY MIKKELSON NORDIC COMPETITION. COMPETITION. (REGN'L). CHUCK MORSE, EXEC ADMIN; US SKI ASSOC & FAR WEST SKI ASSOC.; 1313 W 8TH ST; LOS ANGELES, CA 90017. (#2438-8).

MAR 6, '76. SIERRA MINERS LONGBOARD RACE. COMPETITION, AWARD. (REGN'L). CHUCK MORSE, EXEC. ADMIN; US SKI ASSOC & FAR WEST SKI ASSOC; 1313 W 8TH ST; LOS ANGELES, CA 90017. (#2438-10).

MAY 15, '76. DEDICATION SNOWSHOE THOMPSON STATUE-HONOR NORWEGIAN NATL HOLIDAY. THE CROWN PRINCE OF NORWAY & INTERNATIONAL DIGNITARIES WILL BE PRESENT. AT IN FRONT OF SKISPORT MUSEUM. (LOCAL). CHUCK MORSE, EXEC ADMIN; US SKI ASSOC & FAR WEST SKI ASSOC; 1313 W 8TH ST; LOS ANGELES, CA 90017. (#2438-11).

BOULEVARD

CAMPO MULTI-PURPOSE BUILDING IN BOULEVARD, CA. CONSTRUCTION OF BUILDING TO INCLUDE RECREATION FACILITIES, TRIBAL OFFICES, MEDICAL-DENTAL FACILITIES, CLASSROOMS, LIBRARY, ALCOHOLISM CENTER, RESTROOM, KITCHEN AND LARGE MEETING ROOM. (LOCAL). MS VALACIA THACKER, TRIBAL CHAIRMAN; CAMPO BAND OF MISSION INDIANS; PO BOX 1094; BOULEVARD, CA 92205. (#22847). **ARBA GRANTEE.**

SEPT 11, '76. BICENTENNIAL DEDICATION. FAIR AT CAMPO INDIAN COMMUNITY BLDG, CAMPO INDIAN RESERVATION. (LOCAL). VALACIA C THACKER; CAMPO BAND OF MISSION INDIANS; PO BOX 1094; BOULEVARD, CA 92005. (#200006-475).

BRAWLEY

OCT 8, '75. CATTLE CALL, WESTERN PARADE & RODEO. RODEO IS RCA CALIBER AND THE WINSTON RODEO AWARDS FOR 1975 WILL BE PRESENTED THIS YEAR. (LOCAL). LEWIS BACON, EXEC DIR; BRAWLEY CHAMBER OF COMMERCE; PO BOX 218; BRAWLEY, CA 92227. (#102503-2).

FEB 1, '76. UNITED STATES ARMED FORCES BICENTENNIAL CARAVAN. CARAVAN IS COMPOSED OF EXHIBIT VANS FOR EACH MILITARY SERVICE. PROJECT THEME IS 'HISTORY OF THE ARMED FORCES AND THEIR CONTRIBUTIONS TO THE NATION'. (LOCAL). SHIRLEY PARK, CHMN; US ARMED FORCES EXHIBIT VANS PROJECT; 133 H ST; BRAWLEY, CA 92227. (#1775-313).

BREA

BICENTENNIAL ART IN THE PARK - BREA, CA. CHILDREN WILL BE CREATIVE WITH CHALK, CRAYON AND PAINT; AWARDS WILL BE GIVEN TO ALL PARTICIPANTS. (LOCAL). JUDY VINCITORIO, SECRETARY; BREA COMMUNITY SERVICES & BRAE JUNIOR WOMEN'S CLUB; BREA BLVD; BREA, CA 92621. (#17548).

BICENTENNIAL ESSAY CONTEST - BREA, CA. STUDENTS WILL WRITE ESSAYS ON THE THEME 'IN YOUR OPINION, WHAT IS THE MOST IMPORTANT EVENT IN AMERICAN HISTORY?'. (LOCAL). RETHA HOLBECK, CHAIRMAN; BREA WOMEN'S CLUB; BREA, CA 92621. (#17546).

GAZEBO FOR SENIOR CITIZNS IN BREA, CALIF. GAZEBO TO BE CONSTRUCTED IN CITY HALL PARK FOR USE BY SENIOR CITIZENS AS PART OF CITY'S BICENTENNIAL COMMEMORATION. (LOCAL). MARGERY PAUL, PRESIDENT; SOROPTIMIST CLUB OF BREA; PO BOX 363; BREA, CA 92621. (#2546).

LIBERTY BELL RELOCATION, BREA, CALIF. LIBERTY BELL TO BE PLACED IN APPROPRIATE LOCATION IN CITY AS PART OF BICENTENNIAL COMMIMORATION. (ST-WIDE). CATHERINE MURPHY, DIRECTOR; ROYAL NEIGHBORS OF AMERICA, FULLERTON CAMP 8399; 613 E BIRCH ST; BREA, CA 92621. (#2547).

POPPY SEED DISTRIBUTION PROJ OF BREA, CALIF. POPPY SEEDS WILL BE DISTRIBUTED TO ALL RESIDENT HOMES IN BREA AS PART OF BICENTENNIAL COMMEMORATION. (LOCAL). S A & LOUISE SMITH, DIRECTORS; VFW & AMERICAN LEGION; 639 E ASH; BREA, CA 92621. (#2545).

1776 TREES - PROJ OF BREA, CA. EVERYONE IN COMMUNITY TO PLANT TREES IN ORDER TO OBTAIN GOAL OF 1776 TREES PLANTED BY 1976. (LOCAL). JUDY VINCITORIO, SECRETARY; BEAUTIFICATION COMMITTEE & BREA JUNIOR WOMEN'S CLUB; BREA, CA 92621. (#17547).

NOV 26, '75. BICENTENNIAL THANKSGIVING SERVICE. COMPETITION AT ST ANGELA MERCICI CATHOLIC CHURCH, FIR & WALNUT STS. (LOCAL). JUDY VINCITORIO, SEC; BREA BICENTENNIAL COMMISSION; BREA BICENTENNIAL COMMISSION; BREA, CA 92621. (#103355-1).

FEB 19, '76. BREA CITY BICENTENNIAL BIRTHDAY PARTY. CEREMONY, EXHIBIT, FESTIVAL AT COMMUNITY CENTER, 500 SIEVERS. (LOCAL). JUDY VINCITORIO, SEC; BREA HISTORICAL SOCIETY & BICENTENNIAL COMMITTEE; BREA BICENTENNIAL COMMISSION; BREA, CA 92621. (#103355-2).

APR 3, '76. BICENTENNIAL SYMPHONY CONCERT, RIO HONDO SYMPHONY ORCHESTRA. LIVE PERFORMANCE AT BREA OLINDA HIGH SCHOOL AUDITORIUM, 803 E BIRCH. (LOCAL). JUDY VINCITORIO, SEC; BREA BICENTENNIAL COMMISSION; BREA BICENTENNIAL COMMISSION; BREA, CA 92621. (#103355-3).

MAY 1, '76. UNITED STATES ARMED FORCES BICENTENNIAL CARAVAN. CARAVAN IS COMPOSED OF EXHIBIT VANS FOR EACH MILITARY SERVICE. PROJECT THEME IS ' HISTORY OF THE ARMED FORCES & THEIR CONTRIBUTIONS TO THE NATION'. (LOCAL). MRS LAVETA DAETWEILER; U S ARMED FORCES BICENTENNIAL CARAVAN; 415 S POPLAR; BREA, CA 92621. (#1775-560).

JULY 4, '76. FIREWORKS SPECTACULAR PRECEDED BY UNITED CHURCH CHOIRS. FESTIVAL AT BREA OLINDA HIGH SCHOOL, FOOTBALL FIELD, 803 E BIRCH. (LOCAL). JUDY VINCITORIO, SEC; BREA FIREMAN'S ASSOC; BREA BICENTENNIAL COMMISSION; BREA, CA 92621. (#103355-4).

BRIDGEPORT

SITE PREPARATION FOR RESERVATION HOMES - CA. GRADING AND LANDSCAPING TO BEAUTIFY RESIDENTIAL AREA. (LOCAL). HENRY GLAZIER, TRIBAL CHAIRMAN; BRIDGEPORT INDIAN COLONY; PO BOX 233; BRIDGEPORT, CA 93517. (#22897). **ARBA GRANTEE.**

BRISBANE

BRISBANE HISTORY BOOK, CA. A BRIEF HISTORY OF BRISBANE'S GOVERNMENT & FOLKLORE. (LOCAL). HON ART MONTENEGRO, MAYOR; BRISBANE BICENTENNIAL COMMITTEE; 44 VISITATION AVE; BRISBANE, CA 94005. (#18437).

INDEPENDENCE WALKWAY, BRISBANE, CA. PRESERVATION OF ECOLOGY-SENSITIVE AREA BY PAVING AN INDEPENDENCE WALKWAY. (LOCAL). HON ART MONTENEGRO, MAYOR; BRISBANE BICENTENNIAL COMMITTEE; 44 VISITATION AVE; BRISBANE, CA 94005. (#18438).

MOBILE MUSEUM, BRISBANE, CA. MOBILE MUSEUM DISPLAYING LOCAL INDIAN ARTIFACTS. (LOCAL). HON ART MONTENEGRO, MAYOR; BRISBANE BICENTENNIAL COMMITTEE; 44 VISITATION AVE; BRISBANE, CA 94005. (#18436).

DEC 31, '75. BICENTENNIAL BALL. FESTIVAL AT BRISBANE INN, VISITACION AVE. (LOCAL). ANJA MILLER, CHAIRMAN; FEDERATED WOMEN'S CLUB OF BRISBANE; 224 SIERRA POINT RD; BRISBANE, CA 94005. (#103797-1).

JUNE 3 - 6, '76. WESTERN DAYS BICENTENNIAL CELEBRATION. FESTIVAL, PARADE. (LOCAL). VINCE MARSILL, CHMN; BRISBANE CHAMBER OF COMMERCE; BRISBANE, CA 94005. (#103797-2).

BROWNSVILLE

JULY 5 - 6, '75. FIRST ANNUAL MOUNTAIN FAIR. ACTIVITIES INCLUDE MUSIC, SQUARE DANCING, AUCTIONS, COMPETITIVE GAMES, VARIOUS CRAFT BOOTHS & REFRESHMENTS. AT YUBA FEATHER HEALTH CENTER, WILLOW GLEN & LAPORTE RDS. (LOCAL). DR LEWIS J FERRARI, CHMN; YUBA COUNTY BICENTENNIAL COMMITTEE; 2205 COVILLAUD ST; MARYSVILLE, CA 95901. (#200006-192).

JULY 3 - 4, '76. SECOND ANNUAL MOUNTAIN FAIR. ACTIVITIES INCLUDE MUSIC, AUCTION, GAMES, VARIOUS BOOTHS & REFRESHMENTS. AT YUBA FEATHER HEALTH CENTER, WILLOW GLEN & LAPORTE RD. (LOCAL). DR LEWIS J FERRARI, CHMN; YUBA COUNTY BICENTENNIAL COMMITTEE; 2205 COVILLAUD ST; MARYSVILLE, CA 95901. (#200006-185).

BUENA PARK

OCT 31, '76. KNOTTS BERRY FARM HALLOWEEN HAUNT. FESTIVAL. (LOCAL). DIRECTOR; PUBLICITY OFFICE, KNOTT'S BERRY FARM; 8039 BEACH BLVD; BUENA PARK, CA 90620. (#103416-648).

BUENAVENTURA

MAY 21, '76. UNITED STATES ARMED FORCES BICENTENNIAL CARAVAN. CARAVAN IS COMPOSED OF EXHIBIT VANS FOR EACH MILITARY SERVICE. PROJECT THEME IS ' HISTORY OF THE ARMED FORCES & THEIR CONTRIBUTIONS TO THE NATION'. (LOCAL). FAYE CAMPBELL, CHAIRMAN; U S ARMED FORCES BICENTENNIAL CARAVAN; PO BOX 99; VENTURA, CA 93001. (#1775-572).

BURBANK

JULY 4, '75. ANNUAL JULY 4 PARADE. BURBANK, CALIF, ON PARADE. ANNUAL FOURTH OF JULY PARADE SPONSORED BY EXCHANGE CLUBS & SERVICE CLUBS OF BURBANK, CA WILL CULMINATE IN SUPER-PARADE ON JULY 4, 1976. (LOCAL). STEPHEN H EBERLE; BURBANK BICENTENNIAL COMMITTEE; 632 N ORCHARD DR; BURBANK, CA 91505. (#2285-501).

JAN 2 - FEB 1, '76. ART SHOW. ALL ART WILL BE FROM OUR LOCAL ART GROUPS. AT BURBANK MAIN LIBRARY, GLENOAKS

BURBANK — CONTINUED

& OLIVE. (LOCAL). STEVE EBERLE; BURBANK BICENTENNIAL COMMITTEE; 632 N ORCHARD DR; BURBANK, CA 91506. (#50373-2).

FEB 21, '76. WASHINGTON BIRTHDAY BALL. A COMPLETE COSTUME DINNER DANCE HONORING THE NATIONS FIRST PRESIDENT. SPEACHES BY MAYOR, CONGRESS MEN, ASSEMBLY MEN & ARBA. AT CASTAWAY HARVARD RD BURBANK CA. (LOCAL). MRS. LEE MAPLE; BURBANK BICENTENNIAL COMMITTEE; P.O. BOX 1776; BURBANK, CA 91507. (#50373-1).

JULY 4, '76. SUPER PARADE '76 IN BURBANK. A PARADE WILL TAKE PLACE AND COVER AREA FROM BUENA VISTA PARK UP OLIVE AVE AND TERMINATE AT MCCAMBRIDGE PARK. EXACT TIMES ARE NOT YET DETERMINED. AT FROM BUENA VISTA PARK TO MCCAMBRIDGE PARK. (LOCAL). STEPHEN H EBERLE,CHAIRMAN; BURBANK BICENTENNIAL COMMITTEE; 632 N ORCHARD DR; BURBANK, CA 91505. (#2285-2).

BURLINGAME

AMER REVOLUTION HISTORY EXHIBITS, BURLINGAME, CA. EXHIBITS DEPICTING THE AMERICAN REVOLUTION WILL BE DISPLAYED IN PUBLIC PLACES. (LOCAL). WILLIAM F MCCANN, PRESIDENT; EXHIBIT MEDIA, INC; 1290 BAYSHORE HWY; BURLINGAME, CA 94010. (#12413).

EXHIBITS ON U S HISTORY & PATRIOTISM - CA. U S HISTORY AND PATRIOTIC INSPIRATIONAL EXHIBITS WILL BE MADE AVAILABLE FOR STUDENTS OF ALL AGES THROUGHOUT THE U S. (NAT'L). WILLIAM F MCCANN, PRESIDENT; EXHIBIT MEDIA, INC; 1290 BAYSHORE HWY; BURLINGAME, CA 94010. (#12412).

EXHIBITS ON U S BUSINESS - BURLINGAME, CA. EXHIBITS DEPICTING THE AMERICAN REVOLUTION AND THE HISTORY OF BUSINESS IN THE FREE ENTERPRISE SYSTEM IN THE U S. (REGN'L). WILLIAM F MCCANN, PRESIDENT; EXHIBIT MEDIA, INC; 1290 BAYSHORE HWY; BURLINGAME, CA 94010. (#12414).

HERITAGE FOOT BRIDGE, BURLINGAME, CA. CONSTRUCTION OF A REDWOOD FOOTBRIDGE, 52' X 8' & 12' AT THE HIGHEST POINT OVER THE STREAM. THE BRIDGE ACTS TO PRESERVE THE SOLITUDE OF THE PARK & A SAFE WAY TO CROSS THE CREEK. (LOCAL). LCDR R N ANDRIANO MOORE, COMMANDING OFFICER; NAVAL & MARINE CORPS RESERVE CENTER; COMMODORE DR & SNEATH LA; SAN BRUNO, CA 94066. (#28601).

PLAYGROUND, BURLINGAME, CA. THE CENTER ASSISTED COMMUNITY ACTION GROUPS & PTA TO CONSTRUCT A PLAYGROUND FOR MCKINLEY ELEMENTARY SCHOOL, BY PROVIDING LABOR & PLANNING EXPERTISE. (LOCAL). LCDR R N ANDRIANO MOORE, COMMANDING OFFICER; NAVAL & MARINE CORPS RESERVE CENTER; COMMODORE DR & SNEATH LA; SAN BRUNO, CA 94066. (#28598).

MAR 26 - 27, '75. RE-ENACTMENT OF THE ANZA EXPEDITION. LIVE PERFORMANCE AT BURLINGAME HIGH SCHOOL, CAROLAN AND OAK GROVE AVE. (REGN'L). CAROLE WHITEHILL, COORD; AMERICAN REVOLUTION BICENTENNIAL COMMITTEE OF SAN MATEO COUNTY; 141 BOREL AVE; SAN MATEO, CA 94402. (#200006-85).

BURNEY

JULY 3 - 5, '76. 'BURNEY BASIN DAYS'-ANNUAL PIONEER CELEBRATION. THIS HAS BEEN A CONTINUOUS CELEBRATION SINCE 1954 AND THIS YEAR'S THEME WILL BE BICENTENNIAL. AT VETERANS' HALL, FOOTBALL FIELD, RODEO ARENA & BALL DIAMOND. (LOCAL). L M MORGAN, CHAIRMAN; BURNEY BASIN DAYS COMMITTEE; PO BOX 1103; BURNEY, CA 96013. (#104366-1).

CALIFORNIA CY

NOV 3, '76. UNITED STATES ARMED FORCES BICENTENNIAL CARAVAN. CARAVAN IS COMPOSED OF EXHIBIT VANS FOR EACH MILITARY SERVICE. PROJECT THEME IS 'HISTORY OF THE ARMED FORCES & THEIR CONTRIBUTIONS TO THE NATION'. (LOCAL). MERELE F SMITH; UNITED STATES ARMED FORCES BICENTENNIAL CARAVAN; 8126 CALIFORNIA CY, BLVD PO 2181; CALIFORNIA CY, CA 93505. (#1775-837).

CALIPATRIA

FEB 2, '76. UNITED STATES ARMED FORCES BICENTENNIAL CARAVAN. CARAVAN IS COMPOSED OF EXHIBIT VANS FOR EACH MILITARY SERVICE. PROJECT THEME IS 'HISTORY OF THE ARMED FORCES AND THEIR CONTRIBUTIONS TO THE NATION'. (LOCAL). WILLIAM SORENSEN, CHMN; US ARMED FORCES EXHIBIT VANS PROJECT; 101 N LAKE; CALIPATRIA, CA 92233. (#1775-314).

CAMARILLO

NOV 9, '76. UNITED STATES ARMED FORCES BICENTENNIAL CARAVAN. CARAVAN IS COMPOSED OF EXHIBIT VANS FOR EACH MILITARY SERVICE. PROJECT THEME IS 'HISTORY OF THE ARMED FORCES & THEIR CONTRIBUTIONS TO THE NATION'. (LOCAL). MRS LYNN BENNETT; UNITED STATES ARMED FORCES BICENTENNIAL CARAVAN; PO 452; CAMARILLO, CA 93010. (#1775-840).

CAMPBELL

HISTORICAL OAK TREE PROJECT. 202 YEAR OLD OAK TREE, CALLED QR4, SPLIT, PRESERVED AND STUDIED BY LOCAL STUDENTS WITH LABLED HISTORICAL DATES ON TREE RINGS. READER BOARD DESCRIBES EVENTS. LOCATED AT CAMPBELL LIBRARY. (LOCAL). PHYLLIS B HOFER, CHAIRMAN; CAMPBELL BICENTENNIAL COMMITTEE; 75 N CENTRAL AVE; CAMPBELL, CA 95008. (#29553).

MAY 1 - NOV 15, '76. CREATIVE WRITING CONTEST. RULES: ALL PROSE AND POETRY SUBJECT MATTER MUST BE RELATED TO THE BICENTENNIAL. PROGRAM IS OPEN TO ADULTS & YOUTH. (YOUTH MUST STATE AGE). ALL WRITINGS MUST INCLUDE NAME, ADDRESS, PHONE # & BE AVAILABLE FOR PUBLICATION. AT CAMPBELL CITY HALL, 75 N CENTRAL AVE. (LOCAL). PHYLLIS B HOFER, CHMN; CAMPBELL BICENTENNIAL COMMITTEE; 421 MANCHESTER AVE; CAMPBELL, CA 95008. (#200006-397).

CANOGA PARK

JULY 25, '76. OAK TREE CONTEST. OAK TREE MUST BE HEALTHY AND MUST BE MEASURED BY CIRCUMFERENCE USING RING TREE COUNTING METHOD AND MUST BE IN THE CITY LIMITS. A LAMINATED PLAQUE WILL BE ATTACHED TO THE TREE. THE TREE SELECTED WAS 700 YRS OLD AND MEASURES 32' 11' IN CIRCUMFERENCE. AT ORCUTT RANCH HORTICULTURE CENTER, CANOGA PARK, CA. (LOCAL). MS HELEN TREEND, DIRECTOR; SAVE ORCUTT COMMUNITY, INC; BOX 1383; CANOGA PARK, CA 91304. (#104753-10).

CANYON

MAR 20, '76. GRANDLAND SINGERS BICENTENNIAL SHOW. LIVE PERFORMANCE AT STAKE CENTER, CAMP PLENTY RD, CANYON COUNTRY. (LOCAL). BOBBIE TRUEBLOOD, CHMN; LDS CHURCH & SANTA CLARA BICENTENNIAL COMMITTEE; 23845 W MCBEAN PKWY; VALENCIA, CA 91355. (#104755-6).

MAY 22 - 23, '76. DISCOVERY DAYS, GOLD & OIL. TOURS OF HISTORIC SPOTS, DANCE BAND CONCERT, PICNIC AND GOLD PANNING. AT ELKS LODGE. (LOCAL). BOBBIE TRUEBLOOD, CHMN; ELKS LEGION & SANTA CLARA BICENTENNIAL COMMITTEE; 23845 W MCBEAN PKWY; VALENCIA, CA 91355. (#104755-5).

MAY 30, '76. MEMORIAL DAY SERVICE. CEREMONY AT ELKS LODGE. (LOCAL). BOBBIE TRUEBLOOD, CHMN; ELKS LEGION - MOOSE AND SANTA CLARA BICENTENNIAL COMMITTEE; 23845 W MCBEAN PKWY; VALENCIA, CA 91355. (#104755-4).

JULY 3, '76. STAKE CENTER MORMON CHOIR PATRIOTIC CONCERT. LIVE PERFORMANCE. (LOCAL). BOBBIE TRUEBLOOD, CHMN; LDS CHURCH & SANTA CLARA BICENTENNIAL COMMITTEE; 23845 W MCBEAN PKWY; VALENCIA, CA 91355. (#104755-3).

SEPT 5, '76. LANG GOLDEN SPIKE 100TH ANNIVERSARY CELEBRATION & BARECUE. THE SANTA CLARA BICENTENNIAL COMMITTEE WILL CO-SPONSOR THIS EVENT. (LOCAL). RUTH NEWHALL; SANTA CLARITA VALLEY HISTORICAL SOCIETY & MINT CANYON LIONS CLUB; SIGNAL, 6TH ST; NEWHALL, CA 91321. (#104755-2).

NOV 6, '76. SOUTHERN CALIFORNIA MORMON CHOIR CONCERT. LIVE PERFORMANCE AT STAKE CENTER. (LOCAL). BOBBIE TRUEBLOOD, CHMN; LDS CHURCH & SANTA CLARA BICENTENNIAL COMMITTEE; 23845 W MCBEAN PKWY; VALENCIA, CA 91355. (#104755-1).

CARLSBAD

CARLSBAD SPRING HOLIDAY, A FESTIVAL IN CALIFORNIA. A CITY-WIDE CELEBRATION CULMINATING IN A LARGE PARADE. FLOWER, ART, AND HOBBY SHOWS ARE FEATURED. (LOCAL). WILLIAM NICKLES, MANAGER; CARLSBAD CHAMBER OF COMMERCE; ELM AVE; CARLSBAD, CA 92008. (#6211).

APR 26 - 28, '75. A FLOWER SHOW FEATURING MANY VARIETIES OF LOCALLY-GROWN FLOWERS. PARADE, EXHIBIT. (LOCAL). WILLIAM NICKLES, MANAGER; CARLSBAD CHAMBER OF COMMERCE; ELM AVE; CARLSBAD, CA 92008. (#6211-502).

APR 26 - 28, '75. A HOBBY DISPLAY BY LOCAL RESIDENTS. PARADE, EXHIBIT. (LOCAL). WILLIAM NICKLES, MANAGER; CARLSBAD CHAMBER OF COMMERCE; ELM AVE; CARLSBAD, CA 92008. (#6211-503).

APR 26 - 28, '75. A PAINTING EXHIBIT BY LOCAL AND REGIONAL ARTISTS. PARADE, EXHIBIT. (LOCAL). WILLIAM NICKLES, MANAGER; CARLSBAD CHAMBER OF COMMERCE; ELM AVE; CARLSBAD, CA 92008. (#6211-504).

APR 26 - 28, '75. A PARADE THROUGH DOWNTOWN CARLSBAD WITH MANY BANDS, EVENTS & FLOATS. CARLSBAD SPRING HOLIDAY, A FESTIVAL IN CALIFORNIA. A CITY-WIDE CELEBRATION CULMINATING IN A LARGE PARADE. FLOWER, ART, AND HOBBY SHOWS ARE FEATURED. (LOCAL). WILLIAM NICKLES, MANAGER; CARLSBAD CHAMBER OF COMMERCE; ELM AVE; CARLSBAD, CA 92008. (#6211-501).

JAN 11 - 12, '76. UNITED STATES ARMED FORCES BICENTENNIAL CARAVAN. CARAVAN IS COMPOSED OF EXHIBIT VANS FOR EACH MILITARY SERVICE. PROJECT THEME IS 'HISTORY OF THE ARMED FORCES AND THEIR CONTRIBUTIONS TO THE NATION'. (LOCAL). MRS CONNIE LUEDTKE, SEC; US ARMED FORCES EXHIBIT VANS PROJECT; CARLSBAD CITY HALL; CARLSBAD, CA 92008. (#1775-304).

JUNE 20 - 21, '76. SERIES OF DIFFICULT MOTORCYCLE RACES W/INTERNATIONAL RIDERS. MOTORCYCLE RACES IN CARLSBAD, CALIFORNIA. MOTORCYCLE RACES WITH INTERNATIONALLY KNOWN RIDERS COMPETING FROM VARIOUS FOREIGN COUNTRIES WILL BE DESIGNATED AS THE HANG TEN UNITED STATES GRAND PRIX MOTORCROSS. (INT'L). TRIPPE - COX ASSOCIATES; HANG TEN; 2061 BUSINESS CNTR DR, SUITE 206; IRVINE, CA 92664. (#6745-501).

CARMEL

STUDY COMPARING U S PRESS FREEDOM 1791 & 1976. STUDY DIFFERENCES BETWEEN CONCEPTION OF PRESS FREEDOM AMONG FRAMERS OF FIRST AMENDMENT AND OUR CONCEPTION TODAY, ALSO COMPARE PRESS-PRESIDENCY RELATIONS IN WASH-JEFF ERA AND KENNEDY-FORD PERIOD. (NAT'L). RODERICK B HOLMGREN, PROFFESSOR; UNIV OF CALIFORNIA, DAVIS; 545 SYCAMORE LN, APT 108N; DAVIS, CA 95616. (#5388). **(??).**

MAY 6, '76. NETHERLANDS CHAMBER ORCHESTRA VISITS CARMEL. LIVE PERFORMANCE. (INT'L). WILLIAM SIMONSZ, COORD; NETHERLANDS GOVERNMENT; NETHERLANDS EMBASSY-4200 LINNEAN; WASHINGTON, DC 20008. (#109013-16).

CARMICHAEL

SOUND EXPRESS SEES AMERICA '75 IN CARMICHAEL, CA. SOUND EXPRESS, A SWING CHOIR OF 25 TEENAGERS, PRESENTING A POSITIVE IMAGE OF CALIF YOUTH ON TOUR OF THE USA, WILL BE COORDINATING THEIR PERFORMANCES AND VISITS TO SITES RELEVANT TO THE BICENTENNIAL. (ST-WIDE). MRS JOYCE LORD, DIRECTOR; SOUND EXPRESS PARENTS CLUB OF LA SIERRA HIGH SCHOOL; 5510 LINDA LANE; CARMICHAEL, CA 95608. (#9121).

CARSON VALLEY

MAR 22, '75. HISTORICAL SKI TOUR OF HOPE VALLEY-KIRKWOOD MEADOWS TRAIL. COMPETITION, AWARD, CEREMONY, TOUR. (REGN'L). CHUCK MORSE; US SKI ASSOC & FAR WEST SKI ASSOC; 1313 W 8TH ST; LOS ANGELES, CA 90017. (#2438-504).

MAR '76. HISTORICAL SKI TOUR OF HOPE VALLEY-KIRKWOOD MEADOWS TRAIL. TOURING OF HISTORICAL TRAILS OF PIONEERS OF CALIF. AT SOUTH LAKE TAHOE AREA. (LOCAL). CHUCK MORSE, EXEC ADMIN.; US SKI ASSOC & FAR WEST SKI ASSOC.; 1313 W 8TH ST; LOS ANGELES, CA 90017. (#2438-4).

CASTRO VALLEY

GIRLS OF YESTERYEAR, CASTRO VALLEY, CA. WOMEN WHO HAVE THE TALENT FOR VOICE AND THEATRE AND WANT TO DO SOMETHING ABOUT IT WILL PERFORM. (LOCAL). MAURINE COWELL, DIRECTOR; 5190 CRANE AVE; CASTRO VALLEY, CA 94546. (#13390).

RELOCATION & RESTORATION OF STANTON HOUSE - CA. THE STANTON HOUSE WILL BE RESTORED AND RELOCATED TO MAKE AVAILABLE A LEARNING CENTER FOR CHILDREN. (LOCAL). BETTY ANNABLE, PROJ DIRECTOR; CASTRO VALLEY CHAMBER OF COMMERCE; 3484 VILLAGE DR; CASTRO VALLEY, CA 94546. (#11623).

MAY 2, '76. ADOBE BRICK BUILDING - SEMINAR. SEMINAR AT CASTRO VALLEY ADOBE CENTER, 1099 E ST. (LOCAL). MONTE R HESS, DIRECTOR; CITY OF SAN PABLO; 2021 MARKET ST; SAN PABLO, CA 94806. (#106556-1).

CEDARVILLE

APPLEGATE, LASSEN & NOBELS TRAIL MARKERS - CA. RESEARCH AND PERMANENT MARKING OF THE APPLEGATE, LASSEN & NOBLES EMIGRANT TRAILS IN CALIFORNIA WITH PUBLIC BICENTENNIAL OBSERVANCE. (LOCAL). JAMES LINEBAUGH, VICE PRESIDENT; TRAILS WEST, INC; BOX 151; CEDARVILLE, CA 96104. (#16310).

CENTURY CITY

AMERICAN INDIAN CELEBRATION. A 10-DAY FESTIVAL IN AUGUST 1976 WHICH WILL INVOLVE NATIVE AMERICANS FROM THROUGHOUT THE COUNTRY. IT WILL FEATURE ALL AREAS OF NATIVE HISTORY, CULTURE, AND ARTS. (NAT'L). PEGGY OSTERMAN, PRESIDENT; AMERICAN INDIAN ART AND CULTURAL EXCHANGE; 10100 SANTA MONICA BLVD, #310; LOS ANGELES, CA 90067. (#27290). **ARBA RECOGNIZED.**

JAN - AUG '76. 'SUITE AMERICA', POP-ROCK MUSICAL PRESENTED BY 'YOUNG AMER FOR '76'. THE MUSICAL INTRODUCES THE FIRST 200 YEAR OLD MAN AND TAKES A LOOK AT HIS LIFETIME. (LOCAL). STANFORD R GAMBURG, COORD; YOUNG AMERICA FOR '76; 1888 CENTURY PK EAST, STE 1015; LOS ANGELES, CA 90067. (#102032-1).

CERRITOS

SEPT 1, '75. GRAND LAND SINGERS: 'DISCOVER YOUR AMERICA'. GRAND LAND SINGERS HAS A PROGRAM TO GET THE INDIVIDUAL, FAMILY, THE SCHOOL & ENTIRE COMMUNITY INVOLVED IN THE BICENTENNIAL. THE PROGRAM IS CALLED 'DISCOVER YOUR AMERICA'. AT INST OF RELIGION. (ST-WIDE). RONALD LEE SELLERS; INST OF RELIGION/CHURCH OF JESUS CHRIST OF LATTER DAY SAINTS; 16025 STUDEBAKER RD; CERRITOS, CA 90701. (#102906-1).

CERRITOS — CONTINUED

NOV 1, '75. CAMP FIRE GIRLS DAY AT LOS CERRITOS CENTER. FESTIVAL AT LOS CERRITOS CENTER. (LOCAL). MARY LITTLEFORD, PROJ DIR; LONG BEACH COUNCIL OF CAMP FIRE GIRLS; 7070 E CARSON ST; LONG BEACH, CA 90808. (#200006-3).

NOV 1, '75. GIRL SCOUTS BICENTENNIAL DISPLAY. EXHIBIT AT CERRITOS MALL. (LOCAL). MILDRED FRERKS, COORD; LONG BEACH GIRL SCOUT COUNCIL; 393 LOS ALTOS AVE; LONG BEACH, CA 90814. (#200006-5).

APR 10, '76. UNITED STATES ARMED FORCES BICENTENNIAL CARAVAN. CARAVAN IS COMPOSED OF EXHIBIT VANS FOR EACH MILITARY SERVICE. PROJECT THEME IS ' HISTORY OF THE ARMED FORCES & THEIR CONTRIBUTIONS TO THE NATION'. (LOCAL). MARY MARSHALL, DIRECTOR; U S ARMED FORCES BICENTENNIAL CARAVAN; 19400 S PIONEER BLVD; CERRITOS, CA 90701. (#1775-551).

CHATSWORTH

OCT 2 - 31, '76. 1976 PUMPKIN FESTIVAL. FESTIVAL AT CORNER OF NORDOFF & CANOGA. (LOCAL). JACK FARLEY, COORD; PUMPKIN FESTIVALS OF AMERICA; 1630 JANDO; TOPANGA, CA 90290. (#103416-619).

CHEMEHUEVI

APR 10 - 25, '76. ARTS AND CRAFTS FAIR AND INDIAN OLYMPICS AND GAMES. COMPETITION, FAIR AT CHEMEHUEUI RESERVATION, HAUASU LAKE, CA. (LOCAL). HERB PENCILLE, CHMN; CHEMEHUEUI, INC; 80 SOUTH LAKE, SUITE 821; PASADENA, CA 91101. (#104183-1).

CHERRY VALLEY

MONUMENT & TREE PLANTING - CHERRY VALLEY, CA. A STONE MONUMENT WAS ERECTED AND 2 REDWOOD TREES WERE PLANTED IN COMMEMORATION OF THE BICENTENNIAL. (LOCAL). MARGARET JOHNSTON, CHAIRPERSON; CHERRY VALLEY BICENTENNIAL COMMITTEE; 9634 OAK GLENN RD; CHERRY VALLEY, CA 92223. (#31278).

CHICO

UNIVERSITY MUSEUM PROJECT - CHICO, CALIFORNIA. A SPECIAL COLLECTION OF ARCHAEOLOGICAL ARTIFACTS WILL BE ON DISPLAY AT THE UNIVERSITY MUSEUM. (LOCAL). RICHARD E WILSON, COMMITTEE CHAIRMAN; CHICO STATE UNIV BICENT COMMISSION; 1ST AND NORMAL STS; CHICO, CA 95926. (#10408).

OCT 4, '75. HISTORICAL PAGEANT AND BIDWELL MANSION FAIR. STAR SPANGLED FESTIVAL IS THE THEME OF ANNUAL FIESTA RANCHO CHICO, HONORING CHICO'S FOUNDER GEN JOHN BIDWELL & HIS WIFE, ANNIE E K BIDWELL. LOCAL ORGANIZATIONS SELL ITEMS FROM BOOTHS, CONDUCT TOURS THRU BIDWELL MANSION & COLORFUL EXTRAVAGANZA IN BIDWELL BOWL IN EVENING. AT BIDWELL MANSION & GROUNDS AND BIDWELL BOWL, THE ESPLANADE DOWNTOWN. (LOCAL). MARILYN WARRENS, CHAIRMAN; LAS SENORAS OF THE GREATER CHICO CHAMBER OF COMMERCE; 2190 NORTH AVE; CHICO, CA 95926. (#200006-6).

APR 1 - 4, '76. 'THE DONNER PARTY'. LIVE PERFORMANCE AT READER'S THEATER. (LOCAL). MARILYN WARRENS, COORD; CALIFORNIA STATE UNIVERSITY'S SPEECH & DRAMA DEPT; PO BOX 3038; CHICO, CA 95927. (#102447-3).

APR 1 - 30, '76. PUBLIC SCHOOL PROGRAMS. ASSEMBLIES, PAGEANTS, INT'L FIESTA, MUSICALS, CONCERTS; ON FOLLOWING DAYS ONLY: APRIL 1, 3, 7, 22, 27-30. (LOCAL). MARILYN WARRENS, COORD; CHICO PUBLIC SCHOOLS; PO BOX 3038; CHICO, CA 95927. (#102447-6).

APR 5 - 11, '76. BUTTE COUNTY ENVIRON COUNCIL'S CHATAUQUA. SPECIFIC EMPHASIS PLACED UPON ENVIRONMENTAL EDUCATION. (LOCAL). MARILYN WARRENS, COORD; BUTTE COUNTY ENVIRONMENTAL COUNCIL; PO BOX 3038; CHICO, CA 95927. (#102447-4).

APR 24, '76. CHICO SYMPHONY GUILD POPS CONCERT. LIVE PERFORMANCE AT SILVER DOLLAR FAIRGROUNDS. (LOCAL). MARILYN WARRENS, COORD; CHICO SYMPHONY GUILD; PO BOX 3038; CHICO, CA 95927. (#102447-5).

APR 24, '76. HISTORICAL HOME TOUR & BICENTENNIAL TEA. TOUR OF FIVE OLDER HOMES, HIGH TEA AND BOUTIQUE OF HANDCRAFTS MADE BY MEMBERS. AT 5 HOMES; HIGH TEA AT COMMUNITY CENTER, 545 VALLOMBROSA AVE. (LOCAL). ROSEMARY STAPLETON; ROCKABYE CHAPTER, CHILDRENS' HOME SOCIETY; 19 YALE; CHICO, CA 95926. (#102447-2).

APR 26 - MAY 1, '76. 'GEORGE M' MUSICAL. LIVE PERFORMANCE. (LOCAL). MARILYN WARRENS, COORD; CALIFORNIA STATE UNIVERSITY'S SPEECH & DRAMA DEPT; PO BOX 3038; CHICO, CA 95927. (#102447-7).

MAY 1, '76. 'WE THE PEOPLE, OF CHICO STATE' PIONEER DAY PARADE. FOR & BY NORTHERN CA SCHOOLS & ORGANIZATIONS, CHICO SCHOOLS & CSU AT CHICO ORGANIZATIONS. AT DOWNTOWN CHICO. (LOCAL). MARILYN WARRENS, COORD; CALIFORNIA STATE UNIV; PO BOX 3038; CHICO, CA 95927. (#102447-8).

MAY 1 - 31, '76. 'LET'S COLOR CHICO RED, WHITE AND BLUE'. WORKSHOPS & SUGGESTIONS FOR CITIZENS TO PLANT GARDENS. (LOCAL). MARILYN WARRENS, COORD; CHICO JR WOMEN'S CLUB; PO BOX 3038; CHICO, CA 95927. (#102447-10).

JULY 2 - 3, '76. BIDWELL GENERALS' ANNUAL BARBERSHOP SHOW. LIVE PERFORMANCE AT PERFORMING ARTS CENTER. (LOCAL). MARILYN WARRENS, COORD; CALIFORNIA STATE UNIV; PO BOX 3038; CHICO, CA 95927. (#102447-12).

JULY 2 - 3, '76. OUR HERITAGE HISTORICAL PAGEANT. LIVE PERFORMANCE AT BIDWELL BOWL. (LOCAL). MARILYN WARRENS, COORD; LAS SENORAS OF CHICO; PO BOX 3038; CHICO, CA 95927. (#102447-11).

JULY 3, '76. 'LET FREEDOM RING' PATRIOTIC CEREMONY. CEREMONY AT BIDWELL PARK. (LOCAL). MARILYN WARRENS, COORD; CHICO BICENTENNIAL COMMITTEE; PO BOX 3038; CHICO, CA 95927. (#102447-13).

JULY 3, '76. OLD-FASHIONED INDEPENDENCE DAY CELEBRATION. FEATURING BOOTHS OF FOOD/CRAFTS OF OUR HERITAGE. PART OF CHICO'S GREAT AMERICAN INDEPENDENCE WEEKEND. AT ONE-MILE PICNIC PLAYGROUND, BIDWELL PARK. (LOCAL). MARILYN WARRENS, COORD; GREATER CHICO CHAMBER OF COMMERCE; PO BOX 3038; CHICO, CA 95927. (#102447-14).

JULY 4, '76. BAND CONCERT & DEDICATION OF NEW BANDSTAND. ALSO DURING BAND CONCERT, AWARDS FOR 'WE THE PEOPLE' CONTEST, AND CHICO'S 10 MOST INFLUENTIAL WOMEN WILL BE PRESENTED. AT CITY PLAZA. (LOCAL). MARILYN WARRENS, COORD; DOWNTOWN BUSINESS ASSOC; ARROYO FED WOMEN'S CLUB; CHICO WOMEN'S CLUB; PO BOX 3038; CHICO, CA 95927. (#102447-17).

JULY 4, '76. FIREWORKS SPECTACULAR. FESTIVAL AT MUNICIPAL AIRPORT. (LOCAL). MARILYN WARRENS, COORD; CHICO BICENTENNIAL COMMISSION; PO BOX 3038; CHICO, CA 95927. (#102447-18).

JULY 4, '76. FLY-IN. EXPERIMENTAL AIRCRAFT, AEROBATICS, JUMPING DEMONSTRATIONS. AT RANCHERO AIRPORT. (LOCAL). MARILYN WARRENS, COORD; CHICO BICENTENNIAL COMMISSION; PO BOX 3038; CHICO, CA 95927. (#102447-16).

JULY 4, '76. FREEDOM TO WORSHIP CELEBRATION. CEREMONY. (LOCAL). MARILYN WARRENS, COORD; CHICO COUNCIL OF CHURCHES; PO BOX 3038; CHICO, CA 95927. (#102447-15).

SEPT 7, '76. UNITED STATES ARMED FORCES BICENTENNIAL CARAVAN. CARAVAN IS COMPOSED OF EXHIBIT VANS FOR EACH MILITARY SERVICE. PROJECT THEME IS 'HISTORY OF THE ARMED FORCES & THEIR CONTRIBUTIONS TO THE NATION.'. (LOCAL). MS MARILYN WARRENS, CHMN; UNITED STATES ARMED FORCES BICENTENNIAL CARAVAN; 2190 NORTH AVE.; CHICO, CA 95926. (#1775-714).

CHINA LAKE

PATRIOTIC PAINT SCHEME OF CIA AIRCRAFT - CA. SQUADRON'S CIA AIRCRAFT PAINTED IN PATRIOTIC RED, WHITE AND BLUE PAINT SCHEME. LOCAL CONTEST PUBLICIZED WITH DESIGNER OF WINNING PAINT SCHEME AWARDED PRIZE AND RECOGNITION. (REGN'L). JOHN LESLIE, LT USN PUBLIC AFFAIRS OFFICER; AIR TEST AND EVALUATION SQUADRON FIVE; NAVAL AIR FACILITY; CHINA LAKE, CA 93555. (#29819).

THIS DAY IN NAVAL HISTORY - CHINA LAKE, CA. DAILY LISTING IN POD OF HISTORICAL NAVAL EVENTS SPANNING PAST 200 YRS. (LOCAL). JOHN LESLIE, LT USN PUBLIC AFFAIRS OFFICER; AIR TEST AND EVALUATION SQUADRON FIVE; NAVAL AIR FACILITY; CHINA LAKE, CA 93555. (#29820).

OCT 9, '75 - NOV 20, '76. BICENTENNIAL EVENTS AT CHINA LAKE'S NAVAL WEAPONS CENTER. 10/9-13 US NAVY 200 BIRTHDAY CELEBRATION, WITH EXHIBITS, SHOWS, TOURS, CEREMONIES; 10/30/76 BICENT SALUTE TO THE ARMED FORCES; 11/13 BICENT MUSICAL SALUTE TO AMERICA; 11/20 US MARINE CORPS BIRTHDAY CEREMONIES & FLAG PAGEANT. (LOCAL). H D PARODE, CHMN; NAVAL WEAPONS CENTER; CODE 003, PIO; CHINA LAKE, CA 93555. (#200006-529).

CHINO

MAY 7, '76. UNITED STATES ARMED FORCES BICENTENNIAL CARAVAN. CARAVAN IS COMPOSED OF EXHIBIT VANS FOR EACH MILITARY SERVICE. PROJECT THEME IS ' HISTORY OF THE ARMED FORCES & THEIR CONTRIBUTIONS TO THE NATION'. (LOCAL). BICENTENIAL CHAIRMAN; U S ARMED FORCES BICENTENNIAL CARAVAN; C/O CITY HALL; CHINO, CA 91710. (#1775-563).

CHULA VISTA

BICENTENNIAL LIBRARY OF CHULA VISTA, CALIFORNIA. CHULA VISTA PLANS NEW LIBRARY TO BE LANDMARK FOR BICENTENNIAL YEAR. (LOCAL). SIDNEY CORNELL, CHAIRMAN; CHULA VISTA BICENTENNIAL COMMITTEE; 6586 FRIARS RD, #203; SAN DIEGO, CA 92108. (#2983). **(??).**

JAN 25 - 26, '76. UNITED STATES ARMED FORCES BICENTENNIAL CARAVAN. CARAVAN IS COMPOSED OF EXHIBIT VANS FOR EACH MILITARY SERVICE. PROJECT THEME IS 'HISTORY OF THE ARMED FORCES AND THEIR CONTRIBUTIONS TO THE NATION'. (LOCAL). SIDNEY CORNELL, CHMN; US ARMED FORCES EXHIBIT VANS PROJECT; POB 1087; CHULA VISTA, CA 92012. (#1775-309).

JUNE 3 - 5, '76. 'HALLELUJAH AMERICA' - MUSICAL REVUE. SHOW WILL CONSIST OF VARIOUS SONGS, DANCES & RE-CREATIONS OF EVENTS FROM THE AMERICAN REVOLUTIONARY WAR ERA. AT MAYAN HALL, SOUTHWESTERN COLLEGE. (LOCAL). LYNN STED, COORD; COMMUNITY HOSPITAL OF CHULA VISTA; PO BOX 1297; CHULA VISTA, CA 92012. (#106804-7).

JULY 4, '76. FLOAT W/ THEME 'FREEDOM - 200' ENTERED IN CITY'S BICENTENNIAL PARADE. THE FLOAT CARRYING 'MISS NAVY- SAN DIEGO COUNTY - 1976'. DESIGNED AS AN EARLY AMERICAN SAILING VESSEL, THE FLOAT BORE THE NAME 'FREEDOM200' DRAMATIZING 200 YEARS OF AMERICAN FREEDOM. AT PARADE ROUTE: ALONG THIRD E & FOURTH STS, CHULA VISTA. (LOCAL). JESS F DRUMMER; FORCE/AREA COMMAND STAFF 1021; 1002 CREELMAN LANE; RAMONA, CA 92065. (#200006-524).

CLAREMONT

'A CITY LOOKS AT ITSELF', CLAREMONT, CA. A SERIES OF DISCUSSION GROUPS WITH A LEADER & RECORDER, INVOLVING ALL SEGMENTS OF THE COMMUNITY, EXAMINING THE STRENGTHS & WEAKNESSES OF CLAREMONT & IDENTIFYING GOALS FOR EXCELLENCE IN THE FUTURE. (LOCAL). ED MALAN, CO-CHAIRMAN; CLAREMONT BICENTENNIAL COMMITTEE; CLAREMONT, CA 91711. (#31082).

'HANDS ACROSS THE NATION' - CLAREMONT, CA. A BICENTENNIAL YEAR 'SISTER CITY' ARRANGEMENT BETWEEN CLAREMONT, CA & PRINCETON, NJ. THE CITIES WILL EXCHANGE ARTIFACTS, ART, EXHIBITS, STUDENTS, VISITORS & NATIVE TREES. (LOCAL). WILLIAM DUNSETH, VICE CHAIRMAN; CLAREMONT BICENTENNIAL COMMITTEE; 1845 ANTIOCH RD; CLAREMONT, CA 91711. (#31080).

'OPERATION POPPY SEED' - CLAREMONT, CA. CITY YOUTH DRIED & PLANTED POPPY SEEDS FOR BEAUTIFICATION OF VACANT LOTS PARKS & ROADSIDES. ALSO SHARED SEEDS WITH NEIGHBORING TOWNS & GARDEN CLUBS & WITH SISTER CITY, PRINCETON, NJ. (LOCAL). O N BATCHELLER, COORDINATOR; CLAREMONT BICENTENNIAL COMMITTEE - HORTICULTURE COMMITTEE; 137 W 7TH ST; CLAREMONT, CA 91711. (#31081).

JUNE '75 - AUG '76. CONCERTS IN THE PARKS, AMERICAN MUSIC FORMS AND STYLES. A SUMMER SERIES OF MUSICAL CONCERTS IN THE SEVERAL CITY PARKS OF CLAREMONT. DIXIELAND JAZZ, BARBERSHOP SINGING, SYMPHONY ORCHESTRA, 'BLUE GRASS', 'SOFT ROCK', ETC. HELD ON MONDAY EVENINGS. NO ADMISSION CHARGED & AUDIENCE ENCOURAGED TO BRING PICNIC SUPPERS. AT WHEELER PARK, MEMORIAL PARK, CAHUILLA PARK. (LOCAL). BEULAH R MAXWELL; PERFORMING ARTS COMM OF CLAREMONT BICENTENNIAL COMMITTEE; 146 MARYWOOD AVE; CLAREMONT, CA 91711. (#200006-403).

NOV '75 - MAR '76. 'AMERICAN IMAGE' FILM SERIES (CHAPLIN, KEATON, D W GRIFFITH, ETC). A SERIES OF 27 CLASSIC AMERICAN-MADE MOTION PICTURES SHOWN TO THE COMMUNITY ON SUNDAY EVENINGS FROM NOV 1975 THRU MARCH 1976. EACH FILM SELECTED BECAUSE OF SIGNIFICANT COMMENTARY ON AMERICAN LIFE AND MORES. AT MUDD COMMUNICATIONS BUILDING, SCHOOL OF THEOLOGY. (LOCAL). BEULAH R MAXWELL; PERFORMING ARTS COMMITTEE & ARTS FILM COUNCIL OF SCHOOL OF THEOLOGY; 146 MARYWOOD AVE; CLAREMONT, CA 91711. (#200006-402).

JUNE 4, '76. BICENTENNIAL DANCE CELEBRATION. A PERFORMANCE OF AMERICAN DANCE FORMS, REFLECTING THE INFLUENCE OF ENGLISH, SPANISH & OTHER CULTURES UPON OUR OWN. AUDIENCE PARTICIPATION, AND LESSONS FOLLOWING THE PERFORMANCE. AT TAYLOR HALL. (LOCAL). BEULAH R MAXWELL; PERFORMING ARTS COMMITTEE, CLAREMONT BICENTENNIAL COMMITTEE; 146 MARYWOOD AVE; CLAREMONT, CA 91711. (#200006-401).

CLAYTON

BOY SCOUT HISTORICAL TRAILS BADGE, CLAYTON, CA. BOY SCOUT TROOP #262 PLANS TO ACHIEVE HISTORIC TRAILS BADGE BY TRACING A PORTION OF OLD STAGE COACH ROUTE FROM DANVILLE TO CLAYTON WELLS FARGO. (LOCAL). LLOYD MUNFORT, SCOUT LEADER; BOY SCOUTS OF AMERICA TROOP #262; 5739 LAURELWOOD PL; CONCORD, CA 94521. (#9787).

CLAYTON, CA, 1975 HISTORICAL CALENDAR. THIS HISTORIC CALENDAR WAS COMPILED, RESEARCHED, PHOTOGRAPHED AND PRINTED & BOUND BY LOCAL CITIZENS. (LOCAL). CLAIRE BECKER, PRESIDENT; UPPER CLAYTON VALLEY CORPORATION; 2 KENSTON CT; CLAYTON, CA 94517. (#9785).

COMPARATIVE HISTORY STUDY OF CALIFORNIA, CLAYTON. THE STUDY WILL COVER THE PRIME BICENTENNIAL YEARS & WHAT WAS OCCURING ON THE EAST COAST; THIS WILL BE UTILIZED AS A COURSE OF STUDY FOR AMERICAN HISTORY FOR THE 5TH GRADERS IN LOCAL SCHOOL. (LOCAL). MRS JOYCE MURDOCK, COMMISSIONER; CLAYTON AMERICAN ASSOC OF UNIV WOMEN; 5858 PINE HOLLOW; CLAYTON, CA 94517. (#9784).

HISTORIC BICENTENNIAL QUILT, CLAYTON, CA. THE QUILT WILL CONTAIN PATCHES WITH SIGNATURES OF ALL THE STATE GOVERNORS, THE PRESIDENT AND VICE-PRESIDENT, AND THE OFFICIAL BICENT LOGO WILL BE IN THE CENTER; ALL PATCHES WILL BE RED, BLUE AND WHITE. (ST-WIDE). MRS BARBARA ABBOTT, BICENT COMMISSIONER; CLAYTON WOMAN'S CLUB; 5700 VERNA WAY; CLAYTON, CA 94517. (#9783).

RESTORATION OF HISTORIC JOEL-CLAYTON HOME IN CA. THE ORIGINAL JOEL CLAYTON HOME WILL BE MOVED TO THE CENTER OF CLAYTON WHERE IT WILL BE RESTORED; IT WILL HOUSE THE FUTURE HISTORICAL SOCIETY. (LOCAL). MRS NAN WALLACE, PRESIDENT; CLAYTON HISTORICAL SOCIETY; 6000 MAIN ST; CLAYTON, CA 94517. (#9786).

NOV 7, '75. RESTORED TAVERN RECOGNITION. CEREMONY HONORS THE RESTORATION OF RESTAURANT LA COCOTTE; IT WAS A FORMER GROWLER TAVERN DURING THE COAL-MINING

CLAYTON — CONTINUED

ERA. AT LA COCOTTE RESTAURANT. (LOCAL). GEORGE SALAS, OWNER; CLAYTON BICENTENNIAL COMMISSION & GEORGE SALAS; 6115 MAIN ST; CLAYTON, CA 94517. (#200006-1).

JULY 4, '76. OLD-FASHIONED 4TH OF JULY. THERE WILL BE A REVIVAL OF THE 4TH OF JULY CELEBRATIONS WITH ACTIVITIES DATING AS FAR BACK AS 1896; MAIN EMPHASIS WILL BE ON CHILDREN; GAMES, PARADES AND CONCESSIONS HAVE BEEN PLANNED. (LOCAL). LTC CHARLES A FARREN; CLAYTON 4TH OF JULY COMMITTEE; 33 HERRIMAN; CLAYTON, CA 94517. (#9782-1).

CLOVERDALE

RAILROAD DEPOT BUILDING IN CLOVERDALE, CA. RELOCATE AND PRESERVE 104 YR OLD BUILDING FOR MUSEUM AND ART CENTER. (LOCAL). MARIE HILL, BICENTENNIAL CHAIRMAN; CLOVERDALE BICENTENNIAL COMMITTEE; PO BOX 187; CLOVERDALE, CA 95425. (#8511).

JUNE 14, '75. FLAG DAY FESTIVAL BICENTENNIAL KICKOFF EVENT. FESTIVAL, PARADE, EXHIBIT AT CITRUS FAIR PAVILION. (LOCAL). MARIE HILL; CLOVERDALE BICENTENNIAL COMMITTEE; PO BOX 187; CLOVERDALE, CA 95425. (#50319-2).

SEPT 26 - 27, '75. BICENTENNIAL WAGON VISIT. TOUR AT CLOVERDALE CITY PARK. (LOCAL). MARIE HILL, DIRECTOR; CLOVERDALE BICENT COMMITTEE; PO BOX 187; CLOVERDALE, CA 95425. (#10695-1).

OCT 1, '76. UNITED STATES ARMED FORCES BICENTENNIAL CARAVAN. CARAVAN IS COMPOSED OF EXHIBIT VANS FOR EACH MILITARY SERVICE. PROJECT THEME IS 'HISTORY OF THE ARMED FORCES & THEIR CONTRIBUTIONS TO THE NATION'. (LOCAL). DAVE HOWELL; UNITED STATES ARMED FORCES BICENTENNIAL CARAVAN; 124 N COVERDALE; CLOVERDALE, CA 95425. (#1775-817).

CLOVIS

BICENTENNIAL DECALS - CLOVIS, CA. ADHESIVE DECALS FOR USE ON ENVELOPES OF OUTGOING CITY MAIL. (LOCAL). STANLEY E KING, CHAIRMAN; CITY OF CLOVIS AND CLOVIS BICENTENNIAL COMMITTEE; 533 POLLASKY AVE; CLOVIS, CA 93612. (#20610).

DEDICATION OF NAME PLAQUE. DEDICATE NAME PLAQUE FOR TREASURE-INGMIRE PARK, THE FIRST CITY PARK. (LOCAL). STANLEY E KING, CHAIRMAN; CLOVIS BICENTENNIAL COMMITTEE; 533 POLLASKY AVE; CLOVIS, CA 93612. (#104850-2). **(??).**

FIRE HYDRANT PAINTING - CLOVIS, CA. PAINT FIRE HYDRANTS AS SOLDIERS IN BUSINESS AREA. (LOCAL). ALLEN L GOODMAN; CLOVIS JOBS DAUGHTERS; 533 POLLASKY AVE; CLOVIS, CA 93612. (#20611).

HISTORY LIST AND MAP OF OLD HOMES - CLOVIS, CA. HISTORY LIST AND MAP OF OLD HOMES FOR DISTRIBUTION. (LOCAL). GEORGE KASTNER, MEMBER; CLOVIS BICENTENNIAL COMMITTEE; 533 POLLASKY AVE; CLOVIS, CA 93612. (#20613).

PAINT WATER TOWER - CLOVIS, CA. PAINT WATER TOWER IN DOWNTOWN CLOVIS RED, WHITE AND BLUE WITH '76'. (LOCAL). ALLEN L GOODMAN, CITY MANAGER; CITY OF CLOVIS; 533 POLLASKY AVE; CLOVIS, CA 93612. (#20612).

TOWN MEETING AND PARK. THE ALL-DAY AFFAIR WILL INCLUDE A PICNIC, PROGRAMS AND COMMUNITY SING IN THE EVENING. (LOCAL). STANLEY E KING, CHAIRMAN; CLOVIS BICENTENNIAL COMMITTEE; 533 POLLASKY AVE; CLOVIS, CA 93612. (#104850-3). **(??).**

AUG 22 - 24, '75. NATIONAL MASTERS OUTDOOR DIVING CHAMPIONSHIP. COMPETITION AT CLOVIS HIGH SCHOOL DIVING POOL, 5550 N FOWLER. (NAT'L). STANLEY E KING; NATIONAL AMATEUR ATHLETIC ASSOC; 533 POLLASKY AVE; CLOVIS, CA 93612. (#200006-2).

JULY 4, '76. DEDICATION OF NEW CLOVIS CIVIC CENTER. THE SPACIOUS NEW CIVIC CENTER WILL REPLACE OLD BUILDINGS AND CONSOLIDATE CIVIC SERVICES IN ONE LOCATION. (LOCAL). ALLEN L GOODMAN, MANAGER; CITY OF CLOVIS; 533 POLLASKY AVE; CLOVIS, CA 93612. (#104850-4).

JULY 4, '76. JULY 4TH CELEBRATION. FESTIVAL AT CLOVIS HIGH SCHOOL STADIUM, 5550 N FOWLER. (LOCAL). STANLEY E KING, PROJ DIR; CITY OF CLOVIS AND CLOVIS BICENTENNIAL COMMITTEE; 533 POLLASKY AVE; CLOVIS, CA 93612. (#104850-1).

OCT 16, '76. UNITED STATES ARMED FORCES BICENTENNIAL CARAVAN. CARAVAN IS COMPOSED OF EXHIBIT VANS FOR EACH MILITARY SERVICE. PROJECT THEME IS 'HISTORY OF THE ARMED FORCES & THEIR CONTRIBUTIONS TO THE NATION'. (LOCAL). STAN KING; UNITED STATES ARMED FORCES BICENTENNIAL CARAVAN; CLOVIS CITY HALL; CLOVIS, CA 93612. (#1775-826).

COALINGA

FILMS AND DINNERS ON ETHNIC GROUPS IN AMERICA - CA. DINNERS ARE SERVED TYPICAL OF ETHNIC GROUPS IN AMERICA. THEN FILMS ARE SHOWN OF ETHNICS HOME COUNTRY. (LOCAL). JERRY CASKEY, CHAIRMAN BICENTENNIAL FORUM; WEST HILLS COMMUNITY COLLEGE; 300 CHERRY LANE; COALINGA, CA 93210. (#32306).

MAKING OF PATRIOTIC PLAQUE PERMANENT PLACEMENT - C. STUDENT INVOLVEMENT IN MAKING PERMANENT BRONZED PLAQUE FOR INSTALLATION IN FOYER OF ADMINISTRATION BUILDING. (LOCAL). JERRY CASKEY, CHAIRMAN BICENTENNIAL FORUM; WEST HILLS COLLEGE; 300 CHERRY LANE; COALINGA, CA 93210. (#32307).

JAN 8, '76. PRESENTATION OF BICENTENNIAL FLAG AND PLAQUE. CEREMONY AT FLAGPOLE QUAD. (LOCAL). GERALD C CASKEY; WEST HILLS COLLEGE BICENTENNIAL FORUM; 300 CHERRY LANE; COALINGA, CA 93210. (#200006-414).

AUG 28, '76. VARIETY SHOW. LIVE PERFORMANCE AT SPEECH ARTS BUILDING THEATER. (LOCAL). GERALD C CASKEY; WEST HILLS COLLEGE; 300 CHERRY LANE; COALINGA, CA 93210. (#200006-413).

OCT 18, '76. UNITED STATES ARMED FORCES BICENTENNIAL CARAVAN. CARAVAN IS COMPOSED OF EXHIBIT VANS FOR EACH MILITARY SERVICE. PROJECT THEME IS 'HISTORY OF THE ARMED FORCES & THEIR CONTRIBUTIONS TO THE NATION'. (LOCAL). AUDREY B ACEBEDO; UNITED STATES ARMED FORCES BICENTENNIAL CARAVAN; PO 573-C/O BICENT COMM; COALINGA, CA 93210. (#1775-827).

COLTON

APR 6, '76. UNITED STATES ARMED FORCES BICENTENNIAL CARAVAN. CARAVAN IS COMPOSED OF EXHIBIT VANS FOR EACH MILITARY SERVICE. PROJECT THEME IS ' HISTORY OF THE ARMED FORCES & THEIR CONTRIBUTIONS TO THE NATION'. AT FLEMMING PARK, ON F ST BETWEEN LA CADENA DR AND 7TH STREET. (LOCAL). RANDY JOHNSEN; US ARMED FORCES BICENTENNIAL CARAVAN; COLTON BICENTENNIAL COMM; 650 N LA CADENA DR; COLTON, CA 92324. (#1775-548).

COMMERCE

LIBERTY TREE PLANTING PROJECT, COMMERCE, CA. SEQUOIA TREES WILL BE PLANTED IN REDWOOD PARK, VETERANS MEMORIAL PARK, BANDIHI PARK & AT THE SENIORS CENTER. (LOCAL). LUCY MAESE, COORDINATOR; CITY OF COMMERCE COORDINATING COMMITTEE; 2432 SENTA; COMMERCE, CA 90040. (#28616).

APR 23, '76. YOUTH SALUTES AMERICA. LIVE PERFORMANCE AT GREAT WESTERN EXHIBIT CENTER. (LOCAL). LUCY MAESE, CHAIRMAN; CITY OF COMMERCE COORDINATING COMMITTEE; 2432 SENTA AVE; COMMERCE, CA 90040. (#200006-374).

JULY 4, '76. JULY FOURTH PARADE. FESTIVAL AT ROSEWOOD PARK. (LOCAL). LUCY MAESE, CHAIRMAN; CITY OF COMMERCE BICENTENNIAL COMMITTEE; 2432 SENTA AVE; COMMERCE, CA 90040. (#200006-373).

JULY 13, '76. FLAGPOLE & TIME CAPSULE DEDICATION. CEREMONY AT HERITAGE PARK. (LOCAL). LUCY MAESE, CHAIRMAN; CITY OF COMMERCE COORDINATING COMMITTEE; 2432 SENTA AVE; COMMERCE, CA 90040. (#200006-375).

NOV 7, '76. VETERANS' MEMORIAL PARK DEDICATION. CEREMONY. (LOCAL). LUCY MAESE, CHAIRPERSON; CITY OF COMMERCE COORDINATING COMMITTEE; 2432 SENTA; COMMERCE, CA 90040. (#109330-2).

JULY 4, '77. VIETNAM VETERANS COMMEMORATION. CEREMONY. (LOCAL). LUCY MAESE, CHAIRPERSON; CITY OF COMMERCE COORDINATING COMMITTEE; 2432 SENTA; COMMERCE, CA 90040. (#109330-1).

COMPTON

AUG 15 - 31, '75. 'KINGS & QUEENS TO WHO KNOWS WHAT'. WRITE & PRODUCE THEATRICAL PRESENTATION DEPICTING MINORITY & YOUTH CONTRIBUTIONS TO GROWTH OF AMERICA, ESPECIALLY DURING THE AMERICAN REVOLUTION. SUN 3PM MATINEE. (LOCAL). ROBERT BROWNING; PAUL ROBESON PLAYERS; 401 N BULLIS RD; COMPTON, CA 90221. (#10877-1).

AUG 30, '75. PAUL ROBESON PLAYERS BICENTENNIAL COMMEMORATION. THERE WILL BE A CONCERT, ART SHOW, FASHION SHOW AND A HISTORICAL PLAY 'KINGS AND QUEENS' TO BE PERFORMED BY THE AWARD WINNING PAUL ROBESON PLAYERS AT COMPTON HIGH SCHOOL, 601 S ACACIA. AT COMPTON COLLEGE, 1111 E ARTESIA BLVD. (LOCAL). ROBERT BROWNING, EXEC DIR; PAUL ROBESON PLAYERS; 401 N BULLIS RD; COMPTON, CA 90221. (#101451-1).

JAN 14 - 15, '76. SCREENING OF 'MARTIN LUTHER KING: THE MAN AND THE MARCH'. EXHIBIT. (LOCAL). ULIS C WILLIAMS, CHMN; COMPTON COMMUNITY COLLEGE; 1111 E ARTESIA BLVD; COMPTON, CA 90221. (#200006-342).

APR 25, '76. TRIBUTE TO THE AMERICAN INDIAN. AN OUTDOOR PERFORMANCE OF THE FRED SWEETWATER NATIVE AMERICAN DANCERS. WILL DISPLAY AUTHENTIC TRIBAL COSTUMES & RITUALS WITH AUDIENCE PARTICIPATION INVITED. AT COLLEGE CAMPUS. (LOCAL). ULIS C WILLIAMS, CHMN; COMPTON COMMUNITY COLLEGE BICENTENNIAL COMMITTEE; 1111 E ARTESIA BLVD; COMPTON, CA 90221. (#200006-531).

CONCORD

BICENTENNIAL PARK - CONCORD, CALIFORNIA. A NEW 100 ACRE COMMUNITY PARK DEDICATED AS THE NEWHALL BICENTENNIAL PARK. THE PARK WILL OPEN IN 1976. IT ALREADY FEATURES A VIETNAM VETERAN'S GROVE ON ITS HIGHEST KNOLL. (LOCAL). HALE CAVANAGH, PARK DIRECTOR; CITY OF CONCORD; 1950 PARKSIDE DR; CONCORD, CA 94519. (#5078).

HISTORICAL FLAG EXHIBIT IN CONCORD, CALIFORNIA. A COLLECTION OF 12 HISTORICAL AMERICAN FLAGS WILL BE FLOWN AROUND TODOS SANTOS PLAZA. EACH FLAG WILL HAVE A PERMANENT, BUT MOVABLE, FLAGPOLE AND A DESCRIPTIVE PLAQUE. (LOCAL). JERRY WENTLING, COORDINATOR; CONCORD BICENTENNIAL COMMITTEE; 1950 PARKSIDE DR; CONCORD, CA 94519. (#5077).

LANDMARK PRESERVATION IN CONCORD, CALIF. PRESERVATION AND RESTORATION OF HISTORIC CONCORD BUILDINGS. (LOCAL). CARL JEFFERSON, CHAIRMAN; CONCORD BICENTENNIAL COMMITTEE; 2820 WILLOW PASS; CONCORD, CA 94520. (#2303).

OPEN SPACE PROJECT OF CONCORD, CALIF. PRESERVATION OF LAND FOR OPEN SPACE, EMPHASIZING RURAL HERITAGE AND PLEASING ENVIRONMENT FOR FUTURE GENERATIONS. (LOCAL). CARL JEFFERSON, CHAIRMAN; CONCORD BICENTENNIAL COMMISSION; 2820 WILLOW PASS; CONCORD, CA 94520. (#2304). **(??).**

JULY 4 - 5, '75. PRODUCTION OF AN ORIGINAL MUSICAL WITH COLONIAL THEME. BICENTENNIAL MUSICAL HAPPENING IN CONCORD, CALIF. A LOCAL WRITER-COMPOSER IS WRITING AND WILL PRODUCE A MUSICAL ON A COLONIAL THEME. THE PRODUCTION WILL BE STAGED AT THE CONCORD PAVILION ON JULY 4TH & 5TH, 1975. (LOCAL). DOUG GIEBEL, COMPOSER; CONCORD BICENTENNIAL COMMITTEE; 1950 PARKSIDE DR; CONCORD, CA 94519. (#5079-501).

AUG 26, '76. ISRAELI PHILHARMONIC ORCHESTRA VISITS CONCORD. LIVE PERFORMANCE. (INT'L). URI AHARON BAR-NEV; ISRAELI GOVERNMENT; 1621 21ST ST, NW; WASHINGTON, DC 20008. (#109015-2).

CORNING

SEPT 17, '75. WAGON TRAIN PILGRIMAGE. PARADE, AWARD. (LOCAL). MS DOROTHY CRAIG, CHMN; CORNING BICENTENNIAL COMMITTEE; 816 THOMES AVE; CORNING, CA 96021. (#101751-1).

OCT 12 - 19, '75. HERITAGE WEEK. FESTIVITIES INCLUDE: BALLOON RACE, HOMECOMING, PARADE, FOOTBALL GAME, OLIVE FESTIVAL, FASHION SHOW, MUSICAL, FIESTA, SPECIAL WORSHIP SERVICES, ETC. AT MEMORIAL HALL, AIRPORT, SOLANO ST. (LOCAL). MS DOROTHY CRAIG, CHMN; CORNING BICENTENNIAL COMMITTEE; 816 THOMES AVE; CORNING, CA 96021. (#101750-1).

CORONADO

CORONADO, CA, HISTORICAL TOUR GUIDE BROCHURE. BROCHURE, COMPILED BY 2 LOCAL HISTORIANS, LISTS 86 HISTORIC SITES IN CITY; INCLUDES A MAP & GIVES BRIEF BACKGROUND MATERIAL ON THESE POINTS OF INTEREST. (LOCAL). MRS K E CARLIN, CHAIRMAN, ARTIFACTS & RECORDS; CORONADO HISTORICAL ASSOC, INC; PO BOX 393; CORONADO, CA 92118. (#12323).

DISPLAY CASE FOR NEW PUBLIC LIBRARY, CORONADO, CA. PRESENTATION OF A NEW DISPLAY CASE TO PUBLIC LIBRARY; IT WILL HOUSE DISPLAY OF HISTORICAL ASSOCIATION ARTIFACTS. (LOCAL). MRS KATHERINE CARLIN, CHAIRMAN; CORONADO HISTORICAL ASSOCIATION, INC; PO BOX 393; CORONADO, CA 92118. (#13983).

HISTORICAL SITE TOUR AND BROCHURE. TOUR AT CITYWIDE. (LOCAL). MRS V E CARLIN; CORONADO HISTORICAL ASSN; 1030 GLORIETTA BLVD; CORONADO, CA 92118. (#50626-1).

HOME TOUR BROCHURE, CORONADO, CA. A BROCHURE OF TOUR ROUTE OF SELECTED (86) HOMES OF HISTORICAL INTEREST WITH DESCRIPTIONS, PICTURES AND A MAP DESIGNATING LOCATIONS OF HOMES. (LOCAL). MRS KATHERINE CARLIN, CHAIRMAN; CORONADO HISTORICAL ASSOCIATION, INC; PO BOX 393; CORONADO, CA 92118. (#13985).

INDEPENDENCE PARK IN CORONADO, CALIFORNIA. A 30 ACRE REGIONAL PARK INCLUDING SWIMMING, A BEACH, BIKE PATHS, SPORTS FIELDS, PICNIC AREAS, SENIOR CITIZEN FACILITIES AND LANDSCAPED OPEN SPACE. LOCATION IS AT ENTRANCE TO CITY OF CORONADO. (LOCAL). JACK LOHMAN, DIRECTOR OF COMMUNITY DEVELOPMENT; CITY OF CORONADO; 1825 ST RAND WAY; CORONADO, CA 92118. (#9123).

LANDSCAPING IN CORONADO, CA. REPLACE TREES ON PARKWAY. (LOCAL). M P DAVIS, CHAIRMAN; CORONADO BEAUTIFUL COMMITTEE; 947 ALAMEDA BLVD; CORONADO, CA 92118. (#10624).

ORAL HISTORY PROJECT, CORONADO, CA. TAPED INTERVIEWS OF EARLY CORONADO CITIZENS CONDUCTED BY 'GIFTED CHILDREN'S' ELEMENTARY CLASS. (LOCAL). MRS KATHERINE CARLIN, CHAIRMAN; CORONADO HISTORICAL ASSOCIATION, INC; PO BOX 393; CORONADO, CA 92118. (#13987).

PRESENTATION OF PLAQUES IN CORONADO, CA. BRONZE PLAQUES ARE BEING PLACED ON BUILDINGS AND HOMES OF HISTORICAL OR ARCHITECTURAL SIGNIFICANCE. (LOCAL). MRS KATHERINE CARLIN, CHAIRMAN; CORONADO HISTORICAL ASSOCIATION, INC; PO BOX 393; CORONADO, CA 92118. (#13984).

SLIDES OF CORONADO, CA. EXTENSIVE COLLECTION OF SLIDES MADE FROM OLD PHOTOS SHOWING ALL PHASES OF EARLY LIFE IN CORONADO. (LOCAL). MRS KATHERINE CARLIN, CHAIRMAN; CORONADO HISTORICAL ASSOCIATION, INC; PO BOX 393; CORONADO, CA 92118. (#13986).

SPRECKLES PARK BANDSTAND IN CORONADO, CA. BANDSTAND TO BE BUILT IN PARK FOR CONCERTS & OTHER ACTIVITIES. (LOCAL). MRS ROBERT HOPPE, PRESIDENT; SOROPTIMIST INTERNATIONAL OF CORONADO; 741 CABRILLO AVE; CORONADO, CA 92118. (#10623).

CORONADO — CONTINUED

OCT 10, '75. BICENTENNIAL INAUGURAL CEREMONY. SPECIAL WARFARE STATIC DISPLAYS & FLOAT. AT NAB CORONADO. (LOCAL). JOE T SIEGLER; NAVAL SPECIAL WARFARE GROUP ONE; NAB CORONADO NAVSPECWARGRU ONE; SAN DIEGO, CA 92155. (#200006-508).

OCT 11 - 13, '75. NAVY BICENTENNIAL FAIR SPONSORED BY UDT 11. FAIR, PARADE AT USNAB CORONADO. (LOCAL). CDR CRAIG E DORMAN, CO; UDT ELEVEN; UDT ELEVEN USNAB CORONADO; SAN DIEGO, CA 92155. (#200006-511).

JAN 23 - 24, '76. UNITED STATES ARMED FORCES BICENTENNIAL CARAVAN. CARAVAN IS COMPOSED OF EXHIBIT VANS FOR EACH MILITARY SERVICE. PROJECT THEME IS 'HISTORY OF THE ARMED FORCES AND THEIR CONTRIBUTIONS TO THE NATION'. (LOCAL). MRS ROBT HOPPE, CHMN; US ARMED FORCES EXHIBIT VANS PROJECT; BOX 67; CORONADO, CA 92118. (#1775-308).

APR 15 - MAY 23, '76. ALL MEDIA ART CONTEST FOR SCHOOLCHILDREN. TO DEVELOP AWARENESS OF HERITAGE. OPEN DURING LIBRARY HOURS. JUDGING APRIL 15TH; EXHIBIT MAY 15 - MAY 23RD. AT CORONADO PUBLIC LIBRARY. (LOCAL). MRS FRANK CURTIS; CORONADO ART ASSN; 250 I AVENUE; CORONADO, CA 92118. (#50648-1).

MAY 1, '76. FLOWER SHOW. COMPETITION, EXHIBIT AT SPRECKERS PARK, ORANGE AVE BETWEEN 6TH & 7TH STS.. (LOCAL). CAPT BENNETT WRIGHT; CORONADO FLORAL ASSN; 411 TENTH ST; CORONADO, CA 92118. (#50625-1).

MAY 8, '76. STARS AND STRIPES FASHION SHOW. SLIDE PRESENTATION OF 200 YRS OF AMERICAN FASHIONS, CRAFT TABLE, SIX MODELS WITH AUTHENTIC DRESS FROM 1776 TO 1910, THREE MINUTE ORATION FROM EACH MODEL ABOUT HER DRESS & FAMOUS WOMEN OF HER ERA. AT CORONADO WOMEN'S CLUB. (LOCAL). ILA LAING; CORONADO JUNIOR WOMAN'S CLUB; 337 G AVE; CORONADO, CA 92118. (#50622-2).

MAY 31, '76. MARINE FLAG PAGEANT. CEREMONY AT SPRECKELS PARK BETWEEN 6TH & 7TH ON ORANGE AVE 11:00 AM. (LOCAL). MRS JERRY STRAYER; COLONIAL DAMES OF THE 17TH CENTURY; 1627 MIGUEL AVE; CORONADO, CA 92118. (#50627-1).

MAY '76. CORONETS COSTUME BALL. FESTIVAL AT HOTEL DEL CORONADO BALLROOM. (LOCAL). MRS VIRGINIA GARDNER; CORONETS, AUXILARY TO THE CORONADO PLAYHOUSE; 630 B AVE; CORONADO, CA 92118. (#50623-1).

JUNE 22, '76. SPECIAL WARFARE DEMONSTRATION. DEMONSTRATIONS BY THE NAVY PARACHUTE TEAM, UNDERWATER DEMOLITION TEAMS & SEAL TEAM IN PARACHUTE PRECISION JUMPING AND WATER RESCUE & PARADROP EXERCISES. (LOCAL). JOE T SEIGLER; NAVAL SPECIAL WARFARE GROUP ONE; NAVSPECWARGRU; CORONADO, CA 92155. (#200006-507).

JULY 4, '76. FOURTH OF JULY CELEBRATION. PARADE, NAVY, NAVY SHOW, FIREWORKS, ETC. AT OPEN AIR-ORANGE AVENUE AND GLORIETTA BAY. (LOCAL). WILLARD E. EDER; CITIZENS COMMITTEE FOR CORONADO FOURTH OF JULY CELEBRATION, INC.; BOX 541; CORONADO, CA 92118. (#50617-1).

JULY 4, '76. INVITATIONAL REGATTA - POP COWLEY MEMORIAL BICENTENNIAL RACE. COMPETITION AT YACHT CLUB, STRAND WAY - GLORIETTA BAY. (LOCAL). ADMIRAL JACK COY; CORONADO YACHT CLUB; 681 GUADALUPE AVE; CORONADO, CA 92118. (#50621-1).

JULY 5, '76. CITY OF CORONADO DAY. USN PARACHUTE TEAM DEMONSTRATION; STATIC DISPLAYS; PARADE FLOAT; UDT & SEAL TEAM DEMONSTRATION. (LOCAL). JOE T SEIGLER; CITY OF CORONADO; NAVSPECWARGRU ONE NAB CORONADO; SAN DIEGO, CA 92155. (#200006-506).

JULY 5, '76. CORONADO INDEPENDENCE DAY PARADE & DEMONSTRATION. UDT/SEAL DEMONSTRATION - PARACHUTING. AT USNAR CORONADO. (LOCAL). CDR CRAIG E DORMAN, CO; UDT ELEVEN; UDT ELEVEN USNAB CORONADO; SAN DIEGO, CA 92155. (#200006-505).

JULY 20, '76. INVITATIONAL GOLF TOURNAMENT-THEME: 'HORIZONS OF GOLF'. WOMEN'S GOLF CLUB IS PLANNING INVITATIONAL TOURNAMENT FOR THE BICENTENNIAL. AT CORONADO MUNICIPAL GOLF COURSE. (LOCAL). VET PRASSINOS; CORONADO WOMEN'S GOLF ASSOCIATION; 610 TENTH STREET; CORONADO, CA 92118. (#2976-1).

JULY 24 - 25, '76. SPORTS FESTIVAL. MISC COMPETITIVE SPORTS EVENTS FOR YOUTH. AT OPEN AIR IN PARKS, PLAYGROUNDS AND BEACHES. (LOCAL). CAPTAIN DAVE NASH; CORONADO OPTIMIST CLUB; 845 J AVE; CORONADO, CA 92118. (#50616-1).

AUG 22, '76. SAND CASTLE BUILDING CONTEST. COMPETITION, EXHIBIT AT CENTRAL BEACH. (LOCAL). ILA LAING; CORONADO JUNIOR WOMAN'S CLUB; 337 G AVE; CORONADO, CA 92118. (#50622-1).

NOV 17, '76. HOME TOUR. GUIDED TOUR OF SELECTED CORONADO HOMES. OF 04/22/75. AT CITYWIDE AND COUNTYWIDE. (LOCAL). GLORIA BAILEY; CORONADO WOMAN'S CLUB; 725 ADELLA AVE; CORONADO, CA 92118. (#50620-1).

CORTE MADERA

JULY 3 - 4, '76. LARKSPUR-CORTE MADERA FOURTH OF JULY CELEBRATION. FAIR, FESTIVAL, PARADE AT THROUGHOUT LARKSPUR & CORTE-MADERA. (LOCAL). CAROL PASQUINELLI, DIR; LARKSPUR-CORTE MADERA CHAMBERS OF COMMERCE; 500 TAMALPHAIS; CORTE MADERA, CA 94925. (#103070-1).

COSTA MESA

BICENTENNIAL BOOK ABOUT ORANGE COUNTY, CALIFORNIA. SPECIAL BICENTENNIAL ISSUE OF 'A SLICE OF ORANGE' ON THE HISTORY OF COSTA MESA AND ORANGE COUNTY. (LOCAL). DON BULL, CHAIRMAN; U S BICENTENNIAL COMMITTEE OF COSTA MESA CALIFORNIA; PO BOX 1564; COSTA MESA, CA 92626. (#5831).

BICENTENNIAL GAZETTE PROJ OF COSTA MESA, CA. A QUARTERLY FOCUS ON SPANISH-CALIFORNIA HISTORY AND ITS RELATIONSHIP TO U S HISTORY OF THE REVOLUTIONARY ERA. GAZETTE WILL ALSO GIVE NEWS AND ANNOUNCEMENTS OF BICENTENNIAL ACTIVITIES. (LOCAL). DON BULL, CHAIRMAN; U S BICENTENNIAL COMMITTEE OF COSTA MESA CALIFORNIA; PO BOX 1564; COSTA MESA, CA 92626. (#5836).

ESSAY CONTEST ON CITIZENSHIP IN COSTA MESA, CA. ESSAY CONTEST FOR LOCAL HIGH SCHOOL STUDENTS W/TWO WINNERS RECEIVING TRIP TO WASHINGTON, DC. (LOCAL). DON BULL, CHAIRMAN; U S BICENTENNIAL COMMITTEE OF COSTA MESA CALIFORNIA; PO BOX 1564; COSTA MESA, CA 92626. (#5829).

ESTANCIA ADOBE OIL PAINTING PROJ OF COSTA MESA, CA. OIL PAINTING OF HISTORIC LANDMARK THE ESTANCIA ADOBE DWELLING. THE PAINTING WAS COMMISSIONED FOR THE BICENTENNIAL. (LOCAL). DON BULL, CHAIRMAN; U S BICENTENNIAL COMMITTEE OF COSTA MESA CALIFORNIA; PO BOX 1564; COSTA MESA, CA 92626. (#5837).

LECTURE SERIES ON HISTORY OF SOUTHERN CALIFORNIA. HISTORY SERIES WILL RELATE TO THE REVOLUTIONARY ERA. (LOCAL). DON BULL, CHAIRMAN; U S BICENTENNIAL COMMITTEE OF COSTA MESA CALIFORNIA; PO BOX 1564; COSTA MESA, CA 92626. (#5827).

MOVING PICTURE DISPLAY IN COSTA MESA, CALIFORNIA. DISPLAY OF PHOTOS OF OLD COSTA MESA SET UP AT DIFFERENT TIMES AND PLACES THROUGHOUT THE CITY. (LOCAL). DON BULL, CHAIRMAN; U S BICENTENNIAL COMMITTEE OF COSTA MESA CALIFORNIA; PO BOX 1564; COSTA MESA, CA 92626. (#5830).

MAY 1 - 15, '75. DISPLAY OF OLD ORANGE COUNTY PHOTOGRAPHS. DISPLAYED IN BOOTH AT THE ORANGE COUNTY FAIR. BICENTENNIAL LITERATUTE ALSO AVAILABLE. (LOCAL). DON BULL, CHAIRMAN; U S BICENTENNIAL COMMITTEE OF COSTA MESA CALIFORNIA; PO BOX 1564; COSTA MESA, CA 92626. (#5832-501).

JUNE 21, '75. PRESENT AWARDS TO AMERICANIZATION CLASS. CERTIFICATES AWARDED TO FUTURE CITIZENS OF GRADUATING AMERICANIZATION CLASS. (LOCAL). DON BULL, CHAIRMAN; BICENTENNIAL COMMITTEE OF COSTA MESA CALIFORNIA; PO BOX 1664; COSTA MESA, CA 92626. (#5833-501).

JULY 4, '75. 4TH OF JULY CELEBRATION, WITH FIREWORKS, PICNIC & PARADE. FESTIVAL, LIVE PERFORMANCE, PARADE. (LOCAL). DON BULL, CHAIRMAN; U S BICENTENNIAL COMMITTEE OF COSTA MESA CALIFORNIA; PO BOX 1664; COSTA MESA, CA 92626. (#5835-501).

COTATI

WOMEN'S HISTORY MEDIA PROJECT, COTATI, CA. MULTI-MEDIA PRESENTATION ON WOMEN'S HISTORY WITH EMPHASIS ON CALIFORNIA. (LOCAL). MS SUSAN TELLER, CHAIRMAN; WOMEN'S HISTORY MEDIA GROUP; 615 SCHOOL ST; COTATI, CA 94928. (#9603).

COVINA

AUG 14, '76. CITY OF COVINA, & U S BIRTHDAY PARTY-PICNIC. FESTIVAL AT COVINA CITY PARK. (LOCAL). SURVILLA GRAHAM, CHMN; COVINA BICENTENNIAL COMMITTEE; 1567 E PUENTE; COVINA, CA 91724. (#200006-356).

CP PENDLETON

USMC CAMP PENDELTON HISTORICAL/ECOLOGICAL TOUR, CA. SELF-GUIDE TOUR OF USMC CP PENDELTON & 1ST MARINE DIVISION, OPENED DURING ARMED FORCES WEEK, MAY 8-15. TOUR INCLUDES SPANISH & MEXICAN HISTORICAL SITES, MISSION RUINS & EL CAMINO REAL. (LOCAL). LT COL D W BROWN, DIRECTOR; JOINT PUBLIC AFFAIRS OFFICE; CP PENDELTON, CA 92005. (#25211).

MAY 8 - DEC 31, '76. MARINE CORPS BASE CAMP PENDLETON SELF-GUIDED AUTOMOBILE TOUR. TOUR INCLUDES A STOP AT AN AMPHIBIAN VEHICLE MUSEUM WITH EQUIPMENT PREDATING WORLD WAR 2. AT TOUR COMMENCES AT THE MAIN GATE OFF IS-5 1 MILE NORTH OF OCEANSIDE. (LOCAL). MAJ J H HANSON; MARINE CORPS BASE CAMP PENDLETON - JOINT PUBLIC AFFAIRS OFFICE; CAMP PENDELTN, CA 92055. (#109334-1).

MAY 8 - DEC 31, '76. USMC CAMP PENDLETON HISTORICAL/ECOLOGICAL TOUR. THE FREE TOUR IS OPEN TO THE PUBLIC ALL YEAR OF 1976; RESERVATIONS WILL BE REQUIRED FOR LARGE GROUPS. TOUR FEATURES MANY SPANISH & MEXICAN HISTORICAL SITES INCLUDING LAS FLORES ADOBE & YSIDORA FLATS. AT MARINE CORPS BASE CAMP PENDLETON - ENTER MAIN GATE OFF HWY 5. (LOCAL). COMMUNITY REL'NS OFC; USMC BASE CAMP PENDLETON; JPAO MARINE CORPS BASE; CP PENDLETON, CA 92055. (#25211-1).

JULY 3, '76. 4TH OF JULY BICENTENNIAL CELEBRATION. COMPETITION, FESTIVAL. (LOCAL). R O TILLEY, CHAIRMAN; HEADQUARTERS, 4TH MARINE DIVISION; 312 NEVILLE CIRCLE; CMP PENDLETON, CA 92055. (#200006-393).

CRESCENT CITY

CRESCENT CITY LIGHTHOUSE DISPLAY AND MUSEUM - CA. UPGRADE AND REHABILITATE THE INTERPRETIVE AND MUSEUM DISPLAYS OF THE CRESCENT CITY LIGHTHOUSE, A HISTORIC FACILITY NOW OPEN TO THE PUBLIC AND OPERATED BY THE DEL NORTE COUNTY HISTORICAL SOCIETY. (LOCAL). STEPHEN D VEIRS, PRESIDENT; DEL NORTE COUNTY HISTORICAL SOCIETY; 577 H ST; CRESCENT CITY, CA 95531. (#27419). **ARBA GRANTEE.**

JULY 31 - AUG 1, '76. NATL PK SVC 'PEOPLE OF 1776' PLAYS AT REDWOOD NATL PARK. TRAVELING TROUPE WILL BRING VARIOUS ASPECTS OF COLONIAL LIFE (MILITARY LIFE,, MUSIC, CRAFTS) TO VISITORS IN TWO SECTIONS OF THIS NATIONAL PARK. AT EUREKA & CRESCENT CITY. (REGN'L). REDWOOD NATL PARK; NATIONAL PARK SERVICE; DRAWER N; CRESCENT CITY, CA 95531. (#1469-13).

AUG 20, '76. NATL PK SVC '...A LITTLE LOOK AROUND' VISITS REDWOOD NP. THIS SHORT PROGRAM FEATURES ACTORS PORTRAYING FAMOUS AMERICANS OF THE PAST WHO'VE RETURNED TO SEE AMERICA'S GROWTH. (REGN'L). REDWOOD NATL PK; NATIONAL PARK SERVICE; DRAWER N; CRESCENT CITY, CA 95531. (#5653-40).

CUCAMONGA

THE HISTORY OF CUCAMONGA, CA. THE SAN BERNARDINO COUNTY MUSEUM ASSOCIATION IS SPONSORING THE PUBLICATION OF A BOOK BY ESTHER B BLACK. THE BOOK TRACES THE HISTORY OF THE AREA FROM 'MISSION DAYS' TO PRESENT. (LOCAL). WILLIAM J MANN, CHAIRMAN; SAN BERNARDINO COUNTY BICENTENNIAL COMMITTEE; 2024 ORANGE TREE LN; REDLANDS, CA 92373. (#16361).

CULVER CITY

HERITAGE DISPLAY, CULVER CITY, CALIF. DISPLAY CASES IN FOYER OF LOCAL COUNTY LIBRARY HAVE BEEN MADE AVAILABLE FOR AN ON-GOING DISPLAY FEATURING LOCAL AND NATIONAL HERITAGE FROM APRIL 1974 UNTIL JULY 1976 CHANGED EVERY 3 MONTHS. (LOCAL). DORAL L MCKEE, CHAIRPERSON; HERITAGE GROUP OF CELEBRATION 76 COMMITTEE; BOX 507; CULVER CITY, CA 90230. (#2676).

'A PAST TO REMEMBER', BOOK ON CULVER CITY'S HIST. PAPERBACK BOOK PUBLISHED TO RECOGNIZE CULVER CITY'S HERITAGE IN BUILDING THIS COUNTRY. (LOCAL). DORAL MCKEE, CHAIRMAN; CELEBRATION 76 COMMITTEE; PO BOX 507; CULVER CITY, CA 90230. (#25741).

WOODEN BICENTENNIAL COMMEMORATION COIN-CULVER CITY. A WOODEN COIN TO COMMEMORATE THE USA BICENTENNIAL BY THE CULVER CITY COIN CLUB. (LOCAL). PAUL BORACH, BICENTENNIAL COIN COORDINATOR; CULVER CITY COIN CLUB; 3125 W WASHINGTON BLVD; MARINA DEL RY, CA 90291. (#29124).

FEB 9, '75. 'UP WITH PEOPLE' CONCERT BENEFIT FOR ORTHOPEDIC HOSPITAL. LIVE PERFORMANCE AT VETERANS MEMORIAL AUDITORIUM. (LOCAL). TOM BETTS, PRESIDENT; CULVER CITY JAYCEES & CULVER CITY BICENTENNIAL COMMITTEE; PO BOX 21-35; CULVER CITY, CA 90230. (#103347-1).

JULY 4, '75. 13TH ANNUAL INDEPENDENCE DAY-FIREWORKS SHOW AND DISPLAY. CEREMONY, FESTIVAL AT CULVER CITY HIGH SCHOOL FOOTBALL FIELD AND RELATED FACILITIES. (LOCAL). RICHARD ROSS BRUNDO, CHMN; CULVER CITY EXCHANGE CLUB; 4267 OVERLAND AVE; CULVER CITY, CA 90230. (#200006-4).

MAR 1 - 30, '76. HERITAGE DISPLAY. CHAIRMAN MILDRED KEARNY CALLS ATTENTION TO A GROUP OF EARLY TOOLS & BOOKS BELONGING TO ARNOLD GORDON OF WESTCHESTER, PRES OF THE WESTERN BRANCH OF THE EARLY AMERICAN INDUSTRY ASSOC & MATT MATHESON OF CULVER CITY. AT FOYER OF THE COUNTY LIBRARY. (LOCAL). DORAL MCKEE, COORD; BICENTENNIAL CALENDAR; 10801 MALONY RD; CULVER CITY, CA 90230. (#105925-1).

MAR 13 - MAY 2, '76. BICENTENNIAL POSTAL ART. EXHIBIT AT MUSEUM OF SCIENCE & INDUSTRY. (LOCAL). DORAL MCKEE, COORD; BICENTENNIAL CALENDAR; 10801 MALONY RD; CULVER CITY, CA 90230. (#105925-9).

MAR 17, '76. 'U S ART-A GIFT TO OURSELVES', FILM PRESENTATION. EXHIBIT AT CULVER CITY LIBRARY, 4975 OVERLAND. (LOCAL). DORAL MCKEE, COORD; CELEBRATION '76 COMMITTEE OF CULVER CITY; 10801 MOLONY RD; CULVER CITY, CA 90230. (#104974-1).

MAR 20, '76. JR PROGRAMS BICENTENNIAL CONCERT. ORIGINAL MUSICAL ENTITLED 'DAVEY CROCKETT'; A LARGE CAST OF SINGERS & DANCERS FROM CERRITOS COLLEGE. AUDITORIUM DOORS OPEN AT 12:45. AT ROBERT FROST AUDITORIUM. (LOCAL). DORAL MCKEE, DIRECTOR; BICENTENNIAL CALENDAR; 10801 MOLONY RD; CULVER CITY, CA 90203. (#105925-7).

MAR 21, '76. ARTS AND CRAFTS EXHIBIT. 4TH ANNUAL EXHIBIT; THERE WILL BE A SPECIAL BICENTENNIAL AWARD CATEGORY. AT VETERANS MEMORIAL AUDITORIUM. (LOCAL). DORAL MCKEE, DIRECTOR; CULVER CITY PARKS & RECREATION DEPT & ART ASSOC; 10801 MOLONY RD; CULVER CITY, CA 90230. (#105925-6).

MAR 22, '76. CELEBRATION '76 COMMITTEE. PUBLIC INVITED TO BRING OWN LUNCH, BEVERAGE PROVIDED. AT GARDEN ROOM, VETERANS MEMORIAL BLDG. (LOCAL). DORAL MCKEE, DIRECTOR; BICENTENNIAL CALENDAR; 10801 MOLONY RD; CULVER CITY, CA 90230. (#105925-4).

CULVER CITY — CONTINUED

MAR 22, '76. EARTH DAY. A TOTAL OF 40 TREES HAVE BEEN ALLOTTED TO THE SCHOOLS & WILL BE PLANTED AS A PART OF 'PLANT TREES IN CULVER CITY'. A GROUP WILL BE PLANTED AT TELLEFSON PARK USING MONEY DONATED FOR PUBLIC PLANTINGS. (LOCAL). DORAL MCKEE, DIRECTOR; BICENTENNIAL CALENDAR; 10801 MOLONY RD; CULVER CITY, CA 90230. (#105925-5).

MAR 25 - 26, '76. CULVER CITY UNIFIED SCHOOL DISTRICT BICENTENNIAL CONCERT. A CHORAL PAGEANT ENTITLED 'OUR COUNTRY, TIS OF THEE' COMBINED CHORUS OF 225; ORCHESTRA OF 85; HIGH SCHOOL MARCHING & STAGE BANDS DIRECTED BY DEBORAH CASTRICONE, ELEMENTARY MUSIC SUPERVISOR. AT ROBERT FROST AUDITORIUM. (LOCAL). DORAL MCKEE, COORD; BICENTENNIAL CALENDAR; 10801 MALONY RD; CULVER CITY, CA 90230. (#105925-3).

MAR 31, '76. AMERICAN ISSUES FORUM. 'THE BUSINESS OF AMERICA' LED BY PETER PARENTEAU OF CULVER CITY CHAMBER OF COMMERCE; THIRD IN SERIES OF DISCUSSION MEETINGS WHICH WILL TRACE IMPORTANCE OF FREE ENTERPRISE IN HISTORY OF OUR COUNTRY. AT MULTI-PURPOSE ROOM. (LOCAL). DORAL MCKEE, COORD; BICENTENNIAL CALENDAR; 10801 MALONY RD; CULVER CITY, CA 90230. (#105925-2).

APR 6, '76. WAR-GAMING AS RELATED TO THE REVOLUTIONARY WAR PERIOD. TOM COVENEY, AN EXPERT ON WAR GAMES, WILL SPEAK ON WAR-GAMING AS RELATED TO THE REVOLUTIONARY WAR PERIOD, ILLUSTRATED W/MINIATURE FIGURES & MODELS. AT AT THE LIBRARY, 4975 OVERLAND AVE. (LOCAL). LIBRARIAN; CULVER CITY BRANCH, COUNTY LIBRARY; 4975 OVERLAND AVE; CULVER CITY, CA 90230. (#200006-174).

APR 28, '76. AMERICAN ISSUES FORUM - 'AMERICA IN THE WORLD'. FINAL IN THE SERIES, THIS ONE IS A LOOK AT AMERICA'S FOREIGN POLICY. (LOCAL). DORAL MCKEE, DIRECTOR; CULVER CITY BICENTENNIAL COMMITTEE; 10801 MOLONY ROAD; CULVER CITY, CA 90230. (#106869-1).

MAY 7 - 8, '76. WEST LOS ANGELES COLLEGE HERITAGE FESTIVAL. DANCE FESTIVAL, DISPLAYS, FOOD & FUN. (LOCAL). DR JACKIE IRELAND; WEST LOS ANGELES COLLEGE; CULVER CITY, CA 90230. (#106811-1).

JUNE 2, '76. BICENTENNIAL DANCE RECITAL. PERFORMANCE BY THE CHILDREN'S DANCE CLASS OF THE PARKS & RECREATION DEPT. AT VETERAN'S MEMORIAL AUDITORIUM. (LOCAL). MRS DORAL MCKEE, CHAIRMAN; CULVER CITY BICENTENNIAL COMMITTEE; BOX 507; CULVER CITY, CA 90230. (#200006-314).

JUNE 5, '76. COMMUNITY FLAG DAY PARADE. PARADE, LIVE PERFORMANCE AT VETERANS AUDITORIUM, OVERLAND AVE AT CULVER BLVD. (LOCAL). MRS CY MOHLER, DIR; ELKS LODGE #1917; CULVER CITY, CA 90230. (#103347-2).

JULY 4, '76. DEDICATION OF TREES DONATED TO TREE-PLANTING PROJECT. TREE PLANTING PROJECT OF CULVER CITY, CALIF. LONG TERM REFORESTATION IN URBAN CULVER CITY BY PARK SUPERINTENDENT AND BY OWNERS OF PRIVATE PROPERTY. (LOCAL). ROY WELLS; CITY OF CULVER CITY; CITY HALL; CULVER CITY, CA 90230. (#2287-501).

JULY 4, '76. 13TH ANNUAL EXCHANGE CLUB FIREWORKS DISPLAY. FESTIVAL, LIVE PERFORMANCE AT CULVER CITY HIGH SCHOOL FOOTBALL FIELD. (LOCAL). MRS DORAL MCKEE, CHAIRMAN; CULVER CITY BICENTENNIAL COMMITTEE; BOX 507; CULVER CITY, CA 90230. (#200006-315).

CUPERTINO

HISTORY OF CUPERTINO, CALIFORNIA. A NARRATIVE OF THE CITY'S HISTORY WILL BE COMPILED FROM THE PERIOD OF THE SPANISH EXPLORATION TO THE PRESENT. (LOCAL). WALT WARREN, DIRECTOR CALIFORNIA HISTORY CENTER; DE ANZA COLLEGE; 21250 STEVENS CREEK BLVD; CUPERTINO, CA 95014. (#9985).

TRIANON MANSION RESTORATION IN CUPERTINO, CA. DESIGNED BY WILLIS POLK, THE TRIANON SERVED AS A COUNTRY HOME FOR CHARLES BALDWIN; IT WAS BUILT IN 1895; WHEN RESTORED, THE TRIANON WILL HOUSE THE CALIFORNIA HISTORY CENTER OF DE ANZA COLLEGE. (LOCAL). WALT WARREN, DIRECTOR, CALIFORNIA HISTORY CENTER; DE ANZA COLLEGE; 21250 STEVENS CREEK BLVD; CUPERTINO, CA 95014. (#9984).

MAR 9, '76. LECTURE BY ALAN TOFFLER. THE THEME OF THE LECTURE WILL BE 'THE OUTLINE OF TOMORROW, THE SUPER INDUSTRIAL REVOLUTION.'. AT FLINT CENTER, DEANZA COLLEGE. (LOCAL). STANLEY C BENZ, COUNSELOR; SANT CLARA COUNTY COLLEGE AND UNIVERSITIES CONSORTIUM; SAN JOSE STATE UNIV; SAN JOSE, CA 95192. (#103394-4).

APR 23, '76. ODORI FESTIVAL OF JAPAN VISITS CUPERTINO, CA. LIVE PERFORMANCE AT FLINT CENTER. (INT'L). DIRECTOR; MEL HOWARD PRESENTS; 143 E 27TH ST; NEW YORK, NY 10016. (#108965-9).

NOV 23, '76. DANCE AMERICANA. LIVE PERFORMANCE AT FLINT CENTER, DE ANZA COLLEGE. (LOCAL). ANNETTE MACDONALD, CHMN; SAN JOSE STATE UNIVERSITY & DE ANZA COLLEGE; SAN JOSE, CA 95192. (#104497-1).

DALY CITY

APR 3 - 4, '76. SCOUT AMERICA, 76 -- A BICENTENNIAL CELEBRATION OF GIRL SCOUTING. A REGIONAL CELEBRATION OF GIRL SCOUTING FEATURING BICENTENNIAL ARTS AND 'HIDDEN HEROINES'. AT SERRAMONTE CENTER, DALY CITY, CA 94014 AN ENCLOSED MALL SHOPPING CTR. (LOCAL). ALVIN L. SCHWARZBACH; GS USA SAN FRANCISCO BAY COUNCIL, SAN FRAN & NORTHERN SAN MATEO ASSC; 43 CASTELLEJO STREET; DALY CITY, CA 94015. (#50196-1).

MAY 30 - 31, '76. UNITED STATES ARMED FORCES BICENTENNIAL CARAVAN. CARAVAN IS COMPOSED OF EXHIBIT VANS FOR EACH MILITARY SERVICE. PROJECT THEME IS 'HISTORY OF THE ARMED FORCES AND THEIR CONTRIBUTIONS TO THE NATION. (LOCAL). WILLIAM FLANAGAN; U S ARMED FORCES BICENTENNIAL CARAVAN; 3 SERRAMONTE CENTER; DALY CITY, CA 94015. (#1775-718).

DANA POINT

APR 16 - 17, '76. UNITED STATES ARMED FORCES BICENTENNIAL CARAVAN. CARAVAN IS COMPOSED OF EXHIBIT VANS FOR EACH MILITARY SERVICE. PROJECT THEME IS ' HISTORY OF THE ARMED FORCES & THEIR CONTRIBUTIONS TO THE NATION'. (LOCAL). KATHY THOMPSON, CHAIRMAN; U S ARMED FORCES BICENTENNIAL CARAVAN; BANK OF AMERICA, PO BOX 427; DANA POINT, CA 92629. (#1775-554).

DANVILLE

JUNE 25, '76. UNITED STATES ARMED FORCES BICENTENNIAL CARAVAN. CARAVAN IS COMPOSED OF EXHIBIT VANS FOR EACH MILITARY SERVICE. PROJECT THEME IS 'HISTORY OF THE ARMED FORCES AND THEIR CONTIBUTIONS TO THE NATION. (LOCAL). DAVE STEGMAN; U S ARMED FORCES BICENTENNIAL CARAVAN; BOX 604; DANVILLE, CA 94526. (#1775-721).

DAVIS

'SPECIMEN DAYS', MUSIC COMPOSITION - DAVIS, CA. A CLASSICAL COMPOSITION FOR VOICE AND INSTRUMENT ON TEXT IN FRENCH, GERMAN, ITALIAN, ENGLISH AND SPANISH. (NAT'L). RICHARD SWIFT, COMPOSER; 568 S CAMPUS WAY; DAVIS, CA 95616. (#21551).

DEATH VALLEY

NOV 1, '75 - APR 24, '76. DEATH VALLEY NM PGM ON CULTURE OF THE DEATH VALLEY SHOSHONE INDIAN. TALKS ON SHOSHONE BASKETRY MANUFACTURE AND FOOD PREPARETION, DEMONSTRATIONS OF FOOD PREPARATION TECHNIQUES, AND WALKS THROUGH TULE SPRING AREA, SHOSHONE WINTER CAMP SITE, AND THROUGH MESQUITE AREA. CONTACT FURNACE CREEK VISITOR CENTER FOR DAYS AND TIMES. AT FURNACE CREEK VISITOR CENTER. (REGN'L). DEATH VALLEY NM; NATIONAL PARK SERVICE; DEATH VALLEY, CA 92328. (#6729-156).

NOV 1, '75 - APR 24, '76. DEATH VALLEY NM HISTORY TALKS ON U S GOVT. PRESENTATION OF TALKS ON THE U S GOVERNMENT'S SCIENTIFIC & MILITARY EXPEDITIONS OF 1860, 1861, 1871, 1875, AND 1891. VISITORS SHOULD CONTACT THE FURNACE CREEK VISITOR CENTER FOR SPECIFIC TIMES TALKS ARE GIVEN. AT FURNACE CREEK VISITOR CENTER. (REGN'L). DEATH VALLEY NAT MEM; NATIONAL PARK SERVICE; DEATH VALLEY, CA 92328. (#6730-126).

NOV 1, '75 - APR 24, '76. HISTORICAL TALKS ON THE ECONOMIC HISTORY OF MINING IN DEATH VALLEY. PRESENTATION OF TALKS ON THE ECONOMIC AND LEGAL HISTORY OF MINING IN DEATH VALLEY. VISITORS SHOULD CONTACT THE FURNACE CREEK VISITOR CENTER FOR SPECIFIC TIMES TALKS ARE GIVEN. AT FURNACE CREEK VISITOR CENTER. (REGN'L). DEATH VALLEY NM; NATIONAL PARK SERVICE; DEATH VALLEY, CA 92328. (#6730-142).

DEL MAR

BICENTENNIAL CONSTRUCTION PROJECTS, DEL MAR, CA. HORIZONS '76 PROJECTS TO INCLUDE CONSTRUCTION OF MINI-PARK, PUBLIC TENNIS COURTS, DEVELOPMENT OF SPRINKLER GARDEN & LIGHTING OF PLANTINGS ON MEDIAN STRIP. (LOCAL). TOM PEARSON, CHAIRMAN; DEL MAR BICENTENNIAL COMMITTEE; CITY HALL; DEL MAR, CA 92016. (#21147).

JAN 31, '76. WALKING TOUR OF DEL MAR HISTORIC STRUCTURES. TOUR. (LOCAL). ALICE GOODKIND, CHAIRMAN; LEAGUE OF WOMEN VOTERS; 1535 FOREST WAY; DEL MAR, CA 92014. (#200006-173).

JAN 31 - MAR 15, '76. BICENTENNIAL ESSAY CONTEST. A CONTEST FOR ALL STUDENTS, ELEMENTARY THROUGH HIGH SCHOOL LIVING IN SAN DIEGUITO ON SUBJECT 'SPIRIT OF '76: WORKING TOGETHER IN SAN DIEGUITO' WITH PRIZES IN EACH SCHOOL DISTRICT. (LOCAL). HAL BUTLER, CHAIRMAN; DEL MAR BICENTENNIAL COMMITTEE; CITY HALL; DEL MAR, CA 92012. (#104902-1).

FEB 15 - 22, '76. ARTS FESTIVAL. FESTIVAL, EXHIBIT. (LOCAL). MARGARET HOUGH, CHAIRMAN; DEL MAR BICENTENNIAL COMMITTEE; DEL MAR, CA 92014. (#200006-172).

FEB 20 - MAY 14, '76. FILM FESTIVAL. HEMINGWAY & CHAPLIN FILMS TO BE INCLUDED IN THE SERIES. (LOCAL). BONNIE HOUGH, CHAIRMAN; DEL MAR BICENTENNIAL COMMITTEE; CITY HALL; DEL MAR, CA 92014. (#105019-1).

MAR 13, '76. BICENTENNIAL COSTUME BALL. FESTIVAL. (LOCAL). CHRISTOPHER DINNES, CHMN; TORREY PINES HIGH SCHOOL BICENTENNIAL COMMITTEE; BLACK MOUNTAIN RD; DEL MAR, CA 92014. (#105193-2).

MAR 18 - MAY 20, '76. BICENTENNIAL LECTURE SERIES. MARCH 18: 'REVOLUTION & WILL OF MINORITY SOCIAL & POLITICAL IN CONFLICT'; MAY 20: 'FRUITS OF THE REVOLUTION, POLITICAL, ECONOMIC, INDUSTRIAL'. PURPOSE OF SERIES IS TO GIVE RELEVANCE OF REVOLUTION TO FORCES AMERICANS FACE TODAY. (LOCAL). TOM SHEPARD, CHAIRMAN; SPEAKER'S BUREAU, BICENTENNIAL COMMITTEE OF DEL MAR; CITY HALL; DEL MAR, CA 92014. (#105036-1).

APR 2 - JULY ??, '76. MUSIC FESTIVAL. A GOSPEL CHOIR CONCERT; JAZZ CONCERT; AND A BICENTENNIAL CONCERT OF AMERICAN MUSIC FROM THE REVOLUTION. (LOCAL). BERT TURETLKY, CHAIRMAN; DEL MAR BICENTENNIAL COMMITTEE; CITY HALL; DEL MAR, CA 92014. (#105193-6).

APR 18, '76. PAUL REVERE'S RIDE. RE-ENACTMENT OF PAUL REVERE'S RIDE BY THE DEL MAR BOY SCOUTS CLIMAXING IN BEACH BONFIRE AND COMMUNITY SING. (LOCAL). MRS IRISH DENNIS; BOY SCOUTS TROOP 713; 329 9TH STREET; DEL MAR, CA 92014. (#105193-3).

JUNE 19 - 20, '76. FESTIVAL OF THE FLAGS. A 2-DAY CELEBRATION HONORING OUR SPANISH-AMERICAN HERITAGE. (LOCAL). VIRGINIA IGONDA, CHAIRMAN; DEL MAR BICENTENNIAL COMMITTEE; CITY HALL; DEL MAR, CA 92014. (#105193-4).

JUNE 22 - JULY 5, '76. SOUTHERN CALIFORNIA EXPOSITION. AN ANNUAL CELEBRATION INCLUDING THE WORLD'S LARGEST PERFORMING HORSE SHOW SALUTES CALIFORNIA'S COLORFUL HERITAGE. AT DEL MAR FAIRGROUNDS. (LOCAL). RALPH TREMBLEY, DIRECTOR; SOUTHERN CALIFORNIA EXPOSITION; DEL MAR, CA 92014. (#103416-388).

AUG 8 - 28, '76. ARTS AMERICANA. FREE MULTI-RACIAL PERFORMING WORKSHOP FOR 30 TALENTED YOUNG PEOPLE BETWEEN AGES OF 13 AND 20 FROM THE DEL MAR AREA AND SAN DIEGO COUNTY. (LOCAL). IRIS DINNES, COORDINATOR; ACADEMY OF THE ARTS AT DEL MAR; 329 9TH ST; DEL MAR, CA 92014. (#105193-1).

DELANO

FARM WORKER MUSIC PROJECT - DELANO, CA. PRODUCE A RECORD OF THE SONGS OF PABLO & JUANITA SALUDADO & FRANCISCO GARCIA, FARM WORKERS AND UNITED FARM WORKERS MEMBERS IN DELANO. (LOCAL). PROF D K WILGUS, COORDINATOR; JOHN EDWARDS MEMORIAL FOUNDATION FOLKLORE CENTER, UCLA; 405 HILGARD; LOS ANGELES, CA 90404. (#27324).

OCT 23 - 24, '76. UNITED STATES ARMED FORCES BICENTENNIAL CARAVAN. CARAVAN IS COMPOSED OF EXHIBIT VANS FOR EACH MILITARY SERVICE. PROJECT THEME IS 'HISTORY OF THE ARMED FORCES & THEIR CONTRIBUTIONS TO THE NATION'. (LOCAL). MRS HELEN COLE; UNITED STATES ARMED FORCES BICENTENNIAL CARAVAN; 1804 TERRACE PLACE; DELANO, CA 93215. (#1775-830).

DESERT H SPG

COMMEMORATIVE PLAQUES & LIBERTY BELL - CA. COMMEMORATIVE PLAQUES DEPICTING AMERICAN HISTORY WILL BE PLACED ALONG MAIN ST; A REPLICA OF THE LIBERTY BELL WILL BE INSTALLED AND RUNG ON EVERY AMERICAN HOLIDAY. (LOCAL). WILLIAM A VANGELI, VICE PRESIDENT; CITY OF DESERT HOT SPRINGS; 12065 PALM DR; DESERT H SPG, CA 92240. (#26888).

JULY 3 - 4, '76. BICENTENNIAL PARADE. PARADE AT WARDMAN PARK. (LOCAL). WILLIAM A VANGELI, V-PRES; DESERT HOT SPRINGS CHAMBER OF COMMERCE; 12065 PALM DR; DESERT H SPG, CA 92240. (#200006-170).

JULY 3 - 4, '76. HOMETOWN '76 INTER-COMMUNITY COMPETITION & ENTERTAINMENT. COMPETITION, FESTIVAL, PARADE AT WARDMAN PARK. (LOCAL). WILLIAM A VANGELI, V-PRES; DESERT HOT SPRINGS CHAMBER OF COMMERCE; 12065 PALM DR; DESERT H SPG, CA 92240. (#200006-169).

JULY 4, '76. FOURTH OF JULY BARBEQUE & PICNIC. FESTIVAL AT WARDMAN PARK. (LOCAL). WILLIAM A VANGELI, V-PRES; DESERT HOT SPRINGS CHAMBER OF COMMERCE; 12065 PALM DR; DESERT H SPG, CA 92240. (#200006-168).

DEC 2, '76. UNITED STATES ARMED FORCES BICENTENNIAL CARAVAN. CARAVAN IS COMPOSED OF EXHIBIT VANS FOR EACH MILITARY SERVICE. PROJECT THEME IS 'HISTORY OF THE ARMED FORCES & THEIR CONTRIBUTIONS TO THE NATION'. (LOCAL). JAY CORSINI; UNITED STATES ARMED FORCES BICENTENNIAL CARAVAN; 15021 PALM DR; DESERT HT SPG, CA 92240. (#1775-849).

DINUBA

PAINTING FIRE HYDRANTS - DINUBA, CA. FIRE HYDRANTS IN DINUBA, CUTLER, OROSI & SULTANA WILL BE PAINTED IN A BICENTENNIAL THEME. (LOCAL). GEORGE MADRID, PROJ COORDINATOR; ALTA DISTRICT BICENTENNIAL COMMITTEE & PUBLIC SCHOOLS; 1070 N ALTA AVE; DINUBA, CA 93618. (#26649).

JULY 4, '75. ETHNIC FESTIVAL. ETHNIC DANCES & FOODS, OLD-FASHIONED GAMES & EXHIBITS. AT EL MONTE PARK. (LOCAL). GEORGE MADRID, COORD; ALTA DISTRICT BICENTENNIAL COMMITTEE; 1070 N ALTA AVE; DINUBA, CA 93618. (#200006-171).

MAR 13, '76. PLANTING GIANT SEQUOIA. CEREMONY AT DINUBA MEMORIAL HALL, YETTEM LEARNING CENTER, LEDBETTER PARK. (LOCAL). GEORGE MADRID, CO-CHMN; ALTA DISTRICT BICENT COMMITTEE, GIRL SCOUTS, VERDE VISTA GARDEN CLUB; 1070 N ALTA AVE; DINUBA, CA 93618. (#108905-4).

JULY 3 - 5, '76. JULY 4TH FESTIVAL. THERE WILL BE ETHNIC & AMERICAN FOOD & DANCES, EXHIBITS & GAMES. AT EL MONTE PARK. (LOCAL). GEORGE MADRID, CO-CHMN; ALTA DISTRICT

DINUBA — CONTINUED

BICENTENNIAL COMMITTEE; 1070 N ALTA AVE; DINUBA, CA 93618. (#108905-3).

JULY 4, '76. RE-ENACTMENT OF PAUL REVERE'S RIDE. LIVE PERFORMANCE. (LOCAL). GEORGE MADRID, CO-CHMN; ALTA DISTRICT BICENTENNIAL COMMITTEE; 1070 N ALTA AVE; DINUBA, CA 93618. (#108905-2).

NOV 2, '76. BURY TIME CAPSULE. TIME CAPSULE WILL BE OPENED IN 2076. (LOCAL). GEORGE MADRID, CO-CHMN; ALTA DISTRICT BICENTENNIAL COMMITTEE; DINUBA CITY LIBRARY; DINUBA, CA 93618. (#108905-1).

DISNEYLAND

'AMERICA ON PARADE' - DISNEYLAND, CA. AN ENTERTAINMENT PROGRAM USING STREETS OF DISNEYLAND & DISNEYWORLD AS A STAGE FOR DAILY PARADES EMPHASIZING AMERICA'S PAST, AMERICA'S PEOPLE & DIVERSE ASPECTS OF THE AMERICAN SCENE. (NAT'L). JACK B LINDQUIST, VICE PRESIDENT-MARKETING; WALT DISNEY PRODUCTIONS; 500 BUENA VISTA ST; BURBANK, CA 91503. (#1978). **ARBA RECOGNIZED.**

JUNE 19, '75 - SEPT 6, '76. AMERICA ON PARADE....A SALUTE....A CELEBRATION. 50 UNITS DEPICTING MEMORABLE MOMENTS IN US HISTORY & SALUTES TO OUR NATIONS CREATIONS, PASTTIMES & LIFESTYLES. DOLL-LIKE CHARACTERIZATIONS OF 'PEOPLE OF AMERICA', HIGH SCHOOL & COLLEGE BANDS, SALUTE DIFFERENT STATE EACH WEEK. AT DISNEYLAND. (NAT'L). DISNEYLAND PUBLICITY; WALT DISNEY PRODUCTIONS; 1313 HARBOR BOULEVARD; ANAHEIM, CA 92803. (#50252-1).

DOWNEY

MAY 10 - 11, '76. UNITED STATES ARMED FORCES BICENTENNIAL CARAVAN. CARAVAN IS COMPOSED OF EXHIBIT VANS FOR EACH MILITARY SERVICE. PROJECT THEME IS ' HISTORY OF THE ARMED FORCES & THEIR CONTRIBUTIONS TO THE NATION'. (LOCAL). HENRY OBERNDORF, CHAIRMAN; U S ARMED FORCES BICENTENNIAL CARAVAN; 7810 STEWART & GRAY; DOWNEY, CA 90241. (#1775-566).

DUARTE

CITY OF HOPE NATIONAL MEDICAL CENTER, DUARTE, CA. NATIONAL MEDICAL AND RESEARCH CENTER IS BEING EXPANDED. FREE NONSECTARIAN PATIENT CARE, RESEARCH & POSTGRADUATE EDUCATION IN CANCER, LEUKEMIA, HEART, BLOOD & RESPIRATORY AFFLICTIONS, DIABETES, ETC. (NAT'L). SYDNEY J KEITH, DIRECTOR OF PUBLIC RELATIONS; CITY OF HOPE NATIONAL MEDICAL CENTER; 208 W 8TH ST; LOS ANGELES, CA 90014. (#20114).

DUBLIN

BEEP BASEBALL FOR THE SIGHTLESS, DUBLIN, CA. A BASEBALL GAME AND OTHER ATHLETIC EVENTS FOR THE SIGHTLESS. (ST-WIDE). NEIL MILLER, DIR COMMUNITY RELATIONS/PROGRAM DEV; SIGHTLESS SPORTS, INC; PO BOX 2418; DUBLIN, CA 94566. (#14724).

BICENTENNIAL HEADQUARTERS OF ALAMEDA COUNTY, CA. OLD ST RAYMOND'S CHURCH IN DUBLIN, CALIFORNIA, HAS BEEN RESTORED & NOW HAS COUNTY BICENTENNIAL OFFICE & DISPLAY SPACE. (LOCAL). FRANK M KING, DIRECTOR OF PUBLICITY; ALAMEDA COUNTY BICENTENNIAL COMMISSION; PO BOX 2001; DUBLIN, CA 94566. (#16062).

BOOKING THROUGH THE BICENTENNIAL, DUBLIN, CA. SPECIAL SHELF IN LIBRARY OF BOOKS PERTINENT TO THE REVOLUTIONARY PERIOD. (LOCAL). VIRGINIA BENNETT, LIBRARIAN; FRIENDS OF THE DUBLIN LIBRARY; 6930 VILLAGE PKY; DUBLIN, CA 94566. (#20724).

CALIFORNIA HERITAGE CENTER - DUBLIN. PRESERVE THE HISTORICAL RESOURCES OF STATE OF CA, ALAMEDA CO & COMMUNITY. INCLUDES PIONEER CEMETERY, 1840'S ST RAYMOND'S CHURCH, OLD MURRAY SCHOOL, BLACKSMITH SHOP AND J FALLON HOUSE. (ST-WIDE). JUDY EARL, PRESIDENT; DUBLIN HISTORICAL PRESERVATION ASSOC; PO BOX 2245; DUBLIN, CA 94566. (#27697). **ARBA GRANTEE.**

COLONIAL AMERICA COMMEMORATED, DUBLIN, CA. DISPLAY IN LIBRARY SHOWCASE OF BICENTENNIAL COINS & STAMPS PERTINENT TO COLONIAL AMERICA. (LOCAL). VIRGINIA BENNETT, LIBRARIAN; FRIENDS OF DUBLIN LIBRARY; 6930 VILLAGE PKY; DUBLIN, CA 94566. (#20725).

HORIZONS OF HERITAGE, DUBLIN, CA. ONGOING PURCHASES OF AMERICAN HERITAGE BOOKS FOR PERMANENT LIBRARY COLLECTION. (LOCAL). VIRGINIA BENNETT, LIBRARIAN; FRIENDS OF DUBLIN LIBRARY; 6930 VILLAGE PKY; DUBLIN, CA 94566. (#20723).

PAINTING HOUSE NUMBERS ON CURBS, DUBLIN, CA. SPECIAL RED, WHITE AND BLUE DESIGNS FOR HOUSE NUMBERS AND CURBS. (LOCAL). RITA RICAERO, COORDINATOR; YOUNG AMERICAN PROMOTION AGENCY; 11481 SILVERGATE AVE; DUBLIN, CA 94566. (#20722).

RESTORATION OF THE OLD MURRAY SCHOOL, DUBLIN, CA. PRESERVATION AND RESTORATION OF 119 YEAR OLD SCHOOL. (LOCAL). JUDY EARL, CHAIRMAN; DUBLIN HISTORICAL PRESERVATION ASSOCIATION; 11635 LOS RANCHITOS; DUBLIN, CA 94566. (#20726).

EL CAJON

APR 20, '76. OUTSTANDING STUDENT AWARD & EUCALYPTUS TREE PLANTING. CEREMONY AT VALHALLA HIGH SCHOOL, 1725 HILLSDALE RD. (LOCAL). CAPTAIN LOYD MALAND; SORLANDET LODGE #105, SONS OF NORWAY; 9333 LEMON AVE; LA MESA, CA 92041. (#104427-26).

EL CAMINO

NOV 8 - 19, '76. CARL HAVERLIN/BROADCAST MUSIC, INC, ARCHIVES BICENTENNIAL EXHIBIT. OFFERS A VERSATILE PICTURE OF HISTORY, REGIONAL LIFE & MUSIC FOR OVER 200 YEARS. CONTAINS PRESIDENTIAL LETTERS, LETTERS OF FAMOUS AMERICANS, OLD BOOKS, MANUSCRIPTS, HISTORY OF 'THE STAR SPANGLED BANNER' & COMPOSER AUTOGRAPHS, PLUS SHEET MUSIC OF THE PAST. AT EL CAMINO COLLEGE. (ST-WIDE). DR ROBERT HAAG, PGM MGR; EL CAMINO COLLEGE; EL CAMINO, CA 90506. (#20784-7).

EL CENTRO

'BRAWLEY NEWS' CONTRIBUTIONS TO BICENT - NBMRP. NEWSPAPER HAS CONSISTENTLY GIVEN PAGE-ONE COVERAGE TO LOCAL EVENTS AND PROGRAMS. ALSO CARRIED SERIES ON ORIGINAL COLONIES AND THE AMERICAN ISSUES FORUM. (LOCAL). J R FITCH, EDITOR & PUBLISHER; THE BRAWLEY NEWS; PO BOX 251; EL CENTRO, CA 92227. (#28587).

IMPERIAL VALLEY PRESS BICENTENNIAL COVERAGE -NBMRP. EXTENSIVE COVERAGE OF EVENTS, INCL FRONT PAGE STORIES & PICTUES ON FREEDOM TRAIN & WAGON TRAIN, PLUS LOCAL PROGRAMS. RAN SERIES ON ORIGINAL 13 COLONIES & AMERICAN ISSUES FORUM. (LOCAL). J R FITCH, EDITOR & PUBLISHER; THE IMPERIAL VALLEY PRESS; 205 N 8TH ST; EL CENTRO, CA 92243. (#28518).

JAN 30 - 31, '76. UNITED STATES ARMED FORCES BICENTENNIAL CARAVAN. CARAVAN IS COMPOSED OF EXHIBIT VANS FOR EACH MILITARY SERVICE. PROJECT THEME IS 'HISTORY OF THE ARMED FORCES AND THEIR CONTRIBUTIONS TO THE NATION'. (LOCAL). ROY PERRY; US ARMED FORCES EXHIBIT VANS PROJECT; 1037 SANDALWOOD; EL CENTRO, CA 92243. (#1775-312).

EL CERRITO

JUNE 30, '76. UNITED STATES ARMED FORCES BICENTENNIAL CARAVAN. CARAVAN IS COMPOSED OF EXHIBIT VANS FOR EACH MILITARY SERVICE. PROJECT THEME IS 'HISTORY OF THE ARMED FORCES AND THEIR CONTIBUTIONS TO THE NATION. (LOCAL). MRS KATHLEEN SEABURY; U S ARMED FORCES BICENTENNIAL CARAVAN; MEZZANINE, RM 304, EL CERRITO PL; EL CERRITO, CA 94530. (#1775-723).

JULY 1, '76. UNITED STATES ARMED FORCES BICENTENNIAL CARAVAN. CARAVAN IS COMPOSED OF EXHIBIT VANS FOR EACH MILITARY SERVICE. PROJECT THEME IS 'HISTORY OF THE ARMED FORCES & THEIR CONTRIBUTIONS TO THE NATION.'. (LOCAL). KATHLEEN SEABARY, CHMN; UNITED STATES ARMED FORCES BICENTENNIAL CARAVAN; RM 304, EL CERRITO PLAZA; EL CERRITO, CA 94530. (#1775-683).

SEPT 6, '76. 1976 LABOR DAY PARADE & PICNIC. FESTIVAL AT COMMUNITY CENTER. (LOCAL). A E SCHROEDER, DIRECTOR; EL CERRITO BICENTENNIAL COMMITTEE; CITY HALL; EL CERRITO, CA 94530. (#104029-1).

EL MONTE

COMMUNITY RESOURCE CENTER (CRC) - EL MONTE, CA. VOLUNTEER INVOLVEMENT TO IDENTIFY COMMUNITY PROBLEMS, GATHER FACTS, ANALYZE DATA AND IDENTIFY ANSWERS TO THE PROBLEMS. DISSEMINATE INFORMATION TO ENLIGHTEN THE ELECTORATE & SOLICIT CITIZEN ACTION. (LOCAL). HAPPY CLUFF, PRESIDENT; CITIZEN FOR EL MONTE (CEM); 3901 COGSWELL RD; EL MONTE, CA 91732. (#25660).

EL TORO

MAR 8, '75. ARTS COUNCIL - BICENTENNIAL CONFERENCE, COTO DE CAZA. DISCUSSION OF ROLE ARTS WILL TAKE IN LONG BEACH BICENTENNIAL CELEBRATION. AT COTO DE CAZA COUNTRY CLUB. (LOCAL). CHAIRMAN; LONG BEACH REGIONAL ARTS COUNCIL, ARBC OF LONG BEACH, INC; 555 OCEAN BLVD #718; LONG BEACH, CA 90802. (#200006-73).

ENCINO

AMERICAN HERITAGE SQUARE PROJ IN CALIFORNIA. CREATION OF AN INTERNATIONAL RECREATION CENTER IN THE ENCINO AREA. WILL EXHIBIT PRODUCTS, ENTERTAINMENT, FOLKLORE & FILMS REPRESENTING 21 OR MORE COUNTRIES. (NAT'L). RUDY LINAN, PROJ COORDINATOR; AMERICAN HERITAGE SQUARE TEAM; 6430 SUNSET BLVD; HOLLYWOOD, CA 90028. (#17216).

FLAG DISPLAY - ENCINO, CA. INSTALLATION OF 203 AMERICAN FLAGS ALONG VENTURA BLVD. (LOCAL). C H MOSER, BICENTENNIAL CHAIRMAN; ENCINO CHAMBER OF COMMERCE; 4933 BALBOA BLVD; ENCINO, CA 91316. (#29437).

SEPT 9, '76. DEDICATION OF OAK TREE & CITING BY NAT'L SOCIETY OF ARBORICULTURE. CEREMONY. (LOCAL). C H MOSER, CHAIRMAN; ENCINO CHAMBER OF COMMERCE; 6337 BALBOA BLVD; ENCINO, CA 91316. (#200006-349).

SEPT 17, '76. BICENTENNIAL PARADE. PARADE. (LOCAL). C H MOSER, CHAIRMAN; ENCINO CHAMBER OF COMMERCE; 6337 BALBOA BLVD; ENCINO, CA 91316. (#200006-350).

ESCALON

NEW COMMUNITY PARK OF ESCALON, CALIF. 20 ACRE PARK INCLUDES COMMUNITY SERVICE CENTER DEDICATED 1976 AVAILABLE ALL AGES CONTAIN RECREATIONAL FACILITIES FOR YOUTH TO ELDERLY. DEDICATED AREAS, BY DIFFERENT ORGANIZATIONS. (LOCAL). EARL WILSON, CITY ADMINISTRATOR; CITY OF ESCALON; 1520 2ND ST; ESCALON, CA 95320. (#3314).

JULY 18 - 19, '75. ESCALON NATIONAL BICENTENNIAL SUMMER COUNTRY FAIRE. AWARD, COMPETITION, FAIR, PARADE AT CITY OF ESCALON CITY PARK EL PORTAL SCHOOL-FIRST STREET. (ST-WIDE). HAZEL M BODIN; ESCALON DISTRICT CHAMBER OF COMMERCE; 2315 VINE AVE; ESCALON, CA 95320. (#50456-1).

ESCONDIDO

CALIFORNIA'S CAVALCADE OF BANDS. A SINGLE PERFORMING UNIT OF 1,976 MUSICIANS AND DRILL TEAM MARCHERS FROM 115 CALIFORNIA HIGH SCHOOLS WILL PERFORM IN WASHINGTON, DC, BOSTON, PHILADELPHIA, & NY AT YANKEE STADIUM, CENTRAL PARK & THE UN. (NAT'L). DAVID HARRISON, DIRECTOR, DEPARTMENT OF MUSIC; ORANGE GLEN HIGH SCHOOL 'PATRIOT' BAND; 2200 GLENOROGE RD; ESCONDIDO, CA 92025. (#12232).

CENTER FOR HUMANE EDUCATION, ESCONDIDO, CA. THE CENTER WILL PROVIDE: YEAR 'ROUND CLASSES ON PRESERVING THE ENVIRONMENT, ANIMAL LIFE, CARE AND RESPONSIBILITY OF DOMESTIC ANIMALS & SPACE FOR 4-H & FUTURE FARMER CLUBS. (LOCAL). SID HOLLINS, PRESIDENT; ESCONDIDO HUMANE SOCIETY, INC; 163 E MISSION; ESCONDIDO, CA 92025. (#12230).

CREATE ESCONDIDO CITY MUSEUM, CALIFORNIA. REFURBISH FIRST CITY LIBRARY FOR USE AS A CITY MUSEUM. COLLECT & DISPLAY ARTIFACTS & DOCUMENTS TO ILLUSTRATE HISTORY OF THE AREA. (LOCAL). MRS A A CHURCH, SECRETARY; ESCONDIDO HISTORICAL SOCIETY; PO BOX 263; ESCONDIDO, CA 92025. (#5645).

ESCONDIDO CULTURAL ARTS CENTER IN CA. RELOCATE A LANDMARK BUILDING TO BECOME THE CULTURAL CENTER FOR CONTINUOUS EXHIBITS, FILMS, PERFORMANCES, ART & DANCE CLASSES & HOME OF CIVIC THEATRE TROUPE. (LOCAL). BONNIE HASEMAN, STAFF COORDINATOR; ESCONDIDO CULTURAL ARTS COMMISSION; 100 VALLEY BLVD; ESCONDIDO, CA 92025. (#12231).

ESCONDIDO, CA, BICENTENNIAL EDUCATION FOUNDATION. THIS PROJECT IS TO PERPETUATE THE MEMORY OF MEN & WOMEN WHO ACHIEVED AMERICAN INDEPENDENCE BY ENCOURAGING HISTORICAL RESEARCH OF THE REVOLUTIONARY ERA AND DOCUMENTS PERTAINING TO IT. (LOCAL). YOLANDA A FLEET, TREASURER; ESCONDIDO BICENTENNIAL EDUCATIONAL FOUNDATION, INC; 100 VALLEY BLVD; ESCONDIDO, CA 92025. (#5860).

'FLAGS OVER ESCONDIDO' - CALIFORNIA STUDENT PROJ. HIGH SCHOOL STUDENT BICENTENNIAL COMMITTEE, USING HOMEMAKING, INDUSTRIAL ARTS & OTHER DEPTS, WILL MAKE COPIES OF ALL FLAGS EVER FLOWN IN ESCONDIDO & MAKE STANDARDS FOR DISPLAY. (LOCAL). ALAN FOUCAR, PRINCIPAL; HIGH SCHOOL BICENTENNIAL COMMITTEE; 1535 N BROADWAY; ESCONDIDO, CA 92025. (#5644).

FOSTER AMER REVOLUTION RESEARCH, ESCONDIDO, CA. PERPETUATE SPIRIT OF MEN & WOMEN WHO ACHIEVED AMER INDEPENDENCE BY ENCOURAGING HISTORICAL RESEARCH OF: DECLARATION OF INDEPENDENCE, AMERICAN REVOLUTION AND US CONSTITUTION & AMENDMENTS. (LOCAL). YOLANDA A FLEET, TREASURER; ESCONDIDO BICENTENNIAL EDUCATIONAL FOUNDATION INC; 100 VALLEY BLVD; ESCONDIDO, CA 92025. (#5643).

KIT CARSON MUNICIPAL THEATRE, ESCONDIDO, CALIF. AMPHITHEATRE IN CITY PARK WILL BE DEDICATED TO KIT CARSON, LOCAL HISTORIC PERSONAGE. (LOCAL). MRS YOLANDA FLEET, CHAIRMAN; ESCONDIDO BICENTENNIAL COMMITTEE; RT 3 BOX 606; ESCONDIDO, CA 92027. (#2302). **(??).**

JAN 18 - 19, '76. UNITED STATES ARMED FORCES BICENTENNIAL CARAVAN. CARAVAN IS COMPOSED OF EXHIBIT VANS FOR EACH MILITARY SERVICE. PROJECT THEME IS 'HISTORY OF THE ARMED FORCES AND THEIR CONTRIBUTIONS TO THE NATION'. (LOCAL). YOLANDA FLEET, CHMN; US ARMED FORCES EXHIBIT VANS PROJECT; 3045 FELICITA RD; ESCONDIDO, CA 92025. (#1775-306).

APR 30, '76. NETHERLANDS CHAMBER ORCHESTRA VISITS ESCONDIDO. LIVE PERFORMANCE. (INT'L). WILLIAM SIMONSZ, COORD; NETHERLANDS GOVERNMENT; NETHERLANDS EMBASSY-4200 LINNEAN; WASHINGTON, DC 20008. (#109013-11).

EUREKA

BICENT HERITAGE COURSES AT COLLEGE OF REDWOODS, CA. TWO HERITAGE SERIES TO BE OFFERED: US HERITAGE AS EPITOMIZED BY 1776 AND HERITAGE OF CALIFORNIA'S NORTH COAST COVERING SELECTED ASPECTS OF THE AREA'S HISTORY & CULTURE. CREDIT GIVEN FOR ATTENDANCE. (LOCAL). HAROLD J SNELGROVE, PROJECT COORDINATOR; REDWOODS BICENTENNIAL COMMITTEE; COLLEGE OF THE REDWOODS; EUREKA, CA 95501. (#8195).

EUREKA — CONTINUED

PLANTING TREES IN REDWOOD GROVE IN EUREKA, CA. PLANTING OF 100 REDWOOD TREES WITH BICENTENNIAL PLAQUE AND INSCRIBED REDWOOD LOG. ALSO PROVIDE A DRINKING FOUNTAIN, PICNIC TABLES, FOOTBRIDGE AND PUBLIC RESTROOMS. (LOCAL). HAROLD J SNELGROVE, PROJECT COORDINATOR; REDWOODS BICENTENNIAL COMMITTEE; COLLEGE OF THE REDWOODS; EUREKA, CA 95501. (#8194).

REDWOOD SEEDLING BICENTENNIAL PROJECT - CA. THE COLLEGE OF THE REDWOOD HAS SENT A REDWOOD LIBERTY TREE TO EACH COMMUNITY COLLEGE IN THE U S & TO EACH MEMBER OF THE CALIFORNIA LEGISLATOR AS PART OF ITS BICENTENNIAL OBSERVANCE. (NAT'L). HAROLD J SNELGROVE, COORDINATOR; COLLEGE OF THE REDWOODS; THOMPKINS HILL RD; EUREKA, CA 95501. (#30220).

APR - JUNE '75. BICENT HERITAGE STUDIES AT COLLEGE OF REDWOODS, CA. 6 CLASSES UNDER THE DEPARTMENT HEADING 'BICENTENNIAL HERITAGE' TO BE FEATURED SPRING QUARTER: HERITAGE READERS THEATER, HIST OF CAL, HUMBOLDT HERITAGE TOUR, SPINNING/DYEING, COLONIAL WOMEN & COSTUMES. ALSO: EDUCATIONAL COURSE. (LOCAL). HAROLD J SNELGROVE; REDWOODS BICENTENNIAL COMMITTEE; COLLEGE OF THE REDWOODS; EUREKA, CA 95501. (#8193-1).

SEPT 1, '75 - JUNE 30, '76. REGIONAL AND STATE TOUR OF COMPLETED INDIAN COMIC THEATRE PIECE. TWO-PART THEATER PIECE EXPLORING INDIAN COMIC CHARACTERS IN A COMMEDIA DELL'ARTE FORMAT. (LOCAL). JANE MAZZONE-CLEMENTI; DELL'ARTE, INC; BOX 816 FIRST & H STS; BLUE LAKE, CA 95501. (#5354-502).

OCT 9, '75. EVERYDAY LIFE IN EARLY AMERICA; ART, CRAFTS AND COOKERY. EXHIBIT AT FORUM BLDG, COLLEGE OF THE REDWOODS. (LOCAL). HAROLD SNELGROVE, CHMN; COLLEGE OF THE REDWOODS BICENTENNIAL COMMITTEE; COLLEGE OF THE REDWOODS; EUREKA, CA 95501. (#102326-1).

OCT 30, '75. NORTH COAST KALEIDOSCOPE - HISTORIC HOMES AND PEOPLE. EXHIBIT AT FORUM BUILDING, COLLEGE OF THE REDWOODS. (LOCAL). HAROLD SNELGROVE, CHMN; COLLEGE OF THE REDWOODS BICENTENNIAL COMMITTEE; COLLEGE OF THE REDWOODS; EUREKA, CA 95501. (#102326-2).

NOV 20, '75. THE NATIVE AMERICAN HERITAGE - THE 18TH & 19TH CENTUREIS. EXHIBIT AT FORUM BLDG, COLLEGE OF THE REDWOODS. (LOCAL). HAROLD SNELGROVE, CHMN; COLLEGE OF THE REDWOODS BICENTENNIAL COMMITTEE; COLLEGE OF THE REDWOODS; EUREKA, CA 95501. (#102326-3).

JAN 8, '76. NORTH COAST KALEIDOSCOPE - FAMOUS HOMES & BUILDINGS OF HUMBOLDT CO. EXHIBIT, SEMINAR AT FORUM BUILDING, COLLEGE FO THE REDWOODS. (LOCAL). HAROLD SNELGROVE, CHMN; COLLEGE OF THE REDWOODS BICENTENNIAL COMMITTEE; COLLEGE OF THE REDWOODS; EUREKA, CA 95501. (#102326-4).

JAN 29, '76. GREAT ISSUES OF THE AMERICAN REVOLUTION: RELIGIOUS FREEDOM. SEMINAR AT FORUM BLDG, COLLEGE OF THE REDWOODS. (LOCAL). HAROLD SNELGROVE, CHMN; COLLEGE OF THE REDWOODS BICENTENNIAL COMMITTEE; COLLEGE OF THE REDWOODS; EUREKA, CA 95501. (#102326-5).

FEB 19, '76. GREAT ISSUES OF THE AMER REVOLUTION: WOMEN-A LEGACY OF SUPPRESSION. SEMINAR AT FORUM BLDG, COLLEGE OF THE REDWOODS. (LOCAL). HAROLD SNELGROVE, CHMN; COLLEGE OF THE REDWOODS BICENTENNIAL COMMITTEE; COLLEGE OF THE REDWOODS; EUREKA, CA 95501. (#102326-6).

MAR 11, '76. NORTH COAST KALEIDOSCOPE: LOGGING AND HUMBOLDT BAY. SEMINAR AT FORUM BLDG, COLLEGE OF THE REDWOODS. (LOCAL). HAROLD SNELGROVE, CHMN; COLLEGE OF THE REDWOODS BICENTENNIAL COMMITTEE; COLLEGE OF THE REDWOODS; EUREKA, CA 95501. (#102326-7).

APR 24 - 25, '76. HERITAGE FAIR '76 'THE SPIRIT OF OLD EUREKA'. FAIR CLOSES SUNDAY AT 6PM. AT EXHIBIT BUILDING, REDWOOD ACRES FAIR GROUNDS, PARKING AVAILABLE. (LOCAL). MARILYNN BARTLETT, CHMN; EUREKA BICENTENNIAL COMMISSION & EUREKA HERITAGE SOCIETY; 1210 LONG ST; EUREKA, CA 95501. (#105294-1).

APR 29, '76. THE AMERICAN REVOLUTION: THE HERITAGE OF AMERICAN MUSIC. LIVE PERFORMANCE AT FORUM BLDG, COLLEGE OF THE REDWOODS. (LOCAL). HAROLD SNELGROVE, CHMN; COLLEGE OF THE REDWOODS BICENTENNIAL COMMITTEE; COLLEGE OF THE REDWOODS; EUREKA, CA 95501. (#102326-8).

MAY 9, '76. NETHERLANDS CHAMBER ORCHESTRA VISITS EUREKA. LIVE PERFORMANCE. (INT'L). WILLIAM SIMONSZ, COORD; NETHERLANDS GOVERNMENT; NETHERLANDS EMBASSY-4200 LINNEAN; WASHINGTON, DC 20008. (#109013-19).

MAY 20, '76. NORTH COAST AND AMERICAN REVOLUTION: HERITAGE OF AMERICAN THEATER. LIVE PERFORMANCE AT FORUM BLDG, COLLEGE OF THE REDWOODS. (LOCAL). HAROLD SNELGROVE, CHMN; COLLEGE OF THE REDWOODS BICENTENNIAL COMMITTEE; COLLEGE OF THE REDWOODS; EUREKA, CA 95501. (#102326-9).

JULY 14 - 15, '76. UNITED STATES ARMED FORCES BICENTENNIAL CARAVAN. CARAVAN IS COMPOSED OF EXHIBIT VANS FOR EACH MILITARY SERVICE. PROJECT THEME IS 'HISTORY OF THE ARMED FORCES & THEIR CONTRIBUTIONS TO THE NATION.'. (LOCAL). WILLIAM T DALY, CHMN; UNITED STATES ARMED FORCES BICENTENNIAL CARAVAN; 160 SPRUCE ST; EUREKA, CA 95501. (#1775-689).

EXETER

JULY 4, '76. EXETER CELEBRATION. FESTIVAL AT EXETER LIBRARY AUDITORIUM. (LOCAL). DAWRENCE S GLENN, CHMN; CITY OF EXETER; PO BOX 181; EXETER, CA 93221. (#200006-353).

FAIRFAX

DEDICATION OF THE TOWN'S RECREATION CENTER - CA. THE TOWN IS BUILDING A NEW RECREATION CENTER; THE NEW CENTER WILL BE USED FOR YOUTH PROGRAMS AND FOR COMMUNITY MEETINGS. (LOCAL). WILLIAM E HADEN, CITY ADMINISTRATOR; TOWN OF FAIRFAX; 142 BOLINAS RD; FAIRFAX, CA 94930. (#18083).

ELLIOTT NATURE PRESERVE - FAIRFAX, CA. THE TOWN IS PURCHASING A 45-ACRE PARCEL TO BE USED AS A NATURE PRESERVE. (LOCAL). WILLIAM E HADEN, CITY ADMINISTRATOR; TOWN OF FAIRFAX; 142 BOLINAS RD; FAIRFAX, CA 94930. (#18084).

HONOR GROVE - FAIRFAX, CA. TO RECONSTRUCT THE TOWNS HONOR GROVE; THE HONOR GROVE IS A GROVE. OF REDWOOD TREES WHICH IS USED TO HONOR THE TOWNS VETERANS. (LOCAL). WILLIAM E HADEN, CITY ADMINISTRATOR; TOWN OF FAIRFAX; 142 BOLINAS RD; FAIRFAX, CA 94930. (#18082).

FAIRFIELD

OCT 25, '75. ANNUAL ALL HALLOWS EVE PARADE WITH BICENTENNIAL THEME. PARADE AT MAIN DOWNTOWN AREA. (LOCAL). DOROTHY FUNE, COORDINATOR; FAIRFIELD RECREATION DEPT; 1000 WEBSTER; FAIRFIELD, CA 94533. (#102982-1).

OCT 26 - 27, '75. UNITED STATES ARMED FORCES BICENTENNIAL CARAVAN. THE CARAVAN IS COMPOSED OF EXHIBIT VANS FOR EACH BRANCH OF THE MILITARY SERVICE. THE THEME OF THE EXHIBITION IS 'HISTORY OF THE ARMED FORCES AND THEIR CONTRIBUTION TO THE NATION'. (LOCAL). DOROTHY FUNE, DIRECTOR; U S ARMED FORCES BICENTENNIAL EXHIBIT VANS PROJECT; PO BOX 1776; FAIRFIELD, CA 94533. (#1775-285).

JUNE 13, '76. FLAG DAY CEREMONY. CEREMONY. (LOCAL). DOROTHY FUNE, COORDINATOR; ELKS LODGE; PO BOX 1776; FAIRFIELD, CA 94533. (#102982-3).

JULY 4, '76. ANNUAL FOURTH OF JULY PARADE WITH BICENTENNIAL THEME. PARADE. (LOCAL). DOROTHY FUNE, COORDINATOR; FAIRFIELD RECREATION DEPT; 1000 WEBSTER; FAIRFIELD, CA 94533. (#102982-2).

FALLBROOK

JULY 4, '76. FOURTH OF JULY PICNIC. FESTIVAL AT LIVE OAK PARK. (LOCAL). DON DUSSAULT, CHMN; FALLBROOK CHAMBER OF COMMERCE BICENTENNIAL COMMITTEE; 4782 SLEEPING INDIAN RD; FALLBROOK, CA 92028. (#200006-530).

FOLSOM

THE BICENTENNIAL GROVE OF FOLSOM, CALIF. PLANT A GROVE OF TWENTY CALIF REDWOODS IN CITY PARK. TREES WILL HAVE DONOR-MARKED BRONZE PLAQUE. (LOCAL). ED MITCHEL, PARK DIRECTOR; CITY OF FOLSOM; 50 NATOMA ST; FOLSOM, CA 95630. (#3407).

SIX MELODRAMAS BY THE GASLIGHTERS OF FOLSOM, CALIF. WRITE AND PRODUCE SIX NEW PLAYS ABOUT LIFE IN THE GOLD FIELDS DURING THE 1850 'S. (ST-WIDE). DAN WELTY, OWNER-PRODUCER; SUTTER GASLIGHT THEATER; 720 SUTTER ST; FOLSOM, CA 95630. (#3406).

MAR 14, '75 - MAR 5, '77. MELODRAMA & AFTER-SHOW. GOLD RUSH THEME, 1849 TO 1900. PERIOD ENTERTAINMENT, DRAMA, SONGS, DANCES & SKETCHES. EACH PRODUCTION RUNS 4 MO, YEAR ROUND, EXCEPT EASTER, LABOR DAY & WEEKEND PRIOR TO CHRISTMAS. SUITABLE FOR ALL AGES. 1700 PERFORMANCES, 40 PRODUCTIONS SINCE FEB 1962. AT SUTTER GASLIGHTER THEATER 720 SUTTER ST N/O HIWAY 50 FREE PARKING. (LOCAL). LOUISE K WELTY; FOLSOM BICENTENNIAL COMMITTEE; 1010 FIGUEROA ST; FOLSOM, CA 95630. (#50081-1).

JULY 2 - 6, '75. ANNUAL PROFESSIONAL RODEO AND GIANT FIREWORKS DISPLAY. SPECIAL BICENTENNIAL FIREWORKS DISPLAY NIGHTLY SPECIAL RIDING DRILL TEAMS MOLLY BEE SHOW-75. AT FOLSOM CITY PARK DAN RUSSELL ARENA. (LOCAL). FOLSOM CHAMBER OF COMM; FOLSOM CHAMBER OF COMMERCE; 200 WOOL ST.; FOLSOM, CA 95630. (#50353-1).

JULY 10, '75. UNITED STATES ARMED FORCES BICENTENNIAL CARAVAN. CARAVAN NUMBER FOUR-COMPOSED OF EXHIBIT VANS FOR EACH MILITARY SERVICE. PROJECT THEME IS 'HISTORY OF THE ARMED FORCES & THEIR CONTRIBUTIONS TO THE NATION.'. (LOCAL). DAWN LANDIS; US ARMED FORCES BICENT EXHIBIT VAN PROJECT; KIDS KLOSET, 335 A E BIDWELL ST; FOLSOM, CA 95630. (#1775-146).

JULY 1, '76. ANNUAL PROFESSIONAL RODEO AND GIANT FIREWORKS DISPLAY. SPECIAL BICENTENNIAL FIREWORKS DISPLAY NIGHTLY; SPECIAL RIDING DRILL TEAMS; SPECIAL COUNTRY - WESTERN STAR. AT FOLSOM CITY PARK DAN RUSSELL ARENA. (LOCAL). FOLSOM CHAMBER-COMMERCE; FOLSOM CHAMBER OF COMMERCE.; 200 WOOL ST.; FOLSOM, CA 95630. (#50353-2).

FONTANA

FOUNDING OF HISTORICAL MUSEUM - FONTANA, CA. PROJECT EMPHASIZING ARTIFACTS & HISTORY OF CITY OF FONTANA. (LOCAL). NAT SIMON, CHAIRMAN; FONTANA BICENTENNIAL COMMITTEE; SIERRA AVE; FONTANA, CA 92355. (#17252).

MAY 8, '76. UNITED STATES ARMED FORCES BICENTENNIAL CARAVAN. CARAVAN IS COMPOSED OF EXHIBIT VANS FOR EACH MILITARY SERVICE. PROJECT THEME IS ' HISTORY OF THE ARMED FORCES & THEIR CONTRIBUTIONS TO THE NATION'. AT FONTANA SWUARE - FOOTHILL BLVD & MANGO ST. (LOCAL). DR ROBERT D SPRAGUE, DIR; U S ARMED FORCES BICENTENNIAL CARAVAN; CITY HALL; FONTANA, CA 92335. (#1775-564).

FORBESTOWN

YUBA FEATHER HISTORICAL MUSEUM, FORBESTOWN, CA. COLLECT & PRESERVE ARTIFACTS & MEMORABILIA ASSOCIATED WITH PIONEERS OF THE AREA WHO PLAYED SUCH AN IMPORTANT ROLE IN DEVELOPMENT OF THIS AREA OF YUBA & BUTTE COUNTIES. (LOCAL). ADELE HIGGINS, MUSEUM CHAIRPERSON; YUBA FEATHER HISTORICAL ASSOC; NEW YORK FLAT RD; FORBESTOWN, CA 95941. (#25742).

SEPT 11, '76. DEDICATION OF PIONEER CEMETERY MEMORIAL PARK & YUBA FEATHER MUSEUM. CEREMONY AT YUBA FEATHER MUSEUM. (LOCAL). DR LEWIS J FERRARI, CHMN; YUBA COUNTY BICENTENNIAL COMMITTEE/YUBA FEATHER HISTORICAL MUSEUM; 2205 COVILLAUD; MARYSVILLE, CA 95901. (#109302-1).

FOREST RANCH

MAY 8 - 9, '76. FOREST RANCH COUNTRY FAIR. BOOTHS, GAMES OF OLD, CAKE WALK, WESTERN DANCE, VAUDEVILLE SHOW, HORSE SHOES, SQUARE DANCING. AT PARK AREA. (ST-WIDE). MARILYN WARRENS, COORD; CHICO BICENTENNIAL COMMISSION; PO BOX 3038; CHICO, CA 95927. (#102447-9).

FORT ORD

APR 1, '75 - JULY 31, '76. BICENTENNIAL CARTOON CONTEST. CARTOON TECHNIQUE WORKSHOP, FT ORD, MONTEREY: 2/76 & 5/76; CONTEST FINALISTS EXHIBIT AT CRAFTS GALLERY: 7/1/76 - 7/31/76; AWARDS PRESENTATION, RECEPTION & WINNERS' DINNER: 7/13/76. AT FORT ORD RECREATION CENTER 1. (LOCAL). HARRIET E RICE, DIRECTOR; U S ARMY RECREATION CENTERS, RECREATION SERVICES DIV DPCA; RECREATION CENTER 1, BLDG 4600; FORT ORD, CA 93941. (#103817-1).

FORTUNA

ESTABLISHMENT OF MUSEUM IN FORTUNA, CALIFORNIA. NORTHWESTERN PACIFIC DEPOT BUILT IN 1893 MOVED TO CITY OWNED PARK AND BEING RESTORED AS A MUSEUM. (LOCAL). BETH RUNDELL, CHRMN AND COUNCILWOMAN; FORTUNA BICENTENNIAL COMMITTEE; BOX 811; FORTUNA, CA 95540. (#4527).

MAY 5 - 7, '76. ANTIQUE SHOW. EXHIBIT AT VETERANS BUILDING. (LOCAL). JIMMIE BALLINGER; UNITED METHODIST WOMEN; 587 SPRING ST; FORTUNA, CA 95540. (#50100-2).

JULY 4, '76. ANVIL FIRING. FESTIVAL AT ROHNER PARK. (LOCAL). DONALD KRADER; AMERICAN LEGION; 2789 KENMAR RD; FORTUNA, CA 95540. (#50100-1).

FOSTER CITY

APR 8 - 10, '76. USA THE HILLBARN WAY - A REVUE TO BENEFIT COMMUNITY THEATRE. LIVE PERFORMANCE AT HILLBARN THEATRE, HILLSDALE BLVD. (LOCAL). MRS SPEIGLEMAN, COORD; HILLBARN THEATRE LEAGUE, INC; PO BOX 913; SAN MATEO, CA 94403. (#104952-1).

JUNE 6, '76. RED, WHITE AND BLUE KITEFLY. KITEMAKING WORKSHOPS WILL BE HELD AT 4 RECREATION CENTERS PRIOR TO THE KITEFLY. AT EMPTY LOT AT E HILLSDALE & SHELL. (LOCAL). MAIZIE UNG, COORD; INTERNATIONAL FESTIVAL AND CHINESE CLUB OF FOSTER CITY; 611 N IDAHO ST; SAN MATEO, CA 94401. (#107272-1).

FOUNTAIN VLY

COMMUNITY SCHOOL PROGRAM, FTN VLY SCHOOL DIST, CA. COMMUNITY SCHOOL PROGRAM IS A RECIPIENT OF THE HORIZIONS ON DISPLAY BICENTENNIAL AWARD; THE PROGRAM WILL BE OPEN FOR PUBLIC VIEW AND TOURS; FAMILY ORIENTED EDUCATIONAL & CULTURAL PROGRAMS. (LOCAL). DR PATRICIA CLARK, ADMINISTRATOR; FOUNTAIN VALLEY SCHOOL DISTRICT COMMUNITY SCHOOL PROGRAM; NUMBER ONE LIGHTHOUSE LN; FOUNTAIN VLY, CA 92708. (#20060).

WATER FACTORY 21, FOUNTAIN VALLEY, CALIF. PROTOTYPE WASTE WATER RECYCLING PLANT & SEAWATER DESALTING MODULE. (LOCAL). MRS JAN WILHELM, CHAIRPERSON; FOUNTAIN VALLEY BICENTENNIAL COMMITTEE; 16527 REDWOOD CIR; FOUNTAIN VAL., CA 92708. (#2301). **(??).**

FREMONT

BICENTENNIAL NEWSLETTER, FREMONT, CA. PREPARE A MONTHLY NEWSLETTER FOR TEACHERS THAT WILL INCLUDE A DAY BY DAY CALENDAR OF EVENTS RELATED TO U S HISTORY. (LOCAL). DOLORES ROSE, COORDINATOR; FREMONT UNIFIED SCHOOL DISTRICT; 37802 FREMONT BLVD; FREMONT, CA 94536. (#20731).

BICENTENNIAL SPEAKERS' BUREAU, FREMONT, CA. SEVEN FACULTY MEMBERS TO ADDRESS COMMUNITY GROUPS ON RESPECTIVE

FREMONT — CONTINUED

FIELDS SUCH AS HISTORY, ECONOMICS & THEATER, RELATED TO BICENTENNIAL THEMES. (LOCAL). DIANE BROWN, COMMUNITY SERVICES ASST; OHLONE COLLEGE; 43600 MISSION BLVD; FREMONT, CA 94538. (#14720).

BICENTENNIAL TAPESTRY - PROJ OF FREMONT, CA. CHILDREN HAVE LEARNED DIFFERENT TECHNIQUES OF TAPESTRY AND GAINED AN UNDERSTANDING OF THE SIGNIFICANCE OF THE HISTORY OF THEIR COUNTRY. (LOCAL). MRS NADINE MEYER, TEACHER; MOWRY SCHOOL 5TH GRADE; 4700 CALAVERAS AVE; FREMONT, CA 94536. (#13391).

BUS TRIP TO FREEDOM TRAIN FOR SENIOR CITIZENS, CA. TRANSPORTATION & ADMISSION TO FREEDOM TRAIN TOUR WILL BE PROVIDED FOR SENIOR CITIZENS. (LOCAL). DIANE BROWN, COMMUNITY SERVICES ASST; OHLONE COLLEGE; 43600 MISSION BLVD; FREMONT, CA 94538. (#14717).

COMPLETION OF QUILT WITH HISTORICAL LANDMARKS, CA. QUILT WITH HISTORICAL LANDMARKS WILL BE MADE. (LOCAL). CAROL AMICK, PRESIDENT; COUNTY CLUB OF WASHINGTON TOWNSHIP; 3721 PARISH AVE; FREMONT, CA 94538. (#20729).

DISCUSSION OF 'GONE WITH THE WIND', FREMONT, CA. CLASS DISCUSSION AND COMPARISON OF NOVEL & FILM, FOR A BETTER UNDERSTANDING OF CIVIL WAR & POST WAR RESTORATIONS. (LOCAL). DIANE BROWN, COMMUNITY SERVICES ASST; OHLONE COLLEGE; 43600 MISSION BLVD; FREMONT, CA 94538. (#14718).

GOLD RUSH COUNTRY COURSE AND TOUR, FREMONT, CA. A HISTORY OF THE FORTY-NINERS AND A TOUR THROUGH GOLD RUSH COUNTRY. (LOCAL). DIANE BROWN, COMMUNITY SERVICES ASST; OHLONE COLLEGE; 43600 MISSION BLVD; FREMONT, CA 94538. (#14719).

HISTORY OF FREMONT, CA. DEVELOPING AN UP-TO-DATE HISTORY OF FREMONT AND ITS SCHOOLS FOR USE BY TEACHERS. (LOCAL). PHILIP HOLMES, PROJ DIRECTOR; 37944 FARWELL DR; FREMONT, CA 94536. (#13387).

HISTORY OF THE NILES AREA - FREMONT, CA. THE HISTORY OF THE NILES AREA WILL INSTILL IN THE STUDENTS & COMMUNITY THE RICH HERITAGE FOUND IN THE NILES AREA AND PRIDE IN WHAT WAS DONE BY THE PIONEERS. (LOCAL). WINIFRED ENOS, TEACHER; NILES SCHOOL; 355 HILLVIEW DR; FREMONT, CA 94536. (#13388).

PAINTING A MURAL, FREMONT, CA. A 5' X 18' MURAL DEPICTING TYPE OF STUDENTS AT AMERICAN HIGH. (LOCAL). JOE TRANCHINA, PRINCIPAL; AMERICAN HIGH SCHOOL; 36300 FREMONT BLVD; FREMONT, CA 94536. (#20730).

REDEDICATION OF OUR CLUB HOUSE, FREMONT, CA. CLUB HOUSE BUILT IN 1912; RESTORATION & PAINTING FINISHED IN 1975 ON OUTSIDE; REDECORATING OF INSIDE BY MEMBERS IN 1975 AND 1976. (LOCAL). CAROL AMICK, PRESIDENT; COUNTY CLUB OF WASHINGTON TOWNSHIP; 3721 PARISH AVE; FREMONT, CA 94538. (#20727).

RESTORATION OF THE MISSION SAN JOSE - FREMONT, CA. PROJECT WILL BE TO RESTORE MISSION SAN JOSE BUILT IN 1797; 14TH IN THE CHAIN OF 21 CALIFORNIA MISSIONS. (ST-WIDE). FRANK DONAHOE, CHAIRMAN; COMMITTEE FOR RESTORATION OF MISSION SAN JOSE; 39039 PASEO PADRE; FREMONT, CA 94537. (#11352).

SHINN HISTORICAL PARK RESTORATION, FREMONT, CA. THE PRESERVATION OF AN IMPORTANT HISTORICAL RESOURCE, A 4 1/2 ACRE EARLY CALIFORNIA RANCH. (LOCAL). DR ROBERT FISHER, CHAIRMAN; MISSION PEAK HERITAGE FOUNDATION; PO BOX 3405; FREMONT, CA 94538. (#11362).

WASHINGTON TOWNSHIP HERITAGE - FREMONT, CA. PRESENTATION OF A COURSE ON LOCAL HISTORY AT OHLONE COLLEGE. (LOCAL). PHILIP HOLMES, PROJ DIRECTOR; 42071 CAMINO SANTA BARBARA; FREMONT, CA 94538. (#13386).

WOMAN'S ROLE AT TURN OF CENTURY, FREMONT, CA. AN ORAL HISTORY COLLECTION WILL BE RECORDED FROM INTERVIEWS WITH OLDER WOMEN RESIDENTS. (NAT'L). DIANE BROWN & JOHN BAKER, CO-CHAIRPERSONS; OHLONE COLLEGE; 43600 MISSION BLVD; FREMONT, CA 94532. (#11799).

NOV 8, '75. SPIRIT LEADER COMPETITION. COMPETITION AT AMERICAN HIGH SCHOOL. (LOCAL). PRINCIPAL; AMERICAN HIGH SCHOOL; 36300 FREMONT BLVD; FREMONT, CA 94536. (#200006-72).

JAN 24 - MAR 18, '76. MUSICAL ARTS SERIES. LIVE PERFORMANCE AT EPLER GYM, OHLONE - NEWARK H S. (LOCAL). DIANE BROWN, DIRECTOR; OHLONE COLLEGE COMMUNITY SERVICES; 43600 MISSION BLVD; FREMONT, CA 94537. (#105000-4).

FEB 18, '76. HISTORICAL BUS TOUR. TOUR AT STARTS AT HUB SHOPPING CENTER. (LOCAL). DIANE BROWN, DIRECTOR; OHLONE COLLEGE COMMUNITY SERVICES; 43600 MISSION BLVD; FREMONT, CA 94537. (#105000-5).

MAR 2 - 21, '76. MISSION TRAIL CLASSES AND TOUR. TOUR AT 43600 MISSION BLVD. (LOCAL). DIANE BROWN, DIRECTOR; OHLONE COLLEGE COMMUNITY SERVICES; 43600 MISSION BLVD; FREMONT, CA 94537. (#105000-2).

MAR 12 - 13, '76. MEN'S CONFERENCE. CONFERENCE AT FREMONT CAFETERIA-LECTURE HALL. (LOCAL). DIANE BROWN, DIRECTOR; OHLONE COLLEGE COMMUNITY SERVICES; 43600 MISSION BLVD; FREMONT, CA 94537. (#105000-3).

MAR 21, '76. PHILHARMONIC ORCHESTRA BICENTENNIAL CONCERT. LIVE PERFORMANCE AT AMERICAN HIGH SCHOOL, 36300 FREMONT BLVD - GYMNASIUM. (LOCAL). SUSAN ROSE, PRESIDENT; PHILHARMONIC SOCIETY OF FREMONT-NEWARK; PO BOX 104; FREMONT, CA 94537. (#101076-1).

MAY 22 - 23, '76. SHINN HISTORICAL PARK OPEN HOUSE & TOUR. EXHIBIT AT SHINN HISTORICAL PARK, 1269 PERALTA BLVD. (LOCAL). DR ROBERT FISHER; MISSION PEAK HERITAGE FOUNDATION; PO BOX 3405; FREMONT, CA 94538. (#11362-1).

MAY 22 - 23, '76. 100TH ANNIVERSARY OF THE SHINN HOUSE. CEREMONY, FESTIVAL AT SHINN HOUSE. (LOCAL). CAROL AMICK, PRES; COUNTRY CLUB OF WASHINGTON TWNSHP; ALAMEDA DISTRICT FED OF WOMEN; 3721 PARISH AVE; FREMONT, CA 94538. (#105000-1).

JUNE 4 - 5, '76. PERFORMANCES BY 'THE TOWN CRIERS'. LIVE PERFORMANCE. (LOCAL). E ELDER, SECRETARY; AMERICAN HIGH SCHOOL; 36300 FREMONT BLVD; FREMONT, CA 94536. (#104995-1).

FRESNO

FRESNO, CALIF, HISTORY BOOK. BOOK COMMEMORATING THE HISTORY, PEOPLE, EVENTS, STRUCTURES, ETC, AND HOW THEY INFLUENCED THE FRESNO OF TODAY. (LOCAL). WILLIAM BRIAM, PRINCIPAL ANALYST; FRESNO REGIONAL BICENTENNIAL COORDINATING COMMITTEE; 2326 FRESNO ST; FRESNO, CA 93721. (#3961). **(??).**

MEUX FAMILY HOME RESTORATION IN FRESNO, CALIF. RESTORING THE HOME OF DR T R MEUX, A VICTORIAN STYLE HOUSE BUILT IN 1888 AND OCCUPIED BY THE SAME FAMILY FOR 86 YEARS. (LOCAL). WILLIAM BRIAM, PRINCIPAL ANALYST; FRESNO REGIONAL BICENTENNIAL COORDINATING COMMITTEE; 2326 FRESNO ST; FRESNO, CA 93721. (#4038).

OCT 12 - 19, '75. TRIBUTE TO AMERICAN INDIANS - ART EXHIBIT. AN ART EXHIBIT DEPICTING THE LIFE & HISTORY OF AMERICAN INDIANS WILL BE PRESENTED. THE EXHIBIT OF WORKS BY PROFESSOR WILLIAM MINSCHEW OF CALIFORNIA STATE UNIV UTILIZES VARIOUS ART MEDIA. AT ART BUILDING. (ST-WIDE). BICENTENNIAL PLANNING COM; CALIFORNIA STATE UNIV, FRESNO; SHAW & MAPLE AVE; FRESNO, CA 93740. (#8015-1).

OCT 16 - 25, '75. THE LIBERTY DANCE OF HENRY SPARROW - DRAMA ON THE AMER REVOLUTION. A DRAMA BASED ON ACTUAL WRITINGS AND COLORFUL ANECDOTES FROM THE PERIOD OF THE AMERICAN REVOLUTION WILL BE PRESENTED AT THE CALIFORNIA STATE UNIVERSITY. SLIDES & MUSIC FROM THE PERIOD WILL BE USED. AT LITTLE THEATER, CALIFORNIA STATE UNIV. (LOCAL). BICENTENNIAL PLANNING COM; CALIFORNIA STATE UNIV, FRESNO; SHAW & MAPLE AVE; FRESNO, CA 93740. (#8016-1).

NOV 27 - 29, '75. UNITED STATES ARMED FORCES BICENTENNIAL CARAVAN. THE CARAVAN IS COMPOSED OF EXHIBIT VANS FOR EACH BRANCH OF THE MILITARY SERVICE. THE THEME OF THE EXHIBITION IS 'HISTORY OF THE ARMED FORCES AND THEIR CONTRIBUTION TO THE NATION'. (LOCAL). JAMES DODSON, CHAIRMAN; U S ARMED FORCES BICENTENNIAL EXHIBIT VANS PROJECT; 1221 FULTON MALL, ROOM 431; FRESNO, CA 93721. (#1775-295).

DEC 19 - 21, '75. AMERICAN FREEDOM TRAIN DISPLAY DAYS AT FRESNO. THE AMERICAN FREEDOM TRAIN WILL INCLUDE 10 EXHIBIT CARS & 2 SHOWCASE CARS DEPICTING DIFFERENT PHASES OF THE AMERICAN EXPERIENCE. ITS ARRIVAL WILL SERVE AS A CATALYST FOR LOCAL BICENTENNIAL CELEBRATIONS BY PEOPLE THROUGHOUT THIS NATION. (ST-WIDE). DON MALLICOAT, EDIT SVCS; THE AMERICAN FREEDOM TRAIN FOUNDATION, INC; 5205 LEESBURG PIKE, SUITE 800; BAILEY'S XRDS, VA 22041. (#1776-37).

FEB 23, '76. 'THE BRITISH ARE COMING!' - BRITISH MILITARY BAND PERFORMANCE. TOUR OF MAJOR U S CITIES BY BRITISH MILITARY UNITS AS REPRESENTATIVE OF UNITS INVOLVED IN REVOLUTIONARY WAR CAMPAIGN. AT CONVENTION CENTER ARENA. (INT'L). CHARLES K JONES, PRES; COLUMBIA ARTISTS FESTIVALS CORP; 165 W 57TH ST; NEW YORK, NY 10019. (#6532-25).

JUNE 21, '76. UNIVERSITY OF CALIFORNIA MARCHING BAND PRESENTS 'SPIRIT OF AMERICA'. THIS EVENT IS PART OF A SIX-WEEK PERFORMANCE TOUR OF THE U S BY THE UNIVERSITY OF CALIF MARCHING BAND. SPIRIT OF AMERICA IS A COLLEGIATE MUSICAL REVUE CELEBRATING OUR NATION'S BICENTENNIAL. AT SELLAND ARENA FRESNO CONVENTION CENTER. (ST-WIDE). AL GELLER, CHMN; EAST FRESNO KIWANIS CLUB; 329 VAN NESS AVE; FRESNO, CA 93701. (#10515-7).

JULY 3 - 4, '76. 'FROM RED COATS TO RED PLANET' HISTORICAL PAGEANT. A PAGEANT WRITTEN & PRODUCED BY PROF EDWARD EMANUEL, WHICH WILL COVER THE FULL 200 YEAR BICENTENNIAL PERIOD WITH PARTICIPATION BY HUNDREDS OF COMMUNITY RESIDENTS IN FULL COSTUME. MUSIC, FIREWORKS, TRIBUTES; ALL OUT-OF-DOORS IN GRANDSTAND AREA. AT FRESNO DISTRICT FAIRGROUNDS. (LOCAL). JACQUELINE L RYLE; FRESNO REGIONAL BICENTENNIAL COORDINATING COMM; 2326 FRESNO ST; FRESNO, CA 93721. (#6353-502).

JULY 4, '76. PARADE WITH THEME ON HISTORY & DEVELOPMENT OF FRESNO. PARADE TRACING GROWTH OF FRESNO FROM RAILROAD TOWN OF 1800'S TO THRIVING METROPOLIS OF 1970'S. AT COURTHOUSE PARK. (LOCAL). WILLIAM BRIAM; FRESNO REGIONAL BICENT COORDINATING COMMITTEE; 2326 FRESNO ST; FRESNO, CA 93721. (#3962-1).

JULY 4, '76. PLANTING & DEDICATION OF OFFICIAL BICENT TREE - VIRGINIANA OAK. OPENING, FESTIVAL, CEREMONY AT COURTHOUSE PARK, TULARE & M STS, FRESNO, CA. (LOCAL). JACQUELINE L RYLE; FRESNO REGIONAL BICENTENNIAL COORDINATING COMMITTEE; 2326 FRESNO ST; FRESNO, CA 93721. (#3963-501).

AUG 31 - SEPT 6, '76. BRITISH INVITATIONAL RIFLE MATCH. CEREMONY, COMPETITION, LIVE PERFORMANCE AT FRESNO CALIFORNIA RIFLE RANGE. (REGN'L). BERNARD BALLOUGH; FRESNO RIFLE CLUB; 2213 E RANCHO CULEBRA DR; COUINA, CA 91724. (#107692-1).

OCT 5 - 17, '76. FRESNO DISTRICT FAIR. FAIR AT 1121 CHANCE. (ST-WIDE). RALPH M HINDS, DIR; 21ST DISTRICT AGRICULTURAL ASSOCIATION; 1121 CHANCE AVE; FRESNO, CA 93702. (#106095-32).

FT BRAGG

MAY 10, '76. NETHERLANDS CHAMBER ORCHESTRA VISITS FORT BRAGG. LIVE PERFORMANCE. (INT'L). WILLIAM SIMONSZ, COORD; NETHERLANDS GOVERNMENT; NETHERLANDS EMBASSY-4200 LINNEAN; WASHINGTON, DC 20008. (#109013-20).

FULLERTON

'AMERICA' SERIES FILMS - PROJ OF FULLERTON, CA. 13 FILMS; A PERSONAL HISTORY OF THE U S BY ALISTAR COOKE WILL BE SHOWN EACH MONTH. (LOCAL). MS JEAN NELSON, LIBRARIAN; FULLERTON PUBLIC LIBRARY; 353 W COMMONWEALTH; FULLERTON, CA 92632. (#14873).

ARBORETUM - HERITAGE HOUSE, FULLERTON, CA. 20 ACRE ARBORETUM TO SERVE AS AN ECOLOGICAL PRESERVE FOR NATIVE VEGETATION & A WILDLIFE SANCTUARY. IT FEATURES ONE OF THE ORIGINAL FULLERTON HOUSES OF THE 1890'S, SERVING AS A MUSEUM. (LOCAL). DR DAVID E VAN DEVENTER, CHAIRMAN; CALIFORNIA STATE UNIVERSITY BICENTENNIAL COMMITTEE; 800 N STATE COLLEGE BLVD; FULLERTON, CA 92634. (#18434).

ART IN PUBLIC PLACES - PROJ OF FULLERTON, CA. ENCOURAGE ART IN PUBLIC BUILDINGS & PARKS; COMMITTEE WILL RAISE FUNDS AND COMMISSION ARTISTS. (LOCAL). MRS EDWARD M GINTER, CHAIRPERSON; FULLERTON BICENTENNIAL COMMISSION; 303 W COMMONWEALTH; FULLERTON, CA 92632. (#14875).

ART OF THE 19TH CENTURY, FULLERTON, CA. A SURVEY OF ORANGE COUNTY ART COMPLETED BY AMERICAN ARTISTS IN THE 19TH CENTURY, WILL BE TAKEN. (LOCAL). MRS MARY ANN LYLES, CHAIRMAN; FULLERTON BICENTENNIAL COMMISSION; 331 N JEFFERSON; FULLERTON, CA 92632. (#14877).

ORAL HISTORY - PROJ OF FULLERTON, IL. INTERVIEWS WITH COMMUNITY PIONEERS WILL BE TAPED, TRANSCRIBED, EDITED AND PUBLISHED. (LOCAL). DR DAVID VAN DEVENTER, CHAIRMAN; FULLERTON BICENTENNIAL COMMISSION/CALIFORNIA STATE UNIV; 800 N STATE COLLEGE BLVD; FULLERTON, CA 92634. (#14876).

RESTORATION OF FULLERTON HOME, CA. THE HOME OF FULLERTON'S FIRST DOCTOR HAS BEEN MOVED TO THE ABRORETUM BUILDING AND RESTORED TO 1894 CONDITION. (LOCAL). MRS JO ANN WOODARD, HERITAGE HOUSE CO-ORDINATOR; FULLERTON BICENTENNIAL COMMISSION; 2525 SANTA YSABEL; FULLERTON, CA 92631. (#14878).

RESTORATION OF HILLCREST FOUNTAIN - FULLERTON, CA. A FOUNTAIN BUILT IN 1930, VANDALIZED & INOPERABLE SINCE 1945, WILL BE RESTORED; NEW PUMPS, JETS, LIGHTS AND LANDSCAPING. (LOCAL). MRS EDWARD M GINTER, CHAIRPERSON; FULLERTON BICENTENNIAL COMMISSION; 303 W COMMONWEALTH; FULLERTON, CA 92633. (#14874).

SEPT 13 - OCT 12, '75. REFLECTIONS OF AN ARTIST: FLORENCE ARNOLD. EXHIBIT. (LOCAL). MS DALE RAOUL, CHMN; MUCKENTHALER CULTURAL CENTER; 1201 W MALVEEN; FULLERTON, CA 92633. (#102099-1).

SEPT 26, '75. INTERNATIONAL FOLK BALLET. LIVE PERFORMANCE AT CAMPUS THEATER. (LOCAL). MS AMANDA SMITH, DIR; FULLERTON COLLEGE; 321 E CHAPMAN; FULLERTON, CA 92632. (#102099-2).

SEPT 27 - NOV 30, '75. A TRIBUTE TO LUCY LEWIS, ACOMA POTTER. EXHIBIT. (LOCAL). MRS EDWARD N GINTER, CHMN; MUSEUM OF NORTH ORANGE COUNTY/FULLERTON BICENTENNIAL COMMITTEE; 1816 YERMO PL; FULLERTON, CA 92633. (#102099-3).

OCT 4 - 5, '75. ARTS & CRAFTS FESTIVAL. EXHIBIT, FAIR AT HILLCREST PARK, HARBOR AT BREA AVE. (LOCAL). MRS EDWARD M GINTER, CHMN; FULLERTON BICENTENNIAL COMMISSION & FULLERTON PARK & RECREATION DEPT; 1816 YERMO PL; FULLERTON, CA 92633. (#102099-4).

OCT 11 - NOV 16, '75. THE WORLD OF ARTHUR PUTNAM. EXHIBIT AT 1201 W MALVERN. (LOCAL). MRS EDWARD M GINTER, CHMN; MUCKENTHALER CULTURAL CENTER; 1816 YERMO PL; FULLERTON, CA 92633. (#102099-5).

JAN 16, '76. WALT WHITMAN'S AMERICA. LIVE PERFORMANCE AT PLUMMER AUDITORIUM. (LOCAL). MS AMANDA SMITH, COORD; FULLERTON COLLEGE; 321 E CHAPMAN; FULLERTON, CA 92632. (#102099-6).

MAR 20, '76. FULLERTON TOWN HALL MEETING '76. CONFERENCE AT FULLERTON COLLEGE, 321 E CHAPMAN AVE. (LOCAL). DORIS COVELLI, CHAIRMAN; FULLERTON BICENTENNIAL COMMISSION, FULLERTON COLLEGE; 321 E CHAPMAN; FULLERTON, CA 92635. (#105469-1).

APR 2 - JUNE 30, '76. WOMEN ARTISTS OF THE WEST 1850-1950. EXHIBIT AT 1201 WEST MALVERN. (LOCAL). ALLYSON SANBRIN, COORD; MUCKENTHALER CULTURAL CENTER & FULLERTON BICENTENNIAL COMMISSION; 303 W COMMONWEALTH AVE; FULLERTON, CA 92632. (#104191-2).

APR 8 - 11, '76. HISTORY OF AMERICA AS SEEN THROUGH THE EYES OF BEN FRANKLIN. LIVE PERFORMANCE. (LOCAL). LU ANNE JOHNSON, COORD; FULLERTON CIVIC LIGHT OPERA CO; 1513 W ASH ST; FULLERTON, CA 92633. (#105438-1).

FULLERTON — CONTINUED

APR 24 - 25, '76. THE GREAT AMERICAN SWAP MEET. FESTIVAL AT KIMERLY CLARK ATHLETIC FIELD, STATE COLLEGE BLVD, FULLERTON. (LOCAL). ALLYSON SANBURN, COORD; FULLERTON BICENTENNIAL COMMITTEE; 303 W COMMONWEALTH AVE; FULLERTON, CA 92632. (#105469-2).

APR 28 - 29, '76. UNITED STATES ARMED FORCES BICENTENNIAL CARAVAN. CARAVAN IS COMPOSED OF EXHIBIT VANS FOR EACH MILITARY SERVICE. PROJECT THEME IS ' HISTORY OF THE ARMED FORCES & THEIR CONTRIBUTIONS TO THE NATION'. (LOCAL). ALLISON SANBURN, CHAIRMAN; U S ARMED FORCES BICENTENNIAL CARAVAN; 303 W COMMONWEALTH; FULLERTON, CA 92632. (#1775-559).

MAY 13 - 19, '76. FESTIVAL OF AMERICAN MUSIC. LIVE PERFORMANCE AT MUSIC DEPT, 800 N STATE. (LOCAL). MRS EDWARD M GINTER, CHMN; CALIFORNIA STATE UNIV; 1816 YERMO PL; FULLERTON, CA 92632. (#102099-7).

JUNE 12 - JULY 11, '76. 100 AMERICAN DOLLS, AN EXHIBITION. EXHIBIT AT 1201 W MALVERN. (LOCAL). ALLYSON SANBRIN, COORD; MUCKENTHALER CULTURAL CENTER & FULLERTON BICENTENNIAL COMMISSION; 303 W COMMONWEALTH AVE; FULLERTON, CA 92632. (#104191-1).

JULY 4, '76. INVOLVEMENT DAY. FESTIVAL AT CITY PARKS. (LOCAL). MRS EDWARD M GINTER, CHMN; FULLERTON BICENTENNIAL COMMISSION; 1816 YERMO PL; FULLERTON, CA 92633. (#102099-8).

MAR 19 - APR 24, '77. 'TREASURES OF LONDON' EXHIBITION. 500 YEARS OF BRITISH SILVER ARE REPRESENTED IN THIS EXHIBITION OF 46 ANTIQUE OBJECTS, 46 MODERN PIECES, & 100 PIECES OF MODERN JEWELRY. AT MUCKENTHALER CULTURAL CENTER. (INT'L). EILEEN HARAKAL, COORD; SMITHSONIAN INSTITUTION TRAVELING EXHIBITION SERVICE; 1000 JEFFERSON DR, SW; WASHINGTON, DC 20560. (#26660-2).

SEPT 10 - OCT 16, '77. EXHIBITION OF YUGOSLAV NAIVE ART - SITES. EXHIBIT AT MUCKENTHALER CULTURE CENTER, 1201 W MALVERN. (INT'L). WILLIAM GRAVESMILL, DIR; MUCKENTHALER CULTURE CENTER; 1201 W MALVERN; FULLERTON, CA 92633. (#106777-1).

GALT

LANDSCAPING & DEVELOPING HISTORICAL PARK -GALT, CA. LOCAL PARK UNDERGOING GRADING, WATER PIPE INSTALLATION, & PLANTING AS A GOAL FOR '76. (LOCAL). MRS BAXTER SPERRY, DIRECTOR; AMERICAN REVOLUTION BICENTENNIAL COMMISSION OF GALT; 807 C ST; GALT, CA 95632. (#3553).

RESTORATION OF GALT'S 'OLD TOWN' CALIFORNIA. INCLUDES LANDSCAPING, ERECTING REPLICA OF OLD BANDSTAND, PUTTING IN TABLES & BENCHES IN 4TH ST. PARK. ALSO, HITCHING POSTS, REPLICA OF OLD TOWN WELL, PLAQUES ON HISTORIC BLDGS & DECORATE SIGNS & DOORS. (LOCAL). MRS BAXTER SPERRY, DIRECTOR; AMERICAN REVOLUTION BICENTENNIAL COMMISSION OF GALT; 807 C ST; GALT, CA 95632. (#3348).

JULY 4, '75. DEDICATE BANDSTAND, 4TH OF JULY PICNIC. ERECTING REPLICA OF BANDSTAND, PICNIC FACILITIES IN 4TH ST PARK. HITCHING POSTS, REPLICA OF OLD TOWN WELL. AT 4TH ST PARK BTW B&C STS. GALT CA. (LOCAL). MRS BAXTER SPERRY; AM REV BICEN COMM OF GALT; 807 C ST; GALT, CA 95632. (#3348-1).

JULY 9, '75. UNITED STATES ARMED FORCES BICENTENNIAL CARAVAN. CARAVAN NUMBER FOUR-COMPOSED OF EXHIBIT VANS FOR EACH MILITARY SERVICE. PROJECT THEME IS 'HISTORY OF THE ARMED FORCES & THEIR CONTRIBUTIONS TO THE NATION.'. (LOCAL). MRS LOUISE DOWDELL; US ARMED FORCES BICENT EXHIBIT VAN PROJECT; PO BOX 672; GALT, CA 95632. (#1775-145).

JULY 1 - 31, '76. PAGEANT, MUSIC FESTIVAL. OPENING. (LOCAL). MRS BAXTER SPERRY; AMERICAN REVOLUTION BICENTENNIAL COMMISSION OF GALT; 807 C ST; GALT, CA 95632. (#3348-501).

JULY 4, '76. THIRD ANNUAL 4TH OF JULY TOWN PICNIC. 3RD ANNUAL PICNIC WITH THE NEWLY FORMED GALT COMMUNITY BAND, PERFORMING ON THE NEWLY DEDICATED (MAY 21, 1976) BICENTENNIAL BANDSTAND IN OLD TOWN PARK. AT BICENTENNIAL BANDSTAND IN OLD TOWN PARK. (LOCAL). MRS BAXTER SPERRY, DIR; AMERICAN REVOLUTION BICENTENNIAL COMMISSION OF GALT; 807 C STREET; GALT, CA 95632. (#3553-1).

GARDEN GROVE

BICENTENNIAL MALL & STRUCTURE, GARDEN GROVE, CA. CONSTRUCTION OF A BICENTENNIAL MALL & STRUCTURE LOCATED IN THE CIVIC CENTER COMPLEX. (LOCAL). JOHN BURKE, CHAIRMAN; GARDEN GROVE BICENTENNIAL COMMISSION; 11391 ARCADIA PKWY; GARDEN GROVE, CA 92640. (#18428).

BOLSA GRANDE HIGH SCHOOL BICENTENNIAL TOUR. 1-WK TOUR OF WASHINGTON, DC AREA & OTHER AMERICAN REVOLUTIONARY WAR POINTS OF INTEREST. STUDENTS WILL PERFORM HISTORICAL SONGS FOR AREA GROUPS ALSO. (LOCAL). ERNEST BOTTS; BOLSA GRANDE HIGH SCHOOL; 9401 WESTMINSTER AVE; GARDEN GROVE, CA 92640. (#104118-4). **(??).**

FOREIGN GUESTS IN PRIVATE HOMES PROJECT. AMERICAN FAMILIES HAVE FOREIGN GUESTS IN THEIR HOMES FOR 3 TO 7 DAYS IN 1976. 30 STATES TO PARTICIPATE. (INT'L). TOM MURPHY, DIRECTOR; AMERICAN HOST PROGRAM, INC; SUITE 2100, COMMADORE HOTEL; NEW YORKO, NY 10017. (#263).

NEW CLUBHOUSE FOR BOYS' CLUB, GARDEN GROVE, CA. CONSTRUCTION OF A NEW CLUBHOUSE FOR WEST GARDEN GROVE BOYS' CLUB. (LOCAL). KEN SLIMMER, PROJ DIRECTOR; WEST GARDEN GROVE BOYS CLUB; 6761 KILLARNEY AVE; GARDEN GROVE, CA 92645. (#14713).

PATRIOTIC WEEK. W GARDEN GROVE ELEMENTARY SCHOOLS STUDY & CELEBRATE 20 YR OF AMERICAN HISTORY. (LOCAL). MRS JAN DUNN; WEST GARDEN GROVE ELEMENTARY SCHOOLS; 10331 STANFORD AVE; GARDEN GROVE, CA 92640. (#104118-2). **(??).**

SANTIAGO HIGH SCHOOL COUNTRY FAIR. BICENTENNIAL BOOTHS, DISPLAYS, ETC AT HIGH SCHOOL. (LOCAL). MRS JAN DUNN; SANTIAGO HIGH SCHOOL; 12342 TRASK AVE; GARDEN GROVE, CA 92640. (#104118-1). **(??).**

SPIRIT OF '76 MINI-PARK - GARDEN GROVE, CA. TO EXPAND A NETWORK OF COMMUNITY MINI-PARKS AND GARDENS THROUGHOUT THE CITY OF GARDEN GROVE AND TO HARVEST CROPS GROWN THERE. (LOCAL). JOE MELLO, CHAIRMAN; GARDEN GROVE YOUTH COMMISSION; 11391 ACACIA PKWY; GARDEN GROVE, CA 92640. (#20769). **ARBA GRANTEE.**

JAN 4 - DEC 19, '76. BICENTENNIAL ROLL CALL. EACH STATE WILL BE REPRESENTED BY A DISPLAY. THE HISTORICAL SOCIETY'S NEWSLETTER WILL FEATURE HISTORICAL EVENTS FROM EACH STATE. AT HERITAGE PARK, 12174 EUCLID. (LOCAL). JANET Y NULL, CHAIRMAN; HISTORICAL SOCIETY OF GARDEN GROVE; 12174 EUCLID; GARDEN GROVE, CA 92640. (#14715-1).

FEB 7, '76. SOUNDS OF FREEDOM BICENTENNIAL BALL. THE SOCIETY FOR THE PRESERVATION OF BIG BANDS WILL PROVIDE CONTINUOUS DANCE MUSIC CULLED FROM AMERICAN HISTORY. REFRESHMENTS WILL BE SERVED. AT COMMUNITY MEETING CENTER, 11300 STANFORD. (LOCAL). MELISSA DICKERSON, COORD; CITY OF GARDEN GROVE & GARDEN GROVE BICENTENNIAL COMMISSION; 11391 ACACIA PKY; GARDEN GROVE, CA 92640. (#105095-1).

MAR 6 - APR 24, '76. BICENTENNIAL CRAFTS EXHIBITION. SPECIAL CRAFT AND ANTIQUE EXHIBITION OF TRADITIONAL AMERICAN ARTS & CRAFTS SUCH AS BUTTER CHURNING, BREAD BAKING AND HOMEMADE JAM. AT ARTISAN'S GUILD HALL, 9858 GARDEN GROVE BLVD. (LOCAL). MELISSA DICKERSON, COORD; GARDEN GROVE ARTISANS GUILD; 11391 ACACIA PKY; GARDEN GROVE, CA 92640. (#105095-2).

MAR 27, '76. BICENTENNIAL VARIETY SHOW. LOCAL TALENT IN THE CHURCH INCLUDES: A SHORT LOOK AT ROMEO & JULIET, PIANO RAGTIME, PULIANSIAN DANCERS AND MUCH MORE. AT UNITED METHODIST CHURCH, 12741 MAIN ST. (LOCAL). RUTH KUBBERNESS, CHAIRMAN; GARDEN GROVE HIGH SCHOOL; 11802 MORRIE LANE; GARDEN GROVE, CA 92640. (#105913-1).

APR 3, '76. ORANGE CO SENIOR CITIZENS BICENTENNIAL BALL. FESTIVAL AT GARDEN GROVE COMMUNITY MEETING CENTER; 11300 STANFORD AVE. (LOCAL). JEAN BLOOM/BARB ANDERSON; FIFTY PLUS CLUB OF GARDEN GROVE; 11391 ACACIA PKY; GARDEN GROVE, CA 92640. (#104118-3).

APR 25, '76. BICENTENNIAL SUNDAY. FESTIVAL AT EUCLID PARK ON EUCLID AVE. (LOCAL). MELISSA DICKERSON, COORD; CITY OF GARDEN GROVE, BICENTENNIAL COMMISSION, GIRL SCOUTS; 11391 ACACIA PKY; GARDEN GROVE, CA 92640. (#105095-4).

MAY 1, '76. 'I HEAR AMERICA SINGING'. THIS IS A MUSICAL NARRATIVE PROGRAM ABOUT AMERICAN HISTORY; MARCHES, TRADITIONAL HYMNS AND FOLK SONGS FROM 1776 TO THE PRESENT WILL BE FEATURED. AT DON WASH AUDITORIUM, GARDEN GROVE HIGH SCHOOL, 11271 STANFORD. (LOCAL). MELISSA DICKERSON, COORD; PORTERVILLE COLLEGE, CITY OF GARDEN GROVE BICENTENNIAL COMMISSION; 11391 ACACIA PKY; GARDEN GROVE, CA 92640. (#105095-5).

MAY 28 - 31, '76. STRAWBERRY FESTIVAL. FESTIVAL, PARADE AT GARDEN GROVE PARK. (LOCAL). LAWRENCE CASEY, CHMN; GARDEN GROVE CHAMBER OF COMMERCE; PO BOX 464; GARDEN GROVE, CA 92640. (#103416-339).

NOV 19 - 20, '76. UNITED STATES ARMED FORCES BICENTENNIAL CARAVAN. CARAVAN IS COMPOSED OF EXHIBIT VANS FOR EACH MILITARY SERVICE. PROJECT THEME IS 'HISTORY OF THE ARMED FORCES & THEIR CONTRIBUTIONS TO THE NATION'. (LOCAL). GLEN WEISNER; UNITED STATES ARMED FORCES BICENTENNIAL CARAVAN; 11391 ACHIA; GARDEN GROVE, CA 92640. (#1775-844).

GARDENA

NOV 12 - 13, '76. UNITED STATES ARMED FORCES BICENTENNIAL CARAVAN. CARAVAN IS COMPOSED OF EXHIBIT VANS FOR EACH MILITARY SERVICE. PROJECT THEME IS 'HISTORY OF THE ARMED FORCES & THEIR CONTRIBUTIONS TO THE NATION'. (LOCAL). MRS M JOHNSON; UNITED STATES ARMED FORCES BICENTENNIAL CARAVAN; 15306 ST ANDREWS PLACE; GARDENA, CA 90249. (#1775-841).

GEORGE AFB

AIRCRAFT DISPLAY, GEORGE AFB, CA. THE BICENTENNIAL EMBLEM HAS BEEN PLACED ON THE SIDES OF THREE PERMNENT STATIC DISPLAY AIRCRAFT. (LOCAL). COL WILLIAM H TALLEY, CHAIRMAN; 35 TACTICAL FIGHTER WING; GEORGE AFB, CA 92392. (#32606).

FREEDOM TREE, GEORGE AFB, CA. MOST IMPRESSIVE SELECTED TO REMIND US NATIONS GROW LIKE TREES. PEOPLE LIKE LEAVES CONTRIBUTE TO THAT GROWTH. TREE HAS PLAQUE AT FOOT. (LOCAL). COL WILLIAM H. TALLEY, CHAIRMAN; 35TH TACTICAL FIGHTER WING; GEORGE AFB, CA 92392. (#32608).

NOV 7, '76. OPEN HOUSE WITH USAF THUNDERBIRDS. STATIC DISPLAYS OF BOTH MODERN & VINTAGE AIRCRAFT WILL BE VIEWED. AT GAFB FLIGHT LINE. (LOCAL). COL WILLIAM H TALLEY; 35TH TACTICAL FIGHTER WING; 35TH TACTICAL FIGHTER WING; GEORGE AFB, CA 92392. (#200006-429).

GEYSERVILLE

MUSEUM IN GEYSERVILLE, CA. HISTORICAL EXHIBITS OF OLD GEYSERVILLE PICTURES, LITERATURE & DISHES. (LOCAL). WILMA BRIGGS, DIRECTOR; CHAMBER OF COMMERCE; PO BOX 276; GEYSERVILLE, CA 95441. (#31207).

MAY 1, '76. MAY DAY CELEBRATION. CEREMONY, FESTIVAL AT HOFFMAN GROVE. (LOCAL). WILMA BRIGGS; CHAMBER OF COMMERCE; PO BOX 276; GEYSERVILLE, CA 95441. (#200006-482).

GILROY

MAR 15, '76. 'WHITMAN, WHISLER & TENNESSEE WILLIAMS', LECTURE BY VINCENT PRICE. LIVE PERFORMANCE AT AUDITORIUM, GAVILAN COLLEGE. (LOCAL). STANLEY C BENZ, COUNSELOR; SANT CLARA COUNTY COLLEGE AND UNIVERSITIES CONSORTIUM; SAN JOSE STATE UNIV; SAN JOSE, CA 95192. (#103394-3).

OCT 12, '76. UNITED STATES ARMED FORCES BICENTENNIAL CARAVAN. CARAVAN IS COMPOSED OF EXHIBIT VANS FOR EACH MILITARY SERVICE. PROJECT THEME IS 'HISTORY OF THE ARMED FORCES & THEIR CONTRIBUTIONS TO THE NATION'. (LOCAL). BUTCH HART; UNITED STATES ARMED FORCES BICENTENNIAL CARAVAN; PO 66; GILROY, CA 95020. (#1775-823).

GLEN ELLEN

MAR '76. A VISIT WILL BE PAID TO THE JACK LONDON RANCH. SEMINAR, CEREMONY, TOUR. (LOCAL). DR KEVIN STARR; OAKLAND PUBLIC LIBRARY SAN FRANCISCO LIBRARY; CIVIC CTR; SAN FRANCISCO, CA 94102. (#9835-503).

GLENDALE

FEB 2, '76. JAMES WALKER, ORGANIST - PERFORMANCE. LIVE PERFORMANCE AT FIRST UNITED METHODIST CHURCH OF GLENDALE/BROADWAY AT KENWOOD. (LOCAL). XENIA DESBY, COORD; AMERICAN GUILD OF ORGANISTS, LOS ANGELES CHAPTER; 6234 SCENIC AVE; HOLLYWOOD, CA 90068. (#104525-3).

GLENDORA

BICENTENNIAL BIG TREE PARK, GLENDORA, CA. DEVELOPMENT OF PARK TO PRESERVE OVER 100 YEAR OLD FIG TREE. (LOCAL). DOUG MILLER, CHAIRMAN; GLENDORA BICENTENNIAL COMMITTEE; GLENDORA, CA 91740. (#28611).

GLENDORA HISTORICAL MUSEUM RESTORATION, CA. RESTORATION OF MUSEUM SITE AND CITY HISTORICAL SITE. (LOCAL). DOUG MILLER, COUNCILMAN; GLENDORA HISTORICAL SOCIETY; GLENDORA, CA 91740. (#28610).

RETURN OF THE POPPIES, GLENDORA, CA. POPPIES WERE PLANTED ON 5 ACRES. (ST-WIDE). DOUG MILLER, CHAIRMAN; GLENDORA BICENTENNIAL COMMITTEE; 116 E FOOTHILL BLVD; GLENDORA, CA 91740. (#28612).

SENIOR CITIZENS' HOUSING PROJECT, GLENDORA, CA. PROJECT TO SECURE & ASSIST IN THE DEVELOPMENT OF HOUSING FOR SENIOR CITIZENS. (LOCAL). HAL FRANKS, COORDINATOR; GLENDORA CHURCH HOMES; PO BOX 366; GLENDORA, CA 91740. (#28609).

JAN 10, '76. BICENTENNIAL PARADE. PARADE. (LOCAL). DOUG MILLER, CHAIRMAN; GLENDORA JAYCEES; 116 E FOOTHILL BLVD; GLENDORA, CA 91740. (#200006-379).

JAN 26 - 29, '76. 'I LOVE AMERICA' - MUSICAL. LIVE PERFORMANCE AT GRACE BAPTIST CHURCH, 1515 GLENDORA AVE. (LOCAL). JOHN JACKSON, DIRECTOR; AZUSA & GLENDORA CHOIRS & GLENDORA BICENTENNIAL COMMITTEE; GLENDORA, CA 91740. (#200006-376).

MAY '76. MISS GLENDORA BICENTENNIAL PAGEANT. COMPETITION AT CITY HALL, 116 E FOOTHILL BLVD. (LOCAL). DOUG MILLER, CHAIRMAN; GLENDORA JAYCEES; 116 E FOOTHILL BLVD; GLENDORA, CA 91740. (#200006-378).

JUNE 12, '76. GLENDORA BICENTENNIAL PICNIC. FESTIVAL AT GLENDORA AVENUE, BUSINESS DISTRICT. (LOCAL). JOHN C FIELDS, CHAIRMAN; GLENDORA BICENTENNIAL COMMISSION; GLENDORA, CA 91740. (#200006-380).

OCT 12, '76. BICENTENNIAL FLAG RAISING CEREMONY. CEREMONY AT GLENDORA CITY HALL, 116 E FOOTHILL BLVD. (LOCAL). NICK MOFFITT, COORD; GLENDORA BICENTENNIAL COMMITTEE; GLENDORA, CA 91740. (#109333-1).

GOLETA

FEB 25, '76. DEDICATION OF PLAQUE AT DE ANZA CAMP SITE OF FEB 25, 1776. STATE OF CALIFORNIA HISTORICAL COMMITTEE ACKNOWLEDGED THE APPLICATION BY SANTA BARBARA COUNTY BOARD OF SUPERVISORS IN JULY, 1975; THIS AREA INCLUDED ONE OF LARGEST CONCENTRATIONS OF INDIANS. AT GOLETA BEACH COUNTY PARK. (LOCAL). VIVIAN H OBERN, CHMN; SANTA BARBARA COUNTY BICENTENNIAL COMMITTEE; 4140 MARINA DR; SANTA BARBARA, CA 93110. (#102601-1).

GONZALES

GONZALES TRIBUNE & SOLEDAD BEE BICENT EFFORT-NBMRP. 3 JOINT PROGRAMS:1)EDUCATIONAL SPEAKING TOUR WITH DISPLAY OF HISTORICAL NEWSPAPERS;2)BEE WILL PROMOTE SPECIAL FIESTA FOR DE ANZA TREK & 3)TRIBUNE PROMOTES BICENTENNIAL OF CALIFORNIA'S WINE INDUSTRY. (LOCAL). MARY JO CHISM, EDITOR; GONZALES TRIBUNE; PO BOX 648; GONZALES, CA 93926. (#21294).

GROVER CITY

JULY 5, '76. ALL STATES PICNIC FESTIVAL & GAMES. CEREMONY, FESTIVAL. (LOCAL). CHARLES D NEWTON, CHMN; GROVER CITY BOOSTERS; PO BOX 407; GROVER CITY, CA 93433. (#200006-381).

GUSTINE

FILM ON PORTUGESE FILM FESTIVAL - GUSTINE, CA. PILOT DOCUMENTARY FOR SERIES OF FILMS ON FOLKLORE FESTIVALS IN AMERICA. (NAT'L). RICK FRIEDBERG, PRODUCER; RICK FRIEDBERG PRODUCTIONS; 6238 DEL VALLE DR; LOS ANGELES, CA 90048. (#27952).

HALF MOON BAY

RESTORATION OF THE JAMES JOHNSTON HOUSE - CA. RESTORATION OF AN 1853 HOUSE ON ORIGINAL SITE NEAR HALF MOON BAY TO USE FOR COMMUNITY ACTIVITIES, EDUCATIONAL PURPOSES AND HISTORIC AND AGRICULTURAL DISPLAYS. (LOCAL). STANLEY WALKER, CITY PLANNER; CITY OF HALF MOON BAY; CITY HALL, MAIN ST; HALF MOON BAY, CA 94019. (#9119).

HAVENLY VLY

MAR 2 - 7, '76. WORLD CUP RACE. COMPETITION AT SKI HILL. (REGN'L). PATTY OLSON, CHAIRMAN; FIS WORLD CUP RACE; SOUTH TAHOE, CA 95705. (#200006-167).

HAVILAH

REPLICA OF FIRST PUBLIC SCHOOL IN HAVILAH, CA. A REPLICA OF THE FIRST PUBLIC SCHOOL IN HAVILAH WILL BE BUILT. THE ORIGINAL WAS BUILT IN 1867, SHORTLY AFTER THE FOUNDING OF KERN COUNTY. (LOCAL). CLEONE L SHAW, PRESIDENT; HAVILAH CENTENNIAL GROUP, INC; PO BOX 32; BODFISH, CA 93205. (#28621).

APR 4, '76. COMMEMORATIVE PROGRAM. FESTIVAL, LIVE PERFORMANCE AT KERN COUNTY COURTHOUSE. (LOCAL). CLEONE L SHAW, CHAIRMAN; HAVILAH CENTENNIAL GROUP, INC & HAVILAH COMMUNITY NON-PROFIT GROUP; PO BOX 32; BODFISH, CA 93205. (#200006-371).

HAWAIIAN GDNS

HAWAIIAN GARDENS, CALIFORNIA, HISTORY BOOK. PRINTING A LOCAL HISTORY BOOK OF THE AREA WITH PICTURES. (LOCAL). LEON RICHARDS, CHAIRMAN; CITY OF HAWAIIAN GARDENS; 12134 TILBURY ST; HAWAIIAN GDNS, CA 90716. (#5027).

HAWKINSVILLE

MAR 12 - 14, '76. THIRD ANNUAL HARNESS FESTIVAL. ANNUAL FESTIVAL OF HORSE RACING WITH A PARADE AND ENTERTAINMENT. AT PULASKI COUNTY FAIRGROUNDS. (ST-WIDE). ILENE DAILY, COORD; HAWKINSVILLE HARNESS FESTIVAL; PO BOX 238; HAWKINSVILLE, CA 95836. (#103416-208).

HAWTHORNE

APR 18 - 19, '75. BICENTENNIAL INAUGURAL PROGRAM AND BALL. BICENTENNIAL INAUGURAL PROGRAM AND BALL. PRELUDE MUSIC BY UNITED STATES MARINE CORP BAND, 3RD MARINE AIRCRAFT WING, EL TORO MARINE BASE, CALIFORNIA-VIP IN ATTENDANCE, JOE DOBAL, FEDERAL-STATE RELATIONS DIRECTOR BICENTENNIAL PROGRAM, KENT WILLIAMS WESTERN DIR. AT HAWTHORNE MEMORIAL CENTER 3901 W. EL SEGUNDO BLVD AMPLE PARKING. (LOCAL). JOE MILLER CHAIRMAN; HAWTHORNE BICENTENNIAL COMMITTEE; 4460 W 126 STREET; HAWTHORNE, CA 90250. (#50183-1).

JAN 23, '76. BICENTENNIAL BALL WITH MUSIC BY TEX BENEKE. FESTIVAL AT HAWTHORNE MEMORIAL CENTER, 3901 W EL SEGUNDO BLVD. (LOCAL). JOE MILLER, CHAIRMAN; HAWTHORNE BICENTENNIAL COMMITTEE; 4460 W 126TH ST; HAWTHORNE, CA 90250. (#104287-1).

HAYWARD

ALISTAIR COOKE'S VIDEO SERIES ON AMERICA. PROJECT TO OBTAIN ALISTAIR COOKE'S 13 PART VIDEO TAPE SERIES ON AMERICA AS A PERMANENT ADDITION TO THE CHABOT COLLEGE LEARNING RESOURCES LIBRARY. (LOCAL). DR LEE HINCKLEY, DEAN OF INSTRUCTION; CHABOT COLLEGE OFFICE OF COMMUNITY SERVICES; 25555 HESPERIAN BLVD; HAYWARD, CA 94545. (#6665).

CALIFORNIA STATE UNIVERSITY HAYWARD MUSEUM - CA. CREATION OF A MUSEUM AT CALIFORNIA STATE UNIVERSITY TO BE DESIGNATED THE ALAMEDA COUNTY CLEARING HOUSE FOR HISTORIC & ARCHAEOLOGICAL REMAINS. (ST-WIDE). GEORGE P RODGERS, CHAIRMAN; CALIFORNIA STATE UNIV ANTHROPOLOGY DEPT; 25800 HILLARY; HAYWARD, CA 94542. (#11354).

FIVE BICENTENNIAL BOOKLISTS, HAYWARD, CA. MAKE AVAILABLE TO THE CITIZENS OF ALAMEDA COUNTY A CAREFULLY CHOSEN READING LIST OF THEIR OWN BOOKS RELATING TO BICENTENNIAL TOPICS. (LOCAL). JUDY LEES, CHAIRMAN; ALAMEDA COUNTY LIBRARY; 224 W WINTON AVE; HAYWARD, CA 94544. (#20732).

HALL OF JUSTICE, HAYWARD, CA. HAYWARD HALL OF JUSTICE, A COURT FACILITY OF MUNICIPAL AND SUPERIOR COURT DEPARTMENTS, WILL BE DEDICATED IN 1976. (LOCAL). JEAN WENTE, CHAIRMAN; ALAMEDA COUNTY ART COMMISSION; 5565 TESLA RD; LIVERMORE, CA 94550. (#11361).

LIBERTY TREES IN HAYWARD, CA. REDWOOD SEEDLINGS WILL BE PLANTED AT EACH OF THE 59 HIGH SCHOOLS IN ALAMEDA COUNTY. (LOCAL). MRS JAMES ROSE, CHAIRMAN; PERALTA CHAPTER DAR; 30524 OAKMONT WAY; HAYWARD, CA 94544. (#11358).

PLANT A TREE AT CHABOT COLLEGE, CALIFORNIA. CHABOT COLLEGE STUDENTS WILL PURCHASE AND DONATE TREES AS A LASTING CONTRIBUTION TO THE BEAUTIFICATION OF THE COLLEGE AND COMMUNITY. (LOCAL). DR LEE HINCKLEY, ASSOC DEAN OF INSTRUCTION; ASSOCIATED STUDENTS OF CHABOT COLLEGE; 25555 HESPERIAN BLVD; HAYWARD, CA 94545. (#6664).

JUNE 20 - AUG 30, '75. SUMMER BICENTENNIAL FESTIVAL OF CONCERTS & COURSES. THE BICENTENNIAL FESTIVAL CONSISTS OF NINE MAJOR CONCERTS ORIENTED TO THE BICENTENNIAL, WITH 12 RELATED SHORT COURSES FOR WHICH STUDENTS MAY EARN CREDIT. INCLUDES ARTISTS, MAX MORATH, TEX WILLIAMS, BILL SCHUSTICK & OTHERS. (LOCAL). MISS GAIL JOHNSON; CHABOT COLLEGE; 25555 HESPERIAN BLVD; HAYWARD, CA 94545. (#101075-1).

OCT 9 - 10, '76. HAYWARD CENTENNIALS COMMUNITY QUILT FAIRE '76. 3RD ANNUAL QUILT SHOW TO BE HELD IN THE HAYWARD COMMUNITY. LAST YEAR'S ATTENDANCE TOTALLED 3200. QUILT ENTRIES IN THE FAIRE DATE BACK TO THE AMERICAN REVOLUTION. A DOOR PRIZE QUILT HAS BEEN MADE BY GAIL MOORE QUILT MAKING CLASSES. AT CENTENNIAL HALL, 22292 FOOTHILL BLVD. (LOCAL). GAIL MOORE, DIRECTOR; GAIL MOORE'S QUILT MAKER'S AND HAYWARD FIRST COMMITTEE; 22499 CHARLENE WAY; CASTRO VALLEY, CA 94546. (#105789-1).

HAZLEHURST

TIME CAPSULE - HAZLEHURST, CA. COMMITTEE WILL COLLECT, AUTHENTICATE & PREPARE HISTORY, TO BE PLACED IN 50 YEAR & 100 YEAR CAPSULES. (LOCAL). TAYLOR DOMINY, CHAIRMAN; BICENTENNIAL HISTORICAL COMMITTEE OF HAZLEHURST; DOUGLAS HWY; HAZLEHURST, CA 91539. (#27528).

HEALDSBURG

COMMEMORATIVE FOUNTAIN IN HEALDSBURG, CA. RESTORATION OF BRONZE FOUNTAIN ORIGINALLY INSTALLED AT OAKMOUND CEMETERY IN 1876. (LOCAL). JESSE WILLIS, DIR; AMERICAN LEGION; 1260 CHIQUITA RD; HEALDSBURG, CA 95448. (#19153).

MARKING HISTORIC SITES IN HEALDSBURG, CA. PLACING DESCRIPTIVE MARKERS AT PRINCIPAL HISTORIC SITES IN AREA. (LOCAL). GLEN DAVIS, DIRECTOR; HEALDSBURG KIWANIS CLUB; 301 PLAZA ST; HEALDSBURG, CA 95448. (#19155).

MUSEUM IN HEALDSBURG, CA. ESTABLISHING MUSEUM IN BUILDING PROVIDED BY CITY. (LOCAL). EDWIN LANGHART, CHAIRMAN; HEALDSBURG BICENTENNIAL COMMITTEE; PO BOX 905; HEALDSBURG, CA 95448. (#19154).

ORAL HISTORY IN HEALDSBURG, CA. DEVELOP ORAL HISTORY OF DRY CREEK VALLEY AREA NEAR HEALDSBURG AND CULMINATE IN PUBLICATION. (LOCAL). MRS DON SCHMIDT, PROJ DIRECTOR; DRY CREEK NEIGHBORS CLUB; 5675 DRY CREEK RD; HEALDSBURG, CA 95448. (#19152).

JULY 4, '76. COMMUNITY BARBECUE AND CELEBRATION. FESTIVAL AT VILLA CHANTICLEER. (LOCAL). EDWIN LANGHART, PROJ DIR; HEALDSBURG BICENTENNIAL COMMITTEE; HEALDSBURG, CA 95448. (#104173-1).

JULY 4, '76. MARATHON RE-CREATING POPULAR RUN OF 50 YEARS AGO. COMPETITION, FESTIVAL. (LOCAL). RODNEY W WALLSTRUM, CHMN; CHAMBER OF COMMERCE; 225 LINCOLN ST; HEALDSBURG, CA 95448. (#104173-2).

HEMET

APR 24 - MAY 9, '76. 49TH ANNUAL RAMONA PAGEANT. AN ANNUAL PRODUCTION RETELLS A STORY OF EARLY CALIFORNIA'S HISTORY AND ROMANCE & CONFLICT BETWEEN THE INDIANS AND THE COMING OF THE WHITE MAN. AT RAMONA BOWL. (ST-WIDE). GENERAL MANAGER; RAMONA PAGEANT ASSOC; PO BOX 755; HEMET, CA 92343. (#103416-272).

HOLLISTER

FEB 28 - MAY 1, '76. CAMPFIRE SLIDE PGM AT PINNACLES NM ON MEN AND A MONUMENT. SLIDE PROGRAM TELLS PINNACLES STORY FROM DAYS OF INDIANS TO TOMORROW ON FEB 28-MAR 13, MAR 27-AP 3,AP 17-MAY 1; ALSO AVAILABLE FOR PRESENTATION OFFSITE TO LOCAL SCHOOLS AND ORGANIZATIONS BY ARRANGEMENT WITH PARK STAFF. AT CHALONE CREEK CAMPGROUND, ONE AND A HALF MILES FROM VISITOR CENTER. (REGN'L). PINNACLES NM; NATIONAL PARK SERVICE; PAICINES, CA 95043. (#6730-123).

HOLLYWOOD

'HAPPY BIRTHDAY USA'-RECORD ALBUM - HOLLYWOOD, CA. DOUBLE ALBUM OF 32 SONGS EACH SONG ON A PART OF AMERICAN HISTORY BEGINNING WITH THE MAYFLOWER UP UNTIL TODAY. (NAT'L). RAY RUFFIN AND SEAN DOWNEY, PRODUCERS; HAPPY BIRTHDAY USA; BOX 1746; HOLLYWOOD, CA 90028. (#17863). **ARBA GRANTEE.**

'HAPPY BIRTHDAY USA' PROJECT PACKAGE. AN ALBUM ON THE HISTORY OF AMERICA; A ROAD SHOW, TELEVISION SPECIAL AND HISTORY GUIDES IN THE SCHOOLS. (LOCAL). RAY RUFF, PRESIDENT; HAPPY BIRTHDAY USA; PO BOX 1746; HOLLYWOOD, CA 90028. (#18383).

'...WHO HELP THEMSELVES', FILM PROJ OF CALIFORNIA. FILM PROJECT FOR CALIFORNIA INDUSTRIES FOR THE BLIND; 15-MIN RUNNING TIME. (LOCAL). ROBERT C PETERS, VICE PRESIDENT; PARAMOUNT MOTION PICTURES CORPORATION; 5451 MARATHON ST; HOLLYWOOD, CA 90038. (#9035).

OCT 20 - DEC 31, '75. WAGON TRAIN TOUR & FESTIVAL. FESTIVAL, TOUR AT PO BOX 3539. (REGN'L). M P HAIR, EXEC DIRECTOR; WAGON TRAIN TOUR ASSOCIATION; PO BOX 3539; HOLLYWOOD, CA 90028. (#102007-1).

MAR 19 - 21, '76. BLACKS IN COMMUNICATION. FESTIVAL. (LOCAL). GLORIA PRYOR WALKER; CLARK COLLEGE; 3168 G CANDLEWOOD DRIVE; EAST POINT, GA 30344. (#10875-2).

JULY 4, '76. USA 1976 BIRTHDAY PARTY. NON-PROFIT BICENTENNIAL PROJECT FOR CHILDREN WHO WILL BE 13 ON JULY 4, 1976. WILL ENCOURAGE BIRTHDAY PARTIES TYING IN THE AGE 13 WITH THE ORIGINAL 13 COLONIES. (REGN'L). MILT FORREST, COORDINATOR; USA 1976 BIRTHDAY PARTY; 183 N MARTEL AVE, SUITE 1976; HOLLYWOOD, CA 90036. (#106784-1).

HOLTVILLE

APR 19, '75. INITIAL PROGRAM-FLAG RAISING CEREMONIES-ALL DAY FESTIVITIES. ALL DAY FESTIVITIES-PANCAKE BREAKFAST AT 7:00AM BASEBALL GAME 9:30AM ICE CREAM & CAKE,AND RECREATION 10-2:00PM. BARBQUE 4:30-7:30PM WITH ENTERTAINMENT 4:30-7:30. 8:00PM.PRESENTATION,DEDICATION OF NEW FLAG & FLAG POLE, WITH SPEECHES & CEREMONIES, AND FOLLOWED AT 9:30 PM. AT HOLTVILLE CITY PARK HOLT AVE & US 80 HIGHWAY HOLTVILLE CALIF.. (LOCAL). MARIANNE WILSON; CITY OF HOLTVILLE BICENTENNIAL COMMISSION; 940 ORANGE; HOLTVILLE, CA 92250. (#50104-1).

DEC 5, '75. OLD FASHIONED CHRISTMAS DANCE. FUND RAISING & COMMEMORATIVE TO RAISE MONEY FOR CHAIRS & TABLES FOR ELEMENTARY SCHOOL. AT I U SWISS CLUB, 1585 E WORTHINGTON RD. (LOCAL). SHIRLEY DILLON, COORD; PTA; 538 WOOLDRIDGE; HOLTVILLE, CA 92250. (#200006-71).

DEC 16, '75. ANNUAL PTA CHRISTMAS CONCERT. CHRISTMAS MUSIC & PATRIOTIC MUSIC BY JR HIGH BAND. AT FINLEY AUDITORIUM - 600 BLOCK OF EAST 6TH. (LOCAL). JACK KELLY, DIRECTOR; HOLTVILLE PTA; 845 PINE; HOLTVILLE, CA 92250. (#104161-3).

JAN 12 - 13, '76. PENNSYLVANIA BICENTENNIAL WAGON TRAIN. BAND ESCORT ENTRANCE OF WAGON TRAIN; SILENT MOVIE 'WINNING OF BARBARA WORTH' WILL BE SHOWN AND SCROLL PRESENTATION MADE. (LOCAL). MARIANNE WILSON, DIR; HOLTVILLE BICENTENNIAL COMMISSION; 940 ORANGE; HOLTVILLE, CA 92250. (#104161-2).

JAN 24 - FEB 1, '76. HOLTVILLE ANNUAL CARROT FESTIVAL. ANNUAL HORSE SHOW STARTS THIS WEEK; OTHER ACTIVITIES DURING THE WEEK ARE CARROT COOKING CONTEST, TRACTOR PULL, 4-H LIVESTOCK SHOW, ART SHOW, PARADE ON SATURDAY & A CARNIVAL EACH NIGHT IN BABE RUTH PARK. AT HORSESHOW - E 4TH; PARADE DOWNTOWN; CARNIVAL-BABE RUTH PARK. (LOCAL). MARIANNE WILSON, DIR; HOLTVILLE BICENTENNIAL COMMISSION; 940 ORANGE; HOLTVILLE, CA 92250. (#104161-1).

FEB 3, '76. UNITED STATES ARMED FORCES BICENTENNIAL CARAVAN. CARAVAN IS COMPOSED OF EXHIBIT VANS FOR EACH MILITARY SERVICE. PROJECT THEME IS 'HISTORY OF THE ARMED FORCES AND THEIR CONTRIBUTIONS TO THE NATION'. (LOCAL). ALICE ARMSTRONG, CHMN; US ARMED FORCES EXHIBIT VANS PROJECT; 1945 E EVAN HEWES; HOLTVILLE, CA 92250. (#1775-315).

HOOPA

RESERVATION BEAUTIFICATION AND RESTORATION IN CA. RESTORE OLD VILLAGES, CEREMONIAL GROUNDS AND U S GRANT'S FORMER HOME; REMOVAL OF OLD BUILDINGS & BRUSH; IMPROVE RECREATIONAL AREAS AND HOMES, FENCING AND BEAUTIFICATION OF CEMETERIES. (LOCAL). PETER H MASTEN, JR, CHAIRMAN; HOOPA VALLEY TRIBE; PO BOX 817; HOOPA, CA 95546. (#22852). **ARBA GRANTEE.**

HUNTINGTN BCH

A FILM DOCUMENTARY IN HUNTINGTON BEACH, CA. FILM ON AMERICAN KNOWLEDGE IN MANAGEMENT AND COORDINA-

HUNTINGTN BCH — CONTINUED

TION TECHNIQUES IN PLANNING A HISTORICAL EVENT. (NAT'L). DAVID P GAROFOLO, PRESIDENT; U S BICENTENNIAL CORP OF HUNTINGTON BEACH; PO BOX 190; HUNTINGTN BCH, CA 92648. (#10890).

THE GREAT AMERICAN MARBLE - DANCE PROJ, CA. THE PROJECT IS A DANCE PERFORMANCE DEPICTING A COMPENDIUM OF THE LORE INVOLVING THE GAME OF MARBLES. (LOCAL). JERRY LASCOE, EXEC DIRECTOR; MATTI LASCO DANCE THEATRE COMPANY; 18733 ELMWOOD LN; HUNTINGTN BCH, CA 92646. (#17122).

MAY 1 - JULY 4, '76. COMMUNITY FESTIVALS FOR THE BICENTENNIAL. COMMUNITY FESTIVAL & PARADE, HUNTINGTON BEACH, CAL. FESTIVALS WITH THEME 'PAST TO REMEMBER, FUTURE TO MOLD', FEATURING ORGANIZATIONS CONCERNED WITH THE NEEDS OF YOUTH, THE NEEDY, AND THE AGED. (LOCAL). MARK G HAMMERQUIST; HUNTINGTON BEACH BICENTENNIAL COMMISSION; 20862 FARNSWORTH; HUNTINGTN BCH, CA 92646. (#2298-501).

MAY 9, '76. UNITED STATES ARMED FORCES BICENTENNIAL CARAVAN. CARAVAN IS COMPOSED OF EXHIBIT VANS FOR EACH MILITARY SERVICE. PROJECT THEME IS ' HISTORY OF THE ARMED FORCES & THEIR CONTRIBUTIONS TO THE NATION'. (LOCAL). BILL REED; U S ARMED FORCES BICENTENNIAL CARAVAN; PO BOX 190; HUNTINGTN BCH, CA 92648. (#1775-565).

JULY 4, '76. BICENTENNIAL PARADE. PARADE AT MAIN ST. (LOCAL). WILLIAM G REED, COORD; JAYCEES; 2000 MAIN ST; HUNTINGTN BCH, CA 92648. (#102979-1).

IMPERIAL

NOV 30 - DEC 7, '75. DE ANZA RE-ENACTMENT. TRAIL RIDE FROM COLORADO RIVER IN YUMA, AZ DOWN THE BANKS OF ALL AMERICAN CANAL WILL LAST 3 DAYS; CHRISTMAS PARADE DEC 6 IN EL CENTRO AND BARBEQUE CELEBRATION ON DEC 7 AT IMPERIAL COUNTY FAIRGROUNDS. AT IMPERIAL MID-WINTER FAIRGROUNDS. (LOCAL). PAULINE RICE, CHAIRMAN; IMPERIAL COUNTY BICENTENNIAL COMMISSION; 1101 AIRPORT RD; IMPERIAL, CA 92251. (#103726-1).

IMPERIAL BCH

MINI PARK-IMPERIAL BEACH, CALIFORNIA. A SMALL UNDEVELOPED TRI-ANGLE, LOCATED BETWEEN TWO MAIN HIGHWAYS. PLANS DEVELOPED THROUGH CONTEST IN LOCAL COLLEGE ARCHITECTURAL CLASS. FINANCING BY LOCAL SERVICE CLUBS. (LOCAL). ALICE L BOWLER, CHAIRMAN; IMPERIAL BEACH BICENTENNIAL COMMITTEE; 212 DAISY; IMPERIAL BCH, CA 92032. (#3262).

JULY '75. ALL STATES PICNIC. FESTIVAL AT MARINA VISTA PARK. (ST-WIDE). VIRGINIA BRISSEY; CHAMBER OF COMMERCE; 840 DELAWARE; IMPERIAL BCH, CA 92030. (#50535-1).

JAN 28, '76. UNITED STATES ARMED FORCES BICENTENNIAL CARAVAN. CARAVAN IS COMPOSED OF EXHIBIT VANS FOR EACH MILITARY SERVICE. PROJECT THEME IS 'HISTORY OF THE ARMED FORCES AND THEIR CONTRIBUTIONS TO THE NATION'. (LOCAL). ALICE BOWLER, CHMN; US ARMED FORCES EXHIBIT VANS PROJECT; 212 DAISY; IMPERIAL BEAC, CA 92032. (#1775-311).

JULY 18, '76. CITY'S 20TH BIRTHDAY CO-CELEBRATING WITH THE NATION. OPENING, COMPETITION. (LOCAL). ALICE L BOWLER, CHAIRMAN; IMPERIAL BEACH BICENTENNIAL COMMITTEE; 212 DAISY; IMPERIAL BCH, CA 92032. (#3262-501).

INDIO

DEC 3, '76. UNITED STATES ARMED FORCES BICENTENNIAL CARAVAN. CARAVAN IS COMPOSED OF EXHIBIT VANS FOR EACH MILITARY SERVICE. PROJECT THEME IS 'HISTORY OF THE ARMED FORCES & THEIR CONTRIBUTIONS TO THE NATION'. (LOCAL). JACK R MCCALLUM; UNITED STATES ARMED FORCES BICENTENNIAL CARAVAN; C/O UNITED CALIFORNIA BANK; INDIO, CA 92201. (#1775-850).

INGLEWOOD

AVIATION HISTORY BOOK SERIES - NORTHROP UNIV, CA. PUBLICATION OF A SERIES OF BOOKS BY DAVID D HATFIELD, CURATOR OF THE AMERICAN HALL OF AVIATION - SLATED TO COME OUT MONTLY OVER AN 8 MONTH PERIOD. (ST-WIDE). MRS NAN MCCANDLESS, BICENTENNIAL CHMN; NORTHROP UNIV; 1155 W ARBOR VITAE ST; INGLEWOOD, CA 90306. (#16683).

CITY OPTIONS-INDUSTRIAL DEVELOPMENT GUIDELINES, CA. PREPARATION OF GUIDELINES FOR DIRECTING DEVELOPMENT OF AN INDUSTRIAL AREA WITHIN INGLEWOOD THAT WILL PRODUCE AN INTEGRATED AESTHETIC & EDUCATIONAL ENVIRONMENT. (LOCAL). RALPH H WEBB ASSISTANT CITY ADMINISTRATOR; CITY OF INGLEWOOD; ONE MANCHESTER BLVD; INGLEWOOD, CA 90301. (#2778).

JAN 4 - 10, '76. GRAND OPENING & DEDICATION OF AMERICAN HALL OF AVIATION HISTORY. CEREMONY, OPENING. (LOCAL). JOHN G MOREY, DIRECTOR; NORTHROP UNIVERSITY; 1155 W ARBOR VITAE ST; INGLEWOOD, CA 90306. (#9125-2).

JAN 4, '76 - CONTINUING . AMERICAN HALL OF AVIATION HISTORY EXHIBIT. AQUISITION & DISPLAY OF DOCUMENTS, MEMORABILIA, FILMS, PERSONAL COLLECTIONS, INDUSTRY & AIRLINE RECORDS AND OTHER MATERIALS RELATED TO THE HISTORY OF AVIATION, ITS PAST, PRESENT & FUTURE. (REGN'L). JOHN G MOREY; NORTHROP UNIVERSITY; 1155 W ARBOR VITAE ST; INGLEWOOD, CA 90306. (#9125-1).

IRVINE

'CROOKED PATHS-IMAGES OF THE AMERICAN FUTURE' BOOK. CHARACTERIZES THE PRESENT FERMENT IN SOCIETY AS POLITICAL & SOCIAL CRISES UNFOLD WITHIN A CRISIS OF CULTURE, BY PETER CLECAK, A PHI BETA KAPPA BICENTENNIAL FELLOWSHIP AWARD. (NAT'L). KENNETH M GREENE, SECRETARY; PHI BETA KAPPA; 1811 Q ST, NW; WASHINGTON, DC 20009. (#260).

IRVINE GAZETTE AND UNIVERSAL INTELLIGENCER, CA. BICENTENNIAL NEWSLETTER ON LOCAL EVENTS AND HISTORICAL DATA. (LOCAL). TOBA WHEELER, EDITOR; IRVINE BICENTENNIAL COMMITTEE; 17585 ROCKROSE WAY; IRVINE, CA 92715. (#21541).

RELIGIOUS HERITAGE ESSAY CONTEST. AN ESSAY CONTEST FOR LOCAL STUDENTS ON THE THEME 'WHAT MY RELIGIOUS HERITAGE MEANS TO ME'. (LOCAL). MARILYN ORTON, ADVISOR; IRVINE BICENTENNIAL COMMITTEE; 17612 MANCHESTER; IRVINE, CA 92715. (#105115-1).

MAY 15, '76. IRVINE CONTINENTAL CONGRESS. THE CONTINENTAL CONGRESS WILL BE RE-ENACTED IN COSTUME BY LOCAL RESIDENTS PORTRAYING HISTORICAL FIGURES; CONFERENCE WILL COMMENCE WITH A PRESENTATION ON AMERICAN HISTORY; AN IRVINE BICENTENNIAL DECLARATION WILL BE DRAFTED FOR SIGNATURES ON JULY 4, 1976. AT UNIVERSITY HIGH SCHOOL CAMPUS AND CULVER MULTIPURPOSE ROOMS. (LOCAL). ROBERT B MARTIN, JR, CHMN; IRVINE BICENTENNIAL COMMITTEE; 5792 SIERRA CASA RD; IRVINE, CA 92715. (#105421-2).

JULY 4, '76. A COMMUNITY FOURTH OF JULY. A FOURTH OF JULY PARADE FEATURING CITY COMMUNITY ASSOCIATIONS AND SERVICE GROUPS FOLLOWED BY A FESTIVAL AND FIREWORKS. AT CULVERDALE COMMUNITY PARK. (LOCAL). TERRY MILSTEAD, COORD; IRVINE BICENT COMMITTEE & CULVERDALE COMMMUNITY ASSN; 17591 HASTINGS AVE; IRVINE, CA 92714. (#105421-1).

NOV 21, '76. SPIRITUAL EMPHASIS SUNDAY. AN INTERDENOMINATIONAL WORSHIP SERVICE EMPHASIZING THE SPIRITUAL VALUES OF THE FOUNDING FATHER FOLLOWED BY A THANKSGIVING PICNIC. AT CHRIST COLLEGE GROUNDS. (LOCAL). MARILYN ORTON, COORD; IRVINE BICENTENNIAL COMMITTEE; 17612 MANCHESTER; IRVINE, CA 92714. (#105421-3).

NOV 21 - 22, '76. UNITED STATES ARMED FORCES BICENTENNIAL CARAVAN. CARAVAN IS COMPOSED OF EXHIBIT VANS FOR EACH MILITARY SERVICE. PROJECT THEME IS 'HISTORY OF THE ARMED FORCES & THEIR CONTRIBUTIONS TO THE NATION'. (LOCAL). MARYLIN ORTON; UNITED STATES ARMED FORCES BICENTENNIAL CARAVAN; C/O IRVINE BICENTENNIAL COMM; IRVINE, CA 92664. (#1775-845).

JACKSON

KENNEDY WHEEL MINE MUSEUM IN AMADOR COUNTY, CA. BUILDING TO HOUSE WORKING MINE MODEL AND RELATED GOLD MINE INFORMATION. (LOCAL). MS FISCHER, CITY CLERK; CITY OF JACKSON; JACKSON, CA 95642. (#6270).

JAMUL

JUNE 1 - NOV 30, '76. BICENTENNIAL GRAND HORSE RACE. LIVE PERFORMANCE AT PROPOSED ROUTE WILL BEGIN SOUTH OF JAMESTOWN, NY AND FINISH IN CA. (ST-WIDE). FRAN A FARRELL, COORD; BICENTENNIAL GRAND HORSE RACE; RT 1, BOX 87H; JAMUL, CA 92035. (#104427-12).

JULIAN

HORIZONS '76 PROJECT - JULIAN, CA. A PARK WITH BALLFIELD, PICNIC FACILITIES AND AMPHITHEATRE WAS DEVELOPED. (LOCAL). MARY A WERNER, CHAIRPERSON; JULIAN CHAMBER OF COMMERCE; PO BOX 413; JULIAN, CA 92036. (#32092).

MAY 8 - OCT 17, '76. ART & WEED SHOW-MELODRAMA-4TH OF JULY CELEBRATION-OCT HARVEST FAIR. EXHIBIT, LIVE PERFORMANCE, FESTIVAL AT TOWN HALL-FRANK LANE PARK & ARENA-MAIN ST. (LOCAL). MARY WERNER; CHAMBER OF COMMERCE; PO 787; JULIAN, CA 91036. (#200006-517).

KING CITY

JUNE 9 - 13, '76. PINNACLES NM PARTICIPATES IN SALINAS VALLEY FAIR. DISPLAY BOOTH FEATURING THE SCENIC BEATUTY OF PINNACLES NATIONAL MONUMENT; CONTAINS A BICENTENNIAL EXHIBIT AND SLIDE PROGRAM. AT EXPO BUILDING, SALINAS VALLEY FAIRGROUNDS. (REGN'L). PINNACLES NM; NATIONAL PARK SERVICE; PAICINES, CA 95043. (#6728-253).

KINGSBURG

BICENTENNIAL PARK & REST STOP, KINGSBURG, CALIF. DEVELOP & DEDICATE PARK. ACTIVITIES WILL INCLUDE FOLK FESTIVAL, BAND CONCERTS & FIREWORKS. (LOCAL). EDWIN DACOBS CHAIRMAN; BICENTENNIAL CELEBRATION COMM; 1467 MARION ST; KINGSBURG, CA 93631. (#2588).

JULY 2 - 4, '76. BAND CONCERT, FIREWORKS, PAGEANT & FOLK FESTIVAL. FOLK FESTIVAL, ETHNIC FOOD & ENTERTAINMENT, JULY 2ND AT 6PM. BICENT PARK DEDICATION JULY 3RD, 8PM AT PARK; HISTORICAL PAGEANT ON JULY 3RD AT 8:30; BAND & CHORUS CONCERT, FIREWORKS JULY 4TH AT 8:15 PM. AT FESTIVAL, PAGEANT & CONCERT AT HIGH SCHOOL BOWL. (LOCAL). EDWIN JACOBS, CHAIRMAN; BICENTENNIAL CELEBRATION COMM; 1467 MARION ST; KINGSBURG, CA 93631. (#2588-501).

JULY 2 - 4, '76. DEDICATION NIGHT PARK DEDICATION & PROGRAM OF HISTORICAL EPISODES. BICENTENNIAL CELEBRATION WEEK FOCUSING ON KINGSBURG'S ETHNIC DIVERSITY AND THE CONTRIBUTIONS THESE GROUPS HAVE MADE TO LOCAL, STATE & NATIONAL HISTORY. AT HIGH SCHOOL. (LOCAL). EDWIN E JACOBS, CHAIRMAN; KINGSBURG BICENTENNIAL COMMITTEE; PO BOX 126; KINGSBURG, CA 93631. (#2299-2).

JULY 2 - 4, '76. FIESTA NIGHT; FOOD, MUSIC & DANCE REPRESENTING EACH NATIONALITY. ARTS INCLUDING MUSIC, DANCING AND COOKING SHOW KINGSBURG'S ETHNIC DIVERSITY AND CONTRIBUTIONS MADE TO HISTORY. AT HIGH SCHOOL BOWL IN KINGSBURG. (LOCAL). EDWIN E JACOBS, CHAIRMAN; KINGSBURG BICENTENNIAL COMMITTEE; PO BOX 126; KINGSBURG, CA 93631. (#2299-1).

JULY 4, '76. INDEPENDENCE DAY CELEBRATION, COMMUNITY POTLUCK, SPEECHES, FIREWORKS. DISPLAY OF ETHNIC AND CULTURAL ITEMS, POTLUCK DINNER, SPEECHES RELATING TO HISTORY AND REVOLUTION. CONCLUDING WITH FIREWORKS. AT HIGH SCHOOL AUDITORIUM. (LOCAL). EDWIN E JACOBS, CHAIRMAN; KINGSBURG BICENTENNIAL COMMITTEE; PO BOX 126; KINGSBURG, CA 93631. (#2299-3).

LA CANADA

JUNE 1 - JULY 31, '76. AMERICANA EXHIBIT ON THE REVOLUTIONARY WAR PERIOD. EXHIBIT AT LA CANADA LIBRARY. (LOCAL). MRS RICHARD J FRIEND; LA CANADA LIBRARY; 10253 MARCUS ST; TUJUNGA, CA 91042. (#100658-1).

JULY 4, '76. INDEPENDENCE DAY BICENTENNIAL PARADE. PARADE. (LOCAL). JOHN IVERS, CHAIRMAN; LA CANADA CHAMBER OF COMMERCE; 4710 HILLARD AVE; LA CANADA, CA 91011. (#100656-1).

LA CRESCENTA

BICENTENNIAL FLAG PROGRAM - LA CRESCENTA, CA. A FLAG RAISING CEREMONY AND FLYING THE FOUR FLAGS FOR BICENTENNIAL COMMUNITY (LA CRESCENTA, LA CANADA, MONTROSE & VERUNGO). FLGS WILL BE FLOWN AT VARIOUS COMMUNITY ORGANIZATIONS. (LOCAL). CAROL RUYGROK, PROJ DIRECTOR; CRESCENTA/CANADA VALLEY BICENTENNIAL COMMITTEE; PO BOX 1776; MONTROSE, CA 91020. (#12184).

SCHOOL BELL MONUMENT - PROJ OF LA CRESCENTA, CA. THIS IS THE FIRST SCHOOL BELL IN LA CRESCENTA TO BECOME A MONUMENT. IT WILL BE A MONUMENT TO THE FIRST SCHOOL AND TO THE BICENTENNIAL; BELL WEIGHS 1500 LBS AND WAS IN STORAGE FOR YEARS. (LOCAL). PAMELA WILLIAMS, CHAIRMAN; CRESCENTA/CANADA VALLEY BICENTENNIAL COMMITTEE; PO BOX 1776; MONTROSE, CA 91020. (#12183).

JULY 4, '76. SCHOOL BELL MONUMENT DEDICATION. CEREMONY. (LOCAL). PAMELA WILLIAMS, CHMN; CRESCENTA-CANADA VALLEY BICENTENNIAL COMMITTEE; 9626 LOS OLIVOS AVE; LA CRESCENTA, CA 91214. (#100657-1).

LA HABRA

BEAUTIFICATION & CLEAN-UP CAMPAIGN, LA HABRA, CA. BEAUTIFICATION PROJECT TO INCLUDE, TREE PLANTING IN LOCAL PARK, SETTING UP FLOWER BOXES ALONG LA HABRA BOULEVARD & PAINTING TRASH REEPTACLES IN LOCAL PARK. (LOCAL). RUTH SCHERMITZLER, CHAIRMAN; LA HABRA WOMEN'S CLUB & LA HABRA JUNIOR WOMEN'S CLUB; 200 W GREENWOOD AVE; LA HABRA, CA 90631. (#19372).

CARILLON TOWER OF LA HABRA, CALIFORNIA. 'BELLS OF FREEDOM' CARILLON BELL TOWER WILL BE CONSTRUCTED AT THE CIVIC CENTER. (LOCAL). ESTHER CRAMER, CHAIRMAN; LA HABRA ANNIVERSARY & BICENT COMMITTEE; CIVIC CENTER; LA HABRA, CA 90631. (#10467).

CHILDREN'S MUSEUM OF LA HABRA, CALIFORNIA. ACQUISITION OF HISTORY BOOKS FOR CHILDREN'S MUSEUM, WHICH IS LOCATED IN AN OLD RAILROAD CABOOSE. (LOCAL). ESTHER CRAMER, CHAIRMAN; LA HABRA ANNIVERSARY & BICENT COMMITTEE; CIVIC CENTER; LA HABRA, CA 90631. (#10466).

MEMORIAL PARKS & BEAUTIFICATION, LA HABRA, CALIF. COMMUNITY REDEVELOPMENT PROGRAM, INCLUDING NEW ARBORETUM & TWO MEMORIAL PARKS; ALSO ARBOR DAY TREE PLANTING, STREET LANDSCAPING & GENERAL CLEAN-UP IN FALL 1975 IN PREPARATION FOR SPRING & SUMMER 1976. (LOCAL). MRS ESTHER R CRAMER, CHAIRMAN; LA HABRA BICENTENNIAL COMMITTEE; 600 LINDEN AVE; LA HABRA, CA 90631. (#2307).

DEC 3 - 19, '75. OUR AMERICAN HERITAGE THROUGH SONG AND DANCE. LIVE PERFORMANCE AT FASHION SQUARE, IMPERIAL & BEACH BLVDS. (LOCAL). LEE RIVERA; CITY OF LA HABRA BICENTENNIAL COMMITTEE; CIVIC CENTER; LA HABRA, CA 90631. (#200006-22).

MAR 13, '76. CULTURAL HERITAGE DAY. EXHIBITS, FOODS, DANCES & CRAFTS WILL SHOW THE CONTRIBUTIONS OTHER CULTURES HAVE MADE ON OUR OWN. AT EL CENTRO PARK, CYPRESS & ERNA STS. (LOCAL). MRS MARY E MEYER, CHMN;

LA HABRA — CONTINUED

LA HABRA BICENTENNIAL COMMITTEE; 1060 NANTUCKET; LA HABRA, CA 90631. (#104653-1).

LA HONDA

SAVE 'HERITAGE GROVE' PROJ OF LA HONDA, CA. COUNTY ACQUISITION OF 37 ACRES OF PROPERTY CONTAINING MAGNIFICENT OLD GROWTH REDWOODS FOR INCORPORATION INTO PARK SYSTEM; DEDICATION WITH PLAQUE, LETTER AND BROCHURE. (LOCAL). MRS ANN RADWELL, CAMPAIGN CO-LEADER; CITIZENS EFFORT TO SAVE THE HOLMES GROVE; STAR RTE 3, BOX 56; LA HONDA, CA 94020. (#14543).

LA JOLLA

COURSES BY NEWSPAPER -LECTURES ON AMERICA, S DIEGO. WEEKLY ARTICLES BY DISTIGUISHED WRITERS & TEACHERS ON AMERICA'S HERITAGE AND ITS IMPLICATIONS FOR OUR FUTURE. PUBLISHED IN MANY LOCAL PAPERS, THE COURSE CAN BE FOLLOWED FOR PLEASURE OR TAKEN FOR CREDIT. (NAT'L). CALEB A LEWIS, PROJECT DIRECTOR; COURSES BY NEWSPAPER, UNIV OF CALIFORNIA, SAN DIEGO; PO BOX 109; LA JOLLA, CA 92037. (#2407).

OPEN-SKY STEP-STREET AMPHIPLAZA OF LA JOLLA, CALIF. A STUDY TO INCORPORATE A SLOPING & UPPER-LEVEL CROSS STREET INTO COMUNITY PLAZA SUITABLE FOR PERFORMANCES & COMPATIBLE WITH ADJACENT PROPERTIES. NEA GRANT. (LOCAL). JUDITH MUNK, DIRECTOR; 9530 LA JOLLA SHORES DR; LA JOLLA, CA 92037. (#2397). **(??).**

SEPT 29, '73 - FEB 15, '74. AMERICA & THE FUTURE OF MAN - BICENTENNIAL COURSE BY NEWSPAPER. COURSES BY NEWSPAPER -LECTURES ON AMERICA, S DIEGO. WEEKLY ARTICLES BY DISTIGUISHED WRITERS & TEACHERS ON AMERICA'S HERITAGE AND ITS IMPLICATIONS FOR OUR FUTURE. PUBLISHED IN MANY LOCAL PAPERS, THE COURSE CAN BE FOLLOWED FOR PLEASURE OR TAKEN FOR CREDIT. (NAT'L). CALEB A LEWIS, PROJECT DI; COURSES BY NEWSPAPER, UNIV OF CALIFORNIA, SAN DIEGO; PO BOX 109; LA JOLLA, CA 92037. (#2407-901).

SEPT 29, '74 - JAN 31, '75. IN SEARCH OF THE AMERICAN DREAM - BICENTENNIAL COURSE BY NEWSPAPER. COURSES BY NEWSPAPER -LECTURES ON AMERICA, S DIEGO. WEEKLY ARTICLES BY DISTIGUISHED WRITERS & TEACHERS ON AMERICA'S HERITAGE AND ITS IMPLICATIONS FOR OUR FUTURE. PUBLISHED IN MANY LOCAL PAPERS, THE COURSE CAN BE FOLLOWED FOR PLEASURE OR TAKEN FOR CREDIT. (NAT'L). CALEB A LEWIS, PROJECT DI; COURSES BY NEWSPAPER, UNIV OF CALIFORNIA, SAN DIEGO; PO BOX 109; LA JOLLA, CA 92037. (#2407-902).

LA MESA

MAY 12, '73. HIGH SCHOOL BANDS PARTICIPATE IN WESTERN STATES MUSIC TOURNAMENT. EACH OF 10 CHAMPION BANDS COMPETING, PORTRAYS PAGEANTRY SYMBOLIZING AN EVENT IN ITS STATE'S HISTORY AND LINKED TO 1776 HERITAGE. (NAT'L). JAMES M CULVER; WESTERN STATES MUSIC TOURNAMENT; P.O. BOX 235; LA MESA, CA 92041. (#321-901).

MAY 10, '74. CONCERT & SIGHT-READING COMPETITION AT GROSSMONT HIGH SCHOOL. LA MESA WESTERN STATES MUSIC TOURNAMENT OF CALIF. 10 HIGH SCHOOL BANDS IN MUSIC COMPETITION--CONCERT-SIGHT READING PARADE-FIELD SHOW, PORTRAYING HISTORICAL PAGEANTRY. (ST-WIDE). JAMES M CULVER,EXEC DIR; LA MESA CHAMBER OF COMMERCE; 8155 UNIVERSITY AVE; LA MESA, CA 92041. (#687-901).

MAY 11, '74. PARADE MARCHING COMPETITION AT GROSSMONT SHOPPING CENTER. LA MESA WESTERN STATES MUSIC TOURNAMENT OF CALIF. 10 HIGH SCHOOL BANDS IN MUSIC COMPETITION--CONCERT-SIGHT READING PARADE-FIELD SHOW, PORTRAYING HISTORICAL PAGEANTRY. (ST-WIDE). JAMES M CULVER, EXEC DIR; LA MESA CHAMBER OF COMMERCE; 8155 UNIVERSITY AVE; LA MESA, CA 92041. (#687-902).

MAY 8 - 9, '76. LA MESA WESTERN STATES MUSIC TOURNAMENT OF CALIF. 10 HIGH SCHOOL BANDS IN MUSIC COMPETITION--CONCERT-SIGHT READING PARADE-FIELD SHOW, PORTRAYING HISTORICAL PAGEANTRY. 8 HIGH SCHOOL CHOIRS IN CHORAL COMPETITION. WILL BE FROM 10:00AM TO 11:00PM ON SATURDAY, MAY 9. AT GROSSMONT HIGH SCHOOL AUDITORIUM. (REGN'L). GORDON L AUSTIN; LA MESA CHAMBER OF COMMERCE; 8155 UNIVERSITY AVE; LA MESA, CA 92041. (#687-1).

LA MIRADA

LA MIRADA THEATRE, CA. THE BUILDING WILL BE RENOVATED TO MEET THE NEEDS OF THE COMMUNITY. (LOCAL). HON WIL SIMENDINGER, MAYOR; CITY OF LA MIRADA; 13700 LA MIRADA BLVD, CITY HALL; LA MIRADA, CA 90638. (#23943).

JULY 4, '76. INDEPENDENCE DAY CELEBRATION. FESTIVAL AT LA MIRADA REGIONAL PARK. (LOCAL). C W CAMP, COORDINATOR; LA MIRADA PARKS & RECREATION COMMISSION; 13700 MIRADA BLVD; LA MIRADA, CA 90638. (#107107-1).

LA PUENTE

HISTORIC CALIFORNIA HOME TO BE RESTORED. PARADE AND RESTORATION OF 125 YEAR OLD REED HOME. (LOCAL). EDWARD WADE, CHAIRMAN; LA PUENTE BICENT COMMITTEE; 15917 E MAIN ST; LA PUENTE, CA 91747. (#9796).

RESTORATION OF THE REED HOME - LA PUENTE, CA. RESTORATION OF THE 110 YEAR OLD REED HOME. (LOCAL). ED WADE, CHAIRMAN; LA PUENTE BICENTENNIAL COMMITTEE; 15917 E MAIN ST; LA PUENTE, CA 91747. (#16311).

JULY 5, '76. LA PUENTE ANNIVERSARY-BICENTENNIAL PARADE. PARADE, FAMILY PICNIC, DEDICATION HISTORIC HOME, BARBECUE, FIRE WORKS DISPLAY, SQUARE DANCING. AT CITY-WIDE. (LOCAL). CECIL J ENGLAND; LA PUENTE BICENTENNIAL COMMITTEE; PO BOX 327; LA PUENTE, CA 91747. (#50701-1).

LA VERNE

BICENTENNIAL MEMORIAL GARDEN - LA VERNE, CA. DEVELOPMENT OF THE BICENTENNIAL MEMORIAL GARDEN AT THE UNITED METHODIST CHURCH. (LOCAL). R G HARRIS, CHAIRMAN; LA VERNE BICENTENNIAL COMMITTEE; 2078 BONITA AVE; LA VERNE, CA 91750. (#21834).

LA VERNE, CA, LIBERTY BELL PROJECT. THE CITIZENS HAVE PURCHASED A REPLICA OF THE LIBERTY BELL CASTED BY WHITE CHAPEL FOUNDRY IN ENGLAND, CASTER OF THE ORIGINAL BELL. IT IS ONE OF TWO SUCH BELLS IN CALIFORNIA. (ST-WIDE). R G HARRIS, CHAIRMAN; LA VERNE BICENTENNIAL COMMITTEE; 2078 BONITA AVE; LA VERNE, CA 91750. (#20468).

SISTER CITY PROJECT, LA VERNE, CALIF. LA VERNE ESTABLISHING SISTER CITY RELATIONSHIP WITH COLONIAL CITY OF COMPARABLE SIZE TO TRADE CALIFORNIA MISSION HERITAGE FOR REVOLUTIONARY HERITAGE AND TO EXPAND OUR APPRECIATION OF THESE TWO HISTORIES. (LOCAL). R G HARRIS, CHAIRMAN; LA VERNE BICENTENNIAL COMMITTEE; 2078 BONITA AVE; LA VERNE, CA 91750. (#2297).

LAGUNA BEACH

JULY 16 - AUG 29, '76. 41ST ANNUAL FESTIVAL OF ARTS AND PAGEANT OF THE MASTERS. ART FESTIVAL CELEBRATES BICENTENNIAL WITH VARIETY OF AUDIO-VISUAL DELIGHTS. AT IRVINE BOWL. (LOCAL). SALLY REEVE, COORDINATOR; LAGUNA BEACH FESTIVAL; 650 LAGUNA CANYON RD; LAGUNA BEACH, CA 92651. (#103416-485).

LAKE ELSINORE

APR 7, '76. UNITED STATES ARMED FORCES BICENTENNIAL CARAVAN. CARAVAN IS COMPOSED OF EXHIBIT VANS FOR EACH MILITARY SERVICE. PROJECT THEME IS ' HISTORY OF THE ARMED FORCES & THEIR CONTRIBUTIONS TO THE NATION'. (LOCAL). JOHNNY PEARSON, DIR; U S ARMED FORCES BICENTENNIAL CARAVAN; 805 W HERAALD AVE; LAKE ELSINORE, CA 92330. (#1775-549).

LAKE ISABELLA

JULY 3 - 5, '76. HERITAGE DAYS. A PICNIC AND COMMUNITY DANCE WILL BE FEATURED. AT UFFERT PARK. (LOCAL). JOSEPH NEMISH, CHAIRMAN; ELKS MOOSE AND CHAMBER OF COMMERCE; BOX C; LAKE ISABELLA, CA 93240. (#103718-1).

LAKE TAHOE

JULY 30, '76. UNIVERSITY OF CALIFORNIA MARCHING BAND PRESENTS 'SPIRIT OF AMERICA'. THIS IS PART OF A 6-WEEK PERFORMANCE TOUR OF THE U S; 'SPIRIT OF AMERICA' IS A COLLEGIATE MUSICAL REVIEW CELEBRATING OUR NATION'S BICENTENNIAL; WILL INCLUDE FOLK MUSIC, MARCHING, VAUDEVILLE, ROCK, DIXIELAND, JAZZ, BARBERSHOP & SOLOS. AT SOUTH LAKE TAHOE HIGH SCHOOL GYMNASIUM. (ST-WIDE). JOHN UPTON, DIRECTOR; ROTARY CLUB OF SOUTH LAKE TAHOE; PO BOX 8997; LAKE TAHOE, CA 95731. (#10515-24).

LAKEPORT

HISTORIC LAKEPORT, CA COURTHOUSE TO BECOME MUSEUM. 100 YEAR OLD COURTHOUSE TO BE RESTORED FOR USE AS MUSEUM OF INDIAN & PIONEER ARTIFACTS. BUILDING IS LISTED IN NATIONAL REGISTER OF HISTORIC PLACES. (LOCAL). MS MARION GEOBLE, SECRETARY; OLD COURTHOUSE COMMITTEE; PO BOX 517; LAKEPORT, CA 95453. (#9402).

DEC 15, '75 - CONTINUING . OLD LAKE COUNTY COURTHOUSE RESTORATION. RESTORATION OF CENTURY-OLD COURTHOUSE FOR COUNTY MUSEUM, TO INCLUDE PIONEER & INDIAN ARTIFACTS. BUILDING IS LISTED IN NATIONAL REGISTER OF HISTORICAL PLACES. ALSO: BUILDING/FACILITY/MONUMENT, NEWSPAPER/NEWSLETTER. AT OLD LAKE COUNTY COURT HOUSE. (LOCAL). MARION GEOBLE; LAKE COUNTY BICENTENNIAL COMMISSION; PO BOX 517; LAKEPORT, CA 95453. (#5068-1).

LAKESIDE

BAND CONCERT IN THE PARK - LAKESIDE, CA. BROWN BAG PICNIC AND BAND CONCERT FOR FOURTH OF MONTH, ONE OF SIX CELEBRATIONS, JAN TO JULY. (LOCAL). G ERNESTINE PAINE, CHAIRMAN; LAKESIDE BICENTENNIAL COMMITTEE; PO BOX 522; LAKESIDE, CA 92040. (#31605).

BOATHOUSE RESTORATION - LAKESIDE, CA. RETURNING HISTORIC BOATHOUSE TO SITE IN LAKE IN COUNTY PARK. (LOCAL). G ERNESTINE PAINE, CHAIRMAN; LAKESIDE BICENTENNIAL COMMITTEE; PO BOX 522; LAKESIDE, CA 92040. (#31607).

FIRE HYDRANT PAINTING - LAKESIDE, CA. THE FIRE HYDRANTS IN LAKESIDE WILL BE PAINTED. (LOCAL). CHUCH WHITLOCK, CHAIRMAN; LAKESIDE FIREMEN'S ASSOC; 9726 RIVERVIEW; LAKESIDE, CA 92040. (#31608).

HERITAGE CENTER - LAKESIDE, CA. FURNISHING CENTER FOR HISTORIC DISPLAYS IN PLANNED LIBRARY ADDITION. (LOCAL). G ERNESTINE PAINE, CHAIRMAN; LAKESIDE BICENTENNIAL COMMITTEE; PO BOX 522; LAKESIDE, CA 92040. (#31606).

HISTORICAL PRINTS - LAKESIDE, CA. 3 ORIGINAL PEN AND INK DRAWINGS OF HISTORICAL SITES, BY LOCAL ARTIST JANET SWEEDER. PRINTS ARE LIMITED EDITIONS & PROCEEDS GO TO HORIZON FUND. (LOCAL). GERTRUDE DAVIS, COORDINATOR; LAKESIDE GARDEN CLUB; 12366 LEMONCREST; LAKESIDE, CA 92040. (#31604).

PIONEERING SPIRIT IN WOMEN. RECOGNITION OF LOCAL WOMEN FOR THEIR COMMUNITY SERVICE IN PIONEERING FIELDS. (LOCAL). MAY JOHNSON, COORD; SOROPTIMIST INTERNATIONAL OF LAKESIDE; PO BOX 522; LAKESIDE, CA 92040. (#200006-490).

'RAISE THE MONITOR' - LAKESIDE, CA. THIS IS A HISTORIC SHIP PROJECT ORIGINATING IN CAPE HATTERAS, NC. (NAT'L). BILL DAVIS, COORDINATOR; LAKESIDE HISTORICAL SOCIETY; 12366 LEMONCREST; LAKESIDE, CA 92040. (#31609).

JAN 4, '76. BICENTENNIAL KICK-OFF. ARBA PRESENTATION OF FLAG-CHARTER. AT LINDO LAKE PARK. (LOCAL). ERNESTINE PAINE, CHMN; LAKESIDE BICENTENNIAL COMMITTEE; PO BOX 522; LAKESIDE, CA 29040. (#200006-484).

JAN 20, '76. BICENTENNIAL USA. EXHIBIT AT LAKESIDE JR HIGH AUDITORIUM WOODSIDE AVE. (LOCAL). BILL DAVIS; LAKESIDE HISTORICAL SOCIETY; 12366 LEMONCREST; LAKESIDE, CA 92040. (#200006-479).

MAR 14, '76. PANCAKE DINNER FUND RAISER. FAIR AT VFW HALL 12650 LINDO LANE. (LOCAL). G ERNESTINE PAINE, CHMN; LAKESIDE BICENTENNIAL COMMITTEE; PO BOX 522; LAKESIDE, CA 92040. (#200006-486).

APR 4, '76. SQUARE DANCE. COMPETITION AT VFW HALL 12650 LINDO LANE. (LOCAL). G E PAINE, CHMN; LAKESIDE BICENTENNIAL COMMITTEE; PO BOX 522; LAKESIDE, CA 92040. (#200006-487).

APR 24, '76. BICENTENNIAL PARADE. PARADE AT WOODSIDE & MAINE AVE. (LOCAL). MURIE KIMMSIES; LAKESIDE CHAMBER OF COMMERCE; 12038 WOODSIDE AVE; LAKESIDE, CA 92040. (#200006-483).

JUNE 12, '76. FLAG DAY. RAISED BICENTENNIAL & AMERICAN FLAGS TO MARK BICENTENNIAL COMMUNITY. (LOCAL). G E PAINE, CHAIRMAN; LAKESIDE BICENTENNIAL COMMITTEE; PO BOX 542; LAKESIDE, CA 92040. (#200006-489).

JULY 4, '76. FOURTH OF JULY PICNIC IN THE PARK. PICNIC, GAME AND FOOD BOOTHS, FIREWORKS & DANCING. AT LINDO LAKE PARK. (LOCAL). G ERNESTINE PAINE, CHMN; LAKESIDE BICENTENNIAL COMMITTEE & 25 SERVICE ORGANIZATIONS; PO BOX 522; LAKESIDE, CA 92040. (#200006-485).

NOV 13, '76. BICENTENNIAL BASH. RECOGNITION AWARDS-OLD TIMERS HONORED-POTLUCK DINNER-DANCE. AT VFW HALL 12650 LINDO LANE. (LOCAL). G ERNESTINE PAINE, CHMN; LAKESIDE BICENTENNIAL COMMITTEE; PO BOX 522; LAKESIDE, CA 92040. (#200006-488).

DEC 11, '76. HOME TOUR. EXHIBIT, TOUR AT OPEN DOOR MAINE AVE LAKESIDE. (LOCAL). HARRIET BETCHER; SOROPTIMIST INTERNATIONAL OF LAKESIDE; PO BOX 522; LAKESIDE, CA 92040. (#200006-428).

LAKEWOOD

APR 26 - 27, '76. UNITED STATES ARMED FORCES BICENTENNIAL CARAVAN. CARAVAN IS COMPOSED OF EXHIBIT VANS FOR EACH MILITARY SERVICE. PROJECT THEME IS ' HISTORY OF THE ARMED FORCES & THEIR CONTRIBUTIONS TO THE NATION'. (LOCAL). DON FLEMING, CHAIRMAN; U S ARMED FORCES BICENTENNIAL CARAVAN; 5050 CLARK AVE; LAKEWOOD, CA 90714. (#1775-558).

JULY 4 - 11, '76. 1976 LAKEWOOD PAN AMERICAN FESTIVAL WEEK. 1976 PAN AMERICAN FESTIVAL WEEK, LAKEWOOD, CALIF. THE CITY OF LAKEWOOD, CA WILL JOIN PAN AM FESTIVAL ASSOCIATION IN HONORING OUR LATIN AMERICAN NEIGHBORS FOR THEIR CONTRIBUTIONS TO OUR HERITAGE. (ST-WIDE). STAN JENSEN, CHAIRPERSON; LAKEWOOD BICENTENNIAL COMMITTEE; PO BOX 1776; LAKEWOOD, CA 90714. (#2300-501).

LANCASTER

PRESERVATION OF THE CALIFORNIA POPPY. IN SPRING OF '76 A WILD FLOWER PARK WILL BE ACQUIRED BY THE STATE PARKS FOUNDATION AND TURNED OVER TO THE STATE PARKS DEPARTMENT FOR PRESERVATION OF THE CALIFORNIA POPPY. STATE ARBC ENDORSED. (ST-WIDE). JAMES TRYNER, CHIEF, RESOURCE & MANAGEMENT DIV; CALIFORNIA STATE PARKS DEPARTMENT; 9TH & O STS; SACRAMENTO, CA 95814. (#211).

NOV 5 - 6, '76. UNITED STATES ARMED FORCES BICENTENNIAL CARAVAN. CARAVAN IS COMPOSED OF EXHIBIT VANS FOR EACH MILITARY SERVICE. PROJECT THEME IS 'HISTORY OF THE ARMED FORCES & THEIR CONTRIBUTIONS TO THE NATION'. (LOCAL). WARREN E HUGHES; UNITED STATES ARMED FORCES BICENTENNIAL CARAVAN; 42713 N 21ST W; LANCASTER, CA 93534. (#1775-838).

LARKSPUR

OCT '76. DEDICATION OF CREEKSIDE BICENTENNIAL PARK. DEDICATION OF PARK OF MARSH, NATIVE GRASSES AND RECREATION AREA ON CORTE MADERA CREEK. AT NORTHERLY SIDE OF THE CORTE MADERA CREEK ADJOINING BON AIR ROAD. (LOCAL). MARGARET DEL GRANDE, SEC; COUNTY SERVICE AREA #17 ADVISORY BOARD; 142 ELISEO; GREENBRAE, CA 94904. (#104309-1).

LAYTONVILLE

LAYTONVILLE INDIAN COMMUNITY/CULTURAL CENTER IN CA. CENTER TO ACCOMMODATE TRIBAL AFFAIRS OFFICE, EDUCATIONAL FACILITIES & CULTURAL ACTIVITIES. (LOCAL). BERT SLOANE, JR, TRIBAL CHAIRMAN; LAYTONVILLE CAHTO RANCHERIA; PO BOX 608; LAYTONVILLE, CA 95454. (#22846). **ARBA GRANTEE.**

LE GRAND

COMMUNITY ORGANIZATIONAL EMBLEM STANDARD - CA. A STANDARD WITH A TIME CAPSULE IN ITS BASE, A MARBLE CORNERSTONE AND AN EMBLEM REPRESENTING EACH PARTICIPATING GROUP. (LOCAL). MARY PRINCE, CHAIRMAN; AMERICAN LEGION POST 660 & LE GRAND COMMUNITY GARDEN CLUB; PO BOX 322; LE GRAND, CA 95333. (#31280).

TREE PLANTING - LE GRAND, CA. TREES WILL BE PLANTED AT SCHOOLS, YOSEMITE LAKE AND THE LE GRAND COMMUNITY GARDEN CLUB. (LOCAL). MARY PRINCE, COORDINATOR; LE GRAND COMMUNITY GARDEN CLUB; PO BOX 322; LE GRAND, CA 95333. (#31281).

LEMOORE

BICENTENNIAL ESSAY CONTEST - LEMOORE, CA. STUDENTS PARTICIPATED IN AN ESSAY CONTEST ENTITLED 'THE NEXT TWO HUNDRED YEARS'. THE WINNING ESSAYS WILL BE PUT IN THE TIME CAPSULE WHICH IS TO BE BURIED ON BASE IN DECEMBER 1976. (LOCAL). LCDR G ROSENBERGER, CHAIRMAN; NAVAL AIR STATION; LEMOORE, CA 93245. (#31069).

BICENTENNIAL SCHOLARSHIP - LEMOORE, CA. THE NAVY WIVES CLUB OF AMERICA #225 PRESENTED A $100 SCHOLARSHIP TO A MILITARY DEPENDENT GRADUATED FROM LEMOORE HIGH SCHOOL IN JUNE 1976. (LOCAL). LCDR G ROSENBERGER, CHAIRMAN; NAVAL AIR STATION; LEMOORE, CA 93245. (#31071).

FIRE HYDRANT/DUMPSTER PAINTING CONTEST - CA. A FIREPLUG DECORATING PROGRAM IS DESIGNATED TO BRIGHTEN UP STREETS OF NAS LEMOORE AND TO PROMOTE THE THEME OF 'AMERICA'S HERITAGE'. PRIZES AWARDED FOR BOTH AREAS. (LOCAL). LCDR G ROSENBERGER, CHAIRMAN; NAVAL AIR STATION; LEMOORE, CA 93245. (#31072).

INDIAN COMMUNITY CENTER IN LEMOORE, CA. A MULTI-PURPOSE BUILDING PROVIDING SPACE & ROOMS FOR TRIBAL ACTIVITIES AND PROGRAMS. (LOCAL). CLARENCE ATWELL, JR, TRIBAL CHAIRMAN; SANTA ROSA RANCHERIA; 16300 ALKALI DR; LEMOORE, CA 93245. (#22850). **ARBA GRANTEE.**

LEMOORE OFFICERS' WIVES BICENTENNIAL QUILT - CA. PATCHES DESIGNED AND SEWN BY VARIOUS UNITS AROUND THE AIR STATION GO TO MAKE UP THE BICENTENNIAL QUILT. THESE COULD BE EMBROIDERY, APPLIQUE OR NEEDLEPOINT. (LOCAL). LCDR G ROSENBERGER, CHAIRMAN; NAVAL AIR STATION; LEMOORE, CA 93245. (#31067).

NEUTRA/AKERS ELEMENTARY SCHOOL DRESS UP CONTEST-CA. STUDENTS DRESSED AS THEIR FAVORITE BICENTENNIAL HERO OR HEROINE. THE TEACHER AND MEMBERS OF EACH CLASSROOM SELECTED A WINNER TO REPRESENT THEIR ROOM; FOLLOWED BY A PARADE & PRESENTING WINNERS CERTIFICATES. (LOCAL). LEDR G ROSENBERGER, CHAIRMAN; NAVAL AIR STATION; LEMOORE, CA 93245. (#31065).

SENIOR CITIZEN/HANDICAPPED CHILDREN TOURS - CA. SENIOR CITIZEN GROUPS AND LOCAL AREA SCHOOL GROUPS HAVE TOURED NAS LEMOORE. TO DATE EIGHT TOURS, ABOUT 130 CHILDREN, HAVE BEEN COMPLETED. (LOCAL). LEDR G ROSENBERGER, CHAIRMAN; NAVAL AIR STATION; LEMOORE, CA 93245. (#31066).

STATIC DISPLAYS - LEMOORE, CA. FIVE PEDESTAL MOUNTED AIRCRAFT WERE PAINTED USING A BICENTENNIAL THEME. A PLYWOOD BELL, WITH A RED, WHITE & BLUE BAR ABOVE, AND THE WORDS 'FREEDOM' & '76' WAS MOUNTED ON THE OUTSIDE WALL OF A HANGER. (LOCAL). LCDR G ROSENBERGER, CHAIRMAN; NAVAL AIR STATION; LEMOORE, CA 93245. (#31070).

TIME CAPSULE - LEMOORE, CA. BURYING CAPSULE CONTAINING MEMORABILIA FROM BICENTENNIAL YEAR. THE CAPSULE WILL BE BURIED IN DECEMBER 1976 AND OPENED IN THE YEAR 2076. (LOCAL). LCDR G ROSENBERGER, CHAIRMAN; NAVAL AIR STATION; LEMOORE, CA 93245. (#31073).

THE 1776-1976 BICENTENNIAL STORY PROGRAM - CA. CHILDREN IN TWO CATEGORIES, AGES 6-8 & 9-12 ARE ELIGIBLE TO JOIN IN THE READING CONTEST. PRIZES AND/OR CERTIFICATES WILL BE GIVEN TO EACH ENTRY. (LOCAL). LCDR G ROSENBERGER, CHAIRMAN; NAVAL AIR STATION; LEMOORE, CA 93245. (#31068).

JUNE 5, '76. BICENTENNIAL NAVY PICNIC. A NAVY WIDE PICNIC. CONTESTS INCLUDED, KITE FLYING, BEANBAG THROW, FRISBEE THROW AND A GAME OF 'ANYTHING GOES'. (LOCAL). LCDR G ROSENBERGER, USN; NAVAL AIR STATION; NAVAL AIR STATION; LEMOORE, CA 93245. (#200006-405).

JULY 13, '76. HISTORY THROUGH MUSIC BAND CONCERT. KINGS CO BICENTENNIAL BAND PRESENTED A ONE HOUR CONCERT OF MUSICAL SELECTIONS FROM THE REVOLUTIONARY WAR ERA TO THE PRESENT. (LOCAL). LCDR G ROSENBERGER, USN; NAVAL AIR STATION; NAVAL AIR STATION; LEMOORE, CA 93245. (#200006-406).

NOV 20, '76. MINUTEMAN TURKEY SHOOT. PARTICIPANTS WERE MILITARY PERSONNEL FROM NAS AND MUZZLE LOADER ENTHUSIASTS FROM KINGS CO. (LOCAL). LCDR G ROSENBERGER, USN; NAVAL AIR STATION; NAVAL AIR STATION; LEMOORE, CA 93245. (#200006-407).

LINCOLN

OLD LINCOLN SCHOOL PROJECT - LINCOLN, CA. RESTORATION OF 1890'S SCHOOL BLDG FOR USE AS CLASSROOM, MUSEUM AND COMMUNITY MEETING PLACE. CLASSROOM RESTORED AS HOUSE MUSEUM BUT USED AS PART OF ELEM SCHOOL CURRICULUM. (LOCAL). RICHARD WYATT, PRESIDENT; OLD LINCOLN SCHOOL PROJECT; 641 D ST; LINCOLN, CA 95648. (#24550).

LIVERMORE

HISTORICAL RECORDS INDEX, LIVERMORE, CA. A CHRONOLOGICAL, BIOGRAPHICAL INDEX PERTAINING TO THE HISTORY OF LIVERMORE. (LOCAL). JANET NEWTON, CHAIRMAN; LIVERMORE HERITAGE GUILD; PO BOX 961; LIVERMORE, CA 94550. (#11367).

LIVERMORE HISTORY CENTER, CA. A CENTER CONTAINING HISTORICAL ARTIFACTS AND INFORMATION REGARDING LIVERMORE WILL BE DEVELOPED. (LOCAL). JANET NEWTON, CHAIRMAN; LIVERMORE HERITAGE GUILD & LIVERMORE BICENTENNIAL ORGANIZATION; PO BOX 961; LIVERMORE, CA 94550. (#11359).

PUBLICATION OF HISTORIC PHOTOS OF LIVERMORE, CA. DISSEMINATE INFORMATION ABOUT THE HISTORY OF LIVERMORE BY SELLING SETS OF NOTE CARDS WITH OLD PHOTOS ON THEM. (LOCAL). JANET NEWTON, CHAIRMAN; LIVERMORE BICENTENNIAL ORGANIZATION; PO BOX 1776; LIVERMORE, CA 94550. (#20733).

RECONDITIONING OF THE CALIFORNIA WAGON TRAIN. THE CALIFORNIA WAGON TRAIN IS BEING REFURBISHED FOR THE PILGRIMAGE IN 1976. (ST-WIDE). HAROLD GABRIEL, PROJ COORDINATOR; ALAMEDA COUNTY BICENTENNIAL COMMISSION; PO BOX 623; LIVERMORE, CA 94550. (#20734).

RESTORATION OF MAY SCHOOL IN LIVERMORE, CA. AN OLD SCHOOL WILL BE RESTORED AND STAND AS A VISUAL REMINDER OF THE HISTORY OF THE AREA. (LOCAL). JANET NEWTON, CHAIRMAN; LIVERMORE HERITAGE GUILD & THE BICENTENNIAL COMMITTEE; PO BOX 461; LIVERMORE, CA 94550. (#11521).

STORY OF THE ANZA EXPEDITION - LIVERMORE, CA. A BOOKLET ON THE DE ANZA EXPEDITION OF 1776 WILL BE PUBLISHED AND MADE AVAILABLE AT LOW COST. (ST-WIDE). JANET NEWTON, CHAIRMAN; LIVERMORE HERITAGE GUILD; PO BOX 961; LIVERMORE, CA 94550. (#11622).

LODI

LOCHER TOOL COLLECTION IN LODI, CA. COLLECTION OF 3300 HAND & FOOT POWERED TOOLS DATING FROM 1612. MANY TRADES ARE REPRESENTED INCLUDING LITTLE KNOWN ONES SUCH AS VIOLIN MAKING. COLLECTED BY FLOYD J LOCHER. (ST-WIDE). MRS MEDORA JOHNSON, DIRECTOR; SAN JOAQUIN COUNTY HISTORICAL MUSEUM; 11793 N MICKE GROVE RD; LODI, CA 95240. (#26916). **ARBA GRANTEE.**

OCT 31, '75. UNITED STATES ARMED FORCES BICENTENNIAL CARAVAN. THE CARAVAN IS COMPOSED OF EXHIBIT VANS FOR EACH BRANCH OF THE MILITARY SERVICE. THE THEME OF THE EXHIBITION IS 'HISTORY OF THE ARMED FORCES AND THEIR CONTRIBUTION TO THE NATION'. (LOCAL). VIN BENSON, CHAIRMAN; U S ARMED FORCES BICENTENNIAL EXHIBIT VANS PROJECT; N SACRAMENTO AT LOVIE; LODI, CA 95240. (#1775-288).

JAN 2, '76 - CONTINUING . FLOYD J LOCHER TOOL COLLECTION; A PERMANENT EXHIBIT. COLLECTION OF 3300 HAND & FOOT POWERED TOOLS DATING FROM 1612. ALL TOOLS ARE OF SUPERIOR QUALITY & AREN'T DUPLICATED IN THE COLLECTION. TRADES REPRESENTED ARE CARPENTER, JOINER, CABINETMAKER, SHIPWRIGHT, COACH & CARRIAGE MAKER, ETC. BLACKSMITH & FARRIER TOOLS INCLUDED. AT MICKE GROVE PARK, 11793 N MICKE GROVE RD, LODI, CA. (ST-WIDE). MEDORA JOHNSON, DIR; SAN JOAQUIN COUNTY HISTORICAL MUSEUM; PO BOX 21; LODI, CA 95240. (#26916-1).

LOMITA

ARB FLAG PRESENTATION TO PUBLIC SCHOOLS-LOMITA, CA. FLAGS WERE PRESENTED TO THREE LOCAL SCHOOLS TO TEACH FLAG ETIQUETTE AND BRING SCHOOLS AND LOCAL GOVERNMENT TOGETHER. (LOCAL). HON HAL HALL, MAYOR; LOMITA CITY COUNCIL; 24300 NARBONNE AVE; LOMITA, CA 90717. (#32388).

CITY HALL DISPLAY CASE - LOMITA, CA. DESIGN, GET FUNDING & PROCURE BUILDER FOR DISPLAY CASE TO SHOW LOCAL HISTORY & OTHER COMMUNITY PROJECTS FOR LOMITA CITY HALL. (LOCAL). BARBARA LEARNARD, PRESIDENT; LOMITA HISTORICAL SOCIETY; 24016 BENHILL AVE; LOMITA, CA 90717. (#32391).

FOUNDING OF LOMITA HISTORICAL SOCIETY, LOMITA, CA. ORGANIZATION CREATED TO COLLECT PRESERVE AND DISPLAY HISTORY OF THE CITY OF LOMITA. (LOCAL). BARBARA LEANARD, PRESIDENT; LOMITA HISTORICAL SOCIETY; 24016 BENHILL AVE; LOMITA, CA 90717. (#32392).

LOMITA, CA, LOGO CONTEST. CONTEST FOR A LOCAL ARTIST OR DESIGNER TO CREATE A LOMITA LOGO. (LOCAL). HON HAL HALL, MAYOR; LOMITA CITY COUNCIL; 24300 NARBONNE AVE; LOMITA, CA 90717. (#32387).

LOMITA, CA, MISSIONS TOUR. TOUR BY SENIOR CITIZENS OF CALIFORNIA MISSIONS. (LOCAL). EDMUND ROBERTS, PROJ CHAIRMAN; GOODTIMERS CLUB; 760 W LOMITA BLVD; HARBOR CITY, CA 90710. (#32390).

RAILROAD MUSEUM ANNEX DEDICATED IN LOMITA, CA. EXTENSIVE PARK AREA & BOX CAR FOR MOVIE PRESENTATIONS WAS OPENED WITH DEDICATION CEREMONY BY GOVERNMENT & MUSEUM OFFICIALS. (LOCAL). IRENE LEWIS, COORDINATOR; LOMITA RAILROAD MUSEUM COMMISSION; LOMITA, CA 90717. (#33687).

RECORDS OF LITERATURE FOR BLIND - LOMITA, CA. PURCHASE OF OVER 50 SETS OF RECORDS FOR THE NEW LOMITA LIBRARY OF AMERICAN AND ENGLISH LITERATURE FOR BLIND AND OTHERS. (LOCAL). LINDEN WOOD, PAST-PRESIDENT; HARBOR CITY-LOMITA LIONS CLUB; 2158 256 ST; LOMITA, CA 90717. (#32393).

STUDY ON GOVERNMENT - BOOK, LOMITA, CA. STUDY OF U S GOVERNMENT FROM VIEWPOINT OF CHRISTIAN VALUES. (LOCAL). REV G NELSON STRINGER, PASTOR; WAYSIDE UNITED METHODIST CHURCH; 2083 GUYSON ST; LOMITA, CA 90717. (#32389).

VETERAN PARK DEDICATION IN LOMITA, CA. NEW NEIGHBORHOOD PARK OPENED WITH MEMORIAL TO THOSE WHO SERVED THEIR COUNTRY. (LOCAL). HONORABLE HAL HALL, MAYOR; LOMITA CITY COUNCIL; 24300 NARBONNE AVE; LOMITA, CA 90717. (#33686).

APR 18, '75 - CONTINUING . PAUL REVERE RIDE RECREATION. 5 ELEMENTARY SCHOOLS WERE AUDIENCE FOR A RECREATION OF PAUL REVERE'S RIDE-COSTUMED COLONIAL LADY (HS STUDENT) NARRATED THE EVENT-STUDENTS AUGMENTED PRESENTATION WITH CLASS STUDIES. AT ELEMENTARY SCHOOLS-LOMITA, NORMANT, HARBOR CITY, PRESIDENT, ESHELMAN. (LOCAL). MARGARET ALLEN; LOS ANGELES CITY SCHOOLS AREA A; LOMITA ELEMENTARY SCHOOL; LOMITA, CA 90717. (#200006-467).

AUG 9, '75 - CONTINUING . NEW LOMITA CITY HALL DEDICATION. CEREMONY AT LOMITA CITY HALL 24300 NARBONNE AVE. (LOCAL). MAYOR HAL HALL; LOMITA CITY COUNCIL; 24300 NARBONNE AVE; LOMITA, CA 90717. (#200006-465).

SEPT 21, '75 - CONTINUING . OLD FASHIONED ICE CREAM SOCIAL. FESTIVAL AT LOMITA CITY HALL PATIO 24300 NARBONNE AVE. (LOCAL). BARBARA LEARNARD, PRES; LOMITA HISTORICAL SOCIETY; 24016 BENHILL AVE; LOMITA, CA 90717. (#200006-466).

JULY 4, '76. NATION-WIDE BELL RINGING. COMPETITION. (LOCAL). MAYOR HAL HALL; LOMITA CITY COUNCIL; 24300 NARBONN AVE; LOMITA, CA 90717. (#200006-464).

JULY 5, '76 - CONTINUING . TIME CAPSULE DEDICATION & COMMUNITY PICNIC. CEREMONY, FESTIVAL AT CITY HALL LAWN. (LOCAL). MORRIS VANCE; CITY OF LOMITA; LOMITA CITY HALL 24300 NARBONNE; LOMITA, CA 90717. (#200006-468).

AUG 15, '76 - CONTINUING . MISS SOFTBALL AMERICA BREAKFAST. FUND-RAISING BREAKFAST & CEREMONIES HONORING COACHES, LEADERS & YOUNG ATHLETES. AT LOMITA RECREATION CENTER. (LOCAL). JERRY WILLIAMS; MISS SOFTBALL AMERICA; 1888 WEST 261 ST; LOMITA, CA 90717. (#200006-462).

SEPT 18 - 19, '76. LOMITA JUBILEE JUNCTION '76. FAIR AT LOMITA RECREATION CENTER. (LOCAL). E R BECK; LOMITA CHAMBER OF COMMERCE; 24300 NARBONNE; LOMITA, CA 90717. (#200006-463).

LOMPOC

MISSION MUSIC PROJECT OF CALIFORNIA. RECORD & WRITE A BROCHURE ON THE ORIGIN OF MISSION MUSIC, SERIES OF CONCERTS, RECORDING ON TAPES PLAYED IN MISSIONS, CHURCHES & OTHER LOCATIONS. (ST-WIDE). WILLIAM C DILLINGER, CHIEF OF INFORMATION DIVISION; DEPT OF PARKS & RECREATION; PO BOX 2390; SACRAMENTO, CA 95811. (#1061). **ARBA GRANTEE.**

NOV 27, '75. THE GARDEN THEATRE FESTIVAL. LIVE PERFORMANCE AT LOMPOC PRISON. (LOCAL). WARREN CHRISTENSEN, DIR; THEATRE-IN-PROGRESS; 2625 PORTLAND ST; LOS ANGELES, CA 90007. (#102233-1).

MAY 25, '76. UNITED STATES ARMED FORCES BICENTENNIAL CARAVAN. CARAVAN IS COMPOSED OF EXHIBIT VANS FOR EACH MILITARY SERVICE. PROJECT THEME IS ' HISTORY OF THE ARMED FORCES & THEIR CONTRIBUTIONS TO THE NATION'. (LOCAL). PAUL THOMPSON, CHMN; U S ARMED FORCES BICENTENNIAL CARAVAN; 501 E NORTH AVE; LOMPOC, CA 93436. (#1775-574).

JUNE 25 - 27, '76. LOMPOC VALLEY FLOWER FESTIVAL. A MYRIAD OF SPRINGTIME FLOWERS IN THE WORLD'S LARGEST SEED-PRODUCING AREA CREATES A BACKDROP FOR A WEEKEND FESTIVAL. AT RYON PARK. (LOCAL). BETTY FITTS, CHAIRMAN; LOMPOC CHAMBER OF COMMERCE; LOMPOC, CA 93436. (#103416-387).

LONE PINE

OCT 30, '76. UNITED STATES ARMED FORCES BICENTENNIAL CARAVAN. CARAVAN IS COMPOSED OF EXHIBIT VANS FOR EACH MILITARY SERVICE. PROJECT THEME IS 'HISTORY OF THE ARMED FORCES & THEIR CONTRIBUTIONS TO THE NATION'. (LOCAL). HENRY RAUB; UNITED STATES ARMED FORCES BICENTENNIAL CARAVAN; C/O INYO CO BICENT COMMITTEE; INDEPENDENCE, CA 93526. (#1775-834).

LONG BEACH

ANGLO-AMERICAN WORKSHOPS IN HISTORY 1973-74. TWO CONFERENCES OF BRITISH AND U.S. HISTORIANS & EDUCATIONAL ADMINISTRATORS SEEKING TO DEVELOP A PERMANENT MECHANISM FOR COOPERATION ON MUTUAL PROBLEMS IN EDUCATION (U.S.-1973,U.K.-1974). (INT'L). PROF EUGENE L ASHER, PROJECT DIRECTOR; AMERICAN HISTORICAL ASSN HISTORY EDUCATION PROJECT; DEPT OF HISTORY CALIF STATE UNIV; LONG BEACH, CA 90840. (#2032).

BICENTENNIAL BIKE ROUTE, LONG BEACH, CA. PART OF THE 'PACIFIC COAST BICENTENNIAL ROUTE', PATH TO BE MARKED BY SIGNS; SPONSORED BY THE CALIFORNIA DEPT OF TRANSPORTATION AND THE CITY OF LONG BEACH. (LOCAL). JOHN MANSELL, CITY MANAGER; CITY OF LONG BEACH; CITY HALL; LONG BEACH, CA 90802. (#22394).

BICENTENNIAL CALENDAR - LONG BEACH, CA. THE CALENDAR WILL BE REPRODUCED FROM AN ORIGINAL OIL. (LOCAL). BETTY ANN KIRKPATRICK, PROJECT DIRECTOR; LONG BEACH ART ASSOC; 1491 BRYANT DR; LONG BEACH, CA 90815. (#17206).

BICENTENNIAL DISPLAY - LONG BEACH, CA. 16 CHILDREN AGES 3-16 BUILT YARD DISPLAY WITH LIBERTY BELL, LIGHTS, POSTER-SIZE PICTURES OF BETSY ROSS AND 'SPIRIT OF '76.'. (LOCAL). RICHARD BLISS, COORDINATOR; LONG BEACH BICENTENNIAL COMMISSION; 5450 E HILL ST; LONG BEACH, CA 90815. (#26773).

BICENTENNIAL FLAG PURCHASE FOR SCHOOLS, CA. TO ACQUAINT STUDENTS WITH THE OFFICIAL ARBC FLAG TO BE FLOWN OVER EACH SCHOOL FOR ENTIRE BICENTENNIAL YEAR. (LOCAL). PTA PRESIDENTS OR OFFICERS; LONG BEACH PTA'S; LONG BEACH, CA 90822. (#16939).

BICENTENNIAL FLASH, LONG BEACH, CA. TOASTMISTRESS MEMBERS WILL SPEAK FOR THREE MINUTES AT EACH MEETING ON THE TOPIC BICENTENNIAL FLASH, EVERY 2ND & 4TH THURSDAY THROUGH THE YEAR. (LOCAL). DOROTHY I HERRING, PRESIDENT; LONG BEACH CHAPTER-INTERNATIONAL TOASTMISTRESS CLUB; 6272 SEABREEZE; LONG BEACH, CA 90803. (#17067).

BICENTENNIAL GARDEN, LONG BEACH, CA. RED, WHITE & BLUE GARDEN WILL BE PLANTED IN FRONT OF MINNIE GRANT SCHOOL WITH '76' IN FOCUS. (LOCAL). PAM CINCOLA, PROJ DIRECTOR; MINNIE GANT ELEMENTARY SCHOOL PTA; 1521 GREENBRIER RD; LONG BEACH, CA 90815. (#17068).

BICENTENNIAL PATCHES - LONG BEACH, CA. PATCHES FOR THE TWO ADULT SOFTBALL TEAMS IN THE LONG BEACH SUNDAY MORNING SLOW PITCH LEAGUE. (LOCAL). JOE CLOSE, JR VICE CMDR; VFW POST 1746; 32 E LOUISE ST; LONG BEACH, CA 90805. (#18686).

BICENTENNIAL PRODUCTS CATALOGUE; LONG BEACH, CA. THE BICENTENNIAL CATALOGUE CONTAINS REPRODUCTIONS OF HISTORIC ITEMS. IT IS TO BE PUBLISHED IN 1976. (LOCAL). JAN ERNST ADLMANN, DIRECTOR; LONG BEACH MUSEUM OF ART; 2300 E OCEAN BLVD; LONG BEACH, CA 90803. (#17205).

BICENTENNIAL QUILT, LONG BEACH, CA. A QUILT OF 24 PANELS DEPICTING HISTORY OF LONG BEACH, CA. (LOCAL). VIOLETTE BACHTELLE, SUPERVISOR-CULTURAL ARTS; LONG BEACH RECREATION DEPT - CREATIVE ARTS UNIT; 155 QUEENS WAY LANDING; LONG BEACH, CA 90802. (#17071).

BICENTENNIAL SCHOOL LUNCH MENUS, LONG BEACH, CA. LBUSD FOOD SERVICE PROVIDES A SPECIAL BICENTENNIAL MENU ONCE OR TWICE A MONTH ON HISTORICAL DATES SUCH AS BOSTON TEA PARTY SIGHTING OF PLYMOUTH ROCK, ETC. (LOCAL). DOROTHY WELCH, CHAIRMAN; LONG BEACH UNIFIED SCHOOL DISTRICT; 701 LOCUST AVE; LONG BEACH, CA 90813. (#20217).

BICENTENNIAL THEME FOR COMMUNITY EVENTS - CA. ALL NAPLES IMPROVEMENTS EVENTS IN 1976 WILL EMPHASIZE THE BICENTENNIAL THEME. (LOCAL). SANDRA H DAVIDSON, PRESIDENT; NAPLES IMPROVEMENT ASSOC; 37 NEOPOLITAN LN W; LONG BEACH, CA 90803. (#17204).

BICENTENNIAL TRAVEL SLIDE PRESENTATION - CA. EMPHASIZES DESTINATIONS ASSOCIATED WITH THE CELEBRATION OF THE 200TH ANNIVERSARY OF THE BIRTH OF THIS NATION. (LOCAL). VIVIAN KILEY, COORDINATOR; LONG BEACH KIWIS; LONG BEACH, CA 90806. (#21126).

CALIFORNIA HERITAGE REDISCOVERED - LONG BEACH, CA. CAMPFIRE GIRLS WILL BE VISITING HISTORIC SITES, RESEARCHING HISTORIC LAND GRANTS AND RECORDING ANECDOTES OF SENIOR CITIZENS. (LOCAL). KARIN LEBECQ DUNPHY, EXECUTIVE DIRECTOR; CAMPFIRE GIRLS; 7070 E CARSON ST; LONG BEACH, CA 90808. (#17203).

CAMP FIRE GIRLS MAGAZINE PLAN - LONG BEACH, CA. THE LONG BEACH GIRL SCOUTS WILL SPONSOR A MAGAZINE SUBSCRIPTION RENEWAL PLAN AS A FUND-RAISING EFFORT TO HELP FINANCE THE YEARLY PROGRAM. (LOCAL). MARY LITTLEFORD, PROJ DIRECTOR; LONG BEACH COUNCIL OF CAMP FIRE GIRLS; 7070 E CARSON ST; LONG BEACH, CA 90808. (#18688).

COMMUNICATION '75: REDEDICATION, LONG BEACH, CA. FILM ON LONG BEACH EDUCATIONAL SYSTEM AND GOALS. (LOCAL). HAL LEVICH, ASST DIR INSTRUCTIONAL RESOURCES; LONG BEACH UNIFIED SCHOOL DISTRICT; 201 E 8TH ST; LONG BEACH, CA 90813. (#21968).

A DRIVING TOUR MAP PACKET FOR LONG BEACH, CA. THE PACKET WILL CONTAIN MAPS WITH PLACES OF HISTORICAL INTERESTS AND TOURIST INFORMATION PROPERLY MARKED WILL IDENTIFY CONTEMPORARY STRUCTURES ALONG THE ROUTES. (LOCAL). PHYLLIS POPER, EDITOR OF PACKET; CABRILLO CHAPTER, WOMEN'S ARCHITECTURAL LEAGUE; 2288 ALBURY AVE; LONG BEACH, CA 90815. (#17201).

'EMINENT AMERICANS', LONG BEACH, CA. 20 COPIES OF 'EMINENT AMERICANS' DONATED TO LONG BEACH PUBLIC LIBRARY & 19 COPIES TO THE LONG BEACH UNIFIED SCHOOL DISTRICT IN HONOR OF MAMIE D EISENHOWER. (LOCAL). MRS CHESTER WALLGREN, COORD; 34TH CONGRESSIONAL DISTRICT REPUBLICAN WOMEN FEDERATED; 283 CLAREMONT AVE; LONG BEACH, CA 90803. (#20870).

FLAG PAINTING IN EL DORADO PARK, LONG BEACH, CA. THE U S, BENNINGTON & BICENTENNIAL FLAGS WILL BE PAINTED ON A FLAT WALL IN EL DORADO PARK. (LOCAL). DICK FERRY, PROJ DIRECTOR; RECREATION DIVISION - LONG BEACH SCHOOL DISTRICT; EL DORADO PARK; LONG BEACH, CA 90808. (#17070).

FREEDOM OF THE PRESS: DOCUMENTARY FILM, CA. A 16MM, 25 MINUTE FILM TO BE SHOWN IN LONG BEACH & SURROUNDING AREAS DURING '75 & '76 - NATIONAL VERSION AVAILABLE. (NAT'L). RAY DIPIAZZA, PROJ DIRECTOR; INDEPENDENT PRESS-TELEGRAM; 604 PINE AVE; LONG BEACH, CA 90844. (#17066).

'LAWS FOR YOUTH', LONG BEACH, CA. A BOOKLET DESIGNED TO HELP YOUTH AND PARENTS KNOW THE LAWS THAT EFFECT THEM. (LOCAL). CLIFF BEYERS, PROJ COORDINATOR; LONG BEACH LODGE NO 888-BPO ELKS; 4101 E WILLOW ST; LONG BEACH, CA 90815. (#22395).

LIFE MEMBERSHIP IN VFW TO SPAN-AM WAR VETS - CA. LOCATION OF SURVIVING VETERANS FOR LIFETIME MEMBERSHIP IN THE VFW. (NAT'L). JOE CLOSE, JR VICE CMDR; VFW POST 1746; 32 E LOUISE ST; LONG BEACH, CA 90805. (#18687).

'LONG BEACH AS I REMEMBER IT' BY SENIOR CITIZENS. THE BOOK HONORS SENIOR CITIZENS AND CONTAINS ARTICLES SUBMITTED BY THEM ON THEIR HISTORICAL RECOLLECTIONS OF LONG BEACH. (LOCAL). DONALD E VAN LIEW, DIRECTOR; LAKEWOOD CHAPTER-ORDER OF DEMOLAY; 2372 BELMONT AVE; LONG BEACH, CA 90815. (#17207).

NATIONAL GUARD, COLOR GUARDS, LONG BEACH, CA. AVAILABLE FOR ANY BICENTENNIAL EVENT UPON REQUEST. (LOCAL). LTC RICHARD E THOMAS; CALIF NATIONAL GUARD; 2200 REDONDO; LONG BEACH, CA 90822. (#16942).

RECYCLING DRIVE - LONG BEACH, CA. RAISE MONEY TO PURCHASE TICKETS FOR THE FREEDOM TRAIN AND A $25 HERITAGE CERTIFICATE. (LOCAL). ROSS ALISON, COORDINATOR; SIXTH GRADE CLASSES, PATRICK HENRY SCHOOL; 3720 CANEHILL AVE; LONG BEACH, CA 90808. (#19661).

REDEDICATION OF FREEDOM SHRINE. CEREMONY. (LOCAL). SID BACON, CHAIRMAN; EXCHANGE CLUB OF LONG BEACH; 3935 WALNUT AVE; LONG BEACH, CA 90807. (#103115-4). **(??).**

ROUTE '1776' - LONG BEACH, CA. NEW BUS ROUTE SERVING BELMONT SHORE, BELMONT HEIGHTS & NAPLES. (LOCAL). CHRIS FARELL, PROJ DIRECTOR; LONG BEACH PUBLIC TRANSPORTATION COMPANY; 1300 GARDENIA AVE; LONG BEACH, CA 90813. (#18684).

SALE OF COMMEMORATIVE FLAGS AND POSTERS - CA. THE BICENTENNIAL THEME WILL BE DISPLAYED ON THE MEMORABILIA. (LOCAL). GORDON GETZ, PRESIDENT; LONG BEACH JR CHAMBER OF COMMERCE; 4141 NORSE WAY; LONG BEACH, CA 90808. (#17202).

SALE OF HERITAGE CERTIFICATES, LONG BEACH, CA. NON-TAXABLE, NON-REDEMPTIVE CERTIFICATES WILL BE SOLD TO RAISE MONEY FOR A CLOCK TOWER IN THE NEW CITY HALL COMPLEX AND WILL BE DONATED BY THE LONG BEACH ARBC. (LOCAL). MICHAEL NOTT, CHAIRMAN SALES COMMITTEE; ARBC-LONG BEACH, INC.; 120 E OCEAN BLVD; LONG BEACH, CA 90802. (#17208).

STEEL DRUM BAND, LONG BEACH, CA. CLASSES INSTRUCTING STEEL DRUM TECHNIQUE TO COMMENCE IN OCTOBER. (LOCAL). VI BACHTELLE, SUPERVISOR CULTURAL ARTS; LONG BCH REC DEPT, CITY OF LONG BCH & MYERS BARREL & DRUM CO; 155 QUEENS WAY LANDING; LONG BEACH, CA 90802. (#17069).

SURVEY OF LONG BEACH AREA CHURCH RECORDS, CA. THE CATAGORIES OF RECORDS KEPT, EARLIEST DATE OF SUCH RECORDS, WHERE KEPT AND IF AVAILABLE FOR RESEARCH; LONG BEACH PUBLIC LIBRARY WILL BE THE REPOSITORY FOR THE SURVEY, UPON COMPLETION. (LOCAL). MARTHA HESS, CORRESPONDING SECRETARY; QUESTING HEIRS GENEALOGICAL SOCIETY; PO BOX 15102; LONG BEACH, CA 90815. (#20871).

'WHAT DID GEORGE WASHINGTON REALLY LOOK LIKE', CA. BOYS AND GIRLS 2 TO 12 SUBMITTED ORIGINAL VERSIONS OF GEORGE WASHINGTON PORTRAITS RENDERED IN CRAYONS PAINTS & COLORED PENCILS. (LOCAL). ROBERT G VAN ANTWERP, DIRECTOR; LONG BEACH RECREATION DEPARTMENT; 155 QUEENS WAY LANDING; LONG BEACH, CA 90802. (#21969).

YOUTH BOWLING LEAGUE - LONG BEACH, CA. A YOUTH BOWLING LEAGUE WILL BE SET UP AT THE RED FOX BOWLING ALLEY. (LOCAL). JOE CLOSE, JR VICE CMDR; VFW POST #1746; 32 E LOUISE ST; LONG BEACH, CA 90805. (#18685).

1976 BABY CERTIFICATE AND SAVINGS BOND - CA. PRESENTATION OF CERTIFICATE TO EACH BABY BORN IN 1976; $25.00 U S SAVINGS BOND TO THE FIRST, 200TH & FIRST BORN ON THE 4TH OF JULY. (LOCAL). NORMA KRUEGER, CHAIRMAN; STORK CLUB-NIGHTINGALES, MEMORIAL HOSPITAL; 3861 SUNFLOWER ST; SEAL BEACH, CA 90740. (#18683).

$5 HERITAGE CERTIFICATES TO NEW BORNS - CA. CERTIFICATE PRESENTED TO EACH BABY BORN THE FIRST WEEK IN MAY AT MEMORIAL MEDICAL CENTER. (LOCAL). KAY ROGGEVEEN, COORDINATOR; MEMORIAL MEDICAL CENTER CHILDREN'S AUXILIARY; 269 SAN ANTONIO DR; LONG BEACH, CA 90807. (#25367).

OCT 1 - 31, '73. ANGLO-AMERICAN WORKSHOPS IN HISTORY. TWO CONFERENCES OF BRITISH AND U.S. HISTORIANS & EDUCATIONAL ADMINISTRATORS SEEKING TO DEVELOP A PERMANENT MECHANISM FOR COOPERATION ON MUTUAL PROBLEMS IN EDUCATION. (INT'L). EUGENE L ASHER, PROJ DIR; AMERICAN HISTORICAL ASSN, US DEPT OF STATE, DEPT OF EDUCATION; DEPT HISTORY, CALIF STATE UNIV; LONG BEACH, CA 90840. (#2032-1).

JAN 5, '75. BICENTENNIAL INTERNATIONAL CHILDREN'S CHOIR. LIVE PERFORMANCE. (LOCAL). ZITA REMLEY, CHMN; LONG BEACH EBELL CLUB; 10 1/2 MIRA MAR; LONG BEACH, CA 90803. (#103309-18).

JAN 6, '75. BICENTENNIAL FLAG PRESENTATION - ELKS 888. CEREMONY AT 4101 E WILLOW. (LOCAL). GEN C BEYERS, USA RET; ELKS LODGE 888; 5621 VERNON AVE; LONG BEACH, CA 90815. (#200006-68).

FEB 15, '75. PLAQUE DEDICATION, PUVUNGA INDIAN SITE, RANCHO LOS ALAMITOS. DEDICATION OF MARKER, REFRESHMENTS AND TOUR OF THE RANCHO; FIRST LONG BEACH BICENTENNIAL EVENT. AT RANCHO LOS ALAMITOS. (LOCAL). BILLIE J REISCHE, COORD; SUSAN B ANTHONY CHAPTER - D A R; 3311 RUTH ELAINE DR; LOS ALAMITOS, CA 90720. (#200006-61).

MAR 15, '75. ARMY-NAVY ROTC DRILL COMPETITION. OPEN COMPETITION BETWEEN ARMY AND NAVY AND INTRODUCTION OF OFFICIAL BICENTENNIAL FLAG. AT U S ARMY RESERVE CENTER, 3800 E WILLOW. (LOCAL). COL STOCKWELL, USA RET; ARMY-NAVY ROTC UNITS; 3800 E WILLOW; LONG BEACH, CA 90815. (#200006-46).

APR 5, '75. MUNICIPAL BAND & ALL CITY SCHOOL ORCHESTRA CONCERT. YOUTH CONCERT WITH BICENTENNIAL THEME WILL BE CONDUCTED BY FRED OHLENDORF. AT QUEEN'S SALON ABOARD THE QUEEN MARY. (LOCAL). EVERETT E SIEGRIST, COORD; LONG BEACH MUNICIPAL BAND; 3500 E ANAHEIM; LONG BEACH, CA 90804. (#200006-70).

APR 26, '75. KEEP AMERICA BEAUTIFUL DAY. FESTIVAL AT CITY OF LONG BEACH. (LOCAL). DOROTHY BUERGER; BOY SCOUTS OF AMERICA - LONG BEACH BEAUTIFUL COMMITTEE; 139 LINDERO AVE; LONG BEACH, CA 90803. (#200006-69).

MAY 1, '75. 18TH ANNUAL LAW DAY OBSERVANCE. MEMBERS ONLY AND INVITED GUESTS. THEME - 'AMERICA'S GOAL - JUSTICE THROUGH LAW.'. AT GOLDEN SAILS INN - BANQUET ROOM. (LOCAL). MS NILA ALCOCK; LONG BEACH BAR ASSOC; 444 W OCEAN, SUITE 500; LONG BEACH, CA 90802. (#200006-67).

MAY 11, '75. MOTHER'S DAY BICENTENNIAL CONCERT. SECOND IN A SERIES OF GUEST BANDS FOR BICENTENNIAL CONCERTS. AT BIXBY PARK. (LOCAL). EVERETT E SIEGRIST, COORD; LONG BEACH MUNICIPAL BAND - SAN JOSE HIGH SCHOOL BAND; 3500 E ANAHEIM; LONG BEACH, CA 90804. (#200006-66).

MAY 16 - 18, '75. BICENTENNIAL SEMI-ANNUAL MEETING. DISPLAY SHOWCASE OF 21 SECTIONS-RED, WHITE & BLUE DEPICTING 200 YRS HISTORY IN FORM OF MINIATURE FIGURES AND SCENES. OPEN TO ALL MEMBERS OF THE MASONIC FRATERNITY. AT ROCHELLES CONVENTION CENTER. (LOCAL). JAMES ROBERTSON, COORD; ANCIENT EGYPTIAN ORDER OF SCIOTS - PYRAMIDS #4, 43, & 47; 16511 SOUTH GARFIELD #8-C; PARAMOUNT, CA 90723. (#200006-65).

MAY 22 - 30, '75. BICENTENNIAL CONCERTS FOR LONG BEACH UNIFIED SCHOOL DISTRICT. LIVE PERFORMANCE AT VARIOUS LOCAL ELEMENTARY SCHOOLS. (LOCAL). E E SIEGRIST, DIRECTOR; LONG BEACH MUNICIPAL BAND; 3500 E ANAHEIM; LONG BEACH, CA 90804. (#200006-64).

MAY 26, '75. BICENTENNIAL CONCERT. MEMORIAL DAY SERVICES WILL BE HELD. AT SUNNYSIDE MEMORIAL GARDENS. (LOCAL). E E SIEGRIST, DIRECTOR; LONG BEACH MUNICIPAL BAND - COLOR GUARD FROM US COAST GUARD; 3500 E ANAHEIM; LONG BEACH, CA 90804. (#200006-63).

MAY 28 - JULY ??, '75. BICYCLE RIDE TO WASHINGTON, DC FROM QUEEN MARY-LONG BEACH. ANDY SNINSKY TO RIDE WITH NATIONAL COLORS TO NATION'S CAPITOL ON TEN SPEED BICYCLE, STOPPING AT POSTAL FACILITIES ALONG THE WAY. AT QUEEN MARY. (LOCAL). ANDY SNINSKY, COORD; POST OFFICE WORKERS' UNION; CITY OF LONG BEACH; LONG BEACH, CA 90720. (#200006-62).

JUNE 5 - 8, '75. COIN SHOW. EXHIBIT AT LONG BEACH ARENA. (ST-WIDE). MAURICE M GOULD, CHRMAN; LONG BEACH COIN & STAMP EXPO, TREASURE TROVE CLUB; PO BOX 1500; TUSTIN, CA 92680. (#50753-1).

JUNE 6, '75. BICENTENNIAL MUSIC FOR BAND, ORCHESTRA & CHORUS FOR LBUSD. LIVE PERFORMANCE AT LONG BEACH UNIFIED SCHOOL DISTRICT. (LOCAL). ALICE GALLUP, SUPERVISOR; J C PENNEY CO; 701 LOCUST AVE; LONG BEACH, CA 90813. (#200006-49).

JUNE 6, '75. HONOR SETH HUNTINGTON NIGHT. AWARD DESIGNER OF REVERSE HALF DOLLAR OF BICENTENNIAL COIN. AT LORD NELSON ROOM ABOARD THE QUEEN MARY. (LOCAL). SAM LOPRESTO, DIRECTOR; LONG BEACH COIN AND STAMP SHOW; 309 E OCEAN BLVD; LONG BEACH, CA 90802. (#200006-50).

JUNE 13, '75. PRESENTATION OF OFFICIAL ARBA FLAG TO PRESIDENT S HORN, CSULB. PUBLICITY FOR BICENTENNIAL RECOGNITION ON CSULB CAMPUS, ANNOUNCEMENT OF APPOINTMENT OF IRVINE AHLQUIST AS OFFICIAL BICENTENNIAL REPRESENTATIVE COORDINATOR ON CAMPUS. AT PRESIDENT'S CONFERENCE ROOM,

LONG BEACH — CONTINUED

CA STATE UNIV AT LONG BEACH. (LOCAL). LUCILLE SQUIRE, COORD; LONG BEACH ARBC; 211 GRAND AVE, #203; LONG BEACH, CA 90803. (#200006-48).

JUNE 16, '75. ELKS HONOR OUR FLAG DAY PROGRAM. CEREMONY AT DOME ROOM-ELK'S LODGE, 6101 WILLOW. (LOCAL). CLIFFORD BEYERS, DIR; LONG BEACH ELK'S LODGE #888; 5621 VERNON AVE; LONG BEACH, CA 90815. (#200006-47).

JUNE 23 - AUG 1, '75. THE LITERATURE OF REVOLUTION, 'HONORS SYMPOSIUM', HON X200. SEMINAR AT CSULB CAMPUS, PSYCHOLOGY BLDG, ROOM 234. (LOCAL). BENJAMINE LEVINE, COORD; CSULB-SUMMER CONTINUING SUMMER EDUCATION; 6101 E 7TH ST; LONG BEACH, CA 90840. (#200006-44).

JUNE 23 - AUG 1, '75. PROGRAM IN AMERICAN STUDIES. AN INNOVATIVE TEACHING GRANT PROGRAM INTRODUCTION OF AMERICAN STUDIES INTO THE CLASSROOM. AT CALIF STATE UNIV LONG BEACH. (LOCAL). BEN LEVINE, COORDINATOR; CALIF STATE UNIV LONG BEACH; 6101 E 7TH ST; LONG BEACH, CA 90840. (#200006-43).

JUNE 23 - AUG 1, '75. SPECIAL TOPICS IN AMERICAN CIVILIZATION. SEMINAR AT CSULB CAMPUS, LIBERAL ARTS BLDG 3, ROOM 108. (LOCAL). WILLIAM H WELCH, COORD; CSULB - SUMMER CONTINUING EDUCATION; LONG BEACH, CA 90840. (#200006-45).

JUNE 28, '75. BICENTENNIAL CONCERT AT ALL-AMERICAN CULTURAL DAY. LIVE PERFORMANCE AT ROCKWELL RECREATION CENTER. (LOCAL). EASTER N BEEKLY, COORD; INTERNATIONAL CHILDREN'S CHOIR; PO BOX 5656; LONG BEACH, CA 90840. (#200006-40).

JUNE 29, '75. THE GREAT AMERICAN ALL-CITY PICNIC. FESTIVAL AT EL DORODO PARK. (LOCAL). VIOLETTE BACHTELLE, COORD; LONG BEACH RECREATION DEPT; 155 QUEEN'S WAY; LONG BEACH, CA 90802. (#200006-39).

JUNE - AUG '75. AMERICAN FOLKLORE COURSE. SEMINAR AT 6101 E 7TH ST. (LOCAL). BEN LEVINE, COORDINATOR; CALIF STATE UNIV LONG BEACH; 6101 E 7TH ST; LONG BEACH, CA 90840. (#200006-42).

JUNE - AUG '75. REVOLUTIONARY DOCUMENTS COURSE. SEMINAR AT 6101 E 7TH ST. (LOCAL). BEN LEVINE, COORDINATOR; CALIF STATE UNIV LONG BEACH; 6101 E 7TH ST; LONG BEACH, CA 90840. (#200006-41).

JULY 1 - 10, '75. BICENTENNIAL GIFT DAY. SAVINGS AND LOAN GAVE AWAY AN ALBUM TITLED 'AMERICA SINGS', REVOLUTIONARY THEME. AT 555 E OCEAN BLVD. (LOCAL). SHIRLEY SINSA; FIDELITY FEDERAL SAVINGS & LOAN ASSOC; 555 E OCEAN BLVD; LONG BEACH, CA 90802. (#200006-19).

JULY 2 - 6, '75. BICENTENNIAL BAND CONCERTS. LIVE PERFORMANCE AT VARIOUS LOCAL PARKS. (LOCAL). E E SIEGRIST; LONG BEACH MUNICIPAL BAND; 3500 E ANAHEIM; LONG BEACH, CA 90804. (#200006-18).

JULY 4, '75. SIGNING OF THE DECLARATION OF INDEPENDENCE-PLAY. PLAY DEPICTING THE SCENE IN HISTORY DONE BY LOCAL MEMBERS OF LODGE, PRECEEDED BY A DESSERT PARTY. AT SCOTTISH RITE CATHEDRAL, 855 ELM AVE. (LOCAL). CHARLES J PAYNE, COORD; LONG BEACH SCOTTISH RITE; 855 ELM AVE; LONG BEACH, CA 90802. (#200006-113).

JULY 5, '75. BELMONT SHORE OPENING OF BICENTENNIAL. PANCAKE BREAKFAST-9:00 AM. FLAG PRESENTATION-12:00 NOON. BAND CONCERT. AT GREAT WESTERN SAVINGS AND LOAN PARKING LOT, E 2ND ST. (LOCAL). SANDY SANTA CRUZ, COORD; BELMONT SHORE BUSINESSMEN'S ASSOC; 5209 E 2ND ST; LONG BEACH, CA 90803. (#200006-112).

JULY 14 - 25, '75. BICENTENNIAL THEATRE PRODUCTION WORKSHOP. SEMINAR AT THEATRE ARTS DEPT, CSULB. (LOCAL). RALPH DUCKWALL, COORD; THEATRE ARTS DEPT, CALIFORNIA STATE UNIV, LONG BEACH, CA; 6101 E 7TH ST; LONG BEACH, CA 90840. (#200006-110).

JULY 17, '75. BICENTENNIAL CONCERT: WASHINGTON & OREGON PICNIC. LIVE PERFORMANCE AT BIXBY PARK. (LOCAL). EASTER BEEKLEY, COORD; INTERNATIONAL CHILDREN'S CHOIR; PO BOX 5656; LONG BEACH, CA 90805. (#200006-111).

AUG 17, '75. BICENTENNIAL SAND SCULPTURE CONTEST. COMPETITION. (LOCAL). PATRICIA SIEGRIST, CHMN; ARTS COUNCIL; PO BOX 1776; LONG BEACH, CA 90801. (#100517-1).

AUG 21 - SEPT 19, '75. SMITHSONIAN INSTITUTION EXHIBIT. 'IN THE MINDS AND HEARTS OF THE PEOPLE: PROLOGUE TO THE AMERICAN REVOLUTION, 1760-1774'. AT 6101 E 7TH ST. (LOCAL). IRVING AHLQUIST; CALIF STATE UNIVERSITY LONG BEACH LIBRARY; 6101 E 7TH ST, HISTORY DEPT; LONG BEACH, CA 90840. (#200006-21).

AUG 26, '75. PRESENTATION OF BICENTENNIAL QUILT TO CITY OF LONG BEACH. HISTORICAL SCENES FROM LONG BEACH INCORPORATED INTO AMERICAN BICENTENNIAL QUILT. AT EL DORODO LIBRARY, 2900 STUDEBAKER LONG BEACH. (LOCAL). ROBERT BARRETT; LONG BEACH RECREATIONAL DEPT; 155 QUEEN'S WAY LANDING; LONG BEACH, CA 90802. (#200006-20).

AUG 30 - SEPT 1, '75. VFW BICENTENNIAL BOOTH AT LION'S CLUB FAIR. MEMBERS OF THE POST & THEIR WIVES WILL DRESS IN PATRIOTIC COLORS & DECORATE THE BOOTH ACCORDINGLY. AT HOUGHTON PARK. (LOCAL). JOE CLOSE, JR, VICE CMNDR; VFW POST 1746; 337 E 55TH ST; LONG BEACH, CA 90805. (#101856-1).

SEPT 3, '75. SENIOR CITIZEN HARVEST BICENTENNIAL FAIR. FAIR AT BIXBY PARK LONG BEACH. (LOCAL). GEORGE H TOLL, COORD; LONG BEACH SENIOR CITIZENS; 3632 ROSE AVE; LONG BEACH, CA 90807. (#200006-35).

SEPT 5 - 7, '75. NATIONAL EAGLE SCOUT ASSOCIATION. LIVE PERFORMANCE. (LOCAL). LORAN BURES, COORDINATOR; INTERNATIONAL CITY CHAPTER EAGLE SCOUTS; 244 CORONADO AVE #5; LONG BEACH, CA 90803. (#200006-34).

SEPT 9 - DEC 16, '75. FOLKLORE AND THE AMERICAN REVOLUTIONARY SPIRIT. SEMINAR AT WESTMINSTER HIGH SCHOOL, 14325 GOLDENWEST. (LOCAL). MARILYN ELKINS, COORD; CALIF STATE UNIV LONG BEACH, CONTINUING EDUCATION; 6101 E 7TH ST; LONG BEACH, CA 90840. (#200006-33).

SEPT 15, '75. SALUTE TO LONG BEACH MUNICIPAL BAND BY LB HISTORICAL SOCIETY. LIVE PERFORMANCE, CEREMONY AT BIG HALL, VET'S CLUB HOUSE, 101 E 28TH ST. (LOCAL). ROBERT METZGAR, DIRECTOR; LONG BEACH HISTORICAL SOCIETY; PO BOX 570; LONG BEACH, CA 90801. (#200006-28).

SEPT 17, '75. LIBERTY TREE CEREMONY. CEREMONY LIKENED TO THAT OF ORIGINAL LIBERTY TREE PLANTING; ALSO, LONG BEACH BAND IN CONCERT. AT EL DORADO PARK #3. (LOCAL). MABEL ORNELAS, COORD; DEGREE OF POCAHONTAS-MATTAWA COUNCIL 219; 2025 ORANGE AVE; LONG BEACH, CA 90806. (#200006-32).

SEPT 20, '75. BICENTENNIAL FUND RAISER. FESTIVAL AT WM A WALLACE RES, 4323 CALIFORNIA AVE. (LOCAL). MARGARET GANSSLE, COORD; LEAGUE OF WOMEN VOTERS; 260 SAN REMO DR; LONG BEACH, CA 90803. (#200006-30).

SEPT 20, '75. BICENTENNIAL LUAU OF VETERANS OF FOREIGN WARS. FESTIVAL AT VFW POST AT 32 E LOUISE. (LOCAL). JOE CLOSE, JR, VICE CMNDR; VFW POST 1746; 337 E 55TH ST; LONG BEACH, CA 90805. (#101857-1).

SEPT 20 - OCT 15, '75. AMERICAN TEXTILE TRADITIONS. A CLASS DEALING WITH THE TRADITIONS OF AMERICAN TEXTILES OF THE PAST. AT HOME ECONOMICS BUILDING, ROOM 105. (LOCAL). MARY KEFGEN, COORDINATOR; CALIF STATE UNIV LONG BEACH, CONTINUING EDUCATION; 6101 E 7TH ST; LONG BEACH, CA 90840. (#200006-31).

SEPT 22 - OCT 19, '75. TRANSPARENCY LA-A FRAME OF MIND. EXHIBIT AT GALLERIES A&B. (LOCAL). DIRECTOR; CALIF STATE UNIV LONG BEACH ART GALLERY; 6101 E 7TH ST; LONG BEACH, CA 90840. (#200006-27).

SEPT 28, '75. FORMULA 5000 RACE: PRE-RUNNER GRAND PRIX. COMPETITION, LIVE PERFORMANCE. (LOCAL). PATRICIA SIEGRIST, CHMN; LONG BEACH ARBC; PO BOX 1776; LONG BEACH, CA 90801. (#100519-1).

SEPT 30, '75 - JULY 9, '76. 7-MINUTE LOOK BACKWARD INTO HISTORY. SEMINAR AT 6741 MONTAVA ST. (LOCAL). MAY BERMAN, COORDINATOR; NATIONAL COUNCIL OF JEWISH WOMEN, LONG BEACH SECTION; 2982 DRUID LANE; LOS ALAMITOS, CA 90720. (#200006-25).

SEPT '75 - DEC '76. MUSIC AMERICANA. LONG BEACH MUNICIPAL BAND HOSTS JR & SR HIGH SCHOOL AND YOUTH BANDS IN BICENTENNIAL CONCERTS. AT QUEEN MARY-QUEEN'S SALON. (LOCAL). PATRICIA SIEGRIST, CHMN; LONG BEACH MUNICIPAL BAND; PO BOX 1776; LONG BEACH, CA 90801. (#100518-1).

OCT 9, '75. GENERAL GEORGE S BROWN, USAF CHMN JOINT CHIEF OF STAFFS. CONFERENCE AT ROCHELL'S CONVENTION CENTER, LAKEWOOD BLVD. (LOCAL). M GOLDIE, COORD; ARMED SERVICES COMMISSION, LONG BEACH CHAMBER OF COMMERCE; 50 OCEANGATE; LONG BEACH, CA 90802. (#200006-52).

OCT 11, '75. LONG BEACH SYMPHONY 41ST BICENTENNIAL SEASON OPENING. JOHN BROWNING, PIANIST-SOLOIST, WILL PERFORM. AT LONG BEACH CITY COLLEGE AUDITORIUM. (LOCAL). JOHN L HYER, COORD; LONG BEACH SYMPHONY; 121 LINDEN AVE; LONG BEACH, CA 90802. (#200006-54).

OCT 14, '75. BICENTENNIAL-JR ROTC PROGRAM. CEREMONY AT 1854 NORTH BRITTON DR. (LOCAL). PAM CINCOLA, COORD; MINNIE GANT PTA; 1521 GREENBRIER RD; LONG BEACH, CA 90815. (#200006-60).

OCT 15 - NOV 14, '75. EARLY AMERICAN TOOLS, IMPLEMENTS & DOCUMENTS. EXHIBIT AT LIBRARY. (LOCAL). DR IRVING AHLQUIST; CALIFORNIA STATE UNIV AT LONG BEACH; 6101 E 7TH ST; LONG BEACH, CA 90840. (#103236-1).

OCT 17, '75. BICENTENNIAL AWARDS LUNCHEON. SEN GEORGE DEUKMEJIAN WILL BE THE GUEST SPEAKER. AT INTERNATIONAL BALLROOM--LA FAYETTE HOTEL. (LOCAL). MARGARET GANSSLE, COORD; RETIRED SENIORS VOLUNTEER PROGRAM; 260 SAN REMO DR; LONG BEACH, CA 90803. (#200006-59).

OCT 19, '75. GIRL SCOUTS DEDICATION OF US FLAG. MEMBERS ONLY WILL BE INVITED TO ATTEND. AT 4040 BELLFLOWER BLVD. (LOCAL). MILDRED FRERKS, COORD; GIRL SCOUTS OF AMERICA - LONG BEACH; 393 LOS ALTOS AVE; LONG BEACH, CA 90814. (#200006-58).

OCT 23, '75. NAVY DAY CELEBRATION - BICENTENNIAL OF NAVY. SECRETARY OF NAVY TO BE PRESENT TO KICK-OFF BICENTENNIAL OF NAVY; OPEN TO PUBLIC. AT GOLDEN SAILS. (LOCAL). CAPT J J MEYER; NAVAL GROUPS - CITY OF LONG BEACH; US NAVAL STATION, LONG BEACH; LONG BEACH, CA 90801. (#200006-57).

NOV 1, '75 - SEPT 30, '76. BICENTENNIAL QUILT EXHIBIT. SUNDAY HOURS: 9:30 AM - 5:30 PM. AT BAYSHORE PUBLIC LIBRARY. (LOCAL). VIOLETTE BACHTELLE, COORD; LONG BEACH RECREATION DEPT; 270 E SEASIDE BLVD; LONG BEACH, CA 90802. (#103406-1).

NOV 3 - 26, '75. MICHAEL ANDREWS EXHIBIT. RECEPTION FOR ARTIST NOV 3, 7-9 PM. LECTURE NOV 19, 7 PM-'DIRECTIONS IN CONTEMPORARY PHOTOGRAPHY', BY VAN DEREN COKE. SUNDAY HOURS: 1-4 PM. AT ART GALLERY - CSULB, GALLERY A. (ST-WIDE). CONSTANCE W. GLENN; CA STATE UNIV AT LONG BEACH; 6101 E 7TH ST; LONG BEACH, CA 90840. (#103236-2).

NOV 7, '75. BICENTENNIAL DAY ON CAMPUS. EXHIBIT, FESTIVAL, LIVE PERFORMANCE AT CALIFORNIA STATE UNIVERSITY LONG BEACH CAMPUS. (LOCAL). ALLEN S WHARTON, PROJ DIR; ASSOCIATED STUDENTS, CSULB; 6101 E 7TH ST; LONG BEACH, CA 90840. (#103236-3).

NOV 8, '75. LONG BEACH SYMPHONY 41ST BICENTENNIAL COMMITTEE. ALBERTO BOLET, CONDUCTOR. AT LONG BEACH CITY COLLEGE AUDITORIUM. (LOCAL). JOHN L HYER, PROJ DIR; LONG BEACH SYMPHONY; 121 LINDEN AVE; LONG BEACH, CA 90802. (#103236-4).

NOV 13 - DEC 12, '75. BLACKS IN THE WESTWARD MOVEMENT - EXHIBIT. SMITHSONIAN INSTITUTION EXHIBIT. AT GRAPHICS GALLERY-CA STATE UNIV LONG BEACH. (LOCAL). DR I AHLQUIST; CSULB-LIBRARY; 6101 E 7TH ST; LONG BEACH, CA 90840. (#103236-5).

NOV 17 - DEC 14, '75. LUCAS SAMARAS-PHOTO TRANSFORMATIONS. EXHIBIT NOV 17-DEC 14; LECTURE DEC 1, 7 PM; FILM DEC 1, 7 PM. SUNDAY HOURS 1-4 PM. AT GALLERY B. (ST-WIDE). CINDY CLEARY, CLERK; CSULB-ART GALLERIES; 6101 E 7TH ST; LONG BEACH, CA 90840. (#103236-6).

NOV 18, '75. TICKET SALES KICKOFF-PARADE. PARADE AT 4654 CHARLEMANGE, 1205 FREEMAN, 711 VIAWANDA, & 1835 WILLARD,. (LOCAL). WILLIAM G ORME, EX DIR; BOYS CLUB OF LONG BEACH; 5280 E ARBOR RD; LONG BEACH, CA 90808. (#200006-23).

NOV 22, '75. 'STAR SPANGLED BAND SPECTACULAR'. BANDS AND DRILL TEAMS FROM JORDON HS, LAKEWOOD HS, MILLIKAN HS AND WILSON HS WILL PERFORM. AT VETERAN'S MEMORIAL STADIUM. (LOCAL). DAVID SMOCK, COORD; LONG BEACH CITY COLLEGE AND LOCAL HIGH SCHOOLS; 4901 E CARSON ST; LONG BEACH, CA 90808. (#200006-55).

NOV 22 - 23, '75. BICENTENNIAL CAMPOUT. FESTIVAL AT EL DORODO PARK. (LOCAL). NANCY KENNEDY, PROJ DIR; LONG BEACH COUNCIL OF CAMPFIRE GIRLS; 7070 E CARSON; LONG BEACH, CA 90808. (#103236-7).

NOV 23, '75. A SWEDISH AFTERNOON. PUBLIC WELCOME. AT DOME ROOM, LB ELKS CLUB, 4101 E WILLOW ST. (LOCAL). VERNIS ALLEN, CHMN; VASA, SWEDISH AMERICAN BICENTENNIAL COMMITTEE; 7109 CORALITE AVE; LONG BEACH, CA 90808. (#103309-21).

NOV 24, '75. BICENTENNIAL FAST DAY. CEREMONY AT THROUGHOUT LONG BEACH. (LOCAL). DR DAVID BURCHAM, DIR; AMER REVOLUTION BICENTENNIAL RELIGIOUS COORDINATION COMMITTEE; 607 E 3RD ST; LONG BEACH, CA 90812. (#103236-8).

NOV 26 - DEC 14, '75. THE GREAT QUILT, AN EXHIBIT. QUILT COMPRISED OF 48 12 INCH SQUARES, THE DESIGNS INDIVIDUALLY EXECUTED BY MANY OF AMERICA'S MOST FAMOUS CONTEMPORARY ARTISTS. AT WINDOW GALLERY-CSULB. (LOCAL). CINDY CLEARY, PROJ COORD; CALIF STATE UNIV LONG BEACH ART GALLERIES; 6101 E SEVENTH ST; LONG BEACH, CA 90840. (#102997-1).

DEC 2, '75. COLOR ME RED WHITE AND BLUE - MEN'S FASHION SHOW. EXHIBIT AT GOLDEN SAILS RESTAURANT. (LOCAL). CINDY CLEARY, CHAIRMAN; ST MARY'S HOSPITAL FOUNDATION; 6101 E 7TH ST; LONG BEACH, CA 90840. (#103236-11).

DEC 10 - 31, '75. ANNUAL CHRISTMAS TREE LANE WITH BICENTENNIAL THEME AND DECORATION. EXHIBIT AT DAISY AVE. (LOCAL). ROBERT E KENNEDY, COORD; CITY OF LONG BEACH; 1601 SAN FRANCISCO; LONG BEACH, CA 90813. (#103999-5).

DEC 20 - 21, '75. BICENTENNIAL CHRISTMAS PARADE OF BOATS ON NAPLES CANAL. PARADE. (LOCAL). PATRICIA SIEGRIST, CHMN; LONG BEACH ARBC; PO BOX 1776; LONG BEACH, CA 90801. (#100520-1).

DEC 28, '75. BICENTENNIAL VISITING BAND CONCERT. PATRIOTS' BAND OF FREEDOM HIGH SCHOOL, BETHLEHEM, PA. AT QUEEN'S SALON, QUEEN MARY. (LOCAL). E E SIEGRIST, CHAIRMAN; LONG BEACH ARBC; 3500 E ANAHEIM; LONG BEACH, CA 90804. (#103236-10).

DEC 31, '75. BICENTENNIAL NEW YEAR'S EVE PARTY SPONSORED BY VFW. FESTIVAL AT VFW POST 32, E LOUISE ST. (LOCAL). JOE CLOSE, DIRECTOR; VFW POST 1746; 337 E 5KTH ST; LONG BEACH, CA 90805. (#103309-24).

DEC 31, '75 - JAN 1, '76. REGIONAL ARTS COUNCIL'S BICENTENNIAL NEW YEAR'S EVE EXTRAVAGANZA. FESTIVAL. (LOCAL). PATRICIA SIEGRIST, CHMN; REGIONAL ARTS COUNCIL; PO BOX 1776; LONG BEACH, CA 90801. (#100522-1).

JAN 1 - DEC 31, '76. HISTORICAL AMERICAN MUSIC. CONCERT SEASON PLAYED IN EACH SCHOOL ON REGULARLY SCHEDULED CALENDAR. (LOCAL). PATRICIA SIEGRIST, CHMN; LONG BEACH MUNICIPAL BAND; PO BOX 1776; LONG BEACH, CA 90801. (#100488-1).

JAN 3 - 4, '76. SPECIAL BLESSINGS FOR BICENTENNIAL YEAR 1976. CEREMONY AT CITY OF LONG BEACH. (LOCAL). DR DAVID BURCHAM, CHMN; RELIGIOUS COORDINATION COMMITTEE, LONG BEACH ARBC; 607 E 3RD ST; LONG BEACH, CA 90812. (#103309-19).

JAN 6 - 8, '76. AMERICAN FREEDOM TRAIN DISPLAY DAYS AT LONG BEACH. THE AMERICAN FREEDOM TRAIN WILL INCLUDE 10 EXHIBIT CARS & 2 SHOWCASE CARS DEPICTING DIFFERENT PHASES OF THE AMERICAN EXPERIENCE. ITS ARRIVAL WILL SERVE AS A CATALYST FOR LOCAL BICENTENNIAL CELEBRATIONS BY PEOPLE THROUGHOUT THIS NATION. (ST-WIDE). DON MALLICOAT, EDIT SVCS; THE AMERICAN FREEDOM TRAIN FOUNDATION, INC; 5205 LEESBURG PIKE, SUITE 800; BAILEY'S XRDS, VA 22041. (#1776-85).

JAN 11, '76. AFFIRMATION SERVICE OF JANUARY. CEREMONY AT COVENANT PRESBYTERIAN CHURCH. (LOCAL). REV MICHAEL

LONG BEACH — CONTINUED

NOLIN, DIR; RELIGIOUS COORDINATION COMMITTEE, LONG BEACH ARBC; 607 E 3RD ST; LONG BEACH, CA 90812. (#103309-22).

JAN 16 - 18, '76. BICENTENNIAL MEDIA EXHIBIT & MEDIA CLINIC. EXHIBITION OF MEDIA MATERIALS DEALING WITH ASPECTS OF AMERICA W/ BICENTENNIAL THEME.LECTURES & WORKSHOPS ON THE MEDIA WILL ALSO BE PRESENTED. AT CAL STATE UNIV-LB CAMPUS. (LOCAL). RICHARD J JOHNSON, CHMN; CALIFORNIA STATE UNIV; DEPT OF INSTRUCTIONAL MEDIA; LONG BEACH, CA 90840. (#8263-501).

JAN 17, '76. ANNUAL SOUTHERN LUNCHEON. SPEAKERS: CLINTON O ROSS ON GEN ROBERT E LEE & COM MATTHEW F MAUREY; TOM HOAG ON 'STONEWALL' JACKSON. AT QUEEN MARY. (LOCAL). JEAN RIDDLE, COORD; GENERAL JOE WHEELER CHAPTER-UNITED DAUGHTERS OF THE CONFEDERACY; 3410 CLAREMORE AVE; LONG BEACH, CA 90808. (#200006-164).

JAN 20, '76. ANNUAL GOLDEN BOY AWARD DINNER. AWARD AT LONG BEACH PETROLEUM CLUB. (LOCAL). MAURIE BUGBEE, CHMN; BOYS CLUB OF LONG BEACH; 5280 E ARBOR RD; LONG BEACH, CA 90808. (#103752-1).

JAN 21, '76. DEDICATION OF AMERICAN GOLD STAR MANOR. THE ONLY NATIONAL HOME FOR AMERICAN GOLD STAR MOTHERS. (LOCAL). ED LEONARD, CHAIRMAN; BOARD OF TRUSTEES, AMERICAN GOLD STAR MANOR; 3021 GOLD STAR DR; LONG BEACH, CA 90810. (#104370-4).

JAN 22 - FEB 16, '76. SWEETEN YOUR SPIRIT IN '76 - CAMP FIRE GIRLS CANDY SALE. ANNUAL CANDY SALE: DOOR-TO-DOOR IN RESIDENTIAL AND BUSINESS AREAS, WITH BICENTENNIAL THEME. KICK-OFF: RALLY IN EL DORADO PARK WITH GAMES, REFRESHMENTS, ETC. (LOCAL). NANCY KENNEDY, EXEC DIR; LONG BEACH COUNCIL OF CAMP FIRE GIRLS; 7070 E CARSON; LONG BEACH, CA 90808. (#103309-1).

JAN 23 - 29, '76. BICENTENNIAL SEMINAR: NATIONAL COUNCIL ON YEAR-ROUND EDUCATION. SEMINAR WILL BEGIN ON SUNDAY, JANUARY 25 AT 1:30 PM AND END ON WEDNESDAY, JANUARY 29 AT 5:00 PM. AT QUEEN MARY, PIER J, LONG BEACH. (NAT'L). DR DON E GLINES, DIR; DEPARTMENT OF EDUCATION, STATE OF CALIFORNIA; 721 CAPITOL MALL; SACRAMENTO, CA 95814. (#103309-15).

JAN 24, '76. BICENTENNIAL SALUTE FASHION SHOW. FESTIVAL AT GOLDEN SAILS BANQUET ROOM. (LOCAL). MARLENE SCHAICH, CHMN; ZONTA CLUB; 5200 E 2ND ST; LONG BEACH, CA 90803. (#103752-2).

JAN 24, '76. SALUTE TO AMERICA YOUTH CONCERT. LIVE PERFORMANCE AT LONG BEACH CITY COLLEGE AUDITORIUM. (LOCAL). HELEN BOLDY, CHMN; LONG BEACH SYMPHONY/JUNIOR LEAGUE OF LONG BEACH; 720 PEPPER TREE LN; LONG BEACH, CA 90815. (#103309-16).

JAN 27, '76. BOY SCOUT ANNUAL POT LUCK DINNER AND AWARD CEREMONY. CEREMONY, FESTIVAL AT LONG BEACH ARENA. (LOCAL). DIRECTOR; LB AREA COUNCIL, BOY SCOUTS OF AMERICA; 401 E 37TH ST; LONG BEACH, CA 90807. (#200006-165).

JAN 31, '76. LONG BEACH SYMPHONY 41ST BICENTENNIAL SEASON CONCERT. LIVE PERFORMANCE AT LONG BEACH CITY COLLEGE AUDITORIUM. (LOCAL). JOHN HYER, DIRECTOR; LONG BEACH SYMPHONY; 121 LINDEN AVE; LONG BEACH, CA 90802. (#103309-17).

FEB 3, '76. INTER-FAITH BICENTENNIAL STUDY GROUP-'FREEDOM'. SEMINAR AT ST BARNABAS CHURCH. (LOCAL). CINDY CLEARY, CLERK; ST BARNABAS CHURCH; 3955 ORANGE AVE; LONG BEACH, CA 90807. (#104370-1).

FEB 3, '76. LONG BEACH PTI'S BICENTENNIAL TEA PARTY. FESTIVAL. (LOCAL). HARRIET WILLIAMS, CHMN; LONG BEACH COUNCIL OF PARENTS AND TEACHERS, INC; 259 GRANADA; LONG BEACH, CA 90803. (#103309-9).

FEB 4, '76. SPECIAL BICENTENNIAL PROGRAM. SPEAKER: DR ROBERT H SCHULLER, PASTOR OF GARDEN GROVE COMMUNITY CHURCH--'I AM THE AMERICAN FLAG.'. AT ALLEN CENTER-NAVAL SUPPORT FACILITY. (LOCAL). J B A JOHNSON, DIRECTOR; MILITARY ORDER OF WOLD WARS; 119 MIRA MAR AVE; LONG BEACH, CA 90803. (#104896-1).

FEB 6, '76. 16TH ANNUAL DINNER-DANCE. FESTIVAL AT QUEEN'S SALON--QUEEN MARY. (LOCAL). WARREN HEISSTAND, CHMN; CA SOCIETY OF MUNICIPAL FINANCE OFFICERS; 215 W BROADWAY #302; LONG BEACH, CA 90802. (#105007-2).

FEB 7, '76. THE LONG BEACH ART ASSN BICENTENNIAL TEA PARTY. FUNDS RAISED ENABLE THE GROUP TO AWARD FOUR $150 SCHOLARSHIPS TO GRADUATING HIGH SCHOOL SENIORS. AT FIRST UNITED METHODIST CHURCH, FIFTH ST & PACIFIC AVE. (LOCAL). LBAA GALLERY, COORD; LONG BEACH ART ASSOC; 800 E OCEAN BLVD; LONG BEACH, CA 90803. (#200006-163).

FEB 8, '76. 'FAITH-O-RAMA'. ECUMENICAL RELIGIOUS SERVICE WITH CHURCH LEADERS, GUEST SPEAKER, MUSIC GROUPS, CUB SCOUTS, BOY SCOUTS, EXPLORER SCOUTS & SEA SCOUTS. AT LONG BEACH ELK'S LODGE. (LOCAL). DENNIS GALLAGHER, COORD; ALAMITOS AREA BOY SCOUTS OF AMERICA; 2124 CLARK AVE; LONG BEACH, CA 90815. (#104659-1).

FEB 8, '76. 'UP WITH PEOPLE', BICENTENNIAL SHOW. LIVE PERFORMANCE AT LONG BEACH ARENA. (LOCAL). RAY DIPIAZZA, PROMOT DIR; INDEPENDENT PRESS - TELEGRAM; 604 PINE AVE; LONG BEACH, CA 90844. (#103309-12).

FEB 10, '76. HISTORICAL BICENTENNIAL PLAY. LIVE PERFORMANCE AT 1854 BRITTON DR. (LOCAL). PAM CINCOLA, CHMN; MINNIE GANT PTA; 1521 GREENBRIER RD; LONG BEACH, CA 90815. (#103309-10).

FEB 11, '76. OFFICIAL BICENTENNIAL HERITAGE CERTIFICATE PRESENTATION. PRESENTATION BY WECKFORD MORGAN, CHAIRPERSON OF ARBC-LB, TO 6TH GRADE CLASSES OF PATRICK HENRY SCHOOL. AT SCHOOL AUDITORIUM, 3720 CANEHILL. (LOCAL). LOUIS TRUMBO, COORDINATOR; PATRICK HENRY ELEMENTARY SCHOOL; 3720 CANEHILL; LONG BEACH, CA 90808. (#200006-159).

FEB 14, '76. BICENTENNIAL PANCAKE BREAKFAST. CONFERENCE AT SOCIAL HALL-VET'S PARK. (LOCAL). BETTY BENNETT, PROJ DIR; WRIGLEY BUSINESS & PROFESSIONAL ASSOC; 2612 MAGNOLIA; LONG BEACH, CA 90806. (#103494-1).

FEB 14, '76. PATRIOTIC PARTY--BICENTENNIAL THEME. PURPOSE IS TO DEVELOP PROFICIENCY IN THE PREPARATION & DELIVERY OF SHORT TALKS; TO AQUIRE SKILL IN EXTEMPORANEOUS SPEAKING AND TO CULTIVATE THE HABIT OF ANALYTICAL LISTENING. AT GREAT WESTERN SAVINGS AND LOAN. (LOCAL). ANN M HENDRICK, CHMN; FRIDAY MORNING DISCUSSION CLUB; 2028 'C' CHESTNUT AVE; LONG BEACH, CA 90806. (#103309-11).

FEB 18 - 19, '76. 'INDEPENDENCE & EXPECTATIONS' SYMPOSIUM - MERRILL JENSEN. ON FEB 18 & 19, DR JENSEN, PROFESSOR EMERITUS AT UNIV OF WISCONSIN, WILL SPEAK TO SEVERAL HISTORY CLASSES & AT NOON, FEB 18, WILL GIVE HIS PUBLIC ADDRESS. AT GRADUATE CENTER. (LOCAL). PROF IRVING F AHLQUIST; CALIFORNIA STATE UNIV BICENTENNIAL COORDINATOR; LONG BEACH, CA 90840. (#103752-7).

FEB 18 - APR 28, '76. AMERICAN REVOLUTION BICENTENNIAL SYMPOSIA SERIES. FIVE DISTINGUISHED HISTORIANS FROM UNIVERSITIES ACROSS THE USA WILL DISCUSS VARIOUS ASPECTS OF THE AMERICAN REVOLUTION. THE SYMPOSIA WILL BE OPEN TO THE PUBLIC. AT THE GRADUATE CENTER. (LOCAL). EUGENE L ASHER, CHMN; DEPT OF HISTORY, CALIFORNIA STATE UNIV; 6101 E 7TH ST; LONG BEACH, CA 90840. (#103752-3).

FEB 20 - 28, '76. AMERICAN THEATRE, 'THE MATCHMAKER'. LIVE PERFORMANCE AT UNIVERSITY THEATRE. (LOCAL). RALPH DUCKWALL, CHMN; THEATRE ARTS DEPARTMENT, CALIFORNIA STATE UNIV; 6101 E 7TH ST; LONG BEACH, CA 90840. (#103309-13).

FEB 22, '76. FIRST CHAIR NIGHT CONCERT/LONG BEACH SYMPHONY BICENTENNIAL SEASON. LIVE PERFORMANCE AT LONG BEACH CITY COLLEGE AUDITORIUM. (LOCAL). JOHN HYER, DIRECTOR; LONG BEACH SYMPHONY; 121 LINDEN AVE; LONG BEACH, CA 90802. (#103309-14).

FEB 24, '76. 'FREEDOM PROGRAM'. CHORAL PRESENTATION, BAND, ROTC DRILL TEAM. AT MILIKAN HIGH SCHOOL AUDITORIUM. (LOCAL). JOHN BORDEAUX, COORD; MILIKAN HIGH SCHOOL; 2800 SNOWDEN AVE; LONG BEACH, CA 90815. (#105007-3).

FEB 28, '76. GLOBAL ISSUES AND OPPORTUNITIES. KEYNOTE SESSION, WORKSHOPS, LUNCHEON WITH EUGENE MCCARTHY AS SPEAKER, WRAP UP PANEL AND DISCUSSIONS. AT STUDENT CENTER, 4901 E CARSON. (LOCAL). MRS MARGARET NEE, CHMN; COALITION OF NON-GOVERNMENTAL GROUPS IN LONG BEACH; 2121 E FIRST ST; LONG BEACH, CA 90803. (#105532-1).

FEB - MAR '76. INTERNATIONAL CHILDREN'S CHOIR BICENTENNIAL APPEARANCES. FEB 1-CHAPEL FO FOUR CHAPLAINS; FEB 6-CHILDREN'S HOME SOCIETY BANQUET; FEB 13-BEVERLY HILLS CHAMBER OF COMMERCE BICENTENNIAL BALL; FEB 16-SANTA ANA BOYS CLUB; FEB 17-CHURCH FO RELIGIOUS SCIENCE; MAR 6-ARBOR DAY PROGRAM; MAR 15-FILM FEATURING RAY CHARLES. (LOCAL). EASTER BEEKLEY, COORD; INTERNATIONAL CHILDREN'S CHOIR; PO BOX 5656; LONG BEACH, CA 90805. (#200006-161).

MAR 5 - 13, '76. AMERICAN PLAY - CALIFORNIA STATE UNIV. LIVE PERFORMANCE AT STUDIO THEATRE ON CAMPUS. (LOCAL). R DUCKWALL, CHMN; CAL STATE UNIV THEATRE ARTS DEPT; 6101 E 7TH ST; LONG BEACH, CA 90840. (#100492-1).

MAR 6, '76. LONG BEACH SYMPHONY 41ST BICENTENNIAL SEASON CONCERT. LIVE PERFORMANCE AT LONG BEACH CITY COLLEGE AUDITORIUM. (LOCAL). JOHN HYER, DIRECTOR; LONG BEACH SYMPHONY; 121 LINDEN AVE; LONG BEACH, CA 90802. (#103309-2).

MAR 6, '76. 'WHAT A COUNTRY' - SPEBSQSA PERFORMANCE. LIVE PERFORMANCE AT LAKEWOOD HIGH SCHOOL, 4400 BRIERCREST ST, LAKEWOOD. (LOCAL). CHUCK LOWREY, PROJ CHMN; LONG BEACH CHAPTER SPEBSQSA, INC; 4504 TOLBERT AVE; LONG BEACH, CA 90807. (#105177-1).

MAR 8, '76. 'THE TRUE CAUSES OF THE AMERICAN REVOLUTION' SYMPOSIUM. SYMPOSIUM TO BE GIVEN BY DR PAGE SMITH, PROFESSOR EMERITUS AT UNIV OF CALIFORNIA, SANTA CRUZ. AT GRADUATE CENTER. (LOCAL). PROF IRVING F AHLQUIST; CALIFORNIA STATE UNIV BICENTENNIAL COORDINATOR; LONG BEACH, CA 90840. (#103752-8).

MAR 9, '76. INTER-FAITH BICENTENNIAL STUDY GROUP-'JUSTICE'. SEMINAR AT ST LUKE'S EPISCOPAL CHURCH. (LOCAL). CINDY CLEARY, CLERK; ST LUKE'S CHURCH; 7TH & ATLANTIC; LONG BEACH, CA 90813. (#104370-2).

MAR 12, '76. BICENTENNIAL BALL. FESTIVAL AT ELKS CLUB, WILLOW ST. (LOCAL). JAN SIMONIAN, DIRECTOR; FINE ARTS AFILIATES, CALIFORNIA STATE UNIV; 885 HILLSIDE DR; LONG BEACH, CA 90815. (#103309-3).

MAR 13, '76. BICENTENNIAL BIKE HIKE AND REDEDICATION OF FREEDOM SHRINE. CEREMONY, FESTIVAL AT RANCHO LOS CERRITOS & CAMP FIRE SERVICE CENTER. (LOCAL). DIRECTOR; LONG BEACH COUNCIL OF CAMP FIRE GIRLS, INC; 7070 E CARSON ST; LONG BEACH, CA 90808. (#200006-162).

MAR 13, '76. BICENTENNIAL PARADE. PARADE. (LOCAL). ART NODA, DIRECTOR; WRIGLEY BUSINESS & PROFESSIONAL ASSOCIATION; 2037 PACIFIC AVE; LONG BEACH, CA 90803. (#103309-25).

MAR 13, '76. JR ROTC DRILL COMPETITION. COMPETITION AT U S ARMY RESERVE CENTER, 3800 E WILLOW. (LOCAL). JOHN J GILLESPIE, COORD; LONG BEACH LODGE NO 888, BPO ELKS; 4113 DEL MAR AVE; LONG BEACH, CA 90807. (#200006-156).

MAR 14, '76. BICENTENNIAL GOURMET BRUNCH. FESTIVAL AT BELMONT PLAZA. (LOCAL). DR CANNON, DIRECTOR; LONG BEACH SYMPHONY MEN'S COMMITTEE; LONG BEACH, CA 90815. (#103309-4).

MAR 14 - 21, '76. BICENTENNIAL SERIES CONGRESSIONAL CUP RACE. COMPETITION AT LONG BEACH YACHT CLUB, 6201 APPIAN WAY. (LOCAL). BILL STEUBER, CHMN; LONG BEACH YACHT CLUB; 12172 SILVER FOX RD; LOS ALAMITOS, CA 90720. (#103309-5).

MAR 15 - 22, '76. LONG BEACH INTERNATIONAL AMERICAN CUP & AQUATIC SHOW. COMPETITION AT BELMONT PLAZA POOL. (INT'L). BURT SHAW, CHAIRMAN; AAU; 555 E OCEAN BLVD #718; LONG BEACH, CA 90802. (#105532-2).

MAR 18 - 21, '76. STATE-WIDE HUMAN RELATIONS COMMISSION CONFERENCE. CONFERENCE AT QUEENSWAY HILTON HOTEL. (LOCAL). HARRY LADAS, DIR; LONG BEACH HUMAN RELATIONS COMMISSION; LONG BEACH, CA 90807. (#104496-2).

MAR 19, '76. JR ROTC AWARDS BANQUET AND MILITARY BALL. FESTIVAL, AWARD AT 4101 E WILLOW ST. (LOCAL). JOHN J GILLESPIE, COORD; LONG BEACH LODGE NO 888, BPO ELKS; 4113 DEL MAR AVE; LONG BEACH, CA 90807. (#200006-160).

MAR 19 - 27, '76. AMERICAN THEATRE SERIES-'THE CONTRAST'. LIVE PERFORMANCE AT STUDIO THEATRE. (LOCAL). RALPH DUCKWALL, CHMN; THEATRE ARTS DEPARTMENT, CALIFORNIA STATE UNIV; 6101 E 7TH ST; LONG BEACH, CA 90840. (#103309-6).

MAR 20, '76. MASSING OF THE COLORS. CEREMONY AT ARMY RESERVE CENTER, WILLOW AVE. (LOCAL). JOHN JOHNSON, DIRECTOR; MILITARY ORDER OF WORLD WARS; 119 MIRA MAR AVE; LONG BEACH, CA 90803. (#103309-7).

MAR 20 - 21, '76. NATIONAL DRAG BOAT CHAPIONSHIPS. COMPETITION AT MARINE STADIUM; LONG BEACH. (NAT'L). SKIP SKIBICKI; NATIONAL DRAG BOAT ASSOC; 555 E OCEAN BLVD #718; LONG BEACH, CA 90802. (#103999-2).

MAR 22, '76. 'THE INDIAN & THE BLACK IN THE AMERICAN REVOLUTION' SYMPOSIUM. SYMPOSIUM TO BE GIVEN BY DR GARY NASH, PROFESSOR OF HISTORY AT UCLA. AT GRADUATE CENTER. (LOCAL). PROF IRVING F AHLQUIST; CALIFORNIA STATE UNIV BICENTENNIAL COORINATOR; LONG BEACH, CA 90840. (#103752-9).

MAR 26 - 28, '76. UNITED STATES GRAND PRIX WEST. FORMULA ONE RACING--PRIOR TO RACE, BICENTENNIAL PARADE OF BANDS TO ACCOMPANY EACH RACE CAR WITH FEATURED DRIVER. AT PACIFIC TERRACE CENTER. (INT'L). CHRIS POOK, CHMN; GRAND PRIX ASSOC; 600 E OCEAN BLVD; LONG BEACH, CA 90802. (#103309-8).

MAR 26 - APR 3, '76. AMERICAN MUSICAL PRODUCTION. LIVE PERFORMANCE AT STUDIO THEATRE ON THE CAMPUS.. (LOCAL). R DUCKWALL, CHMN; LONG BEACH ARBC; 6101 E 7TH ST; LONG BEACH, CA 90840. (#100494-1).

MAR 30 - 31, '76. 'THE HEALTH OF THE PRESIDENTS OF THE UNITED STATES'. TALK WILL BE GIVEN BY DR HOWARD WILCOX, MD, ASSOCIATE CHIEF OF STAFF FOR EDUCATION, VETERANS ADMINISTRATION HOSPITAL, SALT LAKE CITY. (LOCAL). PROF IRVING F AHLQUIST; CALIFORNIA STATE UNIV BICENTENNIAL COORDINATOR; LONG BEACH, CA 90840. (#103752-12).

APR 1 - 4, '76. 1976 NATIONAL AAU SENIOR INDOOR SWIMMING CHAMPIONSHIPS. PRELIMS-11:00 AM; FINALS-7:00 PM. AT BELMONT PLAZA OLYMPIC POOL, LONG BEACH. (NAT'L). TOM WITHERSPOON, COORD; AAU; 555 E OCEAN BLVD #718; LONG BEACH, CA 90802. (#106202-1).

APR 2 - 4, '76. BICENTENNIAL ARTS, CRAFTS & HOBBY SHOW. SUNDAY HOURS: 12-6 PM. AT LONG BEACH ARENA. (LOCAL). VI BACHTELLE, CHAIRMAN; LONG BEACH RECREATION DEPARTMENT; 155 QUEEN'S WAY; LONG BEACH, CA 90802. (#103382-20).

APR 5, '76. 'THE DILEMMA OF POWER: BRITTISH STRATEGY AT SEA' SYMPOSIUM. SYMPOSIUM TO BE GIVEN BY DR IRA GRUBER, PROFESSOR OF HISTORY AT RICE UNIV. AT GRADUATE CENTER. (LOCAL). PROF IRVING F AHLQUIST; CALIFORNIA STATE UNIV BICENTENNIAL COORDINATOR; LONG BEACH, CA 90840. (#103752-10).

APR 7 - 9, '76. AMERICAN THEATER FESTIVAL. LIVE PERFORMANCE AT STUDIO THEATRE ON CAMPUS.. (LOCAL). R DUCKWALL, CHMN; CAL STATE UNIV THEATRE ARTS DEPT; 6101 E 7TH ST; LONG BEACH, CA 90840. (#100496-1).

APR 10, '76. MASONIC BICENTENNIAL CELEBRATION. SHOW CONSISTING OF PATRIOTIC PLAY BY SCOTTISH RITE PLAYERS & THE 'GRAND LAND SINGERS'. CHAIRMAN WILL BE CHAIRMAN OF THE LONG BEACH ARBC, WECK MORGAN. AT LONG BEACH ARENA. (LOCAL). RICHARD HARDAGE, COORD; LONG BEACH MASONIC LODGES; 19221 S PIRES AVE; CERRITOS, CA 90701. (#100497-1).

APR 13 - 18, '76. NATIONAL INDOOR SWIMMING CHAMPIONSHIP FOR MEN & WOMEN. COMPETITION AT BELMONT PLAZA OLYMPIC POOL. (NAT'L). SKIP SKIBICKI, PROJ DIR; CITY OF LONG BEACH; 555 E OCEAN BLVD #718; LONG BEACH, CA 90802. (#103382-21).

APR 17, '76. LONG BEACH SYMPHONY BICENTENNIAL CONCERT. LIVE PERFORMANCE AT LONG BEACH CITY COLLEGE AUDITORIUM. (LOCAL). JOHN HYER, CHAIRMAN; LONG BEACH SYMPHONY; 121 LINDEN AVENUE; LONG BEACH, CA 90802. (#103382-22).

LONG BEACH — CONTINUED

APR 21 - 22, '76. CALIFORNIA COUNCIL OF WOMEN'S ARCHITECTURAL LEAGUE CONVENTION. CONFERENCE AT QUEEN'S WAY HILTON. (ST-WIDE). GLENOUS ABSMEIER, CHMN; CALIFORNIA COUNCIL OF WOMEN'S ARCHITECTURAL LEAGUE; 2357 ROCKING HORSE; PALOS VERDE, CA 90274. (#103382-23).

APR 23 - 24, '76. UNITED STATES ARMED FORCES BICENTENNIAL CARAVAN. CARAVAN IS COMPOSED OF EXHIBIT VANS FOR EACH MILITARY SERVICE. PROJECT THEME IS ' HISTORY OF THE ARMED FORCES & THEIR CONTRIBUTIONS TO THE NATION'. SATURDAY HOURS ARE 11 AM - 10 PM. AT ON PINE AVE; 2 UNITS NORTH OF 4TH ST & 2 UNITS SOUTH OF 4TH ST. (LOCAL). VITO ROMANS, CHAIRMAN; U S ARMED FORCES BICENTENNIAL CARAVAN; 320 PINE AVE; LONG BEACH, CA 90802. (#1775-557).

APR 23 - 25, '76. CALIFORNIA WOMEN'S CHORUS BICENTENNIAL CONVENTION. CONFERENCE AT LONG BEACH CITY COLLEGE. (LOCAL). PEG CALLAHAN, CHAIRMAN; CALIFORNIA WOMEN'S CHORUS; 5602 WHITEWOOD; LAKEWOOD, CA 90712. (#103382-25).

APR 23 - 25, '76. PILOT CLUB DISTRICT CONVENTION. CONFERENCE AT QUEEN'S WAY HILTON. (LOCAL). DORIS E HALDEN, CHAIRMAN; PILOT CLUB OF LONG BEACH; 3676 LOMINA AVE; LONG BEACH, CA 90808. (#103382-24).

APR 24, '76. 'OLD FASHIONED PICNIC'. FEATURED EVENTS ARE GAMES, CONCERT BAND, PROGRAM OF PATRIOTIC SINGING, DEMONSTRATIONS OF SQUARE DANCING AND MINUET, CEREMONY HONORING FOUR HIDDEN HEROINES AND BALLOONS. AT ELDORADO PARK #2. (LOCAL). MILDRED FRERKS, COORD; GREATER LONG BEACH GIRL SCOUT COUNCIL; 393 LOS ALTOS AVE; LONG BEACH, CA 90814. (#105638-1).

APR 24, '76. 1976 NATIONAL BEAUTIFICATION DAY. FESTIVAL. (LOCAL). DOROTHY BUERGER, DIRECTOR; BICENTENNIAL BEAUTIFICATION COMMITTEE; 139 LINDERO AVE; LONG BEACH, CA 90803. (#103322-1).

APR 26, '76. GOLD STAR MANOR BICENTENNIAL TEA. ALL DONATIONS TO GO TO HERITAGE CLOCK TOWER PROJECT FUND. AT GOLD STAR MANOR. (LOCAL). ANNA MAERKI, COORDINATOR; GOLD STAR MANOR; 3001 GOLDSTAR DR; LONG BEACH, CA 90810. (#200006-166).

APR 28 - 29, '76. 'HOW OTHERS SEE US: 200 YEARS AFTER' SYMPOSIUM. SYMPOSIUM WILL BE LED BY DR ROBIN WINKS, PROFESSOR OF HISTORY AT YALE UNIVERSITY, FORMER US CULTURAL ATTACHE IN LONDON, AND COORDINATOR OF US STATE DEPARTMENT BICENTENNIAL PROGRAMS. AT 6101 E 7TH ST LONG BEACH. (LOCAL). DR IRV AHLQUIST; DEPARTMENT OF HISTORY--CSULB; 6101 E 7TH ST; LONG BEACH, CA 90840. (#104271-2).

APR 30 - MAY 8, '76. 'SHOWBOAT' AMERICAN MUSIC PRODUCTION SERIES. LIVE PERFORMANCE AT UNIVERSITY THEATRE, CSULB. (LOCAL). R DUCKWALL, PROJ DIRECTOR; THEATRE ARTS DEPT, CSULB; 6101 E 7TH ST; LONG BEACH, CA 90840. (#103382-26).

MAY 1, '76. CREATIVE RANCHO DAY. OPENING AT 6400 BIXBY HILL RD. (LOCAL). MS LONIE BOSSERMAN, CHMN; RANCHO LOS ALAMITOS ACCOCIATES; 12121 CHRISTY; LOS ALAMITOS, CA 90720. (#103382-11).

MAY 1, '76. LONG BEACH SPECIAL OLYMPICS. BASKETBALL, GYMNASTICS, FLOOR HOCKEY, SWIMMING, TRACK & FIELD; THOSE WHO QUALIFY AT THIS LOCAL LEVEL WILL REPRESENT THE CITY IN THE STATE MEET AT UCLA. AT MILLIKAN HIGH SCHOOL. (LOCAL). JEANNIE MILLER, DIRECTOR; LONG BEACH SPECIAL GAMES, INC; 5565 RIVIERA WALK; LONG BEACH, CA 90803. (#106721-1).

MAY 1 - 8, '76. LONG BEACH HERITAGE WEEK. RECREATION OF LIFE IN RANCHO DAYS OF LONG BEACH. AT RANCHO LOS ALAMITOS & RANCHO LOS CERRITOS. (LOCAL). LENA JO SALCITO, PROJ DIR; JUNIOR LEAGUE OF LONG BEACH; 5511 EL CEDRAL ST; LONG BEACH, CA 90815. (#103401-1).

MAY 2, '76. 'CINCO DE MAYO CELEBRATION'. FESTIVAL AT ADMIRAL KIDD PARK, 2125 SANTA FE. (LOCAL). VI BACHTELLE, COORDINATOR; LONG BEACH RECREATION DEPARTMENT; 155 QUEENS WAY LANDING; LONG BEACH, CA 90802. (#200006-36).

MAY 3 - 7, '76. ST MARY MEDICAL CENTER VOLUNTEER AUXILIARY OPEN HOUSE. TOUR AT BAUER HOSPITAL LOBBY. (LOCAL). FRANCI PICKENS, COORD; ST MARY MEDICAL CENTER VOLUNTEER AUXILIARY; 2130 LEES AVE; LONG BEACH, CA 90815. (#200006-37).

MAY 4, '76. BICENTENNIAL CONCERT. LIVE PERFORMANCE AT BETHANY LUTHERAN CHURCH, 4644 CLARK AVE. (LOCAL). SAMUEL P SCHURR, CHMN; AMERICAN GUILD OF ORGANISTS; 4124 MARWICK AVE; LAKEWOOD, CA 90713. (#103382-12).

MAY 4, '76. 'BIRTH OF A NATION', SILENT FILM BY D W GRIFFITH. AMERICAN THEATRE ORGANIST, GAYLORD CARTER, WILL PLAY HIS ORIGINAL SCORE TO ACCOMPANY THE FILM. AT UNIVERSITY THEATRE: CSULB. (LOCAL). SAMUEL SCHURR, COORD; AMERICAN GUILD OF ORGANISTS; 4124 MARWICK; LAKEWOOD, CA 90713. (#105292-1).

MAY 4, '76. INTER-FAITH BICENTENNIAL STUDY GROUP-'UNITY'. SEMINAR AT TEMPLE ISRAEL. (LOCAL). RABBI SIDNEY GUTHMAN; TEMPLE ISRAEL; 3538 E 3RD ST; LONG BEACH, CA 90814. (#104370-3).

MAY 7, '76. TREASURES AND TRIFLES FAIR. FOOD, ARTS & CRAFTS, HANDMADE ITEMS AND MUCH MORE. AT RECREATION COMMUNITY CENTER, 4900 E 7TH ST. (LOCAL). DOROTHY HOLLAND, CHAIRMAN; THE DAMAS CLUB OF LONG BEACH; 6430 EL JARDIN ST; LONG BEACH, CA 90803. (#105059-1).

MAY 8, '76. 'BICENTENNIAL AFFAIR'. FAIR AT HOUGHTON PARK, 6301 MYRTLE AVENUE. (LOCAL). VI BACHTELLE, COORD; LONG BEACH RECREATION DEPARTMENT; 155 QUEENS WAY LANDING; LONG BEACH, CA 90802. (#200006-38).

MAY 8, '76. 'WE'RE RINGING IN THE SOUNDS OF FREEDOM'. LIVE PERFORMANCE AT SAINT ANTHONY HS GYM, 537 ALAMITOS. (LOCAL). COORDINATOR; SAINT ANTHONY HIGH SCHOOL; 650 OLIVE AVE; LONG BEACH, CA 90812. (#200006-109).

MAY 10, '76. BICENTENNIAL ARMED FORCES DAY. CEREMONY AT DOME ROOM, ELKS LODGE, 4101 WILLOW. (LOCAL). CLIFFORD BEYERS, PROJ DIR; LONG BEACH ELKS LODGE #888; 5621 VERNON; LONG BEACH, CA 90815. (#103382-13).

MAY 12, '76. BICENTENNIAL CHORAL CONCERT. LIVE PERFORMANCE AT EBELL CLUB HOUSE AUDITORIUM, 290 CERRITOS AVE. (LOCAL). GRACE BENEDIKTSON, CHMN; WOMEN'S MUSIC CLUB OF LONG BEACH; 7 38TH PLACE; LONG BEACH, CA 90803. (#103382-14).

MAY 12 - 15, '76. CSULB NEW DIRECTIONS ENSEMBLE-PLAYBILL #2. 'THE GOOD DOCTOR' AND 'A KIND OF MAGIC'. AT STUDIO THEATRE, CSULB. (LOCAL). RALPH DUCKWALL, COORD; THEATRE ARTS DEPT, CSULB; 6101 E 7TH ST; LONG BEACH, CA 90840. (#106202-2).

MAY 14, '76. LIBERTY BELL MONUMENT DEDICATION. CEREMONY AT 4101 WILLOW. (LOCAL). CLIFFORD BEYERS, CHAIRMAN; ELKS LODGE #888; 5621 VERNON AVE; LONG BEACH, CA 90815. (#103382-15).

MAY 15, '76. DIE FELDERMAUS. LIVE PERFORMANCE AT LONG BEACH CITY COLLEGE AUDITORIUM. (LOCAL). JOHN HYER, PROJ DIRECTOR; LONG BEACH SYMPHONY; 121 LINDEN AVE; LONG BEACH, CA 90802. (#103382-16).

MAY 16, '76. INTERNATIONAL FESTIVAL. FESTIVAL AT RECREATION PARK. (LOCAL). VIVIAN LINDGREN, CHAIRMAN; WOMEN'S DIVISION-LONG BEACH CHAMBER OF COMMERCE; 857 STEVELY AVE; LONG BEACH, CA 90815. (#103382-17).

MAY 16 - 18, '76. ANCIENT EGYPTIAN ORDER OF SCIOTS-BICENTENNIAL MEETING. CEREMONY AT ROCHELLS. (LOCAL). PATRICIA SIEGRIST, CHMN; LONG BEACH ARBC; 555 E OCEAN BLVD, SUITE 718; LONG BEACH, CA 90802. (#100502-1).

MAY 17, '76. ARMED FORCES NIGHT. SPEAKER: M G FRANK M SCHOBER, COMMANDING GENERAL, CALIFORNIA NATIONAL GUARD. AT 4101 E WILLOW ST. (LOCAL). CLIFF BEYERS, DIRECTOR; LONG BEACH ELKS LODGE #888; 4101 E WILLOW ST; LONG BEACH, CA 90815. (#107034-1).

MAY 17 - JUNE 10, '76. BICENTENNIAL INSTALLATION OF OFFICERS FOR VOLUNTEER GROUPS. CEREMONY AT MEMORIAL HOSPITAL MEDICAL CENTER. (LOCAL). ELLEN BAKER, PROJ DIR; MEMORIAL HOSPITAL MEDICAL CENTER VOLUNTEERS; 2801 ATLANTIC AVE; LONG BEACH, CA 90801. (#103382-10).

MAY 19, '76. SENIOR CITIZENS' DAY AT BIXBY PARK. FESTIVAL AT BIXBY PARK. (LOCAL). GEORGE TOLL, DIR; SENIOR CITIZENS COMMITTEE OF LB-ARBC; 3632 ROSE; LONG BEACH, CA 90807. (#104496-1).

MAY 21 - 23, '76. BICENTENNIAL HARBOR CRUISE. MAY 21, CIVIC & INDUSTRIAL DIGNATARIES FROM 100 SOUTHERN CALIFORNIA CITIES WILL TOUR THE L B HARBOR AND LUNCH ABOARD THE LONG BEACH KING MAY 22-23; FREE HARBOR CRUISES FOR THE GENERAL PUBLIC. AT PORT OF LONG BEACH, LONG BEACH HARBOR. (LOCAL). ROBERT METZGAR, CHAIRMAN; LONG BEACH HARBOR DEPARTMENT & LONG BEACH CHAMBER OF COMMERCE; PO BOX 570; LONG BEACH, CA 90801. (#106654-1).

MAY 22, '76. COORDINATE BODIES OF MASONIC ORDER BICENTENNIAL PARADE. PARADE AT LONG BEACH DOWNTOWN STREETS. (LOCAL). GEREN SPROULL, CHAIRMAN; COORDINATE BODIES-MASONIC ORDER; 23 ZANE AVE; LONG BEACH, CA 90805. (#103382-18).

MAY 22, '76. FRONTIER FREEDOM FAIRE. FAIR AT WARDLOW PARK, 3457 STANBRIDGE. (LOCAL). VI BACHTELLE, COORD; LONG BEACH RECREATION DEPT; 155 QUEENS WAY LANDING; LONG BEACH, CA 90802. (#108077-1).

MAY 22, '76. LAWYERS IN COURTS OVER 200 YEARS. FESTIVAL AT GOLDEN SAILS. (LOCAL). JAN KIGHT, PROJ CHAIRMAN; LAWYERS WIVES; 237 BAYSHORE AVE; LONG BEACH, CA 90803. (#103407-1).

MAY 22, '76. MASONIC BODIES BICENTENNIAL PRESENTATION. LIVE PERFORMANCE AT LONG BEACH ARENA. (LOCAL). GEREN SPROULL, CHAIRMAN; COORDINATE BODIES-MASONIC ORDER-DIVISION 6; 23 ZANE AVE; LONG BEACH, CA 90805. (#103382-19).

MAY 22, '76. 'OUR AMERICAN HERITAGE' - FAIR. FAIR AT DRAKE PARK, 951 MAINE. (LOCAL). VI BACHTELLE, COORD; LONG BEACH RECREATION DEPT; 155 QUEENS WAY LANDING; LONG BEACH, CA 90802. (#108077-2).

MAY 28, '76. PATRICK HENRY DAY. COLONIAL CRAFTS, ACTIVITIES, DANCING, FAIRE AND COSTUMES. AT 3720 CANEHILL AVE. (LOCAL). LOUIS TRUMBO, DIRECTOR; PATRICK HENRY ELEMENTARY SCHOOL; 3720 CANEHILL AVE; LONG BEACH, CA 90808. (#105059-2).

MAY '76. LONG BEACH BEAUTIFUL AWARDS DINNER. CEREMONY, AWARD. (LOCAL). DOROTHY BUERGER, CHMN; LONG BEACH BEAUTIFUL; 139 LINDERO AVE; LONG BEACH, CA 90803. (#103309-26).

JUNE 8 - JULY 16, '76. HERITAGE OF THE AMERICAN REVOLUTION PROGRAM. SEMINAR AT CALIFORNIA STATE UNIV, LONG BEACH. (LOCAL). DR IRVING AHLQUIST; DPET OF HISTORY - CSULB; 6101 E 7TH ST; LONG BEACH, CA 90840. (#107845-1).

JUNE 12, '76. 'HAPPY BIRTHDAY AMERICA'. LIVE PERFORMANCE AT LONG BEACH ELKS DOME AMPHITHEATRE. (LOCAL). BARBARA BOYLAN; BARBARA BOYLAN DANCERS; 3678 OCANA AVENUE; LONG BEACH, CA 90808. (#103309-27).

JUNE 12, '76. SALUTE TO OLD GLORY. LIVE PERFORMANCE AT MILLIKAN HIGH SCHOOL FIELD. (LOCAL). CLIFFORD BEYERS, CHAIRMAN; ELKS & ROTC OF LONG BEACH; 5621 VERNON; LONG BEACH, CA 90815. (#103382-29).

JUNE 12 - 13, '76. NATIONAL DRAG BOAT CHAMPIONSHIPS. COMPETITION AT MARINE STADIUM: LONG BEACH. (NAT'L). SKIP SKIBICKI; NATIONAL DRAG BOAT ASSOC; 555 E OCEAN BLVD #718; LONG BEACH, CA 90802. (#103999-4).

JUNE 15 - JULY 3, '76. AMERICAN THEATRE. LIVE PERFORMANCE AT STUDIO THEATRE ON CAMPUS.. (LOCAL). R DUCKWALL, CHMN; CAL STATE UNIV-LB THEATRE ARTS DEPT; 6101 7TH ST; LONG BEACH, CA 90840. (#100504-1).

JUNE 16 - 20, '76. OLYMPIC SWIMMING TRIALS FOR MEN & WOMEN. COMPETITION AT BELMONT PLAZA OLYMPIC POOL. (LOCAL). SKIP SKIBICKI, PROJ DIR; CITY OF LONG BEACH; 555 E OCEAN BLVD; LONG BEACH, CA 90802. (#103382-30).

JUNE 21 - JULY 9, '76. CRAFTS OF EARLY AMERICA. SEMINAR AT CALIFORNIA STATE UNIV, LONG BEACH. (LOCAL). DR IRVING AHLQUIST; DEPT OF INDUSTRIAL EDUCATION -CSULB; 6101 E 7TH ST; LONG BEACH, CA 90840. (#107845-2).

JUNE 21 - JULY 28, '76. EDUCATION OF UNCLE SAM. SEMINAR AT CALIF STATE UNIV LONG BEACH. (LOCAL). DR IRVING AHLQUIST; DEPT OF EDUCATIONAL PSYCHOLOGY & SOCIAL FOUND. CSULB; 6101 E SEVENTH ST; LONG BEACH, CA 90840. (#107845-7).

JUNE 22 - JULY 15, '76. THE LOS ANGLES INTER-CULTURAL SCENE. SEMINAR AT CALIF STATE UNIV LONG BEACH. (LOCAL). DR IRVING AHLQUIST; DEPT OF COMPARATIVE LITERATURE - CSULB; 6101 E SEVENTH ST; LONG BEACH, CA 90840. (#107845-6).

JUNE 22 - JULY 29, '76. MUSIC FOR THE BICENTENNIAL. SEMINAR AT CALIF STATE UNIV LONG BEACH. (LOCAL). DR IRVING AHLQUIST; DEPT OF MUSIC - CSULB; 6101 E SEVENTH ST; LONG BEACH, CA 90840. (#107845-3).

JUNE 24 - 29, '76. BICENTENNIAL CONVENTION - MUSIC TEACHERS ASSOC OF AMERICA. CONFERENCE AT QUEEN MARY. (ST-WIDE). FLORENCE ZOOK, PROJ DIR; MUSIC TEACHERS' ASSOCIATION OF CALIFORNIA; 6100 BIRKDALE; LONG BEACH, CA 90815. (#103382-31).

JUNE 28 - JULY 16, '76. AMERICA FROM A EUROPEAN PERSPECTIVE IN THE ARTS. SEMINAR AT CALIFORNIA STATE UNIV LONG BEACH. (LOCAL). DR IRVING AHLQUIST; DEPTMENT OF COMPARATIVE LITERATURE-CSULB; 6101 E SEVENTH ST; LONG BEACH, CA 90840. (#107845-4).

JULY 2, '76. BICENTENNIAL FORUM. SEMINAR AT STARR KING PRESBYTERIAN CHURCH, 132 E ARTESIA BLVD. (LOCAL). MRS JOHN HOEPFL, CHMN; CHURCH WOMEN UNITED, LONG BEACH UNIT; 2040 CEDAR AVE; LONG BEACH, CA 90806. (#107554-1).

JULY 3 - 6, '76. GREAT BICENTENNIAL CONGRESS OF THE ARTS FAIR. EXHIBIT, FAIR AT RECREATION PARK, 7TH & PARK STS. (LOCAL). DORIS STOVALL, PROJ DIR; LONG BEACH REGIONAL ARTS COUNCIL, INC; 130 PINE AVENUE #208; LONG BEACH, CA 90802. (#103382-5).

JULY 4, '76. FLAG PRESENTATION TO CITY OF LONG BEACH. CEREMONY AT NEW CIVIC CENTER. (LOCAL). BILLIE REISCHE, PROJ DIR; SUSAN B ANTHONY CHAPTER DAR; 3311 RUTH EALINE DR; LOS ALAMITOS, CA 90740. (#103382-8).

JULY 4, '76. FOURTH OF JULY SHOW & FIREWORKS. FESTIVAL AT VETERAN'S STADIUM. (LOCAL). BOB THOMPSON, PROJ DIR; LONG BEACH FIREFIGHTERS & LONG BEACH ELKS LODGE #888; 100 MAGNOLIA AVE; LONG BEACH, CA 90802. (#103382-7).

JULY 4, '76. TIME CAPSULE FOR LONG BEACH CIVIC CENTER - CEREMONY. CEREMONY AT DEDICATION OF CIVIC CENTER. (LOCAL). ROBERT METZGAR, PROJ DIR; LONG BEACH HISTORICAL SOCIETY; PO BOX 570; LONG BEACH, CA 90801. (#103382-6).

JULY 6 - 8, '76. NATIONAL DRAG BOAT CHAMPIONSHIPS. POSSIBILITY OF BRINGING FORTH 8 BICENTENNIAL SYMBOL FLAGS IN BOATS WITH AMERICAN FLAG IN CENTER, FOR PRE-RACE INTRODUCTION. AT MARINE STADIUM. (REGN'L). SKIP SKIBICKI, DIR; NATIONAL DRAG BOAT ASSOC/SEA FESTIVAL; 555 E OCEAN BLVD, #718; LONG BEACH, CA 90802. (#100510-1).

JULY 7 - 31, '76. AMERICAN THEATRE. LIVE PERFORMANCE AT CALIFORNIA STAE UNIV THEATRE AT LONG BEACH. (LOCAL). R DUCKWALL, CHMN; CAL STATE UNIV-LB THEATRE ARTS DEPT; 6101 E 7TH ST; LONG BEACH, CA 90840. (#100507-1).

JULY 11, '76. WEST SIDE MULTI-CULTURAL FESTIVAL. LIVE PERFORMANCE AT LONG BEACH SPORTS ARENA. (LOCAL). CHARLES ARA; WESTSIDE NEIGHBORHOOD CENTER; 1372 WEST WILLOW ST; LNG BEACH, CA 90810. (#107809-1).

JULY 20 - AUG 27, '76. THE AMERICAN IMAGINATION & THE REVOLUTION. SEMINAR AT CALIF STATE UNIV LONG BEACH. (LOCAL). DR IRVING AHLQUIST; DEPT OF HISTORY - CSULB; 6101 E SEVENTH ST; LONG BEACH, CA 90840. (#107845-5).

JULY 31 - AUG 1, '76. RELIGIOUS ARTS FESTIVAL. ALL FAITHS TO BE REPRESENTED. AT RECREATION PARK. (LOCAL). MIKE MC CLELAN; ARBC RELIGIOUS COORDINATION COMMITTEE; 607 E 3RD ST; LONG BEACH, CA 90812. (#100508-1).

AUG 6 - 8, '76. NATIONAL DRAG BOAT CHAMPIONSHIPS. COMPETITION AT MARINE STADIUM--LONG BEACH. (NAT'L). SKIP SKIBICKI, PROJ DIR; NATIONAL DRAG BOAT ASSOCIATION; 555 E OCEAN BLVD #718; LONG BEACH, CA 90802. (#103382-1).

LONG BEACH — CONTINUED

AUG 7 - 22, '76. BICENTENNIAL INTERNATIONAL SEA FESTIVAL. MODEL SAILBOAT SHOW, SABOT REGATTA, SWIMMING MEETS, HOBIE CAT REGATTA, SCHOONER REGATTA(ANCIENT MARINER), & DRAG BOAT RACES. (LOCAL). SKIP SKIBICKI, DIR; CITY OF LONG BEACH/LONG BEACH CONVENTION & NEWS BUREAU; 555 E OCEAN BLVD, #718; LONG BEACH, CA 90802. (#100509-1).

AUG 9, '76. LAW AND ORDER NIGHT. SPEAKER: RALPH G KORTZ, CHIEF OF POLICE, CITY OF LONG BEACH. AT 4101 E WILLOW ST. (LOCAL). CLIFF BEYERS, DIRECTOR; LONG BEACH ELKS LODGE #888; 4101 E WILLOW ST; LONG BEACH, CA 90815. (#107034-2).

AUG 19, '76. BICENTENNIAL PICNIC. FESTIVAL AT HOUGHTON PARK, NORTH LONG BEACH. (LOCAL). HENRIETTA THOMAS, COORD; NORTH LONG BEACH REAL ESTATE CLUB; 1315 SOUTH ST; LONG BEACH, CA 90805. (#105292-2).

AUG 21 - SEPT 19, '76. 'A BICENTENNIAL SUITE', INTAGLIO & RELIEF PRINTS. 12 COLOR INTAGLIO & RELIEF PRINTS TO CELEBRATE THE BICENTENNIAL. PRINTS DEPICT FAMOUS EVENTS & AMERICANS. PRESENTED IN PORTFOLIO OR FRAMED FOR EXHIBITION. AT CALIFORNIA STATE COLLEGE AT LONG BEACH LIBRARY GALLERY. (LOCAL). HARRIET ZEITLIN, ARTIST; HARRIET ZEITLIN, ARTIST-PRINTMAKER; 202 S SALTAIR AVE; LOS ANGELES, CA 90049. (#23677-3).

AUG 22, '76. SAN FRANCISCO WHEELMEN ROAD RACE - 76 MILES. COMPETITION, EXHIBIT AT JUNIPERO AVENUE BEACH - LONG BEACH, CA. (LOCAL). DORIS STOVALL, EXEC DIR; LONG BEACH REG ARTS COUNCIL - CALIFORNIA INTN'L SEA FESTIVAL; 130 PINE AVE #208; LONG BEACH, CA 90802. (#103382-3).

AUG 27 - SEPT 6, '76. WORLD TOURNAMENT SOFT BALL CHAMPIONSHIP. WILL ASSEMBLE APPROXIMATELY 24 OF THE TOP SOFTBALL TEAMS IN USA WHO WILL PARTICIPATE IN A DOUBLE-LOSS ELIMINATION TOURNAMENT. WINNER TO BE CROWNED NATIONAL CHAMPION. (NAT'L). CHIEF VIRGIL JONES; LONG BEACH FIRE FIGHTERS; 100 MAGNOLIA AVE; LONG BEACH, CA 90802. (#100512-1).

SEPT 13, '76. SALUTE TO CALIFORNIA. SPEAKER: GEORGE SALZER, CURATOR OF RANCHO LOS ALAMITOS MUEUM. AT 4101 E WILLOW ST. (LOCAL). CLIFF BEYERS, DIRECTOR; LONG BEACH ELKS LODGE #888; 4101 E WILLOW ST; LONG BEACH, CA 90815. (#107034-3).

OCT 2 - 3, '76. NATIONAL DRAG BOAT CHAMPIONSHIPS. COMPETITION AT MARINE STADIUM: LONG BEACH. (NAT'L). SKIP SKIBICKI; NATIONAL DRAG BOAT ASSOC; 555 E OCEAN BLVD #718; LONG BEACH, CA 90802. (#103999-3).

OCT 8 - 16, '76. AMERICAN THEATRE PRODUCTION - CAL STATE UNIV, LONG BEACH. LIVE PERFORMANCE AT CALIFORNIA STATE UNIV THEATRE AT LONG BEACH. (LOCAL). PROF RALPH W DUCKWALL; THEATRE ARTS DEPT, CSULB; 6101 E 7TH ST; LONG BEACH, CA 90840. (#100514-1).

OCT 18, '76. DEDICATION OF FLAG ISLAND. CEREMONY AT 4101 E WILLOW ST. (LOCAL). GEN CLIFF BEYERS, COORD; LONG BEACH ELKS LODGE #888; 4101 E WILLOW ST; LONG BEACH, CA 90815. (#109350-1).

NOV 11 - 23, '76. AMERICAN OPERA PRODUCTION. LIVE PERFORMANCE AT UNIVERSITY THEATRE. (LOCAL). RALPH W DUCKWALL; OPERA DEPARTMENT, CALIFORNIA STATE UNIVERSITY LONG BEACH; 6101 E 7TH ST; LONG BEACH, CA 90840. (#103382-28).

NOV 20 - 21, '76. THANKSGIVING PRAYERS-RELIGIOUS HERITAGE FOR THIS NATION. CEREMONY AT LONG BEACH HOUSES OF WORSHIP. (LOCAL). DR DAVID BURCHAM, CHMN; RELIGIOUS COORDINATION COMMITTEE & LONG BEACH AMER REVOL BICENT CO; 607 E 3RD ST; LONG BEACH, CA 90812. (#103382-27).

NOV 22, '76. ISABEL PATTERSON, BICENTENNIAL TOWER DEDICATION. CEREMONY AT BICENTENNIAL TOWER, LONG BEACH CIVIC CENTER COMPLEX. (LOCAL). PATRICIA K SIEGRIST, CHMN; ARBC - LONG BEACH, INC; 555 E OCEAN BLVD, #718; LONG BEACH, CA 90802. (#109452-1).

DEC 3 - 11, '76. AMERICAN THEATRE PRODUCTION - CAL STATE UNIV, LONG BEACH. LIVE PERFORMANCE AT CALIFORNIA STATE UNIV THEATRE AT LONG BEACH. (LOCAL). PROF R DUCKWALL; THEATRE ARTS DEPT, CSULB; 6101 E 7TH ST; LONG BEACH, CA 90840. (#100516-1).

DEC 27, '76. FLAG RETIREMENT PROGRAM. CEREMONY AT 4101 E WILLOW ST. (LOCAL). CLIFF BEYERS, COORD; LONG BEACH ELK'S LODGE #888; 4101 E WILLOW ST; LONG BEACH, CA 90815. (#106489-1).

LOOMIS

HORSE AND BIKE TRAILS - LOOMIS, CA. TRAILS WILL JOIN NATIONAL AND STATE TRAILS TO FACILITATE TRAVEL OUTSIDE THE AREA. (LOCAL). CHARLES P WING, CHAIRMAN; LOOMIS-PENRYN BICENTENNIAL COMMISSION; PO BOX 513; LOOMIS, CA 95650. (#32546).

SEPT 25, '76. BICENTENNIAL PARADE. LARGEST PARADE EVER HELD IN LOOMIS BASIN AREA OF PLACER COUNTY. 2300 PARADE PARTICIPANTS FROM 45 LOCAL ORGANIZATIONS & INDIVIDUALS (AGES: 9 MO OLD TRIPLETS-101 YEAR OLD), GRAND MARSHALL, 180 HORSES PLUS FARM ANIMALS. (LOCAL). CHARLES P WING; LOOMIS PENRYN BICENTENNIAL COMM & LOOMIS AREA CHAMBER OF COMMERCE; PO BOX 457; LINCOLN, CA 95648. (#200006-435).

LOS ALAMITOS

MAY 6 - 7, '76. CIRCUS PINES BIGGEST LITTLE SHOW ON EARTH. CIRCUS WILL INCLUDE: HIGH WIRE ACTS, CLOWNS, ACROBATS, MUSIC, DANCE AND MUCH MORE. AT SOUTH ARENA, 4112 CERRITOS AVE. (LOCAL). GLENN L ODER, DIRECTOR; PINE JUNIOR HIGH SCHOOL & ANAHEIM OPTIMISTS BREAKFAST CLUB; 4112 CERRITOS AVE; LOS ALAMITOS, CA 90720. (#105912-1).

LOS ALTOS

JAN 1, '76. MIDNIGHT RUN. WHILE THE RUNNERS WERE COMPETING, VARIOUS SIDE EVENTS WERE OCCURING SUCH AS PAUL REVERE RIDING AHEAD OF THE RUNNERS WARNING 'THE BRITISH ARE COMING'. AT STREETS OF DOWNTOWN LOS ALTOS. (LOCAL). MARTIN KILKENNY; LOS ALTOS BICENTENNIAL COMMITTEE; 1552 JULIE LANE; LOS ALTOS, CA 94022. (#200006-433).

SEPT 16, '76. 200 YEARS ON PARADE. ATER THE PARADE THE AUDIENCE FOLLOWED THE PARTICIPANTS TO THE LOS ALTOS HS ATHLETIC FIELD TO LISTEN TO 15 OF THE HISTORICAL CHARACTERS SPEAK, FOR INSTANCE, ABRAHAM LINCOLN, GAVE HIS GETTYSBURGH ADDRESS. AT STREETS OF DOWNTOWN LOS ALTOS. (LOCAL). BILL SHINE; LOS ALTOS BICENTENNIAL COMMITTEE; 176 2ND ST; LOS ALTOS, CA 94022. (#200006-434).

LOS ALTOS HLS

DOCUMENTARY OF ANZA TREK IN LOS ALTOS HILLS, CA. FILM DEPICTS RE-ENACTMENT OF ANZA TREK THROUGH LOS ALTOS HILLS. FILM BY KIETH MERRILL & CO. (LOCAL). MS FLORENCE M FAVA, CHAIRMAN; TOWN OF LOS ALTOS HILLS; 26379 FREMONT RD; LOS ALTOS HLS, CA 94022. (#9928).

DOCUMENTATION OF MEXICAN LAND GRANTS IN CAL. AS PART OF A STUDY OF CALIFORNIA HERITAGE, EARLY MEXICAN LAND GRANTS ARE TO BE DOCUMENTED FOR RANCHO LA PURISIMA CONCEPCION & RANCHO SAN ANTONIO. (LOCAL). ROBERT CROWE, TOWN MANAGER; TOWN OF LOS ALTOS HILLS; 26379 FREMONT RD; LOS ALTOS HLS, CA 94022. (#12213).

FILM, 'GREAT AMERICAN COWBOY', TO BE SHOWN IN CA. AN AWARD WINNING FILM, DIRECTED BY KEITH MERRILL. (LOCAL). DR CHASE, DIRECTOR COMMUNITY SERVICES; FOOTHILL COMMUNITY COLLEGE; 12345 S EL MONTE; LOS ALTOS HLS, CA 94022. (#9927).

HISTORY OF LOS ALTOS HILLS, CA - BOOK. HISTORY BOOK WRITTEN BY FLORENCE M FAVA TO BE PUBLISHED. (LOCAL). FLORENCE FAVA, HISTORIAN; G RICHARDS PUBLICATIONS; 4125 WOODSIDE RD; WOODSIDE, CA 94062. (#16218).

PERMANENT HISTORICAL DISPLAY, LOS ALTOS HILLS, CA. THE PURCHASE OF A BUILDING TO HOUSE A DISPLAY OF LOS ALTOS HILLS HISTORY, BEGINNING WITH INDIAN SETTLEMENTS TO PRESENT. (LOCAL). ROBERT CROWE, TOWN MANAGER; TOWN OF LOS ALTOS HILLS; 26379 FREMONT RD; LOS ALTOS HLS, CA 94022. (#12212).

JAN 5 - 31, '76. PHOTO-DOCUMENTATION OF AMERICAN LIFE - EXHIBIT. EXHIBIT AT FOOTHILL COLLEGE LIBRARY. (LOCAL). JOAN GREEN, PROJ DIRECTOR; FOOTHILL COLLEGE; 12345 EL MONTE RD; LOS ALTOS HLS, CA 94022. (#104253-2).

JAN 15 - MAR 11, '76. THE AMERICAN MOSAIC LECTURE SERIES. LECTURES INCLUDE 'AFRICAN CONTRIBUTIONS TO NORTH AMERICAN MUSIC' 'THE SCOTS-IRISH IN AMERICA', 'CHICANO ISSUES', 'JAPANESE ENDURANCE & TENACITY'. AT FORUM BUILDING, ROOM 1. (LOCAL). JOAN GREEN, PROJ DIRECTOR; FOOTHILL COLLEGE FACULTY SENATE; 12345 EL MONTE RD; LOS ALTOS HLS, CA 94022. (#104253-3).

JAN '76. DEDICATION OF PERMANENT HISTORICAL BUILDING. CEREMONY. (LOCAL). CHODI MCREYNOLDS; TOWN OF LOS ALTOS HILLS; 27112 MOODY CT; LOS ALTOS HLS, CA 94022. (#100148-1).

FEB 26 - AUG ??, '76. ALL AMERICAN THEATRE SEASON. LIVE PERFORMANCE AT FOOTHILL COLLEGE THEATRE. (LOCAL). JOAN GREEN, PROJ DIRECTOR; FOOTHILL COLLEGE DRAMA DEPARTMENT; 12345 EL MONTE RD; LOS ALTOS HLS, CA 94022. (#104253-1).

MAR 26, '76. REENACTMENT OF ANZA TREK, FIESTA, PANCAKE BREAKFAST. FESTIVAL AT GARDNER BULLIS SCHOOL 25890 FREMONT ROAD LOS ALTOS HILLS. (LOCAL). CHODI MCREYNOLDS; TOWN OF LOS ALTOS HILLS & LOS ALTOS HILLS HISTORICAL SOCIETY; 27112 MOODY CT; LOS ALTOS HIL, CA 94022. (#50728-1).

LOS ANGELES

AFRO-AMERICAN HISTORY MONTH, LOS ANGELES, CA. MEETINGS STRESSING HISTORICAL ACHIEVEMENTS OF BLACK AMERICANS AND OTHER ETHNIC GROUPS. (LOCAL). MRS VASSIE WRIGHT, COORDINATOR; OUR AUTHORS STUDY CLUB; 3439 5TH AVE; LOS ANGELES, CA 90018. (#23591). **ARBA GRANTEE.**

AMAN FOLK ENSEMBLE IN LOS ANGELES, CA. 'CALIFORNIA MINERS' SUITE' WHICH WILL TRACE THE EVOLUTION OF THE MINERS' FOLK ARTS JUST AFTER 1849. (LOCAL). MICHAEL ALEXANDER, COORDINATOR; AMAN FOLK ENSEMBLE; 15158 MORRISON ST; SHERMAN OAKS, CA 91403. (#12547).

AMERICA TELEVISION SERIES-SCHOOL GUIDE BOOKS - CA. 13-WEEK COLOR DOCUMENTARY ON PERSONAL HISTORY OF U S BY ALISTAIR COOKE WITH SPECIAL TEACHER GUIDE BOOKS FOR JUNIOR & SENIOR HIGH SCHOOL TEACHERS. (LOCAL). C R JAMES, SUPERVISOR; SOUTHERN CALIFORNIA GAS COMPANY; 720 W 8TH ST; LOS ANGELES, CA 90017. (#18804).

'AMERICA 200', CHILDREN'S BOOK, LOS ANGELES. HISTORICAL READER AND COLORING BOOK FOR AGES 7-13. BOOK TRACES AMERICA'S DEVELOPMENT FROM VIKING THROUGH THE SPACE AGE. ARTWORK IS DESIGNED TO SUGGEST ARTISTIC CONTRIBUTIONS BY THE READER. (NAT'L). WAYNE HOWARD, PUBLISHER; HOWARD COMMUNICATIONS; 1888 CENTURY PARK E, SUITE 10; LOS ANGELES, CA 90067. (#9600).

AMERICAN HERITAGE SQUARE. ESTABLISHMENT OF AN HISTORICAL, CULTURAL, RECREATIONAL & ENTERTAINMENT CENTER DEDICATED TO THE HISTORY & VARIED HERITAGE OF THE USA. PROJECT NOT CARRIED OUT DUE TO LACK OF FUNDING. (NAT'L). RUDY LINAN, PRESIDENT; SPANISH SPEAKING MANAGEMENT & CONSTRUCTION CORP; 6430 SUNSET BLVD, SUITE 306; HOLLYWOOD, CA 90028. (#33270). **ARBA RECOGNIZED.**

AMERICAN INDIAN ART AND CULTURAL EXCHANGE, CA. MOBILE TEACHING EXCHANGE PROGRAM INCORPORATING INDIAN ART & CRAFTS. (LOCAL). MS PEGGY OSTERMANN, COORDINATOR; AMERICAN INDIAN ART AND CULTURAL EXCHANGE, INC; 9615 HAINES CANYON; TUJUNGA, CA 91042. (#12549).

'AMERICAN ISSUES' - TV SERIES OF LOS ANGELES. A SERIES OF EIGHT MONTHLY RELIGIOUSLY ORIENTED TELEVISION PRESENTATIONS CONCERNED WITH THE INFLUENCE AND SIGNIFICANCE OF RELIGIOUS FREEDOM IN AMERICA. (LOCAL). RABBI ALFRED WOLF; RELIGIOUS HERITAGE TEAM OF THE LOS ANGELES CITY BICENT COMM; 3663 WILSHIRE BLVD; LOS ANGELES, CA 90010. (#7944).

THE AMERICAN MUSIC PROJECT, LOS ANGELES, CA. YANKEE DOODLE SOCIETY WILL RECONSTRUCT THE LOST ROOTS OF AMERICAN POPULAR MUSIC ON TAPES FOR USE ON RADIO, IN SCHOOLS AND LIBRARIES; AN ARCHIVE THAT WILL SPAN THE YEARS 1770-1900. (ST-WIDE). JOSEPH BYRD, DIRECTOR; THE YANKEE DOODLE SOCIETY; 1003 C ASHLAND AVE; SANTA MONICA, CA 90405. (#12503).

'AMERICA, A PICTURE IN MY MIND' - FILM. A CINEMATIC CELEBRATION FOR THE BICENTENNIAL PORTRAYING AMERICA'S STRUGGLE FOR FREEDOM AND BROTHERHOOD. (NAT'L). DENNIS M GILBERT, MANAGER; PAULIST PRODUCTIONS; PO BOX 1057 PACIFIC PALISADES; LOS ANGELES, CA 90272. (#4801).

ARBA FLAGS - LOS ANGELES, CA. FLY AND DISPLAY OFFICIAL ARBA FLAG AT COMPANY FACILITIES HAVING HIGH PUBLIC VISIBILITY THROUGH DEC, 1976. (LOCAL). C R JAMES, SUPERVISOR; SOUTHERN CALIFORNIA GAS COMPANY; 720 W 8TH ST; LOS ANGELES, CA 90017. (#18812).

ART WORKSHOPS IN LOS ANGELES, CA. DEVELOP ARTISTIC FACILITIES AND PROVIDE INSTITUTIONAL WORKSHOPS & SEMINARS IN THE VISUAL AND COMMUNICATIVE ARTS. (LOCAL). WILLIAM BEJARANO, DIRECTOR; HISPANIC CULTURE HERITAGE TEAM, LOS ANGELES CITY BICENT COMMITTE; 14687 RAYEN, APT 17; PANORAMA CITY, CA 91402. (#12504).

ASIAN AMERICAN & PACIFIC HERITAGE CALENDAR, CA. AN ASIAN AMERICAN & PACIFIC HERITAGE CALENDAR THAT WILL INDICATE HISTORICAL EVENTS, CULTURAL ACTIVITIES, ETHNIC RESTAURANTS, CHURCHES AND LANDMARKS, FAMOUS PEOPLE AND CULTURAL CLASSES. (LOCAL). MR ALAN KUMAMOTO, CHAIRMAN; ASIAN/PACIFIC NATIONS TEAM OF THE LA CITY BICENTENNIAL COMMITTEE; 714 W OLYMPIA BLVD; LOS ANGELES, CA 90015. (#14711).

AUTHENTIC LIVING HISTORICAL DRAMA, LOS ANGELES, CA. SCHOOL AND COMMUNITY CLUB TOUR OF 8 AUTHENTIC LIVING HISTORICAL THEMES ON THE SIGNIFICANT BUT LITTLE KNOWN CONTRIBUTIONS TO FREEDOM BY AMER BLACKS, WOMEN AND LESSER KNOWN PATRIOTS. (LOCAL). JOYCE GOLDMAN, EXEC SECRETARY; SOCIAL ISSUES RESEARCH COUNCIL; 18075 VENTURA BLVD, RM 220; ENCINA, CA 91316. (#23768). **ARBA GRANTEE.**

BICENT CONCERTS BY THE LOS ANGELES PHILHARMONIC. A CHAMBER OPERA BASED ON PLATO'S 'ALLEGORY OF THE CAVE' WILL BE PRESENTED BY MONDAY EVENING CONCERTS. (REGN'L). DORRANCE STALVEY, EXEC DIRECTOR; MONDAY EVENING CONCERTS; 5905 WILSHIRE BLVD; LOS ANGELES, CA 90036. (#6500).

BICENTENNIAL ACTIVITIES OF KLCS-TV -NBMRP. EXTENSIVE PROGRAMMING EFFORT, INCL 'BICENTENNIAL BEAT', COMPOSED & ILLUSTRATED BY STUDENTS; AN ELABORATE PROGRAM SERIES FROM 30 TO 60 MINUTES EACH ON BICENTENNIAL RELATED SUBJECTS, ETC. (LOCAL). DON HESSLER, BICENTENNIAL COORDINATOR; KLCS TELEVISION STATION; 1061 W TEMPLE ST; LOS ANGELES, CA 90012. (#24691).

BICENTENNIAL BLACK ACHIEVEMENT EXHIBIT. EXHIBIT DEPICTING PEOPLE, ISSUES & EVENTS SHAPING BLACK ACHIEVEMENT IN THE UNITED STATES SINCE 1492. (NAT'L). WILLIAM J MCCANN, MUSEUM DIRECTOR; CALIFORNIA MUSEUM OF SCIENCE & INDUSTRY; 700 STATE DR; LOS ANGELES, CA 90037. (#1073). **ARBA RECOGNIZED. ARBA GRANTEE.**

BICENTENNIAL GUIDE TO HISTORICAL SITES IN CA. DEVELOPMENT OF A BOOKLET DESCRIBING 100-200 HISTORICAL SITES IN AND AROUND LOS ANGELES AS A GUIDE FOR CITIZENS, BOTH LOCAL AND VISITING. (LOCAL). MS JEAN POOLE, CHAIRPERSON; HISTORY TEAM, L A CITY BICENTENNIAL COMMITTEE; 1120 OLD MILL RD; SAN MARINO, CA 91108. (#12487).

BICENTENNIAL LAPEL PINS - LOS ANGELES, CA. ARBA LAPEL PINS WILL BE MADE AVAILABLE TO ALL MANAGEMENT PERSONNEL WHO HAVE PUBLIC CONTACT RESPONSIBILITIES. (LOCAL). C R JAMES, SUPERVISOR; SOUTHERN CALIFORNIA GAS COMPANY; 720 W 8TH ST; LOS ANGELES, CA 90017. (#18814).

BICENTENNIAL MUSIC COMPOSITION, CLAREMONT, CA. THE COMMISSION OF A SYMPHONIC WORK FOR WIND ORCHESTRA

LOS ANGELES — CONTINUED

PLAYABLE BY A PROFESSIONAL OR COLLEGE ORCHESTRA. (NAT'L). KARL KOHN, PROFESSOR OF MUSIC; CLAREMONT MUSIC FESTIVAL; THATCHER MUSIC BLDG; CLAREMONT, CA 91711. (#6169).

BICENTENNIAL SALUTE TO DR WILLIAM GRANT STILL. MUSICAL SALUTE TO BLACK CONDUCTOR, WILLIAM GRANT STILL. EVENT TO BE HELD AT THE LOS ANGELES MUSIC CENTER. (REGN'L). FRAN ZONE, PRESIDENT; WILLIAM GRANT STILL FOUNDATION; 417 S HOLT AVE STE 203; LOS ANGELES, CA 90048. (#7817).

'A BICENTENNIAL SUITE' - INTAGLIO & RELIEF PRINTS. 12 COLOR INTAGLIO & RELEIF PRINTS TO CELEBRATE THE BICENTENNIAL DEPICTING FAMOUS EVENTS & AMERICANS. PRESENTED IN PORTFOLIO OR FRAMED FOR EXHIBITION. TO BE SHOWN ACROSS USA & IN INDIA. (INT'L). HARRIET ZEITLIN; 202 S SALTAIR AVE; LOS ANGELES, CA 90049. (#23677).

BIDDY MASON CENTER OF BLACK HISTORY AND ARTS, CA. A HOUSE OCCUPIED BY BLACKS SINCE THE 1800'S WILL BECOME A MAJOR FOCAL POINT OF BLACK CULTURE IN LOS ANGELES; EMPHASIS WILL BE ON ART, CINEMA, MUSIC & FOOD. (LOCAL). DR CARL MARTIN, DIRECTOR; FEDERATION OF BLACK HISTORY AND ARTS, INC; PO BOX 5959A; LOS ANGELES, CA 90059. (#12501).

THE BIRTH OF THE UNITED STATES: 3 PART EXHIBIT. THIS PROJECT INCLUDES 3 EXHIBITS: 'FROM ARGUMENT TO ARMS', 'A PEOPLE'S WAR' AND 'E PLURIBUS UNUM'. (NAT'L). MS SUE HULL, DIRECTOR OF ADMINISTRATION; HUNTINGTON LIBRARY ART GALLERY & BOTANICAL GARDENS; 1151 OXFORD RD; SAN MARINO, CA 91108. (#8262).

CALENDAR OF MUSEUM BICENTENNIAL EVENTS IN CA. A PUBLISHED COMPILATION OF BICENTENNIAL EXHIBITS PLANNED BY EACH MUSEUM, TO INFORM AND ADVISE THE PUBLIC OF TIME, PLACE AND TYPE OF DIVERSIFIED EXHIBITIONS. (LOCAL). MS VIRGINIA KAZOR, CHAIRPERSON; MUSEUM TEAM, L A CITY BICENTENNIAL COMMITTEE; 4804 HOLLYWOOD BLVD; LOS ANGELES, CA 90027. (#12489).

CALIFORNIA CONSERVATION PROJECT. SMOG RESISTANT TREES SUCH AS SIERRA REDWOODS, JEFFERY & SUGAR PINES, WILL BE PLANTED IN THE SAN BERNADINO MOUNTAINS NEAR LOS ANGELES. (LOCAL). ANDY LIPKINS, DIRECTOR; CALIFORNIA CONSERVATION PROJECT; 1745 SELBY AVE #18; LOS ANGELES, CA 90024. (#12492).

CALIFORNIA RANCHO EASTER FIESTA. 'CALIFORNIA RANCHO EASTER FIESTA', A NEW PRODUCTION WHICH WILL RECREATE MUSIC, DANCE AND RELATED ACTIVITIES OF THE RANCHO PERIOD OF 1835. (LOCAL). MICHAEL ALEXANDER, COORDINATOR; AMAN FOLK ENSEMBLE; 15158 MORRISON ST; SHERMAN OAKS, CA 91403. (#12548).

CALIFORNIA STATE OF THE NATION - LOS ANGELES, CA. MULTIMEDIA PRESENTATION ON CALIFORNIA INDUSTRIES. PERMANENT EXHIBIT AT CAL MUSEUM OF SCIENCE AND INDUSTRY, LOS ANGELES; A TRAVELLING EXHIBIT TO SCIENCE MUSEUMS THROUGHOUT U S. (ST-WIDE). WILLIAM J MCCANN, DIRECTOR; CAL MUSEUM OF SCIENCE & INDUSTRY; 700 STATE DR; LOS ANGELES, CA 90037. (#14990). **ARBA GRANTEE.**

CARROLL AVENUE RESTORATION PROJ - LOS ANGELES, CA. A HISTORIC PARK WILL BE CREATED BY MOVING NEARBY VICTORIAN MONUMENTS TO A VACANT LOT ON THE 1300 BLOCK OF CARROLL AVE; THIS AREA HAS THE. HIGHEST DENSITY OF HISTORIC MONUMENTS IN THE CITY. (LOCAL). PLANARIA KNILL, VICE PRESIDENT; CARROLL AVENUE RESTORATION PROJECT; 1320 CARROLL AVE; LOS ANGELES, CA 90017. (#19669).

'CARTE BLANCHE'S' BICENTENNIAL ISSUE - NBMRP. MARCH/APRIL 1976 ISSUE BICENTENNIAL EDITION PRESENTS BOTH HISTORICAL NARRATIVE & CURRENT PROFILES OF 13 FAMED CITIES. SENT MANY FREE COPIES TO SCHOOLS, TEACHERS, CITY AGENCIES & YOUTH ORGANIZATIONS. (NAT'L). J WALTER FLYNN, PUBLISHER & EDITOR; CARTE BLANCHE MAGAZINE; 3460 WILSHIRE BLVD; LOS ANGELES, CA 90010. (#26069).

CHILDREN'S ART FESTIVAL IN LOS ANGELES, CA. CHILDREN AND ADULTS EXPRESS IDENTITY AND NEIGHBORHOOD EXPERIENCES IN ARTISTIC MEDIA; SPONSORED BY JUNIOR ARTS CENTER. (LOCAL). MS CLAIRE DEUSSEN, DIRECTOR; JUNIOR ARTS CENTER, MUNICIPAL ARTS DEPT; 4814 HOLLYWOOD BLVD; LOS ANGELES, CA 90027. (#12495).

'CHRISTOPHER COLUMBUS', MUSIC COMPOSITION - CA. 'CHRISTOPHER COLUMBUS' IS A CLASSICAL MUSIC COMPOSITION CELEBRATING OUR NATIONAL HERITAGE. (LOCAL). EUGENE ZADOR C/O HON T BRADLEY, MAYOR; CITY HALL; LOS ANGELES, CA 90012. (#22147).

'CITY PARKS FOR CITY PEOPLE', SEMINAR. A DIALOGUE ON PLANNING, TRANSPORTATION & HUMAN VALUES FOR SANTA MONICA MOUNTAINS & SEASHORE. (LOCAL). SUSAN NELSON, CHAIRMAN; FRIENDS OF SANTA MONICA MOUNTAINS, PARKS & SEASHORE; 13215 RIVIERA RANCH RD; LOS ANGELES, CA 90049. (#103618-1). **(??).**

COLLEGE AND UNIV STUDENT NATL BICENT PARTICIPATION. CONTRACT WITH UCLA TO CONDUCT SUMMER TASK FORCE IN 1974 WITH TEN STUDENTS FROM DIFFERENT COLLEGES TO DEVELOP PROGRAM RECOMMENDATIONS FOR COLLEGE STUDENTS. HANDBOOK TO BE DEVELOPED & DISTRIBUTED BY ARBA. (NAT'L). DIRECTOR, PROGRAM REVIEW & EVALUATION; AMERICAN REVOLUTION BICENTENNIAL ADMINISTRATION; 2401 E STREET, NW; WASHINGTON, DC 20276. (#2771).

COMMISSIONING OF A NEW MUSICAL COMPOSITION - CA. A CONCERTO WILL BE WRITTEN FOR GUITAR AND CHAMBER ORCHESTRA. (LOCAL). MARTHA T BLAINE, GENERAL MANAGER; LOS ANGELES CHAMBER ORCHESTRA; 1017 N LA CIENGA, SUITE 109A; LOS ANGELES, CA 90069. (#16162).

CONSERVATION OF PHOTOGRAPHS PROJECT OF CALIF. ESTABLISH PRIORITIES FOR ENDANGERED ITEMS. COPY FADING PHOTOGRAPHS. PRINT UNPRINTED NEGATIVES. DUPLICATE NITRATE NEGATIVES. PROVIDE IDENTIFYING PRINTS TO PROTECT PRIMARY MATERIALS FROM OVEREXPOSURE. (LOCAL). HILDA BOHEM, DIRECTOR; NATIONAL ENDOWMENT FOR THE ARTS; 806 15TH ST, NW; WASHINGTON, DC 20506. (#3126). **(??).**

CONSTRUCTIONS FOR PIANO & ORCHESTRA, LOS ANGELES. CONCERT WORK FOR SOLO PIANO AND SYMPHONY ORCHESTRA. (REGN'L). PHILLIP LAMBRO, COMPOSER; NATIONAL ENDOWMENT OF THE ARTS; 1888 CENTURY PARK E, SUITE 10; CENTURY CITY, CA 90067. (#22594).

CULTURAL BUS NETWORK IN LOS ANGELES, CA. BUS NETWORK TO ALLOW VISITORS TO GO AMONG CULTURAL INSTITUTIONS FOR A SINGLE FARE. (LOCAL). MS CAROL SCOTT, DIRECTOR; MUSEUM TEAM OF THE LOS ANGELES CITY BICENTENNIAL COMMITTEE; 5900 WILSHIRE BLVD; LOS ANGELES, CA 90036. (#12550).

CUSTOMER BILLING AND RETURN ENVELOPES - CA. ENVELOPES WITH ARBA LOGO WILL BE MAILED TO 3 MILLION CUSTOMERS EACH MONTH FROM JULY, 1975-DEC, 1976. CUSTOMERS SEE LOGO WHEN THEY OPEN MAIL & WHEN THEY RETURN PAYMENT; COVERS 534 CITIES. (LOCAL). C R JAMES, SUPERVISOR; SOUTHERN CALIFORNIA GAS COMPANY; 720 W 8TH ST; LOS ANGELES, CA 90017. (#18806).

DECALS ON COMPANY VEHICLES - LOS ANGELES, CA. ARBA SYMBOL WILL BE USED ON APROXIMATELY 4200 COMPANY VEHICLES WHICH TRAVEL THROUGHOUT SOUTHERN CALIFORNIA IN 534 CITIES. (LOCAL). C R JAMES, SUPERVISOR; SOUTHERN CALIFORNIA GAS COMPANY; 720 W 8TH ST; LOS ANGELES, CA 90017. (#18808).

ECONOMIC AWARENESS '76, LOS ANGELES, CA. DONATE TO PUBLIC SCHOOLS IN CALIFORNIA A PACKAGE OF 'BLUEBACKS', SIMULATED CURRENCY FOR INSTRUCTIONAL USE, WITH A TEACHER GUIDE PLUS TWO POSTERS SHOWING EARLY U S MONEY. (ST-WIDE). GARY DORAN, PUBLIC AFFAIRS OFFICER; SECURITY PACIFIC NATIONAL BANK; PO BOX 2097, TERMINAL ANNEX; LOS ANGELES, CA 90051. (#16412).

EMPLOYEE BICENTENNIAL BOX LUNCH SERIES - CA. INVITE EMPLOYEES TO SPECIAL BICENTENNIAL PROGRAM ONCE A MONTH SERIES WILL INCLUDE FILMS, EXHIBITS, SPEAKERS, ENTERTAINMENT WITH BICENTENNIAL THEMES. (LOCAL). C R JAMES, SUPERVISOR; SOUTHERN CALIFORNIA GAS COMPANY; 720 W 8TH ST; LOS ANGELES, CA 90017. (#18815).

EMPLOYEE VOLUNTEER-A-DAY - LOS ANGELES, CA. ENCOURAGE ALL EMPLOYEES AND RETIREES TO VOLUNTEER THEIR OWN TIME TO HELP WITH BICENTENNIAL ACTIVITIES & PROJECTS IN THEIR LOCAL COMMUNITIES. (LOCAL). C R JAMES, SUPERVISOR; SOUTHERN CALIFORNIA GAS COMPANY; 720 W 8TH ST; LOS ANGELES, CA 90017. (#18813).

ESTABLISHMENT OF A SWISS STUDIES CHAIR AT USC. THIS PROJECT WILL BE DONE WITH THE ASSISTANCE OF SWISS INSTITUTIONS, BANKS, AND INDUSTRIES. (INT'L). CULTURAL ATTACHE; EMBASSY OF SWITZERLAND; 2900 CATHEDRAL AVE; WASHINGTON, DC 20008. (#32965).

ESTRADA COURTS - LOS ANGELES, CA. 75 VIVID COLORFUL TWO-STORY MURALS HIGHLIGHTING THE SPANISH-AMERICAN EXPERIENCE IN THE U S AND IN LOS ANGELES INCLUDING INDIAN, CHICANO, MEXICAN AMERICAN AND CURRENT CULTURAL THEMES. (LOCAL). MILDRED WONG, MANAGER; HOUSING AUTHORITY OF THE CITY OF LOS ANGELES; 3232 ESTRADA ST; LOS ANGELES, CA 90023. (#20081).

EVENING CONCERT SERIES - LOS ANGELES, CA. 2-HOUR NIGHTLY RADIO PROGRAM WILL REGULARLY HIGHLIGHT HISTORY AND DEVELOPMENT OF AMERICAN CLASSICAL MUSIC. ARBA SYMBOL WILL BE USED ON PROGRAM WHICH GOES TO ABOUT 60,000 CUSTOMERS EACH MONTH. (LOCAL). C R JAMES, SUPERVISOR; SOUTHERN CALIFORNIA GAS COMPANY; 720 W 8TH ST; LOS ANGELES, CA 90017. (#18810).

EXHIBITION OF AUSTRALIAN ABORIGINAL ARTS & CRAFTS. EXHIBIT. (LOCAL). INFORMATION OFFICE; AUSTRALIAN CONSULATE GENERAL; 636 FIFTH AVE; NEW YORK, NY 10020. (#200006-494).

FEATURES ON GREAT ARMENIANS, LOS ANGELES, CA. BICENTENNIAL COLUMN TO BE PUBLISHED IN BOOK FORM ABOUT GREAT ARMENIANS WHO HAVE CONTRIBUTED TO AMERICAN INDUSTRY, EDUCATION, ENGINEERING, ART LEADERSHIP & RELIGION. (LOCAL). ANNE AVAKIAN-BISHOP, BICENT COMMITTEE CHMN; THE ARMENIAN OBSERVIER & THE GREATER LOS ANGELES PRESS CLUB; 4411 LOCKWOOD AVE; LOS ANGELES, CA 90029. (#15667).

FOLK ART AND CONTEMPORARY CRAFT MUSEUM OF S CA. TO CREATE A MUSEUM FOR THE COMMUNITY IN FOLK ART AND CONTEMPORARY CRAFTS. (LOCAL). MS EDITH WYLE, DIRECTOR; FOLK ART AND CONTEMPORARY CRAFT MUSEUM; 5814 WILSHIRE BLVD; LOS ANGELES, CA 90036. (#12553).

GALA DE L'UNION DES ARTISTES. A JOINT BENEFIT PERFORMANCE BY FRENCH L'UNION DES ARTISTS AND THE AMERICAN MOTION PICTURE ACADEMY. (INT'L). DOMINIQUE PERRIN; GALA DE L'UNION DES ARTISTES; 7 RUE HENRI ROCHEFORT; PARIS/ FRANCE. (#104903-1).

GIFTS TO LOS ANGELES FROM KOREA. KOREA WILL PRESENT A 19-TON TRADITIONAL BRONZE KOREAN BELL AND BELFRY TO THE CITY OF LOS ANGELES. (INT'L). OFFICE OF INFORMATION; EMBASSY OF KOREA; 2320 MASSACHUSETTS AVE, NW; WASHINGTON, DC 20008. (#28316).

GOEZ STUDIO MURALS PROGRAM IN CITY OF LOS ANGELES. 1500 MURALS IN BUILDINGS ACROSS THE CITY INVOLVING YOUNG UNRECOGNIZED TALENT. (LOCAL). JOE GONALES, COORDINATOR; HISPANIC CULTURE HERITAGE TEAM; 3757 E FIRST ST; LOS ANGELES, CA 90063. (#12493).

'GOOD MORNING AMERICA', LOS ANGELES. THE PRODUCTION OF A MUSICAL WORK INVOLVING CHORUS MIXED VOICES, NARRATION OF CARL SANDBURG POETRY AND AN ORCHESTRA. (ST-WIDE). DR RICHARD GILMAN, PRESIDENT; OCCIDENTAL COLLEGE; 1600 CAMPUS RD; LOS ANGELES, CA 90041. (#23670).

HALL OF FINANCE AT CALIF MUSEUM OF SCIENCE. A NEW BUILDING THAT WILL HOUSE EXHIBITIONS THAT CONCERN MONEY, ECONOMICS & BANKING WITH SPECIAL EMPHASIS ON THE FREE ENTERPRISE SYSTEM. (ST-WIDE). WILLIAM J MCCANN, MUSEUM DIRECTOR; CALIFORNIA MUSEUM OF SCIENCE AND INDUSTRY; 700 STATE DR, EXPOSITION PK; LOS ANGELES, CA 90037. (#7054).

HIGHLAND PARK MURAL - PROJ OF LOS ANGELES, CA. A HISTORICAL MURAL ON AN EXISTING TELEPHONE DISTRIBUTING STATION TO DIGNIFY THE COMMUNITY'S HERITAGE. (LOCAL). DAVID ANGELO, CHAIRMAN; PACIFIC TELEPHONE CO; 5271 E BEVERLY BLVD; LOS ANGELES, CA 90022. (#14996).

HISTORIC LOS ANGELES GUIDED BUS TOUR. A GUIDED BUS TOUR OF BUILDINGS & SITES OF HISTORIC SIGNIFICANCE TO THE DEVELOPMENT OF LOS ANGELES. (LOCAL). MS JEAN POOLE, HISTORY TEAM OF THE LOS ANGELES CITY BICENT COMM; 1120 OLD MILL RD; SAN MARINO, CA 91108. (#7945).

HISTORICAL AMERICAN FLAGS - LOS ANGELES, CA. REPLICAS OF 7 DIFFERENT AMERICAN FLAGS WILL BE FLOWN AT COMPANY FACILITIES WITH HIGH PUBLIC VISIBILITY. ONE FLAG PER MONTH WILL BE HIGHLIGHTED. (LOCAL). C R JAMES, SUPERVISOR; SOUTHERN CALIFORNIA GAS COMPANY; 720 W 8TH ST; LOS ANGELES, CA 90017. (#18811).

HISTORY AND MEMORABILIA VAN MUSEUM - CA. THE HISTORY AND MEMORABILIA VAN MUSEUM WILL TRAVEL THROUGHOUT AREAS IN SOUTHERN CALIFORNIA MAY 1976 - JUNE 1977. (ST-WIDE). GERALD C NORDSKOG, CHAIRMAN; LOS ANGELES UNIFIED SCHOOL DISTRICT BICENTENNIAL COMMITTEE; 16216 RAYMER ST; VAN NUYS, CA 91406. (#26926). **ARBA GRANTEE.**

'HONOR THE PAST BY PLANTING FOR THE FUTURE' - CA. BROCHURE WITH IDEAS ON PATRIOTIC LANDSCAPING; GIVES TREES, GROUND COVER & SHRUBS WHICH BLOOM IN RED, WHITE & BLUE. (ST-WIDE). DIRECTOR; LOS ANGELES BEAUTIFUL, INC; 404 S BIXEL ST; LOS ANGELES, CA 90017. (#24207).

THE INTERCULTURAL SPIRIT OF '76. INTERNATIONAL DISTRIBUTION OF 760 SUBSCRIPTIONS TO THE PERIODICAL 'REVOLUTIONARY TIMES' & THE 50-MINUTE FILM 'THE GREAT AMERICAN ADVENTURE'. (INT'L). GURDIAL PAUL SINGH, PHD, FOUNDER-PRESIDENT; THE INTERCULTURAL RELIGIOUS FORUM FOUNDATION; 1436 BELFAST DR; LOS ANGELES, CA 90069. (#7878).

LET FREEDOM RING - LOS ANGELES, CA. AN ORATORICAL PROGRAM OF AMERICAN ISSUES FORUM WILL BE PRODUCED. (LOCAL). EUGENE KREMSDORF, CHAIRMAN; DISTRICT 52-TOASTMASTERS, INTERNATIONAL; PO BOX 665; RESEDA, CA 91335. (#18103).

LOCAL HISTORY PROJECT OF LOS ANGELES. ENABLE A LIBRARY TO ORGANIZE & PRESENT LOCAL HISTORY IN A FORMAT WHICH SMALL COMMUNITIES & NEIGHBORHOODS WITH STRONG ETHNIC IDENTITIES CAN USE. (LOCAL). PHILLIP WESLEY; LIBRARY TEAM OF THE LOS ANGELES CITY BICENT COMM; 1000 E VICTORIA ST; DOMINGUEZ HLS, CA 90247. (#7947).

'MEET THE AMERICANS' - LOS ANGELES, CA. A PROGRAM OF BRINGING PEOPLE OF ALL PROFESSIONS FROM FOREIGN COUNTRIES TO SPEND FIVE DAYS TO TWO WEEKS AS GUESTS OF AMERICAN FAMILIES. (INT'L). ELIZABETH R WALTON, ASST DIRECTOR; AMERICAN HOST FOUNDATION; 515 S FLOWER ST, SUITE 2280; LOS ANGELES, CA 90071. (#19051).

MEXICO CITY FEDERAL ARCHIVES MICROFILM PROJECT, CA. THE INVENTORY AND MICROFILMING OF RECORDS HELD IN MEXICO CITY IN THE MEXICAN FEDERAL ARCHIVES WHICH PERTAIN TO CALIFORNIA WHEN IT WAS THE DOMAIN OF SPAIN AND MEXICO. (INT'L). RAUL ACEVES, CHAIRMAN; CALIFORNIA STATE COLLEGE; 1000 E VICTORIA; LOS ANGELES, CA 90747. (#10838).

MIA AND POW PROJECT IN LOS ANGELES, CA. A PUBLIC AWARENESS CAMPAIGN TO ENCOURAGE PEOPLE TO WRITE ELECTED OFFICIALS IN BEHALF OF THOSE THAT ARE STILL PRISONERS OF WAR OR MISSING IN ACTION IN VIETNAM. (NAT'L). STEPHEN R FRANK, DIRECTOR; VOICES IN VITAL AMERICA; 10966 LE CONTE AVE; LOS ANGELES, CA 90024. (#15496).

MINI PARK, 'PLACITA DE DOLORES', LOS ANGELES, CA. MINI-PARK WILL BE CONSTRUCTED AND REPLICA OF MEXICAN BELL WILL BE DONATED BY MEXICAN GOVERNMENT. (LOCAL). JOE GONZALES, COORDINATOR; HISPANIC CULTURE HERITAGE TEAM, LOS ANGELES CITY BICENT COMMITTE; 3757 E FIRST ST; LOS ANGELES, CA 90063. (#12497).

MUSEUM EXHIBIT ON ENERGY - LOS ANGELES, CA. REDESIGN PERMANENT EXHIBIT ON ENERGY ALONG BICENTENNIAL THEME. EXHIBIT AT CALIF MUSEUM OF SCIENCE & INDUSTRY IS VISITED BY APPROXIMATELY 2 MILLION PEOPLE ANNUALLY. (LOCAL). C R JAMES, SUPERVISOR; SOUTHERN CALIFORNIA GAS COMPANY; 720 W 8TH ST; LOS ANGELES, CA 90017. (#18809).

MUSIC FOR CHAMBER ENSEMBLES - LOS ANGELES, CA. COMPOSITIONS FOR MIXED GROUP OF INSTRUMENTS, FOR BRASS QUINTET AND OTHER SMALL COMBINATIONS. (ST-WIDE). DORRANCE STALVEY, DIRECTOR; MONDAY EVENING CONCERTS-LOS ANGELES COUNTY MUSEUM OF ART; 5905 WILSHIRE BLVD; LOS ANGELES, CA 90036. (#22019).

MUSICAL COMPOSITION - LOS ANGELES, CA. MUSIC IS BEING COMPOSED FOR SOLO SINGERS, CHORUS AND INSTRUMENTAL ENSEMBLE. (LOCAL). CLARE J FRANCO, COMPOSER; 200 3RD AVE; VENICE, CA 90291. (#26442).

NATIONAL SPORTS PROGRAMS - LOS ANGELES, CA. NATIONAL SPORTS PROGRAMS WILL BE HELD AT VARIOUS LOCATIONS

LOS ANGELES — CONTINUED

THROUGHOUT THE COUNTRY. (NAT'L). TULLEY N BROWN, CHAIRMAN; DIRECTION SPORTS, INC; 117 W 9TH ST, SUITE 520; LOS ANGELES, CA 90015. (#27940).

NEIGHBORHOOD ARTS CENTERS IN LOS ANGELES, CA. CENTERS IN NEIGHBORHOODS TO SERVE AS THE HUB FOR ALL ART ACTIVITIES; IDENTIFY EXISTING CENTERS AND DEVELOP ADDITIONAL ONES AS NEEDED. (LOCAL). EVE ESHELMAN, PROJ DIRECTOR; UNIV OF SOUTHERN CALIFORNIA AND CITY BICENT ART TEAM; ONE UNIVERSITY PK; LOS ANGELES, CA 90007. (#12499).

'OPERATION S-O-S' IN LOS ANGELES. A DRAMATIC TELEVISION SERIES WILL BE DONE, EMPHASIZING COOPERATION, ITS ROLE IN AMERICAN SUCCESS & THE URGENCY OF ITS EXTENSION INTERNATIONALLY IN THE SERVICE OF HUMAN SURVIVAL. (REGN'L). RODERIC GORNEY, M D; UCLA SCHOOL OF MEDICINE; 760 WESTWOOD PLAZA; LOS ANGELES, CA 90024. (#8584).

'OUR RELIGIOUS HERITAGE IN SOUTHERN CALIF' - BOOK. THE BOOK WILL COVER THE FOLLOWING CATAGORIES: ROMAN CATHOLIC, JEWISH, PROTESTANT, ORTHODOX AND OTHER GREAT EASTERN RELIGIONS & SECTS PECULIAR TO SOUTHERN CALIFORNIA. (LOCAL). ROBERT C WALKER, COORDINATOR; INTERRELIGIOUS COUNCIL OF SOUTHERN CALIFORNIA; 3460 WILSHIRE BLVD, SUITE 1012; LOS ANGELES, CA 90010. (#18805).

PACIFIC 21-PACIFIC NATION CONFERENCE & EXHIBITION. CULTURAL FESTIVAL AND PERFORMANCES BASED ON HERITAGE & TRADITIONS OF PACIFIC NATIONS EXHIBITION. BASED ON LONG RANGE PROMISE OF PACIFIC. INTERNATIONAL CONFERENCES BASED ON TRADE AND BUSINESS IN 21ST CENT. (INT'L). CHRISTINE AULT, MANAGING DIRECTOR; PACIFIC 21 COUNCIL; 10100 SANTA MONICA BLVD; LOS ANGELES, CA 90067. (#1700). **ARBA RECOGNIZED.**

PARK PROJECT IN LOS ANGELES, CA. THE ESTABLISHMENT OF A NEW PARK TO ENHANCE THE COMMUNITY. (LOCAL). DAVID SILVERMAN, PROJ DIRECTOR; COMMUNITY ACTIVITIES TEAM, LOS ANGELES BICENTENNIAL COMMITTEE; 200 N SPRING ST; LOS ANGELES, CA 90012. (#12486).

PICTORIAL HISTORY OF LOS ANGELES BY CITY SCHOOLS. PUBLICATION OF A SCHOOL CHILDREN'S HISTORY OF THE CITY OF LOS ANGELES, EXECUTED BY CITY PUPILS. (LOCAL). GUY JAMIESON, COORDINATOR; LOS ANGELES UNIFIED SCHOOL DISTRICT, BICENTENNIAL COMMITTEE; 450 N GRAND; LOS ANGELES, CA 90038. (#12485).

PLAZA DE LA RAZA MEMORIAL THEATRE, CA. CULTURAL CENTER IN MEMORY OF RUBEN SALAZAR. (LOCAL). FRANK LOPEZ, PROJ DIRECTOR; HISPANIC CULTURE HERITAGE TEAM, L A BICENTENNIAL COMMITTEE; 3540 N MISSION RD; LOS ANGELES, CA 90031. (#12491).

POCKET CALENDARS - LOS ANGELES, CA. PRINT & DISTRIBUTE FREE, 75,000 POCKET CALENDARS. ARBA SYMBOL ON FRONT COVER & HISTORIC THEME THROUGHOUT INSIDE PAGES. (LOCAL). C R JAMES, SUPERVISOR; SOUTHERN CALIFORNIA GAS COMPANY; 720 W 8TH ST; LOS ANGELES, CA 90017. (#18807).

PORTRAITS OF AMERICA'S PRESIDENTS -CA. OIL PORTRAITS OF THE 37 U S PRESIDENTS WITH BIOGRAPHICAL MATERIAL WILL BE DISPLAYED AT SUITABLE LOCATIONS THROUGHOUT SOUTHERN CALIFORNIA THROUGH DEC, 1976. (LOCAL). C R JAMES, SUPERVISOR; SOUTHERN CALIFORNIA GAS COMPANY; 720 W 8TH ST; LOS ANGELES, CA 90017. (#18816).

PRACTICAL ECOLOGY PROGRAM, LOS ANGELES, CA. PROJECT IS A COMMUNITY AND ENVIRONMENT IMPROVEMENT PROGRAM. (LOCAL). MICHAEL J LEAHY, PROGRAM COORDINATOR; PRACTICAL ECOLOGY PROGRAM 'PEP' GROUP ASSOC; 8444 RESEDA BLVD SUITE D; NORTHRIDGE, CA 91324. (#16362).

'PROJECT SIGNATURE' IN LOS ANGELES COUNTY, CA. GATHER SIGNATURES OF PERSONS RESIDING IN L A COUNTY IN CELEBRATION OF BICENTENNIAL. (LOCAL). WILLIAM H MORRIS, PROJ DIRECTOR; WILLIAM H MORRIS PROJECT SIGNATURE ORGANIZATION; 1242 N WESTMORELAND, NO 1; LOS ANGELES, CA 90029. (#15494).

RED, WHITE AND BLUES - CHORAL PRESENTATION IN CA. WOMEN'S CHORAL CELEBRATION OF THE BICENTENNIAL. (LOCAL). JUDITH BERMAN, DIRECTOR; THE MUSART SINGERS; 5358 OSTROM AVE; ENCINO, CA 91316. (#6286).

RESTORATION OF HISTORIC SCHOOLHOUSE IN LOS ANGELES. BUILDING RESTORED FOR CLASSES AND COMMUNITY MEETINGS. (LOCAL). ALBERT C JOHNSON, EXEC DIRECTOR; CALIFORNIA BICENTENNIAL COMMISSION; 1501 8TH ST; SACRAMENTO, CA 95814. (#22845).

RESTORE & FLY 1ST COMMERCIAL PLANE. AMERICAS SENIOR AIRLINE WILL RESTORE THE M-2 BIPLANE & FLY IT OVER THE ORIGINAL ROUTES OF AIRMAIL CONTRACTS, LOS ANGELES-LAS VEGAS-SALT LAKE CITY ON 50TH ANNIVERSARY OF FIRST FLIGHT, APRIL 17, 1976. (NAT'L). RAY SILVIUS, V P OF CORPORATE AFFAIRS; WESTERN AIRLINES INC; 6060 AVION DR; LOS ANGELES, CA 90009. (#6893).

'REVOLUTIONARY TIMES', MAGAZINE. A MAGAZINE SIZED 4 PAGE NEWSPAPER RE-CREATING THE PERIOD 1763-1776. THE PAPER WILL COMMUNICATE BOTH HISTORICAL FACTS & AN UNDERSTANDING OF THE CULTURAL, SOCIAL & ECONOMIC DIMENSIONS OF THE ERA. (NAT'L). DR RICHARD BERTAIN, PRESIDENT; AMERICAN EDUCATIONAL SERVICES; 1720 PONTIUS ST, SUITE 1776; LOS ANGELES, CA 90025. (#5655). **(??).**

'REVOLUTIONARY TIMES' NEWSPAPER COLUMN. 300-WORD NEWSPAPER COLUMN WILL BE PRINTED 3 TIMES WEEKLY, RECOUNTING EVENTS FROM EARLY NEWSPAPERS AND CITING INTERESTING AND RELEVANT NEWS ITEMS FROM POLITICAL, MILITARY, SOCIETY AND HOME-LIFE ASPECTS. (NAT'L). RICHARD BERTAIN, PRESIDENT; AMERICAN EDUCATIONAL SERVICES; 1720 PONTIUS AVE, SUITE 204; LOS ANGELES, CA 90025. (#6235).

RIDE THE BIG RED CARS, LOS ANGELES, CA. THE HISTORY, OPERATIONS, UNUSUAL FACETS AND IMPACT ON SOUTHERN CA OF THE PACIFIC ELECTRIC RAILWAY. THIS EXHIBIT INCLUDES ONE OF THE SURVIVING RED CARS. (LOCAL). WILLIAM J MCCANN, MUSEUM DIRECTOR; CALIFORNIA MUSEUM OF SCIENCE AND INDUSTRY; 700 STATE DR, EXPOSITION PARK; LOS ANGELES, CA 90037. (#16283).

SLIDES ON COINS AND ARMENIAN NUMISMATIC AWARD, CA. COLOR SLIDE LIBRARY ON ARMENIAN ANCIENT AND MEDIEVAL COINS & MODERN PAPER NOTES. ESTABLISHMENT OF SILVER MEDAL AWARD TO THE BEST WRITER OF ARMENIAN NUMISMATIC BOOK TO BE AWARDED ANNUALLY. (NAT'L). Y T NERCESSIAN, SECRETARY; ARMENIAN NUMISMATIC SOCIETY; 8511 BEVERLY PARK PL; PICO RIVERA, CA 90660. (#6204).

THEATRICAL PLAY & FOLLOW-UP PROGRAM IN LOS ANGELES. AN ORIGINAL PLAY WILL BE PERFORMED FOR GRADES 4-6 OF LOS ANGELES SCHOOLS; THERE WILL BE A FOLLOW-UP PROGRAM IN THE CLASSES. (LOCAL). SUSAN GELB, DIRECTOR; CALIFORNIA CREATIVE ARTS; 4201 GLENALBYN DR; LOS ANGELES, CA 90065. (#10851).

TRAINING TV PRODUCTION ON GOOD NEWS IN AMERICA, CA. YOUNG SAINTS TELECOMMUNICATIONS ACADEMY IN WATTS WILL TRAIN YOUNG PEOPLE TO RESEARCH AND PRODUCE TELEVISION PROGRAMING ON POSITIVE ASPECTS OF COMMUNITY ACTION THROUGHOUT THE USA. (LOCAL). THOMAS S ROBERTS, COORDINATOR; THE YOUNG SAINTS ACADEMY; 6216 S MAIN ST; LOS ANGELES, CA 90003. (#23589). **ARBA GRANTEE.**

'TUTANKHAMEN TREASURES' EXHIBIT. EXHIBIT. (INT'L). CULTURAL ATTACHE; ARAB REPUBLIC OF EGYPT; 2310 DECATUR PL; WASHINGTON, DC 20008. (#31906-4). **(??).**

USA FLAG HISTORY CEREMONY IN LOS ANGELES, CA. A MOVING TRIBUTE TO PROUD HERITAGE OF AMERICA'S FLAGS, PERFORMED BY SEVEN MEMBERS OF ENLISTED ADVISORY COUNCIL, LOS ANGELES AIR FORCE STATION, CALIFORNIA. (LOCAL). MONA J BENNETT, CHIEF, COMMUNITY RELATIONS; SPACE AND MISSILE SYSTEMS ORGANIZATION; PO BOX 92960 WORLDWAY POSTAL CTR; LOS ANGELES, CA 90009. (#31034).

A WALK THROUGH A LEGAL COMMUNITY, CA. COLLEGE STUDENTS, LAW STUDENTS OR COMMUNITY VOLUNTEERS WILL LEAD WALKING TOURS THROUGH AGENCIES THAT WORK IN THE FIELD OF LAW AND JUSTICE. (LOCAL). DICK WEINTRAUB, PROJ DIRECTOR; LAW AND JUSTICE TEAM, L A CITY BICENTENNIAL COMMITTEE; 6310 SAN VICENTE; LOS ANGELES, CA 90046. (#12490).

WATTS INDUSTRIAL PARK - LOS ANGELES, CA. TOURS TO SMALL MINORITY MANUFACTURING AND TECHNICAL BUSINESSES WITHIN THE WATTS INDUSTRIAL PARK; BRIEFINGS BY STAFF PERSONS ON STATUS OF MINORITY BUSINESS ENTERPRISE DEVELOPMENT. (LOCAL). FRITZ BASKETT, ADMINISTRATOR, INFORMATION MGT; ECONOMIC RESOURCES CORP; 11633 S ALAMEDA ST; LOS ANGELES, CA 90059. (#20096).

THE WEST COLONY. HUNTINGTON LIBRARY ART GALLERY & BOTANICAL GARDENS. DISPLAY & INTERPRET BOOKS, MANUSCRIPTS, PAINTINGS, PRINTS, SCULPTURES, MAPS & DOCUMENTS RELATING TO THE AMER. REV. & FORMATION OF A NEW NATION. (REGN'L). MS SUE HULL; HUNTINGTON LIBRARY ART GALLERY & BOTANICAL GARDEN; 1151 OXFORD RD; SAN MARINO, CA 91108. (#149-2).

WOMEN IN COLONIAL LITERATURE. A STUDY OF HOW WOMEN ARE PORTRAYED IN COLONIAL LITERATURE AND THE RELATIONSHIP OF SUCH PORTRAYALS TO THE ACTUAL LIVES OF WOMEN IN THE PERIOD. (NAT'L). ANN STANFORD, PROFESSOR OF ENGLISH; CALIFORNIA STATE UNIV, NORTHRIDGE; NORTHRIDGE, CA 91324. (#5390).

200 YEARS OF MEXICAN AMERICAN COOPERATION, A MURAL. A MURAL DEPICTING 200 YEARS OF SHARED BORDERS BETWEEN THE UNITED STATES & MEXICO, JOINT PROGRESS, TECHNOLOGY, LEADERSHIP & DEMOCRATIC PRINCIPLES. (LOCAL). WILLIAM J MCCANN, MUSEUM DIRECTOR; CALIFORNIA MUSEUM OF SCIENCE AND INDUSTRY; 700 STATE DR, EXPOSITION PK; LOS ANGELES, CA 90037. (#7057).

'50 FLYING YEARS' HISTORY OF COMMERCIAL AIRLINE. THE HISTORY OF AMERICA'S SENIOR AIRLINE & THE AIRLINE INDUSTRY, WILL BE AUTHORED BY ROBERT SERLING & PUBLISHED FOR THE 50TH ANNIVERSARY AT THE TIME OF THE BICENTENNIAL, APRIL 17, 1976. (NAT'L). RAY SILVIUS, V P OF CORPORATE AFFAIRS; WESTERN AIRLINES INC; 6060 AVION DRIVE; LOS ANGELES, CA 90009. (#6892).

JAN 1, '74 - JAN 1, '77. PRESIDENTIAL AND STATE CAPITOL SERIES OF PAINTINGS. SERIES OF PAINTINGS, 'PRESIDENTIAL BIRTHPLACES' BY GERALD J. BURNS. THESE PAINTINGS DEPICT THE BIRTHPLACE HOMES AND THE PERIOD OF TIME OF EACH OF OUR HONORED PRESIDENTS. AT GALLERY 666 NORTH COAST HY. LAGUNA BEACH CALIF.. (ST-WIDE). GERALD J BURNS; COLLECTORS CHOICE GALLERY CORNSTALK FOUNDATION; 460 HIGH DRIVE; LAGUNA BEACH, CA 92651. (#3872-1).

APR 1 - 30, '74. NEW CHAMBER WORK BY JOHN ADAMS PERFORMED BY TONE ROADS WEST. NEW AMERICAN MUSIC BY COMPOSER JOHN ADAMS. GRANT/FELLOWSHIP SPONSORED BY NATL ENDOWMENT FOR THE ARTS TO AID IN PERFORMANCES OF NEW MUSIC BY JOHN ADAMS IN LOS ANGELES, ATLANTA, & OTHER AREAS. (ST-WIDE). JOHN ADAMS, DIRECTOR; JOHN ADAMS; ROUTE 1, BOX 44; STOCKBRIDGE, GA 30281. (#1221-901).

OCT 1 - 31, '74. NEW WORK BY JOHN ADAMS PERFORMED BY TONE ROADS WEST. NEW AMERICAN MUSIC BY COMPOSER JOHN ADAMS. GRANT/FELLOWSHIP SPONSORED BY NATL ENDOWMENT FOR THE ARTS TO AID IN PERFORMANCES OF NEW MUSIC BY JOHN ADAMS IN LOS ANGELES, ATLANTA, & OTHER AREAS. (ST-WIDE). JOHN ADAMS, DIRECTOR; JOHN ADAMS; ROUTE 1, BOX 44; STOCKBRIDGE, GA 30281. (#1221-904).

MAY 22 - 23, '75. INTERNATIONAL HERITAGE FAIR OF LOS ANGELES. A 1-3 DAY CELEBRATION, SPOTLIGHTING THE CONTRIBUTIONS OF THE MANY ETHNIC GROUPS LIVING IN LOS ANGELES. AT LOS ANGELES CITY HALL MALL. (LOCAL). OLEH CHAIKOVSKY, CHAIRMAN; INTERNATIONAL HERITAGE TEAM, L A CITY BICENTENNIAL COMMITTEE; 4002 RAND CT; SHERMAN OAKS, CA 91423. (#12488-1).

JUNE 9, '75 - DEC 31, '76. 'THE EAGLE WITHIN' - MULTI-MEDIA PRODUCTION AT BUSCH GARDENS. 15 MINUTE MULTI-SENSORY PRODUCTION OF COLLECTION OF AMERICANS WITH ONE THING IN COMMON: EACH EPITOMIZES USA EXCELLENCE IN SCIENCE, INDUSTRY, THE CRAFTS, ARTS & ATHLETICS; WILL BE SHOWN CONTINUOUSLY. (REGN'L). JOSEPH T FINNIGAN, DIR; FLEISHMAN-HILLARD, INC; ONE MEMORIAL DR; ST LOUIS, MO 63102. (#101234-2).

JULY 1, '75 - DEC 31, '76. HISTORICAL PANORAMA OF AMERICAN DEVELOPMENT IN SONG. LIVE PERFORMANCE. (LOCAL). JUDITH BERMAN, DIRECTOR; THE MUSART SINGERS; 5358 OSTROM AVE; ENCINO, CA 91316. (#6286-501).

JULY 3, '75 - DEC 1, '76. PERFORMANCE OF CHAMBER OPERA BY MONDAY EVENING CONCERTS. A CHAMBER OPERA BASED ON PLATO'S 'ALLEGORY OF THE CAVE' WILL BE PRESENTED. (REGN'L). DORRANCE STALVEY; MONDAY EVENING CONCERTS; 5905 WILSHIRE BLVD; LOS ANGELES, CA 90036. (#6500-502).

JULY 4 - 6, '75. BICENTENNIAL CONCERT FOR NATIONAL EDUCATION ASSOCIATION. LIVE PERFORMANCE AT LA CONVENTION CENTER AND SHRINE AUDITORIUM. (LOCAL). EASTER BEEKLY; INTERNATIONAL CHILDREN'S CHOIR; PO BOX 5656; LONG BEACH, CA 90805. (#200006-17).

JULY 15 - AUG 13, '75. 'USA '76: THE FIRST TWO HUNDRED YEARS' EXHIBIT IN LOS ANGLES, CA. THIS TRAVELING EXHIBIT PREPARED BY THE ARBA WILL TOUR 10 CITIES DURING THE BICENTENNIAL. IT EXPLORES THE CULTURAL AND SCIENTIFIC HERITAGE OF THE USA. AT AEROSPACE BLDG OF CALIF MUSEUM OF SCIENCE & INDUSTRY. (REGN'L). JACK MASEY; AMERICAN REVOLUTION BICENTENNIAL ADMINISTRATION; 2401 E STREET, NW; WASHINGTON, DC 20276. (#5661-503).

AUG 5 - 10, '75. SAN FERNANDO VALLEY GOLDEN DAYS, VALLEY HISTORY AND CULTURE. FESTIVAL. (LOCAL). SANDY BROWN, PROGRAM ASST; RECREATION & PARKS, CITY OF LOS ANGELES; 200 N MAIN, ROOM 1330; LOS ANGELES, CA 90012. (#100802-1).

AUG 14 - NOV 9, '75. EAGLE EYE AND APPLE PIE - GRAPHIC ART EXHIBIT. EXHIBIT. (LOCAL). WILLIAM MCCANN, DIR; CALIFORNIA MUSEUM OF SCIENCE AND INDUSTRY; 700 STATE DR, EXPOSITION PARK; LOS ANGELES, CA 90037. (#102822-1).

AUG 20 - SEPT 20, '75. ART EXHIBIT OF HUNGARIAN FOLKLORE, HISTORY, ART & MUSIC. EXHIBIT AT CALIFORNIA MUSEUM OF SCIENCE AND INDUSTRY. (LOCAL). MARIA FENYES, DIRECTOR; THE WORLD FEDERATION OF HUNGARIAN ARTISTS; 105 S WESTERN AVE; LOS ANGELES, CA 90004. (#102230-1).

SEPT 1, '75 - CONTINUING . '50 FLYING YEARS' - HISTORICAL AVIATION EXHIBIT. AMERICAS SENIOR AIRLINE IS CREATING A MUSEUM OF THE COMMERCIAL AVIATION INDUSTRYS 50 YEARS OF HISTORY. INCLUDED IS THEIR RESTORED ORIGINAL ARIPLANE & HUNDREDS OF SIGNIFICANT ARTIFACTS & RECORDS. (REGN'L). RAY SILVIUS; WESTERN AIRLINES INC; 6060 AVION DRIVE; LOS ANGELES, CA 90009. (#6891-1).

SEPT 7, '75. BICENTENNIAL CRAFTS - DAY IN THE PARK. FAIR. (LOCAL). MS CLARA LOUVIER, DIR; DEPARTMENT OF RECREATION AND PARKS OF LOS ANGELES; 200 N MAIN, ROOM 1330; LOS ANGELES, CA 90012. (#100800-1).

SEPT 12 - OCT 12, '75. L A PERFORMING ARTS FESTIVAL. LIVE PERFORMANCE AT BARNSDALL PARK, 4800 HOLLYWOOD, HOLLYWOOD, CALIF. (LOCAL). WARREN CHRISTENSEN, DIR; THEATRE-IN-PROGRESS; 2625 PORTLAND ST; LOS ANGELES, CA 90007. (#102235-1).

SEPT 28, '75. FERIA DE LOS NINOS, CELEBRATION HONORING THE SPANISH COMMUNITY. FESTIVAL AT HOLLENBECK PARK, 4TH & ST LOUIS. (LOCAL). CLARA LOUVIER, PROJ COORD; CITY OF LOS ANGELES DEPT OF RECREATION AND PARKS; 200 N MAIN, RM 1330; LOS ANGELES, CA 90012. (#102029-1).

OCT 1, '75 - MAY 31, '76. SIX-CONCERT SERIES AT MUSIC CENTER PAVILION. GLENDALE, CA, SYMPHONY HIGHLIGHTING AMER COMPOSERS. THE 1975-76 CONCERT SEASON OF THE GLENDALE, CA SYMPHONY ORCHESTRA WILL BE DEVOTED EXCLUSIVELY TO WORKS BY AMERICAN COMPOSERS. (ST-WIDE). RICHARD F PERRY, MANAGER; GLENDALE SYMPHONY ASSOC; 401 N BRAND BLVD, SUITE 832; GLENDALE, CA 91203. (#2395-501).

OCT 1, '75 - CONTINUING . BLACK ACHIEVEMENT EXHIBIT. EXHIBIT DEPICTING PEOPLE, ISSUES & EVENTS SHAPING BLACK ACHIEVEMENT IN THE UNITED STATES SINCE 1492. (REGN'L). WILLIAM J MCCANN,DIR; CALIFORNIA MUSEUM OF SCIENCE & INDUSTRY; 700 STATE DR; LOS ANGELES, CA 90037. (#1073-1).

OCT 9, '75. LOS ANGELES COUNTY COMMITTEE ON AGING BICENTENNIAL BANQUET. FESTIVAL AT 404 S BIXELL. (LOCAL). GEORGE H TOLL, COORD; LOS ANGELES COUNTY COMMITTEE ON AGING; 3632 ROSE AVE; LONG BEACH, CA 90807. (#200006-53).

OCT 25, '75. FROM THE ANCIENT KINGDOMS. A SYMPHONY ON THE HISTORY OF BLACK PEOPLES FROM THE ANCIENT KINGDOMS TO WATTS - AND BEYOND; HAS BEEN COMMISSIONED. COMPOSED BY HORACE TAPSCOTT. AT LOS ANGELES MUSIC CENTER. (LOCAL). MORR;S EWING; WATTS COMMUNITY SYMPHONY ASSOC; 900 GRAPE ST; LOS ANGELES, CA 90002. (#12500-1).

OCT 27, '75. SYMPHONY CONCERT HONORING DR WILLIAM GRANT STILL. LIVE PERFORMANCE AT MUSIC CENTER, 135 N GRAND AVE. (LOCAL). MS FRAN ZONE, DIRECTOR; DR WILLIAM GRANT

LOS ANGELES — CONTINUED

STILL FOUNDATION; 417 S HOLT, #203; LOS ANGELES, CA 90048. (#102232-1).

OCT 28, '75. MUSICALE PRESENTATION. LIVE PERFORMANCE. (LOCAL). JUDITH BERMAN, DIRECTOR; THE MUSART SINGERS; 5358 OSTROM AVE; ENCINO, CA 91316. (#6286-503).

NOV 1 - 20, '75. BICENTENNIAL CELEBRITY QUILT IN LOS ANGELES, CA. CELEBRITIES FROM MOTION PICTURES, TV, POLITICS AND SPORTS WILL EACH DESIGN, SEW AND AUTOGRAPH A SQUARE FOR A QUILT COMMEMORATING THE BICENTENNIAL TO BE DISPLAYED THROUGHOUT LOS ANGELES. (ST-WIDE). MS BARBARA ROSENSTEIN; LOS ANGELES CITY BICENTENNIAL ORGANIZATION; 10100 SANTA MONICA BLVD, SUITE 2; LOS ANGELES, CA 90067. (#12551-1).

NOV 14, '75 - JAN 11, '76. GREAT AMERICAN FACE BICENTENNIAL EXHIBIT. EXHIBIT AT CA MUSEUM OF SCIENCE & INDUSTRY, SPACE MUSEUM, EXPOSITION PARK. (ST-WIDE). SUE S BROWN, COORD; KINNEY SHOE CORPORATION; 233 BROADWAY, 15TH FLOOR; NEW YORK, NY 10007. (#200006-56).

DEC 1, '75. FIRST PROGRAM OF ALL-AMERICAN BICENTENNIAL. GAYLORD CARTER, ORGANIST, PLAYING FOR SHOWING OF SILENT FILM 'BIRTH OF A NATION'. AT HOLLYWOOD HS. (LOCAL). XENIA A DESBY, DEAN; LOS ANGELES CHAPTER, AMERICAN GUILD OF ORGANISTS; 6234 SCENIC AVE; HOLLYWOOD, CA 90068. (#200006-427).

DEC 1 - 15, '75. THE ANNUAL BILL OF RIGHTS ESSAY CONTEST. AN ESSAY CONTEST ON 'WHAT THE BILL OF RIGHTS MEANS TO ME' IN 300 WORDS OR LESS; 18 ESSAY WINNERS WILL BE HONORED AT A BANQUET. AT ESSAYS WRITTEN AT HOME; SENT TO ENGLISH & HISTORY TEACHERS.. (LOCAL). GLORIA REISS, DIRECTOR; LOS ANGELES HERALD EXAMINER; 11TH & BROADWAY; LOS ANGELES, CA 90015. (#102470-2).

DEC 13, '75. LA FIESTA DE LOS ANGELES PARADE OF LIGHTS. FLOATS, BANDS, EQUESTRIANS, SPECIALTY UNITS. AT FIRST ST & BROADWAY, BROADWAY TO 7TH ST, 7TH ST TO FIGUEROA. (ST-WIDE). VICKY THOMAS, CHAIRMAN; LOS ANGELES JUNIOR CHAMBER OF COMMERCE; 1076 W 7TH ST; LOS ANGELES, CA 90017. (#103618-3).

DEC 28, '75 - JAN 3, '76. SPIRIT OF AMERICA, A PATRIOTIC PAGEANT. LIVE PERFORMANCE AT LOS ANGELES SPORTS ARENA, 3939 S FIGUEROA. (LOCAL). COL GERALD C BURCH, DIR; UNITED STATES ARMY; 10104 WILSHIRE BLVD; LOS ANGELES, CA 90024. (#102030-1).

JAN 3 - 4, '76. CANADA WEEKEND AT DISNEYLAND. PIPERS, HIGHLAND DANCERS & MASSED BRASS BAND. (INT'L). K DE B PERCY; GOVERNMENT OF CANADA; 1746 MASSACHUSETTS AVE, NW; WASHINGTON, DC 20036. (#104880-1).

JAN 14 - APR 14, '76. AUTHENTIC LIVING HISTORICAL DRAMA. SCHOOL AND COMMUNITY CLUB TOUR OF EIGHT HISTORICAL THEMES HAVING SIGNIFICANT BUT LITTLE KNOWN CONTRIBUTIONS TO FREEDOM BY AMER BLACKS, WOMEN AND LESSER KNOWN PATRIOTS. (LOCAL). CONNIE FRIEND, SEC; SOCIAL ISSUES RESEARCH COUNCIL; 18345 VENTURA BLVD; TARZANA, CA 91356. (#23768-1).

JAN 15 - FEB 15, '76. UPBEAT 200 - S F VALLEY MUSIC FESTIVAL - MAYOR'S COMMITTEE. LIVE PERFORMANCE. (LOCAL). JUDITH BERMAN, DIRECTOR; THE MUSART SINGERS; 5358 OSTROM AVE; ENCINO, CA 91316. (#6286-502).

JAN 16 - FEB 17, '76. MANUSCRIPTS OF THE AMERICAN REVOLUTION, EXHIBIT. THE SMITHSONIAN INSTITUTION'S UNIQUE COLLECTION OF ORIGINAL LETTERS AND DOCUMENTS TO BE ON DISPLAY IN FOREST LAWN'S HALL OF LIBERTY. AT HALL OF LIBERTY BLDG. (LOCAL). ROBERT L WHEELER, CHMN; FOREST LAWN MEMORIAL PARK ASSOC; 6300 FOREST LAWN DR; LOS ANGELES, CA 90068. (#103618-2).

JAN 17 - FEB 18, '76. 'RED, WHITE & BLUES'. LIVE PERFORMANCE, FESTIVAL AT TOPANGA PLAZA MALL, WOODLAND HILLS & TEMPLE JUDEA. (LOCAL). JUDITH M BERMAN, DIRECTOR; UPBEAT 200 - SAN FERNANDO VALLEY BICENTENNIAL MUSIC FESTIVAL; 5358 OSTROM AVE; ENCINO, CA 91316. (#200006-158).

JAN 18 - 19, '76. 'PROFILE 76' EASTMAN KODAK CO'S MULTI-MEDIA BICENTENNIAL SHOW. EXHIBIT AT THORNE HALL OCCIDENTAL COLLEGE, 1600 CAMPUS RD. (LOCAL). LLOYD STONE, DIRECTOR; ROCKY'S CAMERA SHOP; 5110 YORK BLVD; LOS ANGELES, CA 90042. (#104514-1).

JAN 24, '76. BICENTENNIAL INTERNATIONAL FOLK DANCE FESTIVAL. BICENTENNIAL FESTIVAL SALUTES ETHNIC GROUPS' CONTRIBUTIONS TO THIS NATION. AT LOS ANGELES MUSIC CENTER, DOROTHY CHANDLER PAVILION. (ST-WIDE). IRWIN PARNES, COORDINATOR; LA MUSIC CENTER; LA MUSIC CENTER; LOS ANGELES, CA 90069. (#103416-86).

JAN 24 - FEB 26, '76. SALUTE TO THE AMERICAN WEST. MIXED MEDIA EXHIBIT ILLUSTRATES LIFE OF THE AMERICAN WESTERN FRONTIER. AT CA MUSEUM OF SCIENCE & INDUSTRY; EDGERTON HALL. (ST-WIDE). JOAN PUMBAULD, COORD; WOMEN ARTISTS OF AMERICAN WEST; 700 STATE ST; LOS ANGELES, CA 90007. (#103416-138).

FEB 8 - 15, '76. AFRO-AMERICAN HISTORY WEEK. DURING AFRO-AMERICAN HISTORY WEEK, A CELEBRATION WILL BE HELD, INCL A PUBLIC MEETING & A VARIOUS PROGRAMS, BOTHE ENTERTAINMENT & EDUCATIONAL. (LOCAL). MRS VASSIE WRIGHT; OUR AUTHORS STUDY CLUB; 3439 5TH AVE; LOS ANGELES, CA 90018. (#5370-501).

FEB 20 - 22, '76. 'THE BRITISH ARE COMING!' - BRITISH MILITARY BAND PERFORMANCE. LIVE PERFORMANCE AT THE FORUM. (INT'L). CHARLES K JONES, PRES; COLUMBIA ARTISTS FESTIVALS CORP; 165 W 57TH ST; NEW YORK, NY 10019. (#6532-23).

FEB 27, '76. ARMENIAN NUMISMATIC MEDAL AWARD. AWARD. (ST-WIDE). Y T NERCESSIAN, SECRETARY; ARMENIAN NUMISMATIC SOCIETY; 8511 BEVERLY PARK PL; PICO RIVERA, CA 90660. (#6204-502).

FEB 28 - JULY 4, '76. 'A BICENTENNIAL SUITE', INTAGLIO & RELIEF PRINTS - TOUR OF LA COUNTY. EXHIBIT, TOUR AT VARIOUS SITES IN THE LOS ANGELES AREA. (LOCAL). HARRIET ZEITLIN, ARTIST; DEPT OF PARKS & RECREATION; 202 S SALTAIR AVE; LOS ANGELES, CA 90049. (#23677-1).

MAR 13, '76. TRI-CHAPTER CONCLAVE - THE UCLA ALL-AMERICAN SYMPOSIUM. 1PM LECTURE ON LEO SOWERBY BY DR R L TUSLER; UCLA MADRIGAL SINGERS DON WEISS, CONDUCTOR, M BRADSHAW, ORGANIST; 2:30 MULTI-CHOICE LECTURE; 4PM UCLA SYMPHONIC WIND ENSEMBLE; 8:30 DANCE DEPT CONCERT, PREMIERE WORK BY PIA GILBERT. AT UCLA, ROYCE HALL; PUBLIC PARKING AT UNIV OF CALIF. (LOCAL). XENIA DESBY, COORD; AMERICAN GUILD OF ORGANISTS, LOS ANGELES CHAPTER; 6234 SCENIC AVE; HOLLYWOOD, CA 90068. (#104525-2).

APR 5, '76. AMERICAN YOUTH SYMPHONY ORCHESTRA CONCERT; MEHLI MEHTA, CONDUCTOR. 2 FULL LENGTH ORGAN CONCERTOS PLAYED BY KEMO SMITH AND MARTHA KOON, YOUNG ARTIST COMPETITION WINNERS OF THE LOS ANGELES CHAPTER. AT FIRST BAPTIST CHURCH OF L A - 760 S WESTMORELAND. (LOCAL). XENIA DESBY, COORD; AMERICAN GUILD OF ORGANISTS, LOS ANGELES CHAPTER; 6234 SCENIC AVE; HOLLYWOOD, CA 90068. (#104525-1).

APR 9, '76. CHORAL CONCERT WITH EMPHASIS ON AMERICAN MUSIC. LIVE PERFORMANCE AT CHAPEL OF THE SACRED HEART/ LOYOLA MARYMOUNT UNIV WESTCHESTER. (LOCAL). RICHARD H TRAME, DIRECTOR; LOYOLA MARYMOUNT UNIVERSITY CHORAL SERIES; 7101 W 80TH ST; LOS ANGELES, CA 90045. (#102965-1).

APR 11, '76. ODORI FESTIVAL OF JAPAN VISITS THE UNIVERSITY OF CALIFORNIA. LIVE PERFORMANCE AT PAULEY PAVILION. (INT'L). DIRECTOR; MEL HOWARD PRESENTS; 143 E 27TH ST; NEW YORK, NY 10016. (#108965-4).

APR 13 - OCT 31, '76. 'THE TRICENTENNIAL' - WHAT CHANGES SHOULD THERE BE?. A CHANCE TO TELL WHAT CHANGES SHOULD BE BY 2076 IN SUCH FIELDS AS ENTERTAINMENT, GOVERNMENT, ECOLOGY, BUSINESS, ENERGY, ETC. ALL IDEAS SHALL BECOME PUBLIC PROPERTY & MAY BE SUBMITTED IN ANY FORMAT. ALL WILL BE ANALYZED & A FULL REPORT WILL BE MADE BY ATLANTIC RICHFIELD. (NAT'L). DIRECTOR, TRICENTENNIAL; ATLANTIC RICHFIELD CO; PO BOX 2076; LOS ANGELES, CA 90053. (#106788-1).

APR 14 - 20, '76. 'TARGET '76' BICENTENNIAL EXPO. 'TARGET '76' WILL HOST A JOB FAIR, BUSINESS & CULTURAL EXPOSITIONS; THE EXPO IS OPEN TO THE PUBLIC, EXHIBITORS & ADVERTISERS. THERE WILL BE A VARIETY OF HISTORICAL & CULTURAL ACTIVITIES WITH CONTINUOUS LIVE ENTERTAINMENT. AT LOS ANGELES CONVENTION CENTER. (REGN'L). EDWARD K BURBAGE, DIR; 'TARGET '76' BICENTENNIAL EXPO; 1305 TREMAINE AVE; LOS ANGELES, CA 90019. (#103006-1).

APR 17, '76. '50 FLYING YEARS' REFLYING OF FIRST FLIGHT ON THE 50TH ANNIVERSARY. THE FULLY RESTORED DOUGLAS M-2 BIPLANE THAT MADE THE ORIGINAL FLIGHT WILL AGAIN FLY THE ROUTE AND PARTICIPATE IN COMMEMORATIVE EVENTS OF AVIATION HISTORY. A LARGE PUBLIC CEREMONY WILL SEE THE FLIGHT OFF AT ITS START IN LOS ANGELES. AT LOS ANGELES INTERNATIONAL AIRPORT. (NAT'L). MR RAY SILVIUS; WESTERN AIRLINES INC; 6060 AVION DRIVE; LOS ANGELES, CA 90009. (#6893-1).

APR 19, '76. CONCERT BY LA CHAMBER ORCHESTRA PRESENTING NEW COMPOSITION. GUITAR CONCERTO TO BE PERFORMED BY PEPE ROMERO. AT MARK TAPER FORUM MUSIC CENTER. (LOCAL). WINIFRED H RUTTER; LOS ANGELES CHAMBER ORCHESTRA; 1777 N VINE STREET, #400; LOS ANGELES, CA 90028. (#16162-1).

MAY 1, '76 - CONTINUING . CALIFORNIA STATE OF THE NATION. MULTI-MEDIA PRESENTATION ON CALIFORNIA INDUSTRIES. PERMANENT EXHIBIT AT THE CAL MUSEUM OF SCIENCE AND INDUSTRY, LOS ANGELES; A TRAVELLING EXHIBIT TO SCIENCE MUSEUMS THROUGHOUT THE U S. AT LOS ANGELES. (ST-WIDE). WILLIAM J MCCANN, DIR; CA MUSEUM OF SCIENCE & INDUSTRY; 700 STATE DR; LOS ANGELES, CA 90037. (#14990-1).

MAY 12, '76. THE ANNUAL AMERICAN HISTORY EXAM. AN ESSAY, MULTIPLE CHOICE, & FILL IN BLANKS EXAM FOR ACADEMICALLY ADVANCED HIGH SCHOOL STUDENTS IN LOS ANGELES AND ORANGE COUNTIES. U S SAVINGS BONDS AND SAVINGS ACCTS AWARDS PRESENTED TO WINNERS. AT 6 TEST CENTERS AT CONVENIENT SCHOOLS. (LOCAL). GLORIA REISS, DIRECTOR; LOS ANGELES HERALD EXAMINER; 11TH & BROADWAY; LOS ANGELES, CA 90015. (#102470-1).

MAY 13 - 14, '76. BRITISH BICENTENNIAL HERITAGE MISSION. 8 BRITISH LEADERS, 5 OF THEM MEMBERS OF THE HOUSE OF LORDS, WILL VISIT THE U S AS PART OF BRITAIN'S OFFICIAL SALUTE TO THE BICENTENNIAL. (INT'L). DIRECTOR; BRITISH EMBASSY; 3100 MASSACHUSETTS AVE, NW; WASHINGTON, DC 20008. (#109043-12).

MAY 16, '76. CHORAL CONCERT WITH EMPHASIS ON AMERICAN MUSIC. LIVE PERFORMANCE AT CHAPEL OF THE SACRED HEART/ LOYOLA MARYMOUNT UNIV WESTCHESTER. (LOCAL). RICHARD H TRAME, DIRECTOR; LOYOLA MARYMOUNT UNIVERSITY CHORAL SERIES; 7101 W 80TH ST; LOS ANGELES, CA 90045. (#102965-2).

MAY 17, '76. THE BICENTENNIAL ART SHOW, AN EXHIBIT OF CULINARY SKILLS BY CHEFS. EXHIBIT AT HOLLYWOOD PALLADIUM, 6215 W SUNSET BLVD. (LOCAL). RICHARD L MORGAN, DIR; THE CHEFS DE CUISINE ASSOC OF CALIFORNIA INC; 607 S PARK VIEW, ELK'S BLDG; LOS ANGELES, CA 90057. (#102063-1).

MAY 22 - 23, '76. INTERNATIONAL HERITAGE FESTIVAL. THE ARTISTIC, LITERARY, CULINARY & MUSICAL TRADITIONS OF THE ETHNIC COMMUNITIES ARE DISPLAYED IN THIS TWO-DAY FESTIVAL. SUNDAY HOURS: 10 AM - 8 PM. AT LOS ANGELES MALL. (LOCAL). DR KITTY CURTIZ; INTERNATIONAL HERITAGE TEAM; LOS ANGELES BICENTENNIAL COMMITTEE; 6380 WILSHIRE BLVD, SUITE 806; LOS ANGELES, CA 90048. (#103416-336).

MAY 25 - JULY 6, '76. HUBERT STOWITTS EXHIBIT. AN ANTHROPOLOGICAL STUDY OF THE FAR EAST WITH PAINTINGS OF THE JAPANESE THEATER, VANISHING CRAFTSMEN OF INDIA, JAPANESE KABUKI DANCERS AND COURT COSTUMES OF ANCIENT CHINA. AT EXPOSITION PARK, 700 STATE DR. (ST-WIDE). WILLIAM J MCCANN; CALIFORNIA MUSEUM OF SCIENCE AND INDUSTRY; 700 STATE DR, EXPOSITION PARK; LOS ANGELES, CA 90037. (#7056-1).

MAY '76. VISIT BY QUEEN MARGRETHE II AND PRINCE HENRICK OF DENMARK. TOUR. (INT'L). BENT SKOU, PRESS OFFICE; DANISH EMBASSY; 3200 WHITEHAVEN PKY, NW; WASHINGTON, DC 20008. (#104972-17).

JUNE 3 - SEPT 30, '76. EXHIBIT OF ANCIENT & MEDIEVAL ARMENIAN COINS & MODERN PAPER NOTES. SLIDES ON COINS AND ARMENIAN NUMISMATIC AWARD, CA. COLOR SLIDE LIBRARY ON ARMENIAN ANCIENT AND MEDIEVAL COINS & MODERN PAPER NOTES. ESTABLISHMENT OF SILVER MEDAL AWARD TO THE BEST WRITER OF ARMENIAN NUMISMATIC BOOK TO BE AWARDED ANNUALLY. (ST-WIDE). Y T NERCESSIAN, SECRETARY; ARMENIAN NUMISMATIC SOCIETY; 8511 BEVERLY PARK PL; PICO RIVERA, CA 90660. (#6204-501).

JUNE 4, '76. LLOYD HOLZGRAF, ORGANIST. CONCERT OF ORGAN COMPOSITIONS BY AMERICAN BORN COMPOSERS. AT FIRST CONGREGATIONAL CHURCH, 540 S COMMONWEALTH, LOS ANGELES. (LOCAL). XENIA DESBY, COORD; AMERICAN GUILD OF ORGANISTS (L A CHAPTER) & 1ST CONGREGATION CHURCH; 6234 SCENIC AVE; HOLLYWOOD, CA 90068. (#104523-1).

JUNE 11 - 13, '76. INTERNATIONAL PHILATELIC EXHIBIT OF STAMPS & RELATED BICENT HISTORY. FANTASTIC SHOW WITH EXHIBITS, DEALERS & FOREIGN GOVERNMENT POST OFFICE COMING FROM AROUND THE WORLD WILL BE LARGEST SHOW EVER HELD IN THE WEST; EXHIBIT WILL STRESS BICENTENNIAL. AT INTERNATIONAL HOTEL, 6225 W CENTURY BLVD; $.50 PER DAY PARKING. (NAT'L). ISRAEL I BICK, EX DIR; INTL STAMP COLLECTORS SOCIETY; BOX 48806; LOS ANGELES, CA 90048. (#100393-1).

JUNE 14 - JULY 4, '76. BICENTENNIAL RELAY OF GOOD WILL. A RUN DEDICATED TO OUR 200TH ANNIVERSARY; THE CITIZENS AND PEACE OFFICERS OF LA & THE U S & CANADIAN OLYMPIANS WILL RUN NON-STOP TO MONTREAL, QUEBEC. AT START OF RACE - THE OLYMPIC TORCH, LA COLISEUM. (INT'L). ROBERT BURKE, PROJ DIR; LA POLICE BOOSTERS, 7-UP CO, S CA GAS, US AAU, CA JC'S, NIKE SHOES; 1880 N ACADEMY DR; LOS ANGELES, CA 90012. (#103618-4).

JUNE 26, '76. AIR FORCE BICENTENNIAL OPEN HOUSE. DEPICTING LATEST ADVANCEMENTS IN THE NATION'S SPACE AND MISSLE SYSTEMS. AT LOS ANGELES AIR FORCE STATION. (LOCAL). LT COL MILTON W KOHUT; AIR FORCE SPACE AND MISSILE SYSTEMS ORGANIZATION; PO BOX 92960 WORLDWAY POSTAL CTR; LOS ANGELES, CA 90009. (#200006-410).

JULY 1 - DEC 31, '76. 'AMERICA DREAMS ON...', BICENTENNIAL SCIENCE & INDUSTRY FAIR. AN EXHIBITION ON AMERICAN VALUES & IDEAS; TOPICS TO INCLUDE EDUCATION, LEISURE TIME, COMMUNICATION, THE STATUS OF WOMEN, WORK ETHIC, QUALITY OF LIFE & AN HISTORICAL & FUTURISTIC LOOK AT THE AMER DREAM. AT EXPOSITION PARK, 700 STATE DR. (REGN'L). WILLIAM J MCCANN; CALIFORNIA MUSEUM OF SCIENCE AND INDUSTRY; 700 STATE DR, EXPOSITION PK; LOS ANGELES, CA 90037. (#7058-1).

JULY 3, '76 - DEC 1, '77. PERFORMANCE OF 'CELEBRATION, SEQUENT II' BY L A PHILHARMONIC. A COMPOSITION FOR ORCHESTRA WILL BE PERFORMED TITLED, ' CELEBRATION, SEQUENT II'. (REGN'L). DORRANCE STALVEY; MONDAY EVENING CONCERTS; 5905 WILSHIRE BLVD; LOS ANGELES, CA 90036. (#6500-501).

JULY 4, '76. 'ALL NATION, ALL PEOPLE' LOS ANGELES COUNTY BICENTENNIAL PARADE. THE LONGEST PARADE IN THE NATION'S HISTORY MARKS THIS CELEBRATION OF AMERICA'S 200TH BIRTHDAY. AT WILSHIRE BLVD. (LOCAL). BILL MCCLELLAND, COORD; LOS ANGELES MUSIC CENTER; 135 N GRAND AVE; LOS ANGELES, CA 90012. (#103416-412).

JULY 4 - AUG 15, '76. THE FABRIC OF A NATION: 19TH CENTURY QUILTS AND QUILTMAKERS. HISTORIC RESEARCH OF FAMILY OWNED QUILTS NOW IN THE GREATER LOS ANGELES AREA. AN EXHIBIT IN 1976 WILL INCLUDE MAPS OF MIGRATION PATTERNS & PHOTOS, AS WELL AS 40 HISTORICALLY DOCUMENTED 19TH CENTURY QUILTS. AT LOS ANGELES MUNICIPAL ART GALLERY, BARNSDALL PARK. (LOCAL). MS SANDI FOX; 1000 W KENSINGTON RD; LOS ANGELES, CA 90026. (#7946-1).

JULY 6 - 8, '76. SCOTTISH NATIONAL ORCHESTRA CHORUS. LIVE PERFORMANCE AT HOLLYWOOD BOWL. (INT'L). CULTURAL AFFAIRS OFFICE; BRITISH EMBASSY; 3100 MASSACHUSETTS AVE, NW; WASHINGTON, DC 20008. (#108960-1).

JULY 6 - 15, '76. JAPANESE YOUTH GOODWILL CRUISE VISITS LOS ANGELES. HOURS ON WEDNESDAY 7 AM TO 9 AM; THURSDAY 4 PM TO 6 PM. (INT'L). MITAKE KATSUBE, COORD; JAPANESE PRIME MINISTER'S OFFICE; OCHANOMIZU WOMEN'S UNIV; TOKYO/JAPAN. (#109014-2).

JULY 11 - 15, '76. NATL FINNISH AMERICAN BICENTENNIAL MEETING AND FESTIVAL. BICENT FESTIVALS WILL BE HELD IN FINNISH-AMERICAN CENTERS LOCATED IN SEVERAL CITIES DURING 1976. (REGN'L). RALPH J JALKANEN, PRES; SUOMI COLLEGE; QUINCY ST; HANCOCK, MI 49930. (#8628-5).

LOS ANGELES — CONTINUED

JULY 24, '76 - CONTINUING . JOINT MUSIC AND DANCE CONCERTS. CONCERTS TO RUN AS AN ONGOING ACTIVITY WITH LOCAL PROFESSIONAL DANCERS, COMPOSERS AND MUSICIANS PARTICIPATING; TO BE GIVEN AS FREE CULTURAL EVENTS FOR THE COMMUNITY. KICK-OFF CONCERT ON SERIES IS 7/24/76 AT OLIVE RECREATION CENTER. AT LOS ANGELES COUNTY FACILITIES. (LOCAL). VALENTINA OUMANSKY, DIR; VALENTINA OUMANSKY DRAMATIC DANCE FOUNDATION, INC.; 14318 CHANDLER BLVD; VAN NUYS, CA 91401. (#104469-1).

AUG 1 - 7, '76. JAPAN-CALIFORNIA ASSOCIATION 1976 MEETING. THE THEME OF THIS EVENT IS 'A LONG LOOK AHEAD AT JAPANESE AND US RELATIONSHIPS'. AT CENTURY CITY HOTEL. (INT'L). DR W B GIBSON, VICE PRES; STANFORD RESEARCH INSTITUTE; MENLO PARK, CA 94025. (#104844-1).

AUG 14, '76. NISEI WEEK FESTIVAL KARATE CHAMPIONSHIP. COMPETITION AT KOYASAN HALL. (ST-WIDE). HIDETAKA NISHIYAMA, COORD; ALL AMERICA KARATE FEDERATION (SOUTHWEST REGION); 1440 W OLYMPIC BLVD; LOS ANGELES, CA 90015. (#109087-1).

AUG 16 - 27, '76. CARL HAVERLIN/BROADCAST MUSIC, INC, ARCHIVES BICENTENNIAL EXHIBIT. OFFERS A VERSATILE PICTURE OF HISTORY, REGIONAL LIFE & MUSIC FOR OVER 200 YEARS. CONTAINS PRESIDENTIAL LETTERS, LETTERS OF FAMOUS AMERICANS, OLD BOOKS, MANUSCRIPTS, HISTORY OF 'THE STAR SPANGLED BANNER' & COMPOSER AUTOGRAPHS, PLUS SHEET MUSIC OF THE PAST. AT CALIFORNIA MUSEUM OF SCIENCE AND INDUSTRY, 700 STATE DR. (ST-WIDE). MICHAEL L MOCK, ASST DIR; CALIFORNIA MUSEUM OF SCIENCE AND INDUSTRY; 700 STATE DR; LOS ANGELES, CA 90037. (#20784-5).

AUG 25, '76. ISRAELI PHILHARMONIC ORCHESTRA VISITS LOS ANGELES. LIVE PERFORMANCE. (INT'L). URI AHARON BAR-NEV; ISRAELI GOVERNMENT; 1621 21ST ST, NW; WASHINGTON, DC 20008. (#109015-1).

AUG 25 - SEPT 19, '76. STAR-SPANGLED HISTORY: DRAWINGS BY J B BEALE - MAGIC LANTERN ARTIST. NATIONAL TRAVELLING EXHIBITION OF 65 ORIGINAL WASH DRAWINGS BY JOSEPH BOGGS BEALE, 19TH CENTURY ILUSTRATOR. SLIDE PRESENTATION. AT CALIFORNIA MUSEUM OF SCIENCE & INDUSTRY, 700 STATE DR. (REGN'L). KAREN HUGHES, PROJ MGR; AMER NATL INSURANCE CO, AMER NATL TOWER OF GALVESTON, TX; RUDER & FINN, 110 E 59TH ST; NEW YORK, NY 10022. (#9820-8).

AUG 28, '76. ISRAELI PHILHARMONIC ORCHESTRA VISITS LOS ANGELES. LIVE PERFORMANCE. (INT'L). URI AHARON BAR-NEV; ISRAELI GOVERNMENT; 1621 21ST ST, NW; WASHINGTON, DC 20008. (#109015-3).

SEPT 4, '76. LOS ANGELES FOUNDERS DAY AND ETHNIC CULTURE FAIR. FESTIVAL, LIVE PERFORMANCE AT LOS ANGELES PLACITA. (LOCAL). EDDIE MAGIC, COORD; LOS ANGELES FOUNDERS CELEBRATION; 98525 ARDMORE; LOS ANGELES, CA 90036. (#103416-574).

SEPT 11, '76. SPIRIT OF '76 SHOW. BETWEEN-THE-GAMES SHOW - A PAGEANTRY OF MUSIC AND DANCE WILL DEPICT THE SPIRIT OF THE AMERICAN REVOLUTION, THE FREEDOM AND DIGNITY OF MAN. AT DODGER STADIUM. (REGN'L). GEORGE M WILLIAMS; NICHIREN SHOSHU ACADEMY; PO BOX 1427; SANTA MONICA, CA 90406. (#108211-1).

SEPT 18, '76. 1976 SOUTHWEST KARATE CHAMPIONSHIP. COMPETITION AT LOS ANGELES CITY COLLEGE MENS GYM. (REGN'L). HIDETAKA NISHIYAMA; HIDETAKE NISHIYAMA; 1440 WEST OLYMPIC BOULEVARD; LOS ANGELES, CA 90015. (#109086-1).

SEPT 19, '76. FESTIVAL OF FAITHS. PRESENTATIONS THROUGH MUSIC AND THE SPOKEN WORD BY THE MAJOR FAITHS REPRESENTED IN THE INTERRELIGIOUS COUNCIL OF SO. CA. AT FIRST UNITED METHODIST CHURCH, LOS ANGELES. (LOCAL). ROBERT C WALKER; INTERRELIGIOUS COUNCIL - L A CITY BICENTENNIAL COMMITTEE; 3460 WILSHIRE BLVD, SUITE 1012; LOS ANGELES, CA 90010. (#12506-1).

SEPT 19, '76. LONDON SCHOOLS SYMPHONY ORCHESTRA. LIVE PERFORMANCE AT HOLLYWOOD BOWL. (INT'L). CULTURAL AFFAIRS OFFICE; BRITISH EMBASSY; 3100 MASSACHUSETTS AVE, NW; WASHINGTON, DC 20008. (#108963-3).

SEPT 30 - NOV 21, '76. 'TWO CENTURIES OF BLACK AMERICAN ART' EXHIBITION. OPEN ON SATURDAYS & SUNDAYS 10:00AM TO 6:00PM. CLOSED THANKSGIVING, CHRISTMAS & NEW YEAR'S DAY. AT LOS ANGELES COUNTY MUSEUM OF ART-FRANCES & ARMAND HAMMER WING. (REGN'L). PUBLIC INFO OFFICE; LOS ANGELES COUNTY MUSEUM OF ART; 5905 WILSHIRE BLVD; LOS ANGELES, CA 90036. (#103416-575).

OCT 1 - 3, '76. ENERGY FAIR '76-CONSUMER SHOW: ENERGY CONSERVATION & ALTERNATIVES. AN ENERGY CAREER CENTER, PROCLAIMED BY MAYOR BRADLEY AS ENERGY FAIR WEEK. SOLAR AND WIND DEMONSTRATIONS IN OUTSIDE SPACE. AT L A CONVENTION CENTER, 1201 S FIGUEROA. (ST-WIDE). SHIRLEY SOLOMON, COORD; ENERGY FAIR, INC; 15915 ASILOMAR BLVD; PAC PALISADES, CA 90272. (#108308-1).

OCT 8 - 10, '76. FAR WEST SKI ASSOC 45TH ANNIVERSARY COMMEMORATION. COMPETITION, CEREMONY AT JACK TAR HOTEL. (REGN'L). CHUCK MORSE, EXEC ADMIN; US SKI ASSOC & FAR WEST SKI ASSOC.; 1313 W 8TH ST.; LOS ANGELES, CA 90017. (#2438-5).

OCT 11, '76. 'THE PROPHET BIRD' - BY KARL KOHN. LIVE PERFORMANCE AT LOS ANGELES COUNTY MUSEUM OF ART IN THE LEO S BING THEATER. (ST-WIDE). DORRANCE STALVEY, DIR; SOUTHERN CALIFORNIA CHAMBER MUSIC SOCIETY; 5905 WILSHIRE BLVD; LOS ANGELES, CA 90036. (#22019-1).

OCT 15 - 31, '76. 'THE WHITE HOUSE' PERFORMED BY THE HERITAGE PLAYERS - CA. HERITAGE PLAYERS WILL PERFORM 'THE WHITE HOUSE', A FULL LENGTH STAGE PRODUCTION. WRITTEN BY A E HOTCHNER. PERFORMANCES ON SAT, SUN & MON. THIS PRODUCTION AT THE REQUEST OF THE MUNICIPAL ARTS DEPT, BUREAU OF MUSIC, CITY OF LOS ANGELES. AT BARNSDALL GALLERY THEATRE, BARNSDALL PARK. (LOCAL). JOHN B MAC DONALD, DIR; HERITAGE PLAYERS; 14956 DICKENS ST; SHERMAN OAKS, CA 91403. (#7844-1).

OCT 16, '76. NAVAL & MARITIME SEAPOWER SYMPOSIUM & DEBATE. A DEBATE FOR LOS ANGELES AREA HIGH SCHOOLS ON THE IMPORTANCE OF SEAPOWER IN THE NEXT 100 YEARS. HIGH SCHOOL DEBATE TEAMS ARE INVITED TO PARTICIPATE & ARE PROVIDED W/FACILITIES FOR RESEARCH ON THE DEBATE QUESTION. (LOCAL). MICHAEL ELDREDGE, LT, USN; NROTC UNIT UCLA; 405 HILGARO AVE; LOS ANGELES, CA 90024. (#109332-1).

NOV 1 - DEC 31, '76. WORLD OF FRANKLIN & JEFFERSON EXHIBIT AT MUSEUM OF ART. AN EXHIBIT OF HISTORICAL MEMORABILIA SPANNING 120 YEARS IN THE LIVES OF FRANKLIN AND JEFFERSON. DESIGNED BY CHARLES EAMES & SHOWN BY USIA OVERSEAS & IN THE UNITED STATES IN 1976 BY THE ARBA. (REGN'L). JACK MASEY; AMERICAN REVOLUTION BICENTENNIAL ADMINISTRATION; 2401 E STREET, NW; WASHINGTON, DC 20276. (#112-506).

NOV 5, '76 - JAN 11, '77. SPANN 200: PARTICIPATION IN A NEW NATION, ROLE OF GERMAN AMERICANS. EXHIBIT AT SPACE MUSEUM, CA MUSEUM OF SCIENCE & INDUSTRY. (ST-WIDE). BUD HOPPS; NATIONAL CARL SCHURZ ASSOC; 700 STATE DR; LOS ANGELES, CA 90037. (#24060-5).

NOV 18 - DEC 23, '76. PACK-IN PAINTERS OF THE AMERICAN WEST. WESTERN AMERICAN LANDSCAPE PAINTS BY ARTISTS WHO 'PACKED-INTO' THE SUBJECT AREAS TO PAINT SPECIFIC SCENES. APPROXIMATELY 30 PAINTINGS FROM PUBLIC AND PRIVATE COLLECTIONS THROUGHOUT THE USA. AT FISHER GALLERY, HARRIS HALL, USC CAMPUS. (LOCAL). DONALD BREWER, DIRECTOR; UNIVERSITY OF SOUTHER CALIFORNIA, UNIVERSITY GALLERIES; 823 EXPOSITION BLVD; LOS ANGELES, CA 90007. (#107875-1).

NOV 22 - DEC 3, '76. CARL HAVERLIN/BROADCAST MUSIC, INC, ARCHIVES BICENTENNIAL EXHIBIT. OFFERS A VERSATILE PICTURE OF HISTORY, REGIONAL LIFE & MUSIC FOR OVER 200 YEARS. CONTAINS PRESIDENTIAL LETTERS, LETTERS OF FAMOUS AMERICANS, OLD BOOKS, MANUSCRIPTS, HISTORY OF 'THE STAR SPANGLED BANNER' & COMPOSER AUTOGRAPHS, PLUS SHEET MUSIC OF THE PAST. AT UNIV OF CALIFORNIA AT LA MUSIC LIBRARY, 1102 SCHOENBERG HALL. (ST-WIDE). MARSHA BERMAN, PGM MGR; UNIV OF CALIFORNIA AT LOS ANGELES; 1102 SCHOENBERG HALL; LOS ANGELES, CA 90024. (#20784-8).

DEC 4, '76. RUN FOR THE HANDICAPPED. COMPETITION AT GRIFFITHS PARK. (LOCAL). ADELL CAMPBELL, CHMN; LOS ANGELES LIVE STEAMERS; 6939 FULLBRIGHT AVE; CHATSWORTH, CA 91311. (#109456-1).

DEC 6 - 20, '76. CARL HAVERLIN/BROADCAST MUSIC, INC, ARCHIVES BICENTENNIAL EXHIBIT. OFFERS A VERSATILE PICTURE OF HISTORY, REGIONAL LIFE & MUSIC FOR OVER 200 YEARS. CONTAINS PRESIDENTIAL LETTERS, LETTERS OF FAMOUS AMERICANS, OLD BOOKS, MANUSCRIPTS, HISTORY OF 'THE STAR SPANGLED BANNER' & COMPOSER AUTOGRAPHS, PLUS SHEET MUSIC OF THE PAST. AT CALIFORNIA STATE UNIV AT LA MUSIC DEPT, 5151 STATE UNIVERSITY DR. (ST-WIDE). DR ROBERT, COORDINATOR; CALIFORNIA STATE UNIV AT LOS ANGELES; 5151 UNIVERSITY DR; LOS ANGELES, CA 90032. (#20784-9).

JAN '77 - CONTINUING . PLANNING AMERICA'S GREAT CITIES, AN EXHIBITION. EXHIBIT, RADIO/TV AT CALIFORNIA MUSEUM OF SCIENCE & INDUSTRY. (REGN'L). MS LEE KIMCHE; ASSOC OF SCIENCE & TECHNOLOGY; 2100 PENNSYLVANIA AVE, NW; WASHINGTON, DC 20037. (#8615-10).

APR 25, '77. 'THE ALLEGORY OF THE CAVE' - BY DORRANCE STALVEY. LIVE PERFORMANCE AT LEO S BING THEATRE AT THE LOS ANGELES COUNTY MUSEUM OF ART. (ST-WIDE). DORRANCE STALVEY, DIR; SOUTHERN CALIFORNIA CHAMBER MUSIC SOCIETY; 5905 WILSHIRE BLVD; LOS ANGELES, CA 90036. (#22019-2).

LOS BANOS

JUNE 22, '76. UNITED STATES ARMED FORCES BICENTENNIAL CARAVAN. CARAVAN IS COMPOSED OF EXHIBIT VANS FOR EACH MILITARY SERVICE. PROJECT THEME IS ' HISTORY OF THE ARMED FORCES & THEIR CONTRIBUTIONS TO THE NATION'. (LOCAL). CHUCK OLSEN, CHAIRMAN; U S ARMED FORCES BICENTENNIAL CARAVAN; PO BOX 1006; LOS BANOS, CA 93635. (#1775-578).

OCT 13, '76. UNITED STATES ARMED FORCES BICENTENNIAL CARAVAN. CARAVAN IS COMPOSED OF EXHIBIT VANS FOR EACH MILITARY SERVICE. PROJECT THEME IS 'HISTORY OF THE ARMED FORCES & THEIR CONTRIBUTIONS TO THE NATION'. (LOCAL). TIM MCNALLY; UNITED STATES ARMED FORCES BICENTENNIAL CARAVAN; C/O LOS BANOS BICENT COM; LOS BANOS, CA 93635. (#1775-824).

LOS GATOS

THE CALIFORNIA RELIEF MAP. MAP, DEVELOPED IN 1924, WILL BE RESTORED & MOUNTED ON TRAILERS FOR EXHIBITION THROUGHOUT THE STATE DURING 1976, THEN PERMANENTLY DISPLAYED BY THE CALIFORNIA STATE FOUNDATION. (ST-WIDE). CALIFORNIA STATE FOUNDATION; CALIFORNIA STATE FOUNDATION; 15879 LOS GATOS BLVD; LOS GATOS, CA 95030. (#7949).

'OUR PEOPLE' FESTIVAL, LOS GATOS, CALIF. THE CITY'S ETHNIC GROUPS WILL DEPICT THEIR HERITAGE IN SONG & DANCE. (LOCAL). DR GEORGE G BRUNTZ, CHAIRPERSON; LOS GATOS BICENTENNIAL COMMITTEE; 17041 LOS ROBLES; LOS GATOS, CA 95030. (#2306).

MAY 1, '76. LOYALTY DAY 1976 - VETERANS OF FOREIGN WARS. CEREMONY AT VASONA LAKE PARK, GROUP CIRCLE AREA, AREA 'C'. (LOCAL). SIDNEY R DESSAUER, CHMN; VETERANS OF FOREIGN WARS, DISTRICT 12; PO BOX 2131; SAN JOSE, CA 95151. (#200006-24).

LOS MOLINOS

BICENTENNIAL CELEBRATION OF LOS MOLINAS, CA. EVENTS INCLUDED FASHION SHOWS, TALENT SHOWS, RELIGIOUS ACTIVITIES, 4TH OF JULY PARADE, LIBERTY BELL EXHIBIT, COLONIAL TEA, PADDLE BOATS AND A BICENTENNIAL MEDAL PRESENTATION. (LOCAL). MERRIL BAUER, BICENT CHAIRMAN; LOS MOLINAS CHAMBER OF COMMERCE; 99 E; LOS MOLINAS, CA 96055. (#32367).

TOWN MEDALLION - LOS MOLINAS, CA. DIE CAST FOR MEDALLION. ONE SIDE, 1856 LOS MOLINAS SESMA MILL; OTHER SIDE, 13 STAR FLAG, FLAGS & PORTAL OF THE PAST AND OF 1976. TO BE SOLD IN NOV & DEC, 1976. (LOCAL). MERRILL BAUER, BICENT CHAIRMAN; LOS MOLINAS VOLUNTEER FIRE DEPT; N SHERWOOD BLVD; LOS MOLINAS, CA 96055. (#32368).

MAR 21 - 28, '76. DEDICATION OF NEW BLDG. SUNDAY SERVICE TRACED THE ORIGIN & DEVELOPMENT OF METHODISM IN THE US. CEREMONY WAS DEDICATION OF NEW CHURCH BUILDING WITH STATE & LOCAL CELEBRACIES PRESENT; FOLLOWED BY A DINNER AT VETS HALL. AT UNITED METHODIST CHURCH, JOSEPHINE & SHERWOOD BLVD. (LOCAL). MERRIL BAUER; LOS MOLINOS UNITED METHODIST CHURCH; 25101 2ND AVE; LOS MOLINOS, CA 96055. (#200006-474).

APR 24, '76. COLONIAL TEA IN COSTUME. CEREMONY AT LOS MOLINOS UNITED METHODIST CHURCH. (LOCAL). MERRIL BAUER; UNITED METHODIST WOMEN; 25101 2ND AVE; LOS MOLINOS, CA 96055. (#200006-472).

MAY 1, '76. FASHIONS-OLD & NEW. LIVE PERFORMANCE AT VETERAN'S MEMORIAL BLDG. (LOCAL). MERRIL BAUER; LOS MOLINOS WOMEN'S CLUB; 25101 2ND AVE; LOS MOLINOS, CA 96055. (#200006-471).

MAY 16, '76. HOME TALENT SHOW. HISTORICAL MUSIC & WOMEN THRU THE YEARS IN SKIT FORM. AT LOS MOLNOS VETERANS MEMORIAL BLDG. (LOCAL). VALENTINO NIELSEN; LOS MOLNOS BUSINESS & PROFESSIONAL WOMEN'S CLUB; 25192 NORTH CENTER; LOS MOLNOS, CA 96055. (#200006-469).

JULY 4, '76. FOURTH OF JULY PARADE & PICNICS. FAIR, PARADE AT N SHERWOOD BLVD. (LOCAL). MERRILL BAUER; LOS MOLINOS FIRE DEPT; 25101 2ND AVE; LOS MOLINOS, CA 96055. (#200006-470).

JULY 4, '76. LIBERTY BELL FLOAT IN 4TH OF JULY PARADE. PARADE AT MAIN ST. (LOCAL). MERRIL BAUER; LOS MOLINOS BUSINESS & PROFESSIONAL WOMEN'S CLUB; 25101 2ND AVE; LOS MOLINOS, CA 96055. (#200006-473).

MADERA

JULY 1 - 5, '76. BICENTENNIAL WEEK. JULY 1-2, MUSICAL 'AMERICA SINGS'; JULY 3, OLD-FASHIONED CELEBRATION AT HISTORICAL PARK; JULY 4 THEME FOR THE DAY 'ONE NATION UNDER GOD'; JULY 5 WAS HORIZONS DAY. (LOCAL). JACK W PORTER, CHAIRMAN; EXCHANGE CLUB OF MADERA; 401 W YOSEMITE AVE; MADERA, CA 93637. (#200006-390).

MALIBU

MAY 16, '76. UNITED STATES ARMED FORCES BICENTENNIAL CARAVAN. CARAVAN IS COMPOSED OF EXHIBIT VANS FOR EACH MILITARY SERVICE. PROJECT THEME IS ' HISTORY OF THE ARMED FORCES & THEIR CONTRIBUTIONS TO THE NATION'. (LOCAL). EDWARD R WEINECKE, DIR; U S ARMED FORCES BICENTENNIAL CARAVAN; 23922 DE VILLE WAY; MALIBU, CA 90265. (#1775-568).

MANTECA

NOV 4, '75. UNITED STATES ARMED FORCES BICENTENNIAL CARAVAN. THE CARAVAN IS COMPOSED OF EXHIBIT VANS FOR EACH BRANCH OF THE MILITARY SERVICE. THE THEME OF THE EXHIBITION IS 'HISTORY OF THE ARMED FORCES AND THEIR CONTRIBUTION TO THE NATION'. (LOCAL). GLAYDS BROCK, CHAIRMAN; U S ARMED FORCES BICENTENNIAL EXHIBIT VANS PROJECT; 166 MAPLE AVE; MANTECA, CA 95336. (#1775-290).

JULY 4, '76. JULY 4TH BICENTENNIAL CELEBRATION. FESTIVAL AT GUS SCHMIEDT FOOTBALL FIELD. (LOCAL). GLADYS BROCK; MANTECA CHAMBER OF COMMERCE; 166 N MAPLE ST; MANTECA, CA 95336. (#106747-2).

OCT 31, '76. BICENTENNIAL PUMPKIN FESTIVAL. THE FESTIVAL WILL INCLUDE A PUMPKIN ROLLING CONTEST & A PIE EATING CONTEST. (PUMPKIN PIE OF COURSE!). (LOCAL). MARVIN BROCCHINI; MANTECA JAYCEES; 417 LOCUST ST; MANTECA, CA 95336. (#106747-1).

MARIN COUNTY

FIRST AID IN SCHOOLS - A BICENTENNIAL PROJECT - CA. A TWO YEAR PROJECT, CULMINATING IN 1976, TO TRAIN MARIN

MARIN COUNTY — CONTINUED

COUNTY PUBLIC & PRIVATE SCHOOL PERSONNEL IN FIRST AID COMPETENCY & TO PROVIDE STUDENTS K-12 OPPORTUNITY TO BE TRAINED IN BASIC/STANDARD FIRST AID. (LOCAL). MARGARET ANDERSON, EXEC DIRECTOR; AMERICAN NATIONAL RED CROSS, MARIN COUNTY CHAPTER; 712 5TH AVE; SAN RAFAEL, CA 94901. (#18081).

MARTINEZ

MUIR NATL HIST SITE--ENVIRONMENTAL LIVING PROJECT. PROJECT TO HELP SCHOOL AGED CHILDREN UNDERSTAND, THROUGH STUDY OF CHINESE IMMIGRANTS, PROBLEMS FACED BY NEW IMMIGRANTS. (LOCAL). SUPERINTENDENT, JOHN MUIR NATL HIST SITE; NATIONAL PARK SERVICE; 4202 ALHAMBRA, AVE; MARTINEZ, CA 94553. (#1466).

MAY 1 - NOV 25, '75. ENVIRONMENTAL LIVING PROGRAM AT JOHN MUIR NHS. THIS PROGRAM WILL HELP CHILDREN UNDERSTAND THROUGH THE STUDY OF CHINESE IMMIGRANTS, PROBLEMS FACED BY NEW IMMIGRANTS TO OUR COUNTRY. (LOCAL). SUPT, JOHN MUIR NHS; NATIONAL PARK SERVICE; 4202 ALHAMBRA AVENUE; MARTINEZ, CA 94553. (#6725-10).

SEPT 1 - OCT 31, '75. VINES & WINES OF CONTRA COSTA COUNTY AT JOHN MUIR NHS. LOCAL COMMERCIAL WINES AND HOME WINE MAKING. AT AT THE MARTINEZ ADOBE WITHIN THE PARK.. (REGN'L). SUPT JOHN MUIR NHS; NATIONAL PARK SERVICE; 4202 ALHAMBRA AVE; MARTINEZ, CA 94553. (#6729-37).

JAN 1 - MAR 31, '76. AN IMMIGRANT SAMPLER -- POLAND AND SCOTLAND. THIS EXHIBIT IS ON DISPLAY AT THE MARTINEZ ADOBE OF THE JOHN MUIR NATIONAL HISTORIC SITE. AT MARTINEZ ADOBE. (REGN'L). JOHN MUIR NHS; NATIONAL PARK SERVICE; 4202 ALHAMBRA AVE; MARTINEZ, CA 94553. (#6729-150).

JAN 1 - DEC 31, '76. TOURS THROUGH HOME OF JOHM MUIR, NATURALIST AND CONSERVATIONIST. TOURS THROUGH JOHN MUIR'S HOME EMPHASIZE HIS CONTRIBUTION TO AMERICA'S HERITAGE IN CONSERVATION. (REGN'L). JOHN MUIR NHS; NATIONAL PARK SERVICE; 4202 ALHAMBRA AVENUE; MARTINEZ, CA 94553. (#6729-179).

FEB 1 - DEC 31, '76. ENVIRONMENTAL LIVING PROGRAM AT JOHN MUIR NHS. SCHOOL CHILDREN LEARN THE PROBLEMS FACED BY CHINESE IMMIGRANTS TO OUR COUNTRY BY ROLE-PLAYING CHINESE FARM LABORERS OF JOHN MUIR'S TIME. OPEN TO SCHOOL GROUPS BY ARRANGEMENT WITH PARK STAFF DURING FEBRUARY THROUGH MAY, AND SEPTEMBER THROUGH DECEMBER 1976. (LOCAL). SUPT, JOHN MUIR NHS; NATIONAL PARK SERVICE; 4202 ALHAMBRA AVENUE; MARTINEZ, CA 94553. (#6725-510).

APR 1 - MAY 31, '76. ALTA CALIFORNIA - MEXICAN CONTRIBUTION EXHIBIT AT JOHN MUIR NHS. THIS EXHIBIT WILL BE ON DISPLAY AT THE MARTINEZ ADOBE OF THE JOHN MUIR NATIONAL HISTORIC SITE. AT MARTINEZ ADOBE. (REGN'L). JOHN MUIR NHS; NATIONAL PARK SERVICE; 4202 ALHAMBRA AVE; MARTINEZ, CA 94553. (#6729-151).

MAY 8, '76. JOHN MUIR NHS -- 'FAVORITE SON,' A MUSICAL PLAY ABOUT JOHN MUIR. THIS ORIGINAL MUSICAL PLAY IS BASED UPON THE LIFE OF JOHN MUIR, NATURALIST AND CONSERVATIONIST, AT THE TURN OF THE CENTURY IN MARTINEZ, CALIFORNIA, AND THE REACTION OF THE TOWNSPEOPLE TO MR. MUIR. AT MARTINEZ JUNIOR HIGH SCHOOL, COUNT & WARREN STS, MARTINEZ, CA. (REGN'L). JOHN MUIR NATL HIST SITE; NATL PK SVC, SIERRA CLUB, JOHN MUIR MEMOIAL ASSN; 4202 ALHAMBRA AVE; MARTINEZ, CA 94553. (#6729-30).

JUNE 1 - AUG 31, '76. EXHIBIT ON INDIANS OF CALIFORNIA AT JOHN MUIR NHS. THIS EXHIBIT WILL BE ON DISPLAY AT THE MARTINEZ ADOBE OF THE JOHN MUIR NATIONAL HISTORIC SITE. AT MARTINEZ ADOBE. (REGN'L). JOHN MUIR NHS; NATIONAL PARK SERVICE; 4202 ALHAMBRA AVE; MARTINEZ, CA 94553. (#6729-152).

JUNE 16 - AUG 18, '76. BROWN BAG BARBEQUES -- EVENING PROGRAMS AT JOHN MUIR NHS. THE PUBLIC IS INVITED TO BRING THEIR OWN HOTDOGS TO FRY OVER THE PARK BARBECUE PIT AND DISCUSS THE PHILOSOPHY OF JOHN MUIR WITH THE PARK HISTORIAN. TO BE HELD ON THREE EVENINGS: JUNE 16, JULY 14, AND AUGUST 18, 19769. AT MARTINEZ ADOBE. (REGN'L). JOHN MUIR NHS; NATIONAL PARK SERVICE; 4202 ALHAMBRA AVE; MARTINEZ, CA 94553. (#6728-254).

JULY 3, '76. 'INDEPENDENCE, ECOLOGY & YOU' SEMINAR AT JOHN MUIR NHS. AT THIS DAY-LONG, OPEN-AIR, WORKSHOP-SEMINAR WILL BE DEMONSTRATIONS OF OLD AND NEW TECHNIQUES WHICH REDUCE HOUSEHOLDERS DEPENDECE ON PESTICIDES, CHEMICAL FERTILIZERS, PLASTICS, FOSSIL FUELS, AND OTHER SCARCE ITEMS. GENERAL PUBLIC IS ENTHUSIASTICALLY INVITED. AT JOHN MUIR NHS, 4202 ALHAMBRA AVE. (REGN'L). JOHN MUIR NHS; NATIONAL PARK SERVICE; 4202 ALHAMBRA AVE; MARTINEZ, CA 94553. (#6725-56).

SEPT 1 - OCT 31, '76. VINES & WINES OF CONTRA COSTA COUNTY AT JOHN MUIR NHS. THIS EXHIBIT OF LOCAL COMMERCIAL WINES AND HOME WINE MAKING WILL BE ON DISPLAY AT THE MARTINEZ ADOBE OF THE JOHN MUIR NATL HIST SITE. AT AT THE MARTINEZ ADOBE WITHIN THE PARK.. (REGN'L). SUPT JOHN MUIR NHS; NATIONAL PARK SERVICE; 4202 ALHAMBRA AVE; MARTINEZ, CA 94553. (#6729-537).

NOV 1 - DEC 31, '76. EXHIBIT ON 19TH CENTURY CHILDREN'S TOYS AND DOLLS AT JOHN MUIR NHS. THIS EXHIBIT WILL BE ON DISPLAY AT THE MARTINEZ ADOBE OF THE JOHN MUIR NATIONAL HISTORIC SITE. AT MARTINEZ ADOBE. (REGN'L). JOHN MUIR NHS; NATIONAL PARK SERVICE; 4202 ALHAMBRA AVE; MARTINEZ, CA 94553. (#6729-153).

MARYSVILLE

BICENTENNIAL AFGHAN - MARYSVILLE, CA. A HAND CROCHETED, 6 FT BY 7 FT AFGHAN WITH MOTIF DONE IN CROSS STITCH EMBROIDERY. CROCHETED AFGHAN MADE BY DOROTHY VICKERS. (LOCAL). DR LEWIS J FERRARI, CHAIRMAN; YUBA COUNTY BICENTENNIAL COMMITTEE; 2205 COVILLAUD ST; MARYSVILLE, CA 95901. (#28263).

BICENTENNIAL BUMPER STICKER, MARYSVILLE, CA. RED, WHITE & BLUE BUMPER STICKER THAT READS '1776, 200 YEARS, 1976, UNITY, STRENGTH, ALLEGIANCE; YUBA COUNTY BICENTENNIAL COMMITTEE'. (LOCAL). DR LEWIS J FERRARI, CHAIRMAN; YUBA COUNTY BICENTENNIAL COMMITTEE; 2205 COVILLAND; MARYSVILLE, CA 95901. (#20873).

BICENTENNIAL HISTORY BEE IN MARYSVILLE, CA. HISTORY BEE ON AMERICAN REVOLUTION SUBJECTS. (LOCAL). DR LEWIS J FERRARI, CHAIRMAN; YUBA COUNTY BICENTENNIAL COMMITTEE; 2205 COVILLAUD; MARYSVILLE, CA 95901. (#20874).

BICENTENNIAL PAINT A PLUG IN MARYSVILLE, CA. HIGH SCHOOL STUDENT TO SUBMIT DESIGNS; JUDGES WILL PICK WINNERS & DESIGNS WILL BE PAINTED ON FIRE PLUGS. (LOCAL). DR LEWIS J FERRARI, CHAIRMAN; YUBA COUNTY BICENTENNIAL COMMITTEE; 2205 COVILLAUD; MARYSVILLE, CA 95901. (#20875).

BICENTENNIAL SCHOOL LUNCH PROGRAM, MARYSVILLE, CA. BICENTENNIAL LUNCH MENU DEPICTING HISTORICAL EVENT ACCOMPANIED BY A LESSON PLAN IN THE CLASSROOM TO LEARN ABOUT HISTORICAL EVENTS, IE BEN FRANKLIN TURKEY WITH GRAVY. (LOCAL). DR LEWIS J FERRARI, SUPERINTENDENT; MARYSVILLE JOINT UNIFIED SCHOOL DISTRICT; 504 J ST; MARYSVILLE, CA 95901. (#22114).

FAMILY NIGHT AT HOME - MARYSVILLE, CA. ONE NIGHT A WEEK WILL BE SET ASIDE FOR A FAMILY NIGHT IN ORDER TO RENEW EMPHASIS ON STRONG FAMILY UNITS. (LOCAL). DR LEWIS J FERRARI, CHAIRMAN; YUBA COUNTY BICENTENNIAL COMMITTEE; 2205 COVILLAUD ST; MARYSVILLE, CA 95901. (#28262).

FLAG IN EVERY HOME, MARYSVILLE, CA. ARBA AND VARIOUS U S FLAGS WERE DISTRIBUTED TO BANKS IN YUBA COUNTY TO BE PUT ON DISPLAY AND SOLD TO PROMOTE PATRIOTISM AND GET AS MANY FLAGS IN HOMES OF CITIZENS AS POSSIBLE. (LOCAL). DR LEWIS J FERRARI, CHAIRMAN; YUBA COUNTY BICENTENNIAL COMMITTEE; 2205 COVILLAUD; MARYSVILLE, CA 95901. (#22112).

HECTOR, THE BICENTENNIAL MOUSE, MARYSVILLE, CA. ONE FT BY TWO FT COLORING BOOK TO INFORM CHILDREN OF THE NOTEWORTHY EVENTS IN THE HISTORY OF THE U S, IN A FORMAT WHICH THEY CAN APPRECIATE. (LOCAL). JOHN COLE, COORDINATOR; TWIN CITIES OPTIMIST; PO BOX 1973; MARYSVILLE, CA 95901. (#22116).

'HISTORY OF THE LINDA-OLIVEHURST AREA' - CA. 'RECLAMATION', HISTORY OF LINDA-OLIVEHURST AREA; THE BOOK IS ABOUT THE PEOPLE OF YUBA COUNTY, THEIR ORIGINS, CULTURE, AND INSTITUTIONS. PUBLISHED BY NORMART PRINTERS, MARYSVILLE, CA. (LOCAL). LOUIE A SMITH, AUTHOR; OLIVEHURST SENIOR CITIZENS ASSOC; 1770 HAMMONTON RD; MARYSVILLE, CA 95901. (#19621).

ONE MAN-ONE VOTE, MARYSVILLE, CA. PROJECT TO INSTILL IN CITIZENS THE IMPORTANCE OF VOTING AND PARTICIPATING IN THE AMERICAN WAY OF LIFE. (LOCAL). DR LEWIS J FERRARI, CHAIRMAN; YUBA COUNTY BICENTENNIAL COMMITTEE; 2205 COVILLAND; MARYSVILLE, CA 95901. (#20590).

PATRIOTIC CITIZEN OF THE MONTH - MARYSVILLE, CA. RECOGNIZE A YUBA COUNTY RESIDENT EACH MONTH WHO HAS MADE A CONTRIBUTION TO COMMUNITY AND PEOPLE IN THE SPIRIT OF COMMUNITY INVOLVEMENT, PATRIOTISM & CITIZENSHIP. (LOCAL). DR LEWIS J FERRARI, CHAIRMAN; YUBA COUNTY BICENTENNIAL COMMITTEE; 504 J STREET; MARYSVILLE, CA 95901. (#19623).

READING OF COLONIAL NEWS TO ROTARY CLUB, CA. EACH WEEK, ROTARY CLUB MEMBERS WILL HEAR A NEWS RELEASE OF THE MOST SIGNIFICANT EVENTS THAT OCCURRED 200 YEARS AGO. (LOCAL). DR LEWIS J FERRARI, CHAIRMAN; YUBA COUNTY BICENTENNIAL COMMITTEE; 2205 COVILLAUD; MARYSVILLE, CA 95901. (#22113).

YUBA COUNTY BICENTENNIAL COMMERATIVE BOOK - CA. PICTORIAL HISTORY OF EACH COMMUNITY IN YUBA COUNTY. (LOCAL). MRS FRANCES MCDOUGAL, CHAIRMAN; YUBA COUNTY HISTORICAL COMMISSION; 203 JOHNSON AVE; MARYSVILLE, CA 95901. (#19622).

YUBA COUNTY BICENTENNIAL MEDALLIONS - CA. OBVERSE DESIGN, A MODIFICATION OF THE SEAL OF YUBA COUNTY TO INCLUDE '1851-125 YEARS-1976'. THE REVERSE DESIGN, A SPECIAL DESIGN, CALIFORNIA SALUTES AMERICAN REVOLUTION BICENTENNIAL. (LOCAL). DR LEWIS FERRARI, CHAIRMAN; YUBA COUNTY BICENTENNIAL COMMITTEE; 2205 COVILLAUD; MARYSVILLE, CA 95901. (#28259).

YUBA COUNTY BICENTENNIAL COMMUNITY SIGNS - CA. FIVE BICENTENNIAL ROADSIGNS INSTALLED AT MAIN HIGHWAYS ENTRANCES TO YUBA COUNTY. FOUR BY EIGHT FOOT SIGNS READING 'WELCOME TO YUBA COUNTY-A BICENTENNIAL COMMUNITY.'. (LOCAL). DR LEWIS J FERRARI, CHAIRMAN; YUBA COUNTY BICENTENNIAL COMMITTEE; 2205 COVILLAUD ST; MARYSVILLE, CA 95901. (#28260).

YUBA COUNTY BICENTENNIAL COMMITTEE MEMBERS, CA. ACTIVE STEERING COMMITTEE FOR ALL AMERICAN REVOLUTION BICENTENNIAL PROJECTS AND EVENTS. LISTING IS IN NATIONAL & STATE ARCHIVES. (LOCAL). DR LEWIS J FERRARI, CHAIRMAN; YUBA COUNTY BICENTENNIAL COMMITTEE; 2205 COVILLAUD; MARYSVILLE, CA 95901. (#32684).

YUBA FEATHER HEALTH CENTER - MARYSVILLE, CA. THE HEALTH CENTER REPRESENTS THE SUCCESSFUL EFFORTS OF INTERESTED CITIZENS IN PROVIDING HEALTH CARE FOR THE COMMUNITY. (LOCAL). DR LEWIS J FERRARI, CHAIRMAN; YUBA COUNTY BICENTENNIAL COMMITTEE; 2205 COVILLAUD ST; MARYSVILLE, CA 95901. (#28261).

MAY 24, '75. YUBA COUNTY BICENTENNIAL INAUGURAL PROGRAM. PICNIC AFTER PROGRAM, MUSIC PROVIDED BY HIGH SCHOOL BAND. AT YUBA COUNTY COURTHOUSE STEPS, SOUTHSIDE, 5TH & B STS. (LOCAL). DR LEWIS J FERRARI; YUBA COUNTY BICENTENNIAL COMMITTEE; 2205 COVILLAUD; MARYSVILLE, CA 95901. (#200006-101).

JUNE 6 - 8, '75. LINDA-OLIVEHURST SPRING FESTIVAL ENTRY. PARADE ENTRY-'MR SPIRIT OF '76', 3 STUDENTS: ROBERT LONG, GARY MILLER & JASON YOUNG. BOOTH: BICENTENNIAL SOUVENIRS. AT THE MALL, 6000 LINDHURST RD. (LOCAL). DR LEWIS J FERRARI, CHMN; YUBA COUNTY BICENTENNIAL COMMITTEE; 2205 COVILLAUD ST; MARYSVILLE, CA 95901. (#200006-191).

JULY 4, '75. JULY 4TH CELEBRATION 1975. SOFTBALL GAMES-BRYANT FIELD 1JTH & C ST AT 1 PM; BOOTHS, BICENTENNIAL SOUVENIRS & BEER. (LOCAL). DR LEWIS J FERRARI, CHMN; YUBA COUNTY BICENTENNIAL COMMITTEE; 2205 COVILLAUD ST; MARYSVILLE, CA 95901. (#200006-193).

AUG 1, '75 - DEC 31, '76. BICENTENNIAL QUILT DISPLAY. ELIZABETH CARROLL'S 2ND GRADE CLASS AT OLIVEHURST ELEMENTARY SCHOOL MADE A QUILT IN HONOR OF THE BICENTENNIAL. MERCHANTS ARE DISPLAYING THE QUILT IN THEIR WINDOWS. AT LINDA MALL, MARYSVILLE. (LOCAL). DR LEWIS J FERRARI, CHMN; YUBA COUNTY BICENTENNIAL COMMITTEE; 2205 COVILLAUD; MARYSVILLE, CA 95901. (#20872-1).

SEPT 9, '75. OFFICIAL ARBA FLAG PRESENTATION & OFFICIAL RECOGNITION. PRESENTED BY MR A JOHNSON, EXECUTIVE DIRECTOR, ARBA OF CALIFORNIA TO YUBA COUNTY BICENTENNIAL COMMITTEE & BOARD OF SUPERVISORS. AT YUBA COUNTY COURTHOUSE, MARYSVILLE, CA. (LOCAL). DR LEWIS J FERRARI; YUBA COUNTY BICENTENNIAL COMMITTEE; 2205 COVILLAND; MARYSVILLE, CA 95901. (#104881-1).

SEPT 15, '75. J C PENNEY BICENTENNIAL MUSIC PRESENTATION - PRESENTED TO SCHOOLS. CEREMONY AT YUBA COUNTY COURTHOUSE, MARYSVILLE, CA. (LOCAL). DR LEWIS J FERRARI; J C PENNEY - YUBA COUNTY BICENTENNIAL COMMITTEE; 2205 COVILLAND; MARYSVILLE, CA 95901. (#104881-2).

SEPT 17, '75. CONSTITUTION DAY PROGRAM-SKITS AND PATRIOTIC SONGS. LIVE PERFORMANCE AT YUBA COLLEGE THEATER, LINDA AVE & BEALE RD. (LOCAL). DR LEWIS J FERRARI; YUBA COUNTY BICENTENNIAL COMMITTEE & MASONIC LODGE; 2205 COVILLAUD; MARYSVILLE, CA 95901. (#200006-104).

OCT 12, '75. RE-ENACTMENT OF THE LANDING OF COLUMBUS. LIVE PERFORMANCE AT ELLIS LAKE, 10TH & B STS. (LOCAL). DR LEWIS J FERRARI; YUBA COUNTY BICENTENNIAL COMMITTEE; 2205 COVILLAUD; MARYSVILLE, CA 95901. (#200006-107).

OCT 12, '75. YUBA COUNTY ETHNIC CULTURE ARTS, CRAFTS, DANCE AND FOOD FAIR. EXHIBIT, FAIR AT ELLIS LAKE PARK, YUBA COUNTY. (LOCAL). DR LEWIS J FERRARI; YUBA COUNTY BICENT COMMITTEE ETHNIC COMMITTEE; 2205 COVILLAUD; MARYSVILLE, CA 95901. (#200006-108).

OCT 25 - 26, '75. HOT AIR BALLOON RACES. MORE THAN 20 HOT AIR BALLOONS ARE SCHEDULED TO PARTICIPATE; TETHERED BALLOON RIDES WILL BE SPONSORED BY AIR EXPO FROM 5-7 PM. AT RIVER BOTTOMS BY 10TH ST BRIDGE. (LOCAL). DR LEWIS J FERRARI, CHMN; YUBA COUNTY BICENTENNIAL COMMITTEE; 2205 COVILLAUD ST; MARYSVILLE, CA 95901. (#200006-194).

OCT 31, '75. BICENTENNIAL HALLOWEEN PARADE-CHILDREN DRESSED IN PATRIOTIC COSTUME. PARADE AT DOWNTOWN MARYSVILLE. (LOCAL). DR LEWIS J FERRARI; MARYSVILLE AREA GENERAL IMPROVEMENT CORPORATION; 2205 COVILLAND; MARYSVILLE, CA 95901. (#104881-3).

NOV 15, '75. LINDA FIREMAN'S ASSOCIATION BICENTENNIAL DANCE. DANCE IS TO RAISE MONEY FOR THE EQUIPMENT AT THE LINDA FIRE DEPT. DANCE WILL HAVE A BICENTENNIAL THEME. MUSIC BY DAVE WHITE & THE COUNTRY TRAVELERS. AT LINDA FIRE DEPT, MILLER DAY HALL, YUBA CO AIRPORT. (LOCAL). DR LEWIS J FERRARI, CHMN; LINDA FIREMAN'S ASSOCIATION DANCE; 2205 COVILLAUD ST; MARYSVILLE, CA 95901. (#200006-195).

DEC 2, '75. YANKEE TUNE-SMITHS. ENGLISH HANDBELLS PLAYED BY STUDENTS FROM BUTTE COMMUNITY COLLEGE. AT PRESBYTERIAN CHURCH, RIDEOUT & SAMPSON. (LOCAL). DR LEWIS J FERRARI; BUTTE COMMUNITY COLLEGE; 2205 COVILLAUD; MARYSVILLE, CA 95901. (#200006-103).

DEC 5, '75. BICENTENNIAL CHRISTMAS PARADE. PARADE AT D ST. (LOCAL). DR LEWIS J FERRARI, CHMN; YUBA COUNTY BICENTENNIAL COMMITTEE; 2205 COVILLAUD ST; MARYSVILLE, CA 95901. (#200006-196).

DEC 31, '75. DRAWING FOR BETSY ROSS CROCHETED FLAG. BETSY ROSS CROCHETED FLAG MADE BY MRS. RUTH SEALE. (LOCAL). DR LEWIS J FERRARI, CHMN; YUBA COUNTY BICENTENNIAL COMMITTEE; 504 J ST; MARYSVILLE, CA 95901. (#200006-154).

DEC 31, '75 - JAN 1, '76. BICENTENNIAL NEW YEAR'S EVE BALL W/ DINNER, ENTERTAINMENT & DANCING. FESTIVAL AT THOROUGHBRED RESTAURANT, LINDA MALL, 6000 LINDHURST. (LOCAL). DR LEWIS J FERRARI; YUBA COUNTY BICENTENNIAL COMMITTEE; 504 J ST; MARYSVILLE, CA 95901. (#200006-102).

JAN 1 - AUG 31, '76. LIBRARY BI-COUNTIES BICENTENNIAL REGALIA. PROGRAMS AND DEMONSTRATIONS WILL CONSTITUTE BULK OF PROGRAMSSPINNING, WEAVING, QUILTING AND CANDLE DIPPING. AT VARIOUS LOCATIONS IN YUBA

MARYSVILLE — CONTINUED

COUNTY. (LOCAL). DR LEWIS J FERRARI, CHMN; YUBA COUNTY LIBRARY/SUTTER COUNTY LIBRARY; 2205 COVILLAUD; MARYSVILLE, CA 95901. (#105922-3).

JAN 2 - DEC 31, '76. AFJROTC BICENTENNIAL CELEBRATION. RE-ENACTMENT OF VARIOUS EVENTS: REVOLUTIONARY WAR BATTLES, SIGNING OF THE DECLARATION OF INDEPENDENCE, PAUL REVERE'S RIDE, SPEECHES, PARADES, COLOR GUARD BY LINDHURST HIGH SCHOOL JR ROTC. (LOCAL). LEWIS J FERRARI, CHMN; YUBA COUNTY BICENTENNIAL COMMITTEE; 2205 COVILLAUD; MARYSVILLE, CA 95901. (#105922-1).

FEB 21 - 22, '76. TWIN CITIES BICENTENNIAL ICE HOCKEY GAME. YUBA FLYERS VS CANADIAN NAVY FLEET PACIFIC CHAMPIONS. TWIN CITIES HOCKEY TEAM IS A NON-PROFIT ORGANIZATION, PROCEEDS WENT TO ICE TIME, THE JUNIOR HOCKEY FUND AND THE CRIPPLE CHILDREN FUND. AT THE ICE ARENA, 1525 C ST. (INT'L). DR LEWIS J FERRARI, CHMN; YUBA COUNTY BICENTENNIAL COMMITTEE; 2205 COVILLAUD ST; MARYSVILLE, CA 95901. (#200006-197).

MAR 13, '76. BICENTENNIAL FASHION SHOW: 'LET HERITAGE RING'. CO-SPONSOR-BETA SIGMA PHI, BEALE AFB. PROGRAM TO INCLUDE A BICENTENIAL CONCERT BY THE 'BEALTONES'. DECORATIONS & DISPLAYS WILL FEATURE COLONIAL ATTIRE & HOUSEHOLD ARTIFACTS. AT ST JOHN'S EPISCOPAL CHURCH. (LOCAL). DR LEWIS J FERRARI, CHMN; YUBA COUNTY BICENTENNIAL COMMITTEE; 2205 COVILLAUD ST; MARYSVILLE, CA 95901. (#200006-198).

APR 4, '76. MARTIN LUTHER KING, JR COMMEMORATION. MUSIC CONCERT BY LOCAL RELIGIOUS GROUPS. MC-REV WES SMITH; CHOIR-ST JOHN'S EPISCOPAL, SOLOIST-ETTA BARBER, COLOR GUARD-BSA TROOP #21, SUB-COMMITTEE CO-CHAIRMAN-ROBERT JOHNSON & DR JAMES MARINER. AT ELLIS LAKE, 9TH & B ST. (LOCAL). DR LEWIS J FERRARI, CHMN; YUBA COUNTY BICENTENNIAL COMMITTEE, ETHNIC SUB-COMMITTEE; 2205 COVILLAUD ST; MARYSVILLE, CA 95901. (#200006-199).

APR 10 - 11, '76. SPRING FESTIVAL. THE BALLET FOLKLORICO OF YUBA COLLEGE TO ASSIST WITH ENTERTAINMENT. AT NOTRE DAME SCHOOL, 715 C ST. (LOCAL). DR LEWIS J FERRARI, CHMN; YUBA COUNTY BICENTENNIAL COMMITTEE & NOTRE DAME SCHOOL; 2205 COVILLAUD ST; MARYSVILLE, CA 95901. (#200006-200).

MAY 1 - 2, '76. BALLET FOLKLORICO: DANCES OF JOLISCO & NORTHERN MEXICO. FOCUS ON MEXICAN HERITAGE OF CALIFORNIA AND RICHNESS OF MEXICAN CULTURE. CORINE ANDREWS, DANCE DIRECTOR. AT YUBA COLLEGE THEATER, N BEALE RD. (LOCAL). DR LEWIS J FERRARI, CHMN; YUBA COLLEGE & YUBA COUNTY BICENTENNIAL COMMITTEE; 2205 COVILLAUD ST; MARYSVILLE, CA 95901. (#200006-201).

MAY 7, '76. YUBA COUNTY BICENTENNIAL HOSTESS CONTEST. A CONTEST TO SELECT OFFICIAL COUNTY HOSTESS FOR THE BICENTENNIAL YEAR. HOSTESS MUST BE KNOWLEDGEABLE IN HISTORY & CURRENT EVENTS. WINNING CONTESTANTS: TISH LITCHFIELD, GAYLE YOSHIMURA, MUFFI WALTZ, MARY WOLTMAN, TERRI LYNN DODSON. (LOCAL). LEWIS J FERRARI, CHMN; YUBA COUNTY BICENTENNIAL COMMITTEE; 2205 COVILLAUD; MARYSVILLE, CA 95901. (#105922-2).

MAY 8, '76. BOY SCOUTS SCOUT-O-RAMA. SEVERAL SKITS WERE PUT ON BY DIFFERENT POSTS. INCLUDING: RE-ENACTMENT OF BATTLE OF BUNKER HILL, THE BOSTON TEA PARTY & INDIAN DANCES. AT MARYSVILLE HIGH SCHOOL FOOTBALL STADIUM. (LOCAL). DR LEWIS J FERRARI, CHMN; YUBA COUNTY BICENTENNIAL COMMITTEE; 2205 COVILLAUD ST; MARYSVILLE, CA 95901. (#200006-202).

MAY 21, '76. YUBA COUNTY SCHOOLS BICENTENNIAL HISTORY BEE. COMPETITION AT LESTA JOUBERT STUDENT CENTER, 18TH & B STS. (LOCAL). DR LEWIS J FERRARI; OPTIMIST CLUB AND YUBA COUNTY BICENTENNIAL COMMISSION; 2205 COVILLAUD ST; MARYSVILLE, CA 95901. (#200006-100).

MAY 24 - 28, '76. 'SING OUT SWEET LAND' - A MUSICAL HISTORY OF THE USA. LIVE PERFORMANCE AT YUBA COLLEGE THEATRE, LINDA CAMPUS. (LOCAL). DON BUTLER, COOR & PROD; YUBA COMMUNITY COLLEGE & YUBA COUNTY BICENTENNIAL COMMITTEE; YUBA COLLEGE; MARYSVILLE, CA 95901. (#108299-1).

MAY 28 - 30, '76. MEMORIAL DAY MUSIC WITH SENIOR CITIZENS. COMMUNITY SHOWCASE OF SENIOR CITIZEN INDIVIDUAL AND SMALL GROUPS ENTERTAINING WITH COUNTRY/WESTERN, BLUEGRASS & OTHER INDIGENOUS MUSIC OF AMERICA. AT YUBA COUNTY COURTHOUSE. (LOCAL). DR LEWIS FERRARI, CHMN; YUBA COUNTY BICENTENNIAL COMMITTEE; 2205 COVILLAUD ST; MARYSVILLE, CA 95901. (#200006-323).

MAY 31, '76. CELEBRATION IN CHURCH HONORING FATHER JUNIPERO SERRA. REVEREND DECLAN O'SULLIVAN WILL CELEBRATE THE MASS W/SPECIAL PROCESSION, MUSIC & GUEST SPEAKER FROM FRANCISCAN ORDER. REV NOEL F MOHOLY. HONOR GUARD-BEALE AFB & COLOR GUARD-KNIGHTS OF COLUMBUS. AT ST JOSEPH'S CATHOLIC CHURCH, 319 7TH ST. (LOCAL). DR LEWIS J FERRARI, CHMN; ST JOSEPH'S CHURCH & NATIVE DAUGHTERS OF THE GOLDEN WEST; 2205 COVILLAUD ST; MARYSVILLE, CA 95901. (#200006-203).

JUNE 12 - 13, '76. YUBA SUTTER AIR EXPO W/PLANE RIDES, PARACHUTISTS & DEMONSTRATIONS. BOOTHS, EXHIBITS & DINNER DANCE. AT YUBA COUNTY AIRPORT. (LOCAL). DR LEWIS J FERRARI, CHMN; YUBA COUNTY BICENTENNIAL COMMITTEE; 2205 COVILLAUD ST; MARYSVILLE, CA 95901. (#200006-204).

JUNE 14, '76. FLAG DAY CEREMONY. RAY SWEENEY, MARYSVILLE EXCHANGE CLUB, WILL PRESENT PROGRAM. YUBA GARDENS SCHOOL BAND WILL PERFORM. COLOR GUARD-BEALE AFB. SERVICE TO INCLUDE COLLECTING USED AMERICAN FLAGS THAT ARE NO LONGER USEABLE TO BE DESTROYED BY FIRE IN THE LAWFUL WAY. AT YUBA COUNTY COURT HOUSE STEPS, 5TH ST. (LOCAL). DR LEWIS J FERRARI, CHMN; YUBA COUNTY BICENTENNIAL COMMITTEE; 2205 COVILLAUD ST; MARYSVILLE, CA 95901. (#200006-205).

JUNE 21 - JULY 4, '76. YUBA SUTTER RELIGIOUS HERITAGE CRUSADE - MOBILE SPACE MUSEUM. COLONEL JAMES IRWIN WILL PRESENT THE STATE FLAG, WHICH HE TOOK TO THE MOON, TO A DIGNITARY; RELIGIOUS AND A VARIETY OF OTHER PROGRAMS. AT MARYSVILLE HIGH SCHOOL GYM, STADIUM, SOUTH AUDITORIUM, 18TH & B. (LOCAL). REV WES SMITH, PROJ DIR; YUBA-SUTTER MINISTERIAL ASSOCIATION; 516 E 16TH ST; MARYSVILLE, CA 95901. (#104445-2).

JULY 3, '76. 'JOINING HANDS ACROSS THE BRIDGE'. SALUTE TO THE FLAG; THE NATIONAL ANTHEM; INTRODUCTION OF THE GRAND MARSHALLS AND OTHER DIGNITARIES; JOINING HANDS ACROSS THE BRIDGE; PRAYER OF THANKSGIVING; 'GOD BLESS AMERICA' GREETING FROM YUBA CO HOSTESS; TRIBUTE TO 'ONE NATION UNDER GOD' & DISMISSAL. AT 5TH ST BRIDGE, FEATHER RIVER. (LOCAL). DR LEWIS J FERRARI, CHMN; YUBA COUNTY BICENTENNIAL COMMITTEE; 2205 COVILLAUD ST; MARYSVILLE, CA 95901. (#200006-181).

JULY 3, '76. PIONEER DAY - 'EARLY SETTLERS HOMECOMING'. RECOGNITION TO PIONEERS, PRESENT & PAST, BOXED-LUNCH PICNIC W/MUSIC & BALLET FOLKLORICO, FIRE DANCE PERFORMED BY BOY SCOUT TROOP #40, RESUME OF EARLY IRISH PIONEERS AND PRESENTATION OF CHINESE COMMUNITY SPECIAL PLAQUE. AT LESTA JOUBERT BLDG, MARYSVILLE HIGH SCHOOL. (LOCAL). DR LEWIS J FERRARI, CHMN; YUBA COUNTY BICENTENNIAL COMMITTEE; 2205 COVILLAUD ST; MARYSVILLE, CA 95901. (#200006-183).

JULY 3, '76. 'SIGNING OF THE DECLARATION OF INDEPENDENCE' - PLAY. A RE-ENACTMENT OF THE SIGNING OF THE DECLARATION OF INDEPENDENCE BY THE TABLE MOUNTAIN LODGE #124 TEAM, PARADISE, CA. AT LESTA JOUBERT BLDG, MARYSVILLE HIGH SCHOOL. (LOCAL). DR LEWIS J FERRARI, CHMN; YUBA COUNTY BICENTENNIAL COMMITTEE; 2205 COVILLAUD ST; MARYSVILLE, CA 95901. (#200006-184).

JULY 3, '76. YUBA-SUTTER BICENTENNIAL PARADE. THE PARADE CONSISTED OF 58 ENTRIES OF VARIOUS TYPES INCLUDING A MISSILE FROM BEALE AFB, THE WELLS FARGO STAGE, A 1924 FIRE-TRUCK & OTHER ANTIQUE CARS, MARCHING UNITS, FLOATS, MOUNTED UNITS, & COSTUMED HISTORIC PERSONALITIES. (LOCAL). DR LEWIS J FERRARI, CHMN; YUBA AND SUTTER COUNTY BICENTENNIAL COMMITTEES; 2205 COVILLAUD ST; MARYSVILLE, CA 95901. (#200006-182).

JULY 3 - 4, '76. 1976 JULY FOURTH CELEBRATION. 2 DAY CELEBRATION: PARADE, BASEBALL GAME, PIONEER'S PICNIC, FIREWORKS, CHURCH SERVICE, 'JOINING OF THE COUNTIES' CEREMONY & REENACTMENTS OF HISTORICAL EVENTS. 7/3: 11 AM - 4 PM, 7/4: 7 AM - 10 PM. (LOCAL). DR LEWIS J FERRARI, CHMN; YUBA COUNTY BICENTENNIAL COMMITTEE; 2205 COVILLAUD ST; MARYSVILLE, CA 95901. (#200006-179).

JULY 4, '76. BASEBALL GAME: 'SAINTS VS SINNERS' - PREACHERS & POLITICIANS. THIS IS THE SECOND ANNUAL JULY 4TH SOFTBALL GAME. THE PERPETUAL TROPHY WAS AWARDED TO THE 'SAINTS' THIS YEAR. AT BRYANT FIELD, 14TH & B ST. (LOCAL). DR LEWIS J FERRARI, CHMN; YUBA COUNTY BICENTENNIAL COMMITTEE; 2205 COVILLAUD ST; MARYSVILLE, CA 95901. (#200006-189).

JULY 4, '76. CHURCH SERVICES, CHURCH WOMEN UNITED OF YUBA AND SUTTER COUNTIES. CEREMONY AT NORTH END OF LAKE ELLIS, B ST. (LOCAL). DR LEWIS J FERRARI, CHMN; YUBA COUNTY BICENTENNIAL COMMITTEE; 2205 COVILLAUD ST; MARYSVILLE, CA 95901. (#200006-186).

JULY 4, '76. MASTER OF CEREMONIES - JULY 4TH CELEBRATION. DR LEWIS J FERRARI WAS MASTER OF CEREMONIES FOR THE FIREWORKS AND MUSIC OF THE JULY 4TH CELEBRATION. HE INTRODUCED GUEST SPEAKERS, LED SINGING OF 'GOD BLESS AMERICA' & ANNOUNCED START OF FIREWORKS. AT LAKE ELLIS, B ST. (LOCAL). DR LEWIS J FERRARI, CHMN; YUBA COUNTY BICENTENNIAL COMMITTEE; 2205 COVILLAUD ST; MARYSVILLE, CA 95901. (#200006-180).

JULY 4, '76. RE-ENACTMENT OF THE 'BATTLE OF LEXINGTON'. LIVE PERFORMANCE AT BRYANT FIELD, 14TH & B ST. (LOCAL). DR LEWIS J FERRARI, CHMN; YUBA COUNTY BICENTENNIAL COMMITTEE; 2205 COVILLAUD ST; MARYSVILLE, CA 95901. (#200006-187).

JULY 4, '76. RE-ENACTMENT OF THE 'BOSTON TEA PARTY'. LIVE PERFORMANCE AT LAKE ELLIS, B ST. (LOCAL). DR LEWIS J FERRARI, CHMN; YUBA COUNTY BICENTENNIAL COMMITTEE; 2205 COVILLAUD ST; MARYSVILLE, CA 95901. (#200006-188).

JULY 4, '76. SQUARE DANCE EXHIBITION. BEALE TWIRLERS; CALLER: DAVE HUGGINS. AT PARKING LOT OF THE COMMUNITY CENTER. (LOCAL). DR LEWIS J FERRARI, CHMN; YUBA COUNTY BICENTENNIAL COMMITTEE; 2205 COVILLAUD ST; MARYSVILLE, CA 95901. (#200006-190).

SEPT 3 - 6, '76. 'COMMUNITY FESTIVAL '76'. SEPT 3: 5 PM - MIDNIGHT; SEPT 4 & 5: NOON - MIDNIGHT; SEPT 6: NOON - 10 PM. AT LONE TREE SCHOOL GROUNDS, BEALE AFB. (LOCAL). DR LEWIS J FERRARI, CHMN; YUBA COUNTY BICENTENNIAL COMMITTEE; 2205 COVILLAUD; MARYSVILLE, CA 95901. (#109303-1).

SEPT 8 - 9, '76. UNITED STATES ARMED FORCES BICENTENNIAL CARAVAN. CARAVAN IS COMPOSED OF EXHIBIT VANS FOR EACH MILITARY SERVICE. PROJECT THEME IS 'HISTORY OF THE ARMED FORCES & THEIR CONTRIBUTIONS TO THE NATION.'. (LOCAL). DR LEWIS J FERRARI, CHMN; UNITED STATES ARMED FORCES BICENTENNIAL CARAVAN; CITY HALL; MARYSVILLE, CA 95901. (#1775-715).

SEPT 11, '76. PIONEER DAY: MOUNTAIN AREA. PROGRAM HONORING THE MOUNTAIN AREA PIONEERS & THEIR DESCENDENTS; PIONEERS WILL BE ASKED TO REGISTER AND WEAR NAME TAGS. WE HOPE THIS EVENT WILL ESTABLISH A PERMANENT RECORD OF EARLY PIONEERS WITH THE YUBA COUNTY BICENTENNIAL CHAIRMAN & COMMITTEE TAKING PART. AT OLD FORBESTOWN SCHOOL. (LOCAL). DR LEWIS FERRARI, CHMN; YUBA COUNTY BICENTENNIAL COMMITTEE; 2205 COVILLAUD; MARYSVILLE, CA 95901. (#200006-328).

SEPT 27 - OCT 2, '76. 'LIBERTY IN LAW' WEEK. CHAIRMEN: MR LYLE GISI & MAJOR MELL LACY WILL LEAD PARTICIPATION IN A WEEK LONG FREE LEGAL CLINIC. A COMBINED EFFORT OF THE LAWYERS FROM MARYSVILLE AND BEALE AIR FORCE BASE. AT THE MALL. (LOCAL). DR LEWIS FERRARI, CHMN; YUBA COUNTY BICENTENNIAL COMMITTEE; 2205 COVILLAUD; MARYSVILLE, CA 95901. (#200006-330).

OCT 1 - 31, '76. 'AMERICA FEST SHOWS AMERICA'S BEST'. ETHNIC ARTS & CRAFTS FAIR, HOT AIR BALLOON RACES, APPLE PIE CONTEST, HALLOWEEN PARADE, ANTIQUE AUTO AND TRANSPORTATION SHOW. AT THROUGHOUT CITY OF MARYSVILLE. (LOCAL). MRS MARLENE SORUM, CHMN; MARYSVILLE AREA GENERAL IMPROVEMENT CORPORATION; 526 C ST; MARYSVILLE, CA 95901. (#104445-1).

OCT 2, '76. CONSTITUTION DAY PROGRAM- SIGNING OF THE DECLARATION OF INDEPENDENCE. RE-ENACTMENT PERFORMED BY THE SCOTTISH RITE PLAYERS AT THE SCOTTISH RITE TEMPLE IN SAN JOSE. WALTER F STEWART IS THE DIRECTOR. 6:30 PM BEAN & SALAD FEED - $2.00 FOR PEOPLE OVER 14, $1.00 FOR 8 - 14, AND FREE FOR CHILDREN UNDER 8. AT YUBA COUNTY COMMUNITY CENTER, 9TH & B STS. (LOCAL). DR LEWIS J FERRARI, CHMN; YUBA COUNTY BICENTENNIAL COMMITTEE & 206TH MASONIC DISTRICT; 2205 COVILLAND; MARYSVILLE, CA 95901. (#200006-421).

OCT 9, '76 - APR 30, '77. 'YUBA COUNTY HISTORICAL MONTH'- HISTORICAL BUS TRIPS. OCT 9, 1976: HILL COUNTRY TOUR; APR 30, 1977: VALLEY COUNTRY TOUR. AT MONTGOMERY WARDS PARKING LOT, 6TH & 9TH ST. (LOCAL). DR LEWIS J FERRARI, CHMN; YUBA COUNTY BICENTENNIAL COMMITTEE & HISTORICAL COMMISSION; 2205 COVILLAUD ST; MARYSVILLE, CA 95901. (#109303-2).

OCT 10, '76. JAPANESE-AMERICAN CITIZENS LEAGUE CULTURE FAIR. BONZAI TREE DISPLAY & CLINIC ON MAINTENANCE & CARE, FASHION & FLOWER SHOW, 'ORIGAMI' ART DEMONSTRATION, LECTURE ON SWORD MAKING, SAND PAINTING DEMONSTRATION, & DOLL EXHIBIT. AT BUDDHIST CHURCH ANNEX, 125 B ST. (LOCAL). DR LEWIS J FERRARI, CHMN; YUBA COUNTY BICENTENNIAL COMMITTEE; 2205 COVILLAND ST; MARYSVILLE, CA 95901. (#200006-425).

OCT 16, '76. BOK KAI TEMPLE BICENTENNIAL PLAQUE DEDICATION. THE BOK KAI TEMPLE HAS BEEN CHOSEN TO RECEIVE A BICENTENNIAL PLAQUE; IT WILL BE RESTORED AND DEDICATED AS A STATE MONUMENT AT THE BOK KAI FESTIVAL. AT BOK KAI TEMPLE. (REGN'L). DR LEWIS J FERRARI, CHMN; YUBA COUNTY BICENTENNIAL COMMITTEE; 2205 COVILLAND; MARYSVILLE, CA 95901. (#20482-1).

OCT 16, '76. COLUMBUS DAY: 2ND ANNUAL RE-ENACTMENT-LANDING OF COLUMBUS & DANCE. LIVE PERFORMANCE, CEREMONY, FESTIVAL AT LAKE ELLIS & COMMUNITY CENTER, 10TH & B ST. (LOCAL). DR LEWIS J FERRARI, CHMN; YUBA COUNTY BICENTENNIAL COMMITTEE; 2205 COVILLAUD; MARYSVILLE, CA 95901. (#109303-3).

OCT 16, '76. ETHNIC FESTIVAL. A COUNTY-WIDE FESTIVAL THAT WILL BRING ABOUT BETTER UNDERSTANDING AND APPRECIATION OF DIFFERENT ETHNIC GROUPS, THEIR CUSTOMS, TRADITIONS AND HERITAGE. AT LAKE ELLIS, MARYSVILLE, CA. (LOCAL). DR LEWIS J FERRARI, CHMN; YUBA COUNTY BICENTENNIAL COMMITTEE; 2205 COVILLAND; MARYSVILLE, CA 95901. (#20483-1).

OCT 22 - 23, '76. READER'S THEATRE PRODUCTION: A E NOTCHNER'S, 'THE WHITE HOUSE'. SPECIAL LIVE THEATER PRESENTATION AS A BICENTENNIAL AND PRE-ELECTION EVENT. AT THE PLAYHOUSE, 629 G ST. (LOCAL). GILBERT READE, COORD; SUTTER BUTTES REGIONAL THEATER/YUBA COUNTY BICENTENNIAL COMMITTEE; 629 G ST; MARYSVILLE, CA 95901. (#108569-1).

DEC 2, '76. APPRECIATION DINNER. AWARD, FESTIVAL AT YUBA COUNTY COMMUNITY CENTER, 9TH & B ST. (LOCAL). DR LEWIS J FERRARI, CHMN; YUBA COUNTY BICENTENNIAL COMMITTEE; 2205 COVILLAUD ST; MARYSVILLE, CA 95901. (#32684-1).

DEC 31, '76. NEW YEAR'S EVE BICENTENNIAL BALL. FESTIVAL AT YUBA COUNTY COMMUNITY CENTER, 9TH & B ST. (LOCAL). DR LEWIS J FERRARI, CHMN; YUBA COUNTY BICENTENNIAL COMMITTEE; 5504 COVILLAUD ST; MARYSVILLE, CA 95901. (#32684-2).

MATHER AFB

BICENTENNIAL PROJECTS AT MATHER AFB, CA. BEAUTIFY GRASS, SHRUBS; BICENT PAINT; DECORATE ROCK; EXCAVATE LAKE; NEW PARK IN WORK AREA; SAVE PICNIC GROUNDS & NAVIGATION MUSEUM. (LOCAL). SSGT JOSEPH C BOYKIN, COORDINATOR; 323D FLYING TRAINING WING, MATHER AFB; SACRAMENTO, CA 95655. (#32205).

APR 11, '76. AIR FAIR '76. LIVE PERFORMANCE, EXHIBIT AT MATHER AFB SACRAMENTO. (LOCAL). OFFICE OF INFORMATION; 323D FLYING TRAINING WING; 323 FLYING TRAINING WING; MATHER AFB, CA 95655. (#200006-432).

OCT 4, '76. FREE SPIRIT FREE COUNTRY. EXHIBIT, FESTIVAL, OPENING AT MATHER AFB, SACRAMENTO, CA. (LOCAL). OFFICE OF INFORMATION; 323D FLYING TRAINING WING; MATHER AFB, CA 95655. (#200006-431).

MCCLELLAN AFB

BUILDING DEDICATION. CEREMONY DEDICATING HEADQUARTERS BUILDING TO THE FIRST COMMANDING OFFICER, CAPTAIN JOHN AUSTIN. AT SACRAMENTO AIR LOGISTICS CENTER. (LOCAL). ALBERT T OLDHAM, MAJ USAF; SACRAMENTO AIR LOGISTICS CENTER; MCCLELLAN AFB, CA 95652. (#200006-491).

HEADQUARTERS BLDG DEDICATION-MCCLELLAN AFB. HEADQUARTERS BUILDING TO BE DEDICATED TO CAPTAIN JOHN AUSTIN, FIRST COMMANDING OFFICER OF THE AIR FORCE BASE. (LOCAL). KENNETH E LAVIN, CHIEF, OFFICE OF INFO; SACRAMENTO AIR LOGISTICS CENTER; MCCLELLAN AFB; SACRAMENTO, CA 95652. (#33266).

JUNE 28, '75. BICENTENNIAL DAY CELEBRATION. SHOWING OF SERVICE EXHIBIT VANS (ARMY, NAVY, AIR FORCE & MARINES). FASHION SHOW OF REVOLUTIONARY COSTUMES. SENTRY DOG DEMONSTRATION & CONCERT BY MCCLELLANAIRES (CHORAL GROUP). AT BASE THEATER PARKING LOT. (LOCAL). LYLE CLARKSON; MCCLELLAN AFB; SACRAMENTO AIR LOGISTICS CENTER; MCCLELLAN AFB, CA 95652. (#200006-457).

AUG 18, '76. BICENTENNIAL OPEN HOUSE AT AIR FORCE BASE. FIRE SUPPRESSION DEMONSTRATION. F106 FLY-OVER. F105 FINAL DEPARTURE. AIO ARRIVAL. SENTRY DOG DEMONSTRATION. RADIO CONTROL MODEL AIRCRAFT. PARAMEDICS SHOW. ACADEMY JUMP TEAM. F111 FLY-OVER. MARCHING BAND. PERFORMANCES BY JAZZ GROUP, BANJO GROUP, CHORAL GROUP & NAVY BAND. AT BASE OPERATIONS & FLIGHT LINE AREA. (LOCAL). LYLE CLARKSON, COORD; SACRAMENTO AIR LOGISTICS CENTER; SACRAMENTO AIR LOGISTICS CENTER; MCCLELLAN AFB, CA 95652. (#33266-1).

MCFARLAND

BICENTENNIAL FIRE HYDRANTS, MCFARLAND, CA. DECORATING AND PAINTING OF FIRE HYDRANTS IN RED, WHITE AND BLUE. (LOCAL). ROBERT MCLAUGHLIN, CHAIRPERSON; MCFARLAND HIGH SCHOOL; PO BOX 575; MCFARLAND, CA 93250. (#28866).

BICENTENNIAL TREE, MCFARLAND, CA. PLANTING AND DEDICATION OF A BICENTENNIAL TREE. (LOCAL). CHUCK TORRES, COORDINATOR; BOY SCOUTS OF AMERICA TROOP 941; 140 FIRST ST; MCFARLAND, CA 93250. (#28865).

DISCOVERY '76, MCFARLAND, CA. SELECTION AND CORRESPONDENCE WITH CHILDREN IN SISTER CITY LOCATED IN ONE OF THE ORIGINAL 13 STATES. (REGN'L). ROBERT MCLAUGHLIN, CHAIRPERSON; MCFARLAND ELEMENTARY SCHOOL; PO BOX 575; MCFARLAND, CA 93250. (#28864).

FREEDOM-PAST, PRESENT AND FUTURE, MCFARLAND, CA. POSTER CONTEST WITH DISPLAY IN LOCAL LIBRARY-THEME OF FREEDOM. (LOCAL). ROBERT MCLAUGHLIN, CHAIRPERSON; MCFARLAND ELEMENTARY SCHOOL; PO BOX 575; MCFARLAND, CA 93250. (#28868).

REMEMBER MCFARLAND, MCFARLAND, CA. SELECTION OF AND HONORING THE OLDEST CITIZEN OF MCFARLAND AND THE RESIDENT OF LONGEST STANDING. (LOCAL). ROBERT MCLAUGHLIN, CHAIRPERSON; MCFARLAND SENIOR CITIZENS; PO BOX 575; MCFARLAND, CA 93250. (#28867).

RESTORATION OF FIRST CITY JAIL, MCFARLAND, CA. RESTORATION & DEDICATION OF THE FIRST CITY JAIL USED IN AREA AS A HISTORICAL SITE. (LOCAL). ROBERT MCLAUGHLIN, CHAIRPERSON; MCFARLAND BICENTENNIAL COMMITTEE; PO BOX 575; MCFARLAND, CA 93250. (#28869).

JULY 3, '76. HAPPY BIRTHDAY AMERICA. PRESENTATION OF BICENTENNIAL ARTIFACTS & FLAG TO CITY OF MCFARLAND; SPEECHES RECOGNIZING AMERICA'S 200TH BIRTHDAY FROM CITY OFFICIALS; FIREWORKS DISPLAY ENDING PROGRAM. AT MCFARLAND HIGH SCHOOL FOOTBALL STADIUM, 350 SHERWOOD AVE. (LOCAL). ROBERT J MCLAUGHLIN, CHMN; CITY OF MCFARLAND; PO BOX 575; MCFARLAND, CA 93250. (#200006-357).

JULY 4 - 10, '76. AMERICAN FLAG WEEK. ENCOURAGING ALL CITIZENS & BUSINESSES TO FLY AMERICAN FLAG FOR 7 DAYS. (LOCAL). ROBERT J MCLAUGHLIN, CHMN; VETERANS OF FOREIGN WARS; 117 FOURTH PLACE; MCFARLAND, CA 93250. (#200006-359).

SEPT 20 - 25, '76. SEPTEMBER WEEK. MCFARLAND HERITAGE WEEK-AGRICULTURE OUR HERITAGE, ENDING WEEK BY CELEBRATING IN COUNTY-WIDE BICENTENNIAL PARADE. (LOCAL). ROBERT MCLAUGHLIN, CHMN; MCFARLAND BICENTENNIAL COMMITTEE; PO BOX 575; MCFARLAND, CA 93250. (#200006-358).

DEC 11, '76. CHRISTMAS PARADE. PARADE AT SECOND ST. (LOCAL). RICHARD CONKLIN, CHMN; CITIZENS ADVISORY COMMITTEE; PO BOX 1488; MCFARLAND, CA 93250. (#109405-1).

MERCED

NOV 9 - 10, '75. UNITED STATES ARMED FORCES BICENTENNIAL CARAVAN. THE CARAVAN IS COMPOSED OF EXHIBIT VANS FOR EACH BRANCH OF THE MILITARY SERVICE. THE THEME OF THE EXHIBITION IS 'HISTORY OF THE ARMED FORCES AND THEIR CONTRIBUTION TO THE NATION'. (LOCAL). ZACK HURRELL, CHAIRMAN; U S ARMED FORCES BICENTENNIAL EXHIBIT VANS PROJECT; 3033 N G ST, PO BOX 739; MERCED, CA 95340. (#1775-294).

MILL VALLEY

CONFLICT BTWN ARCHITECTS & URBAN DESIGNERS STUDY. THE OBJECTIVES OF ARCHITECTS ARE OFTEN AT ODDS WITH THE REQUIREMENTS OF A COHERENT URBAN ENVIRONMENT. THIS STUDY EXPLORES THE NATURE AND ROOT CAUSES OF CONFLICT & SUGGESTS CORRECTIVE MEASURES. NEA GRANT. (NAT'L). RICHARD D HEDMAN, DIRECTOR; 22355 SNORELINE HWY.; MARSHALL, CA 94940. (#2273).

THE CURTIS EXPERIENCE - MILL VALLEY, CA. FILM, SLIDE AND LECTURE ON THE NORTH AMERICAN INDIAN AS DEPICTED BY EDWARD S CURTIS. (LOCAL). KIRK RUDY, VICE-PRESIDENT; NEW WESTERN FRONT; 159 THROCKMORTON; MILL VALLEY, CA 94941. (#24549).

APR 2 - 4, '76. 'A PATCH IN TIME' - QUILT EXHIBIT. EXHIBIT AT MILL VALLEY RECREATION CENTER, 180 CAMINO ALTO. (LOCAL). MARIAN WILKIE, CHMN; MILL VALLEY BICENTENNIAL COMM/MILL VALLEY QUILT AUTHORITY; 27 OAKDALE; MILL VALLEY, CA 94941. (#104073-4).

MILLBRAE

DISTRIBUTION OF HISTORICAL DOCUMENTS - CA. DISTRIBUTION OF COPIES OF THE CONSTITUTION OF THE U S AND OF THE BILL OF RIGHTS IN THEIR ORIGINAL MANUSCRIPT TO ALL STUDENTS IN LOCAL SCHOOLS. (LOCAL). ART LEPORE, CHAIRMAN; MILLBRAE BICENTENNIAL COMMITTEE; 621 MAGNOLIA AVE; MILLBRAE, CA 94030. (#22612).

PAINTING OF LOCAL FIRE HYDRANTS - MILLBRAE, CA. CITY FIRE HYDRANTS WILL BE PAINTED IN PATRIOTIC THEMES AND COLORS BY STUDENTS OF TAYLOR INTERMEDIATE AND ST DUNSTAN'S SCHOOLS. (LOCAL). ART LEPORE, CHAIRMAN; MILLBRAE BICENTENNIAL COMMITTEE; 621 MAGNOLIA AVE; MILLBRAE, CA 94030. (#22614).

POPPY SEEDING - MILLBRAE, CA. THE PLANTING OF POPPY SEEDS ON AS MANY 'RAW' HILLS AS POSSIBLE. (LOCAL). ART LEPORE, CHAIRMAN; MILLBRAE BICENTENNIAL COMMITTEE; 621 MAGNOLIA AVE; MILLBRAE, CA 94030. (#22613).

SISTER-CITY PROGRAM - MILLBRAE, CA. ESTABLISHING A CITY ASSOCIATION WITH IPSWICH, MASSACHUSETTS, AS A STEP TOWARD PROVIDING NATIONAL UNITY AND PURPOSE DURING OUR BICENTENNIAL YEAR. (REGN'L). ARTHUR LEPORE, CHAIRMAN; MILLBRAE BICENTENNIAL COMMITTEE; 621 MAGNOLIA AVE; MILLBRAE, CA 94030. (#23211).

VOTER REGISTRATION CONTEST - MILLBRAE, CA. NATIONWIDE VOTER CONTEST BASED ON THE HIGHEST PERCENTAGE INCREASE IN VOTER REGISTRATION FROM NOVEMBER '75 TO NOVEMBER '76; HIGHEST INCREASE IN VOTER TURN OUT & HIGHEST PERCENTAGE OF VOTER TURN OUT. (LOCAL). VALLI SLATE, EXEC VICE-PRESIDENT; MILLBRAE CHAMBER OF COMMERCE; 5 LA CRUZ AVE; MILLBRAE, CA 94030. (#22611).

OCT 13, '75. RECOGNITION PROGRAM AS A BICENTENNIAL CITY. CAPUCHINO HS BAND, USMC COLOR GUARD, PRESENTATION AND RAISING OF OFFICIAL BICENTENNIAL FLAG, PLEDGE TO FLAG LEAD BY LOCAL BLUE BIRDS AND CUB SCOUTS. AT CITY HALL, 621 MAGNOLIA AVE. (LOCAL). HON BARNEY SPERA, MAYOR; MILLBRAE CITY COUNCIL AND MILLBRAE BICENTENNIAL COMMITTEE; CITY HALL, 621 MAGNOLIA AVE; MILLBRAE, CA 94030. (#200006-106).

APR 9, '76 - CONTINUING . UNVEILING OF PATRIOTIC MURAL AT ST DUNSTAN SCHOOL. CEREMONY, EXHIBIT AT OUTSIDE, AT END OF SCHOOL BUILDING. (LOCAL). BARBARA BACIOCCO, DIR; ST DUNSTAN ELEMENTARY SCHOOL; 1150 MAGNOLIA; MILLBRAE, CA 94030. (#108906-2).

APR 18, '76. EASTER EGG HUNT. COMPETITION AT MILLBRAE PARK AND RECREATION DEPT, 477 LINCOLN CIRCLE. (LOCAL). TERRANCE JEWELL, COORD; MILLBRAE PARK AND RECREATION DEPT; 477 LINCOLN CIRCLE; MILLBRAE, CA 94030. (#106220-4).

MAY 2, '76. ANNUAL BONSAI SHOW. EXHIBIT AT MILLBRAE PARK AND RECREATION DEPT, 477 LINCOLN CIRCLE. (LOCAL). TERRANCE JEWELL, COORD; MILLBRAE PARK AND RECREATION DEPT; 477 LINCOLN CIRCLE; MILLBRAE, CA 94030. (#106220-3).

JUNE 1 - 2, '76. UNITED STATES ARMED FORCES BICENTENNIAL CARAVAN. CARAVAN IS COMPOSED OF EXHIBIT VANS FOR EACH MILITARY SERVICE. PROJECT THEME IS ' HISTORY OF THE ARMED FORCES & THEIR CONTRIBUTIONS TO THE NATION'. (LOCAL). TOLLIO BERTINI, CHAIRMAN; U S ARMED FORCES BICENTENNIAL CARAVAN; 621 MAGNOLIA AVE; MILLBRAE, CA 94030. (#1775-582).

JUNE 12, '76. FESTIVAL OF THE ARTS - BICENTENNIAL CHORAL CONCERT. LIVE PERFORMANCE AT MILLBRAE COMMUNITY UNITED METHODIST CHURCH - 450 CHADBOURNE AVE. (LOCAL). MARY GRIFFIN, COORD; MILLBRAE BICENTENNIAL COMMITTEE; 67 AURA VISTA DR; MILLBRAE, CA 94030. (#106220-5).

JUNE 12, '76. MILLBRAE BICENTENNIAL DAY. FESTIVAL, FAIR AT VICINITY OF CITY HALL, 621 MAGNOLIA AVE. (LOCAL). JANE STEVENS, CHAIRMAN; MILLBRAE BICENTENNIAL COMMITTEE; 1002 CRESTVIEW DR; MILLBRAE, CA 94030. (#106443-1).

JUNE 13, '76. FESTIVAL OF THE ARTS. BICENTENNIAL CHORAL CONCERT-1776 - 1976, ART APPRECIATION DAY, INCLUDES: DRAMA, MUSIC, PHOTOGRAPHY, PAINTING, DANCING AND POETRY. AT MILLBRAE PARK & RECREATION DEPT, 477 LINCOLN CIRCLE. (LOCAL). MARY GRIFFIN, COORD; MILLBRAE BICENTENNIAL COMMITTEE; 67 AURA VISTA DR; MILLBRAE, CA 94030. (#106220-1).

SEPT 4 - 5, '76. MILLBRAE ART AND WINE FESTIVAL. EXHIBIT, FESTIVAL. (LOCAL). VALLI SLATE, PROJ CHMN; MILLBRAE CHAMBER OF COMMERCE; 5 LA CRUZ; MILLBRAE, CA 94030. (#108906-1).

NOV 6, '76. RE-DEDICATION OF PORTOLA CAMP-REGISTERED CA HISTORICAL LANDMARK #27. SIXTEEN TON SERPENTINE STONE (OFFICIAL STATE STONE) WITH A BRONZE PLAQUE PLACED TO RE-DEDICATE THE SITE OF THE FIRST CAMP AFTER THE FIRST WHITE MEN DISCOVERED SAN FRANCISCO BAY. AT WEST END OF HILLCREST BLVD, ENTRANCE TO CAMP SAWYER RD. (LOCAL). MRS ALFRED HALL, COORD; SAN ANDREAS CHAP OF DAR, BICENT COMMITTEE OF MILBRAE; 368 PARAMOUNT DR; MILLBRAE, CA 94030. (#109474-1).

MILPITAS

MAR 31, '76. MILPITAS CEREMONIES-SANTA CLARA COUNTY DE ANZA TREK RE-ENACTMENT. MILPITAS CEREMONIES INCLUDED THE DEDICATION OF A DE ANZA MAVILER, PRESENTATION OF RIBBONS & COLONIAL MAP TO THE EXPEDITION, HIGH SCHOOL BAND, ETC. (LOCAL). RICHARD C AMBROSE; MILPITAS BICENTENNIAL COMMITTEE; 455 E CALAVERAS BLVD; MILPITAS, CA 95035. (#200006-436).

JULY 5, '76. MILPITAS JULY 5TH FIREWORKS DISPLAY. LIVE PERFORMANCE AT PROPOSED JUNIOR COLLEGE SITE, LANDESSAVE/SEQUOIA. (LOCAL). RICHARD C AMBROSE; MILPITAS BICENTENNIAL COMMITTEE; 455 E CALAVERAS BLVD; MILPITAS, CA 95035. (#200006-437).

MINERAL

JUNE 1 - SEPT 30, '76. RECOLLECTIONS OF EARLY PIONEERS RE AREA'S SETTLEMENT AT LASSEN NP. LOCAL RESIDENTS WILL SHARE WITH PARK VISITORS FIRST-HAND RECOLLECTIONS OF EARLY PIONEERS AND SETTLEMENT OF THIS REGION. AT VISTORS CENTER OF LASSEN VOLCANIC NP RT36 BETWEEN REDBLUFF&SUSANVLL. (REGN'L). LASSEN VOLCANIC N P; NATIONAL PARK SERVICE; MINERAL, CA 96063. (#6730-35).

JUNE 15 - SEPT 6, '76. HAT CREEK INDIAN ENCAMPMENT AT LASSEN VOLCANIC NP. FROM 9:00 AM TO 4:00 PM INDIANS FROM THE LOCAL HAT CREEK TRIBE WILL DEMONSTRATE SKILLS AND CRAFTS THAT WERE PRACTICED BY THEIR ANCESTORS AND AT 2:00 PM WILL BE A SPECIAL CULTURAL DEMONSTRATION. AT MANZANITA LAKE. (REGN'L). LASSEN VOLCANIC NP; NATIONAL PARK SERVICE; MINERAL, CA 96063. (#6727-221).

JUNE 15 - SEPT 6, '76. PIONEER WAGON TRAIN ENCAMPMENT AT LASSEN VOLCANIC NP. DEMONSTRATIONS OF PIONEER SKILLS, CRAFTS, & FOLKWAYS OF THE 1850'S. NOBLES' EMIGRANT TRAIL IN THE 1850'S. AT LASSEN VOLCANIC PARK RT 36 BETWEEN REDBLUFF & SUSANVILLE. (REGN'L). LASSEN VOLCANIC NATL PK; NATIONAL PARK SERVICE; MINERAL, CA 96063. (#6727-41).

AUG 4 - 10, '76. LASSEN VOLCANIC NP'S COMMEMORATION AND OPEN HOUSE. PROGRAM WILL INCLUDE DEMONSTRATIONS OF ETHNIC AND FOLK CRAFTS, AND COMMUNITY PARTICIPATION IS INVOLVED. AT LASSEN VOLCANIC PK RT 36 BETWEEN REDBLUFF & SUSANVILLE. (REGN'L). LASSEN VOLCANIC NATL PK; NATIONAL PARK SERVICE; MINERAL, CA 96063. (#6728-74).

AUG 4 - 10, '76. SUMMER INDIAN ENCAMPMENT AT LASSEN VOLCANIC NP. MEMBERS OF THE HAT CREEK INDIAN TRIBE WILL ENCAMP AS THEIR FOREFATHERS HAVE IN THE PAST. AT LASSEN VOLCANIC NP, RT 36, BETWEEN REDBLUFF & SUSANVILLE. (REGN'L). LASSEN VOLCANIC N P; NATIONAL PARK SERVICE; MINERAL, CA 96063. (#6727-43).

MISSION HILLS

JAN 10, '76. BICENTENNIAL DINNER. CEREMONY, FESTIVAL. (LOCAL). BOBBIE TRUEBLOOD, CHMN; SANTA CLARITA VALLEY BICENTENNIAL COMMITTEE; 23845 W MCBEAN PKWY; VALENCIA, CA 91355. (#200006-153).

MODESTO

GREAT VALLEY MUSEUM OF NATURAL HIST, MODESTO, CAL. NATURAL HISTORY MUSEUM TO BE LOCATED ON MODESTO JR COLLEGE NEW WEST CAMPUS. DEDICATED TO STUDY OF CALIF'S GREAT VALLEY. PROGRAM INCLUDES DISPLAY, EDUCATION, RESEARCH FOR THIS UNIQUE BIOLOGICAL ENVIRONMENT. (LOCAL). STAN W ELEMS, MUSEUM DIRECTOR; MODESTO JR COLLEGE FOUNDATION; COLLEGE AVE; MODESTO, CA 95350. (#5141).

SCHOOL CURRICULUM REVISION OF MODESTO, CALIFORNIA. INVOLVING PUBLIC & PRIVATE SCHOOL, JR COLLEGE & UNIVERSITY IN WORKSHOPS ON THE HISTORY, SOCIAL STUDIES, ECONOMIC, AGRICULTURAL, POLITICAL STUDIES DURING 1776 PERIOD. (LOCAL). RICHARD A BELT, CHAIRMAN; STANISLAUS COUNTY BICENTENNIAL COMMITTEE; BOX 1010; MODESTO, CA 95353. (#2977). **(??).**

STANISLAUS COUNTY GOLD RUSH PARK AT LAGRANGE, CA. DEDICATION OF COMPREHENSIVE DEVELOPMENT THAT INCLUDES WILDLIFE PRESERVE WITH BALD EAGLES & SALMON SPAWNING ALSO VISITORS CENTER, GOLD DREDGE, GHOST TOWN, WELLS FARGO BLDG, A JAIL AND A SCHOOL. (ST-WIDE). RICHARD L BELT, CHAIRMAN; STANISLAUS COUNTY BICENTENNIAL COMMITTEE; 1505 10TH ST; MODESTO, CA 95353. (#5142).

NOV 5 - 6, '75. UNITED STATES ARMED FORCES BICENTENNIAL CARAVAN. THE CARAVAN IS COMPOSED OF EXHIBIT VANS FOR EACH BRANCH OF THE MILITARY SERVICE. THE THEME OF THE EXHIBITION IS 'HISTORY OF THE ARMED FORCES AND THEIR CONTRIBUTION TO THE NATION'. (LOCAL). RICHARD A LANG, CHAIRMAN; U S ARMED FORCES BICENTENNIAL EXHIBIT VANS PROJECT; 1330 COLLEGE AVE; MODESTO, CA 95350. (#1775-291).

MONROE

MAR 28 - APR 14, '76. FESTIVAL OF THE ARTS. OPEN HOUSE ON CAMPUS WITH EMPHASIS ON THE ARTS. (LOCAL). MARTHA A MADDEN, DIRECTOR; NORTHEASTERN LOUISIANA UNIV; STUDENT UNION, RM 211; MONROE, LA 71201. (#108161-1).

MONROVIA

BROCHURE - PROJ OF MONROVIA, CA. A LARGE BROCHURE DEPICTING MONROVIA'S PAST, PRESENT AND FUTURE. (LOCAL). MYRON HOTCHKISS, CHAIRMAN; HISTORICAL COMMITTEE FRIENDS OF THE MONROVIA PUBLIC LIBRARY; 321 MYRTLE AVE; MONROVIA, CA 91016. (#14630).

MUSEUM PROJECT OF MONROVIA, CA. A HOME THAT WAS BUILT IN 1887 HAS BEEN GIVEN TO THE HISTORICAL COMMITTEE TO BE USED AS A MUSEUM FOR THE 90-YEAR OLD TOWN OF MONROVIA. (LOCAL). MYRON HOTCHKISS, CHAIRMAN; HISTORICAL COMMITTEE FRIENDS OF THE MONROVIA PUBLIC LIBRARY; 321 S MYRTLE AVE; MONROVIA, CA 91016. (#14629).

SLIDE SHOW ON MONROVIA, CA, HISTORY. A SLIDE SHOW PRESENTATION DEPICTING MONROVIA HISTORY. (LOCAL). MYRON HOTCHKISS, CHAIRMAN; HISTORICAL COMMITTEE FRIENDS OF THE MONROVIA PUBLIC LIBRARY; 321 S MYRTLE AVE; MONROVIA, CA 91016. (#14628).

NOV 3, '75. BUSINESS & PROFESSIONAL WOMEN'S BICENTENNIAL DINNER. DINNER WILL INCLUDE A BICENTENNIAL SPEECH ON LOCAL HISTORY & BICENTENNIAL PLANS; ALSO, A BICENTENNIAL SLIDE SHOW DEPICTING MONROVIA HISTORY. AT DERBY RESTAURANT, ARCADIA. (LOCAL). VIRGINIA MATTERN, CHMN; MONROVIA BUSINESS & PROFESSIONAL WOMEN'S CLUB; 138 MAUNA LOA; MONROVIA, CA 91016. (#101925-1).

MAY 16 - 20, '76. MONROVIA DAYS BICENTENNIAL DAYS CELEBRATION. CELEBRATION BEGINS MAY 16 WITH A CARNIVAL IN THE PARK AND BOOTHS OPERATED BY LOAL CLUBS. AT LIBRARY PARK, MYRTLE & FOOTHILL BLVD. (LOCAL). ROBERT MORRIS, DIRECTOR; MONROVIA DAYS ASSOCIATION; PO BOX 344; MONROVIA, CA 91016. (#101926-1).

MONTEREY

BICENTENNIAL BOOKMOBILE IN MONTEREY, CA. MOBILE LIBRARY TO HAVE A SCHEDULED ROUTE THROUGH CITY; DURING '76 WILL VISIT SCHOOLS AND DISPLAY PICTURES AND SLIDES LOANED BY HISTORICAL SOCIETY AND ART ASSISTANT. (LOCAL). COLIN LUCAS, CHIEF LIBRARIAN; BRUGGEMEYER LIBRARY; 318 S RAMONA AVE; MONTEREY PK, CA 91754. (#9370).

NOV 30, '75 - JUNE 29, '76. RE-ENACT 1776 TREK OF JUAN DE ANZA FROM MEXICO, THRU CALIF.. RE-ENACT 1776 TREK OF JUAN DE ANZA FROM MEXICO AND ARIZONA TO SAN FRANCISCO. CAST TO BE FROM COMMUNITIES VISITED BY THE CARAVAN. (NAT'L). MRS HELEN SHROPSHIRE; CALIFORNIA HERITAGE GUIDES & ARBC OF CALIF; 181 PACIFIC ST; MONTEREY, CA 93940. (#261-1).

DEC 31, '75. YANKEE DOODLE BALL NEW YEARS EVE. PARADE OF NATIONS IN MONTEREY, CALIFORNIA. DIFFERENT ETHNIC GROUPS WILL DISPLAY COSTUMES, DANCE, FOOD, ARTS, CRAFTS AND MUSIC. (LOCAL). HELEN SHROPSHIRE; PARADE OF NATIONS; 181 PACIFIC ST; MONTEREY, CA 93940. (#5896-501).

NOV 5 - 28, '76. 'A BICENTENNIAL SUITE', INTAGLIO & RELIEF PRINTS. 12 COLOR INTAGLIO & RELIEF PRINTS TO CELEBRATE THE BICENTENNIAL. PRINTS DEPICT FAMOUS EVENTS & AMERICANS. PRESENTED IN PORTFOLIO OR FRAMED FOR EXHIBITION. AT MONTEREY PENINSULA MUSEUM OF ART. (LOCAL). HARRIET ZEITLIN, ARTIST; HARRIET ZEITLIN, ARTIST-PRINTMAKER; 202 S SALTAIR AVE; LOS ANGELES, CA 90049. (#23677-4).

MONTEREY PARK

NEW CITY HALL OF MONTEREY PARK, CALIFORNIA. MONTEREY PARK'S CITY HALL WILL BE RE-LOCATED IN A NEWER BUILDING THAT BELONGED TO A LOCAL CORPORATION. (LOCAL). GERALD WEEKS, CITY MANAGER; CITY OF MONTEREY PARK; 320 W NEWMARK AVE; MONTEREY PARK, CA 91754. (#9372).

RESTORATION PROJ OF MONTEREY PARK, CALIFORNIA. A CULTURAL & ARTS CENTER WILL BE MADE FROM AN OLD CALIFORNIA LANDMARK. THE THEME OF THE PROJ IS 'THE BICENTENNIAL SHOULD SERVE TO ILLUMINATE THE GREAT HERITAGE INHERENT IN THE PEOPLE OF THIS COUNTRY.'. (LOCAL). LOUISE DAVIS, CHAIRPERSON; MONTEREY PARK BICENTENNIAL COMMITTEE; PO BOX 1976; MONTEREY PARK, CA 91754. (#9858).

JULY 4, '76. OPENING OF 'HERITAGE FALLS' ARTS & CULTURAL CENTER. CEREMONY, FESTIVAL. (LOCAL). LOUISE DAVIS, CHAIRPERSON; MONTEREY PARK BICENTENNIAL COMMITTEE; PO BOX 1976; MONTEREY PARK, CA 91754. (#9858-501).

NOV 14 - 15, '76. UNITED STATES ARMED FORCES BICENTENNIAL CARAVAN. CARAVAN IS COMPOSED OF EXHIBIT VANS FOR EACH MILITARY SERVICE. PROJECT THEME IS 'HISTORY OF THE ARMED FORCES & THEIR CONTRIBUTIONS TO THE NATION'. (LOCAL). CHMN, MONTEREY BICENT COM; UNITED STATES ARMED FORCES BICENTENNIAL CARAVAN; PO 1976; MONTEREY PARK, CA 91754. (#1775-842).

MONTROSE

BICENTENNIAL COLUMN - PROJ OF MONTROSE, CA. A WEEKLY COLUMN ABOUT BICENTENNIAL EVENTS AND LOCAL AND NATIONAL HISTORY IN THE LARGEST LOCAL NEWSPAPER. (LOCAL). W.B. SCHAFER, CHAIRMAN; CRESCENTA/CANADA VALLEY BICENTENNIAL COMMITTEE; PO BOX 1776; MONTROSE, CA 91020. (#12185).

MORENO

JAN 3 - 4, '76. WAGON TRAIN RECEPTION. CEREMONY, FESTIVAL, PARADE AT MORENO BOYS' HOME. (NAT'L). VAL RUSSO; ARBA; 18156 W COAST BLVD; RIALTO, CA 92376. (#200006-523).

MORGAN HILL

HISTORY OF MORGAN HILL, CA. HISTORY OF MORGAN HILL BE COLLECTED FROM THE 'TIMES' NEWSPAPER. (LOCAL). CAROL JAECH, COORDINATOR; MORGAN HILL BICENTENNIAL COMMITTEE; 17575 PEAK AVE; MORGAN HILL, CA 95037. (#28602).

MICROFILMING OUR TOWN'S HISTORY - CA. $1000 RAISED FROM VARIOUS EVENTS WILL BE USED TO MICROFILM THE HISTORY OF MORGAN HILL FROM NEWSPAPERS DATING BACK TO 1894. (LOCAL). WANDA OAKS, PROJ COORDINATOR; MORGAN HILL BICENTENNIAL COMMITTEE; 17765 LAUREL RD; MORGAN HILL, CA 95037. (#28603).

MOUNT SHASTA

OCT 14, '75. UNITED STATES ARMED FORCES BICENTENNIAL CARAVAN. THE CARAVAN IS COMPOSED OF EXHIBIT VANS FOR EACH BRANCH OF THE MILITARY SERVICE. THE THEME OF THE EXHIBITION IS 'HISTORY OF THE ARMED FORCES AND THEIR CONTRIBUTION TO THE NATION'. (LOCAL). JOE FORNERO, DIRECTOR; U S ARMED FORCES BICENTENNIAL EXHIBIT VANS PROJECT; PO BOX 235; MOUNT SHASTA, CA 96067. (#1775-278).

MOUNTAIN VIEW

CITIZENSHIP AWARDS, MOUNTAIN VIEW, CA. RESIDENTS OF MOUNTAIN VIEW WHO RECIEVE THEIR US CITIZENSHIP IN 1976 WILL RECIEVE A NICKEL-SILVER MEDAL BEARING THE CITY SEAL ON ONE SIDE AND THE CALIFORNIA BICENTENNIAL DESIGN ON THE OTHER. (LOCAL). HELEN EWBANK, REPRESENTATIVE; MOUNTAIN VIEW BICENTENNIAL COMMITTEE AND CITY COUNCIL; PO BOX 1776, 201 S RENGSTORFF; MOUNTAIN VIEW, CA 94042. (#22016).

PAINT-A-PLUG, MOUNTAIN VIEW, CA. RESIDENTS PURCHASE PERMITS & PAINT KITS FOR MINIMAL FEE TO DECORATE FIRE HYDRANTS IN BICENTENNIAL THEME. KITS ARE AVAILABLE AT COMMUNITY CENTER. (LOCAL). HELEN EWBANK, REPRESENTATIVE; MOUNTAIN VIEW BICENTENNIAL COMMITTEE; PO BOX 1776, 201 S RENGSTORFF; MOUNTAIN VIEW, CA 94042. (#22017).

THE PASTORAL DAYS OF MOUNTAIN VIEW, CA. BRIEF HISTORY ON FOUNDING & EARLY DEVELOPMENT OF MOUNTAIN VIEW. MAPS & ORIGINAL PHOTOS. WRITTEN BY DEWITT HOGLE, LOCAL HISTORIAN & SCHOOL TEACHER. PROCEDES TO BE USED TO FUND BICENTENNIAL PROJECTS. (LOCAL). HELEN EWBANK, REPRESENTATIVE; MOUNTAIN VIEW BICENTENNIAL COMMITTEE; PO BOX 1776, 201 S RENGSTORFF; MOUNTAIN VIEW, CA 94042. (#22018).

MAR 30, '76. CELEBRATION OF ARRIVAL OF DE ANZA EXPEDITION. WELCOME OF RIDERS, LIVE BANDS, DEDICATION OF TREK MARKER IN THE PARK, CEREMONY TO HONOR THE CITY'S FOUNDING FATHERS. A LUNCHEON AT THE COMMUNITY CENTER WILL BE HELD UPON ARRIVAL OF THE RIDERS. AT RENGSTORFF PARK, 201 S RENGSTORFF AVE. (LOCAL). HELEN EWBANK, CHAIRMAN; MOUNTAIN VIEW BICENTENNIAL COMMITTEE/DEPT OF PARKS & RECREATION; PO BOX 1776, 201 S RENGSTORFF; MOUNTAIN VIEW, CA 94042. (#105788-1).

MAY 31, '76. MEMORIAL DAY SERVICE. CEREMONY AT PIONEER MEMORIAL PARK, CHURCH ST. (LOCAL). HELEN EWBANK, CHAIRMAN; MOUNTAIN VIEW BICENTENNIAL COMMITTEE/MOUNTAIN MINISTERS; PO BOX 1776, 201 S RENGSTORFF; MOUNTAIN VIEW, CA 94042. (#105788-3).

JULY 4, '76. FOURTH OF JULY GALA BIRTHDAY PARTY. FESTIVITIES WILL INCLUDE: BOOTHS, DRAMATIC PRESENTATIONS, DEDICATION OF TIME CAPSULE AND FIREWORKS. AT RENGSTORFF PARK & MOUNTAIN VIEW COMMUNITY CENTER, 201 S RENGSTORFF. (LOCAL). HELEN EWBANK, CHAIRMAN; MOUNTAIN VIEW BICENTENNIAL COMMITTEE/DEPT OF PARKS & RECREATION; PO BOX 1776, 201 S RENGSTORFF; MOUNTAIN VIEW, CA 94042. (#105788-2).

NOV 21 - 28, '76. PRAYER FOR PEACE WEEK. CONDUCTED BY LOCAL MINISTERS AND RELIGIOUS LEADERS; A SERIES OF SEMINARS AND SERVICES TO SHOW THANKS FOR 200 YEARS OF GOOD LIVING AND OFFER PRAYER FOR CONTINUED BLESSINGS FOR OUR NATION. (LOCAL). HELEN EWBANK, CITY REP; MOUNTAIN VIEW BICENTENNIAL COMMITTEE/MOUNTAIN VIEW MINISTERS; PO BOX 1776, 201 S RENGSTORFF; MOUNTAIN VIEW, CA 94042. (#105788-4).

MSN SAN JOSE

MAR 31, '76. WELCOME OF RIDER RE-ENACTING DE ANZA EXPEDITION. CEREMONY. (LOCAL). MRS JAMES FERENZ, DIR; COMMITTEE FOR RESTORATION MISSION SAN JOSE; PO BOX 3314; MSN SAN JOSE, CA 94538. (#104998-1).

MUIR WOODS

MAR 22 - JUNE 18, '76. MUIR WOODS NM PGM ON AMERICANS, ETHICS, AND ENVIRONMENT. TALKS AND WALKS ON THE HISTORICAL EVOLUTION OF LAND USE PATTERNS IN THE LOCAL AREA AND ITS RELATIONSHIP TO THE STORY OF THE NATION'S LAND AND PEOPLE; AVAILABLE TO LOCAL SCHOOL GROUPS AND ORGANIZATIONS BY ARRANGEMENT WITH PARK STAFF; SLIDE PROGRAMS ALSO AVAILABLE. (REGN'L). MUIR WOODS NM; NATIONAL PARK SERVICE; MILL VALLEY, CA 94941. (#6730-122).

NAPA

OCT 24 - 25, '75. UNITED STATES ARMED FORCES BICENTENNIAL CARAVAN. THE CARAVAN IS COMPOSED OF EXHIBIT VANS FOR EACH BRANCH OF THE MILITARY SERVICE. THE THEME OF THE EXHIBITION IS 'HISTORY OF THE ARMED FORCES AND THEIR CONTRIBUTION TO THE NATION'. (LOCAL). JESS DOUD, DIRECTOR; U S ARMED FORCES BICENTENNIAL EXHIBIT VANS PROJECT; 928 COOMBS ST; NAPA, CA 94558. (#1775-284).

NAS MOFFETT

FLAGS OF THE REVOLUTION IN NAS MOFFETT, CA. PATROL SQUADRON NINETEEN HAS PREPARED AND PRESENTED TO LOCAL COMMUNITY A DISPLAY OF AMERICAN FLAGS OF THE REVOLUTIONARY ERA WITH A HISTORICAL NARRATIVE. (LOCAL). COMMANDING OFFICER/PATROL SQUADRON NINETEEN; UNITED STATES NAVY; PATROL SQUADRON NINETEEN; NAS MOFFETT, CA 94035. (#31127).

JULY 27 - 28, '75. AIR SHOW AND OPEN HOUSE. FLIGHT DEMO BY NAVY BLUE ANGELS AND STATIC DISPLAYS OF FLIGHT VEHICLES FROM HOT AIR BALLOONS THROUGH WWII TO CONTEMPORARY JET COMBAT PATROL AIRCRAFT AND SPACE HARDWARE. (LOCAL). JOHN SHACKLETON, CHAIRMAN; NAVAL AIR STATION; MOFFETT FIELD, CA 94035. (#200006-362).

NATIONAL CITY

BICENTENNIAL MUSIC PROGRAM - NATIONAL CITY, CA. BICENTENNIAL MUSIC PROGRAM AT HISTORIC GRANGER HALL GRANGER HALL WILL BE USED FOR OTHER COMMUNITY FUNCTIONS. (LOCAL). HELEN LAMB, DIRECTOR; SOUTH BAY HISTORICAL SOCIETY; GRANGER HALL, 1700 E 4TH ST; NATIONAL CITY, CA 92050. (#16222).

GRANGER MUSIC HALL IN NATIONAL CITY, CALIFORNIA. THE SOUTH BAY HISTORICAL SOCIETY IS SPONSORING THE RESTORATION OF GRANGER MUSIC HALL FOR CONCERTS, MUSICALS & SHOWS. (LOCAL). HELEN LAMB, CHAIRMAN; SOUTH BAY HISTORICAL SOCIETY; 441 E 7TH ST; NATIONAL CITY, CA 92050. (#6007).

MEET THE AMERICANS HOST PROGRAM OF NATL CITY, CA. A PLAN TO FACILITATE THE TRAVEL OF FOREIGN VISITORS TO NATIONAL CITY AND MAKE THEM FEEL AT HOME WITH ENTERTAINMENT AND INFORMATION. (LOCAL). IDAMAE H KERR, CHAIRMAN; BICENTENNIAL COMMITTEE OF NATIONAL CITY; 1243 NATIONAL AVE; NATIONAL CITY, CA 92050. (#5584). **(??).**

SWEETWATER HEIGHTS BICENT PARK IN NATL CITY, CA. NATIONAL CITY PLANS A PARK & PLAYGROUND IN THE SWEETWATER HEIGHTS AREA. (LOCAL). IDA MAE H KERR, CHAIRMAN; NATIONAL CITY BICENTENNIAL COMMITTEE; 1243 NATIONAL AVE; NATIONAL CITY, CA 92050. (#6008).

MAY 3, '75. BAND COMPETITION. PARADE, LIVE PERFORMANCE, COMPETITION. (LOCAL). EDITH HUGHES, CO-CHAIRMAN; NATIONAL CITY CHAMBER OF COMMERCE; 711 A AVE; NATIONAL CITY, CA 92050. (#5585-501).

JUNE 15, '75. PLAYGROUND & PARK DEDICATION. OPENING. (LOCAL). IDA MAE H KERR, CHAIRMAN; NATIONAL CITY BICENTENNIAL COMMITTEE; 1243 NATIONAL AVE; NATIONAL CITY, CA 92050. (#6008-501).

JAN 27, '76. UNITED STATES ARMED FORCES BICENTENNIAL CARAVAN. CARAVAN IS COMPOSED OF EXHIBIT VANS FOR EACH MILITARY SERVICE. PROJECT THEME IS 'HISTORY OF THE ARMED FORCES AND THEIR CONTRIBUTIONS TO THE NATION'. (LOCAL). IDA MAE KERR, CHMN; US ARMED FORCES EXHIBIT VANS PROJECT; 1243 NATIONAL AVE; NATIONAL CITY, CA 92050. (#1775-310).

MAY 1, '76. BAND COMPETITION. 50 HIGH SCHOOL & SENIOR HIGH SCHOOL BANDS FROM THRUOUT CALIFORNIA WILL PARTICIPATE, ALONG WITH MAJORETTES & DRILL TEAMS. AWARDS CEREMONIES WILL TAKE PLACE IMMEDIATELY FOLLOWING IN KIMBALL PARK BOWL. AT DOWNTOWN NATIONAL CITY. (ST-WIDE). EDITH HUGHES, CO-CHAIRMAN; CITY OF NATIONAL CITY; 2211 HIGHLAND AVE; NATIONAL CITY, CA 92050. (#5585-502).

NEVADA CITY

JAN 2, '75 - DEC 31, '76. BICENTENNIAL MUSEUM. LECTURE TOUR WITH EXHIBITS. AT S YUBA CANAL BLDG 112-1/2 MAIN ST. (LOCAL). HJALMER E BERG, DIRECTOR; NEVADA COUNTY HISTORICAL SOCIETY; PO BOX 1300; NEVADA CITY, CA 95959. (#101084-1).

APR 18, '75 - OCT 15, '76. GOLD COUNTRY HISTORIC TOURS. OPEN ON OTHER DAYS, BY APPOINTMENT. AT 214 MAIN STREET, NEVADA CITY 95959. (LOCAL). HJALMER BERG, COORDINATOR; NEVADA COUNTY HISTORICAL SOCIETY; PO BOX 1300; NEVADA CITY, CA 95959. (#50802-1).

NEW ALMADEN

PERHAM ADOBE RE-PLASTERING, NEW ALMADEN, CA. PRESERVATION AND RESTORATION OF 1854 ADOBE & 1854 LOCALLY MADE BRICK BULMORE HOUSE. (LOCAL). MRS CONSTANCE B PERHAM, OWNER; NEW ALMADEN MUSEUM; 21570 ALMEDEN RD, POB 1; NEW ALMADEN, CA 95042. (#20735).

NEWARK

'NEWARK - ITS FIRST HUNDRED YEARS', CA. PROVIDE PERMANENT RESOURCE BOOK ON HISTORY OF NEWARK, FOR USE IN THE CLASSROOM AS A BASIS FOR STUDY OF CALIFORNIA HISTORY. (LOCAL). SHIRLEY SISK, DIRECTOR; NEWARK DAYS CELEBRATION, INC; 6202 BELLHAVEN PL; NEWARK, CA 94560. (#11364).

SPECIAL BICENTENNIAL BOOK DISPLAY, NEWARK, CA. PROJECT IS TO COLLECT BOOKS FOR A SPECIAL DISPLAY DEALING WITH THE COLONIAL AND REVOLUTIONARY PERIODS. (LOCAL). JOAN M SINEX, BRANCH LIBRARIAN; NEWARK LIBRARY; 37101 NEWARK BLVD; NEWARK, CA 94560. (#20915).

JUNE 23 - 24, '76. UNITED STATES ARMED FORCES BICENTENNIAL CARAVAN. CARAVAN IS COMPOSED OF EXHIBIT VANS FOR EACH MILITARY SERVICE. PROJECT THEME IS ' HISTORY OF THE ARMED FORCES & THEIR CONTRIBUTIONS TO THE NATION'. (LOCAL). BICENT CHMN; U S ARMED FORCES BICENTENNIAL CARAVAN; CITY HALL; NEWARK, CA 94560. (#1775-579).

SEPT 15 - 19, '76. NEWARK DAYS CENTENNIAL-BICENTENNIAL FESTIVAL - '76. FIVE-DAY FESTIVAL FOCUSING ON THE MULTI-ETHNIC HERITAGE OF THE AREA THROUGH DISPLAYS, ART SHOWS, CULTURAL PERFORMANCES, CIRCUS, PARADE, CHILDREN'S SHOWS AND FIREWORKS. AT NEWARK BLVD & CEDAR BLVD. (LOCAL). FRANK SISK, PRESIDENT; NEWARK DAYS CELEBRATION, INC; 6202 BELLHAVEN PL; NEWARK, CA 94560. (#10934-1).

NEWHALL

FEB 6, '76. BICENTENNIAL SONG FESTIVAL. FESTIVAL AT NEWHALL PARK. (LOCAL). BOBBIE TRUEBLOOD, CHMN; LA CO DEPT OF PARKS & RECREATION; SANTA CLARA BICENTENNIAL COMMITTEE; 23845 W MCBEAN PKWY; VALENCIA, CA 91355. (#104753-7).

FEB 10, '76. REPUBLICAN WOMEN'S BICENTENNIAL TEA. FESTIVAL AT FRIENDLY VALLEY AUDITORIUM. (LOCAL). BOBBIE TRUEBLOOD, CHMN; SANTA CLARITA VALLEY REPUBLICAN WOMEN; SANTA CLARA BICENT COMMITTEE; 23845 W MCBEAN PKWY; VALENCIA, CA 91355. (#104753-6).

MAY 30, '76. MENTRYVILLE CELEBRATION. FESTIVAL. (LOCAL). BOBBIE TRUEBLOOD, CHMN; NEWHALL WOMEN'S CLUB & SANTA CLARA BICENTENNIAL COMMITTEE; 23845 W MCBEAN PKWY; VALENCIA, CA 91355. (#104753-5).

JULY 3, '76. CENTENNIAL YOUTH FESTIVAL. EXHIBIT, FESTIVAL AT NEWHALL PARK. (LOCAL). BOBBIE TRUEBLOOD, CHMN; LA CO DEPT OF PARKS & RECREATION; SANTA CLARA BICENTENNIAL COMMITTEE; 23845 W MCBEAN PKWY; VALENCIA, CA 91355. (#104753-4).

JULY 4, '76. BICENTENNIAL FAIR. FAIR AT NEWHALL PARK. (LOCAL). BOBBIE TRUEBLOOD, CHMN; LA CO DEPT OF PARKS & RECREATION; SANTA CLARA BICENTENNIAL COMMITTEE; 23845 W MCBEAN PKWY; VALENCIA, CA 91355. (#104753-3).

JULY 4, '76. 4TH OF JULY BUFFALO BARBECUE. FESTIVAL AT OLPH CHURCH, LYONS AVENUE. (LOCAL). BOBBIE TRUEBLOOD, CHMN; OPTIMISTS CLUB & SANTA CLARA BICENTENNIAL COMMITTEE; 23845 W MCBEAN PKWY; VALENCIA, CA 91355. (#104757-1).

JULY 4, '76. 4TH OF JULY BURGER FRY. FESTIVAL AT VALLEY FED SAVINGS PARKING LOT, NEAR PARADE FORMATION AREA. (LOCAL). BOBBIE TRUEBLOOD, CHMN; NEWHALL ROTARY CLUB & SANTA CLARA BICENTENNIAL COMMITTEE; 23845 W MCBEAN PKWY; VALENCIA, CA 91355. (#104753-2).

JULY 4, '76. 50TH ANNUAL 4TH OF JULY PARADE. PARADE AT DOWNTOWN NEWHALL. (LOCAL). BOBBIE TRUEBLOOD, CHMN; NSV CHAMBER OF COMMERCE & SANTA CLARA BICENTENNIAL COMMITTEE; 23845 W MCBEAN PKWY; VALENCIA, CA 91355. (#104753-1).

SEPT 5, '76. CENTENNIAL RE-ENACTMENT OF DRIVING OF GOLDEN SPIKE. CEREMONY, LIVE PERFORMANCE AT ALONG AND ADJACENT TO SP TRACK AT LANG STATION SITE. (ST-WIDE). WILLIAM T WATSON, CHMN; PACIFIC RAILROAD SOCIETY/RAILWAY AND LOCOMOTIVE HISTORICAL SOCIETY; 1433 11TH ST, #3; SANTA MONICA, CA 90401. (#104753-8).

NEWPORT BEACH

'THE PILGRAM' - NEWPORT BEACH, CA. AUTHENTIC REPLICA FROM REVOLUTIONARY WAR ERA; 118 FOOT SQUARE RIGGER MODELED AFTER 1774 BALTIMORE CLIPPER. THE SHIP WILL SAIL CALIFORNIA PORTS TO BE USED AS TRAINING SHIP FOR YOUTH. (LOCAL). DENNIS HOLLAND, CHAIRMAN; AMERICAN NAUTICAL HERITAGE FOUNDATION; 2000 W PACIFIC COAST HWY; NEWPORT BEACH, CA 92660. (#26937). **ARBA GRANTEE.**

PRIVATE HOUSING, NEWPORT BEACH, CA. A SPECTRUM OF AVAILABLE TYPES OF MARKET-RATE HOUSING AVAILABLE IN THIS COUNTRY IN THE MIDDLE TO UPPER-INCOME RANGE, IN A COMMUNITY NOTED FOR PLANNING AND INNOVATIVE GOVERNANCE IDEAS. (LOCAL). MICHAEL L MANAHAN MANAGER, COMMUNITY RELATIONS; THE IRVINE COMPANY; 550 NEWPORT CENTER DR; NEWPORT, CA 92663. (#20065).

OCT 11, '75. BICENTENNIAL BANQUET. SCANDINAVIAN-AMERICAN SOCIETY IN AMERICA CELEBRATING ITS NATIONAL BIRTHDAY OF 200 YEARS. AT NEWPORTER INN, 1107 JAMBOREE RD. (LOCAL). VERNIS ALLEN, COORD; VASA ORDER OF AMERICA-PACIFIC S/W DISTRICT NO 15; 7109 CORALITE AVE; LONG BEACH, CA 90808. (#200006-96).

FEB 17, '76. 30TH ANNUAL CHARTER DAY LUNCHEON. CONFERENCE AT CAROUSEL ROOM, NEWPORTER INN, 1107 JAMBOREE RD, NEWPORT BEACH. (LOCAL). LORENE MOSS, COORD; NATIONAL COUNCIL OF JEWISH WOMEN, LONG BEACH SECTION; 2842 BRIMHALL DR; LOS ALAMITOS, CA 90720. (#105079-1).

APR 19 - 20, '76. UNITED STATES ARMED FORCES BICENTENNIAL CARAVAN. CARAVAN IS COMPOSED OF EXHIBIT VANS FOR EACH MILITARY SERVICE. PROJECT THEME IS ' HISTORY OF THE ARMED FORCES & THEIR CONTRIBUTIONS TO THE NATION'. (LOCAL). JACK KING, CHAIRMAN; U S ARMED FORCES BICENTENNIAL CARAVAN; 600 IRVINE AVE; NEWPORT BEACH, CA 92660. (#1775-555).

NORTH ISLAND

PAINTING OF MURAL - NORTH ISLAND, CA. MURAL REPRESENTING SPIRIT OF '76 COVERS ENTIRE BACK WALL OF BUILDING. 50-STAR FLAG IS AT ONE END; 13-STAR FLAG IS AT THE OTHER. MURAL IS 55 FT WIDE AND OVER 6 FT LONG. (LOCAL). W G DAVIS, PUBLIC AFFAIRS OFFICER; NAVAL AIR REWORK FACILITY - NAVAL AIR STATION; NORTH ISLAND; SAN DIEGO, CA 92135. (#29016).

NOV 1, '75. BICENTENNIAL OPEN HOUSE. THERE WILL BE A DISPLAY OF F-4 BICENTENNIAL AIRCRAFT AND A PHOTO EXHIBIT. AT BUILDING 245. (LOCAL). W G DAVIS, CO-CHMN; NAVAL AIR REWORK FACILITY; SAN DIEGO, CA 92135. (#200006-367).

NORTHRIDGE

APR 25, '76. CAL-AMERICAN MUSIC FESTIVAL. FESTIVAL AT STATEWIDE. (ST-WIDE). FRANK MCGINNIS; CALIFORNIA ASSOC OF PROFESSIONAL MUSIC TEACHERS, INC; 11001 ETIWANDA; NORTHRIDGE, CA 91324. (#200006-129).

AUG 11 - 15, '76. SAN FERNANDO VALLEY FAIR. FAIR AT DEVONSHIRE DOWNS, 18000 DEVONSHIRE ST, NORTHRIDGE, CALIFORNIA. (LOCAL). ROBERT N STARR, GEN MGR; 51ST DISTRICT AGRICULTURAL ASSOCIATION (STATE OF CALIFORNIA); 11311 CAMARILLO ST; N HOLLYWOOD, CA 91602. (#104512-1).

NORWALK

SPIRIT OF '76: BICENTENNIAL CARAVAN & EXHIBIT - CA. NATIONWIDE CARAVAN TOUR AND HANCRAFTED EXHIBIT DEPICTING THE 1776 HISTORIC ERA. (REGN'L). AL PALLADINO, PROJ DIRECTOR; NORWALK CITIZENS ACTION COUNCIL, INC OF NORWALK; 13722 S PIONEER BLVD; NORWALK, CA 90650. (#20538).

APR 11 - 12, '76. UNITED STATES ARMED FORCES BICENTENNIAL CARAVAN. CARAVAN IS COMPOSED OF EXHIBIT VANS FOR EACH MILITARY SERVICE. PROJECT THEME IS ' HISTORY OF THE ARMED FORCES & THEIR CONTRIBUTIONS TO THE NATION'. (LOCAL). MRS PEG NELSON, CHAIRMAN; U S ARMED FORCES BICENTENNIAL CARAVAN; 12700 NORWALK BLVD; NORWALK, CA 90650. (#1775-552).

NOVATO

BICENTENNIAL CAKES IN NOVATO, CA. CAKES WILL BE BAKED AND DECORATED WITH BICENTENNIAL THEMES. (LOCAL). GERALDINE RICKERT, PROJ DIRECTOR; ICING ARTISTS OF MARIN; 11 HARDING DR; NOVATO, CA 94947. (#18864).

INDIAN VALLEY COLLEGES BICENT STORY THEATRE - CA. DRAMATIZATION OF AMERICAN FOLKTALES FOR PRESENTATION IN ELEMENTARY SCHOOLS. DRAMATIZED THROUGH IMPROVISATION BY COLLEGE STUDENTS. SERVES AS ENRICHMENT, ENTERTAINMENT, EXAMPLE. (LOCAL). DR ERNEST BERG, PRESIDENT; INDIAN VALLEY COLLEGES; IGNACIO BLVD; NOVATO, CA 94947. (#26606).

JUNE 30, '76. UNITED STATES ARMED FORCES BICENTENNIAL CARAVAN. CARAVAN IS COMPOSED OF EXHIBIT VANS FOR EACH MILITARY SERVICE. PROJECT THEME IS ' HISTORY OF THE ARMED FORCES & THEIR CONTRIBUTIONS TO THE NATION'. (LOCAL). BICENT CHMN; U S ARMED FORCES BICENTENNIAL CARAVAN; CITY HALL; NOVATO, CA 94947. (#1775-583).

JULY 10 - 11, '76. UNITED STATES ARMED FORCES BICENTENNIAL CARAVAN. CARAVAN IS COMPOSED OF EXHIBIT VANS FOR EACH MILITARY SERVICE. PROJECT THEME IS 'HISTORY OF THE ARMED FORCES & THEIR CONTRIBUTIONS TO THE NATION.'. (LOCAL). MAYNARD BRIGGS, CHMN; UNITED STATES ARMED FORCES BICENTENNIAL CARAVAN; 2233 OAK KNOLL RD; NOVATO, CA 94947. (#1775-688).

JULY 10 - 25, '76. GREAT AMERICAN SHINDIG & OLD-FASHIONED COUNTRY FAIR. ACTIVITIES RECALL AMERICA'S CENTENNIAL YEAR, HELD ON WEEKENDS. AT BLACK POINT FARM. (LOCAL). ELKE ZEMAN, COORDINATOR; LIVING HISTORY CENTRE; 627 COMMERCIAL ST; SAN FRANCISCO, CA 94911. (#103416-483).

OAKLAND

BICENTENNIAL BROCHURE - OAKLAND, CA. THE BROCHURE WILL ANNOUNCE BICENTENNIAL INSTRUCTIONAL CLASSES AND ACTIVITIES. (LOCAL). GLENNA BRYANT, DIVISIONAL CHAIRPERSON; MERRITT COLLEGE; 12500 CAMPUS DR; OAKLAND, CA 94619. (#14458).

BICENTENNIAL CONCERTS IN OAKLAND, CA. COLLEGE SYMPHONY ORCHESTRA WILL PERFORM WORKS BY AMERICAN COMPOSERS. (LOCAL). DR RANDOLPH HUNT, DIRECTOR; MERRITT COLLEGE; 12500 CAMPUS DR; OAKLAND, CA 94619. (#14455).

BICENTENNIAL CREATIVE ARTS CINEMA SERIES, CA. FILMS WITH LECTURES ON PAST, PRESENT AND FUTURE AMERICAN ISSUES. (LOCAL). DR DONALD P DENEVI, PROGRAM COORDINATOR; MERRITT COLLEGE; 12500 CAMPUS DR; OAKLAND, CA 94619. (#14456).

BICENTENNIAL LECTURE SERIES - OAKLAND, CA. FACULTY AND COMMUNITY LEADERS WILL DISCUSS AMERICAN ISSUES, BOTH PAST AND PRESENT. (LOCAL). DR BENJAMIN J YERGER, DIRECTOR, COMMUNITY SERVICES; MERRITT COLLEGE; 12500 CAMPUS DR; OAKLAND, CA 94619. (#14453).

BICENTENNIAL POETRY SERIES - OAKLAND, CA. READINGS BY LOCAL POETS OF EARLY AMERICAN WORKS. (LOCAL). MS EDITH JENKINS, ENGLISH PROFESSOR; MERRITT COLLEGE; 12500 CAMPUS DR; OAKLAND, CA 94619. (#14454).

DIALOGUE '76 - DOCUMENTARY, OAKLAND, CA. A VIDEO DOCUMENTARY OF SIGNIFICANT CONTRIBUTIONS OF PEOPLE & INSTITUTIONS TO THE SPIRIT OF COMMUNITY LIFE. (LOCAL). PETER ZIEGLER, MEDIA DIRECTOR; PETER ZIEGLER, MEDIA DESIGN; 73-8TH ST; OAKLAND, CA 94607. (#20917).

HISPANIC HERITAGE OF THE SOUTHWEST, OAKLAND, CA. SCHOOL DEMONSTRATIONS WITH A STUDY PACKET; PERFORMED BY ARTISTTEACHERS WHO SING, DANCE & PERFORM VARIOUS ASPECTS OF THE HISPANIC CULTURE & LANGUAGE; A 50-MINUTE MULTICULTURAL INVOLVEMENT. (LOCAL). MARUJA VARGAS, PRESIDENT; DEL ORO CONSERVATORY FOR THE CLASSICAL ARTS OF MUSIC AND DANCE; 3521 GRAND AVE; OAKLAND, CA 94610. (#13193).

HISTORY OF THE JEWS OF ALAMEDA COUNTY, CA. TO DEPICT THE CONTRIBUTIONS & ROLE OF JEWISH PIONEERS FROM 1855 TO PRESENT; TRAVELING PHOTO & TEXT MURAL. (LOCAL). SEYMOUR FROMER, DIRECTOR; JUDAH L MAGNES MEMORIAL MUSEUM; 2911 RUSSELL ST; BERKELEY, CA 94705. (#20916).

HISTORY OF THE ROMAN CATHOLIC CHURCH - OAKLAND, CA. A BOOK ON THE HISTORY OF THE CHURCH FROM DAYS OF THE MISSIONS TO THE PRESENT; IT WILL BE WRITTEN BY DR PETER T CONMY. (LOCAL). THE REVEREND FLOYD BEGIN, BISHOP OF OAKLAND; CATHOLIC DIOCESE OF OAKLAND; 2900 LAKESHORE AVE; OAKLAND, CA 94610. (#11353).

MARIN COUNTY, CALIF, OUTSTANDING WOMEN PROGRAM. COMMEMORATE DISTINGUISHED WOMEN THOUGH STATE PARK MEMORIALS, MEDIA & OTHER MEANS. (LOCAL). GERALDINE L OWENS, GIRL SCOUT REPRESENTATIVE; MARIN COUNTY BICENTENNIAL COMMISSION; 1400 7TH AVE; OAKLAND, CA 94606. (#3900). **(??).**

MINI-PARK & MINI-PARK MANUAL - OAKLAND, CA. PROJECT WILL BE TO PROVIDE RECREATIONAL FACILITIES & ACTIVITIES IN THE ELMHURST NEIGHBORHOOD OF EAST OAKLAND. ALSO ISSUANCE OF A MANUAL TO PROVIDE INFORMATION ON MINI-PARKS FOR OTHER NEIGHBORHOODS. (LOCAL). MARY LEE WIDENER, DIRECTOR; OAKLAND NEIGHBORHOOD HOUSING SERVICES; 1543 98TH AVE; OAKLAND, CA 94603. (#11357).

MUSEUM 'SATELLITES', MERRITT COLLEGE, OAKLAND, CA. ANTHROPOLOGICAL EXHIBITS PRESENTED TO EAST BAY COMMUNITY THROUGH 'SATELLITE' DISPLAY CASES IN PUBLIC PLACES. (LOCAL). MAURICE WOLFE, DIRECTOR; MERRITT COLLEGE ANTHROPOLOGY MUSEUM; 12500 CAMPUS DR; OAKLAND, CA 94619. (#18440).

THE OAKLAND TRIBUNE'S BICENTENNIAL EDITION, CA. SPECIAL SUPPLEMENT IN THE OAKLAND TRIBUNE, SUNDAY JULY 4, 1976, WITH UNUSUAL MATERIAL ABOUT THE TWIN-BICENTENNIALS OF U S INDEPENDENCE AND THE HISPANIC-AMERICAN SETTLEMENT OF THE SAN FRANCISCO BAY AREA. (ST-WIDE). GEORGE ROSS, MANAGING EDITOR; THE OAKLAND TRIBUNE; 401 THIRTEENTH ST; OAKLAND, CA 94623. (#22411).

RESTORATION OF THE STANFORD-CAMRON HOUSE - CA. RESTORATION OF THE LAST REMAINING VICTORIAN MANSION AT LAKE MERRITT IN OAKLAND, CA. (LOCAL). MRS W A SHAW, JR CHAIRMAN; THE STANFORD-CAMRON HOUSE PRESERVATION ASSOC; 261 PERSHING DR; OAKLAND, CA 94611. (#11356).

THE SECRET MUSIC OF OAKLAND, CALIFORNIA 1976. A MUSIC AND THEATER COMPOSITION THAT GIVES THE ARTISTS CONCEPTION OF SOUTHERN URBAN CALIFORNIA. (ST-WIDE). ROBERT ASHLEY, COMPOSER; ARTSERVICES; 463 WEST ST; NEW YORK, NY 10014. (#22431).

OAKLAND — CONTINUED

SERVICE IN THE SPIRIT OF '76, OAKLAND, CA. PROGRAM DESIGNED TO ENCOURAGE YOUTH TO ASSIST THEIR COMMUNITY, PARTICULARLY THE ELDERLY & DISABLED. (LOCAL). EVA PERAKIS, PROJ COORDINATOR; DISABLED AMERICAN VETERANS; 10724 BANCROFT AVE; OAKLAND, CA 94603. (#20918).

SPANISH-CALIFORNIA BICENT PERFORMING ARTS COMPANY. TRAVELING COMPANY TO FOCUS ON SPANISH CULTURAL HERITAGE OF CALIFORNIA; THEY WILL PERFORM EARLY CALIFORNIA DANCE & MUSIC IN CITIES, SCHOOLS & A FIESTA IN '75 & '76. (ST-WIDE). MARUJA YARGAS, DIRECTOR; DEL ORO CONSERVATORY FOR THE CLASSICAL ARTS; 3521 GRAND AVE; OAKLAND, CA 94610. (#11355).

TREE PLANTING - OAKLAND, CA. IN HONOR OF THE BICENTENNIAL, A REDWOOD TREE WILL BE PLANTED. (LOCAL). EMILE LABADIE, PROFESSOR; MERRITT COLLEGE; 12500 CAMPUS DR; OAKLAND, CA 94619. (#14457).

7TH ST CONTAINER SHIPPING PROJECT - OAKLAND, CA. SHIPPING & TRANSPORTATION FACILITIES WILL BE VIEWED FROM PARK OR THROUGH GUIDED GROUP TOURS ACTIVITIES AT MAJOR CONTAINER AND OCEAN SHIPPING TERMINAL. (LOCAL). CHARLES SEIFERT, PUBLIC RELATIONS DIRECTOR; PORT OF OAKLAND; 66 JACK LONDON SQUARE; OAKLAND, CA 94607. (#20093).

JULY 26, '75. ST JAMES EPISCOPAL CHURCH FESTIVAL. FESTIVAL AT 12TH AVE & FOOTHILL, IN PARKING LOT. (LOCAL). GEORGIA HOARD, PROJ DIR; ST JAMES EPISCOPAL CHURCH; 25739 SOTO ROAD; HAYWARD, CA 94544. (#100357-1).

SEPT '75 - DEC '76. BLACK HISTORY LECTURES. A SERIES OF LECTURES ON THE MUCH NEGLECTED HISTORY OF THE AMERICAN BLACK AND HIS CONTRIBUTIONS TO OUR COUNTRY DURING THE PERIOD OF 1770 TO THE PRESENT. AT LIBRARY MUSEUM, 3651 GROVE ST, OAKLAND, CA. (LOCAL). EUGENE P LASARTEMAY; EAST BAY NEGRO HISTORICAL SOCIETY, INC; 3651 GROVE ST; OAKLAND, CA 94609. (#11363-1).

DEC 5 - 8, '75. AMERICAN FREEDOM TRAIN DISPLAY DAYS AT OAKLAND. THE AMERICAN FREEDOM TRAIN WILL INCLUDE 10 EXHIBIT CARS & 2 SHOWCASE CARS DEPICTING DIFFERENT PHASES OF THE AMERICAN EXPERIENCE. ITS ARRIVAL WILL SERVE AS A CATALYST FOR LOCAL BICENTENNIAL CELEBRATIONS BY PEOPLE THROUGHOUT THIS NATION. (ST-WIDE). DON MALLICOAT, EDIT SVCS; THE AMERICAN FREEDOM TRAIN FOUNDATION, INC; 5205 LEESBURG PIKE, SUITE 800; BAILEY'S XRDS, VA 22041. (#1776-83).

FEB 24, '76. 'THE BRITISH ARE COMING!' - BRITISH MILITARY BAND PERFORMANCE. TOUR OF MAJOR U S CITIES BY BRITISH MILITARY UNITS AS REPRESENTATIVE OF UNITS INVOLVED IN REVOLUTIONARY WAR CAMPAIGN. AT COLISEUM COMPLEX. (INT'L). CHARLES K JONES, PRES; COLUMBIA ARTISTS FESTIVALS CORP; 165 W 57TH ST; NEW YORK, NY 10019. (#6532-44).

MAR '76. A TOUR OF JACK LONDON'S EAST BAY RESIDENCES; A RECEPTION & LECTURE. SEMINAR, CEREMONY, TOUR. (LOCAL). DR KEVIN STARR; OAKLAND PUBLIC LIBRARY SAN FRANCISCO LIBRARY; CIVIC CTR; SAN FRANCISCO, CA 94102. (#9835-501).

APR 2, '76. MEXICAN AMERICAN EXTRAVAGANZA. LIVE PERFORMANCE AT PARAMOUNT THEATRE. (LOCAL). JOSE LUIS CORTEZ, DIR; LATIN AMERICAN SERVICES ORGANIZATION; 2368 BLUEBELL DR; LIVERMORE, CA 90042. (#104999-1).

APR 15, '76. ODORI FESTIVAL OF JAPAN VISITS OAKLAND. LIVE PERFORMANCE AT PARAMOUNT THEATRE. (INT'L). DIRECTOR; MEL HOWARD PRESENTS; 143 E 27TH ST; NEW YORK, NY 10016. (#108965-7).

JUNE 3, '76. AUSTRALIAN YOUTH ORCHESTRA CONCERT. LIVE PERFORMANCE. (INT'L). JOHN MAUNDER, DIRECTOR; AUSTRALIAN GOVERNMENT; AUSTRALIAN CG, 636 FIFTH AVENUE; NEW YORK, NY 10020. (#108021-8).

JUNE 6, '76. A SALUTE TO AMERICAN MUSIC BY OAKLAND YOUTH CHOIR. LIVE PERFORMANCE. (LOCAL). JOHN TURPIN, SR MINISTER; FIRST PRESBYTERIAN CHURCH; 2619 BROADWAY; OAKLAND, CA 94612. (#104997-1).

JULY 7 - AUG 21, '77. 'CITIES ON STONE: 19TH C LITHOGRAPHS OF THE URBAN WEST'. EXHIBIT AT OAKLAND MUSEUM OF ART. (ST-WIDE). RON TYLER, HIST CURATOR; AMON CARTER MUSEUM OF WESTERN ART; 3501 CAMP BOWIE BLVD; FORT WORTH, TX 76101. (#15666-4).

OCEANSIDE

AMERICANA ESSAY CONTEST - PROJ OF OCEANSIDE, CA. A THREE-YEAR ESSAY PROGRAM WITH DIFFERENT THEMES FOR EACH YEAR; AWARDS WILL BE GIVEN DURING A SPECIAL LUNCHEON TO THE WINNING STUDENTS. (LOCAL). MIKE STAMBAUGH, DIRECTOR; OCEANSIDE BICENT COMMITTEE; OCEANSIDE, CA 92054. (#9891).

FLAG DISPLAY; AMERICAN LEGION, POST 146 - CA. THE LEGION WILL DISPLAY 150 BANNERS; 300 STREET FLAGS, 4X6 FT; 6 8X12 FT AMERICAN FLAGS AT MAIN INTERSECTIONS; AND 12 AMERICAN REVOLUTION FLAGS AT THE WOMEN'S CLUB. (LOCAL). ALEXANDER H KAPITANSKI, COMMANDER; AMERICAN LEGION, POST 146; 1312 SELMA DR; OCEANSIDE, CA 92054. (#11998).

OCEANSIDE BICENTENNIAL MEDALLION, CALIFORNIA. A MEDALLION HAS BEEN DESIGNED AND A SUPPLY PURCHASED TO BE SOLD. PROCEEDS WILL GO TO OCEANSIDE BICENT COMMITTEE FOR FUTURE PROJECTS. (ST-WIDE). JACK GILMORE, PROJECT DIRECTOR; OCEANSIDE ELKS LODGE; 444 COUNTRY CLUB LANE; OCEANSIDE, CA 92054. (#9892).

JAN 20 - 21, '76. UNITED STATES ARMED FORCES BICENTENNIAL CARAVAN. CARAVAN IS COMPOSED OF EXHIBIT VANS FOR EACH MILITARY SERVICE. PROJECT THEME IS 'HISTORY OF THE ARMED FORCES AND THEIR CONTRIBUTIONS TO THE NATION'. (LOCAL). PHIL FRANKLIN, CHMN; US ARMED FORCES EXHIBIT VANS PROJECT; 1714 S HILL; OCEANSIDE, CA 92054. (#1775-307).

FEB 8 - 15, '76. DISPLAY OF LINCOLN DOCUMENT. DISPLAY OF THE LINCOLN DOCUMENT GIVING RESTORATION OF THE MISSION TO THE CHURCH. IT WAS SIGNED BY LINCOLN SHORTLY BEFORE HIS ASSASSINATION. (LOCAL). MARTIN MCKEON, DIRECTOR; SAN LOUIS REY MISSION; 4050 MISSION AVE; OCEANSIDE, CA 92068. (#9893-1).

APR 2, '76. BILL OF RIGHTS FOR CHILDREN - LECTURE. SEMINAR AT STUDENT UNION PALOMAR COLLEGE, 1140 W MISSION SAN MARCOS. (LOCAL). CARRIE ZIEMAK; MIRACOSTA AND PALOMAR COLLEGES; ONE BARNARD DR; OCEANSIDE, CA 92054. (#104981-12).

APR 3, '76. PUPPET THEATER-BRUNNER PUPPETEERS POPCORN THEATER. LIVE PERFORMANCE AT GYMNASIUM. (LOCAL). CARRIE ZIEMAK; MIRACOSTA COLLEGE; ONE BARNARD DR; OCEANSIDE, CA 92054. (#104981-11).

APR 3, '76. 'REVEL '76', BROWNIE & JR CRAFTS SKILLS PUPPET SHOW. FESTIVAL AT BUDDY TODD PARK. (LOCAL). SHARON MERINGOLO, DIR; GIRL SCOUTS OF UNITED STATES OF AMERICA (GSUSA); 137 HERITAGE; OCEANSIDE, CA 92054. (#104981-13).

APR 7, '76 - CONTINUING . TRAVEL ADVENTURE SERIES - BACK ROADS USA. EXHIBIT, SEMINAR AT CARLSBAD UNION CHURCH, 3175 HARDING ST. (LOCAL). CARRIE ZIEMAK, COORD; MIRACOSTA COLLEGE; ONE BARNARD DR; OCEANSIDE, CA 92054. (#104981-10).

APR 17, '76. CORONATION BALL HELD AT OCEAN COMMUNITY CENTER - $5.00, 7PM-1AM. CORONATION BALL, QUEEN MISS AMERICA, GI FORUM - CA. COMPETITION BETWEEN GIRLS AGES 16-21 FROM OCEAN & CARLSBAD; WILL BE JUDGED ON POISE, BEAUTY & SPEECH; WINNER GOES TO STATE COMPETITION. COMPETITION TO RAISE MONEY FOR COLLEGIATE SCHOLARSHIPS. (LOCAL). FERNANDO ACUNA, SECRETARY; AMERICAN GI FORUM OF U S, OCEANSIDE CHAPTER; PO BOX 1283; OCEANSIDE, CA 92054. (#11994-501).

APR 24, '76. AMAN FOLK ENSEMBLE. LIVE PERFORMANCE AT OCEANSIDE WEST HIGH SCHOOL CAMPUS AUDITORIUM. (LOCAL). R H PIEHL, PROJ COORD; NORTH COUNTY CONCERT ASSOC; 3053 SONJA CT; OCEANSIDE, CA 92054. (#104981-8).

APR 27, '76. AMERICAN ISSUES FORUM - GROWING UP IN AMERICA. SEMINAR AT CAMP PENDLETON LIBRARY. (LOCAL). CARRIE ZIEMAK, COORD; MIRACOSTA COLLEGE; ONE BARNARD DR; OCEANSIDE, CA 92054. (#104981-7).

MAY 2, '76. CHAMBER MUSIC SERIES 'THE AMERICAN EARLY MUSIC ENSEMBLE'. LIVE PERFORMANCE AT FIRST PRESBYTERIAN CHURCH 2001, EL CAMINO REAL. (LOCAL). CARRIE ZIEMAK, COORD; MIRACOSTA COLLEGE; ONE BARNARD DR; OCEANSIDE, CA 92054. (#104981-5).

MAY 23, '76. COMMUNITY CHORUS & ORCHESTRA CONCERT. LIVE PERFORMANCE AT GYMNASIUM. (LOCAL). CARRIE ZIEMAK, COORD; MIRACOSTA COLLEGE; ONE BARNARD DR; OCEANSIDE, CA 92054. (#104981-4).

MAY 27 - 29, '76. 'SWEET CHARITY' - MUSICAL COMEDY. LIVE PERFORMANCE AT LITTLE THEATER ONE BARNARD DR. (LOCAL). CARRIE ZIEMAK, COORD; MIRACOSTA COLLEGE DRAMA DEPT; ONE BARNARD DR; OCEANSIDE, CA 92054. (#104981-3).

JUNE 12, '76. DINNER DANCE & INSTALLATION OF OFFICERS. AMER GI FORUM OF U S INSTALLATION OF OFFICERS - CA. INSTALLATION WILL BE AT A DINNER DANCE TO BE HELD MAY 29, 1976 AT THE OCEANSIDE COMMUNITY CENTER ON THE STRAND. PURPOSE IS TO AWARD $4000 SCHOLARSHIPS TO 27 COLLEGE STUDENTS. (LOCAL). FERNANDO ACUMA, SECRETARY; AMERICAN GI FORUM OF THE U S, OCEANSIDE CHAPTER; PO BOX 1283; OCEANSIDE, CA 92054. (#11996-501).

JULY 3, '76. SOUTHERN CALIFORNIA BICENTENNIAL PARADE PART 2-A LOOK TO THE FUTURE. PARADE. (LOCAL). PHIL FRANKLIN, COORD; OCEANSIDE CHAMBER OF COMMERCE; 1714 S HILL; OCEANSIDE, CA 92054. (#104981-2).

JULY 3, '76 - CONTINUING . 1976 BICENTENNIAL ONE MILLION MILE - THE AMERICAS BIKE-A-THON. BIKE-A-THONE TO GO COAST TO COAST. RIDERS WILL START FROM OCEANSIDE & BE SPONSORED BY VARIOUS GROUPS FROM COAST TO COAST. (NAT'L). DANA J MORRISON, PROJ DIR; OCEANSIDE BICENTENNIAL COMMITTEE; 10002 BURGUNDY PL; ANAHEIM, CA 92804. (#104981-1).

JULY 4, '76. INDEPENDENCE MONTH PARADE. OCEANSIDE INDEPENDENCE MONTH PARADE, CA. PARADE THEME WILL BE BICENTENNIAL, PART 2; IT WILL BE SPONSORED BY THE OCEANSIDE CHAMBER OF COMMERCE. (ST-WIDE). DAVID LAURENT; OCEANSIDE CHAMBER OF COMMERCE; 510 4TH ST; OCEANSIDE, CA 92054. (#11997-501).

JULY 10, '76. STAGE PERFORMANCE - MARIACHI BAND & FOLKLORICO DANCERS. FIESTA AMERICANA - PROJ OF OCEANSIDE, CA. THE MEXICAN FIESTA IS A YEARLY EVENT CONSISTING OF 2 PERFORMANCES HELD IN THE BANDSHELL ON THE STRAND. (LOCAL). FERNANDO ACUNA, SECRETARY; AMERICAN GI FORUM OF THE U S, OCEANSIDE CHAPTER; PO BOX 1283; OCEANSIDE, CA 92054. (#11995-501).

JULY 17 - 18, '76. FIESTA PROJECT. 1976 WILL MARK THE 177TH BIRTHDAY OF THE SAN LUIS REY MISSION. AN EQUESTRIAN RIDE OF THREE DAYS CULMINATES AT THE MISSION. FESTIVAL STARTS AT NOON WITH THE BLESSING OF ANIMALS. WILL ALSO INCLUDE SOME MEXICAN DANCERS, MUSICIANS, AND A BARBEQUE. (LOCAL). MARTIN MCKEON, DIRECTOR; SAN LUIS REY MISSION; 4050 MISSION AVE; OCEANSIDE, CA 96068. (#9895-1).

DEC 19, '76. LAS POSADAS CELEBRATION & PINATA. A RELIGIOUS DRAMATIZATION OF JOSEPH AND MARY'S SEARCH FOR A PLACE TO STAY ON CHRISTMAS EVE. A MEXICAN CELEBRATION BROUGHT INTO CALIFORNIA BY THE MEXICAN PEOPLE. (ST-WIDE). MARTIN MCKEON, DIRECTOR; SAN LUIS REY MISSION; 4050 MISSION AVE; OCEANSIDE, CA 92068. (#9894-1).

OJAI

STRUCTURAL IMPROVEMENTS AT LIBBY BOWL, OJAI, CA. BUILD REST ROOMS AND DRESSING ROOMS TO IMPROVE FACILITIES. (LOCAL). FRANK MCDEVITT, PROJ DIRECTOR; OJAI FESTIVALS, LTD; PO BOX 185; OJAI, CA 93023. (#10798).

JULY 4, '75. INDEPENDENCE DAY CELEBRATION. OLD FASHIONED PICNIC AT SARIZOTTI PARK; PATRIOTIC PGM; ONE HOUR OF FIREWORKS AT DUSK; AND PARADE WITH 120 ENTRIES. PARADE THEME IS, 'A MORE PERFECT UNION.'. AT OJAI AVE; SARZOTTI PARK; HIGH SCHOOL STADIUM. (LOCAL). FRANK MCDEVITT; INDEPENDENCE DAY COMMITTEE; 806 GRAND AVE; OJAI, CA 93023. (#100101-1).

MAY 20, '76. UNITED STATES ARMED FORCES BICENTENNIAL CARAVAN. CARAVAN IS COMPOSED OF EXHIBIT VANS FOR EACH MILITARY SERVICE. PROJECT THEME IS ' HISTORY OF THE ARMED FORCES & THEIR CONTRIBUTIONS TO THE NATION'. (LOCAL). ED ALLEN, CHAIRMAN; U S ARMED FORCES BICENTENNIAL CARAVAN; 1111 N VENTURA ST; OJAI, CA 93023. (#1775-571).

ONTARIO

'THE DAILY REPORT' SPECIAL ISSUES - NBMRP. PAPER BEGAN IN 1975 SERIES OF SPECIAL ISSUES DEALING WITH LATER AMERICAN HISTORY. THIS SERIES COMPLEMENTS ESSAY CONTEST FOR 5TH & 6TH GRADERS WHICH IS SPONSORED BY PAPER'S PARENT COMPANY. (LOCAL). MARGE GROSS, BICENTENNIAL COORDINATOR; THE DAILY REPORT; 212 EAST B ST, BOX 593; ONTARIO, CA 91764. (#25670).

ORANGE

AMERICAN HERITAGE FORUM - ORANGE, CA. SERIES OF LECTURES ON VARIOUS ASPECTS OF AMERICAN CULTURE. ONE LECTURE WILL BE HELD PER MONTH. (LOCAL). BARBARA MULCH, CHAIRMAN; CHAPMAN COLLEGE; 333 N GLASSEN; ORANGE, CA 92666. (#28606).

APR 8, '76. UNITED STATES ARMED FORCES BICENTENNIAL CARAVAN. CARAVAN IS COMPOSED OF EXHIBIT VANS FOR EACH MILITARY SERVICE. PROJECT THEME IS ' HISTORY OF THE ARMED FORCES & THEIR CONTRIBUTIONS TO THE NATION'. (LOCAL). GENE BEYER, DIRECTOR; U S ARMED FORCES BICENTENNIAL CARAVAN; 370 NORTH GALLSEU; ORANGE, CA 92666. (#1775-550).

ORLAND

DEDICATION CEREMONY-PERMANENT MARKER FOR GRANVILLE P SWIFT ADOBE. CEREMONY AT ROADSIDE, 15 MILES N OF ORLAND. (LOCAL). JOANNE OVERTON, CHAIRMAN; ORLAND BICENTENNIAL COMMITTEE; ROUTE 1, BOX 280; ORLAND, CA 95963. (#106445-1).

OROVILLE

AVENUE OF FLAGS IN OROVILLE, CA. AVENUE OF FLAGS AT LOCAL CEMETERY IN MEMORY OF ALL VETERANS. BURIAL FLAGS WILL FLY AROUND VETERANS' PLOTS. (LOCAL). EDWARD R MCQUEEN, SR V COMMANDER; VETERANS COMMITTEE OF OROVILLE; PO BOX 411; PALERMO, CA 95968. (#21361).

CENTENNIAL MURALS - OROVILLE, CA. MURALS, DONE BY THE CENTRAL SCHOOL CHILDREN, WILL PORTRAY SOME ASPECTS OF AMERICANA. (LOCAL). MRS DELL DEMYER, TEACHER; CENTRAL SCHOOL; 2565 MESA AVE; OROVILLE, CA 95965. (#26469).

CLAY ART PROJECT - OROVILLE, CA. CLAY ART PROJECT OF ELEMENTARY SCHOOL CHILDREN FOR OROVILLE CITY PARKING. (LOCAL). JEAN MINASIAN, CHAIRMAN; FRIENDS OF THE PARK; 1370 2ND AVE; OROVILLE, CA 95965. (#13799).

ISHI OF MAIDU INDIAN TRIBE - WOODEN SCULPTURE. SCULPTURE OF THE LAST INDIAN OF THE COUNTY'S MAIDU TRIBE. (LOCAL). MRS JACK MINASIAN, CHAIRMAN; OROVILLE BICENTENNIAL COMMITTEE; 1370 2ND AVE; OROVILLE, CA 95965. (#32676).

JOHNNY APPLESEED BICENTENNIAL PROJECT - CA. PLANTING AND LANDSCAPING PROJECT FOR BIRD STREET SCHOOL. (LOCAL). MRS S GIRDLER, DIRECTOR; BIRD STREET SCHOOL; OROVILLE, CA 95965. (#25467).

MEMORIAL FOR ALL VETERANS IN OROVILLE, CA. MONUMENT IN MEMORY OF ALL VETERANS OF ALL WARS OF THE UNITED STATES. NAMES OF VETERANS OF THIS AREA WILL BE INSCRIBED. (LOCAL). EDWARD R MCQUEEN, SR V COMMANDER; VETERANS COMMITTEE OF OROVILLE; PO BOX 411; PALERMO, CA 95965. (#21362).

SEPT 19, '75. WAGON TREK. WAGON TRAIN CELEBRATION, PIONEER PARADE, BARBECUE AND WESTERN DANCE. (LOCAL). DR J A SIGFRID, DIRECTOR; CSHA REGION II - OROVILLE PAGEANT RIDERS; BOX 322; PALERMO, CA 95968. (#101246-1).

OROVILLE — CONTINUED

OCT 4 - 6, '75. OCTOBERFEST '75. FESTIVAL OF FOOD AND GAMES. (LOCAL). REV PAUL DEGNAN; DIRECTOR; ST THOMAS SCHOOL; 1330 BIRD ST; OROVILLE, CA 95965. (#101244-1).

OCT 20, '75. UNITED STATES ARMED FORCES BICENTENNIAL CARAVAN. THE CARAVAN IS COMPOSED OF EXHIBIT VANS FOR EACH BRANCH OF THE MILITARY SERVICE. THE THEME OF THE EXHIBITION IS 'HISTORY OF THE ARMED FORCES AND THEIR CONTRIBUTION TO THE NATION'. (LOCAL). JACK MINASIAN, DIRECTOR; U S ARMED FORCES BICENTENNIAL EXHIBIT VANS PROJECT; 1370 2ND AVE; OROVILLE, CA 95965. (#1775-282).

APR 10 - JULY 4, '76. BENNINGTON FLAG DISPLAY 'COUNTDOWN '76'. EXHIBIT AT DOWNTOWN. (LOCAL). JOHN DAHLMEIER, DIR; BOY SCOUTS OF AMERICA TROOP 29; 2 ADELAIDE WAY; OROVILLE, CA 95965. (#107971-1).

MAY 7 - 9, '76. FEATHER FIESTA DAYS, CARNIVAL. THREE DAYS OF ACTIVITIES, BOAT FEES ONLY. AT DOWNTOWN, OROVILLE, AFTERBAY & SANK PARK. (LOCAL). MRS JACK MINASIAN, CHMN; MR HANK MC QUOWN; JR CHAMBER OF COMMERCE; 1370 2ND AVE; OROVILLE, CA 95965. (#104813-1).

JULY 4, '76. BOAT FESTIVAL AND PARADE & COUNTRY FAIR. A COMPETITIVE DECORATED BOAT PARADE TO BE AROUND THE SHORES OF OROVILLE DAM DURING DAYLIGHT HOURS. THE LAST BOATS TO PASS THE DAM WILL BE AT DUSK ILLUMINATED BY LIGHTS. AT LAKE OROVILLE, CALIFORNIA STATE PARK. (LOCAL). DELORES L POWERS, CO-CHMN; OMEGA NU - ALPHA BETA; 205 SKYLINE BLVD; OROVILLE, CA 95965. (#101243-1).

JULY 4, '76. DEDICATION OF CITY HALL PARKING LOT WITH WILDFLOWER DISPLAY. A DEDICATION OF CITY HALL PARKING LOT WITH WILDFLOWER DISPLAY AND HISTORIC MURAL 1856-1976. AT CITY HALL PARKING LOT, MONTGOMERY AND LINCOLN. (LOCAL). MRS JACK MINASIAN, CHMN; CITY OF OROVILLE BICENTENNIAL COMMITTEE; 1370 2ND AVE; OROVILLE, CA 95965. (#104813-3).

JULY 4, '76. FOURTH OF JULY COUNTY FAIR. FAIR AT PLAYTOWN USA, 5TH AND POMONA STS. (LOCAL). MRS GERRY THEVEOS, COORD; JUNIOR WOMEN'S CLUB OF OROVILLE; 2078 CAMPBELL AVE; OROVILLE, CA 95965. (#104813-4).

JULY 4, '76 - CONTINUING . 'OUR HERITAGE IN FASHIONS - CHINESE AND AMERICAN'. EXHIBIT OPENED & DEDICATED ON JULY 4, 1976. ILLUSTRATES SOME OF THE HISTORICAL HIGHLIGHTS OF LATE 19TH & EARLY 20TH CENTURIES. WEDNESDAY & THURSDAY HOURS 1PM TO 4:30PM. (LOCAL). MRS JACK MINASIAN, COORD; OROVILLE BICENTENNIAL COMMITTEE; 1735 MONTGOMERY ST; OROVILLE, CA 95965. (#108288-1).

JULY 5, '76 - CONTINUING . CHINESE-AMERICAN CLOTHES EXHIBIT. AUTHENTIC GARMENTS & ARTIFACTS DEPICTING 18 & 19TH CENTURY OUTFITS OF CHINA AND AMERICA; COPY OF CHINESE GARMENT FROM 500 BC INCLUDED. AT CHINESE TEMPLE COMPLEX, BRODERICK ST, OFF MONTGOMERY ST. (LOCAL). MRS JACK MINASIAN, CHMN; CITY OF OROVILLE BICENTENNIAL COMMITTEE; 1370 2ND AVE; OROVILLE, CA 95965. (#104813-6).

SEPT 12, '76. DEDICATION CHINESE TEMPLE COMPLEX ADDITION. AUTHENTIC GARMENTS & ARTIFACTS DEPICTING 18 AND 19 CENTURY OUTFITS OF BOTH COUNTRIES, (CHINA AND AMERICA), CHINESE GARMENT FROM 500BC INCLUDED. AT CHINESE TEMPLE COMPLEX, BRODERICK ST, OFF MONTGOMERY ST. (LOCAL). MRS JACK MINASIAN, CHMN; CITY OF OROVILLE BICENTENNIAL COMMITTEE; 1370 2ND AVE; OROVILLE, CA 95965. (#104813-2).

OWENS VALLEY

JULY 4 - DEC 31, '76. INYO COUNTY PAGEANT. CEREMONY, FESTIVAL, PARADE, LIVE PERFORMANCE. (ST-WIDE). DOROTHY C CRAGEN, CHMN; INYO COUNTY BICENTENNIAL COMMITTEE; INDEPENDENCE, CA 93526. (#100442-1).

OXNARD

MAY 19, '76. UNITED STATES ARMED FORCES BICENTENNIAL CARAVAN. CARAVAN IS COMPOSED OF EXHIBIT VANS FOR EACH MILITARY SERVICE. PROJECT THEME IS ' HISTORY OF THE ARMED FORCES & THEIR CONTRIBUTIONS. (LOCAL). STEVE GERHART, CHAIRMAN; U S ARMED FORCES BICENTENNIAL CARAVAN; CITY HALL; OXNARD, CA 93030. (#1775-570).

PACIFIC BEACH

BICENT MUSIC INFORMATION CENTER, PACIFIC BEACH, CA. A COLLECTION OF AMERICAN MUSIC FROM 1750-1812. INCLUDED ARE ANTHEMS, CAROLS, MADRIGALS, MARCHES & PROCESSIONS. (LOCAL). DR R JAY, PLANNER; PACIFIC BEACH BICENTENNIAL MUSIC INFORMATION CENTER; 880 SAPPHIRE ST; PACIFIC BEACH, CA 92109. (#20455). **ARBA GRANTEE.**

JAN 1 - DEC 31, '76. BICENTENNIAL MUSIC EXHIBIT. AN EXHIBIT OF MUSIC AND MUSICAL INSTRUMENTS (1750-1812) IN AMERICA; COMPOSITIONS AND ARRANGEMENTS OF THE PAST AND PRESENT WILL ALSO BE FEATURED. AT 880 SAPPHIRE ST. (ST-WIDE). DR R JAY, DIRECTOR; PACIFIC BEACH BICENTENNIAL MUSIC INFORMATION CENTER; 880 SAPPHIRE ST; PACIFIC BEACH, CA 92109. (#20455-1).

PACIFIC GROVE

OCT 16, '76. BUTTERFLY FESTIVAL. FESTIVAL, PARADE. (LOCAL). SECRETARY; PACIFIC GROVE CHAMBER OF COMMERCE; PACIFIC GROVE, CA 93950. (#103416-615).

PACIFICA

ARCHAEOLOGICAL INVESTIGATION IN PACIFICA, CA. EXPOSE, DELINEATE AND FURTHER CONFIRM THE MISSION DELORES OUTPOST BUILDINGS ON SANCHEZ ADOBE GROUNDS. DEVELOP HISTORICAL INTERPRETIVE PROGRAM ENCOMPASSING INDIAN, MISSION, SPANISH AND AMERICAN PERIODS. (ST-WIDE). JOHN T BROOKE, JR, DIRECTOR; COUNTY OF SAN MATEO, DEPT OF PARKS AND RECREATION; COUNTY GOVERNMENT CENTER; REDWOOD CITY, CA 94063. (#9120).

SAN FRANCISCO BAY DISCOVERY SITE - PACIFICA, CA. NATIONAL MONUMENT STATUS FOR PARK SITE OF HISTORIC SIGNIFICANCE, GREAT SCENIC BEAUTY & RECREATIONAL VALUE; IT IS NOW A NATIONAL HISTORIC LANDMARK WITH GUIDED TOURS, POSTALS, TALKS & FILM STRIPS. (LOCAL). CARL P MCCARTHY, VICE PRESIDENT; PORTOLA EXPEDITION FOUNDATION; 5 EASTLAKE AVE; PACIFICA, CA 94044. (#22524).

JULY 3 - 5, '76. PACIFICA BICENTENNIAL FIESTA. PIER TO PARK 5 MILE RACE; RED, WHITE & BLUE BALL; KIWAINIS PANCAKE BREAKFAST. AT FRONTIERLAND PARK, YOSEMITE DR. (LOCAL). MRS SHIELA HYMAN, CHMN; CITY OF PACIFICA; 836 STANDISH RD; PACIFICA, CA 94044. (#103797-7).

PAICINES

AUG 24, '76. NATL PK SVC '...A LITTLE LOOK AROUND' VISITS PINNACLES N M. THIS SHORT PROGRAM FEATURES ACTORS PORTRAYING FAMOUS AMERICANS OF THE PAST WHO'VE RETURNED TO SEE AMERICA'S GROWTH. (REGN'L). PINNACLES NATL MON; NATIONAL PARK SERVICE; PAICINES, CA 95043. (#5653-43).

PALA

SEPT 24, '76. INDIAN HERITAGE DAY. DANCING, DEMONSTRATIONS, BASKET WEAVING, COMMUNICATIONS & TAPES. AT CULTURAL BLDG IN PALA. (LOCAL). FRONA LANE, CHAIRMAN; BICENTENNIAL COMMITTEE OF SAN MARCOS; 1400-18 EL NORTE PARKWAY; SAN MARCOS, CA 92069. (#100661-1).

PALM SPRINGS

JAN 24 - FEB 1, '76. PALM SPRINGS DESERT MUSEUM OPENING. GRAND OPENING OF NEW AND PRESTIGIOUS DESERT MUSEUM KICKS OFF A WEEK OF FESTIVITIES SALUTING THE BICENTENNIAL YEAR. AT DESERT MUSEUM AND MUSEUM ST. (LOCAL). LEE CHRISTOPHER, COORD; PALM SPRINGS CONVENTION AND VISTORS BUREAU; PALM SPRINGS DESERT MUSEUM; PALM SPRINGS, CA 92262. (#103416-117).

NOV 29 - 30, '76. UNITED STATES ARMED FORCES BICENTENNIAL CARAVAN. CARAVAN IS COMPOSED OF EXHIBIT VANS FOR EACH MILITARY SERVICE. PROJECT THEME IS 'HISTORY OF THE ARMED FORCES & THEIR CONTRIBUTIONS TO THE NATION'. AT SUNRISE PLAZA. (LOCAL). JOE HEALEY; UNITED STATES ARMED FORCES BICENTENNIAL CARAVAN; 640 E VISTA CHINO; PALM SPRINGS, CA 92262. (#1775-855).

PALO ALTO

OCT 22 - 26, '75. PALO ALTO SYNCON. CONFERENCE. (INT'L). BARBARA HUBBARD, CHMN; THE COMMITTEE FOR THE FUTURE, INC; 2325 PORTER ST, NW; WASHINGTON, DC 20008. (#21698-4).

MAR 13 - 14, '76. CONCLAVE '76 - COMMEMORATION OF 200 YEARS OF FLY FISHING IN USA. CONSERVATION LUNCHEON ON SATURDAY WITH ASST SECRETARY OF THE INTERIOR NATHANIEL REED & SUPERSTAR SATURDAY NIGHT DANCE. DEMONSTRATIONS, EXHIBITS, NEW EQUIPMENT DISPLAYS, & THE BICENTENNIAL COLLECTION OF FEDERATION OF FLY FISHERMAN'S FINEST FLY PLATE DISPLAYS. AT CABANA HYATT HOUSE HOTEL. (REGN'L). MARTY SELDON, CHMN; NORTHERN CALIFORNIA COUNCIL OF FLY FISHING CLUBS; 1146 PULORA CT; SUNNYVALE, CA 94087. (#102065-1).

PANORAMA CITY

OLDEST LIVING VALLYITE SEARCH, PANORAMA CITY, CA. A SEARCH CONDUCTED FOR THE OLDEST LIVING VALLYITES TO BE HONORED WITH A PANORAMA CITY PLAQUE. (LOCAL). MS GEORGIA P LAMB, BICENT CHMN; PANORAMA CHAMBER OF COMMERCE; 8155 VAN NUYS BLVD; PANORAMA CITY, CA 91402. (#15495).

PARAMOUNT

FEB 19, '76. DEDICATION OF FLAGPOLE AND PRESENTATION OF FLAG. THE FLAGPOLE IS 125 FEET HIGH AND THE FLAG IS 30 BY 50 FEET. AT HUNSAKER & ALONDRA BLVD. (LOCAL). MARY M MOSIER, CHAIRMAN; PARAMOUNT CITY BICENTENNIAL COMMITTEE; 15910 ORIZABA; PARAMOUNT, CA 90723. (#200006-152).

PASADENA

TOURNAMENT OF ROSES PARADE - 1975-1976-1977. PUBLIC AWARENESS EFFORT THROUGH USE OF BICENTENNIAL THEMES. EACH FLOAT IN '75 PARADE WILL RELATE TO THE THEME HERITAGE '76. FESTIVAL USA & HORIZONS '76 WILL BE USED FOR 1976 & '77 PAGEANTS. (NAT'L). WILLIAM LAWSON, EXEC DIRECTOR; PASADENA TOURNAMENT OF ROSES ASSOC; 391 SOUTH ORANGE GROVE BOULEVARD; PASADENA, CA 91105. (#3046). **ARBA RECOGNIZED.**

JAN 1, '75. CITY OF LONG BEACH BICENTENNIAL THEME FLOAT, ROSE PARADE. PARADE. (NAT'L). MAYOR; CITY OF LONG BEACH; 205 W BROADWAY; LONG BEACH, CA 90802. (#200006-95).

JAN 1, '75. ROSE PARADE FLOAT. COMPETITION, PARADE. (REGN'L). K C THOMPSON, CHMN; CITY OF SAN DIEGO; 530 B ST; SAN DIEGO, CA 92101. (#200006-334).

JAN 1, '76. BICENTENNIAL WAGON TRAIN PILGRIMAGE TO PENNSYLVANIA AT ROSE BOWL. PARADE. (NAT'L). GEORGE KEEGAN, CHMN; PENNSYLVANIA BICENTENNIAL COMMISSION; FOUR PENN CENTER; PHILADELPHIA, PA 19103. (#2184-2).

JAN 1, '76. CANADIAN BICENTENNIAL SALUTE IN THE 1976 TOURNAMENT OF ROSES PARADE. AN HISTORICAL FIRST, SPONSORED BY THE CITIES OF CALGARY & MONTREAL & PROVINCES OF QUEBEC & NOVA SCOTIA - 2 MARCHING BANDS AND THE ROYAL CANADIAN MOUNTED POLICE RIDERS. (INT'L). KEITH DE B PERCY, COORD; EMBASSY OF CANADA; 1746 MASSACHUSETTS AVE NW; WASHINGTON, DC 20036. (#18824-1).

JAN 1, '76. 'HATS OFF TO AMERICA' - PASADENA ROSE PARADE FLOAT. THEME OF FLOAT IS BICENTENNIAL HORIZONS. (LOCAL). JOHN SNIDELOR, DIRECTOR; CITY OF LONG BEACH; 6101 E 7TH ST; LONG BEACH, CA 90840. (#103309-20).

JAN 1, '76. TOURNAMENT OF ROSES - 1976 THEME OF 'AMERICA, LET'S CELEBRATE!'. PUBLIC AWARENESS EFFORT THROUGH USE OF BICENTENNIAL THEMES. EACH FLOAT IN '75 PARADE WILL RELATE TO THE THEME HERITAGE '76. FESTIVAL USA & HORIZONS '76 WILL BE USED FOR 1975 & '76 PAGEANTS. EACH FLOAT IN PARADE WILL FEATURE BICENTENNIAL THEME. (INT'L). FOREST W (FROSTY) FOSTER; PASADENA TOURNAMENT OF ROSES ASSOCIATION; 391 SO. ORANGE GROVE BLVD.; PASADENA, CA 91105. (#3046-1).

JAN 1 - 2, '76. PARTICIPATION IN THE TOURNAMENT OF ROSES PARADE WITH MAJOR DISPLAY. PARADE, RADIO/TV AT CITY OF PASADENA. (NAT'L). HERBERT R HANDS, MGR; AMERICAN SOCIETY OF CIVIL ENGINEERS; ASCE, 345 E 47TH ST; NEW YORK, NY 10017. (#104250-1).

MAY 4, '76. NETHERLANDS CHAMBER ORCHESTRA VISITS AMBASSADOR COLLEGE. LIVE PERFORMANCE. (INT'L). WILLIAM SIMONSZ, COORD; NETHERLANDS GOVERNMENT; NETHERLANDS EMBASSY-4200 LINNEAN; WASHINGTON, DC 20008. (#109013-15).

JAN 1, '77. FAIRVIEW BAND'S PERFORMANCE IN 1977 ROSE BOWL PARADE. PARADE. (LOCAL). ROBERT E JEFFREY, DIR; FAIRVIEW HIGH SCHOOL BAND; 1515 GREENBRIAR; BOULDER, CO 80303. (#107519-1).

JAN 1, '77. PASADENA TOURNAMENT OF ROSES - 1977 THEME OF 'HORIZONS '76'. PUBLIC AWARENESS EFFORT THROUGH USE OF BICENTENNIAL THEMES. EACH FLOAT IN THE PARADE WILL FEATURE A BICENTENNIAL THEME. (NAT'L). FOREST W (FROSTY) FOSTER; PASADENA TOURNAMENT OF ROSES ASSOC; 391 S ORANGE GROVE BLVD; PASADENA, CA 91105. (#3046-2).

PCFIC PALSADS

THE AMERICAN MUSIC PROJECT OF PACIFIC PALIS, CA. PROGRAM TO RECORD AND BROADCAST PRE-20TH CENTURY AMERICAN MUSIC TO INCLUDE DOCUMENTARIES DEALING WITH AMERICAN MUSIC. (ST-WIDE). CLARE SPARK, DIRECTOR; THE YANKEE DOODLE SOCIETY; 825 BROOKTREE RD; PACIFIC PALIS, CA 90272. (#10881).

BOOK & RECORDINGS ON MUSIC THEORY, CA. A TEXT WITH RECORD EXAMPLES ON THE EXPANSION OF CONTEMPORARY MELODIC & HARMONIC RELATIONSHIPS. (LOCAL). ROY HARRIS, COORDINATOR; 1200 TELLEM DR; PCFIC PALSADS, CA 90272. (#23130).

FEB 17 - 22, '76. 50TH LOS ANGELES OPEN GOLF TOURNAMENT. COMPETITION AT RIVIERA COUNTRY CLUB, 1250 CAPRI DR. (REGN'L). KAREN JENSEN, DIRECTOR; LOS ANGELES JUNIOR CHAMBER OF COMMERCE; 404 S BIXEL ST; LOS ANGELES, CA 90017. (#104513-1).

PERRIS

PERRIS BICENTENNIAL PROJECTS, CA. EACH MONTH'S CELEBRATION WILL BE CENTERED AROUND A DIFFERENT THEME. PROJECTS INCLUDE: CONVERSION OF OLD DEPOT INTO MUSEUM & RESEARCH LIBRARY & BURIAL OF TIME CAPSULE W/RECORD OF YEARS EVENTS. (LOCAL). ROSEMARY EVANS, COORDINATOR; PERRIS VALLEY HISTORIC & MUSEUM ASSOC; 157 PERON ST; PERRIS, CA 92370. (#28608).

PETALUMA

MAY 8 - 15, '76. OPEN HOUSE COAST GUARD TRAINING CENTER. TOUR, EXHIBIT AT COAST GUARD TRAINING CENTER PETALUMA. (LOCAL). ROY G COOK; COAST GUARD TRAINING CENTER PETALUMA; U S COAST GUARD TRACEN; PETALUMA, CA 94952. (#200006-417).

PETALUMA — CONTINUED

JUNE 19, '76. BICENTENNIAL-OLYMPIC DAY. COMPETITION AT COAST GUARD TRAINING CENTER PETALUMA. (LOCAL). ROY G COOK; COAST GUARD TRAINING CENTER PETALUMA, CHIEF PETTY OFFICER ASSOC; U S COAST GUARD TRACEN; PETALUMA, CA 94952. (#200006-416).

PICO RIVERA

BICENTENNIAL PARK IN PICO RIVERA, CA. $1.5 MILLION PARK: TO HAVE 50 CAMPSITES ON 60 ACRES OF LAND. EACH OF THE 50 CAMPSITES HAVE WATER & ELECTRICITY AND HE REST WILL BE A PRIMITIVE STATE. (LOCAL). FRANK TERRAZAS, CHAIRMAN; BICENTENNIAL COMMISSION OF PICO RIVERA; 6615 PASSONS; PICO RIVERA, CA 90660. (#31196).

CHARRO ARENA IN PICO RIVERA, CA. 5000 SEAT MULTIPURPOSE AMPHITHEATRE, EMPHASIZING MEXICAN-AMERICAN HERITAGE TO BE USED BY CHARROS, WHICH IS A MEXICAN RODEO GROUP. IT WILL ALSO BE USED FOR CONCERTS AND EXHIBITIONS. (LOCAL). FRANK TERRAZAS, CHAIRMAN; BICENTENNIAL COMMISSION OF PICO RIVERA; 6615 PASSONS BLVD; PICO RIVERA, CA 90660. (#31197).

JAN 23, '76. HAPPY BIRTHDAY AMERICA. FESTIVAL AT RIVERA PARK. (LOCAL). FRANK TERRAZAS, CHMN; BICENTENNIAL COMMISSION; 6615 PASSONS BLVD; PICO RIVERA, CA 90660. (#200006-452).

FEB 21, '76. BICENTENNIAL COSTUME BALL. FAIR AT LATIN AMERICAN PRESS CLUB. (LOCAL). FRANK TERRAZAS, CHMN; BICENTENNIAL COMMISSION; 6615 PASSONS BLVD; PICO RIVERA, CA 90660. (#200006-455).

FEB 23 - 28, '76. ART CONTEST: 'AMERICA WHY I LOVE HER'. COMPETITION AT ALL PARKS. (LOCAL). FRANK TERRAZAS, CHMN; BICENTENNIAL COMMISSION; 6615 PASSONS BLVD; PICO RIVERA, CA 90660. (#200006-454).

MAR 27, '76. BEN FRANKLIN KITE FAIR. COMPETITION, AWARD AT SMITH PARK. (LOCAL). FRANK TERRAZAS, CHMN; BICENTENNIAL COMMISSION; 6615 PASSONS BLVD; PICO RIVERA, CA 90660. (#200006-453).

APR 9, '76. AMERICANISM DAY. SPEECH CONTEST 'WHAT THE BICENTENNIAL MEANS TO ME' BY HS STUDENTS. AT RODEWAY INN 6540 ROSEMEAD PICO RIVERA. (LOCAL). FRANK TERRAZAS, CHMN; BICENTENNIAL COMMISSION; 6615 PASSONS BLVD; PICO RIVERA, CA 90660. (#200006-443).

APR 12 - 13, '76. EVENING AT EASTER. LIVE PERFORMANCE AT ST HILARY CATHOLIC CHURCH. (LOCAL). FRANK TERRAZAS, CHMN; BICENTENNIAL COMMISSION; 6615 PASSONS BLVD; PICO RIVERA, CA 90660. (#200006-444).

APR 24, '76. MARK TWAIN FESTIVAL. OLD-FASHIONED GAMES & CONTEST BASED ON MARK TWAIN'S NOVELS. AT PICO PARK. (LOCAL). FRANK TERRAZAS, CHMN; BICENTENNIAL COMMISSION; 6615 PASSONS BLVD; PICO RIVERA, CA 90660. (#200006-445).

MAY 1, '76. CINCO DE MAYO FIESTA. FAIR AT SMITH PARK. (LOCAL). FRANK TERRAZAS, CHMN; BICENTENNIAL COMMISSION; 6615 PASSONS BLVD; PICO RIVERA, CA 90660. (#200006-446).

JUNE 12, '76. AN EVENING'S TRIBUTE TO FREEDOM. GRAND MARCH, SPEECH, SINGING & DRAMATIC PRESENTATION. AT EL RANCHO HS STADIUM. (LOCAL). FRANK TERRAZAS, CHMN; BICENTENNIAL COMMISSION; 6615 PASSONS BLVD; PICO RIVERA, CA 90660. (#200006-441).

JUNE 19, '76. ALL AMERICAN BABY SHOW. BABY CONTEST WITH PARTICIPANTS DRESSED IN RED, WHITE & BLUE. AT RIVERA PARK. (LOCAL). FRANK TERRAZAS, CHMN; BICENTENNIAL COMMISSION; 6615 PASSONS BLVD; PICO RIVERA, CA 90660. (#200006-447).

JULY 2 - 5, '76. 4TH OF JULY CARNIVAL & PARADE. CARNIVAL; RIDES; GAMES; ENTERTAINMENT; FIREWORKS. AT SMITH PARK. (LOCAL). FRANK TERRAZAS, CHMN; BICENTENNIAL COMMISSION; 6615 PASSONS BLVD; PICO RIVERA, CA 90660. (#200006-448).

AUG 16 - 20, '76. HUCK FINN SALUTES AMERICA. PARADE, FAIR AT SMITH PARK. (LOCAL). FRANK TERRAZAS, CHMN; BICENTENNIAL COMMISSION; 6615 PASSONS BLVD; PICO RIVERA, CA 90660. (#200006-449).

SEPT 13 - 17, '76. GREAT AMERICAN ATHLETICS FILM FESTIVAL. EXHIBIT AT ALL PARKS. (LOCAL). FRANK TERRAZAS, CHMN; BICENTENNIAL COMMISSION; 6615 PASSONS BLVD; PICO RIVERA, CA 90660. (#200006-450).

OCT 16, '76. CALICO DAZE. FESTIVAL BASED ON THE OLD WEST PRESENTED BY THE CITY'S CHILDREN. AT RIO HONDO PARK. (LOCAL). FRANK TERRAZAS, CHMN; BICENTENNIAL COMMISSION; 6615 PASSONS BLVD; PICO RIVERA, CA 90660. (#200006-451).

NOV 13, '76. DRAMA REVIEW. CHILDREN FROM EACH PARK PRESENT A DRAMA BASED ON AMERICA'S PAST. AT PICO PARK. (LOCAL). FRANK TERRAZAS, CHMN; BICENTENNIAL COMMISSION; 6615 PASSONS BLVD; PICO RIVERA, CA 90660. (#200006-442).

NOV 22 - 23, '76. EVENING AT THANKSGIVING. LIVE PERFORMANCE AT ST HILARY CATHOLIC CHURCH. (LOCAL). FRANK TERRAZAS, CHMN; BICENTENNIAL COMMISSION; 6615 PASSONS BLVD; PICO RIVERA, CA 90660. (#200006-440).

NOV 28, '76. BICENTENNIAL TARDEADA. LIVE PERFORMANCE AT HOT POTATO RESTAURANT WHITTIER BLVD. (LOCAL). FRANK TERRAZAS, CHMN; BICENTENNIAL COMMISSION; 6615 PASSONS; PICO RIVERA, CA 90660. (#200006-438).

DEC 6 - 10, '76. CREATIVE WRITING CONTEST. 25 WORD ESSAY BASED ON THE SENTENCE: 'IF I WERE PRESIDENT...'. (LOCAL). FRANK TERRAZAS, CHMN; BICENTENNIAL COMMISSION; 6615 PASSONS BLVD; PICO RIVERA, CA 90660. (#200006-439).

PIEDMONT

BICENTENNIAL OAK TREE - PIEDMONT, CA. AN OAK TREE COMMEMORATING THE BICENTENNIAL WAS PLANTED ON THE SITE WHERE A HERITAGE OAK TREE ONCE STOOD. (LOCAL). STEVEN EIGENBERG, CHAIRMAN; PIEDMONT BICENTENNIAL COMMITTEE; 120 VISTA AVE; PIEDMONT, CA 94611. (#31320).

JULY 4, '76. 4TH OF JULY PARADE & PUBLIC CELEBRATION. AN ANNUAL EVENT WITH A BICENTENNIAL THEME FOR THIS YEAR'S PARADE & CEREMONY. THE PARADE CONSISTED OF OVER 30 UNITS FOLLOWED BY A CITY PICNIC & SPEECHES. AT LENGTH OF HIGHLAND AVE TO THE COMMUNITY HALL AREA OF PIEDMONT PARK. (LOCAL). KAY CHEATHEM; PIEDMONT RECREATION COMMISSION/CITY OF PIEDMONT; 120 VISTA AVE; PIEDMONT, CA 94611. (#200006-502).

SEPT 26, '76. PIEDMONT ARTS FESTIVAL & BICENTENNIAL CONCERT. AN ANNUAL EVENT, THIS YEAR STAGED WITH A BICENTENNIAL THEME. THIS EVENT INCLUDED ARTS/CRAFTS EXHIBIT, FLOWER/PLANT SALE, ENTERTAINMENT: BICENTENNIAL CONCERT CONDUCTED BY MAESTRO CARMEN DRAGON & FEATURED SOLOIST, PIANIST ROY BOGAS. AT PIEDMONT PARK/PIEDMONT COMMUNITY HALL. (LOCAL). ROBERT C LEEFELDT; CITY OF PIEDMONT/PIEDMONT BEAUTIFICATION FOUNDATION; 120 VISTA AVE; PIEDMONT, CA 94611. (#200006-503).

NOV 26, '76. BENNINGTON FLAG RAISING CEREMONY & PARADE. RAISING OF THE BENNINGTON FLAG AT ALL PUBLIC BUILDINGS & SCHOOLS. A BICENTENNIAL MILITARY COLORGUARD & PIEDMONT HIGH SCHOOL BAND TOOK PART IN THE CEREMONY AT PIEDMONT CITY HALL FOLLOWED BY A PARADE. AT PIEDMONT CITY HALL/ALL PUBLIC SCHOOLS/ALL OTHER PUBLIC BLDGS. (LOCAL). STEVEN EIGENBERG; PIEDMONT BICENTENNIAL COMMITTEE; 120 VISTA AVE; PIEDMONT, CA 94611. (#200006-504).

PINE GROVE

SEPT 25 - 26, '76. DEDICATION OF INDIAN CULTURAL CENTER AT GRINDING ROCK STATE PK. AMADOR COUNTY INDIAN CULTURAL CENTER, CA. MUSEUM AND SCHOOL FOR MIWOK TRIBE TO PRESERVE THEIR CULTURE. INDIANS BUILDING COMPLETE VILLAGE FOR CAMPING. (LOCAL). BEVERLY P RAUH, CHAIRMAN; AMADOR BICENT COMMISSION AND AMADOR CHAMBER OF COMMERCE; PO BOX 596; JACKSON, CA 95642. (#6271-502).

SEPT 25 - 26, '76. DEDICATION OF 'INDIAN DAYS' AT GRINDING ROCKS PARK. OPENING, FESTIVAL, EXHIBIT. (LOCAL). BEVERLY P RAUH, CHAIRMAN; AMADOR COUNTY ARBA; PO BOX 596; JACKSON, CA 95642. (#6271-501).

PITTSBURG

ARTS AND CULTURAL COMMISSION PROJ -PITTSBURG, CA. COMMISSION ESTABLISHED THROUGH CITY ORDINANCE. WILL FOCUS ON BICENTENNIAL RELATED ACTIVITIES-THEN WILL BE ON-GOING COMMISSION FOCUSING ON ARTS AND CULTURAL ACTIVITIES IN COMMUNITY. (LOCAL). REV ALLAN STURTEVANT, CHAIRMAN; PITTSBURG BICENTENNIAL COMMISSION; PO BOX 1776; PITTSBURG, CA 94565. (#3219).

HISTORICAL RECOLLECTIONS BOOK OF PITTSBURG, CALIF. BOOK TO BE PUBLISHED OF PERSONAL RECOLLECTIONS OF LONG-TIME RESIDENTS ABOUT EVENTS IN THE DEVELOPMENT OF THE CITY & SURROUNDING AREA. (LOCAL). REV ALLAN STURTEVANT, CHAIRMAN; PITTSBURG BICENTENNIAL COMMISSION; PO BOX 1776; PITTSBURG, CA 94565. (#3217).

MARINA VIEW PARK OF PITTSBURG, CALIF. COMMUNITY PARK COMMEMORATING COMMERCIAL FISHING ERA IN CITY HISTORY. FOCUS ON FISHING AND OTHER WATER-ORIENTED RECREATIONAL ACTIVITIES & COMPLEMENTS CITY'S MARINA. (LOCAL). REV ALLAN STURTEVANT, CHAIRMAN; PITTSBURG BICENTENNIAL COMMISSION; PO BOX 1776; PITTSBURG, CA 94565. (#3220).

PITTSBURG HISTORICAL LANDMARKS - PITTSBURG, CA. SITE MARKERS AND EXPLANATIVE MAPS & BROCHURES OF HISTORICAL SITES THROUGHOUT THE COMMUNITY. (LOCAL). MRS BESS AFFINITO, CHAIRPERSON; PITTSBURG BICENTENNIAL COMMITTEE/PITTSBURG HISTORICAL SOCIETY; 65 CIVIC AVE; PITTSBURG, CA 94565. (#20771).

PITTSBURG, CALIF, HISTORY PROJECT. PAMPHLET, MAP & BRIEF HISTORY OF PITTSBURG WRITTEN BY LOCAL HISTORIAN, JACK AIELLO. MARKERS WILL BE PLACED TO SHOW POINTS OF INTEREST TO REMIND PITTSBURG RESIDENTS OF THEIR CITY'S RICH HERITAGE. (LOCAL). BESS AFFINITO, CHAIRMAN; PITTSBURG BICENTENNIAL COMMITTEE; PO BOX 1776; PITTSBURG, CA 94565. (#2305).

PITTSBURG, CALIF, BICYCLE PATHS. DEVELOPMENT OF A NETWORK OF BICYCLE PATHS WITHIN THE CITY. TO BE DESIGNED TO TIE IN WITH BICYCLE PATHS IN NEIGHBORING COMMUNITIES. (LOCAL). REV ALLAN STURTEVANT, CHAIRMAN; PITTSBURG BICENTENNIAL COMMISSION; PO BOX 1776; PITTSBURG, CA 94565. (#3215).

SMALL WORLD CHILDREN'S PARK IN PITTSBURG, CALIF. CHILDRENS PARK DESIGNED TO REFLECT HISTORICAL ERAS IN CITY'S DEVELOPMENT; ONE COMPONENT IN PLANNED COMMUNITY PARK KNOWN AS STONEMAN EAST. (LOCAL). REV ALLAN STURTEVANT, CHAIRMAN; PITTSBURG BICENTENNIAL COMMISION; PO BOX 1776; PITTSBURG, CA 94565. (#3221).

JULY 4, '75. DEDICATION CEREMONY OF BICYCLE PATHS. DEVELOPMENT OF A NETWORK OF BICYCLE PATHS WITHIN THE CITY. TO BE DESIGNED TO TIE IN WITH BICYCLE PATHS IN NEIGHBORING COMMUNITIES. (LOCAL). REV ALLAN STURTEVANT; PITTSBURG BICENTENNIAL COMMISSION; PO BOX 1776; PITTSBURG, CA 94565. (#3215-501).

JULY 4, '75. DEDICATION CEREMONY OF MARINA VIEW PARK. MARINA VIEW PARK OF PITTSBURG, CALIF. COMMUNITY PARK COMMEMORATING COMMERCIAL FISHING ERA IN CITY HISTORY. FOCUS ON FISHING AND OTHER WATER-ORIENTED RECREATIONAL ACTIVITIES & COMPLEMENTS CITY'S MARINA. (LOCAL). REV ALLAN STURTEVANT; PITTSBURG BICENTENNIAL COMMISSION; PO BOX 1776; PITTSBURG, CA 94565. (#3220-502).

OCT 15 - 31, '75. COMMEMORATION OF BLESSING OF THE FLEET. MARINA VIEW PARK OF PITTSBURG, CALIF. COMMUNITY PARK COMMEMORATING COMMERCIAL FISHING ERA IN CITY HISTORY. FOCUS ON FISHING AND OTHER WATER-ORIENTED RECREATIONAL ACTIVITIES & COMPLEMENTS CITY'S MARINA. (LOCAL). REV ALLAN STURTEVANT; PITTSBURG BICENTENNIAL COMMISSION; PO BOX 1776; PITTSBURG, CA 94565. (#3220-501).

FEB '76. RIVERVIEW PARK DEDICATION. PICNIC TABLE AND BARBEQUE. AT RIVERVIEW PARK/FOOT OF MONTEZUMA ST/ON-SITE PARKING/FISHING PIER. (LOCAL). CHRIS BEKIARIS; PITTSBURG AMERICAN REVOLUTION BICENTENNIAL COMMISSION; 65 CIVIC AVE; PITTSBURG, CA 94565. (#104240-5).

MAR 20, '76. AMERICA'S MUSIC: CONCERT OF AMERICAN MUSIC. PIANIST: WANDA KRASNOFF, LOS MEDANOS COLLEGE ORCHESTRA. AT LITTLE THEATRE/250 SCHOOL ST PARKING AVAILABLE. (LOCAL). CHRIS BEKIARIS; PITTSBURG AMERICAN REVOLUTUION BICENTENNIAL COMMISSION; 65 CIVIC AVE; PITTSBURG, CA 94565. (#104240-2).

APR 2, '76. DE ANZA TREK TOUR: HISTORICAL RE-CREATION OF DE ANZA EXPLORATION. TOUR. (LOCAL). CHRIS BEKIARIS; PITTSBURG & CONTRA COSTA COUNTY BICENTENNIAL COMMISSION; 65 CIVIC AVE; PITTSBURG, CA 94565. (#104240-1).

JUNE 5, '76. BIKE PATH DEDICATION. CEREMONY AT LELAND RD AT EAST-WEST; HARBOR STREET AND EAST LELAND. (LOCAL). CHRIS BEKIARIS; PITTSBURG AMERICAN REVOLUTION BICENTENNIAL COMMISSION; 65 CIVIC AVE; PITTSBURG, CA 94565. (#104240-6).

JULY 2 - 3, '76. UNITED STATES ARMED FORCES BICENTENNIAL CARAVAN. CARAVAN IS COMPOSED OF EXHIBIT VANS FOR EACH MILITARY SERVICE. PROJECT THEME IS 'HISTORY OF THE ARMED FORCES & THEIR CONTRIBUTIONS TO THE NATION.'. (LOCAL). MRS BESS AFFIRITO, CHMN; UNITED STATES ARMED FORCES BICENTENNIAL CARAVAN; 3701 BROOKSDIE DRIVE; PITTSBURG, CA 94565. (#1775-684).

JULY 4, '76. DEDICATION CEREMONY OF SMALL WORLD CHILDREN'S PARK. JOINT COMMUNITY/CITY PROJECT TO BUILD CHILDREN'S PARK WITH TRAIN, LAGOON, FERRYBOAT, WESTERN THEATRE, PET FARM & GAMES. AT SMALL WORLD PARK, LELAND RD & HARBOR ST. (LOCAL). MRS BESS AFFINITO; PITTSBURG BICENTENNIAL COMMISION; PO BOX 1776; PITTSBURG, CA 94565. (#3221-501).

JULY 4, '76. HAPPY BIRTHDAY AMERICA: A 4TH OF JULY CELEBRATION. COMMUNITY CHURCH SERVICE AT 9 AM, PARADE AT 10 AM, INDEPENDENCE DAY CELEBRATION AT NOON, FIREWORKS AT 10 PM. ALSO ETHNIC MUSIC, FOOD & DRINK; GAMES; MILITARY MANEUVERS & DISPLAYS. AT STONEMAN PARK/E LELAND RD & HARBOR ST/PARKING AVAILABLE. (LOCAL). CHRIS BEKIARIS; PITTSBURG AMERICAN REVOLUTION BICENTENNIAL COMMISSION; 65 CIVIC AVE; PITTSBURG, CA 94565. (#104240-3).

PLACENTIA

BICENTENNIAL MEDALLION PROJECT - PLACENTIA, CA. 2500 ANTIQUED BRONZE MEDALS DEPICTING PLACENTIA'S 50TH ANNIVERSARY AND AMERICA'S 200TH BIRTHDAY WERE STRUCK. (LOCAL). DORIS BLACK, CHAIRMAN; PLACENTIA BICENTENNIAL COMMITTEE; 401 E CHAPMAN; PLACENTIA, CA 92670. (#28913).

FIRST DAY COVER - DECEMBER 2, 1976 - PLACENTIA, CA. 1000 FIRST DAY COVERS WILL BE ISSUED ON DECEMBER 2, 1976 TO COMMEMORATE PLACENTIA'S FIFTIETH BIRTHDAY. (LOCAL). DORIS BLACK, CHAIRMAN; PLACENTIA BICENTENNIAL COMMITTEE; 401 E CHAPMAN; PLACENTIA, CA 92670. (#28912).

JULY 24 - AUG 24, '75. BROWER COLLECTION DISPLAY. EXHIBIT AT PLACENTIA DISTRICT LIBRARY. (LOCAL). JOHN SLOTA, CHAIRMAN; PLACENTIA BICENTENNIAL COMMITTEE; 401E CHAPMAN; PLACENTIA, CA 92670. (#200006-364).

JUNE 14, '76. FLAG DAY CEREMONY. CEREMONY AT PLACENTIA CIVIC CENTER. (LOCAL). LEO COWAN, CHAIRMAN; INTERNATIONAL ORDER OF FORRESTERS; 1707 CARTLEN DR; PLACENTIA, CA 92670. (#200006-363).

JULY 4, '76. JULY 4TH PICNIC & FIREWORKS SHOW. ALL STATES PICNIC; FIVE GROUPS PROVIDED ENTERTAINMENT. AT VALENCIA HIGH SCHOOL STADIUM. (LOCAL). ED HOUSTON, CHAIRMAN; PLACENTIA BICENTENNIAL COMMITTEE; 401 E CHAPMAN; PLACENTIA, CA 92670. (#200006-366).

JULY 30, '76. BICENTENNIAL DRUM & BUGLE CORPS COMPETITION. COMPETITION, LIVE PERFORMANCE AT VALENCIA HIGH SCHOOL STADIUM. (LOCAL). MARV REID, CHAIRMAN; PLACENTIA BICENTENNIAL COMMITTEE; 401 E CHAPMAN; PLACENTIA, CA 92670. (#200006-365).

DEC 3, '76. PLACENTIA 50TH ANNIVERSARY DANCE. FESTIVAL AT ALTA VISTA COUNTRY CLUB. (LOCAL). SUSAN WEBER, COORD; JUNIOR ROUND TABLE OF PLACENTIA; PO BOX 923; PLACENTIA, CA 92670. (#109409-1).

PLACERVILLE

BICENTENNIAL PROJECTS - PLACERVILLE, CA. PROJECTS INCLUDE: PLACING MARKERS ON HISTORICAL BUILDINGS, WRITING COLUMNS FOR LOCAL NEWSPAPER - 'REMINISCING', WORKING WITH SCHOOL GROUPS AND PUBLISHING A BOOKLET ON LOCAL HISTORY. (LOCAL). BETTY HARVEY, PROJ DIRECTOR; HERITAGE ASSOC OF EL DORADO COUNTY; PO BOX 62; PLACERVILLE, CA 95667. (#22795).

RESTORATION PROJECT - PLACERVILLE, CA. A COUNTRY STORE AND OLD BARN WILL BE BUILT AND WE WILL RESTORE THE OLD STAMP MILL; THE STORE WILL BE PART OF THE MUSEUM AND THE STAMP MILL AND BARN WILL BE ON THE MUSEUM GROUNDS. (LOCAL). BRUCE ROBINSON, CURATOR; EL DORADO CO HISTORICAL SOCIETY/EL DORADO CO MUSEUM COMMISSION; 2850 COLD SPRINGS RD; PLACERVILLE, CA 95667. (#21471).

APR 10, '76. FASHION SHOW. COMPETITION, LIVE PERFORMANCE AT EL DORADO COUNTY FAIR GROUNDS MULTIPURPOSE ROOM. (LOCAL). YOLANDA WHITE, PROJ CHMN; UNITED RESCUE GRANGE #450 - CA WOMEN'S ACTIVITIES; PO BOX 412; SHINGLE SPG, CA 95682. (#106171-1).

MAY 7, '76. SUPPER PROGRAM. SUPPER PROGRAMS WITH AMERICAN FOODS, MUSICAL PRESENTATIONS AND PLAY. AT EL DORADO JR ACADEMY, 1900 BROADWAY. (LOCAL). MYRON WHITING, PRINCIPAL; EL DORADO JR ACADEMY; 1900 BROADWAY; PLACERVILLE, CA 95667. (#106171-4).

MAY 27, '76. HERITAGE 200. HERITAGE 200 WILL INCLUDE PARADE, RED WAGON FLOATS, COSTUMES, CONTESTS, SLIDE SHOWS, FOLK MUSIC, CONCERTS, CRAFTS AND OTHER DEMONSTRATIONS. AT FAIR GROUNDS. (LOCAL). ALLEN TUTTLE, COORD; ELDORADO COUNTY OFFICE OF EDUCATION; 337 PLACERVILLE DR; PLACERVILLE, CA 95667. (#106171-6).

JULY 4, '76. SIGNING OF BICENTENNIAL BOOK 'I REMEMBER...'. HARDBOUND BOOK OF 240 PAGES OF STORIES PICTURES & DOCUMENTS SUPPLIED BY DESCENDENTS OF PIONEER FAMILIES. AT EL DORADO COUNTY CHAMBER OF COMMERCE, 542 MAIN ST. (LOCAL). JACKIE BRANCH, MANAGER; EL DORADO COUNTY CHAMBER OF COMMERCE; 542 MAIN ST; PLACERVILLE, CA 95667. (#106171-7).

PLEASANT HILL

FILLINWOOD NATURE CENTER IN PLEASANT HILL, CA. PROJECT ENTAILS THE PRESERVATION & RESTORATION OF WALNUT CREEK; ALSO THE CONVERSION OF AN OLD FARM & SURROUNDING LAND INTO A NEW NATURE CENTER. (LOCAL). BRUCE M HERBERT, PRESIDENT; PLEASANT HILL BICENTENNIAL COMMISSION; PO BOX 1776, 3300 MAIN ST; PLEASANT HILL, CA 94523. (#9859).

HERITAGE TREES FOR PLEASANT HILL, CALIFORNIA. THE COMMUNITY OF PLEASANT HILL WILL JOIN IN AN EFFORT TO PRESERVE OLD TREES AND SET UP A TREE FARM TO ASSURE A CONTINUOUS SUPPLY OF NEW ONES. (LOCAL). BRUCE M HERBERT, PRESIDENT; PLEASANT HILL BICENTENNIAL COMMISSION; PO BOX 1776, 3300 MAIN ST; PLEASANT HILL, CA 94523. (#9860).

SCHOOL HOUSE RESTORATION PROJ OF PLEASANT HILL, CA. AN OLD SCHOOLHOUSE IS BEING RESTORED TO SERVE AS A COMMUNITY MUSEUM AND A MEETING PLACE FOR THE HISTORICAL SOCIETY. (LOCAL). BRUCE M HERBERT, PRESIDENT; PLEASANT HILL BICENTENNIAL COMMISSION; PO BOX 1776, 3300 MAIN ST; PLEASANT HILL, CA 94523. (#9861).

WAR MUSEUM RELOCATION PROJ IN PLEASANT HILL, CA. PLEASANT HILL'S WAR MUSEUM WILL BE MOVED TO A MORE SUITABLE PLACE. (LOCAL). BRUCE M HERBERT, PRESIDENT; PLEASANT HILL BICENTENNIAL COMMISSION; PO BOX 1776, 3300 MAIN ST; PLEASANT HILL, CA 94523. (#9862).

AUG 29 - 30, '75. VISIT OF THE BICENTENNIAL WAGON TRAIN. EXHIBIT, TOUR. (LOCAL). BRUCE M HERBERT, PRES; PLEASANT HILL BICENTENNIAL COMMISSION; PO BOX 1776, 3300 MAIN ST; PLEASANT HILL, CA 94523. (#9859-1).

MAY 7, '76. 'SPIRIT OF 1776', THEATRE AND DINNER PARTY. EXHIBIT, TOUR. (LOCAL). BRUCE M HERBERT, PRES; PLEASANT HILL BICENTENNIAL COMMISSION; PO BOX 1776, 3300 MAIN ST; PLEASANT HILL, CA 94523. (#9859-4).

JUNE 25, '76. UNITED STATES ARMED FORCES BICENTENNIAL CARAVAN. CARAVAN IS COMPOSED OF EXHIBIT VANS FOR EACH MILITARY SERVICE. PROJECT THEME IS ' HISTORY OF THE ARMED FORCES & THEIR CONTRIBUTIONS TO THE NATION'. (LOCAL). H C HAGELIA, CHAIRMAN; U S ARMED FORCES BICENTENNIAL CARAVAN; 2255 CONTRA COSTA BLVD; PLEASANT HILL, CA 94523. (#1775-580).

JUNE 28 - JULY 4, '76. 'WE, THE PEOPLE OF PLEASANT HILL', A WEEK LONG 200TH BIRTHDAY PARTY. FESTIVAL, CEREMONY, PARADE. (LOCAL). BRUCE M HERBERT, PRES; PLEASANT HILL BICENTENNIAL COMMISSION; PO BOX 1776, 3300 MAIN ST; PLEASANT HILL, CA 94523. (#9859-2).

JULY 4, '76. UNITED STATES ARMED FORCES BICENTENNIAL CARAVAN. CARAVAN IS COMPOSED OF EXHIBIT VANS FOR EACH MILITARY SERVICE. PROJECT THEME IS 'HISTORY OF THE ARMED FORCES & THEIR CONTRIBUTIONS TO THE NATION.'. (LOCAL). BRUCE HERBERT, CHMN; UNITED STATES ARMED FORCES BICENTENNIAL CARAVAN; 3300 N MAIN ST; PLEASANT HILL, CA 94523. (#1775-685).

OCT 17, '76. PRESIDENTIAL BICENTENNIAL COMMUNITY DANCE. FESTIVAL. (LOCAL). BRUCE M HERBERT, PRES; PLEASANT HILL BICENTENNIAL COMMISSION; PO BOX 1776, 3300 MAIN ST; PLEASANT HILL, CA 94523. (#9859-3).

PLEASANTON

BICENTENNIAL COMMUNITY BAND, PLEASANTON, CA. CREATION OF BAND FROM MEMBERS OF COMMUNITY TO PLAY BICENTENNIAL MUSIC AT VARIOUS CELEBRATIONS DURING THE BICENTENNIAL. (LOCAL). CHARLOTTE SEVERIN FESTIVAL SUB-COMMITTEE; BICENTENNIAL COMMUNITY BAND; 4513 MIRADOR DR; PLEASANTON, CA 94566. (#14722).

'FREEDOM OF SPEECH 1976'-SPEECHES, PLEASANTON, CA. BICENTENNIAL SPEECHES WILL BE PRESENTED TO ENCOURAGE GROUPS TO PARTICIPATE IN THE BICENTENNIAL. (LOCAL). LEONARD E PRATT, ADMIN LT GOVERNOR; TOASTMASTERS INTERNATIONAL DISTRICT 57; 2371 RAVEN RD; PLEASANTON, CA 94566. (#20919).

JEREMIAH FALLON HOUSE RELOCATION & RESTORATION-CA. PROJECT WILL BE TO RELOCATE, RESTORE & PRESERVE THIS 123-YEAR OLD HOUSE; IT WILL BE USED AS A MUSEUM & AN EDUCATIONAL TOOL. (LOCAL). TANYA CLARK, CO-CHAIRMAN; AMADOR-LIVERMORE VALLEY HISTORICAL SOCIETY; PO BOX 573; PLEASANTON, CA 94566. (#11629).

YOUNG CALIFORNIAN BUILDING, PLEASANTON, CA. BUILDING TO SERVE YOUTH OF ALAMEDA COUNTY, PARTICULARLY 4-H & FUTURE FARMERS OF AMERICA CLUBS. (LOCAL). LEE HALL, MANAGER; ALAMEDA COUNTY FAIR ASSOC; PO BOX 579; PLEASANTON, CA 94566. (#11621).

SEPT 16 - NOV 7, '75. SPIRIT OF '76 POSTER CONTEST. COMPETITION AT PLEASANTTON SCHOOL DISTRICT OFFICE BLDG. (LOCAL). BARBARA JOAN SMITH, CHMN; PLEASANTON PTA AND BOOSTER CLUBS; 2229 CAMINO BRAZOS; PLEASANTON, CA 94566. (#14721-1).

OCT 5, '75. HERITAGE HOME TOUR. TOURS OF PRIVATE AND HISTORICAL HOMES. AT TOUR WILL BEGIN IN DOWNTOWN PLEASANTON. (LOCAL). SANDI SINCLAIR, DIRECTOR; PLEASANTON BICENTENNIAL ORGANIZATION; 4005 STANLEY BLVD; PLEASANTON, CA 94566. (#102038-1).

JUNE 27 - JULY 11, '76. ALAMEDA COUNTY AGRICULTURAL FAIR ASSOCIATION. HORSE RACING, LIVESTOCK SHOW AND AUCTION, EDUCATIONAL & COMMERCIAL EXHIBITS, PROFESSIONAL INFORMATION FROM TV, STAGE AND SCREEN, GIANT MIDWAY, FLORICULTURE, FINE ARTS, MINERAL AND GEM SHOWS ARE THE PLANNED EVENTS. AT CORNER OF PLEASANTON AND BERNAL AVE. (LOCAL). LEE R HALL, SEC-MGR; ALAMEDA COUNTY AGRICULTURAL FAIR ASSOC; PO BOX 579; PLEASANTON, CA 94566. (#106095-2).

POINT MUGU

OCT 16 - 17, '76. BICENTENNIAL AIR SHOW AND OPEN HOUSE. EXHIBIT, LIVE PERFORMANCE AT APPROXIMATELY 60 MILES NORTH OF LOS ANGELES ON COAST HIGHWAY ONE. (REGN'L). PUBLIC RELATIONS OFFICER; NAVY PACIFIC MISSILE TEST CENTER; PACIFIC MISSILE TEST CENTER; POINT MUGU, CA 93042. (#104446-1).

POINT REYES

JULY 1 - DEC 31, '76. MIWOK INDIAN VILLAGE AT POINT REYES NS. REPLICATION OF MIWOK INDIAN TYPE VILLAGE; PUBLIC IS INVITED TO PARTICIPATE IN CONSTRUCTION OF VILLAGE; BUILDING TO BE DONE IN TRADITIONAL FASHION UNDER PROFESSIONAL GUIDANCE; UPON COMPLETION WILL BE SITE OF CULTURAL DEMONSTRATIONS AND HELP PROGRAMS FOR SCHOOL GROUPS. AT BEAR VALLEY HEADQUARTERS -- TRAILHEAD PARKING LOT. (REGN'L). POINT REYES NS; NATIONAL PARK SERVICE; POINT REYES, CA 94956. (#6727-220).

SEPT 25, '76. SIR FRANCIS DRAKE'S CALIFORNIA LANDING SITE SURVEY. CUTTER POINT HARRIS CONDUCTED A COASTAL SURVEY FROM BODEGA BAY TO GOLDEN GATE WITH HISTORIANS FROM THE SIR FRANCIS DRAKE NAVIGATION GUILD, NAT'L PARK SERVICE & CALIF HISTORICAL RESOURCES COMMISSION TO ASCERTAIN THE EXACT LOCATION OF DRAKES' CALIF LANDING. (LOCAL). ARTHUR E BROOKS, CHMN; U S COAST GUARD CUTTER POINT HARRIS (WPB 82376); PO BOX 8; BODEGA BAY, CA 94923. (#200006-394).

POLLOCK PINES

JULY 3 - 4, '76. PONY EXPRESS RE-RUN. THERE WILL BE MARCHING BANDS, SCHOOL BANDS AND BICENTENNIAL FLOATS AND AN ART EXHIBIT & FESTIVAL WILL BE INCLUDED IN THE CELEBRATION. (LOCAL). ALFRED BENTON, MANAGER; POLLOCK PINES CHAMBER OF COMMERCE; PO BOX 95; POLLOCK PINES, CA 95726. (#106171-3).

POMONA

HISTORIC BUILDING RESTORATION OF POMONA, CALIF. RESTORE HISTORIC HOMES AND MAKE THEM MUSEUMS -IST HOME IN VALLEY, AN ADOBE BUILT 1837, 1ST BRICK HOME BUILT 1875. RESTORE DOWNTOWN BUILDINGS FOR ART, ANTIQUE AND BOUTIQUE STORES. (LOCAL). CLEMETT L NEIBEL, CHAIRMAN; POMONA BICENTENNIAL COMMITTEE; CITY HALL P O BOX 660; POMONA, CA 91769. (#2584). **(??).**

LIBERTY GROVE OF TREES, POMONA, CALIF. CONSTITUTE A PARK OF 50 OFFICIAL TREES FROM EACH STATE IN THE UNION SYMBOLIZING LIVING & GROWING TOGETHER. WILL BE EDUCATIONAL AS WELL AS INSPIRING. (LOCAL). CLEMETT L NEIBEL, CHAIRMAN; POMONA BICETENNIAL COMMITTE; CITY HALL PO BOX 660; POMONA, CA 91769. (#2517). **(??).**

POMONA: A CENTENNIAL HISTORY - CA. HISTORY OF POMONA VALLEY WILL BE PUBLISHED. (LOCAL). TONY NAVARRO, ADMIN ASSISTANT; POMONA BICENTENNIAL COMMITTEE; PO BOX 660; POMONA, CA 91769. (#26607).

JUNE 19 - 21, '75. ANNU MEETING OF ALL CALIFORNIA HISTORICAL SOCIETIES. HISTORICAL SOCIETY OF POMONA VALLEY WILL HOST THE CONFERENCE AS ITS WAY TO CELEBRATE POMONA'S CENTENNIAL & NATION'S BICENTENNIAL. (ST-WIDE). MISS ELIZABETH ZILLES; HISTORICAL SOCIETY OF POMONA VALLEY; PO BOX 2473; POMONA, CA 91766. (#2518-501).

JUNE 22, '75. 8TH ANNUAL DEEP PIT BARBECUE. FREE WELLS FARGO STAGE COACH RIDES FOR CHILDREN, POMONA CONCERT, BAND CONCERT, INDIAN AND SPANISH DANCING, BALLET, FOLKLORICO ATZLAN. AT OLD PHILLIPS MANSION GROUNDS 2640 POMONA BLVD. (LOCAL). FRIEDA RIEGER; HISTORICAL SOCIETY OF POMONA VALLEY; 1016 GOTHIC WAY; POMONA, CA 91768. (#50670-1).

AUG 17, '75. RANCHO DE SAN JOSE 6-CITY FIESTA. SALE OF MEXICAN EARLY CALIFORNIA WESTERN FOOD FOLK MEXICAN EARLY CALIFORNIA DANCING MEXICAN WESTERN ENTERTAINERS. AT POMONA CIVIC CENTER PLAZA GAREY AVE MISSION BLVD POMONA. (LOCAL). TONY NAVARRO; BICENTENNIAL COMMITTEES POMONA CLAREMONT LA VERNE CHINO SAN DIMAS; POST OFFICE BOX 660; POMONA, CA 91769. (#50129-1).

DEC 23 - 30, '75. AMERICAN FREEDOM TRAIN DISPLAY DAYS AT POMONA. THE AMERICAN FREEDOM TRAIN WILL INCLUDE 10 EXHIBIT CARS & 2 SHOWCASE CARS DEPICTING DIFFERENT PHASES OF THE AMERICAN EXPERIENCE. ITS ARRIVAL WILL SERVE AS A CATALYST FOR LOCAL BICENTENNIAL CELEBRATIONS BY PEOPLE THROUGHOUT THIS NATION. (ST-WIDE). DON MALLICOAT, EDIT SVCS; THE AMERICAN FREEDOM TRAIN FOUNDATION, INC; 5205 LEESBURG PIKE, SUITE 800; BAILEY'S XRDS, VA 22041. (#1776-84).

SEPT 16 - OCT 2, '76. LOS ANGELES COUNTY FAIR. FAIR. (ST-WIDE). J ROBERT MURRAY, PR; LOS ANGELES COUNTY FAIR ASSOC; PO BOX 2250; POMONA, CA 91766. (#102867-1).

PORT HUENEME

TRIANGLE PARK IN PORT HUENEME, CA. THE U S NAVAL CONSTRUCTION BATTALION CENTER AND HUENEME BEAUTIFUL WILL RESTORE AN OLD DOWNTOWN TRIANGLE AREA OF LAND IN HONOR OF THE BICENTENNIAL. (LOCAL). DOROTHY RAMIREZ, BICENT CHAIRMAN; HUENEME BEAUTIFUL; 220 N MARKET ST; PORT HUENEME, CA 93041. (#16996).

JUNE 30 - JULY 6, '75. PORT HUENEME HARBOR DAYS. FOLLIES, FIREWORKS, BEAUTY CONTEST, CARNIVAL. AT PORT HUENEME RECREATION CENTER 550 PARK AVE. (LOCAL). JAMES DANIELS, GEN CH.; HARBOR DAYS INC. PORT HUENEME, CALIF; 1243 NO. 5TH ST.; PORT HUENEME, CA 93041. (#50788-1).

NOV 15, '75. MARINE CORPS BIRTHDAY BALL. UNIFORM & FLAG PAGEANT. AT SENATOR RICHARD BARD OFFICERS CLUB. (LOCAL). A E INGERSOLL JR, USMCR; I-I STAFF, CO H 2ND BATT, 23RD MARINES, 4TH MAR DIV; MCRTC, BLDG 6, NCBC; PORT HUENEME, CA 93043. (#200006-404).

NOV 22 - 23, '75. CALIFORNIA WAGON TRAIN. THE EVENT WILL INCLUDE AN ALL EQUESTRIAN PARADE, SQUARE DANCE, FOOD BOOTH, DIGNITARIES RECEPTION AND SIGNED SCROLLS TO BE PLACED IN THE WAGON. AT RECREATION CENTER, BUBBLING SPRINGS PARK, 550 PARK AVE. (LOCAL). HON DORILL WRIGHT, MAYOR; PORT HUENEME BICENTENNIAL COMMITTEE; 652 EVERGREEN LN; PORT HUENEME, CA 93041. (#103237-6).

DEC 12, '75. OLD-FASHIONED CHRISTMAS CAROLING. SENIOR CITIZENS FROM AREA REST HOMES WILL BE HONORED AND THE WATER TOWER WILL BE LIT; SANTA CLAUS WILL GIVE GIFTS TO SENIOR CITIZENS & REFRESHMENTS WILL BE SERVED. AT RECREATION CENTER, BUBBLING SPRINGS PARK, 550 PARK AVE. (LOCAL). DOROTHY RAMIREZ, CHMN; PORT HUENEME BICENTENNIAL COMMITTEE; 220 N MARKET ST; PORT HUENEME, CA 93041. (#103237-7).

JAN 9, '76. CITY EMPLOYEE'S PARTY. AWARDS WILL BE GIVEN FOR THE OUTSTANDING EMPLOYEE OF THE YEAR AND FOR THE NUMBER OF YEARS IN SERVICE. AT RECREATION CENTER, BUBBLING SPRINGS PARK, 550 PARK AVE. (LOCAL). HON DORILL WRIGHT, MAYOR; CITY OF PORT HUENEME & PORT HUENEME BICENTENNIAL COMMITTEE; 652 EVERGREEN LN; PORT HUENEME, CA 93041. (#103237-8).

JAN 16, '76. CHAMBER OF COMMERCE INSTALLATION DINNER. AWARD TO CITIZEN OF THE YEAR, HIGH SCHOOL STUDENT, MILITARY PERSON, SENIOR CITIZEN. AT RECREATION CENTER BUBBLING SPRINGS PARK, 550 PARK AVE. (LOCAL). DOROTHY RAMIREZ, CHMN; PORT HUENEME CHAMBER OF COMMERCE & BICENTENNIAL COMMITTEE; 220 N MARKET ST; PORT HUENEME, CA 93041. (#103237-9).

MAR 22, '76. BIRTHDAY PARTY: CITY OF PORT HUENEME. PAINTINGS OF CALIFORNIA MISSIONS TO BE ON DISPLAY; TOURS OF SCHOOL CHILDREN TO VIEW PAINTINGS; RECEPTION HOSTED BY NATIVE DAUGHTERS OF THE GOLDEN WEST. AT CIVIC CENTER, 250 N VENTURA RD, PORT HUENEME. (LOCAL). DOROTHY RAMIREZ, CHMN; PORT HUENEME BICENTENNIAL COMMITTEE; 220 N MARKET ST; PORT HUENEME, CA 93041. (#103237-11).

APR 7, '76. GROUNDBREAKING CEREMONY. GROUNDBREAKING CEREMONIES WILL BE HELD FOR A 120 UNIT SENIOR CITIZEN APARTMENT BUILDING. (LOCAL). HON DORILL WRIGHT, MAYOR; CITY OF PORT HUENEME; 250 N VENTURA RD; PORT HUENEME, CA 93041. (#103237-2).

MAY 1, '76. CINCO DE MAYO FIESTA. YOUTH PARADE INVOLVING PUBLIC SCHOOLS, CHRISTIAN SCHOOLS, U S MARINE CORPS,

PORT HUENEME — CONTINUED

VFW, WONNIE POST, U S NAVY. AT RECREATION CENTER BUBBLING SPRINGS PARK, 550 PARK AVE. (LOCAL). DOROTHY RAMIREZ, CHMN; HUENEME BEAUTIFUL & PORT HUENEME BICENTENNIAL COMMITTEE; 220 N MARKET ST; PORT HUENEME, CA 93041. (#103237-13).

MAY 12, '76. DEDICATION OF SHIP'S BELL, USS GALVESTON AS BICENTENNIAL MEMORIAL. DEDICATED AS A PERMANENT MEMORIAL ON 5/12/76. ABOUT 200 ATTENDED CEREMONY. MEMORIAL NOTES USS GALVESTON WAS FIRST U S NAVY SHIP TO BE EQUIPPED WITH TALOS MISSILE, A PROTOTYPE OF MODERN MISSILRY STILL USED BY THE NAVY TODAY. AT SPACE CITY MALL, NSWSES AREA, SEABEE CENTER. (LOCAL). NICK STRANGIO, CHAIRMAN; NAVAL SHIP WEAPON SYSTEMS ENGINEERING STATION; PORT HUENENE, CA 93043. (#200006-348).

MAY 17, '76. UNITED STATES ARMED FORCES BICENTENNIAL CARAVAN. CARAVAN IS COMPOSED OF EXHIBIT VANS FOR EACH MILITARY SERVICE. PROJECT THEME IS ' HISTORY OF THE ARMED FORCES & THEIR CONTRIBUTIONS TO THE NATION'. (LOCAL). DOROTHY RAMIREZ, CHAIRMAN; U S ARMED FORCES BICENTENNIAL CARAVAN; 410 E SCOTT ST; PORT HUENEME, CA 93041. (#1775-569).

JUNE 26 - JULY 5, '76. PORT HUENEME HARBOR DAYS CELEBRATION. THE THEME IS 'PROUDLY WE HAIL', BEAUTY CONTEST, FESTIVAL, MEN'S FOLLIES, FISHING DERBY, PANCAKE BREAKFAST, NAVY SHIP TOURS, FIREWORKS, BICENTENNIAL BALL AND PARADE. (LOCAL). DR ROBERT KALAYAN, CHMN; PORT HUENEME HABOR DAYS, INC/PORT HUENEME BICENTENNIAL COMMITTEE; 202 E GARDEN GREEN; PORT HUENEME, CA 93041. (#103237-5).

JULY 23, '76. MERCHANT'S NIGHT. MERCHANTS WILL DISPLAY THEIR WARES; THERE WILL BE A SPEAKER AND REFRESHMENTS. AT RECREATION CENTER, BUBBLING SPRINGS PARK, 550 PARK AVE. (LOCAL). DOROTHY RAMIREZ, CHMN; PORT HUENEME BICENTENNIAL COMMITTEE; 220 N MARKET ST; PORT HUENEME, CA 93041. (#103237-4).

SEPT 12, '76. OPEN HOUSE - DE ANZA TRAIL. DISPLAYS OF PHOTOS HISTORICAL LECTURES; TOUR OF DE ANZA TRAIL, BARBE-QUE, MUSIC & DANCING. AT PORT HUENEME MUSEUM, 220 N MARKET ST. (LOCAL). DOROTHY RAMIREZ, CHMN; PORT HUENEME MUSEUM & HISTORICAL SOCIETY & BICENTENNIAL COMMITTEE; 220 N MARKET ST; PORT HUENEME, CA 93041. (#103237-10).

SEPT 22, '76. WALTER B MORANDA PARK DEDICATION. AN 8.3 ACRE ACTIVITY PARK, SITUATED NEAR THE BEACH, WILL INCLUDE TENNIS, BASKETBALL AND VOLLEYBALL COURTS AS WELL AS SOFTBALL FIELDS, SOCCER FIELD, HANDBALL COURTS, HORSESHOE PITS AND A MULTI-PURPOSE BUILDING. (LOCAL). HON DORILL WRIGHT, MAYOR; CITY OF PORT HUENEME; 250 N VENTURA RD; PORT HUENEME, CA 93041. (#103237-1).

PORTERVILLE

VALLEY OAK ACORN SEEDLING NURSERY PROJ OF CALIF. NURSERY TO PRODUCE THOUSANDS OF VALLEY OAKS FOR CITIZENS TO PLANT OVER COUNTY-ALSO REDWOOD SEEDLINGS TO BE PLANTED AS LIBERTY TREES. (LOCAL). RODNEY HOMER, CHAIRMAN; TULARE COUNTY BICENTENNIAL COMMITTEE; 271 E GIBBONS AVE; PORTERVILLE, CA 93257. (#2978).

JUNE 16 - AUG 12, '76. CALIFORNIA GIRLS CHOIR EUROPEAN GOODWILL TOUR. TOUR, LIVE PERFORMANCE. (INT'L). JOHN VAZNAIAN, DIRECTOR; CITY OF PORTERVILLE; 663 MULBERRY AVE; PORTERVILLE, CA 93257. (#108837-1).

JULY 14 - AUG 15, '76. FABULOUS STUDIO BAND TOUR OF THE UNITED STATES. ENGAGEMENTS INCLUDE AMARILLO, DODGE CITY, ST LOUIS, KANSAS CITY, FORDS THEATER, PENTAGON STATE DEPT, JEFFERSON MEMORIAL, ANDREWS AFB, PHILADELPHIA, BOSTON, CHICAGO, OFFUTT AFB, DENVER, SALT LAKE, LAS VEGAS AND PITTSBURGH. (REGN'L). BUCK SHAFFER, DIRECTOR; PORTERVILLE COLLEGE AND PORTERVILLE HIGH; 465 W OLIVE; PORTERVILLE, CA 93257. (#108831-1).

PORTOLA VLY

JULY 4, '76. PORTOLA VALLEY TOWN PICNIC. FESTIVAL. (LOCAL). MRS R H ANDERSON, CHMN; PORTOLA VALLEY BICENTENNIAL COMMITTEE; 134 STONEGATE RD; PORTOLA VLY, CA 94025. (#105107-1).

RAMONA

RESTORATION OF ROMONA TOWN HALL - CA. PROMOTE PUBLIC INTEREST IN THE HISTORY OF TOWN HALL, PUBLICIZE NEEDS FOR RESTORATION AND MAINTENANCE, PROMOTE PROJECT (BICENTENNIAL HERITAGE WEEKEND) DIRECTED TOWARD RAISING FUNDS FOR THIS PURPOSE. (LOCAL). RUTH S MEYER, CHAIRMAN; RAMONA BICENTENNIAL COMMITTEE; PO BOX 1203; RAMONA, CA 92065. (#29438).

MAY 1 - 2, '76. BICENTENNIAL HERITAGE WEEKEND. ANTIQUE EXHIBITS OF VARYING KINDS AT MANY LOCATIONS, HISTORIC BUILDINGS TOUR, SQUARE DANCE AND FOLK DANCE PERFORMANCE, COSTUME CONTEST, OLD-FASHIONED TEA AND WAX MUSEUM AND OTHER EVENTS, FOR BENEFIT OF RAMONA'S HISTORIC TOWN HALL, THE COMMUNITY'S HORIZONS '76 PROJECT. (LOCAL). RUTH S MEYER, CHAIRMAN; RAMONA BICENTENNIAL COMMITTEE; PO BOX 1203; RAMONA, CA 92065. (#200006-351).

JULY 4, '76. COMMUNITY BICENTENNIAL INDEPENDENCE DAY SPIRITUAL CELEBRATION. CEREMONY AT COLLIER PARK. (LOCAL). RUTH MEYER, CHAIRMAN; RAMONA BICENTENNIAL COMMITTEE & RAMONA MINISTERIAL ASSOC; PO BOX 1203; RAMONA, CA 92065. (#200006-343).

RED BLUFF

CHURCH RECOGNITION MONTH - RED BLUFF, CA. THE CHURCH HISTORY WILL BE BROUGHT UP TO DATE. (LOCAL). CHAIRMAN; RED BLUFF BICENTENNIAL COMMISSION; PO BOX 810; RED BLUFF, CA 96080. (#25894).

FILM FESTIVAL IN RED BLUFF, CA. RED BLUFF HIGH SCHOOL WILL VIDEO-TAPE HISTORICAL PLACES AND EVENTS AS A PART OF HIGH SCHOOL SOCIAL SCIENCE CLASS WORK. (LOCAL). CARL L BLOMQUIST, CHAIRMAN; TEHAMA COUNTY BICENTENNIAL COMMITTEE; 1417 COLUSA ST; CORNING, CA 96021. (#14276).

ORAL HISTORY PROJECT - RED BLUFF, CA. A DESCRIPTION OF THE DEPRESSION YEARS WILL BE RECORDED. (LOCAL). RICHARD EGGERS, DIRECTOR; RED BLUFF UNION HIGH SCHOOL; 1260 UNION ST; RED BLUFF, CA 96080. (#25892).

PRESERVATION OF TEHAMA COUNTY'S HISTORY, CA. THE COMMISSION IS PULLING TOGETHER INFORMATION ABOUT PEOPLE, BUILDINGS AND SITES OF HISTORIC INTEREST WHICH IS BEING PUT ON COMPUTER IN SACRAMENTO AS PART OF A STATEWIDE PROJECT. (LOCAL). CARL L BLOMQUIST, CHAIRMAN; TEHAMA COUNTY BICENTENNIAL COMMITTEE; 1417 COLUSA ST; CORNING, CA 96021. (#14274).

RED BLUFF DAILY NEWS CENTENNIAL EDITION - CA. SPECIAL EDITION ON RED BLUFF'S 'YESTERDAYS'. (LOCAL). CHAIRMAN; RED BLUFF BICENTENNIAL COMMISSION; PO BOX 810; RED BLUFF, CA 96080. (#25893).

SERVICE CLUBS WINDOW DISPLAYS - RED BLUFF, CA. DISPLAYS OF HISTORIC ANTIQUES AND WORK BY STUDENTS. (LOCAL). CHAIRMAN; RED BLUFF BICENTENNIAL COMMISSION; PO BOX 810; RED BLUFF, CA 96080. (#25895).

TEHAMA COUNTY AGRICULTURE PROJECT, RED BLUFF, CA. THE DEPARTMENT OF EXTENSION SERVICE WILL BE ASKED TO COORDINATE VISITATION OF SCHOOL CHILDREN WITHIN THE COUNTY AND FROM CITY AREAS TO EXPERIENCE SUCH THINGS AS SHEEP SHEARING AND CATTLE BRANDING. (LOCAL). CARL L BLOMQUIST, CHAIRMAN; TEHAMA COUNTY BICENTENNIAL COMMITTEE; 1417 COLUSA ST; CORNING, CA 96021. (#14275).

TEHAMA COUNTY NOSTALGIA CAVALCADE IN RED BLUFF, CA. TO MAKE TEHAMA COUNTY HERITAGE KNOWN TO ITS OWN PEOPLE AND TOURISTS; TO ENCOURAGE THE PROMOTION OF FESTIVALS TO HIGHLIGHT THE HERITAGE OF THE COUNTY AND OUR COUNTRY; ERECT MONUMENTS OR MARKERS WHERE PROPER. (LOCAL). CARL L BLOMQUIST, CHAIRMAN; TEHAMA COUNTY BICENTENNIAL COMMITTEE; 1417 COLUSA ST; CORNING, CA 96021. (#16359).

WINDOW DISPLAYS - RED BLUFF, CA. ANTIQUES WILL BE DISPLAYED IN STORE WINDOWS. (LOCAL). M HUNT, COORDINATOR; NATIVE DAUGHTERS OF THE GOLDEN WEST; 1200 UNION ST; RED BLUFF, CA 96080. (#25891).

FEB 1, '76. CENTENNIAL FAMILIES HONORED. CEREMONY. (LOCAL). ANDREW OSBORNE, CHAIRMAN; RED BLUFF BICENTENNIAL COMMISSION; 1405 MILLER WAY; RED BLUFF, CA 96080. (#200006-134).

MAR 28, '76. MUSICAL PRESENTATION. LIVE PERFORMANCE AT FIRST CHURCH OF GOD. (LOCAL). REV J A BARBER; FIRST CHURCH OF GOD; S JACKSON & LUTHER RD; RED BLUFF, CA 96080. (#200006-135).

MAR 31, '76. CENTENNIAL CELEBRATION. EXHIBIT, TOUR AT CITY HALL. (LOCAL). ANDREW OSBORNE, COORD; RED BLUFF BICENTENNIAL COMMISSION; 1405 MILLER WAY; RED BLUFF, CA 96080. (#200006-139).

APR 1, '76. BANK OF TEHAMA COUNTY ROBBERY RE-ENACTMENT. LIVE PERFORMANCE AT CROCKER BANK. (LOCAL). ANDREW OSBORNE, COORD; RED BLUFF BICENTENNIAL COMMISSION; 1405 MILLER WAY; RED BLUFF, CA 96080. (#200006-140).

MAY 1 - 2, '76. FIRST CENTENNIAL SOFTBALL TOURNAMENT. COMPETITION AT FREY FIELD. (LOCAL). DIRECTOR; RED BLUFF CHAMBER OF COMMERCE; 100 MAIN ST; RED BLUFF, CA 96080. (#200006-99).

MAY 19, '76. DEDICATION OF SAMUEL AYER PARK. CEREMONY AT DOG ISLAND. (LOCAL). ANDREW OSBORNE, COORD; RED BLUFF CHAMBER OF COMMERCE; 1405 MILLER WAY; RED BLUFF, CA 96081. (#200006-98).

MAY 31, '76. MEMORIAL DAY VETERANS PARADE. PARADE AT MAIN ST. (LOCAL). JIM KENNEDY, COORD; VETERANS OF FOREIGN WARS; 1310 GARDEN AVE; RED BLUFF, CA 96080. (#200006-97).

JUNE '76. CENTENNIAL BUSINESSES HONORED. CEREMONY, CONFERENCE. (LOCAL). MAZOR OSBORNE; RED BLUFF BICENTENNIAL COMMISSION; PO BOX 400; RED BLUFF, CA 96080. (#108351-1).

AUG 11, '76. CENTENNIAL FAMILIES HONORED. CEREMONY. (LOCAL). ANDREW OSBORNE, CHAIRMAN; RED BLUFF BICENTENNIAL COMMISSION; 1405 MILLER WAY; RED BLUFF, CA 96080. (#108366-3).

AUG '76. FRATERNAL GROUPS AND ORGANIZATIONS HONORED. EXHIBIT, CONFERENCE. (LOCAL). MARCER OSBORNE; RED BLUFF BICENTENNIAL COMMISSION; PO BOX 400; RED BLUFF, CA 96080. (#108352-1).

DEC 19, '76. CENTENNIAL PARK DEDICATION. CEREMONY AT PINE AND RIVER ST. (LOCAL). ANDREW OSBORNE, CHAIRMAN; RED BLUFF CHAMBER OF COMMERCE; 1405 MILLER WAY; RED BLUFF, CA 96080. (#108366-2).

DEC 31, '76. TIME CAPSULE. CEREMONY AT TEHAMA COUNTY COURTHOUSE. (LOCAL). ANDREW OSBORNE, CHAIRMAN; RED BLUFF CHAMBER OF COMMERCE; 1405 MILLER WAY; RED BLUFF, CA 96080. (#108366-1).

REDDING

DANCE PROGRAM. AMERICAN DANCE FORMS ARE PRESENTED BY NATIONAL KNOWN PROFESSIONAL DANCE/RESIDENCY COMPANIES. (LOCAL). CRAIG O THOMPSON, COORD; SHASTA COMMUNITY COLLEGE & NATIONAL ENDOWMENT FOR THE ARTS; 1065 N OLD OREGON TRAIL; REDDING, CA 96001. (#104589-3). **(??).**

DISCOVERY SERIES. AMERICAN WORLD TRAVELERS PRESENT AND DISCUSS THEIR EXPLOITS AND HOW THEIR DISCOVERIES RELATE TO FUTURE AMERICAN FOREIGN POLICY. (LOCAL). CRAIG O THOMPSON, COORD; SHASTA COMMUNITY COLLEGE; 1065 N OLD OREGON TRAIL; REDDING, CA 96001. (#104589-4). **(??).**

OCT 15 - 16, '75. UNITED STATES ARMED FORCES BICENTENNIAL CARAVAN. THE CARAVAN IS COMPOSED OF EXHIBIT VANS FOR EACH BRANCH OF THE MILITARY SERVICE. THE THEME OF THE EXHIBITION IS 'HISTORY OF THE ARMED FORCES AND THEIR CONTRIBUTION TO THE NATION'. (LOCAL). BESSIE SANDERS, DIRECTOR; U S ARMED FORCES BICENTENNIAL EXHIBIT VANS PROJECT; BOX 880 SHASTA COUNTY COURTHOUSE; REDDING, CA 96001. (#1775-279).

JUNE 25, '76. GALA OPENING DINNER - 6TH ANNUAL SUMMER FESTIVAL. FESTIVAL ARTISTS JOIN WITH COMMUNITY MEMBERS AND VISITORS FOR A SUMPTUOUS SUMMER DINNER AND ENTERTAINMENT. AT REDDING HILTON INN, HILLTOP DRIVE OFF INTERSTATE 5 & HIGHWAY 44. (LOCAL). CRAIG O THOMPSON, COORD; SHASTA COLLEGE 6TH ANNUAL SUMMER FESTIVAL OF AMERICAN ARTS; 1065 N OLD OREGON TRAIL; REDDING, CA 96001. (#105178-7).

JUNE 25 - AUG 1, '76. SUMMER FESTIVAL OF AMERICAN ARTS. AN OPPORTUNITY FOR COMMUNITY MEMBERS AND VISITORS TO EXPERIENCE VARIOUS FACETS OF THE ARTS. THE FESTIVAL WILL INCLUDE AMERICAN COMEDY, THEATRE, MUSICALS, CHILDREN'S PLAY, ART EXHIBIT, FILM & MUSIC SHOWS. MATINEES ARE AT 2:15 PM. AT SHASTA COLLEGE THEATRE. (LOCAL). CRAIG O THOMPSON, COORD; SHASTA COMMUNITY COLLEGE; 1065 N OLD OREGON TRAIL; REDDING, CA 96001. (#104589-1).

JUNE 26 - 27, '76. AMATEUR FILM FESTIVAL - THE SUMMER FESTIVAL OF AMERICAN ARTS. AMATEUR FILM-MAKERS THROUGHOUT THE U S SUBMIT 8MM AND 16MM ORIGINAL FILMS IN ANIMATION, DOCUMENTARY, HUMOR AND CREATIVE EXPRESSION CATEGORIES; PRIZE MONEY WILL BE AWARDED TO WINNERS & THE GRAND PRIZE WILL INCLUDE A TV SCREENING; THERE IS A SPECIAL BICENT CATEGORY. AT SHASTA COLLEGE THEATRE, 299 EAST TO OLD OREGON TRAIL, PARK SOUTH LOT. (NAT'L). CRAIG O THOMPSON, COORD; SHASTA COLLEGE 6TH ANNUAL SUMMER FESTIVAL OF AMERICAN ARTS; 1065 N OLD OREGON TRAIL; REDDING, CA 96001. (#105178-6).

JUNE 30 - JULY 17, '76. 'TOM SAWYER' - MUSICAL VERSION BY SARA SPENCER. PERFORMANCE TIMES WILL VARY: 9:15 AM, 10:15 AM, 11:15 AM, 1:15 PM & 7:30 PM. AT SHASTA COLLEGE THEATRE, 299 EAST TO OLD OREGON TRAIL, PARK SOUTH LOT. (LOCAL). CRAIG O THOMPSON, COORD; SHASTA COLLEGE 6TH ANNUAL SUMMER FESTIVAL OF AMERICAN ARTS; 1065 N OLD OREGON TRAIL; REDDING, CA 96001. (#105178-5).

JULY 8 - 18, '76. FRANK LOESSER'S 'THE MOST HAPPY FELLA', SUMMER FESTIVAL MUSICAL. BASED ON SIDNEY HOWARD'S 'THEY KNEW WHAT THEY WANTED', THE FRANK LOESSER MUSICAL DESCRIBES THE LEGEND OF A MAIL ORDER BRIDE IN NAPA, CALIFORNIA ABOUT 50 YEARS AGO. A FULLY STAGED PRODUCTION FEATURING SYMPHONY ORCHESTRA AND A CAST OF FORTY. AT SHASTA COLLEGE THEATRE, SOUTH PARKING LOT OFF OLD OREGON TRAIL. (LOCAL). CRAIG O THOMPSON, COORD; SHASTA COLLEGE 6TH ANNUAL SUMMER FESTIVAL OF AMERICAN ARTS; 1065 N OLD OREGON TRAIL; REDDING, CA 96001. (#105178-4).

JULY 11 - 23, '76. 'LIFE WITH FATHER' - COMEDY, SUMMER FESTIVAL PRODUCTION. SEASON SUBSCRIPTIONS AVAILABLE THROUGH JUNE 11TH. AT SHASTA COLLEGE THEATRE, 299 EAST TO OLD OREGON TRAIL, PARK SOUTH LOT. (LOCAL). CRAIG O THOMPSON, COORD; SHASTA COLLEGE 6TH ANNUAL SUMMER FESTIVAL OF AMERICAN ARTS; 1065 N OLD OREGON TRAIL; REDDING, CA 96001. (#105178-3).

JULY 28 - AUG 1, '76. 'THE ME NOBODY KNOWS' A KALEIDOSCOPIC MUSICAL. A KALEIDOSCOPIC MUSICAL FEATURING THE POETIC WRITINGS OF CHILDREN AND DWELLERS OF THE GHETTO, SPOKEN AN SET TO MUSIC. THE PLAY INCLUDES ADDITIONAL POETRY FROM REDDING AREA SCHOOL CHILDREN. THE AUDIENCE WILL FIND ITSELF SURROUNDED BY A MOST UNUSUAL SET. AT SHASTA COLLEGE THEATRE, SOUTH PARKING LOT OFF OLD OREGON TRAIL. (LOCAL). CRAIG O THOMPSON, COORD; SHASTA COLLEGE 6TH ANNUAL SUMMER FESTIVAL OF AMERICAN ARTS; 1065 N OLD OREGON TRAIL; REDDING, CA 96001. (#105178-2).

REDLANDS

JAN 9 - 10, '76. UNITED STATES ARMED FORCES BICENTENNIAL CARAVAN. CARAVAN IS COMPOSED OF EXHIBIT VANS FOR EACH MILITARY SERVICE. PROJECT THEME IS 'HISTORY OF THE ARMED FORCES AND THEIR CONTRIBUTIONS TO THE NATION'.

REDLANDS — CONTINUED

(LOCAL). DR LARRY BURGESS, CHMN; US ARMED FORCES EXHIBIT VANS PROJECT; PO BOX 751; REDLANDS, CA 92373. (#1775-303).

REDONDO BEACH

MAY 4 - 5, '76. UNITED STATES ARMED FORCES BICENTENNIAL CARAVAN. CARAVAN IS COMPOSED OF EXHIBIT VANS FOR EACH MILITARY SERVICE. PROJECT THEME IS ' HISTORY OF THE ARMED FORCES & THEIR CONTRIBUTIONS TO THE NATION'. (LOCAL). A R ALLISON, CHAIRMAN; U S ARMED FORCES BICENTENNIAL CARAVAN; CITY AHLL; REDONDO BEACH, CA 90277. (#1775-562).

REDWOOD CITY

JULY 3 - 5, '76. MULTI-CULTURAL FESTIVAL. FESTIVAL AT FAIR OAKS COMMUNITY CENTER, 2600 MIDDLEFIELD RD. (LOCAL). ANTONIO VILLASENOR, COORD; FAIR OAKS COMMUNITY CENTER; 2600 MIDDLEFIELD RD; REDWOOD CITY, CA 94063. (#106136-1).

RESEDA

INVISIBLE CITIZEN, INCORPORATED - RESEDA, CA. AN UMBRELLA CORPORATION TO INCLUDE HANDICAPPED CITIZENS IN BICENTENNIAL & OTHER ON-GOING PROJECTS. (LOCAL). JYNNY RETZINGER, SECRETARY; THE INVISIBLE CITIZEN, INC; 7635 ETIWANDA AVE; RESEDA, CA 91335. (#30030).

RIALTO

COMMUNITY PROJECT IN RIALTA, CA. COMMUNITY FIREPLUGS WILL BE PAINTED. (LOCAL). VAL RUSSO, CHAIRPERSON; RIALTA BICENTENNIAL COMMITTEE; 2ND & PALM ST; RIALTA, CA 92376. (#30797).

DISPLAY: HISTORICAL BOOKS & MAGAZINES. EXHIBIT AT RIALTO CITY LIBRARY. (LOCAL). FRANK E VOIGHT; HERITAGE COMMITTEE; RIALTO BICENTENNIAL COMMISSION; 175 E HOME ST; RIALTO, CA 92376. (#200006-481).

ESSAY CONTEST - RIALTO, CA. THE THEME IS MARTIN LUTHER KING, JR'S 'I HAVE A DREAM'. (LOCAL). FRANK E VOIGHT, CHAIRMAN; HERITAGE COMMITTEE - RIALTO BICENTENNIAL COMMISSION; 175 E HOME ST; RIALTO, CA 92376. (#31591).

HISTORY OF RIALTO, CA. A HISTORY OF RIALTO, CA IS BEING WRITTEN. COPIES ARE $3.00. (LOCAL). FRANK E VOIGHT, CHAIRMAN; HERITAGE COMMITTEE - RIALTO BICENTENNIAL COMMISSION; 175 E HOME ST; RIALTO, CA 92376. (#31592).

HISTORY OF RIALTO, CA CHURCHES. A HISTORY OF RIALTO, CA CHURCHES IS BEING WRITTEN. COPIES ARE $1.00. (LOCAL). FRANK E VOIGHT, CHAIRMAN; HERITAGE COMMITTEE - RIALTO BICENTENNIAL COMMISSION; 175 E HOME ST; RIALTO, CA 92376. (#31593).

PLAY 'BIRTH CERTIFICATE OF THE UNITED STATES'. LIVE PERFORMANCE. (LOCAL). FRANK E VOIGHT; HERITAGE COMMITTEE, RIALTO BICENTENNIAL COMMISSION; 175 E HOME ST; RIALTO, CA 92376. (#200006-480).

OCT 19, '75 - JULY 4, '76. BICENTENNIAL EVENTS OF RIALTO, CA. 10/19/75 HORSE SHOE CONTEST; 1/10/76 BICENTENNIAL COMMUNITY PARTY; 2/20 LOS COMPADRES COSTUME DANCE; 3/25 BICENT BAND & CHOIR CONCERT; 6/26 CA STARS TALENT SHOW; 7/3-7/4 CELEBRATION & PARADE 'HERITAGE TO HORIZONS'. (LOCAL). VAL RUSSO; RIALTO BICENTENNIAL COMMISSION; 18156 W COAST BLVD; RIALTO, CA 92376. (#200006-527).

RICHMOND

RESTORATION OF WORKS BY JOHN ROEDER, CA. RESTORE NAIVE WORKS BY NATIONALLY RECOGNIZED FOLK ARTIST JOHN ROEDER THAT HAVE BEEN WORN BY TIME, WEATHER AND VANDALS. (LOCAL). J T SOULT, CURATOR; RICHMOND ART CENTER; CIVIC CENTER PLAZA; RICHMOND, CA 94804. (#22451).

MAY 8, '76. NETHERLANDS CHAMBER ORCHESTRA VISITS RICHMOND, CA. LIVE PERFORMANCE. (INT'L). WILLIAM SIMONSZ, COORD; NETHERLANDS GOVERNMENT; NETHERLANDS EMBASSY-4200 LINNEAN; WASHINGTON, DC 20008. (#109013-18).

RIDGECREST

NOV 1, '76. UNITED STATES ARMED FORCES BICENTENNIAL CARAVAN. CARAVAN IS COMPOSED OF EXHIBIT VANS FOR EACH MILITARY SERVICE. PROJECT THEME IS 'HISTORY OF THE ARMED FORCES & THEIR CONTRIBUTIONS TO THE NATION'. (LOCAL). CHMN-RIDGCREST BICENT COM; UNITED STATES ARMED FORCES BICENTENNIAL CARAVAN; RIDGECREST, CA 93555. (#1775-836).

RIPON

OCT 15, '76. UNITED STATES ARMED FORCES BICENTENNIAL CARAVAN. CARAVAN IS COMPOSED OF EXHIBIT VANS FOR EACH MILITARY SERVICE. PROJECT THEME IS 'HISTORY OF THE ARMED FORCES & THEIR CONTRIBUTIONS TO THE NATION'. (LOCAL). MRS C F MULHOLAND; UNITED STATES ARMED FORCES BICENTENNIAL CARAVAN; PO 327; RIPON, CA 95366. (#1775-825).

RIVERBANK

ARBOR TREE-PLANTING CEREMONY: RIVERBANK, CA. PLANTING OF THIRTEEN TREES IN A HUNDRED AND FIFTY FOOT DIAMETER HONORING THE THIRTEEN COLONIES PLUS A FOURTEENTH TREE IN THE CENTER HONORING CALIFORNIA WITH STATE FLAGS AROUND IT IN JACOB MEYER PARK. (LOCAL). HENRI D ETHIER, JR, CHAIRPERSON; RIVERBANK BICENTENNIAL COMMITTEE; 3119 RIVERSIDE DR; RIVERBANK, CA 95367. (#30796).

APR 18 - 19, '75. PAUL REVERE'S RIDE & KICK-OFF BICENTENNIAL DINNER DANCE. A COMPLETE COMMUNITY AFFAIR WITH PAUL REVERE'S RIDE RE-ENACTED, PRESENTATION OF STATE FLAGS OF THE 13 ORIGINAL COLONIES PLUS THE FESTIVAL ASPECTS OF THE DANCE LED TO A WONDERFUL FEELING OF TRUE PATRIOTISM & PRIDE-THE WHOLE FLAG-WAVING BIT!. AT RIVERBANK COMMUNITY CENTER, SANTA FE ST. (LOCAL). HENRI D ETHIER JR; RIVERBANK ARBC; 3119 RIVERSIDE DR; RIVERBANK, CA 95367. (#200006-526).

RIVERSIDE

BICENTENNIAL HISTORY & CALENDAR - RIVERSIDE, CA. WEEKLY PUBLICATION WILL BE CARRIED IN THE PRESS AND ENTERPRISE AS A PUBLIC SERVICE WITH ITEMS OF INTEREST FROM OUR NATIONAL, STATE AND LOCAL HISTORY; INFORMATION ON EXHIBITS, CONTESTS AND PROJECTS. (LOCAL). NORMA SIMPSON, DIRECTOR; RIVERSIDE BICENTENNIAL COMMITTEE; 3900 MAIN ST; RIVERSIDE, CA 92501. (#26894).

BICENTENNIAL PAPER WEIGHTS - RIVERSIDE, CA. GLASS INSULATORS FURNISHED BY PACIFIC TELEPHONE WILL BE PAINTED BY THE SR CITIZENS' ART GUILD AND SOLD BY THE BICENTENNIAL COMMISSION. (LOCAL). NORMA SIMPSON, DIRECTOR; RIVERSIDE BICENTENNIAL COMMITTEE; 3900 MAIN ST; RIVERSIDE, CA 92501. (#26893).

BICENTENNIAL QUILT - RIVERSIDE, CA. PROMINENT RIVERSIDE INDIVIDUALS WILL BE ASKED TO DESIGN, SEW AND AUTOGRAPH A SQUARE COMMEMORATING THE BICENTENNIAL; THE QUILT WILL BE DISPLAYED THROUGHOUT RIVERSIDE. (LOCAL). NORMA SIMPSON, DIRECTOR; RIVERSIDE BICENTENNIAL COMMITTEE; 3900 MAIN ST; RIVERSIDE, CA 92501. (#26892).

BICENTENNIAL RAINCROSS SQUARE HISTORY WALK - CA. A SOROPTOMIST PROJECT; A SERIES OF WALKING STONE PLAQUES ON THE HISTORY OF RIVERSIDE; SUBJECT MATERIAL HAS BEEN DEVELOPED BY TOM PATTERSON, A LOCAL HISTORIAN. (LOCAL). NORMA SIMPSON, DIRECTOR; RIVERSIDE BICENTENNIAL COMMITTEE; 3900 MAIN ST; RIVERSIDE, CA 92501. (#26895).

'PAINT A FIRE PLUG' - RIVERSIDE, CA. THE JURUPA ART CLUB WILL PAINT CITY FIRE PLUGS TO REPRESENT REVOLUTIONARY CHARACTERS. (LOCAL). NORMA SIMPSON, DIRECTOR; RIVERSIDE BICENTENNIAL COMMITTEE; 3900 MAIN ST; RIVERSIDE, CA 92501. (#26896).

PLEDGE OF ALLEGIANCE BOOKLETS - RIVERSIDE, CA. A BOOKLET EXPLAINING & ILLUSTRATING OUR PLEDGE OF ALLEGIANCE AND GEARED TO THE ELEMENTARY GRADES; PUBLICATION OF THE BOOKLET WILL BE PRECEDED BY A SCHOOL-WIDE CONTEST FOR PICTURE ILLUSTRATIONS. (LOCAL). NORMA SIMPSON, DIRECTOR; RIVERSIDE BICENTENNIAL COMMITTEE; 3900 MAIN ST; RIVERSIDE, CA 92501. (#26890).

REVOLUTIONARY REEL. FESTIVAL. (LOCAL). R STOVER, CHAIRMAN; RIVERSIDE COLLEGE; 4800 MAGNOLIA AVE; RIVERSIDE, CA 92506. (#200006-389).

RIVERSIDE, CA, BICENTENNIAL HISTORY. VIRGINIA SUMMERS, WORKING UNDER A HISTORY INTERNSHIP FROM CAL STATE UNIV AT FULLERTON, WILL KEEP A COMPLETE HISTORY ON THE RIVERSIDE BICENTENNIAL AND THE ORGANIZATIONS & INDIVIDUALS INVOLVED. (LOCAL). NORMA SIMPSON, DIRECTOR; RIVERSIDE BICENTENNIAL COMMITTEE; 3900 MAIN ST; RIVERSIDE, CA 92501. (#26897).

OCT 6 - 30, '75. AMERICA'S BICENTENNIAL. EXHIBIT AT COLLEGE LIBRARY. (LOCAL). A C KNOPF, CHAIRMAN; RIVERSIDE CITY COLLEGE; 4800 MAGNOLIA AVE; RIVERSIDE, CA 92506. (#200006-386).

OCT 6 - NOV 15, '75. '200 YEARS BY THE RIVERSIDE'. SEMINAR AT PUBLIC LIBRARY. (LOCAL). A C KNOPF, DIRECTOR; RIVERSIDE CITY COLLEGE & PUBLIC LIBRARY; 4800 MAGNOLIA AVE; RIVERSIDE, CA 92506. (#200006-385).

JAN 2 - 3, '76. CALIFORNIA WAGON TRAIN SHOW. EXHIBIT AT BACK LOT, EVANS PARK, MAGNOLIA AVE & TERRACINA DR. (LOCAL). NORMA SIMPSON, DIRECTOR; RIVERSIDE BICENTENNIAL COMMISSION; 3900 MAIN ST, PO BOX 1776; RIVERSIDE, CA 92501. (#104286-3).

JAN 14, '76. SALUTING OUR NATION'S BICENTENNIAL. LIVE PERFORMANCE AT AUDITORIUM. (LOCAL). A C KNOPF, CHAIRMAN; RIVERSIDE CITY COLLEGE MUSIC DEPT; 4800 MAGNOLIA AVE; RIVERSIDE, CA 92506. (#200006-383).

FEB 6, '76. 'UP WITH PEOPLE'. LIVE PERFORMANCE AT MUNICIPAL AUDITORIUM, 3485 7TH ST. (LOCAL). NORMA SIMPSON, DIRECTOR; RIVERSIDE BICENTENNIAL COMMITTEE; 3900 MAIN, PO BOX 1776; RIVERSIDE, CA 92501. (#104286-6).

FEB 10, '76. EASTMAN KODAK SPECTACULAR. EXHIBIT AT LANDIS AUDITORIUM, RIVERSIDE CITY COLLEGE. (LOCAL). NORMA SIMPSON, DIRECTOR; EASTMAN KODAK, NATIONAL GEOGRAPHIC SOCIETY; 3900 MAIN, PO BOX 1776; RIVERSIDE, CA 92501. (#104286-5).

MAR 18, '76. 'AIRMEN OF NOTE'. LIVE PERFORMANCE AT MUNICIPAL AUDITORIUM, 3485 7TH ST. (LOCAL). NORMA SIMPSON, DIRECTOR; RIVERSIDE BICENTENNIAL COMMISSION; 3900 MAIN, PO BOX 1776; RIVERSIDE, CA 92501. (#104286-7).

MAR 19 - 21, '76. 'GEORGE M' - MUSICAL COMEDY. LIVE PERFORMANCE AT AUDITORIUM. (LOCAL). A C KNOPF, CHAIRMAN; RIVERSIDE CITY COLLEGE; 4800 MAGNOLIA AVE; RIVERSIDE, CA 92506. (#200006-388).

APR 16 - 23, '76. BICENTENNIAL WEEK. FESTIVAL. (LOCAL). NORMA SIMPSON, DIRECTOR; RIVERSIDE BICENTENNIAL COMMISSION; 3900 MAIN, PO BOX 1776; RIVERSIDE, CA 92501. (#104286-2).

APR 21 - 26, '76. UNITED STATES ARMED FORCES BICENTENNIAL CARAVAN. CARAVAN IS COMPOSED OF EXHIBIT VANS FOR EACH MILITARY SERVICE. PROJECT THEME IS ' HISTORY OF THE ARMED FORCES & THEIR CONTRIBUTIONS TO THE NATION'. (LOCAL). NORMAN SIMPSON, DIR; U S ARMED FORCES BICENTENNIAL CARAVAN; PO BOX 1776; RIVERSIDE, CA 92502. (#1775-556).

MAY 1, '76. NETHERLANDS CHAMBER ORCHESTRA VISITS LOMA LINDA UNIV. LIVE PERFORMANCE. (INT'L). WILLIAM SIMONSZ, COORD; NETHERLANDS GOVERNMENT; NETHERLANDS EMBASSY-4200 LINNEAN; WASHINGTON, DC 20008. (#109013-12).

JUNE 23, '76. 'TRAIL IN DANCE' - NATIONAL SQUARE DANCE CONVENTION. FESTIVAL AT MUNICIPAL AUDITORIUM, 3485 7TH ST. (REGN'L). NORMA SIMPSON, DIRECTOR; RIVERSIDE BICENTENNIAL COMMISSION; 3900 MAIN, PO BOX 1776; RIVERSIDE, CA 92501. (#104286-4).

JUNE 26, '76. 'ONE NATION UNDER GOD'. LIVE PERFORMANCE AT MUNICIPAL AUDITORIUM, 3485 7TH ST. (LOCAL). NORMA SIMPSON, DIRECTOR; RIVERSIDE BICENTENNIAL COMMITTEE; 3900 MAIN, PO BOX 1776; RIVERSIDE, CA 92501. (#104286-1).

JULY 4, '76. BICENTENNIAL PARADE. PARADE AT STADIUM & PARKING AREAS. (LOCAL). A C KNOPF, CHAIRMAN; RIVERSIDE CITY COLLEGE & CITY RECREATION DEPT; 4800 MAGNOLIA AVE; RIVERSIDE, CA 92506. (#200006-384).

JULY 4, '76. FOURTH OF JULY OLD-FASHIONED CELEBRATION WITH PARADE. FESTIVAL, PARADE. (LOCAL). NORMA SIMPSON, DIRECTOR; RIVERSIDE BICENTENNIAL COMMISSION; 3900 MAIN, PO BOX 1776; RIVERSIDE, CA 92501. (#104286-8).

AUG 1 - 31, '76. WHAT AMERICA IS?. EXHIBIT AT PUBLIC LIBRARY & LOCAL DAILY NEWSPAPER BUILDING. (LOCAL). A C KNOPF, CHAIRMAN; RIVERSIDE CITY COLLEGE; 4800 MAGNOLIA AVENUE; RIVERSIDE, CA 92506. (#200006-387).

RNCH CORDOVA

EDWARD KELLEY SCHOOL RENOVATION IN CA. RENOVATION OF A 100-YR OLD ONE-ROOM SCHOOL. (LOCAL). PAUL M HAGAN, CHAIRMAN; RANCHO CORDOVA BICENTENNIAL COMMITTEE; 2197 CHASE DR; RNCH CORDOVA, CA 95670. (#29487).

RNCH PLS VRD

HISTORIC & SCENIC MARKERS, RANCHO PALOS VERDES, CA. CONCRETE MARKERS DESIGNATING SITES OF HISTORIC & SCENIC INTEREST & IMPORTANCE IN RANCHO PALOS VERDES. (LOCAL). TOM BANDY, COMMUNITY SERVICES OFFICER; RANCHO PALOS VERDES BICENTENNIAL COMMITTEE; CITY HALL, 30940 HAWTHORNE BLVD; PLS VRD PNSLA, CA 90274. (#28620).

JULY 4, '76. 4TH OF JULY BICENTENNIAL & FIREWORKS CELEBRATION. FESTIVAL AT CITY HALL BUILDINGS & GROUNDS, 30940 HAWTHORNE BLVD. (LOCAL). CHAIRMAN; RANCHO PALOS VERDES BICENTENNIAL COMMITTEE; 30359 HAWTHORNE BLVD; RNCH PLS VRD, CA 90274. (#200006-370).

RNCH SANTA FE

SPECIAL PROJECTS ON AMERICAN HISTORY - CA. FILMS, DRAMATIZATIONS AND EXHIBITS ON HISTORICAL EVENTS. (LOCAL). PRINCIPAL; RANCHO SANTA FE SCHOOL; BOX 809, AVE DE ACACIAS; RNCH SANTA FE, CA 92067. (#28914).

ROHNERT PARK

BICENTENNIAL MURAL TRIBUTE - ROHNERT PARK, CA. AN ARTISTIC PROJECT OF 8 IN-SERVICE TRAINING WORKSHOPS TO INSTRUCT ELEMENTARY SCHOOL TEACHERS IN TECHNIQUES OF CREATING & DEVELOPING HISTORIC MURALS AS A LASTING MEMORIAL TO THE BICENTENNIAL. (LOCAL). ART GRANT, COORDINATOR; CALIFORNIA STATE COLLEGE; 1801 E COTATI AVE; ROHNERT PARK, CA 94928. (#17359).

ROSEMEAD

DINSMOOR HOUSE MONUMENT OF ROSEMEAD, CALIFORNIA. MUSEUM OF EARLY ROSEMEAD AND CALIFORNIA HISTORY AND NEIGHBORHOOD PARK. (LOCAL). HUBERT E FOUTZ, CHAIRMAN; CITY OF ROSEMEAD BICENTENNIAL COMMITTEE; 3824 ROSEMEAD BLVD; ROSEMEAD, CA 91770. (#3303).

NOV 22, '74. PATRIOTIC FLAG PAGEANT-US MARINES AT HIGH SCHOOL& COMMUNITY AUDIT. EXHIBIT. (LOCAL). HUBERT E

ROSEMEAD — CONTINUED

FOUTZ, CHAIRMAN; CITY OF ROSEMEAD BICENTENNIAL COMMITTEE; 3824 ROSEMEAD BLVD; ROSEMEAD, CA 91770. (#3303-901).

JAN 3 - 4, '76. DE ANZA TREK STOPOVER FESTIVAL. OPENING, FESTIVAL, PARADE AT TREK FROM MEXICO TO SAN GABRIEL MISSION. (ST-WIDE). HUBERT E FOUTZ, CHAIRMAN; CITY OF ROSEMEAD BICENTENNIAL COMMITTEE; 3824 ROSEMEAD BLVD; ROSEMEAD, CA 91770. (#3303-502).

FEB 21, '76. DEDICATION OF NEW COMMUNITY CENTER. CEREMONY, LIVE PERFORMANCE. (LOCAL). HUBERT E FOUTZ, CHMN; CITY OF ROSEMEAD BICENTENNIAL COMMITTEE; 3824 ROSEMEAD BLVD; ROSEMEAD, CA 91770. (#3303-503).

FEB 23 - 25, '76. QUILTING DISPLAY AND DEMONSTRATION. EXHIBIT. (LOCAL). HUBERT E FOUTZ, CHMN; BICENT COMMITTEE LADIES & UNIVERSAL SAVINGS & LOAN ASSN; 3824 ROSEMEAD BLVD; ROSEMEAD, CA 91770. (#3303-504).

ROSEVILLE

JULY 7 - 8, '75. UNITED STATES ARMED FORCES BICENTENNIAL CARAVAN. CARAVAN NUMBER FOUR-COMPOSED OF EXHIBIT VANS FOR EACH MILITARY SERVICE. PROJECT THEME IS 'HISTORY OF THE ARMED FORCES & THEIR CONTRIBUTIONS TO THE NATION.'. (LOCAL). MRS MARTA BELISLE; US ARMED FORCES BICENT EXHIBIT VAN PROJECT; 700 VERNON ST; ROSEVILLE, CA 95678. (#1775-144).

S LAKE TAHOE

INDIAN CREEK RESERVIOR, S LAKE TAHOE, CA. AN ADVANCED WASTE WATER TREATMENT SYSTEM THAT HAS PRESERVED THE PURITY OF LAKE TAHOE. (LOCAL). DAVID CALLAHAN, GENERAL MANAGER; SOUTH TAHOE PUBLIC UTILITY DISTRICT; 1275 MEADOW CREST DR; S LAKE TAHOE, CA 95705. (#20029).

S SN FRANCSCO

OCT 3 - 4, '76. UNITED STATES ARMED FORCES BICENTENNIAL CARAVAN. CARAVAN IS COMPOSED OF EXHIBIT VANS FOR EACH MILITARY SERVICE. PROJECT THEME IS 'HISTORY OF THE ARMED FORCES & THEIR CONTRIBUTIONS TO THE NATION'. (LOCAL). WALLACE E PETTIGREW; UNITED STATES ARMED FORCES BICENTENNIAL CARAVAN; CITY HALL S SAN FRANCISCO; S SN FRANCSCO, CA 94080. (#1775-819).

SACRAMENTO

'THE BEAVER' CENTENNIAL BULLETIN PUBLICATION-NBMRP. COLLEGE NEWSPAPER HAS REPRINTED 'THE NATIONAL CENTENNIAL BULLETIN 1776-1876, GIVING INFO ON 1876 CELEBRATION, & DISTRIBUTED IT TO THE COLLEGE & HIGH SCHOOL HISTORY & GOVERNMENT CLASSES IN THE AREA. (LOCAL). HERBERT W BARROWS, JR, MANAGING EDITOR; 'THE BEAVER', AMERICAN RIVER COLLEGE; 4700 COLLEGE OAK DR; SACRAMENTO, CA 95841. (#24694).

BICENTENNIAL COMMEMORATIVE PLAQUE - SACRAMENTO, CA. BRONZE COMMEMORATIVE PLAQUE IN HONOR OF CALIFORNIA AND THE BICENTENNIAL TO BE INSTALLED IN THE LIBRARY AND COURTS BUILDING IN SACRAMENTO. (ST-WIDE). JUNE TUTON, ASSISTANT DIRECTOR; AMERICAN REVOLUTION BICENTENNIAL COMMISSION OF CALIFORNIA; 1501 8TH ST; SACRAMENTO, CA 95814. (#26922). **ARBA GRANTEE.**

'BICYCLING THROUGH THE MOTHER LODE' - CALIFORNIA. TRAVEL GUIDE OF HISTORIC SPOTS RELATED TO CALIFORNIA'S GOLD RUSH ERA BY BICYCLE. (ST-WIDE). WILLIAM PENN MOTT, JR, DEPT DIRECTOR; DEPT OF PARKS & RECREATION; 1416 9TH ST; SACRAMENTO, CA 95814. (#316). **ARBA GRANTEE.**

BILINGUAL BICENTENNIAL COOPERATION CENTERS, CA. CALIFORNIA'S BILINGUAL FOUNDING DOCUMENTS EXHIBITED IN MONTEREY'S COLTON HALL, THE STATE CAPITOL & SACRAMENTO CITY HALL. (ST-WIDE). WALTER FRAME, CHAIRMAN; AMERICAN REVIVAL COMMITTEE; 409 FORUM BLDG; SACRAMENTO, CA 95814. (#15109). **ARBA GRANTEE.**

BOOKLET ON THE GOLD RUSH OF CALIFORNIA. INTERPRETIVE BOOKLET FOR A FLIGHT PATTERN OF THE GOLD RUSH AREA OF CALIFORNIA, WITH DESCRIPTIVE MATERIAL OF THE GOLD COUNTRY. POTENTIAL NOT ONLY FOR THE LOCAL FLYERS BUT CHARTER FLIGHTS MADE AS WELL. (REGN'L). ALBERT C JOHNSON, EXEC DIRECTOR; ARBC OF CALIFORNIA; 1501 8TH ST; SACRAMENTO, CA 95814. (#926). **ARBA GRANTEE.**

CALIFORNIA EDUCATION BICENT PROJ, SACRAMENTO. PROVIDE TECHNICAL ASSISTANCE TO EDUCATIONAL COMMUNITY FOR BICENTENNIAL ACTIVITIES, DEVELOP & DISTRIBUTE INFORMATION PACKETS, PREPARE AND DISTRIBUTE FILM ON ROLE OF EDUCATION IN PROGRESS OF STATE. (ST-WIDE). DR MARCELETT HENRY, CONSULTANT, PGM PLANNING; CALIFORNIA STATE DEPT OF EDUCATION; 721 CAPITOL MALL; SACRAMENTO, CA 95814. (#15331). **ARBA GRANTEE.**

CALIFORNIA HERITAGE IN SONG - SACRAMENTO, CA. RESEARCH OLD CALIFORNIA MUSIC AND LITERATURE; COMMISSION CHORAL ARRANGEMENTS AND ORIGINAL WORKS BASED ON THESE MATERIALS; PERFORM THESE WORKS THROUGHOUT CALIFORNIA. (ST-WIDE). THERESA J MOREHOUSE, PRESIDENT; SACRAMENTO CHORALE; PO BOX 19051; SACRAMENTO, CA 95819. (#9073). **ARBA GRANTEE.**

CALIFORNIA INDEX OF AMERICAN DESIGN, SACRAMENTO. THE CALIFORNIA INDEX, HOUSED IN THE NATIONAL GALLERY OF ART WILL BE PHOTOGRAPHED; SLIDE SETS & DATA SHEETS WILL BE MADE AVAILABLE. THE INDEX WILL BE UPDATED & THE RESULTS WILL BE PUBLISHED. (ST-WIDE). PAMELA MCGUIRE, INTERPRETIVE SPECIALIST; STATE OF CALIFORNIA PARKS & RECREATION; PO BOX 2390; SACRAMENTO, CA 95817. (#18439).

CALIFORNIA'S LITERARY HERITAGE, SACRAMENTO. DISTRIBUTION OF MAPS TRACING CALIFORNIA'S LITERARY HERITAGE TO THE 1500 ENGLISH TEACHERS ATTENDING THE STATEWIDE CONFERENCE. TEACHERS WILL DISPLAY & DISCUSS MAPS IN CLASSROOMS THROUGHOUT THE STATE. (ST-WIDE). EUGENE SOULES, CHAIRMAN; CALIFORNIA ASSOC OF TEACHERS OF ENGLISH; PO BOX 4427; WHITTIER, CA 90607. (#22692). **ARBA GRANTEE.**

CALIF'S TIME-LINE PANORAMIC VIEW OF AMER HISTORY. A CONTRASTING OF IMPORTANT EVENTS OCCURING IN CALIFORNIA WITH THOSE HAPPENING IN THE 13 ORIGINAL STATES DURING THE AMERICAN REVOLUTION ERA, 1769-1783. (ST-WIDE). ALBERT C JOHNSON, EXEC DIRECTOR; ARBC OF CALIFORNIA; 1501 8TH ST; SACRAMENTO, CA 95814. (#315). **ARBA GRANTEE.**

CHARLES CHRISTIAN NAHL; GOLD RUSH PAINTER - CA. AN EXHIBITION OF PAINTINGS, DRAWINGS & PRINTS BY NAHL WHO WAS ACTIVE IN CALIFORNIA DURING 1850 - 78 & CREATED THRU HIS ILLUSTRATIONS & PAINTINGS THE VISUAL IMAGE OF THE GOLD RUSH STILL ACCEPTED TODAY. (ST-WIDE). RICHARD V WEST, DIRECTOR; E B CROCKER ART GALLERY; 216 O ST; SACRAMENTO, CA 95814. (#8728). **ARBA GRANTEE.**

CHINESE HISTORY PROJECT OF CALIFORNIA. DEPICT CONTRIBUTIONS TO CALIFORNIA WAYS OF LIFE, ARCHITECTURE, FOOD CLOTHING AND HORTICULTURE BY CHINESE PIONEERS. (REGN'L). ALBERT C JOHNSON, EXEC DIRECTOR; ARBC OF CALIFORNIA; 1501 8TH ST; SACRAMENTO, CA 95814. (#313).

COMMUNITY CENTER IN SACRAMENTO, CA. CONSTRUCTION OF INDIAN COMMUNITY CENTER. (LOCAL). MARY MAY NORTON, DIRECTOR; CORTINA RANCHERIA; PO BOX 41113; SACRAMENTO, CA 95841. (#22843). **ARBA GRANTEE.**

ELKS HONOR OUR FLAG PROGRAM. T.V., RADIO, NEWS, & BILLBOARD CAMPAIGNS 2-FLAG TRIBUTES BY & FOR STUDENTS DURING SCHOOL YR. 3-LARGE SCALE DRAMATIC COMMUNITY PROGRAMS ON FLAG DAY EACH YEAR. HEAVY EMPHASIS ON YOUTH PARTICIPATION. (NAT'L). YUBI G SEPAROVICH, STATE PRESIDENT; CALIFORNIA-HAWAII ELKS ASSOCIATION; 2028 K ST; SACRAMENTO, CA 95814. (#311).

HISTORIC CIVIL ENGINEERING LANDMARKS OF CALIFORNIA. PUBLICATION OF A BOOKLET LOCATING THE HISTORIC CIVIL ENGINEERING LANDMARKS OF NORTHERN CALIFORNIA FOCUSING UPON THEIR HISTORICAL AND ENGINEERING SIGNIFICANCE. (ST-WIDE). ALAN L PRASUHN, PROF CIVIL ENGINEERING; AMERICAN SOCIETY OF CIVIL ENGINEERS; 6000 J ST; SACRAMENTO, CA 95817. (#9118).

HISTORICAL ENVIRONMENTAL LIVING FOR CHILDREN-CALIF. OVERNIGHT LIVING EXPERIENCE BY CHILDREN AT HISTORIC SITES, RE-ENACTING ACTUAL HISTORIC LIVING ENVIRONMENT. (ST-WIDE). BILL HAUSSLER, VISITOR SERVICES; CALIFORNIA DEPT OF PARKS & RECREATION; 1416 9TH ST; SACRAMENTO, CA 95814. (#1070).

LIBERTY TREES PROJECT OF CALIFORNIA. CALIFORNIA WILL PRESENT REDWOODS TO 13 ORIGINAL COLONIES TO COMMEMORATE LIBERTY TREES PLANTED IN 1773 SHOWING COLONIES' SOLIDARITY. BRO CHURES & FILMS ABOUT REDWOODS & LIFE IN CA. IN 1770'S TO BE PROVIDED. (NAT'L). ALBERT C JOHNSON, EXEC DIRECTOR; ARBC OF CALIFORNIA; 1501 8TH ST; SACRAMENTO, CA 95814. (#928). **ARBA GRANTEE.**

MISSION MUSIC PROJECT OF CALIFORNIA. BROCHURE ON ORIGIN OF MISSION MUSIC DETAILING VARIATIONS REQUIRED TO ENABLE INDIANS TO PLAY INSTRUMENTS IN USE AT THE TIME. INSTRUMENTS RESTORED, PERFORMANCE & RECORDINGS OF MUSIC PLAYED IN CA. MISSIONS. (ST-WIDE). RUSS PORTER, CHIEF OF GRANTS & PLANNING; CALIFORNIA DEPT OF PARKS & RECREATION; PO BOX 2390; SACRAMENTO, CA 95811. (#1106). **ARBA GRANTEE.**

MOTHER LODE SKY TRAIL BOOKLET - CALIFORNIA. BOOKLET FOR PILOTS VIEWING FROM AIR, HISTORIC SPOTS IN ANZA-BORREGO STATE PARK; A TOUR GUIDE AND FLIGHT INSTRUCTION MANUAL. (ST-WIDE). WILLIAM PENN MOTT, JR, DEPT DIRECTOR; DEPT OF PARKS & RECREATION; 1416 9TH ST; SACRAMENTO, CA 95814. (#264).

OLD SACRAMENTO HISTORIC PUBLICATION - CA. A BOOK WILL BE PUBLISHED ON THE HISTORY OF OLD SACRAMENTO. (LOCAL). SAM J BURNS, GENERAL MANAGER; SACRAMENTO CONVENTION & VISITOR'S BUREAU; 1100 14TH ST; SACRAMENTO, CA 95814. (#10765).

OLD SACRAMENTO VISITOR & INFORMATION CENTER - CA. FUNDING COMPLETION OF VISITORS CENTER AT HISTORIC SITE NEAR SACRAMENTO. (LOCAL). SAM J BURNS, PROJ DIRECTOR; SACRAMENTO CONVENTION & VISITORS BUREAU; 1100 14TH ST; SACRAMENTO, CA 95814. (#10756).

PACIFIC COAST BICENTENNIAL BIKEWAY, CA. SIGNS WILL BE PLACED ON A 1,000 MILE BIKEWAY ALONG THE CALIFORNIA COAST; A TOUR GUIDE PACKAGE WILL INCLUDE TOURING & SAFETY INFORMATION AND CA BICYCLING LAWS & RULES. (ST-WIDE). HELY JONES, PUBLIC INFORMATION; CA DEPT OF TRANSPORTATION; 1120 N ST; SACRAMENTO, CA 95814. (#12356). **ARBA GRANTEE.**

RESTORE, DEDICATE & CELEBRATE - OLD SACRAMENTO. DEVEL MUSEUM; DEDICATE PONY EXPRESS STATUE; OLD FASHIONED JULY 4 INCLUDING STREET FAIR, DEDICATION OF STATE RAILROAD MUSEUM, PERIOD PLAYS AT EAGLE THEATRE. (ST-WIDE). RALPH SCURFIELD, DIRECTOR; SACRAMENTO BICENTENNIAL COMMISSION; 2707 K ST; SACRAMENTO, CA 95816. (#2974).

'SACRAMENTO, A PLACE TO REMEMBER' - A FILM IN CA. OLD SACRAMTO, A NATIONAL HISTORIC LANDMARK, IS IN PROCESS OF BEING RESTORED TO THE ERA OF THE CALIFORNIA GOLDRUSH, CIRCA 1849-1870; THE FILM BRINGS THIS ERA BACK TO LIFE. (ST-WIDE). R M STONE, ASST TO EXECUTIVE DIRECTOR; SACRAMENTO HOUSING AND REDEVELOPMENT AGENCY; 630 I ST; SACRAMENTO, CA 95814. (#9857).

SIR FRANCIS DRAKE COMMEMORATION PROJECT, CA. OFFICIAL COMMEMORATION OF 400TH ANNIVERSARY OF DRAKE'S LANDING AND EXPLORATION OF CALIFORNIA IN THE 16TH CENTURY (1579). (LOCAL). WILLIAM L SHAW, PROJ DIRECTOR; SIR FRANCIS DRAKE COMMISSION OF CALIFORNIA; 3701 COLLEGE AVE; SACRAMENTO, CA 95818. (#17097).

SOPHIE COMSTOCK MEMORIAL STATUE OF PONY EXPRESS. STATUE HONORING PONY EXPRESS RIDER AND HORSE AS PERMANENT MEMORIAL IN HISTORIC SECTOR OF SACRAMENTO, WESTERN TERMINUS OF THE PONY EXPRESS. (REGN'L). ALBERT C JOHNSON, EXEC DIRECTOR; ARBC OF CALIFORNIA; 1501 8TH ST; SACRAMENTO, CA 95814. (#326). **ARBA GRANTEE.**

'TWO HUNDRED YEARS OF TECHNICAL PROGRESS' EXPO-CA. ILLUMINATES SCIENTIFIC & TECHNICAL ADVANCEMENTS IN 14 THEMES AFFECTING SOCIETY. CONFERENCE WILL EXAMINE HOW SCIENCE & TECHNOLOGY CAN BE APPLIED TO SOLVING MANY OF SOCIETY'S PROBLEMS. (REGN'L). ROBERT J KUNTZ, PROJECT DIRECTOR; CALIFORNIA ENGINEERING FOUNDATION/CALIFORNIA ARBC; PO BOX 160085; SACRAMENTO, CA 95816. (#21756). **ARBA GRANTEE.**

WE THE PEOPLE - CALIFORNIA VOTERS PROJECT. A NON-PARTISAN VOTERS GUIDE IN OPERATION TO ENCOURAGE VOTER PARTICIPATION IN GOVERNMENT TO BE PUBLISHED FOR 1974 AND 1976 ELECTIONS. SPONSORED BY THE CALIFORNIA CHAMBER OF COMMERCE. (ST-WIDE). JOHN T HAY, EXEC VICE PRESIDENT; CALIFORNIA CHAMBER OF COMMERCE; 455 CAPITOL MALL SUITE 300; SACRAMENTO, CA 95814. (#214).

WESTERN STATES MUSIC TOURNAMENT, SACRAMENTO, CA. COMPETITION IN MUSIC BY YOUTH REPRESENTING THE WESTERN STATES. (REGN'L). MARILYN F LUHARTY, COORDINATOR; LA MESA CHAMBER OF COMMERCE; 8155 UNIVERSITY AVE; SACRAMENTO, CA 92041. (#26948). **ARBA GRANTEE.**

WOMEN ON THE CALIFORNIA MINING FRONTIER. STUDY DIARIES, LETTERS, REMINISCENCES OF WOMEN AT THE CALIFORNIA MINING CAMPS IN THE ROUGH DAYS OF THE GOLD RUSH, CIRCA 1849. (NAT'L). MRS KNAPLUND EAVENSON, INSTRUCTOR; AMERICAN RIVER COLLEGE; SACRAMENTO, CA 95841. (#5389).

JUNE 1, '74. SIMULTANEOUS PLANTING OF REDWOODS IN CALIFORNIA & 13 ORIGINAL STATES. CALIFORNIA WILL PRESENT REDWOODS TO 13 ORIGINAL COLONIES TO COMMEMORATE LIBERTY TREES PLANTED IN 1773 SHOWING COLONIES' SOLIDARITY. BRO CHURES & FILMS ABOUT REDWOODS & LIFE IN CA. IN 1770'S TO BE PROVIDED. (NAT'L). ALBERT C JOHSON, EX DIR; ARBC OF CALIFORNIA; 1501 8TH ST; SACRAMENTO, CA 95814. (#928-901).

APR 29, '75. SACRAMENTO COUNTY BICENTENNIAL KICKOFF DINNER. LIVE PERFORMANCE. (ST-WIDE). MRS JOYCE LORD, DIRECTOR; SOUND EXPRESS PARENTS CLUB OF LA SIERRA HIGH SCHOOL; 5510 LINDA LANE; CARMICHAEL, CA 95608. (#9121-501).

JULY 4 - 6, '75. UNITED STATES ARMED FORCES BICENTENNIAL CARAVAN. CARAVAN NUMBER FOUR-COMPOSED OF EXHIBIT VANS FOR EACH MILITARY SERVICE. PROJECT THEME IS 'HISTORY OF THE ARMED FORCES & THEIR CONTRIBUTIONS TO THE NATION.'. (LOCAL). MS KATHY TEICHROEW; US ARMED FORCES BICENT EXHIBIT VAN PROJECT; 1009 7TH ST; SACRAMENTO, CA 95618. (#1775-143).

SEPT 2, '75 - DEC 30, '76. PHILADELPHIA '76. PERFORMANCES AT: CAMELIA BOWL HUGHES STADIUM DECEMBER 13; OAKLAND RAIDERS GAME DECEMBER 21 AND PIG BOWL JANUARY 10. AT JOHN F KENNEDY HIGH SCHOOL, GLORIA DR. (ST-WIDE). JANE GOULD, CHMN; JOHN F KENNEDY SENIOR HIGH SCHOOL MUSIC BOOSTERS; 46 PARKLITE CR; SACRAMENTO, CA 95831. (#103797-3).

NOV 28 - 30, '75. AMERICAN FREEDOM TRAIN DISPLAY DAYS AT SACRAMENTO. THE AMERICAN FREEDOM TRAIN WILL INCLUDE 10 EXHIBIT CARS & 2 SHOWCASE CARS DEPICTING DIFFERENT PHASES OF THE AMERICAN EXPERIENCE. ITS ARRIVAL WILL SERVE AS A CATALYST FOR LOCAL BICENTENNIAL CELEBRATIONS BY PEOPLE THROUGHOUT THIS NATION. (ST-WIDE). DON MALLICOAT, EDIT SVCS; THE AMERICAN FREEDOM TRAIN FOUNDATION, INC; 5205 LEESBURG PIKE, SUITE 800; BAILEY'S XRDS, VA 22041. (#1776-35).

JAN 31, '76. 'SO PROUDLY WE HAIL'. MODELS WILL PERFORM IN A PAGEANT OF AMERICAN HISTORY, 1776-1976. AT WOODLAKE INN. (LOCAL). MRS ROSE SCHOENMAN, COORD; MERCY HOSPITAL GUILD & SACRAMENTO FLORIST ASSOC; 4690 PARKRIDGE RD; SACRAMENTO, CA 95822. (#102848-1).

FEB 13 - 15, '76. SEMINARS AND WORKSHOPS ON CALIFORNIA AUTHORS; DISTRIBUTE MAPS. LITERARY HERITAGE OF CALIFORNIA - CONVENTION. A CONVENTION OF 2,000 ENGLISH TEACHERS; OBJECTIVE - TO STRESS CALIFORNIA'S LITERARY HERITAGE; DISTRIBUTE CALIFORNIA LITERARY MAPS; AND DISPLAY AND DISCUSS MAPS WITH 2,500 STUDENTS THROUGHOUT STATE. (ST-WIDE). EUGENE SOULES, CHAIRMAN; CALIFORNIA ASSOC OF TEACHERS; PO BOX 4427; WHITTIER, CA 90607. (#9209-501).

APR 3 - 4, '76. PONY EXPRESS ANNIVERSARY CELEBRATION. STATUE HONORING PONY EXPRESS RIDER AND HORSE AS PERMANENT MEMORIAL IN HISTORIC SECTOR OF SACRAMENTO, WESTERN TERMINUS OF THE PONY EXPRESS. STATUE UNVEILING CEREMONY; CONTESTS; MUSIC; HISTORIC DISPLAYS. AT OLD SACRAMENTO HISTORIC AREA. (ST-WIDE). R. M. STONE; OLD SACRAMENTO MERCHANTS ASSOCIATION; 1029 SECOND STREET; SACRAMENTO, CA 95814. (#326-1).

SACRAMENTO — CONTINUED

APR 17, '76. ODORI FESTIVAL OF JAPAN VISITS SACRAMENTO. LIVE PERFORMANCE AT CONVENTION CENTER. (INT'L). DIRECTOR; MEL HOWARD PRESENTS; 143 E 27TH ST; NEW YORK, NY 10016. (#108965-21).

APR 23 - MAY 23, '76. 'OF THEE I SING'. LIVE PERFORMANCE AT EAGLET THEATRE. (LOCAL). CHARLES GOFF, DIRECTOR; SACRAMENTO CIVIC THEATRE; 1419 H ST; SACRAMENTO, CA 95814. (#106962-1).

MAY 14 - 15, '76. WESTERN STATES MUSIC TOURNAMENT. LIVE PERFORMANCE, COMPETITION. (REGN'L). MARILYN F LUHARTY, COORD; LA MESA CHAMBER OF COMMERCE; 8155 UNIVERSITY AVE; LA MESA, CA 92041. (#26948-1).

MAY 25 - SEPT 1, '76. STAGE COACH TOUR. TOUR WILL BEGIN IN ST JOSEPH, MO BY HORSE & STAGE COACH TO SACRAMENTO, CA BY SEPT 1ST; PURPOSE IS TO PROMOTE CUSTER COUNTY, CO AND SELL COMMEMORATIVE COIN. (REGN'L). ALTA FOSTER, COORDINATOR; CITY OF WESTCLIFFE; WESTCLIFFE, CO 81252. (#108684-1).

MAY 28 - 31, '76. 1976 DIXIELAND JUBILEE. APPROXIMATELY 40 JAZZ BANDS, 15 GUEST STARS PLAYING AROUND THE CLOCK IN NIGHT TIME OUTDOOR CONCERTS, AFTERNOON CONCERTS IN 4 SEPARATE LOCATIONS & 18 CABARET SITES. MOST EVENTS ARE STAGED IN HISTORICAL OLD TOWN SACRAMENTO. AT HISTORICAL SECTION, OLD SACRAMENTO. (REGN'L). DR BILL BORCHER; SACRAMENTO TRADITIONAL JAZZ SOCIETY; PO BOX 15604; SACRAMENTO, CA 95813. (#19455-3).

MAY 29 - JUNE 5, '76. UNITED STATES ARMED FORCES BICENTENNIAL CARAVAN. CARAVAN IS COMPOSED OF EXHIBIT VANS FOR EACH MILITARY SERVICE. PROJECT THEME IS ' HISTORY OF THE ARMED FORCES & THEIR CONTRIBUTIONS TO THE NATION'. (LOCAL). RALPH SCURFIELD, CHAIRMAN; U S ARMED FORCES BICENTENNIAL CARAVAN; 2707 K ST; SACRAMENTO, CA 95816. (#1775-576).

JUNE 19, '76. UNIVERSITY OF CALIFORNIA MARCHING BAND PRESENTS 'SPIRIT OF AMERICA'. THIS EVENT IS PART OF A SIX-WEEK PERFORMANCE TOUR OF THE U S BY THE UNIVERSITY OF CALIF MARCHING BAND. SPIRIT OF AMERICA IS A COLLEGIATE MUSICAL REVUE CELEBRATING OUR NATION'S BICENTENNIAL. AT SACRAMENTO HIGH SCHOOL BASKETBALL PAVILION, 2315 34TH ST. (REGN'L). AUBREY PENMAN, CHMN; SACRAMENTO CITY SCHOOLS; 4333 ALDERWOOD WY; SACRAMENTO, CA 95825. (#10515-6).

JULY 3, '76. INDEPENDENCE DAY PARADE AND ACTIVITIES-OLD SACRAMENTO. WESTERN STYLE INDEPENDENCE DAY CELEBRATION-PARADE-STAGE COACH RIDES-CONTESTS-SHOOT OUTS-FIREWORKS-HISTORIC DISPLAYS. AT OLD SACRAMENTO HISTORIC AREA, DOWNTOWN SACRAMENTO. (LOCAL). E S ASTONE; OLD SACRAMENTO CITIZENS AND MERCHANTS ASSOCIATION; 1029 SECOND STREET; SACRAMENTO, CA 95814. (#50437-1).

AUG 20 - SEPT 7, '76. CALIFORNIA STATE FAIR. FAIR AT STATE FAIRGROUNDS-1600 EXPOSITION BLVD, NO ON GROUNDS PARKING. (REGN'L). BARON REED, GEN MGR; STATE DEPT OF PARKS & RECREATION-DIV OF EXPOSITION & STATE FAIR; 1600 EXPOSITION BLVD; SACRAMENTO, CA 95815. (#106095-9).

OCT 18 - 26, '76. 'TWO HUNDRED YEARS OF TECHNICAL PROGRESS'. EXPO WILL ILLUMINATE SCIENTIFIC AND TECHNICAL ADVANCEMENTS IN 14 THEMES AFFECTING SOCIETY. CONFERENCE WILL EXAMINE HOW SCIENCE AND TECHNOLOGY CAN BE APPLIED TO SOLVING MANY OF SOCIETY'S CRITICAL PROBLEMS. AT SACRAMENTO COMMUNITY CONVENTION CENTER, 1100 14TH ST. (REGN'L). ROBERT J KUNTZ, DIR; CAL ENGR FOUNDATION/CAL ARBC/UNIV OF CAL/STANFORD UNIV/CALTECH; PO BOX 160085; SACRAMENTO, CA 95816. (#21756-1).

NOV 1 - 30, '76. WOOD SCULPTURE ART SHOW OF EARLY CALIFORNIA SCENES. WOOD SCULPTURE MADE FROM FOUND MATERIALS (OLD PAINTED WOOD, RUSTED TIN, WINDOW SCREENS) & TREE ROOTS/BARK BECOME SCENES OF THE GOLD COUNTRY, OLD SACRAMENTO, THE CALIFORNIA COAST & NEVADA. AT CROCKER NATL BANK, 400 CAPITOL MALL. (LOCAL). TOM MYERS, PROJ DIRECTOR; PHOTOGRAPHER; 1737 MARKHAM WAY; SACRAMENTO, CA 95818. (#106730-1).

SALINAS

JUNE 6 - JULY 18, '76. BIG MONTH IN STEINBECK COUNTRY. EXHIBIT, FESTIVAL. (LOCAL). DONALD WOLF, CHAIRMAN; SALINAS BICENTENNIAL COMMITTEE; 122 E ALISAI ST; SALINAS, CA 93901. (#200006-392).

SAN ANSELMO

GOLDEN HINDSIGHT BICENTENNIAL 'HERITAGE' PROJ-CA. AN EDUCATIONAL EXPERIENCE FOR FOURTH, FIFTH & SIXTH GRADE STUDENTS, INTERVIEWING SR CITIZENS, TAKING PHOTOS, LAYOUT, WRITING AND EDIT ING INTO A FINISHED PUBLICATION. (LOCAL). BERNIE GRIFF, TEACHER; WADE THOMAS SCHOOL; ROSS AT KENSINGTON; SAN ANSELMO, CA 94960. (#17360).

SAN ARDO

'PORTRAIT OF A TOWN PIONEER', SAN ARDO, CA. A HISTORY OF THE TOWN SAN ARDO WILL BE PUBLISHED. (LOCAL). MRS MICHEL J ORRADRE, CHAIRMAN; SAN ARDO RECREATION CLUB & BICENTENNIAL COMMITTEE; COLLEGE ST; SAN ARDO, CA 93450. (#29563).

JULY 4, '76. 4TH OF JULY PARADE & PICNIC. FESTIVAL, PARADE. (LOCAL). MRS MICHEL J ORRADRE, DIR; SAN ARDO RECREATION CLUB; ST RTE BOX 64; SAN ARDO, CA 93450. (#200006-395).

SAN BERNADINO

BICENT AMPHITHEATER PROJ OF SAN BERNADINO, CAL. THE AMPHITHEATER WILL BE BUILT NEXT TO THE STATE COLLEGE AND IT WILL BE AVAILABLE FOR GENERAL COMMUNITY USE. A 4TH OF JULY PAGEANT IN 1976 IS THE CHRISTENING EVENT. (LOCAL). THELMA PRESS, EXEC DIRECTOR; CITY OF SAN BERNARDINO BICENTENNIAL COMMISSION; 300 NORTH D ST; SAN BERNADINO, CA 92401. (#6018).

BICENTENNIAL ON WHEELS - PROJ OF CALIFORNIA. PROVIDE BUS TRANSPORTATION TO & FROM BICENTENNIAL EVENTS FOR SPECIAL GROUPS. (LOCAL). THELMA PRESS, EXEC DIRECTOR; BICENT COMMISSION OF SAN BERNADINO; 300 NORTH D ST, RM 1776; SAN BERNADINO, CA 92401. (#10740).

FOLKLORE FESTIVAL OF SAN BERNADINO, CALIF. HISTORICAL DANCE/PROGRAM PRESENTION BY ALL GROUPS AT CALIFORNIA ST. COLLEGE-SAN BERNADINO. (LOCAL). THELMA PRESS, EXEC DIRECTOR; CITY OF SAN BERNARDINO BICENTENNIAL COMMISSION; 300 NORTH D ST; SAN BERNADINO, CA 92401. (#2979).

NOV 15, '74 - FEB 18, '76. BETSY ROSS CONTEST FOR CITY FLAG USING CITY BICENTENNIAL LOGO. LIVE PERFORMANCE, FESTIVAL. (LOCAL). THELMA PRESS, EXEC DIR; CITY OF SAN BERNARDINO BICENTENNIAL COMMISSION; 300 NORTH D ST; SAN BERNADINO, CA 92401. (#6018-510).

JAN 1 - 31, '75. NEW COUNTY MUSEUM BUILDING - OFFICIAL OPENING & DEDICATION. OPENING. (LOCAL). DR GERALD A SMITH, DIRECT; SAN BERNARDINO COUNTY MUSEUM AND COMMISSION; 2024 ORANGE TREE LANE; SAN BERNADINO, CA 92373. (#3583-901).

JAN 10, '75 - JUNE 10, '76. TWO HUNDRED YEARS OF PRESIDENTIAL PAPERS (ORIGINAL) EXHIBITED. LIVE PERFORMANCE, FESTIVAL. (LOCAL). THELMA PRESS, EXEC DIR; CITY OF SAN BERNARDINO BICENTENNIAL COMMISSION; 300 NORTH D ST; SAN BERNADINO, CA 92401. (#6018-501).

FEB 1, '75 - JULY 1, '76. LICENSE PLATE CONTEST FOR PLATES RELATING TO BICENTENNIAL. LIVE PERFORMANCE, FESTIVAL. (LOCAL). THELMA PRESS, EXEC DIR; CITY OF SAN BERNARDINO BICENTENNIAL COMMISSION; 300 NORTH D ST; SAN BERNADINO, CA 92401. (#6018-508).

MAR 1, '75 - JUNE 10, '76. ESSAY CONTEST FOR STUDENTS OF ALL AGES ON AMERICA & BICENTENNIAL. LIVE PERFORMANCE, FESTIVAL. (LOCAL). THELMA PRESS, EXEC DIR; CITY OF SAN BERNARDINO BICENTENNIAL COMMISSION; 300 NORTH D ST; SAN BERNADINO, CA 92401. (#6018-507).

MAY 12, '75. PLANTING LIBERTY TREE BY POCAHONTAS WITH PLAQUE IN CITY HALL COMPLEX. BICENT AMPHITHEATER PROJ OF SAN BERNADINO, CAL. THE AMPHITHEATER WILL BE BUILT NEXT TO THE STATE COLLEGE AND IT WILL BE AVAILABLE FOR GENERAL COMMUNITY USE. A 4TH OF JULY PAGEANT IN 1976 IS THE CHRISTENING EVENT. (LOCAL). ROBERT WM PHINNEY; BICENTENNIAL COMMISSION OF SAN BERNARDINO CALIFORNIA; 300 N D ST; SAN BERNADINO, CA 92401. (#6018-505).

JUNE 29 - JULY 6, '75. SERMONS ON THE REVOLUTION IN EACH OF THE SAN BERNADINO CHURCHES. OPENING, LIVE PERFORMANCE, FESTIVAL. (LOCAL). ROBERT WM PHINNEY; BICENTENNIAL COMMISSION OF SAN BERNARDINO CALIFORNIA; 300 N D ST; SAN BERNADINO, CA 92401. (#6018-513).

SEPT 15 - OCT 15, '75. THE PLAY '1776' TO BE PRESENTED IN FALL, 1975 AT CALIFORNIA THEATER. OPENING, LIVE PERFORMANCE, FESTIVAL. (LOCAL). ROBERT WM PHINNEY; BICENTENNIAL COMMISSION OF SAN BERNARDINO CALIFORNIA; 300 N D ST; SAN BERNADINO, CA 92401. (#6018-511).

NOV 21 - 25, '75. FOLKLORE FESTIVAL & BICENTENNIAL FAIR, 5 DAYS BEFORE THANKSGIVING. OPENING, LIVE PERFORMANCE, FESTIVAL. (LOCAL). ROBERT WM PHINNEY; BICENTENNIAL COMMISSION OF SAN BERNARDINO CALIFORNIA; 300 N D ST; SAN BERNADINO, CA 92401. (#6018-512).

DEC 7, '75 - MAR '76. BICENTENNIAL MODEL SHIPBUILDING COMPETITION. MODEL SHIPBUILDING CATEGORIES INCLUDE PLASTIC OR WOOD IN TWO TIME FRAMES - 1776-1890 & 1890-1976. AWARDS FOR EACH CATEGORY WILL BE ANNOUNCED 3/27, ABOARD USS SAN BERNARDINO. BEST OF SHOW TO BE ELIGIBLE FOR EMBARKATION ON THE SHIP FOR A CRUISE TO HAWAII. AT SAN BERNARDINO CONVENTION CENTER/300 N 'D' ST. (LOCAL). CHARLES L FIELD,; USS SAN BERNARDINO (6ST-1189) U S NAVY BICENTENNIAL COMMAND; CITY HALL/300 N 'D' ST; SN BERNARDINO, CA 92418. (#104525-4).

DEC 12 - 14, '75. UNITED STATES ARMED FORCES BICENTENNIAL CARAVAN. THE CARAVAN IS COMPOSED OF EXHIBIT VANS FOR EACH BRANCH OF THE MILITARY SERVICE. THE THEME OF THE EXHIBITION IS 'HISTORY OF THE ARMED FORCES AND THEIR CONTRIBUTION TO THE NATION'. (LOCAL). THELMA PRESS, CHAIRMAN; U S ARMED FORCES BICENTENNIAL EXHIBIT VANS PROJECT; 300 N D ST, ROOM 1776; SAN BERNARDIN, CA 92401. (#1775-301).

FEB 12, '76. A DAY OF FOLKORE AND DANCING AT CENTRAL CITY MALL. LIVE PERFORMANCE, FESTIVAL. (LOCAL). THELMA PRESS, EXEC DIR; CITY OF SAN BERNARDINO BICENTENNIAL COMMISSION; 300 NORTH D ST; SAN BERNADINO, CA 92401. (#6018-506).

FEB 28 - APR 3, '76. TREK OF THE CENTURIES. RECREATING HISTORIC EVENTS ALONG THE 'OLD MOJAVE TRAIL' SUCH AS THE JOURNEY OF FATHER GARCES IN 1776. A PORTION WILL BE DESIGNATED AS A NATIONAL HIKING TRAIL. AT NEW COUNTY MUSEUM, 2024 ORANGE TREE LANE. (LOCAL). DR GERALD A SMITH, DIR; SAN BERNARDINO COUNTY MUSEUM AND COMMISSION; 2024 ORANGE TREE LANE; SAN BERNADINO, CA 92373. (#3583-2).

MAR 11 - 21, '76. 61ST NATIONAL ORANGE SHOW. ANNUAL EXPOSITION SALUTES CITRUS INDUSTRY IN CALIFORNIA; ENTERTAINMENT, RODEO. AT NATIONAL ORANGE SHOW GROUNDS. (REGN'L). BOB RODDICK, COORD; NATIONAL ORANGE SHOW; 689 S E ST; SAN BERNADINO, CA 92408. (#103416-213).

APR 2, '76. A WALKING MARCH COVERING HISTORIC MOJAVE TRAIL. TREK THRU MOJAVE TRAIL - SAN BERNARDINO COUNTY, CA. THE COUNTY MUSEUM WILL SPONSOR A HIKE ALONG THE TRAIL IN MARCH 1976. TO HIGHLIGHT ITS SIGNIFICANT HISTORY. (LOCAL). DR GERALD A SMITH; SAN BERNARDINO COUNTY MUSEUM; 2024 ORANGE TREE LANE; REDLANDS, CA 92373. (#7752-501).

APR 7, '76. USA 200 - A BICENTENNIAL MUSICAL SHOWCASE. 605 STUDENTS PARTICIPATED IN THIS HONOR CHOIR AND BANDS MUSIC OF AMERICAN COMPOSERS ALSO PRESENTED THE NATIONAL ANTHEM AND THE BATTLE HYMN OF THE REPUBLIC, INVOLVING ALL STUDENTS AT ONE TIME. AT SWING AUDITORIUM. (LOCAL). THELMA PRESS, EXEC DIR; CITY OF SAN BERNARDINO BICENTENNIAL COMMISSION; 300 NORTH D ST; SAN BERNADINO, CA 92401. (#6018-502).

MAY 7 - 9, '76. CALICO SPRING FESTIVAL. BARBERSHOP SINGING, SQUARE DANCING AND FIDDLE PLAYING HIGHLIGHT THIS ANNUAL FESTIVAL. CAMPING AVAILABLE. SAT HOURS: 9AM - 12 MIDNITE. SUNDAY HOURS: 9AM - 6PM. AT GHOST TOWN ROAD & I-15, 10 MILES NORTH OF BARSTOW, CA. (REGN'L). DON V TUCKER, COORD; COUNTY OF SAN BERNARDINO, REGIONAL PARKS DEPARTMENT; 825 EAST THIRD ST; SN BERNARDINO, CA 92415. (#103416-265).

JULY 4, '76. ADJUDICATED JULY 4TH PARADE. PARADE, FESTIVAL. (LOCAL). THELMA PRESS, EXEC DIR; CITY OF SAN BERNARDINO BICENTENNIAL COMMISSION; 300 NORTH D ST; SAN BERNADINO, CA 92401. (#6018-503).

JULY 4, '76. PATRIOTS BALL ON JULY 4TH WITH PATRIOT OF THE YEAR. LIVE PERFORMANCE, FESTIVAL. (LOCAL). THELMA PRESS, EXEC DIR; CITY OF SAN BERNARDINO BICENTENNIAL COMMISSION; 300 NORTH D ST; SAN BERNADINO, CA 92401. (#6018-509).

SAN BRUNO

ARTICLES ON REVOLUTION IN STATION NEWSLETTER, CA. MONTHLY ARTICLES & PICTURES ON THE REVOLUTIONARY PERIOD, PEOPLE & PLACES. (LOCAL). LCDR N ANDRIANO MOORE, COMMANDING OFFICER; NAVAL & MARINE CORPS RESERVE CENTER; SAN BRUNO, CA 94066. (#28617).

COLONIAL FLAG DISPLAY, SAN BRUNO, CA. DISPLAY OF FLAGS IN DRILL HALL: BETSY ROSS, BUNKER HILL, STAR SPANGLED BANNER, BENNINGTON, FIRST CONTINENTAL, WASHINGTON CRUISER, GRAND UNION, MOULTRIE, BEDFORD & NAVY JACK. (LOCAL). LCDR R N ANDRIANO MOORE, COMMANDING OFFICER; NAVAL & MARINE CORPS RESERVE CENTER; COMMODORE DR & SNEATH LA; SAN BRUNO, CA 94066. (#28600).

ESSAY & POSTER CONTEST WITH A BICENTENNIAL THEME. AWARD, CEREMONY. (LOCAL). L CURRIE, CHAIRPERSON; SAN BRUNO BICENTENNIAL COMMITTEE; 567 EL CAMINO REAL; SAN BRUNO, CA 94066. (#104213-1). **(??).**

HISTORIC PHOTOGRAPHS DISPLAY, SAN BRUNO, CA. PHOTOGRAPHIC DISPLAY OF REVOLUTIONARY NAVAL HEROES & FAMOUS NAVAL BATTLES. (LOCAL). LCDR R N ANDRIANO MOORE, COMMANDING OFFICER; NAVAL & MARINE CORPS RESERVE CENTER; COMMODORE DR & SNEATH LA; SAN BRUNO, CA 94066. (#28599).

HISTORICAL MARKERS, SAN BRUNO, CA. PERMANENT MARKERS WILL BE INSTALLED ON 11 SELECTED SITES. (LOCAL). L CURRIE, CHAIRPERSON; SAN BRUNO BICENTENNIAL COMMITTEE; 567 EL CAMINO REAL; SAN BRUNO, CA 94066. (#19129).

ORAL HISTORY PROJ - SAN BRUNO, CA. SENIOR CITIZENS WILL PARTICIPATE IN AN ORAL HISTORY PROJECT; THE TAPES WILL BE STORED IN THE LIBRARY. (LOCAL). L CURRIE, CHAIRPERSON; SAN BRUNO BICENTENNIAL COMMITTEE; 567 EL CAMINO REAL; SAN BRUNO, CA 94066. (#19130).

FEB 11, '76. EUGENE ELY'S COMMEMORATIVE PLAQUE DEDICATION. THE PLAQUE PLACED IN TANFORAN SHOPPING CENTER RECOGNIZED THE FIRST SHIPBOARD LANDING MADE ON 2/11-18 FROM LAND TO THE USS PA ANCHORED IN SAN FRANCISCO BAY. IT CONTRIBUTED SIGNIFICANTLY TO NAVAL AVIATION. (LOCAL). CAPT C M HOWE, CHAIRMAN; WESTERN DIV NAV FACILITIES ENGINEERING COMMAND; BOX 727; SAN BRUNO, CA 94066. (#200006-391).

MAR '76. DAY IN THE PARK, A MUSIC, ARTS AND CRAFTS FAIR. FESTIVAL AT SAN BRUNO PARK. (LOCAL). L CURRIE, CHAIRPERSON; SAN BRUNO BICENTENNIAL COMMITTEE; 567 EL CAMINO REAL; SAN BRUNO, CA 94066. (#104187-2).

MAY 22, '76. NAVAL RESERVE BICENTENNIAL BALL. FESTIVAL AT NAVAL AND MARINE CORPS RESERVE CENTER. (LOCAL). MRS JANICE ANDRIANO-MOORE; NAVAL RESERVE OF SAN BRUNO; SAN BRUNO, CA 94066. (#200006-369).

DEC 5, '76. BICENTENNIAL TREE PLANTING. FESTIVAL AT 3 SCHOOL SITES, SAN BRUNO, CRESTMOOR DR, DONNER AVE, SNEATH LN. (LOCAL). L CURRIE, CHAIRPERSON; SAN BRUNO BICENTENNIAL COMMITTEE; 567 EL CAMINO REAL; SAN BRUNO, CA 94066. (#104187-1).

SAN CARLOS

BENNINGTON GROVE - SAN CARLOS, CA. THE REDWOOD GROVE WILL BE PLANTED WITH 13 TREES IN A CIRCLE. (LOCAL). JEAN CANDE, CHAIRMAN; SAN CARLOS BICENTENNIAL COMMITTEE; 133 GARNET; SAN CARLOS, CA 94070. (#14375).

FIRE MUSEUM - SAN CARLOS, CA. AN EARLY CITY HISTORICAL MUSEUM HOUSING PHOTOS, ARTIFACTS AND FIRE EQUIPMENT WILL BE DEDICATED JULY 4, 1976. (LOCAL). BOB WILLIAMSON, CHAIRMAN; SAN CARLOS LIONS CLUB; 365 HILL WAY; SAN CARLOS, CA 94070. (#14376).

OFFICIAL HISTORICAL STATUS OLD - SAN CARLOS, CA. THE ONLY REMAINING HISTORICAL BUILDING WILL BE MARKED WITH A BRASS PLAQUE AND WILL BE GIVEN STATE HISTORICAL RECOGNITION. (LOCAL). MARGARET PRICE, PROJ DIRECTOR; SAN CARLOS BICENTENNIAL COMMITTEE; 300 ELM ST; SAN CARLOS, CA 94070. (#14374).

SEPT 13 - 14, '75. FESTIVAL OF THE ARTS. FESTIVAL, LIVE PERFORMANCE AT CITY HALL PARK, 600 ELM ST. (LOCAL). PAT PLANT, PROJ DIRECTOR; SAN CARLOS FINE ARTS ASSOC; 666 ELM; SAN CARLOS, CA 94070. (#101914-1).

SAN DIEGO

AMERICAN AIRLINES BICENTENNIAL TOURS - CA. CHARTER TOURS TO BOSTON, NEW YORK, PHILADELPHIA AND WASHINGTON, DC. (LOCAL). DAVID H WITT, BICENTENNIAL COORDINATOR; AMERICAN AIRLINES; 222 BROADWAY; SAN DIEGO, CA 92101. (#28373).

AMERICAN BICENTENNIAL PHYSICAL FITNESS PROGRAM-CA. 1, 2 & 3 MILE RUNS AT MISSION BAY PARK WITH PARTICIPATION AS MAIN OBJECTIVE, AWARD INCENTIVES TO ALL PARTICIPATING STAFF, FACULTY AND STUDENTS FROM VARIOUS SCHOOLS; GROUP PHOTO. (LOCAL). FREDERICK J BEIBER, COORDINATOR; AMERICAN BICENTENNIAL PHYSICAL FITNESS PROGRAM; PO BOX 15133; SAN DIEGO, CA 92115. (#28330).

AMERICAN FESTIVAL OF THEATRE ARTS - SAN DIEGO, CA. CREATE NEW THEATRE TO ELEVATE AND FOCUS THEATRE LIFE IN US, CANADA AND MEXICO. (INT'L). JACQUELYN LITTLEFIELD, PRESIDENT; SPRECKLES HIPPODROME THEATRE; 121 BROADWAY; SAN DIEGO, CA 92101. (#28353).

'AMERICAN HERITAGE' SHIP - SAN DIEGO, CA. NEW SHIP TO BE LAUNCHED DURING BICENTENNIAL YEAR. (ST-WIDE). JOHN MURPHY, PRESIDENT; NATIONAL STEEL AND SHIPBUILDING; PO BOX 80278; SAN DIEGO, CA 92138. (#28375).

AMERICAN ISSUES FORUM - SAN DIEGO, CA. FILM AND LECTURE SERIES EXAMINING THOSE ISSUES FUNDAMENTAL TO DEVELOPMENT AND FUTURE OF AMERICAN SOCIETY. (LOCAL). GEORGE COLBURN, COORDINATOR; UNIV OF CALIFORNIA, SAN DIEGO; Q-056; LA JOLLA, CA 92093. (#30236).

AREA COUNCIL MANAGEMENT CLUBS - SAN DIEGO, CA. AN AREA COUNCIL OF MANAGEMENT CLUBS IS BEING FORMED. (LOCAL). BOB CHASE, CHAIRMAN; MANAGEMENT CLUB; 2701 N HARBOR DR; SAN DIEGO, CA 92101. (#30234).

BICENT LECTURE SERIES - SAN DIEGO STATE UNIVERSITY. SERIES OF ANNUAL LECTURES BY OUTSTANDING SCHOLARS OF THE REVOLUTION, SPONSORED BY THE CALIFORNIA STATE UNIVERSITIES AND COLLEGES, WILL BE FREE TO THE PUBLIC. (ST-WIDE). ROBERT DETWEILER, PROFESSOR OF HISTORY; SAN DIEGO STATE UNIV; SAN DIEGO, CA 92182. (#8012).

BICENTENNIAL AIRCRAFT PHOTOGRAPHS - SAN DIEGO, CA. EVOLVING FROM FORMATION FLIGHT SPECIFICALLY FOR THE PURPOSE OF DOING THIS OUR OFFICIAL SQUADRON PHOTO. (LOCAL). RICHARD H PLUSH, LTJG; HELICOPTER COMBAT SUPPORT SQUADRON THREE; NAVAL AIR STATION NORTH ISLAND; SAN DIEGO, CA 92135. (#32112).

BICENTENNIAL ART CONTEST - SAN DIEGO, CA. A CONTEST WAS CONDUCTED TO OBTAIN SUGGESTIONS FOR DECORATING THE SHIP WITH A BICENTENNIAL DESIGN. (LOCAL). CDR DVORNICK, EXEC OFFICER; USS HORNE, CG-30; FPO; SAN FRANCISCO, CA 96601. (#29117).

BICENTENNIAL AWARDS FOR CITIZEN INVOLVEMENT - CA. CERTIFICATES TO CITIZENS WHO PROMOTE BICENTENNIAL ACTIVITIES. (LOCAL). MRS JERRY J STRAYER, COORDINATOR; LINARES CHAPTER, DAR 14TH DISTRICT; 1627 MIGUEL AVE; CORONADO, CA 92118. (#28335).

BICENTENNIAL BIRTHDAY CARD - SAN DIEGO, CA. BIRTHDAY CARD TO USA WHICH WILL BE REPRODUCED ON ONE WALL OF COCACOLA BOTTLING COMPANY PLANT. (LOCAL). DAVID G SMITH, COORDINATOR; COCA-COLA BOTTLING COMPANY; HIGHWAY 94 AT 47TH ST; SAN DIEGO, CA 92102. (#28341).

BICENTENNIAL BULLETINS - SAN DIEGO, CA. BULLETINS DETAILING BICENTENNIAL ACTIVITIES IN SOUTHERN CALIFORNIA. (ST-WIDE). STAN PACKARD, COORDINATOR; AUTOMOBILE CLUB OF SOUTHERN CALIFORNIA; PO BOX 2890, TERMINAL ANNEX; LOS ANGELES, CA 90051. (#28367).

BICENTENNIAL CANNON - SAN DIEGO, CA. 1400-LB CANNON MADE IN CRAFT SHOP; HAS BEEN FIRED TWICE. (LOCAL). A W OLIPHANT, INSTRUCTOR; SNYDER HIGH SCHOOL; 11086 PUEBLA DR; LA MESA, CA 92041. (#28364).

BICENTENNIAL COLOR GUARD, SAN DIEGO, CA. COLOR GUARD AVAILABLE FOR BICENTENNIAL CELEBRATION. (LOCAL). WILLIAM B HOWE, LTUSN; USS DECATUR (DDG-31); FPO; SAN FRANCISCO, CA 96601. (#32406).

BICENTENNIAL CRUISE PLAQUES - SAN DIEGO, CA. USS CHICAGO HAS MADE PLAQUES IN COMMEMORATION OF ALL OVERSEAS DEPLOYMENT CONDUCTED DURING 1976. (INT'L). LT ROBERT L WILSON, COORDINATOR; USS CHICAGO (CG-11); FPO; SAN FRANCISCO, CA 96601. (#29485).

BICENTENNIAL FLAGPOLES, SAN DIEGO, CA. INSTALLATION OF THIRTY ONE FLAGS IN SAN DIEGO. (LOCAL). MARY MADDEN, COORDINATOR; THE SOROPTMIST INTERNATIONAL CLUB; 2219 BANCROFT ST; SAN DIEGO, CA 92113. (#23031).

BICENTENNIAL LIBRARY PROJECT IN SAN DIEGO, CA. PART OF REFERENCE LIBRARY DEDICATED TO BICENTENNIAL-ORIENTED BOOKS & MAGAZINES. DONATIONS REQUESTED FROM COMMAND MEMBERS TO STIMULATE PARTICIPATION. (ST-WIDE). G R SPIDELL, COORDINATOR; NAVMMACPAC; 1220 PACIFIC HWY; SAN DIEGO, CA 92132. (#29488).

BICENTENNIAL LIVING HISTORY COLLECTION - CA. ORAL HISTORY PROGRAM BASED ON INTERVIEWS WITH KEY LIVING PARTICIPANTS IN DEVELOPMENT OF SAN DIEGO. (LOCAL). LONNIE ROWEL, COORDINATOR; EXPLORING FAMILY SCHOOL; 1206 28TH ST; SAN DIEGO, CA 92102. (#28360).

BICENTENNIAL MEAL AT SAN DIEGO PUBLIC SCHOOLS - CA. THE PUBLIC SCHOOLS WILL SERVE A BICENTENNIAL MEAL. (LOCAL). JOAN KLEINHANS, DIETICIAN; SAN DIEGO CITY SCHOOLS; 4100 NORMAL ST; SAN DIEGO, CA 92103. (#28331).

BICENTENNIAL MONUMENT - SAN DIEGO, CA. MONUMENT TO COMMEMORATE NATION'S BICENTENNIAL. (LOCAL). ALBERT A ARNHYM, COORDINATOR; VETERANS ORGANIZATIONS OF SAN DIEGO; 6474 SPEAR ST; SAN DIEGO, CA 92120. (#28336).

BICENTENNIAL PAMPHLET OF USS LEAHY CG-16, CA. BICENTENNIAL PAMPHLET EXPLAINS LEAHY'S ROLE IN MAINTAINING 200 YEARS OF FREEDOM OF THE SEAS. PICTORIAL COVERAGE DEPICTS BICENTENNIAL JACK REVOLUTIONARY WARSHIP AND USS LEAHY. (NAT'L). LTJG CHARLES J DUVEEN, PUBLIC AFFAIRS OFFICER; USS LEAHY (CG-16); FPO; SAN FRANCISCO, CA 96601. (#32340).

BICENTENNIAL PARK PROJECT - SAN DIEGO, CA. DEVELOP PERMANENT PICNIC AND LEISURE AREA WITHIN BALBOA PARK. (LOCAL). DON DAVIS, COORDINATOR; SAN DIEGO JUNIOR CHAMBER OF COMMERCE; 1494 FIFTH AVE; SAN DIEGO, CA 92101. (#28357).

BICENTENNIAL PARISH PICTORIAL DIRECTORY - CA. PICTORIAL DIRECTORY OF PARISH MEMBERS. (LOCAL). REV PATRICK FOX; ST AGNES CHURCH; 1140 EVERGREEN ST; SAN DIEGO, CA 92106. (#28359).

BICENTENNIAL ROSE GARDEN - SAN DIEGO, CA. ESTABLISH A ROSE GARDEN IN SENIOR CITIZENS PARK IN MISSION D'ALCALA AREA. (LOCAL). MISS PATRICIA SULLIVAN, CHAIRMAN; ALPHA IOTA INTERNATIONAL HONORARY BUSINESS SOCIETY; 264 FRAXINELLA ST; ENCINITAS, CA 92114. (#28374).

BICENTENNIAL SCHOOL PROJECTS - SAN DIEGO, CA. SCHOOL DINNERS, SALES BOOTHS, ESSAY CONTESTS, DECORATIONS, BICENTENNIAL FLAG DISPLAYS. (LOCAL). SESLIE CRUSTO, PRESIDENT; JOHN MONTGOMERY JUNIOR HIGH SCHOOL; 2470 ULRIC ST; SAN DIEGO, CA 92111. (#28329).

BICENTENNIAL WAR AGAINST LITTER - SAN DIEGO, CA. PROGRAM GEARED TO CLEANING UP AND BEAUTIFYING CITY. DISTRIBUTION OF CAR LITTER BAGS. (LOCAL). JOYCE COFFEE, EXEC DIRECTOR; WAR AGAINST LITTER COMMITTEE; BALBOA PARK; SAN DIEGO, CA 92101. (#28372).

BICENTENNIAL YEAR CELEBRATION - SAN DIEGO, CA. SERIES OF LUNCHEONS WITH SPEAKERS AND ACTIVITIES DEALING WITH HISTORICAL AND PATRIOTIC ISSUES MONTHLY. (LOCAL). MRS JERRY J STRAYER, CHAIRMAN; LINARES CHAPTER BICENTENNIAL DAR; 1627 MIGUEL AVE; CORONADO, CA 92118. (#28323).

BICENTENNIAL YOUTH ADVISORY BOARD CEREMONY. CEREMONY AT PO BOY 402036 OCEANVIEW BRANCH. (LOCAL). DON DAVIS, COORD; GREATER MIAMI JAYCEES; 1494 5TH AVE; SAN DIEGO, CA 92101. (#104427-6).

BLIND PATH AT CABRILLO MONUMENT - SAN DIEGO, CA. SAFETY PATH FOR HANDICAPPED PERSONS. (LOCAL). SUPERINTENDENT; NATIONAL PARK SERVICE, CABRILLO NATIONAL MONUMENT; PO BOX 6175; SAN DIEGO, CA 92106. (#28347).

BLOOD BANK BICENTENNIAL FLAG - SAN DIEGO, CA. FLAG TO BE FLOWN OVER BLOOD BANK. WHEN FLOWN UPSIDE DOWN IT WILL SERVE AS A DISTRESS SIGNAL TO ALERT DONORS WHEN COMMUNITY BLOOD SUPPLY IS CRITICALLY LOW. (LOCAL). DEL ROBERTS, COORDINATOR; SAN DIEGO BLOOD BANK; 440 UPAS ST; SAN DIEGO, CA 92103. (#28339).

BOY SCOUTS CLEANUP CAMPAIGN - SAN DIEGO, CA. BOY SCOUTS PROJECT TO SAVE RESOURCES, RECYCLE MATERIAL, IMPROVE NATURAL ENVIRONMENT, CONSERVE ENERGY. SOAR PATCH AWARDS FOR PARTICIPANTS. (LOCAL). CHUCK SMITH, COORDINATOR; BOY SCOUTS OF AMERICA; 1207 UPAS ST; SAN DIEGO, CA 92103. (#28342).

'CALL OF THE CALIFORNIAS', SAN DIEGO, CA. A 15 MINUTE FILM PRIMARILY DEVOTED TO SAN DIEGO'S 'FRONTERAS 1976' BICENTENNIAL PROGRAM. (LOCAL). DAL L WATKINS, PRESIDENT; SAN DIEGO CONVENTION AND VISITORS BUREAU; 1200 3RD AVE, SUITE 824; SAN DIEGO, CA 92101. (#10898).

'CAPITOL MADE OF SUGAR' - SAN DIEGO, CA. NATION'S CAPITOL MADE OUT OF SUGAR, SUGAR CUBES AND RHINESTONES. 18 FEET LONG, 6 FEET WIDE, 6 FEET TALL; ENCASED IN GLASS. (LOCAL). BILL MOODY, COORDINATOR; 422 2ND AVE; CHULA VISTA, CA 92010. (#30238).

COSTUMED HOSPITAL VISITS IN SAN DIEGO. COSTUMED MEMBERS OF THIS COMMAND DISTRIBUTED CAKES, COOKIES AND GOOD CHEER TO INPATIENTS AT CORONADO AND CHULA VISTA COMMUNITY HOSPITALS. (LOCAL). LTJG F R RUEHE, PUBLIC AFFAIRS OFFICER; HELICOPTER ANTISUBMARINE SQUADRON (LIGHT) THIRTY THREE; NAS NORTH ISLAND; SAN DIEGO, CA 92135. (#29912).

DECATUR HERITAGE - SAN DIEGO, CA. CONTACT CITIES NAMED DECATUR TO SHARE HERITAGE OF USS DECATUR (DDG31) FIFTH SHIP TO BEAR THE NAME. NAMED AFTER STEPHEN DECATUR. (REGN'L). WILLIAM B HOWE, OPERATIONS OFFICER; USS DECATUR (DDG-31); FPO; SAN FRANCISCO, CA 96601. (#32404).

DECLARATION OF INDEPENDENCE PLAQUES, SAN DIEGO, CA. DECOUPAGED PLAQUES OF DECLARATION OF INDEPENDENCE WILL BE DONATED TO 18 ELEMENTARY SCHOOLS. (LOCAL). ARDYCE JARVIS, CHAIRMAN; CLAIREMONT JUNIOR WOMEN'S CLUB; 5455 VIA BELLO; SAN DIEGO, CA 92111. (#23069).

DISPLAY OF BICENTENNIAL DECALS - SAN DIEGO, CA. DECALS IN PROMINENT PLACE ON AIRCRAFT AND SQUADRON VEHICLES. (LOCAL). RICHARD H PLUSH, LTJG; HELICOPTER COMBAT SUPPORT SQUADRON THREE; NAVAL AIR STATION NORTH ISLAND; SAN DIEGO, CA 92135. (#32113).

DON REED BIG BAND - SAN DIEGO, CA. THE DON REED BIG BAND WILL BE AVAILABLE FOR PERFORMANCES DURING 1976. (LOCAL). DON REED, COORDINATOR; COLLEGIUM MUSICUM; 2808 FIFTH AVE; SAN DIEGO, CA 92103. (#30250).

DONATIONS OF THE PRESIDENT ON EXHIBIT. EXHIBIT AT 525 B ST, ROOM 1717. (LOCAL). RICO JARAMILLO, COORD; PACIFIC TELEPHONE CO; 525 B ST; SAN DIEGO, CA 92101. (#104427-25).

EARLY CENSUSES OF SAN DIEGO COUNTY, CA. CENSUS SHOWING HERITAGE, MIGRATION PATTERNS, LIFESTYLES, FAMILY GROWTHS AND MAPS. (LOCAL). MRS JOHN T ATKINSON, CHAIRPERSON; SAN DIEGO GENEALOGICAL SOCIETY; BALBOA PARK; SAN DIEGO, CA 92101. (#28355).

ESSAY CONTEST - 'WHAT AMERICA MEANS TO ME'. COMPETITION. (LOCAL). SESILIE CROSTO, PRESIDENT; JOHN J MONTGOMERY JR HIGH SCHOOL; 2470 VIRIC ST; SAN DIEGO, CA 92111. (#107328-1).

ESSAY CONTEST - 'CHALLENGE OF CENTURY III. COMPETITION. (LOCAL). ARDYCE JARVIS, CHAIRMAN; CLAIREMONT JR WOMAN'S CLUB; 5455 VIA BELLO; SAN DIEGO, CA 92111. (#107329-1).

AN EVENING WITH KRAZY KAT: SAN DIEGO, CALIFORNIA. A MUSICAL SETTING OF SELECTED MATERIALS BY CARTOONIST GEORGE HARRIMAN WITH SLIDES, 4-CHANNEL TAPE AND LIVE PERFORMERS. EXPERIMENTS IN POSITIONING SOUNDS IN SPACE BY ELECTRONIC PROCESSING & COMPUTERS. (NAT'L). ROGER REYNOLDS, PROFESSOR OF MUSIC; 624 SERPENTINE DR; DEL MAR, CA 92110. (#6593). **(??).**

EVOLUTION OF OLD GLORY - SAN DIEGO, CA. PAGEANT OF FLAGS - FLAGS, DRUMS, COSTUMED MEN. (LOCAL). FRANKLIN G BECK, COMMANDER; LEGION OF HONOR - AL BAHR TEMPLE; 6736 RADCLIFFE DR; SAN DIEGO, CA 92122. (#30180).

'FANFARE' AND 'PERSONAGES 1976' - SAN DIEGO, CA. TWO EXHIBITIONS WITH BICENTENNIAL SUBJECTS, AN ENTIRE YEAR OF SHOWS TO BE DISPLAYED IN SAN DIEGO STATE UNIVERSITY'S LOVE LIBRARY AND TO BE OUT ON LOAN TO OTHER COMMUNITIES. (ST-WIDE). WILLIAM BOWNE, PROJ CHAIRMAN; SAN DIEGO STATE UNIV; 5402 COLLEGE; SAN DIEGO, CA 92115. (#28419).

FEMINIST PEOTRY & GRAPHICS CENTER - SAN DIEGO, CA. EXPAND ARTISTIC OPPORTUNITIES FOR WOMEN THROUGH A POETRY AND GRAPHICS CENTER. (LOCAL). JOYCE NOWER, COORDINATOR; THE FEMINIST POETRY & GRAPHICS CENTER; 2829 BROADWAY; SAN DIEGO, CA 92102. (#24237).

FORTY DOCUMENTS OF OUR AMERICAN HERITAGE - CA. BOOK CONTAINING FORTY PRINCIPLE DOCUMENTS WITH USAGE OF CASSETTE TAPES AS TEACHER GUIDES. (LOCAL). GEN J PAUL HOLLAND, POST COMMANDER IN CHIEF; MILITARY ORDER OF THE WORLD WARS; 11980 ADORNO PL; SAN DIEGO, CA 92128. (#9122).

FOSTER FRIENDSHIP OF PEOPLE IN MEXICO & SAN DIEGO. PROGRAM OF COOPERATIVE EFFORTS BETWEEN PEOPLE OF SAN DIEGO & TIJUANA, MEXICO FOR HISTORIC AND ECOLOGICAL PRESERVATION AND RECOGNITION OF COMMON HERITAGE. (INT'L). ELMER KEEN, PROFESSOR OF GEOGRAPHY; SAN DIEGO STATE UNIV; SAN DIEGO, CA 92182. (#8014).

FREEDOM SHRINE - SAN DIEGO, CA. TWENTY-EIGHT HISTORICAL DOCUMENTS PHOTOGRAPHICALLY REPRODUCED FROM ORIGINALS IN WASHINGTON, DC. (LOCAL). LARRY K ELLIS, COORDINATOR; EXCHANGE CLUB OF MISSION VALLEY; 5375 HEWLETT DR; SAN DIEGO, CA 92115. (#28349).

FRIENDS OF THE HANDICAPPED CHILDREN - CA. CARE VILLAGE, A RESIDENCE/COMMUNITY FOR DEVELOPMENTALLY DISABLED WITH MULTIPLE HANDICAPS OR ONE SEVERLY LIMITING HANDICAP. (LOCAL). WILLIAM G HARTJE, JR, COORDINATOR; FRIENDS OF HANDICAPPED CHILDREN; PO BOX 678; LA JOLLA, CA 92037. (#28352).

'FRONTERAS '76' - REGIONAL PLANNING IN CALIFORNIA. DEFINE SAN DIEGO-TIAJUANA REGION; PROJECT OPTIONS FOR DEVELOPMENT; & PROPOSE SUITABLE POLITICAL MECHANISMS TO ACHIEVE BI-NATIONAL REGIONAL OBJECTIVES. (INT'L). CLIFFORD GROBSTEIN, VICE PRESIDENT; UC/SAN DIEGO, UNIV OF CALIFORNIA; 911 MATTHEWS CAMPUS; SAN DIEGO, CA 92037. (#8569). **ARBA RECOGNIZED.**

'THE GREAT DAY' - SAN DIEGO, CA. CHORAL GROUP AVAILABLE FOR PERFORMANCES. (LOCAL). MARY HORNBERGER, CHAIRMAN; THE GREAT DAY; 5972 MT SOLEDAD RD; LA JOLLA, CA 92037. (#30249).

GREEN SURVIVAL - SAN DIEGO, CA. AN EFFORT TO PROTECT AND IMPROVE THE ENVIRONMENT BY PLANTING TREES & OTHER PLANTS, CLEANING UP NEIGHBORHOODS, PLANTING FLOWER GARDENS IN MUNICIPAL AREAS. (LOCAL). CINDY E CHANDLER, PUBLIC RELATIONS OFFICER; CA ASSOCIATION OF

SAN DIEGO — CONTINUED

NURSERYMEN, SAN DIEGO CHAPTER; 5115 LINDA VISTA RD; SAN DIEGO, CA 92110. (#28327).

HIDDEN HEROINE - SAN DIEGO, CA. PROJECT FOCUSES ON FEMALE CONTRIBUTIONS PAST, PRESENT AND ESPECIALLY FUTURE. (LOCAL). LOUISE GLAGOW, DIRECTOR; GIRL SCOUTS SAN DIEGO-IMPERIAL COUNCIL, INC; 1231 UPAS ST; SAN DIEGO, CA 92103. (#24238).

HIGH SPIRIT HOT AIR BALLOONS - SAN DIEGO, CA. PROGRAM DEPICTING HISTORY AND DEVELOPMENT OF WORLD'S OLDEST FORM OF AVIATION. (LOCAL). JOHN STOKES, COORDINATOR; 7-UP CORPORATION; 3585 TEXAS ST; SAN DIEGO, CA 92116. (#30247).

INTERCULTURAL COUNCIL OF THE ARTS - SAN DIEGO, CA. OUTREACH PROGRAM TO INCREASE COMMUNICATION BETWEEN PERSONS OF DIFFERENT CULTURES. MEANINGFUL AND RELEVANT PROGRAMS USING VISUAL AND PERFORMING ARTS. (LOCAL). RICHARD E WHITE, CHAIRPERSON; SAN DIEGO COUNTY HUMAN RELATIONS COMMISSION; 3730 FIFTH AVE; SAN DIEGO, CA 92103. (#28354).

INVENTORY OF HISTORIC SITES IN SAN DIEGO AREA. CONDUCT A SYSTEMATIC INVENTORY OF SITES IN THE SAN DIEGO AREA OF SIGNIFICANT HISTORIC INTEREST, WHICH SHOULD BE PRESERVED FOR THE COMMUNITY'S HERITAGE. (LOCAL). LARRY FORD, PROFESSOR OF GEOGRAPHY; SAN DIEGO STATE UNIV; SAN DIEGO, CA 92182. (#8013). **(??).**

KCBQ BICENTENNIAL QUESTIONAIRE CONTEST - CA. BOOKLET CONTAINING 200 QUESTIONS DEALING WITH EVENTS WHICH TOOK PLACE DURING THE FORMATION OF OUR COUNTRY; PRIZES TO INCLUDE APPROXIMATELY $5,000 IN SCHOLARSHIPS AND AWARDS. (LOCAL). RUSS WITTBERGER, VICE PRESIDENT; KCBQ RADIO STATION; PO BOX 1629; SAN DIEGO, CA 92112. (#28326).

LAURELS FOR LEADERS - SAN DIEGO, CA. COMMUNITY-WIDE RECOGNITION OF HIGH SCHOOL STUDENT LEADERS. (LOCAL). CHAIRMAN; BOARD OF EDUCATION; 4100 NORMAL ST; SAN DIEGO, CA 92103. (#30237).

LIBERTY TREES - SAN DIEGO, CA. SALE OF LIVE CHRISTMAS TREES TO BE RETURNED TO BOY SCOUTS TO BE PLANTED IN BICENTENNIAL GROVES. (LOCAL). CHUCK SMITH, COORDINATOR; BOY SCOUTS OF AMERICA; 1207 UPAS ST; SAN DIEGO, CA 92103. (#28370).

LIBRARY FOR OFFICERS' WARDROOM - SAN DIEGO, CA. INCLUDES BICENTENNIAL BOOK SERIES AND MANY BOOKS DONATED BY SQUADRON PERSONNEL. (LOCAL). RICHARD H PLUSH, LTJG; HELICOPTER COMBAT SUPPORT SQUADRON THREE; NAVAL AIR STATION NORTH ISLAND; SAN DIEGO, CA 92135. (#32111).

LIFESTREAM '76-2000 - SAN DIEGO, CA. MURAL PRESENTING HISTORY AND BEAUTY OF DYNAMICS IN THE EVOLUTION OF CALIFORNIA. (LOCAL). MOLLY JEAN FEATHERINGILL, EXEC DIRECTOR; ECOLOGY CENTRE, INC; 340 KALIMA ST; SAN DIEGO, CA 92101. (#28365).

LOCAL COLLEGE PROGRAMS - SAN DIEGO, CA. VARIETY OF PROGRAMS PRESENTED BY LOCAL COLLEGES. (LOCAL). GEORGE A COLBURN, COORDINATOR; UNIV OF CALIFORNIA; 4901 MORENA BLVD, SUITE 92117; SAN DIEGO, CA 92117. (#28333).

'LOVE IS THE WAY', PROJ OF SAN DIEGO, CA. THE EMPHASIS OF THIS PROJECT IS ON LOVE AS A DAILY WAY OF LIFE, IN ORDER TO PRESERVE OUR NATIONAL HERITAGE & THE FAMILY UNIT. (LOCAL). KEN & BE HUNT, PROJ COORDINATOR; LOVE IS THE WAY; PO BOX 3210; SAN DIEGO, CA 92103. (#17075).

'THE MAGIC OF AMERICA' - SAN DIEGO, CA. MAGIC SHOW WHICH INTRODUCES CHILDREN TO IDEAS, PEOPLE AND PLACES WHICH MADE AMERICA GREAT; AVAILABLE FOR SCHOOL ASSEMBLIES. (LOCAL). JIM BOBO, MAGICIAN; 6817 BARKER WAY; SAN DIEGO, CA 92119. (#30233).

MARK TWAIN FESTIVAL. FESTIVAL AT SANTEE-LAKESIDE ROTARY CLUB. (LOCAL). DALE RUFFIN, COORD; DALE RUFFIN; PO BOX U26; SANTEE, CA 92171. (#104427-18).

'MEET THE AMERICANS' - SAN DIEGO, CA. PROGRAM TO PROVIDE HOSTS FOR FOREIGN VISITORS. (INT'L). GARY L CAIN, LOCAL CONTACT; AMERICAN HOST FOUNDATION; 9942 CATHERINE AVE; GARDEN GROVE, CA 92641. (#28350).

'MEN OF VISION' - SAN DIEGO, CA. A ROSEWOOD STATUE DEPICTING FRANCISCAN PADRE AND THE MINUTEMEN OF THE REVOLUTION. (LOCAL). MRS F R METTLACH, STATE CHAIRMAN; DAR; 4310 ROLANO DR; SAN DIEGO, CA 92115. (#23210).

MIRAMAR COLLEGE BICENTENNIAL - SAN DIEGO, CA. EXHIBITS OF EARLY AMERICAN FIRE, POLICE & AVIATION EQUIPMENT; MURALS DEPICTING CALIFORNIA BLACK HISTORY; BLUE GRASS MUSIC. (LOCAL). VALLETA H LINNETTE, DEAN OF INSTRUCTION; MIRAMAR COLLEGE; 10440 BLACK MOUNTAIN RD; SAN DIEGO, CA 92126. (#32341).

MOST PATRIOTIC TRASH CAN CONTEST - SAN DIEGO, CA. A TRASH CAN PAINTING CONTEST WAS HELD FOR THE MOST PATRIOTIC TRASH CAN. (LOCAL). VIRGINIA WILSON, CHAIRMAN; CLAIREMONT SQUARE MERCHANTS ASSOC; 6348 CHANDLER DR; SAN DIEGO, CA 92117. (#30241).

MUSEUM ON WHEELS - SAN DIEGO, CA. COLLECTION OF HISTORICAL DATA PERTAINING TO DEVELOPMENT OF WEST TO BE DISPLAYED IN RAILROAD CARS. (LOCAL). CARROL W WAYMON, COORDINATOR; SAN DIEGO HISTORICAL SOCIETY; 1925 K ST; SAN DIEGO, CA 92102. (#28337).

MUSEUM ON WHEELS. EXHIBIT AT 69TH ST AND IMPERIAL AVE. (LOCAL). CARROL W WAYMON, COORD; SOUTHEAST BICENTENNIAL CLEARING HOUSE COMMITTEE; 1925 K ST; SAN DIEGO, CA 92102. (#104427-21). **(??).**

NATIONAL CITIZENS AWARDS - SAN DIEGO, CA. HONOR WORTHY CITIZENS FOR THEIR CONTRIBUTIONS TO THE COMMUNITY. (LOCAL). TOM DARBY, COORDINATOR; SONS OF AMERICAN REVOLUTION; 13043 VIA DEL VALEDOR; SAN DIEGO, CA 92124. (#30239).

NATIONAL NETWORK OF YOUTH ADVISORY BOARDS - CA. FORMATION OF LOCAL YOUTH BOARD TO JOIN NATIONAL NETWORK; BROAD BASED COMMUNICATIONS, EXTENSION OF PARTICIPATORY DEMOCRACY; YOUTH MANPOWER FOR PROJ; INTERPRETATION OF YOUTH NEEDS; LEADERSHIP GROWTH. (ST-WIDE). DON DAVIS, COORDINATOR; JUNIOR CHAMBER OF COMMERCE; 1494 FIFTH AVE; SAN DIEGO, CA 92101. (#28324).

NEW THEATRE FOR AMERICA - PROJECT NOW - CA. DEVELOP ONGOING AMERICAN THEATRE PROGRAMS FOCUSING ON CULTURAL BACKGROUND, ETHNIC HERITAGE AND CONTEMPORARY, EXPERIMENTAL THEATRE WORKS. (LOCAL). CRAIG NOEL, PRODUCING DIRECTOR; OLD GLOBE THEATRE; PO BOX 2171, BALBOA PARK; SAN DIEGO, CA 92112. (#28351).

'NOT FOR OURSELVES ALONE' - FILM - SAN DIEGO, CA. A FILM BASED ON 4 MAJOR CRISIS IN AMERICA'S MILITARY HISTORY: THE AMERICAN REVOLUTION, WAR OF 1812, CIVIL WAR & 2 WORLD WARS. (LOCAL). RICHARD H PLUSH, LTJG; HELICOPTER COMBAT SUPPORT SQUADRON THREE; NAVAL AIR STATION NORTH ISLAND; SAN DIEGO, CA 92135. (#32108).

OUTSTANDING STUDENT AWARD - SAN DIEGO, CA. AWARD TO OUTSTANDING SENIOR AT VALHALLA HIGH SCHOOL. (LOCAL). CAPT LOYD J MALAND, PRESIDENT; SORLANDET LODGE #105, S/N; 9333 LEMON AVE; EL CAJON, CA 92041. (#28343).

PACIFIC BEACH BICENTENNIAL MUSIC INFO CENTER, CA. CREATION OF A BICENTENNIAL CELEBRATION IN MUSIC: SONGS OF THE PREREVOLUTIONARY, REVOLUTIONARY AND EARLY COLONIAL PERIODS. (LOCAL). RUTLEDGE JAY, DIRECTOR; PACIFIC BEACH BICENTENNIAL MUSIC INFO CENTER; 880 SAPHIRE ST; PACIFIC BEACH, CA 92109. (#30181).

PACIFIC SOUTHWEST RAILWAY MUSEUM - SAN DIEGO, CA. STEAM LOCOMOTIVE AND MANSION ON WHEELS PRIVATE PASSENGER CAR; BOTH RESTORED BY MUSEUM VOLUNTEERS. (LOCAL). H CHALMERS KERR, COORDINATOR; PACIFIC SOUTHWEST RAILWAY MUSEUM ASSOCIATION, INC; PO BOX 12096; SAN DIEGO, CA 92112. (#28334).

PICTORIAL HISTORY OF VICTORIAN MANSIONS - CA. PICTORIAL PRESENTATION OF VICTORIAN ERA BUILDINGS IN SAN DIEGO IN BOOK FORM. (LOCAL). WILLIAM M CARTWRIGHT, PRESIDENT; SAVE OUR HERITAGE ORGANIZATION; PO BOX 3571; SAN DIEGO, CA 92103. (#28371).

PICTORIAL HISTORY OF SAN DIEGO, CA. A COLLECTION OF HISTORICAL PHOTOS TO SHOW THE HISTORY OF SAN DIEGO. (LOCAL). DONN F NOBLE, COORDINATOR; 115 JUANITA LANE; EL CAJON, CA 92021. (#30240).

PRESENT OF 6 KOALA BEARS TO THE SAN DIEGO ZOO - CA. SIX KOALA BEARS WERE PRESENTED TO THE PEOPLE OF THE UNITED STATES BY THE PEOPLE OF AUSTRALIA ON JULY 26, 1976 AND ARE HOUSED AT THE SAN DIEGO ZOO. (INT'L). OFFICE OF INFORMATION; AUSTRALIAN EMBASSY; 1601 MASSACHUSETTS AVE, NW; WASHINGTON, DC 20036. (#28444).

PRESIDENTIAL SEAL OF STRAW - SAN DIEGO, CA. 4-FOOT CIRCULAR WOODEN FRAME AROUND PRESIDENTIAL SEAL MADE OF STRAW COLLECTED FROM ALL FIFTY STATES. AVAILABLE FOR DISPLAY. (LOCAL). GEORGE KOSTICK, ARTIST; 5738 ABERNATHY WAY; SAN DIEGO, CA 92117. (#30232).

'THE PRESIDENTS' - SAN DIEGO, CA. INDIVIDUAL AWARD WINNING PORTRAITS OF ALL UNITED STATES PRESIDENTS PRESENTED BY PACIFIC TELEPHONE CO TO COUNTY SUPERINTENDENT OF SCHOOLS FOR DISPLAY. (LOCAL). RICO JARAMILLO, COORDINATOR; PACIFIC TELEPHONE COMPANY; 525 B ST, ROOM 1717; SAN DIEGO, CA 92101. (#28321).

PROFILE 76. EXHIBIT AT 1399 NINTH. (LOCAL). ED KAPRIELIAN, COORD; TRAVELBUG INTERNATIONAL; 1399 9TH AVE; SAN DIEGO, CA 92101. (#104427-5).

REDISCOVERING AMERICA - SAN DIEGO, CA. FILMS ON AMERICA WILL BE PRODUCED. (ST-WIDE). HOWARD MATSON, PRODUCER-MANAGER; COPLEY PRODUCTIONS; 7776 IVANHOE AVE; LA JOLLA, CA 92037. (#28363).

RIVERBOAT REPLICAS - SAN DIEGO, CA. REPLICAS OF 'ROBERT E LEE', 'DELTA QUEEN' AND 'MISSISSIPPI QUEEN', DISPLAY SCENE, NARRATION OF RIVERBOAT LORE AND SOUND FILM. (LOCAL). ROGER S JOHNSEN, COORDINATOR; 8301-349 MISSION GORGE RD; SANTEE, CA 92071. (#30242).

RIVERS OF AMERICA FILM - SAN DIEGO, CA. GROWTH OF NATION AS TIED TO RIVERS OF AMERICA WILL BE SHOWN ON FILM. (LOCAL). MICHAEL SULLIVAN, COORDINATOR; RUEBEN FLEET SPACE CENTER; PO BOX 33303; SAN DIEGO, CA 92101. (#28348).

ROYAL T '76 OFFICIAL BICENTENNIAL VEHICLE - CA. RECALLING NOSTALGIA DESIGN OF EARLIER FAMILIAR CLASSIC PRODUCTS OF THE MODEL T AND CONTINENTAL ERAS WITH A PATRIOTIC MOTIF OF COLOR, WITH STAR DEPICTING THE 13 COLONIES PLUS OFFICIAL SEALS. (ST-WIDE). HANK MANOR, PRES, DESIGNER & BUILDER; ROYAL T '76 CORP; 4664 MERCURY ST; SAN DIEGO, CA 92111. (#26608).

SAN CARLOS TOWN MEETING - SAN DIEGO, CA. SERIES OF MEETINGS REGARDING COMMUNITY DEVELOPMENT AND PROBLEMS. (LOCAL). HENRY WILSON, VICE PRESIDENT; SAN CARLOS COMMUNITY COUNCIL; 6368 LAKE ALTURAS AVE; SAN DIEGO, CA 92119. (#30248).

SAN DIEGO BICENTENNIAL MUSIC FESTIVAL. MUSIC FESTIVAL FEATURING HISTORIC SPANISH & MEXICAN-CALIFORNIA MUSIC & MEXICAN MUSIC NOW. ALSO AMERICAN COMPOSITIONS INFLUENCED BY MEXICAN MUSICAL TRADITIONS. (NAT'L). MARTIN DICKINSON, CHAIRPERSON; SAN DIEGO BICENTENNIAL COMMITTEE; 1200 3RD AVE; SAN DIEGO, CA 92101. (#2982).

SAN DIEGO CENTER FOR PHOTO ART - CA. PERMANENT LOCATION TO HOUSE DISPLAY - BALBOA PARK. (LOCAL). LARRY URRUTIA, COORDINATOR; CENTER FOR PHOTOGRAPHIC ART; 7911 HERSHEL AVE; LA JOLLA, CA 92037. (#28332).

SAN DIEGO CHORALEERS - CA. MIXED CHORUS WILL BE AVAILABLE FOR PERFORMANCES. (LOCAL). ESTHER SEGAL, DIRECTOR; SAN DIEGO COMMUNITY COLLEGE; 3565 EDIWHAR; SAN DIEGO, CA 92123. (#28338).

SAN DIEGO COUNTY HERITAGE PARK, SAN DIEGO, CA. A PARK DEDICATED TO THE PRESERVATION & INTERPRETATION OF VICTORIAN HERITAGE, CONTAINING RESTORED VICTORIAN STRUCTURES & SHOPS LEASED FOR COMMERCIAL OPERATION. (LOCAL). LLOYD T LOWERY, DIRECTOR; SAN DIEGO COUNTY DEPARTMENT OF PARKS & RECREATION; 2454 HERITAGE PARK ROW; SAN DIEGO, CA 92110. (#18433).

SAN DIEGO GIRL SCOUTS BICENTENNIAL ACTIVITIES - CA. SPONSORSHIP OF TREES ALONG NATIVE PLANT TRAIL AT SAN DIEGO WILD ANIMAL PARK; GUIDED TOURS OF TRAIL, 'STAR-SPANGLED '76 DAY CAMP;' PROGRAM OF VISITS TO 3 HISTORICAL SITES; FURTHER STUDIES. (LOCAL). BRENDA WHITSETT, COORDINATOR; GIRL SCOUTS, SAN DIEGO-IMPERIAL COUNCIL, INC; 1231 UPAS ST; SAN DIEGO, CA 92103. (#28376).

SAN DIEGO PUBLIC LIBRARY BICENTENNIAL PROJECT - CA. SPECIAL BOOKS AND COLLECTORS' ITEMS ON DISPLAY ON DIFFERING HISTORICAL & PATRIOTIC THEMES ROTATED MONTHLY; SPECIAL FILMS & PROGRAMS OFFERED; BOOKMARK BOOKLISTS ON THE VARIOUS THEMES. (LOCAL). MARCO THORNE, COORDINATOR; SAN DIEGO PUBLIC LIBRARY; 820 E ST; SAN DIEGO, CA 92101. (#28322).

SAN DIEGO STATE UNIV BICENTENNIAL ACTIVITIES. LECTURES, THEATRE PRODUCTIONS BY AMERICAN AUTHORS, CONCERTS, AMERICAN OPERA; PUBLIC RADIO & TELEVISION PROGRAMMING WITH AMERICAN HISTORICAL IMPORT, LIBRARY DISPLAYS OF MULTI-MEDIA, COMMUNITY SPEAKERS. (LOCAL). GORDEN LEE, PUBLIC AFFAIRS OFFICER; SAN DIEGO STATE UNIV; COLLEGE AVE; SAN DIEGO, CA 92182. (#28328).

SAN DIEGO WILD ANIMAL PARK, CA. ANIMAL PRESERVE, A 200 OF THE FUTURE TO BE DEVELOPED IN SAN DIEGO. (LOCAL). FRED CHILDRESS, OPERATIONS DIRECTOR; SAN DIEGO WILD ANIMAL PARK; ROUTE 1, BOX 725 E; ESCONDIDO, CA 92025. (#20002).

SANTA FE DEPOT RESTORATION - SAN DIEGO, CA. PURCHASE AND REFURBISHING OF EXISTING STRUCTURE FOR USE AS MAIN TRANSIT TERMINAL. TICKETING FACILITY, INFORMATION, HISTORICAL EXHIBITS, RESTAURANT, PEOPLE'S MARKET AND ARTISAN FAIR. (LOCAL). CITY MANAGER; INTERGOVERNMENTAL RELATIONS DIVISION; 202 C ST; SAN DIEGO, CA 92101. (#28344).

SAR SPONSORED MONUMENT - SAN DIEGO, CA. FITTING MEMORIAL TO FOUNDING OF COUNTRY IN CENTER OF BUSINESS ACTIVITY OF DOWNTOWN SAN DIEGO. (LOCAL). TOM DARBY, SECRETARY; SONS OF AMERICAN REVOLUTION, SAN DIEGO CHAPTER; BOX 1776; SAN DIEGO, CA 92112. (#28346).

SENIOR CITIZENS PARK - SAN DIEGO, CA. DEVELOPMENT OF PUBLIC PARK FOR SENIOR CITIZENS. (LOCAL). R F CHASE, PRESIDENT; SAN DIEGO COUNCIL OF THE NATIONAL MANAGEMENT ASSOC; 2701 HARBOR DR; SAN DIEGO, CA 92112. (#28345).

SHERMAN-DOIG HOUSE - SAN DIEGO, CA. RESTORATION OF SAN DIEGO HISTORIC SITE 104. (LOCAL). THEODORE A KRAUSS, PROJ DIRECTOR; SOHO - SAVE OUR HERITAGE ORGANIZATION; 136 W FIR ST; SAN DIEGO, CA 92102. (#24241).

SHOWCASE WRITERS CLUB CONTEST - SAN DIEGO, CA. ANNUAL WRITERS CONTEST FOR ALL SAN DIEGO COUNTY WRITERS. (LOCAL). MARY GIACINTO, COORDINATOR; SHOWCASE WRITERS CLUB; PO BOX 691; LEMON GROVE, CA 92045. (#28356).

SQUADRON HISTORY DISPLAY - SAN DIEGO, CA. FOR NEW OFFICERS' WARDROOM; WILL INCLUDE PICTURES, PLAQUES & INFORMATION ON DEVELOPMENT OF SQUADRON AND AIRCRAFT. (LOCAL). RICHARD H PLUSH, LTJG; HELICOPTER COMBAT SUPPORT SQUADRON THREE; NAVAL AIR STATION NORTH ISLAND; SAN DIEGO, CA 92135. (#32110).

STAGE LINE REVIVAL - SAN DIEGO, CA. REVIVE LOCAL STAGE LINES & ENCOURAGE PUBLIC TRAVEL. (LOCAL). ANNIE URQUHART, COORDINATOR; 9040 WESTHILL RD; LAKESIDE, CA 92040. (#30230).

STUDENT FRONTERAS - SAN DIEGO, CA. PARTICIPATION IN FRONTERAS ON HIGH SCHOOL LEVEL - EXTENDING HANDS ACROSS BORDER TO DEVELOP UNDERSTANDING OF CULTURAL HERITAGES AND TRADITIONS AND PROBLEMS. (LOCAL). RICHARD WHITE, CHAIRMAN; THE BISHOP'S SCHOOLS ART DEPT; PO BOX 1948; LA JOLLA, CA 92037. (#28362).

'THERE WAS A TIME' OIL PAINTING - SAN DIEGO, CA. ORIGINAL OIL PAINTING, 24'X48' DEPICTS TWO PLAINS INDIANS SITTING QUIETLY ON HORSEBACK WHILE A VISION OF THEIR CHANGING WAY OF LIFE APPEARS BEFORE THEM. (LOCAL). LORETTA METZGER, ARTIST; 683 STARBRIGHT LANE; ALPINE, CA 92001. (#30235).

'TOWARD OUR THIRD CENTURY' - CONTEST - CA. ESSAYS, FILMS OR TAPE RECORDINGS SUBMITTED COMPETITIVELY & DEALING WITH AMERICA'S THIRD CENTURY; INDIVIDUAL PERCEPTIONS & RECOMMENDATIONS ON AREAS OF HUMAN CONCERN; NATIONAL PROGRAM; AWARDS $100,000. (NAT'L). ADM EDWARD E GRIMM; WELLS FARGO BANK; 500 BROADWAY; SAN DIEGO, CA 92101. (#28320).

SAN DIEGO — CONTINUED

'TRIMS' PROGRAM FOR CHILDREN - SAN DIEGO, CA. CREATIVE CRAFTS PROGRAM FOR CHILDREN. (LOCAL). MADELINE BARKER, COORDINATOR; SOUTH CLAIREMONT RECREATION CENTER; 2452 BAJA CERRO CIRCLE; SAN DIEGO, CA 92109. (#28358).

U S CLOSED BADMINTON CHAMPIONSHIPS - CA. THE AMERICAN BADMINTON ASSOC IS SPONSORING U S CLOSED BADMINTON CHAMPIONSHIPS. (NAT'L). VIRGINIA B LYON, COORDINATOR; AMERICAN BADMINTON ASSOC; 1330 ALEXANDRIA DR; SAN DIEGO, CA 92107. (#27937).

UNITED STATES AND STATES FLAG DISPLAYS - CA. FLAGS OF THE STATES DISPLAYED ON THE ANNIVERSARY DATE OF THE STATES ADMISSION TO THE UNION, OR DATE OF RATIFICATION; POSTERS WITH ADDITIONAL INFORMATION. (LOCAL). JOHN G MOORE, COORDINATOR; 2129 FINCH LANE; SAN DIEGO, CA 92123. (#30251).

UNITED STATES MARINE CORPS BICENTENNIAL PROJECT-CA. TELEVISION APPEARANCE, USMC DAY, DRESS PARADE, FLAG DISPLAY AND PRODUCTIONS IN HONOR OF THE BICENTENNIAL. (LOCAL). KENNETH J HOUGHTON, MAJOR GENERAL; UNITED STATES MARINE CORPS; MARINE CORPS RECRUIT DEPOT; SAN DIEGO, CA 92140. (#28420).

USA BICENTENNIAL AMATEUR RADIO PROGRAM - CA. BICENTENNIAL SUPPORT PROMOTING USA, VARIOUS STATES, CITIES, HISTORY, ASSETS, PEOPLES BEFORE THE WORLD; FREE OF CHARGE COMMUNICATION AND EDUCATION. (LOCAL). CLIFTON EVANS, CMDR USN RET; INTERNATIONAL AMATEUR RADIO SOCIETY, INC; 3212 MESA VERDE RD; BONITA, CA 92002. (#28325).

USE OF NAVY BAND - SAN DIEGO, CA. THE NAVY BAND SAN DIEGO WILL BE REQUESTED TO PROVIDE A PROGRAM OF COMMEMORATIVE MUSIC FOR BOTH MILITARY & CIVILIAN PERSONNEL ABOARD THE AIR STATION. (LOCAL). AZC CHARLES M SYMONDS; NAVAL AIR STATION NORTH ISLAND; SAN DIEGO, CA 92135. (#32339).

USO BICENTENNIAL ACTIVITIES - SAN DIEGO, CA. DANCES, SWIM PARTIES, SOFTBALL GAMES AND CARNIVALS FOR MILITARY PERSONNEL. (LOCAL). PETER ELKIN, EXEC DIRECTOR; UNITED SERVICE ORGANIZATION, INC; 510 W F ST; SAN DIEGO, CA 92101. (#28368).

USS CHICAGO ON DISPLAY - SAN DIEGO, CA. THE USS CHICAGO HAS PAINTED BICENTENNIAL LOGOS ON PROMINENT TOPSIDE EQUIPMENT, FABRICATED SPECIAL BROW COVERS AND CONSTRUCTED SPECIAL PLAQUE/PICTURE DISPLAYS FOR THE QUARTERDECK. (LOCAL). LT ROBERT L WILSON; USS CHICAGO (CG-11); FPO; SAN FRANCISCO, CA 96601. (#29486).

VOTING FILM: 'HAVE YOUR SAY' - SAN DIEGO, CA. FILM DESCRIBES THE IMPORTANCE OF VOTING. (LOCAL). RICHARD H PLUSH, LTJG; HELICOPTER COMBAT SUPPORT SQUADRON THREE; NAVAL AIR STATION NORTH ISLAND; SAN DIEGO, CA 92135. (#32109).

WELCOME ABOARD PAMPHLET - SAN DIEGO, CA. THE USS HORNE HAS DESIGNED A NEW WELCOME ABOARD PAMPHLET TO REFLECT THE BICENTENNIAL THEME. (LOCAL). CDR DVORNICK, EXEC OFFICER; USS HORNE, CG-30; FPO; SAN FRANCISCO, CA 96601. (#29114).

WOMEN'S POETRY & GRAPHICS CENTER BICENT PROGRAM-CA. POETRY READINGS OF OUTSTANDING CA WOMEN POETS, DEBUT READINGS; STORE FRONT GALLERY DISPLAYS; PUBLICATION OF NEW LOCAL & REGIONAL FEMALE POETS; COMMUNITY SEMINARS; ART FORUMS. (LOCAL). JOYCE NOWER, COORDINATOR; THE GREATER GOLDEN HILL POETRY EXPRESS; 2829 BROADWAY; SAN DIEGO, CA 92102. (#28377).

YANKEE DOODLE DANDY GARDENS - SAN DIEGO, CA. HOME GARDENS PLANTED IN RED, WHITE AND BLUE. 'BETSY ROSS' FLAG FLOWN OVER CAPITOL ON FLAG DAY WILL BE PRESENTED TO MOST OUTSTANDING GARDEN. (LOCAL). MRS RICHARD M ROSALER, COORDINATOR; CLAIREMONT WOMEN'S CLUB; 3612 VISTA DE LA BAHIA; SAN DIEGO, CA 92117. (#28369).

YOUNG HISTORIANS BOOK AND PLAQUE - SAN DIEGO, CA. ESSAYS BY HIGH SCHOOL STUDENTS ABOUT LOCAL PERSONS, PLACES AND EVENTS WITH HISTORICAL VALUE. PARTICIPANTS NAMES WILL BE ENGRAVED ON A BRONZE PLAQUE. (LOCAL). ROGER W HOVLAND, COORDINATOR; LA JOLLA AMERICAN LEGION POST AND AUXILIARY UNIT 275; 5803 SOLEDAD RD; LA JOLLA, CA 92037. (#28366).

1952 SEAGRAVES FIRETRUCK - SAN DIEGO, CA. TRIP FROM SAN DIEGO TO PHILADELPHIA TO PARTICIPATE IN JULY 4 CELEBRATION. (REGN'L). ROGER DEAN MARVIN, COORDINATOR; THE BICENTENNIAL KIDS; 3521 ORANGE AVE; SAN DIEGO, CA 92104. (#30231).

200-YEAR PICTORIAL HISTORY OF THE USA - CA. 5-PIECE WOODEN, FREE STANDING DISPLAY ON ROLLERS, CONSISTING OF FOUR WOODEN PANELS (12'X80') ON A WOODEN BASE (18'X80'). ALSO A SEPARATE 3'X80', ONE-SIDED PANEL. AVAILABLE FOR DISPLAY. (LOCAL). JAMES R LAGACE, ARTIST; 6761 JACKSON DR; SAN DIEGO, CA 92119. (#28340).

300 BUS SALUTE TO BICENTENNIAL, SAN DIEGO, CA. SAN DIEGO TRANSIT SALUTES THE BICENTENNIAL BY DISPLAYING ON EACH 300 STANDARD SIZE BUS, THE OFFICIAL CITY OF SAN DIEGO BICENT SHIELD 'SAN DIEGO - THE FINEST CITY IN THE FINEST COUNTY'. (LOCAL). MARC SANDSTROM, COORDINATOR; SAN DIEGO TRANSIT; PO BOX 2511; SAN DIEGO, CA 92112. (#22119).

MAY 11, '74. HALF-TIME FIELD SHOW AZTEC BOWL, CALIFORNIA STATE UNIVERSITY. LA MESA WESTERN STATES MUSIC TOURNAMENT OF CALIF. 10 HIGH SCHOOL BANDS IN MUSIC COMPETITION--CONCERT-SIGHT READING PARADE-FIELD SHOW, PORTRAYING HISTORICAL PAGEANTRY. (ST-WIDE). JAMES M CULVER, EXEC DIR; LA MESA CHAMBER OF COMMERCE; 8155 UNIVERSITY AVE; LA MESA, CA 92041. (#687-903).

DEC 29, '74 - JAN 19, '75. THE SINGING SAN DIEGANS TOUR. TOUR OF ISRAEL, GREECE, TURKEY & HOLLAND. (INT'L). DAVID M LOOMIS, COORD; THE SINGING SAN DIEGANS; 6775 GLENROY; SAN DIEGO, CA 92120. (#200006-275).

MAR 1, '75 - DEC 31, '76. 'IN APPRECIATION OF THE LAND' PROGRAM ON 200 YEARS IN PARKS. A PROGRAM REGARDING THE IMPORTANCE OF PARKS AND OPEN SPACES IN A MODERN CONTEMPORARY TIME. AT IN THE PARK. (REGN'L). CABRILLO NATL MON; NATIONAL PARK SERVICE; PO BOX 6175; SAN DIEGO, CA 92106. (#6725-6).

JUNE 8 - 14, '75. BICENTENNIAL HERITAGE FESTIVAL - MURALS BY CHICANO ARTISTS. EXHIBIT AT BALBOA PARK. (LOCAL). JUAN FELIPE HERRERA, CHMN; CENTRO CULTURAL DE LA RAZA; PO BOX 92102; SAN DIEGO, CA 92102. (#200006-292).

JUNE 15 - SEPT 1, '75. 'TALE OF 8 LIGHTS' PROGRAM ON POINT LOMA LIGHTHOUSE. A DAY IN THE LIFE OF A LIGHTHOUSE KEEPER SET IN THE PERIOD OF THE THE 1870'S. (REGN'L). SUPT CABRILLO NM; NATIONAL PARK SERVICE; PO BOX 6175; SAN DIEGO, CA 92106. (#6729-36).

JULY 2 - AUG 17, '75. FRONTIER AMERICA THE FAR WEST. 300 HISPANIC, INDIAN & AMER ART OBJECTS FROM 9TH-19TH CENTS. PAINTINGS, PRINTS, PHOTOS & OTHER DECORATIVE & UTILITARIAN OBJECTS DISPLAYED. OVER 2/3 ARE LOANS FROM PRIVATE & PUBLIC USA COLLECTIONS. AT FINE ARTS GALLERY. (REGN'L). JEAN WILLIAMS, PUBLICITY; NATIONAL END FOR THE ARTS & PHILIP MORRIS INC; 479 HUNTINGTON AVE; BOSTON, MA 02115. (#4044-2).

JULY 3, '75. SAN DIEGO BOYS' CHOIR - PERFORMANCE. LIVE PERFORMANCE AT LINDA VISTA RECREATION CENTER, 7064 LEVANT. (LOCAL). RAYMOND H COSSEY, COORD; SAN DIEGO BOYS' CHOIR; 4501 ILLINOIS AVE; SAN DIEGO, CA 92116. (#200006-286).

JULY 4, '75. 'SPIRIT OF THE FOURTH' - OLD-FASHIONED CELEBRATION. PARADE, FESTIVAL, FAIR AT TOWM CENTER, RANCHO BERNARDO & SADDLE CLUB. (LOCAL). COL DAVID B WILLETS, CHMN; SPIRIT OF THE FOURTH; 16574 FELICE DR; SAN DIEGO, CA 92128. (#200006-296).

JULY 7, '75. SAN DIEGO BOYS' CHOIR - PERFORMANCE. LIVE PERFORMANCE AT ORGAN PAVILION, BALBOA PARK. (LOCAL). RAYMOND H COSSEY, COORD; SAN DIEGO BOY'S CHOIR; 4501 ILLINOIS AVE; SAN DIEGO, CA 92116. (#200006-287).

JULY 20, '75. 'REVOLUTIONARY IDEAS' - PATRIOTIC MUSICAL. LIVE PERFORMANCE AT BALBOA PARK'S ORGAN PAVILION. (LOCAL). A L DOMINY, COORD; FIRST BAPTIST CHURCH; 930 10TH AVE; SAN DIEGO, CA 92101. (#200006-288).

AUG 1 - 7, '75. SAN DIEGO STATE UNIVERSITY CLOWNS. OBSERVANCE OF NATIONAL CLOWN WEEK. CLOWNS WILL HAVE GRADUATION CEREMONY, DEMONSTRATIONS, SKITS AND THEY WILL VISIT HOSPITALS. AT SDSU; MISSION VALLEY CENTER. (LOCAL). RICH WISE, COORD; SAN DIEGO STATE UNIV; PO BOX 81496; SAN DIEGO, CA 92138. (#200006-283).

AUG 23 - 24, '75. SAN DIEGO FOLK FAIRE. CULTURAL AND RELIGIOUS HERITAGE THROUGH DANCE, MUSIC, ART, COSTUMES, FOOD AND ARTIFACTS; ANNUAL EVENT. (LOCAL). MRS JULIA H SCHILLING; SAN DIEGO COUNTY ECUMENICAL COUNCIL; 1875 2ND AVE; SAN DIEGO, CA 92101. (#200006-257).

AUG 24 - 30, '75. ANNUAL CONVENTION OF MILITARY ORDER OF THE PURPLE HEART, DEPT OF CA. CONFERENCE, EXHIBIT, FESTIVAL AT THE ROYAL INN AT THE WHARF. (ST-WIDE). KEN RICHARDSON, COORD; MILITARY ORDER OF THE PURPLE HEART, DEPT OF CA; 2913 DUCOMMUN AVE; SAN DIEGO, CA 92122. (#200006-300).

AUG 29, '75. SENIOR SUMMER BALL, SENIOR CITIZENS SUMMER ACTIVITY. FESTIVAL AT BALBOA PARK CLUB BALLROOM. (LOCAL). ART SICK, COORD; SENIOR CITIZENS GROUP; CONFERENCE BLDG, BALBOA PARK; SAN DIEGO, CA 92101. (#200006-304).

AUG 30, '75. LEADERSHIP SEMINAR - STUDENTS OPTIMISTIC FOR FUTURE AMERICA EVENTS. SEMINAR AT LINDA VISTA JUNIOR. (LOCAL). ROSS EDWARD PORTER, COORD; STUDENTS OPTIMISTIC FOR FUTURE AMERICA; 4024 ST JAMES PL; SAN DIEGO, CA 92103. (#200006-302).

SEPT 10 - 11, '75. NATL PK SVC 'PEOPLE OF 1776' (PILOT) VISITS CABRILLO NM. TRAVELING TROUPE WILL BRING VARIOUS ASPECTS OF COLONIAL LIFE (MILITARY LIFE, MUSIC, CRAFTS) TO VISITORS TO THIS NATIONAL PARK SERVICE AREA. (REGN'L). SUPERINTENDENT; NATIONAL PARK SERVICE - CABRILLO NATIONAL MONUMENT; PO BOX 6175; SAN DIEGO, CA 92106. (#1469-203).

SEPT 19, '75. BICENTENNIAL CARNIVAL FOR MILITARY MEN AND WOMEN. FAIR AT 510 W F ST. (LOCAL). PETE ELKIN, COORD; UNITED SERVICE ORGANIZATIONS, INC; 510 W F ST; SAN DIEGO, CA 92101. (#200006-293).

SEPT 21 - 28, '75. CABRILLO FESTIVAL. THIS FESTIVAL WILL FEATURE REENACTMENT OF CABRILLO LANDING AT POINT LOMA; APPROPRIATE CEREMONIES AND ART CONTESTS AT VARIOUS PLACES. OPENING, COMMERATIVE CEREMONIES, HISTORIC SEMINAR TO BE HELD AT THE PARK. AT AT VARIOUS LOCATIONS IN SAN DIEGO, INCLUDING CABRILLO. (REGN'L). SUPT, CABRILLO NM; NATIONAL PARK SERVICE; P.O. BOX 6175; SAN DIEGO, CA 92106. (#6728-560).

SEPT 29 - OCT 10, '75. EAST SAN DIEGO PIONEER DAYS - FESTIVAL WITH HISTORICAL THEME. EXHIBIT, FESTIVAL. (LOCAL). JESS M POLAND, COORD; EAST SAN DIEGO CHAMBER OF COMMERCE; PO BOX 5044; SAN DIEGO, CA 92105. (#200006-311).

OCT 4, '75. SAN DIEGO HERITAGE: HISTORICAL TOURS & SLIDE LECTURE PRESENTATIONS. TOUR, EXHIBIT AT FRIAR'S ROOM-PADRE TRAIL INN, OLD TOWN HISTORIC PARK, SEELEY STABLES. (LOCAL). DR CLARE CRANE, COORD; UCSD EXTENSION & MIRAMAR COLLEGE HISTORY DEPT; SAN DIEGO, CA 92110. (#200006-220).

OCT 10, '75. OLIVE TREE DONATION. FESTIVAL, CEREMONY AT SCOTTISH RITE TEMPLE IN MISSION VALLEY. (LOCAL). REV THEODORE PHILLIPS; GRECIAN HOLIDAY BAZAAR; 4849 BIONA DR; SAN DIEGO, CA 92116. (#200006-87).

OCT 10 - 13, '75. NAVY BICENT BIRTHDAY CELEBRATION SPONSORED BY 11 NAVAL DISTRICT. FESTIVAL AT NAVAL TRAINING CENTER; BROADWAY; BROADWAY PIER. (LOCAL). LT STEVE FRANK, COORD; 11TH NAVAL DISTRICT HEADQUARTERS; SAN DIEGO, CA 92132. (#200006-277).

OCT 12, '75. BICENTENNIAL FLAGS DEDICATION. CEREMONY AT FIRST BAPTIST CHURCH, 930 10TH AVE. (LOCAL). A L DOMINY, COORD; FIRST BAPTIST CHURCH; 930 10TH AVE; SAN DIEGO, CA 92101. (#200006-259).

OCT 12 - 19, '75. POWAY POW-WOW DAYS. COMPETITION, EXHIBIT, FAIR. (LOCAL). TOM POST, COORD; POWAY CHAMBER OF COMMERCE; PO BOX 34; POWAY, CA 92064. (#200006-312).

OCT 14, '75. 'FASHION-TENNIAL' - FUND-RAISING EVENT FOR STUDENT FINANCIAL AID. EXHIBIT AT HILTON INN, MISSION BAY. (LOCAL). MRS JOHN MAZUR, COORD; UNIV OF SAN DIEGO AUXILIARY; 10085 GRANDVIEW DR; LA MESA, CA 92041. (#200006-282).

OCT 18, '75. EUCALYPTUS TREE PLANTING. CEREMONY AT 9333 LEMON AVE. (LOCAL). CAPT LLOYD J MALAND, DIR; SONS OF NORWAY, SORLANDET LODGE #105; 9333 LEMON AVE; LA MESA, CA 92041. (#200006-264).

OCT 19, '75. RAINBOW GIRLS BICENTENNIAL DINNER, CELEBRATION AND PATRIOTIC DINNER. CEREMONY, FESTIVAL AT CHARITY, CLAIRMONT #167, 3849 MARLESTA DR. (LOCAL). LESLIE DERWIN, COORD; INTERNATIONAL ORDER OF THE RAINBOW FOR GIRLS; 3849 MARLESTA DR; SAN DIEGO, CA 92111. (#200006-303).

OCT 26, '75. BICENTENNIAL COMMUNITY CONVENTIONS. EXHIBIT AT 3605 CLAIREMONT DR. (LOCAL). NAN VALERIO, COORD; CLAIREMONT TOWN COUNCIL; PO BOX 17306; SAN DIEGO, CA 92117. (#200006-93).

OCT 26, '75 - APR 11, '76. FOUNDING FATHERS. LIVE PERFORMANCE AT 4190 FRONT ST. (LOCAL). MARY MASCHAL, COORD; UNITARIAN CHURCH; 3601 CONRAD AVE; SAN DIEGO, CA 92117. (#104427-14).

NOV 8, '75. SAN DIEGO HERITAGE: HISTORICAL TOURS & SLIDE LECTURE PRESENTATIONS. TOUR, EXHIBIT AT MISSION SAN DIEGO DE ALCALA, PADRE DAM, MISSION SAN LUIS REY. (LOCAL). DR CLARE CRANE, COORD; UCSD EXTENSION & MIRAMAR COLLEGE HISTORY DEPT; SAN DIEGO, CA 92110. (#200006-221).

NOV 14, '75. THE FAITH OF AMERICA. CEREMONY. (LOCAL). REV LAWRENCE WADDY; SAN DIEGO COUNTY ECUMENICAL CONFERENCE; 743 PROSPECT ST; LA JOLLA, CA 92037. (#200006-79).

NOV 19 - 23, '75. 'THE IRISH ARE COMING' - BICENTENNIAL CARNIVAL. FAIR AT SOUTH CLAIREMONT PARK, 3605 CLAIREMONT DR. (LOCAL). MIKE CAIN, DIRECTOR; SAINT PATRICK'S DAY PARADE ASSOCIATION; 3030 SUNCREST DR, 809; SAN DIEGO, CA 92116. (#200006-218).

NOV 21, '75. OPEN HOUSE. EXHIBIT, TOUR. (LOCAL). PAT POLAKOWSKI, CHMN; NAVAL ELECTRONICS LABORATORY CENTER; 271 CATALINA BLVD; SAN DIEGO, CA 92152. (#200006-382).

NOV 25, '75. LINDBERGH BICENTENNIAL CELEBRATION. EXHIBIT AT LINDBERGH FIELD. (LOCAL). KEITH E HATTER; SAN DIEGO SCANDINAVIAN BICENTENNIAL COMMITTEE; 4346 KANSAS ST; SAN DIEGO, CA 92104. (#200006-78).

NOV 25, '75. SAN DIEGO WOMEN'S ART CENTER. EXHIBIT. (LOCAL). JOYCE NOWER; WOMEN'S POETRY AND GRAPHICS CENTER; 2829 BROADWAY; SAN DIEGO, CA 92129. (#200006-80).

NOV 29, '75. 'SALUTE TO AMERICA' - BAND CONCERTS AND FLAG PAGEANTS. LIVE PERFORMANCE. (LOCAL). MAJ GEN K J HOUGHTON; UNITED STATES MARINE CORPS RECRUIT DEPOT; SAN DIEGO, CA 92140. (#200006-331).

DEC 1, '75 - FEB 1, '76. BICENTENNIAL ESSAY CONTEST. AWARD, COMPETITION AT HALE, MARSTON AND EINSTEIN JR HIGH SCHOOLS. (LOCAL). AROYCE JARVIS, CHMN; CLAIREMONT JUNIOR WOMEN'S CLUB; 5455 VIA BELLO; SAN DIEGO, CA 92111. (#200006-333).

DEC 4, '75. BOBBY SHERMAN YOUTH OPEN. COMPETITION. (LOCAL). LAWRENCE E TOWLE; RANCHO PENASQUITOS TOWN COUNCIL; 14483 PENASQUITOS DR; SAN DIEGO, CA 92129. (#200006-81).

DEC 20, '75. ST STEPHEN'S CHURCH BICENTENNIAL EXTRAVAGANZA. FESTIVAL AT ST STEPHEN'S CHURCH, 5825 IMPERIAL AVE. (LOCAL). MRS GERI WALTERS, COORD; ST STEPHEN'S CHURCH OF GOD IN CHRIST; 1735 WINNET ST; SAN DIEGO, CA 92114. (#200006-270).

DEC 31, '75. PHILIPPINE-AMERICAN NEW YEARS EVE BALL. FESTIVAL. (LOCAL). A B SANTOS, COORD; PHILIPPINE-AMERICAN COMMUNITY; 2926 MARKET ST; SAN DIEGO, CA 92102. (#200006-82).

JAN 1 - FEB 15, '76. 'COLOR THE BUS CONTEST'. COLLEGE STUDENTS ARE ENCOURAGED TO SUBMIT A BICENTENNIAL DESIGN FOR ONE OF OUR TRANSIT BUSES. DEADLINE IS MONDAY, FEB 15, 1976. THE WINNING COLLEGE WILL RECEIVE A TRANSIT BUS AND THE NECESSARY PAINT. THE DESIGNER & A GROUP OF STUDENTS WILL THEN PAINT THE BUS. AT VDSV COLLEGE AVE

SAN DIEGO—CONTINUED

AND MONTAZUMA. (LOCAL). J WARREN MOORE, COORD; SAN DIEGO TRANSIT CORPORATION; SAN DIEGO, CA 92112. (#104427-11).

JAN 1 - JULY 4, '76. RIDE FOR NATURE - CROSS-COUNTRY TRIP ON HORSEBACK. INCLUDES EXCHANGE OF IDEAS & INFORMATION ON THE ENVIRONMENT WHILE ENROUTE. AT ACROSS THE USA. (NAT'L). WILLIAM MARKS; 947 LORING ST; SAN DIEGO, CA 92109. (#200006-422).

JAN 1 - DEC 31, '76. A DAY IN THE LIFE OF THE LIGHT KEEPER'S FAMILY AT CABRILLO NM. DEMONSTRATIONS INCLUDE 19TH CENTURY COOKING ARTS, GARDENING, CHILDREN'S TOYS, AND NAVIGATIONAL AIDS. PROGRAM PRESENTED BY VOLUNTEERS ON IRREGULAR SCHEDULE. VISITORS SHOULD CONTACT PARK FOR DAYS AND TIMES PROGRAM IS GIVEN. AT 200 YDS SOUTH OF CABRILLO MONUMENT. (REGN'L). CABRILLO NATL MON; NATIONAL PARK SERVICE; PO BOX 6175; SAN DIEGO, CA 92106. (#6728-62).

JAN 1 - DEC 31, '76. MISSION SAN DIEGO DE ALCALA 200TH ANNIVERSARY. FOR OBSERVANCE OF NATION'S BICENTENNIAL, THE MISSION WILL BE USED AS A FOCAL POINT. CLOSED CHRISTMAS DAY. AT 10818 SAN DIEGO MISSION RD. (LOCAL). MNSGR I BRENT EAGAN; DIOCESAN OFFICE FOR APOSTOLIC MINISTRY/ ALCALA PARK; PO BOX 80428; SAN DIEGO, CA 92138. (#200006-340).

JAN 1 - DEC 31, '76. SPECIAL MULTIMEDIA BICENTENNIAL PROGRAM AT CABRILLO NM. PRESENTATION OF BICENTENNIAL FILMS AND SLIDE PROGRAMS. VISITORS SHOULD CONTACT PARK FOR DAYS AND TIMES OF PRESENTATION. AT PARK VISITOR CENTER AUDITORIUM. (REGN'L). CABRILLO NM; NATIONAL PARK SERVICE; PO BOX 6175; SAN DIEGO, CA 92106. (#6729-181).

JAN 1 - DEC 31, '76. 'VOYAGE OF DISCOVERY', CABRILLO NM PGM ON SPANISH CONTRIB. THIS IS A FILM PRESENTATION OF THE SPANISH CONTRIBUTION TO THE DISCOVERY OF THE NEW WORLD. PROGRAM IS SHOWN DAILY. VISITORS SHOULD CONTACT PARK FOR TIMES. AT PARK'S VISITOR CENTER AUDITORIUM. (REGN'L). SUPT, CABRILLO NM; NATIONAL PARK SERVICE; P.O. BOX 6175; SAN DIEGO, CA 92106. (#6729-35).

JAN 2 - 12, '76. SAN DIEGO MAIL LINE RE-RUN. COMPETITION AT DEPART FROM OLD TOWN, ARRIVING IN YUMA, ARIZONA. (REGN'L). WAYMON SMITH; THE COMMITTEE FOR THE SAN DIEGO MAIL LINE RE-RUN; 350 SAN FERNANDO ST; SAN DIEGO, CA 92106. (#200006-126).

JAN 3 - 4, '76. 'LOVE IS THE WAY' - RADIO PROGRAM. RADIO/TV. (LOCAL). KEN HUNT, COORD; STATION KLRO FM; PO BOX 3210; SAN DIEGO, CA 92103. (#200006-213).

JAN 4 - 9, '76. 'LET'S TALK ABOUT ANTIQUES' - WEEKLY RADIO PROGRAM. RADIO/TV. (LOCAL). DR CECIL MUNSEY, COORD; RADIO STATION KFSD FM; 13541 WILLOW RUN RD; POWAY, CA 92064. (#200006-212).

JAN 6, '76. COLONIAL DINNER-ESSAY CONTEST. CEREMONY, COMPETITION. (LOCAL). SESLIE CRUSTO, COORD; MONTGOMERY STUDENT BODY ASSOC; 2470 ULRIC ST; SAN DIEGO, CA 92111. (#200006-325).

JAN 8 - DEC 2, '76. LINARES CHAPTER, DAR-MONTHLY LUNCHEONS WITH BICENTENNIAL THEMES. LINARES CHAPTER OF DAR WILL SPONSOR A BICENTENNIAL LUNCHEON EACH MONTH: JAN 8, FEB 5, MAR 4, APR 1, MAY 6, JUNE 3, OCT 7, NOV 4, AND DEC 2ND, 1976. AT PAVILLION ROOM, US GRANT HOTEL; 2ND AND BROADWAY. (LOCAL). MRS JERRY J STRAYER; DAUGHTERS OF THE AMERICAN REVOLUTION; 1627 MIGUEL AVE; CORONADO, CA 92115. (#104427-19).

JAN 10 - JULY 11, '76. FINE ARTS GALLERY EXHIBITS & LECTURES. EXHIBIT, SEMINAR AT FINE ARTS GALLERY, BALBOA PARK. (LOCAL). HENRY G GARDINER, COORD; FINE ARTS GALLERY OF SAN DIEGO; BALBOA PARK, PO BOX 2107; SAN DIEGO, CA 92112. (#200006-269).

JAN 14 - 15, '76. PROFILE '76 - MULTIMEDIA SHOW DEPICTING PEOPLE OF AMERICA. EXHIBIT. (LOCAL). ED KAPRIELIAN, COORD; INTERNATIONAL SOCIETY OF TRAVELBUGS; 1399 NINTH AVE, SUITE 101; SAN DIEGO, CA 92101. (#200006-256).

JAN 14 - 18, '76. AMERICAN FREEDOM TRAIN DISPLAY DAYS AT SAN DIEGO. THE AMERICAN FREEDOM TRAIN WILL INCLUDE 10 EXHIBIT CARS AND 2 SHOW CASE CARS DEPICTING DIFFERENT PHASES OF THE AMERICAN EXPERIENCE. ITS ARRIVAL WILL SERVE AS A CATALYST FOR LOCAL BICENTENNIAL CELEBRATIONS BY PEOPLE THROUGHOUT THIS NATION. (ST-WIDE). SY FREEDMAN, DIR P/R; THE AMERICAN FREEDOM TRAIN FOUNDATION, INC.; 5205 LEESBURG PKE, SUITE 800; BAILEY'S XRDS, VA 22041. (#1776-39).

JAN 15 - 17, '76. UNITED STATES ARMED FORCES BICENTENNIAL CARAVAN. CARAVAN IS COMPOSED OF EXHIBIT VANS FOR EACH MILITARY SERVICE. PROJECT THEME IS 'HISTORY OF THE ARMED FORCES AND THEIR CONTRIBUTIONS TO THE NATION'. (LOCAL). ALBERT A ARNHYM, CHMN; US ARMED FORCES EXHIBIT VANS PROJECT; 6474 SPEAR ST; SAN DIEGO, CA 92120. (#1775-305).

JAN 15 - FEB 28, '76. OUR STORIED PAST EXHIBITION. STEVENGRAPHS, EARLY USA POSTAGE STAMPS, OLD MAPS & RARE BOOKS DEPICT THE HISTORY OF THE UNITED STATES. AT LOBBY OF LIBRARY. (LOCAL). LOIS MACKENZIE, PUBL INFO; SAN DIEGO PUBLIC LIBRARY; 820 E ST; SAN DIEGO, CA 92101. (#200006-322).

JAN 15 - NOV 30, '76. BICENTENNIAL USA - LIBRARY EXHIBIT. EXHIBIT OF RARE BOOKS AND STEVENGRAPHS, STAMPS, GLASS WORK, PHOTOS AND TOYS. (LOCAL). MARCO THORNE, LIBRARIAN; SAN DIEGO PUBLIC LIBRARY; 820 E ST; SAN DIEGO, CA 92101. (#107324-1).

JAN 19 - AUG 1, '76. FEMINIST POETRY & GRAPHICS. EXHIBIT, SEMINAR. (LOCAL). JOYCE NOWER, COORD; FEMINIST POETRY AND GRAPHICS CENTER; 2829 BROADWAY; SAN DIEGO, CA 92102. (#200006-255).

JAN 25 - FEB 27, '76. 'FANFARE' - EXHIBITION OF PAINTINGS BASED ON AMERICAN FLAG. EXHIBIT AT MALCOLM LOVE LIBRARY. (LOCAL). LEE SANDELIN, LIBRARIAN; SAN DIEGO STATE UNIV; 5402 COLLEGE AVE; SAN DIEGO, CA 92115. (#200006-247).

JAN 29, '76. MORMON BATTALION DAY - ENTRANCE OF MORMON BATTALION INTO SAN DIEGO. CEREMONY AT PRESIDIO PARK. (LOCAL). FRANK M BRADSHAW, COORD; CHURCH OF JESUS CHRIST OF LATTER DAY SAINTS; 8905 LA MESA BLVD; SAN DIEGO, CA 92041. (#200006-222).

JAN 31, '76. BEST OF ALL WORLDS SMALL IMAGE ART SHOW - ANNUAL EXHIBITION PREVIEW. EXHIBIT AT BALBOA PARK. (LOCAL). J GARY KORNMAYER, COORD; SPANISH VILLAGE ART CENTER; 3436 PARK W LN; SAN DIEGO, CA 92117. (#200006-278).

JAN 31, '76. THE BICENTENNIAL BASH. FESTIVAL AT BALBOA PARK-SAN DIEGO FINE ARTS GALLERY. (LOCAL). HENRY GARDINER, DIR; FINE ARTS GALLERY; PO BOX 2107; SAN DIEGO, CA 92112. (#104427-15).

FEB 1 - 28, '76. JUNIOR ACHIEVEMENT TRADE FAIR. FAIR AT PARKWAY PLAZA SHOPPING CENTER. (LOCAL). VINCENT R CIRUZZI, COORD; JUNIOR ACHIEVEMENT OF SAN DIEGO, INC; 5315 EL CAJON BLVD; SAN DIEGO, CA 92115. (#200006-308).

FEB 1 - JUNE 1, '76. NAZARETH SCHOOL BICENTENNIAL EXHIBITS. EXHIBIT AT NAZARETH SCHOOL, 10728 SAN DIEGO MISSION RD. (LOCAL). SISTER COLOMBA JOSEPH; NAZARETH SCHOOL; 10728 SAN DIEGO MISSION RD; SAN DIEGO, CA 92108. (#200006-267).

FEB 1 - OCT ??, '76. CROSS COUNTRY RIDE FOR NATURE. LONE CROSS COUNTRY RIDE ACROSS THE U S, STARTING FROM SAN DIEGO AND ENDING IN PHILADELPHIA ON JULY 4, 1976. PURPOSE OF THE TRIP IS TO DISCOVER & MAKE RECORD OF THE UNSPOILED PARTS OF OUR COUNTRY. (LOCAL). BILL MARKS, COORD; BILL MARKS; 947 LORING ST; SAN DIEGO, CA 92109. (#107366-2).

FEB 7 - 8, '76. BICENTENNIAL AIR SHOW. EXHIBIT AT BROWN FIELD. (REGN'L). JOHN CROGHAM, PROJ DIR; CITY OF SAN DIEGO; 3750 JOHN J MONTGOMERY DR; SAN DIEGO, CA 92123. (#104427-3).

FEB 9 - 11, '76. NAZARETH SCHOOL BICENTENNIAL CEREMONY. HOURS ARE 9:30 AM - 2:30 PM; AGAIN AT 7:30 PM. AT 10728 SAN DIEGO MISSION RD. (LOCAL). SISTER COLUMBA JOSEPH; NAZARETH SCHOOL BICENTENNIAL; 10728 SAN DIEGO MISSION RD; SAN DIEGO, CA 92120. (#104427-7).

FEB 14, '76. FLAGPOLE DONATION. CEREMONY AT RUEBEN H FLEET SPACE CENTER, BALBOA PARK. (LOCAL). MRS FRED FOX, COORD; CALIFORNIA FEDERATION OF WOMEN'S CLUBS, SAN DIEGO DISTRICT 25; 4319 NEWPORT AVE; SAN DIEGO, CA 92107. (#200006-280).

FEB 14 - 15, '76. BICENTENNIAL DEDICATION & AIR SHOW. EXHIBIT AT BROWN FIELD. (LOCAL). JOHN CROGHAN, COORD; BICENTENNIAL AIR SHOW COMMITTEE; 3750 J J MONTGOMERY DR; SAN DIEGO, CA 92123. (#200006-219).

FEB 19, '76. 'THE BRITISH ARE COMING!' - BRITISH MILITARY BAND PERFORMANCE. LIVE PERFORMANCE AT SPORTS ARENA. (INT'L). CHARLES K JONES, PRES; COLUMBIA ARTISTS FESTIVALS CORP; 165 W 57TH ST; NEW YORK, NY 10019. (#6532-22).

FEB 19, '76. GROVE OF FLOWERING TREES. CEREMONY AT 2252 CAMINITO PRECIOSA. (LOCAL). STERLING DORMAN, PRES; THE THURSDAY CLUB; 2252 CAMINITO PRECIOSA; LA JOLLA, CA 92037. (#104427-24).

FEB 20 - 22, '76. JUNIOR ACHIEVEMENT HERITAGE FESTIVAL. BOOTHS EXHIBITING PRODUCTS MANUFACTURED BY JUNIOR ACHIEVEMENT COMPANIES. FESTIVAL HAS A BICENTENNIAL THEME. AT PARKWAY PLAZA. (LOCAL). VINCENT R CIRUZZI; JUNIOR ACHIEVEMENT OF SAN DIEGO; 575 PARKWAY PLAZA; EL CAJOW, CA 92020. (#104427-17).

FEB 28, '76. ST DAVID'S DAY - 84TH ANNUAL CELEBRATION. FESTIVAL AT U S GRANT HOTEL - CRYSTAL ROOM. (LOCAL). DILYS HALL, COORD; CAMBRIAN (WELSH) SOCIETY OF SAN DIEGO COUNTY; SAN DIEGO, CA 92101. (#200006-294).

FEB 29, '76. 'MEN OF VISION' - DEDICATION OF STATUES. CEREMONY AT SERRA MUSEUM. (LOCAL). MRS JERRY J STRAYER, DIR; CA STATE SOCIETY OF NATIONAL SOCIETY, DAR; 1627 MIGUEL AVE; CORONADO, CA 92118. (#200006-225).

MAR 1 - 31, '76. EARLY VIEWS OF AMERICAN CITIES. FORE-EDGE PAINTINGS, ENGRAVINGS & ILLUSTRATIONS FROM THE RARE BOOK COLLECTION. AT WANGENHEIM ROOM. (LOCAL). LOIS MACKENZIE, PUBL INFO; SAN DIEGO PUBLIC LIBRARY; 820 E ST; SAN DIEGO, CA 92101. (#200006-320).

MAR 1 - 31, '76. THE FIRST AMERICANS - RARE INDIAN PHOTOS BY EDWARD S CURTIS. EXHIBIT AT LOBBY OF LIBRARY. (LOCAL). LOIS MACKENZIE, PUBL INFO; SAN DIEGO PUBLIC LIBRARY; 820 E ST; SAN DIEGO, CA 92101. (#200006-321).

MAR 1 - MAY 12, '76. AZTEC CHOIR. LIVE PERFORMANCE. (LOCAL). FRANK W ALMOND, COORD; SAN DIEGO STATE UNIV DEPT OF MUSIC; SAN DIEGO, CA 92182. (#200006-339).

MAR 2 - APR 4, '76. 'PERSONAGES OF THE REVOLUTION' - EXHIBITION OF PAINTINGS. EXHIBIT AT MALCOLM LOVE LIBRARY. (LOCAL). LEE SANDELIN, LIBRARIAN; SAN DIEGO STATE UNIV; 5402 COLLEGE AVE; SAN DIEGO, CA 92115. (#200006-246).

MAR 5 - 6, '76. 'LIVING PICTURES' - SCENES FROM SAN DIEGO HISTORY. EXHIBIT AT CASA DEL PRADO, BALBOA PARK. (LOCAL). MRS VIRGINIA LUCAS, COORD; SAN DIEGO COUNTY CONGRESS OF HISTORY; 4250 QUAPAW AVE; SAN DIEGO, CA 92117. (#200006-285).

MAR 7, '76. 'BICENTENNIAL FLAGPOLES' - DEDICATION OF FLAGPOLES. CEREMONY AT INTERNATIONAL AEROSPACE HALL OF FAME. (LOCAL). MRS AUSTIN G MADDEN, DIR; SOROPTOMIST INTERNATIONAL OF SAN DIEGO; 2219 BANCROF ST; SAN DIEGO, CA 92104. (#200006-230).

MAR 8, '76. CHURCH OF LATTER DAY SAINTS FESTIVAL. FESTIVAL AT 2727 DE ANZA RD. (LOCAL). BERT KLEIN, PROJ DIR; CHURCH OF LATTER DAY SAINTS; 2727 DE ANZA RD; SAN DIEGO, CA 92103. (#104427-22).

MAR 9 - JUNE 9, '76. ART & CREATIVE WRITING CONTEST - 'THE AMERICAN WAY OF LIFE'. AWARD. (LOCAL). EUDORA CARLSON, CHAIRMAN; TAFT JR HIGH SCHOOL PTA; 2282 GALAHAD; SAN DIEGO, CA 92123. (#107330-1).

MAR 12 - OCT 31, '76. SAN DIEGO GIRL SCOUTS BICENTENNIAL ACTIVITIES. CEREMONY. (LOCAL). BRENDA L WHITSETT; GIRL SCOUTS SAN DIEGO-IMPERIAL COUNCIL, INC; 1231 UPAS ST; SAN DIEGO, CA 92103. (#104427-13).

MAR 14 - APR 18, '76. LENTEN ART FESTIVAL: ALL MEDIA EXPRESSION OF JESUS' MINISTRY. EXHIBIT AT ST MARK'S UNITED METHODIST CHURCH, 3502 CLAIRMONT DR. (LOCAL). ELIZABETH BRANSCOM, CHMN; ST MARK'S UNITED METHODIST CHURCH; 3502 CLAIRMONT DR; SAN DIEGO, CA 92117. (#200006-251).

MAR 17, '76. THE MAGNIFICANT 37 - FASHION SHOW. LIVE PERFORMANCE AT BALBOA PARK. (LOCAL). HENRY G GARDINER, DIR; FINE ARTS GALLERY OF SAN DIEGO; PO BOX 2107; SAN DIEGO, CA 92112. (#104427-16).

MAR 17, '76. 1ST ANNUAL ST PATRICK'S DAY PARADE IN SAN DIEGO. PARADE AT LAUREL, 6TH AND C ST. (LOCAL). MIKE CAIN, COORD; IRISH AMERICAN CLUB AND IRISH STUDENT UNION; 3030 SUNCREST DR; SAN DIEGO, CA 92107. (#200006-281).

MAR 23 - 26, '76. MOBILE VAN BICENTENNIAL EXHIBIT & SCREEN SHOW. EXHIBIT AT FIESTA COURT, MISSION VALLEY CENTER, 1640 CAMINO DEL RIO. (LOCAL). LINDA CAREY, DIRECTOR; U S ARMY CORPS OF ENGINEERS; 1640 CAMINO DEL RIO, N; SAN DIEGO, CA 92108. (#200006-250).

MAR 26 - 28, '76. SANDICAL BICENTENNIAL EXPO. EXHIBIT AT MASONIC HALL, 1895 CAMINO DEL RIO SOUTH, MISSION VALLEY, S.D.. (LOCAL). ROBERT MORRIS, PROJ DIR; SAN DIEGO PHILATELIC COUNCIL, INC; PO BOX 4223; SAN DIEGO, CA 92104. (#104427-4).

MAR 28, '76. WOMEN'S DAY PROGRAM - THE AMERICAN WOMAN, 1776-1976. LIVE PERFORMANCE AT AUDITORIUM, 4190 FRONT ST. (LOCAL). MARY MASCHAL, COORD; UNITARIAN CHURCH; 3601 CONRAD AVE; SAN DIEGO, CA 92117. (#104427-30).

MAR 28 - APR 28, '76. THE AMERICAN WOMAN ART SHOW. EXHIBIT AT 4190 FRONT ST - BARD HALL. (LOCAL). MARY MASCHAL, COORD; UNITARIAN CHURCH; 3601 CONRAD AVE; SAN DIEGO, CA 92117. (#104427-29).

APR 1 - 30, '76. BICENTENNIAL AUCTION. EXHIBIT. (LOCAL). VIRGINIA WILSON, COORD; 4TH OF JULY COMMITTEE; 6348 CHANDLER DR; SAN DIEGO, CA 92117. (#200006-276).

APR 1 - MAY 29, '76. SENIOR CITIZENS PARADE, PAGEANT AND JAMBOREE. CEREMONY, FESTIVAL, PARADE AT BROADWAY, BALBOA PARK CLUB. (LOCAL). ARTHUR F SWAIN, COORD; THE CEDAR COMMUNITY CENTER; 520 QUINCE ST; SAN DIEGO, CA 92103. (#200006-279).

APR 2 - 4, '76. BICENTENNIAL CERAMIC & POTTERY SHOW. 6TH ANNUAL SHOW - THIS YEAR'S EXHIBIT HAS BICENTENNIAL THEME. AT CRA BUILDING AUDITORIUM; 9115 CLAIREMONT MESA BLVD. (LOCAL). MARGARET HOTELL; CRA CERAMIC CLUB AND MARGARET HOTEL; 1446 COOLIDGE ST; SAN DIEGO, CA 92111. (#106804-4).

APR 3 - MAY 16, '76. 'THE CROSS AND THE SWORD' - ART EXHIBIT. EXHIBIT AT FINE ARTS GALLERY, BALBOA PARK. (LOCAL). HENRY G GARDINER, COORD; FINE ARTS GALLERY OF SAN DIEGO; BALBOA PARK, PO BOX 2107; SAN DIEGO, CA 92112. (#200006-263).

APR 5 - 30, '76. TWO HUNDRED YEARS OF TOYS - CHILD'S PLAY IN AMERICA. DOLLS & TOYS FROM COLONIAL TIMES TO PRESENT. SLIDE PROGRAMS: APRIL 24, 'AMERICA'S HERITAGE OF TOYS'; APRIL 29, 'DOLLS TELL THE STORY OF AMERICA'. AT LOBBY OF LIBRARY. (LOCAL). LOIS MACKENZIE, PUBL INFO; SAN DIEGO PUBLIC LIBRARY; 820 E ST; SAN DIEGO, CA 92101. (#200006-319).

APR 10, '76. 'AMERICAN HERITAGE' - NEW SHIP LAUNCHING. CEREMONY. (REGN'L). JOHN MURPHY, COORD; NATIONAL STEEL AND SHIP BUILDING; PO BOX 80278; SAN DIEGO, CA 92138. (#200006-298).

APR 11, '76. 'DIVIDED WE STAND' - CELEBRATION OF THOMAS JEFFERSON'S BIRTHDAY. LIVE PERFORMANCE AT FIRST UNITARIAN CHURCH, 4190 FRONT ST. (LOCAL). JUDITH BARNEY, COORD; FIRST UNITARIAN CHURCH; 4190 FRONT ST; SAN DIEGO, CA 92103. (#200006-254).

APR 12, '76. 'THE AMERICAN WAY OF LIFE'. ARTS/CRAFTS, PERFORMING ARTS & ESSAY CONTEST. AT 9191 GRAMERCY DR. (LOCAL). EUDORA L CARLSON, CHMN; TAFT JR HIGH SCHOOL PTA; 2282 GALAHAD RD; SAN DIEGO, CA 92123. (#200006-332).

APR 13, '76. ODORI FESTIVAL OF JAPAN VISITS SAN DIEGO. LIVE PERFORMANCE AT CIVIC THEATRE. (INT'L). DIRECTOR; MEL HOWARD PRESENTS; 143 E 27TH ST; NEW YORK, NY 10016. (#108965-5).

SAN DIEGO — CONTINUED

APR 18, '76. BICENTENNIAL EASTER EGG HUNT. FESTIVAL. (LOCAL). DOUGLAS E LETSON, COORD; SAN DIEGO COUNTY; 5364 VAN NUYS PL; SAN DIEGO, CA 92101. (#200006-289).

APR 23 - 25, '76. MORGAN HORSE CLUB SHOW - PARADE COMPETITION IN VARIOUS CLASSES. PARADE, COMPETITION AT DEL MAR FAIRGROUNDS. (LOCAL). TERRY BOND, COORD; SAN DIEGO MORGAN HORSE CLUB; RT 3, BOX 488A; ESCONDIDO, CA 92025. (#200006-217).

APR 24, '76. USS HORNE SHIPS' PICNIC. USS HORNE SHIPS' PICNIC WAS CONDUCTED W/THE THEME 'MAINTAINING OUR NATIONS PROUD TRADITION' DECORATIONS AND ACTIVITIES WERE IN ACCORDANCE WITH THIS THEME. AT ADMIRAL BAKER RECREATION FACILITY. (LOCAL). CDR DVORNICK, CHAIRMAN; USS HORNE, CG-30; FPO; SAN FRANCISCO, CA 96601. (#200006-360).

APR 30, '76. 'BICENTENNIAL PARADE FOR YOUTH'. PARADE AT GREENBRIAR AVE TO WARING RD TO ELDRIDGE ST TO BRUNSWICK AVE. (LOCAL). MRS DIANE STEFFENS, DIR; ALLIED GARDENS JUNIOR WOMEN'S CLUB; 6632 CARTWRIGHT ST; SAN DIEGO, CA 92120. (#200006-227).

MAY 1, '76. COTTAGE OF POLAND. FESTIVAL AT 1934 30TH ST. (LOCAL). JOHN CHOBAN, PROJ DIR; POLISH AMERICAN ASSOC OF SAN DIEGO; 1934 30TH ST; SAN DIEGO, CA 92102. (#104427-20).

MAY 1, '76. MAY BALL. FESTIVAL AT SHERATON ISLAND HOTEL, HARBOR ISLAND. (LOCAL). JOHN CHOBAN, CHMN; POLISH AMERICAN ASSOC OF SAN DIEGO; 1934 30TH ST; SAN DIEGO, CA 92102. (#200006-338).

MAY 1, '76. MERRY MOUNT FESTIVAL - EARLY AMERICAN FUN FAIR. RE-CREATION OF QUINCY, MA IN 1626; NATHANIEL HAWTHORNE'S MERRY MOUNT. AT CHURCH BUILDINGS AND GROUNDS, 4190 FRONT ST. (LOCAL). ALICE SHADER, COORD; UNITARIAN CHURCH; 115 WALNUT ST, APT C; SAN DIEGO, CA 92117. (#104427-31).

MAY 1 - 2, '76. ANTIQUE BOTTLE SHOW. EXHIBIT. (LOCAL). ED MCCANN, COORDINATOR; SAN DIEGO ANTIQUE BOTTLE CLUB; 3970 KANSAS ST; SAN DIEGO, CA 92104. (#106804-5).

MAY 1 - JUNE 30, '76. THE EVENTS OF THE REVOLUTION - EXHIBITION OF PAINTINGS. EXHIBIT AT MALCOLM LOVE LIBRARY, SAN DIEGO STATE UNIV. (LOCAL). WILLIAM BOWNE, COORD; MALCOLM LOVE LIBRARY, SAN DIEGO STATE UNIV; SAN DIEGO, CA 92115. (#200006-237).

MAY 3 - 31, '76. 'EXPRESSION' THE CHICANO IN OUR CULTURE. PAINTINGS, PHOTOGRAPHS & POETRY DEPICT THE MEXICAN-AMERICAN'S REACTION TO HIS ENVIRONMENT. AT LOBBY & CORRIDOR GALLERY OF LIBRARY. (LOCAL). LOIS MACKENZIE, PUBL INFO; SAN DIEGO PUBLIC LIBRARY; 820 E ST; SAN DIEGO, CA 92101. (#200006-318).

MAY 5 - 6, '76. NATL PK SVC '...A LITTLE LOOK AROUND' VISITS CABRILLO NM. THIS SHORT PROGRAM FEATURES ACTORS PORTRAYING FAMOUS AMERICANS OF THE PAST WHO'VE RETURNED TO SEE AMERICA'S GROWTH. AND 9/4 MINUTE MAN NHP IN LEXINGTON. (REGN'L). CABRILLO NATL MON; NATIONAL PARK SERVICE; P.O. BOX 6175; SAN DIEGO, CA 92106. (#5653-51).

MAY 6, '76. TAPIOLA CHILDREN'S CHOIR VISITS SAN DIEGO. LIVE PERFORMANCE. (INT'L). TATU TUCHIKORPI; CONSULATE GENERAL OF FINLAND; 540 MADISON AVE; NEW YORK, NY 10022. (#109041-1).

MAY 6 - 9, '76. 'AMERICA 1976' - PERFORMANCE OF SYMPHONY COMPOSERS' COMPETITION. COMPETITION, LIVE PERFORMANCE AT CIVIC THEATRE, 3RD AND C. (LOCAL). ROBERT CHRISTIAN, COORD; SAN DIEGO SYMPHONY ORCHESTRA ASSOC; PO BOX 3175; SAN DIEGO, CA 92103. (#200006-273).

MAY 6 - 9, '76. THE HOME AND LEISURE SHOW. EXHIBIT AT 233 A ST, SUITE 1007. (LOCAL). A J KIDD; BUREAU OF HOME APPLIANCES; 233 A ST, SUITE 1007; SAN DIEGO, CA 92101. (#104427-8).

MAY 6 - 15, '76. 'PLYMOUTH ROCK: THE FIRST AMERICAN ROCK OPERA'. LIVE PERFORMANCE AT SOUTHWESTERN COLLEGE, CHULA VISTA. (LOCAL). SERGIO A ARIAS, CHMN; CALIFORNIA-PACIFIC COMMUNITY THEATRE, INC; 348 W MARKET, SUITE 102; SAN DIEGO, CA 92101. (#200006-336).

MAY 6 - 16, '76. BICENTENNIAL EXPOSITION. CARNIVAL, CIRCUS, EXHIBITS, ENTERTAINMENT AND 200-MILE MARATHON. AT INTERSECTION OF INTERSTATE, 805 & CLAIREMONT MESA BLVD. (LOCAL). PAT VICK, COORDINATOR; P&G ENTERPRISES; 1251 THIRD AVE, SUITE 203; CHULA VISTA, CA 92011. (#200006-299).

MAY 7, '76. SALUTE TO AMERICA. TICKETS AVAILABLE AT CENTER BOX OFFICE. AT GOLDEN HALL - CIVIC CENTER. (LOCAL). MAJ GEN KENNETH HOUGHTON; MARINE CORPS RECRUIT DEPOT; BARNETT ST; SAN DIEGO, CA 92104. (#106804-2).

MAY 8, '76. BICENTENNIAL DOLL CLUBS SHOW. THERE WILL BE AN ENTIRE ROOM ON DISPLAY WITH DOLLS REPRESENTING HISTORICAL EVENTS, FAMOUS PEOPLE IN AMERICAN HISTORY, & PERIODS OF THE LAST 200 YEARS. WILL ALSO INVOLVE THE SAN DIEGO DOLL CLUB & THE DOLL GUILD OF SAN DIEGO. AT 1895 CAMINO DEL RIO S. (ST-WIDE). ELOISE CHRISTIANSON; EVENING BELLES DOLL CLUB OF CALIFORNIA; 6927 QUEMORY CRT; SAN DIEGO, CA 92105. (#104427-1).

MAY 8, '76. LITTLE MISS LIBERTY & MR INDEPENDENCE CONTEST. COMPETITION AT CLAIREMONT SQUARE. (LOCAL). MRS VIRGINIA WILSON, CHMN; GREATER CLAIREMONT 4TH OF JULY COMMITTEE; 6348 CHANDLER DR; SAN DIEGO, CA 92040. (#200006-424).

MAY 8, '76. SPANISH LANDING MONUMENT AND PLAQUE - DEDICATION. CEREMONY AT SPANISH LANDING PARK, HARBOR DRIVE. (REGN'L). EUGENE K CHAMBERLIN, DIR; E CLAMPUS VITUS, SQUIBOB CHAPTER OF THE CALIF HISTORICAL SOCIETY; 3033 DALE ST; SAN DIEGO, CA 92104. (#200006-244).

MAY 11, '76. SOUTHERN CALIFORNIA BICENTENNIAL MARINE BAND CONCERT. LIVE PERFORMANCE AT GOLDEN HALL 202 C ST SAN DIEGO. (LOCAL). GYSGT R P SEGUIN; CITY OF SAN DIEGO; PUBLIC AFFAIRS OFFICE, M C R D; SAN DIEGO, CA 92140. (#200006-509).

MAY 11 - 12, '76. 'EL CAPITAN': A HISTORIC PLAY. LIVE PERFORMANCE AT ALCALA PARK. (LOCAL). B R VAN VLECK, PROF; UNIV OF SAN DIEGO; SAN DIEGO, CA 92110. (#200006-215).

MAY 13 - 16, '76. FIESTA DE LA PRIMAVERA. EXHIBIT, LIVE PERFORMANCE, TOUR AT OLD TOWN SAN DIEGO. (ST-WIDE). DICK YALE, COORD; SAN DIEGO'S OLD TOWN RETURNS TO THE 'DAYS OF THE DONS.'; 2626 SAN DIEGO AVE; SAN DIEGO, CA 92110. (#103416-314).

MAY 14 - 15, '76. SAN DIEGO SUN HARBOR CHORUS AND QUARTETS. LIVE PERFORMANCE AT CIVIC THEATER. (LOCAL). DONALD W MCAVOY, DIR; SD CHAPTER, SOCIETY FOR PRESERVATION OF BARBERSHOP SINGING IN AMER; CASA DEL PRADO BLDG; SAN DIEGO, CA 92103. (#200006-214).

MAY 15, '76. BOYS CLUB REGIONAL TRACK MEET. OLYMPIC TRACK MEET OF BOYS CLUBS WITH PARADE, FLOATS & AWARDS. FIELD EVENTS START AT 10AM & TRACK EVENTS AT 10:30AM. PARADE COMMENCES AT 9:15AM. AT SAN DIEGO STATE UNIV TRACK & FIELD FACILITY. (LOCAL). JOHN POLOS, COORD; KENSINGTON OPTIMIST CLUB OF SAN DIEGO; 2930 MARCY AVE; SAN DIEGO, CA 92113. (#106804-6).

MAY 15, '76. 200-MILE MARATHON RUN. COMPETITION. (LOCAL). GLENN VAUGHAN, COORD; YOUNG MEN'S CHRISTIAN ORGANIZATION; 1115 8TH AVE; SAN DIEGO, CA 92101. (#200006-306).

MAY 16, '76. BICENTENNIAL EXTRAVAGANZA. LIVE PERFORMANCE AT CIVIC THEATER & COMMUNITY CONCOURSE. (LOCAL). WALTER PORTER; SAN DIEGO COMMUNITY COLLEGE DISTRICT; MIDWAY ADULT 3249 FORDHAM ST; SAN DIEGO, CA 92126. (#200006-476).

MAY 16, '76. OPEN HOUSE ON MILITARY RESERVATION. MANY DIGNITARIES AND CIVIC GROUPS WERE INVITED TO OPEN HOUSE. INVITEES WERE GIVEN A NO-HOST LUNCHEON FOLLOWED BY SLIDE PRESENTATIONS FROM THE NAVAL AIR STATION. THE GROUP THEN TOURED THE USS CONSTELLATION & WATCHED A SIMULATED HELICOPTER WATER RESCUE. AT OPEN AIR ON RESERVATION. (LOCAL). ROBERT M. QUITTNER; NAVAL AIR STATION NORTH ISLAND; PAO, NAVAL AIR STATION, N.I.; SAN DIEGO, CA 92135. (#50618-1).

MAY 17 - 23, '76. NAVY WIVES CONVENTION. CONFERENCE AT US NAVAL TRAINING CENTER. (LOCAL). CAROL OLIVER; NAVY WIVES CLUB OF AMERICA; 1976 SW REGIONAL CONVENTION; NATIONAL CITY, CA 92050. (#104427-28).

MAY 19 - 26, '76. PAN ASIAN WEEK. WEEK-LONG CELEBRATION FOR ALL PAN ASIANS AS THEIR CONTRIBUTION TO THE NATION'S HERITAGE AND FUTURE. (LOCAL). BEVERLY YIP, COORD; UNION OF PAN ASIANS COMMUNITIES; 2952 MARKET ST, SUITE F; SAN DIEGO, CA 92102. (#107748-1).

MAY 22, '76. REGIONAL TRACK MEET. COMPETITION AT SDSU TRACK STADIUM. (LOCAL). ART CURRY, COORD; THE BOYS CLUBS OF SAN DIEGO; 6785 IMPERIAL AVE; SAN DIEGO, CA 92114. (#200006-226).

MAY 27, '76. MEDICAL OFFICERS BICENTENNIAL BALL. FESTIVAL AT HOTEL DEL CORONADO. (LOCAL). CYNTHIA KAIRES, LTJG, NC; NAVAL REGIONAL MEDICAL CENTER; 5706 BALTIMORE DR, APT 342; LA MESA, CA 92041. (#200006-245).

MAY 29 - 31, '76. TOUR OF USS LEAHY & FANTAIL EXHIBIT. TOUR OF USS LEAHY INCLUDING BRIDGE, COMBAT INFORMATION CENTER, MISSILE LAUNCHERS & ENGINE ROOM. FANTAIL EXHIBIT COMPARING AMERICAN FIGHTING SHIP 1776 & MODERN CRUISER 1976. AT USS LEAHY BROADWAY PIER, SAN DIEGO WATERFRONT. (LOCAL). CHARLES J DUVEEN LTJG; USS LEAHY CG-16; USS LEAHY CG-16; FPO SAN FRAN, CA 96601. (#200006-477).

MAY 30, '76. AMERICAN DANCE FESTIVAL. EXHIBIT AT ORGAN PAVILION AND BALBOA PARK BOWL. (LOCAL). LLOYD LICKERT - COORD; SWING DANCE CLUB OF AMERICA; 2926-1/2 LINCOLN AVE; SAN DIEGO, CA 92120. (#200006-274).

MAY 30, '76. 'EIGHT STATE FAIR'. FAIR AT RANCHO BERNARDO SADDLE CLUB, 18009 POMERADO RD. (LOCAL). FAYE GORDINIER, COORD; RANCHO BERNARDO CIVIC ASSOC; 2223 AVENIDA DE LA PLAYA; LA JOLLA, CA 92038. (#200006-242).

MAY 31 - JULY 11, '76. AMERICAN ART SINCE 1945. PAINTINGS & SCULPTURES INCLUDING WORKS BY ALBERS, GORKY, JOHNS, KELLY, DE KOONING, OLDENBURG, POLLOCK, RAUSCHENBERG, ROTHKO, STELLA, WARHOL. ACCOMPANIED BY EDUCATIONAL MATERIALS, SERVICES & CATALOGUE. AT FINE ARTS GALLERY OF SAN DIEGO. (ST-WIDE). LINDA GORDON, PUBL INFO; THE MUSEUM OF MODERN ART; 11 WEST 53RD ST; NEW YORK, NY 10019. (#50519-4).

MAY '76. 200 MILE MARATHON YMCA. COMPETITION. (LOCAL). ROGER MARTIN, PROJ DIR; YMCA; 1115 8TH ST; SAN DIEGO, CA 92101. (#104427-23).

JUNE 1 - 30, '76. NEW ENGLAND GRAVESTONE RUBBINGS. 18TH CENTURY TOMBSTONE ART FROM THE COLLECTION OF DR DAVID LUISI. AT LOBBY OF LIBRARY. (LOCAL). LOIS MACKENZIE, PUBL INFO; SAN DIEGO PUBLIC LIBRARY; 820 E ST; SAN DIEGO, CA 92101. (#200006-317).

JUNE 1 - 30, '76. 18TH CENTURY BOOKBINDINGS. EXHIBIT AT WANGENHEIM ROOM. (LOCAL). LOIS MACKENZIE, PUBL INFO; SAN DIEGO PUBLIC LIBRARY; 820 E ST; SAN DIEGO, CA 92101. (#200006-316).

JUNE 1 - NOV 30, '76. GRAN HORSE RACE - LOCAL ENTRANT. RACE FROM EAST TO WEST COAST; FROM JAMESTOWN, NY TO SACRAMENTO, CA. (REGN'L). FRAN FARRELL; BICENTENNIAL GRAND HORSE RACE, LTD; RT 1, BOX 87H; JAMUL, CA 92035. (#200006-341).

JUNE 3 - 5, '76. 'HALLELUJAH AMERICA' - THEATRICAL PRODUCTION & FUND RAISER. LIVE PERFORMANCE AT MAYAN HALL, SOUTHWESTERN COLLEGE. (LOCAL). LYNN STEDD, COORD; COMMUNITY HOSPITAL OF CHULA VISTA AUXILIARY; PO BOX 1297; CHULA VISTA, CA 92012. (#200006-229).

JUNE 3 - 5, '76. NAVY SHIPS TOUR. TOUR AT BROADWAY PIER. (LOCAL). DIRECTOR; 11TH NAVAL DISTRICT HEADQUARTERS, COMNAVSURFPAC; HARBOR DR; SAN DIEGO, CA 92101. (#200006-241).

JUNE 10, '76. OUTSTANDING STUDENT AWARD. AWARD FOR OUTSTANDING SERVICE TO THE SCHOOL AT VALHALLA HIGH SCHOOL. AWARD CONSISTS OF $100 CHECK PLUS PLAQUE. AT VALHALLA HIGH SCHOOL, 1725 HILLSDALE RD, EL CAJUN, CA. (LOCAL). CAPT LOYD MALAND, PRES; OSONS OF NORWAY, SORLANDT LODGE #105; 9333 LEMON AVE; LA MESA, CA 92041. (#107326-1).

JUNE 11, '76. BICENTENNIAL HOBO DAY. FESTIVAL AT 7055 SKYLINE DR. (LOCAL). CATHERINE CIERI; FULTON ELEMENTARY SCHOOL; 202 SYCHAR RD; SAN DIEGO, CA 92114. (#200006-335).

JUNE 12, '76. BICENTENNIAL DISPLAY. EXHIBIT AT MISSION VALLEY SHOPPING CENTER. (LOCAL). BETTIE BOMPUS, COORD; SAN DIEGO GENEALOGICAL SOCIETY; 4730 COLLEGE AVE; SAN DIEGO, CA 92115. (#104427-27).

JUNE 12, '76. COMMUNITY CONCOURSE FLAG RAISING. FLAG RAISING TO COMMEMORATE PHILLIPINE INDEPENDENCE. AT COMMUNITY CONCOURSE. (LOCAL). MRS JUANITO SANTOS, DIR; COUNCIL OF FILIPINO-AMERICAN ORGANIZATIONS; 2952 MARKET ST; SAN DIEGO, CA 92102. (#200006-231).

JUNE 14, '76. SPIRIT OF VOLUNTEERISM - CELEBRATION OF FLAG DAY. CEREMONY AT MISSION BAY ROOM AT BAHIA HOTEL. (LOCAL). MILLIE M CROM, COORD; SAN DIEGO COUNTY HEART ASSOC; PO BOX 3625; SAN DIEGO, CA 92103. (#200006-236).

JUNE 15 - SEPT 1, '76. 'TALE OF 8 LIGHTS' PROGRAM ON POINT LOMA LIGHTHOUSE. A DAY IN THE LIFE OF A LIGHTHOUSE KEEPER SET IN THE PERIOD OF THE THE 1870'S. (REGN'L). SUPT CABRILLO NM; NATIONAL PARK SERVICE; PO BOX 6175; SAN DIEGO, CA 92106. (#6729-536).

JUNE 23 - JULY 6, '76. MARIUS 99, THE WONDER BULL - CHAMPION AMER BRED CHAROLAIS BULL. EXHIBIT. (LOCAL). ALEX COOKE, COORD; ALEX COOKE; 13085 OLD BARONA RD; LAKESIDE, CA 92040. (#200006-216).

JUNE 24, '76. UNIVERSITY OF CALIFORNIA MARCHING BAND PRESENTS 'SPIRIT OF AMERICA'. THIS EVENT IS PART OF A SIX-WEEK PERFORMANCE TOUR OF THE U S BY THE UNIVERSITY OF CALIF MARCHING BAND. SPIRIT OF AMERICA IS A COLLEGIATE MUSICAL REVUE CELEBRATING OUR NATION'S BICENTENNIAL. TICKETS MAY BE PICKED UP AT FIRST FEDERAL BRANCH OFFICES. AT SAN DIEGO STATE UNIVERSITY AZTEC BOWL. (ST-WIDE). DAN DIERDORFF, COORD; FIRST FEDERAL SAVINGS AND LOAN OF SAN DIEGO; PO BOX 656; SAN DIEGO, CA 92112. (#10515-8).

JUNE 25, '76. 'FROM ONE PATRIOT TO ANOTHER' - COMEDY ON STAGE. LIVE PERFORMANCE AT MT CARMEL CENTER FOR PERFORMING ARTS, RANCHO PENASQUITOS. (LOCAL). WALLACE H TUCKER; C A A S T; PO BOX 266; BONSALL, CA 92003. (#200006-337).

JULY 2 - 5, '76. BICENTENNIAL PIER VISIT. THE SHIP WAS AVAILABLE FOR GENERAL VISITING FROM 1000 TO 1700 DAILY WITH TOUR GUIDES IN REVOLUTIONARY COSTUME. BICENTENNIAL SLIDE PRESENTATIONS AND FILMS WERE SHOWN TO THE GENERAL PUBLIC ONBOARD. AT BROADWAY PIER. (LOCAL). CDR DVORNICK, CHAIRMAN; USS HORNE, CG-30; FPO; SAN FRANCISCO, CA 96601. (#200006-361).

JULY 2 - 29, '76. 'LAND THAT I LOVE', SPECIAL EXHIBITION OF ART ABOUT OUR COUNTRY. EXHIBIT AT KNOWLES GALLERY. (LOCAL). MARY KNOWLES, COORD; KNOWLES ART CENTER; 7420 GIRARD AVE; LA VOLLA, CA 92037. (#200006-239).

JULY 2 - ??, '76. BIKE-A-THON-3500 MILE BICYCLE TRIP. TOUR. (ST-WIDE). DIRECTOR; BICYCLE THE AMERICAS CLUB; 1002 BURGANDY PL; ANAHEIM, CA 92804. (#200006-268).

JULY 3, '76. BICENTENNIAL DANCE FESTIVAL. PROGRAM DEPICTING HISTORIC AND PATRIOTIC EVENTS IN THE NATION'S HISTORY, THROUGH DANCE. (LOCAL). HERBERT L WILKINSON, CHMN; CHURCH OF JESUS CHRIST OF LATTER DAY SAINTS; 820 4TH ST; EL CAJON, CA 92021. (#200006-307).

JULY 3, '76. JULY 3RD FESTIVAL - PICNIC, PROGRAM & DANCE. FESTIVAL AT GAS CLUBHOUSE, 1017 S MOLLISON. (LOCAL). PAUL DEESE, COORD; GERMAN AMERICAN SOCIETIES OF SAN DIEGO, INC; 3737 CAMINO DEL RIO S, #301; SAN DIEGO, CA 92108. (#200006-234).

JULY 3 - 4, '76. INTERNATIONAL BICENTENNIAL FESTIVAL 1976. FESTIVAL. (LOCAL). BRIGITT MEEDER, COORD; GERMAN AMERICAN SOCIETIES OF SAN DIEGO, INC; 1721 PRIMROSE ST; EL CAJON, CA 92020. (#200006-248).

JULY 3 - 5, '76. HELICOPTER STATIC DISPLAY. HSL33 PARTICIPATED IN A BICENTENNIAL OPEN HOUSE ABOARD USS HORNE PROVIDING A SQUADRON SHZF SEASPRITE HELICOPTER & A PILOT TO EXPLAIN THE AIRCRAFT & ITS MISSION TO THE

SAN DIEGO — CONTINUED

PUBLIC. AT USS HORNE FOOT OF BROADWAY PIER. (LOCAL). LTJG F R RUEHE HSL33 PAO; HELICOPTER ANTISUBMARINE SQUADRON (LIGHT); HSL 33 NAS NORTH ISLAND; SAN DIEGO, CA 92135. (#200006-461).

JULY 3 - 25, '76. SAN DIEGO WATERCOLOR EXHIBIT. EXHIBIT AT THE NEW CENTRAL FEDERAL TOWER PLAZA GALLERY, 3RD AVE. (LOCAL). EDWIN H WORDELL, COORD; SAN DIEGO WATERCOLOR SOCIETY; 6251 LORCA DR; SAN DIEGO, CA 92115. (#200006-235).

JULY 4, '76. BAND CONCERT AND NEW CONCERT COMPETITION. COMPETITION, LIVE PERFORMANCE AT ORGAN PAVILION, BALBOA PARK. (LOCAL). JOHN R MCCREA, COORD; SAN DIEGO CONCERT BAND; 8288 LINCOLN AVE; LEMON GROVE, CA 92045. (#200006-228).

JULY 4, '76. HOUSE OF PACIFIC RELATIONS LAWN PROGRAM. LIVE PERFORMANCE AT LAWN OF HOUSE OF PACIFIC RELATIONS, BALBOA PARK. (LOCAL). MRS DELORES FRANK, COORD; UNITED STATES HOUSE, THE HOUSE OF PACIFIC RELATIONS; BALBOA PARK; SAN DIEGO, CA 92104. (#200006-262).

JULY 4, '76. HOUSE OF PUBLIC RELATIONS LAWN PROGRAM. CEREMONY AT BALBOA PARK. (LOCAL). DOLORES FRANK, PROJ DIR; HOUSE OF PUBLIC RELATIONS; SAN DIEGO, CA 92104. (#104427-10).

JULY 4, '76. 'JULY 4 PAGEANT' - FIREWORKS DISPLAY, CHOIRS, BANDS, DRUM & BUGLE. HISTORIC EVENTS OF UNITED STATES HISTORY PORTRAYED IN FIREWORKS AND LIVE PAGEANTRY. AT SAN DIEGO STADIUM. (LOCAL). COORDINATOR; GOD BLESS AMERICA WEEK, INC; PO BOX 670; SAN DIEGO, CA 92112. (#200006-295).

JULY 4, '76. LIBERTY BELL REPLICA - DEDICATION. CEREMONY AT BALBOA PARK. (LOCAL). BOB LANTZ, COORD; UNITED STATES HOUSE; HOUSE OF PACIFIC RELATIONS; SAN DIEGO, CA 92104. (#200006-243).

JULY 4, '76. MCRD PARTICIPATION IN 'GOD BLESS AMERICA' BICENTENNIAL PAGEANT. SAN DIEGO MARINE CORPS RECRUIT DEPOT BAND PLAYED & PRESENTED A PATRIOTIC FLAG PRESENTATION. AT SAN DIEGO STADIUM. (LOCAL). GYSGT R P SEGUIN; SAN DIEGO MARINE CORPS RECRUIT DEPOT; PUBLIC AFFAIRS OFFICE, M C R D; SAN DIEGO, CA 92140. (#200006-510).

JULY 4, '76. RINGING OF THE BELLS: TWO-MINUTE BELL RINGING ON JULY 4TH. CEREMONY. (LOCAL). ADM EDWARD GRIMM, COORD; REGIONAL BICENTENNIAL COMMITTEE; 500 BROADWAY; SAN DIEGO, CA 92101. (#200006-272).

JULY 4, '76. THE SAILING OF THE STAR. THE SAILING OF THE STAR OF INDIA WILL BE A SIGNIFICANT HISTORIC EVENT FOR THE STATE OF CALIFORNIA. SHE IS A THREE MASTED BARK BUILT IN 1863. AT SAN DIEGO HARBOR & HARBOR ENTRANCE. (REGN'L). CARL BOWMAN, PRESIDENT; MARITIME MUSEUM; 1306 N HARBOR DR; SAN DIEGO, CA 92101. (#106804-8).

JULY 4, '76. SCRIPPS RANCH 4TH OF JULY PARADE AND PICNIC. PARADE, FESTIVAL AT IRONWOOD RD TO SCRIPPS RANCH BLVD TO AVIARY DR TO HOYT PARK WEST. (LOCAL). CYNTHIA HUGHES, COORD; SCRIPPS RANCH CIVIC ASSOC; PO BOX 45182; SAN DIEGO, CA 92145. (#200006-238).

JULY 6 - 31, '76. 'AMERICA, AMERICA' PAINTINGS. PAINTINGS ON A BICENTENNIAL THEME FROM THE SOUTHEAST SAN DIEGO ART ASSOCIATION. AT CORRIDOR GALLERY IN LIBRARY. (LOCAL). LOIS MACKENZIE, PUBL INFO; SAN DIEGO PUBLIC LIBRARY; 820 E ST; SAN DIEGO, CA 92101. (#107324-3).

JULY 6 - 31, '76. COLONIAL AMERICA EXHIBITION. ARTIFACTS FROM THE LOCAL DAR COLLECTION, INCLUDING FORT HENRY FLAG OF 1749 & A SWORD USED BY GEORGE WASHINGTON. RARE BOOKS FROM THE LIBRARY'S COLLECTION, INCLUDING HORNBOOKS, NEW ENGLAND PRIMERS, ETC. AT LOBBY OF LIBRARY. (LOCAL). LOIS MACKENZIE, PUBL INFO; SAN DIEGO PUBLIC LIBRARY; 820 E ST; SAN DIEGO, CA 92101. (#107324-2).

JULY 10, '76. YOUNG BRONZE BEAUTY & TALENT PAGEANT, 1969-1976. COMPETITION AT INTERNATIONAL ROOM, EL CORTEZ HOTEL, 7TH & ASH. (LOCAL). ZENOLA MAXIE, COORD; LA MIN'S MODELING & CHARM SCHOOL; 4991 IMPERIAL AVE; SAN DIEGO, CA 92114. (#200006-249).

JULY 15 - 18, '76. FESTIVAL OF THE BELLS. FESTIVAL CELEBRATES THE FOUNDING OF CALIFORNIA'S 1ST MISSION. AT PRESIDIO PARK AND MISSION SAN DIEGO DEL ALCALA. (LOCAL). ELEANOR RATNOR, COORD; SAN DIEGO CONVENTION AND VISITORS BUREAU; 1200 3RD AVE, SUITE 824; SAN DIEGO, CA 92101. (#103416-484).

JULY 16 - 18, '76. TREK TO THE CROSS. CELEBRATION OF SAN DIEGO'S BIRTHDAY WILL CULMINATE W/ THE TREK TO THE CROSS ATOP HILL PRESIDO PARK. (LOCAL). J W PARKER, PRESIDENT; SAN DIEGO HISTORICAL DAY ASSOC; 3966 MASON ST; SAN DIEGO, CA 92110. (#106804-3).

JULY 26, '76. PRESENT OF SIX KOALA BEARS TO THE SAN DIEGO ZOO. SIX KOALA BEARS WERE PRESENTED TO THE PEOPLE OF THE UNITED STATES BY THE PEOPLE OF AUSTRALIA AND WILL BE HOUSED AT THE SAN DIEGO ZOO. AT SAN DIEGO ZOO. (INT'L). OFFICE OF INFORMATION; AUSTRALIAN EMBASSY; 1601 MASSACHUSETTS AVE, NW; WASHINGTON, DC 20036. (#28444-1).

JULY 29, '76. FLAG RAISING - OBSERVANCE OF FIRST AMER FLAG RAISING IN SAN DIEGO. CEREMONY AT OLD TOWN PLAZA. (LOCAL). J W PARKER, COORD; SAN DIEGO COUNTY HISTORICAL DAYS ASSOC; 3966 MASON ST; SAN DIEGO, CA 92110. (#200006-223).

JULY 30 - AUG 1, '76. 20TH NATIONAL CONVENTION AND EXHIBITION - AMER PHILATELIC SOCIETY. EXHIBIT AT U S GRANT HOTEL. (LOCAL). GEORGE B BARBER, PRES; UNIVERSAL SHIP CANCELLATION SOCIETY, CA CHAPTER NO 51; 863 9TH AVE; SAN DIEGO, CA 92101. (#200006-271).

AUG 1 - 7, '76. SAN DIEGO STATE UNIVERSITY CLOWNS. GRADUATION CEREMONY, SKITS, SURPRISES, HOSPITAL VISITS. AT AZTEC CENTER; BALBOA PARK; MISSION VALLEY CENTER. (LOCAL). JIM YANAZIN, COORD; SAN DIEGO STATE UNIV; SAN DIEGO, CA 92138. (#200006-284).

AUG 1 - OCT 30, '76. CONCERTS IN THE PARK. HELD EVERY OTHER WEEK JULY 4 THROUGH OCTOBER 30. AT GOLDEN GATE PARK. (REGN'L). SUPT, GOLDEN GATE NRA; NATIONAL PARK SERVICE; FORT MASON; SAN FRANCISCO, CA 94123. (#6728-564).

AUG 3 - 31, '76. SIGNERS OF THE DECLARATION. EXHIBIT AT WAGENHEIM ROOM. (LOCAL). LOIS MACKENZIE, PUBL INFO; SAN DIEGO PUBLIC LIBRARY; 820 E ST; SAN DIEGO, CA 92101. (#107324-5).

AUG 3 - 31, '76. WORLD WAR I POSTERS. EXHIBIT AT LOBBY OF LIBRARY. (LOCAL). LOIS MACKENZIE, PUBL INFO; SAN DIEGO PUBLIC LIBRARY; 820 E ST; SAN DIEGO, CA 92101. (#107324-4).

AUG 8, '76. 'FESTIVAL USA' - FLAG PAGEANT AND CAVALCADE OF MUSIC. FESTIVAL, LIVE PERFORMANCE AT ORGAN PAVILION, BALBOA PARK. (LOCAL). MARIE FIELDING, COORD; ZONTA CLUB OF SAN DIEGO; 4832 CANTERBERRY DR; SAN DIEGO, CA 92116. (#200006-291).

AUG 13 - 15, '76. GOLFINO GOLF CLUB TOURNEY. COMPETITION AT WHISPERING PALMS COUNTRY CLUB. (LOCAL). WILFREDO L ZAMORA, COORD; FILIPINO AMERICAN GOLF ASSOC; 3072 SKIPPER ST; SAN DIEGO, CA 92123. (#200006-224).

AUG 13 - 20, '76. BILLY GRAHAM CRUSADE - RELIGIOUS CRUSADE. LIVE PERFORMANCE, RADIO/TV AT SAN DIEGO STADIUM, FREE PARKING. (LOCAL). DAN MCKINNON, COORD; KSON RADIO; PO BOX 11368; SAN DIEGO, CA 92111. (#200006-290).

AUG 14 - 15, '76. PHILIPPINE FIESTA, EXHIBITS AND VARIETY SHOW OF FOLK SANCES & SONGS. EXHIBIT, FESTIVAL, LIVE PERFORMANCE AT BALBOA PARK ORGAN PAVILION, BALBOA PARK CLUB. (LOCAL). MRS JUANTIA C SANTOS, DIR; COUNCIL OF PHILIPPINO-AMERICAN ORG OF SAN DIEGO COUNTY, INC; 2952 MARKET ST; SAN DIEGO, CA 92111. (#200006-301).

AUG 16 - 20, '76. 6TH MARINE DIVISION ASSOC CEREMONY. CEREMONY AT TOWN & COUNTRY HOTEL & MCRD BASE. (NAT'L). SHELDON F TYLER; 6TH MARINE DIVISION ASSOCIATION INC; PO BOX 550; SANTEE, CA 92071. (#104427-9).

AUG 29, '76. ISRAELI PHILHARMONIC ORCHESTRA VISITS SAN DIEGO. LIVE PERFORMANCE. (INT'L). URI AHARON BAR-NEV; ISRAELI GOVERNMENT; 1621 21ST ST, NW; WASHINGTON, DC 20008. (#109015-4).

SEPT 1 - 30, '76. HISTORIC LANDMARKS OF SAN DIEGO COUNTY - STONE LITHOGRAPHS BY T WADE. EXHIBIT AT LOBBY OF LIBRARY. (LOCAL). LOIS MACKENZIE, PUBL INFO; SAN DIEGO PUBLIC LIBRARY; 820 E ST; SAN DIEGO, CA 92101. (#107324-7).

SEPT 3 - 6, '76. 'ANCIENT AMERICA - MODERN MAN': A BICENTENNIAL LOOK AT WORLD HISTORY. CONFERENCE AT VERSAILLES ROOM, LITTLE AMERICA WESTGATE HOTEL. (LOCAL). DR MAXINE ASHER, COORD; ANCIENT MEDITERRANEAN RESEARCH ASSOC; 1047 GAYLEY AVE, SUITE 201; LOS ANGELES, CA 90024. (#200006-240).

SEPT 4 - 6, '76. MORMON BATTALION CLEAN-UP PROJECT & PARADE. 600 SCOUTS & LEADERS CLEANED UP TO 70 TONS OF LITTER ON SAT. MONDAY PARADE IN 'OLD TOWN' INCL 50 MEMBERS OF MODERN MORMON BATTALION FROM FORT LEAVENWORTH, CONCLUDED BY GENERAL MEETING WITH HOWARD W HANDER, MBR OF COUNCIL OF 12 APOSTLES, GUEST SPEAKER. AT FIELDS IN MISA MESA & SAN DIEGO'S 'OLD TOWN'. (LOCAL). FRANK M BRADSHAW, COORD; CHURCH OF JESUS CHRIST OF LATTER DAY SAINTS; 8905 LA MESA BLVD; SAN DIEGO, CA 92041. (#200006-496).

SEPT 4 - 12, '76. 'AMERICA'S FINEST CITY WEEK'. CEREMONY, EXHIBIT, FESTIVAL. (LOCAL). PAM PARKS, COORD; CITY OF SAN DIEGO; 202 C ST; SAN DIEGO, CA 92101. (#109286-1).

SEPT 9, '76. COLUMBUS DAY PARADE. PARADE AT DOWN BROADWAY FROM 9TH AVE TO COLUMBIA. (LOCAL). FELIX MOTISI, DIR; UNITED ITALIAN AMERICAN ASSOC; 4747 70TH ST; LA MESA, CA 92041. (#200006-232).

SEPT 10 - 12, '76. 'LET'S WAVE THE FLAG' - PUPPET SHOW. LIVE PERFORMANCE AT BALBOA PARK PUPPET THEATRE. (LOCAL). MARIE HITCHCOCK, COORD; 'LET'S WAVE THE FLAG' - PUPPET COMMITTEE; 3002 HELIX ST; SPRING VALLEY, CA 92077. (#200006-233).

SEPT 15 - 18, '76. 'THE MANY FACES OF MEXICO' - EXHIBIT OF PAINTINGS. 'THE MANY FACES OF MEXICO' EXHIBIT OF PAINTINGS AND LAUNCHING OF NEW SCHOOL BOOK 'JUANITO'S RAILROAD IN THE SKY'. BOTH THE EXHIBIT AND THE NEW BOOK AUTHORED & PAINTED BY VIC HERMAN. THIS WILL BE A MONTHLONG CELEBRATION IN TIJUANA, MEXICO AND SAN DIEGO, CA. AT MAY COMPANY, MISSION VALLEY,SAN DIEGO, CA. (INT'L). VIC HERMAN, COORDINATOR; REPUBLIC OF MEXICO & U S INFORMATION SERVICE; RR 1, 25 SOUTH LANE; DEL MAR, CA 92014. (#107325-1).

SEPT 21 - 28, '76. CABRILLO FESTIVAL. COMMEMORATE DISCOVERY AND EXPLORATION OF WEST COAST OF USA IN 1542 BY JUAN RODRIGUEZ CABRILLO. INCLUDES FLAGRAISING, MUSIC, DANCING, ART SHOW, HISTORICAL SEMINAR, COMMEMORATIVE CEREMONIES, REENACTMENT OF LANDING. HELD AT PARK AND VARIOUS LOCATIONS IN SAN DIEGO. AT AT VARIOUS LOCATIONS IN SAN DIEGO, INCLUDING CABRILLO. (REGN'L). SUPT, CABRILLO NM; CABRILLO FESTIVAL INC.; NATIONAL PARK SERVICE; P.O. BOX 6175; SAN DIEGO, CA 92106. (#6728-60).

SEPT 26, '76. SAN DIEGO SCOTTISH HIGHLAND GAMES. COMPETITION AT BALBOA STADIUM. (LOCAL). JEAN WINSTANLEY, COORD; SAN DIEGO SCOTTISH HIGHLAND GAMES, INC; PO BOX 3662; SAN DIEGO, CA 92103. (#109290-1).

SEPT 27 - 28, '76. TURK MURPHY'S JAZZ BAND AT FT POINT NHS. LIVE PERFORMANCE AT GOLDEN GATE NRA. (REGN'L). SUPT FORT POINT NHS; NATIONAL PARK SERVICE; PO BOX 9167; SAN FRANCISCO, CA 94129. (#6728-567).

OCT 2, '76. AKITA KANTO FESTIVAL. FESTIVAL. (LOCAL). PAULA SULLIVAN, COORD; CENTRAL CITY ASSOCIATION OF SAN DIEGO; 631 HOME TOWER BLDG; SAN DIEGO, CA 92101. (#103416-576).

OCT 3 - 8, '76. SCANDANAVIAN WEEK. FESTIVAL. (LOCAL). DON SKORDAHL, COORD; SCANDANAVIAN WEEK FESTIVAL COMMITTEE; 10069 HAWLEY RD; EL CAJON, CA 92021. (#109285-3).

OCT 4 - 30, '76. BEAUTIFUL AMERICA, BEAUTIFUL PINES-PENCIL DRAWINGS BY T MATSUMOTO. EXHIBIT AT CORRIDOR GALLERY OF LIBRARY. (LOCAL). LOIS MACKENZIE, PUBL INFO; SAN DIEGO PUBLIC LIBRARY; 820 E ST; SAN DIEGO, CA 92101. (#107324-8).

OCT 4 - 30, '76. PRINTING IN 18TH CENTURY AMERICA. EXHIBIT AT WAGENHEIM ROOM. (LOCAL). LOIS MACKENZIE, PUBL INFO; SAN DIEGO PUBLIC LIBRARY; 820 E ST; SAN DIEGO, CA 92101. (#107324-6).

OCT 9 - 11, '76. NAVY DAY PARADE & STATIC DISPLAY & AIR/WATER DEMONSTRATION. UDT/SEAL DEMONSTRATION. AT USNAB CORONADO. (LOCAL). CDR CRAIG E DORMAN, CO; UDT ELEVEN; UDT ELEVEN USNAB CORONADO; SAN DIEGO, CA 92155. (#200006-512).

OCT 9 - 11, '76. U S NAVY'S BIRTHDAY CELEBRATION. CEREMONY, EXHIBIT, TOUR AT BROADWAY PIER, NORTH ISLAND & MIRAMAR NAS. (REGN'L). PUBLIC AFFAIRS OFFICER; U S NAVY LEAGUE; SAN DIEGO, CA 92136. (#103416-616).

OCT 11 - DEC 31, '76. EXHIBIT ON MILITARY HISTORY. EXHIBIT, FAIR AT 1220 PACIFIC HWY. (LOCAL). G R SPIDELL, REP; NAVY MANPOWER & MATERIAL ANALYSIS CENTER, PACIFIC; 1220 PACIFIC HWY; SAN DIEGO, CA 92432. (#109431-1).

OCT 15 - 23, '76. REENACTMENT OF DE ANZA EXPEDITION FROM TUBAC TO CALIFORNIA. LIVE PERFORMANCE. (REGN'L). SUPT, TUMACACORI NM; NATIONAL PARK SERVICE; P.O. BOX 67; TUMACACORI, AZ 85640. (#6728-570).

OCT 23 - 24, '76. BICENTENNIAL AIR SHOW, NAVAL AIR STATION MIRAMAR. OPEN HOUSE & AIR SHOW; FLIGHT DEMONSTRATIONS INCLUDE BLUE ANGELS, NAVY PARACHUTE TEAM & VARIOUS AEROBATIC PERFORMERS. HELICOPTER COMBAT SUPPORT SQUADRON THREE WILL UTILIZE ONE H-46 HELICOPTER AS A JUMP PLATFORM FOR NAVY PARACHUTE TEAM. AT NAVAL AIR STATION MIRAMAR. (LOCAL). TOM SMITH; US NAVY; PUBLIC AFFAIRS OFC-NAS MIRAMAR; SAN DIEGO, CA 92145. (#200006-514).

OCT 29, '76. LECTURE BY CONGRESSMAN BOB WILSON. SEMINAR, LIVE PERFORMANCE AT NAVAL AIR STATION NORTH ISLAND. (LOCAL). RICHARD PLUSH LT J G; HELICOPTER COMBAT SUPPORT SQUADRON THREE; USN PUBLIC AFFAIRS OFCR; SAN DIEGO, CA 92135. (#200006-513).

OCT '76. CONFERENCE ON AMERICAN REVOLUTION STUDIES. SCHOLARS OF EARLY AMERICAN HISTORY, LITERATURE, ART AND SOCIETY WILL PRESENT PUBLIC PAPERS OF RESEARCH AND SCHOLARLY INTERPRETATION AT A CONFERENCE TO BE HELD AT SAN DIEGO STATE UNIVERSITY IN 1976. AT AZTEC CENTER. (REGN'L). ROBERT DETWEILER; SAN DIEGO STATE UNIV; SAN DIEGO, CA 92182. (#8011-1).

NOV 1 - 30, '76. 'PERICLES' OPERA PERFORMANCE. WORK COMMISSIONED BY THE NATL ENDOWMENT FOR THE ARTS. (LOCAL). ALAN HOVHANESS; NATIONAL ENDOWMENT OF ARTS & SAN DIEGO YOUTH SYMPHONY; 25 W HIGHLAND DR; SEATTLE, WA 98119. (#22041-1).

NOV 2 - 30, '76. AMERICAN GEMS & MINERALS EXHIBIT BY SAN DIEGO GEM & MINERAL SOCIETY. EXHIBIT AT LOBBY OF LIBRARY. (LOCAL). LOIS MACKENZIE, PUBL INFO; SAN DIEGO PUBLIC LIBRARY; 820 E ST; SAN DIEGO, CA 92101. (#107324-9).

NOV 20 - 21, '76. FOLK FAIRE 76: COLLAGE OF CULTURES. ETHNIC FOOD SALES; ETHNIC HANDICRAFT SALES; ETHNIC DANCES EVERY HOUR. AT SCOTTISH RITE MEMORIAL CENTER, 1895 CAMINO DEL RIO S. (LOCAL). MRS J HULL SCHILLING; SAN DIEGO COUNTY ECUMENICAL CONFERENCE; 1875 SECOND AVE; SAN DIEGO, CA 92101. (#109473-1).

NOV 28 - DEC 24, '76. DRESS A BICENTENNIAL DOLL - GRAND SHOWING OF CONTEST WINNERS. EXHIBIT AT BALBOA PARK. (LOCAL). ED KAPRIELIAN, COORD; INTERNATIONAL SOCIETY OF TRAVELBUGS; PO BOX 12156; SAN DIEGO, CA 92101. (#109285-2).

SAN FERNANDO

MAY 22, '76. 'A TRIBUTE TO MALCOLM X'. FESTIVAL AT FILMORE PARK, 12506 FILMORE. (LOCAL). RAYMA GREENBERG, CHAIRMAN; L A MISSION COLLEGE; 1101 SAN FERNANDO RD; SAN FERNANDO, CA 91340. (#200006-344).

JUNE 4, '76. COMIC RELIEF, A SERIES OF SHORT PLAYS BY AMERICAN AUTHORS. LIVE PERFORMANCE AT SAN FERNANDO JR HIGH, 130 N BRAND. (LOCAL). BOB BAKER, CHAIRMAN; L A MISSION COLLEGE; 1101 SAN FERNANDO RD; SAN FERNANDO, CA 91340. (#200006-345).

SAN FERNANDO — CONTINUED

JULY 4, '76. SAN FERNANDO VALLEY LOYALTY TO GOD AND COUNTRY PARADE. ALSO SPONSORED BY THE SAN FERNANDO VALLEY LOYALTY PARADE COMMITTEE. AT O'MELVENY AT BRAND BLVD, SAN FERNANDO, CA. (LOCAL). MR DAN F MACKIN; CITY OF SAN FERNANDO BICENTENNIAL COMMITTEE; 117 MACNEIL ST; SAN FERNANDO, CA 91340. (#102504-1).

SAN FRANCISCO

'AMERICAN CAMEOS' - MUSICAL PRODUCTION. ENDORSED BY THE ARBC OF CALIFORNIA, THIS THEATRICAL PRODUCTION WITH AN ORIGINAL MUSICAL SCORE, DEALS WITH THE 'LITTLE PEOPLE' OF THE REVOLUTION WHOM WE HEAR SO LITTLE AB OUT. (NAT'L). DR JEAN DE SLAES BENTRAM, EXEC DIRECTOR; SAN FRANCISCO STATE UNIV; 2 VARELA AVE; SAN FRANCISCO, CA 94132. (#33048).

AMERICAN FARM - SAN FRANCISCO, CA. AN INTERPRETIVE TRAVELING EXHIBITION ON THE HISTORY OF AMERICAN AGRICULTURE. (NAT'L). DR J S HOLLIDAY, DIRECTOR; CALIFORNIA HISTORICAL SOCIETY; 2090 JACKSON ST; SAN FRANCISCO, CA 94109. (#2846). **ARBA RECOGNIZED.**

AMERICANS OF AFRICAN DESCENT. PERFORMANCE BY DANCE TROUPS, DRAMATISTS AND MUSICIANS. (LOCAL). LLOYD D LUCKMANN, PRS; LINCOLN UNIV; 281 MASONIC; SAN FRANCISCO, CA 94118. (#105154-2).

AMERICANS & THE CALIFORNIA DREAM. A FIVE PART TELEVISION SERIES BASED ON AMERICANS & THE CALIFORNIA DREAM BY KEVIN STARR INVESTIGATING THE CALIFORNIA EXPERIENCE AS A REPRESENTATIVE AMERICAN EXPERIENCE NOT AN ISOLATED PHENOMENON. (REGN'L). BILL OSTERHAUS, PRESIDENT; KQED, INC; 1011 BRYANT ST; SAN FRANCISCO, CA 94103. (#7864). **(??).**

AMERICA'S FIRST MEDALS - US MINT. RESTRIKING OF OLD MEDALS IN PEWTER FOR BICENT SERIES OF TEN 1&1/2' MEDALS PRESENTED TO NAVAL & OTHER HEROES. UNIT OF TWO MEDALS WILL BE OFFERED IN 1974 & 1975 AND ONE IN 1976. (NAT'L). ROY C CAHOON ASST DIRECTOR FOR PUBLIC SERVICES; US MINT; 1422 MAIN TREASURY BLDG; WASHINGTON, DC 20220. (#1766).

ANGLE OF REPOSE - OPERA IN SAN FRANCISCO. COMMISSION AND PRODUCE NEW OPERA BASED ON NOVEL, 'ANGLE OF REPOSE', WHICH FOLLOWS GENERATIONS OF A PIONEER AMERICAN FAMILY WHO HELPED DEVELOP THE WEST. (REGN'L). KURT HERBERT ADLER, GEN DIRECTOR; SAN FRANCISCO OPERA ASSOC; WAR MEMORIAL OPERA HOUSE; SAN FRANCISCO, CA 94102. (#8601).

AUDIO POSTCARDS FOR THE BICENTENNIAL - CA. AUDIO POSTCARDS OF HISTORICAL EVENTS; ARBA LICENSE # 76-19-0553. (NAT'L). MARIE LOUSIE STEIN, PROJ MANAGER; AMERECORD CORPORATION; 145 LAUREL ST; SAN FRANCISCO, CA 94118. (#12403).

BICENTENNIAL 7TH FLEET COMMAND CENTER IN CA. RED, WHITE & BLUE TILED DECK INSTALLED & WHITE DRAPES EMBROIDERED WITH BICENTENNIAL SEAL. (LOCAL). LT JA GRAW, DIRECTOR; SEVENTH FLEET; FPO; SAN FRANCISCO, CA 96601. (#30975).

BOOK - CAMPING AROUND CALIFORNIA. GUIDEBOOK TO CAMPGROUNDS/RECREATION AREAS, PARKS AND HISTORICAL PLACES. SHARES THE HOSPITALITY OF CALIFORNIA'S CAMPGROUNDS. (ST-WIDE). JIM CRAIN - CO-AUTHOR; 3149 CALIFORNIA ST, NO 104; SAN FRANCISCO, CA 94115. (#16358).

CABLE CAR MEDAL FOR SAN FRANCISCO'S BICENTENNIAL. STRIKING A NATL MEDAL AUTHORIZED BY CONGRESS FOR SAN FRANCISCO BICENNIAL IN 1976. (NAT'L). PAUL FAY JR, CHAIRMAN; SAN FRANCISCO BICENTENNIAL COMMITTEE; 555 MARKET ST; SAN FRANCISCO, CA 94105. (#2981).

CLASSROOM TEACHING UNIT COMPETITION - CA. UNITS WILL BE BASED ON ONE OR MORE ARTICLES IN THE JANUARY, '76 JOURNAL OF GEOGRAPHY. THE BEST 3 WILL BE PRESENTED AT THE ANNUAL CONFERENCE & RECOGNIZED AT BANQUET & IN THE JOURNAL. (REGN'L). DR CLYDE KOHN, CHAIRMAN; DEPT OF GEOGRAPHY, UNIV OF IOWA; IOWA CITY, IA 52242. (#24876).

COMMEMORATION, FERNANDO DE RIVIERA Y MONCADA - CA. CEREMONY TO COMMEMORATE THE ARRIVAL OF FERNANDO DE RIVIERA AND FATHER FRANCISCO PALOU AT LAKE MERCED; THEY WERE THE FIRST EUROPEANS TO VIEW THE GOLDEN GATE. (ST-WIDE). DR ALBERT SHUMATE, CHAIRMAN, HISTORY COMMITTEE; SAN FRANCISCO TWIN BICENT, INC; 555 MARKET ST; SAN FRANCISCO, CA 94105. (#9838).

COMMUNITY DEVELOPMENT ASSISTANCE, SAN FRANCISCO. PROVIDE TECHNICAL ASSISTANCE TO COMMUNITY ORGANIZATIONS FOR COLLECTIVE ACTION THROUGH COALITIONS IN ADDRESSING COMMON PROBLEMS. (LOCAL). HERB ALLEN, DIRECTOR; REGIONAL YOUNG ADULT PROJECT; 944 MARKET #702; SAN FRANCISCO, CA 94102. (#25155).

CONSTITUTIONAL LAW: A BICENTENNIAL SYMPOSIUM-BOOK. THE AMERICAN EXPERIENCE IN CONSTITUTIONAL DEMOCRACY: A LOOK BACKWARD & A LOOK FORWARD. 4 LECTURES BY NOTED INDIVIDUALS & OTHER SCHOLARLY ARTICLES TO BE PUBLISHED IN HASTINGS CONSTITUTIONAL LAW QUARTERLY. (NAT'L). JULIE BANNERMAN, PUBLICATIONS EDITOR; HASTINGS CONSTITUTIONAL LAW QUARTERLY; 198 MCALLISTER ST; SAN FRANCISCO, CA 94102. (#18629). **ARBA GRANTEE.**

DUORAIL UNDERGROUND ELEVATED - SAN FRANCISCO, CA. FILMS AVAILABLE ON THE BAY AREA RAPID TRANSIT AND INFORMATIONAL BROCHURES ARE ALSO AVAILABLE; THE TELEPHONE INFO SYSTEM WILL BE OPEN FOR TRAVEL INFORMATION. (LOCAL). WILLIAM M MCDOWELL, MANAGER; BAY AREA RAPID TRANSIT DISTRICT; 800 MADISON ST; OAKLAND, CA 94607. (#19335).

EARLY AMERICAN PLAYS FOR RADIO - CA. SAN FRANCISCO STATE UNIV STUDENTS WILL ACT AND PRODUCE SIX EARLY. AMERICAN RADIO PLAYS. (LOCAL). S HYDE, CHMN, BROADCAST COMMUNICATION DEPT; SAN FRANCISCO STATE UNIV; 1600 HOLLOWAY; SAN FRANCISCO, CA 94132. (#18583).

EFFECTS OF LENDING BIASES ON URBAN RESIDENCES -CAL. RESEARCH THE IMPACT OF CURRENT REAL ESTATE LENDING PRACTICES ON THE DECISIONS OF PERSONS CONSIDERING THE PURCHASE AND REHABILITATION OF OLDER, URBAN RESIDENCES. NEA GRANT. (NAT'L). ALAN E ROTHENBERG, PROJ DIRECTOR; FINANCIAL SUPPORT, INC; 2229 DIVISADERO; SAN FRANCISCO, CA 94115. (#2252).

ETHNIC PASTORATE IN THE USA - SAN FRANCISCO, CA. PROPOSAL OF RESOLVING ETHNIC PASTORAL CARE ACCORDING TO THE PAPAL NOTION OF THE LOCAL CHURCH FOR THE NCCB BICENTENNIAL CONGRESS IN DETROIT. (REGN'L). ANDREW N WOZNICKI, PH.D; COMMISSION ON RELIGIOUS AFFAIRS, POLISH AMERICAN COMGRESS; 7313 EMANON; DEARBORN, MI 48126. (#32159).

EXHIBIT: CALIFORNIA 1970-1976. THE EXHIBIT WILL INCLUDE PAINTINGS, SCULPTURE AND MIXED MEDIA. (LOCAL). ARNOLD HERSTAND, PRESIDENT; SAN FRANCISCO ART INSTITUTE; 800 CHESTNUT; SAN FRANCISCO, CA 94133. (#9829).

'I HAVE A DREAM' - ORATORIO IN SAN FRANCISCO. AN AWARD OF $2,000 TO A STUDENT COMPOSING THE BEST ORATORIO BASED ON THE FAMOUS MARTIN LUTHER KING ADDRESS IN 1963. (NAT'L). THEODORE S CONNELLY, DIRECTOR; COMMUNICATIONS LIBRARY; 1535 FRANCISCO ST; SAN FRANCISCO, CA 94123. (#9599).

JACK LONDON'S 100TH ANNIVERSARY IN SAN FRANCISCO. A THREE DAY SYMPOSIUM TO BE HELD IN CELEBRATION OF THE 100TH BIRTHDAY OF JACK LONDON, ONE OF AMERICA'S GREATEST LITERARY FIGURES WHO WAS ALSO A NATIVE SAN FRANCISCAN. (LOCAL). DR KEVIN STARR, CITY LIBRARIAN; OAKLAND PUBLIC LIBRARY SAN FRANCISCO LIBRARY; CIVIC CTR; SAN FRANCISCO, CA 94102. (#9835).

MARINE CORPS COLOR GUARDS - SAN FRANCISCO. FOUR MARINES, TWO IN 1775 UNIFORMS & TWO IN 1975 UNIFORMS, PRESENT COLORS IN PRECISE MILITARY MANNER FOR CEREMONIES AND VARIOUS PUBLIC OCCASIONS. (REGN'L). COL B C STINEMETZ, DISTRICT DIRECTOR; 12TH MARINE CORPS DISTRICT; BLDG 7, USNS TREASURE ISLAND; SAN FRANCISCO, CA 94130. (#12520).

MARITIME EXHIBIT ON THE CALIFORNIA GOLD RUSH. THIS EXHIBIT WILL FEATURE GOLD RUSH AND POST GOLD RUSH TRANSPORTATION TO SAN FRANCISCO. (ST-WIDE). RICHARD M GRIFFITH, EXECUTIVE VICE PRESIDENT; SAN FRANCISCO MARITIME MUSEUM; POLK ST; SAN FRANCISCO, CA 94109. (#17386).

MEETING MISTER IVES - SAN FRANCISCO, CA. A CABARET PRESENTATION GROWING OUT OF THE MUSIC OF AMERICAN COMPOSER CHARLES IVES WILL BE A BICENTENNIAL PROJECT. (LOCAL). KURT HERBERT ADLER, GENERAL DIRECTOR; SPRING OPERA THEATER; WAR MEMORIAL OPERA HOUSE; SAN FRANCISCO, CA 94102. (#8573).

A MILITARY BALL IN SAN FRANCISCO, CA. AN ARMY BALL TO BE HELD ON JUNE 14, 1975 AS PART OF THE COMMEMORATIVE EVENTS OF THE BICENTENNIAL CELEBRATION OF THE FORMATION OF THE ARMY ON JUNE 14, 1775. (LOCAL). ROBERT A JOY, SECRETARY; ASSOC OF THE U S ARMY; PO BOX 9115, PRESIDIO OF S F; SAN FRANCISCO, CA 94129. (#9836).

MULTI-CULTURE PROGRAM, SAN FRANCISCO, CA. A PROGRAM DESIGNED TO STRENGTHEN MUTUAL ETHNIC & CULTURAL UNDERSTANDING & COOPERATION IN SCHOOL SYSTEMS THROUGHOUT THE COUNTRY. THE THEME OF THE PROGRAM IS 'DIFFERENT BUT THE SAME.'. (NAT'L). MARTELLA WILSON, EXEC DIRECTOR; MULTI-CULTURE INSTITUTE; 1900 PIERCE ST; SAN FRANCISCO, CA 94115. (#16369).

MUSIC COMPOSITIONS IN SAN FRANCISCO, CA. DIATRIBE FOR VIOLIN AND PIANO, RHAPSODY FOR CELLO AND PIANO, OCTET FOR MIXED ENSEMBLE. (LOCAL). LASZLO VARGA, COORD; SAN FRANCISCO STATE UNIVERSITY; SAN FRANCISCO, CA 94111. (#28188).

MUSICAL VISIONS OF AMERICA - SAN FRANCISCO, CA. BICENTENNIAL SPECIAL IN SERIES DATING BACK TO 1928, FOUR FILMSTRIPS, AUDIO CASSETTES & TEACHERS' GUIDES PROVIDED FREE TO 16,000 ELEMENTARY/JR H S IN W ROCKY MTN AREA & S W USA THRU 1976. (REGN'L). EDWARD H FRANKLIN, PROJ DIRECTOR; STANDARD OIL COMPANY OF CALIFORNIA; 225 BUSH ST; SAN FRANCISCO, CA 94120. (#16974).

MUSIC: FABLES OF THE ANT - SAN FRANCISCO. A NEW WORK FOR CHAMBER ORCHESTRA SOLOISTS, SPEAKER, ACTORS AND FILM, BASED ON FABLES OF AESOP & OTHERS. THIS WORK SEEKS TO SHATTER CONVENTIONAL WISDOM ON ART AND POLITICS. (NAT'L). MARTIN BRESNICK, LECTURER IN MUSIC; PO BOX 3506; STANFORD, CA 94305. (#6738).

NATIONAL INVENTORY OF NATURAL AREAS - CA. A NATIONAL, REGIONAL, & LOCAL INVENTORY OF GEOLOGICAL, BOTANICAL, & ZOOLOGICAL AREAS BY AMATEUR, PROFESSIONAL, AND GOVERNMENT PERSONNEL. THE DATA COLLECTED WILL BE COMPUTERIZED. (NAT'L). LESLIE HOOD, PROGRAM COORDINATOR; SIERRA CLUB; MILLS TOWER; SAN FRANCISCO, CA 94104. (#119). **ARBA RECOGNIZED.**

NATL CONFERENCE, HISTORY OF THE CHINESE IN USA. NATIONAL CONFERENCE ON LIFE, INFLUENCE AND ROLE OF CHINESE IN U.S. 1776 TO 1960 & REPORT OF FINDINGS IN 1976. (NAT'L). THOMAS W CHINN, CHAIRMAN, BICENTENNIAL ACTIVITY; CHINESE HISTORICAL SOCIETY OF AMERICA; 1050 SANSOME ST - 4TH FLR; SAN FRANCISCO, CA 94111. (#228). **ARBA RECOGNIZED. ARBA GRANTEE.**

NAVY-MARINE CORPS MUSEUM AND MASTER MURAL, CA. NAVY-MARINE CORPS MUSEUM AND MASTER MURAL DEPICTING THE ROLES OF THE NAVY AND MARINE CORPS IN THE PACIFIC; PAST, PRESENT & FUTURE. MURAL DESIGNED BY NY ARTIST, LOWELL NESBITT, ASSISTED BY 14 LOCAL ARTISTS. (REGN'L). LCDR G P VERCESSI, USN, 12ND PUBLIC AFFAIRS OFC; TWELFTH NAVAL DISTRICT/TWELFTH U S MARINE CORPS DISTRICT; BLDG 1, TREASURE ISLAND; SAN FRANCISCO, CA 94130. (#20920).

NEIGHBORHOOD IMPROVEMENT PROJECT OF SAN FRANCISCO. INNER DISTRICT & COMMUNITY COMPETITION TO STIMULATE CITIZENS TO CREATE & RUN PROGRAMS TO IMPROVE THE NEIGHBORHOODS & COMMUNITIES. THERE IS AN AWARDS PROGRAM & A PARADE WINDS UP NEIGHBORHOOD WEEKS. (LOCAL). MICHELLE ANDERSON, COORDINATOR; NEIGHBORHOD BICENTENNIAL CELEBRATION SF PUBLIC LIBRARY; CIVIC CENTER; SAN FRANCISCO, CA 94102. (#9837).

ON LOK SENIOR HEALTH SERVICES - SAN FRANCISCO, CA. COMMUNITY BASED HEALTH CARE FOR THE ELDERLY AS AN ALTERNATIVE TO INSTITUTIONALIZATION. (ST-WIDE). MARIE-LOUISE ANSAK, EXEC DIR; ON LOK SENIOR HEALTH SERVICES; 1490 MASON ST; SAN FRANCISCO, CA 94133. (#20056).

OPERA PROJECT IN SAN FRANCISCO, CALIFORNIA. 'ANGLE OF REPOSE' IS A THREE ACT OPERA COMMISSIONED BY THE SAN FRANCISCO OPERA, BASED ON A NOVEL BY WALLACE STEGNER. THE MUSIC IS COMPOSED BY ANDREW IMBRIE WITH LIBRETTO BY OAKLEY HALL. (REGN'L). KURT HERBERT ADLER, GENERAL DIRECTOR; SAN FRANCISCO OPERA; WAR MEMORIAL OPERA HOUSE; SAN FRANCISCO, CA 94102. (#6574).

POLYNESIAN CULTURAL CENTER OF SAMOA, CA. CENTER IS COMPOSED OF A MUSEUM, ROYAL & SOCIAL HALLS, A CHURCH, AN EDUCATIONAL FACILITY, PLAYGROUND, COURTYARD, LIBRARY, PUBLIC & ROYAL CONVENTIONS ROOM, A GIFT SHOP AND A WORKSHOP. (LOCAL). CHIEF LEULUSOO LEATUTUFU, EXECUTIVE DIRECTOR; SAMOAN CHIEF COUNCIL OF CALIFORNIA; 166THE EMBARCADERO, SUITE 601; SAN FRANCISCO, CA 94105. (#19930).

REGIONAL HISTORIES OF CALIFORNIA. A SERIES OF 10 REGIONAL HISTORIES OF CALIFORNIA, EACH BOOK PRESENTING ECONOMIC, SOCIAL, POLITICAL AND ENVIRONMENTAL HISTORY OF PRESCRIBED AREA. ALSO BOOK ENTITLED 'THE AMERICAN FARM' , IN 1976. (ST-WIDE). DR J S HOLLIDAY, EXEC DIRECTOR; CALIFORNIA HISTORICAL SOCIETY; 2090 JACKSON ST; SAN FRANCISCO, CA 94109. (#12305). **ARBA GRANTEE.**

RENEWAL DISTRICT, SAN FRANCISCO, CA. HISTORICAL PHOTOGRAPHS AND MEMORABILIA RELATING TO OLD SITE USAGE AND PRESENTLY DEVELOPED COMPLEX OF UNIQUE RETAIL AND RESTAURANT FACILITIES. (LOCAL). MS CASSANORA STANLEY, DIRECTOR OF PUBLIC RELATIONS; GHIRADELLI SQUARE; 900 N POINT ST; SAN FRANCISCO, CA 94109. (#20064).

RENOVATION OF SAN FRANCISCO MUSEUM OF ART. TO CONSTRUCT NEW IMPROVED STORAGE FACILITIES FOR WORKS OF ART. (REGN'L). HENRY T HOPKINS, DIRECTOR; SAN FRANCISCO MUSEUM OF ART; VAN NESS AT MCALLISTER; SAN FRANCISCO, CA 94102. (#5365).

RESTORATION OF FRANCIS SCOTT KEY MONUMENT, CA. THE MONUMENT TO FRANCIS SCOTT KEY IN SAN FRANCISCO WILL BE RESTORED AND RELOCATED. (LOCAL). REAR ADMIRAL JOHN HARLLEE, USN (RET), EXEC DIR; SAN FRANCISCO BICENTENNIAL; 555 MARKET ST; SAN FRANCISCO, CA 94105. (#14327). **ARBA GRANTEE.**

SAN MATEO COUNTY HERITAGE SCENES, CA. A LASTING EXHIBIT OF SAN MATEO COUNTY HISTORICAL SCENES IN WATER COLOR AND OIL; WILL BE AVAILABLE TO LOCAL GALLERIES, SCHOOLS AND SHOWS. (LOCAL). ELWOOD HANSEN, ARTIST; BAYVIEW FEDERAL SAVINGS; 2601 MISSION; SAN FRANCISCO, CA 94110. (#19822).

'THE SANTANA: AS TIME GOES BY' FILM, CA. A BOOK AND FILM ON AMERICAN SAILING WITH PARTICULAR EMPHASIS ON THE YACHT, SANTANA. (LOCAL). JEFFREY M GROBART, EXEC PRODUCER; BLINDWOLF PRODUCTIONS; 203 CALIFORNIA ST; SAN FRANCISCO, CA 94111. (#8882).

SILVER EAGLE MARINE FESTIVAL. MARINE FESTIVAL IN SAN FRANCISCO BAY, JUNE 9 - JULY 4, 1976. WILL INCLUDE BOAT RACES, PARADE OF US & FOREIGN NAVAL VESSELS & REGATTA OF SAILING VESSELS 25 YEARS & OLDER. (INT'L). W PATRICK BURKE; SILVER EAGLE COMMITTEE OF THE SAN FRANCISCO TWIN BICENTENNIAL; 555 MARKET ST; SAN FRANCISCO, CA 94105. (#19732). **ARBA RECOGNIZED.**

SS MAINE, DESIGNATED BICENTENNIAL SHIP, CA. ON MAIDEN VOYAGE AND THRU 1976, THE FIRST ROLL-ON ROLL-OFF SHIP TO SERVE U S TO ORIENT, WILL DISPLAY THE BICENTENNIAL SYMBOL, PORT & STARBOARD. THE 684 FT SS MAINE IS ALSO RED, WHITE AND BLUE. (NAT'L). THOMAS P WALSH, P R DIRECTOR; STATES STEAMSHIP COMPANY; 320 CALIFORNIA ST; SAN FRANCISCO, CA 94104. (#26438).

SYMBOL DESIGN COMPETITION IN SAN FRANCISCO, CA. IN HONOR OF THE BICENTENNIAL, THERE WILL BE A LOGO DESIGN COMPETITION. (LOCAL). CHRIS STRITZLINGER, CHMN; SAN FRANCISCO TWIN BICENT, INC; 555 MARKET ST; SAN FRANCISCO, CA 94105. (#9834).

TECHNICAL PRESERVATION SVCS PGM OF NATL TRUST - CA. TECHNICAL SERVICE PROGRAM TO PROVIDE ARCHITECTURAL, PLANNING, LEGAL, AND REAL ESTATE ADVICE FOR THE RETENTION AND REUSE OF EXISTING URBAN ENVIRONMENTS IN THE 13 WESTERN STATES. NEA GRANT. (REGN'L). JOHN L FRISBEE III, REGIONAL DIRECTOR; NATIONAL TRUST FOR HISTORIC PRESERVATION - WEST COAST OFFICE; 802 MONTGOMERY ST; SAN FRANCISCO, CA 94133. (#2344).

TOWARD OUR THIRD CENTURY - CA. CONTEST IN COOPERATION WITH SMITHSONIAN, ASKING AMERICANS TO CONSIDER NEEDS

SAN FRANCISCO — CONTINUED

OF U S IN NEXT CENTURY & PROPOSE ACTION TO BE TAKEN. CONTEST WINNERS ANNOUNCED JULY 4, 1976. (NAT'L). GEORGE CAULFIELD OR KATHLEEN COURTNEY; WELLS FARGO BANK; 464 CALIFORNIA ST; SAN FRANCISCO, CA 94104. (#17214). **ARBA RECOGNIZED.**

U S MARINE CORPS HISTORICAL DISPLAY, SAN FRANCISCO. A 30 FT SEMI TRACTOR-TRAILER VAN CONSISTING OF EXHIBITS COVERING 200 YEARS OF MARINE CORP HISTORY. (LOCAL). COL B C STINEMETZ, DISTRICT DIRECTOR; 12TH MARINE CORPS DIST; BLDG 7, USNS TREASURE ISLAND; SAN FRANCISCO, CA 94130. (#12519).

USS BLUE RIDGE'S BICENTENNIAL PROGRAM - CA. PROGRAM INCLUDES: 30-60 SECOND TV SPOTS & FEATURES; THE RADIO STATION WILL PROVIDE AN INFO SERIES ON THE AMER REVOL; THE NEWSPAPER & PLAN OF THE DAY WILL BE REDESIGNED USING REVOLUTIONARY BACKDROP. (LOCAL). CWO CHARLES C CURTIS, PUBLIC AFFAIRS OFFICER; USS BLUE RIDGE, LCC-19; FPO; SAN FRANCISCO, CA 96601. (#29115).

VICAR OF BRAY-SOLE SURVIVING SHIP OF GOLD RUSH. RESTORE & EXHIBIT ON MOBILE FLOAT, ONLY SURVIVING SHIP OF GOLD RUSH. (ST-WIDE). DAVID NELSON, ASST DIRECTOR; SAN FRANCISCO MARITIME MUSEUM; FOOT OF POLK ST; SAN FRANCISCO, CA 94109. (#1071).

JULY 16, '74 - CONTINUING . COLOR CATV:THE AMERICAN CONNECTION,COLONISTS DISCUSSING REVOLUTION. AMERICAN COLONISTS DISCUSSING ALL ASPECTS OF REVOLUTION.COSTUMES. SETS ARE PERIOD ROOMS IN SAN FRANCISCO'S MUSEUMS:PARIS,LONDON,BERLIN PHILADELPHIA.50 TO 60 HALF-HOUR PROGRAMS ARE PROJECTED TO DATE. FILMS FROM CATV TAPES AVAILABLE TO EDUCATIONAL INSTITUTIONS. (REGN'L). WILLIAM R LUTTON; SONS OF AMERICAN REVOLUTION SF CHAPTER & LINCOLN UNIVERSITY,SF; 2121 BROADWAY; SAN FRANCISCO/CANADA 94115. (#2775-1).

JULY 10 - 12, '75. NATIONAL CONFERENCE ON LIFE, INFLUENCE AND ROLE OF CHINESE IN U.S.. NATIONAL CONFERENCE ON LIFE, INFLUENCE AND ROLE OF CHINESE IN U.S. 1776 TO 1960 & REPORT OF FINDINGS IN 1976. (NAT'L). CHINESE HISTORICAL SOC; CHINESE HISTORICAL SOCIETY OF AMERICA; 1050 SANSOME ST, 4TH FLOOR; SAN FRANCISCO, CA 94111. (#228-1).

AUG 1 - OCT 30, '75. CONCERTS IN THE PARK. ON PARK LAND AT FT BARRY, IN MARIN COUNTY, A SERIES OF ETHNIC PERFORMING ARTS PROGRAMS WILL BE PRESENTED ON AUGUST 2 & 3, AUG 24, SEPT 7, SEPT 28, AND OCT 26 AT 2 PM. AT GOLDEN GATE PARK. (REGN'L). SUPT, GOLDEN GATE NRA; NATIONAL PARK SERVICE; FORT MASON; SAN FRANCISCO, CA 94123. (#6728-64).

AUG 12, '75. NATL PK SVC '...A LITTLE LOOK AROUND' VISITS SAN FRANCISCO. THIS SHORT PROGRAM FEATURES ACTORS PORTRAYING FAMOUS AMERICANS OF THE PAST WHO'VE RETURNED TO SEE AMERICA'S GROWTH. (REGN'L). SUPERINTENDENT; NATIONAL PARK SERVICE - GOLDEN GATE NRA; FORT MASON; SAN FRANCISCO, CA 94123. (#5653-207).

AUG 22 - 29, '75. INTERNATIONAL CONGRESS FOR HISTORICAL SCIENCES. XIVTH INTERNATIONAL CONFERENCE AT WHICH HISTORIANS OFFER DIFFERING PTS. OF VIEW AND CLARIFY THE METHODS & MEANS BEST ADAPTED TO ADVANCING STUDY OF HIST. FIRST TIME OUTSIDE EUROPE. BICENTENNIAL STRESSED. (INT'L). DR RICHARD SCHLATTER; AMERICAN HISTORICAL ASSOCIATION; PROVOST'S OFFICE; NEW BRUNSWICK, NJ 08903. (#158-1).

SEPT 12, '75. A BICENTENNIAL SYMPOSIUM: CONSTITUTIONAL LAW. SEMINAR WILL INVOLVE DISCUSSION OF THE AMERICAN EXPERIENCE IN CONSTITUTIONAL DEMOCRACY; PAST & PRESENT; 4 LECTURES BY NOTED SCHOLARS. (LOCAL). SUZANNE VAUPEL, EDITOR; HASTINGS CONSTITUTIONAL LAW QUARTERLY; 198 MCALLISTER; SAN FRANCISCO, CA 94115. (#102852-1).

SEPT 13, '75. LA MUSICA, PERFORMANCE AT LONE MTN COLLEGE. LIVE PERFORMANCE AT MAIN BUILDING 2800 TURK BLVD CORNER MASONIC; PRKNG ANZA & PARKER. (LOCAL). ELAINE WINTERS; LONE MOUNTAIN COLLEGE; 2800 TURK BOULEVARD; SAN FRANCISCO, CA 94118. (#50702-1).

SEPT 13 - 14, '75. NATL PK SVC 'PEOPLE OF 1776' (PILOT) VISITS GOLDEN GATE NRA. TRAVELING TROUPE WILL BRING VARIOUS ASPECTS OF COLONIAL LIFE (MILITARY LIFE, MUSIC, CRAFTS) TO VISITORS TO THIS NATIONAL PARK SERVICE AREA. (REGN'L). SUPERINTENDENT; NATIONAL PARK SERVICE - GOLDEN GATE NRA; FORT MASON; SAN FRANCISCO, CA 94123. (#1469-202).

OCT 5, '75. 'TREASURE ISLAND 1939', RADIO BROADCAST. 'TREASURE ISLAND' WILL BE BROADCAST AROUND THE WORLD VIA ARMED FORCES RADIO ON OCT 13TH. EVENT IS A RE-CREATION OF OPENING DAY OF 1939 GOLDEN GATE EXPOSITION, A SALUTE TO THE NAVY'S 200TH ANNIVERSARY & A TRIBUTE TO RADIO'S GOLDEN AGE. AT BLDG #2, TREASURE ISLAND. (INT'L). JOHN JENSEN, PROJ COORD; UNITED STATES NAVY, USO-KMPX RADIO; 7 ADELAIDE PL; SAN FRANCISCO, CA 94102. (#102485-1).

NOV 12 - DEC 10, '75. STEFAN MROZEWSKI VERNISAGE & EXHIBIT. AS A RESULT OF THE EXHIBIT USF PUBLISHED MROZEWSKI'S FOLIO ALBUM OF 64 WOODCUTS ON THE TRIUMPHUS BONI SUPER MALUM PRO EVANGELIO SANCTI LUCI (TRIUMPH OF GOOD OVER EVIL ACCORDING TO ST LUKE) FOLLOWED BY A SPECIAL COLLECTION FOR RARE BOOK ROOM. AT UNIVERSITY CENTER MAIN LOUNGE PERKER & GOLDEN GATE. (LOCAL). IRENA MROZEWSKA; UNIVERSITY OF SAN FRANCISCO; 1312 SUNSET LOOP; WALNUT CREEK, CA 94596. (#200006-516).

DEC 3, '75 - MAY 29, '76. SAN FRANCISCO SYMPHONY. LIVE PERFORMANCE AT WAR MEMORIAL OPERA HOUSE. (LOCAL). JOS A SCAFIDI, MANAGER; SAN FRANCISCO SYMPHONY ASSOC; VAN NESS AVE AT GROVE ST; SAN FRANCISCO, CA 94102. (#102850-4).

DEC 10 - 13, '75. AMERICAN FREEDOM TRAIN DISPLAY DAYS AT SAN FRANCISCO. THE AMERICAN FREEDOM TRAIN WILL INCLUDE 10 EXHIBIT CARS & 2 SHOWCASE CARS DEPICTING DIFFERENT PHASES OF THE AMERICAN EXPERIENCE. ITS ARRIVAL WILL SERVE AS A CATALYST FOR LOCAL BICENTENNIAL CELEBRATIONS BY PEOPLE THROUGHOUT THIS NATION. (ST-WIDE). DON MALLICOAT, EDIT SVCS; THE AMERICAN FREEDOM TRAIN FOUNDATION, INC; 5205 LEESBURG PIKE, SUITE 800; BAILEY'S XRDS, VA 22041. (#1776-36).

DEC 20, '75. 'FABLES OF THE ANT' PERFORMED BY NEW MUSIC ENSEMBLE. A NEW WORK FOR CHAMBER ORCHESTRA SOLOISTS, SPEAKER, ACTORS AND FILM, BASED ON FABLES OF AESOP & OTHERS. THIS WORK SEEKS TO SHATTER CONVENTIONAL WISDOM ON ART AND POLITICS. (ST-WIDE). MARTIN BRESNICK; MARTIN BRESWICK; PO BOX 3506; STANFORD, CA 94305. (#6738-501).

DEC 30, '75. CANADIAN SALUTE TO SAN FRANCISCO'S BICENTENNIAL. PARTICIPATING IN THE SALUTE ARE PIPERS & HIGHLAND DANCERS, MASSED ALL CANADIAN BRASS BAND, & TWO WELL KNOWN CANADIAN PERSONALITIES: JOHN ALLAN CAMERON & GENEVIEVE BUJOLD. (INT'L). K DE B PERCY; GOVERNMENT OF CANADA; 1746 MASSACHUSETTS AVE NW; WASHINGTON, DC 20036. (#104880-9).

JAN 1 - DEC 26, '76. THOMAS JEFFERSON AND WINE IN EARLY AMERICA. EXHIBTION OF WINE MAKING IN AMERICA SHOWING JEFFERSONS CONTRIBUTION. SUNDAY HOURS: 12 - 5. AT 633 BEACH STREET - ACROSS FROM THE CANNERY. (NAT'L). ERNEST MITTELBERGER, DIR; THE WINE MUSEUM OF SAN FRANCISCO; 633 BEACH; SAN FRANCISCO, CA 94109. (#105154-4).

JAN 1 - DEC 31, '76. ENVIRONMENTAL LIVING PROGRAM AT FORT POINT NHS. THROUGH ROLE-PLAYING SCHOOL CHILDREN RECREATE THE LIFE OF A CIVIL WAR SOLDIER AT FORT POINT. RESERVATIONS ARE FILLED FOR THE 1976 SCHOOL YEAR. FOR INFORMATION ON THE PROGRAM CONTACT THE PARK. AT UNDER SOUTHERN END OF GOLDEN GATE BRIDGE ON PRESIDIO OF SAN FRAN. (LOCAL). FORT POINT NHS; NATIONAL PARK SERVICE; PRESIDIO OF SF, PO BOX 9167; SAN FRANCISCO, CA 94129. (#6726-67).

JAN 3, '76. CANADIAN SALUTE TO USA BICENTENNIAL AT THE SHRINE FOOTBALL GAME. CEREMONY, LIVE PERFORMANCE. (INT'L). K DE B PERCY; GOVERNMENT OF CANADA AND THE SHRINERS; 1746 MASSACHUSETTS AVE, NW; WASHINGTON, DC 20036. (#104880-3).

JAN 24, '76. DEDICATION OF BICENTENNIAL REDWOODS. AN AVENUE OF 200 CALIFORNIA SEQUOIA GIGANTEA REDWOOD SAPLINGS WILL BE PLANTED ALONG PARK PRESIDIO DR FROM GOLDEN GATE PARK TO LAKE STREET. AT PRESIDIO DRIVE. (ST-WIDE). MRS JEAN MCCLATCHY; CITY OF SAN FRANCISCO; 400 VAN NESS AVE; SAN FRANCISCO, CA 94102. (#103416-18).

FEB 7 - 15, '76. CHINESE NEW YEAR CELEBRATION. THE YEAR OF THE DRAGON WILL BEGIN WITH THE MISS CHINATOWN USA CONTEST AND CLIMAX WITH THE FESTIVE PARADE ON SAT 14TH. (ST-WIDE). MARGE BOOKER, PROJ DIR; SAN FRANCISCO CONVENTION & VISITORS BUREAU; 1390 MARKET ST; SAN FRANCISCO, CA 94102. (#103554-1).

FEB 16, '76. AMERICAN REVOLUTION BICENTENNIAL PROGRAM. A TRIBUTE TO BROTHER GEORGE WASHINGTON, 'A MUSICAL AMERICANA EVENING' WITH BROTHER BURL IVES & FRIENDS. AT CALIFORNIA MASONIC MEMORIAL TEMPLE. (LOCAL). WILLIAM OSBORNE, CO-CHMN; MASONIC MASTERS & WARDENS ASSOC; 1982 48TH AVE; SAN FRANCISCO, CA 94116. (#200006-426).

FEB 19 - APR 29, '76. BICENTENNIAL CONCERT SERIES. LIVE PERFORMANCE AT CHORAL ROOM, ARTS BLDG. (LOCAL). LINDA SQUIRES, CHAIRMAN; CITY COLLEGE OF SAN FRANCISCO; 50 PHELAN; SAN FRANCISCO, CA 94112. (#200006-346).

FEB 25, '76. 'THE BRITISH ARE COMING!' - BRITISH MILITARY BAND PERFORMANCE. TOUR OF MAJOR U S CITIES BY BRITISH MILITARY UNITS AS REPRESENTATIVE OF UNITS INVOLVED IN REVOLUTIONARY WAR CAMPAIGN. AT CIVIC AUDITORIUM. (INT'L). CHARLES K JONES, PRES; COLUMBIA ARTISTS FESTIVALS CORP; 165 W 57TH ST; NEW YORK, NY 10019. (#6532-26).

FEB 29, '76. PRESENTATION OF FLAGS OF 50 STATES TO GRACE CATHEDRAL. ROYAL BRITISH LEGION PRESENTS 50 FLAGS IN HONOR OF SOLIDARITY OF THE BICENTENNIAL. THERE WILL ALSO BE A FAIR ON THE GROUNDS. AT GRACE CATHEDRAL, CALIFORNIA ST. (LOCAL). JEAN MCCLATCHY, CHAIRMAN; BRITISH ROYAL LEGION; 555 MARKET; SAN FRANCISCO, CA 94105. (#103900-3).

MAR 1 - APR 30, '76. EXHIBITION OF PAINTINGS BY PICASSO, BRAQUE & LEGER. THE WORKS EXHIBITED CAME FROM SWISS COLLECTIONS. (INT'L). OFFICE OF INFORMATION; EMBASSY OF SWITZERLAND; 2900 CATHEDRAL AVE; WASHINGTON, DC 20008. (#200006-515).

MAR 1 - DEC 31, '76. U S ARMY BICENTENNIAL MARCHING UNIT. DRESSED IN 1870'S UNIFORMS, THE U S ARMY BICENTENNIAL MARCHING UNIT WILL PERFORM THE FORMAL RETREAT CEREMONY AT FORT POINT; CEREMONY TO BE PRESENTED MONTHLY; VISITORS SHOULD CONTACT PARK FOR SPECIFIC DATES AND TIMES. AT UNDER SOUTHERN END OF GOLDEN GATE BRIDGE ON PRESIDIO OF SAN FRAN. (REGN'L). FORT POINT NHS; NATIONAL PARK SERVICE; ARMY PRESIDIO, SAN FRANCISCO; PRESIDIO OF SF, PO BOX 9167; SAN FRANCISCO, CA 94129. (#6728-257).

MAR 8, '76 - CONTINUING . 'LIVING 1776-1976' - EXHIBIT. A POTPOURRI EXHIBIT OF FAMILY HEIRLOOMS FROM A NUMBER OF SAN FRANCISCO RESIDENTS ON LOAN TO THE MUSEUM FOR THE BICENTENNIAL. AT OLD MINT MUSEUM, 5TH & MISSION ST. (REGN'L). OLGA MELKO, ADMIN OFFICER; BUREAU OF THE MINT, DEPT OF THE TREASURY; 88 5TH ST; SAN FRANCISCO, CA 94103. (#108152-1).

MAR 26 - APR 26, '76. COMMEMORATION OF 10 YEAR ANNIVERSARY OF USS NIAGARA FALLS. PUBLIC VISITED SHIP. GUEST SPEAKERS INCLUDED MAYOR O'LAUGHLIN OF NIAGARA FALLS, NY & MAYOR OF SAN FRANCISCO, CA. (LOCAL). LCDR W O HAGERTY; USS NIAGARA FALLS; USS NIAGARA FALLS (AFS-3); FPO SAN FRAN, CA 96601. (#200006-525).

MAR 27, '76. ANZA SCOUTING PARTY COMMEMORATION. REENACTMENT OF LT COLONEL JUAN BAUTISTA DE ANZA'S EXPEDITION AND FOUNDING OF THE PORT MISSION OF SAN FRANCISCO. (LOCAL). MRS JEAN MCCLATCHY, COORD; SAN FRANCISCO CONVENTION & VISITORS CENTER; 1390 MARKET ST; SAN FRANCISCO, CA 94102. (#103416-20).

MAR 28, '76. RE-ENACTMENT OF ANZA EXPEDITION TO FORT POINT AREA IN 1776. RE-ENACTMENT OF JUAN BAUTISTA DE ANZA'S TAKEOVER OF THE FORT POINT AREA IN 1776 TO ESTABLISH THE PRESIDIO OF SAN FRANCISCO AND MISSION DOLORES FOR SPAIN. AT HILL BEHIND FORT POINT NHS IN THE PRESIDIO OF SAN FRANCISCO. (REGN'L). FORT POINT NHS; NATIONAL PARK SERVICE & BICENTENNIAL COMM & ARMY ASSOCIATION; PRESIDIO OF SF, PO BOX 9167; SAN FRANCISCO, CA 94129. (#6728-256).

MAR 28, '76. SAN FRANCISCO COIN FAIR. EXHIBIT THEME WILL BE 'EAST TO WEST SUNRISE TO SUNSET: 200 YEARS OF COINAGE'. (LOCAL). JOHN SEARS, CHAIRMAN; SAN FRANCISCO COIN CLUB; PO BOX 6028; SAN FRANCISCO, CA 94101. (#105154-3).

MAR 28, '76. WEST COAST PREMIERE RECITAL OF 'CONTINENTAL HARP & BAND REPORT'. LIVE PERFORMANCE. (LOCAL). E C HUBERT, DIRECTOR; GRACE CATHEDRAL; 1051 TAYLOR ST; SAN FRANCISCO, CA 94108. (#105154-6).

MAR '76. CONFERENCE ON JACK LONDON AS A WRITER. A THREE DAY SYMPOSIUM TO BE HELD IN CELEBRATION OF THE 100TH BIRTHDAY OF JACK LONDON, ONE OF AMERICA'S GREATEST LITERARY FIGURES WHO WAS ALSO A NATIVE SAN FRANCISCAN. (LOCAL). DR KEVIN STARR; OAKLAND PUBLIC LIBRARY SAN FRANCISCO LIBRARY; CIVIC CTR; SAN FRANCISCO, CA 94102. (#9835-502).

APR 1 - 30, '76. SAN FRANCISCO CITY FAIR. THIS IS AN OLD FASHIONED FAIR WITH FOOD, ENTERTAINMENT, GAMES AND A BAND. (LOCAL). JEAN MCCLATCHY, CHAIRMAN; SAN FRANCISCO VOLUNTEER BUREAU; 555 MARKET; SAN FRANCISCO, CA 94105. (#103900-2).

APR 1 - SEPT 1, '76. COM-MEDIA '76 EXHIBIT OF SELECTED CHILDREN'S DRAWINGS. INVOLVING CHILDREN'S ART AGES 5-12, THRU LOCAL PARK & RECREATION DEP ARTMENTS, FOCUSING ON CONTRIBUTIONS TO GROWTH OF NATION. SELECTED DRAWINGS TO BE GIVEN TO SMITHSONIAN INST FOLLOWING TV COVERAGE. (LOCAL). THEODORE S CONNELLY; COMMUNICATIONS LIBRARY; 1535 SAN FRANCISCO ST; SAN FRANCISCO, CA 94123. (#1487-501).

APR 1 - DEC 31, '76. INTL CHILDREN'S ART FESTIVAL - EXHIBIT, SLIDE SHOW AND FILM. CHILDREN IN OVER 100 COUNTRIES WILL RENDER PAINTINGS & DESCRIPTIVE TEXTS ON THE BICENTENNIAL THEME 'MY COUNTRY 200 YEARS AGO' WHICH WILL BE MADE AVAILABLE TO ALL INTERESTED PARTIES IN SLIDE AND FILM FORM. (LOCAL). FRED BURROWS, DIRECTOR; ARTIST EMBASSY'S INTERNATIONAL CHILDREN'S ART FESTIVAL; 166 GRANT AVE; SAN FRANCISCO, CA 94108. (#105130-1).

APR 1, '76 - APR 1, '77. SHOWING OF ART COLLECTION ON CATV STATIONS THROUGHOUT COUNTRY. COM-MEDIA '76 - CHILDREN'S RECREATION PROJECT. INVOLVING CHILDREN'S ART AGES 5-12, THRU LOCAL PARK & RECREATION DEP ARTMENTS, FOCUSING ON CONTRIBUTIONS TO GROWTH OF NATION. SELECTED DRAWINGS TO BE GIVEN TO SMITHSONIAN INST FOLLOWING TV COVERAGE. (LOCAL). THEODORE S CONNELLY; COMMUNICATIONS LIBRARY; 1535 SAN FRANCISCO ST; SAN FRANCISCO, CA 94123. (#1487-502).

APR 4 - 10, '76. AUDIO CHAIRS ON MINORITIES VISITS GOLDEN GATE NRA. EXHIBIT AT FORT MASON. (REGN'L). GOLDEN GATE NRA; NATIONAL PARK SERVICE; FORT MASON BLDG 201; SAN FRANCISCO, CA 94123. (#5581-15).

APR 16 - 24, '76. NIHONMACHI CHERRY BLOSSOM FESTIVAL. THE JAPAN CENTER'S PEACE PLAZA AT POST & BUCHANAN ST BECOMES INLAND SEA OF SOUND AND MOVEMENT ON FESTIVAL WEEKENDS WITH FOLK SONGS, DANCE FESTS AND TAIKO CONCERTS, CHILDRENS PROGRAMS, MASTERS OF MARTIAL ARTS. (REGN'L). MARGE BOOKER, PROJ DIR; SAN FRANCISCO CONVENTION & VISITORS BUREAU; 1390 MARKET ST; SAN FRANCISCO, CA 94102. (#103552-1).

APR 17 - 24, '76. SAN FRANCISCO SPECIAL OLYMPICS. TRACK AND FIELD EVENTS WILL BE HELD AT KEZAR AND SWIMMING EVENTS WILL BE HELD AT BALBOA POOL. AT KEZAR STADIUM AND BALBOA POOL. (LOCAL). JEAN MCCLATCHY, CHAIRMAN; JOSEPH P KENNEDY FOUNDATION; 555 MARKET; SAN FRANCISCO, CA 94105. (#103900-1).

APR 17 - JULY 31, '76. 3 CENTURIES OF ART IN AMERICA. 104 PAINTINGS (1670-1967) FROM THE COLLECTION OF JOHN D ROCKEFELLER III WILL BE EXHIBITED; PAINTINGS INCLUDE WORKS BY JOHN SINGLETON COPLEY, ANDREW WYETH AND THOMAS EAKINS. (LOCAL). MRS JEAN MCCLATCHY; THE MUSEUM SOCIETY & ALCOA CORP; GOLDEN GATE PARK; SAN FRANCISCO, CA 94115. (#103416-16).

APR 18 - 22, '76. ODORI FESTIVAL OF JAPAN VISITS SAN FRANCISCO. LIVE PERFORMANCE AT KABUKI THEATER. (INT'L). DIRECTOR; MEL HOWARD PRESENTS; 143 E 27TH ST; NEW YORK, NY 10016. (#108965-8).

SAN FRANCISCO — CONTINUED

APR 21 - MAY 26, '76. BICENTENNIAL FILM FESTIVAL. EXHIBIT AT CITY COLLEGE OF SAN FRANCISCO. (LOCAL). LINDA SQUIRES, CHMN; DRAMA DEPT, CITY COLLEGE OF SAN FRANCISCO; 50 PHELAN AVE; SAN FRANCISCO, CA 94112. (#200006-347).

APR 24 - 25, '76. GOLDEN GATE RUGBY TOURNAMENT. COMPETITION. (LOCAL). AUSTIN BREWIN, CHAIRMAN; SAN FRANCISCO RUGBY CLUB; WARD 53, RM 303, SF GEN HOSPITAL; SAN FRANCISCO, CA 94110. (#105154-1).

APR 25 - 30, '76. CONFERENCE OF INTERNATIONAL ASSOCIATION FOR VOLUNTEER EDUCATION. PROMOTE AND ASSIST IN EDUCATION AND TRAINING OF VOLUNTEERS. CONFERENCE NOT OPEN TO GENERAL PUBLIC. BY INVITATION ONLY. AT HEADQUARTERED AT MEDICAL SOCIETY AUDITORIUM, 250 MASONIC ST. (INT'L). MRS WILLIAM O HETTS; INTERNATIONAL ASSOCIATION FOR VOLUNTEER EDUCATION; 645 WOODSTOCK RD; HILLSBOROUGH, CA 94010. (#104044-1).

APR 27 - MAY 8, '76. AMERICAN HISTORY THEATRE. A HISTORICAL AMERICAN PLAY. (LOCAL). MARTIN SNIPPER, DIRECTOR; SAN FRANCISCO ART COMMISSION; 165 GROVE; SAN FRANCISCO, CA 94102. (#103994-2).

APR 28, '76. BICENTENNIAL DAY. EXHIBIT, FESTIVAL, LIVE PERFORMANCE, SEMINAR. (LOCAL). CLAIRE A MCCAFFERY, ADV; PRESENTATION HIGH SCHOOL; 2350 TURK ST; SAN FRANCISCO, CA 94117. (#105679-1).

APR 30 - MAY 2, '76. FAR WEST SKI ASSOCIATION CONVENTION. CONVENTION IS FROM FRIDAY NOON UNTIL SUNDAY AT 6 PM. AT THE 'TOWN HOUSE' HOTEL; 8TH & MARKET STS, SAN FRANCISCO. (REGN'L). FRED ANDREWS, CHMN; SINGLES LEAGUE (LEAGUE OF SINGLE SKI CLUBS); PO BOX 7724; SAN FRANCISCO, CA 94120. (#103916-2).

MAY 8 - 9, '76. AGING IN AMERICA: A NEW LOOK SEMINAR. SEMINAR. (LOCAL). E C HUBERT, DIRECTOR; GRACE CATHEDRAL; 1051 TAYLOR ST; SAN FRANCISCO, CA 94108. (#105154-5).

MAY 11 - 12, '76. BRITISH BICENTENNIAL HERITAGE MISSION. 8 BRITISH LEADERS, 5 OF THEM MEMBERS OF THE HOUSE OF LORDS, WILL VISIT THE U S AS PART OF BRITAIN'S OFFICIAL SALUTE TO THE BICENTENNIAL. (INT'L). DIRECTOR; BRITISH EMBASSY; 3100 MASSACHUSETTS AVE, NW; WASHINGTON, DC 20008. (#109043-11).

MAY 16 - 22, '76. ARTISTS-IN-THE-PARK BICENT EXHIBIT AT GOLDEN GATE NRA. THIS EXHIBIT CONSISTS OF TWENTY-ONE ORIGINAL PAINTINGS COMMISSIONED THROUGH THE ARTISTS-IN-THE-PARKS PROGRAM; EACH PAINTING IS IDENTIFIED WITH PERSONS, PLACES OR EVENTS OF THE AMERICAN REVOLUTION. AT FORT MASON BUILDING 201, GGNRA HEADQUARTERS BAY & FRANKLIN ST. (REGN'L). GOLDEN GATE NRA; NATIONAL PARK SERVICE; FORT MASON BUILDING 201; SAN FRANCISCO, CA 94123. (#1474-16).

MAY 21 - 23, '76. THE GREAT EARTHQUAKE AND FIRE MUSTER. A NATIONAL GATHERING OF FIRE DEPT'S COMPETING IN HAND PUMPING (18201890), BUCKET BRIGADE, HOSE CART, MOTORIZED PUMPING (1900-1940), PARADE, DISPLAY & OLD-TIME FIREMAN'S BALL. AT CITY HALL - CIVIC CNTR PLAZA - CIVIC AUDITORIUM. (NAT'L). WILLIAM G KOENIG, DIR; ST FRANCIS HOOK & LADDER COMPANY/SAN FRANCISCO FIRE DEPT; 260 GOLDEN GATE AVE; SAN FRANCISCO, CA 94102. (#14566-1).

MAY 26 - JUNE 6, '76. 'AMERICA DREAMS ON...' BICENTENNIAL SCIENCE & INDUSTRY FAIR. EXHIBITION EXAMINES AMER VALUE DILEMMAS & ISSUES FROM PAST TO PRESENT. THE EXHIBITION WILL INCLUDE A SERIES OF SYMPOSIA, SPECIAL EVENTS & PARTICIPATION BY THOSE ATTENDING. AT PIER 2, FORT MASON, GOLDEN GATE NATIONAL RECREATION AREA. (REGN'L). MRS JEAN MCCLATCHY; SAN FRANCISCO TWIN CITY BICENTENNIAL; 555 MARKET ST; SAN FRANCISCO, CA 94105. (#103416-17).

MAY 28 - 30, '76. GOLDEN STATE ROUNDUP. LIVE PERFORMANCE AT CIVIC AUDITORIUM. (ST-WIDE). JEAN MCCLATCHY; NORTHERN CALIFORNIA SQUARE DANCERS ASSOC; 555 MARKET; SAN FRANCISCO, CA 94105. (#103891-5).

MAY '76. VISIT BY QUEEN MARGRETHE II AND PRINCE HENRICK OF DENMARK. TOUR. (INT'L). BENT SKOU, PRESS OFFICE; DANISH EMBASSY; 3200 WHITEHAVEN PKY, NW; WASHINGTON, DC 20008. (#104972-16).

JUNE 1 - SEPT 6, '76. DEMONSTRATIONS OF OLD WEAPONS FIRINGS AT FT POINT NHS. IN COOPERATION WITH THE CIVIL WAR SKIRMISH ASSN, DEMONSTRATIONS OF OLD WEAPONS FIRINGS, INCLUDE CIVIL WAR-TYPE MUSKET AND MUZZLE LOADING CANNON, WILL BE SHOWN ON SPECIFIED WEEKENDS DURING THIS TIME FRAME. (REGN'L). FORT POINT NATL HIST SITE; NATIONAL PARK SERVICE; CIVIL WAR SKIRMISH ASSN; P.O. BOX 9167, PRESIDIO; SAN FRANCISCO, CA 94129. (#6727-79).

JUNE 5, '76. BLAZING PADDLES '76 - 600 MI OCEAN PADDLE, SAN FRANCISCO-SAN DIEGO. OUTRIGGER CLUB IS THE FIRST COMPETITIVE CREW IN COLLEGIATE HISTORY. (ST-WIDE). PETE CAROLAN, COACH; TROJAN OUTRIGGERS CLUB, UNIV OF SOUTHERN CALIFORNIA; 11192 MAGNOLIA AVE; GARDEN GROVE, CA 92641. (#200006-117).

JUNE 9 - JULY 4, '76. SILVER EAGLE INTERNATIONAL REGATTA. THREE-WEEK SERIES OF BOAT RACES-12-METER AMERICA'S CUP CLASS YACHTS, UNLIMITED HYDROPLANE, OCEAN-GOING INBOARDS, MASTER MARINERS.INCLUDES VISIT BY OPERATION SAIL '76-PACIFIC OCEAN SQUARE RIGGERS. AT SAN FRANCISCO BAY. (INT'L). JEAN MCCLATCHY; SAN FRANCISCO TWIN BICENTENNIAL; 555 MARKET STREET; SAN FRANCISCO, CA 94105. (#50774-1).

JUNE 11 - 15, '76. CONFERENCE ON YOUTH NEEDS AND YOUTH EXHIBITION. CONFERENCE, EXHIBIT AT HOLIDAY INN GOLDEN GATEWAY, 1500 VAN NESS AVE. (REGN'L). STUART RADO, EXEC DIR; NATIONAL NETWORK OF YOUTH ADVISORY BOARDS; PO BOX 402036, OCEAN VIEW BRANCH; MIAMI BEACH, FL 33140. (#1536-15).

JUNE 12 - 20, '76. SPANISH WEEK. SPANISH EXHIBITS AND EVENTS. (LOCAL). JOSE ANTONIO DE URBINA; 3600 BAKER ST; SAN FRANCISCO, CA 94123. (#104044-4).

JUNE 17 - 19, '76. CONFERENCE OF CALIFORNIA HISTORICAL SOCIETIES. CONFERENCE AT TOWN HOUSE, MARKET STREET. (ST-WIDE). R COKE WOOD; CONFERENCE OF CALIFORNIA HISTORICAL SOCIETIES; UNIV OF THE PACIFIC; STOCKTON, CA 95211. (#103891-2).

JUNE 18 - 20, '76. CHOREOGRAPHY UNLIMITED. OPPORTUNITY BY BAY AREA CHOREOGRAPHERS TO WORK OUT NEW DANCE IDEAS. SUNDAY HOURS: 2:30PM. AT THEATER 44, 44 PAGE ST, SAN FRANCISCO. (LOCAL). JACK GREEN; PACIFIC DANCE THEATER; 1929 IRVING ST; SAN FRANCISCO, CA 94122. (#107673-1).

JUNE 19 - JULY 31, '76. AMERICA ON PARADE BY THE UNIVERSITY OF CALIFORNIA BAND. PARADE. (REGN'L). JEAN MCCLATCHY, CHAIRMAN; UNIVERSITY OF CALIFORNIA BAND; 555 MARKET; SAN FRANCISCO, CA 94105. (#103900-4).

JUNE 21 - AUG 21, '76. GOLD RUSH RESIDENT CAMP, LIFE AND TIMES OF THE GOLD RUSH ERA. CAMP LODGING FOR 50 CHILDREN. ONE WEEK SESSIONS FOR 10 WEEKS PANNING FOR GOLD. COOKING AND THE LIVING STYLE OF THE GOLD RUSH ERA WILL BE A PART OF SOME OF THE CAMP ACTIVITIES. OTHER INFORMATION WILL BE THE INFLUENCE OF THE DISCOVERY ON THE BAY AREA. AT FORT CRONKHITE JUST NORTH OF SAN FRANCISCO. (LOCAL). GOLDEN GATE NRA; NATIONAL PARK SERVICE; GGNRA FORT MASON BLDG 201; SAN FRANCISCO, CA 94123. (#6729-182).

JUNE 21 - AUG 25, '76. BAY AREA CULTURES RESIDENT CAMP AT FORT POINT NHS. CAMP LODGING FOR 50 CHILDREN; ONE-WEEK SESSIONS FOR 10 WEEKS; STAFFF AND CAMPERS WILL REFLECT THE DIVERSE ETHNIC AND CULTURAL BACKGROUNDS OF THE BAY AREA; IT WILL INCLUDE THE INFLUENCES THOSE CULTURES HAVE MADE IN HISTORY & HOW THEY ARRIVED IN THE BAY AREA. AT FORT BARRY. (LOCAL). GOLDEN GATE NRA; NATIONAL PARK SERVICE; FORT MASON BLDG 201; SAN FRANCISCO, CA 94123. (#6726-66).

JUNE 21 - AUG 25, '76. U S PRESIDENTS RESIDENTS CAMP, HISTORY AND IMPACT OF U S PRESIDENTS. CAMP LODGING; 50 CHILDREN; 1 WEEK SESSIONS; 10 WEEKS. GAMES, PLAY CRAFTS AND OTHER MEDIA WILL BE USED TO ACQUIRE INFORMATION ABOUT 8 PRESIDENTS WHO HAVE INFLUENCED CHANGE IN OUR NATION BY VARIOUS DECISIONS. AT FORT BARRY JUST NORTH OF SAN FRANCISCO. (LOCAL). GOLDEN GATE NRA; NATIONAL PARK SERVICE; FORT MASON BLDG 201; SAN FRANCISCO, CA 94123. (#6729-183).

JUNE 26 - 29, '76. RE-ENACTMENT OF THE ANZA TREK. IN HONOR OF THE BICENTENNIAL, A CEREMONY WILL BE HELD TO COMMEMORATE JUAN BAUTISTA DE ANZA'S SELECTING OF THE SITE FOR THE PRESIDIO. AT PRESIDIO PARADE GROUND. (NAT'L). JEAN MCCLATCHY; SAN FRANCISCO TWIN BICENT, INC; 555 MARKET STREET; SAN FRANCISCO, CA 94105. (#9828-1).

JUNE 26 - JULY 4, '76. FILIPINO AMERICAN FRIENDSHIP WEEK. WEEK LONG ACTIVITIES HIGHLIGHTING FILIPINO CULTURE. (LOCAL). MARY GANOTISE, CHMN; FILIPINO AMERICAN COUNCIL; 5715 DIAMOND HEIGHTS; SAN FRANCISCO, CA 94131. (#103994-3).

JUNE 27, '76. INTERFAITH PARADE AND MUSICALE. PUBLIC MANIFESTATIONS OF ALL RELIGIONS; UNITING, RECOGNIZING THE SAME GOD AS THE ORIGIN OF OUR RIGHTS, ACKNOWLEDGED FOUR TIMES IN THE DECLARATION OF INDEPENDENCE. PARADE IS 2-5PM; MUSIC FESTIVAL IS 5PM. AT DOWNTOWN SAN FRANCISCO & CITY AUDITORIUM. (LOCAL). REV ALFRED BOEDDEKER, DIR; INTERFAITH BICENTENNIAL COMMITTEE; 121 GOLDEN GATE AVE; SAN FRANCISCO, CA 94102. (#104461-1).

JUNE 29, '76. MASS AND CIVIL LUNCHEON. CEREMONY AT MISSION DOLORES. (LOCAL). MRS J APPLEGARTH, CHMN; CALIFORNIA HISTORICAL SOCIETY; 44-21ST AVE; SAN FRANCISCO, CA 94121. (#103916-1).

JUNE 30 - JULY 5, '76. JAPANESE YOUTH GOODWILL CRUISE VISITS SAN FRANCISCO. HOURS ON THURSDAY 12 NOON TO 5:30 PM; SUNDAY 6 PM TO 8 PM. (INT'L). MITAKE KATSUBE; JAPANESE PRIME MINISTER'S OFFICE; OCHANOMIZU WOMEN'S UNIV; TOKYO/JAPAN. (#109014-1).

JUNE 30 - AUG 8, '76. EXPLORATORIUM-THE SPIRIT OF INNOVATION. DISPLAY ON SCIENTIFIC AND TECHNICAL INNOVATION IN AMERICAN CULTURE. WEDNESDAY EVENING HOURS: 7-9:30 PM. AT PALACE OF FINE ARTS, MARINA DIST; 3601 LYON ST. (LOCAL). JUDY M DUGGAN, PROJ COORD; THE EXPLORATORIUM; 3601 LYON; SAN FRANCISCO, CA 94123. (#107521-1).

JULY 1 - 7, '76. IRISH AMERICAN HERITAGE WEEK. FESTIVAL. (LOCAL). JOHN WHOOLEY, CHAIRMAN; IRISH HERITAGE FOUNDATION; 2123 MARKET; SAN FRANCISCO, CA 94114. (#104897-1).

JULY 1 - SEPT 12, '76. TOURS OF FORT POINT NATIONAL HISTORIC SITE. CONSTRUCTED 1853 TO 1861, FORT POINT IS A CLASSIC EXAMPLE OF BRICK FORTS BUILT TO PROTECT THE SEA COASTS AND HARBORS OF THE UNITED STATES. HISTORICAL TOURS CONDUCTED DAILY. AT UNDER SOUTHERN END OF GOLDEN GATE BRIDGE ON PRESIDIO OF SAN FRAN. (REGN'L). FORT POINT NATL HIST SITE; NATIONAL PARK SERVICE; PRESIDEIO OF SF, PO BOX 9167; SAN FRANCISCO, CA 94129. (#6730-125).

JULY 2 - 4, '76. 'SPIRIT OF '76' GEM & MINERAL SHOW. CLOSES 6PM ON 7/4, DISPLAYS, LECTURES & BUS TOUR OF LOCAL EARTHQUAKE FAULTS. EXHIBITS OF ROCK, FOSSILS, MINERALS, JEWELRY AND LAPIDARY WORK; GEMSTONE CARVINGS, PETRIFIED WOOD, FLOURESCENT CRYSTALS, EDUCATIONAL CRYSTALS, EDUCATIONAL CASES SPECIAL EXHIBIT FOR THE BLIND. AT COW PALACE, GENEVA & SANTOS STS. (REGN'L). MRS FAITH RIESEN, CHMN; CALIFORNIA FEDERATION OF MINERALOGICAL SOCIETIES, INC; 295 STONECREST DR; SAN FRANCISCO, CA 94132. (#106447-1).

JULY 4, '76. CITIZENS GRAND PARADE. PARADE. (LOCAL). WALTER NEWMAN, CHAIRMAN; SAN FRANCISCO TWIN BICENT, INC; 555 MARKET ST; SAN FRANCISCO, CA 94105. (#9837-1).

JULY 4, '76. FRANCIS SCOTT KEY MONUMENT DEDICATION. CEREMONY AT GOLDEN GATE PARK. (LOCAL). PEGGY KNAPP, COORDINATOR; SAN FRANCISCO TWIN BICENTENNIAL COMMITTEE; 555 MARKET ST; SAN FRANCISCO, CA 94105. (#102850-5).

JULY 4, '76. OPERATION SAIL - GATHERING OF SHIPS IN SAN FRANCISCO. FESTIVAL. (INT'L). JEAN MCCLATCHY, CHAIRMAN; SILVER EAGLE BICENTENNIAL COMMITTEE; 555 MARKET ST; SAN FRANCISCO, CA 94105. (#104277-3).

JULY 4, '76. S F WHEELMEN ROAD RACE - 76 MILES. COMPETITION. (LOCAL). ROGER WHITE; SAN FRANCISCO WHEELMEN 1025 EVERGLADES PACIFICA CA 94044; 132 GARCES DR; SAN FRANCISCO, CA 94132. (#103891-3).

JULY 7 - 10, '76. 38TH ANNUAL CONVENTION & QUARTET & CHORUS CHAMPIONSHIPS OF SPEBSQSA. SHOWS & PERFORMANCES BY QUARTETS & CHORUSES OF THE SOCIETY FOR THE PRESERVATION & ENCOURAGEMENT OF BARBERSHOP QUARTETS SINGING IN AMERICA & BY LOCAL CHAPTERS THRUOUT USA FOR THE BICENTENNIAL ERA. AT HILTON HOTEL AND COW PALACE. (NAT'L). JOHN KRIZEK, GENERAL CHMN; SOC FOR PRES & ENCOURAGEMENT OF BARBERSHOP QUARTET SINGING IN AMERIC; TRANSAMER CORP, 600 MONTGOMERY; SAN FRANCISCO, CA 94111. (#2450-1).

JULY 16 - 18, '76. WELSH HYMN SINGING FESTIVAL. THIS IS THE 7TH REGIONAL GYMANFA GANU & COVERS ALL OF WESTERN CANADA AND THE US. CONVENTION ACTIVITIES FROM 10 AM - 10 PM FRIDAY AND SATURDAY. WELSH HYMN SINGING FESTIVAL ON SUNDAY ONLY. AT JACT TAR HOTEL, GEARY AND VAN NESS AVENUE. (REGN'L). JOHN R NICHOLS, CHMN; WELSH AMERICAN SOCIETY OF NORTHERN CALIFORNIA; 1777 VALLEY VIEW AVE; BELMONT, CA 94002. (#107521-3).

JULY 18, '76. SPIRIT OF '76 SHOW. BETWEEN-THE-GAMES SHOW - A PAGEANTRY OF MUSIC AND DANCE WILL DEPICT THE SPIRIT OF THE AMERICAN REVOLUTION, THE FREEDOM AND DIGNITY OF MAN. AT CANDLESTICK PARK. (REGN'L). GEORGE M WILLIAMS; NICHIREN SHOSHU ACADEMY; PO BOX 1427; SANTA MONICA, CA 90406. (#108210-1).

JULY 23 - 24, '76. SAMOAN COMMUNITY BICENTENNIAL CELEBRATION. A MULTI-EVENT CELEBRATION WILL FEATURE LONGBOATS & CANOE RACES, SPORTS, DANCING & SINGING, BOXING, ARTS & CRAFTS AND SOCIAL & CULTURAL ACTIVITIES. AT AMAZON-CROCKER PARK, GENEVA & MOSCOW ST. (LOCAL). CHIEF LEULUSOO LEATUTUFU; SAMOAN CHIEF COUNCIL OF CALIFORNIA; 166 THE EMBARCADERO, SUITE 601; SAN FRANCISCO, CA 94105. (#19926-1).

JULY 30 - 31, '76. DORCAS QUILTING BEE AND EXHIBITION. FESTIVAL, EXHIBIT AT 25 LAKE ST (AT ARGUELLO); SAN FRANCISCO. (LOCAL). ALICE ZWANCK, DIRECTOR; ST JOHNS PRESBYTERIAN CHURCH; 25 LAKE ST; SAN FRANCISCO, CA 94118. (#103994-1).

AUG 8, '76. FOLK DANCE FESTIVAL. FESTIVAL AT SUNSET RECREATION CENTER 28TH AVE AND LAWTON ST. (LOCAL). LLOYD FEDERLEIN, DIRECTOR; SAN FRANCISCO COUNCIL OF FOLK DANCE GROUPS; 1658 21ST AVE; SAN FRANCISCO, CA 94122. (#107521-2).

AUG 25 - 27, '76. NATL PK SVC '...A LITTLE LOOK AROUND' VISITS GOLDEN GATE NRA. THIS SHORT PROGRAM FEATURES ACTORS PORTRAYING FAMOUS AMERICANS OF THE PAST WHO'VE RETURNED TO SEE AMERICA'S GROWTH. PERFORMANCES ON 8/25 AT FT POINT; ON 8/27 AT FT. POINT. AT 8/25/76 AT FT POINT; 8/26/76 - DOWN DAY; 8/27/76 AT FT. POINT. (REGN'L). GOLDEN GATE NRA; NATIONAL PARK SERVICE; FORT MASON; SAN FRANCISCO, CA 94123. (#5653-44).

AUG 26 - 29, '76. SAN FRANCISCO COUNTY FAIR FLOWER SHOW SALUTES OUR BICENTENNIAL. ANNUAL COUNTY FAIR FLOWER SHOW-COMPETITIVE EXHIBITS OF FLORICULTURE PARTICIPATION BY COMMUNITY RESIDENTS OFSAN FRANCISCO AND SURROUNDING COUNTIES. EDUCATIONAL HORTICULTURE DISPLAYS, LECTURES & DEMONSTRATIONS; FLORAL PAINTINGS & PERFORMING ARTS SHOWS. AT HALL OF FLOWERS, 9TH AVE & LINCOLN WAY. (ST-WIDE). KARL B MUELLER, CHAIRMAN; SAN FRANCISCO FLOWER SHOW, INC; 1847 34TH AVE; SAN FRANCISCO, CA 94122. (#104988-1).

SEPT 2, '76 - JAN 3, '77. EXHIBIT OF CALIFORNIA ART OF THE 20TH CENTURY. EXHIBITIONS DEPICTING CONTRIBUTION AND INFLUENCE OF CALIFORNIA ARTISTS TO MODERN ART IN THE 20TH CENTURY IN PAINTING, SCULPTURE, PHOTOGRAPHY, GRAPHICS, ARCHITECTURE & FOLK ART. AT SAN FRANCISCO MUSEUM OF MODERN ART. (ST-WIDE). HENRY T HOPKINS, DIR; SAN FRANCISCO MUSEUM OF MODERN ART; VAN NESS AT MCALLISTER; SAN FRANCISCO, CA 94102. (#1557-1).

SEPT 5 - 18, '76. STUDENT ARTISTS EXHIBIT VISITS GOLDEN GATE NRA. THIS ART EXHIBIT CONSISTS OF 18 ORIGINAL PAINTINGS SELECTED FROM ENTRIES IN A NATIONWIDE STUDENT ART CONTEST. EACH PAINTING IS IDENTIFIED WITH PERSON, PLACES, OR EVENTS OF THE AMERICAN REVOLUTION. AT FORT MASON BLDG 201 GGNRA HQ BAY & FRANKLIN STS SAN FRANCISCO. (REGN'L). GOLDEN GATE NRA; NATIONAL PARK SERVICE; FORT MASON BUILDING 201; SAN FRANCISCO, CA 94123. (#1474-17).

SAN FRANCISCO — CONTINUED

SEPT 6 - 17, '76. CARL HAVERLIN/BROADCAST MUSIC, INC, ARCHIVES BICENTENNIAL EXHIBIT. OFFERS A VERSATILE PICTURE OF HISTORY, REGIONAL LIFE & MUSIC FOR OVER 200 YEARS. CONTAINS PRESIDENTIAL LETTERS, LETTERS OF FAMOUS AMERICANS, OLD BOOKS, MANUSCRIPTS, HISTORY OF 'THE STAR SPANGLED BANNER' & COMPOSER AUTOGRAPHS, PLUS SHEET MUSIC OF THE PAST. AT GRACE EPISCOPAL CATHEDRAL, 1051 TAYLOR ST. (ST-WIDE). ERIC HUBERT, PGM MANAGER; GRACE EPISCOPAL CATHEDRAL; 1051 TAYLOR ST; SAN FRANCISCO, CA 94108. (#20784-6).

SEPT 16, '76. CATHOLIC CONFERENCE OF BISHOPS. REVIEW OF CATHOLIC HISTORY. (NAT'L). JOHN T DWYER, PROJ DIR; BICENTENNIAL COMMITTEE ON CATHOLIC HISTORY; 221 VALLEY ST; SAN FRANCISCO, CA 94131. (#104044-3).

SEPT 17, '76. LONDON SCHOOLS SYMPHONY ORCHESTRA. LIVE PERFORMANCE AT MASONIC AUDITORIUM. (INT'L). CULTURAL AFFAIRS OFFICE; BRITISH EMBASSY; 3100 MASSACHUSETTS AVE, NW; WASHINGTON, DC 20008. (#108963-2).

SEPT 24 - 26, '76. AKI MATSURI - 7TH ANNUAL JAPANESE FALL FOLK FESTIVAL. FESTIVAL AT JAPAN CENTER AND JAPANTOWN (NIHONMACHI). (INT'L). LOUISE HANFORD, COORD; NIHONMACHI MERCHANTS ASSOCIATION; 582 MARKET ST; SAN FRANCISCO, CA 94115. (#103416-578).

OCT 3 - 11, '76. COLUMBUS DAY CELEBRATION. FESTIVAL, OPENING. (LOCAL). MARGE BOOKER, PROJ DIR; SAN FRANCISCO CONVENTION & VISITORS BUREAU; 1390 MARKET ST; SAN FRANCISCO, CA 94102. (#103553-1).

OCT 9 - 11, '76. WESTERN BICENTENNIAL FOLK FESTIVAL-WESTERN STATES MUSICAL HERITAGE. THIS FESTIVAL IS A THREE-DAY CELEBRATION OF THE WESTERN UNITED STATES RICH AND DIVERSE MUSICAL HERITAGE WITH MANY ETHNIC AND FOLK STYLES REPRESENTED. (REGN'L). GOLDEN GATE NRA; NATIONAL PARK SERVICE & NATIONAL FOLK FESTIVAL ASSOCCIATION; FORT MASON BLDG 201; SAN FRANCISCO, CA 94123. (#6728-255).

OCT 10 - 12, '76. BICENTENNIAL BIRTHDAY PARTIES & PICNIC. 5 BIRTHDAY BALLS WERE HELD TO CELEBRATE THE 200 YEARS-2 OFFICER, 2 CHIEF PETTY OFFICER & 1 FOR ENLISTED. 10/12 PICNIC FOR ALL HANDS AS PART OF BICENTENNIAL OBSERVANCE. (LOCAL). SPECIAL SERVICES; BICENTENNIAL COMMITTEE; COMNAVSPHIL SUBIC BAY RP; FPO SAN FRAN, CA 96651. (#200006-520).

OCT 11 - NOV 5, '76. STAR-SPANGLED HISTORY: DRAWINGS BY J B BEALE - MAGIC LANTERN ARTIST. NATIONAL TRAVELLING EXHIBITION OF 65 ORIGINAL WASH DRAWINGS BY JOSEPH BOGGS BEALE, A 19TH CENTURY ILLUSTRATOR. SLIDE PRESENTATION. (REGN'L). KAREN HUGHES, PROJ MGR; AMERICAN NATIONAL INSURANCE CO OF GALVESTON, TX; 110 E 59TH ST; NEW YORK, NY 10022. (#9820-9).

OCT 25, '76. 'AMERICA CAMEOS' PREMIERES. LIVE PERFORMANCE AT ARENA THEATER OF SFSU. (LOCAL). DR JEAN DE SALES BERTRAM; SAN FRANCISCO STATE UNIVERSITY; 2 VARELA AVE; SAN FRANCISCO, CA 94132. (#30135-1).

NOV 6 - 30, '76. PERFORMANCE OF NEW AMERICAN OPERA, 'ANGLE OF REPOSE'. COMMISSIONED WORK - COMPOSER: ANDREW IMBRIE, LIBRETTIST: OAKLEY HALL; FROM NOVEL BY WALLACE STEGNER. ORCH,GRND TIER-$18.50;DR CIRCLE-$15.50; BALCONY CIRCLE-$13.00; BALCONY-$9.50-$6.00;BX SEAT$21.00 FRI-SAT EVENING-$19.50;$16.50;$14.00;$10.50-$6.50;$23.00. AT WAR MEMORIAL OPERA HOUSE SAN FRANCISCO CA 94102. (ST-WIDE). KURT HERBERT ADLER; SAN FRANCISCO OPERA; WAR MEMORIAL OPERA HOUSE; SAN FRANCISCO, CA 94102. (#6754-2).

NOV 20, '76 - JAN 30, '77. 'THE HISTORY OF JACOB' - 16 CENTURY FLEMISH TAPESTRIES. EXHIBIT AT THE FINE ARTS MUSEUM OF SAN FRANCISCO. (INT'L). CULTURAL ATTACHE; BELGIAN EMBASSY & ROYAL MUSEUM OF ART & HISTORY; 3330 GARFIELD ST; WASHINGTON, DC 20008. (#31903-1).

NOV 22 - 28, '76. ANNUAL CONFERENCE - NATL COUNCIL FOR GEOGRAPHICAL EDUCATION. THE BEST 3 PAPERS OF THE UNDERGRADUATE PAPER COMPETITION, NATIONAL COUNCIL FOR GEOGRAPHICAL EDUCATION, WILL BE PRESENTED AT THE CONVENTION WITH AWARDS PRESENTED AT THE BANQUET. RECOGNITION IN THE JOURNAL OF GEOGRAPHY. AT HILTON HOTEL, SAN FRANCISCO. (REGN'L). DR LON KELLENBERGER, CHMN; NATIONAL COUNCIL FOR GEOGRAPHIC EDUCATION; 9001 STOCKDALE HWY; BAKERSFIELD, CA 93309. (#24874-1).

NOV 24, '76. THE FUTURE OF CANADIAN-U S RESOURCE RELATIONS. DR ROBERT ADAMS, CANADIAN CONSUL GENERAL - OPENING SESSION ADDRESS OF NCGE ANNUAL CONFERENCE; TO BE INTRODUCED BY HERBERT A AUGUSTINE, ONTARIO PROVINCE MINISTRY OF EDUCATION - PRESIDENT OF THE NCGE. AT HILTON HOTEL CONTINENTAL BALLROOM. (INT'L). DR WILLIAM H WAKE; NATIONAL COUNCIL FOR GEOGRAPHIC EDUCATION; DEPT OF EARTH SC, CA ST COLL; BAKERSFIELD, CA 93309. (#102278-2).

NOV 26, '76. 'SO YOU'RE A GEOGRAPHER? SO WHAT!' - GEOGRAPHIC EDUCATION. DR JAMES ROBERTS, CONSULTING GEOGRAPHER AND NATURAL RESOURCE PLANNER, KEYNOTE ADDRESS OF NCGE ANNUAL CONFERENCE. AT HILTON HOTEL, CONTINENTAL BALLROOM. (INT'L). DR WILLIAM H WAKE; NATIONAL COUNCIL FOR GEOGRAPHIC EDUCATION; DEPT EARTH SC, CA ST COLL; BAKERSFIELD, CA 93309. (#102278-3).

DEC 3, '76. 'AMERICAN CAMEOS' SECOND PERFORMANCE. LIVE PERFORMANCE AT 19TH AVE & SLOAT BLVD. (LOCAL). DR JEAN DE SALES BERTRAM; CALIFORNIA BODIES OF THE SCOTTISH RITE; 2 VARELA AVE; SAN FRANCISCO, CA 94132. (#30135-2).

JAN '77 - CONTINUING . PLANNING AMERICA'S GREAT CITIES, AN EXHIBITION. EXHIBIT, RADIO/TV AT THE EXPLORATORIUM. (REGN'L). MS LEE KIMCHE; ASSOC OF SCIENCE & TECHNOLOGY; 2100 PENNSYLVANIA AVE, NW; WASHINGTON, DC 20037. (#8615-11).

SEPT 10 - NOV 13, '77. BICENTENNIAL ART PROGRAM OF DEPT OF THE INTERIOR. PAINTINGS BY MODERN ARTISTS DEPICTING THE NATURAL & HISTORIC PROPERTIES ADMINISTERED BY THE DEPT OF INTERIOR. AT SAN FRANCISCO MUSEUM OF ART. (REGN'L). MRS JEAN HAWKINS; DEPT OF THE INTERIOR; WASHINGTON, DC 20240. (#1239-7).

SAN GABRIEL

SEPT 3 - 5, '76. LA FIESTA DE SAN GABRIEL. FESTIVAL AT MISSION SAN GABRIEL ARCANGEL GROUNDS. (LOCAL). COORDINATOR; MISSION SAN GABRIEL ARCANGEL; 534 W MISSION DR; SAN GABRIEL, CA 91776. (#103416-573).

SAN JACINTO

MT SAN JACINTO COLLEGE BICENTENNIAL PROGRAM, CA. THE PROGRAM WILL INCLUDE AMERICA SERIES WITH FILMSTRIPS & TAPES, LECTURE SERIES - AMERICAN ISSUES FORUM, AMERICAN TRAVEL SERIES, ART EXHIBIT AND FREEDOM SHRINE. (LOCAL). LOUIS CANTER, DEAN OF ACADEMIC INSTRUCTION; MT SAN JACINTO COLLEGE; 21400 HIGHWAY 79; SAN JACINTO, CA 92383. (#15354).

SAN JOSE

ALLEN ELEM SCHOOL BICENT PROJECTS - SAN JOSE, CA. MURAL WITH SCENES OF AMERICAN HERITAGE PAINTED ON THE WALL. THE SCHOOL HELD A TREE PLANTING. (LOCAL). RON GILPATRICK, PRINCIPAL; ALLEN ELEMENTARY SCHOOL; 5845 ALLEN AVE; SAN JOSE, CA 95123. (#30219).

ALLEN ELEMENTARY SCHOOL PROJECTS - SAN JOSE, CA. THE STUDENTS AT ALLEN ELEMENTARY SCHOOL WILL PAINT A MURAL ON AMERICAN HISTORY, MAKE A PATCHWORK QUILT AND PLANT TREES ON THE SCHOOL GROUNDS. (LOCAL). RON GILPATRICK, PRINCIPAL; ALLEN ELEMENTARY SCHOOL; 5845 ALLEN AVE; SAN JOSE, CA 95123. (#26679).

AN AMERICAN PLEDGE - SAN JOSE, CA. SIGNATURES ARE BEING GATHERED ON PLEDGE FROM PROJECT SUPPORTERS; ON JULY 4TH SIGNED PLEDGES WILL BE BURIED IN A TIME CAPSULE, TO BE OPENED JULY 4, 2076. (LOCAL). 2ND LT HUGO H BAYONA, PROGRAMS OFFICER; CIVIL AIR PATROL/AUXILIARY U S AIR FORCE - PENINSULA GROUP 2; PO BOX 4752; SANTA CLARA, CA 95054. (#22616).

ART MUSEUM RENOVATION & SCULPTURE CT IN SAN JOSE. RENOVATE MUSEUM WHICH IS RICHARDSON ROMANESQUE. BUILDING CONSTRUCTED IN 1892 AS FIRST FEDERAL BUILDING IN CITY. ADD SCULPTURE COURT ON ADJACENT SITE OF CALIFORNIA FIRST STATE HOUSE IN 1849-50. (LOCAL). ALBERT DIXON, DIRECTOR; SAN JOSE MUSEUM OF ART ASSOCIATION; 110 SOUTH MARKET ST; SAN JOSE, CA 95113. (#2831).

'AN ARTIST IN SEARCH OF AMERICA' - SAN JOSE, CA. A PAINTING EXHIBITION ON AMERICA DEPICTING LIFE STYLES & ACTIVITIES OF VARIOUS AGES, GROUPS AND OBJECTS SHOWING A HISTORY OF HUMAN USE. (ST-WIDE). BURNAM SCHAA, CURATOR; ROSICRUCIAN EGYPTIAN MUSEUM; ROSICRUCIAN PARK; SAN JOSE, CA 95191. (#16141).

BANK OF ITALY RECONSTRUCTION - SAN JOSE, CA. RECONSTRUCTION OF THE BANK OF ITALY (LATER THE BANK OF AMERICA). THIS IS THE FIRST OUT-OF-TOWN BRANCH; IT WILL CONTAIN EXHIBITS RELATING TO THE HISTORY OF BANKING. (LOCAL). JOHN ROBERTSON, PROJ DIRECTOR; SAN JOSE HISTORICAL MUSEUM; 635 PHELAN AVE; SAN JOSE, CA 95112. (#23451).

BICENT ECOLOGY PROJ AT SAN JOSE STATE UNIV - CA. LAND USE MAPS ARE BEING PLANNED OF SAN JOSE AND SANTA CLARA COUNTIES SO THAT A COMPARISON CAN BE MADE OF USAGE FROM 1776 TO 1976. (LOCAL). DR STANLEY BENZ, PROJ CHAIRMAN; SAN JOSE STATE UNIV; 125 S 7TH; SAN JOSE, CA 95192. (#11803).

BICENT TREE PLANTING IN SAN JOSE, CALIFORNIA. TO GROW 50,000 TREES FROM SEEDLINGS TO 5 GALLON SIZE & PLANT THEM ON PUBLIC PROPERTY OR GIVE THEM TO CITIZENS WHO WILL PLANT THEM UPON THEIR OWN PROPERTY. (LOCAL). STAN HAUGEN, CIVIL ENGINEER; A P HAMANN; 820 ALVISO ST; SANTA CLARA, CA 95050. (#8819).

BICENTENNIAL CLOCK - SAN JOSE, CA. A CLOCK DEPICTING MONTHS LEFT UNTIL 200TH ANNIVERSARY OF THE NATION AND 200TH ANNIVERSARY OF THE CITY OF SAN JOSE ON NOVEMBER 29, 1977. (LOCAL). T W BLACKWELL, VICE PRESIDENT; GLENDALE FEDERAL SAVINGS & LOAN; 200 W TAYLOR ST; SAN JOSE, CA 95112. (#26680).

BICENTENNIAL COURIER PROJECT - SAN JOSE, CA. STUDENTS TO GO ABROAD AS GOODWILL AMBASSADORS PRESENTING NATIONAL AND LOCAL OFFICIALS WITH GIFTS FROM CALIFORNIA. (ST-WIDE). FENTON AND JUDY KOVIC, CA STATE REPRESENTATIVES; YOUTH FOR UNDERSTANDING; 584 W REMINGTON; SUNNYVALE, CA 94087. (#19970).

BICENTENNIAL LECTURE SERIES-PUBLICATION - CA. A SERIES OF HISTORY LECTURES PERTINENT TO THE HISTORY OF THE U S REVOLUTION. (LOCAL). DR TOM WENDEL, PROF, DEPT OF HIST; SAN JOSE STATE UNIV; 125 S 7TH ST; SAN JOSE, CA 95192. (#17733).

BICENTENNIAL PLAZA - SAN JOSE, CA. TILED MOSAIC PLAZA ILLUSTRATING HISTORY, FAMOUS PEOPLE AND LANDMARKS OF SAN JOSE. (LOCAL). NANCY GOETZ, PERCEPTUAL MOTOR RESOURCE TEACHER; WASHINGTON ELEMENTARY SCHOOL; 100 OAK ST; SAN JOSE, CA 95110. (#17684).

BICENTENNIAL SALE - SAN JOSE, CA. WINE GLASSES AND CARAFES WILL BE SOLD JULY 3-4. (LOCAL). GORDON F LEVY, PROJ COORDINATOR; SAN JOSE CHAMBER OF COMMERCE; PO BOX 6178; SAN JOSE, CA 95150. (#24329).

BICENTENNIAL SCULPTURE COURT - SAN JOSE, CA. PROJECT TO COMMEMORATE THE HISTORIC SIGNIFICANCE OF THE ORIGINAL PLAZA OF 1797, THE SPANISH-MEXICAN PERIOD & THE LOCATION OF CALIFORNIA'S FIRST CAPITOL BUILDING. (LOCAL). ALBERT G DIXON, JR, MUSEUM DIRECTOR; SAN JOSE MUSEUM OF ART ASSOC; 110 S MARKET ST; SAN JOSE, CA 95113. (#10779).

BOOK ON HISTORICAL & ARCHITECTURAL HERITAGE - CA. 'THE VALLEY OF SANTA CLARA: HISTORIC BUILDINGS, 1792-1920' WILL HAVE INFORMATION ON THE VALLEY'S INDIVIDUAL COMMUNITIES, ILLUSTRATED WITH CONTEMPORARY & HISTORICAL PHOTOS, DRAWINGS AND MAPS. (LOCAL). MRS ROBERT SWANSON, PROJ COORDINATOR; JUNIOR LEAGUE OF SAN JOSE; 1010 RUFF DR; SAN JOSE, CA 95110. (#26609).

BRAILLE TRANSCRIPTION PROJECT - SAN JOSE, CA. DEMONSTRATIONS OF BRAILLE WRITER, SAMPLES OF TACTUAL AIDS FOR FOREIGN LANGUAGE, MATH, MENUS AND BRAILLED BICENTENNIAL FLAG. (LOCAL). SYLVIA CASSELL, CHAIRMAN; 6TH DISTRICT, CALIFORNIA STATE PTA; 101 N BASCOM AVE; SAN JOSE, CA 95128. (#23450).

BROCHURE OF SAN JOSE ORGANIZATIONS, CA. AN ILLUSTRATED BROCHURE WILL LIST 100 YEAR OLD ORGANIZATIONS WHICH ARE STILL ACTIVE TODAY; BROCHURE WILL INCLUDE A SUMMARY OF THEIR HISTORY AND ILLUSTRATIONS. (LOCAL). EDWARD S HART, PROJ CHAIRMAN; SAN JOSE BICENTENNIAL COMMISSION; 463 WOOSTER AVE, APT B-6; SAN JOSE, CA 95116. (#24819).

CALIFORNIA RELIEF MAP PROJECT & TOUR. 'CALIFORNIA-PARADISE-IN-PANORAMA' IS THE WORLD'S LARGEST RELIEF MAP. 500 FT LONG & 50 YEARS OLD, IT WILL BE CARRIED ON A 58 COUNTY TOUR IN '76 & ON CONTINUING DISPLAY THEREAFTER. (ST-WIDE). RICHARD P KARNAN, PRESIDENT; CALIFORNIA STATE FOUNDATION; 15879 LOS GATOS BLVD; LOS GATOS, CA 95030. (#8373).

'CENTER FOR TOMORROW', SAN JOSE, CALIF. AN 8-FLOOR BUILDING WILL BE CONSTRUCTED WITH LIVE-IN CONFERENCE FACILITIES FOR CONTINUING EDUCATION. ACTIVITIES CONNECTED WITH SAN JOSE STATE UNIVERSITY. (LOCAL). MIKE NEUFELD, EXEC DIRECTOR; SAN JOSE STATE UNIV ALUMNI ASSOCIATION; 210 E SAN CARLOS ST; SAN JOSE, CA 95192. (#2828).

COMMUNITY INTER-AGENCY ACTION ORGANIZATION, CA. THE COMMUNITY INTER-AGENCY ACTION ORGANIZATION WILL PROVIDE AN EFFECTIVE DELIVERY SYSTEM OF SERVICES TO THE COMMUNITY. (LOCAL). DICK BUSSE, CHAIRMAN; SAN JOSE YOUTH COMMISSION; 151 W MISSION; SAN JOSE, CA 95110. (#21318).

DOMINICAN SISTERS' HERITAGE ROOM, SAN JOSE, CA. A HERITAGE ROOM WILL BE DEVELOPED, CONTAINING IMPORTANT ARTICLES AND ELEMENTS FROM THE DOMINICAN SISTERS' 100 YEAR HISTORY. (LOCAL). SISTER MARY PETER, DIRECTOR OF EDUCATION; DOMINICAN SISTERS, MISSION SAN JOSE; 43326 MISSION BLVD; SAN JOSE, CA 94538. (#20921).

FIREPLUG PROJECT IN SAN JOSE, CA. FIREPLUGS WILL BE PAINTED WITH THEME ' CITY OF MANY FACES'; PLUGS WILL REFLECT VARIOUS ETHNIC GROUPS WHO HELPED CONQUER THE WEST 200 YEARS AGO. (LOCAL). JAMES C MALONE, PROJ CHAIRMAN; THE BANK OF CALIFORNIA; 1700 THE ALAMEDA; SAN JOSE, CA 95126. (#14277).

GOALS FOR CENTURY III IN SAN JOSE, CALIFORNIA. A CITYWIDE FORUM TO BE HELD FOR CITIZEN INPUT ON MAJOR GOALS FOR THE CITY'S THIRD CENTURY WHICH STARTS IN 1977. (LOCAL). CHAIRMAN; CITIZENS' COMMUNITY IMPROVEMENT COMMITTEE; CITY HALL; SAN JOSE, CA 95110. (#2832).

HISTORIC BUILDINGS AT SANTA CLARA, CA. BOOK ON HISTORY & ARCHITECTURE OF THE SANTA CLARA VALLEY AND ITS INDIVIDUAL COMMUNITIES; ILLUSTRATED WITH HISTORICAL AND CONTEMPORARY PHOTOS, DRAWINGS AND MAPS. (LOCAL). MRS ROBERT SWANSON, PROJ COORDINATOR; JUNIOR LEAGUE OF SAN JOSE, INC; 1010 RUFF DR; SAN JOSE, CA 95110. (#25468).

HISTORIC PROJECT IN SAN JOSE, CALIFORNIA. THE RECONSTRUCTION OF 12 BUILDINGS REPRESENTING SAN JOSE FROM 1850 TO 1920. (LOCAL). DONALD DEMERS, MUSEUM DIRECTOR; PARKS AND RECREATION DEPT; 151 W MISSION ST, RM 205; SAN JOSE, CA 95110. (#9451).

HISTORIC WALKING TOUR OF DOWNTOWN SAN JOSE, CA. GUIDED WALKING TOUR OF DOWNTOWN SAN JOSE, WITH EMPHASIS ON HISTORICAL POINTS OF INTEREST AND HISTORY OF SAN JOSE. (LOCAL). KATHIE KEELEY, EXEC DIRECTOR; SAN JOSE CHAMBER OF COMMERCE; 165 W SAN CARLOS ST; SAN JOSE, CA 95114. (#8394).

HISTORICAL RECORDS ON SAN JOSE BICENTENNIAL, CA. A SCRAPBOOK OF NEWS CLIPPINGS AND OTHER PERTINENT BICENTENNIAL MULTI -MEDIA SCRIPT. (LOCAL). EARL FREITAS, HERITAGE CHAIRMAN; SAN JOSE BICENTENNIAL COMMISSION, INC; 165 W SAN CARLOS ST; SAN JOSE, CA 95114. (#18344).

HISTORY OF SAN JOSE BOOK. IN DEPTH TWO VOLUME ILLUSTRATED BOOK ON THE 200 YEAR GROWTH AND DEVELOPMENT OF SAN JOSE, CALIFORNIA. (LOCAL). GENE SAALWAECHTER, DIRECTOR; CITY OF SAN JOSE PARKS & RECREATION DEPT; 151 W MISSION ST; SAN JOSE, CA 95110. (#2833).

SAN JOSE — CONTINUED

ILLUSTRATED HISTORY OF SAN JOSE, CA. 100 PAGE HISTORY OF SAN JOSE ILLUSTRATED WITH PEN-INK DRAWINGS AS SOUVENIR EDITION DURING BICENTENNIAL AS WELL AS EDUCATIONAL USE IN SCHOOLS AND TOURISM. (LOCAL). EDITH BROCKWAY, AUTHOR; ACADEMY PRESS; 5544 COPELAND LANE; SAN JOSE, CA 95124. (#24184).

INTERNATIONAL CHILDREN'S DAY AT HAPPY HOLLOW, CA. A CELEBRATION INVOLVING PERFORMERS OF ALL AGES REPRESENTING DIFFERENT COUNTRIES WITH THEIR COSTUMES, MUSIC & DANCES TO FOSTER THE CONCEPT OF INTERNATIONAL BROTHERHOOD. (ST-WIDE). JOE J HASLEMANN, VICE-PRESIDENT; HAPPY HOLLOW PARK AND BABY ZOO; STORY & SENTER RDS; SAN JOSE, CA 95110. (#13429).

LAND USE MAPS - SAN JOSE STATE UNIV, CA. MAPS WILL COMPARE SANTA CLARA COUNTY LAND USE IN 1776 WITH 1976. HIGH ALTITUDE AND SATELLITE PHOTOGRAPHS WILL BE USED. (LOCAL). STANLEY C BENZ, BICENT CHAIRMAN; SAN JOSE STATE UNIV; 125 S 7TH ST; SAN JOSE, CA 95192. (#17735).

OUTREACH FOR WOMEN, INC, SAN JOSE, CA. RESOURCE CENTER FOR WOMEN IN SANTA CLARA COUNTY TO PROVIDE EMPLOYMENT, EDUCATIONAL INFORMATION & REFERENCE/REFERRAL SERVICES. SPONSOR ED BY A NON PROFIT GRP,(WOMEN'S ACTION COALITION)TO UPGRADE STATUS. (LOCAL). RUTH S FLANAGAN, CHAIRPERSON; OUTREACH FOR WOMEN, INC; 1717 THE ALAMEDA; SAN JOSE, CA 95126. (#18432).

PELLIER PARK - SAN JOSE, CALIFORNIA. A SMALL PARK COMMEMORATING THE FRENCH IMMIGRANT WHO INTRODUCED THE FRENCH PRUNE TO CALIFORNIA WILL BE DESIGNATED ON THE ORIGINAL SITE, NOW STATE LANDMARK # 434. (ST-WIDE). LEONARD MCKAY, COMMISSIONER; HISTORIC LANDMARKS COMMISSION; CITY HALL; SAN JOSE, CA 95110. (#6236).

PEOPLE'S MURAL - SAN JOSE STATE UNIV, CA. HISTORICAL MURAL DEVELOPED AND PAINTED BY SAN JOSE STATE UNIV ART CLASS. (LOCAL). STANLEY C BENZ, BICENT CHAIRMAN; SAN JOSE STATE UNIV; 125 S 7TH ST; SAN JOSE, CA 95192. (#17734).

PERALTA ADOBE PROJECT - SAN JOSE, CA. PROJECT INCLUDES DOCENT TOURS FOR SCHOOL CLASSES AT PERALTA ADOBE & PARK; 2 LARGE DISPLAY KIOSKS WITH PUEBLO MAPS & SCALE MODEL; FILMSTRIP KIT & TEACHER'S GUIDE; RESTORATION CONTRIBUTION. (LOCAL). MRS BRUCE JAMISON, CHAIRMAN; JUNIOR LEAGUE OF SAN JOSE, INC; 217 CERRO CHICO; LOS GATOS, CA 95030. (#14243).

SAKAMOTO SCHOOL SITE DEVELOPMENT PROJECT, CA. PUBLIC BICENTENNIAL TREE GROVE AND PUBLIC PICNIC AREA ON THE SAKAMOTO SCHOOL SITE; PROJECT WILL INCLUDE EMPHASIS ON EDUCATION IN ECOLOGY, HISTORY AND SOCIAL SCIENCES. (LOCAL). DIANA FONG, CHAIRMAN; SAKAMOTO HOME AND SCHOOL CLUB; 6280 SHADELANDS DR; SAN JOSE, CA 95123. (#19734).

SAN JOSE SYMPHONY BICENTENNIAL SEASON. A CONCERT SEASON FEATURING GUEST APPEARANCES OF THE NATION'S GREATEST LIVING COMPOSERS PERFORMING THEIR FINEST CONTEMPORARY WORKS. (REGN'L). DON THOMSON, GENERAL MANAGER; SAN JOSE SYMPHONY ASSOC; ST CLAIRE HOTEL, SUITE 210; SAN JOSE, CA 95113. (#2835).

SAN JOSE, CALIF, HISTORIC PARK. IN A SIX BLOCK HISTORIC PARK, ORIGINAL & RECONSTRUCTED BUILDINGS RECREATE THE SAN JOSE OF 1850-1900. ARTIFACTS OF ORIGINAL STRUCTURES ON EXHIBIT. (LOCAL). GENE SAALWAECHTER, DIRECTOR; CITY OF SAN JOSE PARKS & RECREATION DEPT; 151 W MISSION ST; SAN JOSE, CA 95110. (#2282).

SAN JOSE, CA, BICENT AWARD FOR RADIO AMATEURS. A CERTIFICATE WILL BE AWARDED TO RADIO AMATEURS FOR ACCOMPLISHING TWO-WAY CONTACT WITH A SPECIFIC NUMBER OF SAN JOSE STATIONS. (LOCAL). WILLIAM J VETTE, CHAIRMAN; SANTA CLARA COUNTY AMATEUR RADIO ASSOC; PO BOX 61241; SUNNYVALE, CA 94088. (#23449).

SINO-AMERICAN BICENTENNIAL FESTIVAL, SAN JOSE, CA. CULTURAL EXHIBITS, SEMINARS & FILMS; ALSO MURAL DEPICTING U S HISTORY. (LOCAL). FRANK G LOWE, PRESIDENT; INSTITUTE OF SINO-AMERICAN STUDIES; 2819 CUNNINGHAM AVE; SAN JOSE, CA 95122. (#10971).

SPIRIT OF '76 - SAN JOSE, CA. BOOKLET OF ACTIVITIES FOR CLASSROOM USE BY ELEMENTARY STUDENTS. (LOCAL). JAMES L CASSANI, DIRECTOR; FRANKLIN-MCKINLEY SCHOOL DISTRICT; 400 TULLY RD; SAN JOSE, CA 95112. (#24178).

TREE PLANTING PROJECT: A BIRTHDAY SALUTE, CA. 199 TREES HAVE BEEN PLANTED AT REID-HILLVIEW AIRPORT. A SEEDLING FROM GEO WASHINGTON'S 'INDEPENDENCE TREE' IS SCHEDULED FOR PLANTING JULY 4TH. AN EXTRA TREE ADDED EACH JULY 4TH THEREAFTER. (LOCAL). 2ND LT HUGO H BAYONA, PLANS AND PROGRAMS OFFICER; CIVIL AIR PATROL/ AUXILIARY U S AIR FORCE - PENINSULA GROUP 2; PO BOX 4752; SANTA CLARA, CA 95054. (#22525).

TRINITY CHURCH BELLS, SAN JOSE, CA. PRESENT CHIME OF BELLS WHICH DATE BACK TO 1879 TO BE ENLARGED TO TWO CHIMES. (LOCAL). W B MURDOCK, RECTOR; TRINITY EPISCOPAL CHURCH; 81 N 2ND ST; SAN JOSE, CA 95113. (#13314).

UPDATE U S HISTORY FILMS - SAN JOSE, CA. UTILIZING A TIME-LIFE OFFER WHEREBY LOCAL BUSINESSES MAY BECOME LASTINGLY INVOLVED IN THE BICENTENNIAL THROUGH SPONSORSHIP OF A NEW DOCUMENTARY SERIES OF U S HISTORY FILMS. (LOCAL). BUD HORTON, SUPERVISOR; SAN JOSE UNIFIED SCHOOL DISTRICT; 1605 PARK AVE; SAN JOSE, CA 95126. (#26678).

'WORKING AMERICANS' - SAN JOSE, CA. AMERICAN LABOR, PAST, PRESENT AND FUTURE IN REVIEW THROUGH WORDS, PICTURES AND LIVING DEMONSTRATIONS. (LOCAL). ELEANOR EDMONDSON, PROJ DIRECTOR; SANTA CLARA COUNTY CENTRAL LABOR COUNCIL; 2102 ALMADEN RD; SAN JOSE, CA 95125. (#18626).

1976 BICENTENNIAL BROCHURE OF LICEO CUBANO IN CA. CONTAINS SOME OF USA'S BEST KNOWN SYMBOLS, DOCUMENTS, CEREMONIES, CUSTOMS & IMPORTANT EVENTS OCCURRING SINCE 1492, AS WELL AS A HISTORY OF CUBA. (LOCAL). WALDO C ESTRADA, COORDINATOR; LICEO CUBANO, INC; 2912 CABRILLA AVE; SANTA CLARA, CA 95051. (#28034).

89ERS ANNUAL LUNCHEON HONORING PIONEER FAMILIES. AWARD, PARADE, LIVE PERFORMANCE AT HYATT HOUSE. (LOCAL). DAN R COLETTI, CHAIRMAN; BANK OF AMERICA; 2105 FOREST AVE; SAN JOSE, CA 95128. (#106735-1).

JUNE 1, '74 - JUNE 30, '77. AMERICAN SERIES - 20 EXHIBITIONS ON AMERICAN ART. THREE-YEAR SERIES OF MUSEUM EXHIBITIONS EXPLORING AMERICAN ART FROM COLONIAL DAYS TO THE PRESENT. A HISTORY OF AMERICAN ART (COLONIAL TO PRESENT). AT SAN JOSE MUSEUM OF ART. (LOCAL). ALBERT G DIXON, JR; SAN JOSE MUSEUM OF ART ASSOCIATION; 110 SO MARKET STREET; SAN JOSE, CA 95113. (#2830-1).

APR 1 - OCT 15, '75. GUIDED WALKING TOUR OF HISTORIC SAN JOSE, BY APPOINTMENT. GUIDED WALKING TOUR OF DOWNTOWN SAN JOSE, WITH EMPHASIS ON HISTORICAL POINTS OF INTEREST AND HISTORY OF SAN JOSE. (LOCAL). KATHIE KEELEY; SAN JOSE CHAMBER OF COMMERCE; 165 W SAN CARLOS ST; SAN JOSE, CA 95114. (#8394-501).

MAY 3, '75. SAN JOSE NATIONAL BICENTENNIAL INVITATIONAL TRACK AND FIELD MEET. EXTRAVAGANZA FOR YOUTH THROUGH CLUB LEVEL ATHLETES INCLUDING WOMEN, WITH A SPECIAL, LIMITED SECTION FOR POLITICIANS AND CELEBRITIES. AT BUD WINTER FIELD, S 10TH AND E. ALMA. (NAT'L). WYNN COOK; SAN JOSE SPORTS ASSOCIATION & SAN JOSE MERCURY NEWS; SAN JOSE STATE UNIVERSITY; SAN JOSE, CA 95192. (#50559-1).

JUNE 7, '75. 200 YEARS OF FASHION. FASHION SHOW AND LUNCHEON FEATURING FASHIONS AND STYLES FROM 1776 TO 1976 WITH HISTORICAL HIGHLIGHTS. AT MEDITERRENEAN CENTER, SAN JOSE HYATT HOUSE NEAR HWY 101. (LOCAL). PEGGY HOWARD; DAUGHTERS OF THE AMERICAN REVOLUTION; 2271 WESTMORELAND DRIVE; SAN JOSE, CA 95124. (#50557-1).

JUNE 13, '75 - SEPT '77. 'THE GHOSTS OF MRS WINCHESTER', GOTHIC MUSICAL COMEDY. FULL LENGTH MUSICAL COMEDY TO BE PRESENTED OUTDOORS CABARET STYLEWINE AND CHEESEBOARDS SERVED. PERFORMANCES WILL RUN THURSSAT FROM JUNE TO SEPTEMBER ONLY DURING THE THREE-YEAR PERIOD. AT COURTYARD-WINCHESTER MYSTERY HOUSE. (LOCAL). WINCHESTER MYSTERY HOUSE; HERITAGE PRODUCTIONS; 525 SOUTH WINCHESTER BLVD; SAN JOSE, CA 95128. (#50592-1).

JUNE 14, '75. ELKS' SAN JOSE BICENTENNIAL FLAG DAY PARADE. FLAG DAY PARADE, MARCHING UNITS, DRUM CORPS, DRILL TEAMS, COLOR GUARD, FLOATS, MOUNTED UNITS. ANY UNIT APPROVED BY COMMITTEE. AT PARADE WILL FORM AT FIRST ST AND ST JOHN ST. (LOCAL). LOUIS A ROSSI; SAN JOSE ELKS LODGE NO 522; 1209 B OF A BLDG 1ST & STA CLARA; SAN JOSE, CA 95113. (#50560-1).

OCT 4, '75. TOUCH OF AMERICANA - A MUSICAL REVUE. 4 PART HARMONY-BARBERSHOP, GUEST PERFORMERS SAN FRANCISCO STORM DOOR & WHALE OIL CO. SWEET ADELINES ARE REGIONAL CHAMPIONS & INTL AWARDWINNING GROUP OF 85 WOMEN PERFORMING & SINGING SONGS OF BICENTENNIAL AMERICA. AT SAN JOSE CENTER FOR PERFORMING ARTS, 255 ALMADEN. (LOCAL). ROBERT E QUIGLEY, CHMN; MENTAL HEALTH ASSOC & SWEET ADELINES (MISSION VALLEY CHAPTER); 1572 LAS PADRES BLVD; SANTA CLARA, CA 95050. (#200006-86).

OCT 17 - 25, '75. THEATRE PRODUCTION: 'TEA AND SYMPATHY'. LIVE PERFORMANCE AT UNIVERSITY THEATRE, SAN JOSE STATE UNIV. (LOCAL). STANLEY C BENZ, COORD; THEATRE ARTS DEPARTMENT, SAN JOSE STATE UNIV; SAN JOSE, CA 95192. (#200006-89).

OCT 18 - 25, '75. PERFORMANCE BY ALLAN HOHVANESS OF COMMISSIONED SYMPHONY & LECTURES. SAN JOSE SYMPHONY BICENTENNIAL SEASON. A CONCERT SEASON FEATURING GUEST APPEARANCES OF THE NATION'S GREATEST LIVING COMPOSERS PERFORMING THEIR FINEST CONTEMPORARY WORKS. (REGN'L). DON THOMSON; SAN JOSE SYMPHONY ASSOC; ST CLAIRE HOTEL, SUITE 210; SAN JOSE, CA 95113. (#2835-501).

OCT 24 - 25, '75. SYMPHONY NO. 26 COMMISSIONED BY THE SAN JOSE SYMPHONY ORCHESTRA. LIVE PERFORMANCE. (LOCAL). ALAN HOVHANESS; SAN JOSE SYMPHONY ORCHESTRA; 25 W HIGHLAND DR; SEATTLE, WA 98119. (#6731-2).

NOV 5 - 22, '75. PERFORMANCE AND LECTURE BY JOHN CAGE. SAN JOSE SYMPHONY BICENTENNIAL SEASON. A CONCERT SEASON FEATURING GUEST APPEARANCES OF THE NATION'S GREATEST LIVING COMPOSERS PERFORMING THEIR FINEST CONTEMPORARY WORKS. (REGN'L). DON THOMSON; SAN JOSE SYMPHONY ASSOC; ST CLAIRE HOTEL, SUITE 210; SAN JOSE, CA 95113. (#2835-502).

NOV 12 - 14, '75. CONFERENCE ON SCIENTIFIC & SOCIAL PROBLEMS. CONFERENCE AT UNION BLDG. (LOCAL). STANLEY C BENZ, COUNSELOR; SCIENCE DEPT, SAN JOSE STATE UNIV; SAN JOSE, CA 95192. (#103394-36).

NOV 18, '75. LECTURE-CONCERT: JOHN CAGE AT SJSU. LIVE PERFORMANCE AT CONCERT HALL. (LOCAL). STANLEY C BENZ, COUNSELOR; MUSIC DEPT, SAN JOSE STATE UNIV; SAN JOSE, CA 95192. (#103394-34).

NOV 30 - DEC 6, '75. SYMPHONY PERFORMANCES & LECTURES BY CARLOS CHAVEZ. SAN JOSE SYMPHONY BICENTENNIAL SEASON. A CONCERT SEASON FEATURING GUEST APPEARANCES OF THE NATION'S GREATEST LIVING COMPOSERS PERFORMING THEIR FINEST CONTEMPORARY WORKS. (REGN'L). DON THOMSON; SAN JOSE SYMPHONY ASSOC; ST CLAIRE HOTEL, SUITE 210; SAN JOSE, CA 95113. (#2835-503).

DEC 1, '75 - DEC 31, '76. LIBERTY BELLES AND BOYS PERFORMING CHOIR. CHILDREN 5-13, BUILDING PATRIOTISM THROUGH MUSICAL PERFORMANCES. (LOCAL). NAN HUNTER, DIRECTOR; LIBERTY BELLES AND BOYS; 1140 WHITEMARSH CT; SAN JOSE, CA 95120. (#104527-1).

DEC 2, '75. LECTURE-CONCERT: CARLOS CHAVEZ AT SJSU. LIVE PERFORMANCE AT CONCERT HALL. (LOCAL). STANLEY C BENZ, COUNSELOR; MUSIC DEPT, SAN JOSE STATE UNIV; SAN JOSE, CA 95192. (#103394-33).

DEC 5 - 13, '75. THEATRE PRODUCTION 'BEAUX STRATEGEM'. LIVE PERFORMANCE AT UNIVERSITY THEATRE. (LOCAL). STANLEY C BENZ, COUNSELOR; THEATRE ARTS DEPT, SAN JOSE STATE UNIV; SAN JOSE, CA 95192. (#103394-13).

DEC 9, '75. 'PEOPLE'S MURAL' LECTURE BY DR ALAN BARNETT. LIVE PERFORMANCE AT UNION BLDG. (LOCAL). STANLEY C BENZ, COUNSELOR; HUMANITIES DEPT, SAN JOSE STATE UNIV; SAN JOSE, CA 95192. (#103394-17).

DEC 14 - 17, '75. AMERICAN FREEDOM TRAIN DISPLAY DAYS AT SAN JOSE. THE AMERICAN FREEDOM TRAIN WILL INCLUDE 10 EXHIBIT CARS & 2 SHOWCASE CARS DEPICTING DIFFERENT PHASES OF THE AMERICAN EXPERIENCE. ITS ARRIVAL WILL SERVE AS A CATALYST FOR LOCAL BICENTENNIAL CELEBRATIONS BY PEOPLE THROUGHOUT THIS NATION. (ST-WIDE). SY FREEDMAN, DIR OF P/R; THE AMERICAN FREEDOM TRAIN FOUNDATION; 5205 LEESBURG PIKE, SUITE 800; BAILEY'S XRDS, VA 22041. (#1776-145).

JAN 17 - 18, '76. LIBERTY BELL BALL: A FOLK DANCE FESTIVAL. FESTIVAL AT SAN JOSE CIVIC AUDITORIUM, 145 WEST SAN CARLOS ST. (LOCAL). STEPHEN DRAKE; FOLK DANCE FEDERATION OF CALIFORNIA; 2146 MONTEREY AVE; SANTA CLARA, CA 95060. (#200006-127).

JAN 17 - 24, '76. BALLET PERFORMANCES AND LECTURES BY AARON COPLAND. SAN JOSE SYMPHONY BICENTENNIAL SEASON. A CONCERT SEASON FEATURING GUEST APPEARANCES OF THE NATION'S GREATEST LIVING COMPOSERS PERFORMING THEIR FINEST CONTEMPORARY WORKS. (REGN'L). DON THOMSON; SAN JOSE SYMPHONY ASSOC; ST CLAIRE HOTEL, SUITE 210; SAN JOSE, CA 95113. (#2835-504).

JAN 20, '76. EQUAL RIGHTS AMENDMENT - DEBATE. DEBATE BETWEEN MEMBER OF BWPC & FAMILY PRESERVATION LEAGUE, OPEN TO THE PUBLIC. (LOCAL). SHIRLEY SILVA, PGM CHMN; WILLOW GLEN BUSINESS & PROFESSIONAL WOMENS CLUB; 2010 TULLY RD; SAN JOSE, CA 95122. (#200006-133).

JAN 20, '76. LECTURE-CONCERT: AARON COPLAND AT SJSU. LIVE PERFORMANCE AT CONCERT HALL. (LOCAL). STANLEY C BENZ, COUNSELOR; MUSIC DEPT, SAN JOSE STATE UNIV; SAN JOSE, CA 95192. (#103394-32).

JAN 20 - MAY 15, '76. AMERICAN COMPOSER SERIES. CELEBRATION OF BICENTENNIAL BY BRINGING AMERICA'S BEST KNOWN COMPOSERS FOR LECTURE/PERFORMANCES OF THEIR MAJOR WORKS. VARYING DATES FOR SEMINARS AND PERFORMANCES; SEMINARS GIVEN AT 7:30 PM, PERFORMANCES AT 8:30 PM. AT SEMINAR: SAN JOSE UNIV; PERFORM: SAN JOSE CTR FOR PERFORMING ARTS. (LOCAL). BOB CAULFIELD, GEN MGR; SAN JOSE SYMPHONY ASSOC; SYMPHONY SUITE, ST CLAIRE HOTEL; SAN JOSE, CA 95113. (#103797-6).

JAN 21, '76. BICENTENNIAL MUSICAL PROGRAM/WHITTEMORE AND LOWE PIANISTS. LIVE PERFORMANCE AT SAN JOSE CENTER FOR PERFORMING ARTS. (LOCAL). ALICE CRONKRIGHT, CHMN; SAN JOSE COMMUNITY CONCERT ASSOCIATION; 1461 HAMILTON WAY; SAN JOSE, CA 95123. (#102826-3).

JAN - JULY '76. 'AMERICANA SERIES'. 'DAMN YANKEES'-AUG '75, 'WEST SIDE STORY', MAY '76, '1776', 1976 PERFORMANCES 8:00PM FRIDAY, 3:00PM SATURDAY. AT CENTER FOR PERFORMING ARTS, ALMADEN & W SAN CARLOS PKG BY CIVIC AUD.. (ST-WIDE). JOHN HEALY, JR; SAN JOSE CHILDREN'S MUSICAL THEATER; 3293 VALLEY SQUARE LANE; SAN JOSE, CA 95117. (#50591-1).

FEB 2 - 28, '76. HISTORICAL WATERCOLOR EXHIBITION. PAINTINGS OF RECOGNIZABLE SANTA CLARA VALLEY SITES DATING FROM BEFORE 1920. AT 5420 FAIRWAY DR. (LOCAL). SCOTTY HULQUIST, PROJ DIR; THE SANTA CLARA VALLEY WATERCOLOR SOCIETY; 1759 NAGLEE AVE; SAN JOSE, CA 95126. (#102439-3).

FEB 2 - JULY 31, '76. BICENTENNIAL POSTER ART CONTEST. SAVINGS AWARDS WILL BE GIVEN FOR MEANINGFUL BICENTENNIAL ART PROJECTS; OPEN TO PRIMARY CHILDREN IN SAN JOSE'S OAK GROVE SCHOOL DISTRICT. AT 6233 SANTA TERESA BLVD ON CORNER OF COTTLE ROAD. (LOCAL). BARBARA J HODGES, MGR; SECURITY SAVINGS & LOAN ASSOC; 6233 SANTA TERESA BLVD; SAN JOSE, CA 95119. (#108059-3).

FEB 3, '76. LECTURE-CONCERT, DANLEE MITCHELL AS GUEST ARTIST. LIVE PERFORMANCE AT CONCERT HALL. (LOCAL). STANLEY C BENZ, COUNSELOR; MUSIC DEPT, SAN JOSE STATE UNIV; SAN JOSE, CA 95192. (#103394-31).

FEB 7 - 8, '76. FILATELIC FIESTA. LARGEST FREE ADMISSION EXHIBITION ON WEST COAST. PROVIDES AN OUTLET FOR COLLECTORS NATIONWIDE TO DISPLAY BICENTENNIAL-RELATED STAMPS ILLUSTRATING AMER REVOL OR AMER HERITAGE. HOURS SUNDAY 10:00 AM - 05:00 PM. AT LE BARON HOTEL, 1350 N FIRST ST; NEAR HWY 101; PARKING ADJACENT. (REGN'L). DR L W MARPLE, PRESIDENT; SAN JOSE STAMP CLUB; 12287 VIEWOAK DR; SARATOGA, CA 95070. (#3823-1).

FEB 9 - 15, '76. BLACK CULTURAL WEEK. FESTIVAL AT VARIOUS LOCATIONS IN SAN JOSE. (LOCAL). DR WILLIE L WILLIAMS;

SAN JOSE — CONTINUED

BLACK THEATRE WORKSHOP, INC; 2685 ROSALIND CT; SAN JOSE, CA 95121. (#100706-1).

FEB 10, '76. DJAMARRO CAURO DANCE TROUP. LIVE PERFORMANCE AT STUDENT UNION. (LOCAL). STANLEY C BENZ, COUNSELOR; AFRO-AMERICAN STUDIES DEPT, SAN JOSE STATE UNIV; SAN JOSE, CA 95192. (#103394-16).

FEB 10, '76. 'RESCUING EQUALITY', LECTURE BY JOHN H BUNZEL. LIVE PERFORMANCE AT UNIVERSITY THEATRE, SAN JOSE STATE CAMPUS. (LOCAL). STANLEY C BENZ, COUNSELOR; SANT CLARA COUNTY COLLEGE AND UNIVERSITIES CONSORTIUM; SAN JOSE STATE UNIV; SAN JOSE, CA 95192. (#103394-8).

FEB 11, '76. AFRO AMERICAN ART EXHIBITION. EXHIBIT AT STUDENT UNION, SAN JOSE STATE UNIV. (LOCAL). STANLEY C BENZ, CHMN; AFRO-AMERICAN STUDIES DEPARTMENT SAN JOSE STATE UNIVERSITY; SAN JOSE STATE UNIV; SAN JOSE, CA 95192. (#103399-1).

FEB 12, '76. POETRY AND DRAMATIC READINGS. LIVE PERFORMANCE AT STUDENT UNION. (LOCAL). STANLEY C BENZ, COUNSELOR; AFRO-AMERICAN STUDIES DEPT, SAN JOSE STATE UNIV; SAN JOSE, CA 95192. (#103394-15).

FEB 17, '76. LECTURE BY DR ROBERT MACAFEE BROWN. DR BROWN WILL LECTURE ON 'THE FUTURE OF THEOLOGY, AN ECUMENICAL APPROACH.'. AT LECTURE HALL, SANTA CLARA UNIV. (LOCAL). STANLEY C BENZ, COUNSELOR; SANT CLARA COUNTY COLLEGE AND UNIVERSITIES CONSORTIUM; SAN JOSE STATE UNIV; SAN JOSE, CA 95192. (#103394-7).

FEB 25, '76. READING OF REPRESENTATIVE AMERICAN POEMS. SAN JOSE STATE FACULTY MEMBERS WILL PARTICIPATE IN THE READING. AT STUDENT UNION. (LOCAL). STANLEY C BENZ, COUNSELOR; ENGLISH DEPT, SAN JOSE STATE UNIV; SAN JOSE, CA 95192. (#103394-28).

FEB 25 - MAY 12, '76. BICENTENNIAL POETRY CELEBRATION (READINGS, LECTURES & POETRY AWARDS). READINGS BY 4 MAJOR AMERICAN POETS; LECTURES BY 7 DISTINGUISHED WEST COAST SCHOLARS; NATL POETRY COMPETITION, $1,000 IN AWARDS; COURSES INCORPORATING PUBLIC EVENTS THROUGH ENGLISH & CONTINUING EDUCATION DEPTS, RESIDENCIES BY POETS; LECTURES & PUBLISHED SAN JOSE STUDIES. AT STUDENT UNION BALLROOM (LOMA PRIETA ROOM). (REGN'L). NAOMI CLARK, EXEC CORD; CITY OF SAN JOSE, SAN JOSE STATE UNIV, ASSOCIATED STUDENTS, SJSU; ENG DEPT, SAN JOSE STATE UNIV; SAN JOSE, CA 95070. (#104371-3).

FEB 27 - MAR 6, '76. THEATER PRODUCTION 'BROADWAY'. LIVE PERFORMANCE AT UNIVERSITY THEATRE. (LOCAL). STANLEY C BENZ, COUNSELOR; UNIVERSITY THEATRE; SAN JOSE STATE UNIV; SAN JOSE, CA 95192. (#103394-12).

FEB 28 - MAR 6, '76. MUSICAL PERFORMANCES & LECTURES OF MUSIC BY HARRY PARTCH. SAN JOSE SYMPHONY BICENTENNIAL SEASON. A CONCERT SEASON FEATURING GUEST APPEARANCES OF THE NATION'S GREATEST LIVING COMPOSERS PERFORMING THEIR FINEST CONTEMPORARY WORKS. (LOCAL). DON THOMSON; SAN JOSE SYMPHONY ASSOC; ST CLAIRE HOTEL, SUITE 210; SAN JOSE, CA 95113. (#2835-505).

MAR 1 - APR 30, '76. EXHIBIT: ORGANIZED BASEBALL THE 1ST 100 YEARS. MEMORABILIA RELATED TO MAJOR LEAGUE BASEBALL FROM 1876-1976; MAJOR EMPHASIS WILL BE ON MAJOR LEAGUES, PACIFIC COAST LEAGUE, CALIFORNIA LEAGUE AND LOCAL SEMI PROS. AT MAIN LOBBY, SAN JOSE CITY HALL & MAIN LIBRARY. (LOCAL). JOHN E SPALDING, DIRECTOR; JOHN E SPALDING; 5551 FERN DR; SAN JOSE, CA 95124. (#104982-2).

MAR 2, '76. 'ANTONIA BRICO, A PORTRAIT OF A WOMAN' FILM PRESENTATION. LIVE PERFORMANCE AT SAN JOSE CITY COLLEGE GYMNASIUM. (LOCAL). STANLEY C BENZ, COUNSELOR; SANT CLARA COUNTY COLLEGE AND UNIVERSITIES CONSORTIUM; SAN JOSE STATE UNIV; SAN JOSE, CA 95192. (#103394-6).

MAR 3, '76. LECTURE BY DR ROY HARVEY PEARCE. DR ROY HARVEY PEARCE WILL LECTURE ON 'POETRY OF THE REVOLUTIONARY PERIOD.'. AT STUDENT UNION. (LOCAL). STANLEY C BENZ, COUNSELOR; ENGLISH DEPT, SAN JOSE STATE UNIV; SAN JOSE, CA 95192. (#103394-27).

MAR 5, '76. SYMPHONIC BAND CONCERT, ANTONIA BRICO CONDUCTING. LIVE PERFORMANCE AT SAN JOSE CITY COLLEGE GYMNASIUM. (LOCAL). STANLEY C BENZ, COUNSELOR; SANT CLARA COUNTY COLLEGE AND UNIVERSITIES CONSORTIUM; SAN JOSE STATE UNIV; SAN JOSE, CA 95192. (#103394-5).

MAR 10, '76. LECTURE BY DR ROBERT WOODWARD. THE THEME OF THE LECTURE WILL BE 'POETRY OF THE AMERICAN RENAISSANCE.'. AT STUDENT UNION. (LOCAL). STANLEY C BENZ, COUNSELOR; ENGLISH DEPT, SAN JOSE STATE UNIV; SAN JOSE, CA 95192. (#103394-26).

MAR 14 - APR 28, '76. CURRIER AND IVES EXHIBITION OF ORIGINAL AMERICAN SCENIC LITHOGRAPHS. DRAWING TO BE HELD APRIL 28TH AT 3 PM TO GIVE AWAY 9 SETS OF CURRIER AND IVES PRINTS DEPICTING AMERICAN HERITAGE SCENES; 12 PLATES TO A SET; 2ND PRIZE IS A CURRIER AND IVES 1876 CALENDAR. AT WELLS FARGO BANK, 1ST FLOOR LOBBY, 1900 THE ALAMEDA. (LOCAL). ISAAC P CALDWELL, III; CENTRAL COAST INSURANCE AND FINANCIAL SERVICES; 1922 THE ALAMEDA, #104; SAN JOSE, CA 95126. (#106650-3).

MAR 17, '76. LECTURE BY WILLIAM EVERSON. MR EVERSON WILL LECTURE ON REGIONALISM AND THE EFFECT OF PLACE ON AMERICAN POETRY. AT STUDENT UNION. (LOCAL). STANLEY C BENZ, COUNSELOR; ENGLISH DEPT, SAN JOSE STATE UNIV; SAN JOSE, CA 95192. (#103394-25).

MAR 18, '76. BICENTENNIAL YOUTH MUSIC FESTIVAL. PROGRAM WILL FEATURE BANDS AND CHOIRS FROM 9 HIGH SCHOOLS OF THE EAST SIDE UNION HIGH SCHOOL DISTRICT AND WILL INCLUDE NUMBERS BY A MASSED CHOIR AND AN ALL-STAR HONOR BAND. AT SAN JOSE CENTER FOR THE PERFORMING ARTS. (LOCAL). HENRY C JENSEN, DIR; EAST SIDE UNION HIGH SCHOOL DISTRICT; 12660 N CAPITOL AVE; SAN JOSE, CA 95123. (#102298-1).

MAR 20, '76. FLORES MEXICANAS 1776-1976, QUEEN CONTEST, DANCE, MUSIC & ART. QUEEN CONTEST, MUSIC, DANCING & ART. AT PAVILION BLDG/SANTA CLARA CO FAIRGROUNDS, 344 TULLY RD. (LOCAL). MS MARIE DUPUIS, SEC; SAN JOSE CHAPTER, AMERICAN GI FORUM; 1290 SUNDOWN LN; SAN JOSE, CA 95127. (#100940-1).

MAR 24, '76. POETRY READINGS BY HOWARD NEMERON. LIVE PERFORMANCE AT STUDENT UNION. (LOCAL). STANLEY C BENZ, COUNSELOR; ENGLISH DEPT, SAN JOSE STATE UNIV; SAN JOSE, CA 95192. (#103394-24).

MAR 24 - 26, '76. ANZA EXPEDITION 1976. GILROY MORGAN HILL SAN MARTIN PLAN A BARBECUE AND FIESTA AN EXPEDITION PASSES THROUGH OAK PLANS ACTIVITY AT VA HOSPITAL OR PALO ALTO TREE LOS ALTOS AND LOS ALTOS HILLS MAY HOLD FIESTA. AT CAMP 92 LLAGAS CREEK CAMP 93 STEVENS CREEK. (LOCAL). HELEN SCHROPSCHIRE; CALIFORNIA HERITAGE GUIDES; 181 PACIFIC ST; MONTEREY, CA 93940. (#50699-1).

MAR 27, '76. GIRL SCOUT CAMP FIRE BICENTENNIAL FAIR. EXHIBIT, LIVE PERFORMANCE AT SANTA CLARA COUNTY FAIRGROUNDS. (LOCAL). LUCIA ROTHGEB, COORD; GIRL SCOUTS AND CAMPFIRE GIRLS COUNCILS OF SANTA CLARA COUNTY, CA; 1030 S WINCHESTER BLVD; SAN JOSE, CA 95128. (#103762-1).

MAR 28, '76. SONG TO AMERICA. LIVE PERFORMANCE AT SAN JOSE COMMUNITY THEATER. (LOCAL). WALDO C ESTRADA; LICEO CUBANO INC; 2912 CABRILLA AVE; SANTA CLARA, CA 95051. (#200006-121).

MAR 31, '76. LECTURE ON AMERICAN WOMEN POETS BY ALBERT & BARBARA GELPI. LIVE PERFORMANCE AT STUDENT UNION. (LOCAL). STANLEY C BENZ, COUNSELOR; ENGLISH DEPT, SAN JOSE STATE UNIV; SAN JOSE, CA 95192. (#103394-23).

APR 1, '76 - JULY 4, '77. HISTORICAL WALKING TOUR OF DOWNTOWN SAN JOSE. HISTORICAL WALKING TOURS FOR GROUPS OF TEN TO TWENTY-FIVE BY ADVANCE RESERVATION. AT DOWNTOWN SAN JOSE. (ST-WIDE). KATHIE KEELEY; SAN JOSE CHAMBER OF COMMERCE; 165 W SAN CARLOS STREET; SAN JOSE, CA 95114. (#50590-1).

APR 2 - 10, '76. OPERA PERFORMANCES & LECTURES BY VIRGIL THOMSON. SAN JOSE SYMPHONY BICENTENNIAL SEASON. A CONCERT SEASON FEATURING GUEST APPEARANCES OF THE NATION'S GREATEST LIVING COMPOSERS PERFORMING THEIR FINEST CONTEMPORARY WORKS. (LOCAL). DON THOMSON; SAN JOSE SYMPHONY ASSOC; ST CLAIRE HOTEL, SUITE 210; SAN JOSE, CA 95113. (#2835-506).

APR 2 - 10, '76. THEATRE PRODUCTION 'WHEN YOU COMING BACK RED RYDER?'. LIVE PERFORMANCE AT UNIVERSITY THEATRE. (LOCAL). STANLEY C BENZ, COUNSELOR; THEATRE ARTS DEPT, SAN JOSE STATE UNIV; SAN JOSE STATE UNIV; SAN JOSE, CA 95192. (#103394-11).

APR 2 - 22, '76. 'RACOONS AND APPLETREES' PLAY PRODUCTION. LIVE PERFORMANCE AT IDYLWILD CENTER, 1975 CAMBRIANNA DR. (LOCAL). MYRA DUBOWSKY, DIRECTOR; SAN JOSE PARKS AND RECREATION, JUNIOR THEATER; 5175 UNION AVE; SAN JOSE, CA 95117. (#106734-1).

APR 6, '76. LECTURE-CONCERT, VIRGIL THOMPSON AS GUEST ARTIST. LIVE PERFORMANCE AT CONCERT HALL. (LOCAL). STANLEY C BENZ, COUNSELOR; MUSIC DEPT, SAN JOSE STATE UNIV; SAN JOSE, CA 95192. (#103394-30).

APR 7, '76. POETRY READINGS. LIVE PERFORMANCE AT STUDENT UNION. (LOCAL). STANLEY C BENZ, COUNSELOR; ENGLISH DEPT, SAN JOSE STATE UNIV; SAN JOSE, CA 95192. (#103394-22).

APR 9 - MAY 2, '76. BICENTENNIAL JAZZ FAIRE IV. LIVE PERFORMANCE AT SAN JOSE STATE & PERFORMING ARTS CENTER. (LOCAL). BILL POWERS, PROJ DIR; SANTA CLARA COUNTY MUSIC MERCHANTS ASSOC; 448 WINCHESTER BLVD; SAN JOSE, CA 95128. (#104498-1).

APR 10 - 11, '76. INTER-AMERICAN WOMEN WRITERS CONFERENCE. 'LATIN AMERICAN LITERARY REVIEW' WILL INCLUDE THE FOLLOWING UNIVERSITIES: CABRILLO COLLEGE OF APTOS, CA; STANFORD UNIV, CA; STATE UNIV AT LOS ANGELES; UNIV OF CALIFORNIA AT SANTA CRUZ AND CARNEGIE-MELLON UNIV. AT SAN JOSE STATE UNIV FOREIGN LANGUAGE DEPT. (LOCAL). STANLEY C BENZ, COUNSELOR; FOREIGN LANGUAGE DEPT, SAN JOSE STATE UNIV; SAN JOSE, CA 95192. (#103394-1).

APR 10, '76 - CONTINUING . PHOTOGRAPHY EXHIBIT SHOWING DEVELOPMENT OF PHOTOGRAPHIC PROCESSES. EXHIBIT AT ART BLDG, SAN JOSE STATE UNIV. (LOCAL). STANLEY C BENZ, COUNSELOR; ART DEPT OF SAN JOSE STATE UNIV; SAN JOSE, CA 95192. (#103339-1).

APR 21, '76. AMERICAN ETHNIC POETRY - DR ARNOLD RAMPERSAD. LIVE PERFORMANCE AT STUDENT UNION. (LOCAL). STANLEY C BENZ, COUNSELOR; ENGLISH DEPT, SAN JOSE STATE UNIV; SAN JOSE, CA 95192. (#103394-21).

APR 23, '76. RETIRED SENIOR VOLUNTEER PROGRAM RECOGNITION LUNCHEON. FESTIVAL AT LOUS VILLAGE, 1465 W SAN CARLOS. (LOCAL). CURTIS HANSEN, DIRECTOR; RETIRED SENIOR VOLUNTEER PROGRAM, CITY OF SAN JOSE; 199 N 3RD ST; SAN JOSE, CA 95112. (#106650-1).

APR 23 - MAY 1, '76. SYMPHONY PERFORMANCES & LECTURES BY LOU HARRISON. SAN JOSE SYMPHONY BICENTENNIAL SEASON. A CONCERT SEASON FEATURING GUEST APPEARANCES OF THE NATION'S GREATEST LIVING COMPOSERS PERFORMING THEIR FINEST CONTEMPORARY WORKS. (LOCAL). DON THOMSON; SAN JOSE SYMPHONY ASSOC; ST CLAIRE HOTEL, SUITE 210; SAN JOSE, CA 95113. (#2835-507).

APR 24, '76. RECITAL PERFORMANCE BY LEONTYNE PRICE. SAN JOSE SYMPHONY BICENTENNIAL SEASON. A CONCERT SEASON FEATURING GUEST APPEARANCES OF THE NATION'S GREATEST LIVING COMPOSERS PERFORMING THEIR FINEST CONTEMPORARY WORKS. (LOCAL). DON THOMSON; SAN JOSE SYMPHONY ASSOC; ST CLAIRE HOTEL, SUITE 210; SAN JOSE, CA 95113. (#2835-508).

APR 27, '76. LECTURE-CONCERT, LOU HARRISON AS GUEST ARTIST AT SJSU. LIVE PERFORMANCE AT CONCERT HALL. (LOCAL). STANLEY C BENZ, COUNSELOR; MUSIC DEPT, SAN JOSE STATE UNIV; SAN JOSE, CA 95192. (#103394-29).

APR 28, '76. POETRY READINGS BY GWENDOLYN BROOKS. LIVE PERFORMANCE AT STUDENT UNION. (LOCAL). STANLEY C BENZ, COUNSELOR; ENGLISH DEPT, SAN JOSE STATE UNIV; SAN JOSE, CA 95192. (#103394-20).

MAY 1 - 2, '76. BONSAI CLUB SPRING BONSAI EXHIBITION & CELEBRATION. BONSAI DEMONSTRATIONS BOTH DAYS, DOOR PRIZES AND AFTERNOON TEA. AT SAN JOSE BUDDHIST CHURCH, 640 N 5TH ST. (LOCAL). GEORGE M ITAYA, V-PRES; SAN JOSE BONSAI CLUB; 31 N HARDY AVE; CAMPBELL, CA 95008. (#106650-2).

MAY 5, '76. POETRY READINGS BY WILLIAM EVERSON. LIVE PERFORMANCE AT STUDENT UNION. (LOCAL). STANLEY C BENZ, COUNSELOR; ENGLISH DEPT, SAN JOSE STATE UNIV; SAN JOSE, CA 95192. (#103394-19).

MAY 7 - 15, '76. THEATRE PRODUCTION 'REGINA'. LIVE PERFORMANCE AT UNIVERSITY THEATRE. (LOCAL). STANLEY C BENZ, COUNSELOR; THEATRE ARTS DEPT, SAN JOSE STATE UNIV; SAN JOSE STATE UNIV; SAN JOSE, CA 95192. (#103394-10).

MAY 9 - 10, '76. SANTA CLARA COUNTY ROSE SOCIETY GOLDEN ANNIVERSARY SHOW. SPECIAL GOLD TROPHY TO BE AWARDED TO MARK THE SCC ROSE SOCIETY'S 50TH YEAR. AT LEININGER CENTER KELLEY PARK, SENTER AVE, OCTAGON RM. (LOCAL). STANLEY G BURRIS, DIR; SANTA CLARA COUNTY ROSE SOCIETY; 942 SO CLOVER AVE; SAN JOSE, CA 95128. (#106734-2).

MAY 11, '76. NETHERLANDS CHAMBER ORCHESTRA VISITS SAN JOSE. LIVE PERFORMANCE. (INT'L). WILLIAM SIMONSZ, COORD; NETHERLANDS GOVERNMENT; NETHERLANDS EMBASSY-4200 LINNEAN; WASHINGTON, DC 20008. (#109013-21).

MAY 12, '76. 'RECENT AMERICAN POETRY' BY THOMAS A VOGLER. LIVE PERFORMANCE AT STUDENT UNION. (LOCAL). STANLEY C BENZ, COUNSELOR; ENGLISH DEPT, SAN JOSE STATE UNIV; SAN JOSE, CA 95192. (#103394-18).

MAY 15, '76. COMMUNITY BANQUET HONORING RABBI JOSEPH GITIN. CEREMONY, FESTIVAL AT MEDITERRANEAN ROOM, SAN JOSE HYATT HOUSE. (LOCAL). JOSEPHINE NAYMARK, CHMN; TEMPLE EMANUEL; 230 WOODED VIEW DR; LOS GATOS, CA 95030. (#104699-1).

MAY 17 - 23, '76. BICENTENNIAL WEEK AT NODDIN. EVENTS FOR WEEK INCLUDE CEREMONY FOR TIME CAPSULE, CONCERT AND MUSEUM DISPLAY. AT NODDIN ELEMENTARY SCHOOL, 1755 GILDA WAY. (LOCAL). DIANA J MACMILLAN, COORD; NODDIN ELEMENTARY SCHOOL AND NODDIN HOME AND SCHOOL CLUB; 1756 CHEVALIER DR; SAN JOSE, CA 95124. (#200006-83).

MAY 21, '76. 'TIME' - A MUSICAL COMEDY PLUS A FASHION SHOW OF THE PAST. PLAY TELLING THE COUNTRY'S HISTORY. CAST INCLUDES: CHOIR & ACTORS MADE UP OF 44 KINDERGARTEN THROUGH 6TH GRADERS. AT SCHOOL CAFETERIA, PARKING LOT IN FRONT. (LOCAL). DIANA MACMILLAN, COORD; NODDIN ELEMENTARY SCHOOL, HOME & SCHOOL CLUB & DRAMA GROUP; 1756 CHEVALIER DR; SAN JOSE, CA 95124. (#200006-84).

JUNE 1 - 3, '76. 'THE MOTHER OF US ALL' - CHAMBER OPERA BY V THOMPSON & G STEIN. GETTE LEADER, SUSAN BROWNELL ANTHONY. WORK BRINGS TOGETHER A COLORFULL ASSORTMENT OF CHARACTERS FROM THE PAST, INCLUDING DANIEL WEBS STER, JOHN ADAMS, ULYSSES S GRANT & LILLIAN RUSSELL. AT MONTGOMERY THEATER, MARKET & SAN CARLOS STS. (LOCAL). ROBERT HUBBARD, BUS MGR; PORT COSTA CONCERT CORP; 311 FULTON; PALO ALTO, CA 94301. (#106401-1).

JUNE 11, '76. 'I AM AN AMERICAN'. PROGRAM HONORING ADULT STUDENTS OF VARIOUS ETHNIC ORIGINS WHO HAVE COMPLETED CLASSES IN CITIZENSHIP DURING THE 1975/1976 SCHOOL YEAR. AT SAN JOSE HIGH SCHOOL AUDITORIUM. (LOCAL). ESTHER L STONE, COORD; METROPOLITAN ADULT EDUCATION PROGRAM; 1671 PARK AVE; SAN JOSE, CA 95126. (#200006-324).

JUNE 12 - JULY 28, '76. EXHIBIT: 'AN ARTIST IN SEARCH OF AMERICA' BY JANET KRUSKAMP. MUSEUM HOURS MON, SAT & SUN 12 PM TO 5 PM, 9 AM TO 5 PM ALL OTHER DAYS. AT ROSICRUCIAN-EGYPTIAN MUSEUM & ART GALLERY, PARK & NAGLEE STS. (LOCAL). BURNAM SCHAA, CURATOR; THE ROSICRUCIAN ORDER AMORC; ROSICRUCIAN PARK; SAN JOSE, CA 95191. (#102439-2).

JUNE 13, '76. 'HONOR THE FLAG' - BICENTENNIAL FLAG DAY PARADE. PARADE. (LOCAL). LOUIS A ROSSI, GEN CHMN; SAN JOSE LODGE - 522 BPO ELKS; BANK OF AMER BLDG; SAN JOSE, CA 95113. (#107520-1).

JULY 3, '76. BICENTENNIAL CONCERT BY THE LICEO CUBANO. LIVE PERFORMANCE. (LOCAL). WALDO C ESTRADA, COORD; LICEO CUBANA, INC; 2912 CABRILLA AVE; SANTA CLARA, CA 95051. (#200006-313).

JULY 3, '76. GERMANIA VEREIN BICENTENNIAL CELEBRATION DANCE. FESTIVAL AT GERMANIA HALL. (LOCAL). UTE M LORENZ, EXEC SEC; GERMANIA VEREIN, INC; 261 N 2ND ST; SAN JOSE, CA 95112. (#108832-1).

SAN JOSE — CONTINUED

JULY 3, '76. SUPER VETERANS BICYCLE RACE - OPEN FOR 60 YRS & OLDER. COMPETITION. (REGN'L). ED STEFFANI, PRESIDENT; SAN JOSE BICYCLE CLUB; 17281 EL RANCHO; MONTE SERENO, CA 95030. (#108059-2).

JULY 3 - 4, '76. QUILTING EXHIBIT. DISPLAY OF BICENTENNIAL QUILTS DEPICTING AMERICA FROM THE RESIDENTS' POINT OF VIEW. (LOCAL). ALENA WILLCOXEN, CHWMN; SAN JOSE BICENTENNIAL COMMISSION, INC; 165 W SAN CARLOS ST; SAN JOSE, CA 95113. (#104982-1).

JULY 3 - 4, '76. TAPESTRY 'N TALENT. 2 DAY FESTIVAL UTILIZING MULTI-CULTURAL TALENTS OF COMMUNITY IN HERITAGE, ARTS & CULTURE. THERE WILL BE OVER 10,000 PARTICIPANTS RANGING FROM AGE 6 TO THE OLDEST LIVING CITIZEN. EMPHASIS WILL BE ON THE CONTRIBUTIONS OF ALL CULTURES. AT DOWNTOWN AREA. (LOCAL). BETTY EILER, CHAIRMAN; SAN JOSE BICENTENNIAL COMMISSION & FESTIVAL ARTS TASK FORCE; 165 W SAN CARLOS; SAN JOSE, CA 95114. (#2829-1).

JULY 4, '76. AN AMERICAN PLEDGE - TIME CAPSULE WILL BE BURIED. SIGNED PLEDGES WILL BE BURIED AT REID-HILLVIEW AIRPORT. (LOCAL). LT HUGO H BAYONA, CHMN; CIVIL AIR PATROL/AUXILIARY US AIR FORCE-PENINSULA GROUP 2; PO BOX 4752; SANTA CLARA, CA 95054. (#104982-4).

JULY 4, '76. TREE PLANTING PROJECT: A BIRTHDAY SALUTE. 199 TREES HAVE BEEN PLANTED AT REID-HILLVIEW AIRPORT. THE 200TH TREE WILL BE PLANTED ON THE 4TH OF JULY, AND A CEREMONY WILL BE HELD. AT REID-HILLVIEW AIRPORT. (LOCAL). 2ND LT HUGO H BAYONA; CIVIL AIR PATROL/AUXILIARY U S AIR FORCE - PENINSULA GROUP 2; PO BOX 4752; SANTA CLARA, CA 95054. (#22525-1).

JULY 4 - 5, '76. ART CIRCUS. PAPIER MACHE ANIMALS AND ORIGINAL BICENTENNIAL THEME BANNERS DONE BY ELEMENTARY SCHOOL CHILDREN WILL BE ON EXHIBIT IN THE ARTS FESTIVAL. AT CITY CULTURAL CENTER. (LOCAL). BARBARA CASSIN, TEACHER; CORY ELEMENTARY SCHOOL; 2367 NEWHALL ST; SAN JOSE, CA 95128. (#106221-1).

JULY 11, '76. HISTORICAL BIKE TOUR. TOUR. (LOCAL). R CHARLES STEVENS, PRES; SANTA CLARA VALLEY CLUB; PO BOX 24999; SAN JOSE, CA 95154. (#108924-1).

AUG 14 - 19, '76. THOROBRED LEAGUE BASEBALL WORLD SERIES - NATIONAL COMPETITIN. COMPETITION AT PAL STADIUM. (NAT'L). MIKE PEREIRA, DIRECTOR; J AND J SPORTS; SAN JOSE POLICE ATHLETIC LEAGUE; 1457 W SAN CARLOS; SAN JOSE, CA 95126. (#107520-2).

AUG 15, '76. MOONLIGHT BIKE RALLY. TOUR AT ARCH OF SANTA CLARA COUNTY FAIRGROUNDS. (LOCAL). R CHARLES STEVENS, PRES; SANTA CLARA VALLEY CLUB; PO BOX 24999; SAN JOSE, CA 95154. (#108907-1).

AUG 16 - 22, '76. FIESTA DEL PUEBLO. EXHIBIT, FAIR, FESTIVAL AT VARIOUS LOCATIONS IN SAN JOSE. (LOCAL). JOHN ZAMORA, PROJ DIR; SAN JOSE MEXICAN-AMERICAN CHAMBER OF COMMERCE; 235 E SANTA CLARA ST; SAN JOSE, CA 95113. (#100705-1).

SEPT 4 - 6, '76. AMERICAN RADIO RELAY LEAGUE-PACIFIC DIVISION CONVENTION. MEETING OF AMATEUR RADIO OPERATORS & PERSONS INTERESTED IN RADIO COMMUNICATIONS AS A HOBBY AND PUBLIC SERVICE. CONVENTION WILL FEATURE SPEAKERS AND EXHIBITS PERTAINING TO AMATEUR RADIO; TOURS AND A PROGRAM FOR LADIES AND FAMILIES ALSO INCLUDED. AT SAN JOSE HYATT HOUSE HOTEL, 1740 N FIRST ST. (LOCAL). R W MICHELSON, DIRECTOR; ASSOCIATED RADIO CLUBS OF SAN JOSE & AMERICAN RADIO RELAY LEAGUE; PO BOX 6; SAN JOSE, CA 95103. (#104984-1).

SEPT 27 - OCT 2, '76. SINO-AMERICAN WEEK. EXHIBIT, FESTIVAL, LIVE PERFORMANCE AT SAN JOSE AREA. (LOCAL). FRANK LOWE, PROJ DIRECTOR; CHINESE COMMUNITY IN SAN JOSE; 2819 CUNNINGHAM AVE; SAN JOSE, CA 95122. (#100704-1).

OCT 8 - 10, '76. 20TH ANNUAL JUBILEE CONVENTION - SQUARE DANCE. DEMONSTRATIONS DEPICTING THE HISTORY OF SQUARE DANCING; EXHIBITS & EDUCATIONAL EVENTS WILL ALSO BE FEATURED. AT SANTA CLARA COUNTY FAIRGROUNDS-PAVILION BLDG. (ST-WIDE). BOB FERBER, CHMN; SANTA CLARA VALLEY SQUARE DANCERS ASSOC; PO BOX 1559; LOS GATOS, CA 95030. (#104983-1).

OCT 10 - 11, '76. UNITED STATES ARMED FORCES BICENTENNIAL CARAVAN. CARAVAN IS COMPOSED OF EXHIBIT VANS FOR EACH MILITARY SERVICE. PROJECT THEME IS 'HISTORY OF THE ARMED FORCES & THEIR CONTRIBUTIONS TO THE NATION'. (LOCAL). LOUIS A ROSSI, CHMN; UNITED STATES ARMED FORCES BICENTENNIAL CARAVAN; C/O AMER LEGN, PO BOX 1306; SAN JOSE, CA 95108. (#1775-822).

NOV 4 - 6, '76. THEATREAMERICANA. UNIVERSITY DANCE AND MUSIC DEPTS WILL COMBINE TO PERFORM SEVERAL DANCE WORKS: 1)'THE SHAKERS', RECONSTRUCTED FROM LABANOTATION SCORES, ORIGINAL CHOREOGRAPHY BY DORIS HUMPHREY;2) EXPERIMENTAL JAZZ WORK AND 3) 'JOHNNY APPLESEED', MUSIC BY LOU HARRISON. AT UNIVERSITY THEATRE. (LOCAL). ANNETTE MACDONALD, COORD; SAN JOSE STATE UNIVERSITY THEATRE ARTS DEPT, DANCE FACULTY; SAN JOSE, CA 95192. (#106221-3).

MAR 26 - APR 2, '77. JAPANESE AMERICAN COMMUNITY BICENTENNIAL WEEK. MARTIAL ARTS: KARATE, KENDO, JUDO, HIKIDO & SUMO. FINE ARTS: IKEBANA, DOLL MAKING, BRUSH PAINTING, BONSAI, PRINT MAKING, KOTO, SHAKUHACHI, SHAMISEN, BUYO, MINYO, GAGAKU & TAIKO. PHOTO ESSAY, POTTERY, SCULPTURE, BLOCK PRINTING & SYMPHONIC CONCERT. AT SAN JOSE CNTR FOR THE PERFORMING ARTS, CIVIC AUD, SJ BUDDHIST CHURCH. (LOCAL). RICHARD K TANAKA, CHMN; JAPANESE AMERICAN COMMUNITY; 14811 WHIPPLE CT; SAN JOSE, CA 95127. (#100703-1).

APR 1 - OCT 15, '77. GUIDED WALKING TOUR OF HISTORIC SAN JOSE BY APPOINTMENT. GUIDED WALKING TOUR OF DOWNTOWN SAN JOSE, WITH EMPHASIS ON HISTORICAL POINTS OF INTEREST & HISTORY OF SAN JOSE. (LOCAL). KATHIE KEELEY; SAN JOSE CHAMBER OF COMMERCE; 165 W SAN CARLOS ST; SAN JOSE, CA 95114. (#8394-503).

MAY 5 - 8, '77. 77 RAILS WEST - MODEL RAILROAD CONVENTION. SEMINARS ON THE HISTORY OF RAILROADS IN THE SAN JOSE AREA WILL BE HELD & THERE WILL BE AN ART SHOW OF CLASSIC PAINTINGS & ILLUSTRATIONS; THERE WILL BE OPERATING MODEL RAILROAD DISPLAYS WITH TOY & SCALE TRAINS FROM ALL PERIODS. AT SAN JOSE CIVIC AUDITORIUM & CONVENTION CENTER. (REGN'L). MICHAEL F KOTOWSKI, CHMN; CALIFORNIA MODEL RAILROAD CLUB INC & PACIFIC COAST REGION NMRA; 393 E HAMILTON, SUITE E; CAMPBELL, CA 95008. (#108907-2).

NOV 1 - 30, '77. UPTOWN, DOWNTOWN - ART EXHIBIT. THE ART EXHIBIT WILL FEATURE AREA SCENES FOR THE CITY'S 200TH BIRTHDAY. AT SAN JOSE PUBLIC LIBRARY, 180 W SAN CARLOS ST. (LOCAL). BARBARA CASSIN, ARTIST; BARBARA CASSIN; 2367 NEWHALL ST; SAN JOSE, CA 95128. (#103977-1).

NOV 25, '77. SAN JOSE BICENTENNIAL CHILDREN'S CHRISTMAS PARADE. 10000 PARTICIPANTS, GALA HISTORICAL FLOATS, GIGANTIC BALLOONS. AT DOWNTOWN SAN JOSE. (LOCAL). JOHN F BRANTON; SAN JOSE JAYCEES; 349 SO MONROE ST; SAN JOSE, CA 95128. (#50558-1).

SAN JUAN CAPI

A NEW FLAG FOR SAN JUAN CAPISTRANO, CA. 100 FOOT POLE WITH TWELVE BY TWENTY FOUR FOOT FLAG TO BE PLACED IN CITY. (LOCAL). MRS MURIEL SURLES, CHAIRMAN; SAN JUAN CAPISTRANO BICENTENNIAL COMMITTEE; PO BOX 1776; SN JUN CPSTRN, CA 92675. (#5873). **(??).**

200 BY 1976 PROJECT OF SAN JUAN CAPISTRANO, CA. 200 TREES WILL BE PLANTED WITHIN THE CITY TO COMMEMORATE THE COUNTRY'S BIRTHDAY. (LOCAL). G R DURENBERGER, PRESIDENT; SAN JUAN BEAUTIFUL INCORPORATED; PO BOX 301; SN JUN CPSTRN, CA 92675. (#5872).

JAN 19 - 20, '76. AMERICAN FREEDOM TRAIN DISPLAY DAYS AT SAN JUAN CAPISTRANO. THE AMERICAN FREEDOM TRAIN WILL INCLUDE 10 EXHIBIT CARS & 2 SHOWCASE CARS DEPICTING DIFFERENT PHASES OF THE AMERICAN EXPERIENCE. ITS ARRIVAL WILL SERVE AS A CATALYST FOR LOCAL BICENTENNIAL CELEBRATIONS BY PEOPLE THROUGHOUT THIS NATION. (ST-WIDE). SY FREEDMAN, DIR OF P/R; THE AMERICAN FREEDOM TRAIN FOUNDATION; 5205 LEESBURG PIKE, SUITE 800; BAILEY'S XRDS, VA 22041. (#1776-147).

FEB 15 - MAR 30, '76. OUR NATION'S FIRST LADIES EXHIBIT. COLLECTION OF BEAUTIFUL HANDCRAFTED FIGURINES WEARING GOWNS OF OUR NATIONS FIRST LADIES. AT MAGGIS COUNTRY STORE. (LOCAL). MRS MURIEL E SURLES; SAN JUAN CAPISTRANO BICENTENNIAL COMMITTEE; PO BOX 1776; SN JUN CPSTRN, CA 92675. (#5874-1).

MAR 19, '76. ST JOSEPH'S DAY. THE SCHOOL CHILDREN OF THE MISSION SCHOOL PRESENT A PAGEANT OF OLD SPANISH AND INDIAN DANCES ON ST JOSEPH'S DAY AT THE MISSION. (ST-WIDE). TED CROSSMAN, COORD; MISSION SAN JUAN CAPISTRANO; PO BOX 532; SAN JUAN CAPI, CA 92675. (#105691-1).

MAR 20, '76. FIESTA DE LAS GOLANDRINAS PARADE. RETURN OF SWALLOWS TO MISSION. PARADE IS EQUESTRIAN; NO MOTORED VEHICLES ALLOWED. AT MISSION SAN JUAN CAPISTRANO. (ST-WIDE). TED CROSSMAN, COORD; SAN JUAN CAPISTRANO FIESTA ASS'N; PO BOX 532; SAN JUAN CAPI, CA 92675. (#103416-214).

SAN LEANDRO

BICENTENNIAL STATIONERY IN SAN LEANDRO, CA. BOND PAPER BEARING STATE EMBLEM IN WATER MARK IN HONOR OF THE BICENTENNIAL. (ST-WIDE). HAROLD BUSCH, PRINTING REP; BILLINGS PRINTING AND STATIONERY; 16875 E 14TH ST; SAN LEANDRO, CA 94578. (#11366).

BROOKS-MATHEWS BUILDING, SAN LEANDRO, CA. PRIVATE REDEVELOPMENT OF 6 PROPERTIES WHICH ARE SITUATED IN THE CENTER OF THE CITY. (LOCAL). MRS BARBARA MATHEWS BROOKS, COORDINATOR; WILLIAM MATHEWS AGENCY, INC; 1793 E 14TH ST; SAN LEANDRO, CA 94577. (#20748).

CITY-WIDE BLOOD DRIVE, SAN LEANDRO, CA. ALL FACETS OF SAN LEANDRO WILL BE ENCOURAGED TO DONATE BLOOD AND THUS ESTABLISH AN ACCOUNT AT THE BLOOD BANK TO BENEFIT MEMBERS. (LOCAL). JUNE ROUSE, PRESIDENT; DOCTORS AND SAN LEANDRO MEMORIAL HOSPITALS OF SAN LEANDRO; 2800 BENEDICT DR; SAN LEANDRO, CA 94577. (#13385).

CONSTRUCTION & DEDICATION OF MULFORD LIBRARY, CA. IMPROVED BRANCH LIBRARY FACILITIES WILL BE PROVIDED FOR THE MULFORD MARINA AREA. (LOCAL). STEPHEN D EWING, LIBRARY DIRECTOR; BOARD OF LIBRARY TRUSTEES; 300 ESTUDILLO; SAN LEANDRO, CA 94577. (#20745).

FREEDOM SHRINE IN SAN LEANDRO, CA. A DISPLAY OF COPIES OF THE 28 FREEDOM DOCUMENTS FOR PUBLIC VIEWING. (LOCAL). ROBERT A TUCKNOTT, PRESIDENT; SAN LEANDRO EXCHANGE CLUB; 295 PARK ST; SAN LEANDRO, CA 94578. (#14723).

GETTING IT ALL TOGETHER, PROJ OF SAN LEANDRO, CA. THE SAN LORENZO GARDEN CLUB WILL ENCOURAGE THE BEAUTIFICATION OF COMMUNITIES WITH FLOWERS & PLANTS. (LOCAL). MRS FLO WALKER, PROJ DIRECTOR; SAN LORENZO GARDEN CLUB; 1039 DOUGLAS CT; SAN LEANDRO, CA 94577. (#20753).

LANDSCAPING FOR THE FUTURE, SAN LEANDRO, CA. LANDSCAPING WILL BE DONE TO RESTORE NATURAL AREAS IN SAN LEANDRO TO ITS ORIGINAL BEAUTY. (LOCAL). MRS H W BOLESWORTH, PRESIDENT; COMMUNITY IMPROVEMENT FOR CASA PERALTA; 1044 MARQUETTE WAY; SAN LEANDRO, CA 94577. (#20746).

PLAZA I, REDEVELOPMENT PROJECT, PHASE III PLAN, CA. 2 BLOCKS OF THE OLD COMMERCIAL SALES DISTRICT IN THE HEART OF DOWNTOWN SAN LEANDRO WILL BE REVITALIZED WITH THE CONSTRUCTION OF A NEW RETAIL COMMERCIAL CENTER. (LOCAL). WILLIAM A RUGG, COMMUNITY DEVELOPMENT DIRECTOR; REDEVELOPMENT AGENCY-DEVELOPMENT COMMITTEE-PERALTA LAND ASSOC; 835 E 14TH ST; SAN LEANDRO, CA 94577. (#22592).

REDWOOD LIBERTY TREES PRESERVATION, CA. PRESERVATION OF NATIVE REDWOOD TREES & REPLANTING OF THE FROST DAMAGED AREA ALONG JOAQUIN MILLER ROAD. (LOCAL). MRS ERNEST G DUARTE, DISTRICT IV BICENTENNIAL CHMN; 16 CHAPTERS OF DISTRICT IV DAR, EAST BAY; 1184 LOUISE ST; SAN LEANDRO, CA 94578. (#20751).

ROOSEVELT SCHOOL WALL HANGING, SAN LEANDRO, CA. EACH CLASS WILL SUBMIT ONE PATCH FOR A WALL HANGING. (LOCAL). BRENDA CAMPBELL, SECRETARY; ROOSEVELT ELEMENTARY SCHOOL; 951 DOWLING BLVD; SAN LEANDRO, CA 94577. (#20749).

ROOSEVELT SCHOOL LIVING HISTORY READING PROGRAM-CA. CHILDREN WILL READ & WRITE REPORTS ON CHARACTERS AND EVENTS IN FOUR HISTORICAL TIME PERIODS OF AMERICAN HISTORY. FOUR PROGRAMS WILL BE PRESENTED TO THE SCHOOL. (LOCAL). FRAN HALVERSON, TEACHER; ROOSEVELT SCHOOL; 951 DOWLING BLVD; SAN LEANDRO, CA 94577. (#20750).

SAN LEANDRO BICENTENNIAL BOOK, CA. A BICENTENNIAL BOOK ABOUT SAN LEANDRO WILL BE PUBLISHED. (LOCAL). WILLIAM R RUGG, PROJ COORDINATOR; COMMUNITY DEVELOPMENT OFFICE; 835 E 14TH ST; SAN LEANDRO, CA 94577. (#20752).

1976 PRESERVATION PROGRAM - SAN LEANDRO, CA. FURTHERING OBJECTIVES ON CLUB PLANNING & CIVIC & EDUCATIONAL KNOWLEDGE FOR ALL PEOPLE; THE HISTORY OF THE BUILDING & PROTECTING HISTORICAL PROPERTY. (LOCAL). BESSIE ROBERTS, PRESIDENT; ALTA MIRA CLUB, INC; 1674 MANOR BLVD; SAN LEANDRO, CA 94579. (#13389).

MAR 15, '75. MARTHA WASHINGTON TEA. FESTIVAL AT ALTA MIRA CLUB-561 LAFAYETTE AVE. (LOCAL). MRS ROBERT KOLKMANN, DIR; ALTA MIRA CLUB; 128 BEVERLY AVE; SAN LEANDRO, CA 94577. (#105001-3).

MAY 1 - JUNE 1, '75. BICENTENNIAL COLORING BOOK CONTEST. A COLORING BOOK CONTEST TO BRING TO THE ATTENTION OF 3RD, 4TH & 5TH GRADERS THE EARLY HISTORY OF OUR COUNTRY. (LOCAL). JERRY GREEN, PRESIDENT; PELTON SHOPPING CENTER; 1500 E 14TH ST; SAN LEANDRO, CA 94577. (#13384-1).

SEPT 1, '75 - JUNE 15, '76. REFLECTIONS: AMERICA ON STAGE. LIVE PERFORMANCE AT MARINA AND TEAGARDEN STS.. (ST-WIDE). LARRY J LINDA, CHMN; PACIFIC HIGH SCHOOL; 1201 MARINA BLVD; SAN LEANDRO, CA 94577. (#100360-1).

SEPT 28, '75. BANQUET IN HONOR OF PORTUGUESE HERITAGE & JUAN RODRIGUES CABRILLO. CEREMONY. (LOCAL). FRANK B SILVA, DIRECTOR; CABRILLO CIVIC CLUB NO 11 - ALAMEDA CO; IDES HALL, ANTONIO ST; SAN LEANDRO, CA 94577. (#102069-2).

SEPT 28, '75. RE-ENACTMENT OF THE JUAN RODRIGUES CABRILLO LANDING IN CALIFORNIA. THE FESTIVAL WILL EMPHASIZE THE HERITAGE & CONTRIBUTIONS OF THE PORTUGUESE TO AMERICA. AT SAN LEANDRO MARINA. (LOCAL). FRANK B SILVA, DIRECTOR; CABRILLO CIVIC CLUB NO 11 - ALAMEDA CO; IDES HALL, ANTONIO ST; SAN LEANDRO, CA 94577. (#102069-1).

JAN 26, '76. ANNUAL BIRTHDAY LUNCHEON & BICENTENNIAL CELEBRATION. FESTIVAL. (LOCAL). BESSIE ROBERTS; GENERAL ASSEMBLY & EXECUTIVE BOARD OF ALTA MIRA; 561 LAFAYETTE AVE; SAN LEANDRO, CA 94577. (#200006-132).

FEB 1 - MAR 5, '76. POSTER CONTEST FOR SCHOOL CHILDREN THROUGH 3RD GRADE. PRIZES AWARDED ON APRIL 13, 1976 AT 7:30 PM. (LOCAL). ELEANOR GEMMELL, DIR; SAN LEANDRO EMBLEM CLUB NO 386; PO BOX 767; SAN LEANDRO, CA 94577. (#105001-4).

FEB 12, '76. 200 YEARS OF AMERICAN FASHIONS. FESTIVAL AT BLUE DOLPHIN RESTAURANT. (LOCAL). MRS J WALDO RITTLER, CHMN; ALTA MIRA CLUB; 999 BEGIEL AVE; SAN LEANDRO, CA 94577. (#102070-1).

MAR 14, '76. CELEBRATION OF 200TH BIRTHDAY OF USA ENTERTAINMENT. FESTIVAL. (LOCAL). BESSIE ROBERTS, DIRECTOR; ALTA MIRA CLUB; 561 LAFAYETTE AVE; SAN LEANDRO, CA 94577. (#105001-5).

MAR 20, '76. HAPPY BIRTHDAY USA. FESTIVAL AT BLUE DOLPHIN RESTAURANT. (LOCAL). CARLOS ALMEIDA, DIRECTOR; SUPREME COUNCIL OF PORTUGUESE UNION OF CALIFORNIA; 1120 E 14TH ST; SAN LEANDRO, CA 94577. (#105001-7).

MAR 20, '76. MISS SAN LEANDRO PAGEANT. COMPETITION AT S L JUNIOR CHAMBER. (LOCAL). RUSSEL OOSTHUIZEN, DIR; SAN LEANDRO JR CHAMBER OF COMMERCE; PO BOX 776; SAN LEANDRO, CA 94577. (#105001-6).

MAR '76. HISTORICAL VARIETY SHOW. LIVE PERFORMANCE AT ASHLAND AVE. (LOCAL). LAWRENCE C LEONARD, DIR; EDENDALE JR HIGH; ASHLAND AVE; SAN LORENZO, CA 94580. (#105001-8).

APR 1, '76. RE-ENACTMENT OF THE DE ANZA EXPEDITION. PARADE. (LOCAL). STAN WILSON, DIRECTOR; SAN LEANDRO BICENTENNIAL EXECUTIVE COMMITTEE; 384 W ESTUDILLO AVE; SAN LEANDRO, CA 94577. (#105001-2).

SAN LEANDRO — CONTINUED

JULY 1 - DEC 31, '76. RAILROADS IN CALIFORNIA-U S HISTORY - EXHIBIT. EXHIBIT AT REAR OF RUSSCRAFT HOBBIES STORE, DUTTON AVE EXIT FROM MACARTHUR HWY. (LOCAL). S L DEWOLF, PRES; SAN LEANDRO MODEL RAILROAD CLUB; 685 BANCROFT AVE; SAN LEANDRO, CA 94577. (#20747-1).

OCT 9, '76. BICENTENNIAL COSTUME BALL. FESTIVAL AT VETERANS MEMORIAL BLDG. (LOCAL). EDNA LYLES, COORD; SAN LEANDRO BICENTENNIAL EXECUTIVE COMMITTEE; 384 W ESTUDILLO AVE; SAN LEANDRO, CA 94577. (#105001-1).

SAN LORENZO

EXPLORATION OF THE NEW WORLD - SAN LORENZO, CA. RESEARCH OF EXPLORATION ROUTES OF OUR ANCESTORS. (LOCAL). FRANK MARTELLA, PRINCIPAL; EDENDALE JUNIOR HIGH SCHOOL; 16160 ASHLAND AVE; SAN LORENZO, CA 94580. (#13392).

MCCONAGHY HOUSE RESTORATION IN SAN LORENZO, CA. THE MCCONAGHY HOUSE, AN 1880 VICTORIAN DWELLING WILL BE RESTORED AND OPENED TO THE PUBLIC AS AN EXHIBIT. (LOCAL). LEO J PARNEY, PRESIDENT; HAYWARD AREA HISTORICAL SOCIETY; PO BOX 555; HAYWARD, CA 94543. (#11365).

'OUR HERITAGE', PROJECT OF SAN LORENZO, CA. STUDENTS ARE COORDINATING A DISPLAY OF COSTUMES & AN 8' X 12' MAP DEPICTING EXPLORATIONS AND SHOWING RELATIONSHIP OF THE U S WITH MOTHER COUNTRIES. (LOCAL). LAWRENCE C LEONARD, PROJ COORDINATOR; EDENDALE JR HIGH SCHOOL; ASHLAND AVE; SAN LORENZO, CA 94580. (#20757).

SELLING OF BICENT FLAGS & PATRIOTIC GOODS, CA. GIRL SCOUTS WILL SELL PATRIOTIC GOODS & COLLECT SIGNATURES FOR THE PLEDGE OF REDIFICATION. (LOCAL). MRS RALPH SHERMAN, ASST CHAIRMAN; BICENTENNIAL GIRL SCOUT CADETTE TROOP #1776 OF ST FELICITAS; 17076 VIA PASATIEMPO; SAN LORENZO, CA 94580. (#20754).

'THIS IS OUR LAND' - SAN LORENZO, CA. STUDENTS WILL RESEARCH, DESIGN & CREATE A 7' X 13' MAP OF THE U S IN YARN. (LOCAL). LAWRENCE C LEONARD, PROJ CHAIRMAN; EDENDALE JR HIGH SCHOOL; ASHLAND AVE; SAN LORENZO, CA 94580. (#20756).

UNITED STATES FLAGS, SAN LORENZO, CA. STUDENTS HAVE CONSTRUCTED FELT FLAGS OF U S STATES AND 10 U S HISTORICAL FLAGS. THEY WILL HANG PERMANENTLY IN HALL OF FLAGS. (LOCAL). LAWRENCE C LEONARD, CHAIRMAN; EDENDALE JR HIGH SCHOOL; ASHLAND AVE; SAN LORENZO, CA 94580. (#20755).

AUG 15 - 16, '75. GIRL SCOUT BICENTENNIAL WAGON TRAIN VISITS. FESTIVAL. (LOCAL). BETTY MOOSE, CHMN; GIRL SCOUT TROOP #1776; 1328 VIA EL MONTE; SAN LORENZO, CA 94580. (#104996-1).

SAN LUIS OBIS

APR 21 - 24, '76. POLY ROYAL FESTIVAL 1976. BICENTENNIAL EXHIBITS; PARTICIPATION FROM APPROXIMATELY 50 DEPARTMENTS AND 40 CLUBS; INCLUDES SMITHSONIAN EXHIBITS IN AGRICULTURE AND HUMANITIES; AN ANNUAL FESTIVAL DEDICATED IN 1976 TO THE BICENTENNIAL. (LOCAL). JON M ERICSON, DEAN; CALIFORNIA POLY STATE UNIV; SN LUIS OBSPO, CA 93407. (#103797-4).

SAN MARCOS

JULY 4, '76. A PAST TO REMEMBER, A FUTURE TO MOLD FESTIVAL. FESTIVITIES WILL INCLUDE THE UNVEILING OF HISTORICAL MONUMENT, RINGING ALL CHURCH BELLS, PARADE, FIREWORKS, BANDS, COUNTRY & WESTERN MUSIC AND A COMMUNITY FAMILY HERITAGE PICNIC. AT 'THE BARN' MISSION AT SAN MARCOS BLVD. (LOCAL). FRONA LANE, CHAIRMAN; BICENTENNIAL COMMITTEE OF SAN MARCOS; 1400-18 EL NORTE PKWY; SAN MARCOS, CA 92069. (#12186-1).

NOV 23, '76. PATRIOTIC CONCERT AT PALOMAR. PATRIOTIC CONCERT INCLUDING SAN MARCOS SONG. AT PALOMAR COLLEGE, MISSION BLVD. (LOCAL). FRONA LANE, CHAIRMAN; BICENTENNIAL COMMITTEE OF SAN MARCOS; 1400-18 EL NORTE PARKWAY; SAN MARCOS, CA 92069. (#100660-1).

SAN MARINO

CENTURY OF REVOLUTION BY HUNTINGTON LIBRARY. HUNTINGTON LIBRARY ART GALLERY & BOTANICAL GARDENS. DISPLAY & INTERPRET BOOKS, MANUSCRIPTS, PAINTINGS, PRINTS, SCULPTURES, MAPS & DOCUMENTS RELATING TO THE AMER. REV. & FORMATION OF A NEW NATION. (NAT'L). MS SUE HULL, PROJECT DIRECTOR; HUNTINGTON LIBRARY, ART GALLERY & BOTANICAL GARDENS; 1151 OXFORD RD; SAN MARINO, CA 91108. (#149).

JUNE 1 - NOV 23, '75. THE BIRTH OF THE UNITED STATES: FROM ARGUMENT TO ARMS. CLOSED MAJOR HOLIDAYS AND THE ENTIRE MONTH OF OCTOBER.. AT HUNTINGTON LIBRARY BLDG, 1151 OXFORD RD, SAN MARINO. (REGN'L). MS SUE HULL; HUNTINGTON LIBRARY ART GALLERY& BOTANICAL GARDENS; 1151 OXFORD RD; SAN MARINO, CA 91108. (#149-3).

DEC 1, '75 - MAY 22, '76. THE BIRTH OF THE USA: A PEOPLE'S WAR - EXHIBIT. CLOSED MAJOR HOLIDAYS AND THE ENTIRE MONTH OF OCTOBER. AT HUNTINGTON LIBRARY BLDG, 1151 OXFORD RD, SAN MARINO. (REGN'L). MS SUE HULL; HUNTINGTON LIBRARY ART GALLERY& BOTANICAL GARDENS; 1151 OXFORD RD; SAN MARINO, CA 91108. (#149-4).

JUNE 1 - NOV 21, '76. THE BIRTH OF THE UNITED STATES: E PLURIBUS UNUM - EXHIBIT. CLOSED MAJOR HOLIDAYS AND THE ENTIRE MONTH OF OCTOBER. AT HUNTINGTON LIBRARY BLDG 1151, OXFORD ROAD, SAN MARINO, CA. (REGN'L). MS SUE HULL; HUNTINGTON LIBRARY ART GALLERY & BOTANICAL GARDENS; 1151 OXFORD RD; SAN MARINO, CA 91108. (#149-1).

SAN MATEO

ARTISTIC EXPRESSIONS OF SAN MATEO COUNTY, CA. MURALS AND SCULPTURES OF LOCAL ARTISTS FROM THE LATIN AMERICAN COMMUNITY TO BE EXHIBITED IN SAN MATEO COUNTY. (LOCAL). DANIEL CORREA, CHAIRMAN; LATIN AMERICAN SPANISH SPEAKING ORGANIZATION; 2615 FAIR OAKS AVE; REDWOOD CITY, CA 94063. (#19826).

BAY TREE PARK - PROJ OF SAN MATEO, CA. BAY TREE PARK WILL BE PRESERVED AND WILL INCLUDE A MINI-PARK. (LOCAL). DOROTHY GRIMSBY, CHAIRMAN; BAY TREE CITIZENS LEAGUE; 330 W 20TH AVE; SAN MATEO, CA 94403. (#11976).

BICENTENNIAL BAND WAGON, SAN MATEO, CA. THE COLLEGE OF SAN MATEO SYMPHONIC BAND WILL PRESENT AMERICAN MUSIC AT SHOPPING; CIVIC AND RECREATION CENTERS, AIRPORTS AND SCHOOLS. (LOCAL). LEO BARDES, DIRECTOR; COLLEGE OF SAN MATEO SYMPHONIC BAND; 1700 W HILLSDALE BLVD; SAN MATEO, CA 94402. (#19651).

CALIFORNIA POPPY GOLDEN HILLSIDE PROJECT-SAN MATEO. THE PARK AND RECREATION COMMISSION WILL PLANT POPPIES ON HILLSIDES IN TIME TO TURN THE HILLSIDES GOLDEN BY '76. (LOCAL). MRS FLORENCE RHOADS, PROJ DIRECTOR; SAN MATEO PARK & RECREATION COMMISSION; 330 W 20TH AVE; SAN MATEO, CA 94403. (#11983).

COLONIAL VILLAGE REPRODUCTION, SAN MATEO, CA. NEAR LIFE SIZE COLONIAL VILLAGE OF SIX BOOTHS OR UNITS, W/COLONIAL FACADE; REPLICA OF ERA HOUSES AND SHOPS. (LOCAL). LCDR R N ANDRIANO MOORE, USN, COMMANDING OFFICER; NAVAL AND MARINE CORPS RESERVE CENTER; COMMODORE DRIVE AND SNEATH LANE; SAN BRUNO, CA 94066. (#28618).

COMPOSITION OF BICENTENNIAL MUSIC FOR BAND, CA. COMPOSITION OF 2 WORKS FOR SYMPHONIC BAND TITLED 'PACIFIC PAGEANT' AND 'PRAYER AND PARADE', FOR PERFORMANCE AT SAN FRANCISCO STATE UNIV AND THE UNIV OF CALIFORNIA AT BERKELEY. (LOCAL). JAMES BERDAHL, DIRECTOR, STUDENT MUSICAL ACTIVITY; UNIVERSITY OF CALIFORNIA AT BERKELEY; 53 STUDENT CENTER; BERKELEY, CA 94720. (#25306).

COUNTY SPIRIT OF '76; SAN MATEO, CA. BICENTENNIAL T-SHIRT DESIGN CONTEST - 2000 STUDENTS SENT IN DESIGNS; T-SHIRTS WILL BE SOLD THROUGH SCHOOL PTA. (LOCAL). MARION MENDELSON, PROJECT DIRECTOR; SAN MATEO COUNTY ARTS COUNCIL; 141 BOREL AVE; SAN MATEO, CA 94402. (#19823).

COYOTE POINT MUSEUM FOR ENVIRONMENTAL EDUCATION-CA. MUSEUM TO BE CONSTRUCTED AT COYOTE POINT COUNTY PARK; THREE LEVEL SEGMENTED WOOD FRAME BUILDING; PERMANENT EXHIBITION OF ECOLOGICAL RELATIONSHIPS OF SAN MATEO COUNTY. (LOCAL). MRS LAWRENCE H PETERSON, VICE PRESIDENT; COYOTE POINT MUSEUM ASSOCIATION, BOARD OF TRUSTEES; COYOTE POINT; SAN MATEO, CA 94401. (#11853).

HERITAGE CERTIFICATES - PROJ OF SAN MATEO, CA. HERITAGE CERTIFICATES WILL BE SOLD AS COLLECTORS ITEMS FOR A FUND RAISING DRIVE. (LOCAL). CLAIRE MACK, AIDE; SAN MATEO BICENTENNIAL COMMITTEE; 330 W 20TH AVE; SAN MATEO, CA 94403. (#11977).

HISTORICAL BOOKLET - PROJ OF SAN MATEO, CA. BOOKLET ON BLACK PIONEERS TO BE PUBLISHED. (LOCAL). PENNY WILLIAMS SORRELL, PROJ DIRECTOR; PENNY WILLIAMS SORRELL; 114 N DELAWARE ST; SAN MATEO, CA 94401. (#11981).

HISTORICAL SLIDE SHOW AND DISPLAYS - SAN MATEO, CA. HISTORICAL SLIDE SHOW OF SAN MATEO, THEN AND NOW. (LOCAL). MS LOIS DESALERNOS, CHAIRMAN; PENINSULA COLOR SLIDE CLUB; 6 PINECREST TERRACE; SAN MATEO, CA 94402. (#11974).

HISTORY CALIFORNIA STYLE - SAN MATEO, CA. AN EXHIBIT ON WHEELS THAT WILL DISPLAY THE HISTORY OF SAN MATEO CO THROUGH ARTIFACTS, GRAPHICS AND DEMONSTRATIVE MATERIALS; THE BUS WILL GO TO SCHOOLS AND PARKS. (LOCAL). HERBERT E GARCIA, DIRECTOR; SAN MATEO COUNTY HISTORICAL MUSEUM; 1700 W HILLSDALE BLVD; SAN MATEO, CA 94402. (#19824).

ORIGINAL NEWSPAPER WRITINGS PROJ, SAN MATEO, CALIF. PACKAGE OF ORIGINAL WRITINGS OF EVENTS ANECDOTES & ACTIVITIES 17651789 BEING DEVELOPED FOR PRINTING BY LOCAL NEWSPAPERS. ALSO RECOUNT OF VAST AMOUNT ORIGINAL RESOURCES AVAILABLE LOCALLY & NATIONALLY. (LOCAL). GERALD F DAY, CHAIRMAN; SAN MATEO COUNTY BICENTENNIAL PLANNING COMMITTEE; 141 BOREL AVE; SAN MATEO, CA 94402. (#2980). **(??).**

SAN MATEO COUNTY HISTORIC RESOURCES INVENTORY, CA. HISTORIC FEATURES OF SAN MATEO COUNTY WILL BE CATALOGUED TO PROVIDE READY REFERENCE. (LOCAL). ELIZABETH COONAN, COORDINATOR; SAN MATEO COUNTY HISTORIC SITES ADVISORY COMMITTEE; COYOTE POINT MUSEUM; SAN MATEO, CA 94401. (#19825).

SAN MATEO GARDEN CENTER - CA. HORTICULTURAL CENTER TO BE BUILT IN SAN MATEO. (LOCAL). MRS RANDALL COGNETTA, PRESIDENT; SAN MATEO GARDEN CENTER; 2720 ALAMEDA DE LAS PUIGAS; SAN MATEO, CA 94402. (#11982).

SCRIPPS LEAGUE NEWSPAPERS BICENT SUPPORT - NBMRP. 30-PAPER CHAIN, INCL DAILY HOURNAL'S SPL TABLOID ON AMER ART & HISTORY, DAILY NEWS BROCHURE ON AREA PIONEERS, DAILY CHRONICLE'S FUND RAISING EFFORTS FOR HISTORIC BLDG & SPONSORSHIP OF MILITARY BANDS. (ST-WIDE). E W SCRIPPS, PRESIDENT & CHAIRMAN OF THE BOARD; SCRIPPS LEAGUE NEWSPAPERS; PO BOX 1491; SAN MATEO, CA 94401. (#25550).

STORE PROMOTION - PROJ OF SAN MATEO, CA. BICENTENNIAL DECALS FOR STORE WINDOWS - 'WE SUPPORT SAN MATEO'S BICENTENNIAL CELEBRATION'. (LOCAL). CLAIRE MACK, AIDE; SAN MATEO BICENTENNIAL COMMITTEE; 330 W 20TH AVE; SAN MATEO, CA 94401. (#11978).

TRAIL MARKINGS - PROJ OF SAN MATEO, CA. MARKERS ERECTED IN THE SPOTS WHERE THE SPANISH EXPLORERS STOPPED. (LOCAL). CLAIRE MACK, AIDE; SAN MATEO BICENTENNIAL COMMITTEE; 330 W 20TH AVE; SAN MATEO, CA 94401. (#11973).

WATER QUALITY IMPROVEMENT FACILITY - SAN MATEO, CA. DEDICATION OF THE NEW WATER QUALITY IMPROVEMENT FACILITY. (LOCAL). CLAIRE MACK, AIDE; SAN MATEO BICENTENNIAL COMMITTEE; 330 W 20TH AVE; SAN MATEO, CA 94402. (#11980).

1976 CAVALRY BRIGADE, SAN MATEO, CA. YOUNG HORSEMEN IN CAVALRY UNITS, AVAILABLE FOR BICENTENNIAL EVENTS THROUGHOUT THE COUNTY. (LOCAL). AL LUCAS, DIRECTOR; SAN MATEO COUNTY HORSEMENS ASSOCIATION; 133 MARVA OAKS; WOODSIDE, CA 94062. (#19512).

JUNE 14, '75. MONTGOMERY WARD FLAG DAY CEREMONY - SAN MATEO, CA. THE MONTGOMERY WARD COMPANY WILL PRESENT A FLAG RAISING CEREMONY. (LOCAL). RUSS CAMPBELL; MONTGOMERY WARD CO; 1700 S DELAWARE ST; SAN MATEO, CA 94402. (#11975-1).

JULY 28 - AUG 10, '75. HERITAGE FAIRE - CRAFTS, GAMES, ACTIVITIES OF COLONIAL PERIOD. FAIR, EXHIBIT AT COUNTY FAIR GROUNDS 2495 S DELEWARE SAN MATEO. (LOCAL). BICENTENNIAL COMMITTEE; AMERICAN REVOLUTION BICENTENNIAL COMMITTEE OF SAN MATEO COUNTY; 141 BOREL AVE; SAN MATEO, CA 94402. (#50068-1).

SEPT 10 - 12, '75. THREE DAY CONVENTION & PARADE. PARADE IN HONOR OF CALIFORNIA'S ADMISSION TO THE UNION AS A STATE. (LOCAL). CECIL MORRIS, CHAIRMAN; NATIVE SONS; 516 31ST AVENUE; SAN MATEO, CA 94403. (#11979-501).

FEB 14 - 15, '76. SAN FRANCISCO AREA COMBINED BOTTLE COLLECTORS SHOW AND SALE. EXHIBIT AT 2495 S. DELAWARE ST. (LOCAL). FRED ROSENQUIST, COORD; PENINSULA BOTTLE COLLECTORS, INC; PO BOX 886; BELMONT, CA 94002. (#104564-3).

MAY 2, '76. CHORAL FESTIVAL FEATURING MUSIC OF AMERICA: 1776-1976. LIVE PERFORMANCE AT SAN MATEO HIGH SCHOOL AUDITORIUM. (LOCAL). DR MARIETTA TASSOS, CHMN; SAN MATEO COUNTY CHORAL SOCIETY; 381 PARAMOUNT DR; MILLBRAE, CA 94030. (#105108-1).

MAY 8, '76. TAPIOLA CHILDREN'S CHOIR VISITS SAN MATEO. LIVE PERFORMANCE. (INT'L). TATU TUCHIKORPI; CONSULATE GENERAL OF FINLAND; 540 MADISON AVE; NEW YORK, NY 10022. (#109041-2).

MAY 21 - 30, '76. FESTIVAL AMERICAN ORIGINAL. PAGEANT TITLE WILL BE '1976, THE BEST OF OUR TIMES'. AT SAN MATEO HIGH SCHOOL AUDITORIUM. (LOCAL). CLAIRE MACK, CHAIRMAN; SAN MATEO BICENTENNIAL COMMITTEE; 320 W 20TH; SAN MATEO, CA 94401. (#105271-1).

JULY 26 - AUG 7, '76. SAN MATEO COUNTY FAIR AND FLORAL FIESTA - BICENTENNIAL THEME. FEATURING HERITAGE FAIR, CALIFORNIA HISTORY, THIRTEEN COLONIES SISTER CITY PROGRAM, BICENTENNIAL ENTERTAINMENT, AS WELL AS THE ANNUAL FLORAL FIESTA IN THE HALL OF FLOWERS. AT 2495 S DELAWARE STREET, SAN MATEO. (LOCAL). SAL MILLAN; SAN MATEO COUNTY FAIR; 2495 SOUTH DELAWARE; SAN MATEO, CA 94403. (#104564-1).

OCT 8 - 9, '76. UNITED STATES ARMED FORCES BICENTENNIAL CARAVAN. CARAVAN IS COMPOSED OF EXHIBIT VANS FOR EACH MILITARY SERVICE. PROJECT THEME IS 'HISTORY OF THE ARMED FORCES & THEIR CONTRIBUTIONS TO THE NATION'. (LOCAL). HUGH WAYNE; UNITED STATES ARMED FORCES BICENTENNIAL CARAVAN; 72 3RD AVE; SAN MATEO, CA 94401. (#1775-821).

SAN PABLO

HAPPY BIRTHDAY AMERICA: SAN PABLO, CA. NEWSPAPER ARTICLES OF HISTORICAL INTEREST ON THE CONESTOGA WAGON, SALOONS, THE STATUE OF LIBERTY, RAPID TRANSIT & THE GOLDEN GATE BRIDGE. (LOCAL). NORMA MILLHOLLIN, COORD; MILLHOLLIN'S ANTIQUE IMPORTS; 1847 23RD ST; SAN PABLO, CA 94569. (#23440).

HISTORICAL SKETCH OF SAN PABLO, CA. A HISTORY BOOK WILL BE WRITTEN FOR THE SCHOOL CHILDREN OF SAN PABLO; IT WILL CONTAIN INFORMATION ON LOCAL INDIANS, SPANISH, THE RANCHOS, RELIGIOUS & PATRIOTIC GROWTH AND THE FUTURE OF THE TOWN. (LOCAL). BEVERLY DAHLSTEDT, BICENT CHAIRMAN; SAN PABLO BICENTENNIAL COMMITTEE & HISTORICAL SOCIETY; 1400 MINER AVE; SAN PABLO, CA 94806. (#22389).

RECONSTRUCTION OF ALVARADO HOUSE - SAN PABLO, CA. THE ADOBE WILL BE RECONSTRUCTED ON ITS ORIGINAL SITE USING ORIGINAL PLANS & TIMBERS; SCHOOL CHILDREN WILL HELP MAKE THE ADOBE BRICKS FOR THE HOUSE; IT WILL BE A PART OF THE NEW COMMUNITY CENTER. (LOCAL). MONTY HESS, DIRECTOR; CITY OF SAN PABLO; 2021 MARKET AVE; SAN PABLO, CA 94806. (#23394).

SAN PABLO — CONTINUED

SAN PABLO INFORMATION, CA. EXHIBIT WITH PICTURES AND EXPLANATIONS ABOUT THE CITY'S PUBLIC BUILDINGS AND OTHER IMPORTANT LANDMARKS. (LOCAL). SHARON BULLOCK, BICENTENNIAL CHAIRMAN; BAYVIEW SCHOOL PTA; 3001 16TH ST; SAN PABLO, CA 94806. (#21965).

FEB 19, '76. PTA FOUNDERS DAY MEETING. EXHIBIT AT RIVERSIDE SCHOOL, 1300 AMADOR ST. (LOCAL). CELESTE EVANS, PTA PRES; RIVERSIDE PTA; 5623 CASINO AVE; SAN PABLO, CA 94806. (#200006-123).

FEB 19, '76. TRI-CITIES CHAMBER OF COMMERCE BICENTENNIAL CELEBRATION. DANCING, MUSIC, FOOD, ENTERTAINMENT, COSTUME OPTIONAL. AT SLAV HALL, 5220 GLEN AVE, SAN PABLO, PARKING NEAR HALL. (LOCAL). ROLLY APPLETON, CHAIRMAN; CITIES OF SAN PABLO, EL SOBRANTE & PINOLE CHAMBERS OF COMMERCE; PO BOX 204; SAN PABLO, CA 94806. (#104386-1).

MAR 13, '76. SCHOOL CARNIVAL. FESTIVAL AT 3001 16TH ST. (LOCAL). SHARON BULLOCK; BAYVIEW SCHOOL PTA; 1939 PABLO VISTA AVE; SAN PABLO, CA 94806. (#200006-124).

APR 3, '76. RIVERSIDE ELEMENTARY SCHOOL CARNIVAL. FAIR AT RIVERSIDE SCHOOL, 1300 AMADOR ST. (LOCAL). CELESTE EVANS; RIVERSIDE PTA; 5623 CASINO AVE; SAN PABLO, CA 94806. (#200006-130).

MAY 2, '76. PORTUGESE APPRECIATION DAY. FESTIVAL AT SLAV HALL, 5220 GLENN AVE. (LOCAL). JOYCE WILSON, COORD; CITY OF SAN PABLO; 5220 GLENN AVE; SAN PABLO, CA 94806. (#107145-1).

JUNE 29, '76. UNITED STATES ARMED FORCES BICENTENNIAL CARAVAN. CARAVAN IS COMPOSED OF EXHIBIT VANS FOR EACH MILITARY SERVICE. PROJECT THEME IS 'HISTORY OF THE ARMED FORCES AND THEIR CONTIBUTIONS TO THE NATION. (LOCAL). MRS BEVERLY DAHLSTEDT; U S ARMED FORCES BICENTENNIAL CARAVAN; 1400 MINER AVE; SAN PABLO, CA 94806. (#1775-722).

SAN PEDRO

SEPT 20 - 21, '75. INTERNATIONAL JUBILEE. FESTIVAL. (LOCAL). SANDY BROWN, PROGRAM ASST; RECREATION & PARKS, CITY OF LOS ANGELES; 200 N MAIN, ROOM 1330; LOS ANGELES, CA 90012. (#100799-1).

JULY 20 - 25, '76. YUGOSLAVIAN FOLKLIFE GROUP. 11 MAN MACEDONIAN DANCE GROUP, MARTENEGRAN GROUP GUSLAR, 4 MAN SERBIAN BAND, 3 CROATIN SINGERS, SLOVENE SINGERS & 4 HERZEGORNA SINGERS. (INT'L). MIKE GEGNA, COORDINATOR; HARBOR COLLEGE; SAN PEDRO, CA 90731. (#107124-1).

SAN RAFAEL

AMERICAN DREAM COLLOQUIUM, SAN RAFAEL, CA. TWELVE UNIT INTER-DISCIPLINARY HUMANITIES PROGRAM FOCUSING ON THE AMERICAN EXPERIENCE, PAST, PRESENT AND FUTURE. (LOCAL). J LAWRENCE NORTON, DIRECTOR OF DEVELOPMENT; DOMINICAN COLLEGE; GRAND AVE; SAN RAFAEL, CA 94901. (#16235).

BICENTENNIAL ROOM - PROJ OF SAN RAFAEL, CA. A BICENTENNIAL ROOM WITH A DISPLAY OF CIVIL WAR AND WORLD WAR I UNIFORMS AND APPROPRIATE MEMORABILIA OF THESE TIMES. (LOCAL). ELSIE MAZZINI, PRESIDENT; MARIN COUNTY HISTORICAL SOCIETY; SAN RAFAEL, CA 94901. (#14869). **ARBA GRANTEE.**

BICENTENNIAL SERIES OF HISTORICAL ARTICLES, CA. A SERIES OF ARTICLES BY LOCAL AUTHORS ON MARIN COUNTY AND ATLANTIC COAST SUBJECTS PUBLISHED IN INDEPENDENT JOURNAL NEWSPAPER FOR REMAINDER OF 1975 AND THROUGHOUT THE BICENTENNIAL YEAR. (LOCAL). MICHAEL HUGHES, CHMN, HERITAGE COMMITTEE; MARIN COUNTY AMERICAN REVOLUTION BICENTENNIAL COMMISSION; 810 5TH AVE; SAN RAFAEL, CA 94901. (#16936).

CLEAN THE SCENE - KEEP AMERICA BEAUTIFUL - CA. A PROGRAM OF PARENT, CHILD & TEACHER PARTICIPATION IN CONTESTS & ACTIVITIES AIMED AT DEVELOPING AWARENESS OF OUR LITTER PROBLEM AND MAKING AN EFFORT TO CORRECT IT. (LOCAL). MRS WILLIAM C NEILL, CHAIRMAN; MARIN BRANCH ASSOC OF AMERICAN UNIVERSITY WOMEN; 19 CYPRESS AVE; KENTFIELD, CA 94904. (#18480).

FALKIRK BICENTENNIAL PROJECT - SAN RAFAEL, CA. THE COMPLETION OF VARIOUS RESTORATION PROJECTS & INTERIOR FURNISHING OF FALKIRK, COMMUNITY CULTURAL CENTER, CITY OF SAN RAFAEL. (LOCAL). HELGA EPSTEIN, COMMISSIONER; SAN RAFAEL CULTURAL COMMISSION; PO BOX 60; SAN RAFAEL, CA 94901. (#18385).

INDEPENDENT JOURNAL'S MARIN COUNTY HISTORY - NBMRP. SINCE 1975, PAPER HAS BEEN RUNNING HISTORICAL ARTICLES ON MARIN COUNTY, WHICH WERE ORIGINALLY GIVEN TO LOCAL BICENTENNIAL COMMISSION. (LOCAL). BETH M ASHLEY, BICENTENNIAL COORDINATOR; INDEPENDENT JOURNAL; 1040 B STREET; SAN RAFAEL, CA 94901. (#26911).

MARIN COUNTY BICENTENNIAL FILMS - SAN RAFAEL, CA. USE OF A RESTORED FILM FOOTAGE AND NEWLY SHOT FILM TO PRODUCE SEVERAL 16MM COLOR-SOUND FILMS PRESERVING THE MOVING IMAGERY OF MARIN'S PAST. (LOCAL). DAVID SWINGLE, DIRECTOR; SAN RAFAEL CITY SCHOOLS; 3RD & E ST; SAN RAFAEL, CA 94901. (#14870).

MARIN COUNTY BICENTENNIAL CACHET COMMEMORATIVE, CA. THE MARIN COUNTY BICENTENNIAL SYMBOL WILL BE PRINTED ON ENVELOPES WITH A SPECIALLY DESIGNED CANCELLATION TO BE USED ON JULY 4, 1976 BY THE SAN RAFAEL POST OFFICE. (LOCAL). HOWARD A LEVENSON, CHMN, BICENTENNIAL CACHET PROJ; SAN RAFAEL LIONS CLUB; 975 GRAND AVE; SAN RAFAEL, CA 94901. (#17347).

MARIN COUNTY COMMEMORATIVE BICENT MEDALLION - CA. A ONE AND A HALF INCH, PURE SILVER MEDALLION DEPICTING MARIN COUNTY HERITAGE TO COMMEMORATE THE NATION'S 200TH BIRTHDAY. (LOCAL). BEN FARLATTI, VICE CHAIRMAN; MARIN COUNTY ARBC; 810 5TH AVE; SAN RAPHAEL, CA 94901. (#11631).

SAN RAFAEL WALK BOOK, SAN RAFAEL, CA. BOOKLET OF SKETCHES, MAPS AND TEXT DESCRIBING TOURS OF HISTORIC INTEREST WITHIN THE CITY. (LOCAL). CHRIS CLARKE, DIRECTOR; DOMINICAN COLLEGE; GRAND AVE; SAN RAFAEL, CA 94901. (#16234).

SEARS BICENTENNIAL PHOTO CONTEST - SAN RAFAEL, CA. APRIL THROUGH MAY PHOTO CONTEST; SUBJECT MATTER MUST DEAL WITH BICENTENNIAL THEME; EACH SAN FRANCISCO BAY AREA STORE TO PARTICIPATE. (LOCAL). WARREN J JAEGER, MANAGER; SEARS, ROEBUCK AND CO; 9000 NORTHGATE SHOPPING CENTER; SAN RAFAEL, CA 94903. (#17545).

SPANISH COLONIAL ART IN AMERICA, SAN RAFAEL, CA. COURSE IN SPANISH COLONIAL ART IN AMERICA, EMPHASIS ON EXAMPLES WITHIN THE U S. (LOCAL). CHRIS CLARKE, COORDINATOR; DOMINICAN COLLEGE; SAN RAFAEL, CA 94901. (#16233).

NOV 29, '75 - JULY 5, '76. BICENTENNIAL PERIOD SQUARE DANCE PROGRAM. LIVE PERFORMANCE AT NOVATO HIGH SCHOOL, NOVATO, CA. (LOCAL). HARRY E SHARKEY, DIRECTOR; NORTHERN CALIFORNIA SQUARE DANCE ASSOCIATION & MARIN COUNTY ARBC; 229 KNIGHT ST; SAN RAFAEL, CA 94901. (#103284-1).

JAN 5 - DEC 31, '76. MARIN COUNTY CIVIC CENTER LIBRARY BICENT EXHIBITIONS. 9:00AM-6:00PM ON FRIDAY AND SATURDAY. AT CIVIC CENTER LIBRARY. (LOCAL). VIRGINIA BORLAND, COOR; MARIN COUNTY AMERICAN REVOLUTION BICENTENNIAL COMMISSION; CIVIC CENTER LIBRARY; SAN RAFAEL, CA 94903. (#103081-1).

MAR 19 - 28, '76. BICENTENNIAL ARTS FESTIVAL. FESTIVAL, LIVE PERFORMANCE AT DOMINICAN COLLEGE CAMPUS, GRAND AVE. (LOCAL). J LAWRENCE NORTON, COORD; DOMINICAN COLLEGE; DOMINICAN COLLEGE, GRAND AVE; SAN RAFAEL, CA 94901. (#102794-2).

MAR 19 - 28, '76. SIR FRANCIS DRAKE EXHIBITION. EXHIBIT AT ALEMANY LIBRARY, DOMINICAN COLLEGE CAMPUS. (LOCAL). J LAWRENCE NORTON, COORD; DOMINICAN COLLEGE; DOMINICAN COLLEGE, GRAND AVE; SAN RAFAEL, CA 94901. (#102794-1).

MAR 28, '76. BICENTENNIAL CELEBRATION CONCERT. LIVE PERFORMANCE AT MARIN VETERANS MEMORIAL BLDG, MARIN COUNTY CIVIC CENTER. (LOCAL). THELMA SCHULTZ, GEN MGR; MARIN SYMPHONY ASSOC; BOX 127; SAN RAPHAEL, CA 94902. (#104073-1).

APR 24, '76. 'AMERICA DANCING' - MARIN CIVIC BALLET SPRING CONCERT. LIVE PERFORMANCE AT MARIN VETERANS MEMORIAL AUDITORIUM. (LOCAL). MRS ROBERT KNOX, DIRECTOR; MARIN CIVIC BALLET ASSOC; 100 ELM ST; SAN RAFAEL, CA 94901. (#104073-3).

JUNE 5 - 6, '76. BALLET: AQUACADE OF MARIN - A BICENTENNIAL SALUTE. PROCEEDS TO MARIN-DALE SCHOOL FOR ORTHOPEDICALLY HANDICAPPED CHILDREN. PROGRAM OF SYNCHRONIZED SWIMMING & BALLET REPRESENTING THE HISTORY OF THE USA. AT MCNEAR'S BEACH. (LOCAL). MRS D M SULLIVAN, DIR; BALLET-AQUACADE OF MARIN, INC; 165 ELISED DR; GREENBRAE, CA 94904. (#104073-2).

JULY 1 - 5, '76. MARIN COUNTY BICENTENNIAL FAIR. FAIR AT CIVIC CENTER COMPLEX. (LOCAL). DICK CARTER; MARIN COUNTY AMERICAN REVOLUTION BICENTENNIAL COMMISSION; SAN RAPHAEL, CA 94903. (#100451-1).

JULY 25 - AUG 8, '76. FOREST MEADOWS FESTIVAL OF THE ARTS. FESTIVAL, LIVE PERFORMANCE AT DOMINICAN COLLEGE CAMPUS. (LOCAL). J LAWRENCE NORTON, COORD; DOMINICAN COLLEGE; DOMINICAN COLLEGE, GRAND AVE; SAN RAFAEL, CA 94901. (#102794-3).

NOV 5 - 7, '76. FALKIRK BICENTENNIAL FESTIVAL. FESTIVAL AT 1408 MISSION AVE. (LOCAL). WILLIAM BIELSER, PGM MGR; SAN RAFAEL CULTURAL AFFAIRS COMMISSION; CITY HALL; SAN RAFAEL, CA 94901. (#103783-1).

SANTA ANA

BICENTENNIAL PACIFIC CREST TRAIL HIKE. RE-ENACTMENT OF FIRST EXPLORATION BY TEAMS OF BACKPACKERS OF THE PACIFIC CREST NATIONAL SCENIC TRAIL. BACKPACKERS WILL GO FROM MEXICO TO CANADA TO ENCOURAGE THE COMPLETION OF THE TRAIL. (REGN'L). WARREN L ROGERS, COORD; CAMP RESEARCH FOUNDATION; PO BOX 1907; SANTA ANA, CA 92702. (#108292-1).

CITY OF FLAGS, SANTA ANA, CALIFORNIA. THE CHAMBER OF COMMERCE HAS DESIGNATED SANTA ANA AS THE CITY OF FLAGS AND FLAGS WILL BE FLOWN AT ALL PUBLIC & COMMERCIAL BUILDINGS. BENNINGTON FLAGS WILL BE SOLD THROUGHOUT THE CITY. (LOCAL). BONI OVERN, SECRETARY; SANTA ANA BICENTENNIAL COMMITTEE; 1010 N MAIN, SUITE 515; SANTA ANA, CA 92701. (#10646).

HERITAGE PLAZA IN SANTA ANA, CALIFORNIA. DEVELOPMENT OF PARK AROUND HISTORICAL COURTHOUSE AND RESTORATION OF WAFFLE HOUSE, HOME OF FIRST WOMAN SURGEON IN SANTA ANA. HOUSE WILL BE RELOCATED TO THE PLAZA. (LOCAL). BONI OVERN, SECRETARY; SANTA ANA BICENT COMMITTEE; 1010 N MAIN, SUITE 515; SANTA ANA, CA 92701. (#10644).

MEET THE AMERICANS IN SANTA ANA, CA. FIFTY TO SIXTY HOST FAMILIES IN SANTA ANA FOR VISITORS FROM EUROPE. (LOCAL). BONI OVERN, SECRETARY; SANTA ANA BICENTENNIAL COMMITTEE; 1010 N MAIN, SUITE 515; SANTA ANA, CA 92701. (#10645).

RESTORATION OF DR HOWE WAFFLE/CARRIAGE HOUSE IN CA. RESTORATION OF HOME OF FIRST WOMAN DOCTOR IN ORANGE COUNTY; DEVELOPMENT OF SMALL MEDICAL MUSEUM. (LOCAL). RILEY RHODES, DIRECTOR; SANTA ANA HISTORICAL PRESERVATION SOCIETY; 2002 N MAIN ST; SANTA ANA, CA 92701. (#33307). **ARBA GRANTEE.**

TOASTMASTERS INTERNATIONAL VOLUNTEER FORUM. MEMBERS OF TOASTMASTERS INTERNATIONAL WILL SPEAK ON BEHALF OF BICENT PROJECTS IN THEIR COMMUNITY, WORK WITH YOUTH DEBATES, AND PREPARE AND DELIVER TALKS ON AMERICAN ISSUES FORUM. (NAT'L). BRUCE L ANDERSON, EDITOR; TOASTMASTERS INTERNATIONAL; 2200 N GRAND AVE; SANTA ANA, CA 92711. (#6215).

JULY 2, '75. OLD-FASHIONED INDEPENDENCE DAY CELEBRATION - BROWN BAG LUNCH. THE EVENT INCLUDES PARTICIPATION BY THE MARINE CORP BAND & SPEECHES. AT PLAZA OF THE FLAGS, CIVIC CENTER DR. (LOCAL). BONI DIANE OVERN, SEC; SANTA ANA KIWANIS CLUB; 1010 N MAIN, SUITE 515; SANTA ANA, CA 92701. (#100229-1).

SEPT 2, '75 - MAY '76. PANORAMA OF PERFORMING ARTS - AN AMERICAN HERITAGE. DANCE CONCERTS OF CALIFORNIA, AMERICAN, AFRICAN, INDIAN, JAPANESE & FOLK HERITAGE AND CLASSICAL, DIXIELAND, FOLK, CHORAL & POP MUSIC; RANCHO SANTIAGO HISTORICAL PAPERS WILL BE TRANSLATED FROM SPANISH TO ENGLISH. (LOCAL). STEWART S CASE, DIRECTOR; SANTA ANA COLLEGE, RANCHO SANTIAGO COMMUNITY COLLEGE DISTRICT; 17 & BRISTOL ST; SANTA ANA, CA 92706. (#101836-1).

MAR 13, '76. SAINT PATRICK'S DAY PARADE. THIS YEAR'S PARADE WILL HAVE A BICENTENNIAL THEME. WE ARE LOOKING FOR GROUPS IN HISTORICAL OR ETHNIC COSTUMES TO REPRESENT THE DIVERSIFIED GROUPS THAT HAVE CONTRIBUTED TO AMERICA'S DEVELOPMENT. AT CIVIC CENTER DRIVE AND MAIN STREET. (LOCAL). BONI OVERN, DIRECTOR; THE '17TH OF MARCH' COMMITTEE; 1010 N MAIN, SUITE 515; SANTA ANA, CA 92701. (#104328-1).

APR 3 - 4, '76. EL TORO MARINE AIR STATION BICENTENNIAL OPEN HOUSE AND AIR SHOW. PERFORMANCES BY BLUE ANGELS, GOLDEN KNIGHTS, STUNT FLYERS. ONGOING FILMS, DISPLAYS OF AIRCRAFT, STAGE PRESENTATION OF PERIOD UNIFORMS. AT EL TORO MARINE CORPS AIR STATION. (ST-WIDE). CAPTAIN DIBERNARDO, CHMN; SANTA ANA BICENTENNIAL COMMITTEE; EL TORO AIR STATION; SANTA ANA, CA 92709. (#105847-1).

APR 13 - 14, '76. UNITED STATES ARMED FORCES BICENTENNIAL CARAVAN. CARAVAN IS COMPOSED OF EXHIBIT VANS FOR EACH MILITARY SERVICE. PROJECT THEME IS ' HISTORY OF THE ARMED FORCES & THEIR CONTRIBUTIONS TO THE NATION'. (LOCAL). GENE NORIARTY, CHAIRMAN; U S ARMED FORCES BICENTENNIAL CARAVAN; 1010 N MAIN; SANTA ANA, CA 92701. (#1775-553).

MAY 14 - 16, '76. SPIRITUAL HERITAGE FESTIVAL. AWARDS WILL BE GIVEN FOR THE WINNING ENTRY IN THE NATIONAL ORGAN COMPOSITION COMPETITION. THE FESTIVAL WILL INCLUDE CONCERTS, EXHIBITS, SERMON AND WORSHIP. (LOCAL). ROGER W HICKS, DIRECTOR; FIRST BAPTIST CHURCH OF SANTA ANA; 1010 W 17TH ST; SANTA ANA, CA 92706. (#100838-1).

JUNE 4 - 5, '76. 200 YEARS OF AMERICAN MUSIC-IRVINE MASTER CHORALE. LIVE PERFORMANCE AT PHILLIPS HALL. (LOCAL). STU CASE, COORDINATOR; SANTA ANA BICENTENNIAL COMMITTEE & SANTA ANA COLLEGE; 17TH AT BRISTOL; SANTA ANA, CA 92706. (#108167-5).

JUNE 30, '76. CONTINENTAL SINGERS: ORCHESTRA & VOCAL. BRING YOUR LUNCH AND ENJOY THE SUN AND MUSIC. AT PLAZA OF THE SUN, CIVIC CENTER. (LOCAL). GENE LAUMEISTER, COORD; SANTA ANA BICENTENNIAL COMMITTEE & DOWNTOWN KIWANIS CLUB; 20 CIVIC CENTER PLAZA; SANTA ANA, CA 92701. (#108167-3).

JULY 12 - AUG 27, '76. 'VIBASONICS'. BRING YOUR LUNCH AND ENJOY THE MUSIC OF SANTA ANA'S OWN BICENTENNIAL YOUTH BAND EVERY FRIDAY AT NOON. AT PLAZA OF THE SUN, CIVIC CENTER. (LOCAL). GENE LAUMEISTER, COORD; SANTA ANA PARKS AND RECREATION; 20 CIVIC CENTER PLAZA; SANTA ANA, CA 92701. (#108167-2).

JULY 17, '76. CHARLIE CLARK BICENTENNIAL RUN. 1 MILE, 2 MILE & 10 MILE RACES. WOMEN'S, YOUTH & PUBLIC EMPLOYEES CATEGORIES. BRONZE MEDALS AS PRIZES. 200 RUNNERS EXPECTED, SANTA ANA WINDS BAND WILL PERFORM. AT RUN WILL START AT YMCA ON BROADWAY AND CIVIC CENTER DR. (LOCAL). GENE LAUMEISTER, COORD; SANTA ANA RECREATION AND PARKS, YMCA & BICENTENNIAL COMMITTEE; 20 CIVIC CENTER DR; SANTA ANA, CA 92701. (#108309-1).

JULY 19 - 24, '76. 'LEGEND OF SLEEPY HOLLOW'. DELIGHTFUL PRESENTATION OF CHILDREN'S TRADITIONAL AMERICAN STORY OF THE HEADLESS HORSEMAN. AT CITY HALL ANNEX THEATER. (LOCAL). GENE LAUMEISTER, COORD; SANTA ANA PARKS AND RECREATION DEPARTMENT; 20 CIVIC CENTER PLAZA; SANTA ANA, CA 92701. (#108167-1).

JULY 29 - AUG 7, '76. 'GEORGE M'. KEN BERRY WILL PLAY THE TITLE ROLE OF GEORGE M COHAN. AT PHILLIPS HALL THEATRE. (LOCAL). BOB BLAUSTONE, DIRECTOR; SANTA ANA BICENTENNIAL COMMITTEE & SANTA ANA COLLEGE; 17TH AT BRISTOL; SANTA ANA, CA 92706. (#108167-4).

SANTA ANA — CONTINUED

AUG 14, '76. FIRST BICENTENNIAL ANTIQUE AUTO CLASSIC PARADE & SHOW. SIX MILE ROUTE WITH PARADE TIME OF 45 MINUTES. PRIZES FOR UNIQUE ENTRIES & DASHBOARD PLAQUE FOR ALL ENTRIES. SANTA ANA WINDS BAND TO PERFORM AT LUNCHEON & CHAMPAGNE PARTY AT END OF PARADE. AT SOUTH COAST VILLAGE TO FASHION SQUARE. (ST-WIDE). E R LAUMEISTER, SUPT; RECREATION & PARKS DEPT; 20 CIVIC CENTER PLAZA; SANTA ANA, CA 92701. (#108972-1).

SANTA BARBARA

ACCESS - AN ENVIRONMENTAL PROGRAM - CA. ACTION RESEARCH/PROJECT CONCERNED WITH ENVIRONMENTAL POLICY MAKING AND CITIZEN INVOLVEMENT. PROGRAM GOAL: TO EDUCATE CITIZENS ON USE OF TODAYS TECHNOLOGY TO FACILITATE INVOLVEMENT IN PLANNING THE REGION. (REGN'L). WILLIAM EWALD, PROJECT DIRECTOR; ACCESS; 114 EAST DE LA GUERRA; SANTA BARBARA, CA 93101. (#21699). **ARBA RECOGNIZED.**

BANCORFT'S 'HISTORY OF CALIFORNIA'. REPRINT OF 1883 HISTORY OF CALIFORNIA. 7 VOLUMES COVER CALIFORNIA FROM 1542 - 1890. (ST-WIDE). WALLACE HEBBERD, PUBLISHER; WALLACE HEBBERD, PUBLISHER; 1035 SANTA BARBARA ST; SANTA BARBARA, CA 93102. (#1069).

LOGOTYPE CONTEST OF SANTA BARBARA, CALIFORNIA. LOGOTYPE CONTEST FOR SANTA BARBARA ARBC BY JUNIOR HIGH & HIGH SCHOOLS, COLLEGE, ADULT EDUCATION CLASSES & COMMUNITY AT LARGE. (LOCAL). WARD JENKS, CHAIRMAN; SANTA BARBARA BICENTENNIAL COMMITTEE; 3430 LOS PINOS DR; SANTA BARBARA, CA 93105. (#2984).

'NEW GLORY': FLAG DESIGN & HISTORY - CA. EXHIBITIONS & DISPLAYS INDOORS & OUT, BY ART MUSEUMS & SIMILAR INSTITUTIONS OF WELL-DESIGNED HISTORIC & CONTEMPORARY FLAGS FOR STATES, CITIES, SCHOOLS, ETC. ALSO A NATIONAL FLAG DESIGN COMPETITION. (NAT'L). PAUL CHADBOURNE MILLS, DIRECTOR & CHAIRMAN; SANTA BARBARA MUSEUM OF ART; 1130 STATE ST; SANTA BARBARA, CA 93101. (#2296). **ARBA RECOGNIZED.**

RESTORATION PRESIDIO CHAPEL - SANTA BARBARA, CALIF. SANTA BARBARA PRESIDIO CHAPEL RESTARATION SITE LOCATED IN EL PRESIDIO STATE HISTORIC PARK-OBJECTIVE RESTORATION SPANISH FORT WITH CHAPEL BY ITS BICENT, 1982. PRESIDIO IS REGISTERED NATL HISTORIC PLACE. (LOCAL). LILIAN M FISH, PRESIDENT; SANTA BARBARA TRUST FOR HISTORIC PRESERVATION; PO BOX 388; SANTA BARBARA, CA 93102. (#3497). **ARBA GRANTEE.**

APR 21, '75. ANNUAL SANTA BARBARA BIRTHDAY. RESTORATION PRESIDIO CHAPEL - SANTA BARBARA, CALIF. SANTA BARBARA PRESIDIO CHAPEL RESTARATION SITE LOCATED IN EL PRESIDIO STATE HISTORIC PARK-OBJECTIVE RESTORATION SPANISH FORT WITH CHAPEL BY ITS BICENT, 1982. PRESIDIO IS REGISTERED NATL HISTORIC PLACE. (LOCAL). LILIAN M FISH, PRESIDENT; SANTA BARBARA TRUST FOR HISTORIC PRESERVATION; PO BOX 388; SANTA BARBARA, CA 93102. (#3497-502).

JULY 4, '75. SPIRIT OF 76 ANNUAL PARADE. RESTORATION PRESIDIO CHAPEL - SANTA BARBARA, CALIF. SANTA BARBARA PRESIDIO CHAPEL RESTARATION SITE LOCATED IN EL PRESIDIO STATE HISTORIC PARK-OBJECTIVE RESTORATION SPANISH FORT WITH CHAPEL BY ITS BICENT, 1982. PRESIDIO IS REGISTERED NATL HISTORIC PLACE. (LOCAL). LILIAN M FISH, PRESIDENT; SANTA BARBARA TRUST FOR HISTORIC PRESERVATION; PO BOX 388; SANTA BARBARA, CA 93102. (#3497-504).

AUG 1 - NOV 30, '75. 'NEW GLORY' - NATIONWIDE FLAG HISTORY & DESIGN CONTEST. SEEKS PROPOSALS FOR NEW FLAG DESIGNS FOR CITIES, COUNTIES, STATES, COMMUNITIES, ETHNIC GROUPS & OTHER SUCH ORGANIZATIONS. FOUR REGIONAL JURYINGS WILL BE FOLLOWED NATIONAL JURYING. NATIONAL WINNERS WILL BE MADE UP AS FLAGS & SHOWN IN EXHIBITS ACROSS NATION. (NAT'L). PAUL C MILLS, DIRECTOR; SANTA BARBARA MUSEUM OF ART; 1130 STATE ST; SANTA BARBARA, CA 93101. (#2296-1).

OCT 11, '75. SENIOR CITIZENS BICENTENNIAL FAIRE. FREE HEALTH CHECKS; BLOOD PRESSURE & HEARING; OLD-FASHIONED ARTS & CRAFTS; 20 HEALTH & RESOURCE AGENCIES; CITY COLLEGE GROUPS; ENTERTAINMENT. AT OAK PARK, W ALAMAR AVE & W JUNIPERO ST. (LOCAL). MRS BING DEMETRIUS, CHMN; COMMUNITY ACTION COMMISSION/SANTA BARBARA CITY RECREATION DEPT; PO BOX 1348; SANTA BARBARA, CA 93102. (#102095-1).

OCT 22, '75. BAND CONCERT, U S ARMED FORCES BICENTENNIAL BAND & CHORUS. THEATER & USHERS DONATED BY THE MANAGER, MR BROWN; RECEPTION AFTER SHOW BY PATRIOTIC GROUPS. AT ARLINGTON THEATER, 1317 STATE ST. (LOCAL). CHARLES IRELAND, CHMN; SANTA BARBARA ARBC; 2715 CLINTON TERR; SANTA BARBARA, CA 93105. (#102095-2).

NOV 28 - 30, '75. THE GARDEN THEATRE FESTIVAL. LIVE PERFORMANCE AT SANTA BARBARA FIESTA BOWL. (LOCAL). WARREN CHRISTENSEN, DIR; THEATRE-IN-PROGRESS; 2625 PORTLAND ST; LOS ANGELES, CA 90007. (#102234-1).

DEC 1 - 4, '75. SAINT BARBARA'S DAY OBSERVED EACH YEAR ON DECEMBER 4. RESTORATION PRESIDIO CHAPEL - SANTA BARBARA, CALIF. SANTA BARBARA PRESIDIO CHAPEL RESTARATION SITE LOCATED IN EL PRESIDIO STATE HISTORIC PARK-OBJECTIVE RESTORATION SPANISH FORT WITH CHAPEL BY ITS BICENT, 1982. PRESIDIO IS REGISTERED NATL HISTORIC PLACE. (LOCAL). LILIAN M FISH, PRESIDENT; SANTA BARBARA TRUST FOR HISTORIC PRESERVATION; PO BOX 388; SANTA BARBARA, CA 93102. (#3497-503).

DEC 6 - 7, '75. BICENTENNIAL WAGON TRAIN PILGRIMAGE CALIFORNIA WAGON. BICENTENNIAL WAGON PULLED BY 4 LOCAL BELGIUM DRAFT HORSES IN XMAS PARADE; OUTRIDERS, BICYCLISTS AND HIKERS WILL PRESENT SCROLLS SIGNED BY PEOPLE THROUGHOUT THE COUNTRY. AT ALAMEDA PARK. (LOCAL). MRS VIVIAN H OBERN, CHMN; SANTA BARBARA ARBC; 4140 MARINA DR; SANTA BARBARA, CA 93110. (#102602-1).

JAN 2 - 4, '76. AMERICAN FREEDOM TRAIN DISPLAY DAYS AT SANTA BARBARA. THE AMERICAN FREEDOM TRAIN WILL INCLUDE 10 EXHIBIT CARS & 2 SHOWCASE CARS DEPICTING DIFFERENT PHASES OF THE AMERICAN EXPERIENCE. ITS ARRIVAL WILL SERVE AS A CATALYST FOR LOCAL BICENTENNIAL CELEBRATIONS BY PEOPLE THROUGHOUT THIS NATION. (ST-WIDE). DON MALLICOAT, EDIT SVCS; THE AMERICAN FREEDOM TRAIN FOUNDATION, INC.; 5205 LEESBURG PIKE, SUITE 800; BAILEY'S XRDS, VA 22041. (#1776-38).

FEB 24 - 25, '76. RE-ENACTMENT, DE ANZA TREK MEXICO TO SAN FRANCISCO, 1775-1776. FESTIVAL, LIVE PERFORMANCE, AWARD. (LOCAL). MRS VIVIAN OBERN, CHMN; SANTA BARBARA ARBC; 4140 MARINA DR, HOPE RANCH; SANTA BARBARA, CA 93110. (#261-2).

MAR 26 - 28, '76. SANTA BARBARA INTERNATIONAL ORCHID SHOW. THIRTY TO FORTY ORCHID DISPLAYS: SPECIMENS, THEME GARDENS, & ARRANGEMENTS. AT EARL WARREN SHOWGROUNDS. (REGN'L). ALICE RYPINS, COORD; SANTA BARBARA CHAMBER OF COMMERCE; 919 VERONICA SPRINGS RD; SANTA BARBARA, CA 93105. (#103416-235).

APR 14, '76. ODORI FESTIVAL OF JAPAN VISITS SANTA BARBARA. LIVE PERFORMANCE. (INT'L). DIRECTOR; MEL HOWARD PRODUCTIONS, INC; 143 E 27TH ST; NEW YORK, NY 10016. (#108965-6).

MAY 22 - 23, '76. UNITED STATES ARMED FORCES BICENTENNIAL CARAVAN. CARAVAN IS COMPOSED OF EXHIBIT VANS FOR EACH MILITARY SERVICE. PROJECT THEME IS ' HISTORY OF THE ARMED FORCES & THEIR CONTRIBUTIONS TO THE NATION'. (LOCAL). THEODORE HARDER, CHMN; U S ARMED FORCES BICENTENNIAL CARAVAN; 441 STANLEY DR; SANTA BARBARA, CA 93105. (#1775-573).

MAY 28 - JUNE 12, '76. '1776'; A MUSICAL DRAMATIZATION BY SHERMAN EDWARDS & PETER STONE. LIVE PERFORMANCE AT LOBERO THEATRE 33 E CANON PERDIDO; FREE PARKING. (LOCAL). PAUL W JOHNSON, DIRECTOR; SANTA BARBARA AMERICAN REVOLUTION BICENTENNIAL COMMITTEE; 914 SANTA BARBARA ST; SANTA BARBARA, CA 93101. (#3497-2).

JUNE 26 - JULY 4, '76. 40TH ANNUAL SEMANA NAUTICA. AN EXTENSIVE SPORTS FESTIVAL SALUTES THE BICENTENNIAL WITH MORE THAN 50 EVENTS INCLUDING A 90-MINUTE FIREWORKS DISPLAY. (LOCAL). ALLEN SCMIDT, PRESIDENT; SANTA BARBARA CHAMBER OF COMMERCE; 1301 SANTA BARBARA ST, BOX 299; SANTA BARBARA, CA 93102. (#103416-385).

JULY 4, '76. AERIAL FIREWORKS DISPLAY. LIVE PERFORMANCE AT BEACH & HARBOR AREAS. (LOCAL). R L SHAW, CHAIRMAN; SANTA BARBARA JAYCEES; 2555 CALLE GALICIA; SANTA BARBARA, CA 93109. (#15486-1).

JULY 4, '76. SPIRIT OF '76 PARADE & PATRIOTIC RALLY. FLOAT ENTRIES ARE INVITED; ALL ASPECTS OF THE BICENTENNIAL WILL BE REPRESENTED. AT PARADE WILL BEGIN AT STATE ST. (LOCAL). WARD B JENKS, DIRECTOR; SANTA BARBARA AMERICAN REVOLUTION BICENTENNIAL COMMITTEE; 3430 LOS PINOS DR; SANTA BARBARA, CA 93105. (#3497-3).

SANTA CLARA

'A DIFFERENT DRUMMER' - FILM - SANTA CLARA, CA. FILM COMPARES HISTORICAL EVENTS OF THE EAST TO THOSE OF CALIFORNIA; IT ALSO DEPICTS SANTA CLARA TODAY. READY & AVAILABLE FOR NATIONAL USE. (LOCAL). MORT READ, PROJ DIRECTOR; SANTA CLARA BICENTENNIAL COMMITTEE; 1515 EL CAMINO; SANTA CLARA, CA 95052. (#18620).

USS BICENTENNIAL BATTLESHIP-MIAMI TO NEW YORK. MINIATURE BATTLESHIP CARRIES EXCHANGE OF MAIL FROM LOS ANGELES CHILDREN & MAYOR BRADLEY TO 6 LARGE EAST COAST CITIES; 16MM COLOR FILM WILL BE BROUGHT BACK TO SHARE WITH 66,000 CHILDREN. (REGN'L). PATRICIA GATES, PROJ DIRECTOR; LAND & SEA INTERNATIONAL; 720 LAURELWOOD AVE; SANTA CLARA, CA 95050. (#20772).

DEC 20, '75. CHRISTMAS PAGEANT. EVENTS INCLUDE CANDLELIGHT, CHORAL PROCESSION, NATIVITY SCENE WITH LIVE ANIMALS & PEOPLE, LIVE DRAMATIZATION OF WASHINGTON CROSSING THE DELAWARE, PORTION OF THE NUTCRACKER BALLET, MODERN VERSION OF DICKENS 'CHRISTMAS CAROL' AND MEXICAN-SPANISH CHRISTMAS CELEBRATION. AT CENTRAL PARK. (LOCAL). JEANNIE CURRY, PROJ COORD; SANTA CLARA CHAMBER OF COMMERCE; SANTA CLARA, CA 95052. (#103942-1).

FEB 21 - 22, '76. CHINESE MUSICAL FESTIVAL. THIS EVENT CONSISTS OF A 2-HR MUSICAL PROGRAM COSPONSORED BY SANTA CLARA UNIV CHINESE ALUMNI ASSOC AND INSTITUTE OF SINO-AMERICAN STUDIES AND PERFORMED BY A GROUP OF SINO-AMERICAN VOCALISTS AND MUSICIANS WITH ITS EMPHASIS ON CHINESE MUSIC AND SOME WESTERN SONGS. AT MAYER THEATRE, UNIVERSITY OF SANTA CLARA. (LOCAL). DR SHU-PARK CHAN, CHMN; SANTA CLARA COUNTY BICENTENNIAL CHINESE FESTIVAL COMMITTEE; PO BOX 255; SANTA CLARA, CA 95052. (#102809-1).

MAR 6, '76. 200 YEARS OF AMERICAN FASHION. FASHION SHOW OF EARLY AMERICAN CLOTHES; REFRESHMENTS WILL BE EARLY AMERICAN COOKIES. AT CHURCH OF THE VALLEY, 400 N WINCHESTER. (LOCAL). ANITA GOLLWITZER, CHMN; AMERICAN ASSOC OF UNIVERSITY WOMEN; 6865 BURNSIDE DR; SAN JOSE, CA 95120. (#104699-2).

MAY 2 - 31, '76. 'THE GREAT AMERICAN TRANSCON' BALLOON RACE PROMOTION. A BALLOON NAMED 'THE GREAT AMERICAN TRANSCON' WILL VOYAGE ACROSS THE USA, CARRYING A BANNER UNDERNEATH WITH HEADING 'WE THE UNDERSIGNED ARE PROUD TO BE AMERICANS'. SIGNATURES WILL BE GATHERED AND THE SCROLL WILL BE PRESENTED TO THE PRESIDENT. AT MARRIOTT'S GREAT AMERICA PARK. (NAT'L). STEVE ADAMS, PROJ DIR; GREAT AMERICAN TRANSCONTINENTAL BALLOON RACE; PO BOX 6915; SAN JOSE, CA 95150. (#104044-5).

MAY 29 - OCT 3, '76. MARRIOTT'S 'GREAT AMERICA'. LIVE MUSICAL PERFORMANCES, PARADES AND HISTORICALLY THEMED AND COSTUMED AREAS DEPICTING ERAS IN AMERICA'S PAST. COLONIAL 1776 DRILL TEAM, MARDI GRAS FLOAT, PARADE & VISITING HIGH SCHOOL & COLLEGE BANDS; OPEN WEEKENDS SPRING & FALL; OPEN DAILY DURING SUMMER. AT BESIDE US 101 IN SANTA CLARA, 3 MI NORTH OF SAN JOSE, CA. (REGN'L). JOHN POMIROO; MARRIOTT'S GREAT AMERICA; 1776 GREAT AMERICA PARKWAY; SANTA CLARA, CA 95000. (#103416-341).

JUNE 26 - 27, '76. UNITED STATES ARMED FORCES BICENTENNIAL CARAVAN. CARAVAN IS COMPOSED OF EXHIBIT VANS FOR EACH MILITARY SERVICE. PROJECT THEME IS ' HISTORY OF THE ARMED FORCES & THEIR CONTRIBUTIONS TO THE NATION'. (LOCAL). LARRY J MARSHALLI, CHMN; U S ARMED FORCES BICENTENNIAL CARAVAN; 1954 STAFFORD ST; SANTA CLARA, CA 95050. (#1775-581).

SANTA CRUZ

OLD TOWN CLOCK RESTORATION - SANTA CRUZ, CA. RESTORATION OF OLD TOWN CLOCK TO STAND ON A TOWER AT THE HEAD OF THE DOWNTOWN GARDEN MALL. (LOCAL). ROBERT DARROW, CHAIRMAN; TOWN CLOCK COMMITTEE; PACIFIC AVE & LINCOLN; SANTA CRUZ, CA 95060. (#23909).

REVOLUTIONARY BROADSIDES - SANTA CRUZ, CA. A PEOPLE'S SILKSCREEN WORKSHOP, RUN COOPERATIVELY, WILL PRODUCE CONTEMPORARY POSTER MESSAGES USING AMERICAN REVOL SLOGANS; THE TALENT OF ARTISTS, POETS, WRITERS AND PRINTERS WILL BE COMBINED. (LOCAL). BILL REYNOLDS, PROJ DIRECTOR; MUSEUM WITHOUT WALLS, COUNTY SPIRIT PROGRAM; 710 OCEAN AVE, RM 310; SANTA CRUZ, CA 95060. (#12778).

JUNE 19 - 20, '76. MUSEUM WITHOUT WALLS COUNTY SPIRIT PROGRAM - ART EXHIBIT. JURIED ART SHOW OPEN ONLY TO SANTA CRUZ COUNTY RESIDENTS IN ORDER TO CELEBRATE THE GROWING NUMBER AND EXCEPTIONAL TALENT OF DEDICATED VISUAL ARTISTS WHO HAVE MADE THIS AREA THEIR HOME ENRICHING THIS LOCAL BY THEIR PRESENCE. AT PACIFIC GARDEN MALL. (LOCAL). CLAUDIA BACH, DIRECTOR; MUSEUM WITHOUT WALLS; 701 OCEAN ST; SANTA CRUZ, CA 95060. (#200006-119).

JULY 4, '76. JULY 4TH PARADE & TOWN CLOCK DEDICATION. PARADE, CEREMONY AT PACIFIC AVE. (LOCAL). MRS FERN CONGER, DIRECTOR; SANTA CRUZ CITY BICENTENNIAL COMMITTEE; 231 GLENWOOD AVE; SANTA CRUZ, CA 95060. (#107086-1).

SANTA FE SPG

ANTHOLOGY OF RECOLLECTIONS OF SANTA FE SPRINGS, CA. A HISTORY OF SANTA FE SPRINGS IS BEING PUBLISHED. (LOCAL). NADINE HATHAWAY, CHAIRMAN; BICENTENNIAL COMMISSION OF SANTA FE SPRINGS; 11710 TELEGRAPH RD; SANTA FE SPG, CA 90670. (#29010).

DEC 10, '75. WAGON TRAIN VISITATION. MAYOR GREETED WAGON TRAIN AT CITY LIMITS, ESCORTED ASSEMBLAGE & LOCAL RIDERS TO SCHOOL WHERE COSTUMED CHILDREN PUT ON WELCOMING PROGRAM. CITY HOSTED WAGON PERSONNEL, BICENTENNIAL COMMISSION MEMBERS AND ENTERTAINERS FOR LUNCH. FAIR HELD IN PARK IN THE EVENING. AT LAKEVIEW SCHOOL, HATHAWAY HOME, LOS NISTOS PARK. (LOCAL). NADINE HATHAWAY, CHAIRMAN; BICENTENNIAL COMMISSION OF SANTA FE SPRINGS; 11901 E FLORENCE AVE; SANTA FE SPG, CA 90670. (#200006-368).

SANTA MARIA

APR 18 - DEC 10, '75. BICENTENNIAL EVENTS AT ALLAN HANCOCK COLLEGE APR-DEC '75. 4/18 RE-ENACTMENT OF PAUL REVERE'S RIDE; 10/22 LECTURE: WHERE TO FROM HERE?; 11/2 LOS ANGELES CHAMBER ORCHESTRA CONCERT; 11/7 BAND CONCERT; 11/21 LECTURE: THE EVOLUTION OF THE PRESIDENCY; 12/10 LECTURE: SCIENCE IN THE LAST TWO HUNDRED YEARS. (LOCAL). E C STEVENS; ALLAN HANCOCK COLLEGE; 800 SOUTH COLLEGE DR; SANTA MARIA, CA 93454. (#200006-500).

JAN 13 - MAY 20, '76. BICENTENNIAL EVENTS AT ALLAN HANCOCK COLLEGE JAN-MAY '76. 1/13 UTAH SYMPHONY CONCERT; 1/20 LECTURE: LITERATURE & THE AMER TRADITION; 2/25 LECTURE: EARLY AMERICAN ARTISTS; 3/12 DRAMA PRODUCTION '1776'; 3/24 LECTURE: AMERICA'S HERITAGE-AMERICA'S CHALLENGE; 4/28 ORIGIN OF DECLARATION OF INDEPENDENCE; 5/20 JOHN BIGGS CONCERT. (LOCAL). E C STEVENS; ALLAN HANCOCK COLLEGE; 800 S COLLEGE DR; SANTA MARIA, CA 93454. (#200006-501).

SANTA MONICA

MAY 2 - 3, '76. UNITED STATES ARMED FORCES BICENTENNIAL CARAVAN. CARAVAN IS COMPOSED OF EXHIBIT VANS FOR

SANTA MONICA — CONTINUED

EACH MILITARY SERVICE. PROJECT THEME IS ' HISTORY OF THE ARMED FORCES & THEIR CONTRIBUTIONS TO THE NATION'. (LOCAL). MRS CLO HOOVER, CHAIRMAN; U S ARMED FORCES BICENTENNIAL CARAVAN; 301 OCEAN AVE; SANTA MONICA, CA 90402. (#1775-561).

JUNE 26, '76. 44TH ANNUAL HIGHLAND GATHERING AND GAMES. SCOTS COMPETE IN A VARIETY OF GAMES DURING THIS ANNUAL HIGHLAND GATHERING. COVERS ENTIRE WEST COAST OF US & CANADA. & GUESTS COME ANNUALLY FROM AS FAR NORTH AS BRITISH CO. AT CORSAIR FIELD. (ST-WIDE). MARYLIN HUDSON, COORD; UNITED SCOTTISH SOCIETIES, INC.; PO BOX 22, AMBASSADOR HOTEL; LOS ANGELES, CA 90010. (#103416-386).

NOV 28, '76. '13 STARS ON A BLUE FIELD' AND LANDSCAPE WITH ANGELS. A DRAMATIC MONOLOGUE ON THE REVOLUTIONARY WAR ENTITLED '13 STARS ON A BLUE FIELD' & A MOVIE ON THE HISTORY OF THE GROWTH OF LOS ANGELES WILL BE HELD. AT JOHN ADAMS AUDITORIUM, 2425 16TH ST. (LOCAL). HERBERT RONEY, DEAN; SANTA MONICA COLLEGE - COMMUNITY SERVICES; 1815 PEARL ST; SANTA MONICA, CA 90405. (#109373-1).

SANTA PAULA

PIONEER FOUNTAIN - SANTA PAULA, CA. A FOUNTAIN IS TO BE BUILT IN CITY PARK WITH TILED DEPICTIONS OF CITY LANDMARKS. (LOCAL). MRS J R HENDERSON, CHAIRMAN; SANTA PAULA BICENTENNIAL COMMISSION; 1158 WOODLAND DR; SANTA PAULA, CA 93060. (#32551).

JULY 16 - 18, '76. SANTA PAULA CITROS FESTIVAL AND PARADE. BICENTENNIAL COMMITTEE SPONSORED 'UP WITH PEOPLE' AND THE BALLET 'FOLKLORICO DE MEXICANO' AS CULTURAL EVENTS. AT CIVIC PARK. (LOCAL). MARY ALICE HENDERSON; KIWANIS CLUB & SANTA PAULA BICENTENNIAL COMMITTEE; 1158 WOODLAND DR; SANTA PAULA, CA 93060. (#200006-498).

SANTA ROSA

CUB SCOUT BICENTENNIAL COLOR GUARD, SANTA ROSA, CA. THE CUB SCOUT COLOR GUARD WILL PERFORM AT ALL PATRIOTIC EVENTS. (LOCAL). EDMOND A COLEMAN, DIRECTOR; VFW, AMERICAN LEGION, 40 & 8 SOC, MILITARY ORDER PURPLE HEART; 1713 HAPPY VALLEY RD; SANTA ROSA, CA 95404. (#26358).

SEPT 12 - 13, '76. UNITED STATES ARMED FORCES BICENTENNIAL CARAVAN. CARAVAN IS COMPOSED OF EXHIBIT VANS FOR EACH MILITARY SERVICE. PROJECT THEME IS 'HISTORY OF THE ARMED FORCES & THEIR CONTRIBUTIONS TO THE NATION.'. (LOCAL). DR JOHN F MCGREW, CHMN; UNITED STATES ARMED FORCES BICENTENNIAL CARAVAN; 6980 ANALY AVE; SEBASTOPOL, CA 95472. (#1775-716).

SANTA YNEZ

SANTA YNEZ INDIAN COMMUNITY BUILDING - CA. CONSTRUCTION OF SANTA YNEZ COMMUNITY BUILDING FOR USE FOR MEETING ROOM AND TRIBAL OFFICE. (LOCAL). EDWARD OLIVAS, TRIBAL CHAIRMAN; SANTA YNEZ BAND OF MISSION INDIANS; BOX 517; SANTA YNEZ, CA 93460. (#22848). **ARBA GRANTEE.**

SANTA YNEZ INDIAN CAMPGROUND/WILDLIFE HOME IN CA. CONSTRUCTION OF CAMPSITES, ACCESS ROADS, NATURE TRAILS & SANCTUARY FOR WILDLIFE. (LOCAL). EDWARD OLIVAS, TRIBAL CHAIRMAN; SANTA YNEZ BNAD OF MISSION INDIANS; PO BOX 517; SANTA YNEZ, CA 93460. (#22849). **ARBA GRANTEE.**

SARATOGA

MAR 16, '76. 'LIBERTY: CAN WE AFFORD IT?'. THE LECTURE WILL BE DELIVERED BY ARTHUR GOLDBERG, FORMER JUSTICE ON THE U S SUPREME COURT. AT WEST VALLEY COLLEGE GYMNASIUM. (LOCAL). STANLEY C BENZ, COUNSELOR; SANT CLARA COUNTY COLLEGE AND UNIVERSITIES CONSORTIUM; SAN JOSE STATE UNIV; SAN JOSE, CA 95192. (#103394-2).

SAUGUS

JAN 31, '76. BICENTENNIAL COSTUME BALL. FESTIVAL AT GLASSBLOWERS HALL. (LOCAL). BOBBIE TRUEBLOOD, CHMN; NEWHALL OPTIMISTS CLUB & SANTA CLARA BICENTENNIAL COMMITTEE; 23845 W MCBEAN PKWY; VALENCIA, CA 91355. (#200006-122).

SAUSALITO

REDISCOVER AMERICA -CALIF REHABILITATION PROJECT. A COMMUNITY IMPROVEMENT PROGRAM WHERE HISTORICAL COMMUNITY BUILDINGS ARE REHABILITATED AND USED FOR BENEFICIAL COMMUNITY ACTIVITIES. THE REHABILITATION SUPPORTED BY GRANTS FROM AMERICA THE BEAUTIFUL FUNDS. (ST-WIDE). JAMES ROBERTSON, DIRECTOR; AMERICA THE BEAUTIFUL FUND; 2200 BRIDGEWAY; SAUSALITO, CA 94965. (#213). **(??). ARBA GRANTEE.**

SAUSALITO HISTORICAL ROOM, CA. A HISTORICAL MUSEUM PROVIDING REFERENCE MATERIAL FOR HISTORICAL RESEARCH; PLUS ARTIFACTS. (LOCAL). R. JACK TRACY, HISTORIAN; SAUSALITO HISTORICAL SOCIETY; PO BOX 352; SAUSALITO, CA 94965. (#15886). **ARBA GRANTEE.**

SCOTTS VALLEY

JULY 31 - AUG 7, '76. BICENTENNIAL CAVALCADE OF SANTA CRUZ COUNTY WILD WEST REVIEW. THE ONLY SHOW OF ITS KIND IN CA. THE SOUVENIR PROGRAM IS BEING SOLD FOR $1.00 WITH PROCEEDS FOR 'SANTA CRUZ COUNTY HISTORICAL RESTORATION AND LANDMARKS REVOLVING FUND'. AT 'THE RANCH' 6017 SCOTTS VALLEY DR. (REGN'L). AGNES KNOX LEWIS, COORD; SCOTTS VALLEY BICENTENNIAL CAVALCADE COMMITTEE; 4867 SCOTTS VALLEY DR; SCOTTS VALLEY, CA 95066. (#200006-497).

SEAL BEACH

ANTIQUE FIRE ENGINE MUSEUM IN SEAL BEACH, CA. RESTORE ANTIQUE 1929 FIRE TRUCK TO MINT CONDITION AND BUILD ANTIQUE FIRE ENGINE MUSEUM TO HOUSE IT AND ALL OTHER MEMORABILIA PERTAINING TO THE HISTORY OF THE FIRE DEPT IN THE CITY. (LOCAL). PROCTOR H WEIR, EXEC MANAGER; SEAL BEACH CHAMBER OF COMMERCE; 13820 SEAL BEACH BLVD; SEAL BEACH, CA 90740. (#9124).

OCT 26, '75. BICENTENNIAL CONCERT. LIVE PERFORMANCE AT SEAL BEACH PIER. (LOCAL). E E SIEGRIST, COORD; LONG BEACH MUNICIPAL BAND; 3500 E ANAHEIM; LONG BEACH, CA 90804. (#200006-90).

MAY 15 - 16, '76. BICENTENNIAL OPEN HOUSE 1976. LIVE PERFORMANCE, EXHIBIT AT NAVAL WEAPONS STATION. (LOCAL). C W FLAIG; US NAVY; NAVAL WEAPONS STATION; SEAL BEACH, CA 90740. (#200006-478).

SEASIDE

NEW BICENTENNIAL ROOM IN SEASIDE, CALIFORNIA. A COLLECTION OF LOCAL, COUNTY, STATE AND NATIONAL HISTORICAL DOCUMENTS TO BE HOUSED IN THE NEW CITY LIBRARY CONFERENCE ROOM. (LOCAL). OSCAR LAWSON, CHAIRMAN BICENT COMMITTEE; CITY OF SEASIDE; 440 HARCOURT AVE; SEASIDE, CA 93955. (#9337).

JULY 2, '76. DRUM AND BUGLE CORPS INVITATIONAL FIELD CONTEST. EXHIBIT. (LOCAL). OSCAR LAWSON; CITY OF SEASIDE; 440 HARCOURT AVE; SEASIDE, CA 93955. (#9337-501).

JULY 3, '76. MONTEREY PENINSULA PARADE OF CHAMPIONS - INVITATIONAL PARADE. EXHIBIT. (LOCAL). OSCAR LAWSON; CITY OF SEASIDE; 440 HARCOURT AVE; SEASIDE, CA 93955. (#9337-502).

SEBASTOPOL

MEMORIAL GARDENS IN SEBASTAPOL, CALIFORNIA. RESTORATION OF LUTHER BURBANK EXPERIMENTAL FARM AS A MEMORIAL GARDEN & HORTICULTURAL CENTER, EMPHASIZING BURBANK'S AGRICULTURAL CONTRIBUTIONS AND INTENDED FOR SPECIAL USE BY SELECTED GROUPS. (ST-WIDE). MELVIN DAVIS, CITY MANAGER; CITY OF SEBASTAPOL; CITY HALL; SEBASTAPOL, CA 95472. (#6320). **(??).**

SEPT 14, '76. UNITED STATES ARMED FORCES BICENTENNIAL CARAVAN. CARAVAN IS COMPOSED OF EXHIBIT VANS FOR EACH MILITARY SERVICE. PROJECT THEME IS 'HISTORY OF THE ARMED FORCES & THEIR CONTRIBUTIONS TO THE NATION.'. (LOCAL). BICENTENNIAL CHAIRMAN; UNITED STATES ARMED FORCES BICENTENNIAL CARAVAN; CITY HALL; SEBASTOPOL, CA 95472. (#1775-717).

SHAFTER

MEDALLION CONTEST - PROJ OF SHAFTER, CA. TWO-SIDED MEDALLION, WITH ONE SIDE DEPICTING U S HISTORY AND OTHER SHAFTER HISTORY WHICH WILL ALSO BE USED AS NEW CITY SEAL. CONTEST OPEN TO ALL AGES WITH U S SAVINGS BOND AWARDED FOR EACH SIDE. (LOCAL). HERB HOWELL, PROJ DIRECTOR; CHAMBER OF COMMERCE; PO BOX 1088; SHAFTER, CA 93263. (#12166).

OLD SHAFTER STATIONERY - PROJ OF SHAFTER, CA. STATIONERY ILLUSTRATING SEVERAL HISTORICAL BUILDINGS IN SHAFTER; FOR SALE IN COMMUNITY. (LOCAL). NINA LEIGH, CHAIRMAN; SHAFTER BICENTENNIAL COMMITTEE; 242 PINE ST; SHAFTER, CA 93263. (#12167).

ORAL HISTORY PROJECT OF SHAFTER, CA. AUDIO VISUAL TAPING OF SHAFTER PIONEERS BY HIGH SCHOOL STUDENTS FOR PRESENTATION TO SERVICE CLUBS AND PRESERVATION IN LIBRARY. (LOCAL). NINA LEIGH, CHAIRMAN; SHAFTER WOMAN'S CLUB; PO BOX 663; SHAFTER, CA 93263. (#12164).

SHAFTER MUSEUM - PROJ OF SHAFTER, CA. CONVERT THE OLDEST BUILDING IN SHAFTER INTO A MUSEUM. (LOCAL). PAT RICHARDSON, PRESIDENT; COMMUNITY IMPROVEMENT COUNCIL; 314 WALNUT; SHAFTER, CA 93263. (#12163).

SEPT 3, '75 - JUNE 1, '76. COLORING BOOK CONTEST. CONTEST FOR SCHOOL CHILDREN, GRADE K-3; PICTURES AND STORIES DEPICT AMERICAN HISTORY. AT RICHLAND SCHOOL, 331 SHAFTER AVE. (LOCAL). AL SANDRINI; RICHLAND SCHOOL; 331 N SHAFTER AVE; SHAFTER, CA 93263. (#12165-1).

APR '76. MISS SHAFTER QUEEN PAGEANT. LIVE PERFORMANCE. (LOCAL). BEN GRUNDY, PROJ DIRECTOR; SHAFTER FESTIVAL COMMITTEE & CHAMBER OF COMMERCE; 164 STONE AVE; SHAFTER, CA 93263. (#200006-128).

MAY 15 - 18, '76. SHAFTER POTATO AND COTTON FESTIVAL. PARADE, COMPETITION AT MEMORIAL HALL, STRINGHAM PARK, HUDSON PARK, MANNEL PARK. (LOCAL). BEN GRUNDY, PROJ DIRECTOR; SHAFTER FESTIVAL COMMITTEE, SHAFTER CHAMBER OF COMMERCE; 164 STONE AVE; SHAFTER, CA 93263. (#100641-1).

JULY 4, '76. 4TH OF JULY CELEBRATION. FESTIVAL AT SHAFTER HIGH SCHOOL STADIUM. (LOCAL). BEN GRUNDY, PROJ DIRECTOR; SHAFTER FESTIVAL COMMITTEE, SHAFTER CHAMBER OF COMMERCE; 164 STONE AVE; SHAFTER, CA 93263. (#100641-2).

JULY 17 - 18, '76. JUNIOR RODEO EVENT. COMPETITION. (LOCAL). BEN GRUNDY, PROJ DIRECTOR; SHAFTER FESTIVAL COMMITTEE & CHAMBER OF COMMERCE; 164 STONE AVENUE; SHAFTER, CA 93263. (#100641-3).

OCT '76. RECOGNITION DINNER FOR UNPAID CITY GOVERNMENT INDIVIDUALS. CEREMONY. (LOCAL). BEN GRUNDY, PROJ DIRECTOR; SHAFTER FESTIVAL COMMITTEE & CHAMBER OF COMMERCE; 164 STONE AVENUE; SHAFTER, CA 93263. (#100641-4).

SHINGLE SPG

JUNE 25 - 27, '76. DEDICATION OF MINI PARK 'PLAZA'. DEDICATION OF MINI PARK AND TOT PLAYGROUND ON PROPERTY THAT WAS NEVER DEVELOPED; ALSO, MONUMENT ON PLAZA CAMP SITE. AT MOTHER LODGE DR, EAST OF POST OFFICE. (LOCAL). MYRTLE A BAKER, SECRETARY; SHINGLE SPRINGS IMPROVEMENT ASSOC, INC; PO BOX 248; SHINGLE SPG, CA 95682. (#106171-8).

SIGNAL HILL

ALAMITOS #1 BICENTENNIAL LANDMARK - CA. PLACEMENT OF BICENTENNIAL PLAQUE AT THE SITE OF ALAMITOS #1, THE DISCOVERY WELL IN THE LONG BEACH-SIGNAL HILL OIL FIELD. IT WAS MOST PRODUCTIVE OIL FIELD IN HISTORY. (LOCAL). WILLIAM F MENDENHALL, CHAIRMAN; SIGNAL HILL BICENTENNIAL COMMITTEE; 2175 CHERRY AVE; SIGNAL HILL, CA 90806. (#32057).

BICENTENNIAL FIREPLUG PAINTING - SIGNAL HILL, CA. BICENTENNIAL THEME PAINTING OF CITY FIRE HYDRANTS BY VARIOUS YOUTH AND COMMUNITY GROUPS. (LOCAL). WILLIAM F MENDENHALL, CHAIRMAN; SIGNAL HILL BICENTENNIAL COMMITTEE; 2175 CHERRY AVE; SIGNAL HILL, CA 90806. (#32055).

BICENTENNIAL FLOWER GARDENS - SIGNAL HILL, CA. PLANTING OF BICENTENNIAL THEME FLOWER GARDENS IN CITY PARK BY THE VARIOUS COMMUNITY GROUPS. (LOCAL). WILLIAM F MENDENHALL, CHAIRMAN; SIGNAL HILL BICENTENNIAL COMMITTEE; 2175 CHERRY AVE; SIGNAL HILL, CA 90806. (#32056).

JESSIE NELSON CIRCLE/MONUMENT - SIGNAL HILL, CA. NAMING OF LOCAL STREET IN HONOR OF MRS JESSIE NELSON WHO WAS FIRST MAYOR OF SIGNAL HILL AND PLACEMENT OF APPROPRIATE SIGNS & MONUMENT. (LOCAL). WILLIAM F MENDENHALL, CHAIRMAN; SIGNAL HILL BICENTENNIAL COMMITTEE; 2175 CHERRY AVE; SIGNAL HILL, CA 90806. (#32054).

JUNE 19, '76. 18TH CENTURY COSTUME CONTEST. BICENTENNIAL THEME COSTUME CONTEST AT THE CITY'S ANNUAL ANNIVERSARY CELEBRATION/FIESTA. (LOCAL). WILLIAM MENDENHALL, CHMN; SIGNAL HILL BICENTENNIAL COMMITTEE; 2175 CHERRY AVE; SIGNAL HILL, CA 90806. (#200006-492).

SIMI VALLEY

SIMI VALLEY, CA, BICENT ARBOR AND AMPHITHEATRE. OPEN-AIR ARBOR AND AMPHITHEATRE TO BE BUILT IN COMMUNITY PARK WITH FUNDS RAISED BY WHOLE COMMUNITY TO BE USED BY ALL ARTS AND AGES TO BE DEDICATED JULY 4, 1976. (LOCAL). HON JAMES SMITH, MAYOR; CITY OF SIMI VALLEY BICENTENNIAL COORDINATING COMMITTEE; 3200 COCHRAN ST; SIMI VALLEY, CA 93065. (#16360).

SN JUN BATSTA

MAR 1, '75. LIBRARY PARK HISTORICAL MUSEUM TO BE OPENED TO PUBLIC. PROJECT TO BUILD A MUSEUM, LIBRARY AND PARK FOR USE OF THE COMMUNITY AND VISITORS. EXHIBITS IN THE MUSEUM ARE TO EXPLAIN THE HISTORY OF SAN JUAN BAUTISTA AND SOUTHERN CALIFORNIA. (LOCAL). ENOS SILVA, CHAIRMAN; CITY OF SAN JUAN BAUTISTA; 311 2ND ST; SN JUN BATSTA, CA 95045. (#5898-901).

MAY 28 - 29, '76. UNITED STATES ARMED FORCES BICENTENNIAL CARAVAN. CARAVAN IS COMPOSED OF EXHIBIT VANS FOR EACH MILITARY SERVICE. PROJECT THEME IS 'HISTORY OF THE ARMED FORCES AND THEIR CONTIBUTIONS TO THE NATION. AT PLAZA - SAN JUAN BAUTISTA. (LOCAL). MS ALMA ANDREAZZI, COORD; U S ARMED FORCES BICENTENNIAL CARAVAN; PO BOX 367; SN JUN BATSTA, CA 95045. (#1775-719).

SN LUIS OBSPO

SALE OF BICENTENNIAL MEDALS, SAN LUIS OBISPO, CA. BICENTENNIAL MEDALS WILL BE ON SALE. (LOCAL). HOWARD D MANKINS, CHAIRMAN; CITY OF SAN LUIS OBISPO; RM 220, COURTHOUSE ANNEX; SN LUIS OBSPO, CA 93401. (#32697).

SOLEDAD

SOLEDAD BEE & GONZALES TRIBUNE BICENT EFFORT-NBMRP. 3 JOINT PROGRAMS:1)EDUCATIONAL SPEAKING TOUR WITH DISPLAY OF HISTORICAL NEWSPAPERS;2)BEE WILL PROMOTE SPECIAL FIESTA FOR DE ANZA TREK & 3)TRIBUNE PROMOTES BICENTENNIAL OF CALIFORNIA'S WINE INDUSTRY. (LOCAL). DREW F WEST, EDITOR; SOLEDAD BEE; PO BOX 95; SOLEDAD, CA 93960. (#21288).

SOLVANG

PRINTING OF THE U S CONSTITUTION. GRAPHIC PRINTING OF THE U S CONSTITUTION. BICENTENNIAL LICENSE # 7619-0560. (NAT'L). PAUL NOCAS, PROJ DIRECTOR; DOCUMENT HOUSE; BOX 858; SOLVANG, CA 93463. (#12472).

SEPT 18 - 19, '76. DANISH DAYS. FESTIVAL. (LOCAL). COORDINATOR; SOLVANG CHAMBER OF COMMERCE; SOLVANG, CA 93463. (#103416-577).

SONOMA

NSGA SKAGGS ISLAND ART SHOW, SONOMA, CA. NSGA SKAGGS ISLAND ASSISTED IN PLANNING PHASES & PROVIDED MILITARY GUARDS THROUGHOUT THE MONTH OF JULY. (LOCAL). CW03 J F WHIPPLE, COORDINATOR; SAN FRANCISCO SOLANO MISSION; SONOMA, CA 95476. (#33688).

MAY 15, '76. OPEN HOUSE. BRIEFINGS & TOURS OF THE MILITARY FACILITIES OF NSGA SKAGGS ISLAND SONOMA, CA. (LOCAL). CW03 J F WHIPPLE USN; NAVAL SECURITY GROUP ACTIVITY SKAGGS ISLAND; SONOMA, CA 95476. (#200006-459).

JULY 4, '76. FOURTH OF JULY CELEBRATION AT NSGA SKAGGS ISLAND. INCLUDED AN OLD-FASHIONED PICNIC, ATHLETIC EVENTS, PATRIOTIC SPEECHES & VARIOUS DISPLAYS. OVERALL THEME: OLD-FASHIONED 4TH OF JULY. (LOCAL). CW03 J F WHIPPLE USN; NAVAL SECURITY GROUP ACTIVITY SKAGGS ISLAND; SONOMA, CA 95476. (#200006-460).

OCT 2, '76. UNITED STATES ARMED FORCES BICENTENNIAL CARAVAN. CARAVAN IS COMPOSED OF EXHIBIT VANS FOR EACH MILITARY SERVICE. PROJECT THEME IS 'HISTORY OF THE ARMED FORCES & THEIR CONTRIBUTIONS TO THE NATION'. (LOCAL). MRS JOHN MARSH; UNITED STATES ARMED FORCES BICENTENNIAL CARAVAN; 332 LAS CASTAS CT; SONOMA, CA 95476. (#1775-818).

SONORA

MIWOK INDIAN RECONSTRUCTION-SONORA, CALIF. RECONSTRUCT AN ASSEMBLY HOUSE OF THE MIWOK INDIANS. SURROUNDING THE BLDG WILL BE AN INTERPRETATIVE CENTER -REPRENSATIVE MIWOK STRUCTURES, NATURE TRAIL, ARTIFACTS, DISPLAYS, ETC. (LOCAL). RICHARD L DYER, DIRECTOR; TUOLUMNE COUNTY BICENTENNIAL ORG & COLUMBIA JR COLLEGE; BOX 1849; COLUMBIA, CA 95310. (#3928).

JUNE 17 - 19, '76. TUOLUMNE COUNTY PAGEANT. THE PAGEANT WILL FEATURE MUSIC & DRAMA DESIGNED TO CAPTURE THE UNIQUENESS OF TUOLUMNE COUNTY, CA. (LOCAL). RICHARD L DYER; TUOLUMNE COUNTY ARBC; RT 5, BOX 960; SONORA, CA 95370. (#10859-1).

SOUTH GATE

NOV 11, '75. VETERAN'S MEMORIAL FOUNTAIN DEDICATION. IN HONOR OF THOSE WHO GAVE THEIR LIVES IN THE LAST 4 WARS. (LOCAL). WILLIAM WOTHERSPOON, CHMN; SOUTH GATE CHAMBER OF COMMERCE; PO BOX K; SOUTH GATE, CA 90280. (#103226-1).

SQUAW VALLEY

JAN 10 - 11, '76. PRE-OLYMPIC INTERNATIONAL JUMP & CROSS COUNTRY MEET. COMPETITION. (INT'L). CHUCK MORSE, EXEC ADMIN; US SKI ASSOC & FAR WEST SKI ASSOC; 1313 W 8TH ST; LOS ANGELES, CA 90017. (#2438-7).

STANFORD

MICROFILMING FRANCIS B LOOMIS PAPERS-STANFORD UNIV. NEW MICROFILM EDITION OF PAPERS REFLECTING ONE OF MOST DYNAMIC PERIODS OF AMER HISTORY-ERA OF MONROE DOCTRINE, AMERICAN IMPERIALISM & THEODORE ROOSEVELT. (NAT'L). LYNN M JIMENEZ, EDITOR; DEPT OF SPECIAL COLLECTIONS, THE STANFORD UNIV LIBRARIES; STANFORD, CA 94305. (#13119).

MAR 6, '74. LECTURE VERMONT ROYSTER, AM PRESS & REVOLUTIONARY SOCIETY. DISTINGUISHED LECTURE SERIES ON BICENTENNIAL. 18 DISTINGUISHED SCHOLARS DISCUSS NATURE, FUTURE OF AM REVOLUTION AT NATION'S HISTORIC SITES---TAPED FOR BROADCAST ON PBS IN SPRING 1974. TOPICS COVER REV & SOCIETY, RELIGION, PRESS, LAW, CULTURE, GOV'T. (NAT'L). EARL H VOSS; AMERICAN ENTERPRISE INSTITUTE FOR PUBLIC POLICY RESEARCH; 1150 17TH STREET, N.W.; WASHINGTON, DC 20036. (#1297-910).

SEPT 15, '76. LONDON SCHOOLS SYMPHONY ORCHESTRA. LIVE PERFORMANCE AT STANFORD UNIVERSITY. (INT'L). CULTURAL AFFAIRS OFFICE; BRITISH EMBASSY; 3100 MASSACHUSETTS AVE, NW; WASHINGTON, DC 20008. (#108963-1).

STOCKTON

INDEPENDENCE GROVE, SAN JOAQUIN DELTA COLLEGE PROJ. PROJ TO PLANT 13 COAST SEQUOIAS AND TO ERECT A MARKER WITH A PATRIOTIC QUOTE. ALSO A BETSY ROSS FLAG DEDICATION CEREMONY. (LOCAL). EDWARD A RALEIGH, CHAIRMAN; SAN JOAQUIN DELTA COMMUNITY COLLEGE BICENT COMMITTEE; 5151 PACIFIC AVE; STOCKTON, CA 95207. (#6687).

'JUNIPERO SERRA, PIONEER OF THE CROSS' BOOK - CA. BIOGRAPHICAL STORY OF FATHER SERRA, FIRST PRESIDENT OF FRANCISCAN MISSIONS IN CALIFORNIA. (REGN'L). MRS LA SMITH, PRESIDENT; AUXILIARY TO CALIFORNIA PIONEERS, PIONEER MUSEUM; 1201 N PERSHING AVE; STOCKTON, CA 95203. (#19866).

U S COAST GUARD BOSTEAM 12'S BICENT PROJECT - CA. THROUGHOUT 1976, THIS GROUP TRAVELLED THROUGH CALIFORNIA, NEVADA & UTAH, SETTING UP THEIR BICENT & BOATING SAFETY DISPLYS. (REGN'L). CW03 E F KASUN, COMMANDING OFFICER; USCG BOSTEAM 12 NAVCOMMSTA; ROUGH & READY ISLAND; STOCKTON, CA 95203. (#28619).

SEPT 18, '75. 'THE SMALL WORLD OF MUSIC', CONCERT OF AMERICAN MUSIC. LIVE PERFORMANCE AT CIVIC AUDITORIUM. (LOCAL). GEORGE HARTMAN, DIR; SALVATION ARMY; ROTUNDA CITY HALL; STOCKTON, CA 95202. (#101911-1).

NOV 1 - 2, '75. UNITED STATES ARMED FORCES BICENTENNIAL CARAVAN. THE CARAVAN IS COMPOSED OF EXHIBIT VANS FOR EACH BRANCH OF THE MILITARY SERVICE. THE THEME OF THE EXHIBITION IS 'HISTORY OF THE ARMED FORCES AND THEIR CONTRIBUTION TO THE NATION'. (LOCAL). JOE CRAIG, CHAIRMAN; U S ARMED FORCES BICENTENNIAL EXHIBIT VANS PROJECT; CITY HALL; STOCKTON, CA 95202. (#1775-289).

DEC 1 - 3, '75. AMERICAN FREEDOM TRAIN DISPLAY DAYS AT STOCKTON, CALIFORNIA. THE AMERICAN FREEDOM TRAIN WILL INCLUDE 10 EXHIBIT CARS & 2 SHOWCASE CARS DEPICTING DIFFERENT PHASES OF THE AMERICAN EXPERIENCE. ITS ARRIVAL WILL SERVE AS A CATALYST FOR LOCAL BICENTENNIAL CELEBRATIONS BY PEOPLE THROUGHOUT THIS NATION. (ST-WIDE). SY FREEDMAN, DIR OF P/R; THE AMERICAN FREEDOM TRAIN FOUNDATION; 5205 LEESBURG PIKE, SUITE 800; BAILEY'S XRDS, VA 22041. (#1776-151).

JAN 15 - JULY 4, '76. DRAMA PRESENTATION 'TOM PAINE, 1776 THE PATRIOT'. OPENING, CEREMONY. (LOCAL). EDWARD A RALEIGH; SAN JOAQUIN DELTA COMMUNITY COLLEGE BICENT COMMITTEE; 5151 PACIFIC AVE; STOCKTON, CA 95207. (#6687-501).

JUNE 20, '76. 'SPIRIT OF AMERICA', UNIV OF CALIFORNIA MARCHING BAND. THIS EVENT IS PART OF A SIX-WEEK PERFORMANCE TOUR OF THE USA BY THE UNIV OF CA MARCHING BAND. SPIRIT OF AMERICA IS A COLLEGIATE MUSICAL REVUE CELEBRATING OUR NATION'S BICENTENNIAL, INCLUDING FOLK CONCERT, MARCHING, VAUDEVILLE, ROCK, DIXIELAND, JAZZ, BARBERSHOP, SOLOS, ETC. AT UNIV OF THE PACIFIC MEMORIAL 'TIGER' STADIUM. (LOCAL). JACK SCRAFIELD; THE BOYS' CLUB OF STOCKTON; 303 OLYMPIC CIR, BOY'S CLUB; STOCKTON, CA 95205. (#10515-5).

SUNLAND

JULY 3 - 5, '76. BICENTENNIAL FAIR - ALL-COMMUNITY PICNIC WITH CRAFTS AND PARADE. FIREWORKS AND COMMUNITY DEMONSTRATIONS. AT SUNLAND PARK, FOOTHILL BLVD AT SUNLAND BLVD. (LOCAL). HOWARD FINN, CHAIRMAN; BICENTENNIAL COMMITTEE OF SUNLAND-TUJUNGA; 9801 SHADOW ISLAND DR; SUNLAND, CA 91040. (#104753-9).

SUNNYVALE

BICENTENNIAL AGRICULTURAL PARK, SUNNYVALE, CA. THIS PARK CONTAINS 3 ACRES OF FLORA AND AGRICULTURAL PRODUCTS INDIGENOUS TO THE AREA. THIS IS AN ONGOING PROJECT WITH EXTENSIVE COMMUNITY PARTICIPATION. (LOCAL). DONALD E KORESKI, PROJECT DIRECTOR; SUNNYVALE BICENTENNIAL COMMISSION; COMMUNITY CTR, MANET J CRESCENT; SUNNYVALE, CA 94088. (#16681).

SUNNYVALE, CALIFORNIA PLANTS AN ARBORETUM. THE ARBORETUM WILL FEATURE LOCAL PLANT LIFE INDIGENOUS TO THE AREA. (LOCAL). DONALD E KORESKI, CHAIRPERSON; SUNNYVALE BICENT COMMITTEE; PO BOX 607; SUNNYVALE, CA 94088. (#9365).

JULY 19 - 20, '75. MUSTER FIREFIGHTERS OF SUNNYVALE, CA. FEATURE COMPETITIVE EVENTS TO DISPLAY HISTORIC FIRE FIGHTING SKILLS AND EQUIPMENT. (LOCAL). DONALD F KORESKI; SUNNYVALE BICENT COMMITTEE; PO BOX 607; SUNNYVALE, CA 94088. (#9366-1).

DEC 6, '75. PARADE OF FLAGS. FEATURE FLAGS OF EACH STATE IN JULY 4TH CELEBRATION IN ASSOCIATION WITH NUMEROUS DISPLAYS, EVENTS AND ACTIVITIES. AT DOWNTOWN SHOPPING AREA. (LOCAL). DONALD E KORESKI; SUNNYVALE BICENT COMMITTEE; PO BOX 607; SUNNYVALE, CA 94088. (#9364-1).

JUNE 28 - JULY 31, '76. EXHIBIT OF INDOOR FLYING AMERICAN FLAG - NEW GLORY & MOBILITY '76. THE LIBRARY IS OPEN FROM 9 AM TO 9 PM MONDAY THROUGH FRIDAY; FROM 9 AM TO 5 PM ON SATURDAY AND FROM 1 AM TO 5 PM ON SUNDAY. AT SUNNYVALE PUBLIC LIBRARY, 665 W OLIVE AVE. (LOCAL). MRS M J NISBETT, SUPV; SUNNYVALE PATENT LIBRARY; 665 W OLIVE AVE; SUNNYVALE, CA 94086. (#106468-1).

JULY 4, '76. BICENTENNIAL INDEPENDENCE DAY CELEBRATION. THE CELEBRATION INCLUDES COMMUNITY PICNICS ALL DAY AT SIX PARK SITES AND A FIREWORKS DISPLAY IN THE EVENING. AT LOCAL PARK SITES AND AIRFIELD AREA. (LOCAL). DONALD E KORESKI, DIR; SUNNYVALE BICENTENNIAL COMMISSION; PO BOX 607; SUNNYVALE, CA 94088. (#103007-1).

SUSANVILLE

BICENTENNIAL PROJECTS IN SUSANVILLE, CA. TV SERIES ON LASSEN COUNTY HISTORY; GET OUT THE VOTE; 3-DAY SEMINAR ON HYDROPONICS; COMMUNITY ALERTNESS TOWARDS AN ENVIRONMENTAL FUTURE, CONCERT SERIES; FILM SERIES; PLANTING OF TREES IN STUDENT PATIO. (LOCAL). HARLAN C STAMM, CHAIRMAN; LASSEN COLLEGE; PO BOX 3000; SUSANVILLE, CA 96130. (#33700).

INDIAN COMMUNITY CENTER IN SUSANVILLE, CA. THE CENTER WILL PROVIDE A MEETING PLACE FOR EVERYONE IN THE INDIAN COMMUNITY WITH YOUTH PROGRAMS, HEALTH CARE FOR THE ELDERLY AND RECREATION PROGRAMS. (LOCAL). FREDA C OWENS, CHAIRWOMAN; SUSANVILLE INDIAN RANCHERIA; SUSANVILLE, CA 96130. (#22844). **ARBA GRANTEE.**

JULY 8 - 9, '75. EMERSON LAKE WOMEN'S GOLF CLUB INVITATIONAL TOURNAMENT. COMPETITION. (LOCAL). JEROME GARZA, COORDINATOR; EMERSON LAKE WOMEN'S GOLF CLUB INVITATIONAL TOURNAMENT; EMERSON GOLF CLUB; SUSANVILLE, CA 96130. (#100252-4).

JULY 8 - 18, '75. BICENTENNIAL WAGON TRAIN. TOUR, PARADE AT MAIN ST. (LOCAL). JEROME GARZA; CITY OF SUSANVILLE; 66 N LASSEN ST; SUSANVILLE, CA 96130. (#100551-1).

AUG 13 - 17, '75. LASSEN COUNTY BICENTENNIAL FAIR AND LIVESTOCK SHOW. EXHIBIT, FAIR, PARADE AT LASSEN COUNTY FAIRGROUNDS. (LOCAL). AL MARTIN, CHAIRMAN; LASSEN COUNTY; FAIRGROUNDS OFFICE; SUSANVILLE, CA 96130. (#100252-2).

JULY 4, '76. PICNIC IN THE PARK. FESTIVAL AT CITY PARK. (LOCAL). JEROME GARZA, COORDINATOR; SUSANVILLE ARBC; 66 N LASSEN; SUSANVILLE, CA 96130. (#100252-3).

AUG 18 - 22, '76. LASSEN COUNTY BICENTENNIAL FAIR & LIVESTOCK SHOW. EXHIBIT, FAIR, PARADE AT LASSEN COUNTY FAIRGROUNDS. (LOCAL). AL MARTIN, CHAIRMAN; LASSEN COUNTY; FAIRGROUNDS OFFICE; SUSANVILLE, CA 96130. (#100252-1).

TAFT

BICENTENNIAL TREE PLANTING - TAFT, CA. EACH SCHOOL ON THE WEST SIDE WAS PRESENTED A BICENTENNIAL TREE TO PLANT. (LOCAL). G T MORGAN, CHAIRMAN; TAFT COLLEGE; BOX 22; TAFT, CA 93268. (#29161).

APR 22, '76. SCHOOLS SALUTE THE AMERICAN BICENTENNIAL. LIVE PERFORMANCE AT TAFT HIGH SCHOOL STADIUM. (LOCAL). G T MORGAN, CHAIRMAN; TAFT COLLEGE; BOX ZZ; TAFT, CA 93268. (#200006-352).

TAHOE-DONNER

MAR 1, '75. SKI TRAIL TOUR. COMPETITION, AWARD, CEREMONY, TOUR. (NAT'L). CHUCK MORSE, EXEC ADMIN; US SKI ASSOC & FAR WEST SKI ASSOC; 1313 W 8TH ST; LOS ANGELES, CA 90017. (#2438-902).

MAR 6 - 7, '76. SKI TRAIL TOUR. TOUR AT TRUCKEE, CALIFORNIA. (ST-WIDE). CHUCK MORSE, EXEC ADMIN.; US SKI ASSOCIATION & FAR WEST SKI ASSOCIATION; 1313 W 8TH ST; LOS ANGELES, CA 90017. (#2438-2).

TEHACHAPI

OCT 26, '76. UNITED STATES ARMED FORCES BICENTENNIAL CARAVAN. CARAVAN IS COMPOSED OF EXHIBIT VANS FOR EACH MILITARY SERVICE. PROJECT THEME IS 'HISTORY OF THE ARMED FORCES & THEIR CONTRIBUTIONS TO THE NATION'. (LOCAL). RICHARD E KLEIN; UNITED STATES ARMED FORCES BICENTENNIAL CARAVAN; 314 MELROSE CT; TEHACHAPI, CA 93561. (#1775-832).

TEMECULA

THE VALLEY POST'S BICENTENNIAL SUPPORT PEM-NBMRP. PAPER EMPHASIZED HERITAGE THEMES IN EACH ISSUE, WITH SPECIAL EDITION ON THE BICENTENNIAL ON JUNE 30, 1976. SPONSORED WEEK LONG CELEBRATION & A VARIETY OF CONTESTS, INCL ONE FOR AREA'S BICENTENNIAL FLAG. (LOCAL). KELLY HICKS, MANAGING EDITOR; THE VALLEY POST; PO BOX 156; TEMECULA, CA 92390. (#32953).

THOUSAND OAKS

SCARVES FOR THE BICENTENNIAL. SCARVES BEARING THE OFFICIAL BICENTENNIAL SYMBOL ARBA LICENSE NUMBER 76-19-0605. (NAT'L). ALAN UNGER, PRESIDENT; CATHY ACCESSORIES, INC; 141 TRIUNTO CANYON RD; THOUSAND OAKS, CA 91360. (#21183).

STAGECOACH INN MUSEUM COMPLEX IN THOUSAND OAKS, CA. LIVING MUSEUM REPRESENTING THE 3 MAIN CULTURAL INFLUENCES IN LOCAL HISTORY: NATIVE AMERICAN, LATINO & EARLY SETTLER. EXHIBIT AREAS WILL BE CONNECTED BY MARKED NATURE TRAILS, TYPICAL OF STATE COUNTRYSIDE.

THOUSAND OAKS — CONTINUED

(ST-WIDE). CAROL KEOCHEKIAN, CO-CHAIRMAN; CONEJO VALLEY BICENT COMMITTEE; 2318 SIRIUS ST; THOUSAND OAKS, CA 91360. (#9445).

NOV 7 - 8, '76. UNITED STATES ARMED FORCES BICENTENNIAL CARAVAN. CARAVAN IS COMPOSED OF EXHIBIT VANS FOR EACH MILITARY SERVICE. PROJECT THEME IS 'HISTORY OF THE ARMED FORCES & THEIR CONTRIBUTIONS TO THE NATION'. (LOCAL). MRS FRANCES PRINCE; UNITED STATES ARMED FORCES BICENTENNIAL CARAVAN; 2720 N GRANVILLA; THOUSAND OAKS, CA 91360. (#1775-839).

THREE RIVERS

MAY 1 - 12, '76. ARTISTS-IN-THE-PARK BICENT EXHIBIT AT SEQUOIA-KINGS CANYON NP. THE EXHIBIT CONTAINS 21 ORIGINAL PAINTINGS; COLLECTION REPRESENTS A VARIETY OF TECHNIQUES; EACH WORK IS IDENTIFIED WITH PERSONS, PLACES OR EVENTS IMPORTANT TO THE AMERICAN REVOLUTION. AT TULARE COUNTY MUSEUM, 27000 MOONEY BLVD, VISALIA, CA 93277. (REGN'L). SEQUOIA-KINGS CANYON NP; NATIONAL PARK SERVICE; THREE RIVERS, CA 93271. (#1474-14).

JULY 1 - SEPT 1, '76. 'THEY MADE AMERICA', KINGS CANYON NATIONAL PARK. A SERIES OF OLD-FASHIONED CAMPFIRE PROGRAMS PRESENTING CHARACTERS FROM THE PAST WHO HAVE HELPED SHAPE AMERICA: KIT CARSON, JOHN FREMONT, MARK TWAIN, NANCY KELSEY, JOHN MUIR AND JOAQUIN MURIETTA. AT BETWEEN CAMPGROUNDS 3 AND 4, CEDAR GROVE, KINGS CNAYON NP. (REGN'L). SEQUOIA-KINGS CANYON NP; NATIONAL PARK SERVICE; THREE RIVERS, CA 93271. (#6730-121).

AUG 23, '76. NATL PK SVC '...A LITTLE LOOK AROUND' VISITS SEQUOIA NP. THIS SHORT PROGRAM FEATURES ACTORS PORTRAYING FAMOUS AMERICANS OF THE PAST WHO'VE RETURNED TO SEE AMERICA'S GROWTH. AT AMPHITHEATER WITHIN PARK. (REGN'L). SEQUOIA NATL PK; NATIONAL PARK SERVICE; THREE RIVERS, CA 93271. (#5653-42).

OCT 11 - 25, '76. STUDENT ARTISTS BICENT EXHIBIT AT SEQUOIA-KINGS CANYON NP. THIS ART EXHIBIT CONSISTS OF 18 ORIGINAL PAINTINGS SELECTED FROM ENTRIES IN A NATIONWIDE STUDENT ART CONTEST. EACH PAINTING IS IDENTIFIED WITH PERSON, PLACES, OR EVENTS OF THE AMERICAN REVOLUTION. AT TULARE COUNTY MUSEUM, 27000 MOONEY BLVD. (REGN'L). SEQUOIA-KINGS CANYON NP; NATIONAL PARK SERVICE, SEQUOIA-KINGS CANYON NATIONAL PARK; THREE RIVERS, CA 93271. (#1474-13).

TIBURON

MAY 2, '76. BICENT PROGRAMS AT RICHARDSON BAY WILDLIFE SANCTUARY. ACTIVITIES INCLUDE TOURS OF THE AREA; HOURLY SHOWING 'IT BEGAN WITH BIRDS'; DISPLAYS OF ARTIFACTS RELATING TO COASTAL MIWOK PEOPLES; BAY SHORE STUDIES FOR 4-8 GRADERS. AT 376 GREENWOOD BEACH RD, TIBURON, CA. (LOCAL). JOAN G STANLEY; NATIONAL AUDUBON SOCIETY; MARIN HIST SOCIETY; TIBURON LANDMARKS SOC; 950 THIRD AVE; NEW YORK, NY 10022. (#19976-3).

JULY 8 - 9, '76. UNITED STATES ARMED FORCES BICENTENNIAL CARAVAN. CARAVAN IS COMPOSED OF EXHIBIT VANS FOR EACH MILITARY SERVICE. PROJECT THEME IS 'HISTORY OF THE ARMED FORCES & THEIR CONTRIBUTIONS TO THE NATION.'. (LOCAL). HERBERT WENIG, CHMN; UNITED STATES ARMED FORCES BICENTENNIAL CARAVAN; 65 ROLLING HILLS ROAD; TIBURON, CA 94902. (#1775-687).

TORRANCE

AMERICAN REVOLUTION AND THE BICENTENNIAL - CA. COLLEGE COURSE EXAMINING THE AMERICAN REVOLUTION AND ITS RELEVANCE FOR TODAY'S WORLD. (LOCAL). DR R SHERMAN, PROFESSOR; EL CAMINO COLLEGE; TORRANCE, CA 90506. (#31475).

BUSINESS IN AMERICA - TORRANCE, CA. CHANGING DISPLAYS PROVIDED BY LOCAL BUSINESS FIRMS SALUTING THE BICENTENNIAL. (LOCAL). JOHN MARTINELLI, DEPT OF BUSINESS; EL CAMINO COLLEGE; TORRANCE, CA 90506. (#31474).

FACULTY LECTURE SERIES ON AMERICAN REVOLUTION - CA. EXAMINING THE AMERICAN REVOLUTION AND THE REVOLUTIONARY ERA. (LOCAL). MS NADINE HATH, ASSOC PROF OF HISTORY; EL CAMINO COLLEGE; TORRANCE, CA 90506. (#31477).

FILM SERIES ON AMERICAN SOCIETY - TORRANCE, CA. AMERICAN LIFE AND GROWTH AS SEEN IN MAJOR MOTION PICTURES. (LOCAL). DR ROBERT HAAG, COORDINATOR OF COMMUNITY SERVICES; EL CAMINO COLLEGE; TORRANCE, CA 90506. (#31478).

HISTORY-POLITICAL SCIENCE LECTURE SERIES - CA. AMERICA AT 200 WILL BE DISCUSSED IN THE LECTURES. (LOCAL). DR RICHARD SHERMAN, PROF OF HISTORY; EL CAMINO COLLEGE; TORRANCE, CA 90506. (#31476).

LOCAL HISTORY - TORRANCE, CA. COURSE EXAMINING THE HISTORY OF THE COMMUNITIES SERVED BY EL CAMINO COLLEGE. (LOCAL). DONALD HALEY, DEPT OF HISTORY; EL CAMINO COLLEGE; TORRANCE, CA 90506. (#31472).

ORAL HISTORY PROJECT FOR EL CAMINO COLLEGE, CA. GATHERING INFORMATION FROM FACULTY, STUDENTS, ADMINISTRATORS, & MEMBERS OF THE COMMUNITY CONCERNING THE HISTORY OF EL CAMINO COLLEGE AND ITS ROLE IN THE COMMUNITY. (LOCAL). MS ELIZABETH DIXON, LIBRARIAN; EL CAMINO COLLEGE; TORRANCE, CA 90506. (#31473).

RESEARCH JEWISH AMERICAN HISTORY IN TORRANCE, CA. TO PROVIDE MATERIAL ON JEWISH CONTRIBUTIONS TO AMERICAN DEVELOPMENT AND TO EXAMINE THE JEWISH EXPERIENCE IN AMERICA AND THE REACTION OF JEW AND NON-JEW TO THAT ADVENTURE. (NAT'L). RICHARD P SHERMAN, PROFESSOR OF HISTORY; EL CAMINO COLLEGE; TORRANCE, CA 90506. (#5386).

'A TIME FOR NEW BEGINNINGS', TORRANCE, CA. A DRAMATIC PRESENTATION FEATURING HISTORIC PERSONALITIES SUCH AS GEORGE WASHINGTON. (LOCAL). LEE ROY BRANDES, DOCTOR OF MINISTRY; LUTHERAN CHURCH OF THE GOOD SHEPHERD; 21100 VICTOR; TORRANCE, CA 90503. (#20431).

JAN 1 - DEC 31, '76. 1776 EXHIBITS, MUSIC, SHOWS, COSTUMES, LECTURES, TOURS, GAMES, RIDES. CONTINUOUS SHOWS, RIDES, AND ENTERTAINMENT 215 SPECIALTY SHOPS IN A TURN-OF-THE-CENTURY THEMED ATMOSPHERE. $30,000,000 ENCLOSED AIR CO NDITIONED FACILITY THE ONLY ONE OF ITS KIND IN THE WORLD. AT 19800 HAWTHORNE BLVD. (AT 190TH ST.) TORRANCE, CALIFORNIA. (LOCAL). PAUL E CARLSON; OLD TOWNE MALL & AMUSEMENT PARK; 19800 HAWTHORNE BLVD; TORRANCE, CA 90503. (#50119-1).

MAR 7, '76. A BICENTENNIAL CONCERT BY EL CAMINO COLLEGE MUSIC DEPARTMENT. LIVE PERFORMANCE AT AUDITORIUM. (LOCAL). DR LEWIS HILGEL; EL CAMINO COLLEGE; EL CAMINO COLLEGE MUSIC DEPT; TORRANCE, CA 90506. (#200006-411).

MAR 10, '76. '1776', A MUSICAL PRESENTATION. LIVE PERFORMANCE AT EL CAMINO COLLEGE, 16007 CRENSHAW BLVD. (LOCAL). ROBERT HAAG, DIRECTOR; EL CAMINO COLLEGE; 16007 CRENSHAW BLVD; TORRANCE, CA 90506. (#102231-1).

MAY 14 - 15, '76. UNITED STATES ARMED FORCES BICENTENNIAL CARAVAN. CARAVAN IS COMPOSED OF EXHIBIT VANS FOR EACH MILITARY SERVICE. PROJECT THEME IS ' HISTORY OF THE ARMED FORCES & THEIR CONTRIBUTIONS TO THE NATION'. (LOCAL). DON ARMSON, CHARIAMN; U S ARMED FORCES BICENTENNIAL CARAVAN; 2819 W 182ND ST; REDONDO BEACH, CA 90278. (#1775-567).

NOV 8 - 14, '76. BMI BICENTENNIAL EXHIBIT TOUR. EXHIBIT AT LIBRARY. (LOCAL). DR ROBERT HAAG; EL CAMINO COLLEGE; TORRANCE, CA 90506. (#200006-412).

TRACY

JUNE 21, '76. UNITED STATES ARMED FORCES BICENTENNIAL CARAVAN. CARAVAN IS COMPOSED OF EXHIBIT VANS FOR EACH MILITARY SERVICE. PROJECT THEME IS ' HISTORY OF THE ARMED FORCES & THEIR CONTRIBUTIONS TO THE NATION'. (LOCAL). BICENT CHMN; U S ARMED FORCES BICENTENNIAL CARAVAN; CITY HALL; TRACY, CA 95376. (#1775-577).

TRAVIS AFB

BASE ENTRANCE DESIGN - TRAVIS AFB, CA. THE MAIN GATE AND BILLBOARD WERE PAINTED IN A RED, WHITE AND BLUE BICENTENNIAL THEME. (LOCAL). LT COL ERROL K LOVING; 60 MAW OI; TRAVIS AFB, CA 94535. (#31056).

BICENTENNIAL LOGO DECALS - TRAVIS AFB, CA. BICENTENNIAL LOGO DECALS WILL BE PLACED ON THE TAIL OF ALL WING AIRCRAFT. (LOCAL). LT COL ERROL K LOVING; 60 MAW OI; TRAVIS AFB, CA 94535. (#31061).

CHAPEL PROGRAM - TRAVIS AFB, CA. HISTORIC RE-ENACTMENTS OF SERMONS AND SPEECHES. (LOCAL). LT COL ERROL K LOVING; 60 MAW OI; TRAVIS AFB, CA 94535. (#31060).

FIREPLUG PAINTING - TRAVIS AFB, CA. THE BASE FIREPLUGS WERE PAINTED TO REPRESENT REVOLUTIONARY WAR SOLDIERS, PAUL REVERE AND UNCLE SAM. (LOCAL). LT COL ERROL K LOVING; 60 MAW OI; TRAVIS AFB, CA 94535. (#31058).

LOGOS ON BUILDINGS - TRAVIS AFB, CA. THE 60TH MAW DESIGNED A LOGO AND PAINTED IT ON THE HOSPITAL AND CONTROL TOWER. (LOCAL). LT COL ERROL K LOVING; 60 MAW OI; TRAVIS AFB, CA 94535. (#31057).

TRAVIS AFB DIRECTORY & GUIDE - CA. A WELCOME BROCHURE WITH A HISTORY OF THE BASE WAS GIVEN TO NEW ARRIVALS TO THE BASE. (LOCAL). LT COL ERROL K LOVING; 60 MAW OI; TRAVIS AFB, CA 94535. (#31055).

1776 TREE PLANTING - TRAVIS AFB, CA. 1,776 TREES WERE PLANTED IN THE COMMUNITY. (LOCAL). LT COL ERROL K LOVING; 60 MAW OI; TRAVIS AFB, CA 94535. (#31059).

MAY 15, '76. ARMED FORCES DAY OPEN HOUSE. EXHIBIT, TOUR. (LOCAL). EROL LORING, INFO CHIEF; TRAVIS AIR FORCE BASE; 60TH AIR BASE GROUP/CC; TRAVIS AFB, CA 94535. (#200006-409).

MAY 15, '76. RODEO. LIVE PERFORMANCE. (LOCAL). EROL LORING, INFO CHIEF; TRAVIS AFB SADDLE CLUB; 60TH AIR BASE GROUP/CC; TRAVIS AFB, CA 94535. (#200006-408).

TRINIDAD

TRINIDAD INDIAN HEALTH CENTER IN CA. CONSTRUCTION OF ADDITIONS TO THE TRINIDAD RANCERIA COMMUNITY HEALTH CENTER TO HOUSE ADDITIONAL PATIENTS. (LOCAL). MRS JOY SUNDBERG, TRIBAL CHAIRMAN; TRINIDAD RACHERIA; PO BOX 61; TRINIDAD, CA 95570. (#22851). **ARBA GRANTEE.**

TRONA

OCT 31, '76. UNITED STATES ARMED FORCES BICENTENNIAL CARAVAN. CARAVAN IS COMPOSED OF EXHIBIT VANS FOR EACH MILITARY SERVICE. PROJECT THEME IS 'HISTORY OF THE ARMED FORCES & THEIR CONTRIBUTIONS TO THE NATION'. (LOCAL). HARVEY EASTMAN; UNITED STATES ARMED FORCES BICENTENNIAL CARAVAN; PO 443; TRONA, CA 93562. (#1775-835).

TUJUNGA

COOPERATIVE ENVIRONMENTAL ENHANCEMENT PROJECT, CA. GARDEN CLUBS DONATE CA NATIVE PLANTS TO LOS ANGELES COUNTY FLOOD CONTROL DISTRICT FOR NATURALIZING THE DEBRIS BASINS IN THE SAN FERNANDO VALLEY; THERE ARE 17 DEBRIS AREAS. (LOCAL). MRS EDWARD E HALL, CHAIRMAN; SAN FERNANDO VALLEY DIST OF CALIF GARDEN CLUBS, INC; 6116 DILL PLACE; WOODLAND HILL, CA 91364. (#18104).

TULARE

PATRIOTS CALENDAR IN TULARE, CA. A 1976 CALENDAR HONORING REVOLUTIONARY WAR PATRIOTS. (REGN'L). STELLA W BAILEY, CHAIRWOMAN TULARE CITY ARBC; DAUGHTERS OF THE AMERICAN REVOLUTION; 522 DICKRAN DR; TULARE, CA 93274. (#12532).

OCT 22, '76. UNITED STATES ARMED FORCES BICENTENNIAL CARAVAN. CARAVAN IS COMPOSED OF EXHIBIT VANS FOR EACH MILITARY SERVICE. PROJECT THEME IS 'HISTORY OF THE ARMED FORCES & THEIR CONTRIBUTIONS TO THE NATION'. (LOCAL). MRS STELLA W BAILEY; UNITED STATES ARMED FORCES BICENTENNIAL CARAVAN; 522 DICK RAND DR; TULARE, CA 93274. (#1775-829).

TULELAKE

JUNE 15 - SEPT 1, '75. BICENTENNIAL CAMPFIRE PROGRAMS AT LAVA BEDS NATL MON. LAVA BEDS NM, PRINCIPAL THEATER FOR MODOC INDIAN WAR 1872-73, IS PREPARING EVENING CAMPFIRE PROGRAMS COMPARING THE MODOC INDIAN FIGHTING WITH THE AMERICAN REVOLUTION. AT INDIAN WELL CAMPGROUND, HEADQUARTERS AREA. (REGN'L). SUPT, LAVA BEDS NATL MON; NATIONAL PARK SERVICE; P.O. BOX 867; TULELAKE, CA 96134. (#6730-25).

JUNE 15 - SEPT 1, '76. BICENTENNIAL CAMPFIRE PROGRAMS AT LAVA BEDS NATL MON. LAVA BEDS NM, PRINCIPAL THEATER FOR MODOC INDIAN WAR 1872-73, IS PREPARING EVENING CAMPFIRE PROGRAMS COMPARING THE MODOC INDIAN FIGHTING WITH THE AMERICAN REVOLUTION. AT INDIAN WELL CAMPGROUND, HEADQUARTERS AREA. (REGN'L). SUPT, LAVA BEDS NATL MON; NATIONAL PARK SERVICE; P.O. BOX 867; TULELAKE, CA 96134. (#6730-525).

TURLOCK

NOV 7, '75. UNITED STATES ARMED FORCES BICENTENNIAL CARAVAN. THE CARAVAN IS COMPOSED OF EXHIBIT VANS FOR EACH BRANCH OF THE MILITARY SERVICE. THE THEME OF THE EXHIBITION IS 'HISTORY OF THE ARMED FORCES AND THEIR CONTRIBUTION TO THE NATION'. (LOCAL). WES WALLSTROM, CHAIRMAN; U S ARMED FORCES BICENTENNIAL EXHIBIT VANS PROJECT; 125 N BROADWAY; TURLOCK, CA 95380. (#1775-292).

TUSTIN

HISTORICAL MUSEUM FOR TUSTIN, CALIFORNIA. ESTABLISH MUSEUM PRESERVING LOCAL HISTORY FOR CITIZEN EDUCATION, ENJOYMENT & EDIFICATION. THIS ACCOMPLISHMENT WILL INSTILL PATRIOTIC SPIRIT IN RECALLING LOCAL CONTRIBUTIONS TO OUR COUNTRY'S DEVELOPMENT. (LOCAL). VIVIAN OWEN, CHAIRMAN OF HISTORICAL SOCIETY; TUSTIN AREA US BICENTENNIAL FOUNDATION; PO BOX 1776; TUSTIN, CA 92680. (#4648).

JUNE 1, '75. TUSTIN HERITAGE WALK, A WALKERS GUIDE TO OLDE TUSTIN. PUBLIC CAN BUY BOOKLET AND WALK INDEPENDENTLY THROUGH DOWNTOWN TUSTIN. PURCHASE BOOKLET AT MUSEUM. AT MUSEUM AT 135 W.3RD STREET27. (LOCAL). MRS CHARLES A OWEN; TUSTIN US BICENTENNIAL FOUNDATION; 18671 SAUGUS AV; SANTA ANA, CA 92705. (#50800-1).

JULY 4, '76. DEDICATION OF MEMORIAL. BICENTENNIAL MEMORIAL OF TUSTIN, CALIF. SIGNIFICANT SYMBOL(WISHING WELL) INSPIRING A THEME 'WISHING WELL TO EVERYONE' - A POSITIVE MESSAGE OF A NEW AMERICAN SPIRIT. (LOCAL). TOM KELLY, PRESIDENT; TUSTIN AREA US BICENTENNIAL FOUNDATION; PO BOX 1776; TUSTIN, CA 92680. (#4693-501).

UKIAH

CLASSROOM ACTIVITIES ON APPRECIATION OF AMERICA-CA. THE MAJOR OBJECTIVE IS TO OVERCOME CYNICISM ABOUT AMERICA AND TO COLLECT IDEAS FOR CLASSROOM ACTIVITIES THAT WILL HELP ACCOMPLISH THIS. (LOCAL). ROBERT I HAYDEN, CHAIRMAN; UKIAH UNIFIED SCHOOL DISTRICT; BOX 767; UKIAH, CA 95482. (#18441).

UPLAND

WOMEN IN HISTORY - UPLAND, CA. BIOGRAPHIES OF WOMEN WHO HAVE CONTRIBUTED TO CALIFORNIA HISTORY, COMPILED FOR PLACEMENT IN STATE LIBRARY. (ST-WIDE). BETTY J

UPLAND — CONTINUED

EAGON, PRESIDENT; CALIFORNIA FEDERATION BUSINESS & PROFESSIONAL WOMENS CLUBS; 1400 W 13TH ST, SP131; UPLAND, CA 91786. (#26610).

VACAVILLE

OCT 28 - 29, '75. UNITED STATES ARMED FORCES BICENTENNIAL CARAVAN. THE CARAVAN IS COMPOSED OF EXHIBIT VANS FOR EACH BRANCH OF THE MILITARY SERVICE. THE THEME OF THE EXHIBITION IS 'HISTORY OF THE ARMED FORCES AND THEIR CONTRIBUTION TO THE NATION'. (LOCAL). CLARENCE KRANCZAK, CHMN; U S ARMED FORCES BICENTENNIAL EXHIBIT VANS PROJECT; 750 SCHOOL ST; VACAVILLE, CA 95688. (#1775-286).

MAY 15, '76. SCIENCE, WISDOM AND SURVIVAL: A BICENTENNIAL ISSUES SYMPOSIUM. THE SYMPOSIUM WILL DEAL WITH CURRENT AND FUTURE SOCIAL AND SCIENTIFIC ISSUES FACING THE NATION. INCLUDED ARE EXTENSIVE PRESENTATIONS ON PRO AND CON VIEWS ON PROPOSITION 15 (NUCLEAR INITIATIVE). KEYNOTE ADDRESS: 'WHERE ARE WE GOING IN ENERGY?'. AT VACAVILLE COMMUNITY CENTER. (LOCAL). HARRY WEEKS, PRESIDENT; CALIFORNIA SCIENCE ASSOCIATION; 272 BERRYESSA DR; VACAVILLE, CA 95688. (#200006-528).

VALENCIA

JAN 24, '76. EL PRESIDENTE'S BALL-HONORING SPANISH HERITAGE. CEREMONY AT VALENCIA GOLF CLUBHOUSE. (LOCAL). BOBBIE TRUEBLOOD; SANTA CLARITA VALLEY BOYS CLUB; 23845 W MCBEAN PKWY; VALENCIA, CA 91355. (#200006-116).

APR 19 - 23, '76. LEXINGTON-CONCORD WEEK. FAIR. (LOCAL). BOBBIE TRUEBLOOD, CHMN; COLLEGE OF THE CANYONS & SANTA CLARA BICENTENNIAL COMMITTEE; 23845 W MCBEAN PKWY; VALENCIA, CA 91355. (#103966-1).

JUNE 12, '76. AUCTION OF '76. FAIR, FESTIVAL AT CALIFORNIA INSTITUTE OF THE ARTS. (LOCAL). BOB ROSS, EXEC DIRECTOR; SANTA CLARITA VALLEY BOYS CLUB; PO BOX 822; NEWHALL, CA 91322. (#104754-1).

JULY 4, '76. 4TH OF JULY FIREWORKS SHOW. FESTIVAL. (LOCAL). BOBBIE TRUEBLOOD, CHMN; NEWHALL SIGNAL; SANTA CLARA BICENTENNIAL COMMITTEE; 23845 W MCBEAN PKWY; VALENCIA, CA 91355. (#104756-1).

VALLECITO

FIFES AND DRUMMERS OF OLD CALAVRAS - VALLECITO, CA. AN AUTHENTIC, 20-MAN FIFE & DRUM CORPS REFLECTIVE OF THE FIFERS AND DRUMMERS IN THE MOTHER LODE, CA MILITIA, 1860. MUSIC FROM AUTHENTIC SCORES; EMPHASIS ON PERIOD MUSIC AND THAT OF THE CA GOLD RUSH. (LOCAL). LT COL DONALD E MATTSON, DIRECTOR; FIFES AND DRUMS OF OLD CALAVARAS; PO BOX 193; VALLECITO, CA 95251. (#26921). **ARBA GRANTEE.**

JAN 1, '75 - DEC 31, '76. FIFES & DRUMS OF OLD CALAVARAS, AUTHENTIC MUSICAL GROUP OF 1860'S. THIS AUTHENTIC 20 MAN FIFE & DRUM CORPS IS REFLECTIVE OF THE FIFERS AND DRUMMERS IN THE MOTHER LODE (CIRCA CALIFORNIA-1860). MUSIC IS FROM AUTHENTIC SCORES OF THE GOLD RUSH PERIOD. (LOCAL). LT COL DONALD E MATTSON; FIFES & DRUMS OF OLD CALAVARAS; BICENT COMM OF CALAVERAS COUNTY; PO BOX 193; VALLECITO, CA 95251. (#102847-1).

VALLEJO

ARCHITECTURAL HERITAGE DISTRICT OF VALLEJO, CALIF. PERIOD RESIDENCES OF CITY OF VALLEJO WILL BE RESTORED FOR THE BICENTENNIAL COMMEMORATION. (LOCAL). RICHARD H LEMKE, CHAIRMAN; VALLEJO BICENTENNIAL COMMITTEE; 629 MARIN ST; VALLEJO, CA 94590. (#2985).

VALLEJO NAVAL AND HISTORIC MUSEUM IN CA. THE MUSEUM DEPICTS THE HISTORY OF THE WEST COAST'S FIRST NAVY YARD AND ONE OF CALIFORNIA'S FIRST CAPITALS. (LOCAL). RICHARD H LEMKE, PRESIDENT; VALLEJO NAVAL AND HISTORIC MUSEUM, INC; 734 MARIN ST; VALLEJO, CA 94590. (#10823).

JUNE 14, '76. SOLANO COUNTY FAIR. FAIR AT LOCATED HIGHWAYS I-80 AND CALIF STATE ROUTE 37. (ST-WIDE). RONALD D MILLER, CHAIRMAN; SOLANO COUNTY FAIR; 900 FAIRGROUNDS DR, PO BO 9; VALLEJO, CA 94590. (#106295-1).

JULY 5, '76. UNITED STATES ARMED FORCES BICENTENNIAL CARAVAN. CARAVAN IS COMPOSED OF EXHIBIT VANS FOR EACH MILITARY SERVICE. PROJECT THEME IS 'HISTORY OF THE ARMED FORCES & THEIR CONTRIBUTIONS TO THE NATION.'. AT VALLEJO'S MARINA VISTA BLVD AND PARK. (LOCAL). HON M DOUGLAS, MAYOR; UNITED STATES ARMED FORCES BICENTENNIAL CARAVAN; CITY HALL, 734 MAIN ST; VALLEJO, CA 94590. (#1775-686).

VAN NUYS

THE SPIRIT OF N-76, VAN NUYS, CA. A LIGHT-AIRPLANE FLIGHT THROUGH 48 STATES TO DISCOVER THE AMERICAN SPIRIT AFTER 200 YRS. FLOWN BY K O ECKLAND, ILLUSTRATOR, WHO WILL THEN WRITE A BICENTENNIAL BOOK. (NAT'L). K O ECKLAND, PROJ COORDINATOR; 7013 HASKELL AVE; VAN NUYS, CA 91406. (#12316).

VAN NUYS-DELANO PARK CENTER IN VAN NUYS, CA. A PARK WILL BE DEVELOPED IN THE SPANISH-AMERICAN COMMUNITY OF BARRIO DE VAN NUYS; THE PLAZA AREA WILL EMPHASIZE MEXICAN HERITAGE AND CULTURE. (LOCAL). JOSEPH GONZALES, PROJ DIRECTOR; HISPANIC CULTURE HERITAGE TEAM OF THE LOS ANGELES BICENT COMMITT; 3757 E FIRST ST; LOS ANGELES, CA 90063. (#12496).

MAY 3, '76. NETHERLANDS CHAMBER ORCHESTRA VISITS VAN NUYS. LIVE PERFORMANCE. (INT'L). WILLIAM SIMONSZ, COORD; NETHERLANDS GOVERNMENT; NETHERLANDS EMBASSY-4200 LINNEAN; WASHINGTON, DC 20008. (#109013-14).

VENICE

OCT 30 - 31, '76. 5TH ANNUAL SOUTHERN CALIFORNIA CONFERENCE ON WOMEN & THE LAW. PANEL WORKSHOPS & SPEAKER; HIGHLIGHTS: CHANGING ROLES IN A CHANGING SOCIETY; THE 2ND AMERICAN REVOLUTION; A DIALOGUE BETWEEN THE LEGAL PROFESSION & THE COMMUNITY; FAMILIES, MINORITIES, PROFESSIONS, ENVIRONMENT & GOVERNMENT; ALTERNATIVES FOR WOMEN & MEN. AT UCLA LAW SCHOOL, 405 HILGARD LANE. (ST-WIDE). LORA WEINROTH, COORD; UCLA SCHOOL OF LAW; 38 SUNSET AVE; VENICE, CA 90291. (#106961-1).

VENTURA

CHARLES OUTLAND'S VENTURA COUNTY, CA. A SLIDE SERIES OFFERING OUTLAND'S HISTORICAL PERSPECTIVES ON THE PEOPLE, PLACES AND EVENTS OF THE EARLY DAYS IN VENTURA COUNTY. (LOCAL). BEVERLY STRADER, AUDIO VISUAL LIBRARIAN; VENTURA COUNTY LIBRARY SERVICES; 651 MAIN ST; VENTURA, CA 93001. (#26057).

HISTORIC PARK - PROJ OF VENTURA, CA. HISTORIC PARK ON SITE OF ARCHAEOLOGICAL EXCAVATIONS OF UNCOVERED BLDG FOUNDATIONS BELIEVED TO BE THE ORIGINAL MISSION COMPLEX; EXCAVATION TO BE CONTINUED; MATERIALS FOUND WILL BE AUTHENTICATED. (LOCAL). TOM WHITE, PROJ DIRECTOR; REDEVELOPMENT AGENCY, CITY OF BUENAVENTURA; PO BOX 99, 501 POLI ST; VENTURA, CA 93001. (#12177).

MUSEUM FEATURING PIONEER HISTORY - VENTURA, CA. CONSTRUCTION OF VENTURA HISTORICAL PIONEER MUSEUM NEAR OLD MISSION TO HOUSE EXISTING COLLECTION OF INDIAN ARTIFACTS, FARM IMPLEMENTS AND OTHER MEMORABELIA. (LOCAL). FAYE CAMPBELL, PROJECT COORDINATOR; VENTURA BICENTENNIAL COMMISSION; PO BOX 99; VENTURA, CA 93001. (#15957).

JULY 4, '75. OLD FASHIONED PICNIC IN THE PARK. INCLUDES LIVE MUSIC & TRADITIONAL GAMES. FIREWORKS AFTER SUNDOWN. AT PLAZA PARK IN DOWNTOWN VENTURA. (LOCAL). CHERYL MEADON; CITY PARKS & RECREATION DEPT; 632 E MAIN ST; VENTURA, CA 93001. (#10392-1).

JULY 12 - 15, '75. BICENTENNIAL WAGON VISIT. THIS IS THE CALIFORNIA ELEMENT OF THE BICENTENNIAL WAGON TRAIN PILGRIMAGE TO PENNSYLVANIA. AT DOWNTOWN VENTURA. (LOCAL). ERLAND MYERS, PROJ CHMN; VENTURA ARBC; CITY HALL; VENTURA, CA 93001. (#100550-1).

AUG 2 - 3, '75. SUNNY HORSE SHOW. NON-PROFESSIONAL, ALL BREED HORSE SHOW DEDICATED TO THE YOUNG EQUESTRIAN. AT VENTURA COUNTY FAIR GROUNDS. (LOCAL). MRS K M DUTTWEILER; INDIVIDUAL; 392 SAUL PL; VENTURA, CA 93003. (#100253-1).

OCT 27 - NOV 2, '75. PEOPLEHOOD FESTIVAL. DURING WEEK TEENS WILL HOST A BREAKFAST, CABLE TV PANEL & CAR WASH; WEEK ENDS WITH FESTIVAL FEATURING FOOD BOOTHS, FOLK DANCING, MUSIC & CULTURAL ART; PURPOSE IS FOR ALL PEOPLE TO CELEBRATE TOGETHER. (LOCAL). JUDY TRIEM, PROJ COORD; CHURCHES OF VENTURA; BICENTENNIAL OFFICE BOX 99; VENTURA, CA 93001. (#200006-77).

FEB 21 - 22, '76. BICENTENNIAL CHORUS. A PROFESSIONALLY DIRECTED CHORUS OF LOCAL VOICES PRESENTING A PROGRAM OF TYPICALLY AMERICAN AND PATRIOTIC MUSIC. AT VENTURA HIGH SCHOOL AUDITORIUM, MAIN AND CATALINA. (LOCAL). VICTOR A SWEET; AMER REVOL BICENT COMMISSION OF VENTURA; 843 OLYMPIA; VENTURA, CA 93003. (#100253-3).

MAR 29, '76. SOROPTOMIST CLUB BICENTENNIAL DINNER PROGRAM. DISPLAY OF ARTIFACTS FROM LOCAL ARCHAEOLOGICAL EXPLORATIONS. FIRST IN A SERIES OF BICENTENNIAL THEME DINNERS. AT AMERICAN LEGION HALL. (LOCAL). FAYE CAMPBELL, PROJ COORD; SOROPTOMIST CLUB & VENTURA BICENTENNIAL COMMITTEE; PO BOX 99; VENTURA, CA 93001. (#102715-2).

APR 4, '76. HOMETOWN HERITAGE. DISPLAY OF ORIGINAL ART BY LOCAL ARTISTS ON A LOCAL HERITAGE AND LANDMARK THEME. AT CITY HALL. (LOCAL). FAYE CAMPBELL; BUENAVENTURA ART ASSOC; BICENTENNIAL OFFICE, BOX 99; VENTURA, CA 93001. (#200006-115).

MAY 2, '76. A COLONIAL FAIR. FAIR WILL FEATURE MOVIES, SLIDE SHOWS, DRAMA, COSTUMES, DISPLAYS, ETHNIC FOLK DANCING, MUSIC, GAME BOOTHS FOR CHILDREN, ARTS & CRAFTS, FOOD & FUN. AT VENTURA COUNTY JEWISH COUNCIL TEMPLE BETH TORAH. (LOCAL). FAYE CAMPBELL, PROJ COORD; TEMPLE BETH TORAH; BICENTENNIAL OFFICE, BOX 99; VENTURA, CA 93001. (#104389-1).

MAY 2, '76. PRESENTATION OF COHELEACH'S 'BICENTENNIAL EAGLE' TO CITY. GUY COHELEACH, WORLD REKNOWNED WILDLIFE ARTIST, WILL PRESENT TO THE CITY OF SAN BUENAVENTURA A LITHOGRAPH, 'BICENTENNIAL EAGLE' AT CITY HALL. RECEPTION WILL BE HELD AFTER CEREMONY AT THE ANACAPA GALLERY. AT CITY HALL & ANACAPA GALLERY. (LOCAL). FAYE CAMPBELL, PROJ COORD; ANACAPA GALLERY; BICENTENNIAL OFFICE BOX 99; VENTURA, CA 93001. (#200006-76).

MAY 8, '76. NATL PK SVC '...A LITTLE LOOK AROUND' VISITS CHANNEL ISLANDS NM. THIS SHORT PROGRAM FEATURES ACTORS PORTRAYING FAMOUS AMERICANS OF THE PAST WHO'VE RETURNED TO SEE AMERICA'S GROWTH. AND 9/4 MINUTE MAN NHP IN LEXINGTON. (REGN'L). CHANNEL ISLANDS N MON; NATIONAL PARK SERVICE; 1699 ANCHORS WAY DRIVE; VENTURA, CA 93003. (#5653-52).

MAY 15, '76. SENIOR ADULT DAY. FASHION SHOW, CRAFTS DISPLAY & DEMONSTRATIONS, HOBBY DISPLAYS TO COINCIDE WITH NATIONAL OBSERVANCE OF SENIOR CITIZENS MONTH. AT BUENAVENTURA SHOPPING CENTER. (LOCAL). FAYE CAMPBELL; VENTURA BICENTENNIAL OFFICE; PO BOX 99; VENTURA, CA 93001. (#12178-1).

MAY 16 - 23, '76. HISTORIC PRESERVATION WEEK. WALKING TOUR OF HISTORIC DOWNTOWN VENTURA, ENDING AT CITY HALL FOR REFRESHMENTS & PROGRAM. RUSSELL A RUIZ, HISTORIAN & ARTIST WILL SPEAK ON EARLY VENTURA HISTORY & CERTIFICATES WILL BE PRESENTED TO LANDMARK OWNERS. AT CITY HALL. (LOCAL). MIRIAM MACK, COORD; VENTURA HISTORIC PRESERVATION COMMISSION; BICENTENNIAL OFFICE BOX 99; VENTURA, CA 93001. (#200006-75).

MAY 28, '76. VENTURA & MOORPARK COLLEGES BICENTENNIAL CONCERT. COMBINED COLLEGE CHOIRS SINGING COMPOSITIONS BY PAUL CHIHARA AND CAMPUS COMPOSERS BURNS TAFT, SHELDON MEHR, ALAN HYAMS. AT VENTURA COLLEGE THEATER. (LOCAL). FAYE CAMPBELL, PROJ COORD; VENTURA & MOORPARK COLLEGES; BICENTENNIAL OFFICE BOX 99; VENTURA, CA 93001. (#108442-2).

MAY 29, '76. BICENTENNIAL CONCERT OF AMERICAN MUSIC. SPECIAL CONCERT OF AMERICAN MUSIC BY VENTURA HIGH SCHOOL ORCHESTRA, CHOIR, BAND AND DANCERS (CAST OF 150). AT VENTURA HIGH AUDITORIUM. (LOCAL). FAYE CAMPBELL, PROJ COORD; VENTURA HIGH SCHOOL MUSIC DEPT; BICENTENNIAL OFFICE BOX 99; VENTURA, CA 93001. (#108442-1).

JUNE 9, '76. 'THE PATRIOTS'. PRESENTATION OF A GROUP OF AMERICAN PATRIOTS CREATED BY GEORGE S STUART; EXHIBIT PRESENTS THE DAILY LIVES, ACTIVITIES, CLOTHING AND ACCOMPLISHMENTS OF THESE MEN. AT PLEASANT VALLEY RECREATION CENTER. (LOCAL). JUDY TRIEM, PROJ COORD; VENTURA COUNTY HISTORICAL SOCIETY; BOX 99; VENTURA, CA 93001. (#108166-1).

JULY 3 - 5, '76. 4TH OF JULY BIRTHDAY CELEBRATION. CELEBRATION INCLUDES PARADE, STREET DANCING, ETHNIC, EXCHANGE, MUSIC, GAMES AND DISPLAYS. AT DOWNTOWN VENTURA. (LOCAL). FAYE CAMPBELL, DIRECTOR; CITY OF VENTURA & VENTURA BICENTENNIAL COMMISSION; PO BOX 99; VENTURA, CA 93001. (#102715-1).

JULY 31 - AUG 1, '76. SUNNY 3RD ANNUAL OPEN HORSE SHOW. GRAND ENTRY; ORGANIST WILL PLAY THROUGHOUT SHOW; AVENUE OF FLAGS FROM FAIRGROUND ENTRANCE TO SHOW ARENA; HORN BLOWER WILL CALL IN EACH CLASS; OLD-FASHIONED BAND CONCERT DURING LUNCH HOURS. AT VENTURA COUNTY FAIRGROUNDS. (LOCAL). HELEN DUTTWEILER, COORD; SUNNY 3RD ANNUAL HOUSE SHOW; 392 SAUL PLACE; VENTURA, CA 93003. (#106958-1).

OCT 30 - 31, '76. MUSIC OF AMERICA - BICENTENNIAL CHORUS. HERITAGE, MOODS AND RHYTHMS OF THE AMERICAN PEOPLE BROUGHT BACK BY POPULAR DEMAND; AN ALL VOLUNTEER COMMUNITY CHORUS & ORCHESTRA. SUNDAY HOURS ARE 3 PM TO 5 PM. AT VENTURA HIGH SCHOOL, 2155 E MAIN. (LOCAL). FAYE CAMPBELL, COORD; SAN BUENAVENTURA BICENTENNIAL COMMISSION; PO BOX 99; VENTURA, CA 93001. (#109383-1).

VERNON

MEN'S BICENT COORDINATED BLAZER & SLACKS. MENS BLAZER WITH A LOGO ON THE POCKET & COORDINATED SLACKS. ARBA LICENSE NO 76-19-0516. (NAT'L). HERB PHILLIPS, MANAGER; MR MARK CALIFORNIA; 2528 E 37TH ST; VERNON, CA 90058. (#6567).

VICTORVILLE

COLLEGE BICENTENNIAL PROGRAMS IN VICTORVILLE, CA. PROGRAM CONSISTS OF A LECTURE SERIES & FILMS ON LOCAL & U S HISTORY. (LOCAL). DR ALEX RUDOFF, DEAN OF COMMUNITY SERVICES; VICTOR VALLEY COLLEGE; 18422 BEAR VALLEY RD; VICTORVILLE, CA 92392. (#12288).

JAN 7 - 8, '76. UNITED STATES ARMED FORCES BICENTENNIAL CARAVAN. CARAVAN IS COMPOSED OF EXHIBIT VANS FOR EACH MILITARY SERVICE. PROJECT THEME IS 'HISTORY OF THE ARMED FORCES AND THEIR CONTRIBUTIONS TO THE NATION'. (LOCAL). MRS PEGGY SARTOR, CHMN; US ARMED FORCES EXHIBIT VANS PROJECT; 14657 RODEO DR; VICTORVILLE, CA 92392. (#1775-302).

VIRGINIA LAKE

JUNE 24 - 27, '76. THE GREAT SIERRA NEVADA WILDERNESS EXPEDITION. PRESENT DAY MOUNTAINEERS WILL RE-CREATE LIFESTYLES AND CULTURAL ACTIVITIES OF PIONEERS IN WILDERNESS; EXPEDITION EQUIPPED WITH PERIOD GEAR & PROVISIONS; MEMBERS TO FULLFILL SPECIFIC EXPLORATORY ROLES BASED ON HISTORICAL FACT. AT 10 MI WEST OFF HWY 395 AT CONWAY SUMMIT, CA. (REGN'L). ROBERT C PETERS, COORD; 1ST A HOOVER WILDERNESS VIRGINIA LAKES TOIYABE NATIONAL FOREST P G; 5451 MARATHON ST; LOS ANGELES, CA 90038. (#106051-1).

VISALIA

COLLEGE OF THE SEQUOIAS COMMUNITY SERVICES - CA. EMPHASIS IS ON ENTERTAINMENT IN THE 1976-77 SERIES. ARTISTS RANGING FROM MASTER PUPPETEER JOHN BRUNNER TO 1930'S STYLE SINGER KAY ST GERMAIN WILL PERFORM DURING SERIES FROM SEPTEMBER TO MAY. (LOCAL). STEPHEN W EGGLESTON, CHAIRMAN; COLLEGE OF THE SEQUOIAS BICENTENNIAL COMMITTEE; 1307 S DIVISADERO; VISALIA, CA 93277. (#28605).

COLLEGE OF THE SEQUOIAS BICENTENNIAL PROJECTS, CA. HORIZONS '76, PLANTED 3 SEQUOIA GIGANTEA TREES ON CAMPUS - ONE DESIGNATED AS 'THE LIBERTY TREE', PLANTED ROSE GARDEN WITH NEWLY DEVELOPED 'BICENTENNIAL ROSE'. (LOCAL). STEPHEN W EGGLESTON, CHAIRPERSON; COLLEGE OF THE SEQUOIAS COMMUNITY COLLEGE; 915 S MOONEY BLVD; VISALIA, CA 93277. (#28613).

SELF-HELP ENTERPRISES, VISALIA, CA. SELF-HELP ENTERPRISES PROVIDES HOUSING, MANPOWER TRAINING AND ASSISTANCE TO COMMUNITIES IN WATER & SEWER DEVELOPMENT. (LOCAL). GLORIA WRIGHT, SECRETARY; SELF-HELP ENTERPRISES; 220 S BRIDGE ST; VISALIA, CA 93277. (#20007).

MAR 12 - 28, '76. AUDIO CHAIRS EXHIBIT ON NATIVE AMERICANS, BLACKS AND WOMEN IN 1776. IN THESE SPECIAL LISTENING CHAIRS VISITORS WILL HEAR THREE DIFFERENT TAPE RECORDINGS WHICH DESCRIBE THE ROLES OF WOMEN, BLACKS, AND NATIVE AMERICANS DURING THE REVOLUTIONARY PERIOD. AT TULARE COUNTY MUSEUM, 27000 MOONEY BLVD. (REGN'L). SEQUOIA-KINGS CANYON NP; NATIONAL PARK SERVICE; THREE RIVERS, CA 93271. (#5581-16).

OCT 19 - 20, '76. UNITED STATES ARMED FORCES BICENTENNIAL CARAVAN. CARAVAN IS COMPOSED OF EXHIBIT VANS FOR EACH MILITARY SERVICE. PROJECT THEME IS 'HISTORY OF THE ARMED FORCES & THEIR CONTRIBUTIONS TO THE NATION'. (LOCAL). GARY CHAPPELL; UNITED STATES ARMED FORCES BICENTENNIAL CARAVAN; THE TIMES DELTA; VISALIA, CA 93277. (#1775-828).

VISTA

NOV 26 - 27, '76. UNITED STATES ARMED FORCES BICENTENNIAL CARAVAN. CARAVAN IS COMPOSED OF EXHIBIT VANS FOR EACH MILITARY SERVICE. PROJECT THEME IS 'HISTORY OF THE ARMED FORCES & THEIR CONTRIBUTIONS TO THE NATION'. (LOCAL). SAM KANINAU, CHAIRMAN; UNITED STATES ARMED FORCES BICENTENNIAL CARAVAN; 927 JUDILYN DR; VISTA, CA 92083. (#1775-847).

VOLCANO

INDIAN CULTURAL CENTER IN VOLCANO, CALIFORNIA. GRINDING ROCK STATE PARK WILL FEATURE AN INDIAN INTERPRETIVE HERITAGE CENTER HOUSING MIWOK ARTIFACTS IN RECONSTRUCTED INDIAN VILLAGE. WORKSHOP & STORE WILL DISPLAY INDIAN ARTS & CRAFTS. (ST-WIDE). JAMES MICHAEL DOYLE, HISTORY PRESERVATION; CA DEPT OF PARKS & RECREATION; 1416 9TH ST; SACRAMENTO, CA 95814. (#16127). **ARBA GRANTEE.**

WALNUT

'THE CREATIVE CHALLENGE OF CHANGE' - WALNUT, CA. ESTABLISH A COMMUNITY FORUM FOR CONSIDERATION OF LAND USE & ZONING, PHYSICAL ENVIRONMENT AND CULTURAL DEVELOPMENT OF THE 16 CITIES IN THE MT SAN ANTONIO COMMUNITY COLLEGE DISTRICT. (LOCAL). JOSEPH M ZAGORSKI, CHAIRMAN; MT SAN ANTONIO COLLEGE; 1100 N GRAND AVE; WALNUT, CA 91789. (#24551).

THE VINTAGE YEARS-OUR VALLEY BEFORE 1945, CA. MURAL AND ARTIFACT EXHIBIT OF THE EAST SAN GABRIEL AND POMONA VALLEY BEFORE 1945. BEAUTIFUL 92-PAGE CATALOGUE IS SOLD FOR $2 PER COPY. (LOCAL). JOSEPH M ZAGORSKI, DEAN; COMMUNITY SERVICES - MT SAN ANTONIO COLLEGE; 1100 N GRAND AVE; WALNUT, CA 91789. (#31212).

WALNUT CREEK

WALNUT CREEK, CALIF, COOPERATIVE FARM PROJECT. COOPERATIVE FARM OF SEVEN ACRES WILL BE MANAGER BY THE YOUTH COUNCIL FROM WALNUT CREEK HIGH SCHOOLS. (LOCAL). JEFFREN W PETTIGREW, CHAIRMAN; WALNUT CREEK BICENTENNIAL COMMITTEE; 1445 CIVIC DR; WALNUT CREEK, CA 94596. (#2986). **(??).**

JUNE 21, '75. BICENTENNIAL BAZAAR. FESTIVAL AT CITY BROADWAY PARKING GARAGE. (LOCAL). JEFF PETTEGREW; AM REV BICENTENNIAL COMMISSION OF WALNUT CREEK; 1445 CIVIC DR, CITY HALL; WALNUT CREEK, CA 94596. (#50027-1).

WASCO

OCT 25, '76. UNITED STATES ARMED FORCES BICENTENNIAL CARAVAN. CARAVAN IS COMPOSED OF EXHIBIT VANS FOR EACH MILITARY SERVICE. PROJECT THEME IS 'HISTORY OF THE ARMED FORCES & THEIR CONTRIBUTIONS TO THE NATION'. (LOCAL). JACK CUTNER; UNITED STATES ARMED FORCES BICENTENNIAL CARAVAN; PO 250; WASCO, CA 93280. (#1775-831).

WATSONVILLE

MAY 28 - 30, '76. 12TH ANNUAL ANTIQUE FLY-IN AND AIR SHOW. ANTIQUE AIRCRAFT RECALL THE BEGINNINGS OF AMERICA'S AVIATION INDUSTRY. AT WATSONVILLE MUNICIPAL AIRPORT. (LOCAL). JOHN PAYNE, PROJ DIR; CHAMBER OF COMMERCE; PO BOX 470; WATSONVILLE, CA 95076. (#103416-338).

WEED

BEAUTIFICATION OF WEED CITY, CALIFORNIA. A PLAN TO BEAUTIFY WEED BY PAINTING BUILDINGS, PLANTING TREES, CONSTRUCTING DRINKING FOUNTAINS, TRASH RECEPTACLES AND A CENTRAL MEMORIAL FOUNTAIN. ALSO CREATION OF A MUSEUM TO PROMOTE CULTURE. (LOCAL). MARY C CHANEY, CHAIRMAN; WEED BICENTENNIAL COMMITTEE; RT 1 BOX 1058; WEED, CA 96094. (#5945).

JULY 19 - 20, '75. WEED ITALIAN CARNAVALE. A PLAN TO BEAUTIFY WEED BY PAINTING BUILDINGS, PLANTING TREES, CONSTRUCTING DRINKING FOUNTAINS, TRASH RECEPTACLES AND A CENTRAL MEMORIAL FOUNTAIN. ALSO CREATION OF A MUSEUM TO PROMOTE CULTURE. AT BEL AIR PARK COLLEGE AVE. (LOCAL). MAARTEN LIGTENBERG; WEED CHAMBER OF COMMERCE; 269 MAIN STREET; WEED, CA 96094. (#5945-2).

OCT 13, '75. UNITED STATES ARMED FORCES BICENTENNIAL CARAVAN. THE CARAVAN IS COMPOSED OF EXHIBIT VANS FOR EACH BRANCH OF THE MILITARY SERVICE. THE THEME OF THE EXHIBITION IS 'HISTORY OF THE ARMED FORCES AND THEIR CONTRIBUTION TO THE NATION'. (LOCAL). MARY CHANEY; U S ARMED FORCES BICENTENNIAL EXHIBIT VANS PROJECT; BOX B; WEED, CA 96094. (#1775-277).

JUNE 26, '76. LIBERTY MARCH: JFK MEMORIAL HIKE. 13TH ANNUAL JOHN F KENNEDY MEMORIAL 50 MILE HIKE, SANCTIONED BY HIKERS OF AMERICA, INC. AT START SISKIYOUS COLLEGE. (LOCAL). LEE R FERRERO, PROJ DIR; WEED BICENTENNIAL COMMISSION; 450 COLLEGE AVE; WEED, CA 96094. (#103814-1).

JULY 4, '76. JULY 4TH CELEBRATION. OPENING, FESTIVAL. (LOCAL). MARY C CHANEY, CHAIRMAN; WEED BICENTENNIAL COMMITTEE; RT 1 BOX 1058; WEED, CA 96094. (#5945-501).

SEPT 11, '76. LIBERTY MARCH: JFK MEMORIAL HIKE. 13TH ANNUAL JOHN F KENNEDY MEMORIAL 50 MILE HIKE; SANCTIONED BY HIKERS OF AMERICA, INC. AT START SISKIYOUS COLLEGE. (LOCAL). LEE R FERRERO, PROJ DIR; WEED BICENTENNIAL COMMISSION; 450 COLLEGE AVE; WEED, CA 96094. (#103815-1).

WEST COVINA

APR 29, '76. '1776'-BROADWAY MUSICAL PROFESSIONAL PRODUCTION. LIVE PERFORMANCE AT SAN GABRIEL CIVIC AUDITORIUM, 320 S MISSION DR. (LOCAL). JANET WILLIAMS, COORD; WEST COVINA '76 BICENTENNIAL ASSOCIATION; 1444 W GARVEY AVE; WEST COVINA, CA 91790. (#107136-1).

MAY 13, '76. BICENTENNIAL MUSIC FESTIVAL. LIVE PERFORMANCE AT DISTRICT FIELD, CAMERON AVE. (LOCAL). JANET WILLIAMS, COORD; WEST COVINA UNIFIED SCHOOL DISTRICT; 1444 W GARVEY AVE; WEST COVINA, CA 91790. (#107136-4).

JULY 4, '76. FIRE WORKS SHOW 'HAPPY BIRTHDAY AMERICA'. LIVE PERFORMANCE AT MT SAN ANTONIO COLLEGE STADIUM 1140 S GRAND WALNUT. (LOCAL). ALEX GOODMAN, COORD; CHAMBER OF COMMERCE; 1207 WEST COVINA PKWY; WEST COVINA, CA 91790. (#107136-3).

JULY 5, '76. INDEPENDENCE DAY PARADE. PARADE AT GLENDOVA AVE. (LOCAL). JANET WILLIAMS, COORD; INDEPENDENCE DAY PARADE COMMITTEE; 1444 W GARVEY AVE; WEST COVINA, CA 91790. (#107136-2).

NOV 16 - 17, '76. UNITED STATES ARMED FORCES BICENTENNIAL CARAVAN. CARAVAN IS COMPOSED OF EXHIBIT VANS FOR EACH MILITARY SERVICE. PROJECT THEME IS 'HISTORY OF THE ARMED FORCES & THEIR CONTRIBUTIONS TO THE NATION'. (LOCAL). MRS DECKER; UNITED STATES ARMED FORCES BICENTENNIAL CARAVAN; 2860 E ROSEMARY DR; WEST COVINA, CA 91793. (#1775-843).

WESTMINSTER

JAN 1, '75 - AUG 23, '76. GOD & COUNTRY BELL RINGERS - 'LET FREEDOM RING'. UNIFORMED YOUTH PERFORMING VARIED MUSIC WITH AMERICAN HANDBELLS IN ONE NIGHT STANDS AND EXTENDED TOURING. (REGN'L). DUANE A FORCE, DIRECTOR; GOOD SHEPHERD METHODIST; 8402 VALENCIA DR; WESTMINSTER, CA 92647. (#103034-1).

OCT 15 - DEC 19, '75. ESSAY & THEME CONTESTS. THEME OF LOCAL BICENT TO BE 'WE THE PEOPLE' 1776-1976 FESTIVAL, MUSICAL, PARADE & ESSAY CONTEST INVOLVING STUDENTS OVER 10 YEARS OF AGE IN COMMUNITY. (LOCAL). MRS JOY L NEUGEBAUER; WESTMINSTER BICENTENNIAL COMMITTEE; 8200 WESTMINSTER AVE; WESTMINSTER, CA 92683. (#2987-1).

MAR 25 - 28, '76. 'SING OUT AMERICA' - VARIETY SHOW BENEFIT FOR SCHOLARSHIPS. SEVERAL HUNDRED PARENTS WILL PERFORM IN THIS ANNUAL EVENT WITH ALL PROCEEDS DONATED TO GRADUATING SENIORS. AT COMMUNITY SERVICES AUDITORIUM, 7571 WESTMINSTER AVE. (LOCAL). JUDY DAGENHART, DIRECTOR; WESTMINSTER HIGH SCHOOL PTA; 13272 WHITNEY CIRCLE; WESTMINSTER, CA 92683. (#104832-1).

WHEATLAND

MAY 29, '76. MEMORIAL 'PIONEER DAY'. MEMORIAL SERVICES AT WHEATLAND CEMETERY FOR PIONEERS. A LUNCHEON FOR ALL. A TOUR TO HISTORICAL LANDMARKS, MUSIC AND A DANCE. CO-SPONSORED BY: WHEATLAND HISTORICAL SOCIETY, NATIVE DAUGHTER-GOLDEN WEST #218, GRACE CHURCH EPISCOPAL GUILD. AT WHEATLAND HIGH SCHOOL. (LOCAL). DR LEWIS J FERRARI, CHMN; YUBA COUNTY BICENTENNIAL COMMITTEE; 2205 COVILLAUD ST; MARYSVILLE, CA 95901. (#200006-206).

OCT 23, '76. CELEBRATION: DONNER PARTY TRAIL AT THE POINT OF THE JOHNSON CROSSING. FESTIVAL. (LOCAL). DR LEWIS J FERRARI, CHMN; YUBA COUNTY BICENTENNIAL COMMITTEE & WHEATLAND HISTORICAL SOCIETY; 2205 COVILLAUD; MARYSVILLE, CA 95901. (#109301-1).

WHISKEYTOWN

APR 18 - 24, '76. AUDIO CHAIRS EXHIBIT ON MINORITIES VISITS WHISKEYTOWN NRA. IN THESE SPECIAL LISTENING CHAIRS VISITORS WILL HEAR THREE DIFFERENT TAPE RECORDINGS WHICH DESCRIBE THE ROLES OF WOMEN, BLACKS AND NATIVE AMERICANS IN THE REVOLUTIONARY PERIOD. AT REDDING MUSEUM & ART CENTER, 1701 RIO DR. (REGN'L). WHISKEYTOWN NRA; NATIONAL PARK SERVICE; WISKEYTOWN, CA 96095. (#5581-17).

MAY 30 - JUNE 12, '76. ARTISTS-IN-THE-PARKS BICENT EXHIBIT AT WHISKEYTOWN NRA. TWENTY-ONE ORIGINAL PAINTINGS REPRESENTING VARIOUS ASPECTS OF THE REVOLUTIONARY PERIOD. AT REDDING MUSEUM & ART CENTER, 1701 RIO DR. (REGN'L). SUPERINTENDENT; NATIONAL PARK SERVICE & REDDING MUSEUM & ART CENTER; WHISKEYTOWN NATL RECREATION AREA; WHISKEYTOWN, CA 96095. (#1474-12).

JULY 29, '76. NATL PK SVC 'PEOPLE OF 1776' PLAYS AT WHISKEYTOWN NRA. TRAVELING TROUPE WILL BRING VARIOUS ASPECTS OF COLONIAL LIFE (MILITARY LIFE, MUSIC, CRAFTS) TO VISITORS TO THIS NATIONAL PARK SERVICE AREA. (REGN'L). WHISKEYTOWN NATL REC AREA; NATIONAL PARK SERVICE; P.O. BOX 188; WHISKEYTOWN, CA 96095. (#1469-12).

WHITTIER

MUSICAL COMPOSITION - WHITTIER, CA. FIVE MOVEMENTS WILL BE WRITTEN FOR THE ORCHESTRA. (LOCAL). FREDERICK LESEMANN, PROJ DIRECTOR; NATIONAL ENDOWMENT FOR THE ARTS; 2401 E ST, NW; WASHINGTON, DC 20276. (#21836).

MAY 2, '76. NETHERLANDS CHAMBER ORCHESTRA VISITS WHITTIER. LIVE PERFORMANCE. (INT'L). WILLIAM SIMONSZ, COORD; NETHERLANDS GOVERNMENT; NETHERLANDS EMBASSY-4200 LINNEAN; WASHINGTON, DC 20008. (#109013-13).

JUNE 26 - JULY 11, '76. CAVALIER YOUTH BAND BICENTENNIAL TOUR. BAND WILL TOUR THE EAST COAST, CREATING A ROUSING SPIRIT OF OLD FASHIONED PATRIOTISM. (REGN'L). RAYMOND COLE, COORD; WHITTIER CAVALIER YOUTH BAND, INC; 14444 BRONTE; WHITTIER, CA 90602. (#106442-1).

WILLOWS

BICENTENNIAL PROJECTS - WILLOWS, CA. PROJECTS INCLUDE: COMMEMORATIVE MEDALLION, HISTORIC BROCHURE, MARKER PROJECT AND A FIRST DAY COVER. (LOCAL). CECILE B CRAMER, CHAIRMAN; WILLOWS BICENTENNIAL COMMITTEE; 201 N LASSEN ST; WILLOWS, CA 95988. (#24552).

MUSEUM PROJECT IN WILLOWS, CALIFORNIA. RESTORATION & CONVERSION OF FORMER CITY LIBRARY BLDG BUILT IN 1910 UNDER CARNEGIE GRANT AS A MUSEUM FOR PRESENTATION OF HISTORICAL ARTIFACTS TYPICAL OF THE REGION AND ITS DEVELOPMENT. (LOCAL). FLORENCE EWING, SECRETARY; THE MUSEUM SOCIETY; 336 W WALNUT; WILLOWS, CA 95988. (#5051).

OCT 19, '75. UNITED STATES ARMED FORCES BICENTENNIAL CARAVAN. THE CARAVAN IS COMPOSED OF EXHIBIT VANS FOR EACH BRANCH OF THE MILITARY SERVICE. THE THEME OF THE EXHIBITION IS 'HISTORY OF THE ARMED FORCES AND THEIR CONTRIBUTION TO THE NATION'. (LOCAL). CECILE CRAMER, DIRECTOR; U S ARMED FORCES BICENTENNIAL EXHIBIT VANS PROJECT; RT 1 BOX 510; GLENN, CA 95943. (#1775-281).

MAY 6 - 9, '76. LAMB DERBY, AMATEUR SHOW & QUEEN CONTEST. PARADE, LAMB RACES, LAMB BARBECUE, DANCE AND CARNIVAL. AT WILLOWS VETERANS MEMORIAL HALL, W SYCAMORE ST. (LOCAL). FRANK HANSON, PROJ DIR; WILLOWS LAMB DERBY COMMITTEE; 235 S MURDOCK AVE; WILLOWS, CA 95988. (#103710-1).

MAY 15, '76. BICENTENNIAL CONCERT. LIVE PERFORMANCE AT WILLOWS VETERANS MEMORIAL AUDITORIUM. (LOCAL). PAIGE HAMERNICK, COORD; WILLOWS MINISTERIAL ASSOC; 444 S SHASTA ST; WILLOWS, CA 95988. (#106948-1).

JULY 4, '76. JULY FOURTH CELEBRATION, NATIONAL BICENTENNIAL, WILLOWS CENTENNIAL. FESTIVAL AT JENSEN PARK, WESTSIDE MALL PLAZA, ELKS' CLUB. (LOCAL). CHARLES KNOWLES, CHMN; WILLOWS CHAMBER OF COMMERCE/ BICENTENNIAL COMMITTEE/ AMERICAN LEGION; 135 S TEHAMA ST; WILLOWS, CA 95988. (#106948-2).

SEPT 5, '76. DEDICATION OF HISTORIC PLAQUE FOR THE WILLOWS WATER HOLE. CEREMONY, FESTIVAL AT SITE EAST OF WILLOWS TOWNSITE, RT 162. (LOCAL). FERN ADAMS, COORD; BERRYESSA PARLOR, NATIVE DAUGHTERS OF THE GOLDEN WEST; 439 W LAUREL ST; WILLOWS, CA 95988. (#106948-3).

WILMINGTON

LANDMARK DATES IN LOCAL HISTORY - WILMINGTON, CA. HISTORICAL DATES IN LOCAL HISTORY TO BE PRINTED IN ENGLISH AND SPANISH AND USED AS A MAILER. (LOCAL). MS CAMILLE BAXTER, COORDINATOR; LOS ANGELES HARBOR COLLEGE; 1111 FIGUEROA; WILMINGTON, CA 90744. (#14995).

PHOTO MURALS IN WILMINGTON, CALIFORNIA. EDUCATIONAL PHOTO MURALS OF CIVILIAN & MILITARY PERSONALITIES/EVENTS DEPICTING THE GROWTH OF A CITY & A NATION WILL BE RESTORED & SEEN AT THE BANNING RESIDENCE & MUSEUM, A NATIONAL MONUMENT FACILITY. (LOCAL). MRS RICHARD CALL, PRESIDENT; FRIENDS OF BANNING PARK CORP; 617 N ALTA DR; BEVERLY HILLS, CA 90210. (#8540).

WOFFORD HTS

OCT 8 - 9, '76. EARLY CALIFORNIA DAYS. FESTIVAL AT COMMUNITY PARK. (ST-WIDE). DOROTHY BOLSEN; WOFFORD HEIGHTS IMPROVEMENT; PO BOX 341; WOFFORD HTS, CA 93285. (#103416-618).

WOODLAND

OPERATION OF WOODLAND OPERA HOUSE, CALIFORNIA. BICENT COMM & YOLO COUNTY HISTORICAL SOCIETY TO RESTORE THE HISTORIC OPERA HOUSE. WILL BE THEATRE, MUSICAL & THEATRE ARTS CENTER, LECTURE FOR CIVIC GATHERINGS & MUSEUM. (LOCAL). HARRY L NEEDHAM, CHAIRMAN; WOODLAND BICENTENNIAL COMMITTEE; 422 PENDERGAST; WOODLAND, CA 95695. (#2988).

OCT 21 - 22, '75. UNITED STATES ARMED FORCES BICENTENNIAL CARAVAN. THE CARAVAN IS COMPOSED OF EXHIBIT VANS FOR EACH BRANCH OF THE MILITARY SERVICE. THE THEME OF THE EXHIBITION IS 'HISTORY OF THE ARMED FORCES AND THEIR CONTRIBUTION TO THE NATION'. (LOCAL). BRUCE RIKER, DIRECTOR; U S ARMED FORCES BICENTENNIAL EXHIBIT VANS PROJECT; PO BOX 1443; WOODLAND, CA 95695. (#1775-283).

MAY 16, '76. COMMUNITY PICNIC & FAIR. FESTIVAL AT YOLO COUNTY MUSEUM, 511 GIBSON RD. (LOCAL). EARL BALCH, CHAIRMAN; YOLO COUNTY BICENTENNIAL ADVISORY COMMITTEE; 292 W BEAMER ST; WOODLAND, CA 95695. (#103712-1).

JULY 4, '76. JULY 4TH, 1976 DISPLAY AMERICAN FLAG ON ALL HOMES IN WOODLAND. CITIZEN DISPLAY OF AMER FLAG IN WOODLAND, CALIF. PLAN TO HAVE FLAG ON EVERY HOME IN WOODLAND ON JULY 4TH, 1976 AND ON NATIONAL HOLIDAYS. (LOCAL). HARRY L NEEDHAM, CHAIRMAN; WOODLAND BICENTENNIAL COMMISSION; PO BOX 1976; WOODLAND, CA 95695. (#5054-501).

WOODLAND HLLS

NOV 13, '76. MAZELTOV AMERICA. LIVE PERFORMANCE AT TAFT HIGH SCHOOL AUDITORIUM. (LOCAL). ELEANOR SCHUSTER; TEMPLE EMET OF WOODLAND HILLS; 20400 VENTURA BLVD; WOODLAND HLLS, CA 91364. (#200006-522).

YERMO

OCT 8 - 10, '76. CALICO DAYS. FESTIVAL, PARADE AT CALICO GHOST TOWN. (LOCAL). DON V TUCKER, COORD; SAN BERNARDINO COUNTY REGIONAL PARKS DEPT; 825 E 3RD ST; SN BERNARDINO, CA 92415. (#103416-617).

YORBA LINDA

CITY BEAUTIFICATION PROJECT, YORBA LINDA, CA. BEAUTIFICATION OF THE CITY OF YORBA LINDA. (LOCAL). MILLIE KRANTZ, COORDINATOR; YORBA LINDA BICENTENNIAL COMMITTEE; 19701 CRESTKNOLL; YORBA LINDA, CA 92686. (#32156).

YORBA LINDA COMMUNITY BICENTENNIAL PROJECTS IN CA. DEDICATE COMMUNITY CENTER; LOCAL HISTORY; PRESIDENT DAYS; TREE PLANTING; BIKE RIDES FOR FREEDOM; BICENTENNIAL THEME ESSAY CONTEST; FILM: OUR AMERICAN HERITAGE, 1776', COUNTRY FAIR. (LOCAL). MILLIE KRANTZ, CHAIRMAN; YORBA LINDA BICENTENNIAL COMMITTEE; 19701 CRESTKNOLL; YORBA LINDA, CA 92686. (#32210).

MAY 29, '76. BICENTENNIAL 1776 COUNTRY FAIR. EXHIBITS OF 'OLD TIME' HAND CRAFTS, DISPLAY OF LIVESTOCK BY THE 4-H CLUB & ENTERTAINMENT PROVIDED BY SEVERAL GROUPS. AT NIXON PARK. (LOCAL). MILLIE KRANTZ; YORBA LINDA YODELERS; 19701 CRESTKNOLL; YORBA LINDA, CA 92686. (#200006-430).

YOSEMITE

JUNE 1 - DEC 31, '76. YOSEMITE INDIAN CULTURAL EXHIBITS AT YOSEMITE NP. DISPLAYS AND DEMONSTRATIONS OF NATIVE MIWOK INDIAN SOCIAL AND MATERIAL CULTURE. AT VALLEY DISTRICT BUILDING, YOSEMITE VALLEY. (REGN'L). YOSEMITE NP; NATIONAL PARK SERVICE; PO BOX 577; YOSEMITE, CA 95389. (#6729-148).

JUNE 20 - SEPT 6, '76. LIVING HISTORY PROGRAM AT PIONEER YOSEMITE HISTORY CENTER. ROLE-PLAYING DEMONSTRATORS INVOLVE VISITORS IN TASK-ORIENTED ACTIVITIES AND CONVERSATION WITH THEM ABOUT THE WAY OF LIFE AND EVENTS OF THE PERIOD 1864 THROUGH 1915. AT PIONEER YOSEMITE HISTORY CENTER AT WAWONA. (REGN'L). YOSEMITE NP; NATIONAL PARK SERVICE; PO BOX 577; YOSEMITE, CA 95389. (#6727-219).

JUNE 20 - SEPT 6, '76. SILVER THREADS PGM AT YOSEMITE NP. PARK INTERPRETERS DRESSED AS SILVER MINERS CONDUCT LIVING HISTORY WALKS TO OLD SILVER MINES IN THE TIOGA PASS AREA. DAYS AND TIMES OF THESE WALKS ARE ANNOUNCED IN THE YOSEMITE GUIDE SCHEDULE. (REGN'L). YOSEMITE NP; NATIONAL PARK SERVICE; PO BOX 577; YOSEMITE, CA 95389. (#6727-218).

JUNE 20 - OCT 2, '76. INDIAN CULTURAL PROGRAM AT YOSEMITE NP. THERE WILL BE LIVING HISTORY DEMONSTRATIONS OF NATIVE MIWOK INDIAN DOMESTIC AND CULTURAL CRAFTS. AT INDIAN VILLAGE BEHIND YOSEMITE VALLEY VISITOR CENTER. (REGN'L). YOSEMITE NP; NATIONAL PARK SERVICE; P O BOX 577; YOSEMITE NP, CA 95389. (#6727-232).

AUG 22, '76. NATL PK SVC '...A LITTLE LOOK AROUND' VISITS YOSEMITE NP. THIS SHORT PROGRAM FEATURES ACTORS PORTRAYING FAMOUS AMERICANS OF THE PAST WHO'VE RETURNED TO SEE AMERICA'S GROWTH. AT VILLAGE MALL. (REGN'L). YOSEMITE NATL PK; NATIONAL PARK SERVICE; P.O. BOX 577; YOSEMITE NP, CA 95389. (#5653-41).

SEPT 27 - OCT 8, '76. STUDENT ARTISTS BICENT EXHIBIT AT YOSEMITE NP. THIS ART EXHIBIT CONSISTS OF 18 ORIGINAL PAINTINGS SELECTED FROM ENTRIES IN A NATIONWIDE STUDENT ART CONTEST; EACH PAINTING IS IDENTIFIED WITH PERSONS, PLACES OR EVENTS OF THE AMERICAN REVOLUTION. AT PARK VISITOR CENTER IN YOSEMITE VALLEY. (REGN'L). YOSEMITE NP; NATIONAL PARK SERVICE; PO BOX 577; YOSEMITE, CA 95389. (#1474-15).

YREKA

GREENHORN PARK PROJECT - YREKA, CA. DEVELOPMENT OF A GOLD MINING AREA WITHIN PARK PROJECT WITH MUSEUM, ARTIFACTS AND WORKING GOLD MINING ACTIVITIES. (LOCAL). JAMES L DILLON, CITY MANAGER; CITY OF YREKA; 701 4TH ST; YREKA, CA 96097. (#25181). **ARBA GRANTEE.**

NOV 12, '75. UNITED STATES ARMED FORCES BICENTENNIAL CARAVAN. THE CARAVAN IS COMPOSED OF EXHIBIT VANS FOR EACH BRANCH OF THE MILITARY SERVICE. THE THEME OF THE EXHIBITION IS 'HISTORY OF THE ARMED FORCES AND THEIR CONTRIBUTION TO THE NATION'. (LOCAL). DONNA GOODLAND, CHAIRMAN; U S ARMED FORCES BICENTENNIAL EXHIBIT VANS PROJECT; 701 4TH ST; YREKA, CA 96097. (#1775-276).

29 PALMS

SEPT 7, '75. NATL PK SVC 'PEOPLE OF 1776' (PILOT) VISITS JOSHUA TREE NM. TRAVELING TROUPE WILL BRING VARIOUS ASPECTS OF COLONIAL LIFE (MILITARY LIFE, MUSIC, CRAFTS) TO VISITORS TO THIS NATIONAL PARK SERVICE AREA. (REGN'L). SUPERINTENDENT; NATIONAL PARK SERVICE - JOSHUA TREE NATIONAL MONUMENT; 74485 PALM VISTA DR; 29 PALMS, CA 92277. (#1469-204).

JAN 31 - MAY 30, '76. CONDUCTED TOURS OF HISTORIC KEYS RANCH AT JOSHUA TREE NM. HISTORICAL WALK TRACES USE OF DESERT ALCOVE BY INDIAN INHABITANTS, DESERT CATTLEMEN, GOLD MINERS AND THE HOMESTEADER WHO ESTABLISHED THE DESERT QUEEN RANCH; WEEKDAY TOURS FOR GROUPS BY RESERVATION ONLY. AT DESERT QUEEN RANCH NEAR HIDDEN VALLEY CAMPGROUND. (REGN'L). JOSHUA TREE NATL MON; NATIONAL PARK SERVICE; 74485 PALM VISTA DR; 29 PALMS, CA 92277. (#6729-149).

FEB 29 - MAR 7, '76. AUDIO CHAIRS EXHIBIT ON NATIVE AMERICANS, BLACKS AND WOMEN IN 1776. IN SPECIAL LISTENING CHAIRS VISITORS WILL HEAR THREE DIFFERENT TAPE RECORDINGS WHICH DESCRIBE THE ROLES OF WOMEN, BLACKS, AND NATIVE AMERICANS DURING THE REVOLUTIONARY PERIOD. AT MONUMENT VISITOR CENTER. (REGN'L). JOSHUA TREE NM; NATIONAL PARK SERVICE; 74485 PALM VISTA DR; 29 PALMS, CA 92277. (#5581-14).

MAY 9, '76. NATL PK SVC '...A LITTLE LOOK AROUND' VISITS JOSHUA TREE NM. THIS SHORT PROGRAM FEATURES ACTORS PORTRAYING FAMOUS AMERICANS OF THE PAST WHO'VE RETURNED TO SEE AMERICA'S GROWTH. (REGN'L). JOSHUA TREE NATL MON; NATIONAL PARK SERVICE; 74485 PALM VISTA DRIVE; 29 PALMS, CA 92277. (#5653-53).

JULY 3 - 4, '76. COMPETITION-DEMONSTRATION-PRESENTATION. BICEN CELEBRATION IN CONJUNCTION WITH 4TH OF JULY. FLAG CEREMONY, FIREWORK DISPLAY & COMPETITION. AT LUCKY PARK. (LOCAL). B D THORNBURY; MCB 29 PALMS-SAN BARNERDI COUNTY PARK SERVICE; MCB; 29 PALMS, CA 92278. (#200006-458).

Colorado

Theme: Once in a Hundred

Colorado Centennial-Bicentennial Commission

Established by the Colorado State Legislature in November 1971, Colorado Revised Statutes (1973) 24-80-1101 through 24-80-1108

ARBA Statistics

Officially Recognized
- Communities—188
- Colleges/Universities—13
- Military Installations—6

BINET Projects—1,155
- Events—1,755

1976 Population—2,583,000

Bicentennial Archives

Archives and Public Records
1313 Sherman Street
Denver, Colorado 80203

Membership

Lorna Hart, *chairperson* (November 1971–April 1972)
Floyd Sack, *chairperson* (April 1972–August 1973)
E. L. "Corky" Cartwright, *chairperson* (August 1973–February 1975)
Herrick S. Roth, *chairperson* (February 1975–September 1975)
Joe M. Lacy, *chairperson* (September 1975–)
Joseph R. Albi, *executive director* (1971–73)
G. D. Barrante, *executive director* (1973–)

Commissioner Appointments

December 1971

Roger Walton
Paco Sanchez
Alexis McKinney*
Edwin Eisenach
Floyd M. Sack
Leslie Fowler
Ben Klein
Jerome Rose
Pat Kelly

June 1972

Herrick Roth*
Celena Smith*
William Winkler*
Helene Wentzel
Jean Wren
Donn Conn
Bee Vradenburg

August 1973

E. L. Cartwright
Joe M. Lacy*
Vicki Jeanne Morrison
Andres Neidig
Robert Pulcipher*
Calvin Snyder
Robert Tonsing
Leonard Burch

January 1975

Lincoln Baca*
John Denver
Juanita Gray*
Peggy Hart*
Carlos Lucero
James Poole*
Robert Welborn
Vine DeLoria, Jr.*
William Thayer Tutt*

April 1975

Karen Cobb*

June 1975

Sandra Klug*

January 1976

Sara Harper*

---

* Still serving

Colorado

Although December 1976, the closing month of the 22 month Centennial-Bicentennial year, rolled around all too quickly, historic restorations, ethnic memorials, educational programs and arts celebrations that will become annual events will continue to remind Coloradans of the outstanding achievements of the Centennial-Bicentennial commemoration.

During the Centennial-Bicentennial year, 188 communities, representing all 63 counties, were awarded national recognition as Bicentennial Communities because of the excellence of their observances. All 63 counties received CCBC funding, with almost $2 million in grant money generating over $10 million in projects throughout the state. And Colorado was among the top three states in the nation in total projects and community participation.

The *Community Incentive Program* was devised to spark participation. It permitted communities to finance local commemorations by selecting from a wide spectrum of suggested activities and awarded them up to $750 in grants to stage the projects selected. Through this ingenious program, a total of $191,850 was awarded to 217 communities representing 61 of the state's 63 counties.

The Colorado Centennial-Bicentennial Commission's marketing program, established to sell the Colorado Centennial medal and to license use of the Colorado Centennial logo, earned a million dollars for statewide Centennial-Bicentennial projects and events. The medal, available in bronze, gold-plated bronze and silver, is the only commemorative medal ever authorized by Congress to be struck at the Denver Mint. Sales of this item alone totaled a half million dollars.

Royalties from licensing the logo for use on various Colorado Centennial-Bicentennial souvenirs totaled over $200,000. Sale of jewelry, posters and Colorado Centennial flags yielded gross revenues of $70,000 for Centennial and Bicentennial projects throughout the state.

Programs funded in Colorado include 28 parks, 52 restorations, 29 museums, 30 community centers and facilities, 15 community service programs, 48 festival events and 24 educational programs.

Colorado was the only state to have a fourth thematic area in addition to the *Heritage, Festival* and *Horizons* commemorative themes: that of *Ethnic Minority*. Under it, 50 projects were awarded grants of $277,391, to make Colorado's Centennial-Bicentennial commemoration truly representative of the state's history and all its peoples.

AGUILAR

ADULT EDUCATION FORUM-THE HERITAGE OF FREEDOM, CO. AN ADULT EDUCATION FORUM WILL CONCENTRATE ON THE HERITAGE OF FREEDOM DURING THE CENTENNIAL-BICENTENNIAL COMMEMORATION. (LOCAL). JOE DOSEN, COORDINATOR; AGUILAR CATHOLIC CHURCH; AGUILAR, CO 81020. (#15961).

ANNUAL '76 - SCHOOL YEARBOOK PROJ, AGUILAR, CO. THE AGUILAR HIGH SCHOOL YEARBOOK WILL EMPHASIZE THE CENTENNIALBICENTENNIAL THEME WHICH WILL INCLUDE LOGOS, LETTERING STYLES, AND FORMAT. (LOCAL). JOE DOSEN, COORDINATOR; AGUILAR HIGH SCHOOL YEARBOOK STAFF; AGUILAR, CO 81020. (#15959).

BANK BUILDING RESTORATION - AGUILAR, CO. PURCHASE AND RESTORE THE HISTORIC BANK BUILDING ACROSS FROM TOWN HALL. ALSO, CREATE AN AREA FOR DISPLAY OF CENTENNIAL-BICENTENNIAL ARTIFACTS. (LOCAL). JOE DOSEN, COORDINATOR; AGUILAR TOWN BOARD; AGUILAR, CO 81020. (#15960).

ST ANTHONY'S CHURCH ABSTRACT DISPLAY. THE CHURCH WILL DISPLAY THE ORIGINAL ABSTRACT WHICH DATES BACK TO 1876. (LOCAL). JOSEPH DOSEN, PROJ DIR; ST ANTHONY'S CHURCH; AGUILAR, CO 81020. (#102708-1). (??).

MAY 16 - SEPT 19, '76. RODEO ROPING - TEAM ROPING, CALF ROPING & WILD COW MILKING. OTHER EVENTS ARE BARREL RACING, POLE RACE, GOAT TYING, FLAG RACE, SADDLE RACE & BOOT RACE. AT AQUILAR ROPING ARENA, 3 BLOCKS NORTH OF MAIN & ROMERO. (ST-WIDE). NORMAN D DOSS, MARSHALL; AQUILAR ROPING CLUB; AQUILAR CITY HALL; AQUILAR, CO 81020. (#107019-1).

JULY 4, '76. CENTENNIAL FIREWORKS. FESTIVAL. (LOCAL). HON MIKE RIGGIO, MAYOR; TOWN OF AGUILAR; 101 W MAIN ST; AGUILAR, CO 81020. (#108656-2).

JULY 4, '76. INTERNATIONAL FESTIVAL. THE ETHNIC GROUPS OF AGUILAR WILL HOLD A FESTIVAL W/REPRESENTATIVE FOOD, CRAFTS, DRESS, MUSIC & DANCE. AM TO 6:00PM & FIREWORKS AT STADIUM AT 9:00PM ON JULY 3; BICENTENNIAL PARADE OF OVER 100 UNITS FROM 2:00 TO 7:00PM ON JULY 4. AT CITY HALL, WEASEL BROOK PARK, CLIFTON STADIUM, DOWNTOWN CLIFTON. (LOCAL). HON MIKE RIGGIO, MAYOR; TOWN OF AGUILAR; 101 W MAIN ST; AGUILAR, CO 81020. (#108656-1).

AUG 8, '76. COMMUNITY PARADE: THEME 'JOIN IN FORGING COLORADO'S 2ND CENTURY'. PARADE. (LOCAL). HON MIKE RIGGIO, MAYOR; TOWN OF AGUILAR; 101 W MAIN; AGUILAR, CO 81020. (#108714-1).

AUG 14, '76. PICNIC-DANCE. FESTIVAL AT AGUILAR HIGH SCHOOL GYM, 402 BALSAM ST. (LOCAL). JOSEPHINE LUCERO, COORD; AGUILAR PICNIC COMMITTEE; 319 SPRUCE; AGUILAR, CO 81020. (#107000-1).

AUG 15, '76. AGUILAR DAY PICNIC & REUNION. FESTIVAL, PARADE AT AGUILAR PARK, MAIN ST. (LOCAL). JOSEPHINE LUCERO, COORD; AGUILAR PICNIC COMMITTEE; 319 SPRUCE; AGUILAR, CO 81020. (#107000-2).

AKRON

AKRON TOWN PUMP AND WINDMILL PROJECT OF COLORADO. THE OLD WOODEN WINDMILL AND PUMP PRESENTLY LOCATED ON MAIN STREET WILL BE RELOCATED IN AN AREA OF COMMANDING HONOR AND WILL BE MARKED AND DEDICATED AS A CENTENNIAL-BICENTENNIAL PROJECT. (LOCAL). VALERIA HOLTORF, VICE CHAIRMAN; WASHINGTON COUNTY HISTORICAL SOCIETY; C/O BURDETTE RTE; AKRON, CO 80720. (#4956).

AMPHITHEATER AT HISTORIC FREMONT BUTTE-AKRON, COLO. MAKE FURTHER USE OF HISTORIC SITE AND ENCOURAGE CULTURAL DEVELOPMENT OF THE COMMUNITY BY STAGING PLAYS AND DRAMAS OF ALL TYPES. (LOCAL). EDITH CARLSEN, COORDINATOR; COALITION OF WASHINGTON COUNTY CIVIC GTOUPS; C/O 762 MAIN ST; AKRON, CO 83720. (#4953). (??).

OLD PRAIRIEVIEW SCHOOL RESTORATION IN AKRON, COLO. SCHOOL HAS BEEN MOVED TO A CITY-OWNED LOT TO BE REFURBISHED AND REFINISHED TO PIONEER ERA AND APPROPRIATELY MARKED AND DEDICATED TO THE CENTENNIAL-BICENTENNIAL. (LOCAL). MRS FLOYD STARLIN, COORDINATOR; WASHINGTON COUNTY MUSEUM ASSOC; 150 E FIRST ST; AKRON, CO 80720. (#4955).

PIONEER TRAIL OF WASHINGTON COUNTY, COLO. OVERLAND CONESTOGA TRIP TO HISTORICAL SITES IN THE AREA. (LOCAL). ORVILLE JOHNSON COUNTY COMMISSIONER; NOSTALGIA MADE REAL SOCIETY; WASHINGTON COUNTY COURTHOUSE; AKRON, CO 80720. (#2917).

STEAM LOCOMOTIVE & ROUNDHOUSE RESTORATION IN COLO. PURCHASE & RESTORE HISTORIC ENGINE & ROUNDHOUSE FOR THE CENTENNIALBICENTENNIAL COMMEMORATION. (LOCAL). ORVILLE JOHNSON, COUNTY COMMISSIONER; NOSTALGIA MADE REAL SOCIETY; WASHINGTON COUNTY COURT HOUSE; AKRON, CO 80720. (#2914).

WASHINGTON COUNTY COUNTRY CLUB PK CLUBHOUSE, CO. FURTHER DEVELOPMENT OF PARK AND CLUBHOUSE OF WASHINGTON COUNTY TO BE DEDICATED TO THE SPIRIT OF '76. (LOCAL). DELANO ARNOLD, VICE PRESIDENT; WASHINGTON COUNTY GOLF ASSOCIATION; 622 ELM ST.; AKRON, CO 80720. (#4952).

WASHINGTON COUNTY OPERA HOUSE, COLORADO. PART OF THE OLD HIGH SCHOOL WILL BE USED AS OPERA HOUSE AND AS A FACILITY FOR THE STAGING OF LOCAL HIGH SCHOOL AND COMMUNITY DRAMAS HIGHLIGHTING THE DAYS OF COLORADO AND AMERICAN HISTORY. (LOCAL). ROGER MILNER, COORDINATOR; NOSTALGIA MADE REAL; 565 ASH ST; AKRON, CO 80720. (#4959).

MAR 1, '75. GROUNDBREAKING CEREMONY FOR PARK AND CLUBHOUSE. FURTHER DEVELOPMENT OF PARK AND CLUBHOUSE OF WASHINGTON COUNTY TO BE DEDICATED TO THE SPIRIT OF '76. (REGN'L). DELANO ARNOLD, VICE PRES; WASHINGTON COUNTY GOLF ASSOCIATION; 622 ELM ST.; AKRON, CO 80720. (#4952-901).

APR 1, '75. AUCTION SALE OF WINDMILL BLADES TO BE ENGRAVED WITH BUYER'S NAME. FAIR. (LOCAL). VALERIA HOLTORF; WASHINGTON COUNTY HISTORICAL SOCIETY; C/O BURDETTE RTE; AKRON, CO 80720. (#4956-501).

APR 1, '75. GROUND BREAKING CEREMONY FOR THE NEW AMPHITHEATER. AWARD. (LOCAL). EDITH CARLSEN; COALITION OF WASHINGTON COUNTY CIVIC GTOUPS; C/O 762 MAIN ST; AKRON, CO 83720. (#4953-501).

APR 2, '75. GROUNDBREAKING CEREMONY OF FRONTAGE RENOVATION. OPENING. (LOCAL). ROGER MILNER, COORDINATOR; NOSTALGIA MADE REAL; 565 ASH ST; AKRON, CO 80720. (#4959-501).

MAY 23, '75. DEDICATION & OPEN HOUSE. CEREMONY, OPENING AT ROCK BUILDING, MUSEUM HIWAY 34 E 2ND ST. (LOCAL). MRS FLOYD STARLIN; WASHINGTON COUNTY MUSEUM ASSO.; HENRY ROUTE; AKRON, CO 80720. (#50431-1).

MAY 25, '75. OLD SCHOOL HOUSE OPEN HOUSE DAY WITH PICNIC, PROGRAM & DEDICATION.. OPENING, CEREMONY, EXHIBIT. (LOCAL). MRS FLOYD STARLIN; WASHINGTON COUNTY MUSEUM ASSOC; 150 E FIRST ST; AKRON, CO 80720. (#4955-501).

JULY 4, '75. PRESENTATION CEREMONY. AKRON TOWN PUMP AND WINDMILL PROJECT OF COLORADO. THE OLD WOODEN WINDMILL AND PUMP PRESENTLY LOCATED ON MAIN STREET WILL BE RELOCATED IN AN AREA OF COMMANDING HONOR AND WILL BE MARKED AND DEDICATED AS A CENTENNIAL-BICENTENNIAL PROJECT. (LOCAL). VALERIA HOLTORF; WASHINGTON COUNTY HISTORICAL SOCIETY; C/O BURDETTE RTE; AKRON, CO 80720. (#4956-502).

AUG 1, '75. DEDICATION CEREMONY FOR RENOVATED BANDSTAND. REBUILD AND LOCATE REPLICA OF OLD BANDSTAND FOR SPECIAL PATRIOTIC BAND CONCERTS HIGHLIGHTING MUSIC OF THE NATION FROM 1776 TO 1976 AND LATER FOR CONTEMPORARY MUSIC BAND CONCERTS. (LOCAL). R HEDGES, CHAIRMAN; WASHINGTON COUNTY CHURCHES; C/O 175 W 4TH ST; AKRON, CO 80720. (#4957-501).

DEC 1, '75. FIRST PERFORMANCE BY COMMUNITY DRAMA ORGANIZATION. OPENING, LIVE PERFORMANCE. (LOCAL). ROGER MILNER, COORDINATOR; NOSTALGIA MADE REAL; 565 ASH ST; AKRON, CO 80720. (#4959-502).

MAY 28, '76. DEDICATION OF NEW SOIL & WATER RESEARCH FACILITY. OPENING OF NEW FEDERAL RESEARCH FACILITY BUILT TO PROVIDE MODERN OFFICE & LABORATORY SPACE FOR RESEARCH ON SOIL, WATER PLANT PROBLEMS IN WESTERN CENTRAL GREAT PLAINS REGION. MORNING-OPEN HOUSE, NOON-BAR BE-CUE, AFTERNOON-DEDICATION CEREMONIES. AT 4 MILES E OF AKRON CERE-GRADE SCHOOL AUDITORIUM. (LOCAL). ROME H MICKELSON, COORD; CENTRAL GREAT PLAINS FIELD STATION ADVISORY COMMITTEE; PO BOX K; AKRON, CO 80720. (#107010-1).

JULY 1, '76 - CONTINUING . OPEN HOUSE SHOWING RENOVATION OF PIONEER STORE. THE ORIGINAL PIONEER STORE IN AKRON WILL BE RESTORED AND STOCKED WITH AS MUCH ORIGINAL MERCHANDISE AS POSSIBLE TO MAKE IT RESEMBLE A STORE OF 1876. AT FIRST & MAIN STREETS. (LOCAL). WARREN FRENCH, OWNER; WARREN AND NITA FRENCH; 761 MAIN ST; AKRON, CO 80720. (#4954-501).

JULY 3 - 4, '76. AKRON PARADE AND PICNIC. FESTIVAL. (LOCAL). EDITH D CARLSEN, CHAIRMAN; AKRON BICENTENNIAL COMMITTEE; 762 MAIN ST; AKRON, CO 80720. (#107585-1).

JULY 4, '76. BICENTENNIAL FESTIVAL. FLAG RAISING CEREMONY, COMMUNITY CHURCH SERVICE, COMMUNITY POT LUCK DINNER, CONTESTS, GAMES, FREE COMMUNITY BAR-B-CUE, COMMUNITY PAGEANT FEATURING SKITS, MUSIC & SPECIAL EVENTS. (LOCAL). HON ROGER L MILNER, MAYOR; CITY OF AKRON; 190 MAIN ST; AKRON, CO 80720. (#108657-3).

JULY 4, '76. CENTENNIAL FIREWORKS & COMMUNITY PARADE. EXHIBIT, PARADE. (LOCAL). HON ROGER L MILNER, MAYOR; CITY OF AKRON; 190 MAIN ST; AKRON, CO 80720. (#108657-2).

JULY 4, '76. SENIOR CITIZENS' FESTIVAL. SENIOR CITIZENS' KING & QUEEN CONTEST, HONORING THE OLDEST CITIZENS IN THE COMMUNITY. SPECIAL RECOGNITION WILL BE GIVEN TO THOSE BORN IN 1900. (LOCAL). HON ROGER L MILNER, MAYOR; AMERICAN ASSOC OF RETIRED PERSONS; 190 MAIN ST; AKRON, CO 80720. (#108657-1).

ALAMOSA

ADAMS STATE TRAVELING MUSEUM - ALAMOSA, CO. TRAVELING DISPLAY TO INFORM OTHER COLORADO COMMUNITIES OF SAN LUIS VALLEY HISTORY. (LOCAL). THOMAS G SCHWING, PROJ DIRECTOR; ADAMS STATE COLLEGE/CENTENNIAL-BICENTENNIAL COMMITTEE; ALAMOSA, CO 81101. (#18447).

ALAMOSA COMMUNITY CENTER - ALAMOSA, CO. A COMMUNITY CENTER WITH CONVENTION CENTER, INDOOR SWIMMING POOL AND OFFICE SPACE WILL BE PROVIDED FOR THE COMMUNITY. (LOCAL). THOMAS G SCHWING, PROJ DIRECTOR; ALAMOSO CENTENNIAL-BICENTENNIAL COMMITTEE; ALAMOSA, CO 81101. (#18446).

BOOTH AT SAN LUIS VALLEY FAIR - ALAMOSA, CO. CENTENNIAL-BICENTENNIAL BOOTH TO INFORM THE PUBLIC OF THE HISTORY OF SAN LUIS. (LOCAL). THOMAS G SCHWING, PROJ DIRECTOR; ALAMOSO CENTENNIAL-BICENTENNIAL COMMITTEE; ALAMOSA, CO 81101. (#18445).

CENTENNIAL-BICENTENNIAL SCULPTURE - ALAMOSA, CO. COMMISSIONED SCULPTURE BY ADAMS STATE ART STUDENTS TO REPLACE THE MILITARY GUN IN PARK CENTER. (LOCAL). THOMAS G SCHWING, PROJ DIRECTOR; ADAMS STATE COLLEGE ART DEPT/CENTENNIAL-BICENTENNIAL COMMITTEE; ALAMOSA, CO 81101. (#18444).

COLE PARK RENOVATION - ALAMOSA, CO. PARK CLEANUP AND RIVERFRONT DEVELOPMENT IN CONJUNCTION WITH ARMY CORPS OF ENGINEERS. (LOCAL). THOMAS G SCHWING, PROJ DIRECTOR; ALAMOSO CENTENNIAL-BICENTENNIAL COMMITTEE; ALAMOSA, CO 81101. (#18443).

DISCOVER AMERICA SLIDE PRESENTATION - ALAMOSA, CO. A SLIDE PROGRAM TO HELP COMMUNITY APPRECIATION. (LOCAL). GLORIA ANTHONY, PROJ DIRECTOR; ALAMOSA CENTENNIAL-BICENTENNIAL COMMITTEE; 415 MAIN; ALAMOSA, CO 81101. (#18448).

HISTORICAL MARKER SIGNS - ALAMOSA, CO. MARKERS NOTING HISTORICAL SIGHTS IN THE SAN LUIS VALLEY. (LOCAL). THOMAS G SCHWING, PROJ DIRECTOR; SAN LUIS VALLEY HISTORICAL SOCIETY/CENTENNIAL-BICENTENNIAL COMM; ALAMOSA, CO 81101. (#18451).

HISTORY OF SPANISH SPEAKING PEOPLE - ALAMOSA, CO. SLIDE AND NARRATIVE PRESENTATION OF EARLY SPANISH HISTORY IN THE SAN LUIS VALLEY FOR WIDEST POSSIBLE DISTRIBUTION TO SCHOOLS, MEDIA AND INTERESTED GROUPS. (ST-WIDE). FRANK WHITE, CHAIRMAN; SAN LUIS VALLEY HISTORICAL SOCIETY; PO BOX 982; ALAMOSA, CO 81101. (#25994).

INFORMATION SIGNS - ALAMOSA, CO. INFORMATION SIGNS WILL BE PLACED AT THE CITY'S MAIN ENTRANCES. (LOCAL). ED R WHITE, COORDINATOR; CITY OF ALAMOSA; 700 MAIN ST; ALAMOSA, CO 81101. (#26197).

INSIGNIA CONTEST - ALAMOSA, CO. CONTEST FOR BEST USE OF THE ALAMOSA CENTENNIAL-BICENTENNIAL INSIGNIA IN HOUSEHOLD ACTIVITY. (LOCAL). THOMAS G SCHWING, PROJ DIRECTOR; ALAMOSO CENTENNIAL-BICENTENNIAL COMMITTEE; ALAMOSA, CO 81101. (#18450).

MIKE DAVIS CENTENNIAL-BICENTENNIAL RIDE. TOUR. (LOCAL). ED WHITE, COORDINATOR; CITY OF ALAMOSA; 700 MAIN ST; ALAMOSA, CO 81101. (#108674-1).

PRESIDENTS PROGRAM - ALAMOSA, CO. PROGRAM FOR PUBLIC INFORMATION ON EACH PRESIDENT'S LIFE DURING THE 200-YEAR OBSERVANCE. (LOCAL). DR JOE CARTER, PROJ DIRECTOR; ALAMOSA CENTENNIAL-BICENTENNIAL COMMITTEE; ALAMOSA, CO 81101. (#18452).

RIO GRANDE ARTS CENTER - ALAMOSA, CO. CENTER WILL INCLUDE PROGRAMS IN COMMUNITY THEATRE, MUSIC AND THE ARTS; A NON-PROFIT & TAX EXEMPT ORGANIZATION AND A BOARD WILL DIRECT THE ACTIVITIES; DEDICATED TO THE ADVANCEMENT OF HUMAN ARTS. (LOCAL). JACK COOPER, CHAIRMAN; ALAMOSA ROTARY CLUB; 306 CRESTONE; ALAMOSA, CO 81101. (#20622).

SAN LUIS VALLEY HISTORICAL MUSEUM, ALAMOSA, CO. A TRAVELLING EXHIBIT OF HISTORY OF SAN LUIS VALLEY WILL BE PREPARED AND A 3 DIMENSIONAL MAP OF THE UPPER RIO GRANDE WILL BE REPAIRED. (LOCAL). ROBERT H BUCHANAN, PROJ DIRECTOR; ADAMS STATE COLLEGE; LEARNING RESOURCE CENTER; ALAMOSA, CO 81102. (#16056).

SAN LUIS VALLEY HISTORY DISPLAY - ALAMOSA, CO. PHOTOGRAPHS, SLIDES AND BOOKS SHOWING THE HISTORY OF SAN LUIS VALLEY WILL BE COLLECTED AND DISPLAYED. (LOCAL). THOMAS G SCHWING, PROJ DIRECTOR; SOUTHERN PEAKS LIBRARY/CENTENNIAL BICENTENNIAL COMMITTEE; ALAMOSA, CO 81101. (#18453).

4500-MILE BICENTENNIAL HORSEBACK RIDE, ALAMOSA, CO. TOM DAVIS WILL TRAVEL ON HORSEBACK WITH PACK MULES FROM EL PASO, TX TO FAIRBANKS, AK; A PICTORAL & WRITTEN LOG OF TRIP WILL BE MADE & PRESENTED TO INTERESTED GROUPS. (REGN'L). DR JACK COTTON, PROJ COORDINATOR; ALAMOSA ELKS LODGE; PLACHY HALL; ALAMOSA, CO 81101. (#23075).

50 STATE FLAGPOLES - ALAMOSA, CO. 50 DONATED POLES AND FLAGS TO CIRCLE PARK STATUE; THE FLAGS OF ALL 50 STATES WILL BE FLOWN. (LOCAL). THOMAS G SCHWING, PROJ DIRECTOR; ALAMOSO CENTENNIAL-BICENTENNIAL COMMITTEE; ALAMOSA, CO 81101. (#18449).

SEPT 12 - 16, '75. 16TH OF SEPTEMBER. FESTIVAL. (LOCAL). DR ARNOLD CHAVEZ, COORD; COLORADO CENTENNIAL-BICENTENNIAL COMMISSION; C/O CHAMBER OF COMMERCE; ALAMOSA, CO 81101. (#108817-1).

FEB 6 - 14, '76. RIO GRANDE ARTS CENTER - FINE ARTS FESTIVAL. FESTIVAL TO INCLUDE: 'ANNIE GET YOUR GUN', SCULPTURE, CARICATURE AND WATER COLOR EXHIBITS, MUSIC ON ANCIENT INSTRUMENTS & CONCERTS. AT RIO GRANDE ARTS CENTER, 306 CRESTONE AVE. (LOCAL). JACK COOPER, CHAIRMAN; ALAMOSA ROTARY CLUB; 64 EL RIO DR; ALAMOSA, CO 81101. (#104877-1).

MAY 25 - 26, '76. NATL PK SVC '... A LITTLE LOOK AROUND' VISITS GREAT SAND DUNES NM. THIS SHORT PROGRAM FEATURES ACTORS PORTRAYING FAMOUS AMERICANS OF THE PAST WHO'VE RETURNED TO SEE AMERICA'S GROWTH. (REGN'L). GREAT SAND DUNES NM; NATIONAL PARK SERVICE; P.O. BOX 60; ALAMOSA, CO 81101. (#5653-65).

JUNE 27 - JULY 3, '76. TOPICS IN PIONEERING: TRIP BY HORSE & WAGON, CREED TO ALAMOSA. TOUR. (LOCAL). DON EDEN, COORDINATOR; ADAMS STATE COLLEGE; ALAMOSA, CO 81101. (#108655-4).

JULY 2 - 4, '76. FOLKLORICO FESTIVAL. FESTIVAL. (LOCAL). DR ARNOLD CHAVEZ; COLORADO CENTENNIAL-BICENTENNIAL COMMISSION; C/O CHAMBER OF COMMERCE; ALAMOSA, CO 81101. (#108655-1).

ALAMOSA — CONTINUED

JULY 4, '76. BURIAL OF COMMUNITY TIME CAPSULE. CEREMONY. (LOCAL). ED R WHITE, COORDINATOR; ED R WHITE; 700 MAIN ST; ALAMOSA, CO 81101. (#108655-2).

JULY 4, '76. SENIOR CITIZENS' TALL TALES CONTEST. STORIES WILL BE PUBLISHED. (LOCAL). ED R WHITE, COORDINATOR; ED R WHITE; 700 MAIN ST; ALAMOSA, CO 81101. (#108655-3).

OCT 23, '76. ADAMS STATE COLLEGE HOMECOMING. COMPETITION, FESTIVAL, PARADE AT REX FIELD, MAIN ST, COLLEGE CENTER. (LOCAL). JAMES BLUNDO, PROJ COORD; ADAMS STATE COLLEGE; ALAMOSA, CO 81101. (#108817-2).

ALMA

ALMA MUSEUM PROJECT - ALMA, CO. BUILDING TO HOUSE STEAM POWERED FIRE WAGON AND OTHER ARTIFACTS OF HISTORICAL INTEREST TO THE COMMUNITY. (LOCAL). ERIK SWANSON, PROJ COORDINATOR; ALMA FIRE DEPT; BOX 27; ALMA, CO 80420. (#26182).

MUSEUM PROJ - ALMA, CO. COMMUNITY IS BUILDING A MUSEUM TO HOUSE LOCAL HISTORICAL OBJECTS. (LOCAL). JAMES GRACEY, PROJ DIRECTOR; TOWN OF ALMA; CITY CLERKS OFFICE; ALMA, CO 80420. (#26316).

ANTONITO

ANTONITO, CO, RESTORATION PROJECT. RESTORATION OF NARROW GAUGE CABOOSE #0529. (LOCAL). ROBERT A BURGRAAF, COORDINATOR; CITY OF ANTONITO; PO BOX 463; ANTONITO, CO 81120. (#26140).

CUMBRES & TOLTEC RAILROAD PROJECT OF COLORADO. LIVING MUSEUM OF FORM OF TRANSPORTATION WHICH UNLOCKED RESOURCES OF COLORADO & THE U.S. GRANT MONEY RECEIVED WILL RESTORE DEPOT & ENGINE NO 463 TO REGULAR SERVICE. (ST-WIDE). ROBERT A BURGGRAAF, PROJECT MANAGER; TOWN OF ANTONITO; ANTONITO, CO 81120. (#1326).

JULY 21, '76. DEDICATION & INAUGURAL RUN OF STEAM ENGINE 463 & BARBECUE. EVENT IS SCHEDULED FOR WED JULY 21, IN CASE OF BAD WEATHER EVENT WILL BE HELD ON THUR JULY 22. AT DEDICATION OF ENGINE-ANTONITO, BARBECUE-BIG HORN, COLO. (LOCAL). DENISE ROMERO; SOUTH CONEJOS COUNTY SCHOOL DISTRICT; SUPT OFFICE, ANTONITO PUBLIC SCH; ANTONITO, CO 81120. (#1326-1).

JULY 23, '76. ANTONITO'S BICENTENNIAL COMMUNITY PRESENTATION. FESTIVAL. (LOCAL). MAYOR; TOWN OF ANTONITO; ANTONITO, CO 81120. (#108692-1).

APPLEWOOD

FEB 1 - 15, '76. EXHIBIT OF TRAVELING SHOW OF AMERICAN WATERCOLOR SOCIETY. AMERICAN WATERCOLOR SOCIETY EXHIBITION, COLORADO. A TWO WEEK EXHIBITION OF PAINTINGS FROM THE 108TH ANNUAL WATERCOLOR SOCIETY'S ANNUAL SHOW. AT HOURS: TUES THRU FRI- 9:30-5:00; SAT- 9:30-3:00; SUN- 1:00-4:00.. (LOCAL). WAYNE A WELCH; APPLEWOOD ART GALLERY; 12975 W 24TH PL; APPLEWOOD, CO 80401. (#6825-501).

ARRIBA

JULY 4, '76. CENTENNIAL FIREWORKS. FESTIVAL. (LOCAL). THOMAS L RHULE, COORD; CITY OF ARRIBA; BOX 137; ARRIBA, CO 80804. (#108652-2).

JULY 4, '76. COMMUNITY TIME CAPSULE DEDICATION & BURIAL. TIME CAPSULE TO BE PLACED IN A MONUMENT IN CITY PARK TO BE OPENED IN 2076. AT CITY PARK. (LOCAL). THOMAS L RHULE, COORD; CITY OF ARRIBA; BOX 137; ARRIBA, CO 80804. (#108652-4).

JULY 4, '76. JULY 4TH BICENTENNIAL CELEBRATION. OLD-FASHIONED 4TH OF JULY FESTIVAL WITH BUFFALO BAR-B-CUE, VARIOUS EVENTS, COMMUNITY DANCE IN FIREWORKS. AT TARADO MUSEUM, S OF ARRIBA. (LOCAL). HARVEY K GRIFFITH, CHMN; ARRIBA CENTENNIAL-BICENTENNIAL COMMITTEE; BOX Q; FLAGLER, CO 80815. (#108652-1).

JULY 4, '76. MUSIC PROGRAM. SERIES OF CONCERTS THROUGHOUT DAY INCLUDING SENIOR CITIZENS' BAND. (LOCAL). THOMAS L RHULE, COORD; CITY OF ARRIBA; BOX 137; ARRIBA, CO 80804. (#108652-3).

ARVADA

ALICE S THOMAS PARK, ARVADA, CO. A PARK WITH TENNIS COURTS ATOP A 10 MILLION GALLON POTABLE WATER TANK IS BEING DEVELOPED. (LOCAL). CAPP F SHANKS, JR, CITY MANAGER; CITY OF ARVADA; 8101 RALSTON RD; ARVADA, CO 80002. (#20018).

ARVADA NEIGHBORHOOD PARKS PROJ IN COLORADO. THE CITY OF ARVADA WILL ESTABLISH NEIGHBORHOOD PARKS IN 12 AREAS OF THE COMMUNITY. ALL THE PARKS WILL FEATURE CENTENNIAL-BICENTENNIAL COMMEMORATIVE PLAQUES. (LOCAL). CRAIG KOCIAN, ASST TO CITY MGR; CITY OF ARVADA; 8101 RALSTON RD; ARVADA, CO 80002. (#6838).

ARVADA, COLORADO, CITY BEAUTIFICATION PROJECT. CLEANUP, PAINT-UP, FIX-UP & PLANT-UP IS THE THEME OF ARVADA'S BEAUTIFICATION PROJECT. BUSINESSES WILL FURNISH TRASH BAGS WITH THE CENTBICENT LOGO & CCBC JEWELRY WILL BE GIVEN AS AWARDS. (LOCAL). RAMONA HARRIS, COORDINATOR; ARVADA CHAMBER OF COMMERCE; 7305 GRANDVIEW; ARVADA, CO 80002. (#6840). **(??).**

ARVADA, COLORADO'S KOSHARE INDIAN DANCE FESTIVAL. KOSHARE INDIAN DANCERS WILL PERFORM AT THE POMONA HIGH SCHOOL DURING THE CARNIVAL DAYS. FUNDS RAISED FROM THE CARNIVAL WILL BE USED FOR A COMMUNITY PARK. (LOCAL). DON GARDNER, PRESIDENT; WARDER ELEMENTARY SCHOOL PTA; 7860 CARR DR; ARVADA, CO 80005. (#6842).

ARVADA, COLORADO'S HISTORICAL DISPLAYS PROJ. HISTORICAL DISPLAYS DEPICTING HISTORY OF EARLY ARVADA GOING BACK TO ITS BEGINNING AS A FARM COMMUNITY. DISPLAYS ARE AVAILABLE TO SCHOOL YOUTH AND SERVICE GROUPS IN REGARD TO HERITAGE AND EDUC PROGRAMS. (LOCAL). HAROLD STORM, CHAIRMAN HERITAGE COMMITTEE; ARVADA HISTORICAL SOCIETY; PO BOX 419; ARVADA, CO 80002. (#6844).

BICENTENNIAL SINGERS - ARVADA, CO. 30 5TH GRADERS PRESENT 'LET'S SING ABOUT AMERICA' ADAPTED BY ED TOMCO FROM AN ORIGINAL CANTATA BY RUTH ROBERTS & WILLIAM KATZ. STUDENTS DRESS IN PERIOD COSTUMES & PERFORM GRATIS FOR CLUBS, NURSING HOMES. (LOCAL). ED TOMCO, PROJ DIRECTOR; LAWRENCE ELEMENTARY; 5611 ZEPHYR ST; ARVADA, CO 80002. (#25896).

CENTENNIAL FAMILY WEEK CELEBRATION IN ARVADA, CO. JULY 4TH CELEBRATION IN '75 & '76 WITH CONCERTS, PLAYS & HISTORICAL PAGEANTS IN AREA PARKS WITH EMPHASIS ON FAMILY UNITY. EVENTS WILL INCLUDE FIREWORKS DISPLAY & PET PARADE. (LOCAL). KEN MONTAG, CHAIRMAN; ARVADA YOUTH ACTION COMMITTEE; 7620 GRANDVIEW; ARVADA, CO 80002. (#6833).

COMMEMORATE FIRST GOLD DISCOVERY IN COLORADO. ESTABLISH A PARK AND DEDICATE MONUMENT AND HISTORICAL MARKER AT THE SITE OF THE FIRST GOLD DISCOVERY IN THE STATE. THE SITE OF THIS IMPORTANT DEVELOPMENT IS LOCATED IN ARVADA. (ST-WIDE). HAROLD STORM, HERITAGE CHAIRMAN; ARVADA HISTORICAL SOCIETY; PO BOX 419; ARVADA, CO 80002. (#6831). **(??).**

FILM FESTIVAL. FILMS WILL RECALL SIGNIFICANT EVENTS IN 1ST 100 YEARS OF COLORADO & FIRST 200 YEARS OF U S. (LOCAL). DON CARTER, DIRECTOR; ARVADA CENTER; 6901 WADSWORTH BLVD; ARVADA, CO 80004. (#108818-1).

HACKBERRY PARK BEAUTIFICATION - ARVADA, CO. PICNIC TABLE AND BENCHES TO BE ADDED, FENCE TO BE INSTALLED, SHRUBS, FLOWERS AND TREES TO BE PLANTED, SPRINKLER SYSTEM BEING INSTALLED TO BEAUTIFY AND PRESERVE THIS HISTORIC ARVADA LOCATION. (LOCAL). LUCY ROTH, PROJ DIRECTOR; ARVADA GARDEN CLUB; 7995 ALKIRE ST; ARVADA, CO 80004. (#26210).

HOMESTEADERS CABIN RELOCATION AND RESTORATION, CO. ORIGINAL HOMESTEADERS CABIN, BUILT IN APPROXIMATELY 1870, WILL BE REMOVED FROM BLUNN RANCH TO ARVADA CENTER TO BE RESTORED; AUTHENTICALLY FURNISHED TO GIVE VIEWERS GLIMPSE OF LIFE IN EARLY CO. (LOCAL). IRENE VANCE, CHAIRMAN; ARVADA CENTENNIAL-BICENTENNIAL COMMITTEE; 8101 RALSTON RD; ARVADA, CO 80002. (#26208).

'MORE THAN GOLD' - ARVADA, CO. SECOND BOOK ON HISTORY OF ARVADA BY ARVADA HISTORICAL SOCIETY. BOOK AVAILABLE AT ARVADA HERITAGE PRINTERS, 5603 YUKON ST. (LOCAL). MARCETTA LUTZ, PRESIDENT; ARVADA HISTORICAL SOCIETY; PO BOX 419; ARVADA, CO 80002. (#26211).

OFFICIAL CERTIFICATE FOR ARVADA, CO CENT-BICENT. CERTIFICATE ESPECIALLY DESIGNED TO OFFICIALLY RECOGNIZE ENDORSED CENT-BICENT PROJECTS. CERTIFICATE TO BEAR ARVADA & STATE LOGOS. (LOCAL). BERNIE LAMACH, HORIZONS CHAIRMAN; ARVADA CENTENNIAL - BICENTENNIAL COMMITTEE; 8101 RALSTON RD; ARVADA, CO 80002. (#6832).

PAINT-A-PLUG - ARVADA, CO. HISTORICAL FIGURES AND CENTENNIAL-BICENTENNIAL THEMES WILL BE PAINTED ON THE CITY'S FIRE HYDRANTS. (LOCAL). LEROY SCHRODER, CHAIRMAN; ARVADA CENTENNIAL-BICENTENNIAL COMMITTEE; 8101 RALSTON RD; ARVADA, CO 80004. (#26889).

PUBLISH BOOK ON HISTORY OF ARVADA, COLORADO. BOOK ON ARVADA HISTORY TO BE PUBLISHED BY ARVADA HISTORICAL SOCIETY IN COMMEMORATION OF THE BICENTENNIAL & THE COLORADO CENTENNIAL. BOOK COVER WILL BE RED, WHITE & BLUE. (LOCAL). BRUCE BUELL, PRESIDENT; ARVADA HISTORICAL SOCIETY; 6005 DUDLEY ST; ARVADA, CO 80002. (#6835).

SENIOR CITIZEN VAN - ARVADA, CO. VAN FOR USE BY ALL ARVADA SENIOR CITIZENS PURCHASED WITH VOLUNTEER FUNDS RAISED BY THE ARVADA JEFFERSON KIWANIS-ARVADA CENT-BICENT ALLOCATED $250 TOWARDS PURCHASE OF HYDRAULIC LIFT FOR VAN. (LOCAL). JIM POWELL, PRESIDENT; ARVADA-JEFFERSON KIWANIS; 4713 ROBB ST; WHEAT RIDGE, CO 80033. (#26209).

JAN 1 - DEC 31, '75. HISTORICAL DISPLAYS DEPICTING HISTORY OF ARVADA AS FARM COMMUNITY. HISTORICAL DISPLAYS DEPICTING HISTORY OF EARLY ARVADA GOING BACK TO ITS BEGINNING AS A FARM COMMUNITY. DISPLAYS ARE AVAILABLE TO SCHOOL YOUTH AND SERVICE GROUPS IN REGARD TO HERITAGE AND EDUC PROGRAMS. (LOCAL). HAROLD STORM; ARVADA HISTORICAL SOCIETY; PO BOX 419; ARVADA, CO 80002. (#6844-501).

APR 5, '75. KICK OFF DANCE GALA '76. ARVADA, COLORADO, GALA '76. THE KICK OFF DANCE FOR ARVADA'S CENT-BICENT CELEBRATION WILL FEATURE A BALLET, A BARBER SHOP QUARTET AND A PERFORMANCE OF THE MINUET. (LOCAL). DICK TUERS; ARVADA CENTENNIAL BICENTENNIAL COMMITTEE; 8101 RALSTON RD; ARVADA, CO 80002. (#6839-501).

APR 18, '75. PARK PLAQUE PRESENTATION COMMEMORATING CENT-BICENT. FESTIVAL, LIVE PERFORMANCE. (LOCAL). DON GARDNER, PRESIDENT; WARDER ELEMTARY SCHOOL PARENTS & TEACHER'S ASSOC; 7860 CARR DR; ARVADA, CO 80005. (#6842-503).

APR 18 - 19, '75. AWARDS CEREMONY FOR ART CONTEST ENTRIES. FESTIVAL, LIVE PERFORMANCE. (LOCAL). DON GARDNER, PRESIDENT; WARDER ELEMTARY SCHOOL PARENTS & TEACHER'S ASSOC; 7860 CARR DR; ARVADA, CO 80005. (#6842-502).

APR 18 - 19, '75. KOSHARE INDIAN DANCE PERFORMANCES AT POMONA HIGH. FESTIVAL, LIVE PERFORMANCE. (LOCAL). DON GARDNER, PRESIDENT; WARDER ELEMTARY SCHOOL PARENTS & TEACHER'S ASSOC; 7860 CARR DR; ARVADA, CO 80005. (#6842-501).

MAY 15 - 22, '75. YEA '76 PROGRAM TO ENCOURAGE YOUTH INVOLVEMENT. YOUTH OF EVERY AGE '76 (YEA '76), CENT-BICENT YOUTH GROUP, WILL PRESENT AN EDUCATIONAL PROGRAM TO ELEMENTARY SCHOOL AGE CHILDREN TO ENCOURAGE THEIR INTEREST IN THE CENT-BICENT COMMEMORATION. (LOCAL). DIRK MATHIS, CHAIRMAN; YEA '76; 8101 RALSTON RD; ARVADA, CO 80002. (#6845-501).

JULY 1, '75. SUNSET SHOWS. LIVE PERFORMANCE. (LOCAL). SANDY REILLY, CHMN; ARVADA CENTENNIAL-BICENTENNIAL COMMITTEE; 7620 GRANDVIEW; ARVADA, CO 80005. (#102944-1).

JULY 3 - 5, '75. JULY 4TH FAMILY WEEK CELEBRATION IN ARVADA PARKS. CENTENNIAL FAMILY WEEK CELEBRATION IN ARVADA, CO. JULY 4TH CELEBRATION IN '75 & '76 WITH CONCERTS, PLAYS & HISTORICAL PAGEANTS IN AREA PARKS WITH EMPHASIS ON FAMILY UNITY. EVENTS WILL INCLUDE FIREWORKS DISPLAY & PET PARADE. (LOCAL). KEN MONTAG, CHAIRMAN; ARVADA YOUTH ACTION COMMITTEE; 7620 GRANDVIEW; ARVADA, CO 80002. (#6833-501).

SEPT 4 - 6, '75. ARVADA FALL FESTIVAL-1975. ARVADA, COLORADO'S FALL FESTIVAL. THE ANNUAL FALL FESTIVAL WILL HAVE A CENTENNIAL-BICENTENNIAL THEME WITH CENT-BICENT JEWELRY, ARTS & CRAFTS, PARADES WITH FLOATS AND RED WHITE AND BLUE BOOTHS. (LOCAL). DICK TUERS; ARVADA CHAMBER OF COMMERCE; 7305 GRANDVIEW ST; ARVADA, CO 80002. (#6841-502).

SEPT 6, '75. ARVADA FALL FESTIVAL PARADE WITH CENT-BICENT FLOATS. ARVADA, COLORADO'S FALL FESTIVAL. THE ANNUAL FALL FESTIVAL WILL HAVE A CENTENNIAL-BICENTENNIAL THEME WITH CENT-BICENT JEWELRY, ARTS & CRAFTS, PARADES WITH FLOATS AND RED WHITE AND BLUE BOOTHS. (LOCAL). DICK TUERS; ARVADA CHAMBER OF COMMERCE; 7305 GRANDVIEW ST; ARVADA, CO 80002. (#6841-501).

NOV 7 - 15, '75. 'THE UNSINKABLE MOLLY BROWN'. LIVE PERFORMANCE AT ARVADA HIGH SCHOOL AUDITORIUM. (LOCAL). C THOMAS MCCORMICK, DIR; ARVADA HIGH SCHOOL; 7951 W 65TH AVE; ARVADA, CO 80004. (#200007-1).

JAN 1 - 31, '76. DISPLAYS DEPICTING ARVADA'S FARMING HISTORY. HISTORICAL DISPLAYS DEPICTING HISTORY OF EARLY ARVADA GOING BACK TO ITS BEGINNING AS A FARM COMMUNITY. DISPLAYS ARE AVAILABLE TO SCHOOL YOUTH AND SERVICE GROUPS IN REGARD TO HERITAGE AND EDUC PROGRAMS. (LOCAL). HAROLD STORM; ARVADA HISTORICAL SOCIETY; PO BOX 419; ARVADA, CO 80002. (#6844-502).

JAN 1 - MAR 1, '76. CENT-BICENT THEME ESSAY SCHOLARSHIP CONTEST. AWARD, COMPETITION. (LOCAL). DIRK MATHIS, COORDINATOR; ARVADA CENTENNIAL-BICENTENNIAL COMMISSION; 8101 RALSTON RD; ARVADA, CO 80002. (#6837-501).

JAN 1 - SEPT 11, '76. BEARD GROWING CONTEST. COMPETITION AT ANNUAL HARVEST FESTIVAL, DOWNTOWN ARVADA. (LOCAL). FRED M SCHUTZ, COORD; ARVADA CENTENNIAL-BICENTENNIAL COMMITTEE, INC; 8100 RALSTON RD; ARVADA, CO 80002. (#106998-1).

MAR 13 - 17, '76. 'GEORGE WASHINGTON SLEPT HERE' - A 3 ACT PLAY. A FULL LENGTH 3 ACT PLAY SET IN PA. A CITY FAMILY MOVES TO THE COUNTRY, ONLY TO FIND THAT THE HOUSE THEY BOUGHT DOESN'T MEET THEIR EXPECTATIONS. IT WAS SUPPOSEDLY OCCUPIED BY GEORGE WASHINGTON BUT THEY LEARN IT WAS BENEDICT ARNOLD INSTEAD. AT ARVADA SENIOR HIGH SCHOOL AUDITORIUM. (LOCAL). JAN CONE, PUBLICITY CHMN; ARVADA SENIOR HIGH SCHOOL; 7951 W 65TH AVE; ARVADA, CO 80004. (#200007-2).

MAR 15 - SEPT 11, '76. TENNIS TOURNAMENT WITH BICENT THEME FOR OPENING CEREMONY. 1976 TENNIS TOURNAMENT IN ARVADA, COLORADO. TOURNAMENT TO BE HELD IN NEW TENNIS COMPLEX WILL COMMEMORATE CENTENNIAL & BICENTENNIAL. AT OPENING CEREMONY COPIES OF FLAGS OF THE 13 ORIGINAL STATES WILL BE FLOWN. (LOCAL). CAPP SHANKS, CITY MANAGER; CITY OF ARVADA; 8101 RALSTON RD; ARVADA, CO 80002. (#6834-501).

MAY 13 - 22, '76. '1776' - PLAY PRESENTATION. LIVE PERFORMANCE AT ARVADA HIGH SCHOOL. (LOCAL). C THOMAS MCCORMICK, DIR; ARVADA HIGH SCHOOL; 7951 W 65TH AVE; ARVADA, CO 80004. (#103346-3).

JUNE 15, '76 - CONTINUING . 200 YEARS IN MINIATURE - EXHIBIT. ELABORATE MINIATURE DISPLAY DEPICTING LIFE FROM 1776 TO 1976 WITH EARLY COLONIAL HOME, SOD HOUSE, LACE-STYLE HOUSE, COVERED WAGON, SALT BOX HOUSE, INDIAN TEPEE, LOG CABIN & MODERN SPLIT LEVEL; DISPLAY IS HAND-CRAFTED WITH AUTHENTICITY IN ARCHITECTURE, DESIGN, ETC. (LOCAL). DOROTHY HOLMES, COORD; DOROTHY HOLMES; 7059 PARFET CT; ARVADA, CO 80004. (#108358-1).

JUNE 18, '76. DEDICATION-ARVADA TENNIS CENTER. PRESENTATION OF PLAQUE TO MAYOR FELAND BY ARVADA CENTENNIAL - BICENTENNIAL COMMITTEE. MUSIC BY POMONA HIGH SCHOOL STAGE BAND UNDER THE DIRECTION OF KIRK PRICHARD. AT

ARVADA — CONTINUED

68TH & MILLER ST. (LOCAL). IRENE VANCE, CHMN; ARVADA CENTENNIAL-BICENTENNIAL COMMITTEE; 7058 PARFET CT; ARVADA, CO 80004. (#200007-4).

JUNE 18 - 20, '76. CENTENNIAL '76 CARA ADULT SINGLES TENNIS TOURNAMENT. ANNUAL TENNIS TOURNAMENT WILL BE PART OF DEDICATION CEREMONY FOR ARVADA TENNIS CENTER. RED, WHITE & BLUE TENNIS ATTIRE REQUIRED. TROPHIES WILL BEAR STATE CENTENNIAL LOGO. BOB KURTZ & JOHN RAYBURN OF THE CHANNEL 9 NEWS TEAM WILL CHALLENGE THE CITY COUNCIL. AT ARVADA TENNIS CENTER, 68TH & MILLER ST. (ST-WIDE). IRENE VANCE, CHMN; ARVADA CENTENNIAL-BICENTENNIAL COMMITTEE; 7058 PARFET CT; ARVADA, CO 80004. (#200007-5).

JULY 1 - 4, '76. BONANZA CB-SSB CENTENNIAL JAMBOREE CONVENTION. CONVENTION WILL INCLUDE DISPLAYS, EXHIBITS, LIVE ENTERTAINMENT, DANCES, CENTENNIAL DRESS & BEARD CONTEST, FIREWORKS DISPLAY AND RAFFLES. AT ADAMS COUNTY FAIRGROUNDS, EXHIBIT HALL, DOME, ANNEX. (NAT'L). TED GALLENTINE, PRESIDENT; BONANZA CITIZENS BAND COFFEE BREAK INC; 11677 W 62ND AVE #3; ARVADA, CO 80001. (#19813-1).

JULY 2 - 3, '76. FLEA MARKET/BAZAAR. EXHIBIT, FAIR. (LOCAL). IRENE VANCE, CHAIRMAN; ARVADA CENTENNIAL-BICENTENNIAL COMMITTEE; 8101 RALSTON ROAD; ARVADA, CO 80004. (#108654-3).

JULY 2 - 4, '76. JULY 4TH FAMILY WEEK CELEBRATION IN ARVADA PARKS. CENTENNIAL FAMILY WEEK CELEBRATION IN ARVADA, CO. JULY 4TH CELEBRATION IN '75 & '76 WITH CONCERTS, PLAYS & HISTORICAL PAGEANTS IN AREA PARKS WITH EMPHASIS ON FAMILY UNITY. EVENTS WILL INCLUDE FIREWORKS DISPLAY & PET PARADE. (LOCAL). KEN MONTAG, CHAIRMAN; ARVADA YOUTH ACTION COMMITTEE; 7620 GRANDVIEW; ARVADA, CO 80002. (#6833-502).

JULY 3, '76. PARADE. THEME WILL BE 'WE'VE GOT THE SPIRIT OF 76' & WILL FEATURE LOCAL SERVICE & VETERAN GROUPS, A MOTORCYCLE PATROL, YOUTH ORGANIZATIONS & HIGH SCHOOL BANDS. SECOND ANNUAL PET & DOLL PARADE. (LOCAL). IRENE VANCE, CHAIRMAN; ARVADA CENTENNIAL-BICENTENNIAL COMMITTEE; 8101 RALSTON ROAD; ARVADA, CO 80004. (#108654-4).

JULY 3 - 4, '76. HAPPY BIRTHDAY USA - JULY 4TH CELEBRATION. PARADE W/PET & DOLL SEGMENT, BICENT COLOR GUARD, AMER LEGION MOTOR CYCLE PATROL, YOUTH GROUPS, GAMES, CONTESTS, FLEA MARKET & DEDICATION CEREMONY ON 7/3. FREE CONCERT W/THE NEW CHRISTY MINSTRELS. AT N JEFFERSON COUNTY PARK & ARVADA CENTER. (LOCAL). IRENE VANCE, CHAIRMAN; ARVADA CENTENNIAL-BICENTENNIAL COMMITTEE; 7058 PARFET CT; ARVADA, CO 80004. (#108654-1).

JULY 4, '76. CULTURAL COMMUNITY CENTER DEDICATION. CULTURAL & COMMUNITY CENTER TO INCLUDE A HISTORICAL MUSEUM, THEATER, ART WORKSHOPS & AN ART GALLERY. A PLAQUE WAS PERSENTED TO COMMEMORATE THE CENTENNIAL-BICENTENNIAL CELEBRATION. THE BUILDING OPENED TO THE PUBLIC SEPT 9, 1976. (LOCAL). CAPP SHANKS, CTY MGR; CITY OF ARVADA; 8101 RALSTON RD; ARVADA, CO 80002. (#6836-1).

JULY 24 - 25, '76. BLACK POWDER SHOOT AND PICNIC. DAYS OF THE OLD WEST ARE CELEBRATED WITH FUN AND GAMES FOR THE WHOLE FAMILY. ACTIVITIES INCLUDE RIFLE AND PISTOL MATCHES AND A PICNIC WITH RELAY RACES AND CONTESTS. AT BLUNN RANCH, 18761 W 6TH. (LOCAL). IRENE VANCE, CHAIRMAN; ARVADA CENTENNIAL-BICENTENNIAL COMMITTEE; 8101 RALSTON RD; ARVADA, CO 80004. (#102925-1).

JULY 26 - 27, '76. RIFLE & PISTOL MATCHES. COMPETITION AT 18761 W 66TH ST. (LOCAL). IRENE VANCE, COORDINATOR; ARVADA CENTENNIAL-BICENTENNIAL COMMITTEE; 7058 PARFET; ARVADA, CO 80004. (#108732-2).

JULY 27, '76. 'DAYS OF THE OLD WEST' PICNIC. FREE BLACK POWDER RIFLE AND PISTOL INSTRUCTIONS AND SHOOTING PRIVILEGES FOR THOSE IN COSTUME. AT 18761 W 66TH. (LOCAL). IRENE VANCE, COORDINATOR; ARVADA CENTENNIAL-BICENTENNIAL COMMITTEE; 7058 PARFET; ARVADA, CO 80004. (#108732-3).

JULY 31 - AUG 1, '76. CENTENNIAL '76 BLACK POWDER SHOOT & OLD-FASHIONED PICNIC. ARVADA'S COLORADO DAY CELEBRATION WILL RECAPTURE THE EXCITEMENT OF THE EARLY WEST WITH BLACK POWDER COMPETITION. TOMAHAWK THROWING, GAMES & CONTESTS, TYNTYPE PARLOUR, AUTHENTIC EARLY WEST COSTUMES BAR-B-Q, TUG OF WAR, SQUARE DANCING & BLUE GRASS MUSIC. AT 18761 W 66TH AVE, BLUNN RANCH SOUTH OF RALSTON FILTER PLANT. (LOCAL). IRENE VANCE, COORDINATOR; ARVADA CENTENNIAL-BICENTENNIAL COMMITTEE; 7058 PARFET CT; ARVADA, CO 80004. (#108732-1).

AUG 3, '76. JEFFERSON SYMPHONY ORCHESTRA PREFORMANCE. SEMI-PROFESSIONAL ORCHESTRA TO HONOR THE CITY OF ARVADO; MUSIC OF AMERICA & BY AMERICAN COMPOSERS FEATURED. AT ARVADA AMPHITHEATER. (LOCAL). JACKIE MAXWELL, V-PRES; JEFFERSON SYMPHONY ORCHESTRA; 7720 WESTVIEW DR; LAKEWOOD, CO 80215. (#106609-1).

AUG 29, '76. ARVADA REUNION DAYS AND OLD TIMERS PICNIC. PICNIC FOR SENIOR CITIZENS OF ARVADA; 10 OLDEST RESIDENTS WILL RECEIVE SPECIAL AWARDS; INTERVIEWS ON EARLY SCHOOL DAYS WILL BE TAPED AND PLACED IN PERMANENT FILE WITH OTHER HISTORICAL RECORDS. AT NORTH JEFFCO PARK, 9101 RALSTON RD. (LOCAL). MARCETTA LUTZ, COORD; ARVADA HISTORICAL SOCIETY; PO BOX 419; ARVADA, CO 80004. (#108818-4).

SEPT 1, '76. CENT-BICENT THEME ESSAY CONTEST SCHOLARSHIP AWARD PRESENTATION. AWARD, COMPETITION. (LOCAL). MRS ROBT VANCE; ARVADA CENTENNIAL-BICENTENNIAL COMMISSION; 7058 OWEAR; ARVADA, CO 80002. (#6837-502).

SEPT 9 - 11, '76. ARVADA HARVEST FESTIVAL AND PARADE. FESTIVAL & PARADE THEME THIS YEAR WILL BE 'WE'VE GOT THE SPIRIT OF '76'; FEATURES CENTENNIAL-BICENTENNIAL BOOTHS, FLOATS AND AWARDS. (LOCAL). DICK TUERS, COORD; ARVADA CHAMBER OF COMMERCE AND ARVADA JAYCEES; 7530 GRANDVIEW; ARVADA, CO 80002. (#108818-3).

OCT 1 - DEC 18, '76. PREMIER OF 3 AMER PLAYS BY THE RESIDENT THEATRE PRODUCTION COMPANY. LIVE PERFORMANCE AT ARVADA CENTER, 6901 WADSWORTH BLVD. (LOCAL). EDWARD OSBORN, PRODUCER; ARVADA CENTENNIAL-BICENTENNIAL COMMITTEE; 8101 RALSTON RD; ARVADA, CO 80002. (#107887-1).

OCT 15, '76. COSTUME BALL WITH AWARDS OF SAVINGS BONDS FOR THE BEST COSTUMES. ARVADA CENTER OPENING FESTIVITIES IN ARVADA, CO. FESTIVITIES WILL INCLUDE THE DAYS OF '76 COSTUME BALL WITH SAVINGS BONDS PRESENTED AS PRIZES FOR THE BEST COSTUMES. (LOCAL). HAROLD STORM; ARVADA HISTORICAL SOCIETY; PO BOX 419; ARVADA, CO 80002. (#6843-501).

ASPEN

ASPEN ASHCROFT GHOST TOWN PROJECT OF COLORADO. TO PRESERVE AND RESTORE THE REMAINING BUILDINGS ON THE OLD ASHCROFT TOWN SITE. TO INCLUDE MOVING TWO CABINS TO A SAFER LOCATION AND CREATING A WALKING TOUR OF THE SITE. (LOCAL). RAMONA MARKALUNAS, PRESIDENT; ASPEN HISTORICAL SOCIETY; PO BOX 1323; ASPEN, CO 81611. (#4382). **ARBA GRANTEE.**

ASPEN HISTORIC MARKERS, ASPEN, CO. ALL HISTORIC BUILDING & LOCATIONS WILL HAVE AN OFFICIAL HISTORICAL PLAQUE. (LOCAL). RAMONA MARKALUNAS, PROJ DIRECTOR; CENTENNIAL-BICENTENNIAL COMMITTEE; BOX 4795; ASPEN, CO 81611. (#16396).

ASPEN INSTITUTE PROJECT 2076 SEMINAR. A NATIONAL CONFERENCE ON THE QUALITY OF LIFE IN THE UNITED STATES, NOW & FOR THE FUTURE. (NAT'L). REV JEROME B COLL, HORIZONS CHAIRMAN; MAYOR'S COMMITTEE OF 19 FOR '76; CITY AND COUNTY BUILDING; DENVER, CO 80202. (#1910).

ASPEN INSTITUTE BICENTENNIAL PROGRAM. CENTERING ON THE THEME OF CULTURE & DEMOCRACY IN AMERICA, THE INSTITUTE PLANS REGIONAL & NATIONAL PROGRAMS. (NAT'L). JOHN HUNT, VICE PRESIDENT; ASPEN INSTITUTE FOR HUMANISTIC STUDIES; 717 5TH AVE; NEW YORK, NY 10022. (#6882). **ARBA RECOGNIZED.**

ASPEN, COLORADO, HISTORICAL VIDEO PROJECT. TO PRODUCE SERIES OF HISTORICAL VIDEO TAPES TO PROVIDE VIDEO RECORDING & PLAYBACK CAPABILITIES FOR HISTORICAL USE TO COOPERATE WITH COLO MTN COLLEGE IN WORKSHOPS FOR RESEARCH & WRITING DOCUMENTARIES. (ST-WIDE). CHAIRMAN; ASPEN HISTORICAL SOCIETY; PO BOX 1323; ASPEN, CO 81611. (#4344).

ASPEN, COLO, CARRIAGE HOUSE MUSEUM. A PROJECT TO CONSTRUCT A CARRIAGE HOUSE MUSEUM ON THE GROUNDS OF THE EXISTING STALLARD HOUSE MUSEUM TO EXHIBIT HISTORIC VEHICLES. (LOCAL). RAMONA MARKALUNAS, PRESIDENT; ASPEN HISTORICAL SOCIETY; PO BOX 1323; ASPEN, CO 81611. (#4381).

FORMATION & IMPLEMENTATION OF A BELL CHOIR, CO. FORMATION OF BELL CHOIR TO PERFORM AT CENTENNIAL & CHAPEL CONCERTS. (LOCAL). ELLAMAR PHILLIPS, CHAIRPERSON; RSVP; BOX 242; SNOWMASS, CO 81654. (#26153).

HISTORIC ASPEN, COLO, PRESERVATION PLAN. A PROJECT TO DEVELOP A MASTER PLAN FOR THE HISTORIC PRESERVATION OF THE CITY OF ASPEN. PLAN WOULD INDICATE WHAT SHOULD BE PRESERVED AND WITH WHAT PRIORITIES. (LOCAL). FRED WOODEN, PLANNER; CITY OF ASPEN; BOX V; ASPEN, CO 81611. (#4295).

INDEPENDENCE STAGE TRAIL MARKER, ASPEN, CO. MARKERS FOR HIKERS WILL BE ERECTED ACROSS THE INDEPENDENCE STAGE ROUTE FROM LEADVILLE TO ASPEN. (LOCAL). RAMONA MARKALUNAS, PROJ DIRECTOR; ASPEN HISTORICAL SOCIETY; BOX 4795; ASPEN, CO 81611. (#16397).

LITTLE RED SCHOOLHOUSE, ASPEN, CO. RESTORATION OF PIONEER SCHOOLHOUSE FOR MUSEUM. (LOCAL). MAUREEN WALSH, PROJ DIRECTOR; ROARING FORK CBC; PO BOX 4795; ASPEN, CO 81611. (#19505).

PITKIN COUNTY LIGHT RAIL TRANSIT SYSTEM - CO. A LIGHT RAIL TRANSIT SYSTEM CONNECTING ASPEN WITH SNOWMASS RESORT, OUTLYING SKI AREAS AND AIRPORT THROUGH SCENIC ROUTES. (LOCAL). ALLAN BLOOMQUIST, COUNTY MANAGER; BOARD OF COUNTY COMMISSIONERS OF PITKIN COUNTY; 506 E MAIN; ASPEN, CO 81611. (#16401).

WHEELER OPERA HOUSE RESTORATION IN ASPEN, COLORADO. A PROJECT TO RESTORE THE HISTORIC WHEELER OPERA HOUSE AND TO ERECT A PLAQUE ACKNOWLEDGING THAT THE BUILDING IS ON THE NATIONAL REGISTER OF HISTORIC PLACES. (ST-WIDE). HERB BARTEL, CITY-COUNTY PLANNER; CITY OF ASPEN; BOX V; ASPEN, CO 81611. (#4419).

DEC 8, '75 - MAY 10, '76. AMERICAN ISSUES FORUM LECTURES. ADDITIONAL LECTURES: 1/2/76, 2/23/76, 3/22/76, 4/5/76. TUESDAY & THURSDAY HOURS: 10-9. SUNDAY HOURS: 12-6. AT PITKIN COUNTY LIBRARY. (LOCAL). JULIA KLEVEN, LIBRARIAN; PITKIN COUNTY LIBRARY; 120 E MAIN; ASPEN, CO 81611. (#103315-2).

DEC 12 - 20, '75. ASPEN PRO-SPREE. THIS IS THE FIRST PRO SKI RACE OF THE '76 SEASON. (INT'L). REES JOHNSON, COORDINATOR; ASPEN SKIING CORPORATION; 406 S MILL ST; ASPEN, CO 81611. (#102834-2).

JAN 21 - 25, '76. WINTERSKOL. FESTIVAL, PARADE. (LOCAL). JEAN GREINER, OFFICE MGR; ASPEN CHAMBER OF COMMERCE; 328 E HYMAN AVE; ASPEN, CO 81611. (#103315-4).

MAR 12 - 14, '76. 1976 WORLD CUP. THIS IS THE 30TH ANNIVERSARY OF THE ROCH CUP SKI RACE. (INT'L). REES JOHNSON, COORDINATOR; ASPEN SKIING CORPORATION; 406 S MILL ST; ASPEN, CO 81611. (#102834-1).

JUNE 11 - 13, '76. ASPEN ARTS FESTIVAL. FESTIVAL AT ASPEN CITY MALL & ASPEN BUSINESS BUILDINGS. (LOCAL). PRESIDENT; THE ASPEN FOUNDATION FOR THE ARTS; BOX 4615; ASPEN, CO 81611. (#103315-5).

JUNE 13 - AUG 30, '76. HISTORICAL SOCIETY TOURS. TOUR. (LOCAL). ROMONA MARKALUNAS; HISTORICAL SOCIETY; ASPEN, CO 81611. (#107779-2).

JUNE 15 - JULY 31, '76. ORCHESTRAL CONCERT WITH FEMALE VOICE. 'VISIONS OF TERROR & WONDER', ORCHESTRAL MUSIC. COMPOSITION OF ORCHESTRAL PIECE WITH FEMALE VOICE; EMPLOYING TEXTS FROM OLD AND NEW TESTAMENTS AND KORAN. (LOCAL). RICHARD DUFALLO; ASPEN MUSIC FESTIVAL; ASPEN, CO 81611. (#6276-501).

JUNE 25 - AUG 22, '76. 27TH ANNUAL MUSIC FESTIVAL. MUSICIANS WHO HAVE INSPIRED AMERICANS DURING THE NATION'S 200 YEARS ARE HIGHLIGHTED IN THIS SUMMER-LONG FESTIVAL. AT FESTIVAL TENT. (LOCAL). LYNN FURGUSON, CHAIRMAN; MUSIC ASSOCIATES OF ASPEN, INC; BOX AA; ASPEN, CO 81611. (#103416-392).

JULY 1 - 4, '76. THE ROARING FORK VALLEY FOURTH OF JULY 1976 CELEBRATION. FESTIVAL. (LOCAL). RODDY BURDINE; BICENTENNIAL COMMITTEE, CHAMBER OF COMMERCE & VOLUNTEER FIRE DEPT; BOX 4795; ASPEN, CO 81611. (#107779-3).

JULY 2 - 5, '76. ASPEN MUSIC FESTIVAL: SPECIAL BICENTENNIAL-CENTENNIAL PROGRAM. ONE CONCERT DAILY ON JULY 2, 3, 4 & 5; EMPHASIS ON AMERICAN AND BRITISH COMPOSERS INCLUDING ALL TYPES OF AMERICAN MUSIC; CLASSICAL MUSIC SHOWS AND AMERICAN JAZZ, AND A SEMINAR ON AMERICAN MUSIC WILL ALSO BE PRESENTED. AT ASPEN AMPHITHEATRE, W GILLESPIE AVE. (ST-WIDE). EDGAR B STERN; MUSIC ASSOCIATES OF ASPEN, INC; PO BOX AA; ASPEN, CO 81611. (#2911-1).

JULY 2 - 23, '76. A BICENTENNIAL SHOW OF CONTEMPORARY WEAVING. WEAVING PATTERNS FROM COLONIAL PAST USED IN CONTEMPORARY PIECES INCLUDING SOME CONTEMPORARY RED, WHITE, AND BLUE FOR FUN. ALSO AMERICAN HERITAGE THEMES IN SOME WALL HANGINGS. AT EXTRAORDINARY USUALS SHOP IN NORTH OF NEIL BLDG; ASPEN. (LOCAL). ELAINE NIXON, COORD; FIBERS IN WEAVING; 218 SENTINEL LANE; BOULDER, CO 80302. (#106983-1).

JULY 3, '76. SILVER QUEEN BALL. A SALUTE TO THE BIRTHDAY OF THE NATION. AT THE JEROME HOTEL. (LOCAL). RODDEY BURDINE, CHRMN; ROARING FORK VALLEY CENTENNIAL/BICENTENNIAL COMMITTEE; BOX 4795; ASPEN, CO 81611. (#107779-1).

JULY 4, '76. INDEPENDENCE DAY PARADE. PARADE. (LOCAL). JEAN GREINER, OFFICE MGR; ASPEN CHAMBER OF COMMERCE; 328 E HYMAN AVE; ASPEN, CO 81611. (#103315-3).

JULY 4, '76 - CONTINUING . FILM SERIES RECOGNIZING WOMEN IN HISTORY. EXHIBIT. (LOCAL). E W DUNN, COORDINATOR; CITY OF ASPEN; PO BOX 1323; ASPEN, CO 81611. (#108653-2).

JULY 28 - AUG 21, '76. BALLET WEST. COMPANY SPECIALIZES IN BRINGING BALLET TO THE AMERICAN WEST EMPHASIZING BOTH THE CLASSICS & THE CONTEMPORARY. 1976 PROGRAM WILL FEATURE AMERICAN COMPOSERS AS WELL AS A NEW BALLET BY BRUCE MARKS: 'DON JUAN.'. AT ASPEN HIGH SCHOOL, MAROON CREEK RD. (LOCAL). PATRICIA DASKO, COORD; ASPEN FOUNDATION; BOX 1465; ASPEN, CO 81611. (#103315-6).

AUG 21 - 22, '76. PITKIN COUNTY CENTENNIAL-BICENTENNIAL FAIR. EXHIBITION OF 4-H PROJECTS AND ITEMS MADE BY COMMUNITY MEMBERS WITH EMPHASIS ON EARLY PIONEER HANDICRAFTS AND AGRICULTURAL PRODUCTS; BOOTHS ON HISTORICAL ASPECTS OF COUNTY; ENTERTAINMENT, GAMES, LIVESTOCK. (ST-WIDE). DAVE BOYLE, COORDINATOR; BOARD OF COUNTY COMMISSIONERS OF PITKIN COUNTY; 506 E MAIN ST; ASPEN, CO 81611. (#104553-5).

AULT

COLORADO CHRONICLES - AULT, CO. WRITTEN HISTORY OF COMMUNITY PUT IN LOCAL LIBRARY. (LOCAL). BARBARA SWANSON, CHAIRPERSON; AULT CENT-BICENT COMMITTEE; BOX 67; AULT, CO 80610. (#26170).

HISTORY OF PIONEER HOUSES & BUSINESSES - AULT, CO. DOOR TO DOOR INTERVIEWING, RESEARCHING AND COMMUNITY MEETINGS TO COMPILE INFORMATION ON HISTORY OF HOUSES & BUSINESSES IN THE AREA. (LOCAL). BARBARA SWANSON, CHAIRMAN; AULT CENTENNIAL-BICENTENNIAL COMMISSION; 124 1ST ST, PO BOX 67; AULT, CO 80610. (#24591).

RESTORATION OF LIBERTY PARK - AULT, CO. IMPROVEMENT AND DEVELOPMENT OF TENNIS COURTS, ESTABLISH BASKETBALL HOOP & PLAYGROUND, PLANTING OF LAWN, TREES & FLOWERBEDS; MATERIALS & WORK DONATED BY COMMUNITY MEMBERS. MARKER FOR WORLD WAR I VETERANS. (LOCAL). BARBARA SWANSON, CHAIRMAN; AULT CENTENNIAL-BICENTENNIAL COMMITTEE; 124 1ST ST, PO BOX 67; AULT, CO 80610. (#24590).

AULT — CONTINUED

AUG 13 - 14, '76. ANNUAL FALL FESTIVAL & PARADE. FRIDAY IS CHILDREN'S DAY (GAMES, CONTESTS) & EXHIBIT JUDGING, PARADE AT 11 PM SATURDAY, BOOTHS & EXHIBITS OPEN AFTERNOON & EVENING, COMMUNITY FEED AT 5 PM, FOLLOWED BY DRAWINGS & BINGO. AT PARADE ON MAIN ST, BOOTHS IN PARK, EXHIBITS AT HIGH SCHOOL. (LOCAL). BARBARA SWANSON, COORD; AULT CENTENNIAL-BICENTENNIAL COMMISSION & AULT LIONS CLUB; 124 1ST ST; AULT, CO 80610. (#107008-1).

OCT 1, '76. PARK BEAUTIFICATION DAY. FESTIVAL. (LOCAL). BARBARA SWANSON, COORD; TOWN OF AULT; BOX 67; AULT, CO 80610. (#108819-1).

AURORA

BICENTENNIAL PARK PROMOTION, AURORA, CO. DEVELOPMENT OF THE PARK BY CITIZEN SPONSORSHIP THROUGH DONATION; PARK WILL INCLUDE ARTS & CRAFTS CENTER, CULTURAL ART CENTER, OUTDOOR AMPHITHEATER AND BIKE TRAILS WITH HISTORICAL MARKERS. (LOCAL). ADRIAN HIRSCHMANN, CHAIRMAN; AURORA CENTENNIAL BICENTENNIAL COMMITTEE; 1470 EMPORIA; AURORA, CO 80010. (#21599).

CENTENNIAL SUNDIAL IN AURORA, CO. THIS WILL BE INSTALLED IN THE BICENTENNIAL PARK AS A LASTING REMINDER OF THE COMMEMORATION. (LOCAL). ADRIAN HIRSCHMAN, CHAIRMAN; AURORA CITY PARKS AND RECREATION; AURORA, CO 80010. (#16293).

COAL CREEK SCHOOL MUSEUM IN AURORA, CO. THIS CENTENNIAL-BICENTENNIAL PROJECT WILL CREATE A MUSEUM AT THE COAL CREEK SCHOOL. (LOCAL). ADRIAN B HIRSCHMAN, CHAIRMAN; AURORA HISTORICAL SOCIETY; AURORA, CO 80010. (#16288).

EARLY HISTORY OF AURORA, CO. LOCATE AND INTERVIEW PERSONS WITH PERSONAL KNOWLEDGE OF EARLY AURORA. (LOCAL). ADRIAN HIRSCHMAN, CHAIRMAN; AURORA CENTENNIAL-BICENTENNIAL COMMITTEE; 1470 EMPORIA; AURORA, CO 80010. (#21597).

FIRE HYDRANT PAINTING IN AURORA, CO. THIS PROJECT WILL CONCENTRATE ON PAINTING HYDRANTS TO RESEMBLE HISTORICAL FIGURES SUCH AS THE MINUTE MEN AND MANY OTHERS. (LOCAL). ADRIAN B HIRSCHMAN, CHAIRMAN; SERVICE CLUBS; 6740 A E CEDAR AVE; DENVER, CO 80222. (#16291).

FREE ENTERPRISE PROMOTION, AURORA, CO. SALE OF AURORA PINS SUPERVISED BY DISTRIBUTIVE EDUCATION STUDENTS; PROFIT FROM PINS WILL PAY FOR SUNDIAL IN BICENTENNIAL PARK. (LOCAL). ADRIAN HIRSCHMAN, CHAIRMAN; AURORA CENTENNIAL BICENTENNIAL COMMITTEE; 1470 EMPORIA; AURORA, CO 80010. (#21596).

HISTORIC OLD TOWN IN AURORA, CO. THE CREATION OF OLD TOWN ON PARKER ROAD WILL BE A TRIBUTE TO THE CENTENNIAL-BICENTENNIAL CELEBRATION. (LOCAL). ADRIAN B HIRSCHMAN, CHAIRMAN; AURORA HISTORICAL SOCIETY; AURORA, CO 80010. (#16285).

HISTORICAL SITES IN AURORA, CO. IDENTIFY AND DESIGNATE HISTORIC SITES, HOMES, BUSINESSES AND OTHER BUILDINGS LOCATED IN AURORA; DOCUMENTS AND RECORDS WILL BE KEPT. (LOCAL). ADRIAN HIRSCHMAN, CHAIRMAN; AURORA CENTENNIAL-BICENTENNIAL COMMITTEE; 1470 EMPORIA; AURORA, CO 80010. (#21598).

LANDSCAPING SCHOOL GROUNDS IN AURORA, CO. THE SCHOOL GROUNDS OF VARIOUS SCHOOLS IN THE COMMUNITY WILL BE LANDSCAPED AND TREES PLANTED. (LOCAL). ADRIAN B HIRSCHMAN, CHAIRMAN; PARENT-TEACHERS ASSOC; AURORA, CO 80010. (#16286).

OFFICIAL SYMBOL OF THE CITY OF AURORA, CO. THE CITY OF AURORA WILL ADOPT AN OFFICIAL SYMBOL HONORING THE CENTENNIAL-BICENTENNIAL. (LOCAL). ADRIAN B HIRSCHMAN, CHAIRMAN; CITY OF AURORA; 1470 EMPORIA ST; AURORA, CO 80010. (#16290).

PROJECT FREEDOM IN AURORA, CO. THIS PROJECT WILL TRACE 200 YEARS OF RELIGIOUS FREEDOM FOR THE NATION AND COLORADO DURING THE COMMEMORATION. (LOCAL). ADRIAN B HIRSCHMAN, CHAIRMAN; COUNCIL OF CHURCHES; AURORA, CO 80010. (#16287).

SENIOR CITIZENS HISTORICAL MOMENTS, AURORA, CO. VIGNETTES OF HISTORICAL MOMENTS IN THE LIVES OF THE SENIOR CITIZENS IN THE COMMUNITY. (LOCAL). ADRIAN B HIRSCHMAN, CHAIRMAN; AURORA COUNCIL FOR THE ELDERLY; AURORA, CO 80010. (#16289).

TRANSPORTATION HISTORY, AURORA, CO. COURSE ON THE HISTORY OF TRANSPORTATION IN COLORADO. (LOCAL). H O MULLINS, CHAIRMAN; AURORA TROLLEY COMMISSION, LTD; PO BOX 31784; AURORA, CO 80011. (#24614).

OCT 11, '75. PLAZA DEDICATION AND ARBA CITY DESIGNATION. AWARD, CEREMONY AT COLFAX CONCOURSE. (LOCAL). ADRIAN HIRSCHMAN, COORD; AURORA CENTENNIAL BICENTENNIAL COMMITTEE; 1470 EMPORIA; AURORA, CO 80010. (#200007-189).

NOV 1, '75. SUNDIAL DEDICATION. CEREMONY, LIVE PERFORMANCE AT BICENTENNIAL PARK. (LOCAL). ADRIAN HIRSCHMAN, COORD; AURORA CENTENNIAL BICENTENNIAL COMMITTEE; 1470 EMPORIA; AURORA, CO 80010. (#200007-186).

NOV 24, '75. AURORA QUEEN CORONATION. AN AURORA RESIDENT, AGED 77 WAS CHOSEN AS QUEEN. 13 RUNNERS-UP, AGES 76-91 WERE CHOSEN, ONE TO REPRESENT EACH OF THE 13 COLONIES. AT PAUL C BECK RECREATION CENTER. (LOCAL). ADRIAN HIRSCHMAN, COORD; AURORA CENTENNIAL BICENTENNIAL COMMITTEE; 1470 EMPORIA; AURORA, CO 80010. (#200007-187).

FEB 2, '76. 'GENERATIONS U S' - DRAMATIC VIGNETTES OF U S WOMEN. LIVE PERFORMANCE AT HOFFMAN HEIGHTS, WYATTS CAFETERIA. (LOCAL). PAT KENNING, PROJ DIR; AURORA RETIRED PERSONS; 1153 W SHEPPERD AVE; LITTLETON, CO 80120. (#104851-1).

MAY 14 - 16, '76. SQUARE DANCE FESTIVAL. FESTIVAL AT PAUL BECK RECREATION CENTER. (LOCAL). ADRIAN HIRSCHMAN, CHMN; AURORA CENTENNIAL-BICENTENNIAL COMMITTEE; 1470 EMPORIA; AURORA, CO 80010. (#105456-1).

JULY 4, '76. BICENTENNIAL PARK DEDICATION. CEREMONY. (LOCAL). ADRIAN HIRSCHMAN, COORD; CITY OF AURORA; 1470 EMPORIA ST; AURORA, CO 80010. (#108650-1).

BAILEY

ENTRIKEN CABIN PRESERVATION PROJECT OF COLORADO. RESTORATION AND RELOCATION ON THE ENTRIKEN CABIN; CABIN TO BE MOVED TO MCGRAW HISTORICAL PARK; BAILEY, COLORADO. (ST-WIDE). HAROLD M WARREN, PRESIDENT; PARK COUNTY HISTORICAL SOCIETY; PO BOX 43; BAILEY, CO 80421. (#603). **ARBA GRANTEE.**

AUG 2, '75. PIONEER CELEBRATION. PAGEANT OF COMMUNITY HISTORY, COSTUMES, BLACK POWDER SHOOT, PARADE, CRAFTS & GAMES. (LOCAL). TREVA D CLAPP, COORD; BAILEY PIONEER CELEBRATION ASSOC; ROUTE 1, BOX 347; PINE, CO 80470. (#200007-21).

BASALT

ROARING FORK VALLEY, COLO, OVENS PRESERVATION. A PROJECT TO RESTORE AND PRESERVE THE OLD CHARCOAL OVENS LOCATED IN THE ROARING FORK VALLEY. (LOCAL). GEORGE STRICKER, EXEC DIRECTOR; BOX 728; GLENWOOD SPG, CO 81601. (#4246).

BERTHOUD

BEAUTIFICATION OF CEMETERY - BERTHOUD, CO. PLANTING OF TREES AND COVERING OF DITCH IN NEW, UNLANDSCAPED SECTION OF BERTHOUD TOWN CEMETERY - GREENLAWN CEMETERY. (LOCAL). MRS FRANCES NIELSON, TOWN TRUSTEE; TOWN OF BERTHOUD; 328 MASSACHUSETTS AVE; BERTHOUD, CO 80513. (#26176).

BIOGRAPHIES OF PIONEERS OF BERTHOUD & VALLEY - CO. BIOGRAPHIES OF PIONEERS OF BERTHOUD AND LITTLE THOMPSON VALLEY FROM 1870 TO 1910. MATERIAL FROM DESCENDENTS, NEWSPAPER AND CEMETERY RECORDS FOR APPROX 250 FAMILIES WILL BE PUBLISHED. (LOCAL). DR HELEN FICKEL, LIBRARIAN; BERTHOUD PUBLIC LIBRARY & BERTHOUD WOMEN'S CLUB; 328 MASSACHUSETTS AVE; BERTHOUD, CO 80513. (#26175).

'CENTENNIAL MEMORIES' - ARTICLES & PICTURES, CO. HISTORICAL PICTURES, BIOGRAPHIES AND COMMUNITY HISTORY WILL BE PUBLISHED IN THE LOCAL WEEKLY NEWSPAPER, 'THE BERTHOUD BULLETIN'. (LOCAL). DEE KLINGER, EDITOR; BERTHOUD BULLETIN NEWSPAPER; 349 MOUNTAIN AVE; BERTHOUD, CO 80513. (#26180).

MARKING OF OLD BUILDINGS AND TOURS - CO. BUILDINGS IN BERTHOUD AND OLD BERTHOUD WILL BE DATED. TOURS WILL BE GIVEN TO ALL STUDENTS AND ANY OTHER INTERESTED GROUPS. GUIDES WILL BE FROM AMERICAN ASSOCIATION OF RETIRED PERSONS. (LOCAL). MRS LESTER PECKOVER, PRESIDENT; AMERICAN ASSOCIATION OF RETIRED PERSONS; 880 MASSACHUSETTS AVE; BERTHOUD, CO 80513. (#26179).

SCALE MODEL - BERTHOUD, CO. SCALE MODEL OF BERTHOUD'S MAIN STREET (3RD STREET) IN 1904; CAN BE SEEN AT BERTHOUD FAMILY STORE (316 MOUNTAIN) AND AT ARTS AND CRAFTS FESTIVAL ON MAY 26 & 27 AT HIGH SCHOOL (9TH & MASS). (LOCAL). PAMELA FLOYD, RECREATION DIRECTOR; BERTHOUD ELEMENTARY SCHOOL; BUNYAN AVE; BERTHOUD, CO 80513. (#26178).

TIME CAPSULE TO BE OPENED IN 2076 - BERTHOUD, CO. TIME CAPSULE WILL CONTAIN PICTURES OF PRESENT BUILDINGS AND TOWN OFFICIALS, MAP, NEWSPAPERS AND CATALOGS. TIME CAPSULE WILL BE A SEALED METAL BOX AND WILL BE PLACED IN A SAFE AT BERTHOUD TOWN HALL. (LOCAL). WALTER FERGUSON, COORDINATOR; BERTHOUD CENTENNIAL-BICENTENNIAL COMMITTEE; 711 6TH ST; BERTHOUD, CO 80513. (#26177).

APR 7, '76. 'FOR THE RED, WHITE & BLUE'. PLATTE PARK DRAMA GROUP SPONSORED BY DENVER PARKS AND RECREATION DEPARTMENT W/COVERED DISH SUPPER. AT UNITED METHODIST CHURCH, 9TH & LAKE. (LOCAL). MRS LESTER PECKOVER; AMERICAN ASSOCIATION OF RETIRED PERSONS; 880 MASSACHUSETTS; BERTHOUD, CO 80513. (#200007-14).

JUNE 5, '76. BERTHOUD DAY. PARADE - FLOATS, BANDS, CARS OLD & NEW, HORSES, MOTORCYCLES, FIRE DEPARTMENTS OLD & NEW, CENTENNIAL VEHICLES, PETS & DOLLS. OLD PARK - FREE LUNCH, HAYRIDES, HORSESHOEING DEM, RACES. NEW PARK - DANCE, DRAWINGS, BINGO. AT PARADE: MASSACHUSETTS AVENUE & BOTH PARKS ON 7TH STREET. (ST-WIDE). PAMELA FLOYD, REC DIR; BERTHOUD CHAMBER OF COMMERCE; 1025 2 ST; BERTHOUD, CO 80513. (#200007-13).

JUNE 26 - 27, '76. ARTS & CRAFTS FESTIVAL. EXHIBITS OF LOCAL ARTISTS AND CRAFTSMEN. DISPLAYS OF ART, POTTERY, RELICS, PAINTINGS, ANTIQUES, SCULPTURE OR ARTIFACTS RELATING TO COMMUNITY HISTORY. ALSO BOOTHS DEPICTING LIFE IN EARLY AMERICA. AT BERTHOUD HIGH SCHOOL GYMNASIUM, 950 MASSACHUSETTS, PARKING ON N. (ST-WIDE). MRS ELLIS WYKOFF, COORD; LITTLE 'T' ARTS & CRAFTS FESTIVAL GUILD; 705 7 ST; BERTHOUD, CO 80513. (#200007-12).

BEULAH

CENTENNIAL-BICENTENNIAL SPECIAL PROJECTS, CO. SEVERAL CIVIC GROUPS WILL BE WORKING TOGETHER DURING THE CENTENNIAL YEAR TOWARD THE EDUCATION AND ADVANCEMENT OF THE COMMUNITY. (LOCAL). JOSEPH A SELLERS, DIRECTOR; BEULAH CENTENNIAL-BICENTENNIAL COMMITTEE; ROUTE 1, BOX 75; BEULAH, CO 81023. (#15962).

CENTENNIAL-BICENTENNIAL HISTORICAL MARKER, CO. THE MARKER WILL GIVE PERTINENT INFORMATION CONCERNING STATISTICS IN THE AREA. (LOCAL). EVELYN S ELY, PRESIDENT; HISTORICAL SOCIETY; RT 1 BOX 66; BEULAH, CO 81023. (#15964).

HISTORICAL ILLUSTRATED BOOKLET, BEULAH, CO. THE CONTENTS OF THE BOOKLET WILL CONTAIN HISTORY AND GEOLOGY OF THE AREA WHICH WILL BE OF INTEREST TO MANY DURING THE CENTENNIALBICENTENNIAL YEAR. (LOCAL). EVELYN S ELY, PRESIDENT; HISTORICAL SOCIETY; RT 1 BOX 66; BEULAH, CO 81023. (#15963).

DEC 14, '75. 25TH ANNUAL YULE LOG HUNT. HELD ANNUALLY, IT'S A COMMUNITY CELEBRATION IN HONOR OF AN OLD HOLIDAY TRADITION. OPEN TO ALL AGES. AT HORSESHOE LODGE, PUEBLO MOUNTAIN PARK, RT 1 BOX 49. (LOCAL). ALFRED R KREUSCH, CHMN; BEULAH YULE LOG GROUP; NORTH CREEK RD; BEULAH, CO 81023. (#102814-1).

MAY 1, '76. BEULAH CENTENNIAL-BICENTENNIAL FAIR. ITEMS TO BE MADE BY BEULAH RESIDENTS OF ALL AGES FOR PTO; MONEY MADE WILL BE USED FOR STUDENT BENEFIT. AT BEULAH SCHOOL, CORNER GRAND AND FOX LANE. (LOCAL). MRS THOMAS READY, PRES; BEULAH SCHOOL PTO; 9253 SQUIRREL CREEK RD; BEULAH, CO 81023. (#104854-2).

JUNE 1 - 6, '76. PLANTING TREES FOR TOMORROW. STATE FORESTER DEMONSTRATION INCORPORATING 1876 STATE CONSTITUTIONAL PROVISION AUTHORIZING LAWS FOR PRESERVATION OF OUR FORESTS. AT MOUNTAIN PARK. (LOCAL). MRS JOHN B FARLEY, COORD; FRIENDS OF PARKS & RECREATION; 529 COLORADO AVE; PUEBLO, CO 81004. (#200007-9).

JULY 3, '76. STOMP ON DANCE. FESTIVAL. (LOCAL). DALE ALLEE, COORDINATOR; BEULAH CENTENNIAL-BICENTENNIAL COMMITTEE/BEULAH VALLEY SADDLE CLUB; 4770 WATER BARREL RD S; PUEBLO, CO 81004. (#108648-1).

JULY 4, '76. BICENTENNIAL PARADE. PARADE. (LOCAL). DALE ALLEE, COORDINATOR; BEULAH CENTENNIAL-BICENTENNIAL COMMITTEE; 4770 WATER BARREL RD S; PUEBLO, CO 81004. (#108648-2).

JULY 4, '76. CENTENNIAL-BICENTENNIAL PRESENTATION. CEREMONY AT ARENA. (LOCAL). DR THOMAS W READY; BEULAH CENTENNIAL-BICENTENNIAL COMMITTEE; 9253 SQUIRREL CREEK RD; BEULAH, CO 81023. (#108648-3).

JULY 4, '76. PONY EXPRESS RACE AND PARADE. PARADE, COMPETITION, FESTIVAL. (LOCAL). DALE D ALLA, COORDINATOR; CITY OF BEULAH; 4770 WATER BARREL RD S; S PUEBLO, CO 81004. (#108648-4).

JULY 4 - 5, '76. BEULAH VALLEY SADDLE CLUB ANNUAL 4TH OF JULY RODEO. PONY EXPRESS RACE COVERING 30 MILES WILL BEGIN AT 6:30 AM; BICENTENNIAL PARADE WILL CONSIST OF HORSES, RIDERS, BUGGIES, WAGONS, RODEO CONTESTANTS AND SADDLE CLUB MEMBERS; THE ANNUAL JULY 4TH RODEO WILL FOLLOW THE PARADE. AT BEULAH VALLEY. (LOCAL). DR THOMAS READY, PROJ DIR; BEULAH VALLEY SADDLE CLUB; 9253 SQUIRREL CREEK RD; BEULAH, CO 81023. (#104854-1).

JULY 15 - 31, '76. PRESENTATION OF MELODRAMA AND OLIOS BY LOCAL PERFORMERS. THE OLD FASHIONED MELODRAMA AND OLIOS HAS BEEN PRESENTED ANNUALLY BY THE COMMUNITY FOR TWENTY FIVE YEARS. ALL PROFITS ARE FOR THE COMMUNITY CENTER. AT BEULAH COMMUNITY CENTER. (LOCAL). NORMA KREUSCH, DIR; BEULAH COMMUNITY CENTER; BOX 135; BEULAH, CO 81023. (#102814-3).

JULY 23 - 25, '76. ART SHOW. AN ARTS AND CRAFTS SHOW SET OUT OF DOORS IN THE MOUNTAIN TOWN OF BEULAH. PAINTINGS, SCULPTURE AND CRAFTS OF AREA ARTISTS ARE DISPLAYED FOR VIEWING AND FOR SALE. THERE WILL ALSO BE A SECTION FOR CHILDREN'S ART OF THE AREA. AT MAIN ST. (LOCAL). ELIZABETH WASHINGTON, CHM; BEULAH OUTDOOR ARTS AND CRAFTS SHOW; PO BOX 65; BEULAH, CO 81023. (#102814-4).

JULY 31 - AUG 1, '76. COLORADO DAY. FESTIVAL AT BARBEQUE AT PUEBLO MOUNTAIN PARK, STREET DANCE DOWNTOWN. (LOCAL). R S THOMPSON, CHAIRMAN; COMMITTEE FOR COLORADO DAY; 7695 HWY 76; WEST PUEBLO, CO 81004. (#108693-1).

SEPT 11 - 12, '76. BEULAH HISTORICAL EXHIBIT. A SHOW OF ANTIQUES USED IN THE BUILDING AND GROWTH OF OUR CENTENNIAL VILLAGE WITH LIVE DEMONSTRATIONS OF CRAFTS; AN ANNUAL EVENT. AT BEULAH COMMUNITY CENTER. (LOCAL). EVELYN ELY, DIRECTOR; BEULAH HISTORICAL SOCIETY; RT 1, BOX 66; BEULAH, CO 81023. (#103840-8).

DEC 12, '76. 25TH ANNUAL YULE LOG HUNT. HELD ANNUALLY, IT'S A COMMUNITY CELEBRATION IN HONOR OF AN OLD HOLIDAY TRADITION. OPEN TO ALL AGES. AT HORSESHOE LODGE, PUEBLO MOUNTAIN PARK, RT 1 BOX 49. (LOCAL). ALFRED R KREUSCH, CHMN; BEULAH YULE LOG GROUP; NORTH CREEK RD; BEULAH, CO 81023. (#102814-2).

BLACK HAWK

BLACK HAWK CITY HALL RESTORATION, CO. BLACK HAWK CITY HALL WILL BE RESTORED. (LOCAL). HON FRANCIS OLSON, MAYOR; CITY OF BLACK HAWK; GREGORY ST; BLACK HAWK, CO 80422. (#16385).

LACE HOUSE PROJECT, BLACK HAWK, CO. RESTORATION OF LACE HOUSE FOR USE AS A CITY MUSEUM AS A POINT OF SPECIAL INTEREST IN BLACK HAWK HISTORY. (LOCAL). ROBERT CODIN, CENTENNIAL-BICENTENNIAL CHAIRMAN; CITY OF BLACK HAWK; GREGORY ST; BLACK HAWK, CO 80422. (#16386).

JUNE 1, '75. NATIONAL BIKE RACE DAY. BUSINESS ASSOCIATION WILL SPONSOR THIS ANNUAL EVENT. (LOCAL). ROBERT COPPIN, CHAIRMAN; BLACK HAWK BUSINESS ASSOC; PO BOX 192; BLACK HAWK, CO 80422. (#6777-501).

JUNE 1, '75 - JUNE 1, '76. ARTS AND CRAFTS EXHIBITION. BLACK HAWK ART EXHIBIT AT BLACK HAWK, COLORADO. STUDENTS AND LOCAL ARTISTS AND CRAFTSMEN WILL PUBLICLY EXHIBIT THEIR PROJECTS. (LOCAL). ROBERT COPPIN, CHAIRMAN; BLACK HAWK BUSINESS ASSOC; BLACK HAWK, CO 80422. (#6773-501).

SEPT 9, '75 - MAR 1, '76. HISTORY RESEARCH & THEME WRITING CONTEST. BLACK HAWK HISTORICAL THEME CONTEST IN COLORADO. STUDENT COMPETITION RELATING TO BEST THEME ON BLACK HAWK HISTORY WITH PRIZES AND BEST MATERIAL TO BE USED IN A HISTORICAL BOOKLET. (LOCAL). ROBERT COPPIN, CHAIRMAN; BLACK HAWK CENTENNIAL-BICENTENNIAL COMMISSION; BOX 192; BLACK HAWK, CO 80422. (#6776-501).

BOONE

PUBLICATION OF BOOK ON LOCAL HISTORY, BOONE, CO. CHILDREN WILL INTERVIEW LOCAL CITIZENS & COMPILE A BOOK ON THE HISTORY OF THE AREA. (LOCAL). MRS GLEN FELLMORE, COORDINATOR; 1663 BOONE RD; BOONE, CO 81025. (#26151).

BOULDER

'AUDIO SERIES'-FOLK MUSIC OF COLORADO. AUDIO SERIES-FOLK MUSIC OF COLORADO FROM BEN GRAY LUMPKIN COLLECTION SIXTEEN ONE-HALF HOUR TAPES FOR RADIO BROADCAST AND SCHOOL USE. (ST-WIDE). HOWARD D ROARK, DIRECTOR OF CONTRACTS/GRANTS; REGENTS OF THE UNIV OF COLORADO; BOULDER, CO 80302. (#4285).

BELL CHOIR TOUR AT UNIVERSITY OF COLORADO. ILLUSTRATED LECTURE ON HISTORY OF BELLS, ESPECIALLY LIBERTY BELL. ILLUSTRATIVE EXAMPLES OF BELL LITERATURE OF EARLY AMERICAN COMPOSITIONS PERFORMED BY UNIVERSITY BELL CHOIR. (ST-WIDE). HOWARD D ROARK, DIRECTOR OFFICE OF CONTRACTS/GRANT; REGENTS OF THE UNIV OF COLORADO; BOULDER, CO 80302. (#4286).

BOULDER COUNTY CULTURE CENTER, CO. THIS CENTENNIAL-BICENTENNIAL PROJECT WILL HELP THE CITIES IN BOULDER COUNTY TO START DEVELOPING A FAIR-CULTURE CENTER. (LOCAL). MIKE DEGGE, CHAIRMAN; BOULDER COUNTY CENTENNIAL-BICENTENNIAL COMMISSION; PO BOX 3316; BOULDER, CO 80303. (#14857).

BOULDER HISTORIC PRESERVATION PLAN, CO. A HISTORIC PRESERVATION PLAN WILL BE PREPARED BY PROFESSIONAL & LOCAL PEOPLE. THE PLAN IS TO BE RECORDED & PUBLISHED FOR REGIONAL USE BY COMMUNITIES. (LOCAL). ALAN ZEIGEL, VICE CHAIRMAN; HISTORIC BOULDER, INC; PO BOX 1545; BOULDER, CO 80302. (#16384).

BOULDER LINEAL PARK AND CENTENNIAL TRAIL, CO. A CONCRETE TRAIL ALONG BOULDER CREEK TO ACCOMODATE PEDESTRIANS, BIKES AND WHEELCHAIRS, INCORPORATING RESEEDING VEGETATION TO RECLAIM THE ADJACENT DISTURBED AREAS. (LOCAL). RON DONAHUE, CITY PARKS DIRECTOR; BOULDER CITY PACKS - BOULDER CENT-BICENT COMMISSION; PO BOX 791; BOULDER, CO 80302. (#20296).

BOULDER PERFORMING ARTS CENTER OF COLORADO. PLANNING, DEVELOPING AND CONSTRUCTING A CENTER FOR PERFORMING ARTS TO BE DEDICATED TO CENTENNIAL-BICENTENNIAL WITH A PLAQUE SHOWING HOW CENTER WILL PROMOTE COMMUNITY CULTURAL DEVELOPMENT. (ST-WIDE). C WATSON, CHAIRMAN; FLAGSTAFF ARTS AND CULTURAL EXPERIENCE; C/O 3605 TABLE MESA DRIVE; BOULDER, CO 80302. (#4917).

BOULDER WOMEN'S ORAL HISTORY PROJECT, CO. ELDERLY WOMEN WILL BE INTERVIEWED; THESE INTERVIEWS WILL BE PUBLISHED IN BOOK FORM. (LOCAL). NEWBERN SMITH, CHAIRMAN; BOULDER CENTENNIAL-BICENTENNIAL COMMITTEE; PO BOX 791; BOULDER, CO 80302. (#26302).

BOYS' CLUB OF BOULDER ACTIVITY BUILDING, CO. CONSTRUCTION OF A FACILITY TO HOUSE SHOP, GAME ROOM, LIBRARY, GYM & STAFF OFFICES. (LOCAL). ROBERT TOWNER, PRESIDENT; BOYS' CLUB; PO BOX 2155; BOULDER, CO 80302. (#26295).

THE CENTENNIAL IN SONG. DRAMATIC PRESENTATION OF THE HISTORY OF COLORADO BY MEANS OF 45MINUTE, SPOKEN SCRIPTS INTERJECTED WITH 6 ORIGINAL SELF-ACCOMPANIED SONGS. (LOCAL). PAM STINSON, CHMN; BOULDER CENTENNIAL-BICENTENNIAL COMMISSION; BOULDER, CO 80302. (#103840-3).

CENTENNIAL-BICENTENNIAL SYMPHONIC COMPOSITION, CO. CONTEST TO DEVELOP A CENTENNIAL-BICENTENNIAL SYMPHONIC MUSIC MANUSCRIPT ACCENTING HERITAGE AND CULTURE OF BOULDER AND OTHER PARTS OF COLORADO. (LOCAL). RHEDA BRANDT, MEMBER; BOULDER VALLEY SCHOOL; 792 14TH ST; BOULDER, CO 80302. (#10318).

COLO STUDENT CENTENNIAL-BICENT SYMPHONY CONTEST. CONTEST FOR ALL SCHOOL CHILDREN TO DEVELOP A CENTENNIAL-BICENTENNIAL SYMPHONIC MUSIC MANUSCRIPT ACCENTING HERITAGE AND CULTURE OF BOULDER AND COLORADO. (LOCAL). CLARKE R WATSON, CHAIRMAN; BOULDER CENTENNIAL-BICENTENNIAL COMMISSION; PO BOX 791; BOULDER, CO 80302. (#4115).

COLORADO AND AMERICAN MUSIC MAGAZINE PROJECT. THE COLORADO MUSIC EDUCATORS ASSOCIATION MAGAZINE PUBLISHES SPECIAL COLUMN ON CENTENNIAL-BICENTENNIAL MUSIC RESEARCH. (ST-WIDE). KEVIN J MCCARTHY, EDITOR; COLORADO MUSIC EDUCATORS ASSOCIATION; 165 IRIQUOIS DR; BOULDER, CO 80303. (#4461).

COLORADO CRAFT-IN - STATE ARTS & CRAFTS SHOW. ANNUAL STATE ARTS & CRAFTS SHOW HELD IN BOULDER. (ST-WIDE). E P MCGUIRE, DIRECTOR; COLORADO CRAFT-IN; PINE BROOK HILLS; BOULDER, CO 80302. (#2864). **ARBA GRANTEE.**

COLORADO WOMEN'S RESOURCE BOOK, BOULDER, CO. COMPREHENSIVE COMMUNITY SERVICES GUIDE, FEATURING HISTORICAL CONTRIBUTIONS BY WOMEN IN COLORADO AND COMMEMORATIVE POETRY BY COLORADO WOMEN. (ST-WIDE). JUDITH GOODE, PRESIDENT; TAPROOT INC; PO BOX 3119; BOULDER, CO 80302. (#17428).

COMMEMORATIVE PANELS OF COLORADO RIVER. 6 PANELS DEPICTING REMOTE WILDERNESS SCENES & HISTORICAL FIGURES ON COLORADO RIVER FOR PERMANENT DISPLAY IN MAIN ENTRY OF NEW JUSTICE BUILDING. (LOCAL). PAMELA STINSON, CHAIRPERSON; BOULDER CENTENNIAL-BICENTENNIAL COMMISSION; 1777 BROADWAY; BOULDER, CO 80302. (#26297).

COMMUNITY MURAL PROJECT, BOULDER, CO. SMALL MURALS WITH ARTISTIC SCENES WILL BE PLACED IN PUBLIC BUILDINGS. (LOCAL). NEWBERN SMITH, CHAIRPERSON; BOULDER CENTENNIAL-BICENTENNIAL COMMITTEE; PO BOX 791; BOULDER, CO 80302. (#26301).

CORSICA FESTIVAL CITY FIREMEN'S CELEBRATION - SD. TOURS OF HISTORIC HOMES AND SITES OF BOULDER TO SHOW HERITAGE OF SETTLING FOUNDERS OF AREA. (LOCAL). CLARKE L WATSON, CHAIRMAN; BOULDER CENTENNIAL-BICENTENNIAL COMMITTEE; BOX 791; BOULDER, CO 80302. (#4104).

DESIGN COMPETITIONS - BOULDER, COLORADO. CORPORATE SPONSORS WOULD BE ENCOURAGED TO PROVIDE PRIZES FOR WORKING SOLUTIONS TO FUTURE-ORIENTED DESIGN QUESTIONS. (LOCAL). CLARKE R WATSON, CHAIRMAN; BOULDER CENTENNIAL-BICENTENNIAL COMMISSION; PO BOX 791; BOULDER, CO 80302. (#4102).

EL DORADO SPRINGS ORAL HISTORY PROJECT - CO. THE HISTORY OF EL DORADO SPRINGS, ONE OF THE TOP RESORTS OF THE EARLY 20TH CENTURY, WILL BE RESEARCHED, DOCUMENTED AND STORED IN THE FACILITIES OF THE BOULDER PUBLIC LIBRARY. (LOCAL). LYNN DYBA, CHAIRMAN; BOULDER PUBLIC LIBRARY; BOULDER, CO 80302. (#24609).

EMERGENCY HOUSING FOR WOMEN, BOULDER, CO. PROJECT TO PROVIDE EMERGENCY HOUSING FOR WOMEN W/ OR W/OUT CHILDREN, WHO ARE IN TRANSITION OR A CRISIS SITUATION, FOR 3 DAYS TO 2 WEEKS, OFFERING A SUPPORTIVE ENVIRONMENT FOR CHANGING ROLES. (LOCAL). PAMELA HAMM, COORDINATOR; BOULDER WOMEN'S RESOURCE CENTER; 2750 SPRUCE; BOULDER, CO 80302. (#26136).

FAIRVIEW HIGH SCHOOL BAND PROJECT, BOULDER, CO. THE FAIRVIEW HIGH SCHOOL BAND WILL PARTICIPATE IN THE 1977 ROSE BOWL PARADE. (LOCAL). ROBERT E JEFFREY, DIRECTOR; BOULDER VALLEY SCHOOLS; 1415 TOEDLT DR; BOULDER, CO 80303. (#24078).

FILM RESOURCES INVENTORY FOR COLORADO STATE. PLANS ARE TO MAKE A DESCRIPTION OF ALL NON-PROFIT FILM EXHIBITIONS, FILM CRITICISM, FILM MAKING ORGANIZATIONS, FILM LIBRARIES AND COLLEGE FILM COURSES IN COLORADO FOR PUBLICATION. (ST-WIDE). VIRGIL GRILLO, DIRECTOR; ROCKY MOUNTAIN FILM CENTER; UNIV OF COLORADO, 102 HUNTER BLD; BOULDER, CO 80302. (#6822).

GERMAN HERITAGE MINI-MUSEUMS, BOULDER, CO. SEVERAL TRUNKS WILL BE EQUIPPED TO SERVE AS MINI-MUSEUMS ON GERMAN ETHNIC HERITAGE & AMERICAN FOLKWAYS. TRUNKS WILL BE SENT TO KINDERGARTENS, ELEMENTARY & SECONDARY SCHOOLS. (LOCAL). KLAUS J BARTEL, CHAIRMAN; GERMAN AMERICAN CENTENNIAL-BICENTENNIAL COMMITTEE OF COLORADO; 3650 BERKLEY AVE; BOULDER, CO 80303. (#26298).

GERMAN-AMERICAN TEACHING PACKETS, BOULDER, CO. DESIGN & PRODUCTION OF SELF-CONTAINED KITS ON VARIOUS ASPECTS OF GERMAN HISTORY IN COLORADO FOR USE BY KINDERGARTEN, ELEMENTARY & SECONDARY TEACHERS & COMMUNITY GROUPS. (ST-WIDE). KLAUS BARTEL, CHAIRMAN; GERMAN-AMERICAN CENTENNIAL-BICENTENNIAL COMMITTEE OF COLORADO; 3650 BERKLEY AVE; BOULDER, CO 80303. (#26296).

THE GREAT RACE - PROJ OF BOULDER, CO. IN HONOR OF THE CENTENNIAL-BICENTENNIAL, THERE WILL BE A RACE BETWEEN BOULDER AND LONGMONT TO ENCOURAGE A NEW INVENTION TO USE A NEW FUEL OTHER THAN GAS. (LOCAL). MIKE DEGGE, CHAIRMAN; BOULDER COUNTY CENTENNIAL-BICENTENNIAL COMMISSION; PO BOX 3316; BOULDER, CO 80303. (#15132).

HISTORIC DRAMA PRESENTATION IN BOULDER, COLORADO. PLAYS RECREATING HISTORIC EVENTS OF BOULDER AND OTHER PARTS OF COLORADO WILL BE PRESENTED. (ST-WIDE). HENRY SPALL, PROJ DIR; FLAGSTAFF ARTS AND CULTURAL EXPERIENCE; 2950 BIXBY LN #304; BOULDER, CO 80802. (#10320).

HISTORICAL PUBLIC SERVICE CAMPAIGN, BOULDER, CO. 52 HISTORICAL SPOTS, DEALING WITH COLORADO HISTORY, PAST, PRESENT AND FUTURE, WHICH HAVE BEEN PRODUCED FOR VARIOUS MEDIA OUTLETS WILL BE PRESENTED UNTIL JULY 3, 1976. (ST-WIDE). H H ARNOLD, SECRETARY; UNIV OF COLORADO; BOULDER, CO 80302. (#16407).

'IMPROVING YOUR CITY', BOULDER, CO. CITIZEN PARTICIPATION IN AN ONGOING PROJECT TO PLAN FOR A BETTER COMMUNITY. PROJECT WILL INCLUDE OFFICE EXHIBITS & COMMUNITY AWARENESS EVENTS. (LOCAL). NEWBERN SMITH, COORDINATOR; CITY OF BOULDER; PO BOX 791; BOULDER, CO 80302. (#26299).

LANDSCAPE THE COURT HOUSE SQUARE IN BOULDER, CO. NEW GRASS AND BENCHES WILL BE PLACED IN COURT HOUSE SQUARE FOR THE BENEFIT OF THE SENIOR CITIZENS. (LOCAL). MIKE DEGGE, CHAIRMAN; BOULDER COUNTY CENTENNIAL-BICENTENNIAL COMMISSION; PO BOX 3316; BOULDER, CO 80303. (#14856).

MUSEUM DISPLAY ON WOMEN IN BOULDER HISTORY. A PHOTOGRAPHIC DISPLAY ACCOMPANIED BY SHORT SKETCHES OF EARLY BOULDER WOMEN WHO WERE PIONEERS IN THEIR OCCUPATIONS. DISPLAY IN. (LOCAL). NEWBERN SMITH, CHAIRMAN; BOULDER CENTENNIAL-BICENTENNIAL COMMITTEE; PO BOX 791; BOULDER, CO 80307. (#108673-2).

NARROW-GAGE TRAIN IN BOULDER, COLORADO. RESTORE NARROW-GAGE TRAIN IN CENTRAL PARK. (REGN'L). TOM HOFFMAN, HERITAGE CHMN; PARKS AND RECREATION DEPT; 5378 VALMONT; BOULDER, CO 80302. (#10319).

NATL BICENTENNIAL INTERNSHIP PGM -MOUNTAIN AREA. STUDENT INTERN ASSISTANCE IN DEVELOPING SOCIAL, & ECONOMIC RESOURCES TO SUPPORT LOCALLY INITIATED, STATE AGENCY, AND COMMUNITY BASED BICENTENNIAL PROGRAMMING. (REGN'L). ROBERT HULLINGHORST, PROGRAM DIRECTOR; WESTERN INTERSTATE COMMISSION FOR HIGHER EDUCATION; PO DRAWER P; BOULDER, CO 80302. (#114). **ARBA RECOGNIZED. ARBA GRANTEE.**

OLD TIMERS INTERVIEWS IN BOULDER, COLORADO. RECORDED INTERVIEWS WILL BE HELD WITH LIFE-LONG RESIDENTS OF BOULDER COUNTY; PHOTOS WILL BE INCLUDED. (LOCAL). MIKE DEGGE, CHAIRMAN; BOULDER COUNTY CENTENNIAL-BICENTENNIAL COMMISSION; PO BOX 3316; BOULDER, CO 80303. (#14855).

POLITICAL AWARENESS CONFERENCE FOR WOMEN. ACTIVISTS OF 50 YEARS AGO WILL DISCUSS THEIR POLITICAL & SOCIAL INVOLVEMENT IN BOULDER COUNTY SO THAT TODAY'S WOMAN MAY PLAN MORE EFFECTIVELY FOR THE FUTURE. (LOCAL). NEWBERN SMITH, CHAIRMAN; BOULDER CENTENNIAL-BICENTENNIAL COMMITTEE; PO BOX 791; BOULDER, CO 80307. (#108673-1).

'QUAKING ASPEN' PHOTO BOOK OF ASPEN, COLO. BOOK OF 120 BLACK AND WHITE PHOTOGRAPHIC PLATES OF ASPEN, COLORADO, AND SURROUNDING AREA. (LOCAL). GARY METZ, INSTRUCTOR IN PHOTOGRAPHY; UNIV OF COLORADO, DEPT OF FINE ARTS; FINE ARTS BLDG 104; BOULDER, CO 80302. (#4355). **(??).**

RECIPE BOOK - BOULDER, CO. BOOK WITH OLD RECEIPES OF BOULDER COUNTY AND OF THE 1800'S WILL BE PUBLISHED IN HONOR OF THE CENTENNIAL-BICENTENNIAL CELEBRATION. (LOCAL). MIKE DEGGE, CHAIRMAN; BOULDER COUNTY CENTENNIAL-BICENTENNIAL COMMISSION; PO BOX 3316; BOULDER, CO 80303. (#14854).

RESTORATION OF NARROW-GAGE TRAIN IN BOULDER, COLO. RESTORE AND PROVIDE COVER FOR NARROW-GAGE TRAIN IN BOULDER CENTRAL PARK FOR COMMUNITY ENJOYMENT. (LOCAL). CLARKE R WATSON, CHAIRMAN; BOULDER CENTENNIAL-BICENTENNIAL COMMISSION; PO BOX 791; BOULDER, CO 80302. (#4114).

SERVICE CLUB PICNIC. IN OBSERVANCE OF THE CENTENNIAL-BICENTENNIAL, ALL BOULDER COUNTY SENIOR CITIZENS OVER 100 YEARS OLD WILL BE HONORED BY SERVICE CLUBS AND THE YOUTH. (LOCAL). MIKE DEGGE, CHAIRMAN; BOULDER COUNTY CENTENNIAL-BICENTENNIAL COMMISSION; PO BOX 3316; BOULDER, CO 80303. (#102120-1).

T D A COCKERELL: LETTERS FROM WEST CLIFF, CO. PUBLICATION OF A COLLECTION OF LETTERS BY A YOUNG MAN WHO WAS LATER A PROMINENT COLORADOAN. LETTERS ACCURATELY DEPICT 1880'S LIFE IN THE WET MOUNTAIN VALLEY NEAR WESTCLIFFE. (ST-WIDE). WILLIAM A WEBER, CURATOR; UNIV OF COLORADO MUSEUM; BOULDER, CO 80302. (#4420).

UNIV OF COLORADO HISTORICAL PAGEANT. TO ESTABLISH A MAJOR HISTORICAL PAGEANT FOR THE COLORADO CENTENNIAL BICENTENIAL COMMEMORATION. (ST-WIDE). RICHARD KNAUB, DIRECTOR; UNIV OF COLORADO; UNIVERSITY BLVD; BOULDER, CO 80302. (#2899).

UNIV OF COLORADO FOLK SONG PROJECT. PREPARATON OF FOLK MUSIC OF COLORADO: AUDIO SERIES FOR BROADCAST 16 1/2-HOUR TAPES. (ST-WIDE). WILLIAM KEARNS, PROJECT DIRECTOR; UNIV OF COLORADO, COLLEGE OF MUSIC; BOULDER, CO 80303. (#2909).

AUG 13 - 17, '75. COLORADO CRAFT-IN '75. EXHIBIT, FESTIVAL, LIVE PERFORMANCE, SEMINAR AT MAGNIFICANT MOUNTAINS ABOVE BOULDER WORKSHOPS IN & OUT-OF-DOORS. (ST-WIDE). ELISE MCGUIRE; COLO CENTENNIAL BI-CENTENNIAL & COLO CRAFT-IN LTD.; PINEBROOK HILLS; BOULDER, CO 80302. (#2864-1).

SEPT 1, '75 - CONTINUING . COLORADO EXPLORATION & LIFE ZONES EXHIBIT. THE UNIVERSITY OF COLORADO WILL PRESENT AN EXHIBIT OF TOPOGRAPHY, LIFE ZONES, EXPLORERS AND AGRICULTURAL PRODUCTS OF COLORADO. AT HALL OF LIFE, HENDERSON BLDG. (ST-WIDE). PETER ROBINSON, DIRECTOR; UNIV OF COLORADO MUSEUM; BROADWAY BETWEEN 15TH & 16TH ST; BOULDER, CO 80302. (#6827-1).

BOULDER — CONTINUED

NOV 14, '75. DAVID GRUSIN CENTENNIAL CELEBRATION CONCERT. CU SYMPHONY & A JAZZ GROUP FROM HOLLYWOOD WILL ALSO APPEAR. AT MACKY AUDITORIUM, CU CAMPUS. (LOCAL). CHARLES BYERS, CHAIRMAN; UNIV OF COLORADO, COLLEGE OF MUSIC; BOULDER, CO 80309. (#103315-1).

FEB 25, '76. HAL HOLBROOK IN 'MARK TWAIN TONIGHT'. LIVE PERFORMANCE AT MACKY AUDITORIUM, COLORADO UNIVERSITY, BOULDER CAMPUS. (LOCAL). DIANA HAYMEN, COORDINATOR; BOB GARNER ATTRACTIONS AND COLORADO UNIV CENTENNIAL COMMISSION; PO BOX 18390; DENVER, CO 80218. (#104728-1).

MAR 12, '76. CENTENNIAL - BICENTENNIAL CONCERT. LIVE PERFORMANCE AT UNIV OF CO, MACKY AUDITORIUM/SHUTTLE BUS FROM MUNICIPAL BUILDING LOT. (LOCAL). KERRY O'FLYNN COMERFORD; THE PHILHARMONIC SOCIETY OF BOULDER; PO BOX 826; BOULDER, CO 80302. (#200007-7).

APR 26, '76. NETHERLANDS CHAMBER ORCHESTRA VISITS UNIVERSITY OF COLORADO. LIVE PERFORMANCE. (INT'L). WILLIAM SIMONSZ, COORD; NETHERLANDS GOVERNMENT; NETHERLANDS EMBASSY-4200 LINNEAN; WASHINGTON, DC 20008. (#109013-8).

JUNE 4 - 25, '76. A BICENTENNIAL SHOW OF CONTEMPORARY WEAVING. AMERICAN HERITAGE THEMES IN WALL HANGINGS. WEAVING FROM COLONIAL PAST USED IN CONTEMPORARY PIECES. SOME SPLASHY RED, WHITE AND BLUE PIECES TOO!. AT REGENCY CLUB, MAJESTIC SAVINGS, 1247 PEARL, BOULDER. (LOCAL). ELAINE NIXON, COORD; FIBERS IN WEAVING; 218 SENTINEL LANE; BOULDER, CO 80302. (#106978-14).

JUNE 14 - 15, '76. FLAG DAY CELEBRATION. THE ELKS CLUB IS PRESENTING THEIR FLAG COLLECTION WITH INFORMATION & CEREMONY. AT CROSSROADS SHOPPING CENTER HALL. (LOCAL). THESTA SCOGLAND; BOULDER CENTENNIAL-BICENTENNIAL COMMISSION; 704 MAPLETON AVE; BOULDER, CO 80302. (#200007-8).

JULY 4, '76. FOURTH OF JULY MUSICAL PROGRAM. A PROGRAM OF MUSIC AND MELODRAMA COMMEMORATING THE 4TH OF JULY. AT CENTRAL PARK BANDSHELL. (LOCAL). JAMES CARTER, COORDINATOR; BOULDER CENTENNIAL-BICENTENNIAL COMMISSION; 3305 MOORHEAD; BOULDER, CO 80303. (#108647-1).

JULY 25 - AUG 1, '76. POW WOW DAYS. CELEBRATION WILL INCLUDE FLIGHT DISPLAYS, HORSE SHOWS, RODEO, CARNIVAL ATTRACTIONS, SIDEWALK SALES & A PARADE. (LOCAL). TOM REES, COORDINATOR; BOULDER POW WOW, INC; 783 CYPRESS DR; BOULDER, CO 80303. (#103416-39).

AUG 20 - SEPT 5, '76. 'ZOO STORY' & 'AMERICAN DREAM'. TWO LITERATE, BRILLIANT, UNNERVING & HILARIOUS PLAYS BY ONE OF AMERICA'S MOST ACCLAIMED DRAMATISTS, EDWARD ALBEE, PRESENTED BY BOULDER'S PROFESSIONAL THEATRE COMPANY, THE ACTORS THEATRE. AT UNIVERSITY THEATRE IN BOULDER. (LOCAL). ERNESTINE GEORGIANNA, ADM; THE ACTORS THEATRE; 1336 NORTHRIDGE COURT; BOULDER, CO 80302. (#107170-1).

SEPT 10 - 12, '76. HIGH ALTITUDE CHAMPIONSHIP OUTBOARD BOAT RACES. ONE OF THE LARGEST BOAT RACES ON THE CIRCUIT TODAY, WITH BOATS FROM ALL OVER THE U S, ITALY, AUSTRIA & HAWAII. AT BOULDER RESERVOIR, 3 MI FROM BOULDER ON 116 NE. (INT'L). GARY FUJIKI, CHMN; COLORADO SPEEDBOAT ASSOC; 9650 W 51ST PL #215E; ARVADO, CO 80002. (#107028-5).

OCT 11 - 16, '76. TEACHER WORKSHOP ON COLORADO ETHNIC HISTORY. CONFERENCE AT UNIVERSITY OF COLORADO. (ST-WIDE). KLAUS J BARTEL, DIR; FOREIGN LANGUAGE INFO CENTER OF COLORADO; 130 MCKENNA, UNIV OF COLORADO; BOULDER, CO 80302. (#108813-2).

OCT 15, '76. GERMAN CONTRIBUTIONS TO AMERICAN ARTS, LETTERS & SCIENCES -SYMPOSIUM. SYMPOSIUM ON GERMAN CONTRIBUTIONS TO AMERICAN ARTS, LETTERS, AND SCIENCES OVER THE PAST 200 YEARS. AT UNIVERSITY MEMORIAL CENTER, UNIV OF COLORADO. (ST-WIDE). KLAUS J BARTEL, CHMN; GERMAN-AMERICAN CENTENNIAL-BICENTENNIAL COMMITTEE; 3650 BERKLEY AVE; BOULDER, CO 80303. (#108813-1).

OCT 15 - 17, '76. CENTENNIAL-BICENTENNIAL OCTOBERFEST. SPECIAL SALUTE TO COLORADO ETHNIC GROUPS ON FRIDAY & SATURDAY EVENINGS. AT COLORADO UNIV FIELDHOUSE. (ST-WIDE). KLAUS J BARTEL, CHAIRMAN; GERMAN-AMERICAN CENTENNIAL-BICENTENNIAL COMMITTEE; 3650 BERKLEY AVE; BOULDER, CO 80303. (#109095-1).

NOV 22 - DEC 20, '76. A SENSE OF COMMUNITY - A MODEL APPROACH. THIS PROJECT WILL DEVELOP A SENSE OF COMMUNITY WHILE FOCUSING ON HISTORIC PRESERVATION; THE APPROACH IS THE PRODUCTION & PRESENTATION OF 5 FILMS DRAMATICALLY OUTLINING COMMUNITY ARCHITECTURAL FEATURES. (ST-WIDE). SUSAN LYNTON; BOULDER PUBLIC LIBRARY FOUNDATION; 1000 CANYON BLVD; BOULDER, CO 80302. (#10770-1).

BRANSON

BRANSON CITY JAIL AND PARK, BRANSON, CO. TWO-CELL STONE JAIL IS BEING CLEANED AND RESTORED AND A WATER SYSTEM INSTALLED. THE GROUNDS ARE BEING LANDSCAPED WITH A FENCED PARK, FLOWERS AND PICNIC TABLES PUT IN PLACE. (LOCAL). MISS GESILE MCMILLAN, PROJ DIRECTOR; BRANSON-TRINCHERA LIVESTOCK & HOME EC 4-H CLUBS; BRANSON, CO 81027. (#17421).

FLAGPOLE ERECTION, BRANSON, CO. ERECT FLAGPOLE AT MINIPARK FOR THE BICENTENNIAL. (LOCAL). HON TOM RUSSELL, MAYOR; BRANSON CITY COUNCIL; BRANSON, CO 81027. (#26159).

FT UNION-FT LEAVENWORTH TRAIL MARKER, CO. ERECT MONUMENT MARKING FREIGHT BRANCH OF SANTA FE TRAIL. (LOCAL). RICHARD H LOUDEN, CHAIRMAN; CCBC BRANSON-TRINCHERA; BRANSON, CO 81027. (#26160).

MINI-PARK CONSTRUCTION, BRANSON, CO. TREES WILL BE PLANTED, PICNIC FACILITIES PROVIDED AND THE HISTORIC JAILHOUSE RESTORED FOR PARK AREA. (LOCAL). JOHN F DOHERTY, 4-H LEADER; BRANSON-TRINCHERA 4-H CLUB; TRINCHERA, CO 81081. (#26161).

JUNE 26, '76. BRANSON-TRINCHERA OLDTIMERS REUNION. DAY OF VISITING & REMINISCING. NOON LUNCHEON, AWARDS, PROGRAM, & DANCE AT NIGHT. AT BRANSON GYM. (LOCAL). BILL R LOPEZ, COORD; BRANSON-TRINCHERA OLDTIMERS ASOOCIATION; BRANSON, CO 81027. (#200007-11).

JUNE 26, '76. MUSEUM AWARD PRESENTATION TO MIKE MOCK. AWARD WILL BE MADE DURING PROGRAM OF BRANSON-TRINCHERA OLDTIMER REUNION HONORING MIKE MOCK FOR PRIVATE MUSEUM. AT BRANSON GYM. (LOCAL). RICHARD H LOUDEN, CHMN; BRANSON CENTENNIAL-BICENTENNIAL COMMITTEE; BRANSON, CO 81027. (#200007-10).

BRECKENRIDGE

HISTORICAL EVALUATION & INVENTORY, CO. PHOTOGRAPHS WILL BE TAKEN OF STRUCTURES WITHIN THE ORIGINAL TOWN SITE. THESE PHOTOS WILL BE REVIEWED FOR HISTORICAL VALUE BY OLDER CITIZENS & A HISTORICAL INVENTORY COMPILED. (LOCAL). MAUREEN NICHOLLS, COORDINATOR; BOX 381; BRECKENRIDGE, CO 80424. (#26142).

PUBLICATION OF A HISTORICAL RESTORATION GUIDE, CO. PUBLICATION OF A SIMPLIFIED GUIDE OF 'DO'S & DON'TS' FOR ARCHITECTURAL RESTORATION OF HISTORIC STRUCTURES, TO INSURE COMPATIBILITY BETWEEN ORIGINAL & REPRODUCED STRUCTURE. (LOCAL). MAUREEN NICHOLLS, COORDINATOR; BOX 381; BRECKENRIDGE, CO 80424. (#26141).

MAY 1 - SEPT 10, '75. BEARD GROWING CONTEST. COMPETITION. (LOCAL). MAUREEN NICHOLLS, CHMN; VOLUNTEER FIRE DEPT, BRECKENRIDGE CENTENNIAL-BICENT COMMITTEE; 302 S RIDGE BOX 38; BRECKENRIDGE, CO 80424. (#108688-1).

AUG 10, '75. BRECKENRIDGE'S BICENTENNIAL DAYS. ACTIVITIES INCLUDE A BUFFALO BARBEQUE & PICNIC, COSTUME CONTEST, PARADE, DISPLAY OF ANTIQUE FIRE EQUIPMENT AND MINING CONTEST. (LOCAL). MAUREEN NICHOLLS, COORD; BRECKENRIDGE CENTENNIAL COMMITTEE & VOLUNTEER FIRE DEPARTMENT; 302 S RIDGE, BOX 38; BRECKENRIDGE, CO 80424. (#200007-20).

NOV 15, '75 - APR 15, '76. 'AMERICA '76' - MUSICAL REVUE TRACING AMERICA'S HERITAGE. AFTER APRIL 15 THE SHOW WILL BE BOOKED ON TOURS THROUGHOUT THE U S. ALSO AVAILABLE DURING DAYTIME HOURS AND SUNDAYS. CAST OF 14 PEOPLE INCLUDING LIVE BAND, STARING DAVE THORNTON. AT SINGIN' SADIE'S SALOON, FT MERIBEH BLDG, 200 WASHINGTON. (LOCAL). ALBERT E KUEHNERT, CHMN; AL & BETTY ENTERPRISES; PO BOX 428; BRECKENRIDGE, CO 80424. (#103913-1).

AUG 14 - 15, '76. NO MAN'S LAND HOMECOMING. ANNUAL CELEBRATION SINCE 1936 WHEN ED C JOHNSON RAISED THE U S FLAG IN BRECKENRIDGE AND PROCLAIMED THIS STRIP OF LAND A PART OF COLORADO. (LOCAL). MAUREEN NIHOLLS; TOWN OF BRECKENRIDGE; BOX 381; BRECKENRIDGE, CO 80424. (#108715-1).

BRIGGSDALE

ACQUISITION OF COMMUNITY BUILDING AND MUSEUM - CO. FORMER RURAL SCHOOL BUILDING MOVED INTO BRIGGSDALE ANTICIPATED FOR USE AS COMMUNITY BUILDING, DISPLAY OF HISTORIC OBJECTS & ANTIQUES. (LOCAL). C W ARMAGOST, COORDINATOR; BRIGGSDALE LIONS CLUB; BRIGGSDALE, CO 80611. (#26385).

FARMERS UNION HISTORY OF LOCAL 321 - CO. WRITTEN HISTORY OF LOCAL #321 AT BRIGGSDALE. (LOCAL). MRS AGNES SIEVERS, HISTORIAN; FARMERS UNION, LOCAL 321; RT 1, BOX 78; BRIGGSDALE, CO 80611. (#26381).

HERITAGE PROJECT - BRIGGSDALE, CO. GENEALOGY & FAMILY HISTORY OF 4-H MEMBERS. (LOCAL). MABEL BAXTER, PROJ DIRECTOR; 4-H CLUB; RT 1, BOX 9; BRIGGSDALE, CO 80611. (#26387).

HISOTRY OF BRIGGSDALE BAPTIST CHURCH - CO. HISTORY OF BRIGGSDALE BAPTIST CHURCH FORMATION; LISTING OF EARLY MEMBERS & SERVICE LOCATIONS. (LOCAL). MABEL BAXTER, PROJ DIRECTOR; BRIGGSDALE BAPTIST CHURCH; RT 1, BOX 9; BRIGGSDALE, CO 80611. (#26386).

HISTORIES OF FOSSTON AND OSGOOD, CO. ONCE THRIVING PRAIRIE TOWNS NOW VANISHED; PEOPLE LIVING IN AREA COMPILING HISTORY AT COMMUNITY GATHERINGS. (LOCAL). MRS REUEL BOLIN, CHAIRMAN; BRIGGSDALE CENTENNIAL-BICENTENNIAL COMMISSION; RT 4, BOX 60; BRIGGSDALE, CO 80611. (#26384).

HISTORY OF BRIGGSDALE POSTAL SERVICE - CO. WRITTEN HISTORY WITH PICTURES FOR DISPLAY. (LOCAL). BEULAH PARSONS, COORDINATOR; BRIGGSDALE CENTENNIAL-BICENTENNIAL COMMISSION; BRIGGSDALE, CO 80611. (#26377).

HISTORY OF BRIGGSDALE, CO. 650 SQUARE MILES OF PRAIRIE SURROUNDING BRIGGSDALE IS INCLUDED AS THE BRIGGSDALE COMMUNITY; HISTORY OF THIS AREA BEING COMPILED BY VARIETY OF GROUPS; HISTORY OF AREA POST OFFICE ALSO COMPILED. (LOCAL). REUEL BOLIN, COORDINATOR; BRIGGSDALE CENTENNIAL-BICENTENNIAL COMMISSION; RT 4, BOX 60; BRIGGSDALE, CO 80611. (#26379).

LABELING STREETS IN BRIGGSDALE, CO. STREETS IN THE CITY WILL BE LABELED. (LOCAL). REUEL BOLIN, PROJ DIRECTOR; BRIGGSDALE CENTENNIAL-BICENTENNIAL COMMITTEE; RT 4, BOX 60; BRIGGSDALE, CO 80611. (#26378).

MAPPING OF AREA CHURCHES, SCHOOLS & CEMETERIES -CO. IN 650 SQUARE MILE AREA OF PRAIRIE OLD CHURCHES, CEMETERIES, SCHOOLS, PIONEER TRAILS & HISTORIC SPOTS WILL BE PINPOINTED. (LOCAL). REVEL BOLIN, PROJ DIRECTOR; BRIGGSDALE CENTENNIAL-BICENTENNIAL COMMISSION; RT 4, BOX 60; BRIGGSDALE, CO 80611. (#26383).

MAPPING TOWN OF BRIGGSDALE, CO. ONCE A BOOMING AGRICULTURAL PRAIRIE COMMUNITY WITH POPULATION PEAKS OF 300 BETWEEN 1918 TO 1929; BRIGGSDALE WILL BE MAPPED SHOWING COMMERCIAL & RESIDENTIAL SITES; ALSO MAPPING 1926 & 1976 TOWN. (LOCAL). ELSIE SHELLER, HISTORIAN; BRIGGSDALE CENTENNIAL-BICENTENNIAL COMMISSION; RT 4, BOX 60; BRIGGSDALE, CO 80611. (#26380).

MARKING TOWNSITE OF FOSSTON - BRIGGSDALE, CO. MARKING NOW VANISHED PRAIRIE TOWN WITH MARKER OF CEMENT BLOCKS ONCE MANUFACTURED THERE; ALL THAT REMAINS IS ONE BUILDING, ONCE A GENERAL STORE, NOW A FARM BUREAU MEETING HALL. (LOCAL). MRS REUEL BOLIN, PROJ DIRECTOR; FOSSTON WOMAN'S CLUB; RT 4, BOX 60; BRIGGSDALE, CO 80611. (#26382).

TREE AND SHRUB PLANTING IN BRIGGSDALE, CO. FARM BUREAU TRADITIONALLY PROVIDES TREES AND SHRUBS; EMPHASIS WILL BE ON GREENING THIS PRAIRIE TOWN. (LOCAL). REUEL BOLIN, COORDINATOR; BRIGGSDALE CENTENNIAL-BICENTENNIAL COMMISSION; RT 4, BOX 60; BRIGGSDALE, CO 80611. (#26376).

OCT 12, '75. CONGREGATIONAL CHURCH HARVEST HOME DINNER. FESTIVAL AT BRIGGSDALE CONGREGATIONAL CHURCH. (REGN'L). MRS GEORGE SPEAKER, JR; CONGREGATIONAL LADIES AID; RURAL ROUTE; BRIGGSDALE, CO 80611. (#200007-15).

OCT 14, '75 - APR 14, '76. NATIONAL BICENTENNIAL SCHOOL LUNCH. FESTIVAL AT SCHOOL CAFETERIA. (LOCAL). JUANITA MAYS, MANAGER; SCHOOL LUNCH PROGRAM; BRIGGSDALE, CO 80611. (#200007-16).

DEC 3, '75. 4H ACHIEVEMENT BANQUET. FESTIVAL AT SCHOOL AUDITORIUM. (LOCAL). MABEL BAXTER, COORD; 4H CLUB AND BRIGGSDALE LIONS CLUB; R 1, BOX 9; BRIGGSDALE, CO 80611. (#200007-17).

MAR 13, '76. TALENT SHOW - 'HATS OFF TO AMERICA'. LIVE PERFORMANCE AT SCHOOL AUDITORIUM. (LOCAL). CAROL OPDYKE, COORD; PARENT-TEACHERS CLUB; GROVER, CO 80622. (#200007-18).

JUNE 27, '76. OLD TIMERS PICNIC. FESTIVAL AT BRIGGSDALE PARK. (LOCAL). HENRY HART; BRIGGSDALE CENTENNIAL COMMISSION; ROUTE 1; BRIGGSDALE, CO 80611. (#108812-2).

JULY 18, '76. BRIGGSDALE BAPTIST CHURCH GOLDEN ANNIVERSARY FESTIVAL. FESTIVAL AT BAPTIST CHURCH. (LOCAL). JOAN NELSON; BRIGGSDALE BAPTIST CHURCH CONGREGATION; PO BOX 39; BRIGGSDALE, CO 80611. (#108812-1).

NOV 21, '76. ANNUAL THANKSGIVING DINNER. FESTIVAL AT SCHOOL AUDITORIUM. (LOCAL). C W ARMAGOST, V-PRES; BRIGGSDALE LIONS CLUB; BOX 59; BRIGGSDALE, CO 80611. (#108814-1).

BRIGHTON

ADAMS COUNTY CHURCH RESTORATION - BRIGHTON, CO. PURCHASE AND RESTORATION OF THE FIRST CHURCH BUILDING ERECTED IN BRIGHTON; THE BUILDING WILL BE TURNED OVER TO THE CITY OF BRIGHTON AS A HISTORICAL LANDMARK. (LOCAL). ROY H CARLSON, CHAIRMAN; ADAMS COUNTY HISTORICAL SOCIETY; 9755 HENDERSON RD; BRIGHTON, CO 80601. (#17543).

ADAMS COUNTY CLEAR CREEK TRAIL IN BRIGHTON, CO. 3-MILE HIKE, BIKE AND HORSE TRAIL FROM JUNCTURE OF PLATTE RIVER WEST TO BROADWAY. (LOCAL). JERRY GRANT, COMMISSIONER; ADAMS COUNTY BICENTENNIAL COMMISSION; 4TH & BRIDGE STS; BRIGHTON, CO 80601. (#10310).

ADAMS COUNTY INDOOR ARENA IN BRIGHTON, COLORADO. THE CONSTRUCTION OF AN ARENA TO BE USED FOR ADAMS COUNTY CENTENNIALBICENTENNIAL ACTIVITIES; AND FUTURE SPORTING, CULTURAL AND GENERAL EVENTS. (LOCAL). JERRY GRANT, COMMISSIONER; ADAMS COUNTY GOVERNMENT; 4TH & BRIDGE STS; BRIGHTON, CO 80601. (#10311).

ADAMS COUNTY NATURE PRESERVE IN BRIGHTON, CO. 15-ACRE AREA WITH TRAILS AND INTERPRETIVE INFORMATION ON THE AREA. (LOCAL). FRANK E ALLEN, CHAIRMAN; ADAMS COUNTY CENTENNIAL-BICENTENNIAL COMMITTEE; 10201 RIVERDALE RD, #204; THORNTON, CO 80229. (#10312).

COLORADO CHRONICLES HISTORY - BRIGHTON. A HISTORY OF BRIGHTON AND COLORADO WILL BE PUBLISHED. (LOCAL). LARRY WORTH, PROJ DIRECTOR; 36 S MAIN ST; BRIGHTON, CO 80601. (#26158).

FEB 1 - JULY 1, '76. HISTORICAL DISPLAY. EXHIBIT AT ADAMS COUNTY COURTHOUSE LOBBY. (LOCAL). HATTIE C MCCOY, V-PRES; ADAMS COUNTY HISTORICAL SOCIETY; RT 2 BOX 228H; BRIGHTON, CO 80601. (#107018-1).

JULY 4, '76. FIREWORK DISPLAY. FESTIVAL AT ADAMS COUNTY REGIONAL PARK. (LOCAL). EMI CHIKUMA, COORDINATOR; BRIGHTON FIRE DEPT; 221 S 10TH; BRIGHTON, CO 80601. (#108646-1).

JULY 4, '76. PLATTE RIVER RAFT RACE. COMPETITION, FESTIVAL. (LOCAL). LARRY WORTH, COORD; ADAMS COUNTY HISTORICAL

BRIGHTON — CONTINUED

SOCIETY; E 124TH & HENDERSON RD; BRIGHTON, CO 80601. (#108646-2).

AUG 7, '76. COMMUNITY PARADE. PARADE. (LOCAL). LARRY WORTH; BRIGHTON PARADE COMMITTEE; 36 S MAIN ST; BRIGHTON, CO 80601. (#108816-1).

BROOMFIELD

MAY 14, '76. AMERICA &COLORADO - YE OLD AMERICAN FAIRE. SING ALONGS, STUDENT BOOTHS, SQUARE DANCING, CHOIR PRESENTATIONS; EVENTS WILL AROUSE INTEREST & PRIDE IN THE COMMUNITY & AMERICA. AT EMERALD ELEMENTARY SCHOOL, 755 ELMHURST, BROOMFIELD, CO. (LOCAL). KAREN CARPENTER, DIRECTOR; PARENT-TEACHER ORGANIZATION; 755 ELMHURST; BROOMFIELD, CO 80020. (#107169-1).

BRUSH

BEAUTIFICATION OF LIBRARY PARK, BRUSH, CO. PLANTING OF FLOWERS AND PLACING OF BENCHES TO MAKE PARK MORE USEFUL TO COMMUNITY. (LOCAL). JUDY GUTHRIE, PRESIDENT; BRUSH JAYCEE-ETTES; 1504 EATON ST; BRUSH, CO 80723. (#17438).

BRUSH SUMMER PARKS PROGRAM. HERITAGE PLAYS, MUSICAL CONCERTS, ATHLETIC EVENTS, BEAUTIFICATION TO BE PRESENTED THROUGHOUT SUMMER. (LOCAL). CLAUDE MELTON, CHAIRMAN; BRUSH CENTENNIAL-BICENTENNIAL COMMITTEE; 20 CIRCLE DR; BRUSH, CO 80723. (#33723).

CENTENNIAL-BICENTENNIAL SCRAPBOOK, BRUSH, CO. SCRAPBOOK ASSEMBLED TO PRESERVE THE CENTENNIAL-BICENTENNIAL YEAR TO BE PLACED IN LIBRARY FOR PUBLIC USE. (LOCAL). GEORGE REICHERS, PRESIDENT; SENIOR CITIZENS CENTER; 323 CLAYTON ST; BRUSH, CO 80723. (#17437).

'CHILDREN TELL US ABOUT THE PAST' - BRUSH, CO. 4TH, 5TH & 6TH GRADE STUDENTS ARE COMPILING A HISTORY BOOK. (LOCAL). R PAULSEN, COORDINATOR; BRUSH CENTENNIAL-BICENTENNIAL COMMITTEE; 310 TURNER ST; BRUSH, CO 80723. (#26155).

CHURCH HISTORY, BRUSH, CO. HISTORY OF CHURCHES TO BE MADE INTO A BOOK WITH PICTURES. (LOCAL). HON R PAULSEN, MAYOR; BRUSH CENT-BICENT COMMITTEE; 310 TURNER ST; BRUSH, CO 80723. (#26156).

COMMUNITY TIME CAPSULE, BRUSH, CO. A TIME CAPSULE WITH ARTICLES OF COMMUNITY CULTURE WILL BE BURIED. (LOCAL). HON R PAULSEN, MAYOR; BRUSH CENT-BICENT COMMITTEE; 310 TURNER ST; BRUSH, CO 80723. (#26157).

HISTORY OF THE SUGAR BEET AND CATTLE INDUSTRIES-CO. A COMPREHENSIVE HISTORY OF THE SUGAR BEET AND CATTLE INDUSTRIES TO BE PRESERVED AS A HERITAGE OF TO THE COMMUNITY AND SERVE AS A REMINDER OF THE CENTENNIAL-BICENTENNIAL CELEBRATION. (LOCAL). DONALD M LUNGREN, PROJ DIRECTOR; BRUSH HIGH SCHOOL; 310 TURNER ST; BRUSH, CO 80723. (#15261).

SENIOR CITIZENS CENTER - PROJ OF BRUSH, CO. THIS BUILDING WILL BE A LASTING REMINDER OF THE CENTENNIALBICENTENNIAL CELEBRATION BY HAVING A MEETING PLACE FOR SENIOR CITIZENS IN THE COMMUNITY. (LOCAL). GEORGE H REICHERS, PRESIDENT; SENIOR CITIZENS CENTER; 323 CLAYTON ST; BRUSH, CO 80723. (#15260).

SENIOR HOUSING PROJECT OF BRUSH, CO. AS A REMINDER OF THE CENTENNIAL-BICENTENNIAL CELEBRATION, THE BRUSH HOUSING AUTHORITY WILL SPONSOR LOW COST HOUSING FOR SENIOR CITIZENS. (LOCAL). RAY DANIELSEN, CHAIRMAN; BRUSH HOUSING AUTHORITY; PO BOX 707; BRUSH, CO 80723. (#15259).

SUNBONNETS FOR THE CENTENNIAL-BICENTENNIAL - CO. SUNBONNETS WILL BE SOLD IN HONOR OF THE CENTENNIAL-BICENTENNIAL CELEBRATION. (LOCAL). RUTH HENDERSON, CHAIRPERSON; PED CHAPTER T; 617 HOWARD ST; BRUSH, CO 80723. (#21379).

TAPED INTERVIEWS FOR THE LIBRARY - BRUSH, CO. TAPE RECORDINGS MADE OF INTERVIEWS WITH SENIOR CITIZENS WHO HAVE CONTRIBUTED TO THE AREA; ALSO, IMPORTANT EVENTS SUCH AS LAYING CORNERSTONES. (LOCAL). CAL LEACH, CHAIRMAN; BRUSH LIBRARY BOARD; 411 CARSON ST; BRUSH, CO 80723. (#24568).

JAN 6, '76. SENIOR CITIZENS CENTENNIAL-BICENTENNIAL QUEEN CONTEST. COMPETITION. (LOCAL). GEORGE RIECHERS, COORD; SENIOR CITIZENS GROUP; 323 CLAYTON ST; BRUSH, CO 80723. (#200007-19).

APR 25, '76. COLORADO STATE BB GUN CHAMPIONSHIP MATCHES. COMPETITION AT MORGAN COUNTY FAIRGROUNDS. (ST-WIDE). DONALD HEER; BRUSH JAYCEES-COLORADO JAYCEES; 222 CAMERON ST; BRUSH, CO 80723. (#103310-8).

MAY 31 - SEPT 6, '76. BRUSH SUMMER PARKS PROGRAM. FESTIVAL AT VFW PARK & LIBRARY. (LOCAL). CLAUDE MELTON, CHAIRMAN; BRUSH CENTENNIAL-BICENTENNIAL COMMITTEE; 20 CIRCLE DR; BRUSH, CO 80723. (#106048-1).

JULY 2 - 4, '76. AMATEUR RODEO AND JULY 4TH CELEBRATION. GREASED PIG CONTEST FOR BOYS AND GIRLS AGED 7-11 AND UNDER 7 WILL BE HELD DURING RODEO INTERMISSION. OTHER EVENTS INCLUDE A PARADE AND BARBEQUE. AT MORGAN COUNTY FAIRGROUNDS. (LOCAL). KURT CORNUM, CHAIRMAN; BRUSH RODEO ASSOC; 115 HOSPITAL RD; BRUSH, CO 80723. (#106048-3).

JULY 2 - 4, '76. FIREWORKS JULY 4TH CELEBRATION. FIREWORKS DISPLAY WILL BE HELD AFTER THE RODEO. AT MORGAN COUNTY FAIRGROUNDS. (LOCAL). RALPH SCHILLING, DIRECTOR; BRUSH RODEO ASSOC/BRUSH VOLUNTEER FIRE DEPARTMENT; 1515 EDISON ST; BRUSH, CO 80723. (#106048-6).

JULY 2 - 4, '76. GREASED PIG CATCH. CONTEST IS FOR CHILDREN 7 AND UNDER AND 7-11; IT WILL BE HELD DURING THE RODEO INTERMISSION. (LOCAL). TOBY PADILLA, V-PRES; BRUSH RODEO ASSOC; 921 N COLORADO AVE; BRUSH, CO 80723. (#108811-2).

JULY 2 - 4, '76. RODEO FOLLOWED BY CENTENNIAL FIREWORKS. FESTIVAL. (LOCAL). RAYMOND PAULSEN; BRUSH RODEO COMMITTEE; 310 TURNER ST; BRUSH, CO 80723. (#108811-1).

JULY 3, '76. OUTSTANDING PIONEER AWARD. AWARD AT MORGAN COUNTY FAIRGROUNDS. (LOCAL). DICK LEACH, CHAIRMAN; BRUSH RODEO ASSOC; 333 HARVARD; BRUSH, CO 80723. (#106048-9).

JULY 3 - 4, '76. HY-PLAINS RENDEZVOUS. COMPETITION AT 5 MILES SOUTH OF BRUSH ON HWY 71-FOLLOW THE SIGNS. (LOCAL). JIM SPOTTS, CHAIRMAN; BEAVER CREEK MUZZLE LOADERS; 621 SHERMAN; FT MORGAN, CO 80701. (#106048-5).

JULY 4, '76. CENTENNIAL-BICENTENNIAL WORSHIP SERVICE. CEREMONY AT MORGAN COUNTY FAIRGROUNDS. (LOCAL). NORMAN FREUND, CHAIRMAN; EAST MORGAN COUNTY MINISTERIAL ALLIANCE; 523 CUSTER ST; BRUSH, CO 80723. (#106048-2).

JULY 4, '76. JULY 4TH PARADE. PARADE AT CAMERON ST TO EDMUNDS ST TO CUSTER ST; PARADE FORMS ON MILL ST. (LOCAL). CAL HARDING, CHAIRMAN; BRUSH RODEO ASSOC; 26439 COUNTY RD; BRUSH, CO 80723. (#106048-7).

JULY 4, '76. SENIOR CITIZENS' CENTENNIAL-BICENTENNIAL QUEEN IN PARADE. QUEEN AND HER ATTENDANTS WERE JUDGED ON THEIR ABILITY TO COMMUNICATE AND THEIR PERSONALITIES. QUEEN FLORENCE ROUNDS WILL RIDE ON FLOAT IN 4TH OF JULY PARADE AND WILL REPRESENT SENIOR CITIZENS THROUGHOUT THE YEAR. (LOCAL). GEORGE RIECHERS, CHMN; SENIOR CITIZENS GROUP; 323 CLAYTON; BRUSH, CO 80723. (#107446-3).

AUG 1 - 3, '76. ARTS FESTIVAL. FESTIVAL. (LOCAL). R PAULSEN, DIRECTOR; TOWN OF BRUSH; 310 TURNER ST; BRUSH, CO 80723. (#108955-17).

AUG 12 - 13, '76. RELIVING THE PAST THROUGH PLAYS. LIVE PERFORMANCE. (LOCAL). R PAULSEN, COORDINATOR; CITY OF BRUSH; 310 TURNER ST; BRUSH, CO 80723. (#108649-1).

SEPT 11, '76. MEXICAN FIESTA. MUSIC & DANCING WHICH REFLECTS THE MEXICAN-AMERICAN CULTURE, FOOD, AWARDS, SPEECHES AND A MASS. AT BRUSH ROLLER RINK & MORGAN COUNTY FAIRGROUNDS. (LOCAL). MARY HELEN DELAFUENTE; ST MARY'S CIRCLE & FIESTA TIME IN BRUSH; 422 CLIFTON; BRUSH, CO 80723. (#108676-1).

BUENA VISTA

BICENTENNIAL POSTER & ESSAY CONTEST. COMPETITION. (LOCAL). CLYDE TRAINOR, DIRECTOR; OPTIMIST CLUB; BOX 333; BUENA VISTA, CO 81211. (#107439-1).

CHILDREN'S PARK - BUENA VISTA, CO. AN AREA IN THE LOCAL PARK WILL BE FENCED FOR SMALL CHILDREN WITH TOYS, SLIDES, SWINGS AND SANDBOX. (LOCAL). BEVERLY HERRLE, CHAIRMAN; DELPHI CLUB AND OPTIMIST CLUB; BOX 210; BUENA VISTA, CO 81211. (#24602).

COMMUNITY TIME CAPSULE, BUENA VISTA, CO. 5TH GRADE CLASS HAS STARTED A TIME CAPSULE WHICH WILL BE PRESENTED TO THE BUENA VISTA AREA HERITAGE MUSEUM. (LOCAL). SUSAN KELLY, CHAIRPERSON; BUENA VISTA GRADE SCHOOL; BOX 606; BUENA VISTA, CO 81211. (#26152).

MAY 10, '75. BIKE RIDE - 12 MILES TO YOUNGLIFE RANCH. TOUR. (LOCAL). JACK MANLEY, VIC-PRES; OPTIMIST CLUB; 16920 CO RD 338; BUENA VISITA, CO 81211. (#107154-4).

JUNE 15, '76. SENIOR CITIZENS CELEBRATION. FESTIVAL. (LOCAL). SUZANNE KELLY, COORD; SENIOR CITIZENS; BOX 606; BUENA VISTA, CO 81211. (#200007-6).

JUNE 26, '76. BICENTENNIAL JUNE FESTIVAL. ANNUAL FESTIVAL INVOLVING MERCHANTS, CLUBS & SCHOOLS; SQUARE DANCES, ART EXHIBITS & GAMES. (LOCAL). WILLA PICKREL, CHWMN; CHAMBER OF COMMERCE; 423 PRINCETON AVE; BUENA VISTA, CO 81211. (#107154-2).

JULY 4, '76. GRAND OPENING OF RESTORED COURTHOUSE-MUSEUM. OPENING AT COURTHOUSE BUILDING, 510 E MAIN ST. (LOCAL). SUZANNE KELLY, COORD; BUENA VISTA HERITAGE; BOX 606; BUENA VISTA, CO 81211. (#107004-1).

JULY 4, '76. 4TH OF JULY FIREWORKS DISPLAY. FESTIVAL AT RODEO GROUNDS 3 MILES WEST OF TOWN.. (LOCAL). ED LAMBERT, COORD; AMERICAN LEGION; 430 E MAIN; BUENA VISTA, CO 81211. (#107154-1).

JULY 5, '76 - CONTINUING . MUSEUM EXHIBITS. EXHIBIT AT COURTHOUSE BUILDING, 510 E MAIN ST. (LOCAL). SUZANNE KELLY, COORD; BUENA VISTA HERITAGE; BOX 606; BUENA VISTA, CO 81211. (#107004-2).

JULY 10, '76. ANNUAL OUTDOOR ART FAIR. ART WORK OF HISTORICAL SIGNIFICANCE TO COLORADO. AT CHAPEL IN THE PARK ON HWY 24. (LOCAL). GRACE HUFF, CHWMN; BUENA VISTA FINE ARTS ASSOC; 28483 CO RD 340; BUENA VISTA, CO 81211. (#107154-3).

JULY 10, '76. COMMUNITY PARADE: 'JOIN IN FORGING COLORADO'S 2ND CENTURY'. PARADE. (LOCAL). SUZANNE KELLY, COORD; PARADE COMMITTEE; BOX 606; BUENA VISTA, CO 81211. (#108712-1).

JULY 10 - 11, '76. BICENTENNIAL LIONS CLUB RODEO. COMPETITION, LIVE PERFORMANCE AT BUENA VISTA RODEO GROUNDS. (LOCAL). BILL NELSON, PRESIDENT; BUENA VISTA LIONS CLUB; 537 GANNISON AVE; BUENA VISTA, CO 81211. (#107439-2).

AUG 6 - 8, '76. BICENTENNIAL KAYAK RACES. COMPETITION. (REGN'L). DIANA MAKRIS, SEC; FIBARK BOATING CLUB; 18060 CO RD 162; NATHROP, CO 81211. (#107154-5).

BURLINGTON

CAROUSEL RESTORATION, BURLINGTON, CO. RESTORATION OF KIT CARSON COUNTY OWNED 1905 PHILADELPHIA TOBOGGAN, CAROUSEL & WURLITZER MONSTER MILITARY BAND ORGAN. CREATE MEMORIAL PARK AROUND CAROUSEL SITE. (LOCAL). NORMA PANKRATZ, CORRESPONDING SECRETARY; KIT CARSON COUNTY CENTENNIAL-BICENTENNIAL COMMITTEE; BOX 218; BURLINGTON, CO 80807. (#23663).

COUNTY PARK - KIT CARSON COUNTY, CO. CONSTRUCT COUNTY PARK WHICH WILL BE CONTIGUOUS TO COUNTY FAIRGROUNDS AND ADD TO THE COUNTY DEVELOPMENT AS A REMINDER OF THE CENTENNIALBICENTENNIAL CELEBRATION. (LOCAL). ROBERT MCCLELLAND, PROJ COORDINATOR; FEDERATED AND CIVIC CLUBS OF KIT CARSON COUNTY; RT 1 BOX 60; BURLINGTON, CO 80807. (#15278).

FRONTIER COOKBOOK - KIT CARSON COUNTY, CO. AS A CENTENNIAL-BICENTENNIAL PROJECT, THE COMMITTEE WILL COMPILE ETHNIC-ORIENTED RECEIPES REFLECTING THE BROAD BASED FRONTIER POPULATION WHICH SETTLED THE AREA. (LOCAL). ROBERT MCCLELLAND, CHAIRMAN; KIT CARSON COUNTY CENTENNIAL-BICENTENNIAL COMMITTEE; ROUTE 1 BOX 60; BURLINGTON, CO 80807. (#15277).

NOV 11, '75. UNITED STATES ARMED FORCES BICENTENNIAL CARAVAN. THE CARAVAN IS COMPOSED OF EXHIBIT VANS FOR EACH BRANCH OF THE MILITARY SERVICE. THE THEME OF THE EXHIBITION IS 'HISTORY OF THE ARMED FORCES AND THEIR CONTRIBUTION TO THE NATION'. (LOCAL). JOHN HUDLER, CHMN; U S ARMED FORCES BICENTENNIAL EXHIBIT VANS PROJECT; BURLINGTON, CO 80807. (#1775-247).

JUNE 12, '76. LITTLE BRITCHES ART MART. THE ART MART OFFERS A FESTIVAL APPROACH FOR LOCAL ARTISTS' EXHIBITS. AN EXHIBITION HALL HOUSES FINE ARTS FOR SHOW/SALE WITH ALL-DAY LIVE PERFORMANCES OUTSIDE. FRIENDSHIP, FRIVALITY ARE ENCOURAGED TO WELCOME THE FAMOUS LITTLE BRITCHES RODEO. OPEN TO THE PUBLIC. AT KIT CARSON COUNTY FAIR GROUNDS. (LOCAL). CAROLE ISAAK, COORD; HI PLAINS ARTS COUNCIL; 337 12TH; BURLINGTON, CO 80807. (#107236-2).

AUG 2 - 7, '76. KIT CARSON COUNTY FAIR. 1905 CAROUSEL RIDES FOR $.25. 3 RODEO PERFORMANCES, TRACTOR PULL, TEAM PULL & DEMOLITION DERBY. AT KIT CARSON COUNTY FAIR GROUNDS. (LOCAL). NORMA PANKRATZ; KIT CARSON COUNTY; BOX 218; BURLINGTON, CO 80807. (#107236-1).

AUG 3 - 7, '76. CENTENNIAL EXHIBIT. EXHIBIT AT HOME EC BUILDING, KIT CARSON COUNTY FAIRGROUNDS. (LOCAL). JOYCE MILLER, CHMN; VONA CENTENNIAL BICENTENNIAL COMMITTEE; BOX 116; VONA, CO 80861. (#108815-1).

BYERS

JUNE 12, '76. BICENTENNIAL PARADE & PARK SIGN DEDICATION. PARTICIPATION BY BUSINESSES, CHURCHES, CLUBS & SCHOOL GROUPS. AT END OF PARADE, SIGN WAS DEDICATED AT THE LOCAL PARK BY THE COMMANDER OF LOCAL AMERICAN LEGION, FOLLOWED BY A PICNIC & SOFTBALL GAME AT THE SCHOOL. DANCE IN THE EVENING AT THE AMERICAN LEGION HALL. AT DOWNTOWN BYERS. (LOCAL). CALVIN L GRAVES, CHAIRMAN; BYERS BICENTENNIAL COMMITTEE; PO BOX 112; BYERS, CO 80103. (#200007-199).

CALHAN

AUG 15, '75 - AUG 17, '76. SENIOR CITIZENS' BUS TOURS OF EL PASO COUNTY FAIR. TOUR AT 332 W BIJOU. (LOCAL). BILL LIEB, PROJ MANAGER; PIKES PEAK OR BUST CENTENNIAL COMMITTEE; 1576 KEATON LN; COLORADO SPG, CO 80909. (#10155-1).

JULY 28 - AUG 1, '76. 71ST ANNUAL EL PASO COUNTY FAIR & RODEO. COMPETITION, LIVE PERFORMANCE AT COUNTY FAIR GROUNDS. (LOCAL). HON JOHN L PIEPER, MAYOR; TOWN OF CALHAN; CALHAN, CO 80808. (#108808-1).

CAMPO

AUG 2, '76. OLD-TIME COUNTY FAIR. SUNRISE SERVICE AT THE PARK, PIE-EATING CONTEST, FOAL RACES, SACK RACES, WATERMELON FEED & BASKET DINNER FEATURED. AT MELLS' MEMORIAL PAK. (LOCAL). MRS EDEN; TOWN OF CAMPO; BOX 69; CAMPO, CO 81029. (#108955-19).

CANON CITY

AREA QUILTING BEE AND ANTIQUE EXHIBIT. PUBLIC EXHIBITS OF QUILTS AND DEMONSTRATIONS OF QUILTING ON FRAMES BY GOLDEN AGE CENTER. SPONSOR PLANS INCOMPLETE AS OF 04/14/75. AT FINE ARTS BLDG 212 SO 4TH. (LOCAL). FINE ARTS ASSOCIATION; CANON CITY FINE ARTS ASSOCIATION; P.O. BOX; CANON CITY, CO 81212. (#4113-2).

CANON CITY — CONTINUED

CANON CITY CENTENNIAL PARK IN COLORADO. CITY PARK WITH LAKE, TENNIS, AND PLAYGROUNDS TO BE DEDICATED TO THE 100TH ANNIVERSARY OF COLORADO'S ENTRANCE INTO THE UNITED STATES IN 1876. (LOCAL). HON JOHN GRIFFIN, MAYOR; CITY OF CANON CITY; BOX 711; CANON CITY, CO 81212. (#4943).

CANON CITY COLO, FIRE STATION PROJECT. A NEW FIRE STATION WILL BE CONSTRUCTED TO MEET THE NEEDS OF GROWING COMMUNITY. THIS STATION WILL BE DEDICATED TO THE ACHIEVEMENTS OF THE COMMUNITY FOR '76. (LOCAL). HON JOHN GRIFFIN, MAYOR; CITY OF CANON CITY; BOX 711; CANON CITY, CO 81212. (#4945).

CANON CITY FLOOD CONTROL PROJ OF COLORADO. A CONTROL SYSTEM TO HANDLE MOUNTAIN RUN-OFF FROM THE MOUNTAINS TO THE NORTH OF THE CITY WHICH WILL ENHANCE THE NATURAL CONTOUR OF THE LAND. (LOCAL). HON JOHN GRIFFIN, MAYOR; CITY OF CANON CITY; PO BOX 711; CANON CITY, CO 81212. (#4922). **(??).**

CANON CITY WATER EXPANSION PROJECT OF COLORADO. THIS PROJECT IS TO PROVIDE BETTER WATER QUALITY AND QUANITY TO THE CITIZENS AND WILL ENHANCE THE ECOLOGICAL ATTRACTION OF THE MAN-MADE IMPROVEMENT. (LOCAL). HON JOHN GRIFFIN, MAYOR; CITY OF CANON CITY; BOX 711; CANON CITY, CO 81212. (#4920).

CENTENNIAL TRAILS AT CANON CITY, COLORADO. TRAILS FOR BIKING AND HIKING WILL BE ESTABLISHED TO POINT OUT THE HISTORIC AND SCENIC FEATURES OF THE AREA. (LOCAL). HON JOHN GRIFFIN, MAYOR; CITY OF CANON CITY; BOX 711; CANON CITY, CO 81212. (#4919). **(??).**

RUDD HOME RESTORATION IN CANON CITY, COLO. A PROJECT TO RESTORE THIS HISTORIC TWO STORY STONE BUILDING FOR USE AS A MUSEUM. THE PROJECT INCLUDES REPAIRS & MAINTENANCE TO BLDG, CONSTRUCTING DISPLAY CASES, MOVING ARTIFACTS, SECURITY FEATURES. (LOCAL). P E 'GUS' STANSELL, CHAIRMAN, CANON CITY '76; CANON CITY MUSEUM BOARD AND CITY OF CANON CITY; 810 PINE AVE; CANON CITY, CO 81212. (#4417). **ARBA GRANTEE.**

MAY 3 - 4, '75. BLOSSOM FESTIVAL EXHIBIT OF FINE ARTS & BLOSSOM FESTIVAL WEEKEND. ART EXHIBITED BY LOCAL ARTISTS. FESTIVAL WILL HAVE PARADE DAILY, BAND COMPETITION & FIELD SHOWS BY 40 BANDS FROM 12 STATES. EXHIBIT WILL RUN APPROX FROM MID-APRIL-MID-MAY. AT FINE ARTS CENTER, 5TH ST & ROYAL GORGE BLVD. (ST-WIDE). JOHN GRIFFIN; CITY OF CANON CITY; BOX 711; CANON CITY, CO 81212. (#4105-1).

JUNE 7 - 9, '75. INVITATIONAL SOFT BALL TOURNAMENT. BASEBALL TEAMS FROM DIFFERENT AREAS OF COLORADO ARE INVITED TO COMPETE IN THIS BASEBALL TOURNAMENT WHICH WILL LAST A WEEKEND AND WILL BE DEDICATED TO THE CENTENNIAL. AT JUSTIN FIELD & ROUSE FIELD. (ST-WIDE). P E STANSELL, CHRMN; CANON CITY METRO RECREATION DISTRICT; C/O 810 PINE AVE; CANON CITY, CO 81212. (#4107-1).

JULY 4, '75. 4TH OF JULY FIREWORKS AND CELEBRATION. TRADITIONAL 4TH OF JULY CELEBRATION EMPHASIZING THE 200TH BIRTHDAY OF OUR NATION. AT RODEO GROUNDS. (LOCAL). MEL HAINES; CANON CITY JAYCEES; 632 MYRTLE AVE; CANON CITY, CO 81212. (#4950-1).

JULY 18 - 20, '75. LITTLE BRITCHES RODEO. TRADITIONAL YOUTH ACTIVITY OF RODEO EVENTS SINCE AMERICAN REVOLUTIONARY DAYS. AT RODEO GROUNDS CANON CITY. (ST-WIDE). CHAS PERSINGER; LITTLE BRITCHES RODEO ASS'N; MICANITE ROUTE; CANON CITY, CO 81212. (#4916-1).

AUG 1, '75 - JULY 4, '76. VOTE FOR COLORADO'S STATEHOOD. COMPETITION. (ST-WIDE). JEFF THOMAS, COORD; PIKES PEAK REGION ATTRACTIONS ASSOC; 1050 S 21ST ST; COLORADO SPG, CO 80904. (#108644-1).

APR 17 - 23, '76. JR & SR HIGH SCHOOL ART EXHIBIT. VARIED EXHIBITS OF STUDENT CULTURE, ART & CRAFTWORK. THIS IS IN CONJUNCTION WITH ABBEY SCHOOL FESTIVAL. (LOCAL). CANON CITY PUBLIC SCHOOLS; 11TH & RIVER STS; CANON CITY, CO 81212. (#4109-2).

APR 24 - 30, '76. ABBEY SCHOOL COMMUNITY ART FESTIVAL. EXHIBIT, FESTIVAL AT ABBEY SCHOOL. (ST-WIDE). P E STANSELL, CHRMAN; CANON CITY CENT BICENT COMMITTEE & SCHOOLS; C/O 810 PINE AVE; CANON CITY, CO 81212. (#4112-1).

APR 24 - MAY 15, '76. BLOSSOM FESTIVAL EXHIBIT OF FINE ARTS. COMPETITIVE STATEWIDE EXHIBIT OF PAINTINGS, PRINTS AND SCULPTURE TO BE JUDGED AND AWARDED PRIZES. PART OF CANON CITY BLOSSOM FESTIVAL. AT FINE ARTS BLDG, 212 SO 5TH ST. (ST-WIDE). FINE ARTS ASSOCIATION; CANON CITY FINE ARTS ASSOCIATION; PO BOX 212 SO 5TH; CANON CITY, CO 81212. (#4105-2).

APR 24 - MAY 15, '76. IMPRESSIONS OF AMERICA - TOURING DANCE PRODUCTION. PLAYED IN: CANON CITY, APR 24; COTOPAXI, APR 25; SALIDA, MAY 1; WESTCLIFFE, MAY 8TH; BUENA VISTA, MAY 15TH. DANCE CLUB COMPOSED OF 20 GIRLS. PART OF COLORADO COMMUNITY PROGRAM. (LOCAL). P E STANSELL, COORDINATOR; DANCE TROUPE OF ST SCHOLASTICA SCHOOL; 810 PINE AVE; CANON CITY, CO 81212. (#108678-1).

MAY 1 - 2, '76. MUSIC & BLOSSOM FESTIVAL. VISITING BANDS FROM COLORADO CITIES AND ALL SURROUNDING STATES INVITED FOR THE COMPETITIVE PARADE WITH FLOATS USING THEME THE SPIRIT OF 76. FORTYFIVE BANDS PARTICIPATED IN MAY AND MORE EXPECTED IN '76. CROWD OF 8000 TO 10,000. AT PARADE 15 BLOCKS MAIN ST AND CITIZENS STADIUM. (ST-WIDE). P E STANSELL; CANON CITY JAYCEES; 810 PINE AVE; CANON CITY, CO 81212. (#102868-2).

JUNE 22, '76. DRUMS ALONG THE ROCKIES. BRILLIANT PAGEANTRY FEATURING PRECISION MARCHING EXTRAORDINARY DRUMS & BUGLES, FLAGS IN MOTION & RIFLE MANEUVERS. PATRIOTIC, CLASSICAL & POPULAR MUSIC EMPLOYED. SHOW INCLUDES MADISON SCOUTS, 1975 NATIONAL CHAMPIONS. AT CITIZEN'S STADIUM, COLLEGE AT YALE STS. (LOCAL). BRUCE SHERWOOD, CHAIRMAN; CANON CITY ROTARY CLUB; PO BOX 762; CANON CITY, CO 81212. (#200007-22).

JUNE 22, '76. SPIRIT OF '76 BAND CONCERT. PATRIOTIC CONCERTS AND MANUEVERS AT CITIZENS STADIUM. 'DRUMS ALONG THE ROCKIES', WORLD'S FINEST DRUM & BUGLE CORPS IN REVIEW; COMPETITIVE JUDGING. AT PARKS, CITIZENS STADIUM,HIGH SCHOOL. (ST-WIDE). P E STANSELL, CHRMN; CANON CITY ROTARY CLUB; C/O 810 PINE AVE; CANON CITY, CO 81212. (#4154-1).

JULY 4, '76. DEDICATION AND OPENING OF RUDD HOME. THE RUDD HOME CONTAINS THE LIFE-LONG COLLECTION OF MRS LAURA HUNTLEY. AT RUDD HOME. (LOCAL). P E STANSELL, COORD; CANON CITY '76 COMMISSION; 810 PINE AVE; CANON CITY, CO 81212. (#108644-2).

JULY 4, '76. 4TH OF JULY FIREWORKS AND CELEBRATION. TRADITIONAL 4TH OF JULY CELEBRATION EMPHASIZING THE 200TH BIRTHDAY OF OUR NATION. AT RODEO GROUNDS. (LOCAL). MEL HAINES; CANON CITY JAYCEES; 632 MYRTLE AVE; CANON CITY, CO 81212. (#4950-2).

JULY 4, '76 - CONTINUING . RUDD HOME EXHIBIT. THE RUDD HOME CONTAINS THE LIFE-LONG COLLECTION OF MRS LAURA HUNTLEY. AT RUDD HOME, 612 ROYAL GORGE BLVD, CANON CITY, CO. (ST-WIDE). MR BRIG YOUNG, CURATOR; CANON CITY '76 COMMISSION; 612 ROYAL GORGE BLVD; CANON CITY, CO 81212. (#108356-1).

JULY 9 - 10, '76. THE ROYAL GORGE RODEO. EVENTS INCLUDE WILD COW MILKING, BAREBACK & SADDLE BRONC RIDING, CALF ROPING, BULLDOGGING, CALF ROPING AND ANNUAL PARADE. AT THE ROYAL GORGE RODEO GROUNDS. (LOCAL). ROGER OBERHELMAN, PRES; CANON CITY RODEO ASSOC; 1011 MAIN ST; CANON CITY, CO 81212. (#101435-1).

JULY 30 - AUG 1, '76. LITTLE BRITCHES RODEO. TRADITIONAL YOUTH ACTIVITY OF RODEO EVENTS SINCE AMERICAN REVOLUTIONARY DAYS. AT RODEO GROUNDS, CANON CITY. (ST-WIDE). CHAS PERSINGER; LITTLE BRITCHES RODEO ASS'N; MICANITE ROUTE; CANON CITY, CO 81212. (#4916-2).

AUG 6 - 7, '76. SQUARE DANCE FESTIVAL OF CANON CITY COLORADO. AREA SQUARE DANCE GROUPS WILL PERFORM THIS HERITAGE-ORIENTED DANCE WHICH PROVIDED PIONEER FOREFATHERS WITH FUN AND ENTERTAINMENT. AREA GROUPS SPONSORING THE EVENT ARE GRANDPA'S SQUARES SWINGIN'PIONEERS, ROYAL GORGE PROMENADERS AND SILVER SPURS. AT CITIZENS STADIUM. (ST-WIDE). P.E. STANSELL; CANON CITY SQUARE DANCE CLUBS; 810 PINE AVE.; CANON CITY, CO 81212. (#4944-1).

AUG 13 - 18, '76. 1976 4-H COUNTY FAIR. COUNTY FAIR WHICH IS ONE OF THE LARGEST IN THE STATE WILL FEATURE STYLE SHOE, ALL CLASSES OF HORSE ENTRIES & PERFORMANCE,BICYCLE RODEO, SHEEP & SWINE ENTRIES, WOODWORKING, WILDLIFE, CATTLE, PARADE & SHOWMANSHIP. AT RODEO GROUNDS & 4H BUILDING. (ST-WIDE). P E STANSELL, CHRMN; FREMONT COUNTY 4H FAIR ASSOC; C/O 810 PINE AVE; CANON CITY, CO 81212. (#4110-1).

OCT 1, '76 - APR 1, '77. ENTERTAINMENT INC CONCERT SERIES. STAGE PRODUCTION ONLY. ALL EVENTS BOOKED OUT OF DENVER. 4 OR 5 PER SEASON. AT WASHINGTON SCHOOL AUDITORIUM. (LOCAL). P E STANSELL; CANON CITY '76 COMMISSION; CANON CITY FINE ARTS ASSOC; C/O 810 PINE AVE; CANON CITY, CO 81212. (#4111-1).

NOV 11 - 12, '76. MCKINLEY SCHOOL CENTENNIAL-BICENTENNIAL MELODRAMA. LIVE PERFORMANCE AT MCKINLEY SCHOOL AUDITORIUM, 1240 MCKINLEY AVE. (LOCAL). P E STANSELL, CHAIRMAN; MCKINLEY SCHOOL; 810 PINE AVE; CANON CITY, CO 81212. (#108678-2).

CARBONDALE

'THE BALLAD OF BABY DOE'. LIVE PERFORMANCE. (LOCAL). RICHARD A FLEWELLING, MGR; TOWN OF CARBONDALE; BOX 86; CARBONDALE, CO 81623. (#25760-1).

CASCADE

BEAUTIFICATION PROJ - CASCADE, CO. BEAUTIFY THE AREA BY CLEANING IT UP AND PLANTING RED, WHITE AND BLUE PETUNIAS THROUGHOUT THE TOWN. (LOCAL). PAT KUPKO, CHAIRPERSON; CASCADE WOMANS CLUB; CASCADE, CO 80809. (#26168).

BICYCLE TRAIL - CASCADE, CO. A BICYCLE TRAIL IN CASCADE CHAPITA PARK FOR RECREATION AND SAFETY PURPOSES. (LOCAL). MRS STEVE KAPCHINSKE, CHAIRPERSON; CASCADE HOMEOWNERS ASSOC; 4410 MARTINDALE AVE; CASCADE, CO 80809. (#26167).

HISTORIC LANDMARKS, CASCADE, CO. THE 100 YR OLD EASTHOME HOTEL, THE LAND OFFICE, STATION MASTER'S HOUSE, HOLY ROSARY CHAPEL AND THE PARK PAVILION WILL BE PROVIDED WITH BRASS PLAQUES. (ST-WIDE). ANNIE LEE ROSS, CHAIRPERSON; CASCADE HOME OWNERS ASSOC; CASCADE, CO 80809. (#26163).

RESTORATION OF TOWN PAVILION - CASCADE, CO. VOLUNTEER FIRE DEPT AND UTE PASS ELEMENTARY SCHOOL WILL RESTORE THE TOWN PAVILION BY SEPT 1, 1976. (LOCAL). ANNE FOSTER, CHAIRPERSON; CASCADE FIRE DEPT & UTE PASS ELEMENTARY SCHOOL; CASCADE, CO 80809. (#26165).

UTE INDIAN TRAIL - CASCADE, CO. RESTORATION & MARKING THE UTE INDIAN TRAIL FROM MANITOU SPGS TO CASCADE, CHIPITA PARK BY BOY SCOUTS AND EXPLORERS. (ST-WIDE). JAN PETTIT, COORDINATOR; BOY SCOUTS & EXPLORERS; CASCADE, CO 80809. (#26162).

JULY 18 - AUG 8, '76. COUNTRY FAIR & ICE CREAM SOCIAL. FAIR, FESTIVAL AT PAVILION, CASCADE PARK AT HOLY ROSARY CHAPEL. (ST-WIDE). DEE POWER, COORDINATOR; CASCADE WOMEN'S CLUB; CASCADE, CO 80809. (#108694-1).

CASTLE ROCK

CASTLE ROCK CENTENNIAL PARK - CASTLE ROCK, CO. TENNIS COURT, PICNIC AREA, PLAYGROUND & BALLFIELD ARE THE PLANNED FACILITIES. (LOCAL). A C HALL, CHAIRMAN; CASTLE ROCK CHAMBER OF COMMERCE; PO BOX 282; CASTLE ROCK, CO 80104. (#24628).

CLASS OF '76 FLAG - CASTLE ROCK, CO. THE FLAG WILL BE RED, WHITE AND BLUE AND WILL BE SIGNED BY EVERY CLASS MEMBER; IT WILL BE USED AT HOMECOMING AND AT GRADUATION. (LOCAL). PAULINE HODGES, CHAIRPERSON; DOUGLAS COUNTY CENTENNIAL-BICENTENNIAL COMMITTEE; CASTLE ROCK, CO 80104. (#20616).

DISPLAY CASES - CASTLE ROCK, CO. DISPLAY CASES WILL BE SET UP IN THE DOUGLAS COUNTY PUBLIC LIBRARY TO DISPLAY HISTORICAL RELICS. (LOCAL). PAULINE HODGES, CHAIRPERSON; DOUGLAS COUNTY CENTENNIAL-BICENTENNIAL COMMITTEE; 417 JERRY ST, #304; CASTLE ROCK, CO 80104. (#20615).

PICTURES OF COUNTY OFFICIALS - CASTLE ROCK, CO. PICTURES OF PAST ELECTED OFFICIALS WILL BE HUNG IN THE COURTHOUSE. (LOCAL). PAULINE HODGES, CHAIRPERSON; DOUGLAS COUNTY CENTENNIAL-BICENTENNIAL COMMITTEE; CASTLE ROCK, CO 80104. (#20618).

PUBLICATION OF DOUGLAS CO HISTORY - CO. WRITINGS OF LOCAL HISTORIANS WILL BE COLLECTED AND COMPILED INTO A BOOK. (LOCAL). PAULINE HODGES, CHAIRMAN; DOUGLAS CO CENTENNIAL-BICENTENNIAL COMMITTEE; 417 JERRY ST, #304; CASTLE ROCK, CO 80104. (#24627).

TREE PLANTING ON COURTHOUSE LAWN - CASTLE ROCK, CO. BEAUTIFICATION OF LAWN IN FRONT OF THIS HISTORIC BUILDING. (LOCAL). PAULINE HODGES, CHAIRPERSON; DOUGLAS COUNTY CENTENNIAL-BICENTENNIAL COMMITTEE; CASTLE ROCK, CO 80104. (#20617).

FEB 9 - 13, '76. CENTENNIAL-BICENTENNIAL WEEK. EXHIBIT AT CASTLE ROCK JUNIOR HIGH SCHOOL. (LOCAL). MARGE MCDONALD, COORD; CASTLE ROCK JUNIOR HIGH SCHOOL; 7677 S DATURA CIR; LITTLETON, CO 80120. (#200007-24).

FEB 9 - 13, '76. COSTUME CONTEST - RED, WHITE & BLUE DAY. COMPETITION. (LOCAL). MARGE MCDONALD, TEACHER; DOUGLAS COUNTY JUNIOR HIGH SCHOOL; HIGH SCHOOL RD; CASTLE ROCK, CO 80104. (#107436-5).

FEB 9 - 13, '76. PHOTOGRAPHY CONTEST. REPRESENT THE HISTORY OF COLORADO AND/OR THE U S THROUGH PICTURES. (LOCAL). MARGE MCDONALD, TEACHER; DOUGLAS COUNTY JUNIOR HIGH SCHOOL; HIGH SCHOOL RD; CASTLE ROCK, CO 80104. (#107436-4).

FEB 9 - 13, '76. POSTER CONTEST. DESIGN POSTERS TO REPRESENT THE HISTORY OF COLORADO AND/OR THE U S. (LOCAL). MARGE MCDONALD, TEACHER; DOUGLAS COUNTY JUNIOR HIGH SCHOOL; HIGH SCHOOL RD; CASTLE ROCK, CO 80104. (#107436-3).

FEB 9 - 13, '76. THEME, POETRY & MUSIC CONTEST. REPRESENT OUR HISTORY AND WHAT IT MEANS TO BE AN AMERICAN THROUGH ESSAYS, POEMS AND MUSIC. (LOCAL). MARGE MCDONALD, TEACHER; DOUGLAS COUNTY JUNIOR HIGH SCHOOL; HIGH SCHOOL RD; CASTLE ROCK, CO 80104. (#107436-2).

JULY 4, '76. OLD-FASHIONED SMOKEY HILL DAYS. AN OLD-FASHIONED CELEBRATION OF THE 4TH OF JULY TO BE HELD ON THE OLD SMOKY HILL TRAIL WITH FUN FOR ALL AGES; PONY EXPRESS, RACES AND GREASED PIG CONTEST. (LOCAL). LEROY R NITSCH, V-PRES; DOUGLAS COUNTY JAYCEES; 567 S LAKEGULCH RD; CASTLE ROCK, CO 80104. (#107436-1).

CEDAREDGE

JUNE 25 - 27, '76. EDGE OF THE CEDARS ART FESTIVAL. ART FESTIVAL FOR DELTA COUNTY ARTISTS ONLY. JURIED SHOW OPEN TO THE PUBLIC WITH SEVERAL MEDIAS REPRESENTED. ART WORKS WILL BE ON SALE. AT HUNSICKER SCHOOL ALL-PURPOSE ROOM, N MAIN ST, CEDAREDGE. (LOCAL). MARY LOU HUERKAMP, COORD; ZETA OMICRON CHAPTER, EPSILON SIGMA ALPHA INTERNATIONAL SORORITY; PO BOX 65; AUSTIN, CO 81410. (#107156-1).

JULY 3, '76. CENTENNIAL-BICENTENNIAL FIREWORKS DISPLAY. FESTIVAL AT HART'S BASIN AT ANTELOPE HILL OFF HIGHWAY 65. (LOCAL). THOMAS H HUERKAMP, CHMN; SURFACE CREEK VALLEY CENTENNIAL-BICENTENNIAL COMMITTEE; PO BOX 65; AUSTIN, CO 81410. (#107156-3).

JULY 3, '76. SURFACE CREEK VALLEY CENTENNIAL-BICENTENNIAL SWEETHEART. BEAUTY PAGEANT FOR LADIES 60 YEARS AND OLDER; ENTRANTS MUST WEAR PERIOD COSTUMES AND WILL BE ACCOMPANIED BY MUSIC PERFORMED BY SENIOR CITIZENS. AT CEDAREDGE PARK, W CEDAR MESA ST. (LOCAL). JAN FAGAN, CHAIRMAN; SURFACE CREEK VALLEY CENTENNIAL-BICENTENNIAL COMMITTEE; PO BOX 91; CEDAREDGE, CO 81413. (#107156-2).

JULY 9 - 11, '76. LITTLE BRITCHES RODEO. ONE OF THE OLDEST LITTLE BRITCHES RODEO'S IN THE NATION; ENTRIES WILL RIDE

CEDAREDGE — CONTINUED

BAREBACK, ROPE CALVES, RIDE WILD BULLS, SADDLE BRONC AND MILK WILD COWS. AT CEDAREDGE RODEO GROUNDS, E CEDAR MESA ST. (LOCAL). DON CRAMER, COORDINATOR; SURFACE CREEK VALLEY FESTIVAL ASSOC; PO BOX 494; CEDAREDGE, CO 81413. (#107156-5).

JULY 9 - 11, '76. PARADE, BAR-B-QUE, FIREWORKS. FAIR, PARADE, LIVE PERFORMANCE. (LOCAL). HON ED MARAH, MAYOR; TOWN OF CEDAREDGE; BOX 396; CEDAREDGE, CO 81413. (#108862-1).

JULY 10, '76. LIONS CLUB PANCAKE BREAKFAST. THE PANCAKE BREAKFAST WILL BE THE KICKOFF TO THE DAY'S EVENTS. (LOCAL). DONALD PETERSON, COORD; SURFACE CREEK LIONS CLUB; RT 1, BOX 116A; CEDAREDGE, CO 81413. (#107156-4).

JULY 10, '76. SURFACE CREEK VALLEY FESTIVAL ASSOC BARBEQUE. LOCAL SENIOR CITIZENS WILL BE GUESTS; BOOTHS AND GAMES WILL BE SET UP. AT CEDAREDGE PARK, W CEDAR MESA ST. (LOCAL). DON CRAMER, COORDINATOR; SURFACE CREEK VALLEY FESTIVAL ASSOC; PO BOX 494; CEDAREDGE, CO 81413. (#107156-6).

JULY 10, '76. SURFACE CREEK VALLEY FESTIVAL CENTENNIAL-BICENTENNIAL PARADE. PARADE ENTRIES ARE DRAWN FROM ENTIRE COUNTY; FEATURES WILL BE SENIOR CITIZENS IN VINTAGE TRANSPORTATION. AT STARTS AT HIGH SCHOOL, DOWN 5TH ST TO CEDAR MESA, SOUTH ON MAIN. (LOCAL). DONALD PETERSON, COORD; SURFACE CREEK LIONS CLUB; RT 1, BOX 116A; CEDAREDGE, CO 81413. (#107156-7).

AUG 1, '76. PARADE, BARBEQUE AND FIREWORKS. FAIR, PARADE. (LOCAL). HON ED MARAH, MAYOR; TOWN OF CEDAREDGE; BOX 396; CEDAREDGE, CO 81413. (#108955-20).

CENTER

SAGUACHE COUNTY HEAD START PROGRAM OF COLORADO. BUILDING A COMMUNITY CENTER FOR CIVIC, RECREATION, BUSINESS & LOCAL PURPOSES. FACILITY WILL BE MULTI-PURPOSE, FROM EDUCATION TO PUBLIC MEETINGS. (LOCAL). G D BARRANTE, EXEC DIRECTOR; SAGUACHE COUNTY COMMUNITY COUNCIL; BOX 574; CENTER, CO 81125. (#1993). **ARBA GRANTEE.**

CENTRAL CITY

AMERICAN OPERA FESTIVAL IN COLORADO. COMMISSION, PRODUCE AND WORLD PREMIERE NEW OPERA WESTERN AMERICANA THEME BY A MAJOR AMERICAN COMPOSER TO BE PRESENTED DURING 1976 FESTIVAL WITH 'BALLAD OF BABY DOE' AND 3RD MAJOR AMERICAN WORK. (REGN'L). ROBERT F LOTITO, EXEC DIRECTOR; CENTRAL CITY OPERA HOUSE ASSOC; 910 16TH ST; DENVER, CO 80202. (#4290). **ARBA GRANTEE.**

CENTRAL CITY CENTENNIAL PARK, COLO. TO DEVELOP IN HONOR OF AND NAMED FOR COLORADO'S CENTENNIAL. (LOCAL). RICHARD HICKS, CHAIRMAN; CENTRAL CITY CENTENNIAL-BICENTENNIAL ASSOC; BOX 361; CENTRAL CITY, CO 80427. (#4157). **(??).**

INTERNATIONAL FESTIVAL. MUSIC, DANCING, CUISINE AND CRAFTS OF ALL COLORADO ETHNIC GROUPS; THERE WILL ALSO BE A LIVE SHOW ON COLORADO FASHION IN THE OPERA HOUSE. (LOCAL). B BRANNON, PROJ DIR; INTERNATIONAL FESTIVAL COMMITTEE; PO BOX 247; CENTRAL CITY, CO 80427. (#108675-1).

PIONEERS MONUMENT IN CENTRAL CITY, COLO. ERECTED ON CITY DONATED LAND-A MONUMENT OF NATIVE STONE, WITH TOWN'S HISTORIC BELL & FLAGPOLE. WILL BE DEDICATED TO MEMORY OF THE PIONEERS WHO DEVELOPED CENTRAL CITY. (LOCAL). RICHARD HICKS, CHAIRMAN; CENTRAL CITY CENTENNIAL-BICENTENNIAL ASSOC; BOX 361; CENTRAL CITY, CO 80427. (#4156). **(??).**

RESTORATION OF CENTRAL CITY OPERA HOUSE, COLORADO. THIS PROJECT PROVIDES FOR AN INTERIM CONSULTATION FOR THE RESTORATION OF OPERA HOUSE CEILING ARCH AND TELLER LAD OFFICE. THE OPERA ASSOC IS COMMISSIONING AN OPERA ESPECIALLY FOR CBC IN '76. (ST-WIDE). ED WHITE PROJECT CHAIRMAN; LITTLE KINGDOM HISTORICAL FOUNDATION; CENTRAL CITY, CO 80207. (#4389).

RESTORATION OF WASHINGTON HALL, CENTRAL CITY, CO. RESTORATION OF WASHINGTON HALL, THE OLDEST PUBLIC BUILDING IN COLORADO. (LOCAL). JOHN H O'CONNOR, PROJ DIRECTOR; CITY OF CENTRAL CITY; 117 EUREKA; CENTRAL CITY, CO 80427. (#19503).

AUG 4, '75. COLORADO DAY DINNER. DRAMA OF THE HIGHLIGHTS OF AUNT CLARA BROWNS LIFE, SHE WAS THE FIRST BLACK PIONEER. AT TELLER HOUSE. (LOCAL). RICHARD HICKS, CHRMN; CENTRAL CITY CENT-BICENT ASSOCIATION; BOX 361; CENTRAL CITY, CO 80427. (#4159-1).

DEC 31, '75. NEW YEAR'S EVE TURN-OF-THE CENTURY BALL. DANCING FROM 9 PM TO MIDNIGHT; AT MIDNIGHT: DYNAMITE BLASTS, RINGING OF ALL CHURCH BELLS, FIREWORKS, ILLUMINATION OF CENTRAL CITY HISTORIC MONUMENTS. AT BELVIDERE THEATER, MAIN ST. (LOCAL). RICHARD HICKS, CHMN; CENTRAL CITY CHAPTER OF THE ELKS/CENTENNIAL-BICENTENNIAL COMMITTEE; BOX 361; CENTRAL CITY, CO 80427. (#18526-1).

JAN 31, '76. CHINESE NEW YEAR CELEBRATION. SALUTE TO THE CHINESE CONTRIBUTIONS IN EARLY COLORADO MINING CAMPS. CHINESE DINNER AT 6 PM WITH AUTHENTIC MUSIC AND DECORATIONS; PERFORMANCE OF SHIN-GO-JU-RYU, ART OF SELF-DEFENSE IN DANCE FORM BY THE AMERICAN JUDO COLLEGE OF DENVER AT 8 PM. AT BELVIDERE THEATER, MAIN ST. (LOCAL). RICHARD HICKS, CHMN; CENTRAL CITY CENTENNIAL-BICENTENNIAL COMMITTEE; BOX 361; CENTRAL CITY, CO 80427. (#18526-2).

FEB 28, '76. CENTENNIAL MARDI GRAS. COSTUMES WITH CENTENNIAL-BICENTENNIAL THEMES, ENTERTAINMENT, CONTESTS, DANCING AND PRIZES. AT TOLL GATE, MAIN ST. (LOCAL). RICHARD HICKS, CHMN; CENTRAL CITY CENTENNIAL-BICENTENNIAL COMMITTEE; BOX 361; CENTRAL CITY, CO 80427. (#18526-3).

MAR 13, '76. ELKS CENTENNIAL BALL. OPEN TO ALL; DANCING FROM 9 TIL 2; DANCING CONTEST TO SELECT CENTENNIAL COUPLE AND ANNIVERSARY COUPLE OF '76. AT ELKS HALL, MAIN ST. (LOCAL). RICHARD HICKS, CHMN; CENTRAL CITY CHAPTER OF ELKS/CENTENNIAL-BICENTENNIAL COMMITTEE; BOX 361; CENTRAL CITY, CO 80427. (#18526-4).

APR 17, '76. TURNOVER BALL. SALUTE TO THE GERMAN CONTRIBUTION IN EARLY COLORADO MINING CAMP; DANCING FROM 9 TIL 2; GERMAN FAMILY BAND PLAYING WALTZES, POLKAS, SQUARE AND ROUND DANCES. AT BELVIDERE THEATER, MAIN ST. (LOCAL). RICHARD HICKS, CHMN; CENTRAL CITY CENTENNIAL-BICENTENNIAL COMMITTEE; BOX 361; CENTRAL CITY, CO 80427. (#18526-5).

MAY 8 - 9, '76. GREGORY DAY CELEBRATION. HONORING GREGORY WHO DISCOVERED GOLD IN CENTRAL CITY IN 1859 AND STARTED 'RUSH TO THE ROCKIES' SEARCH FOR GOLD. PARADE-STREET EVENT. AT CITYWIDE. (LOCAL). RICHARD HICKS, CHRMN; CENTRAL CITY CENTENNIAL-BICENTENNIAL COMMITTEE; BOX 361; CENTRAL CITY, CO 80427. (#4120-1).

JUNE 10 - SEPT 6, '76. TELLER HOUSE HOTEL AND OPERA HOUSE TOURS. TOUR AT TELLER HOUSE & OPERA HOUSE. (LOCAL). DAVID EITEMILLER, ASST; CENTRAL CITY OPERA HOUSE ASSOC; 910 16TH ST, SUITE 636; DENVER, CO 80202. (#108643-1).

JUNE 19, '76. SIDEWALK ART FAIR. ALL DAY SIDEWALK ART FAIR; PAINTING, SCULPTURE, CRAFTS, PHOTOGRAPHY. OPEN TO ALL ARTISTS; AWARDS IN ALL CATEGORIES & FOR BEST CENTENNIALBICENTENNIAL THEMES. AT MAIN, EUREKA AND LAWRENCE ST. (LOCAL). RICHARD HICKS, CHMN; CENTRAL CITY CENTENNIAL-BICENTENNIAL COMMITTEE; BOX 361; CENTRAL CITY, CO 80427. (#18526-8).

JULY 1 - AUG 31, '76. FESTIVAL OF AMERICAN OPERA & MUSIC & SPECIAL EVENTS. 20TH ANNIVERSARY PRODUCTION OF 'THE BALLAD OF BABY DOE', MOST NOTED OF AMERICAN OPERAS, FIRST COMMISSIONED BY CENTRAL CITY OPERA. MATINEES AT 2:30PM & TOURS OF THE OPERA HOUSE FROM 10:00AM TO 4:00PM. (REGN'L). ROBERT F LOTITO, EXEC DIR; CENTRAL CITY OPERA HOUSE ASSOC; 910 16TH ST, SUITE 636; DENVER, CO 80202. (#108675-2).

JULY 4, '76. CENTENNIAL FIREWORKS. FESTIVAL. (LOCAL). B BRANNON, COORD; CENTRAL CITY BICENTENNIAL ASSOC; PO BOX 247; CENTRAL CITY, CO 80427. (#108643-2).

JULY 4, '76. INDEPENDENCE DAY FESTIVAL. GAMES AND EVENTS FOR ALL AGES FROM 10 AM TIL 5 PM; STREET DANCE AT 8 PM; FIREWORKS AT 9 PM. AT MAIN ST. (LOCAL). RICHARD HICKS, CHMN; CENTRAL CITY CENTENNIAL-BICENTENNIAL COMMITTEE; BOX 361; CENTRAL CITY, CO 80427. (#18526-9).

JULY 17 - 18, '76. WALKING TOURS OF CENTRAL CITY HISTORIC HOMES & BUILDINGS. TOURS OF INTERESTING HOMES & BUILDINGS RARELY SEEN BY VISITORS. COSTUMED HOSTESSES WILL RECEIVE & GIVE COMMENTARY AT EACH LOCATION. INCLUDED ARE MASONIC HALL AND ODD FELLOWS LODGE. (LOCAL). RICHARD HICKS, CHMN; CENTRAL CITY CENTENNIAL-BICENTENNIAL COMMITTEE; BOX 361; CENTRAL CITY, CO 80427. (#18526-10).

AUG 1, '76. COLORADO DAY: 100 YEARS OF STATEHOOD. PARADE OF BANDS & FLOATS WITH HISTORIC & ETHNIC THEMES AT 2 PM; CITY HALL DEDICATION AT 5 PM; DINNER AT TELLER HOUSE AT 6 PM; SPEAKER IS CENTRAL CITY HISTORIAN, JUDGE LEW CARTER. AT TELLER HOUSE. (LOCAL). RICHARD HICKS, CHMN; CENTRAL CITY CENTENNIAL-BICENTENNIAL COMMITTEE; BOX 361; CENTRAL CITY, CO 80427. (#18526-11).

AUG 2, '76. ETHNIC FESTIVAL. MUSIC, DANCING, CUISINE AND CRAFTS OF ALL COLORADO ETHNIC GROUPS; LIVE SHOW OF COLORADO FASHION IN THE OPERA HOUSE AT 2 PM. (LOCAL). RICHARD HICKS, CHMN; CENTRAL CITY CENTENNIAL-BICENTENNIAL COMMITTEE; BOX 361; CENTRAL CITY, CO 80427. (#18526-12).

AUG 2, '76 - CONTINUING . DRAMATIZATION OF EVENTS IN THE LIFE OF AUNT CLARA BROWN. DRAMA BY EDEN THEATRICAL WORKSHOP ABOUT THE LIFE OF BLACK PIONEER AUNT CLARA BROWN. PERFORMANCE WILL BE DONE WITH CHORAL BRIDGES AND WILL BE HELD IN THE CHURCH THAT AUNT CLARA BROWN HELPED BUILD. AT ST JAMES METHODIST CHURCH, EUREKA ST - ON & OFF STREET PARKING. (ST-WIDE). RICHARD HICKS, CHMN; CENTRAL CITY CENTENNIAL-BICENTENNIAL COMMITTEE; BOX 361; CENTRAL CITY, CO 80427. (#18526-17).

AUG 21, '76. LOU BUNCH DAY. LOU BUNCH, MOST RENOWNED OF CENTRAL CITY'S MADAMS, AND HER GIRL REIGN SUPREME; BED RACE ON MAIN ST AT 4 PM; MADAMS AND MINERS BALL AT TELLER HOUSE AT 9 PM WITH GRAND MARCH TO SELECT & PRESENT TROPHIES TO MADAM OF THE YEAR & GIRL OF THE YEAR. AT TELLER HOUSE. (LOCAL). RICHARD HICKS, CHMN; CENTRAL CITY CENTENNIAL-BICENTENNIAL COMMITTEE; BOX 361; CENTRAL CITY, CO 80427. (#18526-13).

SEPT 11, '76. TOMMY KNOCKER DAY. CELEBRATION HONORING WELSH & CORNISH CONTRIBUTIONS TO THE OLD MINING CAMP; 100 YEAR OLD CUSTOMS & TRADITIONS: ROCK DRILLING CONTEST, HOSE CART RACE, PASTIE SUPPER & WELSH CHOIR. TOMMY KNOCKERS WERE CREATURES OF SUPERSTITION, GREMLINS OF THE MINES. (LOCAL). RICHARD HICKS, CHMN; CENTRAL CITY CENTENNIAL-BICENTENNIAL COMMITTEE; BOX 361; CENTRAL CITY, CO 80427. (#18526-14).

OCT 2, '76. PAT CASEY DAY. PAT CASEY, OUTSTANDING IRISH PERSONALITY OF EARLY CENTRAL CITY, STRUCK IT RICH AFTER ESTABLISHING BAUDY REPUTATION. PUBLIC PROCESSION ALONG CASEY'S ROUTE LED BY BAGPIPERS; IRISH DINNER & EXHIBIT AT 6 PM. AT BELVIDERE THEATER, MAIN ST. (LOCAL). RICHARD HICKS, CHMN; CENTRAL CITY CENTENNIAL-BICENTENNIAL COMMITTEE; BOX 361; CENTRAL CITY, CO 80427. (#18526-15).

DEC 11, '76. WINTERSHIRE CENTENNIAL BALL. ANNUAL WINTERSHIRE BALL; SPECIAL CENTENNIAL YEAR ENDING. DANCING FROM 9 TIL 2; CORONATION OF THE FIRST WINTERSHIRE KING AND QUEEN OF THE NEW CENTURY. AT BELVIDERE THEATER, MAIN ST. (LOCAL). RICHARD HICKS, CHMN; CENTRAL CITY CENTENNIAL-BICENTENNIAL COMMITTEE; BOX 361; CENTRAL CITY, CO 80427. (#18526-16).

CHERRY VALLEY

JULY 28, '75. CENTENNIAL BICENTENNIAL BARBECUE. FESTIVAL. (LOCAL). GEO OHLMAN, COORD; DOUGLAS CO CENTENNIAL BICENTENNIAL COMMITTEE; FRANKTOWN, CO 80116. (#200007-198).

CHEYENNE WLS

JULY 4, '76. 4TH OF JULY FIREWORKS. FESTIVAL. (LOCAL). ELIZABETH E GILBERT, DIR; 4TH OF JULY FIREWORKS COMMITTEE; 151 S 1ST W; CHEYENNE WLS, CO 80816. (#108639-1).

CHIPITA PARK

BEAUTIFY & CLEANUP OF CHIPITA PARK, CO. BEAUTIFICATION OF THE AREA BY CLEANING UP AND PLANTING RED, WHITE & BLUE PETUNIAS IN PUBLIC AND PRIVATE PLACES. (LOCAL). KATY SPILLANE, CHAIRPERSON; CHIPITA PARK HOMEOWNERS ASSOC; 8955 CHIPITA PARK RD; CHIPITA PARK, CO 80811. (#24949).

FILMS ON HISTORIC UTE PASS, CO. OLD FILMS ON UTE PASS, CHIPITA PARK, CASCADE & GREEN MOUNTAIN FALLS WILL BE COLLECTED, STORED AND SHOWN. (LOCAL). LOUIS G FEIL, PRESIDENT; CHIPITA PARK HOMEOWNERS ASSOC; 8955 CHIPITA PARK RD; CHIPITA PARK, CO 80811. (#24948).

SCRAPBOOKS CHIPITA PARK, CO. SCRAPBOOKS WITH NEWSPAPER ARTICLES AND PHOTOGRAPHS PORTRAYING HISTORY OF CASCADE, CHIPITA PARK, GREEN MOUNTAIN FALLS & UTE PASS WILL BE MADE & PLACED IN THE LIBRARY OR MUSEUM. (LOCAL). GERTRUDE GILL, SECRETARY; CHIPITA PARK HOMEOWNERS ASSOC; TIMPA RD; CHIPITA PARK, CO 88011. (#24950).

JUNE 30 - SEPT 25, '76. FILMS ON HISTORIC UTE PASS - FROM 1860 TO PRESENT. EXHIBIT AT NARCROFT HALL, UTE PASS SCHOOL, CHIPITA RD. (LOCAL). LOUIS G FEIL, COORD; CHIPITA PARK HOMEOWNERS ASSOC; 8955 CHIPITA PARK RD; CHIPITA PARK, CO 80811. (#107026-1).

JULY 1 - 11, '76. PIONEER ROOM WITH ANTIQUES & RELATED ITEMS. EXHIBIT AT CHIPITA PARK LODGE, CHIPITA RD. (LOCAL). MARY LOUISE HOEGH, CHMN; CHIPITA PARK HOMEOWNERS ASSOC; 5620 TIMPA RD; CHIPITA PARK, CO 80811. (#106828-1).

JULY 15 - 19, '76. ARTS AND CRAFTS EXHIBIT. EXHIBIT. (LOCAL). MARY LOUISE HAEGH; TOWN OF CHIPITA PARK; 5620 TIMPA RD; CHIPITA PARK, CO 80811. (#108860-1).

COAL CREEK

JUNE 5, '76. CLEANING & REPAIRING COMMUNITY BUILDINGS. REPAINT COMMUNITY BLDG & REPLACE BROKEN WINDOWS. (LOCAL). RUTH FRANKLIN, CHMN; CITY OF COAL CREEK; PO BOX 36; COAL CREEK, CO 81221. (#200007-27).

JULY 3, '76. SENIOR CITIZEN AWARD-FIREWORKS. ORGANIZED GAMES FOR CHILDREN; AWARDS TO BE GIVEN TO ELDEST MALE AND FEMALE CITIZENS; TALKS FROM SENIOR CITIZENS; FIREWORKS IN THE EVENING. (LOCAL). RUTH FRANKLIN, COORD; TOWN COUNCIL; PO BOX 36; COAL CREEK, CO 81221. (#108638-1).

AUG 1, '76. ARTS FESTIVAL & COMMUNITY PICNIC. TOWN INVITED TO DISPLAY ALL ARTS; AWARDS TO BE GIVEN (YOUTH AND ADULT) AT COMMUNITY PICNIC. (LOCAL). RUTH FRANKLIN, DIRECTOR; TOWN OF COAL CREEK; PO BOX 36; COAL CREEK, CO 81221. (#108955-21).

COKEDALE

HISTORY OF COKEDALE BROCHURE; CO. A BROCHURE ON COKEDALE'S PAST AS A MINING & COKE PRODUCING TOWN. (LOCAL). MRS MONA HENNIGH, PUBLICITY CHAIRMAN; TOWN OF COKEDALE; COKEDALE, CO 81032. (#24364).

RESTORATION & BEAUTIFICATION PROJECT, COKEDALE, CO. PROJECT INCLUDES RENOVATION OF HISTORICAL BUILDINGS & BEAUTIFICATION OF THE TOWN. (LOCAL). MRS HARRY HENNIGH, PROJ DIRECTOR; TOWN OF COKEDALE, INC; COKEDALE, CO 81082. (#20528).

JUNE 26 - 27, '76. BUGGY NUTS GET TOGETHER. ON SATURDAY THERE WILL BE COUNTRY DRIVING & PICNIC; ON SUNDAY, COMPETITION DRIVING & JUDGING, AND A PARADE. AT BASEBALL AREA. (LOCAL). GARRY COULTER, COORD; TOWN OF COKEDALE; COKEDALE, CO 81032. (#107033-1).

COKEDALE — CONTINUED

AUG 7 - 8, '76. ARTS & CRAFTS FAIR. FAIR AT ELM ST BETWEEN OLD MERCANTILE, BOARDING HOUSE & SHOWERHOUSE. (LOCAL). MRS L WOODWARD, COORD; TOWN OF COKEDALE; COKEDALE, CO 81032. (#107033-2).

AUG 15, '76. REUNION & BARBEQUE FOR EARLY SETTLERS AND RESIDENTS. FESTIVAL AT TOWN PARK, SPRUCE & PINE STS. (LOCAL). JOHN JOHNSON; TOWN OF COKEDALE; PO BOX 244; COKEDALE, CO 81032. (#108716-1).

COLLBRAN

JULY 3 - 5, '76. 4TH OF JULY CELEBRATION. EVENTS FOR WEEKEND INCLUDE FLAG RAISING CEREMONY, PARADE, 4-H FAIR, LIONS CLUB BAR-B-CUE & DANCE; SUNDAY: CHURCH SERVICE, HORSE SHOW & GYMKHANA. (LOCAL). HOWARD E BRANSON; CITY OF COLLBRAN; CITY HALL; COLLBRAN, CO 81624. (#108637-1).

COLONA

RESTORATION OF BECKWITH GRAVE, COLONA, CO. THE FENCING & RESTORATION OF BECKWITH GRAVE IN COLONA CEMETERY. (LOCAL). CARA MILLER, PROJ DIRECTOR; PRIDE OF THE ROCKIES 4-H CLUB; RTE 2, BOX 263; MONTROSE, CO 81401. (#16395).

COLORADO CITY

JULY 2 - 5, '76. COLORADO CITY CELEBRATION. FRIDAY - DANCE; SAT MORNING - PARADE FROM RYE TO COLORADO CITY, SAT EVENING - DANCE, MIDNIGHT - FIREWORKS; SUNDAY - ALL DENOMINATIONAL CHURCH SERVICE AT FOOTBALL FIELD, NOON - BAR-B-Q, AFTERNOON - GAMES, FIREWORKS AT DUSK; MONDAY - GAMES AND CLEANUP. AT MERBISC CENTER. (LOCAL). MEL HARMON, COORD; COLORADO CITY; PUEBLO ARMY DEPOT; PUEBLO, CO 81003. (#108642-1).

COLORADO SPG

AMERICAN ARCHITECTURE THROUGH CHURCHES - CO. THIS IS A MULTI-MEDIA PRESENTATION WITH PICTURES, SLIDES & CASSETTES OF HISTORIC CHURCHES IN AMERICA AND OUTSTANDING MODERN CHURCHES TO ILLUSTRATE AMERICAN ARCHITECTURE. (LOCAL). PROF ROGER M WILLIAMS, PROJ DIRECTOR; NAZARENE BIBLE COLLEGE; 1111 CHAPMAN DRIVE; COLORADO SPG, CO 80930. (#17419).

AMERICANA GALLERY - AMERICAN NUMISMATIC ASSOC. TO PROVIDE DISPLAY CASES TO BE USED AS MEANS TO INSTITUTE PERMANENT EXHIBIT GALLERY USING EXISTING COLLECTIONS NUMISMATIC MATERIAL RELEVANT TO AMERICAN INDEPENDENCE. (NAT'L). EDWARD C ROCHETTE, EXEC DIRECTOR; AMERICAN NUMISMATIC ASSOCIATION; PO BOX 2366; COLORADO SPG, CO 80901. (#4376). **ARBA GRANTEE.**

ARMY DISPLAY OF PICTURES - COLORADO SPRINGS, CO. SERIES OF 15 PICTURES REPRESENTING THE U S ARMY IN ACTION FROM THE REVOLUTIONARY WAR TO PRESENT PRESENTED TO THE FT CARSON MUSEUM. (LOCAL). JUDY SIBERT, PROJ DIRECTOR; FT CARSON OFFICERS WIVES CLUB; FT CARSON, CO 80913. (#14819).

BICENTENNIAL CHARITY GROUP, COLORADO SPG, CO. OLD NEWSPAPERS WILL BE COLLECTED BY VOLUNTEERS & SOLD TO PROCESSORS, REVENUE WILL GO TO WORTHY NON-PROFIT ORGANIZATIONS. (LOCAL). REV (RET) C F FURGUSON; BICENTENNIAL CHARITY GROUP; 321 E MONUMENT ST; COLORADO SPG, CO 80903. (#19508).

BICENTENNIAL COSTUME BALL. LIVE PERFORMANCE. (LOCAL). SYLVIA STOREY, CHMN; THE COLORADO SPRINGS CHORALE GUILD; 6640 MESEDGE DR; COLORADO SPG, CO 80919. (#102320-3).

BICENTENNIAL TOURS IN COLORADO SPRINGS, CO. A SERIES OF WALKING & BUS TOURS SPONSORED BY THE LOCAL BICENTENNIAL COMMITTEE. (LOCAL). SELMA LIEB; PIKES PEAK OR BUST BY 76 CENTENNIAL-BICENTENNIAL COMMITTEE; 332 W BIJOU; COLORADO SPG, CO 80905. (#15965).

BLACK WHO'S WHO IN COLORADO SPRINGS, CO. PUBLISH ANNUAL BOOKLET IDENTIFYING COLO SPGS RESIDENTS, INCLUDING BACKGROUND & ACHIEVEMENT PROFILES & SNAPSHOTS. PROVIDE POSITIVE MINORITY MODELS & ADDED INCENTIVE TO CHILDREN TO ACHIEVE. (LOCAL). JANETTE COLBERT, PROJ DIRECTOR; 356 KENADY CIRCLE; COLORADO SPG, CO 80910. (#14828).

BONFILS THEATRE TOUR - COLORADO QUEST. A SERIES OF DRAMATIC VIGNETTES PRESENTING COLORADO'S HISTORY THROUGH MUSIC, THEATER & DANCE. (ST-WIDE). GLORIA GROTH, CHAIRMAN; FESTIVAL COMMITTEE - PIKES PEAK CENTENNIAL COMMITTEE; 332 W BIJOU; COLORADO SPG, CO 80905. (#14804).

BUS TOUR OF HISTORIC BUILDINGS IN COLORADO SPG, CO. BUS TOUR OF METRO AREA TO POINT OUT HISTORIC BUILDINGS & POINTS OF INTEREST IN CITY'S DEVELOPMENT. (LOCAL). MS RHODA D WILCOX, COORDINATOR; LANDMARKS PRESERVATION COUNCIL; 1620 E CACHE LE POUDRE; COLORADO SPG, CO 80909. (#8907).

CATALOGUE OF BICENTENNIAL COINS & MEDALS. A COMPREHENSIVE CATALOGUE RELATING TO THE INDEPENDENCE PERIOD 1776 TO 1783, THE CENTENNIAL 1876, AND THE BICENTENNIAL 1976. (NAT'L). E C ROCHETTE, EXEC DIRECTOR; AMERICAN NUMISMATIC ASSOC; 818 N CASCADE; COLORADO SPRG, CO 80903. (#8602).

CCBC SELF GUIDED HISTORY TOURS OF COLORADO. STATEWIDE SYSTEM OF SELFGUIDED HISTORICAL TOURS TO ALL CBC SITES BY ALL MODES OF TRAVEL INCL WALKING, DRIVING, BACKBACK & RECREATIONAL VEHICLES. ALL SEASONS. GROUP OR INDIVIDUALS, PRIVATE OR COMMERCIAL. (ST-WIDE). DAVID HUGHES, PRESIDENT; ENJOY COLORADO; 332 W BIJOU ST; COLORADO SPGS, CO 80903. (#1322). **(??).**

'CELEBRATE '76' - COLORADO SPRINGS, CO. GATHERING THE RESOURCES AND EXPERIENCE OF THE COMMUNITY TO PRESENT A LIVING HISTORY TO THE STUDENTS OF DISTRICT #11 AS REQUESTED BY THEIR TEACHERS. (LOCAL). BARBARA HOOK, CHAIRMAN; SCHOOL VOLUNTEER SERVICES; 1115 N EL PASO ST; COLORADO SPG, CO 80903. (#24625).

CENTENNIAL CALENDAR FOR COLORADO SPRINGS, CO. A DAYBOOK TYPE CALENDAR WITH ENTRIES CITING HISTORICAL EVENTS FROM THE PIKES PEAK REGION, ALSO INCLUDING HISTORIC PHOTOS SHOWING THE CHANGING SCENES. (LOCAL). DR HARVEY L CARTER, PROJ DIRECTOR; 4 CRAGMOR VILLAGE; COLORADO SPG, CO 80907. (#14816).

CENTENNIAL OPTIMIST CLUB HISTORICAL CALENDAR - CO. FUNDRAISING PROJECT; WILL FEATURE CENTENNIAL PROJECTS & CALENDAR OF EVENTS. (LOCAL). HERB SWING, CHAIRMAN; CENTENNIAL OPTIMISTS CLUB; 7060 RAVEN HILLS PL; COLORADO SPG, CO 80919. (#18511).

CENTER PARKWAY LANDSCAPING PROGRAM - CO. DEVELOPMENT & MAINTENANCE OF 14 MILES OF CENTER PARKWAYS. SPECIAL SECTION OF PARKWAY WILL BE A CENTENNIAL PROJECT. (LOCAL). RICHARD C BUERKLE, DIRECTOR; COLORADO SPRINGS PARKS & RECREATION DEPT; 1400 GLEN AVE; COLORADO SPG, CO 80904. (#15582).

CHURCH ARCHITECTURE IN AMERICA - COLORADO SPRINGS. MULTIMEDIA PRESENTATION ON CHURCH ARCHITECTURE SHOWING DEVELOPMENT OF CHURCH BLDG IN 200 YR OF AMER HISTORY; PHOTOS ENLARGED & MOUNTED WITH A DIMENSIONAL EFFECT. (LOCAL). ROGER WILLIAMS, COORDINATOR; NAZARENE BIBLE COLLEGE; 1220 CHAPMAN DR; COLORADO SPG, CO 80930. (#29665).

COLORADO BALLET COMPANY TOURING PROJECT. PRESENT THROUGHOUT COLORADO PERFORMANCES DEALING WITH COLO NATIVE THEMES: ONE ORIGINAL WORK, ONE BY A GUEST CHOREOGRAPHER, AND A THIRD AMERICAN BALLET. (ST-WIDE). ILSE REESE GAHART, EXEC DIRECTOR; COLORADO BALLET COMPANY; 705 WEST BROOKSIDE ST; COLORADO SPG, CO 80906. (#4364).

COLORADO NATL COMMUNITY SCHOOL INVITATIONAL CONF. THEME HOW WE CAN REVITALIZE THE LITTLE RED SCHOOL HOUSE CONCEPT SPONSORED BY NATL, STATE & LOCAL JAYCEES, PTA, SW REGIONAL CNTR FOR COMMUNITY SCHOOL DEVELOPMENT, AZ & COL STATE UNIV, & COL DEPT OF ED. (ST-WIDE). DAVE MAYNARD, SUPERVISOR, COMMUNITY SCHOOLS; CITY OF COLORADO SPRINGS; 316 N WEBER ST; COLORADO SPG, CO 80902. (#2014).

THE COLORADO OPERA FESTIVAL. NINE PERFORMANCES OF THREE MAJOR OPERATIC PRODUCTIONS BY A RESIDENT PROFESSIONAL COMPANY, GIVEN IN ENGLISH AND ACCOMPANIED BY A FULL ORCHESTRA. (LOCAL). MS JANET SPROUSE, ASST MANAGER; THE COLORADO OPERA FESTIVAL; COLORADO COLLEGE; COLORADO SPG, CO 80903. (#8891).

COLORADO OPERA FESTIVAL. NINE PERFORMANCES OF THREE MAJOR OPERATIC PRODUCTIONS BY A RESIDENT PROFESSIONAL COMPANY, GIVEN IN ENGLISH AND ACCOMPANIED BY A FULL ORCHESTRA. (LOCAL). JANET SPROUSE, COORD; THE COLORADO OPERA FESTIVAL; COLORADO COLLEGE; COLORADO SPG, CO 80903. (#108803-1).

COLORADO SPRINGS MURAL CONTEST. A STATEWIDE CONTEST FOR A MURAL TO BE PLACED ON THE WALL OF THE COLORADO SPRINGS FINE ARTS CENTER. SUBJECT MATTER MUST BE HISTORIC COLORADO. (ST-WIDE). RICHARD H RIXON, DIRECTOR; COLORADO SPRINGS FINE ARTS CENTER; 30 WEST DALE ST; COLORADO SPG, CO 80903. (#4366).

COLORADO SPRINGS HOSTS PARADE OF FLAGS. FORMING PARADE MARCHING GROUP WITH ONE FLAG FROM EACH STATE. (ST-WIDE). ANNIE V AVERY, PROJ COORDINATOR; PETERSON FIELD NCO WIVES; PETERSON FLD, CO 80914. (#9284).

'COLORADO SQUARE', COLORADO SPRINGS, CO. CONSTRUCTION OF $14 MILLION OFFICE TOWER & COMMERICAL COMPLEX IN DOWNTOWN COLORADO SPRINGS. (LOCAL). D C WHITE, PROJ COORDINATOR; OXFORD ANSCHUTZ DEVELOPMENT CO; 633 17TH ST, SUITE 2010; DENVER, CO 80202. (#9273).

COLORADO 100 YEARS - COLORADO SPRINGS, CO. PRODUCE A PHOTOGRAPHIC EXHIBITION BY COLLECTING & REPRODUCING OLD PHOTOGRAPHS OF COLORADO. (ST-WIDE). CRISTOFER PULOS, PROJ DIRECTOR; 2517 WHEELER AVE; COLORADO SPG, CO 80904. (#18512).

COMMEMORATIVE MEDAL, COLORADO SPRINGS, CO. PIKES PEAK BY '76 OR BUST CENTENNIAL-BICENTENNIAL CELEBRATION MEDALAVAILABLE NUMBERED OR UNNUMBERED IN GOLD, GOLD-PLATED, SILVER OR BRONZE. (LOCAL). DAVID R HUGHES, CHAIRMAN; PIKES PEAK BY '76 OR BUST CENTENNIAL-BICENTENNIAL COMMITTEE; 7 N TEJON; COLORADO SPG, CO 80903. (#26374).

COMPOSITION FOR COLORADO SPRINGS SYMPHONY. COMMISSIONED WORK BY COMPOSER HAROLD FARBERMAN & LIBRETTIST NANCY WOOD. DESCRIBES PHILISOPHIES OF THE AMERICAN INDIAN COMMON TO ALL TRIBES. CHARLES ANSBACHER, CONDUCTER. (ST-WIDE). BEATRICE W VRADENBURG, MANAGER; COLORADO SPRINGS SYMPHONY ORCHESTRA ASSOC; PO BOX 1692; COLORADO SPG, CO 80901. (#4280). **ARBA GRANTEE.**

A DECADE OF TREES, BEAUTIFICATION PROJ IN COLORADO. A TREE PLANTING PROGRAM WITH TREES AVAILABLE TO RESIDENTS AT A REASONABLE PRICE FOR BEAUTIFICATION OF THE COMMUNITY. (LOCAL). WILLIAM H STOOKEY, CITY FORESTER; CITY PARK & RECREATION DEPT; 1400 GLEN AVE; COLORADO SPG, CO 80903. (#9259).

DELTA SIGMA THETA SCHOLARSHIP IN COLORADO. SCHOLARSHIP FOR MINORITY HIGH SCHOOL STUDENTS TO ATTEND COLLEGE. (ST-WIDE). MS LINDA YOUNG, PRESIDENT; DELTA SIGMA THETA SORORITY, INC; 155 S ACADEMY BLDG; COLORADO SPG, CO 80910. (#9255).

DOCUMENTARY FILM ON COLORADO SPRINGS, CO. THE PROJECT INVOLVES A FIFTY MINUTE DOCUMENTARY FILM ON THE PIKES PEAK REGION EMPHASIZING COLORADO SPRINGS, ITS HISTORY AND DIRECTIONS THE REGION IS TAKING NOW. (ST-WIDE). PAUL FRANKLIN, PRESIDENT; INTERNATIONAL MEDIA SYSTEMS; 7 E BIJOU ST; COLORADO SPG, CO 80901. (#10512).

EARLY COLORADO CHURCHES & PIONEER PREACHERS, CO. PROJECT IS A HERITAGE PROGRAM OF COLORADO PREACHERS AND EARLY CHURCHES; PROGRAM INCLUDES, DISPLAYS & SLIDES. (ST-WIDE). DR RICHARD SPINDLE, CHAIRMAN; NAZARENE BIBLE COLLEGE; 1111 CHAPMAN DR; COLORADO SPG, CO 80930. (#17433).

EL PASO COMM COLLEGE 'CENTENNIAL' CAMPUS - CO. CONSTRUCTION OF NEW CAMPUS OF CAREER-ORIENTED INSTITUTION. EVENTS & ACTIVITIES ACCOMPANYING THE VARIOUS CONSTRUCTION PHASES WILL BE PLANNED TO INCLUDE APPROPRIATE CENTENNIAL-BICENTENNIAL FOCUS. (LOCAL). HELEN ANDERSON, PUBLIC INFORMATION OFFICER; EL PASO COMMUNITY COLLEGE; 2200 W BOTT; COLORADO SPG, CO 80904. (#14347).

EXPLORING COLORADO RIVERS, COLORADO SPGS, CO. A TEACHING GAME TO HELP CHILDREN LEARN THE STRONG SENSE OF PRIDE AND RESPECT FOR THE EFFORTS OF THE EARLY PIONEERS WHO FIRST EXPLORED COLORADO RIVERS. (LOCAL). PATRICIA ANN PEACOCK, PROJ DIRECTOR; DIST #11 COMMUNITY SCHOOLS; 316 N WEBER ST; COLORADO SPG, CO 80903. (#18510).

FARMERS MARKET IN COLORADO SPRINGS, CO. A LOCAL FARMERS' AND GARDENERS' MARKET WILL BE ESTABLISHED. (LOCAL). PATRICIA M WHITE, MARKET MASTER; COLORADO STATE UNIV EXTENSION SERVICE; 27 VERMIJO AVE; COLORADO SPG, CO 80903. (#14859).

FILMS ON PIKE PEAK REGION OF COLORADO. FILM ACCOUNT OF PIKES PEAK REGION AVAILABLE FOR SALE, LEASE OR DONATION TO AD AGENCIES AND EDUCATIONAL INSTITUTIONS; HISTORICALLY, COMMERICIALLY AND EDUCATIONALLY ENTERTAINING. (LOCAL). J MAX FOWLER, EXEC DIRECTOR; ARKANSAS VALLEY ARTISTS; 111 B ST; PUEBLO, CO 81000. (#9280).

FIVE ART SHOWS BY COLORADO SPG ART GUILD IN 1975. ANNUAL SPRING JURIED SHOW; SUMMER SIDEWALK ART SHOW; 31ST ANNUAL OUTDOOR 'BUY' CENTENNIAL I SHOW; ANNUAL FALL JURIED SHOW; AND FIRST ANNUAL WINTER 'BUY' CENTENNIAL II ART SHOW. (ST-WIDE). DOROTHY N MYERS, PUBLIC RELATIONS; COLORADO SPG ART GUILD, INC; 2016 MT VERNON; COLORADO SPG, CO 80909. (#10165).

'FLIGHT OVER COLORADO' FILM. WIDE SCREEN PANORAMA OF FLIGHT OVER AROUND AND THROUGH THE NATURAL AND MAN-MADE WONDERS OF COLORADO AS SEEN FROM A CAMERA MOUNTED IN THE NOSE OF A LOW FLYING JET PLANE AS DONE IN CINERAMA. (ST-WIDE). JAMES R MORRISON, PRESIDENT; ESPIRIT, INC; 3514 NORTH TEJON ST; COLORADO SPG, CO 80933. (#4281).

FOUNTAIN VALLEY CREEK TRAIL, COLORADO SPRINGS. DEVELOP TRAIL ALONG FOUNTAIN CREEK FROM COLORADO SPGS TO FOUNTAIN, COLORADO; INCLUDING PLANTING, LANDSCAPING AND REST AREAS. (ST-WIDE). GEORGE HECHT, PROJ COORDINATOR; EL PASO PARK & RECREATION DISTRICT; 105 E VERMIJO; COLORADO SPG, CO 80903. (#9271).

FOUNTAIN VALLEY HEALTH PROJECT, COLORADO SPG, CO. HEALTH PROJECT ATTACK PLAN AGAINST VENEREAL DISEASE & DRUG ABUSE. (ST-WIDE). DOUGLAS POLLEY, DIRECTOR & CHAIRMAN; FOUNTAIN VALLEY HEALTH PROJECT; APT 2C, 1910 E BIJOU; COLORADO SPG, CO 80909. (#9275).

FUTURE FAIRS - PROJ OF COLORADO SPG, CO. SERIES OF 6 FREE TRAVELING FAIRS THAT MARKS PROGRESS OF INDUSTRY & SHOW INDUSTRIAL TOOLS ALREADY AT HAND TO SOLVE THE PROBLEMS THAT STAND BETWEEN US & THE FUTURE. (LOCAL). DRAKE HIGHTOWER, PRESIDENT; AMERICAN INDUSTRY BICENTENNIAL CORP; 934 PEARL ST; BOULDER, CO 80302. (#14823).

GARDEN OF THE GODS MASTER PLAN - COLORADO SPG, CO. COMPLETE REVIEW OF PRESENT PLAN BY CITIZENS STEERING COMMITTEE. NEW MASTER PLAN WILL CONTROL USE, REDUCE EROSION & INTERPRET NATURAL RESOURCES. PLAN FINALIZED 1975; IMPLEMENTATION 1976. (LOCAL). RICHARD C BUERKLE, DIRECTOR; COLORADO SPRINGS PARKS & RECREATION DEPT; 1400 GLEN AVE; COLORADO SPG, CO 80904. (#15584).

GOLD HILL MESA MINERAL RECLAMATION IN COLORADO. PROJECT TO REFINE & RECLAIM LONG DORMANT GOLD MILL TAILINGS. ALSO OBTAIN EXISTING GOLD, SILVER, SAND FOR GLASS, CLAY & OTHER PRODUCTS; DONE FOR PROFIT, HISTORIC & ECOLOGICAL VALUE, COMMUNITY DEVELOPMENT. (ST-WIDE). DAVID R HUGHES, GENERAL MANAGER; GOLD HILL MESA CORP; 1624 S 21ST ST; COLORADO SPG, CO 80901. (#9264).

THE GRASS ROOTS PEOPLE - COLORADO SPRINGS, CO. PHOTOGRAPHY PROJECT OF THE RURAL PEOPLE OF COLORADO AND THEIR WAY OF LIFE: HOME, FAMILY, WORK AND RECREATION. (ST-WIDE). NANCY WOOD, PROJ DIRECTOR; 825 PASEO RD; COLORADO SPG, CO 80907. (#18513).

'HENRY MCALLISTER AND HIS FRIENDS' PROJ OF COLO. A PROJECT TO PUBLISH A PAPER ENTITLED 'HENRY MCALLISTER AND HIS

COLORADO SPG — CONTINUED

FRIENDS' WRITTEN BY GLADYS BUELER. THE PAPER CONTAINS SHORT VIGNETTES ON WELL KNOWN COLORADO SPRINGS HISTORIC FIGURES. (LOCAL). POLLY KING RUHTENBERG, PR CHAIRMAN; MCALLISTER HOUSE MUSEUM; 69 MARLAND RD; COLORADO SPG, CO 80906. (#4296).

HIGH FLIGHT MOBILE SPACE MUSEUM. MUSEUM HOUSED IN TRAILER WHICH USES APOLLO 15 MOON MISSION AS PRIMARY SUBJECT. HAS MOON ROCK, ASTRONAUT'S SUIT AND APPARATUS USED ON THE MOON. IT IS TRAVELLING AROUND THE UNITED STATES. (NAT'L). L H 'ROCKY' FORSHEY, EXEC VICE PRESIDENT; HIGH FLIGHT FOUNDATION; 5010 EDISON AVE; COLORADO SPG, CO 80915. (#21696). **ARBA RECOGNIZED.**

'HISTORIC AMERICAN FLAG PROJECT', COLORADO SPG, CO. A SPECIFIC AMERICAN FLAG WILL FLY OVER AS MANY U S STATE CAPITALS & FOREIGN CAPITALS AS POSSIBLE IN MEMORY OF PRESIDENT JOHN F KENNEDY. (NAT'L). CHUCK ZIMKAS, JR, MSGT, USAF; 729 DREW DR; WIDEFIELD, CO 80911. (#19509).

HISTORIC PEOPLE & PLACES IN PIKES PEAK REGION-FILM. MOVIETAPE FOR STATEWIDE DISTRIBUTION WILL CONSIST OF HISTORICAL VIGNETTES FEATURING PEOPLE & PLACES IN THE PIKES PEAK REGION FROM 1745 TO 1930. LENGTH OF FILM IS 22 MINUTES. (ST-WIDE). POLLY KING RUHTENBERG, VICE PRESIDENT; FRIENDS OF PIONEERS MUSEUM & CHANNEL 8 PUBLIC SVC NETWORK; 25 WEST KIOWA ST; COLORADO SPG, CO 80902. (#4361).

A HISTORIC VIEW OF THE PIKES PEAK REGION, CO. AN EDUCATIONAL PROGRAM FOR STUDENTS 9-14 WILL PROVIDE INFORMATION ABOUT THE HISTORY OF THE COUNTY; VARIOUS BICENTENNIAL ACTIVITIES WILL DEVELOP PRIDE IN THE PAST. (LOCAL). PEARL ANN SLUTTER, CHAIRMAN; COLORADO STATE UNIV EXTENSION; 27 E VERMIJO; COLORADO SPG, CO 80903. (#14858).

HISTORICAL BOOK SERIES ON PIKES PEAK AREA OF CO. THE 5 BOOKLETS WILL CONTAIN INFORMATION ON HISTORIC HOMES, SITES, EVENTS & HISTORY OF THE PIKES PEAK AREA. TOWNS INCLUDED ARE RAMONA, GLASSTOWN, LAVERNE & MANILOU SPRINGS FROM 1859 TO THE PRESENT. (LOCAL). LUCILLE CUNNINGHAM, PROJ COORDINATOR; PIKES PEAK OR BUST BY 76 CENTENNIAL COMMITTEE; 9 CRESCENT LN; COLORADO SPG, CO 80904. (#9281).

HISTORICAL VIGNETTES - ORAL SUBMISSION. COMPILATION OF WRITTEN ACCTS OF MINORITY ORAL HISTORY BY LONG-TIME RESIDENTS. ACCTS TO BE PRESERVED IN PUBLIC LIBRARY. THIS WILL UNEARTH EARLY COLO PICTURES OF HISTORIC VALUE. (LOCAL). JUANITA MARTIN, PROJ DIRECTOR; 3209 N ILLINOIS AVE; COLORADO SPG, CO 80907. (#14818).

HISTORY OF SCHOOL DISTRICT 20, COLORADO SPG, CO. THIS ACCOUNT, WRITTEN BY CHARLOTTE BROWN, WILL HELP RESIDENTS LEARN THE SCHOOLS, THE COMMUNITY AND THEIR BACKGROUND. (LOCAL). CHARLOTTE BROWN, AUTHOR; AIR ACADEMY SCHOOL DISTRICT #20; COLORADO SPG, CO 80840. (#14812).

INTERSTATE 25 CENTENNIAL PARKWAYS, COLORADO SPG. BEAUTIFICATION OF I-25 ADJOINING LAND THRU IMPLEMENTATION OF MINIPARKS, WALKING PATHS, BICYCLE PATHS AND REST AREAS. (ST-WIDE). MRS FRANCES MORRIS, PROJ DIRECTOR; COLORADO ARBC - HORIZONS COMMITTEE; 6 POPLAR PL; COLORADO SPG, CO 80906. (#9276).

JR LEAGUE'S COMMUNITY CALENDAR OF COLORADO SPRINGS. CALENDAR LISTING COMMUNITY EVENTS AND CENTENNIAL-BICENTENNIAL EVENTS FOR EACH DAY. (LOCAL). MRS LESTER LOO, PROJ COORDINATOR; JR LEAGUE OF COLORADO SPRINGS, INC; 1600 N CASCADE; COLORADO SPG, CO 80903. (#9268).

KKTV/TV'S 'BICENTENNIAL NUGGETS' - NBMRP. KKTV HAS CREATED SERIES OF 56 1-MINUTE SPOTS CALLED 'CENTENNIAL NUGGETS' CELEBRATING COLORADO'S 100TH AS WELL AS NATION'S 200TH ANNIVERSARY. SPONSORED BY SEARS, ROEBUCK & AIRED THROUGHOUT THE STATE. (ST-WIDE). GEORGE JEFFREY, BICENTENNIAL COORDINATOR; KKTV; PO BOX 2110; COLORADO SPGS, CO 80901. (#22606).

LANDSCAPING MEMORIAL PARK, COLORADO SPRINGS, CO. LANDSCAPE NEW ICE CENTER & PARKING AREA W/EVERGREEN TREES, SHRUBS, SHADE TREES & FLOWERING SHRUBS TO ENHANCE THE BEAUTY OF MEMORIAL PARK FOR COMMUNITY ENJOYMENT. (LOCAL). MRS H E HART, CIVIC CHAIRMAN; BROADMOOR GARDEN CLUB; 1260 MESA RD; COLORADO SPG, CO 80906. (#9274).

LIFE IN THE DRY FARMING EASTERN COLORADO PLAINS. TAPE/SLIDE PRESENTATION OF INTERVIEWS ON RURAL LIFE IN THE EASTERN COLORADO DRY FARMING AREAS. (ST-WIDE). BRENDA G HAWLEY, WESTERN HISTORY LIBRARIAN; PENROSE PUBLIC LIBRARY; 20 N CASCADE; COLORADO SPG, CO 80901. (#9269).

A MARK TWAIN CELEBRATION - COLORADO SPRINGS, CO. THEATRE FOR CHILDREN WILL INCLUDE THE FOLLOWING PRESENTATIONS OF GREAT AMERICAN LITERATURE: 'MARK TWAIN', 'HUCK FINN', 'PRINCE AND THE PAUPER' & 'CONNECTICUT YANKEE IN KING ARTHURS COURT.'. (LOCAL). EUGENE W TEDD, DIRECTOR; EL PASO COMMUNITY COLLEGE; 2200 BOTT AVE; COLORADO SPG, CO 80904. (#14810).

MEDICAL HERITAGE HALL OF COLORADO SPRINGS. TO CREATE DISPLAYS FOR MEDICAL HERITAGE SECTION OF PIONEER MUSEUM & TO INCLUDE A MOCK-UP OF AN OLD DOCTORS OFFICE, DISPLAYS OF HISTORICAL EQUIPMENT, DIORAMAS, A TB TENT & MANY OTHER DISPLAYS. (ST-WIDE). MRS DAVID MARTZ, PRESIDENT; WOMEN'S AUXILIARY TO THE EL PASO COUNTY MEDICAL SOCIETY; 980 TIMBER VALLEY RD; COLORADO SPG, CO 80919. (#4418). **ARBA GRANTEE.**

MILITARY-RELATED PUBLIC SERVICE SPOTS, CO. BROADCAST INTERESTING MILITARY EVENTS OF LOCAL INTEREST SIMILAR TO '200 YEARS AGO TODAY.'. (LOCAL). JOHN FOTENOS, CHAIRMAN; MILITARY HERITAGE COMMITTEE; 3846 NUEVO DR; COLORADO SPG, CO 80918. (#14829).

MONTHLY BULLETINS IN COLORADO SPG, CO. A MONTHLY BULLETIN WILL BE PUBLISHED BY NAZARENE BIBLE COLLEGE STUDENTS FEATURING FAMOUS MONTHLY EVENTS IN AMERICAN HISTORY. (LOCAL). JANET S WILLIAMS, PROJ CHAIRPERSON; NAZARENE BIBLE COLLEGE; BOX 4746; COLORADO SPG, CO 80930. (#17432).

NATIONAL CHIN-QUA-PIN DAYS IN COLORADO SPGS. NATIONAL AMERICAN INDIAN DANCE & SONG CONTESTS HELD FOR NATIONAL AWARDS IN MANY CATEGORIES OF TRADITIONAL & ANCIENT REPERTORY OF 42 TRIBES FROM 28 STATES. (NAT'L). WOODROW W PALMER; LONE FEATHER INDIAN COUNCIL, INC; 809 ELLSTON ST; COLORADO SPG, CO 80907. (#8892). **ARBA GRANTEE.**

NEIGHBORHOOD HISTORIES OF COLORADO SPG, CO. RESEARCH & PRESENTATION OF HISTORICAL HERITAGE OF VARIOUS NEIGHBORHOODS FOR PURPOSE OF STIMULATING NEIGHBORHOOD PRIDE. RESIDENTS WILL BE RESEARCHERS & RESOURCES & AUDIENCES. (LOCAL). ERIC SWAB, PROJECT COORDINATOR; URBAN RENEWAL AUTHORITY OF CITY OF COLORADO SPG, CO; 105 E VERMIJO; COLORADO SPG, CO 80901. (#14820).

NEW TOWN - BUST, COLORADO. THE PROJECT INVOLVES THE CHARTER OF THE NEWEST AND SMALLEST TOWN IN COLORADO; TOWN IS LOCATED ON 500 FOOT FRONTAGE OF U S HWY 24 WEST OF CASCADE, CO. (LOCAL). WILLIAM D OSBORNE, PROJ DIRECTOR; PO BOX 338; WOODLAND PARK, CO 80863. (#9270).

NOTECARDS ON FOUR HISTORIC BUILDINGS - CO. INCLUDES GLEN EYRIE, EL PASO COUNTY COURTHOUSE, FIRST CONGREGATIONAL CHURCH & BRIARHURST. PURPOSE TO INCREASE AWARENESS OF 'HISTORIC' BUILDINGS OF BOTH RESIDENTS & VISITORS. (LOCAL). VICKY GOW, CHAIRMAN; LEAGUE OF WOMEN VOTERS; 1907 WARWICK LN; COLORADO SPG, CO 80909. (#14813).

OLD COLORADO CITY PROJECT - COLORADO SPRINGS. REDEVELOPMENT & HISTORICAL REVIVAL OF OLDEST SETTLEMENT IN PIKE'S PEAK REGION: RESTORATION OF STRUCTURES; REENACTMENT OF EVENTS; PUBLICIZING DISTINCT TOWN CHARACTER; ECONOMIC & SOCIAL STIMULUS. (ST-WIDE). DAVID HUGHES, CHAIRMAN; PIKES PEAK OR BUST BY '76 COMMITTEE; F N TEJON; COLORADO SPG, CO 80903. (#20210).

OPEN SPACE PROJECT IN COLORADO SPRINGS, COLORADO. TO SET ASIDE LAND FOR FUTURE DEVELOPMENT OF PARKS, TRAILS & GREENBELT AREA FOR THE COMMUNITY. (LOCAL). MIKE BIRD, COUNCILMAN; CITIZENS FOR OPEN SPACE; C/O MIKE BIRD, CITY HALL; COLORADO SPG, CO 80901. (#9263).

THE OTERO PARK AT THE RIDGE - COLORADO SPG, CO. A 6.5 ACRE PARK WITH WALKWAYS, PLAYING FIELDS, PICNIC AREAS & A TOT LOT; FEATURES NATURAL VEGETATION & PLANTS & FLOWERS NATIVE TO CO; PLANNED WITH COLORADO SPG PARK & RECREATION DEPT. (LOCAL). VIRGINIA L BROST, PROJ DIRECTOR; OTERO SAVINGS AND LOAN ASSOC; 1515 N ACADEMY; COLORADO SPG, CO 80909. (#14826).

PARK DEVELOPMENT PROJECT - COLORADO SPG, CO. SELECTION & DEVELOPMENT OF A PARK BY THE HBA TO BE GIVEN TO THE PARK & REC DEPT. FIRST PARK IS HENRY PARK NAMED AFTER PATRICK HENRY. THIS WILL BE ONGOING THROUGH THE BICENTENNIAL ERA. (LOCAL). ED GENDRON, CHAIRMAN; HOME BUILDERS ASSOC OF METRO COLORADO SPG; 4808 ESCAPARDO WAY; COLORADO SPG, CO 80917. (#14817).

PARK & REC MASTER PLAN (THE NEXT HUNDRED YEARS)-CO. UPON COMPLETION OF PLANNING PROCESS DISPLAY IN LARGE SCALE MAPS & DIAGRAMS PLUS A BROCHURE; WILL INFORM PUBLIC OF PLANNING FOR PARK DEVELOPMENT IN CENTURY III. (LOCAL). RICHARD C BUERKLE, DIRECTOR; COLORADO SPRINGS PARKS & RECREATION DEPT; 1400 GLEN AVE; COLORADO SPG, CO 80904. (#15581).

PHOTO SURVEY AND GUIDE TO ORNAMENTAL IRONWORK-COLO. A PHOTO SURVEY OF 19TH CENTURY IRON FENCES DONE BY HIGH SCHOOL STUDENTS FOR THE PURPOSE OF PUBLISHING A GUIDE FOR WALKING TOURS OF IRONWORK IN COLORADO SPRINGS. (LOCAL). RAYMOND HOFFMAN, PRESIDENT; SPRINGS AREA BEAUTIFUL ASSOCIATION; PO BOX 1300; COLORADO SPGS, CO 80901. (#4375).

PIKES PEAK AREA GEOLOGICAL TOURS IN COLORADO. BROCHURE RELATING GEOLOGICAL HISTORY OF REGION IN CONJUNCTION WITH NUMBERED SIGNPOSTS PROVIDING A SELF-GUIDED TOUR. (ST-WIDE). JACK D THOMPSON, PROJ COORDINATOR; COLORADO SPRINGS MINERALOGICAL SOCIETY; PO BOX 2; COLORADO SPG, CO 80901. (#9267).

PIKES PEAK CENTENNIAL - BICENT QUILT. QUILT OF HISTORICAL SIGNIFICANCE TO THE PIKES PEAK AREA, DESIGNED, WORKED & QUILTED BY WOMEN OF THE PIKES PEAK CHAPTER OF THE EMBROIDERERS' GUILD. (LOCAL). MS ROWEDEAN CONNALLY, PRESIDENT; PIKES PEAK CHAPTER OF NATIONAL EMBROIDERERS' GUILD; 4224 E SAN MIGUEL; COLORADO SPG, CO 80909. (#9253).

PIKES PEAK CENT-BICENT AUTO HILL CLIMB, CO. THIS ANNUAL EVENT DRAWS CARS FROM ACROSS THE NATION. THE 1976 'RACE TO THE CLOUDS' WILL HAVE A CENTENNIAL-BICENTENNIAL THEME. COLORADO SPRINGS CBC AND MANITOU SPRINGS CBC ARE WORKING TOGETHER ON THIS. (NAT'L). JACK VAETH, EXEC DIRECTOR; PIKES PEAK AUTO HILL CLIMB ASSOC, INC; PO BOX 153-80901; COLORADO SPGS, CO 80901. (#6779).

PIKES PEAK REGION HISTORICAL BOOKLETS - CO. A SERIES OF 5 HISTORIC BOOKLETS ON THE PIKES PEAK REGION COVERING: HOMES, HISTORIC SITES, HISTORIC EVENTS, CHURCHES, SATELLITE COMMUNITIES, 1859 TO PRESENT. (ST-WIDE). LUCILLE CUNNINGHAM, CHAIRMAN; HISTORIC SITES COMMITTEE; 9 CRESCENT LN; COLORADO SPG, CO 80904. (#14815).

PIKES-PEAK CENT-BICENT RECIPE COLLECTION, CO. COLLECTION OF AUTHENTIC RECIPES USED OVER THE PAST 200 YEARS BY LOCAL RESIDENTS. THE COLLECTION INCLUDES ANECDOTES, THE USE OF FOOD & THE EVOLUTION OF FOOD & NUTRITION IN THE PAST 200 YEARS. (LOCAL). SHIRLEY K LIPPINCOTT, R D, NUTRITION COMM CHMN; COLORADO SPRINGS DIETETICAS-SOC; 2504 W BIJOU; COLORADO SPG, CO 80904. (#19507).

PIONEER'S MUSEUM OF COLORADO SPRINGS, COLORADO. PIONEER'S MUSEUM IS A STOREHOUSE OF HISTORICAL INFORMATION WHICH IS READILY AVAILABLE TO THE PUBLIC. THIS GRANT WILL BE USED FOR PLANNING OF A PROPOSED EXPANSION. (ST-WIDE). MRS HENRRIETTA PERRY, CURATOR; BOARD OF DIRECTORS, PIONEER MUSEUM; 25 W KIOWA ST; COLORADO SPGS, CO 80902. (#1318).

PRINT DISPLAY COLORADO SPRINGS, CO. THIS IS PART OF A COLLECTION OF PAINTINGS THAT WILL BE AVAILABLE ON A LOAN BASIS TO STUDENTS OF NAZARENE BIBLE COLLEGE. (LOCAL). PROF ROGER WILLIAMS, LIBRARIAN; NAZARENE BIBLE COLLEGE; 1111 CHAPMAN DRIVE; COLORADO SPG, CO 80930. (#17415).

QUEENS CANYON QUARRY - SCAR ON THE MOUNTAIN - CO. CITY OF COLO SPGS WILL ACCEPT LAND OF OPERATING LIMESTONE QUARRY ON SLOPES OF SCENIC FRONT RANGE BACKDROP AFTER QUARRY CLOSES & REVEGETATE FOR PARK OPEN SPACE WITH TREES, SHRUBS & GRASS SEEDS. (LOCAL). RICHARD C BUERKLE, DIRECTOR; COLORADO SPRINGS PARKS & RECREATION DEPT; 1400 GLEN AVE; COLORADO SPG, CO 80904. (#15583).

QUILT TO BE MADE BY SENIOR CITIZENS, COLORADO SPG. PIKES PEAK HISTORICAL QUILT; APPROXIMATELY 30 SQUARES TO FORM A KING SIZE QUILT DEPICTING SPECIFIC EVENTS AND PEOPLE IMPORTANT TO THE HISTORY OF THE PIKES PEAK REGION. (LOCAL). MRS KEN KEENE & MRS T MARTIS, CO-CHAIRMEN; SILVER KEY SERVICES HEADQUARTERS; 731 N CASCADE; COLORADO SPG, CO 80901. (#9278).

RAILROAD DIORAMA OF COLORADO SPRINGS. CONSTRUCTION AND EXHIBIT OF A RAILROAD DIORAMA PORTRAYING THE RAILROADS (IN SCALE) AND THEIR INVOLVEMENT IN THE DEVELOPMENT OF THE COLORADO SPRINGS AND PIKES PEAK REGION. (LOCAL). JOE MUNSON, COORDINATOR; COLORADO CENTRAL MODEL RAILROAD CLUB, INC; 3110 E SAN MINGUEL; COLORADO SPG, CO 80909. (#9252).

RAILROAD SPIKES PROJ - COLORADO SPRINGS, CO. HISTORIC SPIKES REMOVED FROM SANTA FE TRACKS, WILL BE GOLD PLATED, MOUNTED & ACCOMPANIED BY A BOOKLET COVERING HISTORICAL FACTS. MARKETED BY CENTENNIAL JR ACHIEVERS BANK. (ST-WIDE). GORDON EBBE, EXEC DIRECTOR; JUNIOR ACHIEVEMENT OF COLORADO SPRINGS, INC; 201 N WEBER ST; COLORADO SPG, CO 80903. (#14831).

READING IS FUNDAMENTAL PROJECT OF COLORADO SPRINGS. DISTRIBUTION OF 600 BOOKS TO NEEDY CHILDREN. (LOCAL). SALLY CALDWELL, CONTRIBUTION CHAIRMAN; PIKES PEAK JAYCEE-ETTES; 7330 SUGARLOAF TERR; COLORADO SPG, CO 80817. (#14824).

RENOVATION OF TEJON TROLLEY LINE, COLORADO SPG, CO. REINSTALLATION OF TROLLEY LINE THROUGH DOWNTOWN AREA USING AUTHENTIC TROLLEY SYSTEM FOR VISITOR & RESIDENT ATTRACTION. (LOCAL). JOHN HANEY, COORDINATOR; CITIZENS FOR A TEJON TROLLEY; 20 MESA RD; COLORADO SPG, CO 80901. (#9261).

REVERSING ECOLOGICAL DESTRUCTION, PALMER PARK, CO. A REGULAR PROGRAM TO ENHANCE ECOLOGICAL BENEFITS IN A COMMUNITY PARK. (LOCAL). CHARLES MATTHEWS, PROJ DIRECTOR; BOY SCOUTS OF AMERICA; 525 E VINTAH; COLORADO SPG, CO 80903. (#9258).

RURAL SCHOOLS IN EL PASO COUNTY, COLORADO. A BOOKLET ON RURAL SCHOOLS AROUND 1876; INCLUDING PHOTOS, TEXT OF EACH SCHOOL'S HISTORY, PRAIRIE HERITAGE OF ONE ROOM SCHOOLHOUSE AS CENTER OF COMMUNITY LIFE. (LOCAL). LUCILLE CUNNINGHAM, CHAIRMAN, HISTORICAL SITES; PIKES PEAK CENTENNIAL COMMITTEE; 9 CRESCENT LA; COLORADO SPG, CO 80904. (#9283).

SENIOR CLASS BICENTENNIAL PROJECT, COLORADO SPG. BEAUTIFICATION PROJECT WILL INCLUDE THE PLANTING OF TREES ON CAMPUS. (LOCAL). BERNIE MCARDLE & DALE ROSS, CLASS REPRESENTATIVES; NAZARENE BIBLE COLLEGE; 1111 CHAPMAN; COLORADO SPG, CO 80930. (#17336).

SERIES OF PICTURES FOR DISPLAY, COLORADO SPG, CO. 15 PICTURES DEPICTING UNITED STATES FROM REVOLUTIONARY WAR TO TODAY TO BE AVAILABLE FOR DISPLAY TO PUBLIC AT ANY LOCATION UPON REQUEST; CONTACT FORT CARSON OFFICERS WIVES CLUB. (LOCAL). SALLY BUSSEY & JUDY SIBERT, CO-CHAIRMEN; FORT CARSON OFFICERS WIVES CLUB; FORT CARSON, CO 80913. (#9279).

SHOOKS RUN CENTER TASK FORCE IN COLORADO SPRINGS. SOCIAL SERVICE AGENCIES PROVIDING SERVICES FOR LOW INCOME PERSONS. (ST-WIDE). BILL CULPEPPER, COORDINATOR; SHOOKS RUN COALITION; 503 S EL PASO; COLORADO SPG, CO 80907. (#9257).

SIXTH MILITARY HISTORY SYMPOSIUM. THE SYMPOSIUM FOCUSES ON THE AMERICAN REVOLUTION. 300 HISTORIANS ARE EXPECTED AT THE AIR FORCE ACADEMY IN OCTOBER 1974. PROCEEDINGS TO BE PUBLISHED. (NAT'L). MARC HUET, SPECIAL ASSISTANT; DEPT OF DEFENSE; THE PENTAGON, RM 5C-960; WASHINGTON, DC 20330. (#10).

COLORADO SPG — CONTINUED

SOLDIERS OF THE REVOLUTION DISPLAY UNIT - CO. PARADE OR DISPLAY UNIT BASED ON SOLDIERS OF THE REVOLUTION. HEROES OF 76' ALSO CAN SERVE AS HONOR GUARD. (LOCAL). HAROLD G TAYLOR, CONTACT OFFICER; NATIONAL SOJOURNERS, INC; 2214 PASEO RD; COLORADO SPG, CO 80907. (#14814).

SPRING TONIC ARTS & CRAFT SHOW - COLORADO SPG, CO. ANNUAL SPRING SHOW & SALE; EXHIBITS BY MEMBERS IN THREE FIELDS: FINE ARTS, CRAFTS & CULINARY ART. MANY OF THE OLDER ARTS AND CRAFTS WILL BE REVIVED. (LOCAL). TERRY ROERICH, PUBLICITY CHAIRMAN; BLACK FOREST ARTS & CRAFTS GUILD; 5650 BURGESS RD; COLORADO SPG, CO 80908. (#14803).

STATE GOVERNOR'S CONFERENCE, COLORADO SPRINGS, CO. NATIONAL COMMUNITY SCHOOL CONFERENCE AIMING TOWARD MORE COMMUNITY USE & INVOLVEMENT IN SCHOOL FACILITIES. (NAT'L). DAVE MAYNARD, PROJ DIRECTOR; COLORADO SPRINGS JAYCEES; HOLLY SUGAR BLDG; COLORADO SPG, CO 80902. (#14802).

THE STORY OF VAN BRIGGLE'S POTTERY IN COLORADO SPG. A PUBLICATION THAT TRACES AND DESCRIBES THE HISTORY AND DEVELOPMENT OF VAN BRIGGLE'S POTTERY; ALSO CATALOGS HIS POTTERY DESIGNS FROM 1900-1912. (LOCAL). MS ALISON F HAYS, DIR OF PUBLIC RELATIONS; COLORADO SPRINGS FINE ARTS CENTER; COLORADO SPG, CO 80903. (#10325).

SUMMER SYMPHONY - COLORADO SPRINGS, CO. A SERIES OF FREE CONCERTS AND FAMILY ACTIVITIES IN CITY PARKS. (LOCAL). DAVID STRUTHERS, COORDINATOR; COLORADO SPRINGS SYMPHONY; 1600 N CASCADE; COLORADO SPG, CO 80903. (#26375).

SUNBONNETS FOR SALE IN COLORADO SPRINGS, COLORADO. WOMEN OF GATEWAY PRESBYTERIAN CHURCH WILL MAKE & SELL SUNBONNETS FOR WOMEN & GIRLS AT A COST OF $3.00; STRICTLY PROFIT FOR THE CHURCH BUT RECOGNIZED BY HERITAGE COMMITTEE AS A WORTHY PROJECT. (LOCAL). FLORA BELL HULL, PROJ COORDINATOR; GATEWAY UNITED PRESBYTERIAN CHURCH WOMENS ASSOC; 731 CASTLEWOOD RD; COLORADO SPG, CO 80904. (#9277).

SURVEY & GUIDE TO IRON FENCES OF COLORADO SPRINGS. SLIDES, PHOTOS, & WALKING TOURS OF AREA SHOWING EXAMPLES OF 19TH CENTURY IRON WORKS IN FENCES AND GATES IN REGION. DONE MAINLY BY HASSELL IRON WORKS OF COLORADO SPRINGS. (LOCAL). ELAINE FREED, PROJ DIRECTOR; SPRINGS AREA BEAUTIFUL ASSOC; PO BOX 1300; COLORADO SPG, CO 80901. (#9282).

TEJON STREET MALL - COLORADO SPG, CO. PROGRESSIVE CONSTRUCTION OF LIMITED-ACCESS MALL ON 100 N BLOCK OF TEJON IN DOWNTOWN COLORADO SPG. (LOCAL). LAWRENCE OCHS, MAYOR; CITY OF COLORADO SPRINGS; 107 N NEVADA; COLORADO SPG, CO 80901. (#14822).

THREE AMERICAN BALLETS; PERFORMANCES IN COLORADO. THE COLORADO BALLET CO WILL PERFORM 'RODEO', 'COLORADO SUITE' AND 'CONCERTO IN F' FOR THE CENTENNIAL-BICENT CELEBRATION. FOLLOWING THE PERFORMANCE IN COLORADO SPRINGS, THE COMPANY WILL GO TO DENVER. (ST-WIDE). BEN GAHART, MANAGER; COLORADO BALLET CO; 705 W BROOKSIDE ST; COLORADO SPG, CO 80906. (#9254).

TIMBERLINE MOUNTAIN MUSIC FESTIVAL, COLORADO. POPULAR MUSIC CONCERT AND OTHER ARTISTIC AND CULTURAL EVENTS. (LOCAL). GERRY MARTENS, PRESIDENT; GERRY HARTENS INC & DICK CLARK CONCERTS, INC; 2074 CLARKSON ST; DENVER, CO 80205. (#4140).

A TRAVELERS GUIDE TO PIKES PEAK - COLORADO SPG, CO. SMALL BOOK ILLUSTRATING ANECDOTAL NARRATIVE CONCERNING THE PIKES PEAK COG RAILROAD, PIKES PEAK HIGHWAY & BARR TRAIL. (LOCAL). JOHN MCMINN, AUTHOR; BOX 384; CASCADE, CO 80809. (#14811).

TREES FOR TOMORROW PROJ OF COLORADO SPRINGS. PROVIDE TEN THOUSAND DECIDOUS SEEDLINGS TO BE PLANTED IN COLORADO SPRINGS. (LOCAL). MRS EDWARD O'DONNELL, CHAIRPERSON; AUSTIN BLUFFS GARDEN CLUB; 2432 SAM CARLOS CIRCLE; COLORADO SPG, CO 80909. (#4179).

A VILLAGE BLACKSMITH SHOP IN COLORADO SPRINGS, CO. CREATION OF BLACKSMITH SHOP; DEMONSTRATIONS OF TECHNIQUES. (LOCAL). BARRY OLIVER, PROJ COORDINATOR; BARRY OLIVER; 112 E MADISON; COLORADO SPG, CO 80903. (#9272).

'WEST TO COLORADO', ORIGINAL MUSIC - CO. ORIGINAL MUSIC ON 45RPM RECORD - PERTINENT TO THE PEOPLE OF COLORADO. (LOCAL). GILBERT D STONE, COMPOSER; 935 SATURN DR, APT 126; COLORADO SPG, CO 80906. (#24626).

WESTERN MUSEUM OF MINING & INDUSTRY - CO. RESTORATION OF AUTHENTIC MINING EQUIPMENT & CONSTRUCTION, LIGHTING & GRAPHICS CREATING EDUCATIONAL DISPLAYS. (LOCAL). HUGH H C WEED JR, DIRECTOR; WESTERN MUSEUM OF MINING AND INDUSTRY; 1025 NORTHGATE RD; COLORADO SPG, CO 80908. (#14825).

WHITE HOUSE RANCH TRAIL FOR HANDICAPPED - COLORADO. TRAIL FOR HANDICAPPED & BLIND WITH SIGNS IN BRAILLE & PRINT DENOTING FLORA, GEOLOGICAL PHENOMENA & HISTORICAL INFORMATION. (LOCAL). MRS LESTER LOO, PROJ COORDINATOR; JUNIOR LEAGUE OF COLORADO SPRINGS; 1600 N CASCADE; COLORADO SPG, CO 80903. (#9266).

WHITTIER SCHOOL CENTENNIAL QUILT, COLORADO SPG, CO. PRIMARILY A CHILD MADE QUILT. SQUARES ARE APPLIQUED MOTIFS OF COLORADO HISTORICAL SIGNIFICANCE. QUILTING TO BE A COMMUNITY ENDEAVOR ON WESTSIDE COLORADO SPRINGS. (LOCAL). MS BARBARA CARTER; WHITTIER ELEMENTARY SCHOOL; 2904 W KIOWA ST; COLORADO SPG, CO 80904. (#19506).

1975 PARADE OF HOMES - COLORADO SPG, CO. SHOWCASE OF NEW IDEAS IN HOME CONSTRUCTION INCLUDING NEW PRODUCTS & IDEAS PARTICULARLY IN THE FIELD OF RESOURCE CONSTRUCTION. (LOCAL). HANK NORMAN, PROJ DIRECTOR; HOME BUILDERS ASSOC OF METRO COLORADO SPG; 308 W FILLMORE; COLORADO SPG, CO 80907. (#14821).

200 YEARS--200 MILES OF TRAILS. NATL HIKING & SKI TOURING ASSOC PROJ TO HAVE EACH STATE COMMIT TO BUILD 200 MILES OF BICENTENNIAL TRAILS & FOOTPATHS, A CERTAIN PERCENTAGE TO BE ESPECIALLY FOR HANDICAPPED & ELDERLY. (NAT'L). WILLIAM R RUSIN, PRESIDENT; NATIONAL HIKING & SKI TOURING ASSOC; PO BOX 7421; COLORADO SPG, CO 80907. (#4797). **ARBA RECOGNIZED. ARBA GRANTEE.**

6 HISTORICAL AMERICAN FLAGS - COLORADO SPRINGS, CO. BETSY ROSS, BENNINGTON, GADSDEN, STAR-SPANGLED BANNER, MEXICAN WAR AND 50-STAR FLAGS WILL BE EXHIBITED THROUGHOUT THE BICENTENNIAL YEAR AT ALL COLORADO OTERO SAVINGS AND LOAN LOCATIONS. (ST-WIDE). VIRGINIA BROST, ASST VICE-PRESIDENT OF MARKETING; OTERO SAVINGS AND LOAN ASSOC; 1515 N ACADEMY BLVD; COLORADO SPG, CO 80909. (#19663).

OCT 1, '74. SIXTH ANNUAL MILITARY SYMPOSIUM. THE SYMPOSIUM FOCUSES ON THE AMERICAN REVOLUTION. 300 HISTORIANS ARE EXPECTED AT THE AIR FORCE ACADEMY IN OCTOBER 1974. PROCEEDINGS TO BE PUBLISHED. AT U S AIR FORCE ACADEMY. (NAT'L). MARC HUET, SPECIAL ASST,; DEPT OF DEFENSE; THE PENTAGON, ROOM 5C-960; WASHINGTON, DC 20330. (#10-901).

JAN 18, '75 - JULY 4, '77. EXHIBIT OF COINS AND MEDALS RELATING TO FOUNDING OF OUR COUNTRY. EXTENSIVE EXHIBIT OF COINS & MEDALS RELATING TO THE COLONIAL PERIOD. ALSO, CONTINENTAL CURRENCY & FIRST US COINS ON DISPLAY, A THEATER FOR VIEWING FILMS ON COINS, CURRENCY & MEDALS, AND AN EXTENSIVE LIBRARY FOR RESEARCH. AT NATIONAL HEADQUARTERS,-MUSEUM AND LIBRARY, FREE PARKING. (NAT'L). EDWARD C. ROCHETTE; AMERICAN MUMISMATIC ASSOCIATION; 818 N. CASCADE AVENUE; COLORADO SPGS, CO 80903. (#4376-1).

FEB 17, '75. SERTOMA CLUB CENTENNIAL-BICENTENNIAL FREEDOM BANQUET. FREEDOMS ESSAY CONTEST, DISPLAYS, SPEECHES & BANQUET FOR AREA SCHOOLS. RECOGNIZING THE BICENTENNIAL HERITAGE IS THE THEME. (LOCAL). JOE PELTZ, TREASURER; PIKES PEAK SERTOMA CLUB; 2401 W COLORADO AVE; COLORADO SPGS, CO 80904. (#6788-501).

APR 5 - 6, '75. 'SONGS OF THE RIVER'. LIVE PERFORMANCE AT WASSON HIGH SCHOOL AUDITORIUM. (LOCAL). JACK SLOCUM, CHAIRMAN; COLORADO SPRINGS CHAPTER OF BARBERSHOPPERS; 1616 PALMER PARK; COLORADO SPG, CO 80909. (#200007-28).

MAY 3, '75. MUTT SHOW - A MIXED BREED DOG SHOW. COMPETITION AT BOULDER PARK. (LOCAL). PHIL ARKOW, DIRECTOR; THE HUMANE SOCIETY OF THE PIKES PEAK REGION; 633 S 8TH ST; COLORADO SPG, CO 80901. (#200007-29).

MAY 24 - 26, '75. RAMONA FALLS RENDEVOUS: A SHOOT FOR MUZZLELOADERS. MUZZLELOADING SHOOT WITH AUTHENTIC COSTUMES & RIFLES INCLUDING PRIZES, FUN, SHOOTS & ENTERTAINMENT. AT RAMONA FALLS, NEAR CRIPPLE CREEK. (LOCAL). JERRY LEA, CHAIRMAN; COLORADO SPRINGS MUZZLELOADERS, INC; 4950 GALENA; COLORADO SPG, CO 80918. (#200007-30).

MAY 24 - 28, '75. FENCE PAINTING COMPETITION. A PROGRAM OPEN TO PRIMARY THRU HIGH SCHOOL LEVEL STUDENTS TO PAINT HISTORIC SCENES OF THE PIKES PEAK REGION ON THE CONSTRUCTION FENCE SURROUNDING THE OXFORD-ANSCHUTZ 'COLO SQUARE' DEVELOPMENT. AT COLO SQUARE CONSTRUCTION FENCE, PIKES PEAK & NEVADA AVE. (LOCAL). KAREN BOATZ, DIRECTOR; THE COLORADO SPRINGS SUN NEWSPAPER; 103 W COLORADO AVE; COLORADO SPG, CO 80903. (#200007-31).

JUNE 1 - AUG 31, '75. WALKING TOUR - COLORADO COLLEGE. TOUR AT COLORADO COLLEGE, TEJON & CACHE LA POUDRE. (LOCAL). ROY HUGHES, CHAIRMAN; PIKES PEAK OR BUST BY '76 CENTENNIAL-BICENTENNIAL COMMITTEE; 332 W BIJOU; COLORADO SPG, CO 80905. (#200007-32).

JUNE 6, '75. KINDERGARTEN OPERETTA. TWO PRESENTATIONS OF A KINDERGARTEN OPERETTA WITH A BICENTENNIAL THEME, HELD AT FINE ARTS CENTER FOR PARENTS. THERE WILL BE DECORATIONS AND A CAKE WITH CENTENNIAL-BICENTENNIAL THEMES. (LOCAL). ANN NEASE, PROJ DIRECTOR; JUNIOR ACADEMY; 1311 N NEVADA; COLORADO SPG, CO 80902. (#10145-1).

JUNE 9 - SEPT 15, '75. HISTORIC WALKING TOURS OF CRIPPLE CREEK & VICTOR, COLORADO. GUIDED BY KNOWLEDGEABLE INDIVIDUAL. AT 332 W BIJOU. (ST-WIDE). BILL LIEB, CHAIRMAN; PIKES PEAK OR BUST BY 76 CENTENNIAL COMMITTEE - HERITAGE; 1576 KEATON LANE; COLORADO SPG, CO 80909. (#8904-1).

JUNE 15 - OCT 4, '75. TOURS OF PARKS AND RESIDENTIAL AREAS. WALKING TOUR OF TOWN PARK FOR SPRING FLOWERS JUNE 15-AUGUST 1 - BUS TOUR OF RESIDENTIAL AREAS TO ADMIRE FALL COLORS SEPTEMBER 21-OCT 4, BOTH 1975 & 1976. WALKING TOURS JUNE 14, 21, 28/JULY 5 10:00, 2:00 BUS TOURS SEPT 27 & OCT 4. (LOCAL). BILL LIEB, CHAIRMAN; HORTICULTURE SOCIETY; 1576 KEATON LANE; COLORADO SPG, CO 80909. (#8908-1).

JUNE 18 - 22, '75. THE COLORADO OPERA FESTIVAL - 'THE ABDUCTION FROM THE SERAGLIO'. COMPOSED BY N A MOZART & PERFORMED IN ENGLISH. AT ARMSTRONG HALL - COLORADO COLLEGE. (LOCAL). JANET SPROUSE, COORD; THE COLORADO OPERA FESTIVAL; COLORADO COLLEGE; COLO SPGS, CO 80903. (#200007-33).

JUNE 24 - AUG 5, '75. WALKING TOUR OF THE 'TRIANON'. TOUR AT TRIANON-COLORADO SPG SCHOOL 21, BROADMOOR AVE. (LOCAL). ROY HUGHES, CHAIRMAN; PIKES PEAK OR BUST BY '76 CENTENNIAL-BICENTENNIAL COMMITTEE; 332 W BIJOU; COLORADO SPG, CO 80905. (#200007-34).

JUNE 28, '75. BICYCLE & ANTIQUE CAR HISTORICAL TOUR. TOUR OF OLDER HISTORICAL HOMES IN AREA. ANTIQUE CARS PROVIDED FOR SENIOR CITIZENS; BOOKLET FOR SELF-GUIDED TOURS. PICNIC FOLLOWS. AT MONUMENT VALLEY PARK. (LOCAL). CHUCK EICHMAN, COORD; COLORADO SPRINGS DEPT OF PARKS & RECREATION; 1400 GLEN; COLORADO SPG, CO 80904. (#200007-36).

JUNE 28, '75. FARM-CITY DAY. FESTIVAL, TOUR AT NORRIS RANCH. (LOCAL). MRS JOE HATTON, PRES; PIKES PEAK COWBELLES; 1401 WINFIELD; COLORADO SPG, CO 80906. (#200007-35).

JUNE 30, '75. PRESENTATION OF CENTENNIAL DRAWING TO MAYOR. PRESENTATION OF DRAWING BY ARTIST JACK FROST DEPICTING COLORADO CENTENNIAL HISTORY; OLD-FASHIONED SACK LUNCH FOLLOWS; MAYOR WILL THEN PRESENT KEY TO NEW HEADQUARTERS FOR ASSISTANCE LEAGUE. (LOCAL). MRS DON E JOHNSON, COORD; THE ASSISTANCE LEAGUE OF COLORADO SPRINGS; 209 E COSTILLA; COLORADO SPG, CO 80903. (#200007-37).

JULY 1 - AUG 8, '75. CITIZENSHIP EXPERIENCE FOR DENVER DISADVANTAGED YOUTH. A SUMMER CITIZENSHIP EXPERIENCE FOR DISADVANTAGED DENVER YOUTHS. THE PROGRAM IS OPERATED BY USAF ACADEMY CADETS AS A LEADERSHIP PROGRAM. (LOCAL). LT COL R HESS, DIRECTOR; U S AIR FORCE ACADEMY DIRECTORATE OF PLANS & PROGRAMS; COLORADO SPGS, CO 80840. (#6764-501).

JULY 2 - AUG 27, '75. WALKING TOUR OF TUBERCULOSIS SANITARIUM/MT ST FRANCIS CONVENT. TOUR AT MT ST FRANCIS CONVENT, WEST OF I-25 ON WOODMEN VALLEY RD. (LOCAL). ROY HUGHES, CHAIRMAN; PIKES PEAK OR BUST BY '76 CENTENNIAL-BICENTENNIAL COMMITTEE; 332 W BIJOU; COLORADO SPG, CO 80905. (#200007-38).

JULY 3 - SEPT 4, '75. BUS TOUR TO VICTOR & CRIPPLE CREEK. HISTORICAL TOUR WITH GUIDE ON BUS. HELD EVERY THURSDAY THRU SUMMER. AT ACACIA PARK APTS, 104 E PLATTE AVE. (LOCAL). ROY HUGHES, COORD; PIKES PEAK OR BUST BY '76 CENTENNIAL-BICENTENNIAL COMMITTEE; 332 W BIJOU; COLORADO SPG, CO 80905. (#200007-180).

JULY 4, '75. BLACK FOREST DAY. FESTIVAL AT BLACK FOREST COMMUNITY CHURCH. (LOCAL). BARBRO LUNDGREN, COORD; EDUCATIONAL OPPORTUNITIES FOUNDATION; 11205 FAWN; COLORADO SPG, CO 80908. (#200007-39).

JULY 4, '75. PIKES PEAK AUTO HILL CLIMB. 2ND OLDEST AUTO RACE IN US. THIS ANNUAL EVENT DRAWS CARS FROM ACROSS THE NATION. THE 1976 'RACE TO THE CLOUDS' WILL HAVE A CENTENNIAL-BICENTENNIAL THEME. COLORADO SPRINGS CBC AND MANITOU SPRINGS CBC ARE WORKING TOGETHER ON THIS. AT PIKES PEAK MOUNTAIN. (REGN'L). JACK VAETH, EXEC DIRECTOR; PIKES PEAK AUTO HILL CLIMB ASSOC, INC; PO BOX 153; COLORADO SPGS, CO 80901. (#6779-501).

JULY 4 - 6, '75. NATIONAL PROFESSIONAL ART SHOW. WITH THE ASSISTANCE OF THE COLORADO SPRINGS ART SHOWS, INC, COLORADO WILL PRESENT A NATL ART SHOW, FEATURING PROFESSIONAL ARTISTS AND JUDGES. AT HILTON INN, I25 AT GARDEN OF THE GODS RD. (NAT'L). CAROL BOURDO; COLORADO ART SHOWS, INC; 1530 NORTHGATE RD; COLORADO SPG, CO 80906. (#8898-1).

JULY 6, '75. BICENTENNIAL MOTORCYCLE RACE. MOTORCYCLE RACE TO HELP FUND FUTURE BICENT EVENTS. OPEN TO ALL ENTRANTS. AT AZTEC RACEWAY PARK, HWY 94. (LOCAL). GLORIA GROTH, CHMN; PIKES PEAK OR BUST BY '76 FESTIVAL COMMITTEE; 1604 HALLAM AVE; SECURITY, CO 80911. (#8876-1).

JULY 7 - 12, '75. WINDOW DISPLAY CONTEST. A WINDOW DISPLAY CONTEST BY MERCHANTS IN THE DOWNTOWN AREA AND ALSO IN MAJOR SHOPPING CENTERS. THEME IS EITHER CENTENNIAL OR BICENT. PRIZES TO BE AWARDED. AT DOWNTOWN BUSINESS AREA, MAINLY TEJON ST. (LOCAL). RITA MCCLAIN, COORD; CELLULAR PRODUCTS SERVICES; 3125A N EL PASO; COLORADO SPG, CO 80907. (#8886-1).

JULY 9 - 13, '75. THE COLORADO OPERA FESTIVAL. THREE PERFORMANCES OF 'THE TURN OF THE SCREW' BY BENJAMIN BRITTEN. PRODUCED BY A RESIDENT PROFESSIONAL COMPANY, GIVEN IN ENGLISH AND ACCOMPANIED BY A FULL ORCHESTRA. TWO OTHER PRODUCTIONS THIS SUMMER; EVENING PERFORMANCE 8:15, MATINEE 2:30. AT COLORADO COLLEGE, ARMSTRONG HALL. (LOCAL). MS JANET SPROUSE; THE COLORADO OPERA FESTIVAL; COLORADO COLLEGE; COLORADO SPG, CO 80903. (#8891-1).

JULY 12, '75. FESTIVAL OF 'SHAN-KIVE'. DOWNTOWN MERCHANTS PARTICIPATING IN SIDEWALK SALES; ARTS & CRAFTS DISPLAYS, PARADES & BANDS. TEJON ST WILL BE BLOCKED OFF AND AN OLD FASHIONED TROLLEY WILL BE USED. (LOCAL). GLORIA GROTH, CHMN; PIKES PEAK OR BUST BY '76 FESTIVALS COMMITTEE; 1604 HALLAM AVE; COLORADO SPG, CO 80911. (#8888-1).

JULY 16, '75. PIKES PEAK OR BUST RODEO STREET BREAKFAST. STREET BREAKFAST IS KICK-OFF EVENT ANNUALLY TO PUBLICIZE THE PIKES PEAK OR BUST RODEO AND IS THE START OF THE ANNUAL RANGE RIDE. IT IS A JOINT EFFORT OF FORT CARSON AND COMMUNITY - PROCEEDS TO CHARITY. AT PIKES PEAK & TEJON STS. (REGN'L). WILLIAM F BAYNES; CENTENNIAL SERTOMA CLUB; C/O 1730 FOUNTAIN BLVD; COLORADO SPG, CO 80910. (#8895-1).

COLORADO SPG — CONTINUED

JULY 19, '75. FIRST ANNUAL PAINT HORSE SHOW. LIVE PERFORMANCE AT PENROSE EQUESTRIAN STADIUM. (LOCAL). DUKE MCSWAIN, COORDINATOR; WING CIVIL AIR PATROL; PO BOX 1431; COLORADO SPG, CO 80901. (#200007-40).

JULY 19 - 20, '75. PIKES PEAK GEM AND MINERAL SHOW. A DISPLAY OF MINERALS, GEMS, JEWELRY, FOSSILS AND ARTIFACTS. ALSO SHOWN WILL BE A SPECIAL DISPLAY OF ALL PAST PRESIDENTS' COLLECTONS ALONG WITH A SALE AND EXCHANGES BY COLLECTORS. AT CITY AUDITORIUM, KIOWA & WEBER STS. (ST-WIDE). PHILLIP JOHNSON; COLORADO SPRINGS MINERALOGICAL SOCIETY; C/O PO BOX 2; COLORADO SPG, CO 80901. (#8897-1).

JULY 20, '75. QUARTER MIDGET RACING IN COLORADO SPRINGS. QUARTER MIDGET RACING IS A PASTIME FOR THE WHOLE FAMILY. RACING IS LIMITED TO YOUNGSTERS BETWEEN AGES OF 5 AND 15. AT PIKES PEAK SPEEDWAY. (ST-WIDE). MS CHARLOTTE DAVIS; PIKES PEAK QUARTER MIDGET ASSOC; 6878 GRAPEWOOD CIR; COLORADO SPG, CO 80918. (#10135-1).

JULY 22 - SEPT 15, '75. FARMERS MARKET. THE HOURS ON TUESDAY WILL BE 9AM TO 11AM AND THE HOURS ON THURSDAY WILL BE 6PM TO 8PM. AT EL PASO COUNTY COURTHOUSE LAWN - TEJON & CUCHARRAS. (LOCAL). PATRICIA WHITE, PROJ DIR; COLORADO STATE UNIV EXTENSION SERVICE; 27 E VERMIJO; COLORADO SPG, CO 80903. (#102125-1).

JULY 25 - 27, '75. LA FIESTA BONITA. A THREE-DAY CELEBRATION WITH PAGEANT CONTESTANTS, MARIACHI BANDS, BOOTHS SET UP FOR FOOD AND CRAFTS. PRIZES AWARDED FOR AUTHENTIC COSTUMES. MUSICAL PAGEANT FOR 1976 UNDERWAY. AT ACACIA PARK, TEJON & BIJOU STS. (ST-WIDE). JOSE ALVARADO, CHAIRMAN; LOS CABALLEROS DE ANZO; 2518 W BIJOU ST; COLORADO SPG, CO 80904. (#8899-1).

JULY 25 - 27, '75. SCHOOL DISTRICT ELEVEN'S AMERICAN PAGEANT. TWO-HUNDRED YEAR AMERICAN HISTORY DRAMATIZATION THROUGH MUSIC AND READINGS BY JUNIOR HIGH STUDENTS. PUT ON ENTIRELY BY STUDENTS UNDER THE SUPERVISION OF 3 TEACHERS. (LOCAL). BRUCE HUNT, PROJ MGR; SCHOOL DISTRICT 11; 2308 LELARAY; COLORADO SPG, CO 80907. (#8887-1).

JULY 25 - 27, '75. 31ST ANNUAL OUTDOOR ART SHOW. 31ST ANNUAL OUTDOOR SHOW TITLED 'BUY' CENTENNIAL I. MANY ART FORMS WILL BE ON DISPLAY AND FOR SALE. THE HOUSR: FRI 5-10 PM, SAT 12-10 PM AND SUN 12-8 PM. AT HONNEN RINK, CACHE LA POUDRE & CASCADE, COLORADO COLLEGE. (LOCAL). DOROTHY N MYERS, PROJ DIR; COLORADO SPG ART GUILD, INC; 2016 MT VERNON; COLORADO SPG, CO 80909. (#10165-1).

JULY 25 - AUG 2, '75. UNITY CHURCH WALKING TOURS. SLIDE PRESENTATION ON JULY 25 AT 8 PM. TOURS LED BY MS WILCOX. AT 627 N CIRCLE DR. (LOCAL). MS RHODA WILCOX, COORD; UNITY CHURCH; 1620 E CACHE LA POUDRE; COLORADO SPG, CO 80909. (#8906-1).

JULY 30 - AUG 3, '75. THE COLORADO OPERA FESTIVAL. THREE PERFORMANCES OF 'THE TALES OF HOFFMANN' BY JACQUES OFFENBACH. PRODUCED BY A RESIDENT PROFESSIONAL COMPANY, GIVEN IN ENGLISH AND ACCOMPANIED BY A FULL ORCHESTRA. TWO OTHER PRODUCTIONS THIS SUMMER; EVENING PERFORMANCE 8:15, MATINEE 2:30. AT COLORADO COLLEGE, ARMSTRONG HALL. (LOCAL). MS JANET SPROUSE; THE COLORADO OPERA FESTIVAL; COLORADO COLLEGE; COLORADO SPG, CO 80903. (#8891-2).

AUG 1 - 3, '75. VINTAH GARDENS SHOPPING CENTER PROMOTION. A SHOPPING CENTER PROMOTION WITH SQUARE DANCING, INDIAN DANCING, STAGECOACH RIDES, QUICKDRAW SHOOTOUT, COUNTRY-WESTERN BAND AND WELLKNOWN COUNTRY STAR TO PERFORM AT A FREE SHOW. AN ALL-DAY AFFAIR. AT VINTAH GARDENS SHOPPING CENTER, 1810 W VINTAH. (ST-WIDE). JIM FREILINGER, COORD; VINTAH GARDENS MERCHANTS ASSOC; 1810 W VINTAH; COLORADO SPG, CO 80904. (#8878-1).

AUG 1, '75 - JULY 4, '76. 'ELECTION OF AMERICA'S MOST POPULAR PRESIDENT'. COMPETITION. (LOCAL). JEFF THOMAS, EXEC DIR; PIKES PEAK REGIONAL ATTRACTIONS ASSOC; 1050 S 21ST ST; COLORADO SPGS, CO 80904. (#108660-2).

AUG 2, '75. OLD-FASHIONED STREET DANCE. DOWNTOWN STREET (TEJON) OF COLORADO SPRINGS BLOCKED OFF FOR OLD-FASHIONED STREET DANCE FOR ALL RESIDENTS AND VISITORS TO PARTICIPATE IN. AT TEJON ST/DOWNTOWN. (LOCAL). BONNIE FERGUSON, PROJ DIR; EL PASO COUNTY CLERK AND RECORDERS OFFICE; 27 E VERMIJO AVE; COLORADO SPG, CO 80902. (#10163-1).

AUG 2 - 3, '75. TREASURE HUNT AND GOLD PANNING. 3RD ANNUAL TREASURE HUNT ON GOLD HILLS MESA AND GOLD PANNING CONTEST ALONG THE CREEK BELOW. THERE WILL BE INDIAN DANCING AND OTHER FESTIVITIES. AT GOLD HILLS MESA, 1624 S 21ST ST. (ST-WIDE). HUGH HOKENSTAD, PROJ DIR; SANGRE DE CHRISTO ADVENTURERS LEAGUE; PO BOX 6755; COLORADO SPG, CO 80904. (#8875-1).

AUG 4 - 8, '75. 26TH ANNUAL PIKES PEAK AMATEUR GOLF TOURNAMENT. AN AMATEUR GOLF TOURNAMENT OPEN TO ALL INTERESTED GOLFERS REGARDLESS OF SKILLS. AT PATTY JEWETT GOLF COURSE, ESPANOLA & PROSPECT STS. (ST-WIDE). CARL G CROOK, DIR; PATTY JEWETT MEN'S GOLF ASSOC; ESPANOLA & PROSPECT STS; COLORADO SPG, CO 80907. (#8890-1).

AUG 6 - 9, '75. PIKES PEAK OR BUST RODEO. FOUR-DAY RODEO HELD AT PENROSE STADIUM EACH YEAR WITH A LARGE NUMBER OF EVENTS FOR PARTICIPANTS FROM ALL OVER THE U S. ALSO INCLUDED IN THE EVENTS IS A 'PAGEANT PARADE OF THE ROCKIES' WITH FLOATS & QUEEN. MATINEE SHOW AT 2 PM, EVENING SHOW AT 8 PM. AT PENROSE STADIUM. (REGN'L). LEON WILMOT; COLORADO SPG RODEO ASSOC, INC; C/O BROADMOOR HOTEL; COLORADO SPG, CO 80906. (#8896-1).

AUG 16 - 17, '75. INTERNATIONAL HERITAGE DAY. A TWO-DAY CELEBRATION FOR PEOPLE OF ALL NATIONALITIES TO SHARE THEIR HERITAGE: SUCH AS FOOD, ARTS, ENTERTAINMENT AND OTHER CUSTOMS. BANDS PARADE, STREET DANCING, FOOD, CRAFT BOOTHS ETC. AT ACACIA PARK, TEJON & BIJOU STS. (LOCAL). BETSY ACREE, CHMN; PIKES PEAK OR BUST BY '76 FESTIVALS COMMITTEE; 1529 MCKAY WAY; COLORADO SPG, CO 80915. (#10164-1).

AUG 16 - 18, '75. A MARK TWAIN CELEBRATION - 'TOM SAWYER'. LIVE PERFORMANCE AT FINE ARTS CENTER, 30 WEST. (LOCAL). EUGENE W TEDD, CHAIRMAN; EL PASO COMMUNITY COLLEGE; 2200 BOTT AVE; COLORADO SPG, CO 80904. (#200007-41).

AUG 23, '75. BICENTENNIAL SWIM EXTRAVAGANZA. FEATURES SYNCHRONIZED SWIMMING, BICENTENNIAL PAGEANT & MUSIC & DIVING DEMONSTRATION BY OLYMPIC GOLD MEDALIST MICKI KING. AT MUNICIPOOL, 270 S UNION BLVD. (LOCAL). CYNTHIA A LOVE, CHMN; COLORADO SPRINGS DEPT OF PARKS & RECREATION; 1400 GLEN AVE; COLORADO SPG, CO 80904. (#200007-42).

SEPT 1, '75 - DEC 31, '76. CONTINENTAL COLOR GUARD. 3 CADETS WILL WEAR AUTHENTIC REPRODUCTIONS OF CONTINENTAL ARMY UNIFORMS & CARRY BETSY ROSS FLAG, DRUM & FIFE. (LOCAL). CAPT R C EHRHART; USAF ACADEMY - DEPT OF HISTORY; DEPT OF HISTORY; USAF ACADEMY, CO 80840. (#102800-1).

SEPT 2 - 7, '75. PRODUCTION OF '1776'. PRESENTATION OF THE MUSICAL PRODUCTION '1776' BY THE CADET BLUEBARD SOCIETY DURING ACADEMIC YEAR 1975-76. AT ARNOLD HALL, USAF ACADEMY. (LOCAL). CAPT D C SCOTT; USAF ACADEMY BICENTENNIAL COMMITTEE; COLORADO SPGS, CO 80840. (#6723-501).

SEPT 2 - 15, '75. ANNUAL FALL JURIED ART SHOW. ANNUAL FALL JURIED ART SHOW - OPEN TO MEMBERS ONLY; OPEN FOR PUBLIC VIEWING; DONATE PART OF PROCEEDS TO FINE ARTS CENTER. AT COLORADO SPG FINE ARTS CENTER, DALE & CASCADE. (LOCAL). DOROTHY N MYERS, PROJ DIR; COLORADO SPG ART GUILD, INC; 2016 MT VERNON; COLORADO SPG, CO 80909. (#10165-2).

SEPT 13 - 14, '75. SPORT CAR RALLY. A SPORTS CAR RALLY OVER HISTORIC ROUTES NEAR COLORADO SPG; NO LIMITS ON MAKE OF AUTOS; THREE SEPARATE CLASSES WILL BE AVAILABLE TO THE PUBLIC; REGISTRATION 8AM; DEPARTURE 10AM. AT DEPARTURE FROM GARDEN OF THE GODS. (ST-WIDE). CHARLOTTE L DAVIS; PIKES PEAK SPORTS CAR CLUB; 6878 GRAPEWOOD CIR; COLORADO SPG, CO 80918. (#8883-1).

SEPT 15, '75. 'PICK A FASHION' SHOW. FASHION SHOW/BRUNCH WHERE GOODWILL FASHIONS ARE MODELED & SOLD AFTER THE SHOW. FASHIONS OF YESTERYEAR WILL BE INCORPORATED IN THE SHOW & CENT-BICENT DECORATIONS FEATURED. AT ANTLERS HOTEL BALLROOM, CHASE STONE CENTER. (LOCAL). MRS P M SULLIVAN, CHMN; AUXILIARY TO GOODWILL INDUSTRIES OF COLORADO SPRINGS, INC; 313 CHAMBERLIN AVE; COLORADO SPG, CO 80906. (#200007-43).

SEPT 28, '75. BICENTENNIAL REDEDICATION PROGRAM-WEST JR HIGH SCHOOL. REDEDICATION OF SCHOOL TO MARK BICENT & GOLDEN ANNIV OF SCHOOL. PROGRAM TO INCLUDE PUBLIC CONCERT, CORNERSTONE CEREMONY & BICENT FLAG RAISING. (LOCAL). STANLEY GALLOWAY, COORD; WEST JUNIOR HIGH SCHOOL; 1920 W PIKES PEAK; COLORADO SPG, CO 80904. (#102123-1).

SEPT 28, '75 - AUG 31, '76. PLANETARIUM PROGRAMS. LIVE PERFORMANCE AT FALCON STADIUM. (LOCAL). MAJOR ENGLISH; USAF ACADEMY; AHB; USAF ACADEMY, CO 80840. (#102800-7).

OCT 2 - 5, '75. AMERICAN FREEDOM TRAIN DISPLAY DAYS AT COLORADO SPRINGS. THE AMERICAN FREEDOM TRAIN WILL INCLUDE 10 EXHIBIT CARS & 2 SHOWCASE CARS DEPICTING DIFFERENT PHASES OF THE AMERICAN EXPERIENCE. ITS ARRIVAL WILL SERVE AS A CATALYST FOR LOCAL BICENTENNIAL CELEBRATIONS BY PEOPLE THROUGHOUT THIS NATION. (ST-WIDE). DON MALLICOAT, EDIT SVCS; THE AMERICAN FREEDOM TRAIN FOUNDATION, INC; 5205 LEESBURG PIKE, SUITE 800; BAILEY'S XRDS, VA 22041. (#1776-25).

OCT 29 - NOV 1, '75. COMMUNITY SCHOOL CONFERENCE. AN INVITATIONAL CONFERENCE TO AIM TOWARD MORE COMMUNITY USE OF SCHOOL FACILITIES & INVOLVEMENT IN SCHOOL PROGRAMS. AT FOUR SEASONS MOTOR INN. (ST-WIDE). DR RAY PETERSON; COLORADO SPRINGS JAYCEES, STATE PTA & BOARD OF EDUCATION; STATE DEPT OF EDUCATION; DENVER, CO 80203. (#9265-1).

OCT 31 - NOV 2, '75. BLACK FOREST ARTS & CRAFTS FALL SHOW. FALL SHOW AND SALE WITH OLD FASHIONED THEME EXHIBITS BY THE MEMBERS IN THREE FIELDS: FINE ARTS, CRAFTS AND CULINARY ART. REVIVING MANY OF THE ARTS AND CRAFTS; HOURS ARE: FRIDAY AND SATURDAY 9AM TO 9PM AND SUNDAYS 11AM TO 5PM. AT BLACK FOREST COMMUNITY HALL. (ST-WIDE). TERRY ROEHRICH; BLACK FOREST ARTS AND CRAFTS GUILD; 5650 BURGESS RD; COLORADO SPG, CO 80908. (#8881-1).

NOV 1, '75. UNITED STATES ARMED FORCES BICENTENNIAL CARAVAN. THE CARAVAN IS COMPOSED OF EXHIBIT VANS FOR EACH BRANCH OF THE MILITARY SERVICE. THE THEME OF THE EXHIBITION IS 'HISTORY OF THE ARMED FORCES AND THEIR CONTRIBUTION TO THE NATION'. (LOCAL). COL M A MADSEN, CHMN; U S ARMED FORCES BICENTENNIAL EXHIBIT VANS PROJECT; A F ACADEMY; COLORADO SPG, CO 80916. (#1775-242).

NOV 1 - 2, '75. COLORADO CENTENNIAL-BICENTENNIAL MUSIC FESTIVAL TAKES PLACE. A CULTURAL ARTS PROGRAM WITH AN EMPHASIS ON THE CULTURE OF NATIVE AMERICANS. (ST-WIDE). MS BEE VRADENBURG; COLORADO SPRINGS SYMPHONY ORCHESTRA; PO BOX 1692; COLORADO SPG, CO 80901. (#189-501).

NOV 1 - 30, '75. COLLECTION OF EARLY AMERICAN ART PRINTS. EXHIBIT AT LIBRARY, ADMINISTRATION BUILDING. (LOCAL). JANET S WILLIAMS, CHMN; BICENTENNIAL COMMITTEE, NAZARENE BIBLE COLLEGE; BOX 4746; COLORADO SPG, CO 80930. (#103324-3).

NOV 2 - 3, '75. U S ARMED FORCES BICENT CARAVAN. EXHIBIT. (LOCAL). JOHN FOTENOS; MILITARY HERITAGE COMMITTEE; 3846 NUEVO DR; COLORADO SPG, CO 80918. (#100045-1).

NOV 6, '75 - DEC 31, '76. SIX HISTORICAL FLAGS DIPLAY OF OTERO SAVINGS & LOAN ASSOC. A SERIES OF SIX BICENTENNIAL FLAGS WILL BE FLOWN IN FRONT OF EACH OF NINE OFFICES THROUGHOUT THE STATE OF COLORADO, AS AN ON-GOING CONTRIBUTION TO THE BICENTENNIAL. FLYERS ON THE HISTORY OF EACH FLAG ARE AVAILABLE IN THE SAVINGS & LOAN OFFICES. (ST-WIDE). VIRGINIA BROST, VICE-PRES; OTERO SAVINGS & LOAN ASSOCIATION; 1515 N ACADEMY BLVD; COLORADO SPG, CO 80907. (#103384-3).

NOV 8, '75. CENTENNIAL-BICENTENNIAL BARBERSHOP HARMONY SHOW. LIVE PERFORMANCE AT CITY AUDITORIUM - 221 E KIOWA. (LOCAL). DOTTIE KEFFER; COLORADO SPGS CHAPTER OF SWEET ADELINES; 415 YELLOWSTONE; COLORADO SPG, CO 80910. (#102126-1).

NOV 15 - 16, '75. FIRST ANNUAL WINTER ART SHOW. FIRST ANNUAL WINTER ART SHOW ENTITLED 'BUY' CENTENNIAL II; ART WORKS ON DISPLAY FOR SALE TO THE PUBLIC. AT ANTLER'S HOTEL BALLROOM, ANTLER'S PLAZA. (ST-WIDE). DOROTHY N MYERS, PROJ DIR; COLORADO SPG ART GUILD, INC; 2016 MT VERNON; COLORADO SPG, CO 80909. (#10165-3).

NOV 21 - 23, '75. A MARK TWAIN CELEBRATION - 'HUCK FINN'. THEATRE FOR CHILDREN. INTRODUCTION TO LIVE THEATRE PRESENTATIONS OF GREAT AMERICAN LITERATURE. 7:30 FRIDAY; 10AM, 2PM SATURDAY; 3PM SUNDAY. AT FINE ARTS CENTER - 30 WEST DALE. (LOCAL). EUGENE W TEDD, PROJ DIR; EL PASO COMMUNITY COLLEGE; 2200 BOTT AVE; COLORADO SPG, CO 80904. (#102129-1).

NOV 22 - 23, '75. TOURNAMENT OF TABLES. COMPETITION, EXHIBIT AT ANTLERS HOTEL, CASCADE AND PIKE'S PEAK; STREET PARKING & PARK & SHOP. (LOCAL). LORRAINE RORICK, CHMN; COLORADO SPRINGS SYMPHONY GUILD; 1913 N TEJON; COLORADO SPG, CO 80907. (#200007-191).

NOV 23, '75. WALKING TOURS OF HISTORICAL JAZZ ENVIRONMENTS. HOSTS DRESSED IN PERIOD COSTUMES SERVING DIFFERENT FOODS AND DRINK. INCLUDED ARE: BACH SWINGS IN OLD BOSTON, 1875; RAGTIME IN OLD SEDALIA, 1900; NEW ORLEANS TRADITIONAL JAZZ, 1925; MANHATTAN SKYLINE, 1950; ELECTRONIC JAZZ FROM VAIL, 1975. PROCEEDS GO TO SCHOLARSHIPS. AT MEMBERS HOMES. (LOCAL). RICHARD F DONAHUE, PHD; BROADMOOR JAZZ CLUB, INC; 1403 MESA AVE; COLORADO SPG, CO 80906. (#200007-188).

DEC 12, '75. 200 AMERICAN CHRISTMASES - CAROLING. LIVE PERFORMANCE AT STUDENT UNION BLDG, 1111 CHAPMAN DR. (LOCAL). MARTHA GILBERT, CHAIRMAN; WOMEN'S ORGANIZATION, NAZARENE BIBLE COLLEGE, SIGMA CHAPTER; BOX 4746; COLORADO SPG, CO 80930. (#103315-10).

DEC 30, '75 - JAN 1, '76. PIKES PEAK CENTENNIAL-BICENTENNIAL FLAG PLANTING. CLIMB TO TOP OF PIKES PEAK BY ADAMAN CLUB WHO WILL PLANT COLORADO FLAG AND COLORADO CENTENNIAL FLAG ON PEAK ON JAN 1, 1976; ALSO WILL HAVE A LARGE FIREWORKS DISPLAY. AT PIKES PEAK MOUNTAIN TOP. (ST-WIDE). JAMES L BATES, CHAIRMAN; ADAMAN CLUB; 2030 N EL PASO; COLORADO SPG, CO 80907. (#10154-1).

JAN 7 - 11, '76. 1976 U S FIGURE SKATING CHAMPIONSHIPS. THE FINEST FIGURE SKATERS IN THE NATION WILL PERFORM IN COMPETITION AND EXHIBITION. AT BROADMOOR WORLD ARENA. (NAT'L). JANET ALTRICHTER, COORD; U S FIGURE SKATING CHAMPIONSHIPS; BROADMOOR; COLORADO SPG, CO 80901. (#103561-1).

JAN 17, '76. CENTENNIAL-BICENTENNIAL BARBERSHOP HARMONY SHOW. THE SWEET ADELINES, A FEMALE BARBERSHOP GROUP, IS SPONSORING THIS EVENT. AT PALMER HIGH SCHOOL AUDITORIUM. (LOCAL). DOTTIE KEFFER, CHMN; SWEET ADELINES; 415 YELLOWSTONE; COLORADO SPG, CO 80910. (#103346-1).

JAN 17 - MAY 16, '76. 'COUNTDOWN 1976: AMERICA IN SPACE'. PROGRAM OFFERED AT 2 PM AND 3 PM, FREE OF CHARGE, ON WEEKENDS. AT U S AIR FORCE PLANETARIUM. (NAT'L). CAPT ROTHGEB, COORD; U S AIR FORCE ACADEMY; US AIR FORCE ACADEMY; COLORADO SPG, CO 80840. (#103416-240).

JAN 20 - AUG 30, '76. OUTDOOR HISPANIC MURALS. EXHIBIT. (LOCAL). CLARITA TRUJILLO; UNITY COUNCIL; 14 W COSTILLA; COLORADO SPG, CO 80907. (#107023-4).

JAN '76. FORUM: THE FUTURE OF THE CHURCH IN AMERICA. SEMINAR AT STUDENT UNION BUILDING, 1111 CHAPMAN DR. (LOCAL). JANET S WILLIAMS, CHMN; NAZARENE BIBLE COLLEGE; BOX 4746, KNOB HILL STATION; COLORADO SPG, CO 80903. (#103315-15).

FEB 7, '76. MILITARY BALL. A FORMAL MILITARY BALL IS SCHEDULED IN CONNECTION WITH THE UNVEILING OF THE COLORADO BICENTENNIAL/CENTENNIAL MURAL PAINTED BY ACADEMY ARTIST PAUL BAKER DEPICTING COLORADO & US HISTORY FROM THE SPANISH EXPLORERS TO THE SPACE AGE. AT USAF ACADEMY ARNOLD HALL. (ST-WIDE). CAPTAIN JOHN B MOREY; U S AIR FORCE BICENTENNIAL COMMISSION; COLORADO SPGS, CO 80840. (#6763-1).

FEB 14, '76. CENTENNIAL BALL. DRESS WILL BE 1776 COSTUME AND ALL FOOD WILL BE SERVED '1776 STYLE'; WALTZ CLUB

COLORADO SPG — CONTINUED

WILL PERFORM A FLOOR SHOW. AT CHURCH AT OLE BROADMOOR RD & PINE AVE. (LOCAL). SHARON CLAWSON, COORD; CHURCH OF JESUS CHRIST OF THE LATTER DAY SAINTS; 1371 MEARS DR; COLORADO SPG, CO 80915. (#200007-44).

FEB 16 - 22, '76. SERTOMA CLUB AMERICAN HERITAGE PROGRAM & FREEDOM FOUNDATION BANQUET. ESSAY CONTESTS AND AWARDS FOR STUDENTS, PATRIOTIC THEMES. AT FOUR SEASONS MOTEL, I-25 AND HARRISON RD. (LOCAL). JAMES J KEENEY; SERTOMA CLUBS; 418 W COLORADO AVE; COLORADO SPG, CO 80905. (#102114-1).

FEB 21, '76. BICENTENNIAL YOUTH DEBATE, SECTIONAL EVENT. THE USAF ACADEMY WILL HOST THE COLORADO-NEW MEXICO SECTIONAL EVENT OF THE BICENTENNIAL YOUTH DEBATES. PARTICIPANTS FROM THE SIX BYD DISTRICTS IN COLORADO AND NEW MEXICO WILL COMPETE AGAINST EACH OTHER WINNERS WILL COMPETE IN THE SOUTHWEST REGIONAL EVENT IN APRIL '76. AT USAF ACADEMY, FAIRCHILD HALL, THIRD FLOOR LECTINARS. (REGN'L). MAJ ROGER LESTINA, COORD; USAF ACADEMY; USAF ACADEMY/DFEFA; USAF ACADEMY, CO 80840. (#6720-2).

MAR 5, '76. A DAY OF PRAYER OBSERVATION - CHAPEL SERVICE. CEREMONY AT FIRST NAZARENE CHURCH. (LOCAL). DR G B WILLIAMSON; NAZARENE BIBLE COLLEGE; BOX 4746, KNOB HILL STATION; COLORADO SPG, CO 80903. (#103315-14).

MAR 5 - 7, '76. A MARK TWAIN CELEBRATION - 'PRINCE & THE PAUPER'. THEATRE FOR CHILDREN. INTRODUCTION TO LIVE THEATRE PRESENTATIONS OF GREAT AMERICAN LITERATURE. 7:30 FRIDAY; 10AM, 2PM SATURDAY; 3PM SUNDAY. AT FINE ARTS CENTER - 30 WEST DALE. (LOCAL). EUGENE W TEDD, PROJ DIR; EL PASO COMMUNITY COLLEGE; 2200 BOTT AVE; COLORADO SPG, CO 80904. (#102129-3).

MAR 8, '76. EIGHTEENTH HARMON MEMORIAL LECTURE. SPEAKER TO BE PROF EDWARD COFFMAN OF THE UNIV OF WISCONSIN, ON THE TOPIC 'THE YOUNG OFFICER IN THE OLD ARMY'. AT ARNOLD HALL/USAFA. (LOCAL). CAPT CHARLES W SPECHT; USAF ACADEMY; DEPT OF HISTORY; USAF ACADEMY, CO 80840. (#102800-8).

MAR 8 - 14, '76. EARLY DAYS OF NAZARENE BIBLE COLLEGE - PRESIDENT'S EXHIBIT. EXHIBIT AT ADMINISTRATION BUILDING. (LOCAL). DR L S OLIVER, CHAIRMAN; NAZARENE BIBLE COLLEGE; BOX 4746; COLORADO SPG, CO 80930. (#103315-12).

MAR 11 - 14, '76. CHORAL MUSIC PRESENTION. LIVE PERFORMANCE AT BELL TOWER, NAZARENE BIBLE COLLEGE, 1111 CHAPMAN DR. (LOCAL). PROF WILLIS BALDRIDGE; NAZARENE BIBLE COLLEGE; BOX 4746 KNOB HILL STATION; COLORADO SPG, CO 80930. (#103315-8).

MAR 11 - 14, '76. EXHIBIT OF IMPORTANT DOCUMENTS IN AMERICAN HISTORY. EXHIBIT AT POWERS HALL. (LOCAL). JANET S WILLIAMS, CHMN; BICENTENNIAL COMMITTEE, NAZARENE BIBLE COLLEGE; BOX 4746; COLORADO SPG, CO 80930. (#103324-1).

MAR 11 - 14, '76. 'THE STRENGTH OF AMERICA' - AN ART FORMS PRODUCTION. LIFE SIZE FRAME FOR SCRIM; PRESENTATION OF FAMOUS PAINTINGS, AMERICAN MUSIC & LITERATURE ON HISTORICAL EVENTS. AT POWERS HALL, 1111 CHAPMAN DR. (LOCAL). AUDREY WILLIAMSON, CHMN; NAZARENE BIBLE COLLEGE; BOX 476 KNOB HILL STATION; COLORADO SPG, CO 80930. (#103315-9).

MAR 25 - 28, '76. RELIGIOUS DRAMA AND OPEN HOUSE - SPRING 1976. DURING SPRING 1976 A ONE-WEEK OPEN HOUSE AT NAZARENE BIBLE COLLEGE WITH A DRAMA REPRESENTING RELIGION IN AMERICA THROUGH ART, MUSIC & LITERATURE AND A DISPLAY OF OLDER CHURCHES IN COLORADO WITH PHOTOS, SLIDES, PAINTINGS AND SCULPTURE. AT NAZARENE BIBLE COLLEGE CAMPUS, 1220 CHAPMAN DR. (LOCAL). JANET S WILLIAMS, PGM DIR; NAZARENE BIBLE COLLEGE; 1220 CHAPMAN DR; COLORADO SPG, CO 80916. (#8879-1).

MAR 27, '76. BICENTENNIAL COSTUME BALL. THE THEME OF THE BALL WILL BE 200 YEARS OF ENTERTAINMENT IN AMERICA; THOSE ATTENDING WILL DRESS AS THEIR FAVORITE PERFORMING ARTIST. AT THE BROADMOOR HOTEL BALLROOM AND MEZZAZINE. (ST-WIDE). SYLVIA STOREY, CHAIRMAN; COLORADO SPRINGS CHORALE GUILD; 6640 MESEDGE DR; COLORADO SPG, CO 80919. (#102320-1).

APR 16, '76. A DAY OF WITNESS - EMPHASIS: NATIONAL ASSOC OF EVANGELICALS. CEREMONY AT CHAPEL, FIRST NAZARENE CHURCH, 1220 CHAPMAN DR. (LOCAL). DR G B WILLIAMSON, CHMN; NAZARENE BIBLE COLLEGE; NAZARENE BIBLE COLLEGE; COLORADO SPG, CO 80903. (#103315-7).

APR 24, '76. PUPPET SHOW: 'THE MIDNIGHT RIDE OF PAUL REVERE & WILLIAM DAWES'. LIVE PERFORMANCE AT STUDENT UNION, COLLEGE CAMPUS. (LOCAL). DORLEITA REED, CHAIRMAN; NAZARENE BIBLE COLLEGE; BOX 4746; COLORADO SPG, CO 80930. (#103315-16).

MAY 1, '76. CORNERSTONE REDEDICATION & OLD FASHIONED COMMUNITY FUN DAY. CEREMONY, LIVE PERFORMANCE. (LOCAL). MRS BARBARA CARTER; WHITTIER ELEMENTARY SCHOOL; 2904 W KIOWA; COLORADO SPG, CO 80904. (#103955-1).

MAY 7, '76. FILM: 'THE ORDEAL OF JONATHAN EDWARDS'. EXHIBIT AT STUDENT UNION BUILDING, 1111 CHAPMAN DR. (LOCAL). JANET S WILLIAMS, CHMN; NAZARENE BIBLE COLLEGE; BOX 4746; COLORADO SPG, CO 80903. (#103315-13).

MAY 8, '76. GRAND FESTIVAL OF FAITH. AN INTERFAITH EVENT OF MUSIC AND RELIGIOUS DRAMATIZATION WITH COMBINED CHOIRS, ORCHESTRAS AND RELIGIOUS ART, POSSIBLY A PARADE WILL BE INCLUDED IN THIS EVENT. (LOCAL). REV PHILIP L GREEN; CHURCHES OF PIKES PEAK & THE PIKES PEAK OR BUST BY '76 COMMITTEE; 420 N NEVADA; COLORADO SPG, CO 80903. (#8880-1).

MAY 15, '76. OPEN HOUSE & TOURS OF THE ACADEMY FACILITIES. OPEN HOUSE AT THE AIR FORCE ACADEMY ON THE THIRD SATURDAY IN MAY 1976 TO EXPOSE RICH LEARNING RESOURCES AND ALLOW AREA PEOPLE TO UNDERSTAND AND APPRECIATE THE USAF ACADEMY AS A NATL RESOURCE. (REGN'L). COL MADSEN; USAF ACADEMY INFORMATION OFFICE; COLORADO SPGS, CO 80840. (#6769-501).

MAY 15 - 18, '76. THE STRENGTH OF AMERICA FESTIVAL. FESTIVAL OF FAMOUS AMERICAN EVENTS AS PORTRAYED BY AMERICAN ARTISTS, ACCOMPANIED BY READINGS FROM AMERICAN LIT AND CLASSICAL MUSIC. TABLEAU PICTURES IN AUTHENTIC PERIOD COSTUMES. AT POWERS HALL, ACADEMY AND FOUNTAIN. (LOCAL). JANET S WILLIAMS, CHMN; NAZARENE BIBLE COLLEGE; COLORADO SPG, CO 80930. (#200007-207).

MAY 28, '76. COLORADO SPRING CHORALE CONCERT, 'HORA NOVISSINIA'. PERFORMANCE OF 'HORA NOVISSINIA' WRITTEN BY HORATIO PARKER IN 1893. CONDUCTED BY DONALD P JENKINS; ONLY ONE OTHER PERFORMANCE SCHEDULED IN AMERICA DURING BICENT YEAR OF THIS GREAT WORK DESCRIBING THE JOYS OF HEAVEN. AT PALMER HIGH SCHOOL AUDITORIUM, 301 N NEVADA. (REGN'L). SYLVIA STOREY, CHAIRMAN; COLORADO SPRINGS CHORALE; 6640 MESEDGE DR; COLORADO SPG, CO 80919. (#102320-2).

MAY 29 - 30, '76. MEMORIAL DAY MOTOCROSS RACE. A STATE-WIDE MOTO CROSS COMPETITION WILL BE HELD AT AZTEC RACEWAY, IN COLORADO SPRINGS ON MEMORIAL DAY. AT AZTEC PARK 6 MI EAST OF PETERSON FIELD ON HWY 94. (REGN'L). ANTONIO H GONZALEZ; AZTEC RACEWAY PARK AND SPORTS RIDERS ACCOC OF CO; 2014 AFTON WAY; COLORADO SPGS, CO 80909. (#10127-1).

JUNE 1 - 7, '76. SPACE MUSEUM. EXHIBIT AT NAZARENE BIBLE COLLEGE CAMPUS, 1111 CHAPMAN DRIVE. (LOCAL). JANET S WILLIAMS, CHMN; HIGH FLIGHTS; BOX 4746; COLORADO SPG, CO 80930. (#103324-2).

JUNE 11 - 12, '76. 'THE TITLE OF LIBERTY' - A MUSICAL PLAY. LIVE PERFORMANCE AT PALMER HS AUDITORIUM, PLATTE & NEVADA. (LOCAL). LILA TANNER, COORDINATOR; CHURCH OF JESUS CHRIST OF LATTER DAY SAINTS; 4470 S CAREFREE CIRCLE; COLORADO SPG, CO 80917. (#200007-45).

JUNE 13, '76. SUMMER SYMPHONY. AFTERNOON: FINE ARTS CENTER OUTDOOR ARTS FAIR; 7 PM SUMMER SYMPHONY DANCE FESTIVAL; 8 PM SUMMER SYMPHONY. AT MONUMENT VALLEY PARK DALE & MESA. (LOCAL). DAVID STRUTHERS, COORD; COLORADO SPRINGS SYMPHONY; 1600 N CASCADE; COLORADO SPG, CO 80903. (#200007-46).

JUNE 15 - OCT 4, '76. TOURS OF PARKS AND RESIDENTIAL AREAS. WALKING TOUR OF TOWN PARK FOR SPRING FLOWERS JUNE 15-AUGUST 1 - BUS TOUR OF RESIDENTIAL AREAS TO ADMIRE FALL COLORS SEPTEMBER 21-OCT 4, BOTH 1975 & 1976. WALKING TOURS JUNE 14, 21, 28/JULY 5 10:00, 2:00 BUS TOURS SEPT 27 & OCT 4. (LOCAL). BILL LIEB, CHAIRMAN; HORTICULTURE SOCIETY; 1576 KEATON LANE; COLORADO SPG, CO 80909. (#8908-2).

JUNE 16 - 20, '76. DONIZETTI'S 'DON PASQUALE'. MATINEE JUNE 20-2:30 PM. AT ARMSTRONG THEATRE, COLORADO COLLEGE. (LOCAL). JANET SPROUSE, COORD; THE COLORADO OPERA FESTIVAL; COLORADO COLLEGE; COLORADO SPG, CO 80903. (#200007-47).

JUNE 16 - AUG 1, '76. THE COLORADO OPERA FESTIVAL. WEDNESDAY AND FRIDAY EVENING AND SUNDAY MATINEE PERFORMANCES OF 'DON PASQUALE', 'THE SOLDIER'S TALE', 'GIANNI SCHICCHI' AND 'BORIS GODUNON' WILL BE GIVEN IN ENGLISH WITH FULL ORCHESTRA AND DISTINGUISHED VISITING ARTIST SINGERS. AT ARMSTRONG THEATER, CASCADE AT CACHE LA PUDRE ST; FREE PARKING. (LOCAL). JANET SPROUSE, COORD; COLORADO COLLEGE AND THE COLORADO SPG CHORAL SOCIETY; COLORADO SPG, CO 80903. (#108645-3).

JUNE 19, '76. SUMMER SYMPHONY AT BANCROFT PARK. AMERICAN FOLKLORE ARTS & CRAFTS FAIR; SUMMER SYMPHONY FIDDLERS' CONTEST. AT BANCROFT PARK COLORADO & 24TH. (LOCAL). DAVID STRUTHERS, COORD; COLORADO SPRINGS SYMPHONY; 1600 N CASCADE; COLORADO SPG, CO 80903. (#200007-48).

JUNE 19, '76. SUMMER SYMPHONY AT THORNDALE PARK. 7 PM SUMMER SYMPHONY FIESTAO MARIACHI BAND & DANCE TROUPE; 8 PM SUMMER SYMPHONY. AT THORNDALE PARK VINTAH & 23RD. (LOCAL). DAVID STRUTHERS, COORD; COLORADO SPRINGS SYMPHONY; 1600 N CASCADE; COLORADO SPG, CO 80903. (#200007-49).

JUNE 20, '76. SUMMER SYMPHONY AT MEADOWS PARK. AFTERNOON: SUMMER SYMPHONY BLUEGRASS FESTIVAL; 7 P M FAMILY FOLKLORE FESTIVAL; 8 P M SUMMER SYMPHONY. AT MEADOWS PARK (MT WERNER CIRCLE & S EL PASO). (LOCAL). DAVID STRUTHERS, COORD; COLORADO SPRINGS SYMPHONY; 1600 N CASCADE; COLORADO SPG, CO 80903. (#108803-19).

JUNE 25 - 27, '76. NATIONAL CHIN-QUA-PIN DAYS: A NATIONAL NATIVE AMERICAN FESTIVAL. NATIONAL AMERICAN INDIAN DANCE-SONG CONTEST HELD FOR NATIONAL AWARD IN MANY CATEGORIES. AT GARDEN OF THE GODS AREA. (NAT'L). WOODROW W PALMER; LONE FEATHER INDIAN COUNCIL, INC; 809 ELLSTON ST; COLORADO SPG, CO 80907. (#8892-1).

JUNE 26, '76. SUMMER SYMPHONY. 7 PM - NOSTALGIA NIGHT, THE SOUND OF THE BIG BANDS; 8 PM - SUMMER SYMPHONY. AT VILLAGE GREEN IN VILLAGE SEVEN. (LOCAL). DAVID STRUTHERS, COORD; COLORADO SPRINGS SYMPHONY; 1600 N CASCADE; COLORADO SPG, CO 80903. (#108803-13).

JUNE 27, '76. GRAND OPENING OF NATURE TRAIL. INTENDED FOR USE BY ALL, ESPECIALLY BLIND & HANDICAPPED. AT WHITE HOUSE RANCH AREA, GARDEN OF THE GODS. (LOCAL). LESLY HAKS, COORD; JR LEAGUE OF COLORADO SPRINGS; 1600 N CASCADE; COLORADO SPG, CO 80903. (#9266-1).

JUNE 29 - JULY 4, '76. 54TH PIKES PEAK HILL CLIMB - 1976 RACE TO THE CLOUDS. JUNE 29, JUNE 30, JULY 1, PRACTICE 6 A M TO 9 A M; JULY 2, QUALIFYING 6 A M TO 9 A M; JULY 4 RACE DAY AT NOON. AT PIKES PEAK AUTO TOLL ROAD. (LOCAL). SHELDON HARRELL, COORD; PIKES PEAK AUTO HILL CLIMB ASSOC, INC; PALMER HOUSE BEST WESTERN MOTEL; COLORADO SPG, CO 80910. (#6779-1).

JUNE 30, '76. SUMMER SYMPHONY. DOWNTOWN SPECIAL: 'CIRCUS DAY'; NOON: SUMMER SYMPHONY. AT ANTLERS PARK (WEST OF ANTLERS PLAZA). (LOCAL). DAVID STRUTHERS, COORD; COLORADO SPRINGS SYMPHONY; 1600 N CASCADE; COLORADO SPG, CO 80903. (#108803-18).

JUNE 30 - JULY 1, '76. CORY BAND FROM WALES VISITS COLORADO SPRINGS. THIS 38-PIECE BAND, FOUNDED IN 1884, HAS REPRESENTED WALES IN NUMEROUS NATIONAL CONTESTS & IN 1974 WON THE TITLE 'CHAMPION BAND OF GREAT BRITAIN.'. (INT'L). MS EDITH HALL; LYRA ENTERTAINMENT, INC; 16 W 61ST ST; NEW YORK, NY 10023. (#109009-3).

JULY 3, '76. COLORADO CENTENNIAL-BICENTENNIAL MEMORIAL AIR SHOW. FEATURING A TWO HOUR AIR SHOW BY CONFEDERATE AIR FORCE FLYING GROUP OF WORLD WAR II VINTAGE AIRCRAFT. WILL EDUCATE THE PUBLIC OF THE CONTRIBUTION OF AVIATION TO OUR DEVELOPMENT AS A STATE & NATION. AT COLORADO SPRINGS MUNICIPAL AIRPORT. (REGN'L). LT COL TOM STOREY; AREA BUSINESSMEN, SERVICE CLUBS AND MILITARY ORGANIZATIONS; 6640 MESEDGE DR; COLORADO SPGS, CO 80919. (#103918-12).

JULY 3 - 4, '76. REGION 8 STATE'S RACE, QUARTER MIDGET RACING FOR CHILDREN. CONTESTANTS MUST ENTER A REGION STATE'S MEET TO QUALIFY FOR ENTRANCE INTO THE GRAND NATL QUARTER MIDGET RACES. AT 2 MILES OFF HWY 24 ON N MARKSHEFFELL RD, E OF COLORADO SPRINGS. (REGN'L). CHARLOTTE L DAVIS, CHMN; PIKES PEAK QUARTER MIDGET ASSOC; 6878 GRAPEWOOD CIRCLE; COLORADO SPG, CO 80918. (#106988-1).

JULY 3 - 4, '76. 2-DAY SQUARE DANCE JAMBOREE. DANCE FOLLOWING NATL SQUARE DANCE CONVENTION IN CALIFORNIA. SUNDAY HOURS: 2-5 PM. AT WASHINGTON IRVING JR HIGH SCHOOL, 1702 N MURRAY BLVD. (LOCAL). GREGG ANDERSON, CHAIRMAN; COLORADO SPRINGS SQUARE DANCE CALLERS ASS'N; 1331 SUNSET RD; COLORADO SPG, CO 80909. (#102104-1).

JULY 4, '76. A DAY OF WORSHIP & THANKSGIVING. CEREMONY AT BELLTOWER NAZARENE BIBLE COLLEGE, 1111 CHAPMAN DR. (LOCAL). DR G B WILLIAMSON; CHURCH OF THE NAZARENE; BOX 4746; COLORADO SPG, CO 80903. (#103315-11).

JULY 4, '76. FOURTH OF JULY PARADE. PARADE AT PIKES PEAK & NEVADA TO MEMORIAL PARK. (LOCAL). SHELDON HARRELL, COORD; V F W POST 4051; 430 E PIKES PEAK; COLORADO SPG, CO 80901. (#108803-16).

JULY 4, '76. RUNNING CREEK FIELD STATION, ELBERT COUNTY: NATURALISTS DAY. SEMINAR. (LOCAL). ELIZABETH INGRAHAM, COORD; WRIGHT-INGRAHAM INSTITUTE; 1228 TERRACE RD; COLORADO SPG, CO 80904. (#108645-2).

JULY 4, '76. SUMMER SYMPHONY IN THE PARK - FOURTH OF JULY SPECTACULAR. AFTERNOON PICNIC & ACTIVITIES; FAMILY FESTIVAL AT 7 PM; SUMMER SYMPHONY WITH RE-DECLARATION OF INDEPENDENCE, DRAMATIC READINGS, 21-GUN SALUTE AND FIREWORKS BEGINNING AT 8 PM. AT MEMORIAL PARK. (LOCAL). DAVID STRUTHERS, COORD; COLORADO SPRINGS SYMPHONY; 1600 N CASCADE; COLORADO SPG, CO 80903. (#108803-15).

JULY 4, '76. 54TH PIKES PEAK AUTO HILL CLIMB 'RACE TO THE CLOUDS'. SECOND OLDEST SANCTIONED AUTOMOBILE RACE IN THE U S. RACE COVERS 12.5 MILES, FEATURING 156 CURVES ALONG THE DIRT RACE COURSE AND SPEEDS VARY FROM 25 TO 110 MILES PER HOUR. AT PIKES PEAK AUTO TOLL ROAD. (LOCAL). JACK VAETH, EXEC DIR; PIKES PEAK AUTO HILL CLIMB ASSOC, INC; PO BOX 153; COLORADO SPG, CO 80901. (#108645-5).

JULY 7 - 11, '76. STRAVINSKY'S 'THE SOLDIER'S TALE' & PUCCINI'S 'GIANNI SCHICCHI'. JULY 7TH - 8 PM, JULY 9TH - 8 PM, JULY 11TH - 2:30 PM. AT ARMSTRONG THEATER, COLORADO COLLEGE. (LOCAL). JANET SPROUSE, COORD; COLORADO OPERA FESTIVAL; COLORADO COLLEGE; COLORADO SPG, CO 80903. (#108803-14).

JULY 15 - 17, '76. COOLEY FAMILY ASSOC OF AMERICA BIENNIAL MEETING. CONFERENCE AT SATELLITE HOTEL. (REGN'L). MILDRED E COOLEY, PRES; THE COOLEY FAMILY ASSOC OF AMERICA; 160 MIDDLE NECK RD; GREAT NECK, NY 11021. (#200007-181).

JULY 17 - 18, '76. PIKES PEAK GEM AND MINERAL SHOW. A DISPLAY OF MINERALS, GEMS, JEWELRY, FOSSILS AND ARTIFACTS. ALSO SHOWN WILL BE A SPECIAL DISPLAY OF ALL PAST PRESIDENTS' COLLECTONS ALONG WITH A SALE AND EXCHANGES BY COLLECTORS. AT CITY AUDITORIUM, KIOWA & WEBER STS. (REGN'L). BRENDA HAWLEY; COLORADO SPRINGS MINERALOGICAL SOCIETY; 815 E WILLAMETTE; COLORADO SPG, CO 80901. (#8897-2).

JULY 20 - 24, '76. 15TH ANNIVERSARY VINTAGE CHEVROLET MEET & DISPLAY. COMPETITION, EXHIBIT AT FOUR SEASONS MOTOR INN, 2886 CIRCLE DR. (LOCAL). JACK MACY, CHAIRMAN; VINTAGE CHEVROLET CLUB OF AMERICA, INC; 909 N MADISON AVE; ANDERSON, IN 46011. (#108803-17).

JULY 21, '76. PIKES PEAK OR BUST RODEO STREET BREAKFAST. STREET BREAKFAST IS KICK-OFF EVENT ANNUALLY TO PUBLICIZE THE PIKES PEAK OR BUST RODEO AND IS THE START OF THE ANNUAL RANGE RIDE. IT IS A JOINT EFFORT OF FORT CARSON AND COMMUNITY - PROCEEDS TO CHARITY. AT PIKES PEAK & TEJON STS. (ST-WIDE). WILLIAM F BAYNES; CENTENNIAL SERTOMA CLUB; C/O 1730 FOUNTAIN BLVD; COLORADO SPG, CO 80910. (#8895-2).

COLORADO SPG—CONTINUED

JULY 24, '76. TOWN OF ELIZABETH - ELBERT COUNTY GRASSLANDS SEMINAR. SEMINAR AT MAIN ST, ELIZABETH. (LOCAL). BRENDAN DOYLE, COORD; WRIGHT-INGRAHAM INSTITUTE; 1228 TERRACE RD; COLORADO SPG, CO 80904. (#108660-4).

JULY 25 - 31, '76. LA FIESTA BONITA. A THREE-DAY CELEBRATION WITH PAGEANT CONTESTANTS, MARIACHI BANDS, BOOTHS SET UP FOR FOOD AND CRAFTS. PRIZES AWARDED FOR AUTHENTIC COSTUMES. MUSICAL PAGEANT FOR 1976 UNDERWAY. AT ACACIA PARK, TEJON & BIJOU STS. (ST-WIDE). JOSE ALVARADO, CHAIRMAN; LOS CABALLEROS DE ANZO; 2518 W BIJOU ST; COLORADO SPG, CO 80904. (#8899-2).

JULY 28 - AUG 1, '76. MUSSORGSKY'S 'BORIS GUDUNOV'. JULY 28 - 8:00 P M; JULY 30 - 8:00 P M; AUG 1 - 2:30 P M. AT ARMSTRONG THEATRE, COLORADO COLLEGE. (LOCAL). JANET SPROUSE; THE COLORADO OPERA FESTIVAL; COLORADO COLLEGE; COLORADO SPG, CO 80903. (#108803-6).

JULY 31, '76. COLORADO DAY CENTENNIAL EVE ADDRESS. CEREMONY, RADIO/TV. (LOCAL). GLORIA FRANCIS, COORD; PIKES PEAK CENTENNIAL-BICENTENNIAL COMMITTEE; 7 N TEJON ST; COLORADO SPG, CO 80903. (#108803-7).

JULY 31, '76. COLORADO DAY FIREWORKS FROM SUMMIT OF PIKES PEAK. FESTIVAL AT SUMMIT OF PIKES PEAK. (LOCAL). DAVID R HUGHES, COORD; PIKES PEAK OR BUST CENTENNIAL-BICENTENNIAL COMMITTEE; 7 N TEJON; COLORADO SPG, CO 80903. (#108803-9).

JULY 31, '76. COLORADO DAY PIONEER CENTENNIAL BALL. FESTIVAL. (LOCAL). DAVID R HUGHES, COORD; PIKES PEAK OR BUST CENTENNIAL-BICENTENNIAL COMMITTEE; 7 N TEJON; COLORADO SPG, CO 80903. (#108803-8).

JULY 31 - AUG 1, '76. COLORADO DAY CELEBRATION. FESTIVAL. (LOCAL). CHAIRMAN; PIKES PEAK OR BUST '76; 7 N TEJON ST; COLORADO SPGS, CO 80903. (#108660-3).

AUG 1, '76. COLORADO DAY GRAND COMMUNITY CENTENNIAL PICNIC. FESTIVAL AT MONUMENT VALLEY PARK. (LOCAL). DAVID R HUGHES, COORD; PIKES PEAK OR BUST CENTENNIAL-BICENTENNIAL COMMITTEE; 7 N TEJON; COLORADO SPG, CO 80903. (#108803-12).

AUG 1, '76. COLORADO DAY NEIGHBORHOOD PARADES. PARADE AT MONUMENT VALLEY PARK. (LOCAL). GLORIA FRANCIS, COORD; PIKES PEAK OR BUST CENTENNIAL-BICENTENNIAL COMMITTEE; 7 N TEJON ST; COLORADO SPG, CO 80903. (#108803-11).

AUG 1, '76. COLORADO DAY TIME CAPSULE. A RE-DECLARATION SCROLL IS INCLUDED IN THE TIME CAPSULE. AT SUMMIT OF PIKES PEAK. (LOCAL). DAVID R HUGHES, COORD; PIKES PEAK OR BUST CENTENNIAL-BICENTENNIAL COMMITTEE; 7 N TEJON; COLORADO SPG, CO 80903. (#108803-10).

AUG 1, '76. AN EVENING WITH THE MCALLISTERS. A CONCERT ON THE LAWN FEATURING APPROPRIATE MUSIC OF THE PERIOD OF 1876, FEATURING COLONIAL DAMES & FRIENDS WEARING 19TH CENTURY COSTUMES. AT MCALLISTER HOUSE MUSEUM LAWN. (LOCAL). MRS JAMES C BOWERS; MCALLISTER HOUSE CENTENNIAL-BICENTENNIAL COMMITTEE; 423 N CASCADE; COLORADO SPG, CO 80903. (#102072-1).

AUG 1, '76. 21ST INTL PIKES PEAK MARATHON RUN. FOOTRACE TO SUMMIT OF 14,110 FT PIKES PEAK & RETURN. AT START MANITOU SPGS LOG RR DEPOT. (INT'L). RUDY FAHL, COORD; BICENTENNIAL COMMITTEE; 559 PLEASANT VALLEY SHPG CNTR; COLORADO SPG, CO 80904. (#108803-5).

AUG 1 - 31, '76. THE GREAT AMERICAN RODEO-GALLERY EXHIBITS-FILMS-MUSIC. EXHIBIT, FESTIVAL, OPENING AT 30 WEST DALE. (ST-WIDE). RICHARD H RIXON; COLORADO SPRINGS FINE ARTS CENTER; 30 WEST DALE; COLO SPRINGS, CO 80903. (#50065-1).

AUG 4 - 7, '76. PIKES PEAK OR BUST RODEO. FOUR-DAY RODEO HELD AT PENROSE STADIUM EACH YEAR WITH A LARGE NUMBER OF EVENTS FOR PARTICIPANTS FROM ALL OVER THE U S. ALSO INCLUDED IN THE EVENTS IS A 'PAGEANT PARADE OF THE ROCKIES' WITH FLOATS & QUEEN. MATINEE SHOW AT 2 PM, EVENING SHOW AT 8 PM. AT PENROSE STADIUM. (REGN'L). LEON WILMOT; COLORADO SPG RODEO ASSOC, INC; C/O BROADMOOR HOTEL; COLORADO SPG, CO 80906. (#8896-2).

AUG 5, '76. PAGEANT PARADE OF THE ROCKIES. ANNUAL PARADE IN CONJUNCTION WITH PIKES PEAK OR BUST RODEO. AT PARADE STARTS ON NORTH TEJON, DOWNTOWN. (REGN'L). CLAY J BANTA, DIRECTOR; COLORADO SPGS CHAMBER OF COMMERCE; HOLLY SUGAR BLDG; COLORADO SPG, CO 80901. (#102122-1).

AUG 5 - 6, '76. CENTENNIAL CAMEOS FLOWER SHOW. COMPETITION, EXHIBIT AT MASONIC TEMPLE ON PANORAMA. (LOCAL). KATHI O'DONNELL, COORD; AUSTIN BLUFFS GARDEN CLUB; 2432 SAN CARLOS; COLORADO SPG, CO 80910. (#108803-4).

AUG 7, '76. RUNNING CREEK FIELD STATION - ELBERT COUNTY ARCHITECTS SEMINAR. SEMINAR. (LOCAL). ELIZABETH INGRAHAM, COORD; WRIGHT-INGRAHAM INSTITUTE; 1228 TERRACE RD; COLORADO SPG, CO 80904. (#108660-1).

AUG 18, '76. DEDICATION OF NEW COLORADO CENTENNIAL CAMPUS. CEREMONY. (LOCAL). HELEN ANDERSON, CHAIRMAN; EL PASO COMMUNITY COLLEGE; 2200 BOTT ST; COLORADO SPG, CO 80904. (#200007-201).

AUG 20, '76. EDUCATIONAL TOUR. TOUR AT U S AIR FORCE ACADEMY. (LOCAL). MELVIN HARMON, COORD; BPO ELKS LODGE #90; PUEBLO ARMY DEPOT; PUEBLO, CO 81003. (#108726-5).

AUG 20 - 21, '76. UNITED STATES ARMED FORCES BICENTENNIAL CARAVAN. CARAVAN IS COMPOSED OF EXHIBIT VANS FOR EACH MILITARY SERVICE. PROJECT THEME IS 'HISTORY OF THE ARMED FORCES & THEIR CONTRIBUTIONS TO THE NATION.'. (LOCAL). DAVE HUGHES, CHMN; UNITED STATES ARMED FORCES BICENTENNIAL CARAVAN; 9 NORTH TEJON; COLORADO SPG, CO 80903. (#1775-673).

SEPT 1 - OCT 31, '76. EXHIBITION OF NAVAJO BLANKETS, COLORADO SPG FINE ARTS CENTER. EXHIBITION ENTITLED 'BETWEEN TRADITIONS: NAVAJO WEAVING TOWARD THE END OF THE 19TH CENTURY'. EXHIBITION OF NAVAJO BLANKETS. AT COLORADO SPRINGS FINE ARTS CENTER. (REGN'L). KENDRA BOWERS, CURATOR; UNIV OF IOWA, MUSEUM OF ART; COLORADO SPG, CO 80903. (#6548-505).

SEPT 12 - 17, '76. GLIDDEN ANTIQUE CAR TOUR. ANTIQUE CAR TOUR WITH COLORADO SPG, COLORADO AS CENTRAL POINT FOR TOURS OF INTERESTING AND HISTORICAL ATTRACTIONS IN THE PIKES PEAK REGION. TOURS BY 300 ANTIQUE CARS PRIOR TO THE YEAR 1930. AT FOUR SEASONS MOTOR INN. (REGN'L). ROBERT TITTEL, TOUR CHMN; PIKES PEAK CHAPTER OF THE VETERAN MOTOR CAR CLUB OF AMERICA; 424 COLUMBIA RD; COLORADO SPG, CO 80904. (#8901-1).

SEPT 13 - 14, '76. SPORT CAR RALLY. A SPORTS CAR RALLY OVER HISTORIC ROUTES NEAR COLORADO SPG; NO LIMITS ON MAKE OF AUTOS; THREE SEPARATE CLASSES WILL BE AVAILABLE TO THE PUBLIC; REGISTRATION 8AM; DEPARTURE 10AM. (ST-WIDE). CHARLOTTE L DAVIS; PIKES PEAK SPORTS CAR CLUB; 6878 GRAPEWOOD CIR; COLORADO SPG, CO 80918. (#8883-2).

SEPT 20 - 24, '76. BICENTENNIAL NEEDLEWORK DISPLAY. NEEDLE WORK, CROCHET, KNITTING, QUILTING, CREWEL, NEEDLEPOINT. JUDGED ACCORDING TO ABOVE CLASSIFICATION. SPECIAL GROUP-CHILDREN'S DIVISION ACCORDING TO AGE. AT STUDENT UNION, COLLEGE CAMPUS, 1111 CHAPMAN DR. (LOCAL). LINDA SCHOOLING; NAZARENE BIBLE COLLEGE; NAZARENE BIBLE COLLEGE, BOX 4746; COLORADO SPG, CO 80930. (#17420-1).

SEPT 24, '76. 'PIKES PEAK HEALERS', MARSHALL SPRAGUE, BICENTENNIAL LUNCHEON. LECTURE CONCERNS COLORFUL MEDICINE MEN WHO CAME TO COLORADO IN LATE 19TH CENTURY PREACHING GOSPEL OF 'CLIMATOTHERAPY' AS A CURE FOR TUBERCULOSIS. AT BROADMOOR HOTEL. (ST-WIDE). MRS JOHN B FARLEY, COORD; COLORADO MEDICAL SOCIETY AUXILIARY; 529 COLORADO AVE; PUEBLO, CO 81004. (#108803-2).

SEPT 29 - OCT 1, '76. SEVENTH MILITARY HISTORY SYMPOSIUM: THE MILITARY ON THE FRONTIER. LIVE PERFORMANCE, CONFERENCE AT FAIRCHILD HALL. (NAT'L). CAPT DAVID A MILES; USAF ACADEMY; DEPT OF HISTORY; USAF ACADEMY, CO 80840. (#102800-9).

OCT 1 - 2, '76. CENTENNIAL-BICENTENNIAL CHUCKWAGON FESTIVAL. FESTIVAL REUNION OF THE WEST'S TOP CHUCKWAGON STARS. AT FLYING W CHUCKWAGON, 6100 WILSON RD. (ST-WIDE). RUSS WOLFE; FLYING W RANCH; 6100 WILSON RD; COLORADO SPGS, CO 80907. (#9904-1).

NOV 4 - 7, '76. 1976 WESTERN REGION AMER ADVERTISING FEDERATION CONVENTION. THE AMERICAN ADVERTISING FEDERATION'S 1976 WESTERN REGION CONVENTION. (REGN'L). KURT GABEL, CHMN; PIKES PEAK ADVERTISING FEDERATION; BOX 1012; COLORADO SPG, CO 80930. (#102121-1).

NOV 11 - 14, '76. CENTENNIAL-BICENTENNIAL MUSIC FESTIVAL. THE FESTIVAL WILL FEATURE THE CULTURAL CONTRIBUTIONS OF AMERICAN ARTISTS. THE PERFORMANCES ARE THURSDAY AT 8:00 PM, FRIDAY AT 7:30 PM AND SUNDAY AT 3:00 PM. AT PALMER AUDITORIUM. (REGN'L). BEA VRADENBURG, DIRECTOR; COLORADO SPRINGS SYMPHONY ORCHESTRA; PO BOX 1692; COLORADO SPG, CO 80901. (#189-2).

NOV 18 - 20, '76. DEDICATION CONCERT OF BURNS WURLITZER PIPE ORGAN. COMPLETE RESTORATION AND REINSTALLATION OF THE BURNS THEATER ORGAN, A WURLITZER OPUS MADE IN 1927. AT MOUNT ST FRANCIS AUDITORIUM, WOODMEN VALLEY RD. (LOCAL). DAVID N WEESNER; PIKES PEAK AREA THEATRE ORGAN SOCIETY; 19 ARRAWANNA ST; COLORADO SPG, CO 80909. (#9262-1).

COLUMBINE

AMERICAN FLAG DISPLAY - COLUMBINE, CO. VARIOUS EARLY AMERICAN FLAGS MOUNTED ON PLAQUES WILL BE EXHIBITED. EXHIBIT IS AVAILABLE TO SCHOOL, BUSINESSES AND OTHER ORGANIZATIONS IN THE AREA ON MON-FRI, AND TO CHURCHES ON SAT & SUN. (LOCAL). H CHARLES HIRST, COORDINATOR; FLAG DISPLAY COMMITTEE; 7231 S SHERIDAN CT; COLUMBINE, CO 80123. (#26199).

MAY 30 - AUG 29, '76. CONCERTS IN THE PARK. BANDS, ORCHESTRAS & MUSICAL GROUPS WILL BE FEATURED EVERY SUNDAY EVENING; FAMILIES ARE ENCOURAGED TO BRING PICNIC SUPPERS. (LOCAL). H CHARLES HIRST, COORD; CONCERTS IN THE PARK COMMITTEE; 7231 S SHERIDAN CT; COLUMBINE, CO 80123. (#108619-1).

JUNE 11 - 12, '76. STAGE PRODUCTION OF 'GEORGE WASHINGTON SLEPT HERE'. COMMUNITY THEATER PRODUCTION OF 'GEORGE WASHINGTON SLEPT HERE'. THE PERFORMANCE WILL ALSO BE HELD ON JUNE 3 & JUNE 5. AT COLUMBINE HIGH SCHOOL. (LOCAL). H CHARLES HIRST, COORD; COLUMBINE HIGH SCHOOL; 7231 S SHERIDAN CT; COLUMBINE, CO 80123. (#200007-113).

COMMERCE CITY

JULY 4, '76. COMBINED 'FIREWORKS TO MUSIC' FOURTH OF JULY DISPLAY. FIREWORKS DISPLAY WITH COMMUNITY CHORUS AND COMMUNITY BAND SINGING AND PLAYING PATRIOTIC MUSIC. (LOCAL). JAMES R HECK, COORD; FOURTH OF JULY COMMITTEE; PO BOX 159; COMMERCE CITY, CO 80020. (#108640-1).

COPPER MTN

AUG 2 - 7, '76. CENTENNIAL ARTS FESTIVAL. A LEARNING EXPERIENCE IN ARTS OF YESTERYEAR-HISTORIC PRESERVATION THROUGH EDUCATION-RELOCATION OF HISTORIC CABIN AS SUMMER FESTIVAL SIGHT, YEAR-ROUND MUSEUM AND WORKSHOP-SEMINAR LOCATION USE OF ANTIQUE TOOLS AND METHODS IN ARTS OF LIFE 100 YEARS AGO. AT COPPER MTN 'OLLIE LIND CABIN', HWY 91 & 6, 6 MILES WEST OF FRISCO. (ST-WIDE). SUSAN DALEY; COLORADO MTN COLLEGE COPPER MOUNTAIN SUMMIT COUNTY HISTORICAL SOC; BOX 567; FRISCO, CO 80443. (#4433-1).

CORTEZ

COUNTY FAIR AND FACILITIES PROJ OF CORTEZ, COLO. ESTABLISH LOCATION AND CONSTRUCT FACILITIES FOR ANNUAL COUNTY FAIR AND CITY AND COUNTY MEETINGS, EXHIBITIONS AND SOCIAL AFFAIRS. (LOCAL). STANLEY TALCOTT, CHAIRMAN; CORTEZ CENTENNIAL BICENTENNIAL COMMITTEE; C/O BOX 1540; CORTEZ, CO 81321. (#4370). **(??).**

ESCALANTE TRAIL-MONTEZUMA COUNTY, COLORADO. LOCATION AND MARKING OF FOOTTRAIL WHERE ESCALANTE TRAVELED THROUGH MONTEZUMA COUNTY ON HIS TRAVELS IN 1776. (LOCAL). STANLEY TALCOTT, CHAIRMAN; CORTEZ CENTENNIAL BICENTENNIAL COMMITTEE; BOX 1540; CORTEZ, CO 81321. (#4372). **(??).**

HISTORICAL MUSEUM OF CORTEZ, COLORADO. ESTABLISHMENT OF MUSEUM FOR COLLECTION, PRESERVATION AND EXHIBITION OF ITEMS AND ARTIFACTS FOUND IN MONTEZUMA-DOLORES COUNTIES AREA. (LOCAL). STANLEY TALCOTT, CHAIRMAN; MONTELORES HISTORICAL SOCIETY; C/O BOX 1540; CORTEZ, CO 81321. (#4161).

LITTER BASKETS FOR THE CENTENNIAL -CORTEZ, COLO. LITTER BASKETS WITH CENTENNIAL-BICENTENNIAL SYMBOLS TO BE PLACED IN DOWNTOWN CORTEZ. (LOCAL). STANLEY TALCOTT, CHAIRMAN; CORTEZ CENTENNIAL BICENTENNIAL COMMITTEE; BOX 1540; CORTEZ, CO 81321. (#4371).

MAY 21, '76. NATL PK SVC '...A LITTLE LOOK AROUND' VISITS MESA VERDE NP. THIS SHORT PROGRAM FEATURES ACTORS PORTRAYING FAMOUS AMERICANS OF THE PAST WHO'VE RETURNED TO SEE AMERICA'S GROWTH. (REGN'L). MESA VERDE NATL PARK; NATIONAL PARK SERVICE; MESA VERDE NP, CO 81330. (#5653-62).

JUNE 17 - 18, '76. UTE MOUNTAIN ROUNDUP RODEO PARADE. PARADE. (LOCAL). LOUIS C CAUGLEY, COORD; CITY OF CORTEZ; PO BOX 1540; CORTEZ, CO 81321. (#200007-26).

JULY 4, '76. CORTEZ FIREWORKS. FESTIVAL. (LOCAL). C L VANDE VOORDE, CHMN; CORTEZ BICENTENNIAL COMMITTEE; PO BOX 968; CORTEZ, CO 81321. (#107583-1).

JULY 21, '76. NATL PK SVC 'PEOPLE OF 1776' PLAYS AT MESA VERDE NP. TRAVELING TROUPE WILL BRING VARIOUS ASPECTS OF COLONIAL LIFE (MILITARY LIFE, MUSIC, CRAFTS) TO VISITORS TO THIS NATIONAL PARK SERVICE AREA. (REGN'L). MESA VERDE NATL PK; NATIONAL PARK SERVICE; MESA VERDE NP, CO 81330. (#1469-9).

AUG 20 - 22, '76. NATIONAL INTER-TRIBAL GOLF CLASSIC. AMATEUR GOLF TOURNEY OPEN TO ALL WITH INDIAN LINEAGE, A NATIONAL CHAMPIONSHIP. AT CORTEZ MUNICIPAL GOLF COURSE. (NAT'L). BILL STROUD, CHAIRMAN; CORTEZ MUNICIPAL GOLF COURSE MEN'S GOLF ASSOC & INTER TRIBAL COMM; 310 LAPLATA PL; CORTEZ, CO 81321. (#104499-1).

CRAWFORD

COMMUNITY PARK - CRAWFORD, CO. A NEW COMMUNITY PARK WILL BE CONSTRUCTED IN CRAWFORD. (LOCAL). JOHN BAKER, COORDINATOR; TOWN OF CRAWFORD; BOX 223; CRAWFORD, CO 81415. (#26196).

AUG 1 - 3, '76. CHUCK WAGON & ICE CREAM SOCIAL. FESTIVAL. (LOCAL). C B RICHARDSON, COORD; TOWN OF CRAWFORD; BOX 3; CRAWFORD, CO 81415. (#108955-22).

SEPT 6, '76. DEDICATION OF A COMMUNITY PARK. CEREMONY AT WEST END OF TOWN OF CRAWFORD. (LOCAL). W R PITTS; TOWN OF CRAWFORD; PO BOX 182; CRAWFORD, CO 81415. (#26196-1).

SEPT 6, '76. RECOGNITION OF THREE ELDEST CITIZENS. CEREMONY AT PARK AT WEST END OF TOWN OF CRAWFORD. (LOCAL). OTTO PORTER; TOWN OF CRAWFORD; BOX 227; CRAWFORD, CO 81415. (#108809-1).

CREEDE

PEOPLE'S PARK - CREEDE, CO. PARK TO BE BUILT AROUND THE RESTORED DEPOT; THE CITY WILL DONATE DIRT; THE HIGH SCHOOL WILL BUILD TABLES, BENCHES & PLANTERS; THE CITIZENS WILL PLANT GRASS AND TREES. (LOCAL). JENNY INGE, SECRETARY; CREEDE BUSINESSMEN'S ASSOC & ELKS CLUB BPOE #506; BOX 371; CREEDE, CO 81130. (#24016).

APR 18 - 25, '76. CREEDE CLEAN-UP WEEK: TREASURE HUNT, FLEA MARKET & SWAP MEET. FESTIVAL, COMPETITION, EXHIBIT AT COURT HOUSE PARKING LOT, (CITY MAINTENANCE BLDG, IN CASE OF RAIN). (LOCAL). JENNIFER J INGE, COORD; CREEDE BUSINESSMEN'S ASSOC; BOX 371; CREEDE, CO 81130 (#200007-23).

MAY 8 - 16, '76. ARTS & CRAFTS FESTIVAL. ARTS & CRAFTS IN ALL MEDIA DISPLAYED DAILY. DEMONSTRATIONS INCLUDE

CREEDE—CONTINUED

QUILTING, NEEDLEPOINT, POT-THROWING, WEAVING, OLD-TIMERS EXHIBIT, ANTIQUES & ARTIFACTS: OLD TOOLS, FORGOTTEN CRAFTS. NIGHT ACTIVITIES WILL BE PLAYS, TALENT SHOW, SQUARE DANCE, BAND CONCERT. AT CREEDE REPERTORY THEATRE & THE FRENCH RESTAURANT, N CREEDE AVE. (LOCAL). JENNIFER J INGE, COORD; ALPINE ARTISTS ASSOC; BOX 371; CREEDE, CO 81130. (#200007-184).

MAY 22 - 23, '76. HERITAGE WEEKEND: FLAG PRESENTATION AND CONCERT. OLD-FASHIONED HOUSE RAISING TO REBUILD BANDSTAND AS IT ONCE STOOD; COMMUNITY LABOR & POT LUCK LUNCHES; MAY 23: PRESENTATION OF ARBA FLAG AT 4:30 PM, 5:00 PM CONCERT BY SCHOOL BAND; THIS IS THE KICK-OFF EVENT FOR PARK PLANNED AROUND BANDSTAND. AT CREEDE AVE BETWEEN DEPOT & ELKS BLDG. (LOCAL). JENNIFER J INGE, CHMN; ELKS CLUB & RARE THINGS SHOP; BOX 371; CREEDE, CO 81130. (#107908-1).

JULY 3, '76. FOURTH OF JULY CELEBRATION: PARADES MINE CONTESTS, FIREWORKS, DANCE. PARADES 7/3 & 7/4 AT 10AM, SENIOR CITIZEN SELECT QUEEN OF '76 & GENERAL MARSHALL TO RIDE IN PARADES; MINING CONTESTS, HAND & MACHINE EVENTS, LOGGING CONTESTS: 7/3 & 7/4 AT 1-6PM (ONLY 1 OR 2 OTHER SUCH EVENTS LEFT IN THE STATE); FIREWORKS - SUNSET 7/3 & 7/4. (ST-WIDE). BARBARA SPRINGER; CREEDE BUSINESSMEN'S ASSOC; GEN DELIVERY; CREEDE, CO 81130. (#107573-2).

JULY 3 - 9, '76. CREEDE AMERICA. PARADE. (LOCAL). BARBARA SPRINGER, COORD; CREEDE BUSINESS ORGANIZATION; CREEDE, CO 81130. (#107573-1).

CRESTED BUTTE

CENTENNIAL PARK CREATED IN CRESTED BUTTE, CO. CREATION OF A DOWNTOWN MINI-PARK WITH TOURIST FACILITIES, INCLUDING A MAP BOARD, A HISTORY CHART AND OTHER HISTORICAL EXHIBITS. (LOCAL). MARY MCPHERSON, COORDINATOR; CRESTED BUTTE CENTENNIAL-BICENTENNIAL COMMITTEE; BOX 376; CRESTED BUTTE, CO 81224. (#6814).

CITY HALL RESTORATION IN CRESTED BUTTE, COLO. A PROJECT TO RENOVATE AND RESTORE THE OLD CRESTED BUTTE TOWN HALL. (LOCAL). MS PEGGY ROGGENBUCK, MT THEATRE PROJECT COORD; CRESTED BUTTE SOCIETY; PO BOX 55; CRESTED BUTTE, CO 81224. (#4292). **ARBA GRANTEE.**

HERITAGE TRAIL FOR CRESTED BUTTE, COLORADO. PLACES OF HISTORICAL INTEREST WILL BE MARKED WITH SIGNS GIVING A BRIEF DESCRIPTION OF THE PLACE & EVENT. A BROCHURE WILL BE PREPARED FOR PUBLIC DISTRIBUTION. (LOCAL). MARY MCPHERSON, CHAIRPERSON; CRESTED BUTTE CENT-BICENTENNIAL COMMITTEE; BOX 376; CRESTED BUTTE, CO 81224. (#6798).

A LOOK AT THE WOMEN OF CRESTED BUTTE, CO. A SERIES OF INTERVIEWS & SLIDES ON THE ROLE OF CRESTED BUTTE'S WOMEN IN NURTURING A SENSE OF COMMUNITY. (LOCAL). TOWN PLANNER; CITY OF CRESTED BUTTE; BOX 256; CRESTED BUTTE, CO 81224. (#26150).

PUBLIC SUBSCRIPTION OF ART WORKS PROJ OF COLORADO. PRIVATE AND PUBLIC MONIES WILL BE SPENT TO COMMISSION ARTISTS TO DESIGN AND EXECUTE WORKS OF ART FOR DISPLAY IN PUBLIC PLACES. SOME OF THESE WILL BE HISTORICAL IN NATURE. (LOCAL). MARY MCPHERSON, CHAIRPERSON; CRESTED BUTTE ARBA; BOX 376; CRESTED BUTTE, CO 81224. (#6819).

RECREATIONAL & ATHLETIC PROJECTS, CO. THE FOLLOWING ACTIVITIES WILL BE OFFERED: FISHING, RAFTING, HUNTING, HORSEBACK RIDING, KAYAKING, JEEP TOURS, WILDERNESS SKILLS, MOUNTAINEERING, ROCK CLIMBING, NAVIGATION, SKIING, RUGBY & OTHER BALL GAMES. (LOCAL). JOAN L ADAMS, COORDINATOR; CRESTED BUTTE RESORT ASSOC; BOX 565; CRESTED BUTTE, CO 81224. (#26149).

RESTORATION PROJECT IN CRESTED BUTTE, COLORADO. THE RESTORATION OF CRESTED BUTTE'S OLD TOWN HALL, BUILT IN 1883, BUT CONDEMNED IN 1974 FOR FIRE AND SAFETY REASONS, AS A USABLE PUBLIC STRUCTURE AND HOME FOR THE MOUNTAIN THEATER GROUP. (LOCAL). MARY MCPHERSON, CHAIRPERSON; CRESTED BUTTE CENTENNIAL-BICENT COMMITTEE; BOX 376; CRESTED BUTTE, CO 81224. (#6796).

MAR 12 - 14, '76. 4TH ANNUAL NORDIC FEST. SKI TOURING FESTIVAL AND CITIZENS RACE SPONSORED BY CRESTED BUTTE SNOWSHOE & TOBOGGAN CLUB FOUNDED IN 1888. AT THROUGHOUT THE COMMUNITY. (LOCAL). MRS MORGAN QUEAL, CHMN; CRESTED BUTTE SNOWSHOE & TOBOGGAN CLUB; BOX 566; CRESTED BUTTE, CO 81224. (#104656-7).

JUNE 1, '76 - JUNE 30, '77. WALKING TOUR OF HISTORICAL CRESTED BUTTE. TOUR. (LOCAL). S B CRANK, PROJ COORD; TOWN OF CRESTED BUTTE; TOWN HALL; CRESTED BUTTE, CO 81224. (#108672-3).

JUNE 5, '76. GREENING AND CLEANING COLORADO & PICNIC. BACKSLOPE AND SEEDING BY HYDROMULCH OF APPROX 3 TO 5 MILES OF ROADSIDE BANKS WITHIN THE TOWN PRIMARILY ON THE MAIN ROAD THROUGH TOWN AND ROAD CUTS THROUGH HILLSIDES. TO BE FOLLOWED BY A TOWN PICNIC. (LOCAL). JAMES DEAN, COORD; CITY OF CRESTED BUTTE; BOX 669; CRESTED BUTTE, CO 81224. (#200007-25).

JULY 1 - AUG 31, '76. HISTORIC SLIDE SHOW. SHOW EVERY FRIDAY NIGHT THROUGH JULY AND AUGUST. AT RAILROAD DEPOT. (LOCAL). JOAN ADAMS, COORD; TOWN PLANNING COMMITTEE; BOX 256; CRESTED BUTTE, CO 81224. (#108641-2).

JULY 2 - 5, '76. FOURTH OF JULY CELEBRATION. FESTIVAL AT TOWN OF CRESTED BUTTE & ENVIRONS. (REGN'L). JOAN ADAMS, COORDINATOR; RESORT ASSOC; BOX 565; CRESTED BUTTE, CO 81224. (#108641-1).

JULY 3 - 4, '76. CRESTED BUTTE PARADE AND MARATHON. FESTIVAL, PARADE. (LOCAL). SALLY B CRANK, CHAIRMAN; TOWN OF CRESTED BUTTE; PO BOX 256; CRESTED BUTTE, CO 81224. (#107580-1).

JULY 4, '76. FOURTH OF JULY CELEBRATION. AWARD, CEREMONY, COMPETITION, FAIR, PARADE. (LOCAL). SANDY HICKOCK, CHMN; FOURTH OF JULY COMMITTEE; ELK AVE; CRESTED BUTTE, CO 81224. (#102827-2).

JULY 5 - AUG 27, '76. SUMMER ART WORKSHOPS. EXHIBIT AT THE DEPOT. (LOCAL). IRIS LEVIN, CHMN; CRESTED BUTTE SOCIETY INC; BOX 595; CRESTED BUTTE, CO 81224. (#102827-1).

JULY 8 - 11, '76. BICENTENNIAL CARNIVAL. FESTIVAL AT TOWN PARK. (LOCAL). S B CRANK, COORDINATOR; CRESTED BUTTE BUSINESS ASSOC P CRESTED BUTTE RESORT ASSOC; BOX 565; CRESTED BUTTE, CO 81224. (#108739-5).

JULY 12 - 23, '76. CREATIVE MOVEMENT TO ORFF MUSIC OF CHILDREN. ACCREDITED 3 QUARTER HOURS, JUNIORS, SENIORS & GRAD STUDENTS AT UNIV OF N COLORADO AT GREELEY. AT RAILROAD DEPOT. (REGN'L). SALLY CRANK, COORD; CRESTED BUTTE SOCIETY; BOX 427; CRESTED BUTTE, CO 81224. (#108739-1).

JULY 17 - 18, '76. GOLF MARATHON. COMPETITION AT MOUNTAIN PASS. (LOCAL). GEORGE CLAUS, COORD; CRESTED BUTTE BUSINESS ASSOC; BOX 585; CRESTED BUTTE, CO 81224. (#108739-2).

JULY 21, '76. AMERICAN BRASS QUINTET CONCERT. LIVE PERFORMANCE AT CONGREGATIONAL CHURCH. (REGN'L). S B CRANK, COORDINATOR; CRESTED BUTTE SOCIETY, RESORT ASSOCIATION & TOWN OF CRESTED BUTTE; PO BOX 56; CRESTED BUTTE, CO 81224. (#108739-3).

JULY 22 - 23, '76. TAYLOR RESEVOIR OVERNIGHT BICYCLE TRIP. TOUR. (LOCAL). MYLES RADEMAN, PROJ DIR; TOWN OF CRESTED BUTTE; BOX 376 CRESTED BUTTE TOWN HALL; CRESTED BUTTE, CO 81224. (#102827-3).

JULY 24 - 25, '76. HOT AIR BALLOON RACES. COMPETITION, FESTIVAL AT TOWN PARK. (REGN'L). S B CRANK, COORDINATOR; CRESTED BUTTE BUSINESS ASSOC & CRESTED BUTTE RESORT ASSOC; PO BOX 565; CRESTED BUTTE, CO 81224. (#108739-4).

AUG 6 - 7, '76. CHALLENGE DISCOVERY: WILDERNESS AND EDUCATION SEMINAR. SEMINAR AT CRESTED BUTTE RAILROAD DEPOT. (REGN'L). JOAN ADAMS, PROJ DIR; MANKATO STATE COLLEGE; GEN DELIVERY; CRESTED BUTTE, CO 81224. (#102898-1).

AUG 7, '76. HORSEHOE CONTEST. COMPETITION AT TOWN PARK. (LOCAL). MARK CALVE, COORDINATOR; CRESTED BUTTE BUSINESS ASSOC; BOX 502; CRESTED BUTTE, CO 81224. (#108739-6).

AUG 13 - 14, '76. ARTS AND CRAFTS FESTIVAL. EXHIBIT, FESTIVAL, LIVE PERFORMANCE. (LOCAL). MARY MCPHERSON, CHMN; CRESTED BUTTE SOCIETY, INC; PO BOX 466; CRESTED BUTTE, CO 81224. (#102897-1).

AUG 21, '76. ASPEN TO CRESTED BUTTE BICENTENNIAL BICYCLE PEDALTHON. AWARD, CEREMONY, COMPETITION. (LOCAL). MYLES RADEMAN, PROJ DIR; TOWN OF CRESTED BUTTE; BOX 376, CRESTED BUTTE TOWNHALL; CRESTED BUTTE, CO 81224. (#102900-1).

AUG 28 - 29, '76. AMERICAN INDIAN FESTIVAL. AN EXHIBITION OF ARTS & CRAFTS, DANCE & CULTURE OF SEVERAL AMERICAN INDIAN TRIBES. AT TOWN OF CRESTED BUTTE AND ENVIRONS. (REGN'L). BOB GALE, COORD; CRESTED BUTTE RESORT ASSOC; BOX 565; CRESTED BUTTE, CO 81224. (#108806-5).

AUG 28 - 29, '76. MOTOCROSS RACE. MOTORCYCLE MOTOCROSS RACE: NOVICE, B & A, 125CC, 250CC & OPEN. AT AIRPORT. (REGN'L). BOB GALE, COORD; CRESTED BUTTE RESORT ASSOC; BOX 347; CRESTED BUTTE, CO 81224. (#108806-4).

AUG 29, '76. CRESTED BUTTE MOUNTAIN MARATHON AND BARBECUE. A RACE FROM THE TOWN OF CRESTED BUTTE TO THE TOP OF CRESTED BUTTE MOUNTAIN AND BACK. BARBEQUE PICNIC IN THE PARK FOR SURVIVORS AND LONG RANGE SPECTATORS - CONTACT ROY SMITH, BOX 846 CRESTED BUTTE CO, 81224. AT TOWN OF CRESTED BUTTE AND ENVIRONS. (REGN'L). BOB GALE, COORD; CRESTED BUTTE RESORT ASSOC; BOX 565; CRESTED BUTTE, CO 81224. (#108806-3).

SEPT 18 - 19, '76. MOUNTAIN ENDURO. COMPETITION AT CRESTED BUTTE MOUNTAIN. (REGN'L). BOB GALE, COORD; CRESTED BUTTE RESORT ASSOC; BOX 347; CRESTED BUTTE, CO 81224. (#108806-1).

SEPT 25 - 26, '76. FALL COLOR FESTIVAL. WILD WEST SHOW, WESTERN PARADE, SQUARE DANCING & TURKEY SHOOTING. (LOCAL). S B CRANK, COORD; BUSINESSMEN'S ASSOC; BOX 565; CRESTED BUTTE, CO 81224. (#108806-2).

SEPT - OCT '76. ORIGINAL THEATRE PRODUCTION. THE PRODUCTION OF AN ORIGINAL BICENTENNIAL PLAY BY THE CRESTED BUTTE THEATRE TO CELEBRATE THE RENOVATION OF THEIR NEW HOME, THE OLD TOWN HALL. (LOCAL). TOWN PLANNER; TOWN OF CRESTED BUTTE; BOX 256; CRESTED BUTTE, CO 81224. (#108672-2).

JUNE 20 - SEPT 9, '77. MOUNTAIN THEATER PRODUCTION. AN ORIGINAL PRODUCTION WITH MUSIC & DANCE THEMATICALLY ATTUNED TO COLORADO IN THE CENTENNIAL YEAR. (LOCAL). PENNY LAPENTER, COORD; CRESTED BUTTE CENTENNIAL-BICENTENNIAL COMMITTEE; BOX 376; CRESTED BUTTE, CO 81224. (#108672-1).

CRIPPLE CREEK

COLORADO CRAFT-IN. CRAFT-IN IS A COMBINED TOTAL EXPERIENCE IN ALL GRAPHIC VISUAL ARTS, CRAFTS, EDUCATION, HERITAGE, ETHNIC CULTURE, INVOLVING STATEWIDE & NATIONWIDE PARTICIPANTS. FESTIVAL, PAGEANT, CELEBRATION & PUBS. (ST-WIDE). G D BARRANTE, EXEC DIRECTOR; COLORADO CENTENNIAL-BICENTENNIAL COMMISSION; 901 SHERMAN ST, 15TH FLOOR; DENVER, CO 80203. (#2705).

GOLDFIELD CITY HALL AND FIREHOUSE RESTORATION-COLO. TO PRESERVE HISTORIC MINING TOWN CITY HALL & RESTORE AS A COMMUNITY BUILDING AND LOCAL MUSEUM. PART OF HERITAGE OF CRIPPLE CREEK MINING DISTRICT. (ST-WIDE). DAYTON LUMMIS JR, DIRECTOR; CRIPPLE CREEK DISTRICT MUSEUM INC; BOX 475; CRIPPLE CREEK, CO 80813. (#4426). **ARBA GRANTEE.**

THE HISTORY OF CULTURAL ACTIVITIES IN COLO -FILM. A 30 MINUTE DOCUMENTARY RELATING TO THE HISTORY OF CULTURAL ACTIVITIES IN COLORADO. FILM MAY BE USED FOR TV BROADCASTS, AS WELL AS SPECIAL GROUP REQUESTS. (ST-WIDE). DAYTON LUMMIS, DIRECTOR; CRIPPLE CREEK MUSEUM; CRIPPLE CREEK, CO 80813. (#2721). **(??).**

MAY 24 - 26, '75. RAMONA FALLS RENDEZVOUS, A MUZZLE LOADING SHOOT. AUTHENTIC RIFLES & COSTUMES AT THE 1850 RENDEZVOUS SPOT OF RAMONA FALLS, WITH PRIZES & ENTERTAINMENT FOR SPECTATORS & SHOOTERS. (LOCAL). JERRY LEA, SHOOT CHAIRMAN; COLORADO SPRINGS MUZZLE LOADERS INC; 4950 GALENA DR; COLORADO SPG, CO 80918. (#6820-501).

JUNE 1, '75 - SEPT 1, '76. BUS TOUR OF HISTORIC AND SCENIC SITES. BUS TOUR OF GOLD CAMPS. MINE TOUR TO INCLUDE FLUORESCENT FOSSIL BEDS, HIGH-TRAILS SCOUT CAMP, AND ASPEN. FALL TOUR TO DEVELOP AN APPRECIATION OF THE HERITAGE AND HISTORIC PROPERTIES OF THE AREAS TOURED. (LOCAL). BILL LIEB, CHAIRMAN; TOURS COMMITTEE OF THE HERITAGE COMMITTEE; 1576 KEATON LN; COLORADO SPG, CO 80909. (#10140-1).

MAY 29 - 31, '76. RAMONA FALLS RENDEVOUS, A SHOOT FOR MUZZLE LOADERS. A MUZZLE LOADING SHOOT WITH AUTHENTIC COSTUMES AND PRIZES IN CRIPPLE CREEK, CO AT THE 1850 RENDEVOUS SPOT OF RAMONA FALLS WITH PRIZES, FUN, SHOOTS, & ENTERTAINMENT FOR SPECTATORS & SHOOTERS OF COLORADO. AT RAMONA FALLS NEAR CRIPPLE CREEK, COLORADO. (ST-WIDE). JERRY LEA, SHOOT CHMN; COLORADO SPRINGS MUZZLE LOADERS, INC; 4950 GALENA; COLORADO SPG, CO 80918. (#8893-1).

JUNE 26 - 27, '76. DONKEY DERBY DAYS - PARADE & RACES. DONKEY RACE, DRILLING, TOBACCO SPITTIN', GREASED PIG CONTESTS, TREASURE HUNTS, PONY RACES, PARADE-SUN, 6/27, BICENTENNIAL RE-CREATION OF PEARL DEVERE FUNERAL, $250 DONKEY RACE, VICTOR TO CRIPPLE CREEK. AT PARADE & RACES - BENNETT AVE; CONTESTS AT CITY PARK. (ST-WIDE). MARGE PHILLIPS, COORD; CRIPPLE CREEK TWO MILE HIGH CLUB; CRIPPLE CREEK, CO 80813. (#105904-1).

AUG 20 - 22, '76. BICENTENNIAL ARTS & CRAFTS SHOW. EXHIBIT. (REGN'L). HOLLY MERRITIELD, PRES; COLORADO ART SHOWS, INC; PO BOX 609; LITTLETON, CO 80120. (#108057-1).

SEPT 18 - OCT 3, '76. ASPEN-GHOST TOWN GOLD MINE TOURS. FREE JEEP TOURS OF DESERTED GHOST TOWNS IN CRIPPLE CREEK & VICTOR AREAS & HISTORIC TOURS OF CRIPPLE CREEK'S GOLD MINES. HAIR RAISING JEEP JAUNTS OF OLD MINING MULE TRAILS, FOREST OF ASPEN IN BLAZING COLOR. AT STARTING POINT BURNETT AVE. (LOCAL). MARGE PHILLIPS, COORD; TWO MILE HIGH CLUB OF CRIPPLE CREEK; CRIPPLE CREEK, CO 80813. (#105904-2).

CROOK

CROOK, COLO, MUSEUM PROJECT. A PROJECT TO CREATE A MUSEUM IN OLD PRESBYTERIAN CHURCH OF CROOK. PROJECT CALLS FOR INSTALLATION OF SECURITY DEVICIES AND THE CONSTRUC TION OF DISPLAY CASES. (LOCAL). MRS ARMAND MEHL, HERITAGE CHAIRMAN; WOMENS CLUB OF CROOK; CROOK, CO 80726. (#4291).

DE BEQUE

COMMUNITY DEVELOPMENT PROJ - DE BEQUE, CO. THE TOWN'S FIRST PUBLIC BATHROOM WILL BE BUILT. (LOCAL). HON DEL RICKSTREW, MAYOR; CITY OF DE BEQUE; DE BEQUE, CO 81630. (#26174).

FIRE CART RESTORATION, DE BEQUE, CO. A FIRE CART, FIRST USED IN 1900 WILL BE SET UP IN THE PARK. (LOCAL). HON DEL RICKSTREW, MAYOR; CITY OF DE BEQUE; DE BEQUE, CO 81630. (#26173).

JUNE 26, '76. DE BEQUE BICENTENNIAL FESTIVITIES. FESTIVAL. (LOCAL). TERRY N RIGSBY, CHAIRMAN; DE BEQUE CITY GOVERNMENT; 610 CURTIS, BOX 237; DE BEQUE, CO 81630. (#200007-57).

DEER TRAIL

ADDITIONS TO THE CENTENNIAL COMPLEX, CO. RESTROOMS WILL BE ADDED TO THE PARK & MUSEUM. (LOCAL). KATHLEEN REID, COORDINATOR; DEER TRAIL CENTENNIAL-BICENTENNIAL COMMITTEE; BOX 21; DEER TRAIL, CO 80105. (#26172).

CENTENNIAL PARK AND MUSEUM - DEER TRAIL, CO. AN ESTABLISHED PARK WILL BE REDESIGNATED AS THE CENTENNI-

DEER TRAIL—CONTINUED

AL PARK; THE DEER TRAIL HOME HOBBY CLUB WILL BUILD REST ROOMS FUNDED BY DONATIONS. (LOCAL). KATHY REID, PRESIDENT; DEER TRAIL HOME HOBBY CLUB; BOX 21; DEER TRAIL, CO 80105. (#18630).

DEER TRAIL FOURTH OF JULY CELEBRATION, COLORADO. A TRADITIONAL 4TH OF JULY WITH PICNIC, FESTIVAL PROGRAM AND FIREWORKS. ALSO A HISTORICAL PAGEANT. (LOCAL). MS WANDA JOLLY, PRESIDENT; DEER TRAIL RURAL MUSIC CLUB; DEER TRAIL, CO 80105. (#9917).

MOVING AND RESTORING LOG CABIN - DEER TRAIL, CO. WE PLAN TO MOVE ONE AND ONE-HALF STORY LOG CABIN FROM COUNTRY SITE TO MUSEUM GROUNDS IN CITY PARK AND TO RESTORE LOG CABIN. (LOCAL). ETHEL PRICE, PRESIDENT; DEER TRAIL PIONEER HISTORICAL SOCIETY; DEER TRAIL, CO 80105. (#24589).

JUNE 5, '76. DEER TRAIL CHUCKWAGON DAY, ARTS & CRAFTS SHOW. THIS ANNUAL CELEBRATION WILL HONOR THE CENT & BICENT WITH A PERIOD SUPPER MENU OF THE '76 ERA, CRAFTS FAIR AND DEMONSTRATIONS & OLDFASHIONED COSTUMES. AT CENTENNIAL CITY PARK & MUSEUM. (LOCAL). MRS ETHEL V PRICE; DEER TRAIL PIONEER HIST SOCIETY; BOX 1537; DEER TRAIL, CO 80105. (#9916-1).

JUNE 19, '76. DEER TRAIL OLD TIMERS ROUNDUP. ANNUAL BANQUET AND DANCE HONORING THE PIONEERS WHO SETTLED WITHIN A RADIUS OF 50 MILES OF DEER TRAIL 45 OR MORE YEARS AGO. AT SCHOOL GYM. (LOCAL). MARJORIE WOOD, COORD; DEER TRAIL OLD TIMERS; DEER TRAIL, CO 80105. (#200007-50).

JULY 4, '76. 4TH OF JULY CELEBRATION. FESTIVITIES WILL INCLUDE FIREWORKS, POT LUCK DINNER AND MUSICAL ENTERTAINMENT. AT JOCKEY CLUB GROUNDS. (LOCAL). WANDA M JOLLY, PRESIDENT; DEER TRAIL RURAL MUSIC CLUB; DEER TRAIL, CO 80105. (#103111-1).

SEPT 11 - 12, '76. DEER TRAIL RODEO AND RACE MEET AND FESTIVAL. PARADE: SAT 10AM; RODEO & RACE MEET: SAT & SUN 1:30 PM; PUBLIC DANCE SAT NIGHT, SCHOOL GYM - 33RD ANNUAL, COMMEMORATES THE FIRST RODEO IN U S, HELD JULY 4, 1869 AT DEER TRAIL; CHAMPION BRONCO BUSTER OF THE PLAINS WAS NAMED; THIS IS AN AMATEUR RODEO. AT RODEO: DEER TRAIL RODEO GROUNDS; PARADE: FRONT ST; DANCE: SCHOOL GYM. (LOCAL). HARRY L VENTER, SEC; DEER TRAIL JOCKEY CLUB & JOCKEYETTS; TRI-COUNTY TRIBUNE OFFICE; DEER TRAIL, CO 80105. (#9916-3).

OCT 30 - 31, '76. DEER TRAIL TURKEY SHOOT AND BAR-B-QUE. COMPETITION AT DEER TRAIL RODEO GROUNDS. (LOCAL). HARRY L VENTER, DIRECTOR; DEER TRAIL JOCKEY CLUB; TRI-COUNTY TRIBUNE OFFICE; DEER TRAIL, CO 80105. (#9916-2).

DEL NORTE

OLD PICTURE COLLECTION - DEL NORTE, CO. SUMMER OF '76 COLLECTION OF LOCAL PICTURES OF HISTORIC VALUE. (LOCAL). JAY C SCHRADER, COORDINATOR; HISTORICAL SOCIETY; PO BOX M; DEL NORTE, CO 81132. (#26371).

PRESERVATION OF BARLOW & SANDERSON STATION IN COLO. PRESERVE & RESTORE THE BARLOW & SANDERSON STAGE STATION THAT WAS THE FOCAL POINT OF MANY TOURIST S IN 1876. WILL BE OF GREAT INTEREST TO THE TOURISTS OF 76. (ST-WIDE). TOWN MANAGER; BARLOW & SANDERSON STAGE FUND; TOWN HALL; DEL NORTE, CO 81132. (#1068). **ARBA GRANTEE.**

TIME CAPSULE AND FLAGPOLE - DEL NORTE, CO. CONSTRUCTION OF TIME CAPSULE AND COLLECTION OF MATERIALS TO BE ENCLOSED THEREIN. TIME CAPSULE WILL BE CONSTRUCTED AS BASE FOR CENTENNIAL-BICENTENNIAL FLAG POLE. (LOCAL). JAY C SCHRADER, COORDINATOR; TIME CAPSULE COMMITTEE; PO BOX M; DEL NORTE, CO 81132. (#26372).

TOWN BEAUTIFICATION - DEL NORTE, CO. SUMMER 76-PLANT TREES IN TOWN PARK, PUBLIC SCHOOL GROUNDS, AND ENCOURAGE PRIVATE OWNERSHIP BEAUTIFICATION. PROJECT WILL BE IN CONJUNCTION WITH CLASS OF '76 BEAUTIFICATION PROGRAM. (LOCAL). JAY C SCHRADER, COORDINATOR; TOWN OF DEL NORTE; PO BOX M; DEL NORTE, CO 81132. (#26373).

76 LIGHT ON LOOKOUT MOUNTAIN - DEL NORTE, CO. A LIGHT WILL BUILT ON LOOKOUT MOUNTAIN. (LOCAL). JAY C SHRADER, PROJ DIRECTOR; CITY OF DEL NORTE; PO BOX M; DEL NORTE, CO 81132. (#25873).

AUG 20 - 22, '76. COVERED WAGON DAYS. PARADE WITH CENTENNIAL-BICENTENNIAL FLOAT, MUSICAL PROGRAM & EVENTS FOR CHILDREN WILL BE FEATURED DURING THE WEEKEND. (LOCAL). JAY C SCHRADER; COMMITTEE FOR COVERED WAGON DAYS; PO BOX M; DEL NORTE, CO 81132. (#108663-2).

AUG 21, '76. CHILDREN'S PLAY BY CREEDE REPERTORY THEATRE GROUP. LIVE PERFORMANCE. (LOCAL). JAY C SCHRADER, COORD; CREEDE REPERTORY THEATRE GROUP; PO BOX M; DEL NORTE, CO 81132. (#108663-1).

DELTA

ATTACK ON FORT BY INDIANS - PERFORMANCE. LOCAL SCOUTS DRESSED AS INDIANS WILL ATTACK A REPLICA OF AN OLDEN DAY FORT, TO START THE CELEBRATION OF COLORADO STATEHOOD. INDIANS WILL ATTACK FROM THE RIVER IN CANOES. CANOE RACES WILL FOLLOW. (LOCAL). BETTY CRANE, COORD; BOY SCOUTS; 919 GRAND AVE; DELTA, CO 81416. (#108801-1).

CEMETERY FOR VETERANS - PROJ OF DELTA, CO. CREATE A CEMETERY FOR VETERANS WITH SPACE FOR THE COMMUNITY'S TIME CAPSULE. PLANT TREES AND SHRUBS TO HALT EROSION. (LOCAL). BETTY CRANE, CHAIRPERSON; DELTA CENTENNIAL-BICENTENNIAL COMMITTEE; 919 GRAND AVE; DELTA, CO 81416. (#16153).

DELTA COOKBOOK PROJECT - CO. GATHER AND PUT TOGETHER OLD RECIPES. THE COOKBOOK WILL PROVIDE ENJOYABLE READING, BUT THE RECIPES MAY NOT ALL BE USABLE IN A MODERN KITCHEN BECAUSE OF ODD MEASUREMENTS AND INGREDIENTS USED. (LOCAL). HELEN JURCA, PRESIDENT; EPSILON SIGMA ALPHA; RT BOX 140; DELTA, CO 81416. (#16155).

HISTORICAL BOOK - DELTA, CO. A BOOK CONTAINING TRUE STORIES OF THE PAST WILL BE COMPILED. (LOCAL). THELMA R HARE, CHAIRWOMAN; HERITAGE COMMITTEES; RT 1 BOX 309; DELTA, CO 81416. (#26272).

HOSTESS CORPS FOR DELTARADO - DELTA, CO. PROVIDE GENERAL HOSTESSING AT ALL EVENTS FOR DELTARADO DAYS 1975-77. (LOCAL). JUDITH WEISZBROD, PROJ DIRECTOR; COLORADO CHI 545, BETA SIGMA PHI; 304 E 4TH; DELTA, CO 81416. (#16157).

PIECES OF COLORADO - PROJ OF DELTA, CO. A BOOK IS BEING COMPILED OF CULTURAL AND TRADITIONAL STORIES OF THE PAST TO REPRESENT EVERY COUNTY OF COLORADO. (ST-WIDE). THELMA R HARE, CHAIRPERSON; HERITAGE COMMITTEE, DELTA CENTENNIAL-BICENTENNIAL COMMITTEE; RT 1, BOX 309; DELTA, CO 81416. (#16156).

ROSTER OF EMERGENCY INTERPRETORS, DELTA, CO. LISTING OF AREA PEOPLE WHO SPEAK FOREIGN LANGUAGES AND WILL SERVE AS INTERPRETORS FOR RESIDENTS OR TOURISTS IN EMERGENCY SITUATIONS WITH HOSPITAL, DOCTORS, POLICE, AMBULANCE, MOTELS & INFORMATION CENTERS. (LOCAL). JUDITH WEISZBROD, CHAIRWOMAN; COLORADO CHI 545 BETA SIGMA PHI; 304 E 4TH; DELTA, CO 81416. (#16158).

TIME CAPSULE - PROJ OF DELTA, CO. SIGNIFICANT ITEMS REPRESENTATIVE OF THE CENTENNIAL ERA WILL BE COLLECTED AND BURIED IN A TIME CAPSULE TO BE OPENED IN 2076. (LOCAL). TIMOTHY SUKLE, PRESIDENT; DELTA HIGH SCHOOL STUDENT BODY; 822 GRAND AVE; DELTA, CO 81416. (#16154).

JUNE 11, '75. DEDICATION OF CEMETERY. CEREMONY. (LOCAL). BETTY CRANE, COORDINATOR; DELTA CENTENNIAL-BICENTENNIAL COMMITTEE; 919 GRAND AVE; DELTA, CO 81416. (#200007-52).

JULY 21 - 27, '75. 1975 GENERAL HOSTESSING AT ALL EVENTS OF DELTARADO DAYS. FESTIVAL. (LOCAL). JUDITH L WEISZBORD, CHMN; COLO CHI 545 BETA SIGMA PHI; 304 E 4TH; DELTA, CO 81416. (#200007-53).

APR 2 - 4, '76. TRIANGLE THEATER-VALLEY SYMPHONY PRODUCTION OF '1776'. LIVE PERFORMANCE AT DELTA HIGH SCHOOL, 800 GRAND AVE. (LOCAL). BETTY CRANE, COORDINATOR; DELTA TRIANGLE THEATER & VALLEY SYMPHONY; 919 GRAND AVE; DELTA, CO 81416. (#200007-51).

JULY 4, '76. BURIAL OF TIME CAPSULE. CEREMONY. (LOCAL). BETTY G CRANE, CHAIRMAN; DELTA BICENTENNIAL COMMITTEE; 919 GRAND AVE; DELTA, CO 81416. (#107582-1).

JULY 4, '76. FIREWORKS DISPLAY. FESTIVAL. (LOCAL). BETTY CRANE, CHAIRMAN; DELTA FIREWORKS COMMITTEE; 919 GRAND AVE; DELTA, CO 81416. (#108634-1).

JULY 7, '76. MISS DELTA CONTEST. A MISS DELTA WILL BE CHOSEN EACH YEAR TO ACT AS QUEEN AT LOCAL CENTENNIAL AND DELTARADO DAYS FESTIVITIES. (LOCAL). DONNA WIDNER, CHPSN; DELTARADO DAYS COMMITTEE; CHAMBER OF COMMERCE; 224 MAIN ST; DELTA, CO 81416. (#16159-1).

JULY 25 - AUG 1, '76. ARTS FESTIVAL. FESTIVAL TO BE HELD IN CONJUNCTION WITH DELTARADO DAYS CELEBRATION OF COLO STATEHOOD. ALL CRAFTS REPRESENTED IN THIS EVENT. (LOCAL). BETTY G CRANE, PROJ CHMN; ARTS FESTIVAL COMMITTEE; 919 GRAND AVE; DELTA, CO 81416. (#108869-1).

JULY 31, '76. COMMUNITY DELTARADO DAYS PARADE. PARADE. (LOCAL). BETTY CRANE, COORDINATOR; CITY OF DELTA; 919 GRAND AVE; DELTA, CO 81416. (#108695-1).

AUG 1, '76. BURIAL OF TIME CAPSULE. TIME CAPSULE TO BE BURIED IN NEW VETERAN'S CEMETERY. THERE IT WILL REMAIN FOR 100 YRS, FILLED WITH THE THINGS WE USE TODAY AND PICTURES OF OUR HISTORY. (LOCAL). BETTY CRANE, COORD; TOWN OF DELTA; 919 GRAND AVE; DELTA, CO 81416. (#108955-16).

DENVER

AFRO-AMERICAN MUSEUM OF DENVER, COLO. THE ESTABLISHMENT OF A BLACK MUSEUM OF COLORADO'S HISTORIC PAST. THIS MUSEUM WILL EMBODY THE CULTURE OF COLORADO'S EARLY BLACK SETTLERS. (ST-WIDE). PAUL STEWART, DIRECTOR; BLACK WEST FOUNDATION; 3356 LEYDEN ST; DENVER, CO 80205. (#1882).

AIR FORCE HERITAGE MONTH - WINGS OF HISTORY, CO. AIR FORCE HERITAGE IN ART; RARE COLLECTIONS DEPICTING HISTORY OF AVIATION; DATES BACK TO DAEDALUS AND DAVINCI ARTIFACTS THROUGH SPACE AGE. INCLUDES ARTISTS SUCH AS ROCKWELL. (NAT'L). CAPT RONALD T SCONYERS, PR OFFICER; U S AIR FORCE (LOWRY AFB & RECRUITING DET 701) & AIR FORCE ASSOC; 19TH & ST, NCH; DENVER, CO 80202. (#10306).

'AMERICA - THE BICENTENNIAL' CONCERT - CO. A CONCERT OF MUSIC OF AMERICA & THE WEST, MORTON GOULD CONDUCTING. (ST-WIDE). MRS PATRICIA MIDDENDORF, ADMINISTRATIVE ASST; DENVER SYMPHONY ORCHESTRA; 1615 CALIFORNIA ST; DENVER, CO 80202. (#179). **ARBA GRANTEE.**

AMERICAN HISTORY PROGRAMMED LEARNING PROJ - CO. DEVELOPMENT OF A SERIES OF INTERRELATED AND INTERDEPENDENT AMERICAN HISTORY PROGRAMMED SIMULATIONS, TO BE TESTED IN THE CLASSROOM AND MADE AVAILABLE TO THE SCHOOLS. (NAT'L). DR WILLIAM A STEMBLER, PROJ DESIGNER; CENTER FOR RESEARCH AND EDUCATION; 2010 E 17TH AVE; DENVER, CO 80206. (#16403).

AMERICAN INDUSTRY BICENTENNIAL CORPORATION OF COLO. A NATIONAL INDUSTRY EFFORT TO RESTORE PRIDE IN PRESENT INDUSTRIAL ACCOMPLISHMENTS, AND BUILD FAITH IN INDUSTRY'S CAPACITY TO FORGE AHEAD IN SOLVING AMERICA'S FUTURE PROBLEMS. (REGN'L). ERROLL GIDDINGS, SENIOR ADMIN COORDINATOR; COLORADO CENTENNIAL-BICENTENNIAL COMMISSION; 901 SHERMAN ST, 15TH FLOOR; DENVER, CO 80203. (#2718).

AMERICAN ISSUES FORUM COMMUNITY PGM OF DENVER. AMERICAN ISSUES FORUM, INTERSTATE PROGRAM COORDINATED BY STAFF AT UNIVERSITY OF DENVER, WITH PLANNERS IN SIX STATES TO ACTIVATE DIVERSIFIED PROGRAMS FOR COMMUNICATING THE TOPICS ON AMERICA. (REGN'L). ROBERT ROEDER, AMERICAN ISSUES PROJ DIRECTOR; UNIV OF DENVER; DENVER, CO 80210. (#4142).

THE AMERICAN JEWISH EXPERIENCE, DENVER, CO. GOODSTEIN LECTURES ON THE JEWISH EXPERIENCE IN AMERICA. (LOCAL). STANLEY M WAGNER, DIRECTOR; CENTER FOR JUDAIC STUDIES, UNIVERSITY OF DENVER; UNIVERSITY PARK; DENVER, CO 80210. (#16442).

AMERICAN LEGION CENTENNIAL-BICENTENNIAL COMMITTEE. FORMATION OF AN AMERICAN LEGION CENTENNIAL-BICENTENNIAL COMMITTEE TO COORDINATE AND DEVELOP LEGION PROGRAMS IN SUPPORT OF THE STATE CENTENNIAL-BICENTENNIAL. (ST-WIDE). G D BARRANTE, EXEC DIRECTOR; COLORADO CENTENNIAL-BICENTENNIAL COMMISSION; 901 SHERMAN ST 15TH FLOOR; DENVER, CO 80203. (#1965).

AMERICAN MUSIC SERIES OF COLORADO. A SERIES OF PERFORMANCES IN CONNECTION WITH COURSES AT METROPOLITAN STATE COLLEGE WITH EMPHASIS ON LITTLE-KNOWN AMERICAN MUSIC. (ST-WIDE). JERRALD D MCCOLLUM, CHAIRMAN, DEPT OF MUSIC; METROPOLITAN STATE COLLEGE; 250 W 14TH AVE; DENVER, CO 80204. (#4363).

AMERICAN PANORAMA: PAINTINGS: 1730 TO TODAY, CO. 3 MAJOR EXHIBITIONS FROM THE METROPOLITAN MUSEUM OF ART, MUSEUM OF MODERN ART IN NEW YORK & THE PHILLIPS COLLECTION IN WASHINGTON, DC. (REGN'L). THOMAS N MAYTHAM, DIRECTOR; DENVER ART MUSEUM; 100 W 14TH AVE PKWY; DENVER, CO 80204. (#16813). **ARBA GRANTEE.**

ANNIVERSARY SCULPTURE CONTEST. SCULPTURE CONCERNING COLLEGE, STATE AND NATIONAL ANNIVERSARY WILL BE CREATED BY SELECTED MSC STUDENTS; IT WILL BE DEDICATED BY THE COLLEGE TO THE AURARIA SITE DURING AURARIA DAY CELEBRATION. (LOCAL). PAM W CARTER, CHAIRMAN; METROPOLITAN STATE COLLEGE; 250 W 14TH AVE; DENVER, CO 80204. (#102707-1). **(??).**

'ANOTHER CENTURY OF FREEDOM' BROCHURE OF DENVER. BROCHURE FOR AWARENESS, TO INFORM THE YOUTH ON CENTENNIAL - BICENTENNIAL ACTIVITIES. (ST-WIDE). GINA ZARO, CHAIRMAN; CENTENNIAL - BICENTENNIAL AWARENESS COMMITTEE; 1313 TREMONT; DENVER, CO 80204. (#4562).

'ART IN ACTION', COMMUNITY MURALS, DENVER, CO. MURALS OF GLAZED, FIRED, CERAMIC TILES TO ORIENT PEOPLE TO THE MEANING OF PUBLIC ART. A LARGE SCALE PROJECT TO PERMANENTLY ENHANCE THE COMMUNITY. (LOCAL). BARRY ROSE, PROJ DIRECTOR; ART IN ACTION COMMUNITY MURAL PROJECT; 1450 LOGAN ST; DENVER, CO 80203. (#15610).

AURARIN HIGHER EDUCATION CENTER IN DENVER. LANDSCAPE DESIGN FOR 69 ACRE TRI-COLLEGE URBAN CAMPUS. INCLUDED IN THE SITE IS THE NINTH STREET HISTORIC PARK, A BLOCK OF VICTORIAN HOMES TO BE RESTORED FOR ADAPTIVE USE. (LOCAL). G D BARRANTE, EXECUTIVE DIRECTOR; COLORADO CENTENNIAL-BICENTENNIAL COMMISSION; 901 SHERMAN; DENVER, CO 80203. (#3128).

BABI YAR PARK PROJECT OF DENVER. THIS PARK WILL SYMBOLIZE THE SPIRIT OF CONSCIENCE AND CONCERN FOR THE FREEDOM AND DIGNITY OF ALL MEN REGARDLESS OF RELIGIOUS OR OTHER AFFILIATION, RACE, ETHNICITY OR NATIONAL CITICENSHIP. (ST-WIDE). MRS MORRIS GINSBERG, CHAIRWOMAN; MAYOR'S COMMITTEE OF 19 FOR '76; 5801 HAPPY CANYON DR; ENGLEWOOD, CO 80110. (#1949).

'BALLET DENVER' - STATEWIDE TOUR. TRAVELING FROM TOWN TO TOWN, PERFORMING BALLET SHOWS IN THE STYLE OF THE EIGHTEENTH CENTURY. (ST-WIDE). BARBARA HIRSCHFIELD, DIRECTOR; BALLET DENVER; 3955 TENNYSON PL; DENVER, CO 80212. (#2910).

BIBLIOGRAPHY OF BOOKS AND MEDIA, DENVER, CO. PUBLICATION OF A BIBLIOGRAPHY OF BOOKS AND NON-PRINT MEDIA ABOUT COLORADO, INCLUDING ALL SUBJECTS & AGE LEVELS; ESPECIALLY FOR LOCAL SCHOOLS; FREE DISTRIBUTION TO ALL COLORADO SCHOOLS & LIBRARIES. (ST-WIDE). WILLIAM C JONES, CHAIRMAN; COLORADO ASSOC OF SCHOOL LIBRARIANS; 3275 S DAHALIA ST; DENVER, CO 80222. (#10333). **ARBA GRANTEE.**

BICENTENNIAL BOND ISSUE OF DENVER, COLORADO. AS RESULT OF BICENTENNIAL BOND ISSUE, NEW STORM & SANITARY SEWERS, FIRE HQDTRS, POLICE ADMINISTRATION BLDG, & CITY VEHICLES SERVICE CENTER COMPLEX WILL BE CONSTRUCTED. (LOCAL). JOHN HENRY, EXEC OFFICER, DEPT OF PUBLIC WORKS; CITY & COUNTY OF DENVER; COLFAX AVE & BANNOCK ST; DENVER, CO 80202. (#1938).

BICENTENNIAL BRANCH LIBRARIES, PROJECT OF DENVER. THIS PROJECT INVOLVES THE CONSTRUCTION OF TWO BRANCH LIBRA-

DENVER — CONTINUED

RIES AND THE REPLACEMENT OF A LIBRARY IN AN OLDER SECTION OF THE CITY. (LOCAL). JOHN HENRY, EXEC OFFICER, DEPT OF PUBLIC WORKS; CITY & COUNTY OF DENVER; COLFAX AVE & BANNOCK ST; DENVER, CO 80202. (#2021). **(??).**

BICENTENNIAL HERITAGE SONG FESTIVAL - DENVER, CO. ENLISTED MEN AND WOMEN PRESENT SONGS OF THE ARMY FOR MILITARY AND CIVILIAN AUDIENCES. SONGS ARE FROM ALL ERAS - COLONIAL, CIVIL WAR, WW I, WW II, KOREAN AND VIET NAM. (REGN'L). LTC WILLIAM C MARTIN SR, CHAIRMAN; FITZSIMONS ARMY MEDICAL CENTER; DENVER, CO 80240. (#13216).

BICENTENNIAL PERFORMING ARTS CENTER OF DENVER. THIS FACILITY WILL HOST SYMPHONY MUSIC PERFORMANCES AS WELL AS RESIDENT AND TOURING OPERA, BALLET, LYRIC AND EXPERIMENTAL THEATRE. IT IS A RESULT OF A BICENTENNIAL BOND ISSUE. (ST-WIDE). HAROLD COOK, MGR OF PUBLIC WORKS; CITY AND COUNTY BUILDING; RM 379 CITY & COUNTY BLDG; DENVER, CO 80202. (#1989).

BIKECENTENNIAL '76, DENVER, CO. A CROSS COUNTRY BICYCLE TOUR TO TAKE PLACE DURING THE SUMMER OF 1976 IN THE STATE OF COLORADO; TOUR TO JOIN UP WITH A NATIONAL TOURING GROUP. (ST-WIDE). DOROTHY URBAN, REPRESENTATIVE; BIKECENTENNIAL '76 TRANS-AMERICA BICYCLE TRAIL; PO BOX 1034; MISSOULA, MT 59801. (#17426).

BOY SCOUTS BICENTENNIAL PROGRAM - DENVER, CO. A 2-YEAR PROGRAM OF HISTORICAL & COMMUNITY SERVICE; PARTICIPATION ACTIVITIES FOR CUBS, SCOUTS, EXPLORERS, THEIR FAMILIES & FRIENDS. THIS IS A STATE WIDE PROGRAM. (ST-WIDE). ROBERT MEINHOLTZ, SCOUT EXECUTIVE; DENVER AREA COUNCIL BOY SCOUTS OF AMERICA; 2901 W 19TH AVE; DENVER, CO 80204. (#17585).

BOY SCOUTS OF COLO CENTENNIAL ACTIVITIES. DEDICATION OF THEIR ANNUAL SHOW TO THE CENTENNIAL, HISTORIC TRAILS, SERVICE CORP, HISTORIC FLAG CEREMONIES, CAMPOREES AND CAMPFIRE RALLIES AND SPECIAL CENTENNIAL AWARDS. (ST-WIDE). MICHAEL H BARRETT, PRESIDENT; SCOUTS, CUB SCOUTS AND EXPLORERS OF COLORADO; 1375 DELAWARE ST; DENVER, CO 80204. (#4349). **ARBA GRANTEE.**

CAPITOL STAINED GLASS WINDOWS OF COLORADO. PUBLISH A BOOKLET WITH PICTURES AND SHORT BIOGRAPHIES ON THE FAMOUS PEOPLE WHO ARE THE SUBJECTS OF THE 16 STAINED GLASS WINDOWS IN THE STATE CAPITOL BUILDING. (ST-WIDE). MS PEARL WOLFSON, PROJ DIRECTOR; COLORADO CENTENNIAL BICENTENNIAL COMMISSION; 390 BIRCH ST; DENVER, CO 80220. (#4350).

CATHEDRAL OF THE IMMACULATE CONCEPTION CONCERT -CO. SERIES OF REGULAR CARRILON CONCERTS. ORGANIZE ON A NON-DENOMINATION BASIS A GUILD OF CARRILONEURS MADE UP OF COLORADANS FOR PRESENTATION. (ST-WIDE). PAUL RIEDO, DIRECTOR; CATHEDRAL OF IMMACULATE CONCEPTION; 1530 LOGAN; DENVER, CO 80203. (#2884).

CBC LOGO ON STATE LICENSE PLATES FOR 1975 - 1976. STATE LAW AUTHORIZING CBC LOGO, IN COLOR, ON STATE MOTOR VEHICLE. LICENCE PLATES FOR 1975 AND 1976. (ST-WIDE). G D BARRANTE, EXEC DIRECTOR; COLORADO CENTENNIAL-BICENTENNIAL COMMISSION; 901 SHERMAN ST; DENVER, CO 80203. (#2725).

CENTENNIAL-BICENTENNIAL ART HOUSE OF DENVER. OLD BUILDING RESTORED FOR THE PURPOSE OF HOUSING ART OF YOUTH TO DEPICT THERE IDEAS OF THE THIRD CENTURY. (LOCAL). GINA ZARO, CHAIRMAN; CENTENNIAL BICENTENNIAL AWARENESS COMMITTEE; 1313 TREMONT; DENVER, CO 80204. (#4572).

CENTENNIAL-BICENTENNIAL SCHOLARSHIPS - DENVER, CO. TEN HALF-TUITION SCHOLARSHIPS WILL BE AWARDED TO COLORADO RESIDENTS IN HONOR OF THE CENTENNIAL-BICENTENNIAL. (ST-WIDE). JOHN DODSON, DIRECTOR; REGIS COLLEGE; W 50TH & LOWELL; DENVER, CO 80221. (#15262).

CENTENNIAL-BICENTENNIAL ISSUE OF INQUIRY - CO. THE SPRING 1976 ISSUE OF THE BIANNUAL INQUIRY MAGAZINE WILL BE DEVOTED TO THE CENTENNIAL OF COLORADO AND THE BICENTENNIAL OF THE NATION. (REGN'L). TERRY RICH, EDITOR; REGIS COLLEGE; W 50TH & LOWELL; DENVER, CO 80221. (#15264).

THE CENTENNIAL-BICENTENNIAL COLORADO TRAIL, DENVER. THE COLORADO TRAIL, THAT STRETCHES FROM DENVER TO DURANGO, IS A YEAR ROUND TRAIL SYSTEM WHICH ENABLES MAN TO LEARN MORE ABOUT HIMSELF & HIS ENVIRONMENT. (ST-WIDE). PAUL A FITZPATRICK, EXEC DIRECTOR; COLORADO MOUNTAIN TRAILS FOUNDATION; 738 PEARL ST; DENVER, CO 80203. (#17424).

CENTENNIAL-BICENTENNIAL OIL PAINTING - DENVER, CO. PAINTING DEPICTS STATUE OF LIBERTY, LIBERTY BELL, BIBLE, A STAINED GLASS WINDOW, COLORADO STATE FLAG ON ROCKY MOUNTAIN BACKGROUND AND A PRAYER POEM. (LOCAL). WILLIE J BICKHAM, ARTIST; 928 E 25TH AVE; DENVER, CO 80205. (#26260).

CENTENNIAL-BICENTENNIAL TELEVISION SHOW. TORY. (ST-WIDE). DONALD JOHNSON, SEC TREAS; COUNCIL FOR PUBLIC TELEVISION, CHANNEL 6 INC; 1261 GLENARM PL; DENVER, CO 80204. (#108800-4).

CHILDREN'S HISTORY TV SERIES OF COLORADO. DEVELOP AND AIR A 5 TO 10 MINUTE TV SHOW FOR 52 WEEKS STARTING 1975. SCRIPTED & FILMED BY KMGH-TV, CHANNEL 7, DENVER. (ST-WIDE). NOLA CUSTARD, PROJECT DIRECTOR; COLORADO CENTENNIAL-BICENTENNIAL COMMISSION; 901 SHERMAN ST, 15TH FLOOR; DENVER, CO 80237. (#2707).

CLUB 20 - TOURISM PROMOTION PROJECT OF COLORADO. A LARGE GROUP OF PEOPLE INTERESTED IN PROMOTING TOURISM. (ST-WIDE). G D BARRANTE, EXEC DIRECTOR; COLORADO CENTENNIAL-BICENTENNIAL COMMISSION; 901 SHERMAN ST; DENVER, CO 80203. (#1996).

COLLECTION OF LITTLE KNOWN FACTS ABOUT DENVER, CO. PUBLICATION OF A COLLECTION OF CAREFULLY RESEARCHED, UNIQUE, IMPORTANT, INTERESTING HISTORICAL SKETCHES OF PEOPLE & EVENTS IN DENVER OVER THE PAST 100 YEARS. (LOCAL). ANNETTE BRAND, CHAIRMAN; DENVER URBAN OBSERVATORY; BOX A097 E 9TH AVE; DENVER, CO 80220. (#15609).

COLLEGE CAMPUS BEAUTIFICATION PROGRAM, DENVER, CO. PROGRAM INCLUDES ON GOING REHABILITATION OF CAMPUS GROUNDS, TREE PLANTING & DEDICATION OF CENTENNIAL-BICENTENNIAL MEMORIAL PLAQUE. (LOCAL). OLAN COATES, SUPERINTENDENT, BUILDINGS-GROUNDS; COLORADO WOMEN'S COLLEGE; MONTVIEW AND QUEBEC; DENVER, CO 80220. (#20758).

COLONIAL COLOR GUARD & COLONY FLAG DETACHMENT - CO. UNIT PRESENTED BY THE ACTIVE ARMY IN OFFICIAL 1775 ARMY UNIFORMS. CAN BE UTILIZED BY ARMY AND CIVILIAN ORGANIZATIONS FOR VANGUARD OF FREEDOM 75 AND CENTENNIAL/BICENTENNIAL ACTIVITIES. (LOCAL). LTC WILLIAM C MARTIN SR, CHAIRMAN; FITZSIMONS ARMY MEDICAL CENTER; DENVER, CO 80240. (#13215).

COLORADO ARCHITECTURAL HERITAGE, DENVER, CO. A COMPREHENSIVE CHRONICLE OF SIGNIFICANT ARCHITECTURE IN COLORADO THROUGH THE FIRST 100 YEARS OF STATEHOOD; CHRONICLE WILL BE A COLLECTION OF PHOTOGRAPHS. (ST-WIDE). DIETZ LUSK, JR, PRESIDENT; COLORADO SOCIETY OF ARCHITECTS; 1426 LARIMER SQUARE; DENVER, CO 80202. (#17430).

COLORADO CELEBRATION OF THE ARTS- SPREE '76. A THREE DAY CELEBRATION OF THE ARTS IN DENVER. THE FESTIVAL FEATURES LOCAL, STATE AND NATIONAL ARTISTS IN THE PERFORMING, VISUAL AND COMMERCIAL ARTS. (ST-WIDE). STEPHANIE MOORE, COORDINATOR; COLORADO CELEBRATION OF THE ARTS; 1430 LARIMER ST; DENVER, CO 80202. (#27285). **ARBA GRANTEE.**

COLORADO CENTENNIAL VILLAGE. THIS ENDEAVOR WOULD BE ONE IN WHICH ENTERTAINMENT, ADVENTURE, & COMMUNITY CENTER FOR ALL YOUNG AND OLD TO ENJOY. (ST-WIDE). G D BARRANTE, EXEC DIRECTOR; COLORADO CENTENNIAL-BICENTENNIAL COMMISSION; 901 SHERMAN ST 15TH FL; DENVER, CO 80203. (#1954).

COLORADO CENTENNIAL BICENTENNIAL CALENDARS. THE COLORADO CENTENNIAL BICENTENNIAL COMMISSION CALENDAR REPRESENTS OVER 1800 PROJECTS IN EVERY COUNTY OF THE STATE FROM JULY 1 THROUGH DECEMBER 31, 1976. (ST-WIDE). G D BARRANTE, EXEC DIRECTOR; COLORADO CENTENNIAL-BICENTENNIAL COMMISSION; 901 SHERMAN ST,; DENVER, CO 80203. (#2007). **ARBA GRANTEE.**

COLORADO CENTENNIAL GUIDES, DENVER, CO. TO PROVIDE FESTIVE CENTENNIAL TOURS FOR VISITORS TO THE STAFF MUSEUM DURING CENTENNIAL; COSTUMED VOLUNTEER GUIDES WILL BE FEATURED. (ST-WIDE). NANCY MARKHAM, CURATOR; STATE HISTORICAL SOCIETY OF COLORADO; 200 14TH AVE; DENVER, CO 80203. (#17431). **ARBA GRANTEE.**

COLORADO COMMUNITY IN DENVER. A STATEWIDE INCENTIVE PROGRAM WHICH PROVIDES TO EACH COMMUNITY IN THE STATE SMALL GRANTS TO COMPLETE ANY OF A VARIETY OF ACTIVITIES INCLUDING PARADES, PAGEANTS, CLEAN-UPS AND MANY OTHER PROJECTS. (ST-WIDE). RONALD K PIERCE, ASST DIRECTOR FOR PROGRAMS; COLORADO CENTENNIAL-BICENTENNIAL COMMISSION; 901 SHERMAN ST, 15TH FLOOR; DENVER, CO 80203. (#20209).

COLORADO COUNCIL OF CHURCHES BICENT OBSERVANCES. THE OBSERVANCES TO BE HELD IN VARIOUS LOCALITIES WITHIN THE STATE WILL INCLUDE COMMUNITY RELIGIOUS FESTIVALS, DISCUSSIONS ON THE AMER ISSUES FORUM, ECUMENICAL WORSHIP SERVICES ON JULY 4, 1975 ETC. (ST-WIDE). LENA W RIEDEL, ADMINISTRATIVE OFFICER; COLORADO COUNCIL OF CHURCHES; 1313 CLARKSON ST; DENVER, CO 80218. (#6830).

COLORADO CRAFTS WORKSHOPS, DENVER. A SERIES OF WORKSHOPS WILL BE CONDUCTED DURING 1975-76 FOR STUDENTS AND INTERESTED CITIZENS; SEVERAL WORKSHOPS WILL DEAL WITH COLORADO CRAFTS PRACTICED 100 YEARS AGO. (LOCAL). MS KAE LAWLOR, PROJ DIRECTOR; REGIS COLLEGE; W 50TH & LOWELL; DENVER, CO 80221. (#15273).

COLORADO ENVIRONMENTAL DESIGN CONTEST. A STATEWIDE CONTEST, IN CONJUNCTION WITH THE COLORADO CHAPTER OF THE AMERICAN INSTITUTE OF ARCHITECTS WILL OFFER PRIZES FOR THE BEST ENTRIES, ESSAYS, DESIGNS, ETC, REGARDING THE ENVIRONMENT. (ST-WIDE). MS ESTELLE BROWN, COMMITTEE ON ENVIRONMENT; COLORADO CENTENNIAL-BICENTENNIAL COMMISSION; 1575 SHERMAN ST; DENVER, CO 80203. (#363). **ARBA GRANTEE.**

COLORADO FOLK FESTIVAL. FOLK ARTS FESTIVAL INCLUDING MUSIC, DANCE, CULINARY & VISUAL ARTS EMPHASIZING THE CONTRIBUTION OF MANY ETHNIC GROUPS TO BUILDING THE NATION AND THE STATE. (ST-WIDE). VYTS F BELIAJUS, CHAIRMAN; COLORADO FOLK ARTS COUNCIL; PO BOX 1226; DENVER, CO 80201. (#4467).

COLORADO HARD ROCK MINING FOLKLORE STUDY. A STUDY OF SONGS, TALES, SUPERSTITIONS & BELIEFS OF COLORADO MINERS; COLLECTING, CLASSIFYING, CROSS-REFERENCING AND VERIFYING OF MINING LORE OF THE PAST 100 YEARS INCLUDING CURRENT REVIVALS. (ST-WIDE). JACQUELINE J SNYDER, DIRECTOR; METROPOLITAN STATE COLLEGE; 250 W 14TH AVE; DENVER, CO 80204. (#4379). **(??).**

COLORADO HISTORICAL NOVEL CONTEST. AWARD TO BE GIVEN FOR WINNING AUTHOR OF COLORADO HISTORICAL NOVEL. (ST-WIDE). GEORGE D BARRANTE, EXEC DIRECTOR; COLORADO CENTENNIAL-BICENTENNIAL COMMISSION; 901 SHERMAN ST; DENVER, CO 80303. (#1327).

COLORADO LOCAL HISTORY: A DIRECTORY. A PROJECT TO PUBLISH A DIRECTORY TO ALL AVAILABLE LOCAL HISTORY COLLECTIONS IN COLORADO. (ST-WIDE). CAROL JOY, PROJECT DIRECTOR; METROPOLITAN STATE COLLEGE LIBRARY; 250 W 14TH AVE; DENVER, CO 80204. (#4408). **ARBA GRANTEE.**

COLORADO PHOTOGRAPHIC ART CENTER. COMPETITION TO OBTAIN PHOTOGRAPHS OF NATION'S TRANSPORTATION, ARTS, SCIENCES, ETC. (ST-WIDE). HAL GOULD, DIRECTOR; COLORADO PHOTOGRAPHIC ART CENTER; 1301 BANNOCK; DENVER, CO 80202. (#2962).

'COLORADO QUEST' A CENTENNIAL/BICENTENNIAL PLAY. A CELEBRATION OF THE RICH CULTURAL HERITAGE OF COLORADO THROUGH DRAMA, MUSIC, DANCE REACHING MAJOR POPULATION AREAS. DIRECT AUDIENCE PARTICIPATION BY BRINGING IN LOCAL HISTORY. (ST-WIDE). HENRY LOWENSTEIN, PRODUCER-DESIGNER; DENVER CENTER FOR THE PERFORMING ARTS-BONFILS THEATRE DIVISION; E COLFAX AT ELIZABETH; DENVER, CO 80206. (#4466). **ARBA GRANTEE.**

COLORADO SPOTLIGHT HISTORIC FEATURETTE. 60 SECOND FEATURETTES ON EVENTS FROM COLORADO'S PAST THAT OCCURRED DURING THE SAME TIME SPAN, 50-150 YEARS AGO; TO BE AIRED ON RADIO AND TV IN THE COUNTY. (LOCAL). PAM W CARTER, BICENTENNIAL CHAIRMAN; METROPOLITAN STATE COLLEGE; 250 W FOURTEENTH AVE; DENVER, CO 80204. (#19811).

COLORADO STATE HISTORY CONCERT BALLET. A FULL LENGTH ORIGINAL BALLET BASED ON COLORADO HISTORY TO TOUR THE STATE IN 76. (ST-WIDE). NORMA O. WALKER, BUSINESS MANAGER; COLORADO CONCERT BALLET, INC; 3210 E COLFAX; DENVER, CO 80206. (#4468).

COLORADO WATER MONITORING AND RESTORATION. PURCHSE WATER QUALITY MONITORING EQUIPMENT, SPONSOR AND COORDINATE VOLUNTEER GROUPS ESTABLISH AND EDUCATE TEAMS TO COORDINATE STREAM SELECTION TEAMS INSPECT REPORT MONITOR ENFORCEMENT & REMEDIAL ACTION. (ST-WIDE). ROBERT WEAVER, EXEC DIRECTOR; COLO COUNCIL OF TROUT UNLIMITED; 4260 E EVANS; DENVER, CO 80222. (#4118). **(??).**

COLORADO WOMEN: HIDDEN FACES. A PUBLIC DISPLAY ON WOMEN IN COLORADO HISTORY (A SOCIAL HISTORY INCLUDING MINORITY WOMEN) ACCOMPANIED BY PAMPHLETS AND AUDIO-VISUAL PACKAGE TO TOUR STATE IN '76; RELATED MATERIAL USED BEYOND '76. (ST-WIDE). SHERILYN R BRANDENSTEIN, PROJ COORDINATOR; LORETTO HEIGHTS COLLEGE; 3001 S FEDERAL BLVD; DENVER, CO 80236. (#10335).

COLORADO'S CATTLE STORY. MULTI-MEDIA PRESENTATION OF CENTENNIAL-BICENTENNIAL ACTIVITIES IN 1976 AT THE STATE FAIR, STOCK SHOW, COUNTY FAIRS, ETC. (ST-WIDE). GRAHAM SADLER, DIRECTOR; DENVER PUBLIC LIBRARY; 1357 BROADWAY; DENVER, CO 80203. (#2863).

COLORADO'S CENTENNIAL-BICENTENNIAL MEDAL PROJECT. WITH ASSISTANCE OF AMER NUMISMATIC ASSOC & SPECIAL FOUNDATION, C-B-C IS DESIGNING, MINTING & MARKETING OFFICIAL COLORADO MEDAL TO FUND PROJECTS FOR 1976. IN GOLD, BRONZE & SILVER VERSIONS. (ST-WIDE). G D BARRANTE, EXEC DIRECTOR; COLORADO CENTENNIAL-BICENTENNIAL COMMISSION; 901 SHERMAN ST; DENVER, CO 80203. (#2012).

COLORADO'S COLORFUL CHARACTERS. BROAD HISTORY OF COLORADO BROUGHT TOGETHER BY BIOGRAPHIES OF THE STATE'S MOST COLORFUL CHARACTERS. (NAT'L). MRS ALLYNE CHIAPPINI, CHAIRMAN; MAYOR'S COMMITTEE OF 19 FOR '76; PO DRAWER 17-G, TA; DENVER, CO 80217. (#26440).

COLORADO'S MEDAL OF HONOR GROVE AT VALLEY FORGE. PROJECT IS THE RAISING OF FUNDS FOR A MEDAL OF HONOR GROVE AT VALLEY FORGE, BY LOCAL SCHOOLS AND PATRIOTIC GROUPS. (LOCAL). MRS RALPH RATCLIFF, PROJ CHAIRMAN; DENVER AREA WOMEN'S CHAPTER FREEDOMS FOUNDATION AT VALLEY FORGE; 468 S GARFIELD ST; DENVER, CO 80209. (#17425).

CONSERVATION OF ART WORKS - DENVER, CO. CLEANING, RELINING, REPAIR OF PAINTINGS AND SCULPTURE: EUROPEAN, AMERICAN AND SPANISH COLONIAL. (ST-WIDE). THOMAS N MAYTHAM, DIRECTOR; DENVER ART MUSEUM; 100 W 14TH AVE PKY; DENVER, CO 80204. (#21914).

CONSTITUTIONAL LAW VOLUME OF COLORADO. A CAREFULLY RESEARCHED VOLUME ON COLORADO CONSTITUTIONAL LAW. THIS WOULD BE A TREMENDOUS AID TO JUDGES, LAWYERS, LEGISLATORS, PUBLIC OFFICIALS, TEACHERS, STUDENTS & OTHER CITIZENS OF COLORADO. (ST-WIDE). JOHN S CARROLL, STATE REPRESENTATIVE; COLORADO BAR ASSOCIATION; 200 W 14TH AVE; DENVER, CO 80202. (#1325).

CRESTED BUTTE MOUNTAIN THEATRE GROUP OF COLORADO. TOURING SHOW DEPICTING THE CONFLICT BETWEEN CULTURAL & ENVIRONMENTAL VALUES BASED ON PRESENT DAY SOCIAL AND ECONOMIC PRESSURES IN MOUNTAIN COMMUNITIES. (ST-WIDE). PEGGY ROGGENBUCK, PROJECT COORDINATOR; CRESTED BUTTE SOCIETY; DEPOT, E ELK AVE; DENVER, CO 81224. (#2932).

DEAD CAR BODIES-REMOVAL AND RECYCLING PROJ OF COLO. PROJECT ON ENVIRONMENT WITH EMPHASIS ON REMOVAL OF 'DEAD CARS' FROM COLORADO'S STREETS, HIGHWAYS & OUR SCENIC WONDERLAND. TRANSPORTATION OF THESE VEHICLES TO RECYCLING CENTER. (ST-WIDE). ESTELLE BROWN, PROJ DIRECTOR; COLORADO CENTENNIAL-BICENTENNIAL COMMISSION; 901 SHERMAN 15TH FLOOR; DENVER, CO 80202. (#1942).

DENVER ANECDOTES - DENVER, CO. SLICES OF LIFE FROM THE COLORFUL LIVES AND EVENTS IN DENVER'S PAST PRINTED IN THE DENVER POST EDITORIAL SECTION. (ST-WIDE). CATHERINE MOLLECK, CHAIRPERSON; MAYOR'S COMMITTEE OF 19 FOR '76; 1313 TREMONT PL, SUITE 6; DENVER, CO 80204. (#18092).

DENVER — CONTINUED

DENVER CENTENNIAL-BICENTENNIAL BROCHURES. PRINTED PUBLICITY OF DENVER CBC ACTIVITIES FOR MAILING, CITY-WIDE DISTRIBUTION (AIRPORT, GOV'T BUILDINGS, HISTORICAL SITES, POINTS OF INTEREST, MULTI-LINGUAL). (LOCAL). ROBERT J OSMUNDSON, CHAIRMAN; MAYOR'S COMMITTEE OF 19 FOR '76; CITY & COUNTY BLDG; DENVER, CO 80202. (#2023).

DENVER C-B-C BOOK ENDORSEMENT PROJECT. ENDORSEMENT BY MAYOR'S COMMITTEE OF 19 FOR '76 OF BOOKS PERTAINING TO DENVER'S HISTORY, HERITAGE, CULTURE, ETC. (ST-WIDE). ROBERT J OSMUNDSON, CHAIRMAN; MAYOR'S COMMITTEE OF 19 FOR '76; CITY AND COUNTY BUILDING; DENVER, CO 80202. (#1912).

DENVER FAIR AMERICAN 1876 SAILING SHIP PROJECT. WILLIAM BLANNING IS PLANNING TO BUILD AN 1876 STYLE SAILING SHIP AT THE DILLON RESERVOIR, AS PART OF PROJECTED FAIR AMERICAN. (ST-WIDE). G D BARRANTE, EXEC DIRECTOR; COLORADO CENTENNIAL-BICENTENNIAL COMMISSION; 901 SHERMAN ST 15TH FLOOR; DENVER, CO 80203. (#1884).

DENVER INDIAN CENTER COMPLEX. CENTER FOR INDIAN PEOPLE AND FAMILIES FROM RESERVATIONS WHO SEEK TO MAKE A LIFE IN THE URBAN COMMUNITY OF DENVER. (LOCAL). BEN BEZOFF, EXECUTIVE OFFICER; CITY & COUNTY OF DENVER; CITY & COUNTY BLDG, RM 350; DENVER, CO 80202. (#1916).

DENVER LIBRARY CENTENNIAL-BICENTENNIAL EXHIBIT. EXHIBIT OF IMPORTANT DOCUMENTS IN COLORADO HISTORY. (LOCAL). G D BARRANTE, EXEC DIRECTOR; DENVER PUBLIC LIBRARY; 1357 BROADWAY; DENVER, CO 80203. (#1957). **ARBA GRANTEE.**

DENVER PUBLIC LIBRARY NOSTALGIA PROGRAM. PRESENT A PRESENTATION OF EARLY COLORADO CULTURAL LIFE. (ST-WIDE). G D BARRANTE, EXEC DIRECTOR; DENVER PUBLIC LIBRARY; 1357 BROADWAY; DENVER, CO 80203. (#1955).

DENVER SYMPHONY BICENTENNIAL PROJECT. CONCERT SUBTITLED 'MUSIC OF AMERICA & THE WEST' WITH MORTON GOULD CONDUCTING, LEON BATES, PLANIST, AND MICHAEL DOMINICO, DANCER. THE PURPOSE IS TO SECURE AWARENESS STATEWIDE TOWARD CENTEN. ACTIVITIES. (ST-WIDE). DAVID G KENT, GENERAL MANAGER; DENVER SYMPHONY ORCHESTRA; 1615 CALIFORNIA ST; DENVER, CO 80202. (#923). **ARBA GRANTEE.**

DENVER SYMPHONY ALL-AMERICAN PROGRAM. MUSICAL PRESENTATION BY DENVER SYMPHONY ORCHESTRA COMMEMORATING DENVER CENTENNIAL-BICENTENNIAL COMMEMORATION. (LOCAL). ROBERT J OSMUNDSON, CHAIRMAN; MAYOR'S COMMITTEE OF 19 FOR '76; CITY AND COUNTY BUILDING; DENVER, CO 80202. (#1920).

DENVER WINTER OLYMPICS. DENVER WAS SELECTED BY THE INTERNATIONAL OLYMPIC COMMITTEE TO BE HOST CITY FOR THE 1976 WINTER OLYMPIC GAMES. THE CITIZENS OF THE STATE VOTED AGAINST HOLDING THE GAMES THERE IN THE 1972 ELECTIONS. (INT'L). JAMES COTTER, ASST TO THE PRESIDENT; ORGANIZING COMMITTEE FOR THE XII WINTER OLYMPIC GAMES; 1390 LOGAN ST, SUITE 312; DENVER, CO 80203. (#32989). **ARBA RECOGNIZED.**

DENVER 4-H COUNTY COUNCIL FLAG PROJ - DENVER, CO. 4-H COUNCIL WILL SELL FLAGS IN THE DENVER AREA. (LOCAL). SHIRLEY DUADE, COORDINATOR; 4-H COUNCIL; 1300 E VIRGINIA; DENVER, CO 80209. (#26227).

DENVER'S SCOUT CENTENNIAL SERVICE CORPS. SCOUT UNITS OF COLORADO WILL SELECT REPRESENTATIVES TO HANDLE COMMUNITY SERVICE PROJECTS. (LOCAL). GARY SCHRENK, PROJ DIRECTOR; CUB SCOUTS AND EXPLORERS OF COLORADO; 2901 19TH AVE; DENVER, CO 80204. (#16308).

DENVER/COLORADO C-B-C ACTIVITY CALENDAR. CALENDAR OF EVENTS AND ACTIVITIES OF DENVER AND COLORADO C-B-C. (ST-WIDE). ROBERT J OSMUNDSON, CHAIRMAN; MAYOR'S COMMITTEE OF 19 FOR '76; CITY AND COUNTY BUILDING; DENVER, CO 80202. (#1962).

DISCOVER COLORADO PROJECT FOR DENVER GIRLS. CELEBRATE THE CENTENNIAL BY TAKING UNDERPRIVILIGED GIRLS IN DENVER TO VIEW FIRST HAND HISTORICAL AREAS OF THE STATE. (ST-WIDE). DIANE J DVCA, PROJECT DIRECTOR; GIRL'S CLUB OF DENVER; 601 SOUTH IRVING; DENVER, CO 80219. (#4341). **ARBA GRANTEE.**

DO YOU REMEMBER HISTORICAL PROJECT OF DENVER. PROGRAM TO SHARE MEMBERS OF ERAS OF AMERICAN AND DENVER & THEIR RELATIONSHIP TO THOSE EVENTS. (ST-WIDE). G D BARRANTE, EXEC DIRECTOR; DENVER PUBLIC LIBRARY; 1367 BROADWAY; DENVER, CO 80203. (#1947).

DOMINGUEZ-ESCALANTE BICENTENNIAL EXPEDITION - CO. GRANT FUNDS WILL BE USED TO FEED THE 15 MEMBERS OF THE DOMINGUEZESCALANTE BICENTENNIAL EXPEDITION, WHICH WILL COMMEMORATE THE 1776 JOURNEY OF FATHERS DOMINGUEZ & ESCALANTE THROUGH NM, CO, AZ, & UT. (REGN'L). WILLIAM S DALEY, ADMINISTRATOR; DOMINGUEZ-ESCALANTE BICENTENNIAL EXPEDITION; PO BOX 5446; DENVER, CO 80217. (#26685). **ARBA GRANTEE.**

DRUM CORPS INTERNATIONAL. THE DRUM & BUGLE CORPS WILL BE AVAILABLE TO MARCH IN PARADES & COMPETITIONS. (LOCAL). STEVE OGDEN, COORDINATOR; DRUM CORPS INTERNATIONAL; 8715 W 16TH AVE; LAKEWOOD, CO 80215. (#26359).

EASTSIDE CENTENNIAL-BICENTENNIAL HOUSING OF DENVER. NEIGHBORHOOD DEVELOPMENT PROGRAM WILL PROVIDE 499 LOW TO MODERATE INCOME RESIDENTIAL UNITS, INCLUDING 200 UNITS FOR ELDERLY, 50 CONVENTIONAL UNITS, 89 TOWNHOUSES, AND 160 GARDEN APARTMENT UNITS. (LOCAL). HOWARD CONVERSE & HENRY BURGWYN, PLANNERS; CITY & COUNTY OF DENVER; 1445 CLEVELAND PLACE; DENVER, CO 80202. (#1983).

EDEN THEATRICAL WORKSHOP PROJ OF COLORADO. FOSTERING IMPROVED INTERCOMMUNITY AND INTERRACIAL RELATIONS THROUGH A COMMON INTEREST IN THE PERFORMING ARTS AND RELATED CULTURAL ACTIVITIES. (LOCAL). LUCY WALKER, PROJECT COORDINATOR; COLORADO CENTENNIAL-BICENTENNIAL COMMISSION; C/O 504 TROY ST; DENVER, CO 80239. (#2919).

ENVIRONMENT '76 EXHIBIT IN DENVER, CO. JURIED EXHIBITION OF PROPOSED & DEVELOPED PROJECTS FOR IMPROVING ALL ASPECTS OF DENVER SURROUNDINGS THRU CREATION OF A SERIES OF FILMS, BOOKS, PLAYGROUNDS, GARDENS, PHOTOS, ESSAYS, DANCE, ETC. (REGN'L). VICTOR HORNBEIN, PRESIDENT; COLORADO CENTRAL CHAPTER, AMERICAN INSTITUTE OF ARCHITECTS; 1426 LARIMER SQUARE; DENVER, CO 80202. (#52). **ARBA GRANTEE.**

FEED FORWARD - WEEKLY TV SERIES, DENVER, CO. A 15 WEEK TV SERIES ON ENVIRONMENTAL CONCERNS. (ST-WIDE). CHRIS CURTIS, PROG DIRECTOR; KRMA TV; 1261 GLENARM PL; DENVER, CO 80204. (#18614). **ARBA GRANTEE.**

FESTIVAL OF MOUNTAIN AND PLAIN - COLORADO. A 10 DAY FESTIVAL STATEWIDE TO BE HELD ANNUALLY IN DENVER LATE JULY OR AUGUST BEGINNING '75 PARADES PAGEANTS ETHNIC COMMUNITY EXHIBITS AND PROGRAMS INCLUDING 'A NIGHT IN OLD DENVER'. (ST-WIDE). ROBERT RHODES, VICE PRESIDENT; MAYOR'S COMMITTEE OF 19 FOR 76; CITY AND COUNTY BLDG RM 350; DENVER, CO 80202. (#4351).

FIRE DEPARTMENT HDQTS & FIRE STATION, DENVER, COLO. THIS FACILITY WILL COMBINE THE FIRE DEPARTMENT HEADQUARTERS AND A MAJOR FIVE-BAY FIRE STATION. RESULT OF BICENTENNIAL BOND ISSUE. (LOCAL). JOHN HENRY, ADMIN ASST PUBLIC WORKS DEPT; CITY & COUNTY OF DENVER; COLFAX AVE & BANNOCK ST; DENVER, CO 80202. (#1991).

FIRST CITIZENS OF COLORADO PROJECT. SLIDE TAPE EXHIBIT TO DOCUMENT AND HONOR FIRST CITIZENS OF COLORADO. THE CENTENARIAN WHO HAVE LIVED THROUGH THE CHANGES AND CONTRASTS OF THE LAST ONE HUNDRED YEARS. (ST-WIDE). ROBERT MOHL, PLANNER & PHOTOGRAPHER; COLORADO COMMISSION ON AGING; REGENT HALL 34 UNIV OF COLORADO; BOULDER, CO 80302. (#2706). **(??).**

'FIRST OF DENVER ART' CONTEST. 3 PART ART CONTEST FOR METRO STATE STUDENTS RESULTING IN A 3 PIECE MURAL DEPICTING THE THEME OF COLO CENT-BICENT CELEBRATION. CONTEST & MURALS WILL BEGIN 74 & END 76-SCHOLARSHIP FOR EACH PART GIVEN. (ST-WIDE). VONNIE WHEELER, SPECIAL EVENTS DIRECTOR; FIRST NATIONAL BANK OF DENVER; 17TH & WELTON ST; DENVER, CO 80217. (#4279).

FITZSIMONS ARMY MEDICAL CENTER SPEAKERS BUREAU- CO. SPEAKERS WILL BE PROVIDED TO MILITARY AND CIVILIAN ORGANIZATIONS. SEVERAL TITLES WILL BE AVAILABLE. SUBJECTS WILL BE MILITARY, MEDICAL AND GENERAL. (LOCAL). LTC WILLIAM C MARTIN SR, CHAIRMAN; FITZSIMONS ARMY MEDICAL CENTER; DENVER, CO 80240. (#13212).

FLAG GIRL DRUM & BUGLE CORPS. FORMATION OF A MARCHING & PLAYING PRECISION FLAG GIRL UNIT FOR COMPETITION & PARADES. (LOCAL). BILL MOLAND, STATE DIRECTOR OF YOUTH; MOST WORSHIPFULL PRINCE HALL GRAND LODGE F & AM CO & JURISDICTION; 2291 KRAMERIA ST; DENVER, CO 80207. (#26292).

FLAGSTAFF, COLO, ARTS & CULTURAL EXPERIENCE PROJ. DRAMA, COMEDY, CLASSICAL MUSIC, DANCE, ROCK & BLUES, PUPPETRY, OPERA FOLK DANCE, IMPROVISATIONAL THEATER, BLUEGRASS, READINGS: A MAXIMIZATION OF TOTAL COMMUNITY INVOLVEMENT IN THE ARTS. (ST-WIDE). CLARK REED WATSON, COORDINATOR; FLAGSTAFF ARTS & CULTURAL EXPERIENCE; 3605 TABLE MESA DR; BOULDER, CO 80303. (#2862).

FLOWER SHOW AT CURRIGAN HALL. EXHIBIT. (LOCAL). MRS WALTER RUESCH, COORD; COLORADO FEDERATION OF GARDEN CLUBS; DENVER, CO 80222. (#108687-2).

FOCUS ON INDIAN CULTURE, DENVER. HISTORY, CUSTOMS AND ACHIEVEMENTS OF INDIAN PEOPLE IN COLORADO WILL BE PRESENTED TO PUBLIC THROUGH ARTS AND CRAFTS AND EDUCATIONAL PRESENTATIONS. (LOCAL). JOE LOCUST, BOARD CHAIRMAN; DENVER NATIVE AMERICANS UNITED; 2210 E 16TH AVE; DENVER, CO 80206. (#11047). **ARBA GRANTEE.**

'FOR THE RED WHITE & BLUE '76', DENVER, CO. A FULL DISPLAY OF SENIOR CITIZEN ACTIVITIES, A 60 MINUTE MUSICAL AND FORUM FOR AUDIENCE MEMBERS. (ST-WIDE). TOM PROCTOR, CENTER DIRECTOR; PLATT PARK SENIOR CITIZEN CENTER - DENVER PARKS & RECREATION; 1510 S GRANT; DENVER, CO 80210. (#20532).

FORUM CENTER FOR THE ARTS IN DENVER. ORGANIZATION TO FOSTER POTENTIALS OF CHILDREN WHOSE OPPORTUNITIES FOR ARTISTIC EXPRESSION ARE LIMITED. ALSO TO PROVIDE A WELCOMING PLACE TO BE ON A DAILY BASIS. (LOCAL). MIKE GILLIUM, TREASURER; FORUM CENTER FOR THE ARTS; 1570 GILPIN; DENVER, CO 80202. (#2920). **ARBA GRANTEE.**

FRONTIER PARK - DENVER, CO. RESTORATION AND BEAUTIFICATION OF A HISTORIC PARK AND OLD LOG CABIN BUILT IN 1859; AN ALTERNATIVE-EDUCATIONAL EXPERIENCE. (LOCAL). ALAN S WUTH, PROJ DIRECTOR; GRANT JUNIOR HIGH; 1751 S WASHINGTON ST; DENVER, CO 80219. (#18442). **ARBA GRANTEE.**

FUTURES CONFERENCE & FAIR OF COLORADO. A CONFERENCE TO USE THE LESSONS OF THE PAST TO PROJECT AND PREPARE FOR THE FUTURE OF THE STATE. (ST-WIDE). GEORGE BARRANTE, EXEC DIRECTOR; COLORADO CENTENNIAL BICENTENNIAL COMMISSION; 901 SHERMAN ST; DENVER, CO 80203. (#4340).

GREENING OF DENVER PROJECT. ENVIRONMENTAL BEAUTIFICATION PROJECT FOR YOUTH AND CIVIC ORGANIZATIONS. (LOCAL). ROBERT J OSMUNDSON CHAIRMAN; MAYOR'S COMMITTEE OF 19 FOR '76; CITY AND COUNTY BUILDING; DENVER, CO 80202. (#1917).

GREETINGS EXCHANGE WITH NEIGHBORING STATES, CO. BICENTENNIAL GREETINGS FROM CO TO NEIGHBORING STATES, EXCHANGED AT BORDERS. GREETINGS TO CO FROM OTHER STATES WILL BE GIVEN AND BROUGHT TO THE CAPITOL BY MEANS OTHER THAN MOTORIZED VEHICLE. (REGN'L). KIRK SARELL, PROJ CHAIRMAN; COLORADO STATE CHAPTER, ORDER OF DEMOLAY; 6619 W 26TH AVE; DENVER, CO 80214. (#24945).

HARVEY OTIS YOUNG-THE LOST GENIUS-BOOK OF COLORADO. BOOK TO SERVE AS A KEYSTONE IN A REVIVAL OF INTEREST AND INFORMATION ON COLORADO ARTISTS. (ST-WIDE). PATRICIA TRENTON, AUTHOR; DENVER ART MUSEUM; ANCHORAGE WEST/1401 S. OAK KNOLL; PASADENA, CA 91109. (#2761).

HEADSTART MUSIC MAGIC - PROJ OF DENVER, CO. SPECIAL PROGRAM FOR HEADSTART CENTERS AND ELEMENTARY SCHOOLS THROUGH THE MEDIUM OF MUSIC, PUPPETS AND DANCE WITH EMPHASIS ON CULTURAL AND ETHNIC CONTRIBUTIONS OF BLACKS, CHICANOS AND INDIANS. (LOCAL). WATER CHARLES, PROJ DIRECT; COLORADO PHILHARMONIC; BOX 975; EVERGREEN, CO 80439. (#17678). **ARBA GRANTEE.**

HIGH AVENUE OF PRIDE PROJECT OF DENVER. PROPOSES TO HISTORICALLY SHOW ACCOMPLISHMENTS BY MINORITIES. ALSO, TO DEVELOP COMPETITIVE ACTIVITY BY SHOWING THE OPPORTUNITY FOR ACCOMPLISHMENT TO MINORITY YOUTH. (LOCAL). CLARENCE BRISCOE, DIRECTOR; UNITED METHODIST CHURCH HEAD-QUARTERS; C/O 3401 HIGH ST; DENVER, CO 80205. (#2922). **ARBA GRANTEE.**

HISTORICAL ART WORK - DENVER, CO. AN ART WORK REPRESENTATIVE OF COLORADO'S HISTORY WILL BE PRESENTED TO GOVERNOR LAMM AT THE STATE CAPITOL BUILDING. (ST-WIDE). MARIE TRAYNOR, CHAIRPERSON; BETA SIGMA PHI; 3875 S CLARKSON; ENGLEWOOD, CO 80110. (#17540).

HISTORICAL MARKERS PROGRAM OF COLORADO. THERE ARE TWELVE DIFFERENT TYPES OF SIGNS USED FOR MARKING HISTORIC SITES THE HERITAGE COUNCIL WOULD LIKE ONE SIGN DESIGN WHICH WILL BE CONSISTANT, COLORFUL & HIGHLIGHT THE HISTORIC SITES. (ST-WIDE). G D BARRANTE, EXEC DIRECTOR; COLORADO CENTENNIAL-BICENTENNIAL COMMISSION; 901 SHERMAN 15TH FLOOR; DENVER, CO 80203. (#1943).

HISTORY OF HEALTH, P E & RECREATION, COLORADO. THE HISTORY OF HEALTH, PHYSICAL EDUCATION AND RECREATION WILL BE TAUGHT IN PUBLIC SCHOOLS IN EFFORT TO PROMOTE BETTER UNDERSTANDING OF THESE DISCIPLINES. (ST-WIDE). DR JAMES BRYANT, PRESIDENT; COLORADO ASSOCIATION FOR HEALTH, P E AND RECREATION; BOX 25; DENVER, CO 80204. (#17427).

HOMETOWN JOBS 76 PROJECT OF COLORADO. HELP EACH INTERESTED COMMUNITY INITIATE, DEVELOP, FOLLOW THROUGH & COMPLETE A SOUND LOCAL JOB PRODUCING PROJECT BY 1976. (ST-WIDE). CHARLES KORSOSKI, PROJECT DIRECTOR; COLORADO CENTENNIAL BICENTENNIAL COMMISSION; 901 SHERMAN ST; DENVER, CO 80203. (#4337).

HORIZONS FOR YOUTH CONCERTS OF DENVER. A SERIES OF YOUTH ORIENTED ACTIVITIES AND CONCERTS TO BE PRESENTED TO JUNIOR AND SENIOR HIGH SCHOOL STUDENTS IN THE GREATER DENVER AREA, FEATURING MUSIC OF AMERICAN COMPOSERS. (LOCAL). DAVID G KENT, GENERAL MANAGER; DENVER SYMPHONY ORCHESTRA; 1615 CALIFORNIA ST; DENVER, CO 80202. (#4359). **ARBA GRANTEE.**

HOUSING AND HOUSING-RELATED ACTIVITIES OF DENVER. THE CITIZENS OF DENVER APPROVED A BOND ISSUE TO FUND HOUSING AND HOUSING-RELATED ACTIVITIES IN ORDER TO ELIMINATE SLUM AREAS AND TO HELP SOLVE PROBLEM OF INADEQUATE HOUSING. BICENTENNIAL BOND ISSUE. (LOCAL). HOWARD CONYERSE, PLANNER; CITY & COUNTY OF DENVER; COLFAX AVE & BANNOCK ST; DENVER, CO 80202. (#1986).

INTER DIMENSIONS - OUTER EXPRESSIONS, PROJ OF COLO. AUDIO VISUAL SHOW OF BLACK ARTISTS & DESIGNERS. ORIGINAL ART CLOTHES & JEWELRY. A PROJ TO EXHIBIT & PERFORM IN MULTI-MEDIA THE RICH CULTURAL ART HERITAGE OF COLORADO'S BLACK COMMUNITY. (ST-WIDE). JOANNA HOWELL, PROJ DIRECTOR; COLORADO CENTENNIAL-BICENTENNIAL COMMISSION; 901 SHERMAN ST; DENVER, CO 80203. (#1999).

IN-HOUSE ENTERTAINMENT FOR V A HOSPITALS, CO. ENTERTAINMENT WILL BE PROVIDED FOR VETERANS & THEIR FAMILIES AT COLORADO'S 3 V A HOSPITALS. LOCAL ARTISTS WILL PERFORM AT FT LYON; GRAND JUNCTION & DENVER HOSPITALS. (ST-WIDE). MARILYN HELLER, EXEC DIRECTOR; HOSPITAL AUDIENCES, INC; 1510 S GRANT; DENVER, CO 80210. (#20531).

ITALIAN WEEK. A WEEK OF CULTURAL ACTIVITIES MARKING THE CONTRIBUTIONS OF ITALIANS TO AMERICA. MAJOR EVENTS WILL BE ITALIAN NIGHT WITH FOOD & MUSIC, BANQUET & BALL AT REGENCY INN. AT REGENCY INN. (LOCAL). JOE ANTONIO, CHMN; ITALIAN WEEK COMMITTEE; DENVER, CO 80222. (#108687-3).

KALEIDOSCOPE-COLORADO'S COLORFUL CHARACTERS BOOK. BROAD HISTORY OF COLORADO BROUGHT TOGETHER BY BIOGRAPHIES OF THE STATE'S MOST COLORFUL CHARACTERS. (ST-WIDE). GLADYS BUELER, PROJECT DIRECTOR; COLORADO CENTENNIAL-BICENTENNIAL COMMISSION; 901 SHERMAN ST; DENVER, CO 80203. (#2724).

KIT CARSON COUNTRY - A PHOTOGRAPHIC EXHIBIT OF CO. PHOTOGRAPHIC EXHIBIT OF 50 TO 75 COLOR AND BLACK AND WHITE PRINTS OF THE COUNTRY IN COLORADO AND NEW MEXICO WHERE KIT CARSON HUNTED, TRAPPED, EXPLORED, SCOUTED & RANCHED. (REGN'L). MRS AVA WEBBER, SECRETARY; 704 FIFTH; LAS ANIMAS, CO 81054. (#4374).

DENVER — CONTINUED

LAMONT CONCERTS IN DENVER. A SERIES OF CONCERTS HIGHLIGHTING THE MUSICAL LITERATURE OF THIS NATION AND STATE. (LOCAL). ROGER DEXTER FEE, DIRECTOR; UNIV OF DENVER, LAMONT SCHOOL OF MUSIC; UNIVERSITY PARK; DENVER, CO 80210. (#4365).

LIBERTY MARCH 76 OF DENVER, COLORADO. HOST YOUTH CONFERENCES AND HAVE WALKING TOURS BASED ON LOCAL HERITAGE. (LOCAL). CHARLES OZZELLE, STAFF COORDINATION; COLORADO CENTENNIAL BICENTENNIAL COMMISSION; 901 SHERMAN ST; DENVER, CO 80203. (#4338).

LIBRARY MATERIALS FOR THE HANDICAPPED - DENVER, CO. PROJECT WILL BE TO PROVIDE LIBRARY MATERIALS TO BLIND & HANDICAPPED READERS. (LOCAL). DONALD FREEMAN, PROJ DIRECTOR; FRIENDS OF COLORADO LIBRARY FOR THE BLIND & HANDICAPPED; 2030 CHAMPA ST; DENVER, CO 80205. (#20805). **ARBA GRANTEE.**

MARTIN LUTHER KING JR MEMORIAL OF DENVER. PROPOSAL TO ERECT MEMORIAL STATUE TO MARTIN LUTHER KING JR. - TO BE ERECTED PERMANENTLY IN DENVER CITY PARK. (LOCAL). ERROLL GIDDINGS, SENIOR ADMIN COORDINATOR; COLORADO CENTENNIAL-BICENTENNIAL COMMISSION; 901 SHERMAN ST; DENVER, CO 80203. (#2762). **ARBA GRANTEE.**

MATCH BOX UNITS PROJECT OF COLORADO. A PROJECT TO BRING AN UNDERSTANDING OF CITY LIFE AND WHAT MAKES THE CITY WORK AS A WHOLE TO MORE CITIZENS OF COLORADO. (ST-WIDE). G D BARRANTE, EXEC DIRECTOR; COLORADO CENTENNIAL-BICENTENNIAL COMMISSION; 901 SHERMAN ST; DENVER, CO 80203. (#2004).

MCALLISTER PHOTOGRAPHY OF THE COLORADO ROCKIES. A PHOTOGRAPHIC STUDY OF THE 'FACES OF THE COLORADO ROCKIES'. A BLACK AND WHITE DOCUMENTARY OF THE PEOPLES OF THE COLORADO ROCKIES. (ST-WIDE). BRUCE MCALLISTER, PHOTOGRAPHER; 701 MARION ST; DENVER, CO 80218. (#4352).

MEDALLION DESIGN CONTEST OF COLORADO. AWARD FOR WINNING DESIGN OF MEDALLION FOR COLORADO CENTENNIAL-BICENTENNIAL COMMISSION. (ST-WIDE). G D BARRANTE, EXEC DIRECTOR; COLORADO CENTENNIAL-BICENTENNIAL COMMISSION; 901 SHERMAN, 15TH FLR; DENVER, CO 80203. (#1881).

'MEET THE AMERICANS', DENVER, CO. A NATIONAL PROGRAM DESIGNED TO BRING FOREIGN VISITORS INTO AMERICAN HOMES IN ORDER TO GIVE THEM INSIGHTS INTO AMERICAN CULTURE HAS BEEN EXPANDED TO INCLUDE COLORADO AS PART OF ITS SYSTEM. (INT'L). ELIZABETH R WALTON, ASSISTANT DIRECTOR; AMERICAN HOST FOUNDATION; 515 S FLOWER ST; LOS ANGELES, CA 90071. (#16814).

MEMORIAL DAY C-B-C COMMEMORATION, DENVER, COLORADO. TIE IN DENVER C-B-C WITH MEMORIAL DAY CELEBRATIONS. (LOCAL). ROBERT J OSMUNDSON, CHAIRMAN; MAYOR'S COMMITTEE OF 19 FOR'76; CITY & COUNTY BLDG; DENVER, CO 80202. (#2029).

METROPOLITAN SCIENCE CENTER - DENVER, CO. TO RESTORE AND REMODEL THE PAVILION AT CITY PARK FOR USE AS A CENTER FOR RESEARCH AND EDUCATION ABOUT THE ENVIRONMENT THE GENERAL PUBLIC WILL PARTICIPATE IN LECTURES. FIELD TRIPS, SEMINARS, ETC. (ST-WIDE). EVA MCINTOSH, PRESIDENT; METROPOLITAN SCIENCE CENTER; THE PAVILION, CITY PARK; DENVER, CO 80205. (#16503).

METROPOLITAN STATE COLLEGE DISPLAY, DENVER, CO. THE COLLEGE WILL PRODUCE A MOBILE DISPLAY DEPICTING THE TEN-YEAR HISTORY OF MSC AND IT'S PROGRESS AS A COLORADO INSTITUTION OF HIGHER LEARNING IN THE CENTENNIAL-BICENTENNIAL CELEBRATION. (LOCAL). PAM WYNNE CARTER, CHAIRPERSON; ANNIVERSARY COMMITTEE FOR METROPOLITAN STATE COLLEGE; 250 WEST 14TH AVE; DENVER, CO 80204. (#15958).

METROPOLITAN STATE COLLEGE ON THE MOVE WITH COLORADO - A CELEBRATION. MSC'S 10TH ANNIVERSARY WILL COINCIDE WITH THE STATE AND NATIONAL ANNIVERSARY. ACTIVITIES INCLUDE AN ANNIVERSARY CONVOCATION, SCULPTURE PROJECT, MOBILE DISPLAY, MUSIC, AN AURARIA DAY EVENT & A LIBRARY EXHIBIT. (ST-WIDE). PAM W CARTER; METROPOLITAN STATE COLLEGE; 250 W 14TH AVE; DENVER, CO 80204. (#102941-1).

'MINE EYES HAVE SEEN' - DENVER, CO. A ONE MOVEMENT SYMPHONY ENTITLED 'MINE EYES HAVE SEEN', ABOUT THE PARALLELS BETWEEN THE 2 TESTAMENTS IN THE BIBLE AND EVENTS IN AMERCAN HISTORY, WILL BE PERFORMED. (LOCAL). OLEG LOBANOV, MANAGER; DENVER SYMPHONY ORCHESTRA; 1615 CALIFORNIA ST; DENVER, CO 80202. (#25538).

THE MINORITY PHOTOGRAPHERS PROJECT OF DENVER. AN EXPOSITION, EXHIBITION, DOCUMENTATION AND EDUCATION PROJECT ABOUT THE CONTRIBUTIONS OF MINORITY PHOTOGRAPHERS TO THE HISTORY AND PRESENT ACTIVITIES OF PHOTOGRAPHY. (ST-WIDE). WESLEY WADA, DIRECTOR; INSIGHT SCHOOL OF PHOTOGRAPHY; 1266 DOWNING ST; DENVER, CO 80218. (#6772).

MODERN DANCE, THE DEVELOPING AMER ART FORM - COLO. TO BROADEN SCOPE OF DANCE INTEREST STATEWIDE & CREATE AWARENESS OF OUR HERITAGE OF THIS DANCE FORM CCD-SPONSORED DANCE GROUPS PRESENT PERFORMANCES, LECTURES, FILMS & CLASSES THRUOUT STATE. (ST-WIDE). ELIZABETH MANDEVILLE, CHAIRMAN; COLORADO CONTEMPORARY DANCE; PO BOX 6665; DENVER, CO 80206. (#4369).

MONUMENT TO GREAT POLISH-AMERICANS IN DENVER, CO. 20 FT TALL MONUMENT OF GEN PULASKI WITH BRONZE PLAQUES COMMEMORATING POLISH-AMERICANS WHO CONTRIBUTED TO AMER HISTORY & CULTURE WILL BE ERECTED IN PULASKI PARK. (LOCAL). EDWARD J ZALEWSKI, CHAIRMAN; POLISH CLUB OF DENVER; 1660 OGDEN ST; DENVER, CO 80218. (#6823).

MURALS PORTATILES PROJECT OF COLORADO. PROPOSED PAINTING OF TWO MURALS WITH THEMES BASED ON HISTORICAL AND CULTURAL CONTRIBUTIONS TO THE SOUTHWEST. MURALS WILL TOUR VARIOUS INSTITUTIONS THROUGHOUT THE STATE. (ST-WIDE). JACK LANG, EXEC DIRECTOR; LATIN AMERICAN RESEARCH AND SERVICE AGENCY; 1375 DELEWARE; DENVER, CO 80204. (#2923).

A MUSEUM FOR CHILDREN IN DENVER, COLORADO. A MUSEUM FOR CHILDREN IS AN IDEAL WAY COLORADOANS CAN PARTICIPATE & COMMEMORATE THEIR PAST BY LOOKING TO THE FUTURE. THIS MUSEUM WILL BE A CULTURAL INSTITUTION & A PERMANENT ADDITION TO COLORADO. (ST-WIDE). CYNTHIA C KAHN, DIRECTOR; A MUSEUM FOR CHILDREN; 1100 14TH ST, RM 704A; DENVER, CO 80202. (#1324). **ARBA GRANTEE.**

NATIVE AMERICAN HERITAGE-RELIGIOUS CULTURE PARK-CO. COMMEMORATIVE PARK PROPOSED FOR INDIAN POW-WOW GROUND/RELIGIOUS CEREMONIES IN DENVER. (LOCAL). RICHARD TALLBULL, COMMITTEE MEMBER; MAYOR'S COMMITTEE OF 19 FOR '76; CITY AND COUNTY BUILDING; DENVER, CO 80202. (#1911).

NCAA HOCKEY CHAMPIONSHIPS IN DENVER IN 1976. NATIONAL HOCKEY CHAMPIONSHIPS TO BE HELD IN NEW DENVER SPORTS ARENA CREATED BY BICENTENNIAL BOND ISSUE. (NAT'L). UNIVERSITY OF DENVER; MAYOR'S COMMITTEE OF 19 FOR '76; CITY AND COUNTY BUILDING; DENVER, CO 80202. (#1909).

NEEDLEPOINT CENTENNIAL TAPESTRY, DENVER, CO. A NEEDLEPOINT SAMPLER TAPESTRY DEPICTING DENVER'S EARLY HISTORY IS BEING CREATED BY ABOUT 76 DIFFERENT PEOPLE. FINISHED SAMPLER SIZE WILL BE 6X9 FEET. (ST-WIDE). MARILYN FOSTER, CHAIRPERSON; AMERICAN INSTITUTE OF ARCHITECTS, ENVIRONMENT '76; 231 MILWAUKEE; DENVER, CO 80206. (#17538).

NEW DANCE THEATRE TOUR IN COLORADO. COMBINED WINTER TOUR WITH THE COLORADO PHILHARMONIC THE CENTENNIAL BICENTENNIAL THEME WILL BE EXPRESSED THROUGH MUSIC DANCE POETRY PUPETRY IN 12 ENGAGEMENTS IN 12 WESTERN SLOPE COUNTIES. (ST-WIDE). SCHYLEEN QUALLS, VICE PRESIDENT; NEW DANCE THEATRE, INC; 2006 LAWRENCE ST; DENVER, CO 80205. (#4462). **ARBA GRANTEE.**

OPERA FAIR COMPANY OF COLORADO. MOBILE REPERATORY COMPANY OF TEN COLORADO ACTORS-SINGERS TO PRESENT OPERAS TO SCHOOL CHILDREN OF COLORADO'S TARGET-TITLE 3-SCHOOLS. (ST-WIDE). HARRIET LAWYER-DUVALLO; COLORADO CENTENNIAL-BICENTENNIAL COMMISSION; 1080 SHERMAN ST; DENVER, CO 80203. (#2728).

PARKS AND RECREATION PROGRAM OF DENVER. THIS PROJECT INCLUDES FUNDS FOR COMMUNITY PARK DEVELOPMENT, PARK SITE ACQUISITION, COMMUNITY RECREATION CENTERS, BALLFIELD COMPLEXES, TENNIS FACILITIES, HIKE & BIKEWAYS. RESULT OF BICENT. BOND ISSUE. (LOCAL). JOE CIANCIO, MANAGER PARKS & RECREATION DEPT; CITY & COUNTY OF DENVER; COLFAX AVE & BANNOCK ST; DENVER, CO 80202. (#1981).

THE PAYNE EXPEDITION, DENVER TO WASH DC. HORSEBACK RIDE FROM DENVER TO WASHINGTON DC CARRYING PETITIONS FROM COLORADO CITIZENS TO PRESIDENT REQUESTING STATEHOOD IN COMMEMORATION OF CO'S ADMITTANCE TO THE UNION 100 YEARS AGO. (NAT'L). CHARLES V & CATHY PAYNE; MAYOR'S COMMITTEE OF 19 FOR 76; 1313 TREMONT PL SUITE 6; DENVER, CO 80204. (#17212).

PERSONAL SERVICE CENTER PROJ OF DENVER. FUNDING OF AN EXISTING SHOPPE WHICH EMPLOYS ECONOMICALLY LIMITED WOMEN IN AN IRONING SERVICE. IT IS FELT THE OPERATION OF THIS SHOPPE HAS CREATED INTEREST IN SEEKING SOLUTIONS TO UNEMPLOYMENT PROBLEMS. (LOCAL). DOROTHY KING, PROJECT SUPERVISOR; PERSONAL SERVICE CENTER; 2219 E 21ST ST; DENVER, CO 80205. (#2924).

PLATTE AREA RECLAMATION COMMITTEE, PROJ OF COLO. TO MAKE A MULTI-USE AREA OUT OF THE DOWNTOWN SOUTH PLATTE RIVER BASIN IN DENVER. (LOCAL). G D BARRANTE, EXEC DIRECTOR; COLORADO CENTENNIAL-BICENTENNIAL COMMISSION; 901 SHERMAN ST; DENVER, CO 80203. (#1997).

PLATTE RIVER CLEANUP CAMPAIGN,, DENVER, CO. DEVELOPMENT & IMPLEMENTATION OF AN ECOLOGICAL PROJECT WHICH WILL BENEFIT BOTH THE ENVIRONMENT & SEVERAL COLORADO COUNTIES IN JUVENILE CRIME PREVENTION. (LOCAL). JEFF PRYOR, DIRECTOR, COMMUNICATIONS & ACTIVITIES; PARTNERS, INC; 1260 W BAYAUD; DENVER, CO 80223. (#24365).

PLATTE RIVER IMPROVEMENT/WHITE WATER KAYAK CHUTE. DEVELOPMENT OF OUTDOOR RECREATIONAL FACILITIES ALONG PLATTE RIVER SPECIFICALLY A WHITE WATER KAYAK CHUTE. (ST-WIDE). TED MUELLER, PROJ DIRECTOR; COLORADO CENTENNIAL-BICENTENNIAL COMMISSION; 901 SHERMAN ST, 15TH FL; DENVER, CO 80203. (#7816).

PLATTE VALLEY, COLORADO, RENEWAL PLAN. RENEWAL OF THE CENTRAL PLATTE VALLEY IN CONNECTION WITH THE NEW BUILDINGS ETC THAT ARE PLANNED FOR THE CENTENNIAL COMMEMORATION. (LOCAL). JOHN YELENICK, CHAIRMAN; SOUTH PLATTE AREA REDEVELOPMENT COUNCIL; PO BOX 17153 TERMINAL ANNEX; DENVER, CO 80202. (#4404).

PLUS: 'PEOPLE LET'S UNITE FOR SCHOOLS', DENVER, CO. COALITION OF 49 ORGANIZATIONS FORMED TO ASSIST PEACEFUL IMPLEMENTATION OF COURT-ORDERED DESEGREGATION PROMOTING EXCELLENCE OF EDUCATION FOR ALL CHILDREN AND SUPPORT FOR 'POSITIVE PEOPLE'. (LOCAL). THE REVEREND RICHARD S KERR, CHAIRMAN; PLUS - 'PEOPLE, LET'S UNITE FOR SCHOOLS'; 2552 WILLIAMS ST; DENVER, CO 80205. (#20085).

POETRY RECITATION AT OLD FOLKS HOMES - CO. VISIT OLD FOLKS HOMES, NURSING HOMES & SPECIAL SCHOOLS TO RECITE APPROPRIATE AMERICAN POETRY AND READINGS. (LOCAL). GERALD CURTIS, DIRECTOR; 1632 AKRON ST; AURORA, CO 80010. (#26257).

POLICE ADMINISTRATION BUILDING PROJ OF DENVER, CO. THIS FACILITY WILL REPLACE THE PRESENT STRUCTURE AND WILL BE LOCATED WITHIN ONE BLOCK OF THE CITY AND COUNTY BUILDING AND THE COURTS. THIS IS A RESULT OF A BICENTENNIAL BOND ISSUE. (LOCAL). JOHN HENRY, ADMIN ASST PUBLIC WORKS DEPT; CITY & COUNTY OF DENVER; COLFAX AVE & BANNOCK ST; DENVER, CO 80202. (#2001).

'POLISH NATIONAL ALLIANCE' PROJECT OF COLORADO. VISUAL DISPLAY USING PHOTOS AND RESEARCH DATA DEPICTING HISTORY OF THE POLISH COMMUNITY IN COLORADO FROM 1858 TO 1974. (LOCAL). WANDA CUBA, PRESIDENT; ST MARTIN'S GROUP 134; 4839 WASHINGTON ST; DENVER, CO 80216. (#4354).

PRINCE HALL YOUTH GROUP, DENVER, CO. PRINCE HALL YOUTH GROUP DRUM & BUGLE CORP & YOUTH ATHLETIC PROGRAM FOR BOYS 7 TO 18 YEARS OF AGE. (LOCAL). BILL MOLAND, DIRECTOR; MOST WORSHIPFUL PRINCE HALL GRAND LODGE F & AM CO & JURISDICTION; 2291 KRAMERIA; DENVER, CO 80207. (#26304).

PROJECT FORWARD '76 - RELIGIOUS PROJ OF COLORADO. ATMOSPHERE IN OBSERVANCE OF BICENTENNIAL WITH GREATER EMPHASIS ON SPIRITUAL AND RELIGIOUS VALUES.DEEPER APPRECIATION OF THE NUMEROUS CONTRIBUTIONS OF RELIGION TO OUR HERITAGE. (ST-WIDE). G D BARRANTE, EXEC DIRECTOR; COLORADO CENTENNIAL-BICENTENNIAL COMMISSION; 901 SHERMAN ST; DENVER, CO 80203. (#2763).

PROJECT VOTE '76 - DENVER, CO. A NON-PARTISAN PROJECT OT INCREASE PARTICIPATION IN ELECTIONS IN COLORADO THROUGH VOTER EDUCATION AND REGISTRATION ESPECIALLY AMONG YOUTH AND MINORITIES. (ST-WIDE). ROBERT E BOWEN, EXEC DIRECTOR; AMERICAN VOTER EDUCATION FUND, INC; 2952 ZUNI ST; DENVER, CO 80211. (#26370).

PROSPECTUS FOR A MANCOS CANYON INDIAN PARK, COLO. UTE MOUNTAIN TRIBE IS RENOVATING CULTURAL SITES TO CREATE A NEW NATIONAL PARK AND PROVIDE NEEDED INCOME AND EMPLOYMENT TO TRIBE AND ITS MEMBERS. (ST-WIDE). G D BARRANTE, EXEC DIRECTOR; COLORADO CENTENNIAL-BICENTENNIAL COMMISSION; 901 SHERMAN ST 15TH FLOOR; DENVER, CO 80203. (#1961). **(??).**

PUBLICATION OF HISTORIC MAP & BROCHURE OF COLO. A TOP PRIORITY OF THE HERITAGE COUNCIL IS TO PUBLISH AN HISTORIC MAP AND/OR BROCHURE FOR WIDE DISTRIBUTION AT LITTLE OR NO COST. THIS MAP WILL OUTLINE HISTORIC SITES AND SCENIC WONDERS OF THE STATE. (ST-WIDE). G D BARRANTE, PROJECT DIRECTOR; COLORADO CENTENNIAL-BICENTENNIAL COMMISSION; 901 SHERMAN ST; DENVER, CO 80303. (#1323).

PUBLICATION OF INVENTORY OF HISTORIC SITES -COLO. PROJECT TO SUPPORT THE PUBLICATION OF HISTORICAL SITES THROUGHOUT THE STATE. THIS INVENTORY WILL MAKE COLORADOANS MORE AWARE OF THE AVAILABILITY OF THEIR COLORFUL & RICH HERITAGE. (ST-WIDE). G D BARRANTE, EXEC DIRECTOR; COLORADO CENTENNIAL-BICENTENNIAL COMMISSION; 901 SHERMAN ST; DENVER, CO 80203. (#2729).

RACING CHAMPIONSHIPS, DENVER, CO. SPORTS CAR RACING EVENTS WILL TAKE PLACE ACROSS THE COUNTRY. (NAT'L). CAMERON ARGETSINGER, COORDINATOR; SPORTS CAR CLUB OF AMERICA, INC; PO BOX 22467; DENVER, CO 80222. (#27924).

RADIO & TV PROGRAMS - DENVER, CO. RADIO & TELEVISION PROGRAMS WILL BE PRODUCED ON ALL ASPECTS OF THE BICENTENNIAL. (ST-WIDE). LENA W RIEDEL, COORDINATOR; COLORADO COUNCIL OF CHURCHES; 1313 CLARKSON; DENVER, CO 80218. (#26207).

RED WHITE AND BLUEGRASS DANCE MARATHON OF DENVER. DANCE MARATHON LASTING 15 HOURS INCLUDING 7 BANDS AND GAMES AROUND DANCE AREA CONSISTING OF THOSE PLAYED 100 YEARS AGO. (LOCAL). PATTI NATION, COMMITTEE MEMBER; CENTENNIAL - BICENTENNIAL AWARENESS COMMITTEE; 1313 TREMONT; DENVER, CO 80204. (#4566).

REGIONAL AMERICAN ISSUES FORUM, DENVER, CO. CITIZEN PARTICIPATION AND DISCUSSION ON HISTORIC AND CURRENT EVENTS IN AMERICA. (REGN'L). DR ROBERT ROEDER, PROJ CHAIRMAN; REGIONAL AMERICAN ISSUES FORUM, UNIV OF DENVER; 401 MARY REED BLDG; DENVER, CO 80210. (#17429).

REGIONAL PLAYWRITE COMPETITION OF COLORADO. A PROPOSED COMPETITION FOR ONE FULL LENGTH PLAY DEALING WITH A BROAD VIEW OF COLORADO HISTORY. THE WINNING PLAY WILL PERFORM FOR THREE WEEKS AT THE 'CHANGING SCENE' THEATRE IN DENVER. (ST-WIDE). ALFRED BROOKS, PRESIDENT; THE CHANGING SCENE; 1527 1/2 CHAMPA ST; DENVER, CO 80202. (#2764).

REGIS AMERICAN ISSUES FORUM - DENVER, CO. MONTHLY SESSIONS FOR STUDENTS, FACULTY, AND STAFF WILL BE CONDUCTED ON CAMPUS FOLLOWING THE NATIONAL AIF TOPICS. (LOCAL). DR DEBORAH GAENSBAUER, DIRECTOR; REGIS COLLEGE; W 50TH & LOWELL; DENVER, CO 80221. (#15263).

REGIS COLLEGE CENTENNIAL HISTORY (1877-1977) - CO. PUBLICATION OF BOOK TRACING HISTORY OF REGIS COLLEGE FROM ITS BEGINNING IN 1877 IN LAS VEGAS, NEW MEXICO. (LOCAL). DR HARRY STANSELL, HISTORY PROFESSOR; REGIS COLLEGE; W 50TH & LOWELL; DENVER, CO 80221. (#15265).

REPRODUCTIONS OF DECLARATION OF INDEPENDENCE, CO. A FULL COLOR PRINT OF THE DECLARATION OF INDEPENDENCE CREATED BY A DENVER FREELANCE ARTIST, TO BE DISTRIBUTED AS A HANDOUT IN PUBLIC AREAS & BUSINESSES IN DENVER, COLORADO. (LOCAL). L J RUYBAL, COORDINATOR; 1343 ACOMA ST; DENVER, CO 80204. (#6824). **(??).**

DENVER — CONTINUED

SALUTE TO AMERICA. THE SALUTE TO AMERICA WILL FEATURE BAND CONCERTS, MILITARY DISPLAYS, SPEAKERS, MILITARY DINNERS AND BALLS. (LOCAL). WILLIAM C MARTIN, SR; FITZSIMMONS ARMY MEDICAL CENTER; DENVER, CO 80240. (#108800-1).

SALUTE TO SPANISH SURNAMED AMERICANS IN CO HISTORY. PROJECT SALUTES CONTRIBUTIONS OF SPANISH SURNAMED AMERICANS TO COLORADO HISTORY. IT INCLUDES: BAS RELIEF MAP, A SLIDE & CASSETTE PRESSENTATION & SHOWCASE & A DOCUMENTARY FILM. (LOCAL). ANSELMO S JARAMILLO, COMMUNITY RELATIONS DIRECTOR; LATIN AMERICAN RESEARCH & SERVICE AGENCY; 1150 DELAWARE; DENVER, CO 80204. (#26303).

SCOUT HISTORICAL TRAILS PROGRAM, DENVER, CO. ALL COLORADO SCOUTING UNITS ARE IMPLEMENTING THIS TRAIL IMPROVEMENT PROGRAM. (ST-WIDE). GARY SCHRENK, PROJ DIRECTOR; CUB SCOUTS AND EXPLORERS OF COLORADO; 2901 W 19TH AVE; DENVER, CO 80204. (#16307).

SENIOR CITIZEN - YOUTH HOLIDAY PARTY OF DENVER. MAKING AND DISTRIBUTING OF BICENTENNIAL MOTIF CHRISTMAS GIFTS. (LOCAL). KATHY BILLINGS, PROJECT CHAIRMAN; CENTENNIAL - BICENTENNIAL AWARENESS COMMITTEE; 1313 TREMONT; DENVER, CO 80204. (#4563).

SOLAR ENERGY EXHIBITION PROGRAM. TRAVELING EXHIBIT ON SOLAR ENERGY & ACCOMPANYING PROGRAM TO VISIT MAJOR AMERICAN CITIES. A LARGE & SMALL VERSION & GUIDELINES FOR LOCAL PROGRAMS,I.E. WORKSHOPS,LECTURES,FILMS,LOCAL SOLAR INFO GUIDES. (NAT'L). DONALD ROARK, PRESIDENT; AMERICAN INSTITUTE OF ARCHITECTS CENTRAL CHAPTER; 311 DETROIT ST; DENVER, CO 80206. (#7808).

SOUTH PLATTE/CHERRY CREEK REDEVELOPMENT, DENVER. PARK AREA PROPOSED FOR THE AREA INVOLVED. (LOCAL). BEN BEZOFF, EXECUTIVE OFFICER; CITY & COUNTY OF DENVER; ROOM 350 CITY & COUNTY BUILDING; DENVER, CO 80202. (#1964).

SPIRIT OF '76 COLOR GUARD PROJ, DENVER, CO. THE GEORGE WASHINGTON HIGH SCHOOL JROTC PROVIDES 5 MAN COLOR GUARD IN AUTHENTIC COLONIAL UNIFORMS FOR PUBLIC AFFAIRS & BICENTENNIAL EVENTS. (LOCAL). COLONEL L J WEIGEL, DIR OF ARMY INSTRUCTION; DENVER PUBLIC SCHOOLS; 1278 FOX ST; DENVER, CO 80204. (#17469).

SPIRITS OF 76 - PROJ OF DENVER, CO. THE ENLISTED MAN AND WOMAN FROM ARMY UNITS IN METRO-DENVER WHO BEST EXEMPLIFY THE SPIRIT, PATRIOTISM, DEDICATION AND DEVOTION OF THE U S ARMY. (LOCAL). LTC WILLIAM C MARTIN SR, CHAIRMAN; FITZSIMONS ARMY MEDICAL CENTER; DENVER, CO 80240. (#13213).

STADIUM DISPLAY OF CENTENNIAL-BICENTENNIAL LOGO. OFFICIAL LOGO WILL BE DISPLAYED IN MIDDLE OF MILE HIGH STADIUM FOOTBALL FIELD, NEW SPORTS ARENA BASKETBALL COURT, COLISEUM & AUDITORIUM. PLANTING OF ARBA LOGO IN FLOWERBED IN FRONT OF CITY HALL. (ST-WIDE). ROBERT LOCKE, MANAGER DEPT OF GENERAL SERVICES; CITY & COUNTY OF DENVER; COLFAX AVE & BANNOCK ST; DENVER, CO 80202. (#2010).

STAINED GLASS MURAL IN DENVER, COLORADO. STAINED GLASS HISTORY OF COLORADO DEPICTING KEY EVENTS WILL BE COMMISSIONED AS A PORTABLE EXHIBIT WITH ITS OWN LIGHTING AND HANDLING EQUIPMENT. (ST-WIDE). CAROL FRYER, PARTNER; MEMORABILIA & COLORADO ART GLASS WORKS; 1516 BLAKE ST; DENVER, CO 80202. (#6758).

STAMPEDE TO TIMBERLINE - HISTORICAL BOOK OF COLO. OFFICIAL ENDORSEMENT OF MURIEL SIBELL WOLLE'S BOOK ABOUT COLORADO, 'STAMPEDE TO TIMBERLINE'--SWALLOW PRESS, CHICAGO. (ST-WIDE). G D BARRANTE, EXEC DIRECTOR; HERITAGE COUNCIL COLORADO CENTENNIAL-BICENTENNIAL COMMISSION; 901 SHERMAN ST; DENVER, CO 80203. (#4385).

'STANDING ROOM ONLY' SPACE EXHIBIT OF COLORADO. A MULTI-MEDIA TRAVELING DISPLAY UNIT OF 5 ROOMS OF DIMINISHING SIZE TO TOUR COLORADO. THEME: WE HAVE LIMITED PER CAPITA SPACE OVER 200 YRS, BUT STILL HAVE CHOICES FOR FUTURE LAND USES & RESOURCES. (ST-WIDE). CAROL GEORGE, PROJECT DIRECTOR; COLORADO LABOR COUNCIL; 360 ACOMA; DENVER, CO 80223. (#4177).

STAPLETON FIELD, DENVER, PHOTOGRAPHY DISPLAY. FIFTY COLOR PRINTS OF COLORADO LANDSCAPES WOULD BE INSTALLED AT STAPLETON INTERNATIONAL AIRPORT AT MAXIMUM VISIBILITY LOCATIONS, SUCH AS CONCOURSES AND CENTRAL LOBBY AREAS. (LOCAL). JAMES O MILMOE, PHOTOGRAPHER; JAMES O. MILMOE, PHOTOGRAPHER; 14900 CACTUS CIRCLE; GOLDEN, CO 80401. (#4282).

STATE FLAG CEREMONIES BY SCOUTS, DENVER, CO. ALL SCOUTING UNITS OF COLORADO ARE IMPLEMENTING HISTORICAL STATE FLAG CEREMONIES. (ST-WIDE). GARY SCHRENK, PROJ DIRECTOR; CUB SCOUTS AND EXPLORERS OF COLORADO; DENVER, CO 80204. (#16306).

STATEHOUSE TO SCHOOL HOUSE PROJECT OF COLORADO. SOUND/SLIDE PRESENTATION FOR CLASSROOM USE. BRINGS ACTIVITIES OF 3 BRANCHES OF STATE GOVERNMENT TO THE STUDENTS USING CHILDREN AS THE STARS OF THE SEGMENTS. ROLE PLAYING FOR REINFORCEMENT INCLUDED. (ST-WIDE). HENRY KIMBROUGH, ASST TO GOVERNOR; OFFICE OF GOVERNOR AND STATE DEPT OF EDUCATION; STATE CAPITOL BLDG; DENVER, CO 80203. (#2719). **ARBA GRANTEE.**

STATUS OF STATES-PICTORIAL PORTRAIT OF USA IN 1976. A PHOTOGRAPHER'S COMPETITION TO COLLECT PHOTOS OF COLORADO DEPICTING OUR LIFE AND TIMES IN CBC YEAR 1976. ALSO TO ASSEMBLE EXHIBITS FOR CURRENT STATE USA AND PRESERVE SAME FOR USA IN 2076. (ST-WIDE). EUGENE D LANG, PRESIDENT; COLORADO PHOTOGRAPHIC ARTS CENTER; 1301 BANNOCK ST; DENVER, CO 80204. (#2722). **ARBA GRANTEE.**

SUNDIALS WITH BICENTENNIAL SYMBOL. GRANITE SUNDIALS WITH THE BICENTENNIAL SYMBOL. ARBA LICENSE NO 76-19-0547. (NAT'L). ROY ERICKSON, DIRECTOR; ERICKSON MEMORIAL COMPANY; DENVER, CO 80204. (#10417).

THE THIRD GENERATION, DENVER, CO. FOUR, ONE-HOUR TELEVISION PROGRAMS ON THE ELDERLY. (ST-WIDE). DON R FREEMAN, PRODUCER; KRMA-TV, CHANNEL 6; 1261 GLENARM PL; DENVER, CO 80204. (#24941).

THIS IS COLORADO - A TRAVELOGUE. A TRAVELOGUE FOR THEATRICAL RELEASE. (ST-WIDE). G D BARRANTE, EXEC DIRECTOR; COLORADO CENTENNIAL-BICENTENNIAL COMMISSION; 901 SHERMAN ST; DENVER, CO 80203. (#1995).

TRAIN POSTER PROJECT, DENVER, CO. PICTURES OF 1ST TRAIN INTO COLORADO, JUNE 1870 & NEWEST TRAIN ON THE HORIZON TO COLORADO, 1976 AMTRAK WILL BE THE SUBJECT OF A POSTER/BANNER. POSTER IN DENVER UNION TERMINAL IN MARCH. (ST-WIDE). KATHERINE M COMPTON, CHAIRMAN; COMPTON'S ENGINEERS & MERRILL JUNIOR HIGH SCHOOL; 1235 S OGDEN ST; DENVER, CO 80210. (#20213).

TRAINS IN DENVER, CO. BANNER/POSTER OF FIRST TRAIN IN DENVER IN JUNE, 1870 AND THE NEWEST TRAIN IN DENVER, 1976 AMTRAK. (LOCAL). KATHERINE M COMPTON, CHAIRMAN; COMPTON'S ENGINEERS - MERRILL JUNIOR HIGH SCHOOL; 1235 S OGDEN ST; DENVER, CO 80210. (#24938).

TRAVELING ARBA 14-PANEL EXHIBIT PROJECT OF COLO. THIS IS AN EXHIBIT PORTRAYING THE THREE THEME AREAS: HERITAGE '76, FESTIVAL '76, AND HORIZONS '76. IT WILL BE DISPLAYED AT STAPLETON INTERNATIONAL AIRPORT. (ST-WIDE). JOE ALBI, REGIONAL DIRECTOR; REGIONAL OFFICE, FED REGION VIII, ARBA; 1515 CLEVELAND PL, STE 222; DENVER, CO 80202. (#2011).

TRAVELING CULTURAL SHOW IN DENVER, CO. SU TEATRO TOUR; SHOW EMPHASIZES CULTURAL CONCEPTS RELATING TO 'LA FAMILIA', 'CARNALISMO' & HUMAN WORTH & DIGNITY. THE STATEWIDE TOUR SEEKS TO RAISE CULTURAL AWARENESS OF ALL COLORADO'S CITIZENS. (LOCAL). YOLANDA ORTEGA, MEMBER; UNITED MEXICAN-AMERICAN STUDENTS SCHOLARSHIP FUND, INC; 1100 14TH ST; DENVER, CO 80203. (#28191).

'TWO HUNDRED YEARS AGO' - DENVER, CO. A HERITAGE SONG OF AMERICA WITH SLIDE PRESENTATION. (LOCAL). CARRIE COLLINS, COMPOSER; C COLLINS PUBLISHING COMPANY; 5828 E FLORIDA AVE; DENVER, CO 80224. (#26253).

U S ARMY VANGUARD OF FREEDOM '75 CELEBRATION - CO. CELEBRATION OF THE ARMY'S 200TH BIRTHDAY WITH PARADE, OPEN HOUSE, STATIC DISPLAY, CONCERTS, ETC. (REGN'L). LTC WILLIAM C MARTIN SR, CHAIRMAN; FITZSIMONS ARMY MEDICAL CENTER; DENVER, CO 80240. (#13217).

UN DIA CON LA RAZA - DENVER, CO. AN OCCASION FOR ALL COLORADOANS TO PARTICIPATE IN A CELEBRATION COMMEMORATING THE CULTURE AND CONCEPT OF FAMILY (FAMILIA) OF THE MEXICAN-AMERICAN IN COLORADO. (LOCAL). GIL SISNEROS, CHAIRMAN; AMERICAN GI FORUM, SKYLINE CHAPTER; 1120 S DEPEW ST; LAKEWOOD, CO 80226. (#17679). **ARBA GRANTEE.**

UNIVERSITY WITHOUT WALLS OF DENVER. PROPOSING TO GIVE TEN SCHOLARSHIPS TO MINORITY STUDENTS WHO, AS PART OF THEIR STUDIES WOULD BE REQUIRED TO PRODUCE A MAJOR WORK THAT WOULD DEMONSTRATE PAST AND PRESENT CONTRIBUTIONS BY MINORITIES. (LOCAL). ELINOR GREENBURG, DIRECTOR; LORETTO HEIGHTS COLLEGE; 3001 S FEDERAL BLVD; DENVER, CO 80236. (#2921). **ARBA GRANTEE.**

VEHICLE SERVICE CENTER COMPLEX, PROJ OF DENVER CO. THIS FACILITY WILL COMBINE SHOPS OPERATIONS FOR THE PUBLIC WORKS, FIRE, POLICE, AND PARKS AND RECREATION DEPARTMENTS. IT WILL REPLACE THE EXISTING COMPLEXES. RESULT OF BICENTENNIAL BOND ISSUE. (LOCAL). JOHN HENRY, ADMIN ASST PUBLIC WORKS DEPT; CITY & COUNTY OF DENVER; COLFAX AVE & BANNOCK ST; DENVER, CO 80202. (#2003).

VIGNETTES ON LESSER KNOWN HIST AMERICAN WOMEN. AN HR-LONG RESENTATION PERFORMED ON REQUEST FOR GROUPS FOR A MINIMUM FEE OF $25. CAN BE PERFORMED ANYWHERE FROM PRIVATE HOMES TO LARGE AUDITORIUMS. (ST-WIDE). PAT KENNING, PROGRAM DIRECTOR; YOUNG WOMEN'S CHRISTIAN ASSN; 1545 TREMONT PL; DENVER, CO 80202. (#33415).

VOTER REGISTRATION AND VOTER EDUCATION, CO. ENCOURAGEMENT OF VOTER REGISTRATION AND PARTICIPATION IN THE ELECTION PROCESS. PROJECT IS TO COMBAT VOTER APATHY. (LOCAL). LARRY M LOPEZ, DIRECTOR; DENVER ELECTION COMMISSION; 414 14TH ST; DENVER, CO 80802. (#24944).

WARREN VILLAGE -BICENT HOUSING FACILITY OF DENVER. TWO BUILDINGS - A 96 UNIT APARTMENT COMMUNITY FOR LOW TO MODERATE INCOME ONE-PARENT FAMILIES. (LOCAL). JOHN FAHENKROG, DIRECTOR; WARREN VILLAGE, INC; 1323 GILPIN ST; DENVER, CO 80203. (#4117).

WEST SIDE MEXICAN FOLKLORIC DANCE GROUP OF COLO. TO GIVE LOCAL CHILDREN PRIDE IN THEIR ETHNIC BACKGROUND, INCREASE THEIR SELF-IMAGE AND BUILD A BRIDGE OF CULTURAL UNDERSTANDING BETWEEN ETHNIC GROUPS BY INVITING ALL ETHNIC GROUPS TO JOIN. (LOCAL). ERROLL GIDDINGS, SENIOR ADMIN COORDINATOR; COLORADO CENTENNIAL-BICENTENNIAL COMMISSION; 901 SHERMAN ST; DENVER, CO 80203. (#2727). **ARBA GRANTEE.**

WHITE BUFFALO COUNCIL POW-WOW PROJECT OF COLORADO. PROJECT TO ASSIST IN PURCHASE OF COSTUMES TO COMPETE IN INTER-TRIBAL DANCE POW-WOW. FUNDS WILL SUPPLEMENT COUNCIL'S FUNDS & ENHANCE AUTHENTICITY OF POW-WOW. (ST-WIDE). RICHARD TALL BULL, CHAIRMAN; WHITE BUFFALO COUNCIL OF AMERICAN INDIANS; PO BOX 4131 SANTA FE STATION; DENVER, CO 80204. (#2018).

WHO'S WHO IN COLORADO 1976 CENTENNIAL EDITION. BIOGRAPHICAL DIRECTORY OF COLORADO'S LEADING CITIZENS. (ST-WIDE). DANIEL VALDES Y TAPIA, PRESIDENT; WHO'S WHO IN COLORADO, INC; SUITE 320-360 S MONROE; DENVER, CO 80209. (#19750).

'WHY NOT HONOR BARNEY FORD?', DENVER, CO. MEMORALIZATION & PRESERVATION OF MARKER FOR BARNEY L FORD, BLACK PIONEER, CIVIC LEADER AND POLITICIAN OF COLORADO AND THE ROCKY MTN REGION. (REGN'L). KATHRYNE MCKINNEY, CO-CHAIRMAN; BARNEY FORD MEMORIAL ASSOC; PO BOX 8464; DENVER, CO 80201. (#24946).

WILLIAM H MCNICHOLS SPORTS ARENA IN DENVER. FACILITY TO HOST EVENTS SUCH AS HOCKEY, BASKETBALL, ICE SHOWS, AND OTHER PUBLIC GATHERINGS. WILL SEAT MAXIMUM OF 18,000 PEOPLE. RESULT OF BICENTENNIAL BOND ISSUE. OFFICIAL OPENING WAS 10/16/75. (ST-WIDE). BURTON MITCHELL, DEPT OF GENERAL SERVICES; CITY & COUNTY OF DENVER; 1323 CHAMPA; DENVER, CO 80204. (#1968).

7TH AMER HIST SOCIETY OF GERMANS FROM RUSSIA INTL CONFERENCE. CONFERENCE. (INT'L). PHIL B LEGLER, CHMN; THE AMERICAN HISTORICAL SOCIETY OF GERMANS FROM RUSSIA; 680 S ALTON WAY, APT 7-A; DENVER, CO 80231. (#106699-1).

9TH STREET HISTORIC PARK OF DENVER. HISTORIC DENVER PROJECT COMMEMORATING DENVER CENTENNIAL-BICENTENNIAL COMMEMORATION. (LOCAL). BARBARA SUDLER, EXEC DIRECTOR; HISTORIC DENVER, INC; 1015 9TH ST; DENVER, CO 80204. (#1987). **ARBA GRANTEE.**

JULY 1, '73 - DEC 31, '74. ENVIRONMENTAL DESIGN COMPETITION IN COLORADO. A STATEWIDE CONTEST, IN CONJUNCTION WITH THE COLORADO CHAPTER OF THE AMERICAN INSTITUTE OF ARCHITECTS WILL OFFER PRIZES FOR THE BEST ENTRIES, ESSAYS, DESIGNS, ETC, REGARDING THE ENVIRONMENT. (ST-WIDE). MS ESTELLE BROWN; COLORADO CENTENNIAL-BICENTENNIAL COMMISSION; 1575 SHERMAN ST; DENVER, CO 80203. (#363-901).

AUG 19, '73. BICENTENNIAL CONCERT OF AMERICAN MUSIC OPENS IN COLORADO SPRINGS. 'AMERICA - THE BICENTENNIAL' CONCERT. A CONCERT OF MUSIC OF AMERICA & THE WEST, MORTON GOULD CONDUCTING. (ST-WIDE). MRS PATRICIA MIDDENDORF,; DENVER SYMPHONY ORCHESTRA; 1615 CALIFORNIA ST; DENVER, CO 80202. (#179-901).

AUG 6 - 7, '74. WORKSHOP ON THE ARTS. 'DENVER-IT'S CULTURAL DIMENSIONS' PROJECT. WORKSHOP ON THE ARTS, HISTORY, DEVELOPMENT, SUPPORT, & INVOLVEMENT OF DENVERITES. WORKSHOP IS DESIGNED TO INCREASE THE AWARENESS AND LEVEL OF SUPPORT TO THE ARTS. (LOCAL). PEGGY HART, PROGRAM SPECI; DENVER PUBLIC LIBRARY; 1357 BROADWAY; DENVER, CO 80202. (#2760-901).

AUG 19, '74. 'MUSIC OF AMERICA AND THE WEST'. CONCERT SUBTITLED 'MUSIC OF AMERICA & THE WEST' WITH MORTON GOULD CONDUCTING, LEON BATES, PLANIST, AND MICHAEL DOMINICO, DANCER. THE PURPOSE IS TO SECURE AWARENESS STATEWIDE TOWARD CENTEN. ACTIVITIES. (ST-WIDE). DAVID G KENT, GEN MGR; DENVER SYMPHONY ORCHESTRA; 1615 CALIFORNIA ST; DENVER, CO 80202. (#923-901).

JAN 1 - 31, '75. DEDICATION OF DENVER INDIAN CENTER COMPLEX. CENTER FOR INDIAN PEOPLE AND FAMILIES FROM RESERVATIONS WHO SEEK TO MAKE A LIFE IN THE URBAN COMMUNITY OF DENVER. (ST-WIDE). BEN BEZOFF, EXECUTIVE OFF; CITY & COUNTY OF DENVER; CITY & COUNTY BLDG, RM 350; DENVER, CO 80202. (#1916-901).

FEB 20 - 21, '75. ACTION '76 CONFERENCE. CONFERENCE ON EQUAL OPPORTUNITY, EDUCATION, MINORITY EMPLOYMENT & THE DISADVANTAGED. THE CONFERENCE WILL FACILITATE ACTION & COOPERATION BETWEEN BUSINESS AND GOVERNMENT. (ST-WIDE). WAIT ROBERTS, COORDINATOR; METRO DENVER URBAN COALITION, EMPLOYMENT TASK FORCE; 1441 YORK ST; DENVER, CO 80205. (#6800-501).

MAR 17, '75. ST PATRICK'S DAY C-B-C COMMEMORATION PARADE. ST PATRICK'S DAY C-B-C PARADE OF DENVER PARADE WITH DENVER C-B-C THEME AREAS INCORPORATED. (LOCAL). ROBERT J OSMUNDSON, CHMN; MAYOR'S COMMITTEE OF 19 FOR '76; CITY AND COUNTY BUILDING; DENVER, CO 80202. (#1918-901).

APR 4, '75. CITYWIDE PARTY AT CURRIGAN HALL DENVER'S PREMIERE CELEBRATION. MUSIC; ENTERTAINMENT; PAGEANTRY; BUFFET INCLUDING CRAB CLAWS, CHEESE BARBECUED BEEF, A PATRIOTIC SALAD. AT CURRIGAN HALL. (LOCAL). ROSEMARY BARNWELL; MAYOR'S COMMITTEE OF 19 FOR 76; 1313 TREMONT PLACE SUITE 6; DENVER, CO 80203. (#50066-1).

APR 16 - JUNE 1, '75. FRONTIER AMERICA THE FAR WEST. 300 HISPANIC, INDIAN & AMER ART OBJECTS FROM 9TH-19TH CENTS. PAINTINGS, PRINTS, PHOTOS & OTHER DECORATIVE & UTILITARIAN OBJECTS DISPLAYED. OVER 2/3 ARE LOANS FROM PRIVATE & PUBLIC USA COLLECTIONS. AT DENVER ART MUSEUM. (REGN'L). JEAN WILLIAMS, PUBLICITY; NATIONAL END FOR THE ARTS & PHILIP MORRIS INC; 479 HUNTINGTON AVE; BOSTON, MA 02115. (#4044-1).

JUNE 1, '75. SOUTH PLATTE/CHERRY CREEK PARK SITE DEDICATION. OPENING. (LOCAL). BEN BEZOFF; CITY & COUNTY OF DENVER; ROOM 350 CITY & COUNTY BUILDING; DENVER, CO 80202. (#1964-501).

JUNE 5, '75. UNVEILING OF STATUE AT PACO SANCHEZ PARK. MARBLE SCULPTURE DEPICTING OLD MAN, HIS WIFE, A CHILD BEING LED BY PACO WITH INSCRIPTION VENEAN YO LES ENSENERE COMO. LIFE SIZE STATUE IN MEXICO WITH MARBLE FROM ITALY. (LOCAL). LEVI BEALL, DIRECTOR; GOOD AMERICANS ORGANIZATION; 2185 BROADWAY ST; DENVER, CO 80205. (#2723-501).

DENVER — CONTINUED

JUNE 14, '75. U S ARMY VANGUARD OF FREEDOM '75 CELEBRATION - CO. CELEBRATION OF THE ARMY'S 200TH BIRTHDAY WITH PARADE, OPEN HOUSE, STATIC DISPLAY, CONCERTS, ETC. (REGN'L). LTC WILLIAM C MARTIN SR; FITZSIMONS ARMY MEDICAL CENTER; DENVER, CO 80240. (#13217-1).

JUNE 23 - JULY 18, '75. BICENTENNIAL EXHIBITION OF SMITHSONIAN INSTIT HISTORICAL DOCUMENTS. THIRTY HISTORIC LETTERS WILL BE DISPLAYED COVERING THE AMERICAN REVOLUTION THRU THE ELECTION OF GEORGE WASHINGTON. AT FEDERAL BLDG IN DENVER. (REGN'L). ELIZABETH CLINTON; DEPT OF HEALTH, EDUCATION & WELFARE; 1961 STOUT ST; DENVER, CO 80262. (#7908-1).

JUNE 27 - 29, '75. SPREE 75 CELEBRATION OF VISUAL PERFORMING AND COMMERCIAL ARTS. SEMINAR, COMPETITION, EXHIBIT, FESTIVAL, LIVE PERFORMANCE AT THE DENVER ZOO; MUSEUM OF NATURAL HISTORY; PHIPPS AUDITORIUM. (REGN'L). CARL DAHLGREN; THE COLORADO CELEBRATION OF THE ARTS INC; 330 ALBION ST; DENVER, CO 80220. (#50024-1).

JULY 1, '75 - AUG 1, '76. SR CITIZENS PRESENT PATRIOTIC MUSICAL PRODUCTION. SENIOR CITIZENS' DRAMA GROUP, WHICH IS NOW THREE YEARS OLD, HAS PERFORMED 3 MUSICALS & IS TOURING COLORADO DURING THE SUMMER OF '75. (ST-WIDE). THOMAS PROCTOR, CHAIRMAN; DENVER PARKS & RECREATION; 1510 S GRANT ST; DENVER, CO 80210. (#100203-1).

JULY 3, '75. RADIO & TELEVISION HISTORY PROGRAMS SPONSORED BY COLORADO CHURCHES. FESTIVAL, RADIO/TV. (ST-WIDE). LENA W RIEDEL; COLORADO COUNCIL OF CHURCHES; 1313 CLARKSON ST; DENVER, CO 80218. (#6830-503).

JULY 4, '75. ECUMENICAL WORSHIP SERVICES SPONSORED BY CO COUNCIL OF CHURCHES. FESTIVAL, RADIO/TV. (ST-WIDE). LENA W RIEDEL; COLORADO COUNCIL OF CHURCHES; 1313 CLARKSON ST; DENVER, CO 80218. (#6830-502).

JULY 4, '75. OLD-FASHIONED 4TH OF JULY CELEBRATION. PARADE WITH BOOTHS, CIVIC ORGANIZATIONS TO HOST PICNICS, BALL GAMES, RACES, PARK CONCERTS - OLD-FASHIONED NEIGHBORHOOD CELEBRATIONS. RACES, GAMES, MUSIC. AT DENVER CITY PARKS. (LOCAL). ROBERT J OSMUNDSON, CHMN; MAYOR'S COMMITTEE OF 19 FOR '76; CITY AND COUNTY BLDG; DENVER, CO 80202. (#1919-1).

JULY 4, '75 - DEC 31, '76. BICENTENNIAL LIBRARY DISPLAY. EXHIBIT. (LOCAL). DAVID FARR, RES LIBRARIAN; REGIS COLLEGE; W 5/TH & LOWELL; DENVER, CO 80221. (#102323-1).

JULY 6, '75. GROUND BREAKING CEREMONY IN PULASKI PARK. MONUMENT TO GREAT POLISH-AMERICANS IN DENVER, CO. 20 FT TALL MONUMENT OF GEN PULASKI WITH BRONZE PLAQUES COMMEMORATING POLISH-AMERICANS WHO CONTRIBUTED TO AMER HISTORY & CULTURE WILL BE ERECTED IN PULASKI PARK. (LOCAL). EDWARD J ZALEWSKI; POLISH CLUB OF DENVER; 752 S HOLLY ST; DENVER, CO 80218. (#6823-501).

JULY 13, '75 - MAY 29, '76. RADIO-TV PROGRAMS ON AMERICAN ISSUES FORUM. RADIO/TV. (ST-WIDE). LENA W RIEDEL, COORD; COLORADO COUNCIL OF CHURCHES; 1313 CLARKSON ST; DENVER, CO 80218. (#200007-59).

AUG 1, '75. ANNUAL COLO CENTENNIAL-BICENTENNIAL COMMISSION DINNER MEETING. TO PROVIDE COMMUNICATIONS BETWEEN ALL WORKERS OF CBC. MORE THAN 650 VOLUNTEERS AND COMMITTEE MEMBERS WOULD BE INVITED TO A DINNER AT WHICH GOVERNOR WILL BE GUEST SPEAKER. (ST-WIDE). G D BARRANTE; COLORADO CENTENNIAL-BICENTENNIAL COMMISSION; 901 SHERMAN ST, 15TH FLOOR; DENVER, CO 80203. (#2704-501).

AUG 15, '75. WOMEN IN COLORADO HISTORY IN A ONE DAY WORKSHOP. WOMEN IN COLORADO HISTORY WORKSHOP. ONE DAY WORKSHOP TO PROVIDE AN OPPORTUNITY FOR WOMEN IN DENVER AREA TO INVOLVED WITH HISTORIC AND CONTEMPORARY ROLE IN WHICH COLORADO WOMEN HAVE BEEN AND CONTINUE TO BE ACTIVE. (LOCAL). RONALD S BROCKWAY; DEPT OF HISTORY AND GOVERNMENT, REGIS COLLEGE; W 50TH & LOWELL BLVD; DENVER, CO 80207. (#2759-501).

SEPT 1, '75 - JUNE 30, '76. 'DENVER NOW' - YOUTH TALK SHOW. THE PROGRAM, AIRED ON THE FIRST & THIRD MONDAYS OF EACH MONTH, DISCUSSES TOPICS RELEVANT TO YOUTH, WITH THREE ROTATING HIGH SCHOOL MODERATORS. PART OF 'DENVER NOW' WEEKDAY SERIES. AT KWGN-TV STUDIOS, 550 LINCOLN ST. (LOCAL). DAVID ROSENBERG, PRODUCER; YOU AND I PRODUCTIONS; 330 LAFAYETTE ST; DENVER, CO 80218. (#200007-58).

SEPT 14 - OCT 15, '75. 'USA '76: THE FIRST 200 YEARS' - EXHIBIT. THIS TRAVELING EXHIBIT PREPARED BY THE ARBA WILL TOUR 10 CITIES DURING THE BICENTENNIAL. IT EXPLORES THE CULTURAL AND SCIENTIFIC HERITAGE OF THE USA. AT DENVER NATIONAL GUARD ARMORY. (REGN'L). JACK MASEY; AMERICAN REVOLUTION BICENTENNIAL ADMINISTRATION; 2401 E STREET, NW; WASHINGTON, DC 20276. (#5661-504).

SEPT 27 - 29, '75. BIG ORANGE WEEKEND. THE FIRST MAJOR LEAGUE HOCKEY GAME IN DENVER'S NEW MCNICHOLS SPORTS ARENA. AT MCNICHOLS SPORTS ORGANIZATION. (ST-WIDE). JOHN HENRY, CHAIRMAN; DENVER SPURS ORGANIZATION; 3601 S MONACO PKWY; DENVER, CO 80237. (#102579-1).

OCT 1 - DEC 31, '75. EXHIBIT OF TRADITIONAL ARTS AND CRAFTS. HISTORY, CUSTOMS AND ACHIEVEMENTS OF INDIAN PEOPLE IN COLORADO WILL BE PRESENTED TO PUBLIC THROUGH ARTS AND CRAFTS AND EDUCATIONAL PRESENTATIONS. (LOCAL). JOE LOCUST; DENVER NATIVE AMERICANS UNITED; 2210 E 16TH AVE; DENVER, CO 80206. (#11047-501).

OCT 2, '75. MSC FALL ANNIVERSARY CONVOCATION. BICENTENNIAL PROJECT RECOGNITION OPENS COLLEGE'S 10TH ANNIVERSARY YEAR CELEBRATION; SPEAKER ON COLORADO-MSC HISTORY, FACULTY AWARDS AND PRESENTATION OF NEW COLLEGE ANNIVERSARY SONG. AT CENTRE THEATER, 216 16TH ST. (LOCAL). PAM W CARTER, ASST DIR; METROPOLITAN STATE COLLEGE; 250 W 14TH AVE, BOX 14; DENVER, CO 80204. (#200007-60).

OCT 24, '75. ONE HUNDRED YEARS OF COLORADO NUMISMATICS. EXHIBIT DEPICTING HISTORY OF THE EVENTS IN COINAGE & CURRENCY FROM GOLD TO CONSTRUCTION OF PROPOSED NEW DENVER MINT. (LOCAL). LES BLOOM, CHAIRMAN; ROCKY MOUNTAIN STATES COIN SHOW; 2608 RIVER DR; DENVER, CO 80211. (#102578-1).

NOV 7 - 9, '75. UNITED STATES ARMED FORCES BICENTENNIAL CARAVAN. THE CARAVAN IS COMPOSED OF EXHIBIT VANS FOR EACH BRANCH OF THE MILITARY SERVICE. THE THEME OF THE EXHIBITION IS 'HISTORY OF THE ARMED FORCES AND THEIR CONTRIBUTION TO THE NATION'. (LOCAL). ROBERT J OSMUNDSON, CHMN; U S ARMED FORCES BICENTENNIAL EXHIBIT VANS PROJECT; SUITE 6 1313, TREMONT PL; DENVER, CO 80204. (#1775-245).

NOV 8, '75. CHOIR CONCERT FEATURING WORKS OF COLORADO AND AMERICAN COMPOSERS. ONE OF FOUR MAJOR CONCERTS FEATURING LOCAL PROFESSIONAL AND NONPROFESSIONAL PERFORMERS DEDICATED TO THE THEME 'HARMONY OF PEOPLE EXPRESSED THROUGH BEAUTY AND HARMONY OF MUSIC.'. AT FOOTE MUSIC HALL, COLORADO WOMEN'S COLLEGE, MONTVIEW BLVD AND QUEBEC. (LOCAL). CAROL HARRINGTON, CHMN; DENVER CONCERT CHORALE; 900 S QUINCE, #B-811; DENVER, CO 80321. (#200007-194).

NOV 12, '75. THE HISTORY OF BLACK MILITARY ACTIVITY IN COLORADO. 6 LECTURES IN A SERIES COVERING A BROAD SPECTRUM OF COLORADO'S HISTORY. AT RM 207 GLENARM BLDG, 1222 GLENARM PLACE. (ST-WIDE). MARY KARDOES, CHAIRMAN; METROPOLITAN STATE COLLEGE HISTORY CLUB; 250 W 14TH AVE; DENVER, CO 80204. (#102577-1).

NOV 14, '75 - JAN 4, '76. ENVIRONMENT 76 EXHIBIT OF COLORADO AT DENVER ART MUSEUM. JURIED EXHIBITION OF PROPOSED & DEVELOPED PROJECTS FOR IMPROVING ALL ASPECTS OF DENVER SURROUNDINGS THRU CREATION OF A SERIES OF FILMS, BOOKS, PLAYGROUNDS, GARDENS, PHOTOS, ESSAYS, DANCE, ETC. AT DENVER ART MUSEUM. (REGN'L). MARY ANN KOENIG; AMERICAN INSTITUTE OF ARCHITECTS; 1426 LARIMER SQUARE; DENVER, CO 80202. (#52-1).

NOV 15 - 16, '75. SCOUT FESTIVAL '75 - 100 YEARS OF CO HISTORY PORTRAYED BY YOUTH. THE OFFICIAL YOUTH ACTIVITY FOR THE STATE WILL PORTRAY 100 YEARS OF COLORADO PROGRESS; THE THEME IS GATEWAY TO THE CENTENNIAL - MIRACLE ON CHERRY CREEK. AT THE DENVER MERCHANDISE MART, 451 E 58TH AVE. (ST-WIDE). DAN FERGUSON, PROJ DIR; CUB SCOUTS AND EXPLORERS OF COLORADO; 2901 W 19TH AVE; DENVER, CO 80204. (#4349-3).

JAN 1 - DEC 30, '76. COMMUNITY RELIGIOUS FESTIVALS HELD BY LOCAL CHURCHES IN COLORADO. FESTIVAL, RADIO/TV. (ST-WIDE). LENA W RIEDEL; COLORADO COUNCIL OF CHURCHES; 1313 CLARKSON ST; DENVER, CO 80218. (#6830-501).

JAN 1 - DEC 31, '76. PERFORMANCES OF DENVER PUBLIC SCHOOLS DRUM & BUGLE CORPS. LIVE PERFORMANCE. (ST-WIDE). LUCY OTTO, CHAIRPERSON; DENVER PUBLIC SCHOOLS; 900 GRANT; DENVER, CO 80203. (#102941-2).

JAN 1, '76 - CONTINUING . DENVER CIVIC HERITAGE DISPLAY. HISTORIC, ETNNIC, CULTURAL EXHIBITS FOR DENVER C-B-C AREA. AT CITY & COUNTY BLDG, STAPLETON INTL AIRPORT. (LOCAL). ROBERT J OSMUNDSON; MAYOR'S COMMITTEE OF 19 FOR '76; CITY & COUNTY BLDG; DENVER, CO 80202. (#2025-1).

JAN 2 - FEB 28, '76. NATIONAL CHAMPIONSHIP SKATING TO BE HELD AT NEW SPORTS ARENA. NATIONAL FIGURE-SKATING CHAMPIONSHIPS, DENVER 1976. DENVER IS HOSTING NATIONAL FIGURE-SKATING CHAMPIONSHIPS IN NEW SPORT ARENA WHICH IS RESULT OF BICENTENIAL BOND. (NAT'L). MILE-HI FIGURE SKATING; MAYOR'S COMMITTEE OF 19 FOR '76; CITY AND COUNTY BUILDING; DENVER, CO 80202. (#1970-901).

JAN 2 - MAR 1, '76. HERITAGE OF AMERICAN ART: 100 PAINTINGS FROM THE MET. 100 AMER PAINTINGS FROM THE METROPOLITAN MUSEUM OF ART; 1730 - 1930. FREE TOURS OF EXHIBIT & RELATED LECTURES. OPEN DURING REGULAR MUSEUM HOURS. SUNDAY HOURS 1-5PM; WEDNESDAY EVENINGS UNTIL 9 PM. AT 100 W 14TH AVE PKY. (ST-WIDE). LINDA ANDERSON; DENVER ART MUSEUM; 100 W 14TH AVE PKY; DENVER, CO 80204. (#16813-2).

JAN 2 - DEC 31, '76. HISTORY OF POLISH COMMUNITY IN COLO 1858 TO 1975 AUDIOVISUAL DISPLAY. FLEXIBLE AUDIO VISUAL EXHIBIT USING AUDIO FEATURE FOR FIRST TIME IN DENVER PRODUCED BY MOUNTAIN BELL PHONE CO. CANNOT SPECIFY ITEMS 4 5 SINCE EXHIBIT WILL TRAVEL IN DENVER AREA DISPLAYED IN PROMINENT PLACES SUCH AS PHONE CO. LOBBY LIBRARIES MUSEUM SCHOOLS BANKS ETC. AT UNDECIDED. (LOCAL). WANDA CUBA; POLISH NATIONAL ALLIANCE ST MARTINS GROUP 134 DENVER; 2643 UTICA ST; DENVER, CO 80212. (#4354-1).

JAN 3 - DEC 30, '76. COMMUNITY DISCUSSIONS ON THE AMERICAN ISSUES FORUM. CONFERENCE. (ST-WIDE). LENA W RIEDEL, COORD; COLORADO COUNCIL OF CHURCHES; 1313 CLARKSON ST; DENVER, CO 80218. (#108686-1).

JAN 7 - FEB 25, '76. HORIZONS FOR YOUTH CONCERTS. FUNDED BY THE COLORADO CENTENNIAL-BICENTENNIAL COMMISSION. 5 PERFORMANCES. FEBRUARY 25-1:00 PM. AT 3 HIGH SCHOOLS. (ST-WIDE). MONA HOBSON; DENVER SYMPHONY ORCHESTRA; 1615 CALIFORNIA ST; DENVER, CO 80202. (#179-1).

JAN 7 - APR 21, '76. 'FEED FORWARD', AN ENVIRONMENTAL TV SERIES. 15 WEEK ENVIRONMENTAL TV SERIES TO ENGENDER NEW CONCERN AND SENSITIVITY ON PART OF AVERAGE CITIZEN FOR THE REGIONS LIFE SYSTEM AND TO SEE THAT CONCERN DIRECTLY AFFECT THE QUALITY OF LIFE. (ST-WIDE). CHRIS CURTIS, DIRECTOR; KRMA - TV; 1261 GLENARM PL; DENVER, CO 80204. (#103495-1).

JAN 10, '76. DRAMATIC VIGNETTES OF U S WOMEN. LIVE PERFORMANCE AT ROSS CHERRY CREEK LIBRARY, 205 MILWAUKEE. (LOCAL). PAT KENNING, PROJ DIR; DELTA KAPPA GAMMA; 1153 W SHEPPERD AVE; LITTLETON, CO 80120. (#200007-61).

JAN 12 - OCT 30, '76. 'A NEW DAY BEGUN', FINE ARTS PRESENTATION. 12 PRESENTATIONS DEPICTING HISTORIC AND CONTEMPORARY MODES OF BLACK PEOPLE FEATURES: 'LIFT EVERY VOICE' AND 'THE CREATION' BY J W JOHNSON. AT REGENCY INN, 3900 ELATI. (LOCAL). MS EARLIE BELL, PROJ DIR; ZETA ZETA ZETA CHAPTER OF ZETA PHI BETA SORORITY; 2300 S HOLLY PLACE; DENVER, CO 80222. (#108687-1).

JAN 15, '76. DEDICATION OF MARTIN LUTHER KING JR MEMORIAL. PROPOSAL TO ERECT MEMORIAL STATUE TO MARTIN LUTHER KING JR. - TO BE ERRECTED PERMANENTLY IN DENVER CITY PARK. AT CITY PARK. (LOCAL). BILL ROBERTS, COUNCILMAN; MARTIN LUTHER KING FOUNDATION; RM 451 CITY & COUNTY BLDG; DENVER, CO 80202. (#2762-1).

JAN 16 - 24, '76. NATIONAL WESTERN STOCK SHOW FESTIVAL. 20-MINUTE BICENTENNIAL PAGEANT AT NATIONAL WESTERN STOCK SHOW HELD IN DENVER. AT NATIONAL WESTERN STOCK SHOW GROUNDS. (REGN'L). WILLARD SIMMS; NATIONAL WESTERN STOCK SHOW; CITY AND COUNTY BUILDING; DENVER, CO 80202. (#1913-1).

JAN 17 - FEB 1, '76. 'DANDIE DOODLES' - BONFILS THEATRE FOR CHILDREN. A STAR-SPANGLED SALUTE TO '76 WRITTEN BY BEV NEWCOMB; PERFORMANCES AT 1:00 AND 3:30 PM ON JAN 17, 24, 25, 31 AND FEB 1. AT BONFILS THEATRE, COLFAX & ELIZABETH. (LOCAL). DIRECTOR; BONFILS THEATRE; COLFAX & ELIZABETH; DENVER, CO 80206. (#103368-2).

JAN 22, '76. THE CULTURAL TRADITION OF THE AMERICAN JEW. THIS LECTURE IS PART OF A SIX-LECTURE SERIES ON 'THE AMERICAN JEWISH EXPERIENCE.'. AT BOETCHER CENTER AUDITORIUM. (LOCAL). DR STANLEY M WAGNER; UNIVERSITY OF DENVER; 7001 E WALSH PL; DENVER, CO 80224. (#103310-2).

JAN 22, '76. DRAMATIC VIGNETTES OF U S WOMEN. LIVE PERFORMANCE AT BEUCHTEL HOUSE, EVANS & COLUMBINE. (LOCAL). PAT KENNING, PROJ DIR; DENVER UNIV LIBRARY ASSOC; 1153 W SHEPPERD AVE; LITTLETON, CO 80120. (#200007-62).

JAN 23, '76. 'EARLY DENVER AS SEEN THROUGH ITS ARCHITECTURE'. WILLIAM FLICK, FREQUENT LECTURER FOR COLORADO STATE HISTORICAL SOCIETY, PRESENTS A HISTORIC PANORAMA, INCLUDING SLIDES AND MUSIC, OF DENVER'S EARLIEST BEGINNINGS TO THE RECENT RENEWAL OF THE DOWNTOWN AREA. AT RM 207 GLENARM BLDG, 1222 GLENARM PL. (ST-WIDE). MARY KARDOES, DIRECTOR; METRO STATE COLLEGE; 250 W 14TH AVE; DENVER, CO 80204. (#102577-2).

JAN 23 - 24, '76. SIMMENTAL NATIONAL CONVENTION. THIS MEETING, SCHEDULED DURING THE CENTENNIAL STOCK SHOW; BRINGS TOGETHER SIMMENTAL CATTLE BREEDERS FROM ACROSS THE US FOR THEIR ANNUAL CONFERENCE AND STOCK EXHIBIT AND SALE. AT HILTON HOTEL. (NAT'L). MILES DAVIES, CHMN; NATIONAL SIMMENTAL ASSOC; BOX 561; DEER TRAIL, CO 80105. (#102812-1).

JAN 26 - MAR 14, '76. EDWARD WESTON PHOTOGRAPHY RETROSPECTIVE. THE MUSEUM OF MODERN ART IN NEW YORK HAS COMPILED 280 PHOTOGRAPHS BY THIS 20TH CENTURY PHOTOGRAPHER WHOSE WORK RANKS WITH THAT OF STEICHEN AND STEIGLITZ; INCLUDED IN THE DISPLAY ARE SOME OF WESTON'S CLASSICS OF THE AMERICAN WEST. AT DENVER ART MUSEUM, 100 W 14TH AVE. (ST-WIDE). CATHY MCCLAIN, DIRECTOR; DENVER ART MUSEUM; 100 W 14TH AVE; DENVER, CO 80204. (#103325-1).

JAN 27, '76. AMER BASKETBALL ASSOC ALL-STAR GAME IN DENVER IN '76. SPORTS FACILITY TO HOST SUCH EVENTS AS HOCKEY, BASKETBALL, ICE SHOWS, TENNIS, & OTHER PUBLIC GATHERINGS. THIS FACILITY WILL SEAT A MAXIMUM OF 18,000 PEOPLE. NO DETAILS UNTIL PLAYOFFS. AT MCNICHOLS ARENA - SEATS 18,000.. (NAT'L). CARL SCHEER, PRESIDENT; DENVER NUGGETS BASKETBALL CLUB; 1635 CLAY ST; DENVER, CO 80204. (#1968-2).

FEB 1, '76. BICENTENNIAL PARADE OF COLORADO MUSIC. KICK-OFF OF THE CELEBRATION OF THE PARADE OF COLORADO ORIGINAL MUSIC; PRESENTATION OF BRONZE PLAQUE IN HONOR OF PAUL WHITEMAN TO MRS PAUL WHITEMAN. AT WYER AUDITORIUM, DENVER PUBLIC LIBRARY, 14TH & BROADWAY. (LOCAL). RICCARDA F MCQUIE, COORD; COLORADO FEDERATION OF MUSIC CLUBS; 640 GARFIELD ST; DENVER, CO 80206. (#200007-63).

FEB 1 - 8, '76. COLORADO JR MISS PROGRAM & LOCAL COMMUNITY PRELIMINARIES. COMPETITION. (ST-WIDE). MARGARET P MICHLER, DIR; COLORADO JUNIOR MISS SCHOLARSHIP, INC; 3790 S EATON; DENVER, CO 80235. (#103105-1).

FEB 8, '76. BICENTENNIAL PARADE OF COLORADO MUSIC. CONCERT OF ORIGINAL MUSIC BY COLORADO COMPOSERS AS PART OF A SERIES IN CONJUNCTION WITH THE PARADE OF AMERICAN MUSIC. AT LUKENS WING, ST BARNABAS CHURCH, 13TH & VINE. (LOCAL). RICCARDA F MCQUIE, COORD; MUSICIAN'S SOCIETY OF DENVER, INC; 640 GARFIELD ST; DENVER, CO 80206. (#200007-64).

FEB 12, '76. 'GENERATIONS U S' - DRAMATIC VIGNETTES OF U S WOMEN. LIVE PERFORMANCE AT 9TH & CORONA. (LOCAL). PAT KENNING, PROJ DIR; DOORMORE SCHOOL PARENT ED MOTHERS; 1153 W SHEPPERD AVE; LITTLETON, CO 80120. (#104852-1).

DENVER — CONTINUED

FEB 13 - 28, '76. FIRST FIFTY YEARS OF THE CENTURY. FROM THE PHILLIPS COLLECTION, TRACES PAINTING FROM 1900 TO WWII. AT DISCOVERY GALLERY. (LOCAL). LINDA ANDERSON, DIRECTOR; DENVER ART MUSEUM; 100 W 14TH AVE PARKWAY; DENVER, CO 80204. (#103416-140).

FEB 14, '76. WOMEN IN THE 21ST CENTURY SYMPOSIUM. DENVER COMMUNITY ORGANIZATIONS EXPLORE ROLE OF WOMEN IN FUTURE OF AMERICAN FAMILY, EDUCATION, CHURCH AND THE AMERICAN PURSUIT OF HAPPINESS. AT COLORADO WOMEN'S COLLEGE. (LOCAL). IRMGARD VRAGEL, CHAIRMAN; AMERICAN ASSOC OF UNIVERSITY WOMEN -DENVER BRANCH; 3555 E EVANS; DENVER, CO 80210. (#102573-1).

FEB 15, '76. IN-HOUSE ENTERTAINMENT FOR DENVER VA HOSPITAL. LIVE PERFORMANCE AT DENVER VA HOSPITAL. (LOCAL). MARILYN HELLER, COORD; HOSPITAL AUDIENCES, INC; 1510 S GRANT; DENVER, CO 80210. (#200007-65).

FEB 15 - MAR 14, '76. 37 AMERICAN PAINTINGS FROM THE PHILLIPS COLLECTION: 1930-1950. THE 2ND PART OF THIS 3-PART SERIES DEALS WITH AMER ART FROM 1930 TO 1950. EXHIBIT OPEN DURING REGULAR MUSEUM HOURS. AT 100 W 14TH AVE PKY. (LOCAL). CATHY MCCLAIN, PROJ DIR; DENVER ART MUSEUM; 100 W 14TH AVE PKY; DENVER, CO 80204. (#16813-1).

FEB 19 - JULY 4, '76. FOR THE RED WHITE AND BLUE '76. FOR FURTHER PROGRAMMING FOR OLDER PEOPLE, A 60 MINUTE PATRIOTIC MUSICAL, FORUM DISCUSSION FOLLOWS PLAY. (ST-WIDE). TOM PROCTOR, DIRECTOR; DENVER PARKS AND RECREATION, PLATT PARK CENTER; 1510 S GRANT; DENVER, CO 80210. (#104872-2).

FEB 20, '76. COLORADO AUTHOR RECEPTION. RECEPTION AND RECOGNITION CEREMONY TO HONOR OUTSTANDING COLORADO AUTHOR IN BICENTENNIAL YEAR. AT PORTER LIBRARY 7055 E 18TH AVE. (ST-WIDE). LOUISE OTT, COORDINATOR; LIBRARY ASSOC, COLORADO WOMEN'S COLLEGE; COLORADO WOMEN'S COLLEGE; DENVER, CO 80220. (#104993-3).

FEB 20 - 22, '76. 'NO MOTHER TO GUIDE HER'. A MELODRAMA COMPLETE WITH OLIO WHOSE THEME IS 200 YEARS OF AMERICA, SONGS, CORN JOKES, QUICK SKITS; A GRAND BIRTHDAY CELEBRATION. AT SAINT ANDREW SEMINARY, 1050 S BIRCH. (LOCAL). REV B MARK N MATSON CR; SAINT ANDREW SEMINARY; 1050 S BIRCH; DENVER, CO 80222. (#103230-1).

FEB 25, '76. 'THE FIRST EUROPEAN SETTLEMENT IN COLORADO'. DANIEL VALDES, PROFESSOR OF SOCIOLOGY AT METRO STATE, WILL CONDUCT A DISCUSSION OF THE HISPANIC SETTLEMENT'S IMPORTANCE IN COLORADO'S DEVELOPMENT; DR VALDES IS ALSO PUBLISHER/EDITOR OF DENVER-BASED LA LUZ MAGAZINE FOR HISPANOS. AT RM 207 GLENARM BLDG, 1222 GLENARM PL. (ST-WIDE). MARY KARDOES, DIRECTOR; METRO STATE COLLEGE; 250 W 14TH AVE; DENVER, CO 80204. (#102577-3).

FEB 26, '76. THE LITERARY TRADITION OF THE AMERICAN JEW. THIS LECTURE IS PART OF A SIX-LECTURE SERIES ON 'THE AMERICAN JEWISH EXPERIENCE.'. AT BOETCHER CENTER AUDITORIUM. (LOCAL). DR STANLEY M WAGNER; UNIVERSITY OF DENVER; 7001 E WALSH PL; DENVER, CO 80224. (#103310-3).

MAR 1, '76. SCREENING OF FILM ON PUBLIC TV FOR STATE AND NATIONAL IMPACT. 'ISABELLA BIRD', A FILM DOCUMENTARY IN DENVER. DRAMATIZED DOCUMENTARY FILM ON TRAVELS OF ISABELLA BIRD IN COLORADO IN 1873 FOR TV & EDUCATIONAL PURPOSES. (ST-WIDE). CAROL PEARSON, DIRECTOR; WOMEN STUDIES PROGRAM; UNIV OF COLORADO, HILLSIDE BLDG; BOULDER, CO 80302. (#6821-501).

MAR 1 - 31, '76. NCAA HOCKEY CHAMPIONSHIP MATCHES. LIVE PERFORMANCE, RADIO/TV AT CONFINES OF DOWNTOWN AREA. (NAT'L). JOHN HENRY, EXEC OFFICER; DEPT OF PUBLIC WORKS; CITY & COUNTY OF DENVER; COLFAX AVE & BANNOCK STREET; DENVER, CO 80202. (#1968-1).

MAR 1 - JULY 15, '76. 'NOTHING IS LONG AGO - A HISTORY OF COLORADO'. PART 1 OF THIS 2-PART EXHIBIT DEALS WITH THE HISTORY OF COLORADO BEFORE STATEHOOD,1776-1876,OVER 120 MAJOR ITEMS IN TOTAL DISPLAY MOST FROM LIBRARY'S WESTERN HISTORY DEPT, EXHIBIT CATALOG INCLUDES INTRODUCTION WRITTEN BY JAMES MICHENER. AT DENVER PUBLIC LIBRARY, 1357 BROADWAY, DENVER, CO.. (LOCAL). DENVER PUBLIC LIBRARY; 1357 BROADWAY; DENVER, CO 80203. (#1957-1).

MAR 3 - SEPT 8, '76. RAMBLE THROUGH THE ROCKIES - LECTURE & TOUR SERIES. SERIES OF LECTURES, DAY TRIPS & CAMPING TRIPS FOR SENIOR CITIZENS TO GAIN AWARENESS OF COLORADO'S HERITAGE & SCENIC BEAUTY. AT PARK AVE CENTER, 1849 EMERSON ST. (LOCAL). HEIDI EVANS, REC LEADER; DENVER PARKS & RECREATION; 1849 EMERSON ST; DENVER, CO 80218. (#106978-1).

MAR 17, '76. ST PATRICK'S DAY C-B-C COMMEMORATION PARADE. PARADE WITH DENVER C-B-C THEME AREAS INCORPORATED. AT DOWNTOWN DENVER. (LOCAL). ROBERT J OSMUNDSON, CHMN; MAYOR'S COMMITTEE OF 19 FOR '76; CITY AND COUNTY BLDG; DENVER, CO 80202. (#1918-1).

MAR 18, '76. THE SOCIAL TRADITION OF THE AMERICAN JEW. THIS LECTURE IS PART OF A SIX-LECTURE SERIES ON 'THE AMERICAN JEWISH EXPERIENCE.'. AT BOETCHER CENTER AUDITORIUM. (LOCAL). DR STANLEY M WAGNER; UNIVERSITY OF DENVER; 7001 E WALSH PL; DENVER, CO 80224. (#103310-4).

MAR 20, '76. ENGLISH HANDBELL RINGERS' FESTIVAL IN DENVER, CO. ENGLISH HANDBELL RINGERS FROM VARIOUS PARTS OF COLORADO WILL RING MUSIC OF HISTORICAL NATURE AT THE FESTIVAL TO BE HELD IN 1976. THE AMERICAN GUILD OF ENGLISH HANDBELL RINGERS TO SPONSOR THE FESTIVAL. AT GREEN MOUNTAIN HIGH SCHOOL GYM; 13175 GREEN MT DRIVE, LAKEWOOD. (ST-WIDE). JAMES HANSON; AMERICAN GUILD OF ENGLISH HANDBELL RINGERS; 2449 S COLORADO BLVD, APT 17; DENVER, CO 80222. (#6826-1).

MAR 20 - 21, '76. COLORADO CENTENNIAL ARCHERY TOURNAMENT (INDOOR). COMPETITION AT HAL'S ARCHERY LANES, 2200 W ALAMEDA. (ST-WIDE). YVETTE GILL, SEC-TREAS; COLUMBINE BOWMEN, INC; 9130 CLAYTON ST; THORNTON, CO 80229. (#200007-66).

MAR 21, '76. BICENTENNIAL PARADE OF COLORADO MUSIC. CONCERT OF ORIGINAL MUSIC BY COLORADO COMPOSERS AS PART OF A SERIES IN CONJUNCTION WITH THE BICENTENNIAL PARADE OF AMERICAN MUSIC. AT BELLE STANTON THEATER, FEDERAL BLVD. (LOCAL). RICCARDA F MCQUIE, COORD; COLORADO FEDERATION OF MUSIC CLUBS & LORETT HEIGHTS COLLEGE; 640 GARFIELD ST; DENVER, CO 80206. (#200007-67).

MAR 22 - MAY 2, '76. AMERICAN ART SINCE 1945: POSTWAR AMERICAN ART. POSTWAR AMERICAN ART IS SUBJECT OF FINAL SEGMENT OF THIS 3-PART SERIES. PAINTINGS & SCULPTURES INCLUDE WORKS BY ALBERS, GORKY, JOHNS, KELLY, DE KOONING, OLDENBURG, POLLOCK, RAUSCHENBERG, STELLO, & WARHOL. ACCOMPANIED BY EDUCATIONAL MATERIALS & CATALOGUE. AT 100 W 14TH AVE PKY. (LOCAL). CATHY MCCLAIN, PROJ DIR; DENVER ART MUSEUM; 100 W 14TH AVE PKY; DENVER, CO 80204. (#16813-3).

MAR 22 - SEPT 30, '76. ALL SWEDES WEEK BANQUET. BANQUET HONORING CONTRIBUTIONS OF SWEDISH IMMIGRANTS TO U S & COLORADO. (LOCAL). ARTHUR N JACKSON, COORD; 'ALL SWEDES WEEK' COMMITTEE; 3701 E FLORIDA AVE; DENVER, CO 80222. (#106977-1).

MAR 31, '76. 'GHOSTS AT TIMBERLINE'. MURIEL SIBELL WOLLE WILL PRESENT A SHORT SURVEY OF THE DISCOVERY AND MINING OF PRECIOUS METALS IN THE MONTAINS OF COLORADO BETWEEN 1859 AND 1900 AND OF THE CAMPUS AND TOWNS WHICH GREW UP CLOSE TO THE DIGGINGS. AT RM 207 GLENARM BLDG, 1222 GLENARM PL. (ST-WIDE). MARY KARDOES, DIRECTOR; METRO STATE UNIV; 250 W 1JTH AVE; DENVER, CO 80204. (#102577-4).

MAR '76. AMERICAN PAINTING SYMPOSIUM: LITERATURE, HISTORY, PAINTING. SEMINAR AT 100 W 14TH AVE PKY. (ST-WIDE). CATHY MCCLAIN, PROJ DIR; DENVER ART MUSEUM; 100 W 14TH AVE PKY; DENVER, CO 80204. (#16813-4).

APR 1, '76. BASKETBALL GAME TO BE PLAYED IN NEW DENVER SPORTS ARENA. AMER BASKETBALL ASSOC ALL-STAR GAME IN '76, DENVER. AMERICAN BASKETBALL ASSOCIATION ALL-STAR GAME WILL BE HELD IN NEW DENVER SPORTS ARENA CREATED BY BICENTENNIAL BOND. (NAT'L). FRANK GOLDBERG; MAYOR'S COMMITTEE OF 19 FOR '76; CITY & COUNTY BLDG; DENVER, CO 80202. (#1985-901).

APR 1, '76. THE RELIGIOUS TRADITION OF THE AMERICAN JEW. THIS LECTURE IS PART OF A SIX-LECTURE SERIES ON 'THE AMERICAN JEWISH EXPERIENCE.'. AT BOETCHER CENTER AUDITORIUM. (LOCAL). DR STANLEY M WAGNER; UNIVERSITY OF DENVER; 7001 E WALSH PL; DENVER, CO 80224. (#103310-5).

APR 1 - MAY 30, '76. HISTORICAL AMERICAN MUSIC CONCERT SERIES. LIVE PERFORMANCE AT CHEROKEE BLDG, RM 136. (LOCAL). DR JERRALD D MCCOLLUM; METROPOLITAN STATE COLLEGE MUSIC DEPT; METROPOLITAN STATE COLLEGE, B/58; DENVER, CO 80204. (#100583-1).

APR 3 - 4, '76. 8TH ANNUAL SHOW & EXHIBIT OF COLORADO STATE BUTTON SOCIETY. DISPLAYS IN THE CLASSIFICATION OF COMPETITIVE TRAYS OF ANTIQUE AND MODERN BUTTONS IN VARIOUS CATEGORIES. ALL TRAYS ARE MOUNTED AND JUDGED ACCORDING TO THE NATIONAL SOCIETY RULES AS TO SIZE, SHAPE, MATERIAL & TECHNIQUE. MILITARY BUTTONS ARE A SPECIALITY. AT RADIANT CHAPTER BUILDING ASSOC, 225 ACOMA ST. (ST-WIDE). BETHEL M HOUSTON, COORD; COLORADO STATE BUTTON SOCIETY; 1460 ELIZABETH ST; DENVER, CO 80206. (#200007-68).

APR 4, '76. SOLILOQUY TO A MARTYRED HERO. THIS IS A MUSICAL TRIBUTE TO DR MARTIN LUTHER KING, JR. (NAT'L). ALPHONSE ROBINSON; DR MARTIN LUTHER KING PROJ; MAYOR'S COMM OF 19 FOR '76; 2744 GAYLORD; DENVER, CO 80205. (#108426-1).

APR 6, '76. CLASSROOM '76. SEMINAR-LECTURE-DISCUSSION BY COLORADO WOMEN'S COLLEGE FACULTY AND GUEST SPEAKERS ON THE AMERICAN FAMILY FOR THE PAST 200 YEARS. AT HOUSTON FINE ARTS CENTER MONTVIEW AND QUEBEC. (LOCAL). LOUISE OTT, COORDINATOR; LIBRARY ASSOC, COLORADO WOMEN'S COLLEGE; COLORADO WOMEN'S COLLEGE; DENVER, CO 80220. (#104993-1).

APR 8 - JUNE 8, '76. WOMENS INTERNATIONAL BOWLING CONGRESS BICENT CHAMPIONSHIP TOURNAMENT. FESTIVAL AT CELEBRITY SPORTS CENTER/888 S COLORADO BLVD. (INT'L). A W KARCHER, DIRECTOR; WOMENS INTERNATIONAL BOWLING CONGRESS; 5301 S 76TH ST; GREENDALE, WI 53129. (#105633-1).

APR 10, '76. AAU JUNIOR NATIONAL SYNCHRONIZED SWIMMING TEAM CHAMPIONSHIPS. THIS WAS THE FIRST NATIONAL SYNCHRONIZED SWIMMING COMPETITION EVER HELD IN THE ROCKY MOUNTAIN REGION. AT UNIVERSITY OF DENVER POOL. (NAT'L). CAROL TACKETT, MANAGER; SOUTH SUBURBAN TARPONS SYNCHRONIZED TEAM & AAU; 3124 E WEAVER PL; LITTLETON, CO 80121. (#200007-69).

APR 15, '76. IN-HOUSE ENTERTAINMENT FOR DENVER VA HOSPITAL. LIVE PERFORMANCE AT DENVER VA HOSPITAL. (LOCAL). MARILYN HELLER, COORD; HOSPITAL AUDIENCES, INC; 1510 S GRANT; DENVER, CO 80210. (#200007-70).

APR 24, '76. STATEWIDE '76 LITTER REVOLUTION. VOLUNTEER STATEWIDE LITTER CLEANUP WITH INCENTIVES FOR ACTION BEING VOUCHERS FOR MERCHANDISE HIDDEN IN BADLY LITTERED AREAS. (ST-WIDE). BEVERLY FLEMING, EXEC DIR; KEEP COLORADO BEAUTIFUL, INC; 4260 E EVANS; DENVER, CO 80222. (#108254-1).

APR 28, '76. MUSIC IN AMERICA. LIVE PERFORMANCE AT GENERAL CLASSROOM BLDG AUDITORIUM, 2040 S RACE. (LOCAL). ROGER DEXTER FEE, DIR; UNIV OF DENVER, LAMONT SCHOOL OF MUSIC; LAMONT SCHOOL OF MUSIC, D U; DENVER, CO 80210. (#103072-2).

APR 28, '76. 'A SKETCHBOOK OF COLORADO INDIANS'. MICHAEL TAYLOR, CU DENVER CENTER, AND PATTY HARJO, MUSEUM OF NATURAL HISTORY, COMBINE THEIR SCHOLARLY AND CULTURAL BACKGROUNDS TO PRESENT AN INSIGHTFUL OVERVIEW OF COLORADO'S INDIAN HERITAGE YESTERDAY AND TODAY. AT RM 207 GLENARM BLDG, 1222 GLENARM PL. (LOCAL). MARY KARDOES, DIRECTOR; METRO STATE COLLEGE; 250 W 14TH AVE; DENVER, CO 80204. (#102577-5).

APR 29, '76. THE POLITICAL TRADITION OF THE AMERICAN JEW. THIS LECTURE IS PART OF A SIX-LECTURE SERIES ON 'THE AMERICAN JEWISH EXPERIENCE.'. AT BOETCHER CENTER AUDITORIUM. (LOCAL). DR STANLEY M WAGNER; UNIVERSITY OF DENVER; 7001 E WALSH PL; DENVER, CO 80224. (#103310-6).

APR 29 - MAY 2, '76. MOUNTAIN-PLAINS ARTS AND CRAFTS FESTIVAL. ARTS AND CRAFTS DISPLAY AND EXHIBITS; BOOK SALE, MUSIC, GAMES AND THEATER; ETHNIC DANCERS; 40-50 CRAFTSMEN IN BOOTHS; GENERAL ATMOSPHERE OF 1876 FRONTIER VILLAGE RE-CREATED. AT COLORADO WOMEN'S COLLEGE CAMPUS-MONTVIEW AND QUEBEC. (LOCAL). LOUISE OTT, COORDINATOR; LIBRARY ASSOC, COLORADO WOMEN'S COLLEGE; DENVER, CO 80220. (#104993-2).

APR '76 - CONTINUING . A BICENTENNIAL SHOW OF CONTEMPORARY WEAVING. WEAVING PATTERNS FROM COLONIAL PAST USED IN CONTEMPORARY PIECES INCLUDING SOME CONTEMPORAY RED, WHITE & BLUES FOR FUN. (LOCAL). EMMY SPENCER, COORD; FIBERS IN WEAVING; 211 PINE BROOK HILLS; BOULDER, CO 80302. (#106978-6).

MAY 1, '76. US AIR FORCE ACADEMY BAND AND CHORALE CONCERT. CONCERT WITH EMPHASIS ON COLORADO COMPOSERS. AT CURRIGAN EXHIBITION HALL, 13TH AND CHAMPA ST. (ST-WIDE). CATHY MOLLECK, COORD; MAYOR'S COMMITTEE OF 19 FOR '76 AND THE DENVER POST; 1313 TREMONT PL, SUITE 6; DENVER, CO 80204. (#104553-1).

MAY 1 - JUNE 6, '76. STATUS OF THE STATES EXHIBIT - PHOTOGRAPHS OF U S IN 1976. EXHIBIT AT CIVIC CENTER. (LOCAL). JEAN HANN, PROJ CHAIRMAN; COLORADO PHOTOGRAPHIC ARTS EXHIBIT; 1301 BANNOCK ST; DENVER, CO 80204. (#200007-71).

MAY 2 - SEPT 12, '76. CENTRAL DENVER CENTENNIAL-BICENTENNIAL ACTIVITY. SPECIAL FEATURES WILL BE 4 CELEBRATIONS, FILM-SLIDE PRESENTATION, HISTORICAL DISPLAYS AND ARTIFACTS. AT 1690 SHERMAN ST. (LOCAL). RALPH E JOHNSON, CHMN; CENTRAL DENVER COMMUNITY SERVICES & CENTRAL PRESBYTERIAN CHURCH; 3855 S DAHLIA ST; ENGLEWOOD, CO 80110. (#103840-6).

MAY 2 - SEPT 26, '76. FOUR CENTENNIAL-BICENTENNIAL EVENTS. THERE WILL BE 4 CELEBRATIONS FEATURING A FILM & SLIDE PRESENTATION, HISTORICAL DISPLAYS AND ARTIFACTS. (LOCAL). RALPH E JOHNSON, CHAIRMAN; CENTRAL DENVER COMMUNITY SERVICES & CENTRAL PRESBYTERIAN CHURCH; 3855 S DAHLIA ST; DENVER, CO 80110. (#18528-1).

MAY 3, '76. LAW DAY LUNCHEON CEREMONY. CEREMONY AT COSMOPOLITAN HOTEL, 18TH & BROADWAY. (LOCAL). REX DAWSON, SAI; LAW DAY COMMITTEE; 3950 S HOLLY; DENVER, CO 80237. (#107029-1).

MAY 3 - 26, '76. HISTORY OF POLISH COMMUNITY IN COLO 1858 TO 1976 AUD-VIS DISPLAY. OPENING CEREMONY ON MAY 3RD. WILL INCLUDE POLISH YOUTH DANCERS, MASTER OF CEREMONIES STANLEY CUBA OF THE KOSCIUSZKO FOUNDATION IN NEW YORK CITY, AND LOCAL DIGNITARIES. AT COLORADO NAT BANK LOBBY DISPLAY AREA. (LOCAL). WANDA CUBA, CHAIRMAN; POLISH NATIONAL ALLIANCE ST MARTINS GROUP 134; 2643 UTICA ST; DENVER, CO 80212. (#4354-2).

MAY 9 - 15, '76. 27TH INTERNATIONAL SCIENCE AND ENGINEERING FAIR. HIGH SCHOOL SCIENTISTS COMPETE FOR PRIZES; TALK WITH SPECIALIZED JUDGES; EACH STUDENT IS A REGIONAL FAIR WINNER; 3 TO 8 FOREIGN COUNTRIES WILL PARTICIPATE. ALSO SPONSORING ARE THE DENVER POST, NATL BUREAU OF STANDARDS, NATL OCEANIC ADMIN, INST FOR TELECOMM. AT CURRIGAN EXHIBITION HALL, 1323 CHAMPH ST. (INT'L). CALVIN FISHER, DIRECTOR; COLORADO MEDICAL SOCIETY & COLORADO ENGINEERING SOCIETY; 1601 E AVE; DENVER, CO 80218. (#100986-1).

MAY 13 - 30, '76. 'THE CONTRAST' - BONFILS THEATRE. WRITTEN BY ROYALL TYLER, THE PLAY WAS THE FIRST WRITTEN BY AN AMERICAN AND PERFORMED IN AMERICA; THE PLAY WAS SAID TO BE A FAVORITE OF GEORGE WASHINGTON; PERFORMANCES ARE: MAY 13, 14, 15, 20, 21, 22, 28 & 29 AT 8:00 PM; MAY 16, 23 AND 30 AT 2:30 PM. AT BONFILS THEATRE, COLFAX & ELIZABETH. (LOCAL). DIRECTOR; BONFILS THEATRE; COLFAX & ELIZABETH; DENVER, CO 80206. (#103368-1).

MAY 15, '76. OPERATION ROCKY MOUNTAIN EMPIRE: SHERIDAN'S GLORY PIGEON RACE. PIGEON RACE BEGINNING IN SHERIDAN, WY & TERMINATING IN DENVER. (REGN'L). ED JOHNSON, COORD; DENVER RACING PIGEON CLUB; 2601 W JEWELL AVE; DENVER, CO 80219. (#106978-10).

MAY 17 - JUNE 4, '76. STAR-SPANGLED HISTORY: DRAWINGS BY J B BEALE - MAGIC LANTERN ARTIST. NATIONAL TRAVELLING EXHIBITION OF 65 ORIGINAL DRAWINGS BY JOSEPH BOGGS BEALE, A 19TH CENTURY ILLUSTRATOR. A SLIDE PRESENTATION. AT FIRST NATIONAL BANK OF DENVER, 621 SEVENTEENTH ST. (REGN'L). SUE PEARLMAN, PROJ COORD; AMERICAN NATIONAL INSURANCE CO OF GALVESTON, TX; RUDER & FINN, 110 E 59TH ST; NEW YORK, NY 10022. (#9820-6).

DENVER—CONTINUED

MAY 20, '76. THE FUTURE OF THE AMERICAN JEW. THIS LECTURE IS PART OF A SIX-LECTURE SERIES ON 'THE AMERICAN JEWISH EXPERIENCE.'. AT BOETCHER CENTER AUDITORIUM. (LOCAL). DR STANLEY M WAGNER; UNIVERSITY OF DENVER; 7001 E WALSH PL; DENVER, CO 80224. (#103310-7).

MAY 22, '76. OPERATION ROCKY MOUNTAIN EMPIRE: SPRING SALUTE TO THE PRESIDENTS. PIGEON RACE BEGINNING AT MT RUSHMORE, SD & TERMINATING IN DENVER. NATIONWIDE PARTICIPATION, ALL AGES. (REGN'L). ED JOHNSON, COORD; DENVER RACING PIGEON CLUB; 2601 W JEWELL AVE; DENVER, CO 80219. (#106978-8).

MAY 22, '76. OPERATION ROCKY MOUNTAIN EMPIRE: MEMORIAL TO THE OREGON TRAIL. PIGEON RACE BEGINNING AT SCOTTSBLUFF, NE FROM THE OREGON TRAIL MUSEUM & TERMINATING IN DENVER. NATIONWIDE PARTICIPATION, ALL AGES. (REGN'L). ED JOHNSON, COORD; DENVER RACING PIGEON CLUB; 2601 W JEWELL AVE; DENVER, CO 80219. (#106978-9).

MAY 22, '76. YOUTH FESTIVAL '76. PERFORMANCE BY THE HIGHLANDERS, BOYS AGES 8-16, SALUTING OUR HERITAGE AS CITIZENS AND RECOGNIZING THE MANY YOUTH DEVELOPMENT GROUPS IN COLORADO. PERFORMANCE IS THE CULMINATION OF THE HIGHLANDERS PROGRAM YEAR. AT CORKIN THEATER, COLORADO WOMENS' COLLEGE. (LOCAL). EILEEN COLLINS, EXEC DIR; THE HIGHLANDERS; 300 E 4TH AVE; DENVER, CO 80203. (#107445-2).

MAY 23 - JULY 4, '76. EL DORADO: THE GOLD OF ANCIENT COLUMBIA. THIS COLLECTION FROM THE MUSEO DEL 'ORO, BOGOTA, COLUMBIA, IS COMPRISED OF OVER 200 EXAMPLES OF ANCIENT COLOMBIAN GOLD WORK AND CERAMICS DATING FROM 500-1500 AD. THE COLLECTION IS PRESENTED AS A TRIBUTE TO THE CREATIVITY OF SKILLED ARTISANS OF THE AMERICAS. AT DENVER ART MUSEUM, 100 W 14TH AVE. (ST-WIDE). CATHY MCCLAIN, DIRECTOR; DENVER ART MUSEUM; 100 W 14TH AVE; DENVER, CO 80204. (#103327-1).

MAY 27, '76. MEMORIAL DAY TRIBUTE, ANNUAL CHOIR CONCERT WITH FULL ORCHESTRA. ONE OF FOUR MAJOR CONCERTS FEATURING LOCAL PROFESSIONAL AND NONPROFESSIONAL PERFORMERS DEDICATED TO THE THEME 'HARMONY OF PEOPLE EXPRESSED THROUGH BEAUTY AND HARMONY OF MUSIC. AT AUDITORIUM OF FINE ARTS CENTER, LORETTO HEIGHTS, 3001 S FEDERAL. (LOCAL). CAROL HARRINGTON, CHMN; DENVER CONCERT CHORALE; 900 S QUINCE ST, B-811; DENVER, CO 80231. (#17537-1).

MAY 31 - SEPT 30, '76. SYRIAN 49ERS ON PARADE. CEREMONY. (LOCAL). BILL MOLAND, DIRECTOR; MOST WORSHIPFUL PRINCE HALL, GRAND LODGE; 2291 KRAMERIA ST; DENVER, CO 80207. (#108800-8).

MAY '76. A BICENTENNIAL SALUTE TO DUKE ELLINGTON AND ELLA FITZGERALD. A TWO HOUR PERFORMANCE OF COMPOSITIONS WRITTEN BY DUKE ELLINGTON AND MADE POPULAR BY ELLA FITZGERALD. INCLUDING A SLIDE SHOW HISTORY OF ELLINGTON AND FITZGERALD WITH NARRATION. (LOCAL). GENE FIELD; GENE FIELD SINGERS AND JAZZ ORCHESTRA; 747 DILLON, APT 302; AURORA, CO 80012. (#107029-5).

MAY '76. METRO STATE COLLEGE MOVES TO AURARIA. THIS EVENT WILL BE A DEMONSTRATION OF THE FACT THAT MSC IS ON THE MOVE EDUCATIONALLY IN COLORADO. (LOCAL). PAM WYNNE CARTER, CHMN; ANNIVERSARY COMMITTEE FOR METROPOLITAN STATE COLLEGE; 250 W 14TH AVE; DENVER, CO 80204. (#102695-1).

JUNE 1, '76. AUSTRALIAN YOUTH ORCHESTRA CONCERT. LIVE PERFORMANCE. (INT'L). JOHN MAUNDER, DIRECTOR; AUSTRALIAN GOVERNMENT; AUSTRALIAN CG, 636 FIFTH AVENUE; NEW YORK, NY 10020. (#108021-7).

JUNE 2 - DEC 19, '76. 'STATUS OF THE STATES' - EXHIBIT OF PHOTOS OF THE U S IN 1976. EXHIBIT AT CIVIC CENTER, 1301 BANNOCK ST. (LOCAL). JEAN HANN, COORDINATOR; 1301 BANNOCK ST; DENVER, CO 80204. (#108360-2).

JUNE 3 - 5, '76. PRIDE & UNITY '76. EVENTS INCLUDE SENIOR CITIZENS CONFERENCE, LUNCHEON SEMINAR ON ECONOMICS & LABOR, PARADE, BAZAAR & CONTEST FOR MISS BLACK DENVER. (LOCAL). HIAWATHA DAVIS, JR, DIR; EASTSIDE ACTION MOVEMENT; 2855 TREMONT #201; DENVER, CO 80205. (#200007-72).

JUNE 4 - 13, '76. BICENTENNIAL DOG SHOW. 6 CLUBS HELD ALL-BREED DOG SHOW - NUMEROUS SPECIALTY SHOWS FOR ONE BREED WERE ALSO HELD. AT HALL OF EDUCATION, 1325 E 46TH AVE. (ST-WIDE). JACQUES A MACHOL, JR; COLORADO CENTENNIAL CANINE CIRCUIT; 32 S BROADWAY; DENVER, CO 80209. (#200007-73).

JUNE 6, '76. ETHNIC FOLKLIFE FESTIVAL. FOLK SONGS & FOLK DANCES TRADITIONS FOLK ARTS DISPLAYS COSTUMES ETHNIC FOOD BOOTHS EARLY COLORADO DISPLAY UTE INDIAN RESERVATION PRESENTATIONS AND GENERAL FOLK DANCING FOR ALL PROGRAMS FOR 15 MIN EVERY HOUR ALL DAY LONG. AT DENVER UNIV ARENA PARKING AVAILABLE. (ST-WIDE). V F BELIAJUS; COLORADO FOLK ARTS COUNCIL; PO BOX 1226; DENVER, CO 80201. (#50058-1).

JUNE 6, '76. NORTHWEST DENVER NEIGHBORHOOD TOUR. TOUR IS HELD TO FOCUS ATTENTION ON DENVER'S NEIGHBORHOODS, WHY THEY ARE VITAL TO THE CITY, THE DIVERSITY OF ARCHITECTURE, COMMUNITY FACILITIES, RELIGIOUS & CULTURAL INFLUENCES. AT BUSES WILL RUN EVERY 10 MIN FROM MCNICHOLS ARENA TO 16TH & OLAY. (LOCAL). LORETTA CRIPPEN, COORD; LEAGUE OF WOMEN VOTERS OF DENVER; 642 S WILLIAMS; DENVER, CO 80209. (#200007-74).

JUNE 6 - AUG 15, '76. COLORADO CHAUTAUQUA 1976; A TOURING ARTS FESTIVAL. FESTIVAL. (ST-WIDE). DONALD MALMGREN, DIRECTOR; COLORADO COUNCIL OF THE ARTS & HUMANITIES; 1550 LINCOLN ST, ROOM 205; DENVER, CO 80203. (#103072-1).

JUNE 7 - 25, '76. HISTORY OF POLISH COMMUNITY IN COLO 1858 TO 1976 AUD-VIS DISPLAY. WILL INCLUDE POLISH YOUTH GROUP DANCERS, MASTER OF CEREMONIES STANLEY CUBA OF THE KOSCIUSZKO FOUNDATION IN NEW YORK CITY, AND LOCAL DIGNITARIES. AT FIRST NATIONAL BANK 17 & WELTON ST LOBBY EXHIBIT AREA. (LOCAL). WANDA CUBA, CHAIRMAN; POLISH NATIONAL ALLIANCE ST MARTINS GROUP 134; 2643 UTICA ST; DENVER, CO 80212. (#4354-3).

JUNE 13 - 19, '76. SWEDISH ARTS & CRAFTS EXHIBITS. EXHIBIT. (LOCAL). ARTHUR N JACKSON, COORD; 'ALL SWEDES WEEK' COMMITTEE; 3701 E FLORIDA AVE; DENVER, CO 80222. (#106976-1).

JUNE 15, '76. IN-HOUSE ENTERTAINMENT FOR DENVER V A HOSPITAL. LIVE PERFORMANCE AT DENVER V A HOSPITAL. (LOCAL). MARILYN HELLER, CHMN; HOSPITAL AUDIENCES, INC; 1510 S GRANT; DENVER, CO 80210. (#106978-2).

JUNE 18, '76. 'KIRGHIZ MICHAEL & THE BEAUTIFUL AMY OF PFANNENSTIEL'. THE STORY OF MICHAEL HAS LONG EXISTED IN THE FOLKLORE OF GERMAN RUSSIANS. THE TALE WAS FIRST PUBLISHED IN 1861 IN GERMAN. IT IS NOW AN UPDATED PRODUCTION OF MUSIC, DANCE & DRAMA IN ENGLISH, STAGED BY LOCAL TALENT. AT SOUTH HIGH SCHOOL AUDITORIUM, 1700 E LOUISIANA AVE, DENVER. (LOCAL). PHIL B LEGLER, COORD; THE AMERICAN HISTORICAL SOCIETY OF GERMANS FROM RUSSIA; 680 S ALTON WAY, APT 7A; DENVER, CO 80231. (#106994-3).

JUNE 21 - 25, '76. CONFERENCE ON YOUTH NEEDS AND YOUTH EXHIBITION. CONFERENCE, EXHIBIT AT DENVER HILTON, 1550 COURT PL. (REGN'L). STUART RADO, EXEC DIR; NATIONAL NETWORK ADVISORY BOARDS; PO BOX 402036, OCEAN VIEW BRANCH; MIAMI BEACH, FL 33140. (#1536-10).

JUNE 22 - 27, '76. SPREE '76. COLORADO'S CELEBRATION OF THE ARTS SHOWCASES LOCAL, STATE AND NATIONAL ARTISTS IN THE PERFORMING, VISUAL AND COMMERCIAL ARTS. TUES-THRUS ACTIVITIES INCLUDE EXHIBITS IN MUSEUM OF NATURAL HISTORY. FRI-SUN FULL FESTIVITIES THRU PARK AREA. AT DENVER CITY PARK. (ST-WIDE). JOCK BICKERT, CHAIRMAN; COLORADO CELEBRATION OF THE ARTS; 1430 LARIMER #207; DENVER, CO 80207. (#20624-1).

JUNE 25 - 27, '76. COLORADO CELEBRATION OF THE ARTS - SPREE '76. THE FESTIVAL FEATURES LOCAL, STATE AND NATIONAL ARTISTS IN THE PERFORMING, VISUAL AND COMMERCIAL ARTS. (ST-WIDE). STEPHANIE MOORE, COORD; COLORADO CELEBRATION OF THE ARTS; 1430 LARIMER ST; DENVER, CO 80202. (#27285-1).

JUNE 30, '76. ART CONTEST. ARTISTS' CONCEPTION OF WHAT THE COLORADO CENTENNIAL CELEBRATION MEANS TO THEM. (LOCAL). B UKOLOWICZ, COORDINATOR; A NIGHT IN OLD DENVER; 1340 PENNSYLVANIA ST; DENVER, CO 80203. (#108632-4).

JULY 1 - 20, '76. HISTORY OF POLISH COMMUNITY IN COLO 1858 TO 1976 AUD-VIS DISPLAY. WILL INCLUDE POLISH YOUTH GROUP DANCERS, MASTER OF CEREMONIES STANLEY CUBA OF THE KOSCIUSZKO FOUNDATION IN NEW YORK CITY, AND LOCAL DIGNITARIES. AT PUBLIC SERVICE COMPANY; 15TH AT WELTON. (ST-WIDE). WANDA CUBA, CHAIRMAN; POLISH NATIONAL ALLIANCE ST MARTINS GROUP 134; 2643 UTICA ST; DENVER, CO 80212. (#4354-4).

JULY 2, '76. CORY BAND FROM WALES VISITS DENVER. THIS 38-PIECE BAND, FOUNDED IN 1884, HAS REPRESENTED WALES IN NUMEROUS NATIONAL CONTESTS & IN 1974 WON THE TITLE 'CHAMPION BAND OF GREAT BRITAIN.'. (INT'L). MS EDITH HALL; LYRA ENTERTAINMENT, INC; 16 W 61ST ST; NEW YORK, NY 10023. (#109009-4).

JULY 3, '76. INDEPENDENCE DAY PARADE. PARADE WILL FEATURE FLOAT UNITS, BANDS & THE BUDWEISER CLYDESDALE 8 HORSE HITCH. (LOCAL). DON WHITELY; MAYOR'S COMMITTEE OF 19 FOR 76-DENVER; 1313 TREMONT PL #6; DENVER, CO 80204. (#108632-1).

JULY 3 - 4, '76. COLORADO CENTENNIAL ARCHERY TOURNAMENT. ARCHERY TOURNAMENT WITH A BICENTENNIAL THEME OPEN TO ALL ARCHERS IN THE STATE OF COLORADO. AT COLUMBINE TRAILS, 12 MILES W OF SADALIA. (ST-WIDE). YVETTE GILL, SEC-TREAS; COLUMBINE BOWMEN, INC; 9130 CLAYTON ST; THORNTON, CO 80229. (#106978-13).

JULY 4, '76. JULY 4, 1976 DEDICATION AS CENTENNIAL MALL OF DENVER. THERE WILL BE A SPECIAL DEDICATION CEREMONY. THE MALL WILL BE RESTRICTED TO VEHICLES. ONLY PEDESTRIANS WILL BE ALLOWED IN THE MALL WHICH WILL HAVE STATUARY & FOUNTAIN AREAS COMMEMORATING COLORADO'S CENTENNIAL-BICENTENNIAL. AT 16TH STREET IN DOWNTOWN DENVER. (LOCAL). PHIL MILSTEIN, DIR; DOWNTOWN DENVER, INC; GUARANTY NATIONAL BANK BLDG; DENVER, CO 80202. (#1990-1).

JULY 4, '76. PULASKI MONUMENT DEDICATION CEREMONY. MONUMENT TO GREAT POLISH-AMERICANS IN DENVER, CO. 20 FT TALL MONUMENT OF GEN PULASKI WITH BRONZE PLAQUES COMMEMORATING POLISH-AMERICANS WHO CONTRIBUTED TO AMER HISTORY & CULTURE WILL BE ERECTED IN PULASKI PARK. (LOCAL). EDWARD J ZALEWSKI; POLISH CLUB OF DENVER; 752 S HOLLY ST; DENVER, CO 80218. (#6823-502).

JULY 4, '76. THE SPIRIT OF A FOUNDING PEOPLE. A SERIES OF VIGNETTES ON COLORADO'S PAST. AT MCNICHOLS SPORTS ARENA. (LOCAL). SPENCER WREN, COORD; COLORADO COUNCIL OF CHURCHES; DENVER, CO 80204. (#108632-3).

JULY 4 - AUG 14, '76. DENVER MUNICIPAL BAND CONCERTS. FREE CONCERTS BY THE 83 YEAR OLD DENVER MUNICIPAL BAND. RICH IN CULTURAL HERITAGE, BAND PLAYS ALL TYPES OF MUSIC, REPRESENTING MANY ETHNIC GROUPS. EACH CONCERT FEATURES AN INSTRUMENTAL & VOCAL SOLOIST. AT PERMANENT BANDSHELL AT CITY PARK; PORTABLE STAGE AT OTHER PARKS. (LOCAL). C E LENICHECK, COORD; DENVER MUNICIPAL BAND; 3372 S MAGNOLIA ST; DENVER, CO 80224. (#106978-7).

JULY 7 - 21, '76. COLORADO WATERCOLOR SOCIETY ALL WATER-MEDIA SHOW. EXHIBIT AT DENVER BOTANIC GARDENS, 1005 YORK ST. (LOCAL). BEV BASILICATO, CHAIRMAN; COLORADO WATERCOLOR SOCIETY; 1016 S CLAYTON WAY; DENVER, CO 80209. (#108360-4).

JULY 12 - 13, '76. AROUND THE WORLD AUTO RACE VISITS DENVER. 4 AMERICAN AUTOS COMPLETED AN ISTANBUL TO SAN FRANCISCO RACE COVERING 6157 MILES. ENTRIES WERE: 1900 FRANKLIN, 1911 FORD, 1912 ABBOTT AND 1914 DODGE. THE DODGE CARRIED THE EQUIPMENT FOR THE NASA GODDARD SATELLITE TRACKING PROGRAM FROM NEW YORK TO SAN FRANCISCO. (REGN'L). STEVEN POTASH; UNITED STATES COMMITTEE FOR AROUND THE WORLD AUTO RACE; 1701 E 12TH ST; CLEVELAND, OH 44114. (#107029-2).

JULY 15 - 22, '76. CENTRAL STATES GOLF TOURNAMENT AND YOUTH/SCHOLARSHIP PROGRAM. BLACK GOLFERS FROM ACROSS THE COUNTRY WILL COMPETE IN THIS TOURNAMENT; THE ORGANIZATION PROVIDES A JUNIOR GOLF PROGRAM AND 2 FULL 4-YEAR SCHOLARSHIPS FOR GRADUATES OF THE PROGRAM. AT CITY PARK GOLF COURSE. (REGN'L). M A RUTHERFORD, CHMN; CENTRAL STATES GOLF ASSN - EAST DENVER GOLF CLUB HOST; 300 SO CLINTON, #11-D; DENVER, CO 80231. (#103346-2).

JULY 28 - AUG 1, '76. AMERICAN GI FORUM 1976 NATIONAL CONVENTION. CONFERENCE AT REGENCY INN. (NAT'L). JOHN J PADILLA, COORD; AMERICAN GI FORUM OF UNITED STATES; 3098 S IVAN WAY; DENVER, CO 80227. (#108360-5).

JULY 28 - AUG 1, '76. COMMERCE AND INDUSTRY SHOW. EXHIBIT, CONFERENCE AT REGENCY HOTEL, 3900 ELATI ST. (NAT'L). JOHN J PADILLA, CHMN; AMERICAN GI FORUM OF THE U S; 4142 TEJON ST; DENVER, CO 80211. (#108800-9).

JULY 29 - 30, '76. NATL PK SVC '...A LITTLE LOOK AROUND' VISITS DENVER. THIS SHORT PROGRAM FEATURES ACTORS PORTRAYING FAMOUS AMERICANS OF THE PAST WHO'VE RETURNED TO SEE AMERICA'S GROWTH. (REGN'L). RMR BICENT COORDINATOR; NATIONAL PARK SERVICE; P.O. BOX 25287; DENVER, CO 80225. (#5653-27).

JULY 31, '76. 'A NIGHT IN OLD DENVER' - PARADE. PARADE RECALLING COLORADO'S 100 YRS HELD THE DAY BEFORE COLORADO'S CENTENNIAL. MOST PARTICIPANTS IN COSTUME RECALLING AREA'S HISTORICAL, COLORFUL PAST. PARADE KICKS OFF A NIGHT IN OLD DENVER CELEBRATION. AT CIVIC CENTER, 15TH TO STOUT 16TH ST TO BROADWAY TO 14TH AVE. (LOCAL). BOB NIELSEN, CHAIRMAN; HISTORIC DENVER, INC; 3267 QUITMAN; DENVER, CO 80212. (#108360-6).

JULY 31 - AUG 1, '76. THE DUTCHMAN SOCCER TOURNAMENT. ADULT MEN'S TOURNAMENT OF 8 AMATEUR TEAMS FROM BOTH MOUNTAIN & LOCAL COMMUNITIES. AN ANNUAL EVENT INSTITUTED TO PROMOTE RECREATIONAL SOCCER IN THE DENVER METRO AREA DURING THE SUMMER MONTHS. AT FORT LOGAN PARADE GROUND, 4150 S LOWELL BLVD. (LOCAL). W HARGREAVES, COORD; W HARGREAVES; 2323 E LONG AVE; LITTLETON, CO 80122. (#106994-2).

AUG 1, '76. ANTIQUE CAR SHOW. EXHIBIT, FESTIVAL. (ST-WIDE). BRUCE KANTOR, CHMN; COLORADO ASSOC OF LIFE UNDERWRITERS; 1420 LARIMER SQUARE; DENVER, CO 80707. (#103346-4).

AUG 1, '76. CENTENNIAL STEAM POWERED TRAIN OF COLORADO. STEAM POWERED RAILROAD EXCURSION ON UNION-PACIFIC RR FROM DENVER TO LARAMIE, WY; SPECIAL 1 DAY RAILWAY P.O. POSTMARK & CACHET WILL BE ISSUED. LOCAL CELEBATION WITH OUTDOOR LUNCH ETC WHILE TRAIN IS PARKED ON DISPLAY. (REGN'L). KENTON FOREST, AGENT; INTERMOUNTAIN CHAPTER NATIONAL RAILWAY HISTORICAL SOCIETY, INC; PO BOX 5181, TERMINAL ANNEX; DENVER, CO 80217. (#4409-2).

AUG 1, '76. HISTORIC DENVER 9TH STREET PARK DEDICATION & PRESERVATION. CEREMONY GIVING SITE TO STATE AS CENTENNIAL BIRTHDAY GIFT FROM HISTORIC DENVER. AT 9TH ST PARK, 115 9TH ST, AURARIA COLLEGE CAMPUS. (LOCAL). BARBARA KNIGHT, COORD; HISTORIC DENVER, INC; 6051 E DORADO AVE; ENGLEWOOD, CO 80110. (#106994-1).

AUG 1, '76. IN-HOUSE ENTERTAINMENT FOR DENVER V A HOSPITAL. LIVE PERFORMANCE AT DENVER VA HOSPITAL. (LOCAL). MARILYN HELLER, CHMN; HOSPITAL AUDIENCES, INC; 1510 S GRANT; DENVER, CO 80210. (#106978-3).

AUG 1 - 6, '76. FOLKLORAMA INTERNATIONAL CULTURAL FESTIVAL. ITE SPONSORED CITY-WIDE MULTICULTURAL EVENT OF 5 DAY DURATION SCHEDULED FOR AUGUST, '76. SUPPORTED BY INTERNATIONAL CORPORATIONS IN COLORADO FOR MATCHING CCBC FUNDING. (LOCAL). NANCY M HARRINGTON; INSTITUTE OF INTERNATIONAL EDUCATION; E 16TH AT GRANT; DENVER, CO 80203. (#4283-501).

AUG 1 - DEC 15, '76. 'NOTHING IS LONG AGO' - A HISTORY OF COLORADO. EXHIBIT. (LOCAL). LIBRARIAN; DENVER PUBLIC LIBRARY; 1357 BROADWAY; DENVER, CO 80203. (#1957-2).

AUG 2 - 30, '76. HISTORY OF POLISH COMMUNITY IN COLO 1858 TO 1976 AUD-VIS DISPLAY. WILL INCLUDE POLISH YOUTH GROUP DANCERS, MASTER OF CEREMONIES, STANLEY CUBA OF THE KOSCIUSZKO FOUNDATION IN NEW YORK CITY, AND LOCAL DIGNITARIES. AT CENTRAL BANK MEZZANINE EXHIBIT AREA-PRUDENTIAL PLAZA. (LOCAL). WANDA CUBA, CHAIRMAN; POLISH NATIONAL ALLIANCE ST MARTINS GROUP 134; 2643 UTICA ST; DENVER, CO 80212. (#4354-5).

AUG 4 - 7, '76. A NIGHT IN OLD DENVER. A FAMILY FESTIVAL FEATURING FOOD, ENTERTAINMENT, GAMES AND FUN. RE-

DENVER — CONTINUED

CALLS DENVER'S HISTORIC PAST. AT LARIMER SQUARE. (LOCAL). BECKY CUNNINGHAM, COORD; HISTORIC DENVER, INC; 951 S FILLMORE WAY; DENVER, CO 80201. (#108800-5).

AUG 22, '76. UN DIA CON LA RAZA. AN OCCASION FOR ALL COLORADOANS TO PARTICIPATE IN A CELEBRATION COMMEMORATING THE CULTURE AND CONCEPT OF FAMILY (FAMILIA) OF THE MEXICAN-AMERICAN IN COLORADO. AT LAKESIDE AMUSEMENT PARK. (LOCAL). GIL SISNEROS, CHMN; AMERICAN GI FORUM, SKYLINE CHAPTER; 1120 S DEPEW ST; LAKEWOOD, CO 80226. (#17679-1).

AUG 26 - SEPT 5, '76. 'CENTRAL CITY' AN ORIGINAL MUSICAL. AN EXCITING, ROMANTIC MUSICAL-COMEDY RECREATING THE SPIRIT OF CENTRAL CITY DURING THE GOLD FEVER DAYS OF THE TURN OF THE CENTURY. AT LORETTO HEIGHTS COLLEGE CENTER FOR THE PERFORMING ARTS. (ST-WIDE). FATHER DWYER, DIRECTOR; METRO AREA YOUTH SERVICES OF THE ARCHDIOCESE OF DENVER; 463 LOGAN ST; DENVER, CO 80203. (#104872-1).

AUG '76. 'GHOST TOWN'-NARRATIVE DANCE PRESENTATION OF GOLD RUSH ERA. ASSORTED DANCE FORMS SHOW GROWTH OF MINING TOWNS IN GOLD RUSH ERA. SELECTED MUSIC; THREE PERFORMERS. AT LORETTO HEIGHTS COL. BONFILS THEAT 3001 S FEDERAL BLVD DEN PARK AVAL. (ST-WIDE). DIXIE TURNQUIST; PREMIERE DANCE ARTS CO; 714 SO PEARL ST; DENVER, CO 80209. (#4119-1).

SEPT 1, '76 - CONTINUING . HISTORY OF POLISH COMMUNITY IN COLO 1858 TO 1976 AUD-VIS DISPLAY. COLORADO STATE HISTORICAL SOCIETY WILL PLACE EXHIBIT IN PERMANENT HOME IN NEW JUDICIARY HERITAGE BLDG, WHICH WILL ALSO BE THE SOCIETY'S HEADQUARTERS UPON COMPLETION IN 1977. AT NEW JUDICIARY HERITAGE BLDG 14 & BROADWAY. (LOCAL). WANDA CUBA, CHAIRMAN; POLISH NATIONAL ALLIANCE ST MARTINS GROUP 134; 2643 UTICA ST; DENVER, CO 80212. (#4354-6).

SEPT 13 - 25, '76. BIENNIAL NEEDLEWORK EXHIBITION. SUNDAY HOURS: 9AM - 1PM. AT CHERRY CREEK BRANCH, COLUMBIA SAVINGS & LOAN, E 1ST & DETROIT ST. (LOCAL). BEV BASILICATO,CHMN; COLORADO CHAPTER, EMBROIDERERS' GUILD OF AMERICA; 1016 S CLAYTON WAY; DENVER, CO 80209. (#108807-1).

SEPT 17, '76. CITIZENSHIP DAY COMMITTEE RECOGNITION CEREMONY. CEREMONY WILL HONOR & RECOGNIZE NEWLY NATURALIZED CITIZENS IN THE STATE OF COLORADO. (LOCAL). EMILY GRIFFITH, COORD; CITIZENSHIP DAY COMMITTEE; 1250 WELTON ST; DENVER, CO 80204. (#108800-2).

SEPT 19, '76. OPERATION ROCKY MOUNTAIN EMPIRE: ALLIANCE OF THE STATES TO THE UNION. PIGEON RACE BEGINNING IN ALLIANCE, NE & TERMINATING IN DENVER. (REGN'L). ED JOHNSON, COORD; DENVER RACING PIGEON CLUB; 2601 W JEWELL AVE; DENVER, CO 80219. (#106978-12).

SEPT 25 - OCT 3, '76. 7TH ANNUAL OKTOBERFEST. FESTIVAL AT LARIMER SQUARE. (ST-WIDE). LINDA ROHRER, COORD; LARIMER SQUARE ASSOC; 1228 15TH ST; DENVER, CO 88282. (#103416-623).

OCT 3 - 4, '76. OPERATION ROCKY MOUNTAIN EMPIRE: GRANDE FINALE-SALUTE TO PRESIDENTS. PIGEON RACE BEGINNING AT MT RUSHMORE, SD & TERMINATING IN DENVER. NATIONWIDE PARTICIPATION, OPEN TO ALL. (REGN'L). ED JOHNSON, COORD; DENVER RACING PIGEON CLUB; 2601 W JEWELL AVE; DENVER, CO 80219. (#106978-11).

OCT 11, '76. ANNUAL PULASKI DAY COMMEMORATION--BANQUET & BALL. OPENING, CEREMONY. (LOCAL). EDWARD J ZALEWSKI; POLISH CLUB OF DENVER; 752 S HOLLY ST; DENVER, CO 80218. (#6823-503).

OCT 15, '76. IN-HOUSE ENTERTAINMENT FOR DENVER V A HOSPITAL. LIVE PERFORMANCE AT DENVER V A HOSPITAL. (LOCAL). MARILYN HELLER, CHMN; HOSPITAL AUDIENCES, INC; 1510 S GRANT; DENVER, CO 80210. (#106978-4).

OCT 17, '76. CENTENNIAL-BICENTENNIAL HYMN FESTIVAL. LIVE PERFORMANCE AT CENTRAL PRESBYTERIAN CHURCH, SHERMAN ST. (LOCAL). JAMES HANSON, PROJ CHMN; DENVER CHAPTER OF AMERICAN GUILD OF ORGANISTS; 2449 S COLORADO BLVD; DENVER, CO 80222. (#108800-6).

NOV 7 - 20, '76. COLORADO WATERCOLOR SOCIETY ALL-MEDIA SHOW. EXHIBIT AT SOUTH GLEN COLUMBIA SAVINGS & LOAN, E ARAPAHOE RD & S UNIVERSITY. (LOCAL). BEV BASILICATO, CHAIRMAN; COLORADO WATERCOLOR SOCIETY; 1016 S CLAYTON WAY; DENVER, CO 80209. (#108754-1).

DEC 1, '76 - CONTINUING . TURNER MUSEUM DISPLAYS. THE TURNER MUSEUM WILL DISPLAY THE WORKS OF J W TURNER & THOMAS MORAN. OPEN TO THE PUBLIC BEFORE CHRISTMAS, 1976. (ST-WIDE). DOUGLAS GRAHAM, DIRECTOR; GRAHAM'S TURNER MUSEUM AND ART FUND; 924 LOGAN; DENVER, CO 80203. (#103332-1).

DEC 15, '76. IN-HOUSE ENTERTAINMENT FOR DENVER V A HOSPITAL. LIVE PERFORMANCE AT DENVER V A HOSPITAL. (LOCAL). MARILYN HELLER, CHMN; HOSPITAL AUDIENCES, INC; 1510 S GRANT; DENVER, CO 80210. (#106978-5).

DILLON

DILLON CENTENNIAL MEMORIAL AMPHITHEATER-DILLON, CO. AN AMPHITHEATER TO SERVE AS THE FOCAL POINT OF THE COMMUNITY'S ACTTIVITIES, WILL HOUSE LECTURES, CONCERTS & RECITALS. (LOCAL). LORRIE SCHOTTLEUTNER, CHAIRMAN; DILLON CENTENNIAL-BICENTENNIAL COMMITTEE; PO BOX 174; DILLON, CO 80435. (#16394).

ROCKY MOUNTAIN OPEN SLED DOG RACING. ENTRANTS FROM CANADA AND THE U S WILL COMPETE IN RACE; THERE WILL BE SPECIAL EVENTS FOR CHILDREN IN CONJUNCTION WITH DILLON WINTER CARNIVAL. (INT'L). LORRIE SCHOTTLEUTNER; DILLON CENTENNIAL-BICENTENNIAL COMMITTEE; BOX 174; DILLON, CO 80435. (#108799-5).

JULY 1 - 30, '75. SPIRIT OF AMERICA CONCERT. THE PRESENTATION OF CONCERTS CELEBRATING THE SPIRIT OF AMERICA WITH ALL TYPES OF AMERICAN MUSIC. THE PROGRAMS WILL INCLUDE FOLK, JAZZ, ETHNIC, ROCK, SPIRITUALS AND EASY LISTENING MUSIC. (LOCAL). MS GINGER BENDER; COMMUNITY ARTS SYMPHONY; BOX 1222; ENGLEWOOD, CO 80110. (#7724-503).

MAY 30, '76. OPENING DAY TRIBUTE TO OLDER PERSONS. EXHIBIT, OPENING. (LOCAL). NANCY FULTON, CHAIRMAN; SUMMIT HISTORICAL MUSEUM; BOX 336; SILVERTHORNE, CO 80498. (#200007-56).

MAY 30 - SEPT 6, '76. SUMMIT HISTORICAL MUSEUM. MUSEUM IS COMPRISED FO RESTORED 1884 SCHOOLHOUSE, BLACKSMITH SHOP AND GENERAL STORE. AT 403 LA BONTE ST. (LOCAL). NANCY FULTON, CHAIRMAN; SUMMIT HISTORICAL SOCIETY; BOX 336; SILVERTHORNE, CO 80498. (#108799-2).

JUNE 3 - 4, '76. ANNA EMORE DAYS. PARADE, CITIZEN PARTICIPATION; BOAT OWNERS HOLD PARADE OF BOATS ON LAKE DILLON; VOLLEY BALL TOURNAMENT; HORSESHOE CONTEST; BARBECUE CONCERT AT DILLON MEMORIAL AMPHITHEATER; CHURCH SERVICE 9:30 AM. AT DILLON TOWN PARK, CHIEF COLOROW ST. (LOCAL). LORRIE SCHOTTLEUTNER; DILLON CENTENNIAL-BICENTENNIAL COMMITTEE; PO BOX 174; DILLON, CO 80435. (#200007-55).

JUNE 18 - AUG 29, '76. PROGRAMS IN DILLON MEMORIAL AMPHITHEATER. CONCERTS, PLAYS & DANCE RECITALS WILL BE PERFORMED THROUGHOUT THE SUMMER. (LOCAL). LORRIE SCHOTTLEUTNER; DILLON CENTENNIAL-BICENTENNIAL COMMITTEE; PO BOX 174; DILLON, CO 80435. (#108799-6).

JULY 3, '76. ANNA EMORE CAKE DECORATING CONTEST AND AUCTION. AWARD, EXHIBIT AT CONTEST: 403 LA BONTE, AUCTION: DILLON PARK. (LOCAL). NANCY FULTON, CHAIRMAN; SUMMIT HISTORICAL SOCIETY; BOX 336; SILVERTHORNE, CO 80498. (#108799-3).

JULY 4 - 5, '76. DEDICATION CEREMONY AT CENTENNIAL-BICENTENNIAL AMPHITHEATER. CEREMONY AT AMPHITHEATER. (LOCAL). LORRIE SCHOTTLEUTNER; DILLON CENTENNIAL-BICENTENNIAL COMMITTEE; BOX 174; DILLON, CO 80435. (#108633-1).

JULY 24 - 25, '76. CRAFT FAIR. CONCERT BY USAF FALCONNAIRES OF USAF ACADEMY & DILLON MEMORIAL AMPHITHEATER BARBECUE. AT DILLON MALL. (LOCAL). ELSIE SCHULTZ, CHAIRMAN; LAKE DILLON ARTS GUILD; PO BOX 12; DILLON, CO 80435. (#200007-54).

AUG 1, '76. CENTENNIAL QUILT RAFFLE. THE SUMMIT HISTORICAL SOCIETY'S CENTENNIAL QUILT DEPICTING SCENES & BUILDINGS OF THE 1800'S WILL BE RAFFLED OFF TO BENEFIT THE ACTIVITIES OF THE HISTORICAL SOCIETY. (LOCAL). MRS PENNY LEWIS, PRES; SUMMIT HISTORICAL SOCIETY; PO BOX 747; DILLION, CO 80435. (#15966-1).

AUG 7 - 8, '76. ART & MUSIC FESTIVAL. PERFORMANCE BY COMMUNITY ARTS SYMPHONY OF ENGLEWOOD, GORDON PARKS, CONDUCTOR. AT LAKE DILLON MEMORIAL AMPHITHEATER. (LOCAL). LORRIE SCHOTTLEUTNER; DILLON CENTENNIAL-BICENTENNIAL COMMITTEE; PO BOX 174; DILLON, CO 80435. (#108727-1).

AUG 21 - 22, '76. SUMMER FUN TIME. COMPETITION, LIVE PERFORMANCE AT DILLON TOWN PARK, MARINA PARK. (LOCAL). LORRIE SCHOTTLEUTNER; DILLON CENTENNIAL-BICENTENNIAL COMMITTEE; PO BOX 174; DILLON, CO 80435. (#108727-2).

DINOSAUR

JUNE 15 - AUG 25, '75. CAMPFIRE PGMS AT DINOSAUR NM ON LOCAL & REGIONAL HISTORY. ALSO IN 1976. HERE AT A QUARRY OF FOSSIL REMAINS OF ANCIENT ANIMALS VISITORS CAN GAIN AN INSIGHT INTO THE HISTORY OF THIS AREA THROUGHOUT MAN'S TIME AND THROUGH AMERICA'S HISTORY. AT AT SPLIT MOUNTAIN CAMPGROUND. (REGN'L). SUPT, DINOSAUR NATL MON; NATIONAL PARK SERVICE; P.O. BOX 210; DINOSAUR, CO 81610. (#6730-24).

JUNE 15 - AUG 25, '76. CAMPFIRE PGMS AT DINOSAUR NM ON LOCAL & REGIONAL HISTORY. ALSO IN 1976. HERE AT A QUARRY OF FOSSIL REMAINS OF ANCIENT ANIMALS VISITORS CAN GAIN AN INSIGHT INTO THE HISTORY OF THIS AREA THROUGHOUT MAN'S TIME AND THROUGH AMERICA'S HISTORY. AT AT SPLIT MOUNTAIN CAMPGROUND. (REGN'L). SUPT, DINOSAUR NATL MON; NATIONAL PARK SERVICE; P.O. BOX 210; DINOSAUR, CO 81610. (#6730-524).

DOLORES

COLORADO CLEANUP - DOLORES. TRASH CONTAINERS WILL BE PAINTED RED, WHITE AND BLUE AND NEW TOPS WILL BE PURCHASED FOR THEM. THE STREETS WILL BE CLEANED AND WEEDS WILL BE REMOVED. (LOCAL). JUNE L MERRITT, COORDINATOR; BUSINESS & PROFESSIONAL WOMEN & DOLORES CENT-BICENT COMMITTEE; PO BOX 745; DOLORES, CO 81323. (#26186).

JULY 2, '76. CENTENNIAL BIRTHDAY PARTY. THERE WILL BE A BIRTHDAY CAKE FOR EACH STATE IN THE U S. AT TOWN SQUARE. (LOCAL). L B TAYLOR, CHAIRPERSON; DOLORES CENTENNIAL-BICENTENNIAL ORGANIZATION; BOX 745; DOLORES, CO 81323. (#108636-1).

AUG 13, '76. DEDICATION OF DOMINQUES ESCALANTE RUIN. CEREMONY. (LOCAL). CECILE B TAYLOR, CHMN; DOLORES CENTENNIAL-BICENTENNIAL COMMITTEE, BUREAU OF LAND MANAGEMENT; BOX 745; DOLORES, CO 81323. (#108689-1).

DOVE CREEK

JULY 4, '76. BICENTENNIAL PICK & HOE DOMINQUEZ-ESCALANTE TRAIL & CENTER. FAIR. (LOCAL). ROBERT JAMES, CHAIRMAN; PICK & HOE COMMITTEE; BOX 527; DOVE CREEK, CO 81324. (#108635-1).

DURANGO

JOY CABIN RESTORATION IN DURANGO, COLORADO. A PROJECT TO RESTORE THE HISTORIC JOY CABIN TO INCLUDE RECHINKING THE LOGS, CREOSOTING EXTERIOR, REPAIRING ROOF, WHITEWASHING INTERIOR INSTALLING ELECTRIC LIGHTS AND FLOWER BOXES. (LOCAL). CHARLES H GREMMELS, PRESIDENT; FOUR CORNERS MUSEUM ASSOC; 128 FOREST AVE; DURANGO, CO 81301. (#4300).

APR 29 - MAY 22, '76. NATIVE-AMERICAN FESTIVAL - 'WALK IN BEAUTY MY CHILDREN'. FESTIVAL OF INDIAN ARTS, DANCE & MUSIC PERFORMANCES & WORKSHOPS. (LOCAL). KENNETH E BORDNER, COORD; FORT LEWIS COLLEGE; DURANGO, CO 81301. (#106611-1).

JULY 31 - AUG 1, '76. ALUMNI CELEBRATION OF FORT LEWIS STUDENTS WHO ATTENDED 1911 - 1955. FESTIVAL AT FORT LEWIS COLLEGE. (LOCAL). M L CORNELIUS, COORD; FORT LEWIS COLLEGE; DURANGO, CO 81301. (#108696-1).

AUG 24 - 25, '76. UNITED STATES ARMED FORCES BICENTENNIAL CARAVAN. CARAVAN IS COMPOSED OF EXHIBIT VANS FOR EACH MILITARY SERVICE. PROJECT THEME IS 'HISTORY OF THE ARMED FORCES AND THEIR CONTRIBUTIONS TO THE NATION'. (LOCAL). RICHARD ROSKOWINSKI; UNITED STATES ARMED FORCES BICENTENNIAL CARAVAN; PO BOX 221, CITY HALL; DURANGO, CO 81301. (#1775-724).

EADS

EXHIBITION HALL/COMMUNITY CENTER -KIOWA FAIRGROUND. COMMUNITY BUILDING WOULD BE USED PRIMARILY FOR LARGE GROUP ACTIVITIE ADDITIONALLY, THE CENTER WOULD BE USED FOR REGIONAL OR DISTRICT ORGANIZATIONAL MEETINGS IN SOUTHEAST CORNER OF COLORADO. (LOCAL). KAREN FLOYD, DIRECTOR; COLORADO STATE UNIV, COOPERATIVE EXTENSION PROGRAM; PO BOX 97; EADS, CO 81036. (#2918).

HISTORICAL BOOK OF KIOWA COUNTY, COLORADO. COLLECTION OF STORIES AND OTHER MATERIALS DEPICTING COUNTY HISTORY WILL BE PUBLISHED AND SOLD TO PRESERVE THE HERITAGE OF KIOWA COUNTY AND TO HELP FUND PROJECTS. (LOCAL). DORIS ANDERSON, CHMN; KIOWA COUNTY CENTENNIAL-BICENTENNIAL COMMITTEE; TOWNER, CO 81080. (#10315).

WATER VALLEY SCHOOL PRESERVATION IN COLORADO. RESTORE AND FURNISH A ONE-ROOM PRAIRIE SCHOOL TO PRESERVE FOR FUTURE GENERATIONS AN EXAMPLE OF SCHOOLS ON COLORADO'S EASTERN PLAINS DURING THE NINETEENTH CENTURY. (LOCAL). DORIS ANDERSON, COMMITTEE CHAIRMAN; KIOWA COUNTY CENTENNIAL BICENTENNIAL COMMITTEE; TOWNER, CO 81080. (#6848).

JULY 4, '75. 4TH OF JULY FESTIVAL. FESTIVAL. (LOCAL). ALICE WEIL, PROJ DIR; EADS CHAMBER OF COMMERCE; EADS, CO 81036. (#10316-501).

SEPT 11 - 13, '75. KIOWA COUNTY FREE FAIR AND RODEO. A COUNTY HISTORICAL PAGEANT WITH CONTESTS AND CLASSES ON COUNTY HISTORY, TO COMMEMORATE COLORADO'S CENTENNIAL. (LOCAL). GEORGE H ELLICOTT; KIOWA COUNTY FAIR BOARD, CSU EXTENSION SERVICE; BOX 97; EADS, CO 81036. (#10313-501).

EAGLE

BEAUTIFICATION OF BUSINESS DISTRICT, EAGLE, CO. PERMANENT BEAUTIFICATION OF DOWNTOWN BUSINESS DISTRICT THROUGH USE OF TREES, SHRUBS AND FLOWERS; WILL ALSO USE PLANTERS. (LOCAL). DON BOLEN, CHAIRMAN; EAGLE CENTENNIAL-BICENTENNIAL COMMITTEE; PO BOX 378; EAGLE, CO 81631. (#24574).

MAR 1, '76 - CONTINUING . BEARD & PIGTAIL CONTEST. COMPETITION. (LOCAL). KAREN R CLARK, DIRECTOR; TOWN OF EAGLE; BOX 672; EAGLE, CO 81631. (#108794-1).

JUNE 25 - 27, '76. FLIGHT DAYS WITH JR RODEO AND FESTIVAL. COMMEMORATES FLIGHT OF THE EAGLET; WILL HAVE CENTENNIAL-BICENTENNIAL THEME. (ST-WIDE). DON BOLEN, DIECTOR; CHAMBER OF COMMERCE; 201 BROADWAY; EAGLE, CO 81631. (#107153-2).

JUNE 28 - 30, '76. CHAUTAUQUA THEATER GROUP. LIVE PERFORMANCE AT CITY PARK. (LOCAL). KAREN CLARK, COORD; TOWN OF EAGLE; PO BOX 672; EAGLE, CO 81631. (#107153-1).

EATON

'GREENING AND CLEANING' - EATON, CO. YARD WILL BE CLEANED AND FERTILIZED; TREES WILL BE PLANTED, TO BE DEDICATED TO PIONEER FAMILIES AND SENIOR CITIZENS. (LOCAL). BARBARA SCHNEIDER, CHAIRMAN; SEVERANCE PROGRESSIVE CLUB; RT 2, BOX 66; EATON, CO 80615. (#26369).

EATON—CONTINUED

HISTORICAL TRAIL MARKERS - EATON, CO. SIGNS WITH MAPS THAT STATE A BRIEF HISTORY WILL BE PLACED ALONG ROADSIDES MARKING HISTORIC TRAILS, EXPEDITION & STAGECOACH ROUTES AND STOPS & EVENTS THAT OCCURRED NEAR PRESENT COUNTY ROADS. (LOCAL). ED SMILLIE, CHAIRMAN; WELD COUNTY CENTENNIAL-BICENTENNIAL COMMITTEE; 127 ELM; EATON, CO 80615. (#21562).

APR 13, '76. EATON MUSIC CLUB BICENTENNIAL PROGRAM. DONATION TO BE USED FOR BICENTENNIAL PROJECT. AT HIGH SCHOOL AUDITORIUM. (LOCAL). BETY WIDMAIER, COORD; MUSIC CLUB; 515 3RD ST; EATON, CO 80615. (#104182-4).

JUNE 17 - 20, '76. COMMUNITY DAYS. AWARD, COMPETITION, EXHIBIT, PARADE, RADIO/TV AT ALL PURPOSE ROOM, GRADE SCHOOL AUDITORIUM, DOWNTOWN, EATON PARK. (LOCAL). THOMAS DANNAT, COORD; CHAMBER OF COMMERCE; 10 CHEYENNE ST; EATON, CO 80615. (#104182-3).

JUNE 18, '76. HISTORICAL PAGEANT. HOME PAGEANT PRESENTED AT FOOTBALL STADIUM; ENTIRE COMMUNITY PARTICIPATING; DEPICTING THE FIRST 100 YRS OF OUR NATION'S LIFE. (LOCAL). H P CHRISTENSEN, COORD; TOWN OF EATON; BOX 725; EATON, CO 80615. (#200007-78).

JUNE 18, '76. HOMECOMING TEA. FESTIVAL AT METHODIST CHURCH. (LOCAL). PEARL LARSEN, COORD; VARIOUS CLUBS AT THE CHURCH; 323 COTTONWOOD AVE; EATON, CO 80615. (#104182-2).

JUNE 18, '76. 'STARS AND STRIPES IN YOUR EYES' - HISTORICAL PAGEANT. LIVE PERFORMANCE AT L R LEAKE ATHLETIC STADIUM. (LOCAL). MRS ED SMILLIE, CO-CHMN; EATON BICENTENNIAL COMMITTEE; 127 ELM ST; EATON, CO 80615. (#103860-1).

JUNE 18 - 19, '76. ARTS FESTIVAL. ARTS AND CRAFTS FESTIVAL WITH EMPHASIS ON BICENT; SPECIAL BICENT RIBBONS WILL BE AWARDED; SUCH ITEMS AS BICENT SOAP (HOMEMADE) WILL BE ADDED. (LOCAL). H P CHRISTENSEN, COORD; TOWN OF EATON; BOX 725; EATON, CO 80615. (#200007-79).

ECKLEY

SEPT 27, '75. YUMA COUNTY TALENT SHOW WITH A CENTENNIAL-BICENTENNIAL THEME. LIVE PERFORMANCE. (LOCAL). LAUREL A BURTON; YUMA, COLORADO AREANS; YUMA, CO 80759. (#10285-501).

SEPT 4 - 6, '76. ANNUAL OLD SETTLERS' CELEBRATION. FESTIVAL. (LOCAL). JOHN NEWBANKS, COORD; YUMA COUNTY CENTENNIAL-BICENTENNIAL COMMITTEE; ECKLEY, CO 80758. (#106989-1).

EDGEWATER

FILM FESTIVAL. EXHIBIT. (LOCAL). HON DONALD D WISE, MAYOR; CITY OF EDGEWATER; 5845 W 25TH AVE; EDGEWATER, CO 80214. (#108797-1).

JULY 30 - AUG 1, '76. 3 BIRTHDAY CELEBRATIONS: CITY'S 75TH, STATE'S 100TH & NATION'S 200TH. FESTIVAL. (LOCAL). DONALD D WISE, COORD; CITY OF EDGEWATER; 5845 W 25TH AVE; EDGEWATER, CO 80214. (#108697-1).

ELBERT

MAY 21 - 23, '76. CENTENNIAL-BICENTENNIAL STATEWIDE CAMPOREE. 20,000 SCOUTS FROM ALL AREAS OF COLORADO WILL CAMP AND CELEBRATE THE COLORADO CENTENNIAL & BICENTENNIAL OF THE U S. RALLIES AND SPECIAL CENTENNIAL AWARDS. ALSO: NATURAL AREA/PARK/PLANTING, MEDAL. AT PEACEFUL VALLEY SCOUT RANCH, 21 MILES SOUTH OF ELBERT. (ST-WIDE). TERRY SCHWARCK, PROJ DIR; SCOUTS AND EXPLORERS OF COLORADO; 2901 W 19TH AVE; DENVER, CO 80204. (#4349-2).

EMPIRE

BICENTENNIAL CONTESTS. CONTESTS INCLUDE: NAME THE STREET CONTEST, TRASH BARREL PAINTING CONTEST & FIREPLUG DECORATING CONTEST. (LOCAL). DANIEL J DALPES, COORD; CITY OF EMPIRE; BOX 158; EMPIRE, CO 80438. (#108795-2).

CITY CLEANUP & BARBECUE. FESTIVAL. (LOCAL). NINA K AYERS, SEC-TREAS; EMPIRE CENTENNIAL-BICENTENNIAL COMMITTEE & VOLUNTEER FIRE DEPT; PO BOX 67; EMPIRE, CO 80438. (#108795-1).

STREET OF FLAGS - EMPIRE, CO. FLAGS WILL BE HUNG ON THE STREET BETWEEN MEMORIAL DAY AND LABOR DAY, DEPENDING ON THE WEATHER. (LOCAL). DANIEL J DAPES, CHAIRMAN; TOWN OF EMPIRE; BOX 158; EMPIRE, CO 80438. (#26368).

ENGLEWOOD

'CONCERT '76' PROJ OF ENGLEWOOD, COLORADO. 3 CONCERTS ON A POPS LEVEL PROGRAMMED FOR WIDE POPULAR APPEAL AIMED TO EVOKE MEMORIES & CELEBRATE THE MUSIC THAT AMERICANS HAVE ENJOYED THRUOUT THEIR HISTORY -JAZZ, FOLK, SPIRITUAL, & A SLIDE PRODUCTION. (LOCAL). MS GINGER BENDER, PUBLIC RELATIONS; COMMUNITY ARTS SYMPHONY; BOX 1222; ENGLEWOOD, CO 80110. (#4428).

CORNUCOPIA AT CHERRY CREEK, CO. CHERRY CREEK HIGH SCHOOL WILL PARTICIPATE IN CCBC RELATED EDUCATIONAL EXPERIENCES FOR ONE WEEK OF SCHOOL. AN ASSEMBLY PROGRAM WILL INITIATE INTEREST & FACULTY WILL LEARN TO PREPARE CCBC PROGRAMS. (ST-WIDE). TED KEMPTON & JIM STAMPER, SENATES SPONSORS; CHERRY CREEK STUDENT SENATE; 9300 E UNION AVE; ENGLEWOOD, CO 80110. (#16404).

EDUCATION COURSE - ENGLEWOOD, CO. AN EXPERIMENTAL COURSE IN LIVING COLORADO HISTORY. (LOCAL). MAGGIE BOGDON, COORDINATOR; CHERRY CREEK SCHOOLS, ARAPAHOE COUNTY DISTRICT #5; 4700 S YOSEMITE; ENGLEWOOD, CO 80110. (#25897).

'FANFARE '76' MUSICAL COMPOSITION OF COLORADO. SHORT COMMISSIONED MUSICAL COMPOSITIONS--SHORT HIGH SPIRITED AND ALIVE WHICH COULD BE USED BY ANY AND MANY ORCHESTRAS AS OVERTURES AS A SALUTE TO THE CENTENNIAL-BICENT. FOUR FANFARES BY COLO. COMPOSERS. (ST-WIDE). MS GINGER BENDER, PUBLIC RELATIONS; COMMUNITY ARTS SYMPHONY; PO BOX 1222; ENGLEWOOD, CO 80110. (#4353).

THE SCHOOLHOUSE MUSEUM - ENGLEWOOD, CO. AN EDUCATIONAL PROJECT HAS BEEN DESIGNED TO INTRODUCE STUDENTS TO WHAT IT WAS LIKE TO BE A STUDENT IN THE LAST CENTURY; WILL TAKE PLACE IN AN OLD ONE ROOM SCHOOLHOUSE. (LOCAL). JOHN BUCHANON, CHAIRMAN OF SOCIAL STUDIES DEPT; CHERRY CREEK SENIOR HIGH SCHOOL; 9300 E UNION AVE; ENGLEWOOD, CO 80110. (#17644).

SPIRIT OF AMERICA CONCERTS OF ENGLEWOOD, COLORADO. THE PRESENTATION OF CONCERTS CELEBRATING THE SPIRIT OF AMERICA WITH ALL TYPES OF AMERICAN MUSIC. THE PROGRAMS WILL INCLUDE FOLK, JAZZ, ETHNIC, ROCK, SPIRITUALS AND EASY LISTENING MUSIC. (LOCAL). MS GINGER BENDER, PR SPECIALIST; COMMUNITY ARTS SYMPHONY; BOX 1222; ENGLEWOOD, CO 80110. (#7724).

JULY 1 - 30, '75. SPIRIT OF AMERICA CONCERT. THE PRESENTATION OF CONCERTS CELEBRATING THE SPIRIT OF AMERICA WITH ALL TYPES OF AMERICAN MUSIC. THE PROGRAMS WILL INCLUDE FOLK, JAZZ, ETHNIC, ROCK, SPIRITUALS AND EASY LISTENING MUSIC. (LOCAL). MS GINGER BENDER; COMMUNITY ARTS SYMPHONY; BOX 1222; ENGLEWOOD, CO 80110. (#7724-502).

NOV 4 - 5, '75. UNITED STATES ARMED FORCES BICENTENNIAL CARAVAN. THE CARAVAN IS COMPOSED OF EXHIBIT VANS FOR EACH BRANCH OF THE MILITARY SERVICE. THE THEME OF THE EXHIBITION IS 'HISTORY OF THE ARMED FORCES AND THEIR CONTRIBUTION TO THE NATION'. (LOCAL). JOHN SCHAMBOW, CHMN; U S ARMED FORCES BICENTENNIAL EXHIBIT VANS PROJECT; 4565 S IRVING; ENGLEWOOD, CO 80110. (#1775-244).

JULY 1 - 4, '76. TENNIS TOURNAMENT. COMPETITION, LIVE PERFORMANCE. (LOCAL). HAROLD RUST; ENGLEWOOD PARKS & RECREATION DEPT; 3470 S BROADWAY; ENGLEWOOD, CO 80110. (#108629-3).

JULY 2, '76. CHILDREN'S COSTUME PARADE. PARADE. (LOCAL). HAROLD RUST; ENGLEWOOD PARKS & RECREATION DEPT; 3470 S BROADWAY; ENGLEWOOD, CO 80110. (#108629-2).

JULY 2 - 4, '76. RAFT TRIP DOWN COLORADO RIVER. LIVE PERFORMANCE AT MILLER FIELD BLOG. (LOCAL). HAROLD RUST; ENGLEWOOD PARKS & RECREATION DEPT; 3470 S BROADWAY; ENGLEWOOD, CO 80110. (#108629-1).

JULY 2 - 5, '76. FIRE CRACKER SOFTBALL TOURNAMENT. COMPETITION, LIVE PERFORMANCE. (LOCAL). HAROLD RUST; ENGLEWOOD PARKS & RECREATION DEPT; 3470 S BROADWAY; ENGLEWOOD, CO 80110. (#108629-6).

JULY 3, '76. ENGLEWOOD HIGH SCHOOL REUNION OF ALL CLASSES. FESTIVAL AT EHS, STUDENT COMMONS AND FIELD HOUSE. (LOCAL). DOUG HARDER; EHS REUNION OF '76; 4101 S BANNOCK ST; ENGLEWOOD, CO 80110. (#108629-4).

JULY 4, '76. BAND CONTEST. COMPETITION, LIVE PERFORMANCE AT CENTENNIAL PARK. (LOCAL). HAROLD RUST; ENGLEWOOD PARKS & RECREATION DEPT; 3470 S BROADWAY; ENGLEWOOD, CO 80110. (#108629-5).

JULY 14, '76. OPEN HOUSE ARTS & CRAFTS. EXHIBIT, LIVE PERFORMANCE. (LOCAL). HAROLD RUST, COORDINATOR; ENGLEWOOD PARKS & RECREATION DEPT; 3470 S BROADWAY; ENGLEWOOD, CO 80110. (#108698-1).

JULY 30 - AUG 1, '76. YOUTH TENNIS TOURNAMENT. COMPETITION, LIVE PERFORMANCE. (LOCAL). HAROLD RUST; ENGLEWOOD PARKS & RECREATION DEPT; 3470 S BROADWAY; ENGLEWOOD, CO 80110. (#108711-1).

ERIE

BICENTENNIAL FESTIVAL HONORING SENIOR CITIZENS. PARADE, FLAG PRESENTATION, BAR-B-QUE, GAMES & CONTESTS. (LOCAL). JUNE M LEWIS, CHAIRMAN; ERIE CENTENNIAL-BICENTENNIAL COMMITTEE; 3920 WELD CO RD 1; ERIE, CO 80516. (#108796-1).

CLEANUP AND IMPROVEMENT OF TOWN CEMETERY - CO. ALL GROUPS PARTICIPATING IN TOWN CLEANUP WILL HELP IN THE IMPROVEMENT OF THE 100 YEAR OLD CEMETERY. (LOCAL). JUNE M LEWIS, CHAIRPERSON; TOWN IMPROVEMENT COMMITTEE; 3920 WELD COUNTY RD 1; ERIE, CO 80516. (#26367).

GREENING AND CLEANING COLORADO - ERIE. TREES FROM THE FOREST SERVICE WILL BE PLANTED IN THE PARK AND PART OF THE PARK AREA WILL BE SODDED. (LOCAL). JUNE M LEWIS, CHAIRPERSON; TOWN IMPROVEMENT COMMITTEE; 3920 WELD COUNTY RD 1; ERIE, CO 80516. (#26366).

TREE PLANTING - ERIE, CO. 250 TREES WILL BE PLANTED IN THE BALLPARK. (LOCAL). HON HARLAN BROCK, MAYOR; ERIE CENTENNIAL-BICENTENNIAL COMMITTEE AND TOWN OF ERIE; 645 HOLBROOK; ERIE, CO 80516. (#26363).

JUNE 1, '76. 6TH GRADE CBC PRESENTATION. LIVE PERFORMANCE AT ERIE ELEMENTARY SCHOOL. (LOCAL). CHARLES ANDERSON, PRIN; ERIE ELEMENTARY SCHOOL; 4137 N 127; ERIE, CO 80516. (#200007-80).

SEPT 10 - 11, '76. ERIE FESTIVAL. FESTIVAL AT ERIE HS FIELD, ERIE ELEMENTARY SCHOOL VICINITY & STREETS. (LOCAL). JUNE M LEWIS, COORD; ERIE CENTENNIAL-BICENTENNIAL COMMITTEE; 3920 WELD, RD 1; ERIE, CO 80516. (#108955-1).

ESTES PARK

CENTENNIAL MINUTES ON RADIO KSIR, ESTES PARK, CO. A SERIES OF 76 ONE-MINUTE SPOTS IS TO BE AIRED SEQUENTIALLY 6 DAYS A WEEK FOR ONE YEAR. ALL DEAL WITH ESTES PARK'S EARLY HISTORY, ESPECIALLY HOMESTEADERS OF 1875 AND 1876. (LOCAL). BOB GAINES, DIRECTOR; RADIO STATION KSIR; 820 MACGREGOR LANE; ESTES PARK, CO 80517. (#16446).

CENTENNIAL ROOM, ESTES PARK, CO, HISTORIC MUSEUM. AN ADDITION OF ONE LARGE DISPLAY ROOM WITH BASEMENT. (LOCAL). RUTH STAUFFER, PROJ DIRECTOR; ESTES PARK AREA HISTORICAL MUSEUM; 200 4TH ST; ESTES PARK, CO 80517. (#19504).

ESTES PARK TRIBUTE TO FRONTIER SETTLERS. MULTI-MEDIA PROGRAM SHOWING CHARACTER OF COLO PIONEERS AND EARLY SETTLERS BOTH INDIAN AND WHITE. (ST-WIDE). G D BARRANTE, EXEC DIR; COLORADO CENTENNIAL-BICENTENNIAL COMMISSION; 901 SHERMAN STREET, 15TH FLOOR; DENVER, CO 80203. (#1956-1).

ESTES PARK, COLO, FINE ARTS GUILD EXHIBITS. TEN PLANNED PERFORMING ARTS EXHIBITS MUSICAL, THEATRICAL, & ART. (ST-WIDE). MARILYN STEVENS, PRESIDENT; ESTES PARK FINE ARTS GUILD; BOX 1514; ESTES PARK, CO 80517. (#2885).

VIGNETTES OF HOMESTEADERS IN ESTES PARK, CO. A SERIES OF ARTICLES IS BEING WRITTEN ON THE MEN AND WOMEN WHO HOMESTEADED IN ESTES PARK IN 1875-77, INCLUDING EVANS, JAMES, HUPP, MACGREGOR, FERGUSON, CLEAVE, MCCREERY, SPRAGUE AND THEIR FAMILIES. (LOCAL). RUTH STAUFFER, VICE-PRESIDENT; ESTES PARK HISTORICAL MUSEUM, INC; BOX 1961, HIGHWAY 36; ESTES PARK, CO 80517. (#16445).

JUNE 1 - SEPT 1, '75. LIVING HISTORY AT THE WILLIAM WHITE CABIN IN ROCKY MOUNTAIN NP. ADMISSION FEE TO THE PARK. HISTORIAN IN APPROPRIATE PERIOD DRESS LIVE AND WORK AT THE SUMMER HOME OF WILLIAM ALLEN WHITE. ALSO IN '76. AT WILLIAM WHITE CABIN. (REGN'L). SUPT ROCKY MOUNTAIN NP; NATIONAL PARK SERVICE; ESTES PARK, CO 80617. (#6727-20).

JUNE 9 - SEPT 1, '75. LIVING HISTORY AT THE HOLZWARTH RANCH IN ROCKY MOUNTAIN NP. A GUIDED TOUR FROM TIMBER CREEK CAMPGROUND 3 OR 4 TIMES DAILY. FREE TICKETS REQUIRED TO SITE WHERE PEOPLE DEPICTING EARLY LIFE IN AN ISOLATED MOUTAIN VALLEY NEAR THE HEADWATERS OF THE COLORADO RIVER. AT HOLZWARTH HOMESTEAD ONE MILE SOUTH OF TIMBER CREEK CAMPGROUND. (REGN'L). SUPT, ROCKY MOUNTAIN NP; NATIONAL PARK SERVICE; ESTES PARK, CO 80617. (#6727-21).

SEPT 4, '75. ROCKY MOUNTAIN NP REENACTMENT OF 1915 DEDICATION. A SHORT LOW KEYED REDEDICATION OF THE PARK ON THE SAME LOCATION AS ORIGINAL WHICH TOOK PLACE SEPT. 4, 1915. AT LAWN LAKE PARKING AREA. (LOCAL). CH PK NATURALIST; NATIONAL PARK SERVICE; ROCKY MOUNTAIN NATL PARK; ESTES PARK, CO 80517. (#6728-106).

FEB 20 - 21, '76. 'YANKEE-DOODLE: A BALLET IN BLUE JEANS'. LIVE PERFORMANCE AT PARK HIGH SCHOOL, 1500 COMMUNITY DR. (LOCAL). DOLORES DAVIES, COORD; FINE ARTS GUILD; UPPER BROADVIEW; ESTES PARK, CO 80517. (#200007-75).

APR 21, '76. 'THE AMERICAN REVOLUTION, WHY WE FOUGHT', LECTURE. SEMINAR AT MUNICIPAL BUILDING, MACGREGOR LANE AND ELKHORN AVE. (LOCAL). RUTH DEFFENBAUGH, COORD; ESTES PARK PUBLIC LIBRARY; DEVILS GULCH RD; ESTES PARK, CO 80517. (#104745-15).

MAY 30, '76. HANDS ACROSS THE NATION, OPENING OF TRAIL RIDGE ROAD. OPENING OF TRAIL RIDGE ROAD AT CONTINENTAL DIVIDE; MAY BE EARLIER THAN MAY 30 IF SNOW PERMITS. AT MILNER PASS, TOP OF TRAIL RIDGE ROAD. (ST-WIDE). DWIGHT HAMILTON, COORD; ROCKY MOUNTAIN NATIONAL PARK; ESTES PARK, CO 80517. (#104744-1).

JUNE 1 - 5, '76. MUSICAL AND DRAMATIC PRODUCTIONS. 'AMERICAN SCENE, 1776-1976', MUSIC IN COLORADO. A MUSICAL PRODUCTION USING EXCERPTS FROM AMERICAN MUSICALS & OTHER MUSIC THAT IS APPLICABLE TO SPECIFIC PERIODS IN AMERICAN & COLORADO HISTORY. (LOCAL). CHARLES CHAFFIN, CHAIRMAN; FINE ARTS GUILD OF THE ROCKIES; BOX 1514; ESTES PARK, CO 80512. (#7725-501).

JUNE 4, '76. TEA AT THE DUNRAVEN COTTAGE. FESTIVAL, TOUR AT DUNRAVEN COTTAGE ON FISH CREEK RD OFF HWY 36. (LOCAL). MARY HOWARTH, CHAIRMAN; ESTES PARK HISTORICAL SOCIETY; 237 CLEAVE; ESTES PARK, CO 80517. (#200007-76).

JUNE 4 - 19, '76. 'THE AMERICAN SCENE 1776-1976', A MUSICALE. MUSIC FROM 1776-1976; CHORUSES AND SOLOS; DRAMA AND NARRATION. AT PARK SCHOOL THEATER, 1500 COMMUNITY DR. (ST-WIDE). CHARLES CHAFFIN, COORD; FINE ARTS GUILD; DUNRAVEN HEIGHTS; ESTES PARK, CO 80517. (#104745-14).

JUNE 11 - 12, '76. COLORADO SQUARE DANCE FESTIVAL. SQUARE DANCING, OLD AND NEW ROUND DANCING CONTRAST. AT

ESTES PARK — CONTINUED

YMCA OF THE ROCKIES. (LOCAL). VERNA NEWMAN, COORD; COLORADO STATE SQUARE DANCE ASSOC; BOX 177; NIWOT, CO 80544. (#200007-77).

JUNE 18 - 20, '76. BOULDER HUNTER-JUMPER SHOW. COMPETITION, LIVE PERFORMANCE AT STANLEY FIELD, OFF COMMUNITY DRIVE. (ST-WIDE). DICK HILLYER, CHMN; HORSE SHOW COMMITTEE; BOX 1356; ESTES PARK, CO 80517. (#104745-7).

JUNE 19, '76. BICENTENNIAL PARADE OF COLORADO COMPOSERS. ONE OF THE NUMEROUS PERFORMANCES, IN VARIOUS REGIONS OF THE STATE, TAKING CONCERTS OF ORIGINAL MUSIC BY COLORADO COMPOSERS TO THE PEOPLE, PART OF A SERIES IN CONJUNCTION WITH THE BICENTENNIAL PARADE OF AMERICAN MUSIC. AT PARADE-MAIN ST, CONCERT-HIGH SCHOOL AUDITORIUM. (LOCAL). RICCARDA E MCQUIE, COORD; COLORADO FEDERATION OF MUSIC CLUBS; 640 GARFIELD ST; DENVER, CO 80206. (#106991-1).

JUNE 19 - SEPT 6, '76. LIVING HISTORY AT THE WILLIAM WHITE CABIN IN ROCKY MOUNTAIN NP. HISTORIAN IN OLD RANGER UNIFORM LEADS HISTORY WALKS SEVERAL TIMES EACH WEEK WITH WALK CULMINATING AT THE SUMMER HOME OF WILLIAM ALLEN WHITE. AT WILLIAM WHITE CABIN. (REGN'L). SUPT ROCKY MOUNTAIN NP; NATIONAL PARK SERVICE; ESTES PARK, CO 80617. (#6727-520).

JUNE 19 - SEPT 6, '76. LIVING HISTORY AT THE HOLZWARTH RANCH IN ROCKY MOUNTAIN NP. A GUIDED TOUR FROM TIMBER CREEK CAMPGROUND TO SITE WHERE PEOPLE DEPICTING EARLY LIFE IN AN ISOLATED MOUNTAIN VALLEY NEAR THE HEADWATERS OF THE COLORADO RIVER. 3 OR 4 TIMES DAILY; FREE TICKETS REQUIRED. AT HOLZWARTH HOMESTEAD ONE MILE SOUTH OF TIMBER CREEK CAMPGROUND. (REGN'L). SUPT, ROCKY MOUNTAIN NP; NATIONAL PARK SERVICE; ESTES PARK, CO 80617. (#6727-521).

JUNE 27 - 30, '76. COLORADO PHILHARMONIC ORCHESTRA CONCERT AT ROCKY MOUNTAIN NP. PERFORMED OUT-OF-DOORS IN SUPERB MOUNTAIN SETTING. PERFORMANCES ON JUNE 27 AND JUNE 30 ONLY. AT 6/27 STILLWATER CAMPGROUND; 6/30 HIDDEN VALLEY. (REGN'L). ROCKY MOUNTAIN NP; NATIONAL PARK SERVICE; ESTES PARK, CO 80517. (#6728-243).

JUNE 30 - JULY 3, '76. ARABIAN HORSE SHOW. COMPETITION, LIVE PERFORMANCE AT STANLEY FIELD, OFF COMMUNITY DRIVE. (ST-WIDE). DICK HILLYER, CHMN; HORSE SHOW COMMITTEE; BOX 1356; ESTES PARK, CO 80517. (#104745-6).

JULY 4, '76. FIREWORKS AT THE LAKE. CEREMONY, EXHIBIT AT LAKE ESTES, ADJACENT TO VILLAGE. (LOCAL). GENE DYKES, COORD; JAYCEES; 500 ELM; ESTES PARK, CO 80517. (#104745-13).

JULY 4, '76. PERFORMANCE BY CONTINENTAL SINGERS. LIVE PERFORMANCE AT PARK SCHOOL AUDITORIUM. (LOCAL). ESTHER ARNOLD, COORD; FIRST BAPTIST & ESTES PARK CENT-BICENT COMMITTEE; BOX 922; ESTES PARK, CO 80517. (#107005-1).

JULY 5 - 7, '76. CARNIVAL ON INDEPENDENCE DAY. CEREMONY, COMPETITION, FESTIVAL AT YMCA GROUNDS AND ADMINISTRATION BUILDING. (LOCAL). DAVID PRICE, COORD; YMCA OF THE ROCKIES; YMCA ADMINISTRATION BLDG; ASSOC CAMP, CO 80511. (#104745-12).

JULY 5 - AUG 21, '76. SUMMER SEMINARS ON HIST GEOGRAPHY OF COLORADO AT ROCKY MTN NP. OCCUPATION AND USE OF LAND BY SUCCESSIVE GROUPS OF PEOPLE IN COLORADO. FOCUSES ON THE ROCKY MOUNTAIN NATIONAL PARK REGION, PRIMARILY THROUGH FIELD OBSERVATION. COLLEGE CREDIT OFFERED. AT MEET PARK HEADQUARTERS TWO MILES WEST ESTES PARK. (REGN'L). ROCKY MOUNTAIN NP; NATIONAL PARK SERVICE; ESTES PARK, CO 80517. (#6726-61).

JULY 8 - 11, '76. MORGAN HORSE SHOW. COMPETITION, LIVE PERFORMANCE AT STANLEY FIELD, OFF COMMUNITY DRIVE. (ST-WIDE). DICK HILLYER, CHMN; HORSE SHOW COMMITTEE; BOX 1356; ESTES PARK, CO 80517. (#104745-5).

JULY 20 - AUG 20, '76. DOROTHY SCOTT EXHIBIT OF ART 'FIFTY YEARS IN ESTES PARK'. EXHIBIT AT MUNICIPAL BUILDING, MACGREGOR LANE AND ELKHORN AVE. (ST-WIDE). DOROTHY SCOTT, COORD; ESTES PARK HISTORICAL SOCIETY; DEVILS GULCH RD; ESTES PARK, CO 80517. (#104745-11).

JULY 21 - 24, '76. ROOFTOP RODEO, 50TH ANNUAL. MATINEE ON JULY 23, 1976 AT 2:00 PM. AT STANLEY FIELD, OFF COMMUNITY DRIVE. (ST-WIDE). DICK HILLYER, CHMN; HORSE SHOW COMMITTEE; BOX 1356; ESTES PARK, CO 80517. (#104745-4).

AUG 6 - 8, '76. APPALOOSA HORSE SHOW. COMPETITION, LIVE PERFORMANCE AT STANLEY FIELD, OFF COMMUNITY DRIVE. (REGN'L). DICK HILLYER, CHMN; HORSE SHOW COMMITTEE; BOX 1356; ESTES PARK, CO 80517. (#104745-3).

AUG 8, '76. DENVER SYMPHONY ORCHESTRA CONCERT. SYMPHONY ORCHESTRA CONCERT PERFORMED OUTDOORS IN SUPERB MOUNTAIN SETTING. AT HIDDEN VALLEY, 10 MI WEST OF ESTES PARK VILLAGE. (REGN'L). CHIEF PARK NATURALIST; NATIONAL PARK SERVICE, ROCKY MOUNTAIN NP; ROCKY MOUNTAIN NP; ESTES PARK, CO 80217. (#6728-609).

AUG 12 - 13, '76. STYLES THROUGH THE YEARS IN ESTES PARK, A DRAMATIC STYLE SHOW. COSTUMED PERSONS ENACT THE HISTORY OF ESTES PARK - INDIANS, TRAPPERS, HOMESTEADERS, EARL OF DUNRAVEN,M AND F O STANLEY; ALSO SQUARE DANCING AND APPROPRIATE MUSIC. AT PARK SCHOOL THEATER, ON COMMUNITY DRIVE. (ST-WIDE). MARGE WOLPERT, COORD; ESTES PARK HISTORICAL SOCIETY; 440 COLUMBINE AVE; ESTES PARK, CO 80517. (#104745-10).

AUG 14 - 15, '76. PAINT HORSE SHOW. COMPETITION, LIVE PERFORMANCE AT STANLEY FIELD, OFF COMMUNITY DRIVE. (ST-WIDE). DICK HILLYER, CHMN; HORSE SHOW COMMITTEE; BOX 1356; ESTES PARK, CO 80517. (#104745-2).

AUG 31, '76. HISTORIC CRAFT EXHIBIT. EXHIBIT, LIVE PERFORMANCE AT PARK HEADQUARTERS, BEAVER MEADOWS. (ST-WIDE). DWIGHT HAMILTON, COORD; ROCKY MOUNTAIN NATIONAL PARK; ESTES PARK, CO 80517. (#104745-9).

SEPT 6, '76. JACKPOT ROPING. COMPETITION, LIVE PERFORMANCE AT STANLEY FIELD, OFF COMMUNITY DRIVE. (ST-WIDE). DICK HILLYER, COORD; HORSE SHOW COMMITTEE; BOX 1356; ESTES PARK, CO 80517. (#104745-1).

SEPT 25, '76. OLD-FASHIONED FESTIVAL AND FAIR. BEARD-GROWING CONTEST & PIE BAKING CONTEST INCLUDED. AT BOND PARK ON ELKHORN AVE. (LOCAL). ALAN MENCHER, COORD; TRAIL-GAZETTE AND CENTENNIAL COMMISSION OF ESTES PARK; BOX 1707; ESTES PARK, CO 80517. (#104745-8).

EVANS

GREENING AND CLEANING OF COLORADO - EVANS. CLEANUP AND TREE PLANTING IN OPEN SPACE AROUND CITY HALL AND THE SURROUNDING BLOCK. (LOCAL). ALBERT R WEINHOLD, CHAIRMAN; EVANS BICENTENNIAL COMMITTEE; 3221 STATE ST; EVANS, CO 80620. (#26364).

PREPARATION AND PUBLICATION OF EVANS CHRONICLE, CO. THE HISTORY FROM THE 1860'S, WITH THE APPEARANCE OF THE RAILROAD, EARLY COLONISTS, WELLS FARGO AND MORE WILL BE INCLUDED IN THE PUBLICATION. (LOCAL). ALBERT R WEINHOLD, COORDINATOR; EVANS BICENTENNIAL COMMITTEE; 3221 STATE ST; EVANS, CO 80620. (#26365).

JULY '76. ANNUAL TOWN PICNIC WITH OLD-FASHIONED GAMES. FESTIVAL. (LOCAL). ALBERT R WEINHOLD, CHMN; TOWN OF EVANS; 3221 STATE ST; EVANS, CO 80620. (#108798-1).

EVERGREEN

CLEARING HOUSE FOR YOUTH EMPLOYMENT-EVERGREEN, CO. STARTING IN CENTENNIAL YEAR, PROVIDE CENTRAL INFORMATION SOURCE FOR JOBS WANTED AND WORK OFFERED, STRESS COMMUNITY CLEANUP AND BEAUTIFICATION. (LOCAL). L W DAVIS, CHAIRMAN; EVERGREEN CENTENNIAL-BICENTENNIAL ASSOCIATION; PO BOX 97; EVERGREEN, CO 80439. (#15266).

COLORADO PHILHARMONIC TOUR - EVERGREEN. A COMBINED TOUR WITH NEW DANCE THEATRE TO 12 WESTERN SLOPE COMMUNIT IES FEATURING MUSIC DANCE PUPPETRY CHILDREN'S CONCERTS AND WORKSHOPS -ALL ON HISTORIC THEMES. (ST-WIDE). WALTER CHARLES, MUSIC DIRECTOR-CONDUCTOR; COLORADO PHILHARMONIC; PO BOX 975; EVERGREEN, CO 80439. (#4465).

EVERGREEN CENTENNIAL BANDSHELL, EVERGREEN, CO. PROVIDE COMMUNITY FACILITY FOR CONCERTS, PLAYS AND OTHER PUBLIC PRESENTATIONS IN OUTDOOR ENVIRONMENT. (LOCAL). L W DAVIS, CHAIRMAN; EVERGREEN CENTENNIAL-BICENTENNIAL ASSOCIATION; PO BOX 97; EVERGREEN, CO 80439. (#15269).

EVERGREEN CENTENNIAL COMMEMORATIVE BOOK, CO. PRESERVE RECORD OF LOCAL AREA CENTENNIAL-BICENTENNIAL ACTIVITIES TO PROMOTE COMMUNITY CONSCIOUSNESS AND UNITY. (LOCAL). L W DAVIS, CHAIRMAN; EVERGREEN CENTENNIAL-BICENTENNIAL ASSOCIATION; PO BOX 97; EVERGREEN, CO 80439. (#15270).

HEADSTART MUSIC MAGIC - PROJ OF EVERGREEN, CO. SPECIAL PROGRAM FOR HEADSTART CENTERS AND ELEMENTARY SCHOOLS THAT FEATURE THE MEDIUM OF MUSIC, PUPPETS AND DANCE WITH EMPHASIS ON CULTURAL AND ETHNIC CONTRIBUTIONS OF BLACKS, CHICANOS & INDIANS. (LOCAL). WALTER CHARLES, DIRECTOR; COLORADO PHILHARMONIC; BOX 975; EVERGREEN, CO 80439. (#14843).

HIWAN HOMESTEAD IN EVERGREEN, CO. RESTORATION AND DEVELOPMENT OF HISTORIC JEFFERSON COUNTY LANDMARK. (LOCAL). L W DAVIS, CHAIRMAN; EVERGREEN CENTENNIAL-BICENTENNIAL ASSOCIATION; PO BOX 97; EVERGREEN, CO 80439. (#15272).

HOMESTEAD HOUSE MODEL IN EVERGREEN, CO. MODEL OF 1866 LOG HOUSE TO BE USED FOR MUSEUM & CENTER FOR LOCAL HISTORY & CRAFT STUDIES; 17 ROOMS, 3 STORIES. (LOCAL). L A BEARDSLEE, CHAIRMAN; JEFFERSON COUNTY COMMISSIONERS & BICENTENNIAL COMMISSION; COURTHOUSE; GOLDEN, CO 80419. (#11610).

JEFFERSON COUNTY, COLO, HOMESTEAD HOUSE. MINOR MODIFICATIONS TO STRUCTURE FOR PUBLIC USE: OUTFIT SIGNIFICANT ROOMS WITH APPROPRIATE FURNITURE, PROVIDE OPERATING PERSONNEL, DEVELOP PROGRAM FOR CONTINUED USE. COORDINATE CCBC WORK FOR COUNTY. (LOCAL). LYNDON A BEARDSLEE, PROJECT CHAIRMAN; BOARD OF COUNTY COMMISSIONERS; JEFFERSON COUNTY COURTHOUSE; GOLDEN, CO 80419. (#4425).

ORAL HISTORY OF LOCAL PIONEER FAMILIES - CO. OBTAIN AND PRESERVE RECORD OF PIONEER PEOPLE OF COMMUNITY OF EVERGREEN. (LOCAL). L W DAVIS, CHAIRMAN; EVERGREEN CENTENNIAL-BICENTENNIAL ASSOCIATION; PO BOX 97; EVERGREEN, CO 80439. (#15267).

PARADES AND PAGEANTS IN EVERGREEN, CO. PARADES AND PAGEANTS TO STRESS HISTORIC AND MODERN THEMES, CUSTOMS, COSTUMES AND MUSIC DURING THE CENTENNIAL. (LOCAL). L W DAVIS, CHAIRMAN; EVERGREEN CENTENNIAL-BICENTENNIAL ASSOCIATION; PO BOX 97; EVERGREEN, CO 80439. (#15271).

VOLUNTARY REFORESTATION - EVERGREEN, CO. COMMUNITY INVOLVEMENT IN THE PRESERVING AND DEVELOPMENT OF OUR NATURAL ENVIRONMENT-EVERGREENS MOUNTAIN AREA. (LOCAL). L W DAVIS, CHAIRMAN; EVERGREEN CENTENNIAL-BICENTENNIAL ASSOCIATION; PO BOX 97; EVERGREEN, CO 80439. (#15268).

APR 1 - DEC 31, '76. 4 SMITHSONIAN EXHIBITS AT HIWAN HOMESTEAD MUSEUM. EXHIBIT AT JEFFERSON COUNTY MUSEUM - HIWAN HOMESTEAD. (LOCAL). CONNIE FAHNESTOCK, DIR; JEFFERSON COUNTY CENTENNIAL-BICENTENNIAL COMMISSION; RT 3 BOX 2C; EVERGREEN, CO 80439. (#108631-1).

AUG 1, '76. SERIES OF CENTENNIAL MUSICAL & DRAMA CONCERTS. 'POPS AND PATRIOTIC': AN AFTERNOON WITH WALTER CHARLES AND THE COLORADO PHILHARMONIC ORCHESTRA. (LOCAL). JOHN FELLOWS, PRES; EVERGREEN CENTENNIAL-BICENTENNIAL ASSOCIATION; PO BOX 2541; EVERGREEN, CO 80439. (#102324-1).

SEPT 25 - OCT 10, '76. 'PIRATES OF PENZANCE'. LIVE PERFORMANCE. (LOCAL). RUTH SEEBER, COORDINATOR; THE EVERGREEN CHORALE; BOX 440G; EVERGREEN, CO 80439. (#108792-1).

FAIRPLAY

'GREENING AND CLEANING COLORADO' - FAIRPLAY. CLEANUP PROJECT FOR THE ENTIRE TOWN. (LOCAL). LOLA M PIKE, CHAIRPERSON; TOWN OF FAIRPLAY; PO BOX 315; FAIRPLAY, CO 80440. (#26217).

SOUTH PARK CITY MUSEUM - FAIRPLAY, CO. A PROJECT TO CONTINUE THE RESTORATION/PRESERVATION OF SOUTH PARK CITY MUSEUM. TO INCLUDE ERECTING OF PLEXIGLASS PARTITIONS, RESTORING COLLECTIONS AND MAKING NEEDED REPAIRS. (LOCAL). CAROL DAVIS, MANAGER; SOUTH PARK HISTORICAL FOUNDATION; PO BOX 460; FAIRPLAY, CO 80440. (#4383). **ARBA GRANTEE.**

MAY 15 - OCT 15, '76. SOUTH PARK CITY TOUR OF RESTORED MINING TOWN. FACILITY IS A COMPLEX OF 29 BUILDINGS SOME ON THEIR ORIGINAL SITES OTHERS MOVED FROM SURROUNDING GHOST TOWNS. EACH BUILDING HOUSES AN EXHIBIT REPRESENTING PHASES OF LIFE IN A WESTERN MINING TOWN DURING THE 1860'S. MUSEUM IS OPEN TO PUBLIC DAILY BETWEEN MAY 15 & OCT 15. AT CORNER 4TH AND FRONT STS. (LOCAL). CAROL DAVIS, MGR; SOUTH PARK HISTORICAL FOUNDATION INC; BOX 460; FAIRPLAY, CO 80440. (#102817-1).

JULY 4, '76. SENIOR CITIZENS 1976. ICE CREAM SOCIAL TO HONOR SENIOR CITIZENS; THEY WILL ALSO BE IN ANNUAL PARADE. (LOCAL). LOLA M PIKE; SENIOR CITIZENS COMMITTEE; PO BOX 315; FAIRPLAY, CO 80440. (#108626-1).

JULY 25, '76. RELIVING THE PAST - HISTORICAL PLAY. LIVE PERFORMANCE. (LOCAL). LOLA M PIKE, COORDINATOR; TOWN OF FAIRPLAY; PO BOX 315; FAIRPLAY, CO 80440. (#108699-1).

FIRESTONE

CREATE YOUR OWN PROJECT - FIRESTONE, CO. A BICENTENNIAL PARK WILL BE BUILT DURING THE SUMMER OF '76. (LOCAL). MARGARET MACCLOUD, CHAIRPERSON; FIRESTONE BICENTENNIAL COMMITTEE; BOX 100; FIRESTONE, CO 80520. (#26224).

GREENING AND CLEANING COLORADO, FIRESTONE. SUMMER 1976, GENERAL CLEANUP OF TOWN AND LANDSCAPE IN NEW PARK. (LOCAL). MARGARET MACCLOUD, CHAIRPERSON; FIRESTONE BICENTENNIAL COMMITTEE; BOX 100; FIRESTONE, CO 80520. (#26223).

NEW BALLPARK - FIRESTONE, CO. A NEW BALLPARK WILL BE CONSTRUCTED. (LOCAL). MARGARET MCCLOUD, CHAIRPERSON; FIRESTONE BICENTENNIAL COMMITTEE; BOX 100; FIRESTONE, CO 80520. (#26225).

FLAGLER

BROCHURE ON HISTORICAL HIGHLIGHTS OF FLAGLER, CO. HISTORICAL HIGHLIGHTS OF THE FLAGLER AREA WILL BE PUBLISHED IN A BROCHURE-GUIDE. (LOCAL). KENNETH REYHER, PROJ COORDINATOR; FLAGLER BICENTENNIAL COMMITTEE; FLAGLER, CO 80815. (#21533).

COLORADO CHRONICLES, FLAGLER. A HISTORY OF THE FLAGLER AREA IS BEING COMPLETED BY HIGH SCHOOL STUDENTS AND THEIR HISTORY TEACHER FOR PUBLICATION. (LOCAL). TED RILLAHAN, TOWN CLERK; HIGH SCHOOL; FLAGLER, CO 80815. (#26216).

CREATE YOUR OWN PROJECT, FLAGLER, CO. A COMMUNITY BULLETIN BOARD WILL BE PLACED IN THE WINDOW OF FLAGLER NEWSPAPER OFFICE TO DISPLAY ANNOUNCEMENTS AND NOTICES OF INTEREST TO THE LOCAL PEOPLE. FLAGLER SCHOOL SHOP WILL CONSTRUCT BULLETIN BOARD. (LOCAL). TED RILLAHAN, TOWN CLERK; TOWN OF FLAGLER; FLAGLER, CO 80815. (#26215).

GREENING & CLEANING COLORADO - FLAGLER. CLEANUP OF TOPPLED BUILDINGS AND JUNK AREAS; LITTER WILL ALSO BE PICKED UP. (LOCAL). TED RILLAHAN, TOWN CLERK; TOWN OF FLAGLER; FLAGLER, CO 80815. (#26214).

JUNE 17 - 19, '76. BICENTENNIAL CELEBRATION. FESTIVITES INCLUDE A CHAUTAUQUA, ART EXHIBIT, PARADE AND BARBECUE. (LOCAL). HARVEY K GRIFFITH, CHMN; FLAGLER LIONS CLUB; PO BOX Q; FLAGLER, CO 80815. (#105411-2).

JUNE 18 - 19, '76. ARTS FESTIVAL. FESTIVAL, EXHIBIT. (LOCAL). TED RILLAHAN, COORD; TOWN OF FLAGLER; FLAGLER, CO 80815. (#200007-179).

FLAGLER—CONTINUED

JULY 4, '76. ARTS FESTIVAL. FESTIVAL. (LOCAL). TED RILLAHAN, COORD; FLAGLER ARTS FESTIVAL COMMITTEE; FLAGLER, CO 80815. (#108627-1).

JULY 4, '76. COMMUNITY-WIDE WORSHIP SERVICE. CEREMONY. (LOCAL). HARVEY K GRIFFITH, CHMN; FLAGLER BICENTENNIAL COMMITTEE; PO BOX Q; FLAGLER, CO 80815. (#105411-1).

JULY 4, '76. HIGH PLAINS FOURTH OF JULY BICENTENNIAL CELEBRATION. FESTIVAL, PARADE, EXHIBIT AT TARADO MUSEUM, SOUTH OF ARRIBA, CO. (LOCAL). REV HARVEY GRIFFITH, CHMN; FLAGLER CENTENNIAL-BICENTENNIAL COMMITTEE; FLAGLER, CO 80815. (#107586-1).

FLEMING

MUSEUM GROUNDS IMPROVEMENT - FLEMING, CO. A FENCE WILL BE PLACED AROUND THE GROUNDS. (LOCAL). HON LESTER B HARMS, MAYOR; TOWN OF FLEMING; BOX 466; FLEMING, CO 80728. (#26231).

AUG 1, '76. COMMUNITY PICNIC. FESTIVAL. (LOCAL). LESTER B HARMS, CHAIRMAN; TOWN OF FLEMING; BOX 466; FLEMING, CO 80728. (#108955-8).

SEPT 18, '76. FLEMING FESTIVAL - 'FORGING COLORADO'S 2ND CENTURY'. FESTIVAL, PARADE. (LOCAL). LESTER B HARMS, COORD; FLEMING FESTIVAL COMMITTEE; BOX 466; FLEMING, CO 80728. (#108788-1).

FLORENCE

MAR 19 - 21, '76. MUSICAL - 'LI'L ABNER'. LIVE PERFORMANCE AT RIALTO THEATRE, 209 W MAIN ST. (LOCAL). KEN LIVINGSTON, V-PRES; FLORENCE LIONS CLUB; 105 W MAIN ST; FLORENCE, CO 81226. (#200007-83).

MAY 7 - 16, '76. 'THE FIREMAN'S FLAME' - A MELODRAMA WITH MUSIC. SUNDAY PERFORMANCE AT 2:30 PM. AT THE RIALTO THEATRE, 209 W MAIN ST. (LOCAL). KEN LIVINGSTON, VICE CHMN; THE RED BRICK PLAYERS; 105 W MAIN ST; FLORENCE, CO 81226. (#106979-1).

JULY 4, '76. CENTENNIAL FIREWORKS. DAY'S ACTIVITIES BEGIN WITH A STREET PARADE, PROGRAM AT THE PIONEER CITY PARK AND THEN THE FIREWORKS IN THE EVENING. (LOCAL). DARRELL L LINDSEY; COMMITTEE FOR CENTENNIAL FIREWORKS; 605 W 5TH ST; FLORENCE, CO 81226. (#108625-1).

JULY 4, '76. OLD-FASHIONED CELEBRATION. FESTIVAL, PARADE. (LOCAL). BERNICE LANCASTER, CHMN; FLORENCE BICENTENNIAL COMMITTEE; 605 W 5TH ST; FLORENCE, CO 81226. (#107577-1).

AUG 6 - 8, '76. 'HUCKLEBERRY FINN' - CHILDREN'S PLAY. SUNDAY PERFORMANCE AT 2:30 PM. AT THE RIALTO THEATRE, 209 W MAIN ST. (LOCAL). KEN LIVINGSTON, VICE CHMN; THE RED BRICK PLAYERS; 105 W MAIN ST; FLORENCE, CO 81226. (#106979-2).

SEPT 3 - 12, '76. 'SHOW BOAT' - MUSICAL. SUNDAY PERFORMANCE AT 2:30 PM. AT THE RIALTO THEATRE, 209 W MAIN ST. (LOCAL). KEN LIVINGSTON, VICE CHMN; THE RED BRICK PLAYERS; 105 W MAIN ST; FLORENCE, CO 81226. (#106979-4).

SEPT 11, '76. PIONEER DAY CELEBRATION. STREET PARADE AND FREE LUNCH TO ALL PIONEERS WHO HAVE LIVED IN COLORADO 50 YEARS OR MORE. AT PIONEER PARK. (LOCAL). BERNICE LANCASTER, COORD; PIONEER DAY CELEBRATION COMMITTEE; 516 E 3RD STREET; FLORENCE, CO 81226. (#108787-1).

NOV 12 - 20, '76. '1776-1976' - COMEDY & MUSICAL REVUE. SUNDAY PERFORMANCE AT 2:30 PM. AT THE RIALTO THEATRE, 209 W MAIN ST. (LOCAL). KEN LIVINGSTON, VICE CHMN; THE RED BRICK PLAYERS; 105 W MAIN ST; FLORENCE, CO 81226. (#106979-3).

FLORISSANT

JUNE 16 - SEPT 2, '75. 19TH CENTURY MOUNTAIN LIFE AT FLORISSANT FOSSIL BEDS NM. ALSO SUMMER 1976. COSTUMED HISTORIANS PROVIDE A VIGNETTE OF TYPICAL 19TH CENTURY MOUNTAIN FRONTIER LIFE ON AN HISTORIC 1870 HOMESTEAD. THIS PROGRAM IS TENTATIVE. (REGN'L). SUPT FLORISSANT FOSSIL BD; NATIONAL PARK SERVICE; P.O. BOX 185; FLORISSANT, CO 80816. (#6727-32).

JUNE 2 - AUG 28, '76. 19TH CENTURY MOUNTAIN LIFE AT FLORISSANT FOSSIL BEDS NM. PARK INTERPRETERS DEMONSTRATE AND EXPLAIN ARCHITECTURE AND LIVING CONDITIONS IN THE MOUNTAIN WEST IN THE 1880'S. (REGN'L). FLORISSANT FOSSIL BD; NATIONAL PARK SERVICE; P.O. BOX 185; FLORISSANT, CO 80816. (#6727-532).

FORT CARSON

'THE ARMY WIFE IN HISTORY' IN FORT CARSON, CO. A MOBILE NARRATED AND GRAPHIC PRESENTATION FEATURING HISTORICAL COSTUMES, HOMEMAKING AND HOUSEHOLD ITEMS USED BY 'TYPICAL' ARMY WIVES. THE MOBILE IS FOR STATEWIDE USE. (ST-WIDE). MRS SALLY BUSSEY, PRES; OFFICERS' WIVES CLUB; QTRS 22; FORT CARSON, CO 80913. (#10294).

CULTURAL ARTS FESTIVAL IN COLORADO. A 4-DAY FESTIVAL CELEBRATING THE HISTORY, ART, MUSIC AND CULTURAL CONTRIBUTIONS OF ALL AMERICAN ETHNIC GROUPS. IT WILL FEATURE EDUCATIONAL PROGRAM, INDIAN DANCE AND MEXICAN, SPANISH AND BLACK ART. (REGN'L). MAJOR KEN DATE, DIR OF HUMAN RESOURCES; U S ARMY; HQ 4TH INF DIV (M); FT CARSON, CO 80913. (#10289).

FORT CARSON SPEAKERS BUREAU IN COLORADO. 'ESTAB' SPEAKERS BUREAU WILL PROVIDE SPEAKERS FOR CIVIC SERVICES, SOCIAL FUNCTIONS AND FRATERNAL ORGANIZATIONS THROUGHOUT THE REGION. (ST-WIDE). CPT DIANE PAUL; PUBLIC AFFAIRS OFFICE; HQ 4TH INF DIV; FORT CARSON, CO 80913. (#10288).

'HAPPINESS IS A BIRTHDAY' IN FT CARSON, COLORADO. A FLOAT WILL BE ENTERED IN THE COLORADO SPRINGS 'PIKES PEAK OR BUST BY '76' PAGEANT PARADE OF THE ROCKIES, IT WILL HAVE A BIRTHDAY CAKE COMMEMORATING BICENTENNIAL OF THE ARMY AND NATION. (LOCAL). CPT MCGREGOR, DIRECTOR, CIVIL AFFAIRS; UNITED STATES ARMY; HQ 4TH INF DIV (M); FORT CARSON, CO 80913. (#10293).

'HELPING HANDS TO SENIOR CITIZENS' -FT COLLINS, CO. IN COORDINATION WITH COLORADO SPRINGS, SILVER KEY CITIZENS WILL REFURBISH ALBANY HALL, THE SENIOR CITIZEN'S RESIDENCE. (LOCAL). MRS SALLY BUSSEY, PRESIDENT; OFFICERS' WIVES CLUB; QUARTERS 22; FORT CARSON, CO 80913. (#9963).

'HELPING HANDS TO THOSE IN WHEEL CHAIRS' -COLORADO. CONSTRUCTION OF WHEEL CHAIR RAMPS AT ALL PUBLIC BUILDINGS IN FORT CARSON. (LOCAL). MAJOR SCHUMANN, CHAIRMAN; HORIZONS 76 COMMITTEE, FT CARSON BICENT COMMISSION; HQ, 4TH INFANTRY DIV (M); FORT CARSON, CO 80913. (#9965).

HISTORICAL MARKERS IN FORT CARSON, COLORADO. ERECT SIGNS TO COMMEMORATE CIVILIAN FOUNDERS OF CAMP CARSON, INDIAN TRIBES AND PIONEERS MEDAL OF HONOR RECIPIENTS. PAST MILITARY COMMANDERS AND HISTORICAL SITES WILL ALSO BE MARKED. (ST-WIDE). LTC HALL, DIRECTOR; DIRECTOR OF FACILITIES AND ENGINEERING; HQ 4TH INF DIV (M); FORT CARSON, CO 80913. (#10286).

RESTORE ON-POST HISTORICAL GRAVESITES, COLORADO. RESTORE FENCE AND BEAUTIFY SEVEN PIONEER AND INDIAN GRAVESITES WITHIN THE BOUNDARIES OF FORT CARSON. (ST-WIDE). LTC HALL, DIRECTOR; DIRECTOR OF FACILITIES AND ENGINEERING; HQ 4TH INF DIV (M); FORT CARSON, CO 80913. (#10287).

'SUNDAY-IN-THE-PARK CONCERTS' AT FORT CARSON, CO. TWICE-MONTHLY OUTDOOR CONCERTS PRESENTED FROM A GAY NINETIES GAZEBO FEATURING VARIOUS REGIONAL MUSIC GROUPS AND VARIOUS TYPES OF MUSIC; OPEN TO THE PUBLIC & HELD AT THE CHEYENNE SHADOWS SERVICE CLUB. (REGN'L). ROSEMARY ECKLOR, DIR CHEYENNE CLUB; RECREATION SERVICES OFFICE, DPCA; HQ 4TH INF DIV (M); FT CARSON, CO 80913. (#10292).

'1775', NEWSPAPER IN COLORADO. A SPECIAL 16-ISSUE HISTORICAL SUPPLEMENT TO 'THE MOUNTAINEER' POST NEWSPAPER IN FORT CARSON, COLORADO. (REGN'L). IRENE POSNER, COORDINATOR; PUBLIC AFFAIRS OFFICE, COMMAND INFORMATION; HQ 4TH INF DIV (M); FT CARSON, CO 80913. (#10290).

APR 1, '75 - CONTINUING . 'ARMY TOURS THROUGH HISTORY'. PUBLIC TOURS THROUGH THE POST MUSEUM AND OTHER POST FACILITIES FEATURING DISPLAYS AND EXPLANATIONS OF OUR NATIONAL MILITARY PAST. ALSO: FILM/SLIDES. AT FC POST MUSEUM & VISITORS CENTER, O'CONNER & BARKLEY. (ST-WIDE). CPT DIANE PAUL; PUBLIC AFFAIRS OFFICE, POST VISITOR CENTER AND MUSEUM; HQ 4TH INF DIV (M); FT CARSON, CO 80913. (#10291-1).

MAY 26 - AUG 9, '75. 'SUNDAY-IN-THE-PARK CONCERTS'. TWICE-.ZONTHY OUTDOOR CONCERTS PRESENTED FROM A GAY NINETIES TWICE-MONTHLY OUTDOOR CONCERTS PRESENTED FROM A GAY NINETIES GAZEBO TYPES OF MUSIC OPEN TO THE PUBLIC. OPEN TO THE PUBLIC & HELD AT THE CHEYENNE SHADOWS SERVICE CLUB. AT CHEYENNE SHADOWS SERVICE CLUB. (LOCAL). ROSEMARY ECKLOR; RECREATION SERVICES OFFICE, DPCA; HQ 4TH INF DIV (M); FT CARSON, CO 80913. (#10292-501).

AUG 20 - 23, '75. CULTURAL ARTS FESTIVAL. A 4-DAY FESTIVAL CELEBRATING THE HISTORY, ART, MUSIC AND CULTURAL CONTRIBUTIONS OF ALL AMERICAN ETHNIC GROUPS. IT WILL FEATURE EDUCATIONAL PROGRAM, INDIAN DANCE AND MEXICAN, SPANISH AND BLACK ART. (REGN'L). MAJOR KEN DATE; U S ARMY; HQ 4TH INF DIV (M); FT CARSON, CO 80913. (#10289-501).

FORT COLLINS

AVERY HOUSE COOKBOOK IN FT COLLINS, CO. PROJECT IS A CENTENNIAL COOKBOOK WITH OLD FAMILY RECIPES; PROCEEDS FROM BOOK WILL GO TOWARD THE RESTORATION OF HISTORIC AVERY HOUSE. (ST-WIDE). JUNE NEWTON BENNETT, PROJ CHAIRPERSON; DESIGNING TOMMOROW TODAY; 1513 LAKESIDE AVE; FORT COLLINS, CO 80521. (#13916). **ARBA GRANTEE.**

AVERY HOUSE HISTORICAL LANDMARK, FORT COLLINS, CO. EXTERIOR RESTORATION AND STABILIZATION AND RENOVATION OF THE ELECTRICAL PLUMBING AND HEATING SYSTEMS. (ST-WIDE). JUNE BENNETT, PROJ DIRECTOR; POUDRE LANDMARKS FOUNDATION; 1513 LAKESIDE AVE; FORT COLLINS, CO 80521. (#19502).

BUSINESS FOR BEAUTY PROJ OF FORT COLLINS, COLORADO. PROGRAM FOR LOCAL COMMUNITIES TO IMPROVE THE APPEARANCE OF THEIR ESTABLISHMENTS. (ST-WIDE). D V HOLMBERG, CHAIRMAN; GENERAL FEDERATION OF WOMEN'S CLUB; 9025 SOUTH CLAREMONT; CHICAGO, IL 60620. (#4405).

CHILDREN'S ART FESTIVAL. FESTIVAL. (LOCAL). KARL CARSON, CHAIRPERSON; DESIGNING TOMORROW TODAY; 215 S MELDRUM; FORT COLLINS, CO 80522. (#108790-5).

COLORADO ARTIST OUTREACH - MUSICAL PROJECT. TO EXTENT AND ENRICH PUBLIC APPRECIATION FOR THE MUSICAL ARTS. (ST-WIDE). DR ROBERT GARRETSON, SUPERVISOR; COLORADO STATE UNIV; CORNER SHIELDS & PROSPECT STS; FT COLLINS, CO 80521. (#2860).

COLORADO 4-H COMMUNITY PRIDE PROGRAM. 4-H MEMBERS PROMOTE YOUTH AND ADULT INVOLVEMENT WITH OTHER ORGANIZATIONS IN COMMUNITY DEVELOPMENT EFFORTS RELATED TO THE NEEDS OF COLORADO COMMUNITIES. (ST-WIDE). ARTHUR B CARLSON, RESOURCE DIRECTOR; COLORADO 4-H FOUNDATION; 131 AYLESWORTH HALL, CSU; FT COLLINS, CO 80523. (#6799).

COSTUME BALL. FESTIVAL. (LOCAL). KARL CARSON, CHAIRPERSON; DESIGNING TOMORROW TODAY; 215 S MELDRUM; FORT COLLINS, CO 80522. (#108790-7).

FIRE HYDRANT PAINTING - FORT COLLINS, CO. FIRE HYDRANTS WILL BE PAINTED RED, WHITE & BLUE. (LOCAL). KARL CARSON, CHAIRPERSON; DESIGNING TOMORROW TODAY; 215 S MELDRUM; FORT COLLINS, CO 80522. (#26259).

FORT COLLINS YESTERDAYS - CO. THIS BOOK IS A RICHLY ILLUSTRATED HISTORY OF FORT COLLINS FROM PREARMY POST DAYS TO CURRENT TIMES. THE 200 ILLUSTRATIONS INCLUDE RARE PHOTOS. SOME MATERIAL WAS DRAWN FROM INTERVIEWS WITH OLD-TIMERS. (LOCAL). EVADENE B SWANSON, PROJ DIRECTOR; CITY OF FORT COLLINS; 620 MATHEWS, NO 115; FORT COLLINS, CO 80521. (#16249).

FORT COLLINS, COLORADO, HISTORICAL PAGEANT. COMMUNITY COMMEMORATIVE PAGEANT FOCUSING ON AREA HISTORY FOR THE CENTENNIAL OF COLORADO & THE BICENTENNIAL OF THE NATION. (LOCAL). DR KARL CARLSON, CHAIRPERSON; DESIGNING TOMORROW TODAY; 225 S MELDRUM, PO BOX D; FT COLLINS, CO 80522. (#2941).

FORT COLLINS, CO - ARTS CENTER. AUDITORIUM TO SEAT 1200. ART CENTER TO CREATE GALLERY & CLASS AREA FOR COMMUNITY. (LOCAL). ROMERTA F COOK, EXEC DIRECTOR; DESIGNING TOMORROW TODAY; 225 S MELDRUM; FORT COLLINS, CO 80521. (#3552).

FT COLLINS, CO, ARBORETUM. VARIETY OF TREES AND SHRUBS GROWN FOR EXHIBITION AND STUDY IN A SECTION OF MARTINEZ PARK. (LOCAL). DR KARL CARSON, CHAIRMAN; CENTENNIAL-BICENTENNIAL COUNCIL OF DESIGNING TOMORROW, TODAY; 225 S MELDRUM; FT COLLINS, CO 80521. (#24615).

GREEN BELT - OPEN SPACE PROJ OF FT COLLINS, COLO. PLANS TO ACQUIRE & DEVELOP AN OPEN GREEN BELT FOR BEAUTIFICATION & ENJOYMENT OF COMMUNITY. (LOCAL). DR KARL CARSON, CHAIRPERSON; DESIGNING TOMORROW TODAY; 225 S MELDRUM, PO BOX D; FT COLLINS, CO 80522. (#2944).

HISTORICAL MARKER PROJECT - FORT COLLINS, CO. PLACE PERMANENT MARKERS ON HISTORIC BUILDINGS AND SITES. (LOCAL). NONA THAYER, EXEC DIRECTOR; DESIGNING TOMORROW TODAY; 225 S MELDRUM, BOX D; FORT COLLINS, CO 80522. (#26248).

'MOUNTAIN RIVER' BY RICHARD FARQUAR - CO. A COLLECTION OF POEMS & DRAWINGS ABOUT THE NORTHERN COLORADO MOUNTAINS & THE CACHE LA POUDRE RIVER. (ST-WIDE). KARL E CARSON, PROJ COORDINATOR; DESIGNING TOMORROW TODAY; 225 S MELDRUM; FORT COLLINS, CO 80521. (#7726).

NEIGHBORHOOD ROUNDUPS. NEIGHBORHOOD GET TOGETHERS FOR A PICNIC, BRUNCH AND BOX SOCIAL. (LOCAL). NONA THAYER, EXEC DIR; DESIGNING TOMORROW TODAY; 225 S MELDRUM, BOX D; FORT COLLINS, CO 80522. (#108790-1).

POUDRE VALLEY, COLORADO, HISTORICAL TRAIL. BUILD TRAIL ALONG POUDRE RIVER TO TIE IN WITH OTHER TRAILS & HISTORICAL LANDMARKS. (LOCAL). DR KARL CARSON, CHAIRPERSON; DESIGNING TOMORROW TODAY; 225 S MELDRUM, PO BOX D; FT COLLINS, CO 80522. (#2942).

SCHOOL AWARDS. AWARD. (LOCAL). KARL CARSON, CHAIRPERSON; DESIGNING TOMORROW TODAY; 215 S MELDRUM; FORT COLLINS, CO 80522. (#108790-4).

TIME CAPSULE DEDICATION. CEREMONY. (LOCAL). KARL CARSON, CHAIRPERSON; DESIGNING TOMORROW TODAY; 215 S MELDRUM; FORT COLLINS, CO 80522. (#108790-6).

'TRAIN OF THOUGHT' - TRAVELLING CLASSROOM IN COLO. HAVE A TRAIN TRAVEL THROUGH COLORADO WITH INSTUCTORS & HELPERS FOR CLASSES & SEMINARS FOR STUDENTS THRUOUT THE STATE. (ST-WIDE). SARA FRAZIER, DIRECTOR; POUDRE R-1 SCHOOL DISTRICT OF FORT COLLINS; 2407 LA PORTE AVE; FT COLLINS, CO 80521. (#4178).

TREE PLANTING PROGRAM - FT COLLINS, CO. DISEASED ELM TREES WILL BE REPLACED TO BEAUTIFY NEW SUBDIVISIONS. (LOCAL). DR CARL E CARSON, PROJ DIRECTOR; DESIGNING TOMORROW TODAY; 225 MELDRUM, PO BOX D; FT COLLINS, CO 80522. (#14840).

JUNE 14 - 15, '75. FREEDOM SQUARE-A PARK-IN-A-DAY, WORK DAY AND DEDICATION CEREMONY. WORK DAY JUNE 14; PICNIC, DEDICATION JUNE 15. AT NORTH SHIELDS AND VINE STREET. (LOCAL). DESIGNING TOMORROW TODAY; HORIZONS COMMITTEE AND FORT COLLINS JUNIOR CHAMBER OF COMMERCE; 225 SOUTH MELDRUM BOX D; FORT COLLINS, CO 80522. (#50266-1).

JULY 4, '75. COLORADO ARTS FESTIVAL - FIRST TIME HELD OUTSIDE ASPEN. STATEWIDE ARTS FESTIVAL WILL LAUNCH CITY CENTENNIAL-BICENTENNIAL CELEBRATION. (LOCAL). ROMERTA F COOK; DESIGNING TOMORROW TODAY; 225 S MELDRUM; FORT COLLINS, CO 80521. (#3552-501).

JULY 12 - 24, '75. 'FROM THE LAND OF HANGING GRAPES' - PAGEANT OF PONTOTOC COUNTY. FAIR, EXHIBIT AT NEW ART BUILDING COLORADO STATE UNIVERSITY. (LOCAL). DESIGNING

FORT COLLINS — CONTINUED

TOMORROW TODAY; CASA QUASITA CHAPTER OF QUESTERS AND CSV ART DEPARTMENT; 225 SOUTH MELDRUM BOX D; FORT COLLINS, CO 80522. (#50266-3).

JULY 17 - 20, '75. COLORADO PERFORMING ARTS FESTIVAL. JULY 17TH, 18TH, 19TH, 10:00AM-10:00PM; JULY 20TH, 12:00 NOON TO 10:00PM. AT FORT COLLINS HIGH SCHOOL, PARK 1400 REMINGTON. (ST-WIDE). DESIGNING TOMORROW TODAY; FESTIVALS COMMITTEE; 225 SOUTH MELDRUM BOX D; FORT COLLINS, CO 80522. (#2943-1).

FEB 10, '76. BOY SCOUT BLUE AND GOLD BANQUETS. FESTIVAL AT O'DEA SCHOOL GYM. (LOCAL). SANDY COX, CHAIRMAN; O'DEA SCHOOL PTA; 2931 ALAMO ST; FT COLLINS, CO 80521. (#104656-3).

FEB 29, '76. FORT COLLINS SYMPHONY 'STAR SPANGLED SEASON'. LIVE PERFORMANCE AT POUDRE HIGH SCHOOL. (LOCAL). WIL SCHWARTZ, DIRECTOR; FORT COLLINS SYMPHONY; 1117 ROBERTSON ST; FT COLLINS, CO 80521. (#104656-5).

APR 25, '76. FORT COLLINS SYMPHONY 'STAR SPANGLED SEASON'. LIVE PERFORMANCE AT POUDRE HIGH SCHOOL. (LOCAL). WIL SCHWARTZ, DIRECTOR; FORT COLLINS SYMPHONY; 1117 ROBERTSON ST; FT COLLINS, CO 80521. (#104656-4).

MAY 9, '76. BALLET FOLKLORICO NETZAHUALCOYOTL TOUR. LIVE PERFORMANCE AT 326 N WITCOM. (LOCAL). CHICO MARTINEZ, COORD; CHICANO YOUTH ORGANIZATION; 145 2ND ST; FORT COLLINS, CO 80522. (#200007-85).

JUNE 14, '76. FLAG DAY PARADE AND CEREMONY. IF JUNE 14 IS NOT A LEGAL HOLIDAY THE PARADE WILL TAKE PLACE ON JUNE 12. AT 140 E OAK ST. (LOCAL). STUART CASE, CHAIRMAN; ELKS LODGE NO 804; 140 E OAK ST; FT COLLINS, CO 80521. (#104656-2).

JUNE 24, '76. BICENTENNIAL PARADE OF COLORADO MUSIC. CONCERT OF ORIGINAL MUSIC BY COLORADO COMPOSERS, AS PART OF A SERIES IN CONJUNCTION WITH THE BICENTENNIAL PARADE OF AMERICAN MUSIC. AT COLORADO STATE UNIV - MUSIC BUILDING AUDITORIUM. (LOCAL). RICCARDA F MCQUIE, COORD; COLORADO FEDERATION OF MUSIC CLUBS; 640 GARFIELD ST; DENVER, CO 80206. (#106619-1).

JUNE 26, '76. DRUMS ALONG THE ROCKIES. LIVE PERFORMANCE AT FRENCH FIELD. (LOCAL). NONA THAYER, EXEC DIR; DESIGNING TOMORROW TODAY; 225 S MELDRUM, BOX D; FORT COLLINS, CO 80522. (#200007-86).

JUNE 28 - JULY 3, '76. 1976 NATL EXPLORER BICENTENNIAL OLYMPICS. COMPETITION. (NAT'L). ROBERT GLEN, DIRECTOR; NATL COUNCIL OF THE BOY SCOUTS OF AMERICA; RTS 1 & 130; N BRUNSWICK, NJ 08902. (#14018-1).

JULY 3, '76. ARTS X 5. FESTIVAL, LIVE PERFORMANCE AT CITY PARK. (LOCAL). MIMS HARRIS, COORD; FORT COLLINS ARTS AND HUMANITY COUNCIL; 1315 KIRKWOOD DR #903; FORT COLLINS, CO 80521. (#108628-3).

JULY 4, '76. ARBORETUM DEDICATION. THE COMPLETION OF A 2 YEAR PLANTING EFFORT. INCLUDING A VARIETY OF TREES & SHRUBS FOR EXHIBITION AND STUDY IN MARTINEZ PARK. AT MARTINEZ PARK, NORTH OF CHERRY AND MASON STS. (LOCAL). CARL JORGENSEN, CHAIRMAN; FORESTRY DEPT CITY OF FT COLLINS AND CBC COUNCIL OF FT COLLINS; 1445 WHEOBEE ST; FT COLLINS, CO 80521. (#104656-6).

JULY 4, '76. DAY IN THE PARK. FESTIVAL AT CITY PARK. (LOCAL). DR KARL CARSON; FORT COLLINS PARKS & RECREATION DEPT; 225 S MELDRUM BOX D; FORT COLLINS, CO 80522. (#108628-1).

JULY 4, '76. FOURTH OF JULY PARADE FEATURING ANTIQUE CARS. PARADE. (LOCAL). WILLIAM SCHOFFTER, CHMN; JAYCEES; 2301 STANFORD; FT COLLINS, CO 80521. (#104656-1).

JULY 4, '76. GAY 90'S PICNIC. FESTIVAL, LIVE PERFORMANCE. (LOCAL). NONA THAYER, CHAIRMAN; PARKS AND RECREATION, ASSISTANT UNITED BANK, COLUMBIA FEDERAL; 225 S MELDRUM, PO BOX D; FORT COLLINS, CO 80521. (#107578-1).

JULY 4, '76. JULY 4TH FIREWORKS. FESTIVAL AT CITY PARK. (LOCAL). DR KARL CARSON; FORT COLLINS CENT-BICENT COUNCIL & KNIGHTS OF THE ROUNDTABLE CLUB; 225 S MELDRUM BOX D; FORT COLLINS, CO 80522. (#108628-2).

JULY 30 - AUG 2, '76. OUTDOOR HISTORICAL DRAMA. THE OUTDOOR HISTORICAL DRAMA WITH A CAST OF 500 PEOPLE WILL DEPICT THE PAST 100 YEAR HISTORY OF FORT COLLINS AND LARIMER COUNTY. AT ROCKY MOUNTAIN HS STADIUM, 1300 W SWALLOW RD. (LOCAL). JOSEPH T NEWLIN, CHMN; FORT COLLINS CENTENNIAL-BICENTENNIAL COUNCIL; 3212 N SHIELDS ST; FORT COLLINS, CO 80521. (#107014-1).

AUG 27 - 28, '76. FARMERS MARKET. EXHIBIT, FAIR. (LOCAL). FRED KAEHLER, COORDINATOR; DESIGNING TOMORROW TODAY; 1615 WHEDBER; FORT COLLINS, CO 80521. (#108790-8).

OCT 24, '76. FORT COLLINS PUBLIC LIBRARY DEDICATION CEREMONY. BUILD NEW LIBRARY TO REPLACE THE EXISTING ONE. WILL HOUSE FORT COLLINS' HISTORIC ARCHIVES. AT FORT COLLINS PUBLIC LIBRARY. (LOCAL). DESIGNING TOMORROW TODAY; CITY COUNCIL OF FORT COLLINS; 225 SOUTH MELDRUM BOX D; FORT COLLINS, CO 80522. (#2948-1).

NOV 14, '76. HANDBELL CHOIR FESTIVAL. HANDBELL CHOIRS FROM AROUND THE STATE WILL BE INVITED; AN ORIGINAL COMPOSITION USING A COLORADO HISTORY THEME HAS BEEN COMMISSIONED FOR THE FESTIVAL. AT FORT COLLINS HIGH SCHOOL. (LOCAL). MRS ROBERT SLOANE, CHMN; DESIGNING TOMORROW TODAY; 415 S HOWES; FORT COLLINS, CO 80521. (#108790-2).

NOV 21, '76. SYMPHONIC WORK BY GEORGE LYNN FOR FORT COLLINS SYMPHONY. LIVE PERFORMANCE AT POUDRE HIGH SCHOOL AUDITORIUM, 201 IMPALA DR. (LOCAL). WILL SCHWARTZ, DIRECTOR; FORT COLLINS SYMPHONY SOCIETY; 1117 ROBERTSON; FORT COLLINS, CO 80521. (#103840-5).

NOV 24, '76. HANDBELL CHOIR. LIVE PERFORMANCE. (LOCAL). KARL CARSON, COORDINATOR; DESIGNING TOMORROW TODAY; 215 S MELDRUM; FORT COLLINS, CO 80522. (#108790-3).

FORT LUPTON

CENTENNIAL MUSEUM IN FORT LUPTON, CO. HISTORICAL SOCIETY WILL ACQUIRE USE OF VACANT STORE FOR MUSEUM TO BE OPENED DURING RENDEZVOUS DAYS IN SEPT OF '76, TO HOUSE VARIOUS ARTIFACTS RELATIVE TO THE TOWN AND COLORADO'S HISTORY. (LOCAL). NANCY PENFOLD, HISTORIAN; HISTORICAL SOCIETY OF FT LUPTON; RT 2, BOX 186; FORT LUPTON, CO 80621. (#6801).

CENTENNIAL PAPER OF FORT LUPTON, CO. THE DISTRIBUTIVE EDUCATION CLASS OF THE FT LUPTON HIGH SCHOOL WILL REPRODUCE THE CENTENNIAL PAPER FIRST PRODUCED BY THE HIGH SCHOOL JOURNALISM CLASS OF 1936 IN HONOR OF COLORADO'S CENTENNIAL. (LOCAL). BURL VANBUSKIRK, SPONSOR; DISTRIBUTIVE EDUCATION CLASS, FT LUPTON HIGH SCHOOL; 201 S MCKINLEY AVE; FORT LUPTON, CO 80621. (#6803).

CHILDREN'S FISHING POND CREATED, FORT LUPTON, CO. THE AMERICAN LEGION WILL DEVELOP A FISHING POND FOR CHILDREN. IT WILL BE LOCATED ADJACENT TO A PARK. (LOCAL). DONALD K PENFOLD, CLUB REPRESENTATIVE; AMERICAN LEGION; RT 2 BOX 186; FORT LUPTON, CO 80621. (#6811). **(??).**

COSTUMES OF '76 PROJ OF FORT LUPTON, COLORADO. THE WOMEN'S AUXILIARY OF THE FORT LUPTON JAYCEES IS SPONSORING A SALE OF OLD CLOTHING TO RAISE MONEY FOR CENTENNIAL-BICENTENNIAL ACTIVITIES. (LOCAL). MARY ELLEN BAUMGARTNER, CHAIRPERSON; JAYCEE JENS; 305 DEXTOR; FORT LUPTON, CO 80621. (#6846).

FORT LUPTON HISTORICAL REPORT, CO. PREPARATION OF FT LUPTON HISTORICAL MATERIAL FOR PRESENTATION TO LIBRARY. (LOCAL). NANCY PENFOLD, COORDINATOR; CITY OF FORT LUPTON; 3282 CO RD 27; FORT LUPTON, CO 80621. (#26293).

INTERVIEWS WITH OLD TIMERS IN FORT LUPTON, CO. AN ORAL HISTORY PROJECT FACILITATED BY INTERVIEWS WITH SENIOR CITIZENS OF FT LUPTON TO BE PUBLISHED IN LOCAL NEWSPAPERS WHICH WILL HAVE A CENTENNIAL-BICENTENNIAL BANNER. (LOCAL). MRS SALLY MALONEY, COORD; BICENTENNIAL COMMITTEE; 840 HOOVER; FORT LUPTON, CO 80621. (#6809).

NEW FORT LUPTON FLAG TO BE SOLD IN COLORADO. FLAGS WILL BE SOLD & DISTRIBUTED LOCALLY. (LOCAL). HON JOHN MARTIN, MAYOR; CITY OF FORT LUPTON; TOWN HALL, 330 PARK AVE; FORT LUPTON, CO 80621. (#6813).

OFFICIAL TOWN SONG WRITTEN FOR FORT LUPTON, CO. SONG ENTITLED, 'OLD TIMEY TOWN FORT LUPTON' WRITTEN BY MAYOR JOHN B MARTIN, WILL BECOME OFFICIAL TOWN SONG. (LOCAL). HON JOHN MARTIN, MAYOR; 330 PARK AVE; FORT LUPTON, CO 80621. (#6812).

OLD FORT LUPTON PROJECT IN COLORADO. THE OLD FORT LUPTON WALL WILL BE REPAIRED. (LOCAL). NANCY PENFOLD, CHAIRPERSON; FT LUPTON CENTENNIAL-BICENTENNIAL COMMITTEE; RT 2 BOX 186; FORT LUPTON, CO 80621. (#6810).

PARK DEVELOPMENT IN FORT LUPTON, CO. A NEW CITY PARK WILL BE FINISHED WITH GAME AREAS AND NECESSARY LANDSCAPING FOR THE BENEFIT OF THE TOWN CITIZENS AND YOUTH. (LOCAL). MEL BUSH, COORDINATOR; PARKS AND RECREATION DEPARTMENT; TOWN HALL, 330 PARK AVE; FORT LUPTON, CO 80621. (#6805).

SUNBONNETS '76 PROJ OF FORT LUPTON, CO. PRODUCTION & SALE OF OLD-FASHIONED SUNBONNETS DURING THE CENTENNIALBICENTENNIAL YEAR TO RAISE MONEY FOR ACTIVITIES. (LOCAL). NANCY PENFOLD, COORDINATOR; FT LUPTON SENIOR LADIES; C/O RT 2, BOX 186; FORT LUPTON, CO 80621. (#6807).

APR 30, '76. '100 YEAR PLUS 40' PLAY OF FORT LUPTON PRESENTATIONS. '100 YEARS PLUS 40', HISTORY OF FORT LUPTON, CO. AN ORIGINAL PLAY WRITTEN IN 1936 FOR FT LUPTON'S CENTENNIAL WILL BE UPDATED FOR COLORADO'S CENTENNIAL-BICENTENNIAL CELEBRATION. THE PRODUCTION WILL THEN BE STAGED BY LOCAL TALENT. AT FORT LUPTON HIGH SCHOOL GYM. (LOCAL). NANCY PENFOLD; FORT LUPTON CENTENNIAL-BICENTENNIAL COMMITTEE; RT 2, BOX 186; FORT LUPTON, CO 80621. (#6806-501).

JULY 4, '76. FORT LUPTON FOURTH OF JULY PARADE. FESTIVAL, PARADE. (LOCAL). NANCY PENFOLD, CHAIRMAN; FORT LUPTON BICENTENNIAL COMMITTEE; 3282 CO RD 27; FORT LUPTON, CO 80621. (#107569-1).

JULY 4, '76. 4TH OF JULY PICNIC. FESTIVAL AT HIGH SCHOOL FOOTBALL FIELD. (LOCAL). NANCY PENFOLD; FORT LUPTON CENTENNIAL-BICENTENNIAL COMMITTEE; FORT LUPTON, CO 80621. (#108624-1).

SEPT 17 - 19, '76. PARADE & FESTIVAL FOR TRAPPER DAYS. TRAPPER DAYS IN FORT LUPTON, CO. THREE DAYS OF FESTIVITIES TO INCLUDE PARADES, AN ART SHOW GAMES, RACES, A SHOOT-OUT, BEARD CONTEST, DANCES AND FOOD, ALL WITH THE CENTENNIAL-BICENTENNIAL THEME. (LOCAL). JOHN MARTIN; FORT LUPTON CHAMBER OF COMMERCE; 147 S DENVER AVE; FORT LUPTON, CO 80621. (#6808-501).

FORT LYON

JULY 4, '76. IN-HOUSE ENTERTAINMENT FOR FT LYON V A HOSPITAL. LIVE PERFORMANCE AT FT LYON V A HOSPITAL. (LOCAL). MARILYN HELLER, COORD; AUDIENCES, INC; 1510 S GRANT; DENVER, CO 80210. (#106980-1).

AUG 1, '76. IN-HOUSE ENTERTAINMENT FOR FT LYON V A HOSPITAL. LIVE PERFORMANCE AT FT LYON VA HOSPITAL. (LOCAL). MARILYN HELLER, COORD; AUDIENCES, INC; 1510 S GRANT; DENVER, CO 80210. (#106980-2).

FORT MORGAN

CHILDREN'S FUN THEATRE - FORT MORGAN, CO. ANNUAL DRAMA FOR CHILDREN. (LOCAL). JUANITA EICHER, CHAIRMAN; WOMEN'S UNIVERSITY CLUB; 102 ASPEN ST; FORT MORGAN, CO 80701. (#24010).

CULTURAL EXPANSION PROJ - FORT MORGAN, CO. THE BILINGUAL-BICULTURAL PROGRAM WILL BE EXPANDED. (LOCAL). BEVERLY A HALEY, CHAIRPERSON; FORT MORGAN CENTENNIAL-BICENTENNIAL COMMITTEE; 301 WALNUT; FORT MORGAN, CO 80701. (#26242).

INSTALLATION OF MUSEUM EXHIBITS IN FT MORGAN, CO. PROJECT INVOLVING THE INSTALLATION OF EXHIBITS DEPICTING HERITAGE OF MORGAN COUNTY IN THE LOCAL MUSEUM. (LOCAL). MRS BARBARA KEENAN, SECRETARY; FT MORGAN HERITAGE FOUNDATION; PO BOX 184; FT MORGAN, CO 80701. (#10328).

LIBRARY MUSEUM COMPLEX - FORT MORGAN, CO. NEW BUILDING FOR THE PROMOTION OF PUBLICATIONS ON LOCAL HISTORY AND OF SPECIAL LIBRARY AND MUSEUM PROJECTS. (LOCAL). SUE SPENCER, CHAIRMAN; FORT MORGAN HERITAGE FOUNDATION; 612 E BIJOU AVE; FORT MORGAN, CO 80701. (#24011).

NUTRITION-IMPROVEMENT IN QUALITY OF LIFE - CO. ELEMENTARY SCHOOL-WIDE; OF INTEREST TO ALL AGE GROUPS-PURPOSE TO EDUCATE THE CHILDREN TO MAKE WISE NUTRITIONAL CHOICES; TEACHING AIDS FILMS, EXPERIMENTS AND DISCUSSIONS. (LOCAL). KATHY CINK, COORDINATOR; BAKER ELEMENTARY SCHOOL; 300 LAKE ST; FORT MORGAN, CO 80701. (#24009).

SOUTH PLATTE HIKING-BACKPACKING TRAIL - CO. LONG AND SHORT HIKING TRAILS TO PROMOTE INTEREST AND PARTICIPATION IN LOCAL NATURAL BEAUTY. (LOCAL). CHUCK HOBBS, CHAIRMAN; CBC HIKING TRAIL PROJECT; 415 LINCOLN ST; FORT MORGAN, CO 80701. (#23971).

WRITTEN HISTORY PROJECTS OF FT MORGAN, COLO. ONE HISTORICAL PAMPHLET ON FT MORGAN ONE HISTORICAL PICTORIAL MAGAZINE. ONE BOOK ON GERMAN RUSSIAN MIGRATION TO MORGAN COUNTY. ONE ORAL HISTORY AND CRAFT-SKILL GATHERING BOOKLET. (LOCAL). MRS BARBARA KEENAN, SECRETARY; FT MORGAN HERITAGE FOUNDATION; PO BOX 184; FT MORGAN, CO 80701. (#4293). **(??).**

JULY 3 - 4, '76. HY PLAINS RENDEZVOUS. TWO-DAY SHOOTING MEET FOR BLACKPOWDER ENTHUSIASTS - CANNONS, MUSKETS, FLINTLOCKS, PERCUSSION SHOTGUNS, RIFLES, PISTOLS, TOMAHAWKS, & KNIVES; TO INCLUDE ENTIRE FAMILIES. (LOCAL). JIM SPOTTS, COORD; BEAVER CREEK MUZZLE LOADERS; 621 SHERMAN; FT MORGAN, CO 80701. (#107443-1).

JULY 4, '76. JULY 4 '76 CHURCH SERVICE & PICNIC-ICE CREAM SOCIAL - COLORADO. CHURCH SERVICE WILL FOLLOW OLD STYLE OF MEN ON ONE SIDE & WOMEN ON THE OTHER; OLD STYLE DRESS ENCOURAGED; EVERYONE INVITED; ALL DENOMINATIONS. AT CENTRALLY LOCATED CHURCHES & PARK. (LOCAL). REV BOB BIELENBERG; FORT MORGAN MINISTERIAL ALLIANCE; 218 E BEAVER AVE; FORT MORGAN, CO 80701. (#107780-2).

SEPT 9 - 11, '76. FREEDOM FESTIVAL - FORT MORGAN, COLORADO. PARADE, FIREWORKS, CRAFTS, CONCERT, DRAMA, HOME SHOW, CONTESTS, ETC. THIS IS THE BIG EVENT OF THE YEAR!. (LOCAL). DON KOTTWITZ; '76 COMMITTEE OF FT MORGAN CENTENNIAL BICENTENNIAL COMMITTEE; 310 E SIXTH AVE; FORT MORGAN, CO 80701. (#107780-1).

FOUNTAIN

FOUNTAIN VALLEY TRAILS SYSTEM - CO. A TEN MILE STRETCH OF THE FOUNTAIN CREEK BANKS WILL BE DESIGNATED A WILDERNESS TRAIL FOR USE BY OUTDOOR SPORTS ENTHUSIASTS. (LOCAL). HELEN K LARSON, CHAIRPERSON; FOUNTAIN CENTENNIAL-BICENTENNIAL COMMITTEE; 120 E OHIO; FOUNTAIN, CO 80817. (#17057).

JAIL RESTORATION IN FOUNTAIN, COLORADO. RENOVATION OF OLD CITY JAIL AS A '76 BICENTENNIAL PROJECT. (LOCAL). CARLA R BARTELS, CHAIRWOMAN; FOUNTAIN CENTENNIAL-BICENTENNIAL COMMITTEE; 116 S MAIN ST; FOUNTAIN, CO 80817. (#4137).

MOSQUITO CONTROL PROJECT IN FOUNTAIN, COLORADO. CONTROL OF MOSQUITOS BY NATURALISTIC APPROACH. USE OF MOSQUITO LARVA AND PUPA EATING FISH CALLED FUNDULUS, KANSAE, & GAMBUSIA AFFINIS. (LOCAL). CARLA R BARTELS, CHAIRWOMAN; FOUNTAIN CENTENNIAL-BICENTENNIAL COMMITTEE; 116 S MAIN ST; FOUNTAIN, CO 80817. (#4138).

OUTDOOR THEATRE EVENTS FOR FOUNTAIN, CO. THE CITY IS PLANNING SEVERAL EVENTS IN ITS OUTDOOR SERIES INCLUDING A HISTORICAL PAGEANT, CINCO DE MAYO, BAND CONCERTS & PLAYS. (LOCAL). HELEN K LARSON, CHAIRPERSON; FOUNTAIN CENTENNIAL-BICENTENNIAL COMMITTEE; 120 E OHIO; FOUNTAIN, CO 80817. (#17059).

FOUNTAIN — CONTINUED

REGISTRY OF HISTORIC SITES & BLDGS - FOUNTAIN, CO. A LIST OF HISTORIC SITES AND BUILDINGS IN THE CITY OF FOUNTAIN AND ENVIRONS TO BE LISTED IN THE NATIONAL REGISTRY. THE STRUCTURES WILL BE MARKED AS SUCH FOR THE CONVENIENCE OF VISITORS AND RESIDENTS. (LOCAL). HELEN K LARSON, CHAIRPERSON; FOUNTAIN CENTENNIAL-BICENTENNIAL COMMITTEE; 120 E OHIO; FOUNTAIN, CO 80817. (#17058).

JAN 1, '76 - CONTINUING . BICENTENNIAL MUSEUM. ESTABLISH MUSEUM TO HOUSE ARTIFACTS, INFORMATION CONCERNING THE HISTORY OF FOUNTAIN. ALSO: BUILDING/FACILITY/MONUMENT. (LOCAL). HELEN K LARSON, CHAIRMAN; FOUNTAIN CENTENNIAL-BICENTENNIAL COMMITTEE; 116 S MAIN ST; FOUNTAIN, CO 80817. (#4139-1).

MAY 1, '76. CINCO DE MAYO. FEATURED ARE A MARIACHI BAND, MASS MEXICAN-AMERICAN DANCES, FOODS, CRAFTS AND GUEST SPEAKERS. AT METCALF PARK, EAST OF FOUNTAIN ON JIMMY CAMP CREEK. (ST-WIDE). ANNA MARTINEZ, CHAIRMAN; CITY OF FOUNTAIN BICENTENNIAL COMMITTEE; 102 S MAIN; FOUNTAIN, CO 80817. (#103110-1).

MAY 1 - SEPT 6, '76. FOUNTAIN CENTENNIAL-BICENTENNIAL FESTIVAL PROGRAMS. FOUNTAIN CELEBRATES CENTENNIAL-BICENTENNIAL WITH A SCHEDULE OF EVENTS INCLUDING A QUEEN'S PAGEANT, CINCO DE MAYO, 4TH OF JULY, HISTORICAL PAGEANT & FALL FESTIVAL. (LOCAL). HELEN K LARSON, CHAIRMAN; FOUNTAIN CENTENNIAL-BICENTENNIAL COMMITTEE; BOX 252; FOUNTAIN, CO 80817. (#103061-2).

JUNE 25, '76. QUEEN/PIONEER PAGEANT. THE QUEEN/PIONEER PAGEANT IS OPEN TO GIRLS IN FOUNTAIN VLY SCHOOLS 16 TO 18 & TO PIONEERS 70 & OLDER, WHO WILL COMPETE ON STAGE FOR THE HONOR OF REIGNING OVER C-B EVENTS. THE WINNERS WILL TRAVEL TO PROMOTE THESE EVENTS. AT FOUNTAIN HIGH SCHOOL AUDITORIUM, ALABAMA ST, ON SITE PARKING. (LOCAL). H KAY LARSON, PROJ DIR; CHAMBER OF COMMERCE OF FOUNTAIN & CITY OF FOUNTAIN; 120 E OHIO; FOUNTAIN, CO 80817. (#103110-3).

JULY 4, '76. FOUNTAIN POT LUCK PICNIC. FESTIVAL, LIVE PERFORMANCE. (LOCAL). VICKI WOOD, CHAIRMAN; FOUNTAIN BICENTENNIAL COMMITTEE; FOUNTAIN, CO 80817. (#107570-1).

JULY 4, '76. JULY 4TH FAMILY FUN & FIREWORKS DISPLAY. THIS IS A FESTIVAL TO STRESS THE IMPORTANCE OF FAMILY TOGETHERNESS & OUR NATION'S BIRTHDAY. IT WILL FEATURE POT LUCK LUNCHEON/SACK RACES/ DUNKING GAMES/ONE-LEGGED RACES/ETC (NON COMMERCIAL). AT METCALF PARK FOUNTAIN ON JIMMY CAMP CREEK (ON-SITE PARKING). (LOCAL). VICKI WOOD, PROJ DIR; CITY OF FOUNTAIN, FOUNTAIN VALLEY JAYCEES/FOUNTAIN FIREMEN; 102 S MAIN; FOUNTAIN, CO 80817. (#103059-1).

JULY 25 - AUG 2, '76. PIONEER WEEK. RESIDENTS & BUSINESS PERSONS WILL DRESS IN CENTENNIAL-BICENTENNIAL CLOTHING TO PUBLICIZE THE HISTORICAL PAGEANT 7/31 - 8/1. AT THROUGHOUT THE CITY. (LOCAL). H KAY LARSON, CHMN; FOUNTAIN CENTENNIAL-BICENTENNIAL COMMITTEE; 120 E OHIO, PO BOX 698; FOUNTAIN, CO 80817. (#103110-5).

JULY 31 - AUG 1, '76. HISTORICAL PAGEANT. THIS PAGEANT WILL FEATURE LOCAL EL PASO COUNTY COUNTY & U S HISTORICAL EPISODES RANGING FROM A TRAIL DRIVE TO A WORLD WAR II STYLES, MUSIC & DANCES FROM 1776 TO 1976. AT METCALF PARK ON TIMMY CAMP CREEK, ON SITE PARKING. (LOCAL). HELEN K LARSON, PROJ DIR; CITY OF FOUNTAIN & FOUNTAIN CHAMBER OF COMMERCE; 120 E OHIO; FOUNTAIN, CO 80817. (#103110-4).

SEPT 6, '76. FALL FESTIVAL. THIS ANNUAL FESTIVAL FEATURES A STREET BREAKFAST, PARADE, GYMKANA, GAMES, TURKEY SHOOT, BARBEQUE AND DANCING. AT METCALF PARK. (LOCAL). JIM MAYES, DIRECTOR; FOUNTAIN CHAMBER OF COMMERCE; FOUNTAIN, CO 80817. (#103110-2).

FOWLER

SENIOR CITIZENS PROJECTS - FOWLER, CO. TRANSPORTATION IS BEING PROVIDED FOR SENIOR CITIZENS ON ELECTION DAY, TEA & ICE CREAM SOCIAL IS BEING HELD FOR MR FOWLER, PARK WILL BE DEDICATED TO THE SENIOR CITIZENS & NEW TREES WILL BE PLANTED. (LOCAL). BARBARALV SMITH, CHAIRMAN; HERITAGE '76 CENTENNIAL-BICENTENNIAL COMMITTEE; 114 E CRANSTON; FOWLER, CO 81039. (#29279).

JULY 10, '76. LIVING ART SHOW. SPECIAL SHOW & ICE CREAM SOCIAL FOR SENIOR CITIZENS; AWARD FOR BEST BICENTENNIAL THEME FLOAT IN PARADE; SEPARATE FLOAT FOR SENIOR CITIZEN, 'MR FOWLER'. AT PARK SCHOOL, 6TH & GRANT. (LOCAL). BARBARALU SMITH, CHAIRMAN; HERITAGE '76 CENTENNIAL-BICENTENNIAL COMMITTEE; FOWLER, CO 81039. (#200007-203).

AUG 1, '76. COLORADO DAY MUSIC FESTIVAL. FESTIVAL, LIVE PERFORMANCE AT FOWLER HIGH SCHOOL AUDITORIUM. (LOCAL). BARBARALU SMITH, CHAIRMAN; HERITAGE '76 CENTENNIAL-BICENTENNIAL COMMITTEE; FOWLER, CO 81039. (#200007-204).

NOV 27, '76. MUSIC FESTIVAL. LIVE PERFORMANCE AT FOWLER HIGH SCHOOL AUDITORIUM. (LOCAL). BARBARALU SMITH, COORD; HERITAGE '76 CENTENNIAL-BICENTENNIAL COMMITTEE; FOWLER, CO 81039. (#109365-1).

FRANKTOWN

FRANKTOWN CEMETERY PROJECT - CO. RESTORATION OF OLD MARKERS, NEW FENCING, ROAD IMPROVEMENTS, CLEANING AND REPAIR OF WINDMILL. A NEW SIGN WILL ALSO BE ADDED. (LOCAL). EUGENE WHEELER, CHAIRPERSON; FRANKTOWN CENTENNIAL-BICENTENNIAL COMMITTEE; PO BOX 14; FRANKTOWN, CO 80116. (#26362).

APR 29, '75. FRANKTOWN RUSSELLVILLE HERITAGE 1858-1975 HISTORICAL REVIEW. FESTIVAL. (LOCAL). EUGENE WHEELER, COORD; DOUGLAS CO CENTENNIAL BICENTENNIAL COMMITTEE; FRANKTOWN, CO 80116. (#200007-183).

JUNE 29, '75. PANCAKE BREAKFAST. FUND-RAISING EVENT WITH ANTIQUES DISPLAY. AT PIKES PEAK GRANGE HALL, FRANKTOWN, CO. (LOCAL). DORIS B LARREAU, COORD; FRANKTOWN CENTENNIAL-BICENTENNIAL COMMITTEE; BOX 101; FRANKTOWN, CO 80116. (#103793-4).

JULY 27, '75. FRANKTOWN-RUSSELLVILLE GOLDRUSH DAY - 1876-1976. PARADE, FLAG AND ANTIQUE DISPLAYS; PAGEANT WITH NARRATION, BUFFALO BARBEQUE, SINGING & DANCING. AT FRANKTOWN, CO. (LOCAL). DORIS B LARREAU, COORD; FRANKTOWN CENTENNIAL-BICENTENNIAL COMMITTEE; BOX 101; FRANKTOWN, CO 80116. (#103793-5).

OCT 1, '75. FRANKTOWN CENTENNIAL BICENTENNIAL REVIEW. EXHIBIT AT COMMUNITY BUILDING. (LOCAL). DORIS LARREAU, COORD; DOUGLAS CO CENTENNIAL BICENTENNIAL COMMITTEE; BOX 101; FRANKTOWN, CO 80104. (#200007-195).

JUNE 20, '76. FRANKTOWN HERITAGE DAY. FORT CARSON MOUNTED CAVALRY PLATOON & COLOR GUARD, OX TEAM & CART-ANTIQUE CARS, CHUCK WAGON LUNCH, HISTORICAL EXHIBITS. (LOCAL). EUGENE WHEELER, CHAIRMAN; FRANKTOWN CENTENNIAL-BICENTENNIAL COMMITTEE; PO BOX 14; FRANKTOWN, CO 80116. (#200007-84).

JULY 3, '76. HORIZONS FESTIVAL. FESTIVAL, EXHIBIT AT COMMUNITY BUILDING. (LOCAL). DORIS LARREAU, COORD; DOUGLAS COUNTY CENTENNIAL-BICENTENNIAL COMMITTEE; BOX 101; FRANKTOWN, CO 80104. (#106986-1).

FREDERICK

GREENING & CLEANING COLORADO - FREDERICK. NEW MUSEUM WILL BE LANDSCAPED TO ENHANCE THE BEAUTY OF THE COMMUNITY. (LOCAL). MAJORIE A EASTON, CHAIRPERSON; MUSEUM BEAUTIFICATION COMMITTEE; BOX 400; FREDERICKS, CO 80530. (#26233).

FRISCO

'CENTENNIAL ARTS FESTIVAL' OF FRISCO, COLO. SUMMER AND YEAR ROUND WORKSHOPS IN CRAFTS WOULD BE HELD AS CONTINUING EDUCATION IN THE RESTORED 'OLLIE LIND' HOUSE. ALSO TO BE USED AS A MUSEUM FOR SUMMIT COUNTY. (LOCAL). SUE DALEY, DIRECTOR, ADULT EDUCATION; COLORADO MOUNTAIN COLLEGE CONTINUING EDUCATION; TEN MILE CREEK BUILDING BOX 567; FRISCO, CO 80443. (#4433). **ARBA GRANTEE.**

FRISCO CENTENNIAL-BICENTENNIAL VISITORS CENTER, CO. PARK AND VISITOR INFORMATION CENTER PLUS COMMUNITY ACTIVITY CENTER. (LOCAL). MIKE SMITH, CHAIRMAN; FRISCO CENTENNIAL-BICENTENNIAL COMMITTEE; BOX 214; FRISCO, CO 80443. (#24612).

FRUITA

HISTORIC WRITINGS PROJECT, FRUITA, CO. FOXFIRE TYPE ARTICLES TO BE PRINTED IN LOCAL NEWSPAPER & MIMEOGRAPHED JOURNAL. (LOCAL). EARLYNNE BARCUS, COORDINATOR; FRUITA CENTENNIAL-BICENTENNIAL COMMITTEE; BOX 92; FRUITA, CO 81521. (#24362).

TOWN IMPROVEMENT & PARK DEVELOPMENT, FRUITA, CO. THE TOWN IMPROVEMENT COMMITTEE & THE JUNIOR CHAMBER OF COMMERCE WILL SPONSOR A TOWN IMPROVEMENT & PARK DEVELOPED ON CITY PROPERTY; TREES, GRASS, PLAYGROUND EQUIPMENT & PLAYGROUND FACILITIES. (LOCAL). SUSIE OTERO, CHAIRPERSON; TOWN IMPROVEMENT COMMITTEE & JUNIOR CHAMBER OF COMMERCE; 1017 E CAROLINA; FRUITA, CO 81521. (#24361).

JUNE 15 - SEPT 2, '75. TALKS ON MAN AND NATURE IN THE COLORADO NATL MON AREA. LECTURE SERIES, TALKS, SEMINARS & CAMPFIRE PROGRAMS WILL BE GIVEN AT MANY NPS AREAS TO SHOW VISITORS THE ROLE OF THESE VARIOUS PARKS IN THE REVOLUTION AMERICAN HISTORY, & AMERICA'S FUTURE. ADMISSION FEE TO PARK. ANNUAL SUMMER PGM. AT SADDLEHORN CAMPGROUND. (REGN'L). SUPT, COLORADO NM; NATIONAL PARK SERVICE; P.O. BOX 438; FRUITA, CO 81521. (#6730-10).

JUNE 16 - SEPT 2, '75. GUIDED WALK COVERING HISTORY & NATURAL FEATURES OF COLORADO AND UTAH. ADMISSION FEE TO PARK. ANNUAL SUMMER PGM. THIS HALF-MILE GUIDED WALK GOES THROUGH SHEER-WALLED CANYONS, TOWERING MONOLITHS THAT MAKE UP THIS PARK. AT SADDLEHORN HEADQUARTERS AREA. (REGN'L). SUPT, COLORADO NATL MON; NATIONAL PARK SERVICE; P.O. BOX 438; FRUITA, CO 81521. (#6729-5).

JUNE 4, '76. SPIRIT OF '76 DANCE RECITAL. LIVE PERFORMANCE AT FRUITA JUNIOR HIGH SCHOOL. (LOCAL). ELLA NOON, COORDINATOR; TOWN OF FRUITA; 1360 18 1/2 RD; FRUITA, CO 81521. (#200007-81).

JUNE 15 - SEPT 2, '76. TALKS ON MAN AND NATURE IN THE COLORADO NATL MON AREA. LECTURE SERIES, TALKS, SEMINARS & CAMPFIRE PROGRAMS WILL BE GIVEN AT MANY NPS AREAS TO SHOW VISITORS THE ROLE OF THESE VARIOUS PARKS IN THE REVOLUTION AMERICAN HISTORY, & AMERICA'S FUTURE. ADMISSION FEE TO PARK. ANNUAL SUMMER PGM. AT SADDLEHORN CAMPGROUND. (REGN'L). SUPT, COLORADO NM; NATIONAL PARK SERVICE; P.O. BOX 438; FRUITA, CO 81521. (#6730-510).

JUNE 16 - SEPT 2, '76. GUIDED WALK COVERING HISTORY & NATURAL FEATURES OF COLORADO AND UTAH. ADMISSION FEE TO PARK. ANNUAL SUMMER PGM. THIS HALF-MILE GUIDED WALK GOES THROUGH SHEER-WALLED CANYONS, TOWERING MONOLITHS THAT MAKE UP THIS PARK. AT SADDLEHORN HEADQUARTERS AREA. (REGN'L). SUPT, COLORADO NATL MON; NATIONAL PARK SERVICE; P.O. BOX 438; FRUITA, CO 81521. (#6729-505).

JUNE 27, '76. OLD TIMERS PICNIC & PIONEER DAY. FESTIVAL AT FRUITA ARMORY. (LOCAL). MARTIN KELEHER; PIONEERS OF COLORADO; 370 N APPLE; FRUITA, CO 81521. (#200007-82).

JULY 2, '76. FRUITA FIREWORKS DISPLAY. COLORADO FLAG & CCBC LOGO PRESENTED WITH LOCAL FIREWORKS DISPLAY FOR CENTENNIAL & BICENTENNIAL CELEBRATION. AT HWY 340, SOUTH OF COLORADO RIVER. (LOCAL). JOHN BARCUS, COORD; FRUITA VOLUNTEER FIRE DEPARTMENT; PO BOX 794; FRUITA, CO 81521. (#106975-3).

JULY 2 - SEPT 25, '76. ARTS & CRAFTS & PRODUCE DISPLAY. EXHIBIT AT CITY HALL. (LOCAL). BERT HARRISON, COORD; FRUITA CHAMBER OF COMMERCE; PO BOX 92; FRUITA, CO 81521. (#106975-5).

JULY 2 - SEPT 25, '76. BEARD & PIONEER COSTUME CONTEST. JUDGING AT FALL FESTIVAL TO SELECT BEST PERIOD COSTUME & BEST BEARD. AT FRUITA & LOWER VALLEY. (LOCAL). BERT HARRISON, CHMN; FRUITA CENTENNIAL-BICENTENNIAL COMMITTEE; PO BOX 92; FRUITA, CO 81521. (#106975-4).

JULY 2 - SEPT 25, '76. WINDOW AND SHOWCASE DISPLAYS. RELICS, ARTIFACTS & ANTIQUES DISPLAYED IN STORE WINDOWS & SHOWCASES. (LOCAL). BERT HARRISON, CHMN; FRUITA CENTENNIAL-BICENTENNIAL COMMITTEE; 141 S APPLE, PO BOX 92; FRUITA, CO 81521. (#107444-1).

JULY 4, '76. SPIRIT OF '76 DANCE RECITAL. 60 DANCERS, ALL AGES TO PERFORM IN PERIOD COSTUMES. AT FRUITA JR HIGH SCHOOL, 239 N MAPLE. (LOCAL). ELLA MOON, CHAIRPERSON; ELLA MOON DANCE SCHOOL; 1360 18-1/2 RD; FRUITA, CO 81521. (#106975-6).

SEPT 25, '76. COMMUNITY PARADE. PARADE AT DOWNTOWN FRUITA. (LOCAL). ROBERT HARRISON, COORD; FRUITA CHAMBER OF COMMERCE; 141 S APPLE, PO BOX 92; FRUITA, CO 81521. (#106975-2).

SEPT 25, '76. WESTERN BEEF BAR-BE-QUE. FESTIVAL AT CIRCLE PARK SQUARE. (LOCAL). LEONARD WYCKOFF, COORD; FRUITA CHAMBER OF COMMERCE; 105 N PLUM; FRUITA, CO 81521. (#106975-1).

GALETON

RECONSTRUCTION OF SIGN - GALETON, CO. SIGN ORIGINALLY ERECTED FOR WW I & II VETS IN 1946 DETERIORATING; COMMUNITY GROUPS SPONSORING RESTORATION. (LOCAL). CHUCK CARLSON, CHAIRMAN; GALETON CENTENNIAL-BICENTENNIAL COMMITTEE; RT 1, BOX 30; EATON, CO 80615. (#26255).

REDEVELOP COMMUNITY PARK - GALETON, CO. PARK IN CURRENT STATE OF DISREPAIR; REDEVELOPING WILL INCLUDE TRIMMING AND PLANTING OF TREES AND SHRUBS, REPLANTING GRASS, INSTALLATION OF WATERING SYSTEM, FENCING AND PLAYGROUND. (LOCAL). CHUCK CARLSON, CHAIRMAN; GALETON CENTENNIAL-BICENTENNIAL COMMISSION; RT 1, BOX 30; EATON, CO 80615. (#26254).

SCHOOL PATRIOTIC PROGRAMS - GALETON, CO. PROGRAMS WILL EMPHASIZE PARTICIPATION IN GOVERNMENT, CIVIC ACTIVITIES, AMERICAN HERITAGE & IDEALS. (LOCAL). CHUCK CARLSON, COORDINATOR; GALETON CENTENNIAL-BICENTENNIAL COMMITTEE & GRADE SCHOOL; RT 1, BOX 30; EATON, CO 80615. (#26252).

GEORGETOWN

BOWMAN WHITEHOUSE- RESTORATION OF GEORGETOWN, COLO. COMPLETION OF RESTORATION AND PRESERVATION OF THIS HISTORIC HOUSE IN GEORGETOWN, COLORADO. (LOCAL). RON NEELEY, DIRECTOR; GEORGETOWN HISTORICAL SOCIETY; BOX 657; GEORGETOWN, CO 80447. (#2708).

GEORGETOWN ARCHITECTURAL EXHIBITION OF COLORADO. PUBLIC PHOTOGRAPHIC EXHIBITION OF HISTORICAL VICTORIAN ARCHITECTURE IN GEORGETOWN. (LOCAL). RON NEELEY, EXEC DIRECTOR; GEORGETOWN HISTORICAL SOCIETY; BOX 657; GEORGETOWN, CO 80444. (#2711).

GEORGETOWN, COLO, PRESERVATION PLAN. COMPREHENSIVE PLAN DESIGNED TO CONSIDER THE FUTURE RESIDENTIAL AND BUSINESS GROWTH FOR GEORGETOWN. (LOCAL). RON NEELEY, EXEC DIRECTOR; GEORGETOWN HISTORICAL SOCIETY; BOX 657; GEORGETOWN, CO 80444. (#2714).

HAMILL HOUSE RESTORATION OF GEORGETOWN, COLORADO. COMPLETION OF THE RESTORATION AND PRESERVATION OF ONE OF GEORGETOWN COLORADO'S HISTORIC HOUSE AND GROUNDS. (LOCAL). RON NEELEY, EXEC DIRECTOR; GEORGETOWN HISTORICAL SOCIETY; BOX 657; GEORGETOWN, CO 80444. (#2713). **ARBA GRANTEE.**

HOTEL DE PARIS RESTORATION IN GEORGETOWN, COLORADO. A PROJECT TO RESTORE THE HISTORIC HOTEL DE PARIS TO INCLUDE REPAIR OF STRUCTURAL DAMAGE, NEW PLASTERING AND PAINTING BOTH INSIDE AND OUT, REPAIR OF INOPERABLE

GEORGETOWN — CONTINUED

PLUMBING, RECONSTRUCTION OF ROOF, ETC. (LOCAL). ELLEN RAY RIDDLE, CHAIRMAN-HOTEL COMMITTEE; NATIONAL SOCIETY OF COLONIAL DAMES OF AMERICA IN COLORADO; 90 CORONA - APT 1401; DENVER, CO 80218. (#4406). **ARBA GRANTEE.**

TRAPPERS CABIN RESTORATION IN GEORGETOWN, COLORADO. COMPLETION OF RESTORATION OF HISTORIC TRAPPERS CABIN IN GEORGETOWN COLORADO. (LOCAL). RON NEELEY, EXEC DIRECTOR; GEORGETOWN HISTORICAL SOCIETY; BOX 657; GEORGETOWN, CO 80444. (#2712).

JUNE 1 - SEPT 30, '76. RESTORATION HOTEL DE PARIS MUSEUM DEDICATION & OPEN HOUSE. CEREMONY, EXHIBIT AT HOTEL DE PARIS, 409 6TH, GEORGETOWN CO: AMPLE PARKING. (LOCAL). MRS ANDY M RIDDLE; NATIONAL SOCIETY OF COLONIAL DAMES IN STATE OF COLORADO; 90 CORONA APT. 1401; DENVER, CO 80218. (#4406-1).

JUNE 13, '76. NYBRO PARK DEDICATION. DEDICATION OF PARK TO BE NAMED FOR GEORGETOWN'S SISTER CITY IN SWEDEN & HONORING SWEDISH PEOPLE OF GEORGETOWN & CLEAR CREEK COUNTY IMMIGRANTS & THEIR DESCENDANTS. FROM TOWN AFFILIATION ORG. & STATE OFFICIALS. AT CITYWIDE. (LOCAL). ROBERT G BOLANDER; GEORGETOWN HISTORICAL SOCIETY; MASONIC BLDG; GEORGETOWN, CO 80444. (#50513-1).

JUNE 13, '76. SWEDISH MID-SUMMER FESTIVAL. TRADITIONAL SWEDISH MID-SUMMER FESTIVAL WITH DANCING AROUND MAY POLE & ETHNIC DANCERS. AT GEORGETOWN CITY PARK. (LOCAL). ROBERT G BOLANDER, COORD; GEORGETOWN SOCIETY, INC & 'ALL SWEDES WEEK' COMMITTEE; MASONIC BUILDING; GEORGETOWN, CO 80444. (#106992-1).

JULY 4, '76. GEORGETOWN VOLUNTEER FIRE DEPT HOSE CART RACES. SMALL FLAGS FOR CHILDREN, ADVERTISING AND PARTICIPATION AWARDS. (LOCAL). E PLACS, COORDINATOR; GEORGETOWN VOLUNTEER FIRE DEPT; PO BOX 426; GEORGETOWN, CO 80444. (#108616-1).

JULY 4, '76. OLD-FASHIONED FOURTH OF JULY CELEBRATION. 1876 STYLE JULY 4TH TO INCLUDE ORATORY, FIREWORKS, PARADE, MUSIC, AND HORSE CART RACES. AT CITYWIDE. (LOCAL). TED SCHMALZ; GEORGETOWN CHAMBER OF COMMERCE AND VOLUNTEER FIRE DEPARTMENT; BOX 655; GEORGETOWN, CO 80444. (#2709-1).

JULY '76. PARKS DEPT CLEANUP DAY AND ICE CREAM SOCIAL. FESTIVAL. (LOCAL). HON E PLACS, MAYOR; PARKS DEPARTMENT; PO BOX 426; GEORGETOWN, CO 80444. (#108820-1).

AUG 28, '76. GEORGETOWN PRIVATE HOME TOUR. PUBLIC TOURS OF TWELVE HISTORIC GEORGETOWN PRIVATE HOMES. AT VARIOUS HOMES IN GEORGETOWN. (LOCAL). RONALD J NEELY; GEORGETOWN HISTORICAL SOCIETY; BOX 657; GEORGETOWN, CO 80444. (#2710-1).

DEC 6 - 7, '76. GEORGETOWN CHRISTMAS MARKET. TO BE REPEATED 13 & 14 DECEMBER. AT STROUSSE PARK. (LOCAL). KERSTIN GUSTERMAN; CHRISTMAS MARKET COMMITTEE; BOX 546; GEORGETOWN, CO 80444. (#2715-1).

GILCREST

JULY 1 - AUG 15, '76. GILCREST 4-H EXHIBIT DAY FESTIVAL. AWARD, EXHIBIT, FESTIVAL AT SOUTH PLATTE ANGUS FARM, 5 MILES WEST OF LASALLE. (LOCAL). LINDA R RUMSEY, LEADER; GILCREST 4-H; RT 2 BOX 108; LASALLE, CO 80645. (#108621-1).

AUG 1, '76. HOMECOMING REUNION. FESTIVAL AT TOWN PARK. (LOCAL). IRMA COGBURN, CHAIRMAN; GILCREST CENTENNIAL-BICENTENNIAL COMMITTEE; PO BOX 67; GILCREST, CO 80623. (#108955-9).

AUG 1, '76. NEW PARK DEDICATION & NAME SELECTION. AWARD FOR BEST NAME SUBMITTED IN COMMUNITY-WIDE COMPETITION TO BE GIVEN ON COLORADO DAY TO COINCIDE WITH PLANNED COMMUNITY HOMECOMING EVENT. AT GILCREST PARK. (LOCAL). RODNEY BARNES, PROJ CHMN; GILCREST CENTENNIAL-BICENTENNIAL COMMISSION; 830 BIRCH; GILCREST, CO 80623. (#108621-2).

GLENWOOD SPG

DRUMS ALONG THE ROCKIES PROJ OF GLENWOOD SPG, COLO. ANNUAL DRUM & BUGLE CORPS EXHIBITION & COMPETITION. (ST-WIDE). RAYMOND GUERRIE, CHAIRPERSON; GLENWOOD SPRINGS CHAMBER OF COMMERCE CLUB; 714 23RD ST; GLENWOOD SPG, CO 81601. (#2950).

GLENWOOD SPRINGS COMMUNITY THEATRE COLO PLAY PGM. THE DEVELOPMENT OF COMMUNITY THEATRE IN SEVERAL SMALL TOWNS IN NW COLORADO. IT WILL CULMINATE IN A FESTIVAL OF ORIGINAL PLAYS BASED ON THE HISTORIES OF THE RESPECTIVE TOWNS. (ST-WIDE). GEORGE STRICKER, COORDINATOR; GLENWOOD SPRINGS CENTENNIAL-BICENTENNIAL COMMITTEE; CITY HALL; GLENWOOD SPGS, CO 81601. (#4362).

PANCAKE DAY OF GLENWOOD SPRING, COLORADO. CELEBRATION WITH PANCAKE DAY ON MAIN STREET AND ALL-DAY SIDEWALK BAZAAR. (LOCAL). RAYMOND GUERRIE, CHAIRPERSON; KIWANIS CLUB; C/O 714 23RD ST; GLENWOOD SPG, CO 81601. (#2877).

'PERSUNE AND JOSEPHINE'-A COLORADO OPERA. WRITING AND PERFORMING BY UTE INDIANS AND WHITES AN AUTHENTIC OPERA BASED ON LOVE STORY OF PERSUNE AND JOSEPHINE AT MEEKER COLORADO IN 1879 WITH FULL DRAMA, DANCE & MUSIC. PRESENTATIONS THRUOUT STATE. (ST-WIDE). GEORGE STRICKER, DIRECTOR; GLENWOOD SPRINGS CENTENNIAL BICENTENNIAL COMMITTEE; CITY HALL; GLENWOOD SPGS, CO 81601. (#4288).

RECREATION PARK PROJ OF GLENWOOD SPRINGS, COLO. PICNIC & RECREATION FACILITIES IN CONNECTION WITH VISITORS INFORMATION CENTER FOR TOURISTS & AREA RESIDENTS. (LOCAL). RAYMOND GUERRIE, CHAIRPERSON; GLENWOOD SPRINGS CENTENNIAL-BICENTENNIAL COMMISSION; 714 23RD ST; GLENWOOD SPG, CO 81601. (#2954). **(??).**

VISITOR INFORMATION CENTER OF GLENWOOD SPG, COLO. TOURIST INFORMATION CENTER FOR GLENWOOD SPRINGS, WESTERN COLORADO & THE ROCKY MOUNTAIN REGION. (ST-WIDE). RAYMOND GUERRIE, CHAIRPERSON; GLENWOOD SPRINGS CHAMBER OF COMMERCE CLUB; 714 23RD ST; GLENWOOD SPG, CO 81601. (#2952). **(??).**

JULY 4, '75. GLENWOOD SPRINGS OLD FASHIONED 4TH OF JULY. OLD FASHIONED CAR AND CENTENNIAL THEME PARADE, FIREWORKS, PICNICS, GAMES, ETC. AT CITYWIDE. (LOCAL). RAYMOND GUERRIE; GLENWOOD SPRINGS CENTENNIAL-BICENTENNIAL COMMISSION; 714 23RD ST; GLENWOOD SPGS, CO 81601. (#2953-1).

JAN 30 - FEB 1, '76. SKI SPREE. ANNUAL WINTER SKI SHOW AND FESTIVAL. (LOCAL). RAYMOND GUERRIE, CHMN; GLENWOOD CENTENNIAL-BICENTENNIAL COMMISSION; 714 23RD ST; GLENWOOD SPG, CO 81601. (#102110-1).

JUNE 17 - 20, '76. STRAWBERRY DAYS. ANNUAL LOCAL SPRING CELEBRATION WITH A CENTENNIAL THEME. (LOCAL). RAYMOND GUERRIE, CHMN; GLENWOOD CENTENNIAL-BICENTENNIAL COMMISSION; 714 23RD ST; GLENWOOD SPG, CO 81601. (#102109-1).

GOLDEN

CLAY PITS IMPROVEMENT IN GOLDEN, CO. CREATION OF A GEOLOGIC PARK IN A MINED-OUT AREA OF THE CAMPUS AS A LASTING REMINDER OF THE CENTENNIAL-BICENTENNIAL CELEBRATION. (LOCAL). CHARLES S MORRIS, PROJ DIRECTOR; COLORADO SCHOOL OF MINES; 1500 ILLINOIS ST; GOLDEN, CO 80401. (#14069).

COLORADO HISTORIC LEGISLATURE PARK - GOLDEN. LEGISLATURE PARK WITH GAZEBO AND ORIGINAL LANDSCAPING IS BEING CULTIVATED. (LOCAL). GENE CHILD, COORDINATOR; GOLDEN LANDMARKS ASSOC; 1200 ILLINOIS; GOLDEN, CO 80401. (#26202).

COMMUNITY SUPPORT OF BICENTENNIAL IN GOLDEN, CO. SUPPORT OF GOLDEN AREA CENTENNIAL-BICENTENNIAL PROJECTS BY STUDENT ORGANIZATIONS AT COLORADO SCHOOL OF MINES. (LOCAL). CHARLES S MORRIS, PROJ DIRECTOR; COLORADO SCHOOL OF MINES; 1500 ILLINOIS ST; GOLDEN, CO 80401. (#14068).

FOOTHILLS ART CENTER OF GOLDEN, COLORADO. EXTERIOR RESTORATION OF 102 YEAR OLD FIRST PRESBYTERIAN CHURCH OF GOLDEN WHICH HOUSES THE FOOTHILLS ART CENTER - REROOFING, PAINTING, REPLACEMENT OF GUTTERING. (ST-WIDE). MARIAN METSOPOULOS, MANAGER; FOOTHILLS ART CENTER; 15TH & WASHINGTON; GOLDEN, CO 80401. (#1944).

GUY HILL SCHOOL, PROJ OF GOLDEN, CO. MOVE FROM GOLDEN GATE CANYON TO MITCHELL SCHOOL AND USE AS A HERITAGE CENTER FOR CLASSES. (LOCAL). JOANN THISTLEWOOD, PROJ DIRECTOR; STUDENTS OF MITCHELL SCHOOL; 12TH & JACKSON; GOLDEN, CO 80401. (#16390).

HISTORICAL MAP OF JEFFERSON COUNTY, CO. A MAP OF JEFFERSON COUNTY INCLUDING HISTORICAL SITES. (LOCAL). MARY CALHOUN, COORDINATOR; JEFFERSON COUNTY CENTENNIAL-BICENTENNIAL COMMITTEE; 12185 W 29TH PL; LAKEWOOD, CO 80215. (#26290).

JEFFERSON COUNTY'S HISTORY TRAVELING EXHIBIT, CO. ILLUSTRATED TALKS WILL BE PRESENTED AT VARIOUS SCHOOLS THROUGHOUT THE COUNTY DURING THE SCHOOL YEAR. THE TALKS FEATURE JEFFERSON COUNTY'S PAST AND FUTURE. (LOCAL). WILLIAM WHITE, PROJ DIRECTOR; JEFFERSON COUNTY COMMISSIONERS; 1700 ARAPAHOE ST; GOLDEN, CO 80401. (#16443).

MAP OF GOLDEN AND JEFFERSON COUNTIES, CO. JEFFERSON COUNTY HISTORICAL SITES, TRAIL SYSTEMS & PARKS WILL BE SHOWN ON A MAP WHICH INCLUDES HISTORIC AND CULTURAL SITES OF GREATER GOLDEN AS WELL. (LOCAL). MARIAN METSOPOULOS, EXEC DIR; FOOTHILLS ART CENTER, INC; 809 15TH ST; GOLDEN, CO 80401. (#10330).

MINERAL & ENERGY TRAVELING EXHIBIT - CO. HISTORY OF THE MINERALS AND ENERGY INDUSTRY IN COLORADO AND THE ROLE OF THE SCHOOL IN THE CENTENNIAL-BICENTENNIAL CELEBRATION WILL BE THE THEME OF THE EXHIBIT. (LOCAL). CHARLES S MORRIS, PROJ DIRECTOR; COLORADO SCHOOL OF MINES; 1500 ILLINOIS ST; GOLDEN, CO 80401. (#14066).

PATHWAYS PROJECT - GOLDEN, CO. FOOT TRAIL WILL BE DEVELOPED TO BEAVER BROOK AREA IN COOPERATION WITH THE GOLDEN CENTENNIAL-BICENTENNIAL COMMITTEE AS A LASTING REMINDER OF THE CELEBRATION. (LOCAL). CHARLES S MORRIS, PROJ DIRECTOR; COLORADO SCHOOL OF MINES; 1500 ILLINOIS ST; GOLDEN, CO 80401. (#14067).

RED ROCKS STUDENT OUTDOOR CULTURAL CENTER, CO. AN OUTDOOR CULTURAL CENTER MADE UP BASICALLY OF AN AMPHITHEATER AND A GALLERY. THE PROJECT IS SPONSORED, FINANCED & BUILT BY THE STUDENTS. (LOCAL). OWEN G SMITH, VICE PRESIDENT; COMMUNITY COLLEGE OF DENVER - RED ROCKS CAMPUS; 12600 W 6TH AVE; GOLDEN, CO 80401. (#16387).

TREE PLANTING PROJECT IN GOLDEN, CO. TO COMMEMORATE CENTENNIAL-BICENTENNIAL, THERE WILL BE REPLACEMENT OF CAMPUS TREES KILLED BY DUTCH ELM DISEASE. (LOCAL). CHARLES S MORRIS, PROJ DIRECTOR; COLORADO SCHOOL OF MINES; 1500 ILLINOIS ST; GOLDEN, CO 80401. (#14070).

JUNE 1 - 30, '75. PHOTOGRAPHY CONTEST; WINNING PHOTOS TO BE PUBLISHED AS CALENDAR. CENTENNIAL PHOTOGRAPHIC CALENDAR, GOLDEN, COLO A PHOTOGRAPHIC COMPETITION AT FOOTHILLS ART CENTER JUNE '75. PRIZES TO BE AWARDED FOR 12 BEST PHOTOS WINNING PHOTOS WILL BE REPRODUCED ON A CALENDAR INCLUDING HISTORIC DATE INFORMATION ON COLO. HISTORY. (ST-WIDE). GENE CHILD, CHAIRMAN; GOLDEN LANDMARKS ASSOCIATION AND FOOTHILLS ART CENTER; 1200 ILLINOIS; GOLDEN, CO 80401. (#4278-501).

JULY 4 - 6, '75. FESTIVAL DEPICTING HISTORY OF WEST. EXHIBIT AT 1700 ARAPAHOE. (LOCAL). MARY CALHOUN, CHAIRMAN; JEFFERSON COUNTY HISTORICAL COMMISSION; 1700 ARAPAHOE; GOLDEN, CO 80401. (#200007-97).

AUG 17 - SEPT 21, '75. ROCKY MT NATIONAL WATERMEDIA EXHIBITION-COLO CENTENNIAL AWARD. COLORADO CENTENNIAL AWARD TO BE GIVEN TO A COLORADO ARTIST IN THE 1975 ROCKY MOUNTAIN NATIONAL WATERMEDIA EXHIBITION SPONSORED BY THE FOOTHILLS ART CENTER, INC. OPEN SUNDAY 01:00PM-04:00PM. AT 809 15TH STREET GOLDEN COLORADO. (ST-WIDE). MARIAN METSOPOULOS; FOOTHILLS ART CENTER INC; 809 15TH STREET; GOLDEN, CO 80401. (#4289-1).

SEPT 1, '75 - SEPT 1, '76. COMMUNITY SUPPORT OF BICENTENNIAL EVENTS IN GOLDEN COLORADO. SUPPORT OF GOLDEN CENTENNIAL-BICENTENNIAL COMMITTEE PROJECTS BY STUDENTS OF THE COLORADO SCHOOL OF MINES - BEAVER BROOK FOOT TRAIL, ASTOR HOUSE, BUFFALO BILL DAYS, MAP OF HISTORIC GOLDEN, CIVIC PARK, COMMUNITY IMPROVEMENT. (LOCAL). CHARLES S MORRIS, DIR; COLORADO SCHOOL OF MINES; 1500 ILLINOIS ST; GOLDEN, CO 80401. (#102415-2).

NOV 1, '75 - NOV 1, '76. TRAVELING EXHIBIT ON MINING HISTORY. TRAVELING EXHIBIT ON HISTORY OF MINING IN COLORADO AND THE ROLE OF THE COLORADO SCHOOL OF MINES - ILLUSTRATED WITH PHOTOS - WILL TOUR THE STATE FOR ONE YEAR - WILL HIGHLIGHT CENTENNIAL-BICENTENNIAL CELEBRATION. (ST-WIDE). CHARLES S MORRIS, DIR; COLORADO SCHOOL OF MINES; 1500 ILLINOIS ST; GOLDEN, CO 80401. (#102415-1).

APR 2 - 3, '76. ENGINEERS' DAY 1976. STUDENT AND INDUSTRIAL EXHIBITS TO INCLUDE DISPLAYS ON ENERGY AND ECOLOGY; SEMINARS, A SCHOLARSHIP COMPETITION, CONCERT, DANCE, CAMPUS TOURS AND STUDENT CONTESTS. AT GREEN CENTER AND STEINHAUER FIELDHOUSE-CSM CAMPUS. (ST-WIDE). CHARLES S MORRIS, CHMN; ENGINEERS' DAY COMMITTEE ASSOCIATED STUDENTS OF CSM; COLORADO SCHOOL OF MINES; GOLDEN, CO 80401. (#102650-1).

APR 4, '76. JEFFERSON SYMPHONY CONCERT. FOUNDED IN 1953 THIS ALL VOLUNTEER ORCHESTRA IS DESIGNED FOR THE ENTIRE FAMILY. AT GREEN HALL, SCHOOL OF MINES CAMPUS, 16 & ARAPAHOE. (LOCAL). JACKIE MAXWELL; GOLDEN CIVIC ORCHESTRA ASSOC; 7720 WESTVIEW DR; LAKEWOOD, CO 80215. (#200007-98).

MAY 16, '76. JEFFERSON SYMPHONY CONCERT. FOUNDED IN 1953 THIS ALL VOLUNTEER ORCHESTRA IS DESIGNED FOR THE ENTIRE FAMILY. AT GREEN HALL, SCHOOL OF MINES CAMPUS, 16 & ARAPAHOE. (LOCAL). JACKIE MAXWELL, V-PRES; GOLDEN CIVIC ORCHESTRA ASSOC; 7720 WESTVIEW DR; LAKEWOOD, CO 80215. (#107031-3).

JUNE 1, '76. AUSTRALIAN YOUTH ORCHESTRA. LIVE PERFORMANCE AT BUNKER AUDITORIUM. (LOCAL). LEONARD DIGGS, COORD; GOLDEN SYMPHONY YOUTH ORCHESTRA; 6668 VIVIAN ST; ARVADA, CO 80001. (#200007-99).

JUNE 5, '76. SIDEWALK ARTS & CRAFTS SHOW. EXHIBIT, FAIR AT DOWNTOWN GOLDEN. (LOCAL). MARIAN METSOPOULOUS, CHMN; GOLDEN CHAMBER OF COMMERCE AND FOOTHILLS ART CENTER; 809 15TH ST; GOLDEN, CO 80401. (#200007-100).

JUNE 5, '76. SPRING SPORTS FEST. FESTIVAL AT GOLDEN RECREATION CENTER & LIONS PARK - 1015 10TH ST. (LOCAL). C L COURTAD, COORD; GOLDEN CENTENNIAL-BICENTENNIAL COMMITTEE; 623 14TH ST; GOLDEN, CO 80401. (#200007-101).

JUNE 6, '76. CENTENNIAL COLORADO AUTHORS PROGRAM. LIVE PERFORMANCE AT 809 15TH. (LOCAL). KAY MARTIN, COORD; FOOTHILLS ART CENTER; 809 15TH ST; GOLDEN, CO 80401. (#200007-102).

JULY 3 - 4, '76. JEFFERSON COUNTY CENTENNIAL-BICENTENNIAL FESTIVAL OF THE WEST. MIDWAY INCLUDES 50 BOOTHS SHOWING HISTORIC CRAFTS, ARTS & LOCAL LORE & ARENA SHOW ON COLORADO SETTLEMENT OF INDIANS, SPANISH HUNTERS & MINERS, PLUS THE IMMIGRANTS & SETTLERS. SHOW ENDS IN 150 HORSE DRILL BY THE WESTERNAIRES & FIREWORKS. AT JEFFERSON COUNTY FAIRGROUNDS 6TH & INDIANA. (ST-WIDE). MARY CALHOUN, CHMN; JEFFERSON COUNTY; 12185 W 29TH PLACE; LAKEWOOD, CO 80215. (#100050-1).

JULY 4, '76. PATHWAY DEDICATION. OPENING AT NORTH BANK OF CLEAR CREEK CONNECTING CIVIC STRUCTURES & TRAIL. (LOCAL). HENRY HEINS, PROJ DIR; GOLDEN LIONS CLUB; 519 PEERY PARKWAY; GOLDEN, CO 80401. (#108615-1).

JULY 8 - 9, '76. BUFFALO BILL & THE BORDER BANDITS. LIVE PERFORMANCE AT GOLDEN CITY HALL, 911 10TH ST - COMMUNITY ROOM. (LOCAL). RONITA WOOLSEY, COORD; GOLDEN THESPIANS; 1826 SMITH RD; GOLDEN, CO 80401. (#108731-2).

JULY 8 - 10, '76. BUFFALO BILL'S DAYS. FESTIVAL. (LOCAL). VIRGINIA WEIGAND, COORD; GOLDEN CHAMBER OF COMMERCE; 911 10TH; GOLDEN, CO 80401. (#108731-1).

JULY 10, '76. BUFFALO BILL & THE BORDER BANDITS. LIVE PERFORMANCE AT CITY PARK, 10TH & WASHINGTON. (LOCAL).

GOLDEN — CONTINUED

RONITA WOOLSEY, COORD; GOLDEN THESPIANS; 1826 SMITH RD; GOLDEN, CO 80401. (#108731-3).

JULY 10, '76. COLORADO TERRITORIAL LEGISLATURE MEETING SITE 1864-1867. TERRITORIAL LEGISLATURE MET HERE FROM 1864-1867 AT THE LOVELAND BUILDING. AT 1122 WASHINGTON. (LOCAL). C L COURTAD, COORDINATOR; GOLDEN CENTENNIAL-BICENTENNIAL COMMITTEE; 623 14TH ST; GOLDEN, CO 80401. (#108731-5).

JULY 10, '76. DEDICATION OF CHIMNEY GULCH TRAIL. CEREMONY. (LOCAL). DR DIXON SMITH, COORD; GOLDEN OPTIMISTS CLUB; 2060 MT ZION DR; GOLDEN, CO 80401. (#108731-4).

AUG 1, '76. JEFFERSON SYMPHONY CONCERT HONORS CITY OF GOLDEN, COLORADO. FOUNDED IN 1953 THIS ALL VOLUNTEER ORCHESTRA IS DESIGNED FOR THE ENTIRE FAMILY. MUSIC OF AMERICA & AMERICAN COMPOSERS PRESENTED. AT GREEN HALL, SCHOOL OF MINES CAMPUS, 16 & ARAPAHOE. (LOCAL). JACKIE MAXWELL, V-PRES; GOLDEN CIVIC ORCHESTRA ASSOC; 7720 WESTVIEW DR; LAKEWOOD, CO 80215. (#107031-2).

AUG 15, '76. ROCKY MOUNTAIN NATIONAL WATER MEDIA EXHIBITION. EXHIBIT AT FOOTHILLS ART CENTER, 809 15TH. (LOCAL). MARION METSOPOULOAS, DIR; FOOTHILLS ART CENTER; 809 15TH; GOLDEN, CO 80401. (#108731-6).

SEPT 26, '76. CENTENNIAL COLORADO AUTHORS PROGRAMS. COLORADO AUTHOR SUSAN POLIS SCHUTZ WILL BE PRESENT. AT 809 15TH ST. (LOCAL). KAY MARTIN, COORD; FOOTHILLS ART CENTER; 809 15TH ST; GOLDEN, CO 80401. (#108781-4).

OCT 1, '76. COLUMBINE QUILT EXHIBIT. EXHIBIT AT FOOTHILLS ART CENTER, 809-15TH ST. (LOCAL). MARIAN METSOPOULOUS, DIR; EMBROIDER'S GUILD; 809 15TH ST; GOLDEN, CO 80401. (#108781-2).

OCT 17, '76. JEFFERSON SYMPHONY CONCERT. FOUNDED IN 1953, THIS ALL VOLUNTEER ORCHESTRA IS DESIGNED FOR THE ENTIRE FAMILY. AT GREEN HALL, SCHOOL OF MINES CAMPUS, 16 & ARAPAHOE. (LOCAL). JACKIE MAXWELL, V-PRES; GOLDEN CIVIC ORCHESTRA ASSOC; 7720 WESTVIEW DR; LAKEWOOD, CO 80215. (#107031-1).

OCT 24, '76. CENTENNIAL COLORADO AUTHORS PROGRAM. COLORADO AUTHOR FRANCIS L ELNORE WILL BE PRESENT. AT 809 15TH ST. (LOCAL). KAY MARTIN, COORD; FOOTHILLS ART CENTER; 809 15TH ST; GOLDEN, CO 80401. (#108781-1).

NOV 21, '76. CENTENNIAL COLORADO AUTHORS PROGRAM. COLORADO AUTHOR RICHARD PEARL WILL BE PRESENT. AT FOOTHILLS ART CENTER, 809 15TH ST. (LOCAL). KAY MARTIN, COORD; FOOTHILLS ART CENTER; 809 15TH ST; GOLDEN, CO 80401. (#108781-3).

GR SAND DUNES

JUNE 1 - SEPT 1, '75. EVENING CAMPFIRE PROGRAMS WITH CENTENNIAL-BICENTENNIAL SUBJECTS. SUMMER MONTHS 1975, 1976. ADMISSION FEE INTO PARK. GREAT SAND DUNES NM, WITH SOME OF LARGEST & HIGHEST DUNES IN THE US, WILL BE HOSTING THESE CAMPFIRE PROGRAMS. AT CAMPGROUND AMPHITHEATER AT GREAT SAND DUNES NATL MON. (REGN'L). SUPT, GREAT SAND DUNES NM; NATIONAL PARK SERVICE; P.O. BOX 60; ALAMOSA, CO 81101. (#6730-30).

JUNE 10 - SEPT 6, '76. BICENT-CENT EVENING CAMPFIRE PGMS AT GREAT SAND DUNES NM. GREAT SAND DUNES NATL MONUMENT, WITH SOME OF THE LARGEST AND HIGHEST DUNES IN THE UNITED STATES, WILL BE HOSTING THESE CAMPFIRE PROGRAMS. AT CAMPGROUND AMPHITHEATER AT GREAT SAND DUNES NATL MON. (REGN'L). SUPT, GREAT SAND DUNES NM; NATIONAL PARK SERVICE; P.O. BOX 60; ALAMOSA, CO 81101. (#6730-530).

GRANADA

COMMUNITY PARK DEVELOPMENT - GRANADA, CO. THE CITY PARK WILL INCLUDE FIREPLACES, HORSESHOE PITCH, PARK BENCHES AND TABLES AND OVER-NIGHT PARKING. (LOCAL). BESSIE TUCK, CHAIRPERSON; GRANADA CENTENNIAL GROUP; 206 S IRVIN; GRANADA, CO 81041. (#23938).

GRANADA, CO, CENTENNIAL PARK. ACQUIRE LAND & DEVELOP FOR RECREATIONAL PURPOSES WITH TENNIS COURT, SKATING RINK, HORSESHOE COURTS, OUTDOOR BASKETBALL COURTS AND PICNIC AREA. (LOCAL). BESSIE TUCK, CHAIRPERSON; GRANADA BICENTENNIAL GROUP; GRANADA, CO 81041. (#26354).

GRANADA, CO, DISPLAY OF FLAGS. THE SIX FLAGS WHICH HAVE FLOWN OVER THE TERRITORY WILL BE ON PERMANENT DISPLAY. (LOCAL). BESSIE TUCK, CHAIRPERSON; SPEED-WASH & GRANADA BARBERSHOP; GRANADA, CO 81041. (#26356).

GRANADA, CO, HISTORICAL MARKER & FLAG POLE. ERECT A MARKER OUTLINING GRANADA'S HISTORY NOTING POINTS OF INTEREST IN THE AREA; STATE AND NATIONAL FLAG WILL BE FLOWN ON EITHER SIDE OF MARKER. (LOCAL). BESSIE TUCK, CHAIRPERSON; SPEED-WASH & GRANADA BARBERSHOP; GRANADA, CO 81041. (#26355).

PLAYGROUND EQUIPMENT FOR SCHOOL, GRANADA, CO. TWO TENNIS COURTS, ROLLER SKATING RINK AND OUTDOOR BASKETBALL COURT WILL BE ADDED TO THE SCHOOL. (LOCAL). BESSIE TUCK, CHAIRPERSON; GRANADA CENTENNIAL-BICENTENNIAL GROUP; 206 S IRVIN; GRANADA, CO 81041. (#23939).

SOUTH EAST COLORADO TREASURERS - GRANADA. PUBLISH MONTHLY NEWSPAPER FEATURING STORIES OF GRANADA'S FIRST ONE HUNDRED YEARS, THE AREA'S HISTORY & PICTURES OF YESTERYEAR & ITEMS OF LOCAL INTEREST. (LOCAL). FRED NEUHOLD, COORDINATOR; GRANADA AG; GRANADA, CO 81041. (#26357).

JAN 8 - NOV 19, '76. SENIOR CITIZEN 1976. CEREMONY. (LOCAL). BESSIE TUCK; GRANADA CENTENNIAL-BICENTENNIAL COMMITTEE; BOX 37; GRANADA, CO 81041. (#108620-1).

FEB 17 - APR 3, '76. FLAG DISPLAY. FLAG DISPLAY WITH A ROCK FROM EACH OF THE 50 STATES ON THE FLAGPOLE. AT CITY HALL, U S 50. (LOCAL). BESSIE TUCK, CHAIRPERSON; GRANADA CENTENNIAL GROUP; 206 S IRVIN; GRANADA, CO 81041. (#200007-117).

JUNE 18, '76. MELODRAMA. LIVE PERFORMANCE AT GRANADA HIGH SCHOOL AUDITORIUM, 201 S HOISINGTON. (LOCAL). MRS DOROTHY DAWSON, DIR; GRANADA HIGH SCHOOL; 300 E BROADWAY; GRANADA, CO 81041. (#200007-118).

JULY 4, '76. GRANADA CENTENNIAL-BICENTENNIAL PARK DEDICATION. WIENER ROAST, HOME-MADE ICE CREAM & CAKE TO BE SERVED. (LOCAL). BESSIE TUCK; GRANADA CENTENNIAL-BICENTENNIAL COMMITTEE; BOX 37; GRANADA, CO 81041. (#108620-2).

SEPT 16, '76. SPANISH INDEPENDENCE DAY FESTIVAL. HONORING ALL SENIOR CITIZENS OVER 90 YRS OLD. AT SOUTH MAIN STREET. (LOCAL). BESSIE TUCK, CHAIRPERSON; GRANADA CENTENNIAL-BICENTENNIAL GROUP; 206 S IRVIN; GRANADA, CO 81041. (#107114-1).

GRANBY

JULY 4, '76. MUSIC PROGRAMS. CONCERT IN MUNICIAPL PARK AFTER FIREWORKS. AT MUNICIPAL PARK. (LOCAL). JOYCE SCHMIEDBAUER; JULY 4TH CONCERT COMMITTEE; 601 JASPER COURT; GRANBY, CO 80446. (#108623-1).

AUG 3, '76. SENIOR CITIZEN 1976. DINNER GIVEN AND PREPARED BY SENIOR CITIZENS; SERVED IN SENIOR CITIZENS HALL. (LOCAL). JOYCE SCHMIEDBAUER, CHMN; GRANBY SENIOR CITIZEN GROUP; 601 JASPER COURT; GRANBY, CO 80446. (#108786-1).

GRAND LAKE

FILM FESTIVAL - GRAND LAKE, CO. PURCHASE EQUIPMENT FOR SHOWING HISTORIC SLIDES. (LOCAL). KEN ROE, TOWN CLERK; TOWN OF GRAND LAKE; BOX 6; GRAND LAKE, CO 80447. (#26353).

GRAND LAKE, CO SLIDE SHOW. A PROJECT TO CREATE A SLIDE SHOW THROUGH PURCHASE OF A PROJECTOR & TAPE RECORDER TO BE USED BY VISITORS AT THEIR CONVENIENCE. (LOCAL). PATIENCE CAIRNS KEMP, PRES; GRAND LAKE AREA HISTORICAL SOCIETY; 526 CAIRNS AVE; GRAND LAKE, CO 80447. (#10327).

JULY 5 - AUG 28, '75. PUPPET SHOWS BY GIRL SCOUTS. THE GIRLS WILL DO TWO SHOWS: ON WEDNESDAYS, THE HISTORY OF LULU CITY, ONCE A THRIVING GOLD & SILVER MINING TOWN, & ON THURSDAYS, 'THE SHOOTING OF THE COMMISSIONERS, 4 JULY, 1883'. AT TOWN SQUARE OPEN SHELTER. (LOCAL). MRS DEAN SCHIEMANN; GIRL SCOUTS CADETTE TROOP # 251; DRIFTWOOD MOTEL; GRAND LAKE, CO 80447. (#50139-1).

JULY 12 - 13, '75. ARTS AND CRAFTS FESTIVAL AT BUFFALO BARBEQUE G LAKE YESTERDAYS TODAY. WE HAVE HAD BUFFALO BARBECUE FOR MANY YEARS (FISH FRIES BEFORE THAT) PARADE AND BARBEQUE JULY 13 1975 ARTS AND CRAFTS FESTIVAL ADDED THIS YEAR WITH HISTORICAL THEME EXHIBIT AND PARADE: NO ADMISSION PRICE. AT TOWN SQUARE TOWN BUILDING ON GRAND AVE.. (LOCAL). WINTERS, SARA; CHAMBER OF COMMERCE AND G L AREA HISTORICAL SOCIETY; 1307 GRAND AVE.; GRAND LAKE, CO 80447. (#50140-1).

AUG 3, '75. OPEN HOUSE AT KAUFFMAN HOUSE. THIS HOUSE IS AN OLD LOG HOTEL, BUILT IN 1892. THIS PROJECT IS AIMED AT PURCHASING THE BUILDING & RESTORING IT. APPLICATION HAS BEEN MADE FOR LISTING IT ON THE NATIONAL HISTORIC REGISTER. AT KAUFFMAN HOUSE LAKE AVE AT PITKIN ST.. (STWIDE). PATIENCE KEMP; GRAND LAKE AREA HISTORICAL SOCIETY; BOX 544; GRAND LAKE, CO 80447. (#4294-1).

JULY 11, '76. BUFFALO BARBEQUE. BUFFALO WILL BE COOKED IN OUTDOOR PITS AND SERVED WITH ALL THE TRIMMINGS; ENTERTAINMENT INCLUDES BAND CONCERTS, DRILL TEAM EVENTS AND BATON WHIRLING. AT CIRCUS TENT, TOWN SQUARE. (LOCAL). KEN ROE, COORDINATOR; CITY OF GRAND LAKE; BOX 6; GRAND LAKE, CO 80447. (#108700-1).

GRAND VALLEY

PARK IMPROVEMENT PROJECT, GRAND VALLEY, CO. THE PARK ASSOCIATION WILL IMPROVE THE CONDITION OF THE TOWN PARK. (LOCAL). DAVID CRAIG, PRESIDENT; PARK ASSOC; 248 4TH; GRAND VALLEY, CO 81635. (#23076).

DEC 1, '75 - JUNE 15, '76. TOWN SEAL DESIGN CONTEST. A CONTEST, OPEN TO ALL RESIDENTS, TO DESIGN A TOWN SEAL. (LOCAL). ANNA SHADWELL, CHMN; TOWN COUNCIL; 135 E 2ND; GRAND VALLEY, CO 81635. (#106411-1).

APR 6, '76. TOWN NAME CHANGE CEREMONY. AFTER A BALLOT VOTE BY CITIZENS THE TOWN WILL BE RENAMED ITS ORIGINAL NAME, 'PARACHUTE'. (LOCAL). FLOYD MCDANIEL, MAYOR; GRAND VALLEY TOWN COUNCIL; 101 E FRONT ST; GRAND VALLEY, CO 81635. (#106335-1).

AUG 1, '76. GARFIELD COUNTY PIONEER DAY. PRESENTATION OF BICENTENNIAL FLAG TO THE MAYOR; AWARD HONORING OUTSTANDING CITIZEN WILL BE GIVEN. TOWNS INVITED INCLUDE RIFLE, NEW CASTLE, GLENWOOD, SILT AND CARBONDALE. TOWN SEAL AWARD AND OTHERS. AT GRAND VALLEY SCHOOL. (LOCAL). ANNA SHADWELL, CHMN; PIONEER CLUB; 135 2ND ST; GRAND VALLEY, CO 81635. (#108074-1).

SEPT 18 - 19, '76. PARACHUTE REBORN DAYS. PARADE, RODEO, DANCE, ARTS & CRAFTS AND HORTICULTURE DISPLAYS AND STREET GAMES ARE THE SCHEDULED ACTIVITIES. AT RODEO GROUNDS. (LOCAL). DAVID CRAIG, COORD; PARK ASSOC; 248 4TH ST; GRAND VALLEY, CO 81635. (#106335-2).

GREELEY

BACKGROUND HISTORY OF THE UNIV OF NORTHERN COLORADO - LECTURES. LECTURE SERIES BY FRIENDS OF THE LIBRARY ON THE HISTORY OF THE UNIVERSITY OF NORTHERN COLORADO. (LOCAL). JOSEPHINE JONES, CHMN; GREELEY AREA CENTENNIAL-BICENTENNIAL COMMITTEE; GREELEY, CO 80631. (#104284-7).

BICENTENNIAL VILLAGE, GREELEY, CO. UNIVERSITY OF NORTHERN COLORADO WILL PARTICIPATE IN A CITY COUNTY PROJECT: THE RESTORATION OF A HISTORICAL SCHOOL BUILDING. (LOCAL). JOSEPHINE JONES, DIRECTOR; GREELEY AREA CENTENNIAL-BICENTENNIAL COMMITTEE; GREELEY, CO 80631. (#19390).

BOTANICAL GARDENS PROJECT OF GREELEY, COLORADO. A WALKING TOUR THRU GARDENS DEPICTING HOW WATER AFFECTED THE PLAINS. (LOCAL). JOSEPHINE JONES, CHAIRPERSON; GREELEY CENTENNIAL-BICENTENNIAL COMMISSION; 9TH ST & 9TH AVE; GREELEY, CO 80631. (#2903).

BRIDLE PATH PRESERVATION, GREELEY-FT COLLINS AREA. FOLLOWING THE CACHE LA POUDRE RIVER FROM GREELEY TO FT COLLINS, IT HELPS BEAUTIFY & PRESERVE THE SURROUNDING AREA. (LOCAL). JOSEPHINE JONES, CHAIRPERSON; GREELEY CENTENNIAL-BICENTENNIAL COMMISSION; 9TH ST & 9TH AVE; GREELEY, CO 80631. (#2904).

CACHE LA POUDRE GREEN BELT AND TRAIL - GREELEY, CO. GREEN BELT ALONG CACHE LA POUDRE RIVER LINKING CENTENNIAL VILLAGE IN ISLAND GROVE PARK WITH NEARBY AGRICULTURAL LAND. (LOCAL). CHRISTINE KAVALEC, CHAIRMAN; WELD COUNTY CENTENNIAL-BICENTENNIAL COMMITTEE; PO BOX 758; GREELEY, CO 80631. (#21563).

CENTENNIAL-BICENTENNIAL INVOLVEMENT PROJ, CO. WELD COUNTY IS SPONSORING A 'GET INVOLVED' PROJ; IT IS DESIGNED TO CREATE INTEREST & INVOLVEMENT WITHIN THE COUNTY IN THE CELEBRATION; VARIOUS ACTIVITIES ARE PLANNED. (LOCAL). CHRISTINE KAVALEC, CHAIRMAN; WELD COUNTY CENTENNIAL-BICENTENNIAL COMMISSION; 9TH AVE & 10TH ST; GREELEY, CO 80631. (#24579).

THE CHEYENNE INDIAN OF COLORADO, GREELEY, CO. THE UNIVERSITY OF NORTHERN COLORADO MUSEUM WILL HAVE A MUSEUM DISPLAY ON THE CHEYENNE INDIAN IN COLORADO. (LOCAL). JOSEPHINE JONES, DIRECTOR; GREELEY AREA CENTENNIAL-BICENTENNIAL COMMITTEE; GREELEY, CO 80631. (#19391).

'CITY OF GREELEY' - LECTURE SERIES. LECTURE SERIES BY FRIENDS OF THE LIBRARY ON THE HISTORY OF THE GREELEY AREA. (LOCAL). JOSEPHINE JONES, CHMN; GREELEY AREA CENTENNIAL-BICENTENNIAL COMMITTEE; GREELEY, CO 80631. (#104284-6).

COLORADO SCHOOL HISTORY COURSES PROJECT. COURSES ON COLORADO HISTORY AT VARIOUS LEVELS; STUDENT-MADE FILM & OTHER RELATED PROJECTS. (LOCAL). JOSEPHINE JONES, CHAIRPERSON; GREELEY CENTENNIAL-BICENTENNIAL COMMISSION; 9TH ST & 9TH AVE; GREELEY, CO 80631. (#2889).

COMMISSION A CENTENNIAL WORK OF ART -GREELEY, CO. WORK OF ART TO BE DONE BY A LOCAL ARTIST WITH CENTENNIAL THEME. (LOCAL). JOSEPHINE JONES, CHAIRPERSON; GREELEY CENTENNIAL-BICENTENNIAL COMMISSION; 9TH ST & 9TH AVE; GREELEY, CO 80631. (#2894).

COMMISSION PHILHARMONIC WORK FOR GREELEY, COLORADO. A FULL ORCHESTRA & CHOIR WORK TO BE BASED ON A LOCAL THEME FOR THE CENTENNIAL-BICENTENNIAL COMMEMORATION. (LOCAL). JOSEPHINE JONES, CHAIRPERSON; GREELEY CENTENNIAL-BICENTENNIAL COMMISSION; 9TH ST & 9TH AVE; GREELEY, CO 80631. (#2893).

COUNTY-WIDE CENTENNIAL-BICENTENNIAL INVOLVEMENT-CO. GOAL IS TO CREATE CENTENNIAL-BICENTENNIAL AWARENESS AND PROJECTS IN A MAJORITY OF THE TOWNS AND RURAL AREAS. (LOCAL). CHRISTINE KAVALEC, CHAIRMAN; WELD COUNTY CENTENNIAL-BICENTENNIAL COMMISSION; PO BOX 758; GREELEY, CO 80631. (#21561).

HIGH SCHOOL RESTORATION IN GREELEY, COLORADO. RESTORATION OF 1890 HIGHSCHOOL FOR MUSEUM OF HISTORY & PALETHNOLOGY. (LOCAL). JOSEPHINE JONES, CHAIRPERSON; GREELEY CENTENNIAL-BICENTENNIAL COMMISSION; 9TH ST & 9TH AVE; GREELEY, CO 80631. (#2900).

HISTORICAL MARKERS PROJECT OF GREELEY, COLORADO. TRACING & MARKING OF MAJOR PIONEER TRAILS THRU WELD COUNTY & MARKING OF HISTORICAL SITES IN SUITABLE MANNER. (LOCAL). JOSEPHINE JONES, CHAIRPERSON; GREELEY CENTENNIAL-BICENTENNIAL COMMISSION; 9TH ST & 9TH AVE; GREELEY, CO 80631. (#2902).

INDEPENDENCE STAMPEDE. CELEBRATION CONSISTING OF RODEO, PARADE, FIREWORKS, COUNTRY & WESTERN STAGE SHOWS, BARBEQUE, THEATER PRODUCTIONS OF 'MOLLY BROWN' & '1776', HISTORICAL WALKING TOURS, WESTERN ART EXHIBIT, ETC. WRITE BOX CC FOR BROCHURE. SPONSOR PLANS INCOMPLETE AS OF 04/28/75. AT ISLAND GROVE PARK GREELEY CO 14TH AVE C ST.. (LOCAL). RODEO COMMITTEE; INDEPEN-

GREELEY — CONTINUED

DENCE STAMPEDE COMMITTEE; BOX CC; GREELEY, CO 80361. (#2891-1).

LINCOLN PARK RESTORATION PROJ OF GREELEY, COLORADO. HISTORICAL EXPLANATION MARKER TO BE ERECTED, RESTORATION OF PETRIKIN FOUNTAIN & CISTERN COVER, & REPLACEMENT OF TREES. (LOCAL). JOSEPHINE JONES, CHAIRPERSON; GREELEY CENTENNIAL-BICENTENNIAL COMMISSION; 9TH ST & 9TH AVE; GREELEY, CO 80631. (#2901).

ORAL HISTORY OF GREELY, COLORADO. COLLECTION OF ORAL HISTORY AND PHOTOGRAPHS FOR PUBLICATION. (LOCAL). L E TRIPLETT, ASST SUPT; SCHOOL DISTRICT SIX; 815 15 ST; GREELEY, CO 80631. (#10368).

PIONEER VILLAGE IN GREELEY, COLORADO. CONSTRUCTION OF A TYPICAL VILLAGE OF 1870'S USING ORIGINAL & RECONSTRUCTED BUILDINGS FOR USE OF SCHOOL CHILDREN AND OTHERS IN UNDERSTANDING HERITAGE OF NORTHERN COLORADO. (LOCAL). JOSEPHINE JONES, CO-CHAIRMAN; GREELEY AREA CENTENNIAL-BICENTENNIAL COMMITTEE; 2653 52ND AVE CT; GREELEY, CO 80631. (#10366).

SPOON RIVER ANTHOLOGY. LIVE PERFORMANCE. (LOCAL). JOSEPHINE JONES, CHMN; GREELEY AREA CENTENNIAL-BICENTENNIAL COMMITTEE; GREELEY, CO 80631. (#104284-1).

'THREE FRONTIERS OF COLORADO'. LECTURE SERIES BY FRIENDS OF THE LIBRARY ON THE HISTORY OF THE AREA. (LOCAL). JOSEPHINE JONES, CHMN; GREELEY AREA CENTENNIAL-BICENTENNIAL COMMITTEE; GREELEY, CO 80631. (#104284-9).

UNC PERFORMING ARTS: 'ARSENIC AND OLD LACE'. LIVE PERFORMANCE. (LOCAL). JOSEPHINE JONES, CHMN; GREELEY AREA CENTENNIAL-BICENTENNIAL COMMITTEE; GREELEY, CO 80631. (#104284-3).

UNC PERFORMING ARTS: 'OUR TOWN'. LIVE PERFORMANCE. (LOCAL). JOSEPHINE JONES, CHMN; GREELEY AREA CENTENNIAL-BICENTENNIAL COMMITTEE; GREELEY, CO 80631. (#104284-5).

'USE OF NATIVE PLANTS BY INDIANS & SETTLERS' -BOOK. 'THE USE OF NATIVE PLANTS BY INDIANS AND SETTLERS' BY GRETCHEN CUTTS DEMONSTRATES PLANT USAGE PAST, PRESENT AND FUTURE. (REGN'L). JOSEPHINE JONES, CHAIRPERSON; GREELEY CENTENNIAL-BICENTENNIAL COMMISSION; 9TH AVE & 9TH STS; GREELEY, CO 80631. (#2886).

'WILD AND WOOLY WORDS' - LECTURE SERIES. SEMINAR. (LOCAL). JOSEPHINE JONES, CHMN; GREELEY AREA CENTENNIAL-BICENTENNIAL COMMITTEE; GREELEY, CO 80631. (#104284-8).

WILDLIFE SANCTUARY PROJECT OF GREELEY, COLORADO. SET UP A SANCTUARY ON LAND BETWEEN CACHE LA POUDRE RIVER & 5TH AVE. (LOCAL). JOSEPHINE JONES, CHAIRPERSON; GREELEY CENTENNIAL-BICENTENNIAL COMMISSION; 9TH ST & 9TH AVE; GREELEY, CO 80631. (#2890).

WORKSHOP ON COLORADO GEOGRAPHY, GREELEY, CO. UNIVERSITY OF NORTHERN COLORADO OFFERING SUMMER SCHOOL COURSE ON COLORADO GEORGRAPHY WITH A VIEW OF THE NEXT 100 YEARS. (LOCAL). JOSEPHINE JONES, DIRECTOR; GREELEY AREA CENTENNIAL - BICENTENNIAL COMMITTEE; GREELEY, CO 80631. (#19389).

MAY 17, '75. SPRING FLING. 4X8-FT TABLE FOR DISPLAY OF CRAFTS $2 RESERVATION AND FEE DUE WEEK BEFORE REGISTRATION 8AM. DAY OF FESTIVAL. AT LINCOLN PARK, GREELEY CO, 9TH ST, 9TH AVE.. (LOCAL). GAAHC; GREELEY AREA ARTS AND HUMANITIES COUNCIL; BOX 1874; GREELEY, CO 80631. (#50790-1).

OCT 5 - 6, '75. UNITED STATES ARMED FORCES BICENTENNIAL CARAVAN. THE CARAVAN IS COMPOSED OF EXHIBIT VANS FOR EACH BRANCH OF THE MILITARY SERVICE. THE THEME OF THE EXHIBITION IS 'HISTORY OF THE ARMED FORCES AND THEIR CONTRIBUTION TO THE NATION'. (LOCAL). LTC CLIFFORD A BAKER, DIR; U S ARMED FORCES BICENTENNIAL EXHIBIT VANS PROJECT; 2623 52ND AVE; GREELEY, CO 80631. (#1775-238).

NOV 22, '75. FALL FLING. 4X8-FT TABLE FOR DISPLAY OF CRAFT $2.00 RES AND FEE DUE WEEK BEFORE REGISTRATION 8AM DAY OF FESTIVAL. AT GREELEY MALL 17TH AVE, 28TH ST.. (ST-WIDE). GAAHC; GREELEY AREA ARTS AND HUMANITIES COUNCIL; BOX 1874; GREELEY, CO 80631. (#50790-2).

JAN 1 - JUNE 10, '76. CENTENNIAL-BICENTENNIAL INTEGRATED ARTS PROGRAM. CLASSES OF INSTRUCTION TO YOUNGSTERS AT MEEKER SCHOOL (4TH GRADERS). FIELD TRIPS AND DEMONSTRATIONS INCLUDED. (LOCAL). SUSAN DECAMP, DIRECTOR; COMMUNITY CENTER FOR THE CREATIVE ARTS; 1508 8TH ST; GREELEY, CO 80631. (#103840-1).

FEB 12 - 22, '76. WELD COUNTY RED, WHITE & BLUE DAYS. COUNTY-WIDE KICKOFF OF THE CENTENNIAL-BICENTENNIAL. FLAGS WILL BE PRESENTED TO THE COMMUNITIES. GENERAL AWARENESS OF AND INVOLVEMENT IN THE CENTENNIAL-BICENTENNIAL IS ENCOURAGED. AT THROUGHOUT WELD COUNTY. (LOCAL). DAVID ROSENTRATER, COORD; WELD COUNTY CENTENNIAL-BICENTENNIAL COMMITTEE; 2021 CLUBHOUSE DR; GREELEY, CO 80631. (#200007-104).

FEB 27 - MAR 6, '76. UNC PERFORMING ARTS: 'PAINT YOUR WAGON'. THEATRE PERFORMANCE OF A MUSICAL TO COMMEMORATE THE CENTENNIAL OF COLORADO AND THE BICENTENNIAL OF OUR NATION. (LOCAL). JOSEPHINE JONES, CHMN; GREELEY AREA CENTENNIAL-BICENTENNIAL COMMITTEE & UNC PERFORMING ARTS; GREELEY, CO 80631. (#104284-4).

JUNE 26, '76. GRAND OPENING OF AUDUBON NATIVE GARDEN. COLLECTION OF NATIVE PLANTS, TREES & SHRUBS. INTERPRETIVE BUILDINGS; GRAND OPENING, JUNE 26TH. GUIDEBOOK AVAILABLE. AT CENTENNIAL VILLAGE, ISLAND GROVE PARK, GREELEY, CO. (LOCAL). JOAN G STANLEY; GREELEY AUDUBON SOCIETY; 950 3RD AVE; NEW YORK, NY 10022. (#19976-7).

JUNE 26, '76. ISLAND GROVE PARK - CENTENNIAL VILLAGE DEDICATION. GAMES, RACES, CONTEST AND DEDICATION OF CENTENIAL VILLAGE, FIREWORKS AND DANCE. AT ISLAND GROVE PARK. (LOCAL). CHRISTINE KAVALEC, COORD; WELD COUNTY CENTENNIAL-BICENTENNIAL COMMITTEE; PO BOX 758; GREELEY, CO 80631. (#200007-108).

JUNE 26, '76. MEXICAN ADOBE OPENING. OPENING, EXHIBIT. (LOCAL). GEORGE HALL, COORD; WELD COUNTY CENTENNIAL BICENTENNIAL COMMITTEE; 919 7TH ST; GREELEY, CO 80631. (#200007-107).

JUNE 26, '76. PIERCE CAR CARAVAN TO WELD COUNTY FOR COMMUNITY DAY CELEBRATION. CAR CARAVAN OF PIERCE COMMUNITY RESIDENTS WILL LEAVE FROM PIERCE TOWN HALL FOR 16 MILE DRIVE TO ISLAND GROVE PARK IN GREELEY, WHERE CARAVANS FROM THE 29 WELD COUNTY TOWNS WILL MEET FOR PICNIC, CONTESTS, RACES, DEDICATION OF CENTENNIAL VILLAGE. AT ISLAND GROVE PARK IN GREELEY AT NORTH END OF 14TH ST. (LOCAL). CHRISTINE KAVALEE, COORD; PIERCE & WELD CO CENT-BICENT CO & INDEPENDENCE STAMPEDE COMMITTEE; PO BOX 550; GREELEY, CO 80631. (#107009-1).

JUNE 26, '76. TRANSPORTATION FOR WELD COUNTY COMMUNITY DAY. FESTIVAL AT ISLAND GROVE PARK. (LOCAL). PAUL A MARTINEZ, CHMN; GILCREST BICENTENNIAL COMMITTEE; PO BOX 103; GILCREST, CO 80623. (#200007-106).

JUNE 26, '76. WELD COUNTY COMMUNITY DAY. FESTIVAL. (LOCAL). CHRISTINE KAVALEC; WELD COUNTY CENTENNIAL-BICENTENNIAL COMMISSION; 9TH AVE & 10TH ST; GREELEY, CO 80631. (#24579-1).

JUNE 26, '76. WELD COUNTY COMMUNITY DAY BICENTENNIAL RODEO. COMPETITION, FESTIVAL. (LOCAL). CHRISTINE KAVALEC, COORD; WELD COUNTY CENTENNIAL BICENTENNIAL COMMITTEE; PO BOX 758; GREELEY, CO 80631. (#200007-105).

JUNE 27, '76. 'THE UNSINKABLE MOLLY BROWN'. LIVE PERFORMANCE AT GREELEY CENTRAL AUDITORIUM. (LOCAL). CHRISTINE KAVALEC, COORD; GREELEY CHAMBER OF COMMERCE AND GREELEY INDEPENDENCE STAMPEDE; BOX CC; GREELEY, CO 80631. (#200007-109).

JUNE 29, '76. RODEO, WATERMELON RACE AND BUFFALO STAMPEDE. COMPETITION, LIVE PERFORMANCE, FESTIVAL AT ISLAND GROVE PARK. (LOCAL). CHRISTINE KAVALEC, COORD; GREELEY CHAMBER OF COMMERCE & GREELEY INDEPENDENCE STAMPEDE; BOX CC; GREELEY, CO 80631. (#200007-111).

JUNE 29, '76. WESTERN BARBECUE AT INDEPENDENCE STAMPEDE. FESTIVAL AT ISLAND GROVE PARK. (LOCAL). CHRISTINE KAVALEC, COORD; GREELEY CHAMBER OF COMMERCE AND GREELEY INDEPENDENCE STAMPEDE; BOX CC; GREELEY, CO 80631. (#200007-110).

JUNE 29 - JULY 4, '76. INDEPENDENCE STAMPEDE. WRITE BOX CC, GREELEY, CO 80631 FOR BROCHURE. AT ISLAND GROVE PARK GREELEY CO 14TH AVE & E ST.. (REGN'L). J GILBERT HAUSE, PUBL DIR; INDEPENDENCE STAMPEDE COMMITTEE; BOX CC; GREELEY, CO 80631. (#2891-2).

JUNE 30, '76. FAMILY NIGHT & RODEO. COMPETITION, LIVE PERFORMANCE AT ISLAND GROVE PARK. (LOCAL). JOHN CHLANDA, CHAIRMAN; GREELEY INDEPENDENCE STAMPEDE & GREELEY CHAMBER OF COMMERCE; BOX CC; GREELEY, CO 80631. (#108622-1).

JULY 1, '76. SENIOR CITIZEN'S DAY: RODEO, WATERMELON RACE & BUFFALO STAMPEDE. COMPETITION, LIVE PERFORMANCE AT ISLAND GROVE PARK. (LOCAL). JOHN CHLANDA, CHAIRMAN; GREELEY INDEPENDENCE STAMPEDE & GREELEY CHAMBER OF COMMERCE; BOX CC; GREELEY, CO 80631. (#108622-2).

JULY 1 - 4, '76. CENTENNIAL-BICENTENNIAL ART SHOW FOR YOUTH. FEATURES FIRST, SECOND & THIRD PLACE WINNERS IN CENTENNIAL-BICENTENNIAL ART CONTEST FOR ALL GRADE, MIDDLE & HIGH SCHOOL STUDENTS OF WELD COUNTY. WILL RUN CONCURRENTLY WITH GREELEY INDEPENDENCE STAMPEDE. AT ISLAND GROVE PARK. (LOCAL). KAY MCELROY, DIRECTOR; GREELEY ART ASSOC; PO BOX 609; GREELEY, CO 80631. (#108123-1).

JULY 22 - 24, '76. 'SUSANNAH'. LIVE PERFORMANCE AT FRASIER HALL, UNC CAMPUS. (ST-WIDE). OPERA GUILD; UNIVERSITY OF NORTHERN COLORADO, OPERA GUILD; UNIVERSITY OF NORTHERN COLORADO; GREELEY, CO 80639. (#50791-1).

AUG 5 - 7, '76. '1776'. THEATRE PERFORMANCE OF A MUSICAL TO COMMEMORATE THE CENTENNIAL OF COLORADO AND THE BICENTENNIAL OF OUR NATION. AT FRASIER HALL, UNC CAMPUS. (ST-WIDE). PERFORMING ARTS; UNIVERSITY OF NORTHERN COLORADO PERFORMING ARTS; UNIVERSITY OF NORTHERN COLORADO; GREELEY, CO 80639. (#50792-2).

AUG 6 - 10, '76. ANNUAL WELD COUNTY FAIR. DAYS OF '76 THEME FOR ONE OF THE NATION'S LARGEST COUNTY FAIRS, FEATURING 4-H EXHIBITS INVOLVING LIVESTOCK, AGRICULTURE, CANNING, COOKING, SEWING & COMMERCIAL EXHIBITS. AT WELD COUNTY EXHIBITION BUILDING. (ST-WIDE). ELMER ROTHMAN, COORD; WELD COUNTY FAIR BOARD & WELD COUNTY EXTENSION SERVICE; 425 N 15TH AVE; GREELEY, CO 80631. (#107011-1).

GREENWOOD VLG

JULY 31, '76. GREENWOOD VILLAGE CENTENNIAL-BICENTENNIAL FESTIVAL & PICNIC. FESTIVAL. (LOCAL). MRS JOHN LUNT, CHAIRMAN; CITY OF GREENWOOD VILLAGE; 2800 WILLIAMETTE LANE; LITTLETON, CO 80121. (#200007-205).

GRND JUNCTION

COLORADO COUNCIL ON THE ARTS & HUMANITIES. SUPPORT FOR & PROMOTION OF PROJECTS PLANNED & PROJECTS ALREADY UNDER WAY IN CONNECTION WITH THE CENTENNIAL-BICENTENNIAL COMMEMORATION. (ST-WIDE). G D BARRANTE, EXEC DIR; COLORADO CENTENNIAL-BICENTENNIAL COMMISSION; 901 SHERMAN ST; DENVER, CO 80203. (#1998).

COMMUNITY AMPHITHEATRE PROJ OF WEST-CENTRAL COLO. PLANNING & CONSTRUCTING AN OUTDOOR COMMUNITY AMPHITHEATRE FOR PAGEANT DEPICTING HISTORICAL DEVELOPMENT OF AREA, & TO PROVIDE THE WESTERN SLOPE WITH PERMANENT OUTDOOR FACILITY. (ST-WIDE). DON MACKENDRICK, CHAIRPERSON; MESA COUNTY CENTENNIAL-BICENTENNIAL COMMISSION; COUNTY COURT HOUSE; GRND JUNCTION, CO 81501. (#2905).

COMMUNITY FAIRGROUNDS AND GRANDSTAND IN COLORADO. PROJECT TO CONSTRUCT A GRANDSTAND AT THE FAIRGROUNDS IN GRND JUNCTION, COLORADO. (LOCAL). LAWRENCE AUBERT, CHAIRMAN; MESA CO BD OF COMMISSIONERS; BOX 897; GRND JUNCTION, CO 81501. (#5849).

COMMUNITY HISTORY PROJECT OF MESA COUNTY, COLORADO. TO DEVELOP FACILITIES TO GENERATE INTEREST IN THE PIONEER HISTORY OF WEST CENTRAL COLORADO. INCLUDES THE PRESERVATION OF HISTORICAL MATERIALS & POSSIBLE PUBLICATION OF HISTORICAL MONOGRAPHS. (LOCAL). DON MACKENDRICK, CHAIRPERSON; MESA COUNTY CENTENNIAL-BICENTENNIAL COMMISSION; COUNTY COURT HOUSE; GRND JUNCTION, CO 81501. (#2912). **ARBA GRANTEE.**

GRAND JUNCTION AIRPORT TERMINAL, CO. THE BUILDING OF A TERMINAL FOR THE INCREASED AIR TRAFFIC AT GRAND JUNCTION; THE FACILITY WILL BE DEDICATED DURING 1976. (LOCAL). MRS MARIETTA BENGE, COORDINATOR; CITY OF GRAND JUNCTION; 118 HILLCREST MANOR; GRND JUNCTION, CO 81501. (#14838).

HERITAGE BAZAAR. BAZAAR IS A REVIVAL OF EARLY AMERICAN HANDICRAFTS AND ETHNIC ARTS PLUS A PLATFORM FOR INDIVIDUALS & GROUPS TO PARTICIPATE IN THE CENTENNIAL AS A COMMUNITY EFFORT. (LOCAL). MARSHA GOBBO, CHMN; MESA COUNTY CENTENNIAL-BICENTENNIAL COMMITTEE; 127 N 4TH ST; GRND JUNCTION, CO 81501. (#102934-1). **(??).**

MINING-PETROLEUM TABLOID, GRAND JUNCTION, CO. ARTICLES ON OIL SHALING, OIL, GAS, COAL, URANIUM, ZINC, SILVER, & GOLD TO BE PUBLISHED & DISTRIBUTED 9/12/76. (NAT'L). EARL F LAND, COORDINATOR; AMERICAN INSTITUTE OF MINING, METALLURGICAL & PETROLEUM ENGINEER; 2910 FORMAY AVE; GRND JUNCTION, CO 81501. (#27373).

NEW BOYS' CLUB BUILDING OF GRAND JUNCTION, COLO. CONSTRUCTION OF 2-STORY CONCRETE BUILDING TO BE OCCUPIED BY THE GRAND VALLEY BOYS CLUB OF GRAND JCT., COLO. OVER 1000 MINORITY & LOW INCOME BOYS WILL BE MEMBERS OF CLUB & NEW HOME IS NEEDED. (LOCAL). CARL GAUMER, DIRECTOR; BOYS CLUB OF GRAND VALLEY; 601 N FIRST ST; GRND JUNCTION, CO 81501. (#2036). **ARBA GRANTEE.**

PETROGLYPH SURVEY AND PRESERVATION PROJECT - COLO. A PROJECT TO SURVEY RECORD AND PRESERVE THROUGH PHOTOGRAPHY & THRU PERMANENT RECORDS AND ACCURATE CASTS THE PETROGLYPHS OF MESA COUNTY, COLORADO. (ST-WIDE). CARL CONNER; HISTORICAL MUSEUM & INST OF WESTERN COLORADO; 4TH & UTE; GRND JUNCTION, CO 81501. (#2716). **ARBA GRANTEE.**

TURN OF THE CENTURY STREETLIGHTS, GRAND JCT, CO. THE 7TH STREET OLD-FASHIONED STREETLIGHTS PROVIDE A FINISHING TOUCH TO THE RESTORATION OF A 5 BLOCK TRACT IN THE HEART OF TOWN. (LOCAL). HARVEY M ROSE, CITY MANAGER; CITY OF GRAND JUNCTION; 250 N 5 ST; GRAND JCT, CO 81501. (#24575).

WESTERN COLORADO CENTER FOR THE ARTS DEVELOPMENT. DEVELOPMENT OF THE WESTERN COLORADO CENTER FOR THE ARTS. THIS PROJECT IS DESIGNED TO RETAIN WESTERN ART INDIGENOUS TO THE STATE OF COLORADO & SURROUNDING AREA. (ST-WIDE). BILL L BECKWITH, DIRECTOR; WESTERN COLORADO CENTER FOR THE ARTS; 1803 N 7TH ST; GRND JUNCTION, CO 81501. (#1320).

AUG 23, '74 - SEPT 19, '76. CERAMIC AND MACRAME EXHIBIT. EXHIBIT AT MESA COUNTY LIBRARY. (LOCAL). NORMA EISENHAWR, COORD; WESTERN COLORADO POTTERS' GUILD; 1915 LINDA LA; GRND JUNCTION, CO 81501. (#108738-10).

SEPT 1, '74. OPENING OF BOYS CLUB FACILITY. CONSTRUCTION OF 2-STORY CONCRETE BUILDING TO BE OCCUPIED BY THE GRAND VALLEY BOYS CLUB OF GRAND JCT., COLO. OVER 1000 MINORITY & LOW INCOME BOYS WILL BE MEMBERS OF CLUB & NEW HOME IS NEEDED. (LOCAL). CARL GAUMER, DIRECTOR; BOYS CLUB OF GRAND VALLEY; 601 N FIRST ST; GRND JUNCTION, CO 81501. (#2036-901).

JULY 29 - 30, '75. 'OLD WAYS IN THE NEW WORLD' - MEXICAN FOLK GROUP PRESENTATION. THIS MEXICAN FOLK GROUP IS TOURING THE NATION WITH A PERFORMANCE OF MARIACHI MUSIC AND DANCE, JAROCHO MUSIC, ZAPATEADO DANCE PLUS A VOCDUET. THE GROUP PARTICIPATED IN WEEK LONG CULTURAL FESTIVITIES IN WASHINGTON, DC, BEFORE GOING ON TOUR. AT WALTER WALKER THEATER. (LOCAL). KAREN COBB, CHAIRMAN; SMITHSONIAN INSTITUTE; 722 HEMLOCK DR; GRND JUNCTION, CO 81501. (#102102-1).

OCT 31, '75. U S ARMED FORCES BICENTENNIAL BAND PERFORMANCE. LIVE PERFORMANCE AT WALTER WALKER AUDITORIUM, MESA COLLEGE. (LOCAL). B BLACKBURN, DIR; MESA COUNTY CENTENNIAL-BICENTENNIAL COMMITTEE; 1120 NORTH AVE; GRAND JCT, CO 81501. (#102813-1).

GRND JUNCTION—CONTINUED

JAN 5 - 10, '76. MULTI-IMAGE HISTORICAL SLIDE PRESENTATION. A MULTI-IMAGE HISTORICAL SLIDE PRODUCTION THAT WILL INCLUDE HISTORICAL & CONTEMPORARY VISUALS, MUSIC & NARRATION COVERING THE AREA OF WEST CENTRAL COLORADO, PRECOLUMBIAN TIMES TO PRESENT. ALSO: FILM/SLIDES. AT MULTI-PURPOSE BLDG, 100 MAIN ST. (LOCAL). DAN ROBERTS, DIRECTOR; MESA COUNTY CENTENNIAL - BICENTENNIAL; 1120 N MESA COLLEGE; GRND JUNCTION, CO 81501. (#7729-1).

FEB 15 - APR 30, '76. SENIOR CITIZENS HISTORICAL REFLECTIONS CONTEST. COMPETITION. (LOCAL). BARBARA NORRICK, COORD; TOWN OF GRAND JUNCTION; GRND JUNCTION, CO 81501. (#108671-1).

APR 19 - OCT 19, '76. FRESHAZA DAZY BANQUET. FESTIVAL AT HOLIDAY INN. (LOCAL). VIRGINIA FLAGLER, CHMN; WOMENS DIVISION OF THE GRAND JUNCTION CHAMBER OF COMMERCE; 2005 BUNTING; GRND JUNCTION, CO 81501. (#108671-3).

APR 22 - JUNE 20, '76. COLORADO CHRONICLES. A HISTORIC WRITING CONTEST DESIGNED TO CHRONICLE THE HISTORY OF MESA COUNTY. (LOCAL). BARBARA MORRICK, CHWMN; CITY OF GRAND JUNCTION; 250 N 5TH; GRND JUNCTION, CO 81501. (#108822-1).

MAY 21, '76. BICENTENNIAL PARADE OF COLORADO MUSIC. CONCERT OF ORIGINAL MUSIC BY COLORADO COMPOSERS AS PART OF A SERIES IN CONJUNCTION WITH THE BICENTENNIAL PARADE OF AMERICAN MUSIC; MANY PERFORMANCES IN VARIOUS REGIONS OF THE STATE ARE PLANNED. AT AUDITORIUM, MUSIC BLDG, MESA COLLEGE. (ST-WIDE). RICCARDA F MCQUIE, CHMN; COLORADO FEDERATION OF MUSIC CLUBS, INC; 640 GARFIELD ST; DENVER, CO 80206. (#103793-1).

MAY 28 - JUNE 2, '76. NATIONAL JUNIOR COLLEGE ATHLETIC ASSOCIATION BASEBALL TOURNAMENT. COMPETITION AT TWO RIVERS PLAZA & LINCOLN PARK STADIUM. (LOCAL). TOM WORSTER, CHAIRMAN; GRAND JUNCTION CHAMBER OF COMMERCE; 725 ROOD; GRND JUNCTION, CO 81501. (#200007-87).

MAY 29 - JUNE 3, '76. NJCAA MEN'S CHAMPIONSHIP BASEBALL TOURNAMENT. COMPETITION. (LOCAL). SAM SUPLIZIA, COORD; NJCAA; 127 N 4TH; GRND JUNCTION, CO 81501. (#28033-9).

JUNE 1 - AUG 31, '76. GUIDED TRAIL WALK. TOUR AT MESA LAKES RESORT ON GRAND MESA. (LOCAL). SYLVIA BALDWIN, DIRECTOR; MESA LAKES RESORT ON GRAND MESA; MESA, CO 81643. (#108614-1).

JUNE 5 - 6, '76. CENTENNIAL GEM & MINERAL SHOW. EXHIBIT AT TWO RIVERS PLAZA. (LOCAL). GLEN PRYOR, COORDINATOR; GRAND JUNCTION GEM & MINERAL SHOW, INC; 319 MT VIEW ST; GRND JUNCTION, CO 81501. (#200007-88).

JUNE 11 - 13, '76. CLASS OF 1926 50TH REUNION. FESTIVAL, CEREMONY AT HOLIDAY INN. (LOCAL). MRS LEILA KANE; CLASS OF 1926; 175 BELAIR DR; GRND JUNCTION, CO 81501. (#200007-89).

JUNE 11 - 21, '76. HISTORICAL DOCUMENTARY - 'A GOOD MOTHER OF MEN'. EXHIBIT AT WALTER WALKER AUDITORIUM. (LOCAL). MARK WILLIAMS, COORD; MESA COLLEGE VISUAL ARTS DEPT; 250 N 5TH; GRND JUNCTION, CO 81501. (#200007-90).

JUNE 12, '76. PIONEER TEXTILE CRAFTS. EXHIBIT AT GRAND JUNCTION MUSEUM. (LOCAL). BEVERLY GOODRICH, COORD; GRAND JUNCTION MUSEUM; 4TH & UTE; GRND JUNCTION, CO 81501. (#200007-91).

JUNE 19, '76. ALTRUSA COSTUME CONTEST. COMPETITION, LIVE PERFORMANCE. (LOCAL). BEVERLY GOODRICH, CHMN; WOMEN'S DIVISION OF THE CHAMBER OF COMMERCE; 4TH & UTE; GRND JUNCTION, CO 81501. (#200007-92).

JUNE 20, '76. ARTS & CRAFTS. EXHIBIT, FESTIVAL AT MESA COUNTY PUBLIC LIBRARY. (LOCAL). GLENYS GRAY, CHAIRMAN; SENIOR CITIZENS BICENTENNIAL COMMITTEE; 345 OURAY; GRND JUNCTION, CO 81501. (#200007-93).

JUNE 21 - 26, '76. CENTENNIAL YEAR COLORADO STAMPEDE & PARADE. COMPETITION, LIVE PERFORMANCE AT LINCOLN PARK. (LOCAL). VIRGIL VAN DYKE, COORD; MESA COUNTY SHERIFF'S POSSE; 1834 JUNIPER; GRND JUNCTION, CO 81501. (#200007-94).

JUNE 21 - JULY 28, '76. ORIGINAL PAINTINGS EXHIBIT BY GRAND JUNCTION ARTISTS. EXHIBIT AT MESA COUNTY PUBLIC LIBRARY. (LOCAL). CARMA LEMOINE, COORD; MESA COUNTY PUBLIC LIBRARY; 110 MANTEY HEIGHTS DR; GRND JUNCTION, CO 81501. (#108738-7).

JUNE 23 - 26, '76. AUSTRALIAN RODEO RIDERS. TAKING PART IN GRAND JUNCTION RODEO. (INT'L). JOHN MAUNDER, DIRECTOR; AUSTRALIAN GOVERNMENT; AUSTRALIAN CG, 636 FIFTH AVE; NEW YORK, NY 10020. (#108021-14).

JUNE 23 - 27, '76. COLORADO CRAFT-IN-POWDERHORN. CONFERENCE AT GRAND MESA NATIONAL FOREST. (LOCAL). KAREN COBB, COORDINATOR; GRAND MESA NATIONAL FOREST; BOX 1826; GRND JUNCTION, CO 81501. (#200007-95).

JUNE 26, '76. 'A DAY IN 1876'. LIVE PERFORMANCE, FESTIVAL. (LOCAL). MARK WILLIAMS, COORD; CITY OF GRAND JUNCTION; 250 N 5TH ST; GRND JUNCTION, CO 81501. (#200007-96).

JULY 4, '76. ALTRUSA COSTUME CONTEST. COMPETITION AT LINCOLN PARK. (LOCAL). BEVERLY GOODRICH, CHMN; WOMEN'S DIVISION OF THE CHAMBER OF COMMERCE; 4TH & UTE; GRND JUNCTION, CO 81501. (#108614-2).

JULY 4, '76. OLD-FASHIONED PICNIC. FESTIVAL, PARADE. (LOCAL). DON MACKENDRICK, CHAIRMAN; GRAND JUNCTION BICENTENNIAL COMMITTEE; GRAND JCT, CO 81501. (#107576-1).

JULY 4, '76. SPIRIT OF '76 PARADE. PARADE AT LINCOLN PARK & DOWNTOWN. (LOCAL). ALICE DAVIS, CHAIRMAN; WOMEN'S DIVISION OF THE CHAMBER OF COMMERCE; 681 27 1/2 RD; GRND JUNCTION, CO 81501. (#108614-3).

JULY 17 - AUG 14, '76. ART SHOW. EXHIBIT AT WESTERN COLORADO CENTER FOR THE ARTS. (LOCAL). JEAN TODD, COORDINATOR; WESTERN COLORADO CENTER FOR THE ARTS; 1803 N 7TH; GRND JUNCTION, CO 81501. (#108738-4).

JULY 18, '76. ETHNIC COSTUME PICNIC. FESTIVAL AT LINCOLN PARK. (LOCAL). CAROLYN REINSINGER; BAHAI COMMUNITY OF GRAND JUNCTION; 615 AGEANA DR; GRND JUNCTION, CO 81501. (#108738-6).

JULY 27, '76. IN-HOUSE ENTERTAINMENT FOR GRAND JUNCTION V A HOSPITAL. LIVE PERFORMANCE AT GRAND JUNCTION V A HOSPITAL. (LOCAL). MARILYN HELLER, COORD; AUDIENCES, INC; 1510 S GRANT; DENVER, CO 80210. (#106981-2).

JULY 27, '76. SPIRITUAL REVOLUTION IN AMERICA-PROGRAM & ART DISPLAY. LIVE PERFORMANCE, EXHIBIT. (LOCAL). KENNA GALLEGOS, COORD; BAHAI FAITH; 404 GLENWOOD; GRND JUNCTION, CO 81501. (#108738-2).

JULY 29 - AUG 22, '76. HOMESPUN NEEDLECRAFT EXHIBIT. EXHIBIT AT MESA COUNTY LIBRARY. (LOCAL). RUTH MOSS, COORDINATOR; COLORADO BICENTENNIAL COMMITTEE; 964 LAKESIDE CT; GRND JUNCTION, CO 81501. (#108738-1).

JULY 31, '76. TOWN MEETING. CONFERENCE AT TWO RIVERS PLAZA. (LOCAL). BOB QUINBY, COORDINATOR; GRAND JUNCTION KIWANIS; 484 N SHERWOOD; GRND JUNCTION, CO 81501. (#108738-3).

AUG 2 - 4, '76. CHATAUQUA. FESTIVAL, LIVE PERFORMANCE AT LINCOLN PARK. (LOCAL). JIM KYLE, CHMN; ROTARY CLUB; BOX 897; GRND JUNCTION, CO 81501. (#108955-12).

AUG 3 - 5, '76. NEEDLECRAFT DEMONSTRATIONS. THERE WILL BE DEMONSTRATIONS IN HOMESPUN, KNITTING AND CROCHETING BY SPANISH-SPEAKING SENIOR CITIZENS. AT MESA COUNTY LIBRARY. (LOCAL). JUANITA ULIBARRI, COORD; MUSEUM; 538 SOUTH AVE; GRND JUNCTION, CO 81501. (#108784-8).

AUG 6, '76. PYROTECHNICS GUIDE INTERNATIONAL INC FIREWORKS DISPLAY. FIREWORKS WILL LIGHT UP THE SKY OVER GRAND JUNCTION IN THIS GALA DISPLAY. DEMONSTRATION: MUSKETRY, CANNON FIRING, BUGLE CALLS & CAVALRY EQUITATION BY 1ST COLORADO DRAGOONS & INFANTRY. AT VETERANS PARK (URANIUM DOWNS RACETRACK). (ST-WIDE). BILL LAYBORN, CHMN; MESA COUNTY CENTENNIAL-BICENTENNIAL COMMITTEE; 657 20 1/2 RD; GRND JUNCTION, CO 81501. (#102924-1).

AUG 7, '76. BEARD GROWING CONTEST. COMPETITION. (LOCAL). PAT SCHUTZ, COORDINATOR; CITY OF GRAND JUNCTION; 250 5TH ST; GRND JUNCTION, CO 81501. (#108671-2).

AUG 7 - 8, '76. LITTLE BRITCHES RODEO. COMPETITION, FESTIVAL AT URANIUM DOWNS. (ST-WIDE). DALE DEAN, COORDINATOR; MESA COUNTY LITTLE BRITCHES; 345 30 ROAD; GRND JUNCTION, CO 81501. (#108738-9).

AUG 9 - 14, '76. MESA COUNTY FAIR. FAIR AT URANIUM DOWNS. (LOCAL). BILL HUNTLEY, COORD; MESA COUNTY FAIR BOARD; BOX 580; GRND JUNCTION, CO 81501. (#108738-8).

AUG 15, '76. IN-HOUSE ENTERTAINMENT FOR GRAND JUNCTION V A HOSPITAL. LIVE PERFORMANCE AT GRAND JUNCTION V A HOSPITAL. (LOCAL). MARILYN HELLER, COORD; AUDIENCES, INC; 1510 S GRANT; DENVER, CO 80210. (#106981-1).

AUG 20 - 22, '76. SMITHSONIAN INSTITUTION GREEK TOUR. TOUR. (ST-WIDE). MARK WILLIAMS; GRAND JUNCTION BICENTENNIAL COMMITTEE; 250 ST; GRND JUNCTION, CO 81501. (#108738-11).

SEPT 9 - 11, '76. STATE ELKS CONVENTION. CONFERENCE AT TWO RIVERS PLAZA. (ST-WIDE). W A PITTS, COORD; GRAND JUNCTION ELKS LODGE #575; 2626 H RD; GRND JUNCTION, CO 81501. (#108784-15).

SEPT 17 - 18, '76. ART FESTIVAL. EXHIBIT AT ARTIST ENTRY FEE IS $20 - PUBLIC FREE. IS SELLING EXHIBIT. (REGN'L). JOSEPH T SINCLAIR, DIR; GRAND JUNCTION BICENT COMM & GRAND JUNCTION ART FESTIVAL, INC; BOX 2860; GRND JUNCTION, CO 81501. (#108738-12).

SEPT 17 - 18, '76. MINING-PETROLEUM DAYS. OLD & NEW MINING EQUIPMENT WILL BE EXHIBITED. SATURDAY HOURS 10AM - 5:30PM. AT TWO RIVERS PLAZA AND VICINITY. (LOCAL). EARL F LAND; AMERICAN INSTITUTE OF MINING, METALLURGICAL & PETROLEUM ENGINEERS; 2910 FORMAY AVENUE; GRND JUNCTION, CO 81501. (#108784-16).

SEPT 17 - 18, '76. UNITED STATES ARMED FORCES BICENTENNIAL CARAVAN. CARAVAN IS COMPOSED OF EXHIBIT VANS FOR EACH MILITARY SERVICE. PROJECT THEME IS 'HISTORY OF THE ARMED FORCES AND THEIR CONTRIBUTIONS TO THE NATION'. (LOCAL). MARK WILLIAMS; UNITED STATES ARMED FORCES BICENTENNIAL CARAVAN; 250 5TH ST; GRND JUNCTION, CO 81501. (#1775-725).

SEPT 20 - OCT 17, '76. PIONEER PAINTINGS EXHIBIT. ORIGINAL PAINTINGS OF A VARIETY OF HISTORIC SUBJECTS, LANDMARKS AND ANTIQUES. AT MESA COUNTY PUBLIC LIBRARY. (LOCAL). MARK WILLIAMS, COORD; BRUSH AND DALETTE CLUB; 250 N 5TH AVE; GRND JUNCTION, CO 81501. (#108784-13).

SEPT 25, '76. FRUITA COMMUNITY PARADE & BEEF BAR-B-QUE. FESTIVAL, PARADE AT DOWNTOWN. (LOCAL). BERT HARRISON; FRUITA CHAMBER OF COMMERCE; 141 S APPLE; GRND JUNCTION, CO 81521. (#108784-14).

OCT 2, '76. CENTENNIAL STYLE SHOW. THE HISTORICAL MUSEUM & INSTITUTE OF WESTERN COLORADO IS SPONSORING THIS SHOW OF HISTORICAL COSTUMES. AT TWO RIVERS PLAZA, GRAND JUNCTION. (LOCAL). BEVERLY GOODRICH, CHMN; MESA COUNTY CENTENNIAL-BICENTENNIAL COMMITTEE; 4TH UTE AVE; GRND JUNCTION, CO 81501. (#103352-1).

OCT 12 - 16, '76. BASQUE FESTIVAL. FESTIVAL. (REGN'L). JEAN URRUTY, COORD; MESA COUNTY; 465 MESA CT; GRND JUNCTION, CO 81501. (#108784-5).

OCT 18 - NOV 21, '76. WEAVING EXHIBIT. EXHIBIT AT MESA COLLEGE PUBLIC LIBRARY. (LOCAL). GRETCHEN BERING, COORD; MESA WEAVERS' GUILD; 2310 EAST RD; GRND JUNCTION, CO 81501. (#108784-2).

NOV 11, '76. VETERANS' DAY. 132 FLAGS WILL BE ON DISPLAY AROUND THE HOSPITAL. AT VETERANS' HOSPITAL. (LOCAL). AUDREY BAYSINGER, COORD; VOLUNTEERS OF VETERANS' HOSPITAL; 2121 NORTH AVE; GRND JUNCTION, CO 81501. (#108784-6).

NOV 13, '76. POLISH NEW YEAR CELEBRATION. FESTIVAL. (LOCAL). GUY CHERP, COORD; GUY CHERP; BOX 2123; GRND JUNCTION, CO 81501. (#108784-4).

NOV 22 - DEC 19, '76. INDIAN HERITAGE EXHIBIT. EXHIBIT AT MESA COUNTY PUBLIC LIBRARY. (LOCAL). RUTH MOSS, COORD; MESA COUNTY PUBLIC LIBRARY; 964 LAKESIDE CT; GRND JUNCTION, CO 81501. (#108784-3).

DEC 22, '76. LAS POSADAS CELEBRATION - CHRISTMAS EVE IN SPANISH. FESTIVAL AT CATHOLIC CITY CENTER. (LOCAL). JUANITA ULIBARRI; LAS POSADAS CELEBRATION COMMITTEE; 538 SOUTH AVE; GRND JUNCTION, CO 81501. (#108784-12).

GROVER

CEMETERIES IMPROVEMENT - GROVER, CO. THE CEMETERIES IN GROVER WILL BE IMPROVED. (LOCAL). HON F E DUGGAN, MAYOR; CITY OF GROVER; GROVER, CO 80729. (#26361).

HEREFORD & GROVER DOCUMENT PRESERVATION - CO. PRESERVATION AND STORAGE OF HISTORIC DOCUMENTS AND OBJECTS. (LOCAL). HON F E DUGGAN, MAYOR; CITY OF GROVER; GROVER, CO 80729. (#26360).

HISTORY OF GROVER, CO. COLLECT STORIES OF EARLY DAYS AND FAMILY HISTORIES FOR A BOOK. ALSO, TAPE RECORDINGS WILL BE MADE OF INTERVIEWS WITH SENIOR CITIZENS. (LOCAL). ERNESTINE KOENIG, CO-CHAIRMAN; GROVER-HEREFORD BICENTENNIAL COMMISSION; RT 1, BOX 14; GROVER, CO 80729. (#26250).

MEMORY QUILTS - GROVER, CO. TWO PAINTED QUILTS & TWO DUPLICATES HAVE BEEN MADE FOR THE HERITAGE HOUSE; THE 2 DUPLICATES WILL BE SOLD TO RAISE FUNDS FOR THE HOUSE & OTHER PROJECTS. (LOCAL). ERNESTINE KOENIG, CHAIRMAN; GROVER-HEREFORD BICENTENNIAL COMMITTEE; GROVER, CO 80729. (#26256).

JUNE 14 - 17, '76. HEREFORD-GROVER RODEO FESTIVAL. RE-ESTABLISHMENT AND RE-ENACTMENT OF EVENTS FOR RODEO FESTIVAL FROM EARLY DAYS. (LOCAL). F E DUGGAN, COORD; GROVER-HEREFORD BICENTENNIAL COMMITTEE; GROVER, CO 80729. (#200007-115).

JUNE 15 - AUG 30, '76. TIME CAPSULE & TREE PLANTING. CEREMONY AT TOWN HALL, CHATOGA AVE. (LOCAL). HON FRANCIS DUGGAN, MAYOR; GROVER TOWN COUNCIL; GROVER, CO 80729. (#108618-1).

JUNE 19 - 20, '76. GRAND ENTRY LOCAL RCA RODEO. ANNUAL RCA 'EARL ANDERSON MEMORIAL RODEO'. THE GROVER-HEREFORD BICENTENNIAL WILL TAKE PART IN THE GRAND ENTRY. AT RODEO GROUNDS. (ST-WIDE). JACK ANDERSON, COORD; GROVER COMMERCIAL CLUB; RT #1; GROVER, CO 80729. (#200007-116).

SEPT 12, '76. HOBBY 'N' HAPPY DAY. DRAWING FOR HAND-PAINTED CENTENNIAL QUILT WILL BE HELD. (LOCAL). SHIRLEY WIGGIN, COORD; CITY OF GROVER; GROVER, CO 80729. (#108782-1).

GUNNISON

THE BICENTENNIAL FREEDOM CONCEPT - GUNNISON, CO. AS PART OF THE CENTENNIAL-BICENTENNIAL CELEBRATION, THIS PROJECT WILL TRACE CONCEPT OF FREEDOM OVER 200 YEARS, ALLOWING STUDENTS TO EXPRESS THEIR UNDERSTANDING. (LOCAL). CHARLES A PAGE, PROJ DIRECTOR; REIJ SCHOOL DISTRICT; 500 E TOMICHI AVE; GUNNISON, CO 81230. (#15250).

COOPER RECREATION SITE - PROJ OF GUNNISON, CO. AS A CENTENNIAL-BICENTENNIAL PROJECT, PRESERVING THE NAME 'COOPER' ON SITE OF ORIGINAL COOPER RANCH ON GUNNISON RIVER DATING FROM THE 1800'S. (LOCAL). CHARLES A PAGE, PROJ DIRECTOR; CURECANTI NATIONAL RECREATION AREA/ NATIONAL PARK SERVICE; 500 E TOMICHI AVE; GUNNISON, CO 81230. (#15248).

COUNTY ROAD '76 - PROJ OF GUNNISON, CO. RENUMBERING COUNTY ROAD ON QUARTZ CREEK TO #76 AS A REMINDER OF THE PAST AND A DEEPER APPRECIATION OF THE MEANING OF THE CENTENNIALBICENTENNIAL COMMEMORATION. (LOCAL). KENNETH WATTERS, CHAIRMAN; GUNNISON COUNTY BOARD OF COMMISSIONERS; RR; GUNNISON, CO 81230. (#15258).

GUNNISON STREET NAMING PROJECT, CO. SPECIAL TRIPTYCH SHOWS LAND AND SEA BATTLES, AND HONORS LAFAYETTE, WASHINGTON, AND DE GRASSE. (LOCAL). RIAL R LAKE, COORDINATOR; CITY OF GUNNISON; MUNICIPAL BLDG; GUNNISON, CO 81230. (#26291).

GUNNISON — CONTINUED

GUNNISON VALLEY RANCHING MUSEUM - GUNNISON, CO. AS A CENTENNIAL-BICENTENNIAL PROJECT, MULTICASE DISPLAY SHOWING VARIOUS ARTIFACTS, RANCHING, FOREST SERVICE & LIVESTOCK HISTORIES TO PRESENT DAY WITH ILLUSTRATIONS. (LOCAL). CHARLES A PAGE, PROJ DIRECTOR; GUNNISON STOCKGROWERS ASSOC; 500 E TOMICHI AVE; GUNNISON, CO 81230. (#15256).

HERITAGE THROUGH READING - GUNNISON, CO. AS A CENTENNIAL-BICENTENNIAL PROJECT, EXPAND THE HISTORICAL SECTION OF THE GUNNISON COUNTY PUBLIC LIBRARY. (LOCAL). CHARLES A PAGE, PROJ DIRECTOR; GUNNISON COUNTY PUBLIC LIBRARY; 500 E TOMICHI AVE; GUNNISON, CO 81230. (#15255).

THE HISTORY OF GUNNISON COUNTY, CO. A HISTORY OF THE TOWNS, PEOPLE AND EVENTS OF THE GUNNISON RIVER VALLEY IN CENTRAL COLORADO, FROM THE EARLIEST TIMES TO THE PRESENT. (LOCAL). DUANE VANDENBUSCHE, AUTHOR; WESTERN STATE COLLEGE OF COLORADO; GUNNISON, CO 81230. (#10326).

LEGENDS AND TALES OF THE GUNNISON COUNTRY - CO. A CENTENNIAL-BICENTENNIAL PROJECT WILL BE SHORT, TRUE STORIES ABOUT PIONEERS WRITTEN BY STUDENTS. (LOCAL). CHARLES A PAGE, PROJ DIRECTOR; GUNNISON COUNTY HIGH SCHOOL AND RULAND JUNIOR HIGH SCHOOL; 500 E TOMICHI AVE; GUNNISON, CO 81230. (#15254).

LIVING PIONEERS - PROJ OF GUNNISON, CO. TAPED INTERVIEWS OF OLDER RESIDENTS TO PRESERVE THEIR REMEMBRANCES WHICH WILL ADD TO THE MEANING OF THE CENTENNIAL-BICENTENNIAL COMMEMORATION. (LOCAL). CHARLES A PAGE, PROJ COORDINATOR; SENIOR CITIZENS-YOUNG AT HEART CLUB AND GUNNISON COUNTY LIBRARY; 500 E TOMICHI AVE; GUNNISON, CO 81230. (#15253).

NEW RAILROAD MUSEUM - GUNNISON, CO. AS A CENTENNIAL-BICENTENNIAL PROJECT MOVING DENVER AND RIO GRANDE WESTERN DEPOT FROM SARGENTS TO GUNNISON MUSEUM AS ANNEX AND RAILROAD MUSEUM. (LOCAL). CHARLES A PAGE, PROJ DIRECTOR; GUNNISON COUNTY PIONEER AND HISTORICAL SOCIETY; 500 E TOMICHI AVE; GUNNISON, CO 81230. (#15257).

SURVEY OF COUNTY CEMETERIES - GUNNISON, CO. AS A CENTENNIAL-BICENTENNIAL PROJECT, CATALOGING OF ALL MARKERS IN ALL COUNTY CEMETERIES AND PUTTING IN BOOK FORM. (LOCAL). CHARLES A PAGE, PROJ DIRECTOR; LOCAL CHAPTER-DAUGHTERS OF THE AMERICAN REVOLUTION; 500 E TOMICHI AVE; GUNNISON, CO 81230. (#15252).

A TREE FOR THE FUTURE - PROJ OF GUNNISON, CO. AS A REMEMBERANCE OF THE CENTENNIAL-BICENTENNIAL CELEBRATION, THIS PROJECT IS URGING RESIDENTS TO PLANT TREES IN MEMORY OF THE PIONEERS WHO PLANTED TREES IN THE VALLEY IN 1870 AND 1880. (LOCAL). CHARLES A PAGE, PROJ DIRECTOR; GUNNISON IMPROVEMENT ASSOC; 500 E TOMICHI AVE; GUNNISON, CO 81230. (#15249).

20-CIRCLE TOUR MAP - PROJ OF GUNNISON, CO. STRESSING CENTENNIAL-BICENTENNIAL THEME W/HISTORICAL, GEOGRAPHICAL, GEOLOGICAL & RECREATIONAL MAP TO BE PROVIDED FOR RESIDENTS AND VISITORS. (LOCAL). CHARLES A PAGE, PROJ DIRECTOR; GUNNISON COUNTY CHAMBER OF COMMERCE; 500 E TOMICHI AVE; GUNNISON, CO 81230. (#15251).

JUNE 16 - AUG 31, '75. BICENTENNIAL FILM SERIES AT CURECANTI NRA. EXHIBIT AT ELK CREEK VISITOR CENTER. (REGN'L). SUPT, CURECANTI NRA; NATIONAL PARK SERVICE; P.O. BOX 1648; MONTROSE, CO 81401. (#6728-20).

JUNE 16 - AUG 31, '75. WEEKLY GUIDED 'PIONEER LIFE' WALK AND TALK--CURECANTI NRA. TOUR AT ELK CREEK VISITOR CENTER. (REGN'L). SUPT, CURECANTI NRA; NATIONAL PARK SERVICE; P.O. BOX 1648; MONTROSE, CO 81401. (#6729-13).

JUNE 16 - SEPT 1, '75. NIGHTLY CAMPFIRE PGMS ON MAN & ENVIRONS--CURECANTI NRA. ALSO SUMMERS 76 & 77. ONE PROGRAM OF A SERIES BEING PREPARED BY CURECANTI NRA DEALING WITH MAN, NATURAL FEATURES & PROCESSES ALONG THE GUNNISON RIVER IN WESTERN COLORADO. AT ELK CREEK AMPHITHEATER OF CURECANTI NRA. (REGN'L). SUPT, CURECANTI NRA; NATIONAL PARK SERVICE; P.O. BOX 1648; MONTROSE, CO 81401. (#6729-14).

JULY 18, '75 - SEPT 6, '76. GUNNISON VALLEY RANCHING MUSEUM. THE MUSEUM IS A TRIBUTE TO THE AREA'S ECONOMIC HISTORY WITH MULTICASE DISPLAYS SHOWING VARIOUS ARTIFACTS OF RANCHING, FOREST SERVICE AND LIVESTOCK ACTIVITIES IN THE AREA DATING BACK TO THE EARLY DAYS OF SETTLEMENT. AT FOREST BLDG, 216 N COLORADO. (LOCAL). DALE WIDHALM, PROJ COORD; GUNNISON STOCKGROWERS COWBELLES, FOREST SERVICE WSC; 216 N COLORADO; GUNNISON, CO 81230. (#102696-4).

SEPT 15, '75 - JUNE 1, '76. CURECANTI NRA SCHOOL PGM ON PIONEER LIFE ALONG GUNNISON RIVER. MANY AREAS OF THE NATL PARK SYSTEM ARE DEVELOPING PROGRAMS FOR LOCAL SCHOOL GROUPS WHICH WILL GIVE SUCH GROUPS A BETTER UNDERSTANDING OF THE ROLE OF THE PARK & THE NPS IN AMERICA'S HISTORY. UPON REQUEST. AT IN SCHOOLS OF GUNNISON COUNTY. (LOCAL). SUPT, CURECANTI NRA; NATIONAL PARK SERVICE; P.O. BOX 1648; MONTROSE, CO 81401. (#6726-2).

DEC 3, '75 - MAY 5, '76. AMERICAN ISSUES FORUM. SEMINAR AT 307 N WISCONSIN - LIBRARY BLDG. (LOCAL). BONNIE BARIL; GUNNISON COUNTY PUBLIC LIBRARY; 307 N WISCONSIN; GUNNISON, CO 81230. (#104061-2).

FEB 6 - 8, '76. ANNIE GET YOUR GUN - MUSICAL PRODUCTION. PROCEEDS TO WEBSTER HALL & SCHOLARSHIP FUND. AT TAYLOR HALL THEATRE/WESTERN STATE. (LOCAL). BERNARD GOLDBERG; WEBSTER PLAYERS AND WESTERN STATE COLLEGE; 241 N MAIN; GUNNISON, CO 81230. (#104061-3).

MAR 5 - 6, '76. FIREMENS CONCERT AND HONORS BAND. LIVE PERFORMANCE AT TAYLOR HALL THEATRE/WESTERN STATE COLLEGE. (LOCAL). C A PAGE; VOLUNTEER FIRE DEPT AND WESTERN STATE COLLEGE MUSIC DEPT; 500 E TOMICHI AVE; GUNNISON, CO 81230. (#104061-5).

MAR 14, '76. LECTURE: 'SINS OF THE FATHERS - RELIGION & THE AMERICAN REVOLUTION'. SEMINAR AT 107 N IOWA ST. (LOCAL). REV CHARLES DREYER; COMMUNITY CHURCH; 107 N IOWA ST; GUNNISON, CO 81230. (#104061-1).

MAR - MAY '76. MUSICAL PRODUCTION. IN SPRING '76 GUNNISON COMMUNITY COLLEGE DRAMATIC CLUB WILL PRESENT ONE OF THE MAJOR HISTORICAL MUSICALS IN HONOR OF THE CENTENNIALBICENTENNIAL. (LOCAL). BERNARD GOLDBERG, COORD; WEBSTER PLAYERS ASSOC; 241 N MAIN; GUNNISON, CO 81230. (#102696-6).

MAY 31 - SEPT 6, '76. NEW RAILROAD MUSEUM OPENS. THIS CENTENNIAL-BICENTENNIAL PROJECT UNDERTAKES MOVING THE DENVER & RIO GRANDE WESTERN DEPOT FROM SARGENTS TO GUNNISON; DEDICATION IN MAY '76 WILL CELEBRATE THE COMPLETION OF THE PROJECT AND THE OPENING OF THE MUSEUM ANNEX FOR RAILROAD DISPLAYS. AT TOMICHI AVE & ADAMS ST, PIONEER MUSEUM. (LOCAL). B H SNYDER, PROJ DIRECTOR; GUNNISON COUNTY PIONEER & HISTORICAL SOCIETY; 403 N PINE; GUNNISON, CO 81230. (#102696-5).

JUNE 16 - AUG 31, '76. WEEKLY GUIDED 'PIONEER LIFE' WALK AND TALK--CURECANTI NRA. TOUR AT ELK CREEK VISITOR CENTER. (REGN'L). SUPT, CURECANTI NRA; NATIONAL PARK SERVICE; P.O. BOX 1648; MONTROSE, CO 81401. (#6729-513).

JUNE 16 - SEPT 1, '76. NIGHTLY CAMPFIRE PGMS ON MAN & ENVIRONS--CURECANTI NRA. ONE PROGRAM OF A SERIES BEING PREPARED BY CURECANTI NRA DEALING WITH MAN, NATURAL FEATURES AND PROCESSES ALONG THE GUNNISON RIVER IN WESTERN COLORADO. AT ELK CREEK AMPHITHEATER OF CURECANTI NRA. (REGN'L). SUPT, CURECANTI NRA; NATIONAL PARK SERVICE; P.O. BOX 1648; MONTROSE, CO 81401. (#6729-514).

JULY 4, '76. INDEPENDENCE DAY PARADE AND BARBEQUE. THERE WILL BE A BARBEQUE AT 1PM, FOLLOWING THE PARADE. AT TOMICHI AVE & MAIN ST. (LOCAL). CHARLES A PAGE, CHAIRMAN; AMERICAN LEGION & VETERANS OF FOREIGN WARS LOCAL POSTS; 500 E TOMICHI; GUNNISON, CO 81230. (#102696-1).

JULY 4, '76. JULY 4TH FIREWORKS. FESTIVAL AT MOUNTAINEER BOWL, WESTERN STATE COLLEGE. (LOCAL). WHITMAN EASTON, PROJ CHMN; GUNNISON ROTARY CLUB; BOX 60, FIRST NATIONAL BANK; GUNNISON, CO 81230. (#102696-2).

JULY 4, '76. MILITARY TYPE PARADE. PARADE. (LOCAL). GEORGE HEDRICK, JR, COORD; VETERANS OF FOREIGN WAR AND AMERICAN LEGION; 614 W NEW YORK AVE; GUNNISON, CO 81230. (#108617-1).

JULY 14 - 18, '76. CATTLEMEN'S DAYS CELEBRATION. AS A CENTENNIAL-BICENTENNIAL ACTIVITY, THE '76 CELEBRATION WILL CONSIST OF RODEOS, RACES, HORSE SHOWS, JUNIOR LIVESTOCK SHOW AND SALE, PIONEER PARADE AND RELATED ACTIVITIES. AT COUNTY RODEO GROUNDS, S SPRUCE ST. (ST-WIDE). ROGER COTTON, PROJ CHMN; CATTLEMEN'S DAYS ASSOC, INC; BOX 119; GUNNISON, CO 81230. (#102696-7).

JULY 25, '76. ART IN THE PARK. EXHIBIT AT MEMORIAL PARK - TELLER ST & TOMICHI AVE. (LOCAL). MRS R W HARPER; AMERICAN ASSOC OF UNIVERSITY WOMEN; W GUNNISON RURAL ROUTE; GUNNISON, CO 81230. (#104061-4).

AUG 14, '76. ANNUAL FLOWER SHOW. THIS YEAR'S ANNUAL FLOWER SHOW WILL BE DEDICATED TO THE CENTENNIALBICENTENNIAL WITH A PATRIOTIC THEME. AT WEBSTER HALL, 17 N IOWA. (LOCAL). MRS LOUIS MIKKELSON, CHMN; TOP O' THE WORLD GARDEN CLUB; 315 W OHIO ST; GUNNISON, CO 81230. (#102696-3).

HAHNS PEAK

HAHNS PEAK, COLO, AREA RESTORATION PROJECT. RESTORATION AND PRESERVATION OF HISTORIC MINING TOWN SITE, CEMETARY, AND SURROUNDING AREA. (ST-WIDE). MRS W S STEVENSON, CHAIRMAN; HAHNS PEAK HISTORICAL SOCIETY; 1601 N COLLEGE AVE, #98; FORT COLLINS, CO 80428. (#534). **ARBA GRANTEE.**

JULY 5, '75. HAHNS PEAK HISTORIC MINING TOWN PRESENTATION. SLIDE EXHIBIT OF WILD FLOWERS OF NW COLORADO; HISTORICAL PLAYS, OLD STYLE MUSIC & TALENT SHOW; HISTORICAL BOOK REVIEW. AT SCHOOLHOUSE, MAIN ST OF HIWAY 129. (ST-WIDE). RILLA WIGGINS, CHMN; HAHNS PEAK AREA HISTORICAL SOCIETY; 33 W VICTORY WAY; CRAIG, CO 81625. (#534-1).

JULY 19, '75. HAHNS PEAK HISTORIC MINING TOWN PRESENTATION. SLIDE EXHIBIT OF WILD FLOWERS OF NW COLORADO; HISTORICAL PLAYS, OLD STYLE MUSIC & TALENT SHOW; HISTORICAL BOOK REVIEW. AT SCHOOLHOUSE, MAIN ST OF HIWAY 129. (ST-WIDE). RILLA WIGGINS, CHMN; HAHNS PEAK AREA HISTORICAL SOCIETY; 33 W VICTORY WAY; CRAIG, CO 81625. (#534-2).

AUG 2, '75. HAHNS PEAK HISTORIC MINING TOWN PRESENTATION. SLIDE EXHIBIT OF WILD FLOWERS OF NW COLORADO; HISTORICAL PLAYS; OLD STYLE MUSIC & TALENT SHOW; HISTORICAL BOOK REVIEW. AT SCHOOLHOUSE; MAIN ST OF HIWAY 129. (ST-WIDE). RILLA WIGGINS, CHMN; HAHNS PEAK AREA HISTORICAL SOCIETY; 33 W VICTORY WAY; CRAIG, CO 81625. (#534-3).

AUG 16, '75. HAHNS PEAK HISTORIC MINING TOWN PRESENTATION. SLIDE EXHIBIT OF WILD FLOWERS OF NW COLORADO; HISTORICAL PLAYS; OLD STYLE MUSIC & TALENT SHOW; HISTORICAL BOOK REVIEW. AT SCHOOLHOUSE, MAIN ST OF HIWAY 129. (ST-WIDE). RILLA WIGGINS, CHMN; HAHNS PEAK AREA HISTORICAL SOCIETY; 33 W VICTORY WAY; CRAIG, CO 81625. (#534-4).

JULY 3, '76. HAHNS PEAK HISTORIC MINING TOWN PRESENTATION. SLIDE EXHIBIT OF WILD FLOWERS OF NW COLORADO; HISTORICAL PLAYS; OLD STYLE MUSIC & TALENT SHOW; HISTORICAL BOOK REVIEW. AT SCHOOLHOUSE, MAIN ST OF HIWAY 129. (ST-WIDE). RILLA WIGGINS, CHMN; HAHNS PEAK AREA HISTORICAL SOCIETY; 901 SOUTH SPRING; CRAIG, CO 81625. (#534-5).

JULY 17, '76. HAHNS PEAK HISTORIC MINING TOWN PRESENTATION. SLIDE EXHIBIT OF WILD FLOWERS OF NW COLORADO; HISTORICAL PLAYS; OLD STYLE MUSIC & TALENT SHOW; HISTORICAL BOOK REVIEW. AT SCHOOLHOUSE, MAIN ST OF HIWAY 129. (ST-WIDE). RILLA WIGGINS, CHMN; HAHNS PEAK AREA HISTORICAL SOCIETY; 33 W VICTORY WAY; CRAIG, CO 81625. (#534-6).

AUG 7, '76. HAHNS PEAK HISTORIC MINING TOWN PRESENTATION. SLIDE EXHIBIT OF WILD FLOWERS OF NW COLORADO; HISTORICAL PLAYS; OLD STYLE MUSIC & TALENT SHOW; HISTORICAL BOOK REVIEW. AT SCHOOLHOUSE, MAIN ST OF HIWAY 129. (ST-WIDE). RILLA WIGGINS, CHMN; HAHNS PEAK AREA HISTORICAL SOCIETY; 33 W VICTORY WAY; CRAIG, CO 81625. (#534-7).

AUG 21, '76. HAHNS PEAK HISTORIC MINING TOWN PRESENTATION. SLIDE EXHIBIT OF WILD FLOWERS OF NW COLORADO; HISTORICAL PLAYS; OLD STYLE MUSIC & TALENT SHOW; HISTORICAL BOOK REVIEW. AT SCHOOLHOUSE, MAIN ST OF HIWAY 129. (ST-WIDE). RILLA WIGGINS, CHMN.; HAHNS PEAK AREA HISTORICAL SOCIETY; 33 W VICTORY WAY; CRAIG, CO 81625. (#534-8).

HARTMAN

'GREENING & CLEANING COLORADO' - HARTMAN. PAINT FIRE HYDRANTS, CLEANUP TOWN & PARK. (LOCAL). HON W O RANDLE, MAYOR; TOWN OF HARTMAN; HARTMAN, CO 81040. (#26351).

TENNIS COURT - HARTMAN, CO. A TENNIS COURT WILL BE CONSTRUCTED IN THE TOWN PARK. (LOCAL). HON W O RANDLE, MAYOR; TOWN OF HARTMAN; HARTMAN, CO 81043. (#26350).

HAXTUN

CENTENNIAL BULLETIN BOARD OF HAXTUN, COLO. COMMUNITY BULLETIN BOARD TO INFORM CITIZENS OF CENT-BICENT EVENTS AND LATER TO BE USED FOR POSTING OTHER COMMUNITY EVENTS. (LOCAL). G J BENESH, CHAIRMAN; HAXTUN CENTENNIAL-BICENTENNIAL COMMISSION; P O BOX 145; HAXTUN, CO 80731. (#4153).

CENTENNIAL ROADSIDE PARK IN HAXTUN, COLORADO. FINAL DEVELOPMENT OF PARK ON US-6, NAMED CENTENNIAL PARK. PARK WILL HAVE PLAYGROUND, AND COMPLETE FACILITIES FOR THE TRAVELER. WILL ADD SCENIC BEAUTY ALONG ONE OF COLORADO'S ENTERING ROADWAYS. (ST-WIDE). G J BENESH, CHAIRMAN; HAXTUN CENTENNIAL-BICENTENNIAL COMMITTEE; BOX 145; HAXTUN, CO 80731. (#4915).

DAYS OF '76 POSTER CONTEST IN HAXTUN, COLORADO. POSTERS WILL BE SUBMITTED THROUGH SCHOOLS, DEPICTING SCENES OF 1876 AND 1976 IN HONOR OF THE NATION'S BICENTENNIAL AND COLORADO'S CENTENNIAL. (LOCAL). G J BENESH, CHAIRMAN; HAXTUN PUBLIC SCHOOL SYSTEM; C/O BOX 145; HAXTUN, CO 80731. (#4918).

HAXTUN, COLORADO CONFERENCE ON THE FUTURE. THE COMMUNITY PLANS TO ENLIST OUTSIDE EXPERTS TO PROVIDE CONSULTATION AND TO WORK WITH THE COMMUNITY IN SETTING GOALS FOR DEVELOPMENT AND IMPROVEMENT. (LOCAL). G J BENESH, CHAIRMAN; HAXTUN CENTENNIAL-BICENTENNIAL COMMISSION; BOX 145; HAXTUN, CO 80731. (#4914).

SEPT 26 - 27, '75. HARVEST FESTIVAL, 'OUR HERITAGE'. AWARD, FESTIVAL, PARADE AT STREETS OF HAXTUN. (LOCAL). MS BERNICE THOMPSON, CHMN; HAXTUN TOWN BOARD; HAXTUN, CO 80731. (#100202-1).

SEPT 27, '75. CENTENNIAL CORN FESTIVAL. COMMUNITY FESTIVAL WILL HAVE SPIRIT OF '76 THEME. THIS FESTIVAL WILL BE IN THE TRADITION OF THE PIONEER CORN HARVEST FESTIVAL. WILL FEATURE A PARADE. (LOCAL). G J BENESH, CHRMN; HAXTUN CENT-BICENT COMMITTEE; BOX 145; HAXTUN, CO 80731. (#4151-1).

JUNE 19, '76. PAOLI DAY. FESTIVAL. (LOCAL). MRS GALEN BAMFORD, COORD; PHILLIPS COUNTY BICENTENNIAL COMMITTEE; HAXTUN, CO 80731. (#200007-123).

JULY 4, '76. FIREWORKS DISPLAY. FESTIVAL. (LOCAL). MRS GALEN BAMFORD, CHMN; PHILLIPS COUNTY CENTENNIAL-BICENTENNIAL COMMITTEE; HAXTUN, CO 80731. (#108613-2).

JULY 31, '76. OLD-TIME SATURDAY NIGHT. PARADE, SQUARE DANCING, SHORT MELODRAMA AND ICE CREAM SOCIAL. (LOCAL). MRS GALEN BAMFORD, CHMN; PHILLIPS COUNTY CENTENNIAL-BICENTENNIAL COMMITTEE; HAXTUN, CO 80731. (#108613-1).

HAYDEN

HAYDEN VALLEY, COLO, MUSEUM & HOSPITALITY CNTR. HEATING AND REWIRING OF TOWN DEPOT NOW BEING DEVELOPED BY COMMUNITY INTO MUSEUM AND HOSPITALITY CENTER. (ST-WIDE). MARTHA BAIERL, PRESIDENT, HAYDEN HERITAGE CENTER; HAYDEN HERITAGE CENTER; PO BOX 164; HAYDEN, CO 81639. (#379). **(??). ARBA GRANTEE.**

HAYDEN — CONTINUED

HERITAGE CENTER IN HAYDEN, CO. GRAND OPENING OF HAYDEN HERITAGE CENTER ON JUNE 1, 1975. (LOCAL). HENRY ZEHNER, PROJ CHAIRMAN; HAYDEN HERITAGE CENTER; HAYDEN HERITAGE STATION; HAYDEN, CO 81639. (#10375).

TOWN OF HAYDEN, COLORADO, DEPOT PROJECT. CONSTRUCTION OF DISPLAY CASES BUILDING A FENCE AND MODELING THE INTERIOR OF THE DENVER AND RIO GRANDE DEPOT. (LOCAL). MARTHA BALERL, DIRECTOR; HAYDEN MUSEUM; HAYDEN, CO 81639. (#1103). **(??). ARBA GRANTEE.**

JUNE 1, '75. GRAND OPENING OF HAYDEN HERITAGE CENTER. EXHIBIT, OPENING, TOUR AT ABANDONED RIO GRANDE RR STATION SITE OF MUSEUM. (ST-WIDE). JOHN M REAGAN; HAYDEN HERITAGE CENTER; BOX 21; HAYDEN, CO 81639. (#50488-1).

HENDERSON

MAY 5, '76. CENTENNIAL-BICENTENNIAL CINCO DE MAYO FESTIVAL. FESTIVAL, LIVE PERFORMANCE AT ADAMS COUNTY FAIRGROUNDS. (ST-WIDE). ELEANOR GALLEGOS, CHMN; COLORADO STATE UNIV EXTENSION, ADAMS COUNTY; RT 2 BOX 120 P8; BRIGHTON, CO 80601. (#103596-1).

HEREFORD

HEREFORD & GROVER HISTORIC DOCUMENTS - CO. REPRINTING OF DOCUMENTS AND PICTURES OF HISTORICAL VALUE FROM THE PRE-HOMESTEAD AND HOMESTEAD ERA. (LOCAL). HON F E DUGGAN, MAYOR; TOWN OF HEREFORD; HEREFORD GRV, CO 80729. (#26352).

HINSDALE

MEDICAL CENTER FOR LAKE CITY, COLO, AREA. MEDICAL CENTER TO BE BUILT TO IMPROVE THE QUALITY OF LIFE FOR THE INHABITANTS OF LAKE CITY. QUALITY OF LIFE IN AREA. (LOCAL). THOMAS THOMPSON, CO-CHAIRMAN; HINSDALE CENTENNIAL BICENTENNIAL COMMITTEE; BOX 352; LAKE CITY, CO 81235. (#4171).

HOLLY

CENTENNIAL MUSEUM AND PARK - HOLLY, CO. ANTIQUES, SKILLS, ARTS AND PRODUCTS OF LOCAL CREATION AND OWNERSHIP WITH A PARK AREA. (LOCAL). MYRTLE C MILES, CHAIRMAN; HOLLY COMMERCIAL CLUB; BOX 522; HOLLY, CO 81047. (#15592).

FLAGPOLE AND PLANTER - STERLING, CO. BRICK PLANTER AROUND CENTENNIAL-BICENTENNIAL FLAGPOLE. (LOCAL). MYRTLE C MILES, CHAIRMAN; HOLLY COMMERCIAL CLUB; BOX 522; HOLLY, CO 81047. (#15591).

HERITAGE '76 - HOLLY, CO. THE HISTORY OF THE AREA WILL BE COMPILED AS A TRIBUTE TO THE CENTENNIAL-BICENTENNIAL CELBRATION. (LOCAL). MYRTLE C MILES, CHAIRMAN; HOLLY BUSINESS AND PROFESSIONAL WOMENS' CLUB; BOX 522; HOLLY, CO 81047. (#15590).

FEB 1 - JUNE 30, '76. MONTHS OF THE PRESIDENTS - EXHIBIT. EXHIBIT AT ALL BUSINESSES ON MAIN ST & HWY 50. (LOCAL). NOLAMAE ICE, COORD; HOLLY PUBLIC SCHOOLS; 129 S 2ND; HOLLY, CO 81047. (#107012-1).

FEB 22 - 23, '76. MELODRAMA-'SAVED FROM THE FATE OF HER SISTER' & CHERRY PIE SUPPER. LIVE PERFORMANCE, FESTIVAL AT HIGH SCHOOL AUDITORIUM. (LOCAL). NOLAMAE ICE, COORDINATOR; HOLLY BICENTENNIAL COMMITTEE; 129 S 2ND; HOLLY, CO 81047. (#200007-120).

APR 10 - MAY 8, '76. GATEWAY DOWNS PARIMUTUAL HORSERACING - QUARTER HORSES. COMPETITION AT GATEWAY DOWNS RACETRACK, 1 1/2 MILES WEST OF HOLLY ON HWY 50. (LOCAL). MILES VANA, COORD; GATEWAY DOWNS HORSERACING ASSOC; 130 S MAIN; HOLLY, CO 81047. (#107016-3).

JULY 1 - AUG 31, '76. HISTORICAL WINDOW DISPLAY. EXHIBIT. (LOCAL). MILES VANA, PROJ DIR; HOLLY BICENTENNIAL COMMITTEE; 130 S MAIN; HOLLY, CO 81047. (#107016-4).

JULY 4, '76. FIREWORKS AT DARK. FESTIVAL. (LOCAL). HOWARD TEMPLE, COORD; COLORADO STATE UNIV; COUNTY ANNEX; LAMAR, CO 81052. (#108612-1).

JULY 4 - 5, '76. OLD-FASHIONED FOURTH CELEBRATION. CELEBRATION WILL INCLUDE CITY CLEAN-UP; PICNIC IN PARK, CONTESTS AND FIREWORKS. AT CITY PARK, HIGH SCHOOL FOOTBALL FIELD. (LOCAL). VIVIAN AUGUSTINE, COORD; JAYCEES & LIONS CLUB; 201 S 2ND; HOLLY, CO 81047. (#107016-1).

JULY 5, '76. COMMUNITY CLEAN-UP DAY. FESTIVAL. (LOCAL). FLOYD LOWE, CHMN; TOWN OF HOLLY; BOX 458; HOLLY, CO 81047. (#108874-1).

SEPT 23 - 26, '76. HOLLY GATEWAY FAIR - PARADE, BARBECUE & CONTESTS. AWARD, EXHIBIT, FAIR, PARADE AT OLD GYM, GATEWAY DOWNS ARENA. (LOCAL). BOB SMITH, PROJ CHAIRMAN; HOLLY COMMERCIAL CLUB; 200 S MAIN; HOLLY, CO 81047. (#107016-2).

SEPT '76 - CONTINUING . COLORADO CHRONICLES, SCHOOL CHILDREN. COMPETITION. (LOCAL). FLOYD LOWE, COORD; CITY OF HOLLY; PO BOX 458; HOLLY, CO 81047. (#108779-1).

HOLYOKE

CENTENNIAL BULLETIN BOARD OF HOLYOKE, COLO. ERECT COMMUNITY BULLETIN BOARD WITH CENTENNIAL THEME. (LOCAL). CECIL SMITH, CHAIRPERSON; HOLYOKE CENTENNIAL-BICENTENNIAL COMMISSION; 420 S BOWMAN; HOLYOKE, CO 80734. (#2874).

CENTENNIAL COMMUNITY CENTER, HOLYOKE, CO. CENTER INCLUDES BUILDING AND GROUNDS FOR COMMUNITY USE - HOBBY ROOM, CARD AND POOL ROOM, PINBALL AND PING PONG ROOM, KITCHEN AND LARGE MEETING ROOM. (LOCAL). MRS LIDA ORTNER, SECRETARY; CENTENNIAL COMMUNITY CENTER; 410 E KELLOGG; HOLYOKE, CO 80734. (#19812).

COMMUNICATIONS CENTER OF HOLYOKE, COLORADO. PROPOSED MOVE & ENLARGEMENT OF COMMUNICATIONS CENTER LOCATED IN JAIL. ALSO MOVE, ENLARGE & IMPROVE PRESENT JAIL FACILITIES. (LOCAL). HON DARYL KROPP, MAYOR; CITY OF HOLYOKE; 239 E AKRON; HOLYOKE, CO 80734. (#2947).

COMMUNITY HISTORICAL CALENDAR OF HOLYOKE, COLO. PREPARATION AND PRINTING OF A REGIONAL CALENDAR DEPICTING RECORDED HISTORICAL EVENTS IN HOLYOKE, COLORADO. (LOCAL). CECIL SMITH, CHAIRMAN; HOLYOKE CENTENNIAL-BICENTENNIAL COMMISSION; 420 S BOWMAN; HOLYOKE, CO 80734. (#2927).

HISTORIC RESIDENCE RESTORATION IN HOLYOKE, CO. RESTORE OLD LOCAL HOME AND FURNISH IT WITH FURNITURE OF THE PERIOD. (LOCAL). CECIL SMITH, CHAIRMAN; HOLYOKE CENTENNIAL-BICENTENNIAL COMMISSION; 420 S BOWMAN; HOLYOKE, CO 80734. (#14839).

HISTORIC STORY OF PROCESS OF IRRIGATION, COLORADO. A LOCAL DISPLAY DEPICTING HISTORY OF IRRIGATION PROCESS & THE EQUIPMENT INVOLVED. (ST-WIDE). CECIL SMITH, CHAIRMAN; HOLYOKE CENTENNIAL-BICENTENNIAL COMMISSION; 420 S BOWMAN; HOLYOKE, CO 80734. (#2939).

HISTORICAL MUSICAL DRAMA: HOLYOKE, CO, HIGH SCHOOL. LOCAL HIGH SCHOOL PLANS ON WRITING & PRODUCING HISTORICAL MUSICAL DRAMA, WITH A COLORADO STATEHOOD CENTENNIAL THEME. (LOCAL). CECIL SMITH, CHAIRPERSON; HOLYOKE CENTENNIAL-BICENTENNIAL COMMISSION; 420 S BOWMAN; HOLYOKE, CO 80734. (#2933).

HOLYOKE, COLORADO, BANDSTAND PROJECT. PLANS FOR BUILDING COMMUNITY BANDSTAND, CENTRALLY LOCATED FOR THE CONVENIENCE & ENJOYMENT OF THE CITIZENS. (LOCAL). CECIL SMITH, CHAIRMAN; HOLYOKE CENTENNIAL-BICENTENNIAL COMMISSION; 420 S BOWMAN; HOLYOKE, CO 80734. (#2945).

MUSEUM DISPLAY CASES IN HOLYOKE, COLO. BUILD AND INSTALL MUSEUM DISPLAY CASES FOR PRICELESS MAINLY HISTORICAL ITEMS. (LOCAL). CECIL SMITH, CHAIRPERSON; HOLYOKE CENTENNIAL-BICENTENNIAL COMMISSION; 420 S BOWMAN; HOLYOKE, CO 80734. (#2871).

NEW CENTENNIAL HIGH SCHOOL OF HOLYOKE, COLO. PROPOSED PLANS FOR THE BUILDING OF A NEW HIGH SCHOOL TO BE FINISHED IN 1976, COMPLETE WITH CENTENNIAL NAME. (LOCAL). HON DARYL KROPP, MAYOR; CITY OF HOLYOKE; CITY HALL; HOLYOKE, CO 80734. (#2946).

PHILLIPS COUNTY, COLO, MUSEUM EXPANSION. PURCHASE BUILDING, REMODEL & BUILD SHOWCASE DISPLAY AREA FOR HISTORICAL OBJECTS PRESERVED FROM THE PAST. (LOCAL). MRS GALEN BAMFORD, PRESIDENT; PHILLIPS COUNTY HISTORICAL SOCIETY; HAXTUN, CO 80731. (#3890). **ARBA GRANTEE.**

APR 1 - 30, '75. MUSEUM PUBLIC OPENING & SHOWING OF HISTORICAL OBJECTS. OPENING, EXHIBIT, FESTIVAL. (LOCAL). MRS GALEN BAMFORD; PHILLIPS COUNTY HISTORICAL SOCIETY; HAXTUN, CO 80731. (#3890-501).

MAY 30, '75. BAND STAND AND TOWN BAND. CEREMONY, OPENING, LIVE PERFORMANCE AT SOUTH INTEROCEAN AT KELLOGG CITY PARK. (LOCAL). GLADYS BALDWIN; FFA BAND AND MUSIC PARENTS; 325 S PHELAN; HOLYOKE, CO 80734. (#2945-1).

AUG 5 - 7, '75. PHILLIPS COUNTY FAIR & RODEO, 'THE CENTENNIAL COUNTDOWN'. COMPETITION, FAIR, PARADE AT PHILLIPS COUNTY FAIR GROUNDS. (LOCAL). MS BERNICE THOMPSON, CHMN; PHILLIPS COUNTY COMMISSIONERS; HOLYOKE, CO 80734. (#100201-1).

JULY 4, '76. BANDSTAND AND TOWN BAND. CEREMONY, LIVE PERFORMANCE AT 700 S INTEROCEAN, CITY PARK. (LOCAL). GLADYS BALDWIN, COORD; HOLYOKE CENTENNIAL-BICENTENNIAL COMMITTEE; 325 S PHELAN; HOLYOKE, CO 80734. (#200007-119).

JULY 4, '76. BELL RINGING. CEREMONY. (LOCAL). MRS JOHN BALDWIN, COORD; HOLYOKE CENTENNIAL-BICENTENNIAL COMMITTEE; 205 W DENVER; HOLYOKE, CO 80734. (#108611-2).

JULY 4, '76. CENTENNIAL-BICENTENNIAL KING & QUEEN CROWNING. CEREMONY. (LOCAL). MRS JOHN BALDWIN, COORD; HOLYOKE AARP; 205 W DENVER; HOLYOKE, CO 80734. (#108611-3).

JULY 4, '76. FOURTH OF JULY FESTIVAL. SCHEDULED ACTIVITIES ARE A COMMUNITY PICNIC, BELL-RINGING BY THE ENTIRE COMMUNITY, DEDICATION OF TOWN BANDSTAND, LIVE CONCERT AND THE CROWNING OF THE CENTENNIAL-BICENTENNIAL KING AND QUEEN. AT HOLYOKE CITY PARK, 700 S INTEROCEAN. (LOCAL). GLADYS BALDWIN, SEC; CENTENNIAL-BICENTENNIAL COMMITTEE; 325 S PHELAN; HOLYOKE, CO 80734. (#106947-3).

JULY 4, '76. HOLYOKE PICNIC. FESTIVAL. (LOCAL). GLADYS BALDWIN, CHAIRMAN; HOLYOKE CENTENNIAL-BICENTENNIAL COMMITTEE; 205 E DENVER; HOLYOKE, CO 80734. (#107581-1).

JULY 4, '76. TOWN BANDSTAND DEDICATION. BAND CONCERT BY RENEWED HOLYOKE TOWN BAND. (LOCAL). MRS JOHN BALDWIN, COORD; BAND COUNCIL, FFA ORGANIZATION, HOLYOKE CENT-BICENT COMMITTEE; 205 W DENVER; HOLYOKE, CO 80734. (#108611-1).

JULY 31, '76. FIREWORKS DISPLAY. SHOW WILL FEATURE COLORADO '76 LOGO AND FLAG TO CELEBRATE THE COLORADO CENTENNIAL. AT COUNTY FAIRGROUNDS. (LOCAL). GLADYS BALDWIN, SEC; HOLYOKE FIREMEN'S ASSOCIATION; 325 S PHELAN; HOLYOKE, CO 80734. (#108701-1).

AUG 1, '76. CENTENNIAL FIREWORKS. FESTIVAL AT FAIR GROUNDS. (LOCAL). GLADYS BALDWIN, COORD; TOWN OF HOLYOKE; 205 W DENVER; HOLYOKE, CO 80734. (#108955-11).

AUG 1, '76. DEDICATION OF HOMESTEADERS PARK. CEREMONY. (LOCAL). MRS GALEN BAMFORD, CHMN; PHILLIPS COUNTY CENTENNIAL-BICENTENNIAL COMMITTEE; HAXTUN, CO 80731. (#108955-13).

AUG 4, '76. COMMUNITY PARADE. PARADE. (LOCAL). GLADYS BALDWIN, COORD; CITY OF HOLYOKE; 205 W DENVER; HOLYOKE, CO 80734. (#108778-1).

NOV 1, '76. HISTORICAL MUSICAL DRAMA. LIVE PERFORMANCE AT HIGH SCHOOL AUDITORIUM. (LOCAL). GLADYS BALDWIN, SEC; HOLYOKE MUSIC - PARENTS AND STUDENTS; 325 S PHELAN; HOLYOKE, CO 80734. (#106947-2).

HOT SULPHUR

GRAND COUNTY LIBRARY & PIONEER MUSEUM, CO. THE LIBRARY & MUSEUM BUILDING, WHICH WAS THE FIRST COURTHOUSE BEFORE 1890, WILL BE MOVED, ENLARGED & PRESERVED. (LOCAL). IDA SHERIFF, SECRETARY; GRAND COUNTY PIONEER SOCIETY; HOT SULPR SPG, CO 80451. (#18489). **ARBA GRANTEE.**

AUG 28, '76. MOUNTAIN MAN RENDEZVOUS AND FAIR. FAIR CONSISTS OF MUZZLE LOAD SHOOT, A BARBEQUE, MANY GAMES FOR CHILDREN, COSTUME CONTEST AND OTHER ACTIVITIES. AT MUSEUM GROUNDS, SOUTH OF HWY 40 EAST OF TOWN. (LOCAL). JEAN CHENOWETH, DIRECTOR; GRAND COUNTY HISTORICAL ASSOC; BOX 521; JABERNASH, CO 80478. (#104873-1).

HOTCHKISS

HISTORICAL BROCHURE - HOTCHKISS, CO. A HISTORICAL BROCHURE WILL BE PRINTED AND CIRCULATED, BEGINNING ON JUNE 1ST. THE BROCHURE WILL BE USED BY TOURISTS, FOR REUNIONS AND FOR COLORADO DAY. (LOCAL). W ARTHUR WOLVERTON, COORDINATOR; HISTORICAL SOCIETY; RT 1; HOTCHKISS, CO 81419. (#26269).

AUG 7 - 8, '76. DELTA COUNTY FAIR HORSE SHOW. REGISTERED QUARTER HORSE SHOW ON SATURDAY; OPEN HORSE SHOW SUNDAY. AT DELTA COUNTY FAIRGROUNDS, HOTCHKISS, COLORADO. (ST-WIDE). MRS TERI NOEL; DELTA COUNTY FAIR; RT 1; PAONIA, CO 81428. (#104669-2).

AUG 7 - 14, '76. DELTA COUNTY FAIR. FAIR AT DELTA COUNTY FAIRGROUNDS, HOTCHKISS, CO. (ST-WIDE). MR PAUL ELLISON; DELTA COUNTY FAIRBOARD; RR 1, BOX 331; DELTA, CO 81416. (#104669-3).

HUGO

HISTORY OF LINCOLN COUNTY, COLORADO. WRITTEN HISTORY OF LINCOLN COUNTY FROM THE 1860'S TO THE END OF THE HOMESTEAD ERA OF 1920'S IS BEING COMPILED BY MARY OWEN. (LOCAL). GLADYS V WEEDER, CHAIRPERSON; LINCOLN COUNTY CENTENNIAL COMMITTEE; COUNTY BUILDING; HUGO, CO 80821. (#2925).

LINCOLN COUNTY, COLO, HISTORICAL RESTORATION PROJ. RESTORATION OF BUILDINGS, MARK HISTORICAL SPOTS, MARK OLD STAGE COACH ROUTES, WITH POSSIBLE EXCURSIONS OVER THESE ROUTES. (LOCAL). GLADYS K WEEDER, CHAIRPERSON; LINCOLN COUNTY CENTENNIAL COMMITTEE; COUNTY BLDG; HUGO, CO 80821. (#2913).

MAY 15, '75 - MAY 30, '76. PRIZE AWARDS HISTORICAL ESSAY CONTEST IN SCHOOL-COUNTY/REGION PRIZES. CONTEST FOR 7TH-8TH GRADES. PAPER NOT LONGER THAN 1500 WORDS. AWARDS GIVEN EACH YEAR TO WINNERS. A TOP PRIZE AWARDED IN '76 TO ONE OF THE 3 1ST PLACE WINNERS OF '74,'75 & '76 CONTESTS. ORIGINAL RESEARCH ON LOCAL, COUNTY & REGIONAL HISTORY. (LOCAL). MS J R OWEN, CHAIRMAN; CBC REGION #5; HUGO, CO 80821. (#1313-501).

JUNE 12, '76. DEDICATION OF HISTORIC MARKER. CEREMONY TO DEDICATE A PLAQUE WHICH WAS PLACED AT THE SPOT WHERE THE BUILDING USED AS THE COUNTY COURTHOUSE FROM 1893-1905 ONCE STOOD. AT EASTERN SLOPE TELEPHONE BUILDING, HWY 30 & 3RD AVE. (LOCAL). MRS JACK OWEN, COORD; LINCOLN CO HISTORICAL SOCIETY; PO BOX 626; HUGO, CO 80821. (#200007-122).

JUNE 12, '76. HUGO WILD WEST DAYS. COMPETITION, EXHIBIT, LIVE PERFORMANCE AT LINCOLN COUNTY FAIRGROUNDS. (LOCAL). ROBERT UMPHREY, COORD; HUGO ACTION COMMITTEE; HUGO, CO 80821. (#200007-121).

JULY 4, '76. FIREWORKS DISPLAY. FESTIVAL. (LOCAL). MRS JACK OWEN, CHAIRMAN; HUGO FIREWORKS COMMITTEE; HUGO, CO 80821. (#108610-1).

AUG 19 - 21, '76. LINCOLN COUNTY FAIR. COMPETITION, FAIR AT FAIRGROUNDS, 1 MI EAST OF HUGO. (ST-WIDE). CHESTER BROCKWAY; LINCOLN COUNTY; HUGO, CO 80821. (#108717-1).

HYGIENE

JULY 24, '76. THRESHERMAN'S DAY - OLD-FASHIONED THRESHING BEE & DINNER. DEMONSTRATION OF OLD-FASHIONED GRAIN HARVESTING TECHNIQUES: REAPING; SHOCKING; THRESHING USING SEPARATOR POWERED BY STEAM TRACTOR. TRADITIONAL NOON MEAL SERVED OUTDOORS FROM 12 TO 2. RIDES FOR CHILDREN (ANY AGE) ON WAGON TRAIN PULLED BY STEAMER. AT HYGIENE LOCATED 2 MI WEST OF 17TH & MAIN, LONGMONT. (LOCAL). PARKER FOWLER, CHMN; ST VRAIN '76 COMMITTEE & POMONA GRANGE; 8585 HYGIENE RD; LONGMONT, CO 80501. (#108872-1).

IDAHO SPRINGS

ESSAY CONTEST. ESSAY CONTEST FOR 4TH, 5TH & 6TH GRADERS. SUBJECT: ANY PERSON, PLACE OR EVENT OF HISTORICAL INTEREST IN CLEAR CREEK COUNTY. PRIZES WILL BE AWARDED AND A BOOKLET OF THE ESSAYS WILL BE PUBLISHED. (LOCAL). RUTH E FUGATE, COORD; CITY OF IDAHO SPRINGS; PO BOX 1358; IDAHO SPRINGS, CO 80452. (#108776-3).

ESSAY CONTEST & HISTORY BOOKLET, IDAHO SPRINGS, CO. HISTORY WRITING CONTEST BY GRADE SCHOOL STUDENTS WITH BOOKLET ON HISTORY PREPARED BY LOCAL HISTORIAN. (LOCAL). RUTH FUGATE, LIBRARY TRUSTEE; IDAHO SPRINGS FRIENDS OF THE LIBRARY; PO BOX 1358; IDAHO SPRINGS, CO 80452. (#26243).

GOLD RUSH DAYS CELEBRATION. CELEBRATION OF THE HISTORY AND CULTURAL HERITAGE OF IDAHO SPRINGS. (LOCAL). HON JERRY VANCE, MAYOR; CITY OF IDAHO SPRINGS; IDAHO SPRINGS, CO 80452. (#108776-2).

HISTORIC TOUR BOOK OF IDAHO SPRINGS, COLORADO. SELF-GUIDING TOUR BOOK TO HISTORIC SITES IN IDAHO SPRINGS. (LOCAL). ALEXANDER M OLISZEWSKI, CHAIRMAN; CENT-BICENT GOLD RUSH DAYS HISTORIC PRESERVATION COMMITTEE; PO BOX 1472; IDAHO SPRINGS, CO 80452. (#26245).

IMPROVING YOUR TOWN SIGN CONTEST - CO. CONTEST TO DESIGN NEW WELCOME SIGN FOR THE CITY, TO BE CONSTRUCTED AND USED. (LOCAL). HON JERRY VANCE, MAYOR; CITY OF IDAHO SPRINGS; IDAHO SPRINGS, CO 80452. (#26244).

JULY 4, '76. 4TH OF JULY FIREWORKS DISPLAY. DISPLAY INCLUDES MANY BICENT SET PIECES SUCH AS THE AMERICAN AND COLORADO FLAGS, CENT-BICENT LOGO, STATUE OF LIBERTY AND PAUL REVERE. (LOCAL). W L JONES, CHIEF; IDAHO SPRINGS VOLUNTEER FIRE DEPT; PO BOX 356, 1546 MINER ST; IDAHO SPRINGS, CO 80452. (#108609-1).

JULY 30 - AUG 1, '76. 16TH ST ARTS & CRAFTS STREET DISPLAY. DISPLAY OF ARTS AND CRAFTS BY LOCAL ARTISANS WITH CRAFTSPERSONS AVAILABLE FOR DISCUSSIONS WITH VISITORS. (LOCAL). PAUL WINDMUELLER, CHMN; GOLDRUSH ARTS & CRAFTS COMMITTEE - IDAHO SPG CENT-BICENT COMMITTEE; PO BOX 579; IDAHO SPRINGS, CO 80452. (#108776-1).

IGNACIO

SEPT 12 - 14, '75. SOUTHERN UTE TRIBE POW-WOW OF COLORADO. PROJECT TO ASSIST IN PURCHASE OF COSTUMES TO COMPETE IN INTER-TRIBAL DANCE POW-WOW. FUNDS WILL SUPPLEMENT TRIBE'S FUNDS & ENHANCE AUTHENTICITY OF POW-WOW. ALSO: PROGRAM FACILITATION. (ST-WIDE). LEONARD C BURCH, CHAIRMAN; SOUTHERN UTE TRIBE; TRIBAL AFFAIRS BLDG; IGNACIO, CO 81137. (#2016-1).

JULY 23 - 24, '76. IGNACIO/SO UTE TRIBE COMMUNITY BICENTENNIAL FESTIVAL. SAN IGNATIUS HISTORICAL CHURCH CELEBRATION; AN INTER-TRIBAL POW-WOW, PARADE, ARTS/CRAFTS BOOTHS, TRIBAL PROJECTS, RODEO, HORSE RACES, FAMOUS PERSONALITIES & FEATURED SPEAKERS ARE SCHEDULED. AT SKY-UTE DOWNS HORSE CENTER. (LOCAL). LEONARD C BURCH; TOWN OF IGNACIO/SOUTHERN UTE TRIBE; C/O TRIBAL AFFAIRS BLDG; IGNACIO, CO 81137. (#102882-1).

JULY 26 - 27, '76. IGNACIO-SOUTHERN UTE BICENTENNIAL FESTIVAL. FESTIVAL. (LOCAL). RONNIE BAKER, CHAIRMAN; TOWN OF IGNACIO AND SOUTHERN UTE TRIBE; TRIBAL AFFAIRS BLDG; IGNACIO, CO 81137. (#108733-2).

JULY 31 - AUG 1, '76. IGNACIO-SOUTHERN UTE COMMUNITY FESTIVAL. THE IGNACIO SOUTHERN UTE COMMUNITY PROPOSES A FESTIVAL IN '76 WITH THE TRIBE AND THE TOWN OF IGNACIO AND OTHER ETHNIC GROUPS IN THE COMMUNITY TO MAKE THE FESTIVAL AN INTERCULTURAL EVENT OF LASTING BENEFITS TO THE LOCAL RESIDENTS IN THE COMMUNITY. AT SKY-UTE DOWNS & SOUTHERN UTE RESERVATION. (LOCAL). RICHARD FENTZLAFF, COORD4; TOWN OF IGNACIO-SOUTHERN UTE TRIBE; 5 BROWNING AVE; IGNACIO, CO 81137. (#108733-1).

JAMESTOWN

COMMUNITY IMPROVEMENT PROJECT, JAMESTOWN, CO. RE-CREATION OF PARK DESTROYED BY FLOOD. (LOCAL). HON FLORENCE WALKER, MAYOR; CITY OF JAMESTOWN; BOX 273; JAMESTOWN, CO 80455. (#26139).

HISTORY BOOK OF JAMESTOWN, COLORADO. A PROJECT TO PUBLISH AN HISTORICAL BOOKLET ABOUT THE TOWN OF JAMESTOWN. (LOCAL). LORRAINE JOHNSON, CENTENNIAL-BICENTENNIAL CHAIRMAN; TOWN OF JAMESTOWN; JAMESTOWN, CO 80455. (#4297). **(??).**

JAMESTOWN, COLO, PARK PROJECT. A PROJECT TO CREATE A PARK ON A 20 ACRE SITE, FORMERLY A TAILINGS POND. PROJECT INCLUDES BEAUTIFYING AREA AND INSTALLING PLAYGROUND EQUIPMENT, BLEACHERS & PICNIC TABLES. (LOCAL). LORRAINE JOHNSON, CENTENNIAL-BICENTENNIAL CHAIRMAN; TOWN OF JAMESTOWN; JAMESTOWN, CO 80455. (#4299). **(??).**

'PICK AND SHOVEL DAY' IN JAMESTOWN, COLO. AN ANNUAL FOURTH OF JULY CELEBRATION INCLUDING A PANCAKE BREAKFAST, PARADE, GYMKHANA,AND FIREWORKS. (LOCAL). LORRAINE JOHNSON, CENTENNIAL-BICENTENNIAL CHAIRMAN; TOWN OF JAMESTOWN; JAMESTOWN, CO 80455. (#4298).

JULY 4, '75. 'PICK & SHOVEL DAY' FOURTH OF JULY CELEBRATION. 'PICK AND SHOVEL DAY' IN JAMESTOWN, COLO. AN ANNUAL FOURTH OF JULY CELEBRATION INCLUDING A PANCAKE BREAKFAST, PARADE, GYMKHANA,AND FIREWORKS. (LOCAL). LORRAINE JOHNSON; TOWN OF JAMESTOWN; JAMESTOWN, CO 80455. (#4298-501).

JULY 4, '76. CENTENNIAL FIREWORKS. FESTIVAL. (LOCAL). FLORENCE WALKER, COORD; JAMESTOWN FIREWORKS COMMITTEE; BOX 273; JAMESTOWN, CO 80455. (#108608-1).

JULY 4, '76. PICK AND SHOVEL DAY. AN ANNUAL FOURTH OF JULY CELEBRATION INCLUDING A PANCAKE BREAKFAST, PARADE, GYMKHANA,AND FIREWORKS. AT TOWN HALL, CITY PARK. (LOCAL). LORRAINE M JOHNSON; TOWN OF JAMESTOWN, JAMESTOWN PARENT-TEACHER ORG.; PO BOX 157; JAMESTOWN, CO 80455. (#4298-2).

JARRE CANYON

RESTORATION OF INDIAN PARK SCHOOLHOUSE - CO. THE INDIAN PARK SCHOOLHOUSE WILL BE RESTORED AND TURNED INTO A COMMUNITY CENTER. (LOCAL). PAULINE HODGES, CHAIRPERSON; DOUGLAS COUNTY CENTENNIAL-BICENTENNIAL COMMITTEE; CASTLE ROCK, CO 80104. (#24570).

JEFFERSON

BOULDER COUNTY FAIR IN COLORADO. BOULDER COUNTY FAIR EVENT TO BE HELD AT BOULDER COUNTY FAIRGROUNDS; CENTENNIAL - BICENTENNIAL THEME & MOTIF. (LOCAL). ROD AHLBERG, CHAIRMAN; BOULDER COUNTY FAIR COMMITTEE AND LYONS '76 COMMITTEE; 850 FORDHAM; LONGMONT, CO 80501. (#10304).

JOHNSTOWN

IMPROVING OUR TOWN, JOHNSTOWN, CO. PUBLICITY CAMPAIGN MOUNTED IN SPRING TO INVOLVE COMMUNITY PEOPLE IN SUGGESTIONS FOR IMPROVING OUR TOWN. (LOCAL). RAY HAYDEN, COORDINATOR; TOWN OF JOHNSTOWN; RT 1; JOHNSTOWN, CO 80534. (#26219).

SENIOR CITIZEN 1976. HONORING OF SENIOR CITIZENS THROUGH PARTICIPATION IN COMMUNITY DAY PARADE AND 4TH OF JULY FESTIVITIES. (LOCAL). RAY HAYDEN, COORD; SENIOR CITIZEN, INC; RT 1; JOHNSTOWN, CO 80534. (#108777-1).

JUNE 19, '76. CHAMBER OF COMMERCE BARBEQUE. FESTIVAL AT JOHNSON PARISH PARK. (LOCAL). ED SPRENG, PROJ COORD; CHAMBER OF COMMERCE; 903 9TH ST; JOHNSTOWN, CO 80534. (#107023-1).

JUNE 19, '76. 'SPIRIT OF '76' BARBEQUE DAY & PANCAKE BREAKFAST. BARBEQUE DAY WILL INCLUDE PANCAKE BREAKFAST, PARADE & BARBEQUE SUPPER; THEME OF THE DAY IS 'THE SPIRIT OF '76'. AT MASONIC LODGE, MAIN ST & TOWN PARK. (LOCAL). M J FERRIS, CHAIRMAN; VOLUNTEER FIREMEN & ESTRELLITA CLUB; 903 COTTONWOOD DR; JOHNSTOWN, CO 80534. (#107090-1).

JUNE 19, '76. 'SPIRIT OF '76' PARADE & HOBBY SHOW. EXHIBIT, PARADE. (LOCAL). MRS RICHARD WAKEMAN; ESTRELLITA CLUB; 320 KATHLEEN AVE; MILLIKEN, CO 80543. (#107023-2).

JULY 4, '76. FILM FESTIVAL. EVENT FEATURES FILMS, SLIDES & TALKS ABOUT AMERICA, COLORADO AND THE AREA'S HISTORY. (LOCAL). RAY HAYDEN, CHAIRMAN; FILM FESTIVAL COMMITTEE; RT 1; JOHNSTOWN, CO 80534. (#108669-1).

JULESBURG

CENTENNIAL RAILROAD HATS OF FT SEDGWICK, COLO. HATS AUCTIONED OFF TO PROVIDE FUNDS FOR THE MUSEUM & ARE WORN AT ALL OFFICIAL FORT SEDGWICK MUSEUM ACTIVITIES. (LOCAL). CELENA SMITH, CHAIRPERSON; FORT SEDGWICK HISTORICAL SOCIETY; 415 ELM ST; JULESBURG, CO 80737. (#2907).

FORT SEDGWICK DEPOT MUSEUM, JULESBURG, COLORADO. TRAIN DEPOT TO BE RESTORED & RELOCATED FOR USE AS REGIONAL MUSEUM. COLLECTIONS WILL SHOW PIONEER ITEMS & ARTIFACTS OF JULESBURG'S HERITAGE AS 1ST COLORADO COMMUNITY SERVED BY TELEGRAPH RAILROAD, ETC. (ST-WIDE). WALTER R MCKINSTRY, SECRETARY; FORT SEDGWICK HISTORICAL SOCIETY; 320 CEDAR ST; JULESBURG, CO 80737. (#808). **ARBA GRANTEE.**

HISTORIC JULESBURG, COLO, LOCATIONS BOOKLET. FT SEDGWICK HISTORICAL SOCIETY PUBLISHED PAMPHLET FOR SALE ON THE 4 JULESBURG LOCATIONS, AS A GUIDE TO TOURISTS & HISTORIC RECORD. (LOCAL). JEAN WILLIAMSON, PRESIDENT; FORT SEDGWICK HISTORICAL SOCIETY; 515 PINE ST; JULESBURG, CO 80737. (#2906).

REENACTMENT-PONY EXPRESS RIDE, ST LOUIS-SACRAMENTO. THE TOWN OF JULESBURG WILL PARTICIPATE IN THE REENACTMENT OF THE DAYLIGHT PONY EXPRESS RIDE IN 1976. JULESBURG HAS ONE OF THE TWO STATIONS WHICH EXISTED IN COLORADO. (REGN'L). CELENA SMITH, CHAIRPERSON; FORT SEDGWICK HISTORIC SOCIETY; 415 ELM ST; JULESBURG, CO 80737. (#2961). **(??).**

JULY 12, '75. OPENING FT SEDGWICK HISTORICAL MUSEUM, CONVERTED UNION PACIFIC DEPOT. OPENING AT OLD UNION PACIFIC DEPOT. (LOCAL). JEAN WILLIAMSON, PROJ DIR; FT SEDGWICK HISTORICAL SOCIETY; 515 PINE ST; JULESBURG, CO 80737. (#2906-1).

OCT 3, '75. UNITED STATES ARMED FORCES BICENTENNIAL CARAVAN. THE CARAVAN IS COMPOSED OF EXHIBIT VANS FOR EACH BRANCH OF THE MILITARY SERVICE. THE THEME OF THE EXHIBITION IS 'HISTORY OF THE ARMED FORCES AND THEIR CONTRIBUTION TO THE NATION'. (LOCAL). DON WANDLESS, CHMN; U S ARMED FORCES BICENTENNIAL EXHIBIT VANS PROJECT; 804 SYCAMORE ST; JULESBURG, CO 80737. (#1775-236).

JULY 31 - AUG 1, '76. CENTENNIAL COLORADO DAY CELEBRATION. 7/31: BANDS, SPEECHES, ANTIQUE CARS PARADE, VARIETY SHOW, SENIOR CITIZEN AWARDS, COLORADO BIRTHDAY CAKE & FIREWORKS; 8/1 COLORADO DAY ALL-CHURCH SERVICE, FIREMEN WATER FIGHT, OLD-TIME FASHION SHOW, MILKING COW CONTEST AND CRAFTS. AT DICK SCHMITT STADIUM JULESBURG HIGH SCHOOL. (LOCAL). CELENA SMITH, COORD; COLORADO DAY CELEBRATION COUNTY OF SEDGWICK COMMITTEE; 415 ELM ST; JULESBURG, CO 80737. (#108853-1).

KERSEY

'GREENING AND CLEANING COLORADO' - KERSEY. LOCAL 4-H CLUBS BAN TOGETHER TO PLANT TREES THROUGHOUT THE COMMUNITY. (LOCAL). JOSEPHINE KLEIN, COORDINATOR; 4-H CLUBS; RT 4, BOX 213; GREELEY, CO 80631. (#26218).

KIOWA

JULY 17 - 18, '76. KIOWA 1976 CHAMBER OF COMMERCE PONY EXPRESS RACE. COMPETITION AT NEAR ELBERT COUNTY FAIRGROUNDS, KIOWA. (LOCAL). BRANDT C ROBERTS, COORD; KIOWA CHAMBER OF COMMERCE; BOX 192; KIOWA, CO 80117. (#107003-1).

AUG 5 - 8, '76. CENTENNIAL COUNTY FAIR. EXHIBITS, JUDGING AND VIEWING; MARKET SALE, ELBERT COUNTY GYMKHANA AND RODEO, DANCE AND BARBEQUE. AT ELBERT COUNTY FAIRGROUNDS. (ST-WIDE). KATHERINE T RICKART, DIR; ELBERT COUNTY FAIRBOARD; PO BOX 128; SIMLA, CO 80835. (#104672-1).

KIT CARSON

SEPT 2 - 4, '76. RELIVING THE PAST-'MELLA DRAMA'-WESTERN THEME. LIVE PERFORMANCE. (LOCAL). BRUCE ANDERSON, COORD; CHAMBER OF COMMERCE; KIT CARSON, CO 80825. (#108774-3).

SEPT 4, '76. COMMUNITY PARADE. PARADE. (LOCAL). BRUCE ANDERSON, COORD; CHAMBER OF COMMERCE; KIT CARSON, CO 80825. (#108774-1).

SEPT '76. COLORADO CHRONICLES, SCHOOL CHILDREN, COMMUNITY HISTORY. AWARD, CEREMONY. (LOCAL). BRUCE ANDERSON, COORD; CHAMBER OF COMMERCE; KIT CARSON, CO 80825. (#108774-2).

KREMMLING

BUILDING PRESERVATION - KREMMLING, CO. DAN HOARES BLACKSMITH SHOP WILL BE REFURBISHED. (LOCAL). LEO MURRAY, CHAIRMAN; KREMMLING KIWANIS; 100 CENTRAL; KREMMLING, CO 80459. (#24607).

COMPILATION OF CHURCH HISTORY - KREMMLING, CO. ST PETERS CATHOLIC CHURCH HISTORY IS BEING COMPILED BY THE ALTAR AND ROSARY SOCIETY. (LOCAL). JEAN SLOAN, CHAIRPERSON; ST PETERS ALTAR AND ROSARY SOCIETY; KREMMLING, CO 80459. (#24605).

FLAG PRESENTATION. A BENNINGTON FLAG AND A COLORADO CENTENNIAL BANNER WILL BE PRESENTED TO THE TOWN OF KREMMLING. (LOCAL). HERMAN FUNKLER, CHAIRMAN; KREMMLING KIWANIS; 112 N 4TH; KREMMLING, CO 80459. (#107888-1).

PLAQUES FOR HISTORICAL SITES - KREMMLING, CO. RECOGNIZE HISTORICAL SIGNIFICANCE OF BUILDINGS AND SITES BY PLACING PLAQUES ON OR NEAR THE BUILDINGS AND SITES; ALSO, A MAP AND BROCHURE FOR TOURS. (LOCAL). ELDO R GALLAGHER, CHAIRMAN; KREMMLING CENTENNIAL-BICENTENNIAL COMMITTEE; BOX 516; KREMMLING, CO 80459. (#24608).

JUNE 26 - 27, '76. KREMMLING DAYS & KIDS DAY. THEME OF EVENT & PARADE IS 'SPIRIT OF '76' - 1776, 1876 & 1976. (LOCAL). ELDO R GALLAGHER, CHMN; KREMMLING VOLUNTEER FIRE DEPT; BOX 516; KREMMLING, CO 80459. (#107022-2).

SEPT 17 - 19, '76. MIDDLE PARK FAIR. FAIR WILL FEATURE CITIZEN OF THE YEAR AWARD, TRANSPORTATION EXHIBIT AND HONORING PIONEERS OF THE YEAR. AT GRAND COUNTY FAIRGROUNDS. (LOCAL). WHITEY SHERMAN, COORD; MIDDLE PARK FAIR BOARD; DILLON, CO 80435. (#107022-1).

LA JARA

RESTORATION OF WATER TOWER, LA JARA, CO. RESTORATION OF ORIGINAL WOODEN WATER TOWER. (LOCAL). TIM SUTPHEN & TALLY MONDRAGON, CO-CHAIRMEN; LASSO DAYS COMMITTEE & TOWN BOARD; LA JARA CITY HALL; LA JARA, CO 81101. (#26144).

JULY 3, '76. LASSO DAYS FESTIVAL, PAGEANT & BARBEQUE. FESTIVAL, LIVE PERFORMANCE AT RODEO AREA GROUNDS SOUTH OF LA JARA. (LOCAL). TIM SUTPHEN, COORDINATOR; LASSO DAYS COMMITTEE; BOX 426; LA JARA, CO 81101. (#108603-4).

JULY 4, '76. MOTOCROSS RACES & FIREWORKS. COMPETITION, FESTIVAL AT WEST OF LA JARA, PETERSON RD. (LOCAL). HARVEY HOTSTETTER, CHMN; CONEJOS COUNTY CYCLE CLUB; LA JARA SINCLAIR STATION; LA JARA, CO 81101. (#108603-2).

JULY 5, '76. ARTS & ANTIQUE FESTIVAL & PARADE - MR & MRS CITIZEN AWARD. COMPETITION, FESTIVAL, PARADE AT PARADE - MAIN ST; ARTS & ANTIQUE FAIR, CITY PARK; AWARDS, LDS HALL. (LOCAL). TIM SUTPHEN, COORDINATOR; LASSO DAYS COMMITTEE; BOX 426; LA JARA, CO 81101. (#108603-1).

JULY 5, '76. LASSO DAYS 4-H RODEO. COMPETITION, LIVE PERFORMANCE AT COUNTY ARENA. (LOCAL). TIM SUTPHEN, COORDINATOR; LASSO DAYS COMMITTEE; BOX 426; LA JARA, CO 81101. (#108603-3).

LA JUNTA

COLORADO CHRONICLES, LA JUNTA. THE HERITAGE COMMITTEE IS INTERVIEWING ALL OLD SETTLERS IN LA JUNTA, THESE INTERVIEWS WILL BE PUBLISHED IN BOOK FORM. (LOCAL). ALLAN J BENNETT, COORDINATOR; CITY OF LA JUNTA; PO BOX 619; LA JUNTA, CO 81050. (#26289).

CREATION OF A CULTURAL CENTER FOR LA JUNTA, CO. ASSISTANCE IN ESTABLISHING A PERMANENT CULTURAL CENTER FOR LA JUNTA AREA WITH EMPHASIS ON THE PERFORMING ARTS AND VISUAL ARTS. (LOCAL). DONALD L COKER, PRESIDENT; PICKETWIRE PLAYERS; 2411 JOHNSTON DR; LA JUNTA, CO 81050. (#20614).

GREENING & CLEANING COLORADO - LA JUNTA. GIRL & BOY SCOUTS WILL CLEANUP ENTRANCE TO THE CITY; SENIOR CITIZENS WILL PAINT FIREPLUGS RED, WHITE & BLUE. (LOCAL). ALLAN J BENNETT, CHAIRMAN; LA JUNTA CENTENNIAL-BICENTENNIAL COMMITTEE; PO BOX 619; LA JUNTA, CO 81050. (#26234).

NOV 14, '75. UNITED STATES ARMED FORCES BICENTENNIAL CARAVAN. THE CARAVAN IS COMPOSED OF EXHIBIT VANS FOR EACH BRANCH OF THE MILITARY SERVICE. THE THEME OF THE EXHIBITION IS 'HISTORY OF THE ARMED FORCES AND THEIR CONTRIBUTION TO THE NATION'. (LOCAL). ALLAN J BURNETT, CHMN; U S ARMED FORCES BICENTENNIAL EXHIBIT VANS PROJECT; OTERO COUNTY COURTHOUSE; LA JUNTA, CO 81050. (#1775-249).

APR 1 - SEPT 6, '76. BLACKSMITHING, HIDE TANNING & OTHER CRAFTS AT BENT'S OLD FORT. PARK INTERPRETERS IN PERIOD COSTUMES DEMONSTRATED VARIOUS ARTS & CRAFTS IN AN HISTORIC SETTING. AT BENTS OLD FORT NHS, HWY 194. (REGN'L). BENTS OLD FORT NHS; NATIONAL PARK SERVICE; LA JUNTA, CO 81050. (#6727-223).

JULY 20 - 25, '76. 'THE UNSINKABLE MOLLY BROWN'. THE TWO-DAY OUTDOOR FESTIVAL WILL BE JULY 24-25 AND DEDICATION OF BENTS FORT ON JULY 24TH OR 25TH. AT LA JUNTA HIGH SCHOOL THEATRE, 18TH & SMITHLAND. (LOCAL). DONA ALDEA, SECRETARY; PICKETWIRE PLAYERS; 69 CIRCLE DR; LA JUNTA, CO 81050. (#104853-1).

JULY 24, '76. COMMUNITY PARADE. PARADE. (LOCAL). ALLAN J BENNETT, COORD; PARADE COMMITTEE; PO BOX 619; LA JUNTA, CO 81050. (#108691-1).

JULY 25, '76. LA JUNTA OLD SETTLERS FIESTA. FESTIVAL. (LOCAL). SALLY HARDER, COORD; LA JUNTA CENTENNIAL-BICENTENNIAL COMMITTEE; LA JUNTA, CO 81050. (#108868-1).

LA SALLE

CENTENNIAL PARK DEDICATION CEREMONY. DEDICATION OF PLAQUE COMMEMORATING THE CENTENNIAL PARK. DONATION OF PASSIVE RECREATIONAL EQUIPMENT TO THE TOWN RECREATION COMMITTEE. (LOCAL). LARRY W LINDER, CHMN; LA SALLE CENTENNIAL-BICENTENNIAL COMMISSION; BOX 717; LA SALLE, CO 80645. (#108773-1).

COMMUNITY TREE FARM - LA SALLE, CO. THE PURCHASE & MAINTENANCE OF A TREE FARM; GROWING TREES FOR COMMUNITY USE AT SCHOOLS, STREETS AND PRIVATE HOMES. (LOCAL). LARRY W LINDER, CHAIRMAN; LA SALLE CENTENNIAL-BICENTENNIAL COMMITTEE; PO BOX 717; LA SALLE, CO 80643. (#16406).

PRINTING EXPENSE - LA SALLE, CO. WRITTEN HISTORY OF THE BIG BAND AREA WILL BE PUBLISHED. (LOCAL). LARRY W LINDER, CHAIRPERSON; LA SALLE CENTENNIAL-BICENTENNIAL COMMISSION; BOX 717; LA SALLE, CO 80645. (#26221).

LAFAYETTE

CENTENNIAL CANINE CIRCUIT, LAFAYETTE, CO. PROJECT INVOLVES PRESENTATION OF A CONTINUOUS SERIES OF PUREBRED DOG SHOWS THROUGHOUT COLORADO, DURING JUNE OF 1976. (ST-WIDE). JACQUES A MACHAL, PROJ DIRECTOR; COLORADO CENTENNIAL CANINE CIRCUIT; PO BOX 245; LAFAYETTE, CO 80026. (#17423).

FIREHOUSE KITCHEN - LAFAYETTE, CO. RED, WHITE AND BLUE KITCHEN WILL BE USED THROUGHOUT THE YEAR FOR EVENTS INVOLVING ALL THE CITIZENS OF LAFAYETTE. (LOCAL). SHARON V STELSON, COORDINATOR; VOLUNTEER FIREMEN AND AUXILIARY; 201 E SIMPSON; LAFAYETTE, CO 80026. (#26241).

100 YEARS OF FIREFIGHTING AND COOKING - CO. REMODELING OF KITCHEN AT LAFAYETTE FIRE STATION & PAINTING FIRE HYDRANTS RED, WHITE AND BLUE. (LOCAL). CAROL M SADLER, TREASURER; LAFAYETTE FIREMAN'S AUXILIARY; 877 S CARR; LAFAYETTE, CO 80026. (#24620).

MAY 24 - 27, '76. MUSICAL CONCERT 'HAPPY BIRTHDAY USA, HAPPY BIRTHDAY COLORADO'. THIS WILL BE MUSICAL REVUE FROM 1776 ON; SECOND HALF OF CONCERT WILL FEATURE COLORADO HISTORY & MUSIC AND SPECIFICALLY LAFAYETTE; PROGRAM WILL INCLUDE ADULTS FROM THE COMMUNITY. AT LAFAYETTE MIDDLE SCHOOL GYMNASIUM. (LOCAL). CHARLES A KNUTSON; LAFAYETTE ELEMENTARY SCHOOL & PARENT-TEACHER ORGANIZATION; 111 CORAL WAY; BROOMFIELD, CO 80020. (#107024-1).

AUG 1, '76. COLORADO DAYS FESTIVAL FOR LAFAYETTE. FESTIVAL AT FIREHOUSE. (LOCAL). CAROL M SADLER, CHMN; LAFAYETTE VOLUNTEER FIRE DEPT AUXILIARY; 201 E SIMPSON; LAFAYETTE, CO 80026. (#108955-7).

LAKE CITY

CENTENNIAL TENNIS CENTER IN LAKE CITY, COLO. THE BUILDING OF A COMMUNITY TENNIS COURT TO FILL A RECREATIONAL VOID WITH FREE COURT OPEN TO PUBLIC AND NAMED IN HONOR OF COLORADO'S CENTENNIAL. (LOCAL). THOMAS THOMPSON, CO-CHAIRMAN; HINSDALE CENTENNIAL-BICENTENNIAL COMMITTEE; BOX 352; LAKE CITY, CO 81235. (#4165).

'IMPROVING OUR TOWN' - LAKE CITY, CO. PURCHASE OF PARK EQUIPMENT - BENCHES, TRASH CANS AND FIRE PLACE PITS. (LOCAL). WALTER H MCDONALD, PROJ DIRECTOR; TOWN OF LAKE CITY; LAKE CITY, CO 81235. (#26237).

SOUTHWEST COLORADO MOUNTAIN JEEP TOURS. SELF GUIDED JEEP TOURS THROUGH MOUNTAIN PASSES WITH MARKERS AT HISTORICAL POINTS OF INTEREST COMPLETE WITH TAPED COMMENTARY. (ST-WIDE). BILL HALL, PRESIDENT; LAKE CITY CHAMBER OF COMMERCE; BOX 397; LAKE CITY, CO 81235. (#4166).

SOUTHWEST COLORADO HISTORIC SITE MARKING. THE PLACEMENT OF COMMEMORATIVE SIGNS DESCRIBING OLD LANDMARKS FOR BENEFIT OF TOURING PUBLIC. (ST-WIDE). THOMAS THOMPSON, CHAIRMAN; HINSDALE CENTENNIAL-BICENTENNIAL COMMITTEE; BOX 352; LAKE CITY, CO 81235. (#4169).

JULY 4, '75. LAKE CITY, COLO FOURTH OF JULY CELEBRATION. ACTIVITIES IN THE STREETS AND PARKS SUCH AS PARADES, CARNIVALS, SQUAREDANCING AND FIREWORKS. AT COUNTYWIDE. (LOCAL). BILL HALL, PRES; LAKE CITY CHAMBER OF COMMERCE; BOX 397; LAKE CITY, CO 81235. (#4168-1).

JULY 4, '76. COMMUNITY PARADE FOR FOURTH OF JULY CELEBRATION. PARADE. (LOCAL). WALTER H MCDONALD, COORD; 4TH OF JULY FESTIVAL COMMITTEE; LAKE CITY, CO 81235. (#108359-2).

JULY 4, '76. FIREWORKS FOR FOURTH OF JULY CELEBRATION. FESTIVAL. (LOCAL). WALTER H MCDONALD, CHMN; 4TH OF JULY FESTIVAL COMMITTEE; LAKE CITY, CO 81235. (#108359-1).

AUG 2, '76. SENIOR CITIZEN 1976. DINNER ON COLORADO DAY TO HIGHLIGHT THE RESTORATION OF THE SENIOR CITIZENS BUILDING. (LOCAL). WALTER H MCDONALD, COORD; SENIOR CITIZENS; LAKE CITY, CO 81235. (#108955-6).

LAKEWOOD

BELMAR PARK FOCAL POINT IN LAKEWOOD, COLO. TO PLAN AND ESTABLISH APPROPRIATE FOCAL POINT FOR BELMAR PARK IN LAKEWOOD. (LOCAL). MARSHA BROWN, EXEC SECRETARY; LAKEWOOD CENTENNIAL-BICENTENNIAL COMMISSION; 1580 YARROW ST; LAKEWOOD, CO 80215. (#2872). **(??).**

BROTHERS OF THE BUSH, SHAVING PERMITS-LAKEWOOD, CO. SHAVING PERMITS OR BROTHERS OF THE BUSH MEMBERSHIP BADGES WILL BE SOLD TO THOSE WHO OPT TO GROW A BEARD FOR THE CENTENNIAL. PROCEEDS TO BE DONATED TO A VARIETY OF JEFFERSON CITY CHARITIES. (LOCAL). RAY C CUNE, EXEC DIRECTOR; JEFFERSON COUNTY BOARD OF REALTORS; 1675 CARR ST; LAKEWOOD, CO 80215. (#16393).

CENTENNIAL SITES RECOGNITION, JEFFERSON COUNTY, CO. IDENTIFICATION & RECOGNITION OF JEFFERSON COUNTY SITES SIGNIFICANT TO COUNTY HISTORY. (LOCAL). MARY CALHOUN, CHAIRPERSON; JEFFERSON COUNTY CENTENNIAL-BICENTENNIAL COMMISSION; 12185 W 29 PL; LAKEWOOD, CO 80215. (#26145).

CITY OF LAKEWOOD, COLO, FLAG PROJECT. CONDUCT A FLAG CONTEST HAVING VARIOUS CATEGORIES AND PRIZES. THE CHOSEN DESIGN TO BE IMPLEMENTED FOR USE AS OFFICIAL CITY FLAG. (LOCAL). MARSHA BROWN, EXEC SECRETARY; LAKEWOOD CENTENNIAL-BICENTENNIAL COMMISSION; 1580 YARROW ST; LAKEWOOD, CO 80215. (#2930).

GULCH AREA DEVELOPMENT - LAKEWOOD, CO. RESTORE & PRESERVE THE NATURAL ENVIRONMENT OF GULCH AREA ON SCHOOL PROPERTY BY CONSTRUCTING PATHS, LANDSCAPING & HALTING EROSION. (LOCAL). JUDI GIRARD, DIRECTOR; JEFFERSON COUNTY PUBLIC SCHOOLS - CREIGTON JR HIGH; LAKEWOOD, CO 80226. (#26226).

'HISTORY OF LAKEWOOD' BOOKLET OF COLORADO. PRINTED HISTORICAL INFORMATION REGARDING CITY. (LOCAL). MARSHA BROWN, EXEC SECRETARY; LAKEWOOD CENTENNIAL-BICENTENNIAL COMMISSION; 1580 YARROW ST; LAKEWOOD, CO 80215. (#2931).

HONOR GROUP WEEK - PROJECT OF LAKEWOOD, COLORADO. EACH WEEK THRUOUT THE YEAR SET ASIDE IN HONOR OF VARIOUS GROUPS. DETAILED INFORMATION PRINTED & MADE AVAILABLE TO GENERAL PUBLIC, ON A QUARTERLY BASIS OF ALL ACTIVITIES. (LOCAL). V J PARRAHAM, CHAIRPERSON; LAKEWOOD CENTENNIAL-BICENTENNIAL COMMISSION; 1580 YARROW; LAKEWOOD, CO 80215. (#2892).

JEFFERSON COUNTY RESTORATION PROJECT, CO. RESTORATION OF HIWAN CLUB FOR USE AS PIONEER MUSEUM. (LOCAL). MARY C CALHOUN, CHAIRPERSON; JEFFERSON COUNTY CENTENNIAL-BICENTENNIAL COMMISSION; 12185 W 29 PL; LAKEWOOD, CO 80215. (#26146).

JEFFERSON COUNTY ORAL HISTORY PROJECT, CO. INTERVIEWS WITH INDIVIDUALS THROUGHOUT JEFFERSON COUNTY TO BE PRESERVED ON TAPES WHICH WILL BE STORED IN CENTRAL JEFFERSON COUNTY LIBRARY. TAPES WILL BE CATALOGUED & AVAILABLE FOR PUBLIC USE. (LOCAL). MARY CALHOUN, CHAIRPERSON; JEFFERSON COUNTY CENTENNIAL-BICENTENNIAL COMMISSION; LAKEWOOD, CO 80215. (#26305).

LAKEWOOD STONE HOUSE RESTORATION - CO. RESTORATION OF 100 YEAR OLD HOUSE NOW COMMUNITY EYESORE AND HAZARD FOR USE AS COMMUNITY MEETING HOUSE & PARK PLANNING OFFICE THUS PRESERVING AN ARCHITECTURALLY UNIQUE COLO NATL REGISTER STRUCTURE. (ST-WIDE). GARY R MCDONNELL, DIRECTOR PARKS AND RECREATION; CITY OF LAKEWOOD; 1580 YARROW ST; LAKEWOOD, CO 80215. (#16399).

LAKEWOOD, COLO, MUSEUM PROJECT. ESTABLISH MUSEUM WITHIN BELMAR PARK TO HOUSE ARTIFACTS AND HISTORIC ITEMS IMPORTANT IN LAKEWOOD'S HISTORY. BUILDING HAS BEEN ERECTED. (LOCAL). MARSHA BROWN, EXEC SECRETARY; LAKEWOOD CENTENNIAL-BICENTENNIAL COMMISSION; 1580 YARROW ST; LAKEWOOD, CO 80215. (#2873). **(??).**

STAGECOACH HOUSE RESTORATION OF LAKEWOOD, COLO. RESTORATION OF RECENT CITY ACQUISITION OF OLD STAGE COACH HOUSE & PROPERTY. (LOCAL). V J PARRAHAM, CHAIRPERSON; LAKEWOOD CENTENNIAL-BICENTENNIAL COMMISSION; 1580 YARROW; LAKEWOOD, CO 80215. (#2875).

AUG 25 - 28, '75. SLO PITCH SOFTBALL CO-ED TOURNAMENT. COMPETITION AT 200 S KIPLING, LAKEWOOD PARK. (LOCAL). STEVE VAN DEVEERE, DIR; CITY OF LAKEWOOD; 8715 W 16TH AVE; LAKEWOOD, CO 80215. (#16408-6).

JAN 29, '76. DRAMATIC VIGNETTES ON U S WOMEN. LIVE PERFORMANCE AT 12100 W ALAMEDA PKWY. (LOCAL). PAT KENNING, PROJ DIR; LUTHERAN CHURCH OF THE MASTER; 1153 W SHEPPERD AVE; LITTLETON, CO 80120. (#200007-124).

APR 11 - 17, '76. EARTH WEEK - ARBOR DAY CELEBRATION. ARBOR DAY/EARTH WEEK WILL BE OBSERVED BY PLANTING A COLORADO BLUE SPRUCE AND RAISING LAKEWOOD'S NEW FLAG AT THE BELMAR MUSEUM, FORMERLY THE BARN ON THE BONFILS ESTATE (CO-FOUNDER OF THE DENVER POST). AT BELMAR MUSEUM GROUNDS, 777 S WADSWORTH BLVD. (LOCAL). MRS CATHERINE REVIE, CHMN; LAKEWOOD CENTENNIAL-BICENTENNIAL COMMISSION; 1060 S DOVER ST; LAKEWOOD, CO 80226. (#104856-1).

APR 17, '76. SPECIAL OLYMPICS FOR THE HANDICAPPED (TRACK & FIELD). COMPETITION AT LAKEWOOD JUNIOR HIGH SCHOOL TRACK. (NAT'L). TOM HANCOCK; R-I SCHOOLS; 1208 QUAIL ST; LAKEWOOD, CO 80215. (#16408-10).

MAY 8, '76. WRESTLING TOURNAMENT. CONTESTANTS MUST PARTICIPATE IN CLINIC FOR 6 WKS PRIOR TO THE TOURNAMENT. AT GRN MTNS HIGH SCHOOL. (LOCAL). STEVE VAN DEVEER, DIR; CITY OF LAKEWOOD; 8715 W 16TH AVE; LAKEWOOD, CO 80215. (#16408-3).

MAY 15, '76. SPECIAL OLYMPICS FOR THE HANDICAPPED (TRACK & FIELD). COMPETITION AT LAKEWOOD JUNIOR HIGH SCHOOL TRACK; 7655 W 10TH AVE. (LOCAL). PEGGY VAN DEVEERE, DIR; CITY OF LAKEWOOD; 8715 W 16TH AVE; LAKEWOOD, CO 80215. (#16408-5).

JUNE 20 - 26, '76. LAKEWOOD'S INCORPORATION ANNIVERSARY. WEEK OF OLYMPIC-STYLE SPORTS EVENTS. GUEST PRO TOURNAMENTS ENTIRE WEEK OF JUNE 20-26, 1976. AT CITYWIDE. (LOCAL). MRS MARSHA BROWN, EX SEC; LAKEWOOD CENTENNIAL - BICENTENNIAL COMMISSION; 7815 W 16TH AVE; LAKEWOOD, CO 80215. (#3570-1).

JUNE 24 - 25, '76. ANNIVERSARY CELEBRATION OF GOLF TOURNAMENT. JUNE 24 AT FOOTHILLS GOLF COURSE AND JUNE 25TH AT THE APPLEWOOD GOLF COURSE. THE FRIDAY FINAL DAY WILL BE FOLLOWED BY A BUFFET AND PRESENTATION OF AWARDS AT THE APPLEWOOD GOLF COURSE. AT FOOTHILLS GOLF COURSE; APPLEWOOD GOLF COURSE. (LOCAL). TOM HANCOCK, DIR; CITY OF LAKEWOOD; 1209 QUAIL ST; LAKEWOOD, CO 80215. (#2929-1).

JULY 3 - 4, '76. FESTIVAL OF THE WEST. FRONTIER VILLAGE, MIDWAY, GAMES, MUSICAL GROUPS, MELODRAMA, ARENA SHOW DEPICTING HISTORY OF COLORADO. (LOCAL). MARY CALHOUN, CHAIRMAN; LAKEWOOD BICENTENNIAL COMMITTEE; 12185 W 29TH PLACE; LAKEWOOD, CO 80215. (#107572-1).

JULY 4, '76. JULY 4TH FESTIVAL. THE DAY-LONG EVENTS INCLUDE INTERDENOMINATINAL SUNRISE SERVICE, PANCAKE BREAKFAST, PARADE WITH 200 MULTI-STATE ENTRIES, FAIR, FIREWORKS, ENTERTAINMENT (LIVE SHOW). MANY ACTIVITIES ON STADIUM GROUNDS, SOUTH TO & INCLUDING LAKEWOOD PARK. AT PARADE: W ALAMEDA AVE FROM UNION BLVD EAST TO KIPLING. (LOCAL). SUE HUGHEY, COMM CHMN; LAKEWOOD

LAKEWOOD — CONTINUED

CENTENNIAL-BICENTENNIAL COMM & KHOW RADIO STATION; 6801 WEST ELDORADO PLACE; LAKEWOOD, CO 80237. (#104654-1).

JULY 4, '76. TRAP SHOOT. DISPLAYS ARE INCLUDED ALONG WITH SHOOTING DEMONSTRATIONS; EVENTS INCLUDE REGULAR TRAP SHOOTING & A TURKEY SHOOT. AT FOOTHILLS TRAP RANGE, 3803 S CARR. (ST-WIDE). BILL MCGUINE; FOOTHILLS RECREATION DISTRICT; FOOTHILLS TRAP RANGE; LAKEWOOD, CO 80215. (#16408-4).

JULY 8 - 10, '76. BASKETBALL TOURNAMENTS. FOUR AWARDS WILL BE GIVEN IN EACH CLASSIFICATION; CLASSIFICATIONS ARE ONE-ON-ONE, CO-ED AND 2-ON-2; EVERYONE IS INVITED TO PARTICIPATE. AT GRN MTNS HIGH SCHOOL. (LOCAL). STEVE VAN DEVEERE, DIR; CITY OF LAKEWOOD; DEPT OF PARKS & RECREATION; 8715 W 16TH AVE; LAKEWOOD, CO 80215. (#16408-8).

JULY 24, '76. 1776 OLYMPIC. FESTIVAL AT JEFFCO COUNTY FAIRGROUNDS, I-70 AND WEST 6TH. (LOCAL). STEVE LASLEUR, PROJ DIR; LAKEWOOD CO STAKE CHURCH OF JESUS CHRIST OF LATTER DAY SAINTS; 1443 S AMES ST; LAKEWOOD, CO 80226. (#108871-1).

JULY 24 - 25, '76. SWIMMING MEET. AGE GROUP CLASSIFICATIONS WILL BE 10 AND OVER. REGISTRATION IS RESTRICTED TO THOSE SWIMMING CLUBS WITH THE FOOTHILLS SWIMMING ASS'N. AT FOOTHILLS PARK POOL, 2200 S KIPLING ST. (LOCAL). TOM HANCOCK, CHMN; CITY OF LAKEWOOD BICENTENNIAL COMMISSION; 1209 QUAIL ST; LAKEWOOD, CO 80215. (#16408-13).

JULY 24 - 26, '76. GOLF TOURNAMENT. 54 HOLES TO BE PLAYED OVER 3 COURSES, 18 HOLES EACH DAY, HANDICAP BY GROUP; MEN & WOMEN. AT LAKEWOOD JUNIOR HIGH SCHOOL TRACK. (ST-WIDE). JERRY CLAUSSEN, DIRECTOR; CITY OF LAKEWOOD; 655 EVERETT ST; LAKEWOOD, CO 80215. (#16408-11).

JULY 30, '76. 'PLAY-DAY'; DAY LONG ACTIVITIES FOR ELEMENTARY SCHOOL CHILDREN. COMPETITION, FAIR AT MORSE PARK, 20TH ALLISON. (LOCAL). KATHY MCDOWELL, CHAIRMAN; CITY OF LAKEWOOD; 8715 W 16TH AVE; LAKEWOOD, CO 80215. (#16408-1).

JULY 30 - AUG 1, '76. SWIMMING MEET. COMPETITION. (LOCAL). HARV NEELEY, DIRECTOR; CITY OF LAKEWOOD; 200 S KIPLING; LAKEWOOD, CO 80215. (#16408-2).

AUG 1, '76. COLORADO DAY OPEN HOUSE. EXHIBIT AT LAKEWOOD MUSEUM, 400 S WADSWORTH. (LOCAL). RUTH SCHAFFER, COORD; LAKEWOOD CENTENNIAL-BICENTENNIAL COMMITTEE; 13442 W OHIO DR; LAKEWOOD, CO 80228. (#108668-1).

AUG 5, '76. JEFFERSON SYMPHONY ORCHESTRA HONORS LAKEWOOD, CO. SEMI-PROFESSIONAL ORCHESTRA TO HONOR THE CITY OF LAKEWOOD; MUSIC OF AMERICA & BY AMERICAN COMPOSERS FEATURED. AT LAKEWOOD PARK, ALAMEDA & KIPLING; FREE PARKING. (LOCAL). JACKIE MAXWELL, V-PRES; JEFFERSON SYMPHONY ORCHESTRA; 7720 WESTVIEW DR; LAKEWOOD, CO 80215. (#107017-1).

AUG 6 - 8, '76. VOLLEYBALL TOURNAMENT. COURTS WILL BE BOTH SAND AND GRASS; AWARDS FOR 2 TOP PLACES CO-ED; 3 AND 3 DOUBLE ELIMINATION; NO AGE GROUP RESTRICTIONS. (LOCAL). KATHY MCDOWELL, DIRECTOR; CITY OF LAKEWOOD; 8715 W 16TH AVE; LAKEWOOD, CO 80215. (#16408-12).

AUG 13, '76. HORSESHOE TOURNAMENT. AWARD FOR TOP 4 IN 3 CLASSIFICATIONS; JUNIOR-16 & UNDER, ADULT 17-50 AND SENIOR 51 AND OVER. AT MORSE PARK 20TH & CARR ST. (LOCAL). STEVE VAN DEVEERE, DIR; CITY OF LAKEWOOD; 8715 W 16TH AVE; LAKEWOOD, CO 80215. (#16408-9).

AUG 13 - 15, '76. HERITAGE WEEK IN LAKEWOOD, COLORADO. CLOSING TIME ON MONDAY, AUG 15; 7:00 PM SET ASIDE FOR CULTURAL AND HISTORICAL EVENTS. (LOCAL). VERNON PARRAHM; LAKEWOOD CENTENNIAL-BICENTENNIAL COMMISSION; 1545 ROBB ST; LAKEWOOD, CO 80215. (#2928-1).

AUG 21 - SEPT 29, '76. TENNIS TOURNAMENT. TOURNAMENT WILL BE DIVIDED INTO AGE BRACKETS; ENTRY FEE FOR CHILDREN IS $2.00, ADULTS, $3.00; OTHER DIVISIONS ARE BOYS, GIRLS, SINGLES, DOUBLES, MIXED DOUBLES, ETC; PARTICIPANTS ARE LIMITED TO 2 CATEGORIES. AT LOCAL PARKS. (LOCAL). GENEVA ROYAL, DIRECTOR; CITY OF LAKEWOOD; 8715 16TH AVE; LAKEWOOD, CO 80215. (#16408-7).

AUG 22 - 28, '76. ANNIV OF 1ST CITY OFFICIALS. WEEK OF CULTURAL & HISTORICAL EVENTS-INCLUDING PAGENT IN HONOR OF ELECTION OF 1ST CITY OFFICIALS. TO BE HELD AUGUST, 1976. AT SCHOOL AUDITORIUMS CITYWIDE. (LOCAL). MRS MARSHA BROWN, EX SEC; LAKEWOOD CENTENNIAL - BICENTENNIAL COMMISSION; 7815 W 16TH AVE; LAKEWOOD, CO 80215. (#3569-1).

SEPT 1 - 30, '76. FRONTIER ARTS & CRAFTS WITH JEFFCO R-1 SCHOOL DISTRICT. TRAVELING TRUNK EXHIBIT OF HISTORICAL ARTIFACTS FOR SCHOOL CHILDREN IN CONJUNCTION WITH MUSEUM TOURS FOR ELEMENTARY STUDENTS. AT THROUGHOUT JEFFERSON COUNTY R-1 SCHOOL DISTRICT. (LOCAL). BILL WHITE, DIRECTOR; JEFFERSON COUNTY CENTENNIAL-BICENTENNIAL COMMISSION; 1209 QUAIL; LAKEWOOD, CO 80215. (#108775-1).

SEPT 26, '76. MASSING OF THE COLORS. FESTIVAL AT JEFFCO PUBLIC SCHOOLS STADIUM - W SIXTH & KIPLING. (LOCAL). COL L J WEIGEL, COORD; DENVER CHAPTER OF THE MILITARY ORDER OF THE WORLD WARS; 1278 FOX ST; DENVER, CO 80204. (#108770-1).

LAMAR

CENTENNIAL PARK IN LAMAR, COLORADO. CONSTRUCTION OF NEW PARK DEPICTING WESTERN HERITAGE OF SOUTHEAST COLORADO. (LOCAL). KEN MITCHELL, CHRMN, LAMAR CENT-BICENT COMMITTEE; PROWERS COUNTY HISTORICAL SOCIETY; C/O BOX 483; LAMAR, CO 81052. (#4090).

FLAGS OF YESTERYEAR DISPLAY, LAMAR, COLORADO. REPRODUCTIONS OF FLAGS FLOWN OVER UNITED STATES SINCE 1776 TO BE FLOWN AT CENTENNIAL PARK. (LOCAL). KEN MITCHELL, CHAIRMAN; LAMAR CENTENNIAL-BICENTENNIAL COMMITTEE; C/O BOX 483; LAMAR, CO 81052. (#4092).

'A HUNDRED YEARS PLUS' - DOLL EXHIBIT IN LAMAR, CO. DISPLAY AND SHOW OF ANTIQUE DOLLS AND DRESSES OVER THE LAST 100 YEARS FOR PERMANENT DISPLAY IN THE MUSEUM. (LOCAL). KEN MITCHELL, CHAIRMAN; LAMAR CENTENNIAL-BICENTENNIAL COMMITTEE; C/O BOX 483; LAMAR, CO 81052. (#4091).

PIKES COMMEMORATIVE PLAQUE OF LAMAR, COLORADO. PLAQUE WITH CENTENNIAL-BICENTENNIAL SYMBOLS TO BE PLACED ON TOWER COMMEMORATING PIKE'S STOP & CAMP AT WILLOW CREEK ON HIS WAY TO THE ROCKIES. (ST-WIDE). KEN MITCHELL, CHAIRMAN LAMAR CENT-BICENT COMM; PROWERS COUNTY HISTORICAL SOCIETY; C/O BOX 483; LAMAR, CO 81052. (#4197).

PROJECT PRIDE -LAMAR, COLORADO. CLEAN-UP, FIX-UP AND BEAUTIFY THE CITY FOR THE 1976 CELEBRATIONS, INCLUDING PAINTING SENIOR CITIZENS' HOMES. (LOCAL). KEN MITCHELL, CHRMN, LAMAR CENT-BICENT COMMITTEE; LAMAR CHAMBER OF COMMERCE; C/O BOX 483; LAMAR, CO 81052. (#4094). **(??).**

MAY 24, '75 - CONTINUING . WESTERN ARTIFACTS DISPLAY. EXHIBITS OF ARTIFACTS SUCH AS SADDLES, AND 19TH CENTURY CLOTHING. SPONSOR PLANS ARE INCOMPLETE AS OF 04/04/75. AT LOCAL MERCHANTS WINDOWS. (LOCAL). KEN MITCHELL, CHRMN; LAMAR CHAMBER OF COMMERCE; C/O BOX 483; LAMAR, CO 81052. (#4172-1).

NOV 12, '75. UNITED STATES ARMED FORCES BICENTENNIAL CARAVAN. THE CARAVAN IS COMPOSED OF EXHIBIT VANS FOR EACH BRANCH OF THE MILITARY SERVICE. THE THEME OF THE EXHIBITION IS 'HISTORY OF THE ARMED FORCES AND THEIR CONTRIBUTION TO THE NATION'. (LOCAL). KENNETH G MITCHELL, CHMN; U S ARMED FORCES BICENTENNIAL EXHIBIT VANS PROJECT; 1812 S 6TH; LAMAR, CO 81052. (#1775-248).

MAY 22 - 23, '76. LAMAR DAYS '76. CELEBRATION COMMEMORATING THE FOUNDING OF LAMAR TOGETHER WITH THE COLORADO CENTENNIAL AND UNITED STATES BICENTENNIAL CELEBRATIONS. AT CITYWIDE. (LOCAL). KEN MITCHELL, CHRMN; LAMAR CENT-BICENT COMMITTEE; CHAMBER OF COMMERCE, C/O BOX 483; LAMAR, CO 81052. (#4095-1).

JULY 4, '76. BICENTENNIAL FIREWORKS. FESTIVAL. (LOCAL). HOWARD TEMPLE, COORD; COLORADO STATE UNIV; LAMAR, CO 81052. (#108605-1).

JULY 4, '76. LAMAR CELEBRATION. FESTIVAL. (LOCAL). KEN MITCHELL, CHAIRMAN; LAMAR BICENTENNIAL COMMITTEE; PO BOX 483; LAMAR, CO 81052. (#107584-1).

LAS ANIMAS

BENT COUNTY BICENTENNIAL CALENDAR - CO. 1976 CALENDAR WITH PICTURES AND HISTORIC SKETCHES DEPICTING LOCAL AND NATIONAL EVENTS. (LOCAL). STUART COLLINS, CHAIRMAN; BENT COUNTY CENTENNIAL-BICENTENNIAL COMMITTEE; 626 GROVE AVE; LAS ANIMAS, CO 81054. (#26247).

BENT COUNTY COURTHOUSE RESTORATION, CO. RESTORATION OF EXTERIOR OF BENT COUNTY COURTHOUSE TO ITS ORIGINAL STATE. (LOCAL). CLYDE ALBERTSON, CHAIRMAN; BENT COUNTY BOARD OF COMMISSIONERS; 7TH & CARSON STS; LAS ANIMAS, CO 81054. (#26148).

HIGH SCHOOL ART PROJECT - LAS ANIMAS, CO. ART DEPT AT HIGH SCHOOL HAS WRITTEN & ILLUSTRATED A BOOK WHICH CONCEPTUALIZES LIFE IN AMERICA TODAY. (LOCAL). HON ALFRED PUTNAM, MAYOR; CITY OF LAS ANIMAS; PO BOX 468; LAS ANIMAS, CO 81054. (#26222).

LLEWELLYN THOMPSON MEMORIAL - LAS ANIMAS, CO. CREATE A LASTING MEMORIAL TO NATIVE SON, LLEWELLYN THOMPSON. (LOCAL). STUART COLLINS, CHAIRMAN; BENT CO CENTENNIAL-BICENTENNIAL COMMITTEE; 626 GROVE AVE; LOS ANIMAS, CO 81054. (#26262).

OLD BENT'S FORT RESTORATION, LAS ANIMAS, COLO. A PROJECT TO SAVE AND RESTORE BENT'S FORT TO ORIGINAL AND HISTORIC CONDITION. (ST-WIDE). STEPHEN H HART, DIRECTOR; STATE HISTORICAL SOCIETY OF COLORADO; 200 14TH AVE; DENVER, CO 80203. (#1941).

'SOMETHING BETTER' - LAS ANIMAS, CO. ADVANCED ART CLASS AND OTHER STUDENTS OF HIGH SCHOOL JOIN FORCES TO WRITE AND ILLUSTRATE A BOOK COMMEMORATING THE BICENTENNIAL WITH LIGHT AND HUMOROUS FORMAT. (LOCAL). STUART COLLINS, CHAIRMAN; BENT COUNTY CENTENNIAL-BICENTENNIAL COMMITTEE; 626 GROVE AVE; LAS ANIMAS, CO 81054. (#26246).

JUNE 11, '76. SENIOR COLORADOANS DAY. BANQUET; MINIMUM AGE 50; PREFERENCE TO THOSE OVER 65. THEME 'WE STAYED AND MADE THE GRADE.' TEN OUTSTANDING SENIORS WILL BE HONORED. FEATURE SPEAKER, AWARDS PRESENTED BASED ON SEVERAL FACTORS: ACCOMPLISHMENT, INVOLVEMENT, VOLUNTEERING AND PERSONALITY. AT ST MARY'S SCHOOL. (LOCAL). STUART COLLINS, CHMN; BENT COUNTY CENTENNIAL-BICENTENNIAL COMMITTEE; 626 GROVE AVE; LAS ANIMAS, CO 81054. (#200007-128).

JULY 3, '76. BICENTENNIAL CELEBRATION. DOWNTOWN ACTIVITIES, PERIOD DRESS, CONTESTS & SPANISH FIESTA. AT TROJAN FOOTBALL FIELD. (LOCAL). STUART COLLINS, CHAIRMAN; BENT COUNTY CENTENNIAL-BICENTENNIAL COMMITTEE; 626 GROVE AVE; LAS ANIMAS, CO 81054. (#108604-9).

JULY 3, '76. 'SMOKER' - BOXING MATCH BETWEEN YOUTH. COMPETITION. (LOCAL). STUART COLLINS, CHAIRMAN; BENT COUNTY CENTENNIAL-BICENTENNIAL COMMITTEE; 626 GROVE AVE; LAS ANIMAS, CO 81054. (#108604-1).

JULY 3 - 4, '76. SPANISH FIESTA AND FIREWORKS. FESTIVAL, LIVE PERFORMANCE. (LOCAL). STU COLLINS, CHAIRMAN; DOWNTOWN MERCHANTS ASSOC; PO BOX 168; LAS ANIMAS, CO 81054. (#107579-1).

JULY 4, '76. COMMUNITY BREAKFAST. $.76 EACH IN THE SPIRIT OF '76 AND '86. SPECIAL HONOR TO THOSE LIVING IN BENT COUNTY AT LEAST 76 YEARS, FAMILIES WITH MOST MEMBERS, GENERATIONS OR TEENAGERS PRESENT. COSTUME CONTEST. AT TROJAN FOOTBALL FIELD. (LOCAL). STUART COLLINS, CHAIRMAN; BENT COUNTY CENTENNIAL-BICENTENNIAL COMMITTEE; 626 GROVE AVE; LAS ANIMAS, CO 81054. (#108604-3).

JULY 4, '76. DRAMA-'WE THE PEOPLE'. DRAMA PRODUCTION ABOUT THE STRUGGLES OF WRITING THE PREAMBLE TO THE CONSTITUTION; ROLES PLAYED BY LOCAL ACTORS. AT TROJAN FOOTBALL FIELD. (LOCAL). STUART COLLINS, CHAIRMAN; BENT COUNTY CENTENNIAL-BICENTENNIAL COMMITTEE; 626 GROVE AVE; LAS ANIMAS, CO 81054. (#108604-5).

JULY 4, '76. FIREWORKS DISPLAY. JULY 4 FINALE WITH LAS ANIMAS & VA HOSPITAL, FORT LYON COMBINING THEIR FIREWORKS DISPLAYS; WILL EMPHASIZE THE COLORADO CENTENNIAL & WILL INCLUDE THE COLORADO LOGO AND THE STATE FLAG. AT TROJAN FOOTBALL FIELD. (LOCAL). STUART COLLINS, CHAIRMAN; BENT COUNTY CENTENNIAL-BICENTENNIAL COMMITTEE; 626 GROVE AVE; LAS ANIMAS, CO 81054. (#108604-7).

JULY 4, '76. INDIVIDUAL CHURCH COLONIAL WORSHIP. EACH PASTOR WILL CONDUCT IN HIS RESPECTIVE CHURCH A RELIGIOUS SERVICE SIMILAR TO THOSE OF COLONIAL DAYS & OF THEIR RELIGIOUS FAITH AT THEIR USUAL CHURCH HOUR. (LOCAL). STUART COLLINS, CHAIRMAN; BENT COUNTY CENTENNIAL-BICENTENNIAL COMMITTEE; 626 GROVE AVE; LAS ANIMAS, CO 81054. (#108604-4).

JULY 4, '76. PATRIOTIC BAND AND VOCAL CONCERT. PROGRAM OF VOCAL AND INSTRUMENTAL PATRIOTIC MUSIC BY LOCAL PERFORMERS WITH REVOLUTIONARY COLOR GUARD. AT TROJAN FOOTBALL FIELD. (LOCAL). STUART COLLINS, CHAIRMAN; BENT COUNTY CENTENNIAL-BICENTENNIAL COMMITTEE; 626 GROVE AVE; LAS ANIMAS, CO 81054. (#108604-6).

JULY 4, '76. SUNRISE WORSHIP SERVICE. ALL-COMMUNITY, ALL-DENOMINATION SUNRISE WORSHIP SERVICE WILL START A DAY OF SPECIAL JULY 4 EVENTS. AT TROJAN FOOTBALL FIELD. (LOCAL). STUART COLLINS, CHAIRMAN; BENT COUNTY CENTENNIAL-BICENTENNIAL COMMITTEE; 626 GROVE AVE; LAS ANIMAS, CO 81054. (#108604-2).

LEADVILLE

BICENTENNIAL NATURE HIKING TRAIL OF LEADVILLE, CO. TRAIL COVERING 4 MILES OF ABANDONED RIGHT OF WAY OF DENVER AND RIO GRANDE WESTERN R.R. FROM TOP OF TENNESSEE PASS TO MITCHELL CREEK JUNCTION. (LOCAL). BOB RINKER, CHAIRMAN; LAKE COUNTY BICENTENNIAL COMMISSION; C/O 412 7TH ST; LEADVILLE, CO 80461. (#4469). **(??).**

CENTENNIAL NATURE AND HIKING TRAIL-LEADVILLE, CO. TRAIL TO INCLUDE LAST 5 MILES OF ABANDONED COLORADO MIDLAND R.R. GRADE ON EAST SIDE OF HAGERMAN PASS. (LOCAL). BOB RINKER, CHAIRMAN; LAKE COUNTY BICENTENNIAL COMMITTEE; 412 WEST 7TH; LEADVILLE, CO 80461. (#4471).

LAKE COUNTY HISTORIC PAMPHLET -COLORADO. PAMPHLET GUIDE FOR WALKING TOUR OF HISTORIC PAINTS OF INTEREST IN LAKE COUNTY, COLORADO. (LOCAL). BOB RINKER, PROJECT CHAIRMAN; LEADVILLE CHAMBER OF COMMERCE; 412 WEST 7TH ST; LEADVILLE, CO 80461. (#4097). **(??).**

LAKE COUNTY MARKERS OF HISTORIC INTEREST - CO. DESIGNATION BY MARKERS OF HISTORIC SITES IN LAKE COUNTY AREA. (LOCAL). BOB RINKER, CHAIRMAN; LEADVILLE CHAMBER OF COMMERCE; 412 W 7TH ST; LEADVILLE, CO 80461. (#4429). **(??).**

LAKE COUNTY, COLORADO, COMMUNITY PARK. ESTABLISHMENT OF A COMMUNITY PARK FACILITY IN HONOR OF THE CENTENNIAL FOR COMMUNITY BENEFIT. (LOCAL). BOB RINKER, PROJECT DIRECTOR; LEADVILLE JUNIOR CHAMBER OF COMMERCE; 412 WEST 7TH ST; LEADVILLE, CO 80461. (#4099). **(??).**

LEADVILLE, COLO, HERITAGE PARK. A PROJECT TO CREATE A PARK ADJACENT TO THE EXISTING MUSEUM FOR THE DISPLAY OF AN OLD MINER'S CABIN, POPCORN WAGON, MINING CARS, & FOR USE AS A DOWNTOWN PARK. (LOCAL). ROBERT L RINKER, PRESIDENT; LAKE COUNTY CIVIC CENTER ASSOC; PO BOX 962; LEADVILLE, CO 80461. (#4414).

FEB 14 - 16, '75. CRYSTAL CARNIVAL. ICE GOLF, ICE FISHING, ICE AND SNOW SKILL DRIVING CONTEST, SNOWSHOE SOFTBALL GAME, YUGOSLAVIAN FOLK PERFORMERS, SNOWMAN BUILDING CONTEST, SLED AND SKI RACES AND SKI JUMPING WILL BE HELD. (LOCAL). DR MICHAEL G PTACEK, CHMN; LEADVILLE CRYSTAL CARNIVAL ASSOC; 403 HARRISON; LEADVILLE, CO 80461. (#200007-125).

LEADVILLE — CONTINUED

FEB 14 - 16, '76. WINTER CRYSTAL CARNIVAL. FESTIVAL. (LOCAL). DR MIKE PTACEK, COORD; WINTER CRYSTAL CARNIVAL COMMITTEE; BOX 1210; LEADVILLE, CO 80461. (#103416-41).

SEPT '76. HOUSE TOUR. TOUR. (LOCAL). KAREN M DUNN, PRESIDENT; ST VINCENT GENERAL HOSPITAL AUXILLARY; 144 W 9TH; LEADVILLE, CO 80461. (#100361-2).

LIMON

NOV 10, '75. UNITED STATES ARMED FORCES BICENTENNIAL CARAVAN. THE CARAVAN IS COMPOSED OF EXHIBIT VANS FOR EACH BRANCH OF THE MILITARY SERVICE. THE THEME OF THE EXHIBITION IS 'HISTORY OF THE ARMED FORCES AND THEIR CONTRIBUTION TO THE NATION'. (LOCAL). JAMES D STATTON, CHMN; U S ARMED FORCES BICENTENNIAL EXHIBIT VANS PROJECT; BOX 357; LIMON, CO 80828. (#1775-246).

JUNE 30, '76. OLD SCHOOLHOUSE MUSEUM DEDICATION & OPEN HOUSE. EXHIBIT AT D AVE BETWEEN 5TH & 6TH ST. (LOCAL). MRS DOUGLAS STRAUB, CHMN; LIMON TEACHER'S ASSOC & LINCOLN COUNTY HISTORICAL SOCIETY; 783 C AVE; LIMON, CO 80828. (#108602-1).

JULY 3, '76. FIREWORKS. FESTIVAL. (LOCAL). MRS JACK OWEN, DIRECTOR; LIMON FIREWORKS COMMITTEE; HUGO, CO 80821. (#108602-2).

LITTLETON

ARAPAHOE COUNTY HISTORY, CO. A COUNTY HISTORY WILL BE PUBLISHED IN HONOR OF THE CENTENNIALBICENTENNIAL CELEBRATION. (LOCAL). TOM SWEARINGEN, HERITAGE CHAIRMAN; ARAPAHOE COUNTY CENTENNIAL-BICENTENNIAL COMMITTEE; 7100 S PLATTE CANYON RD; LITTLETON, CO 80123. (#14850).

ARAPAHOE COUNTY HISTORIC SITE MARKING, CO. THE HISTORICALLY IMPORTANT COUNTY SITES WILL BE MARKED WITH CENTENNIAL BICENTENNIAL MARKERS. (LOCAL). TOM SWEARINGEN, HERITAGE CHAIRMAN; ARAPAHOE COUNTY CENTENNIAL-BICENTENNIAL COMMITTEE; 7100 S PLATTE CANYON RD; LITTLETON, CO 80123. (#14851).

CENTENNIAL COUNTY - ARAPAHOE COUNTY, CO. THIS PLAN IS TO MAKE ARAPAHOE COUNTY AND ITS CITIES ACTIVE IN THE LEADERSHIP OF ACTIVITIES IN AND FOR THE ENTIRE STATE AS A REMINDER OF THE CENTENNIAL-BICENTENNIAL COMMEMORATION. (LOCAL). PETER D SMYTHE, CHAIRMAN; ARAPAHOE COUNTY CENTENNIAL-BICENTENNIAL COMMITTEE; 7100 S PLATTE CANYON RD; LITTLETON, CO 80123. (#14849).

CENTENNIAL WELCOME CENTER - ARAPAHOE COUNTY, CO. A SPECIAL COLORADO CENTENNIAL INFORMATION CENTER WILL BE SET UP AT ARAPAHOE COUNTY AIRPORT TO WELCOME AND INFORM CENTENNIAL-BICENTENNIAL VISITORS. (LOCAL). PETER D SMYTHE, CHAIRMAN; ARAPAHOE COUNTY CENTENNIAL-BICENTENNIAL COMMITTEE; 7100 S PLATTE CANYON RD; LITTLETON, CO 80123. (#14848).

CONCERTS IN THE PARK. LIVE PERFORMANCE. (LOCAL). ROBERT J MCQUARIE, DIR; CITY OF LITTLETON AND LITTLETON PUBLIC SCHOOLS; 6028 S GALLUP; LITTLETON, CO 80120. (#107155-1).

FLOWER GARDEN AND PARK WITH SCULPTURE - CO. MULTI-ACRE FLORAL GARDEN WITH PRIMARY PROVISIONS FOR SENIOR CITIZENS AND HANDICAPPED TO INCLUDE COMMISSIONED SCULPTURE BY EDGAR BRITTON. (LOCAL). DOUG ROCKNE, PARK PLANNER; SOUTH SUBURBAN PARKS AND RECREATION DISTRICT; 1800 W LITTLETON BLVD; LITTLETON, CO 80120. (#24599).

HISTORICAL FARM - LITTLETON, CO. RESTORED LIVING HISTORY FARM, 1895-1905, WITH COMMUNITY BARN RAISING. (LOCAL). ROBERT J MCQUARIE, DIRECTOR; LITTLETON HISTORICAL MUSEUM; 6028 S GALLUP; LITTLETON, CO 80120. (#24601).

PLAINS CONSERVATION CENTER - ARAPAHOE COUNTY, CO. THE CENTER IS UNDER DEVELOPMENT TO PRESERVE THE PLAINS IN ITS ORIGINAL STATE AND TO SHOW THE USE FOR THE FUTURE AS PART OF THE CENTENNIAL-BICENTENNIAL COMMEMORATION. (LOCAL). TOM LLOYD, PLAINS COMMITTEE CHAIRMAN; ARAPAHOE COUNTY CENTENNIAL-BICENTENNIAL COMMITTEE; 7103 S PLATTE CANYON RD; LITTLETON, CO 80123. (#14847).

RESTORATION OF SANTA FE DEPOT IN LITTLETON, CO. THE PROJECT INVOLVES THE RESTORATION OF THE SANTA FE DEPOT FOR USE AS A COMMUNITY ARTS CENTER. (LOCAL). MRS MILDRED KELLY, PROJECT DIRECTOR; FRIENDS OF THE LIBRARY AND MUSEUM; 6028 S GALLUP; LITTLETON, CO 80120. (#10323).

SOUTH PLATTE PARK - LITTLETON, CO. A 500-ACRE NATURAL PARK ON SOUTH PLATTE RIVER. (LOCAL). CHUCK COWARD, DEPUTY CITY MANAGER; CITY OF LITTLETON; 2450 W MAIN ST; LITTLETON, CO 80120. (#24600).

STAGE COMPANY WAGON, THEATER PROJECT IN COLORADO. THE STAGE COMPANY WAGON IS TO PROVIDE A 9 WEEK SERIES OF COMMUNITY THEATER & MUSICAL PERFORMANCES AT A VARIETY OF COMMUNITY LOCATIONS. (LOCAL). DAVE LORENZ, DIRECTOR; SOUTH SUBURBAN METROPOLITAN RECREATION & PARK DISTRICT; 1800 W LITTLETON BLVD; LITTLETON, CO 80120. (#7728).

YOUTH & COMMUNITY CENTER - LITTLETON, CO. AQUISITION OF OPEN SPACE FOR USE AS PUBLIC PARK & COMMUNITY CENTER; CONSTRUCTION OF SUITABLE FACILITIES FOR RECREATIONAL & CULTURAL USE INCLUDING A YOUTH CENTER. (LOCAL). H CHARLES HIRST, CHAIRMAN; GREATER COLUMBINE CENTENNIAL-BICENTENNIAL COMMITTEE; 7231 S SHERIDAN COURT; LITTLETON, CO 80123. (#16405).

JULY 1 - 30, '75. SPIRIT OF AMERICA CONCERT. THE PRESENTATION OF CONCERTS CELEBRATING THE SPIRIT OF AMERICA WITH ALL TYPES OF AMERICAN MUSIC. THE PROGRAMS WILL INCLUDE FOLK, JAZZ, ETHNIC, ROCK, SPIRITUALS AND EASY LISTENING MUSIC. (LOCAL). MS GINGER BENDER; COMMUNITY ARTS SYMPHONY; BOX 1222; ENGLEWOOD, CO 80110. (#7724-501).

AUG 1 - 2, '75. STAGE COMPANY WAGON THEATER PRESENTATION. LIVE PERFORMANCE AT HARLOW PARK 5101 S LOWELL. (LOCAL). DAVE LORENZ, PROJ DIR; SOUTH SUBURBAN METROPOLITAN RECREATION AND PARK DISTRICT; 1800 W LITTLETON BLVD; LITTLETON, CO 80120. (#7728-5).

AUG 5 - 6, '75. STAGE COMPANY WAGON THEATER PRESENTATION. LIVE PERFORMANCE AT ALICE TERRY PK 4485 S IRVING. (LOCAL). DAVE LORENZ, PROJ DIR; SOUTH SUBURBAN METROPOLITAN RECREATION AND PARK DISTRICT; 1800 W LITTLETON BLVD; LITTLETON, CO 80120. (#7728-4).

AUG 7, '75. STAGE COMPANY WAGON THEATER PRESENTATION. LIVE PERFORMANCE AT ALICE TERRY PARK, 4485 S IRVING & LITTLETON BLVD. (LOCAL). DAVE LORENZ, PROJ CHMN; SOUTH SUBURBAN METROPOLITAN RECREATION & PARK DISTRICT; 1800 W LITTLETON BLVD; LITTLETON, CO 80120. (#7728-3).

AUG 12, '75. STAGE COMPANY WAGON THEATER PRESENTATION. LIVE PERFORMANCE AT STERNE PARK, 5800 S SPOTSWOOD. (LOCAL). DAVE LORENZ, PROJ CHMN; SOUTH SUBURBAN METROPOLITAN RECREATION & PARK DISTRICT; 1800 W LITTLETON BLVD; LITTLETON, CO 80120. (#7728-2).

AUG 14, '75. STAGE COMPANY WAGON THEATER PRESENTATION. LIVE PERFORMANCE AT STERNE PARK, 5800 S SPOTSWOOD. (LOCAL). DAVE LORENZ, PROJ CHMN; SOUTH SUBURBAN METROPOLITAN RECREATION & PARK DISTRICT; 1800 W LITTLETON BLVD; LITTLETON, CO 80120. (#7728-1).

SEPT 3, '75. GENERATIONS U S. LIVE PERFORMANCE. (LOCAL). PAT KENNING, PROG DIR; YWCA; 1153 W SHEPPERD AVE; LITTLETON, CO 80120. (#200007-196).

MAR 27 - JULY 4, '76. SPRING ARTS FESTIVAL. FESTIVAL WILL INCLUDE SATIRICAL MUSICAL PRODUCTION ON LOCAL ISSUES; NUMEROUS SEMINARS & PROGRAMS & A COMMUNITY PICNIC. (ST-WIDE). GERI BRICKLEY, PRES; FRIENDS OF LITTLETON LIBRARY & MUSEUM; 6097 S WINDERMERE WAY; LITTLETON, CO 80120. (#107155-2).

JUNE 26, '76. GREATER COLUMBINE PARADE. MARCHING BANDS, FIRE TRUCKS, ANTIQUE CARS, COLOR GUARDS AND FLOATS WILL BE SEEN IN THIS PARADE. (LOCAL). H CHARLES HIRST, COORD; TOWN OF LITTLETON; 7231 S SHERIDAN CT; LITTLETON, CO 80123. (#200007-114).

JULY 4, '76. FOURTH OF JULY CELEBRATION. FOURTH OF JULY PICNIC TO FEATURE GAMES FOR CHILDREN, BAND CONCERT AND WILL CONCLUDE WITH FIRE WORKS DISPLAY. AT PROGRESS PARK. (LOCAL). DAVE LORENZ, COORDINATOR; SOUTH SUBURBAN PARK DISTRICT AND CITY OF LITTLETON; 1800 W LITTLETON BLVD; LITTLETON, CO 80120. (#107155-3).

JULY 4 - DEC 31, '76. 4 SPECIAL BICENTENNIAL EXHIBITS. 4 EXHIBITS: 'LITTLETON AGRICULTURAL HERITAGE,' 'SUITING EVERYONE: EXHIBIT OF AMERICAN FASHIONS', 'FIVE CRITICAL ELECTIONS', 'SEAT OF AMERICAN INVENTION: HISTORY OF AMERICAN CHAIRS.'. (LOCAL). ROBERT J MCQUARIE, DIR; LITTLETON HISTORICAL MUSEUM; 6028 S GALLUP; LITTLETON, CO 80120. (#107890-1).

AUG 8 - 14, '76. WESTERN WELCOME WEEK. WESTERN WELCOME EVENTS INCLUDE RODEO, PARADE, SIDEWALK ART SHOW AND MANY OTHER ACTIVITIES. AT WEEK-LONG EVENTS IN DIFFERENT LOCATIONS. (ST-WIDE). PHILIP H SWAIM, CHMN; LITTLETON CHAMBER OF COMMERCE; 1695 W STERNE PARKWAY; LITTLETON, CO 80120. (#107155-4).

OCT 16, '76. FALL CRAFTS FAIR. CRAFT FAIR HELD IN LARGE TENT-ONE DAY ONLY. CRAFT DEMONSTRATIONS ON BLACKSMITHING & WEAVING. BAND CONCERT. BOOT HOLDERS SHOULD CALL LITTLETON MUSEUM: (303)7982557 FOR BOTH RENTAL INFORMATION SEVERAL WEEKS IN ADVANCE. AT LITTLETON MUSEUM GROUNDS, 6028 S GALLUP. (LOCAL). ROBERT J MCQUARIE; FRIENDS OF LITTLETON LIBRARY & MUSEUM; 6028 S GALLUP; LITTLETON, CO 80120. (#107155-5).

LOCHBUIE

FORMATION OF CUB SCOUT PACK #241 - CO. LOCHBUIE CUB SCOUT PACK IS NOW OFFICIAL. THE PACK SOLD BICENTENNIAL CALENDARS, THEY DELIVER BI-MONTHLY TOWN NEWSLETTER AND THEY SPONSOR PROJECTS WITH CENTENNIAL-BICENTENNIAL THEMES. (LOCAL). VERNA WEBB, TOWN CLERK; LOCHBUIE CENTENNIAL-BICENTENNIAL COMMITTEE; RT 4, BOX 99; BRIGHTON, CO 80601. (#26191).

'GREENING AND CLEANING' - LOCHBUIE, CO. CREATION OF PARK TO INCLUDE BALLFIELD, PICNIC AREA, SWINGS, NATIVE GRASSES AND LANDSCAPING WILL BE EMPHASIZED. (LOCAL). HON LEO SACK, MAYOR; CITY OF LOCHBUIE; RT 4, BOX 99; BRIGHTON, CO 80601. (#26213).

'IMPROVING OUR TOWN' - LOCHBUIE, CO. STREET IMPROVEMENTS, ESTABLISHMENT OF SEWER SYSTEMS, DEVELOPMENT OF A TOWN PARK AND AN ADDITION FOR TOWN HALL. (LOCAL). HON LEO C SACK, MAYOR; TOWN OF BRIGHTON; RT 4, BOX 99; BRIGHTON, CO 80601. (#26236).

INCORPORATION OF LOCHBUIE, CO. RURAL COMMUNITY, BEGUN IN THE EARLY 1960'S, WISHES INCORPORATION STATUS; TOWN MEETINGS AND STATE PETITIONING BEGUN IN MAY 1974; IT WILL BE FIRST INCORPORATION IN COLORADO IN 50 YEARS. (LOCAL). VERNA WEBB, TOWN CLERK; LOCHBUIE CENTENNIAL-BICENTENNIAL COMMITTEE; RT 4, BOX 99; BRIGHTON, CO 80601. (#26230).

LOCHBUIE PARK, CO. CREATION OF PARK WITH EMPHASIS ON NATIVE GRASSES AND LANDSCAPING, RECREATION AND PICNIC AREAS; WORK DONE THROUGH TOWN GATHERING. (LOCAL). VERNA WEBB, TOWN CLERK; LOCHBUIE CENTENNIAL-BICENTENNIAL COMMITTEE; RT 4 BOX 99; BRIGHTON, CO 80601. (#26229).

'SENIOR CITIZEN - 1976'. HONORING OF AREA SENIOR CITIZEN AT COMMUNITY GATHERING TO COMMEMORATE THE COMPLETION OF PARK. THERE WILL ALSO BE A TREE PLANTING CEREMONY IN HONOR OF A SENIOR CITIZEN. (LOCAL). HON LEO C SACK, MAYOR; CITY OF LOCHBUIE; RT 4, BOX 99; BRIGHTON, CO 80601. (#108772-1).

JULY 3, '76. CENTENNIAL FIREWORKS. FESTIVAL. (LOCAL). LEO C SACK, COORDINATOR; BRIGHTON FIREWORKS COMMITTEE; RT 4, BOX 99; BRIGHTON, CO 80601. (#108607-1).

LOG LANE VIL

DEVELOP COMMUNITY PARK & PLAYGROUND - CO. PLANTS, TREES, SHRUBS, FLOWERS & GRASS WILL BE PLANTED; PLAYGROUND WILL BE FIXED-UP. (LOCAL). PATRICIA A GARVER, TOWN CLERK; TOWN OF FORT MORGAN; PO BOX 912; FORT MORGAN, CO 80701. (#26235).

LONGMONT

CENTENNIAL RIVER PARK IN LONGMONT, CO. PARK DEVELOPMENT ALONG THE RIVER THAT RUNS FROM LONGMONT TO LYONS. (REGN'L). DR FOWLER, CHAIRMAN; LYONS '76 COMMITTEE; 8585 GLENE RD #7; LONGMONT, CO 80501. (#10303).

CENTENNIAL SIGNAGE AND FLAG PROGRAMS - CO. FLAG DISPLAYS ALL YEAR AT ST URAIN 76 CENTER. (LOCAL). F PARKER FOWLER, JR, CHAIRMAN; LONGMONT '76 COMMITTEE; 8585 HYGIENE RD; LONGMONT, CO 80501. (#26190).

LOGO COMPETITION. LOGO COMPETITION TO POST LONGMONT AS A BIRD SANCTUARY. (LOCAL). F PARKER FOWLER, JR, CHMN; LONGMONT '76 COMMITTEE; 8585 HYGIENE RD; LONGMONT, CO 80501. (#108357-1).

LONGMONT CULTURAL CENTER - LONGMONT, CO. THE LONGMONT CULTURAL CENTER WILL BE DEVELOPED AS AN OVERALL PUBLIC USE FACILITY WITH ITS PLANNED COMPLETION DURING THE CENTENNIAL YEAR, 1976. IT WILL BE OPEN TO ST VRAIN VALLEY AND LYONS COMMUNITIES. (LOCAL). F PARKER FOWLER, JR, CHAIRMAN; LONGMONT '76 COMMITTEE; 8585 HYGIENE RD; LONGMONT, CO 80501. (#14842).

RESTORATION OF ROBERT A HAUCK MILKHOUSE, COLORADO. HISTORICAL WATER-COOLED SANDSTONE MILKHOUSE BUILT BY ROBERT A HAUCK IN 1860, WILL BE DISMANTLED AND RECONSTRUCTED IN OLD MILL PARK, TO BE DEDICATED BY DAR & TERRITORIAL DAUGHTERS OF COLORADO. (LOCAL). MRS MARIAN GEICK, PROJ DIR; TERRITORIAL DAUGHTERS OF COLORADO & COLORADO STATE SOC OF USDAR; 3631 W 45TH AVE; DENVER, CO 80211. (#10322).

ST STEPHEN'S CHAPEL PRESERVATION IN LONGMONT, COLO. PROJECT TO PURCHASE THE CHAPEL SITE, RESTORE THE BUILDINGS, DEVELOP A GREEN AREA, PROVIDE A CHAPEL AND MEETING HOUSE FACILITY & DISPLAY CHURCH'S ARTIFACTS FOR THE COMMUNITY. (LOCAL). WARREN MCGAUGHEY, PRESIDENT; ST VRAIN HISTORICAL SOCIETY, INC; PO BOX 705; LONGMONT, CO 80501. (#4423). **ARBA GRANTEE.**

ST VRAIN CENTENNIAL RAILROAD IN COLORADO. STEAM TRAIN REINSTITUTED BETWEEN LONGMONT AND LYONS, COLORADO. (ST-WIDE). MRS VIRGINIA ESTES, CHAIRMAN; LYONS '76 COMMITTEE; 410 TERRY ST; LONGMONT, CO 80501. (#9911).

'TREE-FOR-TREE' - LONGMONT, CO. THE CITY WILL PROVIDE A TREE FOR EVERY TREE PLANTED BY A CITIZEN. THE GOAL IS 20,000 TREES. (LOCAL). F PARKER FOWLER, JR, CHAIRMAN; LONGMONT '76 COMMITTEE; 8585 HYGIENE RD; LONGMONT, CO 80501. (#26188).

SEPT '75 - MAY '76. OPTIMIST CLUB POSTER AND ESSAY CONTEST. A POSTER & ESSAY CONTEST FOR CHILDREN IN 4TH THRU 12TH GRADE. ALL LOCAL CLUB WINNERS WILL COMPETE IN STATE FINALS CONTESTS. CONTESTS WILL HAVE BICENTENNIAL THEME. (ST-WIDE). RICHARD C SCHNEIDER, CHMN; OPTIMIST CLUB OF GUNBARREL; 7292 MT MEEKER RD; LONGMONT, CO 80501. (#102940-1).

OCT 7, '75. UNITED STATES ARMED FORCES BICENTENNIAL CARAVAN. THE CARAVAN IS COMPOSED OF EXHIBIT VANS FOR EACH BRANCH OF THE MILITARY SERVICE. THE THEME OF THE EXHIBITION IS 'HISTORY OF THE ARMED FORCES AND THEIR CONTRIBUTION TO THE NATION'. (LOCAL). F PARKER FOWLER JR, CHMN; U S ARMED FORCES BICENTENNIAL EXHIBIT VANS PROJECT; 8585 HYGIENE RD; LONGMONT, CO 80501. (#1775-239).

JUNE 7 - 8, '76. FLASHBACK: MOUNTAIN MAN ENCAMPMENT. LIVE PERFORMANCE, FESTIVAL AT BARBER PONDS, I-25 AT COLORADO 119. (LOCAL). F PARKER FOWLER, JR; CITY OF LONGMONT; 8585 HYGIENE RD; LONGMONT, CO 80501. (#108601-1).

JUNE 14, '76. FLAG DAY CEREMONY. CEREMONY AT ROOSEVELT PARK. (LOCAL). PARKER FOWLER, CHMN; BPOE (ELKS) & SEROPTIMISTS; 8585 HYGIENE RD; LONGMONT, CO 80501. (#200007-127).

JULY 4 - 5, '76. CENTENNIAL FIREWORKS & IMPACT BRASS & SINGERS. 4TH OF JULY CELEBRATION CONSISTING OF PAGEANTRY, MUSIC AND HISTORICAL RECITATION FOLLOWED BY FIREWORKS AND SET PIECES, INCLUDING, REPRESENTATIONS OF CENTENNIAL & BICENTENNIAL FLAG, REMNANTS AND LOGOS.

LONGMONT — CONTINUED

AT CLARK CENTENNIAL PARK, LASHLEY ST BETWEEN 9TH & MOUNTAIN VIEW. (LOCAL). RAY BARTH, FIRE MARSHALL; CITY OF LONGMONT FIRE DEPT & LONGMONT LIONS CLUB; LONGMONT, CO 80501. (#108601-3).

AUG 1, '76. 'SALUTE TO AMERICA'. PARTICIPATING IN DEDICATION OF HISTORICAL SITE AND FACILITIES WITH SAINT URAIN HISTORICAL SOCIETY, DAR AND 'TERRITORIAL DAUGHTERS OF COLORADO'. AT OLD MILL PARK, SECOND & PRATT ST. (LOCAL). DR PARKER FOWLER, COORD; LONGMONT CHAPTER, SPEBSQSA AND CHICAGO COLONY JAZZ BAND; 8585 HYGIENE RD; LONGMONT, CO 80501. (#108955-5).

AUG 1 - 2, '76. DEDICATION OF ROBERT A HAUCK MILKHOUSE. PARK OPEN TO PUBLIC ON TOUR BASIS MADE BY RESERVATION. (LOCAL). MRS MARIAN GEICK; TERRITORIAL DAUGHTERS OF COLORADO & COLORADO STATE SOC OF NSDAR; 3631 W 45TH AVE; DENVER, CO 80211. (#10322-501).

AUG 7, '76. COUNTY FAIR & PARADE: 'HORIZONS '76, FORGING A SECOND CENTURY'. PARADE, FAIR AT MAIN STREET. (LOCAL). RAY POTTER; KIWANIS CLUB; 1809 ATWOOD; LONGMONT, CO 80501. (#108718-1).

AUG 14, '76. FLASHBACK: THRESHERMEN'S DAY. FESTIVAL, LIVE PERFORMANCE. (LOCAL). F PARKER FOWLER, JR; CITY OF LONGMONT; 8585 HYGIENE RD; LONGMONT, CO 80501. (#108601-2).

AUG 14, '76. PARADE: 'HORIZONS '76: FORGING A SECOND CENTURY'. PARADE. (LOCAL). F PARKER FOWLER, JR, CHMN; KIWANIS CLUB; 8585 HYGIENE RD; LONGMONT, CO 80501. (#108769-2).

AUG 14, '76. 'ST URAIN 2001' TIME CAPSULE. CEREMONY. (LOCAL). F PARKER FOWLER, JR; KIWANIS CLUB; 8585 HYGIENE RD; LONGMONT, CO 80501. (#108769-3).

AUG '76. CHILDREN'S PAGEANT AND FOUNDING FATHERS FESTIVAL. FAIR, LIVE PERFORMANCE. (LOCAL). F PARKER FOWLER, JR, CHMN; 4-H CLUB; 8585 HYGIENE RD; LONGMONT, CO 80501. (#108769-4).

OCT 8 - 10, '76. 'STANDING ROOM ONLY'. A PROJECT OF THE STATE DEPARTMENT OF LOCAL AFFAIRS AND THE COLORADO LABOR COUNCIL TO AWAKEN CONCERN FOR LAND USE AND DEVELOPMENT IN COLORADO. AT THOMPSON PARK, BETWEEN FOURTH AND FIFTH ST ON PRATT ST. (LOCAL). FRAN WRIGHT, COORD; LONGMONT CHAPTER, LEAGUE OF WOMEN VOTERS; 6969 UTE HWY; LONGMONT, CO 80501. (#108769-5).

LOUISVILLE

COAL MINERS MEMORIAL STATUE, LOUISVILLE, CO. ERECTION OF A COAL MINERS' MEMORIAL STATUE TO COMMEMORATE COURAGE & LABOR OF MEN. (ST-WIDE). CAROLYN CONARROE, CHAIRPERSON; LOUISVILLE CENTENNIAL-COMMITTEE; 1131 JEFFERSON AVE; LOUISVILLE, CO 80027. (#20534).

SEPT 6, '76. DEDICATION OF MINERS STATUE. MINERS STATUE HONORS THE MEN AND HERITAGE OF THE INDUSTRY WHICH ESTABLISHED COMMUNITY. AT CITY HALL, 749 MAIN ST. (ST-WIDE). CAROLYN CONARROE, CHMN; HORIZON COMMITTEE, LOUISVILLE CENTENNIAL-BICENTENNIAL COMMITTEE; 1131 JEFFERSON; LOUISVILLE, CO 80027. (#108771-1).

LOUVIERS

TREE REPLACEMENT IN LOUVIERS PARK - LOUVIERS, CO. NEW TREES WILL BE PLANTED IN THE PARK TO REPLACE THE TREES DESTROYED BY DUTCH ELM DISEASE. (LOCAL). JERRY BAKER, PRESIDENT; LOUVIERS PARK ASSOC; LOUVIERS BLVD; LOUVIERS, CO 80131. (#24585).

LOVELAND

BICENTENNIAL PARK, LOVELAND, CO. A BICENTENNIAL PARK WILL BE DEVELOPED IN LOVELAND. (LOCAL). D HEFFINGTON & J MCGUIRE, CO-CHAIRPERSONS; LOVELAND BICENTENNIAL FESTIVAL COMMITTEES; 225 E 10TH ST; LOVELAND, CO 80537. (#20479).

COMMUNITY TIME CAPSULE - LOVELAND, CO. PLACEMENT OF A COMMUNITY TIME CAPSULE IN A PUBLIC BUILDING, TO BE OPENED ON 200TH ANNIVERSARY OF COLORADO STATEHOOD. (LOCAL). HON JEAN A GAINES, MAYOR; TOWN OF LOVELAND; 410 E 5TH ST, PO BOX 419; LOVELAND, CO 80537. (#26220).

LONE TREE SCHOOL & CENTENNIAL PARK - LOVELAND, CO. THE SCHOOL WILL BE MOVED TO A NEW LOCATION AND RESTORED. THE PARK WILL BE LANDSCAPED. (LOCAL). D HEFFINGTON, CO-CHAIRMAN; LOVELAND BICENTENNIAL COMMITTEE; 225 E 10TH ST; LOVELAND, CO 80537. (#24588).

MAY 7 - 9, '76. EARLY AMERICANA ARTS AND CRAFTS FESTIVAL. ARTS & CRAFTS DEMONSTRATIONS, MUSIC, DRAMA, FILMS, FOOD FAIR, DANCE, CONTEST, DISPLAYS, PONY RIDES & BOX SOCIAL. AT LARIMER COUNTY FAIRGROUNDS, SE 5TH AND RAILROAD. (ST-WIDE). MRS FRANK HEFFINGTON, DIR; CITY OF LOVELAND; 225 E 10TH; LOVELAND, CO 80537. (#106259-1).

JULY 4, '76. CENTENNIAL FIREWORKS. FESTIVAL. (LOCAL). JEAN A GAINES, COORD; LOVELAND FIREWORKS COMMITTEE; 410 E 5 ST, PO BOX 419; LOVELAND, CO 80537. (#108606-1).

LOWRY AFB

JUNE 1 - 30, '76. LOWRY AIR FORCE BASE OPEN HOUSE. EXHIBIT, PARADE. (LOCAL). COL RICHARD E LITTLE; UNITED STATES AIR FORCE; BOX 30005; LOWRY AFB, CO 80230. (#101018-1).

OCT '76. DEDICATION OF AIR FORCE ACCOUNTING AND FINANCE CENTER AT LOWRY AFB. CEREMONY, AWARD, OPENING. (LOCAL). COL RICHARD E LITTLE; UNITED STATES AIR FORCE; BOX 30005; LOWRY AFB, CO 80230. (#101021-1).

LUDLOW

COMMUNITY PRIDE PROJECT - LUDLOW, CO. BUILD 5 PICNIC TABLES WITH BENCHES AND MAKE A BOX TO HOLD THE GUEST BOOK; AND 2 NEW TRASH CANS WILL BE OBTAINED. (LOCAL). DALE SIMMONS, CLUB MEMBER; CROSSED ARROWS 4-H CLUB; RT 2 BOX 157; LUDLOW, CO 81082. (#10374).

LYONS

HISTORICAL & PICTORIAL BOOK ABOUT LYONS, CO. BOOK WRITTEN ABOUT LYONS BY OLGA SEYBERT. (LOCAL). HON VAUGHN CARTER, MAYOR; TOWN OF LYONS; PO BOX 78; LYONS, CO 80540. (#26184).

LANDMARKS PROGRAM OF LONGMONT, COLORADO. THE HISTORIC BUILDINGS AND LOCATIONS IN THE CITY WILL BE MARKED WITH APPROPRIATE CENTENNIAL-BICENTENNIAL SIGNS. (LOCAL). MRS VIRGINIA ESTES, CHAIRPERSON; LYONS LANDMARK PRESERVATION COMMITTEE; 410 TERRY ST; LONGMONT, CO 80501. (#10302).

LYONS RAILROAD DEPOT RESTORATION - COLORADO. SAVE HISTORIC LYONS DEPOT AND RETURN IT TO ITS COMMUNITY STATUS FROM PRIVATE OWNERSHIP IN HONOR OF CENTENNIAL-BICENTENNIAL. (LOCAL). MRS VIRGINIA ESTES, CHAIRMAN; SAVE THE DEPOT COMMITTEE; 410 TERRY ST; LONGMONT, CO 80501. (#9910).

JUNE 19 - SEPT 4, '76. SATURDAY SUMMER SQUARE DANCES. FESTIVAL AT LYONS ELEMENTARY GYM, 4TH & STICKNEY. (LOCAL). LAVERN M JOHNSON, COORD; RED ROCK RUMBLERS SQUARE DANCE CLUB; 306 EVANS ST; LYONS, CO 80540. (#107028-3).

MANCOS

CENTENNIAL CENTER OF MANCOS, COLORADO. ESTABLISHMENT OF A LARGER PERMANENT LOCATION FOR MUSEUM TO INCLUDE THIS CENTENNIAL COMMUNITY HALL FOR USE BY ALL. (LOCAL). MRS CARRIE C BAUER, CHAIRPERSON; MANCOS CENTENNIAL-BICENTENNIAL COMMITTEE; BOX 176; MANCOS, CO 81328. (#4163). **(??).**

CENTENNIAL CLEAN-UP - MANCOS, COLORADO. TO HONOR THE CENTIENNIAL THE TOWN STUDENTS WILL COLLECT TONS OF TRASH IN ORDER TO BEAUTIFY THE TOWN. (LOCAL). MRS CARRIE BAUER, CHAIRPERSON; MANCOS CENTENNIAL- BICENTENNIAL COMMITTEE; C/O BOX 176; MANCOS, CO 81328. (#4093).

CENTENNIAL FLAGPOLE OF MANCOS, COLORADO. LIGHTED FLAGPOLE TO BE ERECTED TO CARRY CENTENNIAL AND BICENTENNIAL FLAGS. (LOCAL). MRS CARRIE BAUER, CHAIRPERSON; MANCOS CENTENNIAL-BICENTENNIAL COMMITTEE; C/O BOX 176; MANCOS, CO 81328. (#4162). **(??).**

DOMINGUEZ ESCALANTE TRAIL IN MANCOS, COLORADO. STATE HIGHWAY 184 IS TO BE DESIGNATED, MARKED AND PAVED AS DOMINGUES ESCALANTE TRAIL IN COOPERATION WITH DOLORES COUNTY. (ST-WIDE). CARRIE C BAUER, CHAIRPERSON; MANCOS CENTENNIAL-BICENT COMMITTEE; 113 N MAIN; MANCOS, CO 81328. (#9560).

HISTORICAL TAPE PROJECT - MANCOS, COLO. RECORDING HISTORICAL EVENTS AND INTERVIEWS WITH THE LAST OF THE PIONEER GENERATION IN ORDER TO PRESERVE THE FOLKLORE FOR THE COMING GENERATIONS. (ST-WIDE). MRS CARRIE BAUER, CHAIRPERSON; MANCOS CENTENNIAL- BICENTENNIAL COMMITTEE; C/O BOX 176; MANCOS, CO 81328. (#4089).

MUSEUM FOR MANCOS, COLORADO. A PROJECT TO BUILD A COMMUNITY BUILDING FOR USE AS A MUSEUM. (LOCAL). MRS CLAY V BADER, SECRETARY-TREASURER; MANCOS CENTENNIAL-BICENTENNIAL COMMITTEE; BOX 186; MANCOS, CO 81328. (#4302).

NEW COMMUNITY BUILDING IN MANCOS, COLORADO. THE PROJECT INVOLVES THE BUILDING OF A NEW COMMUNITY BUILDING WHICH WILL HOUSE THE MUSEUM AND LIBRARY; THE BUILDING WILL BE USED FOR ALL COMMUNITY ACTIVITIES. (LOCAL). CARRIE C BAUER, CHAIRPERSON; MANCOS CENTENNIAL-BICENT COMMITTEE; 113 N MAIN; MANCOS, CO 81328. (#9561).

JULY 25 - 27, '75. MANCOS DAYS FESTIVAL. PIONEER QUEEN AT LEAST 65 YEARS OLD, FESTIVAL HONORS PIONEERS OF MANCOS VALLEY.ACTIVITIES INCLUDE PARADES, A DANCE, FISH DERBY, WATER FIGHTS. ACTIVITIES START AT 10:00 EACH MORNING. AT CITYWIDE. (LOCAL). MRS ELLEN HOLSTON, CHRPN; MANCOS CENT-BICENT COMMITTEE; BOX 533; MANCOS, CO 81328. (#4164-1).

JULY 3, '76. DEDICATION OF THE DOMINGUEZ-ESCALANTE HIGHWAY. TO INCLUDE ICE CREAM SOCIAL AND STREET DANCE FOR YOUTHS. AT MAIN ST, TOWN PARK. (LOCAL). MRS JEAN K BADER, SEC; MANCOS CENTENNIAL-BICENTENNIAL COMMITTEE; BOX 186; MANCOS, CO 81328. (#107152-1).

JULY 3 - AUG 1, '76. MANCOS COLORADO DAYS, THEME: ALONG THE DOMINGUEZ TRAIL. EXHIBIT, FESTIVAL AT MANCOS TOWN PARK HIGH SCHOOL AUDITORIUM. (LOCAL). MRS JEAN K BADER, SEC; MANCOS CENTENNIAL-BICENTENNIAL COMMITTEE; BOX 186; MANCOS, CO 81328. (#107152-3).

JULY 4, '76. MANCOS BAND CONCERT. LIVE PERFORMANCE. (LOCAL). CARRIE BAUER, CHAIRMAN; MANCOS BICENTENNIAL COMMITTEE; MANCOS, CO 81328. (#107575-1).

JULY 30 - AUG 1, '76. ARTS FESTIVAL. EXHIBITS OF SPANISH & INDIAN ART, OLD & NEW-PAINTINGS, PHOTOGRAPH OF EARLY MANCOS ANTIQUES. (LOCAL). LYLE C COX, COORD; TOWN OF MANCOS; MANCOS, CO 81328. (#108737-1).

JULY 30 - AUG 1, '76. MUSICAL PROGRAM. PARADE WITH MUSIC EVERYDAY; BAND CONCERT & MUSICAL JULY 31ST. (LOCAL). LYLE C COX, COORDINATOR; TOWN OF MANCOS; MANCOS, CO 81328. (#108737-3).

JULY 31, '76. TOWN BAR-B-QUE & DANCE. FESTIVAL. (LOCAL). LYLE C COX, COORDINATOR; TOWN OF MANCOS; MANCOS, CO 81328. (#108737-2).

AUG 11, '76. DEDICATION OF THE DOMINQUEZ-ESCALANTE HIGHWAY. CEREMONY AT HWY 184, TOWN PARK. (LOCAL). MRS JEAN K BADER, SEC; MANCOS CENTENNIAL-BICENTENNIAL COMMITTEE; BOX 186; MANCOS, CO 81328. (#107152-2).

AUG 11, '76. MANCOS, COLORADO DOMINGUES ESCALANTE FESTIVAL '76. TOUR, CEREMONY AT DEDICATION CEREMONY NEXT TO POST OFFICE. (ST-WIDE). CARRIE C BAUER; MANCOS CENTENNIAL-BICENT COMMITTEE; 113 N MAIN; MANCOS, CO 81328. (#9560-501).

MANITOU SPG

CENTENNIAL-BICENTENNIAL TREE PLANTING PGM, CO. A MANITOU SPRINGS GARDEN OF THE GODS ROTARY CLUB TREE, FLOWER & GARDEN PLANTING PGM IN THE CITY, INCLUDING A 10,000 TREE REFORESTATION PROGRAM IN QUEENS CANYON GRAVEL QUARRY. (LOCAL). MERRILL R CROCKER, PRESIDENT; GARDEN OF THE GODS ROTARY CLUB; 404 EL PASO BLVD; MANITOU SPGS, CO 80829. (#6782).

HISTORIC MANITOU LANDMARKS, COLORADO. IDENTIFY HISTORIC BUILDINGS AND LANDMARKS IN MANITOU SPRINGS FOR THE CENTENNIAL-BICENTENNIAL. (LOCAL). NORIS HUEY, HERITAGE CHAIRPERSON; MANITOU SPRINGS HISTORICAL SOCIETY; 220 ELK PATH; MANITOU SPGS, CO 80829. (#6783). **(??).**

HISTORIC MINERAL SPRINGS, MANITOU SPGS, COLORADO. COMPLETE THE RESTORATION & IDENTIFICATION OF THE, ONCE WORLD FAMOUS, FOURTEEN MINERAL SPRINGS OF MANITOU SPRINGS, COLORADO. (LOCAL). WILLIAM L BAUERS, PRESIDENT; MANITOU SPRINGS RESTORATION GROUP; 205 CRYSTAL HILLS BLVD; MANITOU SPGS, CO 80829. (#6784). **(??).**

MANITOU SPRINGS HISTORICAL MUSEUM, COLORADO. PURCHASE AND DEVELOP DURING THE BICENTENNIAL ERA THE HISTORIC NOLAN HOME AS A NEW MANITOU SPRINGS WESTERN HERITAGE MUSEUM. (LOCAL). NORIS HUEY, HERITAGE CHAIRPERSON; MANITOU SPRINGS HISTORICAL SOCIETY; 220 ELK PATH; MANITOU SPGS, CO 80829. (#6786).

MANITOU'S CENT-BICENT LOGO CONTEST, COLORADO. A DISTRICT WIDE DESIGN COMPETITION TO SELECT THE BEST MANITOU SPRINGS CENTENNIAL-BICENTENNIAL LOGO WITH A $100 PRIZE TO BE AWARDED BY THE CENT-BICENT COMMITTEE. (LOCAL). NORIS HUEY, HERITAGE CHAIRPERSON; MANITOU SPRINGS CENTENNIAL-BICENTENNIAL LOGO COMMITTEE; 220 ELK PATH; MANITOU SPGS, CO 80829. (#6778). **(??).**

MANITOU'S MAGNIFICENT MILE IN COLORADO. A LIGHTED BOARDWALK AND WALKWAY TO BE CONSTRUCTED ALONG FOUNTAIN CREEK IN HONOR OF THE MANITOU SPRINGS CENTENNIAL-BICENTENNIAL. (LOCAL). BILL COPP, CO-CHAIRMAN; MANITOU SPRINGS CENTENNIAL-BICENTENNIAL COMMITTEE; 116 PALISADE CIR; MANITOU SPGS, CO 80829. (#6789). **(??).**

ORAL HISTORY PROGRAM IN MANITOU SPRINGS, CO. HIGH SCHOOL HISTORY STUDENTS WILL CONDUCT TAPE-RECORDED INTERVIEWS WITH AREA RESIDENTS INVOLVING THE HISTORY OF MANITOU SPRINGS. (LOCAL). WILLIAM F PHELPS, JR, CHAIRMAN; MANITOU SPRINGS HIGH SCHOOL HISTORY DEPT; 401 EL MONTE PL; MANITOU SPG, CO 80829. (#15284).

RESTORATION OF UTE PASS WAGON TRAIL, CO. THE HISTORIC UTE PASS WAGON TRAIL WILL BE MARKED AND RESTORED IN HONOR OF THE BICENTENNIAL. (ST-WIDE). WILLIAM L BAURS, PROJ DIRECTOR; MANITOU SPRINGS KIWANIS CLUB; 205 CRYSTAL HILLS BLVD; MANITOU SPG, CO 80829. (#15285).

JULY 4, '75. MANITOU SPRINGS FOURTH OF JULY FIREWORKS FESTIVAL. MANITOU SPRINGS, COLORADO, 4TH OF JULY FIREWORKS. A 'DAYS OF 76' THEME WITH SPECIAL DISPLAYS AND FESTIVAL EVENTS TO BE FEATURES OF THIS MANITOU SPRINGS CENTENNIAL-BICENTENNIAL CELEBRATION. (LOCAL). STEVE HART, CHAIRMAN; MANITOU SPRINGS VOLUNTEER FIRE DEPT; 606 MANITOU AVE; MANITOU SPGS, CO 80829. (#6780-501).

AUG 1, '75 - JULY 4, '76. ELECTION OF AMERICA'S MOST POPULAR PRESIDENT. COMPETITION. (LOCAL). JEFF THOMAS, EXEC DIR; PIKES PEAK REGION ATTRACTIONS ASSOC; 1050 S 21ST ST; COLORADO SPG, CO 80904. (#108704-1).

AUG 17, '75. MANITOU SPRINGS CENTENNIAL-BICENTENNIAL ARTS AND CRAFTS FESTIVAL. ENTERTAINMENT, PERIOD COSTUMES, PRIZES & REFRESHMENTS. AN OUTDOOR EVENT. ARTS AND CRAFTS FESTIVAL WITH ENTERTAINMENT, PERIOD COSTUMES, PRIZES AND REFRESHMENTS. OUTDOOR EVENT. AT SODA SPRINGS PARK, MANITOU SPRINGS. (LOCAL). PAT HUEY, ARTS CHMN; MANITOU SPRINGS HISTORICAL SOCIETY; 220 ELK PATH; MANITOU SPGS, CO 80829. (#6785-501).

AUG 23, '75. 2ND ANNUAL PARADE & PICNIC. PARADE, FESTIVAL AT MANITOU AVENUE. (LOCAL). ARCHIEBALD F ROSS, COORD; MANITOU SPRINGS JAYCEES; 820 SHOSHONE; MANITOU SPGS, CO 80829. (#200007-129).

APR 3, '76. CENTENNIAL-BICENTENNIAL ITM ART SHOW AND SPAGHETTI SUPPER. ARTS AND CRAFTS SHOW, DINNER AND ENTERTAINMENT. AT MANITOU SPRINGS JUNIOR HIGH SCHOOL,

MANITOU SPG — CONTINUED

701 DUCLO AVE. (LOCAL). MARY MARTIN; DISTRICT 14 ITM BOOSTER CLUB; 302 CRYSTAL HILLS BLVD; MANITOU SPGS, CO 80829. (#6787-1).

MAY 28 - NOV 14, '76. MANITOU SPRINGS CENTENNIAL-BICENTENNIAL COMMONWHEEL ART FESTIVALS. DURING MANITOU SPRINGS CENTENNIAL YEAR AND THE NATION'S BICENTENNIAL HISTORIC MANITOU SPRINGS, AS COLORADO'S NEWEST ARTS & CRAFTS CENTER, IS PLANNING ART SHOWS EACH HOLIDAY WEEKEND FROM MEMORIAL DAY THRU VETERANS DAY, NOVEMBER 11TH: A TOTAL OF 6. AT MEMORIAL PARK & MEMORIAL HALL. (ST-WIDE). SOPHIE COWMAN, CHAIRMAN; MANITOU COMMONWHEEL; 903 MANITOU AVE; MANITOU SPGS, CO 80829. (#103918-15).

JUNE 3 - 6, '76. MANITOU SPRINGS CENTENNIAL-BICENTENNIAL HISTORY FAIR. STUDENT, HOBBYIST, CLUB AND SOCIETY HISTORY FESTIVAL AND EXHIBITS. AT MONTCALM CASTLE AND/OR MEMORIAL HALL. (ST-WIDE). NORIS HUEY, CURATOR; MANITOU SPRINGS HISTORICAL SOCIETY; 220 ELK PATH; MANITOU SPGS, CO 80829. (#103918-14).

JUNE 24 - 27, '76. CENTENNIAL-BICENTENNIAL STATEWIDE FIREMAN'S CONVENTION AND FESTIVAL. FESTIVAL IN SODA SPRINGS PARK, PARADE AND CONTESTS. AT MEMORIAL HALL AND SODA SPRINGS PARK. (ST-WIDE). VERNE E WITHAM, CHIEF; MANITOU SPRINGS VOLUNTEER FIRE DEPT; 606 MANITOU AVE; MANITOU SPGS, CO 80829. (#103918-13).

JULY 3 - 4, '76. CENTENNIAL-BICENTENNIAL COMMONWHEEL ART SHOW. ALL-DAY, OUTDOOR MULTI-MEDIA ARTS AND CRAFTS SHOW. AT MEMORIAL PARK. (ST-WIDE). SOPHIE COWMAN, PROJ DIR; COMMONWHEEL ART SOCIETY; 903 MANITOU AVE, MAYBE SHOP; MANITOU SPG, CO 80829. (#102613-1).

JULY 4, '76. CENTENNIAL-BICENTENNIAL FOURTH OF JULY FIREWORKS AND FESTIVAL. FESTIVAL, LIVE PERFORMANCE AT MANITOU SPRINGS AND RED MOUNTAIN. (LOCAL). VERNE A WITHAM, CHIEF; MANITOU SPRINGS VOLUNTEER FIRE DEPT; 606 MANITOU AVE; MANITOU SPGS, CO 80829. (#103918-10).

JULY 4, '76. PIKES PEAK CENTENNIAL-BICENTENNIAL AUTO HILL CLIMB. COMPETITION, RADIO/TV AT PIKES PEAK HIGHWAY. (NAT'L). JACK VAETH; PIKES PEAK HILL CLIMB ASSOC; 526 S NEVADA AVE; COLORADO SPGS, CO 80901. (#103918-11).

JULY 8, '76. MANITOU SPRINGS CENTENNIAL-BICENTENNIAL 100TH ANNIVERSARY BALL. FESTIVAL, LIVE PERFORMANCE AT MONTCALM CASTLE AND/OR MEMORIAL HALL. (LOCAL). BILL COPP, CHAIRMAN; MANITOU SPRINGS CENTENNIAL-BICENTENNIAL COMMITTEE; 116 PALISADE CIRCLE; MANITOU SPGS, CO 80829. (#103918-9).

JULY 17, '76. CENTENNIAL-BICENTENNIAL KIWANIS CLUB PANCAKE DAYS FESTIVAL. PANCAKES, PICNICS, MUSIC AND ENTERTAINMENT. AT SODA SPRINGS PARK. (ST-WIDE). WILLIAM L BAUERS; MANITOU SPRINGS KIWANIS CLUB; 205 CRYSTAL HILLS BLVD; MANITOU SPGS, CO 80829. (#103918-8).

JULY 24, '76. MANITOU SPRINGS CENTENNIAL-BICENTENNIAL HUCK FINN DAYS FESTIVAL. HUCK FINN FISHING CONTESTS, TOM SAWYER AND BECKY SHARP COSTUMES, ENTERTAINMENT AND REFRESHMENTS. AT SCHRYVER PARK AND FOUNTAIN CREEK. (LOCAL). CHARLES SARNER, PRES; MANITOU SPRINGS CHAMBER OF COMMERCE; 354 MANITOU AVE; MANITOU SPGS, CO 80829. (#103918-7).

JULY 31 - AUG 1, '76. CENTENNIAL-BICENTENNIAL GOLD-PANNING CHAMPIONSHIP FESTIVAL. COMPETITION, FESTIVAL AT GOLD HILL MESA, HWY 24 & 21ST ST - COLORADO SPGS. (REGN'L). HUGH HOKENSTAD; PIKES PEAK CHAPTER, GOLD PROSPECTORS ASSOC OF AMERICA; 211 ILLINOIS AVE; MANITOU SPGS, CO 80829. (#103918-5).

JULY 31 - AUG 1, '76. CENTENNIAL-BICENTENNIAL GRAND TREASURE HUNT. FESTIVAL, COMPETITION AT GOLD HILL MESA, HWY 24 AND 21ST ST, COLORADO SPRINGS. (REGN'L). HUGH HOKENSTAD; SANGRE DE CHRISTO ADVENTURE LEAGUE; 211 ILLINOIS AVE; MANITOU SPGS, CO 80829. (#103918-6).

AUG 1, '76. COLORADO DAY CENTENNIAL-BICENTENNIAL FESTIVAL & WALKWAY DEDICATION. DEDICATION OF LANDMARK PLAQUES AT THE CLIFF HOUSE, SPA, NAVAJO HOTEL, CHURCH & MONTCALM CASTLE. ALSO, DEDICATION OF THE CENTENNIAL BICENTENNIAL WALKWAY DURING THE COLORADO DAYS FESTIVAL. AT SODA SPRINGS PARK. (LOCAL). BILL COPP, CHAIRMAN; MANITOU SPRINGS CENTENNIAL-BICENTENNIAL COMMITTEE; 116 PALISADE CIRCLE; MANITOU SPG, CO 80829. (#104245-1).

AUG 1, '76. HISTORIC LANDMARK DEDICATIONS. CEREMONY. (LOCAL). GLEN TRACY WILLIAMS, DIR; HISTORICAL SOCIETY; 606 MANITOU AVE; MANITOU SPG, CO 80829. (#108955-4).

AUG 1, '76. PIKES PEAK CENTENNIAL-BICENTENNIAL MARATHON BARR TRAIL FOOTRACE. 21ST ANNUAL COMPETITION. GOLD, SILVER AND BRONZE OLYMPIC TYPE MEDALS IN ALL COMPETITIONS. BUFFALO BURGERS IN SODA SPRINGS PARK. SOLO BY RAMPART RANGE SERTOMA CLUB. (ST-WIDE). RUDY FAHL, PRESIDENT; RAMPART RANGE SERTOMA CLUB; 2400 W COLORADO AVE; COLORADO SPG, CO 80904. (#9907-501).

AUG 7 - 28, '76. CENTENNIAL-BICENTENNIAL PATRIOTIC CONCERT SERIES (FOUR CONCERTS). VARIETY OF CONCERT MUSIC IN SODA SPRINGS PARK PAVILION. AT SODA SPRINGS PARK PAVILION. (ST-WIDE). G TRACY WILLIAMS, MGR; CITY OF MANITOU SPRINGS AND MUSIC PERFORMANCE TRUST FUND; 606 MANITOU AVE; MANITOU SPGS, CO 80829. (#6781-1).

AUG 14 - 15, '76. PIKES PEAK CENTENNIAL-BICENTENNIAL GUN SHOW. HISTORIC GUNS FROM ALL AREAS OF THE WEST. AT MEMORIAL HALL. (REGN'L). E G MCCUBBIN; PIKES PEAK GUN SHOW ASSOC; 311 MAPLEWOOD; COLORADO SPG, CO 80907. (#102612-1).

AUG 15, '76. CENTENNIAL-BICENTENNIAL ARTS AND CRAFTS FESTIVAL. REGIONAL ARTISTS AND CRAFTSMEN, REFRESHMENTS, PERIOD COSTUMES AND STAGE ENTERTAINMENT. AT SODA SPRINGS PARK. (LOCAL). PAT HUEY, CHAIRMAN; MANITOU SPRINGS HISTORICAL SOCIETY; 220 ELK PATH; MANITOU SPGS, CO 80829. (#103918-3).

SEPT 6, '76. CENTENNIAL-BICENTENNIAL LABOR DAY BUFFALO BAR-B-QUE AND FESTIVAL. ALL-DAY FESTIVAL AND ENTERTAINMENT. MORNING PARADE ON MANITOU AVE. AT SODA SPRINGS PARK. (LOCAL). JAMES J KEENEY, PRESIDENT; RAMPART RANGE SERTOMA CLUB; PO BOX 848; MANITOU SPGS, CO 80829. (#103918-2).

OCT 1 - 3, '76. CENTENNIAL-BICENTENNIAL OCTOBERFEST. GERMAN-AMERICAN OCTOBERFEST FOOD AND BEVERAGES ON THE MANOR LAWNS. GERMAN-AMERICAN CLUBS BANDS AND DANCING; EVENING DINING IN THE MANOR RESTAURANT. AT BRIARHURST ESTATE, 404 MANITOU AVE. (REGN'L). SIGFRIED KRAUSS; BRIARHURT MANOR RESTAURANT; 404 MANITOU AVE; MANITOU SPGS, CO 80829. (#9902-1).

OCT 1 - 3, '76. MANITOU SPRINGS CENTENNIAL-BICENTENNIAL MELODRAMA FESTIVAL. A FESTIVAL REUNION OF MELODRAMA ALUMNI AT THE HISTORIC IRON SPRINGS CHATEAU. AT 444 RUXTON AVE. (LOCAL). DOUG JENSEN, PRODUCER; IRON SPRINGS CHATEAU; 444 RUXTON AVE; MANITOU SPG, CO 80829. (#104030-1).

NOV 11, '76. CENTENNIAL-BICENTENNIAL VETERANS DAY PARADE. VETERANS DAY MOTORCADE PARADE TO WAR MEMORIAL IN MEMORIAL PARK. AT E PIKES PEAK AVE TO MEMORIAL PARK. (LOCAL). DEAN M SORELL, CHAIRMAN; PIKES PEAK VETERANS AND MILITARY COUNCIL; 102 S WEBER; COLORADO SPGS, CO 80901. (#103918-1).

MARBLE

NEW ROAD & BRIDGE TO YULE MARBLE QUARRY, CO. ACCESS TO THE QUARRY WHERE MARBLE FOR TOMB OF UNKNOWN SOLDIER, LINCOLN MEMORIAL, COLORADO MINT & NEW CUSTOM HOUSE WAS QUARRIED, WILL BE MADE AVAILABLE TO THE PUBLIC. (REGN'L). HON LLOYD G BLUE, MAYOR; MARBLE HISTORICAL SOCIETY; BOX 65A STAR ROUTE; MARBLE, CO 81623. (#20533).

RESTORATION OF BELL TOWER & BANDSTAND, MARBLE, CO. RESTORATION OF BELL TOWER & BANDSTAND IN CENTER OF TOWN. THESE STRUCTURES WERE USED FOR COMMUNITY GATHERINGS, FIRE WARNINGS, CELEBRATIONS & NEWS. (LOCAL). HON LLOYD G BLUE, MAYOR; MARBLE HISTORICAL SOCIETY; BOX 65A STAR ROUTE; MARBLE, CO 81623. (#20530).

JULY 31 - AUG 1, '76. ARTS FESTIVAL. A WORKING ART & CRAFT FESTIVAL, EACH EXHIBITOR DEMONSTRATES HIS PARTICULAR CRAFT; PERFORMING ARTS & MARBLE SCULPTURING CONTEST. (LOCAL). LLOYD G BLUE, COORD; ARTS FESTIVAL COMMITTEE; BOX 65A; MARBLE, CO 81623. (#108734-1).

JULY 31 - AUG 1, '76. MUSIC PROGRAMS. FOLK AND BLUE GRASS MUSIC, STREET DANCING, REGIONAL AND TRIBAL MUSIC. (LOCAL). LLOYD G BLUE, COORD; CITY OF MARBLE; BOX 65A; MARBLE, CO 81623. (#108734-3).

JULY 31 - AUG 1, '76. 'RELIVING THE PAST'. RE-CREATION OF HISTORICAL EVENTS PERTAINING TO MARBLE & ENVIRONS; UTE INDIANS WILL PARTICIAPTE WITH TRIBAL DANCES AND PERFORM RITUAL OF REMOVING THE 'CURSE' FROM CRYSTAL VALLEY 1876 DRESS. (LOCAL). LLOYD G BLUE, COORD; CITY OF MARBLE; BOX 65A; MARBLE, CO 81623. (#108734-2).

MCCOY

WATERWHEEL RESTORATION - MCCOY, CO. RESTORATION OF THE LARGEST WATERWHEEL IN THE STATE OF COLORADO; IT IS LOCATED ON THE COLORADO RIVER. (LOCAL). JOHN D COMER, PRESIDENT; COLORADO WATERWHEEL RESTORATION FOUNDATION LTD; 1250 HUMBOLDT ST; DENVER, CO 80203. (#26349).

MEEKER

MEEKER MASSACRE RESTORATION SOLDIERS COMPOUND, CO. ACQUISITION OF LAND TO LOCATE BUILDINGS OF HISTORICAL INTEREST AS ON THE MILITARY POST OF 1880; PROVIDE FOR SHOPS & LOW COST SENIOR CITIZEN HOUSING; FACADE EASEMENTS TO PRESERVE OTHER BUILDINGS. (LOCAL). ELIGE JOSLIN, COORDINATOR; MEEKER CENTENNIAL-BICENTENNIAL COMMITTEE; BOX 268; MEEKER, CO 81641. (#20292).

MEEKER MASSACRE - THORMBURG INCIDENT, CO. ACQUISITION OF LAND AT MILK CREEK BATTLE SITE; LAND IS MARKED BY A MONUMENT AND IS ON THE NATIONAL REGISTER OF HISTORIC PLACES; A PICNIC AREA IS PLANNED FOR THE SITE. (LOCAL). HARTLEY H BLOOMFIELD, CHAIRMAN; MEEKER CENTENNIAL-BICENTENNIAL COMMITTEE; 924 MAIN; MEEKER, CO 81641. (#20293).

MEEKER MASSACRE RESTORATION POWELL PARK, CO. HISTORIC PARK SITE INCLUDING CAMPING FACILITIES WHERE MAJOR JOHN WESLEY POWELL STOPPED DURING HIS EXPLORATION OF THE COLORADO RIVER & ITS TRIBUTARIES. (LOCAL). HARTLEY H BLOOMFIELD, CHAIRMAN; MEEKER CENTENNIAL BI-CENTENNIAL COMMITTEE; 924 MAIN; MEEKER, CO 81641. (#20294).

MEEKER MASSACRE RESTORATION INDIAN AGENCY - CO. ACQUISITION OF 5 ACRES OF LAND & REBUILDING THE INDIAN AGENCY AT THE TIME OF THE MASSACRE. (LOCAL). HARTLEY H BLOOMFIELD, CHAIRMAN; MEEKER CENTENNIAL-BICENTENNIAL COMMITTEE; 924 MAIN; MEEKER, CO 81641. (#20295).

JULY 2, '76. EVENING RODEO. COMPETITION, LIVE PERFORMANCE AT RIO BLANCO COUNTY FAIRGROUNDS. (LOCAL). JUDITH GITCHELL, COORD; MEEKER CENTENNIAL-BICENTENNIAL COMMITTEE; PO BOX E; MEEKER, CO 81641. (#108600-1).

JULY 3 - 4, '76. FOURTH OF JULY PARADE AND BARBECUE. SALUTE THE PIONEERS AND EXPLORERS FROM ESCALANTE TO THE PRESENT; THE PARADE WILL BEGIN AT 10 AM, THE BARBECUE WILL BEGIN AT 1 PM. AT MAIN ST FOR PARADE; CITY PARK FOR BAR-B-QUE. (LOCAL). ALAN JONES, DVM, PRES; RANGE CALL RODEO AND CHAMBER OF COMMERCE; BOX 869; MEEKER, CO 81641. (#104727-3).

JULY 3 - 4, '76. RANGE CALL RODEO. THIS IS THE OLDEST CONTINUOUS RODEO IN COLORADO; JULY 4TH ACTIVITIES WILL BEGIN AT 2:30 PM. AT FAIRGROUNDS; PARKING IN AREA. (LOCAL). ALAN JONES, DVM, PRES; RANGE CALL RODEO AND CHAMBER OF COMMERCE; BOX 869; MEEKER, CO 81641. (#104727-1).

JULY 4, '76. MEEKER MASSACRE PAGEANT. RE-ENACTMENT OF EVENTS LEADING TO THE MEEKER MASSACRE; THE PAGEANT IS A CITIZEN EFFORT TO RELIVE THE PAST FOR 2 1/2 HOURS EACH FOURTH OF JULY. AT FAIRGROUNDS; PARKING IN AREA. (LOCAL). ALAN JONES, DVM, PRES; RANGE CALL RODEO AND CHAMBER OF COMMERCE; BOX 869; MEEKER, CO 81641. (#104727-2).

MERINO

PARK & ICE SKATING RINK PROJ OF MERINO, CO. THE FUTURE FARMERS OF AMERICA ARE PLANNING A PARK & ICE SKATING RINK. TREES & DEBRIS MUST BE REMOVED, A LAND DIKE IS TO BE LEVELED, & LIGHTS ARE TO BE INSTALLED WITH ALL WORK DONE BY FFA STUDENTS. (LOCAL). CHARLES HAUER, SUPT OF SCHOOLS; BUFFALO RE 4 SCHOOL BOARD; MERINO, CO 80741. (#7730).

SEPT 11, '76. OLD-TIME HARVEST DAY FESTIVAL. SLIDE SHOW OF HISTORIC SITES; BOOTHS, STREET GAMES, SPECIALTY FOODS; OLD-FASHIONED DRESS ENCOURAGED. AT MAIN ST. (LOCAL). MRS ROBERT SCHOTT, JR; MERINO BICENTENNIAL CENTENNIAL COMMITTEE; BOX 203; MERINO, CO 80741. (#104083-1).

MESA VERDE

JUNE 15 - SEPT 6, '76. HIGHLIGHTS OF DOMINGUEZ-ESCALANTE EXPEDITION OF 1776. SERIES OF HISTORIC TALKS, SLIDE PROGRAMS, AND TALKS ON THE PREHISTORIC INDIANS OF THE SOUTHWEST; EXHIBITS TO SUPPLEMENT TALKS. AT MORFIELD AMPHITHEATER, MORFIELD CAMPGROUND. (REGN'L). MESA VERDE NM; NATIONAL PARK SERVICE; MESA VERDE, CO 81330. (#6730-115).

MILLIKEN

ARTS FESTIVAL. TOWN & SCHOOL RECORDS WILL BE EXHIBITED AT TOWN HALL AND THERE WILL BE AN ANTIQUE SHOW. (LOCAL). GORDON COOK, CHMN; ARTS FESTIVAL COMMITTEE; 309 JOSEPHINE AVE; MILLIKEN, CO 80543. (#108858-1).

'GREENING AND CLEANING COLORADO' - MILLIKEN. TREES, SHRUBS AND FLOWERS WILL BE PLANTED IN TIME FOR THE ANNUAL BEEF AND BEAN DAY. (LOCAL). GORDON COOK, CHAIRMAN; TOWN IMPROVEMENT COMMITTEE; 309 JOSEPHINE AVE; MILLIKEN, CO 80543. (#25963).

MINTURN

'GREENING AND CLEANING COLORADO' - MINTURN, CO. TREES AND FLOWERS WILL BE PLANTED. (LOCAL). HON HAROLD BELLM, MAYOR; CITY OF MINTURN; PO BOX 381; MINTURN, CO 81645. (#26238).

MONTE VISTA

BOOK ON HISTORY OF SARGENT COMMUNITY - CO. PUBLICATION OF BOOK ON COMPLETE HISTORY OF THE SETTLING & DEVELOPMENT OF THE COMMUNITY. (LOCAL). BETTE B DEACON, CHAIRMAN; SARGENT COMMUNITY CHURCH; 6967 N ROAD 2 E; MONTE VISTA, CO 81144. (#24576).

FIRE HYDRANT PAINTING - MONTE VISTA, CO. DOWNTOWN FIRE HYDRANTS WILL BE PAINTED FIGURES OF HISTORICAL INTEREST. (LOCAL). AMY UHRICH, PROJ CHAIRMAN; CITY OF MONTE VISTA; 3075 SHERMAN AVE; MONTE VISTA, CO 81144. (#26239).

ORAL HISTORY PROJ - MONTE VISTA, CO. ANTHROPOLOGY STUDENTS AT LOCAL HIGH SCHOOL WILL TAPE REMINISCENCES OF 'OLDTIMERS' IN THE COMMUNITY. (LOCAL). AMY UHRICH, PROJ CHAIRMAN; CITY OF MONTE VISTA; 3075 SHERMAN AVE; MONTE VISTA, CO 81144. (#26240).

SARGENT COMMUNITY HISTORY FILM STRIP - CO. A FILM STRIP ABOUT THE LIFE IN THE SARGENT COUNTY FOR THE PAST 60 YEARS; PICTURES INCLUDE OLD PHOTOS OF AGRICULTURE, CHURCH & COMMUNITY LIFE OF THAT PERIOD. (LOCAL). MRS BETTE DEACON, CHAIRMAN; SARGENT COMMUNITY CHURCH; 6967 N RD 2E; MONTE VISTA, CO 81144. (#24586).

SARGENT COMMUNITY SLIDE FILM HISTORY, CO. A SLIDE HISTORY OF THE COMMUNITY WAS PUT TOGETHER. (LOCAL). BETTE B DEACON CHAIRPERSON; SARGENT BICENTENNIAL COMMITTEE; 6967 N ROAD 2 E; MONTE VISTA, CO 81144. (#32615).

MONTE VISTA — CONTINUED

JAN 14, '76. SPIRIT OF '76 DINNER & TALENT SHOW. LIVE PERFORMANCE AT SARGENT SCHOOL. (LOCAL). MRS BETTE DEACON; SARGENT COMMUNITY CHURCH; 5962 E RD 7N; MONTE VISTA, CO 81144. (#200007-130).

JULY 29 - 31, '76. SKI HI STAMPEDE RODEO PARADE. PARADE. (LOCAL). BETTE B DEACON, CHAIRMAN; SARGENT COMMUNITY CHURCH; 5962 EAST RD 7 NORTH; MONTE VISTA, CO 81144. (#107441-1).

AUG 1, '76. COLORADO DAY FIREWORKS DISPLAY. FESTIVAL. (LOCAL). AMY UHRICH, COORD; FESTIVAL COMMITTEE; 3075 SHERMAN AVE; MONTE VISTA, CO 81144. (#108955-2).

AUG 20, '76. TOWN FAIR. A FAIR AT WHICH LOCAL CITIZENS CAN SHOW THEIR WARES & SKILLS. (LOCAL). AMY UHRICH; TOWN OF MONTE VISTA; 3075 SHERMAN AVE; MONTE VISTA, CO 81144. (#108719-1).

MONTROSE

CLUB PROJECT TO RESTORE HISTORICAL GRAVE, CO. HISTORICAL GRAVESITE IS BEING RESTORED WITH RESET STONE AND NEW FENCE. (LOCAL). ROBERT MIDDLETON, 4-H LEADER; PRIDE OF THE ROCKIES 4-H CLUB; RR2; MONTROSE, CO 81401. (#17463).

DOMINGUEZ-ESCALANTE MONUMENT - CO. MONUMENT WILL BE ERECTED TO HONOR DOMINGUEZ-ESCALANTE. (LOCAL). HON ROBERT O STRONG, MAYOR; CITY OF MONTROSE; 433 S FIRST; MONTROSE, CO 81401. (#25990).

FOXFIRE PROJECT-CULTURAL HISTORIES OF COLORADO. OPPORTUNITY FOR HIGH SCHOOL STUDENTS TO UTILIZE CULTURAL HERITAGE AS MOTIVATIONAL FORCE FOR LEARNING BASIC SKILLS & CULTURAL HISTORY OF THE STATE. (ST-WIDE). MARTHA M FRITTS, STAFF; IDEAS; 2525 S DAYTON WAY; DENVER, CO 80231. (#4343). **ARBA GRANTEE.**

MONTROSE RAILWAY DEPOT RESTORATION IN COLORADO. RESTORATION OF RIO GRANDE RAILWAY STATION AND GRAND OPENING. (LOCAL). DORIS HARRINGTON, CHAIRMAN; MONTROSE COUNTY HISTORICAL SOCIETY; 10 POPLAR DR; MONTROSE, CO 81401. (#2751).

SAN JUAN MOUNTAINS MINING TOURS OF COLORADO. AUTO TOURS TO OLD MINES AND GHOST TOWNS IN SAN JUAN MOUNTAINS OF COLORADO FOR 4-WHEEL DRIVE VEHICLES. TOURS STARTING AT 5 LOCATIONS OURAY, SILVERTON, TELLURIDE, LAKE CITY, MONTROSE. (LOCAL). ED NELSON, MANAGER; MONTROSE COUNTY CHAMBER OF COMMERCE; PO BOX 1061; MONTROSE, CO 81401. (#4413).

JUNE 20 - AUG 24, '75. CAMPFIRE PGM ON MAN'S HISTORY IN THE BLACK CANYON OF THE GUNNISON. EVERY SUMMER. PGM WILL FEATURE HISTORY OF THIS SECTION OF THE COLORADO RIVER, INCLUDING ESCALANTE'S VISIT IN 1776. ADMISSION FEE TO THE PARK. AT SOUTH RIM CAMPGROUND IN BLACK CANYON OF GUNNISON NATL MON. (REGN'L). SUPT BLK CNYN OF GUNNISON; NATIONAL PARK SERVICE; 343 S. 10TH STREET; MONTROSE, CO 81401. (#6730-39).

AUG 15, '75 - SEPT 18, '76. 4 WHEEL DRIVE VEHICLE TOURS TO SCENIC HISTORIC SAN JUAN MTN TOWNS. AN HISTORIC DOCUMENTED CONDUCTED TOUR FROM EACH SAN JUAN TOWN SEPT 20 21&13 14 AUG 22 23 & 29 30 USING 4 WHEEL DRIVES TRAIL BIKES TRAIL BIKES, HICKERS, ETC. AT CITIES AND GHOST TOWN MINES OF THE SAN JUAN MTNS. (LOCAL). ED NELSON; LOCAL CITIES AND COUNTIES; PO BOX 1061; MONTROSE, CO 81401. (#50367-1).

MAR 26 - 28, '76. '1776' - THEATRICAL PRODUCTION. LIVE PERFORMANCE AT CIRCLE THEATER, S 12TH ST. (LOCAL). BETTY CRANE, COORD; DELTA TRIANGLE THEATER & VALLEY SYMPHONY; 919 GRAND AVE; DELTA, CO 81416. (#200007-131).

MAY 7 - 8, '76. FOUNDERS' DAY CELEBRATION. EXHIBITS, CONTESTS, SQUARE DANCING, PARADE, FOOD. AT MAIN STREET - DOWNTOWN AREA. (LOCAL). ED NELSON, COORD; MONTROSE CITY/COUNTY CENTENNIAL/BICENTENNIAL COMMITTEE; CHAMBER OF COMMERCE - BOX 1061; MONTROSE, CO 81401. (#104553-3).

MAY 23, '76. NATL PK SVC '...A LITTLE LOOK AROUND' VISITS COLORADO NM. THIS SHORT PROGRAM FEATURES ACTORS PORTRAYING FAMOUS AMERICANS OF THE PAST WHO'VE RETURNED TO SEE AMERICA'S GROWTH. (REGN'L). COLORADO NATL MON; NATIONAL PARK SERVICE; P.O. BOX 1648; MONTROSE, CO 81401. (#5653-64).

JUNE 14 - AUG 24, '76. BLK CNYN OF GUNNISON NM CAMPFIRE PGM ON MAN'S HISTORY IN THE AREA. PROGRAM WILL FEATURE HISTORY OF THIS SECTION OF THE COLORADO RIVER, INCLUDING ESCALANTE'S VISIT IN 1776. AT SOUTH RIM CAMPGROUND IN BLACK CANYON OF GUNNISON NATL MON. (REGN'L). BLK CNYN OF GUNNISON NM; NATIONAL PARK SERVICE; BOX 1648 HWY 50 E; MONTROSE, CO 81401. (#6730-539).

JUNE 15 - SEPT 6, '76. HISTORIC LECTURE SERIES AND GUIDED WALKS. TALKS AND CAMPFIRE PROGRAMS ON THE HISTORY OF COLORADO NATIONAL MONUMENT AND SURROUNDING AREA FROM PREHISTORIC TIMES TO PRESENT. AT COLORADO NATIONAL MONUMENT. (REGN'L). COLORADO NM; NATIONAL PARK SERVICE; FRUITA, CO 81521. (#6730-117).

JUNE 16 - AUG 31, '76. BICENTENNIAL FILM SERIES AT CURECANTI NRA. EXHIBIT AT ELK CREEK VISITOR CENTER, GUNNISON, CO. (REGN'L). SUPT, CURECANTI NRA; NATIONAL PARK SERVICE; P.O. BOX 1648; MONTROSE, CO 81401. (#6728-520).

JULY 4, '76. JULY FOURTH CELEBRATION. FIREWORKS DISPLAY AND BAND CONCERT, CHILDREN'S ACTIVITIES. AT MONTROSE HIGH SCHOOL. (LOCAL). ED NELSON, COORD; ROTARY; CHAMBER OF COMMERCE, BOX 1061; MONTROSE, CO 81401. (#104553-2).

JULY 6 - 31, '76. INDIAN DANCING AT COLORADO NATIONAL MONUMENT. LIVE PERFORMANCE. (REGN'L). COLORADO NM; NATIONAL PARK SERVICE; FRUITA, CO 81521. (#6729-142).

AUG 11 - 15, '76. MONTROSE COUNTY FAIR AND RODEO. FAIR, PARADE AT MAIN AND STOUGH. (ST-WIDE). CINDY GROSKOPF; MONTROSE COUNTY FAIR BOARD; BOX 1061, 550 N TOWNSEND; MONTROSE, CO 81401. (#108720-1).

AUG 13 - 15, '76. MONTE DE ROSES FIESTAS. FESTIVAL AT CITY MARKET. (LOCAL). SAL MAESTAS, DIRECTOR; CITY OF MONTROSE; 309 S CASCADE; MONTROSE, CO 81401. (#103840-7).

AUG 26 - 27, '76. MONTROSE DOMINGUEZ-ESCALANTE CELEBRATION. RE-ENACTMENT OF THE ARRIVAL OF DOMINGUEZ-ESCALANTE IN 1776. THERE WILL BE A DEDICATION CEREMONY AND THE PRESENTATION OF A COIN, REPRESENTING ONE FOUND AT HIS CAMPSITE. AT UTE MUSEUM VICINITY - SOUTH OF MONTROSE. (LOCAL). CINDY GROSKOPF, COORD; MONTROSE COUNTY HISTORICAL SOCIETY; BOX 1061, 550 N TOWNSEND; MONTROSE, CO 81401. (#108768-1).

SEPT 16, '76. UNITED STATES ARMED FORCES BICENTENNIAL CARAVAN. CARAVAN IS COMPOSED OF EXHIBIT VANS FOR EACH MILITARY SERVICE. PROJECT THEME IS 'HISTORY OF THE ARMED FORCES & THEIR CONTRIBUTIONS TO THE NATION.'. (LOCAL). GERRY FLANIGAN, CHMN; UNITED STATES ARMED FORCES BICENTENNIAL CARAVAN; 524 MAIN; MONTROSE, CO 81401. (#1775-676).

MONUMENT

MONUMENT HILL COMMUNITY LIBRARY, MONUMENT,CO. ESTABLISHMENT OF COMMUNITY LIBRARY WITHIN THE AREA OF WOODMOOR/MONUMENT. (LOCAL). MRS DAVID L CLAYTOR, DIRECTOR; MONUMENT HILL COMMUNITY LIBRARY; LAKE WOODMOOR DR; MONUMENT, CO 80132. (#14827).

MORRISON

CENTENNIAL PARK - MORRISON, CO. SIX FIREPLACES, PICNIC TABLES AND RESTROOM FACILITIES WILL BE ADDED TO MORRISON PARK. (LOCAL). HELEN B JORDAN, CHAIRMAN; CENTENNIAL COMMITTEE, RED ROCKS LIONS & DENVER MOUNTAIN PARKS; PO BOX 395; MORRISON, CO 80465. (#24619).

HISTORIC DISTRICT APPLICATION, MORRISON, CO. APPLICATION TO THE NATIONAL REGISTER FOR A HISTORIC DISTRICT. (LOCAL). LORENE HORTON, CHAIRMAN; MORRISON HISTORICAL SOCIETY; PO BOX 251; MORRISON, CO 80465. (#24616).

HISTORICAL CENTENNIAL MUSEUM - MORRISON, CO. THE BUILDING FOR THE CENTENNIAL MUSEUM HAS BEEN SELECTED. (LOCAL). LORENE HORTON, CHAIRMAN; MORRISON HISTORICAL SOCIETY; MORRISON, CO 80465. (#24622).

HISTORICAL WALKING TOUR OF MORRISON, CO. A TOUR GUIDE OF THE HISTORICAL SITES IN MORRISON IS BEING PREPARED. (LOCAL). HELEN B JORDAN, CHAIRMAN; MORRISON CENTENNIAL-BICENTENNIAL COMMITTEE; PO BOX 251; MORRISON, CO 80465. (#24623).

MEMORIAL PLAZA - MORRISON, CO. AN AREA WITH BENCHES WILL BE BUILT IN THE TOWN. (LOCAL). BEULAH HARR, CHAIRMAN; WESTOVER POST VFW; 17372 COLORADO HWY 8; MORRISON, CO 80465. (#24621).

MODERN LACE - MORRISON, CO. RESTORATION OF FRONT OF LAUNDROMAT TO ORIGINAL SANDSTONE FACE. TOWN HALL AND CLERK'S OFFICE WILL BE PAINTED. (LOCAL). BOB HUBBARD, MEMBER; RED ROCKS LION'S CLUB; MORRISON, CO 80465. (#24618).

MORRISON COMMEMORATIVE BELT BUCKLES, CO. BELT BUCKLES ARE BEING MADE FEATURING THE MORRISON SCHOOLHOUSE, BUILT IN 1875. DESIGN IS BY ROLF PAUL, A LOCAL ARTIST. (LOCAL). HELEN B JORDAN, CHAIRMAN; MORRISON CENTENNIAL-BICENTENNIAL COMMITTEE; PO BOX 395; MORRISON, CO 80465. (#24617).

WALKER SQUARE - MORRISON, CO. BEAUTIFICATION OF AREA BETWEEN TOWN HALL AND TOWN CLERKS OFFICE. DEDICATION TO JOHN BRISBIN WALKER WHO DID A GREAT DEAL TO DEVELOP MORRISON'S EARLY HISTORY. (LOCAL). HELEN B JORDAN, CHAIRMAN; CENTENNIAL-BICENTENNIAL COMMITTEE & MORRISON PIONEERS OF '76; PO BOX 395; MORRISON, CO 80465. (#24624).

FEB 23, '76. POSTER CONTEST - CEREMONY. CEREMONY, COMPETITION AT RED ROCK ELEMENTARY SCHOOL. (LOCAL). JUDY WELLS, PROJ DIR; RED ROCK ELEMENTARY SCHOOL, WESTOVER POST CENTENNIAL COMMITTEE; MORRISON, CO 80465. (#200007-146).

JULY 10, '76. MID-CONTINENT HEAVY VARMINT REGIONAL CHAMPIONSHIP. COMPETITION AT TOM PIKE RANCH, NORTH OF MORRISON. (LOCAL). RONALD BEST, COORD; COLORADO BENCH REST SHOOTERS, INC; RT 1 BOX 148; MORRISON, CO 80465. (#108861-1).

JULY 10 - 11, '76. COLORADO/CENTENNIAL STATE BENCH REST CHAMPIONSHIP MATCHES. AWARD, COMPETITION AT TOM PIKE RANCH. (REGN'L). RONALD BEST, SECRETARY; COLORADO BENCH REST SHOOTERS, INC; RT 1 BOX 148; MORRISON, CO 80465. (#107027-1).

JULY 10 - 11, '76. EIGHTH ANNUAL JULY RIFLE MATCHES. COMPETITION AT TOM PIKE RANCH, NORTH OF MORRISON. (LOCAL). RONALD BEST, COORD; COLORADO BENCH REST SHOOTERS, INC; RT 1, BOX 148; MORRISON, CO 80465. (#108861-2).

JULY 11, '76. COMMUNITY PICNIC. FESTIVAL AT MORRISON PARK. (LOCAL). HELEN B JORDAN, CHAIRMAN; MORRISON PIONEERS OF '76 CENTENNIAL-BICENTENNIAL COMMITTEE; PO BOX 395; MORRISON, CO 80465. (#107437-1).

AUG 21 - 22, '76. PIONEER DAYS FESTIVAL & PARADE. FESTIVAL, PARADE AT MAIN ST & PARK AVE. (LOCAL). HELEN B JORDAN, COORD; MORRIS CENTENNIAL-BICENTENNIAL COMMITTEE & RED ROCKS LIONS; PO BOX 251; MORRISON, CO 80465. (#107001-1).

NEW CASTLE

BEAUTIFY NEW CASTLE, CO. CONTESTS FOR IMPROVING & CLEANING UP THE BUSINESS SECTION OF TOWN & FOR HOME IMPROVEMENT PROJECT. (LOCAL). RONALD L BAUSCH; COMMUNITY IMPROVEMENT COMMITTEE; BOX 328; NEW CASTLE, CO 81647. (#26204).

MOUNTAIN RENAMING - NEW CASTLE, CO. 3 MOUNTAINS IN NEW CASTLE WILL BE RENAMED AFTER LEADING CITIZENS. (LOCAL). RONALD L BAUSCH; CITY OF NEW CASTLE; BOX 328; NEW CASTLE, CO 81647. (#26205).

ORAL HISTORY - NEW CASTLE, CO. CASSETTE TAPES OF SENIOR CITIZENS ON EARLY HISTORY OF NEW CASTLE & COLORADO. (LOCAL). RONALD L BAUSCH; GARFIELD COUNTY PUBLIC LIBRARY; BOX 328; NEW CASTLE, CO 81647. (#26203).

JULY 10, '76. ARTS FESTIVAL. DISPLAY OF ARTS & CRAFTS BY LOCAL CITIZENS; PRIZES WILL BE AWARDED IN SEVERAL CATEGORIES. AT GARFIELD COUNTY PUBLIC LIBRARY, 402 W MAIN ST. (LOCAL). RONALD L BAUSCH, COORD; ARTS FESTIVAL COMMITTEE; BOX 328; NEW CASTLE, CO 81647. (#108679-1).

JULY 10, '76. COMMUNITY TIME CAPSULE. RECORDS & PHOTOS OF NEW CASTLE '76 TO BE SEALED IN A TIME CAPSULE TO BE OPENED IN THE YEAR 2000. AT GARFIELD COUNTY PUBLIC LIBRARY. (LOCAL). RONALD L BAUSCH; TIME CAPSULE COMMITTEE; BOX 328; NEW CASTLE, CO 81647. (#108729-1).

JULY 10, '76. HONORING SENIOR CITIZENS. CEREMONY TO HONOR THE OLDEST CITIZEN IN NEW CASTLE. TO BE OPENED IN THE YEAR 2000. AT GARFIELD COUNTY PUBLIC LIBRARY. (LOCAL). RONALD L BAUSCH; SENIOR CITIZENS (RSVP); BOX 328; NEW CASTLE, CO 81647. (#108729-2).

JULY 10, '76. PARADE. TO BE OPENED IN THE YEAR 2000. AT GARFIELD COUNTY PUBLIC LIBRARY. (LOCAL). RONALD L BAUSCH; SENIOR CITIZENS (RSVP); BOX 328; NEW CASTLE, CO 81647. (#108729-4).

JULY 10, '76. 'RELIVING THE PAST'. CONTEST FOR THE BEST & MOST AUTHENTIC OLD COSTUME. TO BE OPENED IN THE YEAR 2000. AT GARFIELD COUNTY PUBLIC LIBRARY. (LOCAL). RONALD L BAUSCH; SENIOR CITIZENS (RSVP); BOX 328; NEW CASTLE, CO 81647. (#108729-3).

JULY 10, '76. WRITING CONTEST. CONTEST FOR THE BEST WRITTEN ENTRY OF HISTORICAL VALUE TO THE TO BE OPENED IN THE YEAR 2000. AT GARFIELD COUNTY PUBLIC LIBRARY. (LOCAL). RONALD L BAUSCH; SENIOR CITIZENS (RSVP); BOX 328; NEW CASTLE, CO 81647. (#108729-5).

NORTHGLENN

ADAMS COUNTY, COLORADO, NATURE PRESERVE. A NATURE PRESERVE ADJOINING THE ADAMS COUNTY FAIRGROUNDS AND ALSO SOME LAND ON THE SOUTH PLATTE RIVER. (LOCAL). ELANOR M WYATT, CO-ORDINATOR; COLORADO CENTENNIAL BICENTENNIAL COMMISSION; 901 SHERMAN ST; DENVER, CO 80203. (#4348). **ARBA GRANTEE.**

AMERICAN BICENTENNIAL COOKBOOK, NORTH GLEN, CO. A COOKBOOK CONTAINING RECIPES FROM THE WIVES OF EVERY GOVERNOR WITH PERTINENT FACTS ABOUT EACH. (NAT'L). WILLIAM A SHEPPARD, JR; AMERICAN BICENTENNIAL COOKBOOK, INC; 10701 MELODY DR; NORTH GLEN, CO 80234. (#16383).

NORTHGLENN, COLORADO, CIVIC GARDENS. SERIES OF GARDENS DEPICTING THE VARIETY OF FLORA IN THE DIFFERENT AREAS OF COLORADO. (LOCAL). ELEANOR M WYATT, CHAIRMAN; NORTHGLENN CIVIC GARDENS COMMITTEE; 10514 KAAMATH; NORTHGLENN, CO 80234. (#4398). **ARBA GRANTEE.**

PARK SIGNS, NORTHGLENN, CO. NEW SIGNS IDENTIFYING ROUTES, THE GARDENS & THE NORTHGLENN CENTENNIAL PARK WILL BE INSTALLED. (LOCAL). ELEANOR M WYATT, PROJ COORDINATOR; CITY OF NORTHGLENN; 10514 KALAMATH; NORTHGLENN, CO 80234. (#26849).

MAY 31, '76. MEMORIAL SERVICE. MEMBERS OF YOUTH SUBCOMMITTEE PRESENT PLAQUE TO NORTHGLENN HIGH SCHOOL TO HONOR THE GRADUATES WHO LOST HTEIR LIVES IN VIETNAM. AT NORTHGLENN HIGH SCHOOL. (LOCAL). DIRECTOR; NORTHGLENN CENTENNIAL-BICENTENNIAL YOUTH SUBCOMMITTEE; NORTHGLENN, CO 80234. (#108680-1).

JUNE 14 - JULY 4, '76. THE CITIZENS' REAFFIRMATION PROGRAM. FESTIVAL, LIVE PERFORMANCE, SEMINAR AT NORTHGLENN MALL. (LOCAL). ELEANOR M WYATT, COORD; NORTHGLENN CENTENNIAL-BICENTENNIAL COMMITTEE; 10514 KALAMATH; NORTHGLENN, CO 80234. (#108599-1).

JUNE 17 - 19, '76. NORTHGLENN FESTIVAL DAYS. ACTIVITIES INCLUDE A PARADE ON 6/19, '1776' PERFORMED BY THE ADAMS COUNTY COMMUNITY THEATER GROUP ON 6/18-19, AN ARTS & CRAFTS BAZAAR ON 6/18-19, AND SENIOR CITIZENS' KING & QUEEN. AT NORTHGLENN MALL. (LOCAL). ELEANOR M WYATT, CHMN; NORTHGLENN CENTENNIAL-BICENTENNIAL COMMISSION; 10514 KALAMATH; NORTHGLENN, CO 80234. (#200007-132).

NORTHGLENN — CONTINUED

JUNE 20, '76. LA FIESTA DE COLOR DANCE GROUP. LIVE PERFORMANCE AT NORTHGLENN COMMUNITY CENTER. (LOCAL). ELEANOR M WYATT, CHMN; NORTHGLENN CENTENNIAL-BICENTENNIAL COMMITTEE; 10514 KALAMATH; NORTHGLENN, CO 80234. (#200007-133).

JUNE 25, '76. CENTENNIAL TEEN DANCE. FESTIVAL AT NORTHGLENN COMMUNITY CENTER. (LOCAL). ELEANOR WYATT, CHMN; NORTHGLENN CENT-BICENT COMMITTEE, PARKS & RECREATION DEPT; 10514 KALAMATH; NORTHGLENN, CO 80234. (#200007-134).

JULY 4, '76. CENTENNIAL FIREWORKS. FESTIVAL AT JAYCEE PARK, IRMA DR AT LEROY DR. (LOCAL). ELEANOR M WYATT, COORD; PARKS & RECREATION DEPT; 10514 KALAMATH; NORTHGLENN, CO 80234. (#108599-2).

JULY 4, '76. 4TH OF JULY FAMILY FUN DAY. FESTIVAL AT WEBSTER LAKE PARK. (LOCAL). ELEANOR M WYATT, COORD; PARKS & RECREATION DEPT; 10514 KALAMATH; NORTHGLENN, CO 80234. (#108599-3).

JULY 13, '76. NORTHGLENN CARNIVAL. FAIR AT WESTVIEW RECREATION CENTER. (LOCAL). ELEANOR M WYATT, CHMN; NORTHGLENN CENTENNIAL-BICENTENNIAL COMMITTEE; 10514 KALAMATH; NORTHGLENN, CO 80234. (#108661-1).

JULY 31 - AUG 1, '76. HISTORIC PHOTO & RELIC DISPLAY. EXHIBIT AT NORTHGLENN COMMUNITY CENTER. (LOCAL). ELEANOR M WYATT, CHMN; NORTHGLENN CENTENNIAL-BICENTENNIAL COMMITTEE; 10514 KALAMATH; NORTHGLENN, CO 80234. (#108661-2).

AUG 1, '76. JIM BRIDGER PRODUCTION. LIVE PERFORMANCE AT NORTHGLENN COMMUNITY CENTER. (LOCAL). ELEANOR M WYATT, COORD; NORTHGLENN CENTENNIAL-BICENTENNIAL COMMITTEE; 10514 KALAMATH; NORTHGLENN, CO 80234. (#108955-27).

AUG 1, '76. PARK DEDICATION & TIME CAPSULE. PHOTOS, NEWSPAPER CLIPPINGS & SIGNATURES WILL BE PUT INTO A TIME CAPSULE BESIDE A LIBERTY BELL AT THE PARK DEDICATION AT 2 PM. AT CENTENNIAL PARK. (LOCAL). ELEANOR M WYATT, COORD; NORTHGLENN CENTENNIAL-BICENTENNIAL COMMITTEE; 10514 KALAMATH; NORTHGLENN, CO 80234. (#108955-29).

AUG 1 - ??, '76. HISTORIC PHOTOS AND RELICS ON DISPLAY. EXHIBIT AT NORTHGLENN COMMUNITY CENTER. (LOCAL). ELEANOR M WYATT, COORD; NORTHGLENN CENTENNIAL-BICENTENNIAL COMMITTEE; 10514 KALAMATH; NORTHGLENN, CO 80234. (#108955-30).

AUG 7, '76. CENTENNIAL PET SHOW. COMPETITION, EXHIBIT AT WEBSTER LAKE PARK. (LOCAL). ELEANOR WYATT; NORTHGLENN CENTENNIAL-BICENTENNIAL COMMITTEE; 10514 KALAMATH; NORTHGLENN, CO 80234. (#108722-1).

NOV 23 - 27, '76. 'STANDING ROOM ONLY'. A PROJECT OF THE STATE DEPARTMENT OF LOCAL AFFAIRS AND THE COLORADO LABOR COUNCIL TO AWAKEN CONCERN FOR LAND USE AND DEVELOPMENT IN COLORADO. AT NORTHGLENN MALL. (LOCAL). ELEANOR M WYATT, COORD; NORTHGLENN CENTENNIAL-BICENTENNIAL COMMITTEE; 10514 KALAMATH; NORTHGLENN, CO 80234. (#108766-1).

NORWOOD

LOG CABIN-KITCHEN, NORWOOD, CO. KITCHEN ADDITION WILL BE USED IN THE ELDERLY NUTRITIONAL PROGRAM. (LOCAL). DOROTHY OLIVER, PRESIDENT; NORWOOD STUDY CLUB; W OF NORWOOD; NORWOOD, CO 81423. (#19814).

SEPT 25, '75. PIONEER DAY PARADE, CROWNING OF QUEEN. CEREMONY, PARADE AT MAIN ST. (LOCAL). DOROTHY OLIVER, COORD; NORWOOD STUDY CLUB; NORWOOD, CO 81423. (#200007-197).

JUNE 16 - OCT 15, '76. SAN JUAN HISTORIC TOURS. TOUR AT INFORMATION BOOTH ON MAIN ST. (LOCAL). DAVIS M WATSON, CHMN; NORWOOD CHAMBER OF COMMERCE; MAIN ST; NORWOOD, CO 81423. (#200007-182).

JULY 4, '76. FLAG POLE DEDICATION AT THE LOG CABIN. DEDICATION OF THE LOG CABIN NEW KITCHEN ADDITION. (LOCAL). JAMES ODLE, COORDINATOR; CENTENNIAL-BICENTENNIAL COMMITTEE OF NORWOOD; PO BOX 127; NORWOOD, CO 81423. (#108598-1).

JULY 4, '76. 4TH OF JULY CELEBRATION. OLD-TIME PICNIC LUNCH WITH STREET SPORTS AND COMMUNITY SING-ALONG. (LOCAL). JAMES ODLE, COORDINATOR; CENTENNIAL-BICENTENNIAL COMMITTEE OF NORWOOD; PO BOX 127; NORWOOD, CO 81423. (#108598-2).

JULY 4 - 9, '76. OPEN HOUSE FOR KITCHEN PROJECT. EXHIBIT, TOUR. (LOCAL). DAVIS M WATSON, CHAIRMAN; CENTENNIAL-BICENTENNIAL COMMITTEE OF NORWOOD; PO BOX 461; NORWOOD, CO 81423. (#108598-3).

JULY 30 - AUG 1, '76. SAN MIGUEL BASIN FAIR AND RODEO. COUNTY FAIR IN CONJUNCTION WITH RODEO; DANCE ON SATURDAY EVENING. AT FAIRGROUNDS SOUTHWEST OF NORWOOD. (LOCAL). GLEN GARDNER, COORD; SAN MIGUEL COUNTY FAIR AND RODEO ASSOCIATION; W OF NORWOOD; NORWOOD, CO 81423. (#104553-4).

AUG 7 - 8, '76. COLORADO COMMEMORATIVE STONE DEDICATION. COMMEMORATIVE STONE MARKS THE CO CENTENNIAL; DEDICATION CEREMONY FOR AUG 7&8 IN CONJUNCTION WITH THE SAN MIQUEL BASIN RODEO. (LOCAL). JAMES ODLE; TOWN OF NORWOOD; PO BOX 127; NORWOOD, CO 81423. (#108721-1).

SEPT 25, '76. PIONEER DAY BREAKFAST AND PARADE. FESTIVAL, PARADE. (LOCAL). DAVIS M WATSON, CHMN; CENTENNIAL-BICENTENNIAL COMMITTEE OF NORWOOD; PO BOX 461; NORWOOD, CO 81423. (#108765-1).

NUCLA

BELL TOWER IN NUCLA, CO. AS A CENTENNIAL-BICENTENNIAL PROJECT, THE TOWN WILL CONSTRUCT A REPLICA OF THE OLD TOWER WHICH WAS A LANDMARK OF THE COMMUNITY FOR MANY YEARS. (LOCAL). JOAN ELLIOT, PROJ MANAGER; WEST END BAND PARENTS; BOX 244; NUCLA, CO 81424. (#14834).

COLLECTING NUCLA'S HISTORICAL ANTIQUES, CO. GATHERING OLD RECIPES, CLOTHES, TOOLS, HOUSEHOLD ITEMS AND STORIES TO COMMEMORATE THE HISTORY FO THE COMMUNITY. (LOCAL). JOAN ELLIOT, PROJ MANAGER; SAN MIGUEL BASIN AND 4-H COUNCIL; BOX 244; NUCLA, CO 81424. (#14833).

COMMUNITY TIME CAPSULE - NUCLA, CO. SEPT 1976 LOCAL NEWSPAPER WILL SUPPLY PHOTOS. TOWN IS BUILDING A NEW MUNICIPAL BUILDING WHICH IS THE PROPOSED LOCATION OF THE TIME CAPSULE BURIAL. (LOCAL). JAN ELLIOT, PROJ COORDINATOR; NUCLA COMMUNITY; NUCLA, CO 81424. (#26183).

CREATION OF FLAG FOR NUCLA, CO. A CONTEST FOR THE BEST FLAG IDEA WILL BE HELD TO HELP INVOLVE SCHOOL CHILDREN IN THE BICENTENNIAL. (LOCAL). JOAN ELLIOT, PROJ MANAGER; NUCLA ELEMENTARY SCHOOL; BOX 244; NUCLA, CO 81424. (#14836).

NATURITA SCHOOLHOUSE RESTORATION IN NUCLA, CO. A PROJECT TO MOVE THE OLD NATURITA SCHOOLHOUSE TO A NEW LOCATION IN NATURITA PARK; BUILDING WOULD HOUSE THE WESTERN MONTROSE COUNTY LIBRARY AND RIMROCKER HISTORICAL SOCIETY MUSEUM. (LOCAL). MRS JEAN ZATTERSON, TREASURER; RIMROCKER HISTORICAL SOCIETY; NUCLA, CO 81424. (#10324).

NUCLA'S HISTORICAL BACKGROUND, CO. TO FURTHER THE CENTENNIAL-BICENTENNIAL CELEBRATION, NUCLA'S HISTORICAL BACKGROUND WILL BE PRESENTED TO THE SCHOOLS. (LOCAL). JOAN ELLIOT, PROJ MANAGER; WEST END TEACHER'S ASSOC; BOX 244; NUCLA, CO 81424. (#14835).

OCT 4, '75. NUCLA'S MARKET DAY. PRODUCE, CRAFTS & CANNED ITEMS WILL BE AUCTIONED. CHILI DINNER SERVED; BAKED GOODS SOLD. AT LAWN OF UNITED CHURCH OF CHRIST, NUCLA. (LOCAL). JOAN ELLIOTT, CHRM; UNITED CHURCH OF CHRIST; BOX 244; NUCLA, CO 81424. (#102106-1).

JUNE 14, '76. DEDICATION CEREMONY IN NUCLA TOWN PARK, FLAG DAY COMMEMORATION. DEDICATION OF THE REPLICA OF THE BELL TOWER IN THE NEW PARK, PRIZES WILL BE AWARDED TO THE WINNER OF THE TOWN FLAG CONTEST. DEDICATION OF PICNIC TABLES & GRILLS BUILT BY H S STUDENTS; FLAG DAY CELEBRATION & COMMEMORATION OF NEWLY PLANTED TREES. AT NUCLA TOWN PARK, SOUTH MAIN ST. (LOCAL). BETTY LANDON, COORD; NUCLA CENTENNIAL-BICENTENNIAL COMMITTEE; 960 GRAPE ST; NUCLA, CO 81424. (#14832-1).

JUNE 14 - 20, '76. NUCLA WATER WEEK. ACTIVITIES INCLUDE KING & QUEEN CONTEST, FILMS, HISTORICAL DISPLAYS, 'HUCK FINN DAY' 6/16; PARADE 6/19; BARBEQUE, FIREWORKS, GAMES, DANCING, TEAM ROPING, SPANISH SONGS & DANCES, FLAG DAY CEREMONY WITH AVENUE OF FLAGS, INDIAN CRAFTS & FOODS-QUILTING EXHIBIT. (LOCAL). MRS JOAN ELLIOT, COORD; NUCLA CENTENNIAL-BICENTENNIAL COMMITTEE; BOX 244; NUCLA, CO 81424. (#200007-135).

JUNE 15 - 17, '76. TOURS OF COLORADO COOPERATIVE COMPANY DITCH. PEOPLE TAKING TOURS WILL FURNISH OWN VEHICLES; LUNCH WILL BE SOLD BY CATHOLIC ALTAR SOCIETY. OLDSTERS WILL ACCOMPANY TOURS GIVING HISTORY OF DITCH. AT COLORADO COOPERATIVE COMPANY DITCH OFFICE, MAIN ST. (LOCAL). BUD BENSON, COORD; COLORADO COOPERATIVE COMPANY; NUCLA, CO 81424. (#14837-1).

OCT 2, '76. NUCLA'S MARKET DAY. IN NUCLA'S HISTORY, AN ANNUAL ACTION WAS HELD EACH FALL TO GIVE FARMER'S A MARKET FOR THEIR PRODUCE. THE NEW MARKET DAY IS BASED ON THAT IDEA. A LUNCH WILL BE SOLD, ALSO BAKED GOODS, ALL KINDS OF PRODUCE, SMALL ANIMALS AND POULTRY AND CANNED GOODS. AT LAWN OF UNITED CHURCH OF CHRIST. (LOCAL). KENT DAHLQUIST, DIRECTOR; UNITED CHURCH OF CHRIST; 1049 MONTANA WAY; NUCLA, CO 81424. (#108141-1).

NUNN

IMPROVING OUR TOWN - NUNN, CO. NEW LAWNS WILL BE PLANTED AND OLD BUILDINGS WILL BE TORN DOWN. (LOCAL). ILA DUBOIS, CHAIRWOMAN; NUNN CENTENNIAL-BICENTENNIAL COMMITTEE; PO BOX 171; NUNN, CO 80468. (#26189).

AUG 28, '76. NUNN HARVEST FESTIVAL. PARADE, GAMES, PICNIC, WHEAT THRESHING. (LOCAL). ILA DUBOIS, COORD; NUNN CENTENNIAL-BICENTENNIAL COMMISSION; BOX 11; NUNN, CO 80648. (#106253-1).

AUG '76. HISTORY OF THE COMMUNITY. THE HISTORY OF NUNN WILL BE READ. (LOCAL). ILA DUBOIS, COORD; HISTORICAL SOCIETY; PO BOX 171; NUNN, CO 80468. (#108764-1).

AUG '76. 'RELIVING THE PAST' - EXHIBIT. THERE WILL BE AN EXHIBIT ON WHEAT THRESHING. (LOCAL). ILA DUBOIS, COORD; HISTORICAL SOCIETY; PO BOX 171; NUNN, CO 80648. (#108764-3).

OLATHE

BROCHURE ON THE HISTORY OF OLATHE, CO. A TOWN BROCHURE W/GENERAL HISTORY & FACTS ABOUT THE COMMUNITY WILL BE PUBLISHED. (LOCAL). RHONDA DALEE, CHAIRMAN; OLATHE CENTENNIAL-BICENTENNIAL COMMITTEE; PO BOX 533; OLATHE, CO 81425. (#28624).

SEPT 11, '76. CENTENNIAL-BICENTENNIAL PARADE, CARNIVAL & PANCAKE SUPPER. FESTIVAL, PARADE AT OLATHE CITY PARK. (LOCAL). RHONDA DALEE, CHAIRMAN; CENTENNIAL-BICENTENNIAL COMMITTEE AND CHAMBER OF COMMERCE; PO BOX 533; OLATHE, CO 81425. (#200007-206).

OLNEY SPRINGS

'GREENING & CLEANING COLORADO' - OLNEY SPRINGS. INDIVIDUALS WILL CLEAN THE OWN YARDS; GROUPS WILL CLEAN ALONG THE STREETS AND PUBLIC AREAS. (LOCAL). BARBARA SANCHEZ, COORDINATOR; TOWN OF OLNEY SPRINGS; BOX 154; OLNEY SPRINGS, CO 81062. (#26899).

HISTORY OF OLNEY SPRINGS, CO. HISTORY OF OLNEY SPRINGS TO BE COMPILED THROUGH CONTACT WITH NUMEROUS SENIOR CITIZENS AND OTHER INTERESTED PARTIES. (LOCAL). DOWNIE BISHOP, COORDINATOR; CITY OF OLNEY SPRINGS; OLNEY SPRINGS, CO 81062. (#26850).

JOHN H COWDEN TWIN LAKES MEMORIAL GARDEN - CO. GARDEN WILL DEPICT THE TWIN LAKES WATER SYSTEM TO BE BUILT ON UNUSED SCHOOL GROUNDS. (LOCAL). TRUMAN J MCCLUNE, COORDINATOR; CITY OF OLNEY SPRINGS; OLNEY SPRINGS, CO 81062. (#25866).

AUG 1, '76. FIREWORKS. FIREWORK DISPLAY AT DEDICATION OF REVAMPED TOWN HALL PARK. (LOCAL). C GALBRAITH, CHMN; TOWN OF OLNEY SPRINGS; OLNEY SPRINGS, CO 81062. (#108955-26).

ORCHARD CITY

COLORADO CHRONICLES - ORCHARD CITY, CO. CEDAREDGE HIGH SCHOOL MEDIA CLASSES RESEARCHING & INTERVIEWING OLD TIMERS OF SURFACE CREEK VALLEY; PUBLISH BOOK AT END OF SCHOOL YEAR. (LOCAL). HON J CLARE DAVIS, MAYOR; CITY OF ORCHARD CITY; PO BOX 21; ORCHARD CITY, CO 81410. (#26347).

JULY 10, '76. SENIOR CITIZEN 1976. GATHER SENIOR CITIZENS FOR FESTIVAL TO HONOR OLDEST MALE & FEMALE; HAVE ALL DRESS IN PERIOD CLOTHING & PARTICIPATE IN EVENTS PERTAINING TO PERIOD; HONOR SURFACE CREEK VALLEY CENT-BICENTENNIAL SWEETHEART. AT CEDAREDGE PARK. (LOCAL). MARY LOU HUERKAMP; SURFACE CREEK VALLEY CENTENNIAL BICENTENNIAL COMMITTEE; P O BOX 65; AUSTIN, CO 81410. (#108705-1).

ORDWAY

PARK IMPROVEMENT - ORDWAY, CO. PARK WILL BE NAMED AND PICNIC TABLES ADDED, SHRUBS PLANTED, BARBEQUE PIT BUILT AND DIRECTIONAL SIGNS ON THE STREETS TO INFORM TRAVELERS. FIRE HYDRANTS WILL BE PAINTED RED, WHITE & BLUE. (LOCAL). JOANNE BAIER, CHAIRMAN; CENTENNIAL-BICENTENNIAL COMMITTEE OF ORDWAY; 725 N MAIN; ORDWAY, CO 81063. (#26258).

JULY 4, '76. FIREWORKS DISPLAY. FESTIVAL AT ORDWAY LANDING STRIP. (LOCAL). JOANNE BAIER, CHAIRMAN; ORDWAY VOLUNTEER FIREMEN; 725 N MAIN ST; ORDWAY, CO 81063. (#108594-1).

OTIS

JULY 3, '76. CHILDREN'S RACES. COMPETITION, FESTIVAL AT WASHINGTON ST. (LOCAL). RONALD S HUEY, SECRETARY; OTIS CENTENNIAL-BICENTENNIAL COMMITTEE; BOX 168; OTIS, CO 80743. (#108596-3).

JULY 3, '76. COMMUNITY PARADE. PARADE AT WASHINGTON ST. (LOCAL). RONALD S HUEY, SECRETARY; OTIS CENTENNIAL-BICENTENNIAL COMMITTEE; BOX 168; OTIS, CO 80743. (#108596-4).

JULY 3, '76. HORSESHOE PITCHING CONTEST. COMPETITION AT BANK PARKING LOT. (LOCAL). RONALD S HUEY, SECRETARY; OTIS CENTENNIAL-BICENTENNIAL COMMITTEE; BOX 168; OTIS, CO 80743. (#108596-2).

JULY 3, '76. SENIOR CITIZENS KING & QUEEN CONTEST AND PARADE. COMPETITION, PARADE AT WASHINGTON ST. (LOCAL). RONALD S HUEY, SECRETARY; OTIS CENTENNIAL-BICENTENNIAL COMMITTEE; BOX 168; OTIS, CO 80743. (#108596-5).

JULY 3 - 4, '76. MUSIC PROGRAM. LIVE PERFORMANCE AT HIGH SCHOOL AUDITORIUM. (LOCAL). RONALD S HUEY, SECRETARY; OTIS CENTENNIAL-BICENTENNIAL COMMITTEE; BOX 168; OTIS, CO 80743. (#108596-1).

JULY 4, '76. CENTENNIAL FIREWORKS. FESTIVAL AT FOOTBALL FIELD. (LOCAL). RONALD S HUEY, SECRETARY; OTIS CENTENNIAL-BICENTENNIAL COMMITTEE & OTIS FIRE DEPT; BOX 168; OTIS, CO 80743. (#108596-6).

OURAY

COLORADO CHRONICLES & ESSAY CONTEST ON HISTORY. SET UP SECTION IN TOWN LIBRARY TO COMMEMORATE AND RECORD MINING DISTRICT & TOWN HISTORY INCLUDING TOM WALSH & CAMP BIRD MINE. (LOCAL). WALDO D BUTLER, CHAIRPERSON; OURAY CENTENNIAL-BICENTENNIAL COMMITTEE; PO BOX 1976; OURAY, CO 81427. (#26348).

'GREENING AND CLEANING COLORADO' - OURAY. THE OLD OURAY DUMP ON U S HWY 550 IS BEING CLEANED AND LANDSCAPED. (LOCAL). JACK L BENHAM, COORDINATOR; CHAMBER OF COMMERCE, CITY COUNCIL & BOY SCOUTS; PO BOX 254; OURAY, CO 81427. (#26267).

HISTORY BOOK OF OURAY, COLORADO. ILLUSTRATED HISTORY BOOK; RECOLLECTIONS OF JUDGE RATHMELL ON EARLY DAYS AS RECORDED IN HIS DIARY AND BY HIS DAUGHTER. (ST-WIDE). JOYCE JORGENSEN; OURAY CENTENNIAL-BICENTENNIAL COMMITTEE; 540 8TH AVENUE; OURAY, CO 81427. (#4121).

REDESIGN CITY PARK, OURAY, CO. CONSTRUCTION OF MULTIPLE USE FACILITIES AT CITY PARK FOR BASEBALL, TENNIS, TRACK, WALKING & BIKE PATHS. ADJACENT TO OUTDOOR SWIMMING POOL AND BATH HOUSE. (LOCAL). ROBERT LARSON, CHMN; CITY OF OURAY; PANORAMIC HEIGHTS; OURAY, CO 81427. (#4124).

RESTORATION OF BUILDING FACADES - OURAY, COLO. REPLACING ORIGINAL DESIGN OF LIBRARY AND CITY HALL WHICH WAS DESTROYED BY FIRE IN 1950 TO FRONT OF PRESENT STRUCTURE. (LOCAL). WALDO D BUTLER, CHAIRMAN; OURAY CENTENNIAL-BICENTENNIAL COMMITTEE; PO BOX 147; OURAY, CO 81427. (#4357).

SPECIAL ARTISTS' ALPINE HOLIDAY - COLORADO. WEEK OF ART COMPETITION WITH SPECIAL HISTORICAL CATEGORY KEYED TO CENTENNIAL IN 1975 AND 1976. (LOCAL). WERNER HENZE, MEMBER; OURAY CENTENNIAL-BICENTENNIAL COMMITTEE; C/O BOX 147; OURAY, CO 81427. (#4356). **ARBA GRANTEE.**

WALSH LIBRARY FACADE RESTORATION - OURAY, COLO. TO RESTORE FACADE OF OURAY CITY HALL AND WALSH LIBRARY BLDG TO ORIGINAL STATE AS REPRODUCTION OF INDEPENDENCE HALL. (ST-WIDE). WALTER RULE, JR, CHAIRMAN; WALSH LIBRARY BLDG RESTORATION CORP; PO BOX 1976; OURAY, CO 81427. (#4422).

JAN 1 - DEC 31, '76. YEAR 'ROUND SPORTS ACTIVITIES ACCELERATED FOR CENTENNIAL YEAR. SWIMMING IN MUNICIPAL POOL, SKI TOURING; DOWNHILL SKIING AT NEARBY RESORTS, SLEIGH RIDES, HAY RIDES, HUNTING, FISHING, JEEP-TOURING, CAMPING, MOUNTAIN CLIMBING, HIKING, HORSEBACK RIDING. SPONSOR PLANS INCOMPLETE AS OF 4-7-75. AT VARIOUS, THROUGHOUT OURAY COUNTY DEPENDING ON ACTIVITY. (LOCAL). ROBERT JINDRA; OURAY COUNTY CHAMBER OF COMMERCE; PO BOX 663; OURAY, CO 81427. (#4122-1).

APR 3, '76. OURAY CENTENNIAL FANCY DRESS BALL. FESTIVAL AT ELKS LODGE HALL. (LOCAL). PATRICIA SOWBY, CHAIRMAN; OURAY CENTENNIAL BALL COMMITTEE; 333 6TH AVE; OURAY, CO 81427. (#105070-1).

MAY 29 - OCT 31, '76. WALKING TOURS OF HISTORIC BUILDINGS DURING OURAY CENTENNIAL YEAR. SELF-GUIDED WALKING TOUR OF VICTORIAN ERA HOMES, BUSINESS & PUBLIC BUILDINGS OF OURAY IN ITS CENTENNIAL YEAR AS A CITY. GUIDE BOOK TO BE AVAILABLE. AT INFORMATON CENTER NEXT TO SWIMMING POOL. (LOCAL). WALTER RULE, JR; OURAY CENTENNIAL BICENTENNIAL COMMITTEE; 615 4TH ST; OURAY, CO 81427. (#4125-1).

JUNE 1 - SEPT 30, '76. COLOR SLIDE SHOWS TO EMPHASIZE HISTORY OF SAN JUAN MTNS, NIGHTLY. NIGHTLY COLOR SLIDE SHOWS TO FEATURE HISTORY OF SAN JUAN MOUNTAINS, OLD MINES AND GHOST TOWNS DURING SUMMER OF OURAY'S AND COLORADO'S CENTENNIAL YEAR. AT WRIGHT OPERA HOUSE BUILDING. (LOCAL). FRANCES KUBOSKE; SAN JUAN SCENIC JEEP TOURS; 512 MAIN STREET; OURAY, CO 81427. (#4127-1).

JULY 3, '76. MINING DAY. LIVE PERFORMANCE, FESTIVAL. (LOCAL). WALDO D BUTLER, COORD; OURAY CENTENNIAL-BICENTENNIAL COMMITTEE; PO BOX 147; OURAY, CO 81427. (#108597-1).

JULY 3 - 4, '76. OLD-FASHIONED INDEPENDENCE DAY CONTESTS AND FESTIVITIES. OLD FASHIONED CONTESTS FOR ALL AGES INCLUDING MINING CONTESTS JULY 3 & FIRE HOSE FIGHTS, STREET GAMES & RACES, FIREWORKS AND FLARE PARADE DOWN SWITCHBACKS OF MOUNTAIN HIGHWAY IN 200 FOUR-WHEEL-DRIVE VEHICLES ON JULY 4. AT MAIN STREET, OURAY CITY PARK, OURAY COUNTY MUSEUM. (LOCAL). DONALD DOUGHERTY; OURAY VOLUNTEER FIRE DEPARTMENT; 790 OAK STREET; OURAY, CO 81427. (#4358-1).

JULY 4, '76. HISTORICAL JULY 4 PARADE COMMEMORATING OURAY'S CENTENNIAL YEAR. PROCESSION OF PACK TRAIN, ORE WAGON, STAGECOACH, HISTORIC FLOATS LED BY HORSEBACK FIGURES REPRESENTING SPANISH EXPLORERS ESCALANTE & DOMINGUEZ WHO PASSED THIS AREA IN 1776. AT MAIN STREET, US HIGHWAY 550. (LOCAL). JACK CLARK, SR; OURAY VOLUNTEER FIRE DEPARTMENT; 790 OAK STREET; OURAY, CO 81427. (#4126-1).

JULY 15 - AUG 19, '76. LECTURE SERIES ON MINING AND METHODS IN THE ROCKIES. SIX WEEKLY MINING HISTORY LECTURES OF SOUTHWESTERN COLORADO ROCKIES TO BE HELD THURSDAYS AT 8PM JULY 15 TO AUG 19 AND TO INCLUDE COLORADO SCHOOL OF MINES TRAVELLING EXHIBIT DURING WEEK OF JULY 15 TO 22, 2PM TO 9PM. AT OURAY CITY HALL AUDITORIUM. (ST-WIDE). WALDO D BUTLER; OURAY CENTENNIAL COMMITTEE; PO BOX 147; OURAY, CO 81427. (#4129-1).

AUG 8 - 14, '76. SPECIAL ARTISTS ALPINE HOLIDAY. ANNUAL WEEK LONG ART COMPETITION AND EXHIBIT TO FEATURE SPECIAL CATEGORY EMPHASIZING HISTORY OF COLORADO AND SAN JUAN MOUNTAINS IN CENTENNIAL YEAR OF COLORADO AND OURAY. AT OURAY HIGH SCHOOL GYMNASIUM. (ST-WIDE). ELAINE MUNZING; OURAY COUNTY ARTS COUNCIL; RURAL ROUTE 1; RIDGWAY, CO 81432. (#4356-1).

SEPT 4 - 6, '76. OURAY COUNTY FAIR & RODEO. COMPETITION, FAIR. (ST-WIDE). ROBERT MIDDLETON, COORD; COUNTY FAIR COMMITTEE; RFD 2, BOX 300; COLONA, CO 81427. (#108763-2).

SEPT 5 - 11, '76. OURAY PORTION OF SAN JUAN HISTORIC TOURS. SELF GUIDED TOURS BY FOUR-WHEEL-DRIVE VEHICLES, TRAIL BIKES, OR BACK PACKING COVERING 6 SEPARATE ROUTES ON SUCCESSIVE WEEKS IN AUG & SEPT OF 1976 TO OLD MINES, GHOST TOWNS, ABANDONED NARROW GAUGE, RAILROAD ROUTES IN 5 COUNTIES OF SAN JUAN MOUNTAINS. AT INFORMATION CENTER BESIDE SWIMMING POOL. (ST-WIDE). ROBERT ZIMMER; OURAY CO BICENTENNIAL COMMITTEE & CHAMBER OF COMMERCE; 6TH AVE & 5TH ST; OURAY, CO 81427. (#4101-1).

SEPT 19 - 26, '76. EXHIBIT OF HISTORIC PHOTOS INCLUDING COLORADO ON GLASS EXHIBIT. EXHIBIT TO FEATURE 100 YEARS OF PHOTOGRAPHY IN SAN JUAN MOUNTAINS TO CELEBRATE CENTENNIAL YEAR FOR OURAY AND COLORADO AND WILL INCLUDE 'COLORADO ON GLASS EXHIBIT' OF STATE HISTORICAL SOCIETY. AT OURAY CITY HALL AUDITORIUM. (ST-WIDE). WALDO D BUTLER; OURAY CENTENNIAL COMMITTEE; PO BOX 147; OURAY, CO 81427. (#4128-1).

PAGOSA SPG

GREENBELT ON THE SAN JUAN RIVER - PAGOSA SPG, CO. CREATION OF A GREENBELT ALONG THE SAN JUAN RIVER. (LOCAL). LOREN W ALEXANDER, CHAIRMAN; PAGOSA SPRINGS CENTENNIAL-BICENTENNIAL COMMITTEE; PO BOX 457; PAGOSA SPG, CO 81147. (#24597).

MARKING OF HISTORICAL SITES - PAGOSA SPRINGS, CO. MARK SCENIC DRIVES AND POINTS OF HISTORIC INTEREST IN PAGOSA SPRINGS. (LOCAL). LOREN W ALEXANDER, CHAIRMAN; PAGOSA SPRINGS CENTENNIAL-BICENTENNIAL COMMITTEE; PO BOX 457; PAGOSA SPG, CO 81147. (#24598).

NARROW GUAGE RAILROAD - PAGOSA SPRINGS, CO. MAPPING OF OLD RAILROAD ROUTES. (LOCAL). EARL MULLINS, CHAIRMAN; SAN JUAN HISTORICAL SOCIETY; PO BOX 456; PAGOSA SPG, CO 81147. (#24596).

PAGOSA HOT SPRING & ORIGINAL FORT LEWIS - CO. COMPILE A HISTORY AND DESIGNATE 'PAGOSA HOT SPRING' AS A HISTORIC SITE; ALSO, FIND AND MARK ANY REMAINS OF THE ORIGINAL FORT LEWIS. (LOCAL). EARL MULLINS, CHAIRMAN; SAN JUAN HISTORICAL SOCIETY; PO BOX 456; PAGOSA SPG, CO 81147. (#24595).

PAGOSA SPRINGS, CO, HISTORICAL MUSEUM. A HISTORICAL MUSEUM WITH VISUAL SLIDE TOUR OF SITES AND A RECORDED COMMENTARY BY OLDTIMERS; WILL ALSO HOUSE HISTORIC ARTIFACTS. (LOCAL). EARL MULLINS, CHAIRMAN; SAN JUAN HISTORICAL SOCIETY; PO BOX 456; PAGOSA SPG, CO 81147. (#24594).

MAY 1 - SEPT 30, '76. CHIMNEY ROCK TOURS. EACH YEAR MORE INDIAN RUINS AT THE SITE ARE BING CLEARED AND RESTORED FOR VIEWING. AT TOWN PARK, OFF U S 160. (LOCAL). LOREN W ALEXANDER, CHMN; PAGOSA SPRINGS CHAMBER OF COMMERCE; PO BOX 457; PAGOSA SPG, CO 81147. (#107171-6).

JUNE 18, '76. SENIOR CITIZEN'S BALL. ACTIVITIES TO INCLUDE HONORING OF ELDEST MAN AND WOMAN. AT TRAILS CLUBHOUSE, OFF U S 160. (LOCAL). LOREN W ALEXANDER, CHMN; SENIOR CITIZENS OF PAGOSA SPRINGS; PO BOX 457; PAGOSA SPG, CO 81147. (#107171-4).

JULY 4, '76. 4TH OF JULY FIREWORKS DISPLAY. FESTIVAL AT CITY PARK, OFF U S 160. (LOCAL). LOREN W ALEXANDER, CHMN; PAGOSA SPRINGS JAYCEES; PO BOX 457; PAGOSA SPG, CO 81147. (#107171-3).

JULY 4, '76. 4TH OF JULY PARADE. PARADE AT MAIN ST. (LOCAL). LOREN W ALEXANDER, CHMN; PAGOSA SPRINGS JAYCEES; PO BOX 457; PAGOSA SPG, CO 81147. (#107171-2).

AUG 1 - 3, '76. RELIVING THE PAST. PAGEANT WILL DEPICT PAST EVENTS PERTAINING TO LOCAL HISTORY. (LOCAL). LOREN W ALEXANDER, COORD; TOWN OF PAGOSA SPRINGS; BOX 457; PAGOSA SPG, CO 81147. (#108955-25).

AUG 5 - 6, '76. ESCALANTE TRAIL SITE DESIGNATION. ON AUGUST 5, 1976 THE ESCALANTE EXPLORATORY EXPEDITION ENTERED COLORADO BY WAY OF ARCHULETA COUNTY; WE WILL DESIGNATE THE TRAIL SITE. (LOCAL). LOREN W ALEXANDER, CHMN; SAN JAUN HISTORICAL SOCIETY; PO BOX 457; PAGOSA SPG, CO 81147. (#107171-5).

AUG 7, '76. HISTORICAL PAGEANT. HAS FOUR SCENES: 1-LEGEND OF HOT SPRINGS; 2-ESCALANTE EXPEDITION; 3-PEIFFER DUEL (BETWEEN COLONEL PEIFFER & THE INDIANS); & 4-PAGOSA SPRINGS IN THE 1920'S. AT ELEMENTARYS SCHOOLS GROUNDS. (LOCAL). LOREN W ALEXANDER, CHMN; PAGOS PLAYERS & FESTIVAL USA COMMITTEE; PO BOX 457; PAGOSA SPG, CO 81147. (#107171-1).

PALISADE

JULY 4, '76. ANNUAL PALISADE FIREMEN'S FOURTH OF JULY CELEBRATION. COMPETITION, FESTIVAL, PARADE AT CITY PARK. (LOCAL). HOMER L SMITH, CHMN; PALISADE VOLUNTEER FIRE DEPT; BOX 631; PALISADE, CO 81526. (#108592-1).

JULY 31, '76. PALISADE PEACH FESTIVAL. FESTIVAL, PARADE AT TOWN PARK. (LOCAL). HOMER L SMITH, CHAIRMAN; PALISADE CHAMBER OF COMMERCE; BOX 631; PALISADE, CO 81526. (#108709-1).

PALMER LAKE

CHRISTMAS STAR ON SUNDANCE MOUNTAIN IN COLORADO. THIS IS A RE-BUILDING OF 5-POINTED STAR, 500' FROM POINT TO POINT, FIRST BUILT IN 1934. THE STAR IS ILLUMINATED EACH YEAR DURING THE MONTH OF DECEMBER. (LOCAL). COLONEL CARL F DUFFNER, CHAIRMAN; PALMER LAKE CENTENNIAL-BICENTENNIAL COMMITTEE; PO BOX 96; PALMER LAKE, CO 80133. (#28623).

PAOLI

CENTENNIAL MEETING HALL OF PAOLI, COLO. REMODELING OF PAOLI TOWN HALL INCLUDING PANELING WALLS, CARPETING, ERECTING OUTSIDE FLOWER BOXES. TOWN HALL WAS FORMERLY THE PAOLI STATE BANK, BUILT IN 1919 AND A POPULAR MEETING PLACE OF AREA TOWNS. (LOCAL). MARILYN MILLER, CHAIRMAN; PAOLI TOWN COUNCIL; BOX 134; PAOLI, CO 80746. (#4485). **(??).**

4-H CENTENNIAL PARK OF PAOLI, COLORADO. TOWN PARK TO BE RE-LANDSCAPED WITH VARIETY OF SHRUBS, FENCING AND PLAYGROUND EQUIPMENT IN HONOR OF CENTENNIAL-BICENTENNIAL. (LOCAL). MELINDA S MILLER, PRESIDENT; 4-H COUNCIL; BOX 134; PAOLI, CO 80746. (#4487).

JUNE 19 - 20, '76. HORSE SHOE PITCHING CONTEST. PAOLI TO SPONSER HORSESHOE PITCHING CONTEST WITH ENTRY FEE AND ADDED PURSE. IT IS HOPED THAT ENTHUSIASM WILL MAKE THIS AN ANNUAL EVENT. AT PAOLI HUSTLERS 4-H CENTENNIAL COMMUNITY PARK. (LOCAL). VERNE E MILLER; PAOLI BICENTENNIAL COMMITTEE; PO BOX 5647; PAOLI, CO 80746. (#4484-1).

JULY 4, '76. FIREWORKS CELEBRATION. FESTIVAL. (LOCAL). MARILYN MILLER, COORD; PAOLI FIREWORKS COMMITTEE; BOX 134; PAOLI, CO 80746. (#108587-1).

PAONIA

CULTURAL INVESTIGATION OF INDIANS - PAONIA, CO. AS LITTLE IS KNOWN OF FORMER RESIDENTS OF THIS AREA, HERITAGE COMMITTEE WILL GATHER & PUBLISH MATERIAL ABOUTS INDIANS FOR SUMMER OF 1976. (LOCAL). WALLACE D EUBANKS, CHAIRPERSON; PAONIA CENTENNIAL-BICENTENNIAL COMMITTEE; DRAWER O; PAONIA, CO 81428. (#26342).

IMPROVEMENT OF HISTORICAL MUSEUM - PAONIA, CO. IMPROVE AND ENLARGE HISTORICAL MUSEUM TO ENABLE LARGER USE BY THE COMMUNITY AND SCHOOLS. (LOCAL). MISS EDNA CAMPBELL, CHAIRMAN; NORTH FORK HISTORICAL SOCIETY; HOTCHKISS, CO 81419. (#18621).

MARKING DOMINGUEZ ESCALANTE EXPEDITION TRAIL - CO. PLACING OF ROAD SIGNS LOCATING CAMPSITES AND ROUTE OF DOMINGUEZ ESCALANTE EXPEDITION OF 1776. (LOCAL). W D EUBANKS, PRESIDENT; NORTH FORK HISTORICAL SOCIETY; PAONIA, CO 81428. (#18622).

TOWN SWIMMING POOL - PAONIA, CO. CONSTRUCTION OF APPROPRIATE SWIMMING-POOL FOR CITIZEN AND STUDENT USE. (LOCAL). CARL CLAY, CHAIRMAN; PAONIA CENTENNIAL-BICENTENNIAL COMMITTEE; PAONIA, CO 81428. (#18623).

JULY 5, '75. OPEN HORSE SHOW. THE SHOW WILL FEATURE GYMKHANA AND HORSE SHOW ACTIVITIES AND 4-H ACTIVITIES. AT SOUTHWEST OF PAONIA ON MATTHEWS LANE AT HORSE PATROL ARENA. (LOCAL). MRS TERI NOEL, COORD; 'THE NORTH FORK BUCKAROOS', PAONIA 4-H HORSE PROJECT CLUB; RT 1; PAONIA, CO 81428. (#103946-1).

FEB 10, '76. PARENT-TEACHERS-STUDENTS ASSOC-CULTURAL ARTS NIGHT. EXHIBIT AT PAONIA HIGH SCHOOL AUDITORIUM. (LOCAL). MRS CLAUDIA KING, PRES; PARENT TEACHERS-STUDENTS ASSOCIATION; PAONIA, CO 81428. (#103946-4).

MAR 1 - JULY 31, '76. EXHIBIT OF ORIGINAL REMINGTON BRONZE SCULPTURE. EXHIBIT AT FIRST NATIONAL BANK, PAONIA, CO. (LOCAL). WALLACE D EUBANKS, CHMN; PAONIA CENTENNIAL-BICENTENNIAL COMMITTEE; DRAWER O; PAONIA, CO 81428. (#108762-1).

APR 1 - AUG 15, '76. ORIGINAL REMINGTON ART EXHIBIT. EXHIBIT AT BANK LOBBY. (LOCAL). LADDIE LIVINGSTON, COORD; FIRST NATIONAL BANK; PAONIA, CO 81428. (#103946-3).

MAY 7, '76. MAY FETE WITH 200 CHILDREN'S VOICES. LIVE PERFORMANCE AT PAONIA HIGH SCHOOL AUDITORIUM. (LOCAL). MRS CLAUDIA KING, COORD; PAONIA PRIMARY SCHOOLS; PAONIA, CO 81428. (#103946-5).

JULY 1 - SEPT ??, '76. PHOTO EXHIBITION. 1500 GLASS NEGATIVES OF LOCAL AREA FROM 1905-1915 WILL BE EXHIBITED. AT NORTH FORK HISTORICAL MUSEUM, PAONIA. (LOCAL). WALLACE D EUBANKS, CHMN; PAONIA CENTENNIAL-BICENTENNIAL COMMITTEE; DRAWER O; PAONIA, CO 81428. (#108824-1).

JULY 2 - 5, '76. PAONIA CENTENNIAL-BICENTENNIAL CHERRY DAY FESTIVAL. JULY 3RD, THE NORTH FORK BUCKAROOS WILL HAVE A PUBLIC DISPLAY ON GRAND AVENUE WHICH WILL BE FREE. AT TOWN WIDE. (LOCAL). CHARLES COLE, PROJ CHMN; PAONIA CHAMBER OF COMMERCE; PAONIA, CO 81428. (#103946-2).

JULY 3, '76. JULY 3RD FESTIVAL. COUNTRY STORE WITH CRAFTS DISPLAYED & FOR SALE, BIKE RODEO, CLOWN TEAM, OPEN HORSE SHOW, MELODRAMA, SQUARE DANCE, ART EXHIBIT

PAONIA — CONTINUED

AND CARNIVAL TO BE FEATURED. (LOCAL). WALLACE D EUBANKS, CHMN; PAONIA CENTENNIAL-BICENTENNIAL COMMITTEE; PO BOX O; PAONIA, CO 81428. (#108590-1).

JULY 4, '76. BICENTENNIAL CARNIVAL. FESTIVAL. (LOCAL). WALLACE D EUBANKS, CHMN; PAONIA CENTENNIAL-BICENTENNIAL COMMITTEE; PO BOX O; PAONIA, CO 81428. (#108590-2).

JULY 4, '76. COMMUNITY SING & PATRIOTIC SPEECH. FESTIVAL. (LOCAL). WALLACE D EUBANKS, CHMN; PAONIA CENTENNIAL-BICENTENNIAL COMMITTEE; PO BOX O; PAONIA, CO 81428. (#108590-7).

JULY 4, '76. FIREWORKS DISPLAY. FESTIVAL. (LOCAL). WALLACE D EUBANKS, CHMN; PAONIA CENTENNIAL-BICENTENNIAL COMMITTEE; PO BOX O; PAONIA, CO 81428. (#108590-6).

JULY 4, '76. HIGH SCHOOL REUNION. FESTIVAL. (LOCAL). WALLACE D EUBANKS, CHMN; PAONIA CENTENNIAL-BICENTENNIAL COMMITTEE; PO BOX O; PAONIA, CO 81428. (#108590-3).

JULY 5, '76. BICENTENNIAL DANCE. FESTIVAL. (LOCAL). WALLACE D EUBANKS, CHMN; PAONIA CENTENNIAL-BICENTENNIAL COMMITTEE; PO BOX O; PAONIA, CO 81428. (#108590-11).

JULY 5, '76. CHUCK WAGON DINNER. FESTIVAL. (LOCAL). WALLACE D EUBANKS, CHMN; PAONIA CENTENNIAL-BICENTENNIAL COMMITTEE; PO BOX O; PAONIA, CO 81428. (#108590-10).

JULY 5, '76. COMMUNITY GAMES. FESTIVAL. (LOCAL). WALLACE D EUBANKS, CHMN; PAONIA CENTENNIAL-BICENTENNIAL COMMITTEE; PO BOX O; PAONIA, CO 81428. (#108590-8).

JULY 5, '76. PANCAKE BREAKFAST. FESTIVAL. (LOCAL). WALLACE D EUBANKS, CHMN; PAONIA CENTENNIAL-BICENTENNIAL COMMITTEE; PO BOX O; PAONIA, CO 81428. (#108590-5).

JULY 5, '76. PARADE. PARADE. (LOCAL). WALLACE D EUBANKS, CHMN; PAONIA CENTENNIAL-BICENTENNIAL COMMITTEE; PO BOX O; PAONIA, CO 81428. (#108590-4).

JULY 5, '76. TALENT SHOW. LIVE PERFORMANCE. (LOCAL). WALLACE D EUBANKS, CHMN; PAONIA CENTENNIAL-BICENTENNIAL COMMITTEE; PO BOX O; PAONIA, CO 81428. (#108590-9).

AUG 4, '76. REGISTERED QUARTER HORSE SHOW. COMPETITION, FESTIVAL AT 4-H RODEO GROUNDS. (ST-WIDE). MRS AUSTIN HALL; NORTH FORK HORSE PATROL; MISSOURI FLATS; CRAWFORD, CO 81415. (#104669-1).

PARKER

PARKER, CO, LIBRARY. THE ORIGINAL METHODIST CHURCH CHAPEL WILL BE MOVED AND CONVERTED INTO A LIBRARY. (LOCAL). PAULINE HODGES, CHAIRPERSON; DOUGLAS COUNTY CENTENNIAL-BICENTENNIAL COMMITTEE; CASTLE ROCK, CO 80104. (#24569).

RESTORATION OF OLD FONDER SCHOOL, PARKER, CO. FIRST SCHOOL IN AREA, A GIFT OF $3000 WAS MADE BY THE PINERY TO HANDLE EXPENSES OF RESTORATION. (LOCAL). PAULINE HODGES, CHAIRPERSON; DOUGLAS COUNTY CENTENNIAL-BICENTENNIAL COMMITTEE; CASTLE ROCK, CO 80104. (#24571).

JULY 4 - 7, '75. PONY EXPRESS RELAY RACE. FESTIVAL. (REGN'L). PAULINE HODGES, CHWMN; DOUGLAS COUNTY CENTENNIAL-BICENTENNIAL COMMITTEE; CASTLE ROCK, CO 80104. (#107885-1).

JULY 4, '76. OLD-FASHIONED 4TH OF JULY CELEBRATED ON THE SMOKEY HILL TRAIL. SMOKEY HILL TRAIL WAS USED AS THE PONY EXPRESS & GENERAL TRAIL FROM THE SOUTHEAST; SOME ACTIVITIES ARE AS FOLLOWS: PONY EXPRESS RACES, GREASED PIG CONTEST, TOBACCO SPITTING, HORSE RIDING, FIREWORKS AND DANCE. AT PINERY ARENA, 7 MILES SOUTH OF PARKE. (LOCAL). LEROY R NITSCH, V-PRES; DOUGLAS COUNTY JAYCEES; 567 S LAKE GULCH RD SEDC; CASTLE ROCK, CO 80104. (#107013-1).

PEETZ

CENTENNI-MENTAL MEMORIES - PEETZ, CO. MURAL WILL BE PAINTED ON ARTS BUILDING WALL, DEPICTING 8 FT FARMER, SUPERIMPOSED ON A MAP. (LOCAL). DOLORES NELSON, CO-CHAIRMAN; 'FOR PEETZ SAKE, LET'S BE CENTENNI-MENTAL'; RD 74 18852; PEETZ, CO 80747. (#26674).

CLEANUP-GREEN UP - PEETZ, CO. PLANTING OF TREES IN LOCAL CEMETERY, CLEANUP OF AREA BY FARMERS UNION, JR VOLUNTEER PAINT UP OF TOWN PARK, TABLES, TRASH BARRELS, FIRE HYDRANTS; LIONS CLUB IN CHARGE OF CEMETERY. (LOCAL). DOLORES NELSON, CO-CHAIRPERSON; 'FOR PEETZ SAKE, LET'S BE CENTENNI-MENTAL'; RD 74 18852; PEETZ, CO 80747. (#26676).

RE-DEDICATION OF STREETS IN VETERAN'S NAMES - CO. AMERICAN LEGION PUT UP NEW STREET SIGNS TO DEDICATE STREETS TO VETERANS. (LOCAL). DOLORES NELSON, CO-CHAIRPERSON; BICENTENNIAL COMMITTEE & AMERICAN LEGION; MAIN ST; PEETZ, CO 80747. (#26675).

AUG 1, '76. ARTS FESTIVAL. DISPLAY PAINTINGS OF LOCAL ARTISTS, EXHIBIT OF ANTIQUES & TOOLS USED BY HOMESTEADERS. (LOCAL). JACOB B ELENZ, COORD; 'FOR PEETZ SAKES LET'S BE CENTENI-MENTAL'; BOX 225; PEETZ, CO 80747. (#108955-49).

AUG 1, '76. AUGUST CELEBRATION. PARADE TO HONOR SENIOR CITIZENS, OLD-FASHIONED GAMES, HORSESHOE CONTEST, COUNTRY STORE, ARTS & CRAFTS AND INDIAN ARTIFACTS EXHIBIT. AT MAIN ST. (LOCAL). DOLORES NELSON, CO-CHMN; PEETZ CENTENNIAL-BICENTENNIAL COMMITTEE; RD 74 18852; PEETZ, CO 80747. (#108921-3).

AUG 1, '76. AUGUST PARADE. RECOGNIZING SENIOR CITIZENS & DRESS THAT WAS COMMON IN EARLY SETTLER DAYS. (LOCAL). JACOB B ELENZ, COORD; TOWN OF PEETZ; BOX 225; PEETZ, CO 80747. (#108955-24).

AUG 1, '76. CLEAN-UP & PAINT-UP DAY. PICK UP TRASH & PAINT WATER-PUMP SHEDS, STOP SIGN POSTS & FIRE HYDRANTS. (LOCAL). JACOB B ELENZ, COORD; TOWN OF PEETZ; BOX 225; PEETZ, CO 80747. (#108955-23).

AUG 1, '76. FLOWER AND VEGETABLE GARDEN DISPLAY. FLOWER & VEGETABLE DISPLAYS AND NEEDLEWORK DEMONSTRATIONS. AT FIRE HOUSE, MAIN ST. (LOCAL). VELMA HAWKINS, COORD; PEETZ GARDEN CLUB; RD 74 18852; PEETZ, CO 80747. (#108921-2).

AUG 1, '76. OLD-TIME SING-A-LONG AND WESTERN DANCE. HONKY TONK PIANO PLAYER, FAKE SHOOTOUT, SING-A-LONG, FRANKIE AND JOHNNY DRAMA, WESTERN SQUARE & ROUND DANCING WILL BE INCLUDED. AT HOT SPOT, MAIN ST. (LOCAL). DON GIANTZ, COORD; BICENTENNIAL COMMITTEE AND HOT SPOT TAVERN; HOT SPOT TAVERN; PEETZ, CO 80747. (#108921-1).

PERRY PARK

AUG 1, '76. BARBEQUE & 4-H HORSE SHOW. FESTIVAL AT PERRY PARK RANCH HEADQUARTERS. (LOCAL). JACK LARUE, COORD; DOUGLAS COUNTY CENTENNIAL-BICENTENNIAL COMMITTEE; 4876 RED ROCK DR; LARKSPUR, CO 80118. (#106987-1).

PETERSON AFB

BICENTENNIAL DISPLAY - PETERSON AFB, CO. FLAG DISPLAY OF 15 ORIGINAL FLAGS FROM THE COLONIAL ERA. (LOCAL). COL EDWARD L ELLIS, BASE COMMANDER; PETERSON FIELD/ENT AFB; 46 AERODW/CVE; PET F/ENT AFB, CO 80914. (#29160).

PIERCE

SIGN COMMEMORATING DENVER PACIFIC RAILROAD - CO. SIGN HONORS THE RAILROAD'S HISTORIC IMPORTANCE IN THE DEVELOPMENT OF PIERCE AND THE PRAIRIE; TOWNSPEOPLE WILL DO AREA LANDSCAPING & PICNIC FACILITIES WILL BE DEVELOPED. (LOCAL). LEONA BRUMFIELD, CHAIRMAN; PIERCE CENTENNIAL-BICENTENNIAL COMMISSION; 5TH & MAIN; PIERCE, CO 80650. (#24587).

FEB 22, '76. BICENTENNIAL FLAG PRESENTATION. PIERCE WILL RECEIVE ITS BICENTENNIAL FLAG DURING A CEREMONY WHICH WILL INCLUDE PERFORMANCES BY SCHOOL CHORUS AND BAND, SPEECH BY SENATOR HANK BROWN. AT HIGH SCHOOL CAFETERIA, 2ND AND JONES. (LOCAL). LEONA BRUMFIELD, CHMN; PIERCE CENTENNIAL-BICENTENNIAL COMMISSION; 5TH AND MAIN; PIERCE, CO 80650. (#200007-145).

JUNE 26, '76. PIERCE COMMUNITY PARADE. PARADE IS FIRST EVENT OF OLD TIMERS' WEEKEND. AT MAIN ST. (LOCAL). JOHN TREINEN, COORD; PIERCE JAYCEES, OLD TIMERS' CLUB, PIERCE CENTENNIAL-BICENTENNIAL COM; 610 FAYE ST; PIERCE, CO 80650. (#106996-2).

JUNE 27, '76. OLD TIMERS' ANNUAL PICNIC. EARLY PIERCE RESIDENTS WILL RE-ENACT EARLY HOMESTEADING DAYS ON THE PRAIRIE. COMMUNITY YOUTH WILL HELP WITH MUSIC. ALL RESIDENTS & FORMER RESIDENTS INVITED. AT HIGH SCHOOL CAFETERIA. (LOCAL). LEONA BRUMFIELD; OLD TIMERS' CLUB; 5TH & MAIN; PIERCE, CO 80650. (#106996-1).

AUG 3, '76. PIERCE CENTENNIAL-BICENTENNIAL SENIOR CITIZEN DAY. DAY OF EXHIBITS AND WORKSHOPS; SENIOR CITIZENS WILL DISPLAY AND SHARE SKILLS AND EXPERIENCES WITH TOWNSPEOPLE AND GUESTS. AT PIERCE COMMUNITY BUILDING. (LOCAL). LEONA BRUMFIELD, CHMN; PIERCE CENTENNIAL-BICENTENNIAL COMMITTEE/STULEDO OLD-TIMERS CLUB; 5TH & MAIN; PIERCE, CO 80631. (#108760-2).

AUG 17, '76. FILM FESTIVAL. EXHIBIT. (LOCAL). LEONA BRUMFIELD; FILM FESTIVAL COMMITTEE; BOX 43; PIERCE, CO 80650. (#108723-1).

SEPT 21, '76. FILM FESTIVAL. EXHIBIT. (LOCAL). LEONA BRUMFIELD, CHMN; PIERCE CENTENNIAL-BICENTENNIAL COMMITTEE; 5TH & MAIN; PIERCE, CO 80650. (#108760-1).

PINE

PINE COMMUNITY CENTER, CO. RESTORATION AND REFURBISHING OF ONE HUNDRED YEAR OLD BUILDING FOR COMMUNITY. (LOCAL). HAZEL HUMPHREYS, PROJ CHAIRMAN; PINE COMMUNITY CIVIC GROUP; PINE, CO 80470. (#26228).

OCT 20, '75 - DEC 31, '76. HISTORICAL EXPOSITION. EXHIBIT. (LOCAL). HAZEL HUMPHREYS, COORD; PINE COMMUNITY CIVIC GROUP; PINE, CO 80470. (#108588-1).

PLATTEVILLE

COMMUNITY BUILDING IN PLATTEVILLE, CO. THIS CENTENNIAL-BICENTENNIAL PROJECT WILL ADD TO THE DEVELOPMENT OF THE COMMUNITY AND BE A LASTING REMINDER OF THE CELEBRATION. (LOCAL). ROGER D PETERSON, CHAIRMAN; PLATTEVILLE CENTENNIAL-BICENTENNIAL COMMITTEE; ROUTE 1, BOX 481; FORT LUPTON, CO 80621. (#14846).

FT VASQUEZ FUR TRADING EXPEDITION, 1976, CO. CANOE TRIP TO KANSAS CITY TO RE-CREATE TRIP MADE BY EARLY FUR TRADERS UNDER THE SAME CONDITIONS. (REGN'L). DON CANNALTE, PUBLIC RELATIONS; UNITED AIRLINES; STAPLETON AIRPORT; DENVER, CO 80207. (#20628).

RENDEZVOUS DAYS - PLATTEVILLE, CO. ART SHOW, DRAMA, PARADE, CAMPFIRE TALK, INDIAN AND LOCAL HISTORY, HISTORIC HOMES TOUR, ENTERTAINMENT, BAR B QUE, GAMES, CHURCH SERVICE TO MARK THE CENTENNIAL-BICENTENNIAL CELEBRATION. (LOCAL). ROGER D PETERSON, CHAIRMAN; PLATTEVILLE CENTENNIAL-BICENTENNIAL COMMITTEE; RT #1, BOX 481; FORT LUPTON, CO 80621. (#17990). **ARBA GRANTEE.**

MAY 27, '75. MISS PLATTEVILLE PAGEANT. CONTEST OPEN TO 4 AGE GROUPS AS A SALUTE TO THE CENTENNIAL-BICENTENNIAL CELEBRATION. (LOCAL). ROGER D PETERSON, CHMN; PLATTEVILLE CENTENNIAL-BICENTENNIAL COMMITTEE; RT 1 BOX 481; FORT LUPTON, CO 80621. (#200007-138).

JULY 14 - 20, '75. PLATTEVILLE RENDEZVOUS DAYS. ACTIVITIES INCLUDE DANCES, ART SHOW, RODEO, BARBEQUE, PARADE, HISTORIC HOMES TOUR, EXHIBITS, CHURCH SERVICES. (ST-WIDE). LLOYD RIGG, PROJ DIR; PLATTEVILLE CITY COUNCIL; 411 GOODRICH AVE; PLATTEVILLE, CO 80651. (#200007-137).

JAN 6, '76. FT VASQUEZ FUR TRADING EXPEDITION 1976 - CANOE TRIP TO KANSAS CITY. CANOE TRIP FROM FT VASQUEZ TO KANSAS CITY TO RE-CREATE FUR TRADING EXPEDITIONS OF EARLY TRAPPERS. AT FT VASQUEZ. (REGN'L). PHIL MAHAFFEY, COORD; UNITED AIR LINES; BOX 269A RT 4; GOLDEN, CO 80401. (#200007-139).

FEB 14, '76. VALENTINES DAY DANCE. FESTIVAL AT PEE WEE'S, 515 MAIN ST. (LOCAL). ROGER D PETERSON, CHMN; PLATTEVILLE CENTENNIAL-BICENTENNIAL COMMITTEE; WELD CO RD 24; FORT LUPTON, CO 80621. (#200007-141).

FEB 16, '76. PLATTEVILLE AMERICAN BICENTENNIAL FLAG CEREMONY. CEREMONY AT MIDDLE SCHOOL GYM, 1004 MAIN ST. (LOCAL). ROGER D PETERSON, CHMN; PLATTEVILLE CENTENNIAL-BICENTENNIAL COMMITTEE; WELD CO RD 24; FORT LUPTON, CO 80621. (#200007-140).

MAY 9 - 15, '76. PLATTEVILLE'S RED, WHITE AND BLUE DAYS. PLATTEVILLE CITIZENS WILL PLANT RED, WHITE & BLUE FLOWERS IN THEIR YARDS AND PLATTEVILLE CENTENNIAL-BICENTENNIAL COMMITTEE WILL PLANT RED, WHITE & BLUE FLOWERS AROUND PUBLIC BUILDINGS SUCH AS TOWN HALL & THE LIBRARY. (LOCAL). ROGER D PETERSON, CHMN; PLATTEVILLE CENTENNIAL-BICENTENNIAL COMMITTEE; 9142 WELD CO RD 24; FORT LUPTON, CO 80621. (#107015-1).

JUNE 5, '76. MISS PLATTEVILLE PAGEANT. COMPETITION, AWARD AT PLATTEVILLE ELEMNTARY SCHOOL, MAIN ST. (LOCAL). ROGER D PETERSON, CHMN; PLATTEVILLE CENTENNIAL-BICENTENNIAL COMMITTEE; 9142 WELD CO RD 24; FORT LUPTON, CO 80621. (#107015-3).

JULY 4, '76. OLD-FASHIONED PICNIC. GAMES, ENTERTAINMENT, CONTESTS & RACES WILL BE FEATURED THROUGHOUT THE DAY. AT LINCOLN PARK. (LOCAL). ROGER D PETERSON, CHMN; PLATTEVILLE CENTENNIAL-BICENTENNIAL COMMITTEE; PO BOX 6; PLATTEVILLE, CO 80651. (#108591-1).

AUG 5 - 14, '76. RENDEZVOUS DAYS, 1976 - PARADE & BARBECUE. THE THEME OF THE PARADE IS 'IN THE SPIRIT OF '76.'. AT PARADE BEGINS AT ELEMENTARY SCHOOL; BARBECUE AT LINCOLN PARK. (LOCAL). ROGER D PETERSON, CHMN; PLATTEVILLE CENTENNIAL-BICENTENNIAL COMMITTEE; WELD CO RD 24; FORT LUPTON, CO 80621. (#107015-2).

PONCHA SPG

RE-NAMING A STREET IN PONCHA SPRINGS, CO. BROWN AVE WILL BE CHANGED TO BURNETT AVE TO HONOR PIONEER FAMILY & LIVING HEIRS OF THAT NAME. (LOCAL). FLORENCE LINDBLOOM, PROJ COORDINATOR; CITY OF PONCHA SPRINGS; PO BOX 142; PONCHA SPG, CO 81424. (#26848).

AUG 1, '76. COMMUNITY PARADE. PARADE. (LOCAL). FLORENCE LINDBLOOM, CHMN; PONCHA SPRINGS FESTIVAL COMMITTEE; PO BOX 142; PONCHA SPG, CO 81242. (#108955-52).

AUG 1, '76. COMMUNITY TIME CAPSULE. CEREMONY. (LOCAL). FLORENCE LINDBLOOM, CHMN; PONCHA SPRINGS FESTIVAL COMMITTEE; PO BOX 142; PONCHA SPG, CO 81242. (#108955-51).

AUG 1, '76. SENIOR CITIZEN 1976. FESTIVAL. (LOCAL). FLORENCE LINDBLOOM, CHMN; PONCHA SPRINGS FESTIVAL COMMITTEE; PO BOX 142; PONCHA SPG, CO 81242. (#108955-50).

PUEBLO

ARKANSAS & FOUNTAIN RIVERS RECREATIONAL TRAILS, CO. TRAILS SYSTEM ALONG THE TWO RIVERS THAT INTERSECT THE CITY OF PUEBLO WITH PRESERVATION OF NATURAL VEGETATION FOR WILD LIFE & RECREATION. (LOCAL). GEORGE R WILLIAMS, DIRECTOR; PUEBLO PARKS AND RECREATION; PUEBLO, CO 81005. (#13965).

BABE RUTH WORLD SERIES - COLORADO HOST. NATL TOURNAMENT INVOLVING PLANNING & COMMITMENTS FROM EACH OF THE BABE RUTH LEAGUES IN THE STATE. TOURNAMENT WILL INVOLVE TEAMS ONLY FROM AGES 13 TO 15. (ST-WIDE). DAVID J NOVAK, CO-HOST PRESIDENT; BABE RUTH WORLD SERIES COMMITTEE; PO BOX 1976; PUEBLO, CO 81001. (#1914). **ARBA GRANTEE.**

BIKE PEDAL & CROSS EXERCISE CIRCUIT OF PUEBLO, CO. A NEW TWO-WHEEL SPORT FOR YOUNG BICYCLISTS, AGES 8 TO 15; TO JUMP OVER HILLS & SPLASH THRU MUD HOLES & SAND TRAPS;

PUEBLO — CONTINUED

EXERCISE CIRCUIT IS PHYSICAL FITNESS FOR EVERYONE. (LOCAL). RICHARD DOERING, PARKS DIRECTOR; CITY PARK OFFICE; PUEBLO BLVD & LEHIGH; PUEBLO, CO 81005. (#10701).

CENTENNIAL LANDSCAPE HOLY ROSARY PARK, PUEBLO, CO. NEW LANDSCAPING OF THE PARK FOR THE CENTENNIAL-BICENTENNIAL. (LOCAL). JOHN PETER ROYBAL, CHAIRMAN; OUR LADY OF HOLY ROSARY PARK; 2207 W 22ND ST; PUEBLO, CO 81004. (#10702).

CENTENNIAL-BICENTENNIAL FILM - PUEBLO, CO. 20-MINUTE FILM REVIEWS THE PRINCIPLES ESTABLISHED BY THE FOUNDING FATHERS. (LOCAL). JOHN WERNA, PROJ CHAIRMAN; FILM COMMITTEE; 302 N SANTA FE; PUEBLO, CO 81003. (#26344).

COLORADO STATE FAIR CENTENNIAL-BICENTENNIAL THEMES. RECOGNITION OF AGRICULTURE, YOUTH, CATTLE INDUSTRY, ART, EDUCATION, SCIENCE, & INDUSTRY TO THE GROWTH OF COLORADO & THE USA. (ST-WIDE). GEORGE SCOTT, MANAGER; COLORADO STATE FAIR BOARD; STATE FAIR; PUEBLO, CO 81003. (#2936).

COLUMBINE CENTENNIAL EXPO CENTER, COLORADO. MULTI-PURPOSE SUPERSTRUCTURE FOR USE BY ALL RESIDENTS OF THE STATE WITH EMPHASIS ON RECREATION, AGRICULTURAL & INDUSTRIAL DISPLAYS & EXHIBITS. (ST-WIDE). GEORGE SCOTT, MANAGER; COLORADO STATE FAIR COMMISSION; STATE FAIRGROUNDS; PUEBLO, CO 81004. (#2937).

CONSTRUCTION OF FORTCADE IN PUEBLO, COLO. DEVELOPMENT OF FRONTIER LOG FORT AT THE COLORADO STATE FAIR FOR CENTENNIAL-BICENTENNIAL CELEBRATION IN 1976. (ST-WIDE). PAUL W COWAN, INFO REPRESENTATIVE; COLORADO STATE FAIR; COLORADO STATE FAIR GROUNDS; PUEBLO, CO 81004. (#1940).

CORWIN MIDDLE SCHOOL BEAUTIFICATION, PUEBLO, CO. IMPROVE SCHOOL APPEARANCE WITH THE ADDITION OF LANDSCAPED PARK AREA AND ADDITIONAL PLAY EQUIPMENT. (LOCAL). GEORGE R WILLIAMS, DIRECTOR; PUEBLO PARKS AND RECREATION; PUEBLO, CO 81005. (#13966).

EASTWOOD SCHOOL BEAUTIFICATION, PUEBLO, CO. IMPROVE SCHOOL APPEARANCE WITH THE ADDITION OF LANDSCAPED PARK AREA AND ADDITIONAL PLAY EQUIPMENT. (LOCAL). GEORGE R WILLIAMS, DIRECTOR; PUEBLO PARKS AND RECREATION; PUEBLO, CO 81005. (#13967).

EL CENTRO DE QUINTO SOL PARK, PUEBLO, CO. OUTDOOR FACILITIES FOR A LARGE VARIETY OF RECREATIONAL ACTIVITIES; PICNICS, HORSESHOES, VOLLEYBALL & BASKETBALL, SERVING AS A COMMUNITY CENTER. (LOCAL). GEORGE R WILLIAMS, DIRECTOR; PUEBLO PARKS AND RECREATION; PUEBLO, CO 81005. (#13970).

FLAGS FOR PUEBLO, COLORADO. EACH CITIZEN & BUSINESS WILL DISPLAY A FLAG EVERY DAY. THIS PROJECT IS DESIGNED TO PROMOTE PATRIOTISM IN PUEBLO. (LOCAL). MRS PRISCILLA SMITH, CHAIRMAN; PUEBLO BEAUTIFUL ASSOC; 7 ROBERTSON RD; PUEBLO, CO 81001. (#9074).

FULTON HEIGHTS SCHOOL BEAUTIFICATION PROJECT, CO. FULTON HEIGHTS SCHOOL WILL DEVELOP A LANDSCAPED PARK AREA AND ACQUIRE ADDITIONAL PLAY EQUIPMENT. (LOCAL). GEORGE R WILLIAMS, PROJ DIRECTOR; PUEBLO PARKS AND RECREATION; PUEBLO, CO 81005. (#13963).

GOODNIGHT SCHOOL BEAUTIFICATION, PUEBLO, CO. A LANDSCAPED AREA AND ADDITIONAL PLAY EQUIPMENT WILL BE ADDED TO THE GOODNIGHT SCHOOL. (LOCAL). GEORGE R WILLIAMS, PROJ DIRECTOR; PUEBLO PARKS AND RECREATION; PUEBLO, CO 81005. (#13960).

HISTORICAL FARMS OF COLORADO. TO RECREATE A FARM OR FARMS AS THEY WERE IN COLORADO'S DISTANT PAST FOR THE PURPOSES OF RECALLING THE HARDSHIPS AND JOYS OF LIFE IN THIS EARLY PERIOD. (ST-WIDE). KERRY PETERSON, PROJECT DIRECTOR; PUEBLO REGIONAL PLANNING COMMISSION; 1 CITY HALL PLACE; PUEBLO, CO 81003. (#4407).

HORSEBACK TRAILS EXPEDITION - PUEBLO, CO. A JOINT PROJECT OF HISTORICAL SOCIETIES AND HORSEMANSHIP GROUPS TO RETRACE ON HORSEBACK THE ROUTES OF THE PIONEERS. (REGN'L). JAY ROBERTS, COORDINATOR; CF & I STEEL CORPORATION; 2100 W 20TH ST; PUEBLO, CO 81003. (#19511).

HYDE PARK SCHOOL BEAUTIFICATION IN PUEBLO, CO. IMPROVE SCHOOL APPEARANCE WITH THE ADDITION OF LANDSCAPED PARK AREA AND ACQUIRE ADDITIONAL PLAYGROUND EQUIPMENT. (LOCAL). GEORGE R WILLIAMS, PROJ DIRECTOR; PUEBLO PARKS AND RECREATION; PUEBLO, CO 81005. (#13964).

INTERNATIONAL CHARRO COMPETITION '76 OF PUEBLO, CO. PROVIDE A PERMANENT CULTURAL AND RECREATIONAL LEARNING CENTER TO RESEARCH AND PRODUCE CULTURAL, HISTORICAL INFORMATION REGARDING THE SOUTHWEST. (REGN'L). HENRY GURULE, COORDINATOR; PUEBLO CHARRO ASSOCIATION; PO BOX 2111; PUEBLO, CO 81004. (#2452). **ARBA GRANTEE.**

INTERNATIONAL HERITAGE - PUEBLO, CO. SENIOR CITIZENS CENTERS WILL PICK A COUNTRY AND RESEARCH CUSTOMS, CULTURE, LANGUAGE, FOODS, ART, MUSIC AND HISTORY. (LOCAL). ESTHER FRETZ, ACTIVITIES PROGRAM COORD; PUEBLO SENIOR CITIZEN RESOURCE DEVELOPMENT; 314 E 7TH; PUEBLO, CO 81003. (#26345).

MINERAL PALACE PARK GREENHOUSE, PUEBLO, CO. MAIN BUILDING IS COMPLETED; THREE GEODESIC DOMES ARE TO BE ADDED TO MAKE A BEAUTIFUL GREENHOUSE COMPLEX. (LOCAL). GEORGE R WILLIAMS, DIRECTOR; PUEBLO PARKS AND RECREATION; PUEBLO, CO 81005. (#13968).

MITCHELL PARK SWIMMING POOL, PUEBLO, CO. A SWIMMING POOL WILL BE BUILT IN MITCHELL PARK; OPPORTUNITIES FOR SWIMMING INSTRUCTIONS & COMPETITION WILL BE AVAILABLE. (LOCAL). GEORGE R WILLIAMS, DIRECTOR; PUEBLO PARKS AND RECREATION; PUEBLO, CO 81005. (#13972).

MOZART FESTIVAL, USA - PUEBLO, COLORADO. OPERAS OF MOZART, CONCERTS, ARTISTS & COMPETITIONS; FROM JANUARY 1975 THRU AUGUST 1976, EMPHASIZING COLORADO CENTENNIAL - USA BICENT. (ST-WIDE). CARMELITA M KEATOR, MANAGER; PUEBLO CIVIC SYMPHONY ASSOC, INC; 1117 LAKE AVE; PUEBLO, CO 81004. (#8597).

PLAZA VERDE PARK, PUEBLO, CO. RECREATIONAL PARK AREA TO BE ADDED TO EXISTING COMMUNITY CENTER WITH PRE-SCHOOL, SENIOR CITIZENS' CENTER AND ACTIVITIES FOR ALL AGES. (LOCAL). GEORGE R WILLIAMS, DIRECTOR; PUEBLO PARKS AND RECREATION; PUEBLO, CO 81005. (#13971).

PUEBLO CHICANO DEMOCRATIC CAUCUS, CO. RESEARCHING, DOCUMENTING & ILLUSTRATING POLITICAL & HISTORICAL ACTIVITIES OF SPANISH-SPEAKING CHICANOS OF PUEBLO COUNTY OVER THE LAST 100 YEARS. (LOCAL). GEORGE AUTOBEE, CHAIRMAN; CHICANO DEMOCRATIC CAUCUS; 1422 PINE; PUEBLO, CO 81004. (#26346).

PUEBLO CIVIC SYMPHONY ASSOC BICENTENNIAL PROJ. ANNUAL MUSIC FESTIVAL WILL COMMEMORATE 200 YEARS OF AMERICAN HISTORY BY INCORPORATING DIVERSE ELEMENTS OF AMERICAN ART TOGETHER WITH WIDE COMMUNITY PARTICIPATION. (REGN'L). MRS CARMELITA KEATOR, MANAGER; PUEBLO CIVIC SYMPHONY ASSOC, INC; 117 LAKE AVE; PUEBLO, CO 81004. (#127). **ARBA RECOGNIZED.**

PUEBLO ICE RINK, CO. A CITY ICE SKATING RINK WILL OPEN THANKSGIVING '75. (LOCAL). GEORGE R WILLIAMS, DIRECTOR; PUEBLO PARKS AND RECREATION; PUEBLO, CO 81005. (#13969).

PUEBLO LIENZO RODEO AREA & PARK IN COLORADO. ESTABLISHMENT AND CONSTRUCTION OF LIENZA-MEXICAN RODEO ARENA TO EMPHASIZE MEXICAN TRADITIONS OF THE SOUTHWEST; ENCOURAGE HORSEMANSHIP, PROVIDE SCHOLARSHIPS, ETC. ONLY SUCH BUILDING IN USA. (ST-WIDE). OTTIE OTTERSON, CHAIRPERSON; PUEBLO CENTENNIAL-BICENTENNIAL COMMISSION; 1 CITY HALL PL; PUEBLO, CO 81003. (#2878).

PUEBLO MOTORSPORTS PARK - PUEBLO, CO. THE PARK WILL CONSIST OF A TWO MILE ROAD COURSE, A QUARTER MIDGET OVAL, A MOTORCYCLE MOTOR CROSS, MOTORCYCLE SHORT TRACK, POLICE PURSUIT COURSE AND A DEFENSIVE DRIVING AREA. (ST-WIDE). BILL DICKY, DIRECTOR; PUEBLO MOTORSPORTS PARK; 3701 BIJON; PUEBLO, CO 81008. (#15489).

PUEBLO SYMPHONY-MINNEQUA OPERA, CO. STORY OF ARRIVAL OF RAILROAD IN COLORADO 1876. BASED ON HISTORICAL FACT. MELTING OF NATIONALITIES: AMERICAN INDIAN, SPANISH, EUROPEAN. LIBRETTO R P DICKEY COMPOSER GERHARD TRACK NOVEL 'BIRTH OF COLORADO'. (ST-WIDE). CARMELITA KEATOR, MANAGER; PUEBLO CIVIC SYMPHONY ASSOCIATION, INC; 1117 LAKE AVE; PUEBLO, CO 81004. (#4464). **ARBA GRANTEE.**

PUEBLO VISITOR CENTER - PROJ OF PUEBLO, CO. OUTDOOR VISITOR INFORMATION CENTER HOUSED IN MISSOURI PACIFIC CABOOSE DONATED BY DEPARTMENT OF TRANSPORTATION TO BE STAFFED BY SCOUT GROUPS. (LOCAL). MS PAULETTE NELSON; BOY SCOUTS OF AMERICA GOD & COUNTRY; 302 NORTH SANTA FE; PUEBLO, CO 81003. (#17358).

RECORDING PATRIOTIC SONGS - PUEBLO, CO. ORIGINAL PATRIOTIC SONGS OF THE STATE & NATION BY BUDDY PRIMA WILL BE RECORDED BY THE PUEBLO SYMPHONY ORCHESTRA. (ST-WIDE). KEN PLONKEY, PRODUCER; 19 ROBERTSON RD; PUEBLO, CO 81001. (#25974).

THE RIDE TO THE BIRTHPLACE OF OUR NATION, CO. A RIDE FROM PUEBLO, COLORADO TO INDEPENDENCE HALL IN PHILADELPHIA ON HORSEBACK IS BEING PLANNED. (NAT'L). MIKE WILLIS, PROJ DIRECTOR; C F & I STEEL CORP, ET AL; PUEBLO, CO 81001. (#19510).

SOMERLIND SCH BEAUTIFICATION PROJECT IN PUEBLO, CO. A LANDSCAPED PARK AREA WILL BE DEVELOPED AT SOMERLID SCHOOL AND ADDITIONAL PLAY EQUIPMENT WILL BE ACQUIRED. (LOCAL). GEORGE R WILLIAMS, PROJ DIRECTOR; PUEBLO PARKS AND RECREATION; PUEBLO, CO 81005. (#13962).

SOUTH COLO STATE COLLEGE CENTENNIAL PIPE ORGAN. DESIGN CONSTRUCT INSTALL 3 MANUAL CONCERT PIPE ORGAN FOR NEW RECITAL HALL AT COLO ST COLLEGE-NO FINE PIPE ORGAN EXISTS IN AREA. WILL BE USED FOR INTERNATIONAL & LOCAL CONCERTS. (ST-WIDE). RODNEY D TOWNLEY DIRECTOR PIPE ORGAN FUND DRIVE; SOUTHERN COLORADO STATE COLLEGE; 2200 N BONFORTE; PUEBLO, CO 81001. (#4346).

SPANN SCHOOL BEAUTIFICATION, PUEBLO, CO. A LANDSCAPED AREA AND ADDITIONAL PLAY EQUIPMENT WILL BE ADDED TO THE SPANN SCHOOL. (LOCAL). GEORGE R WILLIAMS, PROJ DIRECTOR; PUEBLO PARKS AND RECREATION; PUEBLO, CO 81005. (#13961).

WATER BOARD TEST SITE PARK, PUEBLO, CO. PRESENTATION OF PLANT MATERIALS ADAPTED TO DIFFERENT LEVELS OF WATERING; PLANTS SUITABLE FOR LANDSCAPING IN PUEBLO AREA. (LOCAL). LARRY C FONTAINE, EXECUTIVE DIRECTOR; PUEBLO BOARD OF WATER WORKS; 319 W 4TH ST; PUEBLO, CO 81003. (#16482).

YWCA BIKECENTENNIAL PROJECT - PUEBLO, CO. PAINTING & REDECORATING THREE BEDROOMS AND BATHS AT THE PUEBLO YWCA TO SERVE AS A YOUTH HOSTEL FOR NATIONAL AND INTERNATIONAL PARTICIPANTS IN THE BIKECENTENNIAL. (LOCAL). JEAN R WILLIAMS, PRESIDENT; ALTRUSA CLUB OF PUEBLO, INC; 1415 CONSTITUTION; PUEBLO, CO 81001. (#24604).

MAR 15, '75 - DEC 30, '76. CULTURAL HERITAGE DISPLAYS IN PUEBLO, CO. WILL INCLUDE THE DISPLAY OF ARTIFACTS - SEPT 1 TO MAY 31 1PM-4PM; JUNE 1 TO AUG 31 10AM-4PM; HOLIDAYS 2-5PM. SEPT 1-MAY31 1PM-4PM; JUNE 1-AUG 31 10AM-4PM HOLIDAYS 2-5PM. AT 419 WEST 14TH ST, PUEBLO, CO. (LOCAL). MRS HELEN TITUS, MANAGER; PUEBLO METROPOLITAN MUSEUM; 419 W 14TH ST; PUEBLO, CO 81003. (#9507-1).

JULY 4 - 5, '75. OLD FASHIONED 4TH OF JULY CARNIVAL. FESTIVAL AT PUEBLO METROPOLITAN MUSEUM LAWN. (LOCAL). ETHLYN POTESTIO; PUEBLO METROPOLITAN MUSEUM AUXILIARY; 1836 BONFORTE BLVD; PUEBLO, CO 81000. (#7924-1).

OCT 16, '75. PUEBLO SYMPHONY ORCHESTRA - GERHARD TRACK, MUSIC DIRECTOR. SYMPHONY ORCHESTRA CONCERT W/ COLORADOAN EUGENE FODER, INTERNATIONAL VIOLIN WINNER IN MOSCOW 1974: SEASON EMPHASIS ON NATIVE COLORADO AND INTERNATIONAL PERFORMERS & COMPOSERS. AT MEMORIAL HALL, GRAND & UNION EXIT I25, 6TH ST; UNMETERED PARKING. (LOCAL). CARMELITA KEATOR, MANAGER; PUEBLO SYMPHONY ASSOC MOZART FESTIVAL 1976; 1117 LAKE AVE; PUEBLO, CO 81004. (#127-2).

OCT 16, '75 - JUNE 15, '76. MOZART FESTIVAL U S A. ANNUAL MUSIC FESTIVAL WILL COMMEMORATE 200 YEARS OF AMERICAN HISTORY BY INCORPORATING DIVERSE ELEMENTS OF AMERICAN ART TOGETHER WITH WIDE COMMUNITY PARTICIPATION. START & STOP TIMES ARE UNDECIDED. AT MEMORIAL HALL,SANGRE D CRISTO ART & CONFERENCE CENTER. (REGN'L). CARMELITA KEATOR, MANAGER; PUEBLO SYMPHONY ASSOC MOZART FESTIVAL 1976; 117 LAKE AVE, PUEBLO, CO 81004. (#127-1).

OCT 19, '75. EUROPEAN OLD WORLD CHAMBER CONCERT, HAUSMUSIK. VIENNESE CONCERT PIANIST, MICAELA MAIHART TRACK, WITH SELECT CHAMBER STRING AND VOCAL GROUPS. AT PUEBLO METRO MUSEUM, 419 W 14TH ST; UNMETERED PARKING. (ST-WIDE). CARMELITA KEATOR, MANAGER; PUEBLO SYMPHONY ASSOC MOZART FESTIVAL 1976; 1117 LAKE AVE, PUEBLO, CO 81004. (#127-3).

NOV 15 - 16, '75. UNITED STATES ARMED FORCES BICENTENNIAL CARAVAN. THE CARAVAN IS COMPOSED OF EXHIBIT VANS FOR EACH BRANCH OF THE MILITARY SERVICE. THE THEME OF THE EXHIBITION IS 'HISTORY OF THE ARMED FORCES AND THEIR CONTRIBUTION TO THE NATION'. (LOCAL). CHUCK MCKINNEY, CHMN; U S ARMED FORCES BICENTENNIAL EXHIBIT VANS PROJECT; MIDTOWN SHOPPING CENTER; PUEBLO, CO 81003. (#1775-250).

NOV 19, '75. MOZART FESTIVAL 'THIS WORLD' PIANO WORKSHOP WITH JAMES DICK. JAMES DICK PIANO WORKSHOP AND MASTER CLASS; NATIONALLY RENOWNED PIANO CLINICIAN. AT SANGRE DE CRISTO ARTS CENTER THEATRE, 210 N SANTA FE AVE. (ST-WIDE). CARMELITA KEATOR, MANAGER; PUEBLO SYMPHONY ASSOC MOZART FESTIVAL 1976; 1117 LAKE AVE, PUEBLO, CO 81004. (#127-4).

NOV 19, '75. PUEBLO SYMPHONY ORCHESTRA- G TRACK, MUSIC DIR, J DICK, PIANO. 1ST AMERICAN JUDGE IN TSCHKAIKOWSKY COMPETITION IN MOSCOW, 1974. AND 1ST AMERICAN JUDGE IN TSCHKAIKOWSKY COMPETITION IN MOSCOW 1974. AT MEMORIAL HALL, GRAND & UNION EXIT I25, 6TH ST; UNMETERED PARKING. (ST-WIDE). CARMELITA KEATOR, MANAGER; PUEBLO SYMPHONY ASSOC MOZART FESTIVAL 1976; 1117 LAKE AVE; PUEBLO, CO 81004. (#127-5).

NOV 26, '75. MUSIC LIGHTS THE WORLD, PUEBLO YOUTH ORCH & PUEBLO SYMPHONY CHORALE. CITY TURNS ON CHRISTMAS LIGHTS ON THANKSGIVING EVE; THERE WILL BE SPECIAL CEREMONY & CONCERT WITH GERHARD TRACK, MUSIC DIRECTOR. AT SANGRE DE CRISTO ARTS CENTER THEATRE, 210 N SANTA FE AVE. (ST-WIDE). CARMELITA KEATOR, MANAGER; PUEBLO SYMPHONY ASSOC MOZART FESTIVAL 1976; 1117 LAKE AVE; PUEBLO, CO 81004. (#127-6).

DEC 7, '75. 'THIS WORLD' PUEBLO YOUTH SYMPHONY ORCHESTRA CONCERT. CHRISTMAS PROGRAM FOR FAMILIES, WITH SPECIAL CHILDREN'S SECTION OF NARRATED XMAS STORIES; GERHARD TRACK IS MUSICAL DIRECTOR. AT MEMORIAL HALL GRAND & UNION EXIT I25 6TH ST UNMETERED PARKING. (ST-WIDE). CARMELITA KEATOR, MANAGER; PUEBLO SYMPHONY ASSOC MOZART FESTIVAL 1976; 1117 LAKE AVE; PUEBLO, CO 81004 (#127-7).

DEC 20, '75. TIME CAPSULE FOR ICE ARENA. DEDICATION OF ICE ARENA WITH A SPECIAL FLAG CEREMONY; SCROLL OF THOSE ATTENDING WAS KEPT. AT 100 NORTH GRAND AVENUE, PUEBLO, CO 81003. (LOCAL). FRED E WEISBROD; CITY OF PUEBLO; CITY HALL PLACE; PUEBLO, CO 81003. (#200007-142).

DEC 21, '75. HAUSMUSIK OLD-FASHIONED CHRISTMAS. THERE WILL BE INSTRUMENTAL AND VOCAL PERFORMANCES BY ADULTS AND CHILDREN IN A MANSION WITH A DRAWING ROOM SETTING. AT PUEBLO METRO MUSEUM, 419 W 14TH ST, UNMETERED PARKING. (ST-WIDE). CARMELITA KEATOR, MANAGER; PUEBLO SYMPHONY ASSOC MOZART FESTIVAL 1976; 1117 LAKE AVE; PUEBLO, CO 81004. (#127-8).

JAN 9, '76. BIERSTUBE - MOZART FESTIVAL 1976. SINGING & MUSIC. DINING WILL BE FASHIONED AFTER GERMAN BEER FEST IN HISTORIC RAILROAD DEPOT. AT PUEBLO UNION STATION (ST-WIDE). CARMELITA KEATOR, MANAGER; PUEBLO JAYCEES, 1117 LAKE AVE; PUEBLO, CO 81004. (#127-9).

JAN 15, '76. STRING WORKSHOP - J F MULLER GUEST ARTIST. J F MULLER FROM ROTH MUSIC COMPANY WILL INSTRUCT STRING STUDENTS. AT SANGRE DE CRISTO ARTS CENTER THEATRE, 210 N SANTA FE AVE. (ST-WIDE). CARMELITA KEATOR, MANAGER PUEBLO SYMPHONY ASSOC; 1117 LAKE AVE; PUEBLO, CO 81004. (#127-10).

JAN 16, '76. ADVENTURE IN MUSIC CONCERT - MR & MRS OSWALD LEHNERT, PIANO & VIOLIN. INTERNATIONAL MUSIC PROGRAM

PUEBLO — CONTINUED

WITH MR OSWALD LEHNERT, A MEMBER OF PABLO CASALS TRIO, UNIVERSITY OF COLORADO. AT SANGRE DE CRISTO ARTS CENTER THEATRE, 210 N SANTA FE AVE. (ST-WIDE). CARMELITA KEATOR, MANAGER; PUEBLO SYMPHONY ASSOC MOZART FESTIVAL 1976; 1117 LAKE AVE; PUEBLO, CO 81004. (#127-12).

JAN 16 - 17, '76. YOUNG ARTISTS STRING COMPETITION. COMPETITION, LIVE PERFORMANCE AT SANGRE DE CRISTO ARTS CENTER THEATRE, 210 N SANTA FE AVE. (REGN'L). CARMELITA KEATOR, MANAGER; PUEBLO SYMPHONY ASSOC MOZART FESTIVAL 1976; 1117 LAKE AVE; PUEBLO, CO 81004. (#127-11).

JAN 24, '76. '1776' - A MUSICAL PLAY. THE MATINEE FOR CHILDREN WILL BE AT 2:00 PM AND THE EVENING SHOW WILL BE AT 8:00 PM; THE PLAY DEALS WITH THE FOUNDING OF AMERICAN GOVERNMENT. AT MEMORIAL HALL, GRAND & UNION EXIT I25 ON 6TH ST; UNMETERED PARKING. (ST-WIDE). MAGGIE DIVELBISS, DIR; BROADWAY THEATER LEAGUE; 210 N SANTA FE AVE; PUEBLO, CO 81003. (#127-13).

JAN 25, '76. MOZART FESTIVAL OFFICIAL OPENING, GERHARD TRACK MUSIC DIRECTOR. DR KELLNER, AUSTRIAN DIPLOMAT, WILL OFFICIATE. CEREMONY WILL INCLUDE GUEST HIGH SCHOOL CHOIRS FROM COLORADO & NEW MEXICO AND THE PUEBLO YOUTH SYMPHONY. AT MEMORIAL HALL, GRAND & UNION EXIT I25 ON 6TH ST; UNMETERED PARKING. (ST-WIDE). CARMELITA KEATOR, MANAGER; PUEBLO SYMPHONY ASSOC MOZART FESTIVAL 1976; 1117 LAKE AVE; PUEBLO, CO 81004. (#127-14).

JAN 26, '76. HIGH SCHOOL CONCERT - MOZART FESTIVAL 1976. VOCAL AND INSTRUMENTAL CHAMBER CONCERT. AT CENTENNIAL HIGH SCHOOL AUDITORIUM, 2529 MOUNT VIEW DR. (ST-WIDE). DR DUANE STRACHAN, DIR; PUEBLO SCHOOL DISTRICT 60; 102 W ORMAN AVE; PUEBLO, CO 81004. (#127-15).

JAN 29 - 31, '76. MINNEQUA OPERA. STORY OF ARRIVAL OF RAILROAD IN COLORADO, 1876. BASED ON HISTORICAL FACTS OF 'MELTING POT' THEORY: NATIVE AMERICAN, SPANISH & EUROPEAN INFLUENCE. R P DICKEY, LIBRETTO; GERHARD TRACK, COMPOSER. STORY WILL INCLUDE THE BIRTH OF COLORADO. AT MEMORIAL HALL AT GRAND & UNION STS. (LOCAL). CARMELITA M KEATOR; PUEBLO CIVIC SYMPHONY ASSOC, INC; 1117 LAKE AVE; PUEBLO, CO 81004. (#4464-1).

FEB 9 - 17, '76. CHILDREN'S CONCERTS, MOZART FESTIVAL 1976. A PATRIOTIC MUSIC PROGRAM, OPEN TO ALL FIFTH GRADES IN SOUTHERN COLORADO, WILL INCLUDE NARRATION OF COPELAND'S 'PORTRAIT OF LINCOLN' & A NATIONAL ANTHEM. FLAG DISPLAY - U S & ARBA; GERHARD TRACK IS THE MUSIC DIRECTOR. AT 2/9/76 SOUTH HIGH SCHOOL, 2/17/76 EAST HIGH SCHOOL. (ST-WIDE). CARMELITA KEATOR, MANAGER; PUEBLO SYMPHONY ASSOC MOZART FESTIVAL 1976; 1117 LAKE AVE; PUEBLO, CO 81004. (#127-16).

FEB 12 - 14, '76. 'OUR AMERICAN COUSIN' AND THE ASSASSINATION OF LINCOLN. 'OUR AMERICAN COUSIN' WAS BEING PERFORMED AT FORD'S THEATRE THE EVENING THAT LINCOLN WAS SHOT. A SCALE MODEL OF THE STAGE AND LINCOLN'S BOX AT FORD'S IS BEING BUILT. THIS WILL BE A COMEDY AND A DRAMA. AT SANDOVAL MEMORIAL THEATRE - CENTENNIAL HIGH SCHOOL. (LOCAL). GARY E HOLDER, DIRECTOR; CENTENNIAL HIGH SCHOOL DRAMA CLUB; 3825 SHEFFIELD; PUEBLO, CO 81005. (#103956-1).

FEB 22, '76. HAUSMUSIK, PATRIOTIC CHAMBER MUSIC. THE CONCERT WILL INCLUDE BRASS, WOODWINDS, STRINGS AND VOCALS. AT PUEBLO METRO MUSEUM, 419 W 14TH ST; UNMETERED PARKING. (ST-WIDE). CARMELITA KEATOR, MANAGER; PUEBLO SYMPHONY ASSOC MOZART FESTIVAL 1976; 1117 LAKE AVE; PUEBLO, CO 81004. (#127-17).

FEB 22 - 28, '76. PROFESSIONAL ENGINEERS' SALUTE TO THE CENTENNIAL-BICENTENNIAL. RADIO/TV AT CHANNEL 8 TELEVISION (KTSC). (LOCAL). DONALD E COY, CHMN; SOUTHERN CHAPTER OF PROFESSIONAL ENGINEERS OF COLORADO; 211 E D ST; PUEBLO, CO 81003. (#200007-143).

MAR 1 - DEC 25, '76. EXPLORING THE HISTORIC ARKANSAS RIVER WITH ZEBULON PIKE. HISTORIC RIVER TRAIL FROM HOLLY TO LEADVILLE; FOLLOWS THE INTERNATIONAL BOUNDRY LINE BETWEEN THE U S & SPAIN (MEXICO). (ST-WIDE). MRS JOHN B FARLEY, COORD; PUEBLO REGIONAL LIBRARY & HISTORICAL SOCIETY; 529 COLORADO AVE; PUEBLO, CO 81004. (#108593-4).

MAR 5 - 6, '76. SERVICE LEAGUE FOLLIES - GROUP & INDIVIDUAL SONG, DANCE & HUMOR. COMMUNITY INVOLVEMENT OF 100-200 CITIZENS; 14TH 'FOLLIES' IN 40 YEARS; BICENTENNIAL THEME AND TITLE; NO TALENT NECESSARY; JUST IN-/ TEREST AND ENTHUSIASM. AT PUEBLO MEMORIAL AUDITORIUM, UNION ST & CITY HALL ST. (LOCAL). SUSIE ANTON, PROJ COORD; PUEBLO SERVICE LEAGUE; 1925 GREENWOOD; PUEBLO, CO 81003. (#104447-1).

MAR 6, '76. AMERICAN FOLK ARTS AND HERITAGE FAIR. WIDE WORLD OF GIRL SCOUTING. AT SANGRE DE CRISTO ARTS CENTER CONFERENCE AREA 210 N SANTA FE. (LOCAL). LOUISE JONES, DIRECTOR; COLUMBINE GIRL SCOUT COUNCIL, INC; 322 W 5TH ST; PUEBLO, CO 81003. (#100691-1).

MAR 11, '76. PUEBLO SYMPHONY ORCHESTRA, MEISTER & BENDER VOCAL DUO. DIE FLEDERMAUS, AN ARIA BY STRAUSS, WILL BE PERFORMED BY BARBARA MEISTER AND DAVID BENDER, WELL-KNOWN CONCERT ARTISTS AND THE PUEBLO SYMPHONY ORCHESTRA; GERHARD TRACK IS THE MUSIC DIRECTOR. AT MEMORIAL HALL, GRAND & UNION EXIT I25 ON 6TH ST; UNMETERED PARKING. (ST-WIDE). CARMELITA KEATOR, MANAGER; PUEBLO SYMPHONY ASSOC MOZART FESTIVAL 1976; 1117 LAKE AVE; PUEBLO, CO 81004. (#127-18).

MAR 14, '76. FORT EL PUEBLO HISTORIC SITE MARKING P DEDICATION. THIS CEREMONY MARKS THE ORIGINAL SITE OF FT EL PUEBLO. THE MARKER WILL BE MOVED FROM THE SOUTHSIDE OF PUEBLO CITY HALL TO THE ARKANSAS RIVER SITE WHERE THE FORT ACTUALLY STOOD. THE CEREMONY WILL TAKE PLACE DURING THE DAR'S STATE CONVENTION IN PUEBLO. AT PARK AT SITE OF PUEBLO ICE RINK, COURT & FIRST STS. (LOCAL). MRS JOHN B FARLEY, CHMN; ARKANSAS VALLEY CHAPTER DAUGHTERS OF THE AMERICA REVOLUTION; 529 COLORADO AVE; PUEBLO, CO 81004. (#102321-1).

MAR 25 - 27, '76. COLORADO GOLD - CENTENNIAL-BICENTENNIAL THEATRICAL SHOW. MULTI-MEDIA MUSICAL THEATRICAL PERFORMANCE BASED UPON HISTORY LITERATURE AND FOLKLORE OF COLORADO INCLUDING ORIGINAL STATE AND NATIONAL PATRIOTIC SONGS. (ST-WIDE). ELLIE GRUNWALD, DIRECTOR; PUEBLO ARTS COUNCIL; 210 N SANTA FE AVE; PUEBLO, CO 81003. (#104874-1).

MAR 26 - 28, '76. NATIONAL PIANO ENSEMBLE COMPETITION. 3/26: EVENING CONCERT BY WALTZ & KUEMICH, 1 PIANO, 4 HANDS; 3/29: EVENING CONCERT BY THE HADDENS, TWO PIANOS; 3/28 EVENING CONCERT BY COMPETITION WINNERS; FIRST PRIZE: $1,000; SECOND PRIZE: $500; THIRD PRIZE: $250. AT FRANK S HOAG RECITAL HALL, BELMONT CAMPUS. (NAT'L). FRANK CEDRONE, PROJ DIR; UNIV OF SOUTHERN COLORADO, CENTER FOR CREATIVE & PERFORMING ARTS; PUEBLO, CO 81001. (#104041-1).

MAR 27 - 28, '76. SHOW AND TRADE MEET - ANTIQUE BARBED WIRE DISPLAY. EXHIBIT AT 4-H DINING ROOM, COLORADO STATE FAIR GROUNDS, SUMMIT & BEULAH AVE. (ST-WIDE). CHARLIE BRESSAN, DIRECTOR; THE COLORADO WIRE COLLECTOR'S ASSOC; 1720 CLAREMONT; PUEBLO, CO 81005. (#100582-1).

APR 3 - DEC 31, '76. SALUTE TO AMERICA AND COLORADO BARBERSHOP HARMONY SHOW. LIVE PERFORMANCE AT PUEBLO MEMORIAL HALL, CITY HALL - 100 BLK N MAIN ST. (ST-WIDE). W R MCFEDRIES, PRESIDENT; THE PUEBLO SUNSATIONAL CHAPTER OF SPEBQSA, INC; 1615 WABASH AVE; PUEBLO, CO 81004. (#104874-2).

APR 4, '76. PUEBLO YOUTH SYMPHONY SPRING CONCERT 'FROM AMERICA TO AUSTRIA'. GERHARD TRACK IS THE MUSIC DIRECTOR. AT MEMORIAL HALL, GRAND & UNION EXIT I25 ON 6TH ST; UNMETERED PARKING. (ST-WIDE). CARMELITA KEATOR, MANAGER; PUEBLO SYMPHONY ASSOC MOZART FESTIVAL 1976; 1117 LAKE AVE; PUEBLO, CO 81004. (#127-19).

APR 9 - 11, '76. THE LEGEND OF SILVER HEELS. A MODERN BALLET WITH ORIGINAL MUSIC COMPOSED BY ROBERT NARQUIS AND ORIGINAL CHOREOGRAPHY BY MARJORIE DEAN & KEITH WILLIS IS BASED ON COLORADO HISTORY AND LEGEND; IT WILL TOUR PUBLIC SCHOOLS AND SOUTHERN COLORADO. (ST-WIDE). ROCHELLE CHEPOVSKY, PRES; THE PUEBLO CIVIC BALLET COMPANY; 3129 COUNTRY CLUB DR; PUEBLO, CO 81008. (#101677-1).

APR 22, '76. PUEBLO SYMPHONY ORCHESTRA, GERHARD TRACK MUSIC DIRECTOR. THE GUEST PERFORMERS WILL BE A MALE CHOIR FROM BONN, GERMANY AND SOLOIST PATRICK HAYES, OKLAHOMA WINNER IN PIANO COMPETITION, YOUNG ARTISTS MOZART FESTIVAL 1975. AT MEMORIAL HALL, GRAND & UNION EXIT I25 ON 6TH ST; UNMETERED PARKING. (ST-WIDE). CARMELITA KEATOR, MANAGER; PUEBLO SYMPHONY ASSOC MOZART FESTIVAL 1976; 1117 LAKE AVE; PUEBLO, CO 81004. (#127-20).

APR 23 - 25, '76. LULAC STATE CONVENTION. CHICANO CULTURE TEATRO/WORKSHOPS ON EDUCATION, LABOR, BUSINESS, HOUSING AND AGING. AT UNIV OF SOUTHERN COLORADO. (ST-WIDE). MANUEL TRUJILLO, CHMN; LULAC COUNCIL 3008; 1618 IROQUOIS RD; PUEBLO, CO 81001. (#102094-1).

MAY 3 - 6, '76. OUR PAST REVISITED. EXHIBIT AT GYMNASIUM. (LOCAL). CHARLES CARMICHAEL, DIR; VINELAND JUNIOR HIGH SCHOOL; 1132 LANE 36; PUEBLO, CO 81006. (#20619-1).

MAY 8 - 14, '76. WEEK OF THE YOUNG CHILD. A WEEK-LONG CELEBRATION INVOLVING PUEBLO'S CHILDREN & PARENTS WITH COMMUNITY TALENTS & BUSINESSES. (LOCAL). JULIE NEMICK, PROJ CHMN; ALIANZO ASSOC FOR THE EDUCATION OF THE YOUNG CHILD; 24703 COUNTY FARM RD; PUEBLO, CO 81006. (#107025-1).

JUNE 1 - SEPT 30, '76. PUEBLO ARMY DEPOT BICENTENNIAL CELEBRATION. COMMANDER IS BOY SCOUT BICENTENNIAL COORDINATOR, DEPOT PROVIDES EXHIBITS FOR LOCAL FAIRS AND PARADES; PERMANENT BICENTENNIAL FLOAT TO BE CONSTRUCTED; OPEN HOUSE CELEBRATION IN 1976. (ST-WIDE). WILLIAM S FRANCIES, CHMN; PUEBLO ARMY DEPOT CENTENNIAL-BICENTENNIAL COMMITTEE; 47601 PHEASANT CREST; AVONDALE, CO 81002. (#18078-1).

JUNE 7, '76. HISTORICAL FARM, EXHIBITS OF FARMING METHODS, HOME LIFE, IMPLEMENTS. LIVE EXIBITS OF PIONEER CRAFTS AND TRADES, DEMONSTRATIONS OF OLD FARMING TECHNIQUES AND IMPLEMENTS, BUILDINGS RECONSTRUCTED AND FURNISHED AS ORIGINALLY BUILT IN THE FRONT RANGE AREA. PIONEER TRADES DEMONSTRATED AND SOLD AS ORIGINAL ART. AT OLD HONOR FARM SITE, PUEBLO, COLO. (ST-WIDE). DEPT OF PARKS & RECREATIO; DEPT OF PARK & RECREATION; CITY PARK OFFICE; PUEBLO, CO 81004. (#4407-1).

JUNE 13, '76. PUEBLO ELK'S FLAG DAY CEREMONY. PATRIOTIC SALUTE TO HISTORY AND AREAS OF AMERICAN DEVELOPMENT, FLAG DISPLAY AND MUSIC. AT DISTRICT 60 PUBLIC SCHOOL STADIUM, ABRIENDO & CLEVELAND ST. (LOCAL). FRANCES FLECKNER, SEC; ELKS CLUB 426; 426 N SANTA FE AVE; PUEBLO, CO 81003. (#101079-1).

JUNE 22 - 27, '76. 1976 ANNUAL CONFERENCE OF THE NATIONAL ASSOC OF GRUPOS FOLKLORICOS. CONFERENCE, FESTIVAL. (NAT'L). DARRELL BOHLSEN, DIRECTOR; SANGRE DE CRISTO ARTS & CONFERENCE CNETER; 210 N SANTA FE; PUEBLO, CO 81003. (#200007-144).

JUNE 25 - 27, '76. TOP TWENTY CITIZENS' BAND RADIO JAMBOREE. FRIDAY NIGHT SOCIAL; SATURDAY NIGHT DANCE; SUNDAY MORNING SERVICE. AT COLORADO STATE FAIR AGRICULTURAL BUILDING. (NAT'L). JAMES DENNIS, CHMN; STEEL CITY SEARCH & RESCUE; 2041 E EVANS; PUEBLO, CO 81005. (#13939-2).

JULY 2 - 4, '76. FRONTIER DAYS. FESTIVAL AT PUEBLO WEST ARENA. (LOCAL). MEL HARMON, CHAIRMAN; PUEBLO WEST & PUEBLO CENTENNIAL-BICENTENNIAL COMMITTEE; PUEBLO ARMY DEPOT; PUEBLO, CO 81003. (#108593-5).

JULY 3 - 4, '76. 4TH OF JULY CELEBRATION. FOOD, BOOTHS, SYMPHONY CONCERT, GAMES, BEER GARDEN, FILMS, ARTS & CRAFTS SHOW, CONTINUOUS ENTERTAINMENT. TOURS OF THE MUSEUM MAY BE TAKEN. AT PUEBLO METROPOLITAN MUSEUM GROUNDS, 419 W 14TH. (ST-WIDE). ROBERT FINNEY, COORD; PUEBLO METROPOLITAN MUSEUM WOMEN'S AUXILIARY; 419 W 19TH; PUEBLO, CO 81001. (#106999-2).

JULY 4, '76. COMBINED CHURCHES HISTORICAL PAGEANT. BAND CHOIRS & HISTORICAL COSTUMES ARE USED TO DEPICT THE HISTORY OF CHURCHES IN THE U S. AT COLORADO STATE FAIRGROUNDS, JACKSON & SMALL ST. (LOCAL). REV RAY HAWKINS, CHMN; PUEBLO INTERFAITH ASSOC; 1702 BONFORTE BLVD; PUEBLO, CO 81001. (#108593-1).

JULY 4, '76. ECUMENICAL RELIGIOUS PAGEANT. CEREMONY AT COLORADO STATE FAIRGROUNDS. (LOCAL). MEL HARMON, CHAIRMAN; PUEBLO CENTENNIAL-BICENTENNIAL COMMITTEE; PUEBLO ARMY DEPOT; PUEBLO, CO 81003. (#108593-3).

JULY 4, '76. FIREWORKS DISPLAY. FESTIVAL. (LOCAL). MEL HARMON, CHAIRMAN; PUEBLO SERTOMA CLUB & PUEBLO CENTENNIAL COMMITTEE; PUEBLO ARMY DEPOT; PUEBLO, CO 81003. (#108593-2).

JULY 4, '76. PONY EXPRESS RACE. COMPETITION, FESTIVAL AT FROM PUEBLO TO BEULAH. (LOCAL). DALE ALLEE, CHAIRMAN; BEULAH BICENTENNIAL COMMITTEE; 4770 WATER BARREL RD S; PUEBLO, CO 81004. (#108593-6).

JULY 5 - 7, '76. NATIONAL RADIO CB JAMBOREE-COMMUNICATIONS CONVENTION. FRIDAY NIGHT SOCIAL; SATURDAY NIGHT DANCE; SUNDAY MORNING WORSHIP. NATIONWIDE CONVENTION OF TWO-WAY RADIO OPERATORS TO REVIEW COMMUNICATIONS & REVIEW EXISTING PROJECTS TO DETERMINE NEW METHODS OF RELA TING COMMUNITY GOODWILL & BETTER SERVICE TO PUBLIC. (NAT'L). JAMES DENNIS; COLO STATE FAIRGROUNDS AGRICULTURAL BLDG; 2041 E EVANS; PUEBLO, CO 81004. (#13939-1).

AUG 1, '76. DEDICATION CONCERT ON COLORADOS CENTENNIAL BIRTHDAY. FOLLOWED BY A SERIES OF CONCERTS THROUGHOUT THE REMAINDER OF THE YR THIS WILL BE THE FIRST TRUE CONCERT QUALITY PIPE ORGAN IN ARKANSAS VALLEY. AT FRANK S HOAG RECITAL MUSIC RECITAL HALL. (ST-WIDE). RODNEY D TOWNLEY; SOUTHERN COLORADO STATE COLLEGE; 1120 WEST GRANT; PUEBLO, CO 81104. (#4346-1).

AUG 2 - 31, '76. A BICENTENNIAL SHOW OF CONTEMPORARY WEAVING. WEAVING PATTERNS FROM COLONIAL PAST USED IN CONTEMPORARY PIECES, INCLUDING SOME CONTEMPORARY RED, WHITE & BLUE FOR FUN. AT EL PUEBLO MUSEUM, 905 S PRAIRIE AVE. (LOCAL). E R SPENCER, COORDINATOR; FIBERS IN WEAVING; 2040 BALSAM; BOULDER, CO 80302. (#109308-1).

AUG 14, '76. OPENING OF BABE RUTH WORLD SERIES HEADQUARTERS. OPENING, CEREMONY AT RAMADA INN, HWY 50 BYPASS & HUDSON AVE. (LOCAL). MELVIN HARMON, CHAIRMAN; PUEBLO CENTENNIAL-BICENTENNIAL COMMITTEE; PUEBLO ARMY DEPOT; PUEBLO, CO 81003. (#108761-8).

AUG 15, '76. COKE PARTY FOR PRINCESSES & MOTHERS. FESTIVAL. (LOCAL). MELVIN HARMON; PUEBLO CENTENNIAL-BICENTENNIAL COMMITTEE; PUEBLO ARMY DEPOT; PUEBLO, CO 81003. (#108726-7).

AUG 17, '76. HOST FAMILY PLAN SOCIAL HOUR. FESTIVAL AT RAMADA INN, HWY 50 BYPASS & HUDSON AVE. (LOCAL). MELVIN HARMON, COORD; PUEBLO CENT-BICENT COMMITTEE; PUEBLO ARMY DEPOT; PUEBLO, CO 81003. (#108726-8).

AUG 19, '76. TEEN DANCE. FESTIVAL AT SANGRE DE CRISTO FINE ARTS CENTER. (LOCAL). MELVIN HARMON, COORD; PUEBLO CENTENNIAL-BICENTENNIAL COMMITTEE; PUEBLO ARMY DEPOT; PUEBLO, CO 81003. (#108726-6).

AUG 21, '76. MEXICAN HOSPITALITY NIGHT. FESTIVAL AT SANGRE DE CRISTO ARTS & CONFERENCE CENTER. (LOCAL). MELVIN HARMON, COORD; PUEBLO CENTENNIAL-BICENTENNIAL COMMITTEE & EXCHANGE CLUB; PUEBLO ARMY DEPOT; PUEBLO, CO 81003. (#108726-4).

AUG 21, '76. OPENING CEREMONIES - BABE RUTH SERIES. LIVE PERFORMANCE AT RUNYON FIELD. (LOCAL). MELVIN HARMON, COORD; PUEBLO CENTENNIAL-BICENTENNIAL COMMITTEE; PUEBLO ARMY DEPOT; PUEBLO, CO 81003. (#1914-3).

AUG 21, '76. WORLD SERIES PARADE. PARADE AT MEMORIAL HALL TO MAIN ST TO MINERAL PALACE PARK. (LOCAL). MELVIN HARMON, COORD; PUEBLO CENTENNIAL-BICENTENNIAL COMMITTEE; PUEBLO ARMY DEPOT; PUEBLO, CO 81003. (#1914-4).

AUG 21, '76. WORLD SERIES PICNIC. FESTIVAL AT MINERAL PALACE PARK. (LOCAL). MELVIN HARMON, COORD; PUEBLO CENTENNIAL-BICENTENNIAL COMMITTEE; PUEBLO ARMY DEPOT; PUEBLO, CO 81003. (#1914-5).

AUG 21 - 27, '76. 1976 BABE RUTH WORLD SERIES. NATL TOURNAMENT INVOLVING PLANNING & COMMITMENTS FROM EACH OF THE BABE RUTH LEAGUES IN THE STATE. TOURNAMENT WILL INVOLVE TEAMS ONLY FROM AGES 13 TO 15. AT RUNYON FIELD, 400 STANTON ST. (ST-WIDE). DAVID J NOVAK, CO-HOST; COLORADO CENTENNIAL-BICENTENNIAL COMMISSION; PO BOX 1976; DENVER, CO 81002. (#1914-1).

PUEBLO — CONTINUED

AUG 22, '76. HOSPITALITY NIGHT. FESTIVAL AT RAMADA INN. (LOCAL). NORM TRAVIS, COORD; COLORADO BABE RUTH LEAGUES, INC; PUEBLO, CO 81003. (#1914-2).

AUG 23, '76. ADULT GOLF TOURNAMENT. COMPETITION AT CITY PARK GOLF COURSE. (LOCAL). SOL RASO, DIRECTOR; PUEBLO CENTENNIAL-BICENTENNIAL COMMITTEE; PUEBLO, CO 81003. (#108726-1).

AUG 23, '76. ITALIAN HOSPITALITY NIGHT. FESTIVAL AT SANGRE DE CRISTO ARTS & CONFERENCE CENTER. (LOCAL). MELVIN HARMON, COORD; PUEBLO CENTENNIAL-BICENTENNIAL COMMITTEE; PUEBLO ARMY DEPOT; PUEBLO, CO 81003. (#108726-3).

AUG 23, '76. MINIATURE GOLF TOURNAMENT. COMPETITION AT CITY PARK MINIATURE GOLF COURSE. (LOCAL). MELVIN HARMON, COORD; JAYCEES; PUEBLO ARMY DEPOT; PUEBLO, CO 81003. (#108726-2).

AUG 24, '76. BOWLING TOURNAMENT. COMPETITION AT SUNSET PLAZA BOWL-O-MAT & BELMONT LANES. (LOCAL). MELVIN HARMON, CHAIRMAN; PUEBLO CENTENNIAL-BICENTENNIAL COMMITTEE; PUEBLO ARMY DEPOT; PUEBLO, CO 81003. (#108761-12).

AUG 24, '76. HOSPITALITY NIGHT. FESTIVAL, LIVE PERFORMANCE AT HOLIDAY INN. (LOCAL). MELVIN HARMON, CHAIRMAN; PUEBLO CENTENNIAL-BICENTENNIAL COMMITTEE; PUEBLO ARMY DEPOT; PUEBLO, CO 81003. (#108761-11).

AUG 24, '76. LADIES BRUNCH. FESTIVAL AT PUEBLO GOLD & COUNTRY CLUB. (LOCAL). MELVIN HARMON, CHAIRMAN; PUEBLO CENTENNIAL-BICENTENNIAL COMMITTEE; PUEBLO ARMY DEPOT; PUEBLO, CO 81003. (#108761-10).

AUG 24 - 29, '76. FIRST INTERNATIONAL CHARRO COMPETITIONS. AUGUST 24 WILL FEATURE U S VI CHARRO CONGRESO, AUGUST 28 WILL FEATURE CHARRO COMPLETO COMPETITION, AUGUST 29 WILL BE THE FINAL TEAM CHAMPIONSHIPS. A MINIMUM OF 12 ON BOTH MEXICAN AND AMERICAN TEAMS ARE EXPECTED. AT PUEBLO WEST HORSEMAN'S ARENA, GRANDSTAND, COLO STATE FAIRGROUNDS. (INT'L). TED CALANTINO, SEC; PUEBLO CHARRO ASSOC; 108 W 3RD ST; PUEBLO, CO 81003. (#106058-1).

AUG 25, '76. BOJOHN (SLAVIC) HOSPITALITY NIGHT. FESTIVAL, LIVE PERFORMANCE AT SANGRE DE CRISTO ARTS AND CONFERENCE CENTER. (LOCAL). MELVIN HARMON, CHAIRMAN; PUEBLO CENTENNIAL-BICENTENNIAL COMMITTEE; PUEBLO ARMY DEPOT; PUEBLO, CO 81003. (#108761-9).

AUG 25, '76. BUBBLE GUM CONTEST. COMPETITION AT CITY PARK PAVILION. (LOCAL). MELVIN HARMON, CHAIRMAN; PUEBLO CENT-BICENT COM & TOPPS BUBBLE GUM CORPORATION; PUEBLO ARMY DEPOT; PUEBLO, CO 81003. (#108761-16).

AUG 26, '76. HOSPITALITY NIGHT. FESTIVAL AT CHILTON INN. (LOCAL). MELVIN HARMON, CHAIRMAN; PUEBLO CENTENNIAL-BICENTENNIAL COMMITTEE; PUEBLO ARMY DEPOT; PUEBLO, CO 81003. (#108761-14).

AUG 26, '76. SUPER STAR CONTEST. COMPETITION AT RUNYON FIELD. (LOCAL). MELVIN HARMON, CHAIRMAN; PUEBLO CENTENNIAL-BICENTENNIAL COMMITTEE; PUEBLO ARMY DEPOT; PUEBLO, CO 81003. (#108761-15).

AUG 26, '76. WORLD SERIES BANQUET. GUEST SPEAKER: VERNON 'LEFTY' GOMEZ. AT UNIV OF S COLORADO STUDENT CENTER. (LOCAL). MELVIN HARMON, COORD; PUEBLO CENTENNIL-BICENTENNIAL COMMITTEE; PUEBLO ARMY DEPOT; PUEBLO, CO 81003. (#1914-6).

AUG 28 - SEPT 6, '76. COLORADO GOLD DAYS. A MUSICAL SALUTE TO COLORADO & USA; WILL INCLUDE SONGS, DANCES AND STORIES OF COLORADO'S RELATIONSHIP TO THE DEVELOPMENT OF THE USA. AT COLORADO STATE FAIRGROUNDS. (LOCAL). KEN PLONKEY, COORDINATOR; PUEBLO CENTENNIAL-BICENTENNIAL COMMITTEE; 19 ROBERTSON RD; PUEBLO, CO 81001. (#108761-17).

AUG 28 - SEPT 6, '76. COLORADO STATE FAIR AND CENTENNIAL EXPOSITION. RECOGNITION OF AGRICULTURE, YOUTH, CATTLE INDUSTRY, ART EDUCATION, SCIENCE. & TECHNOLOGY, BUSINESS & ECONOMICS, TO GROWTH OF COLORADO AND THE USA. AT STATE FAIRGROUNDS, BEULAH & ARROYO, PUEBLO, CO. (REGN'L). ROBERT J GENTRY; STATE OF COLORADO; STATE FAIRGROUNDS; PUEBLO, CO 81004. (#2936-1).

AUG 28 - SEPT 6, '76. HISTORICAL FARM, EXHIBITS OF FARMING METHODS, HOME LIFE, IMPLEMENTS. TO RECREATE A FARM OR FARMS AS THEY WERE IN COLORADO'S DISTANT PAST FOR THE PURPOSES OF RECALLING THE HARDSHIPS AND JOYS OF LIFE IN THIS EARLY PERIOD. AT OLD HONOR FARM SITE, PUEBLO, COLO. (ST-WIDE). DEPT OF PARKS & RECREATN; DEPT OF PARK & RECREATION; CITY PARK OFFICE; PUEBLO, CO 81004. (#4407-2).

AUG 28 - SEPT 6, '76. SPIRIT OF '76 FIREWORKS SPECTACULAR. FESTIVAL AT STATE FAIRGROUNDS. (ST-WIDE). ROBERT J GENTRY, DIR; THE AMERICAN LEGION, DEPARTMENT OF COLORADO; PUEBLO, CO 81004. (#103113-1).

SEPT 1 - 30, '76. CONCERT MONTH. LIVE PERFORMANCE. (LOCAL). HELEN TITUS, COORDINATOR; CONCERT MONTH COMMITTEE; 419 W 1JTH ST; PUEBLO, CO 81003. (#108761-4).

SEPT 5, '76. CENTENNIAL-BICENTENNIAL AIR FAIR. AIR SHOW WILL INCLUDE EXHIBITION FLIGHTS, PARATROOPERS, SKY WRITING AND STATIC DISPLAYS; PRIVATE PILOTS FROM THROUGHOUT THE U S WILL BE INVITED TO PARTICIPATE. (REGN'L). BOYD DAMKOEHLER, COORD; PUEBLO CENTENNIAL-BICENTENNIAL COMMISSION; 1601 COMMACHE RD; PUEBLO, CO 81001. (#103416-37).

SEPT 5, '76. CENTENNIAL-BICENTENNIAL FALL MUSIC SERIES. LIVE PERFORMANCE. (LOCAL). DARNELL BOHLSEN, COORD; PUEBLO CENTENNIAL-BICENTENNIAL COMMITTEE; 210 N SANTA FE AVE; PUEBLO, CO 81003. (#108761-20).

SEPT 12, '76. CENTENNIAL-BICENTENNIAL FALL MUSIC SERIES. LIVE PERFORMANCE. (LOCAL). DARNELL BOHLSEN, COORD; PUEBLO CENTENNIAL-BICENTENNIAL COMMITTEE; 210 N SANTA FE AVE; PUEBLO, CO 81003. (#108761-19).

SEPT 19, '76. CENTENNIAL-BICENTENNIAL FALL MUSIC SERIES. LIVE PERFORMANCE. (LOCAL). DARNELL BOHLSEN, COORD; PUEBLO CENTENNIAL-BICENTENNIAL COMMITTEE; 210 N SANTA FE AVE; PUEBLO, CO 81003. (#108761-22).

SEPT 26, '76. CENTENNIAL-BICENTENNIAL FALL MUSIC SERIES. LIVE PERFORMANCE. (LOCAL). DARNELL BOHLSEN, COORD; PUEBLO CENTENNIAL-BICENTENNIAL COMMITTEE; 210 N SANTA FE AVE; PUEBLO, CO 81003. (#108761-21).

OCT 17, '76. THE FIRST HAUSMUSIK WITH THE PUEBLO SYMPHONY. LIVE PERFORMANCE. (LOCAL). HELEN TITUS, COORDINATOR; PUEBLO SYMPHONY ORCHESTRA; 419 W 14TH ST; PUEBLO, CO 81003. (#108761-6).

OCT 30 - 31, '76. CAMPFIRE GIRLS BICENT FAIR. SHOWING PUEBLO'S ETHNIC BACKGROUND; CRAFTS, FOOD, COSTUME, DANCE & MUSIC. AT SANGRE DE CRISTO ARTS & CONFERENCE CENTER. (LOCAL). DONNA D CALBER, COORD; PUEBLO CAMP FIRE GIRLS; 705 POLK; PUEBLO, CO 81004. (#108761-3).

NOV 9, '76. MUSEUM'S 9TH ANNIVERSARY PARTY. FESTIVAL. (LOCAL). HELEN TITUS, COORDINATOR; MUSEUM AUXILIARY; 419 W 14TH ST; PUEBLO, CO 81003. (#108761-7).

NOV 10 - 12, '76. TECHNOLOGICAL SYMPOSIUM. EXPOSITION OF HISTORICAL ASPECTS OF TECHNOLOGY 1776-1976, ALSO FUTURE ASPECTS. 9 SEMINARS & 3 MAJOR KEYNOTE ADDRESSES BY NOTABLE INDUSTRIAL & GOVERNMENTAL OFFICIALS ARE PLANNED. AT LIFE SCIENCES AUDITORIUM & UNIV CENTER FACILITIES. (ST-WIDE). ROBERT L SMITH, COORD; UNIV OF SOUTHERN COLORADO; 1820 MAPELWOOD; PUEBLO, CO 81004. (#106999-1).

DEC '76. 'CHRISTMAS WITH THE MUSEUM'. FESTIVAL. (LOCAL). HELEN TITUS, COORDINATOR; MUSEUM AUXILIARY; 419 W 14TH ST; PUEBLO, CO 81003. (#108761-5).

PUEBLO WEST

JUNE 22 - 26, '76. MISS PUEBLO WEST PAGEANT. SELECTING AND CROWNING A QUEEN. AT NATIONAL HORSEMAN ARENA. (ST-WIDE). ERCEL DEWSON, DIRECTOR; PUEBLO WEST CITIZEN ASSOC; PO BOX 7022; PUEBLO WEST, CO 81007. (#104874-6).

JULY 2 - 4, '76. GIRLS' RODEO ASSOC WORLD CHAMPIONSHIP. THIS IS ONE OF THE RICHEST ALL GIRL RODEOS IN HISTORY WITH MORE THAN 200 PARTICIPANTS; PRIZE MONEY WILL BE IN EXCESS OF $25,000. AT NATIONAL HORSEMEN ARENA. (INT'L). PATRICIA MACHUK, CHMN; PUEBLO WEST CITIZEN ASSOC; 146 S GOLFWOOD DR; PUEBLO WEST, CO 81007. (#108589-1).

JULY 2 - 5, '76. CARNIVAL - 'TYPICAL USA FAMILY FUN'. TYPICAL USA FAMILY FUN. AT NATIONAL HORSEMAN ARENA. (ST-WIDE). ERCEL DEWSON, DIRECTOR; PUEBLO WEST CITIZEN ASSOC; PO BOX 7022; PUEBLO WEST, CO 81007. (#104874-9).

JULY 3, '76. EXHIBITS. EXHIBIT AT NATIONAL HORSEMAN ARENA. (LOCAL). ERCEL DEWSON, CHAIRMAN; PUEBLO WEST CITIZEN'S ASSOC; PO 7022; PUEBLO WEST, CO 81007. (#104875-1).

JULY 3, '76. FIREWORKS SHOW. PATRIOTIC DISPLAY, FESTIVAL USA. AT NATIONAL HORSEMAN ARENA. (LOCAL). ERCEL DEWSON, CHAIRMAN; PUEBLO WEST CITIZENS'S ASSOC; PO 7022; PUEBLO WEST, CO 81007. (#104874-12).

JULY 3, '76. FOLK DANCING - PAST, PRESENT AND FUTURE. EXHIBIT OF VARIOUS ETHNIC DANCES OUR PAST AND FUTURE. AT NATIONAL HORSEMAN ARENA. (ST-WIDE). ERCEL DEWSON, DIRECTOR; PUEBLO WEST CITIZEN ASSOC; PO BOX 7022; PUEBLO WEST, CO 81007. (#104874-8).

JULY 3, '76. FOOD FESTIVAL WITH VARIOUS ETHNIC DISHES. SALES OF VARIOUS ETHNIC FOODS. AT NATIONAL HORSEMAN ARENA. (ST-WIDE). ERCEL DEWSON, DIRECTOR; PUEBLO WEST CITIZEN ASSOC; PO BOX 7022; PUEBLO WEST, CO 81007. (#104874-7).

JULY 3, '76. JULY 3RD PARADE. PARADE AT NATIONAL HORSEMAN ARENA. (ST-WIDE). ERCEL DEWSON, DIRECTOR; PUEBLO WEST CITIZEN ASSOC; PO BOX 7022; PUEBLO WEST, CO 81007. (#104874-3).

JULY 3, '76. OLD FASHIONED FAIR. FAIR AT NATIONAL HORSEMAN ARENA. (ST-WIDE). ERCEL DEWSON, DIRECTOR; PUEBLO WEST CITIZEN ASSOC; PO BOX 7022; PUEBLO WEST, CO 81007. (#104874-4).

JULY 3, '76. PROFESSIONAL ENTERTAINMENT - NASHVILLE MUSIC. LIVE PERFORMANCE AT NATIONAL HORSEMAN ARENA. (ST-WIDE). ERCEL DEWSON, DIRECTOR; PUEBLO WEST CITIZEN ASSOC; PO BOX 7022; PUEBLO WEST, CO 81007. (#104874-10).

JULY 3, '76. RODEO AND OLD WESTERN FUN. TYPICAL RODEO EVENTS, OLD WESTERN FUN. AT NATIONAL HORSEMAN ARENA. (ST-WIDE). ERCEL DEWSON, DIRECTOR; PUEBLO WEST CITIZEN ASSOC; PO BOX 7022; PUEBLO WEST, CO 81007. (#104874-5).

JULY 3, '76. SENIOR CITIZENS CHORUS FROM FLINT MICHIGAN. FOUR PART HARMONY CHORUS WILL TOUR COLORADO FOR 6 DAYS; AVERAGE AGE OF MEMBERS IS 73. AT NATIONAL HORSEMAN ARENA. (ST-WIDE). ERCEL DEWSON, DIRECTOR; PUEBLO WEST CITIZEN ASSOC; PO BOX 7022; PUEBLO WEST, CO 81007. (#104874-11).

RAMAH

'CREATE YOUR OWN PROJECT' - RAMAH, CO. REPAIR & REPLACE PLAYGROUND EQUIPMENT IN THE PARK. (LOCAL). VIOLET MCKAY, COORDINATOR; TOWN OF RAMAH; PO BOX 41; RAMAH, CO 80832. (#26898).

JULY 18, '76. TOWN SOCIAL: HAMBURGER FRY IN THE PARK. FESTIVAL AT TOWN PARK. (LOCAL). VIOLET MCKAY, PROJ DIR; TOWN OF RAMAH; PO BOX 141; RAMAH, CO 80832. (#200007-148).

RANGELY

RANGELY'S PRESENT, PAST AND FUTURE PARK, CO. PARK WILL BE LANDSCAPED AND DESCRIPTIVE SIGN WILL BE CONSTRUCTED. (LOCAL). LEONARD W SMITH, COORDINATOR; CITY OF RANGELY; BOX 365; RANGELY, CO 81648. (#26340).

STREET RENAMING - RANGELY, CO. A STREET IN RANGELY WILL BE RENAMED AFTER A LOCAL PERSON AND OTHER PEOPLE WHO HAVE CONTRIBUTED TO THE COMMUNITY WILL BE HONORED BY THE MAYOR. (LOCAL). CECIL LOLLAR, COORDINATOR; RANGELY CENTENNIAL-BICENTENNIAL COMMITTEE; RANGELY, CO 81648. (#26200).

APR 25 - DEC 31, '76. ARTS FESTIVAL. EXHIBIT. (LOCAL). LEONARD W SMITH, COORD; TOWN OF RANGELY; BOX 365; RANGELY, CO 81648. (#108757-1).

RED CLIFF

MUSEUM, RED CLIFF, CO. COLLECT AND DISPLAY-HISTORICAL ITEMS WITH A SPECIAL AREA SET ASIDE FOR MINING RELICS AND HISTORY OF THE EAGLE MINE AT NEARBY GILMAN. (ST-WIDE). PEARL HENDERSON, COORDINATOR; EAGLE COUNTY HISTORICAL SOCIETY; RED CLIFF, CO 81649. (#22554).

RED CLIFF COMMUNITY CENTER, CO. AN OLD SCHOOL BUILDING WILL BE RESTORED, TO HOUSE CITY COUNCIL CHAMBERS, COMMUNITY HALL WITH KITCHEN FACILITIES, A LIBRARY-MUSEUM & A COMMUNITY DAY CARE FACILITY. (LOCAL). HON MANUEL MARTINEZ, MAYOR; TOWN OF REDCLIFF; REDCLIFF, CO 81649. (#16388).

MAY 30, '76. MEMORIAL DAY PICNIC AND OLD-TIMERS REUNION. CEREMONY AT KNOB HILL. (LOCAL). PEARL HENDERSON, COORD; NEIGHBORS OF WOODCRAFT; RED CLIFF, CO 81649. (#106068-1).

JULY 25 - AUG 1, '76. PILGRIMAGE TO MOUNT OF THE HOLY CROSS. PILGRIMAGE CONSISTS OF A WEEK OF DAILY CLIMBS OF NOTCH MOUNTAIN WHERE NOONTIME SERVICES WILL BE HELD, IN FRONT OF THE FAMOUS CROSS (OF SNOW, ON ADJOINING MT OF THE HOLY CROSS), EACH LED BY THE CHURCHES OF A PARTICULAR COMMUNITY IN EAGLE COUNTY. AT TIGIWON LODGE/SOUTH OF MINTORN. (ST-WIDE). REV DON SIMONTON, COORD; TOWN OF RED CLIFF/LOCAL CHURCHES; 2557 W AROSA DR; VAIL, CO 81657. (#106068-2).

SEPT 4, '76. RED CLIFF CENTENNIAL-BICENTENNIAL FIESTA. FESTIVAL, PARADE AT MAIN STREET UNION HALL COMMUNITY CENTER. (LOCAL). MANUEL MARTINEZ, COORD; TOWN OF RED CLIFF; RED CLIFF, CO 81649. (#106068-3).

RICO

COLORADO CHRONICLES - RICO. A SPECIAL EDITION OF THE COLORADO CHRONICLES WILL BE PUBLISHED. (LOCAL). JACK T BURRAN, PROJ DIRECTOR; PO BOX 51; RICO, CO 81332. (#26265).

DOLORES COUNTY, COLO, COURTHOUSE RESTORATION. A PROJECT TO RESTORE THE OLD DOLORES COUNTY COURTHOUSE FOR USE AS A MUSEUM LIBRARY TOWN MEETING HALL AND POSSIBLY A CLINIC. PROJECT WILL REWIRE, REPLASTER & INSTALL NEW LIGHTING. (LOCAL). HON JACK P CURRAN, MAYOR; TOWN OF RICO; PO BOX 56; RICO, CO 81332. (#4416). **ARBA GRANTEE.**

OLD-TIMERS DAY. HONOR THE OLDEST RESIDENT BORN IN RICO; ALSO, DANCE, BARBEQUE AND PARADE. (LOCAL). JACK CURRAN, DIRECTOR; RICO OLD-TIMERS DAY COMMITTEE; PO BOX 51; RICO, CO 81332. (#108758-1).

JUNE 14, '76. BICENTENNIAL FLAG PRESENTATION. AWARD, CEREMONY AT COURT HOUSE. (LOCAL). LONNIE COLE, CHMN; RICO BICENTENNIAL COMMISSION; BOX 237; RICO, CO 81332. (#104164-2).

JULY 4, '76. CENTENNIAL FIREWORKS. FESTIVAL. (LOCAL). JACK CURRAN, PROJ DIR; CITY OF RICO; PO BOX 51; RICO, CO 81332. (#108584-1).

AUG 14, '76. VARIETY SHOW. LIVE PERFORMANCE AT RICO THEATRE. (LOCAL). MARY JAHNKE, CHMN; RICO BICENTENNIAL COMMITTEE; BOX 156; RICO, CO 81332. (#104164-3).

AUG 14 - 15, '76. ARTS AND CRAFTS. EXHIBIT AT RICO PUBLIC SCHOOL LIBRARY ROOM. (LOCAL). DEE JONES, LIBRARIAN; PUBLIC LIBRARY RICO SEWING CLUB; BOX 86; RICO, CO 81332. (#104164-1).

AUG 14 - 15, '76. REVIVAL OF ANNUAL RICO DAZE CELEBRATION. PATRIOTIC FLAG CELEBRATION, RE-DEDICATION OF DELORES CO COURTHOUSE AS A COMMUNITY CENTER, PARADE, ARTS & CRAFTS, VARIETY SHOW, GYMKANA AND INTERTUBE RACES ON DELORES RIVER. (LOCAL). JACK P CURRAN, COORD; RICO DAZE CELEBRATION COMMITTEE; PO BOX 51; RICO, CO 81332. (#108662-1).

RICO — CONTINUED

AUG 15, '76. GYMKANA PARADE. COMPETITION, PARADE AT RICO BALL PARK. (LOCAL). GRADY LEAVELL, CHMN; RICO CHAMBER OF COMMERCE; BOX 144; RICO, CO 81332. (#104164-4).

RIDGWAY

TOWN PARK DEVELOPEMENT - RIDGWAY, CO. INSTALLATION OF ADDITIONAL BUILDINGS IN TOWN PARK FOR FAIR, RODEO AND BARBEQUE. (LOCAL). DIRECTOR; TOWN OF RIDGWAY; PO BOX 242; RIDGWAY, CO 81432. (#25989).

SEPT 4 - 6, '76. OURAY COUNTY FAIR. ACTIVITIES INCLUDE: RODEO, RACE MEET AND BARBEQUE. (ST-WIDE). MARJORIE ISRAEL, CLERK; TOWN BOARD OF TRUSTEES; LENA ST, PO BOX 242; RIDGWAY, CO 81432. (#108361-1).

SEPT 4 - 6, '76. SPECIAL EXHIBITS AT OURAY COUNTY FAIR AND RODEO. ANNUAL COUNTY FAIR AND RODEO TO FEATURE EXHIBITS ON HISTORY OF RANCHING AND AGRICULTURE IN REGION TO CELEBRATE CENTENNIAL YEAR FOR OURAY AND COLORADO, POSSIBLY PARADE OF HORSE-DRAWN VEHICLES AT RODEO. AT OURAY COUNTY FAIR GROUNDS. (ST-WIDE). ROBERT MIDDLETON, CHMN; OURAY COUNTY SHERIFF'S POSSE-4H ORGANIZATION; RFD 2, BOX 300; COLONA, CO 81432. (#4123-1).

RIFLE

'76 YOUTH ENVIRONMENT PROGRAM - RIFLE, CO. HIGH SCHOOL YOUTH WILL WORK ON RESTORATIONS, MARK HISTORIC TRAILS & SITES AND LANDSCAPE & CLEAN UP IN AND AROUND RIFLE AND SURROUNDING COMMUNITIES. (LOCAL). CURT NEUMAN, COMMITTEE DIRECTOR; RIFLE COMMITTEE FOR '76; PO BOX 76; RIFLE, CO 81650. (#17645).

JUNE 25 - 27, '76. CHAUTAUQUA. LIVE PERFORMANCE. (LOCAL). MAJORIE PRICE, COORD; TOWN OF RIFLE; PO BOX 809; RIFLE, CO 81650. (#200007-149).

ROCKVALE

RESTORATION PROJECTS - ROCKVALE, CO. RESTORATION OF EXTERIOR OF OLD SCHOOL BUILDING, COMMUNITY HALL AND OLD FIRE HOSE BELONGING TO THE FIRE DEPT. (LOCAL). JACK D LENNOX, COORDINATOR; BOX 305; ROCKVALE, CO 81244. (#26266).

ROCKY FORD

FAIRGROUNDS IMPROVEMENT - ROCKY FORD, CO. IMPROVEMENTS INCLUDE REPLACEMENT OF RAIL ON RACETRACK, COVERING OF GRANDSTAND AREA, ADDITION OF PUBLIC RESTROOMS AND REPLACEMENT OF 4-H BARN. (LOCAL). KEITH BEATTLE, MANAGER; ARK VALLEY FAIR AND EXPO; 908 ELM AVE; ROCKY FORD, CO 81067. (#24592).

ROCKY FORD WESTERN HISTORY & HERITAGE TRAIL - COLO. BRING TO ATTENTION THE ROLE SOUTHEAST COLORADO PLAYED IN THE HISTORY & DEVELOPMENT OF THE STATE BY DEVELOPING A WESTERN HISTORY AND HERITAGE TRAIL. (LOCAL). ROBERT CAMPBELL, ADMINISTRATIVE DIRECTOR; WESTERN HISTORY & HERITAGE TRAIL; ROUTE #2, BOX 358; ROCK FORD, CO 81067. (#1104). **ARBA GRANTEE.**

ROCKY FORD, COLO, INTL STUDENTS EXCHANGE PROGRAM. A PROGRAM TO BRING STUDENTS FROM OUTSIDE THE USA INTO THE COMMUNITY AND SCHOOLS OF ROCKY FORD IN '76 ON A THREE MONTHS BASIS TO INTRODUCE THE IDEAS OF FESTIVAL USA TO EACH FOREIGN STUDENT. (INT'L). ROBERT E CAMPBELL, CHAIRPERSON; ROCKY FORD HIGH SCHOOL; 601 S 2ND ST; ROCKY FORD, CO 81050. (#2963).

WESTERN HISTORY AND HERITAGE STUDY SEMINAR OF COLO. SEMINARS TO INTRODUCE THE PEOPLE OF ROCKY FORD TO THEIR HISTORIC PAST AND PROMISING FUTURE OF ROCKY FORD. (LOCAL). ROBERT CAMPBELL, ADMINISTRATIVE DIRECTOR; WESTERN HISTORY AND HERITAGE ASSOC; RT #2 BOX 434C; ROCKY FORD, CO 81067. (#2758).

MAR 1 - AUG 31, '76. CENTENNIAL CELEBRATION. FESTIVAL. (LOCAL). ROBERT E CAMPBELL; TOWN OF ROCKY FORD; CITY ADMIN BLDG, S MAIN ST; ROCKY FORD, CO 81067. (#108585-1).

ROGGEN

DISPLAY OF UNITED STATES FLAGS - ROGGEN, CO. THIS HISTORICAL DISPLAY WILL CONTAIN THE FIRST U S FLAG DOWN TO TODAY'S FLAG; COLORADO'S FLAG WILL BE INCLUDED IN DISPLAY WHICH WILL BE OPEN TO THE PUBLIC AT THE GRANGE HALL. (LOCAL). MRS MYRNA WAGNER, PROJ DIRECTOR; KIOWA COMMUNITY CENTENNIAL-BICENTENNIAL COMMITTEE; ROGGEN, CO 80652. (#15276).

FLOAT SPONSORED BY KIOWA UNION SUNDAY SCHOOL, SE WELD-4-H FAIR. FESTIVAL AT HELD IN KEENESBURG, CO. (LOCAL). MRS MYRNA WAGNER, CHMN; KIOWA UNION SUNDAY SCHOOL; ROGGEN, CO 80652. (#102322-1).

HISTORY OF HOMESTEADING FAMILIES IN ROGGEN, CO. AS PART OF THE CENTENNIAL-BICENTENNIAL CELEBRATION, A HISTORY OF FAMILIES WHO HAVE HOMESTEADED IN THE AREA WILL BE COMPILED. (LOCAL). MRS MYRNA WAGNER, PROJ DIRECTOR; HOMESTEAD GRANGE AND BOOSTER CLUB; ROGGEN, CO 80652. (#15274).

MAP OF COMMUNITY - ROGGEN, CO. THIS MAP WILL SHOW THE ORIGINAL HOMESTEAD SITES AND PRESENT OWNERS AS PART OF THE CENTENNIAL OF COLORADO & BICENTENNIAL OF THE NATION. (LOCAL). MRS MYRNA WAGNER, PROJ DIRECTOR; HOMESTEAD GRANGE AND BOOSTER CLUB; ROGGEN, CO 80652. (#15275).

JULY 3, '76. 4TH OF JULY EVE DANCE. FESTIVAL AT GRANGE HALL, 13 MILES SE ROGGEN; PARKING FACILITIES ON GROUNDS. (LOCAL). MRS MYRNA WAGNER, CHPRSN; HOMESTEAD GRANGE; ROGGEN, CO 80652. (#107624-1).

ROMEO

ROMEO EDUCATIONAL/RECREATIONAL CENTER, CO. ESTABLISHMENT OF AN EDUCATIONAL-RECREATIONAL FACILITY FOR THE COMMUNITY. (LOCAL). HON GERTRUDE SALAZAR, MAYOR; ROMEO TOWN COUNCIL; 2ND & BLANCA; ROMEO, CO 81148. (#24363).

JULY 22, '76. FIESTAS DE ROMEO. FESTIVAL: PARADE, MOANING CHURCH SERVICES & ETHNIC PERFORMANCES. (LOCAL). RAYMOND E RAEL, CHAIRMAN; FIESTAS DE ROMEO COMMITTEE; ROMEO, CO 81148. (#108683-1).

RYE

TOWN IMPROVEMENT - RYE, CO. TOWN WILL BE IMPROVED BY BEAUTIFICATION OF HOMES. (LOCAL). HAROLD C PETERSON, COORDINATOR; TOWN IMPROVEMENT COMMITTEE; BOX 129; RYE, CO 81069. (#26274).

JULY 3, '76. MUSICAL & DRAMA PROGRAM. LIVE PERFORMANCE. (LOCAL). HAROLD C PETERSON, COORD; CITY OF RYE; BOX 129; RYE, CO 81069. (#108586-3).

JULY 3, '76. WESTERN DANCE. COMPETITION, FAIR. (LOCAL). HAROLD C PETERSON, COORD; CITY OF RYE; BOX 129; RYE, CO 81069. (#108586-2).

JULY 4, '76. INTERNATIONAL FESTIVAL BAR-B-QUE. FESTIVAL. (LOCAL). HAROLD C PETERSON, COORD; CITY OF RYE; BOX 129; RYE, CO 81069. (#108586-1).

SALIDA

FIB ARK BOAT RACES & PARADE. COMPETITION, PARADE. (LOCAL). EDWARD TOUBER, COORD; CITY OF SALIDA; 122 W 2ND; SALIDA, CO 81201. (#108756-1).

SALIDA AND CHAFFEE COUNTY, COLO, HISTORICAL BOOK. CENTENNIAL-BICENTENNIAL HISTORY OF SALIDA AND CHAFFEE COUNTIES BY LOCAL AUTHOR, STEVE FRAZEE, TO BE MARKETED BY SALIDA MUSEUM ASSOCIATION. (LOCAL). KENNETH ENGLERT, PROJECT DIRECTOR; SALIDA MUSEUM ASSOCIATION; C/O 9095 COUNTY ROAD 120; SALIDA, CO 81201. (#4167). **(??).**

SALIDA MUSEUM PROJECT OF COLORADO. A PROJECT TO BUILD A 40'X100' BUILDING TO BE USED AS A MUSEUM AND A COMMUNITY CENTER. THE BUILDING WILL BE USED FOR ART SHOWS AND OTHER CULTURAL EVENTS AS WELL AS FOR MEETINGS. (LOCAL). MRS SAM RANDOLPH; SALIDA MUSEUM ASSOCIATION; 1401 J STREET; SALIDA, CO 81201. (#4411). **ARBA GRANTEE.**

SPIRIT OF 76 HIGH COUNTRY JEEP TOUR, SALIDA, COLO. A TOUR OF HISTORIC SITES WHICH ARE NOW GHOST TOWNS IN THE HIGHLANDS OF COLORADO. (LOCAL). RALPH WILSON, MANAGER; CHAMBER OF COMMERCE; 123 E ST; SALIDA, CO 81201. (#5946).

1976 LIBRARY FOR THE SALIDA, COLO, SCHOOLS. CREATION OF A SPECIAL LIBRARY BY THE SALIDA SCHOOL SYSTEM TO HOUSE COLORADO HISTORY DOCUMENTS AND BOOKS AND ARTICLES WRITTEN BY THE STUDENTS ON HISTORY EVENTS. (LOCAL). CHARLES MELIEN, SUPERINTENDENT; SALIDA SCHOOL SYSTEM; 146 ADAMS; SALIDA, CO 81201. (#4170).

'76 PAST AND FUTURE - MUSEUM FOR SALIDA, COLO. ESTABLISH A SALIDA MUSEUM AND COMMUNITY CENTER TO HOUSE ARTIFACTS OF AREA & FOR COMMUNITY EVENTS. (LOCAL). ARA RANDOLPH, PRESIDENT; SALIDA MUSEUM ASSOC; 1421 J ST; SALIDA, CO 81201. (#4155).

'76 SALIDA LANDMARKS PROJECT OF COLORADO. BEAUTIFY AND REFOREST TENDERFOOT MOUNTAIN AND DEDICATE SAME TO CITIZENS OF SALIDA IN 2076. (ST-WIDE). GENE POST, PRESIDENT; SALIDA IZAAK WALTON LEAGUE; 1425 E STREET; SALIDA, CO 81201. (#4173). **(??).**

JULY 24 - 25, '75. CENTENNIAL ART SHOW OF SALIDA, COLORADO. THREE ART SHOWS DURING 76. OPEN TO THE PUBLIC. (LOCAL). LORENE ENGLERT; VALLEY ARTIST; SALIDA, CO 81201. (#2717-1).

JAN 1, '76. 'HELLO 1976' - FIREWORKS SALUTE. FESTIVAL AT TENDERFOOT MT. (LOCAL). GLENN VAWSER, CO-CHMN; SALIDA CENTENNIAL-BICENTENNIAL COMMITTEE; 746 D; SALIDA, CO 81201. (#104290-2).

JAN 27 - 28, '76. 1976 HISTORICAL PAGEANT OF SALIDA & CHAFFEE COUNTY. HISTORY PRESENTED IN RELATION TO 25 YEAR SEGMENTS. A SERIES OF HISTORICAL SKITS BACKED WITH MUSICAL GROUPS. NET PROCEEDS TO BE GIVEN TO COMMUNITY PROJECT. AT SALIDA HIGH SCHOOL AUDITORIUM. (LOCAL). MRS WILLIAM RUSH; BETA SIGMA PHI; 1148 F ST; SALIDA, CO 81201. (#2756-1).

MAR 6 - 7, '76. DEDICATION OF COMMUNITY CENTER & HIGH SCHOOL STUDENT ART SHOW. CEREMONY, EXHIBIT. (LOCAL). MRS SAM RANDOLPH, DIR; SALIDA MUSEUM ASSOC; 1401 J ST; SALIDA, CO 81201. (#200007-150).

MAY 28, '76. CEREMONY HONORING OLDEST SENIOR CITIZEN. PUBLIC CELEBRATION OF CLARENCE C BROWN'S 100TH BIRTHDAY. COFFEE AND CAKE WILL BE SERVED. AT SALIDA BUILDING & LOAN MEETING ROOM. (LOCAL). CHARLIE BROWN, COORD; SALIDA BUILDING & LOAN ASSOC; 130 W 2ND; SALIDA, CO 81201. (#107006-1).

JUNE 12 - 13, '76. CENTENNIAL-BICENTENNIAL ART SHOW. EXHIBIT. (LOCAL). SHIRLEY DAVIS, PROJ DIR; VALLEY ARTISTS LEAGUE; 132 E 1ST ST; SALIDA, CO 81201. (#200007-151).

JUNE 12 - JULY 25, '76. VALLEY ARTISTS LEAGUE ART EXHIBIT. OPEN ART SHOW - ALL MEDIA. (LOCAL). SHIRLEY DAVIS, PROJ DIR; VALLEY ARTISTS LEAGUE; 132 E FIRST ST; SALIDA, CO 81201. (#100607-1).

JUNE 18 - 20, '76. SPIRIT OF 76 - KAYACK INTL BOAT RACES. ENLARGED CENTENNIAL-BICENTENNIAL, KAYAK WHITEWATER BOAT RACES WITH A SPIRIT OF 76 AMERICAN FIRST PARADE. SLALOM RACES START AT 11:00 AM ON SAT; 23 MILE DOWN RIVER RACE FROM SALIDA TO COTOPAXI STARTS AT 10 AM ON SUNDAY. AT RIVERSIDE PARK; ARKANSAS RIVER. (LOCAL). ALAN SULZENFUS, COMMADORE; FIB-ARK BOAT RACE COMMITTEE; 222 SOUTH E ST; SALIDA, CO 81201. (#2752-1).

JUNE 18 - 20, '76. 1976 FESTIVAL OF RECREATION: NATIONAL LITTLE BRITCHES RODEO. RODEO EVENTS, QUEEN CONTEST - JR GIRLS 8-13 YEARS; SR GIRLS 14-18 YEARS; 06-19-76 RODEO DANCE; 06-20 CHURCH SERVICE ON HORSEBACK & CONCESSION STAND FOR FOOD. AT HEART OF THE ROCKIES RODEO GROUNDS-COUNTY RD 120-WEST. (LOCAL). LEN KAPUSHION, DIRECTOR; HEART OF THE ROCKIES RECREATION; PO BOX 121; SALIDA, CO 81201. (#2720-2).

JULY 3, '76. 50 MILE ENDURANCE HORSE RIDE. ENDURANCE HORSE RIDE OVER MARKED TRAIL; START & FINISH AT PONDEROSA GUEST RANCH; COURSE TO INCLUDE TRAVEL ON HORSEBACK TO SHAVANO MT & CHALK CREEK AREAS; SPECIAL-CBS AWARD TO EACH PARTICIPANT; ENTRIES ARE NOW BEING ACCEPTED. AT PONDEROSA GUEST RANCH-WEST OF SALIDA. (LOCAL). RICHILIEU CHILDS, DIR; HEART OF THE ROCKIES RECREATION ASSOC; SALIDA, CO 81201. (#2720-4).

JULY 4, '76. WORLD CHAMPIONSHIP BUFFALO CHIP THROWING CONTEST. PART OF 4TH OF JULY EVENTS, FUNDAYS, FIREWORKS DISPLAY, BARBECUE. INDIAN DANCES BY 'CHAVANEAU INDIAN INTERPRETIVE DANCERS' LITTLE BRITCHES RODEO. 50 MILE ENDURANCE RIDE; INDIAN DANCES AT 8 PM. BICENTENNIAL FIREWORKS DISPLAY AT 9 PM. AT RODEO GROUNDS; COUNTY RD 120, WEST OF SALIDA. (REGN'L). LEN KAPUSHION; HEART OF THE ROCKIES RECREATION ASSN INC. (HRRA); PO 121; SALIDA, CO 81201. (#2720-1).

JULY 4, '76. 4TH OF JULY FIREWORKS DISPLAY WITH FLAG DISPLAY. FESTIVAL. (LOCAL). EDWARD TOUBER, COORD; FOURTH OF JULY COMMITTEE; 207 E THIRD ST; SALIDA, CO 81201. (#108690-1).

JULY 18 - SEPT 19, '76. HI COUNTRY JEEP TOURS. TOUR. (LOCAL). RALPH WILSON, DIRECTOR; SALIDA CHAMBER OF COMMERCE; 123 E 3RD; SALIDA, CO 81201. (#104290-1).

AUG 1, '76. CHAFFEE COUNTY CENTENNIAL QUEEN. COMPETITION. (LOCAL). EDWARD TOUBER, CHAIRMAN; SENIOR CITIZENS OF SALIDA; 207 E 3RD ST; SALIDA, CO 81201. (#108955-46).

AUG 1, '76. CHAVANEAUX INDIAN DANCERS. LIVE PERFORMANCE. (LOCAL). EDWARD TOUBER, CHAIRMAN; SALIDA CENTENNIAL-BICENTENNIAL COMMITTEE; 207 E 3RD ST; SALIDA, CO 81201. (#108955-48).

AUG 1, '76. HAPPY BIRTHDAY COLORADO. CROWNING CENTENNIAL QUEEN, A SENIOR CITIZEN; DANCES BY CHAVANEAUX INDIANS, YOUTH BALLET CLASS; ALSO, SPECIAL CHURCH SERVICES ARE PLANNED BY AREA CHURCHES. AT PARK ON HWY 50 ADJACENT TO MUSEUM. (LOCAL). MRS SAM RANDOLPH, COORD; SALIDA CENTENNIAL-BICENTENNIAL COMMITTEE; 1401 J ST; SALIDA, CO 81201. (#108955-47).

SEPT 6, '76. LABOR DAY RODEO AND GYMKAHANA. EVENTS OPEN TO ALL AGE GROUPS; EVENTS SCHEDULED: TEAM ROPING, POLE BENDING, BARRELL RACING, GOAT TYING AND FLAG RACE. AT HEART OF ROCKIES RODEO GROUNDS. (LOCAL). LEN KAPUSHION, DIRECTOR; HEART OF ROCKIES RECREATION ASSOC; PO BOX 121; SALIDA, CO 81201. (#2720-3).

JAN 3, '77. TIME CAPSULE 1976. MATERIAL OF INTEREST OF 1976 TO BE SEALED IN TIME CAPSULE. TIME CAPSULE TO BE OPENED IN 50 YEARS. RESEALED AND OPENED IN 100 YEARS. IT WILL BE STORED IN THE MUSEUM. AT HIGH SCHOOL AUDITORIUM. (LOCAL). MRS SAM RANDOLPH, COORD; HIGH SCHOOL STUDENT COUNCIL; 1401 J ST; SALIDA, CO 81201. (#108751-1).

SAN LUIS

FOXFIRE - PROJ OF SAN LUIS, CO. OPPORTUNITIES FOR HIGH SCHOOL STUDENTS TO UTILIZE CULTURAL HERITAGE AS A MOTIVATION FOR LEARNING BASIC SKILLS. (LOCAL). MARTHA FRITTS, DIRECTOR; IDEAS, INC; 2525 S DAYTON WAY; DENVER, CO 80231. (#14010). **ARBA GRANTEE.**

SAN LUIS, CO, ORAL HISTORY PROJECT. OPPORTUNITIES TO HIGH SCHOOL STUDENTS TO UTILIZE CULTURAL HERITAGE AS MOTIVATIONAL FORCE FOR LEARNING BASIC SKILLS. (LOCAL). MARTHA FRITTS, STAFF; IDEAS; 2525 S DAYTON WAY; DENVER, CO 80231. (#12108).

SARCILLO

SEPT 21, '76. DANCE AND MEMORIAL DEDICATION. HALL TO BE DEDICATED TO ERNEST VIGIL. AT SARCILLO SCHOOL. (LOCAL). VIRGINIA MONTOYA, COORD; SARCILLO SENIOR CITIZENS; RT BOX 370; TRINIDAD, CO 81082. (#108750-2).

SARCILLO — CONTINUED

SEPT 21, '76. SPANISH DINNER. FESTIVAL AT SARCILLO SCHOOL. (LOCAL). JULIA MARTINEZ, PROJ DIR; SARCILLO SENIOR CITIZENS; RTE 1, BOX 1; WESTON, CO 81091. (#108750-1).

SEDALIA

HISTORICAL MARKERS, SEDALIA, CO. MARKERS WILL BE PLACED AT BEAR CANON, NORT AND FLAT'S CEMETERIES, ON OLD WAGON ROAD, GOVERNOR ELIAS AMMON'S HOME AND ON STREET CORNERS IN SEDALIA. (LOCAL). PAULINE HODGES, CHAIRPERSON; DOUGLAS COUNTY CENTENNIAL-BICENTENNIAL COMMITTEE; CASTLE ROCK, CO 80104. (#24580).

NEEDLEPOINT CUSHIONS FOR CHURCH, SEDALIA, CO. 9 COMMUNION RAIL CUSHIONS, RUG AND STOOL WERE PLACED IN ST PHILIP'S EPISCOPAL CHURCH IN SEDALIA, IN MEMORY OF MARGE HANKISON. (LOCAL). REV DON WHITE, PROJ DIRECTOR; ST PHILIP'S GUILD AND ALTAR; SEDALIA, CO 80104. (#24583).

PIONEER COOKBOOK, SEDALIA, CO. OLD AND NEW RECIPES FROM THE PIONEER, CURTIS FAMILY. (LOCAL). GWEN NICHOLS, CHAIRPERSON; SEDALIA-LOUVIERS CENTENNIAL-BICENTENNIAL COMMITTEE; RT 1, BOX 9; SEDALIA, CO 80104. (#24582).

PLANTING TREES IN BEAR CANON CEMETERY, SEDALIA, CO. SPRUCE TREES ARE BEING PLANTED IN THE BEAR CANON CEMETERY. (LOCAL). HENRY H CURTIS, JR, PRESIDENT; SEDALIA COMMUNITY CEMETERY ASSOC; SEDALIA, CO 80104. (#24581).

RURAL CORRAL CENTENNIAL PARK, SEDALIA, CO. PRESERVATION OF SITE OF CATTLE LOADING CHUTES, ROCK QUARRY LOADING AND LUMBER HAULING. (LOCAL). PAULINE HODGES, CHAIRPERSON; DOUGLAS COUNTY CENTENNIAL-BICENTENNIAL COMMITTEE; CASTLE ROCK, CO 80104. (#24584).

JULY 31 - AUG 1, '76. BUFFALO BARBECUE & COLORADO DAY CELEBRATION. FESTIVAL AT CITY OF SEDALIA. (LOCAL). PAULINE HODGES, COORD; DOUGLAS COUNTY CENTENNIAL-BICENTENNIAL COMMITTEE; 417 JERRY ST #304; CASTLE ROCK, CO 80104. (#106985-1).

SEDGWICK

FRIENDSHIP DAY IN SEDGWICK, COLORADO. FRIENDSHIP DAY FOR 1975 & 1976 WILL FEATURE STREET GAMES, EXHIBITS AND EVENTS OF ETHNIC & NATIVE ORIGIN. THERE WILL BE MUSIC, COSTUMES AND DANCING. (LOCAL). DENNIS JOHNSON, CHAIRMAN; SEDGWICK CENTENNIAL-BICENTENNIAL COMMITTEE; SEDGWICK, CO 80749. (#6791).

SEDGWICK HISTORY PROJECT - COLORADO. AN ORAL & WRITTEN HISTORY OF SEDGWICK AREA WILL BE COMPILED WITH THE AID OF YOUTH AND SENIOR CITIZENS; WILL BE PERMANENT PROPERTY OF LIBRARY & AN ON-GOING PROJECT OF SEDGWICK LIBRARY BOARD. (LOCAL). NETA OLSON, LIBRARIAN; SEDGWICK PUBLIC LIBRARY BOARD; SEDGWICK, CO 80749. (#10446).

SEDGWICK, COLORADO CENTENNIAL PARK. THE OTHER HALF OF THE CITY PARK IS TO BE GRASSED AND IMPROVED WITH WATER, RESTROOMS AND OTHER PUBLIC CONVENIENCES. THE PARK WILL BE NAMED AND DEDICATED TO THE CENTENNIAL. (LOCAL). HON ORVILLE FREDRICK, MAYOR; TOWN OF SEDGWICK; MAIN ST; SEDGWICK, CO 80749. (#6793).

AUG 30 - 31, '75. CHILDREN'S RODEO WITH EVENTS SEPARATE FROM ADULT ACTIVITIES. THE HARVEST RODEO AND PARADE IS A TRADITIONAL PIONEER ACTIVITY. IT WILL BE COSTUME AND THEME ORIENTED TOWARDS THE OLD WEST FOR THE 1976 CENTENNIAL-BICENTENNIAL YEAR. (LOCAL). DENNIS JOHNSON; SEDGWICK LIONS CLUB; SEDGWICK, CO 80749. (#6794-501).

AUG 30 - 31, '75. FRIENDSHIP DAY FEATURING MUSIC NATIVE DANCES COSTUMES AND EXHIBITS. JAPANESE, MEXICAN-AMERICAN, GERMAN & OTHER NATIONALITIES, ETHNIC AND RELIGIOUS GROUPS WILL HAVE CULTURAL EXHIBITS AND FOOD BOOTHS. PRESENT NATIVE DANCES AND MUSIC IN SPECIAL COSTUME. AT MAIN STREET. (LOCAL). MRS BILL SAUDER; SEDGWICK CENTENNIAL BI-CENTENNIAL COMMITTEE; 315 MAIN AVENUE; SEDGWICK, CO 80749. (#50487-1).

AUG 30 - 31, '75. HARVEST FALL FESTIVAL 2ND PARADE, ANNUAL WITH CCBC THEME. PARADE FEATURES LOCAL BAND, YOUTH GROUPS, FLOATS, VISITING BANDS ETC FESTIVAL FEATURES AGRICULTURAL EXHIBITS, HOMEMAKING, 4H, SCHOOL AND HISTORICAL AND GENERAL EXHIBITS. STREET GAMES AND CONTESTS. ALUMNI PICNIC, KIDS RODEO, DEMOLITION DERBY. AT SEDGWICK LIONS CLUB-ROOM & MAIN STREET AREA. (LOCAL). MR DEE WEBB; SEDGWICK LIONS CLUB; 322 1 STREET; SEDGWICK, CO 80749. (#50486-3).

AUG 30 - 31, '75. HARVEST RODEO AND DANCE. SPECIAL RAFFLE WINNERS ANNOUNCED-USUALLY BEEF OR BUFFALO HALF. PRICES ARE SUBJECT TO CHANGE. AT RODEO AT SEDGWICK RODEO GROUNDS; DANCE AT SEDGWICK SCHOOL GYMNASIUM. (LOCAL). MR DEE WEBB; SEDGWICK LIONS CLUB; 322 1 STREET; SEDGWICK, CO 80749. (#50486-1).

AUG 28 - 29, '76. FRIENDSHIP DAY FEATURING MUSIC NATIVE DANCES COSTUMES AND EXHIBITS. JAPANESE, MEXICAN AMERICAN, GERMAN AND OTHER NATIONALITIES, ETHNIC AND RELIGIOUS GROUPS WILL HAVE CULTURAL EXHIBITS AND FOOD BOOTHS. PRESENT NATIVE DANCES AND MUSIC IN SPECIAL COSTUME. AT MAIN STREET. (LOCAL). MRS BILL SAUDER; SEDGWICK CENTENNIAL-BICENTENNIAL COMMITTEE; 315 MAIN AVENUE; SEDGWICK, CO 80749. (#50487-2).

AUG 28 - 29, '76. HARVEST FALL FESTIVAL AND PARADE ANNUAL WITH CCBC THEME. PARADE FEATURES LOCAL BAND, YOUTH GROUPS, FLOATS, VISITING BANDS ETC FESTIVAL FEATURES AGRICULTURAL, EXHIBITS, HOMEMAKING, 4H, SCHOOL AND HISTORICAL AND GENERAL EXHIBITS. STREET GAMES AND CONTESTS. ALUMNI PICNIC, KIDS RODEO, DEMOLITION DERBY. AT SEDGWICK LIONS CLUB-ROOM AND MAIN STREET AREA. (LOCAL). MR DEE WEBB; SEDGWICK LIONS CLUB; 322 1 STREET; SEDGWICK, CO 80749. (#50486-4).

AUG 28 - 29, '76. HARVEST RODEO AND DANCE. SPECIAL RAFFLE WINNERS ANNOUNCED-USUALLY BEEF OR BUFFALO HALF. AT RODEO AT SEDGWICK RODEO GROUNDS DANCE AT SEDGWICK SCHOOL GYMNASIUM. (LOCAL). MR DEE WEBB; SEDGWICK LIONS CLUB; 322 1 STREET; SEDGWICK, CO 80749. (#50486-2).

SEGUNDO

CHURCH RESTORATION - SEGUNDO, CO. RESTORE OLD ST IGNACIO CHURCH AS A LASTING REMINDER OF THE CENTENNIAL-BICENTENNIAL CELEBRATION. (LOCAL). M H POOLE, PROJ DIRECTOR; ST IGNATIOUS SOCIETY AND TRINIDAD STATE JUNIOR COLLEGE; TRINIDAD, CO 81082. (#15283).

SEIBERT

GREENING AND CLEANING COLORADO - SEIBERT. GENERAL CLEANUP AND PLANTING WILL BE DONE IN THE SEIBERT AREA. (LOCAL). MARUEL A GEIKEN, COORDINATOR; SEIBERT CENTENNIAL-BICENTENNIAL COMMITTEE; BOX 88; SEIBERT, CO 80834. (#26201).

JULY 4, '76. COMMUNITY TIME CAPSULE. FESTIVAL. (LOCAL). MARUEL A GEIKEN, CHMN; SEIBERT CENTENNIAL-BICENTENNIAL COMMITTEE; BOX 88; SEIBERT, CO 80834. (#108580-2).

JULY '76. SENIOR CITIZEN, 1976. FESTIVAL. (LOCAL). MARUEL A GEIKEN, COORD; SEIBERT CENTENNIAL-BICENTENNIAL COMMITTEE; BOX 88; SEIBERT, CO 80834. (#108580-1).

SEVERANCE

CENTENNIAL QUILT - SEVERANCE, CO. VARIOUS ORGANIZATIONS PARTICIPATED IN QUILT MAKING; IT WILL BE SOLD DURING FUN DAYS. (LOCAL). BARBARA SCHNEIDER, CHAIRMAN; SEVERANCE PROGRESSIVE CLUB; ROUTE 2, BOX 66; EATON, CO 80615. (#26339).

AUG 1, '76. SEVERANCE CENTENNIAL HERITAGE FUN DAY. THE FESTIVAL WILL HONOR SENIOR CITIZENS; EVENTS INCLUDE ICE-CREAM SOCIAL, TREES DEDICATION, FILM FESTIVAL, PIONEER GAMES AND INTERNATIONAL FOOD FESTIVAL. (LOCAL). BARBARA SCHNEIDER, CHMN; SEVERANCE PROGRESSIVE CLUB; RT 2, BOX 66; EATON, CO 80615. (#108752-1).

SILVER CLIFF

AUG 1, '76. CENTENNIAL FIREWORKS. FESTIVAL. (LOCAL). LAWRENCE ENTZ, COORD; TOWN OF SILVER CLIFF; 531 OHIO; SILVER CLIFF, CO 81249. (#108955-36).

AUG 1, '76. MUSIC PROGRAM. LIVE PERFORMANCE. (LOCAL). LAWRENCE ENTZ, COORD; TOWN OF SILVER CLIFF; 531 OHIO; SILVER CLIFF, CO 81249. (#108955-37).

AUG 21 - 22, '76. INTERNATIONAL FESTIVAL. FESTIVAL. (LOCAL). PETER KENNY; TOWN OF SILVER PLUME; C/O TOWN CLERK; SILVER PLUME, CO 80476. (#108724-1).

SILVER PLUME

LITTLE RED CABOOSE RESTORATION OF SILVER PLUME, CO. TO RESTORE AND PRESERVE AN HISTORIC NARROW GAUGE RAILROAD CABOOSE WHICH HAS BECOME A CENTER OF INTEREST FOR LOCAL CULTURAL AWARENESS AS WELL AS A POPULAR TOURIST ATTRACTION. (ST-WIDE). CHERYL BARTON, SECRETARY/TREASURER; PEOPLE FOR SILVER PLUME, INC; PO BOX 935; SILVER PLUME, CO 80476. (#4424). **ARBA GRANTEE.**

SILVER PLUME SCHOOL HOUSE MUSEUM - COLORADO. PURCHASE OF A LOCAL SCHOOL HOUSE TO BE USED AS A MUSEUM AND ALSO AS COMMUNITY CENTER. (LOCAL). PAULINE MARSHALL, PRESIDENT; PEOPLE FOR SILVER PLUME, INC; BOX 935; SILVER PLUME, CO 80476. (#4410). **ARBA GRANTEE.**

JULY 4, '75. JULY 4 ICE CREAM SOCIAL. OLD FASHIONED ICE CREAM SOCIAL WITH OLD TIME BAND. WE ALSO PLAN TO HAVE PRESENATION OF CENTENNIAL-BICENTENNIAL PLAQUES AT THIS TIME. HISTORIC MUSEUM WILL BE OPEN ON THIS DAY AS WELL-ADMISSION $.50. AT SILVER PLUME PARK. (LOCAL). CHERYL BARTON; PEOPLE FOR SILVER PLUME INC; BOX 935; SILVER PLUME, CO 80476. (#50514-1).

JULY 15 - SEPT 1, '75. GEORGE ROWE MUSEUM EXHIBIT OF LOCAL MINING & COMMUNITY LIFE. EXHIBITS LOCAL EARLY MINING AND MOUNTAIN COMMUNITY LIFE. AT SILVER PLUME SCHOOL HOUSE WEST MAIN ST. (LOCAL). CHERYL BARTON; PEOPLE FOR SILVER PLUME INC; BOX 935; SILVER PLUME, CO 80476. (#50536-1).

MAY 29 - 30, '76. GREENING & CLEANING COLORADO. FESTIVAL. (LOCAL). PETER KENNY, COORD; TOWN OF SILVER PLUME; C/O TOWN CLERK; SILVER PLUME, CO 80476. (#200007-155).

JUNE 1 - SEPT 1, '76. SILVER PLUME SCHOOL HOUSE MUSEUM EXHIBIT. EXHIBIT AT SILVER PLUME SCHOOL HOUSE MUSEUM, MAIN ST. (LOCAL). PAULINE MARSHALL; PEOPLE FOR SILVER PLUME, INC; BOX 935; SILVER PLUME, CO 80476. (#4410-1).

JULY 4, '76. CENTENNIAL FIREWORKS. FESTIVAL AT COMMUNITY PARK. (LOCAL). PETER KENNY, PROJ COORD; TOWN OF SILVER PLUME; C/O TOWN CLERK; SILVER PLUME, CO 80476. (#108582-1).

SILVERTHORNE

JULY 10 - 11, '76. BLUE RIVER BOAT RACE. KAYAK & SLALOM RACES ON SATURDAY; DOWNRIVER RACE, 15 MILES LONG, ON SUNDAY. (LOCAL). JOE LACY, CHAIRMAN; SILVERTHORNE FIRE DEPT; PO DRAWER 17-G, TA; DENVER, CO 80217. (#108706-1).

SILVERTON

CENTENNIAL-BICENTENNIAL TREE PLANTING PROJECTS-CO. TREES TO BE PLANTED IN TOWN PARKS IN HONOR OF CENTENNIAL-BICENT COMMEMORATION. (LOCAL). GERALD SWANSON, CHAIRMAN; SILVERTON CENTENNIAL BICENTENNIAL COMMITTEE; C/O 1027 GREENE ST; SILVERTON, CO 81433. (#4134).

DENVER & RIO GRANDE RAILROAD DEPOT RESTORATION. RESTORE THE DEPOT AND TURN INTO A MUSEUM FOR FUTURE USE AND DEVELOP LANSCAPPED PARK FOR COMMUNITY BENEFIT. (LOCAL). ALFRED R KLINKE, CHAIRMAN; SAN JUAN CO HISTORICAL SOCIETY; 767 REESE ST; SILVERTON, CO 81433. (#4131).

HISTORIC JEEP CAVALCADE THRU COLORADO. 5-COUNTY SELF GUIDING JEEP TOUR OF MAPPED HISTORIC SITES. (ST-WIDE). GERALD SWANSON, PRESIDENT; CHAMBER OF COMMERCE; BOX 335; SILVERTON, CO 81433. (#4132).

SILVERTON, COLO, TOWN HALL RESTORATION. RESTORE THE EXTERIOR OF THE TOWN HALL BUILDING IN ORDER TO CELEBRATE THE CENTENNIAL-BICENTENNIAL. (LOCAL). GERALD SWANSON, CHAIRMAN; TOWN OF SILVERTON; C/O 1027 GREENE ST; SILVERTON, CO 81433. (#4174).

MAY 30, '74 - OCT 1, '76. SILVERTON SAN JUAN COUNTY HISTORICAL MUSEUM & ARCHIVES. CONSTRUCTION OF ARCHIVE BLDG FOR PUBLIC RECORDS, PRIVATE DOCUMENTS, AND PAPERS OF COUNTY HISTORY. AT SAN JUAN COUNTY MUS.. (ST-WIDE). ALFRED KLINKE; HISTORICAL SOCIETY OF SILVERTON COLO; 767 REESE ST; SILVERTON, CO 81433. (#1994-1).

MAY 5 - 9, '75. STUDENT LOCAL-MATERIALS CRAFTS FAIR. EXHIBITS OF POTTERY, SCULPTURE, AND VARIOUS ART FORMS PRESENTED BY LOCAL TALENTS. AT SILVERTON PUBLIC SCHOOL. (LOCAL). RUTH S RICHARDSON ASST SC; SCHOOL DISTRICT; C/O SNOWDEN ST; SILVERTON, CO 81433. (#4135-1).

MAY 20, '75 - OCT 1, '76. SILVERTON CHAMBER OF COMMERCE BICENTENNIAL INFORMATION CENTER. CONSTRUCTION OF VISITOR INFORMATION CENTER FOR THE CENTENNIAL-BICENTENNIAL. AT BLAIR STREET. (ST-WIDE). GERALD SWANSON, PRES; SILVERTON CHAMBER OF COMMERCE; 1027 GRECE ST.; SILVERTON, CO 81433. (#4431-1).

JUNE '75. TOWN INCORPORATION CENTENNIAL DINNER. THE GOVERNOR OF COLORADO AND CENTENNIAL COMMITTEE DIGNITARIES WILL HAVE ENTERTAINMNET BY DANCERS & 2 BANDS. OF 04/04/75. AT SILVERTON HS GYM. (LOCAL). GERALD SWANSON, PRES; CHAMBER OF COMMERCE; BOX 335; SILVERTON, CO 81433. (#4133-1).

AUG 15 - 17, '75. MINING DEMONSTRATION WITH EVENTS. RENEWAL OF MINING COMPETITION IN SEVERAL EVENTS AS DONE IN CENTENNIAL ERA BY PROSPECTORS. AT NORTH OF SILVERTON OUTSIDE AREA. (LOCAL). GERALD SWANSON; SILVERTON SAN JOAN COUNTY CENTENNIAL BICENTENNIAL COMMITTEE; 1027 GREENE ST; SILVERTON, CO 81433. (#4483-1).

MAY 3 - 7, '76. STUDENT 'LOCAL MATERIALS' CRAFT FAIR. SCHOOL CHILDREN WILL USE MATERIALS FOUND IN THE LOCAL AREA FOR CRAFTS & PROJECTS RELATING TO THE CENTENNIAL-BICENTENNIAL. AT SCHOOL & MUSIC ROOM. (LOCAL). RUTH S RICHARD, COORD; SCHOOL DISTRICT; SNOWDEN ST; SILVERTON, CO 81433. (#102113-1).

MAY 30 - 31, '76. DEDICATION AND COMMEMORATION: TOWN HALL RESTORATION. CEREMONY. (LOCAL). VINCENT W TOOKEY, COORD; TOWN OF SILVERTON; PO BOX 65; SILVERTON, CO 81433. (#200007-152).

AUG 13 - 15, '76. HARDROCKERS' HOLIDAYS. FESTIVAL AT AT BASE OF MT KENDALL SKITOW ON EAST SIDE OF SILVERTON. (LOCAL). GEORGE D ZANONI, CHMN; HARDROCKERS' HOLIDAYS COMMITTEE; BOX 1876; SILVERTON, CO 81433. (#108736-2).

AUG '76. HERITAGE FAIR. SPECIAL FAMILY TREASURES OF YESTERDAY FOR PUBLIC EXHIBIT. AT LEGION HALL MAIN STREET. (LOCAL). FRANKIE BEABER; SAN JUAN WOMENS CLUB; SILVERTON, CO 81433. (#4430-1).

SNOWMASS

JUNE 15 - SEPT 1, '76. HISTORICAL TOURS SNOWMASS COLORADO. COMPETITION. (LOCAL). JOHN FRANCIS; CENTENNIAL/BICENTENNIAL COMM ROARING FORK VALLEY CO; SNOWMASS RESORT; WEST VILLAGE, CO 81615. (#107808-1).

JULY 30 - AUG 1, '76. CHAUTAUQUA FESTIVAL. CHATAUQUA FESTIVAL HONORING THE ETHNIC HERITAGE OF THE ROARING FORK VALLEY. (LOCAL). JOHN FRANCIS; CENTENNIAL/BICENTENNIAL COMM ROARING FORK VALLEY CO; SNOWMASS RESORT; WEST VILLAGE, CO 81615. (#107808-2).

SNYDER

JULY 24 - 25, '76. SNYDER REUNION & BICENTENNIAL CELEBRATION. CEREMONY, LIVE PERFORMANCE AT IOOF HALL. (LOCAL). MRS MARVIN L RENO, CHMN; SNYDER COMMUNITY COUNCIL

SNYDER—CONTINUED

AND GOLDEN LINKS REBEKAH LODGE #130; 22600 WINCHELL; SNYDER, CO 80750. (#200007-202).

SOUTH FORK

JULY 4, '76. OLD-FASHIONED FAMILY 4TH OF JULY PICNIC. SUNDAY RELIGIOUS SERVICE, BASKET DINNER, RACES & GAMES, FREEZERS OF FROZEN HOMEMADE ICE CREAM. AT THE METHODIST BEAVER CREEK YOUTH CAMP. (LOCAL). BETTE E DEACON, COORD; SARGENT COMMUNITY CHURCH; 5962 E ROAD 7 N; MONTE VISTA, CO 81144. (#107002-1).

STEAMBOAT SPG

CULTURAL DEPOT PROJ OF STEAMBOAT SPRINGS, COLO. RESTORATION AND PRESERVATION OF OLD DEPOT FOR USE AS A MUSEUM, ART GALLERY AND THEATER. DEPOT IMPORTANT TO COMMUNITY. DONE AS MEMORIAM TO THE CENTENNIAL-BICENTENNIAL. (LOCAL). ELEANOR J BLISS, CHAIRPERSON; STEAMBOAT SPR COUNCIL ARTS & HUMANITIES; BOX 697; STEAMBOAT SPG, CO 80477. (#4373).

EDUCATIONAL PLAYS FOR CHILDREN OF COLORADO. THE STROLLING PLAYERS ARE PLANNING A TOUR OF THE ROCKY MOUNTAIN REGION. THE PRODUCTIONS ARE AIMED AT HELPING ELEMENTARY SCHOOL AGE CHILDREN BETTER UNDERSTAND THE HERITAGE OF THE WEST & THE NATION. (ST-WIDE). RON CHITTIM, DIRECTOR; STROLLING PLAYERS; BOX 638; STEAMBOAT SPG, CO 80477. (#6797).

HISTORICAL TOURS MAPS - STEAMBOAT SPG, CO. MAPS WILL BE AVAILABLE SO THAT TOURS OF HISTORIC SITES IN STEAMBOAT SPRINGS CAN BE MADE BY CAR. (LOCAL). MRS PAT GREEN, CHAIRMAN; STEAMBOAT SPRINGS HISTORICAL SOCIETY; BOX 173; STEAMBOAT SPG, CO 80477. (#14841).

HOWELSON HILL RECREATION FACILITIES PROJECT -COLO. IMPROVEMENT OF CITY LAND TO MAKE AVAILABLE TO COMMUNITY BETTER RECREATION FACILITIES INCL ENLARGEMENT AND IMPROVEMENT OF RODEO GROUNDS, BALL FIELDS, COMMUNITY CENTER AND SKI JUMPS RESTORATION. (LOCAL). JOHN FETCHER, CHAIRMAN; WINTER SPORTS CLUB; BOX 5220; STEAMBOAT SPR, CO 80499. (#4427).

NW COLORADO CNTR FOR YOUTH SERVICES PROJ. COORDINATION OF SERVICES TO MEET NEEDS OF CHILDREN AND YOUTH IN NORTHWESTERN COLORADO. (LOCAL). JUDITH S YAMAGUCHI, PROJECT DIRECTOR; COLORADO COMMISSION ON CHILDREN AND YOUTH; PO BOX 1152; STEAMBOAT SPG, CO 80477. (#4345).

STEAMBOAT SPGS, CO, COUNCIL OF ARTS & HUMANITIES. ART FESTIVALS TO BE HELD IN DEPOT & OTHER HISTORIC LANDMARKS. (ST-WIDE). MRS ELEANOR BLISS, PRESIDENT; STEAMBOAT SPRINGS COUNCIL OF ARTS AND HUMANITIES; PO BOX 1913; STEAMBOAT SPG, CO 80477. (#375). **ARBA GRANTEE.**

STEAMBOAT SPRINGS HIGH SCHOOL HISTORY BOOK, CO. HIGH SCHOOL STUDENTS WILL COMPILE EARLY HISTORY OF STEAMBOAT SPRINGS IN COOPERATION WITH ROUTT HISTORICAL SOCIETY, THE PROJECT WILL INCLUDE INTERVIEWING, STUDYING OLD RECORDS & PUBLISHING A BOOK. (ST-WIDE). MRS J C GREEN, PRESIDENT; ROUTT HISTORICAL SOCIETY; BOX 173; STEAMBOAT SPG, CO 80477. (#16392).

THREE WIRE WINTER (FOX FIRE PROJECT) - CO. QUARTERLY MAGAZINE - LOCAL HISTORY AND CRAFTS PUBLISHED BY HIGH SCHOOL STUDENTS. (LOCAL). R GARY WAGGONER, CHAIRMAN; STEAMBOAT SPRINGS '76; BOX 1308; STEAMBOAT SPG, CO 80477. (#26275).

TREAD OF PIONEERS MUSEUM, STEAMBOAT SPRINGS, CO. RENOVATION AND EXPANSION OF TREAD OF PIONEERS MUSEUM. MOVE OF ADDITIONAL COLLECTIONS AND ENHANCED DISPLAY OF ALL ITEMS WHICH CAN NOT BE DISPLAYED NOW. (ST-WIDE). ERNEST 'DUDE' TODDI, DIRECTOR; TREAD OF PIONEERS HISTORICAL COMMISSION; BOX 272; STEAMBOAT SPG, CO 80477. (#1319). **ARBA GRANTEE.**

JUNE 28 - JULY 7, '74. 1974 SUMMER ARTS FESTIVAL. FESTIVAL, EXHIBIT, LIVE PERFORMANCE AT HISTORIC DEPOT & OTHER HISTORICAL LANDMARKS. (ST-WIDE). MRS ELEANOR BLISS, PRES; STEAMBOAT SPRINGS COUNCIL OF ARTS AND HUMANITIES; 39265 ROUTT COUNTY RD; STEAMBOAT SPG, CO 80477. (#375-901).

JUNE 28 - JULY 13, '75. SUMMER ARTS FESTIVAL. DENVER SYMPHONY PERFORMANCE, ART SHOW & SALES, PLAYS, RODEO & 4TH OF JULY PARADE, INCORPORATION CENTENNIAL-BICENTENNIAL THEME. AT CITYWIDE. (LOCAL). ELEANOR J BLISS, CHRPRS; STEAMBOAT SPG COUNCIL ON ARTS & HUMANITIES; BOX 697; STEAMBOAT SPG, CO 80477. (#4136-1).

AUG 1, '75 - JULY 4, '76. BEARD GROWING CONTEST. LOCAL NEWSPAPER SPONSORS BEARD GROWING CONTEST FOR BICENT YEAR. (LOCAL). R GARY WAGGONER, CHMN; STEAMBOAT SPRINGS '76; BOX 1308; STEAMBOAT SPG, CO 80477. (#108581-4).

OCT 11, '75. UNITED STATES ARMED FORCES BICENTENNIAL CARAVAN. THE CARAVAN IS COMPOSED OF EXHIBIT VANS FOR EACH BRANCH OF THE MILITARY SERVICE. THE THEME OF THE EXHIBITION IS 'HISTORY OF THE ARMED FORCES AND THEIR CONTRIBUTION TO THE NATION'. (LOCAL). GARY WAGGONER, CHMN; U S ARMED FORCES BICENTENNIAL EXHIBIT VANS PROJECT; BOX 1308; STEAMBOAT SPG, CO 80477. (#1775-241).

DEC 28, '75. STEAMBOAT SPRINGS WINTER SPORTS EVENTS - OPEN CROSS COUNTRY RACE. COMPETITION. (LOCAL). R GARY WAGGONER, CHMN; STEAMBOAT SPRINGS '76; PO BOX 1308; STEAMBOAT SPG, CO 80477. (#200007-154).

FEB 6 - 8, '76. WINTER CARNIVAL. ANNUAL WINTER EVENT WITH CENTENNIAL-BICENTENNIAL THEME IN 1976. ENTIRE COMMUNITY AND TOURISTS PARTICIPATE IN PARADE, SKI CONTESTS, SKI BAND, JUMPING & SKI RACES, & TORCHLIGHT PROCESSION OF SKIERS IN NIGHT SHOW. AT CITYWIDE. (LOCAL). JOHN FETCHER, CHRMN; WINTER SPORTS CLUB; BOX 5220; STEAMBOAT SPG, CO 80499. (#4175-1).

MAR 12 - 14, '76. NORTH AMERICAN SKI JUMPING CHAMPIONSHIPS-JUMPING OF 90 & 70 METERS. THREE JUMPING EVENTS. COMBINED ON 70 METER, SPECIAL JUMPING ON 70 M. SPECIAL JUMPING ON 90 METER. ON THREE CONSECUTIVE DAYS, FRIDAY, SAT. & SUNDAY. AT HOWELSEN HILL SKI AREA, HOWELSEN PARK. (NAT'L). JOHN R. FETCHER; STEAMBOAT SPRINGS WINTER SPORTS CLUB; BOX 5220; STEAMBOAT VIL, CO 80499. (#50128-1).

JULY 3 - 4, '76. STEAMBOAT SPRINGS ANNUAL RODEO. COMPETITION. (LOCAL). R GARY WAGGONER, CHMN; STEAMBOAT SPRINGS '76; BOX 1308; STEAMBOAT SPG, CO 80477. (#108581-2).

JULY 4, '76. CENTENNIAL FOURTH OF JULY PARADE. PARADE. (LOCAL). R GARY WAGGONER, CHMN; STEAMBOAT SPRINGS '76; BOX 1308; STEAMBOAT SPG, CO 80477. (#108581-1).

JULY 4, '76. FOURTH OF JULY FIREWORKS DISPLAY. FESTIVAL. (LOCAL). R GARY WAGGONER, CHMN; STEAMBOAT SPRINGS '76 & AMERICAN LEGION; BOX 1308; STEAMBOAT SPG, CO 80477. (#108581-3).

JULY 4, '76. PANCAKE BREAKFAST. LIONS CLUB ANNUAL PANCAKE BREAKFAST-CITY PARK OPEN TO EVERYONE AT 6 AM. (LOCAL). R GARY WAGGONER, CHMN; STEAMBOAT SPRINGS '76; BOX 1308; STEAMBOAT SPG, CO 80477. (#108581-5).

JULY 8 - 31, '76. SUMMER ARTS FESTIVAL. THREE WEEKS OF DRAMATIC PERFORMING AND VISUAL ARTS. (LOCAL). R GARY WAGGONER, CHMN; STEAMBOAT SPRINGS '76; BOX 1308; STEAMBOAT SPG, CO 80477. (#108753-3).

AUG 28 - 29, '76. SUMMER LEAGUE SOFTBALL TOURNAMENT. STEAMBOAT SPGS SLOW PITCH SOFTBALL MEN'S AND WOMEN'S LEAGUE TOURNAMENTS. (LOCAL). R GARY WAGGONER, CHMN; STEAMBOAT SPRINGS '76; BOX 1308; STEAMBOAT SPG, CO 80477. (#108753-2).

DEC 17 - 19, '76. STEAMBOAT SPRINGS BICENTENNIAL SKI JUMPING TOURNAMENT. COMPETITION, LIVE PERFORMANCE, RADIO/TV AT HOWELSEN HILL. (REGN'L). JOHN R FETCHER, COORD; STEAMBOAT SPRINGS WINTER SPORTS CLUB; PO BOX 285; STEAMBOAT SPG, CO 80477. (#103957-1).

DEC 23 - 24, '76. ROVING CHRISTMAS TREE. A ROVING CHRISTMAS TREE AND SANTA CLAUS BRINGS A SACK OF GOODIES TO CHILDREN. (LOCAL). R GARY WAGGONER, CHMN; STEAMBOAT SPRINGS '76; BOX 1308; STEAMBOAT SPG, CO 80477. (#108753-1).

STERLING

BAND SHELL AND PICNIC SHELTER - STERLING, CO. OUTDOOR FACILITY FOR ALL GROUPS TO UTILIZE AS PART OF THE CENTENNIAL BICENTENNIAL CELEBRATION. (LOCAL). MARCIA R LUCE, CHAIRMAN; CITY OF STERLING; BOX 590; STERLING, CO 80751. (#15587).

BICENTENNIAL LIBRARY - STERLING, CO. A LIBRARY TO HOUSE PRESENT COLLECTIONS AND TWO PRIVATE COLLECTIONS OF WESTERN BOOKS BEING OFFERED THE CITY OF STERLING. THE PROJECT IS TO PROVIDE A PROPER SETTING AND SECURITY FOR THE BOOKS. (LOCAL). PETER L YOUNGERS, CHAIRMAN; STERLING/LOGAN CENTENNIAL-BICENTENNIAL COMMITTEE; 1418 ADAMS CIRCLE; STERLING, CO 80751. (#16402).

BOOK ON LOGAN COUNTY - STERLING, CO. A HISTORICAL REVIEW OF THE COUNTY IN THIS CENTENNIAL-BICENTENNIAL YEAR. (LOCAL). PETER YOUNGERS, PROJ COORDINATOR; LOGAN COUNTY CENTENNIAL-BICENTENNIAL COUNCIL; 1418 ADAMS CIRCLE; STERLING, CO 80751. (#16258).

CENTENNIAL SQUARE - STERLING, CO. THIS SQUARE IN COMMEMORATION OF CENTENNIAL-BICENTENNIAL CELEBRATION WILL HOUSE LIBRARY, PUBLIC SAFETY BUILDING, CITY HALL AND POLICE STATION. (LOCAL). MARCIA R LUCE, CHAIRMAN; CITY OF STERLING; BOX 590; STERLING, CO 80751. (#15588).

FOXFIRE PROJECT TITLED 'WHISTLEWIND', STERLING, CO. A MAGAZINE AIMED AT PRESERVING NEBRASKA-COLORADO HISTORY, CULTURE & HERITAGE. STORIES ABOUT PEOPLE, HOBBIES, TRADES, RANCHING FOLKLORE AND MUSIC. (REGN'L). PAM BEER AND MARCIA LUCE, ADVISORS; WHISTLEWIND; BOX 1562; STERLING, CO 80751. (#19500).

HERITAGE CENTER - STERLING, CO. A LASTING REMINDER OF THE CENTENNIAL-BICENTENNIAL CELEBRATION WILL BE A COMMUNITY CENTER. (LOCAL). PETER YOUNGERS, PROJ COORDINATOR; LOGAN COUNTY AND CITY OF STERLING; 1418 ADAMS CIRCLE; STERLING, CO 80751. (#16256).

HERITAGE TRAILS IN LOGAN COUNTY, CO. RESTORE AND MAP HISTORICAL TRAILS IN LOGAN COUNTY AS PART OF THE CENTENNIAL-BICENTENNIAL CELEBRATION. (LOCAL). PETER YOUNGERS, PROJ COORDINATOR; LOGAN COUNTY CENTENNIAL-BICENTENNIAL COUNCIL; 1418 ADAMS CIRCLE; STERLING, CO 80751. (#16259).

HEROINES OF THE REVOLUTION. THE SIGNIFICANT ROLE OF WOMEN DURING THE AMERICAN REVOLUTION THAT IS PART OF THE CENTENNIAL-BICENTENNIAL CELEBRATION. (LOCAL). PETER YOUNGERS, PROJ COORDINATOR; DAUGHTERS' OF AMERICAN REVOLUTION; 1418 ADAMS CIRCLE; STERLING, CO 80751. (#16255).

HORIZONS ROOM IN STERLING, CO. ROOM FOR LOGAN COUNTY COMMUNITIES TO EXHIBIT DURING CENTENNIALBICENTENNIAL COMMEMORATION. (LOCAL). PETER YOUNGERS, PROJ COORDINATOR; LOGAN COUNTY CENTENNIAL-BICENTENNIAL COUNCIL; 1418 ADAMS CIRCLE; STERLING, CO 80751. (#16253).

LIBRARY MOMENTO PROJECT IN STERLING, CO. TO PRESENT LIBRARY WITH SOME MOMENTO TO RECALL THE CENTENNIALBICENTENNIAL YEAR. (LOCAL). PETER YOUNGERS, PROJ COORDINATOR; LOGAN COUNTY AND CITY OF STERLING; 1418 ADAMS CIRCLE; STERLING, CO 80751. (#16257).

MONUMENT FOR CENTENNIAL SQUARE - STERLING, CO. A QUIET AREA TO REFLECT AND ENJOY THE BEAUTIES OF COLORADO DURING AND AFTER THE CENTENNIAL AND THE NATION'S BICENTENNIAL. (LOCAL). MARCIA R LUCE, CHAIRMAN; CITY OF STERLING; BOX 590; STERLING, CO 80751. (#15586).

MURALS WITH HISTORICAL THEMES - STERLING, CO. MURALS WITH HISTORICAL THEMES WILL BE PAINTED IN AND ON BUILDINGS IN THE COUNTY. (LOCAL). PETER YOUNGERS, PROJ COORDINATOR; LOGAN COUNTY CENTENNIAL-BICENTENNIAL COUNCIL & AREA HIGH SCHOOLS; 1418 ADAMS CIRCLE; STERLING, CO 80751. (#16252).

PUBLIC SAFETY BUILDING - STERLING, CO. THIS BUILDING WILL HOUSE THE CITY AND RURAL FIRE DEPARTMENTS. IT WILL ALSO SERVE AS A LASTING REMINDER OF THE CENTENNIAL AND THE BICENTENNIAL. (LOCAL). MARCIA R LUCE, CHAIRMAN; CITY OF STERLING; BOX 590; STERLING, CO 80751. (#15589).

SECURITY PAVILION - STERLING, CO. THE PAVILION WILL BE USED FOR CENTENNIAL-BICENTENNIAL EVENTS SUCH AS CONCERTS, PLAYS, ART SHOWS AND COMMUNITY CEREMONIES. (LOCAL). CHARLOTTE O' CONNELL AND MARVIN MCELWAIN, COORD; SECURITY STATE BANK & CITY OF STERLING; PO BOX 590; STERLING, CO 80751. (#19501).

STERLING REGIONAL COLISEUM OF COLORADO. FUNDING OF A STUDY TO DETERMINE FUNDING SOURCES FOR MULTI-PURPOSE COMMUNITY FACILITY FOR ATHLETIC EVENTS TRADE SHOWS CONCERTS CONVENTIONS, AGRICULTURAL EXHIBITS AS WELL AS STOCK SHOWS. (LOCAL). W F HAND, MANAGER; STERLING CHAMBER OF COMMERCE; 113 S 2ND ST; STERLING, CO 80751. (#1952).

TENNANT ART CENTER - STERLING, CO. CENTENNIAL-BICENTENNIAL GALLERY FOR EXHIBITING WESTERN ART. (LOCAL). PETER YOUNGERS, PROJ COORDINATOR; NJC AND LOGAN COUNTY CENTENNIAL-BICENTENNIAL COUNCIL; 1418 ADAMS CIRCLE; STERLING, CO 80751. (#16254).

AUG 1, '75. CENTENNIAL SQUARE DEDICATION. CEREMONY AT CENTENNIAL SQUARE, N 4TH & N 5TH ST. (LOCAL). MARCIA LUCE, CHMN; CITY OF STERLING & STERLING BICENTENNIAL-CENTENNIAL COMMITTEE; BOX 590; STERLING, CO 80751. (#200007-193).

AUG 1, '75. PUBLIC SAFETY BUILDING DEDICATION. CEREMONY. (LOCAL). MARCIA LUCE, CHMN; CITY OF STERLING & STERLING CENTENNIAL-BICENTENNIAL COMMITTEE; BOX K90; STERLING, CO 80751. (#200007-192).

SEPT 2, '75 - MAY 30, '76. SCHOOLS CELEBRATION. ALL-SCHOOL PAGEANT CELEBRATING THE BICENTENNIAL. ALSO WOULD LIKE TO FIND 1-RM SCHOOLHOUSE, MOVE IT TO TOWN & RESTORE IT AS HISTORIC STRUCTURE. (LOCAL). DON WHITE, ASST SUPT; STERLING BICENTENNIAL-CENTENNIAL COMMISSION; 119 N 3RD AVE; STERLING, CO 80751. (#104402-6).

OCT 4, '75. UNITED STATES ARMED FORCES BICENTENNIAL CARAVAN. THE CARAVAN IS COMPOSED OF EXHIBIT VANS FOR EACH BRANCH OF THE MILITARY SERVICE. THE THEME OF THE EXHIBITION IS 'HISTORY OF THE ARMED FORCES AND THEIR CONTRIBUTION TO THE NATION'. (LOCAL). PETER L YOUNGERS, CHMN; U S ARMED FORCES BICENTENNIAL EXHIBIT VANS PROJECT; 1418 ADAMS CIRCLE; STERLING, CO 80751. (#1775-237).

JAN 18, '76. LOGAN CO & STERLING COMMUNITY DESIGNATION CEREMONY. AWARD, CEREMONY AT CITY AUDITORIUM/120 S 4TH. (LOCAL). PETER L YOUNGERS; LOGAN COUNTY & STERLING CO CENTENNIAL-BICENTENNIAL COMMISSION; 1418 ADAMS CIRCLE; STERLING, CO 80751. (#104402-5).

JAN - AUG '76. U S MILITARY CENTENNIAL-BICENTENNIAL DISPLAY. THE DISPLAY WILL SHOW THE MILITARY'S CONTRIBUTIONS TO OUR NATION'S HISTORY. (LOCAL). MARCIA R LUCE, PROJ DIR; CITY OF STERLING; BOX 590; STERLING, CO 80751. (#102651-1).

MAR 4, '76. DENVER SYMPHONY CONCERT. LIVE PERFORMANCE AT THEATRE-NORTHEASTERN JR COLLEGE. (LOCAL). CHRIS PETTEYS, CHMN; LOGAN CO/STERLING CENT-BICENT COMM & NORTHEASTERN JUNIOR COLLEGE; 309 DELMAR; STERLING, CO 80751. (#104402-4).

MAR 4 - 5, '76. DENVER SYMPHONY IN RESIDENCE AT NORTHEASTERN JUNIOR COLLEGE. LIVE PERFORMANCE AT THEATRE-NORTHEASTERN JR COLLEGE CAMPUS. (LOCAL). DOROTHY CORSBERG; NORTHEASTERN JR COLLEGE; NORTHEASTERN JR COLLEGE; STERLING, CO 80751. (#104402-3).

APR 24, '76. TOWN MEETING '76. A DAY-LONG FORUM ON STERLING'S FUTURE. AT STERLING HIGH SCHOOL. (LOCAL). W R WRIGHT, CHMN; STERLING KIWANIS CLUB; 106 GROVE ST, #3 RT; STERLING, CO 80751. (#104402-1).

JUNE 26, '76. CENTENNIAL PARADE. PARADE AT DOWNTOWN STERLING. (LOCAL). HON E FRANKLIN, JR, MAYOR; AMERICAN LEGION & AUXILIARY; PO BOX 454; STERLING, CO 80751. (#102698-1).

JUNE 27 - JULY 3, '76. MISS COLORADO PAGEANT. THE SHOW WILL REVOLVE AROUND THE THEMES OF HERITAGE, FESTIVAL AND HORIZONS; SHARON K RITCHIE, MISS AMERICA 1956, MARILYN VAN DEBUREN, MISS AMERICA 1958 AND REBECCA

STERLING — CONTINUED

KING, MISS AMERICA 1974 WILL BE PERFORMING. AT NJC HUMANITIES BLDG & ELKS LODGE. (ST-WIDE). LEWIS CROUCH, PRESIDENT; MISS COLORADO PAGEANT ASSOC INCORPORATED; S 3RD & ASH ST; STERLING, CO 80751. (#102697-1).

JULY 3 - 4, '76. FOURTH OF JULY CELEBRATION. THE CELEBRATION WILL FEATURE A SPECIAL FIREWORKS DISPLAY, BAND CONCERT AND STREET DANCES INCLUDING DUTCH HOP ROCK & ROLL, POLKA, SQUARE DANCE, WESTERN MUSIC AND MEXICAN MUSIC. AT BALL PARK. (LOCAL). STANLEY GENGLER, COORD; STERLING RECREATION DEPT, CITY OF STERLING; 520 N 3RD AVE; STERLING, CO 80751. (#102699-1).

AUG 1, '76. DEDICATION OF MONUMENT & QUIET AREA FOR CENTENNIAL SQUARE. CEREMONY AT 4TH ST AT CENTENNIAL SQUARE. (LOCAL). MARCIA LUCE, COORD; CITY OF STERLING & STERLING BICENTENNIAL-CENTENNIAL COMMISSION; BOX 590; STERLING, CO 80751. (#15566-1).

AUG 10 - 14, '76. HERITAGE ROOM EXHIBIT OF COMMUNITY HISTORY. EXHIBIT AT LOGAN COUNTY FAIR. (LOCAL). PETER YOUNGERS; LOGAN COUNTY CENTENNIAL-BICENTENNIAL COUNCIL; 1418 ADAMS CIRCLE; STERLING, CO 80751. (#102802-1).

AUG 10 - 14, '76. HORIZONS ROOM AT LOGAN COUNTY FAIR. THE HORIZONS ROOM WILL CONTAIN IDEAS & EXHIBITS FROM EACH COMMUNITY IN LOGAN COUNTY. AT LOGAN COUNTY FAIR GROUNDS & STADIUM. (LOCAL). JIM REED, COORD; LOGAN COUNTY CENTENNIAL-BICENTENNIAL COMMITTEE & LOGAN CO FAIR BOARD; FEDERAL BLDG; STERLING, CO 80751. (#16253-1).

AUG 10 - 14, '76. LOGAN COUNTY FAIR. FAIR, PARADE AT LOGAN COUNTY FAIR GROUNDS & STADIUM. (ST-WIDE). JIM REED, COORD; LOGAN COUNTY FAIR BOARD; FEDERAL BLDG; STERLING, CO 80751. (#104402-2).

STRASBURG

COMANCHE CROSSING MUSEUM PROJECT OF COLORADO. MUSEUM TO BE CONSTRUCTED IN STRASBURG. TOURS WILL INCLUDE FACTUAL STORIES OF PIONEER DAYS, EXHIBITS. HISTORICAL ARTIFACTS, ETC. (LOCAL). EMMA MICHELL, SECRETARY; COMANCHE CROSSING HISTORICAL SOCIETY; STRASBURG, CO 80136. (#1105). **ARBA GRANTEE.**

ELEMENTARY SCHOOL PROJECT - STRASBURG, CO. THE ELEMENTARY SCHOOL WILL SPONSOR A TOWN CLEANUP PROJECT. (LOCAL). DEL HEMPHILL, CHAIRMAN; STRASBURG BICENTENNIAL COMMITTEE; STRASBURG, CO 80136. (#26263).

'GREENING & CLEANING COLORADO' - STRASBURG. THE PARK WILL BE CLEANED UP AND TREES WILL BE PLANTED. (LOCAL). WILLIAM LEGGETT, COORDINATOR; STRASBURG RECREATION DISTRICT; STRASBURG, CO 80136. (#26264).

HAND CARVED & PAINTED REDWOOD SIGNS, CO. HAND CARVED AND PAINTED REDWOOD SIGNS WILL BE DATED AND PLACED ON OLD BUILDINGS. (LOCAL). MRS EMMA MITCHELL, CHAIRMAN; STRASBURG CENTENNIAL-BICENTENNIAL COMMITTEE; RT 1, BOX 75; STRASBURG, CO 80136. (#26270).

HOMETOWN DAYS OF STRASBURG, COLORADO. CELEBRATION TO BRING HOME NATIVE SONS & DAUGHTERS & MAKE THE NEW RESIDENTS AN INTEGRAL PART OF THE COMMUNITY. (LOCAL). EMMA MITCHELL; STRASBURG CENTENNIAL-BICENTENNIAL COMMISSION; ROUTE 1, BOX 75; STRASBURG, CO 80136. (#2934-1).

MARKING OLD STAGE TRAIL & STATIONS - CO. WOODEN SIGNS WILL BE PLACED WHERE TRAILS CROSSED PRESENT ROADS, WHERE LIVING SPRINGS AND KIOWA STATIONS STOOD AND WHERE BOX ELDER STATION WAS. (LOCAL). DONNA HOLCOMB, COORDINATOR; GIRL SCOUTS, BOY SCOUTS & STRASBURG BICENTENNIAL COMMITTEE; STRASBURG, CO 80136. (#26271).

MEMORIAL GARDENS PROJ OF STRASBURG, COLO. PLANTING MATURE TREES, SHRUBS & GRASSES IN NATURAL DISTRICT AS A LIVING, GROWING MEMORIAL TO RESIDENTS & THOSE DEPARTED WHO HAVE MADE OUR COMMUNITY A BETTER PLACE TO LIVE. (LOCAL). EMMA MICHELL, CHAIRPERSON; STRASBURG CENTENNIAL-BICENTENNIAL COMMISSION; ROUTE 1, BOX 75; STRASBURG, CO 80136. (#2949).

NEW POST OFFICE WITH ARBA EMBLEM TO BE DEDICATED. CEREMONY. (LOCAL). MS A ASHWORTH, POSTMASTER; U S GOVT & STRASBURG BICENTENNIAL COMMUNITY; STRASBURG, CO 80136. (#108829-1).

OVERLAND TRAIL - SMOKE HILL TRAIL OF COLORADO. A PROGRAM TO MARK THE ACTUAL SITES OF THE THREE STAGE STATIONS IN LIVING SPRINGS, KIOWA, & BOX ELDER, WITH NARRATIVE BRONZE PLAQUES. (LOCAL). EMMA MICHELL, CHAIRPERSON; STRASBURG CENTENNIAL-BICENTENNIAL COMMISSION; ROUTE 1, BOX 75; STRASBURG, CO 80136. (#2898).

STRASBURG SCHOOLHOUSE - PROJ OF STRASBURG, CO. RESTORATION AND MOVING OF THE SCHOOLHOUSE IN STRASBURG WHICH WAS BUILT IN 1904. (LOCAL). EMMA MICHEL, CHAIRMAN; COMANCHE CROSSING HISTORICAL SOCIETY; STRASBURG, CO 80136. (#14999). **ARBA GRANTEE.**

STREET RENAMING PROJECT - STRASBURG, CO. STREETS FROM MISSOURI AVE TO COLORADO AVE WILL BE RENAMED. (LOCAL). DILLARD REEVES, CHAIRMAN; STRASBURG BICENTENNIAL COMMISSION; STRASBURG, CO 80136. (#26187).

AUG 18, '74. DEDICATION OF COMANCHE MUSEUM. MUSEUM TO BE CONSTRUCTED IN STRASBURG. TOURS WILL INCLUDE FACTUAL STORIES OF PIONEER DAYS, EXHIBITS. HISTORICAL ARTIFACTS, ETC. (LOCAL). EMMA MICHELL, SECRETARY; COMANCHE CROSSING HISTORICAL SOCIETY; STRASBURG, CO 80136. (#1105-901).

NOV 15 - 16, '75. TURKEY SHOOT & BARBECUE. CENTENNIAL-BICENTENNIAL PAGEANT OF STRASBURG, COLO. A DAY TO COMMEMORATE THE NATION'S 200TH & THE STATE'S 100TH ANNIVERSARIES, WITH EMPHASIS ON COMMUNITY CONTRIBUTIONS TO HISTORY OF COLORADO & THE NATION. (LOCAL). EMMA MITCHELL, CHAIRMAN; STRASBURG CENTENNIAL-BICENTENNIAL COMMISSION; ROUTE 1, BOX 75; STRASBURG, CO 80136. (#2935-503).

JUNE 1 - AUG 31, '76. COMANCHE CROSSING MUSEUM EXHIBITS. EXHIBIT. (LOCAL). EMMA MICHELL, CHAIRMAN; COMANCHE CROSSING HISTORICAL SOCIETY; STRASBURG, CO 80136. (#108755-1).

JUNE 27, '76. STRASBURG PRESBY CHURCH 60TH ANNIVERSARY. CEREMONY. (LOCAL). DR S J HANKS, COORD; STRASBURG PRESBY COMMUNITY CHURCH; STRASBURG, CO 80136. (#200007-153).

JULY 4, '76. JULY 4TH CELEBRATION. SOFTBALL GAMES, CONCESSION STANDS, DRAWINGS AND FIREWORKS WILL BE INCLUDED. AT STRASBURG FIREHOUSE. (LOCAL). EMMA MITCHELL, COORD; STRASBURG CENTENNIAL-BICENTENNIAL COMMITTEE & AMERICAN LEGION; STRASBURG, CO 80136. (#108583-1).

AUG 1, '76. COLORADO DAY CELEBRATION - HONOR SENIOR CITIZENS. FESTIVAL. (LOCAL). JAN MONTRAY, COORDINATOR; TRIVALLEY SENIOR CITIZENS; STRASBURG, CO 80156. (#108955-45).

AUG 13, '76. OLD-TIME MEDICINE SHOW. FESTIVAL, LIVE PERFORMANCE AT SCHOOL. (LOCAL). BRUCE RICHTER, COORD; STRASBURG BICENTENNIAL COMMITTEE; STRASBURG, CO 80136. (#108730-3).

AUG 13 - 15, '76. PAGEANT, PARADE, CHURCH SERVICES, ARTS & CRAFTS FAIR, TRAIL MARKING. CENTENNIAL-BICENTENNIAL PAGEANT OF STRASBURG, COLO. A DAY TO COMMEMORATE THE NATION'S 200TH & THE STATE'S 100TH ANNIVERSARIES, WITH EMPHASIS ON COMMUNITY CONTRIBUTIONS TO HISTORY OF COLORADO & THE NATION. ALL OVER TOWN. (LOCAL). EMMA MITCHELL, CHAIRMAN; STRASBURG CENTENNIAL-BICENTENNIAL COMMISSION; ROUTE 1, BOX 75; STRASBURG, CO 80136. (#2935-501).

AUG 14, '76. PARACHUTE DROP. LIVE PERFORMANCE. (LOCAL). GUNNAR HERSKIND, COORD; STRASBURG BICENTENNIAL COMMITTEE & BUCKLEY FIELD AIR NATIONAL GUARD; STRASBURG, CO 80136. (#108730-2).

AUG 14, '76. TIME CAPSULE. CEREMONY. (LOCAL). WILLIAM LEGGETT, COORD; STRASBURG BICENTENNIAL COMMUNITY; STRASBURG, CO 80136. (#108730-1).

AUG 15, '76. RE-ENACTMENT OF JOINING OF RAILS. CEREMONY, LIVE PERFORMANCE. (LOCAL). BRUCE RICHTER, COORD; STRASBURG BICENTENNIAL COMMISSION; STRASBURG, CO 80136. (#108889-1).

OCT 3, '76. NEW HIGH SCHOOL WITH ARBA EMBLEM TO BE DEDICATED. CEREMONY. (LOCAL). WILLIAM LEGGETT, COORD; STRASBURG SCHOOL DISTRICT 31-J & STRASBURG BICENTENNIAL COMMUNITY; STRASBURG, CO 80136. (#108362-1).

NOV 20 - 21, '76. BARBECUE & TURKEY SHOOT. FALL FESTIVAL FEATURING A FREE BARBEQUE, CRAFTSMANSHIP CONTEST, DANCING & A GENERAL FUN CELEBRATION OF COLORADO'S CENTENNIALBICENTENNIAL. AT STRASBURG FIRE DEPT. (LOCAL). EMMA MICHELL, CHAIRPERSON; STRASBURG VOLUNTEER FIRE DEPT; ROUTE 1, BOX 75; STRASBURG, CO 80136. (#2926-2).

STRATTON

RESTORATION OF HISTORICAL MERRY-GO-ROUND, CO. SERVICE CLUBS AND INTEREST GROUPS WILL COLLECT DONATIONS TO RESTORE COUNTY CAROUSEL AS A LASTING REMINDER OF THE CENTENNIAL-BICENTENNIAL CELEBRATION. (LOCAL). IDA BOECKER, CHAIRPERSON; STRATTON CENTENNIAL-BICENTENNIAL ORGANIZATION; STRATTON, CO 80836. (#14853).

STRATTON DAY. THE ENTIRE TOWN WILL ENGAGE IN A VARIETY OF ACTIVITIES WITH A CENTENNIAL-BICENTENNIAL THEME; QUILT DISPLAY, BAND PRESENTATION, PARADE AND A FREE BARBEQUE. (LOCAL). PRESIDENT; ROTARY CLUB, ALUMNI ASSOCIATION; STRATTON, CO 80836. (#102118-1).

SWIMMING POOL IN STRATTON, CO. CITIZENS PARTICIPATING IN EFFORTS TO CONSTRUCT SWIMMING POOL AS A LASTING REMINDER OF CENTENNIAL-BICENTENNIAL CELEBRATION. (LOCAL). HON E L KERL, MAYOR; TOWN OF STRATTON, SWIMMING POOL ASSOC; STRATTON, CO 80836. (#14852).

TELLURIDE

GALLOPING GOOSE RESTORATION OF TELLURIDE, CO. RESTORATION AND PRESERVATION OF THIS TOWN LANDMARK FOR FUTURE GENERATIONS IN HONOR OF CENTENNIAL-BICENTENNIAL. (LOCAL). JERRY MARTIN, CHAIRMAN; TELLURIDE CENTENNIAL - BICENTENNIAL COMMITTEE; BOX 421; TELLURIDE, CO 81435. (#4144). **ARBA GRANTEE.**

HELP LINE FOR CITIZENS IN TELLURIDE, CO. FACILITIES TO IMPLEMENT A TELEPHONE 24-HOUR A DAY HELPLINE FOR BENEFIT OF LOCAL CITIZENS AS PART OF BICENTENNIAL PROJECT. (LOCAL). JERRY MARTIN, CHAIRMAN; FIRST BAPTIST CHURCH; C/O BOX 421; TELLURIDE, CO 81435. (#4145).

HISTORICAL RESOURCE INVENTORY OF TELLURIDE, CO. PRESERVATION OF TOWN HISTORY THROUGH MICROFILMING OF NEWSPAPERS AND PHOTOGRAPHY. (LOCAL). JERRY MARTIN, CHAIRMAN; TELLURIDE HISTORICAL SOCIETY; PO BOX 421; TELLURIDE, CO 81435. (#4146). **(??).**

NATIONAL FILM RESERVE OF TELLURIDE, COLORADO. ESTABLISHMENT OF AN INSTITUTE FOR STORAGE AND STUDY OF FILMS OF COLORADO AND AMERICA IN HONOR OF CENTENNIAL-BICENTENNIAL. (REGN'L). JERRY MARTIN, CHAIRMAN; TELLURIDE CENTENNIAL -BICENTENNIAL COMMITTEE; BOX 421; TELLURIDE, CO 81435. (#4143). **(??).**

TELLURIDE JAIL HOUSE RESTORATION & RELOCATION, CO. OLD JAIL HOUSE, BUILT IN 1880, WILL BE RESTORED AND MOVED TO MAIN STREET TO BE DEDICATED AND MARKED WITH A CENTENNIAL PLAQUE. (LOCAL). JERRY MARTIN, CHAIRMAN; TELLURIDE CENTENNIAL - BICENTENNIAL COMMITTEE; BOX 421; TELLURIDE, CO 81435. (#4148). **ARBA GRANTEE.**

TELLURIDE SENIOR CITIZEN. CEREMONY. (LOCAL). ELVIRA WUNDERLICH, COORD; TOWN OF TELLURIDE; BOX 551; TELLURIDE, CO 81435. (#108682-1).

SEPT '75. COLORIDE NATURE CELEBRATION. TRADITIONAL FALL CELEBRATION OF NATURE'S COLOR CHANGES BY 4 COMMUNITIES IN HONOR OF THE CENTENNIAL-BICENTENNIAL, INCLUDING A RIDE THRU THE PICTURESQUE MOUNTAINS OF TELERIDE. AT COLORIDE TO TELLURIDE. (LOCAL). JERRY MARTIN, CHRMN; TELLURIDE CHAMBER OF COMMERCE; BOX 421; TELLURIDE, CO 81435. (#4196-1).

JUNE 15, '76 - CONTINUING . HISTORIC SAN JUAN TOURS. TOURS OF SCENIC & HISTORIC TOWNS IN SOUTHWESTERN COLORADO WILL BE CONDUCTED; PARTICIPATING TOWNS INCLUDE LAKE CITY, MONTROSE, OURAY, NORWOOD, TELLURIDE & SILVERTON. (LOCAL). JIM BRAND, COORDINATOR; HISTORIC SAN JUAN TOURS; BOX 595; TELLURIDE, CO 81435. (#108823-1).

JUNE 19 - 20, '76. TELLURIDE HIGH SCHOOL REUNION. FESTIVAL. (LOCAL). ELVIRA WUNDERLICH, CHMN; TELLURIDE CENTENNIAL-BICENTENNIAL COMMISSION; TELLURIDE, CO 81435. (#200007-156).

JUNE 19 - 26, '76. SUMMER WORKSHOP IN EARLY MUSIC. CONFERENCE. (LOCAL). BARBARA MARTIN, COORD; AMERICAN RECORD SOCIETY; BOX 821; TELLURIDE, CO 81435. (#200007-157).

JULY 4, '76. NATIONAL BELL RINGING PARTICIPATION. CEREMONY. (LOCAL). ELVIRA WUNDERLICH, CHPSN; TELLURIDE CENTENNIAL-BICENTENNIAL COMMITTEE; PO BOX 421; TELLURIDE, CO 81435. (#200007-211).

JULY 5 - 23, '76. CHAMBER MUSIC FESTIVAL. THE CONCERTS WILL BE HELD ON JULY 5, 11, 16, 19 & 23. (LOCAL). BETH CHRISTENSEN, COORD; TELLURIDE CHAMBER OF COMMERCE; GENERAL DELIVERY; TELLURIDE, CO 81435. (#108577-1).

AUG 1, '76. 'CHILDREN TELL US THE PAST' - DRAMA. LIVE PERFORMANCE. (LOCAL). ELVIRA F WUNDERLICH, CHMN; TELLURIDE CENTENNIAL-BICENTENNIAL COMMITTEE; BOX 551; TELLURIDE, CO 81435. (#108955-43).

AUG 1, '76. MUSIC PROGRAM-CONCERT BY COMMUNITY MUSICIANS. LIVE PERFORMANCE. (LOCAL). ELVIRA F WUNDERLICH, CHMN; TELLURIDE CENTENNIAL-BICENTENNIAL COMMITTEE; BOX 551; TELLURIDE, CO 81435. (#108955-44).

AUG 1, '76. SENIOR CITIZEN PICNIC. FESTIVAL. (LOCAL). ELVIRA F WUNDERLICH, CHMN; TELLURIDE CENTENNIAL-BICENTENNIAL COMMITTEE; BOX 551; TELLURIDE, CO 81435. (#108955-41).

SEPT 3 - 6, '76. TELLURIDE INTERNATIONAL FILM FESTIVAL. MORE THAN 50 FILMS WILL BE SHOWN IN FOUR DIFFERENT THEATERS. THERE WILL BE SEVERAL AMERICAN PREMIERES & SEVERAL WORLD PREMIERES. THREE FILM MAKERS OF WORLD-WIDE REPUTATION WILL BE HONORED. FILM TREASURES FROM AROUND THE WORLD WILL BE SHOWN. AT SHERIDAN OPERA HOUSE. (INT'L). BILL PENCE DIR; NATIONAL FILM PRESERVE LTD; 119 W COLORADO AVE; TELLURIDE, CO 81435. (#103109-1).

NOV 20, '76. OCTAGONAL CLOCK FOR COURT HOUSE. 1863 COURT HOUSE WITH OCTAGONAL SPACES LEFT FOR NEW CLOCK WHICH WAS BOUGHT BY HOLDING VARIOUS FUNDRAISING EVENTS. (LOCAL). ELVIRA F WUNDERLICH, CHMN; TELLURIDE BICENTENNIAL COMMITTEE; TELLURIDE, CO 81435. (#200007-209).

THORNTON

MOUNTAINS, PLAINS AND PLATEAUS - THORNTON, CO. COLORADO HISTORY EXAMINED FROM GEOLOGICAL AND SOCIAL VIEWPOINT AS A CLASS TAUGHT AT THORNTON HIGH SCHOOL. SUMMATION OF INFORMATION WILL BE COMPILED AND A MAP OF HISTORIC POINTS PREPARED. (LOCAL). RICHARD MARCY, SCIENCE TEACHER; THORNTON HIGH SCHOOL; 9451 N WASHINGTON; THORNTON, CO 80229. (#13699). **ARBA GRANTEE.**

PRESERVATION OF DAVID WOLPERT HOUSE, THORNTON, CO. PRESERVATION OF A TWO STORY BRICK HOUSE BUILT BY MINING PIONEER, DAVID WOLPERT; LOCATED AT 9190 RIVERDALE RD EAST OF THORNTON, HOUSE WAS BUILT AROUND 1864. (ST-WIDE). DR ROY H CARLSON, PRESIDENT; ADAMS COUNTY HISTORICAL SOCIETY; RT 2 BOX 120P8; BRIGHTON, CO 80601. (#10331).

NOV 2 - 3, '75. UNITED STATES ARMED FORCES BICENTENNIAL CARAVAN. THE CARAVAN IS COMPOSED OF EXHIBIT VANS FOR EACH BRANCH OF THE MILITARY SERVICE. THE THEME OF THE EXHIBITION IS 'HISTORY OF THE ARMED FORCES AND THEIR CONTRIBUTION TO THE NATION'. (LOCAL). FRANK ALLEN, CHMN; U S ARMED FORCES BICENTENNIAL EXHIBIT VANS PROJECT; 10201 RIVERDALE RD, SPACE 204; THORTON, CO 80229. (#1775-243).

JAN 31, '76. HISTORY OF DANCE. LIVE PERFORMANCE AT NORTH VALLEY SHOPPING CENTER, VALLEY HWY (I-25) & E 8TH AVE. (LOCAL). JEANNE FROMAN, COORD; FROMAN SCHOOL OF DANCE; 9020 FIR DR; THORNTON, CO 80229. (#200007-208).

THORNTON — CONTINUED

FEB 7 - 18, '76. SIGHTS AND SOUNDS OF AMERICA. LIVE DRAMA, MUSIC & DANCE PRESENTATIONS AND DISPLAYS ON AMERICA, 1776-1976. AT NORTH VALLEY SHOPPING CENTER MALL, I-25 & E 84TH AVE. (LOCAL). ROBERT DONALDSON, CHMN; NORTH VALLEY SHOPPING CENTER MERCHANTS ASSOC; PO BOX 29061; THORNTON, CO 80229. (#200007-158).

FEB 20 - 22, '76. INDIAN ARTIFACT SHOW. THE EXHIBIT WILL INCLUDE DISPLAYS OF INDIAN ARTIFACTS, ARCHEOLOGICAL EXCAVATIONS AND PICTOGRAPH RECORDING & RECONSTRUCTION. AT N VALLEY SHOPPING CENTER, 84TH & INTERSTATE HWY 25. (ST-WIDE). HOMER B MCGEORGE, CHMN; DENVER CHAPTER OF THE COLORADO ARCHEOLOGICAL SOCIETY; 5185 BLACKHAWK WAY; DENVER, CO 80239. (#102128-1).

MAY 8, '76. STUDEBAKER DRIVERS CLUB - NORTH VALLEY CENTER STUDEBAKER SHOW. AN EXHIBITION OF STUDEBAKER VEHICLES & PRODUCTS, THE ONLY AMERICAN MANUFACTURER OF HIGHWAY TRANSPORTATION TO CELEBRATE A CENTENNIAL. STUDEBAKER BUILT WAGONS, CARRIAGES, SELF-POWERED AUTOS & MILITARY VEHICLES FROM 1852 TO 1966. AT NORTH VALLEY SHOPPING CENTER MALL; THORNTON, CO. (ST-WIDE). KENNETH E BLUME, COORD; CONESTOGA CHAPTER-STUDEBAKER DRIVERS CLUB INC; 320 W 80TH AVE; DENVER, CO 80221. (#104112-1).

MAY 24, '76. FLAG DESIGN CONTEST. DESIGNING AND MAKING OF NEW CITY FLAG BY THORNTON HIGH SCHOOL STUDENTS & HIGHLAND HIGH SCHOOL STUDENTS, WHICH WILL BE PRESENTED TO THE THORNTON CITY COUNCIL ON THE CITY'S 20TH ANNIVERSARY, MONDAY, MAY 24, 1976. (LOCAL). ROBERT DONALDSON, CHMN; THORNTON CENTENNIAL-BICENTENNIAL COMMITTEE; PO BOX 29061; THORNTON, CO 80229. (#105474-1).

JUNE 12, '76. FLAG DAYS CEREMONIES. SEVERAL MILITARY UNITS ALONG WITH OFFICIAL ADAMS COUNTY CENTENNIALBICENTENNIAL CHORUS PARTICIPATED IN THE CEREMONY. AT NORTH VALLEY SHOPPING CENTER, I-25 AND E 84TH AVE. (LOCAL). ROBERT DONALDSON, CHMN; NORTH VALLEY MERCHANTS ASSOC; PO BOX 29061; THORNTON, CO 80229. (#200007-159).

JUNE 24 - 27, '76. ALMOST ANYTHING GOES. ATHLETIC COMPETITION BETWEEN THE CITIES OF WESTMINSTER, NORTHGLENN & THORNTON PATTERNED AFTER THE TV PROGRAM BEARING THE SAME NAME; THE FINALS ON SUNDAY, JUNE 27TH AT 2 PM. AT THORNTON HIGH SCHOOL STADIUM AT N WASHINGTON ST & E 91ST AVE. (LOCAL). JAY SIMMONS, CHAIRMAN; THORNTON CENTENNIAL-BICENTENNIAL COMMITTEE; PO BOX 29061; THORNTON, CO 80229. (#200007-160).

JUNE 26, '76. FORGING COLORADO'S SECOND CENTURY. STATEWIDE INVITATIONAL PARADE WITH OVER 150 UNITS PARTICIPATING. RAIN DATE: JUNE 27, 1976 AT 1:00 PM. AT FROM N VALLEY SHOPPING CENTER AT 500 E 84TH AVE TO E 92ND AVE. (ST-WIDE). ROBERT DONALDSON, CHMN; THORNTON CENTENNIAL-BICENTENNIAL COMMITTEE; PO BOX 29061; THORNTON, CO 80229. (#105423-2).

JUNE 26, '76. THORNTON CENTENNIAL-BICENTENNIAL PARADE - 1976. PARADE FEATURED OVER 130 UNITS INCLUDING THOSE FROM NEW YORK, FLORIDA & CALIFORNIA AS WELL AS STATEWIDE. INCLUDED 9 BANDS, 35 FLOATS, ANTIQUE CARS, DRILL TEAMS & EQUESTRIAN UNITS; TELEVISION PERSONALITY CARL AKERS WAS GRAND MARSHALL. AT NORTH WASHINGTON ST. (LOCAL). ROBERT DONALDSON, CHMN; THORNTON CENTENNIAL-BICENTENNIAL COMMISSION; PO BOX 29061; THORNTON, CO 80229. (#200007-161).

JULY 4, '76. OLD-FASHIONED FAIR. PIE, CAKE & CHILI CONTEST, SPORTING EVENTS, SINGING GROUPS, FIREWORKS AT 10 PM, SKYDIVERS WILL COME DOWN WITH THE AMERICAN FLAG. NORAD (CANADIAN-U.S.) BAND IN CONCERT. ALSO MUSKET FIRING DEMONSTRATION. AT CITY PARK, EPPINGER BOULEVARD AT GAYLORD STREET. (LOCAL). JAMES LEASE, CHAIRMAN; THORNTON CENTENNIAL-BICENTENNIAL COMMITTEE; THORNTON, CO 80229. (#107574-1).

JULY 4, '76. THORNTON FIREWORKS. FESTIVAL. (LOCAL). JAMES CASTRODALE, COORD; CITY OF THORNTON; 8992 N WASHINGTON; THORNTON, CO 80229. (#108579-1).

JULY 22, '76. CENTENNIAL-BICENTENNIAL MELODRAMA. HISTORY-FILLED MELODRAMA FEATURING VIGNETTES OF EARLY COLORADO AND FLASHING BACK TO COLONIAL EVENTS. AT ELITCH GARDENS, 4620 W 38TH AVE. (LOCAL). JERRY CHETELAT, DIRECTOR; VALLEY VIEW HOSPITAL; 8451 PEARL ST; THORNTON, CO 80229. (#17800-1).

JULY 23 - 25, '76. COLORADO WIRE COLLECTORS SHOW & TRADE MEET. WIRE COLLECTION OF ANTIQUE BARBED WIRE, OLD TOOLS USED FOR FENCING AND RARE WIRE WILL BE SHOWN. AT NORTH VALLEY SHOPPING CENTER, 84TH & I 25. (ST-WIDE). DENNIS D TROEGER, COORD; COLORADO WIRE COLLECTORS; 5224 TITAN CT; DENVER, CO 80239. (#107158-1).

JULY 31, '76. NORTH VALLEY DRUMS ALONG THE ROCKIES - DRUM & BUGLE CORPS SHOW. 7 DRUM & BUGLE CORPS WILL COMPETE AS PART OF A NATIONAL TOUR IN A BICENTENNIAL SPECTACULAR; COMPETING CORPS ARE FROM CONCORD, CA, CASPER, WY, ANAHEIM, CA, GREAT BEND, KS, STOCKTON, CA & AUBURN, WA. AT THORNTON HIGH SCHOOL STADIUM, N WASHINGTON & E 91ST AVE. (REGN'L). DENNIS KUCKLEMAN, COORD; NORTH VALLEY BANK; PO BOX 29061; THORNTON, CO 80229. (#108708-1).

DEC 11, '76. FESTIVAL '76 COSTUME BALL. FESTIVAL AT ADAMS COUNTY FAIRGROUNDS - E 124TH AVE AND MENDERSON RD. (LOCAL). PEGGIE DORR, COORD; THORNTON CENTENNIAL-BICENTENNIAL COMMITTEE; PO BOX 29061; THORNTON, CO 80229. (#105423-1).

TOWAOC

CHIEF JACK HOUSE PARK OF TOWAOC, COLO. DEVELOPMENT OF UTE PARK TO BE NAMED AFTER LAST UTE CHIEF. (ST-WIDE). ERNEST S HOUSE, CHAIRMAN; COLORADO MOUNTAIN UTES CENTENNIAL COMMISSION; ROUTE 1 BOX 22A; CORTEZ, CO 81321. (#4436).

SUN DANCE - UTE RELIGIOUS DANCE PROG OF COLORADO. RELIGIOUS DANCE SHOWING THE YOUNGER UTES THERE IS A SUPREME BEING ASSOCIATED WITH SUN - A BISEXUAL DEITY. (ST-WIDE). ERNEST S HOUSE, CHAIRMAN; COLORADO MOUNTAIN UTES CENTENNIAL COMMITTEE; ROUTE 1-BOX 22A; CORTEZ, CO 81321. (#4488).

UTE MOUNTAIN TRIBE POW-WOW PROJECT OF COLORADO. PROJECT TO ASSIST IN PURCHASE OF COSTUMES TO COMPETE IN INTERTRIBAL DANCE POW-WOW. FUNDS WILL SUPPLEMENT TRIBE'S FUNDS & ENHANCE AUTHENTICITY OF POW-WOW. (ST-WIDE). CHIEF ALBERT WING; UTE MOUNTAIN TRIBE; TOWAOC, CO 81334. (#2017).

UTE MUSEUM OF CORTEZ, COLORADO. MUSEUM SHOWING ARTICLES OF MANCOS CANYON PROJECTS AND UTE TRIBE. (ST-WIDE). ERNEST S HOUSE, CHAIRMAN; COLORADO MOUNTAIN UTES CENTENNIAL COMMITTEE; ROUTE 1-BOX 22A; CORTEZ, CO 81321. (#4096).

WATER FOUNTAIN PROJECT - COLORADO MOUNTAIN UTES. RESTORE FOUNTAIN LOCATED IN GOVERNMENT AND TRIBAL BUILDINGS COMPOUND AND BEAUTIFY AREA. (LOCAL). ERNEST S HOUSE, CHAIRMAN; COLORADO MOUNTAIN UTES CENTENNIAL COMMITTEE; ROUTE 1 BOX 22A; CORTEZ, CO 81321. (#4438). **(??).**

WATER TREATMENT FACILITY FOR COLO UTE RESERVATION. DEVELOPMENT OF WATER SYSTEM OF UTE MOUNTAIN RESERVATION. (LOCAL). ERNEST S HOUSE, CHAIRMAN; COLORADO MOUNTAIN UTES CENTENNIAL COMMISSION; ROUTE 1 BOX 22A; CORTEZ, CO 81321. (#4435).

JUNE 18 - 22, '75. UTE BEAR DANCE FOR SPRING. DANCERS IMITATE THE BEAR IN HIS DANCE, WHICH IS A FEAST, TO WELCOME IN SPRING AND SUMMER. BRING THE TRIBE TOGETHER & PERFORM THE OLDEST DANCE IN THE UTE TRIBE SPRING FESTIVAL DANCE IN THE UTE TRIBE. AT UTE MT. UTE RESERVATION. (REGN'L). ERNEST S HOUSE, CHRMN; COLORADO MT UTES CENT COMMITTEE; ROUTE 1-BOX 22A; CORTEZ, CO 81321. (#4160-1).

TRINCHERA

GOODNIGHT TRAIL MARKER - TRINCHERA, CO. MONUMENT MARKING GOODNIGHT CATTLE TRAIL WILL BE ERECTED. (LOCAL). RICHARD H LOUDEN, CHAIRMAN; BRANSON-TRINCHERA BICENTENNIAL COMMITTEE; BRANSON, CO 81027. (#26181).

TRINIDAD

COMPILE HISTORY OF SPANISH AREA OF COLORADO. IN COMMEMORATION OF THE CENTENNIAL-BICENTENNIAL, A HISTORY OF THE SPANISH PEAKS AREA WILL BE COMPILED AND A PROGRAM WILL BE PRESENTED AT THE STATE LEVEL IN DENVER. (LOCAL). M H POOLE, PROJ DIRECTOR; GULNARE THREE VALLEY 4-H CLUB; TRINIDAD, CO 81082. (#15280).

CORAZON DE TRINIDAD -COLO CONFERENCE ON TOWNS. A NATIONAL CONFERENCE TO CONSIDER THE FUTURE OF SMALL TOWNS, COMMUITY DESIGN & A CENTENNIAL PARK. (ST-WIDE). NORMA BEACH, PROJECT DIRECTOR; TRINIDAD HISTORICAL SOCIETY; 1507 TRINITY; TRINIDAD, CO 81082. (#4342).

HISTORICAL TOUR IN TRINIDAD, CO. HISTORICAL INDIAN SIGHTS, OLD CEMETERIES, HISTORICAL BUILDINGS, LANDMARKS AND GEOGRAPHICAL AREAS WILL BE INCLUDED IN CENTENNIAL-BICENTENNIAL TOUR. (LOCAL). M H POOLE, PROJ DIRECTOR; GULNARE THREE VALLEY 4-H CLUB; TRINIDAD, CO 81082. (#15282).

IMPROVE LUDLOW MONUMENT, TRINIDAD, CO. AS A CENTENNIAL-BICENTENNIAL PROJECT, THE FACILITIES WILL BE IMPROVED BY BUILDING FIVE PICNIC TABLES, BENCHES, TRASH BARRELS AND RESTORED SIGN. (LOCAL). M H POOLE, DIRECTOR; CROSSED ARROW 4-H CLUB; 1611 PINON; TRINIDAD, CO 81082. (#15580).

INSTALL FOUNTAIN ON MUSEUM GROUNDS, CO. RENOVATE AND INSTALL SMALL FOUNTAIN IN GARDEN OF BLOOM HOUSE MUSEUM IN TRINIDAD. (LOCAL). CATHERINE RAYE, PRESIDENT; ALPHA LAMBDA & XI BETA CHI CHAPTERS OF BETA SIGMA PHI SORORITY; 1518 MISSISSIPPI; TRINIDAD, CO 81082. (#26268).

NEW JAYCEE PARK - TRINIDAD, CO. THE TRINIDAD JAYCEES WILL BUILD A NEW DOWNTOWN PARK. (LOCAL). D G SHIER, PROJ CHAIRMAN; TRINIDAD JAYCEES; BOX 268; TRINIDAD, CO 81082. (#24603).

PROGRAMS AND FLAGS PRESENTATIONS IN TRINIDAD, CO. PRESENTATION OF AMERICAN FLAG DECALS AND PATRIOTIC PROGRAMS TO THE PUBLIC AS PART OF THE CENTENNIAL-BICENTENNIAL CELEBRATION. (LOCAL). M H POOLE, PROJ DIRECTOR; GULNARE THREE VALLEY 4-H CLUB; TRINIDAD, CO 81082. (#15279).

RESTORE INDIAN TRADING POST - TRINIDAD, CO. TO MARK HISTORICAL THEME OF CENTENNIAL-BICENTENNIAL CELEBRATION, THE INDIAN TRADING POST WILL BE RESTORED ON THE APISHPA RIVER. (LOCAL). M H POOLE, PROJ DIRECTOR; GULNARE THREE VALLEY 4-H CLUB; TRINIDAD, CO 81082. (#15281).

STYLE REVUE - TRINIDAD, CO. UNIT '76, A STYLE REVUE FOR THE STATE HOME FOR THE AGED AND TRINIDAD HISTORICAL SOCIETY, WILL FEATURE CLOTHING, DANCING AND CRAFTS OF 1776-1876 AND A HISTORICAL RECORD BOOK TO BE COMPLETED. (LOCAL). BILL KING, EXTENSION AGENT/YOUTH; LAS ANI MAS COUNTY 4-H CLUBS; COURTHOUSE; TRINIDAD, CO 81082. (#17422).

'THIS DAY IN HISTORY' - TRINIDAD, CO. THERE WILL BE RESEARCHED & DOCUMENTED HISTORICAL EVENTS OF TRINIDAD AND LAS ANIMAS COUNTY PRESENTED EACH DAY ON RADIO STATION KCRT THROUGHOUT 1976. (LOCAL). GERALD STOKES, CHAIRMAN; CENTENNIAL-BICENTENNIAL COMMITTEE OF TRINIDAD; BOX 2; BONCARBO, CO 81024. (#24611).

TRINIDAD HISTORICAL BOOKLET & TOUR GUIDE, CO. A 40 PAGE ILLUSTRATED HISTORY & TOUR GUIDE OF TRINIDAD. (LOCAL). MRS H L ZUCK, CHAIRMAN; TRINIDAD HISTORICAL SOCIETY; 1208 NEVADA; TRINIDAD, CO 81082. (#16398).

JULY 26, '75. 4-H CLUBS GARMENT SHOW & PLAYS. LIVE PERFORMANCE AT SEBASTIANI GYMNASIUM. (LOCAL). KAY BAZANELLE, COORD; LAS ANIMAS COUNTY 4-H CLUBS; 1003 SAN JUAN; TRINIDAD, CO 81082. (#200007-162).

AUG 20 - NOV 20, '75. CHURCH ART CONTEST & SHOW. PAINTINGS, DRAWINGS & ARTISTIC PHOTOGRAPHS OF CHURCHES IN LAS ANIMAS COUNTY. AT SUNBURST GALLERY, 120 W MAIN. (LOCAL). M H POOLE, PRESIDENT; KIWANIS CLUB AND TRINIDAD ART LEAGUE; 120 W MAIN; TRINIDAD, CO 81082. (#200007-163).

NOV 18, '75. UNITED STATES ARMED FORCES BICENTENNIAL CARAVAN. THE CARAVAN IS COMPOSED OF EXHIBIT VANS FOR EACH BRANCH OF THE MILITARY SERVICE. THE THEME OF THE EXHIBITION IS 'HISTORY OF THE ARMED FORCES AND THEIR CONTRIBUTION TO THE NATION'. (LOCAL). M H POOLE, CHMN; U S ARMED FORCES BICENTENNIAL EXHIBIT VANS PROJECT; ROOM 201, COUNTY COURTHOUSE; TRINIDAD, CO 81082. (#1775-251).

JAN 7, '76 - CONTINUING . ESSAY & POSTER CONTEST. COMPETITION, EXHIBIT. (LOCAL). BILL SEALS, CHAIRMAN; OPTIMIST CLUB; 606 WASHINGTON AVE; TRINIDAD, CO 81082. (#107166-1).

FEB 1, '76. TRINIDAD HISTORICAL SOCIETY BANQUET & PROGRAM. TRINIDAD HISTORICAL SOCIETY HONORS EARLY CITY FATHERS AT THE BANQUET CELEBRATING TRINIDAD'S 100TH BIRTHDAY AS A CITY. MUSICAL PROGRAM ALSO PART OF THE ENTERTAINMENT. AT SEBASTIANI GYMNASIUM. (LOCAL). NORMA BEACH, COORD; TRINIDAD HISTORICAL SOCIETY; 1507 TRINITY; TRINIDAD, CO 81082. (#200007-165).

FEB 1 - 7, '76. TRINIDAD CHARTER WEEK. FESTIVAL. (LOCAL). IVAN WIDOM, COORD; TRINIDAD BI-CENTENNIAL COMMITTEE; 135 N ANIMAS; TRINIDAD, CO 81082. (#200007-166).

FEB 2, '76. STUDENT DAY IN GOVERNMENT. 20 HIGH SCHOOL STUDENTS WILL FILL CITY GOVERNMENT POSITIONS FOR ONE DAY DURING TRINIDAD CHARTER WEEK. THE STUDENTS WILL CHOOSE A MAYOR & SPEND THE DAY LEARNING ABOUT THEIR COUNTERPART'S JOB. THEY WILL PRESENT REPORTS TO THE CITY COUNCIL. (LOCAL). IVAN WIDOM, MANAGER; CITY OF TRINIDAD; CITY HALL; TRINIDAD, CO 81082. (#200007-171).

FEB 2 - 13, '76. FILM 'OLD GLORY' - THE HISTORY OF OUR FLAG. FESTIVAL AT TRINIDAD & LAS ANIMAS COUNTY SCHOOLS. (LOCAL). CATHERINE BEARDEN, DIR; TRINIDAD HISTORICAL SOCIETY; 224 SADDLE RD; TRINIDAD, CO 81082. (#200007-167).

FEB 3, '76. U S AIR FORCE ACADEMY BAND CONCERT. LIVE PERFORMANCE. (LOCAL). IVAN WIDOM, COORD; TOWN OF TRINIDAD; 135 N ANIMAS; TRINIDAD, CO 81082. (#200007-169).

FEB 14 - MAR 6, '76. HISTORICAL STORY HOUR FOR CHILDREN. LOCAL HISTORIANS WILL TELL STORIES OF EARLY HISTORY OF TRINIDAD. THIS IS BEING DONE DURING FEBRUARY DURING THE CITY'S CENTENNIAL CELEBRATION. SOME OF THE STORYTELLERS WILL WEAR COSTUMES & HAVE ARTIFACTS. AT PUBLIC LIBRARY, CHILDREN'S SECTION, 202 N LINDEN ST. (LOCAL). LOUISE HANKS, COORD; AMERICAN ASSOCIATION OF UNIVERSITY WOMEN; 1105 VICTORIA SQUARE; TRINIDAD, CO 81082. (#200007-172).

FEB 22, '76. BI-CENTENNIAL AWARENESS & THINKING DAY. CEREMONY. (LOCAL). LOUISE STEVENSON; GIRL SCOUTS; 2654 AGUILAR DR; TRINIDAD, CO 81082. (#200007-168).

FEB 27 - 28, '76. HISTORICAL QUILT EXHIBIT. HISTORICAL QUILT EXHIBIT, DEMONSTRATING HISTORICAL & MODERN METHODS OF QUILT MAKING. AT SUNBURST GALLERY, 120 W MAIN. (LOCAL). ROSE JEAN DIDERO, CHMN; LAS ANIMAS COUNTY COWBELLS; RFD 1; TRINCHERA, CO 81082. (#200007-170).

MAR 17, '76. BICENTENNIAL MEXICAN DINNER. FESTIVAL. (LOCAL). JOAQUIN RAMIREZ, COORD; CITY OF TRINIDAD; 713 MADISON; TRINIDAD, CO 81082. (#200007-173).

MAR 22 - 23, '76. BICENTENNIAL WAGON TRAIN PILGRIMAGE. SOUTHWEST ROUTE OF BICENTENNIAL WAGON TRAIN PILGRIMAGE TO PA. AT LAS ANIMAS COUNTY FAIRGROUNDS. (LOCAL). WAYNE ARAGON, COORD; TRINIDAD RIDING CLUB; HOEHNE, CO 81082. (#106997-1).

JULY 4, '76. BICENTENNIAL PARK DEDICATION. CEREMONY. (LOCAL). WALTER POIRER, CHAIRMAN; MAYOR'S COUNCIL FOR '76; 302 S CHESTNUT ST; TRINIDAD, CO 81082. (#108578-1).

JULY 4, '76. DEDICATION OF NEW PARK. CEREMONY AT WATER AND LOCUST STREETS. (LOCAL). D G SHIER, PROJ CHMN; TRINIDAD JAYCEES; BOX 268; TRINIDAD, CO 81082. (#107020-2).

TRINIDAD — CONTINUED

JULY 4, '76. FIREWORKS DISPLAY. FESTIVAL. (LOCAL). J R MARTY, COORD; CHAMBER OF COMMERCE (TRINIDAD-LAS ANIMAS COUNTY); 312 NEVADA; TRINIDAD, CO 81082. (#108578-2).

JULY 24, '76. TRINIDAD PICNIC. FAIR. (LOCAL). NORMA BEACH, COORD; TRINIDAD HISTORIC SOCIETY; 1507 TRINITY; TRINIDAD, CO 81082. (#107020-1).

JULY 30 - AUG 1, '76. LITTLE BRITCHES RODEO. FESTIVAL, COMPETITION AT LAS ANIMAS COUNTY FAIRGROUNDS. (LOCAL). FLOYD BARELA, DIRECTOR; LOS AMIGOS RIDING CLUB & TRINIDAD JAYCEES; 601 E FIRST ST; TRINIDAD, CO 81082. (#103346-6).

JULY 31, '76. TRINIDAD HISTORICAL SOCIETY ANNUAL PICNIC AND DINNER. ANNUAL TRINIDAD HISTORICAL SOCIETY PICNIC. ANNUAL TRINIDAD HISTORICAL SOCIETY DINNER. AT PICNIC AT BLOOM MANSION, 300 E MAIN; DINNER AT SEBASTIANI GYM. (LOCAL). JOHN TARABINO, CHAIRMAN; TRINIDAD HISTORICAL SOCIETY; PO BOX 777; TRINIDAD, CO 81082. (#108710-1).

SEPT 3 - 5, '76. ARTS & CRAFTS SHOW AT LAS ANIMAS COUNTY FAIR. EXHIBIT, FESTIVAL AT LAS ANIMAS COUNTY FAIRGROUNDS. (LOCAL). RUBENA MOJICA, DIRECTOR; FISHERS PEAK SENIOR CITIZENS; 430 W BACA; TRINIDAD, CO 81082. (#103346-8).

SEPT 3 - 5, '76. CENTENNIAL FLORAL DISPLAY AT LAS ANIMAS COUNTY FAIR. EXHIBIT, FESTIVAL AT LAS ANIMAS COUNTY FAIRGROUNDS. (LOCAL). HOLLIE ALLEN, CHMN; GARDEN CLUB OF TRINIDAD & HILLSIDE GARDEN CLUB; 1221 ALTA; TRINIDAD, CO 81082. (#103346-7).

SEPT 5 - 7, '76. ANNUAL ROUNDUP AND RODEO. A 3-DAY RODEO WITH A BARBEQUE AND PARADE. AT LAS ANIMAS COUNTY FAIR AND RODEO GROUNDS. (ST-WIDE). HENRY BLACKBURN, CHMN; TRINIDAD ROUNDUP ASSOC; RTE 2, BOX 97; TRINIDAD, CO 81082. (#103346-5).

DEC 3 - 5, '76. 'MOTHER SETON'S DAUGHTERS' - ORIGINAL COPYRIGHTED HISTORIC PLAY. THIS TWO-ACT ORIGINAL PLAY DEALS WITH LOCAL HISTORY AND THE DEVELOPMENT OF THE AREA AND THE SIGNIFICANT ROLE OF RELIGION IN THAT DEVELOPMENT. FIVE PERFORMANCES ARE TO BE GIVEN. DEVELOPMENT. FOUR PERFORMANCES ARE TO BE GIVEN. AT SEBASTIANI GYMNASIUM, ANIMAS STREET. (LOCAL). DOLORES BOSLEY, AUTHOR; HOLY TRINITY COUNCIL OF KNIGHTS OF COLUMBUS; 705 WILLOW; TRINIDAD, CO 81082. (#102950-1).

USAF ACADEMY

AIR FORCE ACADEMY PATRIOTIC BAND CONCERTS. SYMPHONIC CONCERTS, PATRIOTIC THEMES, OPEN TO PUBLIC IN LOCAL AREA; MUSICAL HIGHLIGHTS OF USAFA COMMEMORATION OF BICENTENNIAL YEAR. (LOCAL). CAPT GARY WILSON, INFORMATION OFFICER; U S AIR FORCE ACADEMY OFFICE OF INFORMATION; COLORADO SPG, CO 80840. (#16992).

ARMED FORCES DAY 1976 AT USAF ACADEMY. OPEN HOUSE AT THE AIR FORCE ACADEMY ON THE THIRD SATURDAY IN MAY 1976 TO EXPOSE RICH LEARNING RESOURCES AND ALLOW AREA PEOPLE TO UNDERSTAND AND APPRECIATE THE USAF ACADEMY AS A NATL RESOURCE. (NAT'L). COL MADSEN, OFFICER OF INFORMATION; USAF ACADEMY INFORMATION OFFICE; COLORADO SPGS, CO 80840. (#6769).

BICENTENNIAL ACADEMIC COURSE AT THE USAF ACADEMY. AN INTERDISCIPLINARY COURSE FOCUSING ON THE HERITAGE OF AMERICA. THESE LECTURES MAY BE OPEN TO THE PUBLIC. (LOCAL). LT COL PHILIP CAINE, CHAIRMAN; USAF ACADEMY BICENTENNIAL COMMITTEE; COLORADO SPGS, CO 80840. (#6724).

BICENTENNIAL TRAVELING EXHIBIT AT USAF ACADEMY. AN EXHIBITION DEPICTING THE CONTRIBUTIONS OF THE DEFENSE DEPARTMENT TO THE NATION. THE EXHIBITION WILL BE HOSTED BY THE ACADEMY. (NAT'L). COL MANSEN, INFORMATION OFFICER; USAF ACADEMY OFFICE OF INFORMATION; COLORADO SPG, CO 80840. (#6766).

DISTINGUISHED SPEAKERS PROGRAM AT USAF ACADEMY. SEVERAL DISTINGUISHED SPEAKERS WILL VISIT THE ACADEMY EACH YEAR TO ADDRESS THE CADETS ON A VARIETY OF TOPICS. ONE LECTURE EACH YEAR WILL BE DESIGNATED AS THE BICENTENNIAL LECTURE. (LOCAL). LT COL PHILIP CAINE, CHAIRMAN; USAF ACADEMY BICENTENNIAL COMMISSION; COLORADO SPGS, CO 80840. (#6718).

HARMON MEMORIAL LECTURE AT AIR FORCE ACADEMY. A LECTURE BY A PROMINENT MILITARY HISTORIAN IN MEMORY OF LT GEN HUBERT R HARMON WILL BE GIVEN AT THE ACADEMY IN 1976. THE TEXT OF THE LECTURE WILL BE PUBLISHED. (LOCAL). COL ALFRED F HURLEY, CHAIRMAN; US AIR FORCE ACADEMY BICENTENNIAL COMMITTEE; COLORADO SPGS, CO 80840. (#6715).

ICARUS - MAGAZINE OF CREATIVE WRITING IN CO. ANNUAL PUBLICATION OF USAFA CADET CREATIVE WRITING & PAINTING, TO BE DISTRIBUTED TO APPROXIMATELY 100 CIVILIAN UNIVERSITIES IN USA. (NAT'L). JAMES A GRIMSHAW JR, MAJOR; DEPT OF ENGLISH/FINE ARTS, US AIR FORCE ACADEMY; COLORADO SPG, CO 80840. (#10305).

'MAN-POWER UNLIMITED' PROJ OF USAF ACADEMY. A SUMMER CITIZENSHIP EXPERIENCE FOR DISADVANTAGED DENVER YOUTHS. THE PROGRAM IS OPERATED BY USAF ACADEMY CADETS AS A LEADERSHIP PROGRAM. (LOCAL). LT COL R HESS, DIRECTOR; U S AIR FORCE ACADEMY DIRECTORATE OF PLANS & PROGRAMS; COLORADO SPGS, CO 80840. (#6764).

MEMORIAL FOREST AT USAF ACADEMY. AREAS OF THE ACADEMY ARE DESIGNATED AS MEMORIAL FORESTS. ONE OF THESE AREAS IS TO BE SPECIFICALLY DESIGNATED AS A BICENTENNIAL MEMORIAL FOREST. (LOCAL). COLONEL DONALD R REAVES; DCS/CIVIL ENGINEERING (DE), USAF ACADEMY; COLORADO SPGS, CO 80840. (#6771).

MILITARY BALL AT THE USAF ACADEMY. A FORMAL MILITARY BALL IS SCHEDULED IN CONJUNCTION WITH THE OPENING OF THE USAF ACADEMY WESTERN ARTS FESTIVAL IN JANUARY. THE FESTIVAL IS AIMED AT INCREASED INTERACTION BETWEEN USAFA & THE COMMUNITY. (LOCAL). MAJ N BRUNETTI, CHIEF OF PROTOCOL; U S AIR FORCE BICENTENNIAL COMMISSION; COLORADO SPGS, CO 80840. (#6763).

MURAL OF ACADEMY HISTORY AT THE USAF ACADEMY. A MURAL WILL BE PLACED IN A PROMINENT LOCATION TO SHOW THE HISTORY OF THE SITE OF THE USAF ACADEMY. (ST-WIDE). MAJ B L DOYLE, DEPUTY; USAF ACADEMY BICENTENNIAL COMMITTEE; COLORADO SPGS, CO 80840. (#6717).

NOON PROGRAMS IN THE ARTS AT THE USAF ACADEMY. NOON PROGRAMS PRESENTED TO THE ACADEMY COMMUNITY FEATURING MUSIC BY AMERICAN COMPOSERS, DISCUSSIONS OF AMERICAN ART & LITERATURE AND CONTRIBUTIONS TO AMERICAN CULTURE BY VARIOUS ETHNIC GROUPS. (LOCAL). COL J C GATLIN JR, PROFESSOR; USAF ACADEMY BICENTENNIAL COMMITTEE; COLORADO SPGS, CO 80840. (#6719).

ORAL HISTORY INTERVIEWS PROJ OF USAF ACADEMY. THE HISTORY DEPT OF THE ACADEMY IS PRESENTLY RECORDING THE HISTORY OF AIR POWER & THE US AIR FORCE. TRANSCRIPTS OF THE TAPES ARE DEPOSITED AT THE ACADEMY LIBRARY, COLUMBIA UNIV & MAXWELL AFB. (ST-WIDE). LT COL PHILIP CAINE, CHAIRMAN; DEPT OF HISTORY, USAF ACADEMY; COLORADO SPGS, CO 80840. (#6722).

SCIENCE CONFERENCE ON AMER FUTURE IN COLORADO. US AIR FORCE ACADEMY TO HOST CONFERENCE IN 1976 ON OUR NATION'S FUTURE IN TERMS OF SCIENTIFIC DEVELOPMENT, THE QUALITY OF LIFE, SPACE & AVIATION TECHNOLOGY. (NAT'L). LT COL PHILIP CAINE, COMMITTEE CHAIRMAN; US AIR FORCE ACADEMY BICENTENNIAL COMMITTEE; COLORADO SPGS, CO 80840. (#6714).

U S AIR FORCE ACADEMY TOURS. A PROGRAM OF FORMAL TOURS OF THE USAF ACADEMY THAT WILL SPECIALIZE IN A STRUCTURED EXAMINATION OF THE TOTAL FACILITY. (NAT'L). COL M A MADSEN, DIRECTOR; U S AIR FORCE ACADEMY DIRECTORATE OF INFORMATION; COLORADO SPGS, CO 80840. (#6759).

U S AIR FORCE ACADEMY CENTENNIAL-BICENT FLOAT. THE USAF ACADEMY IS BUILDING A FLOAT WITH A BICENTENNIAL THEME TO BE USED IN CENTENNIAL-BICENTENNIAL FESTIVITIES AROUND THE STATE. (ST-WIDE). COL M A MADSEN, CHIEF INFORMATION OFFICER; U S AIR FORCE ACADEMY DIRECTORATE OF INFORMATION; COLORADO SPGS, CO 80840. (#6761).

U S AIR FORCE ACADEMY DRUM & BUGLE CORPS. PRECISION MARCHING UNIT W/117 CADET MUSICIANS WILL PROVIDE HALF-TIME ENTERTAINMENT DURING USAFA FOOTBALL GAMES AND AT OTHER EVENTS. THIS UNIT INCLUDES A BICENTENNIAL 'CONTINENTAL COLOR GUARD' UNIT. (REGN'L). CAPT GARY WILSON, INFORMATION OFFICER; U S AIR FORCE ACADEMY OFFICE OF INFORMATION; COLORADO SPG, CO 80840. (#16991).

USAF ACADEMY CADET DRILL TEAM. PRECISION MILITARY DRILL TEAM TO PARTICIPATE IN REGIONAL & NATIONAL CENTENNIAL AND BICENTENNIAL EVENTS AROUND THE STATE AND THE NATION. (NAT'L). COMMANDANT OF CADETS, USAF ACADEMY; USAF ACADEMY BICENTENNIAL COMMISSION; COLORADO SPGS, CO 80840. (#6762).

USAF ACADEMY MAJOR SPORTING EVENTS. PLANS TO HOLD MAJOR SPORTING EVENTS WITH A BICENTENNIAL THEME. (NAT'L). CAPT SCHWEITZER, DEPT OF ATHLETICS; USAF ACADEMY BICENTENNIAL COMMISSION; COLORADO SPGS, CO 80840. (#6768).

YOUTH BICENTENNIAL DEBATE AT THE USAF ACADEMY. THE USAF ACADEMY ENGLISH DEPT WILL HOST A SESSION OF THE BICENTENNIAL YOUTH DEBATES. (ST-WIDE). MAJ ROGER H LESTINA; USAF ACADEMY/DFEFA; COLORADO SPGS, CO 80840. (#6720).

'1776', MUSICAL PRODUCTION AT USAF ACADEMY. PRESENTATION OF THE MUSICAL PRODUCTION '1776' BY THE CADET BLUEBARD SOCIETY DURING ACADEMIC YEAR 1975-76. (LOCAL). LT COL PHILIP CAINE, CHAIRMAN; USAF ACADEMY BICENTENNIAL COMMITTEE; COLORADO SPGS, CO 80840. (#6723).

SEPT 1, '75. AIR FORCE ARMY FOOTBALL GAME WITH BICENTENNIAL HALF TIME SHOW. COMPETITION, RADIO/TV, LIVE PERFORMANCE. (NAT'L). CAPT SCHWEITZER; USAF ACADEMY BICENTENNIAL COMMISSION; COLORADO SPGS, CO 80840. (#6768-501).

SEPT 25, '75 - JAN 9, '76. CREATIVE WRITING SYMPOSIUM. CADETS SUBMIT ENTRIES IN POETRY, SHORT STORY, DRAMA, ESSAY & DRAWING CATEGORIES. SELECTED MANUSCRIPTS PUBLISHED IN 'ICARUS', A MAGAZINE OF CREATIVE WRITING. AT FAIRCHILD HALL BLDG 2354. (LOCAL). MAJOR J A GRIMSHAW, JR; UNITED STATES AIR FORCE ACADEMY; DEPT OF ENGLISH & FINE ARTS; USAF ACADEMY, CO 80840. (#102800-2).

SEPT 27, '75. AIR FORCE-UCLA FOOTBALL GAME. COMPETITION AT FALCON STADIUM. (NAT'L). MAJOR ENGLISH; USAF ACADEMY; AHB; USAF ACADEMY, CO 80840. (#102800-6).

OCT 3, '75 - JAN 9, '76. CADET ANNUAL CREATIVE WRITING SYMPOSIUM. SEMINAR. (NAT'L). J A GRIMSHAW, JR, MAJOR; DEPT OF ENGLISH & FINE ARTS; USAF ACADEMY; COLORADO SPG, CO 80840. (#10305-502).

OCT 4, '75. YOUTH BICENTENNIAL DEBATE AT THE USAF ACADEMY. THE USAF ACADEMY ENGLISH DEPT WILL HOST A SESSION OF THE BICENTENNIAL YOUTH DEBATES. (ST-WIDE). MAJ ROGER H LESTINA; USAF ACADEMY/DFEFA; COLORADO SPGS, CO 80840. (#6720-1).

OCT 18, '75. 200TH VARSITY FOOTBALL GAME AIR FORCE-NOTRE DAME. COMPETITION, RADIO/TV, LIVE PERFORMANCE. (NAT'L). CAPT SCHWEITZER; USAF ACADEMY BICENTENNIAL COMMISSION; COLORADO SPGS, CO 80840. (#6768-502).

OCT 25, '75. HIGH SCHOOL BAND DAY AT AF ACADEMY FOOTBALL GAME. COMPETITION, RADIO/TV, LIVE PERFORMANCE. (REGN'L). CAPT SCHWEITZER; USAF ACADEMY BICENTENNIAL COMMISSION; COLORADO SPGS, CO 80840. (#6768-503).

OCT 26, '75. AIR FORCE ACADEMY BAND CONCERT. EVENT IS PART OF A SERIES OF PLANNED USAFA BAND CONCERTS FREE TO THE PUBLIC, HIGHLIGHTING THE ACADEMY'S BICENTENNIAL COMMEMORATION. AT ARNOLD HALL AUDITORIUM. (LOCAL). CAPT GARY WILSON; USAF ACADEMY; U S AIR FORCE ACADEMY; COLORADO SPG, CO 80840. (#16248-1).

NOV 1, '75. U S AIR FORCE ACADEMY VS U S MILITARY ACADEMY FOOTBALL GAME. THE U S AIR FORCE ACADEMY VS THE U S MILITARY ACADEMY GAME HAS BEEN DESIGNATED BY MILITARY CHIEFS AS THE BICENTENNIAL GAME. AT FALCON STADIUM, STADIUM BLVD. (NAT'L). CAPT GARY WILSON, MGR; U S AIR FORCE ACADEMY; COLORADO SPG, CO 80840. (#16247-1).

NOV 11, '75 - DEC 31, '76. DISTINGUISHED SPEAKERS PROGRAM AT THE USAF ACADEMY. SEVERAL DISTINGUISHED SPEAKERS WILL VISIT THE ACADEMY EACH YEAR TO ADDRESS THE CADETS ON A VARIETY OF TOPICS. ONE LECTURE EACH YEAR WILL BE DESIGNATED AS THE BICENTENNIAL LECTURE. AT USAFA FIELD HOUSE. (LOCAL). CAPT J P CASCIANO; USAF ACADEMY BICENTENNIAL COMMISSION; DFPSP; USAFA, CO 80840. (#6718-501).

NOV 19, '75. AIR FORCE - CALIFORNIA FOOTBALL GAME. COMPETITION AT FALCON STADIUM. (NAT'L). MAJOR ENGLISH; USAF ACADEMY; AHB; USAF ACADEMY, CO 80840. (#102800-4).

JAN 1, '76. SCIENCE CONFERENCE ON AMER FUTURE HELD BY US AIR FORCE ACADEMY. US AIR FORCE ACADEMY TO HOST CONFERENCE IN 1976 ON OUR NATION'S FUTURE IN TERMS OF SCIENTIFIC DEVELOPMENT. THE QUALITY OF LIFE, & SPACE & AVIATION TECHNOLOGY. (NAT'L). LT COL PHILIP CAINE; US AIR FORCE ACADEMY BICENTENNIAL COMMITTEE; COLORADO SPGS, CO 80840. (#6714-501).

MAR 10 - 14, '76. AIR FORCE ACADEMY ASSEMBLY. ASSEMBLY IS ANNUAL STUDENT CONFERENCE. TOPIC WILL BE: WOMEN IN THE ECONOMY - A BICENTENNIAL APPRAISAL. A FINAL REPORT, REFLECTING CONCENSUS OF DELEGATES WILL BE PREPARED. AT CADET AREA, USAFA. (REGN'L). CAPTAIN R HAFFA; USAF ACADEMY/THE AMERICAN ASSEMBLY, COLUMBIA UNIV; DFPSP; USAF ACADEMY, CO 80840. (#102800-3).

OCT 7, '76. LECTURE ON ROLE OF MILITARY IN THE DEVELOPMENT OF THE WEST. A LECTURE BY A PROMINENT MILITARY HISTORIAN IN MEMORY OF LT GEN HUBERT R HARMON WILL BE GIVEN AT THE ACADEMY IN 1976. THE TEXT OF THE LECTURE WILL BE PUBLISHED. (REGN'L). COL ALFRED F HURLEY; US AIR FORCE ACADEMY BICENTENNIAL COMMITTEE; COLORADO SPGS, CO 80840. (#6715-501).

VAIL

'ONE HUNDRED YEARS OF SKIING' MUSEUM IN VAIL, CO. A PROJECT TO CREATE A MUSEUM FEATURING HISTORIC AND CONTEMPORARY ARTIFACTS RELATED TO SKIING. (ST-WIDE). HON JOHN DOBSON, MAYOR; TOWN OF VAIL; BOX 100; VAIL, CO 81657. (#4248).

MAR 1 - 28, '76. A BICENTENNIAL SHOW OF CONTEMPORARY WEAVING. WEAVING PATTERNS FROM COLONIAL PAST USED IN CONTEMPORARY PIECES INCLUDING SOME CONTEMPORARY RED, WHITE & BLUE FOR FUN. AT VALLEY FORGE GALLERY. (LOCAL). EMMY SPENCER, COORD; FIBERS IN WEAVING; 211 PINE BROOK HILLS; BOULDER, CO 80302. (#106984-1).

JULY 3 - 9, '76. VAIL-AMERICA WEEK. 7/3: EAGLE VALLEY FAIR & CARNIVAL; 7/4: AMERICA DAY PARADE & FIREWORKS; 7/5: PIONEER DAY RODEO & HORSESHOW; 7/6: CHARLIE VAIL DAY; 7/7: HISTORIC MUSIC & DANCE FESTIVAL; 7/8: ANTIQUE AUCTION & AUTO & BUGGY SHOW; 7/9: GORE VALLEY FISH FRY & FISHING DERBY. (LOCAL). M DALE MCCALL, CHMN; VAIL CENTENNIAL-BICENTENNIAL COMMITTEE; PO BOX 1976; VAIL, CO 81657. (#103913-2).

JULY 26 - AUG 6, '76. CHAUTAUQUA '76 - CONTINUING EDUC FOR NURSES IN LYCEUM TRADITION. SUMMER ADULT EDUCATION IN THE VEIN OF THE EARLY CHAUTAUQUAS. COMBINE EDUCATIONAL AND RECREATIONAL ACTIVITIES FOR THE ENTIRE FAMILY. VACATION WITH AN OPPORTUNITY TO ENJOY THE ROCKY MOUNTAINS. 186 SPEAKERS CONDUCTING 307 SEMINARS, 8:30-11:30 AM / 2:30-5:30 PM DAILY. AT LIONSQUARE LODGE, PO 418. (NAT'L). G CHRISTINE QUINN, COORD; COLORADO NURSES' ASSOC; 5453 E EVANS PL; DENVER, CO 80222. (#108707-1).

JULY 31, '76. CHAUTAUQUA HOEDOWN SQUARE DANCE FOR SQUARE DANCERS. LIVE PERFORMANCE AT MANOR VAIL LODGE-CATILLON ROOM. (ST-WIDE). SALLY POMEROY, PROJ CHMN; COLORADO STATE NURSES ASSOC; WETMORE STAR RT; FLORENCE, CO 81226. (#104876-1).

VILAS

VILAS MUSEUM, CO. RESTORATION OF GENERAL MERCHANDISE STORE TO HOUSE MUSEUM. (LOCAL). JESS HUTCHESS, COORDINATOR; TOWN OF VILAS; BOX 693; VILAS, CO 81087. (#26337).

VINELAND

PUBLICATION OF LOCAL HISTORY - VINELAND, CO. JUNIOR HIGH STUDENTS INTERVIEWED LOCAL RESIDENTS; INFORMATION PUBLISHED IN LOCAL NEWSPAPERS & MAGAZINES. (LOCAL). A H HAYDEN, JR, PROJ DIRECTOR; VINELAND JR HIGH SCHOOL; 1132 LANE 36; PUEBLO, CO 81106. (#26336).

VONA

BOOK ON VONA HISTORY - CO. BOOKS WILL BE PRINTED CONTAINING TEXT AND PHOTOS OF VONA'S HISTORY. MONEY FROM THE SALE OF THE BOOKS WILL GO TO THE VONA FIRE DISTRICT. (LOCAL). JOYCE MILLER, CHAIRPERSON; VONA CENTENNIAL-BICENTENNIAL COMMITTEE; BOX 116; VONA, CO 80861. (#26194).

COMMUNITY SCRAPBOOK - VONA, CO. SCRAPBOOK CONTAINING PICTURES, CLIPPINGS, PHOTOS AND WRITINGS ABOUT VONA'S PAST, PRESENT AND FUTURE IS BEING COMPILED. ITEMS WILL BE PLACED IN THE SCHOOL OR TOWN LIBRARY & KEPT UP TO DATE. (LOCAL). JOYCE MILLER, CHAIRPERSON; VONA CENTENNIAL-BICENTENNIAL COMMITTEE; BOX 116; VONA, CO 80861. (#26193).

IMPROVE ENVIRONMENT PROJECT - VONA, CO. PARTICIPATION IN THE '76 LITTER REVOLUTION; PAINTING WILL ALSO BE DONE AROUND THE COMMUNITY. (LOCAL). JANICE SALMANS, CHAIRMAN; WORTHWHILE HOME DEMONSTRATION CLUB; VONA, CO 80861. (#26195).

OLD NEWS ITEMS PROJECT - VONA, CO. EACH WEEK THE VONA NEWS SECTION OF THE BURLINGTON RECORD FEATURES SOME NEWS ITEMS FROM EARLY DAY VONA AND SEIBERT NEWSPAPERS. (LOCAL). LILA TAYLOR, NEWS CORRESPONDENT; VONA CENTENNIAL-BICENTENNIAL COMMITTEE; VONA, CO 80861. (#26192).

TOWN PARK PROJECT - VONA, CO. PLAN TO PLANT A TREE IN THE SPRING, MAKE PARK BENCHES AND PLANT BULBS THIS FALL. (LOCAL). JOYCE MILLER, CHAIRPERSON; VONA CENTENNIAL-BICENTENNIAL COMMITTEE; BOX 116; VONA, CO 80861. (#26261).

JAN 1 - DEC 30, '76. HISTORIC DISPLAY. EXHIBIT AT HI-PLAINS ELEMENTARY SCHOOL. (LOCAL). JOYCE MILLER, CHAIRPERSON; VONA CENTENNIAL-BICENTENNIAL COMMITTEE; BOX 116; VONA, CO 80861. (#103802-2).

JULY 3 - 4, '76. 4TH OF JULY CELEBRATION. STREET DANCE ON JULY 3RD, COMMUNITY PICNIC ON JULY 4TH WITH STREET GAMES. (LOCAL). JOYCE MILLER, COORD; VONA CENTENNIAL-BICENTENNIAL COMMITTEE; BOX 116; VONA, CO 80861. (#108576-1).

AUG 1, '76. COMMUNITY TIME CAPSULE. TIME CAPSULE TO BE OPENED AUGUST 1, 2076. (LOCAL). ROBERT O EDMUNDS, COORD; TOWN OF VONA; BOX 147; VONA, CO 80861. (#108955-32).

SEPT 6, '76. FUND RAISING FOR MUSCULAR DYSTROPHY. COMPETITION. (LOCAL). JOYCE MILLER, CHMN; VONA CENTENNIAL-BICENTENNIAL COMMITTEE; BOX 116; VONA, CO 80861. (#108748-1).

WALDEN

FLAGPOLE - WALDEN, CO. A FLAGPOLE IS TO BE ERECTED AT THE PIONEER MUSEUM FOR THE PURPOSE OF FLYING THE NATIONAL FLAG AND WORLD WAR I & II FLAGS THAT BELONG TO THE MUSEUM. (LOCAL). ARLETTE PITCHER, COORDINATOR; NORTH PARK CENTENNIAL-BICENTENNIAL COMMITTEE; 360 GRANT; WALDEN, CO 80480. (#26331).

WATERWHEEL - WALDEN, CO. WATERWHEEL WAS USED IN THE LATE 1800'S IN CONNECTION WITH A SAWMILL; IT IS TO BE MOVED TO WALDEN THIS SPRING AND SET IN OUR NEW CITY PARK AS AN HISTORICAL DISPLAY. (LOCAL). MRS NEWELL GEER, CHAIRMAN; NORTH PARK COWBELLES; WALDEN, CO 80480. (#24017).

OCT 9, '75. UNITED STATES ARMED FORCES BICENTENNIAL CARAVAN. THE CARAVAN IS COMPOSED OF EXHIBIT VANS FOR EACH BRANCH OF THE MILITARY SERVICE. THE THEME OF THE EXHIBITION IS 'HISTORY OF THE ARMED FORCES AND THEIR CONTRIBUTION TO THE NATION'. (LOCAL). RUSS BYBEE, CHMN; U S ARMED FORCES BICENTENNIAL EXHIBIT VANS PROJECT; 466 MAIN ST; WALDEN, CO 80480. (#1775-240).

JULY 3 - 4, '76. INDEPENDENCE DAY CELEBRATION. THIS DAY WILL INCLUDE CHILDREN'S GAMES WOODCUTTER'S GAMES A BUFFALO BARBEQUE LIVE MUSIC FOR DANCING - A GENERAL OLD FASHIONED FUN-DAY FOR THE WHOLE FAMILY THE SUNDANCE GUNFIGHTERS WILL PERFORM AFTERNOONS AND EVENINGS. AT 7 UTES LODGE WALDEN FAIR GROUND. (LOCAL). SHEILA POWELL; 7 UTES LODGE VOLUNTEER FIRE DEPT- LOCAL SAWMILLS NPCBC COMM; 2ND & LOGAN ST; WALDEN, CO 80480. (#107809-2).

JULY 11, '76. CENTENNIAL RODEO PARADE. THIS IS AN ANNUAL TWO-DAY ENTERTAINMENT INVOLVING RODEOS, DANCES, BARBEQUES, SIDEWALK SALES, ETC. AT MAIN ST. (ST-WIDE). SHEILA POWELL; VETERANS OF FOREIGN WARS POST 2371; 2ND & LOGAN ST; WALDEN, CO 80480. (#107815-1).

WALSENBURG

CULTURAL ART HERITAGE IN WALSENBURG, COLORADO. EDUCATIONAL PROGRAM DESIGNED TO PROMOTE A SENSE OF AWARENESS IN THE CULTURAL ARTS FIELD BY EXPLORING THE HISTORIC CULTURAL ARTS OF THE AREA. (LOCAL). TANYA HUDSON, COORDINATOR; FREE UNIVERSITY: SPANISH PEAKS MENTAL HEALTH CENTER; 303 W 9TH; WALSENBURG, CO 81089. (#10299).

HERITAGE PARK DEVELOPMENT IN WALSENBURG, CO. DEVELOP A PARK AREA THAT WILL SERVE AS A REST AREA FOR TOURISTS. (LOCAL). MRS SANDY SENZINI, PROJ COORDINATOR; WALSENBURG JUNIOR WOMEN'S CLUB; 115 E CEDER; WALSENBURG, CO 81089. (#9918).

'LAND OF THE HUAJATOLLA' PAGEANT OF COLORADO. A PAGEANT CONSISTING OF A MULTI-MEDIA PRODUCTION OF DANCE, MUSIC, DRAMA & SLIDES BASED ON HISTORY OF SOUTHERN COLORADO AND INVOLVING THE ENTIRE COMMUNITY. (ST-WIDE). LEE JETER, PRESIDENT; ARTS 'N' THINGS ASSOCIATION, INC; BOX 593; WALLSENBURG, CO 81089. (#4463). **ARBA GRANTEE.**

WALSENBURG TRIANGLE IMPROVEMENT IN COLORADO. PLANT TREES, SHRUBS AND FLOWERS AND PLACE A COMMEMORATIVE PLAQUE IN WALSENBURG, COLORADO. (LOCAL). SANDY LENCINI, CHAIRPERSON; WALSENBURG JUNIOR WOMEN'S CLUB; 115 E CEDAR; WALSENBURG, CO 81089. (#10296).

DEC 1, '75 - JULY 31, '76. MUNICIPAL CENTER COMMEMORATION. CEREMONY. (LOCAL). FR JOHN L SULLIVAN, CHMN; WALSENBERG CENT-BICENT COMMITTEE; 502 112 MAIN ST; WALSENBURG, CO 81089. (#108572-1).

JULY 2 - 3, '76. 'LAND OF THE HUAJATOLLA' PAGEANT. A PAGEANT CONSISTING OF A MULTI-MEDIA PRODUCTION OF DANCE MUSIC DRAMA & SLIDES BASED ON HISTORY OF SOUTHERN COLORADO AND INVOLVING THE ENTIRE COMMUNITY. AT FIESTA PARK 10TH AND RUSSELL WALSENBURG COLORADO. (ST-WIDE). LEE JETER; ARTS'N THINGS ASSOCIATION, INC; BOX 593; WALSENBURG, CO 81089. (#4463-1).

WALSH

SEPT 17 - 19, '76. FESTIVAL. FESTIVAL. (LOCAL). THOMAS L UPDYKE, CHMN; FESTIVAL COMMITTEE; BOX 326; WALSH, CO 81090. (#108745-1).

WESTCLIFFE

CUSTER COUNTY, COLO, MEMORIAL PARK. THIS PARK, WHICH IS A MEMORIAL TO THOSE COMMUNITY MEMBERS WHO SERVED IN WORLD WAR II, WILL BE UPDATED TO MEET THE COMMUNITY'S NEEDS. TO BE ACCOMPLISHED IN HONOR OF THE CENTENNIAL AND BICENTENNIAL. (LOCAL). CITY OF ELKHART; CUSTER COUNTY BOARD OF COUNTY COMMISSIONERS; COUNTY COURTHOUSE; WESTCLIFFE, CO 81252. (#4947).

CUSTER COUNTY, COLORADO COMMUNITY YOUTH CENTER. RENOVATING OLD SCHOOL HOUSE AND ESTABLISHMENT OF A COMMUNITY YOUTH CENTER PROVIDING FOCUS POINT FOR CENTENNIAL-BICENTENNIAL ACTIVITIES AND FUTURE RECREATION CIVIC ACTIVITIES FOR AREA YOUTH. (LOCAL). ALISON CLARKE, CHAIRMAN; VALLEY PARK RECREATION AND YOUTH CENTER, INC; C/O MACEY LANE; WESTCLIFFE, CO 81252. (#4948).

OLD WESTCLIFFE SCHOOL RESTORATION - COLORADO. A PROJECT TO RESTORE THE OLD WESTCLIFFE STONE SCHOOLHOUSE WHICH WAS BUILT IN 1891 TO PROVIDE A RECREATION CENTER, MEETING PLACE AND A FOCUS FOR CENTENNIAL-BICENTENNIAL ACTIVITIES. (LOCAL). FRANK PIERCE, COG REPRESENTATIVE; THE VALLEY PARK RECREATION AND YOUTH CENTER INC; PO BOX 92; WESTCLIFFE, CO 81252. (#4415). **ARBA GRANTEE.**

WESTCLIFFE, COLORADO, 1976 STAMPEDE. RODEO, PARADE & DANCING WITH CENTENNIAL-BICENTENNIAL THEME. ACTIVITIES WILL BE ORIENTED TO TRADITIONS OF OUR WESTERN ERA HERITAGE. (LOCAL). A CLARKE, CHAIRMAN; WET MOUNTAIN VALLEY SADDLE CLUB; C/O MACEY LANE; WESTCLIFFE, CO 81252. (#4946).

JULY 3, '76. CUSTER COUNTY FIREMEN'S DANCE. FESTIVAL. (LOCAL). WHITNEY B SULLIVAN, CHMN; CUSTER COUNTY CENTENNIAL-BICENTENNIAL COMMITTEE; PO BOX 307; WESTCLIFFE, CO 81252. (#108574-2).

JULY 4, '76. OLD-FASHIONED 4TH OF JULY. BAND CONCERT, SPEECHES, GAMES, FIREWORKS & A COMMUNITY DINNER. AT MEMORIAL PARK, 400 S 4TH ST. (LOCAL). W B SULLIVAN, CHAIRMAN; CUSTER COUNTY CENTENNIAL BICENTENNIAL COMMITTEE; ROUTE 1 BOX 8A; WESTCLIFFE, CO 81252. (#107021-2).

JULY 9 - 10, '76. MELODRAMA. LIVE PERFORMANCE AT HIGH SCHOOL GYM, MAIN ST. (LOCAL). W B SULLIVAN, CHAIRMAN; CUSTER COUNTY CENTENNIAL BICENTENNIAL COMMITTEE; ROUTE 1 BOX 8A; WESTCLIFFE, CO 81252. (#107021-4).

JULY 9 - 10, '76. MINE TOUR. TOUR OLD SILVER MINES IN THE SILVER CLIFF, QUERIDA AND ROSITA AREA. AT HIGH SCHOOL PARKING LOT, MAIN ST. (LOCAL). W B SULLIVAN, CHAIRMAN; CUSTER COUNTY CENTENNIAL BICENTENNIAL COMMITTEE; ROUTE 1 BOX 8A; WESTCLIFFE, CO 81252. (#107021-6).

JULY 17 - 18, '76. WESTCLIFFE PARADE & STAMPEDE. FESTIVAL, PARADE. (LOCAL). W B SULLIVAN, CHAIRMAN; CUSTER COUNTY CENTENNIAL-BICENTENNIAL COMMITTEE; PO BOX 307; WESTCLIFFE, CO 81252. (#108659-3).

JULY 30 - AUG 8, '76. ART SHOW. EXHIBIT. (LOCAL). W B SULLIVAN, CHAIRMAN; CUSTER COUNTY CENTENNIAL-BICENTENNIAL COMMITTEE; PO BOX 307; WESTCLIFFE, CO 81252. (#108659-1).

JULY 31 - AUG 1, '76. COUNTY FAIR. FAIR. (LOCAL). W B SULLIVAN, CHAIRMAN; CUSTER COUNTY CENTENNIAL-BICENTENNIAL COMMITTEE; PO BOX 307; WESTCLIFFE, CO 81252. (#108659-2).

AUG 1, '76. CENTENNIAL FIREWORKS. FESTIVAL. (LOCAL). W R VICKERMAN, CHMN; TOWN OF WESTCLIFFE; 305 MAIN ST; WESTCLIFFE, CO 81252. (#108955-35).

AUG 1, '76. COLORADO DAY. THERE WILL BE A BAND CONCERT, SPEECHES, FLAG CEREMONY, SEAL THE TIME CAPSULE, HERITAGE FILMS & FIREWORKS. AT MEMORIAL PARK, 400 S 4TH ST. (LOCAL). W B SULLIVAN, CHAIRMAN; CUSTER COUNTY CENTENNIAL BICENTENNIAL COMMITTEE; ROUTE 1 BOX 8A; WESTCLIFFE, CO 81252. (#107021-1).

AUG 1, '76. COMMUNITY TIME CAPSULE WITH RECORDS, PHOTOS & NEWSPAPERS. CEREMONY. (LOCAL). W R VICKERMAN, CHMN; TOWN OF WESTCLIFFE; 305 MAIN ST; WESTCLIFFE, CO 81252. (#108955-33).

AUG 1, '76. FILM FESTIVAL WITH '1776'. FESTIVAL. (LOCAL). W R VICKERMAN, CHMN; TOWN OF WESTCLIFFE; 305 MAIN ST; WESTCLIFFE, CO 81252. (#108955-34).

AUG 1, '76. MUSIC PROGRAM. BAND CONCERT FEATURING PATRIOTIC MUSIC; MUSICIANS WILL COME FROM PUEBLO. (LOCAL). W R VICKERMAN, CHMN; TOWN OF WESTCLIFFE; 305 MAIN ST; WESTCLIFFE, CO 81252. (#108955-38).

AUG 7, '76. MINE TOUR. TOUR OLD SILVER MINES IN THE SILVER CLIFF, QUERIDA AND ROSITA AREA. AT HIGH SCHOOL PARKING LOT, MAIN ST. (LOCAL). W B SULLIVAN, CHAIRMAN; CUSTER COUNTY CENTENNIAL BICENTENNIAL COMMITTEE; ROUTE 1 BOX 8A; WESTCLIFFE, CO 81252. (#107021-5).

AUG 20 - 21, '76. MELODRAMA. LIVE PERFORMANCE AT CUSTER HIGH SCHOOL GYM, MAIN ST. (LOCAL). W B SULLIVAN, CHAIRMAN; CUSTER COUNTY CENTENNIAL BICENTENNIAL COMMITTEE; ROUTE 1 BOX 8A; WESTCLIFFE, CO 81252. (#107021-3).

AUG 20 - 21, '76. MINE TOUR. TOUR OLD SILVER MINES IN THE SILVER CLIFF, QUERIDA AND ROSITA AREA. AT HIGH SCHOOL PARKING LOT, MAIN ST. (LOCAL). W B SULLIVAN, CHAIRMAN; CUSTER COUNTY CENTENNIAL BICENTENNIAL COMMITTEE; ROUTE 1 BOX 8A; WESTCLIFFE, CO 81252. (#107021-7).

SEPT 4, '76. HARVEST FESTIVAL & DANCE. DANCE WILL BEGIN AT 9 PM. (LOCAL). W B SULLIVAN, DIRECTOR; CUSTER COUNTY CENTENNIAL-BICENTENNIAL COMMITTEE; BOX 307; WESTCLIFFE, CO 81252. (#108744-1).

SEPT 18, '76. WETMORE FAIR. FAIR. (LOCAL). W B SULLIVAN, DIRECTOR; CUSTER COUNTY CENTENNIAL-BICENTENNIAL COMMITTEE; BOX 307; WESTCLIFFE, CO 81252. (#108744-2).

NOV 7, '76. LADIES AID BAZAAR. FAIR. (LOCAL). W B SULLIVAN, CHAIRMAN; CUSTER COUNTY CENTENNIAL-BICENTENNIAL COMMITTEE; BOX 307; WESTCLIFFE, CO 81252. (#108825-1).

WESTMINSTER

DISCOVER HISTORIC MOTHERS: PAST - PRESENT, CO. INFORMATION ON COLORADO MOTHERS WHO HAVE CONTRIBUTED TO THE HERITAGE OF THE STATE AND COUNTRY WILL BE SOUGHT. (LOCAL). MRS ODEMAN TOTH, CHAIRMAN; COLORADO AMERICAN MOTHERS COMMITTEE; 7533 RALEIGH ST; WESTMINSTER, CO 80030. (#24613).

WHEAT RIDGE

DECORATIVE STREET SIGNS - WHEAT RIDGE, CO. ORIGINAL STREET NAMES WILL BE POSTED ON SOME OF THE TOWN STREETS AND WILL REMAIN POSTED ALL YEAR. (LOCAL). WARD A HORTON, DIRECTOR; WHEAT RIDGE CENT-BICENT COMMITTEE & DEPT OF PARKS & RECREATION; 4350 GARRISON ST, PO BOX 610; WHEAT RIDGE, CO 80033. (#26185).

WHEAT RIDGE, CO, SOD HOUSE PROJECT. RESTORATION OF UNIQUE SOD DWELLING TO INCLUDE THE CREATION OF A PARK ON THE SITE, THE ESTABLISHMENT OF A MUSEUM IN THE ADJACENT BRICK HOUSE. (LOCAL). WARD A HORTON, DIRECTOR OF PARKS & RECREATION; CITY OF WHEATRIDGE; 4350 GARRISON ST; WHEATRIDGE, CO 80033. (#4421). **ARBA GRANTEE.**

JULY 10, '76. HORSESHOEING DEMONSTRATION. LIVE PERFORMANCE, EXHIBIT AT HISTORICAL PARK, 4610 ROBB ST. (LOCAL). NAOMI K OLSEN, COORD; WHEATRIDGE CENTENNIAL-BICENTENNIAL COMMISSION; 11250 W 38TH AVE; WHEAT RIDGE, CO 80033. (#108658-2).

JULY 10 - AUG 14, '76. WHEAT RIDGE SOD HOUSE EXHIBITS. THE SOD HOUSE HAS BEEN RESTORED AND FURNISHED IN KEEPING WITH THE STYLE OF THE 1880'S. AT HISTORICAL PARK, 4610 ROBB ST. (LOCAL). NAOMI K OLSEN, COORD; WHEATRIDGE CENTENNIAL-BICENTENNIAL COMMISSION; 11250 W 38TH AVE; WHEAT RIDGE, CO 80033. (#108658-1).

JULY 17, '76. LOST KITCHEN ARTS DEMONSTRATION. LIVE PERFORMANCE, EXHIBIT AT HISTORICAL PARK, 4610 ROBB ST. (LOCAL). NAOMI K OLSEN, COORD; WHEATRIDGE CENTENNIAL-BICENTENNIAL COMMISSION; 11250 W 38TH AVE; WHEAT RIDGE, CO 80033. (#108658-4).

JULY 24, '76. NEEDLECRAFT DISPLAY & DEMONSTRATION. EXHIBIT, LIVE PERFORMANCE AT HISTORICAL PARK, 4610 ROBB ST, EXIT I-70 AT WARD, S TO 44, E TO ROBB. (LOCAL). NAOMI K OLSON, COORD; WHEATRIDGE CENTENNIAL-BICENTENNIAL COMMISSION; 11250 W 38TH AVE; WHEAT RIDGE, CO 80033. (#108870-1).

JULY 31, '76. OPEN HOUSE & HISTORICAL DISPLAY. EXHIBIT AT HISTORICAL PARK, 4610 ROBB ST. (LOCAL). NAOMI K OLSEN,

WHEAT RIDGE — CONTINUED

COORD; WHEATRIDGE CENTENNIAL-BICENTENNIAL COMMISSION; 11250 W 38TH AVE; WHEAT RIDGE, CO 80033. (#108658-3).

AUG 1, '76. WHEAT RIDGE-COLORADO DAY CENTENNIAL CELEBRATION. FESTIVAL AT WHEAT RIDGE PARK, 44TH & FIELD ST. (LOCAL). NAOMI K OLSON, CHAIRMAN; WHEAT RIDGE CENT-BICENT COMMISSION & DEPT OF PARKS & RECREATION; 11250 W 38TH AVE; WHEAT RIDGE, CO 80033. (#108955-40).

AUG 5 - 7, '76. PIONEER FASHIONS. LIVE PERFORMANCE AT HISTORICAL PARK, 4610 ROBB ST, EXIT I-70 AT WARD, S TO 44, E TO ROBB. (LOCAL). NAOMI K OLSON, CHMN; WHEAT RIDGE CENTENNIAL-BICENTENNIAL COMMISSION; 11250 W 38TH AVE; WHEAT RIDGE, CO 80033. (#108747-9).

AUG 14, '76. TOOLS OF BYGONE DAYS - EXHIBIT. EXHIBIT AT HISTORICAL PARK, 4610 ROBB ST. (LOCAL). NAOMI K OLSON, CHAIRMAN; WHEATRIDGE CENTENNIAL-BICENTENNIAL COMMISSION; 11250 W 38TH AVE; WHEAT RIDGE, CO 80033. (#108888-1).

AUG 19 - 21, '76. WHEAT RIDGE CARNATION FESTIVAL. CITY WIDE CELEBRATION; BOOTHS, PET & FLOWER SHOWS. 7TH ANNUAL CARNATION FESTIVAL PARADE. AT 38TH & HIGH CT. (LOCAL). NAOMI K OLSON, CHAIRMAN; WHEAT RIDGE CHAMBER OF COMMERCE; 11250 W 38TH AVE; WHEAT RIDGE, CO 80033. (#108888-2).

AUG 28, '76. EARLY WHEAT RIDGE FARMING - DEMONSTRATION. LIVE PERFORMANCE AT HISTORICAL PARK, 4610 ROBB ST, EXIT I-70 AT WARD, S TO 44, E TO ROBB. (LOCAL). NAOMI K OLSON, CHMN; WHEAT RIDGE CENTENNIAL-BICENTENNIAL COMMISSION; 11250 W 38TH AVE; WHEAT RIDGE, CO 80033. (#108747-11).

AUG 28 - DEC 11, '76. WHEAT RIDGE SOD HOUSE. SOD HOUSE HAS BEEN RESTORED WITH THE AID OF A CENTENNIAL-BICENTENNIAL COMMITTEE GRANT; IT WAS BUILT IN 1880 AND IS FURNISHED IN THE MANNER OF THAT ERA. SOD HOUSE WILL BE CLOSED 11/27/76. AT HISTORICAL PARK, 4610 ROBB ST, EXIT I-70 AT WARD, S TO 44, E TO ROBB. (LOCAL). NAOMI K OLSON, CHMN; WHEAT RIDGE CENTENNIAL-BICENTENNIAL COMMISSION; 11250 W 38TH AVE; WHEAT RIDGE, CO 80033. (#108747-17).

SEPT 4, '76. SOAP MAKING & BUTTER CHURNING DEMONSTRATION. LIVE PERFORMANCE AT HISTORICAL PARK, 4610 ROBB ST, EXIT I-70 AT WARD, S TO 44, E TO ROBB. (LOCAL). NAOMI K OLSON, CHMN; WHEAT RIDGE CENTENNIAL-BICENTENNIAL COMMISSION; 11250 W 38TH AVE; WHEAT RIDGE, CO 80033. (#108747-15).

SEPT 11, '76. SPINNING DEMONSTRATION. LIVE PERFORMANCE AT HISTORICAL PARK, 4610 ROBB ST, EXIT I-70 AT WARD, S TO 44, E TO ROBB. (LOCAL). NAOMI K OLSON, CHMN; WHEAT RIDGE CENTENNIAL-BICENTENNIAL COMMISSION; 11250 W 38TH AVE; WHEAT RIDGE, CO 80033. (#108747-14).

SEPT 18, '76. VEGETABLE & FRUIT DRYING - DISPLAY & DEMONSTRATION. EXHIBIT, LIVE PERFORMANCE AT HISTORICAL PARK, 4610 ROBB ST, EXIT I-70 AT WARD, S TO 44, E TO ROBB. (LOCAL). NAOMI K OLSON, CHMN; WHEAT RIDGE CENTENNIAL-BICENTENNIAL COMMISSION; 11250 W 38TH AVE; WHEAT RIDGE, CO 80033. (#108747-12).

SEPT 25, '76. LEATHER CARE DEMONSTRATION AND BIT, BRAND & HARNESS DISPLAY. EXHIBIT, LIVE PERFORMANCE AT HISTORICAL PARK, 4610 ROBB ST, EXIT I-70 AT WARD, S TO 44, E TO ROBB. (LOCAL). NAOMI K OLSON, CHMN; WHEAT RIDGE CENTENNIAL-BICENTENNIAL COMMISSION; 11250 W 38TH AVE; WHEAT RIDGE, CO 80033. (#108747-13).

OCT 2, '76. NEEDLECRAFT DEMONSTRATION & DISPLAY. EXHIBIT, LIVE PERFORMANCE AT HISTORICAL PARK, 4610 ROBB ST, EXIT I-70 AT WARD, S TO 44, E TO ROBB. (LOCAL). NAOMI K OLSON, CHMN; WHEAT RIDGE CENTENNIAL-BICENTENNIAL COMMISSION; 11250 W 38TH AVE; WHEAT RIDGE, CO 80033. (#108747-6).

OCT 9, '76. SEED & HERB DRYING DISPLAY AND DEMONSTRATION. EXHIBIT, LIVE PERFORMANCE AT HISTORICAL PARK, 4610 ROBB ST, EXIT I-70 AT WARD, S TO 44, E TO ROBB. (LOCAL). NAOMI K OLSON, CHMN; WHEAT RIDGE CENTENNIAL-BICENTENNIAL COMMISSION; 11250 W 38TH AVE; WHEAT RIDGE, CO 80033. (#108747-5).

OCT 16, '76. MAKING APPLE CIDER. LIVE PERFORMANCE AT HISTORICAL PARK, 4610 ROBB ST, EXIT I-70 AT WARD, S TO 44, E TO ROBB. (LOCAL). NAOMI K OLSON, CHMN; WHEAT RIDGE CENTENNIAL-BICENTENNIAL COMMISSION; 11250 W 38TH AVE; WHEAT RIDGE, CO 80033. (#108747-4).

OCT 23, '76. JELLY, JAMS & PRESERVING DEMONSTRATION. LIVE PERFORMANCE AT HISTORICAL PARK, 4610 ROBB ST, EXIT I-70 AT WARD, S TO 44, E TO ROBB. (LOCAL). NAOMI K OLSON, CHMN; WHEAT RIDGE CENTENNIAL-BICENTENNIAL COMMISSION; 11250 W 38TH AVE; WHEAT RIDGE, CO 80033. (#108747-2).

OCT 30, '76. PIONEER HALLOWEEN ACTIVITIES. LIVE PERFORMANCE AT HISTORICAL PARK, 4610 ROBB ST, EXIT I-70 AT WARD, S TO 44, E TO ROBB. (LOCAL). NAOMI K OLSON, CHMN; WHEAT RIDGE CENTENNIAL-BICENTENNIAL COMMISSION; 11250 W 38TH AVE; WHEAT RIDGE, CO 80033. (#108747-3).

NOV 6, '76. RUG MAKING, BRAIDING, HOOKING & CROCHETING DEMONSTRATION. EXHIBIT, LIVE PERFORMANCE AT HISTORICAL PARK, 4610 ROBB ST, EXIT I-70 AT WARD, S TO 44, E TO ROBB. (LOCAL). NAOMI K OLSON, CHMN; WHEAT RIDGE CENTENNIAL-BICENTENNIAL COMMISSION; 11250 W 38TH AVE; WHEAT RIDGE, CO 80033. (#108747-1).

NOV 13, '76. WESTERN PIONEER MUSEUM - REMINISCING MENUS AND COOKBOOKS. EXHIBIT AT HISTORICAL PARK, 4610 ROBB ST, EXIT I-70 AT WARD, S TO 44, E TO ROBB. (LOCAL). NAOMI K OLSON, CHMN; WHEAT RIDGE CENTENNIAL-BICENTENNIAL COMMISSION; 11250 W 38TH AVE; WHEAT RIDGE, CO 80033. (#108747-8).

NOV 20, '76. SODHOUSES IN HISTORY. EXHIBIT AT HISTORICAL PARK, 4610 ROBB ST, EXIT I-70 AT WARD, S TO 44, E TO ROBB. (LOCAL). NAOMI K OLSON, CHMN; WHEAT RIDGE CENTENNIAL-BICENTENNIAL COMMISSION; 11250 W 38TH AVE; WHEAT RIDGE, CO 80033. (#108747-7).

DEC 4, '76. OLD-FASHIONED TREE TRIMMING AND HOMEMADE CHRISTMAS ORNAMENTS DISPLAY. EXHIBIT AT HISTORICAL PARK, 4610 ROBB ST, EXIT I-70 AT WARD, S TO 44, E TO ROBB. (LOCAL). NAOMI K OLSON, CHMN; WHEAT RIDGE CENTENNIAL-BICENTENNIAL COMMISSION; 11250 W 38TH AVE; WHEAT RIDGE, CO 80033. (#108747-10).

DEC 11, '76. YULETIDE OPEN HOUSE & SEASONAL BAZAAR. FESTIVAL AT HISTORICAL PARK, 4610 ROBB ST, EXIT I-70 AT WARD, S TO 44, E TO ROBB. (LOCAL). NAOMI K OLSON, CHMN; WHEAT RIDGE CENTENNIAL-BICENTENNIAL COMMISSION; 11250 W 38TH AVE; WHEAT RIDGE, CO 80033. (#108747-16).

WIGGINS

MUSIC PROGRAM. LIVE PERFORMANCE. (LOCAL). GAYLE WEHRER; TOWN OF WIGGINS; PO BOX 2; WIGGINS, CO 80654. (#108742-1).

JUNE 21, '76. WIGGINS' BICENTENNIAL CELEBRATION. ACTIVITIES INCLUDE A GENERAL CLEAN-UP AROUND THE OLD TRAIL SCHOOL MUSEUM, FLAG POLE DEDICATION, COMMUNITY BARBEQUE, SENIOR CITIZEN RECOGNITION, PARADE, BOX SOCIAL DANCE, AND CORNERSTONE PRESERVATION. (LOCAL). GAYLE WEARER, COORD; WIGGINS CENTENNIAL-BICENTENNIAL COMMITTEE; PO BOX 2; WIGGINS, CO 80654. (#200007-176).

WILEY

'GREENING AND CLEANING COLORADO' - WILEY. PROMOTE GENERAL IMPROVED APPEARANCE OF TOWN, BUILD PROTECTIVE FENCE IN PARK, ASSIST IN REMOVAL OF HEAVY TRASH ITEMS, COOPERATE WITH LOCAL UNITS IN PAINTING FIREPLUGS AND PLANTING EVERGREENS. (LOCAL). MRS MILDRED REYHER, CHAIRMAN; COLORADO CENTENNIAL-BICENTENNIAL COMMITTEE OF WILEY; RT 1; WILEY, CO 81092. (#26249).

JULY 3, '76. ETHNIC PICNIC. FESTIVAL AT CITY PARK. (LOCAL). HOWARD TEMPLE, COORD; PIONEERS COUNTY CENTENNIAL COMMITTEE; COLO STATE UNIV-COUNTY ANNEX; LAMAR, CO 81052. (#108571-2).

JULY 3 - 5, '76. CREATE YOUR OWN PROJECT. FESTIVAL AT CITY PARK. (LOCAL). MILDRED REYHER, COORD; COLORADO CENTENNIAL-BICENTENNIAL COMMITTEE; RT 1; WILEY, CO 81092. (#108571-1).

OCT 8 - 9, '76. ARTS FESTIVAL. FESTIVAL. (LOCAL). MRS MILDRED REYHER, CHMN; COLORADO CENTENNIAL-BICENTENNIAL COMMITTEE OF WILEY; RT 1; WILEY, CO 81092. (#108826-1).

WINDSOR

'GREENING & CLEANING COLORADO' - WINDSOR. TREES WILL BE PLANTED IN THE NEW CITY PARK. (LOCAL). KENNETH HENSILKE, TOWN ADMINISTRATOR; TOWN OF WINDSOR; PO BOX 627; WINDSOR, CO 80550. (#26335).

MUSIC PROGRAM. LIVE PERFORMANCE. (LOCAL). ROBERT W HOGAN; TOWN OF WINDSOR; RT 1 BOX 128B; WINDSOR, CO 80550. (#108741-1).

WINDSOR COMMUNITY CENTER IN COLORADO. COMMUNITY BUILDING FOR ALL AGES TO BE USED FOR MEETINGS AND RECREATIONAL ACTIVITIES. (LOCAL). JAMES W MATTHEWS, PRESIDENT; WINDSOR CIVIC COMMITTEE; PO BOX 88; WINDSOR, CO 80550. (#4434).

WINDSOR, CO, DEPOT RESTORATION. WINDSOR WILL RESTORE A DEPOT FOR USE AS A MUSEUM. (LOCAL). ROBERT HOGAN, CHAIRMAN; WINDSOR CIVIC COMMITTEE; PO BOX 88; WINDSOR, CO 80550. (#17542).

AUG 29, '75. JUNIOR MISS PAGEANT FOR NAMING OF HARVEST QUEEN. AWARD, CEREMONY AT WINDSOR HIGH SCHOOL AUDITORIUM W MAIN ST, AMPLE PARKING AT SCHOOL. (LOCAL). SALLY BOESE; WINDSOR CIVIC COMMITTEE INC; PO BOX 1048; WINDSOR, CO 80550. (#4434-3).

AUG 29 - SEPT 1, '75. ANNUAL COMMUNITY HARVEST FESTIVAL. BOATING DISPLAY & WATER ACTIVITIES. ALSO 4H & FFA DISPLAYS INCLUDING TRACTOR PULL, BAKE SALE, CONCESSIONS, AGRICULTURE DISPLAYS. ALSO INCLUDES LABOR DAY PARADE FEATURING LEADING BANDS FROM THE STATE & OUT OF STATE HORSE GROUPS, ANTIQUE CARS, ETC. AT WINDSOR CENTRAL BUSINESS DISTRICT, MAIN ST, OFF STREET PARKING. (LOCAL). ROBERT W HOGAN; WINDSOR CIVIC COMMITTEE INC; RT 1 BOX 128B; WINDSOR, CO 80550. (#4434-2).

AUG 29 - SEPT 1, '75. ANNUAL COMMUNITY ARTS AND CRAFTS FAIR. PRESENT WORK OF LOCAL ARTISTS - HISTORICAL AND CONTEMPORARY. AT WINDSOR SCHOOL SYSTEM - OFF STREET PARKING. (LOCAL). ROBERT W HOGAN, PROJ DIR; WINDSOR CIVIC COMMITTEE INC; RT 1, BOX 128B; WINDSOR, CO 80550. (#4434-4).

AUG 29, '75 - CONTINUING . MUSEUM-DEPOT RESTORATION TOUR DEPICTING COMMUNITY HISTORY. CAPTURING LOCAL, STATE & NAT HISTORICAL DATA OF INTEREST TO ALL GROUPS & DEPICTING ORIGINAL SCENES DISPLAYING LOCAL CULTURE OF THE COMMUNITY; DISPLAY RAILWAY ANTIQUES & MEMORABILIA; TOUR INFORMATION TO WINDSOR COMMUNITY BY CUSTODIAN POINTING OUT HISTORICAL INTERESTS. AT DEPOT - 5TH ST NORTH OFF MAIN ST; OFF STREET PARKING. (LOCAL). ROBERT W HOGAN, PROJ DIR; WINDSOR CIVIC COMMITTEE INC; RT 1 BOX 128B; WINDSOR, CO 80550. (#4434-1).

DEC 19, '75. LOS POSADAS CHRISTMAS FESTIVAL. AMERICAN CAROLING PROCESSION & TRADITIONAL CELEBRATION; CHRISTMAS STORY READING, PINATA CONSTRUCTION, COMMUNITY YULE FEAST & DANCING. AT TOZER SCHOOL MULTI-PURPOSE, RM 501, OAK ST. (LOCAL). ROBERT W HOGAN, PROJ DIR; WINDSOR CIVIC COMMITTEE INC; RT 1 BOX 128B; WINDSOR, CO 80550. (#4434-5).

FEB 22, '76. WINDSOR DEPOT - MUSEUM DEDICATION CEREMONY. DEDICATION CEREMONY WILL OFFICIALLY OPEN MUSEUM. MUSEUM WILL DISPLAY HISTORICAL DATA OF LOCAL, STATE & NATIONAL INTEREST. WILL ALSO DISPLAY CULTURAL & RAILROAD ANTIQUES & MEMORABILIA. AT WINDSOR DEPOT - 5TH ST N, OF MAIN - OFF STREET PARKING. (LOCAL). ROBERT W HOGAN; WINDSOR CIVIC COMMITTEE INC; RT 1 BOX 128B; WINDSOR, CO 80550. (#200007-175).

SEPT 1, '76. COMMUNITY PARADE. PARADE. (LOCAL). ROBERT W HOGAN; TOWN OF WINDSOR; RT 1 BOX, 128B; WINDSOR, CO 80550. (#108741-2).

SEPT 3, '76. ANNUAL HARVEST QUEEN PAGEANT FOR NAMING OF QUEEN. CONTESTANTS JUDGED BY JUNIOR MISS PAGEANT RULES & GUIDELINES & ON TALENT, POISE AND INTERVIEW. AT WINDSOR HIGH SCHOOL AUDITORIUM - W MAIN ST, AMPLE PARKING. (LOCAL). ROBERT W HOGAN, COORD; WINDSOR CIVIC COMMITTEE, INC; RT 1 BOX 128B; WINDSOR, CO 80550. (#4434-7).

SEPT 3 - 6, '76. ANNUAL COMMUNITY HARVEST FESTIVAL. BOATING DISPLAY & WATER ACTIVITIES. ALSO 4H, FFA & VOC AGRICULTURE DISPLAYS INCLUDING TRACTOR PULL, BAKE SALE, CONCESSIONS & AGRICULTURAL DISPLAYS. DEPOT MUSEUM, LABOR DAY PARADE FEATURING STATE & LOCAL BANDS, HORSE GROUPS & ANTIQUE CHAIRS. AT WINDSOR CENTRAL BUSINESS DISTRICT - MAIN ST - OFF STREET PARKING. (LOCAL). ROBERT W HOGAN, COORD; WINDSOR CIVIC COMMITTEE, INC; RT 1, BOX 128B; WINDSOR, CO 80550. (#4434-6).

SEPT 4 - 6, '76. ANNUAL COMMUNITY ARTS & CRAFTS FAIR. PRESENT WORKS OF LOCAL ARTISTS IN THE HISTORICAL & CONTEMPORARY STYLE. AT WINDSOR SCHOOL SYSTEM - W MAIN ST - OFF STREET PARKING. (LOCAL). ROBERT W HOGAN, COORD; WINDSOR CIVIC COMMITTEE, INC; RT 1, BOX 128B; WINDSOR, CO 80550. (#4434-8).

DEC 17, '76. LAS POSADAS - CHRISTMAS FESTIVAL. AMERICAN CAROLING PROCESSION & TRADITIONAL CELEBRATION; CHRISTMAS STORY READING, PINATA BREAKING, COMMUNITY YULE FEAST & DANCING. AT TOZER SCHOOL - MULTI PURPOSE ROOM - 501 OAK ST. (LOCAL). ROBERT W HOGAN, COORD; WINDSOR CIVIC COMMITTEE, INC; RT 1, BOX 128B; WINDSOR, CO 80550. (#4434-9).

WOODLAND PARK

AVENUE OF FLAGS IN WOODLAND PARK, COLO. REPRODUCTIONS OF ALL UNITED STATES FLAGS FROM THE FIRST ONE MADE BY BETSY ROSS TO THE PRESENT 50 STAR FLAG WILL BE DISPLAYED ON MAIN STREET. (LOCAL). JOHN LABBY, CHAIRMAN; LIONS CLUB; C/O STAR RT 1360; WOODLAND PARK, CO 80863. (#4930).

BICENTENNIAL BULLETIN BOARD PROJECT OF COLORADO. COMMUNITY CENTENNIAL-BICENTENNIAL & OTHER ACTIVITIES WILL BE POSTED ON THIS BOARD TO PROMOTE COMMUNITY AWARENESS OF ACTIVITIES. BOARD WILL BE PLACED IN TOWN HALL AND BEAR CENT-BICENT LOGOS. (LOCAL). JOHN LABBY, CHAIRMAN; WOODLAND PARK CENTENNIAL-BICENTENNIAL COMMITTEE; STAR ROUTE 1360; WOODLAND PARK, CO 80863. (#4951).

CENTENNIAL COMMUNITY CENTER OF WOODLAND PARK, CO. TO BE LOCATED IN PARK FOR ICE SKATING ACTIVITIES AND MEETING CENTER FACILITY FOR COMMUNITY SERVICE GROUPS. (LOCAL). JOHN LABBY, CHAIRMAN; COMMUNITY ACTION GROUP - CENTENNIAL BICENTENNIAL CMMITTEE; C/O STAR RT 1360; WOODLAND PARK, CO 80863. (#4396). **(??).**

CENTENNIAL GAZEBO OF WOODLAND PARK, COLORADO. GAZEBO CONSTRUCTED IN THE TOWN'S LAKE FOR THE PURPOSE OF CENTENNIAL CONCERT AND LATER TO BE USED BY HIGH SCHOOL AND CHURCH GROUPS FOR COMMUNITY CONCERTS. (LOCAL). JOHN LABBY, CHAIRMAN; CHAMBER OF COMMERCE - CENTENNIAL BICENTENNIAL COMMITTEE; C/O STAR RT 1360; WOODLAND PARK, CO 80863. (#4397).

CENTENNIAL SWIMMING POOL OF WOODLAWN PARK, COLO. TO CREATE A FACILITY INCORPORATED WITH THE THEME OF '76 FOR THE USE OF SCHOOL STUDENTS AND TOTAL COMMUNITY. (LOCAL). JOHN LABBY, CHAIRMAN; CENTENNIAL BICENTENNIAL COMMITTEE; C/O STAR RT 1360; WOODLAND PARK, CO 80863. (#4391). **(??).**

CENT-BICENT EDITION OF NEWSPAPER, WOODLAND PK, CO. THIS SPECIAL EDITION OF THE TOWN'S PAPER WILL FEATURE PHOTOS AND ARTICLES FROM PAST EDITIONS SHOWING COMMUNITY GROWTH & EVENTS. A COPY WILL BE PLACED IN THE TIME CAPSULE. (LOCAL). JOHN LABBY, CHAIRMAN; UTE PASS COURIER; C/O STAR ROUTE 1360; WOODLAND PARK, CO 80863. (#4949). **(??).**

FESTIVAL WEEK '76 IN WOODLAND PARK, COLORADO. IN ORDER TO CELEBRATE THE CENTENNIAL-BICENTENNIAL A WEEK OF EXCITING FESTIVITIES ARE PLANNED. ACTIVITIES INCLUDE A HORSE

WOODLAND PARK—CONTINUED

RACE THROUGH TOWN, CARNIVAL, PARADE, BUGGY & WAGON DISPLAY, AND WESTERN SHOWS. (LOCAL). JOHN LABBY, CHAIRMAN; WOODLAND PARK CENTENNIAL-BICENTENNIAL COMMISSION; STAR RT 1360; WOODLAND PARK, CO 80863. (#4924).

LANDSCAPING OF WOODLAND PARK, COLORADO. PLANTING OF SHRUBS, TREES & GRASS IN AREAS WHICH NEED BEAUTIFICATION IN HONOR OF THE CENTENNIAL. (LOCAL). JOHN LABBY, CHAIRMAN; 4-H; C/O STAR RT 1360; WOODLAND PARK, CO 80863. (#4927). **(??).**

LOCAL HISTORICAL LANDMARKS -WOODLAWN PARK, COLO. SIGNS DISPLAYING CENTENNIAL-BICENTENNIAL SYMBOLS DESCRIBING THE BUILDINGS AND LOCATIONS OF HISTORICAL VALUE TO OUR COMMUNITY. (LOCAL). JOHN LABBY, CHAIRMAN; WOODLAND PARK HISTORICAL SOCIETY; C/O STAR RT 1360; WOODLAND PARK, CO 80867. (#4390). **(??).**

OLD JAIL RENOVATION OF WOODLAND PARK, COLO. RELOCATE ORIGINAL TOWN JAIL AND PRESERVE THE HISTORIC HERITAGE IN HONOR OF CENTENNIAL-BICENTENNIAL OF COLORADO. (LOCAL). JOHN LABBY, CHAIRMAN; POLICE DEPARTMENT - CENTENNIAL BICENTENNIAL COMMITTEE; C/O STAR RT 1360; WOODLAND PARK, CO 80863. (#4395). **(??).**

OLD PHOTO & MAP COLLECTION OF WOODLAND PARK, COLO. OLD PHOTOS AND MAPS TO BE DISPLAYED IN THE TOWN'S MUNICIPAL BUILDINGS SHOWING WOODLAND PARK AND COLORADO DURING EARY STATEHOOD ERA. (LOCAL). JOHN LABBY, CHMN WOODLAND PARK CENT-BICENT COMM; SENIOR CITIZEN CLUB; C/O STAR RT 1360; WOODLAND PARK, CO 80863. (#4152).

PICNIC FACILITIES IMPROVEMENT, WOODLAND PARK, CO. BICENTENNIAL COMMEMORATIVE IMPROVEMENT OF PICNIC FACILITIES IN TOWN PARKS. (LOCAL). JOHN LABBY, CHAIRMAN; TOWN COUNCIL OF WOODLAND PARK; C/O STAR RT 1360; WOODLAND PARK, CO 80863. (#4931).

PROPOSED CENTENNIAL MONUMENT IN WOODLAND PARK, CO. MONUMENT TO BE ERECTED DEPICTING THE HISTORY OF TELLER COUNTY. (LOCAL). JOHN LABBY, CHAIRMAN; WOODLAND PARK CENTENNIAL-BICENTENNIAL COMMITTEE; STAR RT 1360; WOODLAND PARK, CO 80863. (#4928). **(??).**

RENEWAL OF CEMETERY IN WOODLAND PARK, COLORADO. ESTABLISHING A PERPETUAL CARE FUND TO CARE FOR THE PIONEERS' GRAVES IN HONOR OF CENTENNIAL-BICENTENNIAL. (LOCAL). JOHN LABBY, CHAIRMAN; COMMUNITY ACTION GROUP; C/O STAR RT 1360; WOODLAND PARK, CO 80863. (#4933). **(??).**

ROTARY BEAUTIFICATION IN WOODLAND PARK, COLO. BEAUTIFICATION OF TWO ROTARIES ADJACENT TO MAIN STREET AT HIGHWAY INTERSECTION IN HONOR OF CENTENNIAL-BICENTENNIAL. (LOCAL). JOHN LABBY, CHAIRMAN; LIONS CLUB; C/O STAR RT 1360; WOODLAND PARK, CO 80863. (#4929). **(??).**

WESTERN FRONTAGE ON MAIN ST-WOODLAND PARK, COLO. TO COMPLETE THE WESTERN APPEARANCE ON MAIN STREET OF TOWN TO HELP COMMEMORATE THE CENTENNIAL-BICENTENNIAL. (LOCAL). JOHN LABBY, CHAIRMAN; TOWN COUNCIL - CENTENNIAL BICENTENNIAL COMMITTEE; C/O STAR RT 1360; WOODLAND PARK, CO 80863. (#4394). **(??).**

WOODLAND PK SCHOOL SYSTEM CENT-BICENT PROJ, COLO. STUDENTS OF SCHOOL DISTRICT 2 WILL FORM OWN CENTENNIAL-BICENTENNIAL COMMITTEE TO CONDUCT NUMEROUS HERITAGE, HORIZON & FESTIVAL PROJECTS RELATED TO THE CENTENNIAL-BICENTENNIAL THEMES. (LOCAL). JOHN LABBY, CHAIRMAN; WOODLAND PARK SCHOOL SYSTEM; C/O STAR RT 1360; WOODLAND PARK, CO 80863. (#4923). **(??).**

1976 TIME CAPSULE, WOODLAND PARK, COLORADO. THE TIME CAPSULE WILL INCLUDE WOODLAND PARK CIVIC MATERIALS, AN ARBA FLAG CENTENNIAL-BICENTENNIAL ARTIFACTS FROM 1976 CELEBRATIONS AND OTHER ITEMS OF INTEREST TO 2076 CITIZENS. (LOCAL). JOHN LABBY, CHAIRMAN; WOODLAND PARK CENTENNIAL-BICENTENNIAL COMMITTEE; C/O STAR ROJTE #1360; WOODLAND PARK, CO 80863. (#4800).

JULY 4, '76. JULY 4TH CELEBRATION. 8-12AM, OLD FASHIONED CHURCH SERVICE; 1PM, BAR-B-Q IN MIDLAND PARK; 7:30PM, CENTENNIAL FILM 'ONE NATION UNDER GOD' AT BAPTIST PARK. (LOCAL). BOB BERGMAN, COORD; WOODLAND PARK CENTENNIAL-BICENTENNIAL COMMITTEE; WOODLAND PARK, CO 80863. (#108573-2).

JULY 5, '76. WOODLAND PARK - JULY 5TH CELEBRATION. 10AM - PARADE ON MAIN ST, 1PM - PICNIC AT MIDLAND PARK, 8PM - CAMPFIRE PROGRAM AT RED ROCKS CAMPGROUND. (LOCAL). BOB BERGMAN, COORD; WOODLAND PARK CENTENNIAL-BICENTENNIAL COMMITTEE; WOODLAND PARK, CO 80863. (#108573-1).

JULY 6, '76. CAMPFIRE PROGRAM. FESTIVAL AT RED ROCKS CAMPGROUND. (LOCAL). BOB BERGMAN, CHAIRMAN; WOODLAND PARK CENTENNIAL-BICENTENNIAL COMMITTEE; WOODLAND PARK, CO 80863. (#108735-1).

JULY 7, '76. BICENTENNIAL PLAY BY WOODLAND PARK MIDDLE SCHOOL. THERE WILL ALSO BE A CAMPFIRE PROGRAM AT RED ROCKS CAMPGROUND. AT WOODLAND PARK MIDDLE SCHOOL. (LOCAL). BOB BEGMAN, CHAIRMAN; WOODLAND PARK CENTENNIAL-BICENTENNIAL COMMITTEE; WOODLAND PARK, CO 80863. (#108735-2).

JULY 8, '76. JULY 8TH FESTIVITIES. 2 TO 10 PM - CARNIVAL; 7 PM - WEEKLY BAND CONCERT AT MIDLAND PARK GAZEBO; 7:30 PM - BINGO AT CATHOLIC CHURCH; 8 PM CAMPFIRE PROGRAM AT RED ROCKS CAMPGROUND. (LOCAL). BOB BERGMAN, CHAIRMAN; WOODLAND PARK CENTENNIAL-BICENTENNIAL COMMITTEE; WOODLAND PARK, CO 80863. (#108735-3).

WRAY

BUFFALO BILL CLUB RODEO IN WRAY, CO. THIS IS A YOUTH ORGANIZATION WHICH FEATURES HORSE SHOWS AND LITTLE BRITCHES RODEO WITH A CENTENNIAL-BICENTENNIAL THEME. (LOCAL). TOM LAQUEY, COORDINATOR; BUFFALO BILL CLUB; BOX 385; WRAY, CO 80758. (#14805).

CHAUTAUQUA - WRAY, CO. FESTIVAL ACTIVITY TO COMMEMORATE THE CENTENNIAL-BICENTENNIAL CELEBRATION. (LOCAL). TOM LAQUEY, COORDINATOR; CHAMBER OF COMMERCE AND BICENTENNIAL COMMITTEE; BOX 385; WRAY, CO 80758. (#14807).

MUSEUM PROJECT OF WRAY, COLORADO. A PROJECT TO ERECT A NEW AND LARGER BUILDING TO HOUSE THE LOCAL MUSEUM. (LOCAL). STANLEY E SHAFER, CO COMMISSIONER; YUMA COUNTY HISTORICAL SOCIETY; WRAY, CO 80758. (#4332).

RESTORATION OF OLD MILL RACE OF WRAY, COLO. RESTORE OLD ABANDON WATER WHEEL BUILT AT TURN OF CENTURY IN VICINITY PROPOSED REPUBLICAN RIVER PARK. (LOCAL). THOMAS LAGUEY, JR, COUNTY EXTENSION AGENT; WRAY COUNTY EXTENSION CENTER; WRAY, CO 80758. (#1948).

WRAY RIVERSIDE PARK OF COLORADO. MAKE PARK ON ONE MILE BANKS OF REPUBLICAN RIVER WITH FIVE UNITS. CHILDRENS PLAYS, BARBECUE, CONCERTS, STAGE, FISHING, BICYCLE PATHS, & WALKWAY. (LOCAL). THOMAS LAQUEY, JR, DIRECTOR; COLORADO COUNTY EXTENSION SERVICE; WRAY, CO 80758. (#2009). **ARBA GRANTEE.**

JUNE 13, '76. PUBLIC FLAG DAY CEREMONIES BY WRAY ELKS CLUB. CEREMONY AT WRAY FOOTBALL FIELD. (LOCAL). JIM WISEMAN, COORD; WRAY ELKS CLUB; WRAY, CO 80758. (#200007-174).

JULY 1, '76. HAPPY BIRTHDAY COLORADO. PUBLIC BIRTHDAY PARTY WITH LIVE ENTERTAINMENT WILL BE HELD. AT WRAY CITY PARK. (LOCAL). GILBERT GREEN, COORD; WRAY CENTENNIAL-BICENTENNIAL COMMITTEE; WRAY, CO 80798. (#108575-1).

JULY 3 - 5, '76. WRAY FOURTH OF JULY CELEBRATION. FESTIVAL. (LOCAL). THOMAS LA QUEY, CHMN; WRAY BICENTENNIAL COMMITTEE; PO BOX 385; WRAY, CO 80758. (#107568-1).

JULY 30 - AUG 1, '76. WRAY DAYS - COMMUNITY CELEBRATION WITH CENTENNIAL-BICENTENNIAL THEME. THIS COMMUNITY CELEBRATION FEATURES A PARADE AND COMMUNITY BREAKFAST CENTERED AROUND A CENTENNIAL-BICENTENNIAL THEME. (LOCAL). TOM LAQUEY, CHMN; WRAY CENTENNIAL-BICENTENNIAL COMMITTEE; BOX 385; WRAY, CO 80758. (#103031-2).

JULY 31, '76. BUFFALO BILL'S HORSE CLUB - GYMKHANA FOR YOUTH. THE DAY'S ACTIVITIES WILL INCLUDE: TRADITIONAL RODEO EVENTS, HORSE SHOWS AND SPECIAL EVENTS FOR KIDS. AT TRI-STATE RODEO GROUNDS. (LOCAL). TOM LAQUEY, CHMN; WRAY CENTENNIAL-BICENTENNIAL COMMITTEE; BOX 385; WRAY, CO 80758. (#103031-4).

JULY 31 - AUG 1, '76. COLORADO DAYS. WRAY COMMEMORATES THE STATES CENTENNIAL WITH A WEEKEND OF EVENTS FOR THE ENTIRE COMMUNITY. (LOCAL). TOM LAQUEY, CHMN; WRAY CENTENNIAL-BICENTENNIAL COMMITTEE; BOX 385; WRAY, CO 80758. (#103031-3).

AUG 18 - 19, '76. BEECHER ISLAND CELEBRATION COMMEMORATING FAMOUS INDIAN BATTLE. THERE WILL BE AN OLD-FASHIONED BREAKFAST, BAR-B-QUE, CHURCH SERVICE, INDIAN TALKS, RELIGIOUS SINGING AND GAMES. AT BEECHER ISLAND PARK. (LOCAL). TROIL WELTON, COORD; BEECHER ISLAND ASSOC; WRAY, CO 80758. (#108725-1).

SEPT 18 - 19, '76. BEECHER ISLAND REUNION. THIS WEEKEND ACTIVITY CELEBRATES THE BATTLE OF BEECHER ISLAND WITH CENTENNIAL-BICENTENNIAL GAMES FOR CHILDREN AND ADULTS. AT BEECHER ISLAND BATTLEGROUNDS. (LOCAL). TOM LAQUEY, CHMN; WRAY CENTENNIAL-BICENTENNIAL COMMITTEE; BOX 385; WRAY, CO 80758. (#103031-1).

DEC 1 - 25, '76. OLD-FASHION CHRISTMAS IN BUSINESS DISTRICT. FESTIVAL AT BUSINESS DISTRICT. (LOCAL). GILBERT GREEN, COORD; WRAY CHAMBER OF COMMERCE; WRAY, CO 80758. (#108743-1).

YUMA

'ACTION ON THE PLAINS' BOOK OF YUMA, CO. SALE OF CITY AND COUNTY HISTORY, WITH PROCEEDS GOING TO CREATION OF CENTENNIAL - BICENTENNIAL MUSEUM DISPLAY, ENTITLED 'ACTION ON THE PLAINS.'. (ST-WIDE). MRS LOUIS KORF, COORDINATOR; YUMA COUNTY HISTORICAL SOCIETY; YUMA, CO 80759. (#9912).

CENTENNIAL PICTURE ALBUM - YUMA, CO. A BOOK OF PICTURES OF EARLY DAY YUMA AND COMMUNITY. (LOCAL). MRS LOUIS KORF, PROJ DIRECTOR; YUMA COUNTY HISTORICAL SOCIETY; 114 S BIRCH; YUMA, CO 80759. (#26324).

COLONIAL FIRST GRADE VILLAGE - YUMA, CO. THE FIRST GRADE IS SET UP AS A COLONIAL VILLAGE. THE STUDENTS ARE SEATED IN VILLAGE SQUARE WITH A VILLAGE POST OFFICE, LIBRARY OF CONGRESS, FREEDOM SINGERS AND BETSY ROSS FLAG. (LOCAL). MRS DARLENE KORF, CHAIRMAN; YUMA NORTH GRADE SCHOOL; 519 N ALBANY; YUMA, CO 80759. (#26320).

HERITAGE PLAQUE PROJECT - YUMA, CO. COMMUNITY YOUTH WILL MAKE HERITAGE PLAQUES FOR OLD HOMES AND OTHER HISTORICAL SITES WITH DATE, NAME OF ORIGINAL OWNER & NAME OF PRESENT OWNER. (LOCAL). ROLLIE DEERING, COORDINATOR; YUMA CENTENNIAL-BICENTENNIAL COMMITTEE; 606 S BIRCH; YUMA, CO 80759. (#26321).

HERITAGE SIGN PROJECT - YUMA, CO. HERITAGE SIGNS WILL BE PLACED ON HISTORICAL PROPERTY. (LOCAL). DONALD R STEARNS, PROJ DIRECTOR; YUMA CENTENNIAL-BICENTENNIAL COMMITTEE; 618 S ELM ST; YUMA, CO 80759. (#26326).

HISTORICAL MARKER HONORING FOUNDER OF YUMA, CO. ERECT A HISTORICAL MARKER 3 MILES EAST OF YUMA WHERE THE MAN, YUMA, IS BURIED FOR WHOM THE TOWN IS NAMED. (ST-WIDE). HON DONALD R STARNES, MAYOR; TOWN OF YUMA; 221 S MAIN ST; YUMA, CO 80759. (#9914).

JOHNNY HORIZON-YUMA COMMUNITY CLEANUP - CO. 'LET'S CLEANUP YUMA AND COMMUNITY' IN 1976, THUS COOPERATING WITH KEEP COLORADO AND AMERICA BEAUTIFUL FOR THE 100TH & 200TH BIRTHDAYS OF OUR STATE & NATION. (LOCAL). MRS MARGIE CHANCE, CHAIRPERSON; TOWN OF YUMA; 221 S MAIN; YUMA, CO 80759. (#26322).

LAKE YUMA PROJECT IN COLORADO. A LANDMARK OF YUMA WHICH WAS ONCE A BUFFALO WALLOW, WILL BE CONVERTED INTO AN OUTDOOR RECREATION AREA WITH PICNIC, BOATING AND FISHING FACILITIES. (ST-WIDE). HON DONALD R STARNES, MAYOR; TOWN OF YUMA; BOX 265; YUMA, CO 80759. (#9920).

'MEMORIES' - YUMA, CO. WITH ASSISTANCE OF BOB BROOKS HS COMMUNICATION CLASS, 12 SELECTED RESIDENTS OF LIFE CARE CENTER NURSING HOME WILL BE INTERVIEWED & A HISTORY WILL BE WRITTEN. (LOCAL). PEGGY MCCALL, ACTIVITIES DIRECTOR; LIFE CARE CENTER NURSING HOME; 323 W 9TH AVE; YUMA, CO 80759. (#26251).

OUR RELIGIOUS HERITAGE - YUMA, CO. A RESEARCH PROGRAM ON RELIGIOUS HERITAGE: MAYFLOWER COMPACT, BILL OF RIGHTS, CONSTITUTION, DECLARATION OF INDEPENDENCE AND MUCH MORE TO EXPRESS THAT WE ARE 'ONE NATION, UNDER GOD'. (LOCAL). FAYE ELLEN WINGER, COORDINATOR; YUMA CENTENNIAL-BICENTENNIAL COMMITTEE; 618 S ELM ST; YUMA, CO 80759. (#26323).

SIXTH GRADE FLAGS - YUMA, CO. YUMA SIXTH GRADERS MADE REPLICAS OF EARLY AMERICAN FLAGS AND DISPLAYED THEM IN TOWN LIBRARY AND THE SCHOOL. (LOCAL). NINA STULP, TEACHER; YUMA CENTENNIAL-BICENTENNIAL COMMITTEE; 618 S ELM ST; YUMA, CO 80759. (#26325).

SOD HOUSE IN 1876 STYLE IN YUMA, CO. CONSTRUCT AND AUTHENTICALLY FURNISH A SOD HOUSE IN 1876 STYLE. (ST-WIDE). HON DONALD R STARNES, MAYOR; TOWN OF YUMA; 221 S MAIN; YUMA, CO 80759. (#9915).

YUMA CENTENNIAL PARK IN COLORADO. THE TOWN PARK WILL BE RENAMED 'YUMA CENTENNIAL PARK', AND WILL BECOME THE SITE FOR FUTURE ACTIVITIES. (LOCAL). HON DONALD R STARNES, MAYOR; TOWN OF YUMA; BOX 265; YUMA, CO 80759. (#9919).

YUMA PIONEER NEWSPAPER PROJECT - CO. NEWSPAPER WILL PRINT EARLY DAY PICTURES OF YUMA AND AREA WEEKLY. IT WILL BE IN KEEPING WITH THE CENTENNIAL-BICENTENNIAL THEME, ' A PAST TO REMEMBER'. (LOCAL). ROGER CHANCE, EDITOR; YUMA PIONEER NEWSPAPER; 207 S MAIN; YUMA, CO 80759. (#10295).

AUG 10 - 13, '75. YUMA COUNTY FAIR & PARADE WITH A CENTENNIAL-BICENT THEME. PARADE 8/10, 10:00 AM. EVENING SHOWS: RODEO, COUNTRY WESTERN SHOW, 4-H STYLE SHOW, TRACTOR PULL. WED HOURS 8:00 AM TO 12 NOON. (ST-WIDE). BERNIE BLACH; YUMA CHAMBER OF COMMERCE AND YUMA COUNTY FAIR BOARD; YUMA, CO 80759. (#9924-501).

MAR 28, '76. YUMA ECUMENICAL DINNER. ALL-COMMUNITY CHURCH POT-LUCK SUPPER WITH YUMA AREAN SINGERS PERFORMING A RELIGIOUS HERITAGE MUSICAL; YUMA HOMEMAKER EXTENSION CLUB WILL FURNISH HOMEMADE CHERRY PIE AND ICE CREAM. AT ST JOHN'S CATHOLIC CHURCH. (LOCAL). LINDA FRANK, DIRECTOR; ALTAR & ROSARY SOCIETY; 909 S BUFFALO; YUMA, CO 80759. (#108740-1).

APR 15, '76. ARBOR DAY CENTENNIAL-BICENTENNIAL PROGRAM. YUMA NORTH WILL PLANT 2 MOUNTAIN ASH TREES, WEST SCHOOL 4TH GRADERS WILL EACH PLANT EVERGREENS FOR A WIND BREAK, 5TH GRADERS WILL PLANT A LOCUST TREE, 6TH GRADERS A COLORADO BLUE SPRUCE & THE JUNIOR HIGH SHRUBBERY & 2 TREES. (LOCAL). MRS NINA STULP, CHPRSN; YUMA CENTENNIAL-BICENTENNIAL COMMITTEE; 618 S ELM ST; YUMA, CO 80759. (#200007-177).

MAY 29 - 31, '76. ANNUAL TEENAGE RODEO. ENTRY FEES FOR CONTESTANTS; ADVANCED REGISTRATION NECESSARY. AT RODEO GROUNDS. (ST-WIDE). DALE KIRCHENSCHLAGER, DIR; TOWN OF YUMA TEENAGE RODEO; 221 S MAIN; YUMA, CO 80759. (#102112-1).

JUNE 11 - 13, '76. CHAUTAUQUA CELEBRATION IN 1976. CHAUTAUQUA-SUMMER FESTIVAL IN YUMA, CO. 3-DAY CELEBRATION IN THE SUMMER OF '76 WITH THE BIG TENT FEATURING: PUPPETS, ART, MUSICAL COMEDY, DRAMA, THEATRE, FIESTA MUSIC AND MUCH MORE TO HELP CELEBRATE THE CENTENNIAL-BICENTENNIAL. (LOCAL). MRS STARNES, CHMN; YUMA AREANS; YUMA, CO 80759. (#9923-501).

JULY 4, '76. AIR SHOW. FESTIVAL, LIVE PERFORMANCE. (LOCAL). SHIRLEY M STARNES, CHMN; YUMA CENTENNIAL-BICENTENNIAL COMMITTEE; 618 S ELM ST; YUMA, CO 80759. (#108570-5).

JULY 4, '76. FOURTH OF JULY '76, CENTENNIAL DAY CELEBRATION. FOURTH OF JULY '76 'CENTENNIAL DAY' YUMA, CO. A BIG CELEBRATION WITH A BAR-B-QUE, ARENS PLAY, SQUARE DANCE, COLLECTOR'S FAIR AND FIREWORKS, IN HONOR OF COLORADO'S CENTENNIAL. (LOCAL). LAUREL A BURTON; YUMA AREANS AND YUMA YOUTH; YUMA, CO 80759. (#9922-501).

JULY 4, '76. PATRIOTIC MUSICAL. LIVE PERFORMANCE. (LOCAL). SHIRLEY M STARNES, COORD; YUMA AREANS; 618 S ELM ST; YUMA, CO 80759. (#108570-2).

YUMA — CONTINUED

JULY 4, '76. YUMA WENT (ALMOST EVERYTHING WENT). COMPETITION AT YUMA HIGH SCHOOL FOOTBALL FIELD. (LOCAL). SHIRLEY M STARNES, COORD; YUMA JAYCEES; 618 S ELM; YUMA, CO 80759. (#108570-3).

JULY 4, '76. 1876 CHURCH SERVICES. CEREMONY AT VARIOUS COMMUNITY CHURCHES IN YUMA. (LOCAL). SHIRLEY M STARNES, COORD; YUMA CENTENNIAL-BICENTENNIAL; 618 S ELM ST; YUMA, CO 80759. (#108570-1).

AUG 7 - 11, '76. YUMA COUNTY FAIR & PARADE WITH CENT-BICENT THEME - 1976. PARADE 8/10, 10:00 AM. EVENING SHOWS: RODEO, COUNTRY WESTERN SHOW, 4-H STYLE SHOW, TRACTOR PULL. WED HOURS 8:00 AM TO 12 NOON. (ST-WIDE). BERNIE BLACH; YUMA CHAMBER OF COMMERCE AND YUMA COUNTY FAIR BOARD; YUMA, CO 80759. (#9924-502).

AUG 8, '76. YUMA COUNTY FAIR HISTORICAL PAGEANT - 'TAMING TARNATION'. YUMA COUNTY FAIR HISTORICAL PAGEANT, COLORADO. A SPECIAL CENTENNIAL-BICENTENNIAL SHOW WILL BE HELD AT THE FAIR ON SUNDAY AUGUST 8, 1976. (ST-WIDE). LAUREL A BURTON; YUMA AREANS; YUMA, CO 80759. (#9921-501).

SEPT 1 - NOV 1, '76. YUMA PLATE HISTORICAL PROJECT. FAIR. (LOCAL). SHIRLEY STARNES; YUMA HIGH SCHOOL; 618 S ELM; YUMA, CO 80759. (#108740-2).

SEPT 17 - 19, '76. 'STANDING ROOM ONLY' - EXHIBIT ON LAND USE. STANDING ROOM ONLY IS A 6 CHAMBER EXHIBIT THAT IS HOUSED IN A MOBILE UNIT AND TRAVELS TO DIFFERENT AREAS FOR EXHIBIT. IT TELLS ABOUT OUR LAND FROM THE BEGINNING TO THE PRESENT AND INTO THE FUTURE. AT CITY HALL. (LOCAL). JAY FLAMING, PROJ DIR; YUMA CHAMBER OF COMMERCE; 220 S MAIN; YUMA, CO 80759. (#108740-3).

AMERICAN REVOLUTION BICEN
1776-

CONNECTICUT 1776 1976
THE PROVISION STATE

Connecticut

American Revolution Bicentennial Commission of Connecticut

Commissioned by the State Legislature, July 1971

ARBA Statistics

Officially Recognized
Communities—169
Colleges/Universities—18
Military Installations—10
BINET Projects—417
Events—647
1976 Population—3,117,000

Bicentennial Archives

Connecticut Historical Commission
59 South Prospect Street
Hartford, Connecticut 06106

Connecticut State Library Museum Archives
231 Capitol Avenue
Hartford, Connecticut 06115

Membership

Twelve members appointed by the governor, including state senators or representatives and private citizens.

Eric Hatch, *chairman* (1971-73)
Harlan H. Griswold, *chairman* (1973-76)
Whitney L. Brooks, *vice-chairman* (1971-76)
Philip A. Johnson (1971-75)
Bernhard Knollenberg (1971-72)
Julian H. Norton (1971-73)
Beatrice H. Rosenthal (1971)
Jay W. Jackson (1971-73)
Laura B. MacKenzie (1971-72)
Robert S. Orcutt (1971-73)
Albert E. Van Dusen (1971-76)
Ella F. Wood (1971-73)
Hazel J. Knapp (1972-75)
Nicholas Lenge (1973-76)
Frederick K. Biebel (1973-76)
Bruce L. Morris (1974-76)
Marilyn Schmidt (1973-75)
Richard M. Stewart (1974-75)
Morris I. Budkofsky (1974-75)
Warren B. Fish (1974-76)
Margaret C. Brown (1976)
Berthold Gaster (1976)
Peter J. Kilduff (1976)
John E. Rogers, LHD (1976)
Nancy Spada (1976)

Staff

John W. Shannahan, *director* (1971-76)
George Mackie, *program coordinator* (1970-73)
George W. Cyr, *program coordinator* (1973-76)

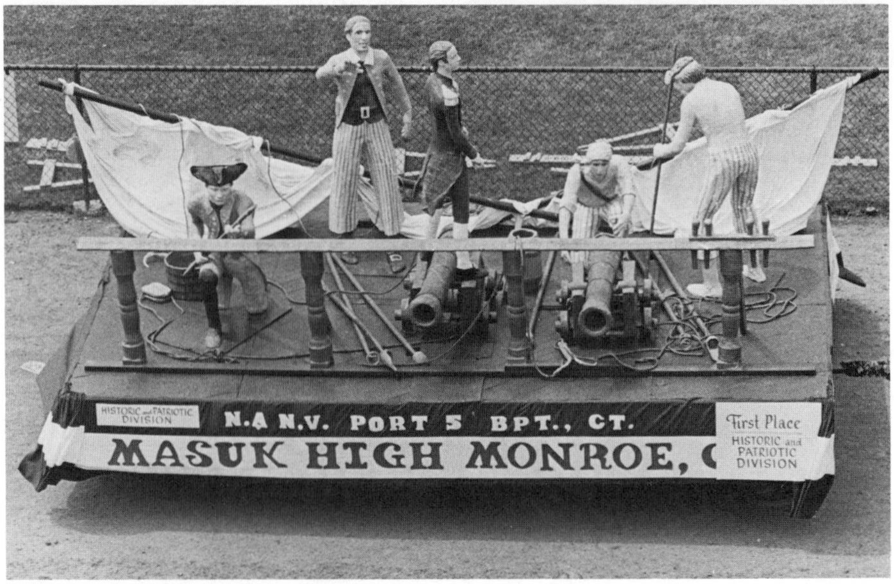

Connecticut

Since the first settlements in 1633, Connecticut has enjoyed a measure of political independence: the *Fundamental Orders* (1638) proclaimed a democratic principle of government based on the will of the people. The *Fundamental Orders* may be the first written constitution of a democratic government; hence, Connecticut calls itself the *Constitution State.*

Connecticut people turned early to manufacturing, making material for every war in which America has fought.

For the Bicentennial, Connecticut commemorated its extensive political and military involvement and its major role in the provisioning of the Continental Army. Her statesmen, Roger Sherman, Silas Deane, Jonathan Trumbull and Oliver Ellsworth, played major roles in uniting the colonies and bringing about their independence. Connecticut provided a large proportion of the courageous men who fought and died in the Battles of Bunker Hill, Saratoga, Long Island and Yorktown. One Connecticut regiment participated in all the hardships of Valley Forge, Morristown and Redding. Among Connecticut's military leaders were Israel Putnam, Thomas Knowlton, David Wooster, Nathan Hale, William Ledyard, Ethan Allen, Seth Warner, Jedediah Huntington, Joseph Spencer, Thomas Grosvenor and, for a time, Benedict Arnold.

The Webb House in Wethersfield and the War Office in Lebanon were sites of strategic planning meetings which altered the course of the war.

The ARBC of Connecticut took a "grassroots" approach to the Bicentennial, encouraging and supporting each city and town in planning an observance that was uniquely its own, springing from the hearts and minds of the citizens. Its goals were to encourage each of the 169 communities to develop appropriate Bicentennial programs, to increase citizen awareness of Connecticut's role in the Revolution, to develop lasting reminders, to provide suitable official statewide observances and celebrations and to attract tourist visitation to Revolutionary War sites. Connecticut was the first state to achieve 100 percent participation in the *Bicentennial Communities Program,* with each of its 169 communities achieving recognition.

At the state level, a series of 40 definitive monographs on Connecticut's role in the Revolution are being published, and an official Bicentennial state highway map is now available.

Old New-Gate Prison in East Granby —a Revolutionary War prison for Tories, the site of the first American chartered copper mine and the first state prison in the U.S.—is being further developed. Viets Tavern, operated by the first warden of the prison, has been purchased, and its restoration is being planned.

Connecticut's permanent contribution to the Bicentennial will be a state museum of Connecticut history.

A statewide Bicentennial cookbook is being published, comprising the best of the local cookbooks.

In November of 1976, a Bicentennial exhibit was presented at the Hartford State Armory showing the efforts of the 169 towns, the schools and 42 state agencies—plus a photographic exhibit of grant projects, an art exhibit and a quilt exhibit. Forty-two hours of continuous entertainment employed over 1,600 entertainers.

The Connecticut Bicentennial Ascension Balloon logged over 90 flights at various locations around the state and represented Connecticut at the National Balloon Race in Indianola, Iowa.

The racing trimaran, *Spirit of America,* represented Connecticut as its official entry in the International One-Man Sailing Race from England to Newport.

The march of General Rochambeau's army across Connecticut was reenacted, a booklet was printed on the Underground Railroad in Connecticut and 20th century pilgrims were honored and a book published about them.

Our monthly calendar of events indicated hundreds of other activities across the state each month, with many ongoing exhibits and festivals. One hundred sixty-nine Lasting Reminder projects were completed by the towns and many more by the state and other organizations. These ranged from books and buildings, bandstands and statues to parks, trails and other projects.

ANSONIA

RESTORATION, GEN DAVID HUMPHREYS HOUSE-ANSONIA, CT. MAJOR REPAIRS TO SILLS AND FOUNDATION: JACK UP HOUSE, REPLACE SILLS, JOISTS, REPAIR FOUNDATION, CORRECT DRAINAGE, DISCONNECT ELL IN REAR FOR STRUCTURAL CHANGES. (LOCAL). DOROTHY LARSON, PRESIDENT; DERBY HISTORICAL SOCIETY; BOX 331; DERBY, CT 06418. (#13655). **ARBA GRANTEE.**

OCT 20 - 26, '75. INTERCULTURAL CREATIVE VEHICLE. PROJECT WILL INCLUDE 129 ETHNIC GROUPS IN A WEEK-LONG CELEBRATION OF FOLK ARTS, DANCE, MUSIC & LANGUAGE; CELEBRATIONS WILL BE HELD IN VALLEY SCHOOLS & ADULT WORKSHOPS. (LOCAL). PATRICIA G EDWARDS; VALLEY ARTS COUNCIL, INC; 350 E MAIN ST; ANSONIA, CT 06401. (#10984-1).

ASHFORD

BICENTENNIAL PROJECTS IN ASHFORD, CT. RESTORE ASHFORD ACADEMY, ONLY TOWN-OWNED 19TH CENT BLDG & BEAUTIFY SURROUNDING SITE. CELEBRATION, JULY 4TH, INCLUDES ARTS & CRAFTS & ETHNIC FESTIVALS. (LOCAL). RICHARD ELIAS, DIRECTOR; ASHFORD BICENTENNIAL COMMISSION & LION'S CLUB; BOX 38; WARRENVILLE, CT 06278. (#102437).

CRAFTS-EDUCATION PROJECT, ASHFORD, CT. COMMUNITY CRAFT CLASSES, FILMS & DISPLAYS BY LOCAL ARTISANS, WEAVING OF AN ORIGINAL BICENTENNIAL TAPESTRY BY ASHFORD ELEMENTARY SCHOOL CHILDREN. (LOCAL). RICHARD F ELINS, CHAIRMAN; ASHFORD BICENTENNIAL COMMISSION & RECREATION COMMISSION; BOX 38; WARRENVILLE, CT 06270. (#15570).

HISTORIC MAP OF ASHFORD, CT. A MAP SHOWING THE HISTORY OF ASHFORD WITH NOTATIONS ON HISTORIC SITES, PATHS, HIGHWAYS & ECONOMIC ACTIVITIES OF THE TOWN DURING THE LAST 260 YEARS. RESEARCH FOR MAP CONDUCTED BY SECONDARY STUDENTS. (ST-WIDE). RICHARD F ELIAS, CHAIRMAN; ASHFORD BICENTENNIAL COMMISSION; BOX 38; WARRENVILLE, CT 06278. (#15571).

OCT 25, '75. HARVEST FESTIVAL SUPPER DANCE WITH ETHNIC EMPHASIS. FESTIVAL AT ASHFORD TOWN HALL - WARRENVILLE, CT - RTE 44. (LOCAL). BARBARA METSACK, COORD; ASHFORD BICENTENNIAL COMMISSION; BOX 38 - TOWN HALL; WARRENVILLE, CT 02678. (#102462-1).

JULY 4, '76. JULY 4TH CELEBRATION. PARADE, CEREMONY, FESTIVAL AT ASHFORD ACADEMY - OLD ASHFORD GREEN - RTE 44. (LOCAL). RICHARD ELIAS, CHMN; ASHFORD BICENTENNIAL COMMISSION; 184D ZAICEK RD; W WILLINGTON, CT 06279. (#102462-2).

AVON

PAVILLION IN RECREATION AREA, AVON, CT. A PAVILLION WILL BE BUILT IN THE TOWN'S RECREATION AREA TO BE USED BY RESIDENTS FOR TOWN FUNCTIONS. (LOCAL). ROBERT BOGINO, COORDINATOR; AVON JAYCEES; 3 SYLVAN ST; AVON, CT 06001. (#22344).

SCALE MODEL OF TOWN OF AVON, CT. A MODEL OF THE TOWN OF AVON IN THE LATE 1800'S. (LOCAL). BARRY RYEBERG, CHMN; AVON HIGH SCHOOL - INDUSTRIAL ARTS DEPT; WEST AVON RD; AVON, CT 06001. (#22345).

SCHOOLHOUSE RESTORATION IN AVON, CT. PINE GROVE SCHOOLHOUSE, BUILT IN 1865, WILL BE RESTORED & PRESERVED AS A LOCAL HISTORIC EXHIBIT. (LOCAL). GEORGE J LEGER, PRESIDENT; AVON HISTORICAL SOCIETY; PO BOX 448; AVON, CT 06001. (#13241). **ARBA GRANTEE.**

OCT 5, '75. AVON FESTIVAL - LOCAL CELEBRATION TO HONOR COMMUNITY LEADERS. CEREMONY, FESTIVAL AT SYCAMORE HILLS RECREATION AREA. (LOCAL). ROBERT AUGUST; AVON BICENTENNIAL STEERING COMMITTEE; OLD FARMS RD; AVON, CT 06001. (#200008-27).

MAY 30, '76. MUSIC, ART & FLOWERS FESTIVAL. FESTIVAL AT AVON HIGH SCHOOL, W AVON ROAD. (LOCAL). JANICE LOEFFLER, PROJ DIR; MUSIC & ART DEPTS OF AVON SCHOOLS; AVON ARTS & CRAFTS ASSOCIATION; 36 HAWLEY HILL; AVON, CT 06001. (#106037-2).

JULY 4 - 5, '76. JULY FOURTH TOWN CELEBRATION. EVENTS INCLUDE GOLF TOURNAMENT, BURIAL OF TIME CAPSULE. TIME CAPSULE, RECEPTION AND TOWN PICNIC. (LOCAL). JANICE LOEFFLER, PROJ DIR; GOLF CLUB OF AVON; TALCOTT MOUNTAIN SCIENCE CENTER; 36 HAWLEY HILL; AVON, CT 06001. (#106037-1).

JULY 21, '76. SWEET ADELINES' CONCERT. LIVE PERFORMANCE AT AVON PARK. (LOCAL). MARY NASON; FARINGTON VALLEY ARTS CENTER; AVON, CT 06001. (#200008-28).

SEPT 19, '76. VOLUNTEER FIRE DEPARTMENT FIELD DAY & BICENTENNIAL CELEBRATION. PARADE ROUTE IS WEST AVON RD. FIELD DAY ACTIVITIES TO START AFTER PARADE. AT AVON HIGH SCHOOL, W AVON RD. (LOCAL). WILLIAM YANDOW, CHMN; AVON VOLUNTEER FIRE DEPT; 86 LAWRENE AVE; AVON, CT 06001. (#106037-3).

OCT 23, '76. BICENTENNIAL BALL. FESTIVAL AT FARMINGTON VALLEY MALL. (LOCAL). MRS ROBERT GORMAN, CHMN; AVON WOMAN'S CLUB; 32 FOX DEN RD; AVON, CT 06001. (#106037-4).

BARKHAMSTED

A FUTURE TO MOLD -PROJ OF BARKHAMSTED, CONN. ESTABLISHING A PERMANENT HOME AND EXHIBIT AREA FOR THE BARKHAMSTED HISTORICAL SOCIETY, INC. (LOCAL). RICHARD G WHEELER, CHAIRMAN; ARB STEERING COMMITTEE OF THE BARKHAMSTED HISTORICAL SOC, INC; RFD 2, OLD NORTH RD; WINSTED, CT 06098. (#2668).

'A PAST TO REMEMBER', BOOK, BARKHAMSTED, CT. PUBLICATION OF A BOOK INCLUDING ESSAYS, DOCUMENTS, PHOTOS, & MAPS ON BARKHAMSTED'S HERITAGE AND LORE FEATURING MAP AND KEY TO OCCUPANCY OF TOWN'S PRE-1918 HOMESTEADS AND PUBLIC SITES. (LOCAL). RICHARD G WHEELER, CHAIRMAN; BARKHAMSTED AMERICAN REVOLUTION BICENTENNIAL STEERING COMMITTEE; BOX 200; PLEASANT VLY, CT 06063. (#11890). **ARBA GRANTEE.**

SEPT 7, '75. OLD HOME DAY. SERIES OF EVENTS INCLUDING PARADE, QUILTING DEMO, & OLD HOME DAY. (LOCAL). RICHARD G WHEELER; BARKHAMSTED ARB STEERING COMMITTEE; RFD 2 OLD NORTH RD; WINSTED, CT 06098. (#2766-3).

DEC 15 - 31, '75. RELEASE OF BOOK, CEREMONY & DEDICATION. PUBLICATION OF A BOOK INCLUDING ESSAYS, DOCUMENTS, PHOTOS, & MAPS ON BARKHAMSTED'S HERITAGE AND LORE FEATURING MAP AND KEY TO OCCUPANCY OF TOWN'S PRE-1918 HOMESTEADS AND PUBLIC SITES. (LOCAL). RICHARD G WHEELER; BARKHAMSTED AMERICAN REVOLUTION BICENTENNIAL STEERING COMMITTEE; BOX 200; PLEASANT VLY, CT 06063. (#11890-501).

MAY 22, '76. OLD NORTH ROAD REVISITED. BUS TOUR OR MOTORCADE ALONG PORTION OF MAJOR REVOLUTIONARY PERIOD ARTERY WITH RE-ENACTMENT VARIOUS EPISODES. TRAVEL BY SECTIONS LASTS THROUGHOUT DAY. SPONSORING TOWNS INCLUDE BARKHAMSTED, COLEBROOK, NEW HARTFORD, NORFOLK & WINCHESTER. AT TOUR VICINITY: RT 44, NEW HARTFORD TO NORFOLK. (LOCAL). R G WHEELER, CHMN; BARKHAMSTED BICENTENNIAL COMMITTEE/INTERTOWN NORTH RD COMMITTEE; RFD 2, OLD NORTH; WINSTED, CT 06098. (#105715-1).

JUNE 18, '76. BARKHAMSTED BICENTENNIAL BALL W/ THE NONNIE JAMES ORCHESTRA. FESTIVAL AT OLYMPIC VILLAGE. (LOCAL). MRS RICHARD WALLACE; PLEASANT VALLEY CHILDREN'S CENTER; RFD 2 WEST HILL; WINSTED, CT 06098. (#106430-1).

JULY 4, '76. ANNUAL JULY 4TH PARADE. PARADE WILL INCLUDE FIRE DEPTS, FLOATS, CHILDREN IN COSTUME, AND A 90-PIECE MARCHING BAND FROM RUSSIA, OHIO. AT CT RT 318 & RT 181. (LOCAL). RICHARD G WHEELER; BARKHAMSTED LIONS CLUB & BARKHAMSTED ARB STEERING COMMITTEE; RFD 2, OLD NORTH ROAD; WINSTED, CT 06098. (#2766-502).

BEACON FALLS

BEACON FALLS HISTORICAL MUSEUM, CT. THE MUSEUM WILL PROVIDE THE TOWNSPEOPLE WITH A PLACE TO PRESERVE ARCHIVES COLLECTED OVER THE YEARS. (LOCAL). JOHN W BETKOSKO, CHAIRMAN; BEACON FALLS BICENTENNIAL COMMITTEE; BEACON FALLS, CT 06403. (#12243). **ARBA GRANTEE.**

BERLIN

BICENTENNIAL PARK PROJECT OF BERLIN, CONN. PARK TO BE LEFT IN ORIGINAL STATE, AS PART OF BERLIN'S CONTRIBUTION TO THE BICENTENNIAL. (LOCAL). HARRISON H SANDERS, CHAIRMAN; BERLIN BICENTINNEL COMMITTEE; TOWN HALL; BERLIN, CT 06037. (#4741).

BETHANY

HISTORICAL MARKING OF HOMES IN BETHANY, CT. 80 HOMES, 18TH & 19TH CENTURY ARCHITECTURE, WILL BE MARKED WITH BRONZE MEDALLIONS ON MAPLE BOARDS TO ENCOURAGE PRESERVATION; SYMBOLIZES BETHANY'S ORIGIN AS A FARMING COMMUNITY. (LOCAL). DWIGHT R JOHNSON, CHAIRMAN; AMERICAN REVOLUTION BICENTENNIAL COMMISSION OF BETHANY; AMITY RD, TOWN HALL; BETHANY, CT 06525. (#13847).

OFFICIAL TOWN SEAL CONTEST - 'LASTING REMINDER'-CT. A CONTEST WAS HELD AND A WINNING ENTRY HAS BEEN CHOSEN FOR THE OFFICIAL TOWN SEAL CONTEST. THE SEAL HAS BECOME THE OFFICIAL TOWN SEAL FOR BETHANY, CT AND WILL BE ON DISPLAY THROUGHOUT 1976. (LOCAL). DWIGHT R JOHNSON, CHAIRMAN; BETHANY ARBC; TOWN HALL, AMITY RD; BETHANY, CT 06525. (#14026).

1834 CENTER SCHOOLHOUSE PROJECT IN BETHANY, CT. THE COMMUNITY'S OLDEST EXISTING SCHOOLHOUSE AND FOCAL POINT OF ITS HERITAGE WILL BE RESTORED AND CONVERTED INTO A MUSEUM, AS A TRIBUTE TO SOCIAL AND ACADEMIC IMAGES AND ARCHITECTURE OF THE 19TH CENTURY. (LOCAL). DWIGHT JOHNSON, CHAIRMAN; BETHANY BICENT COMMISSION; 317 DOWNS ROAD; BETHANY, CT 06525. (#9361).

SEPT 28, '75. CLASS REUNION. BETHANY BICENTENNIAL COMMISSION REQUESTS ALUMNI, PRIOR TO 1935, TO COME TO THE TOWN'S '5 ONE-ROOM SCHOOLHOUSES GET-TOGETHER' AT BETHANY COMMUNITY. AT BETHANY COMMUNITY SCHOOL - NORTH CAMPUS. (LOCAL). DWIGHT R JOHNSON, CHMN; BETHANY BICENTENNIAL COMMISSION; 317 DOWNS RD; BETHANY, CT 06525. (#13683-1).

OCT 25, '75. COUNTRY FAIR. FAIR AT HANGER, OLD BETHANY AIRPORT. (ST-WIDE). E J JOHNSON, SEC; BETHANY BICENTENNIAL COMMISSION; 317 DOWNS RD; BETHANY, CT 06525. (#200008-25).

MAY 1, '76. BICENTENNIAL COSTUME BALL: 1976 KICKOFF IN BETHANY. FESTIVAL AT BETHANY COMMUNITY BLDG, PECK ROAD, BETHANY. (LOCAL). MRS DWIGHT JOHNSON, SEC; BETHANY BICENTENNIAL COMMISSION; 317 DOWNS RD; BETHANY, CT 06525. (#105395-1).

MAY 23, '76. DEDICATION OF GRAVESTONE FOR 8 AMERICAN REVOLUTION SOLDIERS. CEREMONY AT GRAVEYARD. (LOCAL). MRS DWIGHT R JOHNSON, SEC; 'LEARN & DO' - 4-H CLUB; 317 DOWNS RD, RR 2; BETHANY, CT 06525. (#200008-31).

JULY 4, '76. 4TH OF JULY CELEBRATION. PICNIC & GAMES WITH BELL RINGING AT 2 PM. AT BETHANY COMMUNITY BLDG, PECK RD. (LOCAL). DWIGHT R JOHNSON, COORD; BETHANY BICENTENNIAL COMMISSION; 317 DOWNS RD; BETHANY, CT 06525 (#200008-30).

BETHLEHEM

CEMETERY RESTORATION IN BETHLEHEM, CONNECTICUT. OLD CEMETERY DATING BEFORE 1750 WILL BE RESTORED AND IMPROVED. (LOCAL). EDWARD R MILLER PHD, CHAIRMAN; OLD BETHLEM INC; THE GREEN; BETHLEHEM, CT 06751. (#5076).

AN HISTORICAL ABC PRIMER OF BETHLEHEM, CT. AN ALPHABET BOOK OF DRAWINGS & TEXT THAT GIVES THE MAIN HISTORICAL EVENTS OF THE TOWN OF BETHLEHEM USING THE ORIGINAL SPELLING OF THE TOWN. (LOCAL). EDWARD R MILLER, PHD, CHAIRMAN; OLD BETHLEHEM INC; BETHLEHEM, CT 06751. (#13236). **ARBA GRANTEE.**

HISTORICAL DISTRICT OF BETHLEHEM, CONNECTICUT. COLLECTING DATA & DOCUMENTING BUILDINGS AROUND THE GREEN. (LOCAL). EDWARD R MILLER PHD, CHAIRMAN; OLD BETHLEM INC; THE GREEN; BETHLEHEM, CT 06751. (#5075).

JULY 13, '76. UNIVERSITY OF CALIFORNIA MARCHING BAND PRESENTS 'SPIRIT OF AMERICA'. THIS IS PART OF A 6-WEEK PERFORMANCE TOUR OF THE U S; 'SPIRIT OF AMERICA' IS A COLLEGIATE MUSICAL REVIEW CELEBRATING OUR NATION'S BICENTENNIAL; WILL INCLUDE FOLK MUSIC, MARCHING, VAUDEVILLE, ROCK, DIXIELAND, JAZZ, BARBERSHOP & SOLOS. AT FAIR GROUNDS. (ST-WIDE). PAUL JOHNSON, DIR; BETHLEHEM FAIR SOCIETY, INC; BETHLEHEM, CT 06751. (#10515-15).

BLOOMFIELD

DRUMMER BOY STATUE IN BLOOMFIELD, CONNECTICUT. DESIGNED TO LEAVE LASTING REMINDER ON VILLAGE GREEN OF SPIRIT OF THE 1770'S. BROWN DRUMS USED FOR STATUE WERE MANUFACTURED IN BLOOMFIELD DURING REVOLUTIONARY ERA. (LOCAL). JERRY WAGNER, CHAIRMAN; BLOOMFIELD AMERICAN REVOLUTION BICENTENNIAL COMMISSION; 4 CRAIGMORE ROAD; BLOOMFIELD, CT 06002. (#5286). **ARBA GRANTEE.**

BOLTON

DEVELOPMENT OF BIKEWAYS & FOOTPATHS IN BOLTON, CT. TO PROMOTE AND PURSUE THE DEVELOPMENT OF BIKEWAYS IN TOWN AS A FORM OF TRANSPORTATION AND RECREATION. (LOCAL). ILVI JOE-CANNON, CHAIRMAN; BOLTON BICENTENNIAL COMMITTEE; 2 FERNWOOD DR; BOLTON, CT 06040. (#10554).

HISTORICAL SOCIETY IN BOLTON, CT. SOCIETY WILL COLLECT & PRESERVE MEMORABILIA OF THE TOWN. (LOCAL). ILVI JOE-CANNON, CHAIRMAN; BOLTON HISTORICAL SOCIETY; TOWN HALL, BOLTON CENTER RD; BOLTON, CT 06040. (#10556).

BOZRAH

JUNE 5, '76. BOZRAH BICENTENNIAL BALL. FESTIVAL AT MOOSE HALL, FITCHVILLE ROAD, OFF RT 2, EXIT 24, LEFT END OF EXIT. (LOCAL). ABRAHAM FISHBONE, COORD; AMERICAN LEGION POST #138; OLD RT 2; BOZRAH, CT 06334. (#107394-2).

JUNE 20, '76. COLONIAL CHURCH SERVICE. SERVICE WILL INCLUDE MANY FEATURES OF EARLY NEW ENGLAND. BRING BOX LUNCH FOR OUTDOOR PICNIC FOLLOWING THE SERVICE. AT BOZRAH CENTER CONGREGATIONAL CHURCH, RT 163. (LOCAL). REV CLAYTON RICHARDS; BOZRAH CENTER CONGREGATIONAL CHURCH; FITCHVILLE, CT 06334. (#107394-1).

BRANFORD

PROVIDING HISTORICAL BOOKS FOR LIBRARIES - CT. SUPPLY MATERIALS BY PRINTING & DUPLICATING MICROFILMED RECORDS AND HISTORIES NOW IN LOCAL CHURCHES & LIBRARY VAULTS TO MAKE THEM AVAILABLE FOR GENERAL USE. ALSO SOME DIRECT PURCHASES. (LOCAL). THOMAS GROSH, COORDINATOR; BRANFORD HISTORICAL SOCIETY; 421 SHORE DR; BRANFORD, CT 06405. (#12010). **ARBA GRANTEE.**

BRIDGEPORT

BICENTENNIAL VIDEO DOCUMENTATION PROJECT, CT. VIDEO TAPING OF BRIDGEPORT SITES, PEOPLE, EVENTS AND HISTORICAL COLLECTIONS FOR 3 EDITED PROGRAMS TO BE SHOWN IN COMMUNITY GROUPS, SCHOOLS, AND LIBRARY PROGRAMS. (LOCAL). ROSEMARY PALMQUIST, MEDIA LIBRARIAN; BRIDGEPORT PUBLIC LIBRARY; 925 BROAD ST; BRIDGEPORT, CT 06604. (#11886). **ARBA GRANTEE.**

CIVIC CEREMONY - TREE PLANTING. A TREE WILL BE PLANTED IN FRONT COURTYARD WITH A PLAQUE MARKING THE OCCASSION IN WHICH STUDENTS, SCOUTS, VETERANS, CIVIC DIG

BRIDGEPORT — CONTINUED

NITARIES & ADMINISTRATORS CAME TOGETHER & LOOKED WITH IMAGINATION TO THE FUTURE. AT COURTYARD. (LOCAL). MARIAN WENCEK, CHAIRMAN; HOUSATONIC COMMUNITY COLLEGE BICENTENNIAL COMMITTEE; 510 BARNUM AVE; BRIDGEPORT, CT 06608. (#107392-1).

POST PUBLISHING COMPANY'S BICENTENNIAL PROJS-NBMRP. FROM JULY THRU DECEMBER, 1975 RAN WEEKLY SERIES ON SOUTHWESTERN CONNECTICUT TOWNS' PARTICIPATION IN AMER REVOL. PUBLISHED BOOKLET ON AREA'S ROLE IN REVOLUTION. SPECIAL HORIZONS EDITION ON JULY 4, 1976. (LOCAL). JOHN E PFRIEM, PRESIDENT-GENERAL MANAGER; THE POST PUBLISHING COMPANY; 410 STATE ST; BRIDGEPORT, CT 06602. (#27573).

ROLE OF MINORITIES IN U S HISTORY, BRIDGEPORT, CT. BLACK & PUERTO RICAN GROUPS TO CREATE BICENT PROGRAMS TO REFLECT PARTICIPATION IN THE NATION'S DEVELOPMENT. ARTISTS WORKSHOPS, MUSIC EVENTS & OTHER FESTIVITIES TO OCCUR. HISTORICAL PAMPHLET DESIGNED. (LOCAL). GEORGE E PIPKIN, EXECUTIVE DIRECTOR; HALL NEIGHBORHOOD HOUSE; 52 GREEN ST; FAIRFIELD, CT 06608. (#7347). **ARBA GRANTEE.**

JAN 5 - FEB 5, '76. DISTRIBUTION OF VIDEOTAPES TO CITY SCHOOLS. VIDEO TAPING OF BRIDGEPORT SITES, PEOPLE, EVENTS AND HISTORICAL COLLECTIONS FOR 3 EDITED PROGRAMS TO BE SHOWN IN COMMUNITY GROUPS, SCHOOLS, AND LIBRARY PROGRAMS. (LOCAL). ROSEMARY PALMQUIST; BRIDGEPORT PUBLIC LIBRARY; 925 BROAD ST; BRIDGEPORT, CT 06604. (#11886-501).

APR 1, '76. HARAMBEE FIESTA - BLACK & PUERTO RICAN CULTURES EXPRESSED. FESTIVAL. (LOCAL). GEORGE E PIPKIN; HALL NEIGHBORHOOD HOUSE; 52 GREEN ST; FAIRFIELD, CT 06608. (#7347-503).

APR 15 - MAY 15, '76. JOHN SINGER SARGENT A SPIRIT OF CELEBRATION. COMBINED ARTS HERITAGE FESTIVAL, BRIDGEPORT, CT. A 3-YEAR PROGRAM IN ART, FILM AND THEATRE WHICH FOCUSES ON AMERICAN HERITAGE. (REGN'L). REV WILLIAM J FLETCHER; SACRED HEART UNIVERSITY; PARK AVE; BRIDGEPORT, CT 06606. (#11953-501).

APR 30, '76. THIS IS AMERICA DANCE AND PROGRAM OF ETHNIC PERFORMING ARTS. ENTERTAINMENT PROGRAM IN PERFORMING ARTS WILL BE CARRIED OUT BY HCC STUDENTS, HCC MUSIC DEPT; REFRESHMENTS PROVIDED BY STUDENTS OWN ETHNIC CULINARY SPECIALTIES BUFFET; SHORT ADDRESSES BY CIVIC DIGNATARY AND STUDENT GOVT. AT STRATFIELD MOTOR INN, 1241 MAIN ST. (LOCAL). MARION WENCEK, CHAIRMAN; HOUSATONIC COMMUNITY COLLEGE CULTURAL AFFAIRS COMMITTEE; 510 BARNUM AVE; BRIDGEPORT, CT 06608. (#107222-1).

JUNE 25 - JULY 5, '76. BARNUM FESTIVAL '76. 'SALUTE TO AMERICA' PARADE HIGHLIGHTS 11 DAYS OF CIRCUS ACTIVITIES FEATURING CLOWNS, BANDS, ART SHOW, FLEA MARKET, INTERNATIONAL FAIR AND FIREWORKS. (LOCAL). EDAN WHITEMAN, JR, CHMN; BARNUM FESTIVAL; 804 MAIN ST; BRIDGEPORT, CT 06604. (#103416-423).

AUG 10 - 14, '76. BICENTENNIAL/NAVY BIRTHDAY GOOD WILL PORT VISIT. SHIP TOURS WERE GIVEN FOR 3 DAYS. SHIP WAS FOCAL POINT FOR CITY'S CELEBRATION OF NAVY'S 200TH BIRTHDAY. COLONIAL STYLE UNIFORMS WERE WORN BY NAVY RECRUITERS. COMMUNITY OFFICIALS & VARIOUS NAVY GROUPS PARTICIPATED IN THE FESTIVITIES. (ST-WIDE). ENS ROBERT J COX; USS DETECTOR (MSO 429); USS DETECTOR (MSO 429); FPO, NY 09501. (#200008-251).

NOV 1 - DEC 1, '76. CHANNEL 8 TAPE SERIES IN 3 WEEKLY PARTS. VIDEO TAPING OF BRIDGEPORT SITES, PEOPLE, EVENTS AND HISTORICAL COLLECTIONS FOR 3 EDITED PROGRAMS TO BE SHOWN IN COMMUNITY GROUPS, SCHOOLS, AND LIBRARY PROGRAMS. (LOCAL). BERNADETTE BALDINO; BRIDGEPORT PUBLIC LIBRARY; 925 BROAD ST; BRIDGEPORT, CT 06604. (#11886-503).

NOV 23, '76. SENIOR CITIZEN TOUR AND TAPE OF CITY DURING LIBRARY HISTORY FEST. RADIO/TV. (LOCAL). ROSEMARY PALMQUIST; BRIDGEPORT PUBLIC LIBRARY; 925 BROAD ST; BRIDGEPORT, CT 06604. (#11886-504).

DEC 15 - 17, '76. VIEWING & EVALUATION OF TAPES BY CITY INTER-AGENCY GROUP. RADIO/TV. (LOCAL). ROSEMARY PALMQUIST; BRIDGEPORT PUBLIC LIBRARY; 925 BROAD ST; BRIDGEPORT, CT 06604. (#11886-505).

BRIDGEWATER

CONSTRUCTION OF AN OUTDOOR AMPHITHEATER IN CT. CONSTRUCT OUTDOOR AMPHITHEATER TO SEAT 1000 PEOPLE FOR COMMUNITY GATHERINGS. (LOCAL). JOHN W SHANNAHAN, DIRECTOR; CONNECTICUT AMERICAN REVOLUTION BICENTENNIAL COMMISSION; 59 S PROSPECT ST; HARTFORD, CT 06106. (#22832). **ARBA GRANTEE.**

OPEN AIR PAGEANT, BRIDGEWATER, CT. PAGEANT SHOWING CONTRIBUTIONS BY AMERICAN INDIANS AND EARLY SETTLERS TO THE DEVELOPMENT OF WESTERN CONNECTICUT. (LOCAL). ROBERT C TUTHILL, CHAIRMAN; BRIDGEWATER BICENTENNIAL COMMISSION; RFD 1, MAIN ST; BRIDGEWATER, CT 06752. (#25473). **ARBA GRANTEE.**

BRISTOL

BUILD WOODEN BANDSTAND IN PAGE PARK IN BRISTOL, CT. BUILD A BANDSTAND IN A PUBLIC PARK FOR THE ENJOYMENT OF THE PUBLIC AND THE OPPORTUNITY FOR PARTICIPATION BY THE INSTRUMENTALISTS IN THE MANY SCHOOL AND CIVIC BANDS. (LOCAL). GEORGE R PERRY, CHAIRMAN; BRISTOL BICENTENNIAL COMMISSION; PO BOX 1776; BRISTOL, CT 06010. (#7343). **(??). ARBA GRANTEE.**

BUILDERS OF BRISTOL, CT. WEEKLY COLUMN IN THE BRISTOL PRESS TELLING THE STORY OF A MAN OR WOMAN IN BRISTOL'S FIRST 200 YEARS WHO WAS A POSITIVE INFLUENCE ON THE DEVELOPMENT OF THE CITY. (LOCAL). GEORGE R PERRY, CHAIRMAN; BRISTOL BICENTENNIAL COMMISSION; 52 CARMELO RD; BRISTOL, CT 06010. (#13399).

HIKES TO TORY'S DEN - BRISTOL, CONN. HIKE OF ABOUT 2 MILES INTO FORESTED REGION TO REACH A LARGE CAVE CALLED TORY'S DEN, WHERE TORIES HID TO ESCAPE THE HARASSMENT OF THE SONS OF LIBERTY. LEADER OF HIKE EXPLAINS HISTORY OF THE AREA. (LOCAL). GEORGE R PERRY, CHAIRMAN; BRISTOL BICENTENNIAL COMMISSION; 52 CARMELO RD; BRISTOL, CT 06010. (#4668).

HOUSE MARKERS - PROJ OF BRISTOL, CT. WOODEN MARKERS SHOWING DATE OF CONSTRUCTION WILL BE PAINTED & GIVEN GRATIS FOR ANY LOCAL HOUSE BUILT IN 1876 OR EARLIER. (LOCAL). GEORGE R PERRY, PRESIDENT; BRISTOL HISTORICAL SOCIETY; BOX 1393; BRISTOL, CT 06010. (#13400).

MAP OF HISTORIC SITES IN BRISTOL, CONNECTICUT. EXISTING CITY MAP WILL BE MARKED, USING VARIOUS SYMBOLS, TO SHOW THE LOCATION OF HOUSES BUILT IN THE 18TH CENTURY AS WELL AS THE SITES OF HISTORIC EVENTS AND STRUCTURES. (LOCAL). GEORGE R PERRY, CHAIRMAN; BRISTOL BICENTENNIAL COMMISSION; 52 CARMELO RD; BRISTOL, CT 06010. (#4616). **(??).**

REFURBISH ANCIENT TORY CEMETERY IN BRISTOL, CT. RESET FALLEN GRAVESTONES, CLEAN UP GROUNDS, AND REPAIR FENCE AROUND THIS SMALL EPISCOPAL CEMETERY OF THE 18TH CENTURY. (LOCAL). GEORGE R PERRY, CHAIRMAN; BRISTOL BICENTENNIAL COMMISSION; 52 CARMELO RD; BRISTOL, CT 06010. (#4688). **(??).**

WBIS-RADIO YEAR-LONG ORAL HISTORY SERIES - NBMRP. YEAR-LONG SERIES '20 DECADES' BROADCAST TWICE WEEKLY INCL INTERVIEWS WITH LOCAL CITIZENS ON BRISTOL'S PAST, PRESENT, FUTURE; BUILT AROUND MONTHLY BICENT THEMES--BACKGROUND, ETHNIC CONTRIBS, INDUSTRIAL GROW. (LOCAL). RUTH GOODRICH, BICENTENNIAL COORDINATOR; WBIS-RADIO; 1021 FARMINGTON AVE; BRISTOL, CT 06010. (#23263).

SEPT 26, '75. DRAMATIC CHARACTERIZATIONS OF WOMEN IN AMERICAN HISTORY. MISS M TULIS SESSIONS PERFORMED MONOLOGUE CHARACTERIZATIONS OF 7 HISTORIC WOMEN, 4 FIRST LADIES & 3'CONNECTICUT YANKEES'. AT SOUTH SIDE SCHOOL AUDITORIUM. (LOCAL). GEORGE R PERRY, DIRECTOR; GREATER BRISTOL HISTORICAL SOCIETY; 52 CARMELO RD; BRISTOL, CT 06010. (#200008-26).

FEB 21, '76. 'WAY BACK WHEN' - DRAMATIC PRODUCTION. PLAY, SET IN COLONIAL TIMES, PRESENTED BY THE TOURING THEATRE OF THE HARTFORD STAGE COMPANY. AT GIRLS' CLUB GYMNASIUM, 47 UPSON ST. (LOCAL). ROBERT NIELSON, COORD; BRISTOL GIRLS' CLUB ASSOC; 47 UPSON ST; BRISTOL, CT 06010. (#104936-1).

APR 6, '76. BICENTENNIAL CONCERT OF AMERICAN COMPOSERS IN MINIATURE FORM. THIS IS A COMMEMORATIVE TRIBUTE TO THOSE WHO HAVE WORKED IN THE CHURCH FOR THE PAST 200 YEARS; IT FEATURES CLASSICAL PIANIST CAREN GOODIN EVARTS OF THE HARTT COLLEGE OF MUSIC & BALLET DANCER SANDRA CAE GOODIN OF THE FRANCES ALLIS SCHOOL OF BALLET IN CHICAGO. AT AUDITORIUM OF PARISH HOUSE, 35 MAPLE ST, PARKING IN REAR. (LOCAL). MRS AUBREY MURPHY, COORD; WOMENS GUILD OF FIRST CONGREGATIONAL CHURCH; 127 PILGRIM RD; BRISTOL, CT 06010. (#106038-1).

SEPT 19 - OCT 10, '76. BRISTOL CHRYSANTHEMUM FESTIVAL. FESTIVAL AT CIVIC THEATRE. (LOCAL). COORDINATOR; BRISTOL CHAMBER OF COMMERCE; 81 MAIN ST; BRISTOL, CT 06010. (#103416-579).

BROAD BROOK

MAY 21 - 23, '76. FIREMENS' MUSTER & ANTIQUE FIRE EQUIPMENT SHOW. FRIDAY BAND CONCERT BY LOCAL BANDS; SATURDAY PARADE, ANTIQUE FIRE APPARATUS SHOW, FLEA MARKET & SPAGHETTI SUPPER; SUNDAY, FIREMENS' MUSTER & ASSORTED CONTESTS; REFRESHMENTS AVAILABLE ALL DAYS. AT CARNIVAL GROUNDS, CORNER RTS 140/191 (PARKING ON OR NEAR GROUNDS). (LOCAL). KENNETH C YOUNG, COORD; BROAD BROOK FIRE DEPT; 6 DEAN AVE, BOX 515; WAREHOUSE PT, CT 06088. (#105714-1).

BROOKFIELD

BOOKLETS ON BROOKFIELD HISTORY - PROJ OF CT. PAMPHLETS OF 1-10 PAGES WITH PHOTOGRAPHS ON THE HISTORY OF BROOKFIELD, THE PARISH OF NEWBURY FROM 1776, HISTORY OF AREA INDIANS, SCHOOLS, CHURCHES, INDUSTRY AND SOCIAL HISTORY. (LOCAL). HAROLD H TODD, JR, CHAIRMAN; BROOKFIELD BICENTENNIAL COMMISSION; SELECTMAN'S OFFICE; BROOKFIELD, CT 06805. (#14343). **ARBA GRANTEE.**

BURLINGTON

SCHWARZMAN MILL ACQUISITION - BURLINGTON, CT. ACQUISITION OF A BUILDING CONTAINING A GRIST MILL, A CINDER MILL, A SAW MILL & A SHINGLE MILL WHICH DATES FROM COLONIAL TIMES. (LOCAL). ERNEST HUTCHINSON, CHAIRMAN; BURLINGTON BICENTENNIAL COMMISSION; VILLAGE LANE; BURLINGTON, CT 06013. (#16295). **ARBA GRANTEE.**

BYRAM

JUNE 13, '76. SOKOL USA BICENTENNIAL PROGRAM OF DISTRICT JAN FRANCISCI. GYMNASTIC PERFORMANCE BY CHILDREN, TEENAGERS AND ADULTS ON VARIOUS APPARATUS; MASS CALISTHENICS, SPECIAL GROUP AND MODERN GYMNASTIC NUMBERS AND TUMBLING; WILL INCLUDE SLOVAK FOLK DANCE BESEDA AND CONCLUDE WITH A PATRIOTIC FINALE. AT BYRAM SHORE PARK, SHUTTLE FROM SOKOL CLUB, 222 MILL ST. (LOCAL). ANITA VALENTI, DIR; SLOVAK GYMNASTIC UNION, SOKOL OF THE UNITED STATES OF AMERICA; 68 IVY ST; GREENWICH, CT 06830. (#200008-29).

CANTERBURY

EXHIBITS, PRUDENCE CRANDALL HOUSE - CANTERBURY, CT. INSTALLATION OF INTERPRETIVE DISPLAYS WHICH SHOW ROLE OF CONNECTICUT BLACK SOLDIER IN REVOLUTION, HISTORY OF PRUDENCE CRANDALL AND CONTRIBUTIONS OF WOMEN. (ST-WIDE). RICHARD KUNS, SUPERINTENDENT; CONNECTICUT HISTORICAL COMMISSION; 59 S PROSPECT ST; HARTFORD, CT 06106. (#27855). **ARBA GRANTEE.**

CANTON

HIKING TRAIL THROUGH CANTON, CONN. A HIKING TRAIL IS BEING LAID OUT BETWEEN CANTON HIGH SCHOOL AND COLONY ROAD. CANTON JAYCEES ARE IN FULL CHARGE AND WORK HAS STARTED. (LOCAL). DICK WILLIAMS, PROJECT CHAIRMAN; CANTON JAYCEES; CANTON, CT 06019. (#3915).

NOV 15 - DEC 12, '75. 'LIFE IN CANTON IN 1776' - TALK ON COSTUME & ARTIFACTS. SEMINAR AT LOCAL SCHOOLS & CLUBS. (LOCAL). MRS NAOMI LYNCH, V/REGENT; PHOEBE HUMPHREY CHAPTER OF THE DAR; PO BOX 122; COLLINSVILLE, CT 06019. (#200008-32).

CHESHIRE

'OLD HOMES OF CHESHIRE' - CT. PUBLICATION OF A BOOK ENTITLED 'OLD HOMES OF CHESHIRE'. (LOCAL). DR HOWARD OEDEL, CHAIRMAN; CHESHIRE BICENTENNIAL COMMITTEE; 900 N BROOKSVALE RD; CHESHIRE, CT 06410. (#26901).

PUBLICATION - LANDMARKS OF OLD CHESHIRE. UPDATING OF 1894 BOOK 'HISTORIC HOMES OF CHESHIRE'. TO CONTAIN TEXT PHOTOS & WASH DRAWINGS. (LOCAL). DR HOWARD OEDEL, CHAIRMAN BOOK COMMITTEE; CHESHIRE BICENTENNIAL COMMITTEE; 900 N BROOKSVALE RD; CHESHIRE, CT 06410. (#23278).

RESTORATION LOCK 12 FARMINGTON CANAL. DEDICATION LOCK 12 CANAL PARK JULY 4, BEST PRESERVED LOCK ON CANAL, IN OPERATION 1827 TO 1846. THE LOCK IS BEING RESTORED TO OPERATIONAL STATUS. HISTORIC DETAILS PRESERVED - ADJOINING AREA PUBLIC PARK. (LOCAL). E C GUMPRECHT, BICENTENNIAL CHAIRMAN; BICENTENNIAL COMMITTEE & PARK & RECREATION DEPT; 908 S MERIDEN RD, PO BOX 141; CHESHIRE, CT 06410. (#23277).

JAN 10, '76. SANTE FE DRUM CORPS, COLONIAL FASHION SHOW, JR WOMENS CLUB. LIVE PERFORMANCE AT YOUTH CENTER, 559 S MAIN, CHESHIRE. (LOCAL). RAYMOND MCDERMOTT; SANTE FE ANCIENT DRUM CORPS, JR WOMENS CLUB; 95 BEECHER AVE; WATERBURY, CT 06410. (#23278-12).

JAN 22, '76. 'CONNECTICUT IN REVOLUTION', DR HOWARD OEDEL, HISTORY PROF SCSC. SEMINAR AT CHESHIRE PUBLIC LIBRARY. (LOCAL). E C GUMPRECHT; BICENTENNIAL COMMITTEE; 908 S MERIDEN RD; CHESHIRE, CT 06410. (#23278-14).

FEB 6 - 7, '76. MOVIES: 'JOHNNY TREMAINE', ETC. EXHIBIT AT CHESHIRE PUBLIC LIBRARY. (LOCAL). ROBERT TAYLOR; WEST CHESHIRE COMMUNITY CLUB; 1117 PAMELA LN; CHESHIRE, CT 06410. (#23278-13).

FEB 14, '76. WASHINGTON BIRTHDAY COSTUME BALL. FESTIVAL AT WAVERLY INN. (LOCAL). MRS PETER DOMEK; CHESHIRE JUNIOR WOMENS CLUB & BICENTENNIAL COMMITTEE; 499 MOUNTAIN RD; CHESHIRE, CT 06410. (#23278-9).

FEB 26, '76. LECTURE: INVASION OF NEW HAVEN; DR HARMON LEONARD. SEMINAR AT CHESHIRE PUBLIC LIBRARY. (ST-WIDE). EDWARD C GUMPRECHT; BICENTENNIAL COMMITTEE; 908 S MERIDEN RD; CHESHIRE, CT 06410. (#23278-10).

MAR 25, '76. LECTURE: NATHAN HALE; DR THOMAS FARNHAM SCSC. SEMINAR AT CHESHIRE PUBLIC LIBRARY. (LOCAL). EDWARD C GUMPRECHT; BICENTENNIAL COMMITTEE; 908 S MERIDEN RD; CHESIRE, CT 06410. (#23278-11).

APR 22, '76. CONCERT - BICENTENNIAL CHOIR - SOUTHERN CONN STATE COLLEGE. LIVE PERFORMANCE AT CHESHIRE PUBLIC LIBRARY. (LOCAL). E C GUMPRECHT; BICENTENNIAL COMMITTEE; 908 S MERIDEN RD; CHESHIRE, CT 06410. (#23278-8).

MAY 5, '76. BICENTENNIAL LECTURE. SEMINAR AT CHESHIRE PUBLIC LIBRARY. (LOCAL). EDWARD C GRUMPRECHT, DIR; CHESHIRE BICENTENNIAL COMMITTEE; 908 MERIDEN RD; CHESHIRE, CT 06410. (#107143-5).

MAY 5, '76. CACHET FOR STAMP COLLECTORS - HONORING AMOS DOOLITTLE. EXHIBIT. (LOCAL). MRS JOHN PETERSON, DIR; CHESHIRE BICENTENNIAL COMMITTEE; 1335 PECK LN; CHESHIRE, CT 06410. (#107143-6).

MAY 18, '76. CACHET FOR STAMP & HISTORICAL ENVELOPE COLLECTIONS. HONORING AMOS DOOLITTLE - THESE ENVELOPES WILL BE SOLD LOCALLY, THEN STATEWIDE, THEN NATIONALLY. THE ONLY KNOWN PAINTING OF DOOLITTLE IS ENGRAVED ON LEFT

CHESHIRE — CONTINUED

SIDE OF ENVELOPE ALONG WITH PERTINENT DATA. LEXINGTON-CONCORD POSTAGE STAMP PLUS A 3-CENT ONE WILL BE ON IT ALSO. (REGN'L). MRS JOHN PETERSON; BICENTENNIAL COMMITTEE; 1335 PECK LN; CHESHIRE, CT 06410. (#23278-2).

MAY 19, '76. ILLUS LECTURE AMOS DOOLITTLE - KENSETT - RICHARD ULBRICH. SEMINAR AT CHESHIRE PUBLIC LIBRARY. (ST-WIDE). E C GUMPRECHT; BICENTENNIAL COMMITTEE; 908 S MERIDEN RD; CHESHIRE, CT 06410. (#23278-1).

JUNE 10, '76. BICENTENNIAL FLOWER SHOW, 'FAITH OF OUR FATHERS'. EXHIBIT AT FIRST CONGREGATIONAL CHURCH & HISTORICAL SOCIETY. (LOCAL). MRS R T MOKRZRNSKI, COORD; CHESHIRE GARDEN CLUB; 469 CEDAR LN; CHESHIRE, CT 06410. (#107143-8).

JUNE 13, '76. BAND CONCERT AND BOX LUNCH. FESTIVAL AT CHESHIRE GREEN. (LOCAL). THOMAS JACKSON, COORD; CHAMBER OF COMMERCE; 9 S MAIN; CHESHIRE, CT 06410. (#107143-4).

JUNE 24, '76. LECTURE - ILLUST - SIGNERS OF DEC OF INDEP BY PERCY GOODSELL. SEMINAR AT CHESHIRE PUBLIC LIBRARY, MAIN ST. (LOCAL). EDWARD C GUMPRECHT; CHESHIRE BICENTENNIAL COMMITTEE; 908 S MERIDEN RD, PO BOX 141; CHESHIRE, CT 06410. (#23278-5).

JULY 3, '76. DEDICATION BRONZE PLAQUES 3 OLD CEMETERIES NAMES REV SOLDIERS. CEREMONY. (LOCAL). MRS WILLIAM LUCIANI; DAR & BICENTENNIAL COMMITTEE; 22 CEDAR LN; CHESHIRE, CT 06410. (#23278-6).

JULY 4, '76. DEDICATION OF LOCK TWELVE AT HISTORIC CANAL PARK. FESTIVAL. (LOCAL). E C GUMPRECHT, CHMN; CHESHIRE BICENTENNIAL COMMITTEE & PARK & RECREATION DEPT; 908 S MERIDEN RD; CHESHIRE, CT 06410. (#107143-2).

JULY 5, '76. MAMMOTH PARADE. PARADE AT FROM HIGHLAND SCHOOL TO THE HIGH SCHOOL. (LOCAL). HENRY E CARSON, COORD; VETERAN'S COUNCIL; 407 LINCOLN DR; CHESHIRE, CT 06410. (#107143-1).

CHESTER

BOOK ON EARLY ITALIAN COMMUNITY IN CHESTER, CT. A BOOK TRACING THE LINEAGE OF EARLY ITALIAN SETTLERS. (LOCAL). MARY CAPELLINI, CHAIRWOMAN; CHESTER HISTORICAL SOCIETY; 65 MAIN ST; CHESTER, CT 06412. (#12006). **ARBA GRANTEE.**

FILMING OF 1975-1976 ACTIVITIES - CHESTER, CT. FILMING OF 1975-1976 ACTIVITIES FOR THE BICENTENNIAL. (LOCAL). MARY CAPELLINI, CHAIRWOMAN; CHESTER HISTORICAL SOCIETY; 65 MAIN ST; CHESTER, CT 06412. (#12007). **ARBA GRANTEE.**

REPRINTING OF 1936 CENTENNIAL FILM - CHESTER, CT. ORIGINAL FILM HAS BEEN SHOWN MANY TIMES. IT NOW NEEDS COMPLETE RESTORATION. (LOCAL). MARY CAPELLINI, CHAIRWOMAN; CHESTER HISTORICAL SOCIETY; 65 MAIN ST; CHESTER, CT 06412. (#12008). **ARBA GRANTEE.**

SURVEY & BOOK OF OLD HOMES OF CHESTER, CONNECTICUT. A PROGRAM TO RECORD HISTORIC HOUSES, PROVIDE A PERMANENT RECORD OF BUILDINGS & PRESENT AN ENVIRONMENT OF THE TOWN THAT WILL BE A TOOL FOR LONG RANGE PLANNING & PRESERVATION OF HISTORIC STRUCTURES. (LOCAL). ROBERT BLAIR, CO-CHAIRMAN; CHESTER AMERICAN REVOLUTION BICENTENNIAL COMMISSION; TOWN OFFICE BLDG; CHESTER, CT 06412. (#5284). **(??). ARBA GRANTEE.**

COLCHESTER

LIVING HISTORY CENTER - PROJ OF COLCHESTER, CT. A MULTMEDIA RESOURCE CENTER USING FILM, SLIDE & SOUND UNITS AND CLOSED CIRCUIT TV TO CREATE A CONTINUING HISTORY OF THE PAST, PRESENT AND THE FUTURE OF THE COMMUNITY. (LOCAL). ROBERT H RILEY, DIRECTOR; BACON ACADEMY BICENTENNIAL COMMISSION; NORWICH AVE; COLCHESTER, CT 06415. (#13649). **ARBA GRANTEE.**

OUTDOOR PERFORMANCE OR PRESENTATION. 'A DAY IN THE LIFE OF A CONTINENTAL SOLDIER' WILL BE PRESENTED BY A LOCAL, CIVIC, NON-PROFIT ORGANIZATION. (ST-WIDE). WILLIAM DUGUAY, MANAGER; NATHAN HALE ANCIENT FIFES AND DRUMS, INC; BOX 98; COLCHESTER, CT 06415. (#104940-1). **(??).**

COLLINSVILLE

DONATION OF FLAGPOLE, COLLINSVILLE, CT. THE PHOEBE HUMPHREY CHAPTER OF DAR WILL DONATE A POLE AND BRACKET FOR THE CANTON HISTORICAL MUSEUM'S BICENTENNIAL FLAG. (LOCAL). MRS ESTHER K NICHOLS, CHAIRMAN; THE PHOEBE HUMPHREY CHAPTER, DAUGHTERS OF THE AMER REPUBLIC; PO BOX 122; CANTON, CT 06019. (#14879).

RESTORATION OF TOWN HALL & TOWN CENTER - CT. THE TOWN HALL WILL BE REGISTERED IN THE NATIONAL REGISTER OF HISTORIC PLACES AND RESTORED TO ITS ORIGINAL CONDITION; COLLINSVILLE CENTER WILL ALSO BE RESTORED. (LOCAL). ROGER CLARKE, HISTORIAN; TOWN OF CANTON; CANTON, CT 06022. (#27241). **ARBA GRANTEE.**

COLUMBIA

RESTORATION OF MOOR'S INDIAN CHARITY SCHOOL - CT. RESTORE MOOR'S INDIAN CHARITY SCHOOL, FORERUNNER OF DARTMOUTH COLLEGE; BUILDING TO BE USED FOR EDUCATIONAL & HISTORICAL PURPOSES. (LOCAL). DONALD V NELSON, CHAIRMAN; COLUMBIA BICENTENNIAL COMMISSION; EDGARTON RD; COLUMBIA, CT 06237. (#26869). **ARBA GRANTEE.**

CORNWALL

HISTORICAL TOUR MAP OF CORNWALL, CT. MAP WILL DEPICT THE HISTORICAL SITES IN THE CORNWALL AREA. (LOCAL). MRS GUNNAR HOLMES, COORDINATOR; CORNWALL GRANGE; RTS 7 & 45; CORNWALL BR, CT 06754. (#24209).

PUBLICATION OF HEMAN SWIFT BOOKLET, CORNWALL, CT. THIS BOOK WILL BE AVAILABLE ON APRIL 15, 1976. (LOCAL). MRS GUNNAR HOLMES, COORDINATOR; CORNWALL HISTORICAL SOCIETY; RTS 7 & 45; CORNWALL BR, CT 06754. (#24208).

MAY 1 - 30, '76. COSTUME EXHIBIT & FASHION SHOW. EXHIBIT, FESTIVAL AT HUGHES MEMORIAL LIBRARY. (LOCAL). MRS GUNNAR HOLMES, COORD; CORNWALL BICENTENNIAL COMMISSION; RTS 7 & 45; CORNWALL BR, CT 06754. (#106812-5).

MAY 29 - 31, '76. BICENTENNIAL FLOWER SHOW. FLORAL ARRANGEMENTS WILL BE OF REAL, ARTIFICIAL OR DRIED FLOWERS IN RED, WHITE & BLUE. AT CORNWALL TOWN HALL, PINE STREET. (LOCAL). MRS GUNNAR HOLMES, CHMN; CORNWALL HISTORICAL SOCIETY; RTS 7 & 45; CORNWALL BR, CT 06754. (#106812-2).

MAY 30, '76. FESTIVAL WITH HERITAGE THEME. CEREMONY, FESTIVAL, PARADE, EXHIBIT. (LOCAL). MRS GUNNAR HOLMES; CORNWALL BICENTENNIAL ORGANIZATION; ROUTE 4; CORNWALL, CT 06754. (#4698-503).

MAY 30, '76. MEMORIAL DAY PARADE. BICENTENNIAL CELEBRATION OF CORNWALL, CONNECTICUT. SUMMER FESTIVAL OF '76, WITH MEMORIAL DAY PARADE, FAIR, AWARDS, DANCE, HISTORICAL EXHIBITS & CHURCH FESTIVAL. (LOCAL). MRS GUNNAR HOLMES; CORNWALL BICENTENNIAL ORGANIZATION; ROUTE 4; CORNWALL, CT 06754. (#4698-501).

MAY 30, '76. MEMORIAL DAY PRESENTATION OF CITIZENSHIP AWARD. SUMMER FESTIVAL OF '76, WITH MEMORIAL DAY PARADE, FAIR, AWARDS, DANCE, HISTORICAL EXHIBITS & CHURCH FESTIVAL. CHILDREN'S FAIR WILL BE FROM 1-4PM, SPONSORED BY 1ST CHURCH. SUNDAY SCHOOL ADM FREE, RIDES, BOOTHS, COSTUMES, REFRESHMENTS & FROG-JUMPING CONTEST. (LOCAL). MRS GUNNAR HOLMES; CORNWALL BICENTENNIAL ORGANIZATION; VFW; ROUTE 4; CORNWALL, CT 06754. (#4698-502).

MAY 31, '76. CHILDREN'S FAIR. RIDES, BOOTHS, COSTUMES, REFRESHMENTS, FROG-JUMPING CONTEST. (LOCAL). PAULA V HOLMES, COORD; 1ST CHURCH OF CHRIST; RTS 7 & 45; CORNWALL BR, CT 06754. (#106812-6).

JUNE 6 - AUG 29, '76. EXHIBIT-CORNWALL HEIRLOOMS & FOLK ART, 1776-1976. EXHIBIT. (LOCAL). MRS GUNNAR HOLMES, COORD; CORNWALL HISTORICAL SOCIETY; RTS 7 & 45; CORNWALL BR, CT 06754. (#106812-4).

JULY 17, '76. BICENTENNIAL DOLL SHOW & SALE. SPECIAL DISPLAYS, SOME FEATURING DOLLS DRESSED IN BICENTENNIAL COSTUMES. SOME DOLLS FOR SALE. AT MOHAWK SKI LODGE. (LOCAL). MRS HELEN HEDDEN, COORD; CAROUSEL DOLL CLUB; CREAM HILL RD; WEST CORNWALL, CT 06796. (#106812-1).

JULY 18, '76. CORNWALL FIRE DEPARTMENT COSTUME BALL. CEREMONY, FESTIVAL, PARADE, EXHIBIT. (LOCAL). MRS GUNNAR HOLMES; CORNWALL BICENTENNIAL ORGANIZATION; ROUTE 4; CORNWALL, CT 06754. (#4698-504).

AUG 11, '76. BICENTENNIAL WATER SPORTS PROGRAM & PICNIC. FESTIVAL. (LOCAL). MRS GUNNAR HOLMES, COORD; CORNWALL CIVIC CLUB; RTS 7 & 45; CORNWALL BR, CT 06754. (#106812-3).

AUG 16, '76. 150TH ANNIVERSARY FESTIVAL OF 2ND CONGREGATIONAL CHURCH. CEREMONY, FESTIVAL, PARADE, EXHIBIT. (LOCAL). MRS DOROTHY BOUTEILLER; CORNWALL BICENTENNIAL ORGANIZATION; ROUTE 4; CORNWALL, CT 06754. (#4698-505).

COVENTRY

'MUSIC OF THE AMERICAN REVOLUTION' - COVENTRY, CT. A 3-VOLUME SERIES OF 12-INCH LP PHONOGRAPH RECORDS ENTITLED 'THE AMERICAN REVOLUTION'; OVER 60 SELECTIONS FROM THE PERIOD. (REGN'L). RALPH BURNS, TREASURER; NATHAN HALE ANCIENT FIFE & DRUMS, 19TH CT REGIMENT OF FOOT; PO BOX 1776; COVENTRY, CT 06238. (#20714).

NATHAN HALE COMMEMORATIVE MEDAL OF COVENTRY, CT. MEDAL IN COMMEMORATION OF NATHAN HALE, PATRIOT, SPY & HERO OF AMERICAN REVOLUTION; ISSUED BOTH IN SILVER AND IN BRONZE, ONE AND ONE HALF INCH IN DIAMETER. (LOCAL). ELIZABETH RYCHLING, TREASURER; COVENTRY BICENTENNIAL COMMISSION; TOWN OFFICE BLDG, BOX 1976; COVENTRY, CT 06238. (#28180).

'ONE LIFE TO LOSE', A BOOK ABOUT NATHAN HALE - CT. A TEXT BOOK FOR CHILDREN ON THE REVOLUTIONARY WAR HERO, NATHAN HALE. THE BOOK EXPLAINS SELF SACRIFICE, HONOR & PATRIOTISM. (ST-WIDE). ARTHUR W LEIBUNDGUTH, DIRECTOR; ANTIQUARIAN AND LANDMARKS SOCIETY INC OF CONN; 394 MAIN ST; HARTFORD, CT 06103. (#8206). **(??). ARBA GRANTEE.**

OCT 9, '76. 200TH ANNIVERSARY OF HALE HOMESTEAD. CEREMONY, PARADE AT NATHAN HALE HOMESTEAD, SOUTH ST. (ST-WIDE). TRUDY J SCHOBINGER, CHMN; ANTIQUARIUM & LANDMARKS SOCIETY OF CONNECTICUT; 394 MAIN ST; HARTFORD, CT 06103. (#103416-628).

CROMWELL

CROMWELL, CONN, FRISBIE HOUSE RESTORATION PROJECT. RESTORATION OF HOME & GROUNDS. PROVIDING REPOSITORY FOR LOCAL HISTORY CENTER, INCLUDING ARTS & CRAFTS. HEADQUARTERS FOR ACTIVE HISTORICAL SOCIETY. (LOCAL). ANNA DOERING, CHAIRMAN; CROMWELL HISTORICAL SOCIETY; 396 MAIN ST; CROMWELL, CT 06416. (#8811). **ARBA GRANTEE.**

DANBURY

DANBURY, CONN, COMMEMORATIVE MEDALS. SILVER & BRONZE MEDALS COMMEMORATING AMERICAN, BURNING OF DANBURY BY BRITISH IN APRIL, 1777; FOUNDING OF DANBURY IN 1684; INCORPORATION AS CITY IN 1889. (ST-WIDE). ALBERT E HAMILTON, CHAIRMAN; DANBURY '76, INC; C/O CITY HALL, 155 DEER HILL AVE; DANBURY, CT 06810. (#764).

LECTURESHIP PROJECT - DANBURY, CONNECTICUT. LECTURESHIP AT WESTERN CONNECTICUT STATE COLLEGE CREATED TO SERVE AS A REMINDER OF CITIZEN'S RESPONSIBILITY TO MAINTAIN THE LIBERTY DECLARED OURS UNDER THE DECLARATION OF INDEPENDENCE. (ST-WIDE). JACK GARAMELLA, CHAIRMAN; DANBURY AMERICAN REVOLUTION BICENTENNIAL COMMISSION; 66 WEST ST; DANBURY, CT 06810. (#5287). **ARBA GRANTEE.**

MEDALLIC ART CALENDAR WITH BICENTENNIAL SYMBOL. A MEDALLIC ART CALENDAR BEARING THE BICENTENNIAL SYMBOL WILL BE PRODUCED FOR 1976. ARBA LICENSE NO 76-19-0546 (NAT'L). MIKE COOPER, DIR; MEDALLIC ART CO; OLD RIDGEBURY RD; DANBURY, CT 06810. (#10421).

JULY 5 - 16, '76. CARL HAVERLIN/BROADCAST MUSIC, INC, ARCHIVES BICENTENNIAL EXHIBIT. OFFERS A VERSATILE PICTURE OF HISTORY, REGIONAL LIFE & MUSIC FOR OVER 200 YEARS. CONTAINS PRESIDENTIAL LETTERS, LETTERS OF FAMOUS AMERICANS, OLD BOOKS, MANUSCRIPTS, HISTORY OF 'THE STAR SPANGLED BANNER' & COMPOSER AUTOGRAPHS, PLUS SHEET MUSIC OF THE PAST. AT DANBURY SCOTT-FANTON MUSEUM (43 MAIN ST) & HISTORICAL SOCIETY. (ST-WIDE). MRS DOROTHY SCHLING, DIR; DANBURY SCOTT-FANTON MUSEUM & HISTORICAL SOCIETY; 43 MAIN ST; DANBURY, CT 06810. (#20784-10).

OCT 2 - 11, '76. GREAT DANBURY STATE FAIR. 3 HISTORICAL THEME VILLAGES, ANIMALS, GRANDSTAND SHOW, FREE SHOWS, ANTIQUE TOOL DISPLAY, TRANSPORTATION MUSEUM, MODEL T FORD MUSEUM, OX DRAW AND PARADE. AT DANBURY FAIRGROUNDS AT EXIT 3 I-84, JCT OF US 6 & 7. (REGN'L). JOHN H STETSON, CHAIRMAN; DANBURY FAIR, INC; 130 WHITE ST; DANBURY, CT 06810. (#106095-42).

OCT 25, '76. GINO J ARCONTI LECTURESHIP SERIES. LECTURESHIP AT WESTERN CONNECTICUT STATE COLLEGE CREATED TO SERVE AS A REMINDER OF CITIZEN'S RESPONSIBILITY TO MAINTAIN THE LIBERTY DECLARED OURS UNDER THE DECLARATION OF INDEPENDENCE. AT BERKSHIRE AUDITORIUM WESTERN CONN STATE COLL OSBORNE ST. (ST-WIDE). JACK GARAMELLA, CHAIRMAN; DANBURY AMERICAN REVOLUTION BICENTENNIAL COMMISSION; 66 WEST ST; DANBURY, CT 06810. (#5287-1).

DANIELSON

NUTMEG YEAS AND NAYS-VOICES IN DISSENT. THE HISTORICAL PAGEANT WILL FEATURE EVENTS & PERSONALITIES IN CONNECTICUT HISTORY. (LOCAL). JOHN GEARY, PROFESSOR; QUINEBAUG VALLEY COMMUNITY COLLEGE; BOX 449 MAPLE ST; DANIELSON, CT 06239. (#102609-1). **(??).**

PROGRAMS IN EDUCATION, DANIELSON, CT. SPEAKERS SERIES ON CONNECTICUT HISTORY & COMMUNITY COURSE IN LOCAL HISTORY USING COMMUNITY MEMBERS & RESOURCES. (LOCAL). JOHN J GEARY, PROF OF HISTORY; QUINEBAUG VALLEY COMMUNITY COLLEGE; MAPLE ST, BOX 449; DANIELSON, CT 06239. (#15686).

DEC 3, '76. 'THE FREEDOM BELL' - A DRAMATIC PAGEANT. FIFE & DRUM CORPS, A FLAG COLLECTION, CHORAL PROGRAM, AND INTERNATIONAL COSTUMES WITH UNIQUE SETS. AT KILLINGLY HIGH SCHOOL, WESTFIELD. (LOCAL). HOWARD W CURRY, CHMN; KILLINGLY BICENTENNIAL COMMISSION; BEL AIR DR; MOOSUP, CT 06354. (#200008-252).

DARIEN

'TORY HOLE', CONN REVOLUTIONARY WAR HISTORY NOVEL. A REPUBLICATION AS A PAPERBACK WITH A BICENTENNIAL SECTION OF A NOVEL BY CONN WOMAN WRITTEN FOR & ABOUT YOUNG PEOPLE, HERITAGE, TRADITION & LOYALTY. TEXT IS SOUGHT BY ELEMENTARY SCHOOLS. (REGN'L). MRS NOEL A YANEY, VICE CHAIRMAN, TORY HOLE COMM; THE DARIEN COMMUNITY ASSOCIATION, INC; 274 MIDDLE SEX RD; DARIEN, CT 06820. (#23871). **ARBA GRANTEE.**

DEEP RIVER

DEEP RIVER, CONN, 1976 PAGEANT PROJECT. PUBLICATION OF MATERIAL TO BE USED IN 1-DAY PAGEANT CELEBRATION. THE MATERIAL WILL INCLUDE SONG SHEETS, CONTEST APPLICATIONS, STREET & BUILDING DECORATIONS, ETC. (LOCAL). IRWIN CHASE JR, VICE PRESIDENT; DEEP RIVER HISTORICAL SOCIETY; MAIN ST; DEEP RIVER, CT 06417. (#857). **(??). ARBA GRANTEE.**

REPRINTING OF TOWN ACTS OF SAYBROOK, CONNECTICUT. THE PRINTING OF THE ORIGINAL MINUTES OF SAYBROOK TOWN MEETINGS FROM 1774 TO 1784 INCLUDING A REVIEW OF

DEEP RIVER — CONTINUED

LARGER EVENTS TAKING PLACE AT THE SAME TIME & THEIR EFFECT ON THE TOWN AS REFLECTED IN THE TOWN ACTS. (LOCAL). LORRAINE C WALLACE, CHAIRMAN; DEEP RIVER BICENTENNIAL COMMITTEE; WESTBROOK RD; DEEP RIVER, CT 06417. (#8208). **ARBA GRANTEE.**

DERBY

GAZEBO PROJECT - DERBY, CT. A GAZEBO WILL BE BUILT ON THE GREEN TO BE USED FOR ALL SPECIAL OCCASIONS AND MARKED WITH A COMMEMORATIVE PLAQUE. (LOCAL). FRANK H OGLE, CHAIRMAN; DERBY TERCENTENARY & BICENTENNIAL, INC; 300 MAIN ST; DERBY, CT 06418. (#25795). **ARBA GRANTEE.**

HISTORICAL MARKERS - DERBY, CT. METAL MARKERS ON: 1700'S DOCK, INDIAN TRADING POST, ISAAC HULL'S BIRTHPLACE, SHIPBUILDING BOATYARD & VILLAGE GREEN. PLAQUES TO READ: ' A PAST TO REMEMBER, A FUTURE TO MOLD'. (LOCAL). FRANK H OGLE, CHAIRMAN; DERBY TERCENTENARY & BICENTENNIAL, INC; 300 MAIN ST; DERBY, CT 06418. (#25290). **ARBA GRANTEE.**

PLAYGROUND IN DERBY, CT. SITE TO BE SELECTED CENTER OF CITY FOR PLAYGROUND. (LOCAL). FRANK H OGLE, CHAIRMAN; DERBY TERCENTENARY & BICENTENNIAL INC; 300 MAIN; DERBY, CT 06418. (#5939). **(??).**

RESTORATION OF HUMPHRIES HOME IN DERBY, CT. RESTORATION OF THE CENTRAL CHIMNEY OF GENERAL DAVID HUMPHRIES HOME. (LOCAL). DOROTHY LARSON, PRESIDENT; DERBY HISTORICAL SOCIETY; PO BOX 331; DERBY, CT 06418. (#10767).

JULY '76. GAZEBO ON THE GREEN. CEREMONY, OPENING AT DERBY GREEN. (LOCAL). FRANK OGLE, CHAIRMAN; DERBY BICENTENNIAL COMMISSION; PO BOX 90; DERBY, CT 06418. (#103593-1).

DURHAM

'ROOTS', DURHAM, CT. COMMUNITY AND SCHOOL JOIN TOGETHER IN A QUEST FOR ANCESTRAL ROOTS BY STUDYING LOCAL HISTORY, EARLY AMERICAN CRAFTS, LITERATURE, MUSIC, ART AND ARCHITECTURE. (LOCAL). PAULINE DYSON, PROJ DIRECTOR; DURHAM BICENTENNIAL COMMITTEE; TOWN HALL; DURHAM, CT 06422. (#12242). **ARBA GRANTEE.**

E WOODSTOCK

JULY 3 - 5, '76. JULY 4TH JAMBOREE. OLD-FASHIONED FAMILY CELEBRATION - 20TH ANNIVERSARY OF EVENT; WILL INCLUDE: BARBEQUE, FOOD & GAME BOOTHS, ATHLETIC EVENTS, PARADE, BAND CONCERT, SQUARE DANCE DEMONSTRATION, FIRE DEPARTMENT WATER POLO COMPETITION, CAKE WALKS AND TORCH RUNNERS CLOSING CEREMONY. AT PUBLIC GREEN. (LOCAL). LOUISE P JORDAN, DIRECTOR; EAST WOODSTOCK UNITED CHURCH OF CHRIST; RT 2; WOODSTOCK, CT 06281. (#101249-1).

EAST GRANBY

GUIDES TO OLD NEWGATE PRISON - EAST GRANBY, CT. TOUR GUIDES TO THE FIRST STATE PRISON IN CONNECTICUT WILL BE PUBLISHED. (ST-WIDE). RICHARD KUNS, SUPERINTENDENT; CONNECTICUT HISTORICAL COMMISSION; 59 S PROSPECT ST; HARTFORD, CT 06106. (#26738). **ARBA GRANTEE.**

HISTORY OF EAST GRANBY, CT. 300 PAGES OF HISTORY AND 50 ILLUSTRATIONS WILL BE COMPILED TO MAKE UP THE FIRST HISTORY OF EAST GRANBY. (LOCAL). HARVEY FRUCHTER, CHAIRMAN; EAST GRANBY BICENTENNIAL COMMITTEE; PO BOX 1976; EAST GRANBY, CT 06026. (#26737). **ARBA GRANTEE.**

MURALS FOR OLD NEWGATE PRISON - E GRANBY, CT. 6 MURALS DEPICTING THE HISTORY OF THE REVOLUTIONARY WAR PRISON WILL BE INSTALLED IN THE GUARD HOUSE MUSEUM. (LOCAL). JOHN SHANNAHAN, DIRECTOR; CONNECTICUT HISTORICAL COMMISSION; 59 S PROSPECT ST; HARTFORD, CT 06106. (#27353). **ARBA GRANTEE.**

RESTORATION PROJECT - EAST GRANBY, CT. RESTORE OLD REVOLUTIONARY CEMETERY AND PUBLISH A HISTORY OF ITS RESIDENTS. (LOCAL). HARVEY FRUCHTER, CHAIRMAN; EAST GRANBY BICENTENNIAL COMMITTEE; 20 HAMILTON RD; EAST GRANBY, CT 06026. (#13838). **ARBA GRANTEE.**

'SPANNING TIME OLD & NEW' - HOUSE TOUR, CT. HOUSE AND GARDEN TOUR OF BOTH OLD AND NEW HOMES; OLD HOMES MARKED AS A LASTING REMINDER OF THE BICENTENNIAL. (LOCAL). HARVEY FRUCHTER, CHAIRMAN; EAST GRANBY BICENTENNIAL COMMITTEE; PO BOX 1976; EAST GRANBY, CT 06026. (#13850). **ARBA GRANTEE.**

SEPT 18, '75. CONCERT IN RAGTIME. PRE-PERFORMANCE RECEPTION FOR PATRONS 6:30-7:30 WITH REFRESHMENTS. AT COPPERHILL AUDITORIUM. (LOCAL). CHARLES HUNDERLACH, CHMN; EAST GRANBY BICENTENNIAL COMMISSION; 14 MT VERNON DR; EAST GRANBY, CT 06026. (#200008-22).

OCT 1, '75. TOUR OF OLD AND MODERN HOMES. HOUSE AND GARDEN TOUR OF BOTH OLD AND NEW HOMES; OLD HOMES MARKED AS A LASTING REMINDER OF THE BICENTENNIAL. (LOCAL). HARVEY FRUCHTER, CHAIRMAN; EAST GRANBY BICENTENNIAL COMMITTEE; PO BOX 1976; EAST GRANBY, CT 06026. (#13850-501).

OCT 11, '75. HOUSE TOUR. EIGHT HOMES ON TOUR, LUNCHEON AT CONGREGATIONAL CHURCH IN CENTER OF TOWN; COUNTRY STORE; OLD LOOM OPERATION WILL BE DEMONSTRATED. (LOCAL). MRS R GALLUCCIO, CHMN; EAST GRANBY BICENTENNIAL COMMISSION; 25 NUTMEG RD; EAST GRANBY, CT 06026. (#102357-1).

EAST HADDAM

BICENTENNIAL SCHOLARSHIP FUND - EAST HADDAM, CT. ALL FUND RAISING MONIES WILL BE INVESTED WITH THE ANNUAL INTEREST TO BE AWARDED TO A DESERVING HIGH SCHOOL SENIOR EACH YEAR. (LOCAL). DR KARL P STOFKO, CHAIRMAN; EAST HADDAM BICENTENNIAL COMMITTEE; ORCHARD RD; EAST HADDAM, CT 06423. (#32114).

'EAST HADDAM IN 1976' - PA. A PHOTOGRAPHIC COMPETITION WITH RESIDENT AMATEUR PHOTOGRAPHERS TO HELP COMPOSE A PICTORIAL RECORD OF EAST HADDAM IN 1976. PHOTOGRAPHS TO BE PRESERVED FOR FUTURE REFERENCE BY THE HISTORICAL SOCIETY. (LOCAL). DR KARL P STOFKO, CHAIRMAN; EAST HADDAM BICENTENNIAL COMMITTEE; ORCHARD RD; EAST HADDAM, CT 06423. (#32115).

JULY 13, '75. LIBERTY POLE RAISING CEREMONIES. CEREMONIES INCLUDED A PARADE, ENCAMPMENT, SPEECHES, RAISING OF A LIBERTY POLE, DRUM & FIFE CORPS CONCERT, AND REFRESHMENTS. AT NATHAN HALE PARK. (LOCAL). DR KARL P STOFKO, CHMN; EAST HADDAM BICENTENNIAL COMMITTEE; ORCHARD RD; EAST HADDAM, CT 06423. (#200008-73).

SEPT 21, '75. A SALUTE TO THE BICENTENNIAL CONCERT. REV L ALEXANDER HARPER, ON THE HARPSICHORD, AND WESLEY B REED, ON ANCIENT STRINGED INSTRUMENTS, PERFORMED FOR THE TOWN. AT FIRST CHURCH OF CHRIST. (LOCAL). MISS HELEN C COBLEIGH; COLONIAL GUILD, FIRST CHURCH OF CHRIST; TOWN STREET; EAST HADDAM, CT 06423. (#200008-72).

AUG 7, '76. ANTIQUE CARRIAGE RALLY. ACTIVITIES INCLUDED CARRIAGE COMPETITION, COLONIAL DINNER, AND TOUR OF THE HISTORIC VILLAGE. AT JOHNSONVILLE VILLAGE. (LOCAL). DR KARL P STOFKO, CHMN; EAST HADDAM LIONS CLUB; ORCHARD RD; EAST HADDAM, CT 06423. (#200008-71).

AUG 21, '76. AUGUST BICENTENNIAL FESTIVAL. ACTIVITIES INCLUDED TODAY WERE A PARADE, REVOLUTIONARY ENCAMPMENT AND BATTLE REENACTMENT, SPEAKERS, AND REFRESHMENTS. AT MOODUS CENTER. (LOCAL). DR KARL P STOFKO, CHMN; EAST HADDAM BICENTENNIAL COMMITTEE; ORCHARD RD; EAST HADDAM, CT 06423. (#200008-70).

EAST HAMPTON

AUG 7, '76. BICENTENNIAL FESTIVAL. PARADE, BAND CONCERT & BOOTH ACTIVITIES. AT MAIN ST. (LOCAL). ANN R MCLAUGHLIN, SEC; BICENTENNIAL COMMITTEE OF EAST HAMPTON; LAKE DR; EAST HAMPTON, CT 06424. (#106826-1).

EAST HARTFORD

BICENT ACTIVITIES & CELEBRATION IN CONNECTICUT. CONNECTICUT WILL CENTER ITS CELEBRATION AROUND THE 3 BICENT THEMES, HERITAGE, FESTIVAL & HORIZONS. (LOCAL). TERRIE BLACKSTONE, COMMISSION CHAIRPERSON; BICENTENNIAL COMMISSION, TOWN OF EAST HARTFORD; 740 MAIN ST; EAST HARTFORD, CT 06108. (#9575). **ARBA GRANTEE.**

BICENTENNIAL LOGO DESIGN CONTEST. COMPETITION. (LOCAL). TERRYE BLACKSTONE, CHMN; EAST HARTFORD AMERICAN REVOLUTION BICENTENNIAL COMMITTEE; 26 HOLLAND LA; EAST HARTFORD, CT 06118. (#107884-1).

COMMEMORATIVE MEDAL - EAST HARTFORD, CT. THE 6TH CAMPSITE OF ROCHAMBEAU IS PICTURED ON ONE SIDE OF THE MEDAL AND ON THE REVERSE SIDE IS THE INSCRIPTION 'FOR A PRINCIPLE, THE NATION BLED'. (LOCAL). CYNTHIA REDMAN, COORDINATOR; EAST HARTFORD BICENTENNIAL COMMITTEE; 70 HUCKLEBERRY RD; EAST HARTFORD, CT 06118. (#25662).

EAST HARTFORD TOWN FLAG, CT. A TOWN FLAG WILL BE DESIGNED & MANUFACTURED. (LOCAL). TERRYE BLACKSTONE, CHAIRMAN; EAST HARTFORD AMERICAN REVOLUTION BICENTENNIAL COMMITTEE; 26 HOLLAND LA; EAST HARTFORD, CT 06108. (#24368).

EAST HARTFORD, THE COMMUNITY - EDUC COURSE, CT. COURSE ON EAST HARTFORD HISTORY TO BE TAUGHT IN AREA HIGH SCHOOLS. (LOCAL). JOHN LARSON, PROJ COORDINATOR; EAST HARTFORD BOARD OF EDUCATION & EAST HARTFORD ARBC; WOODLAND ST; EAST HARTFORD, CT 06108. (#24369).

HISTORIC BOOKLET - EAST HARTFORD, CT. A BOOKLET CONTAINING A CALENDAR OF EVENTS, A HISTORIC MAP AND A SHORT HISTORY OF THE TOWN WILL BE PUBLISHED. (LOCAL). TERRYE BLACKSTONE, CHAIRMAN; EAST HARTFORD BICENTENNIAL COMMISSION; 720 MAIN ST; EAST HARTFORD, CT 06108. (#25109).

LONG RIVERS COUNCIL BICENTENNIAL ENCAMPMENT - CT. A 3-DAY BOY SCOUT ENCAMPMENT WITH 20,000 SCOUTS PARTICIPATING IN A VARIETY OF BICENTENNIAL THEME ACTIVITIES. (LOCAL). RICHARD L CARLSON, COUNCIL EXEC; LONG RIVER COUNCIL, INC BOY SCOUTS OF AMERICA; 70 FOREST ST; HARTFORD, CT 06105. (#23776). **ARBA GRANTEE.**

MARK & RECORD HISTORICAL BUILDINGS & SITES, CT. DESCRIBE, IDENTIFY WITH PLAQUE & PRODUCE DIRECTORY OF BUILDINGS OF HISTORICAL VINTAGE. (LOCAL). TERRYE BLACKSTONE, CHAIRMAN; EAST HARTFORD AMERICAN REVOLUTION BICENTENNIAL COMMITTEE; 26 HOLLAND LA; EAST HARTFORD, CT 06118. (#24366).

ONE ROOM SCHOOLHOUSE, EAST HARTFORD, CT. RELOCATION, RESTORATION & LANDSCAPING OF ONE ROOM SCHOOLHOUSE. (LOCAL). TERRYE BLACKSTONE, CHAIRMAN; EAST HARTFORD AMERICAN REVOLUTION BICENTENNIAL COMMISSION; 26 HOLLAND LA; EAST HARTFORD, CT 06108. (#24370).

SCHOLASTIC SLOGAN CONTEST. CREATION OF A SLOGAN TO BE ASSOCIATED WITH EAST HARTFORD BICENTENNIAL COMMITTEE. (LOCAL). T BLACKSTONE, CHAIRMAN; EAST HARTFORD BICENTENNIAL COMMITTEE; 740 MAIN ST; EAST HARTFORD, CT 06108. (#107397-1).

TIME CAPSULE, EAST HARTFORD, CT. CAPSULE TO CONTAIN HISTORICAL & BICENTENNIAL MEMORABILIA TO BE OPENED 2001 & RESEALED THEN TO BE OPENED IN 2076. (LOCAL). TERRYE BLACKSTONE, CHAIRMAN; EAST HARTFORD ARBC; 740 MAIN ST; EAST HARTFORD, CT 06108. (#32696).

MAY 3 - 4, '75. LOYALTY DAY PARADE AND ART EXHIBIT. EXHIBIT, PARADE AT ART AT RAYMOND LIB MAIN ST EH PARADE IS TOWN WIDE. (LOCAL). TERRYE BLACKSTONE; VFW AND EAST HARTFORD BICENTENNIAL COMMISSION; TOWN HALL 740 MAIN ST; E HARTFORD, CT 06108. (#50269-1).

OCT 19, '75. COLONIAL DINNER WITH PERIOD DANCE AND MUSIC. FESTIVAL AT EAST HARTFORD ELKS CLUB, ROBERTS ST. (LOCAL). M T BLACKSTONE, CHAIRMAN; EAST HARTFORD AMERICAN REVOLUTION BICENTENNIAL COMMUNITY; 740 MAIN ST; E HARTFORD, CT 06108. (#102134-1).

MAY 12, '76. SPELLING BEE. COMPETITION AT LANGFORD SCHOOL, ALPS DRIVE. (LOCAL). ANTHONY PICANO; EAST HARTFORD BICENTENNIAL COMMISSION; DR LANGFORD SCHOOL ALPS DR; EAST HARTFORD, CT 06108. (#106945-1).

MAY 15, '76. BICENTENNIAL ARTS & CRAFTS ETHNIC FAIR. FAIR, FESTIVAL AT NORTH END PARK, REMINGTON RD. (LOCAL). RAYMOND JOHNSON, COORD; EAST HARTFORD BICENTENNIAL COMMITTEE; 43 FARNHAM DR; EAST HARTFORD, CT 06118. (#106945-4).

MAY 21 - 23, '76. BICENTENNIAL ENCAMPMENT. BOY SCOUTS FROM THE ORIGINAL 13 COLONIES PARTICIPATE IN A FULL JAMBOREE. (REGN'L). RICHARD CARLSON, CHMN; LONG RIVERS COUNCIL; 70 FOREST ST; HARTFORD, CT 06105. (#103416-295).

MAY 22, '76. HOUSE AND GARDEN TOUR. TOUR. (LOCAL). ARLINE KEITHLINE, COORD; EAST HARTFORD BICENTENNIAL COMMITTEE; 9 FULLER AVE; EAST HARTFORD, CT 06108. (#106945-3).

MAY 27, '76. TOWN HALL OPEN HOUSE & YOUTH DAY. TOUR AT TOWN HALL. (LOCAL). MICHAEL VALUK, COORD; EAST HARTFORD BICENTENNIAL COMMITTEE; 740 MAIN ST; EAST HARTFORD, CT 06108. (#106945-2).

MAY 31, '76. MEMORIAL DAY PARADE. PARADE. (LOCAL). TERRYE BLACKSTONE, CHMN; EAST HARTFORD BICENTENNIAL COMMITTEE; EAST HARTFORD, CT 06108. (#200008-18).

JUNE 23 - 24, '76. ROCHAMBEAU COMMEMORATIVE OBSERVANCE. CEREMONY, EXHIBIT AT SILVER LANE. (LOCAL). ANTHONY FORNABI, CHAIRMAN; EAST HARTFORD ARBC; 102 MOHAWK DR; EAST HARTFORD, CT 06108. (#108221-2).

JUNE 27 - 28, '76. CONNECTICUT RIVER CANOE TREK. CEREMONY, EXHIBIT AT CONNECTICUT RIVER, EAST HARTFORD HARBOR. (LOCAL). ALBERT KERLING, COORD; EAST HARTFORD ARBC; 497 TOLLAND ST; EAST HARTFORD, CT 06108. (#108221-1).

JULY 4, '76. COLONIAL FLOWER SHOW. EXHIBIT AT ONE ROOM SCHOOLHOUSE & HUGUENOT HOUSE, 300 BURNSIDE AVE. (LOCAL). GLORIA CRUICKSHANKS, CHMN; EAST HARTFORD BICENTENNIAL COMMITTEE; 23 ROWLAND DR; EAST HARTFORD, CT 06118. (#106945-5).

JULY 4, '76. FIREWORKS DISPLAY. FESTIVAL AT WICKHAM PARK. (LOCAL). TERRYE BLACKSTONE, CHMN; TOWN OF EAST HARTFORD, DEPT OF PARKS; 740 MAIN ST; EAST HARTFORD, CT 06108. (#108157-2).

OCT 2, '76. FORMAL BICENTENNIAL BALL. FESTIVAL AT RAMADA INN, E RIVER DR. (LOCAL). JAMES KERWIN, COORDINATOR; EAST HARTFORD BICENTENNIAL COMMISSION; EAST HARTFORD, CT 06118. (#108157-1).

EAST LYME

SMITH-HARRIS MUSEUM - EAST LYME, CT. ESTABLISH AND EQUIP THE SMITH-HARRIS HOUSE WITH PERIOD FURNISHINGS & ACQUIRE A CATALOG AND MAINTAIN HISTORICAL PUBLICATIONS OF EAST LYME HISTORY. (LOCAL). NORMAN B PECK, CO-CHAIRMAN; EAST LYME AMERICAN REVOLUTION BICENTENNIAL COMMITTEE; PO BOX 3; NIANTIC, CT 06357. (#14562). **ARBA GRANTEE.**

JUNE 12, '76. SALUTE TO THE BICENTENNIAL. EAST LYME SALUTES THE BICENTENNIAL WITH AN EVENING OF AMERICAN MUSIC. (LOCAL). DORE SINGER, COORDINATOR; CITY OF EAST LYME; EAST LYME, CT 06371. (#103416-404).

EAST WINDSOR

FEB 1 - MAY 1, '76. HISTORICAL THEME POSTER CONTEST. PAST HISTORY OF EAST WINDSOR IS CONTEST THEME. 3 AGE GROUPS: 6-12, 13-18, 19 & OVER. TO BE AN INDEPENDENT JUDGING CONTEST, LIMITED TO EAST WINDSOR RESIDENTS OR POST MEMBERS. CASH PRIZES. AT GARDNER ST, WAREHOUSE POINT, CT. (LOCAL). KENNETH C YOUNG, COORD; AMERICAN LEGION WOMENS AUXILIARY UNIT #40 OF EAST WINDSOR; 6 DEAN AVE, BOX 515; WAREHOUSE PT, CT 06088. (#105716-2).

FEB 1 - JULY 4, '76. BEARD AND MUSTACHE CONTEST. LIMITED TO EAST WINDSOR RESIDENTS. MUST BE REGISTERED BY MAY 1ST.

EAST WINDSOR — CONTINUED

AWARDS AND TROPHIES TO BE PRESENTED. AT DEPOT ST. (LOCAL). KENNETH C YOUNG, COORD; THE MUSTACHE CLUB OF THE LIEDERTAFEL SINGING SOCIETY; 6 DEAN AVE, BOX 515; WAREHOUSE PT, CT 06088. (#105716-3).

MAY 15, '76. TOUR OF OLDER HOMES AND LUNCHEON. DISPLAY OF COLONIAL ITEMS AND CRAFTS AT LUNCHEON. AT 74 S MAIN ST/WAREHOUSE POINT, CT. (ST-WIDE). KENNETH C YOUNG, COORD; EAST WINDSOR HIGH SCHOOL BOOSTER CLUB; 6 DEAN AVE, BOX 515; WAREHOUSE PT, CT 06088. (#105716-1).

EASTFORD

20TH CENTURY HISTORY OF EASTFORD, CT. BASED ON ORAL HISTORY, INTERVIEWS AND ARCHIVAL RESEARCH, THE BOOK WILL SHOW THE INFLUENCE OF OUR AMERICAN HERITAGE TOGETHER WITH THE DIFFERENT LIFE STYLES BROUGHT IN BY 20TH CENTURY IMMIGRANTS. (LOCAL). DAGMAR NOLL, SECRETARY; EASTFORD HISTORICAL SOCIETY; PO BOX 113; EASTFORD, CT 06242. (#12265). **ARBA GRANTEE.**

EASTON

EASTON'S LIBRARY'S BICENTENNIAL PROJECTS. READING PGM FOR YOUTH; COLONIAL MUSIC CONCERT; ART, PAINTINGS & ARTIFACTS EXHIBITED; PURCHASE OF BOOKS. (LOCAL). SALLY MUELLER, LIBRARIAN; EASTON BICENTENNIAL COMMITTEE; MOREHOUSE RD; EASTON, CT 06425. (#32634).

PRESERVATION OF 1850 BARN, EASTON, CT. 1850 BARN LOCATED ON TOWN OWNED OPEN SPACE FOR PASSIVE RECREATION AND CONSERVATION PURPOSES. (LOCAL). MRS JOSEPH H HODGSON, CHAIRMAN; EASTON BICENTENNIAL COMMITTEE; 355 CENTER RD; EASTON, CT 06883. (#32632).

SCHOOL TERM PROJECT, EASTON, CT. A SCHOOL TERM PROJECT AT HELEN KELLER MIDDLE SCHOOL. (LOCAL). AL TRIEDEL, CHAIRMAN; HELEN KELLER MIDDLE SCHOOL; 360 SPORT HILL DR; EASTON, CT 06612. (#32633).

ELLINGTON

BICENTENNIAL PARK -ELLINGTON, CONNECTICUT. EXPANSION OF HISTORIC TOWN GREEN TO BE USED AS A PARK. INCLUDED WILL BE A BANDSTAND OF HISTORIC DESIGN WITH COLONIAL LIGHTING. (LOCAL). MRS SALLY A VAUGH, CHAIRMAN; BICENTENNIAL COMMISSION OF ELLINGTON; PO BOX 1776; ELLINGTON, CT 06029. (#3475).

ORGANIZATION OF ELLINGTON PARISH TRAIN BAND -CONN. AN ESSENTIAL PART OF A REVOLUNTIONARY WAR GROUP CONSISTING OF 8-10 FIFERS; 6 DRUMMERS. THE REST OF THE 40 MEN WITH MUSKETS USING MUSIC OF EARLY ELLINGTON RESIDENT, GILES GIBBS. (LOCAL). MRS, SALLY VAUGHN, CHAIRMAN; BICENTENNIAL COMMISSION OF ELLINGTON; P O BOX 1776; ELLINGTON, CT 06029. (#3476).

JULY 4, '75. FOURTH OF JULY PARADE & BOX LUNCH PICNIC. EXPANSION OF HISTORIC TOWN GREEN TO BE USED AS A PARK. INCLUDED WILL BE A BANDSTAND OF HISTORIC DESIGN WITH COLONIAL LIGHTING. THERE WILL BE OLD-FASHION GAMES PUT ON BY THE RECREATION COMMISSION. AT PARADE ROUTES 286 & 140 PICNIC AT BROOKSIDE PARK RT 140. (LOCAL). SALLY VAUGHN; ELLINGTON BICENTENNIAL COMMISSION; 36 MAIN ST; ELLINGTON, CT 06029. (#3475-1).

OCT 11, '75. BICENTENNIAL FREEDOM FESTIVAL. BAND CONCERTS, DANCING & RAISING OF THE LIBERTY BELL. (LOCAL). SALLY VAUGAN, CHAIRPERSON; ELLINGTON BICENTENNIAL COMMISSION; 36 MAIN ST; ELLINGTON, CT 06029. (#102136-1).

OCT 12, '75. BI-SING-TENNIAL: ELLINGTON SINGS OUT. PARADE AT ELLINGTON HIGH SCHOOL, RTE 140. (LOCAL). REV RICHARD BERTRAM; COMBINED CHURCHES OF ELLINGTON; 154 ORCHARD ST; ROCKVILLE, CT 06066. (#102136-2).

FEB 20, '76. PATRIOTS IN PETTICOATS. LIVE PERFORMANCE AT ST LUKE'S PARISH HALL, MAPLE ST. (LOCAL). DONNA VINCENT, CHAIRMAN; ST LUKE'S WOMEN'S GUILD; 9 RASPBERRY LANE; ELLINGTON, CT 06029. (#104932-1).

OCT 16, '76. A DAY IN THE LIFE OF A CONTINENTAL SOLDIER. EXPANSION OF HISTORIC TOWN GREEN TO BE USED AS A PARK. INCLUDED WILL BE A BANDSTAND OF HISTORIC DESIGN WITH COLONIAL LIGHTING. THIS IS A 3 1/2 HR. PROGRAM. AT BROOKSIDE PARK RT. 140 AMPLE PARKING ON PREMISES. (LOCAL). WILLIAM F DUGUAY; ELLINGTON BICENTENNIAL COMMISSION; P O BOX 98; COLCHESTER, CT 06415. (#3475-2).

ENFIELD

BICENTENNIAL SERVICE CENTER FOR CONN SCHOOLS. CLEARINGHOUSE FOR CONNECTICUT SCHOOLS RUN BY STUDENTS AND FACULTY OF ENRICO FERMI HIGH SCHOOL IN ENFIELD AS PART OF THE 'FERMI '76' MODEL PROGRAM TO ASSIST SCHOOLS IN BICENTENNIAL PLANNING. (ST-WIDE). MARK NADEAU, DIRECTOR, FERMI '76; CONNECTICUT ARBC; 59 S PROSPECT ST; HARTFORD, CT 06106. (#2203).

HOUSE RESTORATION OF ENFIELD, CONNECTICUT. RESTORATION OF LATE 1700 PERIOD HOME TO HOUSE PERMANENT & ROTATING EXHIBITS OF HISTORICAL SIGNIFICANCE. (LOCAL). MRS MILO WILCOX, CHAIRMAN; MARTHA A PARSONS MEMORIAL TRUST; 1387 ENFIELD ST; ENFIELD, CT 06082. (#5963).

APR 20, '75. REENACTMENT OF ENFIELD'S CALL TO REVOLUTION. OPENING, EXHIBIT. (LOCAL). MRS MILO WILCOX, CHAIRMAN; MARTHA A PARSONS MEMORIAL TRUST; 1387 ENFIELD ST; ENFIELD, CT 06082. (#5963-501).

OCT 8, '75. FILM, 'PROFILE '76'. EXHIBIT AT FERMI HIGH SCHOOL, MAPLE ST. (LOCAL). EDWARD ALLEN, CHMN; ENFIELD BICENTENNIAL COMMISSION; 18 SCHOOL ST; ENFIELD, CT 06082. (#102356-1).

ESSEX

SCHOONER RACE ON CONNECTICUT RIVER. CONNECTICUT RIVER SCHOONER RACE, REMINISCENT OF THE PAST. (LOCAL). ROBERT WILKERSON, CHAIRMAN; ESSEX BICENTENNIAL COMMITTEE; ESSEX, CT 06426. (#12250). **ARBA GRANTEE.**

TWENTY DECADES OF FREEDOM IN ESSEX, CT. TO PLANT TWENTY TREES FROM ONE END OF TOWN TO THE OTHER; EACH DEDICATED TO A DECADE OF FREEDOM. (LOCAL). ROBERT WILKERSON, CHAIRMAN; ESSEX BICENTENNIAL COMMITTEE; ESSEX, CT 06426. (#12249). **ARBA GRANTEE.**

SEPT 15 - 17, '75. A THREE-DAY SCHOONER RACE. SCHOONER RACE ON CONNECTICUT RIVER. CONNECTICUT RIVER SCHOONER RACE, REMINISCENT OF THE PAST. (LOCAL). ROBERT WILKERSON; ESSEX BICENTENNIAL COMMITTEE; ESSEX, CT 06426. (#12250-501).

FAIRFIELD

ART WORK AND BOOK - FAIRFIELD, CT. 14 LITHOGRAPHIC REPRODUCTIONS OF 'MARINES IN THE REVOLUTION' AND A BOOK, 'MARINES IN THE REVOLUTION', ARE IN THE FAIRFIELD PUBLIC LIBRARY. (LOCAL). LT COL C L OSBORNE, COORDINATOR; VOLUNTEER TRAINING UNIT 1-17, U S MARINE CORPS; 454 VERNA HILL RD; FAIRFIELD, CT 06430. (#29012).

BICENTENNIAL PARTICIPATORY MUSEUM - FAIRFIELD, CT. MUSEUM IN WHICH CHILDREN EXPERIENCE REVOLUTIONARY PERIOD LIFE. (LOCAL). ELIZABETH FITZPATRICK, CHAIRPERSON; FAIRFIELD UNIV; N BENSON RD; FAIRFIELD, CT 06430. (#24133).

BICYCLE TRAILS IN FAIRFIELD, CT. TWO OR MORE TRAILS TO BE MARKED THROUGH FAIRFIELD'S HISTORICAL DISTRICT. (LOCAL). JOHN LEBEDEVITCH, PROJ DIRECTOR; FAIRFIELD JAYCEES; 215 JENIFORD RD; FAIRFIELD, CT 06430. (#13330).

COMMUNICATION ADVANCES - LECTURE & PANEL DISCUSSIONS. SEMINAR. (LOCAL). ELIZABETH FITZPATRICK; FAIRFIELD UNIV; N BENSON RD; FAIRFIELD, CT 06430. (#107824-1). **(??).**

'DOWN IN VILLA PARK' - FAIRFIELD, CT. CHILDREN'S HISTORY BOOK ON THE HUNGARIANS IN FAIRFIELD POINTS TO THE CONTRIBUTIONS THEY HAVE MADE DURING THE PAST 200 YEARS. (LOCAL). STEVEN SZONDY, TREASURER; COLLEGIAL SOCIETY OF HUNGARIAN VETERANS, CT BRANCH INC; 901 KINGS HIGHWAY; FAIRFIELD, CT 06430. (#25349). **ARBA GRANTEE.**

FAIRFIELD IN PHOTOGRAPHS, CT. PHOTO-ARCHIVE OF EARLY PICTURES OF FAIRFIELD TO BE EXHIBITED AND PUBLISHED LATER IN BOOK FORM. (LOCAL). MR BRUCE KERSHNER, PROJ DIRECTOR; FAIRFIELD PUBLIC LIBRARY; 1080 OLD POST RD; FAIRFIELD, CT 06430. (#13328).

PARK BEAUTIFICATION, FAIRFIELD, CT. IMPROVEMENT AND BEAUTIFICATION OF STURGES WILDLIFE PARK. (LOCAL). MRS FRANK THOMPSON, PROJ DIRECTOR; FAIRFIELD WOMEN'S CLUB; 1090 GALLOPING HILL RD; FAIRFIELD, CT 06430. (#13326).

PARTICIPATORY CHILDREN'S MUSEUM - FAIRFIELD, CT. THE MUSEUM WILL PROVIDE AN OPPORTUNITY FOR CHILDREN TO EXPERIENCE THE REVOLUTIONARY PERIOD BY PARTICIPATING IN THE MUSEUM SETTING. (ST-WIDE). BENA KALLICK, DIRECTOR; TEACHERS' CENTER AT FAIRFIELD; N BENSON RD; FAIRFIELD, CT 06430. (#12967).

REDECORATION OF THE OLD ACADEMY, FAIRFIELD, CT. AN EXHIBIT OF EARLY 19TH CENTURY SCHOOL FURNITURE AND RELATED OBJECTS. ALSO REPAIR 96 TOMBSTONES IN THE OLD BURYING GROUND AS PART OF DAR CHAPTER PROJECT. (LOCAL). MRS HUGO KENYON, PROJ DIRECTOR; EUNICE DENNIE BURR CHAPTER OF NSDAR; 15 OSBORN PL; SOUTHPORT, CT 06490. (#13325).

ROLE OF NEWSPAPERS IN THE REVOLUTION - SEMINAR. CHARACTER, STANCE & EFFECT OF CONNECTICUT NEWSPAPERS IN COMMUNICATING REVOLUTIONARY VIEW OF COLONISTS. (LOCAL). ELIZABETH FITZPATRICK; FAIRFIELD UNIV; N BENSON RD; FAIRFIELD, CT 06430. (#107910-1). **(??).**

TREE PLANTING IN FAIRFIELD, CT. TREES WILL BE PLANTED ALONG POST RD & BLACK ROCK TURNPIKE IN FAIRFIELD. (LOCAL). EDWARD GLEASON, PROJ DIRECTOR; CHAMBER OF COMMERCE; 1597 POST RD; FAIRFIELD, CT 06430. (#13329).

WORLD PRESS COVERAGE OF JULY 4, 1976 - CT. BOOK ANALYSING AND INTERPRETING EDITORIALS AND OTHER NEWS OF U S BICENTENNIAL DAY. (LOCAL). ELIZABETH FITZPATRICK, CHAIRPERSON; FAIRFIELD UNIV; N BENSON RD; FAIRFIELD, CT 06430. (#24134).

MAY 1 - JUNE 1, '75. MUSIC WORKSHOP TO REFLECT BLACK HERITAGE & TRADITION. FESTIVAL. (LOCAL). GEORGE E PIPKIN; HALL NEIGHBORHOOD HOUSE; 52 GREEN ST; FAIRFIELD, CT 06608. (#7347-501).

AUG 1, '75. BLACK WRITERS WORKSHOP. FESTIVAL. (LOCAL). GEORGE E PIPKIN; HALL NEIGHBORHOOD HOUSE; 52 GREEN ST; FAIRFIELD, CT 06608. (#7347-502).

SEPT 22, '75. 'THE CRUCIBLE'. LIVE PERFORMANCE AT FAIRFIELD UNIVERSITY PLAYHOUSE. (LOCAL). ELIZABETH FITZPATRICK; FAIRFIELD UNIV BICENTENNIAL COMMITTEE; N BENSON RD; FAIRFIELD, CT 06430. (#107389-2).

JAN 30, '76. SLIDE LECTURE - LIVING AMERICAN SCULPTORS. SEMINAR AT CAMPUS CENTER MEZZANINE. (LOCAL). ELIZABETH FITZPATRICK; FAIRFIELD UNIV BICENTENNIAL COMMITTEE; N BENSON RD; FAIRFIELD, CT 06430. (#107389-1).

FEB 16, '76. 'THE CHANGING FACE OF THE AMERICAN THEATRE' - CLIVE BARNES LECTURE. SEMINAR AT CAMPUS CENTER OAK ROOM. (LOCAL). ELIZABETH FITZPATRICK; FAIRFIELD UNIV BICENTENNIAL COMMITTEE; N BENSON RD; FAIRFIELD, CT 06430. (#107389-5).

MAR 10, '76. LECTURE ON HEALTH IN AMERICA. SEMINAR AT CAMPUS CENTER OAK ROOM. (LOCAL). ELIZABETH FITZPATRICK; FAIRFIELD UNIV BICENTENNIAL COMMITTEE; N BENSON RD; FAIRFIELD, CT 06430. (#107389-6).

MAR 15, '76. 'JOHN & ABIGALE ADAMS - THE EARLY AMERICANS' - PLAY. LIVE PERFORMANCE AT CAMPUS CENTER OAK ROOM. (LOCAL). ELIZABETH FITZPATRICK; FAIRFIELD UNIV BICENTENNIAL COMMITTEE; N BENSON RD; FAIRFIELD, CT 06430. (#107389-3).

MAR 20, '76. BICENTENNIAL BALL. TO RAISE FUNDS TO PRESENT THE TOWN OF FAIRFIELD WITH A BICENTENNIAL GIFT. AT OAK ROOM FAIRFIELD UNIVERSITY. (LOCAL). MRS JEANNE OAKS, DIR; FIFTH WHEEL CLUB OF FAIRFIELD; 70 THORNHILL RD; FAIRFIELD, CT 06430. (#103027-2).

MAR 30, '76. 'THE EXECUTIVE REDCOAT BAND' & 'THE YANKEE TUNESMITHS'. LIVE PERFORMANCE AT GONZAGA AUDITORIUM. (LOCAL). ELIZABETH FITZPATRICK; FAIRFIELD UNIV BICENTENNIAL COMMITTEE; N BENSON RD; FAIRFIELD, CT 06430. (#107389-4).

APR 8, '76. 'FREEDOM TO GROW - FOOD IN AMERICA' - LECTURE. SEMINAR AT CAMPUS CENTER OAK ROOM. (LOCAL). ELIZABETH FITZPATRICK; FAIRFIELD UNIV BICENTENNIAL COMMITTEE; N BENSON RD; FAIRFIELD, CT 06430. (#107389-7).

MAY 12, '76. HISTORIC HOUSE AND GARDEN TOUR. PROCEEDS TO A LOCAL BICENTENNIAL LASTING PROJECT. AT FAIRFIELD SOUTHPORT AREA. (LOCAL). MRS ROBERT JOHNSON, DIR; JUNIOR WOMENS CLUB OF FAIRFIELD; 169 CARRIAGE DR; SOUTHPORT, CT 06490. (#103027-1).

MAY 12 - 22, '76. DOGWOOD FESTIVAL. THE BLOSSOMS OF 30, 000 DOGWOOD TREES PROVIDE THE BACKGROUND FOR A NEW ENGLAND CHURCH FAIR. AT GREENFIELD HILL. (LOCAL). RUTH DENNLER, PRES; GREENFIELD HILL CONGREGATIONAL CHURCH WOMEN'S GUILD; 1597 POST RD; FAIRFIELD, CT 06430. (#103416-316).

MAY 15 - OCT 15, '76. OGDEN HOUSE EXHIBITS. A SERIES OF SPECIAL EVENTS BASED ON LOCAL HISTORY. (LOCAL). FAIRFIELD HIST SOCIETY; FAIRFIELD HISTORICAL SOCIETY; 636 OLD POST RD; FAIRFIELD, CT 06430. (#13327-1).

JUNE 12 - 13, '76. AN OLD FASHIONED COUNTRY FAIR. THE FAIR WILL HONOR HEROINE JULIETTE LOW. AT FAIRFIELD UNIV, N BENSON RD. (LOCAL). MRS RUSSELL HOLMES, CHMN; HOUSATONIC GIRL SCOUTS COUNCIL; 35 HUNTINGTON TPK; BRIDGEPORT, CT 06610. (#102949-1).

JULY 4 - SEPT 21, '76. THE FAIRFIELD COLONIAL SINGERS RECITAL. SERIES OF FOLK AND PERIOD MUSIC RECITALS INCLUDING PERIOD INSTRUMENTS & CHORALE GROUP IN PERIOD COSTUME. AT FAIRFIELD COLONIAL SINGERS, INC.. (LOCAL). MRS BARRY BROWN; AMERICAN PLAYWRITES THEATRE, INC; 110 ORIOLE LANE; FAIRFIELD, CT 06430. (#13331-1).

FALLS VILLAGE

BOOK ON THE HISTORY OF CANAAN, CT - FALLS VILLAGE. HISTORY OF THE TOWN OF CANAAN DURING THE REVOLUTION. (LOCAL). H W FELTON, CHAIRMAN; FALLS VILLAGE BICENTENNIAL COMMITTEE; PROSPECT ST; FALLS VILLAGE, CT 06031. (#29679).

CANAAN, CT DURING THE REVOLUTION - FALLS VILLAGE. DRAMATIC READING ON THE HISTORY OF CANAAN DURING THE REVOLUTION. (LOCAL). H W FELTON, CHAIRMAN; FALLS VILLAGE BICENTENNIAL COMMITTEE & HISTORICAL SOCIETY; PROSPECT ST; FALLS VILLAGE, CT 06031. (#29678).

FALLS VILLAGE COOKBOOK, CT. A COOKBOOK PREPARED BY SENIOR CITIZENS. (LOCAL). H W FELTON, CHAIRMAN; FALLS VILLAGE BICENTENNIAL COMMITTEE; PROSPECT ST; FALLS VILLAGE, CT 06031. (#29680).

FESTIVAL BICENT DAY. INCLUDED ECUMENICAL CHURCH SERVICE, SPORTS, MUSICAL PROGRAM & FAMILY PICNIC. (LOCAL). HAROLD W FELTON, CHMN; BICENTENNIAL COMMITTEE OF FALLS VILLAGE; PROSPECT ST; FALLS VILLAGE, CT 06031. (#200008-43).

PARADE PARTICIPATION IN FALLS VILLAGE, CT. PARADE AND FLOATS IN BICENT CELEBRATION AND FIREMEN'S CARNIVAL. (LOCAL). HAROLD FELTON, CHAIRMAN; FALLS VILLAGE BICENTENNIAL COMMITTEE; PROSPECT ST; FALLS VILLAGE, CT 06031. (#29676).

PLANTED CHARTER OAK TREE IN FALLS VILLAGE, CT. PLANTED CHARTER OAK TREE GIVEN BY STATE. (LOCAL). HOWARD FELTON, CHAIRMAN; FALLS VILLAGE BICENTENNIAL COMMITTEE; PROSPECT ST; FALLS VILLAGE, CT 06031. (#29677).

REDEDICATION OF CENTENNIAL TREE & ERECTION OF MONUMENT. CEREMONY. (LOCAL). H W FELTON, CHMN; BICENTENNIAL COMMITTEE OF FALLS VILLAGE; PROSPECT ST; FALLS VILLAGE, CT 06031. (#200008-250).

SCHOOL CELEBRATION IN FALLS VILLAGE, CT. EACH GRADE IN SCHOOL PRESENTED PROGAM OF OWN DESIGN AND CREATION, RELATING TO AN AMER HISTORICAL EVENT; GIRL SCOUTS PLANTED 13 BLACK WALNUT TREES. (LOCAL). HAROLD FELTON, CHAIRMAN; FALLS VILLAGE BICENTENNIAL COMMITTEE; PROSPECT ST; FALLS VILLAGE, CT 06031. (#29675).

FALLS VILLAGE — CONTINUED

MAY 1, '76. ARTS AND CRAFT FAIR. BETWEEN 40 & 50 CRAFTSMEN WILL DISPLAY & DEMONSTRATE THEIR SKILLS. AT HOUSATONIC VALLEY REGIONAL HIGH SCHOOL. (LOCAL). JOYCE DALEY, DIRECTOR; CORNWALL CHILD CENTER, INC; TOWN RD; W CORNWALL, CT 06796. (#106813-1).

FARMINGTON

BICENTENNIAL NEEDLEWORK CONTEST. PROFESSIONAL JUDGING OF NEEDLE WORK EMPHASIZING THE BICENTENNIAL. CONTEST OPEN TO RESIDENTS OF FARMINGTON, PLAINVILLE & AVON. (LOCAL). BARBARA EYRE, CHAIRMAN; FARMINGTON BICENTENNIAL COMMITTEE; 30 HIGH ST; FARMINGTON, CT 06032. (#107396-1).

CONVERSION OF 18TH CENTURY DWELLING - CT. RENOVATION OF A HANDSOME 18TH CENTURY DWELLING WHICH IS ADJACENT TO THE TOWN HALL AND HIGH SCHOOL TO HOUSE CERTAIN SOCIAL SERVICE AND OTHER ACTIVITIES. (LOCAL). RICHARD M BISSELL, JR, SECRETARY; FARMINGTON BICENTENNIAL COMMITTEE; THE EXCHANGE, FARMINGTON AVE; FARMINGTON, CT 06032. (#18677). **ARBA GRANTEE.**

FARMINGTON COMMEMORATIVE QUILTS AND PILLOWS, CT. 90 VOLUNTEER WOMEN WILL APPLIQUE QUILT BLOCKS OF FARMINGTON SCENES, HOUSES AND PEOPLE FOR INCLUSION INTO TWO QUILTS AND PILLOWS TO BE RAFFLED FOR SUPPORT OF BICENTENNIAL PROJECTS. (LOCAL). RUTH DE GROFF, CHAIRMAN; FARMINGTON BICENTENNIAL COMMITTEE; POPLAR HILL DR; FARMINGTON, CT 06032. (#24372).

FARMINGTON HERITAGE TRAIL, CT. AN EDUCATIONAL PROJECT INVOLVING A SLIDE PRESENTATION, HERITAGE TRAIL GUIDEBOOK, BOOK OF TEN TRADING TALES, THE AFRICAN PRINCE. THE DECLARATION OF INDEPENDENCE TODAY & TEACHER'S GUIDEBOOK. (LOCAL). FRANK AMARA, PROJ DIRECTOR; NOAH WALLACE FUND COMMITTEE; SCHOOL ST; FARMINGTON, CT 06032. (#24371).

FARMINGTON WALKING TOUR MAP AND BROCHURE, CT. PLACES OF HISTORIC INTEREST BRIEFLY DESCRIBED, SOME PICTURED, ALL LOCATIONS DENOTED ON MAPS OF BOTH FARMINGTON AND UNIONVILLE. (LOCAL). JANICE RIEMER, CURATOR; FARMINGTON MUSEUM; HIGH ST; FARMINGTON, CT 06032. (#24373).

WRCH-FM RADIO BICENTENNIAL PROGRAMMING - NBMRP. PRINCIPAL EFFORT WAS IN-DEPTH 30 MINUTE PROGRAM AIRED WEEKLY ENTITLED 'BICENTENNIAL CHRONICLE'. PROGRAM WAS DESIGNED TO PROMOTE THE BICENTENNIAL ACTIVITIES OF CONNECTICUT'S 169 TOWNS & CITIES. (ST-WIDE). LEE MANSON, BICENTENNIAL COORDINATOR; RADIO STATION WRCH-FM; BIRDSEYE RD; FARMINGTON, CT 06032. (#27864).

MAY 15, '76. FARMINGTON BICENTENNIAL BALL. BLACK TIE OR COSTUME. AT THE EXCHANGE, FARMINGTON AVE; PARKING AVAILABLE. (LOCAL). ANN DEMEUSY, COORD; FARMINGTON BICENTENNIAL COMMITTEE; 76 SYLVAN AVE; UNIONVILLE, CT 06085. (#106946-3).

MAY 16, '76. EXHIBIT OF FARMINGTON HISTORY, INTRODUCTION OF WALKING TOUR BROCHURE. FARMINGTON WALKING TOUR MAP AND BROCHURE PREPARED BY JANICE REIMER, CURATOR OF THE FARMINGTON MUSEUM, STANLEY-WHITMAN HOUSE, HIGH ST. AT FARMINGTON VILLAGE LIBRARY, MAIN AND CHURCH STREETS - PARK IN STREET. (LOCAL). ARLINE WHITAKER, COORD; FRIENDS OF THE VILLAGE LIBRARY; HIGH ST; FARMINGTON, CT 06032. (#106946-4).

MAY 21 - 22, '76. FARMINGTON VILLAGE HOUSE AND GARDEN TOUR. TOUR AT FARMINGTON VILLAGE. (LOCAL). BETTY COYKENDALL, COORD; FARMINGTON JUNIOR WOMEN'S CLUB, WOMEN'S CLUB, FARMINGTON GARDEN CLUB; 15 WHISPERING ROD RD; UNIONVILLE, CT 06085. (#106946-5).

MAY 29, '76. FARMINGTON FUN - HOT AIR BALLOONS, SOFTBALL, AAU MARATHON AND GAMES. FAIR AT TUNXIS MEAD RECREATION AREA - MEADOW ROAD - SIGNS POSTED FOR PARKING. (LOCAL). BRUCE TILL, COORD; FARMINGTON BICENTENNIAL COMMITTEE; FARMINGTON TOWN HALL; FARMINGTON, CT 06032. (#106946-2).

JULY 4, '76. COMMEMORATIVE ACADEMIC CHURCH SERVICE - FARMINGTON MEETING HOUSE. ADDRESS TO BE DELIVERED BY WILMARTH LEWIS, INTERNATIONALLY HONORED FARMINGTON HISTORIAN, NOTED FOR HIS LIBRARY AND COLLECTION OF HORACE WALPOLE HOUSED HERE IN FARMINGTON AND PART OF YALE UNIVERSITY. AT FIRST CHURCH OF CHRIST, MAIN ST, FARMINGTON VILLAGE. (LOCAL). WILLIAM LIDGERWOOD, COORD; FARMINGTON HISTORICAL SOCIETY; 29 MOUNTAIN SPRING RD; FARMINGTON, CT 06032. (#106946-1).

OCT 18 - NOV 6, '76. FACES OF FARMINGTON '76 - PHOTOGRAPHY & CREATIVE WRITING CONTEST. PHOTOGRAPHY & CREATIVE WRITING CONTEST RESULTING IN THE PUBLICATION OF A PICTORIAL ESSAY OF FARMINGTON IN 1976. (LOCAL). ANDREW S BRAGET, CHAIRMAN; FARMINGTON BICENTENNIAL COMMITTEE; 221 MAIN ST; FARMINGTON, CT 06032. (#107396-2).

ITCHVILLE

APR 25, '76. BICENTENNIAL SHOW AND FAIR. FAIR AT FIELDS MEMORIAL SCHOOL, ROUTE 163. (LOCAL). MARY CROUCH; BOZRAH BICENTENNIAL COMMISSION; BASHAN HILL RD; ITCHVILLE, CT 06334. (#200008-23).

FRANKLIN

BICENTENNIAL QUILT, FRANKLIN, CT. 30 SQUARES OF QUILT DEPICT HISTORICAL AND PHYSICAL FEATURES OF TOWN OF FRANKLIN; MADE BY FRANKLIN RESIDENTS. (LOCAL). MRS CLARA H BECKWITH, CHAIRMAN; SENIOR CITIZENS & FRANKLIN ARBC; RFD #1; N FRANKLIN, CT 06254. (#32691).

BICENTENNIAL SCROLLS, FRANKLIN, CT. SCROLLS SIGNED BY TOWN RESIDENTS PRESENTED TO WAGONMASTER, BICENTENNIAL WAGON TRAIN DESTINED FOR VALLEY FORGE; INCLUDED IN PERMANENT NATIONAL BICENTENNIAL MUSEUM EXHIBIT. (LOCAL). BARBARA PHILIPP, CHAIRMAN; FRANKLIN ARBC; PAUTIPAUG LANE, RFD 1; N FRANKLIN, CT 06254. (#32690).

BICENTENNIAL TIME CAPSULE, FRANKLIN, CT. CAPSULE DONATED BY FRANKLIN LIONS CLUB. MATERIALS COLLECTED FROM INDIVIDUALS & COMMUNITY ORGANIZATIONS TO BE SEALED & BURIED FALL 1976 FOR OPENING AT NATION'S TRICENTENNIAL, 2076. (LOCAL). REGINALD PARADIN, CHAIRMAN; FRANKLIN LIONS CLUB & FRANKLIN ARBC; SOUTHGATE CIRCLE, RFD 1; N FRANKLIN, CT 06254. (#32693).

FRANKLIN 1976 BICENTENNIAL CALENDAR - CT. FEATURES ORIGINAL PEN & INK DRAWINGS BY FRANKLIN ARTISTS; SCENES SIGNIFICANT IN TOWN'S PAST & PRESENT; NOTATIONS ON DATES PRESENTLY & HISTORICALLY IMPORTANT TO TOWN; INCLUDES SHORT HISTORY OF TOWN. (LOCAL). BARBARA PHILIPP, CHAIRMAN; FRANKLIN ARBC; PAUTIPAUG LANE, RFD 1; N FRANKLIN, CT 06254. (#32688).

LITERATURE, ARTS & CRAFTS CONTEST, FRANKLIN, CT. GRADES K-12, 107 PARTICIPANTS, 118 ENTRIES; SAVINGS BONDS AWARDED AS 1ST PRIZE; CATEGORIES: LITERATURE- ESSAY, STORIES, POEMS; CRAFTS, HANDCRAFTS. (LOCAL). BARBARA PHILIPP, CHAIRMAN; FRANKLIN ARBC; PAUTIPAUG LANE, RFD 1; N FRANKLIN, CT 06254. (#32689).

PLANTING OF CHARTER OAK SEEDLING, FRANKLIN, CT. CHARTER OAK SEEDLING DONATED TO TOWN BY STATE OF CONN & PLANTED BY SUMMBER BIBLE SCHOOL CHILDREN ON GROUNDS OF FRANKLIN CONGREGATIONAL CHURCH. (LOCAL). BARBARA Z PHILIPP, CHAIRMAN; FRANKLIN ARBC; PAUTIPAUG LANE, RFD 1; N FRANKLIN, CT 06254. (#32692).

PLANTING OF WHITE OAK TREE - FRANKLIN, CT. GIRL SCOUTS OFFERED PROGRAM DESCRIBING SIGNIFICANCE OF THE OAK TREE IN THE HISTORY OF CONNECTICUT FOLLOWED BY PLANTING OF A WHITE OAK ON THE GROUNDS OF THE TOWN HALL. PLANTED MAY 3, 1975. (LOCAL). BARBARA PHILIPP, CHAIRMAN; FRANKLIN BICENTENNIAL COMMISSION; PAUTIDAUG LANE, RFD 1; FRANKLIN, CT 06254. (#31985).

MAY 26, '75. MEMORIAL DAY OBSERVANCE. PATRIOTIC CEREMONIES AT TWO LOCAL CEMETERIES. PARADE TO FRANKLIN CONGREGATIONAL CHURCH; FORMAL PATRIOTIC PROGRAM AT CHURCH WITH CITIZEN PARRTICIPATION; COMMUNITY LUNCHEON & FELLLOWSHIP. AT FRANKLIN CEMETERIES; FRANKLIN CONGREGATIONAL CHURCH. (LOCAL). BARBARA PHILIPP, CHMN; FRANKLIN ARBC & TOWN OF FRANKLIN; PAUTIPAUG LN, RFD 1; N FRANKLIN, CT 06254. (#200008-66).

OCT 4, '75. 'WEST FARMS' BICENTENNIAL BALL. COLONIAL DRESS REQUESTED-INCL COLONIAL STYLE BUFFET & DECORATIONS REMINISCENT OF FRANKLIN'S EARLY DAYS AS WEST FARMS OF NORWICHALSO LIVE BAND-FESTIVAL USA THEME. AT FRANKLIN TOWN HALL. (LOCAL). THOMAS SHAKUN, COORD; FRANKLIN ARBC; OLD BALTIC RD, RFD 1; N FRANKLIN, CT 06254. (#200008-69).

NOV 16, '75. BICENTENNIAL EXHIBIT. THEME 'A PAST TO REMEMBER A FUTURE TO MOLD'-APPROX 50 EXHIBITS INCL: 'COLONIAL BAKE SHOPPE'; MOVIES & SLIDES OF OTHER BICENT ACTIVITIES. AT FRANKLIN ELEMENTARY SCHOOL. (LOCAL). BARBARA PHILIPP, CHMN; FRANKLIN ARBC; PAUTIPAUG LN, RFD 1; N FRANKLIN, CT 06254. (#200008-68).

APR 25, '76. SCHOOL-WIDE LITERATURE, ARTS & CRAFTS CONTEST. FOR CHILDREN K THRU 12. 107 PARTICIPANTS, 118 ENTRIES; BICENT THEME. CATEGORIES: LITERATURE-ESSAYS, STORIES, POEMS; ART-ANY MEDIUM; CRAFTS-NEEDLE & HANDICRAFTS. JUDGES WERE PROFESSORS FROM UNIV OF CONN WHO VOLUNTEERED THEIR SERVICES - SUPPORT OF TOWNSPEOPLE. AT FRANKLIN ELEMENTARY SCHOOL-RT 207. (LOCAL). ANN WARD-BARBARA PHILIPP; FRANKLIN ARBC; PAUTIPAUG LN, RFD 1; N FRANKLIN, CT 06254. (#200008-67).

MAY 3, '76. DEDICATION OF FRANKLIN HISTORICAL PLAQUE. PLAQUE TRACES FOUNDING OF FRANKLIN TOWN. INCLUDED SONGS, INVOCATION AND SPEECHES. AT FRANKLIN TOWN HALL. (LOCAL). BARBARA PHILLIP, CHMN; FRANKLIN BICENTENNIAL COMMISSION & HISTORICAL SOCIETY; PAUTIPAUG LN, RFD 1; N FRANKLIN, CT 06254. (#200008-261).

JUNE 30, '76. PRESENTATION OF BICENTENNIAL FLAG & CITATION. JOHN SABINO OF AMERICAN REVOLUTION BICENTENNIAL COMMISSION PRESENTED FLAG & CERTIFICATE TO FRANKLIN FIRST SELECTMAN. SPEAKERS FROM NATIONAL, STATE, & TOWN BICENTENNIAL COMMISSION. AT FRANKLIN TOWN HALL. (LOCAL). BARBARA Z PHILIPP, CHMN; CONN BICENTENNIAL COMMISSION & FRANKLIN BICENTENNIAL COMM; PAUTIPAUG LANE, RFD 1; N FRANKLIN, CT 06254. (#200008-247).

JULY 4, '76. JULY 4TH FRANKLIN BICENTENNIAL CELEBRATION. PROGRAM INCLUDED: PARADE, PATRIOTIC PROGRAM, COMMUNITY PICNIC WITH ACTIVITIES FOR CHILDREN & ADULTS. AT FRANKLIN LIONS RECREATIONAL FIELD-RT 207. (LOCAL). BARBARA Z PHILIPP, CHMN; FRANKLIN ARBC; PAUTIPAUG LN RFD 1; N FRANKLIN, CT 06254. (#200008-64).

OCT 10, '76. FRANKLIN BICENTENNIAL QUILT SHOW. QUILT SHOW EXHIBITED FRANKLIN BICENTENNIAL QUILT AS WELL AS MANY OTHERS MADE BY TOWN & AREA RESIDENTS; REFRESHMENTS SERVED. AT FRANKLIN TOWN HALL. (LOCAL). JEAN CARBONI, COORD; SENIOR CITIZENS-QUILT COMMITTEE-FRANKLIN ARBC; WHIPPOORWILL HOLLOW RD; N FRANKLIN, CT 06254. (#200008-65).

GLASTONBURY

CONNECTICUT BICENTENNIAL HOT AIR BALLOON. HOT AIR BALLOON TO APPEAR AT BICENTENNIAL EVENTS THROUGHOUT THE STATE DURING 1976. (ST-WIDE). WILLIAM MINO, PROJ DIRECTOR; BCTOS; 60 WILLIAMS ST; GLASTONBURY, CT 06033. (#25315). **ARBA GRANTEE.**

OPERATION IRISH-AMERICANS IN THE U S, CT. PROJECT INVOLVES THE CONTRIBUTION OF IRISH & IRISH AMERICANS TO THE GROWTH OF AMERICA. (ST-WIDE). MARGARET RILEY, SECRETARY; CT IRISH-AMERICAN BICENTENNIAL COMMITTEE; 132 COMMERCE ST; GLASTONBURY, CT 06033. (#23827). **ARBA GRANTEE.**

RESTORATION OF WELLES-CHAPMAN TAVERN, CT. RESTORATION OF EXTERIOR OF TAVERN BUILT IN 1776 FOR USE AS COLONIAL LIFE STYLE MUSEUM. THE MUSEUM WILL HOUSE 3000 ARTIFACTS FROM THE ACTUAL TAVERN SITE. (LOCAL). RICHARD BALLARD, CHAIRMAN TAVERN PROJ; HISTORICAL SOCIETY OF GLASTONBURY & BICENTENNIAL COMMITTEE; BOX 46; GLASTONBURY, CT 06033. (#17093). **ARBA GRANTEE.**

18TH CENTURY PRESERVATION IN GLASTONBURY, CONN. RELOCATION OF WELLES TAVERN TO ORIGINAL SITE. (LOCAL). RICHARD BALLARD, PRESIDENT; GLASTONBURY HISTORICAL SOCIETY; 1944 MAIN ST; GLASTONBURY, CT 06033. (#5962).

OCT 4, '75. OLD-FASHIONED BEAN SUPPER IN GLASTONBURY, CT. FOOD AND BEVERAGES SIMILAR TO THE KIND SERVED TO EARLY GLASTONBURY SETTLERS WILL BE SERVED & PERIOD DRESS WILL BE WORN. (LOCAL). BERNICE C BERGERON; AMERICAN LEGION AUXILIARY; 1361 MAIN ST; GLASTONBURY, CT 06033. (#10222-1).

MAR 17, '76. OPERATION IRISH-AMERICANS IN THE U S. EXHIBIT, FESTIVAL, PARADE, TOUR. (ST-WIDE). MARGARET RILEY, SEC; CT IRISH-AMERICAN BICENTENNIAL COMMITTEE; 132 COMMERCE ST; GLASTONBURY, CT 06033. (#23827-1).

APR 10, '76. GLASTONBURY BICENTENNIAL BALL. COSTUME DINNER DANCE FEATURING COSTUMES OF COLONIAL TIMES. AT GLASTONBURY HILLS COUNTRY CLUB. (LOCAL). LIZ TYROL; GLASTONBURY JUNIOR WOMEN'S CLUB; 32 HARDIN LA; GLASTONBURY, CT 06033. (#8821-1).

APR 10, '76. HISTORIC HOUSE TOUR. TOUR OF 12 PRIVATE HOMES; CRAFT DEMONSTRATION & SALE; MUSEUM EXHIBITION. 17TH & 18TH CENTURY REFRESHMENTS AND RECIPES AT EACH HOUSE. AT MUSEUM, GREEN ST. (LOCAL). RICHARD BALLARD, CHMN; HISTORICAL SOCIETY OF GLASTONBURY; 2015 MAIN ST; GLASTONBURY, CT 06033. (#5962-4).

GRANBY

COMMEMORATIVE ORATIONS, 1786-1861 - PROJ OF CT. PUBLICATION OF 4TH OF JULY SELECTED ORATIONS RESEARCHED FROM ORIGINAL MANUSCRIPTS, SPEECH DRAFTS & SOURCES NOT PREVIOUSLY PUBLISHED IN COLLECTED FORMAT, TO BENEFIT SBHS REFERENCE & EDUCATION CENTER. (LOCAL). HARRY R LANSER, PRESIDENT; SALMON BROOK HISTORICAL SOCIETY; 208 SALMON BROOK ST; GRANBY, CT 06035. (#12009). **ARBA GRANTEE.**

JULY 4, '76. FIRE WORKS FESTIVAL. FESTIVAL AT SALMON BROOK PARK. (LOCAL). J R GREENWOOD; BICENTENNIAL CELEBRATION COMMITTEE; TOWN HALL; GRANBY, CT 06035. (#50440-1).

GREENWICH

BICENTENNIAL EXHIBIT - PROJ OF GREENWICH, CT. EXHIBIT WILL FEATURE PHOTOS & PRINTS STRESSING THE HERITAGE & PRACTICE OF SELF-GOVERNMENT. SHOW OPENS AT GREENWICH LIBRARY JAN '76 THEN SHOWN IN OTHER LOCATINS; ALSO MADE INTO A PERMANENT SLIDE SHOW. (LOCAL). MRS F C TANNER, PRESIDENT; THE HISTORICAL SOCIETY OF THE TOWN OF GREENWICH, INC; 39 STRICKLAND RD; COS COB, CT 06807. (#13657). **ARBA GRANTEE.**

CARTOON HISTORY OF AMERICA, GREENWICH, CT. 100 POSTER SIZED DISPLAYS OF U S DEVELOPMENT, AS SEEN THROUGH EYES OF THE NATION'S CARTOONISTS SINCE 1776. THE EXHIBIT WILL BE DUPLICATED FOR TRAVEL; ALSO AVAILABLE ON SLIDES FOR SYNDICATION. (NAT'L). MORT WALKER, PRESIDENT; MUSEUM OF CARTOON ART; 384 FIELD PT RD; GREENWICH, CT 06830. (#11883). **ARBA GRANTEE.**

OUTDOOR SCULPTURE EXHIBIT - GREENWICH, CT. AN EXHIBITION OF LARGE SCALE OUTDOOR SCULPTURE BY MAJOR AMERICAN ARTISTS & PURCHASE OF ONE OR MORE OF THE EXHIBITED SCULPTURES FOR PERMANENT INSTALLATION IN PUBLIC PLACES. (LOCAL). MRS JAMES ANDERSON, PROJ DIRECTOR; GREENWICH ARTS COUNCIL; 101 W PUTNAM AVE; GREENWICH, CT 06830. (#16981). **ARBA GRANTEE.**

RESTORATION OF PUTNAM COTTAGE IN GREENWICH, CT. RESTORATION OF EXTERIOR AND INTERIOR OF 17TH CENTURY KNAPPS TAVERN, NOW PUTNAM COTTAGE. PRESERVATION AND MAINTAINANCE AS MUSEUM. (LOCAL). MRS THOMAS KIRKPATRICK, DIRECTOR; THE ISRAEL PUTNAM HOUSE ASSOC; 243 E PUTNAM AVE; GREENWICH, CT 06830. (#9144). **ARBA GRANTEE.**

SLIDES OF OLD PHOTOGRAPHS & DOCUMENTS, CT. EXHIBITS OF OLD PRINTS AND PHOTOGRAPHS, ENLARGED AND DETAILED HISTORIC MAPS OF GREENWICH AND ADJACENT AREA; TO BE REPRODUCED ON SLIDES WITH AUDIO NARRATIVE FOR SHOWING IN SCHOOLS. (LOCAL). MS FREDERICK TANNER, PRESIDENT;

GREENWICH — CONTINUED

HISTORICAL SOCIETY OF THE TOWN OF GREENWICH; 39 STRICKLAND RD; COS COB, CT 06207. (#22108).

JAN 2, '76. GALA OPENING OF SLIDE SHOW ON HERITAGE & PRACTICE OF SELF-GOVERNMENT. EXHIBIT. (LOCAL). MRS F C TANNER, PRESIDENT; THE HISTORICAL SOCIETY OF THE TOWN OF GREENWICH, INC; 39 STRICKLAND RD; COS COB, CT 06807. (#13657-501).

JAN 5 - FEB 5, '76. EXHIBIT OF OLD PHOTOS, PRINTS, MAPS AND DOCUMENTS. ENLARGED DOCUMENTS & DETAILED HISTORICAL MAPS OF GREENWICH & ADJACENT AREA; REPRODUCED ON SLIDES WITH AUDIO NARRATIVE. EXHIBIT WILL INCLUDE COLLECTION OF OLD PHOTOGRAPHS. WILL BE SHOWN AT OTHER LOCALES DURING 1976, AFTER INITIAL EXHIBIT. AT EXHIBIT HALL OF GREENWICH. (LOCAL). MRS FREDERICK C TANNER; THE HISTORICAL SOCIETY OF THE TOWN OF GREENWICH; BUSH-HOLLEY HOUSE, 39 STRICKLAND; COS COB, CT 06807. (#9146-501).

JAN 25 - JULY 4, '76. EXHIBIT OF CARTOONS-A REVIEW OF HISTORY THRU THE CARTOON. EXHIBIT AT MUSEUM OF CARTOON ART, 384 FIELD PT RD, OFF EXIT 3-NE THRUWAY. (LOCAL). MORT WALKER, COORD; MUSEUM OF CARTOON ART; 384 FIELD PT RD; GREENWICH, CT 06830. (#106943-1).

JUNE 5 - OCT 31, '76. OUTDOOR SCULPTURE EXHIBIT. AN EXHIBITION OF LARGE SCALE OUTDOOR SCULPTURE BY MAJOR AMERICAN ARTISTS. (LOCAL). MRS JAMES ANDERSON, DIR; GREENWICH ARTS COUNCIL; 101 W PUTNAM AVE; GREENWICH, CT 06830. (#16981-1).

JULY 2, '76. 'OPERATION SAIL '76'. TEN 'TALL SHIPS' UNDER 200 FEET IN LENGTH WILL ARRIVE IN CAPTAIN'S HARBOR ON FRIDAY. AT CAPTAIN'S HARBOR. (LOCAL). MRS MCCLENACHAN, COORD; COMBINED YACHT CLUBS OF GREENWICH; 55 NORTH ST; GREENWICH, CT 06830. (#106943-4).

JULY 4, '76. ECUMENICAL FESTIVAL OF WORSHIP - OUTDOOR SERVICE. CEREMONY AT GREENWICH HIGH SCHOOL FIELD, HILLSIDE RD. (LOCAL). THE REV PAUL YINGER; GREENWICH FELLOWSHIP OF CLERGY; 1ST CONGRESSIONAL CHURCH; COS COB, CT 06807. (#106943-3).

JULY 4, '76. YACHT CLUBS EXERCISES ON THE SOUND. LOCAL PARADE OF YACHTS AND REVIEW ON SUNDAY, THE 4TH OF JULY. AT 7PM, ALL BOATS ANCHOR OFF OF ISLAND BEACH FOR EVENING EVENTS WHICH INCLUDE 'MUSIC ON THE SOUND', BAND ON A HOUSEBOAT CIRCULATING AMONG OTHER BOATS. AT 9PM, FIREWORKS AT ISLAND BEACH. AT GREENWICH SHORELINE, LONG ISLAND SOUND. (LOCAL). MRS MCCLENACHAN, COORD; COMBINED YACHT CLUBS OF GREENWICH; 55 NORTH ST; GREENWICH, CT 06830. (#106943-2).

GRISWOLD

SECOND CONGREGATIONAL CHURCH YARD SALE. YARD SALE AS A FUNDRAISER FOR THE BICENTENNIAL COMMISSION. (LOCAL). MRS ROBERT ENGEL; SECOND CONGREGATIONAL CHURCH OF GRISWOLD; EAST MAIN ST; JEWETT CITY, CT 06351. (#200008-75).

MAR 4 - OCT 24, '75. 1975 BICENTENNIAL EVENTS IN GRISWOLD. BICENT CERTIFICATE PRESENTED TO THE TOWN 3/4/75; 4/20 OPENED THE BICENT CELEBRATION WITH PARADE, PERFORMANCES BY LOCAL BANDS, ETC.; 10/24 WAS THE 160TH ANNIVERSARY OF THE TOWN. (LOCAL). SAMUEL CATHCART; GRISWOLD BICENTENNIAL COMMISSION; 99 E MAIN ST; JEWETT CITY, CT 06351. (#200008-82).

SEPT 20, '75. BICENTENNIAL SMORGASBORD. SMORGASBORD SPONSORED AS A FUNDRAISER FOR THE BICENT COMMISSION. AT SOULE ST. (LOCAL). MRS MARTHA MELL, CHMN; JEWETT CITY METHODIST LADIES & RUTHIE REBEKAH LODGE #28; SOULE ST; JEWETT CITY, CT 06351. (#200008-78).

MAY 6 - 7, '76. MUSICAL '1776' PERFORMED. THE HIGHLIGHT OF GRISWOLD'S BICENTENNIAL CELEBRATION, THIS MUSICAL HAD ASSISTANCE FROM THE WHOLE COMMUNITY--LOCAL MERCHANTS DONATED MATERIAL FOR COSTUMES; PARENTS MADE COSTUMES; ART CLASSES DID THE PROGRAMS; HAIRDRESSES DONATED WIGS. AT GRISWOLD ELEMENTARY SCHOOL. (LOCAL). MRS JOHN CURRAN; GRISWOLD ELEMENTARY SCHOOL; SLATER AVE; JEWETT CITY, CT 06351. (#200008-80).

MAY 9 - 15, '76. NURSING HOME WEEK OBSERVANCE. PROGRAM INCLUDED VISITING THE SUMMIT CONVALESCENT HOME, AND PRESENTING A SLIDE SHOW, DISCUSSION, AND REFRESHMENTS. (LOCAL). SAMUEL CATHCART, CHMN; GRISWOLD BICENTENNIAL COMMISSION; 99 E MAIN ST; GRISWOLD, CT 06351. (#200008-76).

MAY 16, '76. BETHEL COMMUNITY UNITED METHODIST CHURCH BICENTENNIAL CELEBRATION. CEREMONY AT BETHEL METHODIST CHURCH RT 165. (LOCAL). MS PATRICIA PELTIER; BETHEL METHODIST CHURCH; RFD #3 BOX 216; NORWICH, CT 06360. (#200008-248).

JULY 1 - 30, '76. DAR OPEN HOUSE. WEEKLY EXHIBIT OF REVOLUTIONARY COLONIAL ARTIFACTS. HOSTESSES WEAR COLONIAL DRESS. (LOCAL). MRS GEORGE NORMAN; DAUGHTERS OF THE AMERICAN REVOLUTION; RFD 1; JEWETT CITY, CT 06351. (#200008-81).

SEPT 26, '76. BAPTIST BICENTENNIAL WORSHIP SERVICE. AMERICAN BAPTIST WOMEN SPONSORED THIS WORSHIP SERVICE WHICH HAD A GUEST SPEAKER SHOW SPOKE ON THE BAPTIST HERITAGE. AN EXHIBIT ON BAPTIST LITERATURE AND PHOTOGRAPHS WAS ALSO DISPLAYED. (LOCAL). MRS SAMUEL CATHCART; AMERICAN BAPTIST CHURCH; 99 E MAIN ST; GRISWOLD, CT 06351. (#200008-74).

GROTON

GROTON HISTORY EXCHANGE, CONNECTICUT. 3 VIDEO DOCUMENTARIES & 50 ORAL HISTORIES ON FT GROSWOLD TO BE MADE AVAILABLE. ALSO EFFORTS TO STIMULATE PUBLIC LIBRARIES TO PRODUCE HIST DOCUMENTS & ORGANIZE AN INTER-LIBRARY EXCHANGE NETWORK. (LOCAL). GRETCHEN HAMMERSTEIN, LIBRARY DIRECTOR; GROTON PUBLIC LIBRARY; FORT HILL RD; GROTON, CT 06340. (#8198). **ARBA GRANTEE.**

HISTORICAL MAP PORTFOLIO, GROTON, CT. PUBLISH PORTFOLIO OF HISTORICAL MAPS OF SOUTHEASTERN CONNECTICUT AREA WITH PARTICULAR EMPHASIS ON DEVELOPMENT AND EVOLUTION OF PRESENT-DAY TOWN OF GROTON; DISTRIBUTE AS AWARDS AND BY SALES. (LOCAL). STEPHEN B LEE, CHAIRMAN; GROTON BICENTENNIAL COMMITTEE; TOWN HALL, FORT HILL RD; GROTON, CT 06340. (#13237). **ARBA GRANTEE.**

HISTORY PROGRAMS IN GROTON, CT. ORAL HISTORY PROGRAM AND HISTORIC LECTURE SERIES, VIDEOTAPED FOR USE BY STUDENTS AND OTHER GROTON RESIDENTS. THE PROGRAM WILL SERVE AS A MEANS OF ENHANCING & PRESERVING LOCAL HISTORY. (LOCAL). GRETCHEN HAMMERSTEIN, LIBRARY DIRECTOR; GROTON PUBLIC LIBRARY & BICENTENNIAL COMMITTEE OF GROTON; FORT HILL RD; GROTON, CT 06340. (#11576).

REHABILITATION OF DINING FACILITY, GROTON, CT. REPLACEMENT OF ALL EQUIPMENT AND INTERIOR FURNISHINGS/FITTINGS IN ON BOARD DINING FACILITY, INCLUDING REDESIGN & COMPLETE REDECORATION TO IMPROVE APPEARANCE AND SANITATION. (LOCAL). LT E F GOODE, USN COMMANDING OFFICER; USS ARD FIVE; FPO; NEW YORK, NY 09501. (#29013).

USS CECIL IN WAR & PEACE - GROTON, CT. GENERAL & GROUP TOURS ON BOARD THE SHIP WITH EXHIBITS & DEMONSTRATIONS. (LOCAL). CHARLES W MONAGHAN, COMMANDER, USN; USS CHARLES P CECIL (DD-835); FPO; NEW YORK, NY 09501. (#29770).

AUG 29 - SEPT 1, '75. BATTLE OF GROTON HEIGHTS: REENACTMENT AND OTHER PROGRAMS. BATTLE REENACTMENT AT SITE OF ORIGINAL ENGAGEMENT BETWEEN H M FORCES UNDER BENEDICT ARNOLD AND LOCAL DEFENDERS UNDER COL LEDYARD; ALSO, HISTORIC HOUSE TOURS, CONCERTS, MARCHING AND MANEUVERS AND OTHER APPROPRIATE PROGRAMS. AT FORT GRISWOLD. (LOCAL). MRS THOMAS ALTHUIS, CHMN; GROTON BANK HISTORICAL ASSOC, GROTON BICENTENNIAL COMMITTEE; 5 MERIDIAN ST; GROTON, CT 06340. (#100433-1).

SEPT 6, '75. ANNIVERSARY OBSERVANCE OF THE BATTLE OF GROTON HEIGHTS. COMMEMORATIVE CEREMONY WITH ADDRESSES MARKING ANNIVERSARY OF 1781 BATTLE OF GROTON HEIGHTS ON THE SITE OF FORT GRISWOLD. AT FORT GRISWOLD. (LOCAL). MRS M V GOODMAN, DIRECTOR; DAR, GROTON BICENTENNIAL COMMITTEE; SAWYER CT; NOANK, CT 06340. (#100433-2).

OCT 11 - 13, '75. AUTUMN FESTIVAL AND COMMEMORATIVE PROGRAMS. A VARIED PROGRAM OF HOUSE TOURS, SPECIAL EVENTS AND COMMEMORATIVE CEREMONIES IN THE ATMOSPHERE OF MARITIME MYSTIC. AT THROUGHOUT THE VILLAGE OF MYSTIC. (LOCAL). MISS BETTY WHEELER, CHMN; MYSTIC RIVER HISTORICAL SOCIETY, GROTON BICENTENNIAL COMMITTEE; 21 W MYSTIC AVE; MYSTIC, CT 06355. (#100433-3).

APR 17, '76. OPENING CEREMONIES FOR THE BICENTENNIAL YEAR. PROGRAM SIMILAR TO INAUGURAL PROGRAM FOR BICENTENNIAL ERA, PATRIOTS DAY 1975, WITH MILITARY UNITS, MUSIC, SPEECHES AND CEREMONY. AT FORT GRISWOLD. (LOCAL). STEPHEN B LEE, CHMN; GROTON BICENTENNIAL COMMITTEE; 44 HILLSIDE AVE; NOANK, CT 06340. (#100433-4).

APR 17, '76. 2ND BICENTENNIAL BALL. CEREMONY, FESTIVAL. (LOCAL). STEPHEN B LEE, CHAIRMAN; GROTON BICENTENNIAL COMMITTEE; TOWN HALL, FORT HILL RD; GROTON, CT 06340. (#13237-503).

JUNE 13, '76. FLAG DAY OBSERVANCE OF THE GROTON LODGE OF ELKS. FLAG CEREMONY AND PAGEANT. AT ELKS LODGE # 2163, SHENNECOSSETT RD. (LOCAL). A K KAYRUKSTIS, CHMN; GROTON LODGE OF ELKS, GROTON BICENTENNIAL COMMITTEE; 65 WILLIAMS ST; NOANK, CT 06340. (#100433-5).

JULY 4, '76. GROTON LODGE OF ELKS BICENTENNIAL INDEPENDENCE DAY OBSERVANCE. FLAG CEREMONY, ADDRESS BY MAYOR; PARADE AND FIREWORKS. AT WASHINGTON PARK. (LOCAL). A K KAYRUKSTIS, CHAIRMAN; GROTON LODGE OF ELKS, GROTON BICENTENNIAL COMMITTEE; 65 WILLIAMS ST; NOANK, CT 06340. (#100433-7).

JULY 5, '76. PIONEER HOSE COMPANY PROGRAMS FOR INDEPENDENCE DAY. FESTIVAL. (LOCAL). STEPHEN LEE, PROJ CHMN; PIONEER HOSE COMPANY, GROTON BICENTENNIAL COMMITTEE; 140 BROAD ST; GROTON, CT 06340. (#100433-6).

JULY 14, '76. FRENCH-AMERICAN DAY. COMMEMORATION CEREMONY OF CONTRIBUTION OF FRANCO-AMERICANS & FRENCH GOVERNMENT TO AMERICAN REVOLUTION ON BASTILLE DAY, 1976. AT FITCH HIGH SCHOOL, FORT HILL. (LOCAL). STEPHEN B LEE, PROJ CHMN; GROTON BICENTENNIAL COMMITTEE; 44 HILLSIDE AVE; NOANK, CT 06340. (#100433-8).

JULY 31 - AUG 1, '76. MIDSUMMER HISTORIC SHIPS & BOATS RENDEZVOUS REGATTA & PARADE. FESTIVAL. (LOCAL). STEPHEN B LEE, CHAIRMAN; GROTON BICENTENNIAL COMMITTEE; TOWN HALL, FORT HILL RD; GROTON, CT 06340. (#13237-507).

AUG '76. OPENING CEREMONY OF REHABILITATED DINING FACILITY. CEREMONY CONSISTED OF RIBBON CUTTING, CAKE CUTTING, REFRESHMENTS SERVED, PHOTOGRAPHIC COVERAGE & ACKNOWLEDGEMENT OF THE VOLUNTEER EFFORTS TO IMPROVE THE DINING FACILITY. AT USS ARD FIVE. (LOCAL). LT E F GOODE, USN; USS ARD FIVE; FPO; NEW YORK, NY 09501 (#29013-1).

SEPT 6, '76. BICENTENNIAL YEAR OBSERVANCE OF THE BATTLE O GROTON HEIGHTS. REENACTMENT OF BATTLE, HISTORIC HOM TOURS, PATRIOTIC ADDRESSES AND OTHER CEREMONIAL OB SERVANCE OF THE ANNIVERSARY OF THE BATTLE OF GROTO HEIGHTS ON SEPT 6, 1781. AT FORT GRISWOLD AND CON TIGUOUS AREAS. (LOCAL). THOMAS ALTHUIS, PROJ DIR GROTON BANK HISTORICAL ASSOC, DAR, GROTON BICENTENN AL COMMITTEE; 5 MERIDIAN ST; GROTON, CT 0634C (#100433-9).

OCT 9 - 11, '76. AUTUMN FESTIVAL & WRAP-UP OF BICENTENNIA YEAR OBSERVANCES IN MYSTIC. FESTIVAL. (LOCAL). STEPHEN LEE, CHAIRMAN; MYSTIC RIVER HISTORICAL SOCIETY; TOW HALL, FORT HILL RD; GROTON, CT 06340. (#13237-509).

DEC 15, '76. BILL OF RIGHTS DAY AND LOCAL CLOSING CEREMON FOR BICENTENNIAL ERA. BILL OF RIGHTS DAY IS A PARTICU LARLY FITTING DAY ON WHICH TO CLOSE THE BICENTENNIA ERA IN GROTON, SINCE IT MARKS THE ATTAINMENT OF THOS RIGHTS FOR WHICH THE SPIRIT OF LIBERTY WAS AROUSE AND THE REVOLUTION WAS FOUGHT. AT AUDITORIUM, FITC HIGH SCHOOL, FORT HILL. (LOCAL). STEPHEN B LEE, CHM GROTON BICENTENNIAL COMMITTEE; 44 HILLSIDE AVE; NOAN CT 06340. (#100433-10).

HAMDEN

BICENTENNIAL INTERNATIONAL CAMPOREE - HAMDEN, CT. CAM ING, TOURING AND HOME HOSPITALITY EXPERIENCE FOR PATROL OF 8 SCOUTS FROM 29 INVITED COUNTRIES TO SHAR WITH U S SCOUTS IN THE 200TH ANNIVERSARY OF THE U (INT'L). EDWARD R OSTROSKY, DISTRICT SCOUT EXEC; QUI NIPIAC COUNCIL OF THE BOY SCOUTS OF AMERICA; 186 WHITNEY AVE; HAMDEN, CT 06460. (#23602). **ARBA GRANTEE.**

JULY 1 - 18, '76. BICENTENNIAL INTERNATIONAL CAMPORE CAMPING, TOURING AND HOME HOSPITALITY EXPERIENCE FO A PATROL OF 8 SCOUTS FROM 29 INVITED COUNTRIES T SHARE WITH U S SCOUTS IN THE 200TH ANNIVERSARY OF TH U S. (INT'L). EDWARD R OSTROSKY, EXEC; QUINNIPIAC COU CIL OF THE BOY SCOUTS OF AMERICA; 1861 WHITNEY AV HAMDEN, CT 06460. (#23602-1).

JULY 21 - 22, '76. UNITED STATES ARMED FORCES BICENTENNIA CARAVAN. CARAVAN IS COMPOSED OF EXHIBIT VANS FO EACH MILITARY SERVICE. PROJECT THEME IS 'HISTORY OF TH ARMED FORCES & THEIR CONTRIBUTIONS TO THE NATION (LOCAL). HERBERT KORTE, CHMN; UNITED STATES ARME FORCES BICENTENNIAL CARAVAN; 3129 WHITNEY AVE; HAM DEN, CT 06247. (#1775-590).

HARTFORD

AMERICAN ART EXHIBITS IN HARTFORD, OCT. SIX EXHIBITS C AMERICAN ART OF THE 18TH, 19TH & 20TH CENTURIES. BEGA JUNE 1975. (LOCAL). HARRISON CROMER, PUBLIC PROGRAM DIRECTOR; WADSWORTH ATHENEUM; 600 MAIN ST; HAR FORD, CT 06103. (#12235).

AMERICAN FILM FESTIVAL - PROJ OF HARTFORD, CT. THE TRINIT CINESTUDIO WILL RUN A SERIES OF POPULAR FILMS INCLU ING DOCUMENTARIES. (LOCAL). LEIGH BRESLAU, CHAIRMA TRINITY COLLEGE BICENTENNIAL COMMISSION; HARTFORD, C 06106. (#13338).

AMERICAN MUSIC, ITS PAST & FUTURE - HARTFORD, CT. AME ICAN MUSIC IN ITS MORE ESOTERIC FORMS WILL BE PE FORMED. (LOCAL). DR CLARENCE BARBER, CHAIRMAN; MUS DEPT; TRINITY COLLEGE; HARTFORD, CT 06106. (#13336).

'THE AMERICAN PRESIDENCY - GEORGE WASHINGTON TO GERA FORD'. EXHIBIT OF PHOTOGRAPHS, CAMPAIGN BUTTONS AN MEMENTOS. AT UNIV OF HARTFORD - CONNECTICUT USA. (S WIDE). DIRECTOR; THE JOHN JUDKYN MEMORIAL, THE DEWI COLLECTION; FRESHFORD MANOR; BATH, AVON/UNITED KIN DOM. (#103992-6).

AMERICAN REVOLUTION IN BRITISH HISTORY - LECTURE. SEMINA (LOCAL). LEIGH BRESLAV, CHAIRMAN; TRINITY COLLEGE; SU MIT ST; HARTFORD, CT 06106. (#107388-9).

AMERICANA EXHIBIT. EXHIBIT. (LOCAL). LEIGH BRESLAV, CHAI MAN; TRINITY COLLEGE; SUMMIT ST; HARTFORD, CT 061C (#107388-8).

AMISTAD HISTORY RESOURCE CENTER - HARTFORD, CT. ESTABLIS MENT OF AN AREA OF AMISTAD HOUSE AS A FACILITY HOUSE VISUAL AND GRAPHIC DEPICTIONS OF THE AMIST STORY. ORIGINALLY, DISPLAY OF PAINTING/COLLAGE/PHOTO RAPHY/SCULPTURE. (LOCAL). CARRIE PERRY, EXECUTI DIRECTOR; AMISTAD HOUSE, INC; 5 CLARK ST; HARTFORD, 06120. (#23609). **ARBA GRANTEE.**

BICENT PGM FACILITATION IN HARTFORD, CONNECTICUT. AN I FORMATION & CLEARING CENTER FOR 29 TOWNS IN GREAT HARTFORD. PROJECTS INCLUDE A BICENT HOTLINE, ARTS RIVER FESTIVAL & OVERSEAS GUEST ACCOMODATION (LOCAL). P MALLET, EXEC DIRECTOR; GREATER HARTFORD AR COUNCIL; 250 CONSTITUTION PLAZA; HARTFORD, CT 061C (#8624).

BICENTENNIAL COOKBOOK - HARTFORD, CT. COMPILATION OF A COOKBOOKS PUBLISHED BY STATE DURING BICENTENNIA TESTING AND SELECTING BEST RECIPES. (ST-WIDE). GEORGE CYR, PROGRAM COORDINATOR; AMERICAN REVOLUTI BICENTENNIAL COMMISSION OF CONNECTICUT; 59 S PROSPE ST; HARTFORD, CT 06106. (#27082). **ARBA GRANTEE.**

HARTFORD — CONTINUED

BICENTENNIAL FILM PROGRAM PROJ IN HARTFORD, CT. A COMPREHENSIVE SURVEY OF AMERICAN CINEMA FROM 1894 TO 1976. FILMS TO BE SHOWN FROM OCT 1975 THRU JUNE 1976. (LOCAL). HARRISON CROMER, PUBLIC PROGRAMS DIRECTOR; WADSWORTH ATHENEUM; 600 MAIN ST; HARTFORD, CT 06103. (#12234).

BICENTENNIAL GUIDE BOOK - HARTFORD, CT. BOOKLET FOR GENERAL PUBLIC DESCRIBING HISTORIC SITES IN CONNECTICUT. (ST-WIDE). BARNEY LASCHEVER, DIRECTOR OF TOURISM; CONNECTICUT DEPARTMENT OF COMMERCE; 210 WASHINGTON ST; HARTFORD, CT 06106. (#27083). **ARBA GRANTEE.**

BICENTENNIAL POSTER CONTEST IN HARTFORD, CT. A CONTEST WILL BE HELD TO PICK A SYMBOL FOR TRINITY COLLEGE'S BICENTENNIAL COMMITTEE. (LOCAL). ROBERT CALE, ARTIST IN RESIDENCE; ART DEPARTMENT, TRINITY COLLEGE; HARTFORD, CT 06106. (#13332).

BLACK MUSIC THROUGH THE AGES - HARTFORD, CT. SPIRITUALS AND AFRICAN MUSIC AS WELL AS OTHER FORMS OF BLACK MUSIC WILL BE PERFORMED BY GUEST ARTISTS. (LOCAL). LEIGH BRESLAU, CHAIRMAN; TRINITY COLLEGE BICENTENNIAL COMMISSION; HARTFORD, CT 06106. (#13346).

BOOKLET ON 20TH CENTURY PILGRIMS - HARTFORD, CT. BIOGRAPHICAL SKETCH ON 20TH CENTURY PILGRIMS HONORED BY CONNECTICUT GATHERED INTO ONE BOOKLET. (ST-WIDE). GEORGE W CYR, PROGRAM COORDINATOR; AMERICAN REVOLUTION BICENTENNIAL COMMISSION OF CONNECTICUT; 59 S PROSPECT ST; HARTFORD, CT 06106. (#27081). **ARBA GRANTEE.**

'THE BRITISH VIEWPOINT OF THE REVOLUTION' - CT. A LECTURE WILL BE GIVEN BY AN HISTORIAN ON THE REVOLUTION AS VIEWED BY THE BRITISH. (LOCAL). LEIGH BRESLAU, CHAIRMAN; TRINITY COLLEGE BICENTENNIAL COMMITTEE; HARTFORD, CT 06106. (#13340).

COMMEMORATIVE PLAQUE - HARTFORD, CT. A COMMEMORATIVE PLAQUE WILL BE PLACED ON THE SPOT OF THE HANGING OF THE ONLY TORY IN CONNECTICUT BY THE FRATERNITY OF ST ANTHONY; THE PLAQUE WILL BE PLACED ON THE 125TH ANNIVERSARY OF THE FRATERNITY. (ST-WIDE). LEIGH BRESLAV, CHAIRPERSON; TRINITY COLLEGE; SUMMIT ST; HARTFORD, CT 06106. (#24135).

COMMEMORATIVE PRESENTATION IN HARTFORD, CT. A PLAQUE WILL BE PUT UP ON CALLOWS HILL TO COMMEMORATE THE EXECUTION OF THE ONLY MURDERED TORY IN CONNECTICUT. (LOCAL). LEIGH BRESLAU, CHAIRMAN; TRINITY COLLEGE BICENTENNIAL COMMISSION; HARTFORD, CT 06106. (#13345).

CONNECTICUT BICENTENNIAL MONOGRAPH SERIES. PUBLICATION OF 35 MONOGRAPHS EDITED BY DR GLENN WEAVER, PROFESSOR OF HISTORY AT TRINITY COLLEGE ON LIFE IN CONNECTICUT DURING THE REVOLUTION. VOLUMES 1-5 AVAILABLE IN 1974. (ST-WIDE). GEORGE W CYR, ACTING PROGRAM COORDINATOR; CONNECTICUT ARBC; 59 S PROSPECT ST; HARTFORD, CT 06106. (#535). **ARBA GRANTEE.**

CONNECTICUT INDIAN ETHNOHISTORY. ESTABLISHMENT OF PERSONAL LIAISON WITH CONNECTICUT INDIANS IN MIDWEST, RESEARCH CONNECTICUT INDIAN ETHNOHISTORY AND CULTURE. (ST-WIDE). BRENDAN KELEHER, INDIAN AFFAIRS COORDINATOR; DEPARTMENT OF ENVIRONMENTAL PROTECTION; 165 CAPITOL AVE; HARTFORD, CT 06115. (#23873). **ARBA GRANTEE.**

CONNECTICUT'S BICENTENNIAL EXHIBIT. AN EXHIBIT OF ARTS & CRAFTS OF THE REVOLUTIONARY ERA. (LOCAL). GEORGE W CYR, CHAIRMAN; AMERICAN REVOLUTION BICENTENNIAL COMMISSION OF CONNECTICUT; 59 S PROSPECT ST; HARTFORD, CT 06106. (#27002). **ARBA GRANTEE.**

'CONNECTICUT'S ROLE IN THE REVOLUTION' - HARTFORD. VARIOUS AUTHORS HAVE BEEN SELECTED TO PREPARE MANUSCRIPTS ON CONNECTICUT'S ROLE IN THE REVOLUTION. 5 WILL BE PUBLISHED EACH YEAR AND OFFERED TO THE PUBLIC. (ST-WIDE). JOHN SHANNAHAN, DIRECTOR; CONNECTICUT HISTORICAL COMMISSION; 59 S PROSPECT ST; HARTFORD, CT 06106. (#26740). **ARBA GRANTEE.**

CONSENT OF THE GOVERNED VOTER REGISTRATION PROJ-CT. VOTER REGISTRATION CAMPAIGN AMONG SPANISH SPEAKING CITIZENS WITH MOBILE UNIT AND TRAINING PROGRAM, ENTERTAINMENT BY IMPACTO BORICUA FOR PROMOTION TO INCREASE PARTICIPATION IN ELECTION '76. (LOCAL). LYNNE O BURFEIND, PRESIDENT; LEAGUE OF WOMEN VOTERS OF HARTFORD; 105 THOMASTON ST; HARTFORD, CT 06112. (#23624). **ARBA GRANTEE.**

COSTUME BALL. FESTIVAL. (LOCAL). LEIGH BRESLAV, CHAIRMAN; TRINITY COLLEGE; SUMMIT ST; HARTFORD, CT 06106. (#107388-4).

COSTUME BALL - HARTFORD, CT. A BALL WILL BE HELD AT THE CLOSE OF OUR BICENTENNIAL CELEBRATION. (LOCAL). LEIGH BRESLAU, CHAIRMAN; TRINITY COLLEGE BICENTENNIAL COMMISSION; HARTFORD, CT 06106. (#13347).

COUNTRY DANCE AND FESTIVAL. LIVE PERFORMANCE, FESTIVAL. (LOCAL). LEIGHTON JAMES, DIRECTOR; GREATER HARTFORD COMMUNITY COLLEGE; 61 WOODLAND ST; HARTFORD, CT 06106. (#107927-2).

ETHNIC MUSIC PERFORMANCE. LIVE PERFORMANCE. (LOCAL). LEIGH BRESLAV, CHAIRMAN; TRINITY COLLEGE; SUMMIT ST; HARTFORD, CT 06106. (#107388-7).

FOLK ARTS AND CRAFTS SHOW. EXHIBIT. (LOCAL). LEIGHTON JAMES, DIRECTOR; GREATER HARTFORD COMMUNITY COLLEGE; 61 WOODLAWN ST; HARTFORD, CT 06016. (#107927-1).

FUTURE PROGRAMS IN THE ART DEPARTMENT - CT. NEW PROGRAMS IN THE ART DEPARTMENT DEALING WITH AMERICAN ART HISTORY. (LOCAL). LEIGH BRESLAV, CHAIRPERSON; TRINITY COLLEGE; SUMMIT ST; HARTFORD, CT 06106. (#24137).

GEN PULASKI MEMORIAL MONUMENT FOR STATE OF CT. STATUE OF GEN CASIMIR PULASKI MOUNTED IN SPIRITED CHARGE POSITION; BRONZE CAST ON LIMESTONE AND GRANITE PEDESTAL ON PULASKI PLAZA, STATUE BY GRANVILLE CARTER. (REGN'L). WALTER PRZECH, GENERAL CHAIRMAN; PULASKI MEMORIAL COMMITTEE OF CT; 60 CHARTER OAK AVE; HARTFORD, CT 06106. (#23824). **ARBA GRANTEE.**

GREAT WOMEN IN CONNECTICUT HISTORY. MONOGRAPH-AUTOBIOGRAPHIES & CONTRIBUTIONS OF 12 GREAT WOMEN IN CT. HISTORY WITH ATTENTION TO DIVERSITY OF INTERESTS & ETHNIC GROUPS. 50 PAGE BOOK. SCHOOL ART CONTEST, 12 RADIO & PRESS RELEASES. (ST-WIDE). SUSAN BUCKNELL, EXEC DIRECTOR; PERMANENT COMMISSION ON THE STATUS OF WOMEN; 6 GRAND ST; HARTFORD, CT 06115. (#23544). **ARBA GRANTEE.**

HISTORIC AND ARCHITECTURAL RESOURCES SURVEY IN CT. A SCAN OF THE STATE OF CONNECTICUT TO IDENTIFY ALL OF OUR HISTORIC BUILDINGS AND BUILDING CLUSTERS WHICH ARE WORTHY OF ADDITIONAL CONSERVATION AND SENSITIVE TREATMENT. (ST-WIDE). JOHN W SHANNAHAN, DIRECTOR; CONNECTICUT HISTORICAL COMMISSION; 59 S PROSPECT ST; HARTFORD, CT 06106. (#22833). **ARBA GRANTEE.**

'THE ITALIANS OF HARTFORD TILL 1900', HARTFORD, CT. BOOK COVERING CULTURAL, SOCIAL, BUSINESS, CIVIC, RELIGIOUS AND POLITICAL PHASES OF THE ITALIANS AND THEIR DESCENDANTS OF THE HARTFORD REGION FROM THE COLONIAL PERIOD TO THE PRESENT. (LOCAL). GENNARO J CAPOBIANCO, PRESIDENT; THE ITALIAN AMERICAN HISTORICAL SOCIETY OF GREATER HARTFORD INC; HARTFORD, CT 06120. (#23825). **ARBA GRANTEE.**

'LECTION DAY' PARADE - HARTFORD CT. A CITY-WIDE CELEBRATION IN THE FORM OF A RE-CREATION OF AN AMERICAN SLAVE TRADITION AND CUSTOM. (LOCAL). DOLLIE MCLEAN, ADMINISTRATIVE DIRECTOR; THE ARTISTS COLLECTIVE, INC; 35 CLARK ST; HARTFORD, CT 06120. (#23826). **ARBA GRANTEE.**

LECTURE ON AMERICAN HISTORY - PROJ OF HARTFORD, CT. MAJOR AMERICAN HISTORIANS WILL BE INVITED TO SPEAK AT TRINITY ON TOPICS OF AMERICAN HISTORY. (LOCAL). BORDEN C PAINTER, DEPARTMENT HEAD; HISTORY DEPARTMENT, TRINITY COLLEGE; HARTFORD, CT 06106. (#13337).

LEWIS & CLARK - LOST & FOUND - HARTFORD, CT. PERFORMANCE IN COMMEMORATION OF THE LEWIS & CLARK EXPEDITION. (LOCAL). JACK MC QUIGGAN, PRODUCER; JFK CENTER FOR THE PERFORMING ARTS & WESLYAN UNIV; BOX AAA; MIDDLETOWN, CT 06457. (#26902). **ARBA GRANTEE.**

MANUSCRIPTS ON CONNECTICUT'S ROLE IN THE REVOL. VARIOUS AUTHORS ARE SELECTED TO PREPARE MANUSCRIPTS ON CONNECTICUT'S ROLE IN THE REVOLUTION; 5 ARE PUBLISHED EACH YEAR AND OFFERED TO THE PUBLIC. (ST-WIDE). ROBERT ORCUTT, COORDINATOR; CONNECTICUT HISTORICAL COMMISSION; 59 S PROSPECT ST; HARTFORD, CT 06106. (#14680). **ARBA GRANTEE.**

MAYOR'S ALL AMERICAN COUNCIL PARADE, CT. THIS PARADE WILL INVOLVE 61 ETHNIC GROUPS OF HARTFORD WITH EACH GROUP DRESSED IN NATIONAL COSTUMES AND BEARING THE FLAGS OF THEIR COUNTRIES OF ORIGIN. (ST-WIDE). HON GEORGE A ATHANSON, MAYOR; MAYOR'S ALL AMERICAN COUNCIL; 550 MAIN ST; HARTFORD, CT 06103. (#23666). **ARBA GRANTEE.**

MELTING POT FESTIVAL IN HARTFORD, CT. FESTIVAL IS DESIGNED TO CELEBRATE THE VARIOUS CONTRIBUTIONS OF DIFFERENT NATIONALITIES TO OUR SOCIETY. (LOCAL). LEIGH BRESLAU, CHAIRMAN; TRINITY COLLEGE BICENTENNIAL COMMISSION; HARTFORD, CT 06106. (#13344).

MUSIC OF THE AMERICAN REVOLUTION IN HARTFORD, CT. RECORDINGS OF POPULAR MUSIC FROM THE PERIOD OF THE AMERICAN REVOLUTION WILL BE DISTRIBUTED TO PUBLIC LIBRARIES AND LOCAL HISTORICAL SOCIETIES; WILL INCLUDE DOCUMENTATION, BIOGRAPHY & RECORDING. (ST-WIDE). MARY ANNA TIEN, DIRECTOR, LIBRARY SERVICE CENTER; CONNECTICUT STATE LIBRARY, DIVISION OF LIBRARY DEVELOPMENT; 231 CAPITOL AVE; HARTFORD, CT 06115. (#15353). **ARBA GRANTEE.**

OLD STATE HOUSE RESTORATION, HARTFORD, CT. REPAIR MAJOR BASEMENT LEAK AND IMPROVE RESTROOM FACILITIES TO MEET VISITOR IMPACT. (ST-WIDE). ROBERT ORCUTT, DIRECTOR; OLD STATE HOUSE ASSOC; 799 MAIN ST; HARTFORD, CT 06103. (#27841). **ARBA GRANTEE.**

PHOTOGRAPHIC RECORD OF BICENTENNIAL IN CT. STILL LIFE, MOTION PICTURE AND VIDRO-TAPE RECORDS OF BICENTENNIAL ACTIVITIES IN CONNECTICUT. (ST-WIDE). GEORGE W CYR, PROGRAM COORDINATOR; AMERICAN REVOLUTION BICENTENNIAL COMMISSION OF CONNECTICUT; 59 S PROSPECT ST; HARTFORD, CT 06106. (#27031). **ARBA GRANTEE.**

PHOTOGRAPHY SHOW OF ARCHITECTURE - HARTFORD, CT. A STUDENT SHOW OF PHOTOGRAPHS OF COLONIAL AND MODERN ARCHITECTURE. (LOCAL). LEIGH BRESLAU, CHAIRMAN; TRINITY COLLEGE BICENTENNIAL COMMISSION; HARTFORD, CT 06106. (#13339).

PLASTIC BICENTENNIAL SYMBOL PINS. MOLDED PLASTIC PIN OF BICENTENNIAL SYMBOL, LICENSE NO 76-19-0567. (NAT'L). MARVIN LEWTAN, PROJ DIRECTOR; LEWTAN INDUSTRIES CORP; 30 HIGH ST; HARTFORD, CT 06101. (#13365).

POSTER CONTEST FOR THE MENTALLY RETARDED - CT. ALL RETARDED INDIVIDUALS IN CONNECTICUT WILL BE ELIGIBLE TO ENTER A CONTEST INVOLVING DRAWING, PAINTING OR PRODUCTION OF A POSTER WITH A HISTORICAL THEME; WINNING POSTER TO BE REPRODUCED FOR DISPLAY. (ST-WIDE). ARTHUR L DUBROW, DIRECTOR; DEPT OF MENTAL RETARDATION; 79 ELM ST; HARTFORD, CT 06105. (#23622). **ARBA GRANTEE.**

PUBLICATIONS ON CT BICENTENNIAL ACTIVITIES. PUBLICATIONS DESCRIBING ACTIVITIES BY CONNECTICUT DURING BICENTENNIAL CELEBRATION. (ST-WIDE). GEORGE W CYR, CPROGRAM COORDINATOR; AMERICAN REVOLUTION BICENTENNIAL COMMISSION OF CONNECTICUT; 59 S PROSPECT ST; HARTFORD, CT 06106. (#27030). **ARBA GRANTEE.**

REENACTMENT ROCHAMBEAU'S MARCH IN HARTFORD, CT. REENACTMENT OF ROCHAMBEAU'S MARCH WITH COLOR GUARDS IN VARIOUS TOWN PARADES. (LOCAL). ARTHUR W MELYCHER, CHAIRMAN; NAVAL & MARINE CORPS RESERVE CENTER; RESERVE RD; HARTFORD, CT 06114. (#31188).

'RESOLVED TO BE FREE' - CONNECTICUT FILM. MOTION PICTURE ON CONNECTICUT'S ROLE IN THE REVOLUTION NARRATED BY KATHERINE HEPBURN; TO BE RELEASED IN EARLY 1975. (ST-WIDE). GEORGE W CYR, ACTING PROGRAM COORDINATOR; CONNECTICUT ARBC; 59 S PROSPECT ST; HARTFORD, CT 06106. (#247).

STATE BICENTENNIAL FORUM ON AGING - HARTFORD, CT. THE CONNECTICUT DEPARTMENT ON AGING WILL SPONSOR A FORUM ON AGING. (ST-WIDE). CHARLES E ODELL, CHAIRMAN; CONNECTICUT DEPT ON AGING; 90 WASHINGTON ST; HARTFORD, CT 06115. (#23626). **ARBA GRANTEE.**

SYMPOSIA ON AMERICAN POLITICS - HARTFORD, CT. THE POLITICAL SCIENCE DEPARTMENT WILL PRESENT A DISCUSSION OF PAST, PRESENT AND FUTURE AMERICAN POLITICS. (REGN'L). DR SAMUEL HENDEL, PROFESSOR OF POLITICAL SCIENCE; POLITICAL SCIENCE DEPT; TRINITY COLLEGE; HARTFORD, CT 06106. (#13350).

THOMPSON'S PREMIER - HARTFORD, CT. CELEBRATION OF THE FUTURE POSSIBILITIES OF THE NATION THROUGH THE STUDY OF MUSIC. (LOCAL). LEIGH BRESLAV, CHAIRPERSON; TRINITY COLLEGE; SUMMIT ST; HARTFORD, CT 06106. (#24136).

TOWN MARKERS - HARTFORD, CT. HISTORICAL MARKERS FOR CONNECTICUT TOWNS DESCRIBING TIME, PLACE AND CIRCUMSTANCES OF TOWN'S FOUNDING. (LOCAL). JOHN SHANNAHAN, DIRECTOR; CONNECTICUT HISTORICAL COMMISSION; 59 S PROSPECT ST; HARTFORD, CT 06106. (#26559). **ARBA GRANTEE.**

TRAVELING EXHIBIT - HARTFORD, CT. PORTABLE EXHIBIT OF BICENTENNIAL IN CONNECTICUT ADAPTABLE TO NEEDS AND INTERESTS OF DIFFERENT COMMUNITIES. (ST-WIDE). GEORGE W CYR, PROGRAM COORDINATOR; AMERICAN REVOLUTION BICENTENNIAL COMMISSION OF CONNECTICUT; 59 S PROSPECT ST; HARTFORD, CT 06106. (#26544). **ARBA GRANTEE.**

TREE PLANTING AND PLAQUE DEDICATION. CEREMONY. (LOCAL). LEIGHTON JAMES, DIRECTOR; GREATER HARTFORD COMMUNITY COLLEGE; 61 WOODLAWN ST; HARTFORD, CT 06160. (#107932-1).

TRINITY PIPES IN CONCERT - HARTFORD, CT. THE TRINITY PIPES, A CHORAL GROUP, WILL PERFORM AMERICAN MUSIC FOR THE COLLEGE COMMUNITY. (LOCAL). LEIGH BRESLAU, CHAIRMAN; TRINITY COLLEGE BICENTENNIAL COMMISSION; HARTFORD, CT 06106. (#13341).

TRUMBULL'S PAINTINGS RESTORATION PROJ OF CONN. RESTORATION OF FIVE PAINTINGS BY JOHN TRUMBULL BY WADSWORTH ATHENEUM OF HARTFORD. (NAT'L). PETER O MARLOW, CHIEF CURATOR; WADSWORTH ATHENEUM; 600 MAIN ST; HARTFORD, CT 06103. (#2039).

UNDERGROUND RAILROAD - HARTFORD, CT. RESEARCH AND MARK SITES OF SLAVE UNDERGROUND RAILROAD IN CONNECTICUT. (ST-WIDE). RICHARD KUNS, SUPERINTENDENT; CONNECTICUT HISTORICAL COMMISSION; 59 S PROSPECT ST; HARTFORD, CT 06106. (#27084). **ARBA GRANTEE.**

URBAN REFORM IN 20TH CENTURY HARTFORD. A HISTORY OF URBAN REFORM IN 20TH CENTURY HARTFORD CONNECTICUT WHICH INCLUDES AN ORAL HISTORY PROJECT CONCERNING THE RECENT ATTEMPT TO BUILD A NEW COMMUNITY IN COVENTRY CONN BY THE HARTFORD PROCESS. (LOCAL). PROF BRUCE M STAVE; DEPT OF HISTORY; UNIV OF CONNECTICUT; STORRS, CT 06268. (#4046).

VIRGIL THOMSON PREMIERE - HARTFORD, CT. VIRGIL THOMSON IS COMPOSING AN ORIGINAL COMPOSITION OF MAJOR LENGTH FOR TRINITY COLLEGE, IT WILL BE PERFORMED BY THE CONCERT CHOIR AND HARTFORD SYMPHONY. (LOCAL). DR JONATHAN REILLY, PROFESSOR OF MUSIC; MUSIC DEPT; TRINITY COLLEGE; HARTFORD, CT 06106. (#13335).

WAGON TRAIN - HARTFORD, CT. EXHIBIT OF CONNECTICUT'S BICENTENNIAL AT SCHOOLS AND FAIRS THROUGHOUT THE STATE. (ST-WIDE). GEORGE W CYR, PROGRAM COORDINATOR; AMERICAN REVOLUTION BICENTENNIAL COMMISSION OF CONNECTICUT; 59 S PROSPECT ST; HARTFORD, CT 06106. (#27032). **ARBA GRANTEE.**

THE WALK, A SELF-GUIDED TOUR OF HARTFORD, CT. A SELF-GUIDED WALKING TOUR OF DOWNTOWN HARTFORD WITH BROCHURES, BANNER MARKERS. (LOCAL). TIMOTHY KEATING & ANN KIEFFER, COORDINATORS; KNOX FOUNDATION; 15 LEWIS ST; HARTFORD, CT 06103. (#16243).

NOV '74 - JAN '75. MARK TWAIN IN HARTFORD, CONN, EXHIBIT. EXHIBITION RELATING TO TWAIN'S HARTFORD YEARS, INCLUDING MEMORABILIA DECORATIVE ARTS, FINE ARTS, ORIGINAL MANUSCRIPTS, ETC. (ST-WIDE). PETER O MARLOW; WADSWORTH ATHENEUM; HARTFORD, CT 06103. (#4402-1).

MAY 1, '75 - CONTINUING . AMERICAN REV AS SEEN BY CURRIER & IVES FROM TRAVELERS COLLECTION. EXHIBIT WILL TRAVEL

HARTFORD — CONTINUED

THROUGH 13 ORIGINAL STATES DURING '75 & '76, THEREAFTER WILL APPEAR IN OTHER STATES. CONSISTS OF 20 ORIGINAL CURRIER & IVES PRINTS MOUNTED IN TEN RED, WHITE & BLUE MODULES. AT VARIOUS. (REGN'L). PAUL D SCHMANSKA; TRAVELERS INSURANCE COMPANIES; 1 TOWER SQ; HARTFORD, CT 06115. (#4473-1).

JULY 1, '75 - JUNE 15, '76. PRESENTATION OF HISTORICAL TOWN MARKERS. THIS IS A STATEWIDE PROJECT TO FURNISH CONNECTICUT TOWNS WITH MARKERS WHICH DESCRIBE THE ORIGINAL SETTLEMENT OF THE TOWN. (LOCAL). R L FRUM, PROJ DIRECTOR; CONNECTICUT HISTORICAL COMMISSION, PLACQUES & MARKERS DIVISION; 59 S PROSPECT ST; HARTFORD, CT 06106. (#103074-1).

AUG 22 - SEPT 7, '75. LOUISIANA TERRITORY OR, LEWIS & CLARK - LOST AND FOUND. LIVE PERFORMANCE AT BUSHNEL PARK. (ST-WIDE). JACK MC QUIGGAN; JFK CENTER FOR THE PERFORMING ARTS AND WESLYAN UNIV; BOX AAA; MIDDLETOWN, CT 06457. (#26902-1).

OCT 1, '75 - JUNE 26, '76. BICENTENNIAL FILM PROGRAM PROJ IN HARTFORD, CT. A COMPREHSIVE SURVEY OF AMERICAN CINEMA FROM 1894 TO 1976. SECOND SHOWING AT 9:30 PM. AT ATHENEUM THEATRE, 25 ATHENEUM SQ N. (ST-WIDE). HARRISON CROMER; WADSWORTH ATHENEUM; 600 MAIN ST; HARTFORD, CT 06103. (#12234-1).

OCT 3 - 4, '75. SYMPOSIUM ON THE BEECHER FAMILY: PORTRAITS OF A 19TH CENTURY FAMILY. CONFERENCE AT THE CONNECTICUT HISTORICAL SOCIETY. (ST-WIDE). MARJORIE HENRY, DIRECTOR; STOWE-DAY FOUNDATION; 77 FOREST ST; HARTFORD, CT 06105. (#100477-1).

OCT 9 - NOV 13, '75. AMERICA: A REVOLUTIONARY SOCIETY - LECTURE SERIES. SEMINAR AT AVERBACH SCIENCE CENTER, 30 ELIZABETH ST. (LOCAL). MRS ELLEN PAULLIN, DIR; HARTFORD COLLEGE FOR WOMEN; 1265 ASYLUM AVE; HARTFORD, CT 06105. (#102245-2).

OCT '75. THE WALK: SELF-GUIDED WALKING TOUR OF DOWNTOWN HARTFORD. BROCHURES, BANNERS AND DIRECTORIES WILL BE MADE AVAILABLE. (LOCAL). T KEATING, CHMN; THE KNOX FOUNDATION; 15 LEWIS ST; HARTFORD, CT 06103. (#102245-1).

NOV 25, '75 - JAN 4, '76. 5 PAINTINGS OF THE REVOLUTION BY JOHN TRUMBULL. EXHIBIT AT 600 MAIN ST. (ST-WIDE). HARRISON CROMER, DIRECTOR; WADSWORTH ATHENEUM; 600 MAIN ST; HARTFORD, CT 06103. (#102318-1).

JAN 5 - MAY 17, '76. HISTORY OF THE U S THROUGH MUSIC. LIVE PERFORMANCE. (LOCAL). LEIGH BRESLAV, CHAIRMAN; TRINITY COLLEGE; SUMMIT ST; HARTFORD, CT 06106. (#107388-2).

JAN 13 - FEB 29, '76. EXHIBIT OF AMERICAN DRESS FROM 3 CENTURIES. EXHIBIT AT 600 MAIN ST. (LOCAL). HARRISON CROMER, DIRECTOR; WADSWORTH ATHENEUM; 600 MAIN ST; HARTFORD, CT 06103. (#102318-4).

JAN 27, '76. 'THE BRITISH ARE COMING!' - BRITISH MILITARY BAND PERFORMANCE. TOUR OF UNITED STATES BY TWO BRITISH REVOLUTIONARY WAR REGIMENTS: THE BLACK WATCH, AND THE ROYAL MARINES. REGTL BANDS TOTALLING APPROX 140 OFFICERS & MEN IN CEREMONIAL UNIFORM. AT CIVIC CENTER. (INT'L). CHARLES K JONES, PRES; COLUMBIA ARTISTS FESTIVAL CORP; 165 W 57TH ST; NEW YORK, NY 10019. (#6532-7).

JAN 27, '76. REVIEW & DRILL. USMC HAS INVITED THE 2ND CONNECTICUT REGIMENT TO APPEAR WITH 42ND HIGHLANDERS & ROYALE MARINES, BOTH ENGLISH GROUPS. THE 2ND CONNECTICUT REGIMENT DRILLS IN COLONIAL UNIFORMS AND FIRES COLONIAL WEAPONS. AT CIVIC CENTER. (NAT'L). EUGENE GUMBS, COORD; USMC; 73 LANTERN HILL RD; LEDYARD, CT 06335. (#200008-19).

JAN 27 - FEB 6, '76. ART EXHIBITS. EXHIBIT. (LOCAL). LEIGH BRESLAV, CHAIRMAN; TRINITY COLLEGE; SUMMIT ST; HARTFORD, CT 06106. (#107388-5).

FEB 1 - MAY 23, '76. 'AMERICA AT THE MOVIES 1930-1947' SERIES. LIVE PERFORMANCE. (LOCAL). LEIGH BRESLAV, CHAIRMAN; TRINITY COLLEGE; SUMMIT ST; HARTFORD, CT 06106. (#107388-3).

MAR 1 - SEPT 30, '76. POSTER CONTEST FOR THE MENTALLY RETARDED. ALL RETARDED INDIVIDUALS IN CONNECTICUT WILL BE ELIGIBLE TO ENTER A CONTEST INVOLVING DRAWING, PAINTING OR PRODUCTION OF A POSTER WITH A HISTORICAL THEME; WINNING POSTER TO BE REPRODUCED FOR DISPLAY. (ST-WIDE). ARTHUR L DUBROW, DIRECTOR; DEPT OF MENTAL RETARDATION; 79 ELM ST; HARTFORD, CT 06105. (#23622-1).

MAR 16 - APR 25, '76. PAINTINGS OF THE HUDSON RIVER SCHOOL: 19TH CENTURY AMER LANDCAPES. EXHIBIT AT 600 MAIN ST. (ST-WIDE). HARRISON CROMER, DIRECTOR; WADSWORTH ATHENEUM; 600 MAIN ST; HARTFORD, CT 06103. (#102318-3).

MAR 19 - 28, '76. 'OKLAHOMA' PLAY SERIES CELEBRATING AMERICAN EXPERIENCE. LIVE PERFORMANCE AT TOWER THEATRE, ASYLUM AVE ENTRANCE. (LOCAL). JOHN SINCLAIR, DIRECTOR; THE PRODUCING GUILD, INC; 450 CAPITOL AVE, BOX 1852; HARTFORD, CT 06101. (#102797-2).

MAR - MAY '76. BICENTENNIAL BIRTHDAY PARTY. FESTIVAL. (LOCAL). LEIGH BRESLAU; TRINITY COLLEGE BICENTENNIAL COMMISSION; HARTFORD, CT 06106. (#13342-1).

APR 1, '76. 'CLASSICS IN THE 18TH CENTURY' BY PROF JOHN C WILLIAMS. SEMINAR. (LOCAL). LEIGH BRESLAV, CHAIRMAN; TRINITY COLLEGE; SUMMIT ST; HARTFORD, CT 06106. (#107388-11).

APR 3, '76. CONCERT SERIES. LIVE PERFORMANCE. (LOCAL). LEIGH BRESLAV, CHAIRMAN; TRINITY COLLEGE; SUMMIT ST; HARTFORD, CT 06106. (#107388-6).

APR 3, '76. PROGRAM OF AMERICAN MUSIC. LIVE PERFORMANCE. (LOCAL). LEIGH BRESLAV, CHAIRMAN; TRINITY COLLEGE; SUMMIT ST; HARTFORD, CT 06106. (#107388-13).

APR 6 - JUNE 30, '76. OPEN HOUSE LECTURE ON BOOKS PRINTED BEFORE 1776. THE WATKINSON COLLECTION OF TRINITY COLLEGE WILL EXHIBIT REVOLUTIONARY & COLONIAL LETTERS, PAPERS, BOOKS & MEMORABILIA TO CORRESPOND WITH OTHER PROGRAMS GIVEN. AT WATKINSON LIBRARY, 300 SUMMIT ST. (LOCAL). MARIAN CLARKE, CURATOR; WATKINSON LIBRARY; TRINITY COLLEGE; HARTFORD, CT 06106. (#13348-1).

APR 22, '76. LECTURE ON THE AMERICAN REVOLUTION. SEMINAR. (LOCAL). LEIGH BRESLAV, CHAIRMAN; TRINITY COLLEGE; SUMMIT ST; HARTFORD, CT 06106. (#107388-14).

APR 22, '76. LECTURE ON 'COLLEGE LIFE IN REVOLUTIONARY AMERICA'. DISTINGUISHED LECTURER FREDERICK RUDOLPH OF WILLIAMS COLLEGE WILL DISCUSS UNDERGRADUATE LIFE IN THE 1700'S. (LOCAL). J RONALD SPENCER; TRINITY COLLEGE; 300 SUMMIT ST/ TRINITY COLLEGE; HARTFORD, CT 06106. (#13349-1).

APR 24, '76. MUSTERS FIFE & DRUM CORPS AND CRAFT FAIR EXHIBIT. PURPOSE IS TO ENLIGHTEN CITIZENS OF CONNECTICUT & ELSEWHERE THAT THERE WERE OVER 5000 BLACK SOLDIERS IN THE REVOLUTIONARY WAR. (LOCAL). LEIGH BRESLAV, CHAIRMAN; TRINITY COLLEGE; 11 RUST HILL RD; WAYLAND, MA 01778. (#107388-1).

APR 26 - MAY 1, '76. BICENTENNIAL FLOWER FESTIVAL. LAST OF A SERIES OF PLAYS CELEBRATING THE AMERICAN EXPERIENCE. AT DOWNTOWN HARTFORD, CIVIC CENTER, SHOPS, PRATT ST, STATE HOUSE. (LOCAL). SANDRA HAMER, MANAGER; DOWNTOWN COUNCIL; 15 LEWIS ST; HARTFORD, CT 06103. (#102245-4).

MAY 1, '76. TRINITY COLLEGE CONCERT CHOIR RECITAL. LIVE PERFORMANCE. (LOCAL). LEIGH BRESLAV, CHAIRMAN; TRINITY COLLEGE; SUMMIT ST; HARTFORD, CT 06106. (#107388-12).

MAY 4 - JUNE 13, '76. AMERICAN COVERLETS. EXHIBIT AT 600 MAIN ST. (LOCAL). HARRISON CROMER, DIRECTOR; WADSWORTH ATHENEUM; 600 MAIN ST; HARTFORD, CT 06103. (#102318-5).

MAY 28, '76. THE TODAY SHOW FEATURES THE STATE OF CONNECTICUT. A CONTINUING WEEKLY SERIES OF PROGRAMS COMMEMORATING EACH STATE. CONNECTICUT WAS ADMITTED INTO THE UNION IN JANUARY, 1788. (NAT'L). STUART SCHULBERG, EX PROD; NATIONAL BROADCASTING CO; 30 ROCKEFELLER PLAZA; NEW YORK, NY 10020. (#7981-27).

JUNE 4 - 13, '76. GREATER HARTFORD CIVIC & ARTS FESTIVAL. VISUAL AND PERORMING ARTS COMBINE IN NEW ENGLAND'S LARGEST OUTDOOR EXPOSITION. AT CONSTITUTION PLAZA & OLD STATE HOUSE. (REGN'L). ART FEST; ART FEST - TRAVELERS INSURANCE COMPANIES; 15 LEWES ST, ROOM 211; HARTFORD, CT 06103. (#103416-345).

JUNE 5, '76. GRISWOLD SCHOOL BAND PARTICIPATES IN HARTFORD PARADE. PARADE. (LOCAL). SAMUEL CATHCART, CHMN; GRISWOLD BICENTENNIAL COMMISSION; 99 E MAIN ST; GRISWOLD, CT 06351. (#200008-77).

JUNE 24, '76. RE-ENACTMENT OF ROCHAMBEAU'S MARCH. COLOR GUARD PRESENTED & VARIOUS PARADES HELD. AT 270 MAIN ST. (LOCAL). JOE EGAN; BICENTENNIAL COMMISSION OF EAST HARTFORD; 270 MAIN ST; HARTFORD, CT 06108. (#200008-259).

JULY 4 - SEPT 12, '76. BICENTENNIAL ART PROGRAM OF DEPT OF THE INTERIOR. PAINTINGS BY MODERN ARTISTS DEPICTING THE NATURAL & HISTORIC PROPERTIES ADMINISTERED BY THE DEPT OF INTERIOR. AT WADSWORTH ANTHENEUM. (REGN'L). MRS JEAN HAWKINS; DEPT OF THE INTERIOR; WASHINGTON, DC 20240. (#1239-10).

SEPT 11 - 12, '76. ENCAMPMENT OF THE BRIGADE OF THE AMERICAN REVOLUTION. AUTHENTIC RE-CREATION OF REVOLUTIONARY WAR MANEUVERS, BATTLES & CAMP LIFE, INCL REALISTIC BATTLES, DRILLS, COOKING & CRAFT ACTIVITIES, BY AUTHENTICALLY COSTUMED & UNIFORMED MEMBERS OF THE BRIGADE. AT BUSHNELL PARK IN DOWNTOWN HARTFORD. (REGN'L). SANDRA HAMER, DIR OF PROM; DOWNTOWN COUNCIL & THE GREATER HARTFORD JAYCEES; 15 LEWIS ST - ROOM 204; HARTFORD, CT 06103. (#108121-1).

SEPT 12, '76. ISRAELI PHILHARMONIC ORCHESTRA VISITS HARTFORD. LIVE PERFORMANCE. (INT'L). URI AHARON BAR-NEV; ISRAELI GOVERNMENT; 1621 21ST ST, NW; WASHINGTON, DC 20008. (#109015-12).

SEPT 25, '76. 'LECTION DAY' PARADE. A CITY-WIDE CELEBRATION IN THE FORM OF A RE-CREATION OF AN AMERICAN SLAVE TRADITION AND CUSTOM. (LOCAL). CLEO GREENE, DIR; GREESON PRODUCTION IN CONJ W/HARTFORD INQUIRER & N HARTFORD COMM; 181 WESTLAND ST; HARTFORD, CT 06120. (#23826-1).

SEPT 28 - NOV 7, '76. EXHIBIT OF GLASS FROM 1500-1950. EXHIBIT AT 600 MAIN ST. (REGN'L). HARRISON CROMER, DIRECTOR; WADSWORTH ATHENEUM; 600 MAIN ST; HARTFORD, CT 06103. (#102318-6).

OCT 28 - 29, '76. STATE BICENTENNIAL FORUM ON AGING. CONFERENCE. (ST-WIDE). CHARLES E ODELL, CHMN; CONNECTICUT DEPT ON AGING; 90 WASHINGTON ST; HARTFORD, CT 06115. (#23626-1).

NOV 1 - 6, '76. BICENTENNIAL EXHIBIT. EXHIBIT AT STATE ARMORY, 360 BROAD ST. (ST-WIDE). GEORGE W CYR, CHMN; AMERICAN REVOLUTION BICENTENNIAL COMMISSION OF CONNECTICUT; 59 S PROSPECT ST; HARTFORD, CT 06106. (#27002-1).

NOV 3 - 6, '76. MINIATURE REPLICA OF HISTORIC COLONIAL HOUSE ON DISPLAY. CT STATE BICENT EXHIBIT STAFFORD JR WOMEN'S CLUB IS LOANING DOLLHOUSE TO BE USED AS THE TOWN OF STRATFORD'S ENTRY. EACH TOWN & CITY IS PERMITTED AN EXHIBIT. AT HARTFORD ARMORY, BROAD ST. (LOCAL). BARBARA OLSEN, COORD; STRAFORD JUNIOR WOMAN'S CLUB; PO BOX 101; STRATFORD, CT 06497. (#200008-44).

HARWINTON

PLANTING OF SEEDLING FROM CHARTER OAK TREE, CT. ORIGINAL SEEDLING FROM THE HISTORIC CHARTER OAK WAS PLANTED IN OLD CENTER CEMETERY. HISTORICAL SOCIETY ESTABLISHED BOUNDS OF OLD CENTER CEMETERY & ERECTED A WROUGHT IRON PICKET FENCE. (LOCAL). MRS BONNIE KOCHISS, PRESIDENT; HARWINTON HISTORICAL SOCIETY; HARWINTON, CT 06790. (#28622).

JUNE 26, '76. BICENTENNIAL PARADE AND PICNIC. FESTIVAL, PARADE AT FAIRGROUNDS. (LOCAL). B L GIOSCIA, CHAIRMAN; HISTORICAL SOCIETY/BICENTENNIAL COMMISSION/PARADE COMMITTEE; NORTH RD; HARWINTON, CT 06790. (#200008-37).

HEBRON

TELEVISION PLAY ABOUT HEBRON, CONNECTICUT. A TV DOCUMENTARY WRITTEN & PRODUCED BY THE AUTHOR OF THE TOWN'S HISTORY. LOCAL CITIZENS WILL BE ACTORS, ACTUAL SITES IN THE TOWN TO BE USED & THE FILM WILL BE AVAILABLE TO SCHOOLS, GROUPS & LIBRARIES. (LOCAL). JOHN SIBUN, CHAIRMAN; HEBRON AMERICAN REVOLUTION BICENTENNIAL COMMISSION; SHADOWSMARK; HEBRON, CT 06248. (#5285). **ARBA GRANTEE.**

HIGGANUM

OLDE SCHOOLHOUSE MEETING PLACE, HIGGANUM, CT. OLD SCHOOL HOUSE PURCHASED AND RESTORED FOR COMMUNITY USE BY ALL LOCAL ORGANIZATIONS. (LOCAL). JOHN W ROGERSON, CHAIRMAN; HIGGANUM ARBC; HIGGANUM, CT 06441. (#32630).

KENT

KENT IRON FURNACE - CT. STABILIZE IRON FURNACE & INTERPRET CONTRIBUTIONS OF IRON INDUSTRY TO REVOLUTIONARY WAR. (LOCAL). RICHARD KUNS, SUPERINTENDENT; CONNECTICUT HISTORICAL COMMISSION; 59 S PROSPECT ST; HARTFORD, CT 06106. (#27896). **ARBA GRANTEE.**

KILLINGLY

TOWN SEAL CONTEST, KILLINGLY, CT. TOWN-WIDE CONTEST TO DESIGN A PERMANENT TOWN SEAL. SEAL WILL REFLECT HISTORY OF TOWN THROUGH APPROPRIATE SYMBOLS. (LOCAL). LOUISA B VIENS, COORDINATOR; KILLINGLY BICENTENNIAL COMMISSION; 68 1/2 FURNACE ST; DANIELSON, CT 06239. (#31499).

LEBANON

RESTORATION OF BROOM FACTORY - LEBANON, CONN. BROOMMAKING MACHINERY IS BEING LOCATED FOR RECENTLY RENOVATED ORIGINAL SMALL BROOM 'FACTORY.' THE LEBANON HISTORICAL SOCIETY IS SPONSORING PROJECT-HOPEFULLY THIS WILL BE A WORKING MUSEUM. (LOCAL). DANA DREW, PAST PRESIDENT; LEBANON HISTORICAL SOCIETY; THE GREEN; LEBANNON, CT 06249. (#3445).

LEDYARD

TRADITIONAL HANDCRAFTED ARTICLES, CT. CREATION OF TRADITIONAL HANDCRAFTED ARTICLES SUCH AS CLOTHING BEAD WORK, BY TRIBAL MEMBERS; THIS IS TO BE A REVITALIZATION OF ANCIENT CRAFT SKILLS. (LOCAL). RICHARD HAYWARD, TRIBAL COUNCIL PRESIDENT; WESTERN PEQUOT TRIBAL COUNCIL; PO BOX 285; STONINGTON, CT 06378. (#23546). **ARBA GRANTEE.**

LISBON

HISTORIC MONUMENT - LISBON, CT. PROCURED AND ERECTED A GRANITE MONUMENT WITH BRONZE PLAQUE DEDICATED TO THE MEN OF LISBON WHO FOUGHT IN THE REVOLUTIONARY WAR. (LOCAL). C H BENKER, CHAIRMAN; ARBC OF LISBON; RFD 2; LISBON, CT 06351. (#32467).

HISTORY OF LISBON, CT. HISTORY OF THE TOWN OF LISBON FROM FIRST SETTLEMENT TO PRESENT, WAS PUBLISHED. (LOCAL). C H BENKER, CHAIRMAN; ARBC OF LISBON; RFD 2; LISBON, CT 06351. (#32465).

PARK - LISBON, CT. DEVELOPMENT OF A 5 ACRE TRACT OF LAND AS A NATURAL AREA FOR EDUCATIONAL AND RECREATIONAL PURPOSES. (LOCAL). C H BENKER, CHAIRMAN; ARBC OF LISBON; RFD 2; LISBON, CT 06351. (#32466).

JAN 11, '76. ARTS AND CRAFTS EXHIBIT. EXHIBIT. (LOCAL). C H BENKER, CHMN; LISBON BICENTENNIAL COMMITTEE; RFD 2; LISBON, CT 06351. (#200008-253).

LISBON — CONTINUED

APR 4, '76. BICENTENNIAL CONCERT. LIVE PERFORMANCE. (LOCAL). C H BENKER, CHMN; LISBON BICENTENNIAL COMMITTEE; RFD 2; LISBON, CT 06351. (#200008-255).

MAY 1, '76. BICENTENNIAL DINNER AND BALL. FESTIVAL. (LOCAL). C H BENKER, CHMN; LISBON BICENTENNIAL COMMITTEE; RFD 2; LISBON, CT 06351. (#200008-254).

LITCHFIELD

THE MELTING OF KING GEORGE: FILM ON LITCHFIELD, CT. A FILM TO BE MADE, BASED ON TALES OF HISTORICAL LITCHFIELD DURING THE REVOLUTIONARY WAR. (LOCAL). ROBERT D COOLEY, FIRST SELECTMAN; LITCHFIELD BICENTENNIAL COMMISSION; TOWN OFFICE BLDG; LITCHFIELD, CT 06759. (#8197). **ARBA GRANTEE.**

WALKING TOUR AND MAP OF HISTORIC LITCHFIELD, CT. RECORDED COMMENTARY AND DESCRIPTIVE MAP AND BROCHURE TO ACCOMPANY WALKING TOUR OF LITCHFIELD'S HISTORIC DISTRICT. (LOCAL). ROBERT COOLEY, FIRST SELECTMAN; TOWN OF LITCHFIELD; LITCHFIELD, CT 06759. (#18678). **ARBA GRANTEE.**

LYME

'PURSUIT OF HAPINESS', A DRAMA IN LYME, CT. A REENACTMENT OF A 1934 PRODUCTION WITH A CONTEMPORARY VIEW ON SOCIAL, FAMILY & RELIGIOUS CUSTOMS OF THE 18TH CENTURY. FOCAL POINT: SCENE FEATURING BUNDLING, RELEVANT TODAY AS IN REVOLUTIONARY TIMES. (LOCAL). MARGARET C BROWN, CHAIRMAN; OLD LYME BICENTENNIAL COMMITTEE; ROUTE 156, HAMBURG COVE; LYME, CT 06371. (#6278).

JULY 4, '75 - JULY 14, '76. 'PURSUIT OF HAPPINESS', A DRAMA SET IN REVOLUTIONARY TIMES. A REENACTMENT OF A 1934 PRODUCTION. PROVIDES A CONTEMPORARY VIEW OF SOCIAL, FAMILY & RELIGIOUS CUSTOMS OF THE 18TH CENTURY. THE FOCAL POINT IS A SCENE FEATURING BUNDLING, RELEVANT TODAY AS IN REVOLUTIONARY TIMES. AT ROUTE 156, HAMBURG COVE. (LOCAL). MARGARET C BROWN; OLD LYME BICENTENNIAL COMMISSION; ROUTE 156, HAMBURG COVE; LYME, CT 06371. (#6278-1).

MADISON

'MADISON, YESTERDAY, TODAY & TOMORROW' IN CT. THE PAMPHLET WILL INCLUDE PROJECTIONS FOR FUTURE RESOURCE NEEDS, LAND USE, POPULATION & GENERAL GROWTH IN MADISON. (LOCAL). JOHN TERRY CHASE, CHAIRMAN; MADISON BICENTENNIAL COMMITTEE; 25 WHITE OAK LANE; MADISON, CT 06443. (#12274). **ARBA GRANTEE.**

DEC '75. COSTUME BALL. 'MADISON, YESTERDAY, TODAY & TOMORROW' IN CT. THE PAMPHLET WILL INCLUDE PROJECTIONS FOR FUTURE RESOURCE NEEDS, LAND USE, POPULATION & GENERAL GROWTH IN MADISON. (LOCAL). JOHN TERRY CHASE; MADISON BICENTENNIAL COMMITTEE; 25 WHITE OAK LANE; MADISON, CT 06443. (#12274-503).

JUNE 14, '76. HISTORICAL SOCIETY OPEN HOUSE TOURS AND LUNCHEON. EXHIBIT. (LOCAL). JOHN TERRY CHASE; MADISON BICENTENNIAL COMMITTEE; 25 WHITE OAK LANE; MADISON, CT 06443. (#12274-502).

JUNE 19, '76. DAR HISTORIC HOUSE TOURS. EXHIBIT. (LOCAL). JOHN TERRY CHASE; MADISON BICENTENNIAL COMMITTEE; 25 WHITE OAK LANE; MADISON, CT 06443. (#12274-504).

JULY 4, '76. JULY 4TH PARADE, FIFE & DRUM CEREMONY AND MEMORIALS. EXHIBIT. (LOCAL). JOHN TERRY CHASE; MADISON BICENTENNIAL COMMITTEE; 25 WHITE OAK LANE; MADISON, CT 06443. (#12274-501).

MANCHESTER

AMERICAN ARTS FESTIVAL, MANCHESTER, CONNECTICUT. FESTIVAL WILL INCLUDE STUDENT, PROFESSIONAL AND LOCAL GROUPS IN PLAY PRODUCTIONS, FILMS SUCH AS, '1776' AND BALLET PERFORMANCE OF 'ALL AMERICANA.'. (ST-WIDE). THOMAS BAVIER, COMMUNITY SERVICE PROGRAM DEVELOPER; MANCHESTER COUNTY COLLEGE BICENTENNIAL COMMITTEE; MANCHESTER COMMUNITY COLLEGE; MANCHESTER, CT 06040. (#10240).

MANCHESTER, CT PRESERVES COMMUNITY HISTORY. MONOGRAPH ON SOUTH MANCHESTER RAILROAD & TRANSCRIPTION OF ORAL HISTORY RELATED TO TRANSITION OF MANCHESTER FROM MILLTOWN TO SUBURB. (LOCAL). THOMAS BAVIER, COMM SERV PROG DEVELOPER; MANCHESTER COLLEGE BICENTENNIAL COMMITTEE; MANCHESTER COMMUNITY COLLEGE; MANCHESTER, CT 06040. (#10241).

'PEOPLE'S PARK', MANCHESTER, CT COMMUNITY COLLEGE. CONSTRUCTION OF AN ECOLOGICALLY CONTROLLED PARK BUILT FROM WOOD IN A WOODED AREA ON THE CAMPUS OF THE COMMUNITY COLLEGE; WILL PROVIDE RECREATIONAL FACILITIES FOR CHILDREN AND ADULTS IN AREA. (LOCAL). THOMAS BAVIER, COMM SERV PROG DEVELOPER; MANCHESTER COMMUNITY COLLEGE BICENTENNIAL COMMITTEE; MANCHESTER COMMUNITY COLLEGE; MANCHESTER, CT 06040. (#10242).

OCT '75. AUTHENTIC COLONIAL DINNER, DONE THROUGH STUDENT RESEARCH. LIVE PERFORMANCE. (ST-WIDE). THOMAS BAVIER; MANCHESTER COUNTY COLLEGE BICENTENNIAL COMMITTEE; MANCHESTER COMMUNITY COLLEGE; MANCHESTER, CT 06040. (#10240-501).

OCT '75. PUBLIC LECTURE BY NEW ENGLAND SCHOLARS ON NEW ENGLAND REVOL HISTORY. SEMINAR. (LOCAL). THOMAS BAVIER; MANCHESTER COLLEGE BICENTENNIAL COMMITTEE; MANCHESTER COMMUNITY COLLEGE; MANCHESTER, CT 06040. (#10241-501).

FEB 13, '76. 'SIR AND WILLIAM PENN' A PLAY BY FISHERMAN'S PLAYERS FROM BOSTON. LIVE PERFORMANCE AT EAST CATHOLIC HIGH SCHOOL, NEW STATE RD. (LOCAL). DAVID CAMPBELL, COORD; UNITED METHODIST CHURCH IN BOLTON AND UNITED METHODIST WOMEN; 1040 BOSTON TURNPIKE; BOLTON, CT 06040. (#200008-17).

APR '76. AUTHENTIC COLONIAL DINNER TO COINCIDE WITH OPENING OF PEOPLE'S PARK. OPENING. (LOCAL). THOMAS BAVIER; MANCHESTER COMMUNITY COLLEGE BICENTENNIAL COMMITTEE; MANCHESTER COMMUNITY COLLEGE; MANCHESTER, CT 06040. (#10242-501).

APR '76. LECTURE ON WOMEN IN CONNECTICUT HISTORY. SEMINAR. (LOCAL). THOMAS BAVIER; MANCHESTER COLLEGE BICENTENNIAL COMMITTEE; MANCHESTER COMMUNITY COLLEGE; MANCHESTER, CT 06040. (#10241-503).

MAY '76. LECTURE BY PROMINENT PUBLIC FIGURE. SEMINAR. (LOCAL). THOMAS BAVIER; MANCHESTER COLLEGE BICENTENNIAL COMMITTEE; MANCHESTER COMMUNITY COLLEGE; MANCHESTER, CT 06040. (#10241-502).

MANSFIELD

AWARENESS AND TRAILS FOR THE FUTURE - CT. A PROGRAM OF HERITAGE AWARENESS FOLLOWED BY THE ESTABLISHMENT OF A NETWORK OF TRAILS TO HISTORIC PLACES AND BUILDINGS AND EVENTS THAT WILL RADIATE FROM A CENTRAL ORIENTATION POINT. (LOCAL). RUDY J FAVRETTI, CHAIRMAN; MANSFIELD BICENTENNIAL COMMITTEE; 1066 MIDDLE TPKE, BOX 403; MANSFIELD, CT 06260. (#13647). **ARBA GRANTEE.**

MAR 1, '75 - DEC 31, '76. NEIGHBORHOOD SEMINARS ON HISTORY AND CULTURE. TOUR, SEMINAR, EXHIBIT, CEREMONY, PARADE. (LOCAL). RUDY J FAVRETTI, CHAIRMAN; MANSFIELD BICENTENNIAL COMMITTEE; 1066 MIDDLE TPKE, BOX 403; MANSFIELD, CT 06260. (#13647-504).

JUNE 1 - OCT 30, '75. HISTORIC TOURS FOR ELDERLY. TOUR, SEMINAR, EXHIBIT, CEREMONY, PARADE. (LOCAL). RUDY J FAVRETTI, CHAIRMAN; MANSFIELD BICENTENNIAL COMMITTEE; 1066 MIDDLE TPKE, BOX 403; MANSFIELD, CT 06260. (#13647-503).

FEB 1 - MAR 30, '76. HISTORIC EXHIBITION. TOUR, SEMINAR, EXHIBIT, CEREMONY, PARADE. (LOCAL). RUDY J FAVRETTI, CHAIRMAN; MANSFIELD BICENTENNIAL COMMITTEE; 1066 MIDDLE TPKE, BOX 403; MANSFIELD, CT 06260. (#13647-501).

JUNE 1 - JULY 30, '76. BICENTENNIAL PAGEANT. TOUR, SEMINAR, EXHIBIT, CEREMONY, PARADE. (LOCAL). RUDY J FAVRETTI, CHAIRMAN; MANSFIELD BICENTENNIAL COMMITTEE; 1066 MIDDLE TPKE, BOX 403; MANSFIELD, CT 06260. (#13647-502).

MARLBOROUGH

'SAVE THE LAKE' STUDY OF MARLBOROUGH, CT. PROJECT TO DETERMINE THE LAKE SITUATION FOR CONTROLLING THE QUALITY OF LAKE TERRAMUGGUS. A TOWN GROUP WILL BE ORGANIZED TO STUDY PROJECT & REPORT ON RESULTS. (LOCAL). FRANCES MACNAUGHT, PROJECT COORDINATOR; SAVE THE LAKE PROJECT; N MAIN ST; MARLBOROUGH, CT 06424. (#32096).

SCHOLARSHIP FOUNDATION OF MARLBOROUGH, CT. TOWN IS ESTABLISHING A BOARD OF TRUSTEES TO ADMINISTER A FOUNDATION WITH INCOME TO BE USED FOR SCHOLARSHIPS WITH POSSIBILITY OF INTEREST RAISING $3000 OR MORE FOR SCHOLARSHIPS. (LOCAL). FRANCES MACNAUGHT, CHAIRMAN; MARLBOROUGH BICENTENNIAL SCHOLARSHIP FOUNDATION; N MAIN ST; MARLBOROUGH, CT 06424. (#32097).

JULY 4, '76. DEDICATION OF FIREPLACE FOR TOWN USE. CEREMONY AT BLISH MEMORIAL PARK. (LOCAL). A BUCKLEY, COORDINATOR; LIONS CLUB; SOUTH RD; MARLBOROUGH, CT 06424. (#105344-2).

JULY 10, '76. TOWN PICNIC. FESTIVAL AT BLISH MEMORIAL PARK. (LOCAL). LINDA HEVENOR, CHAIRMAN; DEMOCRATIC TOWN COMMITTEE; JONES HOLLOW RD; MARLBOROUGH, CT 06424. (#105344-3).

SEPT 19, '76. CELEBRATION OF CREATIVE ARTS. EXHIBIT, FAIR, LIVE PERFORMANCE AT BLISH MEMORIAL PARK. (LOCAL). MARGRET DOYLE, COORD; MARLBOROUGH COMMUNITY ARTS, INC; RR 2, ROBERTS ST; MARLBOROUGH, CT 06424. (#105344-1).

OCT 9, '76. BICENTENNIAL PARADE. PARADE AT MAIN ST, N TO BLIGH PARK. (LOCAL). ZANE ROBERTS, COORDINATOR; AMERICAN LEGION & VOLUNTEER FIRE DEPARTMENT; ROBERTS RD; MARLBOROUGH, CT 06424. (#105344-4).

MERIDEN

GIUFFRIDA PARK PROJECT IN MERIDEN, CONNECTICUT. PARK PROJECT TO PROVIDE ENTRANCE, ROADWAY, PARKING AREA & HIKING TRAILS FOR BEAUTIFUL UNDEVELOPED OPEN SPACE COVERING 500 ACRES. UNSPOILED PARK WILL FACILITATE NATURE STUDEY. (LOCAL). HON JOHN D QUINE, MAYOR; MERIDEN ARBC; CITY HALL; MERIDEN, CT 06450. (#7346). **(??). ARBA GRANTEE.**

FEB 21, '76. BICENTENNIAL COLONIAL COSTUME BALL. FESTIVAL AT MERIDEN SQUARE, LEWIS AVE & MERIDEN CT; HUGE PARKING LOT OFF 66 WEST. (LOCAL). ROSEMARIE KOSIENSKI, DIR; MERIDEN BICENTENNIAL COMMISSION; 7 KENNEDY DR; MERIDEN, CT 06450. (#104658-1).

JUNE 4 - 6, '76. WAGON TRAIN 3-DAY CAMP-OVER. A 3-DAY CAMP OVER WITH NEW ENGLAND CONESTOGA WAGONS WILL INCLUDE ENTERTAINMENT BY WAGON TRAIN GROUP AND MERIDEN UNIT. AT HUBBARD PARK, W MAIN ST. (ST-WIDE). JO PIZZONIA, SECRETARY; MERIDEN BICENTENNIAL COMMISSION; 39 W MAIN ST; MERIDEN, CT 06450. (#105223-1).

JULY 24 - 25, '76. UNITED STATES ARMED FORCES BICENTENNIAL CARAVAN. CARAVAN IS COMPOSED OF EXHIBIT VANS FOR EACH MILITARY SERVICE. PROJECT THEME IS 'HISTORY OF THE ARMED FORCES & THEIR CONTRIBUTIONS TO THE NATION.'. (LOCAL). ANTHONY NOVAK, CHMN; UNITED STATES ARMED FORCES BICENTENNIAL CARAVAN; 39 W MAIN ST, PO BOX 1976; MERIDEN, CT 06540. (#1775-591).

AUG 13 - 15, '76. AMERICAN FREEDOM TRAIN DISPLAY DAYS AT MERIDEN. THE AMERICAN FREEDOM TRAIN WILL INCLUDE 10 EXHIBIT CARS AND 2 SHOWCASE CARS DEPICTING DIFFERENT PHASES OF THE AMERICAN EXPERIENCE. ITS ARRIVAL WILL SERVE AS A CATALYST FOR LOCAL BICENTENNIAL CELEBRATIONS BY PEOPLE THROUGHOUT THIS NATION. (ST-WIDE). SY FREEDMAN, DIR OF P/R; THE AMERICAN FREEDOM TRAIN FOUNDATION, INC; 5205 LEESBURG PIKE, SUITE 800; BAILEY'S XRDS, VA 22041. (#1776-124).

MIDDLETOWN

ETHNIC CELEBRATIONS OF THE ARTS IN MIDDLETOWN, CT. 4 LOCAL CELEBRATIONS, HIGHLIGHTING DANCE CRAFTS, ART, PHOTOGRAPHY, HEIRLOOMS, MUSIC, COMMISSIONED WORKS & FEATURING REPRESENTATIVE WORKS FROM VARIOUS ETHNIC GROUPS. (LOCAL). JOYCE J KIRKPATRICK, CHAIRMAN; MIDDLETOWN COMMISSION ON THE ARTS AND CULTURAL ACTIVITIES; MUNICIPAL BLDG, MAYOR'S OFFICE; MIDDLETOWN, CT 06457. (#11888). **ARBA GRANTEE.**

ORAL HISTORY ETHNIC PROJECT, MIDDLETOWN, CT. ORAL HISTORY PROJECT TO PRESERVE THE ETHNIC HISTORY OF CITIZENS OF MIDDLETOWN CONNECTICUT BY ITS LOCAL LIBRARY AND MEMBERS OF ITS MULTI ETHNIC GROUPS. (LOCAL). SYBIL B PATON, PRESIDENT BOARD OF TRUSTEES; RUSSELL LIBRARY; BROAD ST; MIDDLETOWN, CT 06457. (#23545). **ARBA GRANTEE.**

SEPT 14, '75. CELEBRATION FEATURING BEST OF LOCAL ETHNIC DANCE. 4 LOCAL CELEBRATIONS, HIGHLIGHTING DANCE CRAFTS, ART, PHOTOGRAPHY, HIERLOOMS, MUSIC, COMMISSIONED WORKS & FEATURING REPRESENTATIVE WORKS FROM VARIOUS ETHNIC GROUPS. (LOCAL). JOYCE J KIRKPATRICK; MIDDLETOWN COMMISSION ON THE ARTS AND CULTURAL ACTIVITIES; MUNICIPAL BLDG, MAYOR'S OFFICE; MIDDLETOWN, CT 06457. (#11888-501).

NOV 9, '75. CELEBRATION FEATURING BEST OF LOCAL ETHNIC ART AND PHOTOGRAPHY. FESTIVAL, LIVE PERFORMANCE, OPENING. (LOCAL). JOYCE J KIRKPATRICK; MIDDLETOWN COMMISSION ON THE ARTS AND CULTURAL ACTIVITIES; MUNICIPAL BLDG, MAYOR'S OFFICE; MIDDLETOWN, CT 06457. (#11888-502).

MAR 14, '76. CELEBRATION FEATURING BEST OF LOCAL ETHNIC MUSIC. FESTIVAL, LIVE PERFORMANCE, OPENING. (LOCAL). JOYCE J KIRKPATRICK; MIDDLETOWN COMMISSION ON THE ARTS AND CULTURAL ACTIVITIES; MUNICIPAL BLDG, MAYOR'S OFFICE; MIDDLETOWN, CT 06457. (#11888-503).

MAY 2, '76. ETHNIC WEEKEND AT WESLEYAN UNIVERSITY WITH STATE PERFORMING GROUPS. FESTIVAL, LIVE PERFORMANCE, OPENING. (LOCAL). JOYCE J KIRKPATRICK; MIDDLETOWN COMMISSION ON THE ARTS AND CULTURAL ACTIVITIES; MUNICIPAL BLDG, MAYOR'S OFFICE; MIDDLETOWN, CT 06457. (#11888-505).

JUNE 22, '76. CELEBRATION FEATURING BEST OF COMMISSIONED WORKS AT FESTIVAL. FESTIVAL, LIVE PERFORMANCE, OPENING. (LOCAL). JOYCE J KIRKPATRICK; MIDDLETOWN COMMISSION ON THE ARTS AND CULTURAL ACTIVITIES; MUNICIPAL BLDG, MAYOR'S OFFICE; MIDDLETOWN, CT 06457. (#11888-504).

MILFORD

BLACK HISTORY - MILFORD, CT. COMMEMORATION OF CONNECTICUT'S BLACK REVOLUTIONARY WAR SOLDIERS. (LOCAL). REV CHARLES D WALKER, COORDINATOR; COMM FOR COMMEMORATION OF MILFORD'S BLK REV WAR SOLDIERS; 28 NORTH ST; MILFORD, CT 06460. (#24275). **ARBA GRANTEE.**

FIREPLUG PAINTING - PROJ OF MILFORD, CT. THE FIREPLUGS THROUGHOUT THE CITY WILL BE PAINTED. (LOCAL). EARL GILMORE, PROJ DIRECTOR; MILFORD WOMEN'S CLUB; CITY HALL; MILFORD, CT 06460. (#17947).

HISTORICAL DOCUMENTS ROOM, MILFORD, CONN. GENERATION OF FUNDS TO BE DONATED TOWARDS THE HISTORICAL DOCUMENTS ROOM OF THE NEW MILFORD PUBLIC LIBRARY PRESENTLY UNDER CONSTRUCTION. (LOCAL). MARK D WATERHOUSE; MILFORD BICENTENNIAL OBSERVANCE COMMISSION; DEPT OF COMMUNITY DEVELOPMENT; MILFORD, CT 06460. (#2558).

MILFORD, CT, BICENT AWARENESS EDUCATION PROJECT. COMPREHENSIVE PGM TO ENCOURAGE COMMUNITY-WIDE PARTIC. BY PROVIDING ACTIVITIES TO ALL. FOCUS WILL BE COMMUNITY LEAVING SOMETHING OF IMMEDIATE NEED & LONG RANGE VALUE. (LOCAL). MARK D WATERHOUSE; MILFORD BICENTENNIAL OBSERVANCE COMMISSION; DEPT OF COMMUNITY DEVELOP; MILFORD, CT 06460. (#990). **ARBA GRANTEE.**

MILFORD — CONTINUED

PHOTO-CORPS, MILFORD, CT. A PHOTOGRAPHY COURSE FOR HIGH SCHOOL STUDENTS CONDUCTED BY JOSEPH STUDIO. (LOCAL). JOSEPH HOLT, CHAIRMAN; MILFORD BICENTENNIAL COMMISSION; MILFORD, CT 06460. (#16261).

PRESERVE HISTORIC DOCUMENTS IN MILFORD, CT. PRESERVATION OF IRREPLACEABLE HISTORICAL DOCUMENTS BELONGING TO THE MILFORD PUBLIC LIBRARY THRU REBINDING AND MICROFILMING. TO BE DISPLAYED IN THE HISTORICAL DOCUMENTS ROOM OF THE NEW LIBRARY. (LOCAL). MARK D WATERHOUSE; MILFORD BICENTENNIAL OBSERVANCE COMMISSION; DEPT OF COMMUNITY DEVELOPMENT; MILFORD, CT 06460. (#7344). **ARBA GRANTEE.**

RESTORATION PROJECT, MILFORD, CT. THE RESTORATION OF A 1659 HOUSE TO ITS REBUILT STATE OF 1780. (LOCAL). WILLIAM HOAGLAND, PRESIDENT; MILFORD HISTORICAL SOCIETY, INC; 34 HIGH ST; MILFORD, CT 06460. (#17985). **ARBA GRANTEE.**

SERIES OF HISTORICAL ARTICLES. THE MILFORD BICENTENNIAL COMMISSION WILL PUBLISH A SERIES OF HISTORICAL ARTICLES IN LOCAL NEWSPAPERS. (LOCAL). JAN F NUTT, ASSISTANT; MILFORD BICENTENNIAL COMMISSION; MILFORD, CT 06460. (#16260).

VOTER REGISTRATION, MILFORD, CONN. CONDUCT VOTER REGISTRATION EFFORTS AIMED AT REGISTERING 100% OF ELIGIBLE VOTERS WITH PARTICULAR REFERENCE TO THE NEWLY ELIGIBLE VOTER WHO WILL VOTE FOR THE FIRST TIME IN 1976. (LOCAL). MARK D WATERHOUSE, ASST TO DIRECTOR; MILFORD BICENTENNIAL OBSERVANCE COMMISSION; DEPT OF COMMUNITY DEVELOPMENT; MILFORD, CT 06460. (#2557).

OCT 1, '75 - MAY 31, '76. FILM FESTIVAL. A COMMUNITY ARTS PROJECT. AT CITY HALL. (LOCAL). EARL GILMORE, PROJ DIR; BICENTENNIAL COMMISSION; MILFORD, CT 06460. (#102815-8).

OCT 8 - DEC 20, '75. BICENTENNIAL EXHIBITS OF TRADITIONAL MILFORD SCENES. EXHIBIT AT CITY HALL. (LOCAL). CHARLENE PEET, DIRECTOR; FINE ARTS COUNCIL & MILFORD BICENTENNIAL COMMITTEE; MILFORD, CT 06460. (#102815-1).

JAN 1, '76. HISTORICAL COMMEMORATION. THE EVENT WILL COMMEMORATE 200 PRISONERS WITH SMALL POX WHO WERE LEFT BY THE BRITISH ON THE MILFORD SHORE. AT EELS STOWE HOUSE & CEMETERY. (LOCAL). EARL GILMORE, PROJ DIR; MILFORD BICENTENNIAL COMMITTEE; MILFORD, CT 06460. (#102815-35).

JAN 18, '76. A SALUTE TO CONNECTICUT. LIVE PERFORMANCE AT FIRST UNITED CHURCH OF CHRIST. (LOCAL). EARL GILMORE, PROJ DIR; HERITAGE PRODUCTIONS & MILFORD BICENTENNIAL COMMITTEE; MILFORD, CT 06460. (#102815-36).

FEB 7, '76. FORMATION OF THE MILFORD SHORE GUARD. CEREMONY AT FORT TRUMBULL. (LOCAL). EARL GILMORE, PROJ DIR; MILFORD BICENTENNIAL COMMITTEE; MILFORD, CT 06460. (#102815-37).

MAR 4, '76. BANQUET FOR DECORATED VETERANS. CEREMONY AT CITY HALL. (LOCAL). EARL GILMORE, PROJ DIR; MILFORD BICENTENNIAL COMMITTEE; MILFORD, CT 06460. (#102815-38).

MAR 7 - 14, '76. FINE ARTS EXHIBITION: VARIATIONS OF AMERICA. EXHIBIT AT ON THE GREEN. (LOCAL). MRS WILLIAM GITLITZ, DIR; MILFORD JAYCEES & BICENTENNIAL COMMITTEE; MILFORD, CT 06460. (#102815-39).

MAR 20, '76. THE GREENING OF MILFORD. 1776 TREES WILL BE PLANTED TO BEAUTIFY CITY. AT ON THE GREEN. (LOCAL). EARL GILMORE, PROJ DIR; MILFORD JAYCEES & BICENTENNIAL COMMITTEE; MILFORD, CT 06460. (#102815-40).

MAR 27, '76. SOUND OF FREEDOM CONCERT. CEREMONY WILL TAKE PLACE AFTER THE PARADE. AT ON THE GREEN. (LOCAL). EARL GILMORE, PROJ DIR; MILFORD JAYCEES & BICENTENNIAL COMMITTEE; MILFORD, CT 06460. (#102815-34).

APR 4, '76. MILFORD BICENTENNIAL SYMPHONY ORCHESTRA CONCERT. LIVE PERFORMANCE AT JONATHAN LAW HIGH SCHOOL. (LOCAL). MRS WILLIAM GITLITZ, DIR; MILFORD BICENTENNIAL COMMITTEE; MILFORD, CT 06460. (#102815-33).

APR 24, '76. BOY SCOUTS' JOHNNY HORIZONS CLEANUP PROJECT. A COMMUNITY ECOLOGY PROJECT,. AT THROUGHOUT THE COMMUNITY. (LOCAL). EARL GILMORE, PROJ DIR; BOY SCOUTS OF AMERICA/MILFORD DISTRICT & BICENTENNIAL COMMITTEE; MILFORD, CT 06460. (#102815-5).

APR 28 - MAY 2, '76. BICENTENNIAL ART EXHIBITION. EXHIBIT AT RAVENSWOOD GALLERY. (LOCAL). MARK EINHORN, COORDINATOR; MILFORD BICENTENNIAL COMMITTEE; MILFORD, CT 06460. (#102815-31).

MAY 1, '76. AN EVENING OF BALLET WITH THE NILSSON CONCERT BALLET COMPANY. LIVE PERFORMANCE AT JONATHAN LAW HIGH SCHOOL. (LOCAL). MRS WILLIAM GITLITZ, DIR; NILSSON CONCERT BALLET COMPANY & MILFORD BICENTENNIAL COMMITTEE; MILFORD, CT 06460. (#102815-32).

MAY 2, '76. AMERICAN MUSIC CONCERT. LIVE PERFORMANCE AT FIRST UNITED CHURCH OF CHRIST CONGREGATIONAL. (LOCAL). FRANK MULHEROW, PROJ DIR; FIRST UNITED CHURCH OF CHRIST CONGREGATIONAL & BICENT COMMITTEE; MILFORD, CT 06460. (#102815-29).

MAY 2, '76. BICENTENNIAL STANDARD FLOWER SHOW. COMPETITION AT CENTRAL GRAMMAR SCHOOL. (LOCAL). EARL GILMORE, PROJ DIR; WEPAWAUG GARDEN CLUB & MILFORD BICENTENNIAL COMMITTEE; MILFORD, CT 06460. (#102815-30).

MAY 8, '76. BLACK FOUNDING FATHERS DAY. FESTIVAL AT ON THE GREEN. (LOCAL). EARL GILMORE, PROJ DIR; THE BLACKS OF MILFORD; MILFORD, CT 06460. (#102815-7).

MAY 8, '76. BLACK HISTORY COMMEMORATION OF REVOLUTIONARY WAR SOLDIERS. CEREMONY, EXHIBIT. (ST-WIDE). REV CHARLES D WALKER; COMMITTEE FOR COMMEMORATION OF MILFORD'S BLACK REV WAR SOLDIERS; 28 NORTH ST; MILFORD, CT 06460. (#24275-1).

MAY 8, '76. HISTORIC PAINTING AND SKETCHING TOUR. TOUR. (LOCAL). CHARLENE PEET, DIRECTOR; FINE ARTS COUNCIL & MILFORD BICENTENNIAL COMMITTEE; MILFORD, CT 06460. (#102815-2).

MAY 12 - 16, '76. MUSEUM DAY IN MILFORD. EXHIBIT AT RAVENSWOOD GALLERY. (LOCAL). ANGELO RUSSO, PROJ CHMN; MILFORD BICENTENNIAL COMMITTEE; MILFORD, CT 06460. (#102815-28).

MAY 22, '76. CHILDREN'S ART SHOW. EXHIBIT AT MILFORD GREEN. (LOCAL). EARL GILMORE, PROJ DIR; JAYCEE WIVES & MILFROD BICENTENNIAL COMMITTEE; MILFORD, CT 06460. (#102815-27).

MAY 23, '76. JUNIOR CHORAL FESTIVAL. COMPETITION AT FIRST UNITED CHURCH OF CHRIST CONGREGATIONAL CHURCH. (LOCAL). EARL GILMORE, PROJ DIR; AMER GUILD OF ORGANISTS, BRIDGEPORT CHPT & MILFORD BICENT COMMITTEE; MILFORD, CT 06460. (#102815-26).

MAY 23, '76. UNITED METHODIST DAY. CEREMONY AT MARY TAYLOR MEMORIAL METHODIST CHURCH. (LOCAL). EARL GILMORE, CHMN; MARY TAYLOR MEMORIAL METHODIST CHURCH; CITY HALL; MILFORD, CT 06460. (#103490-2).

MAY 26 - 30, '76. BICENTENNIAL PHOTOGRAPHIC COMPETITION. EXHIBIT AT RAVENSWOOD GALLERY. (LOCAL). EARL GILMORE, PROJ DIR; MILFORD CAMERA CLUB & MILFORD BICENTENNIAL COMMITTEE; MILFORD, CT 06460. (#102815-25).

MAY 29, '76. GREAT MILFORD BICENTENNIAL QUILTING BEE. FESTIVAL AT MILFORD GREEN. (LOCAL). CHARLENE PEET, DIRECTOR; FINE ARTS COUNCIL & MILFORD BICENTENNIAL COMMITTEE; MILFORD, CT 06460. (#102815-3).

MAY 31, '76. MEMORIAL DAY PARADE. PARADE AT MILFORD CENTER. (LOCAL). LAWRENCE CHADBOURNE, CHMN; AMERICAN LEGION POST 196 & MILFORD BICENTENNIAL COMMITTEE; MILFORD, CT 06460. (#102815-24).

MAY 31, '76. MILFORD MONUMENT CEREMONY. CEREMONY WILL TAKE PLACE AFTER THE PARADE. AT ON THE GREEN. (LOCAL). EARL GILMORE, PROJ DIR; MILFORD BICENTENNIAL COMMITTEE; MILFORD, CT 06460. (#102815-6).

JUNE 6, '76. POLISH AMERICAN DAY. FESTIVAL AT FOWLER FIELD. (LOCAL). EDWARD KOZLOWSKI, COORD; MILFORD BICENTENNIAL COMMITTEE; MILFORD, CT 06460. (#102815-23).

JUNE 11 - 12, '76. FIFTH ANNUAL ARTS AND CRAFTS FESTIVAL. FAIR AT MILFORD GREEN. (LOCAL). EARL GILMORE, CHMN; MARY TAYLOR MEMORIAL METHODIST CHURCH; CITY HALL; MILFORD, CT 06460. (#103490-3).

JUNE 12, '76. COLONIAL GAMES. COMPETITION AT MILFORD GREEN. (LOCAL). EARL GILMORE, PROJ DIR; MILFORD BICENTENNIAL COMMITTEE; MILFORD, CT 06460. (#102815-22).

JUNE 13, '76. FLAG DAY PARADE. PARADE AT MILFORD CENTER. (LOCAL). LAWRENCE CHADBOURNE, CHMN; VETERANS OF FOREIGN WARS POST 7788 & MILFORD BICENTENNIAL COMMITTEE; MILFORD, CT 06460. (#102815-21).

JUNE 19, '76. MILFORD RECREATION BICENTENNIAL RUN. COMPETITION AT MILFORD GREEN. (LOCAL). EARL GILMORE, PROJ DIR; MILFORD BICENTENNIAL COMMITTEE; MILFORD, CT 06460. (#102815-20).

JUNE 19, '76. WESTERN BLUE GRASS CONCERT. LIVE PERFORMANCE AT MILFORD GREEN. (LOCAL). EARL GILMORE, PROJ DIR; MILFORD HOUSE OF GUITARS & MILFORD BICENTENNIAL COMMITTEE; MILFORD, CT 06460. (#102815-19).

JUNE 20, '76. FOUNDING FAMILIES DAY. CEREMONY, LIVE PERFORMANCE AT MILFORD GREEN. (LOCAL). EARL GILMORE, PROJ DIR; MILFORD BICENTENNIAL COMMITTEE; MILFORD, CT 06460. (#102815-18).

JUNE 20, '76. 'MISTRESS MERWIN'S RIDE'. LIVE PERFORMANCE AT MILFORD GREEN. (LOCAL). EARL GILMORE, CHMN; MILFORD BICENTENNIAL COMMISSION; CITY HALL; MILFORD, CT 06460. (#103490-1).

JUNE 20, '76. PROMENADE CONCERT. LIVE PERFORMANCE AT MILFORD GREEN. (LOCAL). EARL GILMORE, CHMN; MILFORD BICENTENNIAL COMMISSION; CITY HALL; MILFORD, CT 06460. (#103490-4).

JUNE 26, '76. CANOE RACE ON THE WEPAWAUG. COMPETITION AT WEPAWAUG RIVER. (LOCAL). EARL GILMORE, PROJ DIR; MILFORD BICENTENNIAL COMMITTEE & YMCA; MILFORD, CT 06460. (#102815-17).

JUNE 26, '76. ITALIAN AMERICAN DAY. FESTIVAL. (LOCAL). EARL GILMORE, PROJ DIR; MILFORD BICENTENNIAL COMMITTEE; MILFORD, CT 06460. (#102815-15).

JUNE 27, '76. BICENTENNIAL BICYCLE RODEO. COMPETITION AT MILFORD GREEN. (LOCAL). EARL GILMORE, CHMN; MILFORD POLICE EXPLORER POST 13; CITY HALL; MILFORD, CT 06460. (#103490-5).

JULY 3, '76. FIREWORKS. FESTIVAL AT MILFORD HIGH SCHOOL FIELD. (LOCAL). EARL GILMORE, CHMN; MILFORD LIONS CLUB; CITY HALL; MILFORD, CT 06460. (#103490-6).

JULY 3, '76. PEOPLE REJOICE ON THE GREEN. FESTIVAL AT MILFORD GREEN. (LOCAL). EARL GILMORE, PROJ DIR; MILFORD BICENTENNIAL COMMITTEE & JAYCEES; MILFORD, CT 06460. (#102815-14).

JULY 4, '76. DEDICATION OF NEW LIBRARY. OPENING AT NEW LIBRARY. (LOCAL). EARL GILMORE, PROJ DIR; LIBRARY BOARD & MILFORD BICENTENNIAL COMMITTEE; MILFORD, CT 06460. (#102815-12).

JULY 4, '76. JULY FOURTH CELEBRATION. CEREMONY AT CITY HALL. (LOCAL). EARL GILMORE, PROJ DIR; MILFORD BICENTENNIAL COMMITTEE; MILFORD, CT 06460. (#102815-13).

JULY 4, '76. MEMORIAL SERVICE AT CEMETERY. CEREMONY AT MILFORD CEMETERY. (LOCAL). EARL GILMORE, CHMN; AMERICAN LEGION POST 34; CITY HALL; MILFORD, CT 06460. (#103490-7).

AUG 3 - 5, '76. AMERICAN FREEDOM TRAIN DISPLAY DAYS AT MILFORD. THE AMERICAN FREEDOM TRAIN WILL INCLUDE 10 EXHIBIT CARS AND 2 SHOWCASE CARS DEPICTING DIFFERENT PHASES OF THE AMERICAN EXPERIENCE. ITS ARRIVAL WILL SERVE AS A CATALYST FOR LOCAL BICENTENNIAL CELEBRATIONS BY PEOPLE THROUGHOUT THIS NATION. (ST-WIDE). SY FREEDMAN, DIR OF P/R; THE AMERICAN FREEDOM TRAIN FOUNDATION, INC; 5205 LEESBURG PIKE, SUITE 800; BAILEY'S XRDS, VA 22041. (#1776-123).

AUG 4, '76. JURIED ART SHOW AND PURCHASE AWARD. EXHIBIT AT NEW MILFORD LIBRARY. (LOCAL). CHARLENE PEET, DIRECTOR; FINE ARTS COUNCIL & MILFORD BICENTENNIAL COMMITTEE; MILFORD, CT 06460. (#102815-4).

AUG 21, '76. MILFORD OYSTER DAY FESTIVAL. FESTIVAL AT MILFORD GREEN. (LOCAL). R B GREGORY; MILFORD CHAMBER OF COMMERCE & MILFORD BICENTENNIAL COMMITTEE; PO BOX 452; MILFORD, CT 06460. (#102815-11).

AUG 28, '76. FIFE AND DRUM CORPS MUSTER. FESTIVAL, PARADE AT FOWLER FIELD. (LOCAL). EARL GILMORE, PROJ DIR; MILFORD VOLUNTEER'S ANCIENT FIFE AND DRUM CORPS & BICENT COMMITTEE; MILFORD, CT 06460. (#102815-10).

SEPT 10, '76. ANTIQUE FIRE APPARATUS PARADE & MUSTER. FESTIVAL, PARADE AT EISENHOWER PARK. (LOCAL). RICHARD CODERRE, COORD; ENGINE 260 & MILFORD BICENTENNIAL COMMITTEE; MILFORD, CT 06460. (#102815-9).

MONROE

MASUK HIGH SCHOOL 'SPIRIT OF '76' MARCHING BAND-CT. A PERMANENT LIVING SYMBOL OF OUR NATION'S BICENTENNIAL. BAND WILL PERFORM AT THE TOWN OF MONROE'S CELEBRATION EVENT PLANNED FOR JUNE, 1976. THE HISTORICAL THEME WILL BE EMPHASIZED. (LOCAL). FRANK J MASTRONE, CHAIRMAN; MONROE BICENTENNIAL COMMITTEE; 73 PEPPER ST; MONROE, CT 06468. (#13650). **ARBA GRANTEE.**

JULY 3, '76. JUNIOR OLYMPICS-WOLF PARK TRACK AND FIELD SWIMMING COMPETITION. FESTIVAL, PARADE, LIVE PERFORMANCE. (LOCAL). FRANK J MASTRONE; MONROE BICENTENNIAL COMMITTEE; 73 PEPPER ST; MONROE, CT 06468. (#13650-501).

MONTVILLE

RESTORATION & RELOCATION OF TOLLHOUSE, MONTVL, CT. THE MOUNTVILLE HISTORICAL SOCIETY WILL RESTORE & MOVE HISTORIC TOLLHOUSE FROM RT 32 TO CAMP OAKDALE. (LOCAL). HOWARD BEETHAM, JR, CHAIRMAN; MOUNTVILLE BICENTENNIAL COMMITTEE; 310 NORWICH NEW LONDON TPKE; MOUNTVILLE, CT 06382. (#13239). **ARBA GRANTEE.**

WAR VETERANS MEMORIAL - MONTVILLE, CONNECTICUT. MEMORIAL DEDICATED TO VETERANS OF KOREAN & VIETNAM CONFLICTS. MANY TOWNSMEN SERVED AND DIED FIGHTING FOR FREEDOM. (LOCAL). FRANK KRYSIEWICZ, CHAIRMAN; MONTVILLE AMERICAN REVOLUTION BICENTENNIAL COMMISSION; 12 JEROME AVE; MONTVILLE, CT 06382. (#5288). **ARBA GRANTEE.**

MOOSUP

APR 10, '76. HERITAGE ARTS AND CRAFTS SHOW. EXHIBIT, FESTIVAL AT PLAINFIELD HIGH SCHOOL/RT 12. (LOCAL). HARRY G DENISON, CHMN; PLAINFIELD HISTORICAL SOCIETY; PO BOX 852; MOOSUP, CT 06354. (#105712-1).

MORRIS

'HISTORY OF MORRIS ACADEMY', BOOK PROJ OF CT. A THOROUGHLY RESEARCHED HISTORY OF MORRIS ACADEMY IN LITCHFIELDSOUTH FARMS FROM 1790 - 1888. THE TEXT WILL EMPHASIZE THE INFLUENCE OF THIS PIONEER CO-EDUCATIONAL SCHOOL ON THE COMMUNITY AND TIMES. (LOCAL). MRS LIDA S IVES, CHAIRPERSON; MORRIS BICENTENNIAL COMMITTEE; MORRIS, CT 06763. (#7340). **ARBA GRANTEE.**

MYSTIC

JUNE 19 - 21, '75. BICENTENNIAL INTERPRETIVE WORKSHOP -AMER ASSOC STATE & LOCAL HISTORY. WORKSHOPS AND CONSULTING SERVICES FOR BICENTENNIAL. TWO-DAY REGIONAL PROGRAM FOR VOLUNTEERS, TRUSTEES, AND PROFESSIONAL STAFF OF HISTORICAL SOCIETIES DEALING WITH THE MEANING OF THE REVOLUTION TODAY AND HOW TO CONVEY THAT MEANING TO THE PUBLIC THEY SERVE. (REGN'L). PAMELA JOHNSON; AMER-

MYSTIC—CONTINUED

ICAN ASSOCIATION FOR STATE AND LOCAL HISTORY; 1315 8TH AVE S; NASHVILLE, TN 37203. (#4329-506).

APR 17, '76. BICENTENNIAL BALL. SIMILAR TO 1975 BICENTENNIAL BALL EXCEPT THIS ONE IS A PERIOD COSTUME BALL OF THE LATE 18TH CENTURY, PROCEEDS TO 4-TOWN CEROTON, LEOYARD, STONINGTON, NORTH STONINGTON, BICENTENNIAL COORDINATING COMMITTEE AND ITS PROGRAMS. AT SEAMENS INNE MYSTIC SEAPORT. (LOCAL). PETER STUART, CHMN; MYSTIC ROTARY CLUB/TOWN BICENTENNIAL COMMITTEE; 26 NEW LONDON RD; MYSTIC, CT 06355. (#100435-1).

JULY 4, '76. CENTENNIAL CELEBRATION. MYSTIC SEAPORT CELEBRATES THE BICENTENNIAL BY RECALLING THE ACTIVITIES OF THE CENTENNIAL. (LOCAL). ALBERT LOVER, COORDINATOR; MYSTIC SEAPORT MARITIME MUSEUM; MYSTIC, CT 06355. (#103416-406).

JULY 31 - AUG 1, '76. HISTORIC SHIPS AND BOATS RENDEZVOUS, REGATTA AND PARADE. THIS IS A RENDEZVOUS FOR 'CHARACTER' & ANTIQUE-STYLE BOATS, INCLUDING ELCO CRUISERS, FOR WHICH SPECIAL EVENTS ARE PLANNED AND SAILING CRAFT. RACES AND A PARADE OF PARTICIPANTS ARE PLANNED. AT ALONG MYSTIC RIVER, INCLUDING MOORINGS, MARINAS & MYSTIC SEAPORT. (REGN'L). MS BETTY WHEELER, CHMN; MYSTIC RIVER HISTORICAL SOCIETY/TOWN BICENTENNIAL COMMITTEE; 21 W MYSTIC AVE; MYSTIC, CT 06355. (#100435-2).

SEPT 4 - 7, '76. BICENTENNIAL ART EXHIBIT. EXHIBIT AT R J SCHAEFERBLDG, MYSTIC SEAPORT. (ST-WIDE). ALBERT O LOUER; MYSTIC SEAPORT PUBLIC AFFAIRS; MYSTIC, CT 06355. (#103416-517).

OCT 9 - 11, '76. AUTUMN FESTIVAL AND COMMEMORATIVE PROGRAMS. A VARIED PROGRAM OF TOURS, SPECIAL EVENTS AND COMMEMORATIVE CEREMONIES IN THE ATMOSPHERE OF MARITIME MYSTIC. (ST-WIDE). MISS BETTY WHEELER, CHMN; MYSTIC RIVER HISTORICAL SOCIETY/TOWN BICENTENNIAL COMMITTEE; 21 W MYSTIC AVE; MYSTIC, CT 06355. (#100435-3).

N STONINGTON

BICENTENNIAL VILLAGE GREEN, NORTH STONINGTON, CT. CREATION OF A VILLAGE GREEN ON MAIN STREET WITH HISTORICAL MARKER PLAQUE, FLAGPOLE & FOOTBRIDGE OVER A STREAM, PLUS THE PLANTING OF A CONNECTICUT CHARTER OAK SEEDLING. (LOCAL). GEORGE WALES, CHAIRMAN; NORTH STONINGTON BICENTENNIAL COMMITTEE; 14 OLD COLONY RD; N STONINGTON, CT 06359. (#28628).

MAY 31, '76. MEMORIAL DAY CELEBRATION AND DEDICATION OF VILLAGE GREEN. PARADE, HORSESHOW, DEDICATION OF NEW BICENTENNIAL VILLAGE GREEN AND OLD-FASHIONED STREET DANCE AT THE GREEN. AT MAIN STREET. (LOCAL). GEORGE WALES, CHAIRMAN; NORTH STONINGTON BICENTENNIAL COMMITTEE AND LIONS CLUB; 14 OLD COLONY RD; N STONINGTON, CT 06359. (#200008-38).

AUG 8 - 21, '76. GIRL SCOUT ROUNDUP. A TWO WEEK CAMP FOCUSING ON THE ARTS, NEW TECHNOLOGY AND GIRL TODAY, WOMAN TOMORROW, LOOKING AHEAD TO CHALLANGES AND OPPORTUNITIES FOR GIRLS AND WOMEN; FOR RESIDENT AND DAY PARTICIPANTS. AT LAKE OF ISLES RESERVATION, RT 2, NORTH STONINGTON, CT. (ST-WIDE). BARBARA MILLAR, DIRECTOR; CONNECTICUT TRAILS COUNCIL OF GIRL SCOUTS; 1 STATE ST; NEW HAVEN, CT 06511. (#23625-1).

NAUGATUCK

VOLUNTEER EMERGENCY CENTER IN NAUGATUCK, CT. PROJECT TO ESTABLISH A VOLUNTEER EMERGENCY CENTER TO PROVIDE FIRSTAID FACILITIES, VEHICLES AND EVENTUALLY REFERRAL AND REOURCE FACILITIES. (LOCAL). MISS ALTHEA A LEWIS, CHAIRMAN; NAUGATUCK BICENTENNIAL COMMITTEE; NAUGATUCK, CT 06770. (#10733).

NEW BRITAIN

BICENTENNIAL TREES - PROJ OF NEW BRITAIN, CT. STUDENTS WILL PLANT A GROVE OF TREES IN HONOR OF THE BICENTENNIAL. (LOCAL). DR JOHN G ROMMEL, CHAIRPERSON; CENTRAL CONNECTICUT STATE COLLEGE BICENTENNIAL COMMITTEE; STANLEY ST; NEW BRITAIN, CT 06050. (#12282).

FILMS ON THE AMERICAN REVOLUTION - NEW BRITAIN, CT. A SERIES OF PERIOD AND THEMATIC FILMS ON THE AMERICAN REVOLUTION. (LOCAL). DR JOHN G ROMMEL, CHAIRPERSON; CENTRAL CONNECTICUT STATE COLLEGE BICENTENNIAL COMMITTEE; STANLEY ST; NEW BRITAIN, CT 06050. (#12278).

FREEDOM GROVE - 200 TREES, NEW BRITAIN, IA. A FREEDOM GROVE IN WALNUT HILL PARK OF 200 TREES, ONE FOR EACH YEAR OF THE NATION'S HISTORY. (LOCAL). ANN MARY PUSKARZ, BICENTENNIAL CHAIRPERSON; JUNIOR WOMAN'S CLUB; 35 ROSEMARY LA; NEW BRITAIN, CT 06052. (#24384).

LIBRARY EXHIBITS IN NEW BRITAIN, CT. HISTORIC CULTURAL EXHIBITS AT CENTRAL CONNECTICUT STATE COLLEGE LIBRARY. (LOCAL). DR JOHN G ROMMEL, CHAIRPERSON; CENTRAL CONNECTICUT STATE COLLEGE BICENTENNIAL COMMITTEE; STANLEY ST; NEW BRITAIN, CT 06050. (#12286).

OUR AMERICAN HERITAGE IN ART - NEW BRITAIN, CONN. 'REFLECTIONS OF OUR HERITAGE' - AMERICA AS SEEN THROUGH THE EYES OF HER GREATEST ARTISTS (1730 TO 1974). PRESENTED BY THE NEW BRITAIN MUSEUM OF AMERICAN ART. (ST-WIDE). CHARLES FERGUSON, DIRECTOR; NEW BRITAIN MUSEUM OF AMERICAN ART; 56 LEXINGTON ST; NEW BRITAIN, CT 06052. (#4846).

SHAW'S 'DEVIL'S DISCIPLE' - NEW BRITAIN, CT. THE CENTRAL CONNECTICUT STATE COLLEGE DRAMA DEPARTMENT WILL PRESENT SHAW'S PLAY, 'DEVILS DISCIPLE'. (LOCAL). DR JOHN G ROMMEL, CHAIRPERSON; CENTRAL CONNECTICUT STATE COLLEGE BICENTENNIAL COMMITTEE; STANLEY ST; NEW BRITAIN, CT 06050. (#12284).

SUMMER INSTITUTE ON AMER REVOL IN NEW BRITAIN, CT. 1976 INSTITUTE ON AMER REVOLUTION FOR TEACHERS. (ST-WIDE). DR JOHN G ROMMEL, CHAIRPERSON; CENTRAL CONNECTICUT STATE COLLEGE BICENTENNIAL COMMITTEE; STANLEY ST; NEW BRITAIN, CT 06050. (#12285).

MAY 8 - 18, '75. LOCAL REPERTORY THEATRE PRESENTS '1776'. EXHIBIT. (ST-WIDE). CHARLES FERGUSON; NEW BRITAIN MUSEUM OF AMERICAN ART; 56 LEXINGTON ST; NEW BRITAIN, CT 06052. (#4846-501).

OCT 9 - NOV 16, '75. REFLECTIONS OF OUR HERITAGE - PORTRAITS AND FURNITURE. EXHIBIT AT NEW BRITAIN MUSEUM OF ART, 56 LEXINGTON ST. (LOCAL). CHARLES FERGUSON, DIR; NEW BRITAIN MUSEUM OF ART; 56 LEXINGTON ST; NEW BRITAIN, CT 06052. (#102477-1).

OCT 15, '75. LECTURES ON THE AMERICAN REVOLUTION. FOUR LECTURES DEALING WITH THE MEANING OF THE AMERICAN REVOLUTION IN REGARD TO RELIGION, ART, POLITICS AND CONNECTICUT'S ROLE. AT STUDENT CENTER BALLROOM ANNEX,CCSC. (LOCAL). DR JOHN G ROMMEL; CENTRAL CONNECTICUT STATE COLLEGE BICENTENNIAL COMMITTEE; STANLEY ST; NEW BRITAIN, CT 06050. (#12277-1).

FEB 23 - 27, '76. ART EXHIBIT. BICENTENNIAL ART EXHIBIT FEATURING STUDENT AND FACULTY WORKS. AT STUDENT CENTER BALLROOM,CCSC. (LOCAL). DR JOHN G ROMMEL; CENTRAL CONNECTICUT STATE COLLEGE BICENTENNIAL COMMITTEE; STANLEY ST; NEW BRITAIN, CT 06050. (#12280-1).

APR 14, '76. PANEL ON THE AMERICAN REVOLUTION. EXPLORATION OF TODAY'S PROBLEMS IN LIGHT OF '76 PRINCIPLES. AT STUDENT CENTER BALLROOM ANNEX,CCSC. (LOCAL). DR JOHN G ROMMEL; CENTRAL CONNECTICUT STATE COLLEGE BICENTENNIAL COMMITTEE; STANLEY ST; NEW BRITAIN, CT 06050. (#12279-1).

APR 20, '76. MUSIC CONCERT - CCSC MUSIC DEPT. A BICENTENNIAL MUSIC CONCERT FEATURING ALL-AMERICAN MUSIC. AT WELTE HALL, CCSC. (LOCAL). DR JOHN G ROMMEL; CENTRAL CONNECTICUT STATE COLLEGE DEPT OF MUSIC; STANLEY ST; NEW BRITAIN, CT 06050. (#12281-1).

APR 27, '76. SPRING CONCERT. LIVE PERFORMANCE AT LINCOLN SCHOOL AUDITORIUM, 145 STEELE ST. (LOCAL). GEORGE E SWANSON, COORD; NEW BRITAIN SCHOOL DISTRICT; 145 STEELE ST; NEW BRITAIN, CT 06052. (#200008-15).

APR 28 - MAY 1, '76. ANDERSON'S 'HIGH TOUR'. THE CENTRAL CONNECTICUT STATE COLLEGE DRAMA DEPARTMENT WILL PRESENT ANDERSON'S PLAY ENTITLED 'HIGH TOUR'. AT COLLEGE THEATRE,CCSC. (LOCAL). DR JOHN G ROMMEL; THEATRE DEPT,CCSC; STANLEY ST; NEW BRITAIN, CT 06050. (#12283-1).

APR 29, '76. BICENTENNIAL CELEBRATION - INTERNATIONAL BUFFET & DANCE. FESTIVAL AT VANCE SCHOOL AUDITORIUM. (LOCAL). MISS MARGARET D CENCI; MOTHERS CLUB & SPEAC COMMITTEE; 182 VANCE ST; NEW BRITAIN, CT 06052. (#200008-16).

JUNE 10, '76. NICOLO MARIONETTE SHOW. NICOLO WILL FURNISH PORTABLE STAGE, LIGHTS, SOUND SYSTEM; MARIONETTES ARE 3 1/2' TO 4' TALL FOR GOOD VISIBILITY. SHOW TIMES ARE 3:30 PM AND 7:30 PM. AT WALNUT HILL MUSIC SHELL. (LOCAL). JAMES LEAVENWORTH, COORD; NEW BRITAIN BICENTENNIAL COMMISSION; 29 W MAIN; NEW BRITAIN, CT 06051. (#106483-4).

JUNE 11, '76. ALL CITY JUNIOR HIGH BICENTENNIAL MUSIC FESTIVAL. ALL JUNIOR HIGH STUDENTS WHO ARE IN PERFORMING GROUPS IN THE CITY WILL PARTICIPATE IN A MASS BAND ORCHESTRA AND CHORUS. ALL AMERICAN MUSIC. AT NEW BRITAIN HIGH SCHOOL, 110 MILL ST, NEW BRITAIN. (LOCAL). FREDERICK A JOHNSON, CHMN; SCHOOL DISTRICT OF NEW BRITAIN; 27 HILLSIDE PLACE; NEW BRITAIN, CT 06050. (#107393-1).

JUNE 26, '76. BICENTENNIAL STRAWBERRY FESTIVAL. NEW HORIZONS IS AN ORGANIZATION OF HANDICAPPED INDIVIDUALS. AT NEW BRITIAN MEMORIAL HOSPITAL PLAY GROUND. (LOCAL). ANTHONY ZIENKA, COORD; NEW HORIZONS; CORBIN AVE; NEW BRITAIN, CT 06053. (#106483-1).

JULY 3, '76. SENIOR CITIZENS' JAMBOREE. PROGRAM BASED ON DIXIELAND/SHOWBOAT THEME. AT CAMP SCHOOL, PARK ON STREET, SCHOOL BASEMENT. (LOCAL). MICHAEL LA ROSE, COORD; NEW BRITIAN SENIOR CITIZENS; 15 PROSPECT; NEW BRITIAN, CT 06051. (#106483-3).

NEW CANAAN

'THE ADVERTISER' BICENTENNIAL COVERAGE - NBMRP. 'THE ADVERTISER' CARRIED THE AMERICAN ISSUES FORUM COURSE BY NEWSPAPER & CARRIED ITS OWN 18-MONTH LONG SERIES ON LOCAL HISTORY. (LOCAL). E J CHROSTOWSKI, BICENTENNIAL COORDINATOR; NEW CANAAN ADVERTISER; PO BOX 605; NEW CANAAN, CT 06840. (#27984).

NEW FAIRFIELD

HISTORY OF NEW FAIRFIELD, CT. A PUBLISHED BOOKLET OF THE HISTORY OF NEW FAIRFIELD FROM COLONIAL TIMES TO THE PRESENT. (LOCAL). DR JAMES S MELLETT, CHAIRMAN; NEW FAIRFIELD BICENTENNIAL COMMISSION; TOWN HALL; NEW FAIRFIELD, CT 06810. (#17991). **ARBA GRANTEE.**

TOWN COMMON DEVELOPMENT; NEW FAIRFIELD, CONN. A SMALL PARK NEAR THE TOWN CENTER FEATURING A BANDSTAND WILL BE LANDSCAPED AND DEVELOPED FOR USE BY TOWN RESIDENTS OR VISITORS. (LOCAL). MR IRVING B SIMON, CHAIRMAN; NEW FAIRFIELD BICENTENNIAL COMMISSION; TOWN HALL; NEW FAIRFIELD, CT 06810. (#4728).

TRADITIONAL HOLIDAYS & CRAFTS; NEW FAIRFIELD, CONN. TO RESTORE CONSCIOUSNESS OF OUR AMERICAN HERITAGE BY CELEBRATING TRADITIONAL HOLIDAYS WITH SPECIFIC EVENTS AND BY DEMONSTRATING COLONIAL CRAFTS AND TECHNIQUES. (LOCAL). DR JAMES S MELLETT, CHAIRMAN; NEW FAIRFIELD BICENTENNIAL COMMISSION; TOWN HALL; NEW FAIRFIELD, CT 06810. (#4521).

JULY 4, '75. JULY 4TH PARADE. TRADITIONAL HOLIDAYS & CRAFTS, NEW FAIRFIELD, CONN. TO RESTORE CONSCIOUSNESS OF OUR AMERICAN HERITAGE BY CELEBRATING TRADITIONAL HOLIDAYS WITH SPECIFIC EVENTS AND BY DEMONSTRATING COLONIAL CRAFTS AND TECHNIQUES. (LOCAL). DR JAMES S MELLETT; NEW FAIRFIELD BICENTENNIAL COMMISSION; TOWN HALL; NEW FAIRFIELD, CT 06810. (#4521-501).

NOV 16, '75. BICENTENNIAL BALL. TRADITIONAL HOLIDAYS & CRAFTS, NEW FAIRFIELD, CONN. TO RESTORE CONSCIOUSNESS OF OUR AMERICAN HERITAGE BY CELEBRATING TRADITIONAL HOLIDAYS WITH SPECIFIC EVENTS AND BY DEMONSTRATING COLONIAL CRAFTS AND TECHNIQUES. (LOCAL). DR JAMES S MELLETT; NEW FAIRFIELD BICENTENNIAL COMMISSION; TOWN HALL; NEW FAIRFIELD, CT 06810. (#4521-502).

JULY 15 - 16, '76. UNITED STATES ARMED FORCES BICENTENNIAL CARAVAN. CARAVAN IS COMPOSED OF EXHIBIT VANS FOR EACH MILITARY SERVICE. PROJECT THEME IS 'HISTORY OF THE ARMED FORCES & THEIR CONTRIBUTIONS TO THE NATION.'. (LOCAL). DR JAMES MELLETT, CHMN; UNITED STATES ARMED FORCES BICENTENNIAL CARAVAN; TOWN HALL; NEW FAIRFIELD, CT 06810. (#1775-588).

NEW HARTFORD

YOUTH RECREATIONAL FACILITY - NEW HARTFORD, CT. DEVELOPMENT OF A COMBINATION OUTDOOR BASKETBALL, TENNIS AND ICE SKATING FACILITY IN THE CENTER OF TOWN; FACILITY WILL BE DEDICATED TO THE YOUTH OF TODAY AND TOMORROW. (LOCAL). ROBERT F GRANQUIST, CHAIRMAN; NEW HARTFORD BICENTENNIAL COMMITTEE; TOWN HALL, MAIN ST; NEW HARTFORD, CT 06057. (#23621). **ARBA GRANTEE.**

SEPT 18 - 19, '76. NEW HARTFORD BICENTENNIAL DAYS. EXHIBIT, FESTIVAL AT BROWNS CORNER, STEEL RD. (LOCAL). ROBERT S GRANQUIST, CHMN; NEW HARTFORD BICENTENNIAL COMMISSION; RFD 2; WINSTED, CT 06098. (#109323-1).

NEW HAVEN

AMER ARTS 1750-1800 EXHIBIT IN NEW HAVEN & ENGLAND. A SELECTION OF SOME 200 PAINTINGS; EXAMPLES OF FURNITURE, SILVER, PEWTER, CERAMICS AND TEXTILES PRODUCED IN AMERICA DURING THE REVOLUTIONARY PERIOD, TO BE EXHIBITED IN NEW HAVEN AND LONDON, ENGLAND. (INT'L). ALAN SHESTACK, DIRECTOR; YALE UNIV ART GALLERY; BOX 2006 YALE STATION; NEW HAVEN, CT 06520. (#2135).

BICENTENNIAL BOOK - NEW HAVEN, CT. THE BOOK 'WASHINGTON & GATES: THE BURDEN AND THE CHALLENGE' PROBES THE CONFLICT BETWEEN WASHINGTON & GATES DURING THE AMERICAN REVOLUTION. (NAT'L). MANSON VAN B JENNINGS, PRESIDENT; SOUTHERN CONNECTICUT STATE COLLEGE; 501 CRESCENT ST; NEW HAVEN, CT 06515. (#10763).

BICENTENNIAL OLYMPIAD OF THE ARTS IN NEW HAVEN, CT. NEW HAVEN PLANS ACTIVITIES IN THE ARTS, FUN & PARADES, EXHIBITS OF HISTORICAL INTEREST AND MUCH MORE FOR THEIR BICENT CELEBRATION. (LOCAL). W OGDEN ROSS, CHAIRMAN; NEW HAVEN BICENTENNIAL COMMISSION; 157 CHURCH ST; NEW HAVEN, CT 06510. (#8523).

BOOK ON BRITISH INVASION OF NEW HAVEN, CT. HISTORY OF BRITISH INVASION ON JULY 5, 1779. (LOCAL). THOMAS J FARNHAM, CHAIRMAN, SCSC ARBC; SOUTHERN CONNECTICUT STATE COLLEGE; 501 CRESCENT ST; NEW HAVEN, CT 06515. (#6158).

A BOOK ON VICTORIAN FICTION, NEW HAVEN, CT. THE PROJECT INVOLVES A BOOK ON VICTORIAN FICTION WHICH WILL CENTER ON THE THEME OF REPETITION & WILL HAVE CHAPTERS ON DICKENS, GEORGE ELIOT, TROLLOPE, EMILY BRONTE, CONRAD AND VIRGINIA WOOLF. (NAT'L). PROFESSOR J HILLIS MILLER; YALE UNIV; DEPT OF ENGLISH; NEW HAVEN, CT 06520. (#9839).

COLLEGE COURSE ON THE AMER REVOLUTION, CONNECTICUT. INTERDISCIPLINARY COURSE ON THE REVOLUTIONARY GENERATION. (ST-WIDE). THOMAS J FARNHAM, CHAIRMAN, SCSC ARBC; SOUTHERN CONNECTICUT STATE COLLEGE; 501 CRESCENT ST; NEW HAVEN, CT 06515. (#6163).

CONSERVATION OF IMPORTANT 18TH CENTURY PAINTINGS. CLEANING AND RESTORATION OF MAJOR AMERICAN PAINTINGS OF THE 18TH CENTURY INCL WORKS BY BENJAMIN WEST, RALPH EARL AND COL JOHN TRUMBULL'S DECLARATION OF INDEPENDENCE. (NAT'L). ALAN SHESTACK, DIRECTOR; YALE UNIV ART GALLERY; BOX 2006 YALE STATION; NEW HAVEN, CT 06520. (#2140).

THE CORNER - DOCUMENTARY - NEW HAVEN, CT. A DOCUMENTARY FILM ON BLACK URBAN LIFE AND CULTURE. (LOCAL).

NEW HAVEN — CONTINUED

DIRECTOR; CONNECTICUT COMMITTEE ON THE ARTS; 340 CAPITOL AVE; HARTFORD, CT 06106. (#18627).

ELI WHITNEY GUN FACTORY SITE IN NEW HAVEN, CT. THREE PART PROGRAM DESIGNED TO CREATE A PUBLIC PARK AND MUSEUM OF EARLY AMERICAN INVENTIONS & TECHNOLOGY ON ELI WHITNEY GUN SITE. (LOCAL). J'LENE MAYO, EXEC DIRECTOR; NEW HAVEN BICENTENNIAL COMMITTEE; 157 CHURCH ST; NEW HAVEN, CT 06511. (#10713).

EXHIBIT OF BICENT MATERIALS, NEW HAVEN, CT. HISTORICAL MATERIALS FOR USE OF TEACHERS AND STUDENTS. (LOCAL). RICHARD RAUSCH, DIRECTOR STUDENT SERVICES; SOUTHERN CONNECTICUT STATE COLLEGE; 501 CRESCENT ST; NEW HAVEN, CT 06515. (#6159).

FOURTH INTERNATIONAL CONGRESS ON THE ENLIGHTENMENT. PROJECT INTENDING TO ATTRACT SCHOLARS INTERESTED IN THE INTERDISCIPLINARY STUDY OF THE 18TH CENTURY. THEME-'IN SEARCH OF A NEW WORLD'. (INT'L). PROFESSOR GEORGES MAY, CONGRESS SECRETARY; INTERNATIONAL SOCIETY FOR EIGHTEENTH CENTURY STUDIES; C/O YALE UNIV, 1938 YALE STATION; NEW HAVEN, CT 06520. (#219). **ARBA RECOGNIZED.**

FT NATHAN HALE RESTORATION, WEST HAVEN, CT. RESTORATION OF HISTORIC FORT, SITE OF BRITISH ATTACKS IN 1779 & 1781. EARLIEST FORTIFICATION WAS 1659 & LATEST IN 1863. (LOCAL). LEONARD E ADAMS, EXEC DIRECTOR; FORT NATHAN HALE RESTORATION PROJECTS, INC; 208 GRETA ST, APT 201; WEST HAVEN, CT 06516. (#3945).

GIRL SCOUT ROUNDUP - NEW HAVEN, CT. TWO WEEK CAMP FOCUSSING ON THE ARTS, NEW TECHNOLOGY AND GIRL TODAY WOMAN TOMORROW, LOOKING AHEAD TO CHALLENGES AND OPPORTUNITIES FOR GIRLS AND WOMEN; FOR RESIDENT AND DAY PARTICIPANTS. (ST-WIDE). BARBARA MILLAR, DIRECTOR; CONNECTICUT TRAILS COUNCIL OF GIRL SCOUTS; 1 STATE ST; NEW HAVEN, CT 06511. (#23625). **ARBA GRANTEE.**

HISTORIC DOCUMENTS EDUCATION PUBLICATION OF CONN. REPRODUCE HISTORIC DOCUMENTS RELATING TO AMERICAN REVOLUTIONARY PERIOD, MAPS, LETTERS, DRAWINGS, ETC, TO BE PRODUCED FOR FRAMING. (ST-WIDE). J'LENE MAYO, EXEC DIRECTOR; NEW HAVEN BICENTENNIAL ADVISORY COMMISSION; 157 CHURCH; NEW HAVEN, CT 06510. (#858). **ARBA GRANTEE.**

HISTORY BOOK - NEW HAVEN, CT. A BOOK WILL BE WRITTEN ON THE HISTORY OF CT BLACKS IN THE NATIONAL GUARD. (LOCAL). ERNEST SAUNDERS, DIRECTOR; NEW HAVEN AFRO-AMERICAN HISTORICAL SOCIETY; 444 ORCHARD ST; NEW HAVEN, CT 06511. (#23828). **ARBA GRANTEE.**

HISTORY OF YALE - NEW HAVEN, CT. BICENTENNIAL HISTORY OF ONE OF NINE AMERICAN COLLEGES EXISTING DURING THE REVOLUTION. THIS SHORT HISTORY OF YALE BY GEORGE WILSON PIERSON WILL BE PUBLISHED MAY 15, 1976. COST: $1.00. (REGN'L). ROBIN W WINKS, BICENT CHAIRMAN; YALE UNIV OFFICE OF PUBLIC RELATIONS; WOODBRIDGE HALL; NEW HAVEN, CT 06520. (#19998).

INTERNATIONAL AMERICAN STUDIES SEMINARS. FOREIGN SCHOLARS SPECIALIZING IN AMER STUDIES WILL PARTICIPATE IN SEMINARS IN 5 WORLD CITIES DURING '75. PURPOSE: TO STIMULATE STUDY OF USA ABROAD THROUGH EXCHANGE EXPERIENCE & RESEARCH FINDINGS. (INT'L). ROBERT FORREY, COORDINATOR; BICENTENNIAL COMM ON INTL CONFERENCES OF AMERICANISTS; 70 SACHEM ST, YALE UNIV; NEW HAVEN, CT 06511. (#7916). **ARBA GRANTEE.**

LECTURE SERIES ON THE AMERICAN REVOLUTION,CT. LECTURES ON THE MEANING OF THE AMER REVOLUTION FOR THE FUTURE. (LOCAL). SAMUEL POOR, LYMAN AUDITORIUM DIRECTOR; SOUTHERN CONNECTICUT STATE COLLEGE; 501 CRESCENT ST; NEW HAVEN, CT 06515. (#6157). **(??).**

'MANY-DIMENSIONAL MAN' BOOK. WILL DISCUSS AMERICAN NIHILIST EXPERIENCE AND WHETHER THAT EXPERIENCE CAN FOLLOW A NIETZSCHEAN PATH TOWARDS A CREATIVE RELATIVISM, BY JAMES OGLIVY, UNDER PHI BETA KAPPA GRANT. (NAT'L). KENNETH M GREENE, SECRETARY; PHI BETA KAPPA; 1811 Q ST, NW; WASHINGTON, DC 20009. (#230).

MULTI-MEDIA EXHIBIT ON ETHNIC CULTURE, CT. THE EXHIBIT WILL EXPLORE THE NEW HAVEN AREA ETHNIC HERITAGE THROUGH SLIDES, PHOTOGRAPHS, MUSIC AND ORAL TAPES. (LOCAL). J'LENE MAYO, EXEC DIRECTOR; NEW HAVEN BICENTENNIAL COMMISSION; 157 CHURCH ST; NEW HAVEN, CT 06511. (#21335). **ARBA GRANTEE.**

ORAL HISTORY PROJECT IN NEW HAVEN, CT. DEVELOPMENT OF ORAL HISTORY RECORDS OF VARIOUS ETHNIC GROUPS IN NEW HAVEN, CONNECTICUT. (LOCAL). DOUGLAS ALVES, PRES OF HISTORY CLUB; SOUTHERN CONNECTICUT STATE COLLEGE; 501 CRESCENT ST; NEW HAVEN, CT 06515. (#6160).

PAPERS OF EZRA STILES - NEW HAVEN, CT. EDITING OF PAPERS OF COLONIAL PERIOD PRESIDENT OF YALE. (LOCAL). ROBIN W WINKS, BICENT CHAIRMAN; YALE UNIV LIBRARY MANUSCRIPTS & ARCHIVES; HIGH ST; NEW HAVEN, CT 06520. (#19995).

PARTICIPATION IN OPERATION SAIL - CT. ESCORT OF TALL SHIPS AND FOREIGN VESSELS THROUGH LONG ISLAND SOUND TO NEW YORK CITY FOR FOURTH OF JULY CELEBRATION. (LOCAL). LT JOHN R MCELWAIN, USCG; U S COAST GUARD GROUP, LONG ISLAND SOUND; 120 WOODWARD AVE; NEW HAVEN, CT 06512. (#28928).

PRE-REVOLUTIONARY YALE - NEW HAVEN, CT. SPECIAL TOURS OF COLONIAL AND FEDERAL PERIOD PORTIONS OF CAMPUS. (LOCAL). ROBIN W WINKS, BICENT CHAIRMAN; YALE UNIV; PHELPS GATEWAY; NEW HAVEN, CT 06520. (#19997).

PURCHASE OF ELIHU YALE LETTERS - NEW HAVEN, CT. PURCHASE OF MATERIALS RELATING TO FOUNDING OF YALE COLLEGE. (LOCAL). ROBIN WINKS, BICENT CHAIRMAN; YALE UNIV; 648 YALE STATION; NEW HAVEN, CT 06520. (#20200).

RESTORATION OF HISTORIC STRUCTURE - NEW HAVEN, CT. RESTORATION OF SELECTED STRUCTURES ON THE NEW HAVEN GREEN. (LOCAL). J'LENE MAYO, CHAIRMAN; NEW HAVEN BICENTENNIAL ADVISORY COMMITTEE; 157 CHURCH ST, ROOM 800; NEW HAVEN, CT 06510. (#14545). **ARBA GRANTEE.**

THE SIEGE OF YORKTOWN - NEW HAVEN, CT. REPRODUCTION OF BAUMAN MAP OF SIEGE OF YORKTOWN, ONLY CONTEMPORARY ENGRAVED AMERICAN PLAN OF SIEGE, NOW OWNED BY YALE UNIVERSITY. (REGN'L). ROBIN W WINKS, BICENT CHAIRMAN; YALE UNIV MAP COLLECTION; STERLING MEMORIAL LIBRARY; NEW HAVEN, CT 06520. (#19996).

SONG CYCLE FOR SOPRANO AND CHAMBER ENSEMBLE, CT. SURVEY OF NATIVE AMERICAN CULTURE IN SONG. (REGN'L). FRANK EPSTEIN, GEN DIRECTOR; COLLAGE INC; 186 PLEASANT ST; BROOKLINE, MA 02146. (#23448).

SOUTHERN EDUCATION, 1865-1900 RESEARCH PROJECT. THE IDEOLOGY AND PRACTISE OF SOUTHERN PUBLIC EDUCATION, 1865-1900 A STUDY OF CONFLICTING EXPECTATIONS ABOUT PUBLIC SCHOOLING DURING AND AFTER RECONSTRUCTION, PARTICULARLY BLACK SCHOOLS. (NAT'L). DANIEL W CROFTS, NEH FELLOW; 788 ELM ST; NEW HAVEN, CT 06511. (#4045).

SPECIAL ISSUE OF THE CONNECTICUT REVIEW. ISSUE ON MEANING OF THE AMERICAN REVOLUTION. (NAT'L). BERTRAM SARASON, EDITOR; CONNECTICUT REVIEW; 501 CRESCENT ST; NEW HAVEN, CT 06515. (#6156). **(??).**

WOMEN'S BICENTENNIAL CALENDAR - NEW HAVEN, CT. CITY-WIDE CALENDAR OF ACTIVITIES 1975-76, FOR WOMEN. (LOCAL). ROBIN W WINKS, BICENT CHAIRMAN; YALE UNIV WOMEN'S ORGANIZATION; 6 BROOKHAVEN RD; HAMDEN, CT 06520. (#20202).

YALE AND THE BICENTENNIAL - NEW HAVEN, CT. LEAFLET ON YALE BUILDINGS, BOOKS AND EXHIBITS ON THE BICENTENNIAL FOR FREE PRESENTATION AND MAILING. (LOCAL). ROBIN W WINKS, BICENT CHAIRMAN; YALE UNIV; 648 YALE STATION; NEW HAVEN, CT 06520. (#19999).

YALE UNIV VISITING PROFESSOR FUNDED BY CANADA. THE CANADIAN GOVT HAS SET ASIDE $35,000 TO ESTABLISH A CHAIR AT YALE UNIV. A CANADIAN PROFESSOR WILL JOIN YALE FOR THE ACADEMIC YEAR '76'77. THE GRANT IS SUBJECT TO RENEWAL AFTER AN ANNUAL REVIEW. (INT'L). K DE B PERCY, COORDINATOR; EMBASSY OF CANADA; 1746 MASSACHUSETTS AVE, NW; WASHINGTON, DC 20036. (#20882).

JAN 9 - MAR 27, '75. BICENTENNIAL QUILTING BEE WORKSHOP FAIR HAVEN LIBRARY. A WORKSHOP FOR THE CREATION OF A FAIR HAVEN BICENTENNIAL QUILT COMMORATING PLACES & MOTIFS OF CURRENT & HISTORICAL SIGNIFICANCE TO THE FAIR HAVEN COMMUNITY. ARTISTIC DIRECTOR MARY ALICE BOHN. (LOCAL). PAULA SHEMITZ; FAIR HAVEN LIBRARY; 182 GRAND AVE; NEW HAVEN, CT 06513. (#5668-501).

APR - MAY '75. HISTORY TEACHERS CONFERENCE. MEETINGS TO DISCUSS THE NEW INTERPRETATION OF THE AMERICAN REVOLUTION FOR SECONDARY SCHOOL HISTORY TEACHERS. (LOCAL). ROBIN WINKS, CHAIRMAN; YALE UNIVERSITY BICENTENNIAL COMMITTEE; 648 YALE STATION, ELM ST; NEW HAVEN, CT 06520. (#104634-17).

JULY 13 - 20, '75. 4TH INT'L CONGRESS ON THE ENLIGHTENMENT. PROJECT INTENDING TO ATTRACT SCHOLARS INTERESTED IN THE INTERDISCIPLINARY STUDY OF THE 18TH CENTURY. THEME: 'IN SEARCH OF A NEW WORLD'. (INT'L). PROFESSOR GEORGES MAY; INTERNATIONAL SOCIETY FOR EIGHTEENTH CENTURY STUDIES; 1938 YALE STATION; NEW HAVEN, CT 06520. (#219-1).

SEPT 2 - DEC 15, '75. 'CONNECTICUT LAW AND THE REVOLUTION' - EXHIBIT. EXHIBIT AT STERLING LAW BUILDINGS. (ST-WIDE). ROBIN WINKS, CHAIRMAN; YALE UNIVERSITY BICENTENNIAL COMMITTEE; SCHOOL OF LAW; NEW HAVEN, CT 06520. (#104635-1).

OCT 1, '75 - JUNE 30, '76. ROBYNA NEILSON KETCHUM COLLECTION OF BELLS. EXHIBITION OF BELLS FROM THE COLLECTION OF MRS KETCHUM, DESIGNER OF THE OFFICIAL BICENTENNIAL BELL. (REGN'L). ROBIN WINKS, CHAIRMAN; YALE UNIVERSITY BICENTENNIAL COMMITTEE; 15 HILLHOUSE AVE; NEW HAVEN, CT 06520. (#104634-3).

OCT 1, '75 - OCT 31, '76. MUSIC OF THE REVOLUTION. TOWN-GOWN DINNER AND CONCERT IN THE COSTUME OF DRAWING ROOM MUSIC AS PERFORMED AND SUNG IN COLONIAL NEW ENGLAND IN 1776; CONCERT GROUP THEN TO GO ON TOUR IN STATE UPON REQUEST. (ST-WIDE). ROBIN WINKS, CHAIRMAN; YALE UNIVERSITY BICENTENNIAL COMMITTEE; STOECKEL HALL, WALL ST; NEW HAVEN, CT 06520. (#104634-23).

OCT 21, '75 - NOV 20, '76. BICENTENNIAL THEATRE PRODUCTIONS. 'RICHARD II' - OCT 21-NOV 2, 1975; 'THE STREETS OF NEW YORK' FEB 20-22, 1976; 'RIP VAN WINKLE' - MARCH 11-15, 1976; ' A BICENTENNIAL CELEBRATION' - APRIL 23-25, 1976; 'THE PATRIOTS' OCT 28-30, 1976. (LOCAL). ROBERT KENDALL; SOUTHERN CONNECTICUT STATE COLLEGE; 501 CRESCENT ST; NEW HAVEN, CT 06515. (#6162-1).

NOV 7 - 9, '75. AIR FORCE ACADEMY CADET CHOIR CONCERT. CHOIR CONCERT FRIDAY EVENING AND SACRED MUSIC CONCERT AT 11:00 AM SERVICE OF CENTER CHURCH-ON-THE-GREEN, SUNDAY, NOVEMBER 9. AT LYMAN HALL AUDITORIUM, SOUTHERN CONNECTICUT STATE COLLEGE. (LOCAL). BETH LYONS, CHAIRMAN; YOUNG WOMEN'S CHRISTIAN ASSOCIATION OF NEW HAVEN, INC.; 48 HOWE ST; NEW HAVEN, CT 06511. (#102135-1).

NOV 30, '75. THANKSGIVING INTERFAITH SERVICES. INTERFAITH RELIGIOUS OBSERVANCES ON CAMPUS. (LOCAL). ROBIN WINKS, CHAIRMAN; NEW HAVEN BICENTENNIAL COMMITTEE & YALE UNIV BICENT COMMITTEE; 157 CHURCH ST; NEW HAVEN, CT 06520. (#104634-21).

DEC 1, '75 - JAN 31, '76. BOSTON IN THE EIGHTEENTH CENTURY. A PICTORAL EXHIBITION ON THE EARLY CITY OF BOSTON AND OTHER COLONIAL CITIES. AT STERLING MEMORIAL LIBRARY. (REGN'L). ROBIN WINKS, CHAIRMAN; YALE UNIVERSITY BICENTENNIAL COMMITTEE; STERLING MEMORIAL LIBRARY; NEW HAVEN, CT 06520. (#104632-1).

DEC 1, '75 - JAN 31, '76. 'THE FLAGS OF THE NATION' - EXHIBIT. EXHIBIT AT STERLING MEMORIAL LIBRARY. (ST-WIDE). ROBIN WINKS, CHAIRMAN; YALE UNIVERSITY BICENTENNIAL COMMITTEE; STERLING MEMORIAL LIBRARY; NEW HAVEN, CT 06520. (#104634-18).

JAN 5 - MAR 31, '76. 'BENJAMIN FRANKLIN AND THE REVOLUTION' - EXHIBIT. EXHIBIT OPENING WITH A RECEPTION FOR AUTHORS OF THE WORKS ON FRANKLIN AND THE EDITORS OF HIS PAPERS FOLLOWED BY A 6 MONTHS EXPOSITION; OPENING TO INCLUDE THE FIRST PUBLIC PERFORMANCE OF FRANKLIN'S OWN COMPOSITION HERE. AT STERLING MEMORIAL LIBRARY. (REGN'L). ROBIN WINKS, CHAIRMAN; YALE UNIVERSITY BICENTENNIAL COMMITTEE; 230 STERLING MEMORIAL LIBRARY; NEW HAVEN, CT 06520. (#104634-24).

JAN 5 - MAR 31, '76. IMAGES OF AMERICA BEFORE THE REVOLUTION. EXHIBIT AT BEINECKE RARE BOOK LIBRARY. (REGN'L). ROBIN WINKS, CHAIRMAN; YALE UNIVERSITY BICENTENNIAL COMMITTEE; BEINECKE LIBRARY; NEW HAVEN, CT 06520. (#104634-7).

JAN 26, '76. 'THE BRITISH ARE COMING!' - BRITISH MILITARY BAND PERFORMANCE. TOUR OF UNITED STATES BY TWO BRITISH REVOLUTIONARY WAR REGIMENTS: THE BLACK WATCH, AND THE ROYAL MARINES. REGTL BANDS TOTALLING APPROX 140 OFFICERS & MEN IN CEREMONIAL UNIFORM. AT NEW HAVEN COLISEUM. (INT'L). CHARLES K JONES, PRES; COLUMBIA ARTISTS FESTIVALS CORP; 165 W 57TH ST; NEW YORK, NY 10019. (#6532-6).

FEB 5, '76. EARLY AMERICAN MUSIC PROGRAM. CHORAL MUSIC OF THE REVOLUTIONARY ERA. AT ENGLEMAN HALL, RM 122 E. (LOCAL). PHYLLIS GELINEAU; SOUTHERN CONNECTICUT STATE COLLEGE, DEPARTMENT OF MUSIC; 501 CRESCENT ST; NEW HAVEN, CT 06515. (#6161-1).

FEB 28, '76. GEORGE WASHINGTON'S BIRTHDAY BALL. FESTIVAL AT SHERATON PARK PLAZA BALLROOM. (LOCAL). MRS JOSEPH ROBERTS, CHMN; MILFORD BICENTENNIAL COMMISSION; MILFORD, CT 06460. (#102803-1).

MAR 1 - 31, '76. DAVID BUSHNELL EXHIBIT. EXHIBIT ON DAVID BUSHNELL, UNDERWATER INVENTOR, AND HIS SCIENTIFIC WORK. AT STERLING MEMORIAL LIBRARY. (REGN'L). ROBIN WINKS, CHAIRMAN; YALE UNIVERSITY BICENTENNIAL COMMITTEE; STERLING MEMORIAL LIBRARY; NEW HAVEN, CT 06520. (#104634-8).

MAR 1 - JUNE 30, '76. ALEXIS DE TOCQUEVILLE IN AMERICA. EXHIBIT OF DE TOCQUEVILLE'S PAPERS FROM HIS AMERICAN TOUR. AT BEINECKE LIBRARY. (REGN'L). ROBIN WINKS, CHAIRMAN; YALE UNIVERSITY BICENTENNIAL COMMITTEE; BEINEKE LIBRARY; NEW HAVEN, CT 06520. (#104634-5).

MAR 1 - JUNE 30, '76. TRAVELERS IN AMERICA. EXHIBIT IN THE NAVE OF THE UNIVERSITY LIBRARY ON FOREIGN TRAVELERS IN THE EIGHTEENTH CENTURY. AT STERLING MEMORIAL LIBRARY. (REGN'L). ROBIN WINKS, CHAIRMAN; YALE UNIVERSITY BICENTENNIAL COMMITTEE; STERLING MEMORIAL LIBRARY; NEW HAVEN, CT 06520. (#104634-6).

MAR 1, '76 - CONTINUING . 'YALE COLLEGE LIBRARY AS IT WAS IN 1742' - EXHIBIT. AN EXHIBIT SHOWING THE NATURE OF YALE COLLEGE LIBRARY AT THE TIME OF THE AMERICAN REVOLUTION. AT BEINICKE RARE BOOK & MANUSCRIPT LIBRARY. (REGN'L). ROBIN WINKS, CHAIRMAN; YALE UNIVERSITY BICENTENNIAL COMMITTEE; BEINICKE LIBRARY; NEW HAVEN, CT 06520. (#104634-19).

MAR '76. THE NATIONS THAT MADE US. INTERNATIONAL ARTS, CRAFTS AND FOOD FAIR. AT INTERNATIONAL STUDENT CENTER. (LOCAL). ROBIN WINKS, CHAIRMAN; YALE UNIVERSITY BICENTENNIAL COMMITTEE; 215 PARK ST; NEW HAVEN, CT 06520. (#104634-1).

MAR '76. PRESENTATION TO BRITISH BICENTENNIAL COMMITTEE. PRESENTATION, IN CONJUNCTION WITH THE NEW HAVEN BICENTENNIAL COMMISSION, OF MOMENTOES OF YALE UNIV AND THE CITY OF NEW HAVEN ON OCCASION OF THE VISIT OF CHAIRMAN OF THE BRITISH BICENTENNIAL COMMITTEE. (INT'L). ROBIN WINKS, CHAIRMAN; YALE UNIVERSITY BICENTENNIAL COMMITTEE; 648 YALE STATION; NEW HAVEN, CT 06520. (#104634-11).

APR 3 - MAY 23, '76. AMERICAN ART 1750-1800, 'TOWARDS INDEPENDENCE'. SUNDAY HOURS: 2 - 5 PM. PEWTER, CERAMICS AND TEXTILES PRODUCED IN AMERICA DURING THE REVOLUTIONARY PERIOD, TO BE EXHIBITED IN NEW HAVEN AND LONDON, ENGLAND. AT YALE UNIVERSITY ART GALLERY. (REGN'L). ALAN SHESTACK, DIRECTOR; YALE UNIVERSITY; BOX 2006, YALE STATION; NEW HAVEN, CT 06520. (#2135-1).

APR 4 - 15, '76. FINNISH ARCHITECTURAL EXHIBIT. EXHIBIT AT YALE UNIV. (INT'L). JAAKKO BERGQUIST; FINNISH-AMERICAN BICENTENNIAL COMMITTEE; 1900 24TH ST, NW; WASHINGTON, DC 20008. (#109040-1).

APR 9 - MAY 7, '76. 'THE HOUSE OF MIRTH' BY EDITH WHARTON & CLYDE FITCH. CURTAIN TIMES: TUES 8:00, WED 2:00 & 8:00, THUR 8:00, FRI 8:00, SAT 4:00 & 8:30, SUN 2:00 & 7:30. AT 222 SARGENT DR, NEW HAVEN, CT, EXIT 46 OF CT TPK, FREE PARKING. (ST-WIDE). LONG WHARF THEATRE; 222 SARGENT DR; NEW HAVEN, CT 06511. (#103227-1).

NEW HAVEN — CONTINUED

APR 15, '76 - CONTINUING . 200 YEARS OF AMERICAN INSTRUMENT MAKERS. EXHIBIT OF INSTRUMENTS, 1776-1976. AT DEPARTMENT OF MUSIC - COLLECTION OF MUSICAL INSTRUMENTS. (REGN'L). ROBIN WINKS, CHAIRMAN; YALE UNIVERSITY BICENTENNIAL COMMITTEE; 15 HILLHOUSE AVE; NEW HAVEN, CT 06520. (#104634-2).

MAY 1 - SEPT 30, '76. EXHIBIT: CONNECTICUT NATURAL HABITATS IN 1776. EXHIBITS AND DIORAMAS WILL BE INSTALLED IN THE PEABODY MUSEUM TO ILLUSTRATE THE NATURE OF CONNECTICUT LANDSCAPE IN 1776. AT PEABODY MUSEUM OF NATURAL HISTORY, 170 WHITNEY AVE. (REGN'L). ROBIN WINKS, CHAIRMAN; YALE UNIVERSITY BICENTENNIAL COMMITTEE; 170 WHITNEY AVE; NEW HAVEN, CT 06520. (#104634-13).

MAY 1, '76 - CONTINUING . DUKE ELLINGTON - AN EXHIBITION OF MEMORABILIA. EXHIBITION FOLLOWING ONE SPONSORED BY WASHINGTON, DC BICENTENNIAL COMMITTEE; LARGE AMOUNT OF MEMORABILIA RELATING TO DUKE ELLINGTON. AT YALE SCHOOL OF MUSIC ON WALL STREET. (REGN'L). ROBIN WINKS, CHAIRMAN; YALE UNIVERSITY BICENTENNIAL COMMITTEE; SCHOOL OF MUSIC LIBRARY; NEW HAVEN, CT 06520. (#104633-1).

MAY 6 - 7, '76. BOSTON HISTORICAL MUSICAL PLAY. LIVE PERFORMANCE AT FAIR HAVEN MIDDLE SCHOOL. (LOCAL). THOMAS DONLON, COORD; FAIR HAVEN MIDDLE SCHOOL; 15 SEKELSKY DR; STRATFORD, CT 06497. (#200008-14).

JUNE 1 - SEPT 4, '76. EXHIBIT: MEDICINE IN THE REVOLUTION. EXHIBIT BY THE YALE SCHOOL OF MEDICINE AND THE SCHOOL OF NURSING AND THE YALE-NEW HAVEN HOSPITAL ON THE STATUS OF MEDICAL PRACTICE IN 1776. AT HISTORICAL LIBRARY OF THE YALE MEDICAL SCHOOL. (REGN'L). ROBIN WINKS, CHAIRMAN; YALE UNIVERSITY BICENTENNIAL COMMITTEE; CEDAR ST; NEW HAVEN, CT 06520. (#104634-12).

JUNE 26 - JULY 5, '76. 'THE ETHNIC EXPERIENCE IN NEW HAVEN', EXHIBIT. THE EXHIBIT WILL EXPLORE NEW HAVEN AREA ETHNIC HERITAGE THROUGH SLIDES, PHOTOGRAPHS, MUSIC & ORAL TAPINGS. (LOCAL). J'LENE MAYO, EXEC DIR; NEW HAVEN BICENTENNIAL COMMISSION; 157 CHURCH ST; NEW HAVEN, CT 06511. (#21335-1).

JUNE 26 - JULY 5, '76. NEW HAVEN CIVIC CELEBRATION AND NEW WORLD FESTIVAL. CULTURAL ACCOMPLISHMENTS OF ETHNIC AMERICANS ARE HIGHLIGHTED THROUGH PERFORMING ARTS, PARADE, HISTORICAL PAGEANTRY, EXHIBITS, WORKSHOPS, SPORTS AND MARITIME EVENTS. AT YALE STADIUM, NEW HAVEN GREEN AND HARBORSIDE. (LOCAL). MS J'LENE MAYO, CHAIRMAN; NEW HAVEN BICENTENNIAL COMMISSION; 157 CHURCH ST, ROOM 800; NEW HAVEN, CT 06510. (#103416-422).

JULY 1 - SEPT 3, '76. EXHIBIT: NEW HAVEN AND THE REVOLUTION. EXHIBITS AND CASSETTE TOURS OF HISTORIC NEW HAVEN GREEN PREPARED BY THE NEW HAVEN BICENTENNIAL COMMITTEE IN COOPERATION WITH THE YALE UNIV FACULTY. (REGN'L). ROBIN WINKS, CHAIRMAN; NEW HAVEN BICENTENNIAL COMMITTEE & YALE UNIV BICENT COMMITTEE; 157 CHURCH ST; NEW HAVEN, CT 06520. (#104634-14).

JULY 14, '76. UNIVERSITY OF CALIFORNIA MARCHING BAND PRESENTS 'SPIRIT OF AMERICA'. THIS IS PART OF A 6-WEEK PERFORMANCE TOUR OF THE U S; 'SPIRIT OF AMERICA' IS A COLLEGIATE MUSICAL REVIEW CELEBRATING OUR NATION'S BICENTENNIAL; WILL INCLUDE FOLK MUSIC, MARCHING, VAUDEVILLE, ROCK, DIXIELAND, JAZZ, BARBERSHOP & SOLOS. AT NEW HAVEN GREEN. (ST-WIDE). GENE WEXLER, MANAGER; YALE UNIV BAND; 2139 YALE STATION; NEW HAVEN, CT 06520. (#10515-16).

JULY 15 - 17, '76. KLEINBASLER DRUMMERS & FIFERS FROM SWITZERLAND - LIVE PERFORMANCE. LIVE PERFORMANCE. (INT'L). CHRISTINE BAUMGARTNER; EMBASSY OF SWITZERLAND; 2900 CATHEDRAL AVE, NW; WASHINGTON, DC 20007. (#108956-1).

SEPT 24, '76. SIBELIUS CONCERT GIVEN BY AN EMINENT FINNISH CONDUCTOR AT YALE. LIVE PERFORMANCE. (INT'L). CULTURAL ATTACHE; EMBASSY OF FINLAND; 1900 24TH ST; WASHINGTON, DC 20008. (#200008-83).

NOV '76. FRANCE'S THEATRE OBLIQUE PERFORMS IN NEW HAVEN, CT. LIVE PERFORMANCE. (INT'L). CULTURAL ATTACHE; EMBASSY OF FRANCE; 2535 BELMONT RD; WASHINGTON, DC 20008. (#200008-84).

FEB 27 - 28, '78. 'DREAM' - OPERA. OPERA ON ORIGINAL LIBRETTO, BASED ON CALDERON'S 'LA VIDA ES SUENO'. (LOCAL). HERTA REDLICH, PRODUCER; NEW HAVEN OPERA THEATRE; BLAKE RD; HAMDEN, CT 06438. (#20956-1).

NEW LONDON

BICENT MARKERS/PUBLICATIONS IN NEW LONDON, CT. HISTORICAL MARKERS & PUBLICATION OF BICENT PROGRAM SCRIPTS WILL HELP TO EDUCATE, REDEDICATE & PERMANENTLY MARK THE SIGNIFICANCE OF OUR LOCAL 1976 CELEBRATION. (LOCAL). CAPT PAUL F FOXE, COORDINATOR; NEW LONDON COUNCIL ON ARTS & FESTIVALS, INC; 1111 OCEAN AVE; NEW LONDON, CT 06320. (#8814). **ARBA GRANTEE.**

BICENTENNIAL PLACEMATS - NEW LONDON, CT. DESIGN, PRINT & DISTRIBUTE BICENTENNIAL PLACEMATS TO HOTELS AND RESTAURANTS. (ST-WIDE). HERBERT I MANDEL, CHAIRMAN; CITY OF NEW LONDON BICENTENNIAL COMMITTEE; 70 GREENWAY RD; NEW LONDON, CT 06320. (#18674). **ARBA GRANTEE.**

COMPLETE HISTORIC WALK, NEW LONDON, CT. IDENTIFY, MARK AND PUBLICIZE CONVENIENT 'TRAIL' OF NEW LONDON'S HISTORIC FACILITIES. (LOCAL). HERBERT I MANDEL, CHAIRMAN; CITY OF NEW LONDON BICENTENNIAL COMMITTEE; 70 GREENWAY RD; NEW LONDON, CT 06320. (#18675). **ARBA GRANTEE.**

FORT TRUMBULL WALKING TOURS, CT. WALKING TOURS OF FORT TRUMBULL. (REGN'L). M A TUCCHIO, CHAIRMAN; NAVAL UNDERWATER SYSTEMS CENTER BICENTENNIAL COMMITTEE; FORT TRUMBULL; NEW LONDON, CT 06325. (#28627).

HERITAGE LECTURES AT CONNECTICUT COLLEGE. LECTURES ON NEW LONDON HISTORY UP TO PRESENT DAY. (LOCAL). ROBLEY EVANS, COMMITTEE CHAIRMAN; CONNECTICUT COLLEGE BICENTENNIAL COMMITTEE; NEW LONDON, CT 06320. (#6287).

LOYALTY DAY PARADE - NEW LONDON, CT. NEW LONDON NATIVE WILL BE NATIONAL COMMANDER OF THE VFW IN 1976 AND WILL BE HONORED IN THE PARADE. (ST-WIDE). HERBERT I MANDEL, CHAIRMAN; CITY OF NEW LONDON BICENTENNIAL COMMITTEE; 70 GREENWAY RD; NEW LONDON, CT 06320. (#18672). **ARBA GRANTEE.**

NATHANIEL HEMPSTEAD HOUSE KITCHEN RESTORATION - CT. RESTORATION OF THE KITCHEN IN THE 1759 NATHANIEL HEMPSTEAD HOUSE. (LOCAL). ARTHUR W LEIBUNDGUTH, DIRECTOR; ANTIQUARIAN & LANDMARKS SOCIETY OF CONNECTICUT, INC; 394 MAIN ST; HARTFORD, CT 06103. (#26027). **ARBA GRANTEE.**

NEW LONDON, CT, FIREMEN'S CONVENTION. BICENTENNIAL CELEBRATION IS THE THEME OF THE FIREMENS CONVENTION. (LOCAL). HERBERT I MANDEL, CHAIRMAN; CITY OF NEW LONDON BICENTENNIAL COMMITTEE; 70 GREENWAY RD; NEW LONDON, CT 06320. (#18673). **ARBA GRANTEE.**

PUBLICATION OF HISTORY OF NEW LONDON, CT. HISTORY OF NEW LONDON FROM FOUNDING TO TODAY. (LOCAL). HERBERT I MANDEL, CHAIRMAN; CITY OF NEW LONDON BICENTENNIAL COMMITTEE; 70 GREENWAY RD; NEW LONDON, CT 06320. (#18676). **ARBA GRANTEE.**

SEMINAR ON FREEDOM & RESPONSIBILITY - CT. A SEMINAR ON NEW LONDON HISTORY, BEFORE AND AFTER THE REVOLUTION. (LOCAL). ROBLEY EVANS, CHAIRMAN COMMITTEE; CONNECTICUT COLLEGE; NEW LONDON, CT 06320. (#14541). **ARBA GRANTEE.**

USCG CUTTER EAGLE TALL SHIPS/OPSAIL - CT. CUTTER EAGLE WILL OPERATE IN OPSAIL THROUGHOUT THE SUMMER OF 1976. (INT'L). LT G J WHITING, CHAIRMAN; COAST GUARD ACADEMY; NEW LONDON, CT 06320. (#31637).

SEPT 1, '74 - JUNE 1, '76. DISPLAY OF HISTORIC DOCUMENTS. PRESERVATION AND EXHIBITION OF HISTORICAL DOCUMENTS AT THE COLLEGE LIBRARY. (ST-WIDE). ROBLEY EVANS, CHAIRMAN; CONNECTICUT COLLEGE BICENT COMMITTEE; NEW LONDON, CT 06320. (#6289-501).

JAN 1 - JUNE 30, '76. SIX LECTURES ON CONNECTICUT & NEW LONDON HISTORY. THE NEW LONDON HERITAGE-CONNECTICUT COLLEGE PROJ. LECTURE SERIES & PUBLICATIONS ON NEW LONDON HISTORY. (LOCAL). ROBLEY EVANS, CHAIRMAN; CONNECTICUT COLLEGE BICENTENNIAL COMMITTEE; NEW LONDON, CT 06320. (#6290-501).

JAN 1 - AUG 3, '76. MUSICAL HISTORY NEW LONDON. FESTIVALS: FREEDOM AND RESPONSIBILITY - CT COLLEGE. MUSICAL HISTORY OF TOWN WITH COLLEGE DIRECTION AND PARTICIPATION. (LOCAL). ROBLEY EVANS, CHAIRMAN; CONNECTICUT COLLEGE BICENTENNIAL COMMITTEE; NEW LONDON, CT 06320. (#6288-501).

MAY 2, '76. LOYALTY DAY PARADE. A NEW LONDON NATIVE WILL BE THE NATIONAL COMMANDER OF THE VFW IN 1976 AND WILL BE HONORED IN THE PARADE. (ST-WIDE). HERBERT I MANDEL, CHMN; CITY OF NEW LONDON BICENTENNIAL COMMITTEE; 70 GREENWAY RD; NEW LONDON, CT 06320. (#18672-1).

JUNE 13 - 18, '76. PUPPETEERS OF AMERICA BICENTENNIAL FESTIVAL. FEATURES PERFORMANCES BY OUTSTANDING PROFESSIONAL PUPPETEERS, WORKSHOPS CLASSES FOR BEGINNERS ADVANCED IN ALL FORMS, HAND STRING, ROD, SHADOW PUPPETS FOR PERFORMERS, TEACHERS, THEARPISTS, RELIGIOUS ED TV FILM ENTERTAINMENT, LIBRARY CONSTRUCTION, MANIPULATION, OTHER. AT CONNECTICUT COLLEGE. (ST-WIDE). OLGA STEVENS, EXEC SEC; PUPPETEERS OF AMERICA INC; P OF A BOX 1061; OJAI, CA 93023. (#50605-1).

JULY 5, '76. REDEDICATION OF FORT TRUMBULL AND HMS MATAPAN OPEN HOUSE. SPEAKERS WITH EMPHASIS ON THE HISTORY OF FORT TRUMBULL. PERFORMANCE OF THE 2ND CONN REGIMENT OF THE CONTINENTAL LINE. TOURS OF THE FORT AND HMS MATAPAN. AT FORT TRUMBULL. (LOCAL). MICHAEL A TUCCHIO, CHMN; U S NAVAL UNDERWATER SYSTEMS CENTER/NEW LONDON BICENTENNIAL COMM; 11 LEGENDARY RD; EAST LYME, CT 06333. (#200008-36).

AUG 10 - 12, '76. AMERICAN FREEDOM TRAIN DISPLAY DAYS AT NEW LONDON, CT. THE AMERICAN FREEDOM TRAIN WILL INCLUDE 10 EXHIBIT CARS AND 2 SHOWCASE CARS DEPICTING DIFFERENT PHASES OF THE AMERICAN EXPERIENCE. ITS ARRIVAL WILL SERVE AS A CATALYST FOR LOCAL BICENTENNIAL CELEBRATIONS BY PEOPLE THROUGHOUT THIS NATION. (ST-WIDE). SY FREEDMAN, DIR OF P/R; THE AMERICAN FREEDOM TRAIN FOUNDATION, INC.; 5205 LEESBURG PKE, SUITE 800; BAILEY'S XRDS, VA 22041. (#1776-64).

SEPT 5, '76. RE-ENACTMENT OF SKIRMISH AT FORT TRUMBULL. LIVE PERFORMANCE AT FORT TRUMBULL NEW LONDON CONN. (REGN'L). MICHAEL A TUCCHIO, CHMN; NAVAL UNDERWATER SYSTEMS CENTER; 11 LEGENDARY RD; EAST LYME, CT 06333. (#200008-85).

SEPT 24 - 26, '76. FIREMEN'S CONVENTION. PARADE, CONFERENCE. (ST-WIDE). HERBERT I MANDEL, CHMN; CITY OF NEW LONDON BICENTENNIAL COMMITTEE; 70 GREENWAY RD; NEW LONDON, CT 06320. (#18673-1).

OCT 9 - 10, '76. MILITARY REVIEW & DEDICATION OF THE WASHINGTON PARADE GROUND. ACADEMY 100TH ANNIVERSARY ALUMNI MUSTER WITH ALL LIVING & FORMER COAST GUARD COMMANDANTS AND ACADEMY SUPERINTENDENTS PRESENT. A MILITARY REVIEW AND OPEN HOUSE ALSO HELD. AT HAMILTON HALL, COAST GUARD ACADEMY. (LOCAL). LT GEORGE J WHITING; US COAST GUARD ACADEMY; NEW LONDON, CT 06320. (#200008-258).

FEB 15 - MAR 15, '77. 'AMERICAN NAVAL PRINTS' EXHIBITION OF 65 HISTORIC NAVAL SCENES. EXHIBIT AT LYMAN ALLYN MUSEUM, 100 MOHEGAN AVE. (REGN'L). MRS JOHN A POPE, PRES; INTERNATIONAL EXHIBITIONS FOUNDATION; 1729 H ST, NW - SUITE 310; WASHINGTON, DC 20006. (#109109-1).

NEWINGTON

NEWINGTON HISTORICAL HOME & MUSEUM, CONNECTICUT. HISTORICAL HOME RESTORED FOR USE AS LOCAL MUSEUM AND CULTURAL CNTR. SERVES TO ENHANCE AND GIVE IDENTITY TO COMMUNITY. WILL ALSO BE USED FOR LOCAL MEETINGS OF CULTURAL EDUCATIONAL & CIVIL ORGANIZATIONS. (LOCAL). MRS ESTHER M EDDY, CHAIRMAN; NEWINGTON U S BICENTENNIAL COMMITTEE; TOWN HALL 131 CEDAR ST; NEWINGTON, CT 06111. (#2671). **ARBA GRANTEE.**

PATRIOTIC DOOR DISPLAY PROJECT - NEWINGTON, CT. THE GARDEN CLUB IS TEACHING SENIOR CITIZENS THE ART OF DECORATING DOORS. THE DOORS WILL BE DONE IN RED, WHITE & BLUE AND REMAIN DECORATED FOR ONE MONTH. (LOCAL). PATRICIA GENOVA, COORDINATOR; NEWINGTON RAMBLING ROSE GARDEN CLUB; 179 BROCKETT ST; NEWINGTON, CT 06111. (#17349).

JAN 1 - DEC 31, '76. 'KNOW YOUR TOWN', SLIDE SHOW. EXHIBIT AT TOWN HALL. (LOCAL). PATRICIA GENOVA, COORD; NEWINGTON LEAGUE OF WOMEN VOTERS; 179 BROCKETT ST; NEWINGTON, CT 06111. (#103286-1).

JAN 10, '76. CHORAL CONCERT WITH BICENTENNIAL THEME BY NEWINGTON CHORAL CLUB. LIVE PERFORMANCE AT TOWN HALL. (LOCAL). PATRICIA GENOVA, COORD; NEWINGTON CHORAL CLUB; 179 BROCKETT ST; NEWINGTON, CT 06111. (#103286-2).

JAN 12 - 16, '76. ART & WRITING THEME CONTEST. COMPETITION AT TOWN HALL. (LOCAL). BOB DETORE, PROJ DIRECTOR; NEWINGTON PARKS & RECREATION DEPT; TOWN HALL; NEWINGTON, CT 06111. (#103286-3).

JAN 18, '76. SWIM MEET. COMPETITION AT TOWN HALL. (LOCAL). BOB DETORE, PROJ DIRECTOR; NEWINGTON PARKS & RECREATION DEPT; TOWN HALL; NEWINGTON, CT 06111. (#103286-4).

JAN 19 - 24, '76. WINTER CARNIVAL. FESTIVAL AT TOWN HALL. (LOCAL). BOB DETORE, PROJ DIRECTOR; NEWINGTON PARKS & RECREATION DEPT; TOWN HALL; NEWINGTON, CT 06111. (#103286-5).

FEB 7, '76. OLD-FASHIONED DOLL DAYS. COMPETITION, EXHIBIT AT TOWN HALL. (LOCAL). BOB DETORE, PROJ DIRECTOR; NEWINGTON PARKS & RECREATION DEPT; TOWN HALL; NEWINGTON, CT 06111. (#103286-10).

FEB 15 - 21, '76. LOLLIPOP FAIR, BAKING CONTEST & CHECKERS & CHESS CONTEST. FAIR AT TOWN HALL. (LOCAL). BOB DETORE, PROJ DIRECTOR; NEWINGTON PARKS & RECREATION DEPT; TOWN HALL; NEWINGTON, CT 06111. (#103286-6).

FEB 21, '76. OPENING CEREMONY OF BICENTENNIAL YEAR. COMMEMORATION WILL INCLUDE A COCKTAIL PARTY & A DINNER DANCE. AT INDIAN HILL COUNTRY CLUB. (LOCAL). PATRICIA GENOVA, COORD; NEWINGTON AMERICAN REVOLUTION BICENTENNIAL COMMITTEE; 179 BROCKETT ST; NEWINGTON, CT 06111. (#103286-8).

FEB 22, '76. CHERRY PIE FESTIVAL. FESTIVAL AT CHURCH HALL, CHURCH ST. (LOCAL). PATRICIA GENOVA, COORD; CHURCH OF THE HOLY SPIRIT; 179 BROCKETT ST; NEWINGTON, CT 06111. (#103286-11).

FEB 28, '76. PEACH BASKET AGE BASKETBALL TOURNAMENT. COMPETITION AT TOWN HALL. (LOCAL). BOB DETORE, PROJ DIRECTOR; NEWINGTON PARKS & RECREATION DEPT; TOWN HALL; NEWINGTON, CT 06111. (#103286-12).

MAR 19, '76. CHILDREN'S THEATRE PRODUCTION. LIVE PERFORMANCE AT TOWN HALL. (LOCAL). BOB DETORE, PROJ DIRECTOR; NEWINGTON PARKS & RECREATION DEPT; TOWN HALL; NEWINGTON, CT 06111. (#103286-13).

MAR 20, '76. BICENTENNIAL CULTURE FAIR. EXHIBIT, FAIR AT TOWN HALL. (LOCAL). BOB DETORE, PROJ DIRECTOR; NEWINGTON PARKS & RECREATION DEPT; TOWN HALL; NEWINGTON, CT 06111. (#103286-14).

MAR 25, '76. SADIE HAWKINS DANCE. FESTIVAL AT TOWN HALL. (LOCAL). BOB DETORE, PROJ DIRECTOR; NEWINGTON PARKS & RECREATION DEPT; TOWN HALL; NEWINGTON, CT 06111. (#103286-15).

MAR 27, '76. BADMINTON TOURNAMENT. COMPETITION AT TOWN HALL. (LOCAL). BOB DETORE, PROJ DIRECTOR; NEWINGTON PARKS & RECREATION DEPT; TOWN HALL; NEWINGTON, CT 06111. (#103286-16).

APR 3, '76. FAMILY STYLE ROAST BEEF DINNER. FESTIVAL AT POST HOME, 85 KITTS LA. (LOCAL). FRANCIS CROSSWAY, DIR; JULIAN RUDEK VFW POST #9836 AND AUXILIARY; 85 KITTS LA; NEWINGTON, CT 06111. (#103286-17).

APR 3, '76. OLD-FASHIONED KITE FLY. COMPETITION AT TOWN HALL. (LOCAL). BOB DETORE, PROJ DIRECTOR; NEWINGTON PARKS & RECREATION DEPT; TOWN HALL; NEWINGTON, CT 06111. (#103286-18).

NEWINGTON — CONTINUED

APR 4, '76. LUNCH IN ITALY AND SPAGHETTI DINNER. FESTIVAL AT ST MARY'S CHURCH AUDITORIUM, WILLARD AVE. (LOCAL). ANTHONY GALLICCHIO, CHMN; UNICO NATIONAL; 35 BERKSHIRE DR; NEWINGTON, CT 06111. (#105906-1).

APR 8, '76. BICENTENNIAL ARTS & CRAFTS FAIR. FAIR WILL FEATURE STUDENT DISPLAYS IN ARTS, CRAFTS, INDUSTRIAL ARTS AND HOME ECONOMICS. STUDENTS WILL ALSO DEMONSTRATE CRAFTS SUCH AS POTTERY. AT JOHN WALLACE MIDDLE SCHOOL, HALLERAN RD. (LOCAL). HERBERT SHEPPARD, DIR; JOHN WALLACE MIDDLE SCHOOL; HALLERAN RD; NEWINGTON, CT 06111. (#105822-2).

APR 10, '76. VOLLEY BALL TOURNAMENT. COMPETITION AT TOWN HALL. (LOCAL). BOB DETORE, PROJ DIRECTOR; NEWINGTON PARKS & RECREATION DEPT; TOWN HALL; NEWINGTON, CT 06111. (#103286-21).

APR 11, '76. ECUMENICAL DIALOGUE. SEMINAR AT ST MARY'S CHURCH, WILLARD AVE. (LOCAL). REV CARL EBB; NEWINGTON CLERGY ASSOCIATION; 327 WALSH AVE; NEWINGTON, CT 06111. (#103286-20).

APR 12 - 16, '76. BICENTENNIAL DRAMATIC READING PROGRAM. LIVE PERFORMANCE AT JOHN WALLACE MIDDLE SCHOOL, HALLERAN RD. (LOCAL). HERBERT SHEPPARD, DIR; JOHN WALLACE MIDDLE SCHOOL; HALLERAN RD; NEWINGTON, CT 06111. (#105822-3).

APR 18 - 24, '76. BUSINESS & INDUSTRY EXPOSITION. EXHIBIT AT TOWN HALL. (LOCAL). CRAIG HOLLAND, PRESIDENT; NEWINGTON CHAMBER OF COMMERCE; TOWN HALL; NEWINGTON, CT 06111. (#103286-19).

APR 21, '76. COLONIAL DESSERT CARD PARTY. FESTIVAL AT TOWN HALL - COMMUNITY CENTER. (LOCAL). MRS C DARR, CHAIRMAN; NEWINGTON HISTORICAL SOCIETY; 125 E ROBBINS AVE; NEWINGTON, CT 06111. (#103286-22).

APR 22 - 25, '76. ANTIQUE SHOW. EXHIBIT. (LOCAL). HOWARD DEMING, PROJ DIR; ROTARY CLUB OF NEWINGTON; 135 CENTERWOOD RD; NEWINGTON, CT 06111. (#103286-24).

APR 24, '76. LUMBERJACK DAY. COMPETITION, FAIR, FESTIVAL AT TOWN HALL. (LOCAL). BOB DETORE, PROJ DIRECTOR; NEWINGTON PARKS & RECREATION DEPT; TOWN HALL; NEWINGTON, CT 06111. (#103286-23).

APR 29, '76. FLAG DISPLAY. PHILIP DAIGNAULT'S COLLECTION OF THE 50 STATE FLAGS AND FLAGS OF THE WORLD WILL BE ON DISPLAY. AT JOHN WALLACE MIDDLE SCHOOL, HALLERAN RD. (LOCAL). HERBERT SHEPPARD, DIR; JOHN WALLACE MIDDLE SCHOOL; HALLERAN RD; NEWINGTON, CT 06111. (#105822-5).

APR 29, '76. 'OUR COUNTRY 'TIS OF THEE'. THE PLAY WILL INVOLVE THE ENTIRE SCHOOL; STUDENT SHOWS WILL BE IN THE AFTERNOON ON APRIL 28 & 30. AT JOHN WALLACE MIDDLE SCHOOL, HALLERAN RD. (LOCAL). HERBERT SHEPPARD, DIR; JOHN WALLACE MIDDLE SCHOOL; HALLERAN DR; NEWINGTON, CT 06111. (#105822-1).

APR 30, '76. TIME CAPSULE DEDICATION CEREMONY. EVERY STUDENT WILL PLACE SOMETHING IN THE TIME CAPSULE, EACH GROUP OF STUDENTS HAS A DIFFERENT THEME; ALL STUDENTS AND FACULTY MEMBERS INCLUDING SUPERINTENDENT OF SCHOOLS AND JOHN WALLACE WILL PLACE THEIR SIGNATURES IN THE CAPSULE; THE CAPSULE WILL BE OPENED IN 2001. AT JOHN WALLACE MIDDLE SCHOOL, HALLERAN RD. (LOCAL). HERBERT SHEPPARD, DIR; JOHN WALLACE MIDDLE SCHOOL; HALLERAN RD; NEWINGTON, CT 06111. (#105822-4).

MAY 1 - 31, '76. BICENTENNIAL ACTIVITIES & EVENTS. EXHIBIT, FAIR, CEREMONY AT MARTIN KELLOGG MIDDLE SCHOOL. (LOCAL). LEWIS PILLSBURY, COORD; MARTIN KELLOGG MIDDLE SCHOOL; 30 THOMAS ST; NEWINGTON, CT 06111. (#106944-1).

MAY 2, '76. LOYALTY DAY BICENTENNIAL BREAKFAST. FESTIVAL AT 85 KITTS LN. (LOCAL). FRANCIS CROSSWAY, COORD; JULIAN RUDEK VFW POST #9836 AND AUXILIARY; 85 KITTS LN; NEWINGTON, CT 06111. (#106144-21).

MAY 6 - 8, '76. MUSICAL COMEDY PRODUCTION 'OF THEE I SING'. LIVE PERFORMANCE AT TOWN HALL THEATRE, MILL ST. (LOCAL). TIM GRIFFIN, COORD; THEATRE NEWINGTON; 33 LYONDALE RD; NEWINGTON, CT 06111. (#106144-20).

MAY 8, '76. LITTLE LEAGUE - OPENING CEREMONIES. CEREMONY AT BADGER FIELD. (LOCAL). CHARLES W RUDOLPH; NEWINGTON LITTLE LEAGUE; 98 CEDAR RIDGE RD; NEWINGTON, CT 06111. (#106144-19).

MAY 15, '76. MAY CONCERT. LIVE PERFORMANCE. (LOCAL). RUTH PINGREE, COORD; NEWINGTON CHORAL CLUB; 186 BRENTWOOD RD; NEWINGTON, CT 06111. (#106144-18).

MAY 15, '76. OLD FASHIONED FAIR. THERE WILL BE ARTS & CRAFTS EXHIBITS AND PRIZES FOR HOME CANNING AND QUILTING. AT HOSPITAL GROUNDS - WILLARD AVE. (LOCAL). DR JULIET VILINSKAS, CHMN; VETERANS' HOSPITAL; NEWINGTON, CT 06111. (#106144-17).

MAY 16, '76. GOD AND COUNTRY DAY - EMPHASIS ON PATRIOTISM. SEMINAR AT 505 CHURCH ST. (LOCAL). REV R WINGATE; EMMANUEL GOSPEL CHURCH; 503 CHURCH ST; NEWINGTON, CT 06111. (#106144-16).

MAY 22, '76. DINNER OF THE TIMES - FOOD OF COLONIAL DAYS. FESTIVAL. (LOCAL). PATRICIA GENOVA, COORD; CIVITAN CLUB; 179 BROCKETT ST; NEWINGTON, CT 06111. (#106144-14).

MAY 22, '76. HISTORIC WILDERNESS HIKE - APPALACHIAN TRAIL. TOUR AT BEGIN AT TOWN HALL. (LOCAL). BOB DETORE, COORD; PARK & RECREATION DEPT; NEWINGTON, CT 06111. (#106144-15).

MAY 23, '76. HOUSES - THEN AND NOW. TOUR AT THROUGHOUT TOWN. (LOCAL). MRS J MARCELLINO, COORD; JUNIOR WOMENS' CLUB & NEWINGTON COUNCIL OF GARDEN CLUBS; 187 OLD FARMS DR; NEWINGTON, CT 06111. (#106144-13).

MAY 30, '76. 'MARKET PLACE' CONSISTING OF ANTIQUES, BAZAAR, GAMES & RIDES. OPENING. (LOCAL). MRS ESTHER M EDDY; NEWINGTON U S BICENTENNIAL COMMITTEE; TOWN HALL 131 CEDAR ST; NEWINGTON, CT 06111. (#2671-501).

MAY 30, '76. MEMORIAL DAY SERVICE. THIS EVENT IS ALSO BEING SPONSORED BY THE DISABLED AMERICAN VETERANS CHAPTER 68 AUXILIARY AND THE MAY DAVIS STOTZER POST 117 & AUXILIARY, AMERICAN LEGION. AT CHURCH OF CHRIST CONGREGATION - MAIN ST. (LOCAL). FRANK ZURASKI, COORD; JULIAN RUDEK POST VFW #9836-AMERICAN LEGION; 178 MIAMI AVE; NEWINGTON, CT 06111. (#106144-12).

MAY 30 - JUNE 4, '76. A WEEK-LONG SHOW FEATURING ARTS, CRAFTS & PERFORMING ARTS. OPENING. (LOCAL). MRS ESTHER M EDDY; NEWINGTON U S BICENTENNIAL COMMITTEE; TOWN HALL 131 CEDAR ST; NEWINGTON, CT 06111. (#2671-502).

JUNE 4, '76. FAMILY PICNIC - BICENTENNIAL THEME. FESTIVAL AT SCHOOL GROUNDS, CEDAR ST. (LOCAL). TED RANDICH, COORD; CENTER DISTRICT PTO; 856 MAIN ST; NEWINGTON, CT 06111. (#106144-11).

JUNE 5, '76. OLD TIME FIELD DAY & FAMILY PICNIC - OLD TIME GAMES. LIVE PERFORMANCE AT NEWINGTON PARK. (LOCAL). BOB DETORE, COORD; PARK & RECREATION DEPT; NEWINGTON, CT 06111. (#106144-10).

JUNE 6, '76. SHINDIG IN THE PARK - OPEN SQUARE DANCE. FESTIVAL AT MILL POND PARK. (LOCAL). H MANNING, COORD; NEWINGTON SQUARE DANCE CLUB; 103 WILBUR DR; NEWINGTON, CT 06111. (#106144-9).

JUNE 10 - 13, '76. OLD FASHIONED BEER GARDEN & ENTERTAINMENT. FESTIVAL AT CENTER GREEN. (LOCAL). ALAN HAGER, COORD; NEWINGTON JAYCEES; 7 IVY LN; NEWINGTON, CT 06111. (#106144-8).

JUNE 12, '76. BICENTENNIAL PARADE. OPENING. (LOCAL). MRS ESTHER M EDDY; NEWINGTON U S BICENTENNIAL COMMITTEE; TOWN HALL 131 CEDAR ST; NEWINGTON, CT 06111. (#2671-503).

JUNE 12, '76. CHICKEN BARBECUE. FESTIVAL AT MILL POND PARK. (LOCAL). RALPH HALL, COORD; NEWINGTON GRANGE #44; 36 KIRKHAM ST; NEWINGTON, CT 06111. (#106144-5).

JUNE 12, '76. OPEN HOUSE CELEBRATING REVOLUTIONARY WAR HEROES OF POLISH ORIGIN. FEATURED WILL BE POLISH FOOD, MUSIC & DANCING. AT WILSON AVE. (LOCAL). FRANK ZURASKI, COORD; POLISH AMERICAN CLUB; 178 MIAMI AVE; NEWINGTON, CT 06111. (#106144-4).

JUNE 14, '76. COMMEMORATION OF FLAG DAY. CEREMONY. (LOCAL). FRANK ZURASKI, COORD; AMERICAN LEGION MAY DAVIS STOTZER POST #117; 178 MIAMI AVE; NEWINGTON, CT 06111. (#106144-3).

JUNE 21 - 25, '76. SPORTS CAMP; INSTRUCTION AND DEMONSTRATION. SEMINAR AT TOWN HALL. (LOCAL). BOB DETURE, COORD; PARK & RECREATION DEPT; PARK/RECREATION DEPT, TOWN HALL; NEWINGTON, CT 06111. (#106144-2).

JUNE 26, '76. FIFE & DRUM COMPETITION. LIVE PERFORMANCE AT MILL POND PARK. (LOCAL). NOREEN ADDIS, COORD; NEWINGTON FIFE & DRUM CORPS; NEWINGTON, CT 06111. (#106144-1).

NOV 6, '76. BICENTENNIAL BALL: GRAND FINALE OF NEWINGTON, CT CELEBRATION. OPENING. (LOCAL). MRS ESTHER M EDDY; NEWINGTON U S BICENTENNIAL COMMITTEE; TOWN HALL 131 CEDAR ST; NEWINGTON, CT 06111. (#2671-504).

NOANK

JULY 4, '76. 4TH OF JULY CELEBRATION. BICENTENNIAL PROJECT WILL DEPICT EVENTS OF LOCAL HISTORICAL INTEREST FESTIVE GATHERINGS & ACTIVITIES. ALSO: BOOK/GUIDE/OTHER PUBLICATION. AT NOANK SHIPYARD. (LOCAL). MICHAEL ABEL, PRES; NOANK HISTORICAL SOCIETY; NOANK, CT 06340. (#4189-1).

NORFOLK

BICENTENNIAL CACHET AND COVER IN NORFOLK, CT. A SPECIAL FIRST-DAY COVER BEARING THE SEAL OF THE TOWN AND THREE SPIRIT OF 76 STAMPS AND COMMEMORATING THE DEDICATION OF THE REVOLUTIONARY MONUMENT. (LOCAL). FREDERICK W RIGGS, CHAIRMAN; NORFOLK BICENTENNIAL COMMISSION; WHEELER RD; NORFOLK, CT 06058. (#29673).

HISTORIC UPDATE OF NORFOLK 1900-1976 - CT. A 300-PAGE ILLUSTRATED BOUND BOOK OF THE TOWN'S HISTORY, PRODUCED BY 50 OF THE TOWN'S PROFESSIONAL AND NON-PROFESSIONAL WRITERS. (LOCAL). MS ALICE WALDECKER, COORDINATOR; NORFOLK BICENTENNIAL COMMISSION/NORFOLK HISTORICAL SOCIETY; SHEPARD RD; NORFOLK, CT 06058. (#29674).

NORFOLK NOW AND THEN - CT. A PICTORIAL BOOKLET SHOWING NORFOLK SCENES AND STRUCTURES OF LONG AGO WITH THEIR APPEARANCE TODAY. (LOCAL). ALAN REDFORD, COORDINATOR; NORFOLK HISTORICAL SOCIETY; GREENWOODS RD; NORFOLK, CT 06058. (#29672).

JUNE 6, '76. ECUMENICAL BICENTENNIAL VESPER SERVICE. CEREMONY AT FIRST CHURCH OF CHRIST, CONGREGATONAL NORFOLK TOWN GREEN. (LOCAL). EDWARD QUINLAN, JR; NORFOLK BICENTENNIAL COMMISSION; NORTH ST; NORFOLK, CT 06058. (#200008-41).

JUNE 12, '76. DEDICATION OF REVOLUTIONARY WAR MEMORIAL, HIST LECTURE & EXHIBITS. CEREMONY, EXHIBIT, PARADE AT BUTTERMILK FALLS PARK, VILLAGE GREEN, HISTORICAL MUSEUM. (LOCAL). MRS CARL GABELMANN; NORFOLK BICENTENNIAL COMMISSION & NORFOLK HISTORICAL SOCIETY; LITCHFIELD RD; NORFOLK, CT 06058. (#200008-42).

JULY 3, '76. TRIBUTE TO AN AMERICAN COMPOSER, CHARLES IVES. LIVE PERFORMANCE AT MUSIC SHED, ELLEN BATTELL STOECKEL ESTATE. (ST-WIDE). KEITH WILSON; YALE IN NORFOLK, YALE UNIVERSITY NEW HAVEN; ELLEN BATTELL STOECKEL ESTATE; NORFOLK, CT 06058. (#200008-40).

NORTH CANAAN

JULY 4, '76. ECUMENICAL CHURCH SERVICE AND CHOIR SING - '200 YEARS MUSIC'. HOUSATONIC VALLEY CHORUS, DEDICATION OF NEW FLAG IN E CANAAN. OTHER EVENTS: PARADE, READING-CANAAN DURING REV WAR, OLD COUNTRY STORE, COMMUNITY PICNIC, NEW PARK, FLOWERS PLANTED, CHARTER OAK PLANTED, RAILROAD DAYS, JACK BROWN FAIR BICENTENNIAL BALL, LECTURE, ETC. AT TOWN HALL. (LOCAL). LAURA FREUND, CHAIRMAN; NORTH CANAAN BICENTENNIAL COMMISSION; RFD 1; EAST CANAAN, CT 06024. (#200008-34).

NORTH GRANBY

THE BICENTENNIAL PIANO IN NORTH GRANBY, CT. RE-CREATION OF FIRST PIANO BUILT IN THIS COUNTRY IN 1775 BY JOHN BEHRENT OF PHILADELPHIA. (LOCAL). JANET W HAYES, DIRECTOR; PIANO TECHNICIANS GUILD, INC OF CT; 260 MOUNTAIN RD; NORTH GRANBY, CT 06060. (#33021).

NORTH HAVEN

ESTABLISH CAMPING GROUNDS FOR NORTH HAVEN, CT. FIRST TOWN OWNED CAMPING GROUNDS WILL PROVIDE SAFE OVERNIGHT & DAYTIME CAMPING WITH SUPERVISION & PROTECTION. TOWN EDUCATION, RECREATION & PARK DEPTS TO FOSTER ACTIVITIES, ALSO INVOLVE SCOUT GROUPS. (LOCAL). CAROLANN MUZIO, VICE CHAIRMAN; NORTH HAVEN BICENTENNIAL COMMITTEE - HORIZONS 76; 18 CHURCH ST, PO BOX 1776; NORTH HAVEN, CT 06473. (#7348). **(??). ARBA GRANTEE.**

OCT 13, '76. DEDICATION TOURS & CELEBRATION CEREMONY. OPENING. (LOCAL). CAROLANN MUZIO; NORTH HAVEN BICENTENNIAL COMMITTEE - HORIZONS 76; 18 CHURCH ST, PO BOX 1776; NORTH HAVEN, CT 06473. (#7348-501).

NORWALK

AMERICANA: FILM SERIES, NORWALK, CT. SELECTED FILMS EXPRESSING CURRENTS OF THOUGHTS, CULTURE OR HISTORY WHICH ARE UNIQUELY AMERICAN. OPEN TO COMMUNITY. (LOCAL). PROF ADA LAMBERT, PROJ DIRECTOR; NORWALK COMMUNITY COLLEGE; 333 WILSON AVE; NORWALK, CT 06854. (#17711).

'ARCHAEOLOGY AS AN AVOCATION' - NORWALK, CT. A TRAINING PGM TO GIVE AMATEUR ARCHAEOLOGISTS THE SKILLS NECESSARY TO RESCUE LOCAL PREHISTORY & PRESERVE THE PAST FOR TOMORROW. (LOCAL). LORRAINE OSBORNE, CHAIRWOMAN; NORWALK COMMUNITY COLLEGE BICENTENNIAL COMMITTEE; 333 WILSON AVE; NORWALK, CT 06854. (#17713).

BOOK HISTORY OF NORWALK, CONNECTICUT. HISTORY BOOK OF NORWALK FOR USE IN PRIMARY & SECONDARY SCHOOLS. BOOK WILL COVER THE PERIOD OF HISTORY FROM 1651 TO 1976. (LOCAL). DOUGLAS BORA, CHAIRMAN; NORWALK AMERICAN REVOLUTION BICENTENNIAL COMMISSION; 164 ROWAYTON AVE; NORWALK, CT 06853. (#5290). **ARBA GRANTEE.**

HISTORY OF U S MUSIC, NORWALK, CT. A STUDY OF MUSIC IN THE U S FROM COLONIAL TIMES TO THE PRESENT. (LOCAL). PROF RAYMOND STEWART, PROJ DIRECTOR; NORWALK COMMUNITY COLLEGE; 333 WILSON AVE; NORWALK, CT 06854. (#17712).

WOMEN IN AMERICA THE PAST AND FUTURE - COLLEGE SYMPOSIUM. CONFERENCE. (LOCAL). LORRAINE OSBORNE, CHMN; NORWALK COMMUNITY COLLEGE BICENTENNIAL COMMITTEE; 333 WILSON AVE; NORWALK, CT 06854. (#103395-1).

YANKEE DOODLE HOUSE IN NORWALK, CT. HOUSE IS A REPLICA OF THE THOMAS FITCH HOUSE & PART OF A HISTORIC COMPLEX INCLUDING A TOWN HOUSE, LITTLE RED SCHOOLHOUSE, GOVERNOR FITCH'S HOUSE & THE OLD JAIL. (LOCAL). DOUGLAS A BORA, OFFICE OF THE COMMISSIONER; NORWALK BICENTENNIAL COMMISSION; 164 ROWAYTON AVE; ROYWATON, CT 06853. (#21342). **ARBA GRANTEE.**

NORWICH

BOOK: 'NINE DOLLARS FOR ROOM AND BOARD' - CT. REMINISCENCES OF LEWIS R PECKHAM, CUSTOMS AND EVENTS OF HIS BOYHOOD. (LOCAL). SOPHIE WOODMANSEE, CHAIRMAN; PRESTON HISTORICAL SOCIETY; RFD 3, NORWICH CT; NORWICH, CT 06360. (#20712).

BROCHURES ON NORWICH HERITAGE - NORWICH, CT. 2 BROCHURES, WRITTEN AND SKETCHED BY LOCAL HIGH SCHOOL STUDENTS, WILL BE PRINTED AND DISTRIBUTED BY LOCAL CHAMBER AND MOTELS. (LOCAL). MARIAN K O'KEEFE, CHAIRMAN; NORWICH BICENTENNIAL COMMITTEE; CITY HALL; NORWICH, CT 06360. (#23619). **ARBA GRANTEE.**

NORWICH — CONTINUED

HISTORY OF PRESTON QUILT - NORWICH, CT. EACH BLOCK DEPICTS THE HISTORY OF PRESTON STARTING WITH THE INDIANS AND UP TO SHOWING OUR NEW SCHOOL AND TOWN HALL. (LOCAL). SOPHIE WOODMANSEE, CHAIRMAN; PRESTON HISTORICAL SOCIETY; RFD 3; NORWICH, CT 06360. (#20711).

NORWICH, CONN, DURING THE REVOLUTION PROJECT. FILM STRIP CONSISTING OF 63 PICTURES, MANUSCRIPTS & TAPES DEPICTING LIFE IN NORWICH DURING THE REVOLUTIONARY WAR, TO BE DISTRIBUTED TO THE LOCAL SCHOOL SYSTEM & LIBRARY. (LOCAL). MRS MARIAN K O'KEEFE, CHAIRMAN; NORWICH BICENTENNIAL COMMITTEE; NORWICH CITY HALL, UNION SQUARE; CONNECTICUT, CT 06360. (#2737).

PURCHASE OF INVENTORY OF THOMAS LEFFINGWELL - CT. THE INVENTORY CONCERNS THE HOUSEHOLD EFFECTS OF THOMAS LEFFINGWELL. (LOCAL). MARIAN K O'KEEFE, CHMN; CITY OF NORWICH; CITY HALL; NORWICH, CT 06360. (#15429). **ARBA GRANTEE.**

MAY 4, '75. FIFE & DRUM CORPS PERFORMANCE OF REVOLUTIONARY TIMES. 'A DAY IN THE LIFE OF A CONTINENTAL SOLDIER' - A FIFE & DRUM CORPS PRESENTATION TO BE HELD ON THE TOWN GREEN. GREEN IN MAY 1975. AT TOWN GREEN. (ST-WIDE). MRS MARIAN K O'KEEFE; NORWICH NORWICH BICENTENNIIAL COMMITTEE; NORWICH CITY HALL, UNION SQUARE; NORWICH, CT 06360. (#2738-501).

JUNE 13 - SEPT 20, '75. SUVEY OF AMERICAN GRAPHICS, 1775-1975. MUSEUM IS CLOSED HOLIDAYS. AT 108 CRESCENT ST CAMPUS OF NORWICH FREE ACADEMY. (LOCAL). JOSEPH P GUALTIERI, DIR; THE SLATER MEMORIAL MUSEUM AND CONVERSE ART GALLERY; 108 CRESCENT ST; NORWICH, CT 06360. (#100786-1).

SEPT 25 - NOV 20, '75. 18TH CENTURY REVISITED: 8-WEEK COURSE. SEMINAR AT MOHEGAN COMMUNITY COLLEGE. (ST-WIDE). MS LINDA EDGERTON,COORD; MOHEGAN COMMUNITY COLLEGE AND THE NORWICH BICENTENNIAL COMMITTEE; NORWICH, CT 06360. (#102147-1).

NOV 22, '75. BICENTENNIAL BALL. FESTIVAL AT NORWICH SHERATON, RTE 82. (LOCAL). MRS RIITTA HALEY, CHMN; NORWICH BICENTENNIAL COMMITTEE; CITY HALL; NORWICH, CT 06360. (#102133-1).

DEC 7, '75 - JAN 4, '76. AMERICAN CRAFTS. THE MUSEUM WILL BE OPEN SAT & SUN FROM 2-5 PM, CLOSED HOLIDAYS. AT 108 CRESCENT ST, CAMPUS OF NORWICH FREE ACADEMY. (LOCAL). JOSEPH P GUALTIERI, DIR; THE SLATER MEMORIAL MUSEUM & CONVERSE ART GALLERY; 108 CRESCENT ST; NORWICH, CT 06360. (#100786-3).

JAN 1 - JULY 4, '76. HOUSE RESTORATION AWARD COMPETITION. RESTORATION AWARD PROGRAM, NORWICH, CONN. AWARDS PROGRAM FOR THE BEST RESTORED HOUSES OF THE COLONIAL, FEDERAL & VICTORIAN PERIOD IN NORWICH. (LOCAL). MRS CATHERINE DOROSHEVICH; NORWICH HERITAGE COMMITTEE; AREA CHAMBER OF COMMERCE; CHAMBER OF COMMERCE; NORWICH, CT 06360. (#2739-501).

FEB 15 - MAR 14, '76. VIEWS OF NORWICH, 1776-1976. THE MUSEUM WILL BE OPEN SAT & SUN FROM 2-5 PM, CLOSED HOLIDAYS. AT 108 CRESCENT ST, CAMPUS OF NORWICH FREE ACADEMY. (LOCAL). JOSEPH P GUALTIERI, DIR; THE SLATER MEMORIAL MUSEUM & CONVERSE ART GALLERY; 108 CRESCENT ST; NORWICH, CT 06360. (#100786-2).

JUNE 11 - SEPT 26, '76. AMERICAN HISTORICAL EXHIBITON. CLOSED HOLIDAYS. AT 108 CRESCENT ST, CAMPUS OF NORWICH FREE ACADEMY. (LOCAL). JOSEPH P GUALTIERI, DIR; THE SLATER MEMORIAL MUSEUM & CONVERSE ART GALLERY; 108 CRESCENT ST; NORWICH, CT 06360. (#100786-4).

JULY 26 - 27, '76. UNITED STATES ARMED FORCES BICENTENNIAL CARAVAN. CARAVAN IS COMPOSED OF EXHIBIT VANS FOR EACH MILITARY SERVICE. PROJECT THEME IS 'HISTORY OF THE ARMED FORCES & THEIR CONTRIBUTIONS TO THE NATION.'. AT KELLY JR HIGH SCHOOL, MAHAN DRIVE, NORWICH. (LOCAL). MRS T F O'KEEFE, JR, CHMN; UNITED STATES ARMED FORCES BICENTENNIAL CARAVAN; 5 DUPONT LANE; NORWICH, CT 06360. (#1775-592).

AUG 28, '76. A SETTLER'S DAY IN OLD NORWICHTOWN. FESTIVAL AT NORWICHTOWN GREEN. (ST-WIDE). MARION O'KEEFE, CHMN; OLD SETTLER'S DAY COMMITTEE; NORWICH, CT 06360. (#103416-513).

DEC 12, '76 - JAN 9, '77. CIVIL WAR PERIOD. CLOSED HOLIDAYS. AT 108 CRESCENT ST, CAMPUS OF NORWICH FREE ACADEMY. (LOCAL). JOSEPH P GUALTIERI, DIR; THE SLATER MEMORIAL MUSEUM & CONVERSE ART GALLERY; 108 CRESCENT ST; NORWICH, CT 06360. (#100786-5).

OLD LYME

'A LYME MISCELLANY, 1776-1976', OLD LYME, CT. A BOOK OF POPULAR & SCHOLARY INTEREST ABOUT REVOLUTION INCLUDES ESSAYS BY PROMINENT HISTORIANS AND DOCUMENTARY MATERIAL; ITS OBJECTIVE IS TO RELATE HERITAGE OF THE TOWN & COLONY TO REVOLUTION & PRESENT. (ST-WIDE). MRS JOHN CROSBY BROWN, BICENTENNIAL CHAIRMAN; LYME HISTORICAL SOCIETY; LYME ST; OLD LYME, CT 06371. (#12252). **ARBA GRANTEE.**

A NEW LOOK AT HISTORY PROJECT OF CONN. PROG DESIGNED TO STIMULAE STUDENTS' AWARENESS OF HISTORY IN THEIR DAILY ENVIRONMENT. INCLUDES HISTORY WORK BOOK AND SLIDE PROGRAMS. (ST-WIDE). MRS JOHN CROSBY BROWN, CHAIRMAN; OLD LYME BICENTENNIAL COMMISSION; LYME ST; OLD LYME, CT 06371. (#843). **ARBA GRANTEE.**

MAY 3, '75. MARATHON GIRL SCOUTS WILL PLANT ACORNS FROM CHARTER OAK TREE. FESTIVAL, LIVE PERFORMANCE. (LOCAL). MARGARET C BROWN; OLD LYME BICENTENNIAL COMMITTEE; ROUTE 156, HAMBURG COVE; LYME, CT 06371. (#6278-502).

JULY 12, '75. NATHAN HALE FIFE AND DRUM CORPS - DAY IN LIFE OF CONTINENTAL SOLDIER. FESTIVAL, LIVE PERFORMANCE. (LOCAL). MARGARET C BROWN; OLD LYME BICENTENNIAL COMMITTEE; ROUTE 156, HAMBURG COVE; LYME, CT 06371. (#6278-501).

OLD MYSTIC

LIBRARY ADDITION - OLD MYSTIC, CT. RENOVATE ADJOINING STRUCTURE OF LIBRARY FOR USE AS INDIAN & COLONIAL LIBRARY; RELOCATE FROM STORAGE, REPAIR & CATALOG BOOKS & MANUSCRIPTS FROM THE COLONIAL PERIOD. (LOCAL). WARREN B FISH, V-PRESIDENT; INDIAN & COLONIAL RESEARCH CENTER INC; MAIN ST; OLD MYSTIC, CT 06372. (#26875). **ARBA GRANTEE.**

OLD SAYBROOK

BOOK ON LOCAL HISTORY, OLD SAYBROOK, CONNECTICUT. BOOK WILL COVER PERIOD FROM 1635-1860 & WILL INCLUDE A HISTORY OF FORMER COLONIAL TOWNS. (LOCAL). THOMAS DOYLE JR, CHAIRMAN; OLD SAYBROOK AMERICAN REVOLUTION BICENTENNIAL COMMISSION; PO BOX 1776; OLD SAYBROOK, CT 06475. (#5289). **ARBA GRANTEE.**

GENERAL HART'S HOME RESTORATION - OLD SAYBROOK, CT. ACQUISITION & RESTORATION OF GENERAL WILLIAM HART'S HOME FOR USE AS HEADQUARTERS FOR HISTORICAL SOCIETY MUSEUM & EXHIBIT CENTER, PUBLIC MEETING PLACE FOR LOCAL GROUPS & EDUCATIONAL RESOURCE. (LOCAL). ALEXANDER C HUSBAND, PRESIDENT; OLD SAYBROOK HISTORICAL SOCIETY; 395 MAIN ST; OLD SAYBROOK, CT 06475. (#8812). **ARBA GRANTEE.**

PRESERVATION OF OLD SAYBROOK, CONNECTICUT. HELP IMPROVE SAYBROOKS TOMORROW, OBSERVE, RESTORE YESTERDAY BY PUBLISHING BOOK ON LOCAL HISTORY, PRESERVING OLD FORT & OTHER HISTORICAL LANDMARKS. (LOCAL). THOMAS J DOYLE JR, CHAIRMAN; OLD SAYBROOK BICENTENNIAL COMMITTEE; PO BOX 1776; OLD SAYBROOK, CT 06475. (#4639).

RESTORATION OF COLONIAL KITCHEN, OLD SAYBROOK, CT. PRESERVATION & RESTORATION OF 1767 KITCHEN OF THE GEN W HART HOUSE; WILL BE USED TO DEPICT COLONIAL LIFE AND AS A COMMUNITY ACTIVITY CENTER. (LOCAL). A C HUSBAND, PRESIDENT; OLD SAYBROOK HISTORICAL SOCIETY; PO BOX 4; OLD SAYBROOK, CT 06475. (#13240). **ARBA GRANTEE.**

ONECO

JULY 4, '76. STERLING-VOLUNTOWN INDEPENDENCE DAY PICNIC. FESTIVAL AT EKONK GRANGE #89 & EKONK CONGREGATIONAL CHURCH, RTE #49 TOWN LINE. (LOCAL). MARLENE A COOK, CHAIRMAN; STERLING-VOLUNTOWN BICENTENNIAL COMMITTEES; ROUTE #14A; ONECO, CT 06373. (#200008-35).

OXFORD

CEMETERY REPAIR IN OXFORD, CONNECTICUT. PROVIDE FOR REPAIR OF LOCAL CEMETERY & PROVIDE FOR ITS PERMANENT CARE BY SURVEYING AVAILABLE PLOTS AND GIVING ESTABLISHED CEMETERY GROUP RESPONSIBILITY FOR SALE OF PLOTS AND PERPETUAL CARE DUTIES. (LOCAL). BISHOP W VONWETTBERG, CO-CHAIRMAN; OXFORD BICENT COMMISSION; OXFORD RD; OXFORD, CT 06483. (#9341).

RECORD OF BICENTENNIAL IN OXFORD, CT. THE PROJECT INVOLVES MAKING A RECORD ON FILM, SLIDES AND PHOTOGRAPHS OF THE LOCAL BICENT OBSERVANCE, STRESSING LOCAL HISTORY; THE RECORD WILL BE USED IN SCHOOLS AT A LATER DATE AS AN AUDIO-VISUAL AID. (LOCAL). BISHOP W VONWETTBERG, CO-CHAIRMAN; OXFORD BICENT COMMISSION; OXFORD RD; OXFORD, CT 05483. (#9339).

REGISTRY OF HISTORIC HOMES AND SITES IN OXFORD, CT. MARKING OR REGISTRY OF HISTORIC HOMES AND SITES IN TOWN. (LOCAL). BISHOP W VONWETTBERG, CO-CHAIRMAN; OXFORD BICENT COMMISSION; OXFORD RD; OXFORD, CT 06403. (#9338).

WAR MEMORIAL IN OXFORD, CONNECTICUT. INVESTIGATE AND PLAN FOR MONUMENT TO ALL AMERICAN SOLDIERS FROM ALL AMERICAN CONFLICTS AND WARS; TO BE INCLUDED IN NEW TOWN HALL DEVELOPMENT. (LOCAL). BISHOP W VONWETTBERG, CO-CHAIRMAN; OXFORD BICENT COMMISSION; OXFORD RD; OXFORD, CT 06483. (#9340).

PLAINVILLE

MAY 29, '76. HERITAGE IN THE PARK: A BICENTENNIAL FAIR. FESTIVAL AT NORTON PARK, S WASHINGTON ST. (LOCAL). RUTH HUMMEL, CHMN; PLAINVILLE BICENTENNIAL COMMITTEE; BOX 24; PLAINVILLE, CT 06062. (#200008-260).

MAY 30, '76. DEDICATION OF HISTORIC CENTER. CEREMONY AT 29 PIERCE ST, PLAINVILLE HISTORIC CENTER. (LOCAL). RUTH S HUMMEL, CHMN; PLAINVILLE HISTORICAL SOCIETY, INC; BOX 14; PLAINVILLE, CT 06062. (#200008-63).

PLYMOUTH

COMMEMORATIVE MEDALLION - PLYMOUTH, CT. FOUR MEDALLIONS ARE BEING MADE IN STERLING SILVER, PEWTER, COPPER AND BRONZE WITH THE TOWN SEAL AND THE 6TH REGIMENTAL FLAG ON THEM. (LOCAL). VINCENT A KLIMAS, CHAIRMAN, COIN COMMITTEE; PLYMOUTH BICENTENNIAL COMMISSION; 5 DILION DR; TERRYVILLE, CT 06786. (#17137).

ETHNIC COOKBOOK - PLYMOUTH, CT. THE COOKBOOK WILL CONTAIN ETHNIC RECIPES AND COLONIAL ERA DISHES. (LOCAL). MRS ANN PLOSZAJ, PROJ COORDINATOR; PLYMOUTH BICENTENNIAL COMMITTEE; HIGH ST; TERRYVILLE, CT 06786. (#17135).

HISTORY OF PLYMOUTH, CT. THE HISTORY OF PLYMOUTH FROM 1895 TO THE PRESENT WILL BE PUBLISHED TO SUPPLEMENT THE EXISTING TOWN HISTORY THAT COVERS 1795 TO 1895. (LOCAL). J FRANCIS RYAN, CHAIRMAN; PLYMOUTH BICENTENNIAL COMMITTEE; 8 OAK ST; TERRYVILLE, CT 06786. (#17134).

LASTING BICENTENNIAL MEMORIAL, PLYMOUTH, CONN. PREPARING HISTORY OF PLYMOUTH. MARKING HISTORICAL SITES IN TOWN. ETHNIC SONGS, DANCES & PARADES. HISTORICALLY ILLUSTRATED LECTURES & RELIGIOUS SERVICES. ALSO PREPARING COIN -MEDALLION IN VARIOUS METALS. (LOCAL). J FRANCIS RYAN, DIRECTOR; PLYMOUTH BICENTENNIAL COMMITTEE; 8 OAK ST; TERRYVILLE, CT 06786. (#2582). **ARBA GRANTEE.**

LECTURES & FILMS ON LOCAL HISTORY - PLYMOUTH, CT. FILMS AND LECTURES ON LOCAL HISTORY WILL BE MADE AVAILABLE TO CLUBS SCHOOLS AND CIVIC GROUPS. A PERMANENT TAPE WILL BE PREPARED FOR FUTURE GENERATIONS. (LOCAL). HORACE WHITTIER, HISTORY COMM; PLYMOUTH BICENTENNIAL COMMISSION; 5 MAPLE ST; BRISTOL, CT 06010. (#17136).

JAN 15, '74 - MAR 1, '75. HISTORICAL SLIDE LECTURES. EXHIBIT. (LOCAL). J FRANCIS RYAN, DIRECTOR; PLYMOUTH BICENTENNIAL COMMITTEE; 8 OAK ST; TERRYVILLE, CT 06786. (#2582-902).

MAY 7, '76. INTERNATIONAL ENTERTAINMENT. LIVE PERFORMANCE. (LOCAL). J FRANCIS RYAN, CHMN; PLYMOUTH ARBC; 8 OAK ST; TERRYVILLE, CT 06786. (#200008-13).

MAY 16, '76. BICENTENNIAL DAY IN PLYMOUTH. ACTIVITIES INCLUDE A STAMP SHOW, FLAG DISPLAY AT THE HIGH SCHOOL, ARTS & CRAFTS ON THE VILLAGE GREEN, CONCERT AT ST PAUL'S LUTHERAN CHURCH, HOME TOUR OF 10 HOMES & 2 CHURCHES. (LOCAL). J FRANCIS RYAN, CHMN; PLYMOUTH ARBC; 8 OAK ST; TERRYVILLE, CT 06786. (#200008-12).

MAY 19 - 22, '76. ANTIQUE SHOW AND ARTS & CRAFTS SHOW. EXHIBIT AT E MAIN ELEMENTARY SCHOOL. (LOCAL). J FRANCIS RYAN, CHAIRMAN; PLYMOUTH AMERICAN REVOLUTION BICENTENNIAL COMMITTEE; 8 OAK ST; TERRYVILLE, CT 06786. (#108148-1).

MAY 23, '76. PLYMOUTH BICENTENNIAL TAG SALE ON THE GREEN. VILLAGE GREEN WAS CIVIL WAR TRAINING GROUND. AT PLYMOUTH VILLAGE GREEN. (LOCAL). J FRANCIS RYAN, CHMN; PLYMOUTH ARBC; 8 OAK ST; TERRYVILLE, CT 06786. (#102398-11).

JUNE 20, '76. ECUMENICAL SERVICES ON VILLAGE GREEN. ALSO: COINS, FILM/SLIDES. (LOCAL). J FRANCIS RYAN, DIRECTOR; PLYMOUTH BICENTENNIAL COMMITTEE; 8 OAK ST; TERRYVILLE, CT 06786. (#2582-3).

JULY 4, '76. PARADE - TED KNIGHT, GRAND MARSHALL. LIVE PERFORMANCE AT PLYMOUTH VILLAGE GREEN, ROUTE 6. (LOCAL). J FRANCIS RYAN, CHMN; PLYMOUTH ARBC; 8 OAK ST; TERRYVILLE, CT 06786. (#102398-15).

POMFRET

PERIOD DIARIES IN POMFRET, CONNECTICUT. DECIPHER & PRINT ERA DIARIES OF LEMUEL GROSVENOR, WALTER LYONS AND AARON PUTNAM THAT WERE KEPT DURING THE WAR YEARS. (LOCAL). CHARLES THORPE, CHAIRMAN; POMFRET BICENTENNIAL COMMISSION; PO BOX 1776; POMFRET, CT 06258. (#9617).

MAY 22, '76. MUSTER OF WINDHAM COUNTY TROOPS TO LEXINGTON, CT. FESTIVAL, LIVE PERFORMANCE. (LOCAL). CHARLES THORPE; POMFRET BICENT COMMISSION; BOX 1776; POMFRET, CT 06258. (#9618-1).

PORTLAND

BICENTENNIAL PARK BENCHES, PORTLAND, CT. BENCHES INSTALLED ON MAIN ST AND RECREATIONAL AREAS. (LOCAL). JOHN HAMILTON, PRESIDENT; PORTLAND LIONS CLUB; OLD MARLBOROUGH TPKE; PORTLAND, CT 06480. (#32372).

HISTORY OF PORTLAND, CT. BOOK WRITTEN ON THE HISTORY AND COMMUNITY CULTURE OF PORTLAND. (LOCAL). ALBERT LESHANE, EDITOR; PORTLAND HISTORICAL SOCIETY; OLD MARLBOROUGH TPKE; PORTLAND, CT 06480. (#32370).

'PORTLAND HORIZONS', COMMUNITY NEWSLETTER, CT. COMMUNITY PAPER ON BICENTENNIAL ACTIVITIES IN THE TOWN BY SCHOOLS AND ORGANIZATIONS. (LOCAL). CAROL JOZUS, CHAIRMAN; PORTLAND BICENTENNIAL COMMITTEE; 25 BROOKS LN; PORTLAND, CT 06480. (#32371).

RESTORATION OF CIVIL WAR CANNON - PORTLAND, CT. MONUMENT TO BE MADE OF THE OLD CANNON. (LOCAL). JOHN DILLON, PROJ CHAIRMAN; PORTLAND BICENTENNIAL COMMITTEE; 24 WAVERLY AVE; PORTLAND, CT 06480. (#32373).

STANCLIFF PARK, PORTLAND, CA. PARK AND CHILDREN'S PLAYGROUND IN HONOR OF BICENT CELEBRATION. (LOCAL).

PORTLAND — CONTINUED

HARRIET GROEPER, PARK CHAIRMAN; PORTLAND JUNIOR WOMEN'S CLUB; 643 MAIN ST; PORTLAND, CT 06480. (#32369).

MAY 30, '76. PARADE TO HONOR MEMORIAL DAY & UNITED STATES' BICENTENNIAL. PARADE. (LOCAL). R W ANDERSON, CHMN; AMERICAN LEGION & PORTLAND BICENTENNIAL COMMITTEE; 25 COE AVE; PORTLAND, CT 06480. (#200008-256).

JULY 24, '76. PORTLAND FESTIVAL '76. ACTIVITIES INCLUDED CRAFTS, GAMES, ENTERTAINMENT, & ETHNIC DISPLAYS. AT EXCHANGE CLUB FAIRGROUNDS. (LOCAL). CAROL JOZUS; PORTLAND BICENTENNIAL COMMITTEE; 25 BROOKS LANE; PORTLAND, CT 06480. (#200008-257).

PRESTON

NOV 9, '75. THANKSGIVING CHURCH SERVICE WITH BICENTENNIAL CHOIR. BICENTENNIAL CHOIR WILL SING FIRST AMERICAN HYMNS; ALL WILL DRESS IN 1776 COSTUME. AT LONG SOCIETY CHURCH. (LOCAL). SOPHIE WOODMANSEE, CHMN; PRESTON HISTORICAL SOCIETY; RFD 3; NORWICH, CT 06360. (#200008-11).

MAY 1, '76. POQUETANNECK DAY, EXHIBITS & CHURCH SERVICE. ECUMENICAL BICENTENNIAL CHOIR TO PERFORM AT A PRE-REVOLUTIONARY CHURCH SERVICE, EXHIBITS & DEMONSTRATIONS, BRICKMAKING SHIPBUILDING AND BRASS WORKS, CONCERT BY THE OLD TIME FIDDLERS. AT ST JAMES CHURCH IN POQUETANNECK VILLAGE, RT 2A, PRESTON. (LOCAL). SOPHIE WOODMANSEE, CHMN; PRESTON VFW, CONNECTICUT BRASS CORPS, ST JAMES CHURCH; RFD 3; NORWICH, CT 06360. (#104934-1).

PUTNAM

REPRINT ELLEN LARNED'S 'HISTORY OF WINDHAM CO, CT'. REPRINT CT'S 'BEST COUNTY HISTORY' (A E VAN DUSEN, STATE HISTORIAN) PUBLISHED 1872-1880. 400 SETS FOR GENERAL SALE, 100 TO LIBRARIES, SCHOOLS & COLLEGES. ADD BIOGRAPHICAL NOTE. (LOCAL). MARSHALL E LINDEN, VICE CHAIRMAN; TOWN OF PUTNAM BICENTENNIAL COMMITTEE; TOWN HALL, 126 CHURCH ST; PUTNAM, CT 06260. (#12005). **ARBA GRANTEE.**

JULY 4, '75. ARTS AND CRAFTS SHOW AND SALE. ART CONTEST ENTRIES DISPLAYED. DEMONSTRATION OF EARLY AMERICAN CRAFTS. CONTEST WINNERS TO BE ANNOUNCED. AT PUTNAM SHOPPING CENTER. (LOCAL). LOUISE C PEMDEK; ASPTNOCK HISTORICAL SOCIETY; RFD #1; PUTNAM, CT 06260. (#100118-1).

JUNE 27, '76. ETHNIC FESTIVAL OF CULTURE AWARENESS. THERE WILL BE COSTUMES, MUSIC, DANCING AND A VARIETY OF FOODS. AT KENNEDY DR AREA - ALONG QUINEBAUG RIVER. (LOCAL). CONSTANCE CONNOR, SEC; PUTNAM BICENTENNIAL COMMITTEE; RR 2; PUTNAM, CT 06260. (#108325-1).

REDDING

SECURITY GUARDS FOR PUTNAM MEMORIAL STATE PARK, CT. THREE OFFICIAL PATROLMEN ADDED TO EXISTING STAFF TO PROTECT GROUNDS FROM VANDALS AND TO CONTROL CROWDS. (LOCAL). WILLIAM MILLER, DIRECTOR; DEPARTMENT OF ENVIRONMENTAL PROTECTION; STATE OFFICE BLDG; HARTFORD, CT 06115. (#26779). **ARBA GRANTEE.**

RIDGEFIELD

RIDGEFIELD YOUTH FAIR - RIDGEFIELD, CT. CELEBRATION OF AMERICAN MUSIC AND ART USING 25,000 SCHOOL CHILDREN; THE WILL RE-CREATE 18TH CENTURY IMPLEMENTS, FOOD AND DAILY NECESSITIES. (LOCAL). DENNISON FIALA, CHAIRMAN; RIDGEFIELD BICENTENNIAL COMMISSION; BOX 1776; RIDGEFIELD, CT 06877. (#23620). **ARBA GRANTEE.**

SEPT 27 - 28, '75. HERITAGE PROGRAM: MUSICAL PRESENTATION. PERFORMANCE OF AMERICAN MUSIC & OPERA. SHOW BEGINS AT 8:00 PM ON THE 27TH & 4:00 PM ON THE 28TH. AT KEELER TAVERN GARDEN HOUSE. (ST-WIDE). JANET WHITE, PROJ DIR; DELPHI OPERA GROUP & RIDGEFIELD BICENTENNIAL COMMISSION; 45 W LANE; RIDGEFIELD, CT 06877. (#100466-1).

MAY 22, '76. YOUTH FAIR - 18TH CENTURY MUSIC, DANCES & ART SHOW. THE CHILDREN WILL PLAN AND EXECUTE THIS WHOLE DAY THEMSELVES. AT BALLARD PARK, CENTER OF TOWN, PARKING ALL AROUND. (LOCAL). CHARLES SPIRE, DIRECTOR; RIDGEFIELD BICENTENNIAL COMMISSION; 32 CHERRY LANE; RIDGEFIELD, CT 06877. (#100466-2).

JUNE 26 - 27, '76. COLONIAL COMMON DAYS - TOWNWIDE COLONIAL FESTIVAL. AUTHENTIC AND EXCITING DEMONSTRATIONS, 18TH CENTURY COSTUMES AND PARADE. AT THROUGH THE ENTIRE TOWN, PARKING AS DIRECTED. (LOCAL). TOM PEARSON, PROJ DIR; RIDGEFIELD BICENTENNIAL COMMISSION; 20 OVERLOOK DR; RIDGEFIELD, CT 06877. (#100466-4).

JULY 3, '76. PATRIOT'S BALL. FESTIVAL AT COMMUNITY CENTER. (LOCAL). LEE DICKINSON, CHAIRMAN; RIDGEFIELD BICENTENNIAL COMMISSION; BOX 1776; RIDGEFIELD, CT 06877. (#100466-3).

APR 17, '77. BATTLE OF RIDGEFIELD RE-ENACTMENT. LIVE PERFORMANCE. (LOCAL). T R PEARSON, DIR; RIDGEFIELD BICENTENNIAL COMMISSION; 20 OVERLOOK DR; RIDGEFIELD, CT 06877. (#104115-1).

RIVERTON

SEPT 11, '76. OLD HOME DAY OBSERVANCE. INCLUDES SPEAKER, BARBECUE, MUSIC, EXHIBITS & ATHLETIC EVENTS. AT FAIR GROUNDS, RT 20. (LOCAL). R G WHEELER, COORD; BARKHAMSTED ARB STEERING COMMITTEE; RFD 2, OLD NORTH RD; WINSTED, CT 06098. (#2766-4).

ROXBURY

RENOVATION OF PARK - ROXBURY, CT. CONSTRUCTION OF DRIVEWAY, PARKING LOT, HORSE-RIDING ARENA & PAVILION TO RENOVATE PARK. (LOCAL). ELMER WORTHINGTON, CHAIRMAN; ROXBURY BICENTENNIAL COMMITTEE; TOWN HALL; ROXBURY, CT 06783. (#25056). **ARBA GRANTEE.**

'ROXBURY'S PAST'-GREEN MTN BOYS PROJ OF CT. GREEN MOUNTAIN BOYS, REV ARMY TROOP REACTIVATED. REV TROOP LEADERS FROM ROXBURY, ETHAN ALLEN, & SETH WARNER REPRESENT TOWN IN BICENTENNIAL YEARS. (LOCAL). ELMER WORTHINGTON, CHAIRMAN; ROXBURY BICENTENNIAL COMMITTEE; ROXBURY, CT 06783. (#2550).

OCT 24, '74. ILLUMINATION NIGHT - 'SURRENDER OF CORNWALLIS'. LIVE PERFORMANCE, CEREMONY. (LOCAL). ELMER WORTHINGTON, CHMN; ROXBURY BICENTENNIAL COMMITTEE; ROXBURY, CT 06783. (#2550-901).

MAY 18, '75. CEREMONIES HONORING GEN SETH WARNER. CT GENERAL ASSEMBLY PASSED A BILL MAKING SETH WARNER, COMMANDER OF GREEN MTN BOYS & FIRST GENERAL IN VT MILITIA, A MAJOR GENERAL IN THE CT MILITIA, WAS COL OF CONTINENTAL ARMY BUT HELD NO RANK IN CT MILITIA. MONUMENT ERECTED ON HIS GRAVE IN 1858. AT WARNER'S GRAVE-PARK IN CENTER OF TOWN. (ST-WIDE). ELMER WORTHINGTON; BICENTENNIAL COMMITTEE; BLUE STONE RIDGE; ROXBURY, CT 06783. (#50465-1).

SALEM

FEB 21 - 22, '76. GEORGE WASHINGTON COSTUME BALL. FESTIVAL AT SALEM ELEMENTARY SCHOOL. (LOCAL). D H WORDELL, DIRECTOR; SALEM BICENTENNIAL COMMITTEE; RFD 1 (SALEM); OAKDALE, CT 06370. (#104938-1).

SALISBURY

RENOVATION/PUBLICATION PROJECT: SALISBURY, CT. RENOVATION OF HOLLEY-WILLIAMS HOUSE; PRINTING OF PROGRAMS, DOCUMENTS & ROSTER OF PATRIOTS AND DIARIES OF 18TH & 19TH CENTURY SALISBURY PATRIOTS. (LOCAL). BENJAMIN L BELCHER, CHAIRMAN; SALISBURY ASSOC, INC; TOWN HILL FARM; SALISBURY, CT 06039. (#8813). **(??). ARBA GRANTEE.**

JAN 31 - FEB 1, '76. U S EASTERN SKI JUMP CHAMPIONSHIP. COMPETITION AT SATRE HILL. (REGN'L). MRS AUDREY WHITBECK, DIR; CONNECTICUT DEPT OF COMMERCE; COBBLE RD; SALISBURY, CT 06068. (#103416-101).

SEYMOUR

'SEYMOUR, PAST & PRESENT', HISTORY OF SEYMOUR,CT. AN UPDATE OF SEYMOUR'S HISTORY IN BOOKLET FORM, TO BE USED AT FIFTH GRADE LEVEL, AS PART OF THE HISTORY COURSE. (LOCAL). PAUL HALUSCHAK, PRESIDENT; SEYMOUR BICENTENNIAL COMMISSION; 1 FIRST ST; SEYMOUR, CT 06483. (#11884). **ARBA GRANTEE.**

SHARON

JULY 1 - SEPT 1, '76. 'A YANKEE PEDDLER', A CHILDREN'S MUSICAL. AN ORIGINAL MUSICAL FOR CHILDREN; THE 'PEDDLER'S WAGON' WILL TOUR THROUGHOUT NEW ENGLAND SINGING SONGS, TELLING STORIES AND PLAYING GAMES. THE CHILDREN WILL LEARN AMERICAN HISTORY AND FOLKLORE. ADMISSION & RESERVATIONS VARY WITH LOCAL SPONSORS. AT THROUGHOUT NEW ENGLAND, VARIES WITH LOCAL SPONSOR. (ST-WIDE). TEVIOT B FAIRSERVIS, DIR; KINGS AND COURIERS THEATRE CO; SHARON, CT 06069. (#103917-1).

JULY 24 - 25, '76. BICENTENNIAL RESOLUTION: MAKE PEACE WITH NATURE. 2-DAY CELEBRATION FEATURING TALKS, NATURE WALKS, EXHIBITS AND DEMONSTRATIONS RELATING TO VARIOUS ASPECTS OF OUR NATURAL ENVIRONMENT. AT SHARON AUDUBON CENTER, RTE 4. (LOCAL). JOAN G STANLEY, DIRECTOR; HOUSATONIC AUDUBON SOCIETY; 950 3RD AVE; NEW YORK, NY 10022. (#19976-8).

SHELTON

PLANTING TREES ON MAIN STREET OF SHELTON, CONN. PLANTING OF KWANZEN CHERRY TREES. SPONSORED BY LOCAL BICENTENNIAL COMMISSION & CONSERVATION COMMISSION WITH AID OF PUBLIC WORKS DEPT. (LOCAL). GERTRUDE COOPER, CHAIRMAN; SHELTON BICENTENNIAL COMMISSION; 40 WHITE ST; SHELTON, CT 06460. (#5036).

SIMSBURY

HISTORY OF SIMSBURY, CONN. RE-PRINTING OF THE HISTORY OF SIMSBURY BY DR L I BARBER, ORIGINAL PRINTING 1931- 429 PAGES. INFORMATION ON ALL ASPECTS OF THE FOUNDING & LIFE IN SIMSBURY 1643-1888. A COLLECTOR'S EDITION. (LOCAL). MRS GEORGE STICKLEY, DIRECTOR; ABIGAIL PHELPS CHAPTER, DAR; HOPMEADOW ST; SIMSBURY, CT 06070. (#3459).

JAN 25, '76. CONNECTICUT JUNIOR MISS: SCHOLARSHIP COMPETITION. CONNECTICUT JUNIOR MISS IS OFFICIAL PRELIMINARY FOR AMERICA'S JUNIOR MISS PROGRAM. JUDGING CATEGORIES ARE: YOUTH FITNESS, SCHOLASTIC ACHIEVEMENT, POISE & APPEARANCE, CREATIVE & PERFORMING ARTS AND JUDGES' CONFERENCE. ONLY HIGH SCHOOL SENIOR GIRLS ARE ELIGIBLE. AT SIMSBURY HIGH AUDITORIUM/34 FARMS VILLAGE RD. (ST-WIDE). E K BUCKLAND, PRES; EXCHANGE CLUB OF FARMINGTON, INC; 39 NORTHWOODS RD; FARMINGTON, CT 06032. (#102798-1).

MAY 9 - OCT 15, '76. INDIAN VILLAGE. CONSTRUCTION OF AN AUTHENTIC INDIAN VILLAGE, LONG HOUSE & COLONIAL COMMUNITY GARDEN ON THE GROUNDS OF THE SIMSBURY HISTORICAL SOCIETY AT MASSACOH PLANTATION. ALSO: BUILDING/FACILITY/MONUMENT. AT MEADOW ABOUT 150 YDS BEHIND SIMSBURY HISTORIC CNTR. (LOCAL). CLAVIN FISHER, DIRECTOR; THE SIMSBURY CIVITAN CLUB; NIMROD RD; SIMSBURY, CT 06092. (#3465-1).

JUNE 9, '76. BICENTENNIAL BALL. MAY 9, 1976-OFFICIAL OPENING DATE FOR BICENTENNIAL CELEBRATION IN SIMSBURY. THE DATE IS SIGNIFICANT SINCE ON THAT DATE, 1776, MAJORGEN NOAH PHELPS, A NATIVE SON, SPIED AT FORT TICONDEROGA. LOCATION AND ADMISSION DETAILS NOT YET AVAILABLE. (LOCAL). MRS RONALD F TRENHOLM; SIMSBURY WOMENS CLUB; 8 APPLE LANE; SIMSBURY, CT 06070. (#50151-1).

JULY 4, '76. FOURTH OF JULY 1976 ICE CREAM PARTY AND BAND CONCERT. OPENING. (LOCAL). JACKSON F ENO, CHAIRMAN; SIMSBURY BICENTENNIAL COMMITTE; BOX 1776; SIMSBURY, CT 06070. (#3464-501).

SEPT 5 - 10, '77. OPENING OF RESTORED AMOS R ENO HOUSE AND TOWN LIBRARY. RESTORATION OF THE AMOS R ENO HOUSE-SIMSBURY, CONN. THE RESTORATION OF THE 1822 STRUCTURE WHICH IS THE BIRTHPLACE OF GIFFORD PINCHOT - THE FIRST HEAD OF THE FORESTRY DEPARTMENT AND NOTED CONSERVATIONIST - LIBRARY WILL BE ADDED IN REAR.(24000 SQ FT). (LOCAL). JACKSON F ENO, CHAIRMAN; SIMSBURY BICENTENNIAL COMMITTE; BOX 1776; SIMSBURY, CT 06070. (#3464-502).

SOMERS

MAY 23, '76. SOMERS/SOMERSVILLE SENIOR CITIZENS BICENTENNIAL DAY. A DAYTIME PROGRAM DESIGNED TO HONOR SENIOR CITIZENS DURING THE BICENTENNIAL YEAR WITH A SOCIAL HOUR, DINNER, BARBER SHOP QUARTET, DANCING, AND GIFTS. (LOCAL). JOHN J OBRIEN, DIRECTOR; SOMERS LIONS, ROTARY AND KNIGHTS OF COLUMBUS ORGANIZATIONS; 94 MICHELE DR; SOMERS, CT 06071. (#107142-1).

SOUTH WINDHAM

SEPT 11, '76. SOUTH WINDHAM BICENTENNIAL DAY. FESTIVAL, EXHIBIT, LIVE PERFORMANCE AT GUILFORD SMITH MEMORIAL LIBRARY - UNITED CHURCH OF CHRIST. (LOCAL). SHIRLEY INSALACO, COORD; VILLAGE ORGANIZATIONS OF SOUTH WINDHAM; PIGEON SWAMP RD; SOUTH WINDHAM, CT 06266. (#200008-50).

SOUTHBURY

RESTORATION OF OLD TOWN HALL, SOUTHBURY, CT. OLD FRAME HALL, BUILT IN 1872 & ABANDONED IN 1963 WILL BE RESTORED & SERVE AS THE TOWN HALL. (LOCAL). MICHAEL KENNY, FIRST SELECTMAN; TOWN OF SOUTHBURY BICENTENNIAL COMMITTEE; MAIN ST; SOUTHBURY, CT 06488. (#17092). **ARBA GRANTEE.**

TOWN-WIDE BICENTENNIAL BOND DRIVE FOR 1976 - CT. THE BICENTENNIAL COMMITTEE WILL ATTEMPT TO HAVE EVERY FAMILY IN SOUTHBURY BUY A SAVINGS BOND AND INVEST IN OUR NATION'S FUTURE AS A A PATRIOTIC GESTURE IN SUPPORTING OUR COUNTRY. (LOCAL). GORDON SCHIELKE, CHAIRMAN; SOUTHBURY BICENTENNIAL COMMITTEE & WOMEN'S CLUB OF SOUTHBURY; MAIN ST; SOUTHBURY, CT 06488. (#21500).

FEB 2, '76. PRESENTATION OF BICENTENNIAL FLAG TO SOUTHBURY EAGLES DRUM CORP. CEREMONY. (LOCAL). DOROTHY T ZOKAS, SEC; SOUTHBURY BICENTENNIAL COMMITTEE; SOUTHBURY, CT 06488. (#200008-8).

SPRAGUE

PLANTING CHARTER OAK TREE IN SPRAGUE, CT. PLANTING OF SEEDLING FROM ORIGINAL STATE CHARTER TREE AT ACADEMY OF HOLY FAMILY & SAYLES SCHOOL. (LOCAL). MRS ROSALIE JORCZAK, CHAIRMAN; SPRAGUE BICENTENNIAL COMMITTEE; 198 MAIN ST, RFD #1, BOX 712; BALTIC, CT 06330. (#29671).

OCT 10, '76. FIELD DAY FOR CHILDREN. COMPETITION, FESTIVAL AT BABE BLANCHETTE MEMORIAL FIELD, MAIN ST. (LOCAL). MRS ROSALIE JORCZAK; SPRAGUE BICENTENNIAL COMMITTEE; 198 MAIN ST, RR #1 BOX 712; BALTIC, CT 06330. (#200008-39).

STAFFORD

JAN 31, '76. ELLINGTON BICENTENNIAL BALL. FESTIVAL AT STAFFORD SPEEDWAY RT. 140 STAFFORD SPRINGS AREA PARKING LOT. (LOCAL). PEG CARDIN; ELLINGTON JUNIOR WOMEN'S CLUB; STANDISH ROAD; ELLINGTON, CT 06029. (#50549-1).

STAMFORD

FORT STAMFORD RESTORATION, CONNECTICUT. RESTORATION OF REVOLUTIONARY FORT AND ARCHAEOLOGICAL DIG WITH HISTORICAL RESEARCH TO BECOME A CITY PARK. (ST-WIDE). ELIZABETH G GERSHMAN, EXEC ADMINISTRATOR; FORT STAMFORD RESTORATION INC; 88 SADDLE HILL RD; STAMFORD, CT 06903. (#8560).

'FROM PURITAN TO PATRIOT', HISTORY OF STAMFORD, CT. A SCHOLARLY ANALYSIS OF THE EVOLUTION OF A PURITAN VILLAGE INTO A NEW ENGLAND FRONTIER TOWN CAUGHT ON THE FRONT LINES OF THE REVOLUTION. TEXT BY PROF ESTELLE FEINSTEIN OF THE UNIV OF CONNECTICUT. (LOCAL). THOMAS HUME, CHAIRMAN; STAMFORD BICENTENNIAL COMMITTEE; 66 BROAD ST; STAMFORD, CT 06901. (#17994). **ARBA GRANTEE.**

MOBILE MUSEUM IN STAMFORD, CT. SCHOOL BUS CONVERTED TO MUSEUM. DISPLAYS ARTIFACTS & STUDENT WORK. TOURS SCHOOLS & PUBLIC FUNCTIONS. CHANGING THEMES: BICENTENNIAL, LOCAL/STATE HISTORY, PEOPLE OF USA & SPORTS/RECREATION. (LOCAL). RICHARD C HARPER, COORDINATOR; STAMFORD PUBLIC SCHOOLS; 1500 HIGH RIDGE RD; STAMFORD, CT 06903. (#30185).

STAMFORD, CT, PAST AND PRESENT. PROJECT IS A GUIDE BOOKLET ON THE HISTORY AND DEVELOPMENT OF CITY. (LOCAL). MARGARET PETERS, COORDINATOR; STAMFORD BICENTENNIAL COMMITTEE; ONE LANDMARK SQUARE, BOX 76; STAMFORD, CT 06901. (#20491).

JAN '76. AUDIO-VISUAL PREVIEW - THE HISTORY OF STAMFORD. EXHIBIT. (LOCAL). MARGARET PETERS, COORD; STAMFORD BICENTENNIAL COMMITTEE; ONE LANDMARK SQUARE, BOX 76; STAMFORD, CT 06901. (#200008-10).

FEB 7, '76. TOWN MEETING. CONFERENCE. (LOCAL). MARGARET PETERS, COORD; STAMFORD BICENTENNIAL COMMITTEE; ONE LANDMARK SQUARE BOX 76; STAMFORD, CT 06901. (#104937-1).

JULY 5, '76. ROUND HILL HIGHLAND SCOTTISH GAMES. TRADITIONAL SCOTTISH ACTIVITIES INCLUDE SPORTS, PIPING & DRUMMING. AT R COLHOUN ESTATE, DAVENPORT RIDGE RD. (LOCAL). DAVID BRYSON, COORDINATOR; ROUND HILL HIGHLAND SCOTTISH GAMES ASSOC; PO BOX 271; GREENWICH, CT 06830. (#103416-433).

STERLING HILL

BRONZE PLAQUE, STERLING HILL, CT. TO COMMEMORATE THE HOME OF THE FIRST TOWN MEETING, A PLAQUE READING: 'YE OLDE STAGECOACH TAVERN - HOME OF THE FIRST TOWN MEETING, JUNE 9, 1794', WILL BE ERECTED. (LOCAL). MARLENE A COOK, CHAIRPERSON; STERLING BICENTENNIAL COMMITTEE; RT #14A; ONECO, CT 06373. (#28626).

STONINGTON

SEPT '75 - MAY '76. AMERICAN ISSUES FORUM. FORUM MEETINGS ARE HELD EACH WEDNESDAY. THE SUBJECTS CONFORM APPROXIMATELY WITH THE AMERICAN ISSUES FORUM CALENDAR. (LOCAL). MRS LEE KNEERIM, COORD; ARBC OF STONINGTON; 3 GOLD ST; STONINGTON, CT 06378. (#103865-1).

STORRS

AMERICAN ART EXHIBIT. EXHIBIT. (LOCAL). WILLIAM KENNARD, CHMN; UNIV OF CONNECTICUT BICENTENNIAL COMMITTEE; RT 195; STORRS, CT 06268. (#107390-2). **(??).**

ARTICLE ON AMERICAN PROTEST PRINTS - STORRS, CT. ARTICLE FOR PRINT COLLECTORS NEWSLETTER JULY 1976: 200 YEARS OF AMERICAN PROTEST PRINTS. (LOCAL). WILLIAM KENNARD, CHAIRMAN; UNIV OF CONNECTICUT; RT 195; STORRS, CT 06268. (#24130).

BATTLE RE-ENACTMENT. RE-ENACTMENT OF BATTLE BETWEEN KNOWLTON'S RAIDERS AND GOVERNOR'S FOOT GUARD. (LOCAL). WILLIAM KENNARD, CHMN; UNIV OF CONNECTICUT BICENTENNIAL COMMITTEE; RT 195; STORRS, CT 06268. (#107390-3). **(??).**

BICENTENNIAL GARDEN AND COMMON - STORRS, CT. RE-CREATION OF PERMANENT GARDEN AND COMMON. (LOCAL). WILLIAM KENNARD, CHAIRMAN; UNIV OF CONNECTICUT; RT 195; STORRS, CT 06268. (#24129).

BICENTENNIAL PRIMER TO TRAIN STUDENTS - STORRS, CT. A BICENTENNIAL PRIMER TO TRAIN STUDENTS IN LOCAL HISTORY TECHNIQUES FOR THE REVOLUTIONARY ERA. (ST-WIDE). RICHARD D BROWN, CHAIRMAN; UNIV OF CONNECTICUT; STORRS, CT 06268. (#26031). **ARBA GRANTEE.**

BROCHURE - STORRS, CT. BROCHURE FOR 4-H LEADERS WILL HIGHLIGHT THE BICENTENNIAL. (LOCAL). WILLIAM KENNARD, CHAIRMAN; UNIV OF CONNECTICUT; RT 195; STORRS, CT 06268. (#24128).

CHORAL CONCERT & N-E STRING QUARTET CONCERTS. SERIES OF CONCERTS ON AMERICAN MUSIC OF PAST 200 YEARS. (LOCAL). WILLIAM KENNARD, CHMN; UNIV OF CONNECTICUT BICENTENNIAL COMMITTEE; RT 195; STORRS, CT 06268. (#107390-1). **(??).**

ETHNIC ARTICLES ON CONNECTICUT - HARTOFRD, CT. A GRAPHIC PRESENTATION OF ETHNIC GROUPS IN EACH TOWN IN THE STATE. (ST-WIDE). THOMAS E STEAHR, ASSOCIATE PROFESSOR; DEPT OF AGIECON & RURAL SOC, UNIV OF CONNECTICUT; STORRS, CT 06268. (#23623). **ARBA GRANTEE.**

THE PAPERS OF JONATHAN TRUMBULL, CONNECTICUT. THIS PROJECT STARTED IN 1968, SPONSORED BY THE CONNECTICUT STATE LIBRARY AND THE UNIVERSITY OF CONNECTICUT. ONLY PROJECT DEVOTED TO A CONNECTICUT LEADER OF THE REVOLUTION. (NAT'L). ALBERT E VAN DUSEN, EDITOR; UNIVERSITY OF CONNECTICUT; CAPITOL AVE; STORRS, CT 06268. (#3069). **ARBA GRANTEE.**

RESEARCH ON APPALACHIAN TRAIL EXPEDITION. STUDY OF SOCIO-PSYCHOLOGICAL CHANGES WITHIN MEMBERS OF A GROUP OF COLLEGE STUDENTS RESULTING FROM A 2048 MILE HIKE. VARIABLES ARE SELF-CONCEPT, INTERPERSONAL VALUES & GROUP DYNAMICS. (REGN'L). WARREN DOYLE, EXPEDITION LEADER; UNIVERSITY OF CONNECTICUT; BOX U-93; STORRS, CT 06268. (#7846).

RESTORATION OF MILL TOWN - STORRS, CT. FEASIBILITY STUDY FOR RESTORATION & RECYCLING OF 19TH CENTURY MILL TOWN. (LOCAL). WILLIAM KENNARD, CHAIRMAN; UNIV OF CONNECTICUT; RT 195; STORRS, CT 06268. (#24131).

TOOL COLLECTION - STORRS, CT. COLLECT & COMPILE ANTIQUE FARM IMPLEMENTS & TOOLS FOR STUDY & DISPLAY. (LOCAL). WILLIAM KENNARD, CHAIRMAN; UNIV OF CONNECTICUT; RT 195; STORRS, CT 06268. (#24132).

OCT 7, '76. PERFORMANCE BY ORCHESTRE DE PARIS. LIVE PERFORMANCE AT JORGENSEN AUDITORIUM. (INT'L). INFORMATION OFFICE; COLUMBIA ARTISTS; 165 W 57TH ST; NEW YORK, NY 10019. (#108967-1).

OCT 23 - NOV 21, '76. 'EDVARD MUNCH, THE MAJOR GRAPHICS' EXHIBIT. AN EXHIBITION FROM THE MUNCH MUSEUM IN OSLO BY ONE OF THE GREATEST FIGURES IN MODERN PRINTMAKING. AT WILLIAM BENTON MUSEUM OF ART. (INT'L). EILEEN HARAKAL, COORD; SMITHSONIAN INSTITUTION TRAVELING EXHIBITION SERVICE; 1000 JEFFERSON DR, SW; WASHINGTON, DC 20560. (#26704-11).

STRATFORD

CREATIVE WRITING CONTEST -STRATFORD, CONNECTICUT. THEME TO BE SELECTED BY COMMITTEE, WILL BE RELATED TO THE UPCOMING BICENTENNIAL CELEBRATION. CASH PRIZES TO SEVERAL AGE GROUPS IN LOCAL SCHOOLS DONATED BY COMMUNITY BANKS. (LOCAL). MICHAEL J SWEENEY, VICE PRESIDENT; CITY SAVINGS BANK; 3261 MAIN ST; STRATFORD, CT 06497. (#4685).

HISTORY OF STRATFORD, CT, BICENTENNIAL ACTIVITIES. A PICTORIAL AND WRITTEN RECORD OF ALL OF THE TOWN'S BICENTENNIAL CELEBRATION TO BE PLACED ON DEPOSIT IN STRATFORD HISTORICAL SOCIETY JUDSON HOUSE MUSEUM FOR FUTURE GENERATIONS' READING & VIEWING. (LOCAL). PHILOMENA A KLESPER, CHAIRMAN; STRATFORD BICENTENNIAL COMMITTEE; 2725 MAIN ST; STRATFORD, CT 06497. (#4683).

MINIATURE REPLICA OF HISTORIC COLONIAL HOUSE, CT. DOLLHOUSE REPRODUCTION OF CAPTAIN DAVID JUDSON HOUSE, STRATFORD, CONN; REPLICA COMPLETELY FURNISHED IN GENUINE 18TH CENTURY STYLE. (LOCAL). BARBARA OLSEN, DIRECTOR; STRATFORD JUNIOR WOMEN'S CLUB; PO BOX 101; STRATFORD, CT 06497. (#32683).

SEPT 1 - 30, '75. FESTIVAL WITH EXHIBITS, ENTERTAINMENT, ART, & FOOD. EXHIBITS, ENTERTAINMENT, ART & FOOD SALES BY THE MANY ETHNIC GROUPS IN OUR COMMUNITY. (LOCAL). PHILOMENA A KLESPER, COORD; STRATFORD BICENTENNIAL COMMITTEE; 2725 MAIN ST; STRATFORD, CT 06497. (#4684-501).

JUNE 8 - SEPT 26, '76. AMERICAN SHAKESPEARE FESTIVAL. 'THE WINTER'S TALE', 'THE CRUCIBLE' & 'AS YOU LIKE IT' IN REPERTORY. (REGN'L). DIRECTOR; AMERICAN SHAKESPEARE FESTIVAL; BOX OFFICE ASF; STRATFORD, CT 06497. (#108805-1).

SUFFIELD

BANDSTAND '76 PROJECT OF SUFFIELD, CONN. CONSTRUCT BANDSTAND ON VILLAGE GREEN FOR BICENTENNIAL PERFORMANCES. FOR JULY CELEBRATION IN '76. (LOCAL). ROGER C LOOMIS, CHAIRMAN; AMERICAN BICENTENNIAL COMMISSION OF SUFFIELD; PO BOX 1776; SUFFIELD, CT 06078. (#3417).

COMMEMORATIVE MARKER IN SUFFIELD, CT. A COMMEMORATIVE MARKER WILL BE PLACED ON THE TOWN GREEN. (LOCAL). ROGER C LOOMIS, CHAIRMAN; AMERICAN BICENTENNIAL COMMISSION OF SUFFIELD; PO BOX 1776; SUFFIELD, CT 06078. (#17355).

PRESERVATION HISTORICAL MANUSCRIPTS OF CONNECTICUT. TO PRESERVE PREVIOUSLY LOST MANUSCRIPTS DIARIES AND DOCUMENTS OF THE REVOLUTIONARY WAR PERIOD BY MICROFILM TECHNIQUES. (ST-WIDE). ELINOR BURNHAM, LIBRARIAN; KENT MEMORIAL LIBRARY; 50 N MAIN ST; SUFFIELD, CT 06078. (#828). **ARBA GRANTEE.**

SUFFIELD ORAL HISTORY PROJECT, CT. A COMPILATION OF SUFFIELD'S HISTORY. (LOCAL). ROGER C LOOMIS, CHAIRMAN; AMERICAN BICENTENNIAL COMMISSION OF SUFFIELD; PO BOX 1776; SUFFIELD, CT 06078. (#17356).

THE SUFFIELD SPOON 1776-1976, CT. STERLING SILVER SPOON MODELED AFTER 200 YEAR OLD SPOON BELONGING TO REV EBENEZER GAY OF SUFFIELD, WILL BE ON EXHIBIT. (LOCAL). ROGER C LOOMIS, CHAIRMAN; SUFFIELD BICENTENNIAL COMMITTEE; PO BOX #1776; SUFFIELD, CT 06078. (#22346).

SUFFIELD THE BEAUTIFUL - 1976, CT. PAMPHLET DESCRIBING SUFFIELD'S NATURAL AREAS THAT ARE OPEN TO THE PUBLIC FOR HIKING, ETC. (LOCAL). DAVID SAWYER, CHAIRMAN; SUFFIELD CONSERVATION COMMISSION; 88 S MAIN ST; SUFFIELD, CT 06078. (#22348).

SUFFIELD TOWN MAP, BICENTENNIAL EDITION, CT. RE-ISSUE TOWN MAP WITH COOPERATION OF LOCAL BUSINESSES. (LOCAL). ROGER C LOOMIS, SCOUTMASTER; BOY SCOUT TROOP #160; 500 HALE ST; SUFFIELD, CT 06078. (#22347).

TOWN GREEN BEAUTIFICATION PROJECT, SUFFIELD, CT. TREES & SHRUBS WILL BE PLANTED ON TOWN GREEN. (LOCAL). ROBERT H ALCORN, PROJ DIRECTOR; HELENA SPENCER TREE FUND; 294 S MAIN ST; SUFFIELD, CT 06078. (#17353).

OCT 7 - 30, '75. EASTMAN KODAK'S 'PROFILE '76'. EXHIBIT AT SUFFIELD HIGH SCHOOL AUDITORIUM; MOUNTAIN RD. (LOCAL). ROGER C LOOMIS, CHAIRMAN; AMERICAN BICENTENNIAL COMMISSION OF SUFFIELD & SUFFIELD YMCA; PO BOX 186; WEST SUFFIELD, CT 06093. (#103198-1).

OCT 11, '75. 'THE DECLARATION OF INDEPENDENCE: TRIUMPH OF EFFECTIVE WRITING'. SEMINAR AT TISCH AUDITORIUM, HIGH ST. (LOCAL). PAUL SANDERSON, COORD; SUFFIELD ACADEMY; SUFFIELD, CT 06078. (#200008-3).

NOV 26, '75. BICENTENNIAL EUCUMENICAL THANKSGIVING SERVICE. LIVE PERFORMANCE AT ST JOSEPH'S CHURCH; SOUTH MAIN ST, PARK IN REAR. (LOCAL). REV J GORMAN SMITH, COORD; SUFFIELD COUNCIL OF CHURCHES; HIGH ST; SUFFIELD, CT 06078. (#103865-2).

FEB 19, '76. DISTINGUISHED SERVICE AWARDS NIGHT. ANNUAL DISTINGUISHED SERVICE AWARD AND KICKOFF OF BICENTENNIAL. AT SUFFIELD INN, MOUNTAIN RD. (LOCAL). JOHN G PERMATTEO, DIR; SUFFIELD JAYCEES; 595 N STONE ST; WEST SUFFIELD, CT 06093. (#200008-4).

FEB 27, '76. 'T'WAS NIGHT BEFORE FREEDOM'. LIVE PERFORMANCE AT SUFFIELD HIGH SCHOOL AUDITORIUM, MOUNTAIN RD. (LOCAL). MRS WILLIAM MANN, COORD; SUFFIELD GIRL SCOUT ASSOC; 595 N MAIN ST; SUFFIELD, CT 06078. (#200008-5).

MAR 6, '76. BICENTENNIAL BAND CONCERT. LIVE PERFORMANCE AT SUFFIELD HIGH SCHOOL AUDITORIUM, MOUNTAIN RD. (LOCAL). RAYMOND TANGUAY, COORD; SUFFIELD HIGH SCHOOL BAND; SUFFIELD, CT 06078. (#200008-6).

APR 3, '76. SCOUT BICENTENNIAL SHOW. CUB AND BOY SCOUTS WILL DEMONSTRATE CRAFTS; ALSO FEATURED WILL BE CONNECTICUT'S CONESTOGA WAGON, AMERICAN HISTORY IN FLAGS AND SNET CO'S BICENTENNIAL CARAVAN, 'CONNECTICUT - IT'S ROLE IN THE BIRTH OF OUR NATION.'. AT HATHEWAY HOUSE BARN, S MAIN ST. (LOCAL). ROGER C LOOMIS, CHAIRMAN; BOY SCOUTS AND CUB SCOUTS OF SUFFIELD; 2075 MOUNTAIN RD; WEST SUFFIELD, CT 06093. (#106039-4).

APR 8 - 10, '76. CELEBRATION 'MIME'. THEATRICAL PRESENTATIONS FOR SCHOOL CHILDREN WITH A PUBLIC PROGRAM ON APRIL 10 CALLED 'AMERICAN COLLAGE.'. AT SUFFIELD PUBLIC SCHOOLS AND SUFFIELD HIGH SCHOOL AUDITORIUM. (LOCAL). MRS PAUL SANDERSON, JR; SUFFIELD COUNCIL FOR THE ARTS; N MAIN ST; SUFFIELD, CT 06078. (#106039-5).

APR 10, '76. 'AMERICAN COLLAGE', FOLK MUSIC & DANCE. LIVE PERFORMANCE AT SUFFIELD HIGH SCHOOL AUDITORIUM, MOUNTAIN RD. (LOCAL). MRS PAUL SANDERSON, JR; SUFFIELD COUNCIL FOR THE ARTS; N MAIN ST; SUFFIELD, CT 06078. (#106039-3).

MAY 8, '76. HOUSE AND FARM TOUR. TOUR OF OLD & NEW HOUSES & BARNS, EXHIBITS, LUNCHEON BY RESERVATION ONLY, TIMOTHY SWAN MUSIC FESTIVAL & EARLY AMERICAN MUSIC PROGRAM AT CONGREGATIONAL CHURCH AT 1:30PM, TICKETS AT HATHAWAY HOUSE & KING HOUSE ON S MAIN ST, LUNCHEON AT CONGREGATIONAL CHURCH. AT CONGREGATIONAL CHURCH. (LOCAL). MRS JOHN D GLASS, COORD; SUFFIELD COUNCIL FOR THE ARTS; 96 RANDALL DR; SUFFIELD, CT 06078. (#106039-1).

MAY 8, '76. TIMOTHY SWAN FESTIVAL. PLAYING & SINGING OF MUSIC BY TIMOTHY SWAN, A LOCAL MAN WHOSE MUSIC WAS POPULAR IN THE 1800'S. AT FIRST CHURCH OF CHRIST, HIGH ST. (LOCAL). MRS RAYMOND TANGUAY, DIR; SUFFIELD COUNCIL FOR THE ARTS; 21 RIVERVIEW TERRACE; SUFFIELD, CT 06078. (#106039-2).

JUNE 12, '76. A COLONIAL EXPERIENCE. EVENTS CONSIST OF COLONIAL ACTIVITIES, SCHOOLROOM, FARM ANIMALS; COOKING, HOMEMAKING, GAMES, COLONIAL CRAFTS, ETC. AT SUNRISE PARK, 2075 MOUNTAIN RD. (LOCAL). MRS ROBERT STEWART, CHMN; SUFFIELD PARENTS-TEACHERS ORGANIZATION & AMERICAN BICENTENNIAL COMM; 1230 COPPERHILL RD; WEST SUFFIELD, CT 06093. (#108194-1).

JUNE 25, '76. BICENTENNIAL BALL. FESTIVAL AT SUFFIELD HIGH SCHOOL; MOUNTAIN ROAD; SUFFIELD. (LOCAL). MRS TERRENCE DUNN, COORD; SUFFIELD JAYCEES; 418 N MAIN ST; SUFFIELD, CT 06078. (#108194-2).

JULY 3 - 4, '76. OLD FASHIONED FOURTH OF JULY. PICNIC ON THE GREEN (11:30-1:30); PARADE (2:004:00); ANCIENT MUSTER (4:30-5:00); SUPPER (5:307:00); FIREWORKS (9:00) BEAN SUPPER AND CHURCH SERVICES ON 7 4 AT 11 AM. AT TOWN GREEN - MAIN ST. (LOCAL). ROGER C LOOMIS, CHAIRMAN; AMERICAN BICENTENNIAL COMMISSION OF SUFFIELD; PO BOX 186; W. SUFFIELD, CT 06093. (#3416-1).

TERRYVILLE

FEB 1, '75 - JULY 31, '76. HISTORIC DISPLAYS. EXHIBIT AT MAIN STREET ROUTE 6. (LOCAL). HORACE WHITTIER; THOMASTON SAVINGS BANK TERRYVILLE OFFICE; MAPLE ST; BRISTOL, CT 06786. (#102398-19).

NOV 2, '75. ECUMENICAL CHURCH SERVICES & COLONIAL SUPPER. ADMISSION CHARGE FOR MEAL ONLY 5 TO 7 PM, CHURCH SERVICE 4 PM. AT CONGREGATIONAL CHURCH & CHURCH HALL. (LOCAL). REV JOSEPH SHALOKA, CHMN; PLYMOUTH ARBC; 35 ALLEN ST; TERRYVILLE, CT 06786. (#102398-1).

NOV 22, '75. VARIETY NIGHT. LIVE PERFORMANCE AT HIGH SCHOOL AUDITORIUM. (LOCAL). J FRANCIS RYAN, CHMN; PLYMOUTH ARBC; 8 OAK ST; TERRYVILLE, CT 06786. (#102398-5).

NOV 24, '75. BICENTENNIAL FASHION SHOW 18TH CENTURY COSTUMES. EXHIBIT AT TERRYVILLE HIGH SCHOOL NORTH MAIN STREET. (LOCAL). MRS FELIX BORKOWSKI, CHMN; TOWN OF PLYMOUTH BICENTENNIAL COMMITTEE; AMES AVE; TERRYVILLE, CT 06786. (#102398-18).

FEB 23, '76. FASHION SHOW, COLONIAL AND PRESENT. THEME IS 'NOW & THEN.'. AT HIGH SCHOOL AUDITORIUM. (LOCAL). MRS PATRICIA BORKOWSKI; PLYMOUTH ARBC; 9 AMES ST; TERRYVILLE, CT 06786. (#102398-4).

APR 24, '76. COLONIAL BALL. COLONIAL COSTUMES RECOMMENDED. AT BRISTOL ARENA, N MAIN ST. (LOCAL). FRANCIS GIBB, DIR; TERRYVILLE FIRE DEPT; 5 UNION ST; TERRYVILLE, CT 06786. (#102398-3).

APR 24 - JULY 31, '76. COLONIAL HOME TOURS, COLONIAL PAGEANT, ETHNIC SONG & DANCE FESTIVAL. PAGEANT ON SMALL LAKE, HOME TOURS ON 23 MAY 76, SONG FESTIVAL 7MAY76 PARADE 12 JUN 76, COLONIAL BALL 24 APR 76, STAMP SHOW 16 MAY 76, ANTIQUE DISPLAY 19 MAY 76, BAND CONCERT & PICNIC 4 JULY 76, ECUMENICAL CHURCH SERVICES 13 JUN 76,. AT HIGH SCHOOL AUDITORIUM,. (LOCAL). J FRANCIS RYAN, CHAIRMAN; PLYMOUTH BICENTENNIAL COMMITTEE; 8 OAK ST; TERRYVILLE, CT 06786. (#50233-1).

MAY 7, '76. INTERNATIONAL NIGHT. REPRESENTED WILL BE GERMAN, FRENCH, RUSSIAN, UKRANIAN, SCOTTISH, LITUANIAN, IRISH & ITALIAN GROUPS. AT HIGH SCHOOL AUDITORIUM. (LOCAL). CHARLES DUMOND, DIR; PLYMOUTH ARBC; 617 STAFFORD AVE; BRISTOL, CT 06010. (#102398-2).

MAY 16, '76. HISTORIC FLAG DISPLAY. EXHIBIT AT TERRYVILLE HIGH SCHOOL AUDITORIUM. (LOCAL). ANDREW LUCKX, DIRECTOR; PLYMOUTH ARBC; 5 KING ST; TERRYVILLE, CT 06786. (#102398-6).

MAY 16, '76. PHILATELIC SHOW. HISTORY THRU STAMPS IS THE THEME OF THE SHOW. AT IMMACULATE CONCEPTION CHURCH HALL. (LOCAL). GEORGE TISHON, DIRECTOR; PLYMOUTH ARBC; 1 FAIRMONT AVE; TERRYVILLE, CT 06786. (#102398-7).

MAY 17 - 22, '76. BICENTENNIAL ARTS AND CRAFTS SHOW. EXHIBIT AT HIGH SCHOOL AUDITORIUM. (LOCAL). MS MARYLOU HOFFMAN; PLYMOUTH ARBC; TERRYVILLE HIGH SCHOOL; TERRYVILLE, CT 06780. (#102398-8).

MAY 19 - 22, '76. ANTIQUE DISPLAY. EXHIBIT AT HIGH SCHOOL AUDITORIUM. (LOCAL). RUSSELL BONDESON, DIR; PLYMOUTH ARBC; 149 BOY ST; BRISTOL, CT 06010. (#102398-9).

MAY 23, '76. COLONIAL HOMES, CHURCH AND CONTEMPORARY HOME TOUR. TOUR WILL INCLUDE 8 COLONIAL HOMES, 1 CONTEMPORARY HOME & 1 CHURCH. (LOCAL). MRS ARDEN TOWILL, CHMN; PLYMOUTH ARBC; 41 HARWINTON AVE; PLYMOUTH, CT 06782. (#102398-10).

JUNE 1 - AUG 30, '76. ART SHOW. ONE MAN EXHIBIT OF OIL & WATERCOLOR PAINTINGS ALSO PEN AND INK SKETCHES OF OLD SCENES, HOMES & CHURCHES USED FOR BICENTENNIAL CALENDAR. AT LOCAL BANKS & THE LOCK MUSEUM OF AMERICA, MAIN STREET. (LOCAL). REINHOLDT SCHWANKA, CHMN; PLYMOUTH ARBC; 108 HIGH ST; TERRYVILLE, CT 06786. (#102398-12).

JUNE 12, '76. BICENTENNIAL PARADE. PARADE. (LOCAL). J FRANCIS RYAN, CHMN; PLYMOUTH ARBC; 8 OAK ST; TERRYVILLE, CT 06786. (#102398-13).

JUNE 13, '76. ECUMENICAL CHURCH SERVICE, OUTDOORS. ALL CHURCH GROUPS TO BE RERESENTED. IN CASE OF RAIN - IMMACULATE CONCEPTION CHURCH NEXT TO THE VILLAGE GREEN. AT TERRYVILLE VILLAGE GREEN. (LOCAL). REV JOSEPH SHALOKA, DIR; PLYMOUTH ARBC; 35 ALLEN ST; TERRYVILLE, CT 06786. (#102398-14).

JUNE 19, '76. CHILDREN'S PARADE AND FIELD DAY. PARADE, FESTIVAL AT MAIN ST, RT 6. (LOCAL). J FRANCIS RYAN, CO-CHMN; TOWN OF PLYMOUTH BICENTENNIAL COMMITTEE; 8 OAK ST; TERRYVILLE, CT 06786. (#102398-22).

JULY 10, '76. BICYCLE RACE. COMPETITION. (LOCAL). PAUL SWENTON, DIRECTOR; PLYMOUTH ARBC; WASHINGTON RD; TERRYVILLE, CT 06786. (#102398-16).

JULY 11, '76. COLONIAL PAGEANT - HISTORY OF PLYMOUTH. A GENERAL HISTORY OF PLYMOUTH INCLUDING THE VILLAGES OF TERRYVILLE AND PEQUABUCK. AT LAKE WINFIELD. (LOCAL). J FRANCIS RYAN, CHMN; PLYMOUTH ARBC; 8 OAK ST; TERRYVILLE, CT 06786. (#102398-17).

SEPT 13 - 14, '76. TERRYVILLE COUNTRY FAIR. FAIR AT TOWN HILL ROAD ONE HALF MILE MILE SOUTH OF ROUTE 6. (LOCAL). WAYNE KAMENS, PROJ DIR; TERRYVILLE LIONS CLUB; TERRYVILLE LIONS CLUB; TERRYVILLE, CT 06786. (#102398-20).

THOMASTON

THE STORY OF THOMASTON, CT. PUBLICATION OF A COMPLETE HISTORY OF THOMASTON; ITS ORIGINS AS THE MATTATUCK PLANTATION & NORTHBURY PARISH. (LOCAL). JOSEPH WASSONG, CHAIRMAN; THOMASTON HISTORICAL SOCIETY & THOMASTON BICENTENNIAL COMMITTEE; TOWN HALL; THOMASTON, CT 06787. (#12244). **ARBA GRANTEE.**

TORRINGTON

COE PARK MEMORIAL BUILDING PROJECT, TORRINGTON, CT. COE PARK MEMORIAL BUILDING WILL BE USED AS MULTI-PURPOSE FACILITY FOR CULTURE & RECREATION. (LOCAL). FREDERICK P DALEY, PROJ DIRECTOR; TORRINGTON BICENTENNIAL COMMITTEE; PO BOX 353; TORRINGTON, CT 06790. (#16941). **ARBA GRANTEE.**

ETHNIC HISTORY BOOK, VOLUME II - TORRINGTON, CT. VOLUME II IN A SERIES OF BOOKLETS ON THE HISTORY OF TORRINGTON WILL PORTRAY THE CONTRIBUTIONS OF VARIOUS ETHNIC GROUPS TO THE DEVELOPMENT OF THE CITY. (LOCAL). WHITNEY BROOKS, CHAIRMAN; TORRINGTON BICENTENNIAL COMMITTEE; PO BOX 353; TORRINGTON, CT 06790. (#25038). **ARBA GRANTEE.**

VOL I OF ETHNIC HISTORY OF TORRINGTON, CT. A STUDY OF TORRINGTON'S ETHNIC HISTORY DESIGNED TO RECORD & PROMOTE AN UNDERSTANDING OF TORRINGTON'S ETHNIC HISTORY. (LOCAL). FREDERICK P DALEY, PROJ DIRECTOR; TORRINGTON BICENTENNIAL COMMITTEE; PO BOX 353; TORRINGTON, CT 06790. (#17152). **ARBA GRANTEE.**

SEPT 24 - 25, '74. ETHNIC FAIR - BOOTHS REPRESENTING VARIOUS ETHNIC GROUPS IN CITY. TORRINGTON HERITAGE PROJECT OF CONN. RECOGNITION OF ETHNIC GROUPS IN COMMUNITY. EACH ETHNIC GROUP WILL DISPLAY ARTIFACTS, COSTUMES, MUSIC, DANCE, FOOD, & CULTURE. (LOCAL). JOSEPH E CRAVANZOLA; TORRINGTON BICENTENNIAL COMMITTEE; HOTCHKISS BROTHERS, 199 WATER ST; TORRINGTON, CT 06790. (#2642-901).

AUG 2, '75. FIFE AND DRUM FIELD DAY. ARTS FESTIVAL-CRAFTS, ARTS, HISTORICAL EXHIBITS, WITH DRAMA & MUSIC. INDUSTRY EXHIBITING PRODUCTS PAST & PRESENT. HISTORICAL EXHIBIT IN CIVIC CENTER. PARADE FLOATS DEPICTING LOCAL HISTORY. AT CITYWIDE. (LOCAL). MR JOSEPH E CRABANVOLA; TORRINGTON BICENT COMMITTEE; 192 MAIN ST BOX 373; TORRINGTON, CT 06790. (#3730-7).

AUG 2 - 13, '75. ART FESTIVAL. ARTS FESTIVAL INCLUDES OUTDOOR AND INDOOR EVENTS OUTDOOR COE PARK INDOOR CIVIC CENTER COE PARK TORRINGTON HIGH SCHOOL LITTLE THEATER. AT COE MEMORIAL PARK, RT 202, TORRINGTON. (LOCAL). CATHERINE C CALHOUN; TORRINGTON BICENTENNIAL COMMITTEE; POB 353 192 MAIN ST; TORRINGTON, CT 06790. (#2642-1).

OCT '75. DEDICATION OF NEW CIVIC CENTER. ARTS FESTIVAL-CRAFTS, ARTS, HISTORICAL EXHIBITS, WITH DRAMA & MUSIC. INDUSTRY EXHIBITING PRODUCTS PAST & PRESENT. HISTORICAL EXHIBIT IN CIVIC CENTER. PARADE FLOATS DEPICTING LOCAL HISTORY. SPONSOR PLANS INCOMPLETE AS OF 04-08-75. AT CENTER OF TOWN. (LOCAL). JOSEPH E CRAVANZOLA; TORRINGTON BICENT COMMITTEE; 192 MAIN ST, BOX 353; TORRINGTON, CT 06790. (#3730-6).

JUNE 12 - 13, '76. HERITAGE DAYS & ETHNIC FESTIVAL. ARTS FESTIVAL-CRAFTS, ARTS, HISTORICAL EXHIBITS, WITH DRAMA & MUSIC. AT COE MEMORIAL PARK. (LOCAL). JOSEPH E CRAVANZOLA; TORRINGTON BICENTENNIAL COMMITTEE; 192 MAIN ST, BOX 353; TORRINGTON, CT 06790. (#3730-4).

JUNE 12 - 19, '76. INDUSTRIAL EXHIBITION. LOCAL INDUSTRIES DISPLAY EXAMPLES OF MANUFACTURED ARTICLES - ACTUAL MACHINE WORK. AT COE PARK SO MAIN ST STATE ARMORY. (LOCAL). TORRINGTON COMMITTEE; TORRINGTON BICENTENNIAL COMMITTEE; 192 MAIN ST; TORRINGTON, CT 06790. (#2643-1).

JUNE 14, '76. ELKS' FLAG DAY OBSERVANCE. CEREMONY AT COE MEMORIAL PARK. (LOCAL). JOSEPH E CRAVANZOLA, CHMN; TORRINGTON LODGE, BPOE; 192 MAIN ST, BOX 353; TORRINGTON, CT 06790. (#3730-8).

JUNE 19 - 20, '76. DISPLAY OF 170 FLAGS OF NATIONS. EXHIBIT AT COE MEMORIAL PARK. (LOCAL). JOSEPH E CRAVANZOLA, CHMN; TORRINGTON BICENTENNIAL COMMITTEE; 192 MAIN ST, BOX 353; TORRINGTON, CT 06790. (#3730-9).

JUNE 20, '76. HERITAGE DAYS AND PARADE. PARADE FLOATS DEPICTING LOCAL HISTORY. INDUSTRY EXHIBITING PRODUCTS PAST & PRESENT. HISTORICAL EXHIBIT IN CIVIC CENTER. PARADE FLOATS DEPICTING LOCAL HISTORY. AT COE MEMORIAL PARK. (LOCAL). JOSEPH E CRAVANZOLA; TORRINGTON BICENTENNIAL COMMITTEE; 192 MAIN ST, BOX 353; TORRINGTON, CT 06790. (#3730-5).

JULY 4, '76. JULY 4TH OBSERVANCE - WITH 2:00PM BELL RINGING. CEREMONY, FESTIVAL AT CITY-WIDE. (LOCAL). JOSEPH E CRAVANZOLA, CHMN; TORRINGTON BICENTENNIAL COMMITTEE; 192 MAIN ST, BOX 353; TORRINGTON, CT 06790. (#3730-10).

TRUMBULL

'FROM VALLEY FORGE TO FREEDOM', TRUMBULL, CT. BOOK WILL DEPICT THE LIFE OF BLACK SLAVE NERO HAWLEY, A TOWN RESIDENT WHO OBTAINED FREEDOM BY SERVING WITH CONTINENTAL ARMY; HE LATER ESTABLISHED HIS OWN BUSINESS IN TRUMBULL. (LOCAL). ELWOOD C STANLEY, CHAIRMAN; TRUMBULL AMERICAN REVOLUTION BICENTENNIAL COMMITTEE; TOWN HALL, 5866 MAIN ST; TRUMBULL, CT 06611. (#21339). **ARBA GRANTEE.**

TRADITIONAL HANDCRAFTED ARTICLES - TRUMULL, CT. CREATION OF TRADITIONAL HANDCRAFTED ARTICLES SUCH AS CLOTHING AND BEADWORK BY TRIBAL WOMEN AND CHILDREN; A REVITALIZATION OF ANCIENT CRAFT SKILLS. (LOCAL). AURELIUS PIPER, TRADITIONAL TRIBAL CHIEF; GOLDEN HILL TRIBAL COUNCIL; 427 SHELTON RD; TRUMBULL, CT 06611. (#21873). **ARBA GRANTEE.**

JULY 15, '76 - CONTINUING . TRADITIONAL HANDCRAFTED ARTICLES DISPLAY. CREATION OF TRADITIONAL HANDCRAFTED ARTICLES SUCH AS CLOTHING AND BEADWORK BY TRIBAL WOMEN AND CHILDREN; A REVITALIZATION OF ANCIENT CRAFT SKILLS. AT GOLDEN HILL MUSEUM, GOLDEN HILL RESERVATION, TRUMBULL, CONN. (LOCAL). AURELIUS PIPER, CHIEF; GOLDEN HILL TRIBAL COUNCIL; 427 SHELDON RD; TRUMBULL, CT 06611. (#21873-1).

UNCASVILLE

RELOCATION & RESTORATION OF ROGERS HOUSE - CT. PRESERVATION OF 1740 SALTBOX HOUSE WHICH IS AN EXAMPLE OF EARLY MONTVILLE ARCHITECTURE. (LOCAL). HOWARD R BEETAM, JR, FIRST SELECTMAN; TOWN OF MONTVILLE; UNCASVILLE, CT 06382. (#27080). **ARBA GRANTEE.**

UNION

DATING OF HISTORICAL HOMES AND LANDMARKS. RESEARCH AND COMPILE BRIEF HISTORY OF OLD HOMES AND LANDMARKS AND TO INSTALL DATE PLAQUES ON SAME; RECORD IN SMALL PUBLISHED DESCRIPTIVE BOOKLET. (LOCAL). MARION KINGSBURY, CO-CHAIRMAN; UNION BICENTENNIAL COMMITTEE; 606 BUCKLEY HWY; UNION, CT 06076. (#13238). **ARBA GRANTEE.**

UNIONVILLE

JULY 7, '76. TUNXIS FIREMAN'S CARNIVAL - FIREWORKS DISPLAY. PART OF A WEEK-LONG CARNIVAL BY TUNXIS FIRE DEPARTMENT. AT MAIN STREET, UNIONVILLE CENTER. (LOCAL). JOSEPH LESIAK, CHAIRMAN; TUNXIS HOSE FIRE DEPARTMENT; 1700 FARMINGTON AVE; UNIONVILLE, CT 06085. (#106954-1).

VOLUNTOWN

JULY 24 - AUG 1, '75. BICENTENNIAL FESTIVAL. FESTIVAL AT FESTIVAL FIELD AND TENT MAIN ST. (LOCAL). R I MILLAR, CHAIRMAN; VOLUNTOWN BICENTENNIAL COMMITTEE; RFD #1; VOLUNTOWN, CT 06394. (#200008-1).

JULY 25, '75. VOLUNTOWN BICENTENNIAL PARADE. PARADE AT MAIN STREET. (LOCAL). R I MILLAR, CHAIRMAN; VOLUNTOWN BICENTENNIAL COMMITTEE; RFD #1; VOLUNTOWN, CT 06384. (#200008-2).

JULY 4, '76. INDEPENDENCE DAY PICNIC. FAMILY PICNIC, 200TH BIRTHDAY CAKE, ATHLETIC CONTESTS & BONFIRE. AT LINE CHURCH-EKONK GRANGE, RTE 49. (LOCAL). RAYMOND I MILLAR, CHMN; VOLUNTOWN-STERLING BICENTENNIAL COMMITTEES; RFD #1; VOLUNTOWN, CT 06384. (#104360-1).

WALLINGFORD

PUBLICATION OF HISTORY OF WALLINGFORD, CT. COMPILE AND PUBLISH COMPREHENSIVE HISTORY TO BE USED AS PART OF SCHOOL CURRICULUM AND FOR REFERENCE BY CITIZENS. (LOCAL). ROBERT P BILLINGS, CHAIRMAN; WALLINGFORD BICENTENNIAL COMMISSION; 155 N MAIN ST; WALLINGFORD, CT 06492. (#12264). **ARBA GRANTEE.**

MAY 24 - 27, '76. BICENTENNIAL WEEK IN WALLINGFORD-INDUSTRIAL EXPOSITION. A WEEK OF ACTIVITIES INCLUDING AN INDUSTRIAL EXPOSITION & THE OPENING OF A SMITHSONIAN EXHIBIT HELP WALLINGFORD CELEBRATE THE BICENTENNIAL. AT CHOATE SCHOOL ARENA, CHRISTIAN ST, WALLINGFORD, CT. (ST-WIDE). ROBERT BILLINGS, COORD; BICENTENNIAL WEEK IN WALLINGFORD; PO BOX 76; WALLINGFORD, CT 06492. (#103416-293).

MAY 30 - 31, '76. VETERANS & REDEDICATION DAY & MEMORIAL DAY PARADE. SUNDAY-SPECIAL CHURCH SERVICES; OPEN HOUSE AT VETERANS ORGANIZATIONS & FIREWORKS. MONDAY-PARADE. (LOCAL). ROBERT P BILLINGS, CHMN; WALLINGFORD BICENTENNIAL COMMISSION, INC; PO BOX 76; WALLINGFORD, CT 06492. (#200008-263).

JULY 3 - 4, '76. JULY 4TH WEEKEND CELEBRATION. SATURDAY-MAMMOTH FIREWORKS DISPLAY AT SHEEHAN & MORGAN SCHOOL AREA. SUNDAY-FOURTH OF JULY CEREMONIES INCL BELL RINGERS AT HISTORICAL HOUSE. (LOCAL). ROBERT P BILLINGS, CHMN; WALLINGFORD BICENTENNIAL COMMISSION, INC; PO BOX 76; WALLINGFORD, CT 06492. (#200008-262).

WAREHOUSE PT

JUNE 18, '76. BICENTENNIAL COSTUME BALL. COLONIAL ATTIRE REQUIRED. BUFFET MEAL OPEN BAR 18-PIECE BAND. AT CLEMS RESTAURANT, RT 5, E WINDSOR, CT. (LOCAL). KENNETH C YOUNG, COORD; EAST WINDSOR LIONS CLUB; 6 DEAN AVE, BOX 515; WAREHOUSE PT, CT 06088. (#105713-1).

WASHINGTON

PICTORIAL HISTORY OF WASHINGTON, CT. PHOTOGRAPHIS OF WASHINGTON SINCE THE FIRST CENTENNIAL, TAKEN BY JOSEPH WEST AND OTHERS. (LOCAL). MICHAEL CAROE, PRESIDENT; GUNN MEMORIAL LIBRARY, INC; WASHINGTON GREEN; WASHINGTON, CT 06793. (#11885). **ARBA GRANTEE.**

OCT 24, '75. REENACT ILLUMINATION NIGHT, OCT 24, 1781-CORNWALLIS SURRENDER. BOTH PUBLIC AND PRIVATE BUILDINGS ARE ILLUMINATED WITH OUTDOOR LIGHTING, CANDLES, LANTERNS ETC. CHURCH BELLS RUNG AT 6PM AND 8PM ORIGINAL G. WASHINGTON ILLUMINATION CELEBRATION PROCLAMATION READ FIFE AND DRUM CORPS PLAY AT BONFIRE ENDING AT 8PM. AT CITYWIDE. (LOCAL). TATE BROWN; WASHINGTON AMERICAN REVOLUTIONARY WAR BICENTENIAL COMMISSION; CHURCH HILL; WASHINGTON, CT 06794. (#50285-1).

WATERBURY

GRANITE MEMORIAL - WATERBURY, CT. A MONUMENT TO BE DEDICATED AT CHASE PARK IN COMMEMORATION OF THE PROJECT 'A REVOLUTIONARY REVIEW' PRESENTED BY BOY SCOUT TROOP 28; THE GRANITE MONUMENT WILL HAVE A REPLICA LIBERTY BELL MOUNTED ON IT. (LOCAL). RONALD J CIASULLO, CHAIRMAN; BOY SCOUT TROOP 28, OUR LADY OF MT CARMEL CHURCH; 785 HIGHLAND AVE; WATERBURY, CT 06708. (#23627). **ARBA GRANTEE.**

A REVOLUTIONARY REVIEW - WATERBURY, CT. EXHIBITS ON THE BATTLE OF LEXINGTON, BETSY ROSS, SIGNING OF THE DECLARATION, WASHINGTON AT VALLEY FORGE, ARMY FIELD KITCHEN & HOSPITAL, CONN THE PROVISION STATE & A CEMETERY IN MEMORY OF SOLDIERS. (LOCAL). RONALD J CIASULLO, CHAIRMAN; BOY SCOUT TROOP 28, OUR LADY OF MT CARMEL CHURCH; 785 HIGHLAND AVE; WATERBURY, CT 06708. (#23628). **ARBA GRANTEE.**

ROCHAMBEAU MARCH - WATERBURY, CT. 'ROCHAMBEAU'S ARMY' WILL MARCH FROM JUNE 19TH TO JULY 4, 1976 FROM PROVIDENCE, RI TO VERPLANK, NY. THIS WILL BE A RE-ENACTMENT OF THE MARCH WHEN GEN ROCHAMBEAU MET GEN WASHINGTON IN 1781. (REGN'L). MICHAEL GRANATULE, CHAIRMAN; WATERBURY BICENTENNIAL COMMISSION; GRAND ST; WATERBURY, CT 06702. (#26109). **ARBA GRANTEE.**

JUNE 5 - 6, '76. A REVOLUTIONARY REVIEW. EXHIBITS ON THE BATTLE OF LEXINGTON, BETSY ROSS, SIGNING OF THE DECLARATION, WASHINGTON AT VALLEY FORGE, ARMY FIELD KITCHEN AND HOSPITAL, CONNECTICUT THE PROVISION STATE AND A CEMETERY IN MEMORY OF AREA SOLDIERS. (LOCAL). RONALD J CIASULLO, CHMN; BOY SCOUT TROOP 28, OUR LADY OF MT CARMEL CHURCH; 785 HIGHLAND AVE; WATERBURY, CT 06708. (#23628-1).

JUNE 6, '76. MEMORIAL DEDICATION. A MONUMENT TO BE DEDICATED A CHASE PARK IN COMMEMORATION OF THE PROJECT 'A REVOLUTIONARY REVIEW' PRESENTED BY BOY SCOUT TROOP 28; THE GRANITE MONUMENT WILL HAVE A REPLICA OF THE LIBERTY BELL MOUNTED ON IT. AT CHASE PARK. (LOCAL). RONALD J CIASULLO, CHMN; BOY SCOUT TROOP 28, OUR LADY OF MT CARMEL CHURCH; 785 HIGHLAND AVE; WATERBURY, CT 06708. (#23627-1).

JUNE 19 - JULY 4, '76. RE-ENACTMENT OF ROCHAMBEAU'S MARCH. 'ROCHAMBEAU'S ARMY' WILL MARCH FROM PROVIDENCE, RI TO VERPLANK, NY TO RE-ENACT THE MARCH WHEN GEN ROCHAMBEAU MET GEN WASHINGTON. (LOCAL). MICHAEL GRANATULE, CHMN; WATERBURY BICENTENNIAL COMMISSION; GRAND ST; WATERBURY, CT 06702. (#26109-1).

WATERFORD

MONOGRAPH ON TOWN AND NATIONAL INDEPENDENCE. ILLUSTRATED MONOGRAPH BY SIX HISTORIANS, REVOLUTIONARY VETERANS, HOUSES, RESOURCES, EDUCATION, AND LOCAL INVOLVEMENT IN STRUGGLE FOR NATIONAL AND LOCAL INDEPENDENCE. (LOCAL). CAROL F GATHY, CHAIRMAN; WATERFORD BICENTENNIAL COMMITTEE; 200 BOSTON POST RD; WATERFORD, CT 06385. (#13648). **ARBA GRANTEE.**

SCHOOL RESTORATION OF WATERFORD, CONN. LOCAL SCHOOL WILL BE RESTORED. PROJECT COMPLETION IS EXPECTED IN APRIL '75. (LOCAL). MRS CHARLES WILMOT, PRESIDENT; WATERFORD HISTORICAL SOCIETY; PO BOX 117; WATERFORD, CT 06385. (#3246).

WEST HARTFORD

AMERICAN HISTORY FROM COLONIAL TIMES TO AMERICAN REVOLUTION. FIELD TRIPS TO HISTORIC PLACES IN NEW ENGLAND INCLUDING A TRIP TO WILLIAMSBURG. (LOCAL). SISTER TONI IADAROLA; ST JOSEPH'S COLLEGE BICENTENNIAL COMMITTEE; 1678 ASYLUM AVE; WEST HARTFORD, CT 06117. (#107391-13). **(??).**

ART SCULPTURE AND PAINTING EXHIBIT. EXHIBIT. (ST-WIDE). JANET DISTEFANO, CHAIRMAN; UNIV OF HARTFORD BICENTENNIAL COMMITTEE; 200 BLOOMFIELD AVE BOX #37; W HARTFORD, CT 06117. (#102249-4). **(??).**

ART & LIFE IN AMERICA: 1776-1976. THE COLLEGE HAS AN EXTENSIVE LECTURE COLLECTION BY THE AMERICAN ARTISTS SERIES; FREE OF CHARGE & OPEN TO PUBLIC. (LOCAL). SISTER TONI IADAROLA; ST JOSEPH'S COLLEGE BICENTENNIAL COMMITTEE; 1678 ASYLUM AVE; WEST HARTFORD, CT 06117. (#107391-14). **(??).**

'BEN FRANKLIN' BANQUET - FOOD, COSTUMES & SONG FROM COLONIAL AMERICA. FESTIVAL. (LOCAL). SISTER TONI IADAROLA; ST JOSEPH'S COLLEGE BICENTENNIAL COMMITTEE; 1678 ASYLUM AVE; WEST HARTFORD, CT 06117. (#107391-8). **(??).**

BICENTENNIAL CELEBRATION OF WOMEN IN AMERICAN SOCIETY. SONG, DANCE, DRAMA AND ART DESCRIBING THE IMPACT OF WOMEN ON OUR AMERICAN WAY OF LIFE. (LOCAL). SISTER TONI IADAROLA; ST JOSEPH'S COLLEGE BICENTENNIAL COMMITTEE; 1678 ASYLUM AVE; WEST HARTFORD, CT 06117. (#107391-9). **(??).**

BUS TRIPS TO HISTORICAL SITES - UNIV OF HARTFORD. SCHOOL SPONSORED TRIPS FOR A DAY OR MORE TO HISTORICAL SITES WITHIN THE AREA. (LOCAL). LORI SEIDMAN, COORDINATOR; UNIV OF HARTFORD BICENTENNIAL COMMITTEE; 200 BLOOMFIELD AVE; W HARTFORD, CT 06117. (#16065).

EARLY AMERICAN LITERATURE - W HARTFORD, CT. WEST HARTFORD 1611-1826. (LOCAL). SISTER TONI IADAROLA, BICENTENNIAL CHAIRMAN; ST JOSEPH'S COLLEGE; 1678 ASYLUM AVE; W HARTFORD, CT 06117. (#24406).

EXCAVATION OF REVOLUTIONARY WAR ENCAMPMENT - CT. ARCHAEOLOGICAL EXCAVATION OF CAMPSITE. FIREPLACES KNOWN TO HAVE BEEN USED BY TROOPS DURING REVOLUTIONARY WAR SITE LOCATED IN WEST HARTFORD. (LOCAL). RICHARD M WOODWORTH, CHAIRMAN; WEST HARTFORD BICENTENNIAL COMMISSION; 211 STEELE RD; WEST HARTFORD, CT 06117. (#17993).

FILM SERIES - PROJ OF UNIV OF HARTFORD - CT. FILMS PORTRAYING HISTORICAL TIME PERIODS AND ALSO A SERIES CONVEYING THE HISTORY OF CINEMA. (LOCAL). KEN SIMON, COORDINATOR; FILM COMMITTEE/PROGRAM COUNCIL/UNIV OF HARTFORD; 200 BLOOMFIELD AVE; W HARTFORD, CT 06117. (#15161).

'FROM PARISH TO CITY', HISTORY OF W HARTFORD, CT. A POPULAR PRESENTATION OF WEST HARTFORD'S HISTORY. A SLIDE PRESENTATION TO BE PREPARED BY 20 HIGH SCHOOL STUDENTS FROM RESEARCH DONE BY DR NELSON BURR, HISTORIAN. (LOCAL). NORMAN G FRICKE, TREASURER; WEST HARTFORD SCHOOL DEPARTMENT; 211 STEELE RD; WEST HARTFORD, CT 06117. (#17992). **ARBA GRANTEE.**

HISTORY OF THE UNIVERSITY OF HARTFORD - CT. A HISTORY OF THE ESTABLISHMENT OF THE UNIVERSITY. (LOCAL). JANET DISTEFANO, STUDENT CHAIRPERSON; UNIVERSITY OF HARTFORD BICENTENNIAL; 200 BLOOMFIELD AVE, BOX 370; W HARTFORD, CT 06117. (#15127).

INTERNATIONAL BICENTENNIAL CELEBRATION. THERE WILL BE A DINNER WITH FOODS TYPIFYING VARIOUS ETHNIC GROUPS FOLLOWED BY SONGS AND DANCE. (LOCAL). SISTER TONI IADAROLA; ST JOSEPH'S COLLEGE BICENTENNIAL COMMITTEE; 1678 ASYLUM AVE; WEST HARTFORD, CT 06117. (#107391-12). **(??).**

WHAT WILL WE LOOK LIKE IN OUR TRICENTENNIAL. LECTURE AND DISCUSSION ON PREDICTIONS MADE BY EXPERTS. (LOCAL). SISTER TONI IADAROLA; ST JOSEPH'S COLLEGE BICENTENNIAL COMMITTEE; 1678 ASYLUM AVE; WEST HARTFORD, CT 06117. (#107391-6). **(??).**

WOMEN'S HISTORY - UNIV OF HARTFORD, CT. PRESENTATION OF WOMEN'S ROLE IN HISTORY. (LOCAL). DENISE TRACY, COORDINATOR; WOMEN'S CENTER/UNIV OF HARTFORD; 200 BLOOMFIELD AVE; W HARTFORD, CT 06117. (#16064).

MAR 1 - 31, '75. THE IMMIGRANT EXPERIENCE. AUDIO-VISUAL PRESENTATION OF JEWS, ITALIANS, IRISH AND GERMANS OPEN TO COLLEGE COMMUNITY; DOCUMENTARY PRESENTED TWICE ON CHANNEL 3 & 30. (LOCAL). SISTER TONI IADAROLA; ST JOSEPH'S COLLEGE BICENTENNIAL COMMITTEE; 1678 ASYLUM AVE; WEST HARTFORD, CT 06117. (#107391-2).

OCT 30, '75 - MAY 8, '76. MCAULEY LECTURE SERIES. SPEAKERS: 10/30/75-EDMOND F MORGAN; 11/6/75-RICHARD MORRIS; 2/12/76RICHARD BUSHMAN; 4/8/76-WILLARD M WALLACE; 5/8/76-J H PLUM. (LOCAL). SR TONI IADAROLA, CHMN; ST JOSEPH'S COLLEGE BICENTENNIAL COMMITTEE; 1678 ASYLUM AVE; WEST HARTFORD, CT 06117. (#200008-20).

FEB 12, '76. 'WHY FARMERS FOUGHT IN 1775'. THIS IS ONE OF 5 LECTURES IN A SPECIAL BICENTENNIAL SERIES; LECTURER IS R L BUSHMAN, PROFESSOR OF HISTORY AT BOSTON UNIV. AT HALL HIGH SCHOOL, 975 N MAIN ST. (ST-WIDE). GORDON BENNETT, DIRECTOR; WEST HARTFORD BICENTENNIAL COMMITTEE; 211 STEELE RD - RM 401; WEST HARTFORD, CT 06107. (#104939-1).

APR 1 - 30, '76. BICENTENNIAL CONCERT. THE PROGRAM INCLUDES SPIRITUALS, BALLADS, CIVIL WAR SONGS AND BROADWAY HITS. (LOCAL). SISTER TONI IADAROLA; ST JOSEPH'S COLLEGE BICENTENNIAL COMMITTEE; 1678 ASYLUM AVE; WEST HARTFORD, CT 06117. (#107391-11).

APR 1 - 30, '76. THE NEGRO FROM THE 14TH AMENDMENT TO BLACK POWER. AUDIO-VISUAL PRESENTATION FOR THE ST JOSEPH COLLEGE COMMUNITY. (LOCAL). SISTER TONI IADAROLA; ST JOSEPH'S COLLEGE BICENTENNIAL COMMITTEE; 1678 ASYLUM AVE; WEST HARTFORD, CT 06117. (#107391-1).

APR 20, '76. BEN FRANKLIN KITE CONSTRUCTION AND FLYING CONTEST. COMPETITION, EXHIBIT. (LOCAL). JULIE DEMGEN, ADVISOR; UNIV OF HARTFORD - PROGRAM COUNCIL; 200 BLOOMFIELD AVE GSU; W HARTFORD, CT 06117. (#102249-2).

APR 30, '76. FROM THE NEW FRONTIER TO OUTER SPACE AND BEYOND - LECTURE & SLIDES. SEMINAR. (LOCAL). SISTER TONI IADAROLA; ST JOSEPH'S COLLEGE BICENTENNIAL COMMITTEE; 1678 ASYLUM AVE; WEST HARTFORD, CT 06117. (#107391-7).

MAY 8, '76. NEW ENGLAND HISTORICAL ASSOC MEETING - J H PLUMB SPEAKER. J H PLUMB IS A PROMINET BRITISH HISTORIAN. (REGN'L). SISTER TONI IADAROLA; ST JOSEPH'S COLLEGE BICENTENNIAL COMMITTEE; 1678 ASYLUM AVE; WEST HARTFORD, CT 06117. (#107391-3).

MAY 10 - 15, '76. INDUSTRIAL HERITAGE USA. TWENTY SEVEN EXHIBITS-EACH RELATING TO THE PROGRESS OF AN AMERICAN INDUSTRY. (ST-WIDE). RICHARD WIZE, COORD; WESTFARMS ASSOCIATES; 500 WESTFARMS MALL; FARMINGTON, CT 06012. (#103416-279).

JUNE 12, '76. BICENTENNIAL FAIR. FAIR. (LOCAL). SISTER TONI IADAROLA; ST JOSEPH'S COLLEGE BICENTENNIAL COMMITTEE; 1678 ASYLUM AVE; WEST HARTFORD, CT 06117. (#107391-10).

JUNE 26, '76. SPELLING BEE AT THE NOAH WEBSTER HOMESTEAD. THE 13 ORIGINAL STATES WILL BE REPRESENTED IN THE SPELLING BEE. AT 227 S MAIN ST. (REGN'L). MADELINE MCKERNAN; WEST HARTFORD BICENTENNIAL COMMISSION; 211 STEELE RD; WEST HARTFORD, CT 06117. (#101022-1).

AUG 1 - NOV 30, '76. EXHIBIT OF DEWITT COLLECTION OF ELECTION MEMORABILIA. EXHIBIT. (LOCAL). DR SULLIVAN, CURATOR; UNIVERSITY ADMINISTRATION, UNIVERSITY OF HARTFORD; 200 BLOOMFIELD AVE; W HARTFORD, CT 06117. (#102249-3).

SEPT - NOV '76. WHITHER AMERICAN VALUES. LECTURES AND DISCUSSIONS ON THE SOCIAL, POLITICAL, PHILOSOPHICAL, HISTORICAL AND RELIGIOUS EVOLUTION OF VALUES FROM THE COLONIAL PERIOD TO THE PRESENT DAY. (LOCAL). SISTER TONI IADAROLA; ST JOSEPH'S COLLEGE BICENTENNIAL COMMITTEE; 1678 ASYLUM AVE; WEST HARTFORD, CT 06117. (#107391-5).

OCT 4 - NOV 30, '76. LECTURES BY POLITICAL CANDIDATES. SEMINAR. (LOCAL). JANET DISTEFANO, CHMN; UNIVERSITY OF HARTFORD BICENTENNIAL COMMITTEE; 200 BLOOMFIELD AVE, BOX 370; W HARTFORD, CT 06117. (#102249-1).

WEST HAVEN

JULY 17 - 18, '76. UNITED STATES ARMED FORCES BICENTENNIAL CARAVAN. CARAVAN IS COMPOSED OF EXHIBIT VANS FOR EACH MILITARY SERVICE. PROJECT THEME IS 'HISTORY OF THE ARMED FORCES & THEIR CONTRIBUTIONS TO THE NATION.'. (LOCAL). MICHAEL R HALPIN, DIR; UNITED STATES ARMED FORCES BICENTENNIAL CARAVAN; 270 MAIN ST; WEST HAVEN, CT 06516. (#1775-589).

WEST NEWBURY

APR 20, '75. ECUMENICAL SERVICE. TOLLING OF PAUL REVERE CHURCH BELLS; SERVICE TYPICAL OF REVOLUTIONARY TIME WITH OIL LIGHTS; SOCIAL HOUR; DISPLAY OF ARTIFACTS OF OLD CHURCH; REVOLUTIONARY COSTUMES WILL BE WORN. AT FIRST PARISH COMMUNITY CHURCH, MAIN ST, RT 113. (LOCAL). REV ELIZABETH WALTON; WEST NEWBURY BICENTENNIAL COMMISSION; FARM LN; SEABROOK, NH 03874. (#200024-16).

WESTBROOK

APR 24, '76. COLONIAL FIELD DAY. OVER 20 CORPS WILL BE ON HAND FOR PARADE AND ENCAMPMENT. CRAFTSMEN FROM THROUGHOUT THE NORTHEAST TO DISPLAY AND DEMONSTRATE THEIR WORK. AT TOWN FIELD, BOSTON POST RD, EXIT #65 CONN TURNPIKE. (ST-WIDE). BARRY CLARK, CHMN; WESTBROOK BICENTENNIAL COMMITTEE; WALDRON DR; WESTBROOK, CT 06498. (#103788-1).

AUG 28, '76. NATIONAL ANCIENT MUSTER. LIVE PERFORMANCE AT ATHLETIC FIELD NEAR TOWN HALL. (ST-WIDE). BILL PACE, CHAIRMAN; NATIONAL ANCIENT MUSTER COMMITTEE; CHESTER, CT 06498. (#103416-514).

WESTON

GAZEBO - WESTON, CT. CONSTRUCTION OF GAZEBO OR TOWN BANDSTAND. (LOCAL). G GUIDERA, CHAIRMAN; WESTON BICENTENNIAL COMMITTEE; PO BOX 1776; WESTON, CT 06880. (#20713).

JAN 31, '76. AN EVENING WITH MARK TWAIN. HAL HOLBROOK TYPE EVENING, GAY-NINTIES THEME, CHORAL GROUP ALSO. AT WESTON HIGH SCHOOL AUDITORIUM, OFF WESTON RD. (LOCAL). RICHARD WHITNEY, COORD; WESTON BICENTENNIAL COMMITTEE; 144 GOODHILL RD; WESTON, CT 06880. (#104933-2).

JULY 4, '76. TOWNWIDE FOURTH OF JULY PICNIC. GAMES, FIREWORKS, FOOD, BANDS, COLONIAL MUSTER AND BATTLE. AT WESTON HIGH SCHOOL FIELD. (LOCAL). ELAINE LEWIS, CHAIRMAN; WESTON BICENTENNIAL COMMITTEE; 9 LITTLE FOX LANE; WESTON, CT 06880. (#104933-1).

WESTPORT

'HYAM SOLOMON & THE AMER REVOL', OPERA IN CT. A FOLK OPERA BASED ON THE LIFE OF HYAM SOLOMON, AN AMERICAN PATRIOT OF POLISH JEWISH ORIGIN AND HIS ROLE IN HELPING TO FINANCE THE AMER REVOLUTION. (LOCAL). DR HENRY A SINGER, EXECUTIVE; HUMAN RESOURCES INSTITUTION; 15 IMPERIAL AVE; WESTPORT, CT 06840. (#11882). **ARBA GRANTEE.**

OPERATIC COMPOSITION - WESTPORT, CT. AN OPERA HAS BEEN COMPOSED TO THE DRAMA, 'DONA ROSITA LA SOLTERA O EL LENGUAGE DE LAS FLORES' BY THE SPANISH POET, FEDERICO GARCIA LORCA. (REGN'L). CAROLINE LLOYD, COMPOSER; 3500 GALT OCEAN DRIVE APT 1917; FT LAUDERDALE, FL 33308. (#25853).

WESTPORT — CONTINUED

WESTPORT MINNYBUS SYSTEM, WESTPORT, CT. INNOVATIVE COMMUNITY TRANSPORTATION SYSTEM SERVING THE NEEDS OF A SMALL TOWN. (LOCAL). RICHARD H BRADLEY, EXEC DIRECTOR; WESTPORT TRANSIT DISTRICT; 311 E STATE ST; WESTPORT, CT 06880. (#20075).

JULY 11 - AUG 31, '75. BICENTENNIAL SALUTE TO AMERICAN PLAYWRIGHTS. INCLUDES ROBERT FROST'S 'FIRE & ICE', JULY 11-13; 'HOW DO YOU LIVE WITH LOVE' (A NEW PLAY), JULY 25-27; JOHN STEINBECK'S 'THE LONG VALLEY', AUGUST 8-10; & EVA LE GALLIENE IN 'THE DREAM WATCHER' (A NEW PLAY), AUGUST 29-31. AT EXIT 41 FROM MERRITT PARKWAY. (ST-WIDE). LUCILLE LORTEL, DIRECTOR; WHITE BARN THEATRE; NEWTOWN AVE; WESTPORT, CT 06880. (#100572-1).

SEPT 27, '75. COLONIAL FAIR W/BOOTHS, MUSIC & BICENTENNIAL PROGRAM. COLONIAL LIFE PORTRAYALS & LIVE MUSIC. AT JESSUP GREEN. (LOCAL). RUDRA TAMM, CHAIRMAN; SACRED FIRE; 80 PERRY AVE; NORWALK, CT 06850. (#101295-1).

MAY 29 - 30, '76. WESTPORT HANDCRAFTS FAIR. NEW ENGLAND CRAFTS FAIR FEATURES MORE THAN 85 ARTISTS. AT STAPLES HIGH SCHOOL. (REGN'L). CAROLE DONENFELD; THE WESTPORT-WESTON COOPERATIVE NURSERY SCHOOL; 6 BONNIE BROOK RD; WESTPORT, CT 06880. (#103416-317).

WETHERSFIELD

CONNECTICUT STATE AGENCIES BICENTENNIAL EXHIBIT. AN EXHIBIT FEATURING 200 YEARS OF THE ARTS, SCIENCES, POLITICAL FIGURES & EVENTS RELATED TO THE GROWTH OF DEMOCRACY IN CONNECTICUT. EXHIBIT WILL BE SHOWN AT WEST HARTFORD & HARTFORD ARMORIES. (ST-WIDE). LUCILLE M FOX, CHAIRMAN; STATE OF CONNECTICUT, STATE AGENCY BICENTENNIAL COMMITTEE; 34 WOLCOTT HILL RD, PO DRAWER A; WETHERSFIELD, CT 06109. (#25239). **ARBA GRANTEE.**

WETHERSFIELD, CT IN THE AMERICAN REVOLUTION. PLANS ARE TO PUBLISH TWO BOOKLETS ON WETHERSFIELD, ONE ON MILITARY EVENTS & ONE ON MARITIME EVENTS IN THE AMERICAN REVOLUTION. THESE 60 PAGE BOOKS WILL BE GIVEN TO PARTICIPANTS IN THE HOUSE TOURS. (LOCAL). RONNA LEE REYNOLDS, DIRECTOR; THE WETHERSFIELD HISTORICAL SOCIETY; 150 MAIN ST; WETHERSFIELD, CT 06109. (#7342). **ARBA GRANTEE.**

WILLIMANTIC

RIVER'S PROJECT - WILLIMANTIC, CT. RESTORATION OF RIVER EMBANKMENT AREAS FOR LEISURE & RECREATION. (LOCAL). TERRY WAKEMAN, DIRECTOR; WINDHAM REGIONAL PLANNING AGENCY; 21 CHURCH ST; WILLIMANTIC, CT 06226. (#30204).

TILLSON HOUSE - WILLIMANTIC, CT. RENOVATION OF HISTORIC HOUSE IS TAKING PLACE. (LOCAL). LUCY B CROSBIE, PRESIDENT; WINDHAM HISTORICAL SOCIETY; PO BOX 105; WILLIMANTIC, CT 06226. (#30205).

TOWN MARKER - WILLIMANTIC, CT. A NEW MARKER IS BEING PLACED IN THE CENTER OF TOWN. (LOCAL). DAVID ROTH, COORDINATOR; WINDHAM BICENTENNIAL COMMITTEE; EASTERN CT STATE COLLEGE; WILLIMANTIC, CT 06226. (#30202).

WINDHAM BICENTENNIAL MEDALLION SALE - CT. SALE OF WINDHAM BICENTENNIAL MEDALLIONS IN BRONZE & SILVER. (LOCAL). J EUGENE SMITH, CHAIRMAN; WINDHAM BICENTENNIAL COMMISSION; 905 MAIN ST; WILLIMANTIC, CT 06226. (#30203).

JAN 10 - 12, '75. BICENTENNIAL WORKSHOP ON DISSENT. SEMINAR AT J EUGENE SMITH LIBRARY. (LOCAL). CNTR FOR CONN STUDIES; EASTERN CONNECTICUT STATE COLLEGE; EASTERN CONN STATE COLLEGE; WILLIMANTIC, CT 06226. (#200008-62).

FEB 27, '75. SUFFOLK RESOLVES DEBATE. SEMINAR AT HURLEY HALL, EASTERN CONNECTICUT STATE COLLEGE. (LOCAL). CNTR FOR CONN STUDIES; WINDHAM HIGH SCHOOL; EASTERN CONN STATE COLLEGE; WILLIMANTIC, CT 06226. (#200008-58).

JUNE 13, '75. PRESENTATION OF BICENTENNIAL FLAG. CEREMONY, AWARD AT WINDHAM HIGH SCHOOL. (LOCAL). RUTH RIDGEWAY, MEMBER; WINDHAM BICENTENNIAL COMMISSION; 905 MAIN ST; WILLIMANTIC, CT 06226. (#200008-53).

JUNE 28, '75. BICENTENNIAL WORKSHOP ON DISSENT FOLLOW UP. DISSENT IN AMERICAN HISTORICAL PERSPECTIVE. AT J EUGENE SMITH LIBRARY. (ST-WIDE). CNTR FOR CONN STUDIES; CENTER FOR CONNECTICUT STUDIES, EASTERN CONNECTICUT STATE COLLEGE; EASTERN CONN STATE COLLEGE; WILLIMANTIC, CT 06226. (#200008-57).

SEPT 7, '75. A DAY IN THE LIFE OF A CONTINENTAL SOLDIER. PARADE, LIVE PERFORMANCE, CEREMONY, EXHIBIT AT WINDHAM REGIONAL TECHNICAL SCHOOL FOOTBALL FIELD. (LOCAL). LUCY B CROSBIE, COORD; THE CHRONICLE; CHRONICLE RD; WILLIMANTIC, CT 06226. (#200008-48).

JAN 19, '76. BICENTENNIAL LECTURE SERIES-BRITISH INVASION OF CONN DURING REV WAR. SEMINAR AT WINDHAM HIGH SCHOOL, HIGH ST. (LOCAL). CNTR FOR CONN STUDIES; EASTERN CONNECTICUT STATE COLLEGE; EASTERN CONN STATE COLLEGE; WILLIMANTIC, CT 06226. (#200008-61).

FEB 24, '76. BICENTENNIAL LECTURE SERIES - DAILY LIFE IN COLONIAL CONNECTICUT. SEMINAR AT WINDHAM HIGH SCHOOL, HIGH ST. (LOCAL). CNTR FOR CONN STUDIES; EASTERN CONNECTICUT STATE COLLEGE; EASTERN CONN STATE COLLEGE; WILLIMANTIC, CT 06226. (#200008-60).

APR 20, '76. BICENTENNIAL LECTURE SERIES-NEW ENGLAND BLACKS IN THE REVOLUTION ERA. SEMINAR AT WINDHAM HIGH SCHOOL. (LOCAL). CNTR FOR CONN STUDIES; EASTERN CONNECTICUT STATE COLLEGE; EASTERN CONN STATE COLLEGE; WILLIMANTIC, CT 06226. (#200008-59).

APR 30 - MAY 2, '76. THE AMERICAN DREAM - A DRAMATIZATION. LIVE PERFORMANCE AT SCHOOL AUDITORIUM, VALLEY ST. (LOCAL). REV JOSEPH KUGLER, COORD; ST MARY-ST JOSEPH ELEMENTARY SCHOOL; ST MARY RECTORY - 72 MAPLE AVE; WILLIMANTIC, CT 06226. (#200008-45).

JUNE 13 - 15, '76. FLAG DAY PARADE. PARADE, CEREMONY AT MAIN ST. (LOCAL). ROD VINCELETTE, COORD; ELKS; 198 PLEASANT ST; WILLIMANTIC, CT 06226. (#200008-52).

JUNE 21 - 22, '76. ROCHAMBEAU'S MARCH - WINDHAM TO WILLIMANTIC. PARADE, RADIO/TV AT RECREATION PARK, WILLIMANTIC. (LOCAL). REPL B WHITMORE, COORD; FRANCO AMERICAN CLUB; BRICKTOP RD; WILLIMANTIC, CT 06226. (#200008-46).

JULY 4, '76. HORSESHOE BEND FESTIVAL. FESTIVAL, LIVE PERFORMANCE, RADIO/TV, EXHIBIT AT RECREATION PARK, MAIN ST. (LOCAL). S ANDERSON, COORD; ARBC WINDHAM; PLAINS RD; WINDHAM CNTR, CT 02680. (#200008-51).

MAY 12, '77. FOUNDER'S DAY. CEREMONY, FESTIVAL. (LOCAL). J EUGENE SMITH, CHMN; WINDHAM BICENTENNIAL COMMITTEE; WINDHAM CTR, CT 06280. (#109469-1).

WILLINGTON

JULY 2 - 4, '76. FOURTH OF JULY CELEBRATION. COMPETITION, EXHIBIT, FESTIVAL, PARADE AT TOWN GREEN AND HALL POND IN SOUTH WILLINGTON. (LOCAL). PAUL M MCILVAINE, CHMN; WILLINGTON BICENTENNIAL COMMISSION; RFD 3, DALEVILLE RD; STORRS, CT 06268. (#104935-1).

WILTON

18TH CENTURY DWELLINGS IN WILTON, CT. BOOK-GUIDE OF OLD HOMES IN WILTON. (LOCAL). CYNTHIA JONES, EDITOR; WILTON HISTORICAL SOCIETY; 249 DANBURY RD; WILTON, CT 06897. (#28625).

DEC 4 - 5, '76. BICENTENNIAL BALL. FESTIVAL AT WILTON HIGH SCHOOL FIELD HOUSE, ROUTE 7. (LOCAL). STANLEY GREGORY, COORD; CANNON GRANGE; P O BOX 4; WILTON, CT 06897. (#109335-1).

WINDHAM CNTR

JUNE 23, '74. RE-ENACTMENT OF WINDHAM SHEEP DRIVE TO BOSTON 1774. LIVE PERFORMANCE, CEREMONY, RADIO/TV AT WINDHAM CENTER GREEN & BOSTON COMMON, MASSACHUSETTS. (REGN'L). RUTH RIDGEWAY, MEMBER; WINDHAM REGIONAL TECHNICAL SCHOOL & WINDHAM BICENTENNIAL COMMISSION; 905 MAIN ST; WILLIMANTIC, CT 06226. (#200008-54).

AUG 24, '74. COMMEMORATION OF EIPHALET DYER TO 1ST CONTINENTAL CONGRESS 8/24/1774. CEREMONY, LIVE PERFORMANCE, EXHIBIT, TOUR AT WINDHAM CENTER GREEN, POST OFFICE, LIBRARY, HUNT MUSEUM & DYER HOME. (LOCAL). RUTH RIDGEWAY, MEMBER; WINDHAM BICENTENNIAL COMMISSION; 905 MAIN ST; WILLIMANTIC, CT 06226. (#200008-55).

APR 20, '75. RE-ENACTMENT OF LEXINGTON CONCORD ALARM. LIVE PERFORMANCE, CEREMONY, RADIO/TV AT WINDHAM CENTER GREEN. (LOCAL). RUTH RIDGEWAY, MEMBER; ARBA WINDHAM; 905 MAIN ST; WILLIMANTIC, CT 06226. (#200008-56).

OCT 14, '75. REPLACEMENT OF JOHN CATES MEMORIAL STONE. CEREMONY AT WINDHAM CEMETERY, RTE 203. (LOCAL). FRANCIS E WRIGHT, COORD; WINDHAM HISTORICAL SOCIETY; 201 MANSFIELD AVE; WILLIMANTIC, CT 06226. (#200008-47).

MAY 17 - 21, '76. BICENTENNIAL WEEK AT WINDHAM CENTER SCHOOL. FESTIVAL, EXHIBIT, LIVE PERFORMANCE, CEREMONY, AWARD AT AUDITORIUM. (LOCAL). MRS R L PERRY, COORD; WINDHAM CENTER SCHOOL; 241 NORTH ST; WILLIMANTIC, CT 06226. (#200008-49).

WINDSOR

IMPROVE TOWN GREEN IN WINDSOR, CONNECTICUT. AESTHETICALLY ENHANCE & IMPROVE TOWN GREEN TO PRESERVE & UNIFY THE HISTORIC MONUMENTS OF THE STATE'S FIRST TOWN, SETTLED IN 1633. PARADES, PAGEANTS & OTHER FESTIVITIES TO OCCUR IN '75 & '76. (LOCAL). CAMPBELL B WILSON, CHAIRMAN; AMERICAN REVOLUTION BICENTENNIAL COMMISSION OF WINDSOR; 275 BROAD ST; WINDSOR, CT 06095. (#7345). **ARBA GRANTEE.**

APR 19, '75. REENACTMENT OF SHOT HEARD AROUND THE WORLD. RADES, PAGEANTS & OTHER FESTIVITIES TO OCCUR IN '75 & '76. (LOCAL). CAMPBELL B WILSON; AMERICAN REVOLUTION BICENTENNIAL COMMISSION OF WINDSOR; 275 BROAD ST; WINDSOR, CT 06095. (#7345-501).

FEB 1, '76. DEDICATE TOWN GREEN AND NEW PUBLIC LIBRARY. IMPROVE TOWN GREEN IN WINDSOR, CONNECTICUT. AESTHETICALLY ENHANCE & IMPROVE TOWN GREEN TO PRESERVE & UNIFY THE HISTORIC MONUMENTS OF THE STATE'S FIRST TOWN, SETTLED IN 1633. PARADES, PAGEANTS & OTHER FESTIVITIES TO OCCUR IN '75 & '76. (LOCAL). CAMPBELL B WILSON; AMERICAN REVOLUTION BICENTENNIAL COMMISSION OF WINDSOR; 275 BROAD ST; WINDSOR, CT 06095. (#7345-505).

APR 30 - MAY 22, '76. WINDSOR SHAD DERBY FESTIVAL. ANGLERS IN TRADTIONAL FISHING DERBY CAPTURE SHAD. AT ON THE TOWN GREEN. (ST-WIDE). FRANK PARKER; WINDSOR CHAMBER OF COMMERCE; 176 BROAD ST, PO BOX 144; WINDSOR, CT 06095. (#7345-503).

JULY 1 - 8, '76. INDEPENDENCE DAY CELEBRATION. OPENING, CEREMONY, FESTIVAL. (LOCAL). CAMPBELL B WILSON; AMERICAN REVOLUTION BICENTENNIAL COMMISSION OF WINDSOR; 275 BROAD ST; WINDSOR, CT 06095. (#7345-504).

SEPT 25, '76. BLOCK DANCE. FESTIVAL AT STREET BETWEEN GREEN & POST OFFICE. (LOCAL). C B WILSON, CHAIRMAN; WINDSOR CHAMBER OF COMMERCE; 12 PILGRIM DR; WINDSOR, CT 06095. (#109304-1).

SEPT 25, '76. FAMILY PICNIC & CHICKEN BARBEQUE. FESTIVAL AT TOWN GREEN. (LOCAL). C B WILSON, CHAIRMAN; AMERICAN REVOLUTION BICENTENNIAL COMMISSION OF WINDSOR; 12 PILGRIM DR; WINDSOR, CT 06095. (#109304-3).

SEPT 25, '76. PAGEANT & PARADE. PARADE AT WINDSOR AVE & BROAD ST. (LOCAL). C B WILSON, CHAIRMAN; AMERICAN REVOLUTION BICENTENNIAL COMMISSION OF WINDSOR; 12 PILGRIM DR; WINDSOR, CT 06095. (#109304-2).

OCT 23, '76. PAGEANT - 'A DAY IN THE LIFE OF A CONTINENTAL SOLDIER'. OPENING, CEREMONY, FESTIVAL. (LOCAL). CAMPBELL B WILSON; AMERICAN REVOLUTION BICENTENNIAL COMMISSION OF WINDSOR; 275 BROAD ST; WINDSOR, CT 06095. (#7345-502).

WINDSOR LOCKS

WINDSOR LOCKS, CONN - TOWN OF TRANSPORTATION. THE TOWN OF WINDSOR LOCKS WILL EMPHASIZE ITS CONTRIBUTION TO THE DEVELOPMENT OF OUR NATION BY HIGHLIGHTING THREE MODES OF TRANSPORT CANAL, RAIL, & INTL AIRPORT - THAT MADE THE INDUSTRIAL EAST. (LOCAL). HOWARD J WHITE, CHAIRMAN; AMERICAN REVOLUTION BICENTENNIAL COMMISSION; 76 WEST ST; WINDSOR LOCKS, CT 06096. (#3247).

MAY 8 - JUNE 1, '76. TOUR OF CANAL BY HORSE-DRAWN BARGE. FESTIVAL, EXHIBIT, CEREMONY, PARADE. (LOCAL). HOWARD J WHITE, CHAIRMAN; AMERICAN REVOLUTION BICENTENNIAL COMMISSION; 76 WEST ST; WINDSOR LOCKS, CT 06096. (#3247-507).

MAY 23 - 30, '76. INDUSTRIAL EXHIBITS FEATURING CONTRIBUTIONS TO NATION'S GROWTH. THE TOWN OF WINDSOR LOCKS WILL EMPHASIZE ITS CONTRIBUTION TO THE DEVELOPMENT OF OUR NATION BY HIGHLIGHTING THREE MODES OF TRANSPORT CANAL, RAIL, & INTL AIRPORT - THAT MADE THE INDUSTRIAL EAST. IT FEATURES REPRESENTATIONS OF VARIOUS MFGR COMPANIES IN THE AREA. AT UNION SCHOOL GYM, CHURCH ST. (LOCAL). HOWARD J WHITE, CHMN; AMERICAN REVOLUTION BICENTENNIAL COMMISSION OF WINDSOR LOCKS; 76 WEST ST; WINDSOR LOCKS, CT 06096. (#3247-4).

MAY 28, '76. REDEDICATION CEREMONY, PAGEANT, & ALL FAITH SERVICE TO OPEN PROGRAM. FESTIVAL, EXHIBIT, CEREMONY, PARADE. (LOCAL). HOWARD J WHITE, CHAIRMAN; AMERICAN REVOLUTION BICENTENNIAL COMMISSION; 76 WEST ST; WINDSOR LOCKS, CT 06096. (#3247-506).

MAY 29, '76. PARADE DEPICTING COMMUNITY'S CONTRIBUTION TO U S HISTORY. FESTIVAL, EXHIBIT, CEREMONY, PARADE AT RAIN DATE - 5/30/76.. (LOCAL). HOWARD J WHITE, CHAIRMAN; ARBC OF WINDSOR LOCKS; 76 WEST ST; WINDSOR LOCKS, CT 06096. (#3247-508).

MAY 29 - 30, '76. COSTUME BALL ETHNIC REPRESENTATION OF OUR COMMUNITY HERITAGE. AN ORCHESTRA WILL BE PLAYING. BUFFET SUPPER AT 7:30PM. AT AMERICAN LEGION HALL, SPRING ST. (LOCAL). HOWARD J WHITE, CHMN; AMERICAN REVOLUTION BICENT COMMISSION OF WINDSOR LOCKS; 76 WEST ST; WINDSOR LOCKS, CT 06096. (#3247-5).

MAY 30, '76. COMMUNITY BLOCK DANCE. FESTIVAL, EXHIBIT, CEREMONY, PARADE. (LOCAL). HOWARD J WHITE, CHAIRMAN; AMERICAN REVOLUTION BICENTENNIAL COMMISSION; 76 WEST ST; WINDSOR LOCKS, CT 06096. (#3247-509).

MAY 31, '76. COMMUNITY PICNIC YOUTH CHORAL PRESENTATION AND FIELD DAY. PICNIC FOR PEOPLE OF WINDSOR LOCKS-OLD FASHION COMMUNITY PICNIC FIELD DAY FOR YOUTH OF COMMUNITY, ROAD RUN BLOCK DANCE IN EVENING. ADVANCE TICKET SALE BEGINS APRIL, 1976. AT WINDSOR LOCK HIGH SCHOOL GROUNDS SO ELM ST WINDSOR LOCKS CT 06096. (LOCAL). ROBERT MASSE; AMERICAN REVOLUTION BICENTENNIAL COMMISSION OF WINDSOR LOCKS CT06096; 2 WICKLOW STREET; WINDSOR LOCKS, CT 06096. (#3247-1).

WINSTED

AMERICAN CULTURE FOR STUDENTS FROM SPAIN IN CT. EXCURSIONS, CLASSES IN ENGLISH & AMERICAN CULTURE AND PLANNED ACTIVITIES FOR 40 STUDENTS FROM SPAIN WHO WILL VISIT THIS AREA FOR 4 WEEKS THIS SUMMER. (LOCAL). PETA J HOWARD, FOREIGN STUDY LEAGUE COORDINATOR; NORTHWESTERN CONNECTICUT COMMUNITY COLLEGE; PARK PL; WINSTED, CT 06098. (#15387).

BICENTENNIAL BOOKCOVERS, WINSTED, CT. HISTORICAL THEME & RED, WHITE AND BLUE COVERS ON LITERARY PUBLICATION & CATALOGUE. (LOCAL). EDWARD S GUEST, DEAN OF THE COLLEGE; NORTHWESTERN CONNECTICUT COMMUNITY COLLEGE; PARK PL; WINSTED, CT 06098. (#15384).

BROCHURE ON HISTORIC MONUMENTS, WINSTED, CT. COMPILATION OF A LIST OF HISTORIC LANDMARKS IN NORTHWESTERN CONNECTICUT FOR PUBLICATION. (LOCAL). MILDRED O DUR-

WINSTED — CONTINUED

HAM, BICENTENNIAL CHAIRMAN; NORTHWESTERN CONNECTICUT COMMUNITY COLLEGE; PARK PL; WINSTED, CT 06098. (#15379).

BUS TRIPS TO BOSTON FROM WINSTED, CT. 2 ONE-DAY TRIPS TO THE FREEDOM TRAIL. (LOCAL). EUGENE P FALCO, DIRECTOR OF ACTIVITIES; NORTHWESTERN CONNECTICUT COMMUNITY COLLEGE; PARK PL; WINSTED, CT 06098. (#15385).

CHORALE CONCERTS OF AMERICAN MUSIC. MUSIC FROM THE J C PENNY GIFT VOLUME AND THE AMERICAN THEATER WITH. (LOCAL). ELIZABETH C SONIER, DIR; NORTHWESTERN CONNECTICUT COMMUNITY COLLEGE; PARK PL; WINSTED, CT 06098. (#102384-1).

COMMUNITY SERVICE PROGRAM, WINSTED, CT. LECTURES BY STAFF ON HISTORY, MUSIC, LITERATURE AND RELIGION OF THE REVOLUTIONARY PERIOD. (LOCAL). MILDRED O DURHAM, CHAIRMAN, BICENTENNIAL COMMITTEE; NORTHWESTERN CONNECTICUT COMMUNITY COLLEGE; PARK PL; WINSTED, CT 06098. (#15383).

FILM ON LOCAL HISTORY, WINSTED, CT. RESTORATION OF OLD FILM OF WINSTED FOR PUBLIC VIEWING, TO BE UNDERTAKEN BY THE ALUMNI ASSOCIATION. (LOCAL). MILDRED O DURHAM, COORDINATOR OF ALUMNI AFFAIRS; NORTHWESTERN CONNECTICUT COMMUNITY COLLEGE; PARK PL; WINSTED, CT 06098. (#15388).

FOLK DANCING PROJECT IN WINSTED, CT. EARLY AMERICAN DANCES WILL BE EMPHASIZED IN CLASSES FOR INCLUSION IN MUSIC AND OR THEATRE PROGRAMS. (LOCAL). RICHARD G TRACY, DIRECTOR OF ADMISSIONS; NORTHWESTERN CONNECTICUT COMMUNITY COLLEGE; PARK PL; WINSTED, CT 06098. (#15386).

FUTURE PLANNING CONFERENCE IN WINSTED, CT. ESTABLISHMENT OF A SEMINAR, PANEL DISCUSSION AND GUEST LECTURERS ON FUTURE OF LOCAL AREA. (LOCAL). ARTHUR E PETHYBRIDGE, DIRECTOR OF LIBRARY SERVICES; NORTHWESTERN CONNECTICUT COMMUNITY COLLEGE; PARK PL; WINSTED, CT 06098. (#15377).

HISTORICAL COSTUMING - PROJ OF WINSTED, CT. CREATION OF HISTORICAL COSTUMES TO BE USED IN CONJUNCTION WITH PLANNED PERFORMANCES OR FOR MANNIKIN DISPLAY. (LOCAL). MILDRED O DURHAM, CHAIRMAN; NORTHWESTERN CONNECTICUT COMMUNITY COLLEGE BICENT COMMITTEE; PARK PL; WINSTED, CT 06098. (#15134).

HISTORICAL EXHIBIT IN WINSTED, CT. AMERICAN HISTORY EXHIBIT TO BE DISPLAYED IN CASES IN THE LIBRARY. (LOCAL). ARTHUR E PETHYBRIDGE, DIRECTOR OF LIBRARY SERVICES; NORTHWESTERN CONNECTICUT COMMUNITY COLLEGE; PARK PL; WINSTED, CT 06098. (#15382).

ORAL HISTORY PROJECT, WINSTED, CT. TAPED RECORDINGS OF TOWNSPEOPLES' REMINISCENCES OF PAST. (LOCAL). ARTHUR PETHYBRIDGE, DIRECTOR OF LIBRARY SERVICES; NORTHWESTERN CONNECTICUT COMMUNITY COLLEGE; PARK PL; WINSTED, CT 06098. (#15378).

PANTOMIME IN THE PARK. HISTORIC EVENTS PORTRAYED IN STUDENT CREATED PANTOMINE ACTED OUT IN THE PARK. M. (LOCAL). MILDRED O DURHAM, CHMN; NORTHWESTERN CONNECTICUT COMMUNITY COLLEGE; PARK PL; WINSTED, CT 06098. (#102385-1).

THEATRE PRODUCTION OF HISTORICAL INTEREST, CT. A PLAY DRAWN FROM LOCAL HISTORICAL EVENTS TO BE PRODUCED BY THEATRE WORKSHOP. (LOCAL). JOAN S FLECKENSTEIN, ASST PROF OF THEATRE ARTS; NORTHWESTERN CONNECTICUT COMMUNITY COLLEGE; PARK PL; WINSTED, CT 06098. (#15380).

OCT 5, '74. INTERTOWN QUILTING EXHIBITION BY VIENNA, VA, CHAPT QUILTERS OF AMER. EXHIBIT. (LOCAL). RICHARD G WHEELER, CHMN; ARB STEERING COMMITTEE OF THE BARKHAMSTED HISTORICAL SOC INC; RFD 2, OLD NORTH ROAD; WINSTED, CT 06098. (#2766-901).

MAY 1, '76. FUN DAY. SKILL IN EARLY AMERICAN GAMES DEVELOPED BY STUDENTS FOR FUN DAY. (LOCAL). EUGENE P FALCO, DIRECTOR; NORTHWESTERN CONNECTICUT COMMUNITY COLLEGE BICENTENNIAL COMMITTEE; PARK PL; WINSTED, CT 06098. (#102387-1).

WOLCOTT

RESTORATION OF OLD STONE SCHOOLHOUSE, WOLCOTT, CT. SCHOOL BUILT 1825, OLDEST STONE SCHOOL IN NEW ENGLAND, CURRENTLY A MUSEUM, NEEDS REPAIR; PLAN TO RESTORE BUILDING TO ORIGINAL SCHOOL AS BEGINNING OF WOLCOTT HISTORICAL PARK. (LOCAL). EUGENE DESJARLAIS, PROJ CHAIRMAN; WOLCOTT BICENTENNIAL COMMISSION; WOLCOTT TOWN HALL; WOLCOTT, CT 06716. (#13242). **ARBA GRANTEE.**

WOODBRIDGE

BICENTENNIAL QUILT IN WOODBRIDGE, CT. THE QUILT WILL FEATURE 12 SQUARES DEPICTING SCENES OF HISTORICAL INTEREST TO THE TOWN. (LOCAL). SUSAN B BALDWIN, CHAIRMAN; WOODBRIDGE BICENTENNIAL COMMITTEE; 1015 RACEBROOK RD; WOODBRIDGE, CT 06525. (#15214).

BICENTENNIAL SYMBOL CARDS FOR BUTTON INSERTION. SYMBOL CARDS FOR BUTTON INSERTION WILL BE SOLD TO NON-PROFIT SHELTER WORKSHOPS AND SCHOOLS; ARBA LICENSE NO 76-19-0586. (NAT'L). JACK ALPERT, OWNER; INSTANT BUTTONS MACHINE MANUFACTURING COMPANY; PO BOX 3896 AMITY STATION; WOODBRIDGE, CT 06525. (#17527).

MAY 15, '76. ANTIQUES FESTIVAL. OVER 100 DEALERS TO PARTICIPATE IN THIS YEAR'S ANTIQUE FESTIVAL. AT CENTER SCHOOL GROUNDS, RT 114. (LOCAL). MRS M BALDWIN, CHMN; WOODBRIDGE BICENTENNIAL COMMISSION; 1015 RACEBROOK RD; WOODBRIDGE, CT 06525. (#102355-1).

MAY 22, '76. BICENTENNIAL BALL. FESTIVAL AT UNDER TENT BETWEEN CENTER SCHOOL AND CONGREGATIONAL CHURCH. (LOCAL). MRS MALCOLM BALDWIN, CHMN; WOODBRIDGE BICENTENNIAL COMMISSION; 1015 RACEBROOK RD; WOODBRIDGE, CT 06525. (#102355-2).

JUNE 5, '76. WOODBRIDGE CELEBRATION DAY. 13-GUN SALUTE AT DAWN WILL START OFF ALL-DAY FESTIVITIES; INCLUDED WILL BE A PARADE. AT AMITY HIGH SCHOOL. (LOCAL). MRS MALCOLM BALDWIN, CHMN; WOODBRIDGE BICENTENNIAL COMMISSION; 1015 RAGEBROOK RD; WOODBRIDGE, CT 06525. (#102355-3).

WOODBURY

'WOODBURY, CONN, MEMORIAL COMMON' PROJECT. NATIVE BOULDER WILL BE MOVED TO THE COMMON FOR THE GLEBE HOUSE & EMBEDDED WITH A MEMORIAL PLAQUE TO THOSE WHO SERVED IN THE AMERICAN REVOLUTION. (LOCAL). MRS A CRAIG SHEALY, FIRST SELECTMAN; SELECTMEN'S OFFICE; TOWN OF WOODBURY; WOODBURY, CT 06798. (#1066).

JAN 4, '76. MEMORIAL COMMON DEDICATION. DEDICATION OF PLAQUE. KEYNOTE SPEAKER HARLAN H GRISWOLD, CHAIRMAN OF CONNECTICUT HISTORICAL COMMISSION. AT WEST OF MAIN STREET. (LOCAL). DAVID M NEWELL CHAIRMEN; WOODBURY BICENTENNIAL COMMITTEE; 222 FLANDERS ROAD; WOODBURY, CT 06798. (#1066-1).

WOODSTOCK

AREA INTEREST MAP - WOODSTOCK, CT. PARENT'S WEEKEND MAP OF HISTORICAL SITES OF INTERESTS. (LOCAL). PROF CHARLOTTE A YOUNG, CHAIRMAN; PUBLIC AFFAIRS CLUB, ANNHURST COLLEGE; ROUTE 169; WOODSTOCK, CT 06281. (#20664).

CEMETERY RESTORATION - PROJ OF WOODSTOCK, CT. RESTORATION OF GROUNDS AND EARLY GRAVESTONES. (LOCAL). WILLIAM PERRY, DIRECTOR; SEWEXET GRANGE; WOODSTOCK, CT 06281. (#13801).

COMMON RESTORATION - PROJ OF WOODSTOCK, CT. RESTORE AND LANDSCAPE PUBLIC COMMON WITH MARKERS TO NOTE HISTORIC LANDMARKS IN AREA. (LOCAL). DEBORAH C SHERMAN, CORRESPONDING SECRETARY; WOODSTOCK CONSERVATION COMMISSION; WOODSTOCK, CT 06281. (#13802).

CONCERTS OF AMERICAN MUSIC. MUSIC OF AMERICAN COMPOSERS WITH EMPHASIS ON EARLY AMERICAN MUSIC. (LOCAL). DANIEL GRAVES, DIRECTOR; WOODSTOCK ACADEMY GLEE CLUB AND BAND; WOODSTOCK ACADEMY; WOODSTOCK, CT 06281. (#101247-1).

FLAMENCO DANCING. SPANISH CLUB HIRING ENTERTAINMENT STRESSING CULTURAL CONTRIBUTION. (LOCAL). CHARLOTTE YOUNG, CHMN; SPANISH CLUB, ANNHURST COLLEGE; ROUTE 169; WOODSTOCK, CT 06281. (#104908-3). **(??).**

GERMAN HERITAGE - WOODSTOCK, CT. A FILM ON GERMAN HERITAGE; WILL INCLUDE REFRESHMENTS, SONG AND DANCE. (LOCAL). PROF CHARLOTTE A YOUNG, CHAIRMAN; GERMAN CLUB, ANNHURST COLLEGE; ROUTE 169; WOODSTOCK, CT 06281. (#20665).

HISTORY OF ANNHURST COLLEGE - WOODSTOCK, CT. TAPE INTERVIEWS OF EARLY GRADUATES, ADMINISTRATION AND WRITE UP OF FINDINGS IS THESIS WORK OF A JUNIOR HISTORY MAJOR. (LOCAL). PROF CHARLOTTE A YOUNG, CHAIRMAN; HISTORY DEPT, ANNHURST COLLEGE; ROUTE 169; WOODSTOCK, CT 06281. (#20666).

PHOTOGRAPHIC SURVEY, EARLY BLDGS IN WOODSTOCK, CT. ALL EXTANT BLDGS ON AN 1856 MAP OF WOODSTOCK WILL BE PHOTOGRAPHED. ENLARGED PHOTOS WILL BE FILED AND CATALOGUED FOR FUTURE REFERENCE. AN EXHIBIT WILL BE PREPARED. (LOCAL). MRS ELIZABETH B WOOD, PRESIDENT; WOODSTOCK HISTORICAL SOCIETY; BOX 65; WOODSTOCK, CT 06281. (#11887). **ARBA GRANTEE.**

TREE PLANTING - WOODSTOCK, CT. A BICENTENNIAL TREE WILL BE PLANTED. (LOCAL). PROF CHARLOTTE A YOUNG, CHAIRMAN; ANNHURST BICENTENNIAL COMMITTEE; ROUTE 169; WOODSTOCK, CT 06281. (#20663).

MAY 1, '75. MASS WITH FLAGS. OUTDOOR PATRIOTIC MASS TO CLOSE THE OBSERVANCE. (LOCAL). FATHER DOYLE, CHAPLAIN; ANNHURST COLLEGE; ROUTE 169; WOODSTOCK, CT 06281. (#104908-2).

NOV 22, '75. HOLIDAY FAIR. COLONIAL THEME; HANDMADE GIFTS TO RAISE MONEY FOR CAMPUS CLUBS TO SPONSOR BICENTENNIAL PROJECTS. (LOCAL). CHARLOTTE YOUNG, CHMN; PUBLIC AFFAIRS CLUB, ANNHURST COLLEGE; ROUTE 169; WOODSTOCK, CT 06281. (#104908-1).

APR 24, '76. BICENTENNIAL COSTUME BALL. PERIOD COSTUMES OR SEMI-FORMAL DRESS; APPROPRIATE MUSIC. AT WOODSTOCK ACADEMY ALUMNI FIELD HOUSE - WOODSTOCK HILL, CT. (LOCAL). DEBORAH C SHERMAN, SEC; WOODSTOCK BICENTENNIAL COMMISSION; RT 2; WOODSTOCK, CT 06281. (#101248-1).

MAY 1, '76. PLAY ON PARENTS' WEEKEND ON THE HISTORY OF THE POLYGLOT AMERICAN. NARRATORS-RAGGEDY ANN & ANDY, COLLEGE MASCOTS, EMPHASIZE HOW WE ALL BECAME AMERICANS FROM DIVERSE BACKGROUNDS; ALSO, EMPHASIS ON THE ROLE OF EDUCATION AND MUSIC PERTINENT TO DIFFERENT ETHNIC GROUPS THROUGHOUT HISTORY. AND A QUESTIONING OF WHERE WE WILL GO FROM HERE. AT ANNHURST CULTURAL CENTER. (LOCAL). CHARLOTTE YOUNG, CHMN; ANNHURST COLLEGE BICENTENNIAL COMMITTEE; ROUTE 169; WOODSTOCK, CT 06281. (#104908-5).

OCT 28, '76. FOLK MUSIC OF AMERICA. GUITARIST WILL PLAY AFTER FACULTY BANQUET; COSTUME THEME - COLONIAL AMERICA. AT STUDENT CENTER. (LOCAL). CHARLOTTE YOUNG, CHMN; STUDENT GOVERNMENT, ANNHURST COLLEGE; ROUTE 169; WOODSTOCK, CT 06281. (#104908-4).

THE FIRST STATE

Delaware American Revolution Bicentennial

Delaware

Delaware American Revolution Bicentennial Commission

Established by an act of the General Assembly, signed by Governor Russell W. Peterson on July 1, 1971

Theme: Delaware '76: The First State Builds for a Great Future upon a Proud Past

Subthemes: Historic Delaware, Open House Delaware, Tomorrow's Delaware

ARBA Statistics

Officially Recognized
- Communities—42
- Colleges/Universities—3
- Military Installations—1

BINET Projects—149
- Events—116

1976 Population—582,000

Bicentennial Archives

Hall of Records, Archives
Division of History and Cultural Affairs
Dover, Delaware 19901

Membership

Nine members appointed by the governor; three ex officio nonvoting members representing the State Department of Public Instruction, the State Department of Community Development and Economic Affairs and the Division of Historical and Cultural Affairs, Department of State.

E. A. Trabant, *chairman* (1971-)
Louise L. Prickett (1971-75), *executive director* (1975-)
Muriel F. Cooper (1971-)
Sam Eisenstat (1971-73)
James T. McKinstry (1971-)
M. Catherine Downing (1971-)
William Hughes (1971-72)
Clifton E. Morris (1971-75)
Nathan L. Cohen (1972-)
Samuel L. Shipley (1972-)
Harvey B. Rubenstein (1974-)
Daniel Koch (1975-76)
Norman Borish (1975-)
Kenneth McDowell (1976-)

Ex Officio Members

Howard E. Row (1971-)
Richard L. Murchison (1971-72)
E. Berkeley Tompkins (1971-73)
Ronald M. Finch (1973-75)
Lawrence C. Henry (1975-)
Robert E. Emrich (1973-74)
Bruce N. Saunders (1974-)
John S. Mickey, *executive director* (1973-75), deceased

Delaware

When the Delaware American Revolution Bicentennial Commission set forth its 13 month program, it did so with the intent to create a design for participation by all the state's citizens. When that program came to a close on September 30, 1976 with the sealing of a time capsule in Wilmington's Willingtown Square, the commission could look back and see that it had achieved its goal.

From Claymont in the north to Delmar in the south, Delawareans inspired by the Bicentennial spirit joined in a cooperative outpouring of effort seldom, if ever, seen in time of peace. A total of 55 cities and towns and all three counties became Bicentennial Communities, each planning its own program. While all communities planned programs that honored the past in present celebrations, a sense of the future was much in evidence as they strove to add to their heritage for the benefit of generations to come. Some chose to create museums, others built parks; some, for the first time, published histories. These are but examples; the list is much longer.

Every Bicentennial Community received some financial assistance from the commission through its grants program. Efforts to make the available money go as far as possible led Donald B. Strasburger, the ARBA Region III director, to remark that "Delaware has done *more,* with *less,* than any state in the Union."

Each of the 13 months of Delaware's Bicentennial had its own theme honoring some aspect of the state's life: ethnic heritage, religious heritage, youth and education, commerce, labor and industry, the arts, service organizations, sports, independence and the future—all were saluted in a variety of ways. February 1976 was observed as *Heritage Month,* with costume balls on Washington's Birthday in each of the three counties; the emphasis in June was *See Delaware,* and August was *Open House* month.

The commission was responsible for focusing attention on two days especially significant to the state's history—Separation Day, June 15 and Constitution Day, September 20. On June 15, 1776, the Delaware Assembly declared the state free of the British Crown; on September 20, 1776, Delaware adopted the first constitution ever written by a convention elected for that purpose. Beginning in 1973, the commission sponsored annual observances of these two days.

Delawareans were also inspired by national and international events that touched the state. The *American Freedom Train* made the first stop of its two year run here and drew 70,000 to Delaware Park to see it. A section of the *Wagon Train Pilgrimage to Pennsylvania* encamped in Delaware for three days and attracted thousands more. Delaware was represented in Operation Sail by the *St. Margaret II,* a Newfoundland schooner rebuilt by Nicholas and Donna Benton of New Castle, Delaware.

Perhaps most inspiring of all to Delawareans, and certainly the highlight of the commission's program, was the July 1–2, 1976 reenactment of Caesar Rodney's ride from the John Dickinson Home, located southeast of Dover, to Philadelphia. The purpose was to bring the world's attention to the significance of Rodney's accomplishment and his importance to the cause of American independence. With splendid cooperation from towns along the route, Philadelphia '76 and the Delaware County and Pennsylvania Bicentennial commissions, this goal was achieved. Delaware State Police Captain W. Wallace David, portraying Rodney, made the ride without a hitch, receiving warm applause, accolades and gifts at each of his 16 stops in Delaware and Pennsylvania. Months of planning paid off in this highly successful event.

Contributing much to the success of the Delaware Bicentennial celebration was the active personal interest taken by Governor Sherman W. Tribbitt. He was always available to the commission, kept himself thoroughly informed on Bicentennial planning and, perhaps more than any other governor, used the power of his office to assure a successful celebration.

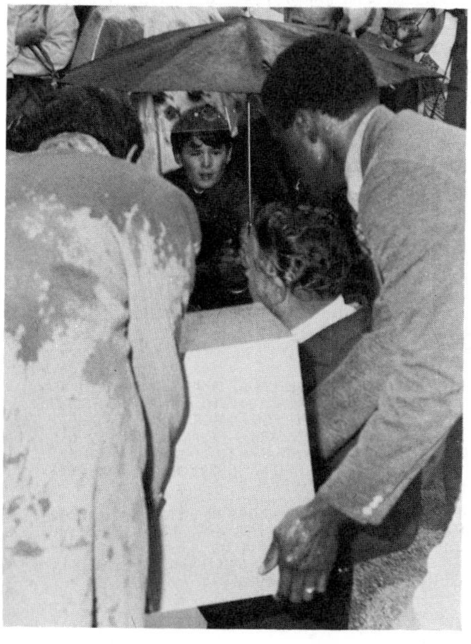

BEAR

CHRISTIANA HISTORICAL DISTRICT SIGNS, DE. ERECTION OF 4 PERMANENT COLONIAL TYPE SIGNS ON THE MAIN HIGHWAYS LEADING TO THE CHRISTIANA HISTORICAL DISTRICT, AND A MAP OF HISTORICAL POINTS OF INTEREST. (LOCAL). JOE G HARPER, CHAIRMAN; CHRISTIANA BICENTENNIAL COMMISSION; BOX 524; BEAR, DE 19701. (#11158). **ARBA GRANTEE.**

BELEFONTE

BELEFONTE BICENTENNIAL MINIPARK, BELEFONTE, DE. PARK COMMEMORATING THE BICENTENNIAL. (LOCAL). HARRY B RAIGN, PRESIDENT COMMISSIONER; TOWN OF BELEFONTE; BELEFONTE, DE 19809. (#21121). **ARBA GRANTEE.**

BETHANY BEACH

BETHANY BEACH COMMUNITY FESTIVAL BANDSTAND - DE. REPLACED BANDSTAND DESTROYED BY COASTAL STORM IN 1962. NEW BANDSTAND LOCATED IN CENTER OF TOWN ADJACENT TO BOARDWALK. DIMENSIONS ARE 26' X 50' AND INCLUDES THREE 30' FLAGPOLES. (LOCAL). ROBERT C MAXWELL, CHAIRMAN; BETHANY BEACH BICENTENNIAL COMMITTEE; BETHANY BEACH, DE 19930. (#27088). **ARBA GRANTEE.**

JULY 4, '76. CHORAL PRESENTATION OF 'I LOVE AMERICA'. PRESENTED BY CHOIR OF ST GEORGE'S UNITED M.E. CHURCH OF CLARKVILLE. AT BANDSTAND - GARFIELD PKWY AND BOARDWALK. (LOCAL). ROBERT C MAXWELL, CHRMN; BETHANY BEACH BICENTENNIAL COMMITTEE; PO BOX 364; BETHANY BEACH, DE 19930. (#107767-1).

JULY 10 - 11, '76. 75TH ANNIVERSARY CELEBRATION OF BETHANY BEACH. HISTORICAL EXHIBITS, ENTERTAINMENT AND REFRESHMENTS WILL BE ON HAND FOR THIS OCCASION. ALSO FEDERAL, STATE AND LOCAL OFFICIALS. AT FIRE HALL; RT 14 AND HOLLYWOOD ST. (LOCAL). ROBERT S MAXWELL, CHRMN; BETHANY BEACH BICENTENNIAL COMMITTEE; PO BOX 364; BETHANY BEACH, DE 19930. (#107767-2).

JULY 11, '76. ECUMENICAL CHURCH SERVICE. CEREMONY AT OCEAN VIEW PARK, OCEAN VIEW. (LOCAL). ROBERT S MAXWELL, CHMN; BETHANY BEACH BICENTENNIAL COMMITTEE; PO BOX 364; BETHANY BEACH, DE 19930. (#107767-3).

JULY 16 - SEPT 4, '76. MUDDYNECK BOY BLUEGRASS MUSIC PRESENTATION. PERFORMANCES ON JULY 16, AUGUST 22 & SEPTEMBER 4. AT BANDSTAND ON BOARDWALK. (LOCAL). ROBERT C MAXWELL, CHMN; BETHANY BEACH BICENTENNIAL COMMITTEE; PO BOX 364; BETHANY BEACH, DE 19930. (#200009-10).

JULY 17 - 24, '76. CONCERT BY US ARMY BAND. LIVE PERFORMANCE AT BANDSTAND AT GARFIELD PARKWAY & BOARDWALK. (LOCAL). ROBERT C MAXWELL; BETHANY BEACH BICENTENNIAL COMMITTEE; PO BOX 364; BETHANY BEACH, DE 19930. (#200009-15).

AUG 5 - SEPT 3, '76. THE DAVIS FAMILY PRESENTS GOSPEL MUSIC. PERFORMANCES ON AUGUST 5, 19, 27, & SEPTEMBER 3. AT BANDSTAND ON BOARDWALK. (LOCAL). ROBERT C MAXWELL, CHMN; BETHANY BEACH BICENTENNIAL COMMITTEE; PO BOX 364; BETHANY BEACH, DE 19930. (#200009-8).

AUG 6 - 21, '76. GOSPEL MUSIC BY THE WELSH FAMILY. LIVE PERFORMANCE AT BANDSTAND - BOARDWALK. (LOCAL). ROBERT MAXWELL, CHMN; BETHANY BEACH BICENTENNIAL COMMITTEE; BOX 364; BETHANY BEACH, DE 19930. (#200009-7).

AUG 26, '76. YOUTH MISSION USA GOSPEL SINGERS PRESENTATION. LIVE PERFORMANCE AT BANDSTAND ON BOARDWALK. (LOCAL). ROBERT C MAXWELL, CHMN; BETHANY BEACH BICENTENNIAL COMMITTEE; PO BOX 364; BETHANY BEACH, DE 19930. (#200009-9).

AUG 28, '76. BARBERSHOP CHORUS & QUARTET. LIVE PERFORMANCE AT BANDSTAND - BOARDWALK. (LOCAL). ROBERT MAXWELL, CHMN; BETHANY BEACH BICENTENNIAL COMMITTEE; BOX 364; BETHANY BEACH, DE 19930. (#200009-6).

SEPT 5, '76. GOSPEL MUSIC BY THE RITTENHOUSE FAMILY. LIVE PERFORMANCE AT BANDSTAND - BOARDWALK. (LOCAL). ROBERT MAXWELL, CHMN; BETHANY BEACH BICENTENNIAL COMMITTEE; BOX 364; BETHANY BEACH, DE 19930. (#200009-5).

BOWERS

A HISTORY OF THE TOWN OF BOWERS, DELAWARE. A HISTORY OF THE TOWN OF BOWERS WILL BE PUBLISHED TO INCREASE LOCAL AWARENESS. (LOCAL). SAMUEL G THOMAS, CHAIRMAN; KENT COUNTY-LEVY COURT BICENT COMMITTEE; THE GREEN; DOVER, DE 19901. (#9757). **ARBA GRANTEE.**

BOWERS BEACH

A HISTORICAL MARITIME MUSEUM AT BOWERS BEACH, DE. PROJECT IS TO ESTABLISH A MUCH NEEDED AND MUCH DESIRED MARITIME MUSEUM TO HELP COMMEMORATE THE HISTORICAL BACKGROUND OF THIS SEAFARING COMMUNITY. (ST-WIDE). SAMUEL G THOMAS, CHAIRMAN; KENT COUNTY-LEVY COURT BICENT COMMITTEE; THE GREEN; DOVER, DE 19901. (#9769). **ARBA GRANTEE.**

JUNE 19, '76. OPENING & DEDICATION OF HISTORICAL MARITIME MUSEUM. OPENING, EXHIBIT AT BOWERS BEACH MARITIME MUSEUM. (LOCAL). EDNA LEMUNYON, CHAIRMAN; BOWRS BEACH BICENTENNIAL MARITIME MUSEUM COMMITTEE; BAY SHORE DR; DOVER, DE 19901. (#9769-1).

JUNE 19, '76 - CONTINUING . BOWERS BEACH MARITIME MUSEUM. EXHIBIT AT BOWERS BEACH MARITIME MUSEUM. (LOCAL). EDNA LEMUNYON, CHAIRMAN; BOWERS BEACH BICENTENNIAL MARITIME MUSEUM COMMITTEE; BAY SHORE DR; BOWERS BEACH, DE 19946. (#103756-2).

CAMDEN-WY

BICENTENNIAL FESTIVAL IN CAMDEN-WYOMING, DELAWARE. THREE-DAY FESTIVAL FEATURING SCHOOL BANDS AND CHOIRS AND A CRAFTS FAIR. (LOCAL). RUSSELL PERRY, PROJ DIRECTOR; CAESAR RODNEY SCHOOL DISTRICT; BOX 188; CAMDEN, DE 19934. (#11162). **ARBA GRANTEE.**

A HISTORY OF THE TOWN OF CAMDEN-WYOMING, DELAWARE. A HISTORY OF THE TOWN OF CAMDEN-WYOMING WILL BE PUBLISHED TO HELP TO INCREASE LOCAL AWARENESS. (LOCAL). SAMUEL G THOMAS, CHAIRMAN; KENT COUNTY-LEVY COURT BICENT COMMITTEE; THE GREEN; DOVER, DE 19901. (#9755). **ARBA GRANTEE.**

NOV 20 - 22, '75. BICENTENNIAL FESTIVAL - THREE DAY MUSIC AND CRAFTS FAIR. FESTIVAL AT CAESAR RODNEY HIGH SCHOOL. (LOCAL). RUSSELL PERRY, DIRECTOR; CAESAR RODNEY SCHOOL DISTRICT; BOX 188; CAMDEN, DE 19934. (#11162-1).

JUNE 27 - JULY 4, '76. CAMDEN-WYOMING BICENTENNIAL CELEBRATION. FESTIVAL, PARADE, TOUR AT CAMDEN WYOMING FIRE CO. (LOCAL). EILEEN H. SIMPSON; CAMDEN WYOMING BICENTENNIAL COMMITTEE; 101 CHOLET CT.; CAMDEN WYOMNG, DE 19934. (#50174-1).

CENTREVILLE

HISTORY OF THE VILLAGE OF CENTREVILLE, DE. A HISTORY OF THE VILLAGE FROM 1776 TO 1976 HAS BEEN WRITTEN. (LOCAL). JOHN H JAMES, CHAIRMAN; CENTREVILLE BICENTENNIAL COMMITTEE; 407 OWLS NEST RD; CENTREVILLE, DE 19807. (#27087). **ARBA GRANTEE.**

CHESWOLD

A HISTORY OF THE TOWN OF CHESWOLD, DELAWARE. A HISTORY OF THE TOWN OF CHESWOLD WILL BE PUBLISHED TO INCREASE THE LOCAL AWARENESS. (LOCAL). SAMUEL G THOMAS, CHAIRMAN; KENT COUNTY-LEVY COURT BICENT COMMITTEE; THE GREEN; DOVER, DE 19901. (#9752). **ARBA GRANTEE.**

CHRISTIANA

A HISTORY OF CHRISTIANA, DE. A CAPSULE HISTORY OF CHRISTIANA, DELAWARE, WRITTEN BY RICHARD RODNEY COOCH WAS PUBLISHED. (LOCAL). RICHARD RODNEY COOCH, MEMBER; CHRISTIANA BICENTENNIAL COMMISSION, INC; 12 E 3RD ST; NEW CASTLE, DE 19720. (#29943).

MAY 8, '76. CHRISTIANA HERITAGE FAIR. EXHIBIT, FESTIVAL. (LOCAL). JOE G HARPER, CHMN; CHRISTIANA BICENTENNIAL COMMISSION, INC; CHAPMAN RD; CHRISTIANA, DE 19702. (#200009-3).

CLAYMONT

'CLAYMONT '76', BICENT PROJECTS IN DELAWARE. VARIOUS COMMUNITY PROJECTS SUCH AS COMMUNITY CALENDAR OF BICENTENNIAL EVENTS, HISTORY OF CLAYMONT, HISTORICAL SITE MARKERS, FEES FOR SPEAKERS, TRAVELING & PRIZE MONEY FOR BANDS FROM SURROUNDING AREAS. (LOCAL). FRANK J FURGELE, SUPERINTENDENT OF SCHOOLS; CLAYMONT SCHOOL COMMUNITY BICENTENNIAL COMMITTEE; GREEN ST; CLAYMONT, DE 19703. (#11044). **ARBA GRANTEE.**

SEPT 21, '75. 'CLAYMONT '76'. COMPETITION, FESTIVAL. (LOCAL). FRANK J FURGELE; CLAYMONT SCHOOL COMMUNITY BICENTENNIAL COMMITTEE; GREEN ST; CLAYMONT, DE 19703. (#11044-1).

OCT 25, '75. ETHNIC CULTURAL CELEBRATION. EXHIBIT. (LOCAL). HOWARD SIMPKINS, JR, CHMN; CLAYMONT BICENTENNIAL COMMITTEE; 7 E DALE RD; WILMINGTON, DE 19810. (#102816-1).

NOV 30, '75. SALUTE TO YOUTH AND EDUCATION; FIELD SHOW OF BANDS. LIVE PERFORMANCE. (LOCAL). HOWARD SIMPKINS, JR, CHMN; CLAYMONT BICENTENNIAL COMMITTEE; 7 E DALE RD; WILMINGTON, DE 19810. (#102816-2).

DEC 21, '75. CHRISTMAS MUSIC FESTIVAL. LIVE PERFORMANCE. (LOCAL). HOWARD SIMPKINS, JR, CHMN; CLAYMONT BICENTENNIAL COMMITTEE; 7 E DALE RD; WILMINGTON, DE 19810. (#102816-3).

FEB 14, '76. GEORGE WASHINGTON BALL - DINNER DANCE. LIVE PERFORMANCE. (LOCAL). HOWARD SIMPKINS, JR, CHMN; CLAYMONT BICENTENNIAL COMMITTEE; 7 E DALE RD; WILMINGTON, DE 19810. (#102816-4).

CLAYTON

A HISTORY OF THE TOWN OF CLAYTON, DELAWARE. A HISTORY OF THE TOWN OF CLAYTON WILL BE PUBLISHED IN ORDER TO INCREASE LOCAL AWARENESS. (LOCAL). SAMUEL G THOMAS, CHAIRMAN; KENT COUNTY-LEVY COURT BICENT COMMITTEE; THE GREEN; DOVER, DE 19901. (#9760). **ARBA GRANTEE.**

DELAWARE CITY

CHESAPEAKE & DELAWARE CANAL LOCKS HISTORIC MARKER. INSTALLATION OF HISTORIC MARKER IN DELAWARE CITY, DE, MARKING IMPORTANT SITES ALONG THE CANAL. (ST-WIDE). ELAINE DERRICKSON, CHAIRMAN; DELAWARE CITY ARBC; 202 ADAMS ST; DELAWARE CITY, DE 19706. (#810). **ARBA GRANTEE.**

FEB 15 - MAR 7, '76. TURKEY SHOOT AT DRAGON RUN. PORT PENN & DELAWARE CITY COMBINED TURKEY SHOOT-SPECIAL BLACK POWDER MUSKET RIFLE EVENT; REFRESHMENTS AVAILABLE. (LOCAL). JULIA L SIDWELL, CHMN; PORT PENN AND DELAWARE CITY BICENTENNIAL COMMITTEES; PORT PENN, DE 19731. (#105012-4).

APR 1, '76. YANKEE DOODLE DANDY EVENING. TICKETS AVAILABLE AT THE PORT PENN BICENTENNIAL COMMISSION OR AT THE DOOR; ENTERTAINMENT, 50-50 DRAWING, A BAZAAR, SURPRISES & FUN FOR THE WHOLE FAMILY. AT GUNNING BEDFORD SCHOOL - DELAWARE CITY, DEL. (LOCAL). JULIA L SIDWELL, COORD; PORT PENN BICENTENNIAL COMMITTEE; PORT PENN, DE 19731. (#105011-1).

MAY 8, '76. FLEA MARKET. FAIR. (LOCAL). MRS GEORGIA BINDER, CHMN; DELAWARE CITY BICENTENNIAL COMMITTEE; DELAWARE CITY, DE 19706. (#105645-3).

MAY 8, '76. HOUSE TOURS. TOUR. (LOCAL). MRS BEVERLY WALTON, CHMN; DELAWARE CITY BICENTENNIAL COMMITTEE; DELAWARE CITY, DE 19706. (#105645-2).

JUNE 5, '76. 150TH BIRTHDAY PARTY. FESTIVAL AT 2ND & WASHINGTON STS. (LOCAL). MS ELAINE DERRICKSON, DIR; DELAWARE CITY BICENTENNIAL COMMITTEE; DELAWARE CITY, DE 19706. (#105645-4).

DELMAR

BICENTENNIAL COOKBOOK - DELMAR, DE. 500 FAVORITE RECIPES OF LOCAL PEOPLE COMPILED INTO A COOKBOOK. (LOCAL). MRS ALVIN S CULVER, CHAIRMAN; DELMAR BICENTENNIAL COMMITTEE; 211 SPRUCE ST; DELMAR, DE 19940. (#29945).

BICENTENNIAL PAVILION PLANNED FOR DELMAR, DELAWARE. A PAVILION IN THE DELMAR TOWN PARK WILL PROMOTE BICENTENNIAL ACTIVITIES IN DELMAR, DELAWARE. (LOCAL). MS MORA I CULVER, CHAIRMAN; DELMAR BICENTENNIAL COMMITTEE; 211 SPRUCE ST; DELMAR, DE 19940. (#9579). **ARBA GRANTEE.**

RESTORE THE OLD RAILROAD HIGHBALL SIGNAL, DELAWARE. RESTORATION & PRESERVATION OF OLD MANUAL RAILROAD SIGNAL IN DELMAR. (LOCAL). WILLIAM C BRITTINGHAM, MAYOR; TOWN OF DELMAR; STATE ST; DELMAR, DE 19940. (#5070).

JAN '76. NEW CENTURY CLUB BICENTENNIAL FASHION SHOW. EXHIBIT AT CAMELOT HALL, STATE ST. (LOCAL). MRS H E WILLIAMS, CHMN; NEW CENTURY CLUB OF DELMAR; 309 E JEWELL ST; DELMAR, DE 19940. (#100693-1).

JULY 4, '76. OLD-FASHIONED PICNIC. FESTIVAL AT TOWNPARK, STATE ST. (LOCAL). MRS ALVIN S CULVER, CHMN; DELMAR BICENTENNIAL COMMITTEE; 211 SPRUCE ST; DELMAR, DE 19940. (#200009-12).

DOVER

BICENTENNIAL EDITION OF DELAWARE RESOURCE GUIDE. THE EXISTING GUIDE WILL BE REPRODUCED AND UPDATED TO BE UTILIZED BY THE EDUCATIONAL COMMUNITY, INTERESTED AGENCIES AND OTHER INDIVIDUALS WHO DESIRE TO LOCATE MATERIALS AND SITES DEALING WITH DELAWARE. (ST-WIDE). DR RANDALL L BROYLES, PROJ DIRECTOR; STATE DEPARTMENT OF PUBLIC INSTRUCTION; TOWNSEND BUILDING; DOVER, DE 19901. (#12004). **ARBA GRANTEE.**

A BICENTENNIAL HISTORY OF KENT COUNTY, DELAWARE. PUBLICATION OF A HISTORY OF KENT COUNTY, DELAWARE FROM 1680 TO THE PRESENT. TEN THOUSAND COPIES WILL BE PUBLISHED AT A NOMINAL COST. A FREE BROCHURE ABOUT THE COUNTY WILL BE MADE AVAILABLE TO THE PUBLIC. (LOCAL). SAMUEL G THOMAS, COORDINATOR; KENT COUNTY LEVY COURT; COURT HOUSE, THE GREEN; DOVER, DE 19901. (#6479). **(??). ARBA GRANTEE.**

BICENTENNIAL ON WHEELS - PROJ OF DOVER, DELAWARE. A MOBILE UNIT WILL SERVE AS AN INFORMATION CENTER AND CARRY BROCHURES, CALENDARS OF EVENTS AND OTHER SOUVENIRS OF THE BICENT. (LOCAL). SAMUEL G THOMAS, CHAIRMAN; KENT COUNTY-LEVY COURT BICENT COMMITTEE; THE GREEN; DOVER, DE 19901. (#9766). **ARBA GRANTEE.**

BICENTENNIAL PARK PROJ OF DOVER, DELAWARE. CONSTRUCT PARK THAT WILL CONSIST OF GARDENS, HISTORIC MEMORIALS, & AN OUTDOOR AMPHITHEATRE FOR PRESENTATION OF BICENTENNIAL PROGRAMS AND FESTIVALS. (LOCAL). DANIEL BLAGG, CHAIRMAN; BICENTENNIAL COMMITTEE OF THE CITY OF DOVER; PO BOX 44; DOVER, DE 19901. (#4243). **(??).**

CAESAR RODNEY RIDE RE-ENACTMENT - DOVER, DE. RE-ENACTMENT OF CAESAR RODNEY'S HISTORIC 80 MILE RIDE TO VOTE TO PUT DELAWARE ON THE SIDE OF INDEPENDENCE. (ST-WIDE). LOUISE L PRICKETT, PROJ DIRECTOR; DELAWARE ARBC; PO BOX 2476; WILMINGTON, DE 19899. (#28536). **ARBA GRANTEE.**

CAPITOL SQUARE DEVELOPMENT PROJ -DOVER, DELAWARE. TRAIL TO BE DEVELOPED AROUND DELAWARE CAPITOL WITH HISTORICAL MONUMENTS TO RELATE HISTORY OF STATE IN SEQUENCE TO BENEFIT SCHOOL GROUPS & VISITORS TO THE CAPITOL ITSELF. (ST-WIDE). DANIEL BLAGG, CHAIRMAN; BICENTENNIAL

DOVER — CONTINUED

COMMITTEE OF THE CITY OF DOVER; PO BOX 44; DOVER, DE 19901. (#4056). **(??).**

COUNTY FAIR - PROJ OF DOVER, DELAWARE. A GRAND FINALE CELEBRATION WILL BRING TOGETHER THE PEOPLE OF THE COUNTY TO SHARE THE TRADITIONS AND CULTURE OF OUR HERITAGE. (LOCAL). SAMUEL G THOMAS, CHAIRMAN; KENT COUNTY-LEVY COURT BICENT COMMITTEE; THE GREEN; DOVER, DE 19901. (#9767). **ARBA GRANTEE.**

DELAWARE STATE COLLEGE SPIRIT OF '76 - DOVER, DE. EXHIBITION FOCUSING ON PAINTINGS AND ARTIFACTS WITH REVOLUTIONARY OR HISTORICAL THEMES PECULIAR TO KENT COUNTY, DE. A SECOND PART WILL BE A BICENTENNIAL BLACK ACHIEVEMENTS EXHIBIT. (ST-WIDE). WINIFRED C HARRIS, PROJ DIRECTOR; DELAWARE STATE COLLEGE; DOVER, DE 19901. (#12090). **ARBA GRANTEE.**

ETHNIC FESTIVAL IN DOVER, DE. DELAWARE'S MANY ETHNIC GROUPS WILL EACH HAVE A DAY FOR CELEBRATION, WITH TRADITIONAL DANCES, FOOD & FOLKWAYS. (LOCAL). WINIFRED C HARRIS, PROJ CHAIRMAN; DELAWARE STATE COLLEGE; DOVER, DE 19901. (#12087). **ARBA GRANTEE.**

GENERAL STORE RESTORATION PROJ -DOVER, DELAWARE. OLD GENL STORE RESTORATION TO BE USED AS BICENT VISITORS CNTR, FUND RAISING STORE & A MUSEUM OF DOVER MERCANTILE EXHIBITS FROM COLONIAL HISTORY TO PRESENT. (LOCAL). DANIEL BLAGG, CHAIRMAN; BICENTENNIAL COMMITTEE OF THE CITY OF DOVER; PO BOX 44; DOVER, DE 19901. (#4059). **(??).**

A HISTORY OF THE TOWN OF DOVER, DELAWARE. A HISTORY OF THE TOWN OF DOVER WILL BE PUBLISHED TO INCREASE LOCAL AWARENESS. (LOCAL). SAMUEL G THOMAS, CHAIRMAN; KENT COUNTY-LEVY COURT BICENT COMMITTEE; THE GREEN; DOVER, DE 19901. (#9758). **ARBA GRANTEE.**

KENT COUNTY FESTIVAL, DE. FESTIVAL, FAIR & TOURING EXHIBITS. (LOCAL). JOHN S MICKEY, PROJ DIRECTOR; DELAWARE AMERICAN REVOLUTION BICENTENNIAL COMMITTEE; PO BOX 2476; WILMINGTON, DE 19899. (#18603). **ARBA GRANTEE.**

LECTURE SERIES ON AMERICAN REVOLUTION, DOVER, DE. FOUR LECTURES BY LEADING AMERICAN SCHOLARS ON THE PAST AND PRESENT SIGNIFICANCE OF THE AMERICAN REVOLUTION AND ITS BICENTENNIAL. (LOCAL). WINIFRED C HARRIS, PROJ CHAIRMAN; DELAWARE STATE COLLEGE; DOVER, DE 19901. (#12086). **ARBA GRANTEE.**

PUBLICATION, 'A VIEW FROM THE PAST', DELAWARE. PUBLICATION OF A HISTORY OF DELAWARE STATE COLLEGE. (LOCAL). WINIFRED C HARRIS, PROJ CHAIRMAN; DELAWARE STATE COLLEGE; DOVER, DE 19901. (#12089). **ARBA GRANTEE.**

PUBLICITY PROJECT - DOVER, DELAWARE. THE FESTIVALS AND EVENTS GOING ON IN THE COUNTY WILL BE PUBLICIZED THROUGH THE NEWSPAPERS, RADIO & EXHIBITS. (LOCAL). SAMUEL G THOMAS, CHAIRMAN; KENT COUNTY-LEVY COURT BICENT COMMITTEE; THE GREEN; DOVER, DE 19901. (#9768). **ARBA GRANTEE.**

RECORDINGS OF REVOLUTIONARY PERIOD SONGS. RECORDINGS OF EARLY AMERICAN SONGS ARBA LICENSE NO 76-19-0628. (NAT'L). JAMES BURROUGHS, PRESIDENT; JAG PRODUCTIONS, INC; 229 S STATE ST; DOVER, DE 19901. (#26063).

SCHOLASTIC DEBATE IN DELAWARE HIGH SCHOOLS-DOVER. A PLANNED PROGRAM IN ORDER TO ACHIEVE GREATER PARTICIPATION OF HIGH SCHOOL STUDENTS IN DEBATE. (LOCAL). RANDALL L BROYLES, PROJ DIRECTOR; DELAWARE DEPARTMENT OF PUBLIC INSTRUCTION; TOWNSEND BUILDING; DOVER, DE 19901. (#11988). **ARBA GRANTEE.**

TWO DRAMATIC PRODUCTIONS IN DOVER, DE. TWO DRAMATIC PRODUCTIONS, ONE A REPRODUCTION OF A PERIOD PLAY, THE OTHER AN EXERCISE IN FOLK THEATER. (LOCAL). WINIFRED C HARRIS, PROJ CHAIRMAN; DELAWARE STATE COLLEGE; DOVER, DE 19901. (#12088). **ARBA GRANTEE.**

1773-1783 PROCEEDINGS OF DELAWARE LEGISLATURE. PUBLICATION OF THE PROCEEDINGS OF THE DELAWARE HOUSE OF REPRESENTATIVES. (ST-WIDE). JOHN S MICKEY, EXEC DIRECTOR; DELAWARE ARBC; PO BOX 2476; WILMINGTON, DE 19899. (#1203). **ARBA GRANTEE.**

OCT 12, '75 - MAY 30, '76. DELAWARE STATE COLLEGE SPIRIT OF '76 EXHIBIT. EXHIBITION FOCUSING ON PAINTINGS AND ARTIFACTS WITH REVOLUTIONARY OR HISTORICAL THEMES PECULIAR TO KENT COUNTY, DE. A SECOND PART WILL BE A BICENTENNIAL BLACK ACHIEVEMENTS EXHIBIT. AT MARTIN LUTHER KING STUDENT CENTER, DELAWARE STATE COLLEGE. (ST-WIDE). WINIFRED C HARRIS; DELAWARE STATE COLLEGE; DOVER, DE 19901. (#12090-1).

OCT 13 - 27, '75. PERIOD DRAMA PRODUCTION. TWO DRAMATIC PRODUCTIONS, ONE A REPRODUCTION OF A PERIOD PLAY, THE OTHER AN EXERCISE IN FOLK THEATER. AT EDUCATION HUMANITIES THEATER. (LOCAL). WINIFRED C HARRIS; DELAWARE STATE COLLEGE; DOVER, DE 19901. (#12088-1).

APR 23, '76. THE TODAY SHOW FEATURES THE STATE OF DELAWARE. A CONTINUING WEEKLY SERIES OF PROGRAMS COMMEMORATING EACH STATE. DELAWARE WAS ADMITTED INTO THE UNION IN DECEMBER, 1787. (NAT'L). STUART SCHULBERG, EX PROD; NATIONAL BROADCASTING CO; 30 ROCKEFELLER PLAZA; NEW YORK, NY 10020. (#7981-31).

MAY 7 - 9, '76. OLD DOVER DAYS. TOURS OF HISTORIC LANDMARKS, PAGEANTRY, CONCERTS, EXHIBITS AND CEREMONIES ARE FEATURED IN FIRST STATE'S CAPITAL. (REGN'L). SUSANNE FOX, CHMN; FRIENDS OF OLD DOVER; PO BOX 44; DOVER, DE 19901. (#103416-298).

MAY 23, '76. CANTATA: 'IN FREEDOM'S LIGHT'. CELEBRATION OF THE BICENTENNIAL THROUGH SONG. AT CONG BETH SHALOM, QUEEN & CLARA ST, DOVER. (LOCAL). RABBI DAVID GEFFEN, DIR; CONGREGATION BETH SHALOM; 18TH & BAYNARD BLVD; WILMINGTON, DE 19802. (#21862-2).

JUNE 9 - 10, '76. UNITED STATES ARMED FORCES BICENTENNIAL CARAVAN. CARAVAN IS COMPOSED OF EXHIBIT VANS FOR EACH MILITARY SERVICE. PROJECT THEME IS ' HISTORY OF THE ARMED FORCES & THEIR CONTRIBUTIONS TO THE NATION'. (LOCAL). DANIEL BLAGG, CHMN; U S ARMED FORCES BICENTENNIAL CARAVAN; 408 S STATE ST; DOVER, DE 19901. (#1775-471).

SEPT 17 - 19, '76. 6TH ANNUAL DELAWARE '500' RACES. LIVE PERFORMANCE, COMPETITION AT DOVER DOWNS INTERNATIONAL SPEEDWAY. (ST-WIDE). DIRECTOR; DOVER DOWNS; DOVER, DE 19901. (#103416-528).

OCT 2 - 3, '76. COUNTY FAIR. A GRAND FINALE CELEBRATION WILL BRING TOGETHER THE PEOPLE OF THE COUNTY TO SHARE THE TRADITIONS AND CULTURE OF OUR HERITAGE. SUNDAY HOURS 10:00 AM - 6:00 PM. AT CAPITAL SQ, DOVER ARMORY, & THE GREEN. (LOCAL). SAMUEL G THOMAS, CHAIRMAN; KENT COUNTY-LEVY COURT BICENT COMMITTEE; THE GREEN; DOVER, DE 19901. (#9767-1).

FARMINGTON

A HISTORY OF THE TOWN OF FARMINGTON, DELAWARE. A HISTORY OF THE TOWN OF FARMINGTON WILL BE PUBLISHED TO INCREASE LOCAL AWARENESS. (LOCAL). SAMUEL G THOMAS, CHAIRMAN; KENT COUNTY-LEVY COURT BICENT COMMITTEE; THE GREEN; DOVER, DE 19901. (#9753). **ARBA GRANTEE.**

FELTON

A HISTORY OF THE TOWN OF FELTON, DELAWARE. A HISTORY OF THE TOWN OF FELTON WILL BE PUBLISHED TO INCREASE LOCAL AWARENESS. (LOCAL). SAMUEL G THOMAS, CHAIRMAN; KENT COUNTY-LEVY COURT BICENT COMMITTEE; THE GREEN; DOVER, DE 19901. (#9762). **ARBA GRANTEE.**

FRANKFORD

SUSSEX HERITAGE 1776 PROJECT - FRANKFORD, DE. RESEARCH, DEVELOP, PRESENT AND PRESERVE ON AUDIO-VISUAL MEDIA A DRAMATIC RE-ENACTMENT OF THE HISTORICAL EVENTS DEPICTING THE COLONIAL HERITAGE OF THE SUSSEX COUNTY AREA. (LOCAL). ROBERT M HYLBERT, DIRECTOR; INDIAN RIVER SCHOOL DISTRICT; RD 2, BOX 236; FRANKFORD, DE 19945. (#11991). **ARBA GRANTEE.**

FREDERICA

A HISTORY OF THE TOWN OF FREDERICA, DELAWARE. A HISTORY OF THE TOWN OF FREDERICA WILL BE PUBLISHED TO INCREASE LOCAL AWARENESS. (LOCAL). SAMUEL G THOMAS, CHAIRMAN; KENT COUNTY-LEVY COURT BICENT COMMITTEE; THE GREEN; DOVER, DE 19901. (#9763). **ARBA GRANTEE.**

GEORGETOWN

COMMISSIONING & PRINTING OF GEORGETOWN HISTORY. GEORGETOWN BICENTENNIAL COMMISSION WILL COMMISSION THE WRITING AND PRINTING OF A HISTORY OF GEORGETOWN IN CONNECTION WITH THEIR HERITAGE 76 PLANS FOR THE BICENTENNIAL. (LOCAL). WILLIAM J WILLIAMS, DIRECTOR; GEORGETOWN BICENTENNIAL COMMITTEE; TOWN HALL; GEORGETOWN, DE 19947. (#1342). **ARBA GRANTEE.**

HISTORY OF GEORGETOWN, DE. 'SIXTEEN MILES FROM ANYWHERE'; COVERS GEORGETOWN'S HISTORY FROM ITS FOUNDING IN 1791 TO 1975. (LOCAL). WILLIAM WILLIAMS, CHAIRMAN; GEORGETOWN BICENTENNIAL COMMITTEE; 238 W PINE; GEORGETOWN, DE 19947. (#29944).

HISTORY OF SUSSEX COUNTY, DELAWARE. THE SUSSEX COUNTY BICENT COMMITTEE IS PRINTING A HISTORY OF THE COUNTY THAT WILL INCLUDE FOLKLORE, LEGENDS AND AN EXTENSIVE MAP OF THE AREA. (LOCAL). JOANN T CONAWAY, SECRETARY; SUSSEX COUNTY BICENTENNIAL COMMITTEE; COURTHOUSE, GEORGETOWN; GEORGETOWN, DE 19947. (#7734).

RECORDING SUSSEX COUNTY ORAL HISTORY, DELAWARE. RECORDING INDIVIDUAL RECOLLECTIONS OF THE COUNTY'S PAST THRU INTERVIEWS. (LOCAL). JOYCE DYER, CO-CHAIRPERSON; SUSSEX COUNTY BICENTENNIAL COMMITTEE; THE COURTHOUSE; GEORGETOWN, DE 19947. (#10340). **ARBA GRANTEE.**

SUSSEX COUNTY BICENT TIME CAPSULE, GEORGETOWN, DE. A TIME CAPSULE CONTAINING ITEMS REPRESENTATIVE OF THE PEOPLE OF SUSSEX COUNTY TO BE BURIED WITH INSTRUCTIONS TO OPEN IN THE YEAR 2076. (ST-WIDE). JOYCE DYER, CO-CHAIRPERSON; SUSSEX COUNTY BICENTENNIAL COMMITTEE; THE COURTHOUSE; GEORGETOWN, DE 19947. (#10342). **ARBA GRANTEE.**

SUSSEX COUNTY FOLKLORE PROJ OF DELAWARE. PAPERBACK BOOKLET OF APPROXIMATELY 50 PAGES ON SUSSEX COUNTY FOLKLORE & LEGENDS. (LOCAL). JOYCE DYER, CO-CHAIRPERSON; SUSSEX COUNTY BICENTENNIAL COMMITTEE; THE COURTHOUSE; GEORGETOWN, DE 19947. (#10339). **ARBA GRANTEE.**

SUSSEX COUNTY HISTORICAL BICENT MAP IN DELAWARE. PRODUCTION OF A COLORED MAP OF SUSSEX COUNTY DIVIDED INTO HUNDREDS, SURROUNDED BY ARTISTS DRAWINGS OF HISTORIC BUILDINGS AND SITES IN THE COUNTY. (LOCAL). JOYCE DYER, CO-CHAIRPERSON; SUSSEX COUNTY BICENTENNIAL COMMITTEE; THE COURTHOUSE; GEORGETOWN, DE 19947. (#10337). **ARBA GRANTEE.**

SUSSEX COUNTY HISTORY GUIDEBOOK, GEORGETOWN, DE. BOOKS OF INFORMATION ON SUSSEX COUNTY HISTORY FROM FIRST SETTLEMENT AT LEWIS IN 1631 TO THE PRESENT. (LOCAL). JOYCE DYER, CO-CHAIRPERSON; SUSSEX COUNTY BICENTENNIAL COMMITTEE; THE COURTHOUSE; GEORGETOWN, DE 19947. (#10338). **ARBA GRANTEE.**

FEB 21, '76. WASHINGTON BIRTHDAY BALL. CEREMONY, FESTIVAL. (LOCAL). JOANN T CONAWAY; SUSSEX COUNTY BICENTENNIAL COMMITTEE; COURTHOUSE, GEORGETOWN; GEORGETOWN, DE 19947. (#7734-502).

NOV 8, '76. SUSSEX TIME CAPSULE. CEREMONY, FESTIVAL. (LOCAL). JOANN T CONAWAY; SUSSEX COUNTY BICENTENNIAL COMMITTEE; COURTHOUSE, GEORGETOWN; GEORGETOWN, DE 19947. (#7734-503).

NOV 8 - 18, '76. MUSICAL PRODUCTION '1776'. LIVE PERFORMANCE. (LOCAL). CAROL EPIFANIO, PRESIDENT; POSSUM POINT PLAYERS; PO BOX 96; GEORGETOWN, DE 19947. (#102022-1).

GREENVILLE

NATURE EDUCATION BOTANY PROJ, GREENVILLE, DE. PROJECT TO FAMILIARIZE STATE CHILDREN WITH NATIVE PLANTS WHICH WERE IMPORTANT TO REVOLUTIONARIES, FARMERS AND INDIANS. (ST-WIDE). LYNN WILLIAMS, CHAIRMAN; DELAWARE NATURE EDUCATION CENTER; BOX 3900; GREENVILLE, DE 19807. (#22370). **ARBA GRANTEE.**

OCT 1 - ??, '77. CONFERENCE ON FRANCO-AMERICAN COMMERCE, 1760 - 1810. EXHIBIT AND CATALOGUE ON HOW FRANCE SAW AMERICA IN REVOLUTION ERA. DOCUMENTS, IMPRINTS, ARTIFACTS & GRAPHICS ON THEMES DECORATIVE ARTS, GOVERNMENT, TRADE, TECHNOLOGY, NATURAL HISTORY & LITERATURE. (REGN'L). DR RICHMOND D WILLIAMS; ELEUTHERIAN MILLS HISTORICAL LIBRARY; GREENVILLE, DE 19807. (#3183-2).

OCT 19 - DEC 14, '77. HOW FRANCE SAW AMERICA, 1765-1815. EXHIBIT AND CATALOGUE ON HOW FRANCE SAW AMERICA IN REVOLUTION ERA. DOCUMENTS, IMPRINTS, ARTIFACTS & GRAPHICS ON THEMES DECORATIVE ARTS, GOVERNMENT, TRADE, TECHNOLOGY, NATURAL HISTORY & LITERATURE. (REGN'L). DR RICHMOND D WILLIAMS; ELEUTHERIAN MILLS HISTORICAL LIBRARY; GREENVILLE, DE 19807. (#3183-1).

HARRINGTON

A HISTORY OF THE TOWN OF HARRINGTON, DELAWARE. TO PROVIDE LOCAL AWARENESS AND INCENTIVES TO CELEBRATE LOCAL HISTORY & HERITAGE. (LOCAL). SAMUEL G THOMAS, CHAIRMAN; KENT COUNTY-LEVY COURT BICENT COMMITTEE; THE GREEN; DOVER, DE 19901. (#9765). **ARBA GRANTEE.**

HARTLY

A HISTORY OF THE TOWN OF HARTLY, DELAWARE. THE HISTORY OF THE TOWN OF HARTLY WILL BE PUBLISHED TO INCREASE AWARENESS OF LOCAL HERITAGE. (LOCAL). SAMUEL G THOMAS, CHAIRMAN; KENT COUNTY-LEVY COURT BICENT COMMITTEE; THE GREEN; DOVER, DE 19901. (#9746). **ARBA GRANTEE.**

HOCKESSIN

BOOK - HOCKESSIN, A PICTORIAL HISTORY - DELAWARE. THIS BOOK IS BY JOE LAKE, JR, AND WAS PUBLISHED IN MAY OF 1976. (LOCAL). LEE MURCH, CHAIRMAN; HOCKESSIN YORKLYN CORNER KETCH; BOX 335, RD 1; HOCKESSIN, DE 19707. (#31951).

PARK DEDICATION - HOCKESSIN, DE. PUBLIC DEDICATION OF A COUNTY PARK IN HOCKESSIN; PRESENTATION OF A PERMANENT MEMORIAL FOR THE PARK; CEREMONY WILL ALSO INCLUDE PRESENTATIONS OF LOCAL HISTORY VIA PAGEANT, TAPE AND PRINTED MATTER. (LOCAL). LEE MURCH, CHAIRMAN; HOCKESSIN YORKLYN CORNER KETCH; BOX 335, RD 1; HOCKESSIN, DE 19707. (#22516). **ARBA GRANTEE.**

PERMANENT MEMORIAL FOR PARK. PROFITS FROM OUR BOOK & 3 DAY CELEBRATION WILL GO TOWARDS A PERMANENT MEMORIAL WHEN THE PARK IS PLANNED. (LOCAL). LEE MURCH, CHAIRMAN; HOCKESSIN YORKLYN CORNER KETCH; BOX 335, RD 1; HOCKESSIN, DE 19707. (#22516-2).

NOV '75. GARDEN TOUR. THE GARDEN TOUR WILL INCLUDE 9 HOMES. (LOCAL). LEE MURCH, CHAIRMAN; HOCKESSIN YORKLYN CORNER KETCH; BOX 335, RD 1; HOCKESSIN, DE 19707. (#22516-4).

NOV '75. LOCAL HISTORY VIA PAGEANT. LIVE PERFORMANCE. (LOCAL). LEE MURCH, CHAIRMAN; HOCKESSIN YORKLYN CORNER KETCH; BOX 335, RD 1; HOCKESSIN, DE 19707. (#22516-3).

JULY 2 - 5, '76. BICENTENNIAL WEEKEND. EVENTS INCLUDE CONVOCATION & CHURCH SOCIAL, YOUTH DAY, PARADE, OUTDOOR DANCE, BICENTENNIAL DINNER DANCE, OX ROAST, ENTERTAINMENT AND BANDS, TRAIN RIDES (WILMINGTON & WESTERN RAILROAD), HAYRIDES, SCOUT EXHIBITS, FLEA MARKET, ARTS & CRAFTS EXHIBIT, INFO CENTER & MORE. (LOCAL). LEE MURCH, CHAIRMAN; HOCKESSIN YORKLYN CORNER HETCH; BOX 335, RD 1; HOCKESSIN, DE 19707. (#22516-5).

HOCKESSIN — CONTINUED

JULY 5, '76. PARK DEDICATION. PUBLIC DEDICATION OF A COUNTY PARK. (LOCAL). LEE MURCH, CHAIRMAN; HOCKESSIN/YORKLYN CORNER KETCH; BOX 335, RD 1; HOCKESSIN, DE 19707. (#22516-1).

HOUSTON

A HISTORY OF THE TOWN OF HOUSTON, DELAWARE. A HISTORY OF THE TOWN OF HOUSTON WILL BE PUBLISHED TO INCREASE LOCAL AWARENESS. (LOCAL). SAMUEL G THOMAS, CHAIRMAN; KENT COUNTY-LEVY COURT BICENT COMMITTEE; THE GREEN; DOVER, DE 19901. (#9761). **ARBA GRANTEE.**

KENTON

A HISTORY OF THE TOWN OF KENTON, DELAWARE. A HISTORY OF THE TOWN OF KENTON WILL BE PUBLISHED TO INCREASE LOCAL AWARENESS. (LOCAL). SAMUEL G THOMAS, CHAIRMAN; KENT COUNTY-LEVY COURT BICENT COMMITTEE; THE GREEN; DOVER, DE 19901. (#9764). **ARBA GRANTEE.**

LAUREL

TOWN SCRAPBOOK ON HISTORY & HERITAGE OF LAUREL, DE. COLLECTIONS OF PICTURES, STORIES, AND HISTORICAL SKETCHES RELATING TO LAUREL, DE, AREAS HISTORY AND HERITAGE. WILL BE PUBLISHED AS A TOWN SCRAPBOOK. (LOCAL). MRS R MEINERSMANN, CHAIRMAN; LAUREL AMERICAN REVOLUTION BICENTENNIAL COMMITTEE; TOWN HALL; LAUREL, DE 19956. (#3214). **(??).**

LEIPSIC

A HISTORY OF THE TOWN OF LEIPSIC, DELAWARE. A HISTORY OF THE TOWN OF LEIPSIC WILL BE PUBLISHED TO INCREASE LOCAL AWARENESS. (LOCAL). SAMUEL G THOMAS, CHAIRMAN; KENT COUNTY-LEVY COURT BICENT COMMITTEE; THE GREEN; DOVER, DE 19901. (#9756). **ARBA GRANTEE.**

JUNE 5 - 6, '76. LEIPSIC BICENTENNIAL CELEBRATION. FESTIVAL. (LOCAL). FRANCES D REMLEY, CHMN; TOWN OF LEIPSIC; RD #4, BOX 324; DOVER, DE 19901. (#200009-4).

LEWES

HIST AREA OF LEWES, DEL, BICENT BEAUTIFICATION. TREES & SHRUBS WILL BE PLANTED TO BEAUTIFY BLDGS OF HIST. SIGNIFICANCE IN HISTORICAL AREA OF LEWES DELAWARE. (ST-WIDE). HON ALFRED A STANGO, MAYOR; LEWES BICENTENNIAL COMMITTEE; LEWES, DE 19958. (#809). **ARBA GRANTEE.**

SUSSEX COUNTY BICENT OPENING FESTIVAL, DELAWARE. LEWIS WILL BE THE SITE FOR THE START OF THE SUSSEX CELEBRATION, FEATURING A PARADE OF FLOATS CARRYING HISTORIC SCENES FROM ALL SUSSEX TOWNS. (LOCAL). JOYCE DYER, CO-CHAIRPERSON; SUSSEX COUNTY BICENTENNIAL COMMITTEE; THE COURTHOUSE; GEORGETOWN, DE 19947. (#10341). **ARBA GRANTEE.**

SEPT 13 - 14, '75. HERITAGE FESTIVAL. PLANS INCLUDE AN OPENING CEREMONY, PARADE, LUNCHEON, SPECIAL CHURCH SERVICES, AND A BOATING SHOW. (LOCAL). JOANN T CONAWAY; SUSSEX COUNTY BICENTENNIAL COMMITTEE; COURTHOUSE, GEORGETOWN; GEORGETOWN, DE 19947. (#7734-501).

LITTLE CREEK

A HISTORY OF THE TOWN OF LITTLE CREEK, DELAWARE. A HISTORY OF THE TOWN OF LITTLE CREEK WILL BE PUBLISHED TO INCREASE LOCAL AWARENESS. (LOCAL). SAMUEL G THOMAS, CHAIRMAN; KENT COUNTY-LEVY COURT BICENT COMMITTEE; THE GREEN; DOVER, DE 19901. (#9748). **ARBA GRANTEE.**

MAGNOLIA

COMMEMORATIVE ITEMS FROM MAGNOLIA, DE. REPRODUCTION CHINA PLATES DEPICTING HISTORICAL SCENES AND NOTE PAPER WITH MAGNOLIA BLOSSOM. (LOCAL). MR HARRY FRESE, ANTIQUE DEALER & MRS E MASSIMILLA; MAGNOLIA BICENTENNIAL COMMITTEE; MAGNOLIA, DE 19962. (#14658).

COMMUNITY DEVELOPMENT PROJECT IN MAGNOLIA, DE. PAINTING COLONIAL SOLDIERS ON TRASH CANS THROUGH TOWN. (LOCAL). MRS BESS DILL, CHAIRPERSON; MAGNOLIA BICENTENNIAL PLANNING COMMITTEE; BOX 23; MAGNOLIA, DE 19962. (#14657).

A HISTORY OF THE TOWN OF MAGNOLIA, DELAWARE. A HISTORY OF THE TOWN OF MAGNOLIA WILL BE PUBLISHED TO INCREASE LOCAL AWARENESS. (LOCAL). SAMUEL G THOMAS, CHAIRMAN; KENT COUNTY-LEVY COURT BICENT COMMITTEE; THE GREEN; DOVER, DE 19901. (#9759). **ARBA GRANTEE.**

NAMESAKE OF MAGNOLIA CELEBRATION, DE. PLANTING OF APPROXIMATLY 50 MAGNOLIA TREES FOR WHICH TOWN IS NAMED. (LOCAL). MRS BESS DILL, CHAIRPERSON; MAGNOLIA BICENTENNIAL COMMITTEE; BOX 23; MAGNOLIA, DE 19901. (#14656).

JUNE 28, '75. ESSAY & BEAUTY CONTEST - WHAT AMERICA MEANS TO ME. COMPETITION, LIVE PERFORMANCE AT MAGNOLIA ELEMENTARY SCHOOL. (LOCAL). MRS BESS DILL, CHMN; MAGNOLIA VOLUNTEER FIRE CO, WOMEN'S AUXILIARY; BOX 23; MAGNOLIA, DE 19962. (#200009-1).

SEPT 27, '75. MAGNOLIA STREET FAIR AND PARADE. FAIR, PARADE AT TOWN OF MAGNOLIA. (LOCAL). GEORGE BARR, DIRECTOR; MAGNOLIA BICENTENNIAL COMMITTEE & MAGNOLIA VOLUNTEER FIRE CO; MAGNOLIA, DE 19962. (#101942-1).

DEC 7, '75. BICENTENNIAL FELLOWSHIP SERVICE. CEREMONY AT MAGNOLIA METHODIST CHURCH, N MAIN ST. (LOCAL). MRS ALVIN WILSON, DIR; MAGNOLIA BICENTENNIAL COMMITTEE & MAGNOLIA UNITED METHODIST CHURCH; KITTS HUMMOCK RD; DOVER, DE 19901. (#101941-1).

FEB 21, '76. SKITS OF GEORGE WASHINGTON'S LIFE. LIVE PERFORMANCE AT MAGNOLIA FELLOWSHIP HALL, N MAIN ST. (LOCAL). MS SANDRA BRYAN, DIR; MAGNOLIA JR MYF OF MAGNOLIA METHODIST CHURCH; 29 N MAIN; MAGNOLIA, DE 19962. (#104114-2).

MAY 2, '76. REVOLUTIONARY PORTRAIT - SONGS OF AMERICAN REVOLUTION. LIVE PERFORMANCE AT MAGNOLIA METHODIST CHURCH, NORTH MAIN, CHURCH PARKING LOT. (LOCAL). JANE BRYAN, DIRECTOR; MAGNOLIA UNITED METHODIST; SENIOR CHOIR; MAGNOLIA, DE 19962. (#104114-1).

MILFORD

BICENTENNIAL PARK OF MILFORD, DELAWARE. TRANSFORMATION OF A VACANT CITY LOT ALONG THE RIVER BANK INTO A PARK DESIGNED FOR SMALL PICNICS AND OTHER RECREATION. (LOCAL). M CATHERINE DOWNING, CHAIRMAN; WILFORD BICENTENNIAL COMMITTEE; 201 S WALNUT ST; MILFORD, DE 19963. (#2741). **ARBA GRANTEE.**

SEPT 21, '75. HISTORIC HOUSE TOUR. BICENTENNIAL PARK OF MILFORD, DELAWARE. TRANSFORMATION OF A VACANT CITY LOT ALONG THE RIVER BANK INTO A PARK DESIGNED FOR SMALL PICNICS AND OTHER RECREATION. (LOCAL). M CATHERINE DOWNING; WILFORD BICENTENNIAL COMMITTEE; 201 S WALNUT ST; MILFORD, DE 19963. (#2741-504).

JAN 1 - 31, '76. HISTORIC EXHIBITS IN STORE WINDOWS. BICENTENNIAL PARK OF MILFORD, DELAWARE. TRANSFORMATION OF A VACANT CITY LOT ALONG THE RIVER BANK INTO A PARK DESIGNED FOR SMALL PICNICS AND OTHER RECREATION. (LOCAL). M CATHERINE DOWNING; WILFORD BICENTENNIAL COMMITTEE; 201 S WALNUT ST; MILFORD, DE 19963. (#2741-505).

APR 25, '76. CONCERT OF PATRIOTIC MUSIC BY LOCAL CHOIR MEMBERS. LIVE PERFORMANCE. (LOCAL). M CATHERINE DOWNING; WILFORD BICENTENNIAL COMMITTEE; 201 S WALNUT ST; MILFORD, DE 19963. (#2741-503).

MAY 28 - 31, '76. FESTIVAL WEEK-END OF PARADE PICNIC SQUARE DANCING FIREWOKS HAYRIDES. 5/28, 7:30-9:30 HAYRIDES, 8-11 PM SQUARE DANCING, WALNUT ST BRIDGE; 5/29, 2PM PARADE AT WALNUT ST, 8:45PM FIREWORKS AT HIGH SCHOOL; 5/30, 1-5PM COMMUNITY PICNIC AT PARSON THORNE MANSION; 5/31, 9:30 AM VETS MEMORIAL SERV, ANNUAL GO-CART RACE AT 1PM, WALNUT ST. AT VARYING TIMES AND LOCATIONS FOR EVENTS. (LOCAL). M CATHERINE DOWNING; MILFORD BICENTENNIAL COMMITTEE; 201 S WALNUT ST; MILFORD, DE 19963. (#2741-501).

JUNE 20, '76. DEDICATION OF BICENTENNIAL PARK. CEREMONY, OPENING. (LOCAL). M CATHERINE DOWNING; MILFORD BICENTENNIAL COMMITTEE; 201 S WALNUT ST; MILFORD, DE 19963. (#2741-506).

MILLSBORO

BEAUTIFICATION U S DUAL ROUTE 113 IN DELAWARE. THE FOLLOWING TREES WILL BE PLANTED ON THE MEDIAN AREA OF ROUTE 113 IN MILLSBORO: THE AMERICAN HOLLY, THE WHITE DOGWOOD, THE WASHIGTON HAWTHORNE AND THE BRADFORD PEAR. (LOCAL). BLANCHE W BARKER, CHAIRMAN; MILLSBORO BICENTENNIAL COMMITTEE; PO BOX 127; MILLSBORO, DE 19966. (#9578). **ARBA GRANTEE.**

CREATION OF MINI-PARK, MILLSBORO, DE. ESTABLISH MINI-PARK WITH REPLICA OF GRISTMILL & WATERWHEEL WITH FLAG POLE & PLANTINGS. (LOCAL). MRS BLANCHE W BAKER, CHAIRMAN; MILLSBORO LIONS CLUB & BICENTENNIAL COMMITTEE; BOX 127; MILLSBORO, DE 19966. (#29998).

HISTORY OF MILLSBORO, DE. RESEARCH & PUBLISH HISTORY OF MILLSBORO. (LOCAL). MRS BLANCHE W BAKER, CHAIRMAN; MILLSBORO BICENTENNIAL COMMITTEE; BOX 127; MILLSBORO, DE 19966. (#30001).

MILLSBORO TOWN SEAL CONTEST - DE. SELECT & ESTABLISH OFFICIAL SEAL FOR MILLSBORO BY CONTEST WITH $100 BOND AS AWARD. (LOCAL). BLANCE W BAKER, CHAIRMAN; MILLSBORO BICENTENNIAL COMMITTEE; BOX 127; MILLSBORO, DE 19966. (#29997).

JAN 26 - 30, '76. COLONIAL HOME LIFE DEMONSTRATION, ARTS & CRAFTS. LIVE PERFORMANCE, EXHIBIT AT EAST ELEMENTARY SCHOOL. (LOCAL). MRS BLANCHE W BAKER, CHMN; MILLSBORO WOMEN'S CIVIC CLUB & BICENTENNIAL COMMITTEE; BOX 127; MILLSBORO, DE 19966. (#200009-13).

JULY 3 - 4, '76. INDEPENDENCE DAY FESTIVAL. FESTIVAL, LIVE PERFORMANCE AT MILLSBORO CUPOLA PARK & MAIN ST. (LOCAL). MRS BLANCHE W BAKER, CHMN; MILLSBORO BICENTENNIAL COMMITTEE; BOX 127; MILLSBORO, DE 19966. (#200009-14).

N BOWERS BCH

BOWERS BEACH MARITIME MUSEUM - DE. MUSEUM ON MARITIME & HISTORY ESTABLISHED TO PRESERVE THE PAST. (LOCAL). JANE BOONE, PRESIDENT; BOWERS BEACH MARITIME MUSEUM, INC; RFD; BOWERS BEACH, DE 19946. (#29946).

NEW CASTLE

AMER WIND SYMPHONY FOR SEPARATION DAY IN DELAWARE. AS PART OF THE 4 DAY SEPARATION DAY CELEBRATION, THE SYMPHONY WILL CONDUCT A WORKSHOP FOR YOUNG PEOPLE AND PLAY A BICENTENNIAL CONCERT IN THE EVENING. (LOCAL). JOHN F KLINGMEYER, CHAIRMAN; NEW CASTLE BICENTENNIAL COMMITTEE; NEW CASTLE, DE 19720. (#6484). **ARBA GRANTEE.**

BICENTENNIAL MINI-PARK, NEW CASTLE, DE. CONSTRUCTION OF A SMALL PARK IN THE CENTER OF TOWN CONTAINING A TOWN BULLETIN BOARD, BENCHES AND PLANTINGS. (LOCAL). DANIEL F WOLCOTT, JR, CO-CHAIRMAN; HISTORIC NEW CASTLE '76; PO BOX 1776; NEW CASTLE, DE 19720. (#25482). **ARBA GRANTEE.**

BICENTENNIAL PROGRAM FOR WILIMINGTON COLLEGE, DE. PROGRAM INCLUDES: ESSAY COMPETITION FOR HIGH SCHOOL STUDENTS, FILM ON COLONIAL & REVOLUTIONARY AMERICA, LECTURE SERIES, BOAT TRIP, AND REPLICATION OF COLONIAL TOYS. (LOCAL). DR ERNEST DIBBLE, CHAIRMAN; WILMINGTON COLLEGE; 320 DUPONT HWY; NEW CASTLE, DE 19720. (#26595). **ARBA GRANTEE.**

HISTORIC LECTURE SERIES, NEW CASTLE, DE. A SERIES OF NINE LECTURES ON HISTORIC TOPICS WILL BE GIVEN AT VARIOUS LOCATIONS IN AND AROUND NEW CASTLE. (LOCAL). DANIEL F WOLCOTT, JR, CO-CHAIRMAN; HISTORIC NEW CASTLE '76; PO BOX 1776; NEW CASTLE, DE 19720. (#25481). **ARBA GRANTEE.**

NEW CASTLE CELEBRATION OF DELAWARE SEPARATION DAY. A 4-DAY FESTIVAL INCLUDING A LARGE PARADE, 2 MUSICAL CONCERTS, (ONE BY THE AMERICAN WIND SYMPHONY), A CRAFTS FAIR & VARIOUS OTHER ACTIVITIES, TO COMMEMORATE SEPARATION FROM ENGLAND, JUNE 15, 1776. (LOCAL). DANIEL F WOLCOTT, JR, CO-CHAIRMAN; HISTORIC NEW CASTLE '76; PO BOX 1776; NEW CASTLE, DE 19720. (#25480). **ARBA GRANTEE.**

TERMINUS FOR THE POWDER PUFF DERBY, NEW CASTLE, DE. END OF POWDER PUFF DERBY TO COINCIDE WITH NEW CASTLE COUNTY'S BICENTENNIAL CELEBRATION JULY 9-14, 1976. (LOCAL). ANNE GRUSSEMEYER, VICE-CHAIRMAN; THE NINETY-NINES, INC; PO BOX 59; NEWARK, DE 19711. (#23672). **ARBA GRANTEE.**

MAY 15, '76. 'A DAY IN OLD NEW CASTLE'. NATION'S OLDEST OPEN HOUSE PROGRAM FEATURES SOME 20 HISTORIC HOMES AND LANDMARKS. AT NEW CASTLE, DE. (LOCAL). CAROL DAVIDSON, CHMN; DAY IN OLD NEW CASTLE COMMITTEE; PO BOX 47; NEW CASTLE, DE 19720. (#103416-301).

JUNE 12 - 15, '76. SEPARATION DAYS. FIREWORKS, ARTS & CRAFTS, FASHION SHOW, FLOWER ARRANGEMENTS, LADIES' LUNCHEON & SUNRISE SERVICES IN BATTERY PARK. THERE WILL ALSO BE A REENACTMENT OF SEPARATION DAY & A PRESENTATION BY THE AMER WOODWIND SYMPHONY FROM A BARGE ON THE DELAWARE RIVER. AT TOWN HALL & COURT HOUSE, DELAWARE & 2ND STS. (LOCAL). DANIEL F WOLCOTT, JR; HISTORIC NEW CASTLE '76; BOX 1776; NEW CASTLE, DE 19720. (#102863-1).

JUNE 15, '76. AMERICAN WIND SYMPHONY FOR SEPARATION DAY. AS PART OF THE 4 DAY SEPARATION DAY CELEBRATION, THE SYMPHONY WILL CONDUCT A WORKSHOP FOR YOUNG PEOPLE AND PLAY A BICENTENNIAL CONCERT IN THE EVENING. AT NEW CASTLE CENTER. (LOCAL). JOHN F KLINGMEYER; NEW CASTLE BICENTENNIAL COMMITTEE; PO BOX 1776; NEW CASTLE, DE 19720. (#6484-1).

JULY 9 - 14, '76. POWDER PUFF DERBY & BICENTENNIAL CELEBRATION. FESTIVAL. (NAT'L). ANNE GRUSSEMEYER, V-CHMN; THE NINETY-NINES, INC; PO BOX 59; NEWARK, DE 19711. (#23672-1).

SEPT 18, '76. DELAWARE'S CONSTITUTION DAY & RE-ENACTMENT OF ADOPTION. WELCOME & BRIEF REMARKS BY THE GOVERNOR & THE CHIEF JUSTICE & THEN A RE-ENACTMENT OF THE ADOPTION OF THE DELAWARE CONSTITUTION BY THE CANDLELIGHT THEATRE CO. FOLLOWING, REFRESHMENTS AVAILABLE ON THE GREEN BY THE NEW CASTLE LIONS CLUB. AT OLD COURT HOUSE STEPS. (ST-WIDE). JOHN S MICKEY, EXEC DIR; DELAWARE BICENTENNIAL FOUNDATION; PO BOX 2476; WILMINGTON, DE 19899. (#200009-11).

NEWARK

AMERICAN MUSIC CONCERTS AT UNIV OF DELAWARE. A SERIES OF CONCERTS BY THE UNIVERSITY STRING QUARTET. (LOCAL). JOHN A MURRAY, CHAIRMAN; UNIV OF DELAWARE BICENTENNIAL COMMITTEE; NEWARK, DE 19711. (#6710).

ANALYSIS OF CHESAPEAKE AND DELAWARE CANAL, DE. STUDY OF FUTURE POTENTIAL OF THE CANAL AS A SHIPPING LANE AND ITS BANKS AS SITES FOR RECREATION; INCLUDES AN ANALYSIS OF TOPOGRAPHY, FAUNA AND FLORA. (ST-WIDE). JOHN A MURRAY, PROJ DIRECTOR; UNIV OF DELAWARE; DIV OF CONTINUING EDUCATION; NEWARK, DE 19711. (#11379). **ARBA GRANTEE.**

CHEMICAL WORLD OF THE FOUNDING FATHERS, NEWARK, DE. RECREATION OF 18TH CENTURY CHEMISTRY EXPERIMENTS; EMPHASIS ON THEIR CONTRIBUTIONS TO 20TH CENTURY SCIENCE. (LOCAL). JOHN A MURRAY, PROJ DIRECTOR; UNIV OF DELAWARE; DIV OF CONTINUING EDUCATION; NEWARK, DE 19711. (#11380). **ARBA GRANTEE.**

NEWARK — CONTINUED

CONCERT TOUR BY UNIVERSITY OF DELAWARE CHOIR. A TOUR OF DELAWARE BY THE UNIVERSITY OF DELAWARE CONCERT CHOIR; PLANNED SELECTIONS INCLUDE MUSIC REPRESENTING ALL THREE BICENTENNIAL THEME AREAS AND COMPOSITIONS BY NATIVE, DELAWARE COMPOSERS. (ST-WIDE). JOHN A MURRAY, PROJ DIRECTOR; UNIV OF DELAWARE; DIV OF CONTINUING EDUCATION; NEWARK, DE 19711. (#11381). **ARBA GRANTEE.**

DELAWARE BICENTENNIAL INTERN PROGRAM. TWO INTERNS ARE TO ASSIST IN THE ENCOURAGEMENT & COORDINATION OF BICENTENNIAL PROGRAMS. THESE PROGRAMS WILL BE COORDINATED BY THE UNIVERSITY OF DELAWARE. (ST-WIDE). JOHN A MURRAY, CHAIRMAN; UNIV OF DELAWARE; NEWARK, DE 19711. (#6480). **ARBA GRANTEE.**

DRAMA SERIES AT THE UNIV OF DELAWARE. A SERIES OF PLAYS WRITTEN BY AMERICAN PLAYWRIGHTS AND SPONSORED BY THE DEPARTMENT OF THEATRE AT THE UNIV OF DELAWARE. (LOCAL). JOHN A MURRAY, CHAIRMAN; UNIV OF DELAWARE BICENTENNIAL COMMITTEE; NEWARK, DE 19711. (#6706).

EDUCATIONAL EXHIBITIONS AT UNIV OF DELAWARE. A SERIES OF EXHIBITIONS IN THE CONTINUING EDUCATION PROGRAM AT THE UNIV OF DELAWARE, THE SUBJECTS OF THE EXHIBITS INCLUDE DELAWARE HISTORY, SPORTS, BLACK HISTORY AND MEDICINE. (LOCAL). JOHN A MURRAY, CHAIRMAN; UNIV OF DELAWARE BICENTENNIAL COMMITTEE; NEWARK, DE 19711. (#6709).

FLORAL SURVEY OF IRON HILL IN NEWARK, DE. PURPOSE IS TO IDENTIFY & RECORD RARE, PLANT SPECIES PRESENT WHEN THE HILL WAS USED AS AN OBSERVATION POST BY GEORGE WASHINGTON. (LOCAL). JOHN A MURRAY, CHAIRMAN; UNIV OF DELAWARE; DIV OF CONTINUING EDUCATION; NEWARK, DE 19711. (#11378). **ARBA GRANTEE.**

HISTORY LECTURES AT UNIV OF DELAWARE. LECTURES ON THE HISTORY OF THE AMERICAN REVOLUTION WILL BE OPEN TO THE PUBLIC AT THE UNIVERSITY OF DELAWARE. (LOCAL). JOHN A MURRAY, CHAIRMAN; UNIV OF DELAWARE BICENTENNIAL COMMITTEE; NEWARK, DE 19711. (#6705).

HISTORY OF THE UNIVERSITY OF DELAWARE. PREPARATION AND STAGING OF AN EXHIBITION AT THE UNIVERSITY OF DELAWARE BY CLASSES IN THE DIVISION OF MUSEUM STUDIES. (LOCAL). JOHN A MURRAY, CHAIRMAN; UNIV OF DELAWARE BICENTENNIAL COMMITTEE; NEWARK, DE 19711. (#6702).

LECTURES FROM DEPT OF MATHEMATICS, UNIV OF DE. A PROGRAM OF LECTURES TO CONSIDER THE RAMIFICATIONS OF ADOPTING THE METRIC SYSTEM. (LOCAL). JOHN A MURRAY, CHAIRMAN; UNIV OF DELAWARE BICENTENNIAL COMMITTEE; NEWARK, DE 19711. (#6704).

LIBRARY EXHIBITIONS AT UNIV OF DELAWARE. A SERIES OF EXHIBITIONS ON DELAWARE AND REVOLUTIONARY WAR HISTORY. (LOCAL). JOHN A MURRAY, CHAIRMAN; UNIV OF DELAWARE BICENTENNIAL COMMITTEE; NEWARK, DE 19711. (#6707).

MUSICAL COMPOSITION AT UNIV OF DELAWARE. ORIGINAL MUSICAL COMPOSITION COMMISSIONED FOR THE DELAWARE SYMPHONIC ORCHESTRA. (ST-WIDE). JOHN A MURRAY, CHAIRMAN; UNIV OF DELAWARE BICENTENNIAL COMMITTEE; NEWARK, DE 19711. (#6711).

NEW CASTLE COUNTY WATER QUALITY MANAGEMENT - DE. A MULTI-JURISDICTIONAL GOVERNMENTAL PROGRAM FOR ENVIRONMENTAL OR WATER RESOURCES PLANNING. (ST-WIDE). MERNA HURD, PROGRAM ADMINISTRATOR; NEW CASTE COUNTY OFFICE OF WATER AND SEWER PLANNING; ONE PEDDLERS VILLAGE; NEWARK, DE 19702. (#20047).

NEW PUBLICATIONS FROM THE UNIV OF DELAWARE PRESS. THE UNIV OF DELAWARE PRESS WILL PUBLISH SEVERAL NEW BOOKS RELATING TO THE AMERICAN REVOLUTION. (ST-WIDE). JOHN A MURRAY, CHAIRMAN; UNIV OF DELAWARE BICENTENNIAL COMMITTEE; NEWARK, DE 19711. (#6708).

NEWARK BICENTENNIAL BEAUTIFICATION PROJ - DELAWARE. BEAUTIFICATION & CLEANUP FOR THE BICENTENNIAL, INCORPORATIONG DOWNTOWN COMPETITIONS, BLOCK BICENTENNIAL BEAUTIFICATION PROJECTS AND PLANTINGS OF TREES AND FLOWERS. (LOCAL). MRS MYRTLE BOWE, CHAIRMAN; NEWARK BICENTENNIAL COMMISSION; GREATER NEWARK SHOPPING CENTER; NEWARK, DE 19711. (#1347). **(??). ARBA GRANTEE.**

SOCIOLOGY SYMPOSIUM AT THE UNIV OF DELAWARE. A DISCUSSION ENTITLED 'THE AMERICAN BICENTENNIAL, WHERE DO WE GO FROM HERE? 1976-2076'. (LOCAL). JOHN A MURRAY, CHAIRMAN; UNIV OF DELAWARE BICENTENNIAL COMMITTEE; NEWARK, DE 19711. (#6703).

UNIVERSITY OF DELAWARE BICENTENNIAL PROGRAM. CONCERTS, LECTURES, SYMPOSIA & PUBLICATIONS BY & FOR THE UNIVERSITY. (ST-WIDE). JOHN A MURRAY, CHMN; UNIV OF DELAWARE BICENTENNIAL COMMITTEE; C/O DIV OF CONTINUING EDUCATION; NEWARK, DE 19771. (#18602). **ARBA GRANTEE.**

JULY 19 - 20, '75. HERITAGE FAIR. MEDIEVAL THEME, ARCHERY TOURNAMENTS, CRAFTS, FOOD, ENTERTAINMENT. AT WHITE CLAY CREEK STATE PARK RT 896 2 MILES NORT OF NEWARK. (ST-WIDE). MYRTLE E BOWE; GREATER NEWARK CHAMBER OF COMMERCE; 250 E MAIN ST; NEWARK, DE 19711. (#50371-1).

JAN 7 - 28, '76. CHEMICAL WORLD OF THE FOUNDING FATHERS: LECTURE SERIES. RE-CREATION OF 18TH CENTURY CHEMISTRY EXPERIMENTS; EMPHASIS ON THEIR CONTRIBUTIONS TO 20TH CENTURY SCIENCE. AT BROWN LABORATORY & CLAYTON HALL. (LOCAL). JOHN J BEER, DIRECTOR; UNIV OF DELAWARE; NEWARK, DE 19711. (#11380-1).

NEWPORT

INSTALLATION OF LASTING MEMORIAL, NEWPORT, DE. INSTALLATION OF A NAVY CANNON & PLANTING OF TREES & SHRUBS IN THE PARK. (LOCAL). HON JOHN S HANNA, JR, MAYOR; NEWPORT BICENTENNIAL COMMISSION; 205 MARSHALL ST; NEWPORT, DE 19804. (#17095). **ARBA GRANTEE.**

OCEAN VIEW

JULY 11, '76. ECUMENICAL CHURCH SERVICE. SERVICE BEING HELD IN CONJUNCTION WITH 'HOMECOMING' CELEBRATION OF THE TOWN COMMISSIONERS. (LOCAL). ROBERT C MAXWELL; BETHANY BEACH BICENTENNIAL COMMITTEE; PO BOX 364; BETHANY BEACH, DE 19930. (#200009-16).

ODESSA

HERITAGE-HORIZON DAY TREE PLANTING - ODESSA, DE. IN CONJUNCTION WITH HERITAGE FESTIVAL, 150 LARGE DOGWOOD TREES WILL BE PLANTED ON THE STREETS OF ODESSA. (LOCAL). HON GANTT W MILLER, MAYOR; COUNCIL OF ODESSA; ODESSA, DE 19730. (#27085). **ARBA GRANTEE.**

DEC 7, '75. CHRISTMAS IN COLONIAL ODESSA DEL.. CHRISTMAS TOUR OF PRIVATE HOMES & MUSEUMS 17THCENTURY TO PRESENT-COLONIAL CRAFTS-(EXHIBITS & SHOP) SPECIAL MUSIC-COLONIAL COSTUMES WORN. DISPLAY ARTS. BY STUDENTS. EMPHASIS ON PRES-RESTOR. OF 19TH CENT CHURCH. AT TOWN OF ODESSA. (LOCAL). MRS JESSE LOVEN; WOMEN'S CLUB OF ODESSA; BOX 155; ODESSA, DE 19730. (#50132-1).

MAY 22, '76. AMERICAN HERITAGE BICENTENNIAL BALL. MUSIC BY SOCIETY'S CHILD; AMERICAN HERITAGE BALL PROGRAMS & DECORATIONS; GOVERNOR & MRS TRIBBITT HAVE BEEN INVITED. AT ODESSA FIRE HALL. (LOCAL). GLORIA E MOFFITT, CHMN; TOWNSEND WOMEN'S CLUB; BOX 203; TOWNSEND, DE 19734. (#105873-1).

PORT PENN

PERMANENT MUSEUM IN PORT PENN, DELAWARE. PURCHASE PROPERTY TO BE USED AS A PERMANENT MUSEUM, TO BE DEDICATED DURING BICENTENNIAL PERIOD. (LOCAL). JULIA L SIDWELL, CHAIRMAN; PORT PENN BICENTENNIAL COMMITTEE; PORT PENN, DE 19731. (#9574). **ARBA GRANTEE.**

FEB 1, '76 - CONTINUING . OPENING OF PORT PENN MUSEUM. MUSEUM OPEN TO PUBLIC ON WEEK-ENDS & DURING WEEK BY APPOINTMENT. (LOCAL). MRS MARGARET ZACHEIS, DIR; PORT PENN BICENTENNIAL COMMITTEE; PORT PENN, DE 19731. (#105012-6).

MAY 22, '76. PORT PENN FESTIVAL. FLEA MARKET, BAZAAR, BOOTHS, REFRESHMENTS; MUSEUM WILL BE OPEN; PARADE STARTS AT 11:00 AM; FREE PARKING; HOME-COOKED FOOD OFFERED IN & LOCATIONS; ENTERTAINMENT DURING THE DAY IN 2 LOCAL CHURCHES. (LOCAL). JULIA L SIDWELL, CHMN; PORT PENN BICENTENNIAL COMMITTEE; PORT PENN, DE 19731. (#105012-7).

AUG 21, '76. BEACH BONANZA. MISS TEENAGE PORT PENN CONTEST WINNER WILL BE CROWNED BY WELL KNOWN PERSONALITY; FLEA MARKET & BAZAAR BOOTHS PLUS REFRESHMENTS; COUNTRY MUSIC FOR DANCING ON BLACK TOP; ADDITIONAL AMUSEUMENT AND WATER ACTI VITY PLANNED; FREE PARKING. AT AUGUSTINE BEACH, ONE MILE SOUTH OF PORT PENN. (LOCAL). JULIA L SIDWELL, CHMN; PORT PENN BICENTENNIAL COMMITTEE; PORT PENN, DE 19731. (#105012-3).

OCT 2 - 30, '76. TURKEY SHOOTS. TURKEY SHOOTS WILL BE HELD ON OCTOBER 2, 9, 16, 23, AND 30TH: REFRESHMENTS WILL BE AVAILABLE. AT OLD CANNERY LOT - PORT PENN, DEL. (LOCAL). JULIA L SIDWELL, CHMN; PORT PENN BICENTENNIAL COMMITTEE; PORT PENN, DE 19731. (#105012-2).

NOV 20, '76. COSTUME BALL. FESTIVAL. (LOCAL). JULIA L SIDWELL, CHMN; PORT PENN BICENTENNIAL COMMITTEE; PORT PENN, DE 19731. (#105012-1).

REHOBOTH BCH

FLAGS OF THE FIFTY STATES IN REHOBOTH BEACH, DEL. SECURE AND DISPLAY THE FLAGS OF OUR 50 STATES ON MAIN AVENUE IN KEEPING WITH THE SLOGAN OF OUR CITY - THE NATION'S SUMMER CAPITAL. (REGN'L). WILLIAM E GREINER, CHAIRMAN; REHOBOTH BEACH BICENTENNIAL COMMITTEE; 305 SCARBOROUGH AVENUE; REHOBOTH BCH, DE 19971. (#26288).

REHOBOTH IN THE SANDS OF TIME. RELOCATE & RESTORE, IN A CITY PARK AREA, ONE OF THE OLDEST DWELLINGS IN REHOBOTH FOR USE AS A MUSEUM-THE MUSEUM-WITH LANDSCAPED GARDENS SURROUNDING IT. WILL SERVE RESIDENTS & VISITORS FOR YRS TO COME. (ST-WIDE). WILLIAM E GREINER, CHAIRMAN; REHOBOTH BEACH BICENTENNIAL COMMITTEE; 305 SCARBOROUGH AVE; REHOBOTH BCH, DE 19971. (#26287).

SEPT 28, '76. CONCERT -UNITED STATE ARMED FORCES BICENTENNIAL BAND AND CHORUS. LIVE PERFORMANCE AT MUNICIPAL BAND STAND, REHOBOTH AVE & BOARDWALK, REHOBOTH BCH, DE. (ST-WIDE). WILLIAM E GREINER, CHMN; REHOBOTH BEACH BICENTENNIAL COMMITTEE; 305 SCARBOROUGH AVE; REHOBOTH BCH, DE 19971. (#26288-1).

RISING SUN

HISTORY OF THE TOWN OF RISING SUN, DELAWARE. A HISTORY OF THE TOWN OF RISING SUN WILL BE PUBLISHED TO INCREASE LOCAL AWARENESS. (LOCAL). SAMUEL G THOMAS, CHAIRMAN; KENT COUNTY-LEVY COURT BICENT COMMITTEE; THE GREEN; DOVER, DE 19901. (#9750). **ARBA GRANTEE.**

SEAFORD

COLLECTION OF COMMUNITY MEMORABILIA - SEAFORD, DE. IN COOPERATION WITH SEAFORD COMMUNITY BICEN COMMITTEE & SEAFORD DISTRICT LIBRARY, HIST SOCIETY HAS STARTED COLLECTION & DISPLAY OF ITEMS PORTRAYING HISTORY OF SEAFORD. (LOCAL). JAMES A KELLEY, CHAIRMAN; SEAFORD COMMUNITY BICENTENNIAL COMMITTEE; R D 2, TIMIHAW ROAD; SEAFORD, DE 19973. (#24018).

INTERVIEWS WITH SENIOR CITIZENS, SEAFORD, DE. SEAFORD SENIOR HIGH SCHOOL SOCIAL STUDIES STUDENTS WILL TAPE INTERVIEWS OF OLDER SENIOR CITIZENS' RECOLLECTIONS OF EVENTS IN THAT COMMUNITY. (LOCAL). JAMES A KELLEY, CHAIRMAN; SEAFORD COMMUNITY BICENTENNIAL COMMITTEE; RD 2, TIMIHAW RD; SEAFORD, DE 19973. (#17094). **ARBA GRANTEE.**

JULY 3 - 5, '76. SEAFORD COMMUNITY HOMECOMING FESTIVAL. SAT 7/3 SPORTS GAMES CONTESTS, AGES6-14 HORSESHOW ARTS & CRAFTS EVE COLONIAL ST DANCE RIVER EXCURSIONS IN AFTERNOON SUN 7/4 REUNIONS CHURCH SERVICES IN AM COMMUNITY SERVICE 7PM MON 7/5 2PM PARADE 7PM FORMAL PROGRAM 9PM FIREWORKS DISPLAY SG&CC. AT SCHOOLS PLAYGROUNDS PARKS FARMS STREETS RIVER ETC. (LOCAL). JAMES A KELLEY; SEAFORD COMMUNITY BICENTENNIAL COMMITTEE; RD2 TIMIHAM RD; SEAFORD, DE 19973. (#107807-1).

SELBYVILLE

MONUMENT TO VETERANS, SELBYVILLE, DE. INSTALLATION AND DEDICATION OF A MONUMENT HONORING VETERANS OF PAST WARS. (LOCAL). RUSSELL D BRITTINGHAM, CHAIRMAN; SELBYVILLE BICENTENNIAL COMMISSION; SELBYVILLE, DE 19975. (#14306). **ARBA GRANTEE.**

TOWN PARK IMPROVEMENT PROGRAM. IMPROVEMENT AND LANDSCAPING OF 4 ACRE PARK IN SELBYVILLE. LOCATED NEXT TO THE TOWN SWIMMING POOL, THE PARK WILL INCLUDE FACILITIES FOR PEOPLE OF ALL AGES. (LOCAL). RUSSELL D BRITTINGHAM, CHAIRMAN; SELBYVILLE BICENTENNIAL COMMISSION; SELBYVILLE, DE 19975. (#14307). **ARBA GRANTEE.**

SMYRNA

BICENTENNIAL BAND, SMYRNA, DE. OPPORTUNITY FOR ADULTS TO CONTINUE THEIR MUSIC THROUGH PARTICIPATION IN A CONCERT BAND DURING AND SUBSEQUENT TO THE CELEBRATION PERIOD. (LOCAL). RICHARD E ENNIS, PUBLIC RELATIONS DIRECTOR; SMYRNA FIRE COMPANY; 351 SUNNYSIDE RD; SMYRNA, DE 19977. (#17326).

COMMEMORATIVE POSTCARDS - SMYRNA, DE. THIS SET OF SIX CARDS DEPICTS SMYRNA'S REVOLUTIONARY WAR HERO, COLONEL ALLEN MCLANE; THE REGULAR PRICE IS $1.25. A CANCELLED STAMP OF DUCK CREEK CROSSROADS COSTS $2.00. (REGN'L). GEORGE L CALEY, PROJ DIRECTOR; SMYRNA BICENTENNIAL COMMITTEE; 5 DELAWARE ST; SMYRNA, DE 19977. (#17381).

A HISTORY OF THE TOWN OF SMYRNA, DELAWARE. A HISTORY OF THE TOWN OF SMYRNA WILL BE PUBLISHED TO INCREASE LOCAL AWARENESS. (LOCAL). SAMUEL G THOMAS, CHAIRMAN; KENT COUNTY-LEVY COURT BICENT COMMITTEE; THE GREEN; DOVER, DE 19901. (#9754). **ARBA GRANTEE.**

MAP OF 35 HISTORIC SITES OF KENT COUNTY, DE. THE FIRST 600 MAPS ARE NUMBERED AND WILL BE AVAILABLE FOR DISTRIBUTION ON OCT 18, 1975. ORDERS ARE BEING TAKEN NOW AND THE PRICE IS $15.00 PER MAP. (ST-WIDE). GEORGE L CALEY, PROJ DIRECTOR; SMYRNA BICENTENNIAL COMMITTEE; 118 S DELAWARE ST; SMYRNA, DE 19977. (#17380).

MUSICAL SALUTE TO 'OUR HERITAGE', WILMINGTON, DE. THE SMYRNA HIGH SCHOOL BAND PLANS TO STAGE A HOMECOMING CELEBRATION WITH 'OUR HERITAGE' AS THE MAIN THEME. (LOCAL). CHARLES V WILLIAMS, SUPERINTENDENT; SMYRNA SCHOOL DISTRICT; 22 S MAIN ST; SMYRNA, DE 19977. (#11156). **ARBA GRANTEE.**

OCT 24, '75. SMYRNA HIGH SCHOOL HOMECOMING. THE SMYRNA HIGH SCHOOL BAND PLANS TO STAGE A HOMECOMING CELEBRATION WITH 'OUR HERITAGE' AS THE MAIN THEME. AT SMYRNA HIGH SCHOOL FOOTBALL STADIUM. (LOCAL). SALLY STERRETT, CHMN; SMYRNA SCHOOL DISTRICT; 22 S MAIN ST; SMYRNA, DE 19977. (#11156-1).

TOWNSEND

BICENTENNIAL CELEBRATION OF TOWNSEND, DELAWARE. CELEBRATIONS, PARADE, CEREMONY & PATRIOTIC SPEECHES FOR NATION'S BICENTENNIAL. (LOCAL). MRS GLORIA E MOFFITT, BICENTENNIAL CHAIRMAN; TOWNSEND WOMEN'S CLUB; BOX 203; TOWNSEND, DE 19734. (#3415).

MAY 25, '75. CHURCH HERITAGE SUNDAY. CELEBRATIONS, PARADE, CEREMONY & PATRIOTIC SPEECHES FOR NATION'S BICENTENNIAL. AT CITYWIDE. (LOCAL). MRS GLORIA E MOF-

TOWNSEND — CONTINUED

FITT; TOWNSEND WOMENS CLUB; BOX 203; TOWNSEND, DE 19734. (#3415-2).

MAY 26, '75. BICENTENNIAL CELEBRATION WITH PARADE, SPEECHES, SCHOOL BAND CONCERT. BICENTENNIAL CELEBRATION OF TOWNSEND, DELAWARE. CELEBRATIONS, PARADE, CEREMONY & PATRIOTIC SPEECHES FOR NATION'S BICENTENNIAL. (LOCAL). MRS GLORIA E MOFFITT; TOWNSEND WOMEN'S CLUB; BOX 203; TOWNSEND, DE 19734. (#3415-503).

OCT 2, '75. BICENTENNIAL FASHION SHOW AT 8:00 PM. BICENTENNIAL CELEBRATION OF TOWNSEND, DELAWARE. CELEBRATIONS, PARADE, CEREMONY & PATRIOTIC SPEECHES FOR NATION'S BICENTENNIAL. (LOCAL). MRS GLORIA E MOFFITT; TOWNSEND WOMEN'S CLUB; BOX 203; TOWNSEND, DE 19734. (#3415-504).

NOV 22, '75. BICENTENNIAL BAZAAR. EXHIBIT AT EMMANUEL METHODIST CHURCH, MAIN ST. (LOCAL). GLORIA MOFFITT, DIR; UNITED METHODIST WOMEN; BOX 203; TOWNSEND, DE 19734. (#103354-1).

MAY 31, '76. BICENTENNIAL DAY '76. GOVERNOR TRIBBITT IS INVITED TO SPEAK AT THE CEREMONY; DELAWARE'S COVERED WAGON TO TAKE PART; DELAWARE NATIONAL GUARD BAND TO MARCH IN PARADE; DISPLAY BY THE LIGHT INFANTRY OF DOVER COLONIAL GROUP. AT MAIN ST. (LOCAL). GLORIA E MOFFITT, CHMN; TOWNSEND WOMEN'S CLUB; BOX 203; TOWNSEND, DE 19734. (#105872-1).

JUNE 12 - 13, '76. UNITED STATES ARMED FORCES BICENTENNIAL CARAVAN. CARAVAN IS COMPOSED OF EXHIBIT VANS FOR EACH MILITARY SERVICE. PROJECT THEME IS ' HISTORY OF THE ARMED FORCES & THEIR CONTRIBUTIONS TO THE NATION'. (LOCAL). MRS FRANK E MOFFITT, CHMN; U S ARMED FORCES BICENTENNIAL CARAVAN; PO BOX 203; TOWNSEND, DE 19734. (#1775-472).

JUNE 13, '76. CHURCH HERITAGE SUNDAY. CEREMONY, FESTIVAL AT TOWN CHURCHES. (LOCAL). GLORIA E MOFFITT, CHMN; TOWNSEND BICENTENNIAL COMMITTEE; BOX 203; TOWNSEND, DE 19734. (#105872-2).

JULY 1, '76. HISTORIC RE-ENACTMENT OF CAESAR RODNEY'S RIDE. LIVE PERFORMANCE AT ROUTE 13 AND ROUTE 896 NEAR BLACKBIRD. (LOCAL). GLORIA E MOFFITT, CHMN; TOWNSEND BICENTENNIAL COMMITTEE; BOX 203; TOWNSEND, DE 19734. (#105872-4).

VIOLA

HISTORY OF THE TOWN OF VIOLA, DELAWARE. A HISTORY OF THE TOWN OF VIOLA WILL BE PUBLISHED TO INCREASE LOCAL AWARENESS. (LOCAL). SAMUEL G THOMAS, CHAIRMAN; KENT COUNTY-LEVY COURT BICENT COMMITTEE; THE GREEN; DOVER, DE 19901. (#9749). **ARBA GRANTEE.**

WILLOW GROVE

A HISTORY OF THE TOWN OF WILLOW GROVE, DELAWARE. A HISTORY OF THE TOWN OF WILLOW GROVE WILL BE PUBLISHED TO INCREASE LOCAL AWARENESS. (LOCAL). SAMUEL G THOMAS, CHAIRMAN; KENT COUNTY-LEVY COURT BICENT COMMITTEE; THE GREEN; DOVER, DE 19901. (#9747). **ARBA GRANTEE.**

WILMINGTON

AMERICAN FILM FESTIVAL IN WILMINGTON, DE. NORTHEAST SCHOOL PLANS AN AMERICAN FILM FESTIVAL TO HELP UNITE AND EXPAND COMMUNITY INTEREST IN THE BICENTENNIAL CELEBRATION. (LOCAL). MURIEL F COOPER, PROJ DIRECTOR; NORTH EAST SCHOOL, WILMINGTON PUBLIC SCHOOL DISTRICT; 5TH AND LOMBARD STS; WILMINGTON, DE 19801. (#11152). **ARBA GRANTEE.**

AMERICAN WIND SYMPHONY WORKSHOP AND CONCERT - DE. THE AMERICAN WIND SYMPHONY ORCHESTRA WILL CONDUCT A WORKSHOP AND PERFORM AT THE CHRISTINA COMMUNITY CENTER. (ST-WIDE). JOHN S MICKEY, CHAIRMAN; DELAWARE ARBC; PO BOX 2476; WILMINGTON, DE 19899. (#13447). **ARBA GRANTEE.**

ANNUAL SPELLING BEE IN WILMINGTON, DE. A SPELLING BEE WHICH SEEKS TO IMPROVE THE LANGUAGE-ARTS SKILLS OF ELEMENTARY SCHOOL CHILDREN WITH MOTIVATIONAL INCENTIVES FOR ATTAINING EXCELLENCE IN ACADEMIC PERFORMANCE. (LOCAL). JOSEPH V WILLIAMS, JR; KAPPA ALPHA PSI FRATERNITY; 3304 WASHINGTON ST; WILMINGTON, DE 19802. (#13643). **ARBA GRANTEE.**

BICENTENNIAL MARIONETTE PLAYS - WILMINGTON, DE. MARIONETTE PLAYS WILL BE PRESENTED IN THE STATE AT VARIOUS SCHOOLS AND INSTITUTIONS. CHILDREN OF ST MARY MAGDALEN SCHOOL WILL MAKE PROPS COSTUMES, ETC AND WILL MANIPULATE THE MARIONETTES. (ST-WIDE). MRS MARIANNE GANDOLFO, INSTRUCTOR; ST MARY MAGDALEN SCHOOL; 7 SHARPLEY RD; WILMINGTON, DE 19803. (#27086). **ARBA GRANTEE.**

BICENTENNIAL METROSCOPE IN WILMINGTON, DE. INTERCULTURAL EDUCATIONAL PROGRAM INVOLVING YOUTH IN VARIOUS AREAS; INCLUDED WILL BE TEACHING MATERIALS SUCH AS CALENDARS, GUIDE BOOKS, SLIDE PRESENTATIONS AND MAPS. (LOCAL). CYNTHIA H BURT, PROGRAM COORDINATOR; DELAWARE STATES ARTS COUNCIL; 1105 MARKET ST; WILMINGTON, DE 19807. (#22834). **ARBA GRANTEE.**

BICENTENNIAL PLAYWRITING CONTEST PROJECT -DELAWARE. PROJECT IS AN ORIGINAL PLAYWRITING CONTEST WITH THEMATIC MATERIAL CONCERNING DELAWARE'S PART IN THE FOUNDING OF THE NATION. (ST-WIDE). MABEL W HENRY, PRESIDENT; DELAWARE THEATRE ASSOCIATION; 99 W PARK PL; NEWARK, DE 19711. (#1341). **ARBA GRANTEE.**

BLACK HERITAGE UNFOLDS IN WILMINGTON, DE. A PRODUCTION OF AN AUDIO-VISUAL PRESENTATION OF THE HISTORY OF THE BLACK PEOPLE OF DELAWARE. (ST-WIDE). MURIEL F COOPER, DISTRICT CHAIRPERSON; WILMINGTON HIGH SCHOOL, WILMINGTON PUBLIC SCHOOL DISTRICT; DUPONT RD; WILMINGTON, DE 19805. (#11153). **ARBA GRANTEE.**

BLACK LIFE AND PEOPLE IN DELAWARE. 10 PAINTINGS DEPICTING BLACK LIFE AND HISTORY WILL BE COMMISSIONED FOR EXHIBITION THROUGHOUT THE STATE. (ST-WIDE). HARMON R CAREY, EXEC DIRECTOR; DEL KING MEMORIAL FOUNDATION, INC; 2414 MARKET ST; WILMINGTON, DE 19802. (#22075). **ARBA GRANTEE.**

BOOK ON OUTSTANDING MOTHERS, DE. BOOK HONORING OUTSTANDING MOTHERS FROM EACH STATE ENTITLED 'MOTHERS OF ACHIEVEMENT IN AMERICAN HISTORY, 1776 - 1976.'. (NAT'L). RUTH M CANN, CHAIRMAN FOR DELAWARE; AMERICAN MOTHERS COMMITTEE; 2401 PENNSYLVANIA AVE; WILMINGTON, DE 19806. (#24730). **ARBA GRANTEE.**

CANTATA: 'IN FREEDOM'S LIGHT' - WILMINGTON, DE. CELEBRATION OF THE BICENTENNIAL THROUGH SONG. (LOCAL). RABBI DAVID GEFFEN, PROJ DIRECTOR; CONGREGATION BETH SHALOM; 18TH & BAYNARD BLVD; WILMINGTON, DE 19802. (#21862). **ARBA GRANTEE.**

'CARCROFT - NOW AND THEN', DE. THE CARCROFT ELEMENTARY SCHOOL WILL INVOLVE THEIR STUDENTS IN AN INQUIRY INTO THE HISTORY OF THEIR FAMILIES, SCHOOL AND COMMUNITY, TO MAKE THEM AWARE OF THEIR HERITAGE. (LOCAL). THOMAS D CHILDREY, PROJ DIRECTOR; MOUNT PLEASANT SCHOOL DISTRICT; 503 CREST RD; WILMINGTON, DE 19803. (#11159). **ARBA GRANTEE.**

CATALOG OF AMER PAINTINGS & SCULPTURE - DELAWARE. RESEARCH & PUBLICATION OF SIGNIFICANT AMERICAN PAINTINGS & SCULPTURE IN THE DELAWARE ART MUSEUM COLLECTION. (NAT'L). ELIZABETH HAWKES, ASSISTANT CURATOR; DELAWARE ART MUSEUM; 2301 KENTMERE PARKWAY; WILMINGTON, DE 19806. (#1570).

'COME ALL', CHILDREN'S BOOK IN WILMINGTON, DE. 'COME ALL', IS A COMPILATION OF ELEMENTARY SCHOOL CHILDREN'S STORIES AND ILLUSTRATIONS, TELLING HOW THEY FEEL ABOUT DIFFERENT ASPECTS OF WILMINGTON, DELAWARE AND AMERICA. (LOCAL). MURIEL F COOPER, PROJ COORDINATOR; WILMINGTON PUBLIC SCHOOL DISTRICT; WILMINGTON, DE 19801. (#11149). **ARBA GRANTEE.**

CONSERVATION - WILMINGTON, DE. CONSERVATION TREATMENT OF WORKS OF ART OF PAPER FROM THE PERMANENT COLLECTION OF THE DELAWARE ART MUSEUM. (LOCAL). ROWLAND ELZEA, CURATOR OF COLLECTIONS; DELAWARE ART MUSEUM; 2301 KENTMERE PKY; WILMINGTON, DE 19806. (#21127).

DELAWARE BICENTENNIAL PARTICIPATION PROGRAM. THEME OF 'DELAWARE '76', ENCOMPASSING TOTAL CELEBRATION WITH STATE OFFICIALLY RECOGNIZED & SUPPORTING EVENTS RELATING TO APPROPRIATE MONTHLY THEMES FROM SEPT. 1975 TO SEPT. 1976. (ST-WIDE). JOHN S MICKEY, EXEC DIRECTOR; DELAWARE ARBC; PO BOX 2476; WILMINGTON, DE 19899. (#942). **ARBA GRANTEE.**

THE DELAWARE OFFICE WORKER IN COLONIAL TIMES. A BOOK DESCRIBING THE TYPICAL CONDITIONS UNDER WHICH OFFICE WORKERS WORKED DURING THE COLONIAL PERIOD IN DELAWARE. (ST-WIDE). WILLIAM G OTT, EXEC VICE-PRESIDENT; GOLDEY BEACOM COLLEGE; 4701 LIMESTONE RD; WILMINGTON, DE 19808. (#11167). **ARBA GRANTEE.**

ETHNIC ENCLAVE - WILMINGTON SQUARE, DELAWARE. REHABILITION OF HISTORIC HOUSES, CNTR FOR PERFORMING ARTS, HISTORY MUSIC, ARTS & CRAFTS REPRESENTING LIVE CONTRIBUTIONS TO WILMINGTON & DELAWARE, REPRESENTING ALL ETHNIC GROUPS IN DELAWARE. (LOCAL). DALE FIELDS, EXEC DIRECTOR; HISTORICAL SOCIETY OF DELAWARE; 505 MARKET ST; WILMINGTON, DE 19801. (#7822).

FESTIVAL USA - PROJ OF WILMINGTON, DE. OLD MILL LANE PTA WILL ORGANIZE A NEIGHBORHOOD FESTIVAL TITLED FESTIVAL USA. THE THEME WILL BE THE RECREATION OF EVENTS LEADING TO AND CULMINATING IN THE AMERICAN REVOLUTION. (LOCAL). ALLEN R DEVER, PRESIDENT; OLD MILL LANE SCHOOL PTA; OLD MILL LANE; WILMINGTON, DE 19803. (#11990). **ARBA GRANTEE.**

FILM SERIES - 'WILMINGTON UP TO NOW' - DE. MOUNT PLEASANT SEVENTH AND EIGHTH GRADE STUDENTS WILL PRODUCE SOUND FILMS TRACING THE HISTORY AND CULTURE OF WILMINGTON. (LOCAL). HAROLD M LEWIS, CHAIRMAN; MOUNT PLEASANT INTERMEDIATE SCHOOL; DUNCAN RD; WILMINGTON, DE 19809. (#13704). **ARBA GRANTEE.**

FOLK HEROES AND LEGENDS OF AMERICA AND DELAWARE. STUDENTS OF BAYARD SCHOOL WILL BECOME INVOLVED IN LEARNING ABOUT THE GROWTH AND DEVELOPMENT OF OUR NATION AND STATE THROUGH LITERATURE, SONGS, DANCE AND DRAMATICS. (LOCAL). MURIEL COOPER, DISTRICT CHAIRPERSON; WILMINGTON PUBLIC SCHOOL DISTRICT; BAYARD MIDDLE SCHOOL; WILMINGTON, DE 19801. (#11151). **ARBA GRANTEE.**

FRANCE VIEWS AMERICA, 1750-1800 -PROJ OF DELAWARE. EXHIBIT AND CATALOGUE ON HOW FRANCE SAW AMERICA IN REVOLUTION ERA. DOCUMENTS, IMPRINTS, ARTIFACTS & GRAPHICS ON THEMES DECORATIVE ARTS, GOVERNMENT, TRADE, TECHNOLOGY, NATURAL HISTORY & LITERATURE. (NAT'L). DR RICHMOND D WILLIAMS, LIBRARY DIRECTOR; ELEUTHERIAN MILLS HISTORICAL LIBRARY; GREENVILLE, DE 19807. (#3183).

HERITAGE 76 - PROJ OF WILMINGTON, DE. A PAGEANT PREPARED BY STUDENTS AND TEACHERS WILL CONSIST OF A FOURTH AND FIFTH GRADE PRESENTATION OF UNITED STATES HISTORY EMPHASIZING THE BUILDING OF THE NATION. (LOCAL). CHARLES T CHRISTINE, PRINCIPAL; OLD MILL LANE ELEMENTARY SCHOOL; OLD MILL LANE; WILMINGTON, DE 19803. (#11989). **ARBA GRANTEE.**

HISTORY OF DELAWARE. DR JOHN A MONROE HAS BEEN COMMISSIONED TO PREPARE A SCHOLARLY HISTORY OF DELAWARE IN CONJUNCTION WITH THE BICENTENNIAL. (ST-WIDE). LOUISE L PRICKETT, EXECUTIVE DIRECTOR; DELAWARE AMERICAN REVOLUTION BICENTENNIAL COMMISSION; PO BOX 2476; WILMINGTON, DE 19899. (#6483). **ARBA GRANTEE.**

A HUMANITIES FESTIVAL TO CELEBRATE THE BICENT, DE. THE FINE ARTS DEPARTMENTS OF THE SCHOOLS WILL DESIGN AND CONSTRUCT RELEVANT PROJECTS INCLUDING ART, SCULPTURE AND WEAVING TO PERMANENTLY COMMEMORATE THE BICENTENNIAL. (LOCAL). CARROLL W BIGGS, SUPERINTENDENT OF SCHOOLS; ALFRED I DUPONT SCHOOL DISTRICT; 4 MT LEBANON RD; WILMINGTON, DE 19803. (#11045). **ARBA GRANTEE.**

LIBERTY AND INDEPENDENCE - WILMINGTON, DE. PUBLICATION ON DELAWARE DURING REVOLUTIONARY PERIOD. (ST-WIDE). LOUISE PRICKETT, COORDINATOR; DELAWARE AMERICAN REVOLUTION BICENTENNIAL COMMISSION; PO BOX 2476; WILMINGTON, DE 19899. (#26925).

MUSIC OF BLACK AND WHITE COMPOSERS IN AMERICA, DE. THE MUSIC OF BLACK AND WHITE AMERICAN COMPOSERS WILL BE PERFORMED & RECORDED BY STUDENTS OF THE WILMINGTON PUBLIC SCHOOL DISTRICT. (LOCAL). MURIEL F COOPER, CHAIRPERSON; WILMINGTON PUBLIC SCHOOL DISTRICT; 1400 WASHINGTON; WILMINGTON, DE 19801. (#11154). **ARBA GRANTEE.**

NEW CASTLE COUNTY BICENTENNIAL PROJECTS. A COMPREHENSIVE PROGRAM FOR THE COUNTY OF NEW CASTLE INCLUDING THE CREATION OF A PARK AT THE REVOLUTIONARY WAR SITE, IRON HILL; A BICENT BAND TWO GALA 4TH OF JULY CELEBRATIONS VARIOUS OTHER EVENTS. (ST-WIDE). BETTY MITCHELL, CHAIRPERSON; NEW CASTLE COUNTY BICENTENNIAL COMMITTEE; 1314 KING ST; WILMINGTON, DE 19801. (#17862). **ARBA GRANTEE.**

OLD SWEDES PARK, WILMINGTON, DE. REDEVELOPMENT OF PARK AREA NEXT TO OLD SWEDES CHURCH, A NATIONAL HISTORIC LANDMARK. (REGN'L). JACK M MCKELVEY, VICAR & SECRETARY; HOLY TRINITY (OLD SWEDES) CHURCH FOUNDATION, INC; 606 CHURCH ST; WILMINGTON, DE 19801. (#22086). **ARBA GRANTEE.**

POLISH DAY CELEBRATION - WILMINGTON, DE. HISTORIC COMMEMORATIVE CELEBRATION EMPHASIZING POLISH HERITAGE IN DELAWARE'S HISTORY. (LOCAL). HELEN KILCZEWSKI, CHAIRMAN; CAPT S MLOTKOWSKI MEMORIAL BRIGADE SOCIETY; 247 PHILADELPHIA PIKE; WILMINGTON, DE 19809. (#22145). **ARBA GRANTEE.**

PRE-RAPHAELITISM & ITS INFLUENCE, WILMINGTON, DE. EXHIBITION EXAMINING THE EFFECTS OF PRE-RAPHAELITE ART ON ENGLISH & AMERICAN FINE & DECORATIVE ART IN THE LAST HALF OF THE 19TH CENTURY. (REGN'L). ROWLAND ELZEA, CURATOR; DELAWARE ART MUSEUM; 2301 KENTMERE PKWY; WILMINGTON, DE 19806. (#6190).

SALUTE TO DELAWARE WOMEN - WILMINGTON, DE. SOFT-BOUND BOOK CONTAINING BIOGRAPHICAL SKETCHES OF ABOUT 150 DELAWARE WOMEN WHO HAVE GAINED A PLACE IN DELAWARE'S HISTORY. (ST-WIDE). DOROTHY HANDE, DIRECTOR; CHESAPEAKE BAY GIRL SCOUT COUNCIL, INC; 1503 W 13TH ST; WILMINGTON, DE 19806. (#20233). **ARBA GRANTEE.**

SHORTLIDGE IN ACTION FOR THE BICENTENNIAL, DE. A MOVIE OF CHILDREN'S ACTIVITIES AT VARIOUS STAGES OF THE TOTAL SCHOOL BICENTENNIAL EFFORT. (LOCAL). MURIEL F COOPER, CHAIRPERSON; WILMINGTON PUBLIC SCHOOL DISTRICT; WILMINGTON, DE 19899. (#11150). **ARBA GRANTEE.**

STANTON COUNTY RESOURCE PROJECT, DE. THE PROJECT INVOLVES LOCATING, COLLECTING, ORGANIZING AND DESSEMINATING INFORMATION ABOUT COMMUNITY HISTORY. (LOCAL). GEORGE K MCDOWELL, PROJ DIRECTOR; STANTON SCHOOL DISTRICT; 1800 LIMESTONE RD; WILMINGTON, DE 19804. (#11895). **ARBA GRANTEE.**

THE VISUAL ARTS, CATALYST FOR LEARNING, DE. AN EXHIBIT OF ART WORK BY CHILDREN OF ALL AGES, PRESENTLY ATTENDING WILMINGTON PUBLIC SCHOOLS. THIS EXHIBIT WILL PROMOTE THE DELAWARE BICENTENNIAL'S 'SALUTE TO YOUTH AND EDUCATION.'. (LOCAL). ROBERT MOORE, SUPERVISOR OF ART EDUCATION; WILMINGTON PUBLIC SCHOOL DISTRICT; 1400 WASHINGTON; WILMINGTON, DE 19899. (#11155). **ARBA GRANTEE.**

WILMINGTON PUBLIC SCHOOLS BICENTENNIAL PROGRAM, DE. DRAMA FILM FESTIVAL, BOOK, RECORDING & ART EXHIBITS THROUGHOUT THE SCHOOL SYSTEM. (LOCAL). JOHN S MICKEY, PROJ DIRECTOR; DELAWARE AMERICAN REVOLUTION BICENTENNIAL COMMITTEE; PO BOX 2476; WILMINGTON, DE 19899. (#18601). **ARBA GRANTEE.**

WORLD PREMIERE OPERA 'LAST OF THE MOHICANS' IN DE. THE OPERA IS BASED ON J FENIMORE COOPER'S NOVEL ABOUT THE FRENCH AND INDIAN WARS. (LOCAL). ERIC W KJELLMARK, JR, PRESIDENT; WILMINGTON OPERA SOCIETY INC; BOX 3553; GREENVILLE, DE 19807. (#10994).

NOV 1 - 3, '73. ROLE OF IMMIGRANTS IN USA INDUSTRIAL DEVELOPMENT - CONFERENCE. FOCUS ON THE ROLE OF IMMIGRANTS IN THE INDUSTRIAL DEVELOPMENT OF THE UNITED STATES, TO BE HELD AT THE ELEVTHERIAN MILLS HISTORICAL LIBRARY. (NAT'L). PHILIP F. MOONEY, ASSISTA; THE BALCH INSTITUTE; 1627 FIDELITY BLDG. 123 S BROAD; PHILADELPHIA, PA 19109. (#295-901).

WILMINGTON — CONTINUED

APR 1 - 4, '75. AMERICAN FREEDOM TRAIN DISPLAY DAYS START AT WILMINGTON, DELAWARE. THE AMERICAN FREEDOM TRAIN WILL INCLUDE 10 EXHIBIT CARS & 2 SHOWCASE CARS DEPICTING DIFFERENT PHASES OF THE AMERICAN EXPERIENCE. ITS ARRIVAL WILL SERVE AS A CATALYST FOR LOCAL BICENTENNIAL CELEBRATIONS BY PEOPLE THROUGHOUT THIS NATION. (ST-WIDE). SY FREEDMAN, DIR OF P/R; THE AMERICAN FREEDOM TRAIN FOUNDATION; 5205 LEESBURG PIKE, SUITE 800; BAILEY'S XRDS, VA 22041. (#1776-135).

APR 23 - MAY 1, '75. BICENTENNIAL PLAYWRITING CONTEST. PROJECT IS AN ORIGINAL PLAYWRITING CONTEST WITH THEMATIC MATERIAL CONCERNING DELAWARE'S PART IN THE FOUNDING OF THE NATION. AT PATCHWORK PLAYHOUSE & DOVER MIDDLE SCHOOL. (ST-WIDE). MABEL W HENRY, PRESIDENT; DELAWARE THEATRE ASSOCIATION; 99 W PARK PL; NEWARK, DE 19711. (#1341-1).

SEPT 3, '75. GALA OPENING OF THE DELAWARE BICENTENNIAL COMMEMORATION. THEME OF 'DELAWARE '76', ENCOMPASSING TOTAL CELEBRATION WITH STATE OFFICIALLY RECOGNIZED & SUPPORTING EVENTS RELATING TO APPROPRIATE MONTHLY THEMES FROM SEPT. 1975 TO SEPT. 1976. (ST-WIDE). MS LOUISE L PRICKETT; DELAWARE ARBC; PO BOX 2476; WILMINGTON, DE 19899. (#942-501).

OCT 1 - 31, '75. SPECIAL PROGRAMS HONORING ETHNIC HERITAGE. DELAWARE BICENTENNIAL PARTICIPATION PROGRAM. THEME OF 'DELAWARE '76', ENCOMPASSING TOTAL CELEBRATION WITH STATE OFFICIALLY RECOGNIZED & SUPPORTING EVENTS RELATING TO APPROPRIATE MONTHLY THEMES FROM SEPT. 1975 TO SEPT. 1976. (ST-WIDE). MS LOUISE L PRICKETT; DELAWARE ARBC; PO BOX 2476; WILMINGTON, DE 19899. (#942-502).

OCT 4, '75. PARADE. PARADE AT FOULK RD & NAAMANS RD. (LOCAL). HAL SCHIFF, COORDINATOR; ALFRED I DUPONT SCHOOL DISTRICT; 4 MT LEBANON RD; WILMINGTON, DE 19803. (#200009-2).

OCT 18, '75. FESTIVAL USA. OLD MILL LANE PTA WILL ORGANIZE A NEIGHBORHOOD FESTIVAL TITLED FESTIVAL USA. THE THEME WILL BE THE RECREATION OF EVENTS LEADING TO AND CULMINATING IN THE AMERICAN REVOLUTION. AT OLD MILL LANE SCHOOL. (LOCAL). TOM MEIER, PRESIDENT; OLD MILL LANE SCHOOL PTA; OLD MILL LANE; WILMINGTON, DE 19803. (#11990-1).

OCT 20 - NOV 9, '75. THE VISUAL ARTS, CATALYST FOR LEARNING, EXHIBIT OF CHILDREN'S WORK. AN EXHIBIT OF ART WORK BY WILMINGTON PUBLIC SCHOOL STUDENTS; IT WILL PROMOTE DE BICENT 'SALUTE TO YOUTH & EDUCATION'. THEME: ART EDUCATION'S CONTRIBUTION TO YOUTH'S GROWTH, KNOWLEDGE & SELF-IMAGE. SAT: 9:30-11 AM; TUES, WED & THURS EVE: 7:30-10 PM. AT DELAWARE ART MUSEUM, EDUCATIONAL WING, 2301 KENTMERE PWY. (LOCAL). ROBERT MOORE, ART SUPV; WILMINGTON PUBLIC SCHOOL DISTRICT; 1400 WASHINGTON; WILMINGTON, DE 19899. (#11155-1).

NOV 1 - 30, '75. SALUTE TO YOUTH & EDUCATION, WITH GIANT YOUTH PARADES IN STATE. DELAWARE BICENTENNIAL PARTICIPATION PROGRAM. THEME OF 'DELAWARE '76', ENCOMPASSING TOTAL CELEBRATION WITH STATE OFFICIALLY RECOGNIZED & SUPPORTING EVENTS RELATING TO APPROPRIATE MONTHLY THEMES FROM SEPT. 1975 TO SEPT. 1976. (ST-WIDE). MS LOUISE L PRICKETT; DELAWARE ARBC; PO BOX 2476; WILMINGTON, DE 19899. (#942-503).

DEC 1 - 31, '75. RELIGIOUS OBSERVANCES, INCL HANDEL'S 'MESSIAH' BY SYMPHONY ORCHESTRA. DELAWARE BICENTENNIAL PARTICIPATION PROGRAM. THEME OF 'DELAWARE '76', ENCOMPASSING TOTAL CELEBRATION WITH STATE OFFICIALLY RECOGNIZED & SUPPORTING EVENTS RELATING TO APPROPRIATE MONTHLY THEMES FROM SEPT. 1975 TO SEPT. 1976. (ST-WIDE). MS LOUISE L PRICKETT; DELAWARE ARBC; PO BOX 2476; WILMINGTON, DE 19899. (#942-504).

FEB 22, '76. WASHINGTON'S BIRTHDAY BALL IN EACH COUNTY OF DELAWARE. DELAWARE BICENTENNIAL PARTICIPATION PROGRAM. THEME OF 'DELAWARE '76', ENCOMPASSING TOTAL CELEBRATION WITH STATE OFFICIALLY RECOGNIZED & SUPPORTING EVENTS RELATING TO APPROPRIATE MONTHLY THEMES FROM SEPT. 1975 TO SEPT. 1976. (ST-WIDE). MS LOUISE L PRICKETT; DELAWARE ARBC; PO BOX 2476; WILMINGTON, DE 19899. (#942-506).

MAR 1 - 31, '76. BICENT HISTORICAL FASHIONS EXTRAVAGANZA-200 YRS OF FASHION IN DEL. DELAWARE BICENTENNIAL PARTICIPATION PROGRAM. THEME OF 'DELAWARE '76', ENCOMPASSING TOTAL CELEBRATION WITH STATE OFFICIALLY RECOGNIZED & SUPPORTING EVENTS RELATING TO APPROPRIATE MONTHLY THEMES FROM SEPT. 1975 TO SEPT. 1976. (ST-WIDE). MS LOUISE L PRICKETT; DELAWARE ARBC; PO BOX 2476; WILMINGTON, DE 19899. (#942-507).

MAR 7, '76. CANTATA: 'IN FREEDOM'S LIGHT'. CELEBRATION OF THE BICENTENNIAL THROUGH SONG. AT BETH SHALOM SYNAGOGUE. (LOCAL). RABBI DAVID GEFFEN, DIR; CONGREGATION BETH SHALOM; 18TH & BAYNARD BLVD; WILMINGTON, DE 19802. (#21862-1).

APR 1 - 30, '76. BICENT FESTIVAL OF THE ARTS, SALUTING ALL ART FORMS. DELAWARE BICENTENNIAL PARTICIPATION PROGRAM. THEME OF 'DELAWARE '76', ENCOMPASSING TOTAL CELEBRATION WITH STATE OFFICIALLY RECOGNIZED & SUPPORTING EVENTS RELATING TO APPROPRIATE MONTHLY THEMES FROM SEPT. 1975 TO SEPT. 1976. (ST-WIDE). MS LOUISE L PRICKETT; DELAWARE ARBC; PO BOX 2476; WILMINGTON, DE 19899. (#942-508).

APR 9 - MAY 30, '76. EXHIBITION OF FINE AND APPLIED ART INFLUENCED BY PRE-RAPHAELITISM. EXHIBITION EXAMINING THE EFFECTS OF PRE-RAPHAELITE ART ON ENGLISH & AMERICAN FINE & DECORATIVE ART IN THE LAST HALF OF THE 19TH CENTURY. (REGN'L). ROWLAND ELZEA, CURATOR; DELAWARE ART MUSEUM; 2301 KENTMERE PKWY; WILMINGTON, DE 19806. (#6190-501).

APR 27 - MAY 27, '76. HUMANITIES FESTIVAL TO CELEBRATE BICENTENNIAL. UNVEILINGS OF SCULPTURES, MIXED MEDIA MURALS, TAPESTRIES, WOOD RELIEF SCULPTURE & QUILTED APPLIQUE. THESE OCCUR AT VARYING DATES AT DIFFERENT DISTRICT HIGH SCHOOLS. A BICENTENNIAL PARADE ON MAY 15, 1976 AS PART OF DIST PTA FAIR. AT VARIOUS HIGH SCHOOLS IN DISTRICT. (LOCAL). CARROLL W BIGGS; ALFRED I DUPONT SCHOOL DISTRICT; 4 MT LEBANON RD; WILMINGTON, DE 19803. (#11045-1).

APR 28, '76. HERITAGE '76 PAGEANT. A PAGEANT PREPARED BY STUDENTS AND TEACHERS WILL CONSIST OF A FOURTH AND FIFTH GRADE PRESENTATION OF UNITED STATES HISTORY EMPHASIZING THE BUILDING OF THE NATION. AT OLD MILL LANE SCHOOL. (LOCAL). CHARLES T CHRISTINE; OLD MILL LANE ELEMENTARY SCHOOL; OLD MILL LANE; WILMINGTON, DE 19803. (#11989-1).

MAY 1 - 31, '76. DELAWARE'S SPORT FESTIVAL WITH AMATEUR GROUPS FROM ALL OVER STATE. DELAWARE BICENTENNIAL PARTICIPATION PROGRAM. THEME OF 'DELAWARE '76', ENCOMPASSING TOTAL CELEBRATION WITH STATE OFFICIALLY RECOGNIZED & SUPPORTING EVENTS RELATING TO APPROPRIATE MONTHLY THEMES FROM SEPT. 1975 TO SEPT. 1976. (ST-WIDE). MS LOUISE L PRICKETT; DELAWARE ARBC; PO BOX 2476; WILMINGTON, DE 19899. (#942-509).

MAY 10, '76 - DEC 31, '77. 'WILMINGTON 1876' - EXHIBIT. OPEN SUNDAYS 1-5; RESERVATIONS REQUIRED FOR GROUP TOURS. AT HAGLEY MUSEUM, RTE 141. (REGN'L). LIBBA SEVISON, CHMN; HAGLEY MUSEUM; GREENVILLE; WILMINGTON, DE 19807. (#103667-1).

MAY 22 - 23, '76. HANDMADE HERITAGE : AN EXPOSITION OF AMERICAN CRAFTS. CRAFTSPEOPLE MARKET THEIR WORK DURING 2-DAY CELEBRATION OF THE HANDMADE OBJECT & ITS CREATION. VISITING ARTISTS, DEMONSTRATIONS; CONCERTS BY THE RED CLAY RAMBLERS, OLD-TIME BAND FROM NORTH CAROLINA. AT CAROUSEL FARM, A NEW CASTLE CO PARK. (ST-WIDE). KATHRYN KERR, COORD; NEW CASTLE COUNTY DEPT OF PARKS & RECREATION; 310 KIAMENSI RD; WILMINGTON, DE 19808. (#106308-1).

JUNE 6, '76. CANTATA: 'IN FREEDOM'S LIGHT'. CELEBRATION OF THE BICENTENNIAL THROUGH SONG. AT WILMINGTON MALL ON MARKET STREET. (LOCAL). RABBI DAVID GEFFEN, DIR; CONGREGATION BETH SHALOM; 18TH & BAYNARD BLVD; WILMINGTON, DE 19802. (#21862-3).

JUNE 8, '76. AMERICCAN WIND SYMPHONY'S FLOATING ARTS CENTER VISITS WILMINGTON. EMBARKING UPON A BICENTENNIAL CULTURAL TOUR, THE WIND SYMPHONY WILL VISIT 76 CITIES BRINGING MUSIC, DANCE, SYMPOSIA AND CHILDREN'S THEATRE TO THE WATERWAYS OF AMERICA DURING ITS 6-MONTHS TOUR. (NAT'L). PAULA BERN; AMERICAN WIND SYMPHONY ORCHESTRA OF WESTERN PA; GATEWAY TOWERS 18G; PITTSBURGH, PA 15222. (#2800-14).

JUNE 12 - 26, '76. WORLD PREMIER OF OPERA 'LAST OF THE MOHICANS'. FOUR PERFORMANCES WILMINGTON; WORLD PREMIER SAT JUNE 12& SIX OTHERS ON JUNE 16, 18, 20; ONE SHOW MILFORD, DEL, JUNE 26. SIX TO COMMEMORATE OPENING OF NEWLY RESTORED GRAND OPERA HOUSE IN WILMINGTON AS WELL AS THE BICENTENNIAL. AT GRAND OPERA HOUSE & MILFORD HIGH SCHOOL. (REGN'L). ERIC W KJELLMARK; WILMINGTON OPERA SOCIETY INC; PO BOX 3553; GREENVILLE, DE 19807. (#8526-1).

JUNE 13, '76. POLISH DAY CELEBRATION. HISTORIC COMMEMORATIVE CELEBRATION EMPHASIZING POLISH HERITAGE IN DELAWARE'S HISTORY. AT FORT DELAWARE PEA PATCH ISLAND, DELAWARE CITY. (LOCAL). HELEN KILCZEWSKI, CHMN; CAPT S MLOTKOWSKI MEMORIAL BRIGADE SOCIETY; 247 PHILADELPHIA PIKE; WILMINGTON, DE 19809. (#22145-1).

JULY 1 - 2, '76. RE-ENACTMENT OF CAESAR RODNEY'S RIDE TO VOTE FOR INDEPENDENCE. DELAWARE BICENTENNIAL PARTICIPATION PROGRAM. THEME OF 'DELAWARE '76', ENCOMPASSING TOTAL CELEBRATION WITH STATE OFFICIALLY RECOGNIZED & SUPPORTING EVENTS RELATING TO APPROPRIATE MONTHLY THEMES FROM SEPT. 1975 TO SEPT. 1976. (ST-WIDE). MS LOUISE L PRICKETT; DELAWARE ARBC; PO BOX 2476; WILMINGTON, DE 19899. (#942-514).

JULY 4, '76. NEW CASTLE COUNTY BICENTENNIAL CELEBRATION - GALA 4TH OF JULY. SPECTACULAR EAST COAST INDEPENDENCE DAY CELEBRATION FEATURES MILITARY DISPLAY, AIR SHOW, AND FIREWORKS. AT GREATER WILMINGTON AIRPORT. (REGN'L). AL CAMPAGNONE, DIR; NEW CASTLE COUNTY BICENTENNIAL COMMITTEE; 1314 KING ST; WILMINGTON, DE 19801. (#17862-1).

JULY 29, '76. SALUTE TO INDEPENDENCE-BICENT SPECTACULAR AT STATE FAIR. DELAWARE BICENTENNIAL PARTICIPATION PROGRAM. THEME OF 'DELAWARE '76', ENCOMPASSING TOTAL CELEBRATION WITH STATE OFFICIALLY RECOGNIZED & SUPPORTING EVENTS RELATING TO APPROPRIATE MONTHLY THEMES FROM SEPT. 1975 TO SEPT. 1976. (ST-WIDE). MS LOUISE L PRICKETT; DELAWARE ARBC; PO BOX 2476; WILMINGTON, DE 19899. (#942-511).

AUG 1 - 31, '76. OPEN HOUSE DELAWARE-FOCUS ON STATE TOURIST ATTRACTIONS. DELAWARE BICENTENNIAL PARTICIPATION PROGRAM. THEME OF 'DELAWARE '76', ENCOMPASSING TOTAL CELEBRATION WITH STATE OFFICIALLY RECOGNIZED & SUPPORTING EVENTS RELATING TO APPROPRIATE MONTHLY THEMES FROM SEPT. 1975 TO SEPT. 1976. (ST-WIDE). MS LOUISE L PRICKETT; DELAWARE ARBC; PO BOX 2476; WILMINGTON, DE 19899. (#942-512).

AUG 25, '76. OLD TIMERS' PICNIC - ENTERTAINMENT FOR SENIOR CITIZENS. NEW CASTLE COUNTY, DELAWARE - OLD TIMERS' PICNIC. ANNUAL PICNIC FOR SENIOR CITIZENS OF DELAWARE. PICNIC LUNCHES, ENTERTAINMENT, CELEBRATION FOR THOSE WITH GOLDEN ANNIVERSARIES. RAIN DATE ON AUGUST 26TH, 1976. (LOCAL). PAMELA DUKE, SUPERVISOR; NEW CASTLE COUNTY DEPT OF PARKS AND RECREATION; 310 KIAMENSI RD; WILMINGTON, DE 19808. (#2815-501).

SEPT 1 - 30, '76. SALUTE TO THE FUTURE-BURIAL OF TIME CAPSULE TO BE OPENED IN 2076. DELAWARE BICENTENNIAL PARTICIPATION PROGRAM. THEME OF 'DELAWARE '76', ENCOMPASSING TOTAL CELEBRATION WITH STATE OFFICIALLY RECOGNIZED & SUPPORTING EVENTS RELATING TO APPROPRIATE MONTHLY THEMES FROM SEPT. 1975 TO SEPT. 1976. (ST-WIDE). MS LOUISE L PRICKETT; DELAWARE ARBC; PO BOX 2476; WILMINGTON, DE 19899. (#942-513).

SEPT 11 - 12, '76. 16TH ANNUAL BRANDYWINE ARTS FESTIVAL. FESTIVAL, EXHIBIT AT JOSEPHINE GARDENS, NORTH BRANDYWINE PARK. (ST-WIDE). DIRECTOR; RECREATION PROMOTION & SERVICE, INC; WILMINGTON, DE 19899. (#103416-526).

WINTERTHUR

CATALOGUE OF AMERICAN FURNITURE. PROJECT TO PRODUCE A DEFINITIVE CATALOGUE OF FURNITURE IN 17TH CENTURY & WILLIAM & MARY STYLES, AT THE WINTERTHUR MUSEUM, THE FORMER HOME OF HENRY FRANCIS DUPONT. (ST-WIDE). IAN M G QUIMBY, EDITOR; THE HENRY FRANCIS DUPONT WINTERTHUR MUSEUM INC; WINTERTHUR, DE 19735. (#6502).

WOODSIDE

A HISTORY OF THE TOWN OF WOODSIDE, DELAWARE. A HISTORY OF THE TOWN OF WOODSIDE WILL BE PUBLISHED TO INCREASE THE LOCAL AWARENESS. (LOCAL). SAMUEL G THOMAS, CHAIRMAN; KENT COUNTY-LEVY COURT BICENT COMMITTEE; THE GREEN; DOVER, DE 19901. (#9751). **ARBA GRANTEE.**

District of Columbia

WASHINGTON 76

District of Columbia Bicentennial Commission and Assembly

Established May 21, 1975 by Mayor's Order 75-106. The commission worked with foundations, corporate and business groups and shared responsibility for the celebration with the assembly, which worked with neighborhood and civic groups.

ARBA Statistics

Officially Recognized
Communities—1
Colleges/Universities—2
Military Installations—8
BINET Projects—640
Events—615
1976 Population—702,000

Bicentennial Archives

Office of the Secretariat
Executive Office of the Mayor
Washington, D.C. 20004

Membership

Commission Board

Adelaide Clark, *president*
Charles Norberg, *vice president*
Elwood Davis
Lee Folger
Patrick Hayes
John Kinard
Bill Lucy

Commission Members

George Apperson
Donald S. Bittinger
Edward Burling, Jr.
Marie Cunningham
Joseph P. Danzansky
Charles T. Duncan
Robert Ewell
Philip Hammer
John W. Hechinger
Ron M. Linton
R. Grayson McGuire, Jr.
Edward Murphy
Mary Pett
Flaxie Pinkett
Dr. Margaret Reuss
Emmett Rice
Charles Richardson
Helen Smith
Chauncey Thomas
James O. Thomas
The Right Reverend John T. Walker
Honorable Walter E. Fauntroy, *ex officio*
Honorable Sterling Tucker, *ex officio*
Honorable Walter E. Washington, *ex officio*

Assembly Officers

Leroy Washington, *chairperson*
Nathaniel Williams
Nathan Brossard
F. J. Payton
Steve Adams
Dick Brown
Daisy Powell
Orrin Cohill
William Carroll
Robert O'Hara

District of Columbia

In 1776, John Adams, commenting on future commemorations of American independence, wrote: "It ought to be commemorated as the day of deliverance, by solemn acts of devotion to God Almighty. It ought to be solemnized with pomp and parade, with shows, games, sports, guns, bells, bonfires, and illuminations, from one end of this continent to the other, from this time forward, forever more."

The celebration of the 200th birthday of the United States in the nation's capital offered all Americans the unprecedented opportunity to reevaluate the country's achievements, to consider the problems confronting us and to reflect upon our aspirations for the future. Not only was it a time for commemoration of our historic beginnings as a nation, but, in order to give real value and continued meaning to those principles by which the United States was founded, the Bicentennial also provided a spiritual reaffirmation.

Following the theme enunciated by President Adams, the Bicentennial celebration in Washington, D.C. focused on festivals and programs that reflected the rich culture and heritage

of our citizens, our city and our country. Exhibitions in Washington's museums and galleries of art, as well as the reenactments of famous events held in Washington's parks, recaptured the history of our country and its people. Bicentennial Washington also offered a series of concerts, songfests, religious meetings and special events on the grounds of the Washington Monument, Lincoln Memorial and Jefferson Memorial . . . songfests, ethnic arts performances and special events in the mini-parks of the city . . . commemorative performing arts productions from around the city, country and world . . . state days, territorial days and international days . . . boat and walking tours to fit every interest . . . and the national Children's Bicentennial Island, to be completed in 1977, an innovative park and recreation area that pioneers in specially designed play areas and facilities for the handicapped.

Bicentennial visitors to the nation's capital were greeted by the city's Junior Ambassadors, a corps of young people with information on where to eat, what to see and how to get places. Visitors were faced with the task of exercising freedom of choice, for in Washington they could explore the capital and the community, the historic and the contemporary, the familiar and the offbeat.

The Bicentennial celebration in the nation's capital came to a climax on the 3rd and 4th of July, 1976, with millions of people throughout the world witnessing in person and on television the special events and ceremonies, the parade and a display of fireworks the likes of which has never before been seen in Washington.

While the District of Columbia was indeed host to the nation, many programs existed for and by the people of the city. Many are ongoing into the third century, and responsibility for them has been moved to appropriate agencies within the D.C. government.

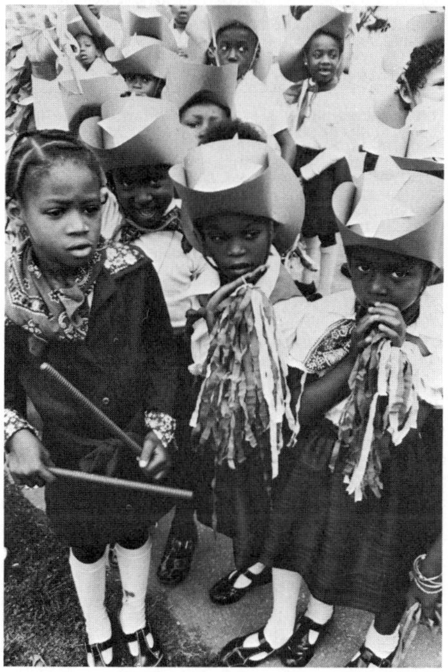

In retrospect, John Adams would have been proud of the manner in which the 200th birthday of American independence was celebrated in the city of Washington, D.C.

BOLLING AFB

MAY 8 - 15, '76. UNITED STATES ARMED FORCES BICENTENNIAL CARAVAN. CARAVAN IS COMPOSED OF EXHIBIT VANS FOR EACH MILITARY SERVICE. PROJECT THEME IS ' HISTORY OF THE ARMED FORCES & THEIR CONTRIBUTIONS TO THE NATION'. (LOCAL). COL MATHEW, USA, CHMN; U S ARMED FORCES BICENTENNIAL CARAVAN; FORT LESLIE J MCNAIR; WASHINGTON, DC 20004. (#1775-461).

WASHINGTON

ABA BANKING HISTORY EXHIBIT AT THE SMITHSONIAN. A WIDE RANGING SPECIAL EXHIBIT ON THE 200-YEAR HISTORY OF BANKING AND BANKING TECHNOLOGY IN THE NATIONAL MUSEUM OF HISTORY & TECHNOLOGY IN WASHINGTON, DC. (NAT'L). MICHAEL DELANEY, ASSOC DIRECTOR OF P/R; AMERICAN BANKERS ASSOC; 1120 CONNECTICUT AVE, NW; WASHINGTON, DC 20036. (#1795).

ABOVE GROUND ARCHAEOLOGY PROGRAM OF THE ARBA. ARBA PUBLICATION THAT DESCRIBES A PROGRAM DEVELOPED FOR JUNIOR AND SENIOR HIGH SCHOOL STUDENTS. THE ACTIVITY INVOLVES THE SEARCH FOR ARTIFACTS & OBJECTS RELATING TO OUR CULTURAL HERITAGE. (NAT'L). SUPERINTENDENT OF DOCUMENTS; US GOVERNMENT PRINTING OFFICE; WASHINGTON, DC 20402. (#1380).

ACADEMIC EXCHANGE FOR AMERICAN & DUTCH SCHOLARS. THE NETHERLANDS GOVERNMENT WILL MAKE FUNDS AVAILABLE FOR AN ACADEMIC EXCHANGE TO COLLABORATE ON A COMPARATIVE STUDY ON RECENT DEVELOPMENTS IN THE UNITED STATES AND THE NETHERLANDS. (INT'L). CULTURAL ATTACHE; EMBASSY OF THE NETHERLANDS; 4200 LINNEAN AVE; WASHINGTON, DC 20008. (#31871).

ADVENTURES IN AMERICAN OPERA PROJECT IN DC. A 45 MINUTE PROGRAM FOR ELEMENTARY SCHOOL CHILDREN TO ACQUAINT THEM WITH OPERA BY GREAT AMERICAN COMPOSERS. (LOCAL). MS CAROL STOWE, ARTISTIC ADMINISTRATOR; OPERA SOCIETY OF WASHINGTON; 2000 P ST, NW; WASHINGTON, DC 20007. (#5621).

ADVISORY SERVICES TO LOCAL HERITAGE ARTS PROJECTS. ADVISORY SERVICES, WORKSHOPS & EDUCATIONAL MATERIALS TO BE PROVIDED FOR COMMUNITY PROGRAMS NATIONALLY. (NAT'L). NANINE BILSKI, PROJECTS DIRECTOR; AMERICA THE BEAUTIFUL FUND; 219 SHOREHAM BLDG; WASHINGTON, DC 20005. (#7943). **ARBA RECOGNIZED. ARBA GRANTEE.**

AGRICULTURAL RESEARCH IN THE UNITED STATES OF AMER. A PUBLICATION FEATURING CONTRIBUTIONS OF AGRICULTURAL RESEARCH IN THE 200 YEARS OF AMERICA'S HISTORY. (NAT'L). ROBERT RATHBONE, DIRECTOR INFORMATION DIVISION; AGRICULTURAL RESEARCH SERVICE, US DEPARTMENT OF AGRICULTURE; 14TH & INDEPENDENCE AVE, SW; WASHINGTON, DC 20250. (#5574).

AHA BICENTENNIAL AWARD FOR FOREIGN SCHOLARS. THE AHA WILL OFFER A PRIZE IN 1976 FOR THE BEST HISTORICAL BOOK OR MANUSCRIPT, IN A LANGUAGE OTHER THAN ENGLISH, ON THE ERA OF THE AMERICAN REVOLUTION. WORK TO BE SUBMITTED BY 12/31/74. (INT'L). OFFICE OF THE EXECUTIVE SECRETARY; AMERICAN HISTORICAL ASSOCIATION; 400 A ST, SE; WASHINGTON, DC 20003. (#1565).

ALL THINGS CONSIDERED - PUBLIC RADIO BROADCASTS. NATIONAL PUBLIC RADIO HAS MADE AVAILABLE TO PUBLIC RADIO STATIONS NATIONWIDE TAPED PROGRAMS OF AMERICAN MUSIC, HISTORY & CULTURE W/ PLANS FOR EXPANDING & EXTENDING THE PROGRAMS FOR '75 & '76. (NAT'L). PRESLEY D HOLMES, VICE PRES; NATIONAL PUBLIC RADIO; 2025 M ST, NW; WASHINGTON, DC 20036. (#2843).

AMER BICENTENNIAL MUSIC PROJ FOR YOUNG PEOPLE - DC. PARTICIPATING SCHOOL GROUPS WILL PERFORM SELECTIONS FROM BICENTENNIAL MUSIC PROJECT UNITS AND SUBMIT PERFORMANCE TAPES FOR EVALUATION BY MUSIC PANEL. AWARDS WILL BE GIVEN FOR OUTSTANDING PERFORMANCES. (NAT'L). DR HAROLD ARBERG, BICENTENNIAL COORDINATOR; DEPT OF HEALTH, EDUCATION & WELFARE, OFFICE OF EDUCATION; 400 MARYLAND AVE, SW; WASHINGTON, DC 20202. (#14844).

AMER FOLK MUSIC RECORDED ANTHOLOGY-LIB OF CONGRESS. SET OF 15 RECORDS WITH ACCOMPANYING TEXT TO PRESENT MAJOR AMER FOLKMUSIC TRADITION FROM LIBRARY OF CONGRESS FOLK SONG ARCHIVE & OTHER COLLECTIONS. ENGLISH & NON-ENGLISH MATERIAL INCLUDED. (NAT'L). JOSEPH HICKERSON, ACTING HEAD; LIBRARY OF CONGRESS, ARCHIVE OF FOLK SONG; 10 FIRST ST SE; WASHINGTON, DC 20540. (#1751).

AMER REVOLUTION EXHIBITION OF LIBRARY OF CONGRESS. MAJOR EXHIBIT IN THE LIBRARY'S GREAT HALL ON THE AMERICAN REVOLUTION WHICH WILL OPEN IN APRIL, 1975. DATE WILL COINCIDE WITH TWO HUNDRETH ANNIVERSARY OF BEGINNING OF AMERICAN REVOLUTION. (NAT'L). DR JAMES HUTSON, BICENTENNIAL COORDINATOR; LIBRARY OF CONGRESS; 10 FIRST ST, SE; WASHINGTON, DC 20540. (#134).

AMER REVOLUTION RESEARCH PROJ - JOHN BIRCH SOCIETY. THE PROJECT INVOLVES RESEARCH ABOUT THE JOHN BIRCH SOCIETY AND ABOUT THE AMERICAN REVOLUTION. (NAT'L). RONALD BERMAN, CHAIRMAN; NATIONAL ENDOWMENT FOR THE HUMANITIES; 806 15TH ST NW; WASHINGTON, DC 20506. (#9844).

AMERICA AS ART -PAINTINGS ON 200 YEARS OF USA. EXHIBIT AT THE NATIONAL COLLECTION OF FINE ARTS EXPLORING THE AMERCAN SCENE FROM THE ARTIST'S POINT OF VIEW OVER 200 YEARS OF PAINTING. (NAT'L). RICHARD N MURRAY, COORDINATOR, AMERICA AS ART; SMITHSONIAN INSTITUTION; NATIONAL COLLECTION OF FINE ARTS; WASHINGTON, DC 20560. (#344).

'AMERICA AT THE MOVIES' - THE ARBA FILM. CREATED & PRODUCED BY THE AMERICAN FILM INSTITUTE FOR THE ARBA, THE FILM TRACES HOW THE USA HAS BEEN PORTRAYED ON THE SCREEN FOR OVER THREE QUARTERS OF A CENTURY. GREAT SCENES FROM NEARLY 100 FILMS. (NAT'L). JACK MASEY, PROJECT DIRECTOR; AMERICAN REVOLUTION BICENTENNIAL ADMINISTRATION; 2401 E STREET, N W; WASHINGTON, DC 20276. (#26650).

AMERICA IN THE INFORMATION AGE, WASHINGTON, DC. THREE-PHASE PROGRAM ON INFORMATION SCIENCE IN AMERICA CONSISTING OF ANALYSIS OF INFORMATION NEEDS & GOALS, CONFERENCE & INFORMATION DISSEMINATION THROUGH EXHIBITS, SEMINAR SERIES AND A TV SHOW. (NAT'L). JAMES W MORENTZ, JR, BICENTENNIAL PROGRAM COORD; AMERICAN SOCIETY FOR INFORMATION SCIENCE; 1155 16TH ST, NW; WASHINGTON, DC 20036. (#19928). **ARBA RECOGNIZED.**

THE AMERICAN BICENTENNIAL FLEET. FLEET OF SHIPS, BARGES AND HISTORIC VESSELS CARRYING DISPLAYS AND PERFORMING GROUPS WITH HERITAGE FESTIVAL AND HORIZONS THEMES. EACH OF 5 FLOTILLAS WILL VISIT EACH OF 60 RIVER, LAKE & OCEAN PORTS. (INT'L). HON HELEN D BENTLEY, CHAIRMAN; THE AMERICAN BICENTENNIAL FLEET, INC; CHAIRMAN'S OFFICE, FED MARITIME; WASHINGTON, DC 20573. (#181). **ARBA RECOGNIZED.**

AMERICAN BICENTENNIAL JAZZ CELEBRATION. PLANS FOR A JAZZ EDUCATIONAL PROGRAM AND A JAZZ FESTIVAL TO TOUR THE US DURING THE BICENTENNIAL ERA TO DRAMATIZE THE HISTORY AND DEVELOPMENT OF THIS ART FORM. (NAT'L). JAZZ PROGRAM COORD, FESTIVAL USA; AMERICAN REVOLUTION BICENTENNIAL ADMINISTRATION; 2401 E STREET, NW; WASHINGTON, DC 20276. (#255).

AMERICAN CRAFTS INVENTORY. A SURVEY TO IDENTIFY CRAFT ENTERPRISES CURRENTLY EXISTING IN ORDER TO STIMULATE THE GROWTH OF THE CRAFT INDUSTRY. (NAT'L). GERALD E ELY, CRAFT SPECIALIST; DEPT OF AGRICULTURE, FARMER COOPERATIVE SERVICE; 500 12TH ST, SW, RM 550; WASHINGTON, DC 20250. (#235).

AMERICAN DESIGN BICENTENNIAL. CELEBRATE THE PAST ACHIEVEMENTS IN AMERICAN DESIGN IN ALL FIELDS OF DESIGN, UTILIZING MANY MEDIA FORMS, AS WELL AS FOCUS ON CURRENT DESIGN NEEDS AND FUTURE DESIGN PROSPECTS. (NAT'L). PAUL SPRINGER, DIRECTOR; AMERICAN DESIGN BICENTENNIAL, INC; 2215 OBSERVATORY PL, NW; WASHINGTON, DC 20007. (#2840). **ARBA RECOGNIZED.**

THE AMERICAN EXPERIENCE EXHIBIT PORTFOLIOS. SERIES OF 24 EXHIBIT PORTFOLIOS SURVEYING THE GROWTH AND DEVELOPMENT OF THE UNITED STATES FROM THE PERIOD OF EXPLORATION AND DISCOVERY TO THE PRESENT DAY. (NAT'L). MRS SUSAN HAMILTON, BICENTENNIAL COORDINATOR; SMITHSONIAN INSTITUTION; 1000 JEFFERSON DR, SW; WASHINGTON, DC 20560. (#339).

'THE AMERICAN FILM HERITAGE'-BOOK, WASHINGTON, DC. A SERIES OF IMPRESSIONS SELECTED BY AMERICAN FILM INSTITUTE BRINGS TO LIFE A WIDE RANGE OF MOVIES, ACTORS & DIRECTORS. CONTRIBUTORS INCLUDE MAJOR FILM CRITICS & EXPERTS. (NAT'L). ALPHONS J HACKL, PUBLISHER; ACROPOLIS BOOKS LTD; 2400 17TH ST, NW; WASHINGTON, DC 20009. (#22465).

THE AMERICAN FREEDOM TRAIN. EXHIBITION TRAIN DRAWN BY STEAM ENGINE DISPLAYING AT 137 CITIES THRU OUT UNITED STATES CARRYING PRECIOUS CARGO REFLECTING THE NATION'S HERITAGE IN AN EXCITING NON-LECTURE FORMAT. (NAT'L). SY FREEDMAN, DIR OF PUBLIC RELATIONS; AMERICAN FREEDOM TRAIN FOUNDATION; 5205 LEESBURG PIKE, SUITE 800; BAILEY'S XRD, VA 22041. (#1776). **ARBA RECOGNIZED.**

AMERICAN HISTORY AND LITERATURE BALLET - DC. LANGSTON HUGHES AND HARRIET TUBMAN WILL BE SUBJECTS FOR THE BALLET. (LOCAL). JAMES A PIPER, COORDINATOR; ANNETTES THEATRE OF DANCE, INC; 329 GALATIN ST, NW; WASHINGTON, DC 20011. (#22887). **ARBA GRANTEE.**

THE AMERICAN INDIAN & INTERNATIONAL LAW. PUBLICATION: COMPENDIUM OF DOCUMENTS, EXPLANATORY NOTES TRACING EVOLUTION OF INTERNATIONAL LAW STATUS OF INDIAN. AREAS INCLUDE: TREATY RIGHTS, SOVEREIGNTY LAND OWNERSHIP, SELF GOVT & PERSONAL RIGHTS. (INT'L). MARILOU M RIGHINI, EDITOR, LEGAL MATERIALS; AMERICAN SOCIETY OF INTERNATIONAL LAW; 2223 MASSACHUSETTS AVE, NW; WASHINGTON, DC 20008. (#8616). **(??).**

'AN AMERICAN INSPIRATION' - SITES EXHIBIT, DC. EXHIBITION WILL SHOW THE SHAKER INFLUENCE ON MODERN DANISH FURNITURE DESIGN. (INT'L). EILEEN HARAKEL, COORDINATOR; SMITHSONIAN INSTITUTION TRAVELING EXHIBITION SERVICE; WASHINGTON, DC 20250. (#28440).

AMERICAN ISSUES FORUM. A CALENDAR OF TOPICS FOR STUDY AND DISCUSSION THROUGHOUT THE BICENTENNIAL YEAR BY THE ENTIRE POPULATION OF THE USA. FORUM WOULD LEAD 'TO A UNIFYING COMMUNITY OF DISCOURSE ACROSS THE WHOLE NATION.'. (NAT'L). OFFICE OF THE CHAIRMAN; NATIONAL ENDOWMENT FOR THE HUMANITIES; 806 15TH ST, NW; WASHINGTON, DC 20506. (#1976). **ARBA RECOGNIZED.**

AMERICAN MERRY-GO-ROUNDS SURVEY. A SURVEY OF EXISTING MERRY-GO-ROUNDS AND THOROUGH RESEARCH INTO THE FACTORIES AND CARVERS WHICH MADE THEM, WOULD GREATLY AID IN THE PRESERVATION AND RESTORATION OF THE 300 PLUS MACHINES THAT STILL EXIST. (NAT'L). BARBARA F CHARLES, PROJECT DIRECTOR; PO BOX 8814; WASHINGTON, DC 20003. (#3750).

AMERICAN MUSIC PROGRAMS IN WASHINGTON, DC. RESEARCH & PREPARATION FOR SPECIAL BICENT AMERICAN MUSIC PROGRAMS. (NAT'L). JILLIAN H POOLE, DIR OF DEVELOPMENT; JOHN F KENNEDY CENTER FOR THE PERFORMING ARTS; WASHINGTON, DC 20566. (#8561). **ARBA RECOGNIZED. ARB GRANTEE.**

'AMERICAN PRINTS FROM WOOD' - SITES PROJECT. THIS TRAVEL ING EXHIBIT IS 120 WOODCUTS AND WOOD ENGRAVING FROM SMITHSONIAN'S COLLECTIONS PLUS A MINI-EXHIBIT O 'HOW A WOODCUT IS MADE.'. (NAT'L). ANDREA STEVENS COORDINATOR; SMITHSONIAN INSTITUTION TRAVELING EX HIBIT SERVICE; WASHINGTON, DC 20560. (#15933).

'THE AMERICAN REVOLUTION: A SELECTED READING LIST'. BIBLIOGRAPHY ON THE AMERICAN REVOLUTION DESIGNED FO THE GENERAL PUBLIC RATHER THAN THE SPECIALIST. (NAT'L DR JAMES HUTSON, BICENTENNIAL COORDINATOR; LIBRARY C CONGRESS; 10 FIRST ST, SE; WASHINGTON, DC 20540. (#100).

AMERICAN REVOLUTION SOURCE MATERIALS. ORIGINAL SOURC MATERIALS OF THE AMERICAN REVOLUTION FROM LIBRARY O CONGRESS COLLECTIONS. INCLUDES A MEMOIR BY JOHN PAL JONES, & JOURNALS OF AN AMERICAN PRIVATEERSMAN & O A BRITISH PRISONER-OF-WAR. (NAT'L). DR JAMES HUTSON BICENTENNIAL COORDINATOR; LIBRARY OF CONGRESS; FIRST ST, SE; WASHINGTON, DC 20540. (#132).

AMERICAN REVOLUTION RESOURCE GUIDES. GUIDES TO TH RESOURCES LOCATED AT THE LIBRARY OF CONGRESS. THOS THOSE ON MANUSCRIPTS, PRINTS & DRAWINGS AR PUBLISHED. WORK ON A GUIDE TO REVOLUTIONARY PERIO MAPS IS IN PROGRESS. (NAT'L). DR JAMES HUTSON, BICENTEN NIAL COORDINATOR; LIBRARY OF CONGRESS; 10 FIRST ST, S WASHINGTON, DC 20540. (#136).

AMERICAN REVOLUTION BICENTENNIAL PHILATELIC AWARDS. TRO PHIES AND CERTIFICATES TO WINNERS IN BICENTENNIAL EX HIBIT CATEGORY AT STAMP SHOWS. (NAT'L). SENIOR PRO GRAM OFFICER, HERITAGE '76; AMERICAN REVOLUTION BICEN TENNIAL ADMINISTRATION; 2401 E STREET, NW; WASHING TON, DC 20276. (#145).

AMERICAN REVOLUTION ROUND TABLE OF WASHINGTON, DC GROUP MEETS MONTHLY FOR DINNER TO HEAR DISTINGUISHE SPEAKERS ON THE MILITARY, NAVAL, ECONOMIC, POLITICAL, SOCIAL ASPECTS & RAMIFICATIONS OF THE AMERICA REVOLUTION. (REGN'L). MRS HELEN A MORRISON, SECRETARY AMERICAN REVOLUTION ROUND TABLE OF THE DISTRICT C COLUMBIA; 5011 RIVER HILL RD; BETHESDA, MD 2001 (#2858).

'AMERICAN REVOLUTION BICENTENNIAL PUBLICATIONS'-DC. A FRE BIBLIOGRAPHY OF PUBLICATIONS, PRINTS AND POSTER PRODUCED BY VARIOUS AGENCIES OF THE U S GOVERNMEN FOR THE BICENTENNIAL WHICH MAY BE PURCHASED THROUG THE GOVERNMENT PRINTING OFFICE. (NAT'L). ASST PUBLI PRINTER, SUPT OF DOCUMENTS; U S GOVERNMENT PRINTIN OFFICE; WASHINGTON, DC 20402. (#28431).

THE AMERICAS - SMITHSONIAN EXHIBIT. EXHIBITION IN RENWIC GALLERY ON THE OTHER COUNTRIES OF THE AMERICAS--TH RICHNESS OF DESIGN, CRAFTS, AND THE DECORATIVE ART DURING THE PERIOD AROUND 1776. (INT'L). LLOYD HERMAN ADMINISTRATOR; SMITHSONIAN INSTITUTION; 1000 JEFFER SON DR, SW; WASHINGTON, DC 20560. (#1768).

AMERICA'S ARCHITECTURAL HERITAGE - SITES. HIGHLIGHTS O ARCHITECTURAL DEVELOPMENT IN THE UNITED STATES FROM 1276 (MESA VERDE) TO 1976, WITH EMPHASIS ON THE LAST 2 YEARS; THERE WILL BE 3 TRAVELING EXHIBITIONS OF PHOTO GRAPHS. (NAT'L). QUINTON HALLETT, PROJ DIRECTOR SMITHSONIAN INSTITUTIN TRAVELING EXHIBITION SERVICES; & I BLDG, RM 2203; WASHINGTON, DC 20560. (#27071).

AMERICA'S HERITAGE PGMS IN THE NATL PARK SYSTEM. AREAS O THE NATIONAL PARK SYSTEM ARE PREPARING BICENTENNIA FILM & SLIDE PROGRAMS, EXHIBITS, DRAMAS, ETC, DEALIN WITH AMERICA'S HERITAGE & THE ROLE THE NATIONAL PAR SYSTEM HAS PLAYED. (NAT'L). BICENTENNIAL COORDINATOR NATIONAL PARK SERVICE; 18TH & C STS, NW; WASHINGTON DC 20240. (#6729).

ANACOSTIA EXHIBITS DESIGN & PRODUCTION LABORATORY. TRAIN ING & PRODUCTION FACILITY CREATING EXHIBITS & RELATE MATERIALS CONCERNING MINORITY GROUP PROBLEMS OF TH CONTEMPORARY AMERICAN SCENE FROM MINORITY PERSPEC TIVE. EXHIBITS WILL BE MOBILE. (LOCAL). MRS SUSAN HAMIL TON, BICENTENNIAL COORDINATOR; SMITHSONIAN INSTITU TION; 1000 JEFFERSON DR, SW; WASHINGTON DC, DC 2056 (#369).

'AND THE BAND PLAYED ON' - SITES PROJECT. EXHIBIT TRACE HISTORY OF BAND IN AMERICA FROM 1776-1976; APPROX MATELY 35 PANELS. (NAT'L). ANDREA STEVENS, COORDINA TOR; SMITHSONIAN INSTITUTION TRAVELING EXHIBIT SERVICE WASHINGTON, DC 20560. (#15932).

ANNALS OF THE BICENTENNIAL 1776-1976 -MONOGRAPHS. OUT STANDING PAPERS DEALING WITH THE NATION'S POLITICAL SOCIAL, AND ECONOMIC HISTORY DURING THE PAST 20 YEARS. MONOGRAPHS SCHEDULED FOR PUBLICATION IN 74 IN CLUDE 3RD PARTY MOVEMENTS, & INFLUENCE OF VEBLEN (NAT'L). M B SCHNAPPER, EDITOR; PUBLIC AFFAIRS PRESS; 41 NEW JERSEY AVE SE; WASHINGTON, DC 20003. (#1289). **(??).**

ANTWERP DRAWINGS & PRINTS OF 16-17 CENTURIES-SITES. EX HIBITION OF 145 DRAWINGS, PRINTS & ALBUMS WHOS THEMES INCLUDE RELIGION, MYTHOLOGY, FANTASY, ALLEGO RY & THE SEA, REPRESENTS WORK OF OVER 50 MASTE DRAFTSMEN ENGRAVERS. (INT'L). EILEEN HARAKAL, COOR DINATOR; SMITHSONIAN INSTITUTION TRAVELING EXHIBITIO SERVICE; WASHINGTON, DC 20560. (#26663).

ARBA COLLEGES & UNIVERSITIES CAMPUS PROGRAM. ELIGIBL COLLEGES & UNIVERSITIES CAMPUSES CAN APPLY FOR OFF CIAL RECOGNITION AFTER ESTABLISHING REPRESENTATIV COMMITTEE, PLANNING OVERALL THEMATIC PGM & RECEIVIN APPROVAL OF CHIEF ADMINISTRATOR. (NAT'L). DIRECTOR

WASHINGTON — CONTINUED

ICENTENNIAL COMMUNITIES DIVISION; AMERICAN REVOLUTION BICENTENNIAL ADMINISTRATION; 2401 E ST, NW; WASHINGTON, DC 20276. (#7894).

RBA COMMEMORATIVE MEDAL ANNUAL SERIES. ANNUAL SALE O PUBLIC OF IDENTICAL BRONZE & SILVER MEDALS. DESIGN Y ARBA, PRODUCED & DISTRIBUTED BY US MINT. PRICE: RONZE $5.00, SILVER $15.00. REVENUE SUPPORTS BICENTENIAL PROJECTS. (NAT'L). SENIOR PROGRAM OFFICER, HERITAGE '6; AMERICAN REVOLUTION BICENTENNIAL ADMINISTRATION; 401 E STREET, NW; WASHINGTON, DC 20276. (#16).

RBA PHILATELIC-NUMISMATIC COMBINATION - THE 'PNC'. ANUAL SALE TO PUBLIC OF COMBINATION BRONZE MEDAL & RST DAY COVER, POSTMARKED AT HISTORIC SITES. RODUCED, DISTRIBUTED WITH COOPERATION OF US MINT & S POSTAL SERVICE. PRICE $5. HELPS SUPPORT ARB PRORAMS. (NAT'L). SENIOR PROGRAM OFFICER, HERITAGE '76; MERICAN REVOLUTION BICENTENNIAL ADMINISTRATION; 401 E STREET, NW; WASHINGTON, DC 20276. (#15).

RBA'S VISITOR SERVICES HANDBOOK FOR COMMUNITIES. A HANDOOK TO BE USED BY COMMUNITIES IN PREPARING TO RECEIVE HE INCREASED NUMBER OF TRAVELERS EXPECTED IN CONNECTION WITH BICENTENNIAL ACTIVIES. (NAT'L). SENIOR PRORAM OFFICER, FESTIVAL USA; AMERICAN REVOLUTION BICENENNIAL ADMINISTRATION; 2401 E STREET, NW; WASHINGON, DC 20276. (#190).

RCHIVE OF SPOKEN COMMUNICATION IN WASHINGTON, DC. RCHIVE WILL PRESERVE RECORDINGS, TAPES, RADIO BROADAST AND VIDEO TAPES OF SPECIFIC EVENTS HELD DURING THE ICENTENNIAL CELEBRATION. (NAT'L). PATRICK KENNICOTT, SST FOR RESEARCH; SPEECH COMMUNICATION ASSOC; 1625 ASSACHUSETTS AVE, NW; WASHINGTON, DC 20036. (#5666). ??).

REA B COMMUNITY MENTAL HEALTH CENTER - DC. DEDICATION ND OPENHOUSE OF THE NEW RESIDENTIAL TREATMENT ACILITY FOR CHILDREN AND YOUTH, AREA B COMMUNITY MENTAL HEALTH CENTER. (LOCAL). ANNIE WOODRIDGE, PREIDENT; AREA B COMMUNITY MENTAL HEALTH CITIZENS' ADISORY COUNCIL; 1125 SPRING RD, NW; WASHINGTON DC, DC 0010. (#26006). **ARBA GRANTEE.**

RGENTINA'S GIFT FOR THE BICENTENNIAL IN DC. THE GOVERNMENT OF ARGENTINA CONTRIBUTED AN OFFICER'S UNIFORM OF HE CEREMONIAL REGIMENT IOF SAN MARTIN. (INT'L). CULURAL ATTACHE; EMBASSY OF THE ARGENTINA; 1600 NEW APSHIRE AVE, NW; WASHINGTON, DC 20009. (#33393).

RLINGTON NATL CEMETERY RENOVATION & CONSTRUCTION. LANS ARE FOR A NEW CHAPEL AND COLUMBARIUM, ADMINISTRATION BUILDING, TOMB FOR AN UNKNOWN SOLDIER ROM THE SE ASIAN CONFLICT, & RENOVATION OF THE AMHITHEATER AREA. (NAT'L). DR DAVID A SMITH; DEPT OF EFENSE BICENTENNIAL OFFICE; THE PENTAGON, RM 1E798; WASHINGTON, DC 20301. (#28).

RMED FORCES INSTALLATIONS & COMMANDS PROGRAM. INOLVE MILITARY INSTALLATIONS THROUGHOUT THE WORLD IN OMMEMORATION OF THE BICENTENNIAL, ESPECIALLY WHEN EASIBLE AT THE LOCAL COMMUNITY LEVEL. (INT'L). DIRECTOR, ICENTENNIAL COMMUNITIES DIVISION; AMERICAN REVOLUTION BICENTENNIAL ADMINISTRATION; 2401 E ST, NW; WASHINGTON, DC 20276. (#7892).

RT EXPOSITION - WASHINGTON, DC. THE WORLD COMMUNITY 'CENTENNIAL ART EXPOSITION WILL FEATURE A VARIETY OF ULTURES. (LOCAL). MRS KASHIF, CHAIRPERSON; NATION OF LAM CREATION COMMITTEE; 1519 4TH ST, NW; WASHINGON, DC 20001. (#26758). **ARBA GRANTEE.**

RTICLES ON US EDUCATION BY DEPT OF HEW. SERIES OF ARTILES IN AMERICAN EDUCATION MAGAZINE HIGHLIGHTING KEY SPECTS OF EDUCATION'S EVOLUTION. (NAT'L). L V GOODMAN, DITOR AMERICAN EDUCATION; DEPT OF HEALTH, EDUCATION WELFARE, OFFICE OF EDUCATION; 400 MARYLAND AVE SW; WASHINGTON, DC 20202. (#1889).

RTISTS-IN-THE PARKS PROJ OF NATL PARK SERVICE. TRAVELING XHIBITS OF THE ART WORKS WHICH ARE BEING PRODUCED BY HE NATIONAL PARK SERVICE'S ARTISTS-IN-THE-PARK PRORAM. THE EXHIBITS WILL TRAVEL TO MUSEUMS AND OTHER TES ACROSS THE COUNTRY. (NAT'L). MANAGER, HARPERS ERRY CENTER; NATIONAL PARK SERVICE; HARPERS FERRY, WV 5425. (#1474).

E ARTS IN WASHINGTON, DC. THE EMPHASIS IN THIS SERIES PROGRAMS WILL BE ON YOUNG BLACK PROFESSIONAL RTISTS. (LOCAL). HARDY FRANKLIN, DIRECTOR; DISTRICT OF OLUMBIA PUBLIC LIBRARY; 901 G ST, NW; WASHINGTON, DC 005. (#22889). **ARBA GRANTEE.**

RTS OF ASIA EXHIBIT OF FREER GALLERY. FREER GALLERY OF ART XHIBIT ON CHINESE, JAPANESE, AND NEAR-EASTERN ART AT IE TIME OF THE BIRTH OF AMERICAN INDEPENDENCE. (INT'L). RS SUSAN HAMILTON, BICENTENNIAL COORDINATOR; MITHSONIAN INSTITUTION; 1000 JEFFERSON DR, SW; ASHINGTON, DC 20560. (#340).

IAN BICENTENNIAL CELEBRATION - WASHINGTON, DC. AMERAANS AND ASIANS WILL PARTICIPATE THROUGH DISTINCTIVE RTS, EDUCATIONAL & COMMUNITY SERVICE ACTIVITIES TO FLECT THE SPIRIT OF '76 NOW AND FOR THE THIRD CENTU. (REGN'L). DR DWAN TAI & ALFRED H LIU, AIA, EXEC RECTORS; ASIAN BENEVOLENT CORPS; 2142 F ST, NW; ASHINGTON, DC 20037. (#20883).

RORA HIGH SCHOOL BAND BICENT TRIP TO WASH, DC. BAND ILL PLAY CONCERT ON ELLIPSE IN DC ON JUNE 22, 1976; SO TO TOUR WASHINGTON & GETTYSBURG AND GIVE 2 CONRTS IN PHILADELPHIA ON JUNE 25, 1976. (REGN'L). MICHAEL KULBA, DIRECTOR; AURORA HIGH SCHOOL BAND; AURORA, NE 68818. (#25801). **ARBA GRANTEE.**

BACKYARD WILDLIFE HABITAT PROGRAM. CONSERVATION PROGRAM WHICH ENCOURAGES FAMILIES WHO ARE HOMEOWNERS TO CREATE AND/OR MAINTAIN A MINIATURE REFUGE ON THEIR PROPERTY. (NAT'L). ROBERT GLOTZHOBER, NATURALIST; NATIONAL WILDLIFE FEDERATION; 1412 16TH ST, NW; WASHINGTON, DC 20036. (#6302). **ARBA RECOGNIZED.**

BAPTIST BICENTENNIAL CONVOCATION IN WASH, DC. A FOUR DAY CONVOCATION ON THE THEME 'BAPTISTS AND THE AMERICAN EXPERIENCE', CONSISTING OF ADDRESSES, PANEL DISCUSSIONS AND A SPECIALLY COMMISSIONED MUSICAL. (NAT'L). JAMES E WOOD, EXECUTIVE DIRECTOR; BAPTIST JOINT COMMITTEE ON PUBLIC AFFAIRS; 200 MARYLAND AVE, NE; WASHINGTON, DC 20002. (#4837).

BELGIAN GUNMAKING & AMERICAN HISTORY - SITES, DC. EXHIBITION ILLUSTRATES RELATIONSHIP BETWEEN AMERICAN & BELGIAN ARMS MANUFACTURERS DURING LAST 200 YEARS, FEATURING VARIETY OF WORLDREKNOWNED LIEGE MARTIAL & SPORTING ARMS. (INT'L). EILEEN HARAKAL, COORDINATOR; SMITHSONIAN INSTITUTION TRAVELING EXHIBITION SERVICE; WASHINGTON, DC 20560. (#26668).

'BELGIUM AND THE UNITED STATES' EXHIBIT - DC. ITS THEME BEING BELGIAN IMMIGRATION TO THE UNITED STATES, THIS EXHIBIT WILL TOUR THE US THROUGH 1977. (INT'L). CULTURAL ATTACHE; EMBASSY OF BELGIUM; 3330 GARFIELD ST; WASHINGTON, DC 20008. (#32961).

BELGIUM PRESENTS ART BOOKS - WASHINGTON, DC. BELGIUM PRESENTS 30 ART BOOKS TO THE DC LIBRARIES. (INT'L). OFFICE OF INFORMATION; BELGIAN EMBASSY; 3330 GARFIELD ST, NW; WASHINGTON, DC 20008. (#28442).

THE BENNINGTON FLAG - WASHINGTON, DC. DECALS OF FIRST OFFICIAL FLAG OF U S WILL BE AVAILABLE TO TRUCKING COMPANIES WHO ARE MEMBERS OF 51 STATE ASSOCIATIONS. (NAT'L). MARY JO LONG, PRESS ASSISTANT; AMERICAN TRUCKING ASSOCIATIONS, INC; 1616 P ST, NW; WASHINGTON, DC 20036. (#20625).

BETHUNE COLLECTION OF BLACK WOMEN'S HISTORY. ESTABLISHMENT OF A HISTORICAL COLLECTION ON WRITTEN & ORAL HISTORICAL MATERIALS & MEMORABILIA ON BLACK WOMEN'S ORGANIZATIONAL AND GROUP EFFORTS. (NAT'L). RUTH A SYKES, SPECIAL ASSISTANT; NATIONAL COUNCIL OF NEGRO WOMEN, INC; 1346 CONNECTICUT AVE NW; WASHINGTON, DC 20036. (#10839). **ARBA RECOGNIZED. ARBA GRANTEE.**

'BETWEEN FRIENDS-ENTRE AMIS', WASHINGTON, DC. A COMMEMORATIVE VOLUME PREPARED BY CANADA'S NATIONAL FILM BOARD ON SHARED TOPOGRAPHY AND BORDERS OF CANADA AND THE UNITED STATES. CONTAINS PHOTOGRAPHS & TEXT. (INT'L). KEITH DE B PERCY, PROJ DIRECTOR; EMBASSY OF CANADA; 1746 MASSACHUSETTS AVE; WASHINGTON, DC 20036. (#18823).

BIBLIOGRAPHY OF AMERICAN ART. A COMPREHENSIVE REFERENCE WORK MAKING AVAILABLE TO SCHOLARS THE PRIMARY DOCUMENTATION REQUIRED FOR SERIOUS RESEARCH IN AMERICAN ART HISTORY. (NAT'L). MRS SUSAN HAMILTON, BICENTENNIAL COORDINATOR; SMITHSONIAN INSTITUTION; 1000 JEFFERSON DR, SW; WASHINGTON, DC 20560. (#77).

BIBLIOGRAPHY OF YUGOSLAV TRANSLATIONS. PUBLICATION OF A BIBLIOGRAPHY OF AMERICAN LITERATURE TRANSLATIONS DONE IN YUGOSLAVIA. (INT'L). CULTURAL OFFICE; EMBASSY OF THE SOCIALIST FEDERAL REPUBLIC OF YUGOSLAVIA; 2401 CALIFORNIA ST, NW; WASHINGTON, DC 20008. (#24416).

BIBLIOGRAPHY, 'CREATING INDEPENDENCE, 1763-1789'. AN INVENTORY AND CATALOGUE OF CHILDREN'S LITERATURE ON AMERICAN REVOLUTION. (NAT'L). DR JAMES HUTSON, BICENTENNIAL COORDINATOR; LIBRARY OF CONGRESS; 10 FIRST ST, SE; WASHINGTON, DC 20540. (#96).

BIBLIOGRAPHY, 'REVOLUTIONARY AMERICA, 1763-1789'. THIS MASSIVE WORK INVENTORIES THE SECONDARY MATERIAL ON THE REVOLUTIONARY PERIOD AND WILL CONTAIN AS MANY AS 20,000 ITEMS. (NAT'L). DR JAMES HUTSON, BICENTENNIAL COORDINATOR; LIBRARY OF CONGRESS; 10 FIRST ST, SE; WASHINGTON, DC 20540. (#129).

BICENT CHRONOLOGY OF AMER AGRICULTURE, 1776-1976. BOOK WITH BIBLIOGRAPHICAL REFERENCE FOR EACH ITEM IN COMPREHENSIVE CHRONOLOGY. (NAT'L). W D RASMUSSEN, HISTORIAN; DEPT OF AGRICULTURE, ECONOMIC RESEARCH SERVICE; 500 12TH ST, SW; WASHINGTON, DC 22050. (#1753).

BICENT ETHNIC/RACIAL COUNCIL CONFERENCE REPORT, DC. DESCRIPTION OF THIS NATIONAL CONFERENCE, POLICY RECOMMENDATIONS ADOPTED AND SUMMARY OF FEDERAL AGENCY PROGRAMS. THIS PUBLICATION IS OUT OF PRINT (10/76). (NAT'L). ETHNIC RACIAL OFFICE; AMERICAN REVOLUTION BICENTENNIAL ADMINISTRATION; 2401 E ST, NW; WASHINGTON, DC 20276. (#28428).

BICENTENNIAL ARTICLES IN 'QUARTERLY JOURNAL'. THE LIBRARY OF CONGRESS DEVOTED THE APRIL, 1972 'QUARTERLY JOURNAL' TO THE PAPERS OF LAFAYETTE. OTHER ARTICLES ON THE REVOLUTION HAVE BEEN PUBLISHED & MORE WILL BE FORTHCOMING. (NAT'L). DR JAMES HUTSON, BICENTENNIAL COORDINATOR; LIBRARY OF CONGRESS; 10 FIRST ST, SE; WASHINGTON, DC 20540. (#139).

BICENTENNIAL ART PROGRAM OF DEPT OF THE INTERIOR. ARTISTS WILL BE COMMISSIONED TO DEPICT THE NATURAL AND HISTORIC PROPERTIES ADMINISTERED BY THE DEPARTMENT OF THE INTERIOR. EXHIBIT WILL OPEN AND TOUR SPRING OF 1976. (NAT'L). MRS JEAN HAWKINS, BICENTENNIAL COORDINATOR; DEPT OF THE INTERIOR; 18TH & C STS NW; WASHINGTON, DC 20240. (#1239).

BICENTENNIAL CELEBRATION OF AMERICAN MUSIC - DC. ALAN & NANCY MANDEL, PIANIST & VIOLINIST, WILL PERFORM CONCERTS THROUGHOUT THE USA AND THE WORLD; MUSIC WILL BE FROM THE REVOLUTIONARY ERA TO THE PRESENT DAY; ALSO LECTURES, TV & RADIO. (LOCAL). SEDGLEY CLAIRE, DIRECTOR; THE SEDGLEY CLAIRE MANAGEMENT; 2524 44TH ST, NW; WASHINGTON, DC 20007. (#16152).

'BICENTENNIAL CITIES'-NEWSLETTER OF CONF OF MAYORS. NEWS OF BICENTENNIAL PLANNING & ACTIVITIES OF USA COMMUNITIES & HOW THOSE PLANS CAN BE USED BY OTHER CITIES. PUBLISHED MONTHLY. (NAT'L). MICHAEL A DINUNZIO, PROJ DIR, BICENT COMMITTEE; US CONFERENCE OF MAYORS; 1620 I ST, NW; WASHINGTON, DC 20006. (#2383).

BICENTENNIAL COINAGE. CHANGE OF US QUARTER, HALF DOLLAR, & DOLLAR COINS TO INCLUDE DATE OF 1776-1976 ON OBVERSE & NEW BICENTENNIAL DESIGNS ON REVERSE OF THE COINS. NEW DESIGN SELECTED IN MARCH 1974. (NAT'L). DIRECTOR, US MINT; BUREAU OF THE MINT; 1500 PENNSYLVANIA AVE, NW; WASHINGTON, DC 20220. (#14).

BICENTENNIAL COMMUNITIES PROGRAM. ANY POLITICAL SUBDIVISION CAN APPLY FOR STATUS AS A BICENTENNIAL COMMUNITY AFTER IT HAS FORMED A REPRESENTATIVE CITIZEN COMMITTEE, PLANNED CITIZEN INVOLVEMENT PROGS & RECEIVED OFFICIAL ENDORSEMENT. (NAT'L). DIRECTOR, BICENTENNIAL COMMUNITIES DIVISION; AMERICAN REVOLUTION BICENTENNIAL ADMINISTRATION; 2401 E STREET, NW; WASHINGTON, DC 20276. (#224).

BICENTENNIAL CONCERT - WASHINGTON, DC. THE JAY BAND HAS BEEN CHOSEN TO REPRESENT MISSOURI AT THE BICENTENNIAL PARADE OF AMERICAN MUSIC APRIL 26, 1976, AT THE KENNEDY CENTER. (REGN'L). JERRY HOOVER, DIRECTOR; JEFFERSON CITY SR HIGH SCHOOL MUSIC DEPT, CONCERT BAND; 609 UNION; JEFFERSON, MO 65101. (#20333). **ARBA GRANTEE.**

BICENTENNIAL CULTURAL ARTS GRANTS. A NEIGHBORHOOD ARTS PROGRAM CONSISTING OF MATCHING GRANTS TO ASSIST SERVICE ORGANIZATIONS WHICH AID A VARIETY OF COMMUNITY CULTURAL ACTIVITIES THROUGH EQUIPMENT LOANS, PUBLICITY, FUND RAISING, ETC. (NAT'L). MR VANTILE WHITFIELD, DIR FOR EXPANSION ARTS PGMS; NATIONAL ENDOWMENT FOR THE ARTS; 806 15TH ST. N.W.; WASHINGTON, DC 20506. (#140).

BICENTENNIAL DANCE ART GRANTS. MATCHING GRANTS TO PROFESSIONAL DANCE COMPANIES TO RESTAGE EXISTING WORKS OR CHOREOGRAPH NEW WORKS BY AMERICAN ARTISTS. (NAT'L). DON ANDERSON, DIRECTOR FOR DANCE PROGRAMS; NATIONAL ENDOWMENT FOR THE ARTS; 806 15TH ST. N.W.; WASHINGTON, DC 20506. (#141).

BICENTENNIAL EAGLE PROJECT. ESTABLISH DATA BANK FOR RESEARCH THAT WILL AID IN PROTECTING BALD EAGLES AND TO LAUNCH EXPANDED PROGRAM OF LAND ACQUISITION TO PURCHASE VITAL EAGLE HABITATS. (NAT'L). JAMES DAVIS, DIR, CREATIVE SERVICES DIVISION; NATIONAL WILDLIFE FEDERATION; 1412 SIXTEENTH ST; WASHINGTON, DC 20036. (#16367). **ARBA RECOGNIZED.**

BICENTENNIAL EDUCATIONAL MATERIAL. BICENTENNIAL EDUCATIONAL MATERIAL PACKAGE; ARBA LICENSE NO 76-19-0617. (NAT'L). MARK JOSEPH, DIRECTOR; AMERICAN SALES AND DISTRIBUTING COMPANY; 1605 35TH ST, NW; WASHINGTON, DC 20007. (#22789).

BICENTENNIAL EDUCATIONAL EXPOSITION, DC. EXHIBITION OF CURRENT PROGRAMS IN OPERATION IN THE PUBLIC SCHOOLS, EDUCATIONAL MATERIALS IN USE IN THE SCHOOLS & A SPECIAL EXHIBIT HIGHLIGHTING HISTORY OF PUBLIC SCHOOL SYSTEMS IN DC. (LOCAL). GORDON OLSON, COORDINATOR; DC PUBLIC SCHOOLS; 415 12TH ST, NW, ROOM 1108; WASHINGTON, DC 20004. (#25628). **ARBA GRANTEE.**

BICENTENNIAL EVENT CALENDAR IN ARBA TIMES. MONTHLY CENTERFOLD CALENDAR IN ARBA'S BICENTENNIAL TIMES TABLOID, TO SHOW SIGNIFICANT EVENTS IN NEXT MONTH PERIOD. MORE EVENT INFO AVAILABLE FROM ARBA'S MASTER CALENDAR SERVICES ON-LINE & PUBS SERVICES. (NAT'L). DIRECTOR, COMMUNICATIONS DIVISION; AMERICAN REVOLUTION BICENTENNIAL ADMINISTRATION; 2401 E ST, NW; WASHINGTON, DC 20276. (#3759).

BICENTENNIAL EVENT PLANNING WORKBOOK. BOOKLET SERVES AS A BASIC RESEARCH & RESOURCE TOOL FOR COMMUNITIES OF ALL SIZES AND VARIETIES. (NAT'L). PROGRAM DIVISION; AMERICAN REVOLUTION BICENTENNIAL ADMINISTRATION; 2401 E ST, NW; WASHINGTON, DC 20276. (#27617).

BICENTENNIAL FILM ON MENTAL RETARDATION - DC. PRODUCTION OF A ONE HOUR FILM ON MENTAL RETARDATION WITH SCENES FROM AROUND THE U S; AWARDS WILL BE PRESENTED TO THOSE WHO HAVE CONTRIBUTED SIGNIFICANTLY IN THE FIELD OF MENTAL RETARDATION. (NAT'L). JAMES JULIANA, DIRECTOR; PRESIDENT'S COMMITTEE ON MENTAL RETARDATION; 7TH & D ST, SW; WASHINGTON, DC 20201. (#23412).

BICENTENNIAL FILM LIST - WASHINGTON, DC. LISTS TITLES AND AVAILABILITY FOR RENTAL AND PURCHASE OF FILMS PERTAINING TO THE BICENTENNIAL AND THE HISTORY OF THE U S. (NAT'L). A V BRANCH; AMERICAN REVOLUTION BICENTENNIAL ADMINISTRATION; 2401 E ST, NW; WASHINGTON, DC 20276. (#28198).

BICENTENNIAL GAMES 'N FUN HANDBOOK, WASHINGTON, DC. 254 SUGGESTIONS, DIRECTIONS & INSTRUCTIONS FOR GAMES, SONGS, CRAFTS, RECIPES, DANCES, PLAYS, READING, PAGEANTS, RECIPES, DECORATIONS, OBSERVANCES & OTHER SPECIAL EVENTS FOR ALL AGES. (LOCAL). ALPHONS J HACKL, PUBLISHER; ACROPOLIS BOOKS LTD; 2400 17TH ST, NW; WASHINGTON, DC 20009. (#22467).

THE BICENTENNIAL INFORMATION NETWORK - BINET. COMPUTERIZED CATALOG OF BICENTENNIAL ACTIVITIES AVAILABLE

WASHINGTON — CONTINUED

NATIONWIDE THRU ON-LINE DATA TERMINALS, PERIODIC PUBLICATIONS & SPECIAL REPORTS. WILL BECOME ARCHIVE OF BICENTENNIAL COMMEMORATION. (INT'L). DIRECTOR, MASTER CALENDAR SERVICES; AMERICAN REVOLUTION BICENTENNIAL ADMINISTRATION; 2401 E STREET, NW; WASHINGTON, DC 20276. (#1973).

BICENTENNIAL INTERNSHIP IN EDUCATION. FREEDOM FROM DEPENDENCE-DEPT HEW SPONSRED PROG PROVIDE GRAD INTERN TEAMS TO STATE EDUC AGENCIES ASSESS ACCOMPLISHMENTS DEFINE PROBLEMS & PLAN SOLUTIONS. ADMIN THRU RESOURCE DEVEL INTERNSHIP PROGRAMS. (NAT'L). DR HAROLD ARBERG, BICENTENNIAL COORDINATOR; DEPT OF HEALTH, EDUCATION & WELFARE, OFFICE OF EDUCATION; 400 MARYLAND AVE, SW; WASHINGTON, DC 20202. (#840). **ARBA RECOGNIZED.**

BICENTENNIAL INTERN PGM IN SCIENCE & TECHNOLOGY. STUDENT INTERNS WILL WORK WITH STATE & LOCAL ORGANIZATIONS ON PROJECTS CONTRIBUTING TO THE PUBLIC UNDERSTANDING OF SCIENCE & TECH. NSF WILL SUPPORT THIS PROGRAM THROUGH MATCHING GRANTS TO NBIP. (NAT'L). RICHARD STEPHENS, PROGRAM OFFICER; NATIONAL SCIENCE FOUNDATION; 1800 G ST, NW; WASHINGTON, DC 20550. (#1522). **ARBA RECOGNIZED.**

BICENTENNIAL LECTURE SERIES - WASHINGTON, DC. LECTURES ON BLACK HISTORY. (LOCAL). VERNARD R GRAY, DIRECTOR; CAFAM-3 INC.; 720 11TH ST, NW; WASHINGTON, DC 20005. (#27266). **ARBA GRANTEE.**

BICENTENNIAL MUSIC COMPOSITION - WASHINGTON, DC. VINCENT PERSICHETTI HAS BEEN COMMISSIONED TO WRITE CHAMBER MUSIC AND MISCELLANEOUS WORKS FOR THE STAGE. (REGN'L). VINCENT PERSICHETTI, COMPOSER; NATIONAL ENDOWMENT FOR THE ARTS; 2401 E ST NW; WASHINGTON, DC 20506. (#21349).

BICENTENNIAL PARADE OF AMERICAN MUSIC. NATL MUSIC COUNCIL SPONSORING 52 STATE MUSIC CONCERTS AT JFK CENTER IN WASHINGTON; 13 WEEK RADIO SERIES IN EACH STATE IN 1976; & PLACING HISTORICAL PLAQUES AT SIGNIFICANT MUSICAL SITES IN EACH STATE. (NAT'L). DR MERLE MONTGOMERY, VICE PRESIDENT; NATIONAL MUSIC COUNCIL; 222 E 80TH ST; NEW YORK, NY 10021. (#4500). **ARBA RECOGNIZED.**

BICENTENNIAL PARADE OF MUSIC, CHEYENNE, WY. WYOMING BAND TO PERFORM AT KENNEDY CENTER, WASHINGTON, DC. (REGN'L). CHARLES PAT HALL, PROJ DIRECTOR; WYOMING BICENTENNIAL COMMITTEE; STATE OFFICE BLDG E; CHEYENNE, WY 82002. (#18606). **ARBA GRANTEE.**

BICENTENNIAL POSTERS OF THE NATL PARK SERVICE. A SERIES OF 6 POSTERS DEPICTING THE FOLLOWING PARKS: ADAMS MINUTE MAN, INDEPENDENCE, SARATOGA, YORKTOWN, STATUE OF LIBERTY. (NAT'L). MANAGER, HARPERS FERRY CENTER; NATIONAL PARK SERVICE; HARPERS FERRY, WV 25425. (#1468).

BICENTENNIAL POSTER SERIES IN WASH, DC. COMMISSION 5 ARTISTS TO DESIGN POSTERS IN COMMEMORATION OF & IN CELEBRATION OF AMERICA'S BICENTENNIAL. (LOCAL). ROY SLADE, DIRECTOR; CORCORAN GALLERY OF ARTS; 17TH & NEW YORK AVE, NW; WASHINGTON, DC 20006. (#8518).

BICENTENNIAL PROGRAM OF WASHINGTON CATHEDRAL. OPENING & DEDICATION OF THE NAVE. ALSO WILL COMMISSION PROJECTS SUCH AS WORKS FOR CHORUS, ORGANISTS & DANCERS. PLAN A SERIES OF LITURGICAL EVENTS & A SUMMER FESTIVAL JUNE-AUG 1976. (NAT'L). R WAYNE DIRKSEN, COORDINATOR; THE WASHINGTON CATHEDRAL; MT ST ALBAN; WASHINGTON, DC 20016. (#5619).

BICENTENNIAL RECORDS OF WASHINGTON, DC. PUBLICATION OF THE RECORDS OF THE COLUMBIA HISTORICAL SOCIETY OF WASHINGTON, DC, TRACING THE DEVELOPMENT OF THE FEDERAL CITY; WILL INCLUDE ROLE PLAYED BY BLACKS & WOMEN IN THAT DEVELOPMENT. (NAT'L). F C ROSENBERGER, PROJ COORDINATOR; COLUMBIA HISTORICAL SOCIETY OF WASHINGTON, DC; 1307 NEW HAMPSHIRE AVE NW; WASHINGTON, DC 20036. (#10721).

BICENTENNIAL REGIONAL TRANSIT NEEDS STUDY. YEAR LONG STUDY BEGUN IN JULY 1972 BY COG & WMATA TO IDENTIFY PERMANENT TRANSIT IMPROVEMENTS NEEDED BY 1976 & SUPPLEMENT LONG RANGE PLANNING FOR THE WASHINGTON, DC METROPOLITAN AREA. (ST-WIDE). PAUL RASMUSEN, URBAN PLANNER; DEPT OF TRANSPORTATION, BICENTENNIAL COORDINATION CNTR; 400 7TH ST, SW; WASHINGTON, DC 20590. (#288).

BICENTENNIAL SALUTE TO THE STATES. EACH STATE & TERRITORY HONORED IN THE DISTRICT OF COLUMBIA ON ONE SPECIFIC DAY IN 1976. DIGNITARIES, CITIZENS & PERFORMING GROUPS FROM EACH STATE & TERRITORY ARE INVITED TO PARTICIPATE. (NAT'L). DR A KNIGHTON STANLEY, EXEC DIRECTOR; OFFICE OF BICENTENNIAL PROGRAMS - DISTRICT OF COLUMBIA; 777 14TH ST, NW; WASHINGTON, DC 20005. (#33271). **ARBA RECOGNIZED.**

BICENTENNIAL SCHOOL PROGRAMS IN NATL PARK SYSTEM. MANY AREAS OF THE NATL PARK SYSTEM ARE DEVELOPING PROGRAMS FOR LOCAL SCHOOL GROUPS WHICH WILL GIVE SUCH GROUPS A BETTER UNDERSTANDING OF THE ROLE OF THE PARK & THE NPS IN AMERICA'S HISTORY. (NAT'L). BICENTENNIAL COORDINATOR; NATIONAL PARK SERVICE; 18TH & C STS, NW; WASHINGTON, DC 20240. (#6726).

BICENTENNIAL SPECIAL OLYMPICS - WASHINGTON, DC. ATHLETIC & RECREATIONAL PROJECT FOR MENTALLY RETARDED CITIZENS; WILL CULMINATE IN A FESTIVE TRACK & FIELD MEET FOR 500 MENTALLY RETARDED CITIZENS. (LOCAL). HARRY F CUSTIS, PRESIDENT; DISTRICT OF COLUMBIA SPECIAL OLYMPICS INC; 5513 CONNECTICUT AVE, NW; WASHINGTON, DC 20015. (#25230). **ARBA GRANTEE.**

BICENTENNIAL TALKS IN THE NATIONAL PARK SERVICE. LECTURE SERIES, TALKS, SEMINARS & CAMPFIRE PROGRAMS WILL BE GIVEN AT MANY NPS AREAS TO SHOW VISITORS THE ROLE OF THESE VARIOUS PARKS IN THE REVOLUTION AMERICAN HISTORY, & AMERICA'S FUTURE. (NAT'L). BICENTENNIAL COORDINATOR; NATIONAL PARK SERVICE; 18TH & C STS, NW; WASHINGTON, DC 20240. (#6730).

BICENTENNIAL THEATER ARTS GRANTS. A PILOT PROJECT CONSISTING OF MATCHING GRANTS TO COMMUNITY ORGANIZATIONS TO SPONSOR RESIDENCY PERFORMANCES AND WORKSHOPS OF 2 OR MORE EXPANSION ART GROUPS. (NAT'L). MR VANTILE WHITFIELD, DIR FOR EXPANSION ARTS PGMS; NATIONAL ENDOWMENT FOR THE ARTS; 806 15TH ST. N.W.; WASHINGTON, DC 20506. (#142).

'BICENTENNIAL TIMES' ARBA'S MONTHLY NEWSPAPER - DC. ARTICLES ON INTERNATIONAL, NATIONAL, REGIONAL, STATE & COMMUNITY PARTICIPATION IN THE BICENTENNIAL AND NEWS OF ARBA PROGRAMS AND ACTIVITIES. TO BE PUBLISHED THROUGH 1976. (NAT'L). OFFICE OF PUBLIC INFORMATION; AMERICAN REVOLUTION BICENTENNIAL ADMINISTRATION; 2401 E ST, NW; WASHINGTON, DC 20276. (#27606).

BICENTENNIAL TOURING THEATER ART GRANTS. MATCHING GRANTS FOR PROFESSIONAL THEATRE COMPANIES TO TOUR COMMUNITIES IN UP TO SEVEN STATES IN 1975-1976. (NAT'L). MRS RUTH MAYLEAS, DIR FOR THEATRE PROGRAMS; NATIONAL ENDOWMENT FOR THE ARTS; 806 15TH ST. N.W.; WASHINGTON, DC 20506. (#143).

BICENTENNIAL TRAVELING EXHIBITIONS, WASHINGTON, DC. FOUR EXHIBITIONS OF AMERICAN ART WHICH ARE PARTICULARLY APPROPRIATE FOR THE BICENTENNIAL. (REGN'L). MRS JOHN A POPE, PRESIDENT; INTERNATIONAL EXHIBITIONS FOUNDATION; 1729 H ST, NW, SUITE 310; WASHINGTON, DC 20005. (#10993).

'BICENTENNIAL TRAVEL INTENTIONS SURVEY - 2' - DC. OCT-NOV 1975, INFORMATION ON ACTUAL CONSUMER TRAVEL PLANS FOR VACATIONS & WEEKEND TRIPS IN 1976, WITH SPECIAL REFERENCE TO BICENT SITES AND EVENTS. PRICE: $12.00. (NAT'L). INFORMATION OFFICER; U S TRAVEL DATA CENTER; 1100 CONNECTICUT AVE, NW; WASHINGTON, DC 20036. (#28426).

BICENTENNIAL WORKSHOP - WASHINGTON, DC. A BICENTENNIAL WORKSHOP WILL BE HELD ON EQUAL EMPLOYMENT OPPORTUNITIES. (REGN'L). BEN SEGAL, SECRETARY; VOICE (VOICE OF INFORMED COMMUNITY EXPRESSION); 4532 49TH ST, NW; WASHINGTON, DC 20016. (#26757). **ARBA GRANTEE.**

BICENTENNIAL YOUTH DEBATES, WASHINGTON DC. NATIONAL PROGRAM OF COMPETITIVE AND COMMUNITY DEBATES ON TOPICS OF HISTORICAL & HUMANISTIC CONCERN. FUNDED BY NATIONAL ENDOWMENT FOR THE HUMANITIES. (NAT'L). RICHARD C HUSEMAN, PROJECT DIRECTOR; SPEECH COMMUNICATION ASSOC; 1625 MASSACHUSETTS AVE, NW; WASHINGTON, DC 20036. (#3057). **ARBA RECOGNIZED. ARBA GRANTEE.**

BICENTENNIALLY RELATED FILM LIST, AR BICENT ADMIN. LIST OF FILMS AVAILABLE TO ORGANIZATIONS & SCHOOLS, EITHER FREE OR RENTAL, ON BICENTENNIAL RELATED SUBJECTS. LIST DIVIDED INTO 3 BICENTENNIAL THEME AREAS, YOUNG PEOPLE, CHILDREN, & GENERAL INTERESTS. (NAT'L). MRS PATRICIA JORDAN, DEPUTY DIR, COMMUNICATIONS; AMERICAN REVOLUTION BICENTENNIAL ADMINISTRATION; 2401 E ST, NW; WASHINGTON, DC 20276. (#2856).

'BICEP' - BICENTENNIAL ENVIRONMENTAL PROGRAM. ENCOURAGES THE COOPERATION OF THE SIX NATIONWIDE VOCATIONAL STUDENT ORGANIZATIONS IN DIVERSE PROJECTS TO IMPROVE THE ENVIRONMENT, BOTH SOCIAL AND PHYSICAL. (NAT'L). ED MILLER, EXEC DIRECTOR; FUTURE BUSINESS LEADERS OF AMERICA; PO BOX 17417-DULLES INTL AIRPORT; WASHINGTON, DC 20041. (#2801). **ARBA RECOGNIZED.**

BIKECENTENNIAL TRAIL & CEREMONY PROJECTS - USDA. COOPERATIVE LOCATION OF CROSS COUNTRY BIKE TRAILS, ARRANGING ANTIPOLLUTION CEREMONIES, & 'HERITAGE & HORIZON' TREES. PROJ SPONSORED BY US FOREST SERVICE. (NAT'L). GLENN A KOVAR, DIRECTOR, SPECIAL PROJECTS; BIKECENTENNIAL & FOREST SERVICE - US DEPARTMENT OF AGRICULTURE; 12TH & INDEPENDENCE AVE, SW; WASHINGTON, DC 20250. (#5568).

BLACK CULTURE CENTER FOR WASH, DC TENANTS ASSOC. THE CENTER WILL OFFER AFRICAN FASHIONS, DANCING & HANDICRAFTS TO FOSTER A HISTORICAL AWARENESS IN THE COMMUNITY. (LOCAL). PATRICIA GANIS, CHAIRWOMAN; CLIFTON TERRACE TENANTS ASSOC; 1312 CLIFTON TERRACE, NW; WASHINGTON, DC 20009. (#8643).

BLACK FILM FESTIVAL - WASH, DC. TEN 1 1/2 - 2 1/2 HR TELEVISION PROGRAMS FEATURING HISTORIC AND CONTEMPORARY FILMS ABOUT THE BLACK EXPERIENCE IN MOTION PICTURES. (NAT'L). MS WALTERENE SWANSTON, PROJ DIRECTOR PRODUCER; WETA TELEVISION; 955 L'ENFANT PLAZA N, SW; WASHINGTON, DC 20024. (#18269).

'BLACKS IN THE REVOLUTIONARY ERA' - SITES PROJECT. 41 COLORFUL EXHIBIT PANELS TRACE BLACK INVOLVEMENT DURING THE 30 YRS THAT STRETCHED FROM THE MARTYRDOM OF CRISPUS ATTUCKS IN 1770 TO THE CONSPIRACY OF GABRIEL PROSSER IN VIRGINIA. (NAT'L). ANDREA STEVENS, COORDINATOR; SMITHSONIAN INSTITUTION TRAVELING EXHIBIT SERVICE; WASHINGTON, DC 20560. (#15925).

'BLACKS IN THE WESTWARD MOVEMENT' - SITES PROJECT. EXHIBIT TRACES THE LITTLE KNOWN BLACK INVOLVEMENT IN THE EXPLORATION AND EXPANSION OF THE U S; 44 FRAMED PANELS CONTAIN TEXT, ILLUSTRATIONS AND GRAPHICS. (NAT'L). ANDREA STEVENS, COORDINATOR; SMITHSONIAN INSTITUTION TRAVELING EXHIBIT SERVICE; WASHINGTON, DC 20560. (#15923).

BONSAI CLUBS INTERNATIONAL CONVENTION, 1976. ANNUA MEMBERSHIP MEETING, PLUS EDUCATIONAL PROGRAMS & DEMONSTRATION OF THE ART OF BONSAI (MINIATURE TREES) HIGHLIGHT WILL BE DEDICATION OF NATIONAL ARBORETUM BONSAI COLLECTION. (INT'L). JAMES R NEWTON, CONVENTION COORDINATOR; BCI '76 & POTOMAC BONSAI ASSOC; PO BO 28308; WASHINGTON, DC 20005. (#2291).

BOOK ON HISTORY OF ROADBUILDING - WASHINGTON, DC. PICTORIAL HISTORY OF ROADBUILDING; 208-PAGE, HARD COVE BOOK; KEY WORDS: TRANSPORTATION, ROADS, HIGHWAYS CONSTRUCTION. (NAT'L). RANDOLPH RUSSELL, ASSISTANT AMERICAN ROADBUILDER'S ASSOCIATION; 525 SCHOOL ST SW; WASHINGTON, DC 20024. (#11540).

BOOKLET ON BANK PUBLIC RELATIONS. SHOWS HOW BANKS CA TIE INTO BANKING CENTENNIAL & U S BICENTENNIAL. (NAT'L) KATIE O' HARA, ASST TO THE DIR OF PUBLIC RELATIONS AMERICAN BANKERS ASSOCIATION; 1120 CONNECTICUT AVE NW; WASHINGTON, DC 20036. (#5632).

BOOKLET ON HISTORY OF FOREST CONSERVATION. REVISION REPRINT AND FIELD DISTRIBUTION OF THE POPULAR BOOKLE ON 'HIGHLIGHTS IN THE HISTORY OF FOREST CONSERVATION (NAT'L). GLENN A KOVAR, CHIEF SPECIAL PROJECTS; DEPT O AGRICULTURE, FOREST SERVICE; 12TH & INDEPENDENCE AVE WASHINGTON, DC 20250. (#1898).

BOOKLET, 'ERDA ENERGY TRAILS' - WASHINGTON, DC. BOOKLE ADVISING TOURISTS OF SITES TO BE VISITED WHERE IMPOR TANT TECHNICAL EVENTS TOOK PLACE. BOOKLET ALSO IN CLUDES MAPS. (NAT'L). CHARLES PELZER, OFFICE OF PUBLI AFFAIRS; ENERGY RESEARCH AND DEVELOPMENT ADMINISTRA TION; WASHINGTON, DC 20545. (#12134).

BOOK: 'AMERICAN RIGHTS HISTORY'. THIS BOOK WILL FOCUS O WHITE & INDIAN REFORM ORGANIZATIONS FROM 1928 T 1976 AS SEEN FROM A HISTORICAL & CULTURAL PERSPECTIV AS AN ASPECT OF AMERICAN POLITICAL & SOCIAL HISTORY (NAT'L). MORTON SOSNA, CHAIRMAN; NATIONAL ENDOWMEN FOR THE HUMANITIES; 805 15TH ST, NW; WASHINGTON, D 20506. (#7310).

THE BOOK: 'EUROPE AND AMERICA' FROM 1820 - DC. REPRINT O THE BOOK 'EUROPE AND AMERICA' FROM 1820 GIVING TH DANISH VIEW OF THE RELATIONSHIP BETWEEN EUROPE AN THE NEW NATION OF AMERICA. (INT'L). NIELS TOFT, PRO DIRECTOR; DANISH EMBASSY; 3200 WHITEHAVEN PKY, NW WASHINGTON, DC 20007. (#20775).

'THE BOSTON MASSACRE' ENGRAVING REPRODUCTION. IN COM MEMORATION OF THE 200TH ANNIVERSARY OF THE BOSTO MASSACRE THE LIBRARY OF CONGRESS ISSUED A COLO REPRODUCTION OF THE FAMOUS PAUL REVERE ENGRAVING O THE EVENT. (NAT'L). DR JAMES HUTSON, BICENTENNIAL COOR DINATOR; LIBRARY OF CONGRESS; 10 FIRST ST, SE; WASHING TON, DC 20540. (#131).

BOYS & GIRLS STATE PROGRAM OF THE AMER LEGION. 1 MONT PROGRAM FOR 300 BOYS & GIRLS INCLUDING IN-SERVIC TRAINING PROGRAM IN U S CONGRESS, OPERATION OF JOIN BOYS & GIRLS NATION IN DC & EVALUATE THE ROLE OF TH CONTINENTAL CONGRESS IN AMER GOVT. (NAT'L). A LEO AN DERSON, CHIEF, VETERANS AFFAIRS; WASH, DC, VA REGIONA OFFICE, RM 1211F; 941 N CAPITOL ST; WASHINGTON, D 20002. (#5617).

BRATTLEBORO, VT, HS BAND TRIP TO WASHINGTON, DC. BRAT TLEBORO HIGH SCHOOL BAND WILL REPRESENT VERMONT I THE 1976 CHERRY BLOSSOM FESTIVAL IN WASHINGTON, DC (REGN'L). J WAYNE CORBEIL, CHAIRMAN; BRATTLEBORO BICEN TENNIAL COMMITTEE; 230 MAIN ST; BRATTLEBORO, VT 0530 (#24894). **ARBA GRANTEE.**

BRITISH PERFORMING GROUPS TOUR THE US IN 1976. THE FO LOWING GROUPS WILL TOUR THE US: ROYAL SHAKESPEAR COMPANY; PROSPECT THEATRE COMPANY; YEHUDI MENUHI SCHOOL; JAYE CONSORT OF VIOLS (TO CHICAGO); NORTHUM BRIAN TRADITIONAL GROUP (TO PHILA, PA). (INT'L). CULTURA ATTACHE; EMBASSY OF GREAT BRITAIN; 3100 MAS SACHUSETTS AVE; WASHINGTON, DC 20008. (#32972).

BROADCAST OF ORCHESTRA PREMIERS & CONCERTS - DC. ORCHES TRA PERFORMANCES, CONCERTS AND WORKS COMMISSIONE BY THE BICENTENNIAL WILL BE BROADCAST. (NAT'L). NORMA KADERLAN, DIRECTOR OF CULTURAL PROGRAMS; NATIONA PUBLIC RADIO; 2025 M ST, NW; WASHINGTON, DC 2003 (#20939).

THE BUFFALO GOODWILL TOUR OF THE USA. 100 CITIES WILL B VISITED BY CARS CARRYING MESSAGES OF CONGRATULATION ON AMERICAN BICENTENNIAL FROM JAPANESE SISTER CITIES (INT'L). TOSHIO YAMAGUCHI, MEMBER; HOUSE OF REPRESEN TATIVES; 409 DIET HOUSE-NAGATACHO CHIYODA; TOKYO JAPAN. (#19349).

BUSINESS BICENTENNIAL PROJECTS CATALOG - DC. LISTING OF NA TIONAL BICENT PROJECTS OFFICIALLY RECOGNIZED BY ARBA I NEED OF ADDITIONAL FINANCIAL ASSISTANCE TO INSUR COMPLETION. OF INTEREST TO BUSINESSES INTERESTED IN SU PORTING BICENT PROJECTS. (NAT'L). RESOURCE DEVELOPMEN DIVISION; AMERICAN REVOLUTION BICENTENNIAL ADMINIS TRATION; 2401 E ST, NW; WASHINGTON, DC 20276. (#28200).

BUSTS OF FRENCH AMER REV WAR HEROS GIVEN TO USA. BUSTS O LAFAYETTE, ROCHAMBEAU, CAVELIER DE LA SALLE, AND AD MIRAL D'ESTAING--FAMOUS REVOLUTIONARY WAS HEROES WILL BE OFFERED TO VARIOUS MUSEUMS & CITIES IN TH UNITED STATES. (INT'L). CULTURAL ATTACHE; EMBASSY O FRANCE; 2535 BELMONT RD; WASHINGTON, DC 2000 (#31900).

CALENDAR OF FOLK FESTIVALS & RELATED EVENTS. ANNUA DETAILED CALENDAR OF FOLK FESTIVALS. (NAT'L). JOSEPH WILSON, EXECUTIVE DIRECTOR; NATIONAL FOLK FESTIVA

WASHINGTON — CONTINUED

SSOC; 1346 CONNECTICUT AVE, NW; WASHINGTON, DC 0036. (#7891).

'CALL FOR ACHIEVEMENT' NATL COMMUNITY GOALS PROJ. PROGRAMS FOR SETTING AND ACHIEVING GOALS IN ALL KINDS OF OMMUNITIES --CITIES, STATES, REGIONS, AND COMMUNITIES F COMMON INTEREST. (NAT'L). SENIOR PROGRAM OFFICER, ORIZONS '76; AMERICAN REVOLUTION BICENTENNIAL ADMINISTRATION; 2401 E STREET, NW; WASHINGTON, DC 20276. #117).

CANADA POST OFFICE ISSUANCE OF COMMEMORATIVE STAMP. ANADA POST OFFICE WILL ISSUE A COMMEMORATIVE STAMP ELEBRATING THE BICENTENNIAL ON JUNE 1, 1976. (INT'L). K E B PERCY, COORDINATOR; EMBASSY OF CANADA; 1746 MASSACHUSETTS AVE, NW; WASHINGTON, DC 20036. (#20737).

CANADIAN BOOK GIFT PROGRAM TO U S COLLEGES - DC. A NATIONWIDE PROGRAM OF BOOK GIFTS FROM THE CANADIAN OVERNMENT TO U S COLLEGES AND UNIVERSITIES HAS BEEN MPLEMENTED DURING THIS BICENTENNIAL YAR. FIRST ECIPIENT WAS JOHNS HOPKINS UNIVERSITY. (INT'L). OFFICE F INFORMATION; CANADIAN EMBASSY; 1746 MASSACHUSETTS AVE, NW; WASHINGTON, DC 20036. (#28443).

CANADIAN FESTIVAL OF THE PERFORMING ARTS, WASH, DC. TWO-WEEK FESTIVAL OF THEATRE, BALLET AND MUSIC. (INT'L). AMANDA MACKENZIE, PUBLIC AFFAIRS COORDINATOR; ANADIAN FESTIVAL FOR THE PERFORMING ARTS-CANADIAN EMBASSY; 1771 N ST, NW; WASHINGTON, DC 20036. (#13694).

CANADIAN FILM FESTIVAL. EXHIBIT AT AMERICAN FILM INSTITUTE, J F KENNEDY CENTER. (INT'L). CULTURAL ATTACHE; ANADIAN EMBASSY; 1746 MASSACHUSETTS AVE; WASHINGTON, DC 20036. (#200010-29).

CANADIAN SCRAPBOOK OF BICENT PROJECTS & EVENTS. A SCRAPBOOK OF ALL CANADIAN PROJECTS & EVENTS WILL BE COMPILED & PRESENTED TO THE PRESIDENT OF THE UNITED STATES BY THE AMBASSADOR OF CANADA AT THE CLOSE FO THE BICENTENNIAL YEAR. (INT'L). K DE B PERCEY, PROJ COORD; EMBASSY OF CANADA; 1746 MASSACHUSETTS AVE, NW; WASHINGTON, DC 20036. (#20494).

CAPITOL INFORMATION CENTER - WASHINGTON, DC. A VISITORS ENTER ON LOWER CAPITOL GROUNDS TO SHOW AWARD WINNING FILM ON WASHINGTON, DC AND TO PROVIDE GENERAL INFORMATION ABOUT THE CONGRESS AN THE DC AREA. (LOCAL). GERALD E COLBERT, DEPUTY DIRECTOR; CENTER FOR MEDIA UNDERSTANDING; 75 HORATIO ST; NEW YORK, NY 0014. (#18237).

CARDIOVASCULAR EXERCISE PROGRAM - DC. A DAILY PROGRAM DESIGNED TO PROMOTE NATIONAL PHYSICAL FITNESS HROUGH CARDIOVASCULAR RESPIRATORY EXERCISE SESSIONS. (ST-WIDE). FREDERICK J BIEBER, PROJ COORDINATOR; SAN DIEGO STATE UNIV; BOX 15133; SAN DIEGO, CA 92115. #14935).

CARTER G WOODSON CENTER BICENT SECTION. THE CENTER, NAMED FOR A FAMOUS BLACK HISTORIAN, WILL CREATE A EFERENCE SECTION TO HOUSE A COLLECTION OF BICENT SOURCE MATERIALS WITH EMPHASIS ON BLACK & OTHER MINORITIES. AVAILABLE TO THE PUBLIC. (NAT'L). J RUPERT ICOTT, EXEC DIRECTOR; ASSOC FOR THE STUDY OF AFRO-AMERICAN LIFE & HISTORY INC; 1401 14TH ST, NW; WASHINGTON, DC 20005. (#8604). **(??).**

'CARTOGRAPHIE IN SWITZERLAND' EXHIBIT IN DC. THIS EXHIBIT WILL BE TOURING THE US UNDER THE AUSPICES OF THE ASSOCIATION OF SCIENCE TECHNOLOGY CENTERS. (INT'L). PAT ORD, PROJECT DIRECTOR; ASSOCIATION OF SCIENCE ECHNOLOGY CENTERS; 2100 PENNSYLVANIA AVE NW; WASHINGTON, DC 20007. (#33394).

CATALOGUE OF THE HOWARD UNIVERSITY ART COLLECTION. THE PHYSICAL CATALOGUING OF THE PERMANENT COLLECTION; RESEARCH AND PREPARATION FOR PUBLICATION OF 2000 AFRICAN AND AFRICAN-AMERICAN ITEMS. NEA GRANT. (ST-WIDE). JEFF R DONALDSON, DIRECTOR; HOWARD UNIV ART GALLERY; 2455 6TH ST, NW; WASHINGTON, DC 20001. #2202).

'CELEBRATION OF AGE', CONFERENCE IN WASHINGTON, DC. NCOA CONFERENCE OF PROMINENT PERSONALITIES SPEAKING ON MAJOR ISSUES CONCERNING AGING, USING SUBJECTS OF BICENTENNIAL-ORIENTED AMERICAN ISSUES FORUM. (NAT'L). JACK OSSOFSKY, EXEC DIRECTOR; NATIONAL COUNCIL ON THE AGING, INC; 1828 L ST, NW; WASHINGTON, DC 20036. #10864).

CEMETERY RESTORATION PROJ OF WASHINGTON, DC. CREATION OF COMMEMORATIVE PARK FROM OLD CEMETERIES IN DC AREA W/COOPERATION OF NATL PARK SVC, CHARITABLE ORGANIZATIONS & PRIVATE DONATIONS. RESEARCH BY THE MOORLAND SPRINGARN RESEARCH CENTER. (LOCAL). MRS VIVIAN ASHTON, PRESIDENT; THE WEE ANGELS, INC; PO BOX 4518; WASHINGTON, DC 20017. (#8647).

THE CENSUS & THE BICENTENNIAL. A BOOKLET HIGHLIGHTING THE HISTORY OF THE US THROUGH ITS CENSUSES DATING BACK TO 1790. IT WILL INCLUDE ALL MAJOR DATES, PLACES & OTHER DATA IN CONNECTION WITH NATIONAL BICENTENNIAL PLANS. (NAT'L). HENRY H SMITH, ACTING CHIEF; BUREAU OF THE CENSUS; DEPARTMENT OF COMMERCE; WASHINGTON, DC 0233. (#173).

CENTENNIAL SAFE IN CUSTODY OF THE US CONGRESS. OPENING & DISPLAY OF A SAFE PRESENTED TO CONGRESS BY MRS CHARLES F DEIHM IN 1876. CONTAINS ITEMS COMMONLY USED & OF PARTICULAR INTEREST TO AMERICANS THEN. SEALED & DONATED DURING CENTENNIAL OBSERVANCE. NAT'L). GEORGE M WHITE, ARCHITECT; US CONGRESS; OFC OF ARCHITECT, US CAPITOL; WASHINGTON, DC 20515. (#83).

CENTENNIAL 1876 EXHIBIT OF SMITHSONIAN INST. AN EXHIBIT RECREATING THE CHARACTER OF THE LATE 19TH CENTURY, & THE SMITHSONIAN'S FIRST NAT'L MUSEUM WHICH HOUSED OBJECTS FROM THE PHILA CENTENNIAL. IN THE ARTS & INDUSTRIES BUILDING. (NAT'L). MRS SUSAN HAMILTON, BICENTENNIAL COORDINATOR; SMITHSONIAN INSTITUTION; 1000 JEFFERSON DR, SW; WASHINGTON, DC 20560. (#74).

CHAIR FOR GERMAN PROFESSOR IN WASHINGTON, DC. ESTABLISHMENT OF A CHAIR FOR A VISITING PROFESSOR AT GEORGETOWN UNIVERSITY IN WASHINGTON, DC, BY THE FEDERAL REPUBLIC OF GERMANY. (INT'L). CULTURAL COUNSELOR; EMBASSY OF THE FEDERAL REPUBLIC OF GERMANY; 4645 RESERVOIR RD, NW; WASHINGTON, DC 20007. (#13695).

CHALLENGE TO TRANSPORTATION - WASHINGTON, DC. FILM OF 25 MINUTES COVERING 200 YEARS OF TRANSPORTATION OF FREIGHT; TO BE USED IN AMERICAN ALBUM SERIES ON SYNDICATED TV STATIONS DURING 1976. (NAT'L). MARY JO LONG, PRESS ASSISTANT; AMERICAN TRUCKING ASSOCIATIONS, INC; 1616 P ST, NW; WASHINGTON, DC 20036. (#20626).

CHALLENGE/RESPONSE PROGRAM. DEVELOPMENT & FREE DISTRIBUTION OF TEN DISCUSSION PAPERS AIMED AT STIMULATING LOCAL THOUGHT & ACTION. TOPICS INCL CITIZEN INVOLVEMENT, ECONOMIC DEVELOPMENT, HEALTH, LEISURE, COMMUNICATIONS, ECOLOGY, ETC. (NAT'L). CHALLENGE/RESPONSE PROGRAM DIRECTOR; DEPT OF HOUSING & URBAN DEVELOPMENT; WASHINGTON, DC 20410. (#33284). **ARBA RECOGNIZED.**

CHAMBER OF COMMERCE OF USA BICENTENNIAL PROGRAM. A TV SERIES OF ONE MINUTE CAPSULE HISTORIES OF MEN & EVENTS IN AMERICAN BUSINESS TO BE DISTRIBUTED AS A PUBLIC SERVICE. (NAT'L). ROBERT H MOXLEY, DIRECTOR OF PROMOTION; CHAMBER OF COMMERCE OF THE USA; 1615 H ST, NW; WASHINGTON, DC 20006. (#32986). **ARBA RECOGNIZED.**

THE CHARLES WILLSON PEALE PAPERS. PUBLICATION IN MICROFICHE & LETTERPRESS OF THE LETTERS, DOCUMENTS, AND PAPERS OF THE REVOLUTIONARY ARTIST AND MUSEUM-KEEPER CHARLES WILLSON PEALE AND THE ARTIST MEMBERS OF HIS IMMEDIATE FAMILY. (NAT'L). DR LILLIAN B MILLER, EDITOR OF C W PEALE PAPERS; NATIONAL PORTRAIT GALLERY - SMITHSONIAN INSTITUTION; F ST AT 8TH, NW; WASHINGTON, DC 20560. (#3749).

CHART OF CHRONOLOGY OF AMER AGRICULTURE 1776-1976. LARGE CHART SHOWING DEVELOPMENT OF AMERICAN AGRICULTURE. (NAT'L). VIVIAN WISER, HISTORIAN; DEPT OF AGRICULTURE, ECONOMIC RESEARCH SERVICE; 500 12TH ST, SW; WASHINGTON, DC 20250. (#1754).

CHARTS--NATL PARK SVC, SUNDAY TIMES OF LONDON. COOPERATION IN PRODUCING CHARTS ON COLONIAL SAILOR, BRITISH SAILOR, COLONIAL SOLDIER, BRITISH SOLDIER, LONDON IN 1776, PHILADELPHIA IN 1776. NPS TO RECEIVE REPRODUCIBLES TO REPRINT BRITISH CHARTS. (INT'L). MANAGER, HARPERS FERRY CENTER; NATIONAL PARK SERVICE; HARPERS FERRY, WV 25425. (#1471).

CHART, 'ERDA ENERGY HISTORY' - WASHINGTON, DC. DESCRIPTIONS AND PICTOGRAMS TRACING EVENTS IN ADVANCEMENTS IN TECHNOLOGY TIED IN WITH CHANGING PRESSURES IN SOCIETY FROM 1776 TO 1976 AND BEYOND TO THE YEAR 2000. (NAT'L). GOVT. FEDERAL; ENERGY RESEARCH AND DEVELOPMENT ADMINISTRATION; WASHINGTON, DC 20545. (#12133).

CHESAPEAKE & OHIO CANAL NHP RESTORATION. THIS PROJECT WILL RESTORE VARIOUS PORTIONS OF THE CANAL FROM WASHINGTON, DC, TO HARPERS FERRY, WEST VIRGINIA. (NAT'L). BICENTENNIAL COORDINATOR, NATIONAL CAPITAL PARKS; NATIONAL PARK SERVICE; 1100 OHIO DR, SW; WASHINGTON, DC 20242. (#333).

CHILDREN'S BICENTENNIAL ISLAND IN WASHINGTON, DC. PARK, PLAYGROUND AND NATURE CENTER FOR CHILDREN, HANDICAPPED AND ELDERLY. (REGN'L). JOSEPH HENSON, PROJ DIRECTOR; DC OFFICE OF BICENTENNIAL PROGRAMS; 1025 15TH ST NW; WASHINGTON, DC 20005. (#10792). **ARBA RECOGNIZED. ARBA GRANTEE.**

THE CHRISTIAN A HERTER LECTURE SERIES - DC. A LECTURE SERIES ON AMERICAN FORIEGN POLICY. (REGN'L). DEA A KLINE, DIRECTOR OF COMMUNITY AFFAIRS; JOHNS HOPKINS UNIV SCHOOL OF ADVANCED INTL STUDIES; 1740 MASSACHUSETTS AVE, NW; WASHINGTON, DC 20036. (#11786).

'CHURCHES AND CATHEDRALS IN SWITZERLAND' EXHIBIT. THIS EXHIBIT WILL BEGIN ITS U S TOUR IN 1976 IN MUSCATINE, IOWA. (INT'L). OFFICE OF INFORMATION; EMBASSY OF SWITZERLAND; 2900 CATHEDRAL AVE; WASHINGTON, DC 20008. (#31922).

CITIZEN ALERT. NATIONWIDE PROGRAM TO TRAIN WOMEN VOLUNTEERS TO AID ECONOMICALLY DISADVANTAGED WOMEN & THEIR FAMILIES UNDERSTAND LOCAL GOVERNMENTAL PRROCESSES & HOW THEIR INVOLVEMENT CAN AFFECT THEIR OWN LIVES. (NAT'L). MARY HALLAREN, EXEC DIRECTOR; WOMEN IN COMMUNITY SERVICE; 1730 RHODE ISLAND AVE, NW; WASHINGTON, DC 20036. (#33283). **ARBA RECOGNIZED.**

CITIZEN INVOLVEMENT NETWORK. A 3-YEAR RESEARCH PROGRAM TO DETERMINE HOW COMMUNITIES CAN USE LOCAL RESOURCES & COOPERATE WITH ONE ANOTHER TO BRING ABOUT DESIRABLE CHANGE. PROGRAM IS TO SUPPORT CITIZEN PARTICIPATION PROJECTS. (NAT'L). JOHN N GENTRY, EXEC DIR; CITIZEN INVOLVEMENT NETWORK; 1211 CONNECTICUT AVE; WASHINGTON, DC 20036. (#23094). **ARBA RECOGNIZED.**

CITIZENS UNITED TO REMOVE BLIGHT - WASHINGTON, DC. CITIZENS UNITED TO REMOVE BLIGHT IS A COMMUNITY IMPROVEMENT PROJECT. (LOCAL). HELEN MITCHELL, PROJ COORDINATOR; OPERATION CURB, OFFICE OF BICENTENNIAL PROGRAMS; 777 14TH ST, NW; WASHINGTON, DC 20005. (#17936). **ARBA GRANTEE.**

CITY CELEBRATION-ANNUAL URBAN FAIR, WASHINGTON, DC. FAIR FEATURING CULTURAL, CREATIVE & PERFORMING ARTS OF THE VARIED COMMUNITIES OF THE NATION'S CAPITAL. (LOCAL). REGINA SAXTON, COORDINATOR; OFFICE OF BICENTENNIAL PROGRAMS; 777 14TH ST, NW; WASHINGTON, DC 20005. (#24893). **ARBA GRANTEE.**

CITY EDGES-DESCRIBING HIST DISTRICTS ACROSS USA. STUDY TO IDENTIFY AND DESCRIBE THE ELEMENTS THAT FORM THE EDGES OF SOME TWENTY EXISTING HISTORIC DISTRICTS ACROSS THE US. TO SERVE AS BASIS FOR A PUBLISHED HANDBOOK. (NAT'L). RUSSELL V KEUNE, DIRECTOR DEPT OF FIELD SERVICES; NATIONAL TRUST FOR HISTORIC PRESERVATION; 740 JACKSON PL, NW; WASHINGTON, DC 20006. (#2417).

CITY HOST: A PROGRAM TO IMPROVE VISITOR SERVICES. A METHODS MANUAL DESIGNED TO ASSIST A COMMUNITY DEVELOPING VISITORS SERVICE PROGRAM. OF INTEREST TO COMMUNITIES WITH POPULATIONS OVER 30,000. (NAT'L). PROGRAMS DIVISION; AMERICAN REVOLUTION BICENTENNIAL ADMINISTRATION; 2401 E ST, NW; WASHINGTON, DC 20276. (#27620).

CITY OUT OF WILDERNESS: WASHINGTON. 28 MINUTE COLOR FILM, 16 & 35MM, ILLUMINATING HISTORY & DEVELOPMENT OF WASHINGTON, DC & US CAPITOL BLDG, WITH FOCUS ON HISTORY & IMPORTANCE OF BLDG. TO BE SHOWN ON CONTINUING BASIS AT NATL VISITOR CNTR. (NAT'L). O B PATTON, EXEC SECRETARY; UNITED STATES CAPITOL HISTORICAL SOCIETY; 200 MARYLAND AVENUE, NE; WASHINGTON, DC 20515. (#3045). **ARBA RECOGNIZED.**

CITY SINGERS BICENTENNIAL TOUR TO WASHINGTON, DC. CONCERT TRACES HISTORY OF U S FROM AMERICAN REVOLUTION TO PRESENT. (REGN'L). RON DREILING, PRESIDENT; GRAND ISLAND CITY SINGERS; 2609 BRAHMA; GRAND ISLAND, NE 68801. (#26551-4).

CITY WITH A PLAN - EXHIBIT ON WASHINGTON, DC. EXHIBITION IN THE ORIGINAL SMITHSONIAN INSTITUTION BUILDING FOCUSING ON THE ARCHITECTURAL AND PLANNING HISTORY OF THE MALL AREA FROM 1776 TO THE PRESENT. (NAT'L). WILCOMB WASHBURN, DIRECTOR, AMERICAN STUDIES; SMITHSONIAN, NCPC, & CFA; 1000 JEFFERSON DR, SW; WASHINGTON, DC 20560. (#1769).

CLEARING HOUSE INFORMATION SYSTEM - WASHINGTON, DC. WRITING AND PUBLICATION OF AN OMNIBUS VISITOR'S BROCHURE. (LOCAL). KATHIE E SAILER, COORDINATOR; BICENTENNIAL COMMISSION OF THE DISTRICT OF COLUMBIA, INC; 1025 15TH ST NW; WASHINGTON, DC 20005. (#13656). **ARBA GRANTEE.**

CLOSE UP: A PROGRAM FOR STUDENTS AND TEACHERS, DC. A PROGRAM OF SEMINARS AND CONFERENCES ON GOVERNMENT & CITIZENSHIP. (LOCAL). GORDON R OLSON, PROGRAM ANALYST; DC PUBLIC SCHOOLS; 415 12TH ST, NW; WASHINGTON, DC 20004. (#24892). **ARBA GRANTEE.**

'CLOTHING AMERICA' - SITES PROJECT. PANEL EXHIBIT ON HISTORY OF READY-MADE CLOTHING IN AMERICA; LOCAL ADDITIONS OF COSTUMES SUGGESTED; 28 ALUMINUM PANELS, READY TO HANG. (NAT'L). ANDREA STEVENS, COORDINATOR; SMITHSONIAN INSTITUTION TRAVELING EXHIBIT SERVICE; WASHINGTON, DC 20560. (#15924).

CNTR FOR DOCUMENTARY STUDY OF AMERICAN REVOLUTION. ESTABLISHED 1971 TO AID SCHOLARLY RESEARCH. DURING THE BICENTENNIAL YEARS THE CENTER WILL PROVIDE INTERESTED PERSONS WITH COPIES OF PREFEDERAL RECORDS & DOCUMENTS, BACKGROUND INFO & ARCHIVES-FINDING AIDS. (NAT'L). KENNETH E HARRIS, CHIEF; CNTR FOR DOCUMENTARY STUDY OF THE AMERICAN REVOLUTION; NATL ARCHIVES & RECORDS SERVICE; WASHINGTON, DC 20408. (#64).

'THE COLLECTED WORKS OF BILLY THE KID'. A PLAY BY CANADIAN PLAYWRIGHT MICHAEL ONDAATJE, PRESENTED IN DC NEW YORK CITY, AND PHILADELPHIA BY THE NEPTUNE THEATER OF HALIFAX. AT FOGER THEATER. (INT'L). CULTURAL ATTACHE; CANADIAN EMBASSY & ROYAL THEATER OF HALIFAX; 1746 MASSACHUSETTS AVE; WASHINGTON, DC 20036. (#200010-31).

THE COMING OF THE AMERICAN ENLIGHTENMENT - BOOK. A STUDY OF THE COMING OF THE AMERICAN ENLIGHTENMENT IN THE LATE SEVENTEENTH AND EARLY EIGHTEENTH CENTURIES WITH A VIEW TO WRITING A BOOK ON THE SUBJECT. (NAT'L). DR JAMES BLESSING, DIRECTOR; NATIONAL ENDOWMENT FOR THE HUMANITIES; 806 15TH ST, NW; WASHINGTON, DC 20506. (#4209). **(??).**

COMMEMORATIVE BANKING STAMP IN 1975. CELEBRATE 200 YEARS OF AMERICAN BANKING BY ISSUANCE OF A COMMEMORATIVE STAMP. (NAT'L). KATIE O' HARA, ASST TO DIR OF PUBLIC RELATIONS; AMERICAN BANKERS ASSOC; 1120 CONNECTICUT AVE, NW; WASHINGTON, DC 20036. (#5630).

COMMITTEE FOR LEAD ELIMINATION ACTION IN DC. THE COMMITTEE FOR LEAD ELIMINATION ACTION IN DC (L E A D) IS WORKING TO ELIMINATE CHILDHOOD LEAD POISONING IN DC THROUGH EDUCATION, HOUSING & HEALTH TASK FORCES. (LOCAL). MRS STEPHANIE KARSTEN, COORDINATOR; COMMITTEE FOR LEAD ELIMINATION ACTION IN DC; 2125 13TH ST, NW; WASHINGTON, DC 20009. (#8640).

COMMUNITY CENTER IN ST MARY'S PARISH, WASH, DC. THE PARISH HALL WILL BE REHABILITATED TO SERVE AS A COMMUNITY CENTER WITH SPECIAL EMPHASIS ON THE ELDERLY & LOW INCOME RESIDENTS OF THE NEIGHBORHOOD. (LOCAL). REV JOHN E WILBUR, RECTOR; ST MARY'S EPISCOPAL CHURCH; 730 23RD ST, NW; WASHINGTON, DC 20037. (#8646).

COMMUNITY PARTICIPATION IN AMERICA'S BICENTENNIAL. COMPILED AS AN IDEA BOOK FOR SISTER CITY COMMUNITIES, BOOKLET DESCRIBES PROJECTS WHICH CAN BE UNDERTAKEN

WASHINGTON — CONTINUED

BY COMMUNITIES IN COMMEMORATION OF THE BICENTENNIAL. (NAT'L). DIRECTOR; SISTER CITIES INTERNATIONAL; 1612 K ST, SUITE 202; WASHINGTON, DC 20006. (#27612).

'COMMUNITY REDISCOVERY '76' - A HOW-TO KIT. A HOW-TO KIT FOR COMMUNITIES TO ASSIST IN DEVELOPING PROJECTS TO IDENTIFY & DRAMATIZE THEIR CULTURAL HERITAGE. OF INTEREST TO GROUPS; NO CHARGE. (NAT'L). PROGRAM DIVISION; AMERICAN REVOLUTION BICENTENNIAL ADMINISTRATION; 2401 E ST, NW; WASHINGTON, DC 20276. (#27619).

COMMUNITY RESOURCE CENTER NOTEBOOK - DC. PROVIDES COMPREHENSIVE HOW-TO ADVICE ON SETTING UP AND RUNNING A COMMUNITY RESOURCE CENTER. OF INTEREST TO GROUPS; NO CHARGE. (NAT'L). DIRECTOR; THE NATIONAL SELF-HELP RESOURCE CENTER; 1800 WISCONSIN AVE, NW; WASHINGTON, DC 20007. (#27618).

COMMUNITY RESOURCE CENTERS (CRC). PROGRAM TO ESTABLISH NATIONWIDE NETWORK OF CRC-PLACES WHERE COMMUNITY RESIDENTS CAN SHARE INFORMATION & SOLVE LOCAL PROBLEMS. TEN MODEL CRC'S WERE CHOSEN & A 'HOW-TO' MANUAL HAS BEEN PREPARED. (NAT'L). SUSAN DAVIS, EXEC DIRECTOR; NATIONAL SELF-HELP RESOURCE CENTER; 1800 WISCONSIN AVE, NW; WASHINGTON, DC 20007. (#33268). **ARBA RECOGNIZED.**

COMMUNITY SERVICES TO INTL VISITORS - 'COSERV'. LANGUAGE, SIGHTSEEING, AND INFORMATION ASSISTANCE TO VISITORS FROM ABROAD IN 88 COMMUNITIES IN THE U.S. HOME HOSPITALITY WHERE POSSIBLE ALL SERVICES PROVIDED BY VOLUNTEERS. (INT'L). ROBERT A AYLWARD, EXEC DIRECTOR; NATL COUNCIL FOR COMMUNITY SERVICES TO INTL VISITORS; 1630 CRESCENT PL, NW; WASHINGTON, DC 20009. (#633).

COMMUNITY SERVICE CNTR FOR THE HEARING IMPAIRED-DC. SERVICES TO DEAF PEOPLE OFFERED BY THE COMMUNITY SERVICE CENTER. (LOCAL). WILLIAM CLAY SAUNDERS, PROJ DIRECTOR; COMMUNITY SERVICE CENTER FOR THE HEARING IMPAIRED; 2010 RHODE ISLAND AVE, NE; WASHINGTON, DC 20018. (#20039).

COMMUNITY SOCCER CLINICS, WASHINGTON, DC. A PROGRAM DESIGNED TO ASSIST COMMUNITY SOCCER CLUBS IN 20 STATES WITH TOP VOLUNTEER SOCCER COACHES RECRUITED FROM LATIN AMERICAN PARTNER COUNTRIES. (INT'L). E DAVID LURIA, ASSOC DIRECTOR; PARTNERS OF THE AMERICAS; 2001 S ST NW; WASHINGTON, DC 20009. (#10727).

COMPLETION OF MARINE CORPS HISTORICAL CENTER - DC. HISTORICAL CENTER IS BEING COMPLETED TO HOUSE THE MARINE CORPS HISTORY AND MUSEUMS DIVISION AND THE MARINE CORPS MUSEUM. (NAT'L). COL F B NIHART, DEPUTY DIRECTOR FOR MUSEUMS; MARINE CORPS HISTORY AND MUSEUMS DIVISION; BLDG 198, WASHINGTON NAVY YARD; WASHINGTON, DC 20374. (#29066).

COMPLIMENTARY BOOK 'DENMARK GETS THE NEWS OF '76'. THE BOOK DESCRIBES HOW DENMARK RECEIVED THE NEWS OF THE DECLARATION OF INDEPENDENCE. (INT'L). NIELS TOFT, PROJ DIRECTOR; DANISH EMBASSY; 3200 WHITEHAVEN PKY, NW; WASHINGTON, DC 20007. (#20776).

COMPREHENSIVE CALENDAR OF BICENT EVENTS: WEST - DC. ONE OF A 2-VOLUME EDITION OF STATE-BY-STATE DETAILS ON LOCAL, STATE, NATIONAL & INTERNATIONAL EVENTS WEST OF THE MISSISSIPPI. AVAILABLE FROM BICENT PUBLICATIONS, SUPT DOCUMENTS, DC 20402. CHARGE. (NAT'L). MASTER CALENDAR SERVICES; AMERICAN REVOLUTION BICENTENNIAL ADMINISTRATION; 2401 E ST, NW; WASHINGTON, DC 20276. (#27610).

COMPREHENSIVE CALENDAR OF BICENT EVENTS: EAST - DC. ONE OF A 2-VOLUME EDITION OF STATE-BY-STATE DETAILS ON LOCAL, STATE, NATIONAL & INTERNATIONAL EVENTS EAST OF THE MISSISSIPPI. AVAILABLE FROM BICENT PUBLICATIONS, SUPT DOCUMENTS, DC 20402. CHARGE. (NAT'L). MASTER CALENDAR SERVICES; AMERICAN REVOLUTION BICENTENNIAL ADMINISTRATION; 2401 E ST, NW; WASHINGTON, DC 20276. (#27611).

COMPUTER-ASSISTED INSTRUCTION PROJ - DC. EDUCATION PROJECT FOR DC PUBLIC SCHOOL STUDENTS. (LOCAL). MILTON WHITE, CHAIRAMN; AFRO-AMERICAN DATANOMICS; 4402 GEORGIA AVE, NW; WASHINGTON, DC 20011. (#22884). **ARBA GRANTEE.**

CONSERVATION OF WORKS OF ART, WASHINGTON, DC. TECHNICAL CONSULTATION ON CONDITION OF WORKS IN THE PHILLIPS COLLECTION AND IMPLEMENTATION OF 2-YEAR CONSERVATION PROGRAM. (REGN'L). RICHARD FRIEDMAN, CURATOR; THE PHILLIPS COLLECTION; 1600 21 ST, NW; WASHINGTON, DC 20009. (#4192).

'CONTINUING REVOLUTION: AMER AGRICULTURE' - SITES. HISTORY AND TECHNOLOGY OF AGRICULTURE IN AMERICAN SOCIETY; 40 PANELS MAKE UP EXHIBITION; LOCAL COLLECTION ADDITIONS ENCOURAGED. (NAT'L). ANDREA STEVENS, COORDINATOR; SMITHSONIAN INSTITUTION TRAVELING EXHIBIT SERVICE; WASHINGTON, DC 20560. (#15922).

COUNT ME IN - NATL DAR HIGH SCHOOL ASSEMBLY PROJ. CONTEMPORARY MULTIMEDIA PRODUCTION TOURING TO HIGH SCHOOLS TO STIMULATE STUDENTS VIA ASSEMBLIES TO WORK IN THEIR SCHOOLS & COMMUNITIES ON ACTIVITIES TO COMMEROATE THE BICENT. 10 TOURING UNITS PLANNED. (NAT'L). DIRECTOR, PROGRAM REVIEW & EVALUATION; AMERICAN REVOLUTION BICENTENNIAL ADMINISTRATION; 2401 E STREET, NW; WASHINGTON, DC 20276. (#2768).

THE COVERDALE COLLECTION OF CANADIAN - SITES, DC. 100 WATERCOLORS, DRAWINGS, PRINTS SHOWING VARIETY OF THEMES OF CANADIAN HISTORY & TOPOGRAPHY AS RECORDED IN THE 18TH AND 19TH CENTURIES. (INT'L). EILEEN HARAKAL, COORDINATOR; SMITHSONIAN INSTITUTION TRAVELING EXHIBITION SERVICE; WASHINGTON, DC 20560. (#26653).

CREATIVE WALLS - WASHINGTON, DC. THE CULTURE AND HISTORY OF THE BLACK COMMUNITY WILL BE FUSED INTO THEMES FOR CREATIVE WALLS. (LOCAL). DONALD S BENJAMIN, ADMINISTRATOR; KUMBA LEARNING CENTER INC; 2506 N ST, SE; WASHINGTON, DC 20019. (#22891). **ARBA GRANTEE.**

CULTURAL VARIETY FOR SCHOOLS. PERFORMANCES & WORKSHOPS FOR ELEM & SECONDARY SCHOOLS - EMPHASIZING MIME & AUDIENCE PARTICIPATION WITH HERITAGE & FUTURE AS SUBJECTS. INCLUDES A MIME HIST OF THE U S, INDIAN RITUALS, MARK TWAIN, ETC. (REGN'L). GARY YOUNG, PRODUCING DIRECTOR; ARCHAESUS PRODUCTIONS INC; 2939 VAN NESS ST, NW #747; WASHINGTON, DC 20008. (#8551).

DANISH BOOK GIFTS - WASHINGTON, DC. TO SUPPORT DANISH STUDIES AT 14 AMERICAN UNIVERSITIES & COLLEGES, BOOK GIFTS OF $1500 EACH PLUS STIPENDS AND EXCHANGE PROFESSORSHIPS WILL BE MADE AVAILABLE. (INT'L). NIELS TOFT, PROJ DIRECTOR; DANISH EMBASSY; 3200 WHITEHAVEN PKY, NW; WASHINGTON, DC 20007. (#20781).

DANISH MUSIC ANTHOLOGY ON RECORDS. SETS OF THE DANISH MUSIC ANTHOLOGY ON RECORDS WILL BE PRESENTED TO 35 AMERICAN CONSERVATORIES. (INT'L). NIELS TOFT, PROJ DIRECTOR; DANISH EMBASSY; 3200 WHITEHAVEN PKY, NW; WASHINGTON, DC 20007. (#20778).

DAR BICENTENNIAL PROGRAM: FOCUS - 1976. PROGRAM OF FIVE PARTS WHICH INCLUDES RESTORATION OF 2 ROOMS AT INDEPENDENCE HALL; DEVELOPMENT & SALE OF 36 MEDALS COMMEMORATING WOMEN OF AMER REVOL; MEMORIAL ROSE GARDEN; A RECORD & OTHER PROJECTS. (NAT'L). MRS ROBERT LACY JACKSON, NATL CHAIRMAN; NATIONAL SOCIETY, DAUGHTERS OF THE AMERICAN REVOLUTION; 1776 D ST, NW; WASHINGTON, DC 20006. (#7896). **ARBA RECOGNIZED.**

DC RECREATION DRUM AND BUGLE CORP. A MUSICAL GROUP OF 125 URBAN YOUTH-15 TO 18 YEARS OF AGE-WHO WILL BE USED AS PERFORMING MUSICAL AMBASSADORS IN CITY AND COMMUNITY BICENTENNIAL FESTIVALS. (LOCAL). RAYMOND GRAY, MUSIC DIRECTOR; DC DEPT OF RECREATION; 3149 16TH ST, NW; WASHINGTON, DC 20010. (#25629). **ARBA GRANTEE.**

DECLARATION OF INTERDEPENDENCE: ED FOR GLOBAL CMTY. NATL EDUCATION ASSOC'S MULTI-PART PROJ WITH THEME OF 'A DECLARATION OF INTERDEPENCE.' INCLUDES PUBS, SATELLITE AS TEACHING TOOL, INTL TEACHER PGM, PEACE STUDIES EXPO, INTL WOMEN'S YEAR IN '75, ETC. (INT'L). MS JANICE COLBERT, BICENTENNIAL COORDINATOR; NATIONAL EDUCATION ASSOCIATION; 1201 16TH ST, NW; WASHINGTON, DC 20036. (#1977). **ARBA RECOGNIZED.**

DEPT OF HEW BICENTENNIAL EXHIBIT. EXHIBIT CENTER FIRST FLOOR HEW SOUTH PORTAL BUILDING. PORTRAYS HEW INVOLVEMENT IN NATION'S HEALTH, EDUCATION, WELFARE. FOCUS ON FUTURE GOALS AND OUTLOOK IN THOSE AREAS. REST AREAS FOR ADULTS, CHILDREN. (NAT'L). ANNE RUSSELL, PROJECT MANAGER; DEPT OF HEALTH, EDUCATION & WELFARE; RM 635G4 - 200 INDEPENDENCE, SW; WASHINGTON, DC 20201. (#1890).

DEPT OF TRANSPORTATION ECE SYMPOSIUM. EUROPEAN CONFERENCE ON URBAN AND TRANS PLANNING AND TOUR OF THE US. (INT'L). RICHARD BOUCHARD, DIR OFF TRANS PLNG ASST; DEPT OF TRANSPORTATION; 400 7TH ST, SW; WASHINGTON, DC 20590. (#1761). **(??).**

DEPT OF TRANSPORTATION/SMITHSONIAN MALL EXHIBIT. DOT PARTICIPATION IN THE FOLK LIFE FESTIVAL ON WASH MALL, SUMMER OF 1976. (NAT'L). RICHARD BOUCHARD, DIR OFF TRANS PLNG ASST; DEPT OF TRANSPORTATION; 400 7TH ST, SW; WASHINGTON, DC 20590. (#1765).

DEPT OF TRANSPORTATION MECCA PROGRAM. PROJECT TO ESTABLISH A CENTER & A HIGHLY COORDINATED SYSTEM OF MEDICAL, TRANSPORTATION, AND COMMUNICATIONS THAT CAN RAPIDLY MOBILIZE CAPABILITIES TO MEET EMERGENCY NEEDS. (NAT'L). RICHARD BOUCHARD, DIR OFF TRANS PLNG ASST; DEPT OF TRANSPORTATION; 400 7TH ST, SW; WASHINGTON, DC 20590. (#1895). **ARBA RECOGNIZED.**

DESIGN IN THE CITY EXHIBIT OF SMITHSONIAN. EXHIBITION IN THE RENWICK GALLERY WHICH WILL FOCUS ATTENTION ON THE CITY-ITS PROMISES AND ITS PROBLEMS-FROM A DESIGN PERSPECTIVE. INCLUDES HISTORICAL & CONTEMPORARY OBJECTS & ACTIVITIES IN WASH, DC. (ST-WIDE). LLOYD HERMAN, ADMINISTRATOR; SMITHSONIAN INSTITUTION; 1000 JEFFERSON DR, SW; WASHINGTON, DC 20560. (#1767).

DIAGNOSTIC TESTING OF PRE-SCHOOL CHILDREN - DC. THIS PROGRAM WILL TEST THE CHILD'S PHYSICAL, SOCIAL, EMOTIONAL AND EDUCATIONAL DEVELOPMENT & PROVIDE FOLLOW-UP TRAINING TO RAISE THE LEVEL OF GROWTH TO THE CHILD'S CHRONOLOGICAL AGE. (LOCAL). YVONNE ALI, PROJ DIRECTOR; NATIONAL CHILD DAY CARE ASSOC; 1200 N CAPITOL ST; WASHINGTON, DC 20002. (#17191).

DIRECTORY FOR BICENTENNIAL PLANNING OF NATL TRUST. LIST OF STATE BICENTENNIAL COMMISSIONS, NATIONAL TRUST ADVISORS, STATE PRESERVATION COORDINATORS, AND STATE HISTORIC PRESERVATION OFFICERS. PRICE $1.50. UPDATED PERIODICALLY. (NAT'L). MRS HELEN BYRD, BICENTENNIAL COORDINATOR; NATL TRUST FOR HISTORIC PRESERVATION; 748 JACKSON PL NW; WASHINGTON, DC 20006. (#1367).

DISCOVER AMERICA WITH THE FIRST AMERICANS PROJECT. DEVELOP AND EXPAND INDIAN-OWNED AND OPERATED TOURS; ESTABLISH FACILITIES ON RESERVATIONS OF INTEREST TO TOURISTS, I.E., NAVAJO SCENIC TOURS; KAH-NEE-TA; OREGON RESORT; SIOUX COUNTRY PACKAGE TOUR. (INT'L). JAMES HAWKINS, SPECIAL ASST FOR INDIAN AFFAIRS; BUREAU OF INDIAN AFFAIRS; DEPARTMENT OF THE INTERIOR; WASHINGTON, DC 20240. (#105).

'DISCOVER BICENTENNIAL AMERICA' NEWS RELEASES. DATO DEVELOPING AN INTENSIVE REGIONAL & NATIONAL CO SUMER-ORIENTED PRINT & BROADCAST MEDIA CAMPAIGN BRING INTO FOCUS THE NATL ASPECTS OF THE BICENTENNIA INCLUDING HIGHLIGHTING TOP EVENTS. (NAT'L). STE KIRSCHNER, PROJECT DIRECTOR; DISCOVER AMERICA TRAV ORGANIZATION - DATO; 1100 CONNECTICUT AVE, N WASHINGTON, DC 20036. (#103416).

'DISCOVER USA: THE BICENTENNIAL TRAVEL GUIDE', DC. CO PREHENSIVE GUIDEBOOK TO THE USA, OVER 200 MAPS PHOTOGRAPHS OF 1,000 PLACES TO VISIT. ALL 50 STATES ONE VOLUME, LISTS 204 LEADING BICENTENNIAL ATTRA TIONS. (NAT'L). ALPHONS J HACKL, PUBLISHER; ACROPOL BOOKS LTD; 2400 17TH ST, NW; WASHINGTON, DC 200 (#22464).

DISTRICT OF COLUMBIA BICENTENNIAL CELEBRATION. NEIGHBC HOOD FESTIVALS BRING TOGETHER CULTURAL & HERITAGE A TIVITIES IN A TWO-DAY CELEBRATION ATTRACTI THOUSANDS OF TOURISTS AND RESIDE NTS. (ST-WID LAWRENCE S STINCHCOMB, PRESIDENT; BICENTENNIAL CO MISSION OF THE DISTRICT OF COLUMBIA, INC; 1025 15TH S NW; WASHINGTON, DC 20005. (#3839).

DOCUMENTARY HIST OF THE 1ST FEDERAL CONGRESS. COLLECTI EDITING AND PUBLISHING 16 VOLUMES OF OFFICIAL RECOR AND UNOFFICIAL SOURCES INCLUDING CONTEMPORA NEWSPAPER ACCOUNTS, PRIVATE LETTERS TO AND FROM CO GRESSMEN, AND DIARIES. (NAT'L). E BERKELEY TOMPKIN EXEC DIRECTOR; NATIONAL HISTORICAL PUBLICATIONS RECORDS COMMISSION; NATIONAL ARCHIVES BLD WASHINGTON, DC 20408. (#2445).

DOROTHY BRONSON SINGERS AS STATE REPRESENTATIVE-NE. S GERS SPONSORED AND SENT TO WASH, DC TO PERFORM STATE REPRESENTATIVES. (LOCAL). MAYRENE GOMPER CHAIRMAN; MITCHELL BICENTENNIAL COMMITTEE; RT MITCHELL, NE 69357. (#30578).

DOWNTOWN THEATRE FESTIVAL, WASHINGTON, DC. DOWNTOV THEATRE PERFORMANCES. (LOCAL). ALICE M DENNE DIRECTOR; WASHINGTON PROJECT FOR THE ARTS; 1227 G NW; WASHINGTON, DC 20005. (#23726). **ARBA GRANTEE.**

'THE DREAM OF AMERICA' - SITES EXHIBIT, DC. EXHIBIT DOC MENTS SWEDISH EMIGRATION TO AMERICA BY EXAMINI THE POLITICAL, SOCIAL & ECONOMIC CONDITIONS OF M 19TH CENTURY SWEDEN, THE JOURNEY TO AMERICA & ADA TATION TO LIFE IN 'THE NEW LAND.'. (INT'L). EILEEN HARAKA COORDINATOR; SMITHSONIAN INSTITUTION TRAVELING E HIBITION SERVICE; WASHINGTON, DC 20560. (#26706).

DUTCH REPUBLIC IN DAYS OF JOHN ADAMS - SITES, DC. THIS E HIBITION DEPICTS THE HISTORY, ART, SCIENCE & SOCIETY 18TH CENTURY HOLLAND. (INT'L). EILEEN HARAKAL, COC DINATOR; SMITHSONIAN INSTITUTION TRAVELING EXHIBITIC SERVICE; WASHINGTON, DC 20560. (#26670).

EAGLE SCOUT BICENTENNIAL CELEBRATION - WASH, DC. COSPC SORS BOY SCOUTS & NATL CAPITAL PARKS. EAGLE SCO CENTER ON MALL SUMMER '76 DURING FOLKLIFE FESTIV WILL PROVIDE VISITOR SERVICES IN DC AREA. APPROX 7 EAGLE SCOUTS NATIONWIDE TO PARTICIPATE. (NAT'L). JOE BANKS, NATIONAL EVENTS DIVISION; BOY SCOUTS OF AME ICA, NATL COUNCIL; N BRUNSWICK, NJ 08902. (#2100).

ECOLOGY 200--OUR CHANGING LAND EXHIBIT. EXHIBIT CHANGES IN THE BIOTA AND LAND FORMS OF WASHINGT DC AS A REFLECTION OF SIMILAR CHANGES OCCURRI THROUGHOUT THE UNITED STATES IN THE MUSEUM OF NAT RAL HISTORY. (NAT'L). MRS SUSAN HAMILTON, BICENTENNI COORDINATOR; SMITHSONIAN INSTITUTION; 1000 JEFFERS DR, SW; WASHINGTON, DC 20560. (#341).

'EDVARD MUNCH, THE MAJOR GRAPHICS' - SITES, DC. AN EXHI TION FROM THE MUNCH MUSEUM IN OSLO BY ONE OF T GREATEST FIGURES IN MODERN PRINTMAKING. (INT'L). EILE HARAKAL, COORDINATOR; SMITHSONIAN INSTITUTI TRAVELING EXHIBITION SERVICE; WASHINGTON, DC 205 (#26704).

EGYPTIAN FILM SERIES IN WASHINGTON, DC. SHAWN AT T AMERICAN FILM FESTIVAL IN KENNEDY CENTER. (INT'L). AHMED M AZZAM; EMBASSY OF THE ARAB REPUBLIC EGYPT; 2200 KALORAMA RD; WASHINGTON, DC 200 (#33397).

ELEMENTARY REPUBLICS OF NEIGHBORHOOD DEMOCRACY. PRODUCE 1) A STATEMENT OF THE CLAIM OF NEIGHBORHO ORGANIZATIONS FOR SELF GOVERNING POWER 2) MOD CHARTERS OF NEIGHBORHOOD ORGANIZATIONS 3) INTERCO NECTED TV PROGRAM OF NEIGHBORHOOD ASSEMBLI (NAT'L). MILTON KOTLER, DIRECTOR; INSTITUTE F NEIGHBORHOOD STUDIES; 1901 QUE ST NW; WASHINGTON, 20009. (#21297).

ELLINGTON MUSIC CENTER IN WASHINGTON, DC. AN INSTITUTI FOR THE CONTINUAL PERPETUATION OF KNOWLEDGE, TRA ING AND PARTICIPATION IN THE JAZZ ARTS. IT WILL ALSO FORD OPPORTUNITIES IN JAZZ FOR STUDENTS, SCHOLARS A LAYMEN. (LOCAL). H BARDONVILLE, DEPUTY DIRECTOR; BICENTENNIAL; 1239 G ST, NW; WASHINGTON, DC 200 (#5620). **(??).**

ENCYCLOPEDIA OF NORTH AMERICAN INDIANS. SUMMARIZI THE PREHISTORY HISTORY & CHANGING CULTURES OF ALL DIAN GROUPS NORTH OF MEXICO, THIS 20 VOLUME SET W BECOME THE STANDARD REFERENCE ON NORTH AMERICAN DIAN HISTORY AND ANTHROPOLOGY. (ST-WIDE). MRS SUS HAMILTON, BICENTENNIAL COORDINATOR; SMITHSONIAN STITUTION; 1000 JEFFERSON DR, SW; WASHINGTON, DC 205 (#103).

WASHINGTON — CONTINUED

ENERGY CONSERVATION PROGRAM - WASHINGTON, DC. A PROGRAM TO PREPARE YOUNGSTERS OF HIGH SCHOOL AGE FOR LEADERSHIP ROLES IN PROMOTING ENERGY CONSERVATION THROUGHOUT THEIR COMMUNITIES; YOUTH TRAINING PROGRAM WILL INVOLVE 12 STATES. (REGN'L). JAMES MERNA, COORDINATOR; BOLTON INSTITUTE; 1835 K ST NW, SUITE 302; WASHINGTON, DC 20006. (#12537).

'ENGLISH DEFENDERS OF AMERICAN FREEDOM, 1774-1778'. FIRST IN SERIES REPRINTING SIGNIFICANT, OUT-OF-PRINT PAMPHLETS FROM THE REVOLUTIONARY PERIOD. OTHER VOLUMES IN PLANNING STAGES. (NAT'L). DR JAMES HUTSON, BICENTENNIAL COORDINATOR; LIBRARY OF CONGRESS; 10 FIRST ST, SE; WASHINGTON, DC 20540. (#130).

ENRICHMENT LAB - WASHINGTON, DC. THE LAB WILL PRESENT THEATRE AND INVOLVE PEOPLE IN THE COMMUNITY IN SEMINARS & DISCUSSION ON THEIR ETHNIC BACKGROUNDS. (LOCAL). GARY YOUNG, PROJECT DIRECTOR; ARCHAESUS PRODUCTIONS, INC; 2939 VAN NESS ST, NW; WASHINGTON, DC 20008. (#22895). **ARBA GRANTEE.**

ENVIRONMENTAL AWARENESS PGMS OF THE NATL PARK SVC. MANY AREAS WITH THE NATIONAL PARK SYSTEM ARE PREPARING PROGRAMS ON AMERICA'S ENVIRONMENT - PAST, PRESENT & FUTURE. (NAT'L). BICENTENNIAL COORDINATOR; NATIONAL PARK SERVICE; 18TH & C STS, NW; WASHINGTON, DC 20240. (#6725).

ENVIRONMENTAL LIVING PROGRAM OF NATL PARK SVC. PGM AIMS AT CREATING AN UNDERSTANDING OF ENVIRONMENT BY LIVING IN & RECREATING NATURAL/CULTURAL ENVIRONS OF THE PAST. EVOLVED FROM COOPERATION NPS, STATES OF CA & AZ. KIT BECOMES AVAILABLE DURING BICENT. (NAT'L). DIVISION OF INTERPRETATION; NATIONAL PARK SERVICE; 18TH & C STS, NW; WASHINGTON, DC 20240. (#6860).

ENVIRONMENTAL STUDY TOUR FOR INTERNATIONAL EXPERTS. FIVE DAY STUDY TOUR TO WILLIAMSBURG AND NORTH CAROLINA FOR ENVIRONMENTAL EXPERTS OF 35 NATIONS FOLLOWING MEETING OF INTERNATL COORDINATING COUNCIL OF UNESCO'S WORLDWIDE MAN AND BIOSPHERE PROGRAM. (INT'L). RAYMOND F KOHN, DIRECTOR, US COMMITTEE; UNITED STATES NATIONAL COMMITTEE FOR MAN AND THE BIOSPHERE; DEPT OF STATE; WASHINGTON, DC 20520. (#2034).

EQUAL OPPORTUNITY PROGRAM. IMPLEMENTATION OF A COMPREHENSIVE PROGRAM TO INCREASE THE SUPPLY OF QUALIFIED AND/OR QUALIFIABLE MINORITY AND WOMEN COLLEGE GRADUATES FOR BUSINESS, EDUCATION AND GOVERNMENT CAREERS. (NAT'L). CYRIL C LING, EXEC VICE-PRESIDENT; AMERICAN ASSEMBLY OF COLLEGIATE SCHOOLS OF BUSINESS; 1755 MASSACHUSETTS AVE, NW; WASHINGTON, DC 20036. (#8617).

EVERYBODY, INC - SPATIAL OPERA IN WASHINGTON, DC. SPATIAL OPERA IN WASHINGTON, DC. (LOCAL). HENRY BRANT, COMPOSER; NATIONAL ENDOWMENT FOR THE ARTS; 2401 E ST, NW; WASHINGTON, DC 20506. (#28182).

'EVERYDAY LIFE IN THE AMERICAN PAST' EXHIBIT. SATELLITE EXHIBIT TO THE SMITHSONIAN'S 'NATION OF NATIONS' EXHIBIT. (NAT'L). MRS SUSAN HAMILTON, BICENTENNIAL COORDINATOR; SMITHSONIAN INSTITUTION; 1000 JEFFERSON DR, SW; WASHINGTON, DC 20560. (#69). **(??).**

THE EVOLUTION OF AMERICAN CULTURE - POSTER EXHIBIT. SERIES OF 16 POSTER-PANEL EXHIBITS ON AMERICAN CULTURE & RELATING TO BOTH SMITHSONIAN COLLECTIONS & COLLECTIONS THROUGHOUT THE COUNTRY. PLANNED FOR TRAVEL & LOCAL COMMUNITY PARTICIPATION. (NAT'L). MRS SUSAN HAMILTON, BICENTENNIAL COORDINATOR; SMITHSONIAN INSTITUTION; 1000 JEFFERSON DR, SW; WASHINGTON, DC 20560. (#303).

EXCHANGE OF SCHOLARS WITH THE NETHERLANDS. AN ACADEMIC EXCHANGE BETWEEN AMERICAN & DUTCH SCHOLARS. (INT'L). PRESS AND CULTURAL SECTION; NETHERLANDS EMBASSY; 4200 LINNEAN AVE, NW; WASHINGTON, DC 20008. (#24415).

EXECUTIVE PROTECTIVE SERVICE BICENT BREAST BADGE. BICENT BREAST BADGE BEING WORN BY ALL MEMBERS OF THE FORCE DURING THE ENTIRE BICENT CALENDAR YEAR, INSTEAD OF REGULARLY ISSUED BADGE, TO CELEBRATE THE 200TH ANNIVERSARY YEAR OF THIS NATION'S BIRTH. (ST-WIDE). EARL A DRESCHER, CHIEF; EXECUTIVE PROTECTIVE SERVICE, US SECRET SERVICE; 1310 L ST, NW; WASHINGTON, DC 20005. (#20598).

EXHIBIT OF AMERICAN JEWISH HISTORY; WASHINGTON, DC. THIS EXHIBIT IS SPONSORED BY BNAI BRITH AND IS ENTITLED 'TO BIGOTRY, NO SANCTION, TO PREJUDICE, NO ASSISTANCE'. (NAT'L). YALE GOLDBERG, DIRECTOR OF ADMINISTRATION; BNAI BRITH; 1640 RHODE ISLAND AVE, NW; WASHINGTON, DC 20036. (#17192).

EXHIBIT OF COSTUMES FROM CANADA'S LE THEATRE DE NOUVEAU MONDE. EXHIBIT AT GRAND FOYER OF THE KENNEDY CENTER. (INT'L). CULTURAL ATTACHE; CANADIAN EMBASSY; 1746 MASSACHUSETTS AVE; WASHINGTON, DC 20036. (#200010-30).

EXHIBIT OF HISTORY OF BLACKS IN AMERICA. AN EXHIBIT DISPLAYING THE BLACK EXPERIENCE IN AMERICA TO BE MOUNTED BY THE NATIONAL PORTRAIT GALLERY OF THE SMITHSONIAN. (NAT'L). MRS SUSAN HAMILTON, BICENTENNIAL COORDINATOR; SMITHSONIAN INSTITUTION; 1000 JEFFERSON DR, SW; WASHINGTON, DC 20560. (#81).

AN EXHIBIT PROJECT IN WASHINGTON, DC. DEPICTS THE IDEAS & IDEALS OF THE MEN & WOMEN INSTRUMENTAL IN THE FORMATION OF THE USA. DESIGNED FOR USE IN DIFFERENT CULTURAL EVENTS IN VARIOUS LOCATIONS THRUOUT THE WORLD. 5 LANGUAGE VERSIONS. (INT'L). MICHAEL SCHNEIDER, ICS/USIA; US INFORMATION AGENCY; 1717 H ST, NW; WASHINGTON, DC 20547. (#21374).

EXHIBITION OF CONTEMPORARY YUGOSLAV PRINTS. EXHIBIT OF 99 PIECES OF GRAPHIC ARTS, INCLUDING LITHOGRAPHS, SEROGRAPHS, ETCHINGS, ENGRAVINGS, AQUATINTS. FROM BIENNIAL GRAPHIC ARTS EXHIBIT HELD IN YUGOSLAVIA IN 1975. (INT'L). JOHN P MULLIGAN; ASSOCIATION OF SCIENCE-TECHNOLOGY CENTERS; 2100 PENNSYLVANIA AVE, NW; WASHINGTON, DC 20037. (#24420).

EXHIBITION OF KLIMT & SCHIELE DRAWINGS - DC. THIS EXHIBITION FROM AUSTRIA WILL TOUR THE US IN 1976. (INT'L). CULTURAL ATTACHE; EMBASSY OF AUSTRIA; 2343 MASSACHUSETTS AVE; WASHINGTON, DC 20008. (#32960).

EXHIBITION OF YUGOSLAV NAIVE ART - SITES. ILLUSTRATES CURRENT DIRECTIONS & EVOLUTION OF NAIVE YUGOSLAV ART. INCL WORKS BY VECENAJ, RABUZIN, SKURJENI, KOVACIC, & LACKOVIC. WOOD SCULPTURES, PAINTINGS, MAPS, FILMS, TAPES ON TRADIT YUGOSLAV MUSIC. (INT'L). REGINA LIPSKY; SMITHSONIAN INSTITUTION TRAVELING EXHIBITION SERVICE; SMITHSONIAN INSTITUTION; WASHINGTON, DC 20560. (#24417).

EXHIBITION-CONTEMPORARY AFRICAN ART IN WASH, DC. TRAVELLING EXHIBITION INCLUDING SCULPTURE PAINTING CERAMICS TEXTILES GRAPHICS DESIGN. DISPLAY OF WORKS WORKSHOPS AND SEMINARS WITH SELECT ED AFRICAN ARTISTS. (INT'L). KOJO FOSU BAIDEN, PROJECT DIRECTOR; COLLEGE OF FINE ARTS, HOWARD UNIV; 2400 6TH ST, NW; WASHINGTON, DC 20001. (#2964). **(??).**

EXHIBIT, SOCIAL SECURITY BENEFITS AND PROTECTION. A MULTIMEDIA EXHIBIT ON SOCIAL SECURITY BENEFITS IN THE NEXT DECADES AND INTO THE 21ST CENTURY INFLATION PROOF BENEFITS AND COMPREHENSIVE COVERAGE. (NAT'L). MILTON WISOFF, CHIEF, AUDIO-VISUAL STAFF; SOCIAL SECURITY ADMINISTRATION; 6401 SECURITY BLVD; BALTIMORE, MD 21235. (#1791).

EXPANSION OF COMMUNITY INFO SERVICES IN WASH, DC. EXISTING SYSTEM WILL BE ENLARGED TO INFORM RESIDENTS AND VISITORS IN 1976 OF BICEN. ACTIVITIES. SYSTEM TO INCLUDE WALK-IN CENTER, EXPANDED NEWSLETTER, VIDEOTAPE PROGRAM, COORDINATION OF LOCAL EVENTS. (ST-WIDE). LAWRENCE S STINCHCOMB, EXEC VICE PRESIDENT; DC BICENTENNIAL COMMISSION; 1239 G ST, NW, 4TH FLOOR; WASHINGTON, DC 20005. (#794). **(??). ARBA GRANTEE.**

EXPERIMENTAL PRISONER RELEASE PROJECT. DEVELOP A PROGRAM DESIGNED TO SEEK EARLY RELEASE OF FIRST OFFENDERS UNDER A COUNCILING PROGRAM WHERE ONE IS TRAINED FOR A SPECIFIC JOB & PROVIDED EMPLOYMENT UPON COMPLETION. (NAT'L). WAYNE J SMITH, EXEC DIRECTOR; FDN FOR THE ADVANCEMENT OF INMATE REHABILITATION & RECREATION; 500 12TH ST, SW, SUITE 810; WASHINGTON, DC 20024. (#266). **(??).**

EXPERIMENTAL THEATER FOR J F KENNEDY CENTER IN DC. JAPAN IS CONTRIBUTING A NEW 500-SEAT EXPERIMENTAL THEATER ON THE TOP FLOOR OF THE KENNEDY CENTER. (INT'L). CULTURAL ATTACHE; EMBASSY OF JAPAN; 2520 MASSACHUSETTS AVE; WASHINGTON, DC 20008. (#33392).

'THE EYE OF THOMAS JEFFERSON' - EXHIBITION IN WASH. EXHIBIT CENTERING ON JEFFERSON'S CONTRIBUTIONS IN ARCHITECTURE, TOWN PLANNING LANDSCAPE GARDENING, LITERATURE IN SOCIETY & THE ARTS DEMONSTRATION OF THE MANY FACETS OF LATE 18TH CENTURY MAN. (INT'L). ROSS WATSON, CURATOR; NATIONAL GALLERY OF ART; 6TH & CONSTITUTION AVE, NW; WASHINGTON, DC 20565. (#684).

FEB 1976 INDEX OF BICENTENNIAL ACTIVITIES. LISTS TITLES OF PROJECTS & EVENTS BY CITY & STATE AND GIVES VOLUME & PAGE NUMBERS IN THE COMPREHENSIVE CALENDARS OF BICENT EVENTS AND MASTER REGISTER OF PROJECTS WHERE DETAILS MAY BE FOUND. (NAT'L). MASTER CALENDAR SERVICES; AMERICAN REVOLUTION BICENTENNIAL ADMINISTRATION; 2401 E ST, NW; WASHINGTON, DC 20276. (#27608).

FEDERAL FORESTRY CENTENNIAL OF DEPT OF AGRICULTURE. CELEBRATION OF 100 YRS OF FEDERAL FORESTRY. EMPHASIS ON CONTRIBUTION TO COUNTRY'S HERITAGE DEVELOPMENT AND PROJECTED HORIZONS. MANY LOCAL AND VARIED EVENTS PLANNED. (NAT'L). GLENN A KOVAR, CHIEF SPECIAL PROJECTS; DEPT OF AGRICULTURE, FOREST SERVICE; 12TH & INDEPENDENCE AVE; WASHINGTON, DC 20250. (#1755).

FEDERAL GOVERNMENT EVOLUTION LECTURE SERIES. THE NATL ARCHIVES IS PREPARING A SERIES OF LECTURES ON THE EVOLUTION OF THE CONCEPTS BEHIND EACH OF THE THREE BRANCHES OF GOVERNMENT. (NAT'L). DR FRANK BURKE, DIRECTOR, EDUCATIONAL PROGRAMS; NATIONAL ARCHIVES AND RECORD SERVICE; 7TH & PENNSYLVANIA AVE, NW; WASHINGTON, DC 20408. (#72).

FEDERALISM SEVENTY-SIX PROJECT. TO BRING ABOUT MORE INFORMED, RESPONSIBLE & ENERGETIC CITIZEN ENGAGE MENT IN THE NATION'S GOVERNANCE, FOSTERING A DEEPER & WIDESPREAD UNDERSTANDING OF THE NATION'S PUBLIC INSTITUTIONS & PROCESSES, ETC. (NAT'L). CARL F STOVER, PRESIDENT; FEDERALISM SEVENTY-SIX; 1900 L ST, NW; WASHINGTON, DC 20036. (#717).

'THE FEDERALIST PAPERS REEXAMINED'. THE INTELLECTUAL, SOCIAL AND POLITICAL FOUNDATIONS OF OUR GOVERNMENT ARE BEING STUDIED IN 6 SMALL SEMINARS. DISCUSSION MATERIALS FROM THE SEMINARS WILL GO TO LOCAL LEAGUES TO STIMULATE SIMILAR PROGRAMS. (NAT'L). HAL LIPPMAN, PROJECT DIRECTOR; LEAGUE OF WOMEN VOTERS EDUCATION FUND; 1730 M STREET, NW; WASHINGTON, DC 20036. (#27289). **ARBA RECOGNIZED.**

FESTIVAL AT THE KENNEDY CENTER, WASHINGTON, DC. THE TOWN AND GOWN THEATER OF THE UNIVERSITY OF ALABAMA WILL SPONSOR A FESTIVAL AT THE KENNEDY CENTER FOR THE PERFORMING ARTS. (REGN'L). JAMES HATCHER, DIRECTOR; UNIV OF ALABAMA - BIRMINGHAM; TOWN AND GOWN THEATER; BIRMINGHAM, AL 35294. (#24729). **ARBA GRANTEE.**

FESTIVAL OF AMERICAN FOLKLIFE. A 12 WEEK FESTIVAL CELEBRATING THE MULTIPLICITY & DIVERSITY OF AMERICAN HERITAGE THROUGH MUSIC, DANCE, CRAFTS & FOOD. THIS IS AN ANNUAL CELEBRATION OF AMERICAN FOLK CULTURES & TRADITIONS. (INT'L). SUSANNE ROSCHWALB, CHIEF, PUBLIC AFFAIRS; SMITHSONIAN INSTITUTION, DIVISION OF PERFORMING ARTS; SUITE 2100, 955 L'ENFANT PLAZA; WASHINGTON, DC 20560. (#111). **ARBA RECOGNIZED.**

FESTIVAL OF AMERICAN MUSIC & DANCE, WASHINGTON. FESTIVAL IN AMERICAN MUSIC AND DANCE, FEATURES BLACKS IN AMERICAN THEATRE, FOLK SONGS AND 3 MUSICALS. (LOCAL). SAMUEL BONDS, DIRECTOR; WOODSON MALE CHORUS AND COMPANY; 1828 S ST, SE; WASHINGTON, DC 20020. (#25930). **ARBA GRANTEE.**

'FESTIVAL USA' THROUGHOUT THE NATIONAL PARK SYSTEM. THROUGHOUT THE NATION, THE NATIONAL PARK SERVICE AREAS ARE COOPERATING WITH LOCAL COMMUNITIES IN PREPARING FESTIVE EVENTS FOR THE BICENTENNIAL. (NAT'L). BICENTENNIAL COORDINATOR; NATIONAL PARK SERVICE; 18TH & C STS, NW; WASHINGTON, DC 20240. (#6728).

FILM ON FINNISH COMMUNITIES IN THE UNITED STATES. A LEADING FINNISH FILM MAKER IS DOING A FILM ON FINNISH COMMUNITIES IN THE UNITED STATES. (INT'L). CULTURAL ATTACHE; EMBASSY OF FINLAND; 1900 24TH ST; WASHINGTON, DC 20008. (#31880).

FILM ON 'MONARCHY AND DEMOCRACY' - WASHINGTON, DC. A DOCUMENTARY FILM, 'MONARCHY AND DEMOCRACY', WILL BE RELEASED IN CONNECTION WITH THE BICENTENNIAL. (INT'L). NIELS TOFT, PROJ DIRECTOR; DANISH EMBASSY; 3200 WHITEHAVEN PKY, NW; WASHINGTON, DC 20007. (#20782).

FILM--'AMERICANS AND THE REVOLUTION'-NATL PARK SVC. INTENDED TO BE INSPIRATIONAL, THIS FILM WILL BE A SIGNIFICANT PORTRAYAL OF THE REVOLUTIONARY PERIOD AS A KIND OF SOCIAL HISTORY OF THE TIMES. TO BE AVAILABLE TO ALL NPS AREAS. (NAT'L). MANAGER, HARPERS FERRY CENTER; NATIONAL PARK SERVICE; HARPERS FERRY, WV 25425. (#1476).

FILM, 'ENERGY USA' - WASHINGTON, DC. MOTION PICTURE ON SWEEP OF AMERICA'S DEVELOPMENT FROM WHEN WE HAD AMPLE ENERGY SOURCES IN 1776 TO THE HEIGHT OF THE INDUSTRIAL REVOLUTION IN 1876 TO PROBLEMS OF 1976 AND HOW ERDA WILL SEEK SOLUTION. (NAT'L). CHARLES PELZER, OFFICE OF PUBLIC AFFAIRS; ENERGY RESEARCH AND DEVELOPMENT ADMINISTRATION; WASHINGTON, DC 20545. (#12132).

'FINNS IN NORTH AMERICA' PUBLICATION. THIS SPECIAL PUBLICATION WRITTEN BY ELOISE ENGEL, WAS DISTRIBUTED BY THE FINNISH EMBASSY. (INT'L). CULTURAL ATTACHE; EMBASSY OF FINLAND; 1900 24TH ST; WASHINGTON, DC 20008. (#33327).

THE FIRST CONTINENTAL CONGRESS PORTRAIT EXHIBIT. AN EXHIBITION BY THE NATIONAL PORTRAIT GALLERY OF THE SMITHSONIAN OF PORTRAITS OF THE DELEGATES TO THE FIRST CONTINENTAL CONGRESS. SLIDE SETS, BOOKLETS, AND OTHER EDUCATIONAL AIDS WILL BE FORTHCOMING. (NAT'L). MRS SUSAN HAMILTON, BICENTENNIAL COORDINATOR; SMITHSONIAN INSTITUTION; 1000 JEFFERSON DR, SW; WASHINGTON, DC 20560. (#82).

'FIVE CRITICAL ELECTIONS' - SITES PROJECT. 35 COLORFUL PANELS DESCRIBE THE ISSUES, CANDIDATES, CAMPAIGNS AND DEVICES USED FOR THE ELECTIONS OF 1800, 1828, 1860, 1896 AND 1936. (NAT'L). ANDREA STEVENS, COORDINATOR; SMITHSONIAN INSTITUTION TRAVELING EXHIBIT SERVICE; WASHINGTON, DC 20560. (#15928).

'FOCUS ON AMERICAN JOURNALISM' - SITES PROJECT. HISTORY OF NEWS REPORTING AND THOSE MEN & MACHINES RESPONSIBLE FOR DEVELOPMENT OF AMERICAN JOURNALISM; 35 FRAMED PANELS. (NAT'L). ANDREA STEVENS, COORDINATOR; SMITHSONIAN INSTITUTION TRAVELING EXHIBIT SERVICE; WASHINGTON, DC 20560. (#15921).

FOLK FESTIVAL USA, WASHINGTON, DC. RADIO SERIES FEATURING AMERICAN FOLK AND TRADITIONAL MUSIC IN LIVE PERFORMANCE SETTING. PROGRAM ORIGINATES FROM VARIOUS CONCERT & FESTIVAL SITES. PRODUCED NATIONWIDE THRU 186 MEMBER STATIONS. (NAT'L). STEVE RATHE, EXEC PRODUCER, FOLK FESTIVAL USA; NATIONAL PUBLIC RADIO; 2025 M STREET, NW; WASHINGTON, DC 20036. (#23295).

FOLK WOODCUTS FROM BRAZIL'S NORTHEAST - SITES, DC. THESE WOODCUTS, USED AS PAMPHLET COVERS, ILLUSTRATE THE FOLK LITERATURE OF THE NORTHEAST REGION OF BRAZIL. (INT'L). EILEEN HARAKAL, COORDINATOR; SMITHSONIAN INSTITUTION TRAVELING EXHIBITION SERVICE; WASHINGTON, DC 20560. (#26651).

FORD'S THEATRE PRODUCTIONS, WASHINGTON, DC. A SERIES OF MUSICALS AND DRAMATIC PLAYS FOR THE BICENTENNIAL AT THE FORD'S THEATRE IN 1976. (REGN'L). ALMA VIATOR, COMMUNICATION DIRECTOR; FORD'S THEATRE; 511 10TH ST, NW; WASHINGTON, DC 20004. (#5606).

FOREIGN OLYMPIC HOSTING - WASHINGTON, DC. FACILITATED APPEARANCE OF 12 FOREIGN OLYMPIC TEAMS PLUS INTERNATIONAL COMPETITIONS FOR HANDICAPPED & HIGH SCHOOL STUDENTS. ALSO SUPPORTED 7 TRACK CLINICS FOR 8 AFRICAN NATIONS IN ETHIOPIA. (INT'L). WILLIAM G MCNAMARA, EXECUTIVE DIRECTOR; AMERICAN COUNCIL ON INTERNATIONAL SPORTS; 817 23RD ST, NW; WASHINGTON, DC 20052. (#32720).

FOREST SERVICE MINI MUSEUMS, VISITOR INFO SERVICE. A VARIETY OF MINI MUSEUMS AT NUMEROUS FOREST SERVICE FACILITIES-INTERPRETIVE MATERIAL ON LOCAL F S AREAS AND THEIR CONTRIBUTION TO HERITAGE AND HORIZONS. (NAT'L). GLENN A KOVAR, CHIEF SPECIAL PROJECTS; DEPT OF AGRICUL-

WASHINGTON — CONTINUED

TURE, FOREST SERVICE; 12TH & INDEPENDENCE AVE, SW; WASHINGTON, DC 20250. (#1758).

FORT LINCOLN NEW TOWN, WASHINGTON, DC. NEW TOWN-IN-TOWN PROVIDING FOR 16,000 LOW & MIDDLE INCOME FAMILIES & ALSO JOBS, COMMERCE, RECREATIONAL FACILITIES, EDUCATIONAL ACTIVITIES, & OTHER URBAN FACILITIES. (ST-WIDE). MARIAN FRYER, ADMIN OFFICER; DC DEPARTMENT OF HOUSING & COMMUNITY DEVELOPMENT; 1325 G ST N W; WASHINGTON, DC 20005. (#188).

FOUR C'S FOR CENTURY III. PROGRAM FOCUSES ON COMMUNITY, CAMPUS, CAMP AND CHARACTER BEAUTIFICATION. COMMUNITY BEAUTIFICATION INCLUDES INDIVIDUAL CHURCHES, VACANT LOTS AND LOCAL AND STATE PARKS. (NAT'L). LEO RANZOLIN, ASSOCIATE YOUTH DIRECTOR; GENERAL CONFERENCE OF SEVENTH-DAY ADVENTISTS; 6840 EASTERN AVE, NW; WASHINGTON, DC 20012. (#4515). **ARBA RECOGNIZED.**

'THE FOURTH PART OF THE WORLD' - SITES EXHIBIT, DC. MAJOR THEME OF THE EXHIBIT IS THE EXPLORATION OF AUSTRALIA WITH EMPHASIS ON SIMILAR DEVELOPMENT IN AMERICAN HISTORY. (INT'L). EILEEN HARAKAL, COORDINATOR; SMITHSONIAN INSTITUTION TRAVELING EXHIBITION SERVICE; WASHINGTON, DC 20560. (#28439).

FOXFIRE PROGRAM. HIGH SCHOOL STUDENTS INTERVIEW OLDER AMERICANS AND WRITE ARTICLES ON THEIR HERITAGE, CRAFTS, ARTS & FOLKLORE FOR PUBLICATION IN FOXFIRETYPE MAGAZINES. (NAT'L). MURRAY DURST, EXEC VICE PRESIDENT; IDEAS - INSTITUTIONAL DEVELOPMENT & ECONOMIC AFFAIRS, INC; 1783 MASSACHUSETTS AVE, NW; WASHINGTON, DC 20036. (#1). **ARBA RECOGNIZED. ARBA GRANTEE.**

THE FREDERICK LAW OLMSTED PAPERS IN WASHINGTON, DC. EDITING FOR PUBLICATION SELECTED LETTERS OF FREDERICK LAW OLMSTED, WRITER ON ANTEBELLUM SOUTH, LANDSCAPE ARCHITECT & CITY PLANNER. COVERS 1822-1903 IN SEVEN VOLUMES. (NAT'L). CHARLES C MCLAUGHLIN, EDITOR IN CHIEF; THE AMERICAN UNIV; MASSACHUSETTS AVE, NW; WASHINGTON, DC 20016. (#5383).

FRENCH POPULAR ART EXHIBITION - SITES, DC. OVER 100 ITEMS FROM THE MUSEE NATIONAL DES ARTS ET TRADITIONS POPULAIRES EXPLORE THE QUESTION 'IS THE TRADITION OF POPULAR ART IN FRANCE UNINTERRUPTED AND WILL IT CONTINUE?'. (INT'L). EILEEN HARAKAL, COORDINATOR; SMITHSONIAN INSTITUTION TRAVELING EXHIBITION SERVICE; WASHINGTON, DC 20560. (#26658).

FRISBEE FOR THE BICENTENNIAL. BICENTENNIAL TOY FLYING SAUCER MADE OF WHITE PLASTIC. ARBA LICENSE NO 76-19-0600. (NAT'L). EDWARD BARRETT, ATTORNEY; LITTLE ANGEL TOY DISTRIBUTOR; 1225 CONNECTICUT AVE, NW; WASHINGTON, DC 20006. (#21178).

'FRITZ WOTRUBA' EXHIBITION - SITES, WASHINGTON, DC. A RETROSPECTIVE EXHIBITION OF AUSTRIA'S GREATEST CONTEMPORARY SCULPTOR; INCLUDES 30 BRONZE SCULPTURES, 15 DRAWINGS, 30 GRAPHICS. (INT'L). EILEEN HARAKAL, COORDINATOR; SMITHSONIAN INSTITUTION TRAVELING EXHIBITION SERVICE; WASHINGTON, DC 20560. (#26665).

'FROM FEW TO HEW' - FILM PROJ OF THE DEPT OF HEW. AN INFORMATION & TRAINING FILM W/ILLUSTRATED TEXT, TRACING THE EVOLUTION OF CONCEPTS INVOLVED IN HEALTH, EDUCATION & WELFARE FROM THE NATION'S FOUNDING TO THE PRESENT & INTO THE FUTURE. (NAT'L). ANNE RUSSELL, PROJ MANAGER; DEPT OF HEALTH, EDUCATION & WELFARE; 330 INDEPENDENCE AVE, SW, #4725N; WASHINGTON, DC 20201. (#1792).

GERMAN RADIO-TV BICENT DOCUMENTARY SERIES - NBMRP. THIS GROUP HAS FILMED ON LOCATION IN THE UNITED STATES FOR BROADCAST IN GERMANY DOCUMENTARIES ON SUCH AS GERMAN IMMIGRANTS TO AMERICA; ALSO MAJOR BICENT EVENTS & RE-ENACTMENTS HAVE ALSO BEEN COVERED. (INT'L). MARYLOU HUMPHREY, BICENTENNIAL COORDINATOR; GERMAN RADIO AND TELEVISION; 3132 M ST, NW; WASHINGTON, DC 20007. (#22797).

GHENT, BELGIUM SPONSORS 'MINI PARK' IN DC. A MINI-PARK WILL BE DEVELOPED IN WASHINGTON AS A BICENTENNIAL GIFT OF THE CITY OF GHENT, BELGIUM. (INT'L). CULTURAL ATTACHE; EMBASSY OF BELGIUM; 3330 GARFIELD ST; WASHINGTON, DC 20008. (#31899).

GIFT FROM DENMARK - WASHINGTON, DC. A MODERNISTIC RELIEF DONE BY THE ROYAL COPENHAGEN PORCELAIN FACTORY WAS GIVEN TO THE KENNEDY CENTER BY DENMARK IN HONOR OF THE U S BICENTENNIAL. PRESENTED MAY 11, 1976 BY THE QUEEN OF DENMARK. (INT'L). CULTURAL ATTACHE; ENBASSY OF DENMARK; 3200 WHITEHAVEN ST; WASHINGTON, DC 20008. (#31925).

GIFT FROM SPAIN - WASHINGTON, DC. AS A PERMANENT CONTRIBUTION HONORING THE U S BICENTENNIAL, A STATUE OF BERNARDO DE GALVEZ WILL BE ERECTED. REPLICAS ARE PLANNED FOR GALVESTON, TX; PENSACOLA, FL; & NEW ORLEANS, LA. (INT'L). CULTURAL ATTACHE; EMBASSY OF SPAIN; 2700 15TH ST; WASHINGTON, DC 20009. (#31926).

GOVERNMENT FILMS ON AMERICAN HISTORY-NATL ARCHIVES. INFORMATION ON THE AVAILABILITY OF FEDERALLY PRODUCED TV MATERIALS. THIS CENTER ACTS AS A CLEARINGHOUSE FOR THE SALE AND RENT OF MANY OF THESE MATERIALS. (NAT'L). JAMES W MOORE, DIRECTOR; NATIONAL AUDIOVISUAL CENTER; NATL ARCHIVES & RECORDS SERVICE; WASHINGTON, DC 20409. (#4314).

THE GREAT AMERICAN INVENTION: A FEDERAL UNION. DOCUMENTARY FILM ON PROBLEMS OF AMERICAN STATES AFTER THE WAR & ON THE CONVENTION TO FORM 'A MORE PERFECT UNION'. HOW THAT THEN UNIQUE UNION SECURED THE AMERICAN HERITAGE & INFLUENCED OTHERS. (NAT'L). JOHN A MATHEWS, CHAIRMAN; CONSORTIUM FOR EDUCATION ON FEDERALISM, INC; 1736 COLUMBIA RD, NW; WASHINGTON, DC 20009. (#8592).

'THE GREAT AMERICAN SCREAM MACHINE' - SITES. EXHIBIT ON HISTORY, TECHNOLOGY AND THRILL OF ROLLER COASTERS; TEXT AND PHOTOGRAPHS MOUNTED ON APPROXIMATELY 50 PANELS, READY TO HANG. (NAT'L). ANDREA STEVENS, COORDINATOR; SMITHSONIAN INSTITUTION TRAVELING EXHIBIT SERVICE; WASHINGTON, DC 20560. (#15930).

'GREAT AMERICA', WASHINGTON, DC. FESTIVAL OF MUSIC 6 EVENINGS A WEEK FROM 06/14/76-09/06/76 AT SYLVAN THEATER IN WASHINGTON, DC; SPONSORED BY MARRIOTT CORPORATION IN COOPERATION WITH THE NATIONAL PARK SERVICE. (NAT'L). T A BURKE, VICE PRESIDENT FOR CORPORATE AFFAIRS; MARRIOTT CORPORATION; 5161 RIVER RD; WASHINGTON, DC 20016. (#12484).

GREAT SEAL OF THE UNITED STATES PUBLICATION. COMMEMORATIVE VOLUME ON HISTORY & SIGNIFICANCE OF THE GREAT SEAL OF THE USA. (NAT'L). FREDRICK AANDAHL, DEPUTY DIRECTOR; DEPT OF STATE, HISTORICAL OFFICE; 2201 C ST NW; WASHINGTON, DC 20520. (#2289).

GREEK AMERICAN CONTRIBUTIONS TO AMERICA EXHIBIT. CONCURRENT EXHIBITS IN 25 AMERICAN CITIES ON THE HISTORY OF GREEK AMERICANS, AND ON THEIR CONTRIBUTIONS TO AMERICA. BOOK & SLIDE-TAPE PRESENTATION TO BE AVAILABLE IN 1976. (NAT'L). GEORGE J LEBER, DIRECTOR; ORDER OF AHEPA (AMER HELLENIC EDUCATIONAL PROGRESSIVE ASSOC); 1422 K ST NW; WASHINGTON, DC 20005. (#2294).

GREEK EXHIBITION-ANTIQUITIES, PLAYS, PHOTO EXHIBIT. A MULTIPHASED EXHIBITION OF CLASSICAL GREEK ANTIQUITIES, THEATRICAL GROUPS PRESENTING ANCIENT AND MODERN GREEK PLAYS, AND PHOTO EXHIBITS DEPICTING THE EXCHANGE OF POLITICAL IDEAS BETWEEN GREECE AND AMERICA. (INT'L). JOHN PERDIKIS, FIRST SECRETARY; GREEK EMBASSY; 2221 MASSACHUSETTS AVE, NW; WASHINGTON, DC 20008. (#113).

GREEN SURVIVAL FOR THE THIRD CENTURY. ENCOURAGES THE PLANTING OF TREES, SHRUBS AND OTHER PLANTS IN EFFORT TO PURIFY THE AIR AND BEAUTIFY THE LAND. TECHNICAL ASSISTANCE AND LEADERSHIP PROVIDED BY THE NURSERY INDUSTRY. (NAT'L). MISS JEAN BLACKBURN, PROJECT DIRECTOR; AMERICAN ASSOCIATION OF NURSERYMEN, INC; 230 SOUTHERN BLDG; WASHINGTON, DC 20005. (#2769). **ARBA RECOGNIZED.**

'A GUDE TO 200 SITES' - HORIZONS ON DISPLAY BOOK. A MAP/BROCHURE IDENTIFYING THE LOCATION & BRIEFLY DESCRIBING THE 200 HORIZONS ON DISPLAY SITES. OF INTEREST TO INDIVIDUALS AND GROUPS; NO CHARGE. (NAT'L). HORIZONS ON DISPLAY; AMERICAN REVOLUTION BICENTENNIAL ADMINISTRATION; 2401 E ST, NW; WASHINGTON, DC 20276. (#27615).

'GUIDE TO RELIGIOUS ACTIVITIES' - WASHINGTON, DC. A LIST OF NATIONAL BICENT PROGRAMS SPONSORED BY RELIGIOUS & INTERRELIGIOUS ORGANIZATIONS THAT HAVE COME TO THE ATTENTION OF ARBA. (NAT'L). PROGRAM DIVISION; AMERICAN REVOLUTION BICENTENNIAL ADMINISTRATION; 2401 E ST, NW; WASHINGTON, DC 20276. (#28427).

GUIDE TO STATE HISTORIC PRESERVATION PROGRAMS. COMPENDIUM OF INFORMATION ON STATE GOVT PROGRAMS THAT IDENTIFY, EVALUATE, RECOGNIZE, PROTECT & PRESERVE ARCHITECTURAL, HISTORICAL, & ARCHEOLOGICAL SITES IMPORTANT IN LOCAL, STATE & NATIONAL HISTORY. (NAT'L). RUSSELL V KEUNE, DIR, DEPT; NATIONAL TRUST FOR HISTORIC PRESERVATION; 740-748 JACKSON PL, NW; WASHINGTON, DC 20006. (#3797).

GUIDES & TECHNICAL PUBLICATIONS ON THE REVOLUTION. THESE GUIDES & AIDS, INTERRELATING DIVERSE RECORDS, WILL ENABLE THE RESEARCHER TO COVER THE ENTIRE SPAN OF SOURCE MATERIALS AVAILABLE, MAKING THE RECORDS OF THE REVOLUTION MORE MEANINGFUL & USEFUL. (NAT'L). KENNETH E HARRIS, CHIEF; CNTR FOR DOCUMENTARY STUDY OF THE AMERICAN REVOLUTION; NATL ARCHIVES & RECORDS SERVICE; WASHINGTON, DC 20408. (#60).

HALL OF AMERICAN MARITIME ENTERPRISE. AN EXHIBIT FEATURING THE PAST, PRESENT & FUTURE OF AMERICAN ENTERPRISE EXPERIENCE. TO BE LOCATED IN THE SMITHSONIAN INSTITUTION'S NATIONAL MUSEUM OF HISTORY & TECHNOLOGY. (NAT'L). DR MELVIN JACKSON, CURATOR OF MARITIME HISTORY; MUSEUM OF SCIENCE & TECHNOLOGY; SMITHSONIAN INSTITUTION; WASHINGTON, DC 20560. (#3). **ARBA RECOGNIZED.**

A HANDBOOK ON AGING - DC. HANDBOOK WILL INCLUDE METHODS TO INVOLVE THE ELDERLY WITH THE BICENTENNIAL. (NAT'L). MARJORIE COLLINS, DIRECTOR OF TRAINING; NATIONAL COUNCIL ON AGING; 1828 L ST, NW; WASHINGTON, DC 20036. (#10832). **ARBA RECOGNIZED.**

'HAPPY BIRTHDAY, USA!'. 4-DAY HOLIDAY FESTIVITIES TO BE BROADCAST NATIONWIDE & TO INCLUDE: HONOR AMERICA DAY GALA & RECEPTION; NATIONAL PAGEANT OF FREEDOM AT US CAPITOL; FIREWORKS; BICENTENNIAL PARADE; & AREA ACTIVITIES. (NAT'L). LAWRENCE S STINCHCOMB, PROJECT DIRECTOR; HAPPY BIRTHDAY, USA!; 1025 15TH ST, NW; WASHINGTON, DC 20005. (#7980). **ARBA RECOGNIZED.**

HEALTH, EDUCATION & WELFARE BICENT EXHIBIT IN DC. THE EXHIBITION PORTRAYS HEW'S INVOLVEMENT IN THE HEALTH, EDUCATION AND WELFARE OF THE NATION. THE FOCUS IS ON THE FUTURE GOALS & OUTLOOK IN THOSE AREAS. EXH CENTER 1ST FLOOR HEW SOUTH PORTAL BUILDING. (NAT'L). ANNE RUSSELL, PROJECT MANAGER; DEPT OF HEALTH, EDUCATION & WELFARE; 330 INDEPENDENCE AVE, SW, #4725N; WASHINGTON, DC 20201. (#8001).

HERITAGE PERFORMANCE & DANCE - WASHINGTON, DC. A HERITAGE PERFORMANCE & DANCE ENTITLED 'FROM WEST AFRICA TO HARLEM'. (LOCAL). FLAVIUS GALIBER, PROJ DIRECTOR; WASHINGTON COMMUNITY SCHOOL OF MUSIC; 22ND & VARNUM ST, NE; WASHINGTON, DC 20018. (#23603). **ARBA GRANTEE.**

'HERITAGE & HORIZON TREES', FOREST SERVICE PROJ. OBTAINING & PLANTING AT APPROPRIATE BICENTENNIAL SITES, SEEDLINGS FROM 200 + YEAR OLD TREES FROM THE 13 ORIGINAL COLONIES ALONG WITH GENETICALLY IMPROVED 'SEEDLINGS OF THE FUTURE'. (NAT'L). GLENN A KOVAR, DIRECTOR, SPECIAL PROJECTS; DEPT OF AGRICULTURE, FOREST SERVICE; 12TH & INDEPENDENCE AVE, SW; WASHINGTON, DC 20250. (#5565).

HERITAGE '76 YOUTH BICENTENNIAL PROGRAM. CREATE AND PRODUCE 30-SECOND RADIO SPOTS BASED ON NATIONAL ISSUES FOR MONTHLY SHOWS; TO BE BROADCAST IN 15 METROPOLITAN AREAS. (REGN'L). SUSAN R HILGERS, PRESIDENT; NATIONAL YOUTH PRO-LIFE COALITION; 235 MASSACHUSETTS AVE, NW; WASHINGTON, DC 20002. (#10973).

HIRSHHORN MUSEUM & SCULPTURE GARDEN IN DC. SCHEDULED TO OPEN BY SUMMER OF 1974. THE MUSEUM WILL HOUSE MORE THAN 7000 WORKS OF ART WITH COLLECTIONS OF PAINTINGS PRIMARILY 20TH CENTURY & WORLD SCULPTURES FROM ANTIQUITY TO PRESENT. (NAT'L). MRS SUSAN HAMILTON, BICENTENNIAL COORDINATOR; SMITHSONIAN INSTITUTION; 1000 JEFFERSON DR, SW; WASHINGTON, DC 20560. (#343).

HISTORIC PRESERVATION BOOK OF GENERAL SVCS ADMIN. BOOK, 'THE GOLDEN AGE OF AMERICAN PUBLIC ARCHITECTURE', THE HISTORY OF THE SUPERVISNG ARCHITECT OF THE TREASURY, YRS 1850-1900 WHEN AMER ARCHITECTURE, UNDER FEDERAL PATRONAGE, FIRST REACHED WORLD NOTICE. (NAT'L). STEVEN RUTTENBAUM, GSA HIST PRES OFFICER; GENERAL SERVICES ADMINISTRATION; 18TH AND F STS, NW; WASHINGTON, DC 20405. (#1897).

HISTORIC RESOURCES & HUMAN ENVIRONMENT STUDY. THIS STUDY WILL DEFINE THE ESSENTIAL COMPONENTS OF OUR HERITAGE AND REQUIREMENTS FOR ITS ADEQUATE PRESERVATION, WILL ASSESS PRESENT PROGRAMS & ADVISE GOVERNMENT OF ITS ROLE IN DEVELOPING FUTURE PROGRAMS. (NAT'L). ROBERT GARVEY, EXECUTIVE SECRETARY; ADVISORY COUNCIL ON HISTORIC PRESERVATION; 1522 K ST, NW, ROOM 403; WASHINGTON, DC 20005. (#148).

HISTORIC TRAILS PROJECT - DEPT OF THE INTERIOR. TO IDENTIFY, MARK AND INTERPRET THREE MAJOR NATIONAL TRAILS--OREGON AND MORMON TRAIL(MIGRATION TO PACIFIC), PONY EXPRESS(POSTAL SERVICE BETWEEN MO. AND CA.) ESCALANTE(SPANISH COLONIZATION IN SOUTHWEST). (NAT'L). JOHN F LANZ, OUTDOOR RECREATION PLANNER; BUREAU OF LAND MANAGEMENT; DEPARTMENT OF THE INTERIOR; WASHINGTON, DC 20240. (#1240).

HISTORICAL PHOTOGRAPHS OF BLACKS - WASH, DC. THE PHOTOGRAPHS WILL PORTRAY BLACKS IN THE FABRIC OF AMERICAN LIFE. PARTICULARLY BLACKS IN WASHINGTON, DC DURING THE EARLY AND MIDDLE 1900'S. PHOTOGRAPHS BY ADDISON N SCURLOCK. (LOCAL). FRANCES FRALIN; CORCORAN GALLERY OF ART; 17TH ST & NEW YORK AVE, NW; WASHINGTON, DC 20006. (#22894). **ARBA GRANTEE.**

'THE HISTORY OF JACOB' - 16 C FLEMISH TAPESTRIES. THIS SERIES OF TAPESTRIES WILL BE ON LOAN FROM THE ROYAL MUSEUM OF ART AND HISTORY IN BRUSSELS TO HOUSTON, BIRMINGHAM, SAN FRANCISCO. (INT'L). CULTURAL ATTACHE; EMBASSY OF BELGIUM; 3330 GARFIELD ST; WASHINGTON, DC 20008. (#31903).

HISTORY OF PUBLIC WORKS IN UNITED STATES 1776-1976. A HISTORY OF THE STRUCTURES AND FACILITIES OF PUBLIC AGENCIES WHICH PROVIDE WATER, POWER, WASTE DISPOSAL, TRANSPORTATION AND SIMILAR SERVICES TO THE UNITED STATES. (NAT'L). DR ELLIS L ARMSTRONG, CHAIRMAN; AMERICAN PUBLIC WORKS ASSOCIATION; 1776 MASSACHUSETTS AVE, NW; WASHINGTON, DC 20036. (#5150).

HISTORY OF US FOREIGN RELATIONS - FILM SERIES. THREE EDUCATIONAL FILMS IN COLOR COVERING US FOREIGN RELATIONS FROM AMERICAN REVOLUTION TO WORLD WAR II. PROJECTED 4TH FILM WILL COVER RECENT DECADES. EMPHASIS ON OUR DIPLOMATIC HERITAGE IN WORLD TODAY. (INT'L). PAUL E AUERSWALD, DIR, OFFICE OF MEDIA SERVICES; DEPT OF STATE; 2201 C ST, NW; WASHINGTON, DC 20520. (#2031).

HISTORY OF WASHINGTON, DC. THE HISTORY WILL FOCUS ON THE FAR NORTH WEST WASHINGTON. (LOCAL). MARGARET MURRAY, NPC 2 CHAIRPERSON; NEIGHBORHOOD PLANNING COUNCIL; 4025 CHESAPEAKE ST, NW; WASHINGTON, DC 20016. (#22896). **ARBA GRANTEE.**

HOME HOSPITALITY SURVEY. A NATIONAL PUBLIC OPINION SURVEY TO STUDY THE ATTITUDES & PREFERENCES TOWARD PROVIDING HOME HOSPITALITY TO FELLOW CITIZENS & FOREIGN VISITORS FOR THE BICENTENNIAL COMMEMORATION. (INT'L). SENIOR PROGRAM OFFICER, FESTIVAL USA; AMERICAN REVOLUTION BICENTENNIAL ADMINISTRATION; 2401 E STREET NW; WASHINGTON, DC 20276. (#253).

'HORIZONS ON DISPLAY'-COMMUNITY DEVELOPMENT PROJ. NATIONAL AND INTERNATIONAL VISIBILITY FOR 200 INNOVATIVE PROJECTS NATIONWIDE WHICH, DUE TO THE COMMUNITY CHALLENGE ADDRESSED, MAKE A STATEMENT OF AMERICA'S CAPACITY TO MEET COMMUNITY NEEDS IN CENTURY 3. (NAT'L). HUGH ALLEN, PROJECT DIRECTOR; DEPT OF HOUSING & URBAN DEVELOPMENT; 1111 18TH ST, NW; WASHINGTON, DC 20036. (#20000). **ARBA RECOGNIZED.**

HORIZONS '76 IDEABOOK - WASHINGTON, DC. DESCRIBES SUCCESSFUL BICENT PROJECTS WHICH CAN BE DUPLICATED BY COMMUNITIES & ORGANIZATIONS. AVAILABLE FROM SUPT

WASHINGTON — CONTINUED

DOCUMENTS IN DC; CHARGE. STOCK # 052-008-00012-3. (NAT'L). PROGRAM DIVISION; AMERICAN REVOLUTION BICENTENNIAL ADMINISTRATION; 2401 E ST, NW; WASHINGTON, DC 20276. (#27616).

HORIZONS '76 SLIDE SHOW - WASHINGTON, DC. A DESCRIPTION OF THE HORIZONS '76 CONCEPT, GIVING EXAMPLES OF SUCH PROJECTS ACROSS THE COUNTRY. (NAT'L). PROGRAM DIVISION CHAIRMAN; AMERICAN REVOLUTION BICENTENNIAL ADMINISTRATION; 2401 E ST, NW; WASHINGTON, DC 20276. (#28430).

HOSPITALITY CENTER IN WASHINGTON, DC. THERE WILL BE A TOUR OF THE CHURCH, DESIGNED BY ARCHITECT, A CLUSS, FOLLOWED BY THE SHOWING OF THE FILM 'CITY OUT OF WILDERNESS', 1975 RUNNER-UP IN ACADEMY AWARDS; REFRESHMENTS WILL BE SERVED. ALSO: FILM/SLIDES. (LOCAL). FRANCES INMAN; CALVARY BAPTIST CHURCH; 8TH & H ST, NW; WASHINGTON, DC 20001. (#13687-1).

HOUSING REDEVELOPMENT IN AREA OF WASHINGTON, DC. CITY GOVT WILL DEMOLISH EXISTING HOUSING PROJ IN HIGHPOINT-BARNABYWASHINGTON HIGHLANDS AREA & SELL TO PRIVATE DEVELOPER FOR TOWNHOUSES. (LOCAL). RUTH WENZEL, SPECIAL ASSISTANT; DC GOVT, OFFICE OF HOUSING; 1170 12TH ST, NW; WASHINGTON, DC 20004. (#5610). **(??).**

THE HOWARD THEATER FOUNDATION OF WASHINGTON, DC. RESTORATION AND REVITALIZATION OF HOWARD THEATER IN WASHINGTON, DC. TO RE-ESTABLISH AND PRESERVE THE HOWARD STAGE AS A VIABLE CULTURAL INSTITUTION AND DOCUMENT ITS HISTORY. (LOCAL). CONNIE L DRUMGOLD, EXEC DIRECTOR; HOWARD THEATER FOUNDATION, INC; 1140 CONNECTICUT AVE, NW; WASHINGTON, DC 20036. (#2841).

HUGH O'BRIAN YOUTH FDN 1976 LEADERSHIP SEMINAR. A LEADERSHIP SEMINAR FOR HIGH SCHOOL SOPHOMORES PROVIDING IN DEPTH HUMANIZED APPRECIATION OF THE SOCIAL, ECONOMIC & TECHNOLOGICAL DEVELOPMENT OF THE NATION & THE OPPORTUNITIES AHEAD IN CENTURY III. (NAT'L). HUGH O'BRIAN, PRESIDENT; HUGH O'BRIAN YOUTH FOUNDATION; PO BOX 1779; BEVERLY HILLS, CA 90213. (#7933). **ARBA RECOGNIZED.**

'HUNGARIAN ART NOUVEAU' - SITES, WASHINGTON DC. THE INSTITUTE FOR CULTURAL RELATIONS IN BUDAPEST IS ORGANIZING THIS EXHIBITION OF APPROXIMATELY 150 OBJECTS DOCUMENTING THE ART NOUVEAU MOVEMENT IN HUNGARY. TOUR TO BEGIN APRIL, 1977. (INT'L). EILEEN HARAKAL, COORDINATOR; SMITHSONIAN INSTITUTION TRAVELING EXHIBITION SERVICE; WASHINGTON, DC 20560. (#28445).

ICONS FROM ORTHODOX CHURCH MUSEUM OF FINLAND-SITES. EXHIBITION OF ICONS REPRESENTING SACRED FIGURES & EVENTS OF EASTERN ORTHODOX CHRISTIANITY ARE FROM MONASTERIES AND PARISHES OF KARELIA IN EASTERN FINLAND. (INT'L). EILEEN HARAKAL, COORDINATOR; SMITHSONIAN INSTITUTION TRAVELING EXHIBITION SERVICE; WASHINGTON, DC 20560. (#26657).

ILLUSTRATED HISTORY 'THE AMERICAN WORKER'. HISTORY OF AMERICAN WORKER'S CONTRIBUTION TO DEVELOPMENT OF AMERICA OVER 200 YEARS. (NAT'L). RICHARD CONN, EXEC DIR BICENTENNIAL OFFICE; DEPT OF LABOR; 200 CONSTITUTION, NW; WASHINGTON, DC 20210. (#1762).

IN SEARCH OF DECLARATION: 2 CENTERS OF DISSENT. AN EXIBIT IN THE NATIONAL PORTRAIT GALLERY OF THE SMITHSONIAN USING A BIOGRAPHICAL APPROACH TO THE AMERICAN REVOLUTION. EDUCATIONAL AIDS WILL BE FORTHCOMING. (NAT'L). MRS SUSAN HAMILTON, BICENTENNIAL COORDINATOR; SMITHSONIAN INSTITUTION; 1000 JEFFERSON DR., S.W.; WASHINGTON, DC 20560. (#26).

IN THE MINDS & THE HEARTS OF PEOPLE - EXHIBIT. AN EXHIBIT CENTERING ON INDIVIDUALS WHO GAVE IMPETUS TO THE CAUSE OF INDEPENDENCE. OPENS APRIL, 1974 AT THE NATIONAL PORTRAIT GALLERY OF THE SMITHSONIAN. GUIDES AND EDUCATIONAL AIDS WILL BE PREPARED. (NAT'L). MRS SUSAN HAMILTON, BICENTENNIAL COORDINATOR; SMITHSONIAN INSTITUTION; 1000 JEFFERSON DR, SW; WASHINGTON, DC 20560. (#95).

INAUGURAL STORY-FROM WASHINGTON TO FORD - SITES. EXHIBITION ILLUSTRATES EVERY PRESIDENTIAL INAUGRATION SINCE WASHINGTON WAS INAUGURATED IN 1789; INCLUDES 40 PANELS. (NAT'L). ANDREA STEVENS, COORDINATOR; SMITHSONIAN INSTITUTION TRAVELING EXHIBIT SERVICE; WASHINGTON, DC 20560. (#15934).

INDEXES TO THE PAPERS OF THE CONTINENTAL CONGRESS. COMPUTER-ASSISTED SUBJECT & NAME INDEXES TO RECORDS OF CONTINENTAL & CONFEDERATION CONGRESSES & THE CONSTITUTIONAL CONVENTION, 1774-1789. PUBL IN 10-12 VOLS IN 1977. FUNDED BY FORD FNDN & NATL ARCHIVES. (NAT'L). JOHN P BUTLER, CNTR FOR DOCUM STUDY OF AMER REVOL; NATIONAL ARCHIVES AND RECORD SERVICE; 6TH & PENNSYLVANIA AVE, NW; WASHINGTON, DC 20408. (#824).

INFORMATION ON FIRE SAFETY EDUCATION - DC. DC FIRE DEPARTMENT WILL PROVIDE FIRE SAFETY INSTURCTIONS. (LOCAL). BURTON W JOHNSON, FIRE CHIEF; DC FIRE DEPARTMENT; 614 H ST, NW; WASHINGTON, DC 20001. (#22886). **ARBA GRANTEE.**

INNER CITY CENTER FOR TECHNOLOGICAL ACTION - DC. COMMUNITY COMPUTER CENTER WILL PROVIDE SUPPLIES FOR NEIGHBORHOOD SMALL BUSINESS, CHURCHES, COMMUNITY ORGANIZATIONS & CAI FOR REMEDIAL EDUCATION & SKILL REINFORCEMENT FOR YOUTH & RESIDENTS. (LOCAL). DR MILTON WHITE, PHD; AFRO-AMERICAN DATANAMICS, INC; 4402 GEORGIA AVE, NW; WASHINGTON, DC 20011. (#10769).

INTERAMERICAN REHABILITATION EXCHANGE. EXCHANGE OF MENTAL RETARDATION EXPERTS FROM 20 STATES WITH LATIN AMERICAN COUNTERPARTS FOR LONG-RANGE COOPERATIVE DEVELOPMENT AND INSTITUTIONAL LINKS. (INT'L). E DAVID LURIA, ASSOC DIRECTOR; PARTNERS OF THE AMERICAS; 2001 S ST NW; WASHINGTON, DC 20009. (#7877).

INTERAMERICAN RURAL YOUTH EXCHANGE. A TECHNICAL EXCHANGE OF 52 RURAL YOUTH LEADERS FROM 8 U S STATES & 9 LATIN AMERICAN COUNTRIES FOR IMPROVED AGRICULTURAL TRAINING AND PRODUCTION. (INT'L). E DAVID LURIA, ASSOC DIRECTOR; PARTNERS OF THE AMERICAS; 2001 S ST, NW; WASHINGTON, DC 20009. (#8542). **ARBA RECOGNIZED. ARBA GRANTEE.**

INTERDISCIPLINARY COURSE ON PERIOD OF REVOLUTION. TO DEVELOP AND TEST AN INTERDISCIPLINARY COURSE ON THE AMERICAN REVOLUTION IN HIGH SCHOOLS. (NAT'L). PRISCILLA R CRANE, DIRECTOR OF DEVELOPMENT; SIDWELL FRIENDS SCHOOL; 3825 WISCONSIN AVE, NW; WASHINGTON, DC 20016. (#19).

INTERIOR DEPT BICENTENNIAL CONSERVATION YEARBOOK. THE BOOK WILL EXAMINE THE NATION'S NATURAL RESOURCES AND LAND POLICIES OVER THE LAST 200 YEARS & HOW THESE POLICIES AFFECTED THE SOCIAL AND ECONOMIC GROWTH OF THE NATION. (NAT'L). VIRGINIA S HART, ASST FOR BICENT AFFAIRS; DEPARTMENT OF THE INTERIOR, OFFICE OF COMMUNICATIONS; 18TH & C STS, NW; WASHINGTON, DC 20240. (#6317).

INTERNATIONAL AUTOMOBILE FEDERATION CONFERENCE. INTERNATIONAL CONFERENCE OF AUTO CLUB INDUSTRY. (INT'L). JOHN U OLIVEAU, EXEC DIRECTOR; AMERICAN AUTOMOBILE ASSOCIATION; 1712 G ST, NW; WASHINGTON, DC 20006. (#270).

INTERNATIONAL AUTOMOBILE TOURING CONFERENCE. INTERNATIONAL CONFERENCE OF TOURING AUTOMOBILE CLUB INDUSTRY. (INT'L). J MAXWELL SMITH, PRESIDENT; AMERICAN AUTO TOURING ALLIANCE; 2040 MARKET ST; PHILADELPHIA, PA 19103. (#271).

INTERNATIONAL BLACKBELT CHAMPIONSHIPS - DC. THE WORLD BLACKBELT LEAGUE IS SPONSORING INTERNATIONAL BLACKBELT CHAMPIONSHIPS. (INT'L). K K CHUNG, COORDINATOR; WORLD BLACKBELT LEAGUE; 2000 L ST, NW, SUITE 101; WASHINGTON, DC 20036. (#27931).

INTERNATIONAL EDUC: LINK FOR HUMAN UNDERSTANDING. PROGRAM TO ASSESS IMPACT OF INTERNATIONAL & CULTURAL EXCHANGE THRU TEN REGIONAL & ONE INTERNATIONAL MEETING FOR FULBRIGHT SCHOLARS. FOREIGN SCHOLARS INVOLVED IN REGIONAL COMMUNITY PROGRAMS. (INT'L). WINSTON E FORREST, JR, PROJECT COORDINATOR; BOARD OF FOREIGN SCHOLARSHIPS; 1709 NEW YORK AVE, NW - #307; WASHINGTON, DC 20006. (#33272). **ARBA RECOGNIZED.**

INTERNATIONAL SALUTE TO THE STATES EXHIBITIONS. MAJOR EXHIBITIONS OF ARTISTIC AND HISTORIC TREASURES FROM NATIONS AROUND THE WORLD WILL CIRCULATE TO US MUSEUMS AND GALLERIES IN SPECIAL TRIBUTE TO THE USA DURING THE BICENTENNIAL. (INT'L). EILEEN HARAKAL, TRAVELING EXHIBITION SERVICE; SMITHSONIAN INSTITUTION; 1000 JEFFERSON DR, SW; WASHINGTON, DC 20560. (#1774).

INTL CALENDAR OF BICENTENNIAL EVENTS - WASH, DC. LISTS EVENTS, DATES AND CITY & STATE LOCATIONS OF INTERNATIONAL BICENT ACTIVITIES TO TAKE PLACE IN THE USA AS ANNOUNCED BY EMBASSIES IN WASHINGTON, DC. (NAT'L). INTERNATIONAL DIVISION; AMERICAN REVOLUTION BICENTENNIAL ADMINISTRATION; 2401 E ST, NW; WASHINGTON, DC 20276. (#27671).

INVENTORY OF AMER PAINTINGS EXECUTED BEFORE 1914. A PROGRAM TO SEARCH AND RECORD THE WHOLE RANGE OF AMERICAN PAINTINGS FROM THE EARLIEST YEARS OF OUR HISTORY TO THE PRESENT CENTURY. (NAT'L). ABIGAIL BOOTH, COORDINATOR BIAP; SMITHSONIAN INSTITUTION; NATIONAL COLLECTION OF FINE ARTS; WASHINGTON, DC 20560. (#76).

IRISH ART EXHIBIT. EXHIBIT. (REGN'L). SEAN D COAKLEY, CHAIRMAN; IRISH-AMERICAN BICENTENNIAL COMMITTEE; SUITE 427, 1825 CONN AVE, NW; WASHINGTON, DC 20009. (#7917-1). **(??).**

IRISH-AMERICAN THEATRICAL PRODUCTION. LIVE PERFORMANCE. (REGN'L). SEAN D COAKLEY, CHAIRMAN; IRISH-AMERICAN BICENTENNIAL COMMITTEE; SUITE 427, 1825 CONN AVE, NW; WASHINGTON, DC 20009. (#7917-4). **(??).**

ISLAMIC FESTIVAL. SOME EGYPTIAN SCHOLARS ARRIVED IN WASHINGTON FOR A 3 DAY CONFERENCE AT THE ISLAMIC CENTER. AT ISLAMIC CENTER. (INT'L). DR AHMED M AZZAM; EMBASSY OF THE ARAB REPUBLIC OF EGYPT; 2200 KALORAMA RD; WASHINGTON, DC 20008. (#200010-52).

JAMAICA SALUTES AMERICA ON ITS BICENTENNIAL. A CONGRATULATORY MESSAGE FROM JAMAICA'S PRIME MINISTER, THE HON MICHAEL MANLEY, WAS FORWARDED TO THE PRESIDENT AND PEOPLE OF THE UNITED STATES. (INT'L). ASTON IRVING, INFORMATION DIRECTOR; EMBASSY OF JAMAICA; 1666 CONNECTICUT AVE; WASHINGTON, DC 20009. (#31886).

JAPAN SALUTES AMERICA ON ITS BICENTENNIAL. CONGRATULATIONS ON THE BICENTENNIAL FROM THE JAPANESE PEOPLE AND A REVIEW OF U S - JAPANESE RELATIONS IN THE FORM OF A NEWSPAPER SUPPLEMENT TO BE PUBLISHED JULY 4, 1976. (INT'L). TERUO HACHIYA, EXECUTIVE DIRECTOR; THE AMERICA-JAPAN SOCIETY, INC; 370 MARUNQUCHI BLDG, CHIYODA-KU; TOKYO/JAPAN. (#16118).

'JAPANESE FLOWERING CHERRY TREES OF WASH, DC'-BOOK. SUBTITLED 'A LIVING SYMBOL OF FRIENDSHIP' & WRITTEN BY ROLAND M JEFFERSON & ALAN M FUSONIE, IT IS THE HISTORY OF THE TIDAL BASIN'S CHERRY TREES. (NAT'L). ROLAND M JEFFERSON, BOTANIST; DEPT OF AGRICULTURE, NATIONAL ARBORETUM; 24TH & R STS, NE; WASHINGTON, DC 20002. (#5570).

JAPANESE PERFORMING ARTS GROUP TOUR THE USA. APRIL 3 - JUNE 2 1976 THE FOLKLORIC DANCE ENSEMBLE WILL TOUR THE US; JULY 11-25 1976, JAPANESE BOYS CHOIR WILL BE IN AMES, IOWA; A BUDOKAN MARTIAL ARTS GROUP WILL GIVE EXHIBITIONS ON KARATE & JUDO. (INT'L). CULTURAL ATTACHE; EMBASSY OF JAPAN; 2520 MASSACHUSETTS AVE; WASHINGTON, DC 20008. (#32975).

JEFFERSON DRAFTS OF DECLARATION OF INDEPENDENCE. DECLARATION'S ADOPTION, INCLUDES RARE JEFFERSON WAFER CENSORING GEORGE III AND THE DUNLAP BROADSIDE. (NAT'L). ALPHONS J HACKL, PUBLISHER; ACROPOLIS BOOKS LTD; 2400 17TH ST, NW; WASHINGTON, DC 20009. (#22466).

JEWISH COMMUNITY SURVEY; WASHINGTON, DC. THE PURPOSE OF THIS SURVEY IS TO DETERMINE THE STATUS OF THE AMERICAN JEWISH COMMUNITY BY STUDYING ITS GOALS FOR THE FUTURE AND ITS ACCOMPLISHMENTS OF THE PAST. (NAT'L). LILY EDELMAN, PROGRAM DIRECTOR; BNAI BRITH; 1640 RHODE ISLAND AVE, NW; WASHINGTON, DC 20036. (#17193).

JOHN J MCCLOY FOUNDATION FOR GERMAN-AMER EXCHANGE. THE PURPOSE OF THE FOUNDATION WILL BE TO FACILITATE STUDY TOURS AND PARTICIPATION IN GERMAN-AMERICAN CONFERENCES BY YOUNG POLITICIANS, JOURNALISTS, LABOR AND BUSINESS REPRESENTATIVES. (INT'L). CULTURAL COUNSELOR; EMBASSY OF THE FEDERAL REPUBLIC OF GERMANY; 4645 RESERVOIR RD, NW; WASHINGTON, DC 20007. (#13692).

JOHNNY HORIZON 76. NATIONAL PROGRAM TITLED 'LET'S CLEAN UP AMERICA FOR OUR 200TH BIRTHDAY'. ENCOURAGES & STIMULATES CITIZEN CLEANUPS, BEAUTIFICATIONS, RECYCLING & CONSERVATION PROJECTS & OTHER ENVIRONMENTAL EFFORTS. (NAT'L). IVAN SCOTT, NATIONAL COORDINATOR; DEPT OF THE INTERIOR; DEP'T OF THE INTERIOR; WASHINGTON, DC 20240. (#115). **ARBA RECOGNIZED.**

'JOURNALS OF CONTINENTAL CONGRESS, 1774-89' INDEX. THE CENTER FOR THE DOCUMENTARY STUDY OF THE AMERICAN REVOLUTION WILL PUBLISH A CONSOLIDATED INDEX TO THE 15 INDICES OF THE 'JOURNALS OF THE CONTINENTAL CONGRESS, 1774-1789'. (NAT'L). KENNETH E HARRIS, CHIEF; CNTR FOR DOCUMENTARY STUDY OF THE AMERICAN REVOLUTION; NATL ARCHIVES & RECORDS SERVICE; WASHINGTON, DC 20408. (#62).

JUNIOR COMMITTEES OF CORRESPONDENCE. COMMITTEE OF CORRESPONDENCE WIL BE ESTABLISHED IN ELEMENTARY SCHOOLS ACROSS THE U S FOR EXCHANGE OF LETTERS BY STUDENTS EXPRESSING THOUGHTS ON PARTICIPATION IN COMMUNITY BICENTENNIAL ACTIVITIES. (NAT'L). GEORGE WHITEMAN PROJ DIR; UNITED STATES POSTAL SERVICE; ROOM 5821; WASHINGTON, DC 20260. (#15318). **ARBA RECOGNIZED.**

KAPITOL KLOWNS PERFORM FOR THE DEAF. TRAIN CLOWNS THRUOUT US TO COMMUNICATE W/ DEAF THRU CLOWNING. ASSIST IN DEVELOPING PGMS FOR BOY & GIRL SCOUTS & COMMUNITY LEADERS WHICH WILL INCREASE THEIR UNDERSTANDING OF DEAF PEOPLE. (REGN'L). BERNARD HAMBURGER, SECRETARY - TREASURER; KAPITOL KLOWNS; 12811 BLUHILL RD; SILVER SPRING, MD 20906. (#11165).

KENNEDY CENTER BICENTENNIAL PROGRAM, DC. KANSAS STATE UNIV RESIDENT STRING QUARTET WILL PERFORM 2 CONCERTS AT THE KENNEDY CENTER. (REGN'L). DR ROBERT STEINBAUER, CHAIRMAN; KANSAS STATE UNIV MUSIC DEPT; MANHATTAN, KS 66506. (#26700). **ARBA GRANTEE.**

KENTUCKY BICENTENNIAL PARADE OF AMERICAN MUSIC. KENTUCKY DAY WILL FEATURE MUSIC BY KENTUCKY COMPOSERS PERFORMED BY KENTUCKY MUSIC GROUPS. (LOCAL). ELIZABETH CLARK, COORDINATOR; NATIONAL FEDERATION OF MUSIC CLUB; 514 COLBY RD; WINCHESTER, KY 40391. (#21808). **ARBA GRANTEE.**

'KNOWLEDGE 2000' -- INTL SYMPOSIA IN '76. SERIES OF 3 INTERNATIONAL SYMPOSIA. EACH WILL FOCUS ON A SPECIFIC DIMENSION OF KNOWLEDGE: THE USES OF KNOWLEDGE; THE GENERATION OF KNOWLEDGE; & COMMUNICATION OF KNOWLEDGE DURING NEXT 25 YEARS. (INT'L). R LYNN CARROLL, EXEC ASSOCIATE; NATIONAL SCIENCE FOUNDATION; 1800 G ST, NW; WASHINGTON, DC 20550. (#6064). **ARBA RECOGNIZED.**

LA COMPAGNIE FOLKLORIQUE FANNY THIBOUT TOURS USA. THIS GROUP FROM BELGIUM WILL TOUR THE SOUTHEASTERN PART OF THE US IN JULY 1976. (INT'L). CULTURAL ATTACHE; EMBASSY OF BELGIUM; 3330 GARFIELD ST; WASHINGTON, DC 20008. (#32978).

LAW DAY 1976 - US DEPT OF JUSTICE. A ONE TIME DISTINCT PROGRAM IN THE U.S. DEPARTMENT OF JUSTICE WHICH WILL DRAMATIZE THE ROLE OF LAW DURING THE REVOLUTIONARY PERIOD AND IN THE ONGOING DEVELOPMENT OF LIFE AND INSTITUTIONS IN THE U.S. (NAT'L). OFFICE OF LEGAL COUNSEL ASSISTANT ATTORNEY GEN'L; DEPT OF JUSTICE; PENNSYLVANIA AVE AT 10TH ST; WASHINGTON, DC 20560. (#1901).

LECTURE ON NUTRITION, W O ATWATER MEMORIAL. A MEMORIAL LECTURESHIP THAT RECOGNIZES DISTINGUISHED ACCOUPLISHMENTS IN HUMAN NUTRITION FOR ADVANCING PUBLIC UNDERSTANDING OF THE ROLE OF SCIENCE IN MEETING WORLD FOOD NEEDS. (INT'L). ROBERT M NELSON, INFORMATION OFFICER; DEPT OF AGRICULTURE, AGRICULTURAL RESEARCH SERVICE; ARS-INFO US DEPT OF AGRICULTURE; WASHINGTON, DC 20250. (#1757).

LETTERS OF THE DELEGATES TO CONGRESS, 1774-1789. UP TO 25 VOLUMES ON THESE LETTERS, ANNOTATED AND CONTAINING AT LEAST 18,000 ITEMS, WILL BE PUBLISHED. TWO VOLUMES READY BY 1976; COMPLETE IN 1991. (NAT'L). DR JAMES HUTSON, BICENTENNIAL COORDINATOR; LIBRARY OF CONGRESS; 10 FIRST ST, SE; WASHINGTON, DC 20540. (#138).

WASHINGTON — CONTINUED

LET'S HAVE A BIRTHDAY PARTY - US DEPT OF AGRICULT. BROCHURE OF IDEAS LOCAL COMMUNITIES USE BY VOLUNTEERS TO TIE IN WITH THEMES OF HERITAGE '76, FESTIVAL USA, & HORIZONS '76. 500,000 COPIES SENT 3000 LOCAL EXTENSION SERVICE OFFICES AND OTHER USDA OUTLETS. (NAT'L). OVID BAY, DIRECTOR OF INFORMATION; DEPT OF AGRICULTURE, EXTENSION SERVICE; 500 12TH ST, SW; WASHINGTON, DC 20250. (#1752).

'LIBERTY AND JUSTICE FOR ALL' - WASHINGTON, DC. LOCAL GROUP DISCUSSIONS AND REGIONAL CONSULTATIONS, LEADING TO A NATIONAL CONFERENCE IN OCT '76; TO ENCOURAGE REFLECTION BY THE AMERICAN CATHOLIC COMMUNITY ON ISSUES OF LIBERTY & JUSTICE TODAY. (NAT'L). MR FRANCIS J BUTLER, EXEC DIRECTOR; NATIONAL CONFERENCE OF CATHOLIC BISHOPS BICENT COMMITTEE; 1312 MASSACHUSETTS AVE, NW; WASHINGTON, DC 20005. (#10960).

LIBERTY BELL FOR SMITHSONIAN DISPLAY - KS. A LIBERTY BELL (6' HIGH, 6' DIAMETER), MADE OF WINTER WHEAT, WILL BE ON DISPLAY AT THE SMITHSONIAN INSTITUTE FOR 2 YEARS AFTER ITS LOCAL PREVIEW IN THE KANSAS AREA. (REGN'L). BEN BOESE, PRESIDENT; MENNONITE IMMIGRANT HISTORICAL FOUNDATION; 223 W GALLE; MOUNDRIDGE, KS 67107. (#20267).

LIBRARY OF CONGRESS HISTORICAL SYMPOSIA. A SERIES OF ANNUAL SYMPOSIA TO BE HELD EACH SPRING THROUGH 1976 ON SUBJECTS CONCERNING THE AMERICAN REVOLUTION. (NAT'L). DR JAMES HUTSON, BICENTENNIAL COORDINATOR; LIBRARY OF CONGRESS; 10 FIRST ST, SE; WASHINGTON, DC 20540. (#2). **ARBA RECOGNIZED.**

LIBRARY PROJ ON THE ARTS - WASHINGTON, DC. INSTRUCTION, EDUCATION AND INFORMATION WILL BE OFFERED BY THE DC PUBLIC LIBRARY. (LOCAL). HARDY R FRANKLIN, DIRECTOR; DISTRICT OF COLUMBIA PUBLIC LIBRARY; 901 G ST, NW; WASHINGTON, DC 20005. (#22892). **ARBA GRANTEE.**

LIBRARY PROJECT FOR THE DEAF - WASHINGTON, DC. THE PROJECT INVOLVES SPECIAL MACHINERY AND INSTRUCTIONS FOR ITS USE, SPECIAL FACILITIES AND PROGRAMS FOR THE DEAF. (LOCAL). HARDY FRANKLIN, DIRECTOR; DISTRICT OF COLUMBIA PUBLIC LIBRARY; 901 G ST, NW; WASHINGTON, DC 20005. (#22893). **ARBA GRANTEE.**

LIFE PORTRAITS OF GEORGE WASHINGTON - DC. AN EXIBIT BY THE NATIONAL PORTRAIT GALLERY OF THE SMITHSONIAN WHICH WILL SHOW LIKENESSES OF WASHINGTON DONE THROUGH THE 1832 CENTENNIAL OF HIS BIRTH. (NAT'L). MRS SUSAN HAMILTON, BICENTENNIAL COORDINATOR; SMITHSONIAN INSTITUTION; 1000 JEFFERSON DR., S.W.; WASHINGTON, DC 20560. (#30).

LUXEMBOURG POPULAR METALWORK - SITES EXHIBIT, DC. AN EXHIBITION, ACCOMPANIED BY SLIDE PROGRAM, OF 19TH CENTURY POPULAR METALWORK AND PHOTOGRAPHIC & TEXT PANELS FROM THE MUSEE DE L'ETAT. A VISUAL IMPRESSION OF TYPICAL 19TH CENTURY LUXEMBOURG KITCHEN. (INT'L). EILEEN HARAKAL, COORDINATOR; SMITHSONIAN INSTITUTION TRAVELING EXHIBITION SERVICE; WASHINGTON, DC 20560. (#26669).

LYNDON B JOHNSON MEMORIAL GROVE ON THE POTOMAC. A PERMANENT MEMORIAL IN WASHINGTON, DC, TO THE 36TH PRESIDENT OF THE UNITED STATES. (NAT'L). NASH CASTRO, CHAIRMAN; COMMITTEE FOR THE LBJ MEMORIAL GROVE ON THE POTOMAC; PO BOX 5557; WASHINGTON, DC 20016. (#2847). **ARBA RECOGNIZED.**

MAGAZINE ON NEIGHBORHOOD CULTURES & PERSONALITIES. THE WESTERN SCHOOL OF ARTS WILL PREPARE A MAGAZINE ON THE HISTORY OF THE PENNSYLVANIA AVE AREA IN WASHINGTON, DC, PERSONAL INTERVIEWS AND MEMORIES WILL BE INCLUDED. (LOCAL). MARGARET STEVENSON, CITYSCAPE ADVISOR; WESTERN SCHOOL OF THE ARTS; 35TH & R ST, NW; WASHINGTON, DC 20007. (#22440). **ARBA GRANTEE.**

MAGAZINES, RADIO BROADCASTS, FILMS & TV - WASH, DC. DIVISIONS OF 'NIRA' HAVE PRODUCED FILMS, TV SPOTS, MAGAZINES AND RADIO BROADCASTS FOR USE WITHIN THE NAVAL COMMUNITY AND OVER COMMERCIAL RADIO STATIONS. (LOCAL). ROBERT W KERR, COORDINATOR; NAVY INTERNAL RELATIONS ACTIVITY; PENTAGON ROOM 2E329; WASHINGTON, DC 20350. (#29421).

MAINE DAY BICENTENNIAL SALUTE TO THE STATES - DC. THE MAINE DAY BICENTENNIAL SALUTE TO THE STATES WILL BE HELD AT THE KENNEDY CENTER IN WASHINGTON. (REGN'L). GERTRUDE KRIGER, PROJ DIRECTOR; MAINE FEDERATION OF MUSIC CLUBS; 98 BEDFORD ST; PORTLAND, ME 04101. (#22281). **ARBA GRANTEE.**

MAN THINKING IN AMERICA-PHI BETA KAPPA STUDIES. SEVEN BOOKS TO BE PUBLISHED ON STUDIES THAT DEAL WITH THE CULTURAL CRISIS OF CONTEMPORARY AMERICA AND TRY TO TRACE PATHS TO A MORE RATIONAL FUTURE. (NAT'L). MRS EVELYN GREENBERG, ASSOCIATE SECRETARY; PHI BETA KAPPA; 1811 Q ST, NW; WASHINGTON, DC 20009. (#147).

MAPS FOR THE VISUALLY HANDICAPPED, WASHINGTON, DC. TWO WASHINGTON MAPS FOR THE BLIND: ONE FOR ORIENTATION TO METROPOLITAN AREA WILL BE WALL SIZE FOR PUBLIC BUILDINGS. ONE OF MALL & ADJACENT AREAS WILL BE PERSONAL SIZE FOR MOBILITY GUIDANCE. (ST-WIDE). C WILLIAM BEETSCHEN, COORDINATOR; DEPT OF THE INTERIOR, GEOLOGICAL SURVEY; NATL CENTER, RM 2A108 MS 512; RESTON, VA 22092. (#2780).

MARINE CORPS PROJECT IN WASHINGTON, DC. FLAG PAGEANTS, BICENT COMMAND PROGRAM, MUSEUM & ART EXHIBITS, SPEAKERS, BAND PERFORMANCES, AIRCRAFT DEMONSTRATIONS & COMMUNITY PARTICIPATION IN VARIOUS EVENTS. (LOCAL). VANCE HUSTON, LT COL; MARINE CORPS HEADQUARTERS (CODE PAB); WASHINGTON, DC 20380. (#29890).

MARKET DAY & COUNTRY FAIR IN THE CITY, WASH, DC. A FESTIVAL STYLED AFTER STATE FAIRS WITH A TOUCH OF THE URBAN MARKET IS PLANNED BY FRIENDSHIP HOUSE. ACTIVITIES INCLUDE ARTS, BAKE SALE, GAMES, DISPLAYS, MUSIC & FOOD. COMMUNITY TO BE INVOLVED. (LOCAL). ERNEST WITHERS, ASST DIRECTOR; FRIENDSHIP HOUSE; 619 D ST, SE; WASHINGTON, DC 20007. (#5605).

'MASSING OF THE COLORS' CEREMONY & SERVICE. LOCAL PATRIOTIC & YOUTH ORGS WITH THEIR COLORS & COLOR GUARDS ARE INVITED TO MARCH TO CHURCH CATHEDRAL OR FACILITY FOR CEREMONY & SERVICES HONORING OUR COUNTRY & FLAG ON SUNDAY NEAREST VETERANS DAY. (NAT'L). M C DEMLER MGEN USAF(RET), CHRMAN BICENT COMMITTEE; MILITARY ORDER OF THE WORLD WARS; 1100 17TH ST, NW; WASHINGTON, DC 20036. (#3110).

MASTER REGISTER OF BICENTENNIAL PROJECTS - DC. LISTS MORE THAN 30,000 LOCAL, STATE, NATIONAL & INTERNATIONAL NONEVENT-ORIENTED ACTIVITIES (IE, BOOKS, PARKS & BLDGS), PLUS DETAILS ON PLANNING ACTIVITIES. (NAT'L). MASTER CALENDAR SERVICES; AMERICAN REVOLUTION BICENTENNIAL ADMINISTRATION; 2401 E ST, NW; WASHINGTON, DC 20276. (#27609).

MCCOOK COLLEGE SINGERS: WHITE HOUSE VISITORS PGM. LIVE PERFORMANCE OF VARIED MUSIC IN WASHINGTON, DC. (REGN'L). CHARLES LAWSON, CHAIRMAN, DEPT OF MUSIC; MCCOOK COLLEGE; 1205 E 3RD ST; MCCOOK, NE 69001. (#25802). **ARBA GRANTEE.**

MEDIA FOR THE BICENTENNIAL IN WASHINGTON, DC. SELECTED U S GOVERNMENT MEDIA APPROPRIATE FOR USE IN BICENTENNIAL ACTIVITIES; PRODUCED BY MANY GOVERNMENT AGENCIES OVER A 40 YEAR SPAN AND REFLECTING AMERICAN SENTIMENT AT THE TIME OF PRODUCTION. (NAT'L). LESLIE M GREENBERG, MARKETING OFFICER; NATIONAL AUDIOVISUAL CENTER, (GSA); WASHINGTON, DC 20409. (#11827).

MEETING HOUSE PRESERVATION ACT. RESTORATION OF ONE NATIONAL REGISTER HISTORIC SITE PER STATE & TERRITORY TO SERVE AS PERMANENT LEGACY AFTER BICENTENNIAL. TO BE USED AS MEETING HOUSES FOR THOSE INTERESTED IN IMPROVING ENVIRONMENT. (NAT'L). HELEN BYRD, BICENTENNIAL COORDINATOR; NATL TRUST FOR HISTORIC PRESERVATION; 748 JACKSON PL, NW; WASHINGTON, DC 20006. (#287). **(??). ARBA RECOGNIZED.**

'MEMO FROM BELGIUM' BICENTENNIAL BOOKLET - DC. A SPECIAL BICENTENNIAL BOOKLET 'MEMO FROM BELGIUM' ON BELGIANS AND THE U S IS AVAILABLE FROM THE BELGIAN EMBASSY. (INT'L). OFFICE OF INFORMATION; BELGIAN EMBASSY; 3330 GARFIELD ST, NW; WASHINGTON, DC 20008. (#28441).

MEXICAN PERFORMING ARTS GROUPS TOUR THE USA. AN ALL-MEXICAN TALENT CIRCUS PLANS TO TOUR THE US IN 1976 WHILE THE STATE OF MEXICO SYMPHONY ORCHESTRA TOURED IN 1975. (INT'L). CULTURAL ATTACHE; EMBASSY OF MEXICO; 2829 16TH ST; WASHINGTON, DC 20009. (#32976).

MICROFILMING NATL ARCHIVES' AMER REVOL RECORDS. THIS PROJECT WILL COMPLETE THE MICROFILMING OF THE MOST SIGNIFICANT MATERIAL IN THE NAT'L ARCHIVES RELATING TO THE AMERICAN REVOLUTION. (NAT'L). KENNETH E HARRIS, CHIEF; CNTR FOR DOCUMENTARY STUDY OF THE AMERICAN REVOLUTION; NATL ARCHIVES & RECORDS SERVICE; WASHINGTON, DC 20408. (#73).

MICRONESIA FILM STUDY - WASHINGTON, DC. PREPARATION OF FILM RECORD OF ASPECTS OF DAILY LIFE & ARTISTIC EXPRESSIONS OF MICRONESIAN PEOPLE. THIS FILM WILL BE PRESERVED AS A PERMANENT CULTURAL RESOURCE. (REGN'L). E RICHARD SORENSON, DIRECTOR; NATIONAL ANTHROPOLOGICAL FILM CENTER/SMITHSONIAN INSTITUTE; WASHINGTON, DC 20560. (#26090).

MILITARY CEREMONIES AND PARADES - WASHINGTON, DC. OVER 1000 BICENTENNIAL CEREMONIES WILL BE HELD IN 1976. THESE CEREMONIES WILL HAVE INCLUDED FROM ONE TO 500 MARINE PARTICIPANTS. (NAT'L). MAJOR H W BUSE, III, OPERATIONS OFFICER; UNITED STATES MARINE CORPS; 8TH & I ST, SE; WASHINGTON, DC 20390. (#29065).

MINNESOTA DAYS IN WASHINGTON, DC. MINNESOTA DAYS WILL BE HELD IN THE KENNEDY CENTER IN JUNE 1976. (REGN'L). RON PETRUCCI, PROJ CHAIRMAN; MINNESOTA AMERICAN REVOLUTION BICENTENNIAL COMMISSION; STATE CAPITOL, RM 12; ST PAUL, MN 55155. (#25653). **ARBA GRANTEE.**

MONOGRAPHS ON THE CONTINUING AMERICAN REVOLUTION. COMMISSIONED MONOGRAPH SERIES ON RESEARCH AND THOUGHT OF PROMINENT COMMUNICATION SCHOLARS ABOUT AMERICAN REVOLUTION AS AN ONGOING FLOW OF IDEAS WHICH SYMBOLIZE AMERICAN EXPERIENCE AND VALUES. (NAT'L). PATRICK KENNICOTT, ASST FOR RESEARCH; SPEECH COMMUNICATION ASSOC; 1625 MASSACHUSETTS AVE, NW; WASHINGTON, DC 20036. (#5662). **(??).**

MULTI-ARTS EXHIBITION IN WASHINGTON, DC. EXHIBITIONS OF DIFFERENT ART FORMS: OIL & WATER COLOR PAINTINGS, WELDED METAL, STONE, WOOD, SCULPTURES, PRINTS, WOOD BLOCK, ETCHINGS, SILK SCREEN, LINOLEUM BLOCKS, LITHOGRAPHS & ALL TYPES OF FINE ART. (REGN'L). HELEN S MASON, DIRECTOR; SMITH MASON GALLERY OF ART INC; 1207 RHODE ISLAND AVE, NW; WASHINGTON, DC 20005. (#6604).

MURALS AND FESTIVITIES - WASHINGTON, DC. SUBJECT OF THE MURALS WILL BE LATINO PEOPLE AT WORK. (LOCAL). LYNN GLIXON, ADMINISTRATOR; WOODROW WILSON INTERNATIONAL CENTER; 1470 IRVING ST, NW; WASHINGTON, DC 20010. (#22885). **ARBA GRANTEE.**

MUSEUM OF AFRICAN ART IN WASHINGTON, DC. EXHIBITION OF 500 WORKS OF TRADITIONAL AFRICAN SCULPTURES & ELISOFON COLOR PHOTOS, TOURS & LECTURES ON AFRICAN CULTURE USING LIBRARY ARCHIVES EXTENSION PROGRAMS. (REGN'L). WARREN M ROBBINS, DIRECTOR; MUSEUM OF AFRICAN ART; 318 A ST, NE; WASHINGTON, DC 20002. (#5353).

MUSIC AND DANCE FROM THE AGE OF JEFFERSON, DC. PERFORMANCES IN THIS PROGRAM ARE AUTHENTIC RE-CREATIONS SPANNING THE MOMENTOUS CHANGES IN MUSIC, DANCES & SOCIAL CUSTOMS FROM 1743, THE YEAR OF JEFFERSON'S BIRTH, TO 1826, THE YEAR OF HIS DATH. (NAT'L). SUSANNE ROSCHWALB, PROJ DIRECTOR; SMITHSONIAN INSTITUTION, DIVISION OF PERFORMING ARTS; L'ENFANT 2100, SW; WASHINGTON, DC 20560. (#18826).

MUSIC FOR ORCHESTRA - WASH, DC. AN ORIGINAL SYMPHONIC WORK FOR ORCHESTRA, 'VOYAGE'. (NAT'L). JOHN HUGGLER, COMPOSER; NATIONAL ENDOWMENT FOR THE ARTS; 2401 E ST, NW; WASHINGTON, DC 20276. (#21961).

MUSICAL CONCERT - WASHINGTON, DC. CONCERT WILL BE HELD IN J F K CENTER FOR THE PERFORMING ARTS, THE ELIPSE AND AT PRESIDENT'S PARK. (LOCAL). RON DREILING, PRESIDENT; GRAND ISLAND CITY SINGERS; 2609 BRAHMA; GRAND ISLAND, NE 68801. (#26551). **ARBA GRANTEE.**

MUSIQUE VIVANTE TO TOUR US UNIVERSITIES. TOUR WIL BEGIN AT THE GEORGE WASHINGTON UNIVERSITY IN OCTOBER 1976. (INT'L). CULTURAL ATTACHE; EMBASSY OF FRANCE; 2535 BELMONT RD; WASHINGTON, DC 20008. (#32979).

'THE MYSTERY OF HOME--CZECHS IN AMERICA'--TV FILM. CZECH EMIGRANTS WILL BE THE SUBJECT OF A SERIES FOR CZECHOSLAVAKIAN TV DOCUMENTARIES. IT WAS FILMED IN PART IN TABOR, SD. (INT'L). OFFICE OF INFORMATION; CZECHOSLOVAKIAN EMBASSY; 3900 LINNEAN AVENUE; WASHINGTON, DC 20008. (#31874).

NATION OF NATIONS INTL EXHIBIT - SMITHSONIAN. AN EXHIBIT OF THE CONTRIBUTIONS A WORLD OF PEOPLE MADE IN CREATING A NEW NATION WITH A NEW IDENTITY. LARGEST EVER PRODUCED BY SMITHSONIAN OCCUPYING THE ENTIRE WEST 2ND FLOOR, MUSEUM OF HISTORY & TECHNOLOGY. (INT'L). MRS SUSAN HAMILTON, BICENTENNIAL COORDINATOR; SMITHSONIAN INSTITUTION; 1000 JEFFERSON DR, SW; WASHINGTON, DC 20560. (#101).

THE NATIONAL AIR AND SPACE MUSEUM. SCHEDULED TO OPEN JULY 1, 1976 THE MUSEUM WILL INCLUDE A SPACEARIUM, EXHIBITS ON THE HISTORY OF FLIGHT & SPACE EXPLORATION, AND A THEATRE WHERE VISITORS SEE AMERICA THROUGH FLIGHT-ORIENTED EYES. (NAT'L). LYNNE MURPHY, PRESS ASSISTANT; NATIONAL AIR & SPACE MUSEUM; SMITHSONIAN INSTITUTION; WASHINGTON, DC 20560. (#123).

NATIONAL ARCHIVES EXHIBIT 'FORMATION OF THE UNION'. THIS EXHIBIT WAS REFURBISHED & INSTALLED IN THE MAIN EXHIBITION HALL OF THE NATIONAL ARCHIVES IN SPRING, 1973. THE FOCAL POINTS ARE THE DECLARATION OF INDEPENDENCE, CONSTITUTION, AND BILL OF RIGHTS. (NAT'L). ALBERT MEISEL, ASST ARCHIVIST FOR EDUC PGMS; NATIONAL ARCHIVES AND RECORD SERVICE; 7TH & PENNSYLVANIA AVE, NW; WASHINGTON, DC 20408. (#55).

NATIONAL ARCHIVES EXHIBIT 'WRITTEN WORD ENDURES'. COMPLETE TITLE OF EXHIBIT IS 'THE WRITTEN WORD ENDURES: DOCUMENTS OF AMERICAN HISTORY'. (NAT'L). ALBERT MEISEL, ASST ARCHIVIST FOR EDUC PGMS; NATIONAL ARCHIVES AND RECORD SERVICE; 7TH & PENNSYLVANIA AVE, NW; WASHINGTON, DC 20408. (#30437).

NATIONAL BICENTENNIAL SERVICE ALLIANCE - NBSA. OFFICIAL ARBA RECOGNITION OF COMMITMENTS BY NATIONAL CIVIC AND SERVICE ORGANIZATIONS TO ESTABLISH BICENTENNIAL LIAISON OFFICE & TO MOUNT A COMMUNICATIONS EFFORT AMONG MEMBERS & SPONSOR PROJECTS. (NAT'L). DEXTER DICKINSON, PROGRAM MANAGER; AMERICAN REVOLUTION BICENTENNIAL ADMINISTRATION; 2401 E ST, NW; WASHINGTON, DC 20276. (#1786).

NATIONAL BICENTENNIAL BUSINESS ALLIANCE - NBBA. NBBA IS OPEN TO ALL BUSINESS ENTITIES INVOLVED, AS A PUBLIC SERVICE, IN MULTISTATE BICENTENNIAL PROGRAMS WHICH ARE IN ADDITION TO THEIR NORMAL BUSINESS OPERATIONS. (NAT'L). PROGRAMS DIVISION (BUSINESS ALLIANCE); AMERICAN REVOLUTION BICENTENNIAL ADMINISTRATION; 2401 E ST, NW; WASHINGTON, DC 20276. (#18394).

NATIONAL BICENTENNIAL HOSPITALITY ALLIANCE - NBHA. NBHA IS OPEN TO ALL NON-PROFIT ORGANIZATIONS W/GROUPS IN 3 OR MORE STATES WHOSE PURPOSE IS SUSTAINED PROGRAMS FOR BRINGING PEOPLE OF DIFFERENT COMMUNITIES & NATIONS TOGETHER FOR UNDERSTANDING. (NAT'L). BICENTENNIAL HOSPITALITY ALLIANCE PROGRAM OFFICE; AMERICAN REVOLUTION BICENTENNIAL ADMINISTRATION; 2401 E ST, NW; WASHINGTON, DC 20276. (#18396).

NATIONAL BICENTENNIAL SPORTS ALLIANCE - NBSA. NBSA IS TO PROMOTE ACTIVE PARTICIPATION IN THE BICENTENNIAL & IS FOR ALL SPORTS & OR ATHLETIC ORGANIZATIONS IN 3 OR MORE STATES WHOSE PRIMARY PURPOSE IS INDIVIDUAL & TEAM ATHLETIC PROGRAMS & EVENTS. (NAT'L). BICENTENNIAL SPORTS ALLIANCE PROGRAM OFFICE; AMERICAN REVOLUTION BICENTENNIAL ADMINISTRATION; 2401 E ST, NW; WASHINGTON, DC 20276. (#18397).

NATIONAL BICENTENNIAL ETHNIC/RACIAL ALLIANCE-NBERA. NBERA IS OPEN TO ALL NON-PROFIT ORGANIZATIONS WHOSE PRIMARY PURPOSE IS TO CONDUCT SUSTAINED PROGRAMS ENCOMPASSING THE PLURALITY, VARIETY & DIVERSITY OF THE AMERICAN SOCIETY & INVOLVEMENT OF ITS PEOPLE. (NAT'L). BICENTENNIAL ETHNIC/RACIAL PROGRAM OFFICE; AMERICAN REVOLUTION BICENTENNIAL ADMINISTRATION; 2401 E ST, NW; WASHINGTON, DC 20276. (#18398).

WASHINGTON — CONTINUED

NATIONAL BICENTENNIAL 'JASS' CELEBRATION. ASSOCIATION OF LOCAL TRADITIONAL (OR DIXIELAND) JAZZ GROUPS SPEARHEADED PARTICIPATION OF MEMBER GROUPS IN BICENTENNIAL ACTIVITIES, WHICH INCLUDED CONCERTS, PRESENTATIONS & EXHIBITS. (NAT'L). RODERICK W CLARKE, DIRECTOR; NATIONAL MUSEUM OF TRADITIONAL JAZZ; SUITE 201, 21 DUPONT CIRCLE; WASHINGTON, DC 20036. (#19455). **ARBA RECOGNIZED.**

NATIONAL BICENTENNIAL MEDIA RECOGNITION PGM -NBMRP. PROGRAM WILL PROVIDE OFFICIAL ARBA RECOGNITION TO MEDIA ORGANIZATIONS WHICH MAKE A SPECIAL BICENTENNIAL EFFORT SUBSTANTIALLY BEYOND THE NORMAL SCOPE IN FURTHERING PUBLIC INTEREST IN THE BICENTENNIAL. (NAT'L). HERBERT E HETU, ASST ADMIN, COMMUN & PUBL AFFAIRS; AMERICAN REVOLUTION BICENTENNIAL ADMINISTRATION; 2401 E ST, NW; WASHINGTON, DC 20276. (#20501).

NATIONAL BONSAI COLLECTION, WASHINGTON, DC. THE NATL ARBORETUM WILL DEVELOP A NATL COLLECTION OF DWARF BONSAI PLANTS OF HISTORIC QUALITY FROM JAPAN & A COLLECTION FROM THE US. (INT'L). JOHN L CREECH, DIRECTOR; DEPT OF AGRICULTURE, NATIONAL ARBORETUM; 24 & R STS, NE; WASHINGTON, DC 20002. (#5571).

NATIONAL CAPITAL PARKS--IMPROVEMENT & DEVELOPMENT. GENERAL IMPROVEMENT & DEVELOPMENT OF PARKS, MONUMENTS, MEMORIALS, & VISITOR FACILITIES IN & AROUND THE NATION'S CAPITAL. SEPARATE ENTRIES ARE IN BINET FOR EACH DESCRIBED PROJECT. (NAT'L). BICENTENNIAL COORDINATOR, NATIONAL CAPITAL PARKS; NATIONAL PARK SERVICE; 1100 OHIO DR, SW; WASHINGTON, DC 20242. (#274).

NATIONAL FOLK FESTIVAL - WASHINGTON, DC. ANNUAL FOLK FESTIVAL SHOWING PERFORMANCE AND CRAFT TRADITIONS WITH NIGHTTIME PERFORMANCES AND DAILY WORKSHOPS HELD AT WOLFTRAP FARM PARK; ALSO FURNISHES TECHNICAL ASSISTANCE TO OTHER FESTIVALS. (REGN'L). LEO BERNACHE, EXEC DIRECTOR; NATIONAL FOLK FESTIVAL ASSOC; 1346 CONNECTICUT AVE; WASHINGTON, DC 20036. (#15970).

NATIONAL GUARD HERITAGE GALLERY. THE GALLERY WILL RELATE THE STORY OF THE MINUTEMEN WHO BORE ARMS IN DEFENSE OF THEIR HOMES AND COMMUNITIES TO ESTABLISH THIS NATION'S FREEDOM; THE GROWTH OF THE NATIONAL GUARD IS ALSO TRACED. (NAT'L). LESLIE H CROSS, COL, US ARMY(RET), ASST CURATOR; HISTORICAL SOCIETY OF THE MILITIA AND NATIONAL GUARD; 1 MASSACHUSETTS AVE, NW; WASHINGTON, DC 20001. (#12654). **ARBA RECOGNIZED.**

NATIONAL HERB GARDEN, WASHINGTON, DC. ESTABLISH NATIONAL HERB GARDEN SHOWING VARIOUS HERB USES: MEDICINAL, CULLINARY, PERFUME, COLONIAL INDIAN & EXPERIMENTAL. WILL BE A PERMANENT COLLECTION. (NAT'L). DR JOHN CREECH, DIRECTOR; DEPT OF AGRICULTURE, NATIONAL ARBORETUM; 24TH & R STS, NE; WASHINGTON, DC 20002. (#5572).

NATIONAL HISTORIC RECORDS PROGRAM. H.R. 15818 SIGNED INTO LAW CREATING NATIONAL HISTORICAL PUBLICATIONS AND RECORDS COMMISSION OF THE NATIONAL ARCHIVES. SUPPORT TO STATES FOR DOCUMENTARY RECORDS PRESERVATION IS THE NEW FUNCTION. (NAT'L). DR E BERKELEY TOMPKINS, EXEC DIRECTOR; NATIONAL HISTORICAL PUBLICATIONS & RECORDS COMMISSION; NATIONAL ARCHIVES BLDG; WASHINGTON, DC 20408. (#4). **ARBA RECOGNIZED.**

NATIONAL HOME BUILDERS MEETING HOUSE ASSISTANCE. ASSISTANCE TO EACH STATE MEETING HOUSE PRESERVATION PROJECT BY STATE AND LOCAL AFFILIATES OF THE NATIONAL ASSOCIATION OF HOME BUILDERS CONSISTING OF TECHNICAL & FINANCIAL CONSULTATION. (NAT'L). WALTER LITWIN, DIR INDUST & INST COMMITTEE; NATIONAL ASSOCIATION OF HOME BUILDERS; 15TH & M ST NW; WASHINGTON, DC 20005. (#7901). **(??). ARBA RECOGNIZED.**

NATIONAL LOW-COST ACCOMODATIONS DIRECTORY. A SURVEY OF EXISTING ACCOMODATIONS & A DESCRIPTION OF THE BASIC CHARACTERISTICS OF EACH FOR EXPECTED INCREASE IN VISITORS, FOREIGN & DOMESTIC, DURING THE COMMEMORATION. (INT'L). SENIOR PROGRAM OFFICER, FESTIVAL USA; AMERICAN REVOLUTION BICENTENNIAL ADMINISTRATION; 2401 E STREET, NW; WASHINGTON, DC 20276. (#163).

NATIONAL MODELS FOR NEIGHBORHOOD IMPROVEMENT - DC. PROJECT IS TO APPLY A MULTIPLE IMPACT PROGRAM TO TWO CITIES FOR THE PURPOSE OF DEVELOPING A VARIETY OF NEIGHBORHOOD IMPROVEMENT MODELS & FROM THESE, A NATIONAL PROTOTYPE. (NAT'L). SARAH AUSTIN, VICE PRESIDENT; NATIONAL URBAN COALITION; 1201 CONNECTICUT AVE; WASHINGTON, DC 20036. (#10775). **ARBA RECOGNIZED. ARBA GRANTEE.**

NATIONAL NEWSPAPER ASSOC BICENTENNIAL SERIES-NBMRP. NNA HAS COMMISSIONED, THRU HISTORY DIVISION OF ASSOC FOR EDUCATION, SEVERAL COLLEGE JOURNALISM PROFESSORS TO PREPARE SERIES ON HISTORY OF NEWSPAPERS IN USA. AVAILABLE TO 12,000 SUBSCRIBERS OF NNA. (NAT'L). THEODORE A SHERRILL, EXEC VICE PRESIDENT; NATIONAL NEWSPAPER ASSOC; 491 NATIONAL PRESS BLDG; WASHINGTON, DC 20045. (#21285).

NATIONAL PARK SERVICE HISTORICAL HANDBOOKS. REVOLUTIONARY PARK HANDBOOKS COWPENS, FT NECESSITY, GEORGE ROGERS CLARK, GUILFORD COURTHOUSE, HOPEWELL VILLAGE, INDEPENDENCE, KINGS MOUNTAIN, MINUTE MAN, MOORES CREEK, MORRISTOWN, SARATOGA, YORKTOWN. (NAT'L). MANAGER, HARPERS FERRY CENTER; NATIONAL PARK SERVICE; HARPERS FERRY, WV 25425. (#1470).

NATIONAL PARK SERVICE--VOLUNTEER IN PARKS PROGRAM. NPS NEEDS VOLUNTEERS IN MANY OF ITS 298 AREAS TO ASSIST IN VISITOR SERVICE ACTIVITIES INCLUDING INTERPRETIVE FUNCTIONS, RESOURCE MGMT., AND OTHER ASPECTS OF PARK OPERATIONS. (NAT'L). CHIEF, VISITOR SERVICES DIVISION; NATIONAL PARK SERVICE; 18TH & C STS NW; WASHINGTON, DC 20240. (#1475).

NATIONAL PARK SERVICE TRAVELING AUDIO CHAIRS. AUDIO CHAIRS WITH INFORMATION ON LITTLE KNOWN FACTS OF MINORITY CONTRIBUTIONS DURING THE REVOLUTIONARY WAR PERIOD WILL TRAVEL THROUGH OUT THE NATL PARK SERVICE SYSTEM. (NAT'L). MANAGER, HARPERS FERRY CENTER; NATIONAL PARK SERVICE; HARPERS FERRY, WV 25425. (#5581).

NATIONAL PARK SERVICE'S LIVING HISTORY PROGRAM. A DRAMATIC & POPULAR ASPECT OF NPS' INTERPRETATION OF THE HISTORIC FEATURES OF A PARK. THESE LIVE PGMS, SUPPLEMENTING OTHER INTERPRETIVE PGMS, DEAL WITH CRAFTS, MILITARY LIFE, OR AMERICAN LIFESTYLES. (NAT'L). BICENTENNIAL COORDINATOR; NATIONAL PARK SERVICE; 18TH & C STS, NW; WASHINGTON, DC 20240. (#6727).

THE NATIONAL RIGHT TO READ EFFORT. A PROGRAM DESIGNED TO INCREASE LITERACY. TO ENSURE THAT 99 PER CENT OF THOSE UNDER 16 AND 90 PER CENT OF THOSE OVER 16, CAN READ BY 1980. (NAT'L). DORIS DEW, PROGRAM SPECIALIST; DEPT OF HEALTH, EDUCATION & WELFARE, OFFICE OF EDUCATION; WASHINGTON, DC 20202. (#2772). **(??).**

NATIONAL SYMPHONY ORCHESTRA COMMISSIONS. THE NATIONAL SYMPHONY, ANTAL DORATI, MUSIC DIRECTOR, HAS AWARDED GRANTS TO ELEVEN COMPOSERS TO CREATE WORKS FOR PERFORMANCE IN HONOR OF THE BICENTENNIAL. THERE WILL BE 12 WORKS COMMISSIONED. (INT'L). WILLIAM L DENTON, MANAGING DIRECTOR; NATIONAL SYMPHONY ORCHESTRA ASSOCIATION; JOHN F KENNEDY CENTER; WASHINGTON, DC 20566. (#1714). **ARBA GRANTEE.**

NATIONAL TRANSPORTATION KIT, WASHINGTON, DC. ANNUAL KIT OF MATERIALS TO TRANSPORTATION AND BUSINESS WRITERS ON HISTORY, CURRENT AND FUTURE STATUS OF TRUCKING INDUSTRY. STATISTICS, FEATURE ARTICLES & SUGGESTIONS FOR COMMUNITY PROJECTS INCLUDED. (NAT'L). MARY JO LONG, PRESS ASSISTANT; AMERICAN TRUCKING ASSOCIATIONS, INC; 1616 P ST, NW; WASHINGTON, DC 20036. (#20627).

NATIONAL VISITOR CENTER DEVELOPMENT--WASHINGTON DC. INCLUDED IN THE VISITOR FACILITIES HERE WILL BE WELCOME AREAS AND THEATERS, LOUNGES, EXHIBITS, & AUDIO-VISUAL EQUIPMENT. GENERAL VISITORS INFORMATION AND TRANSPORTATION HUB. (NAT'L). GENERAL MANAGER, NATIONAL VISITOR CENTER; NATIONAL PARK SERVICE; NATL VISITOR CNTR, UNION STATION; WASHINGTON, DC 20002. (#275).

NATIONWIDE BELL RINGING ON JULY 4, 1976. A NATIONWIDE 2-MINUTE BELL RINGING, SUPPORTED BY ARBA & SANCTIONED BY CONGRESS, WILL TAKE PLACE IN EVERY PART OF THE UNITED STATES AND ITS TERRITORIES ON JULY 4 AT 2:00PM, EDT. (NAT'L). DAN BUSER, COORDINATOR, BICENTENNIAL WEEKEND; AMERICAN REVOLUTION BICENTENNIAL ADMINISTRATION; 2401 E ST, NW; WASHINGTON, DC 20276. (#22798).

NATL CAPITAL PARKS-CIRCLE PARKS IMPROVEMENTS. THIS WILL PROVIDE RECREATION DEVELOPMENT IN THIS SERIES OF PARKS & RECREATION-USE FACILITIES. (REGN'L). BICENTENNIAL COORDINATOR, NATIONAL CAPITAL PARKS; DEPT OF THE INTERIOR; 1100 OHIO DR, SW; WASHINGTON, DC 20240. (#289).

NATL CAPITAL PARKS-ANACOSTIA COMMUNITY PARKS. THIS WILL DEVELOP COMMUNITY FACILITIES IN AN AREA OF GREATEST NEED. WILL INCLUDE RECREATION & CIVIC USE. DEVELOPMENT DESIGNED AS A MODEL IN URBAN OPEN SPACES. (ST-WIDE). BICENTENNIAL COORDINATOR, NATIONAL CAPITAL PARKS; NATIONAL PARK SERVICE; 1100 OHIO DR, SW; WASHINGTON, DC 20242. (#293).

NATL CAPITAL PARKS--NATIONAL SCULPTURE GARDENS. REDESIGNING AREA AT NINTH AND CONSTITUTION AVENUE INTO A VISITOR USE FACILITY INCLUDING ICE SKATING RINK, PAVILION, AND SCULPTURE GARDEN. (NAT'L). BICENTENNIAL COORDINATOR,NATIONAL CAPITAL PARKS; NATIONAL PARK SERVICE; 1100 OHIO DR SW; WASHINGTON, DC 20242. (#1478).

NATL CAPITAL PARKS--IMPROVEMENTS ON THE MALL. THIS WILL INCLUDE REPLACING ROADS ON THE MALL WITH BIKEWAYS AND A ROAD SYSTEM FOR THE TOURMOBILE. ALSO, PROVIDE WALKS FOR CONVENIENT CIRCULATION AMONG MALL ATTRACTIONS. (NAT'L). BICENTENNIAL COORDINATOR,NATIONAL CAPITAL PARKS; NATIONAL PARK SERVICE; 1100 OHIO DR SW; WASHINGTON, DC 20242. (#1479).

NATL CAPITAL PARKS--NATIONWIDE BICEN INFO CENTER. NATIONWIDE 'DISCOVER THE USA' EXHIBIT OF THE NCP/NPS & ARBA. PROVIDE INFO ON, AND MOTIVATE VISITS TO, SITES AND ACTIVITIES OF VISITOR INTEREST THROUGHOUT COUNTRY. LOCATED IN NATIONAL VISITOR CENTER. (NAT'L). BICENTENNIAL COORDINATOR, NATIONAL CAPITAL PARKS; NATIONAL PARK SERVICE; 1100 OHIO DR SW; WASHINGTON, DC 20242. (#1482).

NATL CAPITAL PARKS--MONUMENTS MEMORIALS IMPROVEMNT. INCLUDES REPAIRS TO LINCOLN AND JEFFERSON MEMORIALS AND WASHINGTON MONUMENT, AND FACILITIES GIVING HANDICAPPED VISITORS ACCESS TO THE MEMORIALS. (NAT'L). BICENTENNIAL COORDINATOR, NATIONAL CAPITAL PARKS; NATIONAL PARK SERVICE; 1100 OHIO DR SW; WASHINGTON, DC 20242. (#1483).

NATL CAPITOL PARKS - DEVELOP CONSTITUTION GARDENS. PROVIDE PERMANENT FACILITIES FOR CULTURAL & RECREATIONAL USE IN INFORMAL GARDEN SETTING. TO BE DEVELOPED ON THE MALL NEAR THE LINCOLN MEMORIAL. (NAT'L). BICENTENNIAL COORDINATOR, NATIONAL CAPITAL PARKS; NATIONAL PARK SERVICE; 1100 OHIO DR, SW; WASHINGTON, DC 20240. (#294).

NATL CONGRESS ON VOLUNTEERISM & CITIZENSHIP - 1976. A REPRESENTATIVE CONGRESS OF CONCERNED CITIZENS CONVENED TO DISCUSS AND RESOLVE ISSUES GERMANE TO VOLUNTEERISM. (NAT'L). JAMES I LUCK, EXECUTIVE DIRECTOR; NATIONAL CENTER FOR VOLUNTARY ACTION; 1785 MASS AVE; WASHINGTON, DC 20036. (#7813). **ARBA RECOGNIZED. ARBA GRANTEE.**

NATL PARK GUIDE TO AMER REVOL HISTORIC PLACES. THIS IS AN INEXPENSIVE GUIDEBOOK ON NATIONAL HISTORIC SITES, PARKS, AND LANDMARKS RELATING TO THE REVOLUTION INDEXED BY STATE. COMPREHENSIVE YET USABLE BY THE TOURING PUBLIC. (NAT'L). MANAGER, HARPERS FERRY CENTER; NATIONAL PARK SERVICE; HARPERS FERRY, WV 25425. (#1467).

NATL PARK SERVICE BOOKS ON HISTORIC PERSONALITIES. BOOKS DEALING WITH HISTORIC EVENTS AND PERSONALITES SIGNERS OF THE DECLARATION, SPRING '74; THE PRESIDENTS, SPRING '75; SIGNERS OF THE CONSTITUTION, FALL '75. (NAT'L). MANAGER, HARPERS FERRY CENTER; NATIONAL PARK SERVICE; HARPERS FERRY, WV 25425. (#334).

NATL PARK SERVICE BICENTENNIAL GRANTS-IN-AID PROG. REVOLUTION-RELATED SITES ELIGIBLE TO APPLY FOR AID IN HIST PRESERVATION THROUGH SPECIAL BICENTENNIAL GRANTS-IN-AID PROGRAM. (REGN'L). ASST DIR, ARCHEOL AND HIST PRESERVATION; NATIONAL PARK SERVICE; 18TH & C STS NW; WASHINGTON, DC 20240. (#1472).

NATL PARK SERVICE'S 'INDIAN PRIDE ON THE MOVE'. AN ENTERTAINING EDUCATIONAL TRAVELING EXHIBIT OF SELECTED ARTIFACTS FROM DAVID T VERNON COLLECTION WHICH WILL VISIT RURAL COMMUNITIES & INDIAN RESERVATIONS IN NORTHERN ROCKIES AND UPPER MIDWEST. (NAT'L). MANAGER, HARPERS FERRY CENTER; NATIONAL PARK SERVICE; HARPERS FERRY, WV 25425. (#5177).

NATL PARK SVC, '...A LITTLE LOOK AROUND'. THE NATIONAL PARK SERVICE SPONSORS A SERIES OF PERFORMANCES FEATURING PROFESSIONAL ACTORS PLAYING THE PARTS OF FAMOUS AMERICANS OF THE PAST WHO HAVE RETURNED TO SEE AMERICA'S GROWTH. (NAT'L). MANAGER, HARPERS FERRY CENTER; NATIONAL PARK SERVICE; HARPERS FERRY, WV 25425. (#5653).

NAVAL DOCUMENTS OF THE AMERICAN REVOLUTION. US NAVY HISTORIANS HAVE COMPILED AND EDITED 6 VOLS OF THIS EVENTUAL 10 VOL SERIES. AVAILABLE FROM THE SUPERINTENDENT OF DOCUMENTS, WASHINGTON, DC. (NAT'L). CAPT B C CRAWFORD,SPECIAL ASST BICENTENNIAL; DEPT OF THE NAVY; WASHINGTON, DC 20301. (#29).

NAVAL OBSERVATORY EXHIBIT IN WASHINGTON, DC. BICENTENNIAL EXHIBIT, MUSEUM AND TOUR DEPICTING THE HISTORY OF ASTRONOMY IN THE U S NAVY AND A MOVIE HIGHLIGHTING THE MISSION OF THE NAVAL OBSERVATORY. (NAT'L). ROBERT W RHYNSBURGER, PROJ CHAIRMAN; NAVAL OBSERVATORY; 34TH & MASSACHUSETTS AVE; WASHINGTON, DC 20390. (#12065).

NEA FELLOWSHIP GRANT FOR, WASHINGTON, DC. RECIPIENT OF NEA GRANT WILL BE REQUIRED TO TRANSLATE OPERAS FROM ITALIAN, FRENCH & GERMAN INTO ENGLISH, PREPARE SCORES FOR SINGERS & CONDUCTORS & ASSIST WITH STAGE DIRECTION. (LOCAL). REV WILLIAM C COWLES, PROJ COORDINATOR; NATIONAL ENDOWMENT FOR THE ARTS; WASHINGTON, DC 20506. (#22663).

NEBRASKA BAND MARCHING IN CHERRY BLOSSOM PARADE-DC. YORK HIGH SCHOOL BAND WILL BE THE ONLY REPRESENTATIVE FROM NEBRASKA IN THE CHERRY BLOSSOM FESTIVAL PARADE. (REGN'L). WILLIAM L HARSHBARGER, BAND DIRECTOR; YORK HIGH SCHOOL MARCHING BAND; 1005 DUKE DR; YORK, NE 68467. (#25800). **ARBA GRANTEE.**

NETHERLANDS WIND ENSEMBLE GOES ON TOUR IN THE USA. BETWEEN FEBRUARY 10-28, 1976, THIS GROUP PERFORMED IN CALIFORNIA, MINNESOTA, IOWA, OHIO, RHODE ISLAND, CONNECTICUT, NEW YORK AND NEW HAMPSHIRE. (INT'L). CULTURAL ATTACHE; EMBASSY OF THE NETHERLANDS; 4200 LINNEAN AVE; WASHINGTON, DC 20008. (#32977).

NEW HAMPSHIRE DAY IN THE NATION'S CAPITOL. PRELUDE CONCERT BY MANCHESTER HIGH BAND; PARADE ALONG NEW HAPSHIRE AVENUE; NEW HAMPSHIRE FOLKTALE SKIT; LITTLE RED WAGON PUPPETEER SHOW & PLANTING OF THE OFFICIAL NEW HAMPSHIRE TREE. (REGN'L). GILBERT S CENTER, CHAIRMAN; NEW HAMPSHIRE ARBC; 37 PLEASANT ST; CONCORD, NH 03301. (#19074). **ARBA GRANTEE.**

NEW LIFE, INC, WASHINGTON, DC. NEW LIFE INC, IS A SUMMER DAY CAMP PROGRAM, 8 WEEKS OF ACTIVITY & FUNCTIONAL SKILLS, INCLUDING SUMMER WHEELCHAIR SPORTS LEAGUE FOR 14 TO 21 YEAR OLD DISABLED STUDENTS. (LOCAL). WILLIAM J GREENE, DIRECTOR; NEW LIFE INC; 2300 GOOD HOPE RD, SE; WASHINGTON, DC 20020. (#27723). **ARBA GRANTEE.**

NEWSPAPER CARTOON SERIES ON ELDERLY, DC. VIGNETTES OF AMERICANS 65 & OLDER WHO HAVE MADE CONTRIBUTIONS BOTH DURING AND AFTER THE REVOLUTION; WILL BE DISTRIBUTED TO 7,000 NEWSPAPERS THROUGH THE NATIONAL NEWSPAPER ASSOCIATION. (NAT'L). JACK OSSOTSKY, EXEC DIRECTOR; NATIONAL COUNCIL ON AGING; 1828 L ST, NW; WASHINGTON, DC 20036. (#10723).

THE NINETY-NINES BICENTENNIAL STAR PROGRAM. THE INTERN'L LICENSED WOMEN PILOTS, THE 99S' PROGRAM OF AIR-MARKINGS, CLEANUP-BEAUTIFLYCATION, WOMEN IN WORLD AVIATION & DEDICATION OF THE INTERN'L FOREST OF FRIENDSHIP, JULY 24, 1976, ATCHISON, KANSAS. (INT'L). FAY GILLIS WELLS, GENERAL CHAIRMAN; THE NINETY-NINES, INC; 1220 19TH ST, NW, SUITE 501; WASHINGTON, DC 20006. (#154). **ARBA RECOGNIZED.**

NORTH AMERICAN HERITAGE BICENTENNIAL PROGRAM - DC. THE EDUCATIONAL COMMUNICATION ASSOC IS SPONSORING SEVERAL TOUR-CONFERENCES IN THE HISTORIC AREAS OF VIR-

WASHINGTON — CONTINUED

GINIA AND CANADA. (INT'L). ELLA HARLLEE, PRESIDENT; EDUCATIONAL COMMUNICATION ASSOC; 822 NATIONAL PRESS BLDG; WASHINGTON, DC 20005. (#21923).

NORTHEAST CORRIDOR RAIL IMPROVEMENT PROJECT. THE UPGRADING OF THE NORTHEAST CORRIDOR RAIL LINE & THE ACQUISITION OF NEW VEHICLES FOR HIGH SPEED & QUALITY PASSENGER TRAIN SERVICE BETWEEN WASHINGTON & BOSTON. (REGN'L). STEVEN R BITMEYER, OFF OF RSCH & DEMONSTRATION; DEPT OF TRANSPORTATION; 400 7TH ST, SW; WASHINGTON, DC 20590. (#51).

OAKLAND, NE, BICENTENNIAL CHOIR. 'I LOVE AMERICA' PRESENTED BY OAKLAND BICENTENNIAL CHOIR AS PART OF NEBRASKA'S BICENTENNIAL PARADE OF AMERICAN MUSIC. (REGN'L). EDWIN E HANNA, DIRECTOR; OAKLAND MINISTERIAL ASSOC, FIRST LUTHERAN CHURCH; 601 N DAVIS AVE; OAKLAND, NE 68045. (#27338). **ARBA GRANTEE.**

OFFICIAL DELEGATION FROM THE NETHERLANDS ANTILLES. DURING 1976 THIS DELEGATION WILL BE TOURING PORTIONS OF THE UNITED STATES PRESENTING BICENTENNIAL GIFTS, VISITING GOVERNORS OF ORIGINAL 13 COLONIES, MAYOR OF DC, & OTHERS MAINTAINING SPECIAL RELATIONS. (INT'L). CULTURAL ATTACHE; EMBASSY OF THE NETHERLANDS; 4200 LINNEAN AVE; WASHINGTON, DC 20008. (#31872).

OIAF MILITARY BICENTENNIAL PROMOTION PROJ - NBMRP. OFFICE OF INFO FOR ARMED FORCES PGM INCLUDES FILMS ON ROLE OF ARMED FORCES; POSTERS, BROCHURES, SPOTS, RELEASES, PGMS FOR MILITARY INSTALLATIONS ABRD & PUBLIC/COMMERCIAL BROADCASTERS IN US. (NAT'L). LTC FELIX L CASIPIT, USA; OFFICE OF INFORMATION FOR THE ARMED FORCES (OASD-PA); DEPT OF DEFENSE; WASHINGTON, DC 20305. (#23097).

'OKLAHOMA DAY IN WASHINGTON', DC. A PROJECT OF THE DISTRICT OF COLUMBIA, EXTENDING AN INVITATION TO OK OCT 1-3, 1976, TO PRESENT VISUAL & PERFORMING ARTS REPRESENTING THE VARIED TALENTS OF THE SOONER STATE AT KENNEDY CENTER & DC MONUMENTS. (REGN'L). GLADYS WARREN, CHAIRMAN-DIRECTOR; AMERICAN REVOLUTION BICENTENNIAL AUTHORITY OF OKLAHOMA; 4111 N LINCOLN BLVD, SUITE 5; OKLAHOMA CITY, OK 73105. (#32859). **ARBA GRANTEE.**

OLD ANACOSTIA HISTORIC DISTRICT, WASH DC. PRESERVATION OF HISTORIC DISTRICT AROUND THE FREDERICK DOUGLASS MEMORIAL HOME IN OLD ANACOSTIA. (LOCAL). SAMUEL J PARKER, DIR OF PLANNING; WASHINGTON PLANNING & HOUSING ASSOC; 1225 K ST N. W.; WASHINGTON, DC 20005. (#7875).

OMEGA PSI PHI FRATERNITY BICENTENNIAL MEETING - DC. 1ST BLACK FRATERNITY. FOUNDED AT HOWARD UNIV. WILL HOLD ANNUAL MEETING IN WASHINGTON IN 1976 WITH BICENTENNIAL THEME. WILL INCLUDE BOTH SOCIAL & BUSINESS SESSIONS. (LOCAL). EDWARD A CLEMENT, DISTRICT MARSHALL; WASHINGTON AREA CHAPTERS OMEGA PSI PHI FRATERNITY, INC; 7601 CHESAPEAKE ST; LANDOVER, MD 20785. (#2779).

OPEN HOUSES & FIELD DAYS SPONSORED BY USDA. 1 OR 2 DAY OPEN HOUSES AT SEVERAL LARGER INSTALLATIONS LOCATED IN URBAN AREAS. FIELD DAYS AT 30-50 RESEARCH STATIONS IN FARMING AREAS. (NAT'L). ROBERT RATHBONE, DIRECTOR INFORMATION DIVISION; AGRICULTURAL RESEARCH SERVICE, US DEPARTMENT OF AGRICULTURE; 14TH & INDEPENDENCE AVE, SW; WASHINGTON, DC 20250. (#5575).

OPERATION INDEPENDENCE. DESIGNED TO STIMULATE THE PRIVATE/VOLUNTARY SECTOR TO INITIATE COMMUNITY SERVICES WHICH WILL PROVIDE ALTERNATIVES FOR THE AGING. (NAT'L). MS MARJORIE A COLLINS, ASSOC DIR; THE NATIONAL COUNCIL ON THE AGING, INC; 1828 L ST NW; WASHINGTON, DC 20036. (#7935). **ARBA RECOGNIZED.**

OPERATION OUTREACH: UNDERSTANDING FOR SURVIVAL. PROGRAM IS DESIGNED TO INVOLVE MEMBER INSTITUTIONS AND THEIR COMMUNITIES IN MUTUAL ATTEMPTS TO MEET NEEDS OF THE THIRD CENTURY. (NAT'L). MS SANDI MCLEAN, PROJ DIRECTOR; AMERICAN ASSOCIATION OF STATE COLLEGES AND UNIVERSITIES; ONE DUPONT CIRCLE NW SUITE 700; WASHINGTON, DC 20036. (#3723). **ARBA RECOGNIZED.**

OPERATION WELCOME IN WASHINGTON, DC. IRISH-AMERICAN RESIDENTS WILL PROVIDE FREE ACCOMODATIONS AND ACT AS TOUR GUIDES FOR BICENTENNIAL VISITORS FROM IRELAND. (INT'L). SEAN D COAKLEY, CHAIRMAN; IRISH-AMERICAN BICENTENNIAL COMMITTEE; SUITE 427, 1825 CONNECTICUT AVE; WASHINGTON, DC 20009. (#11168).

ORIENTATION PROGRAMS FOR NATL PARK SERVICE AREAS. UPDATE OR NEW AUDIO-VISUAL PROGRAMS FOR NATL PARK SERVICE BICENTENNIAL AREAS RELATED TO THE REVOLUTION SUCH AS MORRISTOWN, SARATOGA, MOORES CREEK, GUILFORD, & KINGS MTN. (NAT'L). MANAGER, HARPERS FERRY CENTER; NATIONAL PARK SERVICE; HARPERS FERRY, WV 25425. (#5580).

ORIGINAL FOREST HERITAGE SONGS, WASHINGTON, DC. ORIGINAL MUSIC & LYRICS BY VOLUNTEER COMPOSER RAY SCHMIDT DEPICTING COLORFUL ROLE OF FORESTS IN BUILDING AMERICA. SONGS PERFORMED BY THE 'BLUEBERRY WINE' GROUP. PROJECT SPONSORED BY US FOREST SERVICE. (NAT'L). GLENN A KOVAR, DIRECTOR SPECIAL PROJECTS; DEPT OF AGRICULTURE, FOREST SERVICE; 12TH & INDEPENDENCE AVE, SW; WASHINGTON, DC 20250. (#5567).

'OUR CAPITOL, FREEDOM SPEAKS'. HISTORAMA USING CAPITOL BUILDINGS AS FOCAL POINT WITH HISTORICAL NARRATIVE THRU SOUND AND LIGHT. PORTRAY DEVELOPMENT OF CAPITOL FROM LAYING OF FIRST STONE THRU IMPORTANT HISTORICAL EVENTS TODAY. (NAT'L). LYNETTE LAWSON, CAMPAIGN DIRECTOR; US CAPITOL HISTORICAL SOCIETY; 200 MARYLAND AVE, NE; WASHINGTON, DC 20515. (#4570). **ARBA RECOGNIZED.**

'OVERLAND TO OREGON IN 1845' - SITES, DC. SKETCHES, WATERCOLORS, MANUSCRIPT ILLUSTRATIONS BY H J WARRE ON HIS JOURNEY FROM CANADA TO OREGON ARE AMONG THE FEW EXISTING PICTORIAL RECORDS OF THE PACIFIC NORTHWEST IN THE 1840'S. (INT'L). EILEEN HARAKAL, COORDINATOR; SMITHSONIAN INSTITUTION TRAVELING EXHIBITION SERVICE; WASHINGTON, DC 20560. (#26654).

OVERSEAS BICENTENNIAL ACTIVITIES RECOGNITION PGM. EFFORTS OF SUCH ACTIVITIES MUST BE INTENDED TO ADVANCE MUTUAL UNDERSTANDING & COOPERATION THRU ACTIVIES PERTAINING TO THE BICENTENNIAL. PGM CARRIED OUT IN CONJUNCTION WITH US & THE DEPARTMENT OF STATE. (INT'L). INTERNATIONAL AFFAIRS DIVISION; AMERICAN REVOLUTION BICENTENNIAL ADMINISTRATION; 2401 E ST, NW; WASHINGTON, DC 20276. (#18399).

O'NEILL IRISH DANCERS - WASHINGTON, DC. DANCERS TO PERFORM VARIOUS PLACES IN WASHINGTON, DC; SCHEDULE TO BE ARRANGED BY DC OFFICE. REPRESENTING NE IN DC'S SALUTE TO THE STATES AT THE KENNEDY CENTER. (NAT'L). VIVIAN MELENA, DIRECTOR; O'NEILL IRISH DANCERS; BOX 323; O'NEILL, NE 68763. (#27346). **ARBA GRANTEE.**

PAHLAVI SYMPOSIUM, WASHINGTON, DC. A CONFERENCE ON PAST, CURRENT AND FUTURE RELATIONSHIPS OF IRAN AND THE US; ECONOMIC, POLITICAL, SOCIAL, BUSINESS, STRATEGIC, CULTURAL AND FOREIGN POLICIES. (INT'L). DR WB GIBSON, EXECUTIVE VICE PRESIDENT; STANFORD RESEARCH CENTER; 333 RAVENSWOOD AVE; MENLO PARK, CA 94025. (#19927). **(??).**

PARKSIDE REDEVELOPMENT IN NE WASHINGTON, DC. REDEVELOPMENT OF HOUSES, MEDICAL FACILITIES & SHOPPING CENTERS. (LOCAL). MARYLOU BATT, PROJECT MANAGER; DC GOVT, OFFICE OF HOUSING; 1170 12TH ST, NW; WASHINGTON, DC 20004. (#5614). **(??).**

'PARTICIPATION IN A NEW NATION' EXHIBIT. EXHIBITION ON GERMAN IMMIGRATION TO THE UNITED STATES. (INT'L). CULTURAL ATTACHE; GERMAN EMBASSY; 4645 RESERVOIR RD; WASHINGTON, DC 20007. (#31879).

PARTNERS OF THE AMERICAS BICENTENNIAL PROGRAM. PROGRAM TO FOSTER CLOSER RELATIONSHIP BETWEEN PEOPLE OF THE UNITED STATES AND PEOPLE OF LATIN AMERICA THROUGH PERSONAL INVOLVEMENT IN SELF-HELP PROJECTS. (INT'L). E DAVID LURIA, ASSOCIATE DIRECTOR; NATL ASSOC OF THE PARTNERS OF THE ALLIANCE, INC; 2001 S ST, NW; WASHINGTON, DC 20009. (#4569). **ARBA RECOGNIZED.**

'PEOPLE OF 1776' SPONSORED BY NATIONAL PARK SVC. TRAVELING TROUPE WILL BRING VARIOUS ASPECTS OF COLONIAL LIFE (MILITARY LIFE, MUSIC, CRAFTS) TO VISITORS TO SELECTED NPS AREAS DURING 1976. (NAT'L). BICENTENNIAL COORDINATOR, HARPERS FERRY CENTER; NATIONAL PARK SERVICE; HARPERS FERRY, WV 25425. (#1469).

PEOPLE WORK FOR PEOPLE, COMMUNITY IMPROVEMENT - DC. WORK-A-THONS, FUND RAISERS & COMMUNITY IMPROVEMENT PROJECTS WITH PROCEEDS TO GO TO COMMUNITY HEALTH ORGANIZATIONS. (LOCAL). DONNA ANDREWS, EXEC DIR; WASH DC CHAPTER, EPILEPSY FNDTN OF AMERICA; 3800 RESERVOIR RD NW STE B5; WASHINGTON, DC 20007. (#8644).

PERFORMING GROUPS FROM THE FED REPUBLIC OF GERMANY. THE BERLIN OPERA TOURED THE USA IN 1975; GERMAN SAENGERBUND WAS IN PHILADELPHIA IN 1976; AND THE SAARLAND CHAMBER ORCHESTRA WAS IN NEW YORK, AUGUST 1976. (INT'L). CULTURAL ATTACHE; EMBASSY OF THE FEDERAL REPUBLIC OF GERMANY; 4645 RESERVOIR RD; WASHINGTON, DC 20007. (#32974).

'PERIODICAL LITERATURE OF THE AMERICAN REVOLUTION'. BIBLIOGRAPHY OF WRITINGS ON THE REVOLUTIONARY PERIOD WHICH HAVE APPEARED IN PERIODICALS. (NAT'L). DR JAMES HUTSON, BICENTENNIAL COORDINATOR; LIBRARY OF CONGRESS; 10 FIRST ST, SE; WASHINGTON, DC 20540. (#99).

'PERSIAN LOCKS' EXHIBITION - SITES. LOCKS, REPRESENTING OBJECTS FOR PROTECTION & ITEMS OF RELIGIOUS SIGNIFICANCE, ARE FROM THE COLLECTION OF PARVIZ TANAVOLI AND DATE FROM EARLY ISLAMIC PERIOD TO EARLY 20TH CENTURY. (INT'L). EILEEN HARAKAL, COORDINATOR; SMITHSONIAN INSTITUTION TRAVELING EXHIBITION SERVICE; WASHINGTON, DC 20560. (#26662).

PETER MAX PAINTS AMERICA - BOOK, WASHINGTON, DC. 50 NEVER-BEFORE-SEEN ORIGINAL PAINTINGS & ORIGINAL VERSE EXEMPLIFYING THE GRANDEUR OF THE 50 STATES, A DAZZLING COLLECTION OF PERSONAL IMPRESSIONS BY INTERNATIONALLY KNOWN ART INNOVATOR-PETER MAX. (NAT'L). ALPHONS J HACKL, PUBLISHER; ACROPOLIS BOOKS LTD; 2400 17TH ST, NW; WASHINGTON, DC 20009. (#22468).

PHI BETA KAPPA BICENTENNIAL POEM. THE COMMISSIONING OF MELVILLE CANE TO WRITE A POEM COMMEMORATING THE BICENTENNIAL. (NAT'L). KENNETH M GREENE, SECRETARY; PHI BETA KAPPA; 1811 Q ST, NW; WASHINGTON, DC 20009. (#89).

'PHOTOGRAPHING THE FRONTIER' - SITES PROJECT. 38 PANEL EXHIBIT INCLUDES 121 PHOTOGRAPHS OF THE FRONTIER TAKEN WHEN THE WEST WAS YOUNG; MANY IMAGES HAVE NEVER BEFORE BEEN SHOWN PUBLICLY. (NAT'L). ANDREA STEVENS, COORDINATOR; SMITHSONIAN INSTITUTION TRAVELING EXHIBIT SERVICE; WASHINGTON, DC 20560. (#15929).

PHYSICAL FITNESS PROGRAM, WASHINGTON, DC. THE PRESIDENT'S COUNCIL ON PHYSICAL FITNESS WILL SPONSOR VARIOUS PROGRAMS ENHANCING PHYSICAL FITNESS & SPORTS. (NAT'L). C CARSON, COORDINATOR; PRESIDENT'S COUNCIL ON PHYSICAL FITNESS; 400 6TH ST SW, RM3030; WASHINGTON, DC 20201. (#27920).

PICTORIAL HISTORY OF BANKING - BOOK. A BOOK ON THE HISTORY OF BANKING WILL BE PUBLISHED BY THE AMERICAN BANKERS ASSOCIATION IN CONJUNCTION WITH AN EXHIBIT AT THE SMITHSONIAN INSTITUTE. (NAT'L). KATIE O' HARA, ASST TO THE DIR OF PUBLIC RELATIONS; AMERICAN BANKERS ASSOCIATION; 1120 CONNECTICUT AVE, NW; WASHINGTON, DC 20036. (#5631).

'PITSEOLAK: A RETROSPECTIVE' EXHIBITION, SITES, DC. EXHIBITION OF 100 DRAWINGS BY ONE OF CANADA'S LEADING ESKIMO GRAPHIC ARTISTS DEPICTS THE LEGENDS & THE SPIRIT WORLD OF ESKIMO TRADITIONS. (INT'L). EILEEN HARAKAL, COORDINATOR; SMITHSONIAN INSTITUTION TRAVELING EXHIBITION SERVICE; WASHINGTON, DC 20560. (#26655).

PLAN FOR AN INVENTORY OF AMERICAN INDIAN ART. A FEASIBILITY SURVEY, BY THE SMITHSONIAN INSTITUTION, TO DETERMINE THE BEST METHOD TO CONDUCT A COMPREHENSIVE INVENTORY OF INDIAN ART IN THE UNITED STATES. (NAT'L). SENIOR PROGRAM OFFICER, FESTIVAL USA; AMERICAN REVOLUTION BICENTENNIAL ADMINISTRATION; 2401 E STREET, NW; WASHINGTON, DC 20276. (#191).

PLANETARIUM PROJECTOR FOR THE EINSTEIN-SPACEARIUM. THE GIFT OF A SOPHISTICATED PROJECTOR FOR THE PLANETARIUM IN THE NEW AIR AND SPACE MUSEUM OF THE SMITHSONIAN INSTITUTE IN WASHINGTON, DC, BY THE FEDERAL REPUBLIC OF GERMANY. (INT'L). CULTURAL COUNSELOR; EMBASSY OF THE FEDERAL REPUBLIC OF GERMANY; 4645 RESERVOIR RD, NW; WASHINGTON, DC 20007. (#13696).

PLANNING AMERICA'S GREAT CITIES. SHOWS DEVELOPMENT OF USA'S MODERN CITIES FROM EARLY TIMES, WHAT IS HAPPENING IN URBAN PLANNING & FUTURE EXPECTATIONS. PROJECT DEVELOPED BY ASSOC OF SCIENCE & TECHNOLOGY CENTERS. (NAT'L). MRS LEE KIMCHE, EXEC DIRECTOR; ASSOCIATION OF SCIENCE & TECHNOLOGY CENTERS; 2100 PENNSYLVANIA AVE, NW; WASHINGTON, DC 20037. (#5349). **ARBA RECOGNIZED. ARBA GRANTEE.**

PLANNING FOR ANACOSTIA'S HISTORICAL AREAS IN DC. A PROGRAM ENCOURAGING LOCAL CITIZEN INVOLVEMENT IN PROMOTING THE USE AND PRESERVATION OF HISTORICALLY VALUABLE PHYSICAL AND CULTURAL INSTITUTIONS FOR PRESENT DAY USE IN ANACOSTIA, DC. (LOCAL). BOWLES C FORD, EXEC DIRECTOR; WASHINGTON PLANNING AND HOUSING ASSOCIATION; 1225 K ST NW; WASHINGTON, DC 20005. (#2292).

PLANT VARIETIES NAMED FOR BICENT, WASHINGTON, DC. NEW PLANT VARIETIES FROM AGRICULTURAL RESEARCH WILL BE NAMED BY THE US AGRICULTURAL RESEARCH SERVICE FOR THE BICENTENNIAL CELEBRATION. (NAT'L). ROBERT RATHBONE, DIRECTOR, INFORMATION DIVISION; AGRICULTURAL RESEARCH SERVICE, US DEPARTMENT OF AGRICULTURE; 14TH & INDEPENDENCE AVE, SW; WASHINGTON, DC 20250. (#5564).

PLAZA DE SAN MARTIN, GIFT FROM ARGENTINA - DC. UNDER CONSTRUCTION IN WASHINGTON, DC, IS THE NEW PLAZA, ARGENTINA'S MAJOR CONTRIBUTION TO THE U S BICENTENNIAL. THE PLAZA WILL CONTAIN AN EQUESTRIAN STATUE OF GENERAL JOSE DE SAN MARTIN. (INT'L). INFORMATION OFFICE; EMBASSY OF ARGENTINA; 1600 NEW HAMPSHIRE AVE; WASHINGTON, DC 20009. (#27914).

POLITICAL & PATRIOTIC SONGS OF AMERICAN REVOLUTION. PUBLICATION OF THESE PERFORMING EDITIONS WILL MATCH LYRICS PUBLISHED IN NEWSPAPERS BETWEEN 1773-1783 WITH TUNES OF THAT PERIOD, ALLOWING MUSICAL REPERTORIES TO BE CHARACTERIZED. (NAT'L). MS GILLIAN B ANDERSON; 1320 NORTH CAROLINA AVE, NE; WASHINGTON, DC 20002. (#87).

PORT OF ENTRY WELCOME SIGNS FOR BICENTENNIAL. SIGNS WILL BE INSTALLED AT PORTS OF ENTRY TO THE US ALONG THE CANADIAN & MEXICAN BORDERS TO WELCOME BILINGUAL GUESTS. (INT'L). KENT SLEPICKA, ACTING DIR, SPECIAL PROG; GENERAL SERVICES ADMINISTRATION; 18TH AND F STS, NW; WASHINGTON, DC 20405. (#1759).

POSITIVE PASTS & FUTURES IN BLACK ED 1776 - 1976. A RESEARCH PROJECT AIMED AT DEMONSTRATING THE BLACK EXPERIENCE IN EDUCATION FROM 1776 TO 1976. (NAT'L). CHERYL J DOBBINS, EXEC DIRECTOR; POSITIVE FUTURES, INC; 1341 G ST, NW, SUITE 413; WASHINGTON, DC 20005. (#8529). **(??).**

POSTER OF WASHINGTON, DC, MONUMENTS. POSTER OF WASHINGTON, DC MONUMENTS. ARBA LICENSE NO 76-19-0601. (NAT'L). MITCHELL NEWDELMAN, PRESIDENT; NEWDELMAN AND JONSSON; SUITE 301 1555 CONN AVE NW; WASHINGTON, DC 20036. (#21179).

POTOMAC BOAT TOURS IN THE WASHINGTON, DC AREA. SIGHTSEEING TOURS AND GENERAL TRANSPORTATION VIA BATEAU MOUCHE TYPE BOATS ON THE POTOMAC AND ANACOSTIA RIVERS. (LOCAL). WILLEM POLAK, PRESIDENT; POTOMAC BOAT TOURS; 210 THE STRAND - OLD TOWNE; ALEXANDRIA, VA 22314. (#8649).

PRESERVATION FOR THE BICENTENNIAL. INFORMATION TO GUIDE INDIVIDUALS & GROUPS IN PLANNING PRESERVATION PROJECTS INCLUDING FUNDING, PROGRAMS, & PUBLICATIONS ETC. PRICE $3. (NAT'L). MRS HELEN BYRD, BICENTENNIAL COORDINATOR; NATL TRUST FOR HISTORIC PRESERVATION; 748 JACKSON PL NW; WASHINGTON, DC 20006. (#1368). **ARBA RECOGNIZED.**

PRESIDENT'S ENVIRONMENTAL MERIT AWARDS PROGRAM. PROGRAM TO RECOGNIZE, REWARD & ENCOURAGE ENVIRONMENTAL ACTIVITIES BY AMERICAN YOUTH, TO SERVE AS A PERSONAL THANK YOU BY PRESIDENT FORD AND TO CREATE AN AWARENESS OF ENVIRONMENTAL PROBLEMS. (NAT'L). MS JOAN DONNELLY, DIRECTOR; ENVIRONMENTAL PROTECTION AGENCY, PRESIDENTS MERIT AWARDS PGM; 401 M ST, SW, A107-PEMAP; WASHINGTON, DC 20460. (#6428).

THE PRESS & THE AMER REVOLUTION-NEWSPAPER ARTICLES. ANPA HAS PREPARED 64 ILLUSTRATED ARTICLES ON EVENTS & PER-

WASHINGTON — CONTINUED

SONALITIES OF REVOLUTION. WEEKLY RELEASE FROM 4/13/75 TO 7A4/76. UTILIZES MTRLS FROM AMER ANTIQUARIAN SOCIETY. WRITTEN BY DR FRANCIS G WALETT. (NAT'L). STEPHEN E PALMEDO, PROJECT DIRECTOR; AMERICAN NEWSPAPER PUBLISHERS ASSOC; PO BOX 17407 DULLES INTL AIRPORT; WASHINGTON, DC 20041. (#6873). **ARBA RECOGNIZED.**

'PRE-REVOLUTIONARY HISTORY' - SITES PROJECT. 30 PANEL EXHIBIT ENTITLED, 'IN THE MINDS & HEARTS OF THE PEOPLE', TELLS STORY OF PRE-REVOLUTIONARY PERIOD WITH COPIES OF PORTRAITS & DOCUMENTS; REPRESENTS PERSONALITIES WHO MOLDED COURSE OF HISTORY. (NAT'L). ANDREA STEVENS, COORDINATOR; SMITHSONIAN INSTITUTION TRAVELING EXHIBIT SERVICE; WASHINGTON, DC 20560. (#15926).

'PRIVATE GOES PUBLIC' STUDY. WILL STUDY HOW THE SHIFTING LINE BETWEEN 'PUBLIC PERSONS' & PRIVATE INDIVIDUALS IS REDRAWN IN TIMES OF CULTURAL CRISIS. BY JETHRO LIEBERMAN, A PHI BETA KAPPA BICENTENNIAL FELLOWSHIP AWARD . (NAT'L). KENNETH M GREENE, SECRETARY; PHI BETA KAPPA; 1811 Q ST, NW; WASHINGTON, DC 20009. (#259).

'PROFILES OF MERCHANT SEAFARERS' - SITES PROJECT. 14 PANELS DESCRIBE TYPICAL REVOLUTIONARY PERIOD SEAFARERS; DATA DRAWN FROM COMPUTERIZED PASSPORT RECORDS FROM 1793 TO 1849. (NAT'L). ANDREA STEVENS, COORDINATOR; SMITHSONIAN INSTITUTION TRAVELING EXHIBIT SERVICE; WASHINGTON, DC 20560. (#15927).

PROJECT S C A T - WASHINGTON, DC. ACTIVITY TOURS FOR SENIOR CITIZENS. (LOCAL). SANDRA A CONLEY, PROGRAM DIRECTOR; MISSION OF COMMUNITY CONCERN; 3920 SOUTH CAPITOL ST, SE; WASHINGTON, DC 20032. (#22883). **ARBA GRANTEE.**

PUBLIC CITIZEN VISITORS CENTER, WASHINGTON, D C. IN-DEPTH CAPITOL HILL TOURS WRITTEN AND ESCORTED; BIWEEKLY CALENDAR OF CONGRESSIONAL AND GOVERNMENT EVENTS; INFORMATION ON FEDERAL GOVERNMENT AND WASHINGTON, DC; GROUP SEMINARS ON CONSUMERISM. (REGN'L). MIKE HORROCKS, DIRECTOR; PUBLIC CITIZEN VISITORS CENTER; 1200 15TH ST, NW; WASHINGTON, DC 20005. (#20079).

PUBLIC SERVICE IN A DEMOCRACY - WASHINGTON, DC. BRIEF HISTORICAL SURVEY OF DEVELOPMENT OF U S PUBLIC SERVICE. SHORT CAREER BIOGRAPHIES OF OUTSTANDING PUBLIC SERVANTS. PROGRAM OF SEMINARS & CONFERENCES TO ACQUAINT YOUTH WITH GOVERNMENT CONCERN. (LOCAL). DANIEL PRICE, EXEC DIRECTOR; NATIONAL CIVIL SERVICE LEAGUE; 917 15TH ST, NW; WASHINGTON, DC 20005. (#10748).

PUBLICATION OF NATL VOTING & REGISTRATION INFO, DC. PUBLICATION OF INFORMATION & VOTING PROCEDURES FOR ALL STATES, DC, VIRGIN ISLANDS & PUERTO RICO FOR 1976 ELECTIONS. (NAT'L). MARY STONE, PGM OFFICER; LEAGUE OF WOMEN VOTERS EDUCATION FUND; 1730 M ST, NW; WASHINGTON, DC 20036. (#10753).

PUBLICATION 'THE DECLARATION OF INDEPENDENCE'. THE LIBRARY OF CONGRESS AND PRINCETON UNIVERSITY PRESS WILL PUBLISH A REVISED AND ENLARGED EDITION OF PROFESSOR JULIAN BOYD'S DEFINITIVE VOLUME ON 'THE DECLARATION OF INDEPENDENCE'. (NAT'L). DR JAMES HUTSON, BICENTENNIAL COORDINATOR; LIBRARY OF CONGRESS; 10 FIRST ST, SE; WASHINGTON, DC 20540. (#135). **(??).**

QUADRIENNIAL MEETING OF INTL COUNCIL ON ARCHIVES. TO BE HELD IN WASHINGTON AT THE INVITATION OF THE NAT'L ARCHIVES AND THE SOCIETY OF AMERICAN ARCHIVISTS. THE THEME WILL BE 'THE ARCHIVAL REVOLUTION OF OUR TIME'. (INT'L). ALBERT MEISEL, ASST ARCHIVIST FOR EDUC PGMS; NATIONAL ARCHIVES AND RECORD SERVICE; 7TH & PENNSYLVANIA AVE, NW; WASHINGTON, DC 20408. (#67).

QUALITY CHILD CARE SERVICES FOR THE NATION, DC. A PROJECT AIMED AT THE HEALTHY DEVELOPMENT OF CHILDREN WITH THE THEME 'BIRTHDAY PARTIES ARE FOR KIDS'. (NAT'L). CAROLE HEFFELFINGER; DAY CARE & CHILD DEVELOPMENT COUNCIL OF AMER, INC; 622 14TH ST NW; WASHINGTON, DC 20005. (#8642).

'QUESTIONS AND ANSWERS ABOUT THE BICENTENNIAL' -DC. THIS BROCHURE ANSWERS THOSE QUESTIONS MOST FREQUENTLY ASKED ABOUT THE AMERICAN REVOLUTION BICENTENNIAL ADMINISTRATION. OF INTEREST TO INDIVIDUALS AND GROUPS. NO CHARGE. (NAT'L). OFFICE OF PUBLIC INFORMATION; AMERICAN REVOLUTION BICENTENNIAL ADMINISTRATION; 2401 E ST, NW; WASHINGTON, DC 20276. (#27607).

RADIO SERIES SPONSORED BY U S DEPT OF AGRICULTURE. WEEKLY RADIO SERIES HIGHLIGHTING AGRICULTURAL RESEARCH CONTRIBUTIONS TO U S PUBLIC. (NAT'L). ROBERT RATHBONE, DIRECTOR ARS INFORMATION DIVISION; AGRICULTURAL RESEARCH SERVICE, US DEPARTMENT OF AGRICULTURE; 14TH & INDEPENDENCE AVE, SW; WASHINGTON, DC 20250. (#5577).

READING IS FUN-DAMENTAL. MOTIVATES READING BY GETTING BOOKS TO CHILDREN & CHILDREN INTO BOOKS. RIF'S BICENTENNIAL AIM IS TO REACH 5 MILLION CHILDREN WITH 25 MILLION BOOKS BY 1976. (NAT'L). DR SIDNEY NELSON, PRESIDENT; READING IS FUN-DAMENTAL; SMITHSONIAN INST, L'ENFANT 2500; WASHINGTON, DC 20560. (#7936). **ARBA RECOGNIZED.**

REBUS FACSIMILIES PROJECT - LIBRARY OF CONGRESS. PUBLICATION OF A SERIES OF REBUS FACSIMILES WILL BEGIN IN 1973. THE FIRST DEPICTS GREAT BRITAIN AND THE COLONIES AS A MOTHER AND CHILD DISPUTING. OTHERS TO BE PUBLISHED AT REASONABLE INTERVALS. (NAT'L). DR JAMES HUTSON, BICENTENNIAL COORDINATOR; LIBRARY OF CONGRESS; 10 FIRST ST, SE; WASHINGTON, DC 20540. (#75).

RED CROSS VOLUNTEER SERVICES TO THE COMMUNITY, DC. WORKING TO OBTAIN VOLUNTEERS FOR THE NATION'S CAPITAL BICENTENNIAL FUNCTIONS IN COOPERATION WITH THE PARK SERVICE, DEPT OF HUMAN RESOURCES & HAPPY BIRTHDAY USA; SERVICED OVER 56,500 PEOPLE. (LOCAL). MRS W M RYON, CHAIRMAN; AMERICAN RED CROSS; 2025 E ST, NW; WASHINGTON, DC 20006. (#32699).

REGIONAL BICENTENNIAL CLIMATOLOGICAL BROCHURES. DISTRIBUTION OF PAMPHLETS CONTAINING REGIONAL DESCRIPTIONS OF WEATHER IN THE U.S. ALSO INCLUDES WEATHER DATA (PRECIPITATION & TEMPERATURES) FOR PRINCIPAL CITIES FOR TOURISTS. (NAT'L). LEWIS A PITT, SPECIAL PROJECTS STAFF; NATL OCEANIC & ATMOSPHERIC ADMINISTRATION; ENVIRONMENTAL DATA SERVICE; WASHINGTON, DC 20235. (#1513).

RELIGIOUS ART MOBILE EXHIBIT FOR ALL STATES. MOBILE EXHIBITS FEATURING US RELIGIOUS ART OF PAST 200 YEARS INCLUDING FILM SERIES ON ART DEVELOPMENT. 10 VANS, EACH SERVING 5 STATES WILL VISIT SMALLER CITIES & TOWNS AS PART OF RELIGIOUS FESTIVAL. (NAT'L). KENNETH L HANSEN, EXEC VICE PRESIDENT; RELIGIOUS HERITAGE OF AMERICA; 1000 CONNECTICUT AVE, NW; WASHINGTON, DC 20036. (#2378).

'RELIGIOUS LANDMARKS IN AMERICA' - BOOK. 250-PAGE TOUR GUIDE OF 2000 RELIGIOUS SITES AND SHRINES IN THE US. INCLUDES A 50-PAGE HAMMOND ROAD ATLAS WITH KEYED INDEX TO ALL SITES & FULL INFORMATION ON EACH. INTRODUCTION BY LOWELL THOMAS. (NAT'L). KENNETH L HANSEN, EXEC VICE PRESIDENT; RELIGIOUS HERITAGE OF AMERICA; 1000 CONNECTICUT AVE, NW; WASHINGTON, DC 20036. (#2379). **(??).**

RENOVATE SR CITIZENS LIVING FACILITY IN WASH, DC. RENOVATE ARTHUR CAPPER BLDG FOR SENIOR CITIZENS HOUSING. (LOCAL). RUTH WENZEL, SPECIAL ASSISTANT; NATL CAPITAL HOUSING AUTHORITY, OFFICE OF HOUSING PROGRAMS; 1170 12TH ST, NW; WASHINGTON, DC 20004. (#5609). **(??).**

RENOVATION OF FIRE STATION IN WASHINGTON, DC. OLD ENGINE #6 FIRE STATION WILL BE HISTORICAL LANDMARK & COMMUNITY EDUCATIONAL CENTER. (LOCAL). LT PETER MCGALLIARIA, COMMUNITY RELATIONS; OLD ENGINE #6; 438 MASSACHUSETTS AVE, NW; WASHINGTON, DC 20001. (#5615).

RESTORATION OF ABNER CLOUD HOUSE, WASHINGTON, DC. RESTORATION OF PHYSICAL PROPERTY AND RE-ACTIVATION OF GARDEN OF ABNER CLOUD HOUSE WHICH WAS BUILT IN THE YR 1801 ON THE CHESAPEAKE & OHIO CANAL LOCATED AT 3.3 MILEAGE NEAR FLETCHER'S BOAT HOUSE. (REGN'L). MRS JOHN A LOGAN, PRESIDENT; COLONIAL DAMES OF AMERICA, CHAPTER III; 2800 ALBEMARLE ST, NW; WASHINGTON, DC 20008. (#19751).

RESTORATION OF PAINTINGS IN WASHINGTON, DC. CONSERVATION AND RESTORATION OF OVER ONE HUNDRED PAINTINGS FROM THE LATE NINETEENTH CENTURY WHICH BELONG TO THE FREER GALLERY OF ART. (INT'L). DR SUSAN HOBBS, ASST CURATOR, AMERICAN ART; SMITHSONIAN INSTITUTION; WASHINGTON, DC 20560. (#16058).

REVITALIZE OLD ANACOSTIA AREA OF WASHINGTON, DC. DC CITY GOVT PLANS TO REVITALIZE ANACOSTIA BY FOSTERING NATL MONUMENTS, NEW SCHOOLS & HOMES AND ECONOMIC ENTERPRISES. (LOCAL). MARYLOU BATT, PROJECT MANAGER; DC GOVT, OFFICE OF HOUSING; 1170 12TH ST, NW; WASHINGTON, DC 20004. (#5613). **(??).**

REVOLUTIONARY MURALS IN WASHINGTON, DC. REPRODUCING UP TO 180 LARGE COPIES OF EACH OF 50 MURAL DESIGNS ON BICENTENNIAL THEMES; MURALS TO BE PLACED IN SCHOOLS AROUND THE NATION. (NAT'L). SHARON P ALBANO, SEC-TREASURER; REVOLUTIONARY MURALS; 131 RICHLAND CIR; STERLING, VA 22172. (#10720). **ARBA GRANTEE.**

'RIDE ON' BICYCLING EXHIBIT - SITES PROJECT. EXHIBIT THAT TRACES THE HISTORY & TECHNOLOGY OF BICYCLING; INCLUDES ANTIQUE CYCLES, TEXT AND ILLUSTRATIONS ON EXHIBIT PANELS. (NAT'L). ANDREA STEVENS, COORDINATOR; SMITHSONIAN INSTITUTION TRAVELING EXHIBIT SERVICE; WASHINGTON, DC 20560. (#15935).

RINGLING BROTHERS & BARNUM & BAILEY BICENT PROGRAM. PROGRAM TO SALUTE THE BICENTENNIAL & GREAT MOMENTS OF OUR HISTORY, USING TRADITIONAL CIRCUS FORMAT, WITH PATRIOTIC & HISTORIC THEMES IN A VARIETY OF WAYS, BOTH INSIDE & OUTSIDE THE SHOW. (NAT'L). ALLEN J BLOOM, SENIOR VICE PRESIDENT; RINGLING BROTHERS & BARNUM & BAILEY COMBINED SHOWS, INC; 1015 18TH ST, NW; WASHINGTON, DC 20036. (#1770). **ARBA RECOGNIZED.**

RIOT CORRIDOR DEVELOPMENT IN WASHINGTON, DC. REDEVELOPMENT OF INNER-CITY RIOT-DAMAGED AREAS (SHAW,14 ST,H ST & DOWNTOWN) FOR NEW HOUSING & RELATED PUBLIC & COMMERCIAL USES - CREATION OF SOUND, STABLE NEIGHBORHOODS & REVITALIZED DOWNTOWN. (LOCAL). MARIAN M FRYER, ADMIN OFFICER; REDEVELOPMENT LAND AGENCY; 1325 G ST, NW; WASHINGTON, DC 20005. (#292).

SALUTE TO BLACK MEN - WASHINGTON, DC. SPECIAL TRIBUTE TO BLACK MEN IN HISTORY. (LOCAL). BETTY J BROWN, PROJ COORDINATOR; CONCERNED BLACK WOMEN OF METROPOLITAN WASHINGTON; 816 EASLEY ST; SILVER SPRING, MD 20910. (#27854). **ARBA GRANTEE.**

SALUTE TO THE STATES PROGRAM, WASH, DC. HISTORY AND DEVELOPMENT OF STATES CONTRIBUTIONS. CEREMONY ON THE CAPITOL STEPS, PARADE OF MUSIC AT THE KENNEDY CENTER, BEAUTIFICATION PROGRAM ON THE HONORED STATE'S AVENUE. (NAT'L). JAN EICHHORN, PROJ DIRECTOR; OFFICE OF BICENTENNIAL PROGRAMS; 777-14TH ST, NW; WASHINGTON, DC 20005. (#17925). **ARBA GRANTEE.**

'SALZBURGER FESTSPIELE!' EXHIBITION - SITES, DC. AN EXHIBITION OF APPROXIMATELY 24 THEATRICAL COSTUMES FROM THE WORLD-FAMOUS SALZBURG FESTIVAL IN SALZBURG, AUSTRIA. (INT'L). EILEEN HARAKAL, COORDINATOR; SMITHSONIAN INSTITUTION TRAVELING EXHIBITION SERVICE; WASHINGTON, DC 20560. (#26664).

SAVE OUR STREAMS, ADOPT ONE. CITIZENS ADOPT A STREAM SEGMENT AND CONTINUE TO CARE FOR IT AS PART OF A CITIZEN ACTION PROGRAM TO RESTORE AND PROTECT WATERWAYS AND STREAMS. INCLUDES 'WATER WAGON', A TRAVELING DEMO WORKSHOP. (NAT'L). JACK LORENZ, EXEC DIRECTOR; THE IZAAK WALTON LEAGUE OF AMERICA, INC; 1800 N KENT ST, SUITE 806; ARLINGTON, VA 22209. (#12653). **ARBA RECOGNIZED.**

SC PARTICIPATION IN BICENT PARADE AMER MUSIC. ONE OF 52 CONCERTS OF AMERICAN MUSIC TO BE PRESENTED AT KENNEDY CENTER & SPONSORED BY FEDERATION OF MUSIC CLUBS. ENTIRE SERIES KNOWN AS BICENTENNIAL PARADE OF AMERICAN MUSIC. (REGN'L). MRS ROBERT FREEMAN, RECORDING SECRETARY; SOUTH CAROLINA FEDERATION OF MUSIC CLUBS; 3910 KENILWORTH RD; COLUMBIA, SC 29205. (#8750). **ARBA GRANTEE.**

SCHOLARLY CONFERENCES OF THE NATIONAL ARCHIVES. SEMI-ANNUAL SERIES ESTABLISHED IN 1967. BICENTENNIAL THEMES INCLUDE A CONFERENCE ON RESEARCH IN AMERICAN REVOLUTIONARY HISTORY EXPLORING THE 'MEANING' OF THAT ERA. (NAT'L). DR FRANK BURKE, DIRECTOR, EDUCATIONAL PROGRAMS; NATIONAL ARCHIVES AND RECORD SERVICE; 7TH & PENNSYLVANIA AVE, NW; WASHINGTON, DC 20408. (#59).

SCIENCE AND SOCIETY TODAY - NATL LECTURE SERIES. NATIONAL LECTURE SERIES FOR SMALL DEVELOPING ISOLATED COLLEGES SOCIOLOGICAL AND PHILOSOPHICAL ASPECTS OF SCIENCE AND TECHNOLOGY FROM THE HISTORICAL PERSPECTIVE OF THE US WITH WORLDWIDE OUTLOOK. (NAT'L). DR THOMAS HOLME, EXEC DIRECTOR; SIGMA XI, THE SCIENTIFIC RESEARCH SOCIETY OF NORTH AMERICA; 345 WHITNEY AVE; NEW HAVEN, CT 06511. (#2035).

SCIENCE: A RESOURCE FOR HUMANKIND. SYMPOSIUM ON RELATIONSHIP OF SCIENCE & TECHNOLOGY TO SOCIAL & ECONOMIC DEVELOPMENT OF THE WORLD. PARTICIPANTS FROM GENERAL ASSEMBLY OF INTERNATIONAL COUNCIL OF SCIENTIFIC UNIONS-OVER 50 NATIONS THERE. (INT'L). E C ROWAN, SEMINAR COORDINATOR; NATIONAL ACADEMY OF SCIENCES; 2101 CONSTITUTION AVE, NW; WASHINGTON, DC 20418. (#33274). **ARBA RECOGNIZED.**

SCULPTURE BY VENEZUELAN ARTIST ALEJANDRO OTERO. A SCULPTURE BY SR OTERO WILL BE OFFERED THE GOVERNMENT OF THE UNITED STATES OF AMERICA FOR WASHINGTON, DC BY THE GOVERNMENT OF VENEZUELA IN HONOR OF THE BICENTENNIAL. (INT'L). OFFICE OF INFORMATION; EMBASSY OF THE REPUBLIC OF VENEZUELA; 2437 CALIFORNIA ST, NW; WASHINGTON, DC 20008. (#26976).

SCULPTURE ON BLACK AMERICANS, WASHINGTON, DC. 'THE FAMILY TREE OF HOPE', THE LARGEST PIECE OF WOODEN, HAND-CARVED AFRICAN-AMERICAN ART IN THIS COUNTRY, WILL BE EXHIBITED AT THE CARTER BARRON GROUNDS. (REGN'L). DENNIS STROY, JR, PROJ COORDINATOR; D'STROY SCULPTING (WOOD SCULPTURE); 5301 8TH ST NW; WASHINGTON, DC 20011. (#9236).

SE FREEWAY ELEVATION DEVELOPMENT IN WASH, DC. RESEARCH STUDY OF POTENTIAL USE OF AIR SPACE UNDER FREEWAY INTERSECTION OF 7TH & 8TH STREETS SE. (LOCAL). VINCENT DEFOREST, PRESIDENT; AFRO-AMERICAN BICENTENNIAL CORPORATION, INC; 1420 N ST, NW, SUITE 101; WASHINGTON, DC 20005. (#5616). **(??).**

SEED BANK OF ENDANGERED PLANT SPECIES. TO ESTABLISH A SEED BANK OF ENDANGERED PLANT SPECIES TO PRESERVE AND ASSURE THE CONTINUED EXISTENCE OF PLANTS THAT ARE NATIVE TO NORTH AMERICA. (NAT'L). ANTHONY WAYNE SMITH, PRESIDENT; NATIONAL PARKS AND CONSERVATION ASSOCIATION; 1701 18TH ST, NW; WASHINGTON, DC 20009. (#273). **(??).**

SELECTIONS ON AMERICAN REVOLUTION - WASHINGTON, DC. 13 SELECTIONS ON AMER REVOL FROM SECONDARY SCHOOL HISTORY BOOKS OF OTHER NATIONS COMPILED INCLUDING ARGENTINA, CANADA, CHINA, EGYPT, FRANCE, GERMANY, GHANA, GR BRITAIN, INDIA, ISRAEL, JAPAN, MX & USSR. (INT'L). HELEN WIPRUD, PUBLICATIONS OFFICER IDIE; DEPT OF HEALTH, EDUCATION & WELFARE, OFFICE OF EDUCATION; ROB #3, RM 3082 USOE; WASHINGTON, DC 20202. (#26536).

SELF-GOVERNMENT FOR THE DISTRICT OF COLUMBIA. WASHINGTON,D.C. BICENTENNIAL COMMISSION HAS LAUNCHED DRIVE TO BRING SELF-GOVERNMENT TO THE RESIDENTS OF THE DISTRICT OF COLUMBIA. (ST-WIDE). LAWRENCE S STINCHCOMB, EXEC VICE PRESIDENT; DC BICENTENNIAL COMMISSION; 1239 G ST, NW; WASHINGTON, DC 20009. (#212). **(??).**

SELF-PORTRAIT OF AMERICAN ARTISTS. AN EXHIBIT OF PORTRAITS OF AMERICAN ARTISTS IN THE NATIONAL PORTRAIT GALLERY OF THE SMITHSONIAN. (NAT'L). MS SUSAN HAMILTON, BICENTENNIAL COORDINATOR; SMITHSONIAN INSTITUTION; 1000 JEFFERSON DR, SW; WASHINGTON, DC 20560. (#79).

SENTRY POST-BICENT PUBLICATION OF WASHINGTON, DC. A MONTHLY TABLOID NEWSMAGAZINE & COMMUNITY COMMUNICATION MEDIUM REPORTING ON BICENTENNIAL PROGRAMS NOT PROVIDED BY MASS MEDIA. (ST-WIDE). LAWRENCE S STINCHCOMB, PRESIDENT; BICENTENNIAL COMMISSION OF THE DISTRICT OF COLUMBIA, INC; 1025 15TH ST, NW; WASHINGTON, DC 20005. (#3838).

SERVICES TO INTERNATIONAL VISITORS, WASHINGTON, DC. HOSPITALITY, SIGHTSEEING, LANGUAGE AND GENERAL ASSISTANCE TO INTERNATIONAL VISITORS AND FOREIGN DIPLOMATS. (LOCAL). ROBERT G CLEVELAND, PRESIDENT; MERIDIAN HOUSE INTERNATIONAL; 1630 CRESCENT PLACE, NW; WASHINGTON, DC 20009. (#20958).

WASHINGTON — CONTINUED

SHAKESPEARE IN AMERICA. SCHOLARLY MEETINGS, LECTURES, DEBATES, ETC, BY WORLD'S LEADING CRITICS, EDUCATORS, PRODUCERS, RESEARCHERS & THINKERS FROM A VARIETY OF DISCIPLINES FOCUSING ON US ROLE IN PRESERVING ENGL CULTURAL HERITAGE. (INT'L). O B HARDISON, JR, DIRECTOR; FOLGER SHAKESPEARE LIBRARY; 201 E CAPITOL ST, SE; WASHINGTON, DC 20003. (#6883). **ARBA RECOGNIZED.**

SICKLE CELL ANEMIA ERADICATION PROGRAM. AN ADVOCACY PROGRAM AIMED AT SICKLE CELL ANEMIA TO INCLUDE RESEARCH, AN INFORMATION CAMPAIGN, CLEARINGHOUSE, & COUNSELING PROCEDURES. (NAT'L). DR E LEON COOPER, ACTING EXEC DIRECTOR; NATIONAL MEDICAL ASSOCIATION; 2109 E ST, NW; WASHINGTON, DC 20037. (#23). **ARBA RECOGNIZED.**

SIGNIFICANT ARCHITECTURE USA-FROM 1607 TO 1976. A MAJOR EXHIBITION FOR THE MUSEUMS OF THE COUNTRY CORRELATED WITH A THREE-VOLUME PAPERBACK GUIDEBOOK. EXHIBIT SPINE WOULD BE PHOTOS OF NATIONAL ACHIEVEMENT CORRELATED WITH REGIONAL WORKS. (NAT'L). BILL N LACY, DIR, ARCHITECTURE & ENVIRONMENT; NATIONAL ENDOWMENT FOR THE ARTS; 806 15TH ST, NW; WASHINGTON, DC 20506. (#2173).

SILVERWORKS FROM THE RIO DE LA PLATA - SITES, DC. EXHIBITION OF 180 ECCLESIASTICAL & SECULAR SILVER OBJECTS REPRESENTS OUTSTANDING CULTURAL/SOCIAL ASPECTS OF ARGENTINE LIFE DURING 18TH & 19TH CENTURIES. (INT'L). EILEEN HARAKAL, COORDINATOR; SMITHSONIAN INSTITUTION TRAVELING EXHIBITION SERVICE; WASHINGTON, DC 20560. (#26666).

SISTER CITIES PROGRAM. A PRIVATE NONPROFIT NATIONAL ORGANIZATION COORDINATING 420 US CITIES & THEIR AFFILIATED SISTER CITIES IN 61 OTHER COUNTRIES. PROGRAM AIMS TO ENCOURAGE INVOLVEMENT OF WORLD COMMUNITY IN BICENTENNIAL. (INT'L). THOMAS GITTINS, EXEC VICE PRESIDENT; THE TOWN AFFILIATION ASSOCIATION, INC; 1625 K ST, NW; WASHINGTON, DC 20006. (#187). **ARBA RECOGNIZED. ARBA GRANTEE.**

SITES EXHIBIT ON 20 POLISH TEXTILE ARTISTS, DC. 35 WORKS BY INTERNATIONALLY KNOWN ARTISTS & SOME NOT KNOWN OUTSIDE OF POLAND. WORKS FROM THE 60'S & EARLY 70'S AS WELL AS PIECES DONE FOR THIS EXHIBITION. (INT'L). EILEEN HARAKAL, COORDINATOR; SMITHSONIAN INSTITUTION TRAVELING EXHIBITION SERVICE; WASHINGTON, DC 20560. (#26705).

SLIDE PRESENTATION - WASHINGTON, DC. THE SLIDES WILL DEPICT THE HISTORY OF THE NATION'S CAPITOL, A RELATIVELY YOUNG CITY IN AMERICA. (LOCAL). HARDY R FRANKLIN, DIRECTOR; DISTRICT OF COLUMBIA PUBLIC LIBRARY; 901 G ST, NW; WASHINGTON, DC 20005. (#22890). **ARBA GRANTEE.**

SLIDE SHOW ON HISTORY OF SOIL CONSERVATION. THE STORY OF SOIL, WATER & FOREST CONSERVATION FROM COLONIAL TIMES TO THE PRESENT, ILLUSTRATED BY SLIDES MADE FROM OLD PHOTOS, ENGRAVINGS AND PORTRAITS WITH NARRATION AND MUSIC. (NAT'L). HUBERT KELLEY, DIRECTOR, INFORMATION DIVISION; DEPT OF AGRICULTURE, SOIL CONSERVATION SERVICE; 14TH & INDEPENDENCE AVE, SW; WASHINGTON, DC 20250. (#5601).

SLOGANS USA. NATIONWIDE CONTEST TO FIND A SLOGAN TO CATCH THE SPIRIT OF AMERICA TODAY, WHICH WOULD ALSO BE APPROPRIATE FOR THE BICENTENNIAL. TO BRING AMERICANS TO CONSTRUCTIVE THINKING ABOUT THEIR COUNTRY. (NAT'L). MS MARDI DEVOLITES, PROGRAM COORDINATOR; SLOGANS USA; 1401 16TH ST, NW; WASHINGTON, DC 20036. (#1783). **ARBA RECOGNIZED. ARBA GRANTEE.**

SMITHSONIAN INSTIT TRAVELING EXHIBIT OF CANADA. THREE PRESTIGIOUS EXHIBITIONS OF CANADIAN ART, PAINTING, PRINTS AND SCULPTURE WILL BE LOANED FOR TOURS OF THE UNITED STATES. (INT'L). KEITH DE B PERCY, PROJ DIRECTOR; EMBASSY OF CANADA; 1746 MASSACHUSETTS AVE; WASHINGTON, DC 20036. (#18825).

SOUND-SLIDE PRODUCTION ON AGING - WASHINGTON, DC. PROGRAM WILL FOCUS ON ELDERLY PERSONS WHO HAVE CONTRIBUTED SIGNIFICANTLY TO LIFE IN THE U S AFTER REACHING AGE 65; SLIDES AND SOUNDTRACK NARRATION OF 15-20 MINUTES. (NAT'L). JACK OSSOFSKY, EXEC DIRECTOR; NATIONAL COUNCIL ON THE AGING, INC; 1828 L ST, NW; WASHINGTON, DC 20036. (#10862).

SOURCE MATERIALS IN WOMEN'S CONGREGATIONS - DC. A SURVEY OF UNKNOWN & UNUSED SOURCE MATERIALS IN ARCHIVES OF RELIGIOUS CONGREGATIONS OF WOMEN IN THE U S. THE RESEARCHED MATERIAL WILL APPEAR IN A GUIDE TO AID RESEARCH ON AMERICAN WOMEN. (NAT'L). MARY DANIEL TURNER, EXEC DIRECTOR; LEADERSHIP CONFERENCE OF WOMEN RELIGIOUS; 1325 MASSACHUSETTS AVE, NW; WASHINGTON, DC 20005. (#8528).

SPECIAL ISSUES OF 2 DANISH NEWSPAPERS IN THE U S. SPECIAL ISSUES OF THE 2 REMAINING DANISH NEWSPAPERS IN THE U S 'DEN DANSKE PIONEER' AND 'BIEN'. A BOOK FUND WILL BE ESTABLISHED FOR THE CONTINUED PUBLICATION OF THESE 2 NEWSPAPERS. (INT'L). NIELS TOFT, PROJ DIRECTOR; DANISH EMBASSY; 3200 WHITEHAVEN PKY, NW; WASHINGTON, DC 20007. (#20774).

THE SPIRIT OF INNOVATION. SHOWS INFLUENCE OF SCIENCE & TECHNOLOGY ON PROGRESS OF USA & HOW IT ENRICHED & DIVERSIFIED ITS CULTURE. PROJECT DEVELOPED BY ASSOC OF SCIENCE & TECHNOLOGY CENTERS WITH NSF GRANT. (NAT'L). MRS LEE KIMCHE, EXEC DIRECTOR; ASSOCIATION OF SCIENCE & TECHNOLOGY CENTERS; 2100 PENNSYLVANIA AVE, NW; WASHINGTON, DC 20037. (#5344). **ARBA RECOGNIZED.**

SPIRIT OF '76 JOG, WASHINGTON, DC. IN HONOR OF THE BICENTENNIAL, THE NATIONAL JOGGING ASSOCIATION IS SPONSORING A 'SPIRIT OF '76' JOG. (NAT'L). GARY K OLSEN, COORDINATOR; NATIONAL JOGGING ASSOC; 1910 K ST, NW, SUITE 202; WASHINGTON, DC 20006. (#27928).

ST LAWRENCE SEAWAY CORP FLOTILLA EXHIBIT. DEPT OF TRANSPORTATION'S PARTICIPATION IN THE MARITIME ADMINISTRATION'S PROPOSAL FOR A NATIONAL SYSTEM OF BICENTENNIAL FLOATING EXHIBIT BARGES. (NAT'L). RICHARD BOUCHARD, DIR OFF TRANS PLNG ASST; DEPT OF TRANSPORTATION; 400 7TH ST, SW; WASHINGTON, DC 20590. (#1896). **(??).**

'STREETSCAPE' - EQUIPMENT SOURCEBOOK. DESIGN INDEX WILL IMPROVE THE VISUAL APPEAL AND UTILITY OF STREET FURNITURE. IT WILL BE A CATALOG OF STANDARDS, GUIDELINES & EXAMPLES OF SUPERIOR PRODUCTS USED BY PERSONS IN COMMUNITY DEVELOPMENT. (NAT'L). HAROLD LEWIS MALT, PRESIDENT; CENTER FOR DESIGN PLANNING; 3417 1/2 M ST NW; WASHINGTON, DC 20007. (#4970).

'STREETSCAPE', EQUIPMENT SOURCEBOOK 2. SES 2 WILL BE AN ENLARGED REFERENCE COMPENDIUM OF STREET FURNITURE EQUIPMENT SELECTED BY A PROFESSIONAL JURY FOR GREATER UTILITY AND ENHANCEMENT OF AMERICAN PUBLIC SPACES AND THE BUILT ENVIRONMENT. (NAT'L). HAROLD LEWIS MALT, EXEC DIRECTOR; CENTER FOR DESIGN PLANNING; 3417 1/2 M ST, NW; WASHINGTON, DC 20007. (#27633).

STUDY OF BLACK HERITAGE PROJECT. CONTRACT BETWEEN NATL PARK SERVICE AND AFRO-AMERICAN BICENTENNIAL CORPORATION FOR A STUDY RECOMMENDING FOR POSSIBLE DESIGNATION AS LANDMARKS AREAS OF BLACK HERITAGE RELATING TO USA GROWTH & DEVELOP. (NAT'L). ASST DIRECTOR, ARCHAEOLOGY & HIST PRESERVATION; NATIONAL PARK SERVICE; DEPT OF THE INTERIOR; WASHINGTON, DC 20240. (#22).

SUBJECT GUIDE TO ALL PRE-FEDERAL RECORDS. A SINGLE-VOLUME SUBJECT GUIDE TO ALL PRE-FEDERAL RECORDS IN NATIONAL ARCHIVES CUSTODY. (NAT'L). HOWARD H WEHMANN, PROG COORDINATOR; NATIONAL ARCHIVES AND RECORD SERVICE; 7TH & PENNSYLVANIA AVE, NW; WASHINGTON, DC 20408. (#63).

SURVEY OF HISTORICAL NEEDS & OPPORTUNITIES- ARBA. A REPORT TO THE STATE ARBCS ON THE NEEDS AND OPPORTUNITIES IN THE HERITAGE THEME. TO BE READIED FOR THE JANUARY 1975 MEETING IN WASHINGTON, DC OF THESE ORGANIZATIONS. (NAT'L). SENIOR PROGRAM OFFICER, HERITAGE '76; AMERICAN REVOLUTION BICENTENNIAL ADMINISTRATION; 2401 E ST, NW; WASHINGTON, DC 20276. (#3293).

'SWEDISH AMERICA, AN INTRODUCTION' BOOK. AUTHOR, NILS HASSELMO; PUBLISHER, SWEDISH INFORMATION SERVICE. (INT'L). CULTURAL ATTACHE, SWEDISH EMBASSY; SWEDISH INFORMATION SERVICE; 600 NEW HAMPSHIRE AVE; WASHINGTON, DC 20037. (#33412).

SWEDISH CULTURAL GROUPS TOUR THE UNITED STATES. THE STOCKHOLM PHILHARMONIC ORCHESTRA AND THE SWEDISH RADIO CHOIR PERFORMED IN THE UNITED STATES IN 1975: THE ORCHESTRA NOV 15 DEC 7; THE RADIO CHOIR OCT 21 - NOV 18. (INT'L). INFORMATION ATTACHE; EMBASSY OF SWEDEN; 600 NEW HAMPSHIRE AVE; WASHINGTON, DC 20037. (#31921).

'THE SWEDISH HERITAGE IN AMERICA' BOOK. AUTHOR, ALLAN KASTRUP; PUBLISHER, SWEDISH COUNCIL OF AMERICA. (INT'L). CULTURAL ATTACHE, SWEDISH EMBASSY; SWEDISH COUNCIL OF AMERICA; 600 NEW HAMPSHIRE AVE; WASHINGTON, DC 20037. (#33411).

SWISS PERFORMING GROUPS TO TOUR THE USA. AMONG THE GROUPS TO TOUR ARE THE CORPS DE MUSIQUE D'ELITE DE GENEVE & THE CORPS DE MUSIQUE LA LANDWEHR OF FRIBOURG. (INT'L). CULTURAL ATTACHE; EMBASSY OF SWITZERLAND; 2900 CATHEDRAL AVE; WASHINGTON, DC 20008. (#32981).

SYMPOSIA SERIES OF THE NATIONAL ARCHIVES. THE DOCUMENTARY STUDY OF THE AMERICAN REVOLUTION, THE PRESERVATION & RESTORATION OF DOCUMENTS, FINDING AIDS, & DESCRIPTIVE DEVICES, WILL BE TOPICS IN THESE REGULARLY SCHEDULED SYMPOSIA. (NAT'L). ALBERT MEISEL, ASST ARCHIVIST FOR EDUC PGMS; NATIONAL ARCHIVES AND RECORD SERVICE; 7TH & PENNSYLVANIA AVE, NW; WASHINGTON, DC 20408. (#57).

SYMPOSIUM ON YUGOSLAV 20TH CENTURY LITERATURE. SEMINAR. (INT'L). DUJAN STOJKOVIC, SEC; EMBASSY OF THE SOCIALIST FEDERAL REPUBLIC OF YUGOSLAVIA; 2401 CALIFORNIA ST, NW; WASHINGTON, DC 20008. (#106780-1).

SYMPOSIUM 'SCIENCE: A RESOURCE FOR HUMANKIND'. INCIDENT TO GENERAL ASSEMBLY OF ICSU, NAS SYMPOSIUM WILL EXAMINE ROLE OF S&T IN RELATION TO THREE AREAS: ECONOMIC DEVELOPMENT, ENVIRONMENTAL MANAGEMENT; SOCIETAL PROBLEMS OVER BALANCE OF CENTURY. (INT'L). HOWARD LEWIS, SYMPOSIUM COORDINATOR; NATIONAL ACADEMY OF SCIENCES/INTL COUNCIL OF SCIENTIFIC UNIONS; 2101 CONSTITUTION AVE, NW; WASHINGTON, DC 20418. (#27810).

TAKOMA SCHOOL PLAN FOR WASHINGTON, DC. A SHOWCASE SCHOOL PLAN IN WASH.,DC FOR BOTH EDUCATIONAL FACILITIES AND METHODS OF COMMUNITY PARTICIPATION DURING AND AFTER SCHOOL HOURS. (ST-WIDE). LAWRENCE S STINCHCOMB, EXEC VICE PRESIDENT; DC BICENTENNIAL COMMISSION; 1239 G ST, NW; WASHINGTON, DC 20009. (#210). **(??).**

TEEN INVOLVEMENT PROGRAM IN WASHINGTON, DC. ORGANIZATION, TRAINING, IMPLEMENTATION & EVALUATION OF SCHOOL-BASED ALCOHOL & DRUG ABUSE PROGRAM; EARLY PRIMARY PREVENTION PROGRAM USING HIGHSCHOOL STUDENTS AS POSITIVE PEER MODELS AT ELEMENTARY SCH LEVEL. (REGN'L). CHAPLAIN (LTC) CHARLES GIBBS, EDUCATION OFFICER; DEPT OF THE ARMY; RM 1C 731, THE PENTAGON; WASHINGTON, DC 20310. (#13260).

TENLEYTOWN HISTORY PROJ OF WASHINGTON, DC. INTERVIEWS, OLD DOCUMENTS & PHOTOGRAPHS AND RESEARCH WILL BE USED TO WRITE A HISTORY OF THE OLD TENLEYTOWN SECTION OF WASHINGTON. (LOCAL). JUDITH HELM & PRISCILLA MCNEIL; 3728 ALTON PL, NW; WASHINGTON, DC 20016. (#8651).

TERRITORIAL PAPERS PROJ OF NATL ARCHIVES. THE ORDINANCE OF 1787 AND THE EFFECT OF THE TERRITORIAL SYSTEM ON US GROWTH AND DEVELOPMENT WILL BE EXPLORED IN THE BOOKS AND MICROFILMS OF THIS PROJECT. (NAT'L). DR JOHN PORTER BLOOM, TERRITORIAL PAPERS BRANCH; NATIONAL ARCHIVES AND RECORD SERVICE; GENERAL SERVICES ADMINISTRATION; WASHINGTON, DC 20408. (#66).

THEATREPIECE PROJECT IN WASHINGTON, DC. SETTING OF TWO WHITMAN POEMS TO MUSIC FOR SOPRANO AND OBOE, USING 3 SPOTLIGHTS, 2 SLIDE PROJECTORS, 4 SPEAKERS AND TO BE TITLED 'UNSEEN LEAVES'. (NAT'L). FERNANDO LAIRES, PROFESSOR; NATIONAL MUSIC COUNCIL; 2109 BROADWAY; NEW YORK, NY 10023. (#6587).

'THESE ARE YOUR FLAGS, FLY THEM PROUDLY!' - DC. BROCHURE EXPLAINS ORIGIN, PURPOSE & AVAILABILITY OF NATIONAL BICENT FLAG, AND COVERS PROPER FLAG ETIQUETTE. DESIGNED & PRINTED AS A PUBLIC SERVICE BY PEOPLES LIFE INSURANCE COMPANY OF WASHINGTON, DC. (NAT'L). OFFICE OF PUBLIC AFFAIRS; AMERICAN REVOLUTION BICENTENNIAL ADMINISTRATION; 2401 E ST, NW; WASHINGTON, DC 20276. (#27605).

THREE ONE ACT OPERAS ON AMERICAN THEMES. THREE ONE ACT OPERAS ON HAWTHORNE'S 'DR. HEIDIGGER'S EXPERIMENT, CRANE'S 'MAGGIE,' AND MELVILLE'S 'THE BELL TOWER. PRODUCED BY STEPHEN BURTON. (REGN'L). JIM IRELAND, DIRECTOR; NATIONAL ENDOWMENT FOR THE ARTS; 806 15TH ST, NW; WASHINGTON, DC 20506. (#1562). **(??).**

THREE PLAYS FOR CHILDREN IN WASHINGTON, DC. THE PLAYS INCLUDE: 'PAUL REVERE RIDES AGAIN', 'TOM PAINE' & '1776.' (LOCAL). TOM ZELANEY, PRESIDENT; THEATER, ETC; 3739 12TH ST NE; WASHINGTON, DC 20017. (#10995).

TOUR OF FOLKLORE ENSEMBLES 'SOTA', PRISTINA. LIVE PERFORMANCE. (INT'L). CULTURAL OFFICE; EMBASSY OF THE SOCIALIST FEDERAL REPUBLIC OF YUGOSLAVIA; 2410 CALIFORNIA ST, NW; WASHINGTON, DC 20008. (#106767-1). **(??).**

TOUR OF THE ACADEMIC CHOIR 'MIRCE ACEV' - SKOPJE. LIVE PERFORMANCE. (INT'L). DUJAN STOJKOVIC, SEC; EMBASSY OF THE SOCIALIST FEDERAL REPUBLIC OF YUGOSLAVIA; 2410 CALIFORNIA ST, NW; WASHINGTON, DC 20008. (#106469-1).

TOUR OF WASHINGTON, DC. EIGHT INDIAN STUDENTS AND TWO CHAPERONES FROM THE WYOMING INDIAN HIGH SCHOOL WILL TOUR WASHINGTON AREA AND PERFORM THEIR NATIVE DANCES. (REGN'L). TOM SHAKESPEARE, PROJ DIRECTOR; ARAPAHOE INDIAN TRADITIONAL CLUB; BOX 145; ETHETE, WY 82520. (#26108). **ARBA GRANTEE.**

'TOYS FROM SWITZERLAND' - SITES EXHIBIT, DC. A HISTORICAL VIEW OF CHILDREN'S PLAYTINGS AND A STUDY OF THE AESTHETIC & EDUCATIONAL CONSIDERATION IN CONTEMPORARY TOY DESIGN. (INT'L). EILEEN HARAKAL, COORDINATOR; SMITHSONIAN INSTITUTION TRAVELING EXHIBITION SERVICE; WASHINGTON, DC 20560. (#26703).

TRAINING MODEL - TOUR GUIDES FOR THE DISABLED - DC. DEVELOPMENT OF TOUR GUIDE TRAINING MODEL FACILITATING PARTICIPATION BY ELDERLY & HANDICAPPED IN BICENTENNIAL; WASHINGTON, DC IS PROTOTYPE FOR TRAINING MODEL TO BE DISSEMINATED NATIONALLY. (NAT'L). DONALD E HAWKINS, CHAIRMAN; WASHINGTON TRANSPORTATION ALLIANCE; 729 DELAWARE AVE, SW; WASHINGTON, DC 20024. (#10834).

TRAVEL GUIDE TO INFORMATION SERVICES - DC. INCLUDES SOURCES FOR ALL TYPES OF TRAVEL INFORMATION, INCLUDING ACCOMMODATIONS & TRANSPORTATION. AVAILABLE FROM SUPT DOCUMENTS, GPO, WASHINGTON, DC 20402. FEE. (NAT'L). OFFICE OF RESOURCE DEVELOPMENT; AMERICAN REVOLUTION BICENTENNIAL ADMINISTRATION; 2401 E ST, NW; WASHINGTON, DC 20276. (#27670).

TREASURES FROM CYPRUS EXHIBITION - SITES, DC. EXHIBITION OF 180 OBJECTS REFLECTS NEARLY 8000 YEARS OF CYPRIOT ART AND CULTURE DIVIDED INTO 3 CATEGORIES: ANTIQUITIES, MEDIEVAL ART & POPULAR FOLK ART. (INT'L). EILEEN HARAKAL, COORDINATOR; SMITHSONIAN INSTITUTION TRAVELING EXHIBITION SERVICE; WASHINGTON, DC 20560. (#26656).

'TREASURES OF LONDON' EXHIBITION - SITES, DC. 500 YEARS OF BRITISH SILVER ARE REPRESENTED IN EXHIBITION OF 46 ANTIQUE OBJECTS, 46 MODERN PIECES & 100 PIECES OF MODERN JEWELRY. (INT'L). EILEEN HARAKAL, COORDINATOR; SMITHSONIAN INSTITUTION TRAVELING EXHIBITION SERVICE; WASHINGTON, DC 20560. (#26660).

TREASURY DEPARTMENT BICENTENNIAL EXHIBIT. MOBILE STAND-ALONE BOX DISPLAY DEPICTING SCENES FROM EACH OF THE 12 TREASURY BUREAUS IN FULL COLOR PROCESS PRINTING TO BE DISPLAYED IN EACH STATE. (NAT'L). ROBERT A GALPIN, ASSISTANT; DEPT OF THE TREASURY, OFFICE OF THE SECRETARY; 15TH & PENNSYLVANIA, NW; WASHINGTON, DC 20220. (#1892).

TREE PLANTING IN WASHINGTON, DC NEIGHBORHOOD. PLANTING SHRUBS, TREES & FLOWERS IN PUBLIC & PRIVATE PLACES IN THE ADAMS-MORGAN AREA. (LOCAL). EDWARD JACKSON, CHAIRMAN; ADAMS MORGAN ORG ENVIRONMENTAL COMMITTEE; 2431 18TH ST, NW; WASHINGTON, DC 20009. (#5607).

WASHINGTON — CONTINUED

TREES FROM THE NATION'S HISTORY. ENVIRONMENTAL PGM TO COLLECT & DISTRIBUTE SEEDS FROM 4 TREES WHICH PLAYED A PART IN AMER HISTORY, TO BE SOLD AT COST. INCLUDES PLANTING INSTRUCTIONS, HISTORICAL RELEVANCE OF SPECIES, FOREST HERITAGE BOOK. (NAT'L). GEORGE C CHEEK, EXEC VICE PRESIDENT; AMERICAN FOREST INSTITUTE; 1619 MASSACHUSETTS AVE, NW; WASHINGTON, DC 20036. (#118). **ARBA RECOGNIZED.**

TUNISIAN MOSAICS ON TOUR - SITES, WASHINGTON, DC. AN EXHIBITION OF 20 MOSAICS FROM THE ROMAN, VANDAL & BYZANTINE PERIODS REVEAL ASPECTS OF EVERYDAY LIFE. SIX OF THE MOSAICS WERE EXCAVATED AS RECENTLY AS 1964. (INT'L). EILEEN HARAKAL, COORDINATOR; SMITHSONIAN INSTITUTION TRAVELING EXHIBITION SERVICES; WASHINGTON, DC 20560. (#26667).

TUTANKHAMEN TREASURES' EXHIBIT. EXHIBIT ON LOAN FRON EGYPT. (INT'L). CULTURAL ATTACHE; ARAB REPUBLIC OF EGYPT; 2310 DECATUR PL; WASHINGTON, DC 20008. (#31906).

TV HISTORICAL SERIES ON US SCIENCE AND TECHNOLOGY. A SERIES OF BETWEEN 4 AND 13 ONE-HOUR HISTORICAL FILMS ON TECHNOLOGY AND SCIENCE IN AMERICAN LIFE; SPONSORED BY NSF AND SMITHSONIAN; INITIALLY FOR TV, BUT AVAILABLE AS 16MM FILMS THRU TRADE CHANNELS. (NAT'L). EUGENE S FERGUSON, PRINCIPAL INVESTIGATOR; SMITHSONIAN INSTITUTION; 1000 JEFFERSON DR, SW; WASHINGTON, DC 20560. (#533).

TWO CENTURIES OF AMERICAN BANKING - BOOK. BOOK CAPTURES IN MORE THAN 300 PICTURES, GLIMPSES OF THE EVOLUTION OF BANKING IN THE U S. MANY CONTEMPORARY ENGRAVINGS AND OLD PHOTOGRAPHS ADD A VISUAL DIMENSION ENHANCING UNDERSTANDING. (NAT'L). ALPHONS J HACKL, PUBLISHER; ACROPOLIS BOOKS LTD; 2400 17TH ST, NW; WASHINGTON, DC 20009. (#22469).

'THE U S AS SEEN BY FRANCE, 1830-1914' - SITES, DC. THE BIBLIOTHEQUE NATIONALE IN PARIS IS ORGANIZING AN EXHIBITION OF WORKS SHOWING HOW FRANCE SAW AMERICA FROM 1830 TO THE BEGINNING OF WORLD WAR I. (INT'L). EILEEN HARAKAL, COORDINATOR; SMITHSONIAN INSTITUTION TRAVELING EXHIBITION SERVICE; WASHINGTON, DC 20560. (#26659).

UNIFORM PUBLIC INFORMATION SIGNS PROJECT. RECOMMENDED GROUP OF INTERNATIONAL SYMBOLS WILL BE DEVELOPED FOR BICENTENNIAL USE ACROSS THE NATION. (NAT'L). RICHARD BOUCHARD, DIR OFF TRANS PLNG ASST; DEPT OF TRANSPORTATION; 400 7TH ST, SW; WASHINGTON, DC 20590. (#1893).

UNITED METHODIST BUILDING BICENTENNIAL PROJECT. SLIDE SHOW ON UNITED METHODISM IN WASHINGTON AREA; FILMS ON SOCIAL ISSUES; LITERATURE ON CURRENT ISSUES; SPECIAL SERVICES; DRAMATIC PRESENTATIONS & CHOIRS; INFORMATION CNTR FOR CHURCH PERSONS ET AL. (REGN'L). REV DON HOWARD, PROG DIRECTOR; UNITED METHODIST BOARD OF CHURCH & SOCIETY; 100 MARYLAND AVE, N E; WASHINGTON, DC 20002. (#7889).

UNITED STATES ARMED FORCES BICENTENNIAL BAND. A PREMIER MULTI-SERVICE CONCERT BAND THAT WILL SERVE TO HIGHLIGHT THROUGH MUSIC, THE HERITAGE OF THE MILITARY SERVICES. (NAT'L). R E THURSTON, LTCOL, USAF; UNITED STATES ARMED FORCES BICENTENNIAL BAND; FORT MEADE, MD 20755. (#7600).

UNITED STATES DEPT OF AGRICULTURE COOKBOOK. 'AUNT SAMMY'S RADIO RECIPES', THE USDA'S FIRST COOKBOOK WILL BE REISSUED WITH ADDITIONAL NEW RECIPES. (NAT'L). ROBERT RATHBONE, DIRECTOR ARS INFORMATION DIVISION; AGRICULTURAL RESEARCH SERVICE, US DEPARTMENT OF AGRICULTURE; 14TH & INDEPENDENCE AVE, SW; WASHINGTON, DC 20250. (#5573).

UNIV SINGERS IN BICENT CONCERT, WASHINGTON, DC. UNIVERSITY OF MISSOURI SINGERS, CHOSEN TO REPRESENT MO, WILL PERFORM AT THE BICENTENNIAL PARADE OF AMERICAN MUSIC AT THE KENNEDY CENTER IN WASHINGTON, DC. (LOCAL). THOMAS L MILLS, DIRECTOR; UNIV OF MISSOURI; 213 FINE ARTS BLDG; COLUMBIA, MO 65201. (#20453). **ARBA GRANTEE.**

THE URBAN LEAGUE NEWS -- BICENTENNIAL ISSUE - DC. DISTRIBUTION OF MAJOR BICENTENNIAL ESSAYS ON THE BLACK HERITAGE, IN TABLOID FORM, DIRECTLY TO 40,000 RESIDENTS OF THE DISTRICT OF COLUMBIA, THRU INSERTION IN BLACK WEEKLIES. (LOCAL). JOHN L WATKINS, DIRECTOR OF COMMUNICATIONS; WASHINGTON URBAN LEAGUE; 1424 16TH ST, NW; WASHINGTON, DC 20036. (#26938). **ARBA GRANTEE.**

US ARMED FORCES BICENTENNIAL FILM. FILM WILL BE ILLUSTRATIVE OF THE ROLE THE ARMED FORCES HAVE PLAYED IN THE CREATION AND GROWTH OF OUR COUNTRY. (NAT'L). MARC HUET, SPEC ASST BICENT PLANNING; DEPT OF DEFENSE; PENTAGON RM 1E776; WASHINGTON, DC 20301. (#2269).

US ARMY 200TH ANNIVERSARY. THE 200TH ANNIVERSARY OF THE US ARMY WILL OCCUR ON JUNE 14, 1975 AND SPECIAL PROGRAMS AND CEREMONIES THROUGHOUT THE US AND OVERSEAS WILL BE SCHEDULED FOR THE OBSERVANCE. (INT'L). SAMUEL GREEN; OFC, CHIEF OF INFORMATION; DEPT OF THE ARMY; WASHINGTON, DC 20310. (#54).

US COAST GUARD ACTIVITIES FOR THE BICENTENNIAL. VARIOUS COAST GUARD ACTIVITIES AND CONCERTS FOR 1976 ARE CURRENTLY BEING PLANNED. (NAT'L). RICHARD BOUCHARD, DIR OFF TRANS PLNG ASST; DEPT OF TRANSPORTATION; 400 7 ST SW; WASHINGTON, DC 20590. (#1894).

US DEPARTMENT OF STATE BROCHURE. ILLUSTRATED HISTORICAL BOOKLET SUMMARIZING DIPLOMATIC HISTORY OF THE UNITED STATES, PROVIDING INFO ON DEPT OF STATE AND FOREIGN SERVICE PAST & PRESENT - WILL EMPHASIZE DIPLOMATIC HERITAGE FOR WORLD PEACE. (INT'L). PAUL E AUERSWALD, DIR, OFFICE OF MEDIA SERVICES; DEPT OF STATE; 2201 C ST, NW; WASHINGTON, DC 20520. (#2033).

US MARINE CORPS 200TH ANNIVERSARY. THE 200TH ANNIVERSARY OF THE US MARINE CORPS WILL OCCUR ON NOVEMBER 10, 1975 SPECIAL PROGRAMS AND CEREMONIES FOR THE OBSERVANCE WILL BE HELD THROUGHOUT THE USA & OVERSEAS. (INT'L). DR DAVID A SMITH; DEPT OF DEFENSE BICENTENNIAL OFFICE; THE PENTAGON RM 1E798; WASHINGTON, DC 20301. (#104).

US NAVY 200TH ANNIVERSARY. THE 200TH ANNIVERSARY OF THE US NAVY WILL OCCUR ON OCTOBER 13, 1975. SPECIAL PROGRAMS AND CEREMONIES WILL BE SCHEDULED THROUGHOUT THE US AND OVERSEAS FOR THE OBSERVANCE. (INT'L). CAPT B C CRAWFORD, USN; BCO (UNSECNAV); DEPT OF THE NAVY; WASHINGTON, DC 20305. (#53).

US POSTAL SERVICE BICENTENNIAL PROGRAM. PROGRAM TO PROVIDE EXHIBIT SERVICES TO ARBA RECOGNIZED EXPOSITION -INTERPHIL '76 IN 1976 & PHILATELIC SERVICES TO SUPPORT FUND RAISING EFFORTS OF STATE & LOCAL BICENT AGENCIES - 'BICENTENNIAL AWARENESS'. (NAT'L). ROBERT W CACCIA, MANAGER BICENTENNIAL BRANCH; US POSTAL SERVICE; WASHINGTON, DC 20260. (#3716). **ARBA RECOGNIZED.**

'USA '76: THE FIRST TWO HUNDRED YEARS' - EXHIBIT. TRAVELING EXHIBIT PREPARED BY ARBA WILL TOUR SEVERAL CITIES DURING THE BICENTENNIAL. IT EXPLORES THE CULTURAL AND SCIENTIFIC HERITAGE OF THE USA. (NAT'L). JACK MASEY, PROJECT DIRECTOR; AMERICAN REVOLUTION BICENTENNIAL ADMINISTRATION; 2401 E STREET, NW; WASHINGTON, DC 20276. (#5661).

USDA SPONSORED RESEARCH ARTICLES FOR MEDIA. SERIES OF RESEARCH FEATURES FOR METROPOLITAN PAPERS, NATIONAL MAGAZINES AND TV TO ESTABLISH RELATIONSHIPS BETWEEN RESEARCH ACHIEVEMENTS AND CONSUMERS. (NAT'L). ROBERT RATHBONE, DIRECTOR ARS INFORMATION DIVISION; AGRICULTURAL RESEARCH SERVICE, US DEPARTMENT OF AGRICULTURE; 14TH & INDEPENDENCE AVE, SW; WASHINGTON, DC 20250. (#5576).

VARIOUS SPECIAL OLYMPICS GAMES, WASHINGTON, DC. VARIOUS SPECIAL OLYMPIC EVENTS WILL TAKE PLACE IN DIFFERENT LOCATIONS ACROSS THE COUNTRY. (NAT'L). ROBERT M MONTAGUE, PROJ COORDINATOR; SPECIAL OLYMPICS; 1701 K ST, NW; WASHINGTON, DC 20006. (#27921).

VENUS DE MEDICI ON LOAN TO THE UNITED STATES. THE VENUS DE MEDICI IS ON LOAN TO THE NATIONAL GALLERY OF ART IN WASHINGTON DC FOR ITS EXHIBITION 'THE EYE OF THOMAS JEFFERSON'. (INT'L). CULTURAL ATTACHE; ITALIAN EMBASSY; 1601 FULLER ST; WASHINGTON, DC 20009. (#31898).

VETERANS DAY '76, AN EXHIBIT IN WASHINGTON, DC. THE VETERANS ADMIN IS SPONSORING AN EXHIBIT, 'AMERICA'S VETERANS, YESTERDAY, TODAY & TOMORROW'; A WREATH LAYING CEREMONY TELEVISED FROM ARLINGTON CEMETERY; AND SATELLITE TRANSMISSION OF THE EVENTS. (NAT'L). RICHARD GILLESPIE, DIRECTOR; VETERANS DAY NATL COMMITTEE OF THE VETERANS ADMIN; 810 VERMONT AVE, NW; WASHINGTON, DC 20005. (#8650).

VIENNA PHILHARMONIC ORCHESTRA TOURS THE USA. THE ORCHESTRA WILL VISIT NEW YORK, PHILADELPHIA, CHICAGO, AND WASHINGTON, DC, IN MARCH AND APRIL 1976. (INT'L). CULTURAL ATTACHE; EMBASSY OF AUSTRIA; 2343 MASSACHUSETTS AVE; WASHINGTON, DC 20008. (#32971).

VIKING SPACE VEHICLE LANDING ON MARS - 1976. SOFT LANDING OF UNMANNED SPACECRAFT ON THE PLANET MARS ON JULY 20, 1976. SPACECRAFT IS CHRISTENED 'VIKING'. EXPECTED TO TIE-IN WITH OPENING OF NEW NATIONAL AIR & SPACE MUSEUM. (INT'L). JOHN P DONNELLY, ASST ADM FOR PUBLIC AFFAIRS; NATIONAL AERONAUTICS AND SPACE ADMINISTRATION; 400 MARYLAND AVE, SW; WASHINGTON, DC 20546. (#1975).

VISIT OF ISRAEL NAVAL MISSILE BOATS - DC. 'YAFFO & 'TARSHISH' PARTICIPATED IN OPERATION SAIL IN NEW YORK; ALSO VISITED PHILADELPHIA, BALTIMORE & MIAMI. (INT'L). LOUIS D BRANDEIS, DIRECTOR; ZIONIST ORGANIZATION OF AMERICA; 1625 I ST NW; WASHINGTON, DC 20006. (#33287).

'WAKE UP AMERICA' RELAY RIDE- WASHINGTON, DC. 600 MILE RELAY RIDE FROM BOSTON TO WASHINGTON, DC COMMEMORATING 200 ANNIVERSARY OF 'PAUL REVERE'S MIDNIGHT RIDE.'. (NAT'L). MONTE BOURJAILY JR, MANAGING DIRECTOR; THE NEW SPIRIT OF '76 FOUNDATION; 918 16TH ST NW, SUITE 603; WASHINGTON, DC 20006. (#2443).

WALKING TOURS OF WASHINGTON, DC. PROJECT TO INCLUDE WALKING TOURS AND THE DESIGN & PRODUCTION OF SOUVENIR MAPS OF HIGH QUALITY & HISTORIC AUTHENTICITY. (LOCAL). MRS WILLIAM PROXMIRE, CHAIRMAN; WASHINGTON WHIRL-AROUND; 2262 HALL PL, NW; WASHINGTON, DC 20007. (#5618). **(??).**

WALL MURAL FOR CHINESE-AMER COMMUNITY - WASH, DC. THE MURAL WILL DEPICT A HISTORY AND THEME RELEVANT TO CHINESE-AMER PEOPLE AND THEIR HERITAGE. (LOCAL). HARRISON LEE, CHAIRMAN; CHINESE CONSOLIDATED BENEVOLENT ASSOCIATION & EASTERN WIND INC; 803 H ST, NW; WASHINGTON, DC 20005. (#22888). **ARBA GRANTEE.**

WALL MURAL FOR MUSEUM OF AFRICAN ART -WASH, DC. REPRODUCTION OF GEOMETRIC, BRILLIANT MURALS OF THE ZULU VILLAGES OF SOUTH AFRICA ON THE FENCES, WALLS AND GARAGES OF FREDERICK DOUGLASS COURT OF THE MUSEUM OF AFRICAN ART. PROJECT DONE BY WOMEN ARTISTS. (REGN'L). JOYCE A ELLWENGER, DEPUTY DIRECTOR; MUSEUM OF AFRICAN ART; 316 A ST, NE; WASHINGTON, DC 20002. (#8550). **ARBA GRANTEE.**

WASHINGTON HOLIDAYS, WASHINGTON, DC. A NON-SECTARIAN CELEBRATION OF THE MULTI-ETHNIC, MULTI-RELIGIOUS METROPOLITAN POPULATION OF THE LIVING CITY. (LOCAL). A KNIGHTON STANLEY, DIRECTOR; OFFICE OF BICENTENNIAL PROGRAMS; 777 14TH ST, NW; WASHINGTON, DC 20005. (#20289). **ARBA GRANTEE.**

WASHINGTON POST DISPLAY & EDUCATIONAL PGM - NBMRP. CO-SPONSORING A DISPLAY OF A POTTER CYLINDER PRESS IN MAY '76 IN SMITHSONIAN'S 1876 CENTENNIAL EXHIBIT. ALSO DISTRIBUTES FREE EDUCATIONAL MATERIALS TO AREA'S JUNIOR & SENIOR HIGH SCHOOLS. (REGN'L). JOHN M DOWER, VICE PRESIDENT/COMMUNICATIONS; THE WASHINGTON POST; 1150 15TH ST, NW; WASHINGTON, DC 20071. (#20604).

WASHINGTON, DC NEIGHBORHOODS IN TRANSITION. A STUDY OF TWO WASHINGTON NEIGHBORHOODS; MASSACHUSETTS AVE BETWEEN UNION STATION & MT VERNON SQUARE & TENLEYTOWN. (LOCAL). DR JEAN M DABLO, PROJ MANAGER; 4640 VERPLANCK PL, NW; WASHINGTON, DC 20016. (#8641).

'WASHINGTON, DC - THE BICENTENNIAL CITY' -FILM. COLORFUL FILM TRAVELOGUE ON WASHINGTON DC & HISTORIC VIRGINIA THAT TELLS THE STORY OF OUR BEGINNING AS A NATION. (REGN'L). JOHN NUGENT, PRESIDENT; NUGENT PRODUCTIONS; 2951 CASHEL LANE; VIENNA, VA 22180. (#3821).

WASHINGTON, DC, EXPANSION OF COMMUNICATIONS PGM. EXPANSION OF EXISTING COMMUNICATIONS PROGRAM INTO A BROADER COMMUNITY INFORMATION SYSTEM PROJECT. (STWIDE). LAWRENCE S STINCHCOMB, EXEC VICE PRESIDENT; DC BICENTENNIAL COMMISSION; 1239 G ST, NW; WASHINGTON, DC 20005. (#1194). **(??). ARBA GRANTEE.**

WASHINGTON, DC, BICENTENNIAL PROMOTIONAL CAMPAIGN. PROMOTIONAL CAMPAIGN FOR THE ESTIMATED MILLIONS OF VISITORS EXPECTED IN WASHINGTON, DC DURING THE BICENTENNIAL YEAR. (NAT'L). A KNIGHTON STANLEY, EXEC DIRECTOR; OFFICE BICENTENNIAL PROGRAMS; 777 14 ST, NW; WASHINGTON, DC 20005. (#20218). **ARBA GRANTEE.**

'WE HOLD THESE RIGHTS', WASHINGTON, DC. A STUDY OF THE POSSESSIVE INDIVIDUALISM UNDERLYING THE LIBERAL DEMOCRATIC THEORY OF THE CONSTITUTION AND DECLARATION OF INDEPENDENCE, IN A THEATER LABORATORY PIECE. (LOCAL). WES SANDERS, ASST PROFESSOR OF ENGLISH; WELLINGTON RESCUE THEATER COLLECTIVE OF OBERLIN COLLEGE; RICE HALL; OBERLIN, OH 44074. (#10887).

'WE, THE PEOPLE' EXHIBIT OF SMITHSONIAN. EXHIBIT AT NATIONAL MUSEUM OF HISTORY & TECHNOLOGY HIGHLIGHTING THE HISTORY OF THE AMERICAN POLITICAL EXPERIENCE. (NAT'L). MRS SUSAN HAMILTON, BICENTENNIAL COORDINATOR; SMITHSONIAN INSTITUTION; 1000 JEFFERSON DR, SW; WASHINGTON, DC 20560. (#68).

'WE' & 'FACTFINDER FOR THE NATION'-CENSUS FILMS. 'WE'-A FILM ON ALL AMERICANS WITH KEY FINDINGS OF THE 1970 CENSUS. 'FACTFINDER OF THE NATION' IS ON THE CENSUS BUREAU, THE ONLY U. S. GOV'T AGENCY THAT CONTACTS EVERY PERSON IN NATION. (NAT'L). HENRY H SMITH, CHIEF, PUBLIC INFORMATION OFFICE; BUREAU OF THE CENSUS; WASHINGTON, MD 20233. (#569).

WHAT YOU CAN DO: A BICENTENNIAL IDEA BOOK - DC. DESCRIBES 20 WAYS AMERICANS ARE PARTICIPATING IN THE BICENTENNIAL, & ILLUSTRATES A DIVERSITY OF IDEAS FOR COMMEMORATING THE NATION'S 200 ANNIVERSARY. OF INTEREST TO INDIVIDUALS & GROUPS; NO CHARGE. (NAT'L). PROGRAM DIVISION; AMERICAN REVOLUTION BICENTENNIAL ADMINISTRATION; 2401 E ST, NW; WASHINGTON, DC 20276. (#27613).

WHITE HOUSE CONF ON LIBRARIES & INFORMATION SVCS. CONFERENCE ON IMPORTANCE OF LIBRARIES & OTHER INFORMATION SERVICES, DUE TO GROWING IMPORTANCE OF MASS DISSEMINATION OF INFORMATION FOR IMPROVEMENT OF EDUCATION. STATE CONFERENCES, '76-'79, NATL IN 1980. (NAT'L). ALPHONSE F TREZZA, EXECUTIVE DIRECTOR; NATL COMMISSION ON LIBRARIES & INFORMATION SCIENCE; 1717 K ST, NW SUITE 601; WASHINGTON, DC 20036. (#366).

'WILDERNESS AMERICA' OF NATL PARK SERVICE. THIS FILM WILL BRING INTO THE BICENTENNIAL CELEBRATION THOSE PORTIONS OF THE NATION WHOSE EXISTENCE AND CONTRIBUTIONS FOLLOWED THE REVOLUTION. TO BE AVAILABLE TO ALL NPS AREAS. (NAT'L). MANAGER, HARPERS FERRY CENTER; NATIONAL PARK SERVICE; HARPERS FERRY, WV 25425. (#1477).

WMAL RADIO 63 'PRESIDENTIAL PERSPECTIVE' - NBMRP. SERIES, BEGUN IN SEPT '75, BROADCAST DAILY. PROGRAMS ARE DEVOTED TO THE LIFE, TIMES, HISTORY & HUMAN INTEREST STORIES OF A PRESIDENT. WRITTEN & RESEARCHED BY BROADCAST INTERNS & AVAILABLE TO SCHOOLS. (REGN'L). ELLEN MANOWITZ, BICENTENNIAL COORDINATOR; WMAL RADIO 63; 4400 JENNIFER ST; WASHINGTON, DC 20015. (#22602).

WOODLEY PARK COMMUNITY PLAN - WASHINGTON, DC. DEVELOP A PLAN WHICH WILL ACCOMODATE A MORE INTENSIVE RESIDENTIAL & COMMERCIAL DEVELOPMENT IN THE WOODLEY PARK COMMUNITY WHILE ENHANCING ITS EXISTING SOCIAL & PHYSICAL CHARACTERISTICS. (LOCAL). CHARLES SZORADI, DIRECTOR; 1625 K ST, NW; WASHINGTON, DC 20006. (#2253).

WOODSY OWL ANTI-POLLUTION CAMPAIGN - US FOREST SVC. WOODSY OWL, NATIONAL 'WISE USE OF OUR ENVIRONMENT SYMBOL' PLANS VIA CAMPAIGN MATERIAL TO WISH OUR COUNTRY HAPPY BIRTHDAY ENCOURAGING GIFTS OF CLEAN AIR, WATER, BEAUTY, AND QUIET. (NAT'L). GLENN A KOVAR, HEAD SPECIAL PROJECTS; DEPT OF AGRICULTURE, FOREST SERVICE; 12TH & INDEPENDENCE AVE, SW; WASHINGTON, DC 20250. (#2418).

'WORKERS AND ALLIES' - SITES PROJECT. EXHIBIT SURVEYS WOMEN'S PARTICIPATION IN THE TRADE UNION MOVEMENT FROM 1824 TO 1976; TEXT AND PHOTOGRAPHS MOUNTED ON

WASHINGTON — CONTINUED

35 PANELS. (NAT'L). ANDREA STEVENS, COORDINATOR; SMITHSONIAN INSTITUTION TRAVELING EXHIBIT SERVICE; WASHINGTON, DC 20560. (#15931).

WORKING AMERICANS. PROMOTION OF WORKING AMERICAN FESTIVALS THRU SELECTION OF FIVE CITIES TO STAGE MODEL FESTIVALS, REGIONAL HOW-TO WORKSHOPS & PRODUCTION OF EXHIBITS FOR SALE. CO-SPONSORS ARE AFL-CIO, DEPT OF LABOR & ARBA. (NAT'L). CAROLYN JACOBSON, PROJECT DIRECTOR; WORKING AMERICANS BICENTENNIAL PROJECT - AFL-CIO; 815 16TH ST, NW; WASHINGTON, DC 20006. (#33273). **ARBA RECOGNIZED.**

THE WORLD OF CHARLES WILLSON PEALE. IN CONJUNCTION WITH PUBLICATION OF CHARLES WILLSON PEALE'S PAPERS BY THE NATIONAL PORTRAIT GALLERY OF THE SMITHSONIAN AN EXHIBIT OF WORKS WILL BE MOUNTED. (NAT'L). MRS SUSAN HAMILTON, BICENTENNIAL COORDINATOR; SMITHSONIAN INSTITUTION; 1000 JEFFERSON DR., S.W.; WASHINGTON, DC 20560. (#65).

WORLD OF FRANKLIN & JEFFERSON - INTL EXHIBIT. AN EXHIBIT OF HISTORICAL MEMORABILIA SPANNING 120 YEARS IN THE LIVES OF FRANKLIN & JEFFERSON. DESIGNED BY CHARLES EAMES FOR THE ARBA THRU A GRANT FROM IBM & SHOWN BY USIA OVERSEAS. U.S. SHOWING IN 1976. (INT'L). JACK MASEY, DIRECTOR, DESIGN & EXHIBITS; AMERICAN REVOLUTION BICENTENNIAL ADMINISTRATION; 2401 E STREET, NW; WASHINGTON, DC 20276. (#112).

YOUNG WASHINGTONIANS' CULTURAL HERITAGE PROJ - DC. WASHINGTON YOUTH WILL PARTICIPATE IN ORAL HISTORY PROJECTS WHICH CONCENTRATE ON LOCAL CULTURAL GROUPS. (LOCAL). LANA D SMITH, PROJECT DIRECTOR; YOUNG WASHINGTONIANS' CULTURAL HERITAGE PROJECT; 1133 15TH ST, NW; WASHINGTON, DC 20019. (#16729). **ARBA GRANTEE.**

YOUTH CONSERVATION CORPS BICENT ENVIRONMENTAL PROJ. NUMEROUS CONSTRUCTION AND REHABILITATION PROJECTS ON NATIONAL FOREST - STRESSING HERITAGE, HORIZONS AND ESTHETICS. PROJECTS MAY INCLUDE DEDICATION CEREMONIES. (NAT'L). GLENN A KOVAR, CHIEF SPECIAL PROJECTS; DEPT OF AGRICULTURE, FOREST SERVICE; 12TH & INDEPENDENCE AVE; WASHINGTON, DC 20250. (#1900).

YOUTH SOCCER MATCHES - WASHINGTON, DC. THE UNITED STATES YOUTH SOCCER ASSOC IS SPONSORING YOUTH SOCCER MATCHES AT VARIOUS LOCATIONS THROUGHOUT THE COUNTRY. (NAT'L). DONALD GREER, COORDINATOR; UNITED STATES YOUTH SOCCER ASSOC; 1819 H ST, NW; WASHINGTON, DC 20006. (#27932).

YUGOSLAV CULTURAL GROUPS TOUR THE U S. THE SLOVENIAN PHILHARMONIC ORCHESTRA, DUBROVNIK DRAMA ENSEMBLE, AND THEATER GROUP 'GAVELLA' WILL TOUR THE UNITED STATES DURING THE BICENTENNIAL ERA. (INT'L). CULTURAL ATTACHE; EMBASSY OF YUGOSLAVIA; 2410 CALIFORNIA ST; WASHINGTON, DC 20008. (#31919).

1830'S TRAIN BICENTENNIAL PROJECT - DC. DISPLAY & FREE-RIDE OPERATION OF 1830'S TRAIN THROUGHOUT 13 STATES, ALSO IN NATIONAL PARADE IN DC, DECORATED LOCOMOTIVES HONORING SOUTHERN SIGNERS OF DECLARATION OF INDEPENDENCE. (REGN'L). W F GEESLIN, ASST VICE PRESIDENT; SOUTHERN RAILWAY SYSTEM; 920 15TH ST, NW; WASHINGTON, DC 20005. (#26853).

19TH CENTURY MELODRAMA PROJ OF WASHINGTON, DC. THE PLAY WILL RE-CREATE THE AURA OF THE 19TH CENTURY MELODRAMA IN ITS OWN TIME SETTING. THE COMMUNITY WILL BE INVOLVED AND THERE WILL BE LOW TICKET PRICES. (REGN'L). THOMAS ZELANEY, PRESIDENT; THEATRE ETCETERA; 3739 12TH ST, NE; WASHINGTON, DC 20017. (#10966).

1970 CENSUS EXHIBIT. VERY MODERN MOBILE EXHIBIT BASED ON THE 1970 CENSUS OF POPULATION & HOUSING. THE EXHIBIT WILL BE LOCATED IN THE DEP'T OF COMMERCE MAIN LOBBY. (NAT'L). HENRY H SMITH, CHIEF, PUBLIC INFORMATION OFFICE; BUREAU OF CENSUS; WASHINGTON, DC 20233. (#566).

1976 INTL CONFERENCE ON THE USA IN THE WORLD. THEME: THE UNITED STATES IN THE WORLD; 200 YEARS OF AMERICAN CULTURE AND HISTORY AND WHAT DIFFERENCE HAS IT MADE? SPONSORED BY THE AMERICAN STUDIES ASSOC, ACLS & SMITHSONIAN INSTITUTION. (INT'L). PROF ALLEN F DAVIS, EXEC SECRETARY; AMERICAN STUDIES ASSOC, UNIV OF PENNSYLVANIA; 4025 CHESTNUT ST; PHILADELPHIA, PA 19174. (#258).

200 TREES PROJECT, WASHINGTON, DC. EACH LOCAL AND STATE SOCIETY TO PLANT 200 TREES BY 1976. (REGN'L). MRS FRED W KRUEGER, SENIOR NATIONAL PRESIDENT; NATIONAL SOCIETY CHILDREN OF THE AMERICAN REVOLUTION; 1776 D STREET, NW; WASHINGTON, DC 20006. (#20593).

'200 YEARS YOUNG' - A YOUTH PROJECTS GUIDE. DESCRIBES YOUTH PROJECTS & ACTIVITIES ALREADY UNDERWAY, AND GIVES EXAMPLES OF ACTIVITIES YOUNG PEOPLE CAN INITIATE IN COMMEMORATION OF THE BICENTENNIAL. (NAT'L). PROGRAMS DIVISION; AMERICAN REVOLUTION BICENTENNIAL ADMINISTRATION; 2401 E ST, NW; WASHINGTON, DC 20276. (#28199).

3,000 BC LIMESTONE STELE - GIFT OF EGYPTIAN PEOPLE. A 250-POUND LIMESTONE STELE DATING BACK TO 3,000 BC WILL BE A GIFT OF THE EGYPTIAN PEOPLE TO THE AMERICAN PEOPLE. (INT'L). CULTURAL ATTACHE; ARAB REPUBLIC OF EGYPT; 2310 DECATUR PL; WASHINGTON, DC 20008. (#31894).

'40 DOCUMENTS OF OUR AMERICAN HERITAGE' & TAPES. REPRODUCTIONS OF ORIGINAL AMER DOCUMENTS ON 1ST FREEDOM TRAIN('47) & TEACHING GUIDE FOR SCHOOLS. TAPE CASSETTES & LISTENER'S GUIDES RELATE TO 40 DOCUMENTS, SOME PRESIDENTS & OTHER AMERICANS. (NAT'L). M C DEMLER MGEN USAF(RET), CHRMN BICENT COMMITTEE; MILITARY ORDER OF THE WORLD WARS; 1100 17TH ST, NW; WASHINGTON, DC 20036. (#3111).

JAN 1 - SEPT 30, '73. 'POLES IN AMERICAN HISTORY' POSTER CONTEST. POLISH BICENTENNIAL POSTER CONTEST. ENTITLED POLES IN AMERICAN HISTORY, RELATING TO THE CONTRIBUTIONS OF POLISH IMMIGRANTS AND POLISH AMERICANS TO US CULTURAL, SCIENTIFIC & ECONOMIC DEVELOPMENT. ENTRY FEE; CASH PRIZES. (NAT'L). MS ROSE NOWOTARSKA; AMERICAN COUNCIL OF POLISH CULTURAL CLUBS; 3712 FULTON ST., NW; WASHINGTON, DC 20007. (#125-901).

JAN 1, '73 - CONTINUING . 'FORMATION OF THE UNION' EXHIBITION. THIS EXHIBIT WAS REFURBISHED & INSTALLED IN THE MAIN EXHIBITION HALL OF THE NATIONAL ARCHIVES IN SPRING, 1973. THE FOCAL POINTS ARE THE DECLARATION OF INDEPENDENCE, CONSTITUTION, AND BILL OF RIGHTS. AT SUNDAY HOURS: 1:00PM-10:00PM.. (NAT'L). ALBERT MEISEL; NATIONAL ARCHIVES AND RECORD SERVICE G S A; 6TH & PENNSYLVANIA AVE NW; WASHINGTON, DC 20408. (#55-1).

SEPT 14 - 16, '73. NAT'L PHILATELIC EXHIBITION, WITH BICENTENNIAL EXHIBITS. TROPHIES AND CERTIFICATES TO WINNERS IN BICENTENNIAL EXHIBIT CATEGORY AT STAMP SHOWS. (NAT'L). SENIOR OFFICER PROGRAM; AMERICAN REVOLUTION BICENTENNIAL ADMINISTRATION; 2401 E STREET, NW; WASHINGTON, DC 20276. (#145-901).

SEPT 16, '73 - DEC 31, '76. COMMERCE SHOWING OF 2 CENSUS BUREAU FILMS. 'WE'-A FILM ON ALL AMERICANS WITH KEY FINDINGS OF THE 1970 CENSUS. 'FACTFINDER OF THE NATION' IS ON THE CENSUS BUREAU, THE ONLY U. S. GOV'T AGENCY THAT CONTACTS EVERY PERSON IN NATION. (REGN'L). HENRY H SMITH, CHIEF; PUBLIC INFORMATION OFFICE, BUREAU OF THE CENSUS; PUBLIC INFO OFFICE BUREAU OF CEN; WASHINGTON, DC 20233. (#569-1).

SEPT 27 - OCT 1, '73. MEETING OF INT'L COUNCIL ON ARCHIVES.. TO BE HELD IN WASHINGTON AT THE INVITATION OF THE NAT'L ARCHIVES AND THE SOCIETY OF AMERICAN ARCHIVISTS. THE THEME WILL BE 'THE ARCHIVAL REVOLUTION OF OUR TIME'. (INT'L). DR FRANK BURKE, DIRECTOR,; NATIONAL ARCHIVES AND RECORD SERVICE; 7TH & PENNSYLVANIA AVE, NW; WASHINGTON, DC 20408. (#67-901).

OCT 1 - 31, '73. WHITE HOUSE CONFERENCE ON HISTORIC PRESERVATION. HISTORIC RESOURCES & HUMAN ENVIRONMENT STUDY. THIS STUDY WILL DEFINE THE ESSENTIAL COMPONENTS OF OUR HERITAGE AND REQUIREMENTS FOR ITS ADEQUATE PRESERVATION, WILL ASSESS PRESENT PROGRAMS & ADVISE GOVERNMENT OF ITS ROLE IN DEVELOPING FUTURE PROGRAMS. (NAT'L). ROBERT GARVEY, EXECUTIVE; ADVISORY COUNCIL ON HISTORIC PRESERVATION; 1522 K ST, NW, ROOM 403; WASHINGTON, DC 20005. (#148-901).

OCT 1 - 31, '73. 2ND OF OFFICIAL MEDALS TO BE PLACED ON SALE. ANNUAL SALE TO PUBLIC OF IDENTICAL BRONZE & SILVER MEDALS. DESIGN BY ARBA, PRODUCED & DISTRIBUTED BY US MINT. PRICE: BRONZE $5.00, SILVER $15.00. REVENUE SUPPORTS BICENTENNIAL PROJECTS. (NAT'L). SENIOR PROGRAM OFFICER, H; AMERICAN REVOLUTION BICENTENNIAL ADMINISTRATION; 2401 E STREET, NW; WASHINGTON, DC 20276. (#16-901).

OCT 9, '73. LECTURE, DANIEL BOORSTIN, POLITICAL REV & REV IN SCIENCE, TECHNOLOGY. DISTINGUISHED LECTURE SERIES ON BICENTENNIAL. 18 DISTINGUISHED SCHOLARS DISCUSS NATURE, FUTURE OF AM REVOLUTION AT NATION'S HISTORIC SITES---TAPED FOR BROADCAST ON PBS IN SPRING 1974. TOPICS COVER REV & SOCIETY, RELIGION, PRESS, LAW, CULTURE, GOV'T. (NAT'L). EARL H VOSS; AMERICAN ENTERPRISE INSTITUTE FOR PUBLIC POLICY RESEARCH; 1150 17TH STREET, N.W.; WASHINGTON, DC 20036. (#1297-901).

OCT 12, '73. LECTURE, IRVING KRISTOL, AM REV AS A SUCCESSFUL REVOLUTION. DISTINGUISHED LECTURE SERIES ON BICENTENNIAL. 18 DISTINGUISHED SCHOLARS DISCUSS NATURE, FUTURE OF AM REVOLUTION AT NATION'S HISTORIC SITES---TAPED FOR BROADCAST ON PBS IN SPRING 1974. TOPICS COVER REV & SOCIETY, RELIGION, PRESS, LAW, CULTURE, GOV'T. (NAT'L). EARL H VOSS; AMERICAN ENTERPRISE INSTITUTE FOR PUBLIC POLICY RESEARCH; 1150 17TH STREET, N.W.; WASHINGTON, DC 20036. (#1297-902).

DEC 13, '73. LECTURE, ROBERT NISBET, SOCIAL IMPACT OF THE REVOLUTION. DISTINGUISHED LECTURE SERIES ON BICENTENNIAL. 18 DISTINGUISHED SCHOLARS DISCUSS NATURE, FUTURE OF AM REVOLUTION AT NATION'S HISTORIC SITES---TAPED FOR BROADCAST ON PBS IN SPRING 1974. TOPICS COVER REV & SOCIETY, RELIGION, PRESS, LAW, CULTURE, GOV'T. (NAT'L). EARL H VOSS; AMERICAN ENTERPRISE INSTITUTE FOR PUBLIC POLICY RESEARCH; 1150 17TH STREET, N.W.; WASHINGTON, DC 20036. (#1297-905).

DEC 16, '73 - NOV 1, '77. WEEKLY RADIO INTERVIEW. RADIO INTERVIEWS ON US HISTORY AND BICENTENNIAL PROJECTS. EXPECTED GUESTS INCLUDE MEMBERS OF CONGRESS, AMBASSADORS, PROJECT SPOKESMEN. AT CITYWIDE. (REGN'L). MIKE CUTHBERT; WGMS AM-FM RADIO RKO GENERAL; 5100 WISCONSIN AVE NW; WASHINGTON, DC 20016. (#1810-1).

JAN 1, '74 - DEC 31, '76. SERIES OF 16 POSTER-PANEL TRAVELING EXHIBITS ON AMERICAN CULTURE. SERIES OF 16 POSTER-PANEL EXHIBITS ON AMERICAN CULTURE & RELATING TO BOTH SMITHSONIAN COLLECTIONS & COLLECTIONS THROUGHOUT THE COUNTRY. PLANNED FOR TRAVEL & LOCAL COMMUNITY PARTICIPATION. (REGN'L). MRS SUSAN HAMILTON; SMITHSONIAN INSTITUTION; 1000 JEFFERSON DR SW; WASHINGTON, DC 20560. (#303-1).

MAR 1, '74 - CONTINUING . 1970 CENSUS EXHIBIT. VERY MODERN MOBILE EXHIBIT BASED ON THE 1970 CENSUS OF POPULATION & HOUSING. THE EXHIBIT WILL BE LOCATED IN THE DEP'T OF COMMERCE MAIN LOBBY. (REGN'L). HENRY H SMITH, CHIEF; PUBLIC INFORMATION OFFICE, BUREAU OF THE CENSUS; PUBLIC INFO OFFICE BUREAU OF CEN; WASHINGTON, DC 20233. (#566-1).

MAR 13, '74. GROUNDBREAKING CEREMONIES, NATIONAL VISITORS CENTER. INCLUDED IN THE VISITOR FACILITIES HERE WILL BE WELCOME AREAS AND THEATERS, LOUNGES, EXHIBITS, & AUDIO-VISUAL EQUIPMENT. GENERAL VISITORS INFORMATION AND TRANSPORTATION HUB. (NAT'L). GENERAL MANAGER, NATIONAL; NATIONAL PARK SERVICE; NATL VISITOR CNTR, UNION STATION; WASHINGTON, DC 20002. (#275-901).

APR 6 - 12, '74. INT'L CONGRESS COMMEMORATING 6TH CENTENNIAL OF PETRARCH'S DEATH. WORLD PETRARCH CONGRESS. AN INT'L CONGRESS COMMEMORATING THE 6TH CENTENNIAL OF THE DEATH OF FRANCESCO PETRARCH, FATHER OF THE RENAISSANCE AND ONE OF THE FIRST HUMANISTS. HIS LIFE'S INFLUENCE IS MAIN TOPIC OF CONGRESS. (INT'L). ADRIENE SCHWARTZ, COORD; FOLGER SHAKESPEARE LIBRARY; 201 EAST CAPITOL STREET, S.E.; WASHINGTON, DC 20003. (#337-901).

APR 15, '74 - JAN 1, '76. CANTATA FOR SMALL ORCHESTRA ON MARK TWAIN TEXTS BY ROBERT EVETT. NATIONAL SYMPHONY ORCHESTRA COMMISSIONS. THE NATIONAL SYMPHONY, ANTAL DORATI, MUSIC DIRECTOR, HAS AWARDED GRANTS TO ELEVEN COMPOSERS TO CREATE WORKS FOR PERFORMANCE IN HONOR OF THE BICENTENNIAL. THERE WILL BE 12 WORKS COMMISSIONED. (REGN'L). WILLIAM L DENTON; NATIONAL SYMPHONY ORCHESTRA ASSOCIATION; JOHN F KENNEDY CENTER; WASHINGTON, DC 20566. (#1714-903).

APR 15, '74 - JAN 1, '76. A CHORAL WORK BY WILLIAM SCHUMAN. NATIONAL SYMPHONY ORCHESTRA COMMISSIONS. THE NATIONAL SYMPHONY, ANTAL DORATI, MUSIC DIRECTOR, HAS AWARDED GRANTS TO ELEVEN COMPOSERS TO CREATE WORKS FOR PERFORMANCE IN HONOR OF THE BICENTENNIAL. THERE WILL BE 12 WORKS COMMISSIONED. (REGN'L). WILLIAM L DENTON; NATIONAL SYMPHONY ORCHESTRA ASSOCIATION; JOHN F KENNEDY CENTER; WASHINGTON, DC 20566. (#1714-912).

APR 15, '74 - JAN 1, '76. CHORAL WORK ON THEMES OF WILLIAM BILLINGS BY ROBERT RUSSELL BENNETT. NATIONAL SYMPHONY ORCHESTRA COMMISSIONS. THE NATIONAL SYMPHONY, ANTAL DORATI, MUSIC DIRECTOR, HAS AWARDED GRANTS TO ELEVEN COMPOSERS TO CREATE WORKS FOR PERFORMANCE IN HONOR OF THE BICENTENNIAL. THERE WILL BE 12 WORKS COMMISSIONED. (REGN'L). WILLIAM L DENTON; NATIONAL SYMPHONY ORCHESTRA ASSOCIATION; JOHN F KENNEDY CENTER; WASHINGTON, DC 20566. (#1714-909).

APR 15, '74 - JAN 1, '76. ORATORIO 'THE DAYS OF GOD' BY JUAN ORREGO-SALAS. NATIONAL SYMPHONY ORCHESTRA COMMISSIONS. THE NATIONAL SYMPHONY, ANTAL DORATI, MUSIC DIRECTOR, HAS AWARDED GRANTS TO ELEVEN COMPOSERS TO CREATE WORKS FOR PERFORMANCE IN HONOR OF THE BICENTENNIAL. THERE WILL BE 12 WORKS COMMISSIONED. (REGN'L). WILLIAM L DENTON; NATIONAL SYMPHONY ORCHESTRA ASSOCIATION; JOHN F KENNEDY CENTER; WASHINGTON, DC 20566. (#1714-908).

APR 15, '74 - JAN 1, '76. ORCHESTRAL SUITE 'AN ICARIAN CRUCIBLE' BY GENE GUTCHE. LIVE PERFORMANCE. (REGN'L). WILLIAM L DENTON; NATIONAL SYMPHONY ORCHESTRA ASSOCIATION; JOHN F KENNEDY CENTER; WASHINGTON, DC 20566. (#1714-904).

APR 15, '74 - JAN 1, '76. AN ORCHESTRAL WORK BY LUIGI DALLAPICCOLA. NATIONAL SYMPHONY ORCHESTRA COMMISSIONS. THE NATIONAL SYMPHONY, ANTAL DORATI, MUSIC DIRECTOR, HAS AWARDED GRANTS TO ELEVEN COMPOSERS TO CREATE WORKS FOR PERFORMANCE IN HONOR OF THE BICENTENNIAL. THERE WILL BE 12 WORKS COMMISSIONED. (REGN'L). WILLIAM L DENTON; NATIONAL SYMPHONY ORCHESTRA ASSOCIATION; JOHN F KENNEDY CENTER; WASHINGTON, DC 20566. (#1714-902).

APR 15, '74 - JAN 1, '76. ORCHESTRAL WORK BY GUNTHER SCHULLER. NATIONAL SYMPHONY ORCHESTRA COMMISSIONS. THE NATIONAL SYMPHONY, ANTAL DORATI, MUSIC DIRECTOR, HAS AWARDED GRANTS TO ELEVEN COMPOSERS TO CREATE WORKS FOR PERFORMANCE IN HONOR OF THE BICENTENNIAL. THERE WILL BE 12 WORKS COMMISSIONED. (REGN'L). WILLIAM L DENTON; NATIONAL SYMPHONY ORCHESTRA ASSOCIATION; JOHN F KENNEDY CENTER; WASHINGTON, DC 20566. (#1714-910).

APR 15, '74 - JAN 1, '76. PASSACAGLIA FOR ORCHESTRA BY BENJAMIN LEES. NATIONAL SYMPHONY ORCHESTRA COMMISSIONS. THE NATIONAL SYMPHONY, ANTAL DORATI, MUSIC DIRECTOR, HAS AWARDED GRANTS TO ELEVEN COMPOSERS TO CREATE WORKS FOR PERFORMANCE IN HONOR OF THE BICENTENNIAL. THERE WILL BE 12 WORKS COMMISSIONED. (REGN'L). WILLIAM L DENTON; NATIONAL SYMPHONY ORCHESTRA ASSOCIATION; JOHN F KENNEDY CENTER; WASHINGTON, DC 20566. (#1714-906).

APR 15, '74 - JAN 1, '76. SONG CYCLE 'ARIEL' FOR BARITONE & ORCHESTRA. NATIONAL SYMPHONY ORCHESTRA COMMISSIONS. THE NATIONAL SYMPHONY, ANTAL DORATI, MUSIC DIRECTOR, HAS AWARDED GRANTS TO ELEVEN COMPOSERS TO CREATE WORKS FOR PERFORMANCE IN HONOR OF THE BICENTENNIAL. THERE WILL BE 12 WORKS COMMISSIONED. (REGN'L). WILLIAM L DENTON; NATIONAL SYMPHONY ORCHESTRA ASSOCIATION; JOHN F KENNEDY CENTER; WASHINGTON, DC 20566. (#1714-901).

APR 15, '74 - JAN 1, '76. SYMPHONY FOR WIND INSTRUMENTS BY FRANK MARTIN. NATIONAL SYMPHONY ORCHESTRA COMMISSIONS. THE NATIONAL SYMPHONY, ANTAL DORATI, MUSIC DIRECTOR, HAS AWARDED GRANTS TO ELEVEN COMPOSERS TO CREATE WORKS FOR PERFORMANCE IN HONOR OF THE BICENTENNIAL. THERE WILL BE 12 WORKS COMMISSIONED. (REGN'L). WILLIAM L DENTON; NATIONAL SYMPHONY ORCHESTRA AS-

WASHINGTON — CONTINUED

SOCIATION; JOHN F KENNEDY CENTER; WASHINGTON, DC 20566. (#1714-907).

APR 15, '74 - JAN 1, '76. TENTH SYMPHONY,'THE AMERICAN MUSE' BY WILLIAM SCHUMAN. NATIONAL SYMPHONY ORCHESTRA COMMISSIONS. THE NATIONAL SYMPHONY, ANTAL DORATI, MUSIC DIRECTOR, HAS AWARDED GRANTS TO ELEVEN COMPOSERS TO CREATE WORKS FOR PERFORMANCE IN HONOR OF THE BICENTENNIAL. THERE WILL BE 12 WORKS COMMISSIONED. (REGN'L). WILLIAM L DENTON; NATIONAL SYMPHONY ORCHESTRA ASSOCIATION; JOHN F KENNEDY CENTER; WASHINGTON, DC 20566. (#1714-911).

APR 15, '74 - JAN 1, '76. WORK FOR ORCHESTRA AND NARRATOR BY ULYSSES KAY. NATIONAL SYMPHONY ORCHESTRA COMMISSIONS. THE NATIONAL SYMPHONY, ANTAL DORATI, MUSIC DIRECTOR, HAS AWARDED GRANTS TO ELEVEN COMPOSERS TO CREATE WORKS FOR PERFORMANCE IN HONOR OF THE BICENTENNIAL. THERE WILL BE 12 WORKS COMMISSIONED. (REGN'L). WILLIAM L DENTON; NATIONAL SYMPHONY ORCHESTRA ASSOCIATION; JOHN F KENNEDY CENTER; WASHINGTON, DC 20566. (#1714-905).

MAY 1 - 31, '74. SYMPOSIUM ON LEADERSHIP IN THE AMERICAN REVOLUTION. A SERIES OF ANNUAL SYMPOSIA TO BE HELD EACH SPRING THROUGH 1976 ON TOPICS CONCERNING THE AMERICAN REVOLUTION. THE 1974 TOPIC WILL CONCERN LEADERSHIP DURING THE REVOLUTION. (NAT'L). DR JAMES HUTSON; LIBRARY OF CONGRESS; 10 FIRST ST, SE; WASHINGTON, DC 20540. (#2-901).

MAY 1 - JULY 8, '74. OPENING OF NEW HIRSHHORN MUSEUM AND SCULPTURE GARDEN. SCHEDULED TO OPEN BY SUMMER OF 1974. THE MUSEUM WILL HOUSE MORE THAN 7000 WORKS OF ART WITH COLLECTIONS OF PAINTINGS PRIMARILY 20TH CENTURY & WORLD SCULPTURES FROM ANTIQUITY TO PRESENT. (NAT'L). MRS SUSAN HAMILTON; SMITHSONIAN INSTITUTION; 1000 JEFFERSON DR, SW; WASHINGTON, DC 20560. (#343-901).

MAY 15, '74. LECTURE, DANIEL MOYNIHAN, HUMAN WELFARE & PRINCIPLES OF REVOLUTION. DISTINGUISHED LECTURE SERIES ON BICENTENNIAL. 18 DISTINGUISHED SCHOLARS DISCUSS NATURE, FUTURE OF AM REVOLUTION AT NATION'S HISTORIC SITES---TAPED FOR BROADCAST ON PBS IN SPRING 1974. TOPICS COVER REV & SOCIETY, RELIGION, PRESS, LAW, CULTURE, GOV'T. (NAT'L). EARL H VOSS; AMERICAN ENTERPRISE INSTITUTE FOR PUBLIC POLICY RESEARCH; 1150 17TH STREET, N.W.; WASHINGTON, DC 20036. (#1297-916).

MAY 22, '74. LECT CHARLES B MARSHALL, AM FOREIGN POLICY AS DIMENSION OF AM REV. DISTINGUISHED LECTURE SERIES ON BICENTENNIAL. 18 DISTINGUISHED SCHOLARS DISCUSS NATURE, FUTURE OF AM REVOLUTION AT NATION'S HISTORIC SITES---TAPED FOR BROADCAST ON PBS IN SPRING 1974. TOPICS COVER REV & SOCIETY, RELIGION, PRESS, LAW, CULTURE, GOV'T. (NAT'L). EARL H VOSS; AMERICAN ENTERPRISE INSTITUTE FOR PUBLIC POLICY RESEARCH; 1150 17TH STREET, N.W.; WASHINGTON, DC 20036. (#1297-917).

MAY 24 - 25, '74. SCULPTURE ART WORK FRAMED & UNFRAMED CRAFTS FESTIVAL. THE AMERICAN ART & CRAFT FESTIVAL, WASHINGTON, DC. MAN'S PAST, PRESENT & FUTURE IN AMERICAN ART. PAST & PRESENT RESERVED FOR PROFESSIONAL & AMATEUR ARTISTS WORK OF TODAY, WHILE STUDENTS FROM ART SCHOOLS & UNIVERSITY ART DEPTARTMENTS DEPICT FUTURE. (REGN'L). KEITH D BELL; SAINT LUKE'S UNITED METHODIST CHURCH; WISCONSIN AVE & CALVERT ST, NW; WASHINGTON, DC 20007. (#1351-901).

MAY 25, '74. PAUL HILL CHORALE PERFORMANCE IN WASHINGTON, DC. THE AMERICAN ART & CRAFT FESTIVAL, WASHINGTON, DC. MAN'S PAST, PRESENT & FUTURE IN AMERICAN ART. PAST & PRESENT RESERVED FOR PROFESSIONAL & AMATEUR ARTISTS WORK OF TODAY, WHILE STUDENTS FROM ART SCHOOLS & UNIVERSITY ART DEPTARTMENTS DEPICT FUTURE. (REGN'L). KEITH D BELL; SAINT LUKE'S UNITED METHODIST CHURCH; WISCONSIN AVE & CALVERT ST, NW; WASHINGTON, DC 20007. (#1351-902).

JUNE 5, '74. LECTURE, DEAN RUSK, THE AMERICAN REVOLUTION AND THE FUTURE. DISTINGUISHED LECTURE SERIES ON BICENTENNIAL. 18 DISTINGUISHED SCHOLARS DISCUSS NATURE, FUTURE OF AM REVOLUTION AT NATION'S HISTORIC SITES---TAPED FOR BROADCAST ON PBS IN SPRING 1974. TOPICS COVER REV & SOCIETY, RELIGION, PRESS, LAW, CULTURE, GOV'T. (NAT'L). EARL H VOSS; AMERICAN ENTERPRISE INSTITUTE FOR PUBLIC POLICY RESEARCH; 1150 17TH STREET, N.W.; WASHINGTON, DC 20036. (#1297-918).

JUNE 24 - JULY 13, '74. FESTIVAL OF AMERICAN FOLKLIFE 1974. A 12 WEEK FESTIVAL CELEBRATING THE MULTIPLICITY & DIVERSITY OF AMERICAN HERITAGE THROUGH MUSIC, DANCE, CRAFTS & FOOD. THIS IS AN ANNUAL CELEBRATION OF AMERICAN FOLK CULTURES & TRADITIONS. (INT'L). SUSANNE ROSCHWALB, DIR; DIVISION OF PERFORMING ARTS, SMITHSONIAN INSTITUTION; SUITE 2100, 955 L'ENFANT PLAZA; WASHINGTON, DC 20560. (#111-901).

JULY 31, '74. SPIRIT OF 76 PHOTO CONTEST DEADLINE. PRIZES FOR BEST PHOTOS REPRESENTING THE SPIRIT OF AMERICA. SHOW WHAT WHAT AMERICA MEANS TO YOU AS A CITIZEN. (LOCAL). ASHLEY MASON, STAFF ASST; HONORABLE ANGELO RONCALLO; US HOUSE OF REPRESENTATIVES; WASHINGTON, DC 20515. (#2382-901).

SEPT 1, '74 - CONTINUING . SUITING EVERYONE: THE DEMOCRATIZATION OF AMERICAN DRESS. EXHIBIT AT WINTER (9 2-3/30) HOURS: 10:00AM-5:30PM.. (NAT'L). BECKY CLAPP; NAT MUSEUM OF HISTORY AND TECHNOLOGY; 14TH AT CONSTITUTION NW; WASHINGTON, DC 20560. (#50002-5).

OCT 26, '74. NAT'L CONG ON HISTORIC PRESERVATION. HISTORIC RESOURCES & HUMAN ENVIRONMENT STUDY. THIS STUDY WILL DEFINE THE ESSENTIAL COMPONENTS OF OUR HERITAGE AND REQUIREMENTS FOR ITS ADEQUATE PRESERVATION, WILL ASSESS PRESENT PROGRAMS & ADVISE GOVERNMENT OF ITS ROLE IN DEVELOPING FUTURE PROGRAMS. (NAT'L). ROBERT GARVEY, EXEC SEC; ADVISORY COUNCIL ON HISTORIC PRESERVATION; 1522 K ST, NW, ROOM 403; WASHINGTON, DC 20005. (#148-903).

DEC 6, '74. WASHINGTON DC HIGH SCHOOL EDITORS BICENTENNIAL SEMINAR. 1976 STUDIES SEMINARS FOR HIGH SCHOOL EDITORS, PA. NATIONWIDE SERIES OF SEMINARS FOR EDITORS OF SECONDARY SCHOOL NEWSPAPERS ON THE NATION'S FOUNDING PRINCIPLES AND THEIR APPLICABILITY TODAY. (NAT'L). NANETTE JONES, 1976 STUDI; BRYN MAWR COLLEGE; BRYN MAWR, PA 19010. (#3102-903).

JAN 1, '75 - DEC 31, '76. TV SERIES-ONE MINUTE SPOTS: GREAT MEN & MOMENTS OF AMER BUSINESS. FILM 'GREAT MOMENTS & GREAT MEN OF AMER BUSINESS'. TV SERIES OF ONE MINUTE CAPSULE HISTORIES ON THE AMERICAN FREE ENTERPRISE SYSTEM, PAYING TRIBUTE TO BUSINESS & ITS LEADERS. (NAT'L). ARCH N BOOTH, PRESIDENT; CHAMBER OF COMMERCE OF THE USA; 1615 H ST, NW; WASHINGTON, DC 20062. (#2251-501).

JAN 1, '75 - JAN 1, '78. EVERYDAY LIFE IN THE AMERICAN PAST EXHIBIT. SATELLITE EXHIBIT TO THE SMITHSONIAN'S 'NATION OF NATIONS' EXHIBIT. AT SMITHSONIAN INSTITUTION. (NAT'L). MRS SUSAN HAMILTON; SMITHSONIAN INSTITUTION; 1000 JEFFERSON DR SW; WASHINGTON, DC 20560. (#69-1).

JAN 19, '75 - DEC 31, '76. MULTI-ARTS EXHIBITION. EXHIBIT, CEREMONY, AWARD. (REGN'L). JAMES C MASON, PRESIDENT; SMITH MASON GALLERY OF ART INC; 1207 RHODE ISLAND AVE, NW; WASHINGTON, DC 20005. (#6604-501).

APR 1 - NOV 30, '75. THE DYE IS NOW CAST: THE ROAD TO AMERICAN INDEPENDENCE 1774-76. AN EXHIBITION BY THE NATIONAL PORTRAIT GALLERY OF THE SMITHSONIAN OF PORTRAITS OF THE DELEGATES TO THE FIRST CONTINENTAL CONGRESS. SLIDE SETS, BOOKLETS, AND OTHER EDUCATIONAL AIDS WILL BE FORTHCOMING. (NAT'L). MRS SUSAN HAMILTON; SMITHSONIAN INSTITUTION; 1000 JEFFERSON DR SW; WASHINGTON, DC 20560. (#82-1).

APR 14, '75. DENVER UNIV SYMPHONY PERFORMANCE AT JOHN F KENNEDY CENTER. LIVE PERFORMANCE AT JOHN F KENNEDY CENTER. (REGN'L). R R PORTER, COORDINATOR; UNIV OF DENVER SYMPHONY ORCHESTRA; UNIV OF DENVER; DENVER, CO 80120. (#103840-9).

APR 24, '75 - DEC 31, '77. 'TO SET A COUNTRY FREE' EXHIBIT AT LIBRARY OF CONGRESS. MAJOR EXHIBIT IN THE LIBRARY'S GREAT HALL ON THE AMERICAN REVOLUTION WHICH WILL OPEN IN APRIL, '75. DATE WILL COINCIDE WITH TWO HUNDREDTH ANNIVERSARY OF BEGINNING OF AMERICAN REVOLUTION. (NAT'L). DR JAMES HUTSON; LIBRARY OF CONGRESS; 10 FIRST ST SE; WASHINGTON, DC 20540. (#134-1).

APR 25 - 27, '75. SCULPTURE ART WORK FRAMED & UNFRAMED CRAFTS FESTIVAL. THE AMERICAN ART & CRAFT FESTIVAL, WASHINGTON, DC. MAN'S PAST, PRESENT & FUTURE IN AMERICAN ART. PAST & PRESENT RESERVED FOR PROFESSIONAL & AMATEUR ARTISTS WORK OF TODAY, WHILE STUDENTS FROM ART SCHOOLS & UNIVERSITY ART DEPTARTMENTS DEPICT FUTURE. (REGN'L). KEITH D BELL; SAINT LUKE'S UNITED METHODIST CHURCH; WISCONSIN AVE & CALVERT ST, NW; WASHINGTON, DC 20007. (#1351-501).

APR 25 - SEPT 15, '75. MUSEUM OF AFRICAN ART-AFRICAN WEAVING AND TRADITIONAL DRESS. EXHIBIT, TOUR AT 318 A STREET NORTHEAST WASHINGTON DC 20002. (INT'L). NANCY V CROMWELL; MUSEUM OF AFRICAN ART; MUSEUM OF AFRICAN ART 318 'A' NE; WASHINGTON, DC 20002. (#50191-1).

APR 26, '75. PAUL HILL CHORALE PERFORMANCE. THE AMERICAN ART & CRAFT FESTIVAL, WASHINGTON, DC. MAN'S PAST, PRESENT & FUTURE IN AMERICAN ART. PAST & PRESENT RESERVED FOR PROFESSIONAL & AMATEUR ARTISTS WORK OF TODAY, WHILE STUDENTS FROM ART SCHOOLS & UNIVERSITY ART DEPTARTMENTS DEPICT FUTURE. (REGN'L). KEITH D BELL; SAINT LUKE'S UNITED METHODIST CHURCH; WISCONSIN AVE & CALVERT ST, NW; WASHINGTON, DC 20007. (#1351-502).

APR 28, '75. COUNTRY-CITY STYLE FAIR. A FESTIVAL STYLED AFTER STATE FAIRS WITH A TOUCH OF THE URBAN MARKET IS PLANNED BY FRIENDSHIP HOUSE. ACTIVITIES INCLUDE ARTS, BAKE SALE, GAMES, DISPLAYS, MUSIC & FOOD. COMMUNITY TO BE INVOLVED. (LOCAL). ERNEST WITHERS; FRIENDSHIP HOUSE; 619 D ST, SE; WASHINGTON, DC 20007. (#5605-501).

MAY 3, '75. BICENTENNIAL KICKOFF-PROCLAMATION CEREMONY AND CAVALCADE. PROCLAMATION BY MAYOR, PLUS OTHER APPROPRIATE SPEAKERS, D.C. YOUTH ORCHESTRA, REPRESENTATIVES FROM EACH OF NINE D.C. BICENTENNIAL ASSEMBLY'S DELEGATIONS, HIGH SCHOOL BANDS. AT DISTRICT BUILDING AND ELLIPSE, 15TH AND E STREETS, N.W.. (LOCAL). MS PERRI MACHUGH; D.C. BICENTENNIAL COMMISSION; 777 14TH STREET; WASHINGTON, DC 20005. (#3839-1).

MAY 3, '75. EXHIBITION OF EQUINE SPORTS FOR SPIRIT OF '76, WAKE UP AMERICA. A MUSICAL WALK BY THE PARK POLICE HORSES AND ALSO POLO GAME. AT WASHINGTON DC VICINITY. (NAT'L). MONTE BOURJAILY, JR, DIR; THE NEW SPIRIT OF '76' FOUNDATION; 918 16TH ST NW, SUITE 603; WASHINGTON, DC 20006. (#2443-3).

MAY 3, '75. SPIRIT OF '76 PARTICIPANT'S RECEPTION, WAKE UP AMERICA. THE PRESIDENT WILL RECEIVE THE 4H CLUB CHILDREN ON THE SOUTH LAWN OF THE WHITE HOUSE. AT WASH. D.C. VICINITY. (NAT'L). MONTE BOURJAILY, JR, DIR; THE NEW SPIRIT OF '76 FOUNDATION; 918 16TH ST NW, SUITE 603; WASHINGTON, DC 20006. (#2443-2).

MAY 3 - 4, '75. DC BICENTENNIAL KICK-OFF ASIAN/ AMERICAN FESTIVAL. WALL MURAL WORKSHOPS, POETRY READINGS, FOLKSINGING, EXHIBITS, DISPLAY AND A FREE DANCE ON SATURDAY EVENING. AT G STREET BETWEEN 7TH AND 9TH. (LOCAL). MS PERRI MACHUGH; D.C. BICENTENNIAL COMMISSION; 777 14TH STREET; WASHINGTON, DC 20005. (#3839-2).

MAY 4, '75. DC BICENTENNIAL KICK-OFF ALL FAITHS BICENTENNIAL SERVICE. ECUMENICAL SERVICE. AT REHOBOTH BAPTIST CHURCH, 621 ALABAMA AVENUE, S.E.. (LOCAL). MS. PERRI MACHUGH; D.C. BICENTENNIAL COMMISSION; 777 14TH STREET; WASHINGTON, DC 20005. (#3839-3).

MAY 5, '75. DC BICENTENNIAL KICK-OFF GHANA FESTIVAL. FILM, MUSIC BY GHANA CULTURAL ENSEMBLE, DRUM MUSIC, FOOD. AT MALCOLM X PARK, 16TH AND EUCLID, N.W.. (LOCAL). MS. PERRI MACHUGH; D.C. BICENTENNIAL COMMISSION; 777 14TH STREET; WASHINGTON, DC 20005. (#3839-4).

MAY 7, '75. DC BICENTENNIAL KICK-OFF - DELAWARE STATE DAY. CEREMONY ON CAPITOL STEPS, PARADE AND MUSIC, POSTER ART CONTEST DISPLAY. AT CAPITOL STEPS, DELAWARE AVENUE, WATERSIDE MALL. (ST-WIDE). MS PERRI MACHUGH; D.C. BICENTENNIAL COMMISSION; 777 14TH STREET; WASHINGTON, DC 20005. (#3839-5).

MAY 8, '75. DC BICENTENNIAL KICK-OFF SPANISH DAY. ALL DAY ART WORKSHOP OR DEMONSTRATION IN CLAY, WATERCOLOR, DRAWING. AN EVENING FILM, VIDEO TAPE. AT DUPONT CIRCLE. (LOCAL). MS. PERRI MACHUGH; D.C. BICENTENNIAL COMMISSION; 777 14TH STREET; WASHINGTON, DC 20005. (#3839-6).

MAY 8 - 9, '75. SYMPOSIUM ON THE IMPACT OF THE REVOLUTION ABROAD. SEMINAR. (NAT'L). DR JAMES HUTSON; LIBRARY OF CONGRESS; 10 FIRST ST, SE; WASHINGTON, DC 20540. (#2-2).

MAY 17, '75. THE AMERICAN ART & CRAFT FESTIVAL. AREA ARTISTS AND CRAFTSMEN SHOW AND SELL THEIR ARTS AND CRAFTS, SOME BEING POTTERY, QUILTS, PAINTINGS, AND FURNITURE. AT ST LUKES UNITED METHODIST CHURCH; 3655 CALVERT ST,NW DC.PARKING AVAL. (REGN'L). KEITH D BELL; ST LUKES UNITED METHODIST CHURCH; 3822 BENTON ST NW; WASHINGTON, DC 20007. (#1351-3).

MAY 17 - OCT 10, '75. US ARMY 200TH ANNIVERSARY. THE 200TH ANNIVERSARY OF THE US ARMY WILL OCCUR ON JUNE 14, 1975 AND SPECIAL PROGRAMS AND CEREMONIES THROUGHOUT THE US AND OVERSEAS WILL BE SCHEDULED FOR THE OBSERVANCE. (INT'L). SAMUEL GREEN; DEPT OF THE ARMY; OFC OF CHIEF OF PUBLIC INFO; WASHINGTON, DC 20310. (#54-1).

MAY 17 - OCT 10, '75. US NAVY 200TH ANNIVERSARY. THE 200TH ANNIVERSARY OF THE US NAVY WILL OCCUR ON OCTOBER 13, 1975. SPECIAL PROGRAMS AND CEREMONIES WILL BE SCHEDULED AT NAVY ACTIVITIES THROUGHOUT THE US AND OVERSEAS FOR THE OBSERVANCE. (INT'L). CAPT B C CRAWFORD, USN; DEPT OF THE NAVY; COMMONWEALTH BLDG #782; WASHINGTON, DC 20350. (#53-1).

JUNE 4, '75 - JUNE 30, '77. 'WE,THE PEOPLE' EXHIBIT OF SMITHSONIAN. EXHIBIT AT NATIONAL MUSEUM OF HISTORY & TECHNOLOGY HIGHLIGHTING THE HISTORY OF THE AMERICAN POLITICAL EXPERIENCE. WINTER HOURS: 10:00AM TO 5:30PM. (NAT'L). MRS SUSAN HAMILTON; SMITHSONIAN INSTITUTION; 1000 JEFFERSON DR SW; WASHINGTON, DC 20560. (#68-1).

JUNE 22 - 29, '75. WASHINGTON WORKSHOPS. 130 TO 150 LONG BEACH STUDENTS TO ATTEND THIS CONGRESSIONAL SEMINAR TO LEARN FIRST HAND ABOUT GOVERNMENT WORKINGS. AT RESIDENCE AT MOUNT VERNON UNIV. (REGN'L). CHRIS AIKEN; WASHINGTON WORKSHOPS; 3836 OLIVE AVE; LONG BEACH, CA 90807. (#200010-1).

JUNE 25 - JULY 6, '75. FESTIVAL OF AMERICAN FOLKLIFE. ANNUAL CELEBRATION OF AMERICAN FOLK CULTURES & TRADITIONS - FEATURES ETHNIC, INDIAN, LABOR & REGIONAL CRAFTS & MUSICAL TRADITIONS FOUND IN AMERICA. AT WASHINGTON, DC. (NAT'L). RICHARD P LUSHER; DIVISION OF PERFORMING ARTS, SMITHSONIAN INSTITUTION; DIVISION OF PERFORMING ARTS; WASHINGTON, DC 20560. (#111-1).

JULY 1 - AUG 31, '75. PUBLIC AND PRIVATE PERFORMANCES OF SWEET LAND OF LIBERTY PUPPET PLAY. PUPPET MUSICAL SPECTACULAR FOR CHILDREN AND FAMILY. ORIGINAL PLAY & MUSIC BY AMERICAN PUPPET PRODUCTIONS IN AN HISTORICAL MUSICAL PAGEANT. (LOCAL). JAMES A VANDERHAAR; AMERICAN PUPPET PRODUCTIONS; PO BOX 119; MIDDLETOWN, NY 10940. (#4934-502).

JULY 1, '75 - CONTINUING . 20 EXHIBIT PORTFOLIOS ON AMERICAN EXPERIENCE & HISTORY. SERIES OF 20 EXHIBIT PORTFOLIOS SURVEYING THE GROWTH AND DEVELOPMENT OF THE UNITED STATES FROM THE PERIOD OF EXPLORATION AND DISCOVERY TO THE PRESENT DAY. (REGN'L). MRS SUSAN HAMILTON; SMITHSONIAN INSTITUTION; 1000 JEFFERSON DR SW; WASHINGTON, DC 20560. (#339-1).

JULY 2 - 6, '75. NATL PK SVC 'A LITTLE LOOK AROUND' VISITS NATIONAL CAPITAL PARKS. THIS SHORT PROGRAM FEATURES ACTORS PORTRAYING FAMOUS AMERICANS OF THE PAST WHO'VE RETURNED TO SEE AMERICA'S GROWTH. JULY 2 AT FORD'S THEATER; 7 3, WASHINGTON MONUMENT; 7 4, MANASSAS NBP IN VA; 7 5, FT WASHINGTON; 7 6, OXON HILL. (LOCAL). NATL CAPITAL PARKS; NATIONAL PARK SERVICE; 1100 OHIO DR SW; WASHINGTON, DC 20242. (#5653-225).

JULY 3, '75 - FEB 28, '76. 'HER INFINITE VARIETY'-A 200 YEAR RECORD OF AMERICA'S WOMEN. 900A-600P OCT-MAR. AT NATIONAL ARCHIVES EXHIBITION HALL, CONSTITUTION AVE. (NAT'L). VIRGINIA PURDY, DIRECTOR; NATIONAL ARCHIVES; NATIONAL ARCHIVES; WASHINGTON, DC 20408. (#100246-1).

JULY 4, '75. INDEPENDENCE DAY CELEBRATION AT THE WASHINGTON MONUMENT. FESTIVAL AT GROUNDS OF MONUMENT. (NAT'L). OFFICE OF PUBLIC AFFAIRS; NATIONAL CAPITAL

WASHINGTON — CONTINUED

PARKS, NATIONAL PARK SERVICE; 1100 OHIO DRIVE, SW; WASHINGTON, DC 20242. (#6728-72).

JULY 4, '75 - DEC 31, '76. UNITED STATES ARMED FORCES BICENTENNIAL CARAVAN. CARAVAN NUMBER ONE-COMPOSED OF EXHIBIT VANS FOR EACH MILITARY SERVICE. PROJECT THEME IS 'HISTORY OF THE ARMED FORCES & THEIR CONTRIBUTIONS TO THE NATION.'. (LOCAL). MARC HUET SPL ASST-BICENT; US ARMED FORCES BICENT EXHIBIT VAN PROJECT; PENTAGON, RM 1E776; WASHINGTON, DC 20330. (#1775-3).

JULY 27, '75. 200TH BIRTHDAY OF THE US ARMY MEDICAL DEPARTMENT. LARGE EXHIBITION TO SHOW ADVANCES IN ARMY MEDICINE, INCLUDING THE LATEST EQUIPMENT & TECHNIQUES. AT WALTER REED HOSPITAL. (REGN'L). DR CHAUNCEY BLY, USA; US ARMY MEDICAL DEPT; AFIP MEDICAL MUSEUM; WASHINGTON, DC 20306. (#7941-1).

JULY 30 - SEPT 9, '75. MASTER PAINTINGS FROM HERITAGE & STATE RUSSIAN MUSEUM, LENINGRAD. UNPRECEDENTED SHOWING-40 ART TREASURES, 30 WESTERN EUROPEAN OLD MASTERS FROM HERMITAGE & AT LEAST 10 19TH CENTURY WORKS FROM STATE RUSSIAN MUSEUM. OFFICIALLY DESIGNATED BICENTENNIAL ACTIVITY BETWEEN USA & USSR. AFTER 9/1/75, HOURS 10AM-5PM & FROM NOON TO 9PM ON SUNDAYS. (INT'L). MARY W DYER, ASSISTANT; NATIONAL GALLERY OF ART; INFORMATION OFFICE; WASHINGTON, DC 20565. (#100164-1).

AUG 1, '75 - DEC 30, '76. EXHIBIT INCORPORATED INTO DHEW EXHIBIT ON SOCIAL SECURITY PROGRAM. A MULTI-MEDIA EXHIBIT ON SOCIAL SECURITY BENEFITS IN THE NEXT DECADES AND INTO THE 21ST CENTURY INFLATION PROOF BENEFITS AND COMPREHENSIVE COVERAGE. AT NEW SOUTH PORTAL BLDG,3RD & INDEPENDENCE AVE. (REGN'L). MILTON WISOFF; SOCIAL SECURITY ADMINISTRATION; 6401 SECURITY BLVD; BALTIMORE, MD 21235. (#1791-1).

AUG 1, '75 - CONTINUING . ENVIRONMENTAL PROTECTION AGENCY VISITOR CNTR. THIS IS A PERMANENT VISITOR CNTR. GROUP TOURS CAN BE ARRANGED. COLORFUL AUDIO VISUAL EXHIBITS MAKE VIEWERS AWARE OF HOW POLLUTION AND WASTE AFFECT THE QUALITY OF THEIR LIVES AND THE EARTH. AT FIRST FLOOR,WEST TOWER,WATERSIDE MALL.401 M ST SW WASH DC. (REGN'L). JOSEPH B HANDY; ENVIRONMENTAL PROTECTION AGENCY; 401 M ST SW; WASHINGTON, DC 20460. (#100166-1).

AUG 11, '75. MARYLAND BICENTENNIAL CELEBRATION AT KENNEDY CENTER. LIVE PERFORMANCE, RADIO/TV, FESTIVAL. (REGN'L). FERNANDO LAIRES; NATIONAL MUSIC COUNCIL; 2109 BROADWAY; NEW YORK, NY 10023. (#6587-501).

AUG 31 - SEPT 27, '75. 'A NATION OF NATIONS' - THE AMERICAN ISSUES FORUM. TOPICS:AUG 31-SEPT 8 'THE FOUNDING PEOPLE';SEPT 7-13 'TWO CENTURIES OF IMMIGRATION';SEPT 14-20 'OUT OF MANY,ONE';SEPT 21-27 'WE PLEDGE ALLEGIANCE'.AMERICA, BASED ON DREAM OF FREEDOM & WELL-BEING, WAS EMBRACED BY MEN & WOMEN OF MANY TONGUES & TRADITIONS. AT NATION-WIDE TV & RADIO,'COURSES BY NEWSPAPER' & DISCUSSION GROUPS.. (NAT'L). OFFICE OF THE CHAIRMAN; NATIONAL ENDOWMENT FOR THE HUMANITIES; 806 15TH STREET, N. W.; WASHINGTON, DC 20506. (#1976-2).

AUG 31, '75 - MAY 29, '76. AMERICAN ISSUES FORUM. A CALENDAR OF TOPICS FOR STUDY AND DISCUSSION THROUGHOUT THE BICENTENNIAL YEAR BY THE ENTIRE POPULATION OF THE USA. FORUM WOULD LEAD 'TO A UNIFYING COMMUNITY OF DISCOURSE ACROSS THE WHOLE NATION.' DETAILS FOR START & STOP TIMES UNDECIDED. AT DETAILS PENDING. (NAT'L). DR GOODMAN; ENDOWMENT FOR THE HUMANITIES; 806 15TH ST NW; WASHINGTON, DC 20506. (#1976-1).

SEPT 1, '75 - DEC 31, '76. 'LONG LIVE THE PARTY' - A BICENTENNIAL REVIEW BY ALLISON LALAND. MRS LALAND TRACES POLITICAL LIFE IN WHITE HOUSE FROM 1776 TO PRESENT THROUGH THE BANQUET & PARTY KITCHENS, GUEST LISTS, STYLES OF ENTERTAINING & PARLOR GAMES; SHE PRESENTS AN ACCOUNT OF OTHERS ON THE SOCIAL SCENE WHO HAVE PRECEDED HER IN ENTERTAINING IN WASHINGTON DC. (LOCAL). WILLIAM TYSON, CHMN; SHOWCASE ASSOCIATES, INC; 173 FERNBROOK AVE; WYNCOTE, PA 19095. (#100392-1).

SEPT 2, '75 - DEC 31, '76. CASH ROOM MUSEUM & MUSEUM WITHOUT WALLS. OPENING CEREMONIES WILL TAKE PLACE ON SEPT 2, 1975. TREASURY BUREAUS IN FULL COLOR PROCESS PRINTING TO BE DISPLAYED IN EACH STATE. AT MAIN TREASURY BLDG. (NAT'L). EDWARD STOREY, BIC COORD; DEPT OF THE TREASURY; ROOM 2112; WASHINGTON, DC 20222. (#1892-1).

SEPT 4, '75. SOUTH CAROLINA'S BICENT PARADE OF AMERICAN MUSIC. ONE OF 52 CONCERTS FROM EACH U S STATE & TERRITORY TO BE PRESENTED IN WASHINGTON, DC. ENTIRE SERIES KNOWN AS THE BICENTENNIAL PARADE OF AMERICAN MUSIC. BILLED AS 'TWILIGHT CONCERT'. FREE. AT KENNEDY CENTER IN WASHINGTON, DC. (LOCAL). MRS ROBERT FREMAN, SEC; SOUTH CAROLINA FEDERATION OF MUSIC CLUBS; 3910 KENILWORTH RD; COLUMBIA, SC 29205. (#8750-1).

SEPT 13, '75. FIRST BICENTENNIAL SYMPOSIUM OF THE CROATIAN ACADEMY OF AMERICA. A SYMPOSIUM ON SOCIAL & CULTURAL CONTRIBUTIONS OF CROATION AMERICANS TO THE AMERICAN EXPERIENCE. AT SHERATON PARK HOTEL, 2660 WOODLEY RD, NW, WASHINGTON, DC, 20008. (NAT'L). EDWARD S YAMBRUSIC, CHMN; THE CROATIAN ACADEMY OF AMERICA, INC; 4720 MASSACHUSETTS AVE, NW; WASHINGTON, DC 20016. (#101804-1).

SEPT 14, '75. THE CROATIAN ETHNIC FOLK MASS WITH THE TAMBURITZA MUSIC. LIVE PERFORMANCE AT THE NATIONAL SHRINE OF THE IMMACULATE CONCEPTION WASHINGTON DC. (REGN'L). STEVE M CVETETIC, CHMN; CROATIAN CATHOLIC UNION OF USA; 125 W 5TH AVE; GARY, IN 46402. (#100682-1).

SEPT 15, '75 - DEC 31, '76. PORTRAY SIGNIFICANT EVENTS IN 200 YR HISTORY OF BANKING THRU FILM. FILM TO PORTRAY SIGNIFICANT EVENTS IN THE 200 YR HISTORY OF BANKING. (REGN'L). WILL DWINNELL; THE AMERICAN BANKERS ASSOCIATION; 1120 CONNECTICUT AVE, NW; WASHINGTON, DC 20036. (#5604-501).

SEPT 18, '75. BANKING & THE BICENTENNIAL - SPEECH. DESCRIBES BANKING'S ROLE IN FINANCING NATION'S BIRTH & GROWTH. (NAT'L). MICHAEL DELANEY; AMERICAN BANKERS ASSOCIATION; 1120 CONNECTICUT AVE, NW; WASHINGTON, DC 20036. (#5633-1).

SEPT 18, '75 - DEC 31, '76. BANKING IN AMERICA. A WIDE RANGING SPECIAL EXHIBIT ON THE 200-YEAR HISTORY OF BANKING AND BANKING TECHNOLOGY IN THE NATIONAL MUSEUM OF HISTORY & TECHNOLOGY IN WASHINGTON, DC. AT MUSEUM OF HISTORY AND TECHNOLOGY SMITHSONIAN INSTITUTE. (REGN'L). MICHAEL DELANEY; AMERICAN BANKERS ASSOCIATION; 1120 CONNECTICUT AVE NW; WASHINGTON, DC 20036. (#1795-1).

SEPT 21, '75. AMERICAN MUSIC PROGRAMS. RESEARCH & PREPARATION FOR SPECIAL BICENT AMERICAN MUSIC PROGRAMS. (NAT'L). JILLIAN H POOLE; JOHN F KENNEDY CENTER FOR THE PERFORMING ARTS; WASHINGTON, DC 20566. (#8561-1).

SEPT 28 - OCT 25, '75. 'THE LAND OF PLENTY' - THE AMERICAN ISSUES FORUM. TOPICS: SEPT 28-OCT 4 'A SHRINKING FRONTIER'; OCT 5-11 'THE SPRAWLING CITY'; OCT 12-18 'USE & ABUSE IN THE LAND OF PLENTY'; OCT 19-25 'WHO OWNS THE LAND?'.AMERICA AS A PLACE TO BE SETTLED, OWNED, RENTED, PLOWED, PLAYED ON, LIVED IN, SPANNING AN ENTIRE CONTINENT. AT NATION-WIDE TV & RADIO, 'COURSES BY NEWSPAPER' & DISCUSSION GROUPS.. (NAT'L). OFFICE OF THE CHAIRMAN; NATIONAL ENDOWMENT FOR THE HUMANITIES; 806 15TH STREET, N. W.; WASHINGTON, DC 20506. (#1976-3).

OCT 1 - NOV 1, '75. RELIGION & THE ARTIST IN AMERICA ART EXHIBIT OF WESTMORELAND CHURCH. ART EXHIBIT FEATURING PAINTINGS & SCULPTURE BY WASHINGTON AREA ARTISTS ON SPIRITUAL THEMES. INVITATIONAL & JURIED. WORKSHOPS WILL BE CONDUCTED. (REGN'L). ROGER NELSON; WESTMORELAND CONGREGATIONAL CHURCH; 1 WESTMORELAND CIRCLE; WASHINGTON, DC 20016. (#2188-501).

OCT 3 - NOV 30, '75. GRAPHICS EXHIBITION, PORTRAYING YOU, ME, HIM, THEM, PLACES & THINGS. EXHIBIT, CEREMONY, AWARD. (REGN'L). JAMES C MASON, PRESIDENT; SMITH MASON GALLERY OF ART INC; 1207 RHODE ISLAND AVE, NW; WASHINGTON, DC 20005. (#6604-504).

OCT 4, '75. GEORGETOWN COMMUNITY STREET FESTIVAL. ANNUAL EVENT HONORING OUR COUNTRY'S HERITAGE BY CELEBRATING 'ON THE STREETS WHERE WE LIVE'. BOOTHS, GAMES, DRAMA, DANCING, & HISTORICAL DISPLAYS HELD. (LOCAL). ANNE B TURPEAU, PROJ DIR; CHURCHES OF GEORGETOWN; 1334 29TH ST NW; WASHINGTON, DC 20007. (#5611-1).

OCT 9, '75. U S NAVY 200TH BIRTHDAY CEREMONY. CEREMONY AT WASHINGTON NAVY YARD. (REGN'L). ROBERT W KERR, CHAIRMAN; NAVY INTERNAL RELATIONS ACTIVITY; WASHINGTON, DC 20350. (#200010-40).

OCT 10 - 13, '75. ENLISTED NAVAL UNIFORM HISTORY. THE FIRST TOUR WAS CONDUCTED DURING THE CELEBRATION OF THE NAVY'S TWO HUNDREDTH BIRTHDAY. IT WAS CONDUCTED AGAIN FROM 11-16 MAY, 1976 IN CONJUNCTION WITH THE CELEBRATION OF ARMED FORCES WEEK. AT USS GREEN BAY (PG 101). (LOCAL). LT L K ROARK, COORD; USS GREEN BAY (PG 101); FPO; NEW YORK, NY 09501. (#200010-23).

OCT 10 - 20, '75. SOCIETY OF AMERICAN TRAVEL WRITERS 20TH ANNUAL CONVENTION. THE MAIN MEETINGS WILL BE HELD IN BOSTON, PHILADELPHIA & WASHINGTON, DC. IN ADDITION, PRE & POST-MEETING TOURS TO THE BALANCE OF THE 13 ORIGINAL COLONIES WILL BE TAKEN, IN THE SPIRIT OF THE BICENTENNIAL. (NAT'L). CAROLYN PATTERSON; SOCIETY OF AMERICAN TRAVEL WRITERS; 1120 CONNECTICUT AVE, NW; WASHINGTON, DC 20036. (#10951-1).

OCT 12 - 13, '75. CITY CELEBRATION-TWO DAY FAIR BY VARIED COMMUNITIES OF DC. TWO DAY EVENT OVER COLUMBUS DAY WEEKEND FEATURING CULTURAL, CREATIVE & PERFORMING ARTS OF THE VARIED COMMUNITIES OF THE NATION'S CAPITAL. SOMETHING FOR EVERYONE, INCL CHILDREN'S ACTIVITIES, DANCE, DRAMA, MUSIC, ETHNIC FOODS, ARTS & CRAFTS, & EXHIBITS. AT DOWNTOWN 15TH AND E STREETS-DISTRICT BUILDING AND ELLIPSE. (LOCAL). MS. PAT MATHEWS; DISTRICT OF COLUMBIA BICENTENNIAL COMMISSION; 1025 15TH STREET, N.W.; WASHINGTON, DC 20005. (#936-1).

OCT 12 - 17, '75. WASHINGTON CONFERENCE ON LAW OF THE WORLD. DELEGATES FROM MORE THAN 120 NATIONS WILL BE IN ATTENDENCE. CONFERENCE WILL BE LARGEST LAW CONFERENCE EVER HELD. WILL INCLUDE EXHIBITS PREPARED IN CONNECTION WITH THE BICENTENNIAL. AT SHERATON-PARK HOTEL. (INT'L). HAROLD SCOTT, DIRECTOR; WORLD PEACE THROUGH LAW CENTER; 400 HILL BLDG; WASHINGTON, DC 20006. (#7918-1).

OCT 13 - 25, '75. 'THE DEVIL'S DISCIPLE' PLAY. PART OF LARGEST CULTURAL PAGEANT CANADA HAS EVER SENT BEYOND ITS BORDERS & MOST COMPREHENSIVE CULTURAL PROGRAM EVER TO BE STAGED IN THE NATION'S CAPITAL. CANADA'S GIFT TO THE BICENTENNIAL. AT NATIONAL THEATRE. (INT'L). AMANDA MACKENZIE, PUB AFF; BICENTENNIAL FESTIVAL CANADA - CANADIAN EMBASSY; 1771 N ST, NW; WASHINGTON, DC 20036. (#13694-5).

OCT 14 - 19, '75. ROYAL WINNEPEG BALLET. PART OF LARGEST CULTURAL PROJECT CANADA HAS EVER SENT BEYOND ITS BORDERS & MOST COMPREHENSIVE CULTURAL PROGRAM EVER TO BE STAGED IN THE NATION'S CAPITAL. CANADA'S GIFT TO THE BICENTENNIAL. AT J F KENNEDY CENTER FOR THE PERFORMING ARTS - OPERA HOUSE. (INT'L). AMANDA MACKENZIE; BICENTENNIAL FESTIVAL CANADA - CANADIAN EMBASSY; 1771 N ST, NW; WASHINGTON, DC 20036. (#13694-1).

OCT 15, '75. DEDICATION OF SCULPTURE PRESENTATION TO NATIONAL ZOOLOGICAL PARK. CEREMONY, OPENING AT NATIONAL ZOOLOGICAL PARK. (LOCAL). WARREN ILIFF, ASST DIR; THE TWENTIETH CENTURY CLUB & THE SMITHSONIAN INSTITUTION; NATIONAL ZOOLOGICAL PARK; WASHINGTON, DC 20009. (#102363-1).

OCT 17, '75. MONIQUE LEYRAC - CHANTEUSE - FOR BICENTENNIAL FESTIVAL CANADA. PART OF LARGEST CULTURAL PROJECT CANADA HAS EVER SENT BEYOND ITS BORDERS & MOST COMPREHENSIVE CULTURAL PROGRAM EVER TO BE STAGED IN THE NATION'S CAPITAL. CANADA'S GIFT TO THE BICENTENNIAL. AT CONCERT HALL, KENNEDY CENTER. (INT'L). AMANDA F MACKENZIE, COORD; BICENTENNIAL FESTIVAL CANADA - CANADIAN EMBASSY; OFFICE OF INFO, 1771 N ST, NW; WASHINGTON, DC 20036. (#13694-8).

OCT 19, '75. MAUREEN FORRESTER IN RECITAL FOR BICENTENNIAL FESTIVAL CANADA. PART OF LARGEST CULTURAL PROJECT CANADA HAS EVER SENT BEYOND ITS BORDERS & MOST COMPREHENSIVE CULTURAL PROGRAM EVER TO BE STAGED IN THE NATION'S CAPITAL. CANADA'S GIFT TO THE BICENTENNIAL. AT CONCERT HALL, KENNEDY CENTER. (INT'L). AMANDA F MACKENZIE, COORD; BICENTENNIAL FESTIVAL CANADA - CANADIAN EMBASSY; OFFICE OF INFO, 1771 N ST, NW; WASHINGTON, DC 20016. (#13694-7).

OCT 21, '75. BICENTENNIAL PARADE OF AMERICAN MUSIC - NEW HAMPSHIRE SALUTE. A TRIBUTE TO AMERICA'S MUSICAL HERITAGE. EACH STATE WILL HAVE A ONEDAY SALUTE. IT IS JOINTLY SUPPORTED BY THE NATIONAL MUSIC COUNCIL & A GRANT FROM EXXON USA. AT KENNEDY CENTER. (REGN'L). CONRAD SPOHNHOLZ; BICENTENNIAL PARADE OF AMERICAN MUSIC; MACDONALD COLONY; PETERBOUROUGH, NH 03458. (#4500-6).

OCT 21, '75. NEW HAMPSHIRE DAY IN THE NATION'S CAPITOL. PRELUDE CONCERT BY MANCHESTER HIGH BAND; PARADE ALONG NEW HAMPSHIRE AVENUE; NEW HAMPSHIRE FOLKTALE SKIT; LITTLE RED WAGON PUPPETEER SHOW & PLANTING OF THE OFFICIAL NEW HAMPSHIRE TREE. AT KENNEDY CENTER. (REGN'L). GILBERT S CENTER, CHMN; NEW HAMPSHIRE ARBC; 37 PLEASANT ST; CONCORD, NH 03301. (#19074-1).

OCT 22 - 25, '75. 'LA BELLE HELENE' OPERA FOR BICENTENNIAL FESTIVAL CANADA. PART OF LARGEST CULTURAL PROJECT CANADA HAS EVER SENT BEYOND ITS BORDERS & MOST COMPREHENSIVE CULTURAL PROGRAM EVER TO BE STAGED IN THE NATION'S CAPITAL. CANADA'S GIFT TO THE BICENTENNIAL. AT J F KENNEDY CENTER FOR THE PERFORMING ARTS - OPERA HOUSE. (INT'L). AMANDA MACKENZIE; BICENTENNIAL FESTIVAL CANADA - CANADIAN EMBASSY; 1771 N ST, NW; WASHINGTON, DC 20036. (#13694-3).

OCT 23, '75. 'LOUIS RIEL' OPERA FOR BICENTENNIAL FESTIVAL CANADA. PART OF LARGEST CULTURAL PROJECT CANADA HAS EVER SENT BEYOND ITS BORDERS & MOST COMPREHENSIVE CULTURAL PROGRAM EVER TO BE STAGED IN THE NATION'S CAPITAL. CANADA'S GIFT TO THE BICENTENNIAL. AT J F KENNEDY CENTER FOR THE PERFORMING ARTS - OPERA HOUSE. (INT'L). AMANDA MACKENZIE, PUB AFF; BICENTENNIAL FESTIVAL CANADA - CANADIAN EMBASSY; 1771 N ST, NW; WASHINGTON, DC 20036. (#13694-4).

OCT 25, '75. MENDELSSOHN CHOIR FOR BICENTENNIAL FESTIVAL CANADA. PART OF LARGEST CULTURAL PAGEANT CANADA HAS EVER SENT BEYOND ITS BORDERS & MOST COMPREHENSIVE CULTURAL PROGRAM EVER TO BE STAGED IN THE NATION'S CAPITAL. CANADA'S GIFT TO THE BICENTENNIAL. AT J F KENNEDY CENTER FOR THE PERFORMING ARTS - CONCERT HALL. (INT'L). AMANDA MACKENZIE, PUB AFF; BICENTENNIAL FESTIVAL CANADA - CANADIAN EMBASSY; 1771 N ST, NW; WASHINGTON, DC 20036. (#13694-6).

OCT 26, '75. NATIONAL ARTS CENTER ORCHESTRA, WITH LOUIS QUILCO, BARITONE. PART OF THE LARGEST CULTURAL PFOJECT CANADA HAS EVER SENT BEYOND ITS BORDERS & MOST COMPREHENSIVE CULTURAL PROGRAM EVER TO BE STAGED IN THE NATIONS CAPITAL. CANADA'S GIFT FOR THE BICENTENNIAL. AT J F KENNEDY CENTER FOR THE PERFORMING ARTS - CONCERT HALL. (INT'L). AMANDA MACKENZIE; BICENTENNIAL FESTIVAL CANADA - CANADIAN EMBASSY; 1771 N ST, NW; WASHINGTON, DC 20036. (#13694-2).

OCT 26 - NOV 22, '75. 'CERTAIN UNALIENABLE RIGHTS' - THE AMERICAN ISSUES FORUM. TOPICS: OCT 26-NOV 1 'FREEDOM OF SPEECH,ASSEMBLY & RELIGION';NOV 2 -8 'FREEDOM OF THE PRESS'; NOV 9-15 'FREEDOM FROM SEARCH & SEIZURE'; NOV 16-22 'EQUAL PROTECTION UNDER THE LAW'.CONCERNS FREEDOMS THAT NEW REPUBLIC GUARANTEED ITS CITIZENS & AFFECTING OUR EVERYDAY LIVES. AT NATION-WIDE TV & RADIO, 'COURSES BY NEWSPAPER' & DISCUSSION GROUPS. (NAT'L). OFFICE OF THE CHAIRMAN; NATIONAL ENDOWMENT FOR THE HUMANITIES; 806 15TH STREET, N. W.; WASHINGTON, DC 20506. (#1976-4).

OCT 27, '75. KIDS DAY. A CHILDREN'S FESTIVAL. AT THE MALL IN WASHINGTON, DC. (ST-WIDE). PETER SHARE; OFFICE OF BICENTENNIAL PROGRAMS; 777 14TH ST, NW; WASHINGTON, DC 20005. (#103359-1).

OCT '75. BAHAMIAN-AMERICAN HERITAGE PROGRAM. 5-DAY HERITAGE PROGRAM FEATURING AN ART AND HISTORY EXHIBIT AND BAHAMIAN MUSIC AND DANCE. (INT'L). CULTURAL ATTACHE; GOVERNMENT OF THE BAHAMAS; EMBASSY OF GREAT BRITAIN; 3100 MASSACHUSETTS AVE; WASHINGTON, DC 20008. (#200010-24).

NOV 1 - DEC 12, '75. NATL BALLOTING FOR THE WINNER OF BICENTENNIAL SLOGAN CONTEST. SLOGANS USA - BICENTENNIAL

WASHINGTON — CONTINUED

SLOGAN CONTEST. NATIONWIDE CONTEST TO FIND A SLOGAN TO CATCH THE SPIRIT OF AMERICA TODAY, WHICH WOULD ALSO BE APPROPRIATE FOR THE BICENTENNIAL. TO BRING AMERICANS TO CONSTRUCTIVE THINKING ABOUT THEIR COUNTRY. (NAT'L). FRANK INGO; SLOGANS USA; 1401 16TH ST, NW; WASHINGTON, DC 20036. (#1783-502).

NOV 1, '75 - DEC 31, '76. HERITAGE OF AFRICAN ARCHITECTURE, TRAVELING PHOTOGRAPHY EXHIBITION. EXHIBITION OF 500 WORKS OF TRADITIONAL AFRICAN SCULPTURES & ELISOFON COLOR PHOTOS, TOURS & LECTURES ON AFRICAN CULTURE USING LIBRARY ARCHIVES EXTENSION PROGRAMS. (REGN'L). WARREN M ROBBINS; MUSEUM OF AFRICAN ART; 318 A ST, NE; WASHINGTON, DC 20002. (#5353-504).

NOV 2, '75. BICENTENNIAL PARADE OF AMERICAN MUSIC - VIRGINIA SALUTE. A TRIBUTE TO AMERICA'S MUSICAL HERITAGE. EACH STATE WILL HAVE A ONEDAY SALUTE. IT IS JOINTLY SUPPORTED BY THE NATIONAL MUSIC COUNCIL & A GRANT FROM EXXON USA. AT KENNEDY CENTER. (REGN'L). MRS JAMES W MILNE, MGR; BICENTENNIAL PARADE OF AMERICAN MUSIC; 429 ALLISON RD SW; ROANOKE, VA 24016. (#4500-2).

NOV 10 - 11, '75. 'TO SHELTER HUMANITY'-WORLD HOUSING NEEDS & ENVIRONMENT SYMPOSIUM. CONCEIVED AS A PRELUDE TO HABITAT '76, TO BE HELD IN CANADA IN 1976, IT IS AN EFFORT TO ENCOURAGE AN UNDERSTANDING IN THE USA ABOUT THIS WORLD CONCERN. CO-SPONSOR IS THE INTERNATIONAL DEVELOPMENT CONFERENCE (A GROUP OF OVER 100 PRIVATE AGENCIES). AT THE AMERICAN UNIVERSITY CAMPUS. (INT'L). DARRELL RANDALL, CO-CHMN; 'TO SHELTER HUMANITY' - SCHOOL OF INTERNATIONAL SERVICE; THE AMERICAN UNIVERSITY; WASHINGTON, DC 20016. (#31870-1).

NOV 10 - DEC 31, '75. MARINE CORPS ARMED FORCES DAY KICKOFF OF 200 ANNIVERSARY IN 1975. THE 200TH ANNIVERSARY OF THE US MARINE CORPS WILL OCCUR ON NOVEMBER 10, 1975 SPECIAL PROGRAMS AND CEREMONIES FOR THE OBSERVANCE WILL BE HELD THROUGHOUT THE USA & OVERSEAS DURING 1975. (INT'L). LT COL JONATHAN F ABEL; US MARINE CORPS; HQ MARINE CORPS (CODE PAB); WASHINGTON, DC 20380. (#104-1).

NOV 15 - DEC 15, '75. 'IMAGES OF AN ERA' - THE AMERICAN POSTER 1945-1975. LATER TO CIRCULATE THRUOUT USA FROM FEB THRU AUGUST, 1976 & THRU WESTERN EUROPE FROM AUGUST, 1976 TO JUNE, 1977. AMERICAN ARTISTS TO DESIGN A SERIES OF TWELVE ORIGINAL PRINTS BASED ON THE THEME 'AMERICA IN THE THIRD CENTURY' - BY MOBIL OIL CORP. AT CORCORAN GALLERY. (REGN'L). STEVE FINEBERG, DIRECTOR; ART PLANNING CONSULTANTS; 830 3RD AVE; NEW YORK, NY 10022. (#1785-501).

NOV 17, '75. BICENTENNIAL PARADE OF AMERICAN MUSIC - NEW YORK STATE SALUTE. OMERTNATIONAL MUSIC CAMP CHORUS & CONCERT BAND, UNDER DR. MERTON UTGAARD'S, WILL PERFORM IN THE CONCERT HALL. GROUP RECEIVED TOP HONORS AT WORLD MUSIC COMPETITION HELD IN EUROPE 1966 & 1970. AT KENNEDY CENTER. (REGN'L). MARION RICHTER, MGR; NATIONAL MUSIC COUNCIL & EXXON; 31 BRADFORD RD; SCARSDALE, NY 10583. (#4500-3).

NOV 20, '75 - DEC 31, '76. ECOLOGY 200 - OUR CHANGING LAND. EXHIBIT ON CHANGES IN THE LIFE & LAND FORMS AS A REFLECTION OF SIMILAR CHANGES THROUGHOUT THE UNITED STATES. AT MUSEUM OF NATURAL HISTORY. (NAT'L). MRS SUSAN HAMILTON; SMITHSONIAN INSTITUTION; 1000 JEFFERSON DR SW; WASHINGTON, DC 20560. (#341-1).

NOV 21, '75 - JAN 4, '76. AMERICAN POSTER EXHIBITION. 250 POSTERS ILLUSTRATE EVENTS 1945-75. SCHEDULE OF TOUR: CONTEMPOPARTS ARTS MUSEUM, HOUSTON - 02/02 - 03/19; MUSEUM OF SCIENCE & INDUSTRY, CHICAGO, 04/01 - 05/02; GAAY ART GALLERY & STUDY CENTER, NEW YORK UNIV, 05/22 - 06/30. AT CORCORAN GALLERY OF ART. (LOCAL). MARGERY BYERS, DIRECTOR; NATIONAL COLLECTION OF FINE ARTS; WASHINGTON, DC 20560. (#103416-102).

NOV 23 - DEC 20, '75. 'A MORE PERFECT UNION' - THE AMERICAN ISSUES FORUM. TOPICS: NOV 23-29 'IN CONGRESS ASSEMBLED...A REPRESENTATIVE LEGISLATURE'; NOV 30-DEC 6 ' A PRESIDENT: AN ELECTED EXECUTIVE'; DEC 7-13 'THE GOVERNMENT:THE GROWTH OF BEAURACRACY'; DEC 14-20 'BY CONSENT OF THE STATES...'.AMERICAN POLITICAL LIFE RARE,RISKY & FRAGILE. AT NATION-WIDE TV & RADIO,'COURSES BY NEWSPAPER' & DISCUSSION GROUPS. (NAT'L). OFFICE OF THE CHAIRMAN; NATIONAL ENDOWMENT FOR THE HUMANITIES; 806 15TH STREET, N. W.; WASHINGTON, DC 20506. (#1976-5).

DEC 1, '75. BICENTENNIAL PARADE OF AMERICAN MUSIC - NORTH CAROLINA SALUTE. A TRIBUTE TO AMERICA'S MUSICAL HERITAGE. EACH STATE WILL HAVE A ONEDAY SALUTE. IT IS JOINTLY SUPPORTED BY THE NATIONAL MUSIC COUNCIL & A GRANT FROM EXXON USA. AT KENNEDY CENTER. (REGN'L). MRS A M FOUNTAIN, MGR; BICENTENNIAL PARADE OF AMERICAN MUSIC; 2620 MAYVIEW RD; RALEIGH, NC 27607. (#4500-4).

DEC 3 - 5, '75. SHAPE TOMMORROW TOGETHER, KEEP AMER BEAUTIFUL 22ND ANNUAL MEETING. CONFERENCE AT MAYFLOWER HOTEL, K ST & CONNECTICUT AVE, WASHINGTON, DC. (REGN'L). EMILY LEONARD, DIR; KEEP AMERICA BEAUTIFUL INC; 99 PARK AVE; NEW YORK, NY 10016. (#100712-1).

DEC 7, '75 - JAN 1, '76. WASHINGTON HOLIDAYS. FESTIVAL. (LOCAL). A KNIGHTON STANLEY, DIR; OFFICE OF BICENTENNIAL PROGRAMS; 777 14TH ST, NW; WASHINGTON, DC 20005. (#20289-1).

DEC 7, '75 - FEB 15, '76. 'THE EUROPEAN VISION OF AMERICA' - ART EXHIBIT. ORGANIZED BY CLEVELAND MUSEUM OF ART; ILLUSTRATES DEVELOPMENT OF THE VISUAL IMAGE OF USA IN EUROPEAN MINDS FROM THE TIME OF COLUMBUS TO LATE 19TH CENTURY; BRINGS TOGETHER WIDE RANGE OF EUROPEAN WORKS OF ARTS & OTHER OBJECTS, INCL SCULPTURE, TAPESTRIES, EARLY MAPS, ETC. AT NATIONAL GALLERY OF ART. (REGN'L). MARY W DYER, ASSISTANT; REUNION DES MUSEES NATIONAUS DE FRANCE & NATL GALLERY OF ART; INFORMATION OFFICE; WASHINGTON, DC 20565. (#100164-2).

DEC 9, '75. BICENTENNIAL PARADE OF AMERICAN MUSIC - RHODE ISLAND SALUTE. A TRIBUTE TO AMERICA'S MUSICAL HERITAGE. EACH STATE WILL HAVE A ONEDAY SALUTE. IT IS JOINTLY SUPPORTED BY THE NATIONAL MUSIC COUNCIL & A GRANT FROM EXXON USA. AT KENNEDY CENTER. (REGN'L). MISS FLORENCE HOARD, MGR; BICENTENNIAL PARADE OF AMERICAN MUSIC; 19 REDWOOD DR; N PROVIDENCE, RI 02911. (#4500-5).

DEC 15, '75 - DEC 31, '76. ARTS IN ASIA AT THE TIME OF THE REVOLUTION. FREER GALLERY OF ART EXHIBIT ON CHINESE, JAPANESE, AND NEAR-EASTERN ART AT THE TIME OF THE BIRTH OF AMERICAN INDEPENDENCE. (INT'L). MRS SUSAN HAMILTON; SMITHSONIAN INSTITUTION; 1000 JEFFERSON DR SW; WASHINGTON, DC 20560. (#340-1).

DEC 19, '75 - CONTINUING . CARTER G WOODSON COLLECTION 'FATHER OF BLACK HISTORY'. HISTORICAL COLLECTION TO BE LOCATED DOWNTOWN AND TO BE MADE AVAILABLE ESPECIALLY FOR 1976 FOR WASHINGTON, D.C. VISITORS AND THEREAFTER. AT CARTER G. WOODSON CENTER. (REGN'L). J. RUPERT PICOTT; ASSOCIATION FOR THE STUDY OF AFRO-AMERICAN LIFE & HISTORY; 1401 FOURTEENTH STREET N.W.; WASHINGTON, DC 20005. (#50700-1).

DEC 29, '75. PANEL DISCUSSION ON CLASSICAL HUMANITIES IN THE AMER REPUBLIC. A SERIES OF PROGAMS INTENDED TO FOCUS ACADEMIC AND PUBLIC ATTENTION ON THE INFLUENCE OF THE GREEK & LATIN CLASSICS ON THE FOUNDING FATHERS AND THEIR THOUGHT. AT STATLER HILTON, 16TH ST AT K AND L, NW. (REGN'L). R W CARRUBBA, SEC; AMERICAN PHILOLOGICAL ASSOCIATION; 431 432 NORTH BURROWES BLDG; UNIVERSITY PK, PA 16802. (#3746-2).

DEC 31, '75 - JAN 1, '76. RELIGIOUS WOMEN TO OFFICIALLY OPEN BICENTENNIAL YEAR WITH PRAYER. CEREMONY. (REGN'L). REV IMAGENE STEWART; AMERICAN WOMEN'S CLERGY ASSOC; 832 7TH ST, NE; WASHINGTON, DC 20002. (#102411-4).

DEC 31, '75 - JAN 1, '76. TROTWOOD-MADISON BICENTENNIAL HOMECOMING. FESTIVAL, PARADE AT COMMUNITY PARK, S BROADWAY. (ST-WIDE). EMERSON D SHANK, CHMN; TROTWOOD-MADISON BICENTENNIAL, INC; PO BOX 1776; TROTWOOD, OH 45426. (#102411-1).

JAN 1, '76. DEDICATE NATL HERB GARDEN AT NATL ARBORETUM. OPENING, EXHIBIT AT NATIONAL ARBORETUM. (REGN'L). DR JOHN CREECH, DIRECTOR; NATIONAL ARBORETUM & THE HERB SOCIETY OF AMERICA; 24TH & R STS, NE; WASHINGTON, DC 20002. (#5572-501).

JAN 1, '76. PRESENTATION OF AWARDS TO WINNERS OF NATL BICENT SLOGAN CONTEST. SLOGANS USA - BICENTENNIAL SLOGAN CONTEST. NATIONWIDE CONTEST TO FIND A SLOGAN TO CATCH THE SPIRIT OF AMERICA TODAY, WHICH WOULD ALSO BE APPROPRIATE FOR THE BICENTENNIAL. TO BRING AMERICANS TO CONSTRUCTIVE THINKING ABOUT THEIR COUNTRY. (NAT'L). FRANK INGO; SLOGANS USA; 1401 16TH ST, NW; WASHINGTON, DC 20036. (#1783-501).

JAN 1 - APR 25, '76. 'THE BLACK WOMAN' EXHIBIT AT ANACOSTIA NEIGHBORHOOD MUSEUM. EXHIBIT AT ANACOSTIA NEIGHBORHOOD MUSEUM, 2405 MARTIN LUTHER KING AVE, SE. (LOCAL). JIM MAHONEY; SMITHSONIAN INSTITUTION; SMITHSONIAM INSTITUTION; WASHINGTON, DC 20560. (#106374-4).

JAN 1 - OCT 31, '76. EARLY AMERICAN OPERA-BARTON'S 'THE DISAPPOINTMENT'. RECONSTRUCTION AND PERFORMANCE OF THE EARLIEST AMERICAN OPERA, BY ANDREW BARTON -'THE DISAPPOINTMENT'. START & STOP TIMES UNDECIDED. AT LIBRARY OF CONGRESS. (REGN'L). JERALD C GRAVE; EASTMAN SCHOOL OF MUSIC,LIBRARY OF CONGRESS; 26 GIBBS ST; ROCHESTER, NY 14604. (#1673-1).

JAN 1 - DEC 30, '76. DESIGN PRESENTATIONS NATIONWIDE USING VARIOUS MEDIA VISUAL DESIGNS. CELEBRATE THE PAST ACHIEVEMENTS IN AMERICAN DESIGN IN ALL FIELDS OF DESIGN, UTILIZING MANY MEDIA FORMS, AS WELL AS FOCUS ON CURRENT DESIGN NEEDS AND FUTURE DESIGN PROSPECTS. (NAT'L). BILL N LACY; NATIONAL ENDOWMENT FOR THE ARTS; 806 15TH ST NW; WASHINGTON, DC 20506. (#2840-501).

JAN 1 - DEC 31, '76. CULTURAL EXHIBITS OF ITALIAN AMER CONTRIBUTIONS. EXHIBITS, FILMS AND FOLK FESTIVALS PORTRAYING ITALIAN CONTRIBUTIONS IN AMERICA. (REGN'L). NICHOLAS R BELTRANTE; AMERICAN ITALIAN BICENTENNIAL COMMISSION INC; PO BOX 780; WASHINGTON, DC 20044. (#5926-501).

JAN 1 - DEC 31, '76. EXHIBIT OF FIREARMS, UNIFORMS, ACCOUTREMENTS OF REVOLUTION ERA. THIS EXHIBIT, WITH 90-MIN OF AUTHENTIC PERIOD MUSIC, INCL BRITISH CLOTHING, AMERICAN OFFICERS COATS, FIREARMS FROM BOTH SIDES, A COLLECTION OF BUCKLES USED BY AMERICAN OFFICERS (INCL STOCK BUCKLE USED AROUND THE NECK. AT NRA'S MUSEUM AT 16TH & RHODE ISLAND AVE. (REGN'L). DAN ABBEY; NATIONAL RIFLE ASSOC; 16TH & RHODE ISLAND AVE, NW; WASHINGTON, DC 20560. (#106174-1).

JAN 1, '76 - JAN 1, '77. JEWISH CONTRIBUTIONS TO AMERICAN DEMOCRACY. THE ROLE OF JEWS IN THE REVOLUTION; THEIR MILITARY AND ECONOMIC SUPPORT AND THEIR CONTRIBUTIONS TO THE GROWTH OF THE NATION. AT B'NAI B'RITH MUSEUM, 1640 RHODE ISLAND AVE, NW. (NAT'L). YALE GOLDBERG; B'NAI B'RITH; 1640 RHODE ISLAND AVE, NW; WASHINGTON, DC 20005. (#10930-1).

JAN 1, '76 - DEC 31, '77. THE LANGUAGE OF AFRICAN ART: A TRAVELING EXHIBIT OF SCULPTURE. EXHIBITION OF 500 WORKS OF TRADITIONAL AFRICAN SCULPTURES & ELISOFON COLOR PHOTOS, TOURS & LECTURES ON AFRICAN CULTURE USING LIBRARY ARCHIVES EXTENSION PROGRAMS. (REGN'L). WARREN M ROBBINS; MUSEUM OF AFRICAN ART; 318 A ST, NE; WASHINGTON, DC 20002. (#5353-502).

JAN 1, '76 - JAN 1, '80. ITALIAN AMERICA HISTORICAL FILM. LIVE PERFORMANCE. (INT'L). NICHOLAS R BELTRANTE; AMERICAN ITALIAN BICENTENNIAL COMMISSION INC; PO BOX 780; WASHINGTON, DC 20044. (#5926-503).

JAN 1, '76 - CONTINUING . 'THE AMERICAN ADVENTURE' - A FILM PRESENTATION. A 50 MINUTE MULTI-MEDIA SHOW ON THE STORY OF AMERICA WILL BE PRESENTED ON 70' SCREENS. RESTAURANTS, GIFT SHOP, VISITORS CENTER, ETC. MULTI-LINGUAL PRESENTATIONS WILL BE AVAILABLE. THERE WILL BE 29 PERFORMANCES DAILY, WITH 320 IN AUDIENCE (2 THEATERS). AT 13TH & E STS, NW, WASH, DC. (INT'L). PATRICIA BRAY; NATIONAL HERITAGE THEATER; 13TH & E STS, NW; WASHINGTON, DC 20004. (#8913-1).

JAN 1, '76 - CONTINUING . FROM FEW TO HEW - EVOLUTION OF US SOCIAL SERVICES. CONSISTS OF FILM, BOOK & 35MM SLIDE PRESENTATION WITH TAPE. TRACES EVOLUTION OF HEW CONCEPT FROM EARLY PATRIOTS AND REVOLUTIONARY ERA TO TODAY & INTO THE FUTURE. FOR USE IN TEACHING & INFORMATIONAL SITUATIONS. BE AVAILABLE THRU FILM & OTHER NATL & STATE REPOSITORIES. (REGN'L). ANNE RUSSELL; DEPT OF HEALTH, EDUCATION & WELFARE; 330 INDEPENDENCE SW,RM 4741 N; WASHINGTON, DC 20201. (#1792-1).

JAN 1, '76 - CONTINUING . NAVAL OBSERVATORY EXHIBIT. MUSEUM & TOUR DEPICTING THE HISTORY OF ASTRONOMY IN THE US NAVY & A MOVIE HIGHLIGHTING THE MISSION OFF THE NAVAL OBSERVATTORY SPECIAL NIGHT TOURS OFFERED MONTHY; NO PRESCHOOLERS ALLOWED; CLOSED WEEKENDS & HOLIDAYS. AT 34TH & MASS AVE,NW, WASH,D.C.. (NAT'L). VISITOR TOURS,NAVAL OBS; NAVAL OBSERVATORY; NAVAL OBSERVATORY; WASHINGTON, DC 20390. (#12065-1).

JAN 5, '76. BICENTENNIAL PARADE OF AMERICAN MUSIC HONORS VERMONT. LIVE PERFORMANCE AT JOHN F KENNEDY MEMORIAL CENTER. (REGN'L). MRS FLOYD D MEHAN, DIR; BICENTENNIAL PARADE OF AMERICAN MUSIC; BOX 174; DORSET, VT 05151. (#4500-9).

JAN 9, '76. PRESENTATION OF NETHERLANDS ANTILLES' BICENT COIN TO THE WHITE HOUSE. A GOLD COIN ISSUED IN COMMEMORATION OF THE 'ANDREW DORIA' SOLUTE OF NOV 16, 1776, WAS PRESENTED TO A REPRESENTATIVE OF PRESIDENT FORD. AT THE WHITE HOUSE. (INT'L). MISS M H DE BRUIJN; ROYAL NETHERLANDS EMBASSY - GOVT OF NETHERLANDS ANTILLES; 4200 LINNEAN AVE; WASHINGTON, DC 20008. (#31907-1).

JAN 11 - FEB 7, '76. 'WORKING IN AMERICA' - THE AMERICAN ISSUES FORUM. TOPICS: JAN 11-17 'THE AMERICAN WORK ETHIC';JAN 18-24 'ORGANISATION OF THE LABOUR FORCE';JAN 25-31 'THE WELFARE STATE:PROVIDING A LIVELIHOOD'; FEB 1-7 'ENJOYING THE FRUITS OF LABOUR'.OPPORTUNITY DREW MILLIONS TO AMERICA, BUT WHAT IS THE END RESULT TODAY?. AT NATION-WIDE TV & RADIO,'COURSES BY NEWSPAPER' & DISCUSSION GROUPS. (NAT'L). OFFICE OF THE CHAIRMAN; NATIONAL ENDOWMENT FOR THE HUMANITIES; 806 15TH STREET, N.W.; WASHINGTON, DC 20506. (#1976-6).

JAN 12 - 15, '76. BAPTIST NATIONAL BICENTENNIAL CONVOCATION. CONFERENCE, SEMINAR AT SHOREHAM HOTEL, 2500 CALVERT NW. (NAT'L). JOHN W BAKER; BAPTIST JOINT COMMITTEE ON PUBLIC AFFAIRS; 200 MARYLAND AVENUE NE; WASHINGTON, DC 20002. (#50335-1).

JAN 15 - DEC 31, '76. BI-CENT-EX, DEPT OF HEALTH, EDUCATION & WELFARE. DISPLAY CENTER TO HOUSE 25 SEPARATE DISPLAY AREAS. RIBBON-CUTTING CEREMONY FOR BI-CENT-EX 10:30-11:30AM, JAN 15. THESE DISPLAYS WILL BE OPEN FROM 9:00AM TO 5:30PM. WEEKEND OPENINGS BEING CONSIDERED - CHECK AGENCY FOR LATEST DETAILS. AT SOUTH PORTAL BLDG,200 INDEPENDENCE,SW. (NAT'L). ANNE RUSSELL; DEPARTMENT OF HEALTH, EDUCATION & WELFARE; 200 INDEPENDENCE AVE, SW; WASHINGTON, DC 20201. (#1890-1).

JAN 15, '76 - DEC 31, '77. EDWARD BANNISTER 19TH CENT AFRO-AMER ARTIST-TRAVELING EXHIBITION. EXHIBITION OF 500 WORKS OF TRADITIONAL AFRICAN SCULPTURES & ELISOFON COLOR PHOTOS, TOURS & LECTURES ON AFRICAN CULTURE USING LIBRARY ARCHIVES EXTENSION PROGRAMS. (REGN'L). WARREN M ROBBINS; MUSEUM OF AFRICAN ART; 318 A ST, NE; WASHINGTON, DC 20002. (#5353-503).

JAN 17 - DEC 31, '76. AMERICA ON STAGE. THE HISTORY OF AMERICAN THEATER, DANCE, MUSIC AND OTHER THEMES FROM COLONIAL DAYS TO PRESENT WILL BE FEATURED IN THE LARGEST EXHIBIT EVER PRODUCED BY THE KENNEDY CENTER. AT KENNEDY CENTER. (LOCAL). WEB GOLINKIN, PROJ CHMN; IBM CORPORATION; 415 MADISON AVE; NEW YORK, NY 10017. (#103416-10).

JAN 17 - DEC 31, '76. 'TO BIGOTRY NO SANCTION, TO PERSECUTION NO ASSISTANCE' - AN EXHIBIT. INCLUDES AUDIO-VISUAL DISPLAY, FILMS, PHOTOGRAPHS AND MEMORABILIA. AT BNAI BRITH KLUTZNICK MUSEUM. (REGN'L). YALE GOLDBERG, PROJ DIR; BNAI BRITH INTERNATIONAL; 1640 RHODE ISLAND AVE, NW; WASHINGTON, DC 20036. (#103414-1).

JAN 18 - MAR 21, '76. 'SLOGANS USA' BALLOTING & ANNOUNCEMENT OF WINNERS. SIX SLOGANS SELECTED BY THE STATES BICENTENNIAL ORGANIZATIONS WILL BE VOTED ON BY THE PUBLIC. SEND CHOICE ON REGULAR SIZED POSTCARD TO: SLOGANS USA, BOX 1976, WASHINGTON, DC 20013. WINNING SLOGAN WILL BE ANNOUNCED THE FIRST DAY OF SPRING, 1976. (NAT'L). MS MARDI DEVOLITIES; SLOGANS USA; 1401 16TH ST, NW; WASHINGTON, DC 20036. (#1783-3).

JAN 18 - MAR 28, '76. PAINTING EXHIBITION, SIGNIFICANT EVENTS & PERSONAGES, PAST & PRESENT. EXHIBIT, CEREMONY, AWARD. (REGN'L). JAMES C MASON, PRESIDENT; SMITH MASON GAL-

WASHINGTON — CONTINUED

LERY OF ART INC; 1207 RHODE ISLAND AVE, NW; WASHINGTON, DC 20005. (#6604-502).

JAN 19, '76. BICENTENNIAL PARADE OF AMERICAN MUSIC HONORS KENTUCKY. LIVE PERFORMANCE AT JOHN F KENNEDY MEMORIAL CENTER. (REGN'L). MRS GARLAND CLARK, DIR; BICENTENNIAL PARADE OF AMERICAN MUSIC; 514 COLBY RD; WINCHESTER, KY 40391. (#4500-10).

JAN 19 - APR 19, '76. 'IMAGES OF AMERICA' - LECTURE/FILM SERIES. SOCIAL AND FILM HISTORIANS WILL INTRODUCE FEATURES, FAMILIAR AND OBSCURE, AND LEAD DISCUSSIONS ON THEIR SOCIAL SIGNIFICANCE. AT THE JOHN F KENNEDY CENTER FOR THE PERFORMING ARTS. (REGN'L). AMERICAN FILM INSTITUTE; THE KENNEDY CENTER; WASHINGTON, DC 20566. (#105832-1).

JAN 19, '76 - CONTINUING . DISPLAY OF THE CENTENNIAL SAFE DONATED TO THE US CONGRESS. SAFE WAS PRESENTED TO THE CONGRESS BY MRS CHARLES F DEIHM IN 1876. OUTER IRON DOORS WERE OPENED ON JAN 19, 1976, BY THE JOINT COMMITTEE ON THE ARRANGEMENTS FOR COMMEMORATION OF THE BICENTENNIAL. THE SAFE'S CONTENTS MAY BE SEEN THROUGH THE INNER GLASS DOOR. AT EAST FRONT LOBBY OF U S CAPITOL BUILDING, 1ST FLOOR. (NAT'L). GEORGE M WHITE, ARCHITECT; U S CONGRESS; US CAPITOL; WASHINGTON, DC 20515. (#83-3).

JAN 20, '76. OPENING OF THE CENTENNIAL SAFE BY THE US CONGRESS. EXHIBIT AT EAST WING, U S CAPITOL BUILDING. (NAT'L). GEORGE M WHITE, ARCHITECT; U S CONGRESS; OFC OF ARCITECT, US CAPITOL; WASHINGTON, DC 20515. (#83-2).

JAN 24 - SEPT 19, '76. 'THE WASHINGTON ROOM' - FINAL BICENTENNIAL EXHIBITION. FEATURES WORKS OF AREA ARTISTS; PAUL KENNEDY, PHOTOGRAPHER; ED LOVE, SCULPTOR WHOSE PRIMARY MEDIUM IS STEEL; & JOSEPH SHANNON, ARTIST & PAINTER, WITH CONTINUING INVOLVEMENT IN THEME OF 'FISHING'. AT CORCORAN GALLERY, 17TH & NEW YORK AVE, NW. (REGN'L). MARTI MAYO, PUBL RELATION; THE CORCORAN GALLERY OF ART; 17TH & NEW YORK AVE, NW; WASHINGTON, DC 20006. (#109357-1).

JAN 26 - FEB 21, '76. 'RIP VAN WINKLE' BY THE CLARENCE BROWN PROFESSIONAL THEATRE CO. THE THEATER PRODUCTION WILL STAR ANTHONY QUAYLE AND WILL BE PRODUCED BY JOSHUA LOGAN. AT KENNEDY CENTER FOR THE PERFORMING ARTS. (LOCAL). DR RALPH ALLEN, PROJ DIR; GREATER KNOXVILLE AMERICAN REVOLUTION BICENTENNIAL COMMISSION; UNIV OF TN, SPEECH & THEATRE; KNOXVILLE, TN 37916. (#101316-1).

JAN 29, '76. BICENTENNIAL CONCERT. LIVE PERFORMANCE AT LINCOLN MEMORIAL. (LOCAL). DR ANN ACKOUREY, V-PRES; CUMBERLAND COLLEGE; LEBANON, TN 37087. (#200010-12).

JAN 29, '76. 'IT TAKES TIME TO KNOW A COUNTRY'. LIVE PERFORMANCE. (LOCAL). JAMES SYMINGTON, COORD; LEGEND SINGERS; U S HOUSE OF REPRESENTATIVES; WASHINGTON, DC 20515. (#200010-14).

JAN 30, '76. BICENTENNIAL CONCERT. LIVE PERFORMANCE AT LINCOLN MEMORIAL. (LOCAL). DR ANN ACKOUREY, V-PRES; CUMBERLAND COLLEGE; LEBANON, TN 37087. (#200010-11).

JAN 30 - 31, '76. MIDWINTER CONVENTION AND SHOW OF SPEBSQSA. SHOWS & PERFORMANCES BY QUARTETS & CHORUSES OF THE SOCIETY FOR THE PRESERVATION & ENCOURAGEMENT OF BARBERSHOP QUARTETS ACROSS AMERICA & BY LOCAL CHAPTERS THRUOUT USA FOR THE BICENTENNIAL ERA. SPONSOR PLANS INCOMPLETE AS OF 04-02-75. AT JOHN F KENNEDY CONCERT HALL. (NAT'L). HUGH INGRAHAM, DIRECTOR; SOC FOR PRES & ENCOURAGEMENT OF BARBERSHOP QUARTET SINGING; 6315 3RD AVE; KENOSHA, WI 53141. (#2450-2).

JAN 31, '76. PREMIERE OF SHOW TRACING HISTORY OF BARBERSHOP SINGING IN AMERICA. PLAN TO TRACE BARBERSHOP IDIOM FROM EARLY DAYS OF REPUBLIC TO PRESENT. COMPLETE SHOW WITH MUSIC AND SCRIPT TO PREMIERE AT JFK CENTER ON JANUARY 31, 1976. THIS SHOW TO BE DISTRIBUTED TO LOCAL CHAPTERS. (REGN'L). HUGH A INGRAHAM; SOCIETY FOR PRESERVATION & ENCOURAGEMENT OF BARBERSHOP QUARTETS; 6315 3RD AVE; KENOSHA, WI 53141. (#2839-501).

FEB 1 - OCT 17, '76. 'BEHIND THE SCENES AT NCFA' - EXHIBIT. THROUGH PHOTOGRAPHS, GRAPHICS & TEXT, THIS EXHIBITION EXPLAINS THE VARIETY & SCOPE OF THE MUSEUM'S OPERATIONS, EMPHASIZING IMPORTANT CONTRIBUTIONS MADE BY MANY PEOPLE BEHIND THE SCENE. AT NATL COLLECTION OF FINE ARTS, 8 & G ST, NW. (REGN'L). DIRECTOR; SMITHSONIAN INSTITUTION; WASHINGTON, DC 20250. (#108935-1).

FEB 1, '76 - FEB 28, '77. THE BEST OF TURQUOISE JEWELRY, LEATHERCRAFT, POTTERY & CLAY MOLDING. THIS AMERICAN INDIAN JEWELRY COLLECTION FEATURES ONE OF THE MOST UNIQUE TURQUOISE BRACELET COLLECTIONS IN THE U S; LEATHERCRAFTING WILL BE A DEMONSTRATION OF THE LATEST IN PROFESSIONAL, AMATEUR AND BEGINNING TECHNIQUES. AT MAKE SOMEONE HAPPY. (LOCAL). CLINT WALKER, CHAIRMAN; PATRIARCHS OF THE AMERICAN REVOLUTION BICENTENNIAL COMMITTEE; 3216 GEORGIA AVE, NW; WASHINGTON, DC 20010. (#104849-1).

FEB 2, '76. BICENTENNIAL PARADE OF AMERICAN MUSIC HONORS TENNESSEE. LIVE PERFORMANCE AT JOHN F KENNEDY MEMORIAL CENTER. (REGN'L). MISS MARTHA MCCRORY, DIR; BICENTENNIAL PARADE OF AMERICAN MUSIC; UNIV OF THE SOUTH; SEWANEE, TN 37375. (#4500-11).

FEB 8 - MAR 6, '76. 'THE BUSINESS OF AMERICA' - THE AMERICAN ISSUES FORUM. TOPICS:FEB 8-14 'PRIVATE ENTERPRISE IN THE MARKETPLACE';FEB 15-21 EMPIRE BUILDING: CORNERING THE MARKET';FEB 22-28 'SUBSIDISING & REGULATING:CONTROLLING THE ECONOMY';FEB 29-MAR 6 'SELLING THE CONSUMER'.AMERICA IS ALSO A MARKETPLACE,WITH ECONOMIC RAMIFICATIONS. AT NATION-WIDE TV & RADIO, 'COURSES BY NEWSPAPER' & DISCUSSION GROUPS. (NAT'L). OFFICE OF THE CHAIRMAN; NATIONAL ENDOWMENT FOR THE HUMANITIES; 806 15TH STREET,N.W.; WASHINGTON, DC 20506. (#1976-7).

FEB 13, '76. BICENTENNIAL PARADE OF AMERICAN MUSIC HONORS OHIO. LIVE PERFORMANCE AT JOHN F KENNEDY MEMORIAL CENTER. (REGN'L). MRS ROBERT CASEY, DIR; BICENTENNIAL PARADE OF AMERICAN MUSIC; 125 SPIREA DR; DAYTON, OH 45413. (#4500-12).

FEB 14, '76. PERFORMANCE BY THE SWISS MIME COMPANY MUMMENSCHANZ. LIVE PERFORMANCE AT LISNER AUDITORIUM. (INT'L). CULTURAL ATTACHE; EMBASSY OF SWITZERLAND; 2900 CATHEDRAL AVE; WASHINGTON, DC 20008. (#200010-49).

FEB 14 - NOV 15, '76. 'WASHINGTON '76' EXHIBIT AT US POST OFFICE. POSTAL SERVICE ARTIFACTS ON DISPLAY--AN EXHIBIT OF BLACKS ON STAMPS, BICENTENNIAL EVENTS DEPICTED ON STAMPS, AND A REPLICA POST OFFICE. AT N CAPITOL ST & MASSACHUSETTS AVE, NW. (REGN'L). JIM BROWN; US POST OFFICE; OFFICE OF THE POSTMASTER; WASHINGTON, DC 20013. (#106175-1).

FEB 14 - DEC 31, '76. THE NATION'S CAPITAL IN PHOTOGRAPHS, 1976. A VISUAL DOCUMENTARY OF WASHINGTON, DC IN 1976 DONE THROUGH THE PHOTOGRAPHS OF 8 CONTEMPORARY AMERICAN PHOTOGRAPHERS COMMISSIONED BY THE CORCORAN. CATALOGS AVAILABLE. EXHIBITION IS A SERIES OF 8 SOLO EXHIBITIONS STAGED 2 AT A TIME THROUGHOUT BICENTENNIAL YEAR. (NAT'L). FRANCIS HARPER; CORCORAN GALLERY OF ART; 17TH ST & NEW YORK AVE, NW; WASHINGTON, DC 20006. (#8516-1).

FEB 22 - 28, '76. NATIONAL ENGINEERS WEEK. WEEK-LONG OBSERVANCE TO FAMILIARIZE PUBLIC WITH WORK OF ENGINEERS AND THEIR CONTRIBUTIONS TO THE GROWTH OF AMERICA. PARTICIPATION OPPORTUNITIES FOR MANY SEGMENTS OF THE POPULATION. AT NATIONWIDE OBSERVANCE - 50 STATES, 535 CITIES. (NAT'L). LEONARD J ARZT; NATIONAL SOCIETY OF PROFESSIONAL ENGINEERS; 2029 K ST, NW; WASHINGTON, DC 20037. (#12000-1).

FEB 23, '76. BICENTENNIAL PARADE OF AMERICAN MUSIC HONORS WASHINGTON, DC. LIVE PERFORMANCE AT JOHN F KENNEDY MEMORIAL CENTER. (REGN'L). MRS IVA LOUGHLEN GUY, DIR; BICENTENNIAL PARADE OF AMERICAN MUSIC; 3224 MORRISON ST, NW; WASHINGTON, DC 20015. (#4500-13).

FEB 23, '76 - FEB 23, '78. THE FEDERAL CITY: PLANS AND REALITIES. EXHIBITION FOCUSING ON THE ARCHITECTURAL & PLANNING HISTORY OF THE MALL AREA FROM 1776 TO THE PRESENT. AT THE ORIGINAL SMITHSONIAN INSTITUTION BUILDING. (NAT'L). WILCOMB WASHBURN; SMITHSONIAN, NCPC & CFA; 1000 JEFFERSON DR SW; WASHINGTON, DC 20560. (#1769-1).

FEB 25 - OCT 31, '76. SIGNS OF LIFE: SYMBOLS IN THE AMERICAN CITY. THE EXHIBITION WILL EXAMINE THE SYMBOLS & SIGNS IN THE DOMESTIC, COMMERCIAL, & CIVIC SECTORS OF OUR CULTURE; DISCUSSIING THEIR ORIGINS & EVOLUTIONS OVER THE LAST 200 YRS & SUGGESTING THEIR GREATER MEANING AS CULTURAL ARTIFACTS. AT NE CORNER OF 17TH & PENN AVE, NW. (NAT'L). RENWICK GALLERY; SMITHSONIAN INSTITUTION; NATIONAL COLL OF FINE ARTS; WASHINGTON, DC 20560. (#1767-1).

FEB 28, '76. POLISH MIME BALLET THEATRE. LIVE PERFORMANCE AT LISNER AUDITORIUM. (INT'L). CULTURAL ATTACHE; EMBASSY OF POLAND; 2640 16TH ST; WASHINGTON, DC 20009. (#200010-48).

FEB 29 - ??, '76. PRAGUE CHAMBER ORCHESTRA PERFORMS. LIVE PERFORMANCE. (INT'L). CULTURAL ATTACHE; EMBASSY OF CHECKOSLOVAKIA; 3900 LINNEAN AVE; WASHINGTON, DC 20008. (#200010-47).

FEB '76 - CONTINUING . SYMBOLS IN THE CITY. EXHIBIT OF SIGNS & SYMBOLS FROM THE HOME, THE STRIP, & THE STREET. GOAL IS TO DEMONSTRATE THE IMPACT OF DESIGN ELEMENTS ON LIFE-STYLES. AT RENWICK GALLERY. (NAT'L). SUSAN HAMILTON, BIC COOR; SMITHSONIAN INSTITUTION; SMITHSONIAN INSTITUTION RM 231; WASHINGTON, DC 20560. (#7907-3).

MAR 1 - 31, '76. AMERICAN IRISH MONTH. CONTINUING ETHNIC CULTURE IN DANCE, CRAFTS, PAINTING, MUSIC, THEATRE & ATHLETICS; CEREMONIES & EDUCATIONAL EXCHANGES BY AMERICAN IRISH BICENTENNIAL COMMITTEE AFFILIATES AND OTHER IRISH AMERICAN GROUPS. AT MALL AREA IN WASH DC, OTHER US CITIES NOT YET DETERMINED. (INT'L). JOSEPH F O'CONNOR; AMERICAN IRISH BICENTENNIAL COMMITTEE; 1629 K ST NW; WASHINGTON, DC 20006. (#2192-1).

MAR 4, '76. BICENTENNIAL PARADE OF AMERICAN MUSIC HONORS LOUISIANA. LIVE PERFORMANCE AT JOHN F KENNEDY MEMORIAL CENTER. (REGN'L). MRS CLIFTON C SEALE, DIR; BICENTENNIAL PARADE OF AMERICAN MUSIC; 4674 FRANKLIN AVE; NEW ORLEANS, LA 70122. (#4500-14).

MAR 7 - APR 3, '76. 'AMERICA IN THE WORLD' - THE AMERICAN ISSUES FORUM. TOPICS:MAR 7-13 'THE AMERICAN 'DREAM' AMONG NATIONS';MAR 14-20 'THE ECONOMIC DIMENSION';MAR 21-27 ' A POWER IN THE WORLD';MAR 28 -APR 3 'A NATION AMONG NATIONS'.THE CONDUCT OF OUR FOREIGN AFFAIRS PRESENTS CONTRASTS AS DRAMATIC AS ANY IN OUR NATIONAL EXPERIENCE. AT NATION-WIDE TV & RADIO,'COURSES BY NEWSPAPER' & DISCUSSION GROUPS. (NAT'L). OFFICE OF THE CHAIRMAN; NATIONAL ENDOWMENT FOR THE HUMANITIES; 806 15TH STREET, N. W.; WASHINGTON, DC 20506. (#1976-8).

MAR 10, '76. DU SYMPHONY NATIONAL BICENTENNIAL EVENTS. ALSO LOCAL PERFORMANCES & PERFORMANCE AT NME CONFERENCE IN ATLANTIC CITY. AT KENNEDY CENTER. (NAT'L). R RUSSELL PORTER, COORD; UNIV OF DENVER COLLEGE OF ARTS & SCIENCES; UNIV OF DENVER, A & S OFFICE; DENVER, CO 80210. (#200007-178).

MAR 11, '76 - MAR 31, '77. A NATION OF NATIONS. AN EXHIBIT OF THE CONTRIBUTIONS A WORLD OF PEOPLE MADE IN CREATING A NEW NATION WITH A NEW IDENTITY. LARGEST EVER PRODUCED BY SMITHSONIAN OCCUPYING THE ENTIRE WEST 2ND FLOOR, MUSEUM OF HISTORY & TECHNOLOGY. (INT'L). MRS SUSAN HAMILTON; SMITHSONIAN INSTITUTION; 1000 JEFFERSON DR SW; WASHINGTON, DC 20560. (#101-1).

MAR 13 - 17, '76. CAMELBACK HIGH SCHOOL BAND & CHOIR TO PERFORM IN WASHINGTON, DC. BAND WILL TOUR DC AND PARTICIPATE IN ST PATRICKS DAY PARADE ON MARCH 14, 1976; CHOIR IS OFFICIAL PARADE CHOIR AND WILL SING AT THE REVIEW STAND PRECEDING START OF PARADE. CHOIR WILL ALSO GIVE CONCERT IN ST MATTHEWS CHURCH. BAND CONCERTS IN KENNEDY CENTER & ELLIPSE. AT ST PATRICK'S DAY REVIEWING STAND, ST MATTHEWS CHURCH, KENNEDY CENTER. (REGN'L). MARY HERTZKE, PRESIDENT; CAMELBACK HIGH SCHOOL PARENT MUSIC ASSOC; 2149 E LAWRENCE RD; PHOENIX, AZ 85016. (#104249-1).

MAR 13 - JULY 18, '76. EXHIBIT: ART FROM ZAIRE: 100 MASTERWORKS - MUSEUM OF AFRICAN ART. LARGEST AND MOST IMPORTANT LOAN OF TRADITIONAL ART EVER MADE BY AN AFRICAN NATION; SCULPTURE REPRESENTS 26 DIFFERENT CULTURES IN ZAIRE AND HAS BEEN GATHERED FROM THE INSTITUTE OF NATIONAL MUSEUM OF ZAIRE (IMNZ) IN KINSHASA. HOURS 12-5 PM ON WEEKENDS. AT 318 A ST, NE. (INT'L). NANCY CROMWELL, DIRECTOR; MUSEUM OF AFRICAN ART; 318 A ST, NE; WASHINGTON, DC 20002. (#105648-2).

MAR 15, '76. BICENTENNIAL PARADE OF AMERICAN MUSIC HONORS INDIANA. LIVE PERFORMANCE AT JOHN F KENNEDY MEMORIAL CENTER. (REGN'L). MRS HARLEY N EDINGTON; BICENTENNIAL PARADE OF AMERICAN MUSIC; 5201 N NEW JERSEY ST; INDIANAPOLIS, IN 46220. (#4500-15).

MAR 15 - OCT 1, '76. BICENTENNIAL INFORMATION CENTER. FACILITY WILL PROVIDE VISITOR INFORMATION, TRAVELERS AID SVCS FOR HANDICAPPED, INFANT CARE, HOUSING HOTLINE, FOREIGN VISITOR SVC DESK A BOOKSTORE, AND A SEATING AREA. ALSO A DISPLAY AREA FOR PRESIDENTIAL GIFTS. AT IN DEPT OF COMMERCE'S GREAT HALL, ON E ST BETWEEN 14 & 15 STS.. (NAT'L). BICENTENNIAL COORDINATOR; NATIONAL PARK SERVICE; 1100 OHIO DR SW; WASHINGTON, DC 20242. (#1482-1).

MAR 16 - OCT 23, '76. WHITE HOUSE VISITOR PROGRAM. A TICKETING PROGRAM PROVIDING ENTERTAINMENT AND SEATING ON ELIPSE FOR THE CROWDS WAITING TO TOUR THE WHITE HOUSE. VISITORS CAN RELAX AND ENJOY MILITARY BANDS AS WELL AS HIGH SCHOOL AND COLLEGE BANDS AND CHORUSES. AT PRESIDENTS' PARK ELLIPSE. (NAT'L). NATIONAL CAPITAL PARKS; NATIONAL PARK SERVICE; 1100 OHIO DRIVE, SW; WASHINGTON, DC 20242. (#6728-262).

MAR 17, '76. 1976 ST PATRICK'S DAY PARADE. PARADE AT CONSTITUTION AVE, MALL & ELLIPSE. (REGN'L). SEAN D COAKLEY, CHAIRMAN; IRISH-AMERICAN BICENTENNIAL COMMITTEE; SUITE 427, 1825 CONN AVE, NW; WASHINGTON, DC 20009. (#7917-2).

MAR 17 - 18, '76. VISIT BY PRIME MINISTER LIAM COSGRAVE OF IRELAND. CEREMONY. (INT'L). CULTURAL ATTACHE; EMBASSY OF IRELAND; 2234 MASSACHUSETTS AVE; WASHINGTON, DC 20008. (#200010-32).

MAR 18 - 28, '76. 'DREAMS ON RUE STREET' - A COMMUNITY BICENTENNIAL PRODUCTION. THE PLAY CENTERS AROUND THE CONTRIBUTIONS OF BLACK MENIAL WORKERS IN THE BUILDING OF AMERICA. P.S. PRODUCTIONS IS CO-SPONSOR. ON MARCH 20, 21 & 28 WILL BE AT 2:30PM. WILL EMPHASIZE COMMUNITY PARTICIPATION, AS WELL AS FAMED PERFORMERS & LOCAL GROUPS. AT PAUL JR HIGH, 8TH & OGLETHORPE STS, NW. (LOCAL). PRINCIPAL; PAUL JR HIGH COMMUNITY SCHOOL; 8 OGLETHORPE ST, NW; WASHINGTON, DC 20011. (#104798-1).

MAR 20 - 21, '76. 'THE BRITISH ARE COMING!' - BRITISH MILITARY BAND PERFORMANCE. TOUR OF UNITED STATES BY TWO BRITISH REVOLUTIONARY WAR REGIMENTS: THE BLACK WATCH, AND THE ROYAL MARINES. REGTL BANDS TOTALLING APPROX 140 OFFICERS & MEN IN CEREMONIAL UNIFORM. AT DC NATIONAL GUARD ARMORY. (INT'L). CHARLES K JONES, PRES; COLUMBIA ARTISTS FESTIVALS CORP; 165 W 57TH ST; NEW YORK, NY 10019. (#6532-43).

MAR 23, '76. REGIONAL WORKSHOP ON TOURISM FOR CONGRESSMEN & SENATORS. THE METROPOLITAN AREA EXHIBITS EXPLAINING ALL LOCAL INFORMATION IS AVAILABLE TO THE PUBLIC IN THE D C AREA. PROGRAM AIMED AT TOURISM IN WASHINGTON, MARYLAND & VIRGINIA. AT CANNON OFFICE BLDG. (NAT'L). KATE MARTIN, ARCHIVIST; JOINT COMMITTEE ON BICENTENNIAL FOR CONGRESS; 44 COURTHOUSE SQUARE; ROCKVILLE, MD 20850. (#200010-34).

MAR 29, '76. BICENTENNIAL PARADE OF AMERICAN MUSIC HONORS MISSISSIPPI. LIVE PERFORMANCE AT JOHN F KENNEDY MEMORIAL CENTER. (REGN'L). MISS ERNESTINE FERRELL; BICENTENNIAL PARADE OF AMERICAN MUSIC; BOX 771; JACKSON, MS 39205. (#4500-16).

MAR 30 - 31, '76. SAGA OF OLD WEST WITH HASTINGS COLLEGE BAND. LIVE PERFORMANCE AT WHITE HOUSE VISITORS CENTER 3/30 & LINCOLN MEMORIAL POOL 3/31. (LOCAL). DUANE E JOHNSON, DIR; CITY OF HASTINGS; 121 E 13TH; HASTINGS, NE 68901. (#25044-3).

MAR '76. AMERICAN IRISH ART EXHIBIT. AN ART EXHIBITION IN WASHINGTON OF AMERICAN-IRISH AND IRISH PAINTERS FEATURING ALL TYPES OF THIS ART FORM TO PROMOTE THE

WASHINGTON — CONTINUED

ARTISTS BY ALLOWING THEIR WORKS TO BE SOLD AND TO GIVE THEM PUBLIC ATTENTION. AT NOT YET DECIDED. (REGN'L). JOSEPH F O'CONNOR; AMERICAN IRISH BICENTENNIAL COMMITTEE; 1629 K ST NW; WASHINGTON, DC 20006. (#2191-1).

MAR '76. VISIT BY KING HUSSEIN OF JORDAN. CONFERENCE. (INT'L). CULTURAL ATTACHE; EMBASSY OF JORDAN; 2319 WYOMING AVE; WASHINGTON, DC 20008. (#200010-26).

APR 1, '76. WASHINGTON MONUMENT ORIENTATION CENTER OPENING. A GIFT FROM THE EASTMAN KODAK COMPANY TO THE NATION. THE CENTER IS A 300 SEAT THEATRE THAT WILL SHOW A FILM ENTITLED 'WASHINGTON THE MAN'. THE SPECIALLY CREATED 14 MINUTE FILM PRODUCED BY EASTMAN KODAK WILL BE SHOWN FREE OF CHARGE FROM 9AM TO 9PM DAILY ON THE MALL. AT GROUNDS OF THE WASHINGTON MONUMENT. (REGN'L). NATIONAL CAPITAL PARKS; NATIONAL PARK SERVICE; 1100 OHIO DRIVE, SW; WASHINGTON, DC 20042. (#6728-263).

APR 1 - 5, '76. 'HENRY MOORE: PRINTS, 1969-1974' - EXHIBITION. AN EXHIBITION OF LITHOGRAPHS AND PRINTS DONE BY THE ARTIST, HENRY MOORE. AT PHILLIPS GALLERY. (LOCAL). MRS JOHN A POPE, COORD; INTERNATIONAL EXHIBITIONS FOUNDATION; 1729 H ST, NW; WASHINGTON, DC 20006. (#108964-3).

APR 1 - 25, '76. 'I HAVE A DREAM' A PLAY. A MAJOR DRAMATIC WORK OF THE EPIC STRUGGLE OF DR MARTIN LUTHER KING. EVENING PERFORMANCES TUES-THURS & FRI 730P SAT 6P & 930 PM THURS 1PM. AT FORD'S THEATER. (ST-WIDE). DIRECTOR; 511 10TH STREET NW; WASHINGTON, DC 20004. (#104887-2).

APR 1 - JUNE 27, '76. 'MAN MADE MOBILE: THE WESTERN SADDLE' EXHIBITION. EXHIBITION INCLUDES 16 SAMPLES AND 2 SLIDE PRESENTATIONS DEALING WITH THE BEAUTY & VARIETY OFFERED TO AMERICAN SETTLERS. CLOSED ON CHRISTMAS DAY. AT RENWICK GALLERY, 17TH & PENNSYLVANIA AVE, NW. (REGN'L). MARGERY BYERS, PUBL AFF; SMITHSONIAN INSTITUTION, RENWICK GALLERY OF ART; WASHINGTON, DC 20560. (#108936-2).

APR 1 - JULY 11, '76. 'BOXES & BOWLS: DECORATED CONTAINERS BY 19TH CENTURY INDIAN ARTISTS'. AN EXHIBITION OF SIGNIFICANT CREATIVE WORKS BY INDIANS OF NORTH AMERICA. CLOSED ON CHRISTMAS DAY. AT RENWICK GALLERY, 17TH & PENNSYLVANIA AVE, NW. (REGN'L). MARGERY BYERS, PUBL AFF; SMITHSONIAN INSTITUTION, RENWICK GALLERY OF ART; WASHINGTON, DC 20560. (#108936-1).

APR 1 - SEPT 12, '76. LOUISIANA TERRITORY OR LEWIS & CLARK, LOST & FOUND - PERFORMANCE. LIVE PERFORMANCE AT OUTSIDE OF JFK CENTER AND THE AREA NEAR LINCOLN MEMORIAL. (REGN'L). JACK MCQUIGGAN, EXEC. DIR; JFK CENTER FOR THE PERFORMING ARTS AND WESLEYAN UNIV. OF CONNECTICUT; 234 WEST 44TH STREET; NEW YORK, NY 10036. (#50356-1).

APR 1 - DEC 31, '76. WASHINGTON MONUMENT VISITOR CENTER OPEN TO PUBLIC. A GIFT FROM EASTMAN KODAK COMPANY TO THE NATION, A 300-SEAT THEATER THAT WILL SHOW A FILM 'WASHINGTON THE MAN'. THIS SPECIALLY CREATED 14-MINUTE FILM PRODUCED BY EASTMAN KODAK COMPANY WILL BE SHOWN FREE FROM 9 AM TO 9 PM DAILY ON THE MALL. AT GROUNDS OF THE WASHINGTON MONUMENT. (REGN'L). NATIONAL CAPITAL PARKS; NATIONAL PARK SERVICE; 1100 OHIO DRIVE, SW; WASHINGTON, DC 20242. (#6728-264).

APR 2 - 5, '76. MEETING OF FIRST BLACK FRATERNITY WITH A BICENTENNIAL THEME. OMEGA PSI PHI FRATERNITY BICENTENNIAL MEETING - DC. 1ST BLACK FRATERNITY. FOUNDED AT HOWARD UNIV. WILL HOLD ANNUAL MEETING IN WASHINGTON IN 1976 WITH BICENTENNIAL THEME. WILL INCLUDE BOTH SOCIAL & BUSINESS SESSIONS. AT INTERNATIONAL INN, WASHINGTON, DC. (LOCAL). EDWARD A CLEMENT; WASHINGTON AREA CHAPTERS OMEGA PSI PHI FRATERNITY, INC; 7601 CHESAPEAKE ST; LANDOVER, MD 20785. (#2779-501).

APR 2 - 10, '76. DOWNTOWN THEATRE FESTIVAL. LIVE PERFORMANCE. (LOCAL). ALICE M DENNY, DIRECTOR; WASHINGTON PROJECT FOR THE ARTS; 1227 G ST, NW; WASHINGTON, DC 20005. (#23726-1).

APR 3, '76. BICENT GOLF & BOWLING TOURNAMENTS & BUSINESS SESSIONS. GOLD TOURNAMENT AT PRINCE GEORGE'S COUNTY COUNTRY CLUB AT 7:30 AM. BOWLING TOURNAMENT AT BRUNSWICK TEN PIN LANES IN BETHESDA AT 9 AM. AT BRUNSWICK RIVER BOWL TEN PIN LANES, 5225 RIVER RD, BETHESDA, MD. (LOCAL). EDWARD A CLEMENT; WASHINGTON AREA CHAPTERS OMEGA PSI PHI FRATERNITY, INC; 7601 CHESAPEAKE ST; LANDOVER, MD 20785. (#2779-502).

APR 3, '76. CARD PARTY, FASHION SHOW & COCKTAIL HOUR. QUETTE ACTIVITIES: SHOPPING TOUR, CARD PARTY, & HOSPITALITY SUITE. 1ST BLACK FRATERNITY. FOUNDED AT HOWARD UNIV. WILL HOLD ANNUAL MEETING IN WASHINGTON IN 1976 WITH BICENTENNIAL THEME. WILL INCLUDE BOTH SOCIAL & BUSINESS SESSIONS. AT INTERNATIONAL INN, WASHINGTON, DC. (LOCAL). EDWARD A CLEMENT; WASHINGTON AREA CHAPTERS OMEGA PSI PHI FRATERNITY, INC; 7601 CHESAPEAKE ST; LANDOVER, MD 20785. (#2779-504).

APR 3, '76. PERFORMANCE BY LUCIANO PAVAROTTI. LIVE PERFORMANCE AT KENNEDY CENTER. (INT'L). CULTURAL ATTACHE; EMBASSY OF ITALY; 1601 FULLER ST; WASHINGTON, DC 20009. (#200010-44).

APR 3, '76. TALENT HUNT WINNERS PROGRAM (UNDERGRAD ACTIVITIES AT HOWARD UNIV). TALENT HUNT AT INTERNATIONAL INN FROM 7-9 PM. UNDERGRADUATE ACTIVITIES AT HOWARD UNIVERSITY FROM 9AM - 12 NOON. AT TALENT HUNT, INTERNATIONAL INN; UNDERGRAD ACTIVITIES AT HOWARD. (LOCAL). EDWARD A CLEMENT; WASHINGTON AREA CHAPTERS OMEGA PSI PHI FRATERNITY, INC; 7601 CHESAPEAKE ST; LANDOVER, MD 20785. (#2779-503).

APR 3 - 10, '76. HUGH O'BRIAN YOUTH FOUNDATION LEADERSHIP SEMINAR. A LEADERSHIP SEMINAR FOR HIGH SCHOOL SOPHOMORES PROVIDING IN DEPTH HUMANIZED APPRECIATION OF THE SOCIAL, ECONOMIC & TECHNOLOGICAL DEVELOPMENT OF THE NATION & THE OPPORTUNITIES AHEAD IN CENTURY III. AT SHERATON PARK HOTEL, WASH, DC. (INT'L). HUGH O'BRIAN, PRESIDENT; HUGH O'BRIAN YOUTH FOUNDATION; 132 S RODEO DR; BEVERLY HILLS, CA 90212. (#7933-1).

APR 4, '76. BUSINESS SESSION, MEMORIAL SERVICES, TOURS & COCKTAIL HOUR. CHAPEL, FOUNDERS MEMORIAL VISIT & HOSPITALITY HOUR. DR BENJAMIN E MAYS, SPEAKER. AT HOWARD UNIVERSITY, WASHINGTON, DC. (LOCAL). EDWARD A CLEMENT; WASHINGTON AREA CHAPTERS OMEGA PSI PHI FRATERNITY, INC; 7601 CHESAPEAKE ST; LANDOVER, MD 20785. (#2779-505).

APR 4, '76. PERFORMANCE BY I MUSICI DI ROMA. LIVE PERFORMANCE AT KENNEDY CENTER. (INT'L). CULTURAL ATTACHE; EMBASSY OF ITALY; 1601 FULLER ST; WASHINGTON, DC 20009. (#200010-45).

APR 4 - 7, '76. BICENTENNIAL EDUCATIONAL EXPOSITION. EXHIBITION OF CURRENT PROGRAMS IN OPERATION IN THE PUBLIC SCHOOLS, EDUCATIONAL MATERIALS IN USE IN THE SCHOOLS & A SPECIAL EXHIBIT HIGHLIGHTING HISTORY OF PUBLIC SCHOOL SYSTEMS IN DC. ALSO WILL HAVE EVENING EVENTS. (LOCAL). GORDON OLSON, COORD; DC PUBLIC SCHOOLS; 415 12TH ST, NW, RM 1108; WASHINGTON, DC 20004. (#25628-1).

APR 4 - MAY 1, '76. 'GROWING UP IN AMERICA' - THE AMERICAN ISSUES FORUM. TOPICS: APR 4-10 'THE AMERICAN FAMILY'; APR 11-17 'EDUCATION FOR WORK & LIFE'; APR 18-24 'IN GOD WE TRUST'; APR 25-MAY 1 'A SENSE OF BELONGING' A UNIQUE MIXING OF PEOPLES & RELIGION, A VIRGIN LAND, LOFTY IDEALS, A NEW FORM OF GOVT HAVE MOLDED OUR SOCIETY & PEOPLE. AT NATION-WIDE TV & RADIO, 'COURSES BY NEWSPAPER' & DISCUSSION GROUPS. (NAT'L). OFFICE OF THE CHAIRMAN; NATIONAL ENDOWMENT FOR THE HUMANITIES; 806 15TH ST NW; WASHINGTON, DC 20506. (#1976-9).

APR 5, '76. BICENTENNIAL PARADE OF AMERICAN MUSIC HONORS ILLINOIS. LIVE PERFORMANCE AT JOHN F KENNEDY MEMORIAL CENTER. (REGN'L). P GEORGE PRESCOTT, DIR; BICENTENNIAL PARADE OF AMERICAN MUSIC; 9424 THROOP ST; CHICAGO, IL 60620. (#4500-17).

APR 5 - 7, '76. INTERNATIONAL CONFERENCE ON NOISE CONTROL ENGINEERING. CONFERENCE AT SHOREHAM-AMERICANA, WASHINGTON, DC. (INT'L). DR MICHAEL J OSLAC, CHMN; INTER NOISE 76 ARL/PSU; BOX 30; STATE COLLEGE, PA 16801. (#103000-1).

APR 6, '76. LBJ MEMORIAL GROVE DEDICATION. AN OFFICIAL NATIONAL MEMORIAL TO THE LATE PRESIDENT JOHNSON, A GROVE OF WHITE PINES WITH BICYCLE PATHS, WALKING TRAILS AND A STONE MONOLITH. (NAT'L). NATIONAL CAPITAL PARKS; NATIONAL PARK SERVICE; 1100 OHIO DR, SW; WASHINGTON, DC 20042. (#6728-261).

APR 6 - 7, '76. THE MUSIC OF WILLIAM SCHUMAN, SYMPHONY NO 10 & LAMENTATION. LIVE PERFORMANCE AT JOHN F KENNEDY CENTER FOR THE PERFORMING ARTS. (REGN'L). MRS HELEN C SHEERAN, DIR; NATIONAL SYMPHONY ORCHESTRA ASSOC; NATIONAL SYMPHONY ORCHESTRA; WASHINGTON, DC 20566. (#102435-1).

APR 6 - 7, '76. MUSICAL: 'PORGY AND BESS'. THE MUSICAL WILL BE DIRECTED BY MR JAMES HALL. AT PAUL JR HIGH - 8TH & OGLETHORPE STS, NW. (LOCAL). DOROTHY E GASSAWAY; PAUL JR HIGH COMMUNITY SCHOOL; 8TH & OGLETHORPE STS, NW; WASHINGTON, DC 20011. (#102790-1).

APR 9 - NOV 13, '76. 'ABROAD IN AMERICA: VISITORS TO THE NEW NATION, 1776-1914'. EXHIBIT BUILT AROUD 28 FOREIGN VISITORS FROM THE REVOLUTION'S TIME THROUGH 1914 WHO CAME HERE SPECIFICALLY TO LOOK US OVER BUT NOT STAY. THESE ARE THEIR REACTIONS. AT NATL PORTRAIT GALLERY, 8TH & F STS, NW. (NAT'L). JIM MAHONEY; SMITHSONIAN INSTITUTE; SMITHSONIAN INSTITUTE; WASHINGTON, DC 20560. (#106374-2).

APR 10, '76. BRATTLEBORO HS BAND TRIP TO CHERRY BLOSSOM FESTIVAL. PARADE. (LOCAL). J WAYNE CORBEIL, CHAIRMAN; BRATTLEBORO BICENTENNIAL COMMITTEE; 230 MAIN ST; BRATTLEBORO, VT 05301. (#24894-1).

APR 10, '76. CHERRY BLOSSOM PARADE. PARADE AT PENNSYLVANIA AVE. (LOCAL). BOB MIRHALSKI; DOWNTOWN JAYCEES; 1344 G ST, NW; WASHINGTON, DC 20005. (#103416-12).

APR 10 - 11, '76. CATHEDRAL CHORAL SOCIETY CONCERTS. CONCERTS FEATURING MUSIC OF AMERICAN COMPOSER JOHN CORIGLIANO. PART OF BICENTENNIAL PROGRAM OF WASHINGTON CATHEDRAL. AT HOURS: 4/10 - 8:00PM; 4/11 - 4:00PM.. (ST-WIDE). R WAYNE DIRKSEN; THE WASHINGTON CATHEDRAL; MT ST ALBAN; WASHINGTON, DC 20016. (#5619-502).

APR 10 - 16, '76. NATIONAL CHERRY BLOSSOM FESTIVAL. ANNUAL CHERRY BLOSSOM FESTIVAL INCLUDES A PARADE ON 4/10, LIGHTING OF JAPANESE LANTERN AT TIDAL BASIN, A BALL ON 4/10, AND OTHER EVENTS THROUGHOUT THE WEEK. AT CONSTITUTION AVE, 6TH TO 19TH, DOWNTOWN WASHINGTON. (NAT'L). BILL HARSHBARGER, DIR; THE WASHINGTON, DC JAYCEES; 1005 DUKE DR; YORK, NE 68467. (#25800-1).

APR 10, '76 - APR 10, '77. AFRICAN CONTEMPORARY ART EXHIBITION 1976. SEMINARS, WORKSHOPS, LECTURES. EXHIBITION TO TRAVEL. AT HOWARD UNIVERSITY ART DEPARTMENT PARKING A. (REGN'L). ART DEPARTMENT HOWARD UNI; NATIONAL ENDOWMENT FOR THE ARTS HOWARD UNIVERSITY; 2400 6TH ST NW; WASHINGTON, DC 20015. (#2964-1).

APR 11 - 12, '76. FESTIVAL AT KENNEDY CENTER. LIVE PERFORMANCE AT KENNEDY CENTER. (LOCAL). JAMES HATCHER, DIR; UNIV OF ALABAMA-BIRMINGHAM; TOWN & GOWN THEATER; BIRMINGHAM, AL 35294. (#24729-1).

APR 12, '76. BICENTENNIAL PARADE OF AMERICAN MUSIC HONORS ALABAMA. IN THE FOYER: MOBILE JAZZ SYMPHONY, GRISSOM CONCERT BAND & PUPILS FROM THE ALABAMA SCHOOL OF FINE ARTS. IN THE CONCERT HALL: THE BIRMINGHAM CIVIC CHORUS & THE CADEK STRING QUARTET WITH PIANO. AT JOHN F KENNEDY MEMORIAL CENTER. (REGN'L). MRS O R GRIMES, DIR; NATL FEDERATION OF MUSIC CLUBS, NATL MUSIC COUNCIL & EXXON; 601 TURRENTINE AVE; GADSDEN, AL 35901. (#4500-18).

APR 12 - 14, '76. ASIS BICENTENNIAL CONFERENCE - AMERICA IN THE INFORMATION AGE. SYNCON ON INFORMATION & NATIONAL DECISION-MAKING, MOCK CONGRESSIONAL HEARINGS, RATIONAL DEBATE ON FREEDOM OF INFORMATION, AND EXHIBITS & ARTIFACTS OF INFORMATION TECHNOLOGY 1776-1976. NATIONALLY-KNOWN FIGURES FOR KEYNOTES, DEBATE & MOCK HEARING. AT GRAND BALLROOM, SHERATON-PARK HOTEL. CONF. ENDS 12:30 WED.. (NAT'L). JAMES W MORENTZ, JR, ASIS; AMERICAN SOCIETY FOR INFORMATION SCIENCE; 1155 16TH ST NW; WASHINGTON, DC 20036. (#104305-1).

APR 16 - 18, '76. BLACKS IN COMMUNICATION. FESTIVAL. (LOCAL). GLORIA PRYOR WALKER; CLARK COLLEGE; 3168 G CANDLEWOOD DRIVE; EAST POINT, GA 30344. (#10875-5).

APR 16 - JUNE 6, '76. BICENTENNIAL ART PROGRAM OF DEPT OF THE INTERIOR. ARTISTS WILL BE COMMISSIONED TO DEPICT THE NATURAL AND HISTORIC PROPERTIES ADMINISTERED BY THE DEPARTMENT OF THE INTERIOR. EXHIBIT WILL OPEN AND TOUR SPRING OF 1976. AT CORCORAN GALLERY OF ART. (REGN'L). MRS JEAN HAWKINS; DEPT OF THE INTERIOR; 18TH & C STS NW; WASHINGTON, DC 20240. (#1239-1).

APR 17, '76. DEDICATION OF WASHINGTON CATHEDRAL NAVE & WEST ROSE WINDOW. CEREMONY, OPENING, FESTIVAL. (ST-WIDE). R WAYNE DIRKSEN; THE WASHINGTON CATHEDRAL; MT ST ALBANS; WASHINGTON, DC 20016. (#5619-501).

APR 18, '76. NETHERLANDS CHAMBER ORCHESTRA. LIVE PERFORMANCE. (INT'L). DIRECTOR; ROYAL NETHERLANDS EMBASSY; 4200 LINNEAN AVE, NW; WASHINGTON, DC 20008. (#200010-3).

APR 19, '76. BICENTENNIAL PARADE OF AMERICAN MUSIC HONORS MAINE. LIVE PERFORMANCE AT JOHN F KENNEDY MEMORIAL CENTER. (REGN'L). MRS LEWIS H KRIGER, DIR; BICENTENNIAL PARADE OF AMERICAN MUSIC; 98 BEDFORD ST; PORTLAND, ME 04102. (#4500-19).

APR 19, '76. MAINE DAY BICENTENNIAL SALUTE TO THE STATES. LIVE PERFORMANCE. (REGN'L). GERTRUDE KRIGER, DIRECTOR; MAINE FEDERATION OF MUSIC CLUBS; 98 BEDFORD ST; PORTLAND, ME 04101. (#22281-1).

APR 19, '76. PERFORMANCE BY THE DON COSSACKS OF THE RESTOV FOLK DANCE COMPANY. LIVE PERFORMANCE AT KENNEDY CENTER. (INT'L). CULTURAL ATTACHE; EMBASSY OF THE SOVIET UNION; 1125 16TH ST; WASHINGTON, DC 20036. (#200010-50).

APR 20 - 23, '76. MAJOR LECTURES ON SHAKESPEARE & USA. PART OF SHAKESPEARE IN AMERICA PROJ OF THE FOLGER LIBRARY; SCHOLARLY MEETINGS, LECTURES, DEBATES, ETC, BY WORLD'S LEADING CRITICS, EDUCATORS, PRODUCERS, RESEARCHERS & THINKERS FROM A VARIETY OF DISCIPLINES FOCUSING ON US ROLE IN PRESERVING ENGL CULTURAL HERITAGE. AT FOLGER LIBRARY & STATLER HILTON HOTEL. (NAT'L). O B HARDISON; FOLGER SHAKESPEARE LIBRARY; 201 E CAPITOL ST, SE; WASHINGTON, DC 20003. (#6883-502).

APR 20 - 25, '76. SHAKESPEARIAN THEATRE PERFORMANCES AT THE FOLGER THEATER. PART OF SHAKESPEARE IN AMERICA PROJ OF THE FOLGER LIBRARY; SCHOLARLY MEETINGS, LECTURES, DEBATES, ETC, BY WORLD'S LEADING CRITICS, EDUCATORS, PRODUCERS, RESEARCHERS & THINKERS FROM A VARIETY OF DISCIPLINES FOCUSING ON US ROLE IN PRESERVING ENGL CULTURAL HERITAGE. AT SAT & SUN MATINEE AT 2:00PM. (NAT'L). O B HARDISON; FOLGER SHAKESPEARE LIBRARY; 201 E CAPITOL ST, SE; WASHINGTON, DC 20003. (#6883-503).

APR 22, '76. CONCERT AT THE FOLGER SHAKESPEARE LIBRARY. SHAKESPEARE IN AMERICA PROJ OF THE FOLGER LIBRARY. SCHOLARLY MEETINGS, LECTURES, DEBATES, ETC, BY WORLD'S LEADING CRITICS, EDUCATORS, PRODUCERS, RESEARCHERS & THINKERS FROM A VARIETY OF DISCIPLINES FOCUSING ON US ROLE IN PRESERVING ENGL CULTURAL HERITAGE. (INT'L). O B HARDISON; FOLGER SHAKESPEARE LIBRARY; 201 E CAPITOL ST, SE; WASHINGTON, DC 20003. (#6883-504).

APR 22 - 23, '76. '200 YEARS OF AMERICAN WOMEN' SCHOLARLY CONFERENCE. SEMI-ANNUAL SERIES ESTABLISHED IN 1967. BICENTENNIAL THEMES INCLUDE A CONFERENCE ON RESEARCH IN AMERICAN REVOLUTIONARY HISTORY EXPLORING THE 'MEANING' OF THAT ERA. AT NATL ARCHIVES BLDG, 8TH ST & PA AVE, NW, WASH, DCC. (NAT'L). DR MABEL DEUTRICH; NATIONAL ARCHIVES; NATIONAL ARCHIVES; WASHINGTON, DC 20408. (#59-1).

APR 23, '76. ANNUAL SHAKESPEARE BIRTHDAY LECTURE AT FOLGER LIBRARY. SHAKESPEARE IN AMERICA PROJ OF THE FOLGER LIBRARY. SCHOLARLY MEETINGS, LECTURES, DEBATES, ETC, BY WORLD'S LEADING CRITICS, EDUCATORS, PRODUCERS, RESEARCHERS & THINKERS FROM A VARIETY OF DISCIPLINES FOCUSING ON US ROLE IN PRESERVING ENGL CULTURAL HERITAGE. (INT'L). O B HARDISON; FOLGER SHAKESPEARE LIBRARY; 201 E CAPITOL ST, SE; WASHINGTON, DC 20003. (#6883-505).

APR 23, '76 - MAR 31, '77. SHAKESPEARE IN AMERICA EXHIBIT. PART OF SHAKESPEARE IN AMERICA PROJ OF THE FOLGER LIBRARY; SCHOLARLY MEETINGS, LECTURES, DEBATES, ETC, BY WORLD'S LEADING CRITICS, EDUCATORS, PRODUCERS, RESEARCHERS & THINKERS FROM A VARIETY OF DISCIPLINES FOCUSING ON US ROLE IN PRESERVING ENGL CULTURAL HERITAGE. (NAT'L). O B HARDISON; FOLGER SHAKESPEARE LIBRARY; 201 E CAPITOL ST, SE; WASHINGTON, DC 20003. (#6883-501).

WASHINGTON — CONTINUED

APR 25, '76. ELIZABETHAN LITURGY -PART OF INTERNATL SHAKESPEARE FESTIVAL. COINCIDES WITH THE SHAKESPEARE WORLD CONGRESS. LITURGY FROM 1559 PRAYER BOOK. ENGLISH SPEAKING UNION, AMERICAN SHAKESPEARE SOC, INTERNATIONAL SHAKESPEARE SOC, & STRATFORD-ON-AVON TRUST REPRESENTED PART OF BICENTENNIAL PROGRAM OF WASHINGTON CATHEDRAL. (INT'L). R WAYNE DIRKSEN; THE WASHINGTON CATHEDRAL & FOLGER SHAKESPEARE LIBRARY; MT ST ALBAN; WASHINGTON, DC 20016. (#5619-506).

APR 25, '76. MARKET DAY STREET FAIR. FAIR AT MARKET ROW, 7TH ST.S.E.BETWEEN PENN.&N.C.AVES.. (LOCAL). RONALD E COOPER ASSOC DIR; FRIENDSHIP HOUSE ASSOCIATION, INC; 619 D ST, SE; WASHINGTON, DC 20003. (#5605-2).

APR 26, '76. BICENTENNIAL PARADE OF AMERICAN MUSIC HONORS MISSOURI. JEFFERSON CITY HIGH SCHOOL BAND HAS BEEN CHOSEN TO REPRESENT THE STATE OF MISSOURI FOR THE BICENTENNIAL PARADE OF AMERICAN MUSIC. UNIV OF MISSOURI SINGERS WILL ALSO PERFORM. AT JOHN F KENNEDY MEMORIAL CENTER. (REGN'L). MRS ROBERT MENEES, DIR; BICENTENNIAL PARADE OF AMERICAN MUSIC; 55 JANSSEN PL; KANSAS CITY, MO 64109. (#4500-20).

APR 26 - 30, '76. MCCOOK COLLEGE SINGERS: WHITE HOUSE BICENTENNIAL VISITORS PROGRAM. LIVE PERFORMANCE AT PRESIDENT'S PARK, THE ELLIPSE, WASHINGTON, D C. (NAT'L). CHARLES T LAWSON, COORD; MCCOOK COMMUNITY COLLEGE; MCCOOK COMMUNITY COLLEGE; MCCOOK, NE 69001. (#25802-1).

APR 27 - AUG 15, '76. BICENTENNIAL FLAG SERIES SCULPTURES. ENORMOUS FLAG SCULPTURES BY MIMI HERBERT ARE GIANT REPLICAS OF HISTORIC AMERICAN FLAGS EXHIBITED AROUND ENTRANCE ABOVE MAIN STAIRCASE. SUPPORTED BY GRANT FROM FIRESTONE FOUNDATION, M GRUMBACHER, INC WHO DONATED MATERIALS & GULF-RESTON, INC WHO PROVIDED WORKING SPACE. AT 17TH & NEW YORK AVENUE, NW. (REGN'L). ANN CRADDOCK, P/R OFFICE; THE CORCORAN GALLERY OF ART; 17TH & NEW YORK AVE, NW; WASHINGTON, DC 22006. (#108119-4).

APR 28 - MAY 10, '76. MEMORIAL TREE PLANTING AND BICENTENNIAL EXCURSION. THE NEBRASKA STATE TREE WILL BE PLANTED ON THE CAPITOL GROUNDS IN WASHINGTON, DC; ALSO, A BUS TOUR ENROUTE WILL CARRY 96 RESIDENTS AND COVER AS MANY POINTS OF HISTORICAL INTEREST AS POSSIBLE IN TWO WEEKS. AT NATIONAL CAPITOL, WASHINGTON, DC. (REGN'L). EVERETT N REIMERS, DIR; OTOE COUNTY BICENTENNIAL COMMITTEE; 621 3RD CORSO; NEBRASKA CITY, NE 68410. (#17874-1).

APR 30, '76. GEORGE WASHINGTON'S INAUGURATION CEREMONY. CEREMONY AT WASHINGTON MONUMENT GROUNDS. (REGN'L). SPECIAL EVENTS, COORD; NPS, MILITARY DISTRICT OF WASHINGTON, WASHINGTON MONUMENT SOCIETY; 1100 OHIO DR, SW; WASHINGTON, DC 20042. (#6728-265).

APR 30 - NOV 7, '76. AMERICA AS ART. EXHIBIT AT THE NATIONAL COLLECTION OF FINE ARTS EXPLORING THE AMERCAN SCENE FROM THE ARTIST'S POINT OF VIEW OVER 200 YEARS OF PAINTING. (REGN'L). RICHARD N MURRAY; NATIONAL COLLECTION OF FINE ARTS; SMITHSONIAN INSTITUTION; WASHINGTON, DC 20560. (#344-1).

APR '76. DANTE'S INFLUENCE ON AMERICAN WRITERS. A SYMPOSIUM TRACING THE IMPACT AND INFLUENCE OF DANTE'S WORK ON AMER POETS, NOVELISTS AND ESSAYISTS, FROM REVOLUTIONARY WAR TIMES TO THE PRESENT. AT WASHINGTON,D.C.. (NAT'L). DR ANNE PAOLUCCI; THE DANTE SOCIETY OF AMERICA; BOYLSTON HALL - HARVARD UNIV; CAMBRIDGE, MA 02138. (#10946-1).

MAY 1, '76. BRITISH BICENTENNIAL HERITAGE MISSION. 8 BRITISH LEADERS, 5 OF THEM MEMBERS OF THE HOUSE OF LORDS, WILL VISIT THE U S AS PART OF BRITAIN'S OFFICIAL SALUTE TO THE BICENTENNIAL. (INT'L). DIRECTOR; BRITISH EMBASSY; 3100 MASSACHUSETTS AVE, NW; WASHINGTON, DC 20008. (#109043-3).

MAY 1, '76. LAW DAY IN THE USA. THE ACTIVITY WILL BE CELEBRATED NATIONWIDE BY MEMBERS OF THE AMERICAN BAR ASSOCIATION. AT GREAT HALL IN JUSTICE DEPT. (NAT'L). MS CHARLEEN MURPHY; DEPT OF JUSTICE; DEPT OF JUSTICE RM 4213; WASHINGTON, DC 20530. (#1901-1).

MAY 1, '76. ODORI FESTIVAL OF JAPAN VISITS WASHINGTON, DC. LIVE PERFORMANCE AT KENNEDY CENTER. (INT'L). DIRECTOR; MEL HOWARD PRESENTS; 143 E 27TH ST; NEW YORK, NY 10016. (#108965-13).

MAY 1, '76. SALUTE USA 200 BICENTENNIAL BREAKFAST. SENATOR JENNINGS RANDOLPH OF WEST VIRGINIA WILL PRESENT THE AMERICAN FLAG TO THE GEORGE WASHINGTON FAMILY DESCENDANTS. MISS ELIZABETH WASHINGTON HOPKINS WILL ACCEPT THE FLAG. GOVERNOR ENDICOTT PEABODY, FORMER GOVERNOR OF MASSACHUSETTS, WILL GIVE THE OPENING PRAYER. AT WOODNER HOTEL. (NAT'L). COL J FLOYD PARKER, COORD; INTERNATIONAL CROSSROADS - YMCA; 2121 P ST, NW; WASHINGTON, DC 20037. (#105348-1).

MAY 1 - 5, '76. CONVENTION-AMERICAN MOTHERS COMMITTEE BICENTENNIAL. AMERICAN MOTHERS COMMITTEE ANNUAL CONVENTION IN WASH,DC.GALA DINNER MAY WITH CONGRESSMEN AS GUESTS & 100 VOICE MORMON CHOIR FEATURED ENTERTAINMENT.HISTORIC MOTHER FROM EACH STATE ANNOUNCED & AMERICAN MOTHER-1976 NAMED.BICENTENNIAL HISTORY OF MOTHERS OF AMERICA. AT SHOREHAM HOTEL. (NAT'L). MRS DOROTHY LEWIS CHAIRMN; AMERICAN MOTHERS COMMITTEE INC.; 301 PARK AVE THE WALDORF; NEW YORK, NY 10022. (#50695-1).

MAY 1 - 31, '76. PAINTINGS BY GOYA ON DISPLAY AT THE NATIONAL GALLERY OF ART. EIGHT PAINTINGS BY FRANCISCO GOYA WERE LOANED FROM THE PRADO IN MADRID FOR EXHIBIT DURING THE BICENTENNIAL. AT NATIONAL GALLERY OF ART, 7 & CONSTITUTION, NW. (INT'L). INFORMATION COUNSELOR; EMBASSY OF SPAIN; 2700 15TH ST; WASHINGTON, DC 20009. (#200010-36).

MAY 1 - JUNE 27, '76. 'ELEANOR' A PLAY. AN INTIMATE PORTRAIT OF THE COURAGE, CONSCIENCE, & CHARACTER OF ELEANOR ROOSEVELT. EVENING PERFORMANCE TUESTHURS & FRI 730P; SAT 6P & 930; THURS 1P PERFORMANCES. AT FORD'S THEATER. (REGN'L). DIRECTOR; FORD'S THEATRE; 511 10TH STREET NW; WASHINGTON, DC 20004. (#104887-1).

MAY 1 - AUG 31, '76. RELIGIOUS MEETINGS. SEMINAR AT MCPHERSON SQUARE. (REGN'L). JAMES C LUCORE, DIRECTOR; DC BICENT CHRISTIAN HERITAGE CELEBRATION; 777 14TH ST, NW; WASHINGTON, DC 20005. (#107335-14).

MAY 2 - 29, '76. 'LIFE, LIBERTY, & THE PURSUIT OF HAPPINESS' - AMERICAN ISSUES FORUM. TOPICS: MAY2-8 'THE RUGGED INDIVIDUALIST'; MAY 9-15 'THE DREAM OF SUCCESS'; MAY 16-22 'THE PURSUIT OF PLEASURE'; MAY 23-29 'THE FRUITS OF WISDOM'. THESE DREAMS & PURPOSES HAVE ATTRACTED MILLIONS & HELPED INSPIRE THE NATION'S GROWTH & PROSPERITY. AT NATON-WIDE TV & RADIO, 'COURSES BY NEWSPAPER' & DISCUSSION GROUPS. (NAT'L). OFFICE OF THE CHAIRMAN; NATONAL ENDOWMENT FOR THE HUMANITIES; 806 15TH ST NW; WASHINGTON, DC 20506. (#1976-10).

MAY 3, '76. ARKANSAS' BICENTENNIAL PARADE OF AMERICAN MUSIC. THE ARKANSAS FEDERATION OF MUSIC CLUBS WILL SPONSOR ENSEMBLES FROM THE ARKANSAS SYMPHONY AT THE KENNEDY CENTER. THE PROGRAM WILL FEATURE MUSIC & COMPOSERS FROM ARKANSAS. AT KENNEDY CENTER FOR PERFORMING ARTS, MUSIC HALL. (REGN'L). MRS CLIFTON BOND, CHMN; ARKANSAS FEDERATION OF MUSIC CLUBS, INC; 360 SHELTON AVE; MONTICELLO, AR 71655. (#4500-8).

MAY 4, '76. BI-CENTENNIAL CELEBRATION AWARDS DINNER. CEREMONY. (REGN'L). MRS DOROTHY LEWIS; BICENTENNIAL PROJECT, AMERICAN MOTHERS COMMITTEE, INC; 301 PARK AVE; NEW YORK, NY 10022. (#5749-501).

MAY 4 - 5, '76. BRITISH BICENTENNIAL HERITAGE MISSION. 8 BRITISH LEADERS, 5 OF THEM MEMBERS OF THE HOUSE OF LORDS, WILL VISIT THE U S AS PART OF BRITAIN'S OFFICIAL SALUTE TO THE BICENTENNIAL. (INT'L). DIRECTOR; BRITISH EMBASSY; 3100 MASSACHUSETTS AVE, NW; WASHINGTON, DC 20008. (#109043-4).

MAY 5, '76. BICENTENNIAL PARADE OF AMERICAN MUSIC HONORS MICHIGAN. LIVE PERFORMANCE AT JOHN F KENNEDY MEMORIAL CENTER. (REGN'L). MRS RAYMOND REECE, DIR; BICENTENNIAL PARADE OF AMERICAN MUSIC; 18 POPLAR PARK; PLEASANT RDG, MI 48069. (#4500-21).

MAY 6 - 7, '76. SYMPOSIUM ON THE INCOMPLETE OR IMPERFECT REVOLUTION. A SERIES OF ANNUAL SYMPOSIA TO BE HELD EACH SPRING THROUGH 1976 ON TOPICS CONCERNING THE AMERICAN REVOLUTION. THE 1976 TOPIC WILL CONCERN THE INCOMPLETE OR IMPERFECT REVOLUTION. (NAT'L). DR JAMES HUTSON; LIBRARY OF CONGRESS; 10 FIRST ST,SE; WASHINGTON, DC 20540. (#2-3).

MAY 6 - ??, '76. PERFORMANCE BY THE MONTE CARLO NATIONAL ORCHESTRA. LIVE PERFORMANCE AT KENNEDY CENTER. (INT'L). CULTURAL ATTACHE; GOVERNMENT OF MONACO; 2535 BELMONT RD; WASHINGTON, DC 20008. (#200010-46).

MAY 8, '76. 'BICENTENNIAL RED, WHITE & BLUE'. EXHIBIT AT SHILOH BAPTIST CHURCH, 1500 9TH ST, NW. (LOCAL). FLOSSIE A LEE, CHAIRMAN; SHILOH BAPTIST CHURCH CIRCLE LEADERS COUNCIL; 202 11TH ST, SE; WASHINGTON, DC 20003. (#200010-15).

MAY 9 - 15, '76. THE BICENTENNIAL SALUTE TO SMALL BUSINESS. EACH DAY OF CONFERENCE WILL HIGHLIGHT A SALUTE BY DIFFERENT SEGMENTS OF AMERICAN SOCIETY: CONGRESS, TRADE ASSOCIATIONS AND EDUCATIONAL INSTITUTIONS. AT HYATT-REGENCY HOTEL, NEW JERSEY AVE & P ST, NW. (NAT'L). ANTHONY PARKER, COOR; SMALL BUSINESS ADMINISTRATION; 1441 L ST NW, RM 1023; WASHINGTON, DC 20416. (#102361-1).

MAY 10 - 12, '76. EMERGENCY MEDICINE IN THE 3RD CENTURY. FORUM IS TO TAKE PLACE IN 1976 AT CONFERENCE OF THOSE SPECIALISTS TO MEET IN MAY IN WASHINGTON, DC; THIS WILL FOLLOW CLINICAL MEETING IN PITTSBURGH AND MEETING OF ANESTHESIOLOGISTS IN MEXICO CITY. PAPERS PRESENTED AT CONFERENCE WILL BE PUBLISHED IN 1976. (NAT'L). DR WILLIAM R GEMMA, CHMN; DEPARTMENT OF HEALTH, EDUCATION, AND WELFARE; 5600 FISHERS LN; ROCKVILLE, MD 20852. (#14499-1).

MAY 10 - 24, '76. VISIT BY QUEEN MARGRETHE II AND PRINCE HENRICK OF DENMARK. TOUR. (INT'L). BENT SKOU, PRESS OFFICE; DANISH EMBASSY; 3200 WHITEHAVEN PKY, NW; WASHINGTON, DC 20008. (#104972-3).

MAY 10 - DEC 31, '76. HISTORIC TRIALS IN THE U S DIRTRICT COURT. ON DISPLAY ARE A NUMBER OF OLD COURT DOCUMENTS & PHOTOGRAPHS PERTINENT TO NOTEWORTHY CASES TRIED IN THE COURT SINCE ITS CREATION IN 1800. INCLUDED IN DISPLAY ARE DOCUMENTS RELATING TO LINCOLN'S ASSASSINATION CONSPIRACY CASE & GARFIELD'S ASSASSINATION CASE. AT U S COURTHOUSE 3RD & CONSTITUTION AVE, NW FIRST FLOOR CORRIDOR. (LOCAL). HELENE BEALE, MGMT ASST; UNITED STATES DISTRICT COURT FOR THE DISTRICT OF COLUMBIA; 3RD & CONSTITUTION AVE, NW; WASHINGTON, DC 20001. (#108069-1).

MAY 11, '76. BICENTENNIAL PARADE OF AMERICAN MUSIC HONORS WEST VIRGINIA. EACH CONCERT FEATURES MUSIC COMPOSED IN OR ABOUT THE FEATURED STATE PLAYED BY OUTSTANDING MUSICAL GROUPS OR SOLOISTS FROM THAT STATE. AT JOHN F KENNEDY MEMORIAL CENTER. (REGN'L). MRS JOHN MCKENZIE, DIR; NATIONAL MUSIC COUNCIL & EXXON; 602 WOODLAWN AVE; BECKLEY, WV 25801. (#4500-29).

MAY 11, '76. OPENING OF EXHIBIT OF WORKS BY CHRISTIAN GULLAGER. EXHIBIT WILL BE OPENED BY HER MAJESTY QUEEN MARGRETHE II OF DENMARK. AT NATIONAL PORTRAIT GALLERY. (INT'L). NIELS TOFT, PROJ COORD; DANISH BICENTENNIAL COMMITTEE & DANISH EMBASSY; 3200 WHITEHAVEN PKY, NW; WASHINGTON, DC 20008. (#104972-19).

MAY 11 - 17, '76. ROYAL DANISH BALLET BICENTENNIAL TOUR. LIVE PERFORMANCE, TOUR AT KENNEDY CENTER. (INT'L). NIELS TOFT, PROJ COORD; GOVERNMENT OF DENMARK & DANISH EMBASSY; 3200 WHITEHAVEN PKY, NW; WASHINGTON, DC 20008. (#104972-4).

MAY 11 - SEPT 30, '76. EXHIBIT OF WORKS OF DANISH BORN PAINTER, CHRISTIAN GULLAGER. AN EXHIBIT OF 50 PORTRAITS INCLUDING ONE OF GEORGE WASHINGTON. AT NATIONAL PORTRAIT GALLERY. (INT'L). NIELS TOFT, PROJ COORD; DANISH BICENTENNIAL COMMITTEE & DANISH EMBASSY; 3200 WHITEHAVEN PKY, NW; WASHINGTON, DC 20008. (#104972-18).

MAY 11 - DEC 31, '76. EXHIBIT:MASTERPIECES OF AFRICAN ART FROM MUSEUM OF PRIMITIVE ART. SELECTIONS OF TRADITIONAL SCULPTURE FROM THE MUSEUM OF PRIMITIVE ART; THE COLLECTION WILL SUBSEQUENTLY BE INSTALLED IN THE PROJECTED MICHAEL ROCKEFELLER WING OF THE METROPOLITAN MUSEUM OF ART. AT 318 A ST, NE (CAPITOL). (NAT'L). NANCY CROMWELL, PR DIR; MUSEUM OF AFRICAN ART; 318 A ST, NE; WASHINGTON, DC 20002. (#105648-1).

MAY 11, '76 - MAY 11, '78. 1876 - A CENTENNIAL EXHIBITION. THIS EXHIBITION IN THE ARTS & INDUSTRIES BLDG, WILL RECREATE THE CHARACTER OF THE LATE 19TH CENTURY ALONG WITH THE INTERNATIONAL EXHIBITION OF 1876 IN PHILADELPHIA & THE SMITHSONIAN'S FIRST NATIONAL MUSEUM WHICH OPENED IN 1881. (NAT'L). MRS SUSAN HAMILTON; SMITHSONIAN INSTITUTION; 1000 JEFFERSON DR SW; WASHINGTON, DC 20560. (#74-1).

MAY 12, '76. OPENING OF EXHIBIT OF DANISH ARCHITECT, ARNE JACOBSEN. EXHIBIT WILL BE OPENED BY HER MAJESTY QUEEN MARGRETHE II OF DENMARK. AT RENWICK GALLERY. (INT'L). NIELS TOFT, PROJ COORD; DANISH BICENTENNIAL COMMITTEE & DANISH EMBASSY; 3200 WHITEHAVEN PKY, NW; WASHINGTON, DC 20008. (#104972-20).

MAY 12, '76. TAPIOLA CHILDREN'S CHOIR VISITS WASHINGTON, DC. LIVE PERFORMANCE. (INT'L). TATU TUCHIKORPI; CONSULATE GENERAL OF FINLAND; 540 MADISON AVE; NEW YORK, NY 10022. (#109041-3).

MAY 12 - 16, '76. WASHINGTON INTERNATIONAL ART FAIR - WASH-ART '76. OVER 250 10X12 BOOTHS MADE AVAILABLE TO ART DEALERS, ART PUBLISHERS AND THE ART PRESS (NATIONAL & INTERNATIONAL) TO SET UP EXHIBITS. OPPORTUNITY FOR CONTEST BETWEEN DEALERS & WITH THE GENERAL PUBLIC. AT DC NATIONAL GUARD ARMORY, 2001 E CAPITOL ST. (REGN'L). CAROL SUPPLEE, DIRECTOR; FELLUSS GALLERY GROUP; 2121 P ST, NW; WASHINGTON, DC 20036. (#101697-1).

MAY 12 - SEPT 6, '76. GRAND CENTENNIAL PUPPET SHOW. A THREE-PART EXTRAVAGANZA COMPLETE WITH MAGIC, SHADOW PUPPETS AND A PANTOMIME PRESENTATION OF THE CLASSIC 'PUSS IN BOOTS.'. AT PUPPET THEATRE, ARTS AND INDUSTRIES BLDG, 900 JEFFERSON DR, SW. (LOCAL). SUSANNE ROSCHWALB, CHMN; DIVISION OF PERFORMING ARTS, SMITHSONIAN INSTITUTION; 2200 AMTRAK BLDG, L'ENFANT PLAZA; WASHINGTON, DC 20560. (#108006-3).

MAY 12 - SEPT 15, '76. A NAVY BICENTENNIAL SUMMER CEREMONY. A BLEND OF MUSIC AND PAGEANTRY IN HONOR OF OUR GREAT COUNTRY AND THE NAVY THAT SERVES HER. AT ADMIRAL LEUTZE PARK, WASHINGTON NAVY YARD, WASHINGTON, DC. (REGN'L). PUBLIC AFFAIRS OFFICER; COMMANDANT NAVAL DISTRICT OF WASHINGTON, DC; HEADQUARTERS NAVAL DISTRICT; WASHINGTON, DC 20374. (#104698-1).

MAY 13 - JULY 31, '76. DESIGN AND ARCHITECTURE EXHIBIT - DANISH ARCHITECT ARNE JACOBSEN. EXHIBIT AT RENWICK GALLERY. (INT'L). NIELS TOFT, PROJ COORD; DANISH BICENTENNIAL COMMITTEE & DANISH EMBASSY; 3200 WHITEHAVEN PKY, NW; WASHINGTON, DC 20008. (#104972-8).

MAY 14, '76. DENVER UNIV SYMPHONY PERFORMANCE. LIVE PERFORMANCE AT JOHN F KENNEDY CENTER. (REGN'L). R R PORTER, COORD; UNIV OF DENVER SYMPHONY ORCHESTRA; UNIV OF DENVER; DENVER, CO 80120. (#103840-10).

MAY 14 - 16, '76. AMERICAN MUSIC THEATRE. LIVE PERFORMANCE AT LISNER AUDITORIUM. (REGN'L). IAN STRASFOGEZ; OPERA SOCIETY OF WASHINGTON; 2000 P ST. N.W.; WASHINGTON, DC 20036. (#50407-1).

MAY 14 - 16, '76. SMITHSONIAN'S 5TH ANNUAL MUSICAL WEEKEND. LIVE PERFORMANCE. (REGN'L). SUSANNE ROSCHWALB, COORD; SMITHSONIAN INSTITUTION; SMITHSONIAN INSTITUTION; WASHINGTON, DC 20560. (#104487-1).

MAY 15 - JUNE 30, '76. 'AMERICANA' - FILM SERIES ON THE AMERICAN EXPERIENCE. A CONTINUING FILM SERIES FEATURING HIGHLIGHTS OF AMERICAN CINEMA OVER THE PAST FIVE DECADES; TWO, PERFORMANCES NIGHTLY--FOR SPECIFIC TITLES EACH DAY, CONSULT BOX OFFICE (202)785-4600. AT THE JOHN F KENNEDY CENTER FOR THE PERFORMING ARTS. (REGN'L). AMERICAN FILM INSTITUTE; THE KENNEDY CENTER; WASHINGTON, DC 20566. (#107623-1).

WASHINGTON — CONTINUED

MAY 16, '76. LAFAYETTE SQUARE SUNDAY. WILL BE FOR ALL PEOPLE OF WASHINGTON AREA & THEIR GUESTS. AT LAFAYETTE SQUARE. (REGN'L). EDWARD STOREY, BIC COORD; DEPT OF THE TREASURY; ROOM 2112; WASHINGTON, DC 20222. (#1892-3).

MAY 17 - 24, '76. SEVENTH INTER-AMERICAN MUSIC FESTIVAL. 5/17, LOUISVILLE ORCHESTRA AT KENNEDY CTR - 5/18, FESTIVAL ORCHESTRA AT KENNEDY CTR - 5/21, QTT NATL UNIV LA PLATA ARGENTINA AT LIBRARY OF CONGRESS - 5/22 INTER-AMER CHAMB SINGERS AT PAN-AMER UNION; 5/23 HOMAGE TO CASALS AT LISNER AUD; 5/24, PHIL COMPOSER FOR. (LOCAL). DOLORES ROBBINS, COORD; ORGANIZATION OF AMERICAN STATES/MUSIC DIVISION; WASHINGTON, DC 20006. (#106454-1).

MAY 20, '76 - MAY 20, '77. ARTISTS-IMMIGRANTS OF AMERICA: 1876-1976. EXHIBITION WILL EXPLORE THE CONTRIBUTIONS MADE BY IMMIGRANTS & REFUGEE ARTISTS TO THE DEVELOPMENT OF AN AMERICAN ART OF INTERNATIONAL STATURE. AT HIRSHHORN MUSEUM & SCULPTURE GARDEN. (NAT'L). SUSAN HAMILTON, BIC COOR; SMITHSONIAN INSTITUTION; SMITNSONIAN INSTITUTION; WASHINGTON, DC 20560. (#7907-5).

MAY 21 - 22, '76. BICENTENNIAL SPECIAL OLYMPICS. FESTIVE TRACK & FIELD MEET FOR 500 MENTALLY RETARDED CITIZENS. THE OLYMPICS WILL START AT 4:00 PM ON THE 22ND. AT GALLAUDET COLLEGE STADIUM, 7TH & FLORIDA AVE, NE. (LOCAL). HARRY F CUSTIS, PRES; DISTRICT OF COLUMBIA SPECIAL OLYMPICS, INC; 5513 CONNECTICUT AVE, NW; WASHINGTON, DC 20015. (#25230-1).

MAY 21 - 22, '76. 'THREE BRITISH REVOLUTIONS - 1640, 1688, 1776'. PURPOSE IS TO EXAMINE THE AMERICAN REVOLUTION IN THE CONTEXT OF ITS SOCIAL, ECONOMIC, PHILOSOPHICAL & POLITICAL PRECEDENTS IN THE UPHEAVALS OF 17TH-CENTURY BRITAIN. NINE DISTINGUISHED HISTORIANS FROM BOTH SIDES OF THE ATLANTIC WILL ADDRESS THESE QUESTIONS. AT REGISTRATION AT 1:00PM FRIDAY - FOLGER SHAKESPEARE LIBRARY. (INT'L). DR O B HARDISON, JR, DIR; FOLGER INSTITUTE OF RENAISSANCE & 18TH-CENTURY STUDIES; 201 E CAPITOL ST; WASHINGTON, DC 20003. (#108120-1).

MAY 23, '76. INTERNATIONAL SOCCER GAME. COMPETITION AT RFK STADIUM. (INT'L). WASHINGTON DIPLOMATS; 1 TYSON CORNER CTR, SUITE LL1; MCLEAN, VA 22101. (#106617-1).

MAY 24, '76. BICENTENNIAL PARADE OF AMERICAN MUSIC HONORS FLORIDA. LIVE PERFORMANCE AT JOHN F KENNEDY MEMORIAL CENTER. (REGN'L). MRS W A SAUNDERS, DIR; BICENTENNIAL PARADE OF AMERICAN MUSIC; STEPHEN FOSTER MEML, BOX 266; WHITE SPRINGS, FL 32069. (#4500-22).

MAY 24 - SEPT 10, '76. HOSPITALITY SERVICES, FILMS, DEMONSTRATIONS. EXHIBIT, LIVE PERFORMANCE AT WEST POTOMAC PARK. (REGN'L). JAMES C LUCORE, DIRECTOR; BOY SCOUTS OF AMERICA; 777 14TH ST, NW; WASHINGTON, DC 20005. (#107335-13).

MAY 26, '76. BICENTENNIAL PARADE OF AMERICAN MUSIC HONORS TEXAS. TEXAS CITY HIGH SCHOOL BAND HAS BEEN SELECTED TO REPRESENT TEXAS. AT JOHN F KENNEDY MEMORIAL CENTER. (REGN'L). DR KENNETH CUTHBERT, DIR; BICENTENNIAL PARADE OF AMERICAN MUSIC; 1919 MISTYWOOD LN; DENTON, TX 76201. (#4500-23).

MAY 27, '76. EVENING CHORAL SOCIETY CONCERT. CHORUS(250) & SYMPHONY ORCHESTRA(80)--MUSIC OF AMERICAN COMPOSERS, JOHN LA MONTAINE, RICHARD DIRKSEN & LEO SOWERBY. PART OF PROGRAM OF WASHINGTON CATHEDRAL. (ST-WIDE). R WAYNE DIRKSEN; THE WASHINGTON CATHEDRAL; MT ST ALBAN; WASHINGTON, DC 20016. (#5619-509).

MAY 27 - 29, '76. CATHEDRAL FOUNDATION CONVOCATION/OPEN HOUSE EXHIBITS. CRAFTS, STONE CARVING, STAINED GLASS, NEEDLEPOINT, ARCHITECTURE-LECTURES, EXHIBITS. (ST-WIDE). R WAYNE DIRKSEN; THE WASHINGTON CATHEDRAL; MT ST ALBAN; WASHINGTON, DC 20016. (#5619-508).

MAY 28 - 30, '76. XVIII A C I FOREIGN EXCHANGE & MONEY DEALERS CONGRESS. COCKTAIL RECEPTION & BUFFET W/CONCERT AT KENNEDY CENTER, ROUNDTABLE DISCUSSIONS AT THE SHOREHAM HOTEL, BANQUET AT WASHINGTON-HILTON, BAR-B-Q AT GAITHERSBURGH, MD. AT CONSTITUTION HALL. (INT'L). ROBERT F LECLER, V/PRES; FOREX ASSOC OF NORTH AMERICA C/O CONTINENTAL BANK INTERNATIONAL; 1 LIBERTY PLAZA; NEW YORK, NY 10006. (#6578-501).

MAY 28 - NOV 28, '76. '1876: AMERICAN ART OF THE CENTENNIAL' EXHIBIT. COMPANION EXHIBIT TO '1876: A CENTENNIAL EXHIBITION', THIS IS AN EXHIBIT OF ART WORKS & PAINTINGS THAT WERE SHOWN AT THE PHILADELPHIA CENTENNIAL EXPOSITION. AT NATL COLLECTION OF FINE ARTS, 8TH & G STS, NW. (NAT'L). JIM MAHONEY; SMITHSONIAN INSTITUTION; SMITHSONIAN INSTITUTION; WASHINGTON, DC 20560. (#106374-1).

MAY 29, '76. 'AMERICA AWAKES' - BICENTENNIAL PATRIOTIC MUSIC PRESENTATION. LIVE PERFORMANCE AT LISNER AUDITORIUM, GEORGE WASHINGTON UNIV, 2121 I ST, NW. (REGN'L). REV DAVID TURK, COORD; THE WAY, INC; 401 WALNUT DR; ANNAPOLIS, MD 21403. (#108011-1).

MAY 29, '76. PRESENTATION OF PLAQUE & LETTER TO PRESIDENT FORD FROM PRBC. CO-CHAIRMEN JOURNEYED TO WASHINGTON TO PRESENT PLAQUE & LETTER TO PRESIDENT FORD ON BE-HALF OF THE PRBC IN RECOGNITION OF OUR NATION'S 200TH BIRTHDAY. GIFT IS ON DISPLAY AT THE GREAT HALL OF THE COMMERCE BUILDING. AT THE WHITE HOUSE, ROOSEVELT ROOM. (NAT'L). ARLENE M BENNETT, CHMN; PORT ROYAL BICENTENNIAL COMMITTEE & SENATOR THURMOND; PO BOX 100; PORT ROYAL, SC 29935. (#200043-48).

MAY 29 - JUNE 13, '76. OUTDOOR ART FAIR. EXHIBIT AT THE ELLIPSE. (REGN'L). JAMES C LUCORE, DIRECTOR; DC DEPT OF RECREATION & SEARS, ROEBUCK, CO; 777 14TH ST, NW; WASHINGTON, DC 20005. (#107335-1).

MAY 29 - SEPT 15, '76. AMERICAN PAINTINGS FROM THE PHILLIPS COLLECTION - 1900-1950. IN ADDITION TO THE PAINTINGS ABOVE, THERE WILL BE THE AMERICAN PAINTINGS PERMANENTLY ON VIEW. AS ALWAYS, THE COLLECTION OF MODERN ART & ITS SOURCES WILL BE SHOWN. SUNDAY HOURS 2 - 7 PM. AT PHILLIPS COLLECTION, 1600 21ST ST, CORNER OF Q ST, NO PARKING. (REGN'L). PHILLIPS COLLECTION; 1600 21ST ST. N.W.; WASHINGTON, DC 20009. (#50404-1).

MAY 30, '76. KOREAN FOLK ART TROUPE. LIVE PERFORMANCE AT WARNER THEATRE, 13TH & E ST. (INT'L). DIRECTOR; EMBASSY OF KOREA INFORMATION OFFICE; 1414 22ND ST, NW; WASHINGTON, DC 20006. (#108931-1).

MAY 30, '76 - OCT 30, '79. 'NEW GLORY CIRCLE' BICENTENNIAL OUTDOOR GALLERY. 26 LARGE FLAGS AT THE NATIONAL SCULPTURE GARDEN PLUS HOST FLAGS BEING PRESENTED BY THE NATIONAL GALLERY OF ART AND MCDONALD'S RESTAURANTS. GALLERY DEPICTS FLAG HISTORY AND DESIGN. AT ON THE MALL IN WASHINGTON, DC AT 7TH ST. (NAT'L). PAUL CHADBOURNE MILLS; SANTA BARBARA MUSEUM OF ART; 1130 STATE ST; SANTA BARBARA, CA 93101. (#2296-2).

MAY 31, '76. BICENTENNIAL PARADE OF AMERICAN MUSIC HONORS IOWA. LIVE PERFORMANCE AT JOHN F KENNEDY MEMORIAL CENTER. (REGN'L). MRS DOROTHY LOWELL, DIR; BICENTENNIAL PARADE OF AMERICAN MUSIC; BOX 407; FAIRFIELD, IA 52556. (#4500-24).

MAY 31, '76. IOWA DAY PROGRAM AT THE JOHN F KENNEDY CENTER. LUTHER COLLEGE CHOIR WILL PARTICIPATE WITH THE IOWA GROUP AT THE KENNEDY CENTER. (REGN'L). GLEN NELSON, DIRECTOR; LUTHER COLLEGE CHOIR; DECORAH, IA 52101. (#105240-1).

MAY '76. BICENTENNIAL VISIT BY FRENCH PRESIDENT & MADAME GISCARD D'ESTAING. CEREMONY. (INT'L). CULTURAL ATTACHE; EMBASSY OF FRANCE; 2535 BELMONT RD; WASHINGTON, DC 20008. (#200010-33).

MAY '76. COMPAGNIE RENAUD-BARRAULT PERFORMANCE. LIVE PERFORMANCE. (INT'L). CULTURAL ATTACHE; EMBASSY OF FRANCE; 2535 BELMONT RD; WASHINGTON, DC 20008. (#200010-28).

MAY '76. IRAN FILM FESTIVAL. EXHIBIT AT AMERICAN FILM INSTITUTE, J F KENNEDY CENTER. (INT'L). CULTURAL ATTACHE; EMBASSY OF IRAN; 3005 MASSACHUSETTS AVE; WASHINGTON, DC 20008. (#200010-27).

MAY '76. MONTE CARLO NATIONAL ORCHESTRA PERFORMS AT THE KENNEDY CENTER. LIVE PERFORMANCE. (INT'L). CULTURAL ATTACHE; GOVERNMENT OF MONACO; 2535 BELMONT RD; WASHINGTON, DC 20008. (#200010-25).

JUNE 1, '76. FIREWORKS DISPLAY OPENING 'THE EYE OF JEFFERSON' EXHIBITION. AN 18TH CENTURY FIREWORKS DISPLAY, BEING PRODUCED BY A FRENCH FIRM, IS PART OF THE OPENING FESTIVITIES FOR 'THE EYE OF JEFFERSON' EXHIBITION. AT REFLECTING POOL, NEAR GRANT STATUE. (INT'L). W HOWARD ADAMS; NATIONAL GALLERY OF ART; NATIONAL GALLERY OF ART; WASHINGTON, DC 20565. (#684-2).

JUNE 1, '76. SALUTE TO THE STATES - IOWA. CEREMONY AT STEPS OF THE CAPITOL. (REGN'L). JAMES C LUCORE, DIRECTOR; GOVT OF THE DISTRICT OF COLUMBIA; 777 14TH ST, NW; WASHINGTON, DC 20005. (#107332-1).

JUNE 1 - 4, '76. BICENTENNIAL YOUTH DEBATES, WASHINGTON DC. NATIONAL PROGRAM OF COMPETITIVE AND COMMUNITY DEBATES ON TOPICS OF HISTORICAL & HUMANISTIC CONCERN. FUNDED BY NATIONAL ENDOWMENT FOR THE HUMANITIES. AT HISTORIC SITES IN THE D.C. AREA. (NAT'L). RICHARD C HUSEMAN; 1625 MASSACHUSETTS AVE, NW; WASHINGTON, DC 20036. (#3057-1).

JUNE 1 - JULY 30, '76. THE GIRLS' CHOIR OF SANDEFJORD VISITS WASHINGTON. CONCERTS IN KENNEDY CENTER, WASHINGTON CATHEDRAL, FILENE CENTER OF WOLFTRAP FARM PARK, HOLY TRINITY CHURCH, SLIGO CHURCH. (INT'L). PRESS & CULTURAL AFFAIRS; ROYAL NORWEGIAN EMBASSY; 3401 MASSACHUSETTS AVE, NW; WASHINGTON, DC 20007. (#109008-1).

JUNE 1 - AUG 10, '76. PALLADIAN EXHIBIT. UNUSUAL EXHIBIT OF 10 WOODEN MODELS & SUPPORTING PHOTO DISPLAY OF BUILDINGS DESIGNED BY ANDREA PALLADIO, ITALIAN ARCHITECT OF THE LATE RENAISSANCE WHOSE IDEAS STRONGLY INFLUENCED THOS JEFFERSON & 18TH & 19TH CENTURY ARCHITECTS IN USA. AT CORCORAN GALLERY OF ART. (INT'L). ANN CRADDOCK, P/R OFFICE; UNIVERSITY OF VIRGINIA & ITALIAN GOVERNMENT; 17TH & NEW YORK AVE, NW; WASHINGTON, DC 20006. (#109011-2).

JUNE 1 - AUG 31, '76. PROMOTION OF PHYSICAL FITNESS. FESTIVAL, EXHIBIT AT WEST POTOMAC PARK AT 17TH ST. (REGN'L). JAMES C LUCORE, DIRECTOR; AMER BICENT PHYSICAL FITNESS PROGRAM; 777 14TH ST, NW; WASHINGTON, DC 20005. (#107335-12).

JUNE 1 - SEPT 30, '76. CALCULATORS AND COMPUTERS, HISTORY AND RECENT ADVANCES. DISPLAY OF TEXT, EQUIPMENT, & PHOTOGRAPHS OUTLINING THE HISTORY OF CALCULATORS & COMPUTERS SINCE THE 16TH CENTURY & SHOWING THE MOST MODERN ADVANCES IN SPEED & CAPACITY. AT ACADEMY BLDG, 2101 CONSTITUTION AVE, WASHINGTON, DC. (NAT'L). NAS OFFICE OF INFORMATION; NATL ACADEMY OF SCIENCES & NATL ACADEMY OF ENGINEERING; 2101 CONSTITUTION AVE; WASHINGTON, DC 20418. (#107856-1).

JUNE 1 - SEPT 30, '76. SCIENCE, ENGINEERING, MEDICINE IN SERVICE TO THE NATION AND PEOPLE. EXHIBIT HAS TEXT, PICTURES, OTHER DISPLAYS DESCRIBING ROLE OF TWO ACADEMIES, INSTITUTE OF MEDICINE & NATL RESEARCH COUNCIL IN SCIENCE, TECHNOLOGY & PUBLIC POLICY. AT ACADEMY BLDG, 2101 CONSTITUTION AVE, WASHINGTON, DC. (NAT'L). NAS OFFICE OF INFORMATION; NATL ACADEMY OF SCIENCES & NATL ACADEMY OF ENGINEERING; 2101 CONSTITUTION AVE; WASHINGTON, DC 20418. (#107856-2).

JUNE 1, '76 - JUNE 1, '77. MASTERPIECES OF AFRICAN ART, EXHIBIT. EXHIBITION OF 500 WORKS OF TRADITIONAL AFRICAN SCULPTURES & ELISOFON COLOR PHOTOS, TOURS & LECTURES ON AFRICAN CULTURE USING LIBRARY ARCHIVES EXTENSION PROGRAMS. (REGN'L). WARREN M ROBBINS; MUSEUM OF AFRICAN ART; 318 A ST, NE; WASHINGTON, DC 20002. (#5353-501).

JUNE 1, '76 - DEC 31, '77. HOUSING AMERICA EXHIBIT. THERE IS A STANDING AUDIOVISUAL EXHIBIT PLUS A FILM-FESTIVAL WHICH WILL BEGIN THE FIRST WEEK OF MAY, 1976. THE FILMS ARE ON A VARIETY OF SUBJECTS RELATED TO HOME BUILDING (DECORATION, MATERIALS, APPLIANCES, RECYCLING, HISTORY OF HOME BUILDING, ETC). AT 15TH & M ST, NW, THE NATIONAL HOUSING CENTER. (REGN'L). EMILY TURK, DIRECTOR; NATIONAL ASSOCIATION OF HOME BUILDERS; 15TH & M ST, NW; WASHINGTON, DC 20005. (#106731-1).

JUNE 2, '76. ANACOSTIA COMMUNITY PAVILLION DEDICATION. A ROLLER SKATING PAVILLION IN THE TWINING SECTION OF ANACOSTIA COMMUNITY PARK; DEDICATION OF FACILITY. (ST-WIDE). NATIONAL CAPITAL PARKS; NATIONAL PARK SERVICE; 1100 OHIO DIRVE, SW; WASHINGTON, DC 20042. (#293-1).

JUNE 3, '76. BICENTENNIAL WORKSHOP ON EQUAL EMPLOYMENT OPPORTUNITIES. CONFERENCE. (REGN'L). BEN SEGAL, SECRETARY; VOICE (VOICE OF INFORMED COMMUNITY EXPRESSION); 4532 49TH ST, NW; WASHINGTON, DC 20016. (#26757-1).

JUNE 3, '76. BRITISH PARLIAMENT LOANS MAGNA CARTA MANUSCRIPT FOR THE BICENT. A DELEGATION FROM BRITAIN'S PARLIAMENT WILL PRESENT ONE OF THE EARLIEST COPIES OF THE MAGNA CARTA TO THE PEOPLE OF THE UNITED STATES FOR LOAN DURING THE BICENTENNIAL. AT U S CAPITOL BUILDING. (INT'L). WALLACE GREEN, DIRECTOR; JOINT COMMITTEE ON THE ARRANGEMENTS FOR THE BICENTENNIAL; US CAPITOL; WASHINGTON, DC 20515. (#108124-2).

JUNE 3, '76. CEREMONY HONORING CHARLES BONAPARTE. CEREMONY AT DEPT OF JUSTICE BUILDING AUDITORIUM. (REGN'L). VIRGIL PTONE, CHMN; ITALIAN HISTORICAL SOCIETY OF AMERICA; 350 65TH ST, APT 2F; BROOKLYN, NY 11220. (#103715-1).

JUNE 3, '76. DEDICATION OF STATUES BY KING JUAN CARLOS OF SPAIN. IN HONOR OF HIS VISIT TO THE U S DURING THE BICENTENNIAL, THREE STATUES ARE PRESENTED TO THE PEOPLE OF THE USA. AT KENNEDY CENTER & STATE DEPT. (INT'L). DIRECTOR; SPANISH GOVERNMENT; 1100 OHIO DR, SW; WASHINGTON, DC 20242. (#200010-2).

JUNE 3 - 4, '76. MUSICAL BICENTENNIAL CELEBRATION BY ELEMENTARY CHILDREN. LIVE PERFORMANCE AT JEFFERSON MEMORIAL. (REGN'L). JAMES C LUCORE, DIRECTOR; CLUB HEIGHTS ELEMENTARY SCHOOL; 777 14TH ST, NW; WASHINGTON, DC 20005. (#107335-11).

JUNE 3 - SEPT 6, '76. 'THE EYE OF THOMAS JEFFERSON' EXHIBIT. EXHIBIT CENTERING ON JEFFERSON'S CONTRIBUTIONS IN ARCHITECTURE, TOWN PLANNING LANDSCAPE GARDENING, LITERATURE IN SOCIETY & THE ARTS DEMONSTRATION OF THE MANY FACETS OF LATE 18TH CENTURY MAN. AT NATIONAL GALLERY OF ART. (NAT'L). ROSS WATSON, CURATOR; NATIONAL GALLERY OF ART; 6TH & CONSTITUTION AVE, NW; WASHINGTON, DC 20565. (#684-1).

JUNE 3 - DEC 31, '76. 'CHRISTOPHER COLUMBUS & HIS TIME' EXHIBITION. A BICENTENNIAL LOAN OF 39 PRICELESS DOCUMENTS & ARTIFACTS PRESENTED BY THE KING & QUEEN OF SPAIN TO THE UNITED STATES ON JUNE 3, 1976. INCLUDES FIRST LETTER COLUMBUS WROTE IN THE NEW WORLD ON JANUARY 4, 1493, MAPS, BOOKS, A TERRESTIAL GLOBE, WEAPONS, ARMOR, ETC. AT NATIONAL MUSEUM OF HISTORY & TECHNOLOGY. (INT'L). DEPUTY DIRECTOR, MHT; SMITHSONIAN INSTITUTION; 1000 JEFFERSON DRIVE; WASHINGTON, DC 20560. (#108462-1).

JUNE 3, '76 - JUNE 3, '77. COPY OF MAGNA CARTA ON DISPLAY AT US CAPITOL BUILDING. ONE OF THE EARLIEST SURVIVING COPIES OF THE MAGNA CARTA IS ON LOAN FROM THE PEOPLE OF GREAT BRITAIN TO THE PEOPLE OF THE US DURING THE BICENTENNIAL. AT US CAPITOL BUILDING. (INT'L). WALLACE GREEN, DIRECTOR; JOINT COMMITTEE ON THE ARRANGEMENTS FOR THE BICENTENNIAL; US CAPITOL; WASHINGTON, DC 20515. (#108124-3).

JUNE 5, '76. FESTIVAL CELEBRATION FOR THE WASHINGTON DIOCESE. EXHIBITS, GAMES, DEMONSTRATIONS, CONCERTS, ETC. AT WASHINGTON CATHEDRAL. (ST-WIDE). NANCY MONTGOMERY, DIR; COMMUNICATIONS DEPT, WASHINGTON CATHEDRAL; MOUNT SAINT ALBAN; WASHINGTON, DC 20016. (#200010-6).

JUNE 5, '76. NATL PK SVC '...A LITTLE LOOK AROUND' COMES TO FORDS THEATER. THIS SHORT PROGRAM FEATURES ACTORS PLAYING THE PARTS OF FAMOUS AMERICANS OF THE PAST WHO'VE RETURNED TO SEE AMERICA'S GROWTH. SHOWINGS AT THIS NPS SITE. AT IN THEATER. (REGN'L). NCP BICENT COORDINATOR; NATIONAL PARK SERVICE; 1100 OHIO DRIVE, SW; WASHINGTON, DC 20242. (#5653-1).

JUNE 5 - 6, '76. DEDICATIONOF THE WASHINGTON CATHEDRAL NAVE. FESTIVAL EUCHARIST ON SATURDAY & CONVOCATION FOR DEDICATION ON SUNDAY. ECUMENICAL, GOVERNMENT REPRESENTATION BY INVITATION. NATIONAL CHURCH REPRESENTATION: ALL EPISCOPAL BISHOPS, EXECUTIVE COUNCIL, DIOCESE OF WASHINGTON, FOUNDATION SCHOOLS & OTHERS. AT WASHINGTON CATHEDRAL HOURS: 6/5 - 6:00PM; 6/6 - 11:00AM.. (ST-WIDE). NANCY MONTGOMERY, DIR; THE

WASHINGTON — CONTINUED

WASHINGTON CATHEDRAL; MOUNT SAINT ALBANS; WASHINGTON, DC 20016. (#5619-510).

JUNE 6, '76. WASHINGTON SENIOR HIGH SCHOOL CHOIR CONCERT. LIVE PERFORMANCE AT WASHINGTON CATHEDRAL. (REGN'L). NANCY MONTGOMERY, DIR; COMMUNICATIONS DEPT, WASHINGTON CATHEDRAL; MOUNT SAINT ALBANS; WASHINGTON, DC 20016. (#200010-7).

JUNE 6 - 18, '76. NATL PK SVC '...A LITTLE LOOK AROUND' VISITS NATIONAL CAPITAL PARKS. PROGRAM FEATURES ACTORS PLAYING THE PARTS OF FAMOUS AMERICANS OF THE PAST WHO'VE RETURNED TO SEE AMERICA'S GROWTH. 6/6 AT FT. WASHINGTON; 6/8-9 AT WASHINGTON MONUMENT; 6/10 GREAT FALLS, VA; 6/12 MANASSAS; 6/15 HARPERS FERRY; 6/16 ANTIETAM; 6/17-18 C&O CANAL. AT MONUMENT GROUNDS. (REGN'L). NCP BICENT COORDINATOR; NATIONAL PARK SERVICE; 1100 OHIO DRIVE, SW; WASHINGTON, DC 20242. (#5653-2).

JUNE 6 - AUG 31, '76. WATERGATE/JEFFERSON MEMORIAL CONCERTS. CONCERTS PRESENTED BY OFFICIAL BANDS OF THE FOUR BRANCHES OF THE MILITARY. AT AT THE JEFFERSON MEMORIAL. (REGN'L). NCP MALL OPERATIONS; NATIONAL PARK SERVICE; 1100 OHIO DRIVE, SW; WASHINGTON, DC 20242. (#108365-1).

JUNE 7, '76. NORTHFIELD BOYS CHORUS. LIVE PERFORMANCE AT WASHINGTON CATHEDRAL. (REGN'L). NANCY MONTGOMERY, DIR; COMMUNICATIONS DEPT, WASHINGTON CATHEDRAL; MOUNT SAINT ALBANS; WASHINGTON, DC 20016. (#200010-8).

JUNE 7 - 11, '76. DANVILLE HIGH SCHOOL BAND CONCERTS. LIVE PERFORMANCE AT JEFFERSON & LINCOLN MEMORIALS, RAWLINS PARK. (REGN'L). JAMES C LUCORE, DIRECTOR; DANVILLE HIGH SCHOOL BOOSTERS ASSOC; 777 14TH ST, NW; WASHINGTON, DC 20005. (#107335-10).

JUNE 8, '76. CREATIVE SCREEN AT THE RENWICK GALLERY. 3 FILMS IN CONJUNCTION W/'SIGNS OF LIFE' EXHIBITION TO BE SHOWN AT 11, NOON, & 1 PM. FOLMS: 'DOWNTOWNS FOR PEOPLE', 'SKYSCRAPER' AND 'BOOMSVILLE'. AT GRAND SALON OF THE RENWICK, 18TH & PA AVE. (REGN'L). DIRECTOR; SMITHSONIAN INSTITUTION; WASHINGTON, DC 20250. (#200010-16).

JUNE 8 - 20, '76. AUSTRALIAN BALLET PERFORMANCE--'THE MERRY WIDOW'. LIVE PERFORMANCE AT KENNEDY CENTER. (INT'L). JOHN MAUNDER, DIRECTOR; AUSTRALIAN GOVERNMENT; AUSTRALIAN CG, 636 FIFTH AVENUE; NEW YORK, NY 10020. (#107857-2).

JUNE 9, '76. COPENHAGEN BOYS CHOIR, MOGENS WOLDIKE CONDUCTING. LIVE PERFORMANCE AT WASHINGTON CATHEDRAL. (INT'L). NANCY MONTGOMERY, DIR; COMMUNICATIONS DEPT, WASHINGTON CATHEDRAL; MOUNT SAINT ALBAN; WASHINGTON, DC 20016. (#200010-4).

JUNE 11, '76. DEDICATION OF FORT DUPONT ICE SKATING RINK. DEDICATION OF AN INDOOR ICE SKATING RINK IN FORT DUPONT PARK. PART OF OVERALL NCP BICENTENNIAL DEVELOPMENT PROGRAM. (ST-WIDE). NATIONAL CAPITAL PARKS; NATIONAL PARK SERVICE; 1100 OHIO DRIVE, SW; WASHINGTON, DC 20042. (#274-1).

JUNE 11, '76. SALUTE TO THE STATES - INDIANA. CEREMONY AT STEPS OF THE CAPITOL. (REGN'L). JAMES C LUCORE, DIRECTOR; GOVT OF THE DISTRICT OF COLUMBIA; 777 14TH ST, NW; WASHINGTON, DC 20005. (#107332-2).

JUNE 12, '76. BAPTIST PRAISING '76 BICENTENNIAL MUSIC FESTIVAL. GUEST GROUPS SING, CONGREGATIONAL PARTICIPATION. PART OF BICENTENNIAL PROGRAM OF WASHINGTON CATHEDRAL. AT WASHINGTON CATHEDRAL. (REGN'L). JAMES C ALLCOCK; BAPTIST CONVENTION OF MD & CHURCH MUSIC DEPT, SOU BAPTIST CONV; 1313 YORK RD; LUTHERVILLE, MD 21093. (#5619-511).

JUNE 12, '76. BICENTENNIAL FESTIVAL OF PRAISE '76. LIVE PERFORMANCE AT WASHINGTON CATHEDRAL. (REGN'L). NANCY MONTGOMERY, DIR; COMMUNICATIONS DEPT, WASHINGTON CATHEDRAL; MOUNT SAINT ALBANS; WASHINGTON, DC 20016. (#200010-9).

JUNE 12 - 13, '76. CITY CELEBRATION-ANNUAL URBAN FAIR. FAIR. (LOCAL). REGINA SAXTON, COORD; OFFICE OF BICENTENNIAL PROGRAMS; 777 14TH ST, NW; WASHINGTON, DC 20005. (#24893-1).

JUNE 13 - 17, '76. ADVANCING THE HUMANE SOCIETY-NATIONAL CONFERENCE ON SOCIAL WELFARE. THE 103RD ANNUAL FORUM OF THE NCSW-INCLUDES PRE AND POST FORUM INSTI TUTES ON SPECIAL ISSUES; 200 MEETING IN ALL. AT SHERATON PARK HOTEL & SHOREHAM-AMERICANA HOTEL. (NAT'L). MARGARET BERRY, PROJ DIR; NATIONAL CONFERENCE ON SOCIAL WELFARE; 22 W GAY ST; COLUMBUS, OH 43215. (#17188-1).

JUNE 14, '76. COSTUMES FROM GIAN CARLO MENOTTI'S OPERA 'MARTIN'S LIE'. EXHIBIT AT RARE BOOK LIBRARY, WASHINGTON CATHEDRAL. (REGN'L). NANCY MONTGOMERY, DIR; COMMUNICATIONS DEPT, WASHINGTON CATHEDRAL; MOUNT SAINT ALBANS; WASHINGTON, DC 20016. (#200010-10).

JUNE 14 - 15, '76. 'NEW GLORY CIRCLE' DEDICATION & OTHER FLAG DAY CEREMONIES. CEREMONY AT ON THE MALL IN WASHINGTON, DC AT 7TH ST. (NAT'L). PAUL CHADBOURNE MILLS; SANTA BARBARA MUSEUM OF ART; 1130 STATE ST; SANTA BARBARA, CA 93101. (#2296-3).

JUNE 14 - 16, '76. KIN & COMMUNITIES - THE PEOPLING OF AMERICA - WORKSHOP. EXHIBIT, CONFERENCE. (REGN'L). SUSAN HAMILTON; SMITHSONIAN INSTITUTION; SMITHSONIAN INSTITUTION; WASHINGTON, DC 20560. (#7907-2).

JUNE 14 - SEPT 6, '76. 'GREAT AMERICA' PERFORMANCES AT WASHINGTON MONUMENT. PRODUCED BY MARRIOTT CORPORATION AND PRESENTED IN COOPERATION WITH THE NATIONAL PARK SERVICE; AN ORIGINAL MUSICAL THAT DEPICTS THE CHARACTERISTICS OF BOTH THE PEOPLE AND THE LAND OF THE UNITED STATES. AT SYLVAN THEATRE ON GROUNDS OF WASHINGTON MONUMENT. (NAT'L). LOUIS V PRIEBE, DIR; MARRIOTT CORPORATION; NATIONAL PARK SERVICE; 5161 RIVER RD; WASHINGTON, DC 20016. (#12355-1).

JUNE 15, '76. BICENTENNIAL PARADE OF AMERICAN MUSIC HONORS WISCONSIN. MS LEE DOUGHERTY, A NATIONAL FEDERATION OF MUSIC CLUBS WINNER OF THE YOUNG ARTIST AWARD IN WOMEN'S VOICES WILL PERFORRM. AT JOHN F KENNEDY MEMORIAL CENTER. (REGN'L). MISS ALICE WALTER, DIR; NATIONAL MUSIC COUNCIL & EXXON; 501 ORCHARD ST; BURLINGTON, WI 53106. (#4500-25).

JUNE 15, '76. MUSICAL COMPOSITION COMPETITION - STRINGS, CHORUS, SOLO VOICE. CASH PRIZES WILL BE AWARDED TO THE WINNERS OF THIS MUSICAL COMPETITION CONTEST FOR STRING ORCHESTRA, FEMALE CHORUS & SOLO INSTRUMENT OR VOICE. THE FINALS WILL BE A GALA PERFORMANCE AT THE KENNEDY CTR. CASH PRIZES AWARDED. AT KENNEDY CENTER. (LOCAL). CATHERINE STEWART; FRIDAY MORNING MUSIC CLUB, INC; 9525 MILSTEAD DR; BETHESDA, MD 20034. (#8648-1).

JUNE 15, '76. SALUTE TO THE STATES - WISCONSIN. CEREMONY AT STEPS OF THE CAPITOL. (REGN'L). JAMES C LUCORE, DIRECTOR; GOVT OF THE DISTRICT OF COLUMBIA; 777 14TH ST, NW; WASHINGTON, DC 20005. (#107332-3).

JUNE 16 - 17, '76. ANGEL DRILL TEAM PERFORMANCES. LIVE PERFORMANCE AT LINCOLN & JEFFERSON MEMORIALS, RAWLINS PARK. (REGN'L). JAMES C LUCORE, DIRECTOR; ANGEL DRILL TEAM; 777 14TH ST, NW; WASHINGTON, DC 20005. (#107335-8).

JUNE 16 - 20, '76. FIRST WEEK'S EVENTS AT THE FESTIVAL OF AMERICAN FOLKLIFE. SUMMER-LONG FESTIVAL. THIS WEEK'S HIGHLIGHTED PROGRAMS: NORTHEAST REGION OF THE US; GHANA & JAMAICA FEATURED AT AFRICAN DIASPORA; NATIVE AMERICANS OF THE NORTHEAST; ISRAEL & ITALY; AND WORKERS WHO EXTRACT AND SHAPE THINGS. AT ON THE MALL, BETWEEN LINCOLN MEMORIAL & WASHINGTON MONUMENT. (INT'L). SUSANNE ROSCHWALB; SMITHSONIAN INSTITUTION, NATIONAL PARK SERVICE; SMITHSONIAN INSTITUTION; WASHINGTON, DC 20560. (#111-3).

JUNE 16 - JULY 3, '76. 'TWELFTH NIGHT'. LIVE PERFORMANCE AT TRAPIER THEATER - WASHINGTON CATHEDRAL GROUNDS. (REGN'L). TED WALCH, DIRECTOR; SHAKESPEARE & CO - TRAPIER THEATER; ST ALBANS SCHOOL; WASHINGTON, DC 20016. (#108434-1).

JUNE 16 - SEPT 6, '76. FESTIVAL OF AMERICAN FOLKLIFE. DIVISIONS OF FESTIVAL: OLD WAYS IN THE NEW WORLD; NATIVE AMERICANS; WORKING AMERICA; REGIONAL AMERICA; AFRICAN DIASPORA; CHILDREN'S AREA & FAMILY FOLKLORE. FEATURING 30 COUNTRIES & 50 STATES. CO-SPONSORS INCL NATL PARK SERVICE, AMERICAN AIRLINES & GENERAL FOODS. AT NATIONAL MALL BETWEEN WASHINGTON MONUMENT AND LINCOLN MEMORIAL. (INT'L). SUSANNE ROSCHWALB, CHMN; SMITHSONIAN INSTITUTION; DIV PERFORMING ARTS SMITHSONIAN; WASHINGTON, DC 20560. (#111-2).

JUNE 16, '76 - JAN 1, '77. BETWEEN FRIENDS/ENTRE AMIS. CEREMONY. (INT'L). K DE B PERCY, COORD; NATIONAL FILM BOARD OF CANADA & GOVT OF CANADA; 1746 MASSACHUSETTS AVE, NW; WASHINGTON, DC 20036. (#105111-14).

JUNE 17, '76. BICENTENNIAL PARADE OF AMERICAN MUSIC HONORS OREGON. THE REDMOND BAND AND THE SHELDON CHORUS WILL APPEAR IN THE FOYER PRECEEDING THE CONCERT. AT JOHN F KENNEDY MEMORIAL CENTER. (REGN'L). MRS THURSTON LINDVALL; NATIONAL MUSIC COUNCIL & EXXON; 15215 SW 116TH ST; TIGARD, OR 97223. (#4500-28).

JUNE 17 - 19, '76. EVOLVING ROLE & STATUS OF CHINESE-AMERICANS. CONFERENCE, EXHIBIT AT MARVIN CENTER AT GEORGE WASHINGTON UNIVERSITY, 21ST & H STS, NW. (REGN'L). FRANK YIN; ORGANIZATION OF CHINESE-AMERICANS, INC; 2721 WOODEDGE RD; WHEATON, MD 20906. (#108122-1).

JUNE 17 - 24, '76. GIAN CARLO MENOTTI COMMISSIONED OPERA. OPENING EVENT IN SUMMER FESTIVAL '76. TWO OPERAS: 'MARTIN'S LIE' AND 'THE EGG'. PART OF THE BICENTENNIAL PROGRAM OF THE WASHINGTON CATHEDRAL. AT THE WASHINGTON CATHEDRAL. (ST-WIDE). R WAYNE DIRKSEN; THE WASHINGTON CATHEDRAL; MT ST ALBAN; WASHINGTON, DC 20016. (#5619-505).

JUNE 18, '76. SALUTE TO THE STATES - OREGON. CEREMONY AT STEPS OF THE CAPITOL. (REGN'L). JAMES C LUCORE, DIRECTOR; GOVT OF THE DISTRICT OF COLUMBIA; 777 14TH ST, NW; WASHINGTON, DC 20005. (#107332-4).

JUNE 18 - 22, '76. MINNESOTA DAYS IN WASHINGTON, DC. LIVE PERFORMANCE AT KENNEDY CENTER. (REGN'L). RON PETRUCCI, PROJ CHMN; MINNESOTA AMERICAN REVOLUTION BICENTENNIAL COMMISSION; STATE CAPITOL, RM 12; ST PAUL, MN 55155. (#25653-1).

JUNE 19 - 20, '76. IRISH-AMERICAN FOLK FESTIVAL. FESTIVAL, LIVE PERFORMANCE, COMPETITION. (INT'L). SEAN D COAKLEY, CHAIRMAN; IRISH-AMERICAN BICENTENNIAL COMMITTEE; SUITE 427, 1825 CONN AVE, NW; WASHINGTON, DC 20009. (#7917-3).

JUNE 19 - JULY 18, '76. TRANSPORTATION-RIDES ON 'BEST FRIEND', 1830'S LOCOMOTIVE & TRAIN. VISITORS WILL BE GIVEN RIDES ON AN OPERATING REPLICA OF AN 1830'S VINTAGE TRAIN ALONG A SCENIC QUARTER-MILE SIDE TRACK BETWEEN THE C&O CANAL AND THE POTOMAC RIVER IN GEORGETOWN, ON 5 SUMMER WEEKENDS DURING THE BICENTENNIAL YEAR. AT SIDETRACK NEAR INTERSECTION OF WISCONSIN & K ST, IN GEORGETOWN. (LOCAL). W F GEESLIN, DIRECTOR; SOUTHERN RAILWAY SYSTEM; SOUTHERN RAILWAY BOX 1808; WASHINGTON, DC 20013. (#103415-1).

JUNE 19 - JULY 31, '76. 'CONTEMPORARY WASHINGTON ART' SPECIAL SERIES. SERIES OF SPECIAL INSTALLATIONS BY WASHINGTON ARTISTS FEATURING HELENE HERZBRUN, JOHN ROBINSON & ALMA THOMAS. EXHIBITION IS SUPPORTED BY THE MORRIS & GWENDOLYN CAFRITZ FOUNDATION & THE NATL ENDOWMENT FOR THE ARTS. AT 17TH & NEW YORK AVENUE, NW. (REGN'L). ANN CRADDOCK, P/R OFFICE; THE CORCORAN GALLERY OF ART; 17TH & NEW YORK AVE, NW; WASHINGTON, DC 22006. (#108119-3).

JUNE 19 - AUG 15, '76. THE HISTORICAL PHOTOGRAPHS OF ADDISON N SCURLOCK. 130 PHOTOGRAPHS BY BLACK PHOTOGRAPHER, WHO EXTENSIVELY DOCUMENTED THE PRESENCE OF BLACK AMERICANS FROM THE EARLY TO MID-1900'S. 20 OF THE PHOTOS ARE VINTAGE PRINTS, 110 ARE FROM ORIGINAL NEGATIVES. FOCUS IS ON ALL LEVELS OF AMERICAN SOCIETY. (NAT'L). FRANCES FRALIN; CORCORAN GALLERY OF ART; 17TH ST & NEW YORK AVE, NW; WASHINGTON, DC 20006. (#22894-1).

JUNE 21, '76. BICENTENNIAL PARADE OF AMERICAN MUSIC HONORS MINNESOTA. EACH CONCERT FEATURES MUSIC COMPOSED IN OR ABOUT THE FEATURED STATE PLAYED BY OUTSTANDING MUSICAL GROUPS OR SOLOISTS FROM THAT STATE. AT JOHN F KENNEDY MEMORIAL CENTER. (REGN'L). MRS PHILIP ECKMAN, DIR; NATIONAL MUSIC COUNCIL & EXXON; 4720 LONDON RD; DULUTH, MN 55804. (#4500-26).

JUNE 21, '76. WHITE HOUSE VISITORS' PROGRAM ON THE ELLIPSE - TOUR & CONCERT. THE AURORA HIGH SCHOOL BAND WILL PERFORM AT PROGRAM ON THE ELLIPSE. AT WHITE HOUSE ELLIPSE. (REGN'L). MICHAEL KULBA, DIRECTOR; AURORA HIGH SCHOOL BAND, SCHOOL DISTRICT 4R; AURORA, NE 68818. (#25801-1).

JUNE 21 - 25, '76. ECONOMIC COUNCIL OF EUROPE SEMINAR & TOUR. SEMINAR, TOUR. (NAT'L). PAUL RASMUSSEN, COORD; U S DEPT OF TRANSPORTATION; WASHINGTON, DC 20590. (#107333-1).

JUNE 21 - 28, '76. UKRAINIAN WEEK. YOUTH ENCAMPMENT LECTURES, FOLK DANCE, SPORTS EVENTS, CULTURAL PROGRAMS, VISIT TO U S CONGRESS AND TO HISTORICAL SITES. AT PUBLIC PARK TO BE DESIGNATED BY D.C. AUTHORITIES. (NAT'L). IVAN BAZARKO; UKRAINIAN BICENTENNIAL COMMITTEE OF AMERICA; 302 W 13TH ST; NEW YORK, NY 10014. (#7843-1).

JUNE 21 - JULY 11, '76. BICENTENNIAL SEMINAR IN AMERICAN ART/ARCHITECTURE/PERFORMING ARTS. SEMINAR. (LOCAL). DR IRVING AHLQUIST; SCHOOL OF FINE ARTS, CALIFORNIA STATE UNIVERSSITY LONG BEACH; 6101 E SEVENTH STREET; LONG BEACH, CA 90840. (#107845-8).

JUNE 22, '76. CREATIVE SCREEN AT THE RENWICK GALLERY. 3 FILMS IN CONJUNCTION WITH 'SIGNS OF LIFE' EXHIBITION TO BE SHOWN AT 11, NOON & 1 PM. FILMS ARE 'DOWNTOWNS FOR PEOPLE', 'SKYSCRAPERS, AND 'BOOMSVILLE'. AT GRAND SALON OF THE RENWICK GALLERY, 18 & PENNSYLVANIA AVE. (REGN'L). DIRECTOR; SMITHSONIAN INSTITUTION; WASHINGTON, DC 20250. (#200010-18).

JUNE 22, '76. JAZZ CONCERT AT THE RENWICK GALLERY OF ART. THE QUARTET 'CROSSING POINT' WILL BE FEATURED. AT FGRAND SALON OF THE RENWICK GALLERY, 18 & PENNSYLVANIA AVE. (REGN'L). DIRECTOR; SMITHSONIAN INSTITUTION; WASHINGTON, DC 20250. (#200010-17).

JUNE 22, '76. SALUTE TO THE STATES - MINNESOTA. CEREMONY AT STEPS OF THE CAPITOL. (REGN'L). JAMES C LUCORE, DIRECTOR; GOVT OF THE DISTRICT OF COLUMBIA; 777 14TH ST, NW; WASHINGTON, DC 20005. (#107332-5).

JUNE 23 - 27, '76. DANISH FIDDLERS PERFORM AT THE AMERICAN FOLKLIFE FESTIVAL. ANNUAL CELEBRATION OF AMERICAN FOLK CULTURES AND TRADITIONS. AT SMITHSONIAN INSTITUTION. (INT'L). NIELS TOFT, PROJ COORD; DANISH BICENTENNIAL COMMITTEE & DANISH EMBASSY; 3200 WHITEHAVEN PKY, NW; WASHINGTON, DC 20008. (#104972-2).

JUNE 23 - 27, '76. SCANDINAVIAN COUNCIL EVENTS AT AMERICAN FOLKLIFE FESTIVAL. SCANDINAVIAN COOKING & CRAFT DEMONSTRATIONS; VISITING TEAMS OF MUSICIANS & CRAFTSMEN FROM DENMARK, FINLAND, ICELAND, NORWAY AND SWEDEN. AT NATL MALL, REFLECTING POOL AT LINCOLN MEMORIAL. (INT'L). ALAN O MANN, CHAIRMAN; SMITHSONIAN INSTITUTE & NATL PARK SERVICE & SCANDINAVIAN GOVTS; 3806 JOCELYN ST, NW; WASHINGTON, DC 20015. (#106580-1).

JUNE 23 - 27, '76. SECOND WEEK'S EVENTS AT THE FESTIVAL OF AMERICAN FOLKLIFE. SUMMER-LONG FESTIVAL. THIS WEEK'S HIGHLIGHTED PROGRAMS: GREAT LAKES SECTION OF THE US; GHANA & JAMAICA AT THE AFRICAN DIASPORA; NATIVE AMERICANS OF THE GREAT LAKES; SCANDINAVIAN COUNTRIES; AND WORKERS WHO EXTRACT AND SHAPE. AT ON THE MALL, BETWEEN LINCOLN MEMORIAL & WASHINGTON MONUMENT. (INT'L). SUSANNE ROSCHWALB; SMITHSONIAN INSTITUTION, NATIONAL PARK SERVICE; SMITHSONIAN INSTITUTION; WASHINGTON, DC 20560. (#111-4).

JUNE 24 - 25, '76. MUSICAL PRESENTATION OF SPIRIT AND MEANING OF 1976. LIVE PERFORMANCE AT WASHINGTON MONUMENT GROUNDS. (REGN'L). JAMES C LUCORE, DIRECTOR; DEPT OF BAPTIST WOMEN; 777 14TH ST, NW; WASHINGTON, DC 20005. (#107335-6).

JUNE 25, '76 - JAN 9, '77. PORTRAIT MINIATURES FROM PRIVATE COLLECTIONS. A SELECTION OF 125 MINIATURE PORTRAITS FROM SEVERAL PRIVATE COLLECTIONS WILL BE SHOWN IN THE

WASHINGTON — CONTINUED

DORIS M MAGOWAN GALLERY. CLOSED CHRISTMAS DAY. AT NATL COLLECTION OF FINE ARTS, 8TH & G ST, NW. (REGN'L). MARGERY BYERS, PUBL AFF; SMITHSONIAN INSTITUTION, NATIONAL COLLECTION OF FINE ARTS; WASHINGTON, DC 20560. (#108937-1).

JUNE 26, '76. HORIZONS DAY: A DAY TO DISCUSS THIRD CENTURY DIRECTIONS. LAST DAY OF INTERNATIONAL SYNCON IS HORIZONS DAY; LOCAL 'FUTURE ASSEMBLIES' TO OCCUR ACROSS THE NATION TO STUDY DIRECTIONS FOR A BETTER FUTURE; TRAINING SESSION AVAILABLE - CONTACT BEFORE APRIL 20,. (NAT'L). BARBARA MAY HUBBARD, DIR; THE COMMITTEE FOR THE FUTURE, INC; 2325 PORTER ST, NW; WASHINGTON, DC 20008. (#21698-2).

JUNE 26, '76. WREATH-LAYING CEREMONY. CEREMONY AT TARAS SHEVCHENKO MONUMENT & WASHINGTON MONUMENT GROUNDS. (REGN'L). JAMES C LUCORE, DIRECTOR; UKRANIAN CONGRESS COMMITTEE OF AMERICA, INC; 777 14TH ST, NW; WASHINGTON, DC 20005. (#107335-5).

JUNE 26 - JULY 18, '76. 'TREASURES OF LONDON' EXHIBITION. 500 YEARS OF BRITISH SILVER ARE REPRESENTED IN THIS EXHIBITION OF 46 ANTIQUE OBJECTS, 46 MODERN PIECES, & 100 PIECES OF MODERN JEWELRY. AT THE 'CASTLE' OF THE SMITHSONIAN, 900 JEFFERSON DR, SW. (INT'L). EILEEN HARAKAL, COORD; SMITHSONIAN INSTITUTION TRAVELING EXHIBITION SERVICE; 1000 JEFFERSON DR, SW; WASHINGTON, DC 20560. (#26660-3).

JUNE 27, '76. 'AMERICA AT THE MOVIES' - THE ARBA FILM'S WORLD PREMIERE. CREATED & PRODUCED BY THE AMERICAN FILM INSTITUTE FOR THE ARBA, THE FILM TRACES HOW THE USA HAS BEEN PORTRAYED ON THE SCREEN FOR OVER THREE-QUARTERS OF A CENTURY. GREAT SCENES FROM NEARLY 100 FILMS. AT J F KENNEDY MEMORIAL CENTER. (NAT'L). JACK MASEY, PROJ DIRECTOR; AMERICAN REVOLUTION BICENTENNIAL ADMINISTRATION; 2401 E STREET, N W; WASHINGTON, DC 20276. (#26650-1).

JUNE 27, '76. CORY BAND FROM WALES VISITS WASHINGTON, DC. THIS 38-PIECE BAND, FOUNDED IN 1884, HAS REPRESENTED WALES IN NUMEROUS NATIONAL CONTESTS & IN 1974 WON THE TITLE 'CHAMPION BAND OF GREAT BRITAIN.'. (INT'L). MS EDITH HALL; LYRA ENTERTAINMENT, INC; 16 W 61ST ST; NEW YORK, NY 10023. (#109009-1).

JUNE 27, '76. WASHINGTON DIPLOMATS SOCCER GAME. COMPETITION AT RFK STADIUM. (REGN'L). WASHINGTON DIPLOMATS; 1 TYSON CORNER CTR, SUITE LL1; MCLEAN, DC 20003. (#106617-2).

JUNE 27 - JULY 23, '76. PRESIDENTIAL CLASSROOM FOR YOUNG AMERICANS. FOUR SHIPYARD PERSONNEL WERE SENT TO WASHINGTON, DC TO ATTEND THE CLASSROOM. PROVIDING DIRECT EXPOSURE TO THE PEOPLE AND POLICY-MAKING PROCEDURES OF THE FEDERAL GOVERNMENT. (REGN'L). ALFRED WONG, PHNSYD; PEARL HARBOR NAVAL SHIPYARD; FPO, BOX 400; SAN FRANCISCO, CA 96610. (#200014-7).

JUNE 27 - AUG 8, '76. VACATION COLLEGE PROGRAM. WEEK-LONG COURSES, MORNING SEMINARS, RELEVANT FIELD TRIPS, AFTERNOON RECREATIONAL ACTIVITIES, EVENING EVENTS; HOUSING AND CHILD CARE PROVIDED; AMPLE PARKING; 10 MINUTES FROM DOWNTOWN DC. AT MASSACHUSETTS AND NEBRASKA AVE. (REGN'L). DR GERTRUDE EATON; THE AMERICAN UNIVERSITY; THE AMERICAN UNIVERSITY; WASHINGTON, DC 20016. (#103453-1).

JUNE 27 - AUG 31, '76. MIXED MEDIA FOR EDUCATIONAL & HISTORICAL INTERESTS. EXHIBIT, CEREMONY, AWARD. (REGN'L). JAMES C MASON, PRESIDENT; SMITH MASON GALLERY OF ART INC; 1207 RHODE ISLAND AVE, NW; WASHINGTON, DC 20005. (#6604-505).

JUNE 28, '76. BICENTENNIAL PARADE OF AMERICAN MUSIC HONORS CALIFORNIA. EACH CONCERT FEATURES MUSIC COMPOSED IN OR ABOUT THE FEATURED STATE PLAYED BY OUTSTANDING MUSICAL GROUPS OR SOLOISTS FROM THAT STATE. AT JOHN F KENNEDY MEMORIAL CENTER. (REGN'L). MRS NAOMI REYNOLDS, DIR; NATIONAL MUSIC COUNCIL & EXXON; 2130 MANNING AVE; LOS ANGELES, CA 90025. (#4500-27).

JUNE 28 - 30, '76. PARADE & CONCERT OPENING AEROSPACE SMITHSONIAN. CAVALCADE OF BANDS & ORANGE GLEN PATRIOTS, CA. A SINGLE PERFORMING UNIT OF 1,976 MUSICIANS AND DRILL TEAM MARCHERS FROM 115 CALIFORNIA HIGH SCHOOLS WILL PERFORM IN WASHINGTON, DC, BOSTON, PHILADELPHIA, & NY AT YANKEE STADIUM, CENTRAL PARK & THE UN. (REGN'L). DAVID HARRISON; ORANGE GLEN HIGH SCHOOL 'PATRIOT' BAND; 2200 GLENOROGE RD; ESCONDIDO, CA 22025. (#12232-501).

JUNE 28, '76 - CONTINUING . FESTIVAL OF AMERICAN MUSIC AND DANCE. FESTIVAL IN AMERICAN MUSIC AND DANCE FEATURES BLACKS IN AMERICAN THEATRE, FOLK SONGS AND 3 MUSICALS. (LOCAL). SAMUEL BONDS, DIRECTOR; WOODSON MALE CHORUS AND COMPANY; 1828 S ST, SE; WASHINGTON, DC 20020. (#25930-1).

JUNE 29, '76. FIRST BAPTIST CHURCH CHORAL PERFORMANCE. LIVE PERFORMANCE AT LINCOLN MEMORIAL. (REGN'L). JAMES C LUCORE, DIRECTOR; FIRST BAPTIST CHURCH; 777 14TH ST, NW; WASHINGTON, DC 20005. (#107335-3).

JUNE 29, '76. LAKEVIEW ELEMENTARY FIFTH GRADE CHOIR PERFORMANCE. ONLY ELEMENTARY OR JUNIOR HIGH SCHOOL IN USA INVITED TO PERFORM. AT PRESIDENT'S PARK. (LOCAL). MILA GIBSON, CHMN; LAKEVIEW ELEMENTARY SCHOOL, MUSIC EDUCATORS NATIONAL CONFERENCE; 13619 WOODCHESTER; SUGAR LAND, TX 77478. (#200046-384).

JUNE 29, '76. OPENING CONCERT OF FREEDOM WEEK TOUR OF ENGLISH HANDBELL RINGERS. OTHER CONCERTS SCHEDULED FOR PHILADELPHIA, NEW YORK & BOSTON.100 RINGERS,WITH BANNERS & BRASS INSTRUMENTS.PART OF BICENTENNIAL PROGRAM OF NATIONAL CATHEDRAL - LITURGICAL EVENTS & A SUMMER FESTIVAL, JUNE - AUGUST, 1976. AT WASHINGTON NATIONAL CATHEDRAL. (REGN'L). NANCY P TUFTS; THE AMERICAN GUILD OF ENGLISH HANDBELL RINGERS; 12001 RIVERVIEW; OXON HILL, MD 20022. (#5619-512).

JUNE 29, '76. SALUTE TO THE STATES - CALIFORNIA. CEREMONY AT STEPS OF THE CAPITOL. (REGN'L). JAMES C LUCORE, DIRECTOR; GOVT OF THE DISTRICT OF COLUMBIA; 777 14TH ST, NW; WASHINGTON, DC 20005. (#107332-6).

JUNE 29 - JULY 30, '76. 'TUNISIAN MOSAICS' EXHIBITION. THIS EXHIBITION OF 20 MOSAICS FROM THE ROMAN, VANDAL & BYZANTINE PERIODS REVEALS ASPECTS OF EVERYDAY LIFE DURING THOSE TIMES. AT KENNEDY CENTER. (INT'L). EILEEN HARAKAL, COORD; SMITHSONIAN INSTITUTION TRAVELING EXHIBITION SERVICE; 1000 JEFFERSON DR, SW; WASHINGTON, DC 20560. (#26667-1).

JUNE 30 - JULY 2, '76. BICENTENNIAL CONCERTS IN WASHINGTON, DC. LIVE PERFORMANCE AT ELIPSE & PRESIDENT'S PARK. (REGN'L). RONALD L DREILING, PRES; GRAND ISLAND CITY SINGERS; 2609 BRAHMA; GRAND ISLAND, NE 68801. (#26551-2).

JUNE 30 - JULY 5, '76. THIRD WEEK'S EVENTS AT THE FESTIVAL OF AMERICAN FOLKLIFE. SUMMER-LONG FESTIVAL. THIS WEEK'S HIGHLIGHTED PROGRAMS: SOUTHERN SECTION OF THE US; BENIN & HAITI AT THE AFRICAN DIASPORA; NATIVE AMERICANS OF THE SOUTHEAST; FRANCE, CANADA, POLAND; AND WORKERS WHO BUILD. AT ON THE MALL, BETWEEN LINCOLN MEMORIAL & WASHINGTON MONUMENT. (INT'L). SUSANNE ROSCHWALB; SMITHSONIAN INSTITUTION, NATIONAL PARK SERVICE; SMITHSONIAN INSTITUTION; WASHINGTON, DC 20560. (#111-5).

JUNE 30 - DEC 31, '76. MULTIPHASED EXHIBIT OF GREEK ANTIQUITIES, PERFORMING ARTS & CRAFTS. A MULTIPHASED EXHIBITION OF CLASSICAL GREEK ANTIQUITIES, THEATRICAL GROUPS PRESENTING ANCIENT AND MODERN GREEK PLAYS, AND PHOTO EXHIBITS DEPICTING THE EXCHANGE OF POLITICAL IDEAS BETWEEN GREECE AND AMERICA. (INT'L). JOHN PERDIKIS; GREEK EMBASSY; 2221 MASSACHUSETTS AVE NW; WASHINGTON, DC 20008. (#113-1).

JUNE '76. BICENTENNIAL CHOIR TOUR. OFFICIAL HIGH SCHOOL CHOIR TO PERFORM IN PHILADELPHIA & WASHINGTON, DC IN JUNE WITH OFFICIAL HIGH SCHOOL BAND FROM OREGON. ALL MUSIC WRITTEN BY AMERICAN COMPOSERS. (REGN'L). GLENN PATTON, MUSIC DIR; SHELDON HIGH SCHOOL; 1510 MORNINGSIDE DR; EUGENE, OR 97401. (#26716-2).

JUNE '76 - CONTINUING . EXHIBIT - LATIN AMERICAN COUNTRIES IN THE DECADE OF REVOLUTION. DETAILS THE RICHNESS OF DESIGN, CRAFTS, & THE DECORATIVE ARTS. AT RENWICK GALLERY. (NAT'L). SUSAN HAMILTON; SMITHSONIAN INSTITUTION; SMITHSONIAN INSTITUTION; WASHINGTON, DC 20560. (#7907-4).

JULY 1, '76. FORMAL OPENING OF THE CENTENNIAL SAFE IN CUSTODY OF US CONGRESS. OPENING & DISPLAY OF A SAFE PRESENTED TO CONGRESS BY MRS CHARLES F. DEIHM IN 1876. CONTAINS ITEMS COMMONLY USED & OF PARTICULAR INTEREST TO AMERICANS THEN. SEALED & DONATED DURING CENTENNIAL OBSERVANCE. TO BE OPENED BY THE PRESIDENT OF THE UNITED STATES. (NAT'L). GEORGE M WHITE, ARCHITECT; UNITED STATES CONGRESS; US CONGRESS OFC OF ARCHITECT; WASHINGTON, DC 20515. (#83-1).

JULY 1, '76. OPENING OF THE NATIONAL AIR AND SPACE MUSEUM. SCHEDULED TO OPEN JULY 1, 1976 THE MUSEUM WILL INCLUDE A SPACEARIUM, EXHIBITS ON THE HISTORY OF FLIGHT & SPACE EXPLORATION, & A THEATER WHERE VISITORS SEE AMERICA THROUGH FLIGHT-ORIENTED EYES. THE PRESIDENT WILL HAVE BRIEF REMARKS. AT 7TH & INDEPENDENCE AVE. (NAT'L). LYNNE MURPHY, PRESS ASST; NATIONAL AIR & SPACE MUSEUM; SMITHSONIAN INSTITUTION; WASHINGTON, DC 20560. (#123-1).

JULY 1, '76. OPENING OF THE NATIONAL GUARD HERITAGE GALLERY. THE GALLERY WILL RELATE THE STORY OF THE MINUTEMEN WHO BORE ARMS IN DEFENSE OF THEIR HOMES AND COMMUNITIES TO ESTABLISH THIS NATION'S FREEDOM; THE GROWTH OF THE NATIONAL GUARD IS ALSO TRACED. AT NATIONAL GUARD MEMORIAL, MASS AVE NW,WASH D.C.. (NAT'L). JAMES B DERRIN; HISTORICAL SOCIETY OF THE MILITIA AND NATIONAL GUARD; 1 MASSACHUSETTS AVE, NW; WASHINGTON, DC 20001. (#12654-1).

JULY 1, '76. TRIP TO OPENING OF NATIONAL AIR & SPACE MUSEUM. BUS TRIP FROM LANCASTER, PENNSYLVANIA, TO WASHINGTON, DC FOR OPENING AND TOUR OF NATIONAL AIR AND SPACE MUSEUM. AT SMITHSONIAN INSTITUTION, THE MALL. (REGN'L). STEPHEN M COBAUGH, COORD; UNITED STATES SPACE EDUCATION ASSOCIATION; 746 TURNPIKE ROAD; ELIZABETHTOWN, PA 17022. (#106807-1).

JULY 1 - 2, '76. CALIFORNIA CAVALCADE OF BANDS CONCERT & MARCH. LIVE PERFORMANCE AT CAPITOL REFLECTING POOL. (REGN'L). JAMES C LUCORE, DIRECTOR; CALIFORNIA CAVALCADE OF BANDS; 777 14TH ST, NW; WASHINGTON, DC 20005. (#107335-16).

JULY 1 - 4, '76. A SEMINAR ON CHRISTIAN CITIZENSHIP FOR HIGH SCHOOL BOYS. CHRISTIAN CITIZENSHIP 76 PROJECT OF MEMPHIS. AN AMBASSADOR SERVICE SEMINAR FOR SOUTHERN BAPTIST BOYS, AGES 15-18, JULY 1-4, 1976, AT QUALITY INN-CAPITOL HILL, WASHINGTON, DC. (ST-WIDE). CHARLES DOGGETT; SOUTHERN BAPTIST BROTHERHOOD CONVENTION; 1548 POPLAR AVE; MEMPHIS, TN 38104. (#1512-501).

JULY 1 - 5, '76. ANTIQUE SHOW. THE SHOW WILL FEATURE ANTIQUES & COLLECTIBLES, FINE EARLY AMERICAN GLASS, PRIMITIVE AMERICANA, FOLK ART, ANTIQUE FURNITURE & TOOLS & BOTTLES, EARLY ADVERTISEMENTS; DISPLAYS OF HEIRLOOMS FROM THE FREEDOM TRAIN; OVER 400 DEALERS WILL BE REPRESENTED. AT DC ARMORY. (REGN'L). JAMES CASSEL, DIRECTOR; COMMUNICATIONS ASSOC; 3807 RODMAN ST, NW; WASHINGTON, DC 20016. (#107337-5).

JULY 1 - 22, '76. BICENTENNIAL RELIGIOUS EXHIBIT. EXHIBIT AT THE ELLIPSE. (REGN'L). JAMES C LUCORE, DIRECTOR; AMERICAN CHRISTIAN HERITAGE ASSOC; 777 14TH ST, NW; WASHINGTON, DC 20005. (#107335-15).

JULY 1 - DEC 31, '76. THE STORY OF TRADITIONAL JAZZ - BASIS OF AMERICA'S UNIQUE ARTFORM. 4 A-V PRESENTATIONS OF 20 MIN EACH TO TELL STORY OF HOW JAZZ CAME ABOUT, ITS EARLY PIONEERS, HOW IT SPREAD THROUGHOUT THE WORLD; & THE GREAT REVIVAL. CONSISTS OF PROJECTED PHOTOGRAPHS SYNCHRONIZED WITH RECORDED MUSIC & NARRATION, SUPPLEMENTED BY LIVE CONCERTS & PARADE. AT MARTIN LUTHER KING MEMORIAL LIBRARY, 901 G ST, NW. (LOCAL). RODERICK W CLARKE, COORD; NATIONAL MUSEUM OF TRADITIONAL JAZZ, INC; 1204 N EVERGREEN ST; ARLINGTON, VA 22205. (#19455-4).

JULY 1, '76 - DEC 31, '77. SPECIAL 28-MINUTE FILM ON AMERICAN DEVELOPMENT AT AIR & SPACE MUSEUM. FILM, WITH IMAX PROJECTION SYSTEM ON 80X55 FT SCREEN, WILL GIVE NEW PERSPECTIVE ON AMERICA, CONTRASTING TODAY WITH ORIGINS 200 YRS AGO. IS SWIFT PANORAMIC JOURNEY, FILMED MAINLY FROM THE AIR, SHOWING HOW AMERICANS DEVELOPED TRANSPORTATION, CULMINATING IN JOURNEY TO MOON. AT NATIONAL AIR & SPACE MUSEUM THEATER. (NAT'L). RUDDICK C LAWRENCE, V P; CONTINENTAL OIL COMPANY; HIGH RIDGE PARK; STAMFORD, CT 06904. (#123-2).

JULY 1, '76 - CONTINUING . MILITIA & NATL GUARD EXHIBIT - THE MILITIA IN THE REVOLUTIONARY WAR. EXHIBIT DEALS W/STORY OF THE FARMERS, SHOPKEEPERS, BOOKSELLERS, ETC WHO DEFEATED BRITISH REDCOATS AT LEXINGTON-CONCORD, AND WENT ON TO SERVE IN NEARLY EVERY BATTLE TOWARD FREEDOM. OTHER MILITIA/GUARD ARTIFACTS ALSO ON DISPLAY IN THE MEMORIAL BUILDING. AT NATIONAL GUARD MEMORIAL BLDG, ONE MASSACHUSETTS AVE, NW. (NAT'L). L H CROSS, ASST CURATOR; HISTORICAL SOCIETY OF THE MILITIA & NATIONAL GUARD; 1 MASSACHUSETTS AVE, NW; WASHINGTON, DC 20001. (#12654-2).

JULY 2, '76. CONCERT IN J F K CENTER OF PERFORMING ARTS. LIVE PERFORMANCE AT JOHN F KENNEDY CENTER FOR THE PERFORMING ARTS. (REGN'L). RON DREILING, PRES; GRAND ISLAND CITY SINGERS; 2609 BRAHMA; GRAND ISLAND, NE 68801. (#26551-1).

JULY 2, '76. MORMON TABERNACLE CHOIR BICENTENNIAL CONCERT. LIVE PERFORMANCE AT CAPITAL CENTRE, LARGO, MD, EXITS 32E & 33E OFF I-495. (REGN'L). TOM HART, CONCERT CHMN; THE CHURCH OF JESUS CHRIST OF LATTER-DAY SAINTS BICENTENNIAL COMM; CAPITAL CENTRE TICKET OFFICE; LANDOVER, MD 20786. (#104806-2).

JULY 2, '76. VISIT OF HRH CROWN PRINCE HARALD & CROWN PRINCESS SONJA OF NORWAY. PRESENTATION TO PRESIDENT FORD OF THE NORWEGIAN BICENTENNIAL GIFT (DONATION TO THE VINLAND NATIONAL CENTER, MINN.). (INT'L). PRESS & CULTURAL AFFAIRS; ROYAL NORWEGIAN EMBASSY; 3401 MASSACHUSETTS AVE, NW; WASHINGTON, DC 20007. (#108835-4).

JULY 2 - 4, '76. LIBERTY LOBBY BICENTENNIAL CONVENTION. CONFERENCE AT PENTAGON QUALITY INN. (REGN'L). CAROL M DUNN, SECRETARY; LIBERTY LOBBY; 300 INDEPENDENCE AVE, SE; WASHINGTON, DC 20003. (#107866-1).

JULY 2 - 5, '76. JULY 4TH, 1976 HOLIDAY WEEKEND. JULY 2 - METROPOLITAN AREA LOCAL BICENTENNIAL CELEBRATIONS; JULY 3 - SPECIAL PROGRAM AT THE KENNEDY CENTER; JULY 4 - PAGEANT OF FREEDOM. AT CAPITOL, WASHINGTON MONUMENT, MALL & CONSTITUTION AVE. (NAT'L). LAWRENCE S STINCHCOMB; HAPPY BIRTHDAY, USA!; 1025 15TH ST, NW; WASHINGTON, DC 20005. (#7980-1).

JULY 2 - 5, '76. NATIONAL TRIBUTE TO THE CHARTERS OF FREEDOM. DECLARATION OF INDEPENDENCE, CONSTITUTION & BILL OF RIGHTS, WILL BE ON ROUND-THE-CLOCK DISPLAY JULY 2 THRU 5. NATIONALLY TELEVISED CEREMONY LED BY REPRESENTATIVES OF 3 BRANCHES OF THE FEDERAL GOVERNMENT, INCL THE PRESIDENT, TO PAY TRIBUTE. AT NATIONAL ARCHIVES PORTICO & GREAT HALL, CONSTITUTION AVE. (NAT'L). JEAN MCKEE, DEPUTY ADMIN; AMERICAN REVOLUTION BICENTENNIAL ADMINISTRATION; 2401 E ST, NW; WASHINGTON, DC 20276. (#107865-1).

JULY 3, '76. CLEVELAND HIGH SCHOOL BAND IN BICENTENNIAL PARADE. PARADE. (REGN'L). DR DON YATES, SUPT; CLEVELAND CITY SCHOOLS; CLEVELAND, TN 37311. (#200010-19).

JULY 3, '76. GALA COSTUME BALL WITH BICENTENNIAL DIGNITARIES AT ELDORADO CC. THE BAND WILL REPRESENT THE STATE OF IOWA IN PARADE. (REGN'L). DAN PETERSON, DIRECTOR; VALLEY HIGH SCHOOL BAND; 1140 35TH ST; W DES MOINES, IA 50265. (#26611-2).

JULY 3, '76. JULY 3RD PARADE DOWN CONSTITUTION AVENUE. THE PARADE WILL BE MADE UP OF MOTORIZED FLOATS, EACH 20-50 FT LONG, THAT WILL DEPICT AMERICAN HISTORY IN 25-YR SEGMENTS. FLOATS WILL INCLUDE PLATFORMS FOR DANCE & CHORAL PERFORMANCES. STARTS AT 11AM & WILL LAST AT LEAST 2 1 2 HOURS. AT FROM 3RD & CONSTITUTION WESTWARD TO 22ND & CONSTITUTION. (NAT'L). LAWRENCE S STINCHCOMB; HAPPY BIRTHDAY, USA!; 1025 15TH ST, NW; WASHINGTON, DC 20005. (#7980-2).

JULY 3, '76. SINGING ALL DAY ON NEBRASKA DAY. LIVE PERFORMANCE. (REGN'L). RON DREILING, PRES; GRAND ISLAND

WASHINGTON — CONTINUED

CITY SINGERS; 2609 BRAHMA; GRAND ISLAND, NE 68801. (#26551-3).

JULY 3 - 5, '76. NATION DAY OBSERVANCE -LITURGY/FESTIVAL CONCERTS/OPEN HOUSE. TWO DAYS OF COLORFUL, SUITABLE CELEBRATION FOR THE NATION'S 200TH BIRTHDAY. (REGN'L). R WAYNE DIRKSEN; THE WASHINGTON CATHEDRAL; MT ST ALBAN; WASHINGTON, DC 20016. (#5619-513).

JULY 4, '76. BICENTENNIAL SALUTE TO AMERICA - SPECIAL SERVICE. ALL INVITED WHO LOVE GOD AND THIS COUNTRY; OLD-FASHIONED HYMN SINGING AND PRAYERS. AT RADIO CITY MUSIC HALL, 815 V ST, NW. (REGN'L). REV IMAGENE STEWART, DIR; WASHINGTON AREA BICENTENNIAL RELIGIOUS COMMITTEE; 832 7TH ST, NE; WASHINGTON, DC 20002. (#105940-1).

JULY 4, '76. CLEVELAND HIGH SCHOOL BAND PERFORMANCE AT 'HAPPY BIRTHDAY USA'. LIVE PERFORMANCE. (REGN'L). T C HENLEY, CHAIRMAN; CLEVELAND HIGH SCHOOL; CLEVELAND, TN 37311. (#27351-1).

JULY 4, '76. INDEPENDENCE DAY CELEBRATION AT THE WASHINGTON MONUMENT. A GRAND CELEBRATION OF INDEPENDENCE DAY HELD IN THE NATION CAPITAL ON THE MALL WITH SPEECHES, PARADES, PICNICS, FESTIVALS, BANDS, WITH FIREWORKS IN THE EVENING. NATIONAL PARK SERVICE COSPONSORS THIS EVENT WITH A NUMBER OF PRIVATE AND PUBLIC ORGANIZATIONS. AT GROUNDS OF MONUMENT. (NAT'L). NATIONAL CAPITAL PARKS; NATIONAL PARK SERVICE; 1100 OHIO DRIVE, SW; WASHINGTON, DC 20242. (#6728-73).

JULY 4, '76. NATIONAL VISITOR CENTER DEDICATION. GRAND OPENING OF THIS FACILITY DESIGNED TO SERVE BOTH NATIONAL AND INTERNATIONAL VISITORS BY PROVIDING A WIDE VARIETY OF SERVICES AND VISITOR INFORMATION. AT UNION STATION. (INT'L). GENERAL MANAGER; NATIONAL PARK SERVICE; NATL VISITOR CNTR, UNION STATION; WASHINGTON, DC 20002. (#275-1).

JULY 4, '76. PAGEANT OF FREEDOM. UNIVERSITY & MILITARY BANDS WILL PLAY, FOLLOWED BY A MILITARY TORCHLIGHT TATTOO & A BICENTENNIAL ADDRESS BY THE VICE PRESIDENT OF THE UNITED STATES. AT ON THE ELLIPSE. (NAT'L). LAWRENCE S STINCHCOMB; HAPPY BIRTHDAY, USA!; 1025 15TH ST, NW; WASHINGTON, DC 20005. (#7980-3).

JULY 4, '76. RELIGIOUS SERVICE. CEREMONY AT STEPS OF THE REFLECTING POOL, NEAR THE LINCOLN MEMORIAL. (LOCAL). JAMES C LUCORE, DIRECTOR; DC DOWNTOWN CLUSTER OF CHURCHES; 777 14TH ST, NW; WASHINGTON, DC 20005. (#107335-18).

JULY 5, '76. SALUTE TO AMERICA. PROGRAM & FAMILY PICNIC DAY SCHEDULED. (NAT'L). LAWRENCE S STINCHCOMB; HAPPY BIRTHDAY, USA!; 1025 15TH ST, NW; WASHINGTON, DC 20005. (#7980-4).

JULY 5 - 7, '76. JAPANESE YOUTH GOODWILL CRUISE VISITS WASHINGTON, DC. TOUR. (INT'L). MITAKE KATSUBE, COORD; JAPANESE PRIME MINISTER'S OFFICE; OCHANOMIZU WOMEN'S UNIV; TOKYO/JAPAN. (#109014-4).

JULY 5 - DEC 27, '76. 'THE ANACOSTIA STORY' EXHIBIT AT ANACOSTIA NEIGHBORHOOD MUSEUM. THIS EXHIBIT TELLS THE STORY OF ANOCOSTIA'S HISTORY FROM ITS FIRST SETTLEMENT, THROUGH ITS ETHNIC AND OTHER CHANGES. AT ANACOSTIA NEIGHBORHOOD MUSEUM, 2405 MARTIN LUTHER KING AVE, SE. (LOCAL). JIM MAHONEY; SMITHSONIAN INSTITUTE; SMITHSONIAN INSTITUTION; WASHINGTON, DC 20560. (#106374-3).

JULY 6 - AUG 8, '76. SHAKESPEARE SUMMER FESTIVAL OF WASHINGTON -'THE TEMPEST'. WILL TOUR MONTROSE, ROCK CREEK, GREENBELT, ANTIETAM, HARPERS FERRY, GLEN ECHO, PRINCE WILLIAM FOREST PARK, FORT HUNT, FORT WASHINGTON & THE ELLIPSE. CHECK LOCAL NEWSPAPERS FOR DATES OR WRITE SPONSOR. (REGN'L). DIRECTOR; SHAKESPEARE SUMMER FESTIVAL OF WASHINGTON; 1000 6TH ST, SW; WASHINGTON, DC 20024. (#108805-8).

JULY 6 - AUG 31, '76. MOVIE OPEN HOUSE AT INTERIOR DEPARTMENT. SUBJECTS ARE KEYED TO ACTIVITIES OF THE DEPARTMENT OF INTERIOR, AND RANGE FROM WILD RIVERS TO WILD HORSE, TO INDIAN LIFE AND CULTURE, TO OUTER SPACE EXPLORATION. AT INTERIOR DEPT AUDITORIUM, 18 & C ST, NW. (REGN'L). HILMAR SALLEE, COORD; U S DEPARTMENT OF THE INTERIOR; 18 & C ST, NW; WASHINGTON, DC 20240. (#108920-1).

JULY 6, '76 - CONTINUING . BICENTENNIAL INVENTORY OF AMERICAN PAINTINGS. EXHIBIT AT NATL COLLECTION OF FINE ARTS, 9TH & G ST, NW. (NAT'L). SUSAN HAMILTON, DIRECTOR; SMITHSONIAN INSTITUTION; WASHINGTON, DC 20560. (#107336-1).

JULY 7, '76. KOREAN AMERICAN ASSOCIATION PRESENTS EMBROIDERED SCROLL. WON SOON LEE, PRESIDENT OF THE KOREAN AMERICAN ASSN, LED A 4-MEMBER DELEGATION TO WASHINGTON TO PRESENT ARBA ONE OF TWO EMBROIDERED COPIES OF THE DECLARATION OF INDEPENDENCE. THE PRESENTATION WAS MADE BY CONGRESSMAN CALDWELL BUTLER. (INT'L). ELIZABETH J KIRBY; KOREAN AMERICAN ASSOCIATION & ARBA; 2401 E ST; WASHINGTON, DC 20276. (#33399-1).

JULY 7 - 8, '76. VISIT BY HER MAJESTY QUEEN ELIZABETH II OF ENGLAND. CEREMONY. (INT'L). INFORMATION OFFICE; EMBASSY OF THE UNITED KINGDOM; 3100 MASSACHUSETTS AVE, NW; WASHINGTON, DC 20008. (#108943-5).

JULY 7 - 9, '76. NATL FINNISH AMERICAN BICENTENNIAL MEETING & FESTIVAL. BICENT FESTIVALS WILL BE HELD IN FINNISH-AMERICAN CENTERS LOCATED IN SEVERAL CITIES DURING 1976. (REGN'L). RALPH J JALKANEN, PRES; SUOMI COLLEGE; QUINCY ST; HANCOCK, MI 49930. (#8628-4).

JULY 7 - 11, '76. CANADIAN PARTICIPATION IN SMITHSONIAN FOLKLIFE FESTIVAL. FESTIVAL. (INT'L). K DE B PERCY, COORD; EMBASSY OF CANADA; 1746 MASSACHUSETTS AVE, NW; WASHINGTON, DC 20036. (#105111-7).

JULY 7 - 11, '76. FOREIGN VISITOR BONSAI SEMINAR AT INTERNATIONAL CONVENTION. BONSAI CLUBS INTERNATIONAL CONVENTION, 1976. ANNUAL MEMBERSHIP MEETING, PLUS EDUCATIONAL PROGRAMS & DEMONSTRATION OF THE ART OF BONSAI (MINIATURE TREES). HIGHLIGHT WILL BE DEDICATION OF NATIONAL ARBORETUM BONSAI COLLECTION. (INT'L). JAMES R NEWTON; BCI '76 & POTOMAC BONSAI ASSOC; PO BOX 28308; WASHINGTON, DC 20005. (#2291-503).

JULY 7 - 11, '76. FOURTH WEEK'S EVENTS AT THE FESTIVAL OF AMERICAN FOLKLIFE. SUMMER-LONG FESTIVAL. THIS WEEK'S HIGHLIGHTED PROGRAMS: THE UPLAND SOUTH SECTION OF THE US; BENIN & HAITI AT THE AFRICAN DIASPORA; NATIVE AMERICANS OF THE PRAIRIES; GREAT BRITAIN, CANADA, PORTUGAL; AND WORKERS WHO BUILD. AT ON THE MALL, BETWEEN LINCOLN MEMORIAL & WASHINGTON MONUMENT. (INT'L). SUSANNE ROSCHWALB; SMITHSONIAN INSTITUTION, NATIONAL PARK SERVICE; SMITHSONIAN INSTITUTION; WASHINGTON, DC 20560. (#111-6).

JULY 7 - 11, '76. INTERNATIONAL CONVENTION OF BONSAI CLUBS. BONSAI CLUBS INTERNATIONAL CONVENTION, 1976. ANNUAL MEMBERSHIP MEETING, PLUS EDUCATIONAL PROGRAMS & DEMONSTRATION OF THE ART OF BONSAI (MINIATURE TREES). HIGHLIGHT WILL BE DEDICATION OF NATIONAL ARBORETUM BONSAI COLLECTION. AT SHOREHAM-AMERICANA HOTEL. (INT'L). JAMES R NEWTON; BCI '76 & POTOMAC BONSAI ASSOC; PO BOX 28308; WASHINGTON, DC 20005. (#2291-501).

JULY 7 - 24, '76. 'LOVE'S LABOUR'S LOST'. LIVE PERFORMANCE AT TRAPIER THEATER - WASHINGTON CATHEDRAL GROUNDS. (REGN'L). TED WALCH, DIRECTOR; SHAKESPEARE & CO - TRAPIER THEATER; ST ALBANS SCHOOL; WASHINGTON, DC 20016. (#108434-2).

JULY 7 - AUG 15, '76. 'FORGE OF FREEDOM'. THE STORY OF OUR COUNTRY, A DRAMATIC PLAY WITH MUSIC FOR THE ENTIRE FAMILY, AS SEEN BY DAWSON FAMILY DURING THE REVOLUTION, WHOSE LOYALTIES WERE DIVIDED. SATURDAY PERFORMANCES AT 6 & 9:30 PM. MATINEES ON THURSDAY AT 1 PM AND SUNDAYS 3 PM. AT FORD'S THEATRE, 511 10TH ST, NW, WASHINGTON, DC. (REGN'L). BOX OFFICE; FORD'S THEATRE; 511 10TH ST, NW; WASHINGTON, DC 20004. (#104887-3).

JULY 8, '76. GRIMETHORPE COLLIERY BAND FROM ENGLAND VISITS THE BRITISH EMBASSY. THIS BAND WAS FORMED IN 1917 BY A GROUP OF WORKMEN FROM THE COAL MINES WHO LIVED IN THE VILLAGE OF CUDWORTH. (INT'L). MS EDITH HALL; LYRA ENTERTAINMENT, INC; 16 W 61ST ST; NEW YORK, NY 10023. (#109010-4).

JULY 9, '76. DEDICATION OF NATIONAL BONSAI COLLECTION. THE NATL ARBORETUM WILL DEVELOP A NATL COLLECTION OF DWARF BONSAI PLANTS OF HISTORIC QUALITY FROM JAPAN & A COLLECTION FROM THE US. (INT'L). JOHN L CREECH, DIRECTOR; NATIONAL ARBORETUM; 24 & R STS, NE; WASHINGTON, DC 20002. (#5571-2).

JULY 9 - AUG 1, '76. FREDERICK DOUGLASS MOBILE THEATRE PROGRAM. PRODUCTION WILL SHOW THE EVOLUTION OF CIVIL RIGHTS FROM THE FOUNDING OF THE NATION TO THE PRESENT TIME. (LOCAL). SUPT, NCP-EAST; NATIONAL PARK SERVICE; 1100 OHIO DR, SW; WASHINGTON, DC 20042. (#6729-162).

JULY 9 - AUG 31, '76. 'EMILY DICKINSON IN CELEBRATION' BY SUSAN GAILBRAITH. WILL BE PRESENTED AT MATINEE & LATE EVENING PERFORMANCES. TICKET PRICES & DATES FOR THIS PRODUCTION WILL BE AVAILABLE AT BOX OFFICE. AT TRAPIER THEATER - WASHINGTON CATHEDRAL GROUNDS. (REGN'L). TED WALCH, DIRECTOR; SHAKESPEARE & CO - TRAPIER THEATER; ST ALBANS SCHOOL; WASHINGTON, DC 20016. (#108434-5).

JULY 9 - NOV ??, '76. WEDGEWOOD REVOLUTIONARY PERIOD PORTRAITS. EXHIBIT AT NATIONAL PORTRAIT GALLERY, 9TH & F ST, NW. (REGN'L). SUSAN HAMILTON, DIRECTOR; SMITHSONIAN INSTITUTION; WASHINGTON, DC 20560. (#107334-2).

JULY 12, '76. KENNEDY CENTER BICENTENNIAL PROGRAM. KANSAS STATE UNIV RESIDENT STRING QUARTET WILL PERFORM 2 CONCERTS. AT KENNEDY CENTER. (REGN'L). DR ROBERT STEINBAUER; KANSAS STATE UNIV MUSIC DEPT; MANHATTAN, KS 66506. (#26700-1).

JULY 12, '76. PARADE OF AMERICAN MUSIC - KANSAS UNIV BAND CONCERTS. LIVE PERFORMANCE AT JAYHAWK BLVD. (REGN'L). ROBERT FOSTER, CHMN; KANSAS FEDERATION OF MUSIC CLUBS UNIV OF KANSAS; LAWRENCE, KS 66045. (#101840-3).

JULY 13 - 16, '76. '76 INTERNATL CONFERENCE ON ELECTROMAGNETIC COMPATIBILITY. '76 INTERNATL CONF ON ELECTROMAGNETIC COMPATIBILTY. THE INSTITUTE OF ELECTRICAL & ELECTRONICS ENGINEERS PLANS TECHNICAL PAPERS, SOCIAL EVENTS, TOURS OF WASHINGTON, DC AND SPECIAL ACTIVITIES FOR THEIR ANNUAL CONVENTION. AT SHOREHAM AMERICANA HOTEL. (INT'L). WILLIAM C GREEN; INSTITUTE OF ELECTRICAL & ELECTRONICS ENGINEERS; 1625 EYE ST NW; WASHINGTON, DC 20006. (#6427-501).

JULY 14, '76. BICENT DEPARTURE DAY CEREMONIES FOR AMERICAN FIELD SERVICE STUDENTS. DEPARTURE DAY IS THE YEAR-END HIGHLIGHT FOR 2600 AMER FIELD SERVICE STUDENTS FROM ABROAD, WHO HAVE SPENT THE BICENT YEAR IN AMERICAN COMMUNITIES. TENTATIVE PLANS INCLUDE PARTICIPATION BY MEMBERS OF CONGRESS. AT WOLF TRAP FARM PARK, SUBURBAN WASHINGTON, DC. (INT'L). SUSAN EISENHART, ASST DIR; AMERICAN FIELD SERVICE INTL SCHOLARSHIPS; 313 E 43RD ST; NEW YORK, NY 10017. (#8974-1).

JULY 14 - 18, '76. FIFTH WEEK'S EVENTS AT THE FESTIVAL OF AMERICAN FOLKLIFE. SUMMER-LONG FESTIVAL. THIS WEEK'S HIGHLIGHTED PROGRAMS: HEARTLAND REGION OF THE US; LIBERIA, TRINIDAD, TOBAGO AT THE AFRICAN DIASPORA; NATIVE AMERICANS OF THE SOUTHERN PLAINS; YUGOSLAVIA, POLAND; AND WORKERS WHO CLOTHE US. AT ON THE MALL, BETWEEN LINCOLN MEMORIAL & WASHINGTON MONUMENT. (INT'L). MRS SHIRLEY CHERKASKY; SMITHSONIAN INSTITUTION, NATIONAL PARK SERVICE; SMITHSONIAN INSTITUTION; WASHINGTON, DC 20560. (#111-7).

JULY 14 - AUG 31, '76. TORCHLIGHT TATTOOS AT THE JEFFERSON MEMORIAL. LIVE PERFORMANCE AT AT THE JEFFERSON MEMORIAL. (REGN'L). NCP MALL OPERATION; US ARMY & NCP; 1100 OHIO DRIVE, SW; WASHINGTON, DC 20242. (#108365-2).

JULY 14 - DEC 31, '76. 'GREAT AMERICAN FACES' PHOTO EXHIBITION. EXHIBIT AT NATIONAL VISITORS CENTER AT UNION STATION. (NAT'L). SUE S BROWN, COORD; KINNEY SHOE CORPORATION; 233 BROADWAY; NEW YORK, NY 10007. (#19279-1).

JULY 15, '76. DEDICATION OF PLANETARIUM-PROJECTOR SYSTEM FOR AIR & SPACE MUSEUM. CHANCELLOR HELMUT SCHMIDT OF WEST GERMANY WILL PRESENT THE PROJECTOR SYSTEM TO THE UNITED STATES. IN CONNECTION W/THE PRESENTATION, A SERIES OF CONCERTS OF ELECTRONIC MUSIC, FEATURING 'SIRIUS' BY KARL HEINZ STOCKHAUSEN, WILL BE GIVEN. AT AIR & SPACE MUSEUM, 7TH & INDEPENDENCE NW. (INT'L). S DILLON RIPLEY, SEC; THE SMITHSONIAN INSTITUTION; WASHINGTON, DC 20560. (#13696-1).

JULY 15 - 17, '76. WORLD COMMUNITY BICENTENNIAL ART EXPOSITION. EXHIBIT AT INTERNATIONAL INN. (LOCAL). MRS KASHIF, CHAIRPERSON; NATION OF ISLAM CREATION COMMITTEE; 1519 4TH ST, NW; WASHINGTON, DC 20001. (#26758-1).

JULY 15 - AUG 15, '76. HAPPY BIRTHDAY AMERICA FROM THE WORLD OF ISLAM. EXHIBIT AT ISLAMIC CENTER OF WASHINGTON, DC, 2551 MASSACHUSETTS AVE, NW. (REGN'L). DIRECTOR, ISLAM EXHIBIT; THE SUPREME COUNCIL ON ISLAMIC AFFAIRS; 2551 MASSACHUSETTS AVE, NW; WASHINGTON, DC 20008. (#109093-1).

JULY 16 - 18, '76. CANADIAN PARTICIPATION AT NATIONAL FOLK FESTIVAL. THE FESTIVAL WILL BE HELD AT WOLF TRAP FARM PARK. (INT'L). K DE B PERCY, COORD; GOVT OF CANADA; 1746 MASSACHUSETTS AVE, NW; WASHINGTON, DC 20036. (#105111-16).

JULY 16 - AUG 8, '76. 'TOCQUEVILLE!' - A MUSICAL COMEDY. FANCIFUL SATIRE OF 19TH CENTURY FRENCH JOURNALIST ALEXIS DE TOCQUEVILLE'S RETURN TO AMERICAN CONTINENT IN 1976 TO TRAVEL ON A BUS TOUR ACROSS THE UNITED STATES. AT TRINITY THEATRE, 36TH & 'O' STS, NW - MATINEES ON SAT - 2 PM. (REGN'L). NICK GALANTE; TRINITY THEATRE; 36TH & O STS, NW; WASHINGTON, DC 20007. (#108942-1).

JULY 17, '76. DRUM AND BUGLE CORPS COMPETITION. COMPETITION, LIVE PERFORMANCE AT DC ARMORY. (REGN'L). ERNEST MYERS, COORDINATOR; MECCA TEMPLE NUMBER 10; 1721 TAYLOR ST, NE; WASHINGTON, DC 20017. (#107337-7).

JULY 18, '76. VISIT BY EDINBURGH'S ORCHESTRA & CHOIR OF CATHEDRAL ST MARY. LIVE PERFORMANCE AT WASHINGTON CATHEDRAL. (INT'L). J STEVEN WATSON, COORD; CATHEDRAL CHURCH OF ST MARY THE VIRGIN; 17 COLLEGE ST; ST ANDREWS/UNITED KINGDOM. (#109012-8).

JULY 18 - AUG 21, '76. FORT DUPONT THEATER EVENING CONCERTS. LIVE PERFORMANCE. (LOCAL). DIRECTOR; NATIONAL PARK SERVICE; 1100 OHIO DR, SW; WASHINGTON, DC 20242. (#108341-1).

JULY 20, '76. VIKING SPACE VEHICLE LANDING ON MARS - 1976. 'VIKING' UNMANNED SPACECRAFT SOFT LANDING ON PLANET MARS ON JULY 20 TO EXPLORE FOR SIGNS OF LIFE. SIGNAL FROM 'VIKING' IN ORBIT AROUND MARS OPENED THE NATIONAL AIR & SPACE MUSEUM ON JULY 1, 1976, IN PRESCENCE OF PRESIDENT FORD & OTHER DIGNITARIES. AT KENNEDY SPACE CENTER, COCOA BEACH, FLORIDA. (INT'L). JOHN P DONNELLY; NATIONAL AERONAUTICS AND SPACE ADMINISTRATION; 400 MARYLAND AVE SW; WASHINGTON, DC 20546. (#1975-1).

JULY 20 - 23, '76. TOUR OF WASHINGTON, DC. EIGHT INDIAN STUDENTS AND TWO CHAPERONES FROM THE WYOMING INDIAN HIGH SCHOOL WILL TOUR WASHINGTON AREA AND PERFORM THEIR NATIVE DANCES. (LOCAL). TOM SHAKESPEARE, PROJ DIR; ARAPAHOE INDIAN TRADITIONAL CLUB; BOX 145; ETHETE, WY 82520. (#26108-1).

JULY 21 - 25, '76. SIXTH WEEK'S EVENTS AT THE FESTIVAL OF AMERICAN FOLKLIFE. SUMMER-LONG FESTIVAL. THIS WEEK'S HIGHLIGHTED PROGRAMS: WESTERN SECTION OF THE US; LIBERIA, TRINIDAD, TOBAGO AT AFRICAN DIASPORA; NATIVE AMERICANS OF THE NORTHERN PLAINS; BELGIUM, NETHERLANDS, LUXEMBOURG, EGYPT; AND WORKERS WHO CLOTHE US. AT ON THE MALL, BETWEEN LINCOLN MEMORIAL & WASHINGTON MONUMENT. (INT'L). SUSANNE ROSCHWALB; SMITHSONIAN INSTITUTION, NATIONAL PARK SERVICE; SMITHSONIAN INSTITUTION; WASHINGTON, DC 20560. (#111-8).

JULY 22 - 24, '76. LEARNING TECHNOLOGY SYMPOSIUM AND EXPOSITION. PRESENTATIONS ON APPLIED LEARNING TECHNOLOGY AND DEMONSTRATIONS OF ACTUAL LEARNING SYSTEMS DEVICES, MACHINES & TECHNIQUES. AT SHERATON PARK HOTEL. (INT'L). RAYMOND G FOX, PRESIDENT; SOCIETY FOR APPLIED LEARNING TECHNOLOGY; 740 15TH ST, NW, SUITE 700; WASHINGTON, DC 20005. (#2387-1).

JULY 23, '76. COACHES ALL-STAR FOOTBALL GAME. RAIN DATE IS 07 24 76. AT RFK KENNEDY STADIUM. (REGN'L). DR JAMES JONES, DIR; YOUTH OPPORTUNITIES SERVICES; DIST BLDG, 14TH & E ST, NW; WASHINGTON, DC 20004. (#107337-3).

WASHINGTON — CONTINUED

JULY 23, '76. SALUTE TO THE STATES - KANSAS. CEREMONY AT STEPS OF THE CAPITOL. (REGN'L). JAMES C LUCORE, DIRECTOR; GOVT OF THE DISTRICT OF COLUMBIA; 777 14TH ST, NW; WASHINGTON, DC 20005. (#107332-7).

JULY 25, '76. LATINO MURALS & FESTIVALS. FESTIVAL, EXHIBIT AT 1470 IRVING STREET, N W. (LOCAL). LYNN GLIXON, ADMIN; WOODROW WILSON INTERNATIONAL CENTER; 1470 IRVING ST, NW; WASHINGTON, DC 20010. (#22885-1).

JULY 25 - 26, '76. PORTERVILLE PANTHER BAND PERFORMANCE. THE PORTERVILLE PANTHER BAND INVOLVES 200 STUDENTS, ONE FOR EVERY YEAR OF OUR HISTORY; THE BAND WILL TRAVEL TO DIFFERENT CITIES PLAYING IN CONCERTS AND PARADES. (REGN'L). BUCK SHAFFER, DIRECTOR; PORTERVILLE PANTHER BAND; 465 W OLIVE; PORTERVILLE, CA 93257. (#102849-5).

JULY 26, '76. BICENTENNIAL PARADE OF AMERICAN MUSIC HONORS NEVADA. EACH CONCERT FEATURES MUSIC COMPOSED IN OR ABOUT THE FEATURED STATE PLAYED BY OUTSTANDING MUSICAL GROUPS OR SOLOISTS FROM THAT STATE. AT JOHN F KENNEDY MEMORIAL CENTER. (REGN'L). KEN HANLON, DIR; NATIONAL MUSIC COUNCIL & EXXON; UNIV OF LAS VEGAS; LAS VEGAS, NV 89107. (#4500-30).

JULY 26 - 28, '76. 1976 NISEI VETERANS REUNION, WASHINGTON VISITATION. ARLINGTON CEMETERY TOMB OF UNKNOWN SOLDIER CEREMONY AND NISEI GI GRAVES, VISIT CAPITOL HILL-LUNCHEON AND TOUR BY REP SPARK MATSUNAGA, JAPANESE EMBASSY RECEPTION BY HON F TOGO AMBASSADOR OF JAPAN; VIP WHITE HOUSE TOUR, GO FOR BROKE BANQUET AT SHOREHAM AMERICANA HOTEL. AT SHOREHAM AMERICANA HOTEL, 2500 CALVERT ST, NW WASHINGTON, DC. (INT'L). HARRY TAKAGI, COORD; WASHINGTON COMMITTEE FOR NISEI VETERANS REUNION; 6006 DENTON COURT; SPRINGFIELD, VA 22152. (#107632-1).

JULY 26 - 31, '76. SPANISH ETHNIC MINI-FESTIVAL. FESTIVAL. (REGN'L). REGINA SAXTON, COORD; DC OFFICE OF BICENTENNIAL PROGRAMS; 777 14TH ST, NW; WASHINGTON, DC 20005. (#107335-2).

JULY 27, '76. SALUTE TO THE STATES - NEVADA. CEREMONY AT STEPS OF THE CAPITOL. (REGN'L). JAMES C LUCORE, DIRECTOR; GOVT OF THE DISTRICT OF COLUMBIA; 777 14TH ST, NW; WASHINGTON, DC 20005. (#107332-8).

JULY 27 - 31, '76. 'THE COURTSHIP OF MARY JONES' BY ROBERT MANSON MYERS - PREMIERE. LIVE PERFORMANCE AT TRAPIER THEATER - WASHINGTON CATHEDRAL GROUNDS. (REGN'L). TED WALCH, DIRECTOR; SHAKESPEARE & CO - TRAPIER THEATER; ST ALBANS SCHOOL; WASHINGTON, DC 20016. (#108434-3).

JULY 28 - AUG 1, '76. SEVENTH WEEK'S EVENTS AT THE FESTIVAL OF AMERICAN FOLKLIFE. SUMMER-LONG FESTIVAL. THIS WEEK'S HIGHLIGHTED PROGRAMS: PACIFIC NORTHWEST SECTION OF THE US; NIGERIA, BRAZIL AT AFRICAN DIASPORA; NATIVE AMERICANS OF NORTHWEST COAST; GERMANY, PAKISTAN; AND WORKERS IN COMMUNICATIONS, ARTS AND RECREATION. AT ON THE MALL, BETWEEN LINCOLN MEMORIAL & WASHINGTON MONUMENT. (INT'L). SUSANNE ROSCHWALB; SMITHSONIAN INSTITUTION, NATIONAL PARK SERVICE; SMITHSONIAN INSTITUTION; WASHINGTON, DC 20560. (#111-9).

JULY 30 - 31, '76. KOOL JAZZ FESTIVAL. LIVE PERFORMANCE AT RFK KENNEDY STADIUM. (REGN'L). OFIELD DUKES & ASSOC; FESTIVAL PRODUCTIONS, INC; SUITE 716, NATL PRESS BLDG; WASHINGTON, DC 20045. (#107337-2).

JULY 31, '76. JEFFERSON MEMORIAL ELEVATOR & RAMP OPENING. OPENING. (REGN'L). NCP DIV SPECIAL EVENTS; NATIONAL PARK SERVICE; 1100 OHIO DRIVE, SW; WASHINGTON, DC 20242. (#1483-1).

JULY '76. KLEINBASLER DRUMMERS & FIFERS FROM SWITZERLAND - LIVE PERFORMANCE. LIVE PERFORMANCE. (INT'L). CHRISTINE BAUMGARTNER; EMBASSY OF SWITZERLAND; 2900 CATHEDRAL AVE, NW; WASHINGTON, DC 20007. (#108956-4).

JULY '76. SALUTE TO BLACK MEN IN HISTORY. CEREMONY. (LOCAL). BETTY J BROWN, PROJ COORD; CONCERNED BLACK WOMEN OF METROPOLITAN WASHINGTON; 816 EASLEY ST; SILVER SPRING, MD 20910. (#27854-1).

JULY '76 - JUNE 30, '77. 'AMERICA AT THE MOVIES' - THE ARBA FILM SHOWN NATIONWIDE. CREATED & PRODUCED BY THE AMERICAN FILM INSTITUTE FOR THE ARBA, THE FILM TRACES HOW THE USA HAS BEEN PORTRAYED ON THE SCREN FOR OVER THREE-QUARTERS OF A CENTURY. GREAT SCENES FROM NEARLY 100 FILMS. (NAT'L). JACK MASEY, PROJ DIRECTOR; AMERICAN REVOLUTION BICENTENNIAL ADMINISTRATION; 2401 E STREET, N W; WASHINGTON, DC 20276. (#26650-2).

AUG 1, '76. EXHIBIT OF 38 FOOT MEMORIAL TO ALL AMERICA'S VETERANS. ONLY MEMORIAL IN DC TO ALL VETS OF ALL WARS. 12 BRONZE 6 X 5 FOOT PANELS WILL SHOW MILITARY HISTORY OF COUNTRY. STATUE WILL BE 38 FEET HIGH. SCULPTOR SAME AS IWO JIMA FLAG RAISING STATUE. AT VFW MEMORIAL BUILDING, 200 MARYLAND AVE, NE. (NAT'L). T H MARLOW, DIRECTOR; VETERANS OF FOREIGN WARS OF THE U S; 200 MARYLAND AVE, NE; WASHINGTON, DC 20002. (#102062-1).

AUG 1 - 5, '76. O'NEILL IRISH DANCERS TO PERFORM AT SALUTE TO NEBRASKA DAY PROGRAM. LIVE PERFORMANCE AT J F KENNEDY CTR, W CAPITOL TER, JEFFERSON MEM, LINCOLN MEM & MORE. (NAT'L). VIVIAN MELENA, DIRECTOR; O'NEILL IRISH DANCERS; BOX 323; O'NEILL, NE 68763. (#27346-1).

AUG 2, '76. BICENTENNIAL PARADE OF AMERICAN MUSIC HONORS NEBRASKA. ELAIN GROVE, A MEMBER OF THE AMERICAN OLD TIME FIDDLERS ASSN, WILL PLAY IN THE FOYER. AT JOHN F KENNEDY MEMORIAL CENTER. (REGN'L). MRS LLOYD SPIKER, DIR; NATIONAL MUSIC COUNCIL & EXXON; 7209 WASHINGTON; RALSTON, NE 68127. (#4500-31).

AUG 3, '76. FINLAND'S PRESIDENT URHO K KEKKONEN VISITS THE UNITED STATES. TOUR. (INT'L). OFFICER OF INFORMATION; EMBASSY OF FINLAND; 1900 24TH STREET, NW; WASHINGTON, DC 20008. (#200010-20).

AUG 3, '76. PERFORMANCE BY DOROTHY BRONSON SINGERS. LIVE PERFORMANCE AT CONGRESSIONAL DINING HALL, UNITED STATES CAPITAL. (REGN'L). DOROTHY BRONSON, COORD; SCOTTSBLUFF-GERING UNITED CHAMBER OF COMMERCE; 1632 19TH AVE; MITCHELL, NE 69357. (#27349-1).

AUG 3, '76. SALUTE TO THE STATES - NEBRASKA. CEREMONY AT STEPS OF THE CAPITOL. (REGN'L). JAMES C LUCORE, DIRECTOR; GOVT OF THE DISTRICT OF COLUMBIA; 777 14TH ST, NW; WASHINGTON, DC 20005. (#107332-9).

AUG 4 - 8, '76. 'THE BALLAD OF DOCTOR FAUSTUS' BY CHRISTOPHER MARLOWE - PREMIERE. WASHINGTON CATHEDRAL'S COMPOSER IN RESIDENCE, WAYNE DIRKSEN, HAS PLACED MARLOWE'S 'DR FAUSTUS' IN THE GOLD RUSH OF THE AMERICAN WEST WITH MUSIC & ADDITIONAL WORDS. AT TRAPIER THEATER - WASHINGTON CATHEDRAL GROUNDS. (REGN'L). TED WALCH, DIRECTOR; SHAKESPEARE & CO - TRAPIER THEATER; ST ALBANS SCHOOL; WASHINGTON, DC 20016. (#108434-4).

AUG 4 - 8, '76. EIGHTH WEEK'S EVENTS AT THE FESTIVAL OF AMERICAN FOLKLIFE. SUMMER-LONG FESTIVAL. THIS WEEK'S HIGHLIGHTED PROGRAMS: SOUTHWEST REGION OF THE US; NIGERIA & PUERTO RICO AT THE AFRICAN DIASPORA; NATIVE AMERICANS OF THE SOUTHWEST; SPAIN & MEXICO; AND WORKERS IN COMMUNICATIONS, ARTS AND RECREATION. AT ON THE MALL, BETWEEN LINCOLN MEMORIAL & WASHINGTON MONUMENT. (INT'L). SUSANNE ROSCHWALB; SMITHSONIAN INSTITUTION, NATIONAL PARK SERVICE; SMITHSONIAN INSTITUTION; WASHINGTON, DC 20560. (#111-10).

AUG 9, '76. BICENTENNIAL PARADE OF AMERICAN MUSIC HONORS COLORADO. THE GOLD SASH BAND WILL APPEAR IN THE FOYER. A VOCAL & INSTRUMENTAL ENSEMBLE FROM COLORADO UNIV & COLORADO STATE UNIV WILL ALSO PERFORM. AT JOHN F KENNEDY MEMORIAL CENTER. (REGN'L). MRS JESS MCQUIE, DIR; NATIONAL MUSIC COUNCIL & EXXON; 640 GARFIELD ST; DENVER, CO 80206. (#4500-32).

AUG 10, '76. SALUTE TO THE STATES - COLORADO. CEREMONY AT STEPS OF THE CAPITOL. (REGN'L). JAMES C LUCORE, DIRECTOR; GOVT OF THE DISTRICT OF COLUMBIA; 777 14TH ST, NW; WASHINGTON, DC 20005. (#107332-10).

AUG 10 - 12, '76. 'I LOVE AMERICA' PRESENTED BY OAKLAND BICENTENNIAL CHOIR. LIVE PERFORMANCE. (REGN'L). EDWIN E HANNA, DIRECTOR; OAKLAND MINISTERIAL ASSOC, FIRST LUTHERAN CHURCH; 601 N DAVIS AVE; OAKLAND, NE 68045. (#27338-1).

AUG 10 - 14, '76. CONFERENCE ON YOUTH NEEDS AND YOUTH EXHIBITION. CONFERENCE, EXHIBIT AT MARRIOTT TWIN BRIDGES. (REGN'L). STUART RADO, EXEC DIR; NATIONAL NETWORK OF YOUTH ADVISORY BOARDS; PO BOX 402036, OCEAN VIEW BRANCH; MIAMI BEACH, FL 33140. (#1536-13).

AUG 11, '76. CANADIAN INVOLVEMENT AND ASSISTANCE WITH THE LA SALLE EXPEDITION. CANADA'S PARTICIPATION WILL BE PARTLY CEREMONIAL & PARTLY FINANCIAL AS CANADA IS CONTRIBUTING THE SUM OF FIVE THOUSAND DOLLARS FOR THIS EVENT. (INT'L). K DE B PERCY, COORD; LA SALLE EXPEDITION & GOVT OF CANADA; 1746 MASSACHUSETTS AVE, NW; WASHINGTON, DC 20036. (#105111-11).

AUG 11 - 15, '76. NINETH WEEK'S EVENTS AT THE FESTIVAL OF AMERICAN FOLKLIFE. SUMMER-LONG FESTIVAL. THIS WEEK'S HIGHLIGHTED PROGRAMS: TRANSPORTATION; ZAIRE & SURINAM AT THE AFRICAN DIASPORA; NATIVE AMERICANS OF THE PLATEAU; JAPAN & GREECE; AND WORKERS IN PROFESSIONAL & TECHNICAL SKILLS (TRANSPORTATION). AT ON THE MALL, BETWEEN LINCOLN MEMORIAL & WASHINGTON MONUMENT. (INT'L). SUSANNE ROSCHWALB; SMITHSONIAN INSTITUTION, NATIONAL PARK SERVICE; SMITHSONIAN INSTITUTION; WASHINGTON, DC 20560. (#111-11).

AUG 12 - 15, '76. CZECHOSLOVAK SOCIETY OF ARTS & SCIENCES IN AMERICA 8TH CONGRESS. U S ARMY MILITARY BAND CONCERT AUG 12TH AT CAPITOL GROUNDS-EAST WITH PROGRAM BY CZECHOSLOVAK COMPOSERS. AT GEORGETOWN UNIV. (REGN'L). EMIL ROYCO, PROJ CHMN; CZECHOSLOVAK SOCIETY OF ARTS & SCIENCES IN AMERICA, INC; 6612 TULIP HILL TERRACE; WASHINGTON, DC 20016. (#108448-1).

AUG 14 - 15, '76. 'TRUCK ROADEO' SAFE DRIVING CHAMPIONSHIPS. ROADEO FEATURES EXAMPLES OF HISTORIC, MODERN AND FUTURE EQUIPMENT OF TRUCKING AND INDUSTRY, MANY DECORATED WITH A BICENTENNIAL MOTIF. AT LOCAL ROADEO HELD AT SMITHSONIAN FOLKLIFE FESTIVAL.. (REGN'L). MARY JO LONG, ASST; AMERICAN TRUCKING ASSOC, INC; 1616 P ST, NW; WASHINGTON, DC 20036. (#104888-1).

AUG 18 - 22, '76. TENTH WEEK'S EVENTS AT THE FESTIVAL OF AMERICAN FOLKLIFE. SUMMER-LONG FESTIVAL. THIS WEEK'S HIGHLIGHTED PROGRAMS: TRANSPORTATION; ZAIRE & SURINAM AT AFRICAN DIASPORA; NATIVE AMERICANS OF THE BASIN; AUSTRIA & INDIA; AND WORKERS IN PROFESSIONAL & TECHNICAL SKILLS (TRANSPORTATION). AT ON THE MALL, BETWEEN LINCOLN MEMORIAL & WASHINGTON MONUMENT. (INT'L). SUSANNE ROSCHWALB; SMITHSONIAN INSTITUTION, NATIONAL PARK SERVICE; SMITHSONIAN INSTITUTION; WASHINGTON, DC 20560. (#111-12).

AUG 20, '76. HERITAGE EXHIBIT. EXHIBIT. (REGN'L). REGINA SAXTON, COORD; DC OFFICE OF BICENTENNIAL PROGRAMS; 777 14TH ST, NW; WASHINGTON, DC 20005. (#107335-9).

AUG 23, '76. BAND CONCERT & DEDICATION OF BRONZE BUST HONORING JOHN PHILIP SOUSA. CONCERT & DEDICATION CEREMONY ADMITTING JOHN PHILIP SOUSA TO THE HALL OF FAME FOR GREAT AMERICANS. UNVEILING OF BUST OF SOUSA BY KARL GRUPPE, NA. PERFORMANCE BY U S MARINE BAND OF MUSIC BY JOHN PHILIP SOUSA. AT JOHN F KENNEDY CENTER CONCERT HALL. (NAT'L). DR J GRUNDFEST, EXEC DIR; HALL OF FAME FOR GREAT AMERICANS/AMERICAN BANDMASTERS ASSOC; 2 WASHINGTON SQUARE VILLAGE; NEW YORK, NY 10012. (#107160-1).

AUG 23, '76. BICENTENNIAL PARADE OF AMERICAN MUSIC HONORS NORTH DAKOTA. LIVE PERFORMANCE AT JOHN F KENNEDY MEMORIAL CENTER. (REGN'L). DR MERTON UTGAARD, DIR; BICENTENNIAL PARADE OF AMERICAN MUSIC; INTL MUSIC CAMP; BOTTINEAU, ND 58318. (#4500-34).

AUG 23, '76. SOUTH GATE CITY YOUTH BAND CONCERT. LIVE PERFORMANCE AT LINCOLN MEMORIAL AT THE REFLECTING POOL STEPS. (REGN'L). JAMES C LUCORE, DIRECTOR; DC DEPARTMENT OF RECREATION; 777 14TH ST, NW; WASHINGTON, DC 20005. (#107335-19).

AUG 24, '76. SALUTE TO THE STATES - NORTH DAKOTA. CEREMONY AT STEPS OF THE CAPITOL. (REGN'L). JAMES C LUCORE, DIRECTOR; GOVT OF THE DISTRICT OF COLUMBIA; 777 14TH ST, NW; WASHINGTON, DC 20005. (#107332-11).

AUG 25, '76. GOVERNMENT STUDY TOUR - WASHINGTON BRIEFING, DEPT OF STATE & USIA. MAYORS AND COUNCIL MEMBERS OF CALIFORNIA CITIES WILL VISIT SELECTED EUROPEAN CITIES TO STUDY LOCAL GOVERNMENT AND MUNICIPAL PROBLEMS. AT TOWN HALL. (INT'L). GEORGE VOIGT, EXEC DIR; SOUTHPORT BICENTENNIAL COMMITTEE; 2468 HUNTINGTON DR; SAN MARINO, CA 91108. (#23678-1).

AUG 25 - 29, '76. ELEVENTH WEEK'S EVENTS AT THE FESTIVAL OF AMERICAN FOLKLIFE. SUMMER-LONG FESTIVAL. THIS WEEK'S HIGHLIGHTED PROGRAMS: TRANSPORTATION; SENEGAL AT THE AFRICAN DIASPORA; NATIVE AMERICANS OF NORTHERN CALIFORNIA; SWITZERLAND & HUNGARY; AND WORKERS WHO FEED US (TRANSPORTATION). AT ON THE MALL, BETWEEN LINCOLN MEMORIAL & WASHINGTON MONUMENT. (INT'L). SUSANNE ROSCHWALB; SMITHSONIAN INSTITUTION, NATIONAL PARK SERVICE; SMITHSONIAN INSTITUTION; WASHINGTON, DC 20560. (#111-13).

AUG 27 - 29, '76. DEMONSTRATIONS OF COLONIAL & NATL GUARD CEREMONIAL ACTIVITIES. LIVE PERFORMANCE AT WEST POTOMAC PARK. (REGN'L). JAMES C LUCORE, DIRECTOR; NATIONAL GUARD ASSOC OF THE UNITED STATES; 777 14TH ST, NW; WASHINGTON, DC 20005. (#107335-20).

AUG 28, '76. AMERICAN BICENTENNIAL 'TRIBUTE TO THE FOREFATHERS. 9:30-11:30 AM: SPECIAL TRIBUTE TO PRESIDENT & MRS FORD, LAFAYETTE PARK; DANCING & SINGING OF CROATIAN FOLKLRORE; 2-4 PM: CULTURAL FESTIVAL ON THE MALL, MEMORIAL GROUNDS V/CROATIAN MUSIC, FOLK & FOODS. AT LAFAYETTE PARK, MEMORIAL GROUNDS ON THE MALL, ARLINGTON CEMETERY. (NAT'L). EDWARD S YAMBRUSIC, ESQ; CROATIAN CATHOLIC UNION OF USA; 4720 MASSACHUSETTS AVE, NW; WASHINGTON, DC 20016. (#106397-1).

AUG 28 - 29, '76. CAPITOL POWER BOAT RACES. COMPETITION AT WEST POTOMAC PARK. (REGN'L). NCP DIV SPECIAL EVENTS; CAPITOL POWER BOAT ASSN; 1100 OHIO DRIVE, SW; WASHINGTON, DC 20242. (#108365-3).

AUG 29, '76. AMERICAN-CROATIAN BICENTENNIAL 'TRIBUTE TO THE FOREFATHERS'. FROM 10 AM-2 PM-CROATIAN RELIGIOUS FESTIVAL ON THE SHRINE GROUNDS W/ MUSIC, RITUALS CROATIAN FOOD; 2 PM-THE TAMBURITZA, CROATIAN FOLK MASS AT THE UPPER CHURCH OF THE SHRINE, SINGING OF THE CROATIAN MARIAN SONGS WITH ACCOMPANIMENT OF A 100-PIECE TAMBURITZA ORCHESTRA. AT NATIONAL SHRINE OF THE IMMACULATE CONCEPTION. (REGN'L). EDWARD S YAMBRUSIY ESQ; CROATIAN CATHOLIC UNION OF USA; 4720 MASSACHUSETTS AVE, NW; WASHINGTON, DC 20016. (#106397-2).

AUG 31, '76. BICENTENNIAL PARADE OF AMERICAN MUSIC HONORS MONTANA. THE MONTANA WOODWIND QUINTET WILL PERFORM. AT JOHN F KENNEDY MEMORIAL CENTER. (REGN'L). MISS SHARON WEAVER, DIR; NATIONAL MUSIC COUNCIL & EXXON; 1717 9TH AVE, S#12; GREAT FALLS, MT 59405. (#4500-33).

AUG 31, '76. SALUTE TO THE STATES - MONTANA. CEREMONY AT STEPS OF THE CAPITOL. (REGN'L). JAMES C LUCORE, DIRECTOR; GOVT OF THE DISTRICT OF COLUMBIA; 777 14TH ST, NW; WASHINGTON, DC 20005. (#107332-12).

SEPT 1 - 2, '76. THE MAHALLI DANCERS OF IRAN. LIVE PERFORMANCE AT KENNEDY CENTER. (INT'L). OFFICE OF INFORMATION; EMBASSY OF IRAN; 3005 MASSACHUSETTS AVE; WASHINGTON, DC 20008. (#200010-21).

SEPT 1 - 30, '76. A SLIDE PRESENTATION ON 'WASHINGTON, THEN AND NOW'. EXHIBIT. (LOCAL). HARDY R FRANKLIN, DIR; DISTRICT OF COLUMBIA PUBLIC LIBRARY; 901 G ST, NW; WASHINGTON, DC 20005. (#22890-1).

SEPT 3 - 6, '76. FINAL WEEK'S EVENTS AT THE FESTIVAL OF AMERICAN FOLKLIFE. SUMMER-LONG FESTIVAL. THIS WEEK'S HIGHLIGHTED PROGRAMS: TRANSPORTATION; SENEGAL AT THE AFRICAN DIASPORA; NATIVE AMERICANS OF THE ARCTIC; CZECHOSLOVAKIA & ROMANIA; AND WORKERS WHO FEED US (TRANSPORTATION). AT ON THE MALL, BETWEEN LINCOLN MEMORIAL & WASHINGTON MONUMENT. (INT'L). SUSANNE ROSCHWALB; SMITHSONIAN INSTITUTION, NATIONAL PARK SERVICE; SMITHSONIAN INSTITUTION; WASHINGTON, DC 20560. (#111-14).

SEPT 5 - OCT 2, '76. TOUR BY NATIONAL THEATRE OF PARIS OPERA. NATIONAL THEATRE OF PARIS OPERA WILL PUT ON 8 PERFORMANCES AT THE METROPOLITAN OPERA IN NEW YORK AND 7 PERFORMANCES AT THE KENNEDY CENTER IN WASHINGTON, DC. AT KENNEDY CENTER. (INT'L). DIRECTOR; SECRETARIAT D'ETAT A LA CULTURE; 3, RUE VALOIS; PARIS FRANCE. (#23429-2).

WASHINGTON — CONTINUED

SEPT 7 - 10, '76. COMPUTER TECHNICAL CONFERENCE - BICENTENNIAL & HORIZONS THEME. COMPCON '76 WILL CELEBRATE THE 25TH ANNIVERSARY OF THE IEEE COMPUTER SOCIETY. MAJOR SUBJECT OF CONFERENCE IS 'COMPUTERS BY THE MILLION, FOR THE MILLIONS'. ASSESMENT OF IMPACT OF MICRO- & MINI-COMPUTERS ON SCIENCE & INDUSTRY IN CENTURY III. AT HOTEL MAYFLOWER. (ST-WIDE). HARRY HAYMAN, DIR; IEEE COMPUTER SOCIETY; PO BOX 639; SILVER SPRING, MD 20901. (#16800-2).

SEPT 7 - 14, '76. 'INVENTING A NATION'. SHOWN TUESDAY 9/7 & 9/14 AT 11, NOON & 1, THIS FILM PRESENTS BEHINDTHE-SCENE ANECDOTES ABOUT THE WRITING OF THE CONSTITUTION, AND THE SECRET DEBATES INVOLVING JAMES MADISON, GEORGE MASON, & ALEXANDER HAMILTON. CLOSED ON CHRISTMAS DAY. AT GRAND SALON, RENWICK GALLERY OF ART, 17TH & PA AVE, NW. (REGN'L). MARGERY BYERS, PUBL AFF; SMITHSONIAN INSTITUTION; RENWICK GALLERY OF ART; WASHINGTON, DC 20560. (#109159-2).

SEPT 9, '76. BICENTENNIAL PARADE OF AMERICAN MUSIC HONORS SOUTH DAKOTA. EACH CONCERT FEATURES MUSIC COMPOSED IN OR ABOUT THE FEATURED STATE PLAYED BY OUTSTANDING MUSICAL GROUPS OR SOLOISTS FROM THAT STATE. AT JOHN F KENNEDY MEMORIAL CENTER. (REGN'L). MRS USHER ABELL, DIR; NATIONAL MUSIC COUNCIL & EXXON; RFD NO 2; VERMILLION, SD 57069. (#4500-35).

SEPT 9 - 12, '76. NATL PK SVC 'PEOPLE OF 1776' VISITS NATIONAL CAPITAL PARKS. TRAVELING TROUPE WILL BRING VARIOUS ASPECTS OF COLONIAL LIFE (MILITARY LIFE, MUSIC, CRAFTS) TO ROCK CREEK PARK ON 09/09/76, TO MANASSAS NBP ON 09/10/76, TO PRINCE WILLIAM FOREST PARK ON 09/11/76, AND TO G.W. PARKWAY ON 09/12/76. (REGN'L). BICENT. COORD., NCP; NATIONAL PARK SERVICE; 1100 OHIO DRIVE, SW; WASHINGTON, DC 20242. (#1469-23).

SEPT 9, '76 - APR 3, '77. THE DECORATIVE ARTS IN LATIN AMERICA IN THE ERA OF THE REVOLUTION. EXHIBIT AT RENWICK GALLERY OF ART, 18TH & PENNSYLVANIA AVE, NW. (REGN'L). SUSAN HAMILTON, DIRECTOR; SMITHSONIAN INSTITUTION; WASHINGTON, DC 20560. (#107338-1).

SEPT 10, '76. SALUTE TO THE STATES - SOUTH DAKOTA. CEREMONY AT STEPS OF THE CAPITOL. (REGN'L). JAMES C LUCORE, DIRECTOR; GOVT OF THE DISTRICT OF COLUMBIA; 777 14TH ST, NW; WASHINGTON, DC 20005. (#107332-13).

SEPT 10 - 24, '76. EXHIBITION OF YUGOSLAV NAIVE ARTS - SITES. EXHIBIT ILLUSTRATES CURRENT DIRECTIONS & EVOLUTION OF NAIVE YUGOSLAV ART. INCLUDES ART BY VECENAJ, RABUZIN, SKURJENI, KOVACIC & LACKOVIC. WOOD SCULPTURES, PAINTINGS; MAPS, FILMS; TAPES ON TRADITIONAL YUGOSLAV FOLK MUSIC. AT INTERNATIONAL MONETARY FUND BLDG. (REGN'L). REGINA LIPSKY, CHAIRMAN; SMITHSONIAN INSTITUTION TRAVELING EXHIBITION SVC & YUGOSLAVIAN GOVT; WASHINGTON, DC 20560. (#106776-1).

SEPT 12, '76. ROCK CREEK CLASSIC VELO RACES. COMPETITION AT ROCK CREEK PARK. (REGN'L). NCP DIV SPECIAL EVENTS; NATIONAL CAPITOL VELO CLUB; 1100 OHIO DRIVE, SW; WASHINGTON, DC 20242. (#108365-5).

SEPT 13, '76. BICENTENNIAL PARADE OF AMERICAN MUSIC HONORS WASHINGTON. AN ALL-STATE BAND WITH REPRESENTATIVES FROM EACH HIGH SCHOOL IN THE STATE IS SCHEDULED. AT JOHN F KENNEDY MEMORIAL CENTER. (REGN'L). MRS WAYNE HERTZ, DIR; NATIONAL MUSIC COUNCIL & EXXON; 209 E 9TH ST; ELLENSBURG, WA 98926. (#4500-36).

SEPT 13 - 15, '76. 'OCEANS '76' CONFERENCE. TECHNICAL SESSIONS ON OCEAN SCIENCES & TECHNOLOGY; INTERNATIONAL & INTERSOCIETY PARTICIPATION; INDUSTRIAL EXHIBITS; LUNCHEONS, BANQUET, FILM FESTIVAL, SPECIAL EVENTS. AT SHERATON PARK HOTEL. (INT'L). ELIZABETH M WALLACE; MARINE TECHNOLOGY SOCIETY & INST ELECTRICAL & ELECTRONIC ENGINEERS; 1730 M ST NW, SUITE 412; WASHINGTON, DC 20036. (#12533-1).

SEPT 14, '76. SALUTE TO THE STATES - WASHINGTON. CEREMONY AT STEPS OF THE CAPITOL. (REGN'L). JAMES C LUCORE, DIRECTOR; GOVT OF THE DISTRICT OF COLUMBIA; 777 14TH ST, NW; WASHINGTON, DC 20005. (#107332-14).

SEPT 15 - DEC 1, '76. VANCOUVER PLAYHOUSE TOUR OF WESTERN SEABOARD CITIES. IN THE FALL OF 1976, THE CANADIAN GOVERNMENT WILL SPONSOR A TOUR OF THE VANCOUVER PLAYHOUSE TO WESTERN SEABOARD CITIES. (INT'L). K DE B PERCY, COORD; EMBASSY OF CANADA; 1746 MASSACHUSETTS AVE; WASHINGTON, DC 20036. (#104966-3).

SEPT 20, '76. BICENTENNIAL PARADE OF AMERICAN MUSIC HONORS IDAHO. WORKS BY DR ARTHUR SHEPHERD HAVE BEEN SELECTED IN A STATEWIDE PERFORMANCE WITH OTHER IDAHO COMPOSERS. AT JOHN F KENNEDY MEMORIAL CENTER. (REGN'L). MRS RALPH CONSTOCK, DIR; NATIONAL MUSIC COUNCIL & EXXON; 3344 MOUNTAIN VIEW DR; BOISE, ID 83704. (#4500-37).

SEPT 21, '76. SALUTE TO THE STATES - IDAHO. CEREMONY AT STEPS OF THE CAPITOL. (REGN'L). JAMES C LUCORE, DIRECTOR; GOVT OF THE DISTRICT OF COLUMBIA; 777 14TH ST, NW; WASHINGTON, DC 20005. (#107332-15).

SEPT 23 - NOV 14, '76. WASHINGTON PRINT CLUB EXHIBITION. 59 WORKS BY AMERICAN ARTISTS FROM PRIVATE COLLECTION; WILL CONCENTRATE ON 20TH CENTURY ARTISTS. CLOSED ON CHRISTMAS DAY. AT NATIONAL COLLECTION OF FINE ARTS, 8TH & G STREETS, NW. (REGN'L). MARGERY BYERS, PUBL AFF; SMITHSONIAN INSTITUTION; NATL COLLECTION OF FINE ARTS; WASHINGTON, DC 20560. (#109159-1).

SEPT 25 - 26, '76. ARLINGTON HALL STATION BICENTENNIAL WALKATHON. INDIVIDUALS AND FAMILIES WALKING A FOUR OR EIGHT MILE COURSE, COVERING SUCH POINTS OF INTEREST AS LINCOLN MEMORIAL, JEFFERSON MEMORIAL, & WASHINGTON MONUMENT, CAPITAL BLDG, WHITE HOUSE, ETC. INDIVIDUALS COMPLETING THE COURSE WILL BE AWARDED A MEDAL. AT MALL AREA. (LOCAL). GERALD O MURDOCK, COORD; USAG, ARLINGTON HALL STATION; ARLINGTON, VA 22212. (#200010-22).

SEPT 25 - 29, '76. AMERICAN FREEDOM TRAIN DISPLAY DAYS AT WASHINGTON, DC. THE AMERICAN FREEDOM TRAIN WILL INCLUDE 10 EXHIBIT CARS AND 2 SHOWCASE CARS DEPICTING DIFFERENT PHASES OF THE AMERICAN EXPERIENCE. ITS ARRIVAL WILL SERVE AS A CATALYST FOR LOCAL BICENTENNIAL CELEBRATIONS BY PEOPLE THROUGHOUT THIS NATION. AT IN THE PENTAGON BUILDING AREA. (REGN'L). SY FREEDMAN, DIR OF P/R; THE AMERICAN FREEDOM TRAIN FOUNDATION, INC.; 5205 LEESBURG PKE, SUITE 800; BAILEY'S XRDS, VA 22041. (#1776-68).

SEPT 26 - OCT 1, '76. THE UNITED STATES IN THE WORLD INTERNATIONAL CONFERENCE. TO EXPLORE THE INTERACTION BETWEEN THE UNITED STATES & OTHER SOCIETIES IN THE AREAS OF SCIENCE, TECHNOLOGY, SOCIAL & BEHAVIORAL SCIENCES, POLITICS, ECONOMICS & POPULAR CULTURE. BY INVITATION ONLY. SOME EVENTS WILL BE OPEN TO THE PUBLIC. AT SMITHSONIAN INSTITUTION. (INT'L). ALLEN F DAVIS; AMERICAN STUDIES ASSOC & SMITHSONIAN & ACLS; ASA-UNIV OF PENNA 4025 CHESTNUT; PHILADELPHIA, PA 19174. (#258-1).

SEPT 26 - OCT 2, '76. YUGOSLAV FILM WEEK AT THE JOHN F KENNEDY CENTER. EXHIBIT, FESTIVAL AT JOHN F KENNEDY CENTER. (INT'L). MICHAEL WEBB, DIRECTOR; THE AMERICAN FILM INSTITUTE; 2700 F ST, NW; WASHINGTON, DC 20037. (#106773-1).

SEPT 27 - 28, '76. BICENTENNIAL PARADE OF AMERICAN MUSIC HONORS WYOMING. WY PARADE OF AMER MUSIC WAS REPRESENTED BY AN HONOR HIGH SCHOOL BAND WITH AT LEAST 1 MUSICIAN FROM EACH TOWN IN WYOMING, TOTALING 4 DIRECTORS & 127 MUSICIANS. THE CONCERT IN THE CONCERT HALL WAS PLAYED BY FACULTY MEMBERS OF THE UNIV OF WY. CEREMONY & BAND CONCERT, ALSO. AT JOHN F KENNEDY CTR, MON; WEST TERRACE OF NATL CAPITOL, TUES. (REGN'L). MRS FLORENCE HOWAR, DIR; NATL MUSIC COUNCIL/EXXON/WYOMING BICENTENNIAL COMMISSION; 2904 CENTRAL AVE; CHEYENNE, WY 82001. (#4500-38).

SEPT 27 - 28, '76. ISRAELI PHILHARMONIC ORCHESTRA VISITS THE KENNEDY CENTER. LIVE PERFORMANCE. (INT'L). URI AHARON BAR-NEV; ISRAELI GOVERNMENT; 1621 21ST ST, NW; WASHINGTON, DC 20008. (#109015-21).

SEPT 27 - OCT 1, '76. WASHINGTON MEETING OF INTERNATIONAL CONGRESS ON ARCHIVES. SOME 1100 TO 1200 ARCHIVISTS FROM AROUND THE WORLD WILL MEET TO DISCUSS THE PRESERVATION & USE OF OFFICIAL RECORDS FOR HISTORICAL SCHOLARSHIP. AT STATLER HILTON HOTEL 16TH & K STREET NW. (INT'L). DR FRANK BURKE; NATIONAL ARCHIVES & RECORDS SERVICE; NATIONAL ARCHIVES RM 106; WASHINGTON, DC 20408. (#67-1).

SEPT 27 - OCT 2, '76. NATIONAL GUARD HERITAGE ENCAMPMENT. LIVE PERFORMANCE, EXHIBIT AT NATIONAL HERITAGE GALLERY, ONE MASSACHUSETTS AVE, NW. (NAT'L). PAUL L LYTER, CHAIRMAN; NATIONAL GUARD ASSOCIATION OF THE U S; ONE MASSACHUSETTS AVE, NW; WASHINGTON, DC 20001. (#103416-508).

SEPT 27 - NOV 21, '76. 'FIVE PLUS ONE' EXHIBIT OF WASHINGTON ART. FIVE YOUNG, & FOR THE MOST PART UNKNOWN, WASHINGTON PAINTERS, SOUGHT OUT BY CHIEF CURATOR, JANE LIVINGSTON. INCLUDES EXTENSIVE CATALOG. THE 'PLUS ONE' IS CLAUDIA DE MONTE, WHOSE WORK TENDS TO BE AUDIENCE PARTICIPATORY, EMPLOYING HERSELF & FRIENDS AS THE ART MEDIUM. AT CORCORAN GALLERY, 17TH & NEW YORK AVE, NW. (REGN'L). FRANCES FRALIN, PUBL REL; THE CORCORAN GALLERY OF ART; 17TH & NEW YORK AVE, NW; WASHINGTON, DC 20006. (#109357-2).

SEPT 28, '76. SALUTE TO THE STATES - WYOMING. CEREMONY AT STEPS OF THE CAPITOL. (REGN'L). JAMES C LUCORE, DIRECTOR; GOVT OF THE DISTRICT OF COLUMBIA; 777 14TH ST, NW; WASHINGTON, DC 20005. (#107332-16).

SEPT 29 - OCT 1, '76. BETTER INVESTING '76 - INVESTMENT & BUSINESS EDUCATION. INFORMATION & EDUCATION IN STOCK MARKET INVESTING. AT SHOREHAM AMERICANA, 2500 CALVERT ST, NW. (REGN'L). CHARLES E MOORE, JR, DIR; NATIONAL ASSOC OF INVESTMENT CLUBS; 1515 E 11 MILE RD; ROYAL OAK, MI 48067. (#108236-3).

SEPT 29 - OCT 2, '76. 26TH NATIONAL CONVENTION - INVESTMENT EDUCATION. INFORMATION & EDUCATION ON STOCK MARKET INVESTING. AT SHOREHAM AMERICANA, 2500 CALVERT ST, NW. (NAT'L). THOMAS E O'HARA, COORD; NATIONAL ASSOCIATION OF INVESTMENT CLUBS; 1515 E ELEVEN MILE RD; ROYAL OAK, MI 48067. (#108236-1).

SEPT 29 - OCT 2, '76. 7TH CONGRESS WORLD FEDERATION OF INVESTMENT CLUBS. INFORMATION & EDUCATION IN STOCK MARKET INVESTING. AT SHOREHAM AMERICANA, 2500 CALVERT ST. (INT'L). THOMAS E O'HARA, COORD; WORLD FEDERATION OF INVESTMENT CLUBS; 1515 E ELEVEN MILE RD; ROYAL OAK, MI 48067. (#108236-2).

OCT 1, '76. BICENTENNIAL PARADE OF AMERICAN MUSIC HONORS OKLAHOMA. PERFORMERS INCLUDE THE 32 TROMBONE CHOIR, THE UNIVERSITY CHORALE, THE OKLAHOMA YOUTH SYMPHONY, AND YVONNE CHOUTEAU (FAMOUS INDIAN DANCER). INGTON OCT 1, 1976 FROM OKLAHOMA. AT JOHN F KENNEDY MEMORIAL CENTER. (REGN'L). MRS J KNOX BYRUM, DIR; NATIONAL MUSIC COUNCIL & EXXON; 1702 N BROADWAY; SHAWNEE, OK 74801. (#4500-40).

OCT 1, '76. SALUTE TO THE STATES - OKLAHOMA. CEREMONY AT STEPS OF THE CAPITOL. (REGN'L). JAMES C LUCORE, DIRECTOR; GOVT OF THE DISTRICT OF COLUMBIA; 777 14TH ST, NW; WASHINGTON, DC 20005. (#107332-17).

OCT 1, '76. THE TULSA OKLAHOMANS PERFORMING 'THE MUSICAL MOODS OF AMERICA'. LIVE PERFORMANCE AT WASHINGTON, DC. (REGN'L). DON LINDE, COORD; OKLAHOMA BICENTENNIAL AUTHORITY; BOX 45208; TULSA, OK 74145. (#26050-4).

OCT 1 - NOV 28, '76. SCULPTURE: WOOD, WELDED METAL, FIELD STONE & MARBLE. EXHIBIT, CEREMONY, AWARD. (REGN'L). JAMES C MASON, PRESIDENT; SMITH MASON GALLERY OF ART INC; 1207 RHODE ISLAND AVE, NW; WASHINGTON, DC 20005. (#6604-503).

OCT 10, '76. JOUSTING TOURNAMENT. COMPETITION AT POLO FIELD OF WEST POTOMAC PARK. (REGN'L). NCP DIV SPECIAL EVENTS; NATIONAL JOUSTING TOURNAMENT ASSN; 1100 OHIO DRIVE, SW; WASHINGTON, DC 20242. (#108365-7).

OCT 11, '76. COLUMBUS DAY CEREMONIES. CEREMONY, PARADE AT COLUMBUS PLAZA. (REGN'L). NCP DIV SPECIAL EVENTS; KNIGHTS OF COLUMBUS & AMERITO; 1100 OHIO DRIVE, SW; WASHINGTON, DC 20242. (#108365-8).

OCT 11, '76. IRISH GORDA SIOCHAN CHOIR PERFORMANCE & NATIONAL CONCERT BAND. CHOIR WILL PERFORM IN CONJUNCTION WITH THE USA NATIONAL CONCERT BAND OF AMERICA. AT J F KENNEDY CENTER, CONCERT HALL. (INT'L). JOSEPH F O'CONNOR; AMERICAN IRISH BICENTENNIAL COMMITTEE; 1629 K ST NW; WASHINGTON, DC 20006. (#2193-2).

OCT 11 - 13, '76. SYMPOSIUM 'SCIENCE: A RESOURCE FOR HUMANKIND'. 11 OCT, CASE STUDIES OF S&T IN ECONOMIC DEVELOPMENT OF 7 DIVERSE COUNTRIES; 12 OCT SCIENCE & ENVIRONMENTAL MANAGEMENT RE-MONITORING, MODELING, RISK ESTIMATION, ETC; 13 OCT SCIENTIFIC CHALLENGES & OPPORTUNITIES, RE SOCIETAL PROBLEMS OVER BALANCE OF CENTURY. AT AUDITORIUM OF NAS, 2101 CONSTITUTION AVE. (INT'L). HOWARD LEWIS, COORD; NATIONAL ACADEMY OF SCIENCES/INTL COUNCIL OF SCIENTIFIC UNIONS; 2101 CONSTITUTION AVE, NW; WASHINGTON, DC 20418. (#27810-1).

OCT 12, '76. ITALIAN AMERICAN DAY. CEREMONY, FESTIVAL. (REGN'L). NICHOLAS R BELTRANTE; AMERICAN ITALIAN BICENTENNIAL COMMISSION INC; PO BOX 780; WASHINGTON, DC 20044. (#5926-505).

OCT 16, '76. PERFORMANCE BY ORCHESTRA DE PARIS. LIVE PERFORMANCE. (INT'L). CULTURAL ATTACHE; EMBASSY OF FRANCE; 2535 BELMONT RD; WASHINGTON, DC 20008. (#200010-43).

OCT 17, '76. PERFORMANCE BY ORCHESTRE DE PARIS. LIVE PERFORMANCE AT KENNEDY CENTER. (INT'L). INFORMATION OFFICE; COLUMBIA ARTISTS; 165 W 57TH ST; NEW YORK, NY 10019. (#108967-8).

OCT 19 - 20, '76. STEPHEN BURTON'S 'ARIEL'. LIVE PERFORMANCE AT JOHN F KENNEDY CENTER FOR THE PERFORMING ARTS. (REGN'L). WILLIAM L DENTON, COORD; NATIONAL SYMPHONY ORCHESTRA ASSOC; KENNEDY CENTER; WASHINGTON, DC 20566. (#106325-2).

OCT 19, '76 - APR 3, '77. AMERICAS: THE DECORATIVE ARTS IN LATIN AMERICA IN THE ERA OF THE REV. EXHIBITION IN RENWICK GALLERY ON THE OTHER COUNTRIES OF THE AMERICAS--THE RICHNESS OF DESIGN, CRAFTS, AND THE DECORATIVE ARTS DURING THE PERIOD AROUND 1776. CLOSED ONLY ON CHRISTMAS DAY. AT NE. CORNER OF 17TH & PENNSYLVANIA AVE NW. (REGN'L). RENWICK GALLERY; THE SMITHSONIAN INSTITUTION; NATIONAL COLLECTION OF FINE ARTS; WASHINGTON, DC 20560. (#1768-1).

OCT 22, '76. THE TOKYO STRING QUARTET. LIVE PERFORMANCE AT CORCORAN AUDITORIUM, 17TH ST & NEW YORK AVE. (LOCAL). DIRECTOR; CORCORAN GALLERY OF ART; 17TH ST & NEW YORK AVE, NW; WASHINGTON, DC 20006. (#109313-1).

OCT 23, '76 - OCT 23, '77. CANADIAN SMITHSONIAN INSTITUTION TRAVELING EXHIBITION. THREE SELECT CANADIAN EXHIBITIONS OF ART WILL START A NATIONAL TOUR IN OCTOBER '76 & RUN THROUGH 1977. THE COLLECTIONS ARE ENTITLED THE PITSEOLAK COLLECTION, THE COVERDALE COLLECTION AND THE WARRE COLLECTION. (INT'L). K DE B PERCY, COORD; SMITHSONIAN INSTITUTION TRAVELING EXHIBITION SERVICE & CANADIAN GOVT; 1746 MASSACHUSETTS AVE, NW; WASHINGTON, DC 20036. (#105111-9).

OCT 24 - 28, '76. 'ICARUS OPUS 48' - A SUITE IN 4 MOVEMENTS BY GENE GUTCHE. ICARUS OPUS 48 BY GENE GUTCHE, COMMISSIONED BY ANTAL DORATI OF THE NATIONAL SYMPHONY UNDER A BICENTENNIAL GRANT BY THE NATIONAL ENDOWMENT FOR THE ARTS. ICARUS IS A PROGRAMMATIC SUITE IN 4 MOVEMENTS: I COLUMBUS; II THE SEA; III INSURRECTION; IV ISTHMUS. AT JOHN F KENNEDY CENTER FOR THE PERFORMING ARTS. (REGN'L). GENE GUTCHE, COMPOSER; NATIONAL ENDOWMENT FOR THE ARTS; 10 BIRCHWOOD LN; WHITE BEAR LK, MN 55110. (#106782-2).

OCT 26, '76. THE POLITICAL CARTOONIST IN AN ELECTION YEAR: HERBLOCK & OLIPHANT. LIVE PERFORMANCE AT CORCORAN AUDITORIUM, 17TH ST & NEW YORK AVE, NW. (LOCAL). DIRECTOR; CORCORAN GALLERY OF ART; 17TH ST & NEW YORK AVE, NW; WASHINGTON, DC 20006. (#109313-2).

OCT 28 - 30, '76. 'THE DISAPPOINTMENT OR THE FORCE OF CREDULITY' - OPERA. THE LIBRARY OF CONGRESS IN COOPERATION WITH THE EASTMAN SCHOOL OF MUSIC WILL PRODUCE THIS PROGRAM AS A MODERN MUSICAL SCORE FAITHFUL TO THE 18TH CENTURY. AT COOLIDGE AUDITORIUM, LIBRARY OF CONGRESS. (REGN'L). MRS ELIZABETH KEGAN, DIR; LIBRARY OF CONGRESS; RM 110, LIBRARY OF CONGRESS; WASHINGTON, DC 20540. (#102362-1).

WASHINGTON — CONTINUED

OCT '76. TOUR BY FRENCH TROUPE. TOUR OF THEATRE NATIONAL POPULAIRE TO NEW YORK, NY AND WASHINGTON, DC IN OCT 1976; 'TARTUFFE' BY MOLIERE DIRECTED BY ROGER PLANCHON AND 'LA DISPUTE' BY MARIVAUX DIRECTED BY PATRICE CHEREAU. (INT'L). DIRECTOR; SECRETARIAT D'ETAT A LA CULTURE; 3, RUE VALOIS; PARIS/FRANCE. (#23432-2).

NOV 2 - 3, '76. ORREGO-SALAS - 'THE DAYS OF GOD'. LIVE PERFORMANCE AT JOHN F KENNEDY CENTER FOR THE PERFORMING ARTS. (LOCAL). WILLIAM L DENTON, COORD; NATIONAL SYMPHONY ORCHESTRA ASSOC; KENNEDY CENTER; WASHINGTON, DC 20566. (#106325-1).

NOV 4, '76. BICENTENNIAL PARADE OF AMERICAN MUSIC HONORS NEW MEXICO. EACH CONCERT FEATURES MUSIC COMPOSED IN OR ABOUT THE FEATURED STATE PLAYED BY OUTSTANDING MUSICAL GROUPS OR SOLOISTS FROM THAT STATE. AT JOHN F KENNEDY MEMORIAL CENTER. (REGN'L). MISS JEANNE GREALISH, DIR; NATIONAL MUSIC COUNCIL & EXXON; 1226 MORNINGSIDE NE; ALBUQUERQUE, NM 87110. (#4500-41).

NOV 5, '76. SALUTE TO THE STATES - NEW MEXICO. CEREMONY AT STEPS OF THE CAPITOL. (REGN'L). JAMES C LUCORE, DIRECTOR; GOVT OF THE DISTRICT OF COLUMBIA; 777 14TH ST, NW; WASHINGTON, DC 20005. (#107332-18).

NOV 6 - 7, '76. BERLIN PHILHARMONIC ORCHESTRA. LIVE PERFORMANCE AT KENNEDY CENTER FOR THE PERFORMING ARTS, CONCERT HALL. (INT'L). DR J KALKBRENNER, COORD; EMBASSY OF FEDERAL REPUBLIC OF GERMANY; 2700 F ST, NW; WASHINGTON, DC 20037. (#106786-1).

NOV 6 - 7, '76. PERFORMANCES BY THE BERLIN PHILHARMONIC. LIVE PERFORMANCE AT KENNEDY CENTER. (INT'L). CULTURAL ATTACHE; EMBASSY OF THE FEDERAL REPUBLIC OF GERMANY; 4645 RESERVOIR RD; WASHINGTON, DC 20007. (#200010-42).

NOV 8, '76. ARIZONA'S BICENTENNIAL PARADE OF AMERICAN MUSIC. EACH CONCERT FEATURES MUSIC COMPOSED IN OR ABOUT THE FEATURED STATE PLAYED BY OUTSTANDING MUSICAL GROUPS OR SOLOISTS FROM THAT STATE SYMPHONY CONCERT.RECEPTION FOLLOWS,SPONSORED BY ORG OF STATES, D.C. AT JOHN F KENNEDY CENTER. (REGN'L). MRS RUTH RASMUSSEN; NATIONAL MUSIC COUNCIL & EXXON; 401 ROCALLA AVE; AJO, AZ 85321. (#4500-1).

NOV 9, '76. SALUTE TO THE STATES - ARIZONA. CEREMONY AT STEPS OF THE CAPITOL. (REGN'L). JAMES C LUCORE, DIRECTOR; GOVT OF THE DISTRICT OF COLUMBIA; 777 14TH ST, NW; WASHINGTON, DC 20005. (#107332-19).

NOV 11, '76. BICENTENNIAL PARADE OF AMERICAN MUSIC HONORS UTAH. THE BRIGHAM YOUNG UNIV. FOLK DANCES, AND THE OREN HIGH SCHOOL A CAPELLA CHOIR WILL PERFORM. AT JOHN F KENNEDY MEMORIAL CENTER. (REGN'L). MRS J TRACEY WOOTTON, DIR; NATIONAL MUSIC COUNCIL & EXXON; 1650 KENSINGTON AVE; SALT LAKE, UT 84105. (#4500-39).

NOV 12, '76. SALUTE TO THE STATES - UTAH. CEREMONY AT STEPS OF THE CAPITOL. (REGN'L). JAMES C LUCORE, DIRECTOR; GOVT OF THE DISTRICT OF COLUMBIA; 777 14TH ST, NW; WASHINGTON, DC 20005. (#107332-20).

NOV 14 - 18, '76. 'ENERGY FOR TOMORROW'S WORLD'-INTL CONFERENCE ON NUCLEAR POLICY. SEMINAR, CONFERENCE, EXHIBIT AT SHOREHAM AMERICANA HOTEL. (INT'L). CONFERENCE MANAGER; ATOMIC INDUSTRIAL FORUM; 7101 WISCONSIN AVE; WASHINGTON, DC 20014. (#7915-1).

NOV 15, '76. BICENTENNIAL PARADE OF AMERICAN MUSIC HONORS ALASKA. EACH CONCERT FEATURES MUSIC COMPOSED IN OR ABOUT THE FEATURED STATE PLAYED BY OUTSTANDING MUSICAL GROUPS OR SOLOISTS FROM THAT STATE. AT JOHN F KENNEDY MEMORIAL CENTER. (REGN'L). MRS THOMAS B STEWART, DIR; NATIONAL MUSIC COUNCIL & EXXON; 925 CALHOUN; JUNEAU, AK 99801. (#4500-42).

NOV 15, '76 - MAR 15, '77. 'TUTANKHAMEN TREASURES' EXHIBIT. EXHIBIT AT NATIONAL GALLERY OF ART. (INT'L). CULTURAL ATTACHE; ARAB REPUBLIC OF EGYPT; 2310 DECATUR PL; WASHINGTON, DC 20008. (#31906-1).

NOV 16, '76. SALUTE TO THE STATES - ALASKA. CEREMONY AT STEPS OF THE CAPITOL. (REGN'L). JAMES C LUCORE, DIRECTOR; GOVT OF THE DISTRICT OF COLUMBIA; 777 14TH ST, NW; WASHINGTON, DC 20005. (#107332-21).

NOV 18, '76. BICENTENNIAL PARADE OF AMERICAN MUSIC HONORS HAWAII. EACH CONCERT FEATURES MUSIC COMPOSED IN OR ABOUT THE FEATURED STATE PLAYED BY OUTSTANDING MUSICAL GROUPS OR SOLOISTS FROM THAT STATE. AT JOHN F KENNEDY MEMORIAL CENTER. (REGN'L). MISS CHARLENE CHADWICK; NATIONAL MUSIC COUNCIL & EXXON; MUSIC DEPT, U OF H, 2411 DOLE ST; HONOLULU, HI 96822. (#4500-43).

NOV 19, '76. SALUTE TO THE STATES - HAWAII. CEREMONY AT STEPS OF THE CAPITOL. (REGN'L). JAMES C LUCORE, DIRECTOR; GOVT OF THE DISTRICT OF COLUMBIA; 777 14TH ST, NW; WASHINGTON, DC 20005. (#107332-22).

NOV 19 - 20, '76. LONDON PHILHARMONIC ORCHESTRA VISITS WASHINGTON, DC. LIVE PERFORMANCE AT KENNEDY CENTER. (INT'L). CULTURAL AFFAIRS OFFICE; BRITISH EMBASSY; 3100 MASSACHUSETTS AVE, NW; WASHINGTON, DC 20008. (#108958-9).

NOV 19 - 23, '76. NATIONAL CONGRESS ON VOLUNTEERISM & CITIZENSHIP - 1976. A SERIES OF FORUMS IN COMMUNITIES ACROSS THE NATION ON VOLUNTEERISM & ON ISSUES SELECTED BY PARTICIPANTS. LOCAL FORUMS UNTIL MAY 15, 76, DISTRICT FORUMS MAY 15 TO AUGUST 15, & A NATIONAL CONGRESS IN NOVEMBER ARE THE MAJOR EVENTS. AT MARRIOTT TWIN BRIDGES HOTEL, ARLINGTON, VA. (NAT'L). JAMES I LUCK, EXEC DIR; NATIONAL CENTER FOR VOLUNTARY ACTION; 1785 MASSACHUSETTS AVE, NW; WASHINGTON, DC 20036. (#7813-1).

NOV 19 - DEC 5, '76. THEATRE 'THE SCHOOL FOR SCANDAL' BY RICHARD BRINSLEY SHERIDAN. LIVE PERFORMANCE AT HARTKE THEATRE, HAREWOOD RD NE, NORTH OF NATL SHRINE. (LOCAL). DANIEL R HELLER, CHMN; CATHOLIC UNIVERSITY; HAREWOOD RD, NE; WASHINGTON, DC 20064. (#109529-2).

NOV 24 - DEC 31, '76. 'REMEMBER THE LADIES' WOMEN IN AMERICA 1750-1815 EXHIBIT. ART EXHIBITION OF ART AND ARTIFACTS ON THE ROLE AND STATUS OF WOMEN, INCLUDING SECTIONS ON CHILDHOOD, MARRIAGE, DEATH, FASHION, ANDD CREATIVE WOMEN. AT CORCORAN GALLERY OF ART, 17TH & E STS, NW. (REGN'L). ROY SLADE, DIRECTOR; THE PILGRIM SOCIETY; CORCORAN GALLERY OF ART; WASHINGTON, DC 20006. (#107840-3).

NOV '76. FRANCE'S THEATRE OBLIQUE PERFORMS IN WASHINGTON, DC. LIVE PERFORMANCE. (INT'L). CULTURAL ATTACHE; EMBASSY OF FRANCE; 2535 BELMONT RD; WASHINGTON, DC 20008. (#200010-38).

DEC 1, '76. AIRCRAFT PRESENTATION. THE CIVIL AIR PATROL WILL PRESENT TO THE NATIONAL AIR AND SPACE MUSEUM A PROTOTYPE OF THE AIRCRAFT USED BY THE CAP DURING WW II. (NAT'L). LTCOL HERBERT A BABB; CIVIL AIR PATROL; HQ CAP-USAF/01; MAXWELL AFB, AL 36112. (#106487-1).

DEC 7, '76 - MAR 7, '77. EXHIBITION OF AUSTRALIAN ABORIGINAL ARTS & CRAFTS. EXHIBIT, TOUR. (INT'L). JOHN MAUNDER, DIRECTOR; AUSTRALIAN CONSULATE GENERAL; 636 5TH AVE; NEW YORK, NY 10020. (#25728-2).

DEC 10 - 17, '76. THE SPIRIT OF AMERICAN ENGINEERING SHOW. ROLE OF THE ENGINEER IN SOCIETY: PAST, PRESENT & FUTURE WITH INTERNATIONAL CONVOCATION; HISTORICAL PUBLICATION; PROJECT OF PUBLIC AUDIO-VISUAL DISPLAYS; EXHIBITIONS. AT DETAILS UNDECIDED. (NAT'L). NEAL FITZSIMONS, CHMN; ENGINEERING COMMITTEE FOR THE AMERICAN BICENTENNIAL, C/O EJC; 345 E 47TH ST; NEW YORK, NY 10017. (#2042-3).

DEC 16, '76 - JAN 1, '77. CHRISTMAS PAGEANT OF PEACE. EXHIBIT AT THE ELLIPSE, SOUTH SIDE OF THE WHITE HOUSE. (REGN'L). NCP DIV SPECIAL EVENTS; CHRISTMAS PAGEANT OF PEACE INC, DC REC DEPT, & NCP; 1100 OHIO DRIVE; WASHINGTON, DC 20242. (#108365-6).

DEC 21, '76 - JAN 2, '77. DUBLIN'S ABBEY PLAYERS. LIVE PERFORMANCE AT HARTKE THEATER, CATHOLIC UNIVERSITY. (INT'L). JEAN FARRELL; EMBASSY OF IRELAND; 2234 MASSACHUSETTS AVE; WASHINGTON, DC 20008. (#200010-37).

DEC 27 - 30, '76. JUBILEE. FESTIVAL, LIVE PERFORMANCE AT WASHINGTON NATIONAL CATHEDRAL. (REGN'L). BERYL TILBURY; INTERNATIONAL FESTIVALS, INC; 202 E MICHIGAN AVE; KALAMAZOO, MI 49006. (#107233-1).

DEC 31, '76. BICENTENNIAL PARADE SPECIAL TRIBUTE TO JOHN PHILIP SOUSA. EACH CONCERT FEATURES MUSIC COMPOSED IN OR ABOUT THE FEATURED STATE PLAYED BY OUTSTANDING MUSICAL GROUPS OR SOLOISTS FROM THAT STATE. AT JOHN F KENNEDY MEMORIAL CENTER. (REGN'L). DR MERLE MONTGOMERY, DIR; NATIONAL MUSIC COUNCIL & EXXON; 222 E 80TH ST; NEW YORK, NY 10021. (#4500-44).

JAN '77 - CONTINUING . PLANNING AMERICA'S GREAT CITIES, AN EXHIBITION. EXHIBIT, RADIO/TV AT NATIONAL ACADEMY OF SCIENCES. (REGN'L). MS LEE KIMCHE; ASSOC OF SCIENCE & TECHNOLOGY; 2100 PENNSYLVANIA AVE, NW; WASHINGTON, DC 20037. (#8615-4).

FEB 4, '77. PERFORMANCE BY THE LENINGRAD SYMPHONY. LIVE PERFORMANCE AT KENNEDY CENTER. (INT'L). CULTURAL ATTACHE; EMBASSY OF THE SOVIET UNION; 1125 16TH ST; WASHINGTON, DC 20036. (#200010-51).

MAR 4 - 20, '77. 'A MAN FOR ALL SEASONS' BY ROBERT BOLT. LIVE PERFORMANCE AT HARTKE THEATRE, HAREWOOD RD, NE, NORTH OF NAT'L SHRINE. (LOCAL). DANIEL R HELLER, CHMN; CATHOLIC UNIVERSITY; HAREWOOD RD, NE; WASHINGTON, DC 20064. (#109529-1).

MAR 18, '77. PERFORMANCE BY THE TORONTO SYMPHONY. LIVE PERFORMANCE AT KENNEDY CENTER. (INT'L). CULTURAL ATTACHE; EMBASSY OF CANADA; 1746 MASSACHUSETTS AVE; WASHINGTON, DC 20036. (#200010-41).

APR 1 - MAY 1, '77. SILVERWORKS FROM THE RIO DE LA PLATA EXHIBITION. THIS EXHIBITION OF 180 ECCLESIASTICAL & SECULAR SILVER OBJECTS REPRESENTS OUTSTANDING CULTURAL-SOCIAL ASPECTS OF ARGENTINE LIFE DURING THE 18TH & 19TH CENTURIES. (INT'L). EILEEN HARAKAL, COORD; SMITHSONIAN INSTITUTION TRAVELING EXHIBITION SERVICE; 1000 JEFFERSON DR, SW; WASHINGTON, DC 20560. (#26666-1).

JULY 4, '77. PRESENTATION OF CHILDREN'S ART COLLECTION TO SMITHSONIAN INSTITUTION. PRESENTATION TO SMITHSONIAN INST OF SELECTED CHILDRENS' DRAWINGS AGES 5-12, FOCUSING ON CONTRIBUTIONS OF COMMUNICATIONS TO THE GROWTH OF THE NATION. AT SMITHSONIAN INSTITUTE. (REGN'L). THEODORE S CONNELLY, DIR; COMMUNICATIONS LIBRARY; 1535 SAN FRANCISCO STREET; SAN FRANCISCO, CA 94123. (#1487-3).

JULY 4, '77. SPIRIT OF '76 JOG. COMPETITION AT MARSHALL BLDG, 1910 K ST, NW. (INT'L). GARY K OLSEN, COORD; NATIONAL JOGGING ASSOCIATION; 1910 K ST, NW, SUITE 202; WASHINGTON, DC 20006. (#109281-1).

JULY '77 - CONTINUING . 'OUR CAPITOL: FREEDOM SPEAKS' - SOUND & LIGHT HISTORAMA. PRODUCTION WILL CONTINUE INDEFINITELY, THREE SHOWS NIGHTLY, FREE TO ALL VISITORS. AT UNITED STATES CAPITOL BLDG-EAST FRONT. (NAT'L). MR OLIVER PATTON; UNITED STATES CAPITOL HISTORICAL SOCIETY; 200 MARYLAND AVE NE; WASHINGTON, DC 20515. (#4570-1).

OCT 1, '77 - JAN 15, '78. IMPACT OF AFRICAN SCULPTURE ON MODERN ART, MAJOR EXHIBIT & BOOK. EXHIBITION OF 500 WORKS OF TRADITIONAL AFRICAN SCULPTURES & ELISOFON COLOR PHOTOS, TOURS & LECTURES ON AFRICAN CULTURE USING LIBRARY ARCHIVES EXTENSION PROGRAMS. (REGN'L). WARREN M ROBBINS; MUSEUM OF AFRICAN ART; 318 A ST, NE; WASHINGTON, DC 20002. (#5353-505).

AMERICAN REVOLUTION BICENTENNIAL 1776-1976
FLORIDA

Florida

Bicentennial Commission of Florida

Commissioned by House Bill 3974 on April 17, 1970 (effective July 4, 1970)

Theme: Heritage, Festivals, Horizons

ARBA Statistics

Officially Recognized
Communities—179
Colleges/Universities—38
Military Installations—32
BINET Projects—816
Events—1,279
1976 Population—8,421,000

Bicentennial Archives

Division of Archives
History and Records Management
Department of State
The Capitol
Tallahassee, Florida 32304

Membership

Governor Reubin O'D. Askew, *honorary chairman*
Lieutenant Governor J. H. "Jim" Williams, *chairman*
Dick J. Batchelor
Johnnie Ruth Clarke
A. H. "Gus" Craig
James J. Gardener
Jim Glisson
Mattox Hair
Thomas L. Hazouri
Ney C. Landrum
Elvin Martinez
Minerva Mason
Carl C. Mertins, Jr.
W. E. Potter
F. Blair Reeves
Richard R. Renick
Myrna Shevin
Don Shoemaker
Mary Singleton
Bruce A. Smathers
Harold W. Stayman, Jr.
Alan Trask
Edward J. Trombetta
Ralph D. Turlington
William S. Turnbull
Robert Williams
Lori Wilson

Former Members

Tom Adams
George I. Baumgartner
Patricia Born
W. D. Childers
Floyd T. Christian
Henry Dartigalongue
Pat Dodson, deceased
Dorothy Glisson
Jack D. Gordon
Dick Greco
Robert C. Hartnett
Warren S. Henderson
Richard S. Hodes
Beth Johnson
Joe Lang Kershaw
Claude R. Kirk, Jr.
Ray C. Osborne
Julius F. Parker
Carolyn Pearce
Charles Perry
Verle A. Pope, deceased
Samuel Proctor
Ted Randell
Jane Robinson
George E. Saunders
Robert Saunders
Don L. Spicer
Richard Stone
Sherman Winn

Staff

Dr. William R. Adams, *executive director* (1975–77)
Bill Miller, *executive director* (1970–73)
Shelton Kemp, *executive director* (1973–75)
Don Pride, *executive director* (1975)
Bruce McDonald, *acting executive director* (1975)

Florida

The Bicentennial in Florida might have ended with another fireworks extravaganza and left only memories, but a lesson learned from history created a Bicentennial celebration aimed at improving life in the Sunshine State.

Florida's formal involvement in the Bicentennial dates back to 1970, when the Florida Legislature passed a law creating the Florida American Revolution Bicentennial Commission with 28 members and the dream of a flashy celebration.

The history lesson that changed the original dream into a desire to create lasting reminders was presented during the first Bicentennial commission meeting, December 18, 1970, in Tallahassee. The late Pat Dodson, the commission's first chairman, told the commissioners, "Now I think you will remember, we had the Civil War Centennial several years ago and the people who participated learned a great deal." Dodson emphasized that what people learned was what to avoid. "I think there were some regrets, quite frankly. They realized restaging battles and this sort of thing left little behind when it was all over." Dodson said the Civil War celebration amounted to a series of spectacles. And he continued, "The tone of the coming Bicentennial, I think, is somewhat more serious; has far-reaching possibilities in improving the country. . . ."

Since the time of that first meeting, the commission's goal has been to improve the quality of life with projects created on behalf of the Bicentennial.

In 1971, the commission promoted creation of County Action '76 Steering Committees. Using as a model an

Action '76 Committee originated in a pilot project by the citizens of Pensacola in Escambia County, the state commission set up Bicentennial steering committees in Florida's 66 other counties and provided administrative funds for the committees' basic operations. The commission devised means of supplementary funding for committees by offering for sale the governor's Bicentennial medallions and the state's commemorative Bicentennial book, *Born of the Sun.*

As local committees sprang up under the guidance of county steering committees, additional money-raising projects were originated and promoted locally to supplement the state agency's work. The commission and its programs have been operated without state tax dollars. The primary sources of funding for the Florida Bicentennial commission have been pari-mutuel receipts and federal grants.

The Bicentennial commission's projects have been designed to offer statewide benefits. One of the nation's most innovative and lasting projects is the ambitious reproduction of 25 rare, out-of-print books in the Floridiana Facsimile Series. The commission also conceived and funded a series of five annual history symposia that have increased understanding of Florida's colorful past, and they published the symposia findings.

While books and studies of historic places were being prepared, attention was also paid to the historic sites themselves. One of America's most widely publicized and most popular Bicentennial projects has been the *Florida Bicentennial Trail.* The 52 site trail provides a journey from the prehistoric past through the nation's oldest continuous settlement at St. Augustine, which was founded by the Spanish in 1565 and occupied by the British during the Revolutionary War. It ends chronologically with the futuristic Kennedy Space Center.

In addition to a trail Floridians could visit, the commission decided to create a project that would visit Floridians. After opinions of museum experts were reviewed by the Buildings, Exhibits and Graphics Subcommittee, the *American Bicentennial Florida Exhibition* was established in three traveling trailers.

Another means of bringing aspects of the Bicentennial to the people was promoted by the Films Committee, which conceived the motion picture, *Florida On My Mind,* and promoted the commission's production of the film, *Florida: First and Last Frontier.*

Increased involvement of students was encouraged by the Education Committee, created in 1975. Students demonstrated their interest through participation during *Bicentennial Schools Festival Week* in April 1976. More than 700 Florida schools have received commission recognition for projects conducted that week.

The commission never lost sight of its primary goal. The improvement of the quality of life in Florida has remained dominant throughout the past six years of the commission's existence. Commission grants have contributed to funding for more than 50 historical publications, in addition to projects furthering the arts, human services, ecological pursuits, historical restorations and creation of new recreation areas and museums.

It is the nation's Bicentennial that has provided the incentive for the greatest cultural boom in Florida's history. Long after the glow of July 4th fireworks has faded to a spectacular memory, Floridians will continue to benefit from lasting reminders of the Bicentennial birthday.

ALACHUA

MAIN STREET RESTORATION PROJECT - ALCHUA, FL. RESTORATION OF HISTORIC BUILDINGS, PRIMARILY ON MAIN STREET. (LOCAL). JERRY SMITH, PRESIDENT; ALACHUA CHAMBER OF COMMERCE; PO BOX 218; ALACHUA, FL 32615. (#28949).

JUNE 3, '76. ALACHUA BICENTENNIAL CELEBRATION PARADE & HISTORICAL EXHIBITS. PARADE, PICNIC, HISTORIC DISPLAYS & EXHIBITS, GUEST SPEAKERS; FLOAT ENTERED IN ALACHUA COUNTY PARADE WON FIRST PRIZE; FLAG CEREMONY; PRESERVATION AND DISPLAY OF HISTORIC ORDINANCES. AT ALACHUA CITY PARK. (LOCAL). PAULA MARTIN, CHAIRMAN; ALACHUA COMMUNITY CENTENNIAL ORGANIZATION; PO BOX U32; ALACHUA, FL 32615. (#200011-259).

ALTAMONTE SPG

BEAUTIFICATION REPORT IN ALTAMONTE SPRINGS, FL. BICENTENNIAL COMMITTEE RECOMMENDATIONS ON AREAS WHICH THE CITY COULD BEAUTIFY (MUNICIPALLY CONTROLLED) & AREAS WHICH ARE NOT IN COMPLIANCE WITH EXISTING LANDSCAPE ORDINANCES. (LOCAL). CHAIRMAN; ALTAMONTE SPRINGS BICENTENNIAL COMMITTEE; 720 FLORIDA BLVD; ALTAMONTE SPG, FL 32701. (#30784).

COLLAGE AMERICA WALL HANGING IN ALTAMONTE SPG, FL. WALL HANGING DEPICTING 200 MAJOR HISTORICAL EVENTS. FABRIC, CRAFT & QUILTING TECHNIQUES USED. (LOCAL). DELORES E VICKERS, CHAIRMAN; CITY OF ALTAMONTE SPRINGS; ALTAMONTE, FL 32701. (#30783).

MAR 15, '75. RED, WHITE & BLUE REVIEW VAUDEVILLE NIGHT. EACH ACT UTILIZES A PHASE OF AMERICA IN EITHER SONG, DANCE OR ORATION. AT ALTAMONTE SPRINGS CIVIC CENTER AUDITORIUM, SO LONGWOOD AVE. (LOCAL). MS BARBARA MCCLELLAN; ALTAMONTE SPRINGS PLAYERS; PO BOX 557 H2; LONGWOOD, FL 32750. (#200011-307).

MAY 30, '76. AMERICA THE BEAUTIFUL-MEMORIAL DAY PARADE & PLANTING CEREMONY. PLANTING CEREMONY SYMBOLIC REPRESENTATION OF CITY'S EFFORT TO IMPROVE & BEAUTIFY CITY. KEYNOTE SPEAKER & GRAND MARSHALL: COL GLENDON PERKINS. 30 CITIZENS FROM VARIOUS BACKGROUNDS & AREAS PARTICIPATED IN ACTUAL PLANTING ACTIVITIES. AT ALTAMONTE SPRINGS CITY HALL, NEWBERRYPORT AVE. (LOCAL). MS PAT FERNANDEZ; ALTAMONTE SPRINGS BICENTENNIAL COMMITTEE; 539 GREENBRIER BLVD; ALTAMONTE SPG, FL 32701. (#200011-305).

MAY '76. BOY SCOUT CAMPOREE. HISTORICAL WAYS OF LIFE REENACTED INCL CIRCUS LIFE, PIONEERING, FARMING, ETC, PAST & PRESENT. COMPETITIONS AMONG TROUPS-AWARDS. AT ALTAMONTE SPRINGS CIVIC CENTER GROUNDS SO LONDWOOD AVE (OFF 436). (LOCAL). JOHN WAYMAN; BOY SCOUTS OF AMERICA WEKIVA DISTRICT, FLA; 2260 COLDSTREAM AVE; WINTER PARK, FL 32806. (#200011-306).

APALACHICOLA

RANEY HOUSE RESTORATION PROJ OF FLORIDA. RESTORATION OF THE DAVID RANEY HOUSE IN FRANKLIN COUNTY FLORIDA. (LOCAL). HON J J NICHOLS, MAYOR; CITY OF APALACHICOLA; CITY HALL; APALACHICOLA, FL 32320. (#5120). **(??).**

OCT 27 - 30, '76. 13TH ANNUAL FLORIDA SEAFOOD FESTIVAL. FESTIVAL AT BATTERY PARK. (ST-WIDE). JOAN B HOFFMAN, CHMN; APALACHICOLA CHAMBER OF COMMERCE; 90 AVENUE B; APALACHICOLA, FL 32320. (#103416-649).

ARCHER

APR 5, '76. PARADE & CEREMONY. CEREMONY, PARADE AT MULTI-PURPOSE BLDG. (LOCAL). S E BENTON, CHMN; ARCHER BICENTENNIAL COMMITTEE; PO BOX 39; ARCHER, FL 32618. (#200011-267).

JULY 3, '76. JULY 3 PARADE IN ARCHER. PARADE. (LOCAL). S E BENTON, CHMN; ARCHER BICENTENNIAL COMMITTEE; PO BOX 39; ARCHER, FL 32618. (#200011-266).

AUBURNDALE

JULY 1 - 4, '76. 4TH OF JULY CELEBRATION. JULY 1ST & 2ND THERE WILL BE A FIDDLER'S CONVENTION WITH STRING BANDS; JULY 3RD FESTIVITIES INCLUDE: SACK RACES, LOG CHOPPING, TENNIS TOURNAMENT & GOSPEL SINGING; ON JULY 4TH THERE WILL BE A CHURCH SERVICE, LUNCH, CONTEST JUDGING AND DEDICATION OF THE TIME CAPSULE. AT CITY PARK & CITY HALL. (LOCAL). CARL ALLEN, CHAIRMAN; AUBURNDALE BICENTENNIAL COMMITTEE; PO BOX 1776; AUBURNDALE, FL 33823. (#105782-1).

JULY 4, '76. GOD AND COUNTRY SERVICE BICENTENNIAL CELEBRATION. SPECIAL SPEAKERS FROM STATE AND LOCAL GOVERNMENTS; COLOR GUARD TO BE PROVIDED BY THE UNITED STATES ARMED FORCES, MUSIC PROVIDED BY THE LOCAL HIGH SCHOOL BAND. BASKET LUNCH-DINNER AFTER THE PROGRAM. AT CORNER OF BARTOW AND BRIDGERS AVE. (LOCAL). MIKE CLYBURN, MINISTER; AUBURNDALE CHURCH OF THE NAZARENE; PO BOX 728; AUBURNDALE, FL 33823. (#108568-1).

AVALON BEACH

PAINTED FIREHOUSE IN BICENTENNIAL MOTIF, FL. VOLUNTEER FIREMEN PAINTED COMMUNITY FIREHOUSE AND MEETING HALL IN A BICENTENNIAL MOTIF - RED, WHITE & BLUE WITH FLAGS AND DATES. (LOCAL). STANLEY WADNICK, PRESIDENT; AVALON CIVIC LEAGUE, INC; 1335 N 14TH AVE; MILTON, FL 32570. (#21801).

AVON PARK

JAN 9 - NOV ??, '76. BICENTENNIAL HIKE. 2 HIKING STAFFS ARE BEING CARRIED BY FLORIDA TRAIL MEMBERS THE LENGTH OF THE STATE; THE 2 GROUPS WILL MEET IN TALLAHASSEE AND PRESENT THE STAFFS AND A PROCLAMATION TO THE GOVERNOR COMMEMORATING THE EVENT. (ST-WIDE). LARRY HOOPER, DIRECTOR; FLORIDA TRAIL ASSOC, INC; PO BOX 83; AVON PARK, FL 33825. (#108398-1).

BABSON PARK

HISTORY OF BABSON PARK, FL. UNPUBLISHED BOOK ON HISTORY OF AREA INCLUDING A PORTION ON WEBBER COLLEGE. A COPY OF THE HISTORY IS TO BE INCLUDED IN WEBBER LIBRARY. (LOCAL). LOUISE QUINN, AUTHOR; WEBBER COLLEGE; N CROOKED LAKE DR, PO BOX 8; BABSON PARK, FL 33827. (#25603).

HISTORY OF CAMPUS - BABSON PARK, FL. A BOOK BY LOUISE QUINN ON 'HISTORY OF BABSON PARK' WHICH INCLUDES A SECTION ON WEBBER COLLEGE, WILL BE PLACED IN THE LIBRARY; A SECTION OF '76-77 YEARBOOK DEDICATED TO HISTORY OF WEBBER. (LOCAL). MRS LOUISE QUINN, PROJ COORDINATOR; WEBBER COLLEGE; RT A27; BABSON PARK, FL 33827. (#25604).

FEB 19, '76. FLAG PRESENTATION. PRESENTATION FOLLOWED BY PATRIOTIC MUSICAL SELECTIONS AND A FASHION SHOW FEATURING CHANGES IN WOMEN'S FASHIONS OVER LAST 200 YEARS. AT WEBBER COLLEGE DINING ROOM, STUDENT CENTER. (LOCAL). CAROL WILSON, DEAN; BABSON PARK WOMEN'S CLUB; RT A27; BABSON PARK, FL 33827. (#200011-3).

APR 6, '76. SYNCRONIZED SWIM SHOW. WEBBER SYNCHRONIZED SWIM TEAM PRESENTED NUMBERS THAT SALUTED THE AMERICAN SOUND OF MUSIC, INCLUDING 'YANKEE DOODLE DANDY', 'A GRAND OLE FLAG' AND 'DIXIE'. AT WEBBER COLLEGE SWIMMING POOL. (LOCAL). GAIL RENARDSON, COORD; WEBBER FOLLIES; RT A27; BABSON PARK, FL 33827. (#200011-2).

APR 14, '76. HISTORY OF FASHION. ANNUAL SHOW BY THE RETAILING DEPT ENTITLED 'THIS FABULOUS CENTURY', A DRAMATIZED RECAP OF AMERICA'S LAST 100 YEARS WITH A SPOTLIGHT ON FASHION. AT MICHAEL WEBBER AUDITORIUM. (LOCAL). NANCY NYGREN, COORD; RETAILING DEPT; RT A27; BABSON PARK, FL 33827. (#200011-1).

APR 14, '76. PICTORIAL HISTORY OF WEBBER COLLEGE CAMPUS. DRAWINGS & PICTURES OF BABSON PARK IN ITS BEGINNING WILL BE DISPLAYED. AT STUDENT CENTER. (LOCAL). CAROL WILSON, DEAN; WEBBER COLLEGE; RT A27; BABSON PARK, FL 33827. (#108131-1).

OCT '76 - APR '77. INAUGURAL BALL GOWN DISPLAY. A COLLECTION OF REPRODUCTIONS OF GOWNS WORN BY PRESIDENTIAL WIVES WILL BE HOUSED IN GLASS CASES. (LOCAL). CAROL WILSON, DEAN; WEBBER COLLEGE; ROUTE A27; BABSON PARK, FL 33827. (#108205-1).

BAREFOOT BAY

JAN 31, '76. NEW YORK STATE DAY. SOCIAL HOUR, DINNER, DANCING & ENTERTAINMENT. AT BAREFOOT BAY CIVIC CENTER. (REGN'L). HAL BRYANT, PROJ DIRECTOR; NEW YORK STATE COMMITTEE; CHAMBER OF COMMERCE; MELBOURNE, FL 32901. (#104085-9).

BARTOW

RELOCATION OF POLK COUNTY HISTORY MATERIAL IN FLA. DUE TO FIRE HAZARD & INACCESSIBILITY, OUTSTANDING COLLECTIONS OF GENEOLOGY & HISTORY VOLUMES WILL BE RELOCATED FROM THEIR PRESENT COURTHOUSE STORAGE AREA IN FEBRUARY, 1975. (LOCAL). MRS BETTE P LOGAN, EXEC DIRECTOR; POLK COUNTY BICENTENNIAL COMMITTEE; PO BOX 1776; LAKELAND, FL 33802. (#3929).

REPLICA OF FORT BLOUNT, BARTOW, FL. A REPLICA OF THE BLOCKHOUSE BUILT BY FIRST PERMANENT SETTLERS FOR PROTECTION FROM INDIANS, WILL BE BUILT. (LOCAL). LOYAL FRISBIE, CHAIRMAN; BARTOW BICENTENNIAL COMMITTEE; 190 S FLORIDA AVE; BARTOW, FL 33830. (#22138).

APR 18, '75. PAUL REVERE DAY. PARADE, FESTIVAL. (LOCAL). LOYAL FRISBIE; BARTOW BICENTENNIAL COMMITTEE; BOX 120; BARTOW, FL 33830. (#50063-1).

JULY 4, '76. FOURTH OF JULY FAMILY CELEBRATION. FAMILY PICNIC, CHILDREN'S GAMES IN AFTERNOON, JOINT CHURCH SERVICE IN EVENING AND FIREWORKS AT NIGHT. AT MARY HOLLAND PARK AND CIVIC CENTER. (LOCAL). LOYAL FRISBIE, CHAIRMAN; BARTOW BICENTENNIAL COMMITTEE; PO BOX 120; BARTOW, FL 33830. (#105836-1).

BELLE ISLE

PAINT YOUR MAILBOX CONTEST - BELLE ISLE, FL. CITIZENS WERE INVITED TO PAINT THEIR MAILBOXES, EITHER PATRIOTIC OR DECORATIVE AND SUBMIT THEIR ENTRY FOR PRIZES. (LOCAL). MRS MARTHA COOLEY, CHAIRMAN; CITY OF BELLE ISLE; 1600 NELA AVE; BELLE ISLE, FL 32809. (#29443).

MAR 27, '76. BELLE ISLE HERITAGE FESTIVAL. EXHIBIT AT CITY HALL, 1600 NELA AVE. (LOCAL). MRS MARTHA COOLEY, CHMN; CITY OF BELLE ISLE; 2211 CROSS LAKE RD; BELLE ISLE, FL 32809. (#200011-244).

BELLEAIR

MAY 15 - 30, '76. BELLEAIR BICENTENNIAL AMERICANA EXHIBIT. EXHIBIT WILL INCLUDE ANTIQUES, COINS, STAMPS, PICTURES AND PHOTOGRAPHS. (LOCAL). ELLEN KAISER, DIRECTOR; FLORIDA GULF COAST ART CENTER; 222 PONCE DE LEON BLVD; BELLEAIR, FL 33516. (#100449-2).

BEVERLY HILLS

REMEMBRANCE PLAQUE - BEVERLY HILLS, FL. A 4 BY 8 FOOT PLAQUE WITH A 23 BY 25 INCH REPLICA OF THE DECLARATION OF INDEPENDENCE; THE PLAQUE WILL BE SIGNED BY PEOPLE ATTENDING THE BICENTENNIAL CELEBRATION. (LOCAL). HENRY HAHN, CHAIRMAN; LECANTO BICENTENNIAL COMMITTEE; 34 S ADAMS ST; LECANTO, FL 32661. (#25950).

JULY 4, '76. BICENTENNIAL PARADE. PARADE. (LOCAL). HENRY HAHN, CHAIRMAN; LECANTO BICENTENNIAL COMMITTEE; 34 S ADAMS ST; LECANTO, FL 32661. (#108404-1).

BISCAYNE PARK

JULY 2 - 4, '76. INDEPENDENCE DAY CELEBRATION - FLAG CEREMONY AND GRASS ROOTS PARADE. FESTIVAL, PARADE. (LOCAL). SUZANNE VAN GUNDY, CHWMN; BISCAYNE PARK BICENTENNIAL COMMITTEE; 11615 GRIFFING BLVD; BISCAYNE PARK, FL 33161. (#2997-10).

BITHLO

JULY 4, '76. DEDICATION OF CENTER AND OPENING OF THE NATURE TRAILS. A COMMUNITY PROJECT TO CONSTRUCT AND SUPPLY A CENTER TO STUDY MAN'S NATURAL HERITAGE; TO BETTER UNDERSTAND IT AND TO PROVIDE AN INTERDISCIPLINARY EDUCATIONAL SUPPLEMENT FOR TEACHERS AND FAMILIES. AT ENVIRONMENTAL EDUCATIONAL CENTER. (LOCAL). RUSSELL A FISHER; ORANGE AUDUBON SOCIETY; AUDUBON HOUSE, PO BOX 1142; MAITLAND, FL 32751. (#5943-501).

BOCA RATON

CITY OF BOCA RATON 50TH ANNIVERSARY CELEBRATION-FL. PARKS & RECREATION DEPARTMENT SPONSORED MUSICAL, CULTURAL, ATHLETIC & EDUCATIONAL PROGRAMS INVOLVING VARIOUS CIVIC, SOCIAL & CULTURAL ORGANIZATIONS IN THE CITY. (LOCAL). MRS CONNIE NELSON, CHAIRMAN; BOCA RATON BICENTENNIAL COMMITTEE; 201 W PALMETTO RD; BOCA RATON, FL 33432. (#11246).

SPANISH RIVER PARK, BOCA RATON, FL. A FINE EXAMPLE OF A COMMUNITY EFFORT TO SHIELD A NATURAL AREA FROM THE DEVELOPERS' BULLDOZERS; APPROVAL OF A 1.5 MILLION BOND ISSUE IN 1966 HELPED PRESERVE A 46 ACRE OCEANFRONT PARK. (LOCAL). JAMES A RUTHERFORD, PARKS AND RECREATION DIRECTOR; CITY OF BOCA RATON; 201 W PALMETTO PARK RD; BOCA RATON, FL 33432. (#20106).

TREE PLANTINGS, BOCA RATON, FL. TREES WILL BE PLANTED ON CAMPUS TO MARK REVOLUTIONARY EVENTS. (LOCAL). ROGER H MILLER, COORDINATOR; FLORIDA ATLANTIC UNIV; 500 NW 20TH ST; BOCA RATON, FL 33431. (#23495).

AUG 31, '74 - MAY 29, '76. AMERICAN ISSUES FORUM-RADIO SERIES ON GREAT ISSUES 1776-1976. PRESENTED ON RADIO 3 TIMES A WEEK OVER 3 STATIONS, ONE AM & 2 FM. AT LEARNING RESOURCES/TV BUILDING. (LOCAL). DOROTHY H WILKEN; LEARNING RESOURCES DIVISION/FLORIDA ATLANTIC UNIVERSITY; FLORIDA ATLANTIC UNIV; BOCA RATON, FL 33431. (#106683-3).

APR 1, '75 - DEC 31, '76. FREEDOM SHRINE DOCUMENTS; A CAMPUS DISPLAY OF HISTORIC DOCUMENTS. EXHIBIT AT WIMBERLY LIBRARY. (LOCAL). THOMAS MANN, COORDINATOR; FLORIDA ATLANTIC UNIV BICENTENNIAL COMMISSION; 500 NW 20TH ST; BOCA RATON, FL 33431. (#106683-1).

JULY 17 - AUG 17, '75. THEATER SERIES. JULY 17-19, AUGUST 7-9 & 17: 'AH WILDERNESS'; JULY 31, AUGUST 1-3, 14-15: 'THE DEVIL'S DISCIPLE'; JULY 24-26, AUGUST 9-10 & 16: 'SPOON RIVER ANTHOLOGY'. AT UNIVERSITY THEATRE, FLORIDA ATLANTIC UNIV. (LOCAL). JOSEPH CONWAY, COORD; THEATRE DEPARTMENT, COLLEGE OF HUMANITIES, FLORIDA ATLANTIC UNIV; 500 NW 20TH ST; BOCA RATON, FL 33431. (#200011-13).

OCT 3 - 26, '75. ART FESTIVAL 'AMERICA AS WE SEE IT' A PHOTOGRAPHIC PORTRAIT. EXHIBIT AT QUADRANGLE, FLORIDA ATLANTIC UNIV CAMPUS. (LOCAL). SYDNEY TAL MASON, COORD; ART DEPARTMENT COLLEGE OF HUMANITIES, FLORIDA ATLANTIC UNIV; 500 NW 2 TH ST; BOCA RATON, FL 33431. (#200011-14).

MAR 2 - DEC 31, '76. 18TH CENTURY CARTOONS EXHIBIT. CARTOONS DEPICT ENGLISH REACTION TO REVOLUTION AND REVOLUTIONARY ERA MANUSCRIPTS. AT S E WIMBERLY LIBRARY. (LOCAL). THOMAS MANN, DIRECTOR; FLORIDA ATLANTIC UNIV BICENTENNIAL COMMITTEE; 500 N W 20TH ST; BOCA RATON, FL 33431. (#106683-4).

MAR 14, '76. 'MUSIC WE HAVE KNOWN AND LOVED FROM THE WARS' - LIVE PERFORMANCE. LIVE PERFORMANCE AT UNIVERSITY THEATRE, FLORIDA ATLANTIC UNIV. (LOCAL). DR EUGENE CRABB, COORD; MUSIC DEPARTMENT, COLLEGE OF HUMANI-

BOCA RATON — CONTINUED

TIES, FLORIDA ATLANTIC UNIV; 500 NW 20TH ST; BOCA RATON, FL 33431. (#200011-15).

MAY 12, '76. AMERICAN WIND SYMPHONY'S FLOATING ARTS CENTER VISITS BOCA RATON. EMBARKING UPON A BICENTENNIAL CULTURAL TOUR, THE WIND SYMPHONY WILL VISIT 76 CITIES BRINGING MUSIC, DANCE, SYMPOSIA, AND CHILDREN'S THEATER TO THE WATERWAYS OF AMERICA DURING ITS 6-MONTH TOUR. (LOCAL). PAULA BERN, COORDINATOR; AMERICAN WIND SYMPHONY ORCHESTRA OF WESTERN PENNSYLVANIA; GATEWAY TOWERS 18G; PITTSBURGH, PA 15222. (#2800-6).

BONIFAY

VIETNAMESE REFUGEE FAMILY-SPONSOR - BONIFAY, FL. RESETTLEMENT ASSOCIATION WILL CARE FOR FAMILIES UNTIL A JOB AND PLACE TO LIVE ARE AVAILABLE TO THEM. (LOCAL). SIMON J BURTTSCHELL, CHAIRMAN; HOLMES COUNTY BICENTENNIAL ASSOC; PO BOX 1776; BONIFAY, FL 32425. (#15012).

OCT 21 - 25, '75. COUNTY FAIR HERITAGE EXHIBITS. BICENTENNIAL ASSOC WILL AWARD CASH PRIZES FOR BEST HERITAGE EXHIBIT OF FAMILY UNIT AND RELIGEOUS HERITAGE. AT FAIRGROUNDS ON HIGHWAY 90. (LOCAL). SIMON BURTTSCHELL, CHMN; GREATER HOLMES COUNTY FAIR ASSOCIATION; PO BOX 1776; BONIFAY, FL 32425. (#102186-1).

JAN 7 - 8, '76. UNITED STATES ARMED FORCES BICENTENNIAL CARAVAN. CARAVAN IS COMPOSED OF EXHIBIT VANS FOR EACH MILITARY SERVICE. PROJECT THEME IS 'HISTORY OF THE ARMED FORCES AND THEIR CONTRIBUTIONS TO THE NATION'. (LOCAL). SIMON J BURTTSCHELL; US ARMED FORCES BICENTENNIAL EXHIBIT VANS PROJECT; PO BOX 1776; BONIFAY, FL 32425. (#1775-417).

BOYNTON BEACH

DEC 7, '75. BOYNTON BEACH CHAMBER OF COMMERCE BICENTENNIAL PARADE. THE LARGEST LOCAL PARADE AROUND; INVOLVES MANY SURROUNDING COMMUNITIES; ALREADY 25 BANDS AND 150 FLOATS; PARADE ROUTE LINED WITH FLAGS FROM EACH OF THE 50 STATES; ALL SPECTATORS ARE ASKED TO ATTEND IN BICENTENNIAL COSTUME. (LOCAL). KATHERINE HOUGHN, CHMN; BOYNTON BEACH CHAMBER OF COMMERCE; 1114 SE 2ND ST; BOYNTON BEACH, FL 33435. (#103688-1).

BRADENTON

MANATEE VILLAGE HISTORICAL PARK - BRADENTON, FL. RESTORATION OF ORIGINAL HISTORIC COURTHOUSE AND CHURCH TO BE USED AS MUSEUMS; PARK IS BEING IMPROVED FOR TOURIST AND CITIZEN USE. (LOCAL). DOROTHEA DRIGGS, ASST DIRECTOR; MANATEE COUNTY ACTION '76 STEERING COMMITTEE; 8626 CONETTA DR; SARASOTA, FL 33580. (#28270). **ARBA GRANTEE.**

DEC 1 - 31, '75. COMPARISONS OF 16TH CENT SPANISH & 18TH CENT CONT'L SOLDIERS. COSTUMED HISTORIANS DRESSED APPROPRIATELY WILL INFORM THE VISITOR OF THE DIFFERENCE THESE TWO SOLDIERS FACED--WEAPONS, CLOTHING, FOOD. (REGN'L). SUPT, DE SOTO N MEM; NATIONAL PARK SERVICE; P.O. BOX 1377; BRADENTON, FL 33506. (#6729-55).

JAN 1 - SEPT 6, '76. DE SOTO NMEM PGM ON 16TH C SPANISH & 18TH C CONTINENTAL SOLDIERS. COSTUMED INTERPRETERS DRESSED AS 16TH CENTURY SPANISH SOLDIER AND 18TH CENTURY AMERICAN SOLDIER WILL CARRY ON INFORMAL DIALOGUE HIGHLIGHTING THEIR DIFFERENCES--THEIR LIVES, WEAPONS, CLOTHING, AND RATIONS. (REGN'L). SUPT, DE SOTO N MEM; NATIONAL PARK SERVICE; P.O. BOX 1377; BRADENTON, FL 33506. (#6729-555).

JAN 24, '76. UNITED STATES ARMED FORCES BICENTENNIAL CARAVAN. CARAVAN IS COMPOSED OF EXHIBIT VANS FOR EACH MILITARY SERVICE. PROJECT THEME IS 'HISTORY OF THE ARMED FORCES AND THEIR CONTRIBUTIONS TO THE NATION'. (LOCAL). PATTY JONES; US ARMED FORCES BICENTENNIAL EXHIBIT VANS PROJECT; 4808 CORAL BLVD; BRADENTON, FL 33507. (#1775-424).

MAR 21 - 28, '76. DE SOTO CELEBRATION. 50 PLANNED ACTIVITIES CELEBRATE THE HISTORIC HERITAGE OF THE AREA. (ST-WIDE). JOHN C HANSON, COORD; HERNANDO DE SOTO HISTORICAL SOCIETY, INC; 809 14TH ST; BRADENTON, FL 33505. (#103416-126).

MAY 30, '76. FISH FRY AT DE SOTO NATL MEMORIAL. COMMEMORATES ANNIVERSARY OF DE SOTO'S LANDING; LOCAL CATERER PROVIDES FRIED FISH & OTHER FOODS FOR NOMINAL FEE; PARK PERSONNEL GIVE SPECIAL BICENTENNIAL PROGRAMS THROUGHOUT THE DAY. (REGN'L). DE SOTO N MEM; COOPERATING ASSOCIATION & NATIONAL PARK SERVICE; PO BOX 377; BEADENTON, FL 33506. (#6728-215).

BRANDON

JULY 3 - 5, '76. FOURTH OF JULY CELEBRATION. FESTIVAL AT CIVIC CENTER, HIGHWAY 60. (LOCAL). RICHARD SMITH, COORD; BRANDON BICENTENNIAL COMMITTEE; 408 W BRANDON BLVD; BRANDON, FL 33511. (#107260-1).

BRONSON

JULY 4, '76. COMMUNITY CELEBRATION. FESTIVAL AT BRONSON HIGH SCHOOL. (LOCAL). LINDA SHAW, CHMN; BRONSON BICENTENNIAL COMMITTEE; PO BOX 183; BRONSON, FL 32621. (#200011-281).

BROOKSVILLE

AUDIO VISUAL SLIDE PROGRAM - BROOKSVILLE, FL. LOCAL RESIDENTS WILL CONTRIBUTE THEIR RECOLLECTIONS OF THE GROWTH & DEVELOPMENT OF HERNANDO COUNTY; ADDITIONS WILL FOLLOW FOR PERMANENT RECORD OF OUR HISTORY. (LOCAL). COL THOMAS DEEN, JR, CHAIRMAN; HERNANDO COUNTY ACTION '76 COMMITTEE; 1 E JEFFERSON ST; BROOKSVILLE, FL 33512. (#25941).

BICENTENNIAL COLUMN IN BROOKSVILLE, FL. THE LOCAL NEWSPAPER WILL RUN BIWEEKLY ARTICLES ON THE AMERICAN REVOLUTION. (LOCAL). RICHARD J KINNEY, CHAIRPERSON; PASCO-HERNANDO COMMUNITY COLLEGE BICENTENNIAL COMMITTEE; 260 S MAY AVE; BROOKSVILLE, FL 33512. (#11767).

BICENTENNIAL MUSIC IN BROOKSVILLE, FL. COLLEGE STUDENTS WILL BE TAUGHT CLASSES ON MUSIC OF 1776. (LOCAL). RICHARD J KINNEY, CHAIRPERSON; PASCO-HERNANDO COMMUNITY COLLEGE BICENTENNIAL COMMITTEE; 260 S MAY AVE; BROOKSVILLE, FL 33512. (#11758).

BICENTENNIAL RADIO PROGRAMS IN BROOKSVILLE, FL. PROJECT INVOLVES THE RADIO BROADCASTING OF WEEKLY HISTORICAL COURSES. (LOCAL). RICHARD J KINNEY, CHAIRPERSON; PASCO-HERNANDO COMMUNITY COLLEGE BICENTENNIAL COMMITTEE; 260 S MAY AVE; BROOKSVILLE, FL 33512. (#11759).

BROOKSVILLE BEAUTIFICATION - BROOKSVILLE, FL. BEAUTIFICATION WITH TREES AND PLANTS AROUND THE CITY. (LOCAL). LOIS DICK, PRESIDENT; BROOKSVILLE GARDEN CLUB; 513 STAFFORD; BROOKSVILLE, FL 33512. (#19243).

CITY SIGN PROJECT IN BROOKSVILLE, FL. PROJECT ENTAILS THE ERECTING OF A SIGN AT THE ENTRANCE OF THE CITY. (LOCAL). RICHARD J KINNEY, CHAIRPERSON; PASCO-HERNANDO COMMUNITY COLLEGE BICENTENNIAL COMMITTEE; 260 S MAY AVE; BROOKSVILLE, FL 33512. (#11760).

CLASS OF '76 FIFE & DRUM GROUP IN BROOKSVILLE, FL. COLLEGE FIFE AND DRUM GROUP WILL PARTICIPATE IN 4TH OF JULY PARADE. (LOCAL). RICHARD J KINNEY, CHAIRPERSON; PASCO-HERNANDO COMMUNITY COLLEGE BICENTENNIAL COMMITTEE; 260 S MAY AVE; BROOKSVILLE, FL 33512. (#11766).

DOCUMENT SIGNING RE-ENACTMENT IN BROOKSVILLE, FL. THE PROJECT ENTAILS A RE-ENACTMENT OF THE SIGNING OF THE DECLARATION OF INDEPENDENCE. (LOCAL). RICHARD J KINNEY, CHAIRPERSON; PASCO-HERNANDO COMMUNITY COLLEGE BICENTENNIAL COMMITTEE; 260 S MAY AVE; BROOKSVILLE, FL 33512. (#11765).

FAIR EXHIBIT IN BROOKSVILLE, FL. COLLEGE STUDENTS WILL ENTER AN EXHIBIT, WITH A BICENTENNIAL THEME, IN THE FAIR. (LOCAL). RICHARD J KINNEY, CHAIRPERSON; PASCO-HERNADO COMMUNITY COLLEGE BICENTENNIAL COMMITTEE; 260 S MAY AVE; BROOKSVILLE, FL 33512. (#11768).

FLORIDA BICENTENNIAL FLAG SALE IN BROOKSVILLE. PROJECT IS THE SELLING OF BICENTENNIAL FLAGS. (LOCAL). RICHARD J KINNEY, CHAIRPERSON; PASCO-HERNANDO COMMUNITY COLLEGE BICENTENNIAL COMMITTEE; 260 S MAY AVE; BROOKSVILLE, FL 33512. (#11763).

FREEDOM FESTIVAL IN BROOKSVILLE, FL. IN HONOR OF THE BICENTENNIAL, A SOCIAL FESTIVAL WILL BE HELD IN JULY OF '76. (LOCAL). RICHARD J KINNEY, CHAIRPERSON; PASCO-HERNADO COMMUNITY COLLEGE BICENTENNIAL COMMITTEE; 260 S MAY AVE; BROOKSVILLE, FL 33512. (#11762).

HERNANDO COUNTY MUSEUM - BROOKSVILLE, FL. ESTABLISHMENT OF A MUSEUM WHICH WILL HOUSE MANY ITEMS OF HISTORICAL VALUE TO HERNANDO COUNTY. (LOCAL). COL THOMAS DEEN, CHAIRMAN; HERNANDO COUNTY ACTION '76; 1 E JEFFERSON ST; BROOKSVILLE, FL 33512. (#15030).

LECTURE SERIES IN BROOKSVILLE, FL. A MONTHLY LECTURE PRESENTATION ON FAMOUS AMERICANS WILL BE THE EMPHASIS OF THE PROJECT. (LOCAL). RICHARD J KINNEY, CHAIRPERSON; PASCO-HERNADO COMMUNITY COLLEGE BICENTENNIAL COMMITTEE; 260 S MAY AVE; BROOKSVILLE, FL 33512. (#11769).

LIBERTY BELL IN BROOKSVILLE, FL. PLACEMENT OF REPLICA OF LIBERTY BELL IN NEW WING OF THE COUNTY COURTHOUSE. (LOCAL). COL THOMAS DEEN, CHAIRMAN; HERNANDO COUNTY ACTION '76; 1 E JEFFERSON ST; BROOKSVILLE, FL 33512. (#15031).

ORAL HISTORY OF HERNANDO COUNTY, FL. TAPING OF ORAL HISTORY FROM MANY OF THE OLDER RESIDENTS OF HERNANDO COUNTY. (LOCAL). COL THOMAS DEEN, CHAIRMAN; HERNANDO COUNTY ACTION '76; 1 E JEFFERSON ST; BROOKSVILLE, FL 33512. (#15011).

ROBIN'S PARK - BROOKSVILLE, FL. REACTIVATE THE COMPLETION OF ROBIN'S PARK WITH RECREATIONAL FACILITIES FOR AREA RESIDENTS. (LOCAL). TONY KOENIG, PROJ CHAIRMAN; ROBIN'S PARK ASSOC; RT 2 BOX 204; BROOKSVILLE, FL 33512. (#25940).

SPRING HILL BEAUTIFICATION - BROOKSVILLE, FL. THE PROJECT WILL INVOLVE THE BEAUTIFICATION OF SPRING HILL COMMUNITY. (LOCAL). COL THOMAS DEEN, CHAIRMAN; HERNANDO COUNTY ACTION '76; 1 E JEFFERSON ST; BROOKSVILLE, FL 33512. (#15033).

STUDENT LOUNGE DECORATIONS AND FESTIVITIES, FL. THE STUDENT LOUNGE OF PASCO-HERNANDO COMMUNITY COLLEGE WILL BE DECORATED IN RED, WHITE & BLUE. (LOCAL). RICHARD J KINNEY, CHAIRPERSON; PASCO-HERNANDO COMMUNITY COLLEGE BICENTENNIAL COMMITTEE; 260 S MAY AVE; BROOKSVILLE, FL 33512. (#11756).

STUDENT SPEAKERS BUREAU IN BROOKVILLE, FL. PROJECT ENTAILS STUDENT LECTURES TO THE PUBLIC ON AMERICAN HISTORY. (LOCAL). RICHARD J KINNEY, CHAIRPERSON; PASCO-HERNADO COMMUNITY COLLEGE BICENTENNIAL COMMITTEE; 260 S MAY AVE; BROOKSVILLE, FL 33512. (#11757).

VOTER AWARENESS PROJECT IN BROOKSVILLE, FL. PROJECT INVOLVES DISSEMINATING OF VOTER REGISTRATION INFORMATION. (LOCAL). RICHARD J KINNEY, CHAIRPERSON; PASCO-HERNADO COMMUNITY COLLEGE BICENTENNIAL COMMITTEE; 260 S MAY AVE; BROOKSVILLE, FL 33512. (#11761).

VOTER TURNOUT PROJECT IN BROOKSVILLE, FL. PROJECT WILL TRY TO ACHIEVE 100% VOTER TURNOUT IN THE 1976 ELECTION. (LOCAL). COL THOMAS DEEN, CHAIRMAN; HERNANDO COUNTY ACTION '76; 1 E JEFFERSON ST; BROOKSVILLE, FL 33512. (#15032).

OCT 25, '75. BROOKSVILLE WOMEN'S CLUB BICENTENNIAL STYLE SHOW. LIVE PERFORMANCE AT COUNTY AUDITORIUM, COUNTY FAIRGROUNDS, HIGHWAY 41. (LOCAL). MRS ROBERTA KINNER, CHMN; BROOKSVILLE WOMEN'S CLUB; 606 SABRA DR; BROOKSVILLE, FL 33512. (#102181-1).

OCT 31 - NOV 2, '75. SPORTSARAMA. COMPETITION AT COUNTY FAIRGROUNDS, HIGHWAY 41. (LOCAL). RAY MUELLER, CHMN; BROOKSVILLE NOON LIONS CLUB; 467 FOREST AVE; BROOKSVILLE, FL 33512. (#102181-4).

NOV 2, '75. BICENTENNIAL TOURING MEDICINE SHOW. LIVE PERFORMANCE AT COUNTY AUDITORIUM, COUNTY FAIRGROUNDS, HIGHWAY 41. (LOCAL). CLAUDETTE JORDAN, CHMN; BROOKSVILLE NOON LIONS CLUB/SHERIFF'S POSSE; 1 E JEFFERSON ST; BROOKSVILLE, FL 33512. (#102181-2).

DEC 13, '75. BICENTENNIAL CHRISTMAS PARADE. PARADE AT HWY 41 THROUGH BROOKSVILLE ON MAIN ST. (LOCAL). NORMA SHAW, COORD; BROOKSVILLE WOMEN'S CLUB; HWY 50 E; BROOKSVILLE, FL 33512. (#200011-4).

DEC 13, '75. CHRISTMAS TREE FANTASY. EXHIBIT AT COUNTY AUDITORIUM, COUNTY FAIRGROUNDS, HIGHWAY 41. (LOCAL). EVE MOAK, CHAIRMAN; HERNANDO COUNTY ACTION '76 COMMITTEE; 1431 LOCKWOOD ST; SPRING HILL, FL 33512. (#102181-3).

JAN 24 - 25, '76. BROOKSVILLE BICENTENNIAL FESTIVAL OF ARTS. FESTIVAL AT CITY PARK. (LOCAL). CLAUDETTE JORDAN; NOON TIME LIONS CLUB; 1 E JEFFERSON; BROOKSVILLE, FL 33512. (#104241-2).

FEB 20, '76. BICENTENNIAL BAND CONCERT - SPRINGSTEAD JR HIGH SCHOOL BAND. THE FIRST CONCERT OF THE NEW SCHOOL WHICH OPENED IN SEPTEMBER, 1975. AT SPRINGSTEAD JR HIGH SCHOOL AUDITORIUM. (LOCAL). DAVID NAUNANN, DIRECTOR; MUSIC DEPT, SPRINGSTEAD JR HIGH SCHOOL; SPRING HILL, FL 33512. (#200011-5).

FEB 26, '76. BICENTENNIAL BONANZA. THE DRUM & FIFE CORPS WILL BE PARTICIPATING IN ALL BI. EVENTS THRU JULY 4TH AND A PROGRAM INVOLVING OUR FUTURE CITIZENS. AT FELLOWSHIP HALL, FIRST METHODIST CHURCH, BROAD ST. (LOCAL). PAULETT DILL, COORD; JR SERVICE LEAGUE OF BROOKSVILLE; 519 SUMMIT DR; BROOKVILLE, FL 33512. (#200011-6).

MAR 1, '76. BEAUTY PAGEANT AND ESSAY ON MEANING OF SPIRIT OF '76. COMPETITION AT CIVIC AUDITORIUM FAIRGROUNDS HWY 41. (LOCAL). PATTY GRESHAM; BROOKSVILLE LIONS CLUB; 506 NORTH ST; BROOKSVILLE, FL 33512. (#104241-1).

MAR 3, '76. HERNANDO COUNTY SINGS. YOUTH INVOLVEMENT TO BE STRESSED. AT COUNTY CIVIC AUDITORIUM, BROOKSVILLE. (LOCAL). TOM DEEN; HERNANDO CO ACTION '76 COMMITTEE; 1 E JEFFERSON; BROOKSVILLE, FL 33512. (#104241-3).

MAR 30 - 31, '76. FLAG CARRYING SPIRIT OF '76 AMERICAN UNITY PROJECT 41. CROSS COUNTY MARCH PASSING PASSING FLAG ON TO NEIGHBORING COUNTY. AT BEGIN COUNTY LINE HERNANDO PASCO COUNTIES. (LOCAL). HORACE HOWELL, COORD; HERNANDO COUNTY ACTION '76 COMMITTEE; 919 CEDAR DR; BROOKSVILLE, FL 33512. (#104706-1).

MAY 2, '76. NATIONAL MUSIC WEEK - 'MUSIC OPENS NEW VISTAS'. RADIO TV AT WWJB BROADCASTING, 315 MAIN. (LOCAL). MS SHIRLEY DESMOND, CHMN; BROOKSVILLE MUSIC CLUB; U S 19 N; BROOKSVILLE, FL 33512. (#200011-7).

MAY 15, '76. HISTORY OF HERNANDO COUNTY AUDIO-VISUAL SLIDE PRESENTATION. THE HERNANDO COUNTY AUDIO-VISUAL SHOW WILL BE MADE AVAILABLE TO CIVIC CLUBS, LIBRARIES, SCHOOLS AND OTHER ORGANIZATIONS. AT HERNANDO COUNTY CIVIC AUDITORIUM. (LOCAL). NOLEN BRUNSON, COORD; HERNANDO COUNTY BICENTENNIAL ACTION '76 COMMITTEE; 105 N MAIN; BROOKSVILLE, FL 33512. (#200011-8).

MAY 17 - 18, '76. BROOKSVILLE JR HIGH SCHOOL BAND BICENTENNIAL CONCERT. TWO ADVANCED BANDS WILL PRESENT A SPRING CONCERT. AT HERNANDO COUNTY CIVIC AUDITORIUM, HWY 41 S. (LOCAL). AMY S WILSON, COORD; MUSIC DEPARTMENT, BROOKSVILLE JUNIOR HIGH SCHOOL; BROOKSVILLE, FL 33512. (#200011-9).

MAY 20, '76. SYMPHONIC BAND SALUTE TO JOHN PHILIP SOUSA. AT THE ENCOURAGEMENT OF THE ACTION '76 COMMITTEE, THE HERNANDO HIGH SCHOOL BAND WILL PRESENT THIS OUTSTANDING CONCERT; ONE OF A SERIES OF HIGH SCHOOL BAND CONCERTS. AT HERNANDO COUNTY CIVIC AUDITORIUM, HWY 41 S. (LOCAL). STEVE MANUEL, COORD; HERNANDO HIGH SCHOOL BAND DEPT; BROOKSVILLE, FL 33512. (#200011-10).

BROOKSVILLE — CONTINUED

MAY 26, '76. LIBERTY BELL PRESENTATION TO HERNANDO HIGH SCHOOL BY CLASS OF '76. SCHOOL ENROLLMENT PLUS GUESTS AND DIGNITARIES WILL ATTEND THE LIBERTY BELL DONATION TO THE SENIOR CLASS, WHO IN TURN WILL PRESENT IT TO THE SCHOOL. THE BELL WILL BE PLACED IN THE SCHOOL QUADRANGLE AND IT WILL CONTAIN A CAPSULE TO BE OPENED IN 2010. AT HERNANDO HIGH SCHOOL QUADRANGLE AREA. (LOCAL). YVONNE FACIANE, COORD; HERNANDO HIGH SCHOOL SENIOR CLASS; BROOKSVILLE, FL 33512. (#200011-11).

MAY 29, '76. PONY EXPRESS. RE-ENACTMENT - JUNE 2, 1887 PASCO COUNTY WAS CREATED, DIVORCING ITSELF FROM HERNANDO COUNTY. 22 RIDERS WILL RE-ENACT THE PONY EXPRESS DELIVERY OF COPY OF PROCLAMATION TO SAN ANTONIO, PASCO COUNTY. AT COUNTY COURTHOUSE ON MAIN ST - STARTING POINT. (LOCAL). DAN DRUMMOND, COORD; HERNANDO COUNTY 4-H CLUBS; BISHOP LOOP; BROOKSVILLE, FL 33512. (#200011-12).

JUNE 1 - JULY 4, '76. FLORIDA'S NO 1 CRACKER - CONTEST. CONTEST TO DETERMINE FLORIDA'S NO 1 CRACKER; AWARD TO BE GIVEN AT COUNTY FOURTH OF JULY PAGEANT IN BROOKSVILLE. (ST-WIDE). RAD V SCOTT, PROJ COORD; HERNANDO COUNTY SERTOMA CLUB; 3825 SPRING HILL BLVD; SPRING HILL, FL 33512. (#108206-1).

JULY 3, '76. COLONIAL TIMES ART EXHIBIT OF FIRE FIGHTING EQUIPMENT. EXHIBIT AT SPRING HILL COMMUNITY BUILDING. (LOCAL). MARGARETHA GILSTER, CHMN; SPRING HILL ART LEAGUE; 1100 CLAY COURT; SPRING HILL, FL 33512. (#108399-1).

JULY 3, '76. INDEPENDENCE PARADE. 75 FLOATS WILL DEPICT ORGANIZATIONS AND BUSINESSES IN THE COMMUNITY. AT START AT HERNANDO PLAZA AND END AT 1ST & N MAIN. (LOCAL). MS EUNICE COMPTON, COORD; BROOKSVILLE WOMEN'S CLUB; 1630 US 98 NORTH; BROOKSVILLE, FL 33512. (#108399-2).

JULY 3 - 4, '76. FOURTH OF JULY CELEBRATION. COUNTY-WIDE CELEBRATION OF INDEPENDENCE - PARADE, FIREWORKS, PICNICS, ETC. PARADE ON 7/3 AT 10AM. 7/4, OLD TOWN VILLAGE GAMES, FASHION SHOW, MUSIC, BOX LUNCH SOCIAL. (LOCAL). THOMAS J DEEN JR, CHMN; HERNANDO COUNTY ACTION '76 STEERING COMMITTEE; 1 E JEFFERSON ST; BROOKSVILLE, FL 33512. (#102199-1).

JULY 3 - 4, '76. HERNANDO COUNTY BICENTENNIAL PARADE. 7/4, SHOWS, BOOTHS, FIREWORKS. AT HWY 41 N. (LOCAL). EUNICE COMPTON, COORD; BROOKSVILLE WOMEN'S CLUB; US 98 N; BROOKSVILLE, FL 33512. (#105246-1).

JULY 4, '76. BICENTENNIAL MUSIC AND DRAMA PAGEANT. LIVE PERFORMANCE AT STRINGER HILL, U S 98 N. (LOCAL). REV STANLEY JOHNSTON; HERNANDO COUNTY ACTION '76 COMMITTEE; RTE 4, BOX 622A; BROOKSVILLE, FL 33512. (#105246-2).

DEC 11, '76. CHRISTMAS TREE FANTASY BENEFIT FOR HERNANDO CO RETARDED CITIZENS. 2ND ANNUAL CHRISTMAS FANTASY WILL HAVE 29 ORGANIZATIONS DECORATING TREES TO EXHIBIT & WILL SELL MERCHANDISE TO BENEFIT THEIR CIVIC PROGRAMS. ALL TICKET MONEY WILL GO TO THE HERNANDO ASSOC FOR RETARDED CITIZENS, THE FIRST TIME THIS GROUP HAS BEEN RECOGNIZED. AT COUNTY CIVIC AUDITORIUM AND FAIRGROUNDS. (LOCAL). EVE MOAK, CHMN; HERNANDO COUNTY BICENTENNIAL ACTION '76 COMMITTEE & H A R C; 1431 LOCKWOOD; SPRING HILL, FL 33512. (#108890-1).

CALLAHAN

BICENTENNIAL FLAGS - CALLAHAN, FL. OFFICIAL FLORIDA BICENTENNIAL FLAGS WERE PRESENTED TO ALL 5 U S POST OFFICES IN NASSAU COUNTY BY ACTION '76 COMMITTEE IN AUGUST OF 1975. (LOCAL). JIM MOORE, PRESIDENT; NASSAU COUNTY BICENTENNIAL STEERING COMMITTEE; PO BOX 1776; CALLAHAN, FL 32011. (#21266).

BOOK ON NASSAU COUNTY HISTORY - CALLAHAN, FL. A HARDCOVER, 320 PAGE BOOK WITH MAPS, SKETCHES, PHOTOGRAPHS, DOCUMENTS AND A RESEARCHED HISTORY OF NASSAU COUNTY FROM 1583 TO 1930; IT WILL BE ENTITLED 'YESTERDAY'S REFLECTIONS'. (LOCAL). JAN JOHANNES, AUTHOR; NASSAU COUNTY BICENTENNIAL STEERING COMMITTEE; PO BOX 1776; CALLAHAN, FL 32011. (#21269).

FLORIDA BICENTENNIAL FLAGS - CALLAHAN, FL. OFFICIAL STATE BICENTENNIAL FLAGS WILL BE PRESENTED TO EACH PUBLIC SCHOOL IN NASSAU COUNTY DURING AN APPROPRIATE CEREMONY; 12 SCHOOLS INVOLVED. (LOCAL). JIM MOORE, PRESIDENT; NASSAU COUNTY BICENTENNIAL STEERING COMMITTEE; PO BOX 1776; CALLAHAN, FL 32011. (#21268).

HISTORICAL PLACEMATS - CALLAHAN, FL. PLACEMATS SHOWING NASSAU COUNTY'S CONTRIBUTIONS DURING THE AMERICAN REVOLUTIONARY PERIOD WERE PRINTED IN RED, WHITE & BLUE & WILL BE DISTRIBUTED TO ALL RESTAURANTS IN NASSAU COUNTY. (LOCAL). JIM LIBBY, PROJ DIRECTOR; NASSAU COUNTY BICENTENNIAL COMMITTEE; PO BOX 1776; CALLAHAN, FL 32011. (#20763).

YOUTH GROUP - COSTUMED AS 'SPIRIT OF '76', FL. 5 MEMBER GROUP OF SCHOOL CHILDREN DRESSED AS BETSY ROSS, '76 DRUMMERS & FLAUTIST & 2 FLAG BEARERS WILL OPEN CEREMONIES FOR GROUPS & ORGANIZATIONS & MARCH IN PARADES. AVAILABLE FOR BOOKINGS. (LOCAL). MRS JIM LIBBY, MGR & ORIGINATOR OF 'SPIRIT OF '76'; WEST NASSAU COUNTY HISTORICAL SOCIETY; RT 1, BOX 254; CALLAHAN, FL 32011. (#20893).

JULY 3 - 4, '76. FOURTH OF JULY CELEBRATION-FESTIVAL USA. TWO-DAY CELEBRATION BEGINNING WITH PARADE, BEAUTY CONTESTS, OLD-TIME GAMES, BLUEGRASS MUSIC ON JULY 3; PATRIOTIC AND RELIGIOUS MUSIC, BEARD CONTEST, RODEO, FOOD AND FIREWORKS ON JULY 4. FIVE MEMBER SPIRIT OF '76 CHILDREN'S GROUP TO PERFORM. AT NORTHEAST FLORIDA FAIRGROUNDS - US#1 NORTH OF CALLAHAN. (LOCAL). JIM LIBBY, DIRECTOR; WEST NASSAU COUNTY CHAMBER OF COMMERCE; RT 1, BOX 254; CALLAHAN, FL 32011. (#105002-1).

CAPE CORAL

CAPE CORAL BICENT ORGANIZATION'S PROJECTS, FL. MONIES RAISED BY THIS GROUP ASSISTED LOCAL PROGRAMS: BIG JULY 4 CELEBRATION, WORKED W/LOCAL SCHOOLS, FUNDED A BICENT MEETING ROOM IN THE NEW LIBRARY, ASSISTED HIGH SCHOOL BAND W/TRIP TO DC. (LOCAL). GORDON A BERNDT, CHAIRMAN; CAPE CORAL BICENT ORGANIZATION; CAPE CORAL, FL 33904. (#28630).

FEB 14, '76. OLD-FASHIONED ICE CREAM SOCIAL. THIS EVENT INCLUDED A CAKE WALK, RUMMAGE SALE, ETC. PROCEEDS WERE DONATED TO THE BICENTENNIAL. (LOCAL). GORDON A BERNDT, CHMN; FIREMEN'S VOLUNTEER BENEVOLENT SOCIETY; CAPE CORAL, FL 33904. (#200011-260).

CARYVILLE

AUG 21, '76. CARYVILLE FISHING RODEO-WORM FIDDLING CONTEST. FISHING CONTEST, FISH FRY, WORM FIDDLING CONTEST & COMMUNITY SING. (LOCAL). TULLY BRIDENBACK, CHMN; WASHINGTON COUNTY BICENTENNIAL COMMITTEE; PO BOX 4; CHIPLEY, FL 32428. (#102213-1).

CASSELBERRY

MAY 1, '76. BICENTENNIAL FESTIVAL. OLD-FASHIONED FAIR WITH OPENING FLAG CEREMONY AND BAND MUSIC; EVENTS WILL INCLUDE GAMES, RACES FOR YOUNG & OLD, BOOTHS AND FIREWORKS FOLLOWED BY A COMMUNITY DANCE. AT STREET LAKE PARK. (LOCAL). JUDY MATHIAS, PRESIDENT; JUNIOR WOMEN'S CLUB OF CASSELBERRY; 801 N WINTER PARK DR; CASSELBERRY, FL 32707. (#102159-1).

CHATTAHOOCHEE

DEDICATION OF ELLICOTT'S OBSERVATORY. CEREMONY. (LOCAL). DIRECTOR; GADSDEN COUNTY HISTORICAL COMMISSION; PO BOX 550; QUINCY, FL 32351. (#108927-3).

CHIEFLAND

JAN 14, '76. UNITED STATES ARMED FORCES BICENTENNIAL CARAVAN. CARAVAN IS COMPOSED OF EXHIBIT VANS FOR EACH MILITARY SERVICE. PROJECT THEME IS 'HISTORY OF THE ARMED FORCES AND THEIR CONTRIBUTIONS TO THE NATION'. (LOCAL). MRS NORMA M HUTSON; US ARMED FORCES BICENTENNIAL EXHIBIT VANS PROJECT; PO BOX 457; CHIEFLAND, FL 32623. (#1775-420).

CHIPLEY

RESTORATION OF GREEN BERRY BUSH HOME, CHIPLEY, FL. RESTORATION OF THE 100 YEAR OLD HOME, BARN, CEMETERY, CORNCRIB AND WELL. (LOCAL). TULLY BRIDENBACK, CHAIRMAN; WASHINGTON COUNTY BICENTENNIAL COMMITTEE; PO BOX 4; CHIPLEY, FL 32428. (#15048).

THE YOUNG AMERICAN DREAM, CHIPLEY, FL. A GROUP OF YOUNG PEOPLE, WHO PERFORM SONGS OF AMERICAN HISTORY AND REPRESENT THE SPIRIT OF AMERICA'S FUTURE. (LOCAL). TULLY BRIDENBACK, CHAIRWOMAN; WASHINGTON COUNTY ACTION '76 COMMITTEE; PO BOX 4; CHIPLEY, FL 32428. (#15051).

NOV 15, '75. BETSY ROSS AND UNCLE SAM IN MINIATURE, CONTEST. CONTEST ENCOURAGING CHILDREN TO DRESS IN HISTORIC COSTUMES. AT CHIPLEY HIGH SCHOOL STADIUM. (LOCAL). TULLY BRIDENBACK, CHMN; WASHINGTON COUNTY BICENTENNIAL COMMITTEE; PO BOX 4; CHIPLEY, FL 32428. (#102210-1).

APR 9 - 11, '76. ARTS SHOW. EXHIBITS OF LOCAL ARTISTS & PHOTOGRAPHERS PLUS VISITING ART SHOW. AT SUNNY HILLS COMMUNITY CENTER. (LOCAL). TULLY BRIDENBACK, CHMN; WASHINGTON COUNTY BICENTENNIAL COMMITTEE; PO BOX 4; CHIPLEY, FL 32428. (#102210-2).

AUG 21, '76. WASHINGTON COUNTY WATERMELON CONTEST & BEAUTY CONTEST. VARIOUS CONTESTS: WATERMELON, BEAUTY QUEEN, HORSESHOW. AT CHIPLEY HIGH SCHOOL GYM. (LOCAL). TULLY BRIDENBACK, CHMN; WASHINGTON COUNTY BICENTENNIAL COMMITTEE; PO BOX 4; CHIPLEY, FL 32428. (#102210-3).

NOV 5 - 6, '76. WASHINGTON COUNTY FAIR. AN OLD FASHIONED COUNTY FAIR. AT WASHINGTON COUNTY FARM CENTRE. (ST-WIDE). TULLY BRIDENBACK, CHMN; WASHINGTON COUNTY BICENTENNIAL COMMITTEE; PO BOX 4; CHIPLEY, FL 32428. (#102210-4).

DEC 31, '76 - JAN 1, '77. NEW YEAR'S EVE BALL. FAMILY DANCE & FIREWORKS DISPLAY. AT NATIONAL GUARD ARMORY. (LOCAL). TULLY BRIDENBACK, CHMN; WASHINGTON COUNTY BICENTENNIAL COMMITTEE; PO BOX 4; CHIPLEY, FL 32428. (#102210-5).

CHRISTMAS

RESTORATION OF FORT CHRISTMAS- CHRISTMAS, FL. CONSTRUCTION OF A REPLICA OF THE ORIGINAL FORT CHRISTMAS WHICH WAS BUILT IN FOUR DAYS IN 1837; IT WILL BE IN A PARK USED BY THE COMMUNITY OF CHRISTMAS. (LOCAL). ROLFE G ARNHYM, CHAIRMAN; ORANGE COUNTY BICENTENNIAL COMMITTEE; 423 S ORANGE AVE; ORLANDO, FL 32801. (#19643).

CLEARWATER

BICENTENNIAL CALENDAR, CLEARWATER, FL. A 1976 CALENDAR FEATURING PHOTOGRAPHS OF CLEARWATER IN THE LATE 1800'S AND EARLY 1900'S; RED, WHITE AND BLUE COLOR SCHEME; FREE TO CONTRIBUTORS. (LOCAL). JOHN C OSBORN, ASST DIRECTOR; DEPT DEVELOPMENT & COMMUNITY RELATIONS, MORTON F PLANT HOSPITAL; 323 JEFFORDS ST; CLEARWATER, FL 33517. (#18941).

BICENTENNIAL MURAL, 'MY COUNTRY 'TIS OF THEE', FL. A MURAL DEPICTING VARIOUS NATIONAL MONUMENTS WITH LIBERTY THEME. (LOCAL). MARY E HOVER, LIBRARY CHAIRMAN; NORTH WARD ELEMENTARY SCHOOL; 900 N FT HARRISON AVE; CLEARWATER, FL 33515. (#18940).

CLEARWATER MARINE SCIENCE CENTER - CLEARWATER, FL. A MARINE SCIENCE CENTER WHICH WOULD INCLUDE AN AUDITORIUM, LIBRARY AND TEACHING LABORATORY. (LOCAL). MRS MARY MCCORMACK, PROJ DIRECTOR; CLEARWATER MARINE SERVICE CENTER; PO BOX 4662; CLEARWATER, FL 33515. (#15071).

FLAGS OF THE REVOLUTIONARY WAR - CLEARWATER, FL. EACH MONTH UNTIL JULY, 1976 ONE OF 12 REVOLUTIONARY WAR FLAGS WILL BE FLOWN AT THE WAR MEMORIAL NEAR CLEARWATER'S CAUSEWAY. (LOCAL). COL T S WOOD, PROJ DIRECTOR; CLEARWATER RETIRED OFFICER'S CLUB; 109 DRIFTWOOD LANE; CLEARWATER, FL 33540. (#14348).

MOCCASIN NATURE EDUCATION CENTER - CLEARWATER, FL. ESTABLISHMENT OF CLEARWATER'S FIRST MAJOR ENVIRONMENTAL EDUCATION CENTER FOR A BETTER APPRECIATION OF NATURE IN AN AREA WITHIN THE URBAN COMMUNITY. (LOCAL). RICHARD BELL, CHAIRMAN; EAST CLEARWATER ROTARY CLUB; PO BOX 4662; CLEARWATER, FL 33518. (#15070).

OAK TREES - PROJ OF CLEARWATER, FL. BEAUTIFICATION OF GULF TO BAY BLVD BY REPLACING OAK TREES; PROJECT IS BEING SPONSORED BY THE CHILDREN'S PLACE AND URBAN PROPERTY OWNERS. (LOCAL). MRS BARBARA MOORE, CHAIRMAN; THE CHILDREN'S PLACE ELEMENTARY SCHOOL; 202 MCMULLEN BOOTH RD; CLEARWATER, FL 33518. (#15069).

PINELLAS COUNTY HISTORICAL PARK, CLEARWATER, FL. A COUNTY PARK ESTABLISHED FOR HISTORICAL PRESERVATION; SOME OF PINELLAS COUNTY'S OLDEST HOUSES WILL BE MOVED THERE AND WILL HOUSE THE COUNTY MUSEUM. (LOCAL). G LEONARD PUCCI, CHAIRMAN; PINELLAS COUNTY HISTORICAL COMMISSION; 315 HAVEN ST; CLEARWATER, FL 33516. (#15074). **ARBA GRANTEE.**

PINELLAS COUNTY SCHOOLS' BICENTENNIAL GUIDE - FL. A GUIDE TO HELP IN THE BICENTENNIAL CELEBRATION CONTAINING SUGGESNS FOR ACTIVITIES AND PROJECTS FOR TEACHERS AND STUDENTS, ELEMENTARY THROUGH HIGH SCHOOL. (LOCAL). DR JOHN L STILL, CHAIRMAN; PINELLAS COUNTY SCHOOLS' BICENTENNIAL STEERING COMMITTEE; 1960 E DRUID RD; CLEARWATER, FL 33518. (#26612).

RICE'S HERITAGE - CLEARWATER, FL. A 2 STORY, 19TH CENTURY BUILDING FURNISHED WITH 15TH THRU 20TH CENTURY FURNITURE; ALSO, ANTIQUE CAR, FIRE ENGINE, SURRY & RAILROAD STATION EQUIPMENT, BLACKSMITH SHOP. ALL FUNCTIONAL. (LOCAL). SAMUEL ALANSON RICE, PROJ DIRECTOR; RICE'S HERITAGE HOUSE; 1418 N BETTY LN; CLEARWATER, FL 33515. (#22700).

SAFETY VILLAGE - CLEARWATER, FL. A CHILDREN'S PROGRAM OF BICYCLE, AUTOMOBILE, PEDESTRIAN, PLANT AND FIRE SAFETY UTILIZING THE MOST CREATIVE TEACHING AIDS POSSIBLE. (LOCAL). MYRNA Q SMITH, PROJ DIRECTOR; THE JUNIOR WOMAN'S AND THE EXCHANGE CLUBS OF CLEARWATER; 1982 BELLEAIR; CLEARWATER, FL 33516. (#19278).

U S COAST GUARD COLOR GUARD - CLEARWATER, FL. FOUR MAN COLOR GUARD AVAILABLE UPON REQUEST FOR PARTICIPATION IN APPROPRIATE CEREMONIES, PARADES AND OTHER SIGNIFICANT EVENTS. (LOCAL). LT CRAIG JUD, PROJ DIRECTOR; DEPARTMENT OF TRANSPORTATION - U S COAST GUARD; USCG AIR STATION; CLEARWATER, FL 33520. (#32322).

JAN 16 - 18, '76. BICENTENNIAL BAZAAR BY HADASSAH. A NATIONAL TOURING EXHIBIT OF FASHIONS FROM 1850 TO 1950, ENHANCED BY A SERIES OF STYLE SHOWS - 'FROM BUSTLES TO BIKINIS'. FREE TO THE PUBLIC. AT COUNTRYSIDE MALL. (LOCAL). ROY KANE, COORDINATOR; COUNTRYSIDE MALL MERCHANT'S ASSOC; COUNTRYSIDE MALL, 1 OFFICE PARK; CLEARWATER, FL 33515. (#104085-14).

JAN 25, '76. BICENTENNIAL BAZAAR BI HADASSAH. 'KOSHER' AMERICAN STYLE FOOD SERVED ALL DAY; HANDCRAFT AND AMERICAN ANTIQUES ON DISPLAY, MERCHANDISE DONATED BY LOCAL MERCHANTS; HOMEMADE JEWISH CAKES AND PASTRIES FOR SALE; PROCEEDS GO TO CANCER RESEARCH. AT CLEARWATER BEACH CIVIC CENTER. (LOCAL). DORIS D HARDING, COORD; HADASSAH; 1755 ASHTON ABBEY RD; CLEARWATER, FL 33515. (#104255-2).

FEB 5, '76. FRED WARING AND THE PENNSYLVANIANS - MUSIC OF AMERICA, PAST & FUTURE. LIVE PERFORMANCE AT CALVARY BAPTIST CHURCH, 331 CLEVELAND ST. (LOCAL). BILL FOLZ, COORD; CLEARWATER LARGO DUNEDIN BOARD OF REALTORS;

CLEARWATER — CONTINUED

301 PIERCE ST, ROOM 209A; CLEARWATER, FL 33518. (#104085-15).

FEB 22, '76. BICENTENNIAL ARTS FESTIVAL. A JUDGED ART SHOW AWARDING PRIZE MONEY AND RIBBONS. AT MANDALAY PARK; OPPOSITE CLEARWATER YACHT CLUB AND FIRE STATION#2. (LOCAL). VIVIAN RUEGGER, COORD; EDWARD AND JAMES WHITE LADIES AUXILIARY, V F W POST 10304; 1674 YOUNG AVE; CLEARWATER, FL 33516. (#104255-1).

MAR 18 - 28, '76. FUN 'N SUN FESTIVAL. FESTIVAL. (LOCAL). ROBERT KENNEDY, DIRECTOR; CLEARWATER CHAMBER OF COMMERCE; 128 N OSCEOLA AVE; CLEARWATER, FL 33510. (#102165-1).

MAY 6, '76. AMERICAN WIND SYMPHONY'S FLOATING ARTS CENTER VISITS CLEARWATER. EMBARKING UPON A BICENTENNIAL CULTURAL TOUR, THE WIND SYMPHONY WILL VISIT 76 CITIES BRINGING MUSIC, DANCE, SYMPOSIA, AND CHILDREN'S THEATER TO THE WATERWAYS OF AMERICA DURING ITS 6-MONTH TOUR. (LOCAL). PAULA BERN, COORDINATOR; AMERICAN WIND SYMPHONY ORCHESTRA OF WESTERN PENNSYLVANIA; GATEWAY TOWERS 18G; PITTSBURGH, PA 15222. (#2800-4).

JULY 4, '76. KIWANIS STARS & STRIPES FAMILY JUBILEE. FESTIVITIES INCLUDE GAMES, MUSIC & VARIOUS ENTERTAINERS. AT JACK WHITE STADIUM. (LOCAL). TED H ROEPKE, CHAIRMAN; KIWANIS SPRINGTIME; 1709 EMERALD DR; CLEARWATER, FL 33516. (#108333-1).

OCT 29, '76. DEDICATION OF NEW US COAST GUARD AIR STATION. THE NEW AIR STATION IS THE LARGEST COAST GUARD AIR FACILITY IN THE US, WITH OVER 2,000 MILITARY PERSONNEL AND DEPENDENTS. THE STATION OPERATES & MAINTAINS FOUR C-130 AIRCRAFT & FOUR HH3F HELICOPTERS. AT ACROSS AIRFIELD FROM ST PETE - CLEARWATER INT'L AIRPORT. (LOCAL). LT CRAIG JUD; DEPARTMENT OF TRANSPORTATION & U S COAST GUARD; USCG AIR STATION; CLEARWATER, FL 33520. (#200011-296).

CLERMONT

BEAUTIFICATION OF CLERMONT, FL. THE BEAUTIFICATION PROJECT OF THE DOWNTOWN AREA WILL INCLUDE NEW PARK BENCHES, PLANTERS AND FLOWERS. (LOCAL). MRS JONNIE WATSON, PRESIDENT; PROJECT CLERMONT; 1713 VIRGINIA DR; CLERMONT, FL 32711. (#15035).

COOPER MEMORIAL LIBRARY - CLERMONT, FL. AN ADDITION WILL BE MADE TO THE LIBRARY BUILDING. (LOCAL). MRS ALICE TILDEN, CHAIRMAN; COOPER MEMORIAL LIBRARY ASSOC, INC; 549 MAR-NAN-MAR PLACE; CLERMONT, FL 32711. (#15034).

MAY 1, '76. STAND UP FOR AMERICA - PARADE & PATRIOTIC RALLY. A RESERVATION WILL BE REQUIRED FOR PARADE; THE COLORS WILL BE LIMITED TO RED, WHITE & BLUE; THE FLOATS ARE TO BE NON-COMMERCIAL AND NON-POLITICAL. AT DOWNTOWN CLERMONT. (LOCAL). LEON DRUMMOND, CO-CHMN; CLERMONT-MINNEOLA LIONS CLUB; 401 MAIN ST; MINNEOLA, FL 32755. (#102215-1).

CLEWISTON

COMMUNITY PARK DEVELOPMENT - CLEWISTON, FL. REDESIGN EXISTING PARK BY REMOVAL OF BUILDINGS & NEW LANDSCAPING. (LOCAL). CHRIS BROWN, CHAIRMAN; CLEWISTON BICENTENNIAL COMMITTEE; PO BOX 1325; CLEWISTON, FL 33440. (#25942).

200 TREES FOR 200 YEARS - CLEWISTON, FL. TREE PLANTING ALONG MAIN STREET OF COMMUNITY. (LOCAL). CHRIS BROWN, CHAIRMAN; CLEWISTON BICENTENNIAL COMMITTEE; PO BOX 1325; CLEWISTON, FL 33440. (#25943).

JULY 4, '76. JULY 4TH COMMUNITY PICNIC. FESTIVAL AT SUGARLAND PARK. (LOCAL). CHRIS BROWN, DIRECTOR; CLEWISTON BICENTENNIAL COMMITTEE; PO BOX 1325; CLEWISTON, FL 33440. (#108400-1).

COCOA

BCC STUDENT BULLETIN IN COCOA, FL. THE STUDENT BULLETIN OF BREVARD COMMUNITY COLLEGE WILL HAVE A TOWN CRIER LOGO AND FORMAT. (LOCAL). LANE CORVEY, CHAIRMAN; BREVARD COMMUNITY COLLEGE BICENTENNIAL COMMITTEE; 1519 CLEARLAKE RD; COCOA, FL 32922. (#11691).

BCC STUDENT HANDBOOK IN COCOA, FL. HANDBOOK WILL FEATURE PHOTOS OF BREVARD COMMUNITY COLLEGE PERSONNEL IN 1776 COSTUMES, AS WELL AS A FORMAT REMINISCENT OF THE COLONIAL ERA. (LOCAL). LANE CORVEY, CHAIRMAN; BREVARD COMMUNITY COLLEGE BICENTENNIAL COMMITTEE; 1519 CLEARLAKE RD; COCOA, FL 32922. (#11690).

BICENTENNIAL BRIEFS IN COCOA, FL. INFORMATIONAL, HISTORICAL GEM IN SMALL BOX ON FRONT PAGE OF EACH ISSUE OF COLLEGE PAPER. (LOCAL). LANE CORVEY, CHAIRMAN; BREVARD COMMUNITY COLLEGE BICENTENNIAL COMMITTEE; 1519 CLEARLAKE RD; COCOA, FL 32922. (#11692).

BIG BROTHERS OF BREVARD COUNTY, FL. PROGRAM GOAL IS TO HELP YOUNG PEOPLE FROM ONE-PARENT FAMILIES TO DEVELOP VALUES. (LOCAL). CHARLES GOODRICH, PROJ DIRECTOR; BIG BROTHERS OF BREVARD; HOLIDAY OFFICE CENTER; COCOA BEACH, FL 32931. (#19212).

BREVARD COUNTY BICENTENNIAL MONUMENT - FL. A COUNTY BICENTENNIAL MONUMENT FOR COMMEMORATION, COMPLETE WITH TIME CAPSULE. (LOCAL). AGATHA DOERER, PROJECT CHAIRMAN; BREVARD COUNTY BICENTENNIAL COMMITTEE; 318 PEACHTREE ST; COCOA, FL 32922. (#21365).

BREVARD COUNTY, FL, SURVEY. A SURVEY HAS BEEN TAKEN ON THE WANTS & NEEDS OF COUNTY RESIDENTS; IT WILL BE TURNED OVER TO THE COUNTY AND ACTED UPON. (LOCAL). W F HOUSNER, CHAIRMAN; BREVARD COUNTY BICENTENNIAL COMMITTEE; PO BOX 1776; COCOA, FL 32922. (#19218).

BREVARD FINE ARTS COUNCIL - COCOA, FL. THE BREVARD ARTS COUNCIL WILL BE FORMED TO ENLIGHTEN & ENLARGE ARTS IN BREVARD COUNTY. (LOCAL). ROBERT LAUER, PROJ DIRECTOR; BREVARD ARTS COUNCIL; 5 AZALEA DR; COCOA BEACH, FL 32931. (#19213).

BREVARD MUSEUM IN COCOA, FL. DISPLAY AREAS & EDUCATIONAL WING TO BE BUILT. (LOCAL). W F HOUSNER, CHAIRMAN; BREVARD COUNTY BICENTENNIAL COMMITTEE; 318 PEACHTREE ST; COCOA, FL 32922. (#21371).

'CAMPAIGNS: 1776-1976' IN COCOA, FL. SHOW WILL FEATURE CAMPAIGN SPEECHES, SONGS AND FESTIVITIES THAT HAVE MADE AMERICAN ELECTIONS UNIQUE. (LOCAL). LANE CORVEY, CHAIRMAN; BREVARD COMMUNITY COLLEGE BICENTENNIAL COMMITTEE; 1519 CLEARLAKE RD; COCOA, FL 32922. (#11696).

CLEANUP AMERICA PROJECT - COCOA, FLORIDA. NEARLY 1,000 TEEN-AGERS, INCLUDING 30 FROM BRITAIN, WILL VISIT 46 CITIES IN TEAMS, PICKING UP LITTER & PROMOTING SPIRITUAL REVIVAL. THEY WILL TOUR BY BUS, BIKE, CANOE & COVERED WAGON. (LOCAL). ROBERT M BLAND, DIRECTOR; TEEN MISSION, INC; 1108 PEACH TREE; COCOA, FL 32922. (#8755). **ARBA GRANTEE.**

COMMEMORATIVE MEDALLION DISPLAY IN BREVARD CO, FL. SILVER MEDALLIONS FEATURING AMERICA IN SPACE, AMERICAN HISTORY AND OUR FOUNDING FATHERS. (LOCAL). W F HOUSNER, CHAIRMAN; BREVARD COUNTY BICENTENNIAL COMMITTEE; 318 PEACHTREE ST; COCOA, FL 32922. (#21366).

FLAGS OF THE REVOLUTION IN COCOA, FL. COLONIAL FLAG REPRODUCTIONS HAVE BEEN SEWN TO BE FLOWN ON THE THREE CAMPUSES DURING BICENTENNIAL EVENTS & HOLIDAYS. FLAGS WILL BE PERMANENTLY HUNG INDOORS AFTER 1976. (LOCAL). LANE CORVEY, BCC BICENTENNIAL DIRECTOR; BREVARD COMMUNITY COLLEGE; COCOA, FL 32922. (#13761).

FLORAL PLANTING IN COCOA, FL. FLORAL PLANTING WILL BE MADE IN THE FORM OF A FLAG. (LOCAL). BILL TAYLOR, DIRECTOR OF STUDENTS SERVICES; BREVARD COMMUNITY COLLEGE; COCOA, FL 32922. (#13760).

FREEDOM CIRCLE IN COCOA, FL. THE TERRAZO CIRCLE ON EACH CAMPUS TO INCLUDE BICENTENNIAL LOGO AND NUMBERS 1776-1976; THE AREA WILL BE RELANDSCAPED. (LOCAL). LANE CORVEY, CHAIRMAN; BREVARD COMMUNITY COLLEGE BICENTENNIAL COMMITTEE; 1519 CLEARLAKE RD; COCOA, FL 32922. (#11689).

A FREEDOM TREE, COCOA, FL. TREE WILL BE PLANTED ON SCHOOL GROUNDS AND A TIME CAPSULE WILL BE BURIED TO BE RECOVERED AT A CEREMONY IN 2076. (LOCAL). W F HOUSNER, CHAIRMAN; POINSETT MIDDLE SCHOOL; COCOA, FL 32922. (#22360).

HERITAGE PARK IN COCOA, FL. OVERGROWN CITY LOT TURNED INTO PARK WITH LANDSCAPING, FOUNTAIN, WALKS & BENCHES TO BE PROVIDED BY STUDENTS. (LOCAL). LANE CORVEY, DIRECTOR; BREVARD COMMUNITY COLLEGE BICENTENNIAL COMMITTEE; COCOA, FL 32922. (#13762).

INDIAN RIVER JUBILEE IN COCOA, FLORIDA. THE JUBILEE WILL BE A FESTIVAL FOR COMMUNITY ENTERTAINMENT & RECREATION. INCLUDED WILL BE A KARATE DEMONSTRATION, AN AUTO SHOW & OTHER GALA EVENTS. (LOCAL). BILL WOOD, CHAIRMAN; INDIAN RIVER JUBILEE COMMITTEE FOR BREVARD COUNTY; 3220 N COCOA BLVD; COCOA, FL 32922. (#7704).

PIONEER VILLAGE IN COCOA, FL. RECREATION AREA WITH BOAT DOCKS, PICNIC TABLES, SHELTERS, NATURE AND BIKE TRAILS; RE-CREATED EARLY BREVARD SETTLEMENT; AMPHITHEATRE FOR CONCERTS AND LECTURES; IN CLOSE PROXIMITY TO MUSEUM. (LOCAL). W F HOUSNER, CHAIRMAN; BREVARD COUNTY BICENTENNIAL COMMITTEE; 318 PEACHTREE ST; COCOA, FL 32922. (#21368).

REVOLUTIONARY NEWSPAPERS - COCOA, FL. REPRODUCTION OF OLD NEWSPAPERS TO BE DISTRIBUTED TO SCHOOLS. (LOCAL). W F HOUSNER, CHAIRMAN; BREVARD COUNTY BICENTENNIAL COMMITTEE; PO BOX 1776; COCOA, FL 32922. (#19210).

STAR-STUDDED HISTORY IN COCOA, FL. PROJECT INVOLVES A FIVE-FILM SERIES DEPICTING VARIOUS ERAS IN AMERICAN HISTORY AND FEATURING AMERICAN ACTORS OF NOTE. (LOCAL). LANE CORVEY, CHAIRMAN; BREVARD COMMUNITY COLLEGE BICENTENNIAL COMMITTEE; 1519 CLEARLAKE RD; COCOA, FL 32922. (#11693).

TABLE TENTS - COCOA, FL. SIGNS WILL BE PLACED ON RESTAURANTS TO WELCOME GUESTS TO THE COUNTY. (LOCAL). W F HOUSNER, CHAIRMAN; BREVARD COUNTY BICENTENNIAL COMMITTEE; PO BOX 1776; COCOA, FL 32922. (#19211).

TECHNOLOGY DAY. DISPLAY OF CLOTHING, TRANSPORTATION & FOOD DEPICTING TECHNOLOGICAL CHANGES FROM 1774-1974. (LOCAL). W F HOUSNER, CHAIRMAN; POINSETT MIDDLE SCHOOL; COCOA, FL 32922. (#22358-1). **(??).**

'YOU ARE THERE' NEWSPAPER COLUMN IN COCOA, FL. COLUMN IN EACH ISSUE OF THE COLLEGE PAPER TELLING ABOUT PAST HISTORICAL EVENTS AS IF THEY WERE HAPPENING NOW. (LOCAL). LANE CORVEY, CHAIRMAN; BREVARD COMMUNITY COLLEGE BICENTENNIAL COMMITTEE; 1519 CLEARLAKE RD; COCOA, FL 32922. (#11694).

JULY 4, '75. 4TH OF JULY CELEBRATION & HAPPY BIRTHDAY AMERICA PICNIC. WILL INCLUDE PARADES, PICNICS, SPORTS ACTIVITIES & FOOD & ENTERTAINMENT FOR FOLKS OF ALL AGES. (LOCAL). W F HOUSNER, CHAIRMAN; BREVARD COUNTY BICENTENNIAL COMMISSION; 318 PEACH ST; COCOA, FL 32922. (#7714-501).

JULY 4 - 6, '75. FIRECRACKER SOFTBALL COMPETITION. COMPETITION. (LOCAL). PAUL ZENO, CHAIRMAN; BREVARD COUNTY DEPT OF PARKS & RECREATION; 625 E NEW HAVEN AVE; MELBOURNE, FL 32901. (#7713-501).

AUG 30, '75. BICENTENNIAL CANOE REGATTA. IN THE TRADITION OF USING THE SEA FOR LIFE & LEISURE, BREVARD COUNTY WILL HOLD CANOE RACES IN HONOR OF THE BICENTENNIAL. (LOCAL). PAUL ZENO, CHAIRMAN; BREVARD COUNTY DEPT OF PARKS & RECREATION; 625 E NEW HAVEN AVE; MELBOURNE, FL 32901. (#7715-501).

SEPT 5, '75. RALLY 'ROUND THE FLAG. ARBA FLAG PRESENTATION AND AWARD CEREMONY FOR PRIZE WINNING 'HERITAGE PARK' BUILT BY BREVARD COMMUNITY COLLEGE STUDENTS; THERE WILL BE A PICNIC AND AN OLD-FASHIONED SING-ALONG. AT BCC AMPHITHEATRE. (LOCAL). LANE CORVEY, PROJ DIR; BREVARD COMMUNITY COLLEGE; BREVARD COMMUNITY COLLEGE; COCOA, FL 32922. (#101278-1).

SEPT 26, '75. RED, WHITE & BLUE(GRASS) - BLUEGRASS CONCERT. PERFORMANCE BY BLUE GRASS MUSICIANS, RED, WHITE & BLUE (GRASS). AT BCC AMPHITHEATRE. (LOCAL). LANE CORVEY, PROJ DIR; BREVARD COMMUNITY COLLEGE; BREVARD COMMUNITY COLLEGE; COCOA, FL 32922. (#101279-1).

OCT 31, '75. THE BEST OF CANDID CAMERA STARRING ALLEN FUNT. EXHIBIT AT BCC HEALTH CENTER (GYM). (LOCAL). LANE CORVEY, PROJ DIR; BREVARD COMMUNITY COLLEGE; BREVARD COMMUNITY COLLEGE; COCOA, FL 32922. (#101281-1).

NOV 21 - 22, '75. INTERNATIONAL HERITAGE SHOW. MUSIC DANCE DRAMA AND SONG BY ETHNIC GROUPS AND INDIVIDUALS. AT BCC FINE ARTS AUDITORIUM - COCOA CAMPUS. (LOCAL). LANE CORVEY, PROJ DIR; BREVARD COMMUNITY COLLEGE; BREVARD COMMUNITY COLLEGE; COCOA, FL 32922. (#101282-1).

JAN 30, '76. 'YE OLDE TIME VAUDEVILLE'. ANNUAL VARIETY SHOW IN THE STYLE OF ONE OF AMERICA'S MOST FAMOUS PRODUCTION FORMAT, VAUDEVILLE. AT FINE ARTS AUDITORIUM, COCOA CAMPUS. (LOCAL). LANE CORVEY, CHAIRMAN; BREVARD COMMUNITY COLLEGE BICENTENNIAL COMMITTEE; 1519 CLEARLAKE RD; COCOA, FL 32922. (#11695-1).

FEB 11 - 12, '76. UNITED STATES ARMED FORCES BICENTENNIAL CARAVAN. CARAVAN IS COMPOSED OF EXHIBIT VANS FOR EACH MILITARY SERVICE. PROJECT THEME IS 'HISTORY OF THE ARMED FORCES AND THEIR CONTRIBUTIONS TO THE NATION'. (LOCAL). BUD HOUSNER; BICENTENNIAL COMMITTEE; PO BOX 1776; COCOA, FL 32922. (#1775-431).

MAR 8 - 12, '76. CRAFTSMEN'S WEEK. CRAFT DEMONSTRATIONS, FOLK MUSIC, LITERATURE & POETRY PRESENTATIONS; ALSO HELD AT THE AMERICAN COFFEE HOUSE MARCH 12, 8:00 PM. AT AMPHITHEATRE AT BCC. (LOCAL). BILL TAYLOR, COORDINATOR; BREVARD COMMUNITY COLLEGE; BREVARD COMMUNITY COLLEGE; COCOA, FL 32922. (#101285-1).

APR 3 - 11, '76. INDIAN RIVER ORANGE JUBILEE. THE JUBILEE WILL BE A FESTIVAL OR COMMUNITY ENTERTAINMENT AND RECREATION. INCLUDED WILL BE A KARATE DEMONSTRATION, AN AUTO SHOW AND OTHER GALA EVENTS. AT ALL OF CENTRAL BREVARD COUNTY. (LOCAL). BILL WOOD, PROJ DIR; INDIAN RIVER ORANGE JUBILEE COMMITTEE; 15 E MERRITT ISLAND CAUSEWAY; MERRITT ISLE, FL 32952. (#103234-4).

APR 12, '76. PARADE & GRAND BALL. FESTIVAL. (LOCAL). BILL WOOD, CHAIRMAN; INDIAN RIVER JUBILEE COMMITTEE FOR BREVARD COUNTY; 3220 N COCOA BLVD; COCOA, FL 32922. (#7704-504).

MAY 16, '76. AMERICAN WIND SYMPHONY'S FLOATING ARTS CENTER VISITS COCOA. EMBARKING UPON A BICENTENNIAL CULTURAL TOUR, THE WIND SYMPHONY WILL VISIT 76 CITIES BRINGING MUSIC, DANCE, SYMPOSIA, AND CHILDREN'S THEATER TO THE WATERWAYS OF AMERICA DURING ITS 6-MONTH TOUR. (LOCAL). PAULA BERN, COORDINATOR; AMERICAN WIND SYMPHONY ORCHESTRA OF WESTERN PENNSYLVANIA; GATEWAY TOWERS 18G; PITTSBURGH, PA 15222. (#2800-8).

MAY 30, '76. MEMORIAL DAY CEREMONIES. CEREMONY AT FLORIDA MEMORIAL GARDENS SOUTH US1 COCOA. (LOCAL). JOHN METZLER, CHAIRMAN; BREVARD COUNTY BICENTENNIAL COMMITTEE; 160 ORANGE LN; MERRITT ISLE, FL 32952. (#104085-7).

JUNE 14 - JULY 31, '76. BICENTENNIAL '76 DECORATION CONTEST. BICENTENNIAL DECORATING CONTEST FOR SMALL BUSINESS, DEPT STORES AND MALLS. (LOCAL). W F HOUSNER, CHAIRMAN; BREVARD COUNTY BICENTENNIAL COMMITTEE; PO BOX 1776; COCOA, FL 32922. (#104228-1).

JULY 4, '76. WORLD-WIDE GREETINGS FROM BREVARD COUNTY, FLORIDA. A MESSAGE OF GREETINGS IN 5 LANGUAGES WILL BE BROADCAST WORLD-WIDE VIA THE OSCAR SATELLITE. (INT'L). W F HOUSNER, CHAIRMAN; BREVARD COUNTY BICENTENNIAL COMMITTEE; PO BOX 1776; COCOA, FL 32922. (#108403-1).

COCOA BEACH

APOLLO COMMEMORATIVE SCHOLARSHIP FUND - FL. 2 ANNUAL SCHOLARSHIPS: ONE FOR HUMANITIES, ONE FOR SCIENCE. (ST-WIDE). RON MORGAN, CHAIRMAN; MOONWALK COMMITTEE; 416 CARMINE DR; COCOA BEACH, FL 32931. (#19216).

COCOA BEACH — CONTINUED

POSTER MATS FOR THE BICENTENNIAL. SERIES OF MATS COMMEMORATING HISTORIC EVENTS IN FIELDS OF MEDICINE, LIBERTY, INDUSTRY, AND SPORTS. BICENTENNIAL LICENSE # 76-19-0564. (NAT'L). PAUL WOLFE, PROJ DIRECTOR; WORLD SALES ORGANIZATIONS, INC; 1615 N ATLANTIC AVE; COCO BEACH, FL 32931. (#12476).

OCT 2 - 4, '75. STAR SPANGLED '75. LIVE PERFORMANCE AT SURFSIDE PLAYHOUSE, RAMR RD. (LOCAL). MRS PETER ANDERSEN, CHMN; COCOA BEACH JUNIOR WOMEN'S CLUB; 118 SURF DR; COCOA BEACH, FL 32931. (#200011-16).

OCT 22 - 26, '75. INTERNATIONAL SYNCON CONFERENCE. INVOLVING APPROXIMATELY 600 PEOPLE FROM THE WORLD COMMUNITY OF VARYING BACKGROUNDS TO DISCUSS & SEEK SOLUTIONS TO WORLD PROBLEMS. THE SYNCON WILL HAVE WORLDWIDE SATELLITE BROADCASTS. (INT'L). BARBARA HUBBARD, CHMN; THE COMMITTEE FOR THE FUTURE, INC; 2325 PORTER ST, NW; WASHINGTON, DC 20008. (#21698-3).

OCT 25, '75. COCOA BEACH WOMAN'S CLUB COLONIAL BALL. FESTIVAL AT ATLANTIS BEACH MOTEL CONVENTION CENTER. (LOCAL). MRS RODNEY KETCHAM, CHMN; COCOA BEACH WOMAN'S CLUB; 441 BLAKEY BLVD; COCOA BEACH, FL 32931. (#102983-9).

DEC 31, '75. NEW YEAR'S EVE CELEBRATION. FESTIVAL AT ATLANTIS BEACH MOTEL CONVENTION CENTER. (LOCAL). AGATHA I DOERER, CHMN; BREVARD COUNTY BICENTENNIAL COMMITTEE; 10 WILLOW GREEN DR; COCOA BEACH, FL 32931. (#102983-11).

APR 13, '76. WATER SKIING & SAILBOAT REGATTA INVOLVING COCOA BEACH & MIAMI. FESTIVAL. (LOCAL). BILL WOOD, CHAIRMAN; INDIAN RIVER JUBILEE COMMITTEE FOR BREVARD COUNTY; 3220 N COCOA BLVD; COCOA, FL 32922. (#7704-505).

JULY 4, '76. FOURTH OF JULY PARTY. FESTIVAL AT CITY HALL, ORLANDO AVE. (LOCAL). MYRON M STEVENS, CHMN; COCOA BEACH BICENTENNIAL COMMITTEEE; 1980 N ATLANTIC; COCOA BEACH, FL 32931. (#102983-8).

JULY 16 - 20, '76. MOONWALK FESTIVAL. MOONWALK BREAKFAST AT KENNEDY SPACE CENTER 7/16/76; MOONWALK BANQUET COCOA BEACH 7/20/76; VARIED ATHLETIC EVENTS. AT VARIOUS LOCATIONS. (LOCAL). RON MORGAN, PROJ DIR; BREVARD BICENTENNIAL COMMITTEE; 416 CARMINE DR; COCOA BEACH, FL 32931. (#104085-5).

COCONUT CREEK

GAZEBO COMMEMORATING BICENTENNIAL YEAR IN FL. A PERMANENT STRUCTURE IN DONALDSON PARK. (LOCAL). THERESA MERENDINO, CO-CHAIRMAN; BICENTENNIAL COMMITTEE OF COCONUT CREEK; 341 NW 42 AVE; COCONUT CREEK, FL 33066. (#30808).

OCT 22 - 23, '76. BICENTENNIAL BALL. CEREMONY AT STARLIGHT BALLROOM 5460 N STATE RD 7 TAMARAC, FL. (LOCAL). THERESA MERENDINO; COCONUT CREEK BICENTENNIAL COMMITTEE; 341 NW 42 AVE; COCONUT CREEK, FL 33066. (#200011-314).

COCONUT GROVE

JULY 4, '75. BLACK GROVE PARADE. FOURTH OF JULY EXTRAVAGANZA OF MIAMI. EVERY YEAR, EACH OF THE 26 MUNICIPALITIES IN THE DADE COUNTY AREA WILL HOLD EVENTS & MANY COUNTY-WIDE ACTIVITIES SUCH AS A MASS SWEARING IN CEREMONY FOR NEW CITIZENS. (LOCAL). MS NORMA HUNT; THIRD CENTURY USA; PO BOX 1976; MIAMI, FL 33101. (#2997-503).

COOPER CITY

COOPER CITY BEAUTIFICATION PROJECT, FL. TREES WILL BE PLANTED ON ALL OF THE MAIN STREETS IN COOPER CITY. (LOCAL). JAMES TINCOMB, PRESIDENT; AMERICAN LEGION; 4903 SW 90 TERRACE; COOPER CITY, FL 33314. (#17999).

NOV 2, '75. ARTS & CRAFTS FESTIVAL AND CITY EMBLEM CONTEST. COMPETITION, FESTIVAL AT CITY HALL, 9090 SW 50TH PL. (LOCAL). SHARON BERKOWITZ, SEC; CIVIC ASSOC; 9090 SW 5 TH PL; COOPER CITY, FL 33314. (#200011-17).

CORAL GABLES

CLEAN ENERGY RESEARCH INST - CORAL GABLES, FLORIDA. PROMOTES THE USE OF CLEAN, SYNTHETIC ENERGY SOURCES TO REPLACE FOSSIL FUELS. COORDINATES AND IMPLEMENTS RESEARCH. ORGANIZES INTL CONFERENCES ON ENERGY-RELATED PROBLEMS & PUBLISHES TECHNICAL BOOKS. (INT'L). T NEJAT VEZIROGLU, DIRECTOR; UNIV OF MIAMI CLEAN ENERGY RESEARCH INSTITUTE; PO BOX 248294; CORAL GABLES, FL 33124. (#5270).

DEDICATION-ALBERT PICK HALL, CENTER FOR ADVANCED INTERNATL STUDIES. CEREMONY. (LOCAL). DR MOSE L HARVEY, DIR; UNIV OF MIAMI - CENTER FOR ADVANCED INTERNATIONAL STUDIES; PO BOX 248073; CORAL GABLES, FL 33124. (#106124-1).

HYDROGEN ENERGY FUNDAMENTALS, UNIV OF MIAMI, FL. PURPOSE OF HYDROGEN ENERGY FOCUSED SYMPOSIUM COURSE IS TO PROVIDE A FOUNDATION FOR, AND TO ADD TECHNOLOGICAL PERSPECTIVE TO, THE FIELD FOR WORKERS AND RESEARCHERS INVOLVED IN THE CLEAN ENERGY FIELD. (INT'L). T NEJAT VEZIROGLU, DIRECTOR; CLEAN ENERGY INSTITUTE, UNIV OF MIAMI; PO BOX 248294; CORAL GABLES, FL 33124. (#16297). **ARBA GRANTEE.**

THE POWER OF PRINT IN AMERICAN HISTORY, FL. SEVEN SCHOLARLY BOOKS WILL BE SHOWN AROUND THE WORLD. UNIV OF MIAMI BOOKS ARE IN THE USIA SELECTION OF SCHOLARLY PRESS PUBLISHING ON AMERICAN HISTORY, BIOGRAPHY AND LITERATURE. (INT'L). ROBERT I FUERST, PROJECT DIRECTOR; UNIVERSITY OF MIAMI PRESS; PO BOX 249088; CORAL GABLES, FL 33124. (#22494).

PROGRAMS FOR WOMEN, CORAL GABLES, FL. COURSES FOR WOMEN AIMED AT GUIDING THEM TO REACH THEIR FULL POTENTIAL. (LOCAL). SHERRY POUND, CHAIRMAN; UNIV OF MIAMI, SCHOOL OF CONTINUING STUDIES; PO BOX 248073; CORAL GABLES, FL 33124. (#22493).

RESTORATION OF THE CORAL GABLES HOUSE - FLORIDA. RESTORATION OF MANOR TO BE COMPLETED IN 1976. MANOR WILL BE A SIGNIFICANT ADDITION TO THE HERITAGE OF DADE COUNTY. (LOCAL). W L PHILBRICK, PRESIDENT; MERRICK MANOR FOUNDATION INC; 837 PONCE DE LEON BLVD; CORAL GABLES, FL 33134. (#5197).

SEPT 1, '75 - MAY 29, '76. AMERICAN ISSUES FORUM. FORUM SPONSORED BY STUDENT HONORARY, OMICRON KAPPA DELTA, TO ENGAGE LOCAL LEADERS & STUDENTS TO DISCUSS LOCAL & NATIONAL ISSUES. (LOCAL). MARK TUCKER, COORD; OMICRON KAPPA DELTA; STUDENT UNION BLDG; CORAL GABLES, FL 33124. (#106124-5).

SEPT 15, '75 - MAY 16, '76. 'THE ALL AMERICAN SEASON' - 11 AMERICAN ART EXHIBITIONS. HOURS SAT: 10AM - 5PM. SUNDAY HOURS: 2-5PM. AT 1301 MILLER DR; CORAL GABLES, FL. (ST-WIDE). JOHN BARATTE, DIR; UNIV OF MIAMI; UNIV OF MIAMI - LOWE ART MUSEUM; CORAL GABLES, FL 33124. (#106124-6).

NOV 1 - 8, '75. UNIVERSITY OF MIAMI BICENTENNIAL HOMECOMING. CEREMONY, PARADE, LIVE PERFORMANCE AT UNIV OF MIAMI, CORAL GABLES & MIRACLE MILE. (LOCAL). LARRY HERRUP, CHAIRPERSON; UNIV OF MIAMI; PO BOX 248146, UNIV OF MIAMI; CORAL GABLES, FL 33124. (#100256-5).

DEC 5 - 6, '75. JUNIOR ORANGE BOWL FOOTBALL. COMPETITION AT CORAL GABLES YOUTH CENTER. (LOCAL). DANIEL S MCNAMARA, CHMN; ORANGE BOWL COMMITTEE; PO BOX 350748; MIAMI, FL 33135. (#1548-3).

DEC 8 - 13, '75. AMERICAN BICENTENNIAL FLORIDA EXHIBIT. EXHIBIT, RADIO/TV AT UNIV PARK ON UNIV DRIVE. (LOCAL). ANITA BJORK; THIRD CENTURY, USA; PO BOX 451976; MIAMI, FL 33145. (#100225-4).

DEC 20 - 24, '75. JUNIOR ORANGE BOWL TENNIS TOURNAMENT. COMPETITION AT SALVADORE PARK, CORAL GABLES. (LOCAL). DANIEL S MCNAMARA, CHMN; ORANGE BOWL COMMITTEE; PO BOX 350748; MIAMI, FL 33135. (#1548-4).

DEC 26 - 29, '75. JUNIOR ORANGE BOWL GOLF TOURNAMENT. COMPETITION AT BILTMORE GOLF COURSE. (LOCAL). DANIEL S MCNAMARA, DIR; ORANGE BOWL COMMITTEE; PO BOX 350748; MIAMI, FL 33135. (#1548-6).

DEC 26 - 29, '75. JUNIOR ORANGE BOWL BOWLING TOURNAMENT. COMPETITION AT COLISEUM LANES, CORAL GABLES. (LOCAL). DANIEL S MCNAMARA, CHMN; ORANGE BOWL COMMITTEE; PO BOX 350748; MIAMI, FL 33135. (#1548-7).

DEC 29, '75. JUNIOR ORANGE BOWL PARADE. PARADE AT DOWNTOWN CORAL GABLES. (LOCAL). DANIEL S MCNAMARA, CHMN; ORANGE BOWL COMMITTEE; PO BOX 350748; MIAMI, FL 33135. (#1548-11).

JAN 1, '76 - CONTINUING . RELIGION IN AMERICAN LIFE. AMERICAN ISSUE FORUM FOCUSING ON RELIGIOUS ASPECT OF EACH ISSUE. 50 MINUTES PER WEEK. AT CLASSROOMS IN UNIV OF MIAMI. (LOCAL). DR W IVAN HOY, CHMN; UNIV OF MIAMI - DEPT OF RELIGION; CORAL GABLES, FL 33124. (#106098-1).

JAN 8 - APR 16, '76. UNIVERSITY OF MIAMI CINEMA CLUB BICENTENNIAL FILM SERIES. RADIO/TV AT LEARNING CENTER BUILDING ON CAMPUS. (LOCAL). OSCAR R MUNOZ, CHAIRMAN; UNIVERSITY OF MIAMI CINEMA CLUB; PO BOX 2480128; CORAL GABLES, FL 33124. (#104566-6).

JAN 30 - 31, '76. ETHNIC TORCHLIGHT PARADE & CELEBRATION. FESTIVAL, PARADE. (LOCAL). GORDON A BERNOT, CHMN; CAPE CORAL BICENTENNIAL COMMITTEE & THE GERMAN AMERICAN CLUB; 4131 SE 3RD AVE; CAPE CORAL, FL 33904. (#200011-316).

FEB 1 - 26, '76. FORUM OF AMERICAN INTELLECT: MONTH LONG SERIES OF LECTURES. SEMINAR. (LOCAL). DR EVELYN HELMICK,DIR; UNIV OF MIAMI - AMERICAN STUDIES PROGRAM; PO BOX 248073; CORAL GABLES, FL 33124. (#106124-4).

MAR 6 - 28, '76. DECORATOR'S SHOW HOUSE '76. SUNDAY HOURS: 1-5PM; OPEN WEDNESDAY EVENINGS: 7-9:30 PM. AT 7401 OLD CUTLER RD. (LOCAL). MRS L PANKEY, CHWMN; THE JUNIOR LEAGUE OF MIAMI, INC; 1227 CATALONIA; CORAL GABLES, FL 33134. (#104566-4).

MAY 8 - NOV 21, '76. ART OF AMERICAN INDIAN. SAT HOURS: 10AM - 5PM; SUNDAY HOURS: 2-5 PM. AT 1301 MILLER DR, CORAL GABLES. (ST-WIDE). JOHN BARATTE, DIR; UNIV OF MIAMI; UNIV OF MIAMI- LOWE ART MUSEUM; CORAL GABLES, FL 33124. (#107852-2).

MAY 17 - 20, '76. AMERICA THROUGH MUSIC. LIVE PERFORMANCE AT DADE COUNTY AUDITORIUM. (LOCAL). MRS HAROLD NORMAN, JR; PRELUDE COMMITTEE, WOMENS GUILD OF THE GREATER MIAMI PHILHARMONIC; 731 SALDANO; CORAL GABLES, FL 33143. (#103165-1).

MAY 26 - JULY 31, '76. LAUGH WITH AMERICA THROUGH DRAMA. 5 COMEDIES DEPICTING DIFFERENT AMERICAN LIFE-STYLES; 5 PLAYS ARE: 'DAMN YANKEES', 'I REMEMBER MAMA', 'MR ROBERTS', 'GIRLS IN 509' AND 'GEORGE M'. (LOCAL). ROBERT ANKROM, MANAGER; UNIV OF MIAMI - RING THEATER; BOX 248273; CORAL GABLES, FL 33124. (#106124-3).

MAY 28 - JULY 11, '76. DESIGN THE NEXT 200. SAT HOURS: 10AM - 5PM; SUNDAY HOURS: 2-5 PM. AT 1301 MILLER DR, CORAL GABLES. (ST-WIDE). JOHN BARATTE, DIR; UNIV OF MIAMI; UNIV OF MIAMI- LOWE ART MUSEUM; CORAL GABLES, FL 33124. (#107852-3).

MAY 31 - JUNE 21, '76. TUBA TOUR '76. A TEN PERSON TUBA ENSEMBLE ON A 21-DAY TOUR OF EUROPE. (LOCAL). CONSTANCE WELDON, CHMN; TUBISTS UNIVERSAL BROTHERHOOD ASSOC; UNIV OF MIAMI MUSIC SCHOOL; CORAL GABLES, FL 33124. (#104566-12).

JUNE 30 - JULY 3, '76. BICENTENNIAL CONFERENCE ON 'THIRD CENTURY, USA' EARLY CHILDHOOD EDUC. COLLEGES AND UNIVERSITIES WILL BE INVITED TO DISPLAY INFORMATION CONCERNING PROGRAMS AND RESEARCH RELATED TO THE EDUCATION OF YOUNG CHILDREN WHICH ARE CURRENTLY IN PROGRESS AT THEIR INSTITUTIONS. INTEGRATIVE SEMINARS WILL BE HELD BY FORMER COLLEAGUES OF KEN WANN. AT WHITTEN STUDENT UNION, UNIV OF MIAMI; CORAL GABLES, FL 33124. (REGN'L). DR BETTY ROWEN, COORD; UNIV OF MIAMI - SCHOOL OF EDUCATION; 5934 SW 34 ST; MIAMI, FL 33155. (#106124-2).

JULY 4, '76. INDEPENDENCE DAY CELEBRATION - TRACK & FIELD, FIREWORKS & DISPLAYS. FESTIVAL AT CORAL GABLES YOUTH CENTER. (LOCAL). KEN SMITH, DIRECTOR; CITY OF CORAL GABLES; 405 BILTMORE WAY; CORAL GABLES, FL 33134. (#2997-16).

JULY 4, '76. TIME CAPSULE BURIAL. CEREMONY AT NEW CORAL GABLES POLICE & FIRE STATION. (LOCAL). KEN SMITH, DIRECTOR; CITY OF CORAL GABLES; 405 BILTMORE WAY; CORAL GABLES, FL 33134. (#2997-15).

JULY 23 - AUG 15, '76. PROFESSIONAL WOMEN ARTISTS OF FLORIDA. SAT HOURS: 10AM - 5PM. SUNDAY HOURS: 2-5 PM. AT 1301 MILLER DR, CORAL GABLES. (ST-WIDE). JOHN BARATTE, DIR; UNIV OF MIAMI; UNIV OF MIAMI -LOWE ART MUSEUM; CORAL GABLES, FL 33124. (#107852-1).

DEC 6 - 8, '76. SOLAR COOLING & HEATING - A NATIONAL FORUM. DISCUSSION OF ECONOMIC ASPECTS, ENVIRONMENTAL EFFECTS AND GOV'T POLICIES. OBJECTIVE TO ACHIEVE THE WIDESPREAD UTILIZATION OF SOLAR ENERGY FOR COOLING AND HEATING OF SCHOOL BLDGS AS WELL AS OTHER SIMILAR BUILDINGS. (NAT'L). T NEJAT VEZIROGLU; UNIV OF MIAMI CLEAN ENERGY RESEARCH INSTITUTE; PO BOX 248294; CORAL GABLES, FL 33124. (#5270-2).

CORAL SPRINGS

CORAL SPRINGS ORCHID PARK IN CORAL SPRINGS, FL. PARK DISPLAYING EXAMPLES OF TROPICAL FLORIDA ECOSYSTEMS ALONG PATHS INTENDED TO EDUCATE PEOPLE CONCERNING ENDANGERED LANDS, ESPECIALLY NATIVE ORCHIDS AND OTHER NATIVE PLANTS. (LOCAL). MRS RICHARD MARINACE, PRESIDENT; CSWC ORCHID AND HORTICULTURAL PARK, INC; 4011 NW 75 WAY; CORAL SPRINGS, FL 33065. (#16502).

NATURE PARK TO PRESERVE RARE PLANT LIFE IN FLORIDA. DEVELOP 30 ACRE PARK TO PRESERVE RARE TROPICAL PLANTS AND TREES IN NATURAL STATE; INSTALL NATURE TRAILS, CATWALKS, TREE IDENTIFICATION SIGNS & OTHER CONVENIENCES FOR FAMILY USE. (ST-WIDE). JOHN A DOW, CHAIRMAN; CITY OF CORAL SPRINGS BICENT COMMITTEE; 9429 W SAMPLE RD; CORAL SPRINGS, FL 33065. (#10802).

FEB 5 - 6, '76. UNITED STATES ARMED FORCES BICENTENNIAL CARAVAN. CARAVAN IS COMPOSED OF EXHIBIT VANS FOR EACH MILITARY SERVICE. PROJECT THEME IS 'HISTORY OF THE ARMED FORCES AND THEIR CONTRIBUTIONS TO THE NATION'. (LOCAL). JOHN A DOW JR; CORAL SPRINGS BICENTENNIAL COMMITTEE; 9429 WEST SAMPLE ROAD; CORAL SPRINGS, FL 33065. (#1775-429).

CPE CANAVERAL

INTERNATIONAL SYNCON. OVER 200 REPRESENTATIVES FROM AROUND THE WORLD WILL EXAMINE HUMANITY'S OPPORTUNITIES FOR THE FUTURE IN MEETING BASIC NEEDS & EXPLORING SOLUTIONS TO WORLD PROBLEMS. (INT'L). BARBARA M HUBBARD, CHAIRMAN; THE COMMITTEE FOR THE FUTURE; 2325 PORTER ST, NW; WASHINGTON, DC 20008. (#21698). **ARBA RECOGNIZED. ARBA GRANTEE.**

'THIRD CENTURY AMERICA' SCIENCE & TECHNOLOGY EXPO. AN OVERVIEW OF AMERICA'S ENERGY, PAST AND FUTURE, FEATURING EXHIBITS ON SOLAR, FOSSIL FUELS, FUSION AND FISSION; WILL INCLUDE BICENTENNIAL FENERGY FILMS & POSTER & OTHER PUBLICATIONS. (INT'L). EDWIN E STOKELY, OFFICE OF PUBLIC AFFAIRS; ENERGY RESEARCH AND DEVELOPMENT ADMINISTRATION; WASHINGTON, DC 20545. (#19656).

MAY 24 - 26, '75. SAIL BOAT RACING. OCEAN REGATTA AT MELBOURNE, FLORIDA. CATAMARANS & OCEAN SAILING VESSELS WILL COMPETE. (LOCAL). PAUL ZENO, CHAIRMAN; BREVARD COUNTY PARKS AND RECREATION DEPT; 625 E NEW HAVEN AVE; MELBOURNE, FL 33901. (#7708-501).

MAY 30 - SEPT 7, '76. 'THIRD CENTURY AMERICA'-SCIENCE & TECHNOLOGY EXPOSITION. THIS WILL BE THE MOST COMPREHENSIVE FEDERAL & INDUSTRIAL EXHIBITION ON SCIENCE & TECHNOLOGY FOR THE BICENTENNIAL. INCLUDES THE ARBA MULTI-MEDIA EXHIBITION 'USA '76: THE FIRST TWO HUNDRED YEARS'. AT NASA SPACE FACILITIES AT CAPE CANAVERAL. (INT'L). MR M ROSS, DEP DIR; UNITED STATES GOVERNMENT; KENNEDY SPACE CENTER; NASA, FL 32899. (#19656-1).

CPE CANAVERAL—CONTINUED

JUNE 23 - 26, '76. INTERNATIONAL SYNCON. OVER 200 REPRESENTATIVES FROM AROUND THE WORLD WILL EXAMINE HUMANITY'S OPPORTUNITIES FOR THE FUTURE IN MEETING BASIC NEEDS & EXPLORING SOLUTIONS TO WORLD PROBLEMS. LAST DAY KNOWN AS HORIZONS DAY; LOCAL COMMUNITIES IN NATION MEET TOO-PHONE RESULTS TO SYNCON. AT CAPE CANAVARAL - SCIENCE & TECHNOLOGY EXHIBITION. (INT'L). BARBARA M HUBBARD, CHMN; THE COMMITTEE FOR THE FUTURE; 2325 PORTER ST, NW; WASHINGTON, DC 20008. (#21698-1).

CRAWFORDVILLE

JULY 4, '76. DEDICATION OF WAKULLA COUNTY COURTHOUSE. CEREMONY AT OLD COUNTY COURTHOUSE, ONE BLOCK W OF 319. (LOCAL). MRS ELLA JEAN WEHUNT; WAKULLA COUNTY ACTION '76 STEERING COMMITTEE; PO BOX 442; PANACEA, FL 32346. (#108393-1).

CROSS CITY

APR 1 - 30, '76. FILMS ON AMERICA. FILMS ON AMERICAN HISTORY & ECOLOGY. (LOCAL). LLOYD JONES, PRINCIPAL; ANDERSON ELEMENTARY SCHOOL; CROSS CITY, FL 32628. (#105827-1).

JULY 4, '76. COMBINED ARTS DISPLAY - FESTIVAL - ALL AGES. ATHLETIC EVENTS ALL DAY; MUSICAL PROGRAM IN EVENING WITH AWARDS, PARADE & EXHIBITS; CENTRAL SPEAKER; CHARGE FOR EVENING - PATRIOTIC MUSICAL SUNG BY COMMUNITY CHOIR AND AN OUTSIDE GROUP. AT BALL FIELD, AUDITORIUM, CITY STREETS. (LOCAL). MARIE C SMITH, CHMN; CROSS CITY BICENTENNIAL COMMISSION; PO BOX 536; CROSS CITY, FL 32628. (#104837-1).

CRYSTAL RIVER

RESTORATION OF PARK AREA - CRYSTAL RIVER, FL. FACILITIES WILL BE PUT IN PLACE TO FORM AN ATTRACTIVE PARK AREA. (LOCAL). JAMES M SMITH, SECRETARY; CRYSTAL RIVER BICENTENNIAL PARK COMMITTEE; 117 N HIGHWAY 19; CRYSTAL RIVER, FL 32629. (#29169).

DADE CITY

BICENTENNIAL BENCH PAINTING - DADE CITY, FL. ALL THE BENCHES ON CAMPUS WILL BE PAINTED RED, WHITE & BLUE WITH PLENTY OF STARS. (LOCAL). RICHARD A MCGINNIS, CHAIRMAN; PASCO - HERNANDO COMMUNITY COLLEGE - EAST; 2401 ST HWY 41 N; DADE CITY, FL 33525. (#15723).

BICENTENNIAL GARDEN - DADE CITY, FL. CONSTRUCTION OF A PERMANENT BICENTENNIAL GARDEN ON CAMPUS. (LOCAL). RICHARD A MCGINNIS, CHAIRMAN; PASLO-HERNANDO COMMUNITY COLLEGE/EAST; 2401 ST HWY 41 N; DADE CITY, FL 33525. (#15724).

BICENTENNIAL PICNIC AREA IN DADE CITY, FL. A PICNIC AREA WILL BE DEVELOPED ON CAMPUS IN HONOR OF THE BICENTENNIAL. (LOCAL). RICHARD A MCGINNIS, CHAIRMAN; PASLO-HERNANDO COMMUNITY COLLEGE/EAST; 2401 ST HWY 41 N; DADE CITY, FL 33525. (#15725).

BICENTENNIAL WALK-RUN MARATHON IN DADE CITY, FL. A MARATHON WALK-RUN IS TO BE HELD TO HELP RAISE MONEY TO BEAUTIFY THE CAMPUS. (LOCAL). RICHARD A MCGINNIS, CHAIRMAN; PASCO - HERNANDO COMMUNITY COLLEGE - EAST; 2401 ST HWY 41 N; DADE CITY, FL 33525. (#15721).

A FLAG IN EVERY HOME IN DADE CITY, FL. THE STUDENTS WILL SELL FLAGS TO FACILITATE BICENT PROGRAMS ON THE CAMPUS. (LOCAL). RICHARD A MCGINNIS, CHAIRMAN; PASCO - HERNANDO COMMUNITY COLLEGE - EAST; 2401 ST HWY 41 N; DADE CITY, FL 33525. (#15719).

HISTORIC HIKE THROUGH PASCO COUNTY, FL. HIKERS WILL VIEW HISTORIC LANDMARKS ON THEIR TREK ACROSS PASCO COUNTY. (LOCAL). RICHARD A MCGINNIS, CHAIRMAN; PASCO - HERNANDO COMMUNITY COLLEGE - EAST; 2401 ST HWY 41 N; DADE CITY, FL 33525. (#15720).

HISTORICAL COMMENTARY IN DADE CITY, FL. PRINCIPAL OF RODNEY B COX ELEMENTARY SCHOOL TO GIVE BI-WEEKLY HISTORICAL COMMENTARY ON AMERICA, USING RECORDED SPEECHES & MUSIC. (LOCAL). CHARLES E.A. LEASE, PRINCIPAL; RODNEY B COX ELEMENTARY SCHOOL; 201 W MAIN AVE; DADE CITY, FL 33525. (#20206).

LOCAL HISTORY PROJECT AT PASCO-HERNANDO COL-FL. THE HISTORY OF THE COUNTY WILL BE RESEARCHED, OLDER RESIDENTS ARE TO BE INTERVIEWED, FINDINGS WILL BE WRITTEN FOR THE BICENTENNIAL. (LOCAL). RICHARD A MCGINNIS, CHAIRMAN; PASCO - HERNANDO COMMUNITY COLLEGE - EAST; 2401 ST HWY 41 N; DADE CITY, FL 33525. (#15722).

VOTING DRIVE - DADE CITY, FL. HELP SUPPORT A 100% VOTING DRIVE IN 1976 ON CAMPUS AND THROUGHOUT THE COMMUNITY. (LOCAL). RICHARD A MCGINNIS, CHAIRMAN; PASLO-HERNANDO COMMUNITY COLLEGE/EAST; 2401 ST HWY 41 N; DADE CITY, FL 33525. (#15726).

DEC 8, '75 - JULY 2, '76. DISPLAY OF HISTORICAL ARTIFACTS & IMPORTANT DOCUMENTS. EXHIBIT. (LOCAL). RICHARD A MCGINNIS, CHMN; PASLO-HERNANDO COMMUNITY COLLEGE/EAST; 2401 ST HWY 41 N; DADE CITY, FL 33525. (#102616-1).

JULY 3, '76. AMERICAN FAMILY DAY PICNIC. PICNIC ON CAMPUS. (LOCAL). RICHARD A MCGINNIS, CHM; PASCO-HERNANDO COMMUNITY COLLEGE/EAST CAMPUS BICENTENNIAL COMMITTEE; 2401 ST HWY 41 N; DADE CITY, FL 33525. (#102510-1).

DAYTONA BEACH

BEAUTIFICATION PROJECT OF DAYTONA BEACH, FL. A PROGRAM IMPLEMENTING FLOWER GROWING AND LANDSCAPING AT RESIDENCES, PLACES OF BUSINESS, ALONG ROADWAYS, IN PARKS AND ELSEWHERE THROUGHOUT THE COUNTY. (LOCAL). ALYS CLANCY, BEAUTIFICATION CHAIRMAN; VOLUSIA COUNTY GARDEN CLUBS; 123 UNIVERSITY BLVD; DAYTONA BEACH, FL 32018. (#15042).

'BICENTENNIAL HOUSE' - DAYTONA BEACH, FLORIDA. A FUND RAISING CAMPAIGN TO BUILD 'BICENTENNIAL HOUSE', PERMANANT HOME OF HALIFAX HISTORICAL SOCIETY & MUSEUM. EXPECT TO BE COMPLETED EARLY IN 1977 AT THE COLLEGE CAMPUS ON VOLUSIA AVENUE. (LOCAL). MRS CHARLES JOHN NORDQUIST; HALIFAX HISTORICAL SOCIETY & DAYTONA BEACH COMMUNITY COLLEGE; 119 N PENINSULA DR; DAYTONA BEACH, FL 32018. (#29927).

BICENTENNIAL ISSUE OF 'THE BAGPIPER', FL. A COMMEMORATIVE ISSUE OF THE STUDENT NEWSPAPER FEATURING ARTICLES ON LOCAL HISTORY AND LANDMARKS. (LOCAL). MIRIAM BLICKMAN, COORDINATOR; DAYTONA BEACH COMMUNITY COLLEGE; PO BOX 1111; DAYTONA BEACH, FL 32015. (#26904).

BIKE TRAILS - DAYTONA BEACH, FL. A CONTINUING PROJECT TO BUILD A NETWORK OF AT LEAST 200 MILES OF SAFE BIKE PATHS THROUGHOUT VOLUSIA COUNTY AND THE HALIFAX AREA. (LOCAL). JOHN HOLLOW, COORDINATOR; VOLUSIA COUNTY ACTION '76; 250 MIDWAY; DAYTONA BEACH, FL 33015. (#28472).

BOOK: HISTORY OF VOLUSIA COUNTY IN FLORIDA. A REVISED HISTORY OF VOLUSIA COUNTY WILL BE WRITTEN IN BOOK FORM BY A PROFESSIONALLY QUALIFIED HISTORIAN. (LOCAL). LOUISE BENSON, CHAIRMAN; JUNIOR SERVICE LEAGUE OF DAYTONA BEACH; 122 S PALMETTO AVE; DAYTONA BEACH, FL 32015. (#7743).

CAMPUS CLINICAL MEDICAL SERVICE - DAYTONA BCH, FL. A CAMPUS CLINICAL MEDICAL SERVICE WILL BE SET UP FOR STUDENTS AT DAYTONA BEACH COMMUNITY COLLEGE. (LOCAL). MIRIAM F BLICKMAN, COORDINATOR; DAYTONA BEACH COMMUNITY COLLEGE; PO BOX 111; DAYTONA BEACH, FL 32015. (#24802).

DRAMA: 'PAGEANT OF BLACK AMERICA' IN FLORIDA. AN OUTDOOR MUSICAL DRAMA ON THE HISTORY OF BLACK AFRICANS IN AMERICA FROM THE BEGINNINGS OF THE SLAVE TRADE TO THE PRESENT, WILL BE PERFORMED BY A LOCAL CAST IN DAYTONA BEACH IN 1976. (LOCAL). BEUNYCE CUNNINGHAM, PAGEANT CHAIRMAN; VOLUSIA COUNTY ACTION '76 BICENTENNIAL COMMITTEE; PO BOX 1671, 250 MIDWAY; DAYTONA BEACH, FL 32015. (#7745).

DRUM & FIFE CORPS - DAYTONA BEACH, FL. THE GROUP IS PATTERNED AFTER THOSE OF COLONIAL TIMES; IT IS AVAILABLE FOR ALL COUNTY AFFAIRS. (LOCAL). GENIE HODGES, COORDINATOR; ORMOND BEACH BICENTENNIAL COMMITTEE; 115 ARLINGTON WAY; ORMOND BEACH, FL 32074. (#28474).

FEASIBILITY STUDY FOR CONVENTION CENTER IN FLORIDA. THE FEASIBILITY OF DEVELOPING A MUCH NEEDED MULTI-PURPOSE CONVENTION AND CIVIC CENTER IS BEING STUDIED BY THE DAYTONA BEACH AREA CHAMBER OF COMMERCE. (LOCAL). JAMES BULLION, HEAD OF FEASIBILITY STUDY; DAYTONA BEACH AREA CHAMBER OF COMMERCE; CITY ISLAND; DAYTONA BEACH, FL 32014. (#7751). **(??).**

HALIFAX RIVER CLEANUP - DAYTONA BEACH, FL. A LONG RANGE PROGRAM TO KEEP OUR WATERS CLEAN. (LOCAL). DREW MURPHY, CHAIRMAN; HORIZONS '76; 1620 CRESCENT RIDGE RD; DAYTONA BEACH, FL 32018. (#28477).

HANDICAPPED REHABILITATION CENTER & SCHOOL - FL. A SPECIALIZED EDUCATIONAL FACILITY IS BEING CONSTRUCTED TO PROVIDE TRAINING FOR MULTI-PHYSICALLY HANDICAPPED PEOPLE TO ENABLE THEM TO BECOME SELF-SUFFICIENT AND EMPLOYABLE. (LOCAL). MILLARD CONKLIN, CHAIRMAN; DAYTONA BEACH LIONS CLUB; 116 SEABREEZE BLVD; DAYTONA BEACH, FL 32015. (#28475).

JOHNNY HORIZON '76 CLEANUP PROGRAM - FL. MASS CLEANUP OF HIGHWAYS IN VOLUSIA AND FLAGLER COUNTIES. (LOCAL). DAVID LEETE, DIRECTOR; DAYTONA BEACH JAYCEES; 140 S GRANDVIEW AVE; DAYTONA BEACH, FL 32015. (#28470).

'OLD KINGS ROAD' PROJECT OF VOLUSIA COUNTY, FL. THE OLD KINGS ROAD, A HISTORICAL LANDMARK OF FLORIDA, IS TO BE IDENTIFIED, APPROPRIATELY MARKED & PUBLICIZED. PROJECT IS IN COOPERATION WITH 4 COUNTIES FOR COMPLETE RECONSTRUCTION OF THE ROAD. (ST-WIDE). LOUISE BENSON, CHAIRMAN; VOLUSIA COUNTY ACTION '76 BICENTENNIAL COMMITTEE; 216 BONNER AVE; DAYTONA BEACH, FL 32018. (#7770).

ORMOND BY THE SEA PARK - DAYTONA BEACH, FL. DEVELOPMENT OF A PARK WITH RECREATIONAL AND PLAYGROUND FACILITIES. (LOCAL). GEORGE FOGLE, CHAIRMAN; FESTIVAL USA; 8 OCEAN EDGE DR; ORMOND BEACH, FL 32074. (#28471).

PAINTING OF FIREPLUGS - DAYTONA BEACH, FL. FIREPLUGS WILL BE PAINTED RED, WHITE & BLUE IN ONE OF 7 DIFFERENT COLONIAL DESIGNS. (LOCAL). SARAH SIGEL, COORDINATOR; ART LEAGUE; 2829 S PENINSULA DR; DAYTONA BEACH, FL 32018. (#28466).

PEABODY AUDITORIUM FUND RAISING PROJECT IN FLORIDA. PROJECT TO RAISE MONEY FOR IMPROVEMENTS OF PEABODY AUDITORIUM IN PREPARATION FOR BICENTENNIAL YEAR PERFORMANCES. (LOCAL). DREW MURPHY, CHAIRMAN; VOLUSIA COUNTY CITIZENS COMMITTEE FOR PEABODY AUDITORIUM; 901 6TH ST; DAYTONA BEACH, FL 32018. (#7750).

PICTORIAL HISTORY OF VOLUSIA COUNTY, FL. PICTORIAL HISTORY WRITTEN & EDITED BY HENRY WATSON, CHAIRMAN OF THE SOCIAL SCIENCES DEPARTMENT. THE BOOK SELLS FOR $7.50. (LOCAL). MIRIAM F BLICKMAN, COORDINATOR; VOLUSIA COUNTY HISTORICAL ASSOC; PO BOX 1111; DAYTONA BEACH, FL 32015. (#24082).

RELOCATION OF THE HALIFAX HISTORICAL SOCIETY - FL. MORE SPACE AND ADEQUATE HOUSING ARE NEEDED TO PRESERVE THE EAST VOLUSIA AREA. PROJECT TO FIND A NEW SUITABLE HOME FOR THE HALIFAX HISTORICAL SOCIETY. (LOCAL). HAZELLE FENTY, PRESIDENT; HALIFAX HISTORICAL SOCIETY; 224 1/2 S BEACH ST; DAYTONA BEACH, FL 32014. (#15044).

REPRINT OF FIRST HALIFAX AREA NEWSPAPER - FL. THE FIRST ISSUE OF THE HALIFAX REPORTER WILL BE REPRINTED. (LOCAL). JIM HILLIARD, DIRECTOR; HALIFAX REPORTER; 37 CORBIN AVE; ORMOND BEACH, FL 32074. (#28467).

RESTORATION OF RIVERFRONT DEPOT - FL. COMPLETE REPLACEMENT OF 12 FT X 30 FT LANDING DOCK WITH CONCRETE DOCK, REPLACEMENT OF FLOOR BEAMS AND CLEANUP OF 650 FT RIVERFRONT PARK. (LOCAL). JOHN P DOWNING, PRESIDENT; WILBUR IMPROVEMENT ASSOC; 3911 S ATLANTIC AVE; DAYTONA BEACH, FL 32019. (#29019).

'SAVE OUR SCHOOL' - DAYTONA BEACH, FL. 'SOS' PROJECT TO RESTORE 105-YEAR OLD SCHOOL FOR USE AS A MUSEUM. (LOCAL). DORIS DICKEY, RECREATION DIRECTOR; CITY OF PORT ORANGE; 707 RIDGEWOOD AVE; PORT ORANGE, FL 32019. (#28473).

SOLID WASTE DISPOSAL - DAYTONA BEACH, FL. INAUGURATION OF EFFICIENT MODERN METHODS FOR CONVERSION OF TRASH & SOLID WASTES INTO FERTILIZER AND RECYCLE METALS. (LOCAL). DREW MURPHY, CHAIRMAN; HORIZONS '76; 1620 CRESCENT RIDGE RD; DAYTONA BEACH, FL 32015. (#28476).

SUITCASE '76 - DAYTONA BEACH, FL. A PRESENTATION ON LOCAL ENVIRONMENT AND CULTURE USING MUSIC & FILM. (LOCAL). WILLIAM NAPOLI, COORDINATOR; HERITAGE & JR SERVICE LEAGUE; 805 CANDLEWOOD; ORMOND BEACH, FL 32015. (#28468).

TALKING BOOKS FOR THE BLIND - DAYTONA BEACH, FL. THE NEW FLORIDIANA FACSIMILE SERIES, PUBLICATIONS OF RARE, OUT-OFPRINT BOOKS OF 450 YEARS OF FLORIDA HISTORY WILL BE REPRODUCED INTO TALKING BOOKS TO ENABLE BLIND PERSONS TO RECALL THEIR HERITAGE. (LOCAL). DONALD J. WEBER, DIRECTOR; TALKING BOOK LIBRARY; P.O. BOX 2299; DAYTONA BEACH, FL 32014. (#15043).

TRAVELLING EXHIBITS PROGRAM IN VOLUSIA COUNTY, FL. MOBILE EXHIBITS PROVIDED BY MILITARY & OTHERS TOURED U S. INCLUDED WAS AN ARCHITECTURAL EXHIBIT. (ST-WIDE). GEN GEORGE FOGLE, FESTIVAL CHAIRMAN; VOLUSIA COUNTY ACTION '76 BICENTENNIAL COMMITTEE; 8 OCEAN EDGE DR; ORMOND BEACH, FL 32074. (#7748).

VOLUSIA CO HISTORICAL ASSOC BLDG - DAYTONA BCH, FL. THE VOLUSIA CO HISTORICAL ASSOC BUILDING WILL BE LOCATED ON THE DAYTONA BEACH COMMUNITY COLLEGE CAMPUS. (LOCAL). MIRIAM F BLICKMAN, COORDINATOR; DAYTONA BEACH COMMUNITY COLLEGE & VOLUSIA CO HISTORICAL ASSOC; PO BOX 111; DAYTONA BEACH, FL 32015. (#24803).

VOLUSIA LANDMARK PROJECT, FLORIDA. A PAMPHLET TO PUBLICIZE HISTORICAL PTS OF INTEREST IN VOLUSIA CO WILL BE DEVELOPED ALONG WITH SUGGESTED TOURS AND SCHEDULES. (LOCAL). DORIS HOUSEHOLDER, REPRESENTATIVE; AMERICAN ASSOC OF UNIV WOMEN; 1476 N PENINSULA; DAYTONA BEACH, FL 32018. (#7740).

VOTER REGISTRATION DRIVE - DAYTONA BEACH, FL. A CONCENTRATED EFFORT TO ENCOURAGE EVERYONE TO REGISTER AND VOTE. (LOCAL). CECILE MCGINNIS, COORDINATOR; LEAGUE OF WOMEN VOTERS; 5612 BRIARWOOD AVE, PORT ORANGE, FL 32019. (#28460).

'WATERWAY OF FLAGS' - DAYTONA BEACH, FL. HOMEOWNERS & BUSINESSES ON HALIFAX RIVER WILL BE ENCOURAGED TO FLY FLAGS. (LOCAL). PALMERA GLICKLER, PRES; DEMOCRATIC WOMEN'S CLUB OF HALIFAX AREA; 328 AUBURN DR; DAYTONA BEACH, FL 32015. (#28479).

YOUTH BICENTENNIAL PARK, DAYTONA BEACH, FL. A RECREATION AND CONSERVATION PARK OF 200 ACRES FOR SCIENCE STUDY, ENVIRONMENTAL EDUCATION AND APPRECIATION OF A TRUE NATURAL AREA. (LOCAL). WILLIAM R GOMON, CHAIRMAN; VOLUSIA COUNTY ACTION '76 STEERING COMMITTEE; PO BOX 1671; DAYTONA BEACH, FL 32015. (#25088). **ARBA GRANTEE.**

YOUTH DEBATES - DAYTONA BEACH, FL. A NATIONWIDE PROGRAM INVOLVING SECONDARY AND COLLEGE STUDENTS TO COMPETE IN DEBATES ON AMERICAN HISTORY; MONETARY & SCHOLARSHIP AWARDS. (REGN'L). DR LYMAN J LAUGHTON, CHAIRMAN; ELKS LODGE & VOLUSIA COUNTY ACTION '76; 340 APACHE TRAIL; ORMOND BEACH, FL 32074. (#28478).

1976 CALENDAR - DAYTONA BEACH, FL. A 1976 CALENDAR LISTING ALL BICENTENNIAL EVENTS IN VOLUSIA COUNTY. (LOCAL). CHAIRMAN; PALMETTO WOMEN'S CLUB; 1000 S BEACH ST; DAYTONA BEACH, FL 32015. (#28469).

MAY 4 - 10, '75. FLORIDA'S BICENT EXHIBIT. MOBILE EXHIBITS PROVIDED BY THE COUNTY BICENT COMMITTEE, ACTION '76, WILL TOUR THE AREA THROUGH 1977. INCLUDED WILL BE A FLORIDA AMERICAN BICENT TRAVELLING EXHIBIT & AN ARCHITECTURAL EXHIBIT. (ST-WIDE). GEN GEORGE FOGLE; VOLUSIA COUNTY ACTION '76 BICENTENNIAL COMMITTEE; PO BOX 1671, 250 MIDWAY; DAYTONA BEACH, FL 32015. (#7748-502).

DAYTONA BEACH — CONTINUED

DEC 31, '75 - JAN 4, '76. FREEDOM FESTIVAL - WEEK OF SQUARE & ROUND DANCING. LIVE PERFORMANCE. (LOCAL). ROLAND G DION, COORD; DIXIE SQUARES, SQUARE DANCE CLUB; 1395 JARECKI AVE; HOLLY HILL, FL 32017. (#7747-501).

JAN 18 - APR 25, '76. AMERICAN ISSUES FORUM-WESH-/TV NEWS JOURNAL COURSE. 13-HALF HOUR SUNDAY TV PANELS ON WESH PLUS ARTICLES IN LOCAL NEWSPAPER IN ADDITION TO TEXT TO BE USED FOR BICENTENNIAL COURSE. IDEA CONCEIVED BY NATIONAL ENDOWMENT OFR THE HUMANITIES. (LOCAL). MIRIAM F BLICKMAN, COORD; DAYTONA BEACH COMMUNITY COLLEGE; PO BOX 1111; DAYTONA BEACH, FL 32015. (#200011-18).

JAN 28 - 30, '76. CANADIAN CHURCH TRIBUTE TO AMER BICENT: MUSIC & RELIGIOUS RALLY. CANADA - U S FRIENDSHIP PROJ IN DAYTONA BEACH, FL. TO FURTHER FRIENDLY RELATIONS OF CANADA & THE U S, A PERFORMANCE WILL BE GIVEN BY THE HUSTLERS' BIBLE CLASS FROM TORONTO AS A TRIBUTE TO AMERICA'S 200TH BIRTHDAY THRU MUSIC & RELIGIOUS RALLY. AT 3140 S ATLANTIC AVE. (LOCAL). REV WALLACE POMPLUN; DRIVE-IN CHRISTIAN CHURCH; 3140 S ATLANTIC AVE; DAYTONA BEACH, FL 32018. (#7746-501).

JAN 31 - FEB 1, '76. 24 HOURS OF DAYTONA WORLD CHAMPIONSHIP SPORTS CAR ROAD RACE. COMPETITION AT DAYTONA INTERNATIONAL SPEEDWAY. (INT'L). JIM FOSTER, PR VICE-PRES; INTERNATIONAL MOTOR SPORTS ASSOCIATION-FIA; 1801 SPEEDWAY BLVD; DAYTONA BEACH, FL 32015. (#103390-3).

JAN 31 - FEB 15, '76. SPEED WEEKS 1976. COMPETITION AT DAYTONA INTERNATIONAL SPEEDWAY. (INT'L). JIM FOSTER, PR VICE-PRES; NASCAR, IMSA, ARCA, IROC, FIA; 1801 SPEEDWAY BLVD; DAYTONA BEACH, FL 32015. (#103390-1).

FEB 2, '76. DECLARATION - BICENTENNIAL MUSICAL. LIVE PERFORMANCE AT HUMANITIES AUDITORIUM. (LOCAL). MIRIAM F BLICKMAN, COORD; DAYTONA BEACH COMMUNITY COLLEGE; PO BOX 1111; DAYTONA BEACH, FL 32015. (#200011-19).

FEB 15, '76. DAYTONA 500 NASCAR-FIA WINSTON CUP GRAND NATIONAL STOCK CAR RACE. COMPETITION AT DAYTONA INTERNATIONAL SPEEDWAY. (INT'L). JIM FOSTER, PR VICE-PRES; NATIONAL ASSOCIATION FOR STOCK CAR AUTO RACING-FIA; 1801 SPEEDWAY BLVD; DAYTONA BEACH, FL 32015. (#103390-4).

FEB 17 - 18, '76. UNITED STATES ARMED FORCES BICENTENNIAL CARAVAN. CARAVAN IS COMPOSED OF EXHIBIT VANS FOR EACH MILITARY SERVICE. PROJECT THEME IS 'HISTORY OF THE ARMED FORCES AND THEIR CONTRIBUTIONS TO THE NATION'. (LOCAL). BILL COMAN; US ARMED FORCES BICENTENNIAL EXHIBIT VANS PROJECT; PO BOX 1671; DAYTONA BEACH, FL 32015. (#1775-433).

FEB 22 - 28, '76. NATIONAL SOCIETY OF PROFESSIONAL ENGINEERS CONVENTION. THEME: '200 YEARS OF ENGINEERING'. WORKSHOPS, PRESENTATION AT AREA SCHOOLS, LECTURES, MOBILE DISPLAYS. AT DAYTONA BEACH COMMUNITY COLEGE CAMPUS. (LOCAL). MIRIAM F BLICKMAN, COORD; NATIONAL SOCIETY OF PROFESSIONAL ENGINEERS, FLORIDA CHAPTER; PO BOX 1111; DAYTONA BEACH, FL 32015. (#200011-20).

MAR 1 - 7, '76. 1976 DAYTONA MOTORCYCLE CLASSICS. COMPETITION AT DAYTONA INTERNATIONAL SPEEDWAY. (INT'L). JIM FOSTER, PR VICE-PRES; AMERICAN MTORCYCLE ASSOCIATION, FIM; 1801 SPEEDWAY BLVD; DAYTONA BEACH, FL 32015. (#103390-2).

MAR 2 - 20, '76. BICENTENNIAL CONVOCATION: LECTURE - 'WOMEN IN THE REVOLUTION'. LECTURE BY PAUL ENGK. AT HUMANITIES AUDITORIUM, DBCC. (LOCAL). MIRIAM F BLICKMAN, COORD; DAYTONA BEACH COMMUNITY COLLEGE; PO BOX 1111; DAYTONA BEACH, FL 32015. (#200011-21).

MAR 6, '76. DAYTONA SUPER SERIES OF MOTO-CROSS. COMPETITION AT DAYTONA INTERNATIONAL SPEEDWAY. (INT'L). JIM FOSTER, PR VICE-PRES; AMERICAN MOTORCYCLE ASSOCIATION; 1801 SPEEDWAY BLVD; DAYTONA BEACH, FL 32015. (#103390-5).

MAR 7, '76. DAYTONA 200 AMERICAN MOTORCYCLE ASSOCIATION EXPERT ROAD RACE. COMPETITION AT DAYTONA INTERNATIONAL SPEEDWAY. (INT'L). JIM FOSTER, PR VICE-PRES; AMERICAN MOTORCYCLE ASSOCIATION-FIM; 1801 SPEEDWAY BLVD; DAYTONA BEACH, FL 32015. (#103390-6).

MAR 20, '76. MUSIC OF GEORGE GERSHWIN - CONCERT. LIVE PERFORMANCE AT HUMANITIES AUDITORIUM. (LOCAL). MIRIAM F BLICKMAN, COORD; DAYTONA BEACH COMMUNITY COLLEGE; PO BOX 1111; DAYTONA BEACH, FL 32015. (#200011-22).

APR 2 - 10, '76. 'SHOW BOAT' - DBCC SPRING MUSICAL. LIVE PERFORMANCE AT HUMANITIES AUDITORIUM. (LOCAL). MIRIAM F BLICKMAN, COORD; DAYTONA BEACH COMMUNITY COLLEGE; PO BOX 1111; DAYTONA BEACH, FL 32015. (#200011-23).

APR 9, '76. BICENTENNIAL BANQUET. FESTIVAL AT STUDENT CENTER-DBCC. (LOCAL). MIRIAM F BLICKMAN, COORD; DBCC & YOLUSIA COUNTY ACTION '76 BICENTENNIAL COMMITTEE; PO BOX 1111; DAYTONA BEACH, FL 32015. (#200011-25).

MAY 29 - 30, '76. FLORIDA BICENTENNIAL ARCHERY FESTIVAL. A MILITARY BAND AND PARADE OF ARCHERS WILL HIGHLIGHT THE FESTIVAL. IT IS AN OLYMPIC PREPARATION, INTERNATIONAL FITA STAR TOURNAMENT. 300 ARCHERS WILL BE IN LINE WITH AWARDS AND TROPHIES GIVEN. SPECIAL BICENTENNIAL AWARDS WILL BE GIVEN. AT DAYTONA INTERNATIONAL SPEEDWAY. (REGN'L). JOEL SAYERS, CHAIRMAN; DAYTONA BEACH ARCHERY CLUB; 1812 N ATLANTIC AVE; DAYTONA BEACH, FL 32018. (#102207-1).

MAY 30, '76. MEMORIAL DAY CEREMONY-BANDS, PARADE FIRING SQUAD, AND SPEECHS. CEREMONY, PARADE. (LOCAL). BILL GOMON, CHMN; VOLUSIA COUNTY ACTION'76 BICENTENNIAL COMMITTEE; PO BOX 1671, 250 MIDWAY; DAYTONA BEACH, FL 32015. (#7744-501).

JUNE 14, '76. FLAG DAY-FLAG RECOGNITION THROUGHOUT VOLUSIA COUNTY. CEREMONY, PARADE. (LOCAL). BILL GOMON, CHMN; VOLUSIA COUNTY ACTION'76 BICENTENNIAL COMMITTEE; PO BOX 1671, 250 MIDWAY; DAYTONA BEACH, FL 32015. (#7744-503).

JULY 3 - 4, '76. FIRECRACKER 400 CONGRESSIONAL MEDAL OF HONOR NASAR STOCK CAR RACE. COMPETITION AT DAYTONA INTERNATIONAL SPEEDWAY. (INT'L). JIM FOSTER, PR VICE-PRES; NATIONAL ASSOCIATION FOR STOCK CAR AUTO RACING - FIA; 1801 SPEEDWAY BLVD; DAYTONA BEACH, FL 32015. (#103390-7).

JULY 3 - 4, '76. JULY 4, 1976 GALA INDEPENDENCE CELEBRATIONS. STREET PARADE, YACHTING EVENTS, NAUTICAL FLAG RAISING, BOAT PARADE, SAILBOAT RACES, FIRECRACKER 400, NATURALIZATION CEREMONIES AND MUCH MORE. (LOCAL). GEORGE FOGLE, CHMN; FESTIVALS USA; 8 OCEAN EDGE DR; ORMOND BEACH, FL 32074. (#200011-221).

JULY '76. ARCHERY FESTIVAL. COMBINATION OF 4 STATE & REGIONAL ARCHERY TOURNAMENTS INTO A NATIONAL CELEBRATION FOR PROFESSIONAL AND AMATEUR ARCHERS. (REGN'L). JOEL SAYERS, CHMN; FLORIDA BICENTENNIAL ARCHERY FESTIVAL; 1812 N ATLANTIC AVE; DAYTONA BEACH, FL 32019. (#200011-222).

JULY '76. FLORIDA PATRIOTS PROGRAM. A RECOGNITION CEREMONY HONORING FLORIDIANS NOMINATED BY THEIR ASSOCIATES FOR THEIR ACCOMPLISHMENTS. (LOCAL). GEORGE FOGLE, CHMN; FESTIVALS USA; 8 OCEAN EDGE DR; ORMOND BEACH, FL 32074. (#200011-220).

OCT 27, '76. VETERANS DAY CEREMONIES AT PARKS, AMER LEGION, CEMETERIES AND VFW. CEREMONY, PARADE. (LOCAL). COL SEDGLEY THORNBURY; VOLUSIA COUNTY ACTION'76 BICENTENNIAL COMMITTEE; PO BOX 1671, 250 MIDWAY; DAYTONA BEACH, FL 32015. (#7744-502).

NOV 10, '76. U S ARMED FORCES BICENTENNIAL BAND & CHORUS. LIVE PERFORMANCE AT PEABODY AUDITORIUM. (LOCAL). MARGE LAUGHTON, DIRECTOR; VOLUSIA ACTION '76; PO BOX 1671; DAYTONA BEACH, FL 32015. (#109531-1).

MAR 26 - 27, '77. ANTIQUE BOTTLE COLLECTORS EXHIBITION. EXHIBIT AT VOLUSIA COUNTY FAIRGROUNDS/INTERSECTION I-4 & FLA 44. (LOCAL). BILL DREGGORS, COORD; M T BOTTLE COLLECTORS ASSOC; RT 3, BOX 566; DELAND, FL 32720. (#200011-219).

DEFUNIAK SPG

CHAUTAUQUA AUDITORIUM RESTORATION, FL. THE HISTORICAL AUDITORIUM WILL BE RESTORED. (LOCAL). JOHN E CREEL, CHAIRMAN; WALTON COUNTY BICENTENNIAL COMMITTEE; NELSON AVE; DEFUNIAK SPG, FL 32433. (#15039).

COMMUNITY CENTER IN FLOWERSVIEW AREA, FL. RENOVATION OF COMMUNITY BUILDING IN FLOWERSVIEW AREA. (LOCAL). JOHN E CREEL, CHAIRMAN; WALTON COUNTY BICENTENNIAL COMMITTEE; NELSON AVE; DEFUNIAK SPG, FL 32433. (#15041).

S WALTON COMMUNITY CENTER & FIRE STATION, FL. A COMMUNITY CENTER & FIRE STATION WILL BE BUILT IN S WALTON COUNTY. (LOCAL). JOHN E CREEL, CHAIRMAN; WALTON COUNTY BICENTENNIAL COMMITTEE; NELSON AVE; DEFUNIAK SPG, FL 32433. (#15040).

MAY 30, '75 - MAY 30, '76. DINNER THEATRE. LIVE PERFORMANCE AT DEFUNIAK COUNTRY CLUB. (LOCAL). JOHN E CREEL, CHAIRMAN; WALTON COUNTY BICENTENNIAL COMMITTEE; PO BOX 548; DEFUNIAK SPG, FL 32433. (#102206-1).

JULY 2, '76. CHAUTAUQUA '76. EXHIBIT, FESTIVAL, PARADE AT LAKE DEFUNIAK PARK AND CHAUTAUQUA AUDITORIUM. (LOCAL). JOHN E CREEL, CHMN; WALTON COUNTY BICENTENNIAL COMMITTEE; PO BOX 548; DEFUNIAK SPG, FL 32433. (#102205-1).

DELAND

VOLUSIA COUNTY BIKE TRAIL PROJECT: DELAND, FLORIDA. PROJECT TO GET NETWORK OF BIKE-WAYS ESTABLISHED THROUGHOUT THE COUNTY FOR THE GROWING NUMBER OF CITIZENS WHO ENJOY THIS POPULAR FORM OF EXERCISE AND POLLUTION-FREE MEANS OF TRANSPORTATION. (LOCAL). JOHN HOLLON, CHAIRMAN; VOLUSIA COUNTY PUBLIC WORKS; 136 N FLORIDA AVE; DELAND, FL 32720. (#6253). **(??).**

VOLUSIA COUNTY ECOLOGY PROJECT - FLORIDA. PROJECT WILL RESTORE ECOLOGICAL BALANCE OF LOCAL WATERS, STUDY FEASIBILITY FOR DISCOURAGEMENT OF LITTERING, CONVERSION OF SOLID WASTE INTO SUPER SOIL, PLANT TREES & BEAUTIFICATION PROGRAM. (LOCAL). DREW MURPHY, CHAIRMAN; NEWS JOURNAL; PO BOX 431; DAYTONA BEACH, FL 32014. (#6254). **(??).**

VOLUSIA COUNTY PARKS PROJECT: DELAND, FLORIDA. TO CREATE & DEVELOP A RECREATION & CONSERVATION YOUTH PARK FOR USE & EDUCATION OF SCHOOL CHILDREN. (LOCAL). MRS JO DAVIDSON, CHAIRMAN; NEWS JOURNAL; PO BOX 431; DAYTONA BEACH, FL 32014. (#6252).

VOLUSIA COUNTY VOTER REGISTRATION, FLORIDA. AIM TO GET 100% VOTER TURN-OUT, TO FAMILIARIZE MORE PEOPLE WITH VOTING PROCEDURE AND TO BE A 100% REGISTERED CO. (LOCAL). GEORGE FOGLE, CHAIRMAN; VOLUSIA CO ACTION '76 BICENTENNIAL COMMITTEE; PO BOX 1671 250 MIDWAY; DAYTONA BEACH, FL 32015. (#6255).

APR 29 - MAY 4, '75. FLORIDA'S BICENT MOBILE EXHIBIT-THE STORY OF FLORIDA, PAST & PRESENT. MOBILE EXHIBITS PROVIDED BY THE COUNTY BICENT COMMITTEE, ACTION '76, WILL TOUR THE AREA THROUGH 1977. INCLUDED WILL BE A FLORIDA/AMERICAN BICENT TRAVELLING EXHIBIT & AN ARCHITECTURAL EXHIBIT. (ST-WIDE). GEN GEORGE FOGLE; VOLUSIA COUNTY ACTION '76 BICENTENNIAL COMMITTEE; PO BOX 1671, 250 MIDWAY; DAYTONA BEACH, FL 32015. (#7748-501).

JULY 4, '76. NATURALIZATION CEREMONY. CEREMONY AT EDMUNDS ACTIVITIES CENTER, STETSON UNIV. (INT'L). CHIEF JUDGE; CIVIC ASSOCIATIONS; 7TH JUDICIAL CIRCLE; DELAND, FL 32720. (#109346-1).

NOV 4 - 14, '76. VOLUSIA COUNTY FAIR. FAIR AT DELAND FAIRGROUNDS. (LOCAL). BETTY BAGGETT, COORD; VOLUSIA COUNTY ACTION '76; 1118 JARCANDA; DAYTONA BEACH, FL 32018. (#109347-1).

DELRAY BEACH

SW FOURTH AVE RECREATION PARK, DELRAY BEACH, FL. TO PROVIDE THE CITIZENS ADEQUATE RECREATIONAL FACILITIES, BALL PARK, HANDBALL COURTS AND CHILDREN'S PLAYGROUND. (LOCAL). J ELDON MARRIOTT, CITY MANAGER; PARKS AND RECREATION DEPT; CITY OF DELRAY BEACH; DELRAY BEACH, FL 33444. (#22838). **ARBA GRANTEE.**

DELTONA

JULY 2 - 4, '76. BICENTENNIAL VILLAGE: 200 YEARS OF PROGRESS. 8 SECTIONS: ARTS & CRAFTS SHOW WITH CRAFTSMEN IN ACTION, HISTORICAL SKITS, GAY 90'S TAVERN WITH DANCING, YOUTH GAMES & RIDES, RACES AND SPORTING EVENTS, LUNCHEON FACILITIES, FIREWORKS ON JULY 4TH ONLY. AT NEXT TO DELTONA INN AT ENTRANCE TO DELTONA FROM INTERSTATE 4. (LOCAL). MARGARET E THOMAS, CHMN; DELTONA BICENTENNIAL COMMITTEE; 1168 BRIARWOOD AVE; DELTONA, FL 32763. (#106322-1).

JULY 4, '76. DEDICATION OF COMMEMORATIVE BRONZE PLAQUE. INSCRIBED PLAQUE DEDICATED TO DELTONANS FOR THEIR CONTRIBUTION TO THE BICENTENNIAL EFFORT. AT PUBLIC LIBRARY, PROVIDENCE BLVD, DELTONA, FL. (LOCAL). MARGARET E THOMAS, CHMN; DELTONA BICENTENNIAL COMMITTEE; 1168 BRIARWOOD AVE; DELTONA, FL 32763. (#106322-3).

JULY 4, '76. FREEDOMS OF AMERICA PARADE. THEME FLOATS ON FREEDOMS IN BILL OF RIGHTS & CONSTITUTION. ALSO MANY HISTORICAL MOMENTS & PERSONALITIES, WITH MUSIC & MARCHING UNITS. FLOAT ENTRIES INFO: DR CLUDE MEADE, SAXTON BLVD, DELTONA, FL. AT PROVIDENCE BOULEVARD IN DELTONA, PARKING ON SIDE STREETS. (LOCAL). MARGARET E THOMAS, CHMN; DELTONA BICENTENNIAL COMMITTEE; 1168 BRIARWOOD AVE; DELTONA, FL 32763. (#106322-2).

DISNEY WORLD

JUNE 7, '75 - SEPT 6, '76. AMERICA ON PARADE AT WALT DISNEY WORLD. 50 UNITS DEPICTING MEMORABLE MOMENTS IN US HISTORY & SALUTES TO OUR NATIONS CREATIONS, PASTTIMES & LIFESTYLES. DOLL-LIKE CHARACTERIZATIONS OF 'PEOPLE OF AMERICA', HIGH SCHOOL & COLLEGE BANDS, SALUTE DIFFERENT STATE EACH WEEK. AT WALT DISNEY WORLD, NEAR ORLANDO, FL. (NAT'L). JACK B. LINDQUIST; WALT DISNEY PRODUCTIONS; 1313 HARBOR BLVD.; ANAHEIM, CA 92803. (#50252-2).

JUNE 30 - JULY 7, '76. LITTLE ROCK, IOWA BAND TO MARCH AT DISNEY WORLD. DATE OF THE PARADES IS 4 JULY. STUDENTS WILL ALSO TOUR THE GREAT SMOKY MOUNTAINS NATIONAL PARK AND ST AUGUSTINE, NATION'S OLDEST CITY. MARCHED IN 2 PARADES: 2 PM PARADE ON JULY 4TH AND 9 PM PARADE ON JULY 5TH. AT DISNEY WORLD, FLORIDA. (REGN'L). BYRON K PERRINE, DIRECTOR; LITTLE ROCK SCHOOL & MUSIC BOOSTERS; LITTLE ROCK, IA 51243. (#107688-11).

DUNEDIN

DUNEDIN BICENTENNIAL COMMUNITY POOL - FL. BUILDING A POOL FOR RECREATIONAL AS WELL AS COMPETITIVE PURPOSES FOR ALL PEOPLE LIVING IN AND AROUND THE DUNEDIN AREA. (LOCAL). BARBARA NELSON, CHAIRMAN; DUNEDIN BI-COM, INC; 903 MICHIGAN; DUNEDIN, FL 33528. (#15072).

MAR 18 - 20, '76. 10TH ANNUAL HIGHLAND GAMES AND FESTIVAL. SCOTTISH TOWN SALUTES ITS HERITAGE THROUGH CELEBRATION OF MUSIC, DANCES & GAMES. (ST-WIDE). ROBERT LONGSTREET, COORD; DUNEDIN HIGHLAND GAMES FESTIVAL; PO BOX 507; DUNEDIN, FL 33528. (#103416-210).

EATONVILLE

EATONVILLE PARK - EATONVILLE, FL. AN AREA FOR EATONVILLE TOWN RESIDENTS TO BE ABLE TO ENJOY OUTDOOR PICNICS, MEETINGS OR CIVIC ACTIVITIES SUCH AS FORUMS, YOUTH PROGRAMS AND CONCERTS. (LOCAL). ROLFE G ARNHYM, CHAIRMAN; ORANGE COUNTY BICENTENNIAL COMMITTEE; 423 S ORANGE AVE; ORLANDO, FL 32801. (#19644).

EBRO

MAY 15, '76. DOG SHOW AND RACE. DOG OBEDIENCE CONFIRMATION AND GREYHOUND RACES. AT DOG TRACK. (LOCAL). TULLY BRIDENBACK, CHMN; WASHINGTON COUNTY BICENTENNIAL COMMITTEE; PO BOX 4; CHIPLEY, FL 32428. (#102211-1).

EDGEWATER

PAINTING FIREPLUGS IN EDGEWATER, FL. PAINTED FIREPLUGS IN PATRIOTIC COLORS & THEMES. (LOCAL). PATRICIA M GOODSON, CHAIRMAN; EDGEWATER BICENTENNIAL COMMITTEE; 1820 LIME TREE DR; EDGEWATER, FL 32032. (#31183).

VOLUNTEER RESCUE SQUAD IN EDGEWATER, FL. ORGANIZATION OF VOLUNTEER RESCUE SQUAD FOR WELFARE OF PRESENT AND FUTURE NOW OPERATIONAL WITH EMERGENCY MEDICAL TECHNICIANS AND TRUCK. (LOCAL). PATRICIA M GOODSON, SECRETARY; EDGEWATER VOLUNTEER EMERGENCY RESCUE COMMITTEE; PO BOX 333; EDGEWATER, FL 32032. (#31182).

JULY 3 - 4, '76. COMMUNITY 4TH OF JULY CELEBRATION. FESTIVAL AT COMMUNITY CENTER PIER, RIVERSIDE DRIVE & E PARK AVE. (LOCAL). PATRICIA GOODSON, CHMN; EDGEWATER VOLUNTEER FIRE DEPARTMENT; 1820 LIME TREE DR; EDGEWATER, FL 32032. (#200011-282).

EGLIN AFB

NOV 20, '76. BICENTENNIAL OPEN HOUSE '76. EXHIBIT, TOUR, LIVE PERFORMANCE AT ELGIN AFB FLIGHTLINE. (LOCAL). CAPT DICK OLIVER, CHMN; ARMAMENT DEVELOPMENT & TEST CENTER; EGLIN AFB, FL 32542. (#200011-257).

EL PORTAL

FEB 12 - 15, '76. 'YESTERDAY AND TOMORROW', PAGEANT AND FESTIVAL. FESTIVAL, LIVE PERFORMANCE AT EL PORTAL VILLAGE HALL. (LOCAL). HON FORREST BOWEN, MAYOR; VILLAGE OF EL PORTAL; 500 NE 87TH ST; MIAMI, FL 33138. (#200011-26).

EUSTIS

LITTLE LEAGUE COMPLEX IN EUSTIS, FL. LITTLE LEAGUE AND RELATED ATHLETIC FIELDS WILL BE CONSTRUCTED IN HONOR OF THE BICENTENNIAL. (LOCAL). ALBERT MICKLER, PRES; EUSTIS LITTLE LEAGUE; 312 PALM AVE; EUSTIS, FL 32726. (#15036).

FEB 16 - 21, '76. GEORGE WASHINGTON'S BIRTHDAY FESTIVAL. EXHIBIT, FAIR, FESTIVAL, PARADE AT DOWNTOWN EUSTIS & FERRAN PARK. (LOCAL). DICK MULLINS, EXEC SEC; EUSTIS CHAMBER OF COMMERCE; 601 N SHORE DR; EUSTIS, FL 32726. (#102203-1).

FLORAL CITY

RECREATION CENTER IMPROVEMENTS - FLORAL CITY, FL. CONSTRUCTION OF OUTDOOR SHUFFLEBOARD COURTS, PLAYGROUND EQUIPMENT & PICNIC AREA WITH B-B-Q PITS AND CENTRAL AIR CONDITIONING FOR COMMUNITY BUILDING USED BY RESIDENTS. (LOCAL). MRS ICEAL RICH, SECRETARY-TREASURER; FLORAL CITY BICENTENNIAL COMMITTEE; RT 1, BOX 219R; FLORAL CITY, FL 32636. (#25993).

FORT MYERS

JUNIOR MUSEUM AND PLANETARIUM OF LEE COUNTY, FL. MUSEUM HAS BOARDWALKS, NATURE TRAILS AND A PICNIC AREA. THE PURPOSE IS EXHIBITION, PRESERVATION AND TEACHING OF SW FLORIDA'S NATURAL AND HUMAN HISTORY. (LOCAL). ROBIN C BROWN, PRESIDENT; FT MYERS JUNIOR MUSEUM & PLANETARIUM BOARD; 2121 W FIRST ST; FT MYERS, FL 33901. (#27008). **ARBA GRANTEE.**

'TWO CENTURIES IN PERSPECTIVE', TV SERIES - FL. ETV SERIES PRODUCED BY SOCIAL SCIENCES FACULTY WITH PROGRAMMING DIRECTED TOWARD HISTORICAL & SOCIAL ISSUES. (LOCAL). NANETTE J SMITH, CHAIRMAN; EDISON COMMUNITY COLLEGE BICENTENNIAL COMMITTEE; COLLEGE PARKWAY; FT MYERS, FL 33901. (#15704).

JAN 22 - OCT 15, '76. AMERICAN FILM CLASSICS. JAN 22ND, 'ADAMS RIB'; FEB 10TH, 'EDISON THE MAN'; MAR 5TH, 'IT HAPPENED ONE NIGHT'; MAY 20TH, 'GUYS AND DOLLS'; JUNE 18TH, 'SHOWBOAT'; JULY 21ST, 'AMERICA: THE NATION IN FILMS'; AUG 20TH, 'TOM SAWYER'; SEP 24 'GRAPES OF WRATH'; OCT 15TH, 'GOLDEN AGE OF COMEDY'. (LOCAL). NANETTE J SMITH, CHAIRMAN; EDISON COMMUNITY COLLEGE BICENTENNIAL COMMITTEE; COLLEGE PARKWAY; FT MYERS, FL 33901. (#102516-2).

JAN 27 - 28, '76. UNITED STATES ARMED FORCES BICENTENNIAL CARAVAN. CARAVAN IS COMPOSED OF EXHIBIT VANS FOR EACH MILITARY SERVICE. PROJECT THEME IS 'HISTORY OF THE ARMED FORCES AND THEIR CONTRIBUTIONS TO THE NATION'. (LOCAL). WILLIAM C SMITH; US ARMED FORCES BICENTENNIAL EXHIBIT VANS PROJECT; PO BOX 88; FORT MEYERS, FL 33902. (#1775-426).

JAN 30 - DEC 9, '76. AMERICA IN MUSIC. JAN 30, CONCERT, CLASSIC: ELENA NIKOLAIDI; FEB 16, GEN CONCERT, MAC FRAMPTON; MAR 28TH, GEN CONCERT, ECC CHORALE; JUNE 2ND, LECTURE-CONCERT, NASH NOBLE; AND DEC 9TH, GENERAL CONCERT, ECC CHORALE. (LOCAL). NANETTE J SMITH, CHMN; EDISON COMMUNITY COLLEGE BICENTENNIAL COMMITTEE; COLLEGE PKWY; FT MYERS, FL 33901. (#102515-6).

FEB 7 - 14, '76. EDISON PAGEANT OF LIGHT. GALA CELEBRATION COMMEMORATES BIRTHDAY OF INVENTOR WHO MAINTAINED WINTER HOME HERE WITH A PARADE, PARTIES, RACES AND DANCES. THE VONDA KAY VAN DYKE TICKETS ARE $5.50, $6.50 & $7.50.). (LOCAL). MARGIE B WILLIS, COORD; EDISON PAGEANT OF LIGHT; PO BOX 1311; FORT MYERS, FL 33902. (#103416-139).

FEB 10, '76. TOWARD TECHNOLOGY'S THIRD CENTURY. DEDICATION OF NEW TECHNICAL BUILDING TO THE FUTURE OF SOUTHWEST FLORIDA AND ADVANCING TECHNOLOGY; PARTICIPATION OF MEMBERS OF FAMILY OF THOMAS ALVA EDISON. AT ON CAMPUS. (LOCAL). NANETTE J SMITH, CHMN; EDISON COMMUNITY COLLEGE BICENTENNIAL COMMITTEE; COLLEGE PKWY; FT MYERS, FL 33901. (#102515-1).

FEB 16, '76. AMERICA'S HISTORY IN MUSIC. CONCERT BY MAC FRAMPTON. AT SEVEN LAKES AUDITORIUM. (LOCAL). NANETTE J SMITH, CHMN; EDISON COMMUNITY COLLEGE BICENTENNIAL COMMITTEE; COLLEGE PKWY; FT MYERS, FL 33901. (#102515-2).

MAR 26 - DEC 5, '76. BICENTENNIAL DRAMA FESTIVAL. TWO STUDENT DRAMA PRODUCTIONS WILL BE HELD, THE BEST IN AMERICAN DRAMA. MAR 26-30, 'LOOK HOMEWARD ANGEL'; DEC 1-5, 'LADY IN THE DARK'. (LOCAL). NANETTE J SMITH, CHMN; EDISON COMMUNITY COLLEGE BICENTENNIAL COMMITTEE; COLLEGE PKWY; FT MYERS, FL 33901. (#102515-5).

APR 15 - 17, '76. CONTRIBUTIONS OF BLACK CULTURE. THE EVENT WILL FOCUS ON ARTHUR HALL DANCER, WITH FLORIDA ARTS COUNCIL WORKSHOPS, PERFORMANCES AND EXHIBITS OF AFRICAN ART PRINTS. (LOCAL). NANETTE J SMITH, CHAIRMAN; EDISON COMMUNITY COLLEGE BICENTENNIAL COMMITTEE; COLLEGE PARKWAY; FT MYERS, FL 33901. (#102516-1).

JULY 1 - 31, '76. TWO CENTURIES IN AMERICAN ART. EXHIBITS WITH LECTURES, FILMS, PROGRAMS FROM RINGLING MUSEUM OF ART. AT ON CAMPUS. (LOCAL). NANETTE J SMITH, CHMN; EDISON COMMUNITY COLLEGE BICENTENNIAL COMMITTEE; COLLEGE PKWY; FT MYERS, FL 33901. (#102515-3).

JULY 3, '76. INDEPENDENCE DAY CELEBRATION. FEATURING POLK COUNTY BICENTENNIAL MEDICINE SHOW, SPORTS, ACTIVITIES PICNIC; ENTIRE COMMUNITY INVITED. AT ON CAMPUS. (LOCAL). NANETTE J SMITH, CHMN; EDISON COMMUNITY COLLEGE BICENTENNIAL COMMITTEE; COLLEGE PKWY; FT MYERS, FL 33901. (#102515-4).

JULY 6, '76. TIME CAPSULE DEDICATION CEREMONY. CEREMONY AT FT MYERS CITY HALL, 2200 2ND ST, PARKING IN DOWNTOWN AREA. (LOCAL). WADE SCAFFE, CHAIRMAN; FORT MYERS BICENTENNIAL COMMITTEE; 2200 2ND ST; FORT MYERS, FL 33902. (#107112-1).

FORT WHITE

APR 5 - 10, '76. FORT WHITE COMMUNITY SCHOOL FESTIVAL. SCHOOL 1776 DAY; DRESS ACCORDING TO REVOLUTIONARY DAYS. SIXTH GRADE PLAY; SCHOOL AND COMMUNITY DISPLAY OF LIFE FOR PAST 200 YEARS. AT FORT WHITE PUBLIC SCHOOL. (LOCAL). HON CARLOS MAXWELL, MAYOR; COLUMBIA COUNTY ACTION '76 COMMITTEE; CITY HALL; FORT WHITE, FL 32038. (#200011-27).

FRNANDINA BCH

RESTORATION OF BUSINESS SECTION - FL. CENTRE STREET, OLD & PRESENT BUSINESS AREA, RESTORED & REVITALIZED TO VICTORIAN & 1890HS ERA ARCHITECTURE AND GENERAL ATMOSPHERE; 8BLOCK AREA; SOME WORK STILL IN PROGRESS. (LOCAL). ANDY ALLAN III, CHAIRMAN; CENTRE STREET MERCHANTS ASSOC; BOX 472; FRNANDINA BCH, FL 32034. (#21267).

APR 30 - MAY 2, '76. 13TH ANNUAL SHRIMP BOAT FESTIVAL. 13TH ANNUAL FESTIVAL, RECOGNIZING BIRTHPLACE OF SHRIMPING INDUSTRY; ARTS & CRAFTS SHOW, BEARD CONTEST, BEAUTY CONTEST, FOOD BOOTHS WITH SEAFOOD SPECIALTIES, COUNTRY FOLK FESTIVAL, PARADE & PIRATES LANDING; ALSO SHRIMP BOAT RACES AND DRIVING TOUR OF OLD HOMES. AT CENTRE ST, TO AMELIA RIVER. (REGN'L). DON ROBERTS, DIRECTOR; CHAMBER OF COMMERCE FISHERMANS ASSN ARTS & CRAFTS ASSN; 102 CENTRE ST; FRNANDINA BCH, FL 32034. (#105632-1).

FROSTPROOF

RENOVATION OF DEPOT - FROSTPROOF, FL. THE DEPOT WILL BE RENOVATED INTO A COMMUNITY-RECREATION HALL; IT WILL BE AN INDOOR OUTDOOR FACILITY WITH DANCE FLOOR, WORK AREA FOR CLASSES, BAR-B-QUE PIT, GARDEN PARK AREA & OFFICE SPACE. (LOCAL). DAN H RUHL, JR, TREASURER; FROSTPROOF BICENTENNIAL COMMITTEE; 47 W WALL ST; FROSTPROOF, FL 33843. (#24861).

'THERE'S ONLY ONE FROSTPROOF' - BOOK, FL. THE BOOK WILL INCLUDE FAMILY HISTORIES AND HISTORICAL PICTURES; IT WILL BE PUBLISHED IN BOTH HARDBACK AND PAPERBACK. (LOCAL). DAN H RUHL, JR, TREASURER; FROSTPROOF BICENTENNIAL COMMITTEE; 47 W WALL ST; FROSTPROOF, FL 33843. (#24860).

FT JEFFERSON

MAY 25 - DEC 31, '75. EVENING PGMS ON ROLE OF THE DRY TORTUGAS IN 18TH CENTURY. ALSO IN 1976. FT JEFFERSON, THE LARGEST ALL-MASONRY FORTIFICATION IN WESTERN WORLD, WAS BUILT FOR CONTROL OF THE FLORIDA STRAITS. AT FT JEFFERSON IS LOCATED OFF KEY WEST, FL. (REGN'L). SUPT, EVERGLADES NP; NATIONAL PARK SERVICE; P.O. BOX 279; HOMESTEAD, FL 33030. (#6730-9).

JAN 1 - DEC 31, '76. FT JEFFERSON NM PGM ON ROLE OF DRY TORTUGAS AS PIRATES'S HAVEN. SLIDE PROGRAM IN EVENINGS DEALING WITH NATURAL LIFE IN THIS AREA. FT JEFFERSON IS ACCESSIBLE ONLY BY BOAT OR AMPHIBIOUS AIRCRAFT. (REGN'L). FORT JEFFERSON NM; NATIONAL PARK SERVICE; C/O U S COAST GUARD BASE; KEY WEST, FL 33040. (#6730-101).

JAN 1 - DEC 31, '76. FT JEFFERSON NM EVEN PGM - DRY TORTUGAS IN 18TH CENTURY. FORT JEFFERSON, THE LARGEST ALL-MASONRY FORTIFICATION IN THE WESTERN WORLD, WAS BUILT FOR CONTROL OF THE FLORIDA STRAITS. FT JEFFERSON IS ACCESSIBLE ONLY BY BOAT OR AMPHIBIOUS AIRCRAFT. AT FT JEFFERSON IS LOCATED APP. 75 MILES OFF KEY WEST, FL.. (REGN'L). EVERGLADES NATL PK; NATIONAL PARK SERVICE; P.O. BOX 279; HOMESTEAD, FL 33030. (#6730-509).

FT LAUDERDALE

ART CONTEST & SHOW - FT LAUDERDALE, FL. THE ART CONTEST & SHOW WILL FEATURE INTERPRETIVE PHOTOGRAPHY. (LOCAL). CYNTHIA E RUSH, CHAIRMAN; BREWARD COUNTY HISTORICAL COMMISSION; 201 SE 6 ST; FT LAUDERDALE, FL 33304. (#20305).

BICENTENNIAL COMPETITIONS IN FT LAUDERDALE, FL. COUNTY-WIDE COMPETITIONS IN AREAS OF ART, MUSIC, CREATIVE WRITING, SPEECH AND ATHLETICS. (LOCAL). DR ROY A CHURCH, CHAIRMAN; BROWARD COMMUNITY COLLEGE BICENTENNIAL COMMITTEE; 1000 COCONUT DRIVE BLVD; POMPANO, FL 33066. (#15731).

BICENTENNIAL CONTESTS - FT LAUDERDALE, FL. LETTERS CONTEST SUBJECT IS: A BICENTENNIAL THEME; ESSAY CONTEST SUBJECT IS: ONE PARTICULAR WOMAN'S ROLE IN THE AMERICAN REVOLUTION; MUSIC, ORIGINAL COMPOSITION. (LOCAL). MARGARETTE PARKER, CHAIRMAN; FT LAUDERDALE BRANCH OF NATIONAL LEAGUE OF AMERICAN PEN WOMEN; 3100 N E 49TH ST, APT 809; FT LAUDERDALE, FL 33308. (#19569).

BICENTENNIAL FLORIDA TRAVEL STUDY PROGRAM. DEVELOPMENT OF A BICENTENNIAL NON-CREDIT AND/OR CREDIT COURSE WHICH WILL TOUR THE STATE IN A HISTORICAL STUDY FRAMEWORK. (LOCAL). DR ROY A CHURCH, CHAIRMAN; BROWARD COMMUNITY COLLEGE BICENTENNIAL COMMITTEE; 1000 COCONUT DRIVE BLVD; POMPANO, FL 33066. (#15732).

THE COLONIALS - FT LAUDERDALE, FL. GROUP CONSISTS OF A COLOR GUARD WITH 26 BOYS DRESSED IN COLONIAL COSTUMES CARRYING 18 MUSKETS & A FIFE & DRUM CORPS OF 10 BOYS; THEY ARE AVAILABLE AT NO CHARGE EXCEPT EXPENSES IF TRAVEL OUTSIDE AREA. (ST-WIDE). ZEKE LANDIS, PROJ DIRECTOR; SCOUTMASTERS' CAMPOREE COMMITTEE, NEW RIVER DISTRICT; 4210 SW 74TH AVE; DAVIE, FL 33314. (#20925).

COUNCIL FOR INTERNATIONAL VISITORS - FL. A FORT LAUDERDALE BRANCH OF THE ALREADY ESTABLISHED MIAMI CHAPTER; TO ENCOURAGE BETTER RELATIONS BETWEEN LOCAL CITIZENS AND FOREIGN VISITORS. (LOCAL). LAURA WARD, COORDINATOR; CITY OF FORT LAUDERDALE BICENTENNIAL COMMITTEE; PO BOX 14250; FT LAUDERDALE, FL 33302. (#19571).

EDUCATIONAL CONTINUUM, FT LAUDERDALE, FL. AN INTERDISCIPLINARY PARTICIPATORY PROGRAM FOR ALL AGES; TO BE HOUSED IN FORT LAUDERDALE'S OLDEST EXISTING HOTEL WHICH IS CURRENTLY IN THE RESTORATION PROCESS. (ST-WIDE). MRS R O POWELL, CHMN CONTINUUM BOARD OF DIRECTORS; JUNIOR LEAGUE OF FORT LAUDERDALE, INC; 229 SW 2ND AVE; FT LAUDERDALE, FL 33301. (#15673).

ESTABLISHMENT OF 'CHORD', FT LAUDERDALE, FL. THE ESTABLISHING OF CHORD, A RESIDENCE FOR FEMALE FIRST & 2ND OFFENDERS, AGES 13-17 YEARS, REFERRED THROUGH DIVISION OF FAMILY SERVICES. (LOCAL). MRS WILLIAMS JOYNER, PRESIDENT; CHORD, INC; 535 N VICTORICIA PARK RD; FT LAUDERDALE, FL 33301. (#15685).

FIRE HYDRANT DECORATING - FT LAUDERDALE, FL. ART STUDENTS FROM FOUR AREA HIGHSCHOOLS TO DECORATE HYDRANTS IN A PATRIOTIC FREESTYLE DESIGN. (LOCAL). MISS ANNE VANDERSLICE, PROJ COORDINATOR; FORT LAUDERDALE BICENTENNIAL OFFICE; PO BOX 14250; FT LAUDERDALE, FL 33302. (#17998).

FLORENCE C HARDY MEMORIAL PORTABLE DISPLAY CASE-FL. A PANORAMIC HISTORY OF FORT LAUDERDALE UNDER 200 SQUARE FEET OF PORTABLE DISPLAY SPACE. (LOCAL). MRS MARJORIE PATTERSON, EXEC DIRECTOR; FORT LAUDERDALE HISTORICAL SOCIETY; 850 NE 12TH AVE; FT LAUDERDALE, FL 33304. (#15484).

FORT LAUDERDALE RECIPES, BOOK, FL. 3RD PRINTING, FOR THE BICENTENNIAL OF A BOOK ON FORT LAUDERDALE HISTORY WITH A LISTING OF TROPICAL FRUITS, NUTS & RECIPES OF EARLY SETTLERS. (LOCAL). MRS MARJORIE PATTERSON, CHAIRMAN; FORT LAUDERDALE HISTORICAL SOCIETY; 850 NE 12TH AVE EXTENDED; FT LAUDERDALE, FL 33304. (#15674).

HISTORICAL WALL HANGINGS, FT LAUDERDALE, FL. 3' X 5' NEEDLEPOINT WALL HANGING DEPICTING HISTORICAL SCENES OF BROWARD AND PALM BEACH COUNTIES (15 SCENES). (LOCAL). MRS GEORGE C FRENCH, JR, PRESIDENT; GOLDCOAST NEEDLEARTS GUILD; 2848 NE 35TH CT; FT LAUDERDALE, FL 33308. (#15672).

'THE LEWIS FAMILY - FT LAUDERDALE, FL. A 5'X2'X2' TRAVELING DISPLAY FEATURING APPLEHEAD DOLLS; DEPICTS LIFE AND THE AREA WHERE THE LEWIS FAMILY SETTLED IN 1793. (LOCAL). MRS CARL CUNNINGHAM, PROJ DIRECTOR; BROWARD COUNTY BICENTENNIAL COMMITTEE; 1223 S W 18TH AVE; FT LAUDERDALE, FL 33312. (#19567).

NEEDLEPOINT DESIGN OF FIRST SCHOOLHOUSE. AN ORIGINAL NEEDLEPOINT DESIGN OF ONE ROOM SCHOOLHOUSE BUILT IN 1899. (LOCAL). MRS HILDA FLOWERS, PROJ DIRECTOR;

FT LAUDERDALE — CONTINUED

BROWARD COUNTY RETIRED TEACHERS ASSOC; 108 S E 14TH ST; FT LAUDERDALE, FL 33316. (#19568).

ORIGINAL ART COMMISSION - FT LAUDERDALE, FL. INDIVIDUALS WILL BE COMMISSIONED TO RAISE MONEY TO PURCHASE AN ORIGINAL ART WORK AS A BICENTENNIAL MEMORIAL. (LOCAL). DR ROY A CHURCH, CHAIRMAN; BROWARD COMMUNITY COLLEGE BICENTENNIAL COMMITTEE; 1000 COCONUT CREEK BLVD; POMPANO, FL 33066. (#15730).

PERFORMING ARTS COMPLEX - FT LAUDERDALE, FL. AN ARTS COMPLEX WILL BE CONSTRUCTED IN HONOR OF THE BICENTENNIAL. (LOCAL). DR ROY A CHURCH, CHAIRMAN; BROWARD COMMUNITY COLLEGE BICENTENNIAL COMMITTEE; 1000 COCONUT CREEK BLVD; POMPANO, FL 33066. (#15729).

REBUILDING AND RESTORATION OF THE UNICORN, FL. A BRIG BEING READIED FOR THE TALL SHIPS RACE 1976 -PART OF OPERATION SAIL -PERSONNEL ON THE PROJECT ARE FROM THE FLORIDA OCEAN SCIENCES INSTITUTE: A REHABILITATION GROUP FOR MALE JUVENILE OFFENDERS. (LOCAL). MISS JANE WILLIAMS, PROJ COORDINATOR; UNICORN, INC; 775 TAYLOR LN; DANIA, FL 33004. (#15669).

RECONSTRUCTION OF FIRST SCHOOLHOUSE - FL. RECONSTRUCTION OF ONE ROOM SCHOOLHOUSE BUILT IN 1899. (LOCAL). MRS FRAN HILLIARD, CHAIRMAN; BROWARD COUNTY BICENTENNIAL COMMITTEE; 448 BONTONA AVE; FT LAUDERDALE, FL 33301. (#19566).

RESTORATION AND RENOVATION OF NEW RIVER INN, FL. RESTORATION OF CITY'S OLDEST EXISTING HOTEL; BUILT IN 1905. (LOCAL). MR ROGER GERMAIN, PROJ COORDINATOR; CITY OF FORT LAUDERDALE, PLANNING DEPARTMENT; 100 N ANDREWS AVE; FT LAUDERDALE, FL 33302. (#15684).

ROBERT H BUBIER MEMORIAL PARK - FT LAUDERDALE, FL. A RIVERFRONT PARK IN THE HEART OF DOWNTOWN AREA; PLANNED AS A LASTING REMINDER FOR THE BICENTENNIAL. THE CONCEPT WAS ORIGINATED BY A BICENTENNIAL SUB-COMMITTEE. (LOCAL). BILL KIRILOFF, ADMINISTRATIVE ASSISTANT; CITY OF FORT LAUDERDALE, OFFICE OF THE CITY MANAGER; PO BOX 14250; FT LAUDERDALE, FL 33302. (#19564).

SELF GUIDED CITY TOUR, FT LAUDERDALE, FL. COMBINES FLORA, HERITAGE, NEW AND OLD LANDMARKS AND SPOTS OF BEAUTY. (LOCAL). LAURA WARD, COORDINATOR; CITY OF FORT LAUDERDALE BICENTENNIAL COMMITTEE; PO BOX 14250; FT LAUDERDALE, FL 33302. (#19565).

SELF-GUIDED TOUR SIGN DESIGN CONTEST - FL. A CONTEST TO DESIGN TRAIL MARKER TO BE USED FOR SELF-GUIDED CITY TOUR. (LOCAL). LAURA WARD, COORDINATOR; CITY OF FORT LAUDERDALE BICENTENNIAL COMMITTEE; PO BOX 14250; FT LAUDERDALE, FL 33302. (#19570).

STEAM TRAIN TO THE PAST, FT LAUDERDALE, FL. ON PERMANENT DISPLAY IS THE 'FERDINAND MAGELLAND'; IT WAS BUILT FOR EXCLUSIVE USSE OF U S PRESIDENTS. (LOCAL). ROSS B PETRIE, CHAIRMAN; GOLD COAST RAILROAD, INC; 3398 SW 9TH AVE; FT LAUDERDALE, FL 33315. (#29983).

TOWN MEETINGS PROJECT IN FT LAUDERDALE, FL. ACTIVITIES TO INCLUDE TRAVELING ROAD SHOW, AMERICANA FESTIVAL, PROGRAMS BY COMMUNITY SERVICE ORGANIZATIONS, BICENTENNIAL COMPETITIONS, HEALTH FAIRS, VOTER REGISTRATION AND TOWN MEETING. (LOCAL). DR ROY A CHURCH, CHAIRMAN; BROWARD COMMUNITY COLLEGE BICENTENNIAL COMMITTEE; 1000 COCONUT CREEK BLVD; POMPANO, FL 33066. (#15728).

TRAVELING ART EXHIBIT PROJECT IN FT LAUD, FL. PROJECT IS THE DEVELOPING OF VISUAL ART EXHIBIT OF LOCAL PROFESSIONAL ARTISTS' WORKS; EXHIBIT WILL TRAVEL THROUGHOUT BROWARD COUNTY ON A SCHEDULED BASIS IN ACCORD WITH LOCAL BICENTENNIAL CELEBRATIONS. (LOCAL). VELMA RIEBLING & JANICE KEMP, CO-CHAIRPERSON; BROWAR COUNTY BICENTENNIAL COMMITTEE; VISUAL ARTS COMMITTEE; PO BOX 9507; FT LAUD, FL 33310. (#16501).

JULY 3 - 6, '75. 16TH ANNUAL FORT LAUDERDALE SUMMER BOAT SHOW. AMERICA'S ONLY MAJOR SUMMER BOAT SHOW. A COMMUNITY SPONSORED EVENT DESIGNED TO BENEFIT BOTH RESIDENTS AND TOURISTS. A FITTING, PATRIOTIC TRIBUTE FROM THE YACHTING CAPITAL OF THE WORLDD. AT DOWNTOWN MUNICIPAL MARINA, FT. LAUDERDALE, FLA.. (REGN'L). JOE SCHABO, VP; MARINE INDUSTRIES ASSN. OF BROWARD COUNTY, FLA.; 411 S.W. 31 AVE.; FT LAUDERDALE, FL 33312. (#50382-1).

JULY 4, '75. OLD FASHIONED FOURTH OF JULY CELEBRATION. PARADE, AWARD, CEREMONY, COMPETITION, FESTIVAL AT HOLIDAY PARK. (LOCAL). NAN S. HUTCHISON; BRO. CO. WOMENS CHAP. FREEDOMS FOUNDATION OF VALLEY FORGE; 13 SW 16 ST.; FT LAUDERDALE, FL 33315. (#50822-1).

OCT 7, '75 - APR 21, '76. BICENTENNIAL CONCERT SEASON. THE SYMPHONY WILL HIGHLIGHT ALL AMERICAN BORN GUEST ARTISTS. AT WAR MEMORIAL AUDITORIUM - 800 NE 8TH ST. (LOCAL). HERBERT W BROMBERG, DIR; FORT LAUDERDALE SYMPHONY ORCHESTRA ASSOCIATION; 450 E LAS OLAS BLVD; FT LAUDERDALE, FL 33301. (#103517-11).

OCT 10 - 13, '75. CELEBRATE THE NAVY'S 200TH BIRTHDAY. A FOUR DAY CELEBRATION WITH BRITISH AND AMERICAN SHIPS IN PORT. EVENTS INCLUDE WELCOMING BY BANDS, RECEPTIONS, DINNERS, COOKOUTS, COMPETITIVE GAMES, RELIGIOUS EXCHANGE, TOURS, ENTERTAINING IN PRIVATE HOMES AND LOCAL CITIZEN INVOLVEMENT. AT PORT EVERGLADES. (LOCAL). STEVE FREID, COORDINATOR; FT LAUDERDALE NAVY LEAGUE, FT LAUDERDALE BICENTENNIAL COMMITTEE; 90 ABACUS SYSTEMS, PO BOX 4558; FT LAUDERDALE, FL 33304. (#102417-3).

OCT 25, '75. BICYCLE RALLY. A BICYCLE RALLY TO EMPHASIZE IMPORTANCE OF CLEANER AIR (PART OF CLEANER AIR WEEK); ENTERTAINMENT & SPEECHES; BIKE DEOCRATING CONTEST & SPECIAL APPEARANCE BY MISS USA. AT HOLIDAY PARK. (LOCAL). MISS ANN VANDERSLICE, DIR; AMERICAN LUNG ASSOC AND FORT LAUDERDALE BICENTENNIAL COMMITTEE; PO BOX 14250; FT LAUDERDALE, FL 33302. (#200011-28).

NOV 7, '75. HOLIDAY CRAFTS FAIR. FAIR AT SUNRISE SHOPPING CENTER; 2400 E SUNRISE BLVD. (LOCAL). MRS JOHN STEPHENS, COOR; FT LAUDERDALE JUNIOR SYMPHONY GUILD; 18 S E 10TH AVE; FT LAUDERDALE, FL 33301. (#102417-2).

NOV 14 - 16, '75. PROMENADE SALUTES AMERICA. EXHIBIT, FESTIVAL, LIVE PERFORMANCE, PARADE AT POMPANO PARK HARNESS TRACK, RACETRACK RD. (LOCAL). MRS JAMES HYATT, CHMN; BEAUX ARTS OF THE FT LAUDERDALE MUSEUM OF THE ARTS; 5778 NE 17TH AVE; FT LAUDERDALE, FL 33334. (#101077-1).

FEB 6 - MAR 6, '76. PHOTOGRAPHY SHOW & CONTEST ON BROWARD COUNTY. COMPETITION. (LOCAL). CARYL BUCNIS, CURATOR; BROWARD COUNTY HISTORICAL COMMISSION; 201 SE 6TH ST; FT LAUDERDALE, FL 33301. (#102607-1).

FEB 10 - MAR 7, '76. 'AMERICANA' FROM THE CHASE MANHATTEN NATIONAL BANK COLLECTION. EXHIBIT AT 426 EAST LAS OLAS. (LOCAL). GEORGE BOLGE, DIRECTOR; FORT LAUDERDALE MUSEUM OF THE ARTS; 426 E LAS OLAS; FT LAUDERDALE, FL 33301. (#103410-1).

FEB 20 - 22, '76. SCOUTMASTERS' CAMPOREE - HERITAGE '76. FESTIVAL AT HOLIDAY PARK AND LOCKHART STADIUM. (LOCAL). ZEKE LANDIS, CHMN; NEW RIVER BOY SCOUTS COUNCIL; 4210 S W 74TH AVE; DAVIE, FL 33314. (#102417-4).

MAR 9, '76. 'WOMEN OF '76: A TAPESTRY OF RESEARCH'. PROCEEDS GO TO SPONSOR SCHOLARSHIPS FOR BROWARD COMMUNITY COLLEGE STUDENTS. SCHOLARSHIPS AWARDED TO WINNERS OF BICENTENNIAL CONTESTS IN ART, LETTERS & MUSIC. AT GOVERNOR'S CLUB & HOTEL. (LOCAL). MARGARETTE PARKER, CHMN; FT LAUDERDALE BRANCH, NATIONAL LEAGUE OF AMERICAN PEN WOMEN; 3100 NE 49TH ST; FT LAUDERDALE, FL 33308. (#104312-2).

MAR 11 - 12, '76. PINE CREST SCHOOL MOCK CONVENTION. CONVENTION ON ONE OF AMERICA'S ESSENTIAL POLITICAL PROCESSES, BIPARTISIAN IN NATURE, SPONSORED BY THE STUDENT BICENTENNIAL COMMITTEE. THE 6-MONTH PROJECT WILL CULMINATE IN A OCK CONVENTION; NATIONAL ADVISORY COMMITTEE WILL INCLUDE U S SENATORS & REPS. AT PINE CREST SCHOOL GYM, FORT LAUDERDALE. (LOCAL). A G BARBER JR, CHMN; PINE CREST PREPARATORY SCHOOL STUDENT BICENTENNIAL COMMITTEE; 1501 NE 62ND ST; FT LAUDERDALE, FL 33334. (#102198-1).

MAR 25 - 26, '76. GLASS & STONEWARE EXHIBIT. AND TOMORROW. 3/25 DEBATE: THE CHANGING RELATIONSHIPS OF GOV'T BY HON JAMES C CORMAN & HON PAUL LAXALT. 3/26 AT 8 PM LECTURE: MR MAX LERNER ON 'THE CHANGING AMERICAN ETHIC'. AT THE UNIVERSITY CENTER, UTC. (LOCAL). DENNIS DUKE, CHMN; ANTIQUE BOTTLE COLLECTORS ASSOC OF FLORIDA; 320 FLORIDA AVE; FT LAUDERDALE, FL 33312. (#102197-1).

MAR 27, '76. BICENTENNIAL STREET DANCE. HIGHLIGHTING AMERICANA ON NORTH BANK OF RIVER; ETHNIC CULTURES ON SOUTH BANK OF RIVER. AT NORTH AND SOUTH BANKS OF NEW RIVER - DOWNTOWN. (LOCAL). MS MARY COPELAND, COORD; FORT LAUDERDALE BICENTENNIAL COMMITTEE; 820 SE 6TH CT; FT LAUDERDALE, FL 33302. (#104312-1).

MAR 27 - 28, '76. LAS OLAS ARTS FESTIVAL. ARTS AND CRAFTS FESTIVAL WITH NATIONAL RECOGNITION. (ST-WIDE). MRS KATY DARR, DIRECTOR; BEAUX ARTS AND FRIENDS OF THE FORT LAUDERDALE MUSEUM OF THE ARTS; PO BOX 2211; FT LAUDERDALE, FL 33303. (#103517-8).

APR 2 - 3, '76. PLANTATION JUNIOR WOMEN'S CLUB CABARET - BICENTENNIAL '76. ORIGINAL MUSICAL ACTS; AFTER PERFORMANCE AREA IS CLEARED FOR DANCING. AT WAR MEMORIAL AUDITORIUM, 800 NE 8TH ST. (LOCAL). MRS BARBARA SANTORO, DIR; PLANTATION JUNIOR WOMEN'S CLUB; 681 N FIG TREE LN; PLANTATION, FL 33317. (#103517-10).

APR 30, '76. BICENTENNIAL BALL. FESTIVAL AT STARLIGHT BALLROOM, 5460 N STATE RD 7. (LOCAL). ELSIE JANE STASKA, COORD; BICENTENNIAL COMMITTEE OF SUNRISE; 1720 NW 60TH AVE; SUNRISE, FL 33313. (#200011-196).

MAY 1 - 8, '76. 'SING OUT SWEET LAND', MUSICAL DRAMA. LIVE PERFORMANCE AT PARKER PLAYHOUSE, 707 N E 8TH ST. (LOCAL). MRS JAMES E NALL, COOR; FORT LAUDERDALE CHILDREN'S THEATRE; 716 N E 25TH WY; FT LAUDERDALE, FL 33304. (#102417-1).

MAY 14 - 16, '76. A MUSICAL SALUTE TO AMERICA. CHORAL, ORCHESTRAL AND SOLO MUSICAL CONCERT PRINCIPALLY USING MUSIC COMMISSIONED FOR THE BICENTENNIAL BY J C PENNEY. AT WAR MEMORIAL AUDITORIUM - 800 NE 8TH ST. (LOCAL). N NEVIN ACTON, II; GREATER FORT LAUDERDALE SYMPHONY CHORUS; 1318 SE 1ST AVE; FT LAUDERDALE, FL 33316. (#102417-7).

MAY 27 - 31, '76. ANGEL DERBY '76 - ALL WOMEN'S INTERNATIONAL AIR RACE. AN ALL WOMEN INTERNATIONAL AIR RACE TO BEGIN IN CANADA FROM A POINT ASSOCIATED WITH AMERICAN REVOLUTION AND OVERFLYING HISTORICAL SITES ASSOCIATED WITH THE REVOLUTION ENROUTE TO FORT LAUDERDALE. AT FORT LAUDERDALE EXECUTIVE AIRPORT. (INT'L). VIRGINIA BRITT, PROJ DIR; ALL WOMEN'S INTERNATIONAL AIR RACE, INC; 5555 N W 15TH AVE; FT LAUDERDALE, FL 33309. (#100692-1).

JULY 1 - 5, '76. MARINE INDUSTRIES ASSOCIATION SUMMER BOAT SHOW. PATRIOTIC BOAT PARADE OPENS THE SHOW; THURSDAY HOURS: 5 PM-10 PM, FRIDAY-SUNDAY HOURS: 12 PM-10 PM, MONDAY HOURS: 12 PM-8 PM. AT MUNICIPAL DOCKS, SOUTH NEW RIVER DR. (REGN'L). JOE SCHABO, COORDINATOR; MARINE INDUSTRIES ASSOCIATION; 411 SW 31ST AVE; FT LAUDERDALE, FL 33302. (#105355-1).

JULY 4, '76. BCC'S JULY 4TH CELEBRATION. FESTIVAL AT FT LAUDERDALE. (LOCAL). ROY A CHURCH, CHM; BROWARD COMMUNITY COLLEGE BICENTENNIAL COMMITTEE; 1000 COCONUT BLVD; POMPANO, FL 33066. (#102509-1).

JULY 4, '76. JULY 4TH BOAT PARADE & SUNRISE RELIGIOUS SERVICE. 250 PRIVATE YACHTS & BOATS DECORATED WITH BICENTENNIAL THEME WILL PARADE THE LENGTH OF THE COUNTY. AT INTERCOSTAL WATERWAY IN BROWARD COUNTY. (LOCAL). KAYE PEARSON, COORDINATOR; THE BROWARD MINUTEMEN; 528 RIVIERA ISLE; FT LAUDERDALE, FL 33301. (#105352-2).

JULY 4, '76. OLD-FASHIONED FOURTH OF JULY CELEBRATION. THE EVENTS FOR THE DAY INCLUDE A PARADE, PICNIC, ENTERTAINMENT, CONTESTS, AWARDS, BOOTHS, CONCESSIONS & REFRESHMENTS. AT HOLIDAY PARK. (LOCAL). NAN S HUTCHISON, PRES; BROWARD COUNTY WOMENS CHAPTER FREEDOMS FOUNDATION AT VALLEY FORGE; 13 SW 16TH ST; FT LAUDERDALE, FL 30015. (#105355-2).

JULY 4, '76. SALUTE TO AMERICA. A MAMMOTH AERIAL FIREWORKS DISPLAY FROM 10 BARGES ALONG 25 MILE BROWARD COUNTY COASTLINE. U S NAVY, AIR FORCE & BRITISH WILL PARTICIPATE. AN 800 VOICE CHOIR WILL PERFORM WITH LIVE RADIO/TV COVERAGE. AT ATLANTIC OCEAN OFF BROWARD COUNTY BEACHES. (LOCAL). LARRY EDGE, COORD; THE BROWARD MINUTEMEN; 32 E LAS OLAS BLVD; FT LAUDERDALE, FL 33301. (#105352-1).

OCT 1 - 31, '76. 'HENRY MOORE: PRINTS, 1969-1974' - EXHIBITION. AN EXHIBITION OF LITHOGRAPHS AND PRINTS DONE BY THE ARTIST, HENRY MOORE. (LOCAL). MRS JOHN A POPE, COORD; INTERNATIONAL EXHIBITIONS FOUNDATION; 1729 H ST, NW; WASHINGTON, DC 20006. (#108964-1).

DEC 20 - 23, '76. AMERICAN FREEDOM TRAIN DISPLAY DAYS AT FORT LAUDERDALE. THE AMERICAN FREEDOM TRAIN INCLUDES 10 EXHIBIT CARS & 2 SHOW CASE CARS DEPICTING DIFFERENT PHASES OF THE AMERICAN EXPERIENCE. ITS ARRIVAL WILL SERVE AS A CATALYST FOR LOCAL BICENTENNIAL CELEBRATIONS BY PEOPLE THROUGHOUT THIS NATION. (ST-WIDE). SY FREEDMAN, DIR OF P/R; THE AMERICAN FREEDOM TRAIN FOUNDATION; 5205 LEESBURG PIKE, SUITE 800; BAILEY'S XRDS, VA 22041. (#1776-113).

FT MYERS BCH

BICENTENNIAL SCHOLARSHIPS - FL. THE CHAMBER OF COMMERCE WILL AWARD BICENTENNIAL SCHOLARSHIPS TO LOCAL YOUTHS. (LOCAL). K KNAUFF, CHAIRPERSON; CHAMBER OF COMMERCE; SAN CARLOS BLVD; FT MYERS BCH, FL 33931. (#29020).

FT PIERCE

DRAMA PRESENTATION. HISTORICAL OUTDOOR STAGECRAFT COURSE WILL CO-PRODUCE A BICENTENNIAL DRAMA PRESENTATION DEPICTING LOCAL DEVELOPMENT AND THE HISTORY OF FT PIERCE-ST LUCIE COUNTY AND FLORIDA EAST COAST. (LOCAL). MRS ADA C WILLIAMS, DIR; INDIAN RIVER COMMUNITY COLLEGE; 3209 VIRGINIA AVE; FT PIERCE, FL 33450. (#22044-1).

FLORIDA'S FUTURE - EXHIBIT. DISPLAY OF MODELS FOR GROWTH POTENTIAL OF COLLEGE, BUSINESS AND RECREATION AREAS IN THE COLLEGE DISTRICT; INCLUDES COLLEGE MASTER PLAN FOR CAMPUS CIRCA 2000. (LOCAL). REGINALD WOODALL, CHMN; INDIAN RIVER COMMUNITY COLLEGE; 3209 VIRGINIA AVE; FT PIERCE, FL 33450. (#105797-2). **(??).**

PLASTIC BICENTENNIAL SYMBOL PLAQUES. 36' PLASTIC PLAQUE BEARING OFFICIAL BICENTENNIAL SYMBOL ARBA LICENSE NO 76-19-0603. (NAT'L). DAVID STUART, PRESIDENT; WORLD OF PLASTICS, INC; 3206 ENTERPRISE; FT PIERCE, FL 33450. (#21181).

FEB 10 - 14, '76. SPECIAL STUDENT BICENTENNIAL ACTIVITIES. DANCES, INTRAMURAL EVENTS AND POST SEASON INVITATIONAL TOURNAMENT W SPECIAL DECORATIVE EFFECTS TO COMMEMORATE THE BICENTENNIAL. (LOCAL). MS ADELLA GROVE, CHAIRMAN; INDIAN RIVER COMMUNITY COLLEGE; 3209 VIRGINIA AVE; FT PIERCE, FL 33450. (#105797-1).

MAR 1 - JULY 14, '76. DISPLAY OF DOCUMENTS DEPICTING FOUR-COUNTY HISTORY. LIBRARY DISPLAY OF DOCUMENTS AND NEWS ARTICLES DEPICTING HISTORICAL HIGHLIGHTS OF THE FOUR-COUNTY AREA SERVED BY THE COLLEGE, HOURS ON MON - THURS: 8AM-9PM. HOURS ON FRI: 8AM-5PM. AT CHARLES S MILEY LEARNING RESOURCES CTR, INDIAN RIVER COMMUNITY COLL. (LOCAL). DR RUDOLPH WIDMAN, CHMN; INDIAN RIVER COMMUNITY COLLEGE; 3209 VIRGINIA AVE; FT PIERCE, FL 33450. (#105812-1).

JUNE 4 - JULY 31, '76. DISPLAY OF HISTORICAL DOCUMENTS ON U S HISTORICAL EVENTS. DOCUMENTS OF U S HISTORICAL EVENTS: THE DECLARATION OF INDEPENDENCE, BILL OF RIGHTS AND WORLD WAR II ARMISTICE WILL BE ON DISPLAY. (LOCAL). JOHN W MUIR, CHAIRMAN; INDIAN RIVER COMMUNITY COLLEGE; 3209 VIRGINIA AVE; FT PIERCE, FL 33450. (#105816-1).

FT WALTON BCH

SPIRIT OF '76 IN FORT WALTON BEACH, FL. A BRONZE STATUE OF AM WILLARDS FAMOUS STATUE. IDEA DEVELOPED BY HURL-

FT WALTON BCH — CONTINUED

BERT BICENTENNIAL COMMITTEE & PASSED TO FT WALTON BICENTENNIAL COMMITTEE FOR IMPLEMENTATION. (LOCAL). KATE BAGLEY, CHAIRPERSON; FT WALTON BEACH BICENTENNIAL COMMITTEE; CITY HALL; FT WALTON BCH, FL 32548. (#29871).

JAN 5 - 6, '76. UNITED STATES ARMED FORCES BICENTENNIAL CARAVAN. CARAVAN IS COMPOSED OF EXHIBIT VANS FOR EACH MILITARY SERVICE. PROJECT THEME IS 'HISTORY OF THE ARMED FORCES AND THEIR CONTRIBUTIONS TO THE NATION'. AT FORT WALTON BEACH CIVIC CENTER. (LOCAL). CAPT DICK OLIVER USAF; US ARMED FORCES BICENTENNIAL EXHIBIT VANS PROJECT; ADTC/OI; ELGIN AFB, FL 32542. (#1775-416).

GAINESVILLE

ALBERT LAESSLE MEDAL FUND - GAINESVILLE, FL. FUND WILL RAISE MONEY TO PRESERVE A MEDAL DESIGNED & MODELED BY ALBERT LAESSLE IN 1931. COPIES WILL BE OFFERED FOR SALE TO FINANCE DONATIONS OF COPIES OF THE MEDAL TO 14 USA MUSEUMS. (REGN'L). THOMAS M OLMSTED, PAST PRES; GAINESVILLE COIN CLUB/ALBERT LAESSLE MEDAL FUND; PO BOX 13012; GAINESVILLE, FL 32604. (#19637).

AMERICAN HERITAGE DISPLAYS - GAINESVILLE, FL. SANTA FE COMMUNITY COLLEGE WILL ORGANIZE AND PRESENT A SERIES OF COMMUNITY AND EDUCATIONAL DISPLAYS OF AMERICANA: ANTIQUES, PERIOD CLOTHING, GRAPHICS, MOMENTOS, COINS, MEDALS AND PHOTOS. (LOCAL). ROBERT A HAWK, CHAIRMAN; SANTA FE COMMUNITY COLLEGE BICENTENNIAL COMMITTEE; 3000 NE 83RD ST; GAINESVILLE, FL 32601. (#15742).

AMERICAN HISTORY: A SPECIAL PRESENTATION, FL. HISTORICAL STUDIES FACULTY WILL OFFER A UNIQUE SERIES OF AMERICAN HISTORY COURSES THAT PRESENT A TOPICAL EXAMINATION OF THE AMERICAN PAST THROUGH INNOVATIVE MULTI-DISCIPLINARY FORMAT. (LOCAL). ROBERT A HAWK, CHAIRMAN; SANTA FE COMMUNITY COLLEGE BICENTENNIAL COMMITTEE; 3000 NE 83RD ST; GAINESVILLE, FL 32601. (#15743).

THE AMERICAN VETERANS & THE BICENTENNIAL - FL. HISTORY OF VETERANS AFFAIRS POLICY. (LOCAL). MALCOLM RANDALL, PROJ DIRECTOR; VETERANS ADMINISTRATION HOSPITAL; ARCHER RD; GAINESVILLE, FL 32602. (#17910).

BARRIER FREE DESIGN 1976 - GAINESVILLE, FL. SURVEYS OF THE COMMUNITY TO ELIMINATE BARRIERS WHICH PREVENT DISABLED PEOPLE FROM MOVING FREELY ABOUT. (LOCAL). KARL LUNDGREN, PROJ DIRECTOR; GAINESVILLE BICENTENNIAL COMMITTEE; 300 W UNIVERSITY AVE; WINDSOR, FL 32601. (#21116).

BEAUTIFICATION OF OLD CITY PARK - GAINESVILLE, FL. PLANS CALL FOR AN IRRIGATION SYSTEM AND LANDSCAPING. (LOCAL). LE VERN SEARCY, PROJ CHAIRMAN; PILOT CLUB OF GAINESVILLE; 1126 NW 11TH AVE; GAINESVILLE, FL 32601. (#19638).

BICENTENNIAL CALENDAR - UNIV OF FLORIDA. THE CALENDAR REFLECTS AT LEAST ONE BICENTENNIAL ACTIVITY PER MONTH TO BE PRESENTED BY AN INSTITUTE OF FOOD AND AGRICULTURAL SCIENCES UNIT DURING 1976. (LOCAL). A F CRIBBETT, PROJ DIRECTOR; INSTITUTE OF FOOD & AGRICULTURAL SCIENCES; UNIV OF FLORIDA; GAINESVILLE, FL 32611. (#10267).

BICENTENNIAL DISPLAY CABINET, GAINESVILLE, FL. BICENTENNIAL DISPLAY CABINET TO CONTAIN VALUABLE DOCUMENTS AND OTHER MEMORABILIA OF ALACHUA COUNTY IN THE SCHOOL ADMINISTRATION BUILDING. (LOCAL). N J HILL, PROJ DIRECTOR; SCHOOL BOARD OF ALACHUA COUNTY; 1817 E UNIVERSITY AVE; GAINESVILLE, FL 32601. (#21117).

BICENTENNIAL HISTORICAL BOOKS; GAINESVILLE, FL. BOOKS WITH BICENTENNIAL THEME ARE BEING DONATED TO SANTA FE REGIONAL LIBRARY. (LOCAL). MRS B W AMES, PROJ DIRECTOR; AMERICAN ASSOC OF UNIVERSITY WOMEN; 1610 NW 24TH ST; GAINESVILLE, FL 32601. (#17908).

BICENTENNIAL MUSIC PROGRAMMING, UNIV OF FLORIDA. EVERY SOLOIST OR MUSIC GROUP WILL BE URGED TO INCLUDE AT LEAST ONE AMERICAN WORK IN WHATEVER PROGRAM IS PERFORMED. (LOCAL). DR DONALD MCGLOTHLIN, PROFESSOR; UNIV OF FLORIDA DEPT OF MUSIC; UNIV OF FLORIDA; GAINESVILLE, FL 32611. (#10263).

BICENTENNIAL NEWSLETTER - GAINESVILLE, FL. SANTA FE COMMUNITY COLLEGE BICENTENNIAL COMMITTEE TO PUBLISH MONTHLY NEWSLETTER TO CONTAIN CALENDAR OF BICENT EVENTS WITH HISTORICAL ANECDOTES AND INFORMATIONAL BACKGROUND STORIES. (LOCAL). ROBERT A HAWK, CHAIRMAN; SANTA FE COMMUNITY COLLEGE BICENTENNIAL COMMISSION; 3000 NE 83RD ST; GAINESVILLE, FL 32601. (#15740).

CALENDAR OF SPANISH DOCUMENTS, GAINESVILLE, FL. PROJECT IS A CALENDAR OF SPANISH DOCUMENTS IN P K YOUNGE LIBRARY OF FLORIDA HISTORY PERTAINING TO FLORIDA'S 1ST & 2ND SPANISH PERIODS. INFORMATION WILL BE INTERNATIONALLY DISSEMINATED. (INT'L). MS ELIZABETH ALEXANDER, PROJ CHAIRMAN; UNIV OF FLORIDA LIBRARIES; UNIV OF FLORIDA; GAINESVILLE, FL 32611. (#10247).

CALENDAR ON HISTORY AND NOSTALGIA; GAINESVILLE, FL. A 52 WEEK ENGAGEMENT CALENDAR WITH 4 PHOTOGRAPH FOR EACH WEEK DEPICTING A SCENE OF LOCAL BUILDINGS OR SCENES OF LOCAL INTEREST, EITHER HISTORICALLY OR NOSTALGICALLY. (LOCAL). JOYCE ANNE MERRITT, PROJ CHAIRMAN; GAINESVILLE WOMENS CLUB; 2809 W UNIVERSITY AVE; GAINESVILLE, FL 32601. (#17913).

COLLEGE SCHOLARSHIPS - GAINESVILLE, FL. A SCHOLARSHIP WILL BE GIVEN TO A STUDENT AT THE UNIV OF FLORIDA. IT WILL BE NAMED 'THE SPIRIT OF '76'. (LOCAL). CLYDE BOYLES, BICENTENNIAL CHAIRMAN; GAINESVILLE CHARTER CHAPTER-AMERICAN BUSINESS WOMEN'S ASSOC; 308 NW 14TH AVE; GAINESVILLE, FL 32601. (#19639).

DISTRIBUTION OF FOUNDING DOCUMENTS - FL. THE DECLARATION OF INDEPENDENCE & THE BILL OF RIGHTS ARE BEING REPRODUCED SO THAT EVERYONE MAY HAVE A COPY. (LOCAL). VIRGINIA SUE GANN, PRESIDENT; GAINESVILLE BICENTENNIAL VOLUNTEERS, INC; 1105 W UNIVERSITY AVE; GAINESVILLE, FL 32601. (#19337).

DOWNTOWN PLAZA DEVELOPMENT PROJ - GAINESVILLE, FL. DOWNTOWN PLAZA TO FUNCTION AS CENTER OF INTERACTION FOR PERSONNEL IN SURROUNDING AGENCIES. (LOCAL). NORMAN BOWMAN, DIRECTOR; CITY OF GAINESVILLE; PO BOX 490; GAINESVILLE, FL 32602. (#17903).

FLORIDA COLLEGE TEACHERS OF HISTORY ANNUAL MEETING. STRONG BICENTENNIAL EMPHASIS WILL BE GIVEN TO THIS MEETING OF THE FLORIDA COLLEGE TEACHERS OF HISTORY. (ST-WIDE). DR ELDON R TURNER, PROFESSOR; UNIV OF FLORIDA DEPARTMENT OF HISTORY; UNIV OF FLORIDA; GAINESVILLE, FL 32611. (#10266).

'FLORIDA'S LIVING TREASURE' -FILM ON AGRICULTURE. HISTORY OF DEVELOPMENT OF AGRICULTURE TECHNOLOGY & VITAL ROLE TECHNOLOGY HAS PLAYED IN THE DEVELOPMENT OF FLORIDA'S AGRICULTURE. FILM AVAILABLE FOR NATIONWIDE USE. (ST-WIDE). A F CRIBBETT, PROJECT DIRECTOR; INSTITUTE OF FOOD AND AGRICULTURAL SCIENCES; UNIV OF FLORIDA; GAINESVILLE, FL 32611. (#10269).

FLOWERING TREE AND SHRUB CAMPAIGN; GAINESVILLE, FL. CONDUCTING PUBLICITY CAMPAIGN TO MAKE CITIZENS AWARE OF THE PART PLANTING MORE FLOWERING TREES AND SHRUBS IN THEIR OWN YARDS CAN PLAY IN BEAUTIFICATION OF GAINESVILLE. (LOCAL). JAMES B GAHAN, CHAIRMAN; CITY BEAUTIFICATION BOARD; 3845 SW 3RD AVE; GAINESVILLE, FL 32607. (#17905).

GIRL SCOUTS FIRE HYDRANT PAINTING PROJ, FL. GIRL SCOUTS PAINTED FIRE HYDRANTS ALONG CENTRAL ROADS RED WHITE AND BLUE; EACH TROOP DECIDED ON THEIR OWN INDIVIDUAL DESIGN. (LOCAL). KARIN K REDERSEN, PROJ COORDINATOR; GAINESVILLE BICENTENNIAL COMMITTEE & LOCAL GIRL SCOUT TROOPS; 2370 SW ARCHER RD APT 4; GAINESVILLE, FL 32608. (#17646).

GRAND OLD GUARD WEEKEND AT UNIVERSITY OF FLORIDA. GRAND OLD GUARD WEEKEND DURING FOOTBALL SEASON TO HONOR MEMBERS OF THE CLASS OF 1926. (ST-WIDE). JEANETTE BLEVINS, DIRECTOR; DEVELOPMENT AND ALUMNI AFFAIRS; UNIV OF FLORIDA; GAINESVILLE, FL 32611. (#10277).

LAW FOR WOMEN - A SHORT COURSE IN GAINESVILLE, FL. THE PROJECT INVOLVES A SHORT COURSE ABOUT LAW FOR WOMEN; THE TOPICS COVERED WILL INCLUDE WILLS, DIVORCE, WORKING WOMEN AND OWNERSHIP OF PROPERTY. (LOCAL). MRS REID POOLE, CHAIRMAN; UNIVERSITY WOMEN'S CLUB; UNIV OF FLORIDA; GAINESVILLE, FL 32611. (#10249).

LOCAL HISTORY OF MEDICINE - GAINESVILLE, FL. DISPLAY OF DRESSED MANNAKINS IN NURSING COSTUMES OF OLD & NEW, FILM SLIDE SHOW PICTURES & DOCUMENTS SHOWING GROWTH OF LOCAL HOSPITAL. (LOCAL). MRS R H SHARPE, CHAIRMAN; ALACHUA GENERAL HOSPITAL AUX; 605 SW 9TH ST; GAINESVILLE, FL 32601. (#17909).

MEMORIAL PARK AND FREEDOM SHRINE - GAINESVILLE, FL. SANTA FE COMMUNITY COLLEGE MEMORIAL PARK AND FREEDOM SHRINE TO BE CONSTRUCTED; WILL INCLUDE EXTENSIVE LANDSCAPING AND BUILDING OF 'LIBERTY TREE AND FREEDOM OF SPEECH' PODIUM. (LOCAL). ROBERT A HAWK, CHAIRMAN; SANTA FE COMMUNITY COLLEGE BICENTENNIAL COMMITTEE; 3000 NW 83RD ST; GAINESVILLE, FL 32601. (#15739).

MULTI-MEDIA PRODUCTION, UNIV OF FLORIDA. INSTITUTE OF FOOD & AGRICULTURAL SCIENCES EDITORIAL DEPT CREATED A MULTI-MEDIA PRODUCTION & FILM, FOCUSING ON EARLY RESEARCH AND TECHNOLOGY. (ST-WIDE). A F CRIBBETT, PROJ DIRECTOR; INSTITUTE OF FOOD & AGRICULTURAL SCIENCES - EDITORIAL DEPT; UNIV OF FLORIDA; GAINESVILLE, FL 32611. (#10276).

A NEW COURSE AT UNIV OF FLORIDA IN GAINESVILLE. IN COOPERATION WITH THE HISTORY DEPARTMENT, A MEMBER OF THE UNIV HISTORY OF LATIN AMERICA FACULTY WILL OFFER A COURSE IN 1976 TO BE ENTITLED 'TWO CENTURIES OF U S/LATIN AMERICAN RELATIONS. (LOCAL). CAPT RAYMOND J TONER, PROFESSOR; CENTER FOR LATIN AMERICAN STUDIES; UNIV OF FLORIDA; GAINESVILLE, FL 32611. (#10259).

NORTHEAST COMMUNITY CENTER; GAINESVILLE, FL. A COMMUNITY CENTER WITH LEISURE AND RECREATIONAL FACILITIES AND DAY CARE CENTER IS BEING BUILT. (LOCAL). GENE LIDDON, DIRECTOR; CITY OF GAINESVILLE; PO BOX 490; GAINESVILLE, FL 32602. (#17904).

ORAL HISTORY OF EDUCATION; ALACHUA COUNTY, FL. COUNTY RETIRED TEACHERS HAVE RECORDED THE HISTORY OF EDUCATION IN AREA ON CASSETTE TAPES AND PRESENTED THEM TO SANTA FE REGIONAL LIBRARY FOR PUBLIC REFERENCE USE. (LOCAL). GRACE STEVENS & DAPHNE WILLIAMS, CO-CHAIRPERSONS; ALACHUA COUNTY RETIRED TEACHERS ASSOC; 546 NE 6TH AVE; GAINESVILLE, FL 32601. (#17914).

PARADOX OF FREEDOM, AMER HERITAGE PROGRAM - FL. HISTORY & HUMANITIES DEPARTMENTS ARE DEVELOPING A SERIES OF AMERICAN HERITAGE PRESENTATIONS TO BE OFFERED TO INTERESTED GROUPS & SCHOOLS. (LOCAL). ROBERT A HAWK, CHAIRMAN; SANTA FE COMMUNITY COLLEGE BICENTENNIAL COMMITTEE; 3000 NE 83RD ST; GAINESVILLE, FL 32601. (#15738).

PIONEER FARM AT GAINESVILLE, FLORIDA. RECREATION OF THE RURAL LIFESTYLE OF THIS AREA IN THE 1800'S. AN OUTDOOR MUSEUM INCLUDING FARM HOUSES, OUTBUILDINGS, SAWMILL, CANE PRESSES, TOBACCO BARN AND OTHER RELATED OBJECTS. (LOCAL). R A KENDZIOR, CHAIRMAN; ALACHUA COUNTY BICENTENNIAL; PO BOX 12659; GAINESVILLE, FL 32604. (#5143).

POLICE HEADQUARTERS BEAUTIFICATION PROJECT IN FL. PAINTING, PLANTING & CLEAN-UP OF POLICE BUILDING. (LOCAL). B HAROLD FARMER, CITY MANAGER; CITY OF GAINESVILLE; PO BOX 490; GAINESVILLE, FL 32602. (#22836). **ARBA GRANTEE.**

'POWER OF ONE VOTE - YOUR VOTE' - GAINESVILLE, FL. A STATEWIDE PROMOTION IN SHOPPING CENTERS, THROUGH CONTESTS, ESSAYS, POSTERS & POETRY REFLECTING INSTANCES WHERE EITHER ONE VOTE OR A SMALL PERCENTAGE OF VOTES BECAME A DECISIVE FACTOR IN HISTORY. (ST-WIDE). SHARON POLK, CHAIRMAN; FLORIDA STATE MANAGERS & PROMOTION DIRECTORS ASSOC; 2552 1/2 NW 13TH ST; GAINESVILLE, FL 32601. (#24230).

THE PRESIDENT'S MUSIC FESTIVAL IN GAINESVILLE, FL. THE PROJECT INVOLVES SIX MAJOR CONCERTS: THE NEW ORLEANS SYMPHONY ORCHESTRA WILL GUEST FOR 3 PERFORMANCES, ONE IN CONCERT WITH THE COUNTY YOUTH ORCHESTRA AND CHORUS. (LOCAL). DR DONALD MCGLOTHLIN, PROF; UNIV OF FLORIDA DEPT OF MUSIC; UNIV OF FLORIDA; GAINESVILLE, FL 32611. (#10264).

REKINDLE PRIDE IN OUR NATION'S FLAG - FL. THIS PROGRAM IS DESIGNED TO INSPIRE PRIDE IN OUR NATION'S FLAG; PLANS ARE BEING MADE TO ACQUIRE A SUPPLY OF FLAGS WITH BOOKLETS ON THE PROPER USAGE. (LOCAL). VIRGINIA SUE GANN, PRESIDENT; GAINESVILLE BICENTENNIAL VOLUNTEERS, INC; 1105 W UNIVERSITY AVE; GAINESVILLE, FL 32601. (#19336).

RENOVATION OF OLD SAFE - GAINESVILLE, FL. RENOVATION OF THE FIRST SAFE USED BY THE FIRST NATIONAL BANK HERE IN GAINESVILLE; IT WILL BE PLACED ON DISPLAY IN OUR OFFICES. (LOCAL). VIRGINIA SUE GANN, PRESIDENT; GAINESVILLE BICENTENNIAL VOLUNTEERS, INC; 1105 W UNIVERSITY AVE; GAINESVILLE, FL 32602. (#19338).

RENOVATION OF UNIVERSITY FACILITIES, FLORIDA. THE PROJECT INVOLVES COMPLETION OF RENOVATION OF UNIVERSITY AUDITORIUM AND ANDERSON MEMORIAL ORGAN FOR BICENTENNIAL MUSICAL EVENTS. (LOCAL). DR DONALD MCGLOTHLIN, PROFESSOR; UNIV OF FLORIDA DEPARTMENT OF MUSIC; UNIV OF FLORIDA; GAINESVILLE, FL 32611. (#10262).

RURAL MINI-ARTS TOUR - GAINESVILLE, FL. SANTA FE COMMUNITY COLLEGE WILL SPONSOR A RURAL MINI-ARTS TOUR. (LOCAL). ROBERT A HAWK, CHAIRMAN; SANTA FE COMMUNITY COLLEGE BICENTENNIAL COMMITTEE; 3000 NE 83RD ST; GAINESVILLE, FL 32601. (#15741).

SANTA FE COMMUNITY COLLEGE ARTS FESTIVAL. ARTS FESTIVAL TO HAVE OVER 400 EXHIBITORS. ALSO TO INCLUDE A FILM SERIES, DEDICATION OF NEW ART GALLERY, AND DONATION OF AMERICAN GRAPHICS AND FINE ARTS MATERIAL. AT ON CAMPUS. (LOCAL). ROBERT A HAWK, CHMN; SANTA FE COMMUNITY COLLEGE BICENTENNIAL COMMITTEE; 3000 NE 83RD ST; GAINESVILLE, FL 32601. (#102507-1).

SANTA FE COMMUNITY COLLEGE CELEBRATES NATION'S INTERNATIONAL ORIGINS. A CELEBRATION OF ETHNIC & CULTURAL HERITAGE. ONE DAY PROGRAM FEATURING SAMPLES OF COSTUMES, GAMES, MUSIC, DANCE & FOOD FROM VARIOUS ETHNIC/CULTURAL GROUPS REPRESENTED ON CAMPUS. AT ON CAMPUS. (LOCAL). ROBERT A HAWK, CHMN; SANTA FE COMMUNITY COLLEGE BICENTENNIAL COMMITTEE; 3000 NE 83RD ST; GAINESVILLE, FL 32601. (#102507-2). **(??).**

SANTA FE COMMUNITY COLLEGE CHILDREN'S THEATRE. GROUP TO PRESENT UNIQUE SERIES OF CHILDREN'S THEATRE ACTIVITIES TO SCHOOLS AND OTHER LOCAL GROUPS. (LOCAL). ROBERT A HAWK, CHMN; SANTA FE COMMUNITY COLLEGE BICENTENNIAL COMMITTEE; 3000 NE 83RD ST; GAINESVILLE, FL 32601. (#102507-4). **(??).**

SERIES OF PANEL DISCUSSIONS IN GAINESVILLE, FL. THE PROJECT INVOLVES FOUR SESSIONS - HUMANITIES, SOCIOLOGY, BIOLOGICAL SCIENCES AND PHYSICAL SCIENCES; SCIENTISTS WOULD BE INVOLVED IN THIRD CENTURY-TYPE PROGRAMS. (LOCAL). DR ARTHUR FUNK, PROFESSOR; COLLEGE OF ARTS AND SCIENCES; UNIV OF FLORIDA; GAINESVILLE, FL 32611. (#10257).

SPANISH MISSION IN GAINESVILLE, FL. LOCATE EXACT SITE OF SAN FRANCISCO SPANISH MISSION DESTROYED IN 1602; MISSION PART OF CHAIN OF SPANISH MISSION STATIONS FROM ST AUGUSTINE TO PENSACOLA; MISSION TO BE PRESERVED AS NAT'L LANDMARK. (ST-WIDE). REV WILLIAM E SHEA, PROJ CHAIRMAN; HIGHLANDS PRESBYTERIAN CHURCH; 1001 NE 16TH AVE; GAINESVILLE, FL 32601. (#17911).

SPECIAL HISTORY COURSE AT UNIV OF FLORIDA. 'REVOLUTIONARY IDEAS IN AMERICAN CULTURE' - THE COURSE IS CONCERNED WITH REVOLUTIONARY THOUGHT AND ACTION IN THE UNITED STATES (BROADER THAN JUST 18TH CENTURY). (LOCAL). DR ELDON R TURNER, PROFESSOR; DEPARTMENT OF HISTORY; UNIV OF FLORIDA; GAINESVILLE, FL 32611. (#10265).

A SPECIAL ISSUE OF ALUMNI MAGAZINE, UNIV OF FL. A SPECIAL ISSUE OF UNIV OF FLORIDA ALUMNI MAGAZINE FEATURES THE BICENTENNIAL AND HISTORIC EVENTS RELATING TO THE UNIVERSITY. (ST-WIDE). JEANETTE BLEVINS, DIRECTOR; DEVELOPMENT AND ALUMNI AFFAIRS; UNIV OF FLORIDA; GAINESVILLE, FL 32611. (#10255).

THOMAS CENTER RESTORATION AND REHABILITATION - FL. RESTORATION OF 1920'S HOTEL LISTED IN THE NATIONAL REGISTER OF HISTORIC PLACES AS A GOVERNMENT AND CULTURAL CENTER. (LOCAL). R HAROLD FARMER, CITY MANAGER; CITY OF GAINESVILLE; PO BOX 490; GAINESVILLE, FL 32602. (#17912).

GAINESVILLE — CONTINUED

VOTER ALERT IN GAINESVILLE, FL. PROJECT ENTAILS REGISTERING VOTERS, PREPARING & PUBLISHING VOTER'S GUIDE & CITIZEN'S HANDBOOK, PARTICIPATING IN NATURALIZATION CEREMONIES AND OTHER ACTIVITIES. (LOCAL). MRS JOHN K MAHON & MRS WALDO FISHER, CO-CHMN; LEAGUE OF WOMEN VOTERS OF GAINESVILLE; 4129 SW 2ND AVE; GAINESVILLE, FL 32607. (#17906).

4-H CLUB HERITAGE PROJECT, UNIV OF FLORIDA. AT THE ANNUAL 4-H CONGRESS, THE EVENTS INCLUDE HISTORIC SLIDES, HERITAGE SPEAKERS, FASHION REVUE, SHARE-THE-FUN SHOW, BANQUET, ARCHIVE WORKSHOPS, A SHORT COURSE ON CITIZENSHIP & SALE, FREEDOM DOCUMENTS. (ST-WIDE). RUTH MILTON, PROJ DIR; STATE 4-H CLUB & INSTITUTE OF FOOD & AGRICULTURAL SCIENCES; UNIV OF FLORIDA; GAINESVILLE, FL 32611. (#10268).

4-H COMMUNITY PRIDE PROGRAM IN GAINESVILLE, FL. 4-H'ERS FROM 55 COUNTIES WILL PARTICIPATE IN A CLEANUP CAMPAIGN; THE PROJECT INCLUDES PUBLIC LANDSCAPING, ECOLOGY STUDIES, CEMETERY RESTORATIONS, RESTORATION OF HISTORIC BUILDINGS, ETC. (ST-WIDE). RUTH MILTON, CHAIRMAN; 4-H DEPT - INSTITUTE OF FOOD & AGRICULTURAL SCIENCES; UNIV OF FLORIDA; GAINESVILLE, FL 32611. (#10250).

MAR 15 - 17, '75. MEDICAL GUILD ANNUAL ANTIQUE FAIR. MEDICAL GUILD ANNUAL ANTIQUE FAIR IS ORIENTED TO BICENTENNIAL YEAR; PLAN TO INVOLVE BUSINESS COMMUNITY IN MANY DISPLAYS OF ALL VARIETY OF ITEMS BELONGING TO THE PAST. (LOCAL). MRS CHANDLER STETSON JR; MEDICAL GUILD; UNIV OF FLORIDA; GAINESVILLE, FL 32611. (#10248-1).

JULY 28, '75. GIANT BIRTHDAY PARTY AT STATE 4-H CLUB CONGRESS. FAIR, COMPETITION, SEMINAR. (ST-WIDE). RUTH MILTON; STATE 4-H DEPT, INSTITUTE OF FOOD & AGRICULTURAL SCIENCES; UNIV OF FLORIDA; GAINESVILLE, FL 32611. (#10270-505).

JULY 28 - 29, '75. STATE 4-H SHARE THE FUN PROGRAM AT STATE 4-H CONGRESS. FAIR, COMPETITION, SEMINAR. (ST-WIDE). RUTH MILTON; STATE 4-H DEPT, INSTITUTE OF FOOD & AGRICULTURAL SCIENCES; UNIV OF FLORIDA; GAINESVILLE, FL 32611. (#10270-501).

JULY 28 - AUG 1, '75. FASHION REVUE, SHARE-THE-FUN SHOW, BANQUET. CONFERENCE, FESTIVAL, LIVE PERFORMANCE. (ST-WIDE). RUTH MILTON, PROJ DIR; STATE 4-H CLUB & INSTITUTE OF FOOD & AGRICULTURAL SCIENCES; UNIV OF FLORIDA; GAINESVILLE, FL 32611. (#10268-503).

JULY 28 - AUG 1, '75. PATRIOTIC KEYNOTE SPEAKERS AT THE CONGRESS ASSEMBLY MEETING. FAIR, COMPETITION, SEMINAR. (ST-WIDE). RUTH MILTON; STATE 4-H DEPT, INSTITUTE OF FOOD & AGRICULTURAL SCIENCES; UNIV OF FLORIDA; GAINESVILLE, FL 32611. (#10270-503).

JULY 28 - AUG 1, '75. SLIDE PRESENTATION DEPICTING HISTORY OF 4-H IN FLORIDA. AT THE ANNUAL 4-H CONGRESS, THE EVENTS INCLUDE HISTORIC SLIDES, HERITAGE SPEAKERS, FASHION REVUE, SHARE-THE-FUN SHOW, BANQUET, ARCHIVE WORKSHOPS, A SHORT COURSE ON CITIZENSHIP & SALE, FREEDOM DOCUMENTS. (ST-WIDE). RUTH MILTON, PROJ DIR; STATE 4-H CLUB & INSTITUTE OF FOOD & AGRICULTURAL SCIENCES; UNIV OF FLORIDA; GAINESVILLE, FL 32611. (#10268-501).

JULY 28 - AUG 1, '75. SPEAKERS - RELATING TO AMERICAN HERITAGE. CONFERENCE, FESTIVAL, LIVE PERFORMANCE. (ST-WIDE). RUTH MILTON, PROJ DIR; STATE 4-H CLUB & INSTITUTE OF FOOD & AGRICULTURAL SCIENCES; UNIV OF FLORIDA; GAINESVILLE, FL 32611. (#10268-502).

JULY 28 - AUG 1, '75. WORKSHOPS - HOW TO USE ARCHIVES IN LOCAL COMMUNITIES. CONFERENCE, FESTIVAL, LIVE PERFORMANCE. (ST-WIDE). RUTH MILTON, PROJ DIR; STATE 4-H CLUB & INSTITUTE OF FOOD & AGRICULTURAL SCIENCES; UNIV OF FLORIDA; GAINESVILLE, FL 32611. (#10268-504).

JULY 29 - 30, '75. STATE 4-H CLUB FASHION REVUE AT 4-H CLUB CONGRESS. FAIR, COMPETITION, SEMINAR. (ST-WIDE). RUTH MILTON; STATE 4-H DEPT, INSTITUTE OF FOOD & AGRICULTURAL SCIENCES; UNIV OF FLORIDA; GAINESVILLE, FL 32611. (#10270-502).

AUG 30, '75. BANQUET HONORING BICENTENNIAL AT 4-H CONGRESS. FAIR, COMPETITION, SEMINAR. (ST-WIDE). RUTH MILTON; STATE 4-H DEPT, INSTITUTE OF FOOD & AGRICULTURAL SCIENCES; UNIV OF FLORIDA; GAINESVILLE, FL 32611. (#10270-504).

OCT 4 - 5, '75. ROOM OF BICENTENNIAL QUILTS AT 2ND ANNUAL QUILT EXHIBIT. EXHIBIT AT COX'S CARRIAGE HOUSE, 3215 NW 13TH ST. (LOCAL). THOMAS M OLMSTEAD, DIR; GAINESVILLE QUILTING ASSOC; PO BOX 13012; GAINESVILLE, FL 32604. (#200011-30).

OCT 23, '75. INTERNATIONAL WOMEN'S YEAR LUNCHEON. FESTIVAL AT REITZ STUDENT UNION BLDG, UNIV OF FLORIDA CAMPUS, PARKING ADJACENT. (LOCAL). CHARLOTTE A YATES, CHMN; ALTRUSA, AMERICAN ASSOC OF UNIV WOMEN, JR WOMEN'S CLUB; 4929 NW 41ST ST; GAINESVILLE, FL 32601. (#200011-29).

NOV 8, '75 - NOV '76. 'HISTORY BEGINS AT HOME' - MULTIMEDIA PRESENTATION. A MULTIMEDIA PRESENTATION USING SLIDES, ACTING & NARRATION; GIVEN AT SCHOOLS, CLUBS, & COMMUNITY ORGANIZATIONS & COUNTY FAIR. (LOCAL). CAROLYN L HUFTY, DIRECTOR; HARMONY 4-H CLUB/ALACHUA COUNTY EXTENSION SERVICE; RTE 1, BOX 415; NEWBERRY, FL 32669. (#104610-6).

NOV 15, '75. BICENTENNIAL POETRY CONTEST. THE GAINESVILLE BICENTENNIAL STEERING COMMITTEE CONSENTED TO ACT AS JUDGES. THREE WINNERS WILL BE AWARDED PRIZES OF SAVINGS BONDS. (LOCAL). MRS WILLIAM H CLEMENTS; GAINESVILLE JUNIOR WOMAN'S CLUB, ARTS DEPARTMENT; 2223 NW 21ST PL; GAINESVILLE, FL 32605. (#200011-32).

NOV 29 - 30, '75. FRATERNAL ORDER OF POLICE BICENTENNIAL WORLD CHAMPIONSHIP RODEO. COMPETITION, LIVE PERFORMANCE AT CITIZENS FIELD, WALDO RD & NE 8TH AVE. (LOCAL). KATHY MCDONALD, COORD; FRATERNAL ORDER OF POLICE & ALACHUA COUNTY BICENTENNIAL COMMITTEE; 3000 E UNIVERSITY AVE; GAINESVILLE, FL 32601. (#200011-31).

JAN 1 - DEC 31, '76. BICENT FLAG DISPLAY AT ATLANTIC FIRST NATL BANK. PARKING DECK DISPLAY OF 8 FLAGS: BRITISH, FRENCH, SPANISH, USA, CONFEDERATE, FLORIDA, BICENT & BENNINGTON. (LOCAL). L K CANNON, JR, V-PRES; ATLANTIC FIRST NATIONAL BANK OF GAINESVILLE; 104 N MAIN ST; GAINESVILLE, FL 32601. (#107340-1).

JAN 2 - JUNE 30, '76. BLACKS IN THE MILITARY: THE AMERICAN REVOLUTION TO VIETNAM. SEMINAR AT INSTITUTE OF BLACK CULTURE, 1510 NW UNIVERSITY AVE. (LOCAL). WILLIAM SIMMONS, DIRECTOR; INSTITUTE OF BLACK CULTURE; 1510 NW UNIVERSITY AVE; GAINESVILLE, FL 32601. (#104610-5).

JAN 19 - 23, '76. AMERICA THE BEAUTIFUL FLORAL ARRANGEMENTS. EXHIBIT AT FLORIDA STATE MUSEUM, UNIV OF FLORIDA CAMPUS. (LOCAL). MRS JAMES MILAM, CHMN; FOUR SEASONS GARDEN CLUB; 4104 NW 13TH PL; GAINESVILLE, FL 32605. (#200011-35).

JAN 22 - JULY ??, '76. PARTS OF OUR PAST - HISTORICAL DISPLAYS. SERIES OF HISTORICAL DISPLAYS, FEATURING LOCAL, STATE AND NATIONAL OBJECTS, WILL BE EXHIBITED. AT GAINESVILLE CITY HALL, 200 E UNIVERSITY AVE. (LOCAL). HELEN ELLERBE, HISTORIAN; ALACHUA COUNTY HISTORICAL SOCIETY; 918 S W 8TH LANE; GAINESVILLE, FL 32601. (#106040-2).

JAN 23 - 24, '76. 1976 FLORIDA DIVISION LIBERAL ARTS INSTITUTE, NSA. ANNUAL INSTITUTE FOR SECRETARIES SPONSORED BY GAINESVILLE CHAPTER OF THE NATIONAL SECRETARIES ASSOC, INTERNATIONAL. MEMBERS OF NSA AND AREA SECRETARIES ARE INVITED; TOUR OF FLORIDA STATE MUSEUM, ATTENDANCE OF LITTLE THEATRE PERFORMANCE, SPEAKERS AND FILM PRESENTATIONS. AT FLAGLER INN, 1250 W UNIVERSITY AVE. (ST-WIDE). MRS MARGARET V LINDSEY; FLORIDA DIVISION & GAINESVILLE CHAPTER OF THE NSA; 425 N W 79TH DR; GAINESVILLE, FL 32601. (#103470-2).

JAN 24 - 25, '76. DESOTO HISTORICAL TRAIL - ORANGE LAKE TO GAINESVILLE. TOUR AT HIKE FROM ORANGE LAKE TO GAINESVILLE - APPROX 22 MILES. (LOCAL). DOYLE HAYES, SCOUTMASTER; MANATEE COUNTY CITIZENS BICENTENNIAL COMMITTEE; 715 NW 12TH AVE; GAINESVILLE, FL 32601. (#200011-36).

JAN 31 - FEB 1, '76. DESOTO HISTORICAL TRAIL - GAINESVILLE TO UNION CITY. TOUR AT HIKE FROM GAINESVILLE TO UNION COUNTY - APPROX 24 MILES. (LOCAL). DOYLE HAYES, SCOUTMASTER; MANATEE COUNTY CITIZENS BICENTENNIAL COMMITTEE; 715 NW 12TH AVE; GAINESVILLE, FL 32601. (#200011-34).

FEB 13, '76. 'OUR TOWN HAS GROWING PAINS'. LIVE PERFORMANCE AT GAINESVILLE WOMEN'S CLUBHOUSE, W UNIVERSITY AVE. (LOCAL). MARTHA BALLARD CODY, CHMN; GAINESVILLE WOMEN'S CLUB; 1831 NE 7TH TERR; GAINESVILLE, FL 32601. (#103470-1).

FEB 14, '76. BICENTENNIAL DOLL SHOW AND COMPETITION. A CHILD MAY ENTER ONLY ONE DOLL IN COMPETITION WITH OTHER CHILDREN THRU 18 YEARS OF AGE IN ONE OF 12 CATEGORIES INCLUDING 'BEST OF SHOW' AWARD. AT GAINESVILLE MALL, NW 13TH ST. (LOCAL). MRS HAROLD STRINGER, DIR; DOLL-INGS OF GAINESVILLE; 922 NW 36TH DR; GAINESVILLE, FL 32605. (#104610-3).

FEB 15 - MAR 31, '76. UNIVERSITY ART GALLERY EXHIBIT OF LATIN AMERICAN ART & ARTIFACTS. PROJECT INVOLVES ACQUISITION OF LATIN AMERICAN ARTIFACTS REPRESENTING LATIN AMERICAN COUNTRIES & CULTURES; DISPLAYED ON CAMPUS DURING 1976 & OTHER COLLEGES THROUGHOUT SOUTHEASTERN UNITED STATES. ALSO INVOLVES ACQUISITION OF LATIN AMERICAN PHOTOGRAPHS. AT UNIVERSITY GALLERY. (REGN'L). ROY CRAVEN, DIRECTOR; UNIV OF FLORIDA - CENTER FOR LATIN AMERICAN STUDIES; UNIV OF FLORIDA; GAINESVILLE, FL 32611. (#10258-1).

FEB 21, '76. BICENTENNIAL POPS. LIVE PERFORMANCE AT GAINESVILLE WOMEN'S CLUB, 2809 W UNIVERSITY AVE. (LOCAL). JUDITH BRECHNER, CHMN; B'NAI ISRAEL SISTERHOOD; 415D NW 39TH RD; GAINESVILLE, FL 32607. (#200011-37).

FEB 28, '76. OLD-FASHIONED POLITICAL RALLY. THERE WILL ALSO BE A CHICKEN BAR-B-QUE. AT ALACHUA COUNTY FAIRGROUNDS. (LOCAL). BUD IRBY, CHAIRMAN; GAINESVILLE JAYCEES; 2913 NW 45TH AVE; GAINESVILLE, FL 32605. (#104610-4).

MAR 1 - 2, '76. ANNUAL CONFERENCE OF CENTER FOR LATIN AMERICAN STUDIES. THE 26TH ANNUAL CONFERENCE OF THE CENTER FOR LATIN AMERICAN STUDIES WILL BE ON THE THEME 'THE FLORIDA BORDERLANDS DURING THE AGE OF THE AMERICAN REVOLUTION'. AT J WAYNE REITZ UNION. (INT'L). DR TERRY L MCCOY; CENTER FOR LATIN AMERICAN STUDIES; 319 LGH UNIV OF FLORIDA; GAINESVILLE, FL 32611. (#10260-1).

MAR 1 - 31, '76. ARTS & CRAFTS SHOW. JUDGES WILL BE INDIVIDUALS FROM THE COMMUNITY WHO ARE RECOGNIZED FOR THEIR CONTRIBUTIONS IN THE FIELD OF ARTS & CRAFTS. AT VA HOSPITAL AUDITORIUM; PARKING IN VISITORS AREA. (LOCAL). METTA L BAXTER, COORD; V A HOSPITAL BICENTENNIAL COMMITTEE; GAINESVILLE, FL 32602. (#200011-38).

MAR 1 - 31, '76. FLAGS OVER FLORIDA FLOWN AT 1ST FLORIDA SAVINGS & LOAN. EXHIBIT OF 6 FLAGS THAT HAVE FLOWN OVER FLORIDA FROM 1513-1976. AT MAIN OFFICE, 515 N MAIN ST, FREE PARKING. (LOCAL). CAROLYN F DURST, DIR; FIRST FLORIDA SAVINGS AND LOAN ASSOC; PO BOX 968, 515 N MAIN ST; GAINESVILLE, FL 32602. (#106040-1).

MAR 6, '76. SPRING PILGRIMAGE - TO RAISE INTEREST IN HISTORIC PRESERVATION. A BICENTENNIAL SPRING PILGRIMAGE AND LUMINAIRE TO RAISE INTEREST IN HISTORIC PRESERVATION AND FORM THE W.R. THOMAS ENDOWMENT FOR EDUCATIONAL AND BEAUTIFICATION PROJECTS. AT THOMAS CENTER, CHURCHES, AND HOMES. (LOCAL). MRS FRANK E MALONEY, CHMN; GAINSVILLE GARDEN CLUB/WOMEN'S CLUB/HISTORIC GAIN. INC.; 1823 N W 10TH AVE; GAINESVILLE, FL 32605. (#103470-4).

MAR 6 - 21, '76. PRESIDENTS FIFTH ANNUAL FESTIVAL OF MUSIC. WORLD RENOWNED GUEST ARTISTS APPEAR WITH UNIVERSITY MUSIC ENSEMBLES ORCHESTRA. AT REITZ UNION BALLROOM. (LOCAL). DONALD MCGLOTHLIN, CHMN; UNIVERSITY OF FLORIDA; UNIV OF FLORIDA, DEPT OF MUSIC; GAINESVILLE, FL 32601. (#102498-1).

MAR 21, '76. MARINE CORPS PARADE. CEREMONY, PARADE AT CITIZEN FIELD. (LOCAL). CECIL D COX, SR, PROJ DIR; CITY OF GAINESVILLE & VETERANS OF FOREIGN WAR, PACT 2811; 1514 NE 8TH ST; GAINESVILLE, FL 32601. (#105122-1).

MAR 26 - 27, '76. BICENTENNIAL RELAYS. COMPETITION AT UNIV OF FLORIDA TRACK - SE CORNER, SW 2ND AVE & 23RD ST. (LOCAL). JIMMY CARNES, PROJ DIR; UNIV OF FLORIDA ATHLETIC DEPT; GAINESVILLE, FL 32601. (#101002-1).

APR 3 - 4, '76. SPRING ARTS FESTIVAL. FESTIVAL AT NE 1ST ST. (LOCAL). KAREN BEACH, DIRECTOR; SANTA FE COMMUNITY COLLEGE; PO BOX 1187; GAINESVILLE, FL 32602. (#103470-3).

APR 9 - 10, '76. 1976 FLORIDA COLLEGE TEACHERS OF HISTORY CONFERENCE. CONFERENCE GUEST SPEAKERS WILL BE: DR GEORGE E MOWRY, FORMER PRES OF THE ORGANIZATION OF AMER HISTORIANS, FRI AT 8:00 PM; BILL ADAMS, DIR OF STATE BICENT, SAT MORNING AND FORMER GOV LEROY COLLINS AT 1:00 PM LUNCHEON; SERIES OF SESSIONS ON BLACKS, WOMEN AND CIVIL LIBERTIES. AT FLAGLER INN, UNIVERSITY AVE AND 13TH ST. (ST-WIDE). PROF DAVID COLBURN, DIR; FLORIDA COLLEGE TEACHERS OF HISTORY; UNIV OF FLORIDA-DEPT OF SOC SCI; GAINESVILLE, FL 32611. (#104780-3).

APR 25, '76. VETERANS' ADMINISTRATION EMPLOYEES BICENTENNIAL PICNIC AND PLAYDAY. FESTIVAL AT US ARMY RESERVE CENTER GROUNDS, 1125 NE 8TH AVE. (LOCAL). METTA L BAXTER, CHMN; VA HOSPITAL BICENTENNIAL COMMITTEE; GAINESVILLE, FL 32669. (#200011-39).

MAY 13, '76. CONVOCATION & SPECIAL FACULTY AWARD. IFAS STUDENT AGRICULTURAL SCHOLARSHIP & LEADERSHIP CONVOCATION, DEDICATED TO BICENT, TO HONOR AN OUTSTANDING PAST FACULTY MEMBER. A MARKER WILL BE PLACED IN LANDSCAPED AREA OF AGRICULTURAL COMPLEX. AT JWREITZ UNION, UNIV OF FLORIDA. (ST-WIDE). A F CRIBBETT; INSTITUTE OF FOOD & AGRICULTURAL SCIENCES-STUDENT COUNCIL; UNIV OF FLORIDA; GAINESVILLE, FL 32611. (#10271-1).

MAY 14, '76. STUDENT'S ARTS AND CRAFTS EXHIBITION. EXHIBIT AT EAST SIDE HIGH MALL AREA. (LOCAL). MIKE OYENARTE, TEACHER; EAST SIDE HIGH SCHOOL; 1245 SE 45 TERRACE; GAINESVILLE, FL 32601. (#106040-4).

MAY 21, '76. MINI-ARTS FESTIVAL. EXHIBIT, FESTIVAL. (LOCAL). BETTY J GROSS, DIRECTOR; SMOKEY BEAR PARK PRESCHOOL AND KINDERGARTEN; 2500 NE 15TH ST; GAINESVILLE, FL 32601. (#200011-40).

MAY 21 - 22, '76. ANNUAL EXHIBIT OF SCHOOL ART. EXHIBIT AT GAINESVILLE MALL. (LOCAL). THADDEUS S GRIMES, DIR; ALACHUA COUNTY ART TEACHERS ASSOC; 1817 E UNIVERSITY AVE; GAINESVILLE, FL 32601. (#200011-41).

JUNE 4, '76. POETRY READING. FESTIVAL, LIVE PERFORMANCE AT FIRST ALLIANCE MISSIONARY CHURCH, 2500 NE 15TH ST. (LOCAL). BETTY J GROSS, DIR; GAINESVILLE POETRY ASSOC; 3502 NW 10TH AVE; GAINESVILLE, FL 32605. (#200011-42).

JUNE 11 - AUG 20, '76. HAPPY BIRTHDAY TO U S - SUMMER READING PROGRAM. FESTIVAL AT SANTA FE REGIONAL LIBRARY. (LOCAL). LINDA BOYLES, LIBRARIAN; SANTA FE REGIONAL LIBRARY; 222 E UNIVERSITY AVE; GAINESVILLE, FL 32601. (#106798-1).

JUNE 14 - JULY 9, '76. HISTORIC FLAGS OF THE EARLY UNITED STATES. EXHIBIT AT MAIN OFFICE, 515 N MAIN ST, FREE PARKING. (LOCAL). CAROLYN F DURST, DIR; FIRST FLORIDA SAVINGS AND LOAN ASSOC; PO BOX 968, 515 N MAIN ST; GAINESVILLE, FL 32608. (#106040-3).

JULY 3, '76. FREEDOM PARADE FEATURING 100 UNITS. PARADE AT WEST UNIVERSITY AVE. (LOCAL). RICHARD DUDLEY, DIRECTOR; ALACHUA COUNTY BICENTENNIAL COMMITTEE; PO BOX 12659; GAINESVILLE, FL 32604. (#104780-2).

JULY 4, '76. ALACHUA COUNTY BICENTENNIAL BEARD GROWING CONTEST. THIS CONTEST IS OPEN TO RESIDENTS OF ALACHUA COUNTY ONLY; PRIZES WILL BE AWARDED FOR 1ST, 2ND AND 3RD PLACE IN EACH CATEGORY. AT FAIRGROUNDS, NE 39TH AVE. (LOCAL). LT GENE WATSON, PROJ CHMN; FRATERNAL ORDER OF POLICE, GATOR LODGE 67; UNIV POLICE DEPT, UNIV OF FL; GAINESVILLE, FL 32601. (#105122-2).

JULY 4, '76. CENTENARIAN CELEBRATION. AWARDS WILL BE PRESENTED IN RECOGNITION OF RESIDENTS AGE 100 OR OVER. (LOCAL). GRACE KNIGHT, COORDINATOR; GAINESVILLE AMER ASSOC OF RETIRED PERSONS #363; 23 NW 20TH DR; GAINESVILLE, FL 32603. (#104610-2).

JULY 4, '76. OLE FASHIONED FOURTH OF JULY CELEBRATION. FESTIVAL WILL FEATURE GAMES, COMPETITIONS, EXHIBITS, ENTERTAINMENT, DANCING AND FOOD. AT ALACHUA COUNTY

GAINESVILLE — CONTINUED

FAIRGROUNDS, N WALDO ROAD. (LOCAL). MARY ANN GREEN, DIRECTOR; ALACHUA COUNTY BICENTENNIAL COMMITTEE; PO BOX 12659; GAINESVILLE, FL 32604. (#104780-1).

JULY 26 - 27, '76. STATE 4-H SHARE THE FUN PROGRAM AT STATE 4-H CONGRESS. FAIR, COMPETITION, SEMINAR. (ST-WIDE). RUTH MILTON; STATE 4-H DEPT, INSTITUTE OF FOOD & AGRICULTURAL SCIENCES; UNIV OF FLORIDA; GAINESVILLE, FL 32611. (#10270-507).

JULY 26 - 30, '76. PATRIOTIC KEYNOTE SPEAKERS AT THE CONGRESS ASSEMBLY MEETING. FAIR, COMPETITION, SEMINAR. (ST-WIDE). RUTH MILTON; STATE 4-H DEPT, INSTITUTE OF FOOD & AGRICULTURAL SCIENCES; UNIV OF FLORIDA; GAINESVILLE, FL 32611. (#10270-509).

JULY 28, '76. STATE 4-H CLUB FASHION REVUE AT 4-H CLUB CONGRESS. FAIR, COMPETITION, SEMINAR. (ST-WIDE). RUTH MILTON; STATE 4-H DEPT, INSTITUTE OF FOOD & AGRICULTURAL SCIENCES; UNIV OF FLORIDA; GAINESVILLE, FL 32611. (#10270-508).

NOV '76. SANTA FE COMMUNITY COLLEGE FESTIVAL OF THE PERFORMING ARTS. A WIDE SELECTION OF DRAMATIC AND MUSICAL PERFORMANCES BY COLLEGE & COMMUNITY GROUPS AND INDIVIDUALS. AT ON CAMPUS. (LOCAL). ROBERT A HAWK, CHMN; SANTA FE COMMUNITY COLLEGE BICENTENNIAL COMMITTEE; 3000 NE 83RD ST; GAINESVILLE, FL 32601. (#102507-3).

DEC 15 - 19, '76. ENERGY AWARENESS WEEK. DISPLAY OF HAND GENERATOR, MODEL OF NUCLEAR PLANT; INCREASE PUBLIC AWARENESS OF ENERGY PROBLEMS, PRESENT THE OUTLOOK FOR THE FUTURE, AND PRESENT PROBLEMS IN PRODUCING ADEQUATE ENERGY FOR TOMORROW'S NEEDS. AT GAINESVILLE MALL. (LOCAL). PAULA JONES, COORD; REGIONAL UTILITIES BOARD; 200 E UNIV, PO BOX 490; GAINESVILLE, FL 32601. (#200011-33).

GOULDS

'WE ARE A COMPOSITE OF THEM ALL' - GOULDS, FL. A YEAR-LONG FESTIVAL WHERE PUPILS WILL PARTICIPATE IN A SIGNIFICANT EXPERIENCE IN WHICH THEY WILL REALIZE THEY ARE CITIZENS & THAT ALTERNATE LIFE STYLES TO THOSE THEY OBSERVE DAILY ARE POSSIBLE. (LOCAL). ELIZABETH A COLLINS, PRINCIPAL; PINE VILLA ELEMENTARY SCHOOL; 21799 S W 117 COURT; GOULDS, FL 33141. (#17178).

GRANT

FEB 15 - 16, '76. ANNUAL SEAFOOD FESTIVAL. ANNUAL SEAFOOD FESTIVAL IN GRANT, FLORIDA. AN ANNUAL CELEBRATION OF THE BOUNTY OF THE OCEAN, OVER THREE THOUSAND MEALS WILL BE SERVED IN TWO DAYS. (LOCAL). RONNIE SENNE, CHAIRMAN; GRANT SEAFOOD ASSOC; GRANT, FL 32949. (#7698-501).

GREEN CV SPG

BEARD GROWING CONTEST. OFFICERS OF LAW ENFORCEMENT AGENCIES OF CLAY COUNTY TO PARTICIPATE; PERMITS TO SHAVE OR GROW A BEARD TO BE SOLD TO MEMBERS WITH PROCEEDS GOING TO COUNTY BICENTENNIAL STEERING COMMITTEE. (LOCAL). PAUL R BESELER, JR, TREAS; FRATERNAL ORDER OF POLICE - LODGE 104; BOX 1331; GREEN CV SPG, FL 32043. (#106743-4).

BEAUTIFICATION AT CHAMBER OF COMMERCE BLDG. SHRUBBERY TO BE PLANTED AROUND THE CLAY COUNTY CHAMBER OF COMMERCE BUILDING. (LOCAL). MRS MYRTICE TRUETT, PRESIDENT; JAPONICA GARDEN CLUB; SUSAN DR; GREEN CV SPG, FL 32043. (#24867).

CIVIC BEAUTIFICATION - GREEN COVE SPRINGS, FL. FIRST BEAUTIFICATION PROJECT INVOLVES LANDSCAPING A TRIANGLE OF LAND AT INTERSECTION OF HWY 17 AND PALMETTO AVE. (LOCAL). MRS JOSEPH MCKENZIE, PRESIDENT; VILLAGE IMPROVEMENT ASSOC; PO BOX 696; GREEN CV SPG, FL 32043. (#24527).

CLAY COUNTY BOOKLET; GREEN COVE SPRINGS, FL. AN INFORMATIVE BOOKLET ABOUT THE CLAY COUNTY AREA FOR USE BY VISITORS, RESIDENTS AND BUSINESSES IN THE COUNTY. (LOCAL). VICTOR ZIEGLER, PRESIDENT; CLAY COUNTY CHAMBER OF COMMERCE; HIGHWAY 17; GREEN CV SPG, FL 32043. (#18015).

COURTHOUSE & MUSEUM GROUNDS BEAUTIFICATION, FL. OLD COURTHOUSE AND HISTORIC MUSEUM GROUNDS WILL HAVE SHRUBS TRIMMED AS WELL AS NEW ONES ADDED; BEDS OF RED, WHITE & BLUE PETUNIAS WILL BE PLANTED AROUND THE OLD COURTHOUSE. (LOCAL). MRS RALPH MONTE, PRESIDENT; FOUNDERS GARDEN CLUB; PO BOX 1423; GREEN CV SPG, FL 32043. (#24868).

FLAG DONATIONS - GREEN COVE SPRINGS, FL. TWO FLAGS, THE U S FLAG AND THE FLORIDA STATE FLAG, HAVE BEEN GIVEN TO THE CLAY COUNTY PUBLIC LIBRARY IN GREEN COVE SPRINGS. (LOCAL). MRS JOSEPH MCKENZIE, PRESIDENT; VILLAGE IMPROVEMENT ASSOC; PO BOX 696; GREEN CV SPG, FL 32043. (#24528).

HANDMADE QUILT - GREEN COVE SPRINGS, FL. A QUILT WILL BE CONSTRUCTED OF SQUARES MADE BY INDIVIDUAL MEMBERS OF THE CLUB; RED, WHITE & BLUE COLORS; QUILT WILL BE GIVEN TO CLAY COUNTY HISTORICAL MUSEUM'S PERMANENT COLLECTION. (LOCAL). MRS JESSE GODBOLD, PRESIDENT; JUNIOR WOMEN'S CLUB OF GREEN COVE SPRINGS; 205 PARK ST; GREEN CV SPG, FL 32043. (#24181).

HERITAGE STUDY PROJECT - GREEN COVE SPRINGS, FL. THE 6 WEEK COMMUNITY STUDY COURSE WILL FOCUS ON VARIOUS ERAS OF LOCAL, STATE & NATIONAL HISTORY WITH DISCUSSIONS IN OPEN PUBLIC FORUM; LIBRARY MATERIALS TO BE UTILIZED. (LOCAL). JIM GAINEY, CHAIRMAN; GREEN COVE SPRINGS BICENTENNIAL COMMITTEE & CITY OF GREEN CV SPG; CITY HALL, 229 E WALNUT ST; GREEN CV SPG, FL 32043. (#24863).

HISTORY OF CLAY COUNTY, GREEN COVE SPRINGS, FL. AN IN-DEPTH WORK ON THE HISTORY OF CLAY COUNTY & ITS PEOPLE WILL BE WRITTEN BY DR FRED BLAKEY. THE WORK IS COMMISSIONED BY THE COUNTY BOARD OF COMMISSIONERS. (LOCAL). THOMAS D RYAN, JR, CHAIRMAN; CLAY COUNTY HISTORICAL COMMISSION; 2000 CORPORATE SQUARE; JACKSONVILLE, FL 32216. (#18014).

INTERVIEWS WITH SENIOR CITIZENS, GREEN CV SPG, FL. INTERVIEWS WITH LONG-ESTABLISHED CITIZENS OF THE COMMUNITY WILL BE TAPED IN AN EFFORT TO CAPTURE THEIR RECOLLECTIONS OF OUR HISTORIC PAST; TAPES WILL BE PERMANENTLY STORED IN CLAY COUNTY LIBRARY. (LOCAL). JIM GAINEY, CHAIRMAN; GREEN COVE SPRINGS BICENTENNIAL COMMITTEE & CITY OF GREEN CV SPG; CITY HALL, 229 E WALNUT ST; GREEN CV SPG, FL 32043. (#24869).

LANDSCAPING OF HIGHWAY MEDIAN - GREEN CV SPG, FL. LANDSCAPING OF THE HIGHWAY MEDIAN NORTH OF WAGER'S STANDARD STATION AT THE INTERSECTION OF ORANGE & MAGNOLIA. (LOCAL). MRS JESSE GODBOLD, PRESIDENT; JUNIOR WOMEN'S CLUB OF GREEN COVE SPRINGS; 205 PARK ST; GREEN CV SPG, FL 32043. (#24182).

OLD NEWSPAPER AND PHOTO REPRINTS, FL. OLD NEWS STORIES & PHOTOS REPRINTED AT REGULAR INTERVALS IN CURRENT EDITIONS OF SPONSORING NEWSPAPERS. (LOCAL). JAMES WILSON, PUBLISHER; CLAY COUNTY CRESCENT; 806 W WALNUT ST; GREEN CV SPG, FL 32043. (#18013).

PRE-DELINQUENT RETARDED WORKSHOP, FL. A NEWLY ESTABLISHED RESIDENTIAL TREATMENT PROGRAM FOR RETARDED BOYS, 12-16 YEARS OF AGE, TO TRAIN THEM SOCIALLY & OCCUPATIONALLY. 'CHANCE': CHILDREN HAVE A NEED FOR CREATIVE EDUCATION. (LOCAL). MISS TERI MEEHAN, C.H.A.N.C.E. DIR; CLAY COUNTY ASSOC FOR THE RETARDED; PO BOX 1041; GREEN CV SPG, FL 32043. (#18011).

RESTORATION & PRESERVATION OF CLUBHOUSE - FL. A 10-YEAR PROGRAM DEDICATED TO BICENTENNIAL FOR COMPLETE RENOVATION OF CLUB'S QUARTERS, PLUS PRESERVATION OF HISTORIC CLUB DOCUMENTS DATING BACK TO LATE 1800'S, AS WELL AS PRESERVING ALL MEMORABILIA. (LOCAL). MRS T R ROSAKRANSE, CHAIRMAN; VILLAGE IMPROVEMENT ASSOC; HIBERNIA ROUTE; GRN COVE SPG, FL 32043. (#18935).

WORK ACTIVITIES PROGRAM - GREEN COVE SPRINGS, FL. A NEWLY ESTABLISHED WORK-ACTIVITIES PROGRAM FOR RETARDED PERSONS, AGED 18 YRS & OLDER. ACTIVITIES INCLUDE: COOKING, HORTICULTURE, WOODEN PLANTER ASSEMBLY, BOWLING & SUMMER CAMPING PROGRAM. (LOCAL). MISS NANCY KEATING, PROJ DIRECTOR; CLAY COUNTY ASSOC FOR THE RETARDED; 1107 MIDDLEBURG AVE; GREEN CV SPG, FL 32043. (#18010).

DEC 1 - 5, '75. PRESENTATION OF BICENTENNIAL ALMANACS. BICENTENNIAL ALMANACS WILL BE PRESENTED TO CUAY COUNTY PUBLIC LIBRARY AND EACH SCHOOL LIBRARY IN GREEN COVE SPRINGS. (LOCAL). MRS JESSE GODBOLD, PRES; JUNIOR WOMEN'S CLUB OF GREEN COVE SPRINGS; 205 PARK ST; GREEN CV SPG, FL 32043. (#106746-1).

JAN 31, '76. PARADE AND CEREMONY - SCROLL PRESENTATIONS. AT THE END OF PARADE IN A CEREMONY AT THE MUSEUM, WOMEN'S CLUBS FROM KEYSTONE & GREEN COVE SPRINGS WILL PRESENT THEIR SIGNED SCROLLS TO 4-H MEMBERS FOR LATER DELIVERY TO THE FLORIDA WAGON TRAIN; HORSEMEN WILL ACT AS OUTRIDERS FOR PARADE & WAGON TRAIN. AT CLAY CO HISTORICAL MUSEUM, WALNUT ST. (LOCAL). JESSE GODBOLD, CHAIRMAN; BLACK CREEK HORSEMEN'S ASSOC/GREEN COVE SPRINGS WOMENS CLUB; 205 PARK ST; GRN COVE SPG, FL 32043. (#104898-1).

MAR 1 - APR 5, '76. ESSAY CONTEST. ESSAY CONTEST FOR CLAY COUNTY SCHOOL CHILDREN; ESSAYS MUST DEAL WITH AMERICAN HERITAGE; $100.00 TOTAL PRIZE MONEY. (LOCAL). JAMES WILSON, PUBLISHER; CLAY COUNTY CRESCENT; 806 W WALNUT ST; GRN COVE SPG, FL 32043. (#103517-30).

JULY 3, '76. 'FAMILY FROLICS'. A FULL DAY'S PROGRAM INCLUDING PARADE, BEARD CONTEST, LADIES' DRESS CONTEST, CHILDREN'S ACTIVITIES, SQUARE DANCE AND FIREWORKS. AT SPRING PARK, ONE BLOCK EAST OF HWY 17 BEHIND CITY HALL. (LOCAL). JIM GAINEY, CHAIRMAN; CITY OF GREEN COVE SPRINGS, GREEN COVE SPRINGS BICENT COMMITTEE; 299 E WALNUT ST; GREEN CV SPG, FL 32043. (#107622-1).

GULF BREEZE

SYMPOSIUM ON AMERICAN FAMILY IN GULF BREEZE, FL. WORKSHOP SPONSORED BY FACULTY OF HISTORY, SOCIOLOGY AND PSYCHOLOGY. (LOCAL). JAMES MCGOVERN, CHAIRMAN; THE UNIV OF WEST FLORIDA BICENTENNIAL COMMITTEE; 2721 BAY ST; GULF BREEZE, FL 32561. (#11676).

JUNE 1 - AUG 30, '75. PGMS ON INFLUENCES OF GERMANS, FRENCH, BRITISH & SPANISH IN FLORIDA. THESE TALKS WILL COVER THE INFLUENCES OF THE VARIOUS INHABITANTS THROUGHOUT FLORIDA'S HISTORY AND THE ROLE OF THESE INFLUENCES IN THE HISTORY OF THE UNITED STATES AS WELL AS FLORIDA. AT CAMPGROUND #4, CEDAR GROVE, KINGS CANYON NP. (REGN'L). SUPT, GULF ISLANDS NS; NATIONAL PARK SERVICE; P.O. BOX 100; GULF BREEZE, FL 32561. (#6730-43).

MAY 1 - DEC 31, '76. ART CONTEST--AMERICA'S ENVIRONMENT IN 3RD CENTURY--GULF IS NS. MANY AREAS OF THE NATL PARK SYSTEM ARE DEVELOPING PROGRAMS FOR LOCAL SCHOOL GROUPS WHICH WILL GIVE SUCH GROUPS A BETTER UNDERSTANDING OF THE ROLE OF THE PARK & THE NPS IN AMERICA'S HISTORY. IN CONJUNCTION WITH LOCAL SCHOOL SYSTEMS. AT AT PARK HEADQUARTERS AT FT PICKENS, FL.. (LOCAL). SUPT, GULF ISLANDS NS; NATIONAL PARK SERVICE; P.O. BOX 100; GULF BREEZE, FL 32561. (#6726-1).

MAY 1 - DEC 31, '76. GULF ISLANDS NS LOCAL HISTORY PHOTO CONTEST. THIS PHOTO CONTEST'S AIM IS TO INVOLVE THE COMMUNITY IN REDISCOVERING PENSACOLA'S PAST. AFTER CONTEST, EXHIBIT WILL BE HELD WITHIN GULF ISLANDS NATL SEASHORE. AT AT HEADQUARTERS AT FT PICKENS, FL. (LOCAL). SUPT GULF ISLANDS NS; NATIONAL PARK SERVICE; P.O. BOX 100; GULF BREEZE, FL 32561. (#6728-16).

JUNE 1 - AUG 30, '76. PGMS ON INFLUENCES OF GERMANS, FRENCH, BRITISH & SPANISH IN FLORIDA. THESE TALKS WILL COVER THE INFLUENCES OF THE VARIOUS INHABITANTS THROUGHOUT FLORIDA'S HISTORY AND THE ROLE OF THESE INFLUENCES IN THE HISTORY OF THE UNITED STATES AS WELL AS FLORIDA. AT CAMPGROUND #4, CEDAR GROVE, KINGS CANYON NP. (REGN'L). SUPT, GULF ISLANDS NS; NATIONAL PARK SERVICE; P.O. BOX 100; GULF BREEZE, FL 32561. (#6730-543).

GULFPORT

BOOK, HISTORY OF GULFPORT - FL. HISTORY AND PICTURES FROM BEGINNING OF AREA UNTIL PRESENT TIME. (LOCAL). MRS J F JOHNSON, CHAIRMAN; CITY OF GULFPORT BICENTENNIAL COMMITTEE; 5012 17TH AVE SO; GULFPORT, FL 33707. (#32116).

JAN 11, '76. GULFPORT'S BICENTENNIAL KICKOFF PARADE, PROGRAM & BAND CONCERT. AMONG THE ACTIVITIES SCHEDULED WERE A PARADE, PRESENTATION OF BICENT COMMUNITY CERTIFICATE, BAND CONCERT BY BOCA CIEGA HIGH SCHOOL BAND, AND PRESENTATION OF A COIN COLLECTION TO THE LIBRARY. AT THROUGHOUT THE CITY OF GULFPORT. (LOCAL). MRS J F JOHNSON; CITY OF GULFPORT BICENTENNIAL COMMITTEE; 5012 17TH AVE S; GULFPORT, FL 33707. (#200011-299).

FEB 22, '76. MT VERNONAIRES PRESENTS A WASHINGTON BIRTHDAY CHORAL CONCERT. LIVE PERFORMANCE AT COMMUNITY CENTER, 5730 SHORE BLVD S. (LOCAL). MRS J F JOHNSON; CITY OF GULFPORT BICENTENNIAL COMMITTEE; 5012 17TH AVE S; GULFPORT, FL 33707. (#200011-301).

MAR 7, '76. DEDICATION OF JAY P CLYMER CITY PARK. CITY OF GULFPORT DEVELOPED THE PARK & NAMED IT FOR THE MAYOR. CIVIC CLUBS & ORGANIZATIONS DONATED MANY THINGS FOR THE PARK--FLAG POLE & FLAG, SUNDIAL, TREES & SHRUBS, WEATHERVANE, ETC. DISSTON MIDDLE SCHOOL'S BAND PROVIDED MUSIC DURING THE CEREMONIES. AT BEACH BLVD, BETWEEN 22ND & 23RD AVES S. (LOCAL). MRS J F JOHNSON; CITY OF GULFPORT; 5012 17TH AVE S; GULFPORT, FL 33707. (#200011-300).

JULY 4, '76. JULY 4TH FESTIVAL. AMONG THE DAY'S MANY ACTIVITIES WERE A BOAT PARADE WITH PRIZES & FUN (6:30 PM) AND FIREWORKS (9 PM). AT GULFPORT BEACH. (LOCAL). MRS J F JOHNSON, CHMN; CITY OF GULFPORT BICENTENNIAL COMMITTEE; 5012 17TH AVE S; GULFPORT, FL 33707. (#200011-284).

SEPT 6, '76. LABOR DAY FESTIVITIES. AMONG THE ACTIVITIES: FISH FRY (12-2 PM); BEAUTY PAGEANT (2-4 PM), GAMES FOR CHILDREN ALL AFTERNOON; EVENING FISH FRY (4-6 PM); DEDICATION OF L T MCCARTHY FIRE ADMIN BLDG (10 AM). (LOCAL). MRS J F JOHNSON, CHMN; CITY OF GULFPORT & GULFPORT LIONS CLUB; 5012 17TH AVE S; GULFPORT, FL 33707. (#200011-285).

NOV 5 - 7, '76. ANTIQUE CAR SHOW AND ARTS & CRAFTS FAIR. ANTIQUE CARS (100), ARTS & CRAFTS, BAND CONCERT BY BOCA CIEGA HIGH SCHOOL BAND, FASHION SHOW OF ANTIQUE CLOTHES & FLEA MARKET. AT JAY P CLYMER PARK, BEACH BLVD BETWEEN 22ND AVE S & 25TH AVE S. (LOCAL). MRS J F JOHNSON, DIR; CITY OF GULFPORT; 5012 17TH AVE S; GULFPORT, FL 33707. (#109522-2).

NOV 21 - 23, '76. HERITAGE WEEK. CITIZENS OF CITY WILL PUT THEIR ANTIQUES ON DISPLAY FOR PUBLIC. RUSSIAN & CZECHOSLOVAKIAN & SQUARE DANCE EXHIBITIONS. ELEM SCHOOL HOLIDAY PROGRAM WILL BE PRESENTED. AT COMMUNITY CENTER, 5730 SHORE BLVD S. (LOCAL). MRS J F JOHNSON, CHAIRMAN; CITY OF GULFPORT BICENTENNIAL COMMITTEE; 5012 17TH AVE S; GULFPORT, FL 33707. (#109522-1).

HALLANDALE

AN OLD-FASHIONED TOWN MEETING. TO DEVELOP THE AWARENESS OF THE QUALITY OF LIFE IN THE CITY OF HALLANDALE. (LOCAL). EMILIO F MENDILLO; BICENTENNIAL COMMITTEE; 501 SE 1ST AVE; HALLANDALE, FL 33009. (#200011-311).

MAR 1 - 7, '76. STAR-SPANGLED WEEK. QUEEN CONTEST, DEBATES, GARDEN CLUB ART SHOW, SALUTE TO SR CITIZENS, FLAG CEREMONY, CRAFTS ENDING WITH OLD FASHIONED TOWN MEETING. AT HALLANDALE RECREATION CENTER. (LOCAL). EMILIO F MENDILLO; BICENTENNIAL COMMITTEE; 501 SE 1ST AVE; HALLANDALE, FL 33009. (#200011-310).

HARBOR CITY

PRIMITIVE AMERICAN VILLAGE - HARBOR CITY, FL. PLANS ARE BEING MADE TO CONSTRUCT A PRIMITIVE AMERICAN VILLAGE. (LOCAL). W F HOUSNER, CHAIRMAN; HARBOR CITY ELEMENTARY SCHOOL/BREVARD CO BICENTENNIAL COMMITTEE; MELBOURNE, FL 32901. (#21463).

HAWTHORNE

BICENTENNIAL DENOMINATIONAL CONFERENCE. CONFERENCE. (LOCAL). REV WESCOAT HOLLOWAY, DIR; HAWTHORNE MINISTERIAL ASSOC; PO BOX 415; HAWTHORNE, FL 32640. (#105121-2).

FLAG PROJ IN HAWTHORNE, FL. HOMES AND PLACES OF BUSINESS ARE BEING ENCOURAGED TO FLY THE U S FLAG THROUGH JULY 4TH; WILL BE AN ONGOING PROJECT. (LOCAL). ANNIE MAE PHILLIPS, FACULTY CHMN; HAWTHORNE HIGH SCHOOL; PO BOX 46; HAWTHORNE, FL 32640. (#20373).

PICTURE POST CARDS OF HISTORIC HAWTHORNE, FL. OLD SCENES OF HAWTHORNE REPRODUCED AS POST CARDS. (LOCAL). KATHY DUNN, CHAIRMAN; HAWTHORNE CHAMBER OF COMMERCE; PO BOX 1087; HAWTHORNE, FL 32640. (#21115).

PLANTING TREES ON CAMPUS, HAWTHORNE, FL. TREES WILL BE SOLD TO SCHOOL CLASSES, CLUBS AND ORGANIZATIONS TO PLANT IN HONOR OF BICENTENNIAL. (LOCAL). FRANCES LOVE, MEDIA SPECIALIST; HAWTHORNE HIGH SCHOOL LIBRARY CLUB; HAWTHORNE, FL 32640. (#20372).

JULY 4, '75. COMMUNITY BICENTENNIAL WORSHIP SERVICE. CEREMONY AT HAWTHORNE HIGH SCHOOL AUDITORIUM. (LOCAL). REV WESCOAT HOLLOWAY; HAWTHORNE MINISTERIAL ASSOC; PO BOX 415; HAWTHORNE, FL 32640. (#200011-43).

JAN 19 - 21, '76. CHILDREN'S ART IN THE MALL - 'HAPPY BIRTHDAY USA'. EXHIBIT AT GAINESVILLE MALL. (LOCAL). MRS BEN CAMPEN, CHAIRMAN; ALACHUA COUNTY ELEMENTARY SCHOOLS & GAINESVILLE JR WOMEN'S CLUB; PO BOX 183; HAWTHORNE, FL 32640. (#200011-44).

APR 5 - 10, '76. SPRING ART SHOW CELEBRATING BICENTENNIAL '76. EXHIBIT AT HAWTHORNE LIBRARY, JOHNSON ST. (LOCAL). MARY MOORE, LIBRARIAN; HAWTHORNE LIBRARY; PO BOX 242; HAWTHORNE, FL 32640. (#105121-1).

HIALEAH

YMCA THIRD CENTURY DAY CAMP IN HIALEAH, FL. DAY CAMP SITE BEING DEVELOPED TO SUPPORT YMCA PROGRAMS WHICH HELP DEVELOP THE CHARACTER AND PERSONALITIES OF OUR YOUTH. (LOCAL). NEAL W ALLEN, EXEC DIR; YMCA HIALEAH - MIAMI SPRINGS BRANCH; 4300 PALM AVE; HIALEAH, FL 33012. (#10528).

NOV 24 - 29, '75. AMERICAN BICENTENNIAL FLORIDA EXHIBIT. EXHIBIT, RADIO/TV AT WESTLAND MALL, NW 103RD ST. (LOCAL). ANITA BJORK; THIRD CENTURY, USA; PO BOX 451976; MIAMI, FL 33145. (#100225-3).

MAR 20 - 21, '76. MIAMI RIVER TRASH BASH: A REMOVAL OF SUNKEN OBJECTS AND LITTER. FESTIVAL. (LOCAL). TOM HOMBERGER, DIRECTOR; MIAMI RIVER INTER-CITY BOARD; 265 W 25 ST; HIALEAH, FL 33010. (#5198-1).

APR 23 - 25, '76. ANNUAL MIAMI RIVER REGATTA. COMPETITION, FESTIVAL AT UPPER RIVER - HIALEAH, MIAMI SPRINGS. (LOCAL). TOM HOMBERGER, DIRECTOR; MIAMI RIVER INNER - CITY BOARD; 265 W 25TH ST; HIALEAH, FL 33010. (#5198-3).

MAY 20, '76. HIALEAH BICENTENNIAL MODEL AIRPLANE MEET - HAND LAUNCHED GLIDERS. COMPETITION, EXHIBIT AT 5987 E 7TH AVE. (LOCAL). HELEN ANDREWS, COORD; AMELIA EARHART SCHOOL & CITY OF HIALEAH; 51 E 43RD ST; HIALEAH, FL 33013. (#108150-1).

JULY 4, '76. INDEPENDENCE DAY BAR-B-QUE AND FIREWORKS DISPLAY. FESTIVAL AT MILANDER STADIUM. (LOCAL). RUSS MARCHNER, DIRECTOR; CITY OF HIALEAH; 501 PALM AVE; HIALEAH, FL 33011. (#2997-17).

HIGH SPRINGS

'GOOD OLD DAYS' - PLACEMENT FLOWER SHOW. AWARD, COMPETITION, EXHIBIT AT HOME OF MR & MRS RAPHORD FARRINGTON, 30 NE FIRST AVE. (LOCAL). MRS WYNDELL EVERETT; HIGH SPRINGS GARDEN CLUB; HIGH SPRINGS, FL 32643. (#107968-1). **(??).**

HILLIARD

PICTORIAL HISTORY OF NASSAU COUNTY, FL. THE HISTORY BOOK WILL CONTAIN 200 PICTURES DEPICTING LIFE IN NASSAU COUNTY FROM 1875-1930; IT WILL DESCRIBE HOW EACH COMMUNITY ACQUIRED ITS NAME AND DEVELOPED. (LOCAL). JAN H JOHANNES, SR, AUTHOR; NASSAU COUNTY BICENTENNIAL STEERING COMMITTEE; BOX 1776; CALLAHAN, FL 32046. (#15038).

HOLLYWOOD

OKALEE VILLAGE INTERIOR RESTORATION, HOLLYWOOD, FL. RENOVATE OKALEE INDIAN VILLAGE AND CONSTRUCT DRIVEWAY IMPROVEMENT ON THE RESERVATION. (LOCAL). HOWARD H TOMMIE, TRIBAL CHAIRMAN; SEMINOLE TRIBE OF FLORIDA - TRIBAL COUNCIL; 6073 STIRLING RD; HOLLYWOOD, FL 33024. (#21195). **ARBA GRANTEE.**

FEB 15, '75. UNITED STATES NAVY BAND CONCERT. NET PROCEEDS WILL GO TO NAVY LEAGUE YOUTH PROGRAM; MATINEE PERFORMANCE AT 2 PM ON 2/15 FOR STUDENT BAND MEMBERS. AT SOUTH BROWARD HIGH SCHOOL AUDITORIUM, 1901 N FEDERAL HWY. (LOCAL). JOHN T WULFF; HOLLYWOOD COUNCIL OF THE NAVY LEAGUE OF THE US; 5100 POLK ST; HOLLYWOOD, FL 33021. (#200011-45).

OCT 18 - 19, '75. 'PIONEER DAYS'. AN EXHIBITION OF HISTORICAL MATERIALS HONORING BROWARD COUNTY'S 60TH ANNIVERSARY. HOURS 10/19: 1:30PM-6:00PM. AT HOLLYWOOD HILLS HIGH SCHOOL, 5400 STIRLING RD. (LOCAL). DON CUDDY, COORDINATOR; GREATER HOLLYWOOD BICENTENNIAL TASK FORCE; BOX 2345; HOLLYWOOD, FL 33022. (#102167-1).

OCT 25, '75. DEDICATION OF BIKE PATH. CEREMONY. (LOCAL). DON CUDDY, COORDINATOR; GREATER HOLLYWOOD BICENTENNIAL TASK FORCE; BOX 2345; HOLLYWOOD, FL 33022. (#102167-2).

NOV 2, '75. RECEPTION AT ART AND CULTURAL CENTER. CEREMONY, EXHIBIT AT 1301 SO OCEAN DR. (LOCAL). DON CUDDY, COORDINATOR; GREATER HOLLYWOOD BICENTENNIAL TASK FORCE; BOX 2345; HOLLYWOOD, FL 33022. (#102865-1).

NOV 8, '75. 50TH BIRTHDAY PARADE & PARTY. PARADE, FESTIVAL. (LOCAL). DON CUDDY, COORDINATOR; GREATER HOLLYWOOD BICENTENNIAL TASK FORCE; BOX 2345; HOLLYWOOD, FL 33022. (#102167-3).

NOV 22 - 23, '75. 7 LIVELY ARTS YOUNG CIRCLE ARTS & CRAFTS SHOW. EXHIBIT. (LOCAL). DON CUDDY, COORDINATOR; GREATER HOLLYWOOD BICENTENNIAL TASK FORCE; BOX 2345; HOLLYWOOD, FL 33022. (#102167-4).

OCT 9 - 10, '76. BROWARD COUNTY BICENTENNIAL PIONEER DAYS EXPOSITION. EXHIBIT, FESTIVAL AT PORT EVERGLADES PASSENGER TERMINAL. (LOCAL). CYNTHIA E RUSH, COORD; BROWARD COUNTY HISTORICAL COMMISSION & PORT EVERGLADES AUTHORITY; 201 SE 6TH ST, RM 800; FT LAUDERDALE, FL 33301. (#102419-1).

HOMESTEAD

GIVE YOUR COUNTRY A BIRTHDAY PRESENT, FL. EVERY STUDENT AND TEACHER WILL GIVE A BIRTHDAY GIFT TO AMERICA THROUGH SOME FORM OF SERVICE TO THE SCHOOL, COMMUNITY, STATE OR NATION. AT END OF YEAR, BIRTHDAY BOOK TO BE SENT TO U S PRESIDENT. (LOCAL). EDWARD E COMBIE, CHAIRMAN; HOMESTEAD JUNIOR HIGH SCHOOL; 650 NW 2ND AVE; HOMESTEAD, FL 33030. (#21870).

HOMESTEAD CENTER FOR THE ARTS - HOMESTEAD, FL. ACQUISITION & CONSTRUCTION OF A BUILDING TO HOUSE ART MUSEUM AND WORKSHOP ROOMS AS WELL AS QUARTERS AND FACILITIES FOR MUSIC, DRAMA AND DANCE. (LOCAL). MRS LOIS JOHNSTON, PRESIDENT; HOMESTEAD ART CLUB; PO BOX 1441; HOMESTEAD, FL 33030. (#24808).

NATIONAL BICYCLING CENTER, HOMESTEAD, FLORIDA. THIS CENTER WILL PROMOTE MORE & SAFER BICYCLING AND PROVIDE SAFETY LITERATURE, INSTRUCTION & LECTURES. A HOBBY SHOP IS INCLUDED. (NAT'L). GEORGE S FICHTER, PRESIDENT; NATIONAL BICYCLING FOUNDATION, INC; PO BOX 1368; HOMESTEAD, FL 33030. (#5199).

OCT 6 - 11, '75. AMERICAN BICENTENNIAL FLORIDA EXHIBIT. EXHIBIT, RADIO/TV AT HARRIS FIELD, 1034 NE 8 ST. (LOCAL). ANITA BJORD; THIRD CENTURY USA; PO BOX 451976; MIAMI, FL 33145. (#100225-1).

JAN 1 - DEC 31, '76. PROGRAM ABOUT ACCELERATION OF CHANGE DURING THE PAST 200 YRS. INTERPRETERS WILL PRESENT PROGRAMS THROUGHOUT PARK WHICH EMPHASIZE THEME OF ACCELERATED CHANGE DURING PAST 200 YEARS AND ROLE OUR NATIONAL HERITAGE PLAYED. AT EVERGLADES NATIONAL PARK. (REGN'L). SUPT EVERGLADES NP; NATIONAL PARK SERVICE; PO BOX 279; HOMESTEAD, FL 33030. (#6729-571).

FEB 3 - 8, '76. SOUTH DADE COUNTRY FAIR. FAIR AT TOM J HARRIS FIELD. (LOCAL). KEITH CONNER, CHAIRMAN; HOMESTEAD BICENTENNIAL COMMITTEE; 790 HOMESTEAD BLVD; HOMESTEAD, FL 33030. (#104566-3).

MAY 15 - 16, '76. ARMED FORCES DAY '76. EXHIBIT, FESTIVAL AT OPALOCLCA AIRFIELD. (LOCAL). LT COL E CARDENAS, DIR; ARMED FORCES BICENTENNIAL COUNCIL OF GREATER MIAMI; 31ST ADA BRIG; HOMESTEAD AFB, FL 33030. (#104566-10).

JUNE 13, '76. HOMESTEAD FLAG DAY OBSERVANCE AND OUTDOOR BAND CONCERT. CEREMONY, LIVE PERFORMANCE AT CITY HALL. (LOCAL). KEITH CONNER, CHAIRPERSON; CITY OF HOMESTEAD AND THE HOMESTEAD BICENTENNIAL COMMITTEE; 790 HOMESTEAD BLVD; HOMESTEAD, FL 33030. (#107551-1).

JULY 4, '76. INDEPENDENCE DAY PICNIC, COUNTRY BAND JAMBOREE AND FIREWORKS DISPLAY. FESTIVAL AT HARRIS FIELD. (LOCAL). KEITH CONNOR, DIRECTOR; CITY OF HOMESTEAD AND THE HOMESTEAD BICENTENNIAL COMMITTEE; 790 HOMESTEAD BLVD; HOMESTEAD, FL 33030. (#2997-19).

HOMESTEAD AFB

HOMESTEAD AIR FORCE BASE OPEN HOUSE IN FLORIDA. IN 1975 THIS ANNUAL EVENT WILL PLACE PARTICULAR EMPHASIS ON THE PART THAT THE ARMED FORCES HAVE PLAYED IN THE DEVELOPMENT OF OUR COUNTRY, AS WELL AS THE 200TH BIRTHDAY OF THE ARMY, NAVY & MARINE CORPS. (LOCAL). CAPT MIKE GALLAGHER, INFORMATION OFFICER; HOMESTEAD AIR FORCE BASE; 31ST TAC FW; HAFB, FL 33030. (#5231).

NOV 8, '75. AIR FORCE BASE OPEN HOUSE. IN 1975 THIS ANNUAL EVENT WILL PLACE PARTICULAR EMPHASIS ON THE PART THAT THE ARMED FORCES HAVE PLAYED IN THE DEVELOPMENT OF OUR COUNTRY, AS WELL AS THE 200TH BIRTHDAY OF THE ARMY, NAVY & MARINE CORPS. AT HOMESTEAD AIR FORCE BASE, FLIGHT LINE AREA. (LOCAL). CAPT MIKE GALLAGHER; HOMESTEAD AIR FORCE BASE; 31ST TAC FW; HAFB, FL 33030. (#5231-1).

NOV 27, '76. HOMESTEAD AIR FORCE BASE OPEN HOUSE. IN 1976 THIS ANNUAL EVENT WILL PLACE PARTICULAR EMPHASIS ON THE PART THE AIR FORCE HAS PLAYED IN THE DEVELOPMENT OF OUR COUNTRY AS WELL AS THE 200TH BIRTHDAY OF THE ARMY, NAVY & MARINE CORPS. AT HOMESTEAD AIR FORCE BASE. (ST-WIDE). CAPT MIKE GALLAGHER; ARMED FORCES BICENTENNIAL COUNCIL OF GREATER MIAMI; OFFICE OF INFORMATION; HOMESTEAD AFB, FL 33030. (#104052-1).

HURLBURT FLD

BICENTENNIAL OBSERVANCE PLAN IN HURLBURT FLD, FL. A PLAN CALLING FOR ALL UNITS ON HURLBURT FLD TO COMPLETE ONE BICENTENNIAL PROJECT WITH AN AMERICAN REVOLUTION THEME. BASE IMPROVEMENTS YOUTH ACTIVITIES & PICNIC AREAS WERE CONTRIBUTED. (LOCAL). CAPT JOHN WEAVER, JR; 1ST SPECIAL OPERATIONS WING/101; HURLBURT FLD, FL 32544. (#29870).

INDEPENDENCE ROAD/HERITAGE GATE IN FL. COMPLETION OF A NEW ROAD LINKING HURLBURT FLD & GREATER FT WALTON BEACH COMMUNITIES. NEW ROAD SAVES 15 MINUTE DRIVE TIME & A NEW MILITARY GATE TO HURLBURTFIELD OPENED. (LOCAL). CAPT JOHN WEAVER, JR; 1ST SPECIAL OPERATIONS WING/01; HURLBURT FLD, FL 32544. (#29872).

APR 23 - 25, '76. JUMPFEST '76. A MILITARY PARACHUTING DEMONSTRATION AND COMPETITION INVOLVING OVER 300 MILITARY PARACHUTISTS. EVENT HELD IN CONJUNCTION WITH A MILITARY OPEN HOUSE AT HURLBURT FIELD. AT HURLBURT FIELD, PARACHUTE DEMONSTRATION AREA. (REGN'L). CAPT JOHN V O WEAVER, JR; 1ST SPECIAL OPERATIONS WING (TAC); HURLBURT FLD, FL 32544. (#200011-287).

JUNE 26, '76. FESTIVAL DAYS. A FESTIVAL DESIGNED TO GATHER ART & RECREATION TOGETHER IN CELEBRATING OUR COUNTRY'S 200TH BIRTHDAY. WAS BEGINNING OF BICENTE EVENTS WEEK IN FT WALTON BEACH AREA. AT HURLBURT FIELD AIR PARK. (LOCAL). CAPT JOHN V O WEAVER, JR; 1ST SPECIAL OPERATIONS WING (TAC); HURLBURT FLD, FL 32544. (#200011-286).

INDIALANTIC

'AMERICAN KNOW HOW', WINDOW DISPLAYS, FL. WINDOW DISPLAYS TO ILLUSTRATE THE PART EACH BUSINESS HAS PLAYED IN THE AMERICAN STORY; WINDOWS WILL BE JUDGED & AWARDS WILL BE PRSENTED AT JULY 4TH AWARDS PARTY. (LOCAL). PHIL POWELL, CO-CHAIRMAN; INDIALANTIC MERCHANTS ASSOCIATION; INDIALANTIC, FL 32935. (#18002).

BICENTENNIAL EVENTS SIGNS & FLAGPOLES PROJ, FL. 3 SIGNS AT 3 MAIN ENTRANCE ROADS TO TOWN EACH WITH FLAGPOLE & BETSY ROSS FLAG - SCHEDULE OF EVENTS POSTED MONTHLY. (LOCAL). RUTH WERMUTH, PROJ CHAIRMAN; BICENTENNIAL COMMITTEE & INDIALANTIC IMPROVEMENT ASSOCIATION; 205 TAMPA AVE; INDIALANTIC, FL 32903. (#17647).

BICENTENNIAL MEMORIAL GAZEBO, INDIALANTIC, FL. LASTING REMINDER WITH MEMORIAL PLAQUE - WILL PROVIDE SITE FOR FUTURE CIVIC & CULTURAL EVENTS. (LOCAL). ROBERTO ROMARION, CHAIRMAN; INDIALANTIC-BY-THE-SEA BICENTENNIAL COMMITTEE; 303 12TH TERRACE; INDIALANTIC, FL 32903. (#17648).

THE TOWN CRIER, BICENTENNIAL NEWSLETTER, FL. INDIALANTIC-BY-THE-SEA BICENTENNIAL COMMITTEE NEWSLETTER TO BE DISTRIBUTED PERIODICALLY TO COMMUNITY TO INFORM & INVOLVE CITIZENS & VISITORS IN COMMITTEE ACTIVITIES & EVENTS. (LOCAL). PHIL POWELL, CO-CHAIRMAN; INDIALANTIC-BY-THE-SEA BICENTENNIAL COMMITTEE; 235 FIRST AVE; INDIALANTIC, FL 32903. (#18000).

OCT 25, '75. TOWN FESTIVAL DAY - SURF FESTIVAL/PARADE/MISS BICENTENNIAL PAGEANT. PARADE STARTS 10AM ON BOARDWALK; SURF CONTEST FOLLOWS ON BEACH; MISS BICENTENNIAL TEENAGER PAGEANT BEGINS 7 PM - BALLET INTERLUDE; SCHOLARSHIP AWARDS. AT PALMS OCEAN INN-501 NORTH A1A HIGHWAY INDIALANTIC - BOARDWALK. (LOCAL). PHIL POWELL, CO-CHAIRMAN; INDIALANTIC-BY-THE-SEA BICENTENNIAL COMMITTEE; 235 FIRST AVE; INDIALANTIC, FL 32903. (#103517-17).

NOV 3, '75 - JULY 4, '76. BICENTENNIAL EXHIBIT OF HISTORICAL AMERICANA. THE EVENT WILL CHANGE PERIODICALLY. AT FIRST FEDERAL OF BREVARD, 5TH AVE. (LOCAL). LES BARLOW, TOWN MGR; INDIALANTIC BICENTENNIAL COMMITTEE; 216 5TH AVE; INDIALANTIC, FL 32903. (#103409-1).

FEB 14, '76. '76 MUSIC DAY DANCE. FUND-RAISING EVENT FOR GAZEBO FUND. (LOCAL). PHIL POWELL, DIRECTOR; INDIALANTIC-BY-THE-SEA BICENTENNIAL COMMITTEE; 235 FIRST AVE; INDIALANTIC, FL 32903. (#103517-20).

APR 23 - 25, '76. INDIALANTIC ART SHOW & BICENTENNIAL AWARDS. SPECIAL AWARDS TO WORKS BY BREVARD COUNTY ARTISTS BEST DEPICTING EACH OF THE 3 BICENTENNIAL THEMES. AT ON STREET ALONG 5TH AVE. (LOCAL). BERNICE AMMERMAN, DIR; INDIALANTIC ART SHOW COMMITTEE; 401 MICHIGAN AVE; INDIALANTIC, FL 32903. (#103517-21).

JULY 4, '76. BICENTENNIAL PARADE & AWARDS PARTY. FLOATS TO ISSUSTRATE HISTORIC SCENES OVER PAST 200 YEARS FROM

INDIALANTIC — CONTINUED

REVOL TO SPACE PROGRAM; EVENING AWARDS PARTY WILL CONCLUDE BICENTENNIAL. AT TO START AT BOARDWALK & FIFTH AVE. (LOCAL). PHIL POWELL, CO-CHAIRMAN; INDIALANTIC BICENTENNIAL COMMITTEE; 235 FIRST AVE; INDIALANTIC, FL 32903. (#103517-22).

INDIANTOWN

JULY 2 - 5, '76. DIXIE STATES BICENTENNIAL FAIR AND EXPOSITION. BLUE GRASS MUSIC, SKY-DIVING, BEAUTY CONTESTS, FAIR AND MIDWAY, CAMPING, FLY-IN-CIRCLE T AIRPORT. AT BURT REYNOLDS ARENA. (REGN'L). GREGORY BEAN, PROMOTER; DOWN HOME PRODUCTIONS, INC; PO BOX 2327; W PALM BEACH, FL 33402. (#105362-1).

INDIN HBR BCH

BICENTENNIAL MEMORIAL PARK - INDIAN HARBOR, FL. A MEMORIAL AT INDIAN HARBOR BEACH COMMUNITY CENTER INCLUDES WATERFALL, 4 PLAQUES, FLOWER GARDEN, FLAG POLE & TIME CAPSULE CONSTRUCTION BY BOY SCOUT TROOP 376. (LOCAL). MARTIN C PERTL, CHAIRMAN; INDIAN HARBOR BEACH BICENTENNIAL COMMITTEE; 555 DESOTO PARKWAY; INDIAN HARBOR, FL 32937. (#25951).

OCEAN BREEZE PLAYGROUND, INDIAN HARBOR BEACH, FL. DEVELOP A SCHOOL PLAYGROUND FOR OCEAN BREEZE ELEMENTARY SCHOOL AT INDIAN HARBOUR BEACH. (LOCAL). W F HOUSNER, CHAIRMAN; BREVARD SCHOOL SYSTEM; INDIN HBR BCH, FL 32935. (#22359).

OCEAN FRONT RECREATION AREA, FL. COMMUNITY RECREATION AREA TO BE OPENED OCT 1, 1975. (LOCAL). MARTIN C PERTL, COORDINATOR; CITY RECREATION DEPT; 535 DE SOTO PKWY; INDIN HBR BCH, FL 32937. (#16934).

U S FLAG & DECAL PROJECT OF INDIAN HARBOUR BCH, FL. PROJECT TO SELL U S FLAGS & DECALS TO CITY RESIDENTS. (LOCAL). MARTIN C PERTL, CHAIRMAN; CITY RECREATION ADVIS; INDIN HBR BCH, FL 32937. (#17088).

1776 TREES - INDIAN HARBOUR BEACH, FL. 1776 TREES PLANTED IN THE CITY BY RESIDENTS AND BUSINESSES. (LOCAL). MARTIN C PERTL, COORDINATOR; CITY BEAUTIFICATION BOARD; 555 DESOTO PKWY; INDIN HBR BCH, FL 32937. (#16933).

JAN 1, '76. OPENING OF OCEAN BREEZE PLAYGROUND AREA. OPENING AT OCEAN BREEZE ELEMENTARY SCHOOL. (LOCAL). MARTIN C PERTL, CHAIRMAN; INDIAN HARBOR BEACH BICENT COMMITTEE & BREVARD CO SCHOOL SYSTEM; 555 DESOTO PKY; INDIN HBR BCH, FL 32937. (#103066-1).

JUNE 1, '76. DEDICATION OF HIDDEN LAKE CITY PARK. A RECREATIONAL AREA AND THEATRE ARE BEING CONSTRUCTED; IT WILL BE DEDICATED TO THE EARLY SETTLERS. (LOCAL). MARTIN C PERTL, CHAIRMAN; INDIAN HARBOR BEACH BICENTENNIAL COMMITTEE; 555 DESOTO PKWY; INDIN HBR BCH, FL 32937. (#103066-2).

JULY 4, '76. BICENTENNIAL FESTIVAL '76. FESTIVAL, PARADE, LIVE PERFORMANCE AT PARK BEACH FRONT. (LOCAL). MARTIN C PERTL, CHAIRMAN; CITY RECREATION DEPT & INDIAN HARBOR BEACH BICENTENNIAL COMMITTEE; 555 DESOTO PKY; INDIN HBR BCH, FL 32937. (#103066-3).

INVERNESS

CITRUS COUNTY HISTORY BOOK - INVERNESS, FL. THE CITRUS COUNTY HISTORY BOOK WILL RECOUNT ALL FACETS OF THE PAST; HAMPTON DUNN IS THE EDITOR. (LOCAL). DAVID S ARTHURS, PUBLISHER; CITRUS COUNTY PUBLISHING COMPANY; 103 N APOPKA AVE, PO BOX 65; INVERNESS, FL 32650. (#15037).

OCT 18 - 19, '75. ANNUAL CITRUS COUNTY CANOE RACE, CRUISE, AND REGATTA. THE SOUTH'S FOREMOST CANOE AND KYAK EVENT. A WEEKEND OF COMPETITION, CRUISING AND SOCIAL GATHERINGS FOR CANOESTS FROM THROUGHOUT NORTH AMERICA. AT WITHLACOOCHEE RIVER AND STATE ROAD 44. (ST-WIDE). DAVID S ARTHURS; CITRUS COUNTY CHAMBER OF COMMERCE; BOX 65; INVERNESS, FL 32650. (#50208-3).

NOV 1, '75. CITRUS COUNTY FESTIVAL OF THE ARTS (ANNUAL). JUDGED ARTS AND CRAFTS SHOW-$1000 MINIMUM PRIZE MONEY-DANCE, MUSICAL AND PERFORMING ARTS ON STAGE ON THE COURTHOUSE SQUARE-NOTED AMERICAN ARTIST IS ANNUAL FEATURED ARTIST. AT COURTHOUSE SQUARE INVERNESS, FL. (ST-WIDE). DAVID S ARTHURS; CITRUS COUNTY ART LEAGUE & CITRUS COUNTY CHAMBER OF COMMERCE; BOX 65; INVERNESS, FL 32650. (#50208-1).

MAR 8 - 12, '76. CITRUS COUNTY FAIR. FAIR AT COUNTY FAIR GROUNDS SOUTH OF INVERNESS ON US 41. (LOCAL). ARTHUR ALSTON; CITRUS COUNTY FAIR ASSOCIATION; RT1 BOX 6; INVERNESS, FL 32650. (#50628-1).

OCT 16 - 17, '76. ANNUAL CITRUS COUNTY CANOE RACE, CRUISE AND REGATTA. THE SOUTHEAST U.S. FOREMOST CANOE AND KAYAK EVENT. A WEEKEND OF COMPETION,CRUSING AND SOCIAL GATHERINGS FOR CANOESTS FROM THROUGHOUT NORTH AMERICA. AT WITHLACOOCHEE RIVER AND STATE ROAD 44. (REGN'L). DAVID S ARTHURS; CITRUS COUNTY CHAMBER OF COMMERCE; BOX 65; INVERNESS, FL 32650. (#50208-4).

NOV 6, '76. ANNUAL CITRUS COUNTY FESTIVAL OF THE ARTS. JUDGED ARTS AND CRAFTS SHOW-$1000 MINIMUM PRIZE MONEY-DANCE MUSICAL AND PERFORMING ARTS ON STAGE ON THE COURTHOUSE SQUARE-NOTED ARTIST IS ANNUAL FEATURED ARTIST. AT COURTHOUSE SQUARE, INVERNESS, FL. (ST-WIDE). DAVID S ARTHURS; CITRUS COUNTY ART LEAGUE AND CITRUS COUNTY CHAMBER OF COMMERCE; BOX 65; INVERNESS, FL 32650. (#50208-2).

MAR 7 - 12, '77. CITRUS COUNTY FAIR. FAIR AT COUNTY FAIR GROUNDS, SOUTH OF INVERNESS ON US 41. (ST-WIDE). ARTHUR ALSTON; CITRUS COUNTY FAIR ASSOCIATION; RT 1, BOX 6; INVERNESS, FL 32650. (#50628-2).

JACKSONVILLE

THE AMERICAN HERITAGE MERIT BADGE - FL. EARNING THIS BADGE WILL TEACH THE SCOUT ABOUT THE EARLY AND CONTINUAL HISTORY OF OUR NATION: ITS TRADITIONS, ITS ASPIRATIONS AND ITS GOALS UTILIZING NATIONAL BOY SCOUT STANDARDS. (LOCAL). DEBORAH J EPSTEIN, ADMIN ASSISTANT; JACKSONVILLE ARBC/BOY SCOUTS OF AMERICA; 2113 HENDRICKS AVE; JACKSONVILLE, FL 32207. (#22432).

BEADS, SEEDS AND TREES, 'JOHNNY HORIZON', FL. ENVIRONMENTAL PROGRAM, TREE PLANTING AND BACHELOR'S BUTTONS, EARNING BEADS TOWARD BICENTENNIAL MERIT BADGES. (LOCAL). DEBBIE EPSTEIN, ADMINISTRATIVE ASSISTANT; ABCJ/ CAMP FIRE GIRLS, INC; JOHNNY HORIZONS PROGRAM/ABCJ; 2113 HENDRICKS AVE; JACKSONVILLE, FL 32207. (#22417).

BENNINGTON FLAGS - JACKSONVILLE, FL. BENNINGTON FLAGS WILL BE DISTRIBUTED TO EACH HIGH SCHOOL IN DUVAL COUNTY; LITERATURE RELATING TO THE HISTORY OF THE FLAG WILL ALSO BE DISTRIBUTED. (LOCAL). DEBORAH J EPSTEIN, ADMIN ASSISTANT; JACKSONVILLE ARBC/U S STEEL CORPORATION; 2113 HENDRICKS AVE; JACKSONVILLE, FL 32207. (#22435).

BICENTENNIAL EVENT IN JACKSONVILLE, FL. FORT CAROLINE CELEBRATION. (INT'L). DEBORAH J EPSTEIN, COORD; BICENTENNIAL COMMISSION OF JACKSONVILLE & U S NAVY; 2113 HENDRICKS AVE, SUITE 206; JACKSONVILLE, FL 32207. (#106799).

BICENTENNIAL HOME OF THE FUTURE, JACKSONVILLE, FL. DEVELOPMENT OF LOW ENERGY HOUSING IN JACKSONVILLE. (LOCAL). DON PRIDE, EXEC DIRECTOR; AMERICAN BICENTENNIAL COMMISSION OF JACKSONVILLE; PO BOX 10207; JACKSONVILLE, FL 32207. (#13837). **ARBA GRANTEE.**

BICENTENNIAL MARKER OF BATTLE OF THOMAS CREEK - FL. ERECTING A MARKER AT SITE WHERE BATTLE WAS FOUGHT MAY 15, 1777, NEAR COWFORD AT JUNCTION OF THOMAS CREEK & NASSAU RIVER. (ST-WIDE). DEBBE EPSTEIN, COORDINATOR; CHILDREN OF THE AMERICAN REVOLUTION-PRINCESS MALEE CHAP/ABCJ; 2113 HENDRICKS AVE, SUITE 206; JACKSONVILLE, FL 32207. (#11348).

BICENTENNIAL QUILT, JACKSONVILLE, FL. WILL PRODUCE THIS CITY'S BICENTENNIAL COMMUNITY QUILT; ANYONE OR A GROUP IS ELIGIBLE TO SUBMIT DESIGNS FOR ALL OR PART; CLASSES IN QUILT-MAKING FOR ALL OF COMMUNITY. (LOCAL). DEBORAH J EPSTEIN, ADMINISTRATIVE ASSISTANT; LEMOYNE CHAPTER OF EMBROIDERERS GUILD OF AMERICA/ABCJ; 2113 HENDRICKS AVE; JACKSONVILLE, FL 32207. (#22419).

BICENTENNIAL TREE PLANTING PROGRAM - FL. MARINE RESERVES WITH ASSISTANCE FROM HIGH SCHOOL STUDENTS WILL PLANT 200 TREES ON THE CAMPUSES OF THE THREE COUNTY HIGH SCHOOLS BY JULY 4, 1976. (LOCAL). MAJOR JOE ALEXANDER, PROJ DIRECTOR; U S MARINE RESERVES; NAS BOX 44, BLDG 411; JACKSONVILLE, FL 32212. (#18934).

'CLEANUP AMERICA FOR OUR 200TH BIRTHDAY' - FL. CITY-WIDE ENVIRONMENTAL AWARENESS PROGRAMS IN CONJUNCTION WITH THE JOHNNY HORIZONS '76 PROGRAM. (LOCAL). DEBORAH J EPSTEIN, ADMIN ASSISTANT; JACKSONVILLE ARBC/ JOHNNY HORIZONS '76; 2113 HENDRICKS AVE; JACKSONVILLE, FL 32207. (#22430).

CRASH! - CHILDREN'S REVOLUTION FOR SAFER HOMES- FL. A PROGRAM OF ACTIVITIES FOR YOUNGSTERS; PLANNED WITH POLICE AND THE FIRE DEPT; THEME IS: 'A SAFER HOME FOR A SAFER AMERICA.'. (LOCAL). DEBORAH J EPSTEIN, ADMIN ASSISTANT; DUVAL CO COUNCIL OF CAMP FIRE GIRLS, INC/ ABCJ; 2113 HENDRICKS AVE, SUITE 206; JACKSONVILLE, FL 32207. (#24233).

DUVAL COUNTY SCHOOLS' PROJECTS & EVENTS - FL. EACH SCHOOL IN DUVAL COUNTY WILL COMMEMORATE THE BICENTENNIAL WITH SPECIAL PROJECTS AND EVENTS. (LOCAL). DEBORAH J EPSTEIN, ADMIN ASSISTANT; JACKSONVILLE ARBC DUVAL COUNTY SCHOOLS; 2113 HENDRICKS AVE; JACKSONVILLE, FL 32207. (#22428).

ENGINEERING ACHIEVEMENT MARKERS - JACKSONVILLE, FL. MARKERS DEPICTING ENGINEERING ACHIEVEMENTS OF A HISTORICAL NATURE INCLUDING BUILDINGS, MACHINERY AND TRANSPORTATION. (LOCAL). DEBORAH J EPSTEIN, ADMIN ASSISTANT; JACKSONVILLE ARBC JACKSONVILLE TRANSPORTATION AUTHORITY; 2113 HENDRICKS AVE; JACKSONVILLE, FL 32207. (#22437).

FLY YOUR FLAG - JACKSONVILLE, FL. SQUADRON PURCHASED, SOLD AND ENCOURAGED DISPLAYS OF THE AMERICAN FLAG. (LOCAL). LCDR W G MATTON, COORDINATOR; PATROL SQUADRON 56; NAVAL AIR STATION; JACKSONVILLE, FL 32212. (#29448).

FREEDOM NEWSSTANDS, JACKSONVILLE, FL. NEWSPAPER STANDS DECORATED AND MARKED, DEPICTING HISTORIC SPOTS OF INTEREST IN DUVAL COUNTY; THEY ARE MARKED WITH BRONZE PLAQUES. (ST-WIDE). DEBBIE EPSTEIN, ADMINISTRATIVE ASSISTANT; JACKSONVILLE BICENTENNIAL COMMITTEE; FLORIDA PUBLISHING COMPANY; 2113 HENDRICKS AVE; JACKSONVILLE, FL 32207. (#22416).

'GET OUT AND VOTE IN '76' - JACKSONVILLE, FL. MAJOR CAMPAIGN, CO-SPONSORED BY STUDENTS AT FLORIDA JUNIOR COLLEGE, TO REGISTER 200,000 VOTERS FOR THE 1976 ELECTIONS IN DUVAL COUNTY. (LOCAL). DEBORAH J EPSTEIN, ADMIN ASSISTANT; JACKSONVILLE ARBC/FLORIDA JUNIOR COLLEGE; 2113 HENDRICKS AVE; JACKSONVILLE, FL 32207. (#22429).

'GUIDE FOR THE HANDICAPPED', JACKSONVILLE, FL. BOOKLETS, 10,000 COPIES TO BE DISTRIBUTED TO HANDICAPPED CITIZENS OF JACKSONVILLE; HORIZONS '76 'PROVIDING A BETTER QUALITY OF LIFE FOR ALL AMERICANS IN 1976.'. (LOCAL). DEBBIE EPSTEIN, ADMINISTRATIVE ASSISTANT; JUNIOR LEAGUE OF JACKSONVILLE/JACKSONVILLE BICENT COMMITTEE; 2113 HENDRICKS AVE; JACKSONVILLE, FL 32207. (#22422).

HISTORIC MARKERS IN ST JOHNS BLUFF, JACKSONVLE, FL. PLACEMENT OF MARKERS COMMEMORATING THE FOUNDING OF FORT CAROLINE AND ST JOHNS BLUFF AREA, THE FIRST SETTLEMENT IN AMERICA. (REGN'L). DEBBIE EPSTEIN, ADMINISTRATIVE ASSISTANT; JACKSONVILLE BICENTENNIAL COMMITTEE; ST JOHN BLUFF HIST ASSOC; 2113 HENDRICKS AVE; SUITE 206; JACKSONVILLE, FL 32207. (#22413).

HISTORIC TRAILS BROCHURE, JACKSONVILLE, FL. HISTORIC SPOTS IN DUVAL COUNTY AND INNER CITY OF JACKSONVILLE DEPICTED IN BROCHURE TO BE DISTRIBUTED TO ALL SCHOOL STUDENTS IN DUVAL COUNTY. (ST-WIDE). DEBBIE J EPSTEIN, ADMINISTRATIVE ASSISTANT; JACKSONVILLE BICENTENNIAL COMMITTEE; 2113 HENDRICKS AVE, SUITE 206; JACKSONVILLE, FL 32207. (#22418).

A HISTORY OF JEWISH COMMUNITY, JACKSONVILLE, FL. HISTORY RESEARCHED UNDER THE GUIDANCE AND DIRECTION OF DR SAMUEL PROCTOR OF THE UNIVERSITY OF FLORIDA. (LOCAL). DEBORAH J EPSTEIN, ADMINISTRATIVE ASSISTANT; JACKSONVILLE CHAPTER OF HADASSAH/JACKSONVILLE BICENTENNIAL COM; 2113 HENDRICKS AVE; JACKSONVILLE, FL 32207. (#22420).

JACKSONVILLE, FL, ARMED FORCES BANQUET. THE 679TH RADAR SQUADRON NAVAL AIR STATION WILL PARTICIPATE IN THE ARMED FORCES BANQUET. THE CHIEF OF NAVAL OPERATIONS, ADMIRAL HOLLOWAY, III, WILL BE PRESENT. (LOCAL). PAUL T GARDNER, MAJOR, USAF; 679TH RADAR SQUADRON NAVAL AIR STATION; BUILDING 658; JACKSONVILLE, FL 32212. (#29595).

JOHNNY HORIZON '76 PROJECT OF JACKSONVILLE, FL. CITYWIDE PROGRAM TO CLEAN UP AMERICA: ECOLOGY EMPHASIS, WILDLIFE PRESENTATION, ENVIRONMENTAL AWARENESS & HYGIENE PROGRAMS INVOLVING ALL CITIZENS. (LOCAL). DEBORAH J EPSTEIN, ADMIN ASSISTANT; JACKSONVILLE BICENT COMMISSION; 2113 HENDRICKS AVE, SUITE 206; JACKSONVILLE, FL 32207. (#9954).

JOSEPH E LEE MEMORIAL LIBRARY MUSEUM, JACKSONVILLE. THE COMMUNITY CENTER, LIBRARY & MUSEUM, COMMEMORATING JOSEPH E LEE, WILL HOUSE HISTORICAL DOCUMENTS OF THE TIME; JOSEPH E LEE WAS 1ST BLACK REPUBLICAN LEADER IN FLORIDA FROM JACKSONVILLE IN 1873. (LOCAL). DEBORAH J EPSTEIN, ADMIN ASSISTANT; CITIZENS FOR COMMUNITY ACTION & JACKSONVILLE BICENT COMMISSION; 2113 HENDRICKS AVE, SUITE 206; JACKSONVILLE, FL 32207. (#9955).

'LEARN TO READ' - JACKSONVILLE, FL. PROGRAM INVOLVES RAISING THE LITERACY RATE IN DUVAL COUNTY IN 1976 THROUGH THE 'LEARN TO READ' PROGRAM UTILIZING AMERICAN WORKS AND LITERATURE; 200 VOLUNTEER TUTORS WILL ASSIST. (LOCAL). DEBORAH J EPSTEIN, ADMIN ASSISTANT; JACKSONVILLE ARBC/LEARN TO READ, INC; 2113 HENDRICKS AVE; JACKSONVILLE, FL 32207. (#22424).

LECTURES ON HISTORY OF SCIENTIFIC DISCIPLINES. A SERIES OF TALKS ON THE HISTORY AND SIGNIFICANCE OF THE VARIOUS SCIENCE DISCIPLINES; LEADING SCIENTISTS IN THE STATE WILL PRESENT THE TALKS. (LOCAL). DR J S BROWDER, CHAIRMAN; DIVISION OF SCIENCE AND MATHEMATICS, JACKSONVILLE UNIV; JACKSONVILLE UNIV; JACKSONVILLE, FL 32211. (#102521-1). **(??).**

MANDARIN PATRIARCH OAKS - JACKSONVILLE, FL. CITY COUNCIL RESOLUTION DESIGNATING MADARIN RD AS MANDARIN PARKWAY AND ALL THE OLD OAK TREES ALONG AND WITHIN THE RIGHT-OF-WAY AS PATRIARCH OAKS. (LOCAL). DEBORAH J EPSTEIN, ADMIN ASSISTANT; MANDARIN GARDEN CLUB ABCJ; 2113 HENDRICKS AVE, SUITE 206; JACKSONVILLE, FL 32207. (#24234).

MARINE BARRACKS BICENTENNIAL FLAG PAGEANT - FL. A PRESENTATION OF A BICENTENNIAL UNIFORM AND FLAG PAGEANT FEATURING 14 PERIODS IN OUR FLAG'S HISTORY & 14 PERIODS OF THE HISTORY OF THE MARINE CORPS UNIFORM ACCOMPANIED BY A HISTORICAL NARRATION & MUSIC. (NAT'L). MAJ JOHN C CREGAN, EXEC OFFICER; MARINE BARRACKS; NAVAL AIR STATION; JACKSONVILLE, FL 32212. (#29445).

MARINE CORPS HISTORICAL FLAG PAGEANT. LIVING DISPLAY OF HISTORICAL DEVELOPMENT OF U S FLAG; 14 MEN, EACH IN APPROPRIATE UNIFORM FOR THE FLAG HE CARRIES. ACCOMPANIED BY NARRATION & MARTIAL MUSIC; COVERS 1770'S TO PRESENT. (LOCAL). MAJOR JOE ALEXANDER; UNITED STATES MARINE CORPS; NAVAL AIR STA BOX 44, BLDG 411; JACKSONVILLE, FL 32212. (#104085-2).

NAS' GET OUT AND VOTE - JACKSONVILLE, FL. CAMPAIGN TO ENCOURAGE VOTING WAS CONDUCTED. (LOCAL). LCDR W G MATTON, COORDINATOR; PATROL SQUADRON 56; NAVAL AIR STATION; JACKSONVILLE, FL 32212. (#29450).

NATIONAL SECRETARIES ASSOC HISTORY PROJECT - FL. A HISTORY OF SECRETARIES AND CLERICAL WORKERS IN JACKSONVILLE WILL BE PUBLISHED. (LOCAL). DEBORAH J EPSTEIN, ADMIN ASSISTANT; JACKSONVILLE ARBC NATIONAL SECRETARIES ASSOC; 2113 HENDRICKS AVE; JACKSONVILLE, FL 32207. (#22427).

JACKSONVILLE — CONTINUED

NEPTUNE BEACH CITY HALL RESTORATION, FL. RESTORATION OF ORIGINAL NEPTUNE BEACH CITY HALL AS A BICENTENNIAL MEMORIAL. (LOCAL). DEBORAH J EPSTEIN, ADMIN ASSISTANT; BOY SCOUT TROOP #326; 2800 SUNI-PINES BLVD; JACKSONVILLE, FL 32207. (#25255).

ORAL HISTORY SEMINAR & WORKSHOP, JACKSONVILLE, FL. DR S PROCTOR WILL LECTURE & LEAD A WORKSHOP ON METHODS USED IN THE COLLECTION OF DATA & RESEARCH IN ORAL HISTORY, PROGRAM TO INCLUDE AN EXHIBIT OF HISTORICAL MATERIALS. (LOCAL). DR JOAN CARVER, CHAIRMAN BICENTENNIAL; JACKSONVILLE UNIVERSITY & JACKSONVILLE HISTORICAL SOCIETY; JACKSONVILLE, FL 32211. (#15701).

ORIGINAL MUSICAL COMPOSITION TO PATRIOTIC THEME,FL. ARTIST IN RESIDENCE, WILLIAM HOSKINS WILL COMPOSE AN ORIGINAL WORK TO AN EXISTING AMERICAN POEM OR AN ORIGINAL PATRIOTIC POEM BY A STUDENT. (ST-WIDE). JOAN CARVER, CHAIRMAN BICENTENNIAL COMMITTEE; COLLEGE OF FINE ARTS JACKSONVILLE UNIV; JACKSONVILLE, FL 32211. (#15698).

OUR AMERICAN HERITAGE, JACKSONVILLE, FL. RADIO VIGNETTES RUN DAILY OF AMERICAN HISTORY DURING THE 200TH YEAR; ANNOUNCEMENTS OF UPCOMING ABCJ ACTIVITIES AND JACKSONVILLE HISTORY. (LOCAL). DEBORAH J EPSTEIN, ADMINISTRATIVE ASSISTANT; WMBR RADIO AND JACKSONVILLE BICENTENNIAL COMMITTEE; 2113 HENDRICKS AVE; JACKSONVILLE, FL 32207. (#22414).

PAGEANT AMERICA: PLAYS PRODUCED AT UNIV IN FLORIDA. FOUR COSTUMED PERIOD PLAYS WILL BE WRITTEN, PRODUCED & CAST BY STUDENTS AND FACULTY OF THE UNIVERSITY OF NORTH FLORIDA. EACH PLAY CONCERNS A HISTORICAL EVENT. (LOCAL). LEONARD BURNS, VICE CHAIRPERSON; BICENTENNIAL COMMITTEE, UNIV OF NORTH FLORIDA; PO BOX 17074, POTTSBURG STATION; JACKSONVILLE, FL 32216. (#8682).

PAINTING OF STATION NURSERY PLAYGROUND - FL. PAINTED PLAYGROUND EQUIPMENT IN RED, WHITE AND BLUE. (LOCAL). LCDR W G MATTON, COORDINATOR; PATROL SQUADRON 56; NAVAL AIR STATION; JACKSONVILLE, FL 32212. (#29449).

PATRIOTIC FIREPLUGS, JACKSONVILLE, FL. PAINTING OF FIREPLUGS, CITY-WIDE. (LOCAL). DEBBIE EPSTEIN, ADMINISTRATIVE ASSISTANT; BOLD CITY JAYCEES/JACKSONVILLE BICENTENNIAL COMMITTEE; 2113 HENDRICKS AVE; JACKSONVILLE, FL 32207. (#22421).

PATRIOTIC MUSIC BY JACKSONVILLE UNIV DOLPHINAIRES. JACKSONVILLE UNIVERSITY DOLPHINAIRES WILL PERFORM A PATRIOTIC MUSIC REVIEW OF SONG & DANCE FOR SERVICE ORGANIZATIONS. (LOCAL). DEAN F KINNE, DEAN; COLLEGE OF FINE ARTS, JACKSONVILLE UNIV; JACKSONVILLE, FL 32211. (#15697).

PHYSICAL FITNESS CLINICS HELD FOR YOUTH IN FLORIDA. THE UNIVERSITY OF NORTH FLORIDA'S PHYSICAL EDUCATION & ATHLETIC DEPARTMENTS WILL HOLD HEALTH & PHYSICAL FITNESS CLINICS IN 1976, PARTICULARLY FOR SCHOOL CHILDREN. PURPOSE TO FOSTER HEALTHIER ADULTS. (LOCAL). RICHARD REISINGER, PROJ COORDINATOR; UNIV OF NORTH FLORIDA, BICENTENNIAL COMMITTEE; PO BOX 17074, POTTSBURG STATION; JACKSONVILLE, FL 32216. (#8684).

PIONEER HOMESTEAD RESTORATION - JACKSONVILLE, FL. THE JACKSONVILLE CHILDREN'S MUSEUM WILL RESTORE THE PIONEER HOMESTEAD. (LOCAL). DORIS L WHITMORE, DIRECTOR; JACKSONVILLE CHILDREN'S MUSEUM; 1025 GULF LIFE DR; JACKSONVILLE, FL 32207. (#28269). **ARBA GRANTEE.**

PRESERVATION OF TREE HILL - JACKSONVILLE, FL. EDUCATIONAL TOURS ON TREE HILL EMPHASIZING THE NATURAL HERITAGE OF THE JACKSONVILLE AREA. (LOCAL). DEBORAH J EPSTEIN, ADMIN ASSISTANT; JACKSONVILLE ARBC/THE PRESERVATION ASSOC FOR TREE HILL, INC; 2113 HENDRICKS AVE; JACKSONVILLE, FL 32207. (#22433).

PRESERVATION OF EARLY FLORIDA RECORDS - FL. THE MINUTES OF THE OLD PROVIDENCE BAPTIST CHURCH, ESTABLISHED IN 1833, WILL BE PUBLISHED IN BOOK FORM AND PRESENTED TO THE JACKSONVILLE GENEALOGICAL SOCIETY WORKSHOP '76. (LOCAL). DEBORAH J EPSTEIN, ADMIN ASSISTANT; JACKSONVILLE GENEALOGICAL SOCIETY/ABCJ; 2113 HENDRICKS AVE, SUITE 206; JACKSONVILLE, FL 32207. (#24852).

RESEARCH ON ST JOHN'S TOWN, JACKSONVILLE, FL. ORIGINAL RESEARCH AND MAPPING OF ST JOHN'S TOWN, A SEVENTEENTH CENTURY TOWN ON THE ST JOHN'S RIVER. LITTLE PREVIOUS RESEARCH HAS BEEN DONE ON THE TOWN. (LOCAL). DR JAMES OLSON, ASST PROFESSOR OF HISTORY; PHI ALPHA THETA, HISTORY HONORARY SOCIETY; JACKSONVILLE, FL 32211. (#15700).

RIVERSIDE-AVONDALE RESTORATION PROJECTS - FL. HOME RESTORATIONS IN THE RIVERSIDE-AVONDALE AREA OF JACKSONVILLE AS WELL AS NEIGHBORHOOD IMPROVEMENTS AND BEAUTIFICATION PROJECTS. (LOCAL). DEBORAH J EPSTEIN, ADMIN ASSISTANT; JACKSONVILLE ARBC/RIVERSIDE-AVONDALE PRESERVATION ASSOC; 2113 HENDRICKS AVE; JACKSONVILLE, FL 32207. (#22426).

'THE RIVER, THE ROAD AND THE REVOLUTION', FL. DEPICTING JACKSONVILLE'S HISTORICAL SIGNIFICANCE RELATING TO THE KINGS ROAD, ST JOHNS RIVER AND THE AMERICAN REVOLUTION; REVOLUTIONARY WAR PERIOD CABIN RECONSTRUCTED ON MUSEUM GROUND. (LOCAL). DEBBIE EPSTEIN, ADMINISTRATIVE ASSISTANT; JACKSONVILLE CHILDREN'S MUSEUM JACKSONVILLE BICENT COMMITTEE; 2113 HENDRICKS AVE; JACKSONVILLE, FL 32207. (#22423).

SPECIAL EXHIBITS AT JACKSONVILLE, FL. SPECIAL DISPLAYS RELATED TO BICENTENNIAL TO BE DISPLAYED THROUGHOUT THE YEAR. (LOCAL). JOAN CARVER, CHAIRMAN BICENTENNIAL COMMITTEE; LIBRARY OF JACKSONVILLE UNIV; JACKSONVILLE, FL 32211. (#15699).

SPIRIT OF '76 - JACKSONVILLE, FL. A PATCH EARNED BY THE GIRL SCOUTS OF AMERICA. (LOCAL). DEBORAH J EPSTEIN, ADMIN ASSISTANT; GIRL SCOUTS OF AMERICA, GATEWAY COUNCIL/ ABCJ; 2113 HENDRICKS AVE, SUITE 206; JACKSONVILLE, FL 32207. (#24235).

SPIRIT SPECIALS - JACKSONVILLE, FL. RED, WHITE AND BLUE MINI BUSES WILL BE USED AS PART OF MASS TRANSIT IN DUVAL COUNTY. (LOCAL). DEBORAH J EPSTEIN, ADMIN ASSISTANT; JACKSONVILLE ARBC/JACKSONVILLE TRANSPORTATION AUTHORITY; 2113 HENDRICKS AVE; JACKSONVILLE, FL 32207. (#22425).

SYMPOSIUM ON AMERICAN WOMEN IN JACKSONVILLE, FL. THE UNIVERSITY OF NORTH FLORIDA WILL HOLD A SYMPOSIUM IN 1976 ON WOMEN'S STRUGGLE FOR EQUAL RIGHTS. LECTURES & FILMS WILL FOCUS ON FUTURE GOALS OF WOMEN. (LOCAL). ELLYN DAVEPORT, PROJ COORDINATOR; UNIV OF NORTH FLORIDA, BICENTENNIAL COMMITTEE; PO BOX 17074, POTTSBURG STATION; JACKSONVILLE, FL 32216. (#8685).

TABLETALK DISCUSSION SERIES ON CONTEMPORARY ISSUES. A MONTHLY LUNCHEON DISCUSSION WILL FOCUS ON ISSUES FACING OUR NATION IN THE REMAINDER OF THE 20TH CENTURY - POPULATION PROBLEMS, HUMAN FREEDOM ETC. (LOCAL). JOAN CARVER, CHAIRMAN; JACKSONVILLE UNIV BICENTENNIAL COMMITTEE; JACKSONVILLE UNIV; JACKSONVILLE, FL 32211. (#102530-1). **(??).**

TOYS FOR TOTS - JACKSONVILLE, FL. ANNUAL PROJECT THIS YEAR DEDICATED TO THE BICENTENNIAL AND EXPANDED TO REACH MORE AREAS AND GREATER NUMBERS OF CHILDREN. (LOCAL). MAJOR JOE ALEXANDER, PROJ DIRECTOR; U S MARINE CORPS RESERVES; NAS BOX 44, BLDG 411; JACKSONVILLE, FL 32212. (#18936).

TREE PLANTING - JACKSONVILLE, FL. TWO TREES WERE PLANTED AT THE RADAR SITE. (LOCAL). PAUL T GARDNER, MAJOR, USAF; 679TH RADAR SQUADRON NAVAL AIR STATION; BUILDING 658; JACKSONVILLE, FL 32212. (#29594).

TRICENTENNIAL FUND '2076', JACKSONVILLE, FL. 100 CITIZENS FROM JACKSONVILLE CONTRIBUTING $2076 TOWARD JACKSONVILLE TRICENTENNIAL CELEBRATION. FUNDS TO BE PLACED IN SPECIAL BANK ACCOUNT WITH MEMENTOS, POEMS ETC. (LOCAL). DEBBIE EPSTEIN, ADMINISTRATIVE ASST; JACKSONVILLE BICENTENNIAL COMMITTEE; 2113 HENDRICKS AVE SUIT, 206; JACKSONVILLE, FL 32207. (#29942).

WMBR RADIO CONTRIBUTIONS TO BICENTENNIAL - NBMRP. BICENTENNIAL PROGRAMMING INCLUDED PSA'S FOR LOCAL COMMUNITIES, INTERVIEW PROGRAMS & FEATURES INCLUDING NEWSCAST COVERAGE OF PERSONALITIES, ACTIVITIES & EVENTS. (LOCAL). TOM DAREN, BICENTENNIAL COORINATOR; RADIO STATION WMBR; 138 WAMSLEY RD, PO BOX 6877; JACKSONVILLE, FL 32205. (#28310).

WVOJ RADIO'S 'AN AMERICAN IDEA' - NBMRP. STATION PURCHASED SYNDICATED BICENTENNIAL PROGRAM 'AN AMERICAN IDEA' & BROADCAST 18 SUCH FEATURES EACH WEEK. PROMOTED A VARIETY OF LOCAL BICENTENNIAL EVENTS. (LOCAL). R T OLDENBURG, BICENTENNIAL COORDINATOR; RADIO STATION WVOJ; 1435 ELLIS RD SOUTH; JACKSONVILLE, FL 32205. (#28309).

'200 YEARS BEFORE THE MAST' - SLIDE SHOW, FL. A NAVY SLIDE PRESENTATION ON NAVAL HISTORY FROM ITS INCEPTION UNTIL THE PRESENT. (LOCAL). DALE SUMMERS, PETTY OFFICER, FIRST CLASS; NAVAL AIR RESERVE UNIT; PO BOX 4, NAVAL AIR STATION; JACKSONVILLE, FL 32212. (#31312).

'200 YEARS IN AMERICA', BOOK - JACKSONVILLE, FL. HISTORY OF THE MIGRATION OF ENGLISH & IRISH IMMIGRANTS TO THIS COUNTRY BEGINNING IN 1775; DEALS WITH TRIALS & TRIBULATIONS THEY ENCOUNTERED AND ESTABLISHMENT OF THE CATHOLIC EDUCATIONAL SYSTEM. (ST-WIDE). DEBORAH J EPSTEIN, ADMINISTRATIVE ASSISTANT; ST PAUL'S GUILD - ST PAUL CATHOLIC CHURCH / ABCJ; 2113 HENDRICKS AVE SUITE 206; JACKSONVILLE, FL 32207. (#22415).

MAY 3 - 8, '75. FLORIDA BICENTENNIAL EXHIBIT. 3 TRAVELING VANS ON DISPLAY, WALK-THROUGH EXHIBIT OF FLORIDA AND BICENTENNIAL BAND FEATURED. (ST-WIDE). DEBORAH J EPSTEIN, COORD; AMERICAN BICENT COMMISSION OF JACKSONVILLE FL BICENT COMMISSION; 2113 HENDRICKS AVE, SUITE 206; JACKSONVILLE, FL 32207. (#200011-52).

MAY 17, '75. ARMED FORCES DAY/BICENTENNIAL LUNCHEON. A NO-HOST FORMAL LUNCHEON PRECEDING ARMED FORCES DAY ACTIVITIES OPEN TO PUBLIC. CONGRESSMEN CHARLES E BENNETT & WILLIAM V CHAPPELL WILL BE FEATURED SPEAKERS. AT HILTON HOTEL BALLROOM, 565 S MAIN ST JACKSONVILLE. (LOCAL). DEBORAH J EPSTEIN; ABJC US ARMY NAVY MARINE CORPS COAST GUARD AIR FORCE; 2113 HENDRICKS AVE SUITE 206; JACKSONVILLE, FL 32207. (#50819-1).

MAY 17, '75. ARMED FORCES DAY AMERICAN BICENTENNIAL COMMISSION OF JAX KICKOFF DAY. A JOINT NON-COMPETITIVE NON-COMMERCIAL EXPOSITION FEATURING FREE DIS PLAYS EXHIBITS & DEMONSTRATIONS BY US ARMY, NAVY, MARINE CORP, COAST GUARD, AIR FORCE IN A SALUTE TO THE 200TH BIRTHDAY OF AMERICA. AT PARKING LOT ON COASTLINE DR & LITTLE THEATRE PORTION OF AUDITORIUM. (ST-WIDE). 2113 HENDRICKS AVE, SUITE; US ARMY, NAVY, MARINE CORPS, COAST GUARD, AIR FORCE ABCJ; 206; JACKSONVILLE, FL 32207. (#50819-2).

MAY 26, '75. MEMORIAL DAY CEREMONIES, EVERGREEN CEMETERY. MEMORIAL DAY OBSERVATION AT FLAG POLE AT EVERGREEN CEMETERY MAIN ST & WINONA DR A DAY OF REMEMBRANCE HONORING THOSE WHO FOUGHT & DIED IN DEFENSE OF AMERICAN INTERNAL FREEDOMS. AT EVERGREEN CEMETERY 4535 MAIN STREET JACKSONVILLE FL. (LOCAL). DEBORAH J EPSTEIN; ABCJ, VETERANS PATRIOTIC OBSERVANCE COMMITTEE; 2113 HENDRICKS AVE, SUITE 206; JACKSONVILLE, FL 32207. (#50821-1).

JULY 1 - 30, '75. BICENTENNIAL ART SHOW & CONTEST AT FT CAROLINE N MEM. COMPETITION, EXHIBIT. (LOCAL). SUPT, FT CAROLINE N MEM; NATIONAL PARK SERVICE; 12713 FORT CAROLINE ROAD; JACKSONVILLE, FL 32225. (#6728-88).

JULY 4, '75. JACKSONVILLE, FLA HOSTS FIRST ANNUAL CHILDREN'S PARADE. PARADE LIMITED TO SCHOOL AGE YOUTH. FLOATS WILL DEPICT BICENT THEMES & WILL BE HAND-DRAWN. CHILDREN WILL BE DRESSED IN COSTUMES RELATING TO BICENT THEMES. AT MARKET ST & COASTLINE DR, W ON COASTLINE DR. (LOCAL). DEBORAH J EPSTEIN; JACKSONVILLE RECREATION DEPT & JAYCEES; 2113 HENDRICKS AVE, SUITE 206; JACKSONVILLE, FL 32207. (#100140-1).

JULY 4 - 6, '75. ARTS FOURTH. SUMMER ART FESTIVAL TO INCLUDE GRAPHIC ARTS, FINE ARTS, THE PERFORMING ARTS (BALLET AND THEATER), A MULTI-ETHNIC FOOD FESTIVAL AND CRAFTS DEMONSTRATIONS. AT CIVIC AUDITORIUM. (LOCAL). DEBBE J EPSTEIN, ASST; ARTS ASSEMBLY OF JAX, INC/ARBCJ/ CITY OF JACKSONVILLE; 2113 HENDRICKS AVE - SUITE 206; JACKSONVILLE, FL 32207. (#100584-1).

SEPT 1 - DEC 15, '75. PLAYWRITING CONTEST. SIXTH ANNUAL PLAYWRITING CONTEST WILL BE HELD; THIS YEAR, SCRIPTS APPROPRIATE TO THE BICENTENNIAL WILL BE EMPHASIZED. (LOCAL). FRANCES KINNE, DEAN; THEATRE ARTS DEPT; JACKSONVILLE UNIV; JACKSONVILLE, FL 32211. (#102527-1).

SEPT 2, '75 - JUNE 1, '76. JUNIOR-SENIOR HIGH SCHOOL CONCERTS BY JAX SYMPHONY. CONCERT THEME: SALUTE TO THE AMERICAN REVOLUTIN BICENTENNIAL. (LOCAL). DEBORAH J EPSTEIN, ASST; ABCJ & JACKSONVILLE SYMPHONY ASSOCIATION; 2113 HENDRICKS AVE, SUITE 206; JACKSONVILLE, FL 32207. (#106094-1).

OCT 3, '75. DAY OF URBANIZATION. THE DAY OF URBANIZATION WILL FOCUS ON OLD & NEW PATTERNS OF PARTICIPATION IN THE GOVERNING OF THE CITY; EMPHASIS ON THE MIX OF PUBLIC AND PRIVATE IN THE ADVISORY AND REGULATORY BOARDS; SPEAKERS WILL BE THOSE IN THE GOVERNMENT. AT GOODING AUDITORIUM AND WOLFSON STUDENT CENTER. (LOCAL). JOAN S CARVER, CHAIRMAN; SOCIAL SCIENCE DIVISION, JACKSONVILLE UNIV; JACKSONVILLE UNIV; JACKSONVILLE, FL 32211. (#102532-1).

OCT 4 - 6, '75. ARTS ARGY WEEKEND. ARTS ARGY WEEKEND WILL FEATURE ALL ARTS ACTIVITIES ON CAMPUS; WILL EMPHASIZE CRAFT DEMONSTRATIONS, CONCERTS, BODY PAINTING AND CONTEMPORARY AMERICAN DANCE. AT COLLEGE OF FINE ARTS, PHILLIPS BUILDING, SWISHER AUDITORIUM. (LOCAL). FRANCES KINNE, DEAN; COLLEGE OF FINE ARTS; JACKSONVILLE, FL 32211. (#102528-1).

OCT 16 - 17, '75. COLLOQUIUM: RELIGION IN THE AMERICAN EXPERIENCE. A TWO DAY COLLOQUIUM DESIGNED TO PROVIDE A PERSPECTIVE ON THE PECULIAR HISTORY OF RELIGION IN THE U S & RELIGION'S PLACE IN THE NATION'S FUTURE. PROGRAMS WILL FOCUS ON CATHOLIC, JEWISH, FEMALE AND BLACK PERSPECTIVE ON RELIGION IN THE AMERICAN EXPERIENCE. AT SWISHER & GOODING AUDITORIUMS, WOLFSON STUDENT CENTER. (LOCAL). JOAN CARVER, CHAIRMAN; JACKSONVILLE UNIV BICENTENNIAL COMMITTEE & DEPT OF RELIGION; JACKSONVILLE UNIV; JACKSONVILLE, FL 32211. (#102520-1).

OCT 24 - NOV 1, '75. 'THE CHILDREN'S HOUR'. LIVE PERFORMANCE AT SWISHER AUDITORIUM. (LOCAL). FRANCES KINNE, DEAN; THEATRE ARTS DEPT, COLLEGE OF FINE ARTS; JACKSONVILLE, FL 32211. (#102528-3).

NOV 20 - DEC 7, '75. AMERICAN MUSIC CONCERTS. THE ORCHESTRA WILL HAVE AN ALL-AMERICAN MUSIC SEASON FOR 1975-76; THERE WILL BE 2 FULL LENGTH CONCERTS WITH SOLOISTS AND A JOINT CONCERT WITH JACKSONVILLE UNIV CHORUS WHICH WILL BE PRESENTED ON CAMPUS AND ON TOUR. AT SWISHER AUDITORIUM. (LOCAL). FRANCES KINNE, DEAN; COLLEGE OF FINE ARTS; JACKSONVILLE UNIV; JACKSONVILLE, FL 32211. (#102522-1).

DEC 7, '75. CONCERTS OF AMERICAN MUSIC BY CHAMBER ORCHESTRA. 2 CONCERTS OF SMALLER WORKS BY AMERICAN COMPOSERS WILL BE PRESENTED BY THE JACKSONVILLE CHAMBER ORCHESTRA. AT RECITAL HALL. (LOCAL). FRANCES KINNE, DEAN; COLLEGE OF FINE ARTS; JACKSONVILLE UNIV; JACKSONVILLE, FL 32211. (#102523-1).

DEC 11 - 13, '75. 'AMAHL AND THE NIGHT VISITORS' - AN AMERICAN OPERA. AMAHL AND THE NIGHT VISITORS WILL BE PRESENTED IN DECEMBER 1975 BY THE JACKSONVILLE UNIVERSITY OPERA WORKSHOP. AT SWISHER AUDITORIUM. (LOCAL). FRANCES KINNE, DEAN; COLLEGE OF FINE ARTS; JACKSONVILLE UNIV; JACKSONVILLE, FL 32211. (#102524-1).

JAN 1 - MAY 7, '76. BICENTENNIAL ART SERIES. COMPETITION. (LOCAL). DEBORAH J EPSTEIN, ASST; KENT THEATRES & WAPE RADIO JACKSONVILLE ARBC; 2113 HENDRICKS AVE, SUITE 206; JACKSONVILLE, FL 32207. (#107321-1).

JAN 1 - DEC 31, '76. IMPACT '76 - 'HERE'S LIFE, JACKSONVILLE'. SEMINAR WILL HAVE CHRISTIAN SPIRITUAL EMPHASIS - HOW TO LIVE AND SHARE THE CHRISTIAN LIFE. (LOCAL). DEBORAH J EPSTEIN, COORD; IMPACT '76, BICENTENNIAL COMMISSION OF JACKSONVILLE; 2113 HENDRICKS AVE, SUITE 206; JACKSONVILLE, FL 32207. (#106799-11).

JAN 1 - DEC 31, '76. STUDENT-FACULTY ART EXHIBIT AT UNIV OF N FLORIDA. A STUDENT-FACULTY ART SHOW, USING MODERN ART AND GRAPHIC TECHNIQUES TO INTERPRET WHAT AMERICA MEANS TO TODAY'S SOCIETY, WILL BE PERMANENTLY EXHIBITED AT THE UNIVERSITY OF NORTH FLORIDA. EXHIBIT OF

JACKSONVILLE — CONTINUED

MODERN ART & GRAPHICS BY STUDENTS AND FACULTY. (LOCAL). LEONARD BURNS; UNIV OF NORTH FLORIDA; PO BOX 17074, POTTSBURG STATION; JACKSONVILLE, FL 32216. (#8679-1).

JAN 15 - 20, '76. US CORPS OF ENGINEERS BICENTENNIAL EXHIBIT. A MULTI-IMAGE, MULTI-SCREEN AND SOUND EXHIBIT ILLUSTRATING HOW A WATER RESOURCE PROJECT IS DEVELOPED FROM 'NEED TO DEED' AND THE WORKINGS OF AN AMERICAN HYDROELECTRIC DAM. AT REGENCY SQUARE, ARLINGTON EXPRESSWAY. (LOCAL). DEBORAH J EPSTEIN, COORD; AMERICAN BICENT COMMISSION OF JACKSONVILLE/REGENCY SQUARE MERCHANTS; 2113 HENDRICKS AVE, SUITE 206; JACKSONVILLE, FL 32207. (#200011-54).

JAN 20 - 22, '76. CRAFTS & HOBBY EXHIBIT AT UNIV OF N FLORIDA. TYPICAL HOBBIES - BOTTLES, COIN & STAMP COLLECTIONS & CRAFTS - WILL BE EXHIBITED BY THE UNIVERSITY OF NORTH FLORIDA DURING 1976. BOTTLE, COIN, STAMP & CRAFTS EXHIBIT. (LOCAL). LEONARD BURNS; UNIV OF NORTH FLORIDA; PO BOX 17074, POTTSBURG STATION; JACKSONVILLE, FL 32216. (#8686-1).

JAN 24, '76. CONSERVATION DAY. CONSERVATION DAY INCLUDES TREE PLANTING, BRUSH CLEARING & JOHNNY HORIZONS PROGRAM. AT CAMP SHANDS, ECHOCKOTEE & JOHNSON. (LOCAL). DEBORAH J EPSTEIN, COORD; AMERICAN BICENT COMMISSION OF JACKSONVL/N FLORIDA COUNCIL BOY SCOUTS; 2113 HENDRICKS AVE, SUITE 206; JACKSONVILLE, FL 32207. (#200011-53).

JAN 27 - 29, '76. FOREIGN POLICY SYMPOSIUM. THE SYMPOSIUM WILL DEAL WITH NEW DIRECTIONS IN AMERICAN FOREIGN POLICY. (LOCAL). JOAN CARVER, CHAIRMAN; JACKSONVILLE UNIV BICENT COMMITTEE & DIVISION OF SOCIAL SCIENCES; JACKSONVILLE UNIV; JACKSONVILLE, FL 32211. (#102529-1).

JAN 28, '76. JOSEPH E LEE MEMORIAL LIBRARY AND MUSEUM DEDICATION. DEDICATION OF STATE'S LARGEST & MOST COMPREHENSIVE DEPOSITORY OF RECORDS DOCUMENTING THE HISTORY & CULTURE OF FLORIDA'S BLACKS. AT 1424 E 7TH ST. (ST-WIDE). DEBBIE EPSTEIN, COORD; JACKSONVILLE BICENTENNIAL COMMITTEE/CITIZENS FOR COMMUNITY ACTION; 2113 HENDRICKS AVE; JACKSONVILLE, FL 32207. (#9955-1).

FEB 1, '76. 'THE JEW IN AMERICAN LIFE', LECTURE BY DR STANLEY F CHYET. DR S F CHYET, PROFESSOR OF AMERICAN JEWISH HISTORY AT HEBREW UNION COLLEGE, WILL SPEAK ON THE INSTITUTE OF JUDAISM, NOW IN ITS 30TH YEAR. AT 8727 SAN JOSE BLVD. (LOCAL). DEBORAH J EPSTEIN, COORD; AMERICAN BICENT COMMISSION OF JACKSONVL/CONGREGATION AHAVATH CHESED; 2113 HENDRICKS AVE, SUITE 206; JACKSONVILLE, FL 32207. (#200011-57).

FEB 1 - JULY 4, '76. BEARD GROWING CONTEST. BEARD GROWING CONTEST TO GENERATE ENTHUSIASM FOR THE BICENTENNIAL YEAR; CONTEST WILL BE JUDGED AT THE 4TH OF JULY PAGEANT. (LOCAL). DEBORAH J EPSTEIN, ASST; JACKSONVILLE ARBC/FRATERNAL ORDER OF POLICE; 2113 HENDRICKS AVE; JACKSONVILLE, FL 32207. (#105884-1).

FEB 2, '76. 'JUDAISM IN AMERICAN LIFE'. 30TH ANNUAL CLERGY INSTITUTE ON JUDAISM FEATURES VARIOUS LECTURES. AT 8727 SAN JOSE BLVD. (LOCAL). DEBORAH J EPSTEIN, COORD; AMERICAN BICENT COMMISSION OF JACKSONVL/CONGREGATION AHAVATH CHESED; 2113 HENDRICKS AVE, SUITE 206; JACKSONVILLE, FL 32207. (#200011-56).

FEB 5, '76. BICENTENNIAL FILM SERIES 'IN COLD BLOOD'. DISCUSSION LEADER IS NORMAN POLLOCK, ASST PROFESSOR OF SOCIOLOGY. AT GOODING AUDITORIUM, JACKSONVILLE UNIV. (LOCAL). DEBORAH J EPSTEIN, COORD; AMERICAN BICENT COMMISSION OF JACKSONVILLE/JACKSONVILLE UNIV; 2113 HENDRICKS AVE, SUITE 206; JACKSONVILLE, FL 32207. (#200011-62).

FEB 7 - 8, '76. 'THE CRUCIBLE' BY ROBERT WARD. OPERA BASED ON PLAY ABOUT WITCH HUNT & TRIALS IN SALEM, MA, 1692. AT CIVIC AUDITORIUM, WATER ST. (LOCAL). DEBORAH J EPSTEIN, COORD; AMERICAN BICENT COMMISSION OF JACKSONVIL/OPERA REPERTORY GROUP, INC; 2113 HENDRICKS AVE, SUITE 206; JACKSONVILLE, FL 32207. (#200011-60).

FEB 9, '76. 'NO GREATER LOVE'. IN A SALUTE TO HOSPITALIZED VETERANS, LETTERS WERE SENT TO ALL HOSPITALIZED VETERANS IN U S HOSPITALS; LOCAL VETERANS RECEIVED THEIR LETTERS IN PERSON. AT CAMPFIRE OFFICE. (LOCAL). DEBORAH J EPSTEIN, COORD; AMERICAN BICENT COMMISSION OF JACKSONVILLE/CAMP FIRE GIRLS, INC; 2113 HENDRICKS AVE, SUITE 206; JACKSONVILLE, FL 32207. (#200011-59).

FEB 9 - 13, '76. A BLACK CULTURE & AWARENESS WEEK EMPHASIZING LOCAL CONTRIBUTIONS. ONE WEEK OF FILMS, SEMINARS, LECTURES AND EXHIBITS ON THE BLACK INFLUENCE IN AMERICA WITH SPECIAL EMPHASIS ON CONTRIBUTIONS OF LOCAL BLACK LEADERS OF THE JACKSONVILLE AREA. (LOCAL). LEONARD M BURNS; BLACK STUDENT UNION; PO BOX 17074, POTTSBURG STATION; JACKSONVILLE, FL 32216. (#8674-1).

FEB 11 - 14, '76. INDUSTRIAL HERITAGE USA. HISTORY OF INDUSTRY & INVENTIONS FEATURED; INCLUDES PRICELESS EXHIBITS FROM GREENFIELD VILLAGE AND HENRY FORD MUSEUM; 27 LARGE DISPLAY CASES ON VIEW TO THE PUBLIC. AT REGENCY SQUARE. (LOCAL). DEBORAH J EPSTEIN, COORD; AMERICAN BICENT COMMISSION OF JACKSONVL/REGENCY SQUARE SHOPPING CTR; 2113 HENDRICKS AVE, SUITE 206; JACKSONVILLE, FL 32207. (#200011-58).

FEB 13 - 15, '76. 2ND ANNUAL TREATY OAK LONG RIFLES RENDEZVOUS & MUZZLE LOADING SHOOT. COMPETITION, EXHIBIT AT GATEWAY RIFLE AND PISTOL CLUB. (LOCAL). DEBORAH J EPSTEIN, COORD; AMERICAN BICENT COMMISSION OF JACKSONVL/TREATY OAK LONG RIFLE ASSOC; 2113 HENDRICKS AVE, SUITE 206; JACKSONVILLE, FL 32207. (#200011-61).

FEB 15 - 22, '76. BROTHERHOOD WEEK. REDEDICATION OF BROTHERHOOD HERITAGE TO FOCUS CITY-WIDE ATTENTION UPON OUR HERITAGE AND TO PROMOTE REDEDICATION TO BROTHERHOOD IN THE FINEST AMERICAN TRADITION; LECTURES IN CHURCHES, SYNAGOGUES AND SCHOOLS. AT 754 GULF LIFE TOWER. (LOCAL). DEBORAH J EPSTEIN, COORD; AMERICAN BICENT COMMISSION OF JACKSONVL/NATL CONF CHRISTIANS & JEWS; 2113 HENDRICKS AVE, SUITE 206; JACKSONVILLE, FL 32207. (#200011-67).

FEB 16, '76. CANDLELIGHT SALUTE TO WOMEN IN AMERICAN HISTORY. 21 GIRL SCOUTS WILL HONOR AN OUTSTANDING WOMAN BY LIGHTING A CANDLE AND DELIVERING A SHORT SPEECH ON HER LIFE. AT ST CATHERINE EPISCOPAL CHURCH. (LOCAL). DEBORAH J EPSTEIN, COORD; AMERICAN BICENT COMMISSION OF JACKSONVILLE/GIRL SCOUT TROOP #98; 2113 HENDRICKS AVE, SUITE 206; JACKSONVILLE, FL 32207. (#200011-66).

FEB 19, '76. JACKSONVILLE UNIV BICENTENNIAL FILM SERIES. DISCUSSION LEADER-MS BETTY WINSTEAD, JACKSONVILLE UNIVERSITY SOCIOLOGIST. AT GOODING AUDITORIUM, JACKSONVILLE UNIV. (LOCAL). DEBORAH J EPSTEIN, COORD; AMERICAN BICENT COMMISSION OF JACKSONVILLE/JACKSONVILLE UNIV; 2113 HENDRICKS AVE, SUITE 206; JACKSONVILLE, FL 32207. (#200011-65).

FEB 21 - 23, '76. UNITED STATES ARMED FORCES BICENTENNIAL CARAVAN. CARAVAN IS COMPOSED OF EXHIBIT VANS FOR EACH MILITARY SERVICE. PROJECT THEME IS 'HISTORY OF THE ARMED FORCES AND THEIR CONTRIBUTIONS TO THE NATION'. (LOCAL). MS DEBBIE EPSTEIN; BICENTENNIAL COMMISSION OF JACKSONVILLE; 2113 HENDRICKS; JACKSONVILLE, FL 32207. (#1775-435).

FEB 24, '76. JACKSONVILLE UNIV CHAMBER ORCHESTRA CONCERT. AMERICAN WORKS. AT PHILLIPS RECITAL HALL, JACKSONVILLE UNIV. (LOCAL). DEBORAH J EPSTEIN, COORD; AMERICAN BICENT COMMISSION OF JACKSONVILLE/JACKSONVILLE UNIV; 2113 HENDRICKS AVE, SUITE 206; JACKSONVILLE, FL 32207. (#200011-64).

FEB 26, '76. 'SUBSIDIES & REGULATIONS CONTROLLING THE ECONOMY'. FEATURED SPEAKER IS DR ROBERT F LANZILLOTTI, DEAN OF COLLEGE OF BUSINESS ADMINISTRATION, UNIV OF FLORIDA. AT GOODING AUDITORIUM, JACKSONVILLE UNIV. (LOCAL). DEBORAH J EPSTEIN, COORD; AMERICAN BICENT COMMISSION OF JACKSONVILLE/JACKSONVILLE UNIV; 2113 HENDRICKS AVE, SUITE 206; JACKSONVILLE, FL 32207. (#200011-63).

FEB 26 - 28, '76. 'A BAG OF TRICKS'. LIVE PERFORMANCE AT SWISHER AUDITORIUM. (LOCAL). FRANCES KINNE, DEAN; THEATRE ARTS DEPT, COLLEGE OF FINE ARTS; JACKSONVILLE, FL 32211. (#102528-1).

FEB 26 - 29, '76. JACKSONVILLE HOME AND PATIO SHOW. BICENTENNIAL THEME FEATURING 600 LB BIRTHDAY CAKE AND REPLICA OF EARLY 1800 SOUTHERN MANSION. EXHIBIT OF ANTIQUES, HOME PRODUCTS AND SERVICES. AT CIVIC AUDITORIUM & EXHIBIT HALL. (LOCAL). DEBORAH J EPSTEIN, COORD; AMERICAN BICENT COMMISSION OF JACKSONVILLE/PARAGON PRODUCTIONS; 2113 HENDRICKS AVE, SUITE 206; JACKSONVILLE, FL 32207. (#200011-68).

MAR 1, '76. AMERICA COMES OF AGE IN PHYSICAL SCIENCES. SPEAKER WILL BE DR STANLEY BALLARD, PROFESSOR OF PHYSICS, UNIV OF FLORIDA. AT JACKSONVILLE UNIV. (LOCAL). DEBORAH J EPSTEIN, COORD; DIVISION OF SCIENCE AND MATH, JACKSONVILLE UNIV/ABC OF JACKSONVILLE; 2113 HENDRICKS AVE, SUITE 206; JACKSONVILLE, FL 32207. (#200011-74).

MAR 3, '76. NUCLEAR POWER IN THE ENERGY CRISIS. SPEAKER WILL BE DR EDWARD CARROLL, PROFESSOR OF NUCLEAR ENGINEERING, UNIV OF FLORIDA. AT JACKSONVILLE UNIV. (LOCAL). DEBORAH J EPSTEIN, COORD; DIVISION OF SCIENCE AND MATH, JACKSONVILLE UNIV/ ABC OF JACKSONVILLE; 2113 HENDRICKS AVE, SUITE 206; JACKSONVILLE, FL 32207. (#200011-75).

MAR 7, '76. CONCERT BY JACKSONVILLE UNIV ORCHESTRA. LIVE PERFORMANCE AT SWISHER AUDITORIUM, JACKSONVILLE UNIV. (LOCAL). DEBORAH J EPSTEIN, COORD; COLLEGE OF FINE ARTS, JACKSONVILLE UNIV/BICENT COMMISSION JACKSONVL; 2113 HENDRICKS AVE, SUITE 206; JACKSONVILLE, FL 32207. (#200011-76).

MAR 9, '76. SYMPOSIUM ON THE GROWTH NEEDS OF JACKSONVILLE, FL. PRESENT & FUTURE TRANSPORTATION, FUEL AND GROWTH NEEDS TO BE EVALUATED. (LOCAL). HAROLD SNIDER; UNIV OF NORTH FLORIDA; PO BOX 17074, POTTSBURG STATION; JACKSONVILLE, FL 32216. (#8677-1).

MAR 9 - 15, '76. CAMP FIRE GIRLS 66TH BIRTHDAY. RECOGNITION CEREMONIES OF NATIONAL AS WELL AS LOCAL FOUNDERS OF CAMP FIRE GIRLS. (LOCAL). DEBORAH J EPSTEIN, COORD; AMERICAN BICENT COMMISSION OF JACKSONVILLE/CAMP FIRE GIRLS, INC; 2113 HENDRICKS AVE, SUITE 206; JACKSONVILLE, FL 32207. (#200011-77).

MAR 9 - 29, '76. GREAT DECISIONS-DISCUSSION SERIES. DISCUSSIONS ON VARIOUS ASPECTS OF AMERICAN FOREIGN POLICY WILL BE HELD EVERY MONDAY EVENING FOR EIGHT WEEKS BEGINNING FEB 9 AND ENDING MARCH 29. AT DOODING AUDITORIUM, JACKSONVILLE UNIV. (LOCAL). DEBORAH J EPSTEIN, ASST; JACKSONVILLE UNIVERSITY, JACKSONVILLE UNITED NATIONS ASSOC & ABCJ; 2113 HENDRICKS AVE, SUITE 206; JACKSONVILLE, FL 32207. (#106094-24).

MAR 10, '76. 'TELEPHONE CENTENNIAL' - TELEPHONE PIONEERS OF AMERICA. RECOGNITION OF AMERICAN ASTRONAUTS, MARKING OF 1ST TELEPHONE BLDG & FIRST CABLE CROSSING OF ST JOHNS. AT JACOBS BLDG, 400 CHURCH ST. (LOCAL). DEBORAH J EPSTEIN, COORD; AMERICAN BICENT COMMISSION OF JACKSONVL TELEPHONE PIONEERS OF AMER; 2113 HENDRICKS AVE, SUITE 206; JACKSONVILLE, FL 32207. (#200011-80).

MAR 11, '76. BICENT FILM SERIES THE 'GRAPES OF WRATH' WITH DISCUSSION. FESTIVAL, SEMINAR AT GOODING AUDITORIUM, JACKSONVILLE UNIV. (LOCAL). DEBORAH J EPSTEIN, COORD; JACKSONVILLE UNIV/AMERICAN BICENT COMMISSION OF JACKSONVILLE; 2113 HENDRICKS AVE, SUITE 206; JACKSONVILLE, FL 32207. (#200011-70).

MAR 12, '76. 'SALUTE '76' - JONES COLLEGE GOLF TOURNAMENT. PARTICIPANTS INCLUDE STUDENTS, STAFF, FACULTY & ALUMNI OF COLLEGE AS WELL AS INVITED GUESTS. COLLEGE OFFERS SPECIAL PRIZES TO PARTICIPANTS WHOSE FINAL TOURNAMENT SCORE IS 76, EITHER GROSS OR HANDICAP. AT MAYPORT NAVAL STATION. (LOCAL). DEBORAH J EPSTEIN, COORD; AMERICAN BICENT COMMISSION OF JACKSONVILLE/JONES COLLEGE; 2113 HENDRICKS AVE, SUITE 206; JACKSONVILLE, FL 32207. (#200011-79).

MAR 13, '76. HIDDEN HEROINES - GIRL SCOUT SALUTE TO AMERICAN BICENTENNIAL. GIRL SCOUTS WILL PREPARE EXHIBITS OF HEROINES, BOTH WELL-KNOWN AND 'HIDDEN' OF THE PAST 200 YEARS. WIVES OF EACH PRESIDENT FROM WASHINGTON TO FORD WILL BE DEPICTED BY A GIRL SCOUT DRESSED IN AN AUTHENTIC INAUGURAL GOWN COSTUME. AT REGENCY SQUARE MALL. (LOCAL). DEBORAH J EPSTEIN, COORD; AMERICAN BICENT COMMISSION OF JACKSONVL/ARLINGTON-LONE STAR GIRL SCT; 2113 HENDRICKS AVE, SUITE 206; JACKSONVILLE, FL 32207. (#200011-83).

MAR 13 - 14, '76. 'BICENTENNIAL SAIL' OF HISTORIC SHIP VISITS FORT CAROLINE N MEM. HISTORIC FISHING SCHOONER 'MARY E', SAILING THE ATLANTIC COAST, WILL STOP AT THIS NATIONAL PARK SERVICE AREA, PROVIDING SHIPBOARD PROGRAMS TO VISITORS TO THIS AREA. (REGN'L). FORT CAROLINE NATL MEM; SEA VENTURES, INC. & NATIONAL PARK SERVICE; 12713 FORT CAROLINE ROAD; JACKSONVILLE, FL 32225. (#7960-3).

MAR 14 - 21, '76. 'BIBS FOR BABY BLUE BIRDS'. BIBS BEING PRESENTED TO BICENTENNIAL BABIES BORN IN LOCAL HOSPITALS DURING CAMP FIRE GIRLS BIRTHDAY WEEK, WITH AN INVITATION TO JOIN CAMP FIRE AT AGE 6; BIBS MADE BY CLUB MEMBERS. AT 2001 ART MUSEUM DR. (LOCAL). DEBORAH J EPSTEIN, COORD; AMERICAN BICENT COMMISSION OF JACKSONVILLE/CAMP FIRE GIRLS, INC; 2113 HENDRICKS AVE, SUITE 206; JACKSONVILLE, FL 32207. (#200011-78).

MAR 15, '76. CONCERT BY JACKSONVILLE UNIV CHORUS. LIVE PERFORMANCE AT PHILLIPS RECITAL HALL, JACKSONVILLE UNIV. (LOCAL). DEBORAH J EPSTEIN, COORD; COLLEGE OF FINE ARTS, JACKSONVILLE UNIV/ABC OF JACKSONVILLE; 2113 HENDRICKS AVE, SUITE 206; JACKSONVILLE, FL 32207. (#200011-71).

MAR 22, '76. 'GEORGE WASHINGTON'S BIRTHDAY TEA'. A JOINT ANNUAL CELEBRATION OF THE REGENTS COUNCIL OF NORTHEAST FL. AT 515 PONTE VEDRA BLVD. (LOCAL). DEBORAH J EPSTEIN, COORD; AMERICAN BICENT COMMISSION OF JACKSONVL/ST JOHNS RIVER CHAPTER DAR; 2113 HENDRICKS AVE, SUITE 206; JACKSONVILLE, FL 32207. (#200011-72).

MAR 24, '76. AMERICAN CANCER SOCIETY'S 7TH ANNUAL FASHION SHOW. BICENTENNIAL FASHIONS THROUGHOUT THE 200 YEAR HISTORY OF AMERICA FEATURED. AT HILTON HOTEL. (LOCAL). DEBORAH J EPSTEIN, COORD; AMERICAN BICENT COMMISSION OF JACKSONVILLE/AMERICAN CANCER SOCIETY; 2113 HENDRICKS AVE, SUITE 206; JACKSONVILLE, FL 32207. (#200011-73).

MAR 25 - 27, '76. 'THE DEVIL'S DISCIPLE' BY G B SHAW. COMEDY BASED ON EVENTS LEADING TO SARATOGA, 1777. AT SWISHER AUDITORIUM, JACKSONVILLE UNIV. (LOCAL). DEBORAH J EPSTEIN, COORD; AMERICAN BICENT COMMISSION OF JACKSONVILLE/JACKSONVL UNIV; 2113 HENDRICKS AVE, SUITE 206; JACKSONVILLE, FL 32207. (#200011-81).

MAR 26, '76. 'ECHOES OF 1776'. WOMAN'S CLUB OF JACKSONVILLE WILL JOIN THE PRINCESS ISSENA CHAPTER & THE ST JOHNS RIVER CHAPTER DAR IN A DINNER THEATRE THAT WILL PRESENT A PLAY ON HOW THE DAR WAS FORMED. AT WOMAN'S CLUB OF JACKSONVILLE. (LOCAL). DEBORAH J EPSTEIN, COORD; AMERICAN BICENT COMMISSION OF JACKSONVL/ST JOHNS RIVER CHAPTER DAR; 2113 HENDRICKS AVE, SUITE 206; JACKSONVILLE, FL 32207. (#200011-69).

MAR 31, '76. MULTI-PURPOSE BANK IN THE LAST HALF OF THE 70'S - SEMINAR. SPEAKER WILL BE GUY BOTTS, CHAIRMAN OF BOARD BARNETT BANKS. AT GOODING AUDITORIUM-JACKSONVILLE UNIV. (LOCAL). DEBORAH J EPSTEIN, ASST; DIVISION OF BUSINESS-JACKSONVILLE UNIV ABCJ; 2113 HENDRICKS AVE, SUITE 206; JACKSONVILLE, FL 32207. (#106094-19).

MAR 31 - MAY 2, '76. KENT BICENTENNIAL PORTFOLIO. EXHIBITION OF CONTEMPORARY AMERICAN PRINTS & SCULPTURE INCLUDING 'SPIRIT OF INDEPENDENCE' AND THE TRANSWORLD ART BICENTENNIAL PORTFOLIO 'AN AMERICAN PORTRAIT, 1776-1976.'. AT 829 RIVERSIDE AVE. (LOCAL). DEBORAH J EPSTEIN, COORD; AMERICAN BICENT COMMISSION OF JACKSONVILLE/CUMMEL GALLERY OF ART; 2113 HENDRICKS AVE, SUITE 206; JACKSONVILLE, FL 32207. (#200011-82).

APR 1, '76. BICENTENNIAL FILM SERIES - & DISCUSSION - 'BIRTH OF A NATION'. DISCUSSION WILL BE LED BY DR FREDERICK ALDRIDGE, PROF OF HISTORY. AT GOODING AUDITORIUM-JACKSONVILLE UNIV. (LOCAL). DEBORAH J EPSTEIN, ASST; JACKSONVILLE UNIVERSITY & ABCJ; 2113 HENDRICKS AVE, SUITE 206; JACKSONVILLE, FL 32207. (#106094-27).

APR 1, '76. INSURANCE WOMEN OF JACKSONVILLE - HISTORICAL EXHIBIT. HISTORY OF INSURANCE INDUSTRY IN FLORIDA. DISPLAY CASES DEPITING HIGHLIGHTS OF HISTORY BASED ON EXTENSIVE RESEARCH. AT INDEPENDENT SQUARE - BLDG LOBBY. (LOCAL). DEBORAH J EPSTEIN, ASST; ABCJ & INSURANCE WOMEN OF JACKSONVILLE; 2113 HENDRICKS AVE, SUITE 106; JACKSONVILLE, FL 32207. (#106094-20).

JACKSONVILLE — CONTINUED

APR 1 - 4, '76. SPRINGS ARTS FESTIVAL '76. EXHIBIT OF 10 MAJOR WORKS OF ART PRESENTED BY METROOLITAN MUSEUM OF ART IN NEW YORK (ON LOAN). 20 MAJOR FESTIVALS DURING 4 DAY EXHIBIT. (LOCAL). DEBORAH J EPSTEIN, ASST; ABCJ & ARTS ASSEMBLY; 2113 HENDRICKS AVE, SUITE 20L; JACKSONVILLE, FL 32207. (#106094-26).

APR 3, '76. 'STARS & STRIPES FOREVER' - ORANGE PARK MARDI GRAS PARADE. PARADE FEATURES BICENTENNIAL TWIRLING CORPS 'LINDA THOMAS ALL STARS' & ALL STAR COLOR GUARD, MARCHING UNIT, FLOATS AND MUSIC. AT US HIGHWAY 17. (LOCAL). DEBORAH J EPSTEIN, COORD; AMERICAN BICENT COMMISSION OF JACKSONVILLE/ORANGE PARK BAND ASSOC; 2113 HENDRICKS AVE SUITE 206; JACKSONVILLE, FL 32207. (#200011-95).

APR 6 - 7, '76. LIFE AND WORK OF WILLIAM FAULKNER-LECTURE AND SLIDE PRESENTATION. SPEAKERS ARE JAMES FAULKNER, NEPHEW OF THE NOVELIST & DR JOSEPH BLOTNER FROM UNIV FO MICHIGAN. AT GOODING AUDITORIUM, JACKSONVILLE. (LOCAL). DEBORAH J EPSTEIN, ASST; DIVISION OF HUMANITIES JACKSONVILLE UNIVERSITY & ABCJ; 2113 HENDRICKS AVE, SUITE 206; JACKSONVILLE, FL 32207. (#106094-25).

APR 8 - 10, '76. 'A MATCH FOR GENERAL SHERMAN' AN ORIGINAL PLAY. LIVE PERFORMANCE AT SWISHER AUDITORIUM-JACKSONVILLE UNIV. (LOCAL). DEBORAH J EPSTEIN, ASST; COLLEGE OF FINE ARTS-JACKSONVILLE UNIV /ABCJ; 2113 HENDRICKS AVE, SUITE 206; JACKSONVILLE, FL 32207. (#106094-21).

APR 11, '76. '76 SALUTE - A TRIBUTE TO AMERICA'S MUSIC. 90-MINUTE PROGRAM FEATURES 200 YEARS OF AMERICAN MUSIC PERFORMED BY U S CONTINENTAL ARMY BAND. PATROL SQUADRON 56 FURNISHED THE COLOR GUARD FOR THE CONCERT. AT 1 RIVERSIDE AVE - JAX. (LOCAL). DEBORAH J EPSTEIN, COORD; ABC OF JACKSONVILLE/JACKSONVILLE JOURNAL/ PATROL SQUADRON 56; 2113 HENDRICKS AVE SUITE 206; JACKSONVILLE, FL 32207. (#200011-94).

APR 12 - 30, '76. 'WE THE PEOPLE' PHOTOGRAPHY EXHIBIT. PHOTOGRAPHS FROM STATE OF FLORIDA PHOTOGRAPHIC ARCHIVES EXHIBITED; INCLUDES COPIES OF DAGUERREOTYPES DATING FROM THE 1840'S AND OF AMBROTYPES AND PHOTOPRINTS FROM GLASS PLATE NEGATIVES. AT CHILDREN'S MUSEUM. (LOCAL). DEBORAH J EPSTEIN; AMERICAN BICENTENNIAL COMMISSION OF JACKSONVILLE; 2113 HENDRICKS AVE SUITE 206; JACKSONVILLE, FL 32207. (#200011-96).

APR 18, '76. ECOLOGY NATURE WALK AT THE UNIV OF N FLORIDA. AN ECOLOGY WALK AND OBSERVANCE WILL BE HELD IN CONJUNCTION WITH EARTH WEEK IN 1976 AT THE UNIVERSITY OF NORTH FLORIDA WILDLIFE PRESERVE. AT WILDLIFE PRESERVE. (LOCAL). ROBERT LOFTIN, PHD; UNIV OF NORTH FLORIDA; PO BOX 17074, POTTSBURG STATION; JACKSONVILLE, FL 32216. (#8687-1).

APR 21, '76. 'BYGONES' AN EARLY AMERICAN FLOWER SHOW. LOG CABIN, CLUBHOUSE, EARLY AMERICAN DRESSES, FURNITURE, FLOWERS & CRAFTS. AT GARDEN CITY CLUB HOUSE - LEM TURNER ROAD. (LOCAL). DEBORAH J EPSTEIN, ASST; ABCJ & SOULANGEANA CIRCLE-GARDEN CLUB OF JACKSONVILLE; 2113 HENDRICKS AVE, SUITE 206; JACKSONVILLE, FL 32207. (#106094-15).

APR 21 - 23, '76. BLUES FESTIVAL & WORKSHOP OF OLD TIME BLUES ARTISTS. CONCERTS, LECTURES, DISCUSSIONS & WORKSHOPS - VIDEO-TAPED AND MADE AVAILABLE AT A LATER DATE. (LOCAL). LEONARD M BURNS; UNIV OF NORTH FLORIDA; PO BOX 17074, POTTSBURG STATION; JACKSONVILLE, FL 32216. (#8676-1).

APR 22 - 24, '76. THE VILLAGE ART GROUP 'CREATES' FOR CANCER. THIS IS THE 11TH ANNUAL SPRING EXHIBITION AND SALE OF DRAWINGS AND PAINTINGS; PROCEEDS WILL GO TO THE 1976 AMERICAN CANCER CRUSADE. AT SEABOARD COASTLINE BLDG. (LOCAL). DEBORAH J EPSTEIN, COORD; VILLAGE ART GROUP & BICENTENNIAL COMMISSION OF JACKSONVILLE; 2113 HENDRICKS AVE, SUITE 206; JACKSONVILLE, FL 32207. (#106799-2).

APR 24, '76. 'MY COUNTRY 'TIS OF THEE' - FLOWER SHOW. THE THREE ARTISTIC CATEGORIES IN THE FLOWER SHOW ARE INTERPRETING 'AMERICA - PAST, PRESENT AND FUTURE'; OVER 300 SPECIMENS OF FLOWERS WILL BE EXHIBITED; PARTICIPANTS WILL BE THE FEDERATED MEMBERS OF THE GARDEN CLUB OF JACKSONVILLE. AT RAY GREEN CENTER, LEONID RD. (LOCAL). DEBORAH J EPSTEIN, COORD; CHERRY LAUREL GARDEN CIRCLE, BICENTENNIAL COMMISSION OF JACKSONVILLE; 2113 HENDRICKS AVE, SUITE 206; JACKSONVILLE, FL 32207. (#106799-4).

APR 24, '76. YANKEE DOODLE FAIR. RE-CREATION OF PIONEER VILLAGE, BOOTHS CREATED TO REPRESENT VILLAGE SCENE OF MERCHANTS SELLING THEIR HANDCRAFTED ARTICLES. AT CHILDREN'S MUSEUM - 1025 GULF DR. (LOCAL). DEBORAH J EPSTEIN, ASST; ABCJ & WOMEN'S GUILD OF JACKSONVILLE CHILDREN'S MUSEUM; 2113 HENDRICKS AVE, SUITE 206; JACKSONVILLE, FL 32207. (#106094-22).

APR 24 - 25, '76. ROSE SHOW ' LAND THAT WE LOVE'. JACKSONVILLE ROSE SOCIETY PRESENTING THEIR COLLECTIONS OF FLOWRS SPECIFICALLY ROSES. AT GARDEN CLUB OF JACKSONVILLE, 1005 RIVERSIDE AVE. (LOCAL). DEBORAH J EPSTEIN, ASST; ABCJ & JACKSONVILLE ROSE SOCIETY; 2113 HENDRICKS AVE, SUITE 20L; JACKSONVILLE, FL 32207. (#106094-23).

APR 25 - MAY 16, '76. DESIGNER'S SHOWCASE. LOCAL HOME HAD EACH ROOM DECORATED BY A DIFFERENT INTERIOR DECORATOR; THE HOUSE WAS A CLINIC WHICH WAS RESTORED TO PRIVATE RESIDENCE. AT 2821 RIVERSIDE AVE. (LOCAL). DEBORAH J EPSTEIN, COORD; AMERICAN BICENT COMMISSION OF JACKSONVILLE & SYMPHONY GUILD; 2113 HENDRICKS AVE, SUITE 206; JACKSONVILLE, FL 32207. (#200011-88).

APR 27 - 29, '76. 15TH ANNUAL MILITARY DEPENDENTS CHAMPIONSHIP GOLF TOURNAMENT. WOMEN DEPENDENTS OF MILITARY FROM THE U S, BOTH ACTIVE AND RETIRED WILL COMPETE IN 54 HOLE MEDAL GOLF TOURNAMENT; BANQUETS LIMITED TO. AT NAVAL AIR STATION GOLF COURSE. (REGN'L). DEBORAH J EPSTEIN, COORD; BICENTENNIAL COMMISSION OF JACKSONVILLE & U S NAVY; 2113 HENDRICKS AVE, SUITE 206; JACKSONVILLE, FL 32207. (#106799-3).

APR 27 - MAY 2, '76. FORT CAROLINE CELEBRATION. WAR SHIPS 'LE BOURDONNAIS' & 'LE PICARD' TO BE DOCKED & OPEN TO THE PUBLIC AT SEABORAD COSTLINE BLDG; FRENCH AMBASSADORE JACQUES KOSCIUSKO-MORIZET WILL PRESENT ORIGINAL DOCUMENTS TO FT CAROLINE MEMORIAL MUSEUM ON MAY 1ST AT 10:30 AM. AT FT CAROLINE MEMOMORIAL MUSEUM. (INT'L). DEBORAH J EPSTEIN, COORD; BICENTENNIAL COMMISSION OF JACKSONVILLE & U S NAVY; 2113 HENDRICKS AVE, SUITE 206; JACKSONVILLE, FL 32207. (#106799-1).

APR 29 - MAY 1, '76. REGIONAL ART EXHIBITS. TWO EXHIBITS WILL BE HELD. ART WORK IS ESPECIALLY REFLECTIVE OF CRAFTS OF THE AREA, CHOSEN FROM THE FLORIDA FEDERATION OF ART COLLECTION AND THE WEAVERS GUILD. (ST-WIDE). FRANCES KINNE, DEAN; JACKSONVILLE UNIV BICENTENNIAL COMMITTEE/COLLEGE OF FINE ARTS; JACKSONVILLE UNIV; JACKSONVILLE, FL 32211. (#102526-1).

APR 29 - MAY 7, '76. AMERICAN BICENTENNIAL ENGLISH HERITAGE TOUR. JOURNEY INTO HISTORY WITH A GUIDED TOUR TO ENGLAND; TRIP TO EXPLORE AMERICAN HERITAGE IN ENGLAND. (INT'L). DEBORAH J EPSTEIN, COORD; WOMEN'S GUILD, BICENTENNIAL COMMISSION OF JACKSONVILLE; 2113 HENDRICKS AVE, SUITE 206; JACKSONVILLE, FL 32207. (#106799-6).

APR 29 - MAY 10, '76. OP SAIL '76 WITH VESSEL 'UNICORN'. THE 'UNICORN' IS A SQUARE RIGGED VESSEL, 146 FT LONG X 121 FT TALL. AT CIVIC AUDITORIUM. (LOCAL). DEBORAH J EPSTEIN, COORD; AMERICAN BICENT COMMISSION OF JACKSONVILLE/OP SAIL '76; 2113 HENDRICKS AVE SUITE 206; JACKSONVILLE, FL 32207. (#200011-93).

APR 30 - MAY 1, '76. BICENTENNIAL WORKSHOP-GENALOGICAL STUDY OF FAMILY LINES. BEGINS AT 9 AM ON SATURDAY. AT QUALITY INN NORTH - BROWARD ROOM. (LOCAL). DEBORAH J EPSTEIN, ASST; ABCJ & JACKSONVILLE GENEALOGICAL SOCIETY; 2113 HENDRICKS AVE, SUITE 206; JACKSONVILLE, FL 32207. (#106094-16).

APR 30 - MAY 1, '76. DROP-IN ART CONFERENCE. A DROP-IN ART CONFERENCE HOSTING SECONDARY TEACHERS AND STUDENTS WILL FEATURE WORKSHOPS IN SEVERAL KINDS OF MEDIA SUCH AS JEWELRY, GLASS-BLOWING AND PAINTING. (LOCAL). FRANCES KINNE, DEAN; COLLEGE OF FINE ARTS, JACKSONVILLE UNIVERSITY; JACKSONVILLE UNIV; JACKSONVILLE, FL 32211. (#102525-1).

MAY 1 - 2, '76. 'WAYS OF YESTERYEAR'. PLANTING EDIBLE FOODS & HERBS GROWN IN COLONIAL DAYS, JUNIOR HORTICULTURE SHOW (KINDERGARDEN THRU 6TH GRADE) AND DEMONSTRATIONS OF COLONIAL LIFE FEATURED AT CHILDREN'S MUSEUM. AT JACKSONVILLE CHILDREN'S MUSEUM. (LOCAL). DEBORAH J EPSTEIN, COORD; AMERICAN BICENT COMMISSION OF JACKSONVILLE/GARDEN CLUB OF JACKSONVL; 2113 HENDRICKS AVE, SUITE 206; JACKSONVILLE, FL 32207. (#200011-89).

MAY 3 - 7, '76. SYMPOSIUM ON THE ADVANCEMENT OF THE AMERICAN WOMAN. LECTURE & FILM ON EQUAL RIGHTS FOR WOMEN FROM PIONEER DAYS TO PRESENT & FUTURE. (LOCAL). ELLYN DAVENPORT; UNIV OF NORTH FLORIDA; PO BOX 17074, POTTSBURG STATION; JACKSONVILLE, FL 32216. (#8684-1).

MAY 7, '76. JACKSONVILLE BOY'S CHOIR - SPRING CONCERT. PATRIOTIC MUSIC SOME OF WHICH WAS WRITTEN BY MRS JACKIE HAND, A LOCAL MUSIC WRITER - SINGING BY JAY BOYS CHOIR. AT ASSUMPTION SCHOOL AUDITORIUM. (LOCAL). DEBORAH J EPSTEIN, COORD; AMERICAN BICENT COMMISSION OF JACKSONVILLE/JACKSONVILLE BOY'S CHOIR; 2113 HENDRICKS AVE SUITE 206; JACKSONVILLE, FL 32207. (#200011-92).

MAY 8, '76. ANTIQUE CLASSIC AUTOMBOILE SHOW. VEHICLES ON DISPLAY WILL BE JUDGED FOR AUTHENTICITY; CAR GAMES TIMED, POTATO SPEARING. 13 CLASSES OF CARS WILL BE JUDGED. AT 125. (LOCAL). DEBORAH J EPSTEIN, ASST; ABCJ & N E FLORIDA REGION ANTIQUE AUTOMOBILE; 2113 HENDRICKS AVE, SUITE 206; JACKSONVILLE, FL 32207. (#106094-9).

MAY 8, '76. BICENTENNIAL EXPOSITION BOY SCOUTS OF AMERICA. EXHIBIT, FESTIVAL AT GATOR BOWL. (LOCAL). DEBORAH J EPSTEIN, ASST; ABCJ & BOY SCOUTS OF AMERICA; 2113 HENDRICKS AVE, SUITE 206; JACKSONVILLE, FL 32207. (#106094-18).

MAY 8, '76. MR & MRS SENIOR CITIZENS TALENT CONTEST. THE CONTEST WILL HAVE A BICENTENNIAL THEME AND WILL FEATURE THE CROWNING OF MR & MRS BICENTENNIAL SENIOR CITIZEN. AT 5714 ARLINGTON RD. (LOCAL). DEBORAH J EPSTEIN, COORD; ARLINGTON'S WOMEN'S CLUB, BICENTENNIAL COMMISSION OF JACKSONVILLE; 2113 HENDRICKS AVE, SUITE 206; JACKSONVILLE, FL 32207. (#106799-7).

MAY 8 - 9, '76. RAP RESTORATION: WALKING & RIDING TOUR OF HOMES. TOUR AT 1520 BARRS ST. (LOCAL). DEBORAH J EPSTEIN, COORD; AMERICAN BICENT COMMISSION OF JACKSONVL RIVERSIDE-AVONDALE PRESERVTN; 2113 HENDRICKS AVE, SUITE 206; JACKSONVILLE, FL 32207. (#200011-84).

MAY 9, '76. GREATER JACKSONVILLE YOUTH SYMPHONY. THE SYMPHONY FEATURES OUTSTANDING ORCHESTRA STUDENTS FROM THE VARIOUS SENIOR HIGH SCHOOLS IN THE SCHOOL SYSTEM. (LOCAL). DEBORAH J EPSTEIN, COORD; AMERICAN BICENT COMMISSION OF JACKSONVILLE DUVAL COUNTY SCHOOL BOARD; 2113 HENDRICKS AVE SUITE 206; JACKSONVILLE, FL 32207. (#200011-91).

MAY 10 - 13, '76. 'PEOPLE TO PEOPLE'. AN EXHIBIT OF SURVIVAL EQUIPMENT, INCLUDING A MK-12 LIFE RAFT, FULLY INFLATED WITH ALL SURVIVAL VEST AND ASSOCIATED EQUIPMENT AND A CASSETTE FILM PRESENTATION SHOWING VARIOUS ASPECTS OF THE PATROL AVIATION COMMUNITY. AT NORMANDY MALL. (LOCAL). W G MATTON, CHAIRMAN; PATROL SQUADRON FIFTY SIX; JACKSONVILLE, FL 32212. (#200011-248).

MAY 14 - 15, '76. AMERICAN BICENTENNIAL SPEECH CONTEST. CONTEST FEATURED ORIGINAL ORATIONS WITH AMERICAN/ PATRIOTIC THEMES. AT 8101 BEACH BLVD. (LOCAL). DEBORAH J EPSTEIN, COORD; AMERICAN BICENT COMMISSION OF JACKSONVILLE/SALAAM CLUB OF JACKSONVL; 2113 HENDRICKS AVE, SUITE 206; JACKSONVILLE, FL 32207. (#200011-87).

MAY 15, '76. MARINE CORPS INVITATIONAL JR ROTC DRILL MEET. HIGH SCHOOL STUDENTS, BOTH BOYS & GIRLS, WILL PARTICIPATE IN THE ROTC DRILL TEAM COMPETITION; TEAMS WILL HAVE 20 MINUTES TO PERFORM BOTH STANDARD AND FANCY DRILL; JUDGES WILL GRADE QUANTITATIVELY FROM A STANDARD CHECKLIST. AT NAVAL AIR STATION. (LOCAL). DEBORAH J EPSTEIN, COORD; MARINE CORPS RESERVE & BICENTENNIAL COMMISSION OF JACKSONVILLE; 2113 HENDRICKS AVE, SUITE 206; JACKSONVILLE, FL 32207. (#106799-5).

MAY 15, '76. PATRIOTIC POEM OR SONG CONTEST. ALL STUDENTS IN GRADES 7 THRU 12 WILL BE URGED TO PARTICIPATE; EMPHASIS WILL BE ON PATRIOTIC SONGS AND POEMS; AWARDS WILL BE GIVEN ON EACH GRADE LEVEL. (LOCAL). DEBORAH J EPSTEIN, ASST; JACKSONVILLE ARBC/NORTH FLORIDA CHRISTIAN MUSIC WRITERS ASSOC; 2113 HENDRICKS AVE; JACKSONVILLE, FL 32207. (#105704-1).

MAY 15, '76. PHILIPPINE SALUTE TO JACKSONVILLE. THE DINNER-DANCE WILL FEATURE FOLK DANCES AND PRINCIPLE ADDRESS BY THE PHILIPPINE AMBASSADOR, HON EDUARDO ROMUALDEZ. AT INDEPENDENT LIFE BLDG. (LOCAL). DEBORAH J EPSTEIN, COORD; AMERICAN BICENT COMMISSION OF JACKSONVL/FILIPINO-AMERICAN CLUB; 2113 HENDRICKS AVE, SUITE 206; JACKSONVILLE, FL 32207. (#200011-86).

MAY 15 - 16, '76. CORK & CLEAVER BICENTENNIAL TENNIS TOURNAMENT. MIXED DOUBLES AMATEUR OPEN TENNIS TOURNAMENT; AWARDS GIVEN AT COMPLETION OF TOURNAMENT. TOURNAMENT IS OPEN TO THE PUBLIC. (LOCAL). DEBORAH J EPSTEIN, COORD; JACKSONVILLE BICENTENNIAL COMMITTEE & CORK & CLEAVER CLUB; 2113 HENDRICKS AVE, SUITE 206; JACKSONVILLE, FL 32207. (#107738-1).

MAY 15 - 16, '76. SPRING ART FESTIVAL. ART EXHIBITS, CRAFT DEMONSTRATIONS, RIBBONS AWARDED FOR PAINTING, CRAFTS, PHOTO & HOME CRAFTS-BOTH PROFESSIONAL & AMATEUR. AT FIRST GAURANTY BANK - 1234 KING ST. (LOCAL). DEBORAH J EPSTEIN, COORD; RIVERSIDE-AVONDALE PRESERVATION - ABCJ; 2113 HENDRICKS AVE, SUITE 206; JACKSONVILLE, FL 32207. (#107739-1).

MAY 17 - 22, '76. FLORIDA BICENTENNIAL EXHIBIT. WALK-THROUGH EXHIBIT OF FLORIDA HISTORY DEVELOPMENT, BANDS & SURROUNDING ACTIVITIES. AT JACKSONVILLE BEACH. (LOCAL). DEBORAH J EPSTEIN, SST; ABCJ & FLORIDA BICENTENNIAL COMMISSION; 2113 HENDRICKS AVE, SUITE 206; JACKSONVILLE, FL 32207. (#106094-17).

MAY 21, '76. GRAND COUNCIL FIRE - ANNUAL RECOGNITION CEREMONY. AWARD, CEREMONY AT 2001 ART MUSEUM DR. (LOCAL). DEBORAH J EPSTEIN, ASST; ABCJ & CAMPFIRE GIRLS, INC; 2113 HENDRICKS AVE, SUITE 206; JACKSONVILLE, FL 32207. (#106094-12).

MAY 25, '76. CRUISE & DINNER - CHANGE OF COMMAND. CEREMONIAL DINNER & CRUISE FOR HELICOPTER COMBAT SUPPORT SQUADRON 2, CHANGE OF COMMAND. AT US NAVAL AIR STATION. (LOCAL). DEBORAH J EPSTEIN, COORD; AMERICAN BICENT COMMISSION OF JACKSONVL/HELICOPTER COMBAT SUPPORT 2; 2113 HENDRICKS AVE, SUITE 206; JACKSONVILLE, FL 32207. (#200011-90).

MAY 26, '76. MEMORIAL DAY CEREMONY. MEMORIAL DAY OBSERVATION AT FLAG POLE AT EVERGREEN CEMETERY. A DAY OF REMEMBERANCE HONORING THOSE WHO FOUGHT & DIED IN DEFENSE OF AMERICAN FREEDOM. AT EVERGREEN CEMETERY, 4535 MAIN ST. (LOCAL). DEBORAH J EPSTEIN, ASST; ABCJ & VETERAN'S PATRIOTIC OBSERVATION COMMITTEE; 2113 HENDRICKS AVE, SUITE 206; JACKSONVILLE, FL 32207. (#106094-13).

MAY 27 - 30, '76. OPERATION SAIL '76 - TOUR OF BLUENOSE II. BLUENOSE II, A FAMOUS CANADIAN FISHING SCHOONER, WILL BE OPEN TO THE PUBLIC FOR VIEWING. AT SCL BLDG, DOWNTOWN JACKSONVILLE (DOCK). (LOCAL). DEBORAH J EPSTEIN; OPERATION SAIL '76 & CANADIAN TOURISM COMMISSION; 2113 HENDRICKS AVE, SUITE 206; JACKSONVILLE, FL 32207. (#107970-5).

MAY 28 - 30, '76. 1976 PHYSICIANS SEMINAR. CONTINUING EDUCATION PROGRAM ON RESPIRATORY DISEASE FOR PHYSICIANS, REGISTERED NURSES & THERAPISTS. AT TURTLE INN, ATLANTIC BEACH. (ST-WIDE). DEBORAH J EPSTEIN; FLORIDA LUNG ASSOC & BICENTENNIAL COMMISSION OF JACKSONVILLE; 2113 HENDRICKS AVE, SUITE 206; JACKSONVILLE, FL 32207. (#107970-7).

MAY '76. ARMED FORCES DAY 1976. DISPLAYS, EXHIBITS & PERFORMANCES REPRESENTATIVE OF ALL BRANCHES OF THE ARMED FORCES-ACTIVE AND RESERVES-SHIP TOURS, BAND PERFORMANCES, AIR SHOWS & MILITARY DEMONSTRATIONS. AT CITY AUDITORIUM AND FACILITIES ON COASTLINE DR. (LOCAL). DEBORAH J EPSTEIN, CHMN; AMERICAN REVOLUTION BICENTENNIAL COMM & ALL BRANCHES OF ARMED FORCES; 2113 HENDRICKS AVE, SUITE 206; JACKSONVILLE, FL 32207. (#103393-8).

JACKSONVILLE — CONTINUED

JUNE 2, '76. HAPPY BIRTHDAY AMERICA. ACTIVITIES INCLUDE PUPPET SHOW, SKIT ON CHARACTERS & EVENTS OF THE PAST, CRAFTS WITH BICENTENNIAL THEME AND A PROGRAM TO HELP GENERATE AN INTEREST IN AMERICA, IN THE BOYS CLUB MEMBERS. AT 11TH & LIBERTY ST. (LOCAL). DEBORAH J EPSTEIN, COORD; BOYS CLUB OF AMERICA & BICENTENNIAL COMMITTEE; 2113 HENDRICKS AVE, SUITE 206; JACKSONVILLE, FL 32207. (#200011-225).

JUNE 8 - 12, '76. BICENTENNIAL EXHIBITION OF NORMAN ROCKWELL ART WORK. EXHIBIT OF OVER 500 PIECES OF ROCKWELL ART AS A PORTRAYAL OF AMERICAN LIFE. AT ROOSEVELT BLVD AT SAN JUAN. (LOCAL). DEBORAH J EPSTEIN; ROOSEVELT MALL MERCHANTS ASSOC & BICENT COMMISSION OF JACKSONVILLE; 2113 HENDRICKS AVE, SUITE 206; JACKSONVILLE, FL 30207. (#107970-6).

JUNE 11 - 20, '76. SUWANNEE RIVER RAFT RACE. COMPETITION, FESTIVAL. (LOCAL). DEBORAH J EPSTEIN, ASST; JACKSONVILLE ARBC/NORTH FLORIDA BOY SCOUTS; 2113 HENDRICKS, SUITE 206; JACKSONVILLE, FL 32207. (#106076-1).

JUNE 13, '76. CELEBRATION OF EBENEZER'S HISTORY, 1864-1976. CEREMONY WILL EMPHASIZE THE SIGNIFICANCE & CHALLENGE OF THE GREAT HERITAGE OF OUR NATION - CORNERSTONE LAYING & DEDICATION SERVICE. AT 9114 NORFOLK BLVD. (LOCAL). DEBORAH J EPSTEIN; EBENEZER UNITED METHODIST CHURCH, BICENT COMMISSION OF JACKSONVILLE; 2113 HENDRICKS AVE, SUITE 206; JACKSONVILLE, FL 32207. (#107970-4).

JUNE 14, '76. BICENTENNIAL FLAG DAY. DEDICATION AND OPENING OF BICENTENNIAL FLAG PAVILLION FEATURING FLAGS FROM ALL 50 STATES AND VARIOUS TERRITORIES OF U S. FLAG MUSEUM OPENING, BANDS, PARADES & FLAG RAISING CEREMONIES. AT BICENTENNIAL FLAG PAVILLION - JACKSONVILLE BEACH. (LOCAL). DEBORAH J EPSTEIN, CHMN; JAX BEACH CHAMBER OF COMMERCE, GARDEN CLUB, ABCJ; 2113 HENDRICKS AVE, SUITE 206; JACKSONVILLE, FL 32207. (#103393-2).

JUNE 17 - 20, '76. 56TH ANNUAL CONVENTION OF BUSINESS & PROFESSIONAL WOMEN. 56TH ANNUAL STATE CONVENTION OF FLORIDA FEDERATIN OF BUSINESS AND PROFESSIONAL WOMEN'S CLUB, INC. WOMEN FROM 117 BPW CLUBS IN THE STATE WILL BE IN ATTENDANCE. THEME: BICENTENNIAL PERSPECTIVE FOR WOMEN. AT HILTON HOTEL. (LOCAL). DEBORAH J EPSTEIN, ASST; ABCJ & JACKSONVILLE BUSINESS & PROFESSIONAL WOMEN'S CLUB; 2113 HENDRICKS AVE, SUITE 206; JACKSONVILLE, FL 32207. (#106094-14).

JUNE 18, '76. HOSPITAL CORPS ANNUAL BALL. THE BALL IS BEING HELD TO HONOR THE NAVY HOSPITAL CORPSMEN WHO, THROUGHOUT THE YEARS, HAVE DEVOTED THEIR TIME TO CARE FOR THE ILL. AT CANDLELIGHT ROOM. (LOCAL). DEBORAH J EPSTEIN, ASST; NAVAL REGIONAL MEDICAL CENTER/ABCJ; 2113 HENDRICKS AVE, SUITE 206; JACKSONVILLE, FL 32207. (#108402-2).

JUNE 19, '76. 'OUR TOUR OF HOMES'. AWARD WINNING HOMES; THE TOUR OF HOMES WILL INCLUDE RESIDENCES THAT HAVE APPEARED IN HOME & GARDEN, NEW YORK TIMES, FLORIDA ARCHITECT, ETC. AT BEACH AREA. (LOCAL). DEBORAH J EPSTEIN, ASST; PABLO PILOT CLUB/ABCJ; 2113 HENDRICKS AVE, SUITE 206; JACKSONVILLE, FL 32207. (#108402-1).

JUNE 19 - 20, '76. CANOE TRIP DOWN THE SUWANNEE - CLEANUP TRIP. OVERNIGHT CANOE TRIP COMBINED WITH CLEANUP PROGRAM. AT SUWANNEE RIVER. (LOCAL). DEBORAH J EPSTEIN, ASST; ABCJ & SIERRA CLUB; 2113 HENDRICKS AVE, SUITE 206; JACKSONVILLE, FL 32207. (#106094-8).

JUNE 20, '76. FT CAROLINE - ST JOHN'S BLUFF 1564 COMMEMORATIVE WEEK. WEEK LONG EVENTS, FORT TOURS, SCENIC TRAILS, DEDICATION OF SIGNS; THE COMMEMORATIVE WEEK WILL FEATURE A DIFFERENT EVENT OR TOUR EACH DAY, THE FEATURE BEING A SERVICE TO 'FREEDOM OF RELIGION'. AT FT CAROLINE NATIONAL PARK. (LOCAL). DEBORAH J EPSTEIN, ASST; ABCJ & ST JOHN'S BLUFF HISTORICAL SOCIETY; 2113 HENDRICKS AVE, SUITE 206; JACKSONVILLE, FL 32207. (#106094-7).

JUNE 26, '76. BUS TOUR TO HISTORICAL SITES. BUS TOUR TO FT CAROLINE, MAYPORT AND KINGSLEY PLANTATION TO STUDY EARLY HISTORY OF JACKSONVILLE; FOR AARP MEMBERS NOT TAKING BUS TOUR, DENA SNODGRASS WILL SPEAK ON PATRIOTS IN PETTICOATS.'. AT RIVERSIDE PRESIDENT APTS, 1045 OAK ST. (LOCAL). DEBORAH J EPSTEIN; RIVERSIDE CHAPTER #1361 AARP, BICENT COMMISSION OF JACKSONVILLE; 2113 HENDRICKS AVE, SUITE 206; JACKSONVILLE, FL 32207. (#107970-1).

JULY 1 - 30, '76. BICENTENNIAL ART SHOW & CONTEST AT FT CAROLINE N MEM. ORIGINAL ART WORK WILL BE FEATURED. (REGN'L). DE SOTO N MEM; COOPERATING ASSOCIATION & NATIONAL PARK SERVICE; 12713 FORT CAROLINE ROAD; JACKSONVILLE, FL 32225. (#6728-588).

JULY 2 - 5, '76. ARTS FOURTH 1976; ART & CULTURAL FESTIVAL. ONLY MAJOR ART & CULTURAL FESTIVAL IN STATE OF FLORIDA DURING SUMMER OF 76 ARTS & CRAFTS EXHIBIT, MULTI ETHNIC FOOD FESTIVAL, BALLET & THEATRE PRODUCTIONS, WATER DEMONSTRATIONS AND DISPLAYS. AT CIVIC AUDITORIUM. (LOCAL). DEBORAH J EPSTEIN, COORD; AMERICAN BICENTENNIAL COMMISSION OF JACKSONVILLE; 2113 HENDRICKS AVE, SUITE 206; JACKSONVILLE, FL 32207. (#103393-4).

JULY 2 - 6, '76. KINGS ROAD HIKE. 4 DAY HIKE BY BOY SCOUTS RETRACING STEPS OF FOREFATHERS ON FLORIDA'S FIRST HIGHWAY. AT KING ROAD. (LOCAL). DEBORAH J EPSTEIN, ASST; ABCJ & NORTH FLORIDA COUNCIL-BOY SCOUTS OF AMERICA; 2113 HENDRICKS AVE, SUITE 206; JACKSONVILLE, FL 32207. (#106094-10).

JULY 4, '76. BOLD CITY 1976 AMERICAN BICENTENNIAL BICYCLE RACE. 6-MILE COURSE; RACES FOR MEMBERS OF THE U S CYCLING FEDERATION; RACES & RACERS CLASSIFIED BY AGE; WILL ALSO FEATURE NOVICE CLASSES FOR NON-UCFC RIDERS. AT GULF LIFE BUILDING. (LOCAL). DEBORAH J EPSTEIN, ASST; NORTH FLORIDA ROAD CLUB/ABCJ; 2113 HENDRICKS AVE, SUITE 206; JACKSONVILLE, FL 32207. (#108402-3).

JULY 4, '76. FOURTH OF JULY PICNIC. OLD-FASHIONED PICNIC WITH FOLLOWING ACTIVITIES: WATERMELON EATING CONTEST, CONTESTS, BAND CONCERT AND SPEAKER. AT BOONE PARK. (LOCAL). DEBORAH J EPSTEIN, COORD; RIVERSIDE AVONDALE PRESERVATION, BICENT COMMISSION OF JACKSONVILLE; 2113 HENDRICKS AVE, SUITE 206; JACKSONVILLE, FL 32207. (#106799-9).

JULY 4, '76. INDEPENDENCE DAY CELEBRATION. ART EXHIBIT, PARADE, MULTI-ETHNIC FOOD, BALLET AND THEATRE PRESENTATIONS CELEBRATE NATION'S BIRTHDAY. PARADE AT 7PM; FIREWORKS AFTER. (LOCAL). DEBBE EPSTEIN, COORD; AMERICAN BICENTENNIAL COMMISSION OF JACKSONVILLE; 2113 HENDRICKS AVE SUITE 206; JACKSONVILLE, FL 32207. (#103416-166).

JULY 4, '76. 4TH OF JULY BAR-B-Q. ANNUAL 4TH OF JULY CELEBRATION WITH BAR-B-Q & HAMBURGER PLATE. FUND RAISING PROJECT TO RAISE MONEY FOR THE HANDICAPPED PEOPLE WHO RESIDE AT THE BETHESDA CENTER. AT SEARS, ROEBUCK & CO PARKING LOT. (LOCAL). DEBORAH J EPSTEIN, COORD; BETHESDA CLUB, INC & JACKSONVILLE BICENTENNIAL COMMITTEE; 2113 HENDRICKS AVE, SUITE 206; JACKSONVILLE, FL 32207. (#108892-1).

JULY 6, '76. BLOOD BANK DRIVE. PART OF THE JACKSONVILLE BICENTENNIAL COMMITTEE 'BLEED FOR AMERICA' PROJECT. AT HILTON HOTEL. (LOCAL). DEBORAH J EPSTEIN, COORD; ROTARY CLUB OF SOUTH JACKSONVILLE & BICENTENNIAL COMMITTEE; 2113 HENDRICKS AVE, SUITE 206; JACKSONVILLE, FL 32207. (#108892-2).

JULY 11, '76. BICENTENNIAL DOG FAIR. EXHIBITS ON VARIOUS FACETS OF DOGDOM OVER THE PAST 200 YEARS BOOTHS SNOWING THE AMERICAN DOG IN MEDICINE, WAR & COMPANIONSHIP; DEMONSTRATION OF TRAINING. AT BICENTENNIAL FLAG PAVILLION. (LOCAL). DEBORAH J EPSTEIN, ASST; ABCJ & K-9 OBEDIENCE CLUB OF JACKSONVILLE/K-9 DRILL TEAM OF JAX, INC; 2113 HENDRICKS AVE, SUITE 206; JACKSONVILLE, FL 32207. (#106094-28).

JULY 18, '76. 'DAYS TO REMEMBER' AT CAMP ECHOCKOTEE. REUNION & CELEBRATION OF FOUNDING OF CAMP ECHOCKOTEE. AT 2512 DOCTORS LAKE DR, ORANGE PARK. (LOCAL). DEBORAH J EPSTEIN, ASST; ABCJ & NORTH FLORIDA COUNCIL BSA; 2113 HENDRICKS AVE, SUITE 206; JACKSONVILLE, FL 32207. (#106094-11).

JULY 23, '76. OPERATION SAIL TO DISPLAY FLOTILLA OF WORLD'S SAILING VESSELS. EXHIBIT AT ST JOHNS RIVER. (INT'L). DEBORAH J EPSTEIN, COORD; JACKSONVILLE BICENTENNIAL COMMITTEE/PORT OF AUTHORITY; 2113 HENDRICKS AVE, SUITE 206; JACKSONVILLE, FL 32207. (#109-9).

AUG 1 - 31, '76. BICENTENNIAL 'HOME OF THE FUTURE'. TO RESEARCH POSSIBLE ALTERNATIVE ENERGY SYSTEMS SUCH AS SUN, WIND, METHANE GAS; AND TO REPORT ON THE PRACTICALITY OR NET ENERGY OF SUCH SYSTEMS FOR RESIDENTIAL APPLICATION. PROTOTYPICAL HOUSE TO BE DESIGNED & OPEN FOR EXHIBIT. AT THE WOODS DEVELOPMENT, ATLANTIC BLVD. (ST-WIDE). DEBORAH J EPSTEIN, COORD; JACKSONVILLE & FLORIDA BICENTENNIAL COMMISSIONS/HOMEBUILDERS ASSOC; 2113 HENDRICKS AVE, SUITE 206; JACKSONVILLE, FL 32207. (#13837-1).

AUG 27 - 29, '76. DIXIE CLASSIC CHAMPIONSHIP RODEO. BICENTENNIAL THEME RODEO FEATURING BRONCO BUSTING, STEER WRESTLING, BULL RIDING, BAREBACK RIDING AND CALF ROPING. EVENT IS STAGED TO RAISE MONEY FOR LOCAL CHARITY. AT JACKSONVILLE COLISEUM. (LOCAL). DEBORAH J EPSTEIN, COORD; JACKSONVILLE JAYCEES & BICENTENNIAL COMMITTEE; 2113 HENDRICKS AVE, SUITE 206; JACKSONVILLE, FL 32207. (#200011-226).

SEPT 2 - 6, '76. NATIONAL SLOW PITCH SOFTBALL TOURNAMENT. COMPETITION AT JACKSONVILLE DREW PARK. (REGN'L). DEBORAH J EPSTEIN, ASST; JACKSONVILLE BICENTENNIAL COMMITTEE; 2113 HENDRICKS AVE, SUITE 206; JACKSONVILLE, FL 32207. (#200011-241).

SEPT 11, '76. BICENTENNIAL SALUTE TO JACKSONVILLE'S SENIOR CITIZENS. IN RECOGNITION OF THE ROLE OF SR CITIZENS AS BUILDERS, CULTIVATORS AND DEVELOPERS OF JACKSONVILLE; LIVE ENTERTAINMENT AND BACK YARD COOKOUT. AT HOGAN'S CREEK TOWER, 1320 BROAD ST. (LOCAL). DEBORAH J EPSTEIN, ASST; JACKSONVILLE BICENTENNIAL COMMITTEE; 2113 HENDRICKS AVE, SUITE 206; JACKSONVILLE, FL 32207. (#200011-239).

SEPT 11 - 12, '76. AMERICAN INDIAN FESTIVAL. HONORING INDIAN TRIBES OF AMERICA WITH CRAFTS, HISTORICAL DISPLAYS AND INDIAN DINNER. AT 2246 BLANDING BLVD. (ST-WIDE). DEBORAH J EPSTEIN, COORD; LAKE SHORE UNITED METHODIST CHURCH, BICENT COMMISSION OF JACKSONVL; 2113 HENDRICKS AVE, SUITE 206; JACKSONVILLE, FL 32207. (#106799-10).

SEPT 15 - OCT 30, '76. BOLD CITYFEST. FAIR. (LOCAL). IVAN CLARE, COORD; BOLD CITYFEST, INC; 220 E BAY ST, ROOM 107; JACKSONVILLE, FL 32202. (#103416-572).

SEPT 18 - 19, '76. BICENTENNIAL TENNIS TOURNAMENT. COMPETITION. (LOCAL). DEBORAH J EPSTEIN, ASST; JACKSONVILLE BICENTENNIAL COMMITTEE; 2113 HENDRICKS AVE, SUITE 206; JACKSONVILLE, FL 32207. (#200011-240).

SEPT 21, '76. MENTAL HEALTH SYMPOSIUM AT UNIV OF N FLORIDA. A SYMPOSIUM & WORKSHOPS ON THE MENTAL HEALTH OF AMERICANS, SPONSORED BY THE UNIVERSITY OF NORTH FLORIDA, WILL BE HELD IN JACKSONVILLE IN 1976. PARTICIPANTS TO INCLUDE STUDENTS, FACULTY & GUEST LECTURERS. INVOLVES STUDENTS, FACULTY & COMMUNITY W/GUEST LECTURERS. (LOCAL). LEONARD BURNS; UNIV OF NORTH FLORIDA; PO BOX 17074, POTTSBURG STATION; JACKSONVILLE, FL 32216. (#8683-1).

SEPT 23, '76. BICENTENNIAL BROTHERHOOD AWARDS BANQUET. KEYNOTE SPEAKER - JESSE OWENS, OLYMPIC GOLD MEDALIST; HONOREE PRIME F OSBORN. AT HOTEL ROBERT MEYER. (LOCAL). DEBORAH J EPSTEIN, ASST; JACKSONVILLE BICENTENNIAL COMMITTEE; 2113 HENDRICKS AVE, SUITE 206; JACKSONVILLE, FL 32207. (#200011-238).

SEPT 25 - 27, '76. FLORIDA LIMITED STEAM LOCOMOTIVE TRIP. TRAIN TRIP ON STEAM LOCOMOTIVE FROM JACKSONVILLE, THROUGH OKEFENOKEE NATIONAL FOREST TO VALDOSTA, GA. AT SIMPSON YARD. (LOCAL). DEBORAH J EPSTEIN, CHMN; JACKSONVILLE CHAPTER OF NATIONAL RAILWAY HISTORICAL SOCIETY; 2113 HENDRICKS AVE, SUITE 206; JACKSONVILLE, FL 32207. (#108892-3).

OCT 2 - NOV 7, '76. 'TREASURES OF LONDON' EXHIBITION. EXHIBIT. (INT'L). EILEEN HARAKAL, COORD; SMITHSONIAN INSTITUTION TRAVELING EXHIBITION SERVICE; 1000 JEFFERSON DR, SW; WASHINGTON, DC 20560. (#26660-4).

OCT 6, '76. AMERICAN SHAKESPEARE THEATRE FESTIVAL. 'AS YOU LIKE IT' & 'THE WINTERS TALE' PRESENTED BY THE AMERICAN SHAKESPEARE THEATRE OF STATFORD. AT CIVIC AUDITORIUM. (LOCAL). DEBORAH J EPSTEIN, ASST; JACKSONVILLE THEATRE & JACKSONVILLE ART MUSEUM; 2113 HENDRICKS AVE; JACKSONVILLE, FL 32207. (#200011-278).

OCT 8, '76. BOY SCOUTS OF AMERICA - 'ANNUAL FALL ENCAMPMENT' - BICENT EMPHASIS. 3 DAY ENCAMPMENT INVOLVING CUB SCOUTS, BOY SCOUTS, EXPLORERS AND ADULTS. WEEKEND WILL HAVE BICENTENNIAL THEME WITH HIGHLIGHTS BEING A CAMPFIRE PROGRAM ON SATURDAY NIGHT, SCOUT PRODUCED SKILL-O-RAMA, MERIT-BADGE FAIR, RELIGIOUS SERVICES ON SUNDAY. AT CAMP BLANDING. (LOCAL). DEBORAH J EPSTEIN, ASST; ABCJ & NORTH FLORIDA COUNCIL-BOY SCOUTS OF AMERICA; 2113 HENDRICKS AVE, SUITE 206; JACKSONVILLE, FL 32207. (#106094-2).

OCT 20 - 30, '76. GREATER JACKSONVILLE FAIR. FAIR AT GATOR BOWL SPORTS COMPLEX. (ST-WIDE). C L RAINES, GEN MGR; GREATER JACKSONVILLE FAIR ASSOC, INC; 1400 E DUVAL ST; JACKSONVILLE, FL 32202. (#106095-14).

OCT 24, '76. NAVY 201ST BIRTHDAY. COMMEMORATION CEREMONIES HONORING NAVY ON 201ST BIRTHDAY & LOCAL BASES ACTIVITIES. (ST-WIDE). DEBORAH J EPSTEIN, ASST; ABCJ/U S NAVY-NAS-JAX, NAS-CECIL FIELD, NAS-MAYPORT; 2113 HENDRICKS AVE, SUITE 206; JACKSONVILLE, FL 32207. (#106094-3).

OCT '76. KINGS ROAD MARKER DEDICATION. DEDICATION OF BRONZE CAST MARKERS PLACED AT 11 SPECIFIC LOCATIONS ALONG HISTORIC KINGS ROAD, THE FIRST HIGHWAY INTO THE STATE OF FLORIDA. (LOCAL). DEBORAH J EPSTEIN, ASST; JACKSONVILLE ARBC/ROTARY CLUB OF SOUTH JACKSONVILLE; 2113 HENDRICKS AVE; JACKSONVILLE, FL 32207. (#22436-1).

NOV 10, '76. MARINE CORPS 201ST BIRTHDAY. COMMEMORATION CEREMONIES HONORING LOCAL MARINE UNITS ON 201ST BIRTH201ST BIRTHDAY OF U S MARINE CORPS. AT NAS JACKSONVILLE. (LOCAL). DEBORAH J EPSTEIN, ASST; ABCJ/U S MARINES; 2113 HENDRICKS AVE, SUITE 206; JACKSONVILLE, FL 32207. (#106094-4).

NOV 10 - 14, '76. DISCOVER AMERICA TRAVEL SHOWCASE. EXHIBIT OF 27 MODULE DISPLAY UNITS DEPICTING ALL 50 STATES. DISPLAYS FEATURE CITIES & STATES WITH HISTORICAL ARTIFACTS FROM MUSEUMS. AT NORMANDY MALL. (LOCAL). DEBBE EPSTEIN, ADMIN ASST; PARAGON PRODUCTIONS; 2113 HENDRICKS AVE, SUITE 206; JACKSONVILLE, FL 32207. (#109481-1).

NOV 11, '76. VETERAN'S DAY PARADE. PARADE SALUTING & HONORING VETERANS OF AMERICAN ARMED SERVICES. AT DOWNTOWN JACKSONVILLE. (LOCAL). DEBORAH J EPSTEIN, ASST; ABCJ/CITY OF JACKSONVILLE VETERAN'S PATRIOTIC OBSERVANCE COMMITTEE; 2113 HENDRICKS AVE, SUITE 206; JACKSONVILLE, FL 32207. (#106094-5).

NOV 13 - 14, '76. 'SUSANNAH' - OPERA SALUTE TO AMERICA'S BICENTENNIAL. PRESENTED FOR THE CITY OF JACKSONVILLE IN SALUTE TO AMERICAN OPERA DURING THE BICENTENNIAL YEAR. PERFORMANCE AT 8:15 PM ALSO. AT CIVIC AUDITORIUM. (LOCAL). DEBORAH J EPSTEIN, ASST; ABCJ & OPERA REPERTORY GROUP, INC; 2113 HENDRICKS AVE, SUITE 206; JACKSONVILLE, FL 32207. (#106094-6).

NOV 23, '76. MARKER DEDICATION OF INDEPENDENCE ISLE. DEDICATION OF ISLAND IN THE CAMPUS LAKE AS INDEPENDENCE ISLAND ON THE ANNIVERSARY OF PLYMOUTH ROCK. (LOCAL). HAROLD SNIDER; UNIV OF NORTH FLORIDA; PO BOX 17074, POTTSBURG STATION; JACKSONVILLE, FL 32216. (#8678-1).

NOV 24 - 29, '76. AMERICAN FREEDOM TRAIN DISPLAY DAYS AT JACKSONVILLE. THE AMERICAN FREEDOM TRAIN WILL INCLUDE 10 EXHIBIT CARS AND 2 SHOWCASE CARS DEPICTING DIFFERENT PHASES OF THE AMERICAN EXPERIENCE. ITS ARRIVAL WILL SERVE AS A CATALYST FOR LOCAL BICENTENNIAL CELEBRATIONS BY PEOPLE THROUGHOUT THIS NATION. (ST-WIDE). SY FREEDMAN, DIR OF P.R; THE AMERICAN FREEDOM TRAIN FOUNDATION, INC.; 5205 LEESBURG PKE, SUITE 800; BAILEY'S XRDS, VA 22041. (#1776-77).

NOV 29 - DEC 22, '76. CARL HAVERLIN/BROADCAST MUSIC, INC, ARCHIVES BICENTENNIAL EXHIBIT. OFFERS A VERSATILE PICTURE

JACKSONVILLE — CONTINUED

OF HISTORY, REGIONAL LIFE & MUSIC FOR OVER 200 YEARS. CONTAINS PRESIDENTIAL LETTERS, LETTERS OF FAMOUS AMERICANS, OLD BOOKS, MANUSCRIPTS, HISTORY OF 'THE STAR SPANGLED BANNER' & COMPOSER AUTOGRAPHS, PLUS SHEET MUSIC OF THE PAST. AT COLLEGE OF FINE ARTS - ART DEPT. (ST-WIDE). DR NANCY THOMAS, COORD; JACKSONVILLE UNIVERSITY; UNIVERSITY BLVD N; JACKSONVILLE, FL 32211. (#20784-13).

DEC 1 - 25, '76. 'TOYS FOR TOTS' - A BICENTENNIAL TOY LIBRARY. CITY-WIDE PROGRAMS TO COLLECT USABLE EDUCATION-ORIENTED TOYS TO BE DONATED FOR DUVAL COUNTY'S RETARDED CITIZENS; AND TO ESTABLISH A TOY LIBRARY FOR THE NEEDY, 'PROVIDING A BETTER LIFE FOR ALL AMERICANS'. AT CITY-WIDE. (LOCAL). DEBORAH J EPSTEIN, COORD; JACKSONVILLE BICENTENNIAL COMMITTEE/US MARINES/DUVAL ASSOC; 2113 HENDRICKS AVE/SUITE 206; JACKSONVILLE, FL 32207. (#18936-1).

JASPER

COMPLETE HISTORY OF HAMILTON CO - JASPER, FL. HERITAGE '76 WILL WRITE, COMPILE AND PUBLISH A HISTORY OF HAMILTON CO, FLORIDA. COPIES TO BE PLACED IN SCHOOLS, LIBRARY & PRESENTED TO STATE BICENTENNIAL COMMISSION. (LOCAL). LORAINE KIEFER, CHAIRMAN; HAMILTON CO BICENTENNIAL COMMITTEE; 413 CENTRAL AVE; JASPER, FL 32052. (#25996).

PLACE MARKERS IN OLD CEMETERIES & OLD HOUSES - FL. A MAP GUIDING THE WAY & EXPLAINING THE HISTORY WILL BE PROVIDED FOR THE MARKERS. (LOCAL). LORAINE KIEFER, CHAIRMAN; HAMILTON COUNTY BICENTENNIAL COMMISSION; BOX 54; JASPER, FL 32052. (#25997).

OCT 10, '75. FILMS ON FLORIDA'S BICENTENNIAL TRAIL. EXHIBIT. (LOCAL). LORRAINE KIEFER, COORD; THE WOMEN'S CLUB OF JASPER FOR THE BICENTENNIAL; 413 CENTRAL AVE; JASPER, FL 32052. (#108367-4).

FEB 1, '76. FLAG DISPLAY. EXHIBIT. (LOCAL). MRS LORAINE KIEFER, CHMN; CITY OF JASPER; 413 CENTRAL AVE; JASPER, FL 32052. (#200011-46).

JENSEN BEACH

SEPT 15 - NOV 11, '75. UNCLE SAM AND BETSY ROSS ESSAY CONTEST. COMPETITION AT JENSEN BEACH CHAMBER OF COMMERCE, 51 COMMERCIAL ST. (LOCAL). MRS BARBARA TOROW, CHMN; JENSEN BEACH BICENTENNIAL COMMITTEE; 51 COMMERCIAL ST; JENSEN BEACH, FL 33457. (#200011-47).

FEB 8, '76. GARDEN CLUB WALK. HORTICULTURE EXHIBIT AT COMMUNITY CENTER, JENSEN BEACH, PLUS TOUR OF OLDER HOMES & TWO OLDEST CHURCHES IN JENSEN BEACH AREA. REFRESHMENTS SERVED AT ALL SAINTS EPISCOPAL CHURCH, OLDEST ORIGINAL CHURCH IN MARTIN COUNTY. AT TOUR OF HISTORIC AND OLDER HOMES IN JENSEN BEACH AREA. (LOCAL). IRENE STEPHENSON, COORD; JENSEN BEACH GARDEN CLUB; 4344 NE SKYLINE DR; JENSEN BEACH, FL 33457. (#200011-48).

FEB 13 - 15, '76. FOLK CRAFT & MUSIC FESTIVAL PLUS OPEN HOUSE. A 3-DAY FESTIVAL: FRIDAY IS OPEN HOUSE & TOUR; SAT & SUN EVERYONE INVITED TO SET UP DISPLAYS OF ARTS & CRAFTS FOR DISPLAYS & SALE. BLUE GRASS MUSIC SAT & SUN. AT FIT CAMPUS, INDIAN RIVER DRIVE. (LOCAL). JANIS MIRANDA, PROJ COORD; FLORIDA INSTITUTE OF TECHNOLOGY; JENSEN BEACH, FL 33457. (#200011-49).

FEB 15, '76. GOD AND COUNTRY DAY. THEME RING IT AGAIN, PRINCIPAL SPEAKER WILL BE AN ASTRONAUT TO BE NAMED BY NASA. BAND, CHORAL GROUPS AND VOCAL SOLOISTS. MASSING OF THE COLORS OF MANY ORGANIZATIONS. AT MARTIN COUNTY HIGH SCHOOL GYM, SR76 / MILE WEST, US1 STUART, FL. (LOCAL). REV FRANK R ALVAREZ; ALL SAINTS PE CHURCH, JENSEN BEACH POST & THE AMERICAN LEGION; 108 PATRICIAN BLVD; JENSEN BEACH, FL 33457. (#104085-16).

FEB 23, '76. BICENTENNIAL DINNERS. A SERIES OF DINNERS BY LOCAL CHEFS & RETIRED CHEFS FROM THEIR OWN COUNTRIES BEGINNING WITH FRENCH, ENDING WITH AMERICAN TO SHOW HOW OTHER COUNTRIES HAVE INFLUENCED AMERICAN LOOKING; LIMITED TO FIFTY INDIVIDUALS EACH DINNER. FEB CHEF ANDRE GIRARD. AT HOLIDAY INN OCEANSIDE, TIFFANY ROOM. (LOCAL). JACK KLETT, COORD; JENSEN BEACH BICENTENNIAL COMMITTEE; 232 N INDIAN RIVER DR; JENSEN BEACH, FL 33457. (#200011-50).

FEB 25, '76. RE-AWAKENING THE REVOLUTION-PATRIOTISM FOR A NATION UNDER GOD. SPEAKER: DR HARRELL BECK, STAFF, BOSTON UNIV SCHOOL OF THEOLOGY. AT JENSEN BEACH COMMUNITY CHURCH, SKYLINE DR. (LOCAL). REV D CLARK THOMPSON; MINISTRIAL ASSOCIATION OF MARTIN COUNTY & TRINITY METHODIST CHURCH; 140 ARCH ST; JENSEN BEACH, FL 33457. (#200011-51).

JULY 4, '76. FOURTH OF JULY PARADE. SECOND ANNUAL FOURTH OF JULY PARADE IN JENSEN BEACH HISTORY INSPIRED BY THE BICENTENNIAL FESTIVITIES IN 1975. AT DOWNTOWN JENSEN BEACH, INDIAN RIVER DRIVE TO CAUSEWAY. (LOCAL). ANDRA WEBB, COORD; JENSEN BEACH OPTIMIST CLUB AUXILIARY; 229 HYLINE DR; JENSEN BEACH, FL 33457. (#105361-1).

JULY 4, '76. 200TH BIRTHDAY CELEBRATION. THERE WILL BE GAMES, FISHING AND PICNIC, CLIMAXED BY A FIREWORKS DISPLAY EXTRAVAGANZA. AT JENSEN BEACH CAUSEWAY. (LOCAL). BARBARA TOROW, COORD; JENSEN BEACH CHAMBER OF COMMERCE; 51 COMMERCIAL ST; JENSEN BEACH, FL 33457. (#105361-2).

OCT 10, '76. LEIF ERIKSON DAY. FESTIVAL AT BEACH AREA. (LOCAL). RICHARD CAMPBELL, COORD; JENSEN BEACH CHAMBER OF COMMERCE; PO BOX 787; JENSEN BEACH, FL 33457. (#103416-633).

JUPITER

TOURS OF JUPITER LIGHTHOUSE - FL. PAMPHLET ON HISTORY OF LIGHTHOUSE & AREA. TOURS TO PUBLIC ON SUNDAY. GROUP TOURS AS SCHEDULED. PROJECT SPONSORED BY USCG AND LOXAHCHEE HISTORICAL SOCIETY. (LOCAL). COMMANDING OFFICER; USCG LORAN A/C STATION; PO BOX 997; JUPITER, FL 33458. (#29451).

KEY BISCAYNE

DEC 27, '75 - DEC 31, '76. AMERICAN LIBERTY TRAIN. HISTORICAL RAILWAY EXHIBIT. (LOCAL). K GORDON MURRAY, PRES; TRANS-INTERNATIONAL FILMS, INC; 104 CRANDON BLVD; KEY BISCAYNE, FL 33149. (#101423-1).

KEY WEST

FORT ZACHARY TAYLOR PROJECT IN KEY WEST, FL. NAVAL AIR STATION KEY WEST ORGANIZED A CLEANUP CAMPAIGN AT FT TAYLOR IN CONJUNCTION WITH OTHER LOCAL MILITARY SERVICES BEFORE THE FT WAS TURNED OVER TO THE STATE OF FLORIDA. (LOCAL). HOWARD ENGLAND, FT TAYLOR CURATOR; NAVAL AIR STATION KEY WEST; KEY WEST, FL 33040. (#29874).

'KEY WEST, FL, AS IT WAS'. RECORDING CONVERSATIONS WITH PEOPLE WHO WERE BORN HERE & KNOW THE TRUE OLD KEY WEST. (LOCAL). MRS MARY MALONE, PROJ COORDINATOR; WOMAN'S CLUB; 1108 SOUTH ST; KEY WEST, FL 33040. (#15068).

NAS KEY WEST NAVAL AIR EXHIBIT - FL. A CEREMONY & EXHIBIT IN HONOR OF ARMED FORCES. (LOCAL). LT MARY PERRI CRAWFORD; KEY WEST OFFICERS CLUB; 938 WHITEHEAD ST; KEY WEST, FL 33040. (#28231).

NAS KEY WEST'S MILITARY LIGHTHOUSE MUSEUM PROJECT. EXHIBIT CREATED ON THE HISTORY OF NAVAL AVIATION IN THE KEY WEST AREA ON DISPLAY PERMANENTLY AT THE KEY WEST MILITARY LIGHTHOUSE MUSEUM; ALSO, ALL MILITARY EXHIBITS ON DISPLAY REFURBISHED BY SPONSOR. (LOCAL). FLORENCE FULLER, CHAIRMAN; MILITARY LIGHTHOUSE MUSEUM; 938 WHITEHEAD ST; KEY WEST, FL 33040. (#29873).

OPERATION SENTINEL - PROJ OF KEY WEST, FL. REPOPULATION OF PALMS BY PLANTING 10,000 ON THE ISLAND BY JULY, '76. (LOCAL). MRS MERILL MCCOY, CHAIRMAN; KEY WEST GARDEN CLUB; 88 HILTON HAVEN; KEY WEST, FL 33040. (#15067).

PAINTING OF FIREPLUGS, KEY WEST, FL. FIREPLUGS ARE BEING PAINTED RED, WHITE AND BLUE WITH FACES OF LOCAL POLITICIANS ADDED. (LOCAL). ROSE MARIBONA, PRESIDENT; KEY WEST FIREFIGHTERS AUXILIARY; 1202 ROYAL ST; KEY WEST, FL 33040. (#22015).

PICTORIAL HISTORY: NAVAL AIR STATION KEY WEST, FL. PICTORIAL HISTORY OF NAVAL AIR STATION KEY WEST DISPLAYED AS PART OF TRAVELING STATE EXHIBIT SEP 22-27, 1975. (LOCAL). LT MARY CRAWFORD, PUBLIC AFFAIRS OFFICER; NAVAL AIR STATION KEY WEST; KEY WEST, FL 33040. (#29875).

PROJECT DOWNTOWN '76 - KEY WEST, FL. THE FACELIFTING OF OLD BUILDINGS, THE WIDENING OF SIDEWALKS, EXTENSIVE PLANTING AND BEAUTIFICATION OF DUVAL STREET. (LOCAL). HON CHARLES MCCOY, MAYOR; KEY WEST CITY COMMISSION; ANGELA & SIMONTON ST; KEY WEST, FL 33040. (#15066).

SEPT 22 - 27, '75. PICTORIAL HISTORY OF KEY WEST NAVAL AIR STATION. EXHIBIT AT KEY PLAZA WEST. (LOCAL). MARY P CRAWFORD, LT USN; NAVAL AIR STATION; NAS KEY WEST, FL 33040. (#200011-291).

SEPT 22 - 27, '75. PRESIDENTIAL PORTRAIT EXHIBIT. EXHIBIT AT E MARTELLO TOWER MUSEUM, S ROOSEVELT BLVD. (LOCAL). MRS SANDRA HIGGS, SEC; MONROE COUNTY BICENTENNIAL COMMITTEE; 518 DUVAL ST, SAN CARLOS BLDG; KEY WEST, FL 33040. (#102162-1).

OCT 30 - NOV 3, '75. EXHIBIT OF LUNAR SAMPLES. LUNAR SAMPLES TRANSPORTED TO KEY WEST BY NAS PERSONNEL, ALSO SUPPLIED SECURITY FORCE TO GUARD EXHIBIT. AT MILITARY LIGHTHOUSE MUSEUM. (LOCAL). FLORENCE FULLER, CHMN; KEY WEST ART & HISTORICAL SOCIETY; KEY WEST, FL 33040. (#200011-293).

NOV 8, '75. NAVAL AIR STATION BLUE ANGELS BICENTENNIAL AIR SHOW. LIVE PERFORMANCE AT BOCA CHICA FIELD. (LOCAL). MARY P CRAWFORD, LT USN; NAVAL AIR STATION; NAS KEY WEST, FL 33040. (#200011-292).

JAN 3, '76. BICENTENNIAL BALL. FESTIVAL AT E MARTELLO TOWERS, S ROOSEVELT BLVD. (LOCAL). CAROLYN BLACKWELL, COORD; MONROE COUNTY BICENTENNIAL COMMITTEE; 48 KEY HAVEN RD; KEY WEST, FL 33040. (#102162-3).

JAN 8 - 10, '76. BLUE WATER SAILBOAT RACE. COMPETITION AT MALLORY SQUARE OVERLOOKING OCEAN. (REGN'L). DOUG MERRILL, CHAIRMAN; CHAMBER OF COMMERCE & KEY WEST HOSPITALITY COMMITTEE; OLD MALLORY SQUARE; KEY WEST, FL 33040. (#102162-2).

JAN 23 - 30, '76. YACHT RACE. KEY WEST TO FT LAUDERDALE YACHT RACE. AT NAVAL AIR STATION KEY WEST, HARRY TRUMAN ANNEX. (LOCAL). DOUG MERRILL, CHMN; KEY WEST HOSPITALITY COMMITTEE & KEY WEST CHAMBER OF COMMERCE; ISLANDER VILLAGE - HUKILAN; KEY WEST, FL 33040. (#200011-290).

JAN 30 - FEB 1, '76. KEY WEST SIDEWALK ART SHOW. EXHIBIT AT MALLORY SQUARE, FRONT ST. (LOCAL). DELLA VAN DER KLOOT, PRES; KEY WEST ART CENTER; 301 FRONT ST; KEY WEST, FL 33040. (#102162-5).

JAN 31, '76. BICENTENNIAL FARO NIGHT. FESTIVAL AT MALLORY SQUARE CONVENTION CENTER, FRONT ST. (LOCAL). JOHN B KNOWLES, PROJ DIR; DISABLED AMERICAN VETERANS; PO BOX 930; KEY WEST, FL 33040. (#102162-6).

JAN 31, '76. CORONATION BALL. COMPETITION, FESTIVAL AT KEY WESTER, SAINTS & SINNERS ROOM. (LOCAL). JANET HILL, CHAIRMAN; KEY WEST JUNIOR WOMAN'S CLUB; 525 WHITEHEAD ST; KEY WEST, FL 33040. (#102162-4).

FEB 7, '76. STAR SPANGLED SPECTACULAR. EXHIBIT, FESTIVAL AT MALLORY SQUARE, FRONT ST, OLD TOWN KEY WEST. (LOCAL). JACK HENDERSON, PROJ DIR; BOY SCOUTS; KEY WEST, FL 33040. (#102162-7).

FEB 12, '76. DEDICATION OF HISTORIC CUSTOM HOUSE. CEREMONY AT HISTORIC CUSTOM HOUSE/CLINTON SQUARE. (LOCAL). SANDRA HIGGS, EXEC SEC; OLD ISLAND RESTORATION FOUNDATION/BICENTENNIAL COMMITTEE; 1107 THOMPSON ST; KEY WEST, FL 33040. (#200011-100).

FEB 12 - 15, '76. ANTIQUE SHOW. EXHIBIT AT COMMUNITY CENTER, MALLORY SQUARE. (LOCAL). AL BROWN, PGM MGR; OLD ISLAND RESTORATION FOUNDATION; 2101 SEIDENBERG AVE; KEY WEST, FL 33040. (#102162-9).

FEB 21, '76. PANCAKE BREAKFAST. FESTIVAL AT COMMUNITY CENTER, MALLORY SQUARE. (LOCAL). MEL FRUTH, CHMN; HI-NOON LION'S CLUB; 2022 STAPLES AVE; KEY WEST, FL 33040. (#102162-11).

FEB 21, '76. SOUTH OF THE BORDER NIGHT. FESTIVAL AT COMMUNITY CENTER, MALLORY SQUARE. (LOCAL). TONY CASTILLO, CHMN; JAYCEES; 305 VIRGINIA ST; KEY WEST, FL 33040. (#102162-10).

FEB 27 - 29, '76. ISLAND HERITAGE '76. EXHIBIT AT WEST MARTELLO TOWERS, ATLANTIC BOULEVARD. (LOCAL). EVA NEWHOUSE, COORD; KEY WEST GARDEN CLUB; 620 EATON ST; KEY WEST, FL 33040. (#200011-99).

FEB 27 - 29, '76. SIDEWALK CRAFT SHOW. EXHIBIT AT MALLORY SQUARE. (LOCAL). MALCOM ROSS, CHMN; KEY CRAFT CENTER, 520 FRONT ST; KEY WEST, FL 33040. (#102162-12).

FEB 28, '76. CONCH SHELL BLOWING CONTEST. COMPETITION AT COMMUNITY CENTER, MALLORY SQUARE. (LOCAL). FRANCIS SMITH, CHMN; OLD ISLAND RESTORATION FOUNDATION; 1818 HARRIS AVE; KEY WEST, FL 33040. (#102162-8).

FEB '76. BICENTENNIAL PARADE. THIS BIGGEST PARADE KEY WEST HAS EVER SEEN WITH FLOATS AND MARCHING UNITS (LOCAL). ANTHONY NILES, CHMN; KEY WEST BICENTENNIAL COMMITTEE; 2431 SEIDENBURG AVE; KEY WEST, FL 33040 (#102162-13).

APR 5, '76. THE JUNKANOOS - ISLAND MUSICIANS' TROUPE PLAYING BAHAMIAN RHYTHMS. LIVE PERFORMANCE AT CAMPUS BREEZEWAY, STOCK ISLAND, FKCC. (LOCAL). ROBERT R CARON, CHMN; FLORIDA KEYS COMMUNITY COLLEGE; KEY WEST, FL 33040. (#200011-103).

APR 5 - 9, '76. DISPLAY OF ARTIST'S DRAWINGS OF COLLEGE'S FUTURE HUMANITIES' BLDG. EXHIBIT AT CAMPUS BREEZEWAY STOCK ISLAND, FKCC. (LOCAL). ROBERT R CARON, CHMN, FLORIDA KEYS COMMUNITY COLLEGE; KEY WEST, FL 33040. (#200011-101).

APR 5 - 9, '76. KEY WEST-AS IT WAS. LIVE PERFORMANCE AT CAMPUS BREEZEWAY, STOCK ISLAND, FKCC. (LOCAL). ROBERT R CARON, CHMN; FLORIDA KEYS COMMUNITY COLLEGE; KEY WEST, FL 33040. (#200011-102).

APR 6, '76. FLORIDA KEYS COMMUNITY COLLEGE CHORUS AND PIANIST PRESENTATION. LIVE PERFORMANCE AT CAMPUS BREEZEWAY, STOCK ISLAND. (LOCAL). ROBERT R CARON, CHMN; FLORIDA KEYS COMMUNITY COLLEGE; KEY WEST, FL 33040. (#200011-107).

APR 6 - 7, '76. ARTS & CRAFTS FESTIVAL. EXHIBIT, FESTIVAL AT CAMPUS BREEZEWAY, STOCK ISLAND. (LOCAL). ROBERT R CARON, CHMN; FLORIDA KEYS COMMUNITY COLLEGE; KEY WEST, FL 33040. (#200011-105).

APR 6 - 9, '76. NOSTALGIC HOLLYWOOD FILM FESTIVAL. FESTIVAL AT CAMPUS BREEZEWAY, STOCK ISLAND. (LOCAL). ROBERT R CARON, CHMN; FLORIDA KEYS COMMUNITY COLLEGE; KEY WEST, FL 33040. (#200011-106).

APR 7, '76. MUSIC FESTIVAL. LIVE PERFORMANCE AT CAMPUS BREEZEWAY, STOCK ISLAND. (LOCAL). ROBERT R CARON CHMN; FLORIDA KEYS COMMUNITY COLLEGE; KEY WEST, FL 33040. (#200011-108).

APR 9, '76. BOZA'S COMPARSA - ISLAND MUSICIANS-DANCERS WITH CUBAN RHYTHMS. LIVE PERFORMANCE AT CAMPUS BREEZEWAY, STOCK ISLAND CAMPUS, FKCC. (LOCAL). ROBERT R CARON, CHMN; FLORIDA KEYS COMMUNITY COLLEGE; KEY WEST, FL 33040. (#200011-110).

APR 9, '76. STUDENT PICNIC & BARBECUE. FESTIVAL AT CAMPUS BREEZEWAY, STOCK ISLAND. (LOCAL). ROBERT R CARON CHMN; FLORIDA KEYS COMMUNITY COLLEGE; KEY WEST, FL 33040. (#200011-109).

MAY 14, '76. KEY WEST NAVAL AIR STATION BICENTENNIAL COMMAND DESIGNATION CEREMONY. MAYOR CHARLES MCCOY PRESENTED CAPT ROBERT LOVELACE, COMMANDING OFFICER OF NAVAL AIR STATION, WITH OFFICIAL BICENTENNIAL CERTIFICATE ON BEHALF OF THE BICENTENNIAL ADMINISTRATION

KEY WEST — CONTINUED

AT BOCA CHICA KEY. (LOCAL). MARY P CRAWFORD, LT USN; NAVAL AIR STATION; NAS KEY WEST, FL 33040. (#200011-289).

JUNE 14, '76. ANNUAL ELKS FLAG CEREMONY. CEREMONY AT ELKS CLUB, 313 DUVAL ST. (LOCAL). RICK GUTTERY, CHAIRMAN; BPO ELKS CLUB; 3728 PAULA AVE; KEY WEST, FL 33040. (#105784-3).

JULY 3 - 5, '76. JULY FOURTH CELEBRATION. A 3-DAY CELEBRATION: SATURDAY, FIELD EVENTS FOR ALL AGES; SUNDAY, CHURCH SERVICE, BELL RINGING AT 2 PM; MONDAY, PARADE AND FIREWORKS BEGINNING AT 7 PM. (LOCAL). SANDRA HIGGS, EXEC SEC; MONROE COUNTY BICENTENNIAL COMMITTEE; PO BOX 1176, 402 WALL ST; KEY WEST, FL 33040. (#105784-2).

JULY 5, '76. 'THIS IS OUR COUNTRY' - PARADE. THE LARGEST PARADE KEY WEST HAS YET TO EXPERIENCE; THERE WILL BE MARCHING UNITS FROM NAVAL AIR STATION, FLOATS, AND BANDS WITH PARTICIPATION FROM EVERY WALK OF LIFE. (LOCAL). ANTHONY NILES, CHAIRMAN; MONROE COUNTY BICENTENNIAL COMMITTEE; 2431 SEIDENBERG AVE; KEY WEST, FL 33040. (#105784-1).

KEYSTONE HTS

THEME '76 PARK - KEYSTONE HEIGHTS, FL. A MULTI-PURPOSE RECREATIONAL PARK, ONE FULL CITY BLOCK IN SIZE, TO CONTAIN TENNIS COURTS, BASKETBALL COURTS, SHUFFLEBOARD A TINY TOTS PLAYGROUND, LIGHTED SCENIC PATHS, BENCHES & BURIED TIME CAPSULE. (LOCAL). HON CHARLES HEAD, MAYOR; CITY OF KEYSTONE HEIGHTS; LAWRENCE BLVD; KEYSTONE HTS, FL 32656. (#24870).

JULY 2 - 4, '76. JULY 4TH WEEKEND ACTIVITIES. STREET DANCE, BEARD CONCERT, COSTUME CONTEST AND REFRESHMENT BOOTHS. AT ON THE BEACH. (LOCAL). MRS C B BULLOCK, JR, CHMN; CITY OF KEYSTONE HEIGHTS; KEYSTONE HTS, FL 32656. (#107037-1).

JULY 4, '76. BELLAMY TRAIL COMMEMORATIVE MARKER DEDICATION. CEREMONY. (LOCAL). EARL ECKFORD, COORD; KEYSTONE HEIGHTS LIONS CLUB; PO BOX 121; KEYSTONE HTS, FL 32656. (#106797-1).

KISSIMMEE

ART AND HISTORICAL BUILDINGS, KISSIMMEE, FL. INCREASE THE SIZE OF PRESENT FACILITY WITH TWO WING ADDITIONS, ONE A MUSEUM AND ONE AN ART BUILDING. (LOCAL). WALTER G WATKINS, PRES; OSCEOLA COUNTY ART AND CULTURE CENTER INC; PO BOX 1195; KISSIMMEE, FL 32741. (#21955). **ARBA GRANTEE.**

OSCEOLA SUN'S BICENTENNIAL SERIES - NBMRP. THE SUN HAS PUBLISHED 70 WEEKLY ARTICLES ON FLORIDA'S HISTORY; & IS CURRENTLY PUBLISHING A WEEKLY SERIES ON THE COUNTRY'S HISTORY. (LOCAL). KENNETH B GUTHRIE, EDITOR; OSCEOLA SUN; 700 W VINE ST, PO BOX 1677; KISSIMMEE, FL 32741. (#25417).

FEB 18, '76. KISSIMMEE VALLEY LIVESTOCK SHOW - OPENING CEREMONY. SILVER SPURS QUEEN CUT RIBBON TO OPEN SHOW AND OSCEOLA HIGH SCHOOL BAND AND DENN-JOHN MIDDLE SCHOOL COLOR GUARD PARTICIPATED IN THE CEREMONY. ST CLOUD HIGH SCHOOL DECORATED GROUNDS & BLDGS WITH HANDMADE EARLY AMERICAN FLAGS WITH DESCRIPTIVE MARKERS. AT COUNTY AGRICULTURE CENTER, RT 192. (LOCAL). HELEN THOMAS, CO-CHMN; KISSIMMEE VALLEY LIVESTOCK SHOW BOARD; 804 NEPTUNE RD; KISSIMMEE, FL 32741. (#200011-97).

FEB 20 - 22, '76. SILVER SPURS RODEO. COMPETITION, LIVE PERFORMANCE AT SILVER SPURS ARENA, ROUTE 192 BETWEEN KISSIMMEE & ST CLOUD. (LOCAL). MIKE BAST, COORD; SILVER SPURS RIDING CLUB; PO BOX 1909; KISSIMMEE, FL 32741. (#200011-98).

MAR 28, '76. COMMUNITY PORTRAYAL OF ABC TELEVISION'S 'ALMOST ANYTHING GOES'. COMMUNITY INVOLVEMENT EVENT BASED ON ABC TELEVISION'S FUN-FILLED PROGRAM; 10 LOCAL TEAMS VYING FOR FUN & ENTERTAINING THE COMMUNITY. (LOCAL). MIKE WILLIAMS, CHAIRMAN; KISSIMMEE-ST CLOUD JAYCEES & OSCEOLA COUNTY BICENTENNIAL COMMITTEE; PO BOX 519; KISSIMMEE, FL 32741. (#105783-1).

JULY 2 - 4, '76. BICENTENNIAL FESTIVAL. HOURS FOR THE FESTIVAL: JULY 2, 3-8 PM; JULY 3, 3-8 PM; JULY 4, NOON - 7 PM. AT COUNTY AGRICULTURAL CENTER, ROUTE 192, BETWEEN KISSIMMEE & ST CLOUD. (LOCAL). MRS JULIA SHARPLESS, SEC; OSCEOLA COUNTY BICENTENNIAL COMMITTEE; 2226 W ORANGE BLVD; KISSIMMEE, FL 32741. (#105783-2).

JULY 16 - 31, '76. 'BELOVED LAND, MY HOME - THE OSCEOLA STORY' - DRAMA. HISTORICAL DRAMA, RESEARCHED AND WRITTEN BY LOCAL AUTHOR, KENNETH DUNCAN. DIRECTED BY RON MULLINS. TECHNICAL ASSISTANCE & CAST PARTICIPATION BY SEMINOLE INDIANS. AT CO AGRICULTURAL CENTER, RT U S 192. (LOCAL). GEORGE E BEAUCHAMP, COORD; OSCEOLA COUNTY BICENTENNIAL COMMITTEE & OSCEOLA PLAYERS; 2220 W ORANGE BLVD; KISSIMMEE, FL 32741. (#200011-227).

NOV 13 - 14, '76. CENTRAL FLORIDA AIR FAIR - DEMONSTRATIONS BY ARMED FORCES TEAMS. DEMONSTRATIONS BY USAF THUNDERBIRDS, USA GOLDEN KNIGHTS, USA SILVER EAGLES, USMC HARRIER VSTOL, CIVILIAN RED BARONS, HOT AIR BALLOON RACE, EXHIBITS OF ANTIQUE & MODERN MILITARY & CIVILIAN AIRCRAFT. AT KISSIMMEE AIRPORT. (ST-WIDE). KEN GUTHRIE, CHMN; ROTARY CLUB; 708 ROBERT ST; KISSIMMEE, FL 32741. (#108395-1).

LA BELLE

APR 5 - 9, '76. AMERICAN HISTORY WEEK. AMERICAN HISTORY WEEK INVOLVING ENTIRE SCHOOL FOR ONE WEEK; FEATURING PARADE, WINDOW DISPLAYS, HISTORIC PLAY, ETHNIC FOODS, PATRIOTIC MUSIC. AT LA BELLE ELEMENTARY SCHOOL. (LOCAL). JEAN RASMUSSEN, COORD; LA BELLE ELEMENTARY SCHOOL; PO BOX 67; LA BELLE, FL 33935. (#200011-111).

JULY 4, '76. JULY 4TH COMMUNITY PICNIC. FREE BARBEQUE, GAMES, BAND, COMMUNITY SING AND FIREWORKS AFTER DARK. AT BARRON PARK. (LOCAL). JOE THOMAS, DIRECTOR; LA BELLE BICENTENNIAL COMMITTEE; PO BOX 176; LA BELLE, FL 33935. (#108401-1).

LAKE ALFRED

EXHIBIT ON COLONIAL COOKERY. MODEL COLONIAL KITCHEN, FOOD PREPARED & SERVED IN COLONIAL FASHION. (LOCAL). HERRITTA MCGFIFF; FRIENDLY GARDEN CLUB OF LAKE ALFRED; 685 GRAPEFRUIT AVE; LAKE ALFRED, FL 33850. (#200011-279).

HISTORICAL MARKER, LAKE ALFRED, FL. LAND MARKED FOR HISTORICAL FORT CUMMINGS, SITE OF PEACE BETWEEN THE INDIAN AND WHITE MAN. (LOCAL). RICHARD MEESE, PROJ CHAIRMAN; LIONS CLUB; 485 W PIERCE; LAKE ALFRED, FL 38850. (#32399).

JULY 4, '76. JULY 4TH CELEBRATION. PARADE, FUN & FOOD BOOTHS, HISTORY EXHIBIT & FIREWORKS. AT LIONS PARK YOUTH BLDG. (LOCAL). NELL BEDDYFELD, CHMN; LAKE ALFRED BICENTENNIAL COMMITTEE; PO BOX 1304; LAKE ALFRED, FL 33850. (#200011-280).

LAKE CITY

BICYCLE TRAILS FOR LAKE CITY, FLORIDA. INSTALL BIKE LANE ALONG NEW FOUR LANE HWY, BAYA AVE, FROM LAKE CITY TO COMMUNITY COLLEGE. FORMULATE MASTER PLAN FOR BIKE TRAILS BETWEEN ALL LOCAL SCHOOLS. (LOCAL). VIRGINIA H BISHOP, CHAIRMAN; COLUMBIA COUNTY ACTION 76 COMMITTEE; 2003 S FIRST ST; LAKE CITY, FL 32055. (#8390).

CEMETERY RESTORATION-DEDICATION - LAKE CITY, FL. RESTORATION, COMMEMORATION AND DEDICATION OF MEMORIAL CEMETERY. 21 GROUPS LEARNED CEMETERY HISTORY IN RELATION TO COUNTY, STATE AND NATION. (LOCAL). NETTIE OZAKI, PROJ CHAIRMAN; AMERICAN LEGION AND GIRL SCOUTS; 742 DESOTO DR; LAKE CITY, FL 32055. (#25946).

COLUMBIA COUNTY HISTORY - LAKE CITY, FL. PROVIDE PROFESSIONALLY WRITTEN HISTORY OF COLUMBIA COUNTY. (LOCAL). NETTIE OZAKI, PRESIDENT; COLUMBIA COUNTY HISTORICAL SOCIETY; 742 DESOTO CIRCLE; LAKE CITY, FL 32055. (#25947).

ENVIRONMENTAL STUDY AREA - LAKE CITY, FL. CREATE ENVIRONMENTAL STUDY AREA IN WOODS ADJACENT TO SCHOOL, BURY TIME CAPSULE & PRESENT PAGEANT OF LOCAL HISTORY. (LOCAL). LUCY LANE, COORDINATOR; SUMMERS ELEMENTARY SCHOOL; MCFARLANE AVE; LAKE CITY, FL 32055. (#25945).

FINE ARTS COUNCIL - LAKE CITY, FL. ESTABLISH FINE ARTS COUNCIL FOR LAKE CITY-COLUMBIA COUNTY. (LOCAL). LILY DEMAS, PRESIDENT; LAKE CITY-COLUMBIA COUNTY FINE ARTS COUNCIL; CITY HALL; LAKE CITY, FL 32055. (#25948).

MAY 10, '75. WALKATHON ALONG PROPOSED BICYCLE TRAILS. OPENING. (LOCAL). VIRGINIA H BISHOP; COLUMBIA COUNTY ACTION 76 COMMITTEE; 2003 S FIRST ST; LAKE CITY, FL 32055. (#8390-501).

NOV 8, '75. DEDICATION OF RESTORED CEMETERY. CEREMONY. (LOCAL). NETTIE OZAKI, PROJ CHMN; AMERICAN LEGION AND GIRL SCOUTS; 742 DESOTO DR; LAKE CITY, FL 32055. (#25946-1).

JAN 23 - 24, '76. '1776' PLAY. LIVE PERFORMANCE AT TISON AUDITORIUM. (LOCAL). LILY DEMAS, CHAIRMAN; LAKE CITY-COLUMBIA COUNTY FINE ARTS COUNCIL; PO BOX 1776; LAKE CITY, FL 32055. (#200011-113).

APR 7, '76. BURIAL OF TIME CAPSULE & PAGEANT OF LOCAL HISTORY. CEREMONY, LIVE PERFORMANCE. (LOCAL). LUCY LANE, COORD; SUMMERS ELEMENTARY SCHOOL; MCFARLANE AVE; LAKE CITY, FL 32055. (#25945-1).

APR 25 - MAY 1, '76. 'WEEK OF EXCELLENCE'. MAYOR PROCLAIMED WEEK OF EXCELLENCE ASKING EVERY CITIZEN TO DO HIS BEST IN WHATEVER JOB, DUTY OR PROFESSION. (LOCAL). SUNNY SHACKELFORD, CHMN; COLUMBIA COUNTY ACTION '76 COMMITTEE; PO BOX 1776; LAKE CITY, FL 32055. (#200011-112).

MAY 3, '76. SCHOOL ESSAY. ESSAY CONTEST FOR HIGH SCHOOL SENIORS. THE SUBJECT IS 'THE WAY IT WAS'. THE PRIZE IS $100.00. (LOCAL). FREDA PICKENS, COORD; COLUMBIA COUNTY '76 COMMITTEE; PO BOX 1776; LAKE CITY, FL 32055. (#108367-3).

JUNE 15, '76. DEDICATION OF PARK TO BICENTENNIAL AND BAND CONCERT. ESTABLISHMENT AND DEDICATION OF PUBLIC PARK ON SHORE OF LAKE ALLIGATOR WITH COOPERATION OF COUNTY COMMISSION & FLORIDA GAME COMMISSION. (LOCAL). VIRGINIA H BISHOP; COLUMBIA COUNTY ACTION 76 COMMITTEE; 2003 S FIRST ST; LAKE CITY, FL 32055. (#8389-501).

JUNE 15, '76. DEDICATION OF TRAILS TO BICENTENNIAL. OPENING. (LOCAL). VIRGINIA H BISHOP; COLUMBIA COUNTY ACTION 76 COMMITTEE; 2003 S FIRST ST; LAKE CITY, FL 32055. (#8390-502).

JULY 2 - 4, '76. FOURTH OF JULY CELEBRATION. PARADE, SPEECHES, CONTESTS, SIDEWALK ART SHOW, STREET DANCE, FOOD & FIREWORKS. AT OLUSTEE PARK, LAKE CITY. (LOCAL). DOUG TANNENBAUM, CHMN; LAKE CITY JAYCEES; 320 NORTH MARION ST; LAKE CITY, FL 32055. (#105248-1).

JULY 4, '76. DEDICATION OF LIBRARY - MUSEUM COMPLEX TO BICENTENNIAL. OPENING, CEREMONY. (LOCAL). VIRGINIA H BISHOP; COLUMBIA COUNTY ACTION 76 COMMITTEE; 2003 S FIRST ST; LAKE CITY, FL 32055. (#8388-501).

NOV 30 - DEC 1, '76. UNITED STATES ARMED FORCES BICENTENNIAL CARAVAN. CARAVAN IS COMPOSED OF EXHIBIT VANS FOR EACH MILITARY SERVICE. PROJECT THEME IS 'HISTORY OF THE ARMED FORCES & THEIR CONTRIBUTIONS TO THE NATION'. (LOCAL). MRS VIRGINIA BISHOP; UNITED STATES ARMED FORCES BICENTENNIAL CARAVAN; PO BOX 1298; LAKE CITY, FL 32055. (#1775-781).

LAKE MARY

HISTORY BOOK ON LAKE MARY, FL. A HISTORY OF THE TOWN WAS WRITTEN AND PUBLISHED. (LOCAL). DON JACKSON, CHAIRMAN; LAKE MARY BICENTENNIAL COMMITTEE; PO BOX 327; LAKE MARY, FL 32746. (#32213).

LAKE MARY'S CIVIC CENTER - FL. A NEW CIVIC CENTER BUILDING WILL BE DEVELOPED. (LOCAL). DON JACKSON, COORDINATOR; LAKE MARY BICENTENNIAL COMMITTEE; BOX 327; LAKE MARY, FL 32746. (#32214).

JUNE 10, '75. FLAG PRESENTATION & RAISING. CEREMONY AT LAKE MARY ELEMENTARY SCHOOL. (LOCAL). MRS S FOWLER; LAKE MARY BICENTENNIAL COMMITTEE; PO BOX 581; LAKE MARY, FL 32746. (#200011-297).

MAY 26 - SEPT 18, '76. LAKE MARY'S BICENTENNIAL CELEBRATION. ACTIVITIES INCLUDED A CEREMONY, PARADE, ARTS & CRAFTS DISPLAYS AND SALES. AT LAKE MARY'S CITY HALL AND ELEMENTARY SCHOOL. (LOCAL). MRS S FOWLER; LAKE MARY BICENTENNIAL COMMITTEE; PO BOX 581; LAKE MARY, FL 32746. (#200011-298).

LAKE PARK

'GRAND FINALLY DANCE' - LAKE PARK, FL. FINAL PROJECT FOR THE BICENTENNIAL IN LAKE PARK. (LOCAL). JAMES OWENS, CHAIRMAN; LAKE PARK BICENTENNIAL COMMITTEE; 700 OLD DIXIE HWY; LAKE PARK, FL 33403. (#31966).

LAKE WALES

MUSEUM & ART GALLERY - LAKE WALES, FL. THE MUSEUM WILL REFLECT THE HISTORY OF THE COMMUNITY AND OUR NATIONAL HERITAGE; IT WILL ALSO HOUSE AN ART GALLERY FOR DISPLAY OF COMMUNITY ART & TO SERVE AS A COMMUNITY MEETING CENTER. (LOCAL). MRS MIMI HARDMAN, CHAIRMAN; LAKE WALES BICENTENNIAL COMMITTEE; 230 E PARK AVE; LAKE WALES, FL 33853. (#23438).

PIONEER ROOM DISPLAY - LAKE WALES, FL. A PERMANENT SECTION IN LIBRARY WHICH CONTAINS CHURCH OF GOD HISTORY. (LOCAL). NINA RATZLAFF, HEAD LIBRARIAN; WARNER SOUTHERN COLLEGE LIBRARY; HWY 27 S; LAKE WALES, FL 33853. (#25609).

DEC 6, '75. CHRISTMAS PARADE FLOAT. FLOAT WAS PLANNED & DECORATED BY STUDENTS IN RETAILING DEPT. THEME OF FLOAT 'FIRST CHRISTMAS IN A NEW NATION' DEPICTING EARLY AMERICAN CHRISTMAS SCENE WITH STUDENTS WEARING REPRODUCTIONS OF EARLY AMERICAN COSTUMES AND ANTIQUES FOR PROPS ON FLOAT. (LOCAL). CAROL WILSON, DEAN; LAKE WALES CHAMBER OF COMMERCE; RT H27; BABSON PARK, FL 33827. (#200011-114).

MAR 8 - 12, '76. INDIAN HISTORY DISPLAY. DISPLAY OF ARTIFACTS, 102 PAINTINGS OF INDIAN CHIEFS BY KENNETH RED OWL, OTHER PAINTINGS BY LEVI BLACK BEAR WITH SCRIPT EXPLAINING THE PAINTINGS. AT WARNER SOUTHERN COLLEGE CHAPEL. (LOCAL). EMILY SHARP, DIRECTOR; WARNER SOUTHERN COLLEGE & THE EARL BAILEYS; RT 3, BOX 800; LAKE WALES, FL 33853. (#200011-119).

MAR 20, '76. 'THE BIRTH OF A NATION'. PRESENTATION WITH STATE FLAGS, NAVY BAND OF ORLANDO, 50 STATE FLAG TEAM AND WARNER SOUTHERN SINGERS. AT WARNER SOUTHERN COLLEGE CHAPEL. (LOCAL). EMILY SHARP, DIRECTOR; WARNER SOUTHERN COLLEGE; RT 3, BOX 800; LAKE WALES, FL 33853. (#200011-120).

APR 10, '76. ART SHOW. EXHIBIT AT DOWNTOWN LAKE WALES. (LOCAL). MRS MIMI REID HARDMAN; AMERICAN ASSOC OF UNIVERSITY WOMEN; 230 E PARK AVE; LAKE WALES, FL 33853. (#200011-117).

APR 10, '76. PIONEER DAYS. EXHIBIT AT MARKETPLACE - STATION MUSEUM. (LOCAL). MRS MIMI REID HARDMAN; LAKE WALES BICENTENNIAL COMMITTEE; 230 E PARK AVE; LAKE WALES, FL 33853. (#200011-118).

APR 11, '76. FLORIDA CHAMBER PLAYERS CONCERT. LIVE PERFORMANCE AT LAKE WALES HIGH SCHOOL. (LOCAL). MRS MIMI REID HARDMAN; LAKE WALES BICENTENNIAL COMMITTEE; 230 E PARK AVE; LAKE WALES, FL 33853. (#200011-116).

APR 18, '76. EASTER BICENTENNIAL SUNRISE SERVICE. SERVICE 4 18 76 ONLY ORGAN MUSIC SINGING SPEAKING. AT GARDEN BEHIND RESIDENCE. (LOCAL). JAMES R HARPER; UNIVERSAL LIFE BAPTIST CHURCH; 1021 S SCENIC DR; LAKE WALES, FL 33853. (#200011-115).

LAKE WALES — CONTINUED

APR 23, '76. COLLEGE CHAPEL PRESENTATION. THE READING OF SEGMENTS OF HISTORICAL DOCUMENTS. AT WARNER SOUTHERN COLLEGE CHAPEL. (LOCAL). EMILY SHARP, DIRECTOR; WARNER SOUTHERN COLLEGE, COMMUNICATIONS DEPT; RT 3 BOX 800; LAKE WALES, FL 33853. (#200011-121).

MAY 1 - 20, '76. LIBRARY DISPLAY. THE DISPLAY WILL FEATURE BOOKS ABOUT THE HISTORY OF OUR NATION, INDIANS AND THE PRESIDENTS. (LOCAL). NINA RATZLAFF, LIBRARIAN; WARNER SOUTHERN COLLEGE LIBRARY; HWY 27 S; LAKE WALES, FL 33853. (#108132-1).

LAKE WORTH

LAKE WORTH PLAYHOUSE FACILITY RENOVATION - FL. RENOVATION OF NEWLY ACQUIRED THEATRE BY LAKE WORTH PLAYHOUSE FOR A DRAMA AND PERFORMING ARTS CENTER. (LOCAL). CHAIRMAN; PALM BEACH COUNTY BICENTENNIAL COMMITTEE; 730 N COUNTRY RD; PALM BEACH, FL 33480. (#13652). **ARBA GRANTEE.**

VIDEO-TAPED HISTORY PROGRAM - LAKE WORTH, FL. THE PROGRAMS WILL FEATURE NATIONAL, STATE AND LOCAL PERSONS, PLACES AND EVENTS. (LOCAL). EDWIN PUGH, CHAIRMAN; PALM BEACH JUNIOR COLLEGE BICENTENNIAL COMMITTEE; 4200 CONGRESS BLVD; LAKE WORTH, FL 33460. (#15744).

OCT 24, '75 - MAY 17, '76. AMERICAN ISSUES FORUM EVENTS. SCHEDULED FOR 10/24, 11/3 & 12/12/75; 1/29, 2/23, 3/26, 4/30 & 5/17/76. AT PALM BEACH JUNIOR COLLEGE AUDITORIUM. (LOCAL). DR ERROLL HICKS; PALM BEACH JUNIOR COLLEGE BICENTENNIAL COMMITTEE; 4200 CONGRESS AVE; LAKE WORTH, FL 33461. (#102506-9).

DEC 2, '75. AMERICAN JAZZ FESTIVAL. LIVE PERFORMANCE AT P B J C MAIN CAMPUS. (LOCAL). EDWIN V PUGH, CHAIRMAN; PALM BEACH JR COLLEGE BICENTENNIAL COMMITTEE; 4200 CONGRESS AVE; LAKE WORTH, FL 33461. (#102506-15).

JAN 9, '76. HISTORIC MARKER DEDICATION. PLAQUE: PBJC OLDEST PUBLIC JUNIOR COLLEGE IN STATE. AT ON CAMPUS. (LOCAL). EDWIN V PUGH, CHMN; PALM BEACH JR COLLEGE BICENTENNIAL COMMITTEE; 4200 CONGRESS AVE; LAKE WORTH, FL 33460. (#102506-5).

JAN 10, '76. 'COMMON SENSE' DAY. 200 YEARS OF 'COMMON SENSE' - PLAY, DEBATE, MUSIC. AT ON CAMPUS. (LOCAL). EDWIN V PUGH, CHMN; PALM BEACH JR COLLEGE BICENTENNIAL COMMITTEE; 4200 CONGRESS AVE; LAKE WORTH, FL 33460. (#102506-6).

JAN 10 - 19, '76. FLORIDA BICENTENNIAL WAGON DAYS. PARADE. (LOCAL). EDWIN V PUGH, CHAIRMAN; PALM BEACH JR COLLEGE BICENTENNIAL COMMITTEE; 4200 CONGRESS AVE; LAKE WORTH, FL 33461. (#102506-14).

JAN 15, '76. MARTIN LUTHER KING DAY. CEREMONY AT PBJC STUDENT CENTER. (LOCAL). EDWIN V PUGH, CHMN; PALM BEACH JR COLLEGE BICENTENNIAL COMMITTEE; 4200 CONGRESS AVE; LAKE WORTH, FL 33461. (#102506-2).

JAN 16, '76. ARBOR DAY. CEREMONY AT BOTANICAL PARK. (LOCAL). EDWIN V PUGH, CHMN; PALM BEACH JR COLLEGE BICENTENNIAL COMMITTEE; 4200 CONGRESS AVE; LAKE WORTH, FL 33461. (#102506-3).

JAN 19, '76. ROBERT E LEE DAY. CEREMONY AT PBJC LIBRARY & GROUNDS. (LOCAL). EDWIN V PUGH, CHMN; PALM BEACH JR COLLEGE BICENTENNIAL COMMITTEE; 4200 CONGRESS AVE; LAKE WORTH, FL 33461. (#102506-4).

FEB 7 - 8, '76. UNITED STATES ARMED FORCES BICENTENNIAL CARAVAN. CARAVAN IS COMPOSED OF EXHIBIT VANS FOR EACH MILITARY SERVICE. PROJECT THEME IS 'HISTORY OF THE ARMED FORCES AND THEIR CONTRIBUTIONS TO THE NATION'. (LOCAL). CARL L JACOBSON; US ARMED FORCES BICENTENNIAL EXHIBIT VANS PROJECT; 5701 CINNAMEN DR; W PALM BEACH, FL 33406. (#1775-430).

FEB 12, '76. LINCOLN'S BIRTHDAY CELEBRATION. CEREMONY AT PBJC STUDENT CENTER. (LOCAL). EDWIN V PUGH, CHMN; PALM BEACH JR COLLEGE BICENTENNIAL COMMITTEE; 4200 CONGRESS AVE; LAKE WORTH, FL 33461. (#102506-7).

FEB 20 - 21, '76. SECOND NATIONAL EXOSOCIOLOGY SYMPOSIUM. ADDRESS BY DR J ALLEN HYNEK, PROF OF ASTRONOMY, NORTHWESTERN UNIV, AND FORMER ADVISOR TO USAF ON UNIDENTIFIED FLYING OBJECTS. AT PBJC AUDITORIUM ON 2/20 AND HOLIDAY INN, PALM BEACH ON 2/21. (NAT'L). DR RICHARD YINGER; PALM BEACH JR COLLEGE BICENT COMMITTEE & NATL EXOSOCIOLOGY ASSOC; 4200 CONGRESS AVE; LAKE WORTH, FL 33461. (#102506-8).

MAR 17, '76. ST PATRICKS DAY MINORITIES DAY. FESTIVAL AT PBJC AUDITORIUM. (LOCAL). EDWIN V PUGH, CHAIRMAN; PALM BEACH JR COLLEGE BICENTENNIAL COMMITTEE; 4200 CONGRESS AVE; LAKE WORTH, FL 33461. (#103334-4).

APR 7 - 9, '76. BICENTENNIAL EXTRAVAGANZA. LIVE PERFORMANCE AT PALM BEACH JR COLLEGE AUDITORIUM. (LOCAL). EDWIN V PUGH, CHAIRMAN; PALM BEACH JR COLLEGE BICENTENNIAL COMMITTEE & AREA SCHOOLS; 4200 CONGRESS AVE; LAKE WORTH, FL 33461. (#102506-13).

JUNE 3, '76. JEFFERSON DAVIS BIRTHDAY. CEREMONY AT PBJC STUDENT CENTER. (LOCAL). EDWIN V PUGH, CHAIRMAN; PALM BEACH JR COLLEGE BICENTENNIAL COMMITTEE; 4200 CONGRESS AVE; LAKE WORTH, FL 33461. (#103334-3).

JUNE 14, '76. FLAG DAY. CEREMONY, FESTIVAL AT SUNSHINE COURT, MAIN CAMPUS. (LOCAL). EDWIN V PUGH, CHAIRMAN; PALM BEACH JR COLLEGE BICENTENNIAL COMMITTEE; 4200 CONGRESS AVE; LAKE WORTH, FL 33461. (#103334-2).

AUG 1 - 4, '76. NATL FINNISH AMERICAN BICENTENNIAL MEETING AND FESTIVAL. BICENT FESTIVALS WILL BE HELD IN FINNISH-AMERICAN CENTERS LOCATED IN SEVERAL CITIES DURING 1976. (REGN'L). RALPH J JALKANEN, PRES; SUOMI COLLEGE; QUINCY ST; HANCOCK, MI 49930. (#8628-6).

SEPT 17, '76. RET SIGER DAY. SEMINAR AT PALM BEACH JR COLLEGE AUDITORIUM. (LOCAL). EDWIN V PUGH, CHAIRMAN; PALM BEACH JR COLLEGE BICENTENNIAL COMMITTEE; 4200 CONGRESS AVE; LAKE WORTH, FL 33461. (#102506-11).

SEPT 22, '76. NATHAN HALE DAY. READER'S THEATRE PLAY: 'THE HERO WITHOUT A COUNTRY', BY E V PUGH; PRESENTATION OF 'HALE FAREWELL LETTERS'; CONTEST WINNERS TO BE ANNOUNCED. AT PALM BEACH JUNIOR COLLEGE, STUDENT CENTER. (LOCAL). EDWIN V PUGH, PROJ DIR; PALM BEACH BICENTENNIAL COMMITTEE; 4200 CONGRESS AVE; LAKE WORTH, FL 33461. (#102506-10).

DEC 15, '76. BILL OF RIGHTS DAY. CEREMONY AT PBJC STUDENT CENTER & CLASSROOMS. (LOCAL). EDWIN V PUGH, CHAIRMAN; PALM BEACH JR COLLEGE BICENTENNIAL COMMITTEE; 4200 CONGRESS AVE; LAKE WORTH, FL 33461. (#103334-1).

LAKELAND

CAMPUS BEAUTIFICATION - LAKELAND, FL. PLANT LIVE OAK TREES AND HOLLY TREES TO COMMEMORATE THE 13 COLONIES; IMPROVE THE ENVIRONMENT FOR THE FUTURE. (LOCAL). LARRY DURRENCE, PROJ DIRECTOR; FLORIDA SOUTHERN COLLEGE BICENTENNIAL COMMITTEE; LAKELAND, FL 33802. (#22039).

HISTORIC MARKER FOR FLORIDA SOUTHERN COLLEGE. A MARKER WILL BE ERECTED COMMEMORATING THE NAMING OF FLORIDA SOUTHERN COLLEGE AS A NATIONAL HISTORIC SITE. (LOCAL). LARRY DURRENCE, PROJ DIRECTOR; FLORIDA SOUTHERN COLLEGE; LAKELAND, FL 33802. (#22038).

HISTORIC MARKER PROJECT - LAKELAND, FL. PLAN TO PLACE HISTORIC MARKERS ON ONE OR MORE OF THE SITES WHERE FLORIDA SOUTHERN COLLEGE WAS LOCATED BEFORE MOVING TO LAKELAND. (ST-WIDE). LARRY DURRENCE, PROJ DIRECTOR; FLORIDA SOUTHERN COLLEGE BICENTENNIAL COMMITTEE; LAKELAND, FL 33802. (#22040).

THE LIBERTY LINER IN POLK COUNTY, FLORIDA. A MOBILE MUSEUM THAT WILL TOUR POLK COUNTY SCHOOLS & COMMUNITY CENTERS EXHIBITING ARTS, CRAFTS & ITEMS OF HISTORIC INTEREST RELATING TO THE SPIRIT OF THE BICENTENNIAL IN 1976. (LOCAL). JACI HANSON, RESOURCE SPECIALIST; POLK COUNTY BICENTENNIAL COMMITTEE; PO BOX 1776; LAKELAND, FL 33802. (#8638).

MUSEUM RESTORATION - LAKELAND, FL. RESTORATION OF THE FRANK LLOYD WRIGHT MUSEUM. (LOCAL). LARRY DURRENCE, PROJ DIRECTOR; FLORIDA SOUTHERN COLLEGE; LAKELAND, FL 33802. (#22037).

SPIRIT OF 76 PARADE IN LAKELAND, FLORIDA. GALA BICENTENNIAL PARADE TO CELEBRATE THE SPIRIT OF '76. (LOCAL). ROBERT F EPPERSON, PROJ COORDINATOR; LAKELAND BICENTENNIAL COMMITTEE; PO BOX 1776; LAKELAND, FL 33802. (#8652).

VOTE CHALLENGE PROJECT IN LAKELAND, FLORIDA. PROJECT CHALLENGES ALL FLORIDA COUNTIES TO COMPETE FOR HIGHEST PERCENTAGE OF VOTER TURNOUT IN 1976 ELECTIONS. (LOCAL). MRS RICHARD CONIBEAR; POLK COUNTY BICENT COMMITTEE; BOX 1776; LAKELAND, FL 33802. (#8808).

JULY 4, '75 - SEPT 1, '76. BICENTENNIAL TOURING MEDICINE SHOW. THIS UPDATED VERSION OF AN OLD-TIME MEDICINE SHOW IS AVAILABLE TO BICENTENNIAL EVENTS AS AN ADDED ATTRACTION TO THEIR LOCAL EVENT AND THE $500 FEE COVERS SHOW EXPENSES. AT TWO 32 FOOT LONG SEMI-VANS.. (ST-WIDE). BETTE LOGAN; POLK COUNTY BICENTENNIAL COMMITTEE; PO BOX 1776; LAKELAND, FL 33803. (#102981-2).

SEPT 25 - 28, '75. 'GEORGE M' PLAY. LIVE PERFORMANCE AT BUCKNER THEATER. (LOCAL). MEL WOOTEN, COORDINATOR; FLORIDA SOUTHERN COLLEGE; LAKELAND, FL 33802. (#200011-122).

OCT 2 - 5, '75. CONGRESSIONAL MEDAL OF HONOR SOCIETY CONVENTION 1975. 3-DAY CONVENTION IN 1975 IN LAKELAND, FLORIDA. (NAT'L). BETTE LOGAN; POLK COUNTY BICENTENNIAL COMMITTEE; LAKELAND, FL 33801. (#4769-501).

OCT 8, '75. 'THE WORLD OF BENJAMIN FRANKLIN'. LIVE PERFORMANCE AT BRANSCOMB AUDITORIUM. (LOCAL). LARRY DURRENCE, ASST PROF; FLORIDA SOUTHERN COLLEGE; 1611 SALESBERRY ST; LAKELAND, FL 33803. (#200011-123).

JAN 16, '76. 'A LINCOLN PORTRAIT'. LIVE PERFORMANCE AT BRANSCOMB AUDITORIUM. (LOCAL). JULIANA JORDAN, CHAIRMAN; LAKELAND CONCERT ASSOC & FLORIDA SOUTHERN COLLEGE; LAKELAND, FL 33802. (#200011-125).

JAN 21, '76. 'ROOTS' PLAY. LIVE PERFORMANCE AT BRANSCOMB AUDITORIUM. (LOCAL). DAVID TALLEY, COORDINATOR; FLORIDA SOUTHERN COLLEGE; LAKELAND, FL 33802. (#200011-126).

JAN 22, '76. '1776' PLAY. LIVE PERFORMANCE AT BRANSCOMB AUDITORIUM. (LOCAL). JULIANA JORDAN, CHAIRMAN; FLORIDA SOUTHERN COLLEGE; LAKELAND, FL 33802. (#200011-124).

FEB 5, '76. 'VIRGIL FOX'. LIVE PERFORMANCE AT BRANSCOMB AUDITORIUM. (LOCAL). JULIANA JORDAN, CHAIRMAN; FLORIDA SOUTHERN COLLEGE; LAKELAND, FL 33802. (#200011-127).

FEB 18 - 21, '76. ANNUAL FOUNDER'S WEEK AT FLORIDA SOUTHERN COLLEGE. SEVERAL CEREMONIES TO CELEBRATE THE HISTORY OF FLORIDA SOUTHERN COLLEGE. (LOCAL). SAM LUCE, DIRECTOR; FLORIDA SOUTHERN COLLEGE BICENTENNIAL COMMITTEE, LAKELAND, FL 33802. (#105795-5).

FEB 20 - 22, '76. WASHINGTON'S BIRTHDAY PARTY. EXHIBIT, FESTIVAL AT LAKELAND CIVIC CENTER BOX Q LAKELAND FLA 33802. (LOCAL). BETH MASON; LAKELAND BICENTENNIAL COMMITTEE; 1404 BRIARWOOD LANE; LAKELAND, FL 33803 (#50390-1).

FEB 21 - 22, '76. EXPO AMERICANA. A GEORGE WASHINGTON BIRTHDAY PARTY WILL FEATURE DEMONSTRATIONS & TEACHING OF EARLY/RURAL AMERICAN ARTISAN SKILLS BY CRAFTSMEN IN AUTHENTIC COSTUME. SPECIAL COLLECTIONS OF EARLY AMERICANA TO BE SHOWN. ALSO: EDUCATIONAL COURSE. AT LAKELAND CIVIC CENTER, 800 W LEMON. (LOCAL) DIAL JACKSON, CO-CHAIRMAN; LAKELAND BICENT COMMITTEE; 2301 HAWTHORNE TRAIL; LAKELAND, FL 33803. (#8793-1).

MAR 12 - 14, '76. LONGHORN WORLD CHAMPIONSHIP RODEO. TOP AMERICAN, CANADIAN AND AUSTRALIAN COWBOYS AND COWGIRLS WILL COMPETE FOR WORLD CHAMPIONSHIP POINTS IN SEX COMPETITIVE EVENTS. INCLUDES BICENTENNIAL OPENING PAGEANT, RODEO CLOWNS AND SPECIALTY PERFORMERS AT LAKELAND CIVIC CENTER ARENA. (ST-WIDE). BRUCE LEHRKE, PROJ CHMN; LONGHORN RODEO COMPANY; PO BOX 8280; NASHVILLE, TN 37207. (#104574-1).

MAR 31, '76. INTERNATIONAL STRING QUARTET. LIVE PERFORMANCE AT BRANSCOMB AUDITORIUM. (LOCAL). JULIANA JORDAN, COORD; FLORIDA SOUTHERN COLLEGE FESTIVAL OF FINE ARTS; LAKELAND, FL 33802. (#105795-3).

APR 9 - 11, '76. 'THE MUSIC MAN'. LIVE PERFORMANCE AT BRANSCOMB AUDITORIUM. (LOCAL). MEL WOOTEN, DIRECTOR, FLORIDA SOUTHERN COLLEGE BICENTENNIAL COMMITTEE; LAKELAND, FL 33802. (#105795-4).

APR 14, '76. STUDENT FACULTY WORK-DAY. A WORK-DAY TO IMPROVE UNDERSTANDING AND COMMUNICATION BETWEEN FACULTY AND STUDENTS; THEY WILL ALSO BEAUTIFY THE CAMPUS. (LOCAL). LARRY DURRENCE, DIRECTOR; FLORIDA SOUTHERN COLLEGE STUDENT GOVERNMENT; LAKELAND, FL 33802. (#105777-1).

JULY 3, '76. BICENTENNIAL PARADE. A PARADE TO CELEBRATE THE NATION'S 200TH BIRTHDAY. (LOCAL). MRS R F MASON, CHMN; LAKELAND BICENTENNIAL COMMITTEE; LAKELAND, FL 33802. (#102191-1).

JULY 3, '76. POLK COUNTY MUSIC & ART FESTIVAL. SCHOOL CHILDREN WILL MAKE THEIR CONTRIBUTION TO THE CELEBRATION THROUGH MUSIC & ART. (LOCAL). MRS R F MASON, CHMN; LAKELAND BICENTENNIAL COMMITTEE; LAKELAND, FL 33802. (#102190-1).

DEC 6 - 8, '76. AMERICAN FREEDOM TRAIN DISPLAY DAYS AT LAKELAND. THE AMERICAN FREEDOM TRAIN INCLUDES 10 EXHIBIT CARS & 2 SHOW CASE CARS DEPICTING DIFFERENT PHASES OF THE AMERICAN EXPERIENCE. ITS ARRIVAL WILL SERVE AS A CATALYST FOR LOCAL BICENTENNIAL CELEBRATIONS BY PEOPLE THROUGHOUT THIS NATION. (ST-WIDE). SY FREEDMAN, DIR OF P/R; THE AMERICAN FREEDOM TRAIN FOUNDATION; 5205 LEESBURG PIKE, SUITE 800; BAILEY'S XRDS, VA 22041. (#1776-109).

LAND OF LAKES

CHRISTMAS TREE, LAND OF LAKES, FL. STUDENTS WILL RESEARCH THE COLONIAL PERIOD AND DECORATE A CHRISTMAS TREE IN THE STYLE OF THAT ERA. (LOCAL). MADELINE HAYES, TEACHER; ADULT EDUCATION-PASCO COUNTY; US 41; LAND OF LAKES, FL 33539. (#20959).

COOKBOOK, LAND OF LAKES, FL. COOKBOOK WITH GREAT AMERICAN RECIPES. (LOCAL). MADELINE HAYES, TEACHERS; PASCO COUNTY-ADULT EDUCATION; US 41; LAND OF LAKES, FL 33539. (#20960).

OCT '75. BICENTENNIAL DESIGN CONTEST. A $25.00 U S SAVINGS BOND WILL BE GIVEN AS THE AWARD TO THE STUDENT IN THE COUNTY SCHOOL SYSTEM WHOSE DESIGN IS CHOSEN AS THE OFFICIAL BICENTENNIAL LOGO FOR THE COUNTY. (LOCAL). CLARE BARNARD, CHMN; PASCO COUNTY ACTION '76 STEERING COMMITTEE; PO BOX 1776; LAND O'LAKES, FL 33539. (#102200-1).

LARGO

JULY 2, '76. SECOND ANNUAL CHILDREN'S PARADE. PARADE AT PARKVIEW LANE IN PARKVIEW, ESTATES SUBDIVISION. (LOCAL). RAMON G FLOREZ, CHMN; PATRIOTIC KREWE OF LARGO; 1230 16 CT SW; LARGO, FL 33540. (#108075-1).

JULY 2, '76. 2ND ANNUAL CHILDREN'S PATRIOTIC KREW OF LARGO. FESTIVAL, PARADE AT PARK VIEW STATE SUBDIVISION, PARKVIEW LANE. (LOCAL). RAMON G FLOREZ, CHMN; PATRIOTIC KREW OF LARGO; 1230 16TH CT SW; LARGO, FL 33540. (#108060-1).

JULY 3, '76. PATRIOTIC PARADE & BALL. FESTIVAL, PARADE AT LARGO CIVIC AUDITORIUM. (LOCAL). RAMON FLOREZ, CHMN; PATRIOTIC KREWE; LARGO, FL 33540. (#108336-1).

JULY 4, '76. ALL DAY PICNIC. BRING OWN LUNCH; FESTIVITIES OPEN TO PUBLIC; WILL HAVE JUDGING OF BEARD & MOUSTACHE CONTEST AND BURIAL OF TIME CAPSULE. AT HIGHLAND RECREATIONAL COMPLEX. (LOCAL). THOMAS FEASTER, CHAIRMAN; LARGO BICENTENNIAL COMMITTEE; 137 E OVERBROOK; LARGO, FL 33540. (#108336-2).

LAUDERDALE LK

NEW COMMUNITY CENTER IN LAUDERDALE LAKES, FL. A NEW COMMUNITY CENTER WILL BE BUILT IN LAUDERDALE LAKES, FL. (LOCAL). PINKY HERMAN, CHAIRMAN; LAUDERDALE LAKES BICENTENNIAL COMMISSION; 4300 NW 36 ST; LDRDLE LAKES, FL 33319. (#15670).

LEESBURG

CITIZEN AWARENESS SOUND FILMSTRIPS AND LECTURE, FL. AUDIO VISUAL MATERIALS ON PRESIDENCY, CONGRESS, THE SUPREME COURT AND GOVERNMENTAL AGENCIES. PRESENTATION TO COLLEGE AND COMMUNITY GROUPS. (LOCAL). DR EDWARD JACKSON, CHAIRMAN; SOCIAL SCIENCE DEPT; LAKE-SUMTER COMMUNITY COLLEGE; LEESBURG, FL 32748. (#17020).

FILM FESTIVAL - LEESBURG, FL. EARLY FILMS OF MOVIE PIONEERS WHICH MARKED THE BEGINNING OF AN ERA. (LOCAL). DOUGLAS TRABERT, DIRECTOR; MEDIA CENTER; LAKE-SUMTER COMMUNITY COLLEGE; LEESBURG, FL 32748. (#17013).

FLAG RAISING CEREMONY & DISPLAY OF ORIGINAL 13 STATES FLAGS. CEREMONY. (LOCAL). MICHAEL BAKICH, PRES; LAKE SUMTER COMMUNITY COLLEGE BICENTENNIAL COMMITTEE; LAKE SUMTER COMMUNITY COLLEGE; LEESBURG, FL 32748. (#103097-3). **(??).**

HISTORIC BRIEFS IN STUDENT BULLETIN - LEESBURG, FL. BRIEF HISTORIC ARTICLE TO APPEAR IN EACH ISSUE OF STUDENT BULLETIN PUBLISHED BIWEEKLY. (LOCAL). JEAN SNEED, PROJ DIRECTOR; LAKE-SUMTER COMMUNITY COLLEGE; LEESBURG, FL 32748. (#17018).

HISTORIC BRIEFS IN STUDENT NEWSPAPER- LEESBURG, FL. BRIEF HISTORIC ARTICLE TO APPEAR IN EACH ISSUE OF THE ANGLER, STUDENT NEWSPAPER. (LOCAL). BILL BRADFORD, PROJ DIRECTOR; LAKE-SUMTER COMMUNITY COLLEGE; LEESBURG, FL 32748. (#17019).

HISTORICAL FLAG DISPLAY - LEESBURG, FL. EARLY COLONIAL, 13 ORIGINAL STATE AND EVOLUTIONARY DISPLAY OF THE NATIONAL FLAG FROM GRAND UNION TO 50 STATE FLAGS. (LOCAL). HELEN C SERGESON, LIBRARIAN; LAKE-SUMTER COMMUNITY COLLEGE, LEARNING RESOURCES CENTER; LEESBURG, FL 32748. (#17015).

HISTORICAL SOUND FILMSTRIPS - LEESBURG, FL. COLLEGE AUDIO VISUAL MATERIALS ON HISTORICAL, SOCIOLOGICAL AND ECOLOGICAL THEMES TO BE SHOWN IN COLLEGE AND OFF CAMPUS FOR CIVIC AND COMMUNITY GROUPS. CONTINUING PROJECT THROUGHOUT THE YEAR. (LOCAL). WALTER J BRYDE, CHAIRMAN; LAKE-SUMTER COMMUNITY COLLEGE BICENTENNIAL COMMITTEE; LAKE-SUMTER COMMUNITY COLLEGE; LEESBURG, FL 32748. (#17010).

SHOWCASE DISPLAYS AT LAKE-SUMPTER COLLEGE, FL. ITEMS OF HISTORICAL INTEREST DISPLAYED BY LEARNING RESOURCE CENTER. (LOCAL). HELEN C SERGESON, LIBRARIAN; LAKE-SUMTER COMMUNITY COLLEGE; LEESBURG, FL 32748. (#17014).

STUDENT HANDBOOK - LAKE SUMPTER COLLEGE, FL. COVER DECORATED IN BICENTENNIAL THEME. (LOCAL). MICHAEL J BAKICH, PRESIDENT; STUDENT GOVERNMENT; LAKE SUMTER COMMUNITY COLLEGE; LEESBURG, FL 32748. (#17022).

STUDENT UNION DECORATIONS - LEESBURG, FL. RED, WHITE AND BLUE THEME FOR 76. (LOCAL). MICHAEL J BAKICH, PRESIDENT; STUDENT GOVERNMENT; LAKE SUMTER COMMUNITY COLLEGE; LEESBURG, FL 32748. (#17021).

THEME FOR YEARBOOK-MAGAZINE, LEESBURG, FL. HISTORIC THEME FOR YEARBOOK-MAGAZINE. (LOCAL). BETH PARRISH, PROJ DIRECTOR; LAKE-SUMTER COMMUNITY COLLEGE; LEESBURG, FL 32748. (#17017).

TIME CAPSULE IN NOVEMBER, 1976 - LEESBURG, FL. RECORDS, PAPERS, CLIPPINGS, CRAFTS & MEMORABILIA IN CAPSULE AT PERMANENT LOCATION IN COMMUNITY. FIRST ANNIVERSARY OF HAWTHORNE COMMUNITY. (LOCAL). DR JAMES F CORWIN, CHAIRMAN; HAWTHORNE COMMUNITY; 528 PALO VERDE DR; LEESBURG, FL 32748. (#25995).

VOTER REGISTRATION CAMPAIGN - LEESBURG, FL. CAMPAIGN TO REGISTER COLLEGE STUDENTS TO VOTE. (LOCAL). BILL BRADFORD, PROJ DIRECTOR; LAKE-SUMTER COMMUNITY COLLEGE; LEESBURG, FL 32748. (#17016).

NOV 1 - DEC 31, '75. BICENTENNIAL POSTER CONTEST AND EXHIBIT. CONTEST ENTRIES TO BE EXHIBITED IN LIBRARY. CASH PRIZES. EXHIBIT AVAILABLE FOR LOAN TO COMMUNITY CENTERS DURING 1976. AT LIBRARY GALLERY. (LOCAL). JANET KING, DIRECTOR; LAKE SUMTER COMMUNITY COLLEGE BICENTENNIAL COMMITTEE; LAKE SUMTER COMMUNITY COLLEGE; LEESBURG, FL 32748. (#103097-5).

NOV 2, '75. HISTORICAL MURAL OF LEESBURG UNVEILING. AN EIGHT PART MURAL BY ARTIST SID SMITH, DEPICTING THE HIGHLIGHTS OF LEESBURG'S PAST & PRESENT. AT BANQUET ROOM OF THE COMMUNITY BUILDING. (LOCAL). MRS PAULINE BEYERS, CHMN; MURAL COMMITTEE OF LEESBURG COMMUNITY; 704 BOYLE ST; LEESBURG, FL 32748. (#200011-128).

NOV 22, '75. BICENTENNIAL YOUTH DEBATE. COMPETITION AT LEESBURG HIGH SCHOOL. (LOCAL). MS JACQUELYN COLLAR, DIR; LEESBURG LIONS CLUB; 1535 NORMANDY WAY; LEESBURG, FL 32748. (#200011-129).

NOV 26, '75. THE NEGRO IN AMERICA, 1619-1865, A FILM HISTORY. EXHIBIT AT BLDG 'A'. (LOCAL). WALTER J BRYDE; LAKE-SUMTER COMMUNITY COLLEGE SOCIAL SCIENCE DIVISION; LAKE-SUMTER COMMUNITY COLLEGE; LEESBURG, FL 32748. (#102995-1).

DEC 8, '75. THE TRUE STORY OF THE CIVIL WAR, A FILM SHOWING. ACADEMY AWARD MOTION PICTURE. AT BLDG A. (LOCAL). WALTER J BRYDE, DIR; SOCIAL-SCIENCE DIVISION; LAKE-SUMTER COMMUNITY COLLEGE; LEESBURG, FL 32748. (#102998-1).

JAN 17, '76. JOHN CHAPPELL PERFORMS MARK TWAIN ON STAGE. LIVE PERFORMANCE AT GYM. (LOCAL). MRS MARY RUTH TAYLOR, DIR; LAKE SUMTER COMMUNITY COLLEGE BICENTENNIAL COMMITTEE & STUDENT GOV'T; LEESBURG, FL 32748. (#200011-130).

MAR 28 - JULY 4, '76. BICENTENNIAL WAGON TRAIN FROM LEESBURG TO VALLEY FORGE. TOUR. (REGN'L). MRS GWENDOLYN BLACK, CHMN; HAWTHORNE COMMUNITY; 125 JACARANDA; LEESBURG, FL 32748. (#108367-6).

MAR 29, '76. STAGE PLAY: 'THE CONSTITUTIONAL CONVENTION'. PLAY IS TO BE WRITTEN AND PRODUCED BY FACULTY; FACULTY SERVED AS ACTORS. (LOCAL). DAVID PAYNE, DIR; LAKE SUMTER COMMUNITY COLLEGE BICENTENNIAL COMMITTEE; LAKE SUMTER COMMUNITY COLLEGE; LEESBURG, FL 32748. (#103097-7).

APR 3, '76. MAC FRAMPTON TRIO - AMERICANA THEME MUSIC. LIVE PERFORMANCE AT GYM. (LOCAL). MRS M R TAYLOR, CHAIRMAN; LAKE SUMTER COMMUNITY COLLEGE LYCEUM COMMITTEE; LEESBURG, FL 32748. (#200011-138).

APR 4, '76. HAWTHORNE CHORUS PERFORMANCE. LIVE PERFORMANCE AT AUDITORIUM. (LOCAL). DR JAMES F CORWIN, CHMN; HAWTHORNE COMMUNITY CLUB; 528 PALO VERDE DR; LEESBURG, FL 32748. (#200011-137).

APR 4 - 10, '76. BICENTENNIAL WEEK ON CAMPUS. CELEBRATION TO INCLUDE MUSICAL PROGRAMS, EXHIBITS AND PATRIOTIC EVENTS; CELEBRATION IS PART OF STATEWIDE FESTIVAL. (LOCAL). MICHAEL J BAKICH, PRES; LAKE SUMTER COMMUNITY COLLEGE BICENTENNIAL COMMITTEE; LAKE SUMTER COMMUNITY COLLEGE; LEESBURG, FL 32748. (#103097-1).

APR 5, '76. HISTORICAL DOCUMENTS EXHIBIT. EXHIBIT AT AUDITORIUM. (LOCAL). DR JAMES CORWIN, CHMN; HAWTHORNE COMMUNITY CLUB; 528 PALO VERDE DR; LEESBURG, FL 32748. (#200011-135).

APR 6, '76. BICENTENNIAL MOVIE & FLAG DEMONSTRATION. FLAG DEMONSTRATION BY BOY SCOUT TROOP #313; COLONIAL, REVOLUTION, WW I & II FLAGS. AT AUDITORIUM. (LOCAL). REV CARL ELDER, COORD; HAWTHORNE COMMUNITY CLUB; 233 PALO VERDE DR; LEESBURG, FL 32748. (#200011-134).

APR 6, '76. 'FLEECE TO SHAWL' - COLONIAL DYING, SPINNING & WEAVING. LIVE PERFORMANCE AT AUDITORIUM. (LOCAL). MRS BETTY ALEXANDER, CHMN; HAWTHORNE COMMUNITY CLUB; 1430 MONTICELLO BLVD; ST PETERSBURG, FL 33703. (#200011-136).

APR 8, '76. BICENTENNIAL SQUARE DANCE. HISTORIC DANCES & QUADRILLE VIRGINIA REEL BY CIRCLE EIGHT RETIREMENT GROUP. AT AUDITORIUM. (LOCAL). DR JAMES F CORWIN, CHMN; HAWTHORNE COMMUNITY CLUB; 528 PALO VERDE DR; LEESBURG, FL 32748. (#200011-133).

APR 9, '76. HISTORICAL BOOK REVIEW. LIVE PERFORMANCE AT AUDITORIUM. (LOCAL). MRS VIRGINIA SIMON, CHMN; HAWTHORNE COMMUNITY CLUB; 140 PALO VERE DR; LEESBURG, FL 32748. (#200011-132).

APR 9, '76. 'OUR AMERICAN HERITAGE' - MUSICAL PRESENTATION. LIVE PERFORMANCE AT AUDITORIUM. (LOCAL). MRS HELEN K STARR, COORD; HAWTHORNE COMMUNITY CLUB; 522 PALO VERDE DR; LEESBURG, FL 32748. (#200011-131).

JUNE 27, '76. BICENTENNIAL PLANTING AND DEDICATION. DEDICATION OF HAWTHORNE PLANTS NEAR OLD OAK TREE. PLAQUE WILL BE INSTALLED. AT AVOCADO COVE - HAWTHORNE COMMUNITY. (LOCAL). DR JAMES F CORWIN, CHMN; HAWTHORNE COMMUNITY; 528 PALO VERDE DR; LEESBURG, FL 32748. (#108347-1).

JUNE '76. DEDICATION OF NEW FINE ARTS BUILDING. CEREMONY, EXHIBIT AT AUDITORIUM NEW FINE ARTS BUILDING. (LOCAL). DOUGLAS TRABERT, DIRECTOR; LAKE SUMTER COMMUNITY COLLEGE BICENTENNIAL COMMITTEE; LAKE SUMTER COMMUNITY COLLEGE; LEESBURG, FL 32748. (#103097-6).

JULY 4, '76. 'OUR AMERICAN HERITAGE' - EXHIBIT. DISPLAY OF ANTIQUES AND DISTRIBUTION OF COOKBOOKS. PLANTING OF LIBERTY TREE. (LOCAL). BETSY B COLEMAN, CHMN; WOMEN'S CLUB OF LEESBURG; 700 S 9TH ST; LEESBURG, FL 32748. (#108367-5).

JULY 4, '76. UNVEILING MONUMENT & FLAG HONORING ALL LOST IN WAR. CEREMONY AT VENETIAN GARDENS. (LOCAL). GEORGE H RAST, CHAIRMAN; LEESBURG LIONS CLUB; 1303 S 9TH ST; LEESBURG, FL 32748. (#108396-2).

JULY 5, '76. CHARTER DAYS - 101ST ANNIVERSARY. FESTIVAL AT VENETIAN GARDENS. (LOCAL). JACK A FRIEDRICH, CHMN; CITY OF LEESBURG; LEESBURG, FL 32748. (#108396-1).

OCT 24, '76. BICENTENNIAL MUSICAL PROGRAM. LIVE PERFORMANCE. (LOCAL). ERVIN GATLIN, MUSIC DIR; LAKE SUMTER COMMUNITY COLLEGE BICENTENNIAL COMMITTEE; LAKE SUMTER COMMUNITY COLLEGE; LEESBURG, FL 32748. (#103097-8).

OCT 24, '76. DEDICATION OF NEW AUDITORIUM WITH COMMEMORATIVE BICENTENNIAL PLAQUE. OTHER EVENTS IN CONNECTION WITH THIS ITEM INCLUDE MOVIE '1776' AND ORIGINAL PLAY ON THE CONSTITUTIONAL CONVENTION OF 1787. ALSO ART DISPLAY, NATIONAL GUARD UNIT: TROOPING OF COLORS; MASS COMMUNITY BAND; COLLEGE STAGE BAND AND CHORAL GROUPS. AT LSCC FINE ARTS BLDG. (LOCAL). JAMES RENNIE, PROJ DIR; LAKE SUMTER COMMUNITY COLLEGE BICENTENNIAL COMMITTEE; LAKE SUMTER COMMUNITY COLLEGE; LEESBURG, FL 32748. (#103097-2).

NOV '76. DEDICATION OF TIME CAPSULE TO HAWTHORNE COMMUNITY. CEREMONY. (LOCAL). DR JAMES F CORWIN, CHMN; HAWTHORNE COMMUNITY; 528 PALO VERDE DR; LEESBURG, FL 32748. (#25993-1).

LEHIGH ACRES

AMERICAN HERITAGE ROOM-LEHIGH ACRES LIBRARY, FL. AN AMERICAN HERITAGE ROOM FOR A PERMANENT COLLECTION OF PHOTOS DEVOTED TO FAMOUS AMERICAN HISTORICAL SITES & PERSONALITIES. (LOCAL). ROBERT B ROBERTS, CHAIRMAN; LEHIGH ACRES BICENTENNIAL COMMITTEE; 1517 HUNTDALE ST; LEHIGH ACRES, FL 33936. (#11245).

BICENTENNIAL BOOK EXHIBIT, LEHIGH ACRES, FL. BICENTENNIAL BOOK EXHIBIT, FEATURING AMERICAN COLONIAL & REVOLUTIONARY HISTORY AT LEHIGH ACRES PUBLIC LIBRARY. (LOCAL). ROBERT B ROBERTS, CHAIRMAN; LEHIGH ACRES BICENTENNIAL COMMITTEE; 1301 HOMESTEAD RD; LEHIGH ACRES, FL 33936. (#20629).

BICENTENNIAL PHOTO DISPLAY - PROJ OF FL. A PHOTOGRAPHIC DISPLAY OF COLONIAL HISTORY AND THE AMERICAN REVOLUTION. (LOCAL). ROBERT B ROBERTS, CHAIRMAN; LEHIGH ACRES BICENTENNIAL COMMITTEE; 1517 HUNTDALE ST; LEHIGH ACRES, FL 33936. (#11242).

FILMS, ON THE AMERICAN REVOLUTION - FL. FILMS ON THE AMERICAN REVOLUTION WILL BE PRODUCED. (LOCAL). ROBERT B ROBERTS, CHAIRMAN; LEHIGH ACRES BICENTENNIAL COMMITTEE; 1517 HUNTDALE ST; LEHIGH ACRES, FL 33936. (#11243).

LIBRARY EXPANSION, LEHIGH ACRES, FL. THE LEHIGH ACRES PUBLIC LIBRARY WILL BE EXPANDED & AN AMERICAN HERITAGE MUSEUM & MEETING ROOM WILL BE ADDED. (LOCAL). ROBERT B ROBERTS, CHAIRMAN; LEHIGH ACRES BICENTENNIAL COMMITTEE; 1301 HOMESTEAD RD; LEHIGH ACRES, FL 33936. (#20630).

MILITARY PHOTO & PAINTING EXHIBIT-LEHIGH ACRES, FL. AMERICAN HISTORY DISPLAYS DELINEATING AMERICAN REVOLUTION, MARINES, NAVY AND AIR FORCE. AT SUNSHINE MALL. (LOCAL). ROBERT B ROBERTS, CHAIRMAN; LEHIGH ACRES BICENTENNIAL COMMITTEE; 1301 HOMESTEAD RD; LEHIGH ACRES, FL 33936. (#20631).

PAINTING OF FIRE HYDRANTS - LEHIGH ACRES, FL. PAINTING OF COMMUNITY'S FIRE HYDRANTS TO RESEMBLE CONTINENTAL SOLDIERS AND DRUMMERS BY THE D A V AND VFW. (LOCAL). ROBERT B ROBERTS, CHAIRMAN; LEHIGH ACRES BICENTENNIAL COMMITTEE; 1301 HOMESTEAD RD; LEHIGH ACRES, FL 33936. (#19365).

NOV 11, '75. BICENTENNIAL MOVIES: FUND-RAISING FOR LIBRARY EXPANSION. FILM TO BE PRESENTED IS 'THE LAST KING OF AMERICA' WITH PETER USTINOV AND ERIC SEVAREID. MOVIE IS APPROXIMATELY ONE HOUR LONG. SECOND FILM, ONE HALF HOUR LONG, WILL BE DECIDED UPON AT LATER DATE. AT AUDITORIUM, JOEL BLVD. (LOCAL). ROBERT B ROBERTS, CHMN; BICENTENNIAL COMMITTEE AND LITERARY STUDY GROUP; 1517 HUNTDALE ST; LEHIGH ACRES, FL 33936. (#11242-2).

MAR 7 - 13, '76. LEHIGH ACRES SPRING BICENTENNIAL FESTIVAL. OTHER FACILITY LOCATIONS; COMMUNITY BLDG, HOMESTEAD RD; FESTIVAL GROUNDS AND GAZEBO, REAR OF LIBRARY; LAST DAY OF FESTIVAL WILL FEATURE PARADE WITH MANY BANDS AND FLOATS; FESTIVAL WILL INCLUDE BANDS, ORCHESTRAS, CHORAL GROUPS & AMERICAN HERITAGE EXHIBITS. AT AUDITORIUM, JOEL BLVD; LIBRARY, HOMESTEAD RD; CHARM CIR, JOEL BLVD. (LOCAL). CHARLES MATHENY, CHMN; LEHIGH ACRES SPRING FESTIVAL, INC; PO BOX 747; LEHIGH ACRES, FL 33936. (#100235-1).

MAY 24 - JUNE 4, '76. CARL HAVERLIN/BROADCAST MUSIC, INC, ARCHIVES BICENTENNIAL EXHIBIT. OFFERS A VERSATILE PICTURE OF HISTORY, REGIONAL LIFE & MUSIC FOR OVER 200 YEARS. CONTAINS PRESIDENTIAL LETTERS, LETTERS OF FAMOUS AMERICANS, OLD BOOKS, MANUSCRIPTS, HISTORY OF 'THE STAR SPANGLED BANNER' & COMPOSER AUTOGRAPHS, PLUS SHEET MUSIC OF THE PAST. (ST-WIDE). RUSSELL YANCEY, COORD; LEHIGH BICENTENNIAL SPRING FESTIVAL; 1130 HOMESTEAD RD; LEHIGH ACRES, FL 33936. (#20784-12).

LIGHTHOUSE PT

PARADE & BICENTENNIAL CELEBRATION. A BIRTHDAY PARTY FOR USA'S 200 YEARS & LIGHTHOUSE POINT'S 20TH ANNIVERSARY. (LOCAL). P JOHN FIDEL, CHAIRMAN; LIGHTHOUSE POINT RECREATION DEPT; 2200 NE 38TH ST; LIGHTHOUSE PT, FL 33064. (#200011-265).

JAN 1 - JUNE 1, '76. ESSAY CONTEST. COMPETITION. (LOCAL). JOHN TRUDEL, CHAIRMAN; CITY OF LIGHTHOUSE POINT BICENTENNIAL COMMITTEE; 2200 NE 38TH ST; LIGHTHOUSE PT, FL 33064. (#200011-264).

LIVE OAK

JULY 3 - 4, '76. IRA RODEO. LIVE PERFORMANCE, COMPETITION AT RODEO ARENA, SUWANNEE COUNTY FAIRGROUND. (LOCAL). LARRY SNIDER, SECRETARY; SUWANNEE COUNTY CATTLEMAN ASSOC; 601 N HOUSTON AVE; LIVE OAK, FL 32060. (#105837-1).

LK BUENA VIS

MAY 6 - 9, '76. THE BATTLE OF THE CORAL SEA REUNION. OPEN TO PARTICIPANTS IN BATTLE OF CORAL SEA DURING WORLD WAR

LK BUENA VIS — CONTINUED

II. AT WALT DISNEY WORLD, CONTEMPORARY HOTEL. (INT'L). W H MORSE, CHAIRMAN; THE BATTLE OF THE CORAL SEA ASSOCIATION; DRAWER A; KISSIMMEE, FL 32741. (#106744-1).

JUNE 17 - 20, '76. 'BICENTENNIAL MEDICINE 1776-1976: 3RD ANNUAL G H PAFF SEMINAR. PROVIDING 12 POSTGRADUATE CREDIT HOURS FOR MEDICAL SCHOOL ALUMNI. AT ROYAL PLAZA, 1905 PREVIEW BLVD. (NAT'L). FRAN KOENIG, CHAIRMAN; UNIV OF MIAMI MEDICAL SCHOOL ALUMNI ASSOC; PO BOX 520875; MIAMI, FL 33152. (#107552-1).

LONGBOAT KEY

JULY 3 - 5, '76. 3-DAY 4TH OF JULY CELEBRATION. EVENTS ARE: BOAT PARADE, JULY 3; PATRIOTIC SERVICES, JULY 4; PARADE & OLD-FASHIONED 4TH JULY PICNIC. AT TOWN HALL. (LOCAL). LT GEN R M MONTEGOMERY; LONGBOAT KEY BICENTENNIAL COMMITTEE; PO BOX 93; LONGBOAT KEY, FL 33548. (#200011-243).

JULY 3 - 5, '76. 4TH OF JULY WEEKEND CELEBRATION. JULY 3: BOAT PARADE COVERING 30 MILES, WITH 1ST 13 BOATS CARRYING BANNERS OF 13 ORIGINAL COLONIES; JULY 4: PATRIOTIC PGM & BICENTENNIAL PARK DEDICATION; JULY 5: HUGE PARADE OF RED, WHITE & BLUE CARS & FLOATS, FOLLOWED BY OLD FASHIONED JULY 4 PICNIC, SHOWS & FIREWORKS. AT ENTIRE LONGBOAT KEY AREA & SURROUNDING WATERS. (LOCAL). LT GEN R M MONTGOMERY; LONGBOAT KEY BICENTENNIAL COMMITTEE; PO BOX 1776; LONGBOAT KEY, FL 33548. (#200011-283).

LONGWOOD

RESTORATION OF HISTORIC BRADLEE/MCINTYRE HOUSE-FL. RESTORATION OF HISTORIC BLDG IN LONGWOOD HISTORIC DISTRICT WHICH INCLUDES LONGWOOD VILLAGE INN, INSIDE/OUTSIDE HOUSE IN HISTORIC DISTRICT. (LOCAL). MRS ROBERT BRADFORD, PROJ DIRECTOR; CENTRAL FLORIDA SOCIETY FOR HISTORICAL PRESERVATION; PO BOX 500; LONGWOOD, FL 32750. (#15061).

LUTZ

JULY 4, '76. FOURTH OF JULY CELEBRATION. FESTIVAL WILL CONSIST OF A PARADE, BALL GAMES, RACES, PICNIC AND ICE CREAM SOCIAL; THE FIRE DEPT WILL HAVE A WATER FIGHT; A COUNTRY-MUSIC BAND WILL PERFORM & FIREWORKS; COMMITTEE WILL PERFORM HISTORIC PAGEANT. AT CORNER OF VAN DYKE RD AND DALE MABRY EXIT. (LOCAL). JOHN W DOUGHERTY, CHMN; LUTZ BICENTENNIAL COMMITTEE; RT 2 BOX 1212; LUTZ, FL 33549. (#107259-1).

MACDILL AFB

MACDILL AFB GYMNASIUM, FL. THE BASE GYM AT MACDILL AFB WAS DEDICATED IN HONOR OF THE BICENTENNIAL, A PLAQUE WAS PLACED IN THE ENTRANCE FOYER, DEDICATING THE FACILITY TO THE FIGHTING MEN & WOMEN OF AMERICA'S FUTURE. (LOCAL). ROBERT G ANDREWS, CHIEF; 56TFW OFFICE OF INFORMATION; MACDILL AFB, FL 33608. (#28629).

NOV 9, '75. MACDILL AFB BICENTENNIAL COMMEMORATIVE OPEN HOUSE & AIR SHOW. EXHIBIT, TOUR AT BASE FLIGHTLINE. (LOCAL). CAPT ROBERT G ANDREWS; 56TH TFW OFFICE OF INFORMATION; 56TFW OFFICE OF INFORMATION; MACDILL AFB, FL 33608. (#200011-261).

MARGATE

MARGATE BICENTENNIAL PARK, FL. 20 ACRE NATURAL PARK WITH A 2 ACRE LAKE FOR BOATING & FISHING WITH TENNIS COURTS, PICNIC AREAS, AMPHITHEATRE, BICYCLE MOTOCROSS & MINIATURE GOLF COURSE. (LOCAL). ROBERT S YOUNGBLOOD, DEPUTY CHAIRMAN; MARGATE BICENTENNIAL COMMITTEE; 6130 W ATLANTIC BLVD; MARGATE, FL 33063. (#15675).

MARIANNA

COURTHOUSE BASEMENT RENOVATION - MARIANNA, FL. CLEANING OF BASEMENT AND FILING OF DOCUMENTS THAT DATE BACK TO THE LATE 1700'S. (LOCAL). SARA BRUCE HARRIS, CHAIRMAN; JACKSON COUNTY HERITAGE ASSOC; RT 1, BOX 137; MARIANNA, FL 32446. (#25991).

JACKSON COUNTY LIBRARY - MARIANNA, FL. CONSTRUCTION OF NEW LIBRARY FOR JACKSON COUNTY IS BEING PLANNED. (LOCAL). CLAUDE REESE, PRESIDENT; JACKSON COUNTY BICENTENNIAL COMMITTEE; E LAFAYETTE ST; MARIANNA, FL 32446. (#25992).

MAR 20, '76. LIBERTY DAY PARADE. PARADE AT HWY 90. (LOCAL). MRS ANN RAHAL, CHAIRMAN; MINISTERIAL ASSOC & MARIANNA BICENTENNIAL COMMITTEE; MARIANNA, FL 32446. (#200011-140).

APR 24 - 25, '76. BICENTENNIAL TOUR OF HOMES. TOUR AT MARIANNA WOMEN'S CLUB, N CALEDONIA. (LOCAL). MRS ROBERT CRISP, CHMN; JACKSON COUNTY HERITAGE ASSOC; MAGNOLIA RD; MARIANNA, FL 32446. (#200011-141).

JULY 4, '76. JULY 4TH CELEBRATION. FESTIVAL WILL INCLUDE PICNIC, CHURCH SERVICES, FIREWORKS, GAMES & CRAFTS. AT NORTH OF POZIER SCHOOL, OPEN FIELD ON KYNESVILLE HWY. (LOCAL). MRS ANN RAHAL, SECRETARY; JACKSON CO BICENTENNIAL COMMITTEE; MARIANNA, FL 32446. (#108397-1).

SEPT 27, '76. HANGING CEREMONY: PORTRAIT OF GOVERNOR MILTON. PORTRAIT OF GOVERNOR MILTON WILL BE HUNG IN COURTHOUSE AND CEREMONY WILL BE HELD. MILTON WAS GOVERNOR OF FLORIDA DURING THE WAR BETWEEN THE STATES. THERE WILL BE AN OUTSTANDING SPEAKER AND AN UNVEILING OF THE PORTRAIT BY TWO DESCENDANTS. AT JACKSON COUNTY COURT HOUSE LOBBY. (LOCAL). FLOIE PACKARD, CHMN; JACKSON CO HERITAGE ASSOC & BICENTENNIAL COMM AT A JOINT MEETING; 242 LAFAYETTE ST; MARIANNA, FL 32446. (#108350-1).

MELBOURNE

BICENTENNIAL TREES SOLD - MELBOURNE, FL. TREES SOLD TO PURCHASE WELCOME SIGNS FOR CITY BICENTENNIAL CELEBRATION. (LOCAL). ELINOR M GETTYS, CHAIRPERSON; MELBOURNE BICENTENNIAL COMMITTEE; PO BOX 3000; MELBOURNE, FL 32901. (#15768).

BOTANICAL GARDENS CEREMONY IN MELBOURNE, IL. A BICENTENNIAL PLAQUE WILL BE PLACED IN THE BOTANICAL GARDENS. (LOCAL). TOM NUGENT, CHAIRMAN; FLORIDA INSTITUTE OF TECHNOLOGY BICENTENNIAL COMMITTEE; PO BOX 1150; MELBOURNE, FL 32901. (#11770).

BREVARD SCHOOLHOUSE RENOVATION - MELBOURNE, FL. PROJECT WILL INCLUDE REFURBISHMENT OF EXISTING BUILDING TO ENHANCE IT FOR VISITORS; WILL ALSO INCLUDE BICENTENNIAL MEMORIAL PLAQUE. (LOCAL). TOM NUGENT, CHAIRMAN; FLORIDA INSTITUTE OF TECHNOLOGY BICENTENNIAL COMMITTEE; PO BOX 1150; MELBOURNE, FL 32901. (#11771).

CREATION & FOUNDING OF 'SPACE UNIVERSITY' - FL. VISUAL MATERIALS ON DEVELOPMENT OF THE FLORIDA INSTITUTE OF TECHNOLOGY AND ENGINEERING TECHNOLOGY. (LOCAL). TOM NUGENT, CHAIRMAN; FLORIDA INSTITUTE OF TECHNOLOGY BICENTENNIAL COMMITTEE; PO BOX 1150; MELBOURNE, FL 32901. (#11772).

DRIVE FOR PENNIES, MELBOURN, FL. A DRIVE FOR A PENNY FOR EVERY SOLDIER WHO FOUGHT FOR THE CAUSE OF FREEDOM IN THE REVOLUTION; STUDENT PARTICIPATION AWARDS TO BE GIVEN. (LOCAL). W F HOUSNER, CHAIRMAN; HOOVER JR HIGH SCHOOL; MELBOURNE, FL 32901. (#22362).

ENTRANCE SIGN PROJECT IN MELBOURNE, FL. ATTRACTIVE, LANDSCAPED WELCOME SIGNS WILL BE PLACED AT 8 MAJOR ENTRANCES TO THE CITY; THE SIGNS WILL BE MADE FROM COQUINA ROCK AND CYPRESS. (LOCAL). ELINOR GETTYS, CHAIRMAN; MELBOURNE AREA BICENTENNIAL COMMITTEE; 2210 S COUNTRY CLUB RD; MELBOURNE, FL 32901. (#15023).

HACIENDA GIRLS' RANCH - MELBOURNE, FL. THE HACIENDA GIRLS' RANCH WILL BE A HOME FOR HOMELESS GIRLS. (LOCAL). DR RICHARD DEEB, PROJ DIRECTOR; HACIENDA GIRLS' RANCH, INC; 455 MINUTEMAN CAUSEWAY; COCOA BEACH, FL 32931. (#19217).

INDIAN RIVER LAND - PROJ OF MELBOURNE, FL. PLAYS ON AIS INDIAN'S CULTURE AND HISTORY. (LOCAL). TOM NUGENT, CHAIRMAN; FLORIDA INSTITUTE OF TECHNOLOGY BICENTENNIAL COMMITTEE; PO BOX 1150; MELBOURNE, FL 32901. (#11732).

INJURED WILDLIFE SANCTUARY EDUCATION & RESEARCH-FL. ENVIRONMENTAL EDUCATION, WILDLIFE DISEASE RESEARCH AND REHABILITATION OF INJURED WILDLIFE. (ST-WIDE). W F HOUSER, CHAIRMAN; BREVARD COUNTY BICENTENNIAL COMMITTEE; PO BOX 1776; COCOA, FL 32922. (#13651). **ARBA GRANTEE.**

LIBRARY DISPLAY - PROJ MELBOURNE, FL. A SPECIAL SECTION FOR BICENTENNIAL MATERIAL WILL BE PUT ASIDE IN THE LIBRARY. (LOCAL). TOM NUGENT, CHAIRMAN; FLORIDA INSTITUTE OF TECHNOLOGY BICENTENNIAL COMMITTEE; PO BOX 1150; MELBOURNE, FL 32901. (#11773).

NATURE TOURS OF ERNA NIXON HAMMOCK, MELBOURNE, FL. BICENTENNIAL TOURS OF WILDLIFE PRESERVE IN MELBOURNE VILLAGE BY APPT. (LOCAL). ERNA NIXON, PROJ DIRECTOR; MELBOURNE BICENTENNIAL COMMITTEE; PO BOX 3000; MELBOURNE, FL 32901. (#15769).

PARK DEVELOPMENT - MELBOURNE, FL. PRESERVATION OF 52 ACRES OF NATURAL FLORIDA FLORA WITH APPROXIMATELY 2000 FEET OF BOARDWALK. (LOCAL). JAMES VENCILL, CHAIRMAN; SOUTH BREVARD JUNIOR SERVICE LEAGUE; 2500 PARKWAY DR; MELBOURNE, FL 32935. (#32698).

PUBLICATION OF BICENT MATERIALS, MELBOURNE, FL. PUBLICATION OF MATERIALS COVERING 200 YEARS COMMEMORATING THE CITY, ITS SCHOOLS AND NATURAL ENVIRONMENT. (LOCAL). ELINOR M GETTYS, CHAIRPERSON; MELBOURNE BICENTENNIAL COMMITTEE; PO BOX 3000; MELBOURNE, FL 32901. (#15766).

RADIO PROGRAMS - PROJ OF MELBOURNE, FL. HISTORICAL SPOTS AND MUSIC WILL BE PRESENTED OVER THE CAMPUS RADIO STATION. (LOCAL). TOM NUGENT, CHAIRMAN; FLA INSTITUTE OF TECHNOLOGY BICENTENNIAL COMMITTEE; PO BOX 1150; MELBOURNE, FL 32901. (#11776).

SKETCHES OF EARLY MELBOURNE, FL. SKETCH BOOK PUBLISHED DEPICTING LATE 19TH CEN SCENES OF EARLY MELBOURNE. (LOCAL). ELINOR M GETTYS, CHAIRPERSON; MELBOURNE BICENTENNIAL COMMITTEE; PO BOX 3000; MELBOURNE, FL 32901. (#15767).

WASHINGTON'S BIRTHDAY PARADE - MELBOURNE, FL. PARADE AND CEREMONIES TO COMMEMORATE GEORGE WASHINGTON'S BIRTHDAY. (LOCAL). TOM NUGENT, CHAIRMAN; FLA INSTITUTE OF TECHNOLOGY BICENTENNIAL COMMITTEE; PO BOX 1150; MELBOURNE, FL 32901. (#11775).

WELCOME SIGNS - MELBOURNE, FL. ATTRACTIVE WELCOME SIGNS WILL BE PLACED AT EACH ENTRANCE TO THE CITY. (LOCAL). ELINOR GETTYS, CHAIRMAN; MELBOURNE BICENTENNIAL COMMITTEE; 2210 S COUNTRY CLUB RD; MELBOURNE, FL 32901. (#19219).

MAR 1, '75 - APR 30, '76. SUPERSTARS FOR THE BICENTENNIAL. ATHLETIC COMPETITIONS TO DETERMINE THE BICENTENNIAL SUPERSTARS. AT HOOVER JR HIGH SCHOOL. (LOCAL). PAUL ZENO, COORD; DISTRICT 3 PARKS & RECREATION; 625 E NEW HAVEN AVE; MELBOURNE, FL 32901. (#200011-294).

MAY 1 - 30, '75. YOUTH DECATHALON. SUPERSTAR DECATHALON IN MELBOURNE, FLORIDA. A DECATHALON COVERING ALL MAJOR EVENTS IN SPORTS. IT WILL BE DIVIDED AMONG ELEMENTARY, JUNIOR & SENIOR HIGH SCHOOL STUDENTS. (LOCAL). PAUL ZENO, CHAIRMAN; BREVARD COUNTY PARKS AND RECREATION DEPT; 625 E NEW HAVEN AVE; MELBOURNE, FL 33901. (#6446-501).

MAY 16, '75. PERFORMING HORSES TOURING FLORIDA. APPEARANCE OF ROYAL LIPPIZZAN STALLIONS IN FL. THE ROYAL LIPPIZZAN HORSES WILL BE TOURING FLORIDA. (ST-WIDE). P J POPOVICH, MD; ROTORY CLUB OF MELBOURNE; PO BOX 997; MELBOURNE, FL 32901. (#7703-501).

MAY 20, '75. ARCHERY MEET & EXHIBITION. A COMPETITIVE EVENTS FOR AMATEUR ARCHERY ENTHUSIASTS. (LOCAL). PAUL ZENO, CHAIRMAN; BREVARD COUNTY PARKS & RECREATION DEPT; 625 E NEW HAVEN AVE; MELBOURNE, FL 33901. (#7705-501).

MAY 30, '75. BREVARD COUNTY VETERANS MEMORIAL SERVICE. CEREMONY. (LOCAL). JOHN COOPER, COORD; FOUNTAINHEAD MEMORIAL PARK INC; MELBOURNE, FL 32901. (#7709-501).

JUNE 14, '75. HONOR AMERICA DAYS. PRESENTATION OF VALLEY FORGE FREEDOM FOUNDATION AWARDS. (LOCAL). JOHN COOPER, COORD; HONOR AMERICA COMMITTEE; PO BOX 1776; MELBOURNE, FL 32901. (#7710-501).

JUNE 28, '75. OCEAN SWIMMING COMPETITION. COMPETITION. (LOCAL). PAUL ZENO, CHAIRMAN; BREVARD COUNTY DEPT OF PARKS & RECREATION; 625 E NEW HAVEN AVE; MELBOURNE, FL 32901. (#7712-501).

OCT 10, '75. SPANISH HERITAGE DAY. FESTIVAL. (LOCAL). JOANNE NICHOLSON, COORD; BREVARD COMMUNITY COLLEGE; BREVARD COMMUNITY COLLEGE; MELBOURNE, FL 32935. (#101280-1).

NOV 11, '75. VETERANS DAY PARADE. PARADE AT BREVARD AVENUE. (LOCAL). JNO O COOPER, PROJ DIR; BREVARD COUNTY BICENTENNIAL COMMITTEE; PO BOX 1776; MELBOURNE, FL 32901. (#103234-5).

NOV 24, '75. COLONISTS' THANKSGIVING DINNER. A COLONIAL DINNER WITH PARTICIPANTS DRESSED AS COLONISTS & INDIANS. AT SOUTH CAMPUS LAWN. (LOCAL). JOANNE NICHOLSON, COORD; BREVARD COMMUNITY COLLEGE; BREVARD COMMUNITY COLLEGE; MELBOURNE, FL 32935. (#101283-1).

DEC 27, '75 - JAN 4, '76. BICENTENNIAL TENNIS TOURNAMENT. COMPETITION AT FEE AVENUE TENNIS COURTS. (ST-WIDE). E M GETTYS, CHAIRPERSON; MELBOURNE BICENTENNIAL & CITY OF MELBOURNE; PO BOX 3000; MELBOURNE, FL 32901. (#102557-1).

JAN 9 - FEB 9, '76. SUPER STAR DECATHLON - VARIED SPORTS EVENTS FOR ALL AGES. COMPETITION. (LOCAL). PAUL ZENO, COORDINATOR; BREVARD COUNTY PARKS & RECREATION DEPT; 625 E NEW HAVEN AVE; MELBOURNE, FL 32901. (#104085-11).

JAN 16 - 17, '76. BICENTENNIAL FAIR. FAIR AT MELBOURNE CIVIC AUDITORIUM & WELLS PARK. (LOCAL). E M GETTYS, CHAIRPERSON; MELBOURNE BICENTENNIAL & CITY OF MELBOURNE; PO BOX 3000; MELBOURNE, FL 32901. (#102557-2).

MAR 1, '76. CLYDESDALE HORSES. PARADE. (LOCAL). W F HOUSNER, CHMN; BREVARD COUNTY BICENTENNIAL COMMITTEE; 318 PEACHTREE ST; COCOA, FL 32922. (#105359-1).

MAR 1 - 5, '76. CRAFTSMEN'S WEEK. CRAFT DEMONSTRATIONS, FOLK MUSIC, LITERATURE & POETRY PRESENTATIONS; ALSO HELD AT THE AMERICAN COFFEE HOUSE MARCH 5, 8:00 PM. AT BCC STUDENT CENTER & UPPER PATIO. (LOCAL). JOANNE NICHOLSON, COORD; BREVARD COMMUNITY COLLEGE; BREVARD COMMUNITY COLLEGE; MELBOURNE, FL 32935. (#101284-1).

APR 11, '76. BREVARD PATRIOTS DAY. ENLISTMENT OF LOCAL YOUTH INTO ARMED FORCES PARADE AND CEREMONY. AT PARADE ON BABCOCK BLVD, CEREMONIES AT MUNICIPAL AUDITORIUM. (LOCAL). JNO O COOPER, LT COL RET; BREVARD COUNTY BICENTENNIAL COMMITTEE; PO BOX 1776; MELBOURNE, FL 32901. (#104085-13).

MAY 9, '76. 'SPIRIT OF '76', CONCERT OF RELIGIOUS MUSIC W/ E COX DIRECTING. LIVE PERFORMANCE AT MELBOURNE CIVIC AUDITORIUM. (LOCAL). E M GETTYS, CHAIRPERSON; MELBOURNE BICENTENNIAL & CITY OF MELBOURNE; PO BOX 3000; MELBOURNE, FL 32901. (#102557-3).

NOV 11, '76. ARMED FORCES BICENTENNIAL BAND. LIVE PERFORMANCE AT MELBOURNE AUDITORIUM. (LOCAL). JNO COOPER, LTC, USA, RET; BREVARD COUNTY BICENTENNIAL COMMITTEE; PO BOX 1776; MELBOURNE, FL 32901. (#105359-2).

MELBOURNE BCH

JUNE 6, '76. COMMEMORATION OF FOUNDING OF MELBOURNE BEACH. THE CELEBRATION WILL COMMEMORATE THE 93RD BIRTHDAY OF FOUNDING OF MELBOURNE BCH AS A PINEAPPLE

MELBOURNE BCH — CONTINUED

PLANTATION; PROGRAM WILL STRESS ADVANTAGES OF COMMUNITY AS QUIET, PROGRESSIVE, RESIDENTIAL AREA. AT TOWN HALL, OCEAN AVE. (LOCAL). COLONEL ROBERT G MATTE; TOWN OF MELBOURNE BEACH; 450 SANDY KEY; MELBOURNE BCH, FL 32951. (#107967-1).

MERRITT ISLE

'BEAUTIFY THE ISLAND FOR '76', MERRITT IS, FL. CONTEST FOR IMPROVEMENT OF MERRITT ISLAND SUBDIVISIONS; THE GARDEN CLUB WILL PROVIDE ASSISTANCE IN THE PLANNING & SELECTION OF PLANTS TO THOSE WHO REQUIRE HELP. (LOCAL). W F HOUSNER, PROJ CHAIRMAN; MERRITT ISLAND GARDEN CLUB; P.O. BOX 1776; COCOA, FL 32952. (#22363).

TEEN MISSIONS, INC IN MERRITT ISLAND, FL. PROJECT TO CLEAN UP AMERICA BOTH SPIRITUALLY & PHYSICALLY. (LOCAL). ROBERT BLAND, DIRECTOR; BREVARD COUNTY BICENTENNIAL COMMITTEE; 318 PEACHTREE ST; COCOA, FL 32922. (#21369).

JAN 6, '76. BICENTENNIAL MEMORABILIA EXTRAVAGANZA - DISPLAYS OF EARLY AMER LIFE. EXHIBIT AT KIWANIS ISLAND ON MERRITT ISLAND. (LOCAL). SUE BLEDSOE, COORD; HOME EXTENSION SERVICE; 1125 W KING ST; COCOA, FL 32922. (#104085-10).

FEB 11, '76. MEDICINE SHOW TOURING POLK COUNTY BICENTENNIAL EXHIBIT. LIVE PERFORMANCE AT KIWANIS ISLAND. (LOCAL). RAY MULBERRY, PROJ DIR; BREVARD COUNTY BICENTENNIAL COMMITTEE; 450 BRIGHTWATERS BLVD; COCOA BEACH, FL 32931. (#103234-6).

FEB 11 - 12, '76. LINCOLN'S BIRTHDAY CELEBRATION ARMED FORCES BICENTENNIAL EXHIBIT. EXHIBIT AT KIWANIS ISLAND. (ST-WIDE). RAY MULBERRY, PROJ DIR; BREVARD COUNTY BICENTENNIAL COMMITTEE; 450 BRIGHTWATERS BLVD; COCOA BEACH, FL 32931. (#103234-3).

MAR 15, '76. JUNIOR OYLMPICS. JUNIOR OLYMPICS AT MERRITT ISLAND, FLORIDA. A MAJOR SPORTS EVENT FOR YOUTH. (REGN'L). PAUL ZENO, CHAIRMAN; BREVARD COUNTY PARKS AND RECREATION DEPT; 625 E NEW HAVEN AVE; MELBOURNE, FL 33901. (#7702-501).

JULY 2 - 5, '76. FIRECRACKER SOFTBALL TOURNAMENT. SLOW-PITCH SOFTBALL TOURNAMENT FOR TEAMS THROUGHOUT SOUTHEASTERN USA DOUBLE ELIMINATION TOURNAMENT. AT KIWANIS ISLAND ON MERRITT ISLAND. (LOCAL). PAUL ZENO, PROJ DIRECTOR; BREVARD COUNTY BICENTENNIAL COMMITTEE; 625 E NEW HAVEN AVE; MELBOURNE, FL 32901. (#104085-6).

MIAMI

THE AFRO-AMERICAN IN FLORIDA, MIAMI. PROJECT IS A BIBLIOGRAPHY THAT DEPICTS THE INVOLVEMENT OF AFROAMERICANS IN FLORIDA'S DEVELOPMENT, IT WILL SUPPLEMENT OTHER DRAMATIC & SCHOLARLY EFFORTS. (LOCAL). MS JACQUELINE C BLACKLEDGE; MIAMI-DADE PUBLIC LIBRARY, DIXIE PARK BRANCH; 350 NW 13TH ST; MIAMI, FL 33136. (#13377).

ALL SAINTS EPISCOPAL CHURCH BICENTENNIAL PGM, FL. CONSTRUCTION OF TOWER & BELL TOWER, MINI-PARK, PICNIC AREA WITH THE ENLARGEMENT OF EXISTING PARKING FACILITY, BEAUTIFICATION OF GROUNDS WITH TREES & GARDEN. (LOCAL). R F MAX SALVADOR, RECTOR; ALL SAINTS EPISCOPAL CHURCH; 1023 SW 27TH AVE; MIAMI, FL 33135. (#16237).

AMERICAN BICENT FLORIDA EXHIBITION, MIAMI, FL. EXHIBITION WILL ENHANCE THE AWARENESS AMONG ALL FLORIDIANS OF THE STATE'S PAST, PRESENT AND FUTURE. (ST-WIDE). GAIL MORANTZ, PROJ CHAIRMAN; THIRD CENTURY USA; PO BOX 451976; MIAMI, FL 33125. (#10534).

AMERICAN HERITAGE ART SHOWS - MIAMI, FL. MONTHLY ART SHOWS WILL PROMOTE ART IN FLORIDA AND THROUGHOUT THE NATION. (LOCAL). HENRY HALAM, PROJ DIRECTOR; HARVEY W SEEDS POST #29, THE AMERICAN LEGION; 6445 NE 7TH AVE; MIAMI, FL 33138. (#12368).

THE AMERICAN JEWISH EXPERIENCE - MIAMI, FL. THE EXPERIENCE OF AMERICAN JEWS WILL BE EXPLORED IN THE CONTEXT OF THE BICENTENNIAL CELEBRATION. (LOCAL). NATALIE B LYONS, PROJECT DIRECTOR; MIAMI CHAPTER OF HADASSAH; 4200 BISCAYNE BLVD; MIAMI, FL 33137. (#16730).

AMERICAN STUDIES - PROJ OF BISCAYNE COLLEGE, FL. AN AMERICAN STUDIES PROGRAM WILL BE OFFERED. (LOCAL). DR HELEN JACOBSTEIN, CO-CHAIRPERSON; BISCAYNE COLLEGE BICENTENNIAL COMMITTEE; 16400 NW 32ND AVE; MIAMI, FL 33054. (#11671).

AMERICAN STUDIES PROGRAM, MIAMI, FL. AMERICAN STUDIES-INTEGRATED STUDY OF AMERICAN HISTORY, LITERATURE, SOCIOLOGY, PHILOSOPHY, RELIGION, FINE ARTS, POLITICAL SCIENCE, GEOGRAPHY, AN ONGOING CURRICULUM. (LOCAL). SR EILEEN RICE, CHAIRPERSON, SOICAL SCIENCES DEPT; BARRY COLLEGE; 11300 NE SECOND AVE; MIAMI SHORES, FL 33161. (#21135).

ARCH CREEK ARCHAEOLOGICAL MUSEUM BRIDGE PROJ, FL. DEVELOPMENT OF THE ARCH CREEK ARCHEOLOGICAL SITE INTO A MINI-MUSEUM AND EDUCATIONAL RESOURCE CENTER. (LOCAL). MRS ADELE VANSEIVER, JR, CHAIRMAN; COMMUNITY IN PROGRESS COMMITTEE; 90 NE 210 ST; MIAMI, FL 33162. (#19832).

'AREYTO' - PUERTO RICAN MUSICAL IN MIAMI, FL. MUSICAL PROGRAM REPRESENTS PUERTO RICAN FOLKLORE FROM PRE-SPANISH COLONIZATION TO PRESENT; SPANISH, INDIAN & AFRICAN CULTURES SHOWN IN MUSIC AND DANCE. (LOCAL). MERCEDES BALSEIRO, CHAIRMAN; THIRD CENTURY'S HISPANIC AMERICAN COMMITTEE; PO BOX 45-1976; MIAMI, FL 33145. (#12371).

ART FESTIVAL SITE RENOVATION IN MIAMI. RENOVATION OF ART FESTIVAL SITE, INCLUDING CLEANUP, LANDSCAPING, RENOVATION & CONSTRUCTION OF BUILDINGS & DISPLAY BOOTH. (ST-WIDE). BUFFALO TIGER, CHAIRMAN; MICCOSUKEE TRIBE OF INDIANS OF FLORIDA; PO BOX 440021, TAMIAMI STATION; MIAMI, FL 33144. (#22837). **ARBA GRANTEE.**

ARTIST-IN-RESIDENCE DANCE PROGRAM, MIAMI, FLORIDA. DANCE EDUCATION PROGRAM IN 'LITTLE HAVANA', MIAMI'S SPANISH-SPEAKING COMMUNITY, TO PRESERVE CULTURAL TRADITIONS. THE PROGRAM INCLUDES: LESSONS, DEMONSTRATIONS AND PERFORMANCES. (LOCAL). MARIA E TORANO, VICE PRESIDENT; CUBAN CULTURAL FOUNDATION; 16101 S W 99TH AVE; MIAMI, FL 33157. (#9104).

BALLET CONCERTO COMPANY OF MIAMI. BALLET CONCERTO TO GIVE A SERIES OF PERFOMACES AT VARIOUS LOCATIONS IN THE DADE COUNTY AREA. TWELVE PRESENTATIONS IN '76. WILL PROMOTE ONE OF THE FINE ARTS WITH EMPHASIS ON OUR YOUTH. (LOCAL). EDUARDO MORE, PRESIDENT; CUBAN CULTURAL FOUNDATION, INC; 3410 CORAL WAY; MIAMI, FL 33143. (#2995).

BICENT BOOK COLLECTION FOR MIAMI-DADE C C. BOOKS ON LOCAL AND NATIONAL HISTORY WILL BE PLACED IN THE MIAMI-DADE COMMUNITY COLLEGE LIBRARY. (LOCAL). MS JO E DEWAR, DIRECTOR; MIAMI-DADE COMMUNITY COLLEGE; 11011 SW 104TH ST; MIAMI, FL 33176. (#24801).

BICENT BOOKS FOR BISCAYNE COLLEGE. A BOOK SHELF WILL BE SET ASIDE IN THE LIBRARY FOR BICENTENNIAL BOOKS. (LOCAL). DR HELEN JACOBSTEIN, CO-CHAIRPERSON; BISCAYNE COLLEGE BICENTENNIAL COMMITTEE; 16400 NW 32ND AVE; MIAMI, FL 33054. (#11666).

BICENTENNIAL CHRONICLE PROJECT OF MIAMI, FLA. NEWS OF THAT TIME. NEWS OF THAT TIME, TO APPEAR REGULARLY IN A DAILY NEWSPAPER. (LOCAL). LIBBY MORELY; THIRD CENTURY USA; PO BOX 011976; MIAMI, FL 33101. (#1539).

BICENTENNIAL CHURCH BELL ACQUISITION PROJECT, FL. CONGREGATION IS SEARCHING FOR BELL TO INSTALL IN BELL TOWER TO BEGIN RINGING ON JULY 4TH; ATTEMPTING TO LOCATE BELL IN NEW ENGLAND, AT KENDALL UNITED METHODIST CHURCH. (LOCAL). HARRY L JORDAN, JR, PROJECT COORDINATOR; E F JOHNSON CO; 3301 NW 82ND AVE; MIAMI, FL 33122. (#21867).

BICENTENNIAL YOUTH DEBATES IN MIAMI SCHOOLS. AN EDUCATIONAL COURSE ON THE ROLE OF DEBATE IN AMERICAN LIFE & THE CONTRIBUTION OF DEBATE TO THE INDIVIDUAL. THE COURSE WILL MAKE DEBATE A VEHICLE FOR EXAMINING BICENTENNIAL ISSUES. (LOCAL). LOUISE HARNS, DISTRICT DIRECTOR; DADE COUNTY PUBLIC SCHOOL BICENTENNIAL OFFICE; 150 NE 19TH ST; MIAMI, FL 33132. (#12276).

BICENTENNIAL - MY - CENTENNIAL; MIAMI, FL. A YEAR LONG PROGRAM WHICH WILL HAVE THE STUDENTS OF VILLAGE GREEN ELEMENTARY SCHOOL PARTICIPATING IN MANY DIFFERENT BICENTENNIAL ACTIVITIES. (LOCAL). MARY ANN FABER, COORDINATOR; VILLAGE GREEN ELEMENTARY; 12265 SW 34TH ST; MIAMI, FL 33145. (#18333).

BIRD ROAD LANDSCAPING PROJECT, MIAMI, FL. LANDSCAPING OF THE MEDIAN AREAS OF BIRD RD BETWEEN SW 82 AVE AND SW 87 AVE. (LOCAL). JANICE RASKIN, PROJ CHAIRMAN; SOUTHWEST GARDEN CLUB; 8541 SW 36 ST; MIAMI, FL 33155. (#18852).

BISCAYNE COLLEGE SUPPORT OF BICENT YOUTH DEBATES. PROJECT WILL INCLUDE STUDENT PARTICIPATION DEBATES SUCH AS THE LINCOLN-DOUGLAS DEBATE. (LOCAL). DR HELEN JACOBSTEIN, CO-CHAIRPERSON; BISCAYNE COLLEGE BICENTENNIAL COMMITTEE; 16400 NW 32ND AVE; MIAMI, FL 33054. (#11665).

BLACK MURAL PROGRAM - MIAMI, FL. PROJECT ENGAGES YOUNG BLACK ARTISTS IN THE PAINTING OF MURALS FOCUSING ON BLACK HISTORY. (LOCAL). MOE ABETTY, ASST DIRECTOR; HUD-DADE COUNTY; 1401 NW 7TH ST; MIAMI, FL 33136. (#24809).

'BUEN VECINO', FREE ENGLISH AND SPANISH CLASSES-FL. THROUGH CLASSES IN ENGLISH & SPANISH, INDIVIDUALS IN GREATER MIAMI'S BILINGUAL COMMUNITY ARE ABLE TO DEVELOP A BETTER FRIENDSHIP, COOPERATION AND UNDERSTANDING OF LANGUAGE AND CULTURAL TRAITS. (LOCAL). EDWARDO S RIVAS, PROFESSOR; MIAMI SENIOR HIGH SCHOOL; 2450 SW FIRST ST; MIAMI, FL 33135. (#24806).

CHARLES IVES CENTENNIAL MUSIC FESTIVAL, MIAMI, FL. PERFORM ALL WORKS OF AMERICA'S FIRST GREAT COMPOSER IN GR. MIAMI. STRESS IMPORTANCE OF EXPRESSING AMERICAN NATIONALISM IN THE ARTS, HIGHLIGHTING CONTRIBUTION OF AMERICAN MUSICIANS TO WORLD CULTURE. (NAT'L). F WARREN O'REILLY, ADMINISTRATOR; THIRD CENTURY USA; 1451 N BAYSHORE DR; MIAMI, FL 33132. (#245).

CITIZEN INVOLVEMENT PROGRAM, MIAMI, FL. AN INNOVATIVE PROGRAM THAT ENGAGES CITIZENS IN PRIORITY SETTING, USING THE COMMUNITY SCHOOL AS A BASE; CONTINUES AFTER 1976. (LOCAL). RUTH SHACK, EDUCATION CHAIRPERSON; THIRD CENTURY USA; PO BOX 45-1976; MIAMI, FL 33145. (#21869).

'THE COMMONER IN THE BRAZILIAN WORLD', MIAMI, FL. PUBLICATIONS BY RECOGNIZED HISTORIANS IN THE U S & BRAZIL FOCUSING ON THE PATTERNS OF IMMIGRATION INTO BRAZIL. (LOCAL). DR GLEN A GOEKE, CHAIRMAN; FIU-USA BICENTENNIAL MEETING; TAMIAMI TRAIL; MIAMI, FL 33199. (#15693).

COMMUNITY LINKAGE SYSTEM-BIKEPATHS & WALKWAYS, FLA. PEDESTRIAN WALKWAY LINKING RECREATIONAL CULTURAL & OTHER PUBLIC FACILITIES IN FLORIDA COMMUNITIES. NEA GRANT. (LOCAL). HORACE MORRIS, EXEC DIRECTOR; METROPOLITAN DADE COUNTY; 73 W FLAGLER ST; MIAMI, FL 33130. (#3116). **(??).**

COUNTY-WIDE CLEAN UP CAMPAIGN OF DADE CO, FLA. TO BEGIN IN ALL DADE COUNTY PARKS IN THE SUMMER OF 74, THIS CAMPAIGN WILL CONTINUE THROUGH 1976 & EXTEND TO ALL AREAS OF THE COUNTY. (LOCAL). MRS BETTY LASCH, SPECIAL BICENT COMMITTEE; DADE COUNTY FEDERATION OF WOMEN'S CLUBS; 345 NE 100TH ST; MIAMI, FL 33138. (#1550).

COURSE ON AMERICAN PHILOSOPHERS, MIAMI, FL. COURSE ON CHIEF AMERICAN PHILOSOPHICAL THINKERS. (LOCAL). DR RONALD URITUS, CHAIRMAN; PHILOPSOPHY DEPT, BARRY COLLEGE; 11300 NE SECOND AVE; MIAMI SHORES, FL 33161. (#21136).

A CRAFT WORKSHOP FOR SENIOR CITIZENS, MIAMI, FL. SENIOR CITIZENS TO PROVIDE A COMMUNITY SERVICE PROJECT IN WHICH THEY WILL FABRICATE EDUCATIONAL MATERIAL FOR MIGRANT CHILDREN. (LOCAL). DR GLENN A GOERKE, CHAIRMAN; FIU-USA BICENTENNIAL MEETING; TAMIAMI TRAIL; MIAMI, FL 33199. (#15691).

CUBAN MUSEUM OF ARTS AND CULTURE IN MIAMI. A NEW MUSEUM WHICH WILL COLLECT AND DISPLAY ALL WORKS OF ART, HISTORIC DOCUMENTS, ARTICLES & RELICS THAT SPEAK OF CUBAN CULTURE & HERITAGE. (LOCAL). OFELIA TABARES DE FERNAND, TREASURER; CUBAN MUSEUM OF ART & CULTURE INC; 1861 SW 36 AVE; MIAMI, FL 33145. (#3001).

DADE CO CHORUS & ORCHESTRA OF HANDICAPPED IN MIAMI. HANDICAPPED INDIVIDUALS OF ALL AGES TO PERFORM WITH ORCHESTRAS & IN CHORUSES, PLAYING IN THE PARKS AND OTHER FACILITIES FOR THE BICENT PERIOD. (LOCAL). HELEN B WOLFENSTEIN, PROJ DIR; MIAMI ASSOC OF LIFE UNDERWRITERS; 12700 BISCAYNE BLVD; MIAMI, FL 33161. (#10526).

DADE COUNTY, FL, STUDY SEMINAR. INDEPENDENT STUDY & SEMINAR PROGRAM IN WHICH STUDENTS STUDY METROPOLITAN & MUNICIPAL PLANNING BOARDS TO ASSESS THE AGENCIES' PROGRAMS AND GOALS. WILL INCLUDE ALL DADE COUNTY'S COLLEGES. (LOCAL). RUTH SHACK, CHWMN, EDUCATION PANEL; THIRD CENTURY USA; 1174 NE 110 ST; N MIAMI, FL 33161. (#10530).

DESIGN AND ARCHITECTURE 200 & BEYOND, MIAMI, FL. AN EXHIBIT WHICH WILL BE A FUTURISTIC LOOK INTO THE NEXT 100 YEARS IN SOUTH FLORIDA, AS VIEWED BY ARCHITECTS AND ARTISTS. (LOCAL). CHARLES PAWLEY, DIRECTOR; 3011 SW 28 LN; MIAMI, FL 33133. (#18851).

'DOCUMENTS OF FREEDOM', MIAMI, FL. THIS PROJECT ENCOURAGES CITIZENS TO EXAMINE THOSE DOCUMENTS THAT PROTECT MINORITY RIGHTS. DOCUMENTS INCLUDE: DECLARATION OF INDEPENDENCE, 13TH, 14TH & 15TH AMENDMENTS & THE CIVIL RIGHTS ACT OF 1964. (LOCAL). DR ROBERT T CUMMINGS, PROJ DIRECTOR; THIRD CENTURY USA; PO BOX 451976; MIAMI, FL 33145. (#25574).

EARLY AMERICANA - A BICENTENNIAL MURAL, MIAMI, FL. A MURAL WITH AN AMERICAN THEME WILL BE PREPARED BY THE CHILDREN OF THE GRANT CENTER FOR RETARDED, EMOTIONALLY DISTURBED & LEARNING DISABLED CHILDREN. (LOCAL). RICHARD PRITIKIN, PROJ DIRECTOR; PROJECT SCHEDULING COMPANY; 9033 BISCAYNE BLVD; MIAMI, FL 33138. (#19829).

ENGLISH OPERA SERIES OF MIAMI, FLA. ALL OPERAS PRODUCED BY THE GREATER MIAMI OPERA ASSOC WILL HAVE PERFORMANCES IN THE ORIGINAL LANGUAGE & IN ENGLISH. THE ENGLISH SHOWSWILL BE AVAILABLE AT POPULAR PRICES FOR THE GENERAL PUBLIC. (LOCAL). WARREN BROOME, ADMINISTRATOR; THE GREATER MIAMI OPERA ASSOC; 1200 CORAL WAY; MIAMI, FL 33129. (#1535).

ESSAY CONTEST-IMPORTANCIA DE LA CULTURA HISPANA. 2000 WD SPANISH ESSAY CONTEST AMONG HIGH SCHOOL & COLLEGE STUDENTS. THEME IS CULTURAL ISSUE OF INTEREST TO YOUTH. PRIZE IS TRIP TO SPANISH-SPEAKING COUNTRY. (LOCAL). WILLIAM ALEXANDER, CAPTAIN; EASTERN AIRLINES; MIAMI INTERNATIONAL AIRPORT; MIAMI, FL 33148. (#3004).

EXTERIOR SENSORY LEARNING ENVIRONMENT (ESLE). FACILITY FOR SEVERELY HANDICAPPED CHILD THAT PROVIDES PLAY/LEARNING AIDS. RECREATION AREA WILL CONTRIBUTE TO THERAPEUTIC, PHYSICAL RESTORATION AND SENSORY LEARNING ASPECTS OF THE MULTI-HANDICAPPED. (NAT'L). PAUL A ROTHMAN, DIRECTOR GRANTS; THIRD CENTURY U S A; BOX 45-1976; MIAMI, FL 33101. (#3843). **ARBA RECOGNIZED. ARBA GRANTEE.**

FESTIVAL OF AMERICAN MUSIC IN MIAMI, FLA. TO ENCOURAGE ALL MUSICAL ORGANIZATIONS, TEACHERS, SCHOOLS, ETC TO PLAY CONCERTS, RECITALS, & PROGRAMS THAT INCLUDE MUSIC BY AMERICAN COMPOSERS. (LOCAL). LUCAS DREW, CHAIRMAN; THIRD CENTURY USA; PO BOX 011976; MIAMI, FL 33101. (#1538).

FILM SERIES - PROJ OF BISCAYNE COLLEGE, MIAMI, FL. SERIES WILL INCLUDE HISTORICAL, POLITICAL & SOCIOLOGICAL FILMS. (LOCAL). DR HELEN JACOBSTEIN, CO-CHAIRPERSON; BISCAYNE COLLEGE BICENTENNIAL COMMITTEE; 16400 NW 32ND AVE; MIAMI, FL 33054. (#11669).

FLY OLD GLORY IN MIAMI, FL. HAVE ALL HOMES FLY AMERICAN FLAG ON JULY 4 IN LARGE AREA CANVASSED BY BOY SCOUT TROOP 457; FLAGS WILL BE OFFERED FOR SALE. (LOCAL). GLENN GIBBS, PROJ DIRECTOR; TROOP 457 BOY SCOUTS OF AMERICA; 5695 N KENDALL DR; MIAMI, FL 33156. (#12366).

'FOR YOUR FREEDOM AND OURS', A TV PROGRAM - FL. A FILM CONCEIVED AS A BICENTENNIAL SALUTE TO THE AMERICANS WHO SHED THEIR BLOOD FOR THE FREEDOM OF EUROPE IN WW

MIAMI — CONTINUED

II. (LOCAL). CHRISTOPHER PERZANOWSKI, DIRECTOR; AMERICAN INSTITUTE OF POLISH CULTURE; 1000 BRICKELL AVE; MIAMI, FL 33143. (#24804).

FOUR FREEDOMS FESTIVAL IN MIAMI, FLORIDA. A FAIR & FESTIVAL REFLECTING 18TH CENTURY ARTS, TRADES, MUSIC AND GENERAL LIFE WITH SPECIAL EMPHASIS ON THE FREEDOM OF WORSHIP. (LOCAL). REV JOHN PALMER, YOUTH COORDINATOR; YOUTH COMMISSION, EPISCOPALIAN DIOCESE OF SE FLORIDA; 464 NE 16TH ST; MIAMI, FL 33132. (#6189).

FOURTH OF JULY EXTRAVAGANZA OF MIAMI. EVERY YEAR, EACH OF THE 26 MUNICIPALITIES IN THE DADE COUNTY AREA WILL HOLD EVENTS & MANY COUNTY-WIDE ACTIVITIES SUCH AS A MASS SWEARING IN CEREMONY FOR NEW CITIZENS. (LOCAL). MS NORMA HUNT, CHAIRPRSN SPECIAL EVENTS PANEL; THIRD CENTURY USA; PO BOX 1976; MIAMI, FL 33101. (#2997).

THE FUSION DANCE COMPANY RESIDENCY PROJECT - FL. THIS PROJECT WILL INTRODUCE MODERN DANCE TO OVER 60,000 DADE COUNTY SCHOOL CHILDREN. (LOCAL). WILLIAM LORD, MANAGER; FUSION DANCE COMPANY; 4137 MALAGA AVE; MIAMI, FL 33133. (#17115).

GREAT EXPRESSWAY LANDSCAPING PROJECT - MIAMI, FL. THE GEL PROJECT INVOLVES PLANTING TREES TO BUFFER HOMES FROM NOISE & AIR POLLUTION; THE DEPT OF TRANSPORTATION IS COOPERATING WITH CITIZENS ON THE PROJECT. (LOCAL). LESLIE JAY GROSS, PRESIDENT; KENDALE HOMEOWNERS ASSOC, INC; 19 W FLAGLER ST, SUITE M-102; MIAMI, FL 33130. (#12372).

HEMISPHERIC CONGRESS FOR WOMEN '76. TO BRING TOGETHER WOMEN'S GROUPS IN THIS HEMISPHERE FOR AN EXCHANGE OF IDEAS. TO EXPOSE, SHARE, & MAKE WOMEN AWARE AS THEY CONTRIBUTE TO THEIR OWN COUNTRY'S DEVELOPMENT & TO THE HEMISPHERE. (INT'L). GUI GOUVAERT, EXEC DIRECTOR; HEMISPHERIC CONGRESS FOR WOMEN, '76 INC; 10 BISCAYNE BLVD, SUITE 200; MIAMI, FL 33132. (#1529). **ARBA RECOGNIZED.**

THE HERITAGE TRAIL - PUBLICATION, MIAMI, FL. A PUBLICATION COMPILED FOR SALE TO THE PUBLIC, LISTING & EXPLAINING HISTORICAL SITES THROUGHOUT DADE COUNTY. (LOCAL). JOHN GIBSON, PRESIDENT; DADE HERITAGE TRUST; 177 OCEAN DR; KEY BISCAYNE, FL 33149. (#16239).

HERSTORY/DADE COUNTY- FLORIDA. BY VARIOUS EVENTS PROMOTE THE SIGNIFICANT CONTRIBUTIONS MADE IN AREA BY WOMEN-WRITE ENCYCLOPEDIA, PRODUCE PLAYS, POSTERS, PAGEANTS. INITIAL RESEARCH WILL DEAL WITH WOMEN'S CONTRIBUTIONS TO DADE COUNTY. (LOCAL). RUTH BRADDOCK, CO-COORDINATOR; HERSTORY; 7801 SW 134TH ST; MIAMI, FL 33156. (#3002).

HIGH SCHOOL POSTER CONTEST, MIAMI, FLORIDA. THE THEME FOR THIS CONTEST IS TO PROMOTE THE BICENTENNIAL, THE FIRST PLACE DESIGN WILL BE PRINTED AND DISPLAYED WHEREVER POSSIBLE. (ST-WIDE). JO BAXTER, ACCOUNTS REPRESENTATIVE; DONNELLY ADVERTISING; 5220 BISCAYNE BLVD; MIAMI, FL 33137. (#5208).

HISPANIC INFLUENCE IN FLORIDA YESTERDAY & TODAY. TO DEVELOP A NATIONAL DEMONSTRATION MODEL IN TRANSFORMING A GHETTO INTO A HEALTHY CITY BY 1976. GOALS INCLUDE ERADICATION OF PROBLEMS; UNDEREMPLOYMENT, DRUG ABUSE, SUBSTANDARD HOUSING, ETC. (LOCAL). WALTER GREEN, PRESIDENT; BLACK GROVE INC; 3565 GRAND AVE; MIAMI, FL 33133. (#1551).

HISPANIC INFLUENCE IN FLORIDA'S PUBLICATIONS. COMPILED INTO SINGLE PUBLICATION ALL OF THE HISPANIC INFLUENCE IN THE HISTORY OF FLORIDA. TO BE WRITTEN IN SPANISH WITH ENGLISH TRANSALATION. DISTRIBUTED AROUND SPANISH SPEAKING COUNTRIES. (ST-WIDE). DR JOSE BALSEIRO; THIRD CENTURY USA; PO BOX 1976; MIAMI, FL 33101. (#2996).

HISTORIC SCHOOLS ENTER THE THIRD CENTURY STUDY -FL. AN INDEPTH STUDY OF TWO HISTORICALLY SIGNIFICANT SCHOOLS WHICH HAVE MAINTAINED ACADEMIC EXCELLENCE. IT WILL SUPPORT THE DEMOCRATIC PROCESS OF PUBLIC ED. AND BRING FORTH THE LEADERS OF THE THIRD CENTURY. (LOCAL). JANET MCALILY, VP DADE COUNTY PTA COUNCIL; COCONUT GROVE PTA & GEO WASH CARVER PTA; 2025 S E COFFEE ST; MIAMI, FL 33133. (#1534). **(??).**

HISTORICAL MARKER PROGRAM, FLORIDA. THIS PROGRAM IS A SERIES OF MARKERS PLACED ON SITES WHICH HAVE PLAYED A MAJOR ROLE IN FLORIDA'S HISTORY. (ST-WIDE). MS MARTY GRAFTON, CHRPSN HISTORY & COMMEMORATIONS; HISTORICAL ASSOC OF SOUTH FLORIDA; 800 DOUGLAS ENTRANCE; CORAL GABLES, FL 33134. (#3000).

HUMANITARIAN PHYSICAL FITNESS AWARD - MIAMI, FL. AWARDS FOR THE YOUNG PEOPLE OF DADE COUNTY IN THE FIELD OF PHYSICAL FITNESS FOR HUMANITARIAN CAUSES & IMPROVING THE QUALITY OF LIFE AND EDUCATION OF THE COUNTY. (LOCAL). RICHARD L JOHNSON, CHAIRMAN; FLORIDA DIABETES ASSOC, INC; 8751 SW 192ND ST; MIAMI, FL 33157. (#18342).

IMPROVING THE QUALITY OF LIFE - 1976; MIAMI, FL. A YEAR LONG SERIES OF EVENTS, EXHIBITS & PROJECTS THAT WILL MAKE THE STUDENTS MORE AWARE OF ECOLOGY AND THE QUALITY OF LIFE. (LOCAL). MRS RONALD TEICHNER, CHAIRMAN; PINECREST ELEMENTARY SCHOOL; 10250 SW 57 AVE; MIAMI, FL 33156. (#18334).

INTERNATIONAL FOLK FESTIVAL OF MIAMI, FLA. THIS MIAMI FESTIVAL ENCOMPASSES FOLK MUSIC, ARTS & CRAFTS, FOOD OF ALL NATIONS & ETHNIC GROUPS. INCLUDES REGATTA, BICYCLE TOUR, CHESSTOURNAMENT, AND A PARADE OF NATIONS. (INT'L). MORTY FREEDMAN, DIRECTOR; CITY OF MIAMI; 2539 S BAYSHORE DR; MIAMI, FL 33129. (#1528).

LECTURE ON CUBA'S ROLE IN AMER REVOLUTION -MIAMI. LECTURE BY EDWARD J TEJERA, AUTHOR OF 'CUBAN HELP TO THE USA'S FIGHT FOR INDEPENDENCE.'. (LOCAL). FLORINDA ALZAGA, PROJ CHAIRMAN; CUBAN WOMEN'S CLUB; 2023 SW FIRST ST; MIAMI, FL 33135. (#10533).

LECTURE SERIES FOR LATIN COMMUNITY - MIAMI, FL. MONTHLY CONFERENCES ABOUT AMERICAN HISTORY; RADIO SPEECHES; AND BROCHURE. (LOCAL). DR MANUEL G MARINAS, VICE PRESIDENT; YMCA-INTERNATIONAL JOSE MARTI; 450 SW 16 AVE; MIAMI, FL 33135. (#13394).

A LIFETIME OF EDUCATION - COMMUNITY SCHOOLS, MIAMI. TO MAKE EVERY SCHOOL A COMMUNITY SCHOOL, TO INTEGRATE THE MANY RESOURCES EXISTING IN THE COMMUNITY & ENCOURAGE NEW ONES & TO ELIMINATE DUPLICATION IN SERVICES & OFFER MORE. (ST-WIDE). MRS MARGE PEARLSON, CHAIRPERSON; THIRD CENTURY COMMMITTEE FOR COMMUNITY EDUCATION; 6400 SW 129 TERRACE; MIAMI, FL 33156. (#1545).

LUMMUS ISLAND CAMPING EXPERIENCE, MIAMI, FL. A YEAR LONG CAMPING EXPERIENCE UTILIZING THE PIONEER CONCEPT OF ESTABLISHING A NEW FACILITY ON PREVIOUSLY UNUSED LAND; PROJECT WILL INVOLVE MANY YOUTH GROUPS IN AN INNER CITY CAMPOUT. (ST-WIDE). RONALD A PHILLIPPO, SCOUT EXECUTIVE; SOUTH FLORIDA COUNCIL, INC & BOY SCOUTS OF AMERICA; 2960 CORAL WY; MIAMI, FL 33145. (#13373).

MARTIN LUTHER KING BLVD IMPROVEMENTS IN MIAMI. IMPROVEMENT OF 62ND ST INTO TOTAL LINEAR PARK COMMUNITY INVOLVING EDUCATION, HOUSING, CULTURAL, & ECONOMIC DEVELOPMENT OF AREA. (LOCAL). MRS ATHALIE RANGE, CHAIRMAN; DR M L KING BLVD DEVELOPMENT CORP C/O MODEL CITIES PROGRAM; 5959 NW 35TH AVE; MIAMI, FL 33142. (#3006). **(??).**

A MENTAL HEALTH DOCUMENTARY, MIAMI, FL. A FILM WHICH IS AN EDUCATIONAL DEVICE USED TO CREATE A MODEL FOR DEVELOPING A UNIFIED, CITY WIDE MENTAL HEALTH SYSTEM. (LOCAL). DAVE EASTON, PROJ DIRECTOR; THE MENTAL HEALTH ASSOC OF DADE COUNTY, INC; 800 BRICKELL PLAZA; MIAMI, FL 33131. (#18853).

MIAMI DADE COMMUNITY COLLEGE ART GALLERY, FL. EXHIBITIONS FEATURING AMERICAN ARTISTS WHICH INCLUDES BOTH HISTORIC AND CONTEMPORARY FORMS OF ART. (LOCAL). TOM HOROWITZ, PROJ DIRECTOR; MIAMI-DADE COMMUNITY COLLEGE; 11011 SW 104 ST; MIAMI, FL 33176. (#18520).

MIAMI EDISON '76 HIGH SCHOOL PROJECT. TO SHOW MIAMI SENIOR HIGH AS A MODEL COMMUNITY SCHOOL BY INVITING THE COMMUNITY INTO THE SCHOOL TO CELEBRATE HERITAGE '76. THE AIM IS TO UNITE THE SCHOOL IN A MAJOR HORIZONS '76 PROJECT. (LOCAL). JUDITH S GREENE, PRINCIPAL; MIAMI EDISON SENIOR HIGH SCHOOL; 6101 NW 2ND AVE; MIAMI, FL 33127. (#1526).

MIAMI RIVER 'TRASH BASH' & REGATTA IN FLORIDA. PROJECT INVOLVES REMOVING SUNKEN OBJECTS ETC FROM THE RIVER & TRASH & LITTER FROM THE UPLAND. 60 DAYS LATER A WATER FESTIVAL & REGATTA WILL BE HELD IN CELEBRATION OF THE CLEAN-UP. (LOCAL). TOM HOMBERGER, DIRECTOR; MIAMI RIVER INTER-CITY BOARD; 180 W 7TH ST; HIALEAH, FL 33012. (#5198).

MIAMI, FLORIDA'S TRIBUTE TO NATION'S BICENTENNIAL. IN COMMEMORATION OF OUR NATION'S BICENTENNIAL, A SERIES OF 12 PICTURES IN COLLAGE DEPICTING INCIDENTS AND EVENTS IN U.S. HISTORY HAVE BEEN CREATED TO BE PLACED ON DISPLAY FOR AUDIENCES OF ALL AGES. (LOCAL). MS DOROTHY B COLE, COORDINATOR; THIRD CENTURY USA; 1039 W 46TH ST; MIAMI, FL 33140. (#5201).

MIAMI'S MUSEUM OF SCIENCE'S 76 EXPANSION PGM. NEW DISPLAYS, FACILITIES, & SPECIAL PGMS HIGHLIGHTING CENTRAL & LATIN-AMERICAN COUNTRIES & S FLORIDA'S CULTURAL, SOCIAL AND INDUSTRAIL DEVELOPMENTS. (REGN'L). GEORGE SINGER; MUSEUM OF SCIENCE; 3280 S MIAMI AVE; MIAMI, FL 33129. (#5209).

MIAMI'S 'THE GREEN CIRCLE PROGRAM, INC'. A PROGRAM TO HELP CHILDREN DEVELOP A POSITIVE ATTITUDE ABOUT THEMSELVES & OTHERS ALONG WITH POSITIVE INTERRACIAL & CROSS-CULTURAL RELATIONSHIPS. (LOCAL). ANITA SHERMAN, PROJ DIR; PANEL OF AMERICAN WOMEN; 19901 NE 21 AVE; N MIAMI BEACH, FL 33162. (#10529).

NARRATIVE BIBLIOGRAPHIES, MIAMI, FL. NARRATIVE BIBLIOGRAPHIES IN SUPPORT OF SELECTED TOPICS ON AMERICAN ISSUES FORUM LIST. (ST-WIDE). SISTER ANN BERNARD GOEDDEKE, OP; BARRY COLLEGE LIBRARY; 11300 NE 2ND AVE; MIAMI SHORES, FL 33161. (#21138).

NARRATIVE BIBLIOGRAPHIES OF AMERICAN ISSUES, FL. COMPILED BIBLIOGRAPHIES WHICH WILL BE DISTRIBUTED TO COINCIDE WITH THE SCHEDULE OF THE AMERICAN ISSUES FORUM SO THAT PARTICIPANTS MAY BECOME MORE KNOWLEDGEABLE. (LOCAL). SISTER ANN BERNARD GOEDDEKE; BARRY COLLEGE; 11300 NE 2ND AVE; MIAMI, FL 33161. (#21866).

NATIONAL NETWORK OF YOUTH ADVISORY BOARDS - FL. TO UNITE EXISTING & NEW YOUTH ADVISORY BOARDS OF CITIES ACROSS THE NATION, TO EXCHANGE INFO & IDEAS BETWEEN AMERICA'S YOUTH, TO HOLD MEETINGS AS A EXTENSION OF THE WHITE HOUSE CONFERENCE ON YOUTH. (NAT'L). STUART RADO, EXTERNAL VICE PRESIDENT; GREATER MIAMI JAYCEES; PO BOX 402036; MIAMI BEACH, FL 33140. (#1536).

NEIGHBORHOODS '76 - DADE COUNTY, FLORIDA. ESTABLISH COMMITTEE IN EACH DADE CO. MUNICIPALITY WHICH WOULD ESTABLISH MAJOR BICENT GOAL AND CATALOG THIRD CENTURY CONCERNS. (LOCAL). CHUCIL NEWCOMB, CHAIRMAN COMMUNITY CORDINATION; THIRD CENTURY USA; PO BOX 01-1976; MIAMI, FL 33101. (#2998).

NEW BROADWAY PRODUCTIONS - PROJ OF MIAMI, FL. LIVE THEATRICAL ENTERTAINMENT TO THE SOUTH FLORIDA AREA ON A TOURING BASIS; VISITING CONDOMINIUMS AND SENIOR CENTERS, THE PROGRAMS ARE DESIGNED TO PROMOTE AN UNDERSTANDING OF AMERICAN THEATRE. (LOCAL). ROBERT M HOLTZMAN, PROJ DIRECTOR; NEW BROADWAY PRODUCTIONS; 111 S E 7TH ST; MIAMI, FL 33131. (#17179).

'ONE NATION UNDER GOD' CHORAL SERVICE, MIAMI, FL. AN INTERDENOMINATIONAL SERVICE COMMEMORATING OUR RELIGIOUS HERITAGE WILL BE SUNG BY 20 CHOIRS. PLANS INCLUDE NEW ANTHEMS & THE READING OF WINNING ESSAY, 'RELIGION IN THE THIRD CENTURY'. (LOCAL). REV AUGUST KLING, CHAIRMAN; THIRD CENTURY'S RELIGION COMMITTEE; 609 BRICKELL AVE; MIAMI, FL 33131. (#5229).

OPEN HOUSE - MIAMI, FL. THERE WILL BE AN OPEN HOUSE OF THE SUBTROPICAL HORTICULTURE RESEARCH STATION IN OCTOBER, 1976. (LOCAL). DR A K BURDITT, JR, PROJ CHAIRMAN; DEPT OF AGRICULTURE, SUBTROPICAL HORTICULTURE RESEARCH STATION; 13601 OLD CUTLER RD; MIAMI, FL 33158. (#24639).

ORANGE BOWL FESTIVAL & PAGEANT - 42ND ANNUAL. THE 1976 ORANGE BOWL FESTIVAL WILL HAVE A TOTAL BICENTENNIAL THEME, INCLUDING THE PARADE, HALFTIME, & ALL ACTIVITIES. WILL BE TELEVISED NATIONWIDE ON DEC. 31, 1975. (NAT'L). DANIEL S MCNAMARA, MANAGER; ORANGE BOWL COMMITTEE; 1400 NW 4TH ST (GATE 7); MIAMI, FL 33135. (#1548). **ARBA RECOGNIZED.**

THE PARADOXES OF THE BILL OF RIGHTS AT MIAMI, FL. A PHOTOGRAPHIC EXHIBIT DEPICTING PARADOXES IN THE BILL OF RIGHTS. CAPTIONS WILL BE DRAWN FROM QUOTES OF THE FOUNDING FATHERS. A PANEL OF HUMANISTS WILL DISCUSS THEM IN PUBLIC FORUMS. (LOCAL). MANUEL MENDOZA, ASSOCIATE PROFESSOR; MIAMI-DADE COMMUNITY COLLEGE; 8110 SW 73RD AVE, APT 3; MIAMI, FL 33143. (#5200).

PATRICK HENRY - FIREBAND OF LIBERTY. AN INTERPRETIVE THEATRE STYLE PRESENTATION ON PATRICK HENRY'S LIFE. (LOCAL). DR PAULA MILTON, DIRECTOR; INTERPRETIVE READERS' ASSOC & MIAMI-DADE COMMUNITY COLLEGE NORTH; 11380 NW 27TH AVE; MIAMI, FL 33167. (#106523-2). **(??).**

PLANET OCEAN - MIAMI, FL. MUSEUM PRESENTING DISCOVERIES ABOUT THE OCEAN, DECISIONS ON CONSERVING CONTENTS. SEVEN THEMES USING MULTI-MEDIA PRESENTATIONS & MECHANICAL TECHNIQUES DRAMATIZING THE OCEAN. (NAT'L). F G WALTON SMITH, PRESIDENT; INTERNATIONAL OCEANOGRAPHIC FOUNDATION; 10 RICKENBACKER CAUSEWAY, VA KEY; MIAMI, FL 33149. (#3011). **ARBA RECOGNIZED.**

POLISH FOLK CELEBRATION. CELEBRATION WILL INCLUDE WOMEN IN POLISH FOLK DRESS, POLISH PASTRY & POLISH FOLK MUSIC. (ST-WIDE). LILLIAN J MICIAK, CHMN; POLISH NATIONAL ALLIANCE HOME; 2144 N E 2ND AVE; MIAMI, FL 33137. (#5192-1).

PROPAGATION OF TREES FOR NEW DADE COUNTY ZOO IN FL. PROPAGATION OF 200,000 TREES & SHRUBS TO LANDSCAPE NEW ZOO WHEN IT IS COMPLETED. ALL PLANTS MUST BE INDIGENOUS TO TROPICAL AFRICA, INDIA OR ASIA. VOLUNTEER EFFORT. (LOCAL). TH STRAUSE, ZOO DESIGNER; CRANDON PARK ZOO; 4000 CRANDON BLVD; KEY BISCAYNE, FL 33149. (#5217).

PUBLICATION, HISPANIC INFLUENCE IN STATE OF FLA. THIS PUBLICATION WILL BE THE COMPILATION OF RESEARCH ON THE HISPANIC INFLUENCE IN FLA FROM 400 YEARS AGO TO THE PRESENT. THE PUBLICATION WILL BE WRITTEN IN SPANISH, WITH TRANSLATION TO ENGLISH. (INT'L). DR JOSE BALSEIRO, PROFESSOR; THIRD CENTURY USA; PO BOX 011976; MIAMI, FL 33143. (#1552).

'READ ON AMERICA', MIAMI, FL. A PROJECT DESIGNED TO MOTIVATE STUDENTS TO READ ABOUT OUR COUNTRY, ITS PATRIOTS, ITS HISTORY, ITS PROBLEMS & THE CREATIVE EFFORTS OF ITS PEOPLE. (LOCAL). LOUISE HARMS, PROJ DIRECTOR; DADE COUNTY SCHOOLS BICENTENNIAL OFFICE; 144 BISCAYNE BLVD; MIAMI, FL 33132. (#19830).

REDLANDS SCHOOL - HISTORICAL SITE, MIAMI, FL. RESTORATION OF REDLANDS SCHOOL TO ACQUAINT THE COMMUNITY & SCHOOL CHILDREN WITH FACTS ABOUT THE SCHOOL'S HERITAGE. (LOCAL). CAROLE FINK, PROJ DIRECTOR; REDLANDS CITIZEN ASSOCIATION; 13395 SW 200 ST; MIAMI, FL 33177. (#19831).

RENOVATION & BEAUTIFICATION OF SW 8 ST IN MIAMI. RENOVATE AREA WHERE CURAN EXILES HAVE SETTLED. DEVELOP AREA INTO TOURIST ATTRACTION. (LOCAL). NILLY GORT, VICE TREASURER; LATIN CHAMBER OF COMMERCE; 601 SW 22 AVE; MIAMI, FL 33125. (#3007).

REPRINT & FACSIMILE SERIES PROJECT OF MIAMI, FLA. TO REPRINT RARE, OUT-OF-PRINT BOOKS RELATING TO SOUTH FLORIDA HISTORY WITH FOREWARDS, CORRECTIONS, NOTES, ETC. PRINTED FOR A SPECIAL BICENTENNIAL EDITION. (ST-WIDE). MRS THOMAS T SHIVERICK, CHAIRPERSON; HISTORICAL ASSOC OF SOUTHERN FLORIDA, INC; 3280 S MIAMI AVE BLDG B; MIAMI, FL 33137. (#1540).

RX FOR CREATIVITY - BISCAYNE COLLEGE, MIAMI, FL. A COURSE ON FREEDOM VS COERSION WILL BE OFFERED. (LOCAL). DR HELEN JACOBSTEIN, CO-CHAIRPERSON; BISCAYNE COLLEGE BICENTENNIAL COMMITTEE; 16400 NW 32ND AVE; MIAMI, FL 33054. (#11668).

SATURDAY IN THE PARK - PROJ OF MIAMI, FL. MUSICAL CONCERT SERIES OF 10 FREE PERFORMANCES AT 7 DADE COUNTY PARKS. (LOCAL). ROD E GLAUBMANS, PROJ DIRECTOR; PERFORMING ARTS FOR COMMUNITY & EDUCATION, INC; 4709 NW 7TH ST; MIAMI, FL 33126. (#13379).

MIAMI — CONTINUED

SOCIOLOGICAL GRADUATE COURSES IN MIAMI, FL. A GRADUATE LEVEL COURSE DISCUSSES TRANSCENDANT VIEWS OF MAN AND HIS SOCIETY. IT ALSO SHOWS ADMINISTRATORS HOW TO RECOGNIZE EARLY WARNING SIGNALS OF CHANGE. (LOCAL). DR JAY MENDELL, ASSOC PROFESSOR; FLORIDA INTERNATIONAL UNIV; TAMIAMI TRAIL; MIAMI, FL 33199. (#10532).

SPANISH TRAINING VESSEL VISITS TO MIAMI, FLORIDA. AS AN OFFICIAL SPANISH SALUTE TO GREATER MIAMI'S PARTICIPATION IN THE BICENTENNIAL, THE VESSEL, 'JUAN SEBASTIAN ELCANO' WILL MAKE A 5 DAY VISIT IN APRIL, 1975. (INT'L). DON VICENTE RAMIREZ-MONTESINOS, CONSUL GEN; GOVERMENT OF SPAIN; 8550 PONCE DE LEON BLVD; CORAL GABLES, FL 33134. (#5195).

SPECIAL BICENTENNIAL EDITION - MIAMI, FL. A SPECIAL EDITION OF THE CAMPUS NEWSPAPER, 'FALCON TIMES', WILL BE PUBLISHED. (LOCAL). JOSE QUEVADO, PROJ CHAIRMAN; MIAMI DADE COMMUNITY COLLEGE; 11380 NW 27TH AVE; MIAMI, FL 33167. (#27059).

SPECIAL LIBRARY COLLECTION, MIAMI, FL. SPECIAL COLLECTION OF PRINT MATERIALS ON FLORIDA AND CATHOLIC HISTORY IN THE U S. (ST-WIDE). SISTER ANN BERNARD GOEDDEKE, O P; BARRY COLLEGE LIBRARY; 11300 NE SECOND AVE; MIAMI SHORES, FL 33161. (#21137).

SPECIAL LIBRARY COLLECTION, MIAMI, FL. AN ANNOTATED LIST OF OUT-OF-PRINT AND NOT READILY AVAILABLE BOOKS IN A SPECIAL COLLECTION ON FLORIDA AND THE HISTORY OF THE CATHOLIC CHURCH IN THE U S; AVAILABLE AT THE BARRY COLLEGE LIBRARY. (LOCAL). SISTER ANN BERNARD GOEDDEKE, OP; BARRY COLLEGE; 11300 NE 2ND AVE; MIAMI, FL 33161. (#21865).

STUDENT GOVT FALL FESTIVAL SALUTES THE BICENTENNIAL. A DAY-LONG FESTIVAL OF PLANNED ACTIVITIES RELATED TO THE BICENTENNIAL THEME; THIS IS THE KICK-OFF OF THE FIU SCHOOL YEAR. AT FLORIDA INTERNATIONAL UNIV. (LOCAL). DR GLENN A GOERKE, CHMN; FIU-USA BICENTENNIAL MEETING; TAMIAMI TRAIL; MIAMI, FL 33199. (#102535-1).

STUDENTS IN GOVT & BUSINESS PROJECT OF FLORIDA. SELECT ELEMEN & HIGH SCHOOL STUDENTS TO SPEND SEMESTER AS INTERN TO GOVT OR BUSINESS OFFICIAL IN ORDER TO UNDERSTAND RELATIONSHIPS AMONG GOVT, BUSINESS & CITIZENS. (LOCAL). RUTH SHACK, CHAIRPERSON EDUCATION PANEL; THIRD CENTURY USA; PO BOX 011976; MIAMI, FL 33101. (#3003).

'TEQUESTA', PUBLICATION, MIAMI, FL. YEARLY PUBLICATION OF THE HISTORICAL ASSOCIATION OF SOUTHERN FL; SUBJECT IN THIS BICENTENNIAL ISSUE WILL DESCRIBE FLORIDA'S ROLE IN AMERICAN HISTORY, 200 YEARS AGO. (ST-WIDE). DR CARLTON TEBEAU, COORDINATOR; UNIVERSITY OF MIAMI; 307 ALEDO AVE; CORAL GABLES, FL 33134. (#21871).

THIRD CENTURY GREENS PROGRAM IN MIAMI, FL. CONSTRUCT PARKS UNDER AND ADJACENT TO EXPRESSWAYS IN DADE COUNTY. (LOCAL). R RAY GOODE, CHAIRMAN; DADE MONROE COUNTIES MANPOWER PLANNING CONSORTIUM; 1399 NW 17TH AVE; MIAMI, FL 33125. (#22835). **ARBA GRANTEE.**

THIRD CENTURY HORIZONS, MIAMI, FL. AN UMBRELLA ORGANIZATION FOR GREATER MIAMI WILL INITIATE & MOTIVATE PARTICIPATION IN ENVIRONMENTAL IMPROVEMENT & COORDINATE TREE PLANTING PROJECTS. (LOCAL). MRS JAMES CONNOLY, CHAIRPERSON; THIRD CENTURY HORIZONS; 12800 SW 82 AVE; MIAMI, FL 33156. (#16238).

TOURING BROADWAY PRODUCTIONS - MIAMI, FL. NEW BROADWAY PRODUCTIONS IS PLANNING TO BRING LIVE THEATRICAL ENTERTAINMENT TO THE SOUTH FLORIDA AREA ON A TOURING BASIS. THE PLAYERS WILL BE VISITING SENIOR CITIZENS AND OTHERS. (LOCAL). ROBERT HOLTZMAN, DIRECTOR; NEW BROADWAY PRODUCTIONS; 111 SE 7TH; SUITE #104; MIAMI, FL 33131. (#16066).

TOURNAMENT OF THE AMERICAS - MIAMI, FL. SPORTS TOURNAMENTS FOR TOTAL FAMILY INVOLVEMENT; WILL BRING TOGETHER FAMILIES OF SPANISH ORIGIN WITH AMERICANS TO PROMOTE MUTUAL UNDERSTANDING. (LOCAL). WILLIAM ALEXANDER, COORDINATOR; GAMMACOLOR; 3496 NW 7TH ST; MIAMI, FL 33125. (#12369).

TREE PLANTING IN MIAMI, FL. 78 ROYAL POINCIANAS AND 16 TABEUIA PALLIDA TREES WILL BE PLANTED TO BEAUTIFY THE COMMUNITY & HELP CONTROL AIR POLLUTION. (LOCAL). MRS THOMAS KOWALSKI, PROJ DIRECTOR; VILLAGE OF KENDALE GARDEN CLUB; 9710 SW 104TH CT; MIAMI, FL 33176. (#12373).

TWO CENTURIES OF AMERICAN HISTORY, MIAMI, FLORIDA. OUTSTANDING EVENTS OF THE U S WAR OF INDEPENDENCE PRESENTED THRU GRAPHIC ARTS TO THE BILINGUAL COMMUNITY OF DADE COUNTY. AMERICAN HISTORY REVEALED VIA CONFERENCES, PAINTINGS ETC. (LOCAL). PROF QSVALDO AGUIRRE, PRESIDENT EDITORIAL AMER; SOCIEDAD ESP DE CUBAN EN EL EXILE; 6401 NW 36TH ST; MIAMI, FL 33130. (#5203).

VALUES IN AMERICAN SOCIETY - CONFERENCE. CONFERENCE AT 11380 NW 27TH AVE. (LOCAL). DR CHAS ASBURY, ASST DIR; MIAMI-DADE COMMUNITY COLLEGE, NORTH CAMPUS; 11380 NW 27TH AVE; MIAMI, FL 33167. (#106523-1). **(??).**

VALUES IN THE POST WOODSTOCK GENERATION, MIAMI, FL. GRADUATE-LEVEL COURSE AT FIU DISCUSSING TRANSCENDENT VIEWS OF MAN & HIS SOCIETY. (LOCAL). DR GLENN A GOERKE, CHAIRMAN; FIU-USA BICENTENNIAL MEETING; TAMIAMI TRAIL; MIAMI, FL 33199. (#15694).

THE VILLAGERS BOOK OF OUTSTANDING HOMES OF MIAMI. THE BOOK TRACES MIAMI'S RESIDENTIAL ARCHITECTURE FROM THE FIRST HOME BUILT IN MIAMI TO THE PRESENT WITH EMPHASIS ON THE HISTORICAL SIGNIFICANCE AS REFLECTED IN THE DIFFERENT STYLES. (LOCAL). MARGARET KUNZ, PRESIDENT; THE VILLAGERS; 18490 S W 83RD AVE; MIAMI, FL 33157. (#17176).

VISUAL ARTS IN THE 3RD CENTURY EXHIBITS - MIAMI. CONTINUOUS EXHIBITIONS & ART-RELATED ACTIVITIES WILL PLAY A MAJOR ROLE IN THE BICENTENNIAL ACTIVITIES OF THE GREATER MIAMI AREA. (LOCAL). ERIKA KING, COORDINATOR CULTURAL EVENTS PANEL; THIRD CENTURY USA; 3112 COMMODORE PLAZA; MIAMI, FL 33133. (#9066).

VISUAL ARTS PROGRAM FOR MIAMI SCHOOLS - FL. A SERIES OF VISUAL ART WORKSHOPS DESIGNED TO EXPAND PARTICIPATION BY YOUTH IN PAINTING, SCULPTURE & CRAFTS, TO BE HELD AT HIGH-DENSITY, LOW-INCOME SCHOOLS. (LOCAL). ESTHER SHRAGO, ART DIR; COMMUNITY ART ALLIANCE, INC; 2035 NE 201 TERRACE; MIAMI, FL 33179. (#10521).

'THE VOICE OF FIU', MIAMI, FL. RADIO BROADCASTS TO FOSTER BETTER UNDERSTANDING AMONG NATIONS OF THE WORLD IN GENERAL AND AMONG THE AMERICAS. (LOCAL). DR GLENN A GOERKE, CHAIRMAN; FIU-USA BICENTENNIAL MEETING; TAMIAMI TRAIL; MIAMI, FL 33199. (#15692).

WALL HANGING: 'LIFE IN SOUTHERN FLORIDA'. CREWEL-EMBROIDERED WALL HANGING DESIGNED AND HANDCRAFTED BY CADETTE GIRL SCOUT TROOP 429 AS A GIFT TO FLORIDA HOUSE IN WASHINGTON, D C. (LOCAL). MRS CLINTON ANDERSON, LEADER; GIRL SCOUT COUNCIL OF TROPICAL FLORIDA; 3001 PONCE DE LEON BLVD; CORAL GABLES, FL 33134. (#9103).

'WOMEN IN ART' SHOW OF MIAMI, FLA. FORTY WOMEN ARTISTS WILL EXHIBIT THEIR WORK - PAINTING, GRAPHICS, SCULPTURE, ETC. THEME THEIR EXPRESSION OF THE TIMES. (ST-WIDE). ERIKA KING, ART CONSULTANT; WOMEN ARTISTS IT'S TIME - WAIT; 4060 HARDIE; COCO GROVE, FL 33133. (#1525).

OCT 6, '72 - JUNE '77. LUNCHTIME LIVELY ARTS SERIES. FEATURES AMERICAN COMPOSERS & DRAMATIC PRODUCTIONS WITH A BICENTENNIAL THEME. AT DOWNTOWN CAMPUS, PATIO. (LOCAL). RUTH GREENFIELD, PROJ DIR; MIAMI-DADE COMMUNITY COLLEGE; 300 NE 2ND AVE; MIAMI, FL 33132. (#107972-1).

SEPT 1, '74 - JUNE 30, '77. EASTERN AIRLINES BICENTENNIAL LITERARY CONTEST. 2000 WORD SPANISH ESSAY CONTEST AMONG HIGH SCHOOL STUDENTS. THEME IS A CULTURAL ISSUE RELATED TO THE AMERICAN REVOLUTION. PRIZE IS A TRIP TO A SPANISH SPEAKING COUNTRY. (LOCAL). MARIA ELENA TORANO, COORD; EASTERN AIRLINES; EASTERN AIRLINES-MIAMI INTL APT; MIAMI, FL 33148. (#102556-1).

OCT 1, '74 - MAY 19, '75. IVES MUSIC FESTIVAL IN DADE, BROWARD & PALM BEACH COUNTIES, FLA. PERFORM ALL WORKS OF AMERICA'S FIRST GREAT COMPOSER IN GR. MIAMI. STRESS IMPORTANCE OF EXPRESSING AMERICAN NATIONALISM IN THE ARTS, HIGHLIGHTING CONNTRIBUTION OF AMERICAN MUSICIANS TO WORLD CULTURE. (NAT'L). F WARREN O'REILLY; THIRD CENTURY USA UNIV OF MIAMI; 1451 N BAYSHORE DR; MIAMI, FL 33132. (#245-1).

OCT 16, '74 - DEC 31, '76. FREEDOM '76 BICENT TYPEFACE DESIGN COMPETITION. A COMPETITION, WITH $2000 IN PRIZE MONEY, OPEN TO STUDENTS & PROFESSIONALS TO DESIGN A NEW TYPEFACE TO CELEBRATE THE BICENTENNIAL TO HONOR THE ROLE PLAYED BY THE PRINTED WORD IN OUR HERITAGE. (NAT'L). ELI BARRY; VISUAL GRAPHICS CORP; 1400 NE 125TH ST; MIAMI, FL 33161. (#1544-1).

OCT 20, '74. IVES CENTENNIAL GALA CONCERT. PERFORM ALL WORKS OF AMERICA'S FIRST GREAT COMPOSER IN GR. MIAMI. STRESS IMPORTANCE OF EXPRESSING AMERICAN NATIONALISM IN THE ARTS, HIGHLIGHTING CONTRIBUTION OF AMERICAN MUSICIANS TO WORLD CULTURE. AT GUSMAN PHILHARMONIC HALL. (NAT'L). F WARREN O'REILLY, ADMIN; THIRD CENTURY USA; 1451 N BAYSHORE DR; MIAMI, FL 33132. (#245-902).

NOV 1, '74 - FEB 15, '75. POSTER CONTEST DISPLAY & JUDGING FOR THE BICENTENNIAL. THIRD CENTURY'S BICENTENNIAL POSTER CONTEST -FL. POSTER CONTEST THEME OF WHICH IS AMER REVOL OR BICENT CELEBRATION CASH PRIZES AWARDED TO 5 LEVELS OF PROFICIENCY. ENTRIES DISPLAYED DURING 76. (LOCAL). NORMA HUNT, CHAIRPERSON; MIAMI CARPENTERS UNION; 700 S ALHAMBRA CIRCLE; CORAL GABLES, FL 33146. (#2990-901).

DEC 1, '74. BICYCLE MARATHON. A SIX-HOUR BICYCLE MARATHON HELD YEARLY FOR FUN & PHYSICAL FITNESS. (ST-WIDE). BASHA SCHLAZER, REC PROGR; CITY OF MIAMI; 2600 S BAYSHORE DR; DINNER KEY, FL 33133. (#1531-901).

FEB 16, '75. BICENTENNIAL KICK-OFF IN SOUTH FLORIDA-A SALUTE TO AMERICAN FASHION. A TWO WEEK SERIES OF EVENTS ON THE THEMES OF AMERICAN CRAFTS & ARTISANS & A SALUTE TO AMERICAN FASHION WILL BE PRESENTED IN DISPLAYS OF MUSIC, COSTUMES, EXHIBITS & DEMONSTRATIONS. (LOCAL). JEANNIE NICHOLL; JORDAN MARSH; 1501 BISCAYNE BLVD; MIAMI, FL 33132. (#5228-901).

FEB 16, '75. BICENTENNIAL RUNNING MARATHON. GREATER MIAMI'S INVITATIONAL MARATHON. 26.3 MI COURSE WILL TEST RUNNERS' PHYSICAL ENDURANCE. HAS AAU SANCTION. (LOCAL). BASHA SCHLAZAR; CITY OF MIAMI; PO BOX 330-708; MIAMI, FL 33133. (#2991-901).

FEB 17 - 26, '75. A TWO WEEK DISPLAY OF CRAFTS & FASHIONS. A TWO WEEK SERIES OF EVENTS ON THE THEMES OF AMERICAN CRAFTS & ARTISANS & A SALUTE TO AMERICAN FASHION WILL BE PRESENTED IN DISPLAYS OF MUSIC, COSTUMES, EXHIBITS & DEMONSTRATIONS. (LOCAL). JEANNIE NICHOLL; JORDAN MARSH; 1501 BISCAYNE BLVD; MIAMI, FL 33132. (#5228-902).

MAR 17 - JUNE 28, '75. USS BICENTENNIAL BATTLESHIP - FROM MIAMI TO NEW YORK. TOUR, EXHIBIT. (REGN'L). CECIL GATES, COORDINATOR; LAND & SEA INTERNATIONAL, INTECH, INC & JOHNSON OUTBOARD MOTORS; 22942 DOLOROSA ST; WOODLAND HILL, CA 91364. (#200011-143).

APR 25 - 26, '75. COMMUNITY SYMPOSIUM. PARTICULAR REFERENCE TO THE GREEK-JEWISH-ITALIAN & POLISH AMERICANS PRESENTED IN CONJUNCTION THE NATIONAL ENDOWMENT FOR THE HUMANITIES & FLORIDA ENDOWMENT FOR THE HUMANITIES. AT PNA HOME 2144 NE 2 AVE MIAMI FL. (ST-WIDE). DR EDWARD D WYNOT; POLISH AMERICAN CONGRESS FLORIDA DIVISION; 2915 HUNTINGTON DR.; TALLAHASSEE, FL 32303. (#50185-1).

APR 27 - MAY 2, '75. VISIT OF SPANISH TRAINING VESSEL 'JUAN SEBASTIAN ELCANO'. AS AN OFFICIAL SPANISH SALUTE TO GREATER MIAMI'S PARTICIPATION IN THE BICENTENNIAL, THE VESSEL, 'JUAN SEBASTIAN ELCANO' WILL MAKE A 5 DAY VISIT IN APRIL, 1975. (INT'L). DON VICENTE RAMIREZ-MONTE; GOVERMENT OF SPAIN; 8550 PONCE DE LEON BLVD; CORAL GABLES, FL 33134. (#5195-501).

MAY 23 - 24, '75. PRESENTATION OF 'JOSEPHINE', A SPANISH-AMERICAN MUSICAL COMEDY. ORIGINAL SPANISH-AMERICAN PLAY WRITTEN BY TWO CUBAN AMERICANS ABOUT A LOVE AFFAIR BETWEEN TWO PEOPLE OF DIFFERENT ETHNIC & CULTURAL BACKGROUNDS. AT DADE COUNTY AUDITORIUM, MIAMI, FL. (LOCAL). OSVALDO FARRES, AUTHOR; OSVALDO FARRES AND PEDRO ROMAN; 6871 S W 32ND TERRACE; MIAMI, FL 33155. (#5210-501).

MAY 25, '75. INTERNATIONAL BALL DURING INTERNATIONAL FOLK FESTIVAL. INTERNATIONAL FOLK FESTIVAL OF MIAMI, FLA. THIS MIAMI FESTIVAL ENCOMPASSES FOLK MUSIC, ARTS & CRAFTS, FOOD OF ALL NATIONS & ETHNIC GROUPS. INCLUDES REGATTA, BICYCLE TOUR, CHESSTOURNAMENT, AND A PARADE OF NATIONS. (INT'L). MORTY FREEDMAN, DIRECTOR; CITY OF MIAMI; 2539 S BAYSHORE DR; MIAMI, FL 33129. (#1528-501).

MAY 26, '75. INTERNATIONAL SOCCER TOURNAMENT. INTERNATIONAL FOLK FESTIVAL OF MIAMI, FLA. THIS MIAMI FESTIVAL ENCOMPASSES FOLK MUSIC, ARTS & CRAFTS, FOOD OF ALL NATIONS & ETHNIC GROUPS. INCLUDES REGATTA, BICYCLE TOUR, CHESSTOURNAMENT, AND A PARADE OF NATIONS. (INT'L). MORTY FREEDMAN, DIRECTOR; CITY OF MIAMI; 2539 S BAYSHORE DR; MIAMI, FL 33129. (#1528-502).

MAY 27 - 30, '75. INTERNATIONAL TRAVEL FILM SHOW. INTERNATIONAL FOLK FESTIVAL OF MIAMI, FLA. THIS MIAMI FESTIVAL ENCOMPASSES FOLK MUSIC, ARTS & CRAFTS, FOOD OF ALL NATIONS & ETHNIC GROUPS. INCLUDES REGATTA, BICYCLE TOUR, CHESSTOURNAMENT, AND A PARADE OF NATIONS. (INT'L). MORTY FREEDMAN, DIRECTOR; CITY OF MIAMI; 2539 S BAYSHORE DR; MIAMI, FL 33129. (#1528-504).

MAY 27 - JUNE 1, '75. FINE ARTS & CRAFTS EXHIBITS AT INTERNATIONAL FOLK FESTIVAL. INTERNATIONAL FOLK FESTIVAL OF MIAMI, FLA. THIS MIAMI FESTIVAL ENCOMPASSES FOLK MUSIC, ARTS & CRAFTS, FOOD OF ALL NATIONS & ETHNIC GROUPS. INCLUDES REGATTA, BICYCLE TOUR, CHESSTOURNAMENT, AND A PARADE OF NATIONS. (INT'L). MORTY FREEDMAN, DIRECTOR; CITY OF MIAMI; 2539 S BAYSHORE DR; MIAMI, FL 33129. (#1528-503).

MAY 28, '75. INTERNATIONAL COSTUME SHOW. INTERNATIONAL FOLK FESTIVAL OF MIAMI, FLA. THIS MIAMI FESTIVAL ENCOMPASSES FOLK MUSIC, ARTS & CRAFTS, FOOD OF ALL NATIONS & ETHNIC GROUPS. INCLUDES REGATTA, BICYCLE TOUR, CHESSTOURNAMENT, AND A PARADE OF NATIONS. (INT'L). MORTY FREEDMAN, DIRECTOR; CITY OF MIAMI; 2539 S BAYSHORE DR; MIAMI, FL 33129. (#1528-505).

MAY 28 - JUNE 1, '75. SINGERS, DANCERS & INSTRUMENTALISTS AT INTL FOLK FESTIVAL. INTERNATIONAL FOLK FESTIVAL OF MIAMI, FLA. THIS MIAMI FESTIVAL ENCOMPASSES FOLK MUSIC, ARTS & CRAFTS, FOOD OF ALL NATIONS & ETHNIC GROUPS. INCLUDES REGATTA, BICYCLE TOUR, CHESSTOURNAMENT, AND A PARADE OF NATIONS. (INT'L). MORTY FREEDMAN, DIRECTOR; CITY OF MIAMI; 2539 S BAYSHORE DR; MIAMI, FL 33129. (#1528-506).

MAY 29 - JUNE 1, '75. FOODS OF THE NATIONS FEAST. INTERNATIONAL FOLK FESTIVAL OF MIAMI, FLA. THIS MIAMI FESTIVAL ENCOMPASSES FOLK MUSIC, ARTS & CRAFTS, FOOD OF ALL NATIONS & ETHNIC GROUPS. INCLUDES REGATTA, BICYCLE TOUR, CHESSTOURNAMENT, AND A PARADE OF NATIONS. (INT'L). MORTY FREEDMAN, DIRECTOR; CITY OF MIAMI; 2539 S BAYSHORE DR; MIAMI, FL 33129. (#1528-507).

MAY 29 - JUNE 1, '75. INTERNATIONAL BAZAAR. INTERNATIONAL FOLK FESTIVAL OF MIAMI, FLA. THIS MIAMI FESTIVAL ENCOMPASSES FOLK MUSIC, ARTS & CRAFTS, FOOD OF ALL NATIONS & ETHNIC GROUPS. INCLUDES REGATTA, BICYCLE TOUR, CHESSTOURNAMENT, AND A PARADE OF NATIONS. (INT'L). MORTY FREEDMAN, DIRECTOR; CITY OF MIAMI; 2539 S BAYSHORE DR; MIAMI, FL 33129. (#1528-508).

MAY 31, '75. PARADE OF NATIONS AT INTERNATIONAL FOLK FESTIVAL. INTERNATIONAL FOLK FESTIVAL OF MIAMI, FLA. THIS MIAMI FESTIVAL ENCOMPASSES FOLK MUSIC, ARTS & CRAFTS, FOOD OF ALL NATIONS & ETHNIC GROUPS. INCLUDES REGATTA, BICYCLE TOUR, CHESSTOURNAMENT, AND A PARADE OF NATIONS. (INT'L). MORTY FREEDMAN, DIRECTOR; CITY OF MIAMI; 2539 S BAYSHORE DR; MIAMI, FL 33129. (#1528-509).

JULY 4, '75. BICYCLE DECORATING CONTEST - JEFFERSON NAT'L BANK KENDALL. FOURTH OF JULY EXTRAVAGANZA OF MIAMI. EVERY YEAR, EACH OF THE 26 MUNICIPALITIES IN THE DADE COUNTY AREA WILL HOLD EVENTS & MANY COUNTY-WIDE ACTIVITIES SUCH AS A MASS SWEARING IN CEREMONY FOR NEW CITIZENS. (LOCAL). MS NORMA HUNT; THIRD CENTURY USA; PO BOX 1976; MIAMI, FL 33101. (#2997-504).

JULY 4, '75. KEY BISCAYNE 4TH OF JULY PARADE. FOURTH OF JULY EXTRAVAGANZA OF MIAMI. EVERY YEAR, EACH OF THE 26 MUNICIPALITIES IN THE DADE COUNTY AREA WILL HOLD EVENTS &

MIAMI — CONTINUED

MANY COUNTY-WIDE ACTIVITIES SUCH AS A MASS SWEARING IN CEREMONY FOR NEW CITIZENS. (LOCAL). MS NORMA HUNT; THIRD CENTURY USA; PO BOX 1976; MIAMI, FL 33101. (#2997-501).

JULY 12, '75. AMERICAN HERITAGE FESTIVAL. EXHIBIT, FESTIVAL AT CUTLER RIDGE REGIONAL SHOPPING CENTER, 20259 S DIXIE HWY. (LOCAL). CHARLES E COOPER, CHMN; SOUTH DADE CITIZEN'S BICENT COMMITTEE; 9921 SW 165 TERRACE; MIAMI, FL 33157. (#100549-1).

JULY 27 - AUG 8, '75. HEMISPHERIC CONGRESS FOR WOMEN '75. CONFERENCE AT SHERATON FOUR AMBASSADORS, BRICKELL AVE. (INT'L). GUI GOUVAERT, EXEC DIR; UNITED STATES COMMITTEE OF COOPERATION; 10 BISCAYNE BLVD, SUITE 200; MIAMI, FL 33132. (#200011-217).

JULY 29, '75. AMERICAN ISSUES FORUM, MIAMI, FL. PARTICIPATION ON THE LOCAL LEVEL IN THE NATIONAL AMERICAN ISSUES FORUM BY ENCOURAGING COMMUNITY ORGANIZATIONS TO ADOPT ONE OF THE THEMES IN DISCUSSIONS. (LOCAL). GLENN GOERKE; FLORIDA INTERNATIONAL UNIV; TAMIAMI TRAIL; MIAMI, FL 33199. (#12367-1).

AUG 8 - 12, '75. VISIT OF 'CHRISTIAN RADICH' - NORWEGIAN SAILING VESSEL. EXHIBIT. (LOCAL). ADM I J STEPHENS,; CHRISTIAN RADICH HOSPITALITY COMMITTEE; 1 SE 3RD AVE, C/O FIRST FEDERAL; MIAMI, FL 33131. (#100256-1).

SEPT 15 - DEC 1, '75. GEORGE C MARSHALL ESSAY CONTEST. COMPETITION. (LOCAL). DR CHARLES ASBURY; MIAMI-DADE COMMUNITY COLLEGE, GEORGE C MARSHALL RESEARCH FOUNDATION; 11380 NW 27TH AVE; MIAMI, FL 33167. (#200011-147).

SEPT 20, '75. FALL FESTIVAL SALUTES THE BICENTENNIAL. FESTIVAL AT FLORIDA INTERNATIONAL TAMIAMI CAMPUS. (LOCAL). JOSE EIRIZ, COORD; FLORIDA INTERNATIONAL UNIV STUDENT GOVERNMENT ASSOC; FIU-TAMIAMI TRAIL; MIAMI, FL 33141. (#200011-148).

SEPT 26, '75. BOSTON TEA PARTY: IMPROVISATIONAL MUSICAL REVUE OF AMERICAN HISTORY. LIVE PERFORMANCE. (LOCAL). JOHN ZEIEN, COORD; MIAMI-DADE COMMUNITY COLLEGE-SOUTH CAMPUS; 11011 SW 104TH ST; MIAMI, FL 33176. (#200011-144).

OCT 2, '75 - JUNE 30, '76. A YEAR OF AMERICAN MUSIC. SERIES OF MUSICAL PROGRAMS TO BE PRESENTED TO THE GENERAL PUBLIC THROUGHOUT 1975-76; WILL BE CENTERED AROUND AMERICAN COMPOSERS. AT FLORIDA INTERNATIONAL UNIV. (LOCAL). DR GLENN A GOERKE, CHMN; FIU-USA BICENTENNIAL MEETING; TAMIAMI TRAIL; MIAMI, FL 33199. (#102535-3).

OCT 6 - 12, '75. HISPANIC HERITAGE WEEK. A WEEK OF CULTURAL CEREMONIES AND ACTIVITIES TO HIGHLIGHT THE HISPANIC HERITAGE OF DADE COUNTY. (LOCAL). J A OJEDA JR; METROPOLITAN DADE COUNTY; 73 WEST FLAGLER ST RM 911; MIAMI, FL 33130. (#50072-1).

OCT 11 - 12, '75. SOCCER OPENING DAY: 75-76 SEASON SALUTE TO THE BICENTENNIAL. COMPETITION, PARADE AT CURTIS PARK, NW 30TH ST. (LOCAL). ALBERT F COLLARD; FLORIDA STATE SOCCER ASSOC; MIAMI INTL AIRPORT; MIAMI, FL 33148. (#102791-4).

NOV 8 - 9, '75. TOUR OF COCONUT GROVE BICYCLE RACE. EACH RACE HAS SEVERAL EVENTS FOR RIDER OF VARYING AGES AND ABILITY. DISTANCES RANGE FROM ONE TO 50 MILES. ALSO: BOOK/GUIDE/OTHER PUBLICATION. AT DOWNTOWN COCONUT GROVE. (LOCAL). DAVID BALKIN; COCONUT GROVE BICYCLE CLUB; 3043 GRAND AVE; MIAMI, FL 33133. (#2992-1).

NOV 13, '75. COLONIAL AMERICAN DINNER. 40 FOOT TREE LIT WITH LANTERNS REPRESENTING THE LIBERTY TREE. MENU: AUTHENTIC FARE FROM COLONIAL WILLIAMSBURG COOK BOOK. ALL PARTICIPANTS WILL BE COSTUMED APPROPRIATELY. AT BAY FRONT AUDITORIUM. (LOCAL). REV JOHN M PALMER; THE EPISCOPAL DIOCESE OF SOUTHEAST FLORIDA, THE YOUTH COMMISSION; 464 NE 16TH ST; MIAMI, FL 33132. (#50676-5).

NOV 14, '75. AWARDS TO SCHOOL CHILDREN FOR ART, MUSIC & DRAMA, BOX LUNCH ON GREEN. FESTIVAL, AWARD, CEREMONY, LIVE PERFORMANCE. (LOCAL). REV JOHN PALMER; YOUTH COMMISSION, EPISCOPALIAN DIOCESE OF SE FLORIDA; 464 NE 16TH ST; MIAMI, FL 33132. (#6189-502).

NOV 14, '75. EVENSONG-POSSIBLE GUEST PREACHER BISHOP OF LONDON. FOUR FREEDOMS FESTIVAL IN MIAMI, FLORIDA. A FAIR & FESTIVAL REFLECTING 18TH CENTURY ARTS, TRADES, MUSIC AND GENERAL LIFE WITH SPECIAL EMPHASIS ON THE FREEDOM OF WORSHIP. (LOCAL). REV JOHN PALMER; YOUTH COMMISSION, EPISCOPALIAN DIOCESE OF SE FLORIDA; 464 NE 16TH ST; MIAMI, FL 33132. (#6189-503).

NOV 14 - 15, '75. FOUR FREEDOMS FESTIVAL--A COLONIAL FAIR (PERIOD MUSIC, GAMES, FOOD). REVOLUTIONARY PERIOD BROUGHT TO LIFE IN CATHEDRAL SETTING. DRAMA, DANCING, MUSIC; EXHIBITS OF PERIOD ARTS & CRAFTS; GAMES; FOODS. PARTICIPATION BY ARTISANS, TRADESMEN, FOOD VENDORS. APPROPRIATE CONTESTS: HORSESHOES, PIE EATING, HOOP ROLLING. AT TRINITY CATHEDRAL, 464 N.E. 16 ST., MIAMI, FL. PARKING ADJACENT.. (REGN'L). REV. JOHN M. PALMER; THE EPISCOPAL DIOCESE OF SOUTHEAST FLORIDA, THE YOUTH COMMISSION; 464 N.E. 16 ST.; MIAMI, FL 33132. (#50676-1).

NOV 16, '75. BICENTENNIAL SERVICE, THE RIGHT REV GERALD ELLISON, BISHOP OF LONDON. CEREMONY AT TRINITY EPISCOPAL CATHEDRAL, 464 N E 16TH ST. (LOCAL). REV JOHN M PALMER; THE EPISCOPAL DIOCESE OF SOUTHEAST FLORIDA, THE YOUTH COMMISSION; 464 NE 16TH ST; MIAMI, FL 33132. (#102067-1).

NOV 30 - DEC 6, '75. A SALUTE TO THE BLACK HERITAGE - 200 YEARS PLUS. FESTIVAL, PARADE, RADIO/TV AT DADE COUNTY AUDITORIUM, ORANGE BOWL. (ST-WIDE). CLINTON E BROWN, CHAIRMAN; FAMU MIAMI ALUMNI CHAPTER AND FLORIDA A&M UNIVERSITY; 19200 NW 19TH AVE; MIAMI, FL 33055. (#103285-5).

DEC 6 - 7, '75. FIRST FLORIDA CONFERENCE ON ART THERAPY. CONFERENCE AT UNIVERSITY OF MIAMI, FLAMINGO BALLROOM. (LOCAL). MRS IRA CUTLER, COORD; AMERICAN ART THERAPY ASSOC, INC; 12940 SW 73RD AVE; MIAMI, FL 33156. (#200011-145).

DEC 7, '75. PHOTOGRAPHY EXPOSED. EXHIBIT AT ENCHANTED FOREST, NE 135 ST & 16TH AVE. (LOCAL). STEPHEN P EVANS; THIRD CENTURY USA; 10625 SW 60TH ST; MIAMI, FL 33173. (#102791-1).

DEC 14, '75. FASHION, THE AMERICAN WAY OF LIFE - PAST AND PRESENT. MUSIC, COMMENTARY & FASHIONS ILLUSTRATING AMER FASHION PAST AND PRESENT AND REASONS FOR THE TRENDS. AT 777 NW 72ND AVE. (LOCAL). MS JAY KINZER, DIRECTOR; THE FASHION GROUP INC OF MIAMI; 777 NW 72ND AVE; MIAMI, FL 33126. (#1541-1).

DEC 22, '75 - JAN 4, '76. AMERICAN BICENTENNIAL FLORIDA EXHIBIT. EXHIBIT, RADIO/TV AT SE 2ND ST & BISCAYNE BLVD. (LOCAL). ANITA BJORK; THIRD CENTURY, USA; PO BOX 451976; MIAMI, FL 33145. (#100225-6).

DEC 27 - 29, '75. JUNIOR ORANGE BOWL SOCCER TOURNAMENT. COMPETITION AT DADE SOUTH COMMUNITY COLLEGE. (LOCAL). DANIEL S MCNAMARA, CHMN; ORANGE BOWL COMMITTEE; PO BOX 350748; MIAMI, FL 33135. (#1548-8).

DEC 28, '75. ORANGE BOWL NAVY-SAILING REGATTA. COMPETITION AT BISCAYNE BAY OFF KEY BISCAYNE. (LOCAL). DANIEL S MCNAMARA, CHMN; ORANGE BOWL COMMITTEE; PO BOX 350748; MIAMI, FL 33135. (#1548-9).

DEC 29, '75. ORANGE BOWL PRAYER BREAKFAST. CONFERENCE AT DUPONT PLAZA HOTEL. (LOCAL). DANIEL S MCNAMARA, DIR; ORANGE BOWL COMMITTEE; PO BOX 350748; MIAMI, FL 33135. (#1548-10).

DEC 31, '75. KING ORANGE JAMBOREE BICENTENNIAL PARADE - ODYSSEY TO FREEDOM. PARADE AT BISCAYNE BLVD. (ST-WIDE). DANIEL S MCNAMARA, CHMN; ORANGE BOWL COMMITTEE; PO BOX 350758; MIAMI, FL 33135. (#1548-12).

DEC 31, '75. ORANGE BOWL FESTIVAL '76. THE 1976 ORANGE BOWL FESTIVAL WILL HAVE A TOTAL BICENTENNIAL THEME, INCLUDING THE PARADE, HALFTIME, & ALL ACTIVITIES. WILL BE TELEVISED NATIONWIDE ON DEC. 31, 1975. (NAT'L). DANIEL S MCNAMARA, MGR; ORANGE BOWL COMMITTEE; 1400 NW 4TH ST; MIAMI, FL 33135. (#1548-1).

JAN 1, '76. 42ND ANNUAL ORANGE BOWL FOOTBALL CLASSIC. COMPETITION AT MIAMI ORANGE BOWL. (NAT'L). DANIEL S MCNAMARA, CHMN; ORANGE BOWL COMMITTEE; PO BOX 350748; MIAMI, FL 33135. (#1548-2).

JAN 2 - JULY 31, '76. 'FLORIDA: HERITAGE & HORIZONS' - CONCERT SERIES. A CONCERT SERIES FROM JAN TO JULY, 1976 EXEMPLIFYING MIAMI'S CULTURAL AND ETHNIC CONTRIBUTIONS TO FLORIDA. THROUGH A COMBINATION OF MODERN DANCE, MUSIC & A MULTIMEDIA PROGRAM. (ST-WIDE). WILLIAM P LORD, DIR; FUSION - THE MODERN DANCE COMPANY OF MIAMI, INC; 4137 MALAGA AVE; CORAL GABLES, FL 33133. (#5223-1).

JAN 5 - 30, '76. EXHIBITION OF AMERICAN PRINTMAKERS. EXHIBIT AT LIBRARY GALLERY, 115TH ST. (LOCAL). JOSEPH M RUFFO, COORD; DIVISION OF FINE ARTS, BARRY COLLEGE; 11300 NE 2ND AVE; MIAMI SHORES, FL 33161. (#200011-149).

JAN 17, '76. 'OTELLO': A DRAMATIC ITALIAN OPERA. ALL OPERAS PRODUCED BY THE GREATER MIAMI OPERA ASSOC WILL HAVE PERFORMANCES IN THE ORIGINAL LANGUAGE & IN ENGLISH. THE ENGLISH SHOWSWILL BE AVAILABLE AT POPULAR PRICES FOR THE GENERAL PUBLIC. AT DADE COUNTY AUDITORIUM, 2901 W FLAGLER, MIAMI. (LOCAL). WARREN BROOME; THE GREATER MIAMI OPERA ASSOC; 1200 CORAL; MIAMI, FL 33129. (#1535-5).

JAN 18, '76. SUPERBOWL X - PROFESSIONAL FOOTBALL CHAMPIONSHIP GAME. TENTH ANNUAL SUPERBOWL WILL HAVE BICENTENNIAL EMPHASIS IN THEME AND PRODUCTION. (NAT'L). LOU PRICE, DIRECTOR; CITY OF MIAMI DEPT OF PUBLICITY & TOURISM; 499 BISCAYNE BLVD; MIAMI, FL 33132. (#1549-1).

JAN 21, '76. 'OTELLO': A DRAMATIC ITALIAN OPERA. ALL OPERAS PRODUCED BY THE GREATER MIAMI OPERA ASSOC WILL HAVE PERFORMANCES IN THE ORIGINAL LANGUAGE & IN ENGLISH. THE ENGLISH SHOWSWILL BE AVAILABLE AT POPULAR PRICES FOR THE GENERAL PUBLIC. AT DADE COUNTY AUDITORIUM. (LOCAL). WARREN BROOME; THE GREATER MIAMI OPERA ASSOC.; 1200 CORAL WAY; MIAMI, FL 33129. (#1535-6).

JAN 24, '76. 'OTELLO': A DRAMATIC ITALIAN OPERA. ALL OPERAS PRODUCED BY THE GREATER MIAMI OPERA ASSOC WILL HAVE PERFORMANCES IN THE ORIGINAL LANGUAGE & IN ENGLISH. THE ENGLISH SHOWSWILL BE AVAILABLE AT POPULAR PRICES FOR THE GENERAL PUBLIC. AT MIAMI BEACH THEATRE OF PERFORMING ARTS. (LOCAL). WARREN BROOME; THE GREATER MIAMI OPERA ASSOC.; 1200 CORAL WAY; MIAMI, FL 33129. (#1535-7).

JAN 24 - JULY 4, '76. BICENTENNIAL AMATEUR RADIO QSL CONTEST. AMATEURS OUTSIDE OF MIAMI WILL COMPETE FOR QSL CARDS, WHICH PROVE CONTACT WITH A MIAMI STATION; THE WINNER MUST HAVE MORE QSL CARDS THAN ANY OTHER HAM OPERATORS. THE MAYOR OF THE CITY OF MIAMI WILL KICK OFF THE CONTEST ON JAN 24, 1976. AT MIAMI AUDITORIUM AND AMATEUR WORLD RADIO PUBLICATIONS. (INT'L). STEVEN KAPLAN, PROJ DIR; DADE COUNTY AMATEUR RADIO SERVICE CORPS; 17111 NE 6TH AVE; N MIAMI BEACH, FL 33162. (#103285-2).

JAN 25, '76. MIAMI'S BICYCLE MARATHON. ANNUAL FUN & FITNESS DAY-LONG OUTING INCLUDING CYCLING, MUSIC, & PICNICS. AT BISCAYNE BLVD, SW 2ND ST TO NW 4TH ST, INCLUDING CHOPIN PLAZA.. (LOCAL). BASHA SCHLAZAR, DIRECTOR; DEPT OF PARKS & RECREATION, MIAMI & PEPSI-COLA CO; PO BOX 330-708; MIAMI, FL 33133. (#3008-1).

JAN 25 - APR 7, '76. BICENTENNIAL CLASSICAL OPERA SERIES OF MIAMI. INCLUDES 'OTHELLO', 'DON PASQUALE', 'THAIS', 'TOSCA', IN BOTH ENGLISH & ITALIAN PERFORMANCES. THERE WILL BE A TOTAL OF 23 PERFORMANCES. FOR DETAILS & DATES, CONTACT WALTER PALEVODA. AT DADE COUNTY AUDITORIUM & MIAMI BEACH THEATRE OF THE PERFORMING ARTS. (ST-WIDE). ROBERT HERMAN, GEN MGR; GREATER MIAMI OPERA ASSOC; 1200 CORAL WAY; MIAMI, FL 33145. (#1535-1).

JAN 28 - APR 1, '76. AMERICAN ISSUES FORUM. FACULTY DISCUSSION SERIES ON AMERICAN ISSUES FORUM TOPICS; FACULTY MEMBERS WITH EXPERTISE IN TOPICS UNDER DISCUSSION WILL PRESENT SEMINARS FOR THE CAMPUS COMMUNITY. (LOCAL). DR CHARLES SEVICK; BARRY COLLEGE; 11300 NE 2ND AVE; MIAMI, FL 33161. (#105156-3).

JAN 29, '76. 'WHO'S AFRAID OF VIRGINIA WOOLF?', THEATRE PRODUCTION. LIVE PERFORMANCE AT FLORIDA INTERNATIONAL UNIV. (LOCAL). DR GLENN A GOERKE, CHMN; FIU-USA BICENTENNIAL MEETING; TAMIAMI TRAIL; MIAMI, FL 33199. (#102535-2).

JAN 31 - FEB 2, '76. UNITED STATES ARMED FORCES BICENTENNIAL CARAVAN. CARAVAN IS COMPOSED OF EXHIBIT VANS FOR EACH MILITARY SERVICE. PROJECT THEME IS 'HISTORY OF THE ARMED FORCES AND THEIR CONTRIBUTIONS TO THE NATION'. AT DINNER KEY. (LOCAL). BONNY BLACK; US ARMED FORCES BICENTENNIAL EXHIBIT VANS PROJECT; BOX 01-1976; MIAMI, FL 33101. (#1775-428).

FEB 2 - 27, '76. BLACK PIONEERS PHOTOGRAPHIC ARCHIVES & ORAL HISTORY COLLECTION. GUIDED TOUR OF GALLERY INCLUDES SPECIAL EXHIBIT OF PHOTOGRAPHS & A SLIDE PRESENTATION RELATING EXPERIENCES OF EARLY BLACK SETTLERS IN DADE COUNTY FROM 1896 TO 1946. EXHIBIT WILL INCLUDE TAPE RECORDINGS. AT HISTORICAL MUSEUM OF SOUTHERN FLORIDA. (LOCAL). PAUL HANSOM, CONSULTANT; THE SCHOOL BOARD OF DADE COUNTY, FLORIDA; 1444 BISCAYNE BLVD, SUITE 309; MIAMI, FL 33132. (#50525-1).

FEB 6 - 8, '76. 'ACT ONE' - A THEATRICAL PRODUCTION. A THEATRICAL PRODUCTION TO BE PRESENTED AT BISCAYNE COLLEGE. (LOCAL). DR HELEN JACOBSTEIN; BISCAYNE COLLEGE BICENTENNIAL COMMITTEE; 16400 NW 32ND AVE; MIAMI, FL 33054. (#11670-1).

FEB 6 - 8, '76. BISCAYNE COLLEGE BICENTENNIAL BASH. PROJECT WILL INCLUDE A WEEKEND CELEBRATION IN FEBRUARY 1976. AT BISCAYNE COLLEGE CAMPUS. (LOCAL). DR HELEN JACOBSTEIN; BISCAYNE COLLEGE BICENTENNIAL COMMITTEE; 16400 NW 32ND AVE; MIAMI, FL 33054. (#11667-1).

FEB 9 - 16, '76. 'MARY MCLEOD BETHUNE', ESSAY, POSTER, POEM OR POETRY CONTEST. COMPETITION AT DADE COUNTY SCHOOLS, ELEMENTARY, JUNIOR HIGH, SENIOR HIGH. (LOCAL). EUNICE LIBERTY, PRESIDENT; NATIONAL COUNCIL OF NEGRO WOMEN, GREATER MIAMI; 1797 NW 52ND ST; MIAMI, FL 33140. (#200011-150).

FEB 10 - 13, '76. BLACK EXPRESSION WEEK - ART AND CULTURE EXHIBITION. EXHIBIT. (LOCAL). H CLAYTON HAMILTON, PRES; UNITED BLACK STUDENTS OF MIAMI DADE COMMUNITY COLLEGE SOUTH; 1011 SW 104TH ST; MIAMI, FL 33156. (#200011-151).

FEB 12, '76. 'ANILLOS PARA UNA DAMA' - PLAY. LIVE PERFORMANCE AT SAA. (LOCAL). SALVADOR UGARTE, COORD; 'LAS MASCARAS' THEATRE; 957 SW 27TH AVE; MIAMI, FL 33135. (#200011-152).

FEB 13 - 15, '76. COCONUT GROVE ARTS FESTIVAL. THREE DAY SIDEWALK ART SHOW WITH EMPHASIS ON BICENTENNIAL IN 1976. THIS ANNUAL EVENT, LARGEST IN THE COUNTRY, ATTRACTS ARTISTS FROM ACROSS THE COUNTRY AND FROM OTHER NATIONS. AT MCFARLANE COMMODORE PLAZA, MIAMI'S MAIN STREET. (REGN'L). MAYSIE BELLER; COCUNUT GROVE ASSOCIATION, INC; PO BOX 757; COCONUT GROVE, FL 33133. (#2999-1).

FEB 16, '76. 'DON PASQUALE': AN ITALIAN COMEDY OPERA. ALL OPERAS PRODUCED BY THE GREATER MIAMI OPERA ASSOC WILL HAVE PERFORMANCES IN THE ORIGINAL LANGUAGE & IN ENGLISH. THE ENGLISH SHOWSWILL BE AVAILABLE AT POPULAR PRICES FOR THE GENERAL PUBLIC. AT DADE COUNTY AUDITORIUM, 2901 W FLAGLER, MIAMI. (LOCAL). WARREN BROOME; THE GREATER MIAMI OPERA ASSOC.; 1200 CORAL WAY; MIAMI, FL 33129. (#1535-8).

FEB 18, '76. 'DON PASQUALE': AN ITALIAN COMEDY OPERA. ALL OPERAS PRODUCED BY THE GREATER MIAMI OPERA ASSOC WILL HAVE PERFORMANCES IN THE ORIGINAL LANGUAGE & IN ENGLISH. THE ENGLISH SHOWSWILL BE AVAILABLE AT POPULAR PRICES FOR THE GENERAL PUBLIC. AT THE MIAMI THEATRE OF THE PERFORMING ARTS. (LOCAL). WARREN BROOME; THE GREATER MIAMI OPERA ASSOC.; 1200 CORAL WAY; MIAMI, FL 33129. (#1535-13).

FEB 19, '76. 'A CANCER UPDATE' - SEMINAR. EXHIBIT, SEMINAR AT MAILMAN CENTER, UNIVERSITY OF MIAMI, JACKSON MEMORIAL. (LOCAL). LARRY STRUM, COORD; COMPREHENSIVE CANCER CENTER FOR THE STATE OF FLORIDA; 1400 NW 10TH AVE; MIAMI, FL 33136. (#200011-153).

FEB 19, '76 - CONTINUING . POLITICS ON PARADE. FORUM PROGRAM WILL BE COMPOSED OF CANDIDATES FOR PUBLIC OFFICE. (LOCAL). DR CHAS ASBURY, ASST DIR; MIAMI-DADE COMMUNITY COLLEGE, NORTH CAMPUS; 11380 NW 27TH AVE; MIAMI, FL 33167. (#106436-1).

MIAMI — CONTINUED

FEB 21, '76. 'AMERICAN WOMAN - ON THE GO FROM 1776-1976'. SHOW FEATURING WOMEN MODELING AUTHENTIC PERIOD DRESS; NARRATIVE POINTING OUT INTERESTING FACTS ABOUT AMERICAN WOMEN - THEIR CUSTOMS, HOME LIFE AND PROGRESS THROUGHOUT OUR 200-YEAR HISTORY. AT CUTLER RIDGE SHOPPING CENTER. (LOCAL). MRS EARL F WARFORD, CHMN; 7 FEDERATED WOMEN'S CLUBS; 9635 DOMINICAN DR; MIAMI, FL 33189. (#101024-1).

FEB 21, '76. 'DON PASQUALE': AN ITALIAN COMEDY OPERA. ALL OPERAS PRODUCED BY THE GREATER MIAMI OPERA ASSOC WILL HAVE PERFORMANCES IN THE ORIGINAL LANGUAGE & IN ENGLISH. THE ENGLISH SHOWSWILL BE AVAILABLE AT POPULAR PRICES FOR THE GENERAL PUBLIC. AT THE DADE COUNTY AUDITORIUM. (LOCAL). WARREN BROOME; THE GREATER MIAMI OPERA ASSOC; 1200 CORAL WAY; MIAMI, FL 33129. (#1535-9).

FEB 21 - 22, '76. CAMPUS JAMBOREE '76. ANNUAL CAMPUS FESTIVAL; 1976 THEME WILL BE A BICENTENNIAL CELEBRATION. (LOCAL). BRIDGET DAVIS, CHAIRMAN; STUDENT GOVERNMENT ASSOC, BARRY COLLEGE; 11300 NE 2ND AVE; MIAMI, FL 33161. (#105156-5).

FEB 22, '76. 'DON PASQUALE'; AN ENGLISH FAMILY, COMEDY OPERA. THIS IS A COMEDY OPERA, PERFORMED IN THE ENGLISH LANGUAGE FOR THE ENJOYMENT OF THE AMERICAN ENGLISH-SPEAKING FAMILY. AT DADE COUNTY AUDITORIUM 2901 W FLAGLER. (LOCAL). WARREN BROOME; THE GREATER MIAMI OPERA ASSOC.; 1200 CORAL WAY; MIAMI, FL 33129. (#1535-2).

FEB 22 - 29, '76. 'YESTERDAY'S CRAFTS ALIVE TODAY, FOR TOMORROW', EXHIBITION. EXHIBIT. (ST-WIDE). EISIE KRONENFIELD, INST; ELDERLY SERVICE DIVISION-IMPACT PROGRAM; 140 W FLAGLER ST; MIAMI, FL 33130. (#200011-154).

FEB 23 - 27, '76. BICENTENNIAL WEEK - ELEMENTARY SCHOOL PROGRAM. PARADE, LIVE PERFORMANCE AT SCHOOL AND SURROUNDING NEIGHBORHOOD. (LOCAL). PAULA CALLAHAN, COORD; EDISON PARK ELEMENTARY SCHOOL; 500 NW 67TH ST; MIAMI, FL 33150. (#200011-155).

FEB 25, '76. BICENTENNIAL SHOW THROUGH HISTORY. LIVE PERFORMANCE AT SCHOOL FOOTBALL FIELD. (LOCAL). MIMI MEYERSON, COORD; ROCKWAY ELEMENTARY; 2790 SW 93RD COURT; MIAMI, FL 33156. (#200011-156).

MAR 2, '76. 'FIRST LADIES ON PARADE' - PRESENTATION OF INAUGURAL BALL GOWNS. EXHIBIT AT DUPONT PLAZA. (LOCAL). BILL STECKLY; WESTMINSTER CHRISTIAN SCHOOL; 6855 SW 152ND ST; MIAMI, FL 33157. (#105578-1).

MAR 6, '76. MARCH OF DIMES SUPERWALK '76. FESTIVAL AT THE ROUTE STARTS AT THE ORANGE BOWL. (LOCAL). DEE TALTY, CHMN; MARCH OF DIMES; 2917 NW 7TH ST; MIAMI, FL 33125. (#104566-13).

MAR 8, '76. 'THAIS': A FRENCH OPERA. ALL OPERAS PRODUCED BY THE GREATER MIAMI OPERA ASSOC WILL HAVE PERFORMANCES IN THE ORIGINAL LANGUAGE & IN ENGLISH. THE ENGLISH SHOWSWILL BE AVAILABLE AT POPULAR PRICES FOR THE GENERAL PUBLIC. AT THE DADE COUNTY AUDITORIUM. (LOCAL). WARREN BROOME; THE GREATER MIAMI OPERA ASSOC.; 1200 CORAL WAY; MIAMI, FL 33129. (#1535-11).

MAR 8 - 14, '76. 1976 DORAL EASTERN OPEN GOLF TOURNAMENT. COMPETITION AT 'BLUE MONSTER' COURSE, DORAL COUNTRY CLUB. (REGN'L). JOHN DEROSE, CHMN; EASTERN AIRLINES AND DORAL COUNTRY CLUB; MIAMI INTERNATIONAL AIRPORT; MIAMI, FL 33148. (#105578-3).

MAR 10, '76. 'THAIS': A FRENCH OPERA. ALL OPERAS PRODUCED BY THE GREATER MIAMI OPERA ASSOC WILL HAVE PERFORMANCES IN THE ORIGINAL LANGUAGE & IN ENGLISH. THE ENGLISH SHOWSWILL BE AVAILABLE AT POPULAR PRICES FOR THE GENERAL PUBLIC. AT THE MIAMI BEACH THEATRE OF PERFORMING ARTS. (LOCAL). WARREN BROOME; THE GREATER MIAMI OPERA ASSOC.; 1200 CORAL WAY; MIAMI, FL 33129. (#1535-12).

MAR 11 - 15, '76. BICENTENNIAL MURAL DISPLAY - MURAL PAINTED ON GROUND. EXHIBIT. (LOCAL). JORGE PUPO, PROJ CHMN; MIAMI-DADE COMMUNITY COLLEGE; 300 NE 2ND AVE; MIAMI, FL 33132. (#200011-157).

MAR 12 - 13, '76. 'RING IT AGAIN SAM' - THEATRE PERFORMANCE. LIVE PERFORMANCE AT GUSSMAN CULTURAL CENTER FOR THE PERFORMING ARTS. (LOCAL). MILLICENT CALLOBRE, CHWMN; CORAL GABLES JUNIOR WOMEN'S CLUB; 2351 SW 23RD AVE; MIAMI, FL 33145. (#104566-14).

MAR 13, '76. PERIWINKLE BICENTENNIAL FUN DAY. FESTIVAL AT GRIFFING PARK, NE 123RD ST & W DIXIE HWY. (LOCAL). SUE DAUBERT, COORD; GIRL SCOUT COUNCIL OF TROPICAL FLORIDA, INC; 1110 NW 129TH ST; MIAMI, FL 33168. (#200011-158).

MAR 13, '76. 'THAIS': A FRENCH OPERA. ALL OPERAS PRODUCED BY THE GREATER MIAMI OPERA ASSOC WILL HAVE PERFORMANCES IN THE ORIGINAL LANGUAGE & IN ENGLISH. THE ENGLISH SHOWSWILL BE AVAILABLE AT POPULAR PRICES FOR THE GENERAL PUBLIC. AT THE DADE COUNTY AUDITORIUM. (LOCAL). WARREN BROOME; THE GREATER MIAMI OPERA ASSOC.; 120 CORAL WAY; MIAMI, FL 33129. (#1535-10).

MAR 13 - 14, '76. HOME FURNISHING INDUSTRY BICENTENNIAL CELEBRATION. MANY FESTIVITIES TO PROMOTE CONSUMER AWARENESS AND EDUCATION. SUNDAY HOURS: 12:00 PM TO 7:00PM. AT 39TH & 40TH STS - FROM N MIAMI AVE TO NE 2ND AVE. (ST-WIDE). BOB RUBINSTEIN, DIR; AMERICAN SOCIETY OF INTERIOR DESIGNERS; 3801 N MIAMI AVE; MIAMI, FL 33137. (#102799-1).

MAR 14, '76. 'THAIS'; AN ENGLISH OPERA PERFORMANCE. ALL OPERAS PRODUCED BY THE GREATER MIAMI OPERA ASSOC WILL HAVE PERFORMANCES IN THE ORIGINAL LANGUAGE & IN ENGLISH. THE ENGLISH SHOWSWILL BE AVAILABLE AT POPULAR PRICES FOR THE GENERAL PUBLIC. THIS CAN BE DESCRIBED AS AN EXOCTIC OPERA PERFORMED IN ENGLISH. AT DADE COUNTY AUDITORIUM, 2901 W FLAGLER, MIAMI. (LOCAL). WARREN BROOME; THE GREATER MIAMI OPERA ASSOC; 1200 CORAL WAY; MIAMI, FL 33129. (#1535-3).

MAR 16, '76. 'SO PROUDLY WE HAIL', A BICENTENNIAL CELEBRATION. FESTIVAL, CEREMONY AT SCHOOL CAFETERIA. (LOCAL). IRMA KOFF, COORDINATOR; BANYAN ELEMENTARY SCHOOL; 3060 SW 85TH AVE; MIAMI, FL 33155. (#103843-22).

MAR 18 - 28, '76. THIRD CENTURY USA YOUTH FAIR. EXHIBITS MUST CONSIST OF YOUTH COMMUNICATING TO YOUTH ABOUT THEIR HOPES & FEARS OF THE FUTURE, LEARNING NEW SKILLS, OCCUPATIONS AND LIFESTYLES. EXHIBITS MAY INCLUDE MODELS & MACHINES. AT YOUTH FAIRGROUNDS, 10901 CORAL WAY. (REGN'L). BONNY BLACK, DIRECTOR; DADE COUNTY YOUTH FAIR; 3361 S W 3RD AVE; MIAMI, FL 33145. (#5215-1).

MAR 20, '76. 'BLACK EXPO': EXHIBITION OF BLACK BUSINESS ACHIEVEMENT. EXHIBIT AT FLORIDA MEMORIAL COLLEGE, NW 42ND AVE. (LOCAL). GAYLENE PERRAULT, COORD; CITIZEN'S UNITED AGAINST SICKLE CELL DISEASE; 800 BRICKELL PLAZA; MIAMI, FL 33131. (#200011-159).

MAR 20 - 21, '76. 'MAZOWSZE' - A POLISH FOLKLORE DANCE GROUP. LIVE PERFORMANCE AT DADE COUNTY AUDITORIUM, 2901 W FLAGLER ST. (LOCAL). BLANKA ROSENSTIAL, CHMN; AMERICAN INSTITUTE OF POLISH CULTURE; 1000 BRICKELL AVE, SUITE 1110; MIAMI, FL 33131. (#100256-3).

MAR 21 - 22, '76. MAZOWSZE FOLKLORIC DANCE GROUP. LIVE PERFORMANCE. (INT'L). CULTURAL ATTACHE; EMBASSY OF POLAND; 2640 16TH ST; WASHINGTON, DC 20009. (#200011-315).

MAR 24 - 27, '76. '76 NATIONAL GOLDEN GLOVES TOURNAMENT OF CHAMPIONS. 32 FRANCHISE HOLDERS FROM US COMPETING FOR 1976 GOLDEN GLOVES TITLE. CHAMPIONS WILL BE PROSPECTS FOR US IN THE OLYMPICS. AT 2600 S BAYSHORE DR. (NAT'L). RICK LEE, DIRECTOR; GOLDEN GLOVES ALUMNI ASSOC; 2600 S BAYSHORE DR; MIAMI, FL 33133. (#2989-1).

MAR 26 - 27, '76. ANNUAL SOUTHERN BADMINTON ASSOCIATION - OPEN CHAMPIONSHIPS. COMPETITION AT MIAMI DADE JR COLLEGE - KENNEDY GYM. (LOCAL). W A GRAHAM, COORD; THE GRAHAM COMPANY; 14200 NW 60TH AVE; MIAMI LAKES, FL 33014. (#103285-4).

APR 1 - 10, '76. 'GUYS AND DOLLS' THEATRE PRODUCTION. LIVE PERFORMANCE AT PAWLEY CREATIVE ARTS CENTER, ROOM 5121. (LOCAL). JOHN ALEXANDER; MIAMI DADE COMMUNITY COLLEGE; 11380 NW 27 AVE; MIAMI, FL 33167. (#200011-160).

APR 3, '76. CONVOCATION ON GROWING UP IN AMERICA. FORUM ON PROBLEMS OF BICULTURAL IDENTITY ENCOUNTERED BY AMERICAN YOUTH OF MINORITY DESCENT IN MIAMI. WILL EXPLORE THE QUESTIONS: IS THERE A MAJORITY? WHEN HAS ONE GROWN UP?. (LOCAL). SISTER CLARE BEAUBIEN; BARRY COLLEGE DEPT OF FAMILY AND CONSUMER SCIENCE; 11300 NE 2ND AVE; MIAMI, FL 33161. (#105156-4).

APR 3 - JUNE 19, '76. 'MENTAL HEALTH IS FOR EVERYONE' - SEMINAR SERIES. SEMINAR AT FIU-DEUXIEME MAISON; CHILDREN'S PSYCHIATRIC CENTER, INC. (LOCAL). MS ANN FORTEZA, DIR; THE CHILDREN'S PSYCHIATRIC CENTER, INC; 901 NW 17TH ST; MIAMI, FL 33136. (#104566-11).

APR 5, '76. 'TOSCA': AN ITALIAN OPERA. ALL OPERAS PRODUCED BY THE GREATER MIAMI OPERA ASSOC WILL HAVE PERFORMANCES IN THE ORIGINAL LANGUAGE & IN ENGLISH. THE ENGLISH SHOWSWILL BE AVAILABLE AT POPULAR PRICES FOR THE GENERAL PUBLIC. AT THE DADE COUNTY AUDITORIUM. (LOCAL). WARREN BROOME; THE GREATER MIAMI OPERA ASSOC; 1200 CORAL WAY; MIAMI, FL 33129. (#1535-14).

APR 7, '76. 'TOSCA': AN ITALIAN OPERA. ALL OPERAS PRODUCED BY THE GREATER MIAMI OPERA ASSOC WILL HAVE PERFORMANCES IN THE ORIGINAL LANGUAGE & IN ENGLISH. THE ENGLISH SHOWSWILL BE AVAILABLE AT POPULAR PRICES FOR THE GENERAL PUBLIC. AT THE MIAMI BEACH OF THE PERFORMING ARTS. (LOCAL). WARREN BROOME; THE GREATER MIAMI OPERA ASSOC; 1200 CORAL WAY; MIAMI, FL 33129. (#1535-16).

APR 10, '76. 'TOSCA': AN ITALIAN OPERA. ALL OPERAS PRODUCED BY THE GREATER MIAMI OPERA ASSOC WILL HAVE PERFORMANCES IN THE ORIGINAL LANGUAGE & IN ENGLISH. THE ENGLISH SHOWSWILL BE AVAILABLE AT POPULAR PRICES FOR THE GENERAL PUBLIC. AT THE DADE COUNTY AUDITORIUM. (LOCAL). WARREN BROOME; THE GREATER MIAMI OPERA ASSOC; 1200 CORAL WAY; MIAMI, FL 33129. (#1535-15).

APR 11, '76. 'TOSCA'; AN ENGLISH OPERA PERFORMANCE. ALL OPERAS PRODUCED BY THE GREATER MIAMI OPERA ASSOC WILL HAVE PERFORMANCES IN THE ORIGINAL LANGUAGE & IN ENGLISH. THE ENGLISH SHOWSWILL BE AVAILABLE AT POPULAR PRICES FOR THE GENERAL PUBLIC. AT DADE COUNTY AUDITORIUM, 2901 W FLAGLER, MIAMI. (LOCAL). WARREN BROOME; THE GREATER MIAMI OPERA ASSOC; 1200 CORAL WAY; MIAMI, FL 33129. (#1535-4).

APR 16 - 17, '76. 9TH ANNUAL INTERNATIONAL PRAM CHAMPIONSHIP. COMPETITION AT KEY BISCAYNE YACHT CLUB. (INT'L). PETE FERGUSON, COORD; KEY BISCAYNE YACHT CLUB; 10205 COLLINS AVE; BAL HARBOUR, FL 33154. (#200011-161).

APR 17, '76. BICENTENNIAL BOOK CHARACTER PARADE. PARADE. (LOCAL). CATHERINE CONDUITTE; CUTLER RIDGE LIBRARY; 20239-D S, DIXIE HWY; MIAMI, FL 33157. (#105578-4).

APR 22 - 25, '76. STAMPOREE '76 USA - NATIONAL STAMP EXHIBITION. NATL STAMP EXIBITION WITH PARTICIPATION OF VISITORS, EXHIBITS FROM OVERSEAS. ANNUAL SPRING MEET, FLA FEDRTN STAMP CLUBS. FOREIGN POSTAL ADMINISTRATIONS PARTICIPATION, FIRST DAYS OF ISSUES, SOUVENIRSS, COURT OF HONOR, ATTRACTIVE CATALOGUE, BANQUETS, AWARDS. AT HOTEL EVERGLADES, 244 BISCAYNE BLVD; AMPLE PARKINNG OFF/ON STREET. (NAT'L). AGUSTIN J. CANTENS, CHRMN; THE CUBAN PHILATELIC SOCIETY OF MIAMI; P.O. BOX 45-0055 SHENANDOAH STA; MIAMI, FL 33145. (#1537-1).

APR 30 - MAY 1, '76. WESLEY MINSTREL & VARIETY SHOW. LIVE PERFORMANCE AT DADE COUNTY AUDITORIUM. (LOCAL). LIB CONNALLY, DIRECTOR; WESLEY AND TRINITY CLASSES OF FIRST UNITED METHODIST CHURCH; 4550 SW 64 CT; MIAMI, FL 33155. (#100256-4).

MAY 1, '76. FARM LIFE 200 YEARS AGO - AN EXHIBITION. EXHIBIT AT CUTLER RIDGE REGIONAL SHOPPING CENTER. (LOCAL). ELIZABETH LIGON, COORD; SOUTH FLORIDA CHAPTER, CYSTIC FIBROSIS FOUNDATION; 16501 SW 102 PLACE; MIAMI, FL 33157. (#104070-70).

MAY 2 - 7, '76. 'OLDER AMERICAN MONTH' BICENTENNIAL CELEBRATION. CEREMONY, EXHIBIT AT JACK ORR PLAZA. (LOCAL). CLARA BRASWELL, COORD; DADE COUNTY IMPACT PROGRAM, ELDERLY SERVICES DIVISION; 550 NW 5TH ST; MIAMI, FL 33128. (#200011-162).

MAY 9 - JUNE 12, '76. INTERNATIONAL FOLK FESTIVAL - 'THE WORLD OF MIAMI'. INCLUDES INTL DOLL SHOW, YOUTH SOCCER TOURNAMENT, PARADE OF NATIONS, BICYCLE RACES, INTL FILM PGM, NATIVE COSTUME SHOWS, FOOD OF THE NATIONS BOOTHS, FOLKLORIC BALLET & MUSIC PGMS & AMERICAN FOLK MUSIC JAMBOREE. PARTICIPANTS FROM MANY FOREIGN NATIONS WILL ENTERTAIN. AT BAYFRONT PARK AUDITORIUM, & DOWNTOWN MIAMI. (INT'L). MORTY FREEDMAN, GEN CHMN; INTERNATIONAL FOLK FESTIVAL COMMITTEE; 2539 S BAYSHORE DR; MIAMI, FL 33133. (#106169-1).

MAY 15, '76. MIAMI SUNSHINE CLASSIC TRACK AND FIELD MEET. COMPETITION AT MIAMI DADE COMMUNITY COLLEGE-NORTH CAMPUS STADIUM. (ST-WIDE). THOMAS BROWN, CHAIRMAN; RICHMOND-PERRINE OPTIMIST CLUB, INC; 14375 BOGGS DR; MIAMI, FL 33176. (#107737-1).

MAY 24 - 28, '76. BICENTENNIAL AMERICAN HERITAGE WEEK. 'OUR AMERICAN HERITAGE - A STAR SPANGLED EXTRAVAGANZA'. AT SAA. (LOCAL). CLAIRE-FRANCES WHITEHURST; MIAMI SENIOR ADULT EDUCATION CENTER; 2450 SW 1ST ST; MIAMI, FL 33135. (#108117-1).

MAY 31, '76. MIAMI BLACK PIONEERS MEMORIAL SERVICE. CEREMONY AT LINCOLN MEMORIAL PARK. (LOCAL). ELLEN D JOHNSON, DIRECTOR; MANAGEMENT AND OFFICERS AND DIRECTORS OF LINCOLN MEMORIAL PARK, INC; 3001 NW 46TH ST; MIAMI, FL 33142. (#104566-2).

JUNE 2, '76. 'THE BREEDERS', A DRAMATIC PLAY. PLAY TELLING THE STORY OF SLAVERY & ITS DEVASTATING EFFECTS ON THE BLACK RACE. PERFORMANCE INCLUDES MUSIC, DANCE AND DRAMA FROM THE BLACK CULTURAL HERITAGE. (LOCAL). JACQUELINE HARDY, MGR; MIAMI NORTHWESTERN HIGH SCHOOL PERFORMING & VISUAL ARTS CENTER; 7007 NW 12 AVE; MIAMI, FL 33150. (#108002-1).

JUNE 5, '76. NATIONAL ASTHMA CENTER: BICENTENNIAL AWARDS LUNCHEON. AWARD, CEREMONY AT MARRIOTT HOTEL. (LOCAL). GAYLE PAPPAS; NATIONAL ASTHMA CENTER - GIFT OF LIFE CHAPTER; 8251 SW 129 AVE; MIAMI, FL 33183. (#102791-5).

JUNE 14, '76. 1976 FLAG DAY CELEBRATION. CEREMONY, EXHIBIT AT DADE COUNTY COURTHOUSE, 73 W FLAGLER ST. (LOCAL). LINDA STECKLEY, CHMN; THIRD CENTURY USA; 8129 SW 81ST COURT; MIAMI, FL 33145. (#108192-1).

JUNE 25 - 30, '76. NATL EDUCATION ASSOC NATIONAL CONVENTION. NATL EDUCATION ASSOC'S MULTI-PART PROJ WITH THEME OF 'A DECLARATION OF INTERDEPENCE.' INCLUDES PUBS, SATELLITE AS TEACHING TOOL, INTL TEACHER PGM, PEACE STUDIES EXPO, INTL WOMEN'S YEAR IN '75, ETC. TEACHER ART & PHOTOGRAPHY EXHIBITIONS, CRAFTS EXPO. AT MIAMI BEACH CONVENTION CENTER. (NAT'L). MS JANICE COLBERT; NATIONAL EDUCATION ASSOCIATION; 1201 16TH ST, NW; WASHINGTON, DC 20036. (#1977-1).

JUNE 30 - JULY 3, '76. SHOWCASE OF PROGRAMS FOR EARLY CHILDHOOD EDUCATION. CONFEREES INCLUDE LEADERS IN FIELD OF EARLY CHILDHOOD EDUCATION; EXHIBITS INVITED FROM INSTITUTIONS STUDYING PHASES OF EARLY CHILDHOOD EDUCATION; FACULTY OF UNIV OF MIAMI SCHOOL OF EDUCATION TO SERVE AS CONFERENCE COMMITTEE. AT STUDENT UNION BLDG & DORM LOUNGES, UNIV OF MIAMI. (REGN'L). DR BETTY ROWEN, CHMN; UNIV OF MIAMI SCHOOL OF EDUCATION; SCHOOL OF ED, UNIV OF MIAMI; MIAMI, FL 33124. (#101025-1).

JULY 4, '76. 'BICENTENNIAL CELEBRATIONS IN OUR PARKS' IN CONTINENTAL PARK. FESTIVAL AT CONTINENTAL PARK, 10000 SW 82ND AVE. (LOCAL). BILL BUSHA, DIRECTOR; DADE COUNTY PARK AND RECREATION DEPARTMENT; 10000 SW 82ND AVE; MIAMI, FL 33165. (#2997-12).

JULY 4, '76. 'BICENTENNIAL CELEBRATIONS IN OUR PARKS' IN TAMIAMI PARK. FESTIVAL AT TAMIAMI PARK AND YOUTH FAIR BUILDING, 10901 SW 24TH ST. (LOCAL). BILL SCHLAMAN, COORD; DADE COUNTY PARKS AND RECREATION DEPARTMENT; 11201 SW 24TH ST; MIAMI, FL 33165. (#2997-13).

JULY 4, '76. BICENTENNIAL PARK DEDICATION AND OLD-FASHIONED PICNIC. CEREMONY, FESTIVAL AT BICENTENNIAL PARK ON BISCAYNE BLVD. (LOCAL). NORA SWAN, CHAIRPERSON; CITY OF MIAMI BICENTENNIAL COMMITTEE; 1317 SW 36TH AVE; MIAMI, FL 33145. (#2997-11).

JULY 4, '76. FOURTH OF JULY PICNIC AND DANCE. FESTIVAL AT 1250 NW 22ND AVE. (LOCAL). EUGENE MROZKOWSKI, DIR; POLISH LEGION OF AMERICAN VETERANS, USA; 1250 NW 22ND AVE; MIAMI, FL 33125. (#2997-7).

MIAMI — CONTINUED

JULY 4, '76. FOURTH OF JULY SWEARING-IN CEREMONIES FOR NEW CITIZENS. FOURTH OF JULY EXTRAVAGANZA OF MIAMI. EVERY YEAR, EACH OF THE 26 MUNICIPALITIES IN THE DADE COUNTY AREA WILL HOLD EVENTS & MANY COUNTY-WIDE ACTIVITIES SUCH AS A MASS SWEARING IN CEREMONY FOR NEW CITIZENS. (LOCAL). MS JAY KINZER; THIRD CENTURY USA; 9200 SW 64TH ST; MIAMI, FL 33143. (#2997-502).

JULY 4, '76. INDEPENDENCE DAY PARADE AND FAMILY SPORTS ACTIVITIES. FESTIVAL, PARADE. (LOCAL). MARIO VARELA, DIRECTOR; CLUB DE LAS AMERICAS; 8500 SW 8TH ST; MIAMI, FL 33144. (#2997-6).

JULY 4, '76. 'INTER-DEPENDENCE' DAY DANCE. FESTIVAL AT THE PLAYHOUSE, MIAMI SPRINGS VILLA, 500 DEER RUN. (LOCAL). MARTIN LISTOWSKY, DIR; YOUNG PROFESSIONALS; 4401 PRAIRIE AVE; MIAMI BEACH, FL 33140. (#2997-20).

JULY 4, '76. KENDALE LAKES INDEPENDENCE DAY. FESTIVAL, PARADE AT NEW KENDALE LAKES ELEMENTARY SCHOOL AND PARK SITE. (LOCAL). LINDA PALMER, DIRECTOR; KENDALE LAKES BICENTENNIAL COMMITTEE; 14195 SW 87TH ST; MIAMI, FL 33183. (#104566-7).

JULY 4, '76. ONE NATION UNDER GOD. AN INTERDENOMINATIONAL CHORAL SERVICE COMMEMORATING OUR RELIGIOUS HERITAGE DRAMATICALLY ENHANCED BY THE OUTDOOR ATMOSPHERE OF DOWNTOWN MIAMI AT SUNRISE IN BICENTENNIAL PARK. AT BICENTENNIAL PARK, BISCAYNE BOULEVARD. (LOCAL). REVEREND AUGUST KLING; INTERFAITH ADVISORY COMMITTEE; 609 BRICKELL AVENUE; MIAMI, FL 33131. (#50438-1).

JULY 4, '76. 'THIS IS MY COUNTRY'. FAIR, PARADE AT MORNINGSIDE PARK. (LOCAL). PATRICIA A LUCEY, CHMN; MACTOWN; 6250 NE 1ST PL; MIAMI, FL 33138. (#103782-1).

JULY 8 - 18, '76. '1776' - A PLAY PRODUCTION. A MUSICAL PRODUCTION OF PLAY '1776' BASED ON BOOK BY PETER STONE, WINNER OF SEVERAL AWARDS. REVIEWER OF NY PRODUCTION DESCRIBES IT AS HIGHLY ORIGINAL, WARM, HUMAN, FUNNY & MOVING. MIAMI'S PRODUCTION FEATURES COUNTY SCHOOL STUDENTS IN CAST AND ALL PHASES OF STAGING. AT GUSMAN PHILHARMONIC HALL, 174 E FLAGLER ST - (PARKING ADJACENT). (LOCAL). MISS A LOUISE HARMS; DADE COUNTY PUBLIC SCHOOLS; 150 NE 19TH ST; MIAMI, FL 33132. (#100930-1).

JULY 23, '76. 'OVERTOWN BICENTENNIAL '76', PARADE, MURAL DEDICATION & SPORTS DAY. FESTIVAL, PARADE. (LOCAL). MATTIE LANDERS, COORD; CULTURAL ADVISORY COUNCIL OF OVERTOWN; 470 NW 11TH ST; MIAMI, FL 33144. (#200011-237).

JULY 24 - 25, '76. BICENTENNIAL ROWING REGATTA. ROWING CLUBS IN FL AND SCHOOLS FROM THE EAST COAST AND PERHAPS 10 CREWS FROM LATIN AMERICA WILL PARTICIPATE IN THE REGATTA. AT MIAMI MARINE STADIUM/RICKENBACKER CAUSEWAY. (INT'L). CESAR H ODIO; MIAMI ROWING CLUB; PO BOX 2544; HIALEAH, FL 33012. (#102791-3).

JULY 29 - AUG 1, '76. INTER-AMERICAN BANKERS CONVENTION. CONFERENCE AT DORAL COUNTRY CLUB. (ST-WIDE). EVELIO W LEY, DIRECTOR; BANKING ADVISORY BOARD OF THE LATIN CHAMBER OF COMMERCE; 120 N BISCAYNE BLVD, SUITE 2502; MIAMI, FL 33131. (#104566-5).

JULY 31 - AUG 8, '76. 'SEA '76' - GREATER MIAMI'S WATER FESTIVAL. SEA '76 WILL COORDINATE ALL WATER BICENT ACTIVITIES IN GREATER MIAMI AREA. WILL INCLUDE VISIT OF SHIPS IN OPSAIL '76, NAVY BLUE ANGELS, VISIT OF US & FOREIGN SHIPS, REGATTAS, FISHING RODEO, WATERSHOWS, SEA CIRCUS & PARADE OF SHIPS, INCLUDING FOREIGN NAVAL SHIPS. AT BISCAYNE BAY. (INT'L). PAUL ANDRE, CHMN; SEA '76, MARINE COUNCIL OF GREATER MIAMI & ARMED FORCES COUNCIL; PO BOX 405-1976; MIAMI, FL 33145. (#5226-1).

AUG 5 - 8, '76. HEMISPHERIC CONFERENCE FOR WOMEN '76. TO BRING TOGETHER WOMEN'S GROUPS IN THIS HEMISPHERE FOR AN EXCHANGE OF IDEAS. TO EXPOSE, SHARE, & MAKE WOMEN AWARE AS THEY CONTRIBUTE TO THEIR OWN COUNTRY'S DEVELOPMENT & TO THE HEMISPHERE. AT FONTAINBLEAU HOTEL. (INT'L). GUI GOUVAERT; HEMISPHERIC CONGRESS FOR WOMEN '76, INC; 10 BISCAYNE BLVD, SUITE 200; MIAMI, FL 33132. (#1529-1).

AUG 16 - 20, '76. 60TH ANNUAL AMERICAN FEDERATION OF TEACHERS CONVENTION. CONFERENCE AT AMERICANA HOTEL - HEADQUARTERS & 7 OTHER HOTELS. (NAT'L). MURRAY SISSELMAN, COORD; UNITED TEACHERS OF DADE; 1809 BRICKELL AVE; MIAMI, FL 33129. (#107550-1).

SEPT 11, '76. BETHUNE-COOKMAN COLLEGE BICENTENNIAL FOOTBALL CLASSIC. GAMES IS BETHUNE-COOKMAN VS TEXAS SOUTHERN UNIVERSITY. AT ORANGE BOWL STADIUM. (LOCAL). J L JONES, CHAIRMAN; MIAMI DADE ALUMNI ASSOC, BETHUNE-COOKMAN COLLEGE; PO BOX 207 NW BRANCH; MIAMI, FL 33147. (#107550-4).

SEPT 20 - 21, '76. ISRAELI PHILHARMONIC ORCHESTRA VISITS MIAMI. LIVE PERFORMANCE. (INT'L). URI AHARON BAR-NEV; ISRAELI GOVERNMENT; 1621 21ST ST, NW; WASHINGTON, DC 20008. (#109015-18).

OCT 10 - 17, '76. HISPANIC HERITAGE WEEK. AN ANNUAL WEEK OF FESTIVITIES COMMEMORATING S FLORIDA'S HISPANIC HERITAGE TO FAMILIARIZE RESIDENTS & VISITORS WITH ITS HISTORIC TRADITION & BICULTURAL RICHNESS. (ST-WIDE). JOSE ANTONIO OJEDA; HISPANIC HERITAGE WEEK COMMITTEE; 73 W FLAGLER ST; MIAMI, FL 33130. (#5211-1).

NOV 2 - 7, '76. AMERICAN ROSE SOCIETY NATIONAL MEET/DISPLAY OF THOUSANDS OF ROSES. SHOW WILL BE ON NOVEMBER 4 & 5. AT FOUR AMBASSADORS HOTEL, 801 S BAYSHORE DR. (NAT'L). MRS S M GREENE, CHAIRMAN; TROPICAL ROSE SOCIETY OF GREATER MIAMI; 1036 S GREENWAY DR; CORAL GABLES, FL 33134. (#100750-1).

NOV 9, '76. 'THE WORLD PROTEIN SHORTAGE', SIGMA XI BICENTENNIAL LECTURE. SEMINAR AT WIEGAND 116E AND W OR AUDITORIUM AT BARRY COLLEGE. (LOCAL). SR JOHN KAREN FREI, PROF; BARRY COLLEGE; 11300 NE 2ND AVE; MIAMI, FL 33161. (#107550-3).

NOV 11 - 14, '76. AMERICAN CRAFTS COUNCIL SE REGIONAL ASSEMBLY & EXHIBITION. EXHIBIT, SEMINAR AT WORKSHOPS-UNIV OF MIAMI; EXHIBITION-METROPOLITAN ART CENTER. (REGN'L). MARGARET PELTON, CHMN; SE REGIONAL ASSEMBLY, AMERICAN CRAFTS COUNCIL; 11011 SW 104TH ST; MIAMI, FL 33176. (#104566-8).

NOV 11 - 14, '76. NATIONAL ALLIANCE OF BLACK SCHOOL EDUCATORS, 4TH ANNUAL CONFERENCE. CONFERENCE AT SHERATON-FOUR AMBASSADORS HOTEL. (NAT'L). J L JONES, CHAIRMAN; NATL ALLIANCE OF BLACK SCHOOL EDUCATORS; PO BOX 470190; MIAMI, FL 33147. (#107550-5).

DEC 3, '76. 'PRE-CLASSIC KWANZA PARADE,' A SALUTE TO THE AMERICAN MARCHING BAND. 'PRE-CLASSIC KWANZA PARADE (& BICENT SALUTE TO THE AMERICAN MARCHING BAND)'. (LOCAL). DORAN G COOPER, COORD; CULTURAL ADVISORY COUNCIL OF OVERTOWN; 1026 NW 2ND AVE; MIAMI, FL 33136. (#109500-1).

DEC 3 - 12, '76. WORLD AMATEUR JAI-ALAI CHAMPIONSHIPS. COMPETITION INVOLVING PLAYERS FROM SPAIN, FRANCE, MEXICO & THE PHILIPPINES. AT MIAMI JAI-ALAI FRONTON. (INT'L). ROBERT GROSSBERG; US AMATEUR JAI-ALAI PLAYERS ASSOC; 100 SE 2ND AVE; MIAMI, FL 33131. (#102791-2).

DEC 6, '76. ANNUAL BICYCLE MARATHON. REGISTRATION OUTSIDE OF THE LIBRARY. REGISTRATION USUALLY STARTS ABOUT 9:00AM. AT DOWNTOWN; BISCAYNE BLVD.. (REGN'L). BASHA SCHLAZER; CITY OF MIAMI; 2600 S BAYSHORE DRIVE; DINNER KEY, FL 33133. (#1531-3).

DEC 26 - 31, '76. AMERICAN FREEDOM TRAIN DISPLAY DAYS AT MIAMI. THE AMERICAN FREEDOM TRAIN WILL INCLUDE 10 EXHIBIT CARS AND 2 SHOWCASE CARS DEPICTING DIFFERENT PHASES OF THE AMERICAN EXPERIENCE. ITS ARRIVAL WILL SERVE AS A CATALYST FOR LOCAL BICENTENNIAL CELEBRATIONS BY PEOPLE THROUGHOUT THIS NATION. (ST-WIDE). SY FREEDMAN, DIR OF P/R; THE AMERICAN FREEDOM TRAIN FOUNDATION, INC.; 5205 LEESBURG PKE, SUITE 800; BAILEY'S XRDS, VA 22041. (#1776-80).

MIAMI BEACH

CHABAD HOUSE MOBILE CENTER - MIAMI BEACH, FL. UNIT WILL VISIT UNIVERSITIES, HEBREW SCHOOLS, SYNAGOGUES AND JEWISH CENTERS THROUGHOUT SOUTH FLORIDA TO PROMOTE JEWISH EDUCATION AND HISTORY. (LOCAL). RABBI DAVID ELIEZRIE, DIRECTOR; CENTRAL ORGANIZATION FOR JEWISH EDUCATION; 1401 ALTON RD; MIAMI BEACH, FL 33139. (#24805).

MAR 3 - 5, '75. HYDROGEN ENERGY FUNDAMENTALS SYMPOSIUM COURSE. PROMOTES THE USE OF CLEAN, SYNTHETIC ENERGY SOURCES TO REPLACE FOSSIL FUELS. COORDINATES AND IMPLEMENTS RESEARCH. ORGANIZES INTERNATL CONFERENCES ON ENERGY-RELATED PROBLEMS & PUBLISHES TECHNICAL BOOKS. (INT'L). T NEJAT VEZIROGLU, DIRECT; UNIV OF MIAMI CLEAN ENERGY RESEARCH INSTITUTE; PO BOX 248294; CORAL GABLES, FL 33124. (#5270-901).

DEC 1 - 6, '75. AMERICAN BICENTENNIAL FLORIDA EXHIBIT. EXHIBIT, RADIO/TV AT SW CORNER OF THE 163RD ST SHOPPING CENTER. (LOCAL). ANITA BJORK; THIRD CENTURY, USA; PO BOX 451976; MIAMI, FL 33145. (#100225-2).

DEC 16 - 21, '75. SUNSHINE CUP MATCHES AND THE SPIRIT OF '76. TENNIS MATCHES INVOLVING TWO MALE JUNIOR TEAMS FROM 38 NATIONS. AT FLAMINGO PARK. (NAT'L). EDDIE HERR; PEOPLE TO PEOPLE SPORTS COMMITTEE & THE MIAMI BEACH TENNIS ASSOC; PO BOX 390704; MIAMI BEACH, FL 33139. (#103285-3).

DEC 22 - 29, '75. WORLD JUNIOR TENNIS TOURNAMENT. COMPETITION AT FLAMINGO PARK, MIAMI BEACH. (LOCAL). DANIEL S MCNAMARA, CHMN; ORANGE BOWL COMMITTEE; PO BOX 350748; MIAMI, FL 33135. (#1548-5).

JAN 3, '76. THE MARCH OF MEDICINE - A BALL SALUTING 200 YEARS OF MEDICINE. FESTIVAL, LIVE PERFORMANCE AT FONTAINEBLEAU HOTEL BALLROOM, MIAMI BEACH. (LOCAL). RICHARD ELIAS, MD, CHMN; MIAMI HEART INSTITUTE'S DEVELOPMENT FUND CORPS; 4701 N MERIDIAN AVE; MIAMI BEACH, FL 33140. (#100256-6).

JAN 8 - 11, '76. MIAMI BEACH INTERNATIONAL MID-WINTER BICENTENNIAL COIN CONVENTION. EXHIBIT FEATURING PRE-REVOLUTION TO PRESENT US COPPER, SILVER, GOLD, COINAGE & CURRENCY, RARE FOREIGN COINS, RARE MEDALS & TOKENS, AWARDS PRIZES, SPECIAL FL 'COUNTERFEIT DETECTION SEMINAR' CONDUCTED BY PRES OF AMER NUMISMATIC ASSOC, OTHER EDUCATIONAL SEMINARS AVAILABLE. AT DEAUVILLE HOTEL, ON THE OCEAN AT 67TH ST. (INT'L). PHILIP WALTON, CHMN; SOUTH FLORIDA COIN CLUB INC; 915 MIDDLE RIVER DR - SUITE 408; FT LAUDERDL, FL 33304. (#102808-1).

JAN 31, '76. 'THE LIBERTY BELL' MUSICAL PRODUCTION. LIVE PERFORMANCE AT THEATRE OF PERFORMING ARTS MIAMI BEACH CONVENTION HALL. (LOCAL). TRUXE LEOIN, DRAMA DIR; TEMPLE EMANU EL, 1701 WASHINGTON AVE, MIAMI BEACH, FLA, 33139; 1701 WASHINGTON AVE; MIAMI BEACH, FL 33139. (#50420-1).

FEB 6 - 8, '76. SECOND OUTDOOR FESTIVAL OF THE ARTS. AN OUTDOOR ART SHOW FEATURING PAINTING, GRAPHICS & DRAWING, CRAFTS, SCULPTURE & PHOTOGRAPHY. SUNDAY HRS: 10 AM - 6 PM. AT CONVENTION CENTER, JACKIE GLEASON DR. (LOCAL). CHARLES CINNAMON, DIR; CITY OF MIAMI BEACH FINE ARTS BOARD; PO BOX BIN 39000; MIAMI BEACH, FL 33139. (#10527-1).

FEB 25 - 29, '76. INTL SYMPOSIUM - 'TRENDS, OCULAR TREATMENT'. SEMINAR AT EDEN ROC HOTEL, MIAMI BEACH. (INT'L). OLGA FERRER, MD, DIRECTOR; HORACIO FERRER EYE INSTITUTE; 1889 S BAYSHORE DR; MIAMI, FL 33133. (#101026-1).

MAR 1 - 3, '76. 2ND INTERNATIONAL HYDROGEN ENERGY CONFERENCE. PROMOTES THE USE OF CLEAN, SYNTHETIC ENERGY SOURCES TO REPLACE FOSSIL FUELS. COORDINATES AND IMPLEMENTS RESEARCH. ORGANIZES INTERNATL CONFERENCES ON ENERGY-RELATED PROBLEMS & PUBLISHES TECHNICAL BOOKS. AT HYATT HOUSE HOTEL MIAMI BEACH FL. (INT'L). T NEJAT VEZIROGLU; UNIVERSITY OF MIAMI; CLEAN ENERGY RESEARCH INST. UM; CORAL GABLES, FL 33124. (#5270-1).

MAR 6 - 7, '76. 'THE LIBERTY BELL', A MUSICAL. A MUSICAL EXTRAVAGANZA IN HONOR OF THE BICENTENNIAL WILL SHOW JEWISH INVOLVEMENT IN THE BUILDING OF THIS COUNTRY. AT FRIEDLAND BALLROOM. (LOCAL). TRIXIE LEVIN, DIR; TEMPLE EMANU-EL; 1701 WASHINGTON AVE; MIAMI BEACH, FL 33139. (#5214-1).

MAY 20 - 24, '76. MIAMI BEACH INTERNATIONAL FLOWER SHOW - THEME: THE NEW LAND. A FLOWER SHOW OF GARDEN, HORTICULTURAL AND ARTISTIC ARRANGEMENTS & DAILY HOW-TO LECTURES. AT MIAMI BCH CONV CENTER, 1700 WASHINGTON AVE. (INT'L). WINNIE STONE; NATL COUNCIL STATE GARDEN CLUBS,INC & MIAMI BEACH TOURIST DEV AUTH; 8640 SW 108 ST; MIAMI, FL 33156. (#1530-1).

JULY 4 - 23, '76. A MUSICAL 'HOORAY USA!'. MUSICAL PANORAMA OF AMERICAN HISTORY WILL INCLUDE SONGS, PAGEANTRY, DANCES IN AMERICA'S 200 YEARS. ONE 2-HR SHOW PER NIGHT. AT MIAMI BEACH CONVENTION CENTER. (NAT'L). CHAMBER OF COMMERCE; GREATER MIAMI CHAMBER OF COMMERCE; MIAMI BCH TOURIST DEVEL AUTHORITY; 1200 BISCAYNE BLVD; MIAMI, FL 33132. (#103416-6).

JULY 13 - 18, '76. 'A MUSICAL JUBILEE' - PLAY. LIVE PERFORMANCE. (LOCAL). CHARLES CINNAMON, COORD; MIAMI BEACH THEATRE OF THE PERFORMING ARTS; 1700 WASHINGTON AVE; MIAMI BEACH, FL 33139. (#200011-236).

JULY 13 - AUG 21, '76. SHAKESPEARE BY THE SEA PERFORMANCES. 'HAMLET' & 'MUCH ADO ABOUT NOTHING' WILL BE PERFORMED. AT NORTH SHORE COMMUNITY CENTER, OUTDOORS. (REGN'L). IVAN KIVITT; MIAMI BEACH TOURIST DEVELOPMENT AUTHORITY; 235 ALCAZAR; CORAL GABLES, FL 33134. (#50163-1).

JULY 20 - 25, '76. 'GONE WITH THE WIND' - PLAY. LIVE PERFORMANCE. (LOCAL). CHARLES CINNAMON, COORD; MIAMI BEACH THEATRE OF THE PERFORMING ARTS; 1700 WASHINGTON AVE; MIAMI BEACH, FL 33139. (#200011-235).

JULY 27 - AUG 1, '76. 'NORMAN, IS THAT YOU?' - PLAY. LIVE PERFORMANCE. (LOCAL). CHARLES CINNAMON, COORD; MIAMI BEACH THEATRE OF THE PERFORMING ARTS; 1700 WASHINGTON AVE; MIAMI BEACH, FL 33139. (#200011-234).

AUG 3 - 8, '76. 'MAME' - PLAY. LIVE PERFORMANCE. (LOCAL). CHARLES CINNAMON, COORD; MIAMI BEACH THEATRE OF THE PERFORMING ARTS; 1700 WASHINGTON AVE; MIAMI BEACH, FL 33139. (#200011-233).

AUG 10 - 15, '76. 'THAT CHAMPIONSHIP SEASON' - PLAY. LIVE PERFORMANCE. (LOCAL). CHARLES CINNAMON, COORD; MIAMI BEACH THEATRE OF THE PERFORMING ARTS; 1700 WASHINGTON AVE; MIAMI BEACH, FL 33139. (#200011-232).

AUG 17 - 22, '76. 'JOHN BROWN'S BODY' - PLAY. LIVE PERFORMANCE. (LOCAL). CHARLES CINNAMON, COORD; MIAMI BEACH THEATRE OF THE PERFORMING ARTS; 1700 WASHINGTON AVE; MIAMI BEACH, FL 33139. (#200011-230).

AUG 24 - 29, '76. 'THE KING AND I' - PLAY. LIVE PERFORMANCE. (LOCAL). CHARLES CINNAMON, COORD; MIAMI BEACH THEATRE OF THE PERFORMING ARTS; 1700 WASHINGTON AVE; MIAMI BEACH, FL 33139. (#200011-231).

AUG 27 - SEPT 1, '76. CONFERENCE ON YOUTH NEEDS AND YOUTH EXHIBITION. CONFERENCE, EXHIBIT AT CARILLON HOTEL. (REGN'L). STUART RADO, EXEC DIR; NATIONAL NETWORK OF YOUTH ADVISORY BOARDS; PO BOX 402036, OCEAN VIEW BRANCH; MIAMI BEACH, FL 33140. (#1536-6).

AUG 31 - SEPT 5, '76. 'FUNNY GIRL' - PLAY. LIVE PERFORMANCE. (LOCAL). CHARLES CINNAMON, COORD; MIAMI BEACH THEATRE OF THE PERFORMING ARTS; 1700 WASHINGTON AVE; MIAMI BEACH, FL 33139. (#200011-229).

MIAMI SHORES

FEB 22, '75. BICENTENNIAL MASS AND INTERNATIONAL DAY. CEREMONY. (LOCAL). REV NEAL MCDERMOTT; METANOIA, BARRY COLLEGE; 11300 NE 2ND AVE; MIAMI SHORES, FL 33161. (#200011-164).

APR 10 - 11, '76. TROPICANA NITE, 'A LATIN SALUTE TO THE BICENTENNIAL'. LIVE PERFORMANCE AT BARRY COLLEGE, THOMPSON HALL CAFETERIA. (LOCAL). ILEANA ARANGO, PRESIDENT; ST ROSE OF LIMA SPANISH CLUB, BARRY COLLEGE; PO BOX 698; MIAMI SHORES, FL 33161. (#200011-165).

MIAMI SPRINGS

MIAMI SPRINGS INTERNATIONAL SWIM MEET. COMPETITION TAKES PLACE IN AUGUST EACH YEAR WITH 300 SWIMMERS

MIAMI SPRINGS—CONTINUED

FROM 12 FOREIGN COUNTRIES. NICKNAMED THE 'FRIENDSHIP MEET' IT PROMOTES GOOD SPORTSMANSHIP & UNDERSTANDING OF OTHER NATIONALITIES. (INT'L). PRESIDENT; MIAMI SPRINGS SWIM ASSOC; PO BOX 66-84; MIAMI SPRINGS, FL 33166. (#2994).

1976 RE-ENACTMENT OF 1ST CONTINENTAL CONGRESS. A RE-ENACTMENT OF THE FIRST CONTINENTAL CONGRESS TO COMPARE THE ISSUES OF THEN AND NOW, TO APPLY THE GOALS OF THAT CONGRESS TO OUR PRESENT ERA AND FOCUS ATTENTION ON THE ORIGINS OF OUR GOVERNMENT. (LOCAL). CINDY STARRETT, PRESIDENT; SOCIAL STUDIES SENATE CLUB MIAMI SPRINGS SENIOR HIGH SCHOOL; 751 DOVE AVENUE; MIAMI SPRINGS, FL 33166. (#5191).

AUG 7 - 9, '75. INTERNATIONAL SWIM MEET. COMPETITION TAKES PLACE IN AUGUST EACH YEAR WITH 300 SWIMMERS FROM 12 FOREIGN COUNTRIES. NICKNAMED THE 'FRIENDSHIP MEET' IT PROMOTES GOOD SPORTSMANSHIP & UNDERSTANDING OF OTHER NATIONALITIES. AT MIAMI SPRG MUNICIPAL POOL - 1401 WESTWARD DR. (INT'L). PAT NALL, PUBLICITY CHMN; MIAMI SPRG SWIMMING ASSOC; 156 CORYDON DR; MIAMI SPRINGS, FL 33166. (#100581-1).

MAR 12, '76. 'A NIGHT IN '76' - SPIRITUAL OUTREACH MEETING, NON-SECTARIAN. CEREMONY AT MIAMI SPRINGS VILLAS PLAYHOUSE RESTAURANT. (LOCAL). MRS H HENRY PHELPS, CHMN; MIAMI NORTH, CHRISTIAN WOMEN'S CLUB; 660 NE 98TH ST; MIAMI SHORES, FL 33138. (#105579-1).

APR 9, '76. RIBS 'N ROAST, 26TH ANNUAL JOURNALISTS' POLITICAL SATIRE. FESTIVAL AT MIAMI SPRINGS VILLAS. (LOCAL). JACK KASSEWITZ, EDITOR; SOCIETY OF PROFESSIONAL JOURNALISTS; PO BOX 615; MIAMI, FL 33152. (#200011-166).

APR 25, '76. ANNUAL MIAMI RIVER REGATTA - DEDICATION OF NEW BIKE PATH. AWARD, CEREMONY, COMPETITION, OPENING AT MIAMI SPRINGS BRIDGE AT 4TH AVE, EAST SIDE OF RIVER. (LOCAL). TOM HOMBERGER, DIRECTOR; MIAMI RIVER INNER-CITY BOARD; 265 W 25TH ST; HIALEAH, FL 33010. (#5198-2).

MAY 16, '76. 'WHICH WAY AMERICA?' - A MUSICAL PRODUCTION. LIVE PERFORMANCE. (LOCAL). SHIRLEY CARY, CHAIRMAN; MIAMI SPRINGS FIRST PRESBYTERIAN CHURCH; 16205 W PRESTWICH PL; MIAMI LAKES, FL 33014. (#107712-1).

JULY 3 - 4, '76. INDEPENDENCE DAY PARADE, BAR-B-QUE AND FIREWORKS. FESTIVAL, PARADE AT PARADE-CURTIS PKY, BAR-B-QUE-MIAMI SPRINGS REC FIELD & GOLF COURSE. (LOCAL). JOHN CAVALIER, DIRECTOR; MIAMI SPRINGS BICENTENNIAL COMMITTEE; 1090 RED BIRD AVE; MIAMI SPRINGS, FL 33166. (#2997-18).

MIDDLEBURG

CEMETERY RESTORATION AND IMPROVEMENT, FL. 2 ACRES OF CHURCH CEMETERY WILL BE RESTORED AND IMPROVED. (LOCAL). THE REVEREND TOM VINCETT, PROJ CHAIRMAN; UNITED METHODIST CHURCH; MIDDLEBURG, FL 32068. (#18012).

PRECISION DRILL TEAM - MIDDLEBURG, FL. 12 RIDERS ON HORSEBACK WILL PERFORM SEVERAL PATTERNS IN A BICENTENNIAL PROGRAM. (LOCAL). DONALD AKINS, TEAM CAPTAIN; BLACK CREEK HORSEMEN'S ASSOC; 4033 PINTO RD; MIDDLEBURG, FL 32068. (#25944).

FEB 28, '76. BOARD ROOM DEDICATION. BOARD ROOM OF CLAY COUNTY SHRINE CLUB DEDICATED TO MEMORY OF GENERAL JONATHAN WAINWRIGHT. ROOM WILL HOUSE A PERMANENT COLLECTION OF MEMORABILIA FROM GENERAL WAINWRIGHT'S LIFE. (LOCAL). CHUCK POLATTY, COORD; CLAY COUNTY SHRINE CLUB; STATE ROAD 209; MIDDLEBURG, FL 32068. (#200011-167).

JULY 2, '76. BICENTENNIAL BALL. A COUNTY-WIDE SEMI-FORMAL BALL WILL BE OPEN TO ALL RESIDENTS; THE BALL, A PART OF THE JULY 4TH CELEBRATION, WILL INCLUDE GUEST SPEAKER AND MARINE CORPS FLAG PAGEANT; PROFITS WILL GO TO THE SHRINERS BURN HOSPITAL. AT CLUB HOUSE, STATE ROAD 209. ADEQUATE FREE PARKING. (LOCAL). LEWIS PARRISH, COORD; CLAY COUNTY SHRINE CLUB/CLAY COUNTY BICENTENNIAL COMMITTEE; 301 DOW COURT; GREEN CV SPG, FL 32043. (#106743-5).

MILTON

ANDREW JACKSON TREE AND PARK - MILTON, FL. PERMANENT PLAQUE AND PARK FOR RECREATION INSTALLED AT FLORIDATOWN, WHERE JACKSON CAMPED ENROUTE TO TAKE PENSACOLA. (LOCAL). WARREN WEEKS, COMMITTEE CHAIRMAN; ACTION '76 STEERING COMMITTEE; PO BOX 604; MILTON, FL 32570. (#15018).

BICENTENNIAL NEWSPAPER COLUMN - MILTON, FL. TWICE WEEKLY COLUMN ON THE BICENTENNIAL WILL APPEAR IN THE LOCAL PAPER. (LOCAL). CHARLIE SOMERBY, EDITOR; MILTON GAZETTE; MILTON, FL 32570. (#15013).

'BORN TO SERVE' - MILTON, FL. BOOK - A 3-GENERATION STORY ON THE ROSASCO FAMILY OF SANTA ROSA CO AND NORTHWEST FLORIDA. AUTHOR, JANE E RICHARDS, DID EXTENSIVE RESEARCH ON LUMBERING, SHIPPING, EXPORT, BUILDING & FINANCE. (LOCAL). JANE E RICHARDS, AUTHOR; ACTION '76 COMMITTEE; PO BOX 604; MILTON, FL 32570. (#26436).

FLAG DAY EVERYDAY, MILTON, FL. CITIZENS ARE URGED TO DISPLAY AMERICAN FLAGS ALONG WITH USING RED, WHITE & BLUE TO SERVE AS A REMINDER OF OUR PATRIOTIC HERITAGE. (LOCAL). DIANE BATES, COMMITTEE CHAIRMAN; PILOT CLUB; 203 OAK; MILTON, FL 32570. (#15014).

HALFTIME FOOTBALL PROGRAMS - PROJ OF MILTON, FL. THE HIGH SCHOOL BAND WILL PERFORM AT FOOTBALL HALFTIME SHOWS. (LOCAL). J E HAWTHORNE, CHAIRMAN; ACTION '76 BICENTENNIAL COMMITTEE; PAGE, FL 32570. (#15121).

HISTORICAL POINTS OF INTEREST MAP, MILTON, FL. HISTORICAL POINTS OF INTEREST WILL BE LOCATED ON NEW COUNTY MAP FOR TOURISTS & SCHOOLS; IT WILL BE DISTRIBUTED BY THE LOCAL CHAMBER OF COMMERCE. (LOCAL). TOM SUTHER, MANAGER; CHAMBER OF COMMERCE; WILLINGS ST; MILTON, FL 32570. (#15016).

HISTORICAL TOUR OF SANTA ROSA COUNTY, FL. ESTABLISH HISTORICAL TOUR THROUGHOUT COUNTY WITH DESCRIPTIVE INFORMATION CONCERNING EACH HISTORICAL SITE. (LOCAL). GUY THOMPSON, COMMITTEE CHAIRMAN; ACTION BICENTENNIAL YOUTH GROUP; PO BOX 604; MILTON, FL 32570. (#15017).

HISTORY OF SANTA ROSA COUNTY, FL. A LOCAL HISTORIAN, AIDED BY LOCAL CITIZENS, HAS WRITTEN & PUBLISHED A HISTORY OF SANTA ROSA COUNTY. (LOCAL). WARREN WEEKS, COMMITTEE CHAIRMAN; ACTION '76 BICENTENNIAL COMMITTEE; PO BOX 604; MILTON, FL 32570. (#15019).

MINUTEMAN FIREPLUGS IN MILTON, FL. FIREPLUGS WILL BE PAINTED IN THE IMAGE OF MINUTEMEN. (LOCAL). DEAN TINSLEY, CHAIRMAN; AVALON CIVIC LEAGUE, INC & AVALON FARMERETTES; ROUTE 7; MILTON, FL 32570. (#15119).

MINUTEMEN FOR 1976 - MILTON, FL. HIGH SCHOOL SENIORS FROM THE CLASS OF '76 WILL BE ORGANIZED INTO A MINUTEMAN SUPPORT GROUP. (LOCAL). GUY THOMPSON, COMMITTEE CHAIRMAN; ACTION '76 COMMITTEE; 704 PARK, APT B; MILTON, FL 32570. (#15015).

NEW MUSEUM IN MILTON, FL. THE OLD L&N RAILROAD STATION WILL BE CONVERTED INTO A NEW MUSEUM. (LOCAL). REV ROBERT COWLING, PROJ DIRECTOR; SANTA ROSA COUNTY HISTORICAL ASSOC; 302 OAK ST; MILTON, FL 32570. (#15020).

PAINTED LITTER BARRELS - MILTON, FL. LITTER BARRELS THROUGHOUT THE COUNTY WILL BE PAINTED. (LOCAL). MARGARET M PITTS, AGENT; 4-H CLUBS; PO BOX 152; MILTON, FL 32570. (#15021).

TIME CAPSULE FOR 2076 - MILTON, FL. MATERIAL ON MILTON AND SANTA ROSA COUNTY IN 1976 WILL BE ENCASED IN A TIME CAPSULE FOR 2076. (LOCAL). WILLIAM S ROSASCO, CHAIRMAN; ACTION '76 BICENTENNIAL COMMITTEE OF SANTA ROSA COUNTY; PO BOX 604; MILTON, FL 32570. (#25602).

OCT 15, '75. FREEDOM ESSAY CONTEST. A $50 SAVINGS BOND PRESENTED TO EACH FIRST PLACE WINNER AND A $25 SAVINGS BOND TO EACH 2ND PLACE WINNER. A CERTIFICATE IS GIVEN TO EACH STUDENT TO ENTERS THE CONTEST. (LOCAL). BERNICE RIVENBECK, CHMN; PILOT CLUB OF MILTON; PO BOX 107; MILTON, FL 32570. (#102189-2).

JULY 2, '76. BICENTENNIAL PARADE. PARADE AT MILTON HIGH SCHOOL TO SIX FLAGS SHOPPING PLAZA. (LOCAL). JANIS ALLEN, CHAIRMAN; ACTION BICENTENNIAL COMMITTEE; 110 TICONDEROGA ST; MILTON, FL 32570. (#108891-1).

JULY 2, '76. TORCHES OF FREEDOM PAGEANT. PAGEANT DEPICTING THE HISTORY OF THE U S UP TO 1776 ENDING WITH THE SIGNING OF THE DECLARATION OF INDEPENDENCE. LARGE CAST USING LOCAL CLUB MEMBERS; EACH GROUP TO STAGE ONE SCENE. AT LOCAL HIGH SCHOOL FOOTBALL STADIUM. (LOCAL). MRS GRACE MCKINNEY; ACTION '76 BICENTENNIAL STEERING COMMITTEE; 902 LARK STREET; MILTON, FL 32570. (#102189-1).

JULY 2 - 5, '76. BICENTENNIAL FESTIVAL. FESTIVAL. (LOCAL). JOHN NESBIT, CHMN; KIWANIS CLUB; ROUTE 8, BOX 172; MILTON, FL 32570. (#102188-1).

JULY 4, '76. BEARD CONTEST. REGISTRATION OF CONTESTANTS, PRIOR TO COMPETITION, ON POSTERS. AT SANTA ROSA COUNTY COURTHOUSE. (LOCAL). CAPTAIN KEN HASSETT; ACTION 76 STEERING COMMITTEE; NAS WHITING FIELD; MILTON, FL 32570. (#106205-1).

JULY 4, '76. BELL RINGING CEREMONY. CEREMONY WILL COINCIDE WITH NATIONAL BELL RINGING CEREMONY, USING ALL FACILITIES POSSIBLE. (LOCAL). W S ROSASEO, CHMN; ACTION '76 BICENTENNIAL COMMITTEE; PO BOX 604; MILTON, FL 32570. (#108202-1).

JULY 4, '76. BICENTENNIAL HISTORICAL ART SHOW. EXHIBIT AT MILTON COLLEGE CENTER. (LOCAL). DOROTHY MORTEWSON, CHMN; AVALON CIVIC LEAGUE, INC; SAN MIQUEL ST; MILTON, FL 32570. (#102189-4).

JULY 5, '76. FUNDAY AFTER SUNDAY - PICNIC & OLD FASHIONED BARRELL RACES. FESTIVAL AT CARPENTER PARK. (LOCAL). W S ROSASCO, III, CHMN; ACTION '76 STEERING COMMITTEE; PO BOX 604; MILTON, FL 32570. (#106205-2).

MT DORA

SHIP 'BRIG FREEDOM' RESTORATION PROJ OF FLORIDA. CONVERT EXISTING HULL TO AUTHENTIC REV ERA BRIG THEN VISIT CITIES IN NORTH CENTRAL AMERICA & CARIBBEAN. FIRST EXHIBIT AS A COLONIAL ERA SHIPYARD THEN AS A COLONIAL ERA SHIP. 2 MASTED, 80 FT LONG. (INT'L). MR & MRS EDW C POULSEN, PRESIDENT & VICE PRESIDENT; SOCIETY OF THE 'BRIG FREEDOM'; PO BX 1255; MT DORA, FL 32757. (#2441).

MT PLEASANT

JAN 1 - DEC 31, '76. JOSHUA DAVIS HOUSE TOUR. ONE OF THE OLDEST WOODEN STRUCTURES IN NORTH FLORIDA, CIRCA 1824; A TOUR WILL BE GIVEN WITH TAPED MUSIC AND NARRATION. AT 40 MILES WEST OF TALLAHASSEE, FLA ON US HWY 90. (REGN'L). DAVID A AVANT, JR; TALLAHASSEE CHAPTER, SONS OF AMERICAN REVOLUTION; BOX 1711; TALLAHASSEE, FL 32302. (#16935-1).

MULBERRY

MULBERRY, FL, BICENTENNIAL PARK - 1901 - 1976. 200 TREES WILL BE PLANTED IN THE CENTER OF THE PARK WITH NAMES OF CITIZENS ENGRAVED ON PLAQUE. TIME CAPSULE BURIAL IN DEC '76 TO BE OPENED 100 YRS HENCE. (LOCAL). HON CARL M ELLIS, MAYOR; MULBERRY BICENTENNIAL COMMITTEE; 606 N FIRST AVE; MULBERRY, FL 33860. (#29806).

N BAY VILLAGE

NORTH BAY VILLAGE JEWISH CENTER - FL. A TEMPLE SEATING 500 W/CLASSROOMS TO BE USED FOR RELIGIOUS, SOCIAL & AS A COMMUNITY AND CULTURAL CENTER. (LOCAL). RUDOLPH HIRSCH, CHAIRMAN; N BAY VILLAGE BICENTENNIAL COMMITTEE; 7504 JEWEL AVE; N BAY VILLAGE, FL 33141. (#24807).

JULY 4, '76. NORTH BAY VILLAGE BICENTENNIAL BIRTHDAY PARTY CELEBRATION. FESTIVAL AT TREASURE ISLAND ELEMENTARY SCHOOL AND GROUNDS OF WCKT-TV. (LOCAL). DR S L SWARTZ, DIR; CITY OF NORTH BAY VILLAGE; 7621 MIAMI VIEW DR; N BAY ISLAND, FL 33141. (#2997-5).

N LAUDERDALE

BICENTENNIAL PARK IN NORTH LAUDERDALE, FL. LOCAL PARK TO BE DEVELOPED INTO A PICNIC PARK WITH COVERED PAVILION, BAND STAND, TABLES, BENCHES, TREES, STORAGE AREA & BARBEQUE PITS. (LOCAL). LOUIS TAFUM, CHAIRMAN; BICENTENNIAL COMMITTEE OF NORTH LAUDERDALE; 6601 BOULEVARD OF CHAMPIONS; N LAUDERDALE, FL 33068. (#15683).

HISTORICAL PRESENTATION. THE HISTORICAL PROGRAM WILL FEATURE A GRAPHIC PRESIDENTIAL ART DISPLAY. (LOCAL). LOUIS TAFRIN, CHAIRMAN; BICENTENNIAL COMMITTEE OF NORTH LAUDERDALE; 6601 BLVD OF CHAMPIONS; N LAUDERDALE, FL 33068. (#102608-1). **(??).**

PRESIDENTIAL BREAKFAST. FESTIVAL AT CITY HALL ANNEX. (LOCAL). LOU TAFURI, CHAIRMAN; BICENTENNIAL COMMITTEE OF N LAUDERDALE; 6564 SW 8TH PL; N LAUDERDALE, FL 33068. (#102417-6). **(??).**

FEB '76. BICENTENNIAL COSTUME BALL. FESTIVAL. (LOCAL). LOUIS TAFURI, CHMN; BICENTENNIAL COMMITTEE OF N LAUDERDALE; 6564 SW 8TH PL; N LAUDERDALE, FL 33068. (#102417-8).

N MIAMI BEACH

NOV 11, '75. VETERANS DAY PARADE. PARADE, COMPETITION. (LOCAL). HERMAN CAPLAN, COORD; CITY OF N MIAMI BEACH AND N MIAMI BEACH CHAMBER OF COMMERCE; 3700 NW 62ND ST; MIAMI, FL 33147. (#200011-168).

MAR 31, '76. BICENTENNIAL ITALIAN AWARENESS NIGHT WITH FILM. FESTIVAL, RADIO/TV AT WASHINGTON FEDERAL SAVING & LOAN ASSOC, 167TH ST. (LOCAL). VINCENT CONTE, PROJ COORD; UNICO NATIONAL; 421 NE 145TH ST; N MIAMI BEACH, FL 33161. (#200011-169).

OCT 14 - 27, '76. MEDICAL HERITAGE PROGRAM. EXHIBIT AT PARKWAY GENERAL HOSPITAL. (LOCAL). FRAN GUGGENHEIM, COORD; PARKWAY GENERAL HOSPITAL; 160 NW 170TH ST; N MIAMI BEACH, FL 33169. (#200011-277).

N PALM BEACH

BICENTENNIAL BANDSTAND - N PALM BEACH, FL. CONSTRUCTION OF AN OLD FASHION BANDSTAND AS A BICENTENNIAL MEMORIAL. PROJECT INCLUDED PLANNING, FUNDING, CONSTRUCTION, LANDSCAPING, AND A DEDICATION CEREMONY WITH THE PALM BEACH COUNTY COMMUNITY BAND. (LOCAL). H MALLORY PRIVETT, JR, CHAIRMAN; NORTH PALM BEACH BICENTENNIAL COMMITTEE; 501 U S HWY #1; N PALM BEACH, FL 33408. (#29444).

JULY 3 - 5, '76. 200TH BIRTHDAY WEEKEND. FESTIVAL AT NORTH PALM BEACH COUNTRY CLUB. (LOCAL). H MALLORY PRIVETT, JR; NORTH PALM BEACH BICENTENNIAL COMMITTEE; 724 NIGHTHAWK WAY; N PALM BEACH, FL 33408. (#200011-245).

NAPLES

COLLIER COUNTY MUSEUM AND ARCHIVES - FLORIDA. 7000 SQ FT MUSEUM AND ARCHIVES TO HOUSE PRESENT COLLECTION OF COUNTY HISTORY BOOKS, PAPERS, TAPED INTERVIEWS, PHOTOS, FOSSILS, INDIAN RELICS & VALUABLE ARTIFACTS. (LOCAL). GEORGE HUNTOON, PRESIDENT; COLLIER COUNTY HISTORICAL SOCIETY; 3990 TAMIAMI TRAIL NORTH; NAPLES, FL 33940. (#3927).

JAN 29, '76. UNITED STATES ARMED FORCES BICENTENNIAL CARAVAN. CARAVAN IS COMPOSED OF EXHIBIT VANS FOR EACH MILITARY SERVICE. PROJECT THEME IS 'HISTORY OF THE ARMED FORCES AND THEIR CONTRIBUTIONS TO THE NATION'. (LOCAL). BEN H ANDERSON; US ARMED FORCES BICENTENNIAL EXHIBIT VANS PROJECT; 3300 GULF SHORE BLVD N; NAPLES, FL 33940. (#1775-427).

NEWPORT RICHY

'THE AMERICAN EXPERIENCE', NEWPORT RICHEY, FL. THE COLLEGE WILL SPONSOR ONE OF THE SMITHSONIAN'S TRAVELING EXHIBITS. (LOCAL). DIANE M PARKER, CHAIRMAN; PASCO - HERNANDO COMMUNITY COLLEGE - WEST; 1510 SOUTH BLVD; NEWPORT RICHY, FL 33525. (#15710).

ARTS & CRAFTS AND MUSIC SHOW. PROGRAM PRESENTED AT PASCO COUNTY FAIR WITH BICENTENNIAL THEME. SLIDE PRESENTATION OF HISTORIC EVENTS & PEOPLE, NARRATED BY STUDENTS. RICHEY ELEMENTARY STUDENTS MADE LARGE CLOTH FLAGS REPRESENTING EACH STATE WITH AN OUTLINE MAP, STATE BIRD & FLOWER DRAWN IN. (LOCAL). KAREN CRUMBLEY, TEACHER; RICHEY ELEMENTARY SCHOOL; 800 N MADISON; NEW PT RICHEY, FL 33552. (#20205-1).

BICENTENNIAL FILM SERIES - NEWPORT RICHEY, FL. FILM SERIES WILL COVER THE HISTORY OF MOVIES & MOVIE MAKING. (LOCAL). DIANE M PARKER, CHAIRMAN; PASCO - HERNANDO COMMUNITY COLLEGE - WEST; 1510 SOUTH BLVD; NEWPORT RICHY, FL 33525. (#15718).

BOOK MOBILE, NEWPORT RICHY, FL. LIBRARY ON WHEELS TO SERVE RURAL AREA. (LOCAL). JIM DRYDEN, CHAIRMAN; WEST PASCO COUNTY BICENTENNIAL COMMITTEE; 407 W MAIN ST; NEWPORT RICHY, FL 33552. (#22365).

'FASHIONS THROUGH THE YEARS'. STUDENTS WILL MODEL 22 FASHIONS DATING FROM THE TIME OF MARTHA WASHINGTON TO THE PRESENT; COMMUNITY IS INVITED TO ATTEND. AT ON CAMPUS. (LOCAL). DIANE M PARKER, CHM; PASCO-HERNANDO COMMUNITY COLLEGE/WEST CAMPUS BICENTENNIAL COMMITTEE; 1510 SOUTH BLVD; NEWPT RICHEY, FL 33525. (#102511-2). **(??).**

GET OUT AND VOTE '76 - NEWPORT RICHEY, FL. VETERANS CLUB ON CAMPUS WILL ENCOURAGE ALL CITIZENS TO REGISTER & VOTE. (LOCAL). DIANE M PARKER, CHAIRMAN; PASCO - HERNANDO COMMUNITY COLLEGE - WEST; 1510 SOUTH BLVD; NEWPORT RICHY, FL 33525. (#15715).

'HISTORICAL DATES TO REMEMBER', NEWPORT RICHEY, FL. A STUDENT TAPED RADIO SERIES USING '200 YEARS AGO' THEME. (LOCAL). DIANE M PARKER, CHAIRMAN; PASCO - HERNANDO COMMUNITY COLLEGE - WEST; 1510 SOUTH BLVD; NEWPORT RICHY, FL 33525. (#15712).

HISTORICAL SITES IN NEWPORT RICHEY, FL. SITES OF LOCAL AND HISTORICAL INTEREST ARE TO BE APPROPRIATELY MARKED. (LOCAL). DIANE M PARKER, CHAIRMAN; PASCO - HERNANDO COMMUNITY COLLEGE - WEST; 1510 SOUTH BLVD; NEWPORT RICHY, FL 33525. (#15714).

KEEP THE SPIRIT OF '76 - NEWPORT RICHEY, FL. THE LEARNING RESOURCE CENTER WILL BE REDONE IN THE SPIRIT OF '76. (LOCAL). DIANE M PARKER, CHAIRMAN; PASCO - HERNANDO COMMUNITY COLLEGE - WEST; 1510 SOUTH BLVD; NEWPORT RICHY, FL 33525. (#15709).

OPEN HOUSE IN COMMEMORATIVE ROOM - FL. HISTORICAL ARTIFACTS WILL BE ON DISPLAY AND THEIR WILL BE A CONTINUOUSLY RUNNING VIDEO TAPE. (LOCAL). DIANE M PARKER, CHAIRMAN; PASCO - HERNANDO COMMUNITY COLLEGE - WEST; 1510 SOUTH BLVD; NEWPORT RICHY, FL 33525. (#15717).

'REMEMBER OUR BICENTENNIAL CELEBRATION' - FL. PHOTO-JOURNALISTS WILL RECORD THE BICENTENNIAL EVENTS OF THE CAMPUS TO BE PUT INTO A SCRAPBOOK. (LOCAL). DIANE M PARKER, CHAIRMAN; PASCO - HERNANDO COMMUNITY COLLEGE - WEST; 1510 SOUTH BLVD; NEWPORT RICHY, FL 33525. (#15716).

'REMEMBER WHEN?' CHRISTMAS CELEBRATION. LOCAL HISTORY WILL BE DISCUSSED BY CITIZENS THROUGH GROUP DISCUSSIONS, FILMS, FAMILY ALBUMS AND A SERIES SHORT LECTURES. (LOCAL). DIANE M PARKER, CHAIRMAN; PASCO - HERNANDO COMMUNITY COLLEGE - WEST; 1510 SOUTH BLVD; NEWPORT RICHY, FL 33525. (#15713).

'WE, THE PEOPLE...', PROJ OF NEWPORT RICHEY, FL. A DUPLICATE COPY OF THE DECLARATION OF INDEPENDENCE, OMITTING ALL SIGNITURES SO THAT FACULTY, STAFF, STUDENTS AND COMMUNITY TO SIGN. (LOCAL). DIANE M PARKER, CHAIRMAN; PASCO - HERNANDO COMMUNITY COLLEGE - WEST; 1510 SOUTH BLVD; NEWPORT RICHY, FL 33525. (#15711).

OCT 10, '75 - DEC 17, '76. HISTORICAL ESSAY CONTEST. COMPETITION. (LOCAL). JULIE OBENRADER, COORD; WEST PASCO HISTORICAL SOCIETY; 117 E TENNESSEE AVE; NW PRT RICHEY, FL 33552. (#106745-1).

DEC '75. NEW WEST CAMPUS DEDICATION AND FLAG RAISING CEREMONY. CEREMONY AT ON CAMPUS. (LOCAL). DIANE M PARKER, CHM; PASCO-HERNANDO COMMUNITY COLLEGE/WEST CAMPUS BICENTENNIAL COMMITTEE; 1510 SOUTH BLVD; NEWPT RICHEY, FL 33525. (#102511-4).

JAN 15 - 16, '76. UNITED STATES ARMED FORCES BICENTENNIAL CARAVAN. CARAVAN IS COMPOSED OF EXHIBIT VANS FOR EACH MILITARY SERVICE. PROJECT THEME IS 'HISTORY OF THE ARMED FORCES AND THEIR CONTRIBUTIONS TO THE NATION'. (LOCAL). EARL MEYER; US ARMED FORCES BICENTENNIAL EXHIBIT VANS PROJECT; 718 OAKHILL RD; NEW PORT RICH, FL 33552. (#1775-421).

MAR 5 - 14, '76. CHASCO FESTIVAL. STUDENTS WILL DESIGN A FLOAT, WITH A BICENTENNIAL THEME, AND ENTER IT IN VARIOUS PARADES. (LOCAL). DIANE M PARKER, CHMN; PASCO-HERNANDO COMMUNITY COLLEGE/WEST CAMPUS BICENTENNIAL COMMITTEE; 1510 SOUTH BLVD; NEWPT RICHEY, FL 33525. (#102994-1).

MAY '76. OUTSIDE BAZAAR. FAIR AT ON CAMPUS. (LOCAL). DIANE M PARKER, CHM; PASCO-HERNANDO COMMUNITY COLLEGE/WEST CAMPUS BICENTENNIAL COMMITTEE; 1510 SOUTH BLVD; NEWPT RICHEY, FL 33525. (#102511-5).

JUNE 13, '76. 'THE STORY OF OLD GLORY' - PAGEANT OF FLAGS. A COPY OF EACH FLAG FLOWN OVER THE PAST 200 YEARS WILL BE PRESENTED WITH MUSIC & DRESS OF EACH ERA. 19 FLAGS WILL BE USED TO DEPICT THE DEVELOPMENT OF OUR FLAG. TABLEAUS WILL RECREATE OUTSTANDING EVENTS IN HISTORY OF OUR FLAG. AT GULF HIGH SCHOOL GYM, NEW PORT RICHEY, FLORIDA. (LOCAL). MARIO BATTISTA, COORD; THE AMERICAN LEGION, PARADISE POST #79; DEPT OF FLORIDA; 710 SAN MARCO DR; PORT RICHEY, FL 33568. (#106044-1).

NICEVILLE

COLLEGE CATALOG - NICEVILLE, FL. COMMEMORATE OUR COUNTRY'S 200TH BIRTHDAY BY PROMOTING EDUCATIONAL OPPORTUNITIES IN THE OWJC DISTRICT. (LOCAL). J E MCCRACKEN, PRESIDENT; OKALOOSA-WALTON JUNIOR COLLEGE; COLLEGE BLVD; NICEVILLE, FL 32578. (#24524).

GRADUATION: BICENTENNIAL DIPLOMAS - NICEVILLE, FL. BICENTENNIAL DIPLOMAS WILL PROVIDE FOR A VERY SPECIAL GRADUATION FOR 1976. (LOCAL). R D WILSON, DEAN OF STUDENTS; OKALOOSA-WALTON JUNIOR COLLEGE; COLLEGE BLVD; NICEVILLE, FL 32578. (#24526).

STATIONERY - NICEVILLE, FL. STATIONERY TO BE USED FROM ALL OFFICES OF OWJC TO CORRESPOND WITH THE PUBLIC. (LOCAL). VICTORIA LAWRENCE, ASSISTANT; OKALOOSA-WALTON JUNIOR COLLEGE; COLLEGE BLVD; NICEVILLE, FL 32578. (#24525).

AUG 25, '75 - JUNE 30, '76. LYCEUM PROGRAMS - GEORGE WASHINGTON, ALPHA OMEGA, 1776. SPECIAL EMPHASIS ON USA WITHIN ON-GOING SERIES. AT AUDITORIUM. (LOCAL). GEORGE CASTLE; OKALOOSA-WALTON JUNIOR COLLEGE; NICEVILLE, FL 32578. (#107038-3).

MAR 19 - 20, '76. 'GHOST OF THE DUNES' (A MELODRAMA). ORIGINAL, CREATIVE CONTRIBUTION TO LOCAL AREA. PREMIER OF LOCALLY PRODUCED, LOCAL COLOR EPIC DRAMA MELODRAMA. AT AUDITORIUM. (LOCAL). J LA ROCHE, PROJ CHMN; OKALOOSA-WALTON JUNIOR COLLEGE; NICEVILLE, FL 32578. (#200011-170).

APR 8 - 10, '76. AMERICAN ARTS FESTIVAL. A DECLARATION BY OKALOOSA-WALTON JUNIOR COLLEGE OF ITS FAITH IN AND COMMITMENT TO OUR AMERICAN HERITAGE. AT OKALOOSA-WALTON JUNIOR COLLEGE CAMPUS. (LOCAL). HOSMER ROBERSON, COORD; OKALOOSA-WALTON JUNIOR COLLEGE; COLLEGE BLVD; NICEVILLE, FL 32578. (#200011-171).

OCT 4 - 8, '76. OKALOOSA AND WALTON COUNTY FAIRS. FAIR AT FAIRGROUNDS IN FORT WALTON BEACH AND IN DEFUNIAK SPRINGS. (ST-WIDE). JAMES RHOADES; OKALOOSA-WALTON JUNIOR COLLEGE; COLLEGE BLVD; NICEVILLE, FL 32578. (#107038-5).

NOV 21, '76 - APR 11, '77. COMMUNITY CONCERT SERIES. SERVICE TO THE COMMUNITY THROUGH AVAILABILITY OF FACILITIES AND ARRANGEMENTS. AT AUDITORIUM. (LOCAL). J RHOADES & A MORTON; OKALOOSA-WALTON JUNIOR COLLEGE; NICEVILLE, FL 32578. (#107038-1).

NORTH MIAMI

ART IN PUBLIC PLACES, EXHIBIT, N MIAMI, FL. AN EXHIBIT BY OUTDOOR ADVERTISING OF POEMS WRITTEN BY CHILDREN PARTICIPATING IN THE SOUTH FLORIDA 'POETS-IN-THE SCHOOLS' PROGRAM AND OTHER VISUAL WORKS BY PROMINENT ARTISTS IN THE COMMUNITY. (LOCAL). JEFFREY KNAPP, PROJ DIRECTOR; INTERNATIONAL INSTITUTE FOR CREATIVE COMMUNICATION; 14699 NE 18 AVE; N MIAMI, FL 33181. (#19833).

BICENTENNIAL QUINMESTER PROGRAM IN N MIAMI, FLA. PROGRAM INITIATED IN N MIAMI SENIOR HIGH SCHOOLS THAT REQUIRES EACH STUDENT TO COMPLETE THREE RESEARCH PAPERS IN THE AREAS OF PAST, PRESENT & FUTURE DURING FOUR OF THE FIVE QUINS. (LOCAL). MIRIAM GERSTEIN, INSTRUCTOR; NORTH MIAMI BEACH SENIOR HIGH SCHOOL; 1247 NE 167TH ST; N MIAMI BEACH, FL 33162. (#5188). **(??).**

DEC 18 - 20, '75. THE MIAMI WINTER NATIONAL MARCHING BAND CONTEST. HIGH SCHOOL BANDS COMPETE ANNUALLY IN MIAMI TO COMMEMORATE BICENTENNIAL. PARADE TO BE HELD IN NORTH MIAMI. AT MIAMI-DADE JR COLLEGE STADIUM. (NAT'L). IRV GREENE; NORTH MIAMI MUSIC PATRONS; 14965 NE 6TH AVE; NORTH MIAMI, FL 33161. (#5204-1).

MAR 25 - 28, '76. FESTIVAL '76 - PERFORMING AND VISUAL ARTS FESTIVAL. FESTIVAL. (ST-WIDE). PATRICIA BOURQUIN, COORD; THE SOCIETY OF THE ARTS; 1365 NE 139TH ST; NORTH MIAMI, FL 33161. (#103030-1).

JULY 4, '76. INDEPENDENCE DAY WATER ACTIVITIES. LIVE PERFORMANCE AT SASSO AND NORTH MIAMI MUNICIPAL POOLS. (LOCAL). VIRGINIA DIFEDERICO, DIR; CITY OF NORTH MIAMI; 776 NE 125TH ST; NORTH MIAMI, FL 33161. (#2997-14).

NW SMYRNA BCH

MAY 17 - 24, '75. FLORIDA'S BICENT EXHIBIT. MOBILE EXHIBITS PROVIDED BY THE COUNTY BICENT COMMITTEE, ACTION '76, WILL TOUR THE AREA THROUGH 1977. INCLUDED WILL BE A FLORIDA/AMERICAN BICENT TRAVELLING EXHIBIT & AN ARCHITECTURAL EXHIBIT. (ST-WIDE). GEN GEORGE FOGLE; VOLUSIA COUNTY ACTION '76 BICENTENNIAL COMMITTEE; PO BOX 1671, 250 MIDWAY; DAYTONA BEACH, FL 32015. (#7748-503).

JUNE 28 - JULY 4, '76. NEW SMYRNA BEACH BICENTENNIAL SEASIDE FIESTA. WEEK LONG CELEBRATION; DISPLAYS, EXHIBITS, BLOCK PARTIES AND DANCES; FIESTA ENDS AT STADIUM WITH OLD FASHIONED 4TH OF JULY CELEBRATION, GAMES, MUSIC, REFRESHMENTS, COMPETITIVE SPORTS, HORSE SHOW; 4TH OF JULY ACTIVITY STARTS AT NOON AND ENDS AT 5:00 PM. AT FLAGLER AVE FROM N CAUSEWAY TO OCEAN, ENDING AT STADIUM. (LOCAL). JIM POWELL, CHMN; NEW SMYRNA BEACH BICENTENNIAL COMMITTEE; 511 DOUGLAS ST; NW SMYRNA BCH, FL 32609. (#104777-1).

OAKLAND PARK

HISTORICAL MUSEUM - OAKLAND PARK, FL. RELOCATION AND RESTORATION OF 40 YEAR OLD HOUSE TO BE USED AS A MUSEUM. (LOCAL). JOHN P TOROK, COUNCILMAN; CITY OF OAKLAND PARK BICENTENNIAL COMMITTEE; 3650 NE 12 AVE; OAKLAND PARK, FL 33334. (#29442).

OCT 23, '76. CITYWIDE RUMMAGE SALE. RUMMAGE SALE BEING HELD TO HELP FUND THE RESTORATION & RELOCATION OF THE HISTORICAL MUSEUM. (LOCAL). JOHN P TOROK, COUNCILMAN; CITY OF OAKLAND PARK BICENTENNIAL COMMITTEE; 3650 NE 12 AVE; OAKLAND PARK, FL 33334. (#109372-1).

OCALA

DEC 2 - 4, '76. UNITED STATES ARMED FORCES BICENTENNIAL CARAVAN. CARAVAN IS COMPOSED OF EXHIBIT VANS FOR EACH MILITARY SERVICE. PROJECT THEME IS 'HISTORY OF THE ARMED FORCES & THEIR CONTRIBUTIONS TO THE NATION'. (LOCAL). JOHN R HUGLI, JR; UNITED STATES ARMED FORCES BICENTENNIAL CARAVAN; PO BOX 1210; OCALA, FL 32670. (#1775-782).

OCOEE

DEC 5, '75. OCOEE CHRISTMAS PARADE. AT 4:30 PM, THE NAVY BAND, HEROES OF '76, CITY OFFICIALS AND HIGH SCHOOL BANDS WILL MARCH FROM STORY RD THROUGH THE CENTER OF OCOEE. AT DOWNTOWN OCOEE. (LOCAL). JACQUELINE AMRHEIN, SEC; OCOEE BICENTENNIAL COMMITTEE; 423 S ORANGE AVE; ORLANDO, FL 32801. (#200011-179).

OKEECHOBEE

OKEECHOBEE, FL, PARK BEAUTIFICATION PROJECT. BEAUTIFICATION OF HISTORIC FLAGLER PARK HAS BEEN PLANNED; REARRANGEMENT OF PRESENT VEGATATION; PLANTING OF FLOWERING TREES AND IRRIGATION. (LOCAL). ROY HOPKE, PROJ DIRECTOR; FLORIDA DEPT OF AGRICULTURE, DIVISION OF FORESTRY; RT 2, BOX 200; OKECHOBEE, FL 33472. (#17283).

OKEECHOBEE'S FIRST SCHOOL HOUSE PROJECT -FL. PURCHASE AND RESTORATION OF ORIGINAL SCHOOL HOUSE. SCHOOL TO BE USED AS MUSEUM AND FOCAL POINT OF FRONTIER PARK. (LOCAL). ANNIE B RAULERSON, PRESIDENT; OKEECHOBEE HISTORICAL SOCIETY; 201 N W 2ND ST; OKEECHOBEE, FL 33472. (#17285).

PUBLIC FISHING PIER - OKEECHOBEE, FL. TO CONSTRUCT A PUBLIC FISHING PIER TO BE USED BY RESIDENTS AND NONRESIDENTS, FACILITY WOULD EXPAND RECREATION AND HELP ECONOMY OF THE AREA. (LOCAL). MARGARET AGER, PROJ DIRECTOR; OKEECHOBEE BICENTENNIAL '76 STEERING COMMITTEE; 802 S W 3RD AVE; OKEECHOBEE, FL 33472. (#17284).

JULY 3 - 4, '76. OLD-FASHIONED 4TH CELEBRATION. CELEBRATION WILL INCLUDE GAMES/FOOD BOOTHS/ARTS & CRAFTS/CONTESTS/ TOURNAMENTS/PARADE/SOMETHING TO INVOLVE EVERYONE. AT DOWNTOWN FLAGLER PK. (LOCAL). MARGARET AGER, EXEC DIR; OKEECHOBEE CO 76 BICENTENNIAL STEERING COMMITTEE; 802 SW 3RD AVE; OKEECHOBEE, FL 33472. (#103255-2).

OKLAWAHA

WITS END FARM BICENTENNIAL CROSS COUNTRY RIDE, FL. A COAST TO COAST RIDE TO PUBLICIZE NEED AND PROMOTE ESTABLISHMENT OF MULTIPURPOSE TRAILS IN US; 3 HORSEMEN RIDE 30 MILES A DAY MEETING EACH NIGHT; CAMPER PULLING TRAILER WITH HAY AND SPARE HORSES. (REGN'L). MARGO ATWOOD, TRAIL BOSS; WITS END FARM; OKLAWAHA, FL 32679. (#19929).

OLDSMAR

OLDSMAR RECREATION CENTER - OLDSMAR, FL. AS OF NOW OLDSMAR HAS NO RECREATIONAL CENTER. THIS WILL PROVIDE A PLACE FOR THE WHOLE COMMUNITY TO USE FOR DANCES OR MEETINGS OR TO OFFER RECREATIONAL ACTIVITIES. (LOCAL). MRS HELEN MANNING, CHAIRPERSON; OLDSMAR BICENTENNIAL COMMITTEE; 1819 DRIFTWOOD CIRCLE S; OLDSMAR, FL 33557. (#15073).

JULY 3, '76. FATHER-SON AND MOTHER-DAUGHTER BALL GAME. COMPETITION AT R E OLDS PARK. (LOCAL). ELLA CAMPOLI, COORD; OLDSMAR BICENTENNIAL COMMITTEE; PO BOX 613; OLDSMAR, FL 33557. (#108335-6).

JULY 5, '76. ARTS & CRAFTS SHOW. EXHIBIT, FESTIVAL AT R E OLDS PARK. (LOCAL). ELLA CAMPOLI, COORD; OLDSMAR BICENTENNIAL COMMITTEE; PO BOX 613; OLDSMAR, FL 33557. (#108335-5).

OLDSMAR — CONTINUED

JULY 6, '76. OLD-FASHIONED ICE CREAM SOCIAL WITH CAKE WALK & AUCTION. FESTIVAL AT R E OLDS PARK. (LOCAL). ELLA CAMPOLI, COORD; OLDSMAR BICENTENNIAL COMMITTEE; PO BOX 613; OLDSMAR, FL 33557. (#108335-2).

JULY 8, '76. STREET SQUARE DANCE. FESTIVAL AT STATE STREET. (LOCAL). ELLA CAMPOLI, COORD; OLDSMAR BICENTENNIAL COMMITTEE; PO BOX 613; OLDSMAR, FL 33557. (#108335-3).

JULY 10, '76. OLDSMAR'S BICENTENNIAL PARADE & PET SHOW. PARADE, FESTIVAL AT R E OLDS PARK. (LOCAL). ELLA CAMPOLI, COORD; OLDSMAR BICENTENNIAL COMMITTEE; PO BOX 613; OLDSMAR, FL 33537. (#108335-1).

JULY 11, '76. SUNDAY MUSICALE. LIVE PERFORMANCE AT R E OLDS PARK. (LOCAL). ELLA CAMPOLI, COORD; OLDSMAR BICENTENNIAL COMMITTEE; PO BOX 613; OLDSMAR, FL 33557. (#108335-4).

OPA-LOCKA

OPA-LOCKA, FL, WOMAN'S CLUB BICENTENNIAL PROJECT. A LIVING PICTURE DEPICTING THE COURAGEOUS CHARACTER OF THE AMERICAN WOMAN IN SUPPORT OF HER HUSBAND, HER CHILDREN AND HER COUNTRY. (LOCAL). MRS BARNEY B BURNETT, CHAIRPERSON; OPA-LOCKA WOMENS CLUB; 1146 JANN AVE; OPA-LOCKA, FL 33054. (#17177).

JULY 4, '76. INDEPENDENCE DAY PARADE AND SPORTS PROGRAM. FESTIVAL, PARADE AT OPA-LOCKA BLVD AND SHERBONDY PARK. (LOCAL). ROBERT A FRAZIER, COORD; OPA-LOCKA BICENTENNIAL COMMITTEE; 780 W SUPERIOR ST; OPA-LOCKA, FL 33054. (#2997-9).

ORANGE PARK

BICENTENNIAL CALENDAR, ORANGE PARK, FL. A JOINT FUND-RAISING PROJECT OF THE LAKESIDE ELEMENTARY & MIDDLE SCHOOLS; EACH MONTH DEPICTS A HISTORICAL EVENT ASSOCIATED WITH THAT MONTH. PICTURES ARE STUDENTS' WINNING ENTRIES OF FALL ART CONTEST. (LOCAL). MRS RICHARD TYMICK, CO-CHAIRMAN; LAKESIDE ELEMENTARY & LAKESIDE MIDDLE SCHOOLS PFA; 1234 ARDEN AVE; ORANGE PARK, FL 32073. (#19984).

BICENTENNIAL COOKBOOK - ORANGE PARK, FL. COOKBOOK FEATURING RECIPES FROM PARENTS, GRANDPARENTS AND CHILDREN. AVAILABLE AFTER END OF OCTOBER FOR GENERAL SALES. (LOCAL). MRS EARLYMAE EDWARDS, PTA BICENTENNIAL CHAIRMAN; ORANGE PARK ELEMENTARY SCHOOL PTA; 431 CLINTON DR; ORANGE PARK, FL 32073. (#18005).

BICENTENNIAL LIVE OAK TREES - ORANGE PARK, FL. IDENTIFY AND GIVE SPECIAL RECOGNITION TO 200 YEAR OLD LIVE OAK TREES THROUGHOUT CLAY COUNTY. (LOCAL). MRS GORDON SANDRIDGE, COORDINATOR; ORANGE PARK ENVIRONMENTAL QUALITY BOARD; 2764 HOLLY POINT RD W; ORANGE PARK, FL 32073. (#24865).

BICENTENNIAL NIGHT. AUTHENTIC FAMILY DINNER SERVED TO PTA MEMBERS & THEIR FAMILIES. BICENT ORIENTED ENTERTAINMENT, INCLUDING GUEST SPEAKER HARRIS T REMLEY. (LOCAL). MRS EARLYMAE P EDWARDS; ORANGE PARK ELEMENTARY SCHOOL PTA; PLAINFIELD AVE; ORANGE PARK, FL 32073. (#106743-1).

BOOK REVIEW. A BOOK REVIEW & DRAMATIZATION BY MRS MARION CONNOR ON SUBJECT PERTINENT TO THE BICENTENNIAL YEAR. (LOCAL). MRS W H MADDOX, JR, PRES; FRIENDS OF THE ORANGE PARK LIBRARY; 1222 S LAKE VIEW DR; ORANGE PARK, FL 32073. (#20632-1).

CEMETERY RESTORATION AND BEAUTIFICATION, FL. CEMETERY TO BE RENOVATED AND BEAUTIFIED; NEW ENTRANCE GATES TO BE ERECTED AND LANDSCAPED. (LOCAL). MRS GORDON SANDRIDGE, CHAIRMAN; O P CIVIC BEAUTIFICATION COMMITTEE & HUMMINGBIRD GARD CIRCLE; 2764 HOLLY POINT RD W; ORANGE PARK, FL 32073. (#18003).

CHURCH RESTORATION - ORANGE PARK, FL. ORANGE PARK'S OLDEST CHURCH, PRESENTLY BEING USED AS A STORAGE AREA BY THE OWNER, IS TO BE RETURNED TO THE MEMBERS OF ST CATHERINE'S PARISH, RESTORED, AND BECOME A SHRINE FOR THE PUBLIC. (LOCAL). FATHER EDWARD ROONEY, PASTOR; ST CATHERINE'S CATHOLIC CHURCH; 1649 KINGSLEY AVE; ORANGE PARK, FL 32073. (#18007).

COUNTY-WIDE BEARD GROWING CONTEST. OPEN TO ALL. CASH PRIZES FOR BEST 3 ALL-AROUND BEARDS. TROPHIES TO 7 'LOOK ALIKE' WINNERS, MOST LIKE BEARDS FO 7 HISTORIC PERSONALITIES WITH 3 SPECIAL PRIZES TO FRATERNAL ORDER OF POLICE, LODGE 104. (LOCAL). A H TEBAULT, EDITOR; 'CLAY TODAY'; 1564 KINGLEY AVE; ORANGE PARK, FL 32073. (#106743-2).

ESSAY CONTEST, ORANGE PARK, FL. ESSAY CONTEST FOR ORANGE PARK HIGH SCHOOL STUDENTS, THE THEME IS: 'FUTURE WAY IN THE USA.' STUDENTS WILL GIVE VIEWS ON GOVERNMENT, HOME LIFE, ECOLOGY & ECONOMICS. (LOCAL). ROBERT E FORD, PRESIDENT; BELLAIR-MEADOWBROOK CIVIC LEAGUE, INC; 470 MADEIRA DR; ORANGE PARK, FL 32073. (#20633).

FLY THE FLAG CAMPAIGN - ORANGE PARK, FL. DESIGNED TO ENCOURAGE ALL RESIDENTS & BUSINESS ESTABLISHMENTS TO PROCURE & DISPLAY THE AMERICAN FLAG ON A DAILY BASIS, ESPECIALLY ON HOLIDAYS OF NATIONAL SIGNIFICANCE. (LOCAL). MRS E L DECROSTA, ADMIN ASSISTANT; CLAY COUNTY BICENTENNIAL STEERING COMMITTEE; PO BOX 1776; ORANGE PARK, FL 32073. (#24657).

FOLKSINGERS - TOM & MICHAEL MOORE, ORANGE PARK, FL. THE STEERING COMMITTEE HAS ENDORSED THE MOORES FOR PARTICIPATION IN CLAY COUNTY'S PERFORMING ARTS GROUP, WHICH IS SPONSORED BY THE COMMITTEE; THE DUO SINGS TRADITIONAL AMERICAN FOLK SONGS. (LOCAL). MRS E L DECROSTA, ADMINISTRATIVE ASSISTANT; CLAY COUNTY BICENTENNIAL STEERING COMMITTEE; BOX 1776; ORANGE PARK, FL 32073. (#22139).

HERITAGE HALL - ORANGE PARK, FL. REDECORATING OF SCHOOL CORRIDORS IN BICENT THEME. HERITAGE HALL IS LOCATED IN FRONT CORRIDOR AND FEATURES PORTRAITS OF PRESIDENTS, HISTORICAL DOCUMENTS, FLAG FLOWN OVER U S CAPITOL & OTHER HIST ITEMS. (LOCAL). DONALD A SOHM, PRINCIPAL; ORANGE PARK ELEMENTARY SCHOOL; PLAINFIELD AVE; ORANGE PARK, FL 32073. (#18006).

HIGHWAY BEAUTIFICATION - ORANGE PARK, FL. A PLAN TO IMPROVE THE LANDSCAPING ON THE MAIN BUSINESS STREET, HWY 17, IN ORANGE PARK AND TO ENCOURAGE AND WORK WITH LOCAL BUSINESSES TO LANDSCAPE AND BEAUTIFY THEIR PROPERTIES ALONG THIS SAME HIGHWAY. (LOCAL). MRS H W MARTENS, PROJ DIRECTOR; HANDS COMMITTEE OF ORANGE PARK GARDEN CLUB; 2763 HOLLY POINT RD EAST; ORANGE PARK, FL 32073. (#18009).

HISTORY OF CLAY COUNTY CHURCHES - FL. EACH MONTH THE HISTORY OF A DIFFERENT RELIGIOUS DENOMINATION IN CLAY COUNTY IS RESEARCHED, WRITTEN & PRESENTED, BOTH AT THE SPONSOR'S MONTHLY MEETING & AS A FEATURED ARTICLE IN A LOCAL NEWSPAPER. (LOCAL). MRS CAMERON BABBITT, PRESIDENT; ORANGE PARK WOMEN'S CLUB; 2840 BIRCHWOOD DR; ORANGE PARK, FL 32073. (#18004).

LANDSCAPING OF YOUTH POOL. LANDSCAPE PLANTINGS TO BE PUT AROUND RECENTLY OPENED YOUTH POOL. (LOCAL). MRS GORDON SANDRIDGE, BICENTENNIAL CHAIRMAN; ORANGE PARK GARDEN CLUB; 2764 HOLLY POINT RD, WEST; ORANGE PARK, FL 32073. (#18008).

'LIBERTY TREE', ORANGE PARK, FL. A SINGLE TREE WILL BE PLANTED IN ORANGE PARK BY THE ORANGE PARK GARDEN CLUB. A PLAQUE WILL BE PLACED AT THE SITE, DESIGNATING IT AS A 'LIBERTY TREE' IN COMMEMORATION OF THE BICENTENNIAL. (LOCAL). MRS L R LEDBETTER, CHMN, BIRDS & CONSERVATION; ORANGE PARK GARDEN CLUB; 2714 WOODLAND DR; ORANGE PARK, FL 32073. (#19983).

LIVE OAK SEEDLING GIVE-AWAY PROGRAM, FL. HUNDREDS OF SEEDLINGS WERE GIVEN AWAY ON FLORIDA ARBOR DAY; PACKETS OF FLOWERING TREES WERE SOLD AT A NOMINAL PRICE. (LOCAL). MRS GORDON SANDRIDGE, CHAIRMAN; CIVIC BEAUTIFICATION COMMITTEE OF TOWN OF ORANGE PARK; 2764 HOLLY POINT RD W; ORANGE PARK, FL 32073. (#24866).

TOWN HALL SQUARE LANDSCAPING - ORANGE PARK, FL. LANDSCAPING TO INCLUDE NEW SHRUBBERY, CORNER RED, WHITE & BLUE PLANTING & INSTALLATION OF REDWOOD BENCHES. (LOCAL). MRS GORDON SANDRIDGE, PROJ CHAIRMAN; ORANGE PARK CIVIC BEAUTIFICATION COMMITTEE & GARDEN CLUB; 2764 HOLLY POINT RD W; ORANGE PARK, FL 32073. (#24864).

FEB 1, '75 - MAY '76. 'ROGER WILLIAMS AND MARY'. A 'READERS THEATRE' PLAY, FEATURING A CAST OF 3, DEALING WITH ONE MAN'S SEARCH FOR FREEDOM OF WORSHIP IN THE NEW WORLD SETTLEMENT IN MASSACHUSETTS. (LOCAL). MRS GEORGE CENTER, DIR; ORANGE PARK COMMUNITY THEATRE - DRAMA TRIO; 2531 ELBOW RD; ORANGE PARK, FL 32073. (#104900-2).

FEB 27 - MAR 16, '76. 'I LOVE AMERICA' CHORAL PROGRAM. FEB 27, 1976: AT MIDDLEBURG ELEMENTARY SCHOOL, 8-9 PM. MAR 5, 1976: GREENCOVE SPRINGS HIGH SCHOOL, 8-9 PM. MAR 16, 1976: ORANGE PARK MORMON CHURCH, 8-9 PM. (LOCAL). MRS R A PATTERSON, CHMN; CLAY COUNTY BICENTENNIAL STEERING COMMITTEE; 2886 RIVER OAK DR; ORANGE PARK, FL 32073. (#103517-31).

MAR 6 - 7, '76. FLOWER SHOW AND TOUR OF HOMES. TOUR HOMES AVAILABLE AT OFFICE PAVILION. AT OFFICE PAVILION, 2301 PARK AVE. (LOCAL). MRS J N HELLMUTH, PRES; ORANGE PARK GARDEN CLUB; 1454 RIVER RD; ORANGE PARK, FL 32073. (#103517-34).

MAR 18, '76. 'WHAT AMERICAN DO YOU MOST ADMIRE AND WHY?' - ESSAY CONTEST. CEREMONY, COMPETITION. (LOCAL). MARCIA RHEA, REPORTER; CLAY COUNTY COMMUNITY NEWS OF THE FLORIDA TIMES UNION; 1 RIVERSIDE AVE; JACKSONVILLE, FL 32202. (#200011-175).

MAR 19 - 21, '76. CLAY FESTIVAL '76 - A COUNTY-WIDE ARTS AND CRAFTS FESTIVAL. OPEN 11 AM TO 8 PM, FRIDAY; 10 AM TO 8 PM SATURDAY; 12 PM TO 4 PM SUNDAY. ENTRANCE FEE OF $5.00 TO THOSE WISHING TO SELL THEIR ENTRY. AT ORANGE PARK KENNEL CLUB, US HWY 17. (LOCAL). MRS R A PATTERSON, CHMN; CLAY COUNTY BICENTENNIAL STEERING COMMITTEE; 2886 RIVER OAK DR; ORANGE PARK, FL 32073. (#103517-32).

MAR 31, '76. MARDI GRAS QUEEN'S PAGEANT. COMPETITION AT ORANGE PARK HIGH SCHOOL CAFETERIA, 2300 KINGSLEY AVE; FREE PARKING. (LOCAL). REDDICK LYONS, COORD; BAND PARENTS ASSOC OF THE ORANGE PARK HIGH SCHOOL; 3317 HOLLYCREST BLVD; ORANGE PARK, FL 32073. (#200011-176).

APR 3, '76. MARDI GRAS PARADE AND FESTIVAL. PARADE FORMS AT 10:00 AM AT THE ORANGE PARK KENNEL CLUB; STARTS AT 11 AM. PROCEEDS SOUTH ON HWY 17 TO THE ORANGE PARK TOWN HALL. THERE WILL BE GAMES, MUSIC, AND A CHICKEN BARBECUE DINNER FROM 11 AM TO 6 PM. (LOCAL). REDDICK LYONS, COORD; BAND PARENTS ASSOC OF ORANGE PARK HIGH SCHOOL; 3317 HOLLYCREST BLVD; ORANGE PARK, FL 32073. (#200011-177).

APR 22 - 24, '76. PATRIOTIC DANCE PROGRAM. DANCE PROGRAM WITH A PATRIOTIC THEME, 1/2 HOUR LONG, CHOREOGRAPHED & DIRECTED BY MISS TRUDY SIGMAN OF ORANGE PARK, FLA. APR 22, 1976: LAKESIDE MIDDLE SCHOOL, 8 PM. APR 24, 1976: RIVERSIDE CHURCH APARTMENTS, 1 PM. (LOCAL). MRS R A PATTERSON, CHMN; CLAY COUNTRY BICENTENNIAL STEERING COMMITTEE; 2886 RIVER OAK DR; ORANGE PARK, FL 32073. (#103517-33).

APR 26 - 30, '76. 'SPIRIT OF '76' - POP MUSICAL PRODUCTION. MAJOR POP MUSIC PRODUCTION INVOLVING MUSIC DEPT OF LOCAL HIGH SCHOOL IN TRIBUTE TO THE BICENT. (LOCAL). NOAH SRYGLEY, DIRECTOR; ORANGE PARK HIGH SCHOOL MUSIC DEPT; 2300 KINGSLEY AVE; ORANGE PARK, FL 32073. (#106743-3).

JUNE 4, '76. STARLIGHT SYMPHONETTE. LIVE PERFORMANCE AT CLUB CONTINENTAL GARDENS. (LOCAL). MRS GORDON SANDRIDGE, DIR; ORANGE PARK 'FRIENDS' OF THE LIBRARY; 2764 HOLLY POINT RD W; ORANGE PARK, FL 32073. (#103517-35).

JULY 4, '76. JULY FOURTH CELEBRATION. ACTIVITIES TO INCLUDE BAND MUSIC, SHORT PATRIOTIC SPEECHES, OUTDOOR PICNIC, SQUARE DANCE AND FIREWORKS. AT ORANGE PARK KENNEL CLUB, HWY 17 & WELLS RD. (LOCAL). JOHN HELLMUTH, CHAIRMAN; TOWN OF ORANGE PARK, ORANGE PARK BICENTENNIAL COMMITTEE; 1454 RIVER RD; ORANGE PARK, FL 32073. (#107621-2).

JULY 4, '76. NEW LIBRARY DEDICATION. CEREMONY AT PLAINFIELD AVE, ONE BLOCK SOUTH OF KINGSLEY AVE. (LOCAL). MRS JOSEPH I TRIPLETT III; FRIENDS OF THE ORANGE PARK LIBRARY; 2512 GRASSHOPPER LANE; ORANGE PARK, FL 32073. (#107621-1).

ORLANDO

APOPKA HIGH SCHOOL PROJECTS - ORLANDO, FL. THE STUDENT BODY WILL CONTRIBUTE A BICENTENNIAL MEMORIAL TO THE SCHOOL; ALSO, CREATIVE WRITING ASSEMBLY PROGRAMS; COLOR DAYS OF BICENTENNIAL SIGNIFICANCE; WILL FUND ACTIVITIES BY SELLING TOYS. (LOCAL). ROLFE G ARNHYM, CHAIRMAN; ORANGE COUNTY BICENTENNIAL COMMITTEE; 423 S ORANGE AVE; ORLANDO, FL 32801. (#20269).

BICENTENNIAL COOKBOOK - ORLANDO, FL. THE BOOK CONTAINS OLD AND NEW ORIGINAL RECIPES WHICH ARE SIMPLIFIED AND UPDATED FOR TODAY'S MODERN APPLIANCES. (LOCAL). ROLFE G ARNHYM, CHAIRMAN; ORANGE COUNTY BICENTENNIAL COMMITTEE; 423 S ORANGE AVE; ORLANDO, FL 32801. (#17200).

BICENTENNIAL DOCUMENTARY FILMS IN ORLANDO, FLORIDA. A SERIES OF FILMS WILL BE MADE ABOUT BICENTENNIAL ACTIVITIES; THERE WILL BE NO CHARGE FOR SHOWINGS TO GROUPS OR CLUBS. (ST-WIDE). TIM ADAMS, PRESIDENT, WHO IS WHO OF ORLANDO; FLORIDA, INCORPORATED, T M, S M; PO BOX 1172, MONTE CARLO TRAIL; ORLANDO, FL 32802. (#10149).

BICENTENNIAL MUSICAL PROGRAM BASED ON EARLY AMERICAN COMPOSITIONS. LIVE PERFORMANCE. (LOCAL). JERRELL SHOFNER, CHMN; FTU BICENTENNIAL COMMITTEE; PO BOX 25000; ORLANDO, FL 32816. (#102508-1). **(??).**

BICENTENNIAL PARADE. PARADE AT WYMORE VOCATIONAL TECHNICAL CENTER. (LOCAL). ROLFE G ARNHYM, CHAIRMAN; ORANGE COUNTY BICENTENNIAL COMMITTEE; 423 S ORANGE AVE; ORLANDO, FL 32801. (#103235-2). **(??).**

BICENTENNIAL RADIO SERIES - ORLANDO, FL. A SERIES OF 52 RADIO PROGRAMS ON REVOLUTIONARY TOPICS FOR WEEKLY DISSEMINATION BY FTU'S RADIO NETWORK. (LOCAL). JERRELL H SHOFNER, CHAIRMAN; FTU BICENTENNIAL COMMITTEE; PO BOX 25000; ORLANDO, FL 32816. (#15735).

BICENTENNIAL YOUTH DEBATES - ORLANDO, FL. DEBATES BY HIGH SCHOOL STUDENTS ON SPECIFIC THEMES RELATING TO OUR HERITAGE; THIS IS PART OF THE NATIONAL PROGRAM. (LOCAL). JERRELL H SHOFNER, CHAIRMAN; FTU BICENTENNIAL COMMITTEE; PO BOX 25000; ORLANDO, FL 32816. (#15734).

BOONE HIGH SCHOOL PROJECT - ORLANDO, FL. STUDENTS WILL PURCHASE 'SPIRIT OF '76' CLASS RINGS; PROGRAMS AND ASSEMBLIES WITH BICENTENNIAL THEMES WILL BE GIVEN BY BAND, CHORUS AND BRAVETTES DANCE TEAM. (LOCAL). ROLFE G ARNHYM, CHAIRMAN; ORANGE COUNTY BICENTENNIAL COMMITTEE; 423 S ORANGE AVE; ORLANDO, FL 32801. (#20255).

CAMPUS LANDSCAPING, ORLANDO, FL. IN HONOR OF THE BICENTENNIAL, MINIATURE HEDGES WILL BE LANDSCAPED ON CAMPUS OF WYMORE VOCATIONAL TECHNICAL CENTER. (LOCAL). ROLFE G ARNHYM, CHAIRMAN; ORANGE COUNTY BICENTENNIAL COMMITTEE; 423 S ORANGE AVE; ORLANDO, FL 32801. (#16938).

COLONIAL HIGH SCHOOL BICENTENNIAL PROJECTS, FL. SCHOOL TO DONATE BANNER TO CITY FOR DISPLAY; MURALS FOR SCHOOL BEING DRAWN WHICH DEPICT HISTORIC EVENTS; THE FROM AND YEARBOOK WILL HAVE A BICENTENNIAL THEME. (LOCAL). ROLFE G ARNHYM, CHAIRMAN; ORANGE COUNTY BICENTENNIAL COMMITTEE; 423 S ORANGE AVE; ORLANDO, FL 32801. (#19640).

COMMEMORATIVE INDIAN PLAQUE - ORLANDO, FL. DAR PURCHASED A 3' X 5' BRONZE RELIEF PLAQUE (CIRCA 1900) DEPICTING THE AMERICAN INDIAN CORN DANCE; IT WILL BE INSTALLED AT ORLANDO PUBLIC LIBRARY. (LOCAL). ROLFE G ARNHYM, CHAIRMAN; ORANGE COUNTY BICENTENNIAL COMMITTEE; 423 S ORANGE AVE; ORLANDO, FL 32801. (#20256).

DAILY HISTORIC ANNOUNCEMENTS, ORLANDO, FL. HISTORIC ANNOUNCEMENTS TO BE MADE DAILY OVER THE INTERCON AT WYMORE VOCATIONAL TECHNICAL CENTER. (LOCAL). ROLFE G

ORLANDO — CONTINUED

ARNHYM, CHAIRMAN; ORANGE COUNTY BICENTENNIAL COMMITTEE; 423 S ORANGE AVE; ORLANDO, FL 32801. (#17140).

EDGEWATER HIGH SCHOOL HISTORICAL PROJECTS - FL. FREEDOM TREE TO BE PLANTED, PLAQUE PRESENTED, SHORT NARRATIVES OF HISTORIC EVENTS WILL BE WRITTEN, SPECIAL DISPLAYS WILL BE EXHIBITED IN THE MEDIA ROOM & STUDENTS WILL WORK ON BICENT CLASS PROJECTS. (LOCAL). ROLFE G ARNHYM, CHAIRMAN; ORANGE COUNTY BICENTENNIAL COMMITTEE; 423 S ORANGE AVE; ORLANDO, FL 32801. (#19641).

ESSAY CONTEST ON AMERICAN HISTORY; ORLANDO, FL. THE THEME OF THIS ESSAY CONTEST IS 'TWO HUNDRED YEARS OF FREEDOM'. THE CONTEST IS BEING SPONSORED FOR ELEMENTARY AND JUNIOR HIGH STUDENTS WHO LIVE IN WINTER PARK PINES. (LOCAL). ROLFE G ARNHYM, CHAIRMAN; ORANGE COUNTY BICENTENNIAL COMMITTEE; 423 S ORANGE AVE; ORLANDO, FL 32801. (#17195).

EVANS HIGH SCHOOL PROJECTS - ORLANDO, FL. BICENTENNIAL HOMECOMING; FIRE HYDRANTS ON CAMPUS WILL BE PAINTED IN THE FORM OF COLONIAL FIGURES; SCHOOL FAIR SPONSORED BY BICENTENNIAL CLUB WITH EXHIBITS OF HISTORICAL PATTERNS. (LOCAL). ROLFE G ARNHYM, CHAIRMAN; ORANGE COUNTY BICENTENNIAL COMMITTEE; 423 S ORANGE AVE; ORLANDO, FL 32809. (#20270).

HAND-CARVED WHITE HOUSE IN MINIATURE. COMPLETED HANDMADE REPLICA OF WHITE HOUSE DONE. ROOMS ARE FURNISHED TO EXACT DETAIL. EXHIBIT WILL TRAVEL THROUGHOUT U.S. (NAT'L). JOHN E ZWEIFEL, PRESIDENT; ZWEIFEL INTERNATIONAL; 8967 EASTERLING DR; ORLANDO, FL 32811. (#17319). **ARBA RECOGNIZED.**

HISTORICAL BOOK ON CENTRAL FLORIDA. THIS BOOK IS FILLED WITH HISTORICAL MEMORABILIA DATING FROM 1875 1975. THE BOOK IS ENTITLED 'MORE THAN A MEMORY'. (LOCAL). ROLFE G ARNHYM, CHAIRMAN; ORANGE COUNTY BICENTENNIAL COMMITTEE; 423 S ORANGE AVE; ORLANDO, FL 32801. (#17198).

HISTORY OF ORANGE COUNTY - ORLANDO, FL. THIS BOOK CONTAINS HISTORICAL INFORMATION ON THE DEVELOPMENT OF ORANGE COUNTY. (LOCAL). ROLFE G ARNHYM, CHAIRMAN; ORANGE COUNTY BICENTENNIAL COMMITTEE; 423 S ORANGE AVE; ORLANDO, FL 32801. (#17199).

JONES HIGH SCHOOL PROJECTS - ORLANDO, FL. COMMEMORATIVE PAVILLION TO BE USED AS A STUDENT MEETING PLACE; THE CHORUS & BAND WILL HAVE PATRIOTIC PRESENTATIONS ON EVENTS IN HISTORY. (LOCAL). ROLFE G ARNHYM, CHAIRMAN; ORANGE COUNTY BICENTENNIAL COMMITTEE; 423 S ORANGE AVE; ORLANDO, FL 32801. (#20260).

LAKEVIEW HIGH SCHOOL BICENTENNIAL PROJECTS, FL. PROJECTS INCLUDE: MAKING A FILM TO SHOW HISTORY OF FORMER SCHOOLS, PLACING A TIME CAPSULE IN THE CORNERSTONE OF NEW BUILDING & RAISING MONEY FOR LANDSCAPING OF NEW BUILDING. (LOCAL). ROLFE G ARNHYM, CHAIRMAN; ORANGE COUNTY BICENTENNIAL COMMITTEE; 423 S ORANGE AVE; ORLANDO, FL 32801. (#16987).

MOVIE ON FLORIDA HISTORY - ORLANDO. USING STUDENT TALENT AND A SCRIPT VERIFIED BY QUALIFIED HISTORIANS, THE MOVIE WILL FEATURE IMPORTANT PLACES IN EARLY FLORIDA HISTORY. (LOCAL). JERRELL H SHOFNER, CHAIRMAN; FTU BICENTENNIAL COMMITTEE; PO BOX 25000; ORLANDO, FL 32816. (#15737).

NAVAL TRAINING CENTER PROVIDES BICENT SUPPORT - FL. SUPPORT PROVIDED FOR MILITARY & CIVILIAN EVENTS THROUGHOUT CENTRAL FLORIDA; PERFORMANCES BY SUCH NTC GROUPS AS NAVY BAND ORLANDO, WOMEN'S DRILL TEAM & NTC SPEAKERS BUREAU. (LOCAL). JERRY R RYAN, LT (USN); NAVAL TRAINING CENTER; PUBLIC AFFAIRS OFFICE; ORLANDO, FL 32813. (#29446).

OAK RIDGE HIGH SCHOOL PROJECTS - ORLANDO, FL. FLAGS OF 13 COLONIES WILL BE FLOWN FOR SPECIAL DAY AT SCHOOL; SPIRIT OF '76 TIME CAPSULE WILL BE PLACED IN THE NEW BUILDING; DONATION OF FLAGPOLE AND COURSES ON HISTORICAL EVENTS & PERSONS. (LOCAL). ROLFE G ARNHYM, CHAIRMAN; ORANGE COUNTY BICENTENNIAL COMMITTEE; 423 S ORANGE AVE; ORLANDO, FL 32801. (#20254).

ORAL HISTORY OF CENTRAL FLORIDA, ORLANDO, FL. A SERIES OF TAPED INTERVIEWS WITH PEOPLE IN THE COMMUNITY; WILL ILLUMINATE THE AREA'S PAST DEVELOPMENT. (LOCAL). EUGENE ROACH, INSTRUCTOR; VALENCIA COMMUNITY COLLEGE; PO BOX 3028; ORLANDO, FL 32802. (#25083).

ORLANDO, FLORIDA'S COMMUNITY DEVELOPEMENT. PLANNING PROGRAM FOR CENTRAL CITY NEIGHBORHOOD TO INCLUDE RESTORATION OF HISTORIC BUILDINGS, SCULPTURE, PUBLIC & PRIVATE RECOGNITION OF DEVELOPMENT, PARKS AND GREENWAYS AND A TIME CAPSULE. (LOCAL). JERRY NAPIER, DIRECTOR OF PLANNING; CITY OF ORLANDO; 400 S ORANGE AVE; ORLANDO, FL 32801. (#5280).

RESTORATION OF 1915 LAFRANCE PUMPER, ORLANDO, FL. RESTORE A 1915 LAFRANCE FIRE ENGINE TO ITS ORIGINAL CONDITION FOR THE HISTORICAL AND EDUCATIONAL BENEFIT OF THE CITIZENS OF CENTRAL FLORIDA. (LOCAL). ROLFE G ARNHYM, CHAIRMAN; ORANGE COUNTY BICENTENNIAL COMMITTEE; 423 S ORANGE AVE; ORLANDO, FL 32801. (#19642).

SCHOOL ESSAYS AND POETRY ON PATRIOTISM - FL. BOTH PROJECTS WILL EMPHASIZE PATRIOTISM AND WILL INVOLVE THE COMMUNITY IN WINTER GARDEN. THE BEST PROJECTS WILL BE PUBLISHED IN THE LOCAL NEWSPAPERS. (LOCAL). ROLFE G ARNHYM, CHAIRMAN; ORANGE COUNTY BICENTENNIAL COMMITTEE; 423 S ORANGE AVE; ORLANDO, FL 32801. (#17196).

TOWN HALL MEETINGS. MEETINGS OF A CROSS SECTION OF AREA POPULATION TO ENCOURAGE COMMUNITY EFFORTS TO IMPROVE THE QUALITY OF LIFE IN THE AREA. PROCEEDINGS OF MEETINGS WILL BE PUBLISHED. (LOCAL). DR OLIN R FISCHER, DIR; VALENCIA COMMUNITY COLLEGE - COMMUNITY INSTITUTE RESOURCES; PO BOX 3028; ORLANDO, FL 32802. (#107828-1). **(??).**

WASHINGTON SHORES RECREATION CENTER DEDICATION; FL. AN ADDITION TO THE EXISTING FACILITY WILL BE CONSTRUCTED AND DEDICATED TO THE BICENTENNIAL. (LOCAL). ROLFE G ARNHYM, CHAIRMAN; ORANGE COUNTY BICENTENNIAL COMMITTEE; 423 S ORANGE AVE; ORLANDO, FL 32801. (#17197).

WINTER PARK HIGH SCHOOL PROJECTS - ORLANDO, FL. SUBSCRIPTION TO SMITHSONIAN REVIEW FOR THE LIBRARY; COLONIAL FAIR BY CLUBS & CLASSES; BATTLE RE-ENACTMENT WITH THEME OF '76 AND BICENTENNIAL DANCE. (LOCAL). ROLFE G ARNHYM, CHAIRMAN; ORANGE COUNTY BICENTENNIAL COMMITTEE; 423 S ORANGE AVE; ORLANDO, FL 32801. (#20253).

18TH CENTURY FLORIDA, EDUCATIONAL COURSE - ORLANDO. A SCHOLARLY PROGRAM ON THE BRITISH IN FLORIDA DURING THE REVOLUTIONARY PERIOD. (LOCAL). JERRELL H SHOFNER, CHAIRMAN; FTU BICENTENNIAL COMMITTEE; PO BOX 25000; ORLANDO, FL 32816. (#15733).

MAR 22 - 23, '74. '18TH CENTURY FLORIDA LIFE ALONG THE FRONTIER' SYMPOSIUM. THIRD ANNUAL FLORIDA BICENTENNIAL SYMPOSIUM. THEME: EIGHTEENTH CENTURY FLORIDA: HER PEOPLE AND THEIR ACTIVITIES. TO BE HELD AT THE FLORIDA TECHNOLOGICAL UNIVERSITY. (ST-WIDE). RONALD L NEWELL, COORD FO; FLORIDA TECHNOLOGICAL UNIVERSITY; BOX 2500; ORLANDO, FL 32186. (#332-901).

JULY 4, '75 - JULY 4, '76. YANKEE DOODLE WHALE AT SEA WORLD. SEA WORLD OF FLORIDA FEATURES SHAMU THE KILLER WHALE PERFORMING BEHAVIORS NEVER BEFORE ACCOMPLISHED BY MARINE MAMMALS AND INCORPORATES THE BICENTENNIAL THEME; SETS DESIGNED AND WRITTEN IN HOLLYWOOD; ORIGINAL COSTUMING; MUSIC BY LES BAXTER. AT SEA WORLD, OFF INTERSTATE 4, ORLANDO FLORIDA. (REGN'L). LT COL ROLFE G ARNHYM; ORANGE COUNTY BICENTENNIAL COMMITTEE; 423 S ORANGE AVE; ORLANDO, FL 32801. (#102201-1).

SEPT 14 - 18, '75. ANNUAL CONFERENCE - NATIONAL EXTENSION HOMEMAKERS' COUNCIL. INCLUDES WORKSHOPS,EDUCATIONAL & LEARNING SESSIONS. AT SHERATON TOWERS HOTEL. (NAT'L). MRS JOSEPH ABBOTT; NATIONAL EXTENSION HOMEMEKERS COUNCIL; 3001 ESTERO BLVD, BOX 40; FT MYERS, FL 33931. (#100108-1).

OCT 23 - 25, '75. 'OF MICE AND MEN' - PLAY BY JOHN STEINBECK. LIVE PERFORMANCE AT SCIENCE AUDITORIUM THEATRE. (LOCAL). DR DAVID MAYS, PROJ DIR; FLORIDA TECHNOLOGICAL UNIV THEATRE; PO BOX 25000; ORLANDO, FL 32816. (#200011-172).

DEC 4 - 6, '75. FLORIDA TECH UNIV PRESENTS, 'THE NIGHT THOREAU SPENT IN JAIL'. LIVE PERFORMANCE AT SCIENCE AUDITORIUM THEATRE. (LOCAL). DR DAVID MAYS, PROJ DIR; FLORIDA TECHNOLOGICAL UNIVERSITY THEATRE; PO BOX 25000; ORLANDO, FL 32816. (#103517-26).

DEC 13, '75. JAYCEES CHRISTMAS PARADE. BETWEEN 80 AND 100 UNITS WITH APPROXIMATELY 23 BANDS, HORSE UNITS AND GRAND MARSHALL KIRBY GRANT WILL TAKE PART IN THE JAYCEES CHRISTMAS PARADE WHOSE THEME THIS YEAR IS 'GOD BLESS AMERICA.'. AT DOWNTOWN ORLANDO. (LOCAL). DIRECTOR; ORLANDO JAYCEES; 423 S ORANGE AVE; ORLANDO, FL 32801. (#200011-173).

FEB 4, '76. DEDICATION OF COMMEMORATIVE INDIAN PLAQUE AT LIBRARY. COMMEMORATIVE INDIAN PLAQUE, FLORIDA. 3X5 BRONZE PLAQUE (CIRCA 1900) DEPICTING AMERICAN INDIAN CORN DANCE IN 5' RELIEF TO BE INSTALLED IN ORLANDO PUBLIC LIBRARY & A PLAQUE CITING DEDICATION; OLDEST CHURCH HISTORIES PLACED IN LIBRARIES. (LOCAL). MRS JAMES L STRAIT; DAUGHTERS OF THE AMERICAN REVOLUTION; 1921 VIA VENETIA; WINTER PARK, FL 32789. (#5941-501).

FEB 12 - 14, '76. PRESENTATION OF 'OF THEE I SING' - MUSICAL BY G KAUFMAN & M PYSKIND. LIVE PERFORMANCE AT SCIENCE AUDITORIUM THEATRE. (LOCAL). DR DAVID MAYS, PROJ DIR; FLORIDA TECHNOLOGICAL UNIVERSITY THEATRE; PO BOX 25000; ORLANDO, FL 32816. (#103517-23).

FEB 13 - 15, '76. UNITED STATES ARMED FORCES BICENTENNIAL CARAVAN. CARAVAN IS COMPOSED OF EXHIBIT VANS FOR EACH MILITARY SERVICE. PROJECT THEME IS 'HISTORY OF THE ARMED FORCES AND THEIR CONTRIBUTIONS TO THE NATION'. (LOCAL). ROLFE K ARNHYM; US ARMED FORCES BICENTENNIAL EXHIBIT VANS PROJECT; SUITE 6 423 S ORANGE AVE; ORLANDO, FL 32802. (#1775-432).

FEB 23 - MAR 6, '76. CENTRAL FLORIDA FAIR. ONE OF NATION'S BIGGEST CELEBRATIONS FEATURING EXHIBITS, ENVIRONMENTAL AND CULTURAL PROGRAMS. (LOCAL). ROLFE G ARNHYM, CHAIRMAN; ORANGE COUNTY BICENTENNIAL COMMITTEE; 423 S ORANGE AVE; ORLANDO, FL 32801. (#104609-3).

MAR 11 - 13, '76. 'A WILLIAMS QUARTET' - 4 PLAYS BY TENNESSEE WILLIAMS. LIVE PERFORMANCE AT SCIENCE AUDITORIUM THEATRE. (LOCAL). DR DAVID MAYS, PROJ DIR; FLORIDA TECHNOLOGICAL UNIVERSITY THEATRE; PO BOX 25000; ORLANDO, FL 32816. (#103517-24).

MAR 18, '76. BICENTENNIAL LUNCHEON. LUNCH ABD PRESENTATION OF FILM 'THE AMERICAN PARADE - WE THE WOMEN' CELEBRATING THE 200 YEARS OF PROGRESS OF THE AMERICAN WOMAN. AT JOHN YOUNG MUSEUM. (LOCAL). MS BEATRICE ETTINGER, DIR; VALENCIA COMMUNITY COLLEGE; PO BOX 3028; ORLANDO, FL 32802. (#107323-1).

MAR 27, '76. BELLE ISLE FREE FOR ALL. THERE WILL BE ENTERTAINMENT THROUGHOUT THE DAY, STREET SQUARE DANCING, FAMILY FILMS & REFRESHMENTS. AT BELLE ISLE PARK. (LOCAL). ROLFE G ARNHYM, COORD; ORANGE COUNTY BICENTENNIAL COMMITTEE; 423 S ORANGE AVE; ORLANDO, FL 32801. (#200011-174).

MAY 1, '76. FESTIVAL USA. CENTRAL FLORIDA COUNCIL OF BOY SCOUTS, INCLUDING ALL TROOPS & PACKS OF THE COUNCIL WILL PARTICIPATE IN SCOUT PROJECTS, CONTESTS AND DEMONSTRATIONS CULMINATING IN A JOINT PARADE IN THE TANGERINE BOWL. AT TANGERINE BOWL & EOLA PARK. (LOCAL). JACQUELINE AMRHEIN, SEC; ORANGE COUNTY BICENTENNIAL COMMITTEE; 423 S ORANGE AVE; ORLANDO, FL 32801. (#104609-1).

MAY 1 - 2, '76. FLORIDA TECH UNIV PRESENTS, 'THE WIZARD OF OZ'. LIVE PERFORMANCE AT SCIENCE AUDITORIUM THEATRE. (LOCAL). DR DAVID MAYS, PROJ DIR; FLORIDA TECHNOLOGICAL UNIVERSITY THEATRE; PO BOX 25000; ORLANDO, FL 32816. (#103517-25).

MAY 1 - 9, '76. DIMENSIONS '76. A NINE DAY ARTS FESTIVAL DISPLAYING PAINTINGS, CRAFTS, SCIENCES, ENTERTAINMENT, DANCING, CONCESSION BOOTHS, SOMETHING FOR THE WHOLE FAMILY. AT LOCH HAVEN ART CENTER, 2416 N MILLS AVE. (LOCAL). JACQUELINE AMRHEIN; ORANGE COUNTY BICENTENNIAL COMMITTEE; 423 S ORANGE AVE; ORLANDO, FL 32801. (#103398-1).

MAY 1 - JUNE 11, '76. FLORIDAWORLD MUSIC FESTIVAL. FESTIVAL, LIVE PERFORMANCE AT LAKELAND CIVIC AUDITORIUM. (LOCAL). LYNNE SORLIE; INTERNATIONAL FESTIVALS, INC; 202 E MICHIGAN AVE; KALAMAZOO, MI 49006. (#107233-2).

MAY 6 - 18, '76. FLORIDAWORLD CHORAL FESTIVAL. FESTIVAL, LIVE PERFORMANCE AT BRANSCOMB AUDITORIUM, FLORIDA SOUTHERN COLLEGE. (LOCAL). MICHAEL RADER; INTERNATIONAL FESTIVALS, INC; 202 E MICHIGAN AVE; KALAMAZOO, MI 49006. (#107233-3).

JUNE 3 - 5, '76. FLORIDA TECH UNIV PRESENTS 'ANOTHER PART OF THE FOREST'. LIVE PERFORMANCE AT SCIENCE AUDITORIUM THEATRE. (LOCAL). DR DAVID MAYS, PROJ DIR; FLORIDA TECHNOLOGICAL UNIVERSITY THEATRE; PO BOX 25000; ORLANDO, FL 32816. (#103517-27).

JUNE 9 - 13, '76. 4 DAY BICENTENNIAL PLAY FESTIVAL. LIVE PERFORMANCE AT EDITH BUSH CIVIC THEATRE, LOCH HAVEN PARK. (LOCAL). ROLFE G ARNHYM, CHAIRMAN; ORANGE COUNTY BICENTENNIAL COMMITTEE; 423 S ORANGE AVE; ORLANDO, FL 32801. (#103235-1).

JUNE 17 - 20, '76. THIRD ANNUAL GEORGE F PAFF ALUMNI SEMINAR. THE COURSE WILL OFFER 12 POSTGRADUATE CREDIT HOURS. (LOCAL). FRAN KOENIG, ASSOC DIR; UNIV OF MIAMI SCHOOL OF MEDICINE ALUMNI ASSOC; PO BOX 520875; MIAMI, FL 33152. (#108349-1).

JULY 4, '76. CENTRAL H S BAND PARTICIPATION IN BICENTENNIAL PARADE. PARADE, TOUR AT DISNEYWORLD. (REGN'L). JAMES BLALOCK, COORD; CENTRAL HIGH SCHOOL; MANCHESTER, TN 37355. (#200011-223).

JULY 4, '76. INDEPENDENCE CELEBRATION. FIVE HOURS OF CONTINUOUS ENTERTAINMENT WITH A LARGE ORCHESTRA FOR FINE LISTENING MUSIC AND A COUNTRY GROUP WITH PROFESSIONAL SQUARE DANCERS, SMALL SINGING GROUPS, FOOD CONCESSIONS & FIREWORKS. PICNIC IN PARK 4-9 PM. BRING OWN LUNCH. AT LAKE EOLA PARK; ROSALIND AVE. (LOCAL). JACQUELINE AMRHEIN, SEC; ORANGE COUNTY BICENTENNIAL COMMITTEE; 423 S ORANGE AVE; ORLANDO, FL 32801. (#103393-6).

AUG 4, '76. ORLANDO'S 101ST ANNIVERSARY CELEBRATION. CEREMONY WILL INCLUDE THE NAVY BAND, RAISING OF THE COLORS, THE STATE DRILL TEAM, FIFE & DRUM CORP, A PARADE TO ROSIE O' GRADY'S FOR LUNCH. AT BEARDALL PARK. (LOCAL). JACQUELINE AMPHEIN, SEC; ORANGE COUNTY BICENTENNIAL COMMITTEE; 423 S ORANGE AVE; ORLANDO, FL 32801. (#103393-7).

OCT 3 - 30, '76. 'A STITCH IN TIME' - NEEDLECRAFT EXHIBIT. AN EXHIBIT OF NEEDLECRAFT IN TRADITIONAL TECHNIQUES OF CREWEL, NEEDLEPOINT, PETITPOINT AND BARGELLO; BOTH TRADITIONAL AND CONTEMPORARY DESIGNS. (LOCAL). MS QURENTIA THROM, CHMN; VALENCIA COMMUNITY COLLEGE ART DEPT; PO BOX 3028; ORLANDO, FL 32802. (#107322-1).

NOV 13 - 14, '76. FIESTA IN THE PARK. 425 ARTS & CRAFTS BOOTHS WITH A BICENTENNIAL THEME WILL BE SET UP IN EOLA PARK WITH ENTERTAINMENT AT THE BANDSHELL. AT EOLA PARK, ROSALIND AVE. (LOCAL). JACQUELINE AMRHEIN, SEC; ORANGE COUNTY BICENTENNIAL COMMITTEE; 423 S ORANGE AVE; ORLANDO, FL 32801. (#104609-2).

DEC 1 - 5, '76. AMERICAN FREEDOM TRAIN DISPLAY DAYS AT ORLANDO. THE AMERICAN FREEDOM TRAIN WILL INCLUDE 10 EXHIBIT CARS AND 2 SHOWCASE CARS DEPICTING DIFFERENT PHASES OF THE AMERICAN EXPERIENCE. ITS ARRIVAL WILL SERVE AS A CATALYST FOR LOCAL BICENTENNIAL CELEBRATIONS BY PEOPLE THROUGHOUT THIS NATION. (ST-WIDE). SY FREEDMAN, DIR OF P/R; THE AMERICAN FREEDOM TRAIN FOUNDATION, INC.; 5205 LEESBURG PKE, SUITE 800; BAILEY'S XRDS, VA 22041. (#1776-78).

OSPREY

HISTORICAL & NATURAL SCIENCE CENTER, OSPREY, FL. ESTABLISH HISTORICAL & SCIENTIFIC TEACHING CENTER IN ORDER TO PRESERVE AN AREA OF SARASOTA COUNTY CONTAINING INDIAN MOUNDS FROM 2150 BC TO 1000 AD. (LOCAL). MRS CW LONSDALE, CHAIRMAN; SARASOTA COUNTY HISTORICAL & NATURAL SCIENCE CENTER, INC; 84 N WASHINGTON DR; SARASOTA, FL 33577. (#24728). **ARBA GRANTEE.**

OVIEDO

ECOLOGICAL STUDIES BUILDING - PROJ OF OVIEDO, FL. PROVIDE AN ECOLOGICAL STUDIES BUILDING, SITUATED IN A NATURAL CLEARING, FOR FORMAL AND INFORMAL EDUCATION IN WATER, SOIL, WEATHER, WILDLIFE AND FLORA. USED FOR DISPLAYS, LABORATORY WORK, FILM ETC. (LOCAL). CLAIRE KOSHAR, PRESIDENT; CITRUS COUNCIL OF GIRL SCOUTS; PO BOX 637; WINTER PARK, FL 32789. (#15062).

HISTORY OF OVIEDO, FLA, 1860-1976. SOCIAL, POLITICAL AND ECONOMIC HISTORY OF OVIEDO BEGINNING IN 1860. (LOCAL). DR RICHARD ADICKS, CHAIRMAN; OVIEDO HISTORICAL SOCIETY; LAKE CHARM; OVIEDO, FL 32765. (#15056).

LECONTES 'SOIL AND CLIMATE OF EAST FLORIDA' - FL. EDITION OF MANUSCRIPT REPORT, 'THE SOIL AND CLIMATE OF EAST FLORIDA' WRITTEN IN 1822 BY CAPT JOHN LACONTE, U S FARMY. (LOCAL). DR RICHARD ADICKS, CHAIRMAN; OVIEDO HISTORICAL SOCIETY; LAKE CHARM; OVIEDO, FL 32765. (#15057).

MEDIA CENTER OVIEDO HIGH SCHOOL - OVIEDO, FL. VISUAL DISPLAY TO PROVIDE CONTINUOUS UPDATING OF U S CABINET MEMBERS INCLUDING INFO ABOUT OFFICE AND INCUMBENT. (LOCAL). VIRGINIA MIKLER, PROJ DIRECTOR; OVIEDO HIGH SCHOOL; 601 KING ST; OVIEDO, FL 32765. (#15054).

PAHOKEE

BICENTENNIAL BIKE PATH IN PAHOKEE, FLORIDA. A BIKE PATH 12 BEING CONSTRUCTED THROUGH AND AROUND THE CITY GIVING SCENIC VIEW OF THE CITY AS WELL AS OUR 730 SQUARE MILE LAKE. (LOCAL). C R WEATHERINGTON, ROTARY BICENTENNIAL REP; PAHOKEE ROTARY CLUB; PAHOKEE, FL 33476. (#9805).

COUNTRY FAIR IN PAHOKEE, FLORIDA. OLD-FASHIONED COUNTRY FAIR WILL TAKE PLACE IN CITY PARK, 7/4/76 WITH BOOTHS EXHIBITING EARLY AMERICAN ARTS & CRAFTS. ALSO FOOD CONCESSIONS & GAMES. (LOCAL). MS ANNICE NORMAN, BICENT REP; BUSINESS & PROFESSIONAL WOMEN; BOX 288; PAHOKEE, FL 33476. (#9803).

FLAG DAY HELD IN PAHOKEE, FLORIDA. PAHOKEE ELKS CLUB WILL HOLD SPECIAL FLAG CEREMONY JUNE 6, 1976 WHICH IS OPEN TO PUBLIC. (LOCAL). DALE ALLEN, CITY BICENT REP; PAHOKEE ELKS CLUB; 619 E MAIN ST; PAHOKEE, FL 33476. (#9801).

HERITAGE CELEBRATION IN PAHOKEE, FLORIDA. DAY-LONG ATHLETIC CONTESTS, BOAT RACES AND CARNIVAL, ENDING WITH FIREWORKS OVER PAHOKEE HARBOR ON LAKE OKEECHOBEE. (LOCAL). MRS V HARRINGTON, SECRETARY; PAHOKEE CHAMBER OF COMMERCE; 100 E MAIN ST; PAHOKEE, FL 33746. (#10369).

OBSERVATION TOWER IN PAHOKEE, FLORIDA. 125 FT TOWER OVERLOOKING LAKE OKEECHOBEE & PAHOKEE HARBOR WILL BE BUILT. (LOCAL). DUNCAN PADGETT, PROJ DIRECTOR; PAHOKEE LIONS CLUB; 1381 E MAIN ST; PAHOKEE, FL 33476. (#9806).

PAINT-A-PLUG PROJECT IN PAHOKEE, FLORIDA. FIRE PLUGS THROUGHOUT THE CITY WILL BE PAINTED TO RESEMBLE REVOLUTIONARY WAR FIGURES. (LOCAL). WYONIA CUMMINGS, SPONSOR; PAHOKEE HIGH SCHOOL BICENT; 130 E MAIN ST; PAHOKEE, FL 33476. (#9807).

WAR MEMORIAL IN FLORIDA. MONUMENT WITH BRONZE PLAQUE LISTING NAMES OF ALL PAHOKEE CITIZENS WHO HAVE GIVEN THEIR LIVES IN THE SERVICE OF THEIR COUNTRY TO BE ERECTED IN MEMORIAL PARK ON BEACON POINT ROAD. (LOCAL). DAVID CUNNINGHAM, BICENT REP; MASONIC LODGE; PAHOKEE, FL 33476. (#9804).

SEPT 11 - 14, '75. PAHOKEE, FL EXHIBITS OF STATE HISTORY. 3-TRAILER CARAVAN WITH ARTIFACTS, PHOTOGRAPHY & ANIMATED DISPLAYS WILL DEPICT FLORIDA'S PAST, PRESENT & FUTURE; EXHIBIT TO RUN FROM SEPT 11-14. (LOCAL). MS WYONIA CUMMINGS; PAHOKEE BICENT COMMITTEE; 291 BANYAN AVE; PAHOKEE, FL 33476. (#9802-1).

JULY 4, '76. FIREWORKS DISPLAY & FUN & GAMES CONTEST. FESTIVAL AT HOOVER DIKE ON L OKEECHOBEE, HIGHWAY 441. (LOCAL). VERONICA HARRINGTON, CHMN; PAHOKEE CHAMBER OF COMMERCE; 115 E MAIN ST; PAHOKEE, FL 33476. (#102554-1).

PALATKA

BICENTENNIAL CAMPING INSIGNIA FOR FLORIDA CAMPERS. CAMPERS INSIGNIA OR PATCH FOR FLORIDA GOOD SAM CAMPERS HONORING BICENTENNIAL. (ST-WIDE). MARTHA C HUDSON, FLORIDA STATE DIRECTOR; GOOD SAM CLUB OF FLORIDA; 1504 PROSPECT ST; PALATKA, FL 32077. (#20606).

BICENTENNIAL CHORUS - 'SONGS OF AMERICA'. LIVE PERFORMANCE. (LOCAL). DICK WESTBURY, CHAIRMAN; PUTNAM COUNTY ACTION '76; PO BOX 234; PALATKA, FL 32077. (#103517-12). **(??).**

BILL OF RIGHTS PROGRAM - PALATKA, FL. STARTING FEB 27, EVERY TWO WEEKS ONE ARTICLE OF THE BILL OF RIGHTS WILL BE HIGHLIGHTED BY REPRINTING THE ARTICLE AND PRINTING A COMMENT BY PROMINENT CITIZENS TO EXPLAIN AND EDUCATE ON ITS UNIQUENESS. (LOCAL). KERRY N DUNNING, BICENTENNIAL CHAIRMAN; PALATKA JUNIOR WOMANS CLUB; 101 W ST JOHNS TERRACE; EAST PALATKA, FL 32031. (#17996).

'THE RIVER FLOWS NORTH' - BOOK, PALATKA, FL. HISTORY OF PUTNAM COUNTY, FLORIDA TO BE PUBLISHED. (LOCAL). PUTNAM COUNTY ACTION '76 STEERING COMMITTEE; HISTORICAL MANUSCRIPT SUBCOMMITTEE-PUTNAM CO ACTION '76 CO; PO BOX 1976; PALATKA, FL 32077. (#28631).

NOV 10, '75. AMERICAN REVOLUTION ERA PERSONALITIES. LIVE PERFORMANCE AT MOSELEY ELEM SCHOOL CAFETERIA, 1001 HUSSON AVE. (LOCAL). MRS CLARICE KENNEDY, DIR1; WILLIAM D MOSELEY ELEMENTARY SCHOOL PARENT TEACHER ORGANIZATION; 001 HUSSON AVE; PALATKA, FL 32077. (#200011-182).

NOV 17 - 28, '75. BICENTENNIAL COSTUME CONTEST. EACH CIVIC CLUB IN PUTNAM WILL BE ASKED TO SPONSOR A MEMBER; GENERAL PUBLIC WILL DECIDE WINNER; ALL PROCEEDS WILL GO TO THE CLUB WITH THE WINNING COSTUME, FOR USE IN A BICENTENNIAL PROJECT. CONTESTANTS WILL BE FEATURED IN JAYCEE PARADE AND IN THE STAR SPANGLED FOLLIES. AT BELK HUDSON STORE, ST JOHN'S AVE. (LOCAL). KERRY N DUNNING, COORD; PALATKA JUNIOR WOMEN'S CLUB; 101 W ST JOHN'S TER; E PALATKA, FL 32031. (#200011-183).

NOV 20, '75. PUTNAM COUNTY HISTORICAL SOCIETY CHORUS PERFORMANCE. THIS WILL BE THE DEBUT OF THE 125 MEMBER CHORUS. AT CIVIC CENTER RAVINE GARDENS. (LOCAL). MRS C S MARVIN, CHMN; PUTNAM COUNTY ACTION '76; PO BOX 234; PALATKA, FL 32077. (#200011-184).

NOV 25, '75. PUTNAM COUNTY MINISTRIAL THANKSGIVING SERVICES. LIVE PERFORMANCE AT FELLOWSHIP HALL-ST JAMES UNITED METHODIST CHURCH. (LOCAL). MRS C S MARVIN, CHAIRMAN; PUTNAM COUNTY ACTION '76; PO BOX 234; PALATKA, FL 32077. (#103517-15).

NOV 28, '75. ANNUAL CHRISTMAS PARADE & THE OFFICIAL BEGINNING OF XMAS SEASON. CHRISTMAS AND PATRIOTIC SONGS, ANNUAL CHRISTMAS PARADE & PRIZES. PARADE SPONSORED BY JAYCEES OF PALATKA. AT COURTHOUSE LAWN, ST JOHN AVE. (LOCAL). MRS C S MARVIN, CHAIRMAN; PUTNAM COUNTY ACTION '76; PO BOX 234; PALATKA, FL 32077. (#103517-14).

DEC 5 - 6, '75. STAR SPANGLED FOLLIES. COMMUNITY MEMBERS WILL BE ON STAGE AND BACKSTAGE. FOLLIES WILL BE DIRECTED BY PROFESSIONAL COMPANY. ALL FUND WILL BE RTURNED TO THE COMMUNITY IN THE FORM OF SCHOLARSHIPS & RECREATIONAL BICENTENNIAL PROJECTS. AT ST JOHN'S RIVER JUNIOR COLLEGE AUDITORIUM. (LOCAL). KERRY N DUNNING, CHMN; PALATKA JUNIOR WOMEN'S CLUB; 101 W ST JOHNS TERR; E PALATKA, FL 32031. (#103517-36).

DEC 9, '75. CONCERT FOR SENIOR CITIZENS FEATURING XMAS & PATRIOTIC SONGS. LIVE PERFORMANCE AT LAKESHORE NURSING HOME, CRESENT CITY, FL. (LOCAL). MRS C S MARVIN, CHAIRMAN; PUTNAM COUNTY ACTION '76; PO BOX 234; PALATKA, FL 32077. (#103517-13).

JAN 29 - DEC 31, '76. PUTNAM COUNTY BICENTENNIAL CHORUS. FOR THE BICENTENNIAL THE CHORUS WILL PERFORM ON SPECIAL OCCASIONS INCLUDING EASTER, MEMORIAL DAY, FLAG DAY, THE 4TH OF JULY, CHRISTMAS & OTHER TIMES. AT VARIOUS LOCATIONS IN PUTNAM COUNTY. (LOCAL). MRS C S MARVIN, CHAIRMAN; PUTNAM COUNTY COMMUNITY ACTION '76; PO BOX 234; PALATKA, FL 32077. (#109309-1).

JUNE 12 - 28, '76. CAMPER CARAVANS FROM PUTNAM COUNTY, FL TO FREDERICK, MD. CARAVAN ADMISSION RESTRICTED TO MEMBERS OF GOOD SAM CLUB OF FLORIDA; TOUR HISTORIC SITES FROM FLORIDA TO MARYLAND; CARAVAN TO END AT NATIONAL GOOD SAM 'SAMBOREE' AT FREDERICK. AT PUTNAM COUNTY FAIRGROUNDS, US 17, SOUTH OF PALATKA, FLA.. (REGN'L). MARTHA C HUDSON, DIR; GOOD SAM CLUB OF FLORIDA; 1504 PROSPECT ST; PALATKA, FL 32077. (#104838-1).

JULY 4, '76. COSTUME CONTEST. ADULT & CHILDREN CATEGORIES WITH WINNERS IN EACH RECEIVING AMERICAN FLAGS DONATED BY LOCAL CIVIC GROUPS. CERTIFICATE PRESENTED TO ALL CONTESTANTS BY PUTNAM CO FESTIVAL COMMITTEE. AT RIVERFRONT & CITY PARK. (LOCAL). KERRY N DUNNING, CHMN; PALATKA JR WOMEN'S CLUB & BICENTENNIAL FESTIVAL COMMITTEE; 101 W ST JOHNS TER; E PALATKA, FL 32031. (#200011-242).

PALM BEACH

NOV 11, '75. ARMISTICE DAY. CEREMONY AT HENRY MORRISON FLAGLER MUSEUM. (LOCAL). EDWIN V PUGH, CHMN; PBJC BICENT COMM, HIST SOC OF PALM BCH & ENGLISH SPEAKING UNION; 4200 CONGRESS AVE; LAKE WORTH, FL 33461. (#102506-1).

MAY 14, '76. FLORIDA AMERICAN REVOLUTION BICENTENNIAL COMMITTEE MEETING. CONFERENCE AT HENRY MORRISON FLAGER MUSEUM, PALM BEACH. (ST-WIDE). EDWIN V PUGH, CHAIRMAN; PALM BEACH JR COLLEGE BICENTENNIAL COMMITTEE; 4200 CONGRESS AVE; LAKE WORTH, FL 33461. (#102506-12).

DEC 17 - 19, '76. AMERICAN FREEDOM TRAIN DISPLAY DAYS AT PALM BEACH. THE AMERICAN FREEDOM TRAIN INCLUDES 10 EXHIBIT CARS & 2 SHOW CASE CARS DEPICTING DIFFERENT PHASES OF THE AMERICAN EXPERIENCE. ITS ARRIVAL WILL SERVE AS A CATALYST FOR LOCAL BICENTENNIAL CELEBRATIONS BY PEOPLE THROUGHOUT THIS NATION. (ST-WIDE). SY FREEDMAN, DIR OF P/R; THE AMERICAN FREEDOM TRAIN FOUNDATION; 5205 LEESBURG PIKE, SUITE 800; BAILEY'S XRDS, VA 22041. (#1776-111).

PANACEA

HISTORICAL MARKER - MAGNOLIA, FL. A HISTORICAL MARKER WILL BE PLACED IN MAGNOLIA, WHICH WAS FOUNDED JULY 4, 1827 BY THE HAMLIN BROTHERS, WHO SET OUT FROM MAINE. (LOCAL). MRS ELLA JEAN WEHUNT, CHAIRPERSON; WAKULLA COUNTY ACTION '76 STEERING COMMITTEE; PO BOX 442; PANACEA, FL 32346. (#15047).

HISTORY OF WAKULLA COUNTY, FL. THE BOOK WILL CONTAIN THE HISTORY OF WAKULLA COUNTY, WHICH WAS SECTIONED FROM LEON COUNTY IN 1843; IT WILL CONTAIN DESCRIPTIONS OF THE TOWN OF MAGNOLIA, MAJOR INDUSTRIES & HISTORICAL POINTS OF INTEREST. (LOCAL). MRS ELIZABETH SMITH, HISTORIAN; WAKULLA COUNTY ACTION '76 STEERING COMMITTEE; PO BOX 442; PANACEA, FL 32346. (#15046).

RESTORATION OF OLD WOODEN COUNTY COURTHOUSE - FL. BUILT IN 1893, THIS IS THE LAST WOODEN COURTHOUSE IN USE; IT WILL BE RESTORED. (LOCAL). MRS ELLA JEAN WEHUNT, CHAIRPERSON; WAKULLA COUNTY ACTION '76 STEERING COMMITTEE; PO BOX 442; PANACEA, FL 32346. (#15045).

JAN 12, '76. UNITED STATES ARMED FORCES BICENTENNIAL CARAVAN. CARAVAN IS COMPOSED OF EXHIBIT VANS FOR EACH MILITARY SERVICE. PROJECT THEME IS 'HISTORY OF THE ARMED FORCES AND THEIR CONTRIBUTIONS TO THE NATION'. AT WAKULLA HIGH SCHOOL. (LOCAL). MRS ELLA J WEHUNT; US ARMED FORCES BICENTENNIAL EXHIBIT VANS PROJECT; PO BOX 442; PANACEA, FL 32346. (#1775-419).

AUG 30, '76. BLUE CRAB FESTIVAL. FESTIVAL AT WATERFRONT, PANACEA BAY, ONE BLOCK E OF HWY 98. (REGN'L). MONROE TAYLOR, CHAIRMAN; PANACEA CHAMBERS OF COMMERCE; PANACEA, FL 32346. (#102209-1).

PANAMA CITY

BAY COUNTY HERITAGE TRAIL - PANAMA CITY, FL. ALL SITES OF HISTORICAL INTEREST IN BAY COUNTY WILL BE MARKED BY THE COUNTY BICENTENNIAL ORG.WITH METAL SIGNS; THE SAME SITES WILL BE INCORPORATED INTO 'HISTORICAL TRAIL MAP'PRINTED & DIST. TO PUBLIC. (LOCAL). BOB HUGHES, CHAIRMAN; BAY COUNTY ACTION '76; PO BOX 1638; PANAMA CITY, FL 32401. (#15029).

BICENTENNIAL BROADCASTS, PANAMA CITY, FL. THE COLLEGE STATION 'WKGC'-FM WILL ACT AS THE 'BICENTENNIAL SENTINEL'. (LOCAL). RONALD CLYDE JOHNSON, CHAIRMAN; GULF COAST COLLEGE BICENTENNIAL COMMITTEE; 5230 W HIGHWAY 98; PANAMA CITY, FL 32401. (#15702).

BICENTENNIAL HERITAGE LIBRARY - PANAMA CITY, FL. RECORDING HISTORY OF BAY COUNTY FROM RESIDENTS & PURCHASING REPRINTS OF OLD BOOKS. (LOCAL). JANE PATTON, LIBRARIAN; BAY COUNTY LIBRARY; MARINA; PANAMA CITY, FL 32401. (#25952).

CHILDREN'S THEATER. LIVE PERFORMANCE. (LOCAL). LYNN SOUTHALL, COORD; BAY COUNTY SCHOOL SYSTEM; PANAMA CITY, FL 32401. (#108367-1).

COLLEGE STATIONERY PROJ OF GULF COAST COL - FL. STATIONERY WILL REFLECT HISTORICAL FEATURES. (LOCAL). RONALD CLYDE JOHNSON, CHAIRMAN; GULF COAST COLLEGE BICENTENNIAL COMMITTEE; 5230 W HWY 98; PANAMA CITY, FL 32401. (#15703).

PIONEER FLORIDA - PANAMA CITY, FL. CENTURY-OLD LOG CABIN WITH AUTHENTIC FURNISHINGS WILL FEATURE THE FOLLOWING ACTIVITIES: CANE GRINDING, BLACKSMITH DEMONSTRATION, CANDLEMAKING AND OTHER CRAFTS. (LOCAL). J ROBERT HUGHES, CHAIRMAN; BAY COUNTY ACTION '76 COMMITTEE; PO BOX 1638; PANAMA CITY, FL 32401. (#15022).

19TH CENTURY FLORIDA PIONEER FARM. DEVELOPMENT AND EXPANSION OF 19TH CENTURY FLORIDA PIONEER FARM. THE COMPLEX CONTAINS AGRICULTURAL IMPLEMENTS & SYSTEMS OF THE 19TH CENTURY. (ST-WIDE). T ROBERT HUGHES, CHAIRMAN; BAY COUNTY BICENTENNIAL COMMITTEE; PO BOX 1638; PANAMA CITY, FL 32401. (#16820). **ARBA GRANTEE.**

DEC 2, '75. 'CELEBRATION USA'. A BICENTENNIAL THEATER PRODUCTION BY THE NATIONAL THEATRE CORPS OF NEW YORK WILL BE SEEN BY 2ND THROUGH 5TH GRADERS. AT MUNICIPAL AUDITORIUM. (LOCAL). BOB HUGHES, DIRECTOR; BAY COUNTY SCHOOL SYSTEM/ACTION '76 COMMITTEE; PO BOX 1638; PANAMA CITY, FL 32401. (#102166-1).

JAN 26, '76. GOVERNMENTAL SEMINAR. MORNING SEMINAR WITH STUDENTS & LOCAL GOV'T OFFICIALS; AFTERNOON PRESENTATION BY DR DONALD FREEMAN, POLI SCI PROF FROM UNIV OF WEST FLORIDA; EVENING ADDRESS BY GOVERNOR RONALD REAGAN. (LOCAL). RONALD CLYDE JOHNSON, DIR; GULF COAST COLLEGE BICENTENNIAL COMMITTEE; 5230 W HIGHWAY 98; PANAMA CITY, FL 32401. (#102517-1).

APR 1 - 10, '76. '1776', A MUSICAL. LIVE PERFORMANCE AT FINE ARTS AUDITORIUM. (LOCAL). NORMAN HAIR, COORD; GULF COAST COMMUNITY COLLEGE, FINE ARTS DIVISION; 5230 W HWY 98; PANAMA CITY, FL 32401. (#104642-3).

MAY 1 - 2, '76. OLD TOWN DAYS FESTIVAL. FESTIVAL AT PANAMA CITY MARINA. (LOCAL). J ROBERT HUGHES, COORD; BAY COUNTY ACTION '76 COMMITTEE; PO BOX 1638; PANAMA CITY, FL 32401. (#200011-187).

MAY 4, '76. AMERICAN WIND SYMPHONY'S FLOATING ARTS CENTER VISITS PANAMA CITY. EMBARKING UPON A BICENTENNIAL CULTURAL TOUR, THE WIND SYMPHONY WILL VISIT 76 CITIES BRINGING MUSIC, DANCE, SYMPOSIA, AND CHILDREN'S. (LOCAL). PAULA BERN, COORDINATOR; AMERICAN WIND SYMPHONY ORCHESTRA OF WESTERN PENNSYLVANIA; GATEWAY TOWERS 18G; PITTSBURGH, PA 15222. (#2800-3).

SEPT 12 - 29, '76. PHOTOGRAPHIC EXHIBIT OF FLORIDA'S HISTORIC ARCHITECTURE. EXHIBIT AT FINE ARTS AUDITORIUM GALLERY. (LOCAL). IAN C BAKER, DIR OF P/R; GULF COAST COMMUNITY COLLEGE; PANAMA CITY, FL 32401. (#102518-2).

PANAMA CITY — CONTINUED

SEPT 27 - OCT 2, '76. BAY COUNTY FAIR. FAIR AT BAY COUNTY FAIRGROUNDS, SHERMAN AVE & 15TH ST, HWY 98 BYPASS. (ST-WIDE). SANDY HENDRICKS, MANAGER; BAY COUNTY FAIR ASSOC; PO BOX 68; PANAMA CITY, FL 32401. (#106095-50).

OCT 19, '76. LRC DEDICATION, LIBERTY BELL, FREEDOM SHRINE. REDEDICATION OF FREEDOM SHRINE AND LIBERTY BELL REPLICA ALONG WITH DEDICATION OF NEW BUILDING IN WHICH THEY WILL BE DISPLAYED. (LOCAL). IAN C BARKER, DIR COL REL; GULF COAST COLLEGE BICENTENNIAL COMMITTEE; 5230 W HIGHWAY 98; PANAMA CITY, FL 32401. (#102518-1).

PASCO COUNTY

HISTORICAL ESSAY CONTEST IN PASCO COUNTY, FL. 6TH GRADE STUDENTS IN PASCO COUNTY SCHOOLS TO PARTICIPATE; SPONSORED BY W PASCO HISTORICAL SOCIETY, INC. (LOCAL). JULIE J OBENREDER, PRESIDENT; W PASCO HISTORICAL SOCIETY, INC; 117 E TENNESSEE AVE; NEW PT RICHEY, FL 33552. (#20204).

PATRICK AFB

APR 12, '76. OPEN HOUSE AT PATRICK AFB W/ THUNDERBIRDS. FESTIVAL. (LOCAL). BILL WOOD, CHAIRMAN; INDIAN RIVER JUBILEE COMMITTEE FOR BREVARD COUNTY; 3220 N COCOA BLVD; COCOA, FL 32922. (#7704-503).

PAXTON

CITY OF PAXTON, FLORIDA, COMMUNITY CENTER. BUILDING, PARKING, PICNIC AREA ON 5 ACRE SITE TO BE DEVELOPED AS A COMMUNITY CENTER BY REMODELING BUILDING AND ADDING RECREATION FACILITIES. (LOCAL). HON DR SHERMAN JOHNSON, MAYOR PRO-TEM; TOWN OF PAXTON; PO BOX 1186; PAXTON, FL 32538. (#3589).

MAR 1 - 15, '76. ARTS AND CRAFTS EXHIBIT. FESTIVAL AT WELCOME STATION, HWY 331. (LOCAL). HON DR SHERMAN JOHNSON; TOWN OF PAXTON; PO BOX 1186; PAXTON, FL 32538. (#3589-1).

PEMBROKE PINE

JAN 24, '76. PEMBROKE PINES DAY - 17TH ANNIVERSARY PARADE AND CARNIVAL. FAIR, PARADE AT NORTH PERRY RECREATION CENTER, 7600 PINES BLVD. (LOCAL). ALEX FERNANDEZ, CHMN; PEMBROKE PINES BICENTENNIAL COMMITTEE; 321 NW 98TH AVE; PEMBROKE PINE, FL 33024. (#200011-180).

MAY 31 - JUNE 6, '76. BICENTENNIAL WEEK. FESTIVAL, PARADE AT PERRY RECREATION CENTER, 7600 PINES BLVD. (LOCAL). ALEX FERNANDEZ, CHAIRMAN; PEMBROKE PINES BICENTENNIAL COMMITTEE; 321 N W 98TH AVE; PEMBROKE PNES, FL 33024. (#104642-2).

PENNEY FARMS

OCT 25 - 26, '75. 50TH ANNIVERSARY CELEBRATION. SATURDAY - DEDICATION OF NEW SHELTERED CARE FACILITY; SUNDAY - WORSHIP SERVICE AND HISTORICAL PAGEANT. AT PENNEY FARMS COMMUNITY, CHAPEL & GROUNDS. (LOCAL). REV PAUL HAGEN, COORD; PENNEY FARMS RETIREMENT COMMUNITY; QUADRANGLE N; PENNEY FARMS, FL 32079. (#200011-181).

PENSACOLA

AMERICAN FLAG DISPLAY, PENSACOLA, FL. DISTRIBUTION OF THE AMERICAN FLAG FOR DISPLAY AT HOME IN THE COMMUNITY. (LOCAL). ROBERT TAYLOR, BICENTENNIAL PROJ OFFICER; NAVAL TECHNICAL TRAINING CENTER; PENSACOLA, FL 32511. (#29756).

ART EXHIBIT IN PENSACOLA, FL. GALLERY SET UP TO REPRESENT 'AMERICA IN 1776, 1876, 1976'. (LOCAL). JAMES MCGOVERN, CHAIRMAN; THE UNIV OF WEST FLORIDA BICENTENNIAL COMMITTEE; 2721 BAY ST; GULF BREEZE, FL 32561. (#11678).

BANANA SCHOOL, 15 YEARS LATER - PENSACOLA, FL. NEWSPAPER ARTICLE PREPARED AS SPECIAL BICENTENNIAL FEATURE OF STATION NEWSPAPER. DESCRIBES BASIC NAVAL AVIATION OBSERVER SCHOOL (BNAO THUS BANANA) AND THE CHANGES IN ITS 15 YEAR HISTORY. (LOCAL). LTJG BERNIECE K JONES, PUBLIC AFFAIRS OFFICER; TRAINING SQUADRON TEN; NAVAL AIR STATION; PENSACOLA, FL 32508. (#29222).

BICENTENNIAL BEAUTIFICATION & TREE PLANTING - FL. PLANTING OF TREES FOR BEAUTIFICATION; TREES WILL BE GIVEN AWAY FREE FOR PUBLIC PLANTING IN ALL AREAS OF THE COUNTY. (LOCAL). BOB PHILLIPS, PROJ DIRECTOR; ST REGIS PAPER COMPANY; PO BOX 87; CANTONMENT, FL 32501. (#20830).

BICENTENNIAL LECTURE SERIES IN PENSACOLA, FL. TEN LECTURES ON HISTORICAL & CONTEMPORARY THEMES DURING THE WINTER OF 1976. (LOCAL). JAMES MCGOVERN, CHAIRMAN; THE UNIV OF WEST FLORIDA BICENTENNIAL COMMITTEE; 2721 BAY ST; GULF BREEZE, FL 32561. (#11674).

BICENTENNIAL T-39D SABRELINER AIRCRAFT. ONE SQUADRON T-39D AIRCRAFT WAS PAINTED IN A BLUE AND WHITE BICENTENNIAL COLOR SCHEME. THE HANDPAINTED EAGLE ON THE VERTICAL STABILIZER BEARS A BANNER PROCLAIMING 'OUR RIGHTS, OUR LIBERTIES'. (REGN'L). LTJG BERNIECE K JONES, PUBLIC AFFAIRS OFFICER; TRAINING SQUADRON TEN; NAVAL AIR STATION; PENSACOLA, FL 32508. (#29221).

BLACK FESTIVAL WEEK IN PENSACOLA, FL. THEME - 'BLACK CONTRIBUTION TO AMERICAN HISTORY'. (LOCAL). JAMES MCGOVERN, CHAIRMAN; THE UNIV OF WEST FLORIDA BICENTENNIAL COMMITTEE; 2721 BAY ST; GULF BREEZE, FL 32561. (#11681).

BUMPER STICKERS - PENSACOLA, FL. AUTOMOBILE STICKERS DEPICTING THE NAVY'S 200TH YEARS OF SERVICE. (LOCAL). ROBERT TAYLOR, BICENTENNIAL PROJ OFFICER; NAVAL TECHNICAL TRAINING CENTER; PENSACOLA, FL 32511. (#29758).

CINEMA EVENT IN PENSACOLA, FL. THE LYCEUM CINEMA COMMITTEE WILL SELECT A FILM WITH AN AMERICAN THEME FOR FALL '75. (LOCAL). JAMES MCGOVERN, CHAIRMAN; THE UNIV OF WEST FLORIDA BICENTENNIAL COMMITTEE; 2721 BAY ST; GULF BREEZE, FL 32561. (#11685).

EXHIBIT OF HISTORY OF NAVAL FLIGHT OFFICER - FL. EXHIBIT USES 16 SCALE MODEL AIRCRAFT AND 6 PHOTOS PLUS BRIEF NARRATIVES TO DESCRIBE THE EMERGENCE AND INCREASING IMPORTANCE OF THE NAVAL FLIGHT OFFICER IN NAVAL AVIATION. (LOCAL). LTJG BERNIECE K JONES, PUBLIC AFFAIRS OFFICER; TRAINING SQUADRON TEN; NAVAL AIR STATION; PENSACOLA, FL 32508. (#29220).

GREAT AMERICANS PROJ - W PENSACOLA, FL. THIRD GRADE STUDENTS WILL CHOOSE GREAT AMERICANS & EACH OF THE 4 CLASSROOMS WILL CONSTRUCT A 4' MODEL, TO BE DISPLAYED AT STRATEGIC LOCATIONS AROUND THE SCHOOL. (LOCAL). ERNEST THORNE, PRINCIPAL, W PENSACOLA ELEM SCHOOL; ESCAMBIA COUNTY SCHOOL BOARD; 215 W GARDEN ST; PENSACOLA, FL 32501. (#18821).

GULF COAST CONFERENCE IN PENSACOLA, FL. THE CONFERENCE WILL DEAL WITH THE CULTURAL LEGACY OF THE GULF COAST. (LOCAL). JAMES MCGOVERN, CHAIRMAN; THE UNIV OF WEST FLORIDA BICENTENNIAL COMMITTEE; 2721 BAY ST; GULF BREEZE, FL 32561. (#11683).

HISTORICAL TOUR IN PENSACOLA, FL. VISITS TO ST AUGUSTINE, SAVANNAH, CHARLESTON, KITTY HAWK, WILLIAMSBURG AND WASHINGTON, DC WILL BE PART OF WINTER '76 TOUR. (REGN'L). JAMES MCGOVERN, CHAIRMAN; THE UNIV OF WEST FLORIDA BICENTENNIAL COMMITTEE; 2721 BAY ST; GULF BREEZE, FL 32561. (#11679).

ILLUSTRATED GUIDE TO TREES & SHRUBS, PENSACOLA, FL. BRIEF DESCRIPTION OF 17 COMMON TREES & SHRUBS FOUND IN THE SEVILLE SQUARE HISTORIC DISTRICT, SUPPLEMENTED BY PEN & INK DRAWINGS OF EACH PLANT. (LOCAL). JANICE P HOLMLAND, CURATOR; HISTORIC PENSACOLA PRESERVATION BOARD; 205 E ZARAGOZA ST; PENSACOLA, FL 32501. (#24047).

LECTURE IN PENSACOLA, FL. LECTURE ON HISTORY OF AMERICAN MEDICINE. (LOCAL). JAMES MCGOVERN, CHAIRMAN; THE UNIV OF WEST FLORIDA BICENTENNIAL COMMITTEE; 2721 BAY ST; GULF BREEZE, FL 32561. (#11686).

MEDICAL CENTER DEDICATION CEREMONY. DEDICATION OF NAVAL AEROSPACE & REGIONAL MEDICAL CENTER. (LOCAL). LT W LAMBERT, CHAIRMAN; NAVAL AEROSPACE AND REGIONAL MEDICAL CENTER; PENSACOLA, FL 32512. (#200011-256).

NAVAL AIR TRAINING COMMAND PAGEANT OF FLAGS. A LIVE PERFORMANCE ON HISTORY OF FLAG USING ALL FLAGS THAT HAVE BEEN USED IN U S HISTORY IN CONJUNCTION WITH OTHER LIVE PERFORMERS IN REPRESENTATIVE PERIOD MILITARY UNIFORMS. AT NAVAL AVIATION MEMORIAL CHAPEL, NAS. (LOCAL). CAPT P R CRAVEN, CHAIRMAN; NAVAL AVIATION SCHOOLS COMMAND; PENSACOLA, FL 32508. (#200011-263).

NEW COLLEGE COURSES IN PENSACOLA, FL. THREE COURSES AT UNIVERSITY OF WEST FLORIDA SUMMER QUARTER '75 WILL BE OFFERED ON THE SIGNIFICANCE OF AMERICAN REVOLUTIONARY EXPERIENCE. (LOCAL). JAMES MCGOVERN, CHAIRMAN; THE UNIV OF WEST FLORIDA BICENTENNIAL COMMITTEE; 2721 BAY ST; GULF BREEZE, FL 32561. (#11688).

NTTC CORRY STATION BICENTENNIAL MURAL, FL. LARGE FREEDOM MURAL ON TRAINING BUILDING DEPICTING NAVY ANCHOR BACKDROPPED W/NATIONAL ENSIGN BALANCED ON EITHER SIDE WITH SHINGING BICENTENNIAL SYMBOL. (LOCAL). ROBERT TAYLOR, BICENTENNIAL PROJ OFFICER; NAVAL TECHNICAL TRAINING CENTER; PENSACOLA, FL 32511. (#29759).

PAST TO '76, NEW COURSE IN PENSACOLA, FL. INTERDISCIPLINARY COURSE WILL BE OFFERED WINTER '76. (LOCAL). JAMES MCGOVERN, CHAIRMAN; THE UNIV OF WEST FLORIDA BICENTENNIAL COMMITTEE; 2721 BAY ST; GULF BREEZE, FL 32561. (#11680).

RECONSTRUCTION OF THE TIVOLI HIGH HOUSE - FLORIDA. THE FINAL PHASE OF THE TIVOLI HIGH HOUSE RECONSTRUCTION IN THE HISTORIC DISTRICT OF PENSACOLA. (ST-WIDE). SHELTON KEMP, EXEC DIRECTOR; BICENTENNIAL COMMISSION OF FLORIDA; PO BOX 10207; TALLAHASSEE, FL 32303. (#8717). **ARBA GRANTEE.**

SALVATION ARMY BEAUTIFICATION PROJ, PENSACOLA, FL. BEAUTIFICATION OF NEW SALVATION ARMY GROUNDS BY PLANTING RED, WHITE & BLUE FLOWERS & TREES REPRESENTING THE 13 ORIGINAL COLONIES. (LOCAL). MRS J C KNEPTON, CHAIRMAN; PENSACOLA FEDERATED GARDEN CLUBS, HANDS COMMITTEE; 1900 N 9TH AVE; PENSACOLA, FL 32503. (#18822).

SERIES OF BICENTENNIAL EVENTS AT NAS PENSACOLA, FL. MOCK SEA BATTLE USING FLOATING REPLICAS OF REVOLUTIONARY WAR; ALSO A SEALED TIME CAPSULE WHICH IS SCHEDULED TO BE OPENED ON NATION'S TRICENTENNIAL; HISTORICAL ARTIFACTS IN U S NAVAL AVIATION MUSEUM. (LOCAL). CDR B J MCGEE, SENIOR ASSISTANT SUPPLY OFFICER; NAVAL AIR STATION - SUPPLY DEPT; BLDG 603-3; PENSACOLA, FL 32508. (#30807).

SLIDE LECTURE - NROTC IN PENSACOLA, FL. HISTORY OF NAVAL AVIATION THROUGH A FILM & SLIDE LECTURE. (LOCAL). JAMES MCGOVERN, CHAIRMAN; THE UNIV OF WEST FLORIDA BICENTENNIAL COMMITTEE; 2721 BAY ST; GULF BREEZE, FL 32561. (#11677).

SPIRIT OF '76 STATIONERY - PENSACOLA, FL. NAVY OFFICIAL STATIONERY IMPRINTED W/GHOST IMAGE OF 'SPIRIT OF '76'. (LOCAL). ROBERT TAYLOR, BICENTENNIAL PROJ OFFICER; NAVAL TECHNICAL TRAINING CENTER; PENSACOLA, FL 32511. (#29757).

SYMPOSIUM ON AMERICAN EDUCATION IN PENSACOLA, FL. THE SYMPOSIUM WILL BE ON A COMPARISON OF EDUCATION - 1776 TO 1976. (LOCAL). JAMES MCGOVERN, CHAIRMAN; THE UNIV OF WEST FLORIDA BICENTENNIAL COMMITTEE; 2721 BAY ST; GULF BREEZE, FL 32561. (#11675).

THEATRE PRESENTATION IN PENSACOLA, FL. THE PROGRAM INVOLVES A SLIDE PRESENTATION WITH A BICENTENNIAL THEME. (LOCAL). JAMES MCGOVERN, CHAIRMAN; THE UNIV OF WEST FLORIDA BICENTENNIAL COMMITTEE; 2721 BAY ST; GULF BREEZE, FL 32561. (#11682).

TIVOLI HIGH HOUSE RECONSTRUCTION IN PENSACOLA, FL. RECONSTRUCTION OF THE HISTORIC TIVOLI HIGH HOUSE, OR CASENAVE HOUSE, (1805) AND ITS INTERPRETATION AS A SITE ON FLA'S BICENTENNIAL TRAIL. IT WILL VISUALLY ASSIST IN SHOWING FLORIDA'S PAST. (ST-WIDE). JAMES W MOODY, JR, DIRECTOR; HISTORIC PENSACOLA PRESERVATION BOARD; 200 E ZARAGOZA ST; PENSACOLA, FL 32501. (#166). **ARBA GRANTEE.**

U S NAVAL AVIATION MUSEUM IN PENSACOLA, FL. MUSEUM OFFERS PANORAMA OF NAVAL AVIATION HISTORY FROM 1911 TO SPACE AGE, INCLUDING NC-4 FLYING BOAT, 1ST PLANE TO CROSS AN OCEAN IN 1919 & SKYLAB COMMAND MODULE WHICH ORBITED EARTH IN 1973 WITH NAVY CREW. (LOCAL). B J MCGEE, COMMANDER; NAVAL AIR STATION - SUPPLY DEPT; BLDG 603-3; PENSACOLA, FL 32508. (#30806).

16 BICENTENNIAL CRUISES IN PENSACOLA, FL. SELECTED PATRIOTIC, YOUTH, SOCIAL & COMMUNITY GROUPS INVITED TO WITNESS SHIPBOARD & CARRIER OPERATIONS & DISPLAYS OF NAVAL HISTORY DURING A DAY AT SEA ABOARD THE USS LEXINGTON. (REGN'L). PUBLIC AFFAIRS OFFICER; USS LEXINGTON CUT 16, NAVAL AIR STATION; PENSACOLA, FL 32508. (#33046).

SEPT 5, '75. WILLIAM BARTRUM DAY. NATURE TRAILS AT UNIV OF WEST FLORIDA WILL BE DEDICATED. (LOCAL). MRS C BLANCHARD, COORD; DEEP SOUTH REGION OF NATIONAL COUNCIL OF STATE GARDEN CLUBS; 4001 MENENDEZ DR; PENSACOLA, FL 32503. (#101859-1).

SEPT 15 - 16, '75. CHAPPY JAMES RECOGNITION DAY. GENERAL 'CHAPPY' JAMES HAS BEEN NAMED COMMANDER OF NORRAD AND IS THE FIRST BLACK OFFICER TO RECEIVE 4 STAR STATUS IN HISTORY. PENSACOLA IS HOSTING MANY EVENTS AROUND HIS 2 DAY STAY. AT WASHINGTON HIGH SCHOOL, PALAFOX ST & SEVILLE SQUARE. (LOCAL). WALLACE KING, COORD; CHAMBER OF COMMERCE; 107 E ROMAND ST; PENSACOLA, FL 32503. (#101860-1).

OCT 10, '75. NAVY BIRTHDAY OPEN HOUSE. OPEN HOUSE FOR SQUADRON MEMBERS, STUDENTS & DEPENDENTS CONSISTING OF AWARDS CEREMONY, NAVAL FLIGHT OFFICER EXHIBIT, DISPLAY OF HISTORICAL POSTERS & TOUR OF SQUADRON. REFRESHMENTS WERE SERVED. AT U S NAVAL AIR STATION. (LOCAL). LTJG B K JONES, CHAIRMAN; TRAINING SQUADRON TEN, NAVAL AIR STATION; PENSACOLA, FL 32508. (#200011-258).

OCT 10, '75. NAVY DAY BALL. FESTIVAL AT DINING FACILITY - CORRY STATION. (LOCAL). ROBERT TAYLOR, PROJ OFC; NAVAL TECHNICAL TRAINING CENTER CORRY STATION; NTTC CORRY STATION; PENSACOLA, FL 32511. (#200011-273).

OCT 11, '75 - FEB 10, '76. '200 YEARS', MULTIMEDIA PRODUCTION SHOWING HISTORY OF U S NAVY. EXHIBIT. (LOCAL). CAPT P R CRAVEN; NAVAL AVIATION SCHOOLS COMMAND; PENSACOLA, FL 32508. (#200011-262).

OCT 13 - 19, '75. HISTORY OF NAVY MEDICINE - EXHIBIT. EXHIBIT AT PENSACOLA INTERSTATE FAIRGROUNDS. (LOCAL). LT W J LAMBERT, CHAIRMAN; NAVAL AEROSPACE AND REGIONAL MEDICAL CENTER; PENSACOLA, FL 32512. (#200011-255).

OCT 13 - 19, '75. INTERSTATE FAIR. MILITARY EDUCATION TRAINING ON COMMUNICATIONS. AT INTERSTATE FAIRGROUNDS MILITARY EXHIBITS. (ST-WIDE). ROBERT TAYLOR; NAVAL TECHNICAL TRAINING CENTER; NTTC CORRY STATION; PENSACOLA, FL 32511. (#200011-274).

OCT 19, '75. 50TH ANNIVERSARY - JAYCEE BICENTENNIAL DISTRICT CAUCUS. CONFERENCE AT BARRANCAS BEACHHOUSE. (LOCAL). NELSON WELLBORN, PRES; ESCAMBIA BAY JAYCEES; 10 COLBY LANE; PENSACOLA, FL 32506. (#102218-1).

NOV 8, '75. ANNUAL ESCAMBIA COUNTY JUNIOR MISS PROGRAM. AWARD, CEREMONY, LIVE PERFORMANCE AT PENSACOLA HIGH SCHOOL AUDITORIUM, 300 N JORDAN, PARKING AVAILABLE. (LOCAL). ELIZABETH ARCENAUX; PENSACOLA JAYCEETTES; 3081 ROTHCHILD DR; PENSACOLA, FL 32503. (#103233-5).

NOV 9, '75. BICENTENNIAL MASSING OF THE COLORS. CEREMONY AT ESCAMBIA HIGH SCHOOL STADIUM. (LOCAL). WYATT JOHNSON, CHMN; MILITARY ORDER OF THE WORLD WARS; PO BOX 797; PENSACOLA, FL 32504. (#103233-3).

NOV 10, '75. BICENTENNIAL VESPER SERVICES. CEREMONY, TOUR AT CHURCH OF THE ANNUNCIATION 1720 W GARDEN ST PENSACOLA FLORIDA. (LOCAL). STELLA KRITSELIS, CHMN; HELLENIC FESTIVAL WEEK; 8644 MEADOWBROOK DR; PENSACOLA, FL 32504. (#102955-4).

PENSACOLA — CONTINUED

NOV 11 - DEC 7, '75. HELLENIC FESTIVAL ART CENTER SHOW. EXHIBIT AT PENSACOLA ART CENTER 407 S JEFFERSON ST PENSACOLA FLORIDA. (ST-WIDE). MRS DOE PAPPAS, CO-CHMN; HELLENIC FESTIVAL WEEK; 3411 CONNELL DR; PENSACOLA, FL 32503. (#102955-2).

NOV 12, '75. CULTURAL ACTIVITY - MME ELENA NIKOLAIDI - MEZZO SOPRANO. LIVE PERFORMANCE AT PENSACOLA JUNIOR COLLEGE FINE ARTS AUDITORIUM. (LOCAL). MISS LIANNA MARKS, CHMN; HELLENIC FESTIVAL WEEK; 4002 MARLANE DR; PENSACOLA, FL 32506. (#102955-6).

NOV 12, '75. FASHION SHOW LUNCHEON. LIVE PERFORMANCE AT SEVILLE QUARTERS/130 E GOVERNMENT ST. (ST-WIDE). MISS GLORIANNE KRITSELIS; HELLENIC FESTIVAL WEEK; 8644 MEADOWBROOK DRIVE; PENSACOLA, FL 32504. (#102955-1).

NOV 12, '75. FASHION SHOW LUNCHEON. FESTIVAL AT SEVILLE QUARTERS, 130 E GOVERNMENT ST. (ST-WIDE). GLORIANNE KRITSELIS, DIR; HELLENIC FESTIVAL WEEK; 8644 MEADOWBROOK DR; PENSACOLA, FL 32504. (#102983-6).

NOV 13, '75. AMERICA '76 FILM LECTURE SERIES. SEMINAR AT WOODHAM HIGH SCHOOL AUDITORIUM. (LOCAL). W L UMPHLETT, CHMN; UNIV OF WEST FLORIDA; PENSACOLA, FL 32504. (#103233-4).

NOV 13, '75. HELLENIC FESTIVAL GALA. LIVE PERFORMANCE AT SCENIC HILLS COUNTRY CLUB. (LOCAL). MRS ANTHONY PAPADELIAS; HELLENIC FESTIVAL WEEK; 2851 BANQUOIS TRAIL; PENSACOLA, FL 32503. (#102955-5).

NOV 30, '75. SALVATION ARMY DEDICATION CEREMONY. CEREMONY AT NEW SALVATION ARMY BUILDING. (ST-WIDE). MAJOR OTIS STREET, COORD; SALVATION ARMY; 1501 N Q ST; PENSACOLA, FL 32505. (#200011-185).

JAN 1 - JULY 4, '76. PENSACOLA-ESCAMBIA FESTIVAL 76. PENSACOLA-ESCAMBIA BICENTENNIAL 1976 PROJ OF FLA. CITIZENS ACTION 5 YEAR GOAL PROGRAM 1971-1976. (LOCAL). WARREN M BRIGGS; ACTION 76; BOX 550; PENSACOLA, FL 32593. (#5899-501).

JAN 3 - 4, '76. UNITED STATES ARMED FORCES BICENTENNIAL CARAVAN. CARAVAN IS COMPOSED OF EXHIBIT VANS FOR EACH MILITARY SERVICE. PROJECT THEME IS 'HISTORY OF THE ARMED FORCES AND THEIR CONTRIBUTIONS TO THE NATION'. (LOCAL). WARREN M BRIGGS; ACTION 76 OF PENSACOLA; PO BOX 550; PENSACOLA, FL 32593. (#1775-415).

JAN 19, '76. AMERICA '76 FILM LECTURE SERIES. SEMINAR AT WOODHAM HIGH SCHOOL AUDITORIUM. (LOCAL). W L UMPHLETT, DIRECTOR; UNIV OF WEST FLORIDA/COMMUNITY SCHOOL SCHOOLS OF PENSACOLA; PENSACOLA, FL 32504. (#103233-2).

JAN 22 - 24, '76. EPISCOPAL DIOCESE CONVENTION OF THE CENTRAL GULF COAST. CONFERENCE AT 3200 N 12TH AVE. (LOCAL). REV LAVAN B DAVIS, DIR; SAINT CHRISTOPHER'S EPISCOPAL CHURCH; PO BOX 2235; PENSACOLA, FL 32501. (#102218-2).

FEB 4, '76. AMERICA '76 FILM LECTURE SERIES. SEMINAR. (LOCAL). W L UMPHLETT, DIRECTOR; PENSACOLA, FL 32504. (#103233-1).

MAR 15 - 26, '76. NATIONAL SECURITY SEMINAR. THE THEME OF THE SEMINAR IS NATIONAL SECURITY. AT PENSACOLA JUNIOR COLLEGE. (NAT'L). WALLACE KING, PROJ DIR; CHAMBER OF COMMERCE & PENSACOLA CHAPTER OF THE NAVY LEAGUE; 107 E ROMANO ST; PENSACOLA, FL 32501. (#101862-1).

MAR 19 - 20, '76. HISTORICAL SYMPOSIUM - '18TH CENTURY FLORIDA'. '18TH CENTURY FLORIDA; THE IMPACT OF THE AMERICAN REVOLUTION', FIFTH IN A SERIES SPONSORED ANNUALLY BY THE BICENTENNIAL COMMISSION. AT UNIV OF WEST FLORIDA CAMPUS. (LOCAL). JED MONGEON, CHMN; BICENTENNIAL COMMISSION OF FLORIDA; UNIV OF W FLA - CONTINUING ED; PENSACOLA, FL 32504. (#103393-1).

APR 2 - 4, '76. GULF COAST COUNCIL BICENTENNIAL ENCAMPMENT. CEREMONY, EXHIBIT, LIVE PERFORMANCE AT NETPDC ELLYSON FIELD, USE GATE ON HWY 90 ONLY. (LOCAL). BEN ARCENEAUX, FIELD DIR; GULF COAST COUNCIL BOY SCOUTS OF AMERICA; 5745 N 9TH AVE; PENSACOLA, FL 32503. (#102148-1).

APR 8 - 9, '76. PROFILE '76 BY EASTMAN KODAK. A 10,000 MILE PANORAMA OF PEOPLE, PLACES AND IDEAS FOR THE BICENT. AT PENSACOLA MUNICIPAL AUDITORIUM. (LOCAL). BOB MEAGHER, CHAIRMAN; PENSACOLA NEWS JOURNAL; 101 E ROMANO ST; PENSACOLA, FL 32501. (#102024-1).

APR 24, '76. JUNIOR LEAGUE BICENTENNIAL PARTY. FESTIVAL AT L & N RAILROAD TERMINAL. (LOCAL). MRS VINCENT WHIBBS, CHMN; PENSACOLA JUNIOR LEAGUE; PENSACOLA, FL 32503. (#102983-4).

MAY 1, '76. PREVIEW OF '76. FESTIVITIES WILL INCLUDE DEMONSTRATIONS, EXHIBITS, CEREMONIES AND PERFORMANCES DEPICTING LIFE IN '76 IN THE HOME, THE ARTS, OCCUPATIONS AND AMUSEMENTS TO BE PRESENTED BY THE GIRL SCOUTS IN THE AREA. AT SEVILLE SQUARE. (LOCAL). MARY JO WELLS, DIRECTOR; NORTHWEST FLORIDA GIRL SCOUT COUNCIL, INC; 4755A OLD SPANISH TRAIL RD; PENSACOLA, FL 32504. (#102164-1).

MAY 1 - 31, '76. NEW GLORY COLONIAL AND REVOLUTIONARY ERA FLAGS. EXHIBIT AT HISPANIC HISTORIC MUSEUM. (LOCAL). RUSSEL E BELOUS, COORD; UNIVERSITY MALL MERCHANTS ASSOC; 200 E ZARRAGOSSA ST; PENSACOLA, FL 32501. (#107276-2).

MAY 2, '76. AMERICAN WIND SYMPHONY'S FLOATING ARTS CENTER VISITS PENSACOLA. EMBARKING UPON A BICENTENNIAL CULTURAL TOUR, THE WIND SYMPHONY WILL VISIT 76 CITIES BRINGING MUSIC, DANCE, SYMPOSIA, AND CHILDREN'S THEATER TO THE WATERWAYS OF AMERICA DURING ITS 6-MONTH TOUR. (LOCAL). PAULA BERN, COORDINATOR; AMERICAN WIND SYMPHONY ORCHESTRA OF WESTERN PENNSYLVANIA; GATEWAY TOWERS 18G; PITTSBURGH, PA 15222. (#2800-2).

MAY 12 - 15, '76. NATL FRATERNITY OF MILITARY PILOTS, ORDER OF DAEDALIANS. INCLUDES CONFERENCES, SEMINARS, BANQUETS, GOLF TOURNEYS & A CRUISE ABOARD THE USS LEXINGTON. AT U S NAVAL AIR STATION. (NAT'L). DICK OLNEY, SR, PROJ DIR; SHANGRI-LA FLIGHT #21; PO BOX 3377; PENSACOLA, FL 32506. (#102615-1).

MAY 13 - 15, '76. ARMED FORCES WEEK. LIVE PERFORMANCE AT UNIVERSITY MALL. (LOCAL). ROBERT TAYLOR; NAVAL TECHNICAL TRAINING CENTER; NTTC CORRY STATION; PENSACOLA, FL 32511. (#200011-275).

JUNE 10 - 12, '76. USS LEXINGTON CVT-16 BICENTENNIAL GUEST AND DEPENDENTS CRUISES. EXHIBIT, TOUR AT NAVAL AIR STATION. (LOCAL). CDR WILLIAM E TURLEY, USN; USS LEXINGTON CVT-16; USS LEXINGTON (CVT-16) NAS; PENSACOLA, FL 32508. (#30805-1).

JUNE 25 - 27, '76. LION'S CLUB BICENTENNIAL RODEO. COMPETITION, LIVE PERFORMANCE AT ASHTON BROSNAHAM RECREATION CENTER, TEN HILE RD. (ST-WIDE). GEORGE SIZEMORE, CHMN; ENSLEY LIONS CLUB & W PENSACOLA LIONS CLUB; 4535 CHRISTY DR; PENSACOLA, FL 32504. (#102983-7).

JUNE 27 - JULY 5, '76. FIESTA OF FIVE FLAGS. THEME OF 'SALUTE TO US OF A', RE-ENACTMENT OF DE LUNA LANDING, PARADE, CORONATION OF DE LUNA & QUEEN, SPONSORS' BALL, ART SHOW, BIKE RACE, AN EVENING AT SEVILLE SQUARE. (LOCAL). DREX POYNTER, EXEC DIR; FIESTA OF FIVE FLAGS COMMISSION INC; PO BOX 1943; PENSACOLA, FL 32589. (#103393-3).

JULY 2, '76. PENSACOLA DELUNE PARADE. PARADE AT DOWNTOWN. (LOCAL). ROBERT TAYLOR; NAVAL TECHNICAL TRAINING CENTER; NTTC CORRY STATION; PENSACOLA, FL 32511. (#200011-276).

JULY 3, '76. JULY 4TH PICNIC CELEBRATION. FESTIVAL AT PICNIC GROUNDS, CORRY STATION. (LOCAL). ROBERT TAYLOR, PROJ OFC; NAVAL TECHNICAL TRAINING CENTER CORRY STATION; NTTC CORRY STATION; PENSACOLA, FL 32511. (#200011-271).

JULY 5, '76. BICENTENNIAL PARADE. PARADE AT DOWNTOWN. (LOCAL). ROBERT TAYLOR, PROJ OFC; NAVAL TECHNICAL TRAINING CENTER; NTTC CORRY STATION; PENSACOLA, FL 32511. (#200011-272).

JULY 5, '76. MOCK SEA BATTLE. UTILIZED PONTOON BARGES DISGUISED TO RESEMBLE 1776 WARSHIPS-1 AMERICAN & 1 BRITISH. THIS BATTLE WILL BE THE FINAL & MAJOR EVENT OF AN ALL DAY CELEBRATION OF SMALLER EVENTS & CLIMAXED WITH A GIGANTIC FIREWORKS DISPLAY. AT PENSACOLA BAY BETWEEN FT PICKENS & FT BARRANCUS. (LOCAL). CDR BJ MCGEE; NAVAL AIR STATION PENASCOLA; SUPPLY DEPT BLDG 603-3 NAS; PENSACOLA, FL 32508. (#200011-312).

AUG 27, '76. SEALED TIME CAPSULE TO BE OPENED ON THE TRICENTENNIAL. THE CAPSULE CONTAINS PRESENT DAY NAVY UNIFORMS, REGULATIONS & ITEMS SLECTED TO DEPICT WHAT THE NAVY EMPLOYEE USES IN HIS DAILY WORK, STAPLERS, PAPER CLIPS, PENCILS, ETC. ALSO MANY GENERAL USE ITEMS TO GIVE THE PEOPLE OF THE FUTURE A GLIMPSE INTO THE PAST. AT US NAVAL AVIATION MUSEUM, DUNCAN RD & TAYLOR RD. (LOCAL). CDR BJ MCGEE; NAVAL AIR STATION PENSACOLA; SUPPLY DEPT BLDG 603-3 NAS; PENSACOLA, FL 32508. (#200011-313).

OCT 1 - 3, '76. BELLVIEW JUNCTION WESTERN ROUNDUP. LIVE PERFORMANCE AT BELLVIEW JUNCTION 6 MILES NORTHWEST OF PENSACOLA ON SAUFLEY FIELD RD. (ST-WIDE). BILL MATHERS, COORD; PENSACOLA-ESCAMBIA DEVELOPMENT COMMISSION; 803 N PALAFOX ST; PENSACOLA, FL 32501. (#103416-571).

OCT 18 - 24, '76. PENSACOLA INTERSTATE FAIR, INC - COUNTY FAIR & EDUCATIONAL EXPO. TOP NAME ENTERTAINMENT ON 2 STAGES, POPULAR COUNTRY & WESTERN MUSIC, ALL EXHIBITS ARE FREE, OVER 100 ACRES OF EDUCATION AND ENTERTAINMENT. AT FAIR GROUNDS, US HWY-90, MOBILE HWY AT PINE FOREST RD. (REGN'L). JOHN E FRENKEL, JR, MGR; PENSACOLA INTERSTATE FAIR, INC; PO BOX 255; PENSACOLA, FL 32592. (#106095-4).

NOV 6 - 7, '76. GREAT GULF COAST FESTIVAL. FESTIVAL AT SEVILLE SQUARE. (REGN'L). CORNELIA HARBISON, COORD; PENSACOLA ARTS COUNCIL & PENSACOLA NEWS-JOURNAL; PENSACOLA, FL 32501. (#107276-1).

PERRY

NEWS ARTICLES, TAYLOR COUNTY, FL - OUR HERITAGE. TAYLOR COUNTY HISTORY, BEGINNING WITH INDIANS UP TO PRESENT, WILL BE FEATURED IN WEEKLY ARTICLES IN TWO LOCAL NEWSPAPERS. (LOCAL). EVELYN WILLIAMS, BICENTENNIAL CHAIRMAN; TAYLOR COUNTY ACTION '76 STEERING COMMITTEE; PO BOX 892; PERRY, FL 32347. (#22364).

JULY 5, '76. ROOTS FOR TOMORROW - 2-HOUR FAMILY EVENT WITH PICNIC AND PLAY. CEREMONY, EXHIBIT, FESTIVAL, LIVE PERFORMANCE AT FLORIDA FOREST FESTIVAL PARK AND HALL, HIGHWAY 19 SOUTH. (LOCAL). EVELYN WILLIAMS, CHMN; TAYLOR COUNTY '76 ACTION COMMITTEE; PO BOX 892; PERRY, FL 32347. (#106043-1).

OCT 18 - 23, '76. FLORIDA FOREST FESTIVAL. FESTIVAL. (ST-WIDE). ANNETTE AARON, CHMN; PERRY CHAMBER OF COMMERCE; PERRY, FL 32347. (#103416-650).

PINELLAS PARK

HISTORY OF CITY IN PINELLAS PARK, FL. HISTORY OF LOCAL AREA PREPARED BY WOMENS CLUB INCLUDING OLD PHOTOS, NEWSPAPER ADS & LICENSES. (LOCAL). RITA ROTH, CHAIRMAN; PINELLAS PARK BICENTENNIAL COMMITTEE; 5100 PARK BLVD; PINELLAS PARK, FL 33565. (#32265).

PARK COMPLETION IN PINELLAS PARK, FL. COMPLETION & DEDICATION OF PARK WITH FLAG RAISING & COMMEMORATIVE PERMANENT SIGNS. (LOCAL). RITA ROTH, CHAIRMAN; PINELLAS PARK BICENTENNIAL COMMITTEE; 5100 PARK BLVD; PINELLAS PARK, FL 33565. (#32264).

PLANT CITY

WPLA RADIO BICENTENNIAL PROGRAMMING - NBMRP. WPLA, PLANT CITY, SERVING A BICENTENNIAL COMMUNITY. LOCAL & COUNTY HISTORY VIGNETTES ARE BROADCAST IN COOPERATION WITH HISTORICAL SOCIETY. (LOCAL). AL BERRY, GENERAL MANAGER; WPLA RADIO; DRAWER J; PLANT CITY, FL 33566. (#21758).

FEB 26 - MAR 6, '76. FLORIDA STRAWBERRY FESTIVAL & HILLSBOROUGH COUNTY FAIR. 41ST ANNUAL FESTIVAL SALUTES BICENTENNIAL WITH SPECIAL PROGRAMS, GRAND PARADE, SENIOR CITIZEN DAY & KIDS DAY. (ST-WIDE). LOUISE GIBBS, MANAGER; FLORIDA STRAWBERRY FESTIVAL ASSOC & HILLSBOROUGH COUNTY FAIR, INC; PO BOX 832; PLANT CITY, FL 33566. (#103416-169).

JULY 3, '76. FOURTH OF JULY CELEBRATION. BARBEQUE, SQUARE DANCE, ART EXHIBITS, CONCESSIONS; A GENERAL CELEBRATION AND PAGEANTRY. AT STATE FARMERS MARKET. (LOCAL). RICHARD ELSTON, DIRECTOR; PLANT CITY JAYCEES; BOX 1329; PLANT CITY, FL 33566. (#105834-1).

PLANTATION

'ADOPT A PLUG', PLANTATION, FL. PAINTING OF FIRE HYDRANTS IN PATRIOTIC COLORS AND THEMES. FAMILIES AND CIVIC GROUPS WILL BE ASKED TO 'ADOPT A PLUG.'. (LOCAL). MRS SHARON LEVENDOSKI, PRESIDENT; PLANTATION JUNIOR WOMEN'S CLUB; 1111 NW 74TH WAY; PLANTATION, FL 33317. (#15678).

BOTANICAL GARDEN, PLANTATION, FL. BOTANICAL GARDEN BEING DEVELOPED ON A TWO ACRE TRACT ADJACENT TO PLANTATION LIBRARY. THE GARDEN WILL CONTAIN A SLAT HOUSE AND BE LANDSCAPED BY THE WINNING DESIGN FROM BROWARD COMMUNITY COLLEGE. (LOCAL). MRS ROY ARMSTRONG & MRS CLARENCE BELLER, CO-CHMN; BAYBERRY GARDEN CIRCLE & PLANTATION ORCHID SOCIETY; 875 NW 65 AVE; PLANTATION, FL 33317. (#18945).

GAZEBO BANDSTAND, PLANTATION, FL. 40' DIAMETER GAZEBO-STYLE BANDSTAND TO BE ERECTED ON CITY OWNED PROPERTY IN A COLONIAL SETTING WHERE FREE CONCERTS WILL BE HELD. (LOCAL). RICHARD O'BRIEN, CHAIRMAN; PLANTATION BICENTENNIAL COMMITTEE; 921 SW 75TH AVE; PLANTATION, FL 33316. (#15676).

HISTORICAL NEEDLEPOINT RUG, PLANTATION, FL. AN ARTIST IS DESIGNING 20 12' SQUARES DEPICTING PLANTATION HISTORY. 20 LOCAL WOMEN WILL COMPLETE THEM IN NEEDLEPOINT. THIS IS TO BE USED AS A RUG IN THE RESTORED PETER'S HOME. (LOCAL). MRS DOROTHY O'HARE, CHAIRMAN; PLANTATION HISTORICAL SOCIETY; 841 OLEANDER DR; PLANTATION, FL 33317. (#15681).

HISTORICAL QUILT, PLANTATION, FL. 40 SIXTH GRADE CHILDREN OF ST GREGORY SCHOOL RESEARCHED, DESIGNED & EMBROIDERED A 40 SQUARE BICENTENNIAL QUILT TO BE PRESENTED TO MAYOR VELTRI FOR THE PETER'S HOME AND MUSEUM. (LOCAL). MRS PAUL WANEK, PROJ DIRECTOR; ST GREGORY SCHOOL; 200 UNIVERSITY DR; PLANTATION, FL 33317. (#15680).

MARKING OF PLANTATION POLICE CARS, FL. ALL POLICE CARS IN THE CITY WILL BE MARKED WITH A DECAL OF THE BICENTENNIAL SYMBOL. (LOCAL). MRS DON ALLEN, PROJ DIRECTOR; CITY OF PLANTATION POLICE DEPARTMENT; 7051 NW 4TH ST; PLANTATION, FL 33317. (#15682).

PAINTING OF LITTER CANS IN PLANTATION, FL. LITTER CANS WILL BE PAINTED IN PATRIOTIC THEMES BY 300 GIRLS, AGES 11-13. THESE ARE TO BE USED IN ALL PUBLIC PARKS & FACILITIES. (LOCAL). MRS SHARON LEVENDOWSKI, CHAIRMAN; PLANTATION JUNIOR MISS CLUB; 1111 NW 74TH WAY; PLANTATION, FL 33317. (#15677).

PLANTATION BICENTENNIAL MARCH - FL. AN ORIGINAL COMPOSITION BY ANTHONY ABANNAT TO BE GIVEN TO THE CITY. IT HAS BEEN ARRANGED AND PUBLISHED FOR USE BY MUSICAL GROUPS. (LOCAL). RICHARD O'BRIEN, CHAIRMAN; PLANTATION BICENTENNIAL COMMITTEE; 921 SW 75TH AVE; PLANTATION, FL 33316. (#15679).

PLANTATION SHOW ARENA, FT LAUDERDALE, FL. STANDARD HORSE SHOW RING TO BE CONSTRUCTED IN A FIVE ACRE PARK; INCLUDES PICNIC GROUNDS, CONCESSION STAND, RESTROOMS, PADDOCKS AND A WARM-UP RING. (LOCAL). MRS JUNE QUINN, PROJ DIRECTOR; PLANTATION ACRES HORSEMAN ASSOC; PO BOX 8954; FT LAUDERDALE, FL 33310. (#18944).

SEPT 17, '75. PLANTATION PATRIOTS BICENTENNIAL BREAKFAST. FESTIVAL AT JACARUNDA COUNTRY CLUB PLANTATION. (LOCAL). RICHARD O'BRIEN, COORD; PLANTATION BICENTENNIAL GROUP AND GULFSTREAM DEVELOPMENT; 921 SW 75TH AVE; PLANTATION, FL 33316. (#200011-188).

PLANTATION — CONTINUED

NOV 9, '75 - JULY 4, '76. CONCERT SERIES- NINE IN BICENTENNIAL SERIES. CONCERT DATES: NOV 9, DEC 7, JAN 11, FEB 14, MAR 14, APR 25, MAY 16, JUNE 27 AND JULY 4. AT BANDSTAND-BICENTENNIAL PARK. (LOCAL). RICHARD O'BRIEN, DIRECTOR; PLANTATION BICENTENNIAL COMMITTEE; 921 SW 75TH AVE; PLANTATION, FL 33316. (#102420-4).

NOV 12, '75. AAUW BICENTENNIAL GOURMET TASTER AND AUCTION. THIRD ANNUAL AAUW GOURMET TASTER AND AUCTION. FUNDS GO TO JANE BOSER MEMORIAL FUND. MEMBERS PREPARE DISH FOR 'TASTING'-RECIPES ARE SOLD TO BE ADDED TO PREVIOUS YEAR'S COLLECTION. GROUP WILL PRESENT OFFICIAL ARBA FLAG TO BE USED IN DEICKE AUDITORIUM. AT DEICKE AUDITORIUM, CYPRESS RD. (LOCAL). MRS WAYNE WARD, COORD; AMERICAN ASSOC OF UNIVERSITY WOMEN-PLANTATION BRANCH; 5261 SW 4TH ST; PLANTATION, FL 33317. (#200011-189).

FEB 14, '76. RED, WHITE AND BLUE, I LOVE YOU - FLOWER SHOW. EXHIBIT AT DEICKE AUDITORIUM, CYPRESS ROAD, PLANTATION, FL. (LOCAL). MRS KELLY BENNETT; BAYBERRY GARDEN CIRCLE; 7490 NW 12TH ST; PLANTATION, FL 33313. (#104085-18).

APR 2 - 3, '76. SPIRIT OF '76 - ANNUAL VARIETY SHOW & CABARET. FESTIVAL, LIVE PERFORMANCE AT WAR MEMORIAL AUDITORIUM IN FT LAUDERDALE. (LOCAL). MRS S LEVENDONSKI, CHWMN; PLANTATION JR WOMEN; 1111 NW 74TH WAY; PLANTATION, FL 33317. (#102420-2).

APR 10, '76. PLANTATION DAYS - ANNUAL FESTIVAL WITH BICENTENNIAL THEME. LOCAL CIVIC GROUPS, SCHOOLS AND CHURCHES HAVE GAME/PRIZE BOOTHS; CONCERTS ARE GIVEN HOURLY, DANCES PERFORMED; A TRUE COMMUNITY FESTIVAL. AT DEICKE AUDITORIUM-HOFFMAN PARK. (LOCAL). MRS HOMER ARMITAGE, DIR; PLANTATION WOMENS CLUB; 6000 ROSE TERRACE; PLANTATION, FL 33317. (#102420-3).

POMPANO BEACH

THE SUN-SENTINEL BICENT PGM, POMPANO BEACH - NBMRP. SINCE OCTOBER, 1975, HAS RUN WEEKLY SERIES ON EACH STATE. IS ALSO PROVIDING PROMINENT COVERAGE OF LOCAL BICENTENNIAL ACTIVITIES. (LOCAL). WILLIAM A MULLEN, EDITOR; THE SUN-SENTINEL; PO BOX 1390; POMPANO BEACH, FL 33061. (#21748).

SEPT 6, '76. DEDICATION OF TRADEWIND PARK AS A BICENTENNIAL PARK. THE PARK WILL BE A TYPICAL HORSE FARM WITH A MUSEUM OF HORSE RACING TROPHIES. AT VINKEMULDER RD. (LOCAL). HELEN K BARNHOUSE, CHMN; AMERICAN BICENTENNIAL COMMISSION OF BROWARD COUNTY; 2750 NE 8TH AVE; POMPANO BEACH, FL 33064. (#108195-2).

NOV 20, '76. OLYMPICS FOR EXCEPTIONAL CHILDREN. COMPETITION. (LOCAL). HELEN K BARNHOUSE, CHMN; AMERICAN BICENTENNIAL COMMISSION OF BROWARD COUNTY; 2750 NE 8TH AVE; POMPANO BEACH, FL 33064. (#108195-1).

PONCE INLET

PONCE INLET LIGHTHOUSE RESTORATION, FLORIDA. PONCE INLET LIGHTHOUSE WILL BE RESTORED TO SAME CONDITION AS WHEN OPENED IN 1886 WITH A RECEPTION AREA AND A MUSEUM. THE LIGHTHOUSE KEEPERS HOME WILL BE FURNISHED AS ORIGINAL & LANDSCAPING ALSO DONE. (LOCAL). ANN POTTS, HEAD OF RESTORATION COMMITTEE; RESTORATION COMMITTEE FOR PONCE INLET LIGHTHOUSE; SAILFISH DR; PONCE INLET, FL 32018. (#7739).

PONTE VENDRA

HISTORY CLASS PROJECTS - PONTE VENDRA, FL. PONTE VEDRA-PALM VALLEY SCHOOL HISTORY CLASS TO SPOTLIGHT SOME PATRIOTIC HISTORICAL FACT THRU SONGS, ESSAYS, PICTURES & COSTUMES. (LOCAL). MRS RUTH HOSS, LIBRARIAN; PONTE VEDRA-PALM VALLEY SCHOOL; BOX 86; PONTE VEDRA, FL 32084. (#15001).

PORT ORANGE

MAY 29, '76. 13 STAR FESTIVAL COMMUNITY PROJECT FOR RESTORATION OF OLD SCHOOL. $1,700 WAS RAISED FOR THE RESTORATION OF THE PORT ORANGE, ONE ROOM SCHOOL HOUSE. AT CITY PROPERTY ON USI WHERE OLD SCHOOL IS NOW STANDING. (LOCAL). MARY SOLANA; SOS-SAVE OUR SCHOOL; NIXON LANE; PORT ORANGE, FL 32019. (#200011-270).

OCT 15, '76. PRESENTATION OF FLAGS & STANDS TO SPRUCE CREEK HIGH SCHOOL. CEREMONY AT SPRUCE CREEK HIGH SCHOOL. (LOCAL). DR LYMAN J LAUGHTON; VOLUSIA ACTION '76 AND ELKS LODGE 1141; 340 APACHE TRAIL; ORMOND BEACH, FL 32074. (#109349-1).

PORT ST JOE

JAN 10 - 11, '76. UNITED STATES ARMED FORCES BICENTENNIAL CARAVAN. CARAVAN IS COMPOSED OF EXHIBIT VANS FOR EACH MILITARY SERVICE. PROJECT THEME IS 'HISTORY OF THE ARMED FORCES AND THEIR CONTRIBUTIONS TO THE NATION'. (LOCAL). R H ELLZEY; US ARMED FORCES BICENTENNIAL EXHIBIT VANS PROJECT; PO BOX 250; PORT ST JOE, FL 32456. (#1775-418).

PRT CHARLOTTE

CHARLOTTE COUNTY CULTURAL CENTER EXPANSION, FL. ADDITIONS TO CURRENT CULTURAL CENTER TO BE COMPLETED BY DECEMBER OF 1976. (LOCAL). GEORGE LANE, JR, EXEC DIRECTOR; CHARLOTTE COUNTY ACTION '76 COMMITTEE; 75 TAYLOR ST; PUNTA GORDA, FL 33950. (#15052).

JUNE 14, '76. FLAG DAY FESTIVAL. SEVERAL HUNDRED PEOPLE PARTICIPATING, INCLUDING AMERICAN LEGION, COUNTY POLICE, BOY SCOUTS, GIRL SCOUTS, SCHOOL BANDS & GUEST SPEAKERS. AT ELKS CLUB. (LOCAL). GEORGE ATKINS, CHAIRMAN; CHARLOTTE COUNTY ACTION '76 COMMITTEE; 95 TAYLOR ST; PUNTA GORDA, FL 33950. (#102156-1).

PT EVERGLADES

OCT 9 - 10, '76. PIONEER DAYS 1976 AMERICAN HISTORY EXHIBIT. EXHIBIT INCLUDES: PICTURES & MAPS OF AMERICAN REVOLUTIONARY WAR CAMPAIGNS, ENGLISH & FRENCH MAP OF MAJOR ANDRE'S ROUTE BEFORE CAPTURE, PICTURES OF FLAGS & U S PRESIDENTS & MAP SHOWING FORTS ALONG HUDSON RIVER. AT PORT EVERGLADES BUILDING 24. (LOCAL). BROWARD HISTORICAL COMM; BROWARD CO HISTORICAL COMM & PORT EVERGLADES AUTHORITY; 201 S E 6 STREET RM 800; FT LAUDERDALE, FL 33301. (#106693-1).

QUINCY

BICENTENNIAL ARTS & CRAFTS FESTIVAL. SECOND ANNUAL CULTURAL & INDUSTRIAL ARTS & CRAFTS FESTIVAL. (LOCAL). ALEXANDER L HINSON, CHMN; GADSDEN COUNTY ACTION '76 STEERING COMMITTEE; 121 N MADISON; QUINCY, FL 32351. (#108927-1).

FEB 13, '76. CARTER - PARRAMORE BICENTENNIAL ASSEMBLY. COLOR GUARD FLAG PRESENTATION, SONGS BY THE CHORUS, FILM - 'FLORIDA ON MY MIND', PLAY - 'CONSPIRACY AT VALLEY FORGE' BY REVEREND SUMPTER'S CLASS AND INTRODUCTORY REMARKS FROM THE SOCIAL STUDIES DEPARTMENT. AT 631 S STEWART ST. (LOCAL). BERNARD KAPLIN, COORD; CARTER - PARRAMORE HIGH SCHOOL; CARTER - PARRAMORE HIGH SCHOOL; QUINCY, FL 32351. (#200011-190).

MAY 2, '76. OLD PHILADELPHIA CHURCH BICENTENNIAL FESTIVAL. HOMECOMING CELEBRATION INCLUDING COSTUMES AND FOOD APPROPRIATE TO THE 1820'S. INDIVIDUALS AND GROUPS ARRIVED BY MULE AND WAGON, HORSEBACK AND SURREY. AT OLD PHILADELPHIA CHURCH, 5 MILES FROM QUINCY. (LOCAL). COORDINATOR; FIRST PRESBYTERIAN CHURCH; QUINCY, FL 32351. (#108927-2).

SAN ANTONIO

OCT 18, '75. RATTLESNAKE FESTIVAL & INTL CHAMPIONSHIP GOPHER RACE. THIS YEAR'S EMPHASIS OF 9TH ANNUAL FESTIVAL IS A TRAVELING MEDICINE SHOW. THERE WILL BE AN ARTS & CRAFTS DIVISION & HOT AIR BALLOONS ALONG WITH A 50 FOOT TRACK FOR LAND TORTOISES RACES. FOOD WILL BE AVAILABLE. AT CITY PARK - 3 MILES EAST OF I-75 ON STATE ROAD 52.. (REGN'L). EDDIE HERRMANN, CHMN; SAN ANTONIO JAYCEES; 214 ELM ST; SAN ANTONIO F, FL 33576. (#101032-1).

JULY 3, '76. FULL STEAM AHEAD - OPENING OF RAILROAD EXHIBIT. OPENING OF EXHIBIT OF PASSENGER CARRYING TRAIN. AT RR STATION, RAILROAD AVE. (LOCAL). ROBERT MOST, CHAIRMAN; SAN ANTONIO AREA BICENTENNIAL COMMITTEE; 564 BOSPHORUS AVE; TAMPA, FL 33606. (#105360-2).

JULY 3, '76 - CONTINUING . FULL STEAM AHEAD - RAILROAD EXHIBIT. TRILBY, SAN ANTONIO & CYPRESS RAILROAD EXCURSION TRAIN ON EXHIBIT. AT RR STATION, RAILROAD AVE. (LOCAL). ROBERT MOST, CHAIRMAN; SAN ANTONIO BICENTENNIAL COMMITTEE; 564 BOSPHORUS AVE; TAMPA, FL 33606. (#105360-1).

SANFORD

COMMEMORATIVE WALK - PROJ OF SANFORD, FL. JOURNEY ALONG EASTERN SEABOARD TO PHILADELPHIA TRAVELING BACKROADS TO GATHER FOLKLORE, SONGS, RECIPES AND PHOTOGRAPHS OF OLDEN TIMES FROM OLD FOLKS TO INSURE PRESERVATION FOR THE FUTURE. (REGN'L). MRS W F GIELOW, CHAIRMAN; SEMINOLE COUNTY ACTION '76 COMMITTEE; 400 E FIRST ST; SANFORD, FL 32711. (#15065).

LAKEFRONT BEAUTIFICATION - PROJ OF SANFORD, FL. BEAUTIFICATION OF 1.8 MILES OF SEA WALL PARK STRIP ALONG LAKE MONROE A PERMANENT PLAQUE WILL BE INSTALLED IN AN APPROPRIATE PLACE FOR FUTURE GENERATIONS TO KNOW IT AS A TRIBUTE TO 76. (LOCAL). MRS W F GIELOW, CHAIRMAN; SEMINOLE COUNTY ACTION 76 COMMITTEE; PO BOX 1523; SANFORD, FL 32771. (#15064).

'LAW AND THE LAYMAN'. LAW WEEK DEVOTED TO TOUR AND LECTURES BY JUDICIAL REPS AT COUNTY COURT FOR ALL SEMINOLE COUNTY STUDENTS. (LOCAL). R BARNETT, CHAIRMAN; BICENTENNIAL EDUCATION COMMITTEE; 202 W COMMERCIAL ST; SANFORD, FL 32771. (#15058-1).

MURALS OF EARLY SANFORD, FL. PAINT MURALS DEPICTING EARLY DAYS IN SEMINOLE COUNTY FLORIDA ON EXTERNAL WALLS OF DOWNTOWN STORES. (LOCAL). FRAN BOWDEN, COORDINATOR; SEMINOLE COUNTY SCHOOLS; 200 W COMMERCIAL ST; SANFORD, FL 32771. (#15055).

OPTIMIST CANTEEN - BICENT MOTIVATION PGM, FL. RECOGNITION/AWARD PROGRAM FOR DETAINEES AT SEMINOLE REGIONAL JUVENILE DETENTION CENTER. PARTICIPANTS PRESENT FREE REDEMPTION CARDS AT OPTIMIST CANTEEN DURING EVENING OPTIMIST HOUR. (LOCAL). J E EISELIEN, PROJ DIRECTOR; COUNTY ACTION '76 COMMITTEE; 115 LAUREL DR; SANFORD, FL 32771. (#15053).

SEMINOLE COUNTY VETERANS MEMORIAL - SANFORD, FL. BUILD A FUNCTIONAL MONUMENT TO HONOR SEMINOLE COUNTY VETERANS. (LOCAL). BERNARD G GUILLAUME, PROJ DIRECTOR; ACTION '76 COMMITTEE SEMINOLE COUNTY; 400 E FIRST ST; SANFORD, FL 32771. (#15063).

SENIOR CITIZENS BENCHES AND RAMPS - SANFORD, FL. CONSTRUCT BENCHES MARKED WITH BICENT LOGO AND STREET CORNER RAMPS FOR USE BY SENIOR CITIZENS ALONG MAIN ST. (LOCAL). MRS JOHN HARRISON, CHAIRMAN; SENIOR CITIZENS CLUB; PO BOX 2122; SANFORD, FL 32771. (#15059).

NOV 9 - 15, '75. 'GOLDEN AGE OLYMPICS'. COMPETITION WILL INCLUDE TRACK & FIELD, ARTS & CRAFTS, BOWLING, TENNIS, GOLF, SHUFFLEBOARD, ETC; WILL CULMINATE IN A DINNER DANCE AWARDS NIGHT. (ST-WIDE). JOHN HORNER, EXEC MANAGER; CHAMBER OF COMMERCE & SEMINOLE COUNTY ACTION '76 COMMITTEE; PO DRAWER CC; SANFORD, FL 32771. (#102248-1).

JAN 2 - DEC 31, '76. BICENTENNIAL BAND. 200 YOUNG MUSICIANS FROM SEMINOLE COUNTY HIGH SCHOOLS WILL PERFORM AT BICENTENNIAL ACTIVITIES THROUGH 1976. (LOCAL). KATHY BUKUR, CHAIRMAN; SEMINOLE COUNTY ACTION '76 PAGEANTRY COMMITTEE; 100 IDLEWYLD DR; SANFORD, FL 32771. (#102160-1).

FEB '76. BLACK FESTIVAL WEEK. THE FESTIVAL WEEK WILL INCLUDE A PARADE, MUSIC, SKITS AND SPEECHES. AT SANFORD CIVIC CENTER. (LOCAL). ALFREDA WALLACE, CHAIRMAN; SEMINOLE COUNTY ACTION '76 BICENTENNIAL COMMITTEE; 400 E FIRST ST; SANFORD, FL 32771. (#102161-1).

MAR 15, '76. PIONEER DAYS, GIRL SCOUT DEMONSTRATION OF EARLY DAY SKILLS. DEMONSTRATION OF PIONEER SKILLS OF QUILTING, BUTTER CHURNING, ICE CREAM MAKING, BLACK SMITHING ETC; A HIDDEN HEROINE, ONE OF EARLY DAY GIRL SCOUT LEADERS STILL ALIVE, WILL BE SPECIAL GUEST. AT FT MELLON PARK. (LOCAL). DOREEN FREEMAN, PROJ DIR; CITRUS COUNCIL OF GIRL SCOUTS; 461 MELLONVILLE AVE; SANFORD, FL 32771. (#102157-1).

MAY 7 - 9, '76. HISTORICAL PAGEANT. THE PAGEANT WILL DEPICT THE HISTORY OF SANFORD IN SONG, DANCE, SKIT AND NARRATIVE; THERE WILL BE THE PRESENTATION OF A ONE ACT PLAY THE WINNER OF A PLAY WRITING CONTEST AMONG HIGH SCHOOL AND JUNIOR COLLEGE STUDENTS. AT SANFORD CIVIC AUDITORIUM, 401 E SEMINOLE BLVD. (LOCAL). BETTYE SMITH, PROJ COORD; SANFORD MUTUAL CONCERT ASSOC; 119 UPSALA RD; SANFORD, FL 32771. (#102158-1).

NOV 7 - 13, '76. 'GOLDEN AGE OLYMPICS'. COMPETITION WILL INCLUDE TRACK & FIELD, ARTS & CRAFTS, BOWLING, TENNIS, GOLF, SHUFFLEBOARD, ETC; WILL CULMINATE IN A DINNER DANCE AWARDS NIGHT. (ST-WIDE). JOHN HORNER, EXEC MANAGER; CHAMBER OF COMMERCE & SEMINOLE COUNTY ACTION '76 COMMITTEE; PO DRAWER CC; SANFORD, FL 32771. (#102248-2).

DEC 5 - 7, '76. UNITED STATES ARMED FORCES BICENTENNIAL CARAVAN. CARAVAN IS COMPOSED OF EXHIBIT VANS FOR EACH MILITARY SERVICE. PROJECT THEME IS 'HISTORY OF THE ARMED FORCES & THEIR CONTRIBUTIONS TO THE NATION'. (LOCAL). JOHN C HORNER; UNITED STATES ARMED FORCES BICENTENNIAL CARAVAN; 400 E FIRST ST; SANFORD, FL 32771. (#1775-783).

SANIBEL

BICENTENNIAL ART COMPETITION & EXHIBITION, FL. ART LEAGUE MEMBERS & ARTISTS SUBMITTED ART WORKS IN ALL MEDIUMS OF LOCAL ISLAND HISTORIC LANDMARKS. PRIZES: BICENTENNIAL SILVER DOLLARS. (LOCAL). BARBARA A SCHUMACHER, CO-CHAIRMAN; SANIBEL BICENTENNIAL COMMITTEE & CAPTIVA CIVIC ART LEAGUE; SANIBEL, FL 33957. (#31527).

BICENTENNIAL ISLAND HISTORY SUPPLEMENT, FL. A SERIES ON SANIBEL ISLAND HISTORY, PUBLISHED MONTHLY IN THE ISLAND REPORTER NEWSPAPER & REISSUED AS A BROCHURE DURING THE JULY 4 FESTIVAL WEEKEND. (LOCAL). ANNE J MARSH, CO-CHAIRMAN; SANIBEL BICENTENNIAL COMMITTEE/ BANK OF THE ISLAND; 1699 PERIWINKLE WAY; SANIBEL, FL 33957. (#31525).

BICENTENNIAL STUDENT GOVERNMENT COMPETITION, FL. ESSAY CONTEST WITH WINNERS BECOMING CITY GOVERNMENT OFFICIALS FOR A DAY. (LOCAL). ANNE MARSH, PROJ CHAIRMAN; CITY OF SANIBEL; SANIBEL, FL 33957. (#31528).

OLD ISLANDS PHOTO COPYING PROJECT, SANIBEL, FL. OLD ISLAND PHOTOS WERE COPIED, TO BE PRESERVED & PLACED ON FILE AT SANIBEL LIBRARY FOR PUBLIC USE. (LOCAL). BARBARA A SCHUMACHER, CO-CHAIRMAN; SANIBEL BICENTENNIAL COMMITTEE & PUBLIC LIBRARY BOARD; PO DRAWER R; SANIBEL, FL 33957. (#31526).

RESTORATION & PRESERVATION OF SANIBEL CEMETERY, FL. CLEANING OF CEMETERY, LOCATION & MARKING OF LOST GRAVE SITES, RESTORATION OF OLD TOMBSTONES. (LOCAL). COORDINATOR; HISTORICAL PRESERVATION COMMITTEE OF THE CITY OF SANIBEL; PERIWINKLE PL; SANIBEL, FL 33957. (#31524).

FEB 12 - 13, '76. BICENTENNIAL ARTS & CRAFTS FAIR. EARLY AMERICAN CRAFT DEMONSTRATIONS WERE GIVEN AT THIS ANNUAL CONTEMPORARY CRAFTS SHOW. AT SANIBEL COMMUNITY HOUSE. (LOCAL). BARBARA SCHUMACHER; SANIBEL PUBLIC LIBRARY & SANIBEL BICENTENNIAL COMMITTEE; 3716 PECTIN CT; SANIBEL IS, FL 33957. (#200011-302).

SANIBEL — CONTINUED

JULY 2 - 4, '76. JULY 4 WEEKEND IN SANIBEL ISLAND. ACTIVITIES INCLUDED A PARADE, FISH FRY SPONSORED BY THE AMERICAN LEGION, ECUMENICAL SUNRISE SERVICE, FAMILY PICNIC AND GAMES, AND A TEEN DANCE. (LOCAL). BARBARA SCHUMACHER; SANIBEL BICENTENNIAL COMMITTEE; 3716 PECTIN CT; SANIBEL IS, FL 33957. (#200011-295).

SARASOTA

SEPT 23, '76. ISRAELI PHILHARMONIC ORCHESTRA VISITS SARASOTA. LIVE PERFORMANCE. (INT'L). URI AHARON BAR-NEV; ISRAELI GOVERNMENT; 1621 21ST ST, NW; WASHINGTON, DC 20008. (#109015-20).

DEC 13 - 15, '76. AMERICAN FREEDOM TRAIN DISPLAY DAYS AT SARASOTA. THE AMERICAN FREEDOM TRAIN INCLUDES 10 EXHIBIT CARS & 2 SHOW CASE CARS DEPICTING DIFFERENT PHASES OF THE AMERICAN EXPERIENCE. ITS ARRIVAL WILL SERVE AS A CATALYST FOR LOCAL BICENTENNIAL CELEBRATIONS BY PEOPLE THROUGHOUT THIS NATION. (ST-WIDE). SY FREEDMAN, DIR OF P/R; THE AMERICAN FREEDOM TRAIN FOUNDATION; 5205 LEESBURG PIKE, SUITE 800; BAILEY'S XRDS, VA 22041. (#1776-110).

SEMINOLE

OCT 21, '75 - JULY 30, '76. HISTORICAL AND RELIGIOUS EVENTS. FESTIVAL, PARADE, LIVE PERFORMANCE AT SEMINOLE HIGH SCHOOL. (LOCAL). B G GUILLAME, CHMN; SEMINOLE AREA BICENTENNIAL COMMITTEE; 6701 SEMINOLE BLVD; SEMINOLE, FL 33542. (#200011-191).

JAN 30 - FEB 29, '76. SEMINOLE HIGH SCHOOL BICENTENNIAL HAPPENINGS. JAN 30 - SUN COAST STRING BAND CONCERT; FEB 28-29 - 'THE WAY IT WAS', A HISTORICAL PAGEANT. (LOCAL). B G GUILLAUME, CHMN; SEMINOLE AREA BICENTENNIAL COMMITTEE; 6701 SEMINOLE BLVD; SEMINOLE, FL 33542. (#103738-1).

MAR 12 - 20, '76. PAGEANT AND POW WOW. MAR 12 - SEMINOLE FIREMEN VS PINELLAS COUNTY SHERIFF DEPUTIES, A FOOTBALL GAME; MAR 13 - MR SEMINOLE BANQUET; MAR 14 - POW WOW COMM VS SEMINOLE FIREMEN, WRESTLING; MAR 19 - SPIRIT OF AMERICA, PRES FORD'S HONOR GUARD; MAR 20 - POW WOW AND FLORIDA RANGERS. (LOCAL). B G GUILLAUME, CHMN; SEMINOLE AREA BICENTENNIAL COMMITTEE; 6701 SEMINOLE BLVD; SEMINOLE, FL 33542. (#103738-2).

JULY 4, '76. BICENTENNIAL CHURCH SERVICES. CEREMONY. (LOCAL). B G GUILLAUME, CHMN; SEMINOLE AREA BICENTENNIAL COMMITTEE; 6701 SEMINOLE BLVD; SEMINOLE, FL 33542. (#103738-3).

JULY 4, '76. LAKE SEMINOLE PRESBYTERIAN CHURCH MUSIC PROGRAM. FESTIVAL. (LOCAL). BERNARD GUILLAUME, CHMN; LAKE SEMINOLE PRESBYTERIAN CHURCH; 8050 SEMINOLE MALL, SUITE 345; SEMINOLE, FL 33542. (#108334-1).

JULY 4, '76. LUNCHEON-MUSIC PROGRAM. SENATOR CHILES WILL BE GUEST SPEAKER; NATIONAL BELL RINGING WILL BE OBSERVED. AT FIRE STATION. (LOCAL). BERNARD GUILLAUME, CHMN; SEMINOLE BICENTENNIAL COMMITTEE & LOCAL CHURCHES; 8050 SEMINOLE MALL, SUITE 345; SEMINOLE, FL 33542. (#108334-2).

SHARPES

APR 6 - 13, '76. MOTO CROSS RACE. FESTIVAL. (LOCAL). BILL WOOD, CHAIRMAN; INDIAN RIVER JUBILEE COMMITTEE FOR BREVARD COUNTY; 3220 N COCOA BLVD; COCOA, FL 32922. (#7704-502).

SOPCHOPPY

JULY 3 - 4, '76. WAKULLA COUNTY 4TH OF JULY CELEBRATION. ACTIVITIES INCLUDE FLYING CIRCUS, PARADE, COUNTRY MUSIC, FLAG CEREMONY, SKY DIVERS, FIREWORKS; ON THE 4TH AFTER CHURCH, DEDICATION OF OLD 1893 COURT HOUSE. AT ELEMENTARY SCHOOL, 2 BLOCKS SOUTH OF HIGHWAY 319 IN CENTER OF TOWN. (LOCAL). BILL STEPHENS, PROJ CHMN; SOPCHOPPY 4TH OF JULY ASSOCIATION; CITY OF SOPCHOPPY, ACTION '76; TOWN HALL; SOPCHOPPY, FL 32358. (#105354-1).

SOUTH BAY

SOUTH BAY, FL BEAUTIFICATION. A LIGHTED WATERFALL FOUNTAIN WAS INSTALLED IN THE PARK AND A LOCAL YOUTH GROUP PAINTED 20 LITTER BARRELS RED, WHITE AND BLUE. (LOCAL). ESTHER H WALKER, SECRETARY-TREASURER; SOUTH BAY BICENTENNIAL COMMITTEE; PALM BEACH RD; SOUTH BAY, FL 33493. (#29447).

SOUTH BAY, FL, BICENTENNIAL PARK. A TRIANGLE IN THE TOWN'S CENTER HAS BEEN FILLED & SODDED, A FOUNTAIN HAS BEEN BUILT & A FLAG POLE HAS BEEN ERECTED, ALONG WITH A 'HAPPY BIRTHDAY USA' SIGN. (LOCAL). ESTHER H WALKER, CHAIRMAN; CITY OF SOUTH BAY BICENTENNIAL COMMITTEE; 270 SE 3RD AVE; SOUTH BAY, FL 33493. (#29138).

JULY 4, '76. BIRTHDAY PARTY FOR OUR NATION. LARGE HAPPY BIRTHDAY USA CUTOUT LETTERS 8 FT TALL COVERING 100 FT. 13 ORIGINAL STATE FLAGS PAINTED ON 4 X 8 SIGNBOARD, THE MOST SPECTACULAR DISPLAY IN FLORIDA, BAND MUSIC, & SPEECHES FROM LOCAL OFFICIALS WERE PART OF THIS ACTIVITY. AT HOOVER DYKE. (LOCAL). ESTHER H WALKER, CHAIRMAN; CITY OF SOUTH BAY BICENTENNIAL COMMITTEE; 270 SE 3RD AVE; SOUTH BAY, FL 33493. (#200011-246).

SOUTH DAYTONA

HALIFAX HISTORICAL SOCIETY MUSEUM, S DAYTONA, FL. CONSTRUCTION OF A MUSEUM OF LOCAL MEMORABILIA. (LOCAL). GEORGE W WAITE, OD; SOUTH DAYTONA BICENTENNIAL COMMITTEE; 2447 S RIDGEWOOD AVE; SOUTH DAYTONA, FL 32019. (#31087).

PAINTING OF CITY FIRE HYDRANTS - SOUTH DAYTONA, FL. CITY FIRE HYDRANTS WERE PAINTED RED, WHITE & BLUE. (LOCAL). GEORGE W WAITE, OD; SOUTH DAYTONA BICENTENNIAL COMMITTEE; 2447 S RIDGEWOOD AVE; SOUTH DAYTONA, FL 32019. (#31085).

TOWN CRIER, SOUTH DAYTONA, FL. A CITY EMPLOYEE DELIVERED THE MAYOR'S LETTER TO AREA RESIDENTS, USING A DECORATED CITY SCOOTER. THE SCOOTER WAS USED IN AREA PARADES WITH A COMMITTEE MEMBER AS DRIVER. (LOCAL). GEORGE W WALTE, OD; SOUTH DAYTONA BICENTENNIAL COMMITTEE; 2447 S RIDGEWOOD AVE; SOUTH DAYTONA, FL 32019. (#31086).

MAY 1 - 10, '76. ART CONTEST FOR CHILDREN 6-12. COMPETITION AT SUNSHINE MALL. (LOCAL). GEORGE W WAITE, OD; SOUTH DAYTONA BICENTENNIAL COMMITTEE; 2447 S RIDGEWOOD AVE; SOUTH DAYTONA, FL 32019. (#200011-268).

JULY 2, '76. BICENTENNIAL PICNIC. FESTIVAL AT BICENTENNIAL PARK. (LOCAL). GEORGE W WAITE, OD; SOUTH DAYTONA BICENTENNIAL COMMITTEE; 2447 S RIDGEWOOD AVE; SOUTH DAYTONA, FL 32019. (#200011-269).

SOUTH MIAMI

IN AND AROUND SOUTH MIAMI - BOOKLET, FL. A 100 PAGE BOOKLET WITH HISTORY OF THE CITY OF SOUTH MIAMI, INDIAN LORE, FLORIDA HISTORY AND INTERVIEWS WITH OLD TIME SETTLERS. (LOCAL). ED CORLEY, CHAIRPERSON; SOUTH MIAMI BICENTENNIAL COMMITTEE; SOUTH MIAMI, FL 33162. (#21868).

FEB 15, '75. SOUTH MIAMI BICYCLE RACE. COMPETITION. (ST-WIDE). NICK ARKON, COORD; MACK CYCLE SHOP OF SOUTH MIAMI; SOUTH MIAMI, FL 33145. (#200011-194).

DEC 22 - 27, '75. AMERICAN BICENTENNIAL FLORIDA EXHIBIT. EXHIBIT, RADIO/TV AT CITY HALL, 6130 SUNSET DR. (LOCAL). ANITA BJORK; THIRD CENTURY, USA; PO BOX 451976; MIAMI, FL 33145. (#100225-5).

MAR 13, '76. ST PATRICK'S DAY BICENTENNIAL PARADE. PARADE AT SUNSET DR; U S 1 TO RED RD. (LOCAL). ED CORLEY, CHAIRPERSON; CITY OF SOUTH MIAMI; SOUTH MIAMI, FL 33157. (#105580-3).

MAY 4, '76. SENIOR CLASS, SOUTH MIAMI SENIOR HIGH SCHOOL, SCHOLARSHIP LUNCHEON. AWARD, CEREMONY AT HOLIDAY INN, S DIXIE HWY. (LOCAL). ED CORLEY, CHAIRPERSON; SOUTH MIAMI BICENTENNIAL COMMITTEE; SOUTH MIAMI, FL 33157. (#105580-2).

MAY 14 - 15, '76. SOUTH MIAMI HOSPITAL SPIRIT OF '76 HEALTH FAIR. EXHIBIT, FAIR AT SOUTH MIAMI HOSPITAL, SW 62ND AVE AND S DIXIE HWY. (LOCAL). ED CORLEY; SOUTH MIAMI BICENTENNIAL COMMITTEE; 5764 SW 77TH TERRACE; SOUTH MIAMI, FL 33143. (#105580-1).

JULY 4, '76. INDEPENDENCE DAY CELEBRATION - FIREWORKS, MUSIC AND GAMES. FESTIVAL AT S MIAMI JUNIOR HIGH SCHOOL ATHLETIC FIELD. (LOCAL). ED CORLEY, DIRECTOR; CITY OF SOUTH MIAMI BICENTENNIAL COMMITTEE; 5764 SW 77TH TERR; SOUTH MIAMI, FL 33143. (#2997-8).

SPRING HILL

1776 MEMBERSHIP DRIVE - SPRING HILL, FL. THE SPRING HILL CIVIC CLUB IS STRIVING FOR A MEMBERSHIP OF 1,776 BY THE END OF THE BICENTENNIAL YEAR. ALL DUES WILL GO FOR COMMUNITY IMPROVEMENT. (LOCAL). JERRY WEXLER, MEMBERSHIP CHAIRMAN; SPRING HILL CIVIC CLUB; 1480 SPRING HILL DR; SPRING HILL, FL 33512. (#25939).

DEC 7, '75. CHRISTMAS PARADE. PARADE AT SPRING HILL BLVD, KENLAKE AVE. (LOCAL). GLADYS READING, COORD; NORTH DELTA CHAPTER BETA SIGMA PHI SORORITY; 1144 HARCROSS CT; SPRING HILL, FL 33512. (#200011-192).

MAR 15, '76. RELIGIOUS HERITAGE. CONFERENCE AT 1ST UNITED METHODIST CHURCH, 2600 SPRING HILL DR, SPRING HILL, FL. (LOCAL). WAYNE S BERRY, PRES; MEN'S CLUB, FIRST UNITED METHODIST CHURCH; 1312 HOLLYHOCK LN; SPRING HILL, FL 33512. (#104705-1).

JUNE 6 - JULY 4, '76. COLONIAL CHURCH LIFE - OUR HERITAGE AS EPISCOPALIANS. 5 SERMONS USING 1662 PRAYER BOOK, THE AUTHORIZED FORM OF WORSHIP IN 1776. AT ST ANDREW'S EPISCOPAL CHURCH, DELTONA BLVD & FOUNDER RD. (LOCAL). ERNEST L BENNETT, VICAR; ST ANDREW'S EPISCOPAL CHURCH; SPRING HILL, FL 33512. (#108399-4).

JULY 3, '76. BICENTENNIAL CELEBRATION IN SPRING HILL. FESTIVAL AT SPRING HILL RECREATION CENTER. (LOCAL). RUSSELL KIRK, CHAIRMAN; SPRING HILL CIVIC CLUB; 585 TRELLIS ST; SPRING HILL, FL 33512. (#108399-3).

ST AUGUSTINE

AMERICAN FLAGS TO FLY IN ST AUGUSTINE, FL. PROVIDING FLAGS TO RESIDENTS AT COST. PERIODIC ARTICLES TO APPEAR IN NEWSPAPER URGING RESIDENTS TO DISPLAY FLAGS, TO BE PURCHASED FROM NEWSPAPER OR BICENTENNIAL OFFICE. (LOCAL). ROBERT E MARTIN, GENERAL MANAGER; THE ST AUGUSTINE RECORD; PO BOX 1630; ST AUGUSTINE, FL 32084. (#18939).

BICENTENNIAL MURAL, ST AUGUSTINE, FL. THE PAINTING OF A MURAL ON SCHOOL CAFETERIA WALL DEPICTING FLORIDA HISTORY & AMERICAN BICENTENNIAL SCENES. (LOCAL). MISS ROBERTA P MCALOON, ART TEACHER; HASTINGS HIGH SCHOOL; 59 N ST AUGUSTINE BLVD; ST AUGUSTINE, FL 32084. (#15005).

BICENTENNIAL MUSICAL PRODUCTION - FL. BICENTENNIAL MUSICAL PRODUCTION WITH COSTUMES INVOLVING 100 CHILDREN. (LOCAL). MRS HARRIETTE NOELL, PRINCIPAL; EVELYN HAMBLEN ELEMENTARY SCHOOL; 16 ISABEL ST; ST AUGUSTINE, FL 32084. (#18937).

BICENTENNIAL WREATH, ST AUGUSTINE, FL. SORORITY MEMBERS TO SELL WREATHS TO FINANCE CONTRIBUTION TO LIBRARIES OF FIFTH AND SIXTH GRADE CENTERS. (LOCAL). MS SUZANNE BIGGS, PROJ COORDINATOR; RHO TAU CHAPTER OF BETA SIGMA PHI SORORITY; 306 SANTANDER ST; ST AUGUSTINE, FL 32084. (#22352).

BIRTHDAY CARD TO AMERICA - ST AUGUSTINE, FL. THIRD GRADERS SENDING BIRTHDAY CARD TO AMERICA C/O PRESIDENT FORD FROM THE NATION'S OLDEST CITY. (LOCAL). MRS DOROTHY BEALE, TEACHER; FULLERWOOD ELEMENTARY SCHOOL; 10 HILDRETH DR; ST AUGUSTINE, FL 32084. (#24548).

CATALOGING OF CEMETERIES, ST AUGUSTINE, FL. THE BOARD FO REALTORS WILL UNDERTAKE THE CATALOGING OF CEMETERIES IN ST AUGUSTINE, NAMELY THE TOLOMATO AND HUGUENOT. (LOCAL). PIERRE D THOMPSON, CHAIRMAN; ST AUGUSTINE BOARD OF REALTORS; PO BOX 1067; ST AUGUSTINE, FL 32084. (#15007).

CHAMBER OF COMMERCE INTERIOR REFURBISHMENT - FL. STATE & NATIONAL INTERIOR DECORATOR EXPERTS TO WORK WITH PILOT CLUB & CHAMBER OFFICIALS FOR REFURBISHING & IMPROVEMENTS. (LOCAL). MISS ANNE L CARLING, CHAIRMAN; PILOT CLUB OF ST AUGUSTINE; PO BOX 1603; ST AUGUSTINE, FL 32084. (#15002).

COLONIAL CRAFTS & DRESS REVUE - ST AUGUSTINE, FL. THE COLONIAL CRAFT DIVISION WILL BE OPEN TO ALL COUNTY TEENAGERS. THE 4-H CLUBS WILL PARADE FOR DRESS REVUE. (LOCAL). MRS E L COOKSEY, PROJ DIRECTOR; 4H CLUBS/HAPPY HOMEMAKERS; PO BOX 1047; ST AUGUSTINE, FL 32084. (#18938).

CONFERENCE ON AMERICAN LOYALISTS. A TWO-DAY MEETING OF SEMINARS ON THE ROLE OF THE AMERICAN LOYALIST DURING THE REVOLUTION. (NAT'L). WERNER BRAATZ, CHAIRMAN; CONFERENCE GROUP FOR SOCIAL AND ADMINISTRATIVE HISTORY; PO BOX 1293; OSHKOSH, WI 54901. (#277).

'A CONSTITUTION FOR THE FUTURE', ST AUGUSTINE, FL. POLITICAL SCIENCE SEMINAR ON CONSTITUTIONAL THEORY. (LOCAL). THOMAS GRAHAM, CHAIRMAN; FLAGLER COLLEGE BICENTENNIAL COMMITTEE; KING ST; ST AUGUSTINE, FL 32084. (#15705).

ECHO HOUSE, ST AUGUSTINE, FL. A LIBRARY SECTION ON BLACK LITERATURE WILL BE DEVELOPED. (LOCAL). MALCOLM L STEPHENS, JR, CHAIRMAN; ST AUGUSTINE'S BICENTENNIAL COMMITTEE & ECHO HOUSE INC; PO BOX 1776; ST AUGUSTINE, FL 32084. (#15008).

EXHIBITION OF FAMILY HEIRLOOMS. EXHIBIT. (LOCAL). DARLENE JOHNS, SECRETARY; ST GEORGE PHARMACY; 121 ST GEORGE ST; ST AUGUSTINE, FL 32084. (#108203-1).

FILM 'LEGACY AMERICANA-LEGACY ST AUGUSTINE', FL. FILM RELEASED BY EASTMAN KODAK TO EDUCATIONAL TV NETWORKS AND INDIVIDUAL STATIONS AS PART OF ITS BICENTENNIAL SERIES. (LOCAL). TOM KING, MANAGER; CHAMBER OF COMMERCE; 10 CASTILLO DR; ST AUGUSTINE, FL 32084. (#22350).

FLAGLER HOSPITAL RENOVATIONS, ST AUGUSTINE, FL. A COVERED CANOPY FOR ENTRANCE TO HOSPITAL, ALSO RENOVATION OF EMERGENCY ROOM. (LOCAL). MRS BILLY B KELLY, SECRETARY; FLAGLER HOSPITAL AUXILIARY; 310 ARPIEKA AVE; ST AUGUSTINE, FL 32084. (#22355).

FOURTH GRADERS - PROJ OF ST AUGUSTINE, FL. FOUR BOYS OF R B HUNT SCHOOL IN REVOLUTIONARY MILITARY UNIFORMS WILL RAISE BRITISH UNION JACK FLAG EACH FRIDAY. (LOCAL). BILL MIGNON, PRINCIPAL; R B HUNT ELEMENTARY SCHOOL; 825 MAGNOLIA DR; ST AUGUSTINE, FL 32084. (#15003).

HISTORIC MARKER 'HOTEL PONCE DE LEON', FL. STATE HISTORIC MARKER PROGRAM. (LOCAL). THOMAS GRAHAM, CHAIRMAN; FLAGLER COLLEGE BICENTENNIAL COMMITTEE; KING ST; ST AUGUSTINE, FL 32084. (#15707).

HISTORIC WALKING & DRIVING GUIDE, ST AUGUSTN, FL. PUBLISH BOOKLET CONTAINING HISTORIC WALKING AND DRIVING TOURS OF ST AUGUSTINE AND NORTHEAST FLORIDA. NAME OF BOOKLET: 'TURN LEFT AT THE PLAZA'. (ST-WIDE). MRS FREDERICK H KENT, PROJ DIRECTOR; NATIONAL SOCIETY OF COLONIAL DAMES OF AMERICA IN FLORIDA; 2970 ST JOHNS AVE; JACKSONVILLE, FL 32205. (#18218).

JULINGTON CREEK ELEMENTARY SCHOOL ACTIVITIES - FL. SCHOOL PLANS TO RECORD STORIES OF RESIDENTS OF MANDARIN AREA, TO CONSTRUCT A BICENTENNIAL DOLL HOUSE AND PLANT AN AMERICAN HOLLY TREE. (LOCAL). SARA MCDANIEL,

ST AUGUSTINE — CONTINUED

PROJ DIRECTOR; JULINGTON CREEK ELEMENTARY SCHOOL; RT 6, BOX 450; ST AUGUSTINE, FL 32084. (#24232).

KINGS ROAD COMMEMORATIVE MARCH, ST AUGUSTINE, FL. BOY SCOUTS FROM 5 COUNTIES WILL HIKE THE ORIGINAL ROUTE; ONE GROUP WILL START FROM ST MARY'S RIVER & THE OTHER GROUP WILL START FROM NEW SMYRNE - THEY WILL MEET IN ST AUGUSTINE. (ST-WIDE). MALCOLM L STEPHENS, JR, CHAIRMAN; ST AUGUSTINE'S BICENTENNIAL COMMITTEE; PO BOX 1776; ST AUGUSTINE, FL 32084. (#15009).

MURAL IN LUNCH ROOMS, ST AUGUSTINE, FL. ART DEPT PLANS TO PAINT MURAL IN LUNCH ROOMS AT HIGH SCHOOL. (LOCAL). LATONA LESTER, INSTRUCTOR; ST AUGUSTINE HIGH SCHOOL ART DEPT; N VARELLA AVE; ST AUGUSTINE, FL 32084. (#22353).

NEWSPAPER TABLOID ACCOUNT OF CELEBRATION, FL. A NEWSPAPER ACCOUNT OF THE NATION'S 200TH ANNIVERSARY AND HOW ST AUGUSTINE CELEBRATED IT. THIS ACCOUNT WILL BE IN THE FORM OF A TABLOID NEWSPAPER CONTAINING PHOTOS & STORIES OF THE CELEBRATION. (LOCAL). ROBERT MARTIN, GENERAL MANAGER; ST AUGUSTINE RECORD; PO BOX 1630; ST AUGUSTINE, FL 32084. (#18220).

ORAL HISTORY PROGRAM AT FLAGLER COLLEGE - FL. THIS PROGRAM WILL BE CONDUCTED BY STUDENTS & FACULTY. (LOCAL). THOMAS GRAHAM, CHAIRMAN; FLAGLER COLLEGE BICENTENNIAL COMMITTEE; KING ST; ST AUGUSTINE, FL 32084. (#15708).

'PATRIOTISM & FAITH IN GOVERNMENT' PROJ OF FLORIDA. STUDY PRE-REVOLUTIONARY HISTORICAL BACKGROUND, DEVELOPMENT OF COMMUNITY MEETING HALL; EXAMINE HERITAGE BY RESTORATION-INTERPRETATION; RECOGNIZE RELATIONSHIP BETWEEN COUNTRIES OF ANCESTRY & UNITED STATES. (ST-WIDE). BRIG GEN RALPH W COOPER JR RET, EXEC DIRECTOR; ST AUGUSTINE'S COMMITTEE FOR THE NATIONAL BICENTENNIAL INC; 9 KING ST PO BOX 1776; ST AUGUSTINE, FL 32084. (#4217).

PRESENTATION ON AMERICANISM & PATRIOTISM, FL. ASHLAR LODGE ,98 WILL PRESENT ITS AMERICANISM PROGRAM. (LOCAL). HARRY WALDRON, WORSHIPFUL MASTER; ASHLAR LODGE #98; ST AUGUSTINE, FL 32084. (#15006).

PUBLIC LIBRARY COLONIAL ROOMS RESTORATION, FL. RESTORATION & DECORATION OF CLUB'S MEETING ROOMS WITH A COLONIAL THEME. (LOCAL). MALCOLM L STEPHENS, CHAIRMAN; ST AUGUSTINE'S BICENT COMMITTEE & MARIA JEFFERSON CHAPTER DAR; ST AUGUSTINE, FL 32084. (#15010).

RENOVATION OF LEAGUE MEETING ROOM, FL. JUNIOR SERVICE LEAGUE TO RENOVATE THEIR QUARTERS IN PUBLIC LIBRARY. (LOCAL). MRS MELVINE BUTLER, PRESIDENT; JUNIOR SERVICE LEAGUE; 1500 SHORE DR; ST AUGUSTINE, FL 32084. (#15004).

REVOLUTIONARY ERA DOCUMENTS EXHIBIT - FL. ORIGINAL DOCUMENTS IN ST AUGUSTINE. (LOCAL). THOMAS GRAHAM, CHAIRMAN; FLAGLER COLLEGE BICENTENNIAL COMMITTEE; KING ST; ST AUGUSTINE, FL 32084. (#15706).

SHOW WAGON, ST AUGUSTINE, FL. CONSTRUCTION OF A 'SHOW WAGON' FOR PRESENTATION OF PLAYLETS, SKITS, AND MUSICAL PRESENTATIONS, WITHIN THE RESTORED AREA AND DOWNTOWN PLAZA DURING THE BICENTENNIAL YEAR AND AFTERWARDS. (LOCAL). TOM RAHNER, PROJ COORDINATOR; ST AUGUSTINE LITTLE THEATRE; 67 LIGHTHOUSE AVE; ST AUGUSTINE, FL 32084. (#18219).

SOCIETY OF HISTORIC FLORIDA MILITIA, ST AUGUSTINE. RE-CREATING MILITARY UNITS WHICH SERVED IN ST AUGUSTINE. THERE WILL BE AUTHENTIC CAMPING, BATTLE RE-ENACTMENTS, PARADES, WEEKLY VOLUNTEER DRILLS AT FORT ST MARK IN ST AUGUSTINE. (LOCAL). ROBERT HALL, ADJUTANT; SOCIETY OF HISTORIC FLORIDA MILITIA; 42 SPANISH ST; ST AUGUSTINE, FL 32084. (#22349).

ST AUGUSTINE BICENTENNIAL CHOIR TRIP ABROAD, FL. MUSICAL AND EDUCATIONAL TOUR OF ENGLAND AND SCOTLAND. (INT'L). WAYNE JORANLIEN, CHOIR DIRECTOR; ST AUGUSTINE BICENTENNIAL CHOIR; ZAMORA ST; ST AUGUSTINE, FL 32084. (#22351).

TRAVELING EXHIBIT-TEACHING MATERIALS, FL. TRAVELING EXHIBIT OF TEACHING MATERIALS OF 200 YEARS AGO, INCLUDING SLATES, PENCILS, REPLICAS OF TEXTBOOKS, ANTIQUE BOOKS, PICTURES OF SCHOOLS AND REPRODUCTION OF HORN BOOK. (LOCAL). MRS DON ROBINSON, PROJ COORDINATOR; ST JOHNS COUNTY READING COUNCIL; 326 MINORCA AVE; ST AUGUSTINE, FL 32084. (#22354).

WEBSTER 6TH GRADE CENTER DISPLAYS. DISPLAY OF A COLONIAL VILLAGE AND NEW BOOKS; ALSO, USE OF SOUND FILM STRIPS AND TAPES AS WELL AS A BICENTENNIAL THEATRE. (LOCAL). ROGER COFFEE, PRINCIPAL; WEBSTER 6TH GRADE CENTER; PO BOX 528; ST AUGUSTINE, FL 32084. (#107838-1).

FEB 10, '74 - APR 8, '75. MINORCAN MIGRATION,TRANSPORTATION OF STATUE FROM SPAIN,DEDICATION. 'PATRIOTISM & FAITH IN GOVERNMENT' PROJ OF FLORIDA. STUDY PRE-REVOLUTIONARY HISTORICAL BACKGROUND, DEVELOPMENT OF COMMUNITY MEETING HALL; EXAMINE HERITAGE BY RESTORATION-INTERPRETATION; RECOGNIZE RELATIONSHIP BETWEEN COUNTRIES OF ANCESTRY & UNITED STATES. (ST-WIDE). BRIG GEN RALPH W COOPER J; ST AUGUSTINE'S COMMITTEE FOR THE NATIONAL BICENTENNIAL INC; 9 KING ST PO BOX 1776; ST AUGUSTINE, FL 32084. (#4217-501).

APR 1, '75 - JULY 4, '76. BICENTENNIAL CELEBRATION WITH MUSIC, COLORFUL PAGEANT, ETC. OPENING, FESTIVAL, TOUR, CEREMONY. (ST-WIDE). BRIG GEN RALPH W COOPER J; ST AUGUSTINE'S COMMITTEE FOR THE NATIONAL BICENTENNIAL INC; 9 KING ST PO BOX 1776; ST AUGUSTINE, FL 32084. (#4217-502).

APR 13, '75 - CONTINUING . 'ST AUGUSTINE '76' HOBI CAT JOURNEY. THE STATE OF FLORIDA, AROUND HONDURAS, THROUGH THE PANAMA CANAL, ALONG THE CALIFORNIA COAST TO HUNTINGTON BEACH, CALIFORNIA. (REGN'L). DAVID BECK, DIRECTOR; ST AUGUSTINE BICENTENNIAL COMMITTEE; PO BOX 1776; ST AUGUSTINE, FL 32084. (#102184-1).

JULY 3 - 4, '75. 'THE YOUNG AMERICAN DREAM'. FESTIVAL, LIVE PERFORMANCE AT ST AUGUSTINE BANDSHELL. (LOCAL). EVELYN SAPP, CHMN; ST AUGUSTINE BICENTENNIAL COMMITTEE; PO BOX 04; CHIPLEY, FL 32428. (#103713-2).

JULY 28, '75. BALLET FOLKLORICO AREYTO - FESTIVE PUERTO RICAN DANCES. LIVE PERFORMANCE AT FL SCHOOL FOR DEAF & BLIND AUDITORIUM. (LOCAL). RALPH W COOPER, EXEC DIR; ST AUGUSTINE BICENTENNIAL COMMITTEE; PO BOX 1776; ST AUGUSTINE, FL 32084. (#200011-197).

AUG 26, '75. ILLUMINATION AND FLYING OF FLAG. CEREMONY, EXHIBIT AT MARINE ST. (LOCAL). DELL R STEWART, COORD; ST AUGUSTINE NATIONAL CEMETERY; 104 MARINE ST; ST AUGUSTINE, FL 32084. (#200011-198).

OCT 18, '75. PERIOD DRESS COSTUME BALL. FESTIVAL AT ST AUGUSTINE SHORES RECREATION CENTER. (LOCAL). MRS ROBERT MATHIS, COORD; JUNIOR SERVICE LEAGUE; 100 SANTA MONICA AVE; ST AUGUSTINE, FL 32084. (#200011-199).

OCT '75. FALL CARNIVAL. THIS CARNIVAL, BICENTENNIAL THEMED, WILL BE PLANNED WHEN STUDENTS RETURN TO SCHOOL IN THE FALL. AT ON CAMPUS. (LOCAL). THOMAS GRAHAM, CHMN; FLAGLER COLLEGE BICENTENNIAL COMMITTEE; KING ST; ST AUGUSTINE, FL 32084. (#102512-1).

OCT '75. PARENTS' WEEKEND. THE ANNUAL PARENT'S WEEKEND WILL INCLUDE A RECEPTION, A TOUR OF THE CAMPUS, AND PATRIOTIC SKITS WITH A BICENTENNIAL THEME. AT ON CAMPUS. (LOCAL). THOMAS GRAHAM, CHMN; FLAGLER COLLEGE BICENTENNIAL COMMITTEE; KING ST; ST AUGUSTINE, FL 32084. (#102512-2).

NOV 24, '75. COOKING CONTEST FOR '76. BAKING CONTEST WITH 4 CATEGORIES: BEST ORIGINAL POTATO, CABBAGE, SEAFOOD AND BEST BICENTENNIAL (A RECIPE HANDED DOWN IN THE FAMILY). (LOCAL). ANNE L CARLING, EDITOR; ST AUGUSTINE RECORD AND HOME ECONOMICS CLUB; PO BOX 1630; ST AUGUSTINE, FL 32084. (#200011-200).

JAN 1 - DEC 31, '76. 18TH CENTURY BRITISH SOLDIERS AT CASTILLO DE SAN MARCOS IN FLA. ADMISSION FEE TO THE PARK. COSTUMED HISTORIANS WILL TELL/SHOW THE STORY OF THE CASTILLO DURING ENGLAND'S OWNERSHIP OF FLORIDA (17631784) AND OF THE LOYALIST FOLLOWING OF ITS INHABITANTS. (REGN'L). CASTILLO DE SAN MARCOS NM; NATIONAL PARK SERVICE; NO 1 CASTILLO DRIVE; ST AUGUSTINE, FL 32084. (#6727-8).

FEB 6, '76 - CONTINUING . FORMAL DEDICATION OF GREEK ORTHODOX SHRINE. NATL SHRINE OF ST PHOTIOS HONORING FIRST GROUP OF GREEK IMMIGRANTS TO ARRIVE IN THE NEW WORLD IN 1768. RESTORATION OF ORIGINAL BUILDING OF 1740 & CONSTRUCTION OF A GREEK ORTHODOX CHAPEL. (REGN'L). ERNEST A VILLAS; GREEK ORTHODOX ARCHDIOCESE OF NORTH AND SOUTH AMERICA; 8 E 79TH ST; NEW YORK, NY 10021. (#6900-501).

FEB 19 - 20, '76. UNITED STATES ARMED FORCES BICENTENNIAL CARAVAN. CARAVAN IS COMPOSED OF EXHIBIT VANS FOR EACH MILITARY SERVICE. PROJECT THEME IS 'HISTORY OF THE ARMED FORCES AND THEIR CONTRIBUTIONS TO THE NATION'. AT COMMUNITY CENTER AT CHAMB OF COMMERCE, ST AUGUSTINE, FL. (LOCAL). GENERAL RALPH COOPER; US ARMED FORCES BICENTENNIAL EXHIBIT VANS PROJECT; PO BOX 1776; ST AUGUSTINE, FL 32084. (#1775-434).

MAR 11, '76. 'BICENTENNIAL SAIL' OF HISTORIC SHIP VISITS CASTILLO DE SAN MARCOS. HISTORIC FISHING SCHOONER 'MARY E', SAILING THE ATLANTIC COAST, WILL STOP AT THIS NATIONAL PARK SERVICE AREA, PROVIDING SHIPBOARD PROGRAMS TO VISITORS TO THIS AREA. (REGN'L). CASTILLO DE SAN MARCOS NM; SEA VENTURES, INC. & NATIONAL PARK SERVICE; 1 CASTILLO DRIVE; ST AUGUSTINE, FL 32084. (#7960-2).

MAR 13, '76. BAND CONCERT. CEREMONY, LIVE PERFORMANCE AT BAY FRONT BAND SHELL. (LOCAL). RALPH COOPER, COORD; FERNANDINA BEACH JUNIOR HIGH SCHOOL & BICENTENNIAL COMMITTEE; ST AUGUSTINE, FL 32084. (#200011-201).

MAR 27, '76. STUDENT ART SHOW. EXHIBIT AT ST AUGUSTINE PLAZA. (LOCAL). MS ROBERTA MCALOON, COORD; ST JOHNS COUNTY ART EDUCATION ASSOC; 59 N ST AUGUSTINE BLVD; ST AUGUSTINE, FL 32084. (#200011-202).

APR 9 - 11, '76. ARTS & CRAFT FESTIVAL. COMPETITION, EXHIBIT. (LOCAL). RALPH COOPER, COORD; ST AUGUSTINE BICENTENNIAL COMMITTEE, ARTS & CRAFTS COUNCIL; PO BOX 1776; ST AUGUSTINE, FL 32084. (#106041-2).

APR 9 - 18, '76. ST AUGUSTINE EASTER WEEK FESTIVAL. EVENTS DURING THE WEEK ARE BLESSING OF THE FLEET (SHRIMP BOATS) AND PARADE OF CARRIAGES, WITH HORSE-DRAWN CARRIAGES, BANDS & FLOATS; THE PARADE WILL CONTAIN APPROX 150 UNITS. (LOCAL). CHARLES COLEE, DIRECTOR; ST AUGUSTINE AND ST JOHN COUNTY CHAMBER OF COMMERCE; 44 BAY VIEW DR; ST AUGUSTINE, FL 32084. (#103416-260).

APR 11, '76. BAND CONCERT. PARADE AT CASTILLO DE SAN MARCOS NATIONAL MONUMENT. (LOCAL). RALPH COOPER, COORD; ST AUGUSTINE BICENTENNIAL COMMITTEE & EASTER WEEK FESTIVAL; PO BOX 1776; ST AUGUSTINE, FL 32084. (#106041-4).

APR 24 - 25, '76. FLOWER SHOW. EXHIBIT AT MARK LANCE ARMORY. (LOCAL). RALPH COOPER, COORD; ST AUGUSTINE BICENT COMMITTEE, PRESIDENT'S COUNCIL OF GARDEN CLUBS; PO BOX 1776; ST AUGUSTINE, FL 32084. (#106041-6).

MAY 1, '76. MAY DAY FESTIVAL. CROOKSHANK ELEMENTARY SCHOOL PLANS MAY DAY FESTIVAL WITH MORNING FLAG CEREMONIES AND BEAUTIFICATION OF SCHOOL GROUNDS. (LOCAL). GLEN SMITH, PRINCIPAL; CROOKSHANK ELEMENTARY SCHOOL; N WHITNEY ST; ST AUGUSTINE, FL 32084. (#106041-7).

MAY 7 - 9, '76. SCOUT SHOW. CEREMONY AT FRANCIS FIELD. (LOCAL). RALPH COOPER, COORD; ST AUGUSTINE BICENTENNIAL COMMITTEE & BOY SCOUTS OF AMERICA; PO BOX 1776; ST AUGUSTINE, FL 32084. (#106041-3).

MAY 28 - 29, '76. TELEPHONE PIONEERS OF AMERICA. AN ANNUAL ASSEMBLY TO ESTABLISH IMAGE OF PRIDE IN COUNTY AND FURTHER HISTORICAL BACKGROUND. AT SOUTHERN BELL BLDG. (LOCAL). WENDELL E CLARDY, MGR; TELEPHONE PIONEERS OF AMERICA, NORTH FLA CHAPTER #39; 58 CHARLOTTE ST; ST AUGUSTINE, FL 32084. (#102185-1).

JUNE 25 - SEPT 5, '76. 'CROSS & SWORD'. THE 2-HOUR STAGE PRESENTATION DEALING WITH THE FIRST PERMANENT COLONY. THE OFFICIAL STATE PLAY OF FLORIDA. AT ST AUGUSTINE AMPHITHEATRE, SOUTH OF CITY LIMITS ON RT A1A.. (REGN'L). JERRY ALLEN, GEN MANAGER; CROSS & SWORD, INC; PO BOX 1965; ST AUGUSTINE, FL 32084. (#103416-11).

JUNE 27, '76. 'VOICES OF LIBERTY' PROGRAM. PRODUCED BY ASHLAR LODGE 98, F & AM, AN EMOTIONAL PATRIOTIC PROGRAM ON THE COUNTRY'S FOUNDING. LIGHTING & SOUND WILL INCLUDE PYROTECHNICS. AT ST AUGUSTINE AMPHITHEATRE. (ST-WIDE). RALPH COOPER, EXEC DIR; ST AUGUSTINE COMMITTEE FOR THE NATIONAL BICENTENNIAL, INC; P O BOX 1776; ST AUGUSTINE, FL 32084. (#106041-10).

JULY 2, '76. NATL PK SVC '...A LITTLE LOOK AROUND' VISITS CASTILLO DE SAN MARCOS. THIS SHORT PROGRAM FEATURES ACTORS PORTRAYING FAMOUS AMERICANS OF THE PAST WHO'VE RETURNED TO SEE AMERICA'S PROGRESS. (REGN'L). CASTILLO DE SAN MARCOS NM; NATIONAL PARK SERVICE; 1 CASTILLO DRIVE; ST AUGUSTINE, FL 32084. (#5653-88).

JULY 3, '76. BICENTENNIAL PARADE. PARADE AT ON CAMPUS. (LOCAL). THOMAS GRAHAM, CHMN; FLAGLER COLLEGE BICENTENNIAL COMMITTEE; KING ST; ST AUGUSTINE, FL 32084. (#102514-1).

JULY 4, '76. JULY 4TH FIREWORKS CELEBRATION. FESTIVAL AT CASTILLO DE SAN MARCOS FORT. (LOCAL). RALPH COOPER, COORD; ST AUGUSTINE BICENTENNIAL COMMITTEE & JAYCEES; PO BOX 1776; ST AUGUSTINE, FL 32084. (#106041-5).

JULY 4, '76. MINISTERIAL ALLIANCE. CEREMONY AT CROSS AND SWORD AMPHITHEATRE. (LOCAL). RALPH COOPER, COORD; ST AUGUSTINE BICENT COMMITTEE & ST AUGUSTINE MINISTERIAL ALLIANCE; PO BOX 1776; ST AUGUSTINE, FL 32084. (#106041-9).

JULY 4, '76. NATIONWIDE BELL RINGING PARTICIPATION. PARTICIPATION IN THE BELL RINGING, WHISTLE & HORN BLOWING COMMEMORATING THE SIGNING OF THE DECLARATION OF INDEPENDENCE. (REGN'L). RALPH COOPER, EXEC DIR; ST AUGUSTINE COMMITTEE FOR THE NATIONAL BICENTENNIAL, INC; P O BOX 1776; ST AUGUSTINE, FL 32084. (#106041-11).

AUG 18 - 21, '76. 'DAYS IN SPAIN' FIESTA. DARING SWORDFIGHTS, TWIRLING DANCERS PERFORMING TO RHYTHMIC CLICK OF CASTANETS AND FIERY SPANISH MUSIC, EXCITING STAGE SHOWS, SERENADES FROM BALCONIES GRACING PICTURESQUE GOVERNMENT HOUSE AND COLORFULLY COSTUMED STROLLING MUSICIANS. AT PLAZA ON KING ST. (ST-WIDE). GEN R W COOPER, JR; ST AUGUSTINE JAYCEES; BICENTENNIAL COMMITTEE BOX 1776; ST AUGUSTINE, FL 32084. (#103393-5).

SEPT 8, '76. ST AUGUSTINE OFFICIAL BIRTHDATE CELEBRATION. NARRATED REENACTMENT CEREMONY; LIVE PERFORMANCE; PERIOD DRESSED SPANISH SOLDIERS AND SETTLERS FOUNDING SETTLEMENT IN 1565. AT ST AUGUSTINE, MISSION OF NOMBRE DE DIOS. (LOCAL). MAYOR'S OFFICE; CITY OF ST AUGUSTINE, CATHOLIC CHURCH & SEVERAL AGENCIES & ORGS.; ST AUGUSTINE, FL 32084. (#103416-537).

OCT 16, '76. CHORAL CONCERT - INSPIRATIONAL & PATRIOTIC MUSIC. LIVE PERFORMANCE AT CONVENT GROUNDS. (LOCAL). SISTER MARIE THERESE, SSJ; SISTERS OF ST JOSEPH; 241 ST GEORGE ST; ST AUGUSTINE, FL 32084. (#106041-8).

ST CLOUD

MAR 13, '76. 'IN GOD WE TRUST', MUSICAL FESTIVAL. THE JOYFUL SOUNDS CHOIR WILL PERFORM. AT VETERAN'S PARK, RT 192. (LOCAL). MRS BERTHA CHASE, COORD; FIRST CHRISTIAN CHURCH OF SAINT CLOUD; FIRST CHRISTIAN CHURCH; SAINT CLOUD, FL 32769. (#200011-193).

ST MARKS

DEC 6 - 7, '75. FIESTA DE SAN MARCOS DE APALACHE. THIS HOLIDAY CELEBRATES THE LANDING OF NARVAEZ & THE FIRST CHRISTMAS IN THE NEW WORLD. THE FORT DE APALACHE HAS BEEN RECONSTRUCTED AND A MUSEUM HAS BEEN ADDED TO THE SPOT. THIS FORT IS ON THE BICENTENNIAL TRAIL. AT WEST SIDE OF TOWN. (LOCAL). HENRY WILLIAMS, CHAIRMAN; FIESTA DE SAN MARCOS DE APALACHE, INC; PO BOX 296; ST MARKS, FL 32355. (#102208-1).

ST PETERSBURG

BICENTENNIAL BUGGY TOUR IN ST PETERSBURG, FL. A GUIDED, 1 1/2 HOUR RIDING TOUR WILL FEATURE ST PETE'S WATERFRONT AND DOWNTOWN HISTORICAL SITES. (LOCAL). CHARLOTTE HUBBARD, PROJ DIRECTOR; PIKELLAS COUNTY BICENTENNIAL COMMITTEE; 115 HAVEN ST; ST PETERSBURG, FL 33516. (#15026).

BICENTENNIAL PARK IN ST PETERSBURG, FL. THE SOUTH MOLE WATERFRONT PROPERTY WILL BE DEVELOPED AS A BICENTENNIAL PARK & AN OUTDOOR SCULPTURE OR SUNDIAL CREATED BY A LOCAL ARTIST WILL BE PLACED IN THE PARK AS A MONUMENT TO THE BICENTENNIAL. (LOCAL). PAT MASON, COORDINATOR; ST PETERSBURG BICENTENNIAL COMMITTEE; 300 2ND AVE NE; ST PETERSBURG, FL 33701. (#11832).

BOYD HILL NATURE TRAIL ANIMAL EXHIBIT IN FLORIDA. HIRING OF A ZOO CONSULTANT TO ADVISE ON REDEVELOPMENT OF ANIMAL EXHIBIT. (ST-WIDE). PAT MASON, PROJ COORDINATOR; ST PETERSBURG BICENT COMMITTEE; 175 5TH ST N; ST PETERSBURG, FL 33731. (#9397).

A HISTORY OF ST PETERSBURG, FL. A COMPREHENSIVE HISTORY OF THE CITY WILL BE PUBLISHED IN PAPERBACK FORM AND WILL BE AVAILABLE IN JULY 1976; IT WILL CONTAIN ILLUSTRATIONS OF PAST AND PRESENT BUILDINGS. (LOCAL). PAT MASON, COORDINATOR; ST PETERSBURG BICENTENNIAL COMMITTEE; 300 2ND AVE NE; ST PETERSBURG, FL 33701. (#11835).

MUSEUM SECURITY SURVEY IN ST PETERSBURG, FLORIDA. SECURITY SURVEY TO BE TAKEN ON THE CARE & PRESERVATION OF THE MUSEUM'S COLLECTION. (LOCAL). ALAN DUBOIS, ASST DIR; MUSEUM OF FINE ARTS; ST PETERSBURG, FL 33701. (#10524).

NATURE PARK ZOO BEAUTIFICATION, ST PETERSBURG, FL. BOYD HILL NATURE PARK, ONE OF THE GREATEST RECREATIONAL RESOURCES IN THE AREA, WILL BE PRESERVED IN ITS NATURAL STATE. (LOCAL). PAT MASON, COORDINATOR; ST PETERSBURG BICENTENNIAL COMMITTEE; 300 2ND AVE NE; ST PETERSBURG, FL 33701. (#11831).

SUNDIAL IN THE PARK - ST PETERSBURG, FLORIDA. IN HONOUR OF THE BICENTENNIAL A LARGE PUBLIC ART WORK WILL BE PLACED IN THE BICENTENNIAL PARK. (LOCAL). MRS PAT MASON, BICENT COORDINATOR; ST PETERSBURG BICENT COMMITTEE; 175 5TH ST N; ST PETERSBURG, FL 33731. (#9394).

WILLIAMS PARK BANDSHELL EXPANSION, FL. THE ORIGINAL ARCHITECT FOR THE WILLIAMS PARK BANDSHELL WILL DRAW PLANS FOR ENLARGING THE STAGE. (LOCAL). PAT MASON, COORDINATOR; ST PETERSBURG BICENTENNIAL COMMITTEE; 300 2ND AVE NE; ST PETERSBURG, FL 33701. (#11833).

SEPT 25, '75 - JUNE 30, '76. BICENTENNIAL BUGGY TOURS. A GUIDED HOUR & A HALF TOUR OF ST PETERSBURG'S WATERFRONT & DOWNTOWN HISTORICAL SITES WITH VOLUNTEER GUIDES FROM THE JR WOMENS CLUB. THE TOUR WILL EMPHASIZE BOTH THE CITY'S NATURAL BEAUTY AND HISTORY. AT STARTS AT BOUNTY PARKING LOT -345-2ND AVE N E. (LOCAL). PAT MASON, BICENT COORD; ST PETERSBURG BICENTENNIAL COMMITTEE; 300-2ND AVE N E; ST PETERSBURG, FL 33701. (#103396-1).

SEPT 27 - OCT 10, '75. ST PETERSBURG HISTORICAL PAGEANT. AN OUTDOOR PAGEANT OF THE PINNELLAS PENINSULA AND ST PETERSBURG HISTORY. AT BOUNTY PARKING LOT, 345 2ND AVE NE. (LOCAL). PAT MASON, COORDINATOR; ST PETERSBURG BICENTENNIAL COMMITTEE; 300 2ND AVE N E; ST PETERSBURG, FL 33701. (#100484-1).

OCT 13, '75 - JUNE 13, '76. THE ST PETE STORY. TRAVELLING HISTORICAL PROGRAM FOR ST PETE ELEMENTARY SCHOOLS. WILL INCLUDE PUPPET & PICTURE SHOWS, MODELS, AND ARTIFACTS, ON VIDEOTAPE. (LOCAL). PAT MASON; PINELLAS COUNTY BICENTENNIAL COMMITTEE; PO BOX 2842; ST PETERSBURG, FL 33751. (#102193-1).

JAN 1 - DEC 31, '76. TYRONE BICENTENNIAL MUSEUM. SEVERAL AREA ARCHAEOLGICAL, HISTORICAL AND ENVIRONMENTAL GROUPS WILL MOUNT A CHANGING DISPLAY THROUGHOUT THE YEAR. SUNDAY HOURS WILL BE 12:00PM - 6:00PM. (LOCAL). MILDRED SCHUTT, CHMN; PINELLAS COUNTY BICENTENNIAL COMMITTEE; 115 HAVEN ST; ST PETERSBURG, FL 33516. (#102194-1).

JAN 2 - 3, '76. BICENTENNIAL TOWN MEETING. MEETINGS WILL SERVE AS A SHOWCASE OF CITY SERVICES, PLANS, PAST PROJECTS AND FUTURE NEEDS. AT BAYFRONT CENTER, 400 1ST ST S. (LOCAL). PAT MASON, COORDINATOR; ST PETERSBURG BICENTENNIAL COMMITTEE; 300 2ND AVE N E; ST PETERSBURG, FL 33701. (#100484-3).

JAN 17 - 18, '76. UNITED STATES ARMED FORCES BICENTENNIAL CARAVAN. CARAVAN IS COMPOSED OF EXHIBIT VANS FOR EACH MILITARY SERVICE. PROJECT THEME IS 'HISTORY OF THE ARMED FORCES AND THEIR CONTRIBUTIONS TO THE NATION'. (LOCAL). MRS PAT MASON; US ARMED FORCES BICENTENNIAL EXHIBIT VANS PROJECT; PO BOX 2842; ST PETERSBURG, FL 33731. (#1775-422).

FEB 20 - 22, '76. THE ST PETERSBURG FOLK FAIR. ETHNIC GROUPS WILL PRODUCE FOLK FAIR HIGHLIGHTING CONTRIBUTIONS THEY HAVE MADE TO COUNTRY'S CULTURE & TRADITIONS. WILL CONTAIN DISPLAYS OF ETHNIC GROUPS, DANCE AND MUSICAL PERFORMANCE, FOOD, ETC. AT BAYFRONT CENTER, 400 FIRST ST S. (LOCAL). PAT MASON, COORDINATOR; ST PETERSBURG BICENTENNIAL COMMITTEE; 300 2ND AVE N E; ST PETERSBURG, FL 33701. (#100484-4).

MAR 1 - 31, '76. HISTORICAL PAGEANT ON LOCAL HISTORY. A PAGEANT ON LOCAL HISTORY FROM THE DISCOVERY BY THE SPANISH UP TO RECENT TIMES. (LOCAL). PAT MASON, COORDINATOR; ST PETERSBURG BICENT COMMITTEE; 175 5 ST N; ST PETERSBURG, FL 33731. (#9391-1).

MAR 24 - APR 5, '76. FESTIVAL OF THE STATES. SOUTH'S LARGEST CIVIC CELEBRATION INCLUDES BAND CONCERTS, EXHIBITS, PARADES, ETC. (REGN'L). ELAINE CAMPBELL, COORD; THE SUNCOASTERS AND ST PETERSBURG FESTIVAL OF STATES; PO BOX 1731; ST PETERSBURG, FL 33731. (#103416-106).

MAR 27 - 28, '76. THE BICENTENNIAL LIVING HISTORY AND CULTURAL ARTS FAIR. A CRAFTS EXHIBIT FEATURING CRAFTS IN EXISTENCE AT THE FOUNDING OF OUR NATION; ARTISTS WILL DEMONSTRATE ARTS OF CANDLE-MAKING, POTTERY, WEAVING, SILVERSMITHING AND QUILTING. AT STRAUB WATERFRONT PARK. (LOCAL). PAT MASON, COORDINATOR; ST PETERSBURG BICENTENNIAL COMMITTEE; 300 2ND AVE N E; ST PETERSBURG, FL 33701. (#100484-7).

MAR 29, '76. NATIONAL FLAG PAGEANT. THIS PAGEANT WILL ALSO TOUR THE UNITED STATES IN SPRING, 1976. AT WILLIAMS PARK BANDSHELL, 2ND AVE, NORTH BETWEEN 3RD & 4TH ST. (LOCAL). PAT MASON, COORDINATOR; ST PETERSBURG BICENTENNIAL COMMITTEE; 300 2ND AVE N E; ST PETERSBURG, FL 33701. (#100484-5).

APR 2, '76. NAVAL ORIENTATION TOUR. THE USS DORMINANT HELD NAVAL ORIENTATION TOUR FOR 90 JNROTC MIDSHIPMEN; EMPHASIS PLACED ON MINE WARFARE TECHNIQUES BOTH PAST & PRESENT. (LOCAL). LLDR M SMEDLEY, CHAIRMAN; USS DOMINANT (MSO 431); BAYBORO HBR, FL 33517. (#200011-252).

APR 22, '76. YOUTH FLAIR BICENTENNIAL MUSEUM. WILL FEATURE YOUTH CREATIVITY THROUGH EXHIBITS, PERFORMANCES, AND DISPLAYS, ALL WITH A BICENTENNIAL THEME. AT BAYFRONT CENTER, 400 1ST ST S. (LOCAL). PAT MASON, COORDINATOR; ST PETERSBURG BICENTENNIAL COMMITTEE; 300 2ND AVE N E; ST PETERSBURG, FL 33701. (#100484-6).

MAY 20, '76. NAVAL ORIENTATION TOUR. A NAVAL ORIENTATION TOUR FOUR ELEMENTARY SCHOOL CHILDREN. (LOCAL). LCDR LO SMEDLEY, CHAIRMAN; USS DOMINANT (MSO 431); BAYBORO HBR, FL 33517. (#200011-251).

MAY 28, '76. FLAG RAISING. HONOR GUARD RAISED FLAG AT ELEMENTARY SCHOOL. (LOCAL). LCDR M SMEDLEY, CHAIRMAN; USS DOMINANT (MSO 431); BAYBORO HBR, FL 33517. (#200011-253).

MAY 28, '76. NAVAL ORIENTATION TOUR. USS DOMINANT HELD NAVAL ORIENTATION TOUR FOR ELEMENTARY SCHOOL CHILDREN. (LOCAL). LCDR M SMEDLEY, CHAIRMAN; USS DOMINANT (MSO 431); BAYBORO HBR, FL 33517. (#200011-254).

JULY 4, '76. BICENTENNIAL FESTIVAL. ENTERTAINMENT: COLONIAL GAMES, OBSERVE NATIONAL BELL RINGING, 21-GUN SALUTE BY COAST GUARD, 13-GUN SALUTE BY COUNTY, MUSICAL CONCERT WITH 3 BANDS AT 6:30 PM, JAYCEES RE-ENACT BOSTON TEA PARTY, WATER SKI SHOW AND FIREWORKS. AT STROBE PARK. (LOCAL). PAT MASON, PROJ DIR; ST PETERSBURG BICENTENNIAL COMMITTEE AND PARKS & RECREATION DEPT; PO BOX 2842; ST PETERSBURG, FL 33731. (#108337-1).

JULY 4, '76. COMMUNITY BIBLE CHURCH OF SEMINOLE, JULY 4TH CELEBRATION. CEREMONY AT ST PETERSBURG BAYFRONT CENTER. (LOCAL). REV MELS CARBONELL; COMMUNITY BIBLE CHURCH OF SEMINOLE; 6262 62ND AVE N; ST PETERSBURG, FL 33565. (#102169-1).

JULY 4 - 5, '76. A BIRTHDAY CELEBRATION AND TRACK MEET. EXHIBIT, FESTIVAL, PARADE, LIVE PERFORMANCE AT STRAUB PARK & SORENO PARK. (LOCAL). PATRICIA MASON, COORD; ST PETERSBURG BICENTENNIAL COMMITTEE & CITY PARKS & RECREATION DEPT; 300 2ND AVE NE; ST PETERSBURG, FL 33701. (#105358-1).

AUG 22, '76. NAVAL ORIENTATION CRUISE. ON 22 AUG, 1976, NAVAL ORIENTATION CRUISE ABOARD AN OCEAN GOIN MINESWEEP FOR CIVIC LEADERS & MEMBERS OF THE COMMUNITY. IT LASTED 6 HOURS, GAVE AN INSIGHT INTO PAST & PRESENT NAVAL AFFAIRS. (LOCAL). LCDR W SMEDLEY, CHAIRMAN; USS DOMINANT (MSO 431); BAYBORO HBR, FL 33517. (#200011-249).

SEPT 28, '76. NAVAL ORIENTATION TOUR. NAVAL ORIENTATION TOURS WER HELD FOR ELEMENTARY SCHOOL CHILDREN. (LOCAL). LCDR W SMEDLEY, CHAIRMAN; USS DOMINANT (MSO 431); BAYBORO HBR, FL 33517. (#200011-250).

OCT 23, '76. LIVING HISTORY & CULTURAL ARTS FAIR. PERFORMANCES OF CRAFTSMEN AND ARTISTS INCLUDING POTTERS, WEAVERS, SILVERSMITHS AND PRINTERS. AT EAST BAYFRONT CENTER PARKING LOT. (LOCAL). MRS PAT MASON; ST PETERSBURG BICENT COMMITTEE; 175 5TH ST N; ST PETERSBURG, FL 33731. (#9389-1).

DEC 9 - 12, '76. AMERICAN FREEDOM TRAIN DISPLAY DAYS AT ST PETERSBURG. THE AMERICAN FREEDOM TRAIN INCLUDES 10 EXHIBIT CARS & 2 SHOW CASE CARS DEPICTING DIFFERENT PHASES OF THE AMERICAN EXPERIENCE. ITS ARRIVAL WILL SERVE AS A CATALYST FOR LOCAL BICENTENNIAL CELEBRATIONS BY PEOPLE THROUGHOUT THIS NATION. (ST-WIDE). SY FREEDMAN, DIR OF P R; THE AMERICAN FREEDOM TRAIN FOUNDATION; 5205 LEESBURG PIKE, SUITE 800; BAILEY'S XRDS, VA 22041. (#1776-114).

OCT 1 - 30, '77. 'EDVARD MUNCH, THE MAJOR GRAPHICS' EXHIBIT. AN EXHIBITION FROM THE MUNCH MUSEUM IN OSLO BY ONE OF THE GREATEST FIGURES IN MODERN PRINTMAKING. (INT'L). EILEEN HARAKAL, COORD; SMITHSONIAN INSTITUTION TRAVELING EXHIBITION SERVICE; 1000 JEFFERSON DR, SW; WASHINGTON, DC 20560. (#26704-10).

STARKE

OLD BRADFORD COURTHOUSE RESTORATION - STARKE, FL. THE OLD COURTHOUSE WILL BE TURNED INTO A COUNTY MUSEUM. (LOCAL). ELZIE S SANDERS, CHAIRMAN; BRADFORD COUNTY ACTION '76 COMMITTEE; PO BOX 68; STARKE, FL 32091. (#25597).

JULY 3 - 4, '76. 4TH OF JULY FAIR & TIME CAPSULE BURIAL. FAIR ON JULY 3, AND BURIAL OF TIME CAPSULE ON JULY 4. AT COUNTY FAIRGROUNDS. (LOCAL). ELZIE S SANDERS, CHAIRMAN; BRADFORD BICENT '76' ACTION COMMITTEE; PO BOX 68; STARKE, FL 32091. (#108414-1).

STUART

DOWNTOWN BEAUTIFICATION, STUART, FL. LANDSCAPING, PLANTING TREES AND SHRUBS AND BEAUTIFYING THE OLDER DOWNTOWN SECTION OF STUART THROUGH CREATION OF PARKS AND NATURAL PLANTINGS. (LOCAL). DR DAVID M MACMILLAN, PROJ DIRECTOR; EXCHANGE CLUB OF STUART; 416 BALBOA; STUART, FL 33494. (#18943).

RESTORATION OF HOUSE OF REFUGE, STUART, FL. COMPLETE RESTORATION OF GILBERT'S BAR HOUSE OF REFUGE, MARTIN COUNTY'S OLDEST AND MOST HISTORIC BUILDING AUTHORIZED BY U S CONGRESS IN 1875. (ST-WIDE). MRS JANET HUTCHINSON, DIRECTOR; MARTIN COUNTY HISTORICAL SOCIETY; 888 N E MACARUHUR BLVD; STUART, FL 33494. (#18942).

SEPT 25, '75 - APR 25, '76. BICENTENNIAL ART CONTEST AND EXHIBIT. THE THEME OF THE COMPETITION IS 'WHAT MY COUNTRY MEANS TO ME'; AWARDS IN 3 GRADE CATEGORIES; 1ST PRIZE $25 SAVINGS BOND, 2ND PRIZE $10 BICENTENNIAL SILVER DOLLARS, 3RD PRIZE $5 BICENTENNIAL DOLLARS, $2 BICENTENNIAL DOLLARS. AT ELLIOTT MUSEUM, 888 NE MACARTHUR BLVD. (LOCAL). VICTORIA S JOHNSON, PRES; ART ASSOCIATES OF MARTIN COUNTY; PO BOX 65; JENSEN BEACH, FL 33457. (#104901-1).

FEB 11, '76. 'HAPPY BIRTHDAY USA' - PAGEANT. A PAGEANT DESIGNED TO DEPICT THE HISTORICAL DEVELOPMENT OF AMERICAN HISTORY FROM THE PRE-REVOLUTIONARY PERIOD TO THE PRESENT DAY. AT LONG FIELD, STUART MIDDLE SCHOOL, E OCEAN BOULEVARD. (LOCAL). WILLIE J THOMPSON; MARTIN COUNTY BOARD OF PUBLIC INSTRUCTION; PO BOX 278; PALM CITY, FL 33490. (#104085-1).

MAR 8 - 13, '76. 17 IN '76, THE 17TH ANNUAL MARTIN COUNTY FAIR. FAIR AT SOUTH DIXIE HIGHWAY. (LOCAL). JOHN WILSE, PRESIDENT; MARTIN COUNTY FAIR ASSOCIATION, INC; PO BOX 1196; STUART, FL 33494. (#104607-1).

MAY 30, '76. BICENTENNIAL PARADE. PARADE AT STUART CENTRAL BUSINESS DISTRICT. (LOCAL). HOWARD B HARSHBARGER; STUART BICENTENNIAL COMMITTEE; 2600 SE OCEAN BLVD; STUART, FL 33494. (#104901-2).

SUN CITY CNTR

NEW BOOKS FOR LIBRARY, SUN CITY CENTER, IN. BOOKS IN LARGE PRINT WILL BE ADDED TO THE LIBRARY'S COLLECTION. (LOCAL). OLAF M LOYTTY, CHAIRMAN; SUN CITY BICENTENNIAL COMMITTEE & SUN CITY CIVIC ASSOC; 1510 HERON DR; SUN CITY CNTR, FL 33570. (#28632).

SUNRISE

AMERICAN HERITAGE COOKBOOK - SUNRISE, FL. RECIPES WILL BE GATHERED FROM LOCAL RESIDENTS & A COOKBOOK WILL BE WRITTEN. (LOCAL). CAROL DEFILIPPO; BICENTENNIAL COMMITTEE OF SUNRISE; 5990 NW 18TH COURT; SUNRISE, FL 33313. (#24021).

BICENTENNIAL WINDOW OF THE MONTH IN SUNRISE, FL. EACH MONTH A SPECIAL BUSINESS IN SUNRISE WILL BE CHOSEN TO DISPLAY ANTIQUES & BICENTENNIAL MEMORABILIA. (LOCAL). ELSIE J STASKA, CHAIRMAN; SUNRISE BICENTENNIAL COMMITTEE; 1277 SUNSET STRIP; SUNRISE, FL 33313. (#15671).

FLAGS OF THE 13 STATES - SUNRISE, FL. 13 FLAGS WILL BE ON DISPLAY AT THE CITY LIBRARY. (LOCAL). BARBARA OUTTRIM, CHAIRMAN; BICENTENNIAL COMMITTEE OF SUNRISE; 1720 NW 60TH AVE; SUNRISE, FL 33313. (#24015).

FLAME OF FREEDOM - SUNRISE, FL. FLAME OF FREEDOM WILL BE LIT EVERY EVENING FOR ETERNITIES. FIRST LIT & DEDICATED ON DEC 9, 1975. TIME CAPSULE PLACED INSIDE TO BE OPENED IN 2076, INCLUDES SCROLL OF SUNRISE 'PIONEERS' & VITAL PAPERS. (LOCAL). E J STASKA, CHAIRMAN; BICENTENNIAL COMMITTEE OF SUNRISE; 1277 SUNSET STRIP, CITY HALL; SUNRISE, FL 33313. (#20926).

INFINITE QUINTESSENCE - SCULPTURE, SUNRISE, FL. A SCULPTURE OF AN EAGLE WITH STEEL WINGS OUTSPREAD BUILT ON 3 TRIANGLES DEPICTING LIFE, LIBERTY & PURSUIT OF HAPPINESS. (LOCAL). GENE PALOWSKY, CHAIRMAN; BICENTENNIAL COMMITTEE OF SUNRISE; 1720 NW 60TH AVE; SUNRISE, FL 33313. (#24020).

UPSIDE DOWN HOUSE MODEL - SUNRISE, FL. A FULL-SIZE 3 BEDROOM HOME COMPLETELY BUILT UPSIDE DOWN WAS TORN DOWN IN 1961; A MODEL OF THIS HOME WILL BE BUILT. (LOCAL). WALT GREEN, CHAIRMAN; BICENTENNIAL COMMITTEE OF SUNRISE; 1720 NW 60TH AVE; SUNRISE, FL 33313. (#23952).

FEB 14, '76. FIFTY'S DANCE. THE DANCE WILL FEATURE MUSIC & DRESS OF THE FIFTIES. (LOCAL). ROBERT LABELLE, CHAIRMAN; SUNRISE BICENTENNIAL YOUTH COMMITTEE; 6701 NW 21ST ST; SUNRISE, FL 33313. (#105357-3).

FEB 21, '76. U S NAVY BAND PERFORMANCE. THIS EVENT IS THE FORERUNNER TO THE NEW 4000 SEAT SUNRISE CULTURAL

SUNRISE — CONTINUED

CENTER. AT PIPER HIGH SCHOOL, 8000 NW 43 PL. (LOCAL). ELSIE JANE STASKA, COORD; BICENTENNIAL COMMITTEE OF SUNRISE; 1720 NW 60TH AVE; SUNRISE, FL 33313. (#200011-195).

MAR 21 - 28, '76. ARTS & CRAFTS HOBBY SHOW. EXHIBIT AT RECREATION CENTER, 1720 NW 60TH AVE. (LOCAL). J GELORMINE, CHAIRMAN; BICENTENNIAL COMMITTEE OF SUNRISE; 2101 NW 73RD AVE; SUNRISE, FL 33313. (#102418-1).

APR 19, '76. PIPER HIGH SINGERS PRESENT 'AMERICA, OUR CORNER OF THE SKY'. DELIGHTFUL MUSIC COMMEMORATES THE BICENTENNIAL WITH 200 YEARS OF MUSIC; $1 OF THE PROCEEDS WILL GO TO THE BICENTENNIAL COMMITTEE AND $1 WILL GO TO THE SINGERS. AT PIPER HIGH SCHOOL AUDITORIUM, UNIV DRIVE & NW 44TH ST. (LOCAL). ROBERT DAGGETT, COORD; BICENTENNIAL COMMITTEE OF SUNRISE; 8000 NW 43RD PL; SUNRISE, FL 33322. (#105357-5).

SEPT 27 - OCT 2, '76. BROWARD COMMUNITY COLLEGE COMES TO SUNRISE. EXHIBITS & PROGRAM INVOLVING WHOLE COMMUNITY, CULMINATES IN TOWN MEETING. SEVERAL AFFAIRS DURING THE WEEK LONG EVENT WILL BE HELD IN THE OPEN BALL PARK AREA 66TH & SUNSET STRIP. (LOCAL). ELSIE J STASKA; BICENTENNIAL COMMITTEE OF SUNRISE; 1720 NW 60TH AVE; SUNRISE, FL 33313. (#105357-6).

SURFSIDE

MAR 22 - 27, '76. SURFSIDE'S CANADA WEEK - SALUTE TO AMERICA'S BICENTENNIAL. CITY OF SURFSIDE'S ANNUAL SALUTE TO CANADA WEEK TO HAVE EMPHASIS ON 200 YEARS OF GOODWILL BETWEEN U S & CANADA; THE GOAL TO ESTABLISH A MUSEUM DEPICTING AMERICAN-CANADIAN CULTURE, TRADITIONS & CUSTOMS IN AN INTERNATIONAL ATMOSPHERE. AT SURFSIDE COMMUNITY CENTER, 9301 COLLINS AVE, SURFSIDE. (INT'L). SHIRLEY LEFCOURT; SURFSIDE TOURIST BOARD; 9301 COLLINS AVE; SURFSIDE, FL 33154. (#101027-1).

TALLAHASSEE

'ACTION 76' PROJECT OF TALLAHASSEE, FL. ORGANIZATION OF GROUPS AT THE LOCAL LEVEL TO ASSURE TOTAL INVOLVEMENT OF COMMUNITIES IN THE BICENTENNIAL OBSERVANCES AND IMPROVE THE QUALITY OF LIFE OF THE CITY. (ST-WIDE). SHELTON KEMP, EXEC DIRECTOR; FLORIDA BICENTENNIAL COMMISSION; 504 E JEFFERSON ST; TALLAHASSEE, FL 32301. (#196).

AMERICAN WIND SYMPHONY ORCHESTRA, FL. BROAD ARRAY OF ARTISTIC ENDEAVORS TO MAJOR SEGMENTS OF FLORIDA PROVIDING MUSIC, PAINTINGS AND SCULPTURE. (REGN'L). WILLIAM R ADAMS, DIRECTOR; BICENTENNIAL COMMISSION OF FLORIDA; PO BOX 10207; TALLAHASSEE, FL 32301. (#19084). **ARBA GRANTEE.**

BICENTENNIAL COMMUNITY DEVELOPMENT PROJ - FL. THE ARTS COUNCIL SPONSORS A PROGRAM OF FINE ARTS IN AREA SCHOOLS. IN CONJUNCTION WITH THE BICENTENNIAL COMMISSION IT WILL BE SPONSORING A 'CITY SPIRIT PROGRAM' AND AN ARTS MONTH. (LOCAL). UNI S THOMAS, PRESIDENT; TALLAHASSEE ARTS COUNCIL, INC; 1520 HIGH ROAD; TALLAHASSEE, FL 32304. (#23270).

BICENTENNIAL RADIO SPOTS - TALLAHASSEE, FL. CONTEMPORARY AND HISTORICAL DOCUMENTARIES ON A SERIES OF 30-SECOND RADIO PRESENTATIONS. (LOCAL). ROBERT ALLEN, DIRECTOR; FLORIDA A & M UNIV; SOUTH BLVD; TALLAHASSEE, FL 32307. (#22033).

BICENTENNIAL UNIVERSITY CALENDAR - TALLAHASSEE, FL. UNIVERSITY CITIZEN'S CALENDAR SHOWING IMPORTANT HISTORICAL EVENTS AND DATES AND UNIVERSITY ACTIVITIES WITH SPECIAL EMPHASIS ON BICENTENNIAL PROJECTS AND PROGRAMS. (LOCAL). LT ANDREW PETRUSKA, PROJ DIRECTOR; FLORIDA A & M UNIV; SOUTH BLVD; TALLAHASSEE, FL 32307. (#22034).

BLACK FLORIDIAN ARCHIVE CENTER AT TALLAHASSEE. PRESERVE THE LETTERS AND PAPERS OF BLACK FLORIDIANS AT FLORIDA A&M UNIV. (ST-WIDE). DR B L PERRY, PRESIDENT; FLORIDA A & M UNIV; BOX 165; TALLAHASSEE, FL 32307. (#19940). **ARBA GRANTEE.**

BLACK HISTORY WEEK - TALLAHASSEE, FL. ANNUAL RECOGNITION OF AND FOCUS ON BLACKS IN THE U S; IMPACT AND CONTRIBUTIONS. (LOCAL). PROF JAMES EATON, CHAIRMAN; FLORIDA A & M UNIV; SOUTH BLVD; TALLAHASSEE, FL 32307. (#22035).

CITY SPIRIT, TALLAHASSEE, FL. IDENTIFYING & MOBILIZING COMMUNITY RESOURCES TO PROVIDE A RICHER QUALITY OF LIFE THROUGH THE ARTS; INTEGRATE ARTS ACTIVITIES INTO THE LIFE OF THE COMMUNITY. (LOCAL). DANIEL H MACDONALD, EXECUTIVE DIRECTOR; CHAMBER OF COMMERCE; PO BOX 1639; TALLAHASSEE, FL 32301. (#22312).

COLLECTION OF MEMORABILIA - TALLAHASSEE, FL. MEMORABILIA SUCH AS LETTERS, PAPERS, COSTUMES & RECORDS ARE BEING COLLECTED FOR RESEARCH, TEACHING AND PRESERVATION; MANY DEPARTMENTS IN THE UNIVERSITY ARE PARTICIPATING IN THE COLLECTION. (LOCAL). JOAN MORRIS, CURATOR; FLORIDA STATE UNIV LIBRARY; TALLAHASSEE, FL 32306. (#24862).

FBC'S BICENTENNIAL TRAVELING EXHIBITION. TRAVELING EXHIBIT W/HERITAGE, FESTIVAL & HORIZONS 76 THEMES. STOPS AT ALL MAJOR STATE FESTIVALS AND SCHEDULED STOPS AT OVER 100 COMMUNITIES. (ST-WIDE). SHELTON KEMP, EXEC DIRECTOR; BICENTENNIAL COMMISSION OF FLORIDA; SUITE 205 110, N MAGNOLIA ST; TALLAHASSEE, FL 32301. (#6195). **ARBA GRANTEE.**

FL STATE MUSEUM BICENTENNIAL EXHIBIT. AN EXHIBIT TO TOUR FLORIDA DURING THE BICENTENNIAL ERA DEPICTING THE HISTORY, PEOPLE, FLORA AND FAUNA OF FLORIDA. (ST-WIDE). VINCENT GABIANELLI, PROJECT DIRECTOR; FLORIDA STATE MUSEUM; MUSEUM RD; GAINSVILLE, FL 32601. (#249).

FLORIDA BICENTENNIAL TRAIL. MARKINGS OF OVER 100 HISTORICAL SITES IN FLORIDA RANGING FRAOM SAINT AUGUSTINE, THE OLDEST, TO KENNEDY SPACE CENTER, THE NEWEST. IN ADDITION, DEVELOPMENT OF NEW SITES IS INCLUDED IN THIS PROJECT. (ST-WIDE). SHELTON KEMP, EXEC DIRECTOR; FLORIDA BICENTENNIAL COMMISSION; 504 E JEFFERSON ST; TALLAHASSEE, FL 32301. (#248).

FLORIDA STATE UNIV HISTORICAL SOCIETY. THE SOCIETY IS DESIGNED TO CREATE INCREASED INTEREST IN HISTORY THROUGH SPEAKERS, TOURS, AWARDS AND CONFERENCES. (LOCAL). WILLIAM W ROGERS, ADVISOR; FLORIDA STATE UNIV HISTORICAL SOCIETY; #79 BELLAMY BLDG; TALLAHASSEE, FL 32306. (#24850).

FLORIDIANA FACSIMILIE SERIES, TALLAHASSEE. PUBLICATION OF RARE OUT OF PRINT BOOKS RELATING TO FLORIDA AND THE NATIONAL HERITAGE. (ST-WIDE). DON PRIDE, EXEC DIRECTOR; BICENTENNIAL COMMISSION OF FLORIDA; 110 N MAGNOLIA, SUITE 105; TALLAHASSEE, FL 32301. (#8376). **ARBA GRANTEE.**

'GAL YOUNG UN', FILM, TALLAHASSEE, FL. A NARRATIVE FILM BASED ON THE MARJORIE KINAW RAWLINGS SHORT STORY OF THE SAME TITLE TO BE DONE BY VICTOR NUNEZ, AN INDEPENDENT FILMMAKER. (NAT'L). JAMES E MENGEL, SPECIAL PROJECTS COORDINATOR; FINE ARTS COUNCIL OF FLORIDA; DEPT OF STATE THE CAPITOL; TALLAHASSEE, FL 32304. (#26437).

MILITARY COLOR GUARD - TALLAHASSEE, FL. AROTC COLOR GUARD IN REVOLUTIONARY GARB TO BE AVAILABLE FOR USE AT APPROPRIATE EVENTS AND PROGRAMS. (LOCAL). COLONEL HERBERT PARKER, PROJ DIRECTOR; FLORIDA A & M UNIV; SOUTH BLVD; TALLAHASSEE, FL 32307. (#20948).

ROLE OF THE BLACK CHURCH IN AMERICAN SOCIETY - FL. RESTORATION & RE-LOCATION OF A RURAL BLACK CHURCH AT THE SITE OF THE TALLAHASSEE JUNIOR MUSEUM. (LOCAL). DR JERRY CHANCE, CHAIRMAN; FLORIDA A & M UNIV; SOUTH BLVD; TALLAHASSEE, FL 32307. (#22036).

THE SEED - FLORIDA DRUG REHABILITATION PROJECT. A DRUG REHABILITATION PROGRAM ADOPTED BY THE FLORIDA B.C. BASED ON THE PREMISE: YOUNG PEOPLE CAN HELP THEMSELVES THROUGH THEIR PEER PRESSURES. (ST-WIDE). SHELTON KEMP, EXEC DIRECTOR; FLORIDA BICENTENNIAL COMMISSION; 504 E JEFFERSON ST; TALLAHASSEE, FL 32301. (#197).

TALLAHASSEE, FL, JUNIOR MUSEUM. A LIVING 1800'S PIONEER FARM: LOG CABIN, BARNS, BLACKSMITH SHOP, OUTBUILDINGS, GARDENS AND LIVESTOCK. SPECIAL PROGRAMS FEATURE DEMONSTRATIONS OF PIONEER CRAFTS & ACTIVITIES. (LOCAL). SAM KATES, DIRECTOR; TALLAHASSEE JUNIOR MUSEUM; 3945 MUSEUM DR; TALLAHASSEE, FL 32304. (#20044).

JULY 7 - 12, '75. THE FLORIDA EXHIBITION. AN AUDIO-VISUAL GRAPHICS DISPLAY THAT TELLS THE STORY OF FLORIDA PAST, PRESENT & FUTURE. (LOCAL). W F HOUSNER; BICENTENNIAL COMMISSION OF FLORIDA; PO BOX 1776; COCOA, FL 32922. (#6195-3).

AUG 11 - 14, '75. CITIZENSHIP COURSE - SPEAKERS ON HERITAGE THEME, TOUR STATE ARCHIVE. CONFERENCE, FESTIVAL, LIVE PERFORMANCE. (ST-WIDE). RUTH MILTON, PROJ DIR; STATE 4-H CLUB & INSTITUTE OF FOOD & AGRICULTURAL SCIENCES; UNIV OF FLORIDA; GAINESVILLE, FL 32611. (#10268-505).

FEB 20, '76. THE TODAY SHOW FEATURES THE STATE OF FLORIDA. A CONTINUING WEEKLY SERIES OF PROGRAMS COMMEMORATING EACH STATE. FLORIDA WAS ADMITTED INTO THE UNION IN MARCH, 1845. (NAT'L). STUART SCHULBERG, EX PROD; NATIONAL BROADCASTING CO; 30 ROCKEFELLER PLAZA; NEW YORK, NY 10020. (#7981-13).

MAR 4 - 10, '76. 'GODSPELL' - MUSICAL PLAY. LIVE PERFORMANCE AT FINE ARTS BUILDING, TENNESSEE & COPELAND ST. (LOCAL). THEA KATOPODY, COORD; SCHOOL OF THEATER; FLORIDA STATE UNIV; TALLAHASSEE, FL 32306. (#200011-204).

MAR 20 - APR 4, '76. SPRINGTIME TALLAHASSEE. BICENTENNIAL THEME INTERWOVEN THROUGH EVENTS PAYING TRIBUTE TO FOUNDING OF FLORIDA AND TALLAHASSEE AND THEIR 5 HISTORICAL ERAS: SPANISH, AMERICAN TERRITORIAL, ANTEBELLUM STATEHOOD, WAR & RECONSTRUCTION, AND TWENTIETH CENTURY. (ST-WIDE). ROBERT C FOSTER, SEC; SPRINGTIME TALLAHASSEE, INC; PO BOX 3123; TALLAHASSEE, FL 32303. (#103416-246).

MAR 31, '76. FLORIDA A & M BICENTENNIAL CONVOCATION. UNIVERSITY PUBLIC CONVOCATION IN OBSERVANCE OF THE BICENTENNIAL AND PRESENTING SPECIAL AWARDS TO 3 OUTSTANDING AMERICANS. AT LEE HALL AUDITORIUM, SOUTH BLVD, STREET PARKING ADJACENT TO BLVD. (LOCAL). DR CHARLES U SMITH, CHMN; FLORIDA A & M UNIV; SOUTH BLVD; TALLAHASSEE, FL 32307. (#105794-1).

APR 1 - DEC 31, '76. 'WE THE PEOPLE' - AN EXHIBIT TOURING FLORIDA. AN EXHIBIT OF PHOTOGRAPHS OF FLORIDIANS AT WORK & PLAY FROM 1845 TO THE PRESENT; PHOTOS ARE FROM THE FLORIDA STATE UNIVERSITY PHOTOGRAPHIC ARCHIVES. EXHIBITS ARE AVAILABLE TO BANKS AND TO OTHER EXHIBITORS. 2 SETS OF 33 PRINTS ARE TOURING SIMULTANEOUSLY. (ST-WIDE). MRS JOAN MORRIS, CURATOR; FLORIDA STATE UNIV; TALLAHASSEE, FL 32306. (#107942-1).

APR 4 - 10, '76. BICENTENNIAL SCHOOLS FESTIVAL WEEK. A WEEK CELEBRATING THE BICENTENNIAL IN ALL SCHOOLS, KINDERGARTEN THROUGH COLLEGE SCHOOLS CELEBRATING WILL BE RECOGNIZED BY THE COMMISSION. THROUGHOUT ENTIRE STATE OF FLORIDA. (ST-WIDE). GLENDA FULMER, COORD; BICENTENNIAL COMMISSION OF FLORIDA; PO BOX 10207; TALLAHASSEE, FL 32301. (#104330-1).

APR 15, '76. LECTURE: EARLY U S COINAGE. DISCUSSION OF INFLUENCES FROM OTHER COUNTRIES ON THE BEGINNINGS OF U S COINAGE, ITS DESIGN & MINTING. AT TALLAXHASSEE FEDERAL, N MONROE ST. (LOCAL). D B PETTENGILL, PRES; CAPITAL CITY COIN CLUB; PO BOX 2072; TALLAHASSEE, FL 32304. (#106204-1).

APR 15 - 24, '76. 'TIME OF YOUR LIFE' - PLAY. LIVE PERFORMANCE AT FINE ARTS BUILDING, TENNESSEE & COPELAND ST. (LOCAL). THEA KATOPODY, COORD; SCHOOL OF THEATER; FLORIDA STATE UNIV; TALLAHASSEE, FL 32306. (#200011-205).

MAY 3 - 5, '76. BICENTENNIAL SPRING SEMINARS. SPECIAL PRESENTATION OF THIS ANNUAL UNIVERSITY EVENT UTILIZING OUTSTANDING HUMANISTS, SCHOLARS AND EXECUTIVES TO ASSESS AMERICA'S PRESENT AND TO PROJECT THE FUTURE. (LOCAL). DR VICTORIA E WARNER, DIR; FLORIDA A & M UNIV; SOUTH BLVD; TALLAHASSEE, FL 32307. (#105794-3).

MAY 17 - 23, '76. EMANCIPATION WEEK CELEBRATION. COOPERATION WITH LEON COUNTY BICENTENNIAL EFFORT AND THE LOCAL COMMUNITY IN A WEEK-LONG CELEBRATION OF THE EMANCIPATION PROCLAMATION. (LOCAL). DR CHARLES U SMITH, CHMN; FLORIDA A & M UNIV; SOUTH BLVD; TALLAHASSEE, FL 32307. (#105794-2).

MAY 20 - 29, '76. BORN YESTERDAY, FROM SERIES OF AMERICAN PLAYS WITH FREEDOM THEME. LIVE PERFORMANCE AT FINE ARTS BUILDING, TENNESSEE & COPELAND STS. (LOCAL). THEA KATOPODY, COORD; SCHOOL OF THEATRE, FLORIDA STATE UNIV; TALLAHASSEE, FL 32306. (#107740-1).

JULY 4, '76. FOURTH OF JULY CELEBRATION. FESTIVAL, CEREMONY, PARADE, LIVE PERFORMANCE AT TALLAHASSEE FAIRGROUNDS. (ST-WIDE). DAISY FLORY, CHAIRMAN; FLORIDA STATE UNIV BICENTENNIAL COMMITTEE; WESTCOTT BLDG; TALLAHASSEE, FL 32306. (#107619-2).

JULY 7 - 17, '76. 'THE GLASS MENAGERIE' - PLAY. LIVE PERFORMANCE AT FINE ARTS BLDG, TENNESSEE & COPELAND ST. (LOCAL). THEA KATOPODY, CHAIRMAN; FLORIDA STATE UNIV SCHOOL OF THEATRE; TALLAHASSEE, FL 32306. (#107619-3).

NOV 10 - 13, '76. FLORA - EARLY AMERICAN OPERA. LIVE PERFORMANCE AT STUDIO AUDITORIUM, WILLIAMS BLDG. (LOCAL). LOUISE WEICHELT; SCHOOL OF MUSIC & SCHOOL OF THEATRE, FLORIDA STATE UNIV; TALLAHASSEE, FL 32306. (#108207-1).

NOV 20 - 22, '76. AMERICAN FREEDOM DISPLAY DAYS AT TALLAHASSEE, FL. THE AMERICAN FREEDOM TRAIN INCLUDES 10 EXHIBIT CARS & 2 SHOW CASE CARS DEPICTING DIFFERENT PHASES OF THE AMERICAN EXPERIENCE. ITS ARRIVAL WILL SERVE AS A CATALYST FOR LOCAL BICENTENNIAL CELEBRATIONS BY PEOPLE THROUGHOUT THIS NATION. (ST-WIDE). SY FREEDMAN, DIR OF P/R; THE AMERICAN FREEDOM TRAIN FOUNDATION; 5205 LEESBURG PIKE, SUITE 800; BAILEY'S XRDS, VA 22041. (#1776-108).

NOV 20 - DEC 6, '76. 'THE DIARY OF ANNE FRANK' - PLAY. LIVE PERFORMANCE AT FINE ARTS BUILDING, TENNESSEE & COPELAND ST. (LOCAL). THEA KATOPODY, COORD; SCHOOL OF THEATER; FLORIDA STATE UNIV; TALLAHASSEE, FL 32306. (#200011-203).

TAMPA

THE AMERICAN MYTH. THE WEEK-LONG CONFERENCE WILL FOCUS ON THE AMERICAN MYTH IN THE POP AND TRADITIONAL ARTS. (LOCAL). W MORRIS, BICENT CHAIRMAN; UNIV OF SOUTH FLORIDA BICENTENNIAL COMMITTEE; TAMPA, FL 33620. (#103098-2). **(??).**

BICENTENNIAL LIBRARY DISPLAYS. EXHIBIT. (LOCAL). J DOBBICK, LIBRARIAN; UNIV OF SOUTH FLORIDA; TAMPA, FL 33620. (#103098-1). **(??).**

BUILDING RENOVATION AT UNIV OF TAMPA, FL. RENOVATION OF FORMER FLORIDA STATE FAIR CONSERVATION INTO UNIVERSITY OF TAMPA ROTC BUILDING TO BE DECORATED & NAMED THE 'HERITAGE '76' BUILDING. (LOCAL). DALE FRIEND, CHAIRMAN; UNIVERSITY OF TAMPA BICENTENNIAL COMMITTEE; 401 W KENNEDY AVE; TAMPA, FL 33606. (#15696).

DEDICATION OF USF BICENTENNIAL LIBRARY. A NEW LIBRARY AT THE UNIVERSITY WILL BE DEDICATED TO THE BICENTENNIAL. (LOCAL). J VICKREY, PROJ COORDINATOR; UNIV OF SOUTH FLORIDA; TAMPA, FL 33620. (#17023).

LIBRARY DISPLAYS IN TAMPA, FL. IN HONOR OF THE BICENTENNIAL, THE LIBRARY WILL HAVE CHANGING DISPLAYS ON AMERICA. (LOCAL). J DOBBICK, SPECIAL COLLECTIONS LIBRARIAN; UNIV OF SOUTH FLORIDA; TAMPA, FL 33620. (#16504).

MERLE KELCE LIBRARY BICENTENNIAL COLLECTION, FL. THE UNIVERSITY OF TAMPA LIBRARY WILL BEGIN A COLLECTION OF MEMORABILIA OF THE BICENTENNIAL. (LOCAL). DALE FRIEND, CHAIRMAN; UNIVERSITY OF TAMPA BICENTENNIAL COMMITTEE; 401 W KENNEDY RD; TAMPA, FL 33606. (#15695).

SEMINAR ON THIRD CENTURY HILLSBOROUGH - FL. THIS IS A SERIES OF OPEN-ENDED CULTURAL EVENTS THAT WILL STIMULATE AUDIENCES TO DISCUSS THE NEXT CENTURY'S CULTURAL LIFE IN A POST INDUSTRIAL AND LEISURE ORIENTED SOCIETY. (LOCAL). RAYMOND C MESLER JR, EXECUTIVE DIRECTOR; ARTS COUNCIL OF TAMPA-HILLSBOROUGH COUNTY; 512 N FLORIDA AVE; TAMPA, FL 33602. (#17210).

'WE THE PEOPLE' - LIVE PERFORMANCE, TAMPA, FL. A SPECIAL BICENTENNIAL PRESENTATION WITH ORIGINAL STAGING. (REGN'L). C G CALDWELL, COORDINATOR; FLORIDA COLLEGE; TEMPLE TER, FL 33617. (#31091).

JUNE 9, '75 - DEC 31, '76. 'THE EAGLE WITHIN' - MULTI-MEDIA PRODUCTION AT BUSCH GARDENS. 15 MINUTE MULTI-SENSORY

TAMPA — CONTINUED

PRODUCTION OF COLLECTION OF AMERICANS WITH ONE THING IN COMMON: EACH EPITOMIZES USA EXCELLENCE IN SCIENCE, INDUSTRY, THE CRAFTS, ARTS & ATHLETICS; WILL BE SHOWN CONTINUOUSLY. (REGN'L). JOSEPH T FINNIGAN, DIR; FLEISHMAN-HILLARD, INC; ONE MEMORIAL DR; ST LOUIS, MO 63102. (#101234-1).

SEPT '75 - MAY '76. BICENTENNIAL MONTHLY SEMINARS. MONTHLY SEMINARS ON AMERICAN CULTURE, SCIENCE, ART, LITERATURE, SOCIAL PROGRESS, RELIGION, LAW, GOVERNMENT, BUSINESS & EDUCATION. (LOCAL). W MORRIS, CHMN; UNIV OF SOUTH FLORIDA BICENTENNIAL COMMITTEE; TAMPA, FL 33620. (#102983-12).

JAN 13 - DEC 31, '76. BICENTENNIAL GUIDED TOURS OF THE FORMER HENRY B PLANT HOTEL. TOUR AT 401 W KENNEDY BLVD FREE LOCAL PARKING. (LOCAL). D E FRIEND; UNIVERSITY OF TAMPA WOMEN'S CLUB; 401 W KENNEDY BLVD; TAMPA, FL 33609. (#104398-1).

JAN 21 - 22, '76. UNITED STATES ARMED FORCES BICENTENNIAL CARAVAN. CARAVAN IS COMPOSED OF EXHIBIT VANS FOR EACH MILITARY SERVICE. PROJECT THEME IS 'HISTORY OF THE ARMED FORCES AND THEIR CONTRIBUTIONS TO THE NATION'. (LOCAL). FRED LEAREY; US ARMED FORCES BICENTENNIAL EXHIBIT VANS PROJECT; PO BOX 610; TAMPA, FL 33601. (#1775-423).

FEB 9 - 12, '76. GASPARILLA PIRATE INVASION & PARADE. FESTIVAL WITH BICENTENNIAL EMPHASIS COMMEMORATES FABLED BUCANEER JOSE GASPAR WITH INVASION, PARADE, FEASTS, DANCING & MERRIMENT. (LOCAL). FRANK J COLLINS, COORD; GASPARILLA; PO BOX 1514; TAMPA, FL 33601. (#103416-141).

MAR 18, '76. PRESIDENT'S HONOR GUARD. CEREMONY, LIVE PERFORMANCE AT PLANT HIGH SCHOOL STADIUM, 2415 S HIMES AVE. (LOCAL). KAREN FUSON, COORD; GREATER TAMPA BICENTENNIAL COUNCIL; PO BOX 420; TAMPA, FL 33601. (#200011-206).

MAR 25, '76. AMERICA TODAY. A KODAK MULTI-MEDIA PRESENTATION INVOLVING SLIDES, FILM AND SOUND, WHICH FOCUSES ON AMERICA'S ACHIEVEMENTS TODAY, AS WITNESSED THROUGH INDIVIDUAL PERSONALITY PORTRAITS. AT CURTIS HIXON CONVENTION CENTER, 600 ASHLEY ST. (LOCAL). KAREN FUSON, CHAIRMAN; GREATER TAMPA BICENTENNIAL COUNCIL, UNIV OF SOUTH FLORIDA; PO BOX 420; TAMPA, FL 33601. (#105833-4).

MAR 26 - 27, '76. BICENTENNIAL PROFILE '76. UNIV OF SOUTHERN FLORIDA AND EASTMAN KODAK WILL PRESENT THIS MULTIMEDIA EVENT ABOUT AMERICA. AT MCKAY AUDITORIUM. (LOCAL). CAESAR GONZMART, JR, CHMN; BICENTENNIAL COMMITTEE OF HILSBOROUGH COUNTY; PO BOX 1381; TAMPA, FL 33606. (#102723-1).

MAR '76. BICENTENNIAL WEEKEND AT UNIVERSITY OF TAMPA. WEEKEND TO INCLUDE SMALL COLLEGE ATMOSPHERE AS PART OF THE AMERICAN HERITAGE, SHOW CHORUS DURING HOMECOMING WEEKEND, CARNIVAL FOR UNDERPRIVILEGED CHILDREN AND TOURS THROUGH MUSEUM AND UNIVERSITY. AT MCKAY AUDITORIUM. (LOCAL). DALE FRIEND, CHAIRMAN; UNIV OF TAMPA BICENTENNIAL COMMITTEE; 401 W KENNEDY BLVD; TAMPA, FL 33606. (#102534-1).

APR 17, '76. JOHNNY HORIZON ENVIRONMENTAL BENEFIT CONCERT. JOHNNY HORIZON '76 ENVIRONMENTAL AWARENESS AND ACTION PROGRAM WITH THE DEPT OF INTERIOR WILL PRESENT A BENEFIT CONCERT ON APRIL 17, AT CURTIS HIXON HALL. PROCEEDS GO TO THE ENVIRONMENTAL CENTER AT COCKROACH BAY. AT CURTIS HIXON CONVENTION CENTER, TAMPA, FLA. (LOCAL). JACKIE BROWN, COORD; FL FEDERATION BUS & PROFESSIONAL WOMEN, DISTRICT 7; 4304 KNIGHTS AVE; TAMPA, FL 33611. (#104839-1).

MAY 7, '76. AMERICAN WIND SYMPHONY'S FLOATING ARTS CENTER VISITS TAMPA. EMBARKING UPON A BICENTENNIAL CULTURAL TOUR, THE WIND SYMPHONY WILL VISIT 76 CITIES BRINGING MUSIC, DANCE, SYMPOSIA, AND CHILDREN'S THEATER TO THE WATERWAYS OF AMERICA DURING ITS 6-MONTH TOUR. AT BARGE ON HILLSBOROUGH RIVER. (LOCAL). ROBERT GRONLUND; AMERICAN WIND SYMPHONY ORCHESTRA OF WESTERN PENNSYLVANIA; 401 W KENNEDY BLVD; TAMPA, FL 33601. (#2800-5).

MAY 15, '76. BICENTENNIAL EDUCATION SHOWCASE. AN EDUCATIONAL SHOWCASE INCLUDING EXHIBITS FROM MOST AREA SCHOOLS AND PERFORMANCES BY THEIR MUSICAL, DANCE AND THEATRE GROUPS. BICENTENNIAL THEME 'LOOKING FORWARD TO OUR THIRD CENTURY.'. AT JEFFERSON HIGH SCHOOL, 4401 CYPRESS ST. (LOCAL). KAREN FUSON, INFO DIR; GREATER TAMPA BICENTENNIAL COUNCIL; PO BOX 420; TAMPA, FL 33601. (#105833-2).

MAY 29, '76. BICENTENNIAL MILITARY PARADE. A MILITARY PARADE WILL BEGIN WITH TRADITIONAL MASSING OF THE COLORS (TO BLESS THEM) AND RESULT IN A STATIC DISPLAY. INSTALATIONS HAVE BEEN INVITED FROM THROUGHOUT THE SOUTHEAST. AT BAYSHORE BLVD. (LOCAL). KAREN FUSON, COORDINATOR; GREATER TAMPA BICENTENNIAL COUNCIL; PO BOX 420; TAMPA, FL 33601. (#107258-1).

JULY 4, '76. FOURTH OF JULY CELEBRATION. THE UNIVERSITY WILL BE THE SITE OF AN 1890'S STYLE PICNIC, COMPLETE WITH MUSIC GROUPS OF ALL TYPES, BALLOON VENDORS, ATHLETIC COMPETITIONS, ETC. AT UNIV OF TAMPA, 401 E KENNEDY BLVD ON HILLSBOROUGH RIVER. (LOCAL). KAREN FUSON, INFO DIR; GREATER TAMPA BICENTENNIAL COUNCIL; PO BOX 420; TAMPA, FL 33601. (#105833-1).

JULY 4, '76. FOURTH OF JULY SUNRISE SERVICE. SPEAKERS WILL ADDRESS CONGREGATION GATHERED ALONG THE RIVER FROM PLANT PARK (THE SITE OF THE AREA'S FIRST SUNRISE SERVICE). GEN. HAYES WILL SPEAK AND MUSIC WILL BE PROVIDED. AT UNIV OF TAMPA'S PLANT PARK, 401 W KENNEDY BLVD ON HILLS RIVER. (LOCAL). KAREN FUSON, INFO DIR; GREATER TAMPA BICENTENNIAL COUNCIL; PO BOX 420; TAMPA, FL 33601. (#105833-6).

SEPT 17 - OCT 15, '76. SILVERWORKS FROM THE RIO DE LA PLATA EXHIBITION. THIS EXHIBITION OF 180 ECCLESIASTICAL & SECULAR SILVER OBJECTS REPRESENTS OUTSTANDING CULTURAL-SOCIAL ASPECTS OF ARGENTINE LIFE DURING THE 18TH & 19TH CENTURIES. AT CURTIS HIXON HALL. (INT'L). EILEEN HARAKAL, COORD; SMITHSONIAN INSTITUTION TRAVELING EXHIBITION SERVICE; 1000 JEFFERSON DR, SW; WASHINGTON, DC 20560. (#26666-2).

DEC 1, '76 - CONTINUING . 3RD CENTURY AMER SCULPTURE COMPETITION - TAMPA, FL. NATIONAL SCULPTURE COMPETITION & EXHIBITION ON BIENNIAL OR TRIENNIAL BASIS. (NAT'L). RAYMOND C MESLER; ARTS COUNCIL OF TAMPA - HILLSBOROUGH COUNTY; 512 N FLORIDA AVE; TAMPA, FL 33602. (#10874-1).

JUNE 3 - 11, '77. SALUTE TO LATIN AMERICA. THE CULTURAL CONTRIBUTIONS OF 27 LATIN AMERICAN COUNTRIES TO THE HERITAGE OF THE USA WILL BE ON EXHIBITION AND WILL BE HONORED BY CULTURAL GROUPS OF THE USA. AT CURTIS HIXON CONVENTION CENTER, 600 ASHLEY. (LOCAL). MIKE MAYFIELD; HILLSBOROUGH COUNTY MUSEUM & FRIENDS OF THE MUSEUM, INC; 1101 E RIVER CV, BOX 8311; TAMPA, FL 33674. (#109094-1).

TARPON SPG

FEB 27 - MAR 14, '76. BICENTENNIAL EORTI: 'HAPPY BIRTHDAY, USA'. EORTI IS A GREEK WORD MEANING HOLIDAY CELEBRATION; FEATURING TRUE TALES OF TARPON SPRINGS. AT SPONGE EXCHANGE ON SPONGE DOCKS. (REGN'L). CLIFFORD M FUGIT, CHMN; TARPON SPRINGS CENTENNIAL AMERICAN REVOLUTION BICENTENNIAL COMMITTEE; 112 S PINELLAS AVE; TARPON SPG, FL 33589. (#104267-1).

FEB 27 - MAR 14, '76. TARPON SPRINGS CENTENNIAL PAGEANT. A MIXTURE OF TAPRON SPRINGS HISTORY & AMERICAN HISTORY WITH MUSIC & PERFORMANCE BY LOCAL PEOPLE. AT SPONG EXCHANGE, THEATRE IN THE ROUND. (LOCAL). ELANE MCGRATH, CHRM; CITY OF TARPON SPRINGS; 1300 RIVERSIDE DR; TARPON SPG, FL 33589. (#102168-1).

TAVARES

LAKE COUNTY COURTHOUSE - TAVARES, FL. A NEW CIRCULAR COURTHOUSE DEDICATED TO SERVE THE PEOPLE AND AS A MEMORIAL TO THE BICENTENNIAL. (LOCAL). J CARL SMITH, EXEC VICE PRESIDENT; LAKE COUNTY CHAMBER OF COMMERCE; 2101 HWY 452 S; EUSTIS, FL 32726. (#24180).

TAVARES CIVIC GROUPS BICENTENNIAL PROJECTS, FL. COMMUNITY PARK BENCHES WERE PAINTED RED, WHITE & BLUE. HIGH SCHOOL ART CLASSES PAINTED MURALS TO BE DISPLAYED DOWNTOWN. MIDDLE SCHOOL STUDENTS PAINTED FIRE PLUGS, LOCAL PARK WAS RENOVATED. (LOCAL). MARY JO BROWN, COORDINATOR; CIVIC CLUBS OF TAVARES; 424 ST CLAIR ABRAMS AVE; TAVARES, FL 32778. (#26905).

T-SHIRTS WITH THE BICENTENNIAL SYMBOL. T-SHIRT WITH BICENTENNIAL SYMBOL, LICENSE NO 76-19-0569. (NAT'L). G H MASSEY, PROJ DIRECTOR; SHARP SHIRTS, INC; RT #1, BOX 146B; TAVARES, FL 32778. (#13363).

DEC 6, '75. DEDICATION OF RENOVATED OLD SEABOARD COASTLINE RAILWAY STATION. CEREMONY. (LOCAL). MARY JO BROWN, CHPRSN; CIVIC CLUBS OF TAVARES; 424 ST CLAIR; TAVARES, FL 32778. (#200011-218).

JULY 4, '76. OLD-FASHIONED PICNIC. FESTIVAL AT TAVARES WOOTEN PARK, ST CLAIR ABRAMS. (LOCAL). MARY JO BROWN, CHAIRMAN; TAVARES BICENTENNIAL COUNCIL; 424 ST CLAIR ABRAMS; TAVARES, FL 32778. (#200011-224).

TEMPLE TER

BOOK: 'OUR RESTORATION HERITAGE', FL. BOOK COMPOSED OF LECTURES IN A SPECIAL SERIES IN JANUARY 1976 AT THE COLLEGE DEALING WITH AMERICAN RELIGIONS HERITAGE AMONG DISCIPLES OF CHRIST AND TIED TO THE BICENTENNIAL THEME. (NAT'L). ROLAND LEWIS, DEAN OF INSTRUCTION; FLORIDA COLLEGE; GLEN ARVEN AVE; TEMPLE TER, FL 33617. (#31092).

JULY 4, '76. FOURTH OF JULY CELEBRATION. MILITARY DISPLAY, SKYDIVERS, MOVIES, DANCE, FOOD, GAMES AND ENTERTAINMENT CULMINATING WITH A FIREWORKS DISPLAY. AT RIVER HILLS DR. (LOCAL). RALPH LUPTON, CHAIRMAN; TEMPLE TERRACE CHAMBER OF COMMERCE; 8745 OVERLOOK DR; TEMPLE TER, FL 33617. (#105835-1).

TITUSVILLE

BICENTENNIAL COOKBOOK, TITUSVILLE, FL. WILL INCLUDE COLLECTION OF RECIPES FROM 1700'S AND 1800'S. (LOCAL). W G LYERLY, CHAIRMAN; NORTH BREVARD AREA BICENTENNIAL COMMITTEE; TITUSVILLE SCHOOLS; 2000 S WASHINGTON AVE; TITUSVILLE, FL 32780. (#20795).

BICENTENNIAL MEMORIAL MINI-PARK - TITUSVILLE, FL. A BICENTENNIAL MINI-PARK WILL BE DEVELOPED BY THE INDIAN RIVER WITH RUSTIC AND SPACE-AGE THEMES. (LOCAL). CHARLES PALMER, PROJ DIRECTOR; BREVARD COUNTY BICENTENNIAL COMMITTEE; 2247 COUNTRY CLUB RD; TITUSVILLE, FL 32780. (#19214).

BICENTENNIAL PARK IN TITUSVILLE, FL. A BICENTENNIAL PARK ON THE SCHOOL GROUNDS IS PLANNED. LIBERTY TREES TO BE PLANTED, PICNIC TABLES TO BE DONATED, AND A TIME CAPSULE WILL BE BURIED IN THE PARK. (LOCAL). W F HOUSNER, CHAIRMAN; SOUTH LAKE ELEMENTARY SCHOOL; BREVARD COUNTY BICENT COMMITTEE; TITUSVILLE, FL 32780. (#22361).

BICENTENNIAL SPEAKER - TITUSVILLE, FL. A BICENTENNIAL SPEAKERS SERVICE WILL BE MADE AVAILABLE. (LOCAL). W G LYERLY, CHAIRMAN; NORTH BREVARD AREA BICENTENNIAL COMMITTEE; 2000 S WASHINGTON AVE; TITUSVILLE, FL 32780. (#20499).

BICENTENNIAL TREE TREASURE TRUNK - TITUSVILLE, FL. A LIVING, CONTINUING PROJECT TO INCREASE HISTORIC AND ENVIRONMENTAL IMPORTANCE OF TREES. (LOCAL). W G LYERLY, CHAIRMAN; NORTH BREVARD BICENTENNIAL COMMITTEE; 2000 S WASHINGTON AVE; TITUSVILLE, FL 32780. (#20498).

DECORATIVE FIRE HYDRANTS, TITUSVILLE, FL. PAINTED FIRE HYDRANTS ON CITY'S MAIN THROUGHPASS IN BRIGHT & PATRIOTIC COLORS OF EARLY AMERICAN FIGURES. (LOCAL). TITUSVILLE ART LEAGUE; NORTH BREVARD AREA BICENTENNIAL COMMITTEE, TITUSVILLE ART LEAGUE; 2000 S WASHINGTON AVE; TITUSVILLE, FL 32780. (#20797).

FLAG DISPLAY, TITUSVILLE, FL. COUNTY WIDE EFFORT TO HAVE EVERY HOME & BUSINESS FLY THE AMERICAN FLAG. (LOCAL). W G LYERLY, CHAIRMAN; NORTH BREVARD BICENTENNIAL COMMITTEE; 2000 S WASHINGTON AVE; TITUSVILLE, FL 32780. (#20794).

HISTORICAL SITE MARKERS - TITUSVILLE, FL. PLAQUES WILL BE PLACED AT MANY HISTORIC HOMES & LOCATIONS. (LOCAL). JAMES C HENDRIX, CHAIRMAN; NORTH BREVARD AREA BICENTENNIAL COMMITTEE; 2000 S WASHINGTON AVE; TITUSVILLE, FL 32780. (#26012).

HISTORICAL U S FLAGS - TITUSVILLE, FL. EACH COUNCIL MEMBER HAS MADE A FLAG REPRESENTING ONE OF THE ORIGINAL FLAGS WHICH HAVE BEEN A SYMBOL OF THIS NATION SINCE ITS BIRTH. (LOCAL). W G LYERLY, CHAIRMAN; NORTH BREVARD AREA BICENTENNIAL COMMITTEE; RIVERVIEW SCHOOL; 2000 S WASHINGTON AVE; TITUSVILLE, FL 32780. (#20793).

INDIAN RIVER FESTIVAL. FESTIVAL. (LOCAL). DON SEARLE, CHAIRMAN; INDIAN RIVER FESTIVAL & NORTH BREVARD AREA BICENTENNIAL COMMITTEE; 25 E MAIN; TITUSVILLE, FL 32780. (#108429-1).

LIBRARY - TITUSVILLE, FL. FEATURING BOOKS SELECTED FOR SCHOOL LIBRARY TO CELEBRATE BIRTHDAY OF COUNTRY. (LOCAL). W G LYERLY, CHAIRMAN; NORTH BREVARD AREA BICENTENNIAL COMMITTEE; MADISON MIDDLE SCHOOL; 2000 S WASHINGTON AVE; TITUSVILLE, FL 32780. (#20792).

'MY COUNTRY 'TIS OF THEE' - OPERETTA. LIVE PERFORMANCE AT SOUTH LAKE ELEMENTARY SCHOOL. (LOCAL). W G LYERLY, CHAIRMAN; NORTH BREVARD AREA BICENTENNIAL COMMITTEE; 2000 S WASHINGTON AVE; TITUSVILLE, FL 32780. (#105015-1).

PIONEER DAYS. PHOTO CONTEST, SKITS AND PIONEER DAYS STUDY OF ARTS & CRAFTS. (LOCAL). W G LYERLY, CHAIRMAN; NORTH BREVARD AREA BICENTENNIAL COMMITTEE; 2000 S WASHINGTON AVE; TITUSVILLE, FL 32780. (#105014-1).

'PROJECT CIVIC CONCERN', TITUSVILLE, FL. MONTHLY AWARD OF A BICENTENNIAL BANNER TO THE BUSINESS & RESIDENCE WITH MOST IMPROVED APPEARANCE & LANDSCAPING DURING A PARTICULAR MONTH. (LOCAL). W G LYERLY, CHAIRMAN; BICENTENNIAL BEAUTIFICATION COMMITTEE, N BREVARD PUBLIC LIBRARY; 2000 S WASHINGTON AVE; TITUSVILLE, FL 32780. (#20796).

SAFETY TOWN, TITUSVILLE, FL. A STATE GRANT IN THE AMOUNT OF $1250.00 HAS BEEN APPROVED FOR COMPLETION OF THE PROJECT WHICH CONSISTS OF A MINIATURE COMMUNITY TO TEACH PRE-SCHOOL & ELEMENTARY CHILDREN SAFETY IN THEIR COMMUNITY. (LOCAL). W G LYERLY, CHAIRMAN; NORTH BREVARD AREA BICENTENNIAL COMMITTEE, PILOT CLUB; 2000 S WASHINGTON AVE; TITUSVILLE, FL 32780. (#20798).

SISTER CITY FOR TITUSVILLE, FL. ATTEMPTING TO FORM A SISTER CITY AFFILIATION WITH BAIKENOR WHICH IS GEOGRAPHICALLY LOCATED NEXT TO THE RUSSIAN COSMO-DOME. (LOCAL). W G LYERLY, CHAIRMAN; NORTH BREVARD AREA BICENTENNIAL COMMITTEE; 2000 S WASHINGTON AVE; TITUSVILLE, FL 32780. (#20791).

THOMAS JEFFERSON MEMORIAL GARDEN - FL. IN HONOR OF THOMAS JEFFERSON, PLAQUE WILL BE PLACED & A HERB GARDEN IS TO BE PLANTED AT THE NORTH BREVARD PUBLIC LIBRARY. (LOCAL). JAMES C HENDRIX, CHAIRMAN; NORTH BREVARD NATURAL GARDENING & NUTRITION GROUP; 1540 THORNTON AVE; TITUSVILLE, FL 32780. (#26011).

TITUSVILLE, FL, COMMUNITY GARDEN. A COMMUNITY GARDEN FOR SENIOR CITIZENS, LOW INCOME AND FIXED INCOME CITIZENS TO PLANT AND CARE FOR THEIR OWN PLANTS. (LOCAL). JAMES C HENDRIX, CHAIRMAN; NORTH BREVARD NATURAL GARDENING & NUTRITION GROUP; 1540 THORNTON AVE; TITUSVILLE, FL 32780. (#26010).

WUESTHOFF NATURE PARK, TITUSVILLE, FL. APPLICATION HAS BEEN MADE FOR MATCHING FUNDS TO CREATE A NATURE AND RECREATION PARK IN THE CURRENTLY EXISTING WUESTHOFF PARK. (LOCAL). W G LYERLY, CHAIRMAN; NORTH BREVARD AREA BICENTENNIAL COMMISSION - BEAUTIFICATION; 2000 S WASHINGTON AVE; TITUSVILLE, FL 32780. (#20799).

MAY 14 - 18, '75. APOLLO SOFTBALL TOURNAMENT FOR COUNTY SOFTBALL CHAMPIONSHIP. COMPETITION. (LOCAL). PAUL ZENO,

TITUSVILLE — CONTINUED

CHAIRMAN; BREVARD COUNTY DEPART OF PARKS & RECREATION; 625 E NEW HAVEN AVE; MELBOURNE, FL 33901. (#7707-501).

JUNE 30 - JULY 3, '75. BICENTENNIAL SPORTS ACTIVITIES WEEK. COMPETITION. (LOCAL). PAUL ZENO, CHAIRMAN; BREVARD COUNTY DEPT OF PARKS & RECREATION; 625 E NEW HAVEN AVE; MELBOURNE, FL 32901. (#7711-501).

MAR 8, '76. 'BICENTENNIAL SAIL' OF HISTORIC SHIP VISITS CANAVERAL N.S.. HISTORIC FISHING SCHOONER 'MARY E', SAILING THE ATLANTIC COAST, WILL STOP AT THIS NATIONAL PARK SERVICE AREA AND PROVIDE SHIPBOARD PROGRAMS TO VISITORS TO THIS AREA. (REGN'L). CANAVERAL NATL SEASHORE; SEA VENTURES, INC. & NATIONAL PARK SERVICE; P.O. BOX 2583; TITUSVILLE, FL 32780. (#7960-1).

MAR 15 - 19, '76. CRAFTSMEN'S WEEK. CRAFT DEMONSTRATIONS, FOLK MUSIC, LITERATURE & POETRY PRESENTATIONS; ALSO HELD AT THE AMERICAN COFFEE HOUSE MARCH 19, 8:00 PM. AT BCC STUDENT CENTER. (LOCAL). LANE CORVEY, COORDINATOR; BREVARD COMMUNITY COLLEGE; BREVARD COMMUNITY COLLEGE; COCOA, FL 32922. (#101286-1).

APR 27, '76. PARADE & ENLISTMENT CEREMONIES. PATRIOTS DAY PARADE IN TITUSVILLE, FLORIDA. A PARADE AND RECOGNITION CEREMONIES OF YOUTH IN THE COUNTY WHO HAVE ENLISTED INTO THE ARMY, THE AIR FORCE, THE MARINES, THE NAVY & THE COAST GUARD. (LOCAL). CHARLES PALMER; BREVARD COUNTY BICENTENNIAL COMMITTEE; TITUSVILLE, FL 32780. (#7706-501).

APR 27, '76. PATRIOTS DAY PARADE. PARADE AT 2000 S WASHINGTON AVE. (LOCAL). CHARLES A PALMER, CHMN; NORTH BREVARD AREA BICENTENNIAL COMMITTEE; 2247 COUNTRY CLUB DR; TITUSVILLE, FL 32780. (#7706-1).

JULY 2, '76. JULY 2ND CELEBRATION. EVENTS INCLUDE CELEBRITY DUNKING, STREET DANCING, JAZZ CONCERT, COUNTRY WESTERN MUSIC AND SQUARE DANCING. AM TO 6:00PM & FIREWORKS AT STADIUM AT 9:00PM ON JULY 3; BICENTENNIAL PARADE OF OVER 100 UNITS FROM 2:00 TO 7:00PM ON JULY 4. AT CITY HALL, WEASEL BROOK PARK, CLIFTON STADIUM, DOWNTOWN CLIFTON. (LOCAL). DONN SEARLE, CHAIRMAN; NORTH BREVARD AREA BICENTENNIAL COMMITTEE; 25 E MAIN ST; TITUSVILLE, FL 32780. (#108125-1).

JULY 2 - 5, '76. INDEPENDENCE FESTIVITIES. VARIETY OF RECREATION ACTIVITIES HIGHLIGHT THIS SPACE COMMUNITY'S INDEPENDENCE CELEBRATION. AT THROUGHOUT TOWN. (LOCAL). BILL LYERLY, EXEC DIR; TITUSVILLE CHAMBER OF COMMERCE; PO BOX 880; TITUSVILLE, FL 32780. (#103416-427).

JULY 3, '76. JULY 3RD CELEBRATION. EVENTS INCLUDE TROUT TOURNAMENT, PARADE, FASHION SHOW WITH COSTUME JUDGING, REGATTA & WATER SKI SHOW & ATHLETIC TOURNAMENTS. (LOCAL). DONN SEARLE, CHAIRMAN; NORTH BREVARD AREA BICENTENNIAL COMMITTEE; 25 E MAIN ST; TITUSVILLE, FL 32780. (#108427-1).

JULY 4, '76. FOURTH OF JULY FESTIVITIES. EVENTS INCLUDE SUNRISE SERVICE, JAYCEES PANCAKE BREAKFAST, BLUEGRASS MUSIC CONCERT, CONTESTS, ROSIE O'GRADY'S DIXIELAND BAND CONCERT, FIREWORKS & COSTUME BALL JULY 5TH. (LOCAL). DONN SEARLE, CHAIRMAN; NORTH BREVARD AREA BICENTENNIAL COMMITTEE; 25 E MAIN ST; TITUSVILLE, FL 32780. (#108428-1).

DEC 5, '76. LITTLE MR & MISS BICENTENNIAL CONTEST. COMPETITION AT MIRACLE CITY MALL, 2500 S WASHINGTON AVE. (LOCAL). ANNETTE MCCALLUM; SUNSHINE HOMEMAKERS CLUB; 2225 S PARK AVE; TITUSVILLE, FL 32780. (#7706-2).

TYNDALL AFB

WORLD-WIDE AIR DEFENSE WEAPONS MEET (WILLIAM TELL). LIVE PERFORMANCE. (LOCAL). GARY W DOOLEY; TYNDALL AFB; 2807 KINGSWOOD DR; PANAMA CITY, FL 32401. (#200011-309).

JUNE 5 - 6, '76. TYNDALL PIONEER DAYS. THOMAS BROGDON IN CIVIL WAR MOTIF-SQUARE DANCE-ALMOST ANYTHING GOESGAMES & CRAZY STUNTS-CHUCK WAGON DINNER & HOEDOWN-AMERICANA FASHION SHOW & OVERNIGHT CAMPING-SUNDAY CHURCH SERVICE-PICNIC-DEBATES-FIRE BRIGADE DEMONSTRATION. AT TYNDALL AFB HDQRS BLDG TO TYNDALL OLD TOWN GROUNDS. (LOCAL). GARY W DOOLEY; TYNDALL AFB BICENTENNIAL COMMITTEE; 2807 KINGSWOOD DR; PANAMA CITY, FL 32401. (#200011-308).

VALPARAISO

BICENTENNIAL CORNER - VALPARAISO, FL. WEEKLY COLUMN IN LOCAL PAPER CONCERNING VARIOUS ASPECTS OF COLONIAL LIFE. (LOCAL). JEANINE M SCOTT, CHAIRMAN; NICEVILLE - VALPARAISO JUNIOR WOMAN'S CLUB; PO BOX 37; VALPARAISO, FL 32580. (#27595).

LECTURE & DISPLAY SERIES - VALPARAISO, FL. DISPLAY OF BOOKS; ART WORKS OF EACH PERIOD OF AMERICAN HISTORY. WITH EACH DISPLAY; A SLIDE LECTURE WAS PRESENTED IN CONJUNCTION WITH EACH DISPLAY. (LOCAL). LOUISE FITZGARRALD, COORDINATOR; VALPARAISO COMMUNITY LIBRARY; HWY 85; VALPARAISO, FL 32580. (#27597).

MARINE LIFE MUSEUM - VALPARAISO, FL. MUSEUM CONTAINING LIVE AND PRESERVED SPECIMENS OF MARINE LIFE FOUND BY SHRIMP BOATS AND FISHING BOATS IN LOCAL WATERS. (LOCAL). W FRANCIS SPENCE, CHAIRMAN; NICEVILLE - VALPARAISO CHAMBER OF COMMERCE; 153 EDGE AVE; VALPARAISO, FL 32580. (#27596).

MEDIAN SEGMENT BEAUTIFICATION - VALPARAISO, FL. PLANTED ONE LARGE MEDIAN TRIANGLE AND COORDINATED WITH THE FL DOT AND SEVERAL OTHER CIVIC CLUBS TO LANDSCAPE ALL THE MEDIAN SEGMENTS ON THE MAIN ROAD RUNNING THRU NICEVILLE & VALPARAISO. (LOCAL). REBECCA CORNETTE, CHAIRMAN; NICEVILLE - VALPARAISO JUNIOR WOMAN'S CLUB; PO BOX 277; VALPARAISO, FL 32580. (#27598).

PAINTING FIREPLUGS - VALPARAISO, FL. THE BICENTENNIAL COMMITTEE OF THE NICEVILLE - VALPARAISO JR WOMAN'S CLUB PAINTED ALL THE FIREPLUGS ON THE MAIN HIGHWAY RUNNING THRU NICEVILLE - VALPARAISO TO RESEMBLE REVOLUTIONARY SOLDIERS. (LOCAL). JEANINE M SCOTT, CHAIRMAN; NICEVILLE - VALPARAISO JUNIOR WOMAN'S CLUB; PO BOX 277; VALPARAISO, FL 32580. (#27599).

VENICE

JAN 25, '76. UNITED STATES ARMED FORCES BICENTENNIAL CARAVAN. CARAVAN IS COMPOSED OF EXHIBIT VANS FOR EACH MILITARY SERVICE. PROJECT THEME IS 'HISTORY OF THE ARMED FORCES AND THEIR CONTRIBUTIONS TO THE NATION'. (LOCAL). WILLIAM C MCFARLAND; US ARMED FORCES BICENTENNIAL EXHIBIT VANS PROJECT; PO BOX 937; VENICE, FL 33595. (#1775-425).

VERNON

MOSS HILL CHURCH BICENTENNIAL PROJECT, VERNON, FL. THE CHURCH WILL BE DESIGNATED AS PART OF THE BICENTENNIAL TRAIL IN FLORIDA. (LOCAL). TULLY BRIDENBACK, CHAIRWOMAN; WASHINGTON COUNTY ACTION '76 COMMITTEE; PO BOX 4; CHIPLEY, FL 32428. (#15049).

RAISING & RESTORATION OF MILLERS' FERRY, FL. THE FERRY WILL BE RAISED & PUT BACK INTO SERVICE. (LOCAL). TULLY BRIDENBACK, CHAIRWOMAN; WASHINGTON COUNTY ACTION '76 COMMITTEE; PO BOX 4; CHIPLEY, FL 32428. (#15050).

JULY 3 - 4, '76. JULY 4TH FESTIVAL. THE EVENTS WILL INCLUDE A PARADE, PICNIC, BASEBALL GAME, SKULLING RACE AND HORSESHOE PITCHING CONTEST. (LOCAL). TULLY BRIDENBACK, CHMN; WASHINGTON COUNTY BICENTENNIAL COMMITTEE; PO BOX 4; CHIPLEY, FL 32428. (#102214-1).

VERO BEACH

RESTORATION OF VERO BEACH WOMAN'S CLUB HOUSE, FL. THE OLDEST PUBLIC BUILDING, BUILT BY THE CLUB TO HOUSE THE ORIGINAL PUBLIC LIBRARY IN 1916, WILL BE RESTORED WITH A NEW ROOF, PLUMBING & WIRING AS WELL AS REDECORATION OF INSIDE AND A NEW GARDEN. (LOCAL). IRENE C MENSER, CO-CHAIRMAN; INDIAN RIVER BICENTENNIAL COMMITTEE; PO BOX 6296; VERO BEACH, FL 32960. (#15028).

W PALM BEACH

HERITAGE MUSIC FESTIVAL - WEST PALM BEACH, FL. THE PALM BEACH COUNTY ACTION '76 STEERING COMMITTEE IS SPONSORING A HERITAGE MUSIC FESTIVAL. (LOCAL). MRS E M RAY, VICE CHAIRMAN; PALM BEACH COUNTY ACTION '76 STEERING COMMITTEE; 5450 ESSEX CT; W APLM BEACH, FL 33405. (#27286). **ARBA GRANTEE.**

JAN 16 - FEB 14, '76. EXHIBIT- 'USA '76: THE FIRST 200 YEARS' IN WEST PALM BEACH, FLORIDA. THIS TRAVELING EXHIBIT PREPARED BY THE ARBA WILL TOUR 10 CITIES DURING THE BICENTENNIAL. IT EXPLORES THE CULTURAL AND SCIENTIFIC HERITAGE OF THE USA. (REGN'L). JACK MASEY; AMERICAN REVOLUTION BICENTENNIAL ADMINISTRATION; 2401 E STREET, NW; WASHINGTON, DC 20276. (#5661-506).

JAN 23 - FEB 1, '76. SOUTH FLORIDA FAIR & EXPOSITION. FAIR'S THEME: SAY HAPPY BIRTHDAY, AMERICAO MEMBER OF FLORIDA ARBA. AT FAIRGROUNDS, 9067 SOUTHERN BLVD. (ST-WIDE). WILLIAM C OCHS, CHMN; FESTIVAL COMMITTEE; PO BOX 15915; W PALM BEACH, FL 33406. (#200011-216).

MAY 14, '76. AMERICAN WIND SYMPHONY'S FLOATING ARTS CENTER VISITS W PALM BEACH. EMBARKING UPON A BICENTENNIAL CULTURAL TOUR, THE WIND SYMPHONY WILL VISIT 76 CITIES BRINGING MUSIC, DANCE, SYMPOSIA, AND CHILDREN'S THEATER TO THE WATERWAYS OF AMERICA DURING ITS 6-MONTH TOUR. (LOCAL). PAULA BERN, COORDINATOR; AMERICAN WIND SYMPHONY ORCHESTRA OF WESTERN PENNSYLVANIA; GATEWAY TOWERS 18G; PITTSBURGH, PA 15222. (#2800-7).

JULY 3 - 4, '76. 4TH OF JULY CELEBRATION. THE PARADE WILL ORIGINATE NEAR THE STADIUM & CONTINUE ON PALM BEACH LAKES BLVD TO THE WATER FRONT; FIREWORKS WILL BEGIN AT DUSK ON FLAGLER DRIVE AT THE WATERFRONT. AT MUNICIPAL STADIUM. (LOCAL). GWEN HANLEY, PROJ DIR; WEST PALM BEACH BICENTENNIAL COMMITTEE; 108 CIEMATIS ST; W PALM BEACH, FL 33401. (#105356-1).

SEPT 22 - ??, '76. ISRAELI PHILHARMONIC ORCHESTRA VISITS WEST PALM BEACH. LIVE PERFORMANCE. (INT'L). URI AHARON BARNEV; ISRAELI GOVERNMENT; 1621 21ST ST, NW; WASHINGTON, DC 20008. (#109015-19).

OCT 8, '76. HERITAGE MUSIC FESTIVAL. HISTORY THROUGH MUSIC - CLASSICS TO ROCK. AT WEST PALM BEACH AUDITORIUM. (LOCAL). MRS E M REY, VICE CHMN; PALM BEACH COUNTY ACTION '76 STEERING COMMITTEE; 5450 ESSEX CT; W PALM BEACH, FL 33405. (#27286-1).

WALDO

PROJECT '76 PARK, WALDO, FL. A RECREATIONAL FACILITY WILL BE ADDED TO WALDO AREA WITH PLAYGROUND EQUIPMENT, SHUFFLEBOARD COURT, GAMES, PARK BENCHES, SHRUBBERY, SHADE TREES, WATER FOUNTAIN & BATHROOM FACILITIES. (LOCAL). NELL BOSDWICK, CHAIRPERSON; WALDO BICENTENNIAL COMMITTEE; PO DRAWER B; WALDO, FL 32601. (#25254).

FEB 12, '76. WALDO'S ABE DAY. IN MEMORY OF ABRAHAM LINCOLN'S BIRTHDAY, THERE WILL BE A RAIL-SPLITTING CONTEST, APPLE PEELING, WOOD SAWING, SPITTING CONTESTS; ENTRANCE FEE $.50-ADULTS & $.25-CHILDREN. COFFEE, HOT CHOCOLATE, COOKIES AND DOUGHNUTS WILL BE AVAILABLE. WINNERS WILL RECEIVE TROPHIES. AT WALDO BASKETBALL COURT, HWY 24 N. (LOCAL). NELL E BOSTWICK, CHMN; WALDO BICENTENNIAL COMMITTEE; RT 1, BOX 46; GAINESVILLE, FL 32601. (#200011-207).

FEB 20, '76. OLD FASHIONED BARN DANCE. FOLK & SQUARE DANCING AND VIRGINIA REELS; OLD FASHIONED DRESS, LIVE ENTERTAINEMENT BY BAND, TROPHY FOR MALE AND FEMALE WITH MOST OLD FASHIONED OUTFITS. AT WALDO FIRE DEPARTMENT BUILDING. (LOCAL). NELL BOSTWICK, CHMN; WALDO BICENTENNIAL COMMITTEE; RT 1, BOX 46; GAINESVILLE, FL 32601. (#200011-208).

MAY 1, '76. WALDO'S MAY DAY FESTIVAL. FESTIVAL AT WALDO BASKETBALL COURT, HWY 24 N. (LOCAL). NELL E BOSTWICK, CHMN; WALDO BICENTENNIAL COMMITTEE; RT 1, BOX 46; GAINESVILLE, FL 32601. (#200011-209).

JUNE 19, '76. WATERMELON FESTIVAL. WATERMELON EATING AND SEED SPITTING CONTEST, COSTUME CONTEST, BEARD CONTEST, FISH FRY, BICENTENNIAL PRESIDENT AND FIRST LADY CONTEST, OLD FASHIONED DANCING DEMONSTRATION AND A STREET DANCE. AT BASKETBALL COURT, HWY 24, NORTH WALDO 71. (LOCAL). NELL E BOSTWICK, CHMN; WALDO BICENTENNIAL COMMITTEE; RT 1, BOX 46; GAINESVILLE, FL 32601. (#200011-210).

WAUCHULA

STREET DECORATION PROJ - BICENT THEME, FL. STREETS WILL BE DECORATED WITH '76 THEME IN RED, WHITE AND BLUE AND BICENTENNIAL FLAGS WILL BE PLACED ON UTILITY POLES. (LOCAL). CURTIS EZELLE, CHAIRMAN; HARDEE COUNTY BICENTENNIAL COMMITTEE & WAUCHULA KIWANIS; WAUCHULA, FL 33873. (#16204).

MAR 7, '76. HARDEE COUNTY PIONEER DAY CELEBRATION WITH MISS AMERICA. MISS AMERICA WILL BE THE MAIN SPEAKER AT AN ALL DAY PIONEER DAY CELEBRATION; SENATOR LAWTON CHILES WILL BE PRESENT ALSO. (LOCAL). CURTIS EZELLE, DIRECTOR; HARDEE COUNTY BICENTENNIAL COMMISSION; BOX 445; WAUCHULA, FL 33873. (#102787-1).

SEPT 21, '76. GOD AND COUNTRY SERVICE. CEREMONY. (LOCAL). CURTIS EZELL, DIRECTOR; HARDEE COUNTY BICENTENNIAL COMMITTEE; BOX 445; WACHULA, FL 33873. (#102787-2).

WAUSAU

AUG 6, '75. WAUSAU FUNDAY. FESTIVAL AT MAIN ST, HWY 77. (LOCAL). TULLY BRIDENBACK, CHMN; WAUSAU COMMUNITY DEVELOPMENT CLUB; PO BOX 4; CHIPLEY, FL 32428. (#200011-214).

WEST MIAMI

MAY 31, '76. 9TH ANNUAL MEMORIAL DAY PARADE. PARADE, FESTIVAL AT PARADE STARTS 5901 SW 16 ST, CONCERT AT PARK ON SW 16TH ST & 5TH AVE. (LOCAL). JIM SLAUGHTER, GEN CHMN; WEST MIAMI MEMORIAL DAY OBSERVANCE COMMITTEE; 6120 SW 16TH TERR; MIAMI, FL 33155. (#100748-1).

WHITE SPRINGS

SERIES OF AMERICAN FOLK MUSIC, WHITE SPRINGS, FL. A SERIES OF LIVE FOLK MUSIC PERFORMANCES. (LOCAL). LORRAINE KIEFER, COORDINATOR; STEPHEN FOSTER MEMORIAL; PO BOX 54; JASPER, FL 32052. (#28275). **ARBA GRANTEE.**

MAR 13, '76. '1776'. MUSICAL DRAMA 1776. AT AMPHITHEATER, STEPHEN FOSTER CENTER. (ST-WIDE). LILY DEMAS, COORD; LAKE CITY-COLUMBIA COUNTY FINE ARTS COUNCIL; PO BOX 1776; LAKE CITY, FL 32055. (#200011-215).

JULY 4, '76. FOURTH OF JULY CELEBRATION. FESTIVAL. (LOCAL). LORAINE KIEFER, CHMN; ACTION '76 COMMITTEE; 413 CENTRAL; WHITE SPRINGS, FL 32052. (#108394-1).

WILLISTON

BEAUTIFICATION, WILLISTON, FL. RED-WHITE-BLUE PLANTING AT PUBLIC BUILDINGS, POST OFFICE, WOMAN'S CLUB AND POTTED PLANTS ON STREETS. PERMANENT PLANTING OF TREES, SHRUBS, AZEALA, DAY LILLIES, ETC. (LOCAL). BARBARA SAPP, CHAIRMAN; WILLISTON BICENTENNIAL COMMITTEE; PO BOX Q; WILLISTON, FL 32696. (#31255).

CITY PARK, WILLISTON, FL. DEVELOP CITY PARK FROM WATER RETAINING AREA. BUILT PICNIC AREA, TENNIS COURTS, PLAYGROUND EQUIPMENT, LANDSCAPE, PLACED ANCIENT OIL BURNING GENERATOR IN PARK. (LOCAL). MARY WHEELER, CHAIRMAN; WILLISTON BICENTENNIAL COMMITTEE; PO BOX Q; WILLISTON, FL 32696. (#28244).

WILLISTON — CONTINUED

CREATION OF VILLAGE GREEN, WILLISTON, FL. UTILIZED A RAILROAD TRACK STRIP LOCATED IN CENTER OF TOWN FOR A PARKING LOT WITH FLOWER BEDS, GRASS, TREES & FOUNTAIN. (LOCAL). KATHREN WHEELER, CHAIRMAN; HISTORICAL & BEAUTIFICATION COMMITTEE; WILLISTON, FL 32696. (#31256).

FIRE STATION, WILLISTON, FL. BUILT NEW BUILDING TO HOUSE FIRETRUCKS WITH REVENUE SHARING MONEY. (LOCAL). DONALD TANNER, SUPERINTENDANT; WILLISTON BICENTENNIAL COMMITTEE; PO BOX Q; WILLISTON, FL 32696. (#28245).

FLAG HISTORY & PROTOCOL POSTER, WILLISTON, FL. POSTERS DONATED BY US MARINE CORP PLACED IN WINDOWS OF BUSINESS ESTABLISHMENTS & SCHOOLS. (LOCAL). BESS E WILLIAMS, CHMN; WILLISTON BICENTENNIAL COMMITTEE; WILLISTON, FL 32696. (#31257).

FURNISHING OF COMMUNITY CENTER, WILLISTON, FL. CENTER WAS FURNISHED WITH CHAIRS, CURTAINS AND OTHER FURNISHINGS. (LOCAL). BARBARA SAPP, CHAIRMAN; AARP AND POT POURRIE HOMEMAKING CLUB; WILLISTON, FL 32696. (#31254).

MURAL, WILLISTON, FL. MURAL DEPICTING BUGLE, FIFE & DRUM CORP WITH FLORIDA FLORA IN BACKGROUND BY LOCAL ARTIST, SIZE 8X16. HUNG FEB 20, 1976 ON WALL OF COMMUNITY CENTER OF THE CITY HALL. (LOCAL). BARBARA SAPP, CHAIRMAN; WILLISTON BICENTENNIAL COMMITTEE; PO BOX Q; WILLISTON, FL 32696. (#31252).

PAINTING OF HYDRANTS, WILLISTON, FL. CITY HYDRANTS PAINTED BY CHURCH YOUNG PEOPLE TO REPRESENT UNCLE SAM AND MINUTEMEN. (LOCAL). BESS E WILLIAMS, CHMN; WILLISTON BICENTENNIAL COMMITTEE; PO BOX Q; WILLISTON, FL 32696. (#31253).

POLICE HEADQUARTERS, WILLISTON, FL. COMPLETELY REMODELED OLD UNUSED JAIL INTO MODERN POLICE & COMMUNICATIONS CENTER WITH 24 HOUR SERVICE. NEW FACILITY FIRST TO BE USED EXCLUSIVELY AS POLICE HEADQUARTERS. (LOCAL). HON JACK HOY, MAYOR; WILLISTON BICENTENNIAL COMMITTEE; PO BOX 1776; WILLISTON, FL 32696. (#28246).

SPIRIT OF 1776-1976, WILLISTON, FL. FOLDED FLAG TOUCHED BY EACH SCHOOL CHILD GRADES THRU 8TH; CARRIED BY BSA FROM CITY TO ARCHER, FLA. PATRIOTIC SERVICES HELD ON ENTRY TO CITY FOLLOWED BY REFRESHMENTS & PARADE. VFW ASSISTED IN CEREMONIES. (LOCAL). BESS E WILLIAMS, CHMN; WILLISTON BICENTENNIAL COMMITTEE; PO BOX Q; WILLISTON, FL 32696. (#31251).

WILLISTON COMMUNITY CENTER, WILLISTON, FL. REMODELING OLD CITY HALL INTO MUCH NEEDED COMMUNITY CENTER FOR USE BY ALL ORGANIZATIONS AND GROUPS IN THE COMMUNITY. (LOCAL). C R BEVERLY, PRESIDENT; WILLISTON BICENTENNIAL COMMITTEE; PO BOX Q; WILLISTON, FL 32696. (#28247).

FEB 15 - OCT 25, '75. BICENTENNIAL EVENTS IN WILLISTON, 1975. 2/15, ELEMENTARY SCHOOL ART SHOW; 4/3 'I LOVE AMERICA' CANTATA; 4/17 PAUL REVERE DAY; 4/18-28 REVOLUTIONARY WAR PLAY; 10/25 PEANUT FESTIVAL; LEVY COUNTY BICENTENNIAL FAIR. (LOCAL). BESS E WILLIAMS, CHMN; WILLISTON BICENTENNIAL COMMITTEE & OTHER LOCAL GROUPS; PO BOX Q; WILLISTON, FL 32696. (#200011-303).

FEB 22, '75. DEDICATION OF WILLISTON COMMUNITY CENTER. CEREMONY. (LOCAL). C R BEVERLY, COORD; WILLISTON BICENTENNIAL COMMITTEE; WILLISTON, FL 32696. (#31261-1).

APR 5, '75. DEDICATION OF WILLISTON FIRE STATION. CEREMONY. (LOCAL). DONALD TANNER, SUPT; WILLISTON BICENTENNIAL COMMITTEE; WILLISTON, FL 32696. (#31259-1).

APR 5, '75. DEDICATION OF WILLISTON POLICE HEADQUARTERS. CEREMONY. (LOCAL). JACK HOY, COORD; WILLISTON BICENTENNIAL COMMITTEE; WILLISTON, FL 32696. (#31260-1).

FEB 22 - APR 10, '76. BICENTENNIAL EVENTS IN WILLISTON, FEBRUARY - APRIL, 1976. 2/22, HEART FUND DAY; 4/5-6, MINI ARTS & CRAFTS SHOW; 4/5 PRESENTATION OF BICENT CERTIFICATE & FLAG; 4/5-10, FESTIVAL '76 WEEK, WITH CANTATA, EXHIBITS, FISH FRY, RELIGIOUS SERVICES, ETC. (LOCAL). BESS E WILLIAMS, CHMN; WILLISTON BICENTENNIAL COMMITTEE & OTHER LOCAL GROUPS; PO BOX Q; WILLISTON, FL 32696. (#200011-304).

JULY 4, '76. 4TH OF JULY DEDICATION OF CITY PARK. CEREMONY. (LOCAL). BESS E WILLIAMS, CHMN; WILLISTON BICENTENNIAL COMMITTEE; WILLISTON, FL 32696. (#31258-1).

WILTON MANORS

BICENTENNIAL COMMITTEE OF WILTON MANORS, FL. ORGANIZATIONS, SCHOOLS, CHURCHES AND BUSINESS PEOPLE WILL GET TOGETHER FOR THIS PROJECT. (LOCAL). MRS GERALD F THOMPSON, CHAIRMAN; BICENTENNIAL COMMITTEE OF WILTON MANORS; 2633 NE 3RD AVE; WILTON MANORS, FL 33334. (#15784).

COLOHATCHEE NATURAL PARK, WILTON MANORS, FL. NATURAL PARK DEVELOPED AS RECREATION CENTER WITHOUT DISTURBING WILDLIFE AND TREES. (ST-WIDE). FRANK STARLING, CITY ADMINISTRATOR; CITY OF WILTON MANORS; 524 NE 21 CT; WILTON MANORS, FL 33305. (#15763).

COMMUNITY BICENTENNIAL QUILT, WILTON MANORS, FL. WILTON MANORS RESIDENTS WILL DESIGN & MAKE A SQUARE TO BE INCORPORATED INTO A QUILT TO BE ON DISPLAY & PRESENTED TO THE WILTON MANORS HISTORICAL SOCIETY FOR PERMANENT DISPLAY. (LOCAL). MRS RALPH TORTORA, COORDINATOR; WILTON MANORS BICENTENNIAL COMMITTEE; 2633 N E 3RD AVE; WILTON MANORS, FL 33334. (#25252).

HISTORY OF WILTON MANORS, FL. HISTORICAL ACHIEVEMENTS OF CITY PIONEERS CODIFIED IN CITY HISTORICAL BOOK. (LOCAL). ALICE SARGENT, PRESIDENT OF FRIENDS; FRIENDS OF THE LIBRARY AND HISTORICAL SOCIETY; 700 NE 21ST DR; WILTON MANORS, FL 33305. (#15765).

'TOWN MEETING ON WHEELS', WILTON MANORS, FL. A SURVEY WILL BE TAKEN ON ISSUES PERTINENT TO IMPROVING THE QUALITY OF LIFE IN AMERICA. (LOCAL). MARCIA STAFFORD, DIRECTOR; BROWARD COMMUNITY COLLEGE; 500 NE 25TH ST; WILTON MANORS, FL 33305. (#25251).

WILTON MANORS BICENTENNIAL FLAG, FL. THE WILTON MANORS BICENTENNIAL FLAG IS CURRENTLY BEING MADE. IT WILL BE PRESENTED TO THE MAYOR AT A CEREMONY & WILL BE HUNG AT CITY CHAMBERS. THE FLAG WAS DESIGNED BY LESLIE ROWNTREE. (LOCAL). JANE MOREY, COORDINATOR; WILTON MANORS MOTHERS COUNCIL; 2429 NE 7TH AVE; WILTON MANORS, FL 33305. (#25253).

WILTON MANORS HISTORICAL SOCIETY, FL. EXHIBIT DEPICTING BROWARD COUNTY HISTORICAL SITES, RECORDS, AND PIONEER ACHIEVEMENTS. (ST-WIDE). MRS GERALD F THOMPSON, PRESIDENT; WILTON MANORS HISTORICAL SOCIETY; 2633 N E 3RD AVE; WILTON MANORS, FL 33334. (#15764).

WILTON MANORS MEMORIAL PARK, FL. MEMORIAL PARK ON MILTON DR TO COMMEMORATE MILITARY PERSONNEL AND BICENTENNIAL. (LOCAL). EUGENE METZGER, CHAIRMAN; BEAUTIFICATION ASSOC; 2957 NW 12TH AVE; WILTON MANORS, FL 33310. (#15762).

OCT 25, '75. FRIENDS OF THE WILTON MANORS LIBRARY ANNUAL BOOK SALE. SPECIAL SECTION WILL BE SET UP FOR VALUABLE OLD BOOKS-SPECIALIST COMING TO APPRAISE AND HELP MARK PRICES. ANYONE CARING TO DONATE BOOKS MAY LEAVE THEN AT THE FIRE HALL EACH SATURDAY UNTIL SALE DATE. AT WILTON MANORS FIRE HALL, 22 ST & WILTON DR. (LOCAL). MRS ALICE SARGENT, COORD; FRIENDS OF THE LIBRARY WILTON MANORS; 700 NE 21 DR; WILTON MANORS, FL 33305. (#200011-213).

NOV 21, '75. BICENTENNIAL THANKSGIVING DINNER. POT-LUCK OLD FASHIONED THANKSGIVING DINNER; PLAN INTERESTING PROGRAM COMMEMORATING THE FIRST THANKSGIVING. AT KIWANIS CLUB/2749 N E 14 AVE. (LOCAL). ALICE SARGENT, PROJ DIR; WILTON MANORS FRIENDS OF THE LIBRARY; 700 N E 21 DR; WILTON MANORS, FL 33305. (#102566-1).

JAN 18, '76. ANNUAL ART & HOBBY SHOW HONORING OUR BICENTENNIAL. POSTER CONTEST/ELEMENTARY SCHOOL DEPICTING BICENTENNIAL AWARDS/EXHIBITS-PAINTING/SCULPTURE/CRAFTS/PLANTS/LEATHER/METAL/CAKES/HAND SEWING ETC. AT HAGEN PARK RECREATION HALL-ADJACENT TO CITY HALL 524 NE 21 COURT. (LOCAL). ALICE SARGENT, PROJ DIR; FRIENDS OF THE LIBRARY & W M SINAWIKS; 700 N E 21 DR; WILTON MANORS, FL 33305. (#102566-2).

APR 26 - MAY 1, '76. TOWN MEETING ON WHEELS. CONFERENCE AT CITY HALL, HAGEN PARK, W M SCHOOL. (LOCAL). MARCIA STAFFORD, COORD; BROWARD COMMUNITY COLLEGE; 500 NE 25TH ST; WILTON MANORS, FL 33305. (#200011-212).

JULY 17, '76. COLOHATCHEE BIRTHDAY PARTY, U S A. FESTIVAL AT COLOHATCHEE NATURAL PARK, 15TH AVE, AMPLE PARKING. (LOCAL). MRS ARTHUR WELLING, COORD; WILTON MANORS BICENTENNIAL COMMITTEE; 2608 N W 5TH AVE; WILTON MANORS, FL 33310. (#200011-228).

WINDERMERE

APR 25 - MAY 1, '76. HERITAGE AND HONOR AMERICA WEEK. A LOOK AT OUR HERITAGE AND CELEBRATION OF THE BICENTENNIAL AND WINDERMERE'S 51ST BIRTHDAY; WILL INCLUDE RELIGIOUS FESTIVAL, MERCHANTS DAY, COMMUNITY DAY, ANNIVERSARY DAY, PIONEER DAY AND HONOR AMERICA DAY. (LOCAL). ROLFE G ARNHYM, CHAIRMAN; ORANGE COUNTY BICENTENNIAL COMMITTEE; 423 S ORANGE AVE; ORLANDO, FL 32801. (#104608-1).

WINTER HAVEN

POOL OF PROGRAMS-SPEAKER'S BUREAU, FL. FILE OF OVER 50 PROGRAMS COVERING 4 THEME AREAS: REVOLUTIONARY PERIOD, AMERICANA, FLORIDA & WINTER HAVEN; THERE WILL BE SPEAKERS, ART, BOOK REVIEWS, EXHIBITS & DEMONSTRATIONS. (LOCAL). THELMA OENNING, CHAIRMAN; WINTER HAVEN BICENTENNIAL COMMITTEE; 815 6TH ST; WINTER HAVEN, FL 33880. (#15024).

TABLE DECORATIONS - WINTER HAVEN, FL. 12 CONESTOGA WAGONS AND 1 LARGE WAGON TO BE USED FOR BANQUETS AND LUNCHEON TABLE DECORATIONS; WAGONS MADE BY ROBERT GREENWALD, LOCAL ARTIST & CRAFTSMAN. (LOCAL). THELMA OENNING, CHAIRMAN; WINTER HAVEN BICENTENNIAL COMMITTEE; 815 6TH ST; WINTER HAVEN, FL 33880. (#15025).

MAR 17 - 21, '76. AMERICANA WEEK, A CELEBRATION OF AMERICAN HERITAGE. FESTIVAL ACTIVITIES INCLUDE A MUSICAL PANORAMA, BEARD GROWING CONTEST TALENT COMPETITION, FLOWER & FASHION SHOWS & THE RE-ENACTMENT THE BATTLE OF CONCORD. (LOCAL). BILL SUTTON, CHAIRMAN; BICENTENNIAL COMMITTEE - CITY OF WINTER HAVEN; PO BOX 1776; WINTER HAVEN, FL 33880. (#103416-73).

MAY 1 - 9, '76. FLORIDA WEEK, A WEEK DEDICATED TO FLORIDA'S HERITAGE. EXHIBIT, FESTIVAL. (ST-WIDE). SUNNY FRANKLIN, EXEC DIR; WINTER HAVEN BICENTENNIAL COMMITTEE; 316 W CENTRAL; WINTER HAVEN, FL 33880. (#104330-4).

JUNE 1 - 30, '76. CYPRESS GARDENS FESTIVAL MONTH. ACTIVITIES CELEBRATE THE BICENTENNIAL WITH A MONTH LONG FESTIVAL. AT CYPRESS GARDENS. (LOCAL). BERT LACEY, CHAIRMAN; CYPRESS GARDENS; WINTER HAVEN, FL 33880. (#103416-358).

JULY 3 - 4, '76. INDEPENDENCE DAY CELEBRATION. SATURDAY: GAMES, PICNIC AND FIREWORKS; SUNDAY: COMMUNITY CHURCH SERVICE. (LOCAL). SUNNY FRANKLIN, EXEC DIR; WINTER HAVEN BICENTENNIAL COMMITTEE; 316 W CENTRAL AVE; WINTER HAVEN, FL 33880. (#104330-2).

FEB 11 - 19, '77. CITRUS MACHINERY, PRODUCTS & MIDWAY. EXHIBIT, FESTIVAL. (LOCAL). DAVID R HINTON, GEN MGR; FLORIDA CITRUS SHOWCASE; 100 CYPRESS GARDENS BLVD, SW; WINTER HAVEN, FL 33880. (#108070-1).

WINTER PARK

DEC 6, '75. ANNUAL WINTER PARK CHRISTMAS PARADE. PARADE AT PARK AVE. (LOCAL). GRANT HUNT, CHMN; PARK AVENUE MERCHANTS ASSOC AND WINTER PARK JAYCEES; 750 S ORLANDO AVE; WINTER PARK, FL 32789. (#200011-211).

FEB 8 - 15, '76. FREEDOM WEEK CELEBRATION. FREEDOM WEEK WILL BEGIN & END WITH A RALLY AT SHOWALTER FIELD. THE CELEBRATION WILL GO ON ALL WEEK; BEGINNING RALLY AT 2/8 AT 2-4 PM AND ENDING RALLY ON 2/15 AT 2-3 PM. AT SHOWALTER FIELD, VARIOUS POINTS AND BUSINESS FIRMS. (ST-WIDE). GRANT HUNT, BICENT CHMN; WINTER PARK CHAMBER OF COMMERCE; 750 S ORLANDO AVE; WINTER PARK, FL 32789. (#104002-5).

MAR 19 - 21, '76. ANNUAL SIDEWALK ART FESTIVAL. FESTIVAL AT PARK AVE. (LOCAL). GRANT HUNT, CHMN; WINTER PARK ART FESTIVAL COMMITTEE; 750 S ORLANDO AVE; WINTER PARK, FL 32789. (#104354-1).

MAY 15, '76. ARMED FORCES DAY CELEBRATION. PARADE AT PARK AVENUE AND U S NAVAL TRAINING CENTER. (LOCAL). GRANT HUNT, BICENT CHMN; YMCA; 750 S ORLANDO AVE; WINTER PARK, FL 32789. (#104002-2).

OCT 16 - 17, '76. WINTER PARK FOUNDERS DAY CELEBRATION. FESTIVAL, PARADE, LIVE PERFORMANCE AT VARIOUS POINTS THROUGHOUT WINTER PARK; CENTERED IN CENTRAL PARK. (LOCAL). GRANT HUNT, BICENT CHMN; WINTER PARK JAYCEES; 750 S ORLANDO AVE; WINTER PARK, FL 32789. (#104002-1).

WINTER SPG

COMMUNITY PARK & BUILDING - WINTER SPRINGS, FL. CONSTRUCTION OF COMMUNITY BLDG AND OPEN PAVILLION, CLEAR 12 ACRE PARK AREA AND ESTABLISH PICNIC AREAS & NATURE TRAILS IN NATURAL FOREST; RENOVATE EXISTING SPORTS FACILITIES & INSTALL '76 MONUMENT. (LOCAL). JOHN DANIELS, COUNCILMAN; COMMUNITY ASSOCIATION/CITY OF WINTER SPRINGS; 1027 ANTELOPE TRAIL; WINTER SPG, FL 32701. (#15060).

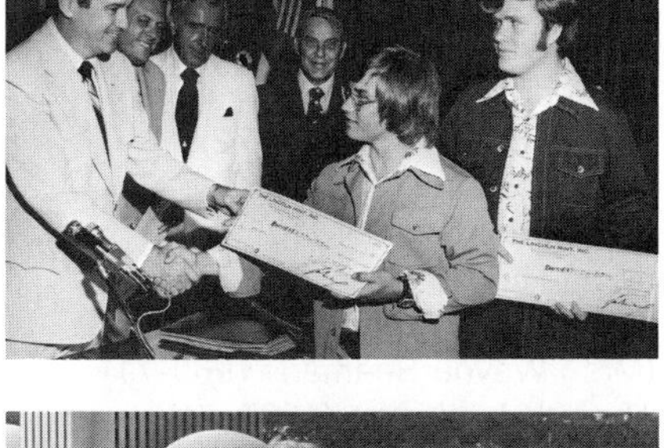

Georgia

Theme: 200 Years of Georgia Days to Remember

Georgia Commission for the National Bicentennial Celebration

Commissioned by the State Legislature in April 1969 by House Resolution No. 251-705; recreated and reestablished by the State Legislature in March 1973 by House Bill 926, Act No. 187

ARBA Statistics

Officially Recognized
Communities—145
Colleges/Universities—23
Military Installations—12
BINET Projects—777
Events—739
1976 Population—4,970,000

Bicentennial Archives

Department of Archives and History
330 Capitol Avenue, S.E.
Atlanta, Georgia 30334

Membership

Harold Clarke (1969-70)
Alan Gaynor (1969-73, 1975-)
Reginald Maxwell, Jr. (1969-70)
Richard M. Scarlett (1969-70)
Albert Thompson (1969-72)
John R. Riley (1969-)
Billy Adams (1969-72)
Jack Hardy (1969-70)
William Searcy (1969-72)
Edward Zipperer (1969-74)
W. B. Withers (1969-71, 1973-)
Jim Aldredge (1969-71)
Leodel Coleman (1969-72)
Ed Y. Chapin (1969-71)
C. S. "Bo" Coogler (1969-72)
(Mrs.) Harold Tuthill (1969-70)
Dr. Kenneth Coleman (1969-)
(Mrs.) Wayne Seaman (1969-71)
Thomas Linthicum (1969-71)
Ernest Key (1969-72)
Clifford M. Clarke (1969-75)
Edward W. Hiles (1969-70)
Martha Cooper (1971)
Bert Hamilton (1972-)
(Mrs.) Gerald Fling (1972)
Trammell Carmichael (1972-)
G. Harold Northrop (1972-)
J. C. Porterfield (1972)
Roy Chalker, Jr. (1972-76)
Jack Williams (1972)
E. Vince Moyer (1973-74)
Arthur Gignilliat (1971-)
Donald Fraser (1973-74)
Canute Richardson (1973-74)
Frank Underwood (1973-)
Frank Pruet (1973-74)
(Mrs.) Arthur Waite (1973-)
W. David Padgett (1973-75)
Dr. William Gabard (1973-)
William E. Blair (1973-)
Joseph H. Brown (1973-)
A. Lester Henderson (1973-)
George A. Mercer (1973-)
Paul Raymon (1973-74)
Vernon Martin (1973-)
Frank Bailey, Jr. (1975-)
Billy Milford (1975-)
Floyd Hudgins (1975-)
Gene Dyson (1975-)
John Melton (1975-)
Sue Jackson (1975-)
Jean Hendrix (1975-)
E. G. Summers (1975-)
Mell Traylor (1975-)
Preston B. Lewis, Jr. (1975-)
Dr. James C. Bonner (1975-)
John Adams (1975-)
Richard A. Dent (1975-)
John Hawkins (1975-)
H. Franklin Fling (1975-)
Janet Merritt (1971-72)
Matthew Mulherin (1971-72)
Ben W. Fortson, Jr. (1969-)
Lou Truman (1969-75)
Carroll Hart (1969-)
Mary Gregory Jewett (1969-75)
George Busbee (1975-)
Zell Miller (1975-)
Tom Murphy (1975-)
Tommy Irvin (1975-)
George Beattie (1973-75)
John Bitterman (1975-)
Dr. Jack Nix (1973-)
Milton Folds (1975-)
Joe D. Tanner (1973-)
Downing Musgrove (1973-75)
Thomas Moreland (1975-)
James McIntyre, Jr. (1973-)
Dr. George L. Simpson, Jr. (1973-)
Colonel J. H. Cofer (1975-)
Major General Billy M. Jones (1975-)
Arthur Bolton (1969-72)

Staff

A. K. Johnson, Jr., *executive director* (1973-)

Georgia

Georgia, an "American original," is indeed a better place to live, to visit and to experience as a result of its people-oriented participation in our nation's Bicentennial.

Cities and towns across the state united in a commitment to bring all elements of a community together, working toward common goals. To achieve these goals, 196 local Bicentennial committees were established around the state. Parks were built, new libraries constructed, restorations completed—the entire community participated.

"People participation" was the key element to the success of the state's major Bicentennial project, the *Georgia Heritage Special.* This unique traveling rail exhibit was designed by University of Georgia art and interior design students and featured displays and stories of colonial Georgia history. The train was staffed by retired senior volunteers from throughout the state. Over 250,000 Georgians in 27 communities viewed the train during its six month tour. The Heritage Special got everyone involved and helped the Georgia Bicentennial commission realize its dream of taking the Bicentennial to the people.

The Bicentennial also provided Georgians a unique opportunity to examine and appreciate the past, assess the present and plan for the future. Georgia Archives Traveling Exhibit Service (GATES) was established to provide exhibits on various topics relating to colonial Georgia. DISCOVERY involved students and teachers in folklore and local history projects. Our heritage was commemorated with the reinterment in Augusta of Colonel William Few, one of Georgia's two signers of the Constitution.

The present was celebrated with a festive opening day of the 1976 Georgia General Assembly, featuring costumed legislators and historical vignettes and speeches by Governor George D. Busbee and ARBA Administrator John W. Warner. Major shopping malls sponsored Bicentennial exhibits and displays. Citizens participated in the traditional parades, barbecues and other activities.

Commitment '76 asked individuals, businesses, civic clubs and other organizations to plan for the future by accomplishing something worthwhile as their gift to America on her 200th birthday. High school seniors set goals for America's third century at a Bicentennial Youth Congress. A drive to register 200,000 new voters by 1976 was endorsed. College students got involved through the *Bicentennial Intern Program* and earned college credit for work on Bicentennial projects. Participation in Bicentennial activities earned youngsters a patch through the *Georgia '76er* program.

People became involved, and an overview of how they participated is found in the documentary film, *For Generations to Come.*

Georgians of today, like their forefathers, take active roles in the events that shape their lives. Through thousands of programs at both the state and community level, they accepted the challenge of the Bicentennial—to make century three USA an even better place to live.

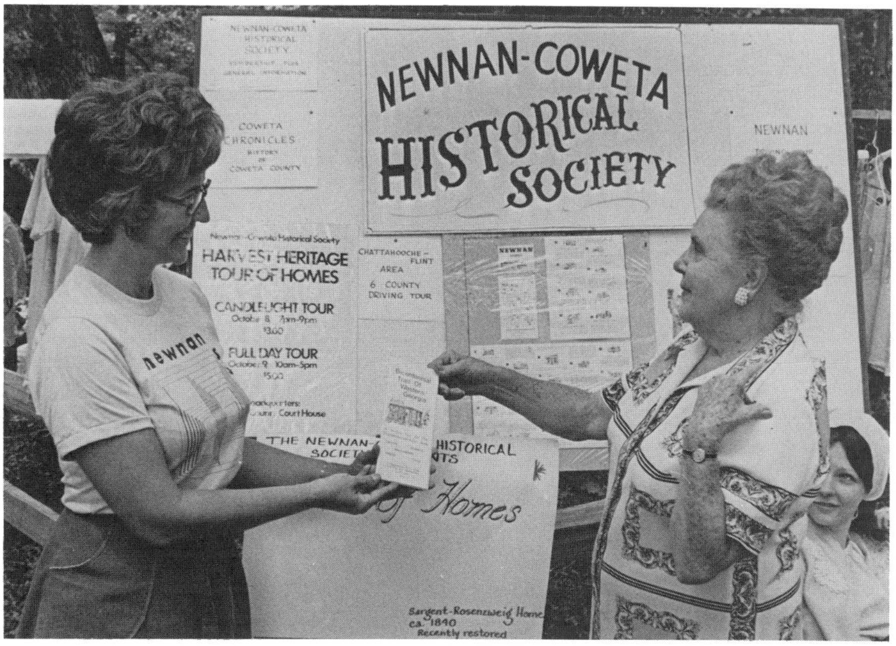

ADAIRSVILLE

AUG 30 - SEPT 1, '75. THE GREAT LOCOMOTIVE CHASE FESTIVAL. FESTIVAL, LIVE PERFORMANCE AT PUBLIC SQUARE, ADAIRSVILLE. (REGN'L). DOT QUILLIAN, CHAIRPERSON; ADAIRSVILLE SHRINE CLUB; BOX 70; CARTERSVILLE, GA 30120. (#102074-1).

ALAMO

FLAG DISPLAY - ALAMO, GA. DISPLAY OF 13 ORIGINAL STATE FLAGS, THE BENNINGTON FLAG & THE U S FLAG DURING 1976. (LOCAL). THOMAS OWENS, CHAIRMAN; CITY OF ALAMO; PO BOX 577; ALAMO, GA 30411. (#23781). **ARBA GRANTEE.**

ALBANY

AMERICANA: FILMS, LECTURES & RECITALS FEATURING AMERICAN AUTHORS. SEMINAR, LIVE PERFORMANCE. (LOCAL). ROBERT E CARLILE, COORD; ALBANY JUNIOR COLLEGE; 2400 GILLIONVILLE RD; ALBANY, GA 31707. (#106435-2).

BICENTENNIAL FLAG PAGEANT, ALBANY, GA. THE U S MARINE CORPS WILL PARTICIPATE IN A BICENTENNIAL SALUTE TO THE U S FLAG. (LOCAL). JAMES J ST CLAIR, PROJ COORDINATOR; U S MARINE CORPS; HQ BN MCLSB LANT; ALBANY, GA 31704. (#29681).

BLACK FOCUS 2000 - ALBANY STATE COLLEGE - GA. COLLECTION OF BOOKS WRITTEN BY BLACKS ABOUT GEORGIA TO BE ADDED TO CONTINUOUSLY SO AS TO ENCOURAGE BLACK STUDENTS IN THE FIELD OF LITERATURE. (LOCAL). MRS LAURA TRIPLETT, PROJ DIRECTOR; ALBANY STATE COLLEGE BICENTENNIAL COMMITTEE; COLLEGE DR; ALBANY, GA 31705. (#13608).

BLACK MUSIC COLLECTION - ALBANY STATE COLLEGE - GA. MUSIC COMPOSED BY BLACKS IN THE U S WILL BE PUT IN A PERMANENT, GROWING COLLECTION. (LOCAL). MRS LAURA TRIPLETT, PROJ DIRECTOR; ALBANY STATE COLLEGE BICENTENNIAL COMMITTEE; COLLEGE DR; ALBANY, GA 31705. (#13606).

CHRISTMAS CONCERT - ALBANY STATE COLLEGE. ALBANY STATE COLLEGE & ALBANY JR COLLEGE WILL COMBINE THEIR TALENTS IN A JOINT CONCERT AT THE MUNICIPAL BUILDING IN ALBANY. (LOCAL). MRS LAURA TRIPLETT, PROJ DIRECTOR; ALBANY STATE COLLEGE BICENTENNIAL COMMITTEE; COLLEGE DR; ALBANY, GA 31705. (#13604).

FESTIVAL OF ARTS - ALBANY STATE COLLEGE - GA. NATIVE FOLK DANCES, ART, SYMPHONY CONCERTS, DRAMATIC PRESENTATIONS AND CRAFT EXPOSITIONS. (LOCAL). MRS LAURA TRIPLETT, PROJ DIRECTOR; ALBANY STATE COLLEGE BICENTENNIAL COMMITTEE; COLLEGE DR; ALBANY, GA 31705. (#13609).

LECTURE COURSE: 'WE, THE INHERITORS', ALBANY, GA. FIVE LECTURES ON PRINCIPLES OF REVOLUTION, INCLUDING: ROOTS OF IDEOLOGY, MEANING OF INDEPENDENCE, FRAMING OF CONSTITUTION, IMPACT OF AMERICAN REVOLUTION & THE CONTINUING REVOLUTION IN AMERICA TODAY. (LOCAL). STELLA DAVIS, CHAIRMAN; ALBANY-DOUGHERTY COUNTY BICENTENNIAL COMMITTEE; PO BOX 308; ALBANY, GA 31702. (#11008). **ARBA GRANTEE.**

MODE 1975-76 - ALBANY, GA. MAGAZINE COVERS SPECIALLY DESIGNED WITH BICENTENNIAL THEME AND MESSAGES FROM ELECTED OFFICIALS. (LOCAL). J LARRY CREAMER, COORDINATOR STUDENT ACTIVITIES; ALBANY JUNIOR COLLEGE; 2400 GILLIONVILLE RD; ALBANY, GA 31707. (#23329).

MUSICAL BICENTENNIAL CELEBRATION FEATURING AMERICAN COMPOSERS. LIVE PERFORMANCE. (LOCAL). F DALE GRABILL, DIRECTOR; ALBANY JUNIOR COLLEGE SYMPHONIC BAND; 2400 GILLIONVILLE RD; ALBANY, GA 31707. (#106521-2). **(??).**

NATIONAL PECAN FESTIVAL IN ALBANY, GA. THE NATIONAL PECAN FESTIVAL IN ALBANY, GA WILL INCLUDE A HISTORY OF PECANS. (LOCAL). MRS SARA TERRELL, PROJ DIRECTOR; NATIONAL PECAN FESTIVAL INC; PO BOX 308; ALBANY, GA 31702. (#13849).

OPEN AIR CONCERT - ALBANY STATE COLLEGE - GA. RAY CHARLES & RAY STEVENS WILL PERFORM AT THE OPEN AIR FESTIVAL. (LOCAL). MRS LAURA TRIPLETT, PROJ DIRECTOR; ALBANY STATE COLLEGE BICENTENNIAL COMMITTEE; COLLEGE DR; ALBANY, GA 31705. (#13607).

PHI THETA KAPPA STATE CONVENTION. ALBANY JUNIOR COLLEGE PLAYS HOST TO PHI THETA KAPPA STATE CONVENTION WITH A SERIES OF BICENTENNIAL PROGRAMS. (ST-WIDE). BRADFORD SEARS, ADVISOR; ALBANY JUNIOR COLLEGE & PHI THETA KAPPA; 2400 GILLIONVILLE RD; ALBANY, GA 31707. (#106521-3). **(??).**

STUDENT HANDBOOK - ALBANY, GA. 1975-76 STUDENT HANDBOOK WILL FEATURE PHOTOGRAPHS OF STUDENTS VISITING HISTORICAL SITES IN PHILADELPHIA. (LOCAL). J LARRY CREAMER, COORDINATOR STUDENT ACTIVITIES; ALBANY JUNIOR COLLEGE; 2400 GILLIONVILLE RD; ALBANY, GA 31707. (#23330).

A STUDY OF JULIAN L HARRIS. A BIOGRAPHICAL STUDY OF JOURNALIST JULIAN L HARRIS, 1874-1963. (NAT'L). RONALD BERMAN CHAIRMAN; NATIONAL ENDOWMENT FOR THE HUMANITIES; 806 15TH ST, NW; WASHINGTON, DC 20506. (#4234). **(??).**

'THIS IS OUR COUNTRY' - HOMECOMING - ALBANY, GA. GAME, PARADE, DECORATIONS, FLOATS & BALLS WILL CENTER AROUND THE BICENTENNIAL THEME. (LOCAL). MRS LAURA TRIPLETT, PROJ DIRECTOR; ALBANY STATE COLLEGE BICENTENNIAL COMMITTEE; COLLEGE DR; ALBANY, GA 31705. (#13605).

'1776' - PROJ OF ALBANY STATE COLLEGE - GA. BROADWAY MUSICAL CONCERNING THE SIGNING OF THE CONSTITUTION WILL BE PRESENTED. (LOCAL). MRS LAURA TRIPLETT, PROJ DIRECTOR; ALBANY STATE COLLEGE BICENTENNIAL COMMITTEE; COLLEGE DR; ALBANY, GA 31705. (#13610).

SEPT 18 - 21, '75. ARTS & CRAFTS, COOKING CONTEST AND WOMEN'S GOLF TOURNAMENT. FESTIVAL, PARADE, EXHIBIT. (LOCAL). MRS SARA TERRELL; NATIONAL PECAN FESTIVAL INC; PO BOX 308; ALBANY, GA 31702. (#13849-501).

SEPT 18 - 21, '75. NATIONAL PECAN FESTIVAL. FESTIVAL. (LOCAL). MRS SARA TERRELL, CHMN; NATIONAL PECAN FESTIVAL, INC; PO BOX 308; ALBANY, GA 31702. (#101888-1).

SEPT 19, '75. MEETING OF PECAN GROWERS - LUNCH & FASHION SHOW. THE NATIONAL PECAN FESTIVAL IN ALBANY, GA WILL INCLUDE A HISTORY OF PECANS. (LOCAL). MRS SARA TERRELL; NATIONAL PECAN FESTIVAL INC; PO BOX 308; ALBANY, GA 31702. (#13849-502).

SEPT 20, '75. PARADE, ANTIQUE CAR SHOW AND MEN'S GOLF TOURNAMENT. FESTIVAL, PARADE, EXHIBIT. (LOCAL). MRS SARA TERRELL; NATIONAL PECAN FESTIVAL INC; PO BOX 308; ALBANY, GA 31702. (#13849-503).

DEC 9, '75 - FEB 3, '76. 'WE THE INHERITORS' - HERITAGE PROGRAMS. ROBIN WINKS: 12/9/75; ALBERT SAYE: 1/13/76; GWENDOLEN CARTER: 2/3/76. AT 1/13/76 - ALBANY HIGH SCHOOL; 2/3/76 - WESTOVER HIGH SCHOOL.. (LOCAL). STELLA DAVIS, CHAIRMAN; ALBANY-DOUGHERTY BICENTENNIAL COMMITTEE; 501 N SLAPPEY BLVD; ALBANY, GA 31702. (#103709-2).

DEC 12, '75. ALBANY STATE/ALBANY JR COLLEGE CHRISTMAS CONCERT. LIVE PERFORMANCE. (LOCAL). LAURA TRIPLETT; ALBANY STATE COLLEGE BICENTENNIAL COMMITTEE; COLLEGE DRIVE; ALBANY, GA 31705. (#104018-1).

JAN 30 - 31, '76. MUSICAL 1776. LIVE PERFORMANCE. (LOCAL). LAURA TRIPLETT; ALBANY STATE COLLEGE BICENTENNIAL COMMITTEE; COLLEGE DRIVE; ALBANY, GA 31705. (#104018-2).

FEB 3, '76. FROM INDEPENDENCE TO INTERDEPENDENCE. CLASS VISITS AND A LECTURE & DISCUSSION BY AN AMERICAN POLITICAL SCIENTIST. (LOCAL). DAVID HEWETT, PROJ CHMN; ALBANY JUNIOR COLLEGE; 2400 GILLIONVILLE RD; ALBANY, GA 31707. (#106435-1).

FEB 23 - 27, '76. HISTORICAL SPEECHES. SPEECHES TO BE PRESENTED BY SPEECH & DRAMA STUDENTS. (LOCAL). LAURA TRIPLETT; ALBANY STATE COLLEGE BICENTENNIAL COMMITTEE; COLLEGE DRIVE; ALBANY, GA 31705. (#104018-3).

FEB '76. MISS AMERICA PAGEANT PRELIMINARY W/ THIS IS OUR COUNTRY THEME. COMPETITION, FESTIVAL. (LOCAL). J LARRY CREAMER, COORD; ALBANY JUNIOR COLLEGE STUDENT GOVERNMENT ASSOC; 2400 GILLIONVILLE RD; ALBANY, GA 31707. (#106521-1).

MAR 19, '76. OPEN AIR CONCERT. PERFORMANCES BY RAY CHARLES & RAY STEVENS. (LOCAL). LAURA TRIPLETT; ALBANY STATE COLLEGE BICENTENNIAL COMMITTEE; COLLEGE DRIVE; ALBANY, GA 31705. (#104018-4).

APR 1 - 29, '76. 'IN SEARCH OF LIBERTY' - 5 BICENTENNIAL STUDIES. THESE FIVE STUDIES ARE DESIGNED TO STIMULATE THOUGHT & DIALOGUE. EACH STUDY IS DESIGNED TO GIVE PARTICIPANTS THE OPPORTUNITY TO HEAR AN OUTSTANDING LECTURER, TO REACT TO COMMENTS OF AN INFORMED PANEL, & TO SHARE IN THE PERSONAL REFLECTIONS OF THOSE ATTENDING. AT ROOM 205, COLLEGE UNION BLDG, ALBANY JUNIOR COLLEGE. (LOCAL). PROF WILLIAM MUGLESTON; ALBANY JUNIOR COLLEGE; 2400 GILLIONVILLE RD; ALBANY, GA 31707. (#106521-4).

APR 14 - 16, '76. FESTIVAL OF BLACK CULTURE. THE VARIOUS DEPARTMENTS ON CAMPUS DESIGNED TO ILLUSTRATE DIFFERENT ELEMENTS OF BLACK CULTURE IN AMERICA WILL COOPERATE ON THIS EFFORT. AT CUL DE SAC AND THE COLLEGE MALL COLLEGE DRIVE. (LOCAL). LAURA TRIPLETT; ALBANY STATE COLLEGE BICENTENNIAL COMMITTEE; COLLEGE DRIVE; ALBANY, GA 31705. (#104018-5).

APR 14 - 18, '76. HERITAGE SPECIAL - TRAIN TOUR. TRAVELING RAIL EXHIBIT EMPHASIZING COLONIAL & REVOLUTIONARY GEORGIA HISTORY, CRAFTS & LIFESTYLE OF GEORGIA COLONISTS. EXHIBITS WILL BE DISPLAYED WITH COMBINATION OF SIGHT & SOUND ACTIVITY. (ST-WIDE). RON HENRY, COORDINATOR; GEORGIA AGRIRAMA DEVELOPMENT AUTHORITY/GEORGIA BICENTENNIAL; 8TH ST A I 75; TIFTON, GA 31794. (#7999-23).

JULY 4, '76. 'ONE NATION UNDER GOD' - ECUMENICAL SERVICE. SERVICE HONORING FREEDOM OF RELIGION. AT STADIUM. (LOCAL). REV CHARLES DONNELL, CHMN; MINISTERIAL ASSOCIATION; 216 W EDGEWATER DR; ALBANY, GA 31707. (#103709-1).

JULY 5, '76. PARADE FOR INDEPENDENCE. PARADE. (LOCAL). EDWARD FREEMAN, PROJ DIR; DOUGHERTY KIWANIS CLUB; 100 N WASHINGTON ST; ALBANY, GA 31701. (#103709-3).

OCT 1 - 5, '76. HERITAGE SPECIAL - TRAIN TOUR. TRAVELING RAIL EXHIBIT EMPHASIZING COLONIAL AND REVOLUTIONARY GEORGIA HISTORY, CRAFTS & LIFESTYLE OF GEORGIA COLONISTS. EXHIBITS WILL BE DISPLAYED WITH COMBINATION OF SIGHT & SOUND ACTIVITY. AT DEPOT. (LOCAL). RON HENRY, DIRECTOR; GEORGIA BICENTENNIAL COMMISSION; 1776 PEACHTREE NW, ROOM 520 S; ATLANTA, GA 30309. (#7999-32).

DEC 9 - 10, '76. UNITED STATES ARMED FORCES BICENTENNIAL CARAVAN. CARAVAN IS COMPOSED OF EXHIBIT VANS FOR EACH MILITARY SERVICE. PROJECT THEME IS 'HISTORY OF THE ARMED FORCES & THEIR CONTRIBUTIONS TO THE NATION'. AT MIDTOWN SHOPPING CENTER PARKING LOT, CORNER OF SLAPPEY BLVD & BROAD. (LOCAL). WILLIAM I WILLIAMS; MILITARY AFFAIRS COMM OF THE ALBANY CHAMBER OF COMMERCE; PO BOX 308; ALBANY, GA 31702. (#1775-784).

ALPHARETTA

THE COLONISTS APPEAR IN ALPHARETTA, GEORGIA. THE COLONISTS MUSIC GROUP WILL PERFORM EARLY AMERICAN MUSIC ON DULCIMER, ETC. (LOCAL). LEON COLE, JR, DIRECTOR; MILTON HIGH SCHOOL; ALPHARETTA, GA 30201. (#10168). **ARBA GRANTEE.**

HISTORY OF ALPHARETTA, GA. A PRINTED BOOKLET COVERING THE HISTORY OF ALPHARETTA FROM 1831-1976. (LOCAL). CLEO CUNNINGHAM, COORDINATOR; ALPHARETTA WOMAN'S CLUB; 134 COLD CREEK DR; ALPHARETTA, GA 30201. (#22059).

LOG CABIN RESTORATION, ALPHARETTA, GA. RESTORED LOG CABIN ON MILTON AVENUE IS NOW OPEN TO THE PUBLIC FOR TOURS. CONTAINS HISTORICAL OBJECTS PERTAINING TO OUR HERITAGE. (LOCAL). CLEO CUNNINGHAM, COORDINATOR; ALPHARETTA WOMAN'S CLUB; 134 COLD CREEK DR; ALPHARETTA, GA 30201. (#22058).

MINI-PARK IN ALPHARETTA, GA. RESTORING THE SITE OF THE OLD HOTEL WHICH WAS BUILT IN 1903 INTO A MINI-PARK; FLOWERS AND TREES WILL BE PLANTED, BENCHES AND A BANDSTAND CONSTRUCTED AND A COMMEMORATIVE MARKER WILL BE ERECTED. (LOCAL). CLEO CUNNINGHAM, COORDINATOR; ALPHARETTA WOMAN'S CLUB; 134 COLD CREEK DR; ALPHARETTA, GA 30201. (#22060).

NOV 25, '75 - NOV 26, '76. SWISS DAIRY OPERATION AND FESTIVAL. FESTIVAL. (ST-WIDE). A K JOHNSON, EXEC DIR; GEORGIA COMMISSION FOR THE NATIONAL BICENTENNIAL CELEBRATION; 1776 PEACHTREE ST; ATLANTA, GA 30309. (#26429-5).

MAY 29, '76. BICENTENNIAL PARADE & FESTIVAL. FESTIVAL INCLUDES ARTS & CRAFTS, GAMES, FOOD, MUSIC AND THE FINALE, 'I LOVE AMERICA' PRESENTED BY CRABAPPLE BABTIST CHURCH CHOIR AT 9 PM WITH FIREWORKS. AT FOLLOWING PARADE, ALL ACTIVITIES HELD AT WILLS PARK. (LOCAL). CLEO CUNNINGHAM, COORD; ALPHARETTA WOMAN'S CLUB; CITY OF ALPHARETTA; 134 COLD CREEK DR; ALPHARETTA, GA 30201. (#105811-1).

MAY 30, '76. SUNDAY NIGHT CHURCH SERVICES. ALL CHOIRS AND CHURCHES TOGETHER FOR WORSHIP AT 7:30 PM AT MILTON HIGH SCHOOL STADIUM TO CLOSE THE FESTIVITIES OF ALPHARETTA'S BICENTENNIAL CELEBRATION. AT MILTON HIGH SCHOOL STADIUM. (LOCAL). CLEO CUNNINGHAM, COORD; ALPHARETTA WOMAN'S CLUB; CITY OF ALPHARETTA; 134 COLD CREEK DR; ALPHARETTA, GA 30201. (#105811-2).

ANDERSONVILLE

ANDERSONVILLE HISTORIC MARKERS, GA. PREPARATION OF HISTORICAL MARKERS FOR SELECTED SITES IN HISTORIC ANDERSONVILLE WITH DOCUMENTED SIGNIFICANCE; WILL AID TOURISTS. (LOCAL). HON LEWIS EASTERLIN, MAYOR; CITY OF ANDERSONVILLE; PO BOX 36; ANDERSONVILLE, GA 31711. (#26959). **ARBA GRANTEE.**

JAN 1 - DEC 31, '76. PICTURE DISPLAY OF AREA FROM PAST TO PRESENT-ANDERSONVILLE NHS. THESE TALKS DEAL WITH THE MOVEMENT FOR INDEPENDENCE AND THE AMERICAN REVOLUTION, AND RELEVANCE OF THOSE IDEAS & CONCEPTS TO MODERN TIMES. (REGN'L). ANDERSONVILLE NHP; NATIONAL PARK SERVICE; ANDERSONVILLE, GA 31711. (#6730-107).

JUNE 29, '76. NATL PK SVC '...A LITTLE LOOK AROUND' VISITS ANDERSONVILLE NHS. THIS SHORT PROGRAM FEATURES ACTORS PORTRAYING FAMOUS AMERICANS OF THE PAST WHO'VE RETURNED TO SEE AMERICA'S PROGRESS. (REGN'L). ANDERSONVILLE N H S; NATIONAL PARK SERVICE; ANDERSONVILLE, GA 31711. (#5653-86).

OCT 2 - 3, '76. HISTORIC FAIR. FESTIVAL, PARADE, FAIR. (LOCAL). DIRECTOR; SUMTER COUNTY BICENTENNIAL COMMITTEE & CHAMBER OF COMMERCE; AMERICUS, GA 31709. (#109414-1).

ARLINGTON

ARLINGTON BICENTENNIAL PARK OF GEORGIA. BICENTENNIAL PARK WITH RECREATION FACILITIES, AMPHITHEATER ETC., TO SERVE AS A FOCAL POINT FOR COMMUNITY ACTIVITIES. (LOCAL). MRS L MITCHELL CONNER, CHAIRMAN; ARLINGTON BICENTENNIAL COMMISSION; PO BOX 310, 218 HIGHLAND AVE; ARLINGTON, GA 31713. (#693). **ARBA GRANTEE.**

MAY 1 - 2, '76. 45TH ANNUAL MAY FESTIVAL. FESTIVAL, PARADE, EXHIBIT AT DOWNTOWN ARLINGTON AND LORO TURNER BOSTWICK PARK. (LOCAL). MRS L MITCHELL CONNER; ARLINGTON HORIZON CLUB; PO BOX 310; ARLINGTON, GA 31313. (#50311-1).

ASHBURN

PRESERVATION OF 'THE WIREGRASS FARMER', GA. MICROFILMING & ENCASING IN PLASTIC OLD, HISTORICAL COPIES OF THE LOCAL NEWSPAPER 'THE WIREGRASS FARMER.'. (LOCAL). J E SEGO, CHAIRMAN; TURNER COUNTY COMMISSION; TURNER COUNTY COURTHOUSE; ASHBURN, GA 31714. (#25685). **ARBA GRANTEE.**

NOV 23 - 24, '76. UNITED STATES ARMED FORCES BICENTENNIAL CARAVAN. CARAVAN IS COMPOSED OF EXHIBIT VANS FOR EACH MILITARY SERVICE. PROJECT THEME IS 'HISTORY OF THE ARMED FORCES & THEIR CONTRIBUTIONS TO THE NATION'. (LOCAL). JIM WILLAFORD; UNITED STATES ARMED FORCES BICENTENNIAL CARAVAN; PO BOX 111; ASHBURN, GA 31714. (#1775-779).

ATHENS

BANNER HERALD-NEWS SPECIAL HIST EDITION - NBMRP. 80-PAGE SPECIAL EDITION W/ 7 SECTIONS, EACH DEALING WITH DIFFERENT ERA OF NORTHEAST GEORGIA HISTORY FROM 1776. ENTIRE STAFF RESEARCHED THE INFORMATION FOR EDITION, WHICH WAS A YEAR IN THE MAKING. (LOCAL). MARK SMITH, BICENTENNIAL COORDINATOR; THE ATHENS BANNER HERALD-THE DAILY NEWS; ONE PRESS PLACE; ATHENS, GA 30601. (#23285).

BICENTENNIAL POSTER PROGRAM, ATHENS, GA. A POSTER FOR EACH BICENTENNIAL THEME WILL BE SELECTED FROM ENTRIES SUBMITTED BY GEORGIA ART STUDENTS. A TRAVELING EXHIBIT OF WINNING ENTRIES WILL TOUR THE STATE. REPRINTS WILL BE AVAILABLE TO PUBLIC. (ST-WIDE). MINA WHITE, PUBLICATIONS COORDINATOR; GEORGIA COMMISSION FOR THE NATIONAL BICENTENNIAL CELEBRATION; 1776 PEACHTREE ST, 520 S WING; ATLANTA, GA 30309. (#12251). **ARBA GRANTEE.**

COLONIAL RECORDS OF THE STATE OF GEORGIA. TWO VOLUME PUBLICATION OF THE ORIGINAL PAPERS OF GOVERNORS REYNOLDS, ELLIS, WRIGHT & OTHERS (1757-1763), EDITED BY KENNETH COLEMAN & MILTON READY & PUBLISHED BY THE UNIVERSITY OF GA PRESS. (ST-WIDE). A K JOHNSON, JR, DIRECTOR; GEORGIA COMMISSION FOR THE NATIONAL BICENTENNIAL CELEBRATION; SUITE 520, 1776 PEACHTREE ST NW; ATLANTA, GA 30309. (#32705).

FIRE HYDRANTS - PROJ OF ATHENS, GA. PAINTING OF HYDRANTS ON THE MAJOR THOROUGHFARES OF ATHENS. (LOCAL). MS GINNY PARKER, CAPTAIN; CLARKE CENTRAL HIGH SCHOOL BAND AUXILIARY CORPS; 321 HAMPTON COURT; ATHENS, GA 30601. (#15478).

GEORGIA COLLECTION AT OCONEE COUNTY LIBRARY. COLLECTION OF BOOKS & OTHER MATERIAL ON GEORGIA HISTORY WITH A HISTORY OF EACH COUNTY IN THE STATE; ALSO, A HISTORY ON THE 13 ORIGINAL AND THE 50 STATES. (LOCAL). MRS J S IVY, JR, CHAIRMAN; OCONEE COUNTY LIBRARY BOARD; 860 ROCK INWOOD DR; ATHENS, GA 30601. (#27288). **ARBA GRANTEE.**

GREEN SURVIVAL - PROJ OF ATHENS, GA. GREEN SURVIVAL IS AN ENVIRONMENTAL ACTION PROGRAM DEMONSTRATING TO INDIVIDUALS THAT THERE ARE MANY THING THEY CAN DO TO IMPROVE THEIR ENVIRONMENT AND HOW PLANTS PLAY A VITAL ROLE TO OUR ECOSYSTEM. (LOCAL). WILBUR MULL, PROJ DIRECTOR; CLASSIC NURSERY; BELMONT RD; ATHENS, GA 30601. (#15476).

ORAL HISTORY PROJECT, ATHENS, GA. STUDENTS WILL TAPE RECOLLECTIONS OF OLDER CITIZENS. (LOCAL). JEANETTE LUND, PRESIDENT; ATHENS-CLARKE HERITAGE FOUNDATION; 280 E DOUGHERTY; ATHENS, GA 30601. (#17144). **ARBA GRANTEE.**

TREES AT DUDLEY PARK - PROJ OF ATHENS, GA. CHICOPEE MILLS' EMPLOYEES WILL PLANT TREES AROUND THE SHELTER AT DUDLEY PARK. THE SHELTER IS USED BY SENIOR CITIZENS PARTICIPATING IN THE FREE LUNCH PROGRAM. THE PARK IS ON LAND DONATED BY CHICOPEE. (LOCAL). CLYDE PARKER, INDUSTRIAL RELATIONS MANAGER; CHICOPEE MILLS; PO BOX 672; ATHENS, GA 30601. (#15477).

MAY 25, '74. NEW WORK BY JOHN ADAMS PERFORMED BY ANNE MCFARLAND, PICC. & COMPOSER. NEW AMERICAN MUSIC BY COMPOSER JOHN ADAMS. GRANT/FELLOWSHIP SPONSORED BY NATL ENDOWMENT FOR THE ARTS TO AID IN PERFORMANCES OF NEW MUSIC BY JOHN ADAMS IN LOS ANGELES, ATLANTA, & OTHER AREAS. (ST-WIDE). JOHN ADAMS, DIRECTOR; JOHN ADAMS; ROUTE 1, BOX 44; STOCKBRIDGE, GA 30281. (#1221-903).

SEPT '75 - MAY '76. AMERICAN ISSUES FORUM. A SERIES OF DISCUSSIONS ON THE MAIN PROBLEMS FACING AMERICA; THEY WILL TAKE PLACE EVERY SECOND MONDAY OF EACH MONTH - SEPTEMBER THRU MAY; THEY WILL ALSO BE BROADCAST ON THE RADIO. (LOCAL). CAROLINE STROBEL, CHMN; ATHENS LEAGUE OF WOMEN VOTERS/WGAV RADIO STATION; 620 RIVERMONT RD; ATHENS, GA 30601. (#102430-4).

OCT 1 - 2, '75. EXPO '75: OPPORTUNITIES IN NORTHEAST GEORGIA. DISPLAYS AND EXHBITS HIGHLIGHTING HOW GOOD IT IS TO LIVE AND WORK IN NORTH EAST GEORGIA. THERE WILL ALSO BE LIVE ENTERTAINMENT. AT UNIV OF GEORGIA COLISEUM. (LOCAL). CLYDE PARKER, CHMN; ATHENS AREA CHAMBER OF COMMERCE; PO BOX 672; ATHENS, GA 30601. (#102430-7).

FEB 13 - 15, '76. THE AMERICAN REVOLUTION; ITS CAUSES AND EFFECTS. THE SEMINAR WILL CONSIST OF TWO KEYNOTE SPEECHES, 8 SMALL DISCUSSION GROUPS, TWO ADDITIONAL GENERAL SPEAKERS, FILMS AND DISPLAYS. AT GEORGIA CENTER FOR CONTINUING EDUCATION. (ST-WIDE). TYUS BUTLER; UNIVERSITY OF GEORGIA ALUMNI SOCIETY; ALUMNI HOUSE; ATHENS, GA 30602. (#104384-1).

APR 1 - 2, '76. TWO HUNDRED YEARS OF AMERICAN DANCE. THE PROGRAM WILL RE-CREATE THE INAUGURAL BALLS OF 6 U S PRESIDENTS FROM WASHINGTON TO COOLIDGE. THE COSTUMES, DANCES AND MUSIC WILL BE HISTORICALLY ACCURATE AND BRIEF CONTEMPORARY DESCRIPTIONS OF THE TIMES WILL ACCOMPANY EACH SEGMENT. AT FINE ARTS AUDITORIUM, UNIV OF GEORGIA. (ST-WIDE). DR JACKSON KESLER; PERIOD DANCE GROUP OF THE UNIV OF GEORGIA; DRAMA DEPT; ATHENS, GA 30602. (#104384-2).

APR 19 - 23, '76. COLONIAL FOOD IN MODERN DRESS. THE OPEN HOUSE WILL FEATURE TOURS OF THE RESEARCH FACILITY, EXHIBITS HIGHLIGHTING THE DIFFERENCES BETWEEN COLONIAL AND MODERN FOOD, AND A MULTI-SCREEN PRESENTATION ON 'AGRICULTURAL RESEARCH-DREAMS THAT LIVE FOR LIFE.' SEN HERMAN TALMADGE WILL DELIVER A KEYNOTE ADDRESS. AT RUSSELL RESEARCH CENTER, COLLEGE STATION RD. (LOCAL). DR DOUGLAS HAMM; RICHARD RUSSELL RESEARCH CENTER; RUSSELL RESEARCH CENTER; ATHENS, GA 30601. (#104384-3).

MAY 4, '76. CLARKE COUNTY SCHOOLS PAGEANT. THE PAGEANT WILL FEATURE STUDENTS FROM ALL CLARKE COUNTY SCHOOLS IN A MUSICAL TRIBUTE TO THE HISTORY OF AMERICA, GEORGIA AND CLARKE COUNTY. AT UNIV OF GA COLISEUM. (LOCAL). MRS SHERRY MALONE; CLARKE COUNTY SCHOOL SYSTEM; HILSMAN MIDDLE SCHOOL; ATHENS, GA 30601. (#104384-4).

MAY 10 - 14, '76. THE COUNTRY SCENE: A RE-CREATION OF THE ATHENS CIRCA 1840. THIS WEEK-LONG EXHIBIT WILL FEATURE A RE-CREATION OF A COUNTRY HOME AND A COUNTRY STORE TO HIGHLIGHT OLDER AMERICANS MONTH. AN AUDIOVISUAL PRESENTATION ON THE HISTORY OF CLARKE COUNTY WILL BE SHOWN AND ARTWORK WILL BE DISPLAYED. AT MAGNOLIA SENIOR CENTER, HULL ST. (LOCAL). MRS LINDA VESELY; ATHENS COMMUNITY COUNCIL ON AGING AND ATHENS KIWANIS CLUB; MAGNOLIA SENIOR CENTER, HULL ST; ATHENS, GA 30601. (#104384-5).

JULY 3, '76. COMMERCE AND INTERNATIONAL DAY. EXHIBITS WILL HIGHLIGHT THE CONTRIBUTIONS OF BUSINESS, INDUSTRY AND PEOPLE OF VARIOUS NATIONALITIES TO AMERICA. (LOCAL). MS BETH BUTLER; ATHENS-CLARKE COUNTY BICENTENNIAL COMMISSION; 404 JEFFERSON RIVER RD; ATHENS, GA 30601. (#104384-8).

JULY 3 - 10, '76. FESTIVAL WEEK. EACH DAY OF FESTIVAL WEEK WILL FOCUS ON A DIFFERENT ASPECT OF AMERICAN LIFE. WEEK WILL INCLUDE RELIGIOUS FREEDOM DAY, CELEBRATION DAY, BLACK AWARENESS DAY, CHILDREN'S DAY, EDUCATION DAY, RURAL LIFE DAY AND AMERICAN FOLKLIFE DAY. DETAILS ARE LISTED SEPARATELY. AT VARIOUS LOCATIONS IN CLARKE COUNTY. (LOCAL). MRS JILL READ; ATHENS-CLARKE COUNTY BICENTENNIAL COMMISSION; HOMEPLACE, 1676 S LUMPKIN ST; ATHENS, GA 30601. (#104384-7).

JULY 4, '76. RELIGIOUS FREEDOM DAY. A VARIETY OF RELIGIOUS SERVICES WILL BE PERFORMED DURING THE DAY AT MEMORIAL PARK TO SHOW THE FAITHS, BELIEFS AND CUSTOMS THAT MAKE UP AMERICA. AT MEMORIAL PARK. (LOCAL). REV CLAUDE MCBRIDE; ATHENS-CLARKE COUNTY BICENTENNIAL COMMISSION; 1690 S MILLEDGE AVE; ATHENS, GA 30601. (#104384-9).

JULY 5, '76. CELEBRATION DAY. THE HIGHLIGHTS OF THE DAY WILL BE A PARADE, WITH FLOATS DEPICTING AMERICAN HISTORY AND A FIREWORKS DISPLAY. (LOCAL). DAVID WEATHERFORD; ATHENS-CLARKE COUNTY BICENTENNIAL COMMISSION; 490 ROBERT RD; ATHENS, GA 30601. (#104384-10).

JULY 6, '76. BLACK AWARENESS DAY. THIS DAY WILL HIGHLIGHT THE ACHIEVEMENTS AND CONTRIBUTIONS OF BLACK AMERICANS. A VARIETY OF PERFORMANCES AND EXHIBITS ARE PLANNED. AT DUDLEY PARK. (LOCAL). MRS CLARA GAY; ATHENS-CLARKE COUNTY BICENTENNIAL COMMISSION; 1990 TIMOTHY RD; ATHENS, GA 30601. (#104384-11).

JULY 7, '76. CHILDREN'S DAY. THE HIGHLIGHT OF THE DAY WILL BE A YOUTH CONGRESS. VARIETY OF ACTIVITIES WILL BE PROVIDED FOR CHILDREN OF ALL AGES. AT VARIOUS LOCATIONS IN ATHENS. (LOCAL). MRS CAROLYN STROBEL; ATHENS-CLARKE COUNTY BICENTENNIAL COMMISSION; 620 RIVERMONT DR; ATHENS, GA 30601. (#104384-12).

JULY 8, '76. EDUCATION DAY. A VARIETY OF PERFORMANCES AND EXHIBITS HIGHLIGHTING THE UNIVERSITY OF GEORGIA ARE PLANNED. AT UNIV OF GA. (LOCAL). DR AUBREY LAND; ATHENS-CLARKE COUNTY BICENTENNIAL COMMISSION; LECONTE HALL, UNIV OF GA; ATHENS, GA 30602. (#104384-13).

JULY 10, '76. AMERICAN FOLKLIFE DAY. A VARIETY OF AMERICAN FOLK ARTS AND CRAFTS WILL BE ON DISPLAY. AT CENTRAL CITY PARK. (LOCAL). DON OLIVER, CHAIRMAN; ATHENS-CLARKE COUNTY BICENTENNIAL COMMISSION; MEMORIAL PARK; ATHENS, GA 30601. (#104384-15).

ATLANTA

ABC MEDALLION - ATLANTA, GA. ISSUE A COMMEMORATIVE MEDAL FOR THE CELEBRATION OF THE NATIONAL BICENTENNIAL. (ST-WIDE). MS ESTELLE FORD GREENE, CHAIRMAN; THE ATLANTA BICENTENNIAL COMMISSION; 225 PEACHTREE ST, NE; ATLANTA, GA 30303. (#24164).

ACQUISITION OF SIGNIFICANT ENDANGERED SITES IN GA. AQUISITION OF ADDITIONAL SIGNIFICANT & ENDANGERED SITES IMPORTANT TO GEORGIA'S NATURAL & CULTURAL HERITAGE THROUGH THE CONTINUED EFFORTS OF THE GEORGIA HERITAGE TRUST. (ST-WIDE). JIM OATES, CHIEF RECREATION & PLANNING SECTION; GEORGIA DEPT OF NATURAL RESOURCES; 270 WASHINGTON ST SW; ATLANTA, GA 30334. (#587). **(??).**

ADDRESSES OF GOVERNORS TO GEORGIA GENERAL ASSEMBLY. PUBLICATION OF ADDRESSES OF GOVERNORS TO THE GEORGIA GENERAL ASSEMBLY, 1800-1900 & ADDITIONAL VOLUMES OF UNPUBLISHED COLONIAL RECORDS OF GEORGIA. (ST-WIDE). JACKIE M ERNEY, BICENTENNIAL COORDINATOR; GEORGIA DEPT OF ARCHIVES & HISTORY; 330 CAPITOL AVE; ATLANTA, GA 30334. (#621). **(??).**

'AFRO AMERICAN '76' - ATLANTA, GA. THE BOOK DEALS WITH THE EXPLORATION AND COLONIZATION OF AMERICA FOR SECONDARY STUDENTS. (REGN'L). JOE ELLIS, PROJ CHAIRMAN; ATLANTA BICENTENNIAL COMMISSION; 1465 NORTHSIDE DR NW, SUITE 74; ATLANTA, GA 30308. (#26646).

AMER REVOLUTION IN GEORGIA BOOKLETS. SERIES OF 13 BOOKLETS ON VARIOUS ASPECTS OF THE AMERICAN REVOLUTION IN GEORGIA TO BE MADE AVAILABLE TO ALL SCHOOLS IN GEORGIA. FIRST 3 HAVE BEEN PUBLISHED, ON SALE, $2.00 PER SET. (ST-WIDE). A K JOHNSON, EXEC DIRECTOR; GEORGIA COMMISSION FOR THE NATIONAL BICENTENNIAL CELEBRATION; 1776 PEACHTREE, SOUTH WING; ATLANTA, GA 30309. (#588).

AN AMERICAN IDEA - ATLANTA, GA. PLAY 2-3 MINUTE BACKGROUND OF AN AMERICAN FIGURE SUCH AS EDGAR ALLEN POE OR THE ORIGIN OF 'UNCLE SAM' AS WELL AS AMERICAN INDUSTRIALISTS. (LOCAL). MS ELAINE BRADLEY, CHAIRMAN; WLTA RADIO; 1459 PEACHTREE ST NE; ATLANTA, GA 30309. (#24172).

ARCHIVES OF SCIENCE AND TECHNOLOGY - GEORGIA TECH. AN ARCHIVE OF SCIENCE TECHNOLOGY AND ARCHITECTURE COMPRISING PERSONAL PAPERS, DESIGNS, DRAWINGS, ARCHITECTURAL PLANS AND PHOTOGRAPHS. (LOCAL). DR JAMES E BRITTAIN, ASSOCIATE PROFESSOR; GEORGIA TECH BICENTENNIAL COMMITTEE; 325 NORTH AVE; ATLANTA, GA 30332. (#17002).

ART IN THE PARK - ATLANTA, GA. HIGH MUSEUM HAS COMMISSIONED THE INTERNATIONALLY FAMOUS AMERICAN ARTIST, ISAMU NAGUCHI, TO DESIGN A PERMANENT CHILDREN'S SCULPTURE PLAYGROUND FOR PIEDMONT PARK. (LOCAL). MS CHERYL HOBSON, COORDINATOR; HIGH MUSEUM OF ART, CITY OF ATLANTA; 1280 PEACHTREE ST, NE; ATLANTA, GA 30309. (#24169).

ARTISTS IN ACTION - ATLANTA, GA. DEMONSTRATIONS BY SCULPTORS, POTTERS AND PAINTERS IN THE MINI-PARK WITH DIALOGUE AND PARTICIPATION; WORKSHOP FOLLOWING. (LOCAL). GERRY POWELL, PRESIDENT; ATLANTA ARTISTS CLUB; 3099 PEACHTREE RD; ATLANTA, GA 30305. (#22622). **ARBA GRANTEE.**

ARTS COUNCIL CENTER IN ATLANTA. ARTS COUNCIL CENTER WILL PROVIDE WORKSHOP FOR ALL ARTISTS THUS ENCOURAGING INTERDEPENDENT RELATIONSHIP. (LOCAL). MS GWEN BECK, PROJ COORDINATOR; ATLANTA ARTS COUNCIL; 820 PEACHTREE CNTR, S TOWER; ATLANTA, GA 30303. (#8943).

ATLANTA BICENTENNIAL MEDAL. A COMMEMORATIVE ITEM DEPICTING OLD ATLANTA WITH FUTURE ATLANTA. (LOCAL). BILL PUGH, EXEC DIRECTOR; ATLANTA BICENT COMMISSION; 820 PEACHTREE CNTR, S TOWER; ATLANTA, GA 30303. (#8934).

ATLANTA MIXED CHORUS OF ATLANTA, GEORGIA. PLANS ARE TO FORM A PERMANENT MIXED CHORUS TO PERFORM AT MUSICAL EVENTS IN THE ATLANTA AREA. (LOCAL). GEORGE GOODWIN, PROJ COORDINATOR; ATLANTA CHRISTIAN COUNCIL; 820 PEACHTREE CENTER, S TOWER; ATLANTA, GA 30303. (#8942).

ATLANTA MODEL CITIES EDUCATION COMPLEX, GA. MULTI-PURPOSE COMPLEX WITH SCHOOLS, NEIGHBORHOOD FACILITIES, PARKS, RECREATION FACILITIES IN ONE LOCATION. (LOCAL). MYRA B PEABODY, COMMUNITY AFFAIRS DIRECTOR; DEPT OF COMMUNITY AND HUMAN DEVELOPMENT; 100 MITCHELL ST, SW; ATLANTA, GA 30303. (#20022).

ATLANTA: AN AFRO-AMERICAN PERCEPTION - ATLANTA, GA. ACCOMPLISHED AND DEVELOPING BLACK ARTISTS IN ATLANTA WILL BE RECRUITED TO ATTEND WORKSHOPS AND WORK ON PAINTINGS. FOCUS WILL BE ON CAPTURING ATLANTA ON CANVAS AS PERCEIVED BY AFRO-AMERICANS. (LOCAL). MS SANDRA L SWANS, COORDINATOR; NEIGHBORHOOD ARTS CENTER, INC; 252 GEORGIA AVE SW; ATLANTA, GA 30312. (#24158).

BICENTENNIAL DECALS, AUTO & BIKE LICENSE PLATES. DECALS, AUTO & BIKE LICENSE PLATES WITH THE BICENTENNIAL SYMBOL. ARBA LICENSE NO 76-19-0515. (NAT'L). STEPHEN SCHMIDT, JR, MANAGER; DIXIE SEAL AND STAMP CO; PO BOX 54616; ATLANTA, GA 30308. (#6553).

BICENTENNIAL EDUCATIONAL TV PROGRAMS OF GEORGIA. DEVELOPMENT OF 8 BICENTENNIAL PROGRAMS FOR EARLY ELEMENTARY GRADES. (ST-WIDE). ANNE RAYMOND, DIRECTOR, PUBLICATIONS SERVICE; GEORGIA DEPT OF EDUCATION; 103 STATE OFFICE BLDG; ATLANTA, GA 30334. (#652).

BICENTENNIAL EXPOSITION IN ATLANTA, GA. IN AUGUST 1975, A BICENTENNIAL EXPOSITION WILL BE HELD IN LENNOX SQUARE; EXHIBIT INCLUDES CRAFT DEMONSTRATIONS, LIVE PERFORMANCES BY BANDS, CHORAL & DANCE GROUPS AND EXHIBITS. (ST-WIDE). MINA WHITE, PUBLICATIONS COORDINATOR; GEORGIA COMMISSION FOR THE NATIONAL BICENTENNIAL CELEBRATION; 1776 PEACHTREE, 520 SOUTH WING; ATLANTA, GA 30309. (#13446). **ARBA GRANTEE.**

BICENTENNIAL HIGHWAY MAPS OF GEORGIA. REVISION OF 1975-76 STATE HIGHWAY MAPS TO INCLUDE PICTURES & OTHER DATA RELATED TO HISTORICALLY SIGNIFICANT PLACES AND BUILDINGS WITH EMPHASIS ON THE COLONIAL & REVOLUTIONARY PERIOD. (ST-WIDE). BOB KIRK, TRANSPORTATION PLANNING ENGINEER; GEORGIA DEPT OF TRANSPORTATION; 2 CAPITOL SQUARE; ATLANTA, GA 30334. (#669).

'BICENTENNIAL MAGAZINE' - ATLANTA, GA. STUDENT PUBLICATION FEATURING PROJECTS SUCH AS INTERVIEWS & PHOTOS OF OLD ATLANTA RESIDENTS & RESEARCH PROJECTS ABOUT ATLANTA'S HISTORY AND DEVELOPMENT. (LOCAL). SISTER BARBARA M SITKO, COORDINATOR; ST PIUS X HIGH SCHOOL; 2674 JOHNSON RD NE; ATLANTA, GA 30345. (#24189).

BICENTENNIAL MULTI-MEDIA SHOW, ATLANTA, GA. 300 SLIDES (16MM FILM) PROGRAMMED TO A 35 MINUTE, TAPED NARRATION OF MUSIC COVERING 200 YEARS OF AMERICAN HISTORY, PROJECTED ONTO THREE SCREENS SIMULTANEOUSLY. (LOCAL). JEANNETTE ABI-NADER, DIRECTOR OF MEDIA SERVICES; ST PIUS X HIGH SCHOOL; 2674 JOHNSON RD, NE; ATLANTA, GA 30345. (#22305). **ARBA GRANTEE.**

BICENTENNIAL PATCHES AND EMBLEMS OF ATLANTA. DEVELOPMENT AND PURCHASE OF BICENTENNIAL YOUTH PATCHES, LAPEL EMBLEMS AND DECALS. (ST-WIDE). A K JOHNSON, JR, EXEC DIRECTOR; GEORGIA COMMISSION FOR THE NATIONAL BICENTENNIAL CELEBRATION; 1776 PEACHTREE RD, NW; ATLANTA, GA 30309. (#9634). **ARBA GRANTEE.**

BICENTENNIAL PSALM CONCERT, GA. THANKSGIVING PERFORMANCE OF PSALM SETTINGS BY CONTEMPORARY AMERICAN COMPOSERS. SECOND IN A SERIES OF BICENTENNIAL CONCERTS RECOGNIZING AMER CONTRIBUTIONS TO THE FIELD OF

ATLANTA — CONTINUED

CHORAL MUSIC. ALSO IN DUNWOODY. (LOCAL). THOMAS L SCHWARTZ, DIRECTOR; CHORAL GUILD OF ATLANTA; 124 PEACHTREE MEMORIAL DR #4; ATLANTA, GA 30309. (#20496). **ARBA GRANTEE.**

BICENTENNIAL THEME PLAYS - ATLANTA, GA. CREATION & PRODUCTION OF TWO BICENTENNIAL PLAYS FOR A TOUR OF SCHOOLS ACROSS GEORGIA. (ST-WIDE). DAVID BISHOP, MANAGING DIRECTOR; ALLIANCE THEATRE CO; ATLANTA ARTS ALLIANCE; 15 16TH ST, NE; ATLANTA, GA 30309. (#17477). **ARBA GRANTEE.**

BICENTENNIAL TRAVEL PROMOTION PROGRAM, ATLANTA, GA. PROMOTIONAL PROGRAM TO STIMULATE TRAVEL TO SOUTHERN STATES DURING THE BICENT THROUGH A VARIETY OF MATERIALS AVAILABLE TO THE PUBLIC. (REGN'L). BILL S BARNES, PRESIDENT; SOUTHERN TRAVEL DIRECTORS COUNCIL; 235 PEACHTREE ST, NE; ATLANTA, GA 30303. (#10977).

BLACK PERSPECTIVE IN AMERICAN ISSUES FORUM. EMPHASIS IS GIVEN TO POSITIVE PARTICIPATION IN THE BICENTENNIAL BY BLACKS, EXTOLLING THE RECORD OF CITIZENSHIP AWARENESS, PATRIOTISM & COMMUNITY SERVICE. (LOCAL). DR BLANTON E BLACK, CHMN; MORRIS BROWN COLLEGE; 643 HUNTER ST; ATLANTA, GA 30314. (#108063-1).

BLACK SYMPHONIC COMPOSERS - ATLANTA, GA. RECORDS WILL BE MADE FEATURING MUSIC BY BLACK COMPOSERS. (REGN'L). JOANN MCCLINTON, PROJ CHAIRMAN; ATLANTA BICENTENNIAL COMMISSION; 820 PEACHTREE CENTER, S TOWER; ATLANTA, GA 30303. (#26645).

CALENDAR OF EVENTS - ATLANTA, GA. COMPILATION AND PUBLICATION OF ALL LOCAL BICENTENNIAL EVENTS. (LOCAL). MS ESTELLE FORD GREENE, CHAIRMAN; ATLANTA BICENTENNIAL COMMISSION; 225 PEACHTREE ST NE; ATLANTA, GA 31303. (#24160).

CARROLL ST RESTORATION PROJECT, GA. UPGRADE AND BEAUTIFY CARROLL ST BY REPAIRING HOUSES, CREATING GREEN SPACE AND DEVELOPING EXISTING AND NEW BUSINESSES. (LOCAL). ESTHER LEFEVER, EXEC DIRECTOR; THE PATCH, INC; 242 CARROLL ST, SE; ATLANTA, GA 30312. (#24724). **ARBA GRANTEE.**

CATALOG AFRO-AMERICAN ART COLLECTION, ATLANTA, GA. PUBLISHED CATALOG OF THE ATLANTA UNIVERSITY ART COLLECTION, THE LARGEST COLLECTION OF BLACK ART IN AMERICA. (NAT'L). CASPER L JORDON, UNIV LIBRARIAN; ATLANTA UNIV BICENTENNIAL COMMITTEE; 223 CHESTNUT ST SW; ATLANTA, GA 30314. (#25519).

CHINESE CULTURE CENTER, ATLANTA, GA. THE CHINESE-AMERICAN INSTITUTE, INC WISHES TO ESTABLISH A CULTURAL CENTER AT 386 NORTH AVE, NE, FOR GATHERINGS OF CHINESE-AMERICANS IN GEORGIA. (LOCAL). PING CHUNG, PRESIDENT; CHINESE-AMERICAN INSTITUTE, INC; 386 NORTH AVE, NE; ATLANTA, GA 30308. (#22074). **ARBA GRANTEE.**

'THE CLARK COLLEGE LEGACY' - ATLANTA, GA. THE BOOK DETAILS THE HISTORY OF ATLANTA'S CLARK COLLEGE WHICH IS 106 YEARS OLD. (LOCAL). DR JAMES P BRAWLEY, PRESIDENT EMERITUS; CLARK COLLEGE; 240 CHESTNUT ST SW; ATLANTA, GA 30314. (#26647).

CLASSIFYING ALL STATE PARKS & HISTORIC SITES IN GA. PRELIMINARY STUDY OF ALL STATE PARKS AND HISTORIC SITES TO CLASSIFY EACH ACCORDING TO OPTIMUM POTENTIAL AS AN HISTORICAL, SCENIC, OR RECREATION FACILITY. (ST-WIDE). JIM OATES, CHIEF RECREATION & PLANNING SECTION; GEORGIA DEPT OF NATURAL RESOURCES; 270 WASHINGTON ST SW; ATLANTA, GA 30334. (#595). **(??).**

COL ROBERT ALSTON HOME - ATLANTA, GA. COL ROBERT ALSTON'S HOME WILL BE PLACED ON THE NATIONAL REGISTER. (LOCAL). CHARLES M LESTER, DIRECTOR; EAST LAKE NEIGHBORS COMMUNITY ASSOC; 2869 ALSTON DR; ATLANTA, GA 30317. (#24162).

CONSTRUCTION OF MUSEUM AND PARK IN ATLANTA. PLANS TO BUILD A MUSEUM OF ARCHEOLOGY IN A PARK SETTING, ADJACENT TO THE MARTIN LUTHER KING, JR MEMORIAL. (LOCAL). GEORGE GOODWIN, PROJ COORDINATOR; ATLANTA BICENT COMMISSION; 820 PEACHTREE CENTER, S TOWER; ATLANTA, GA 30303. (#8944).

COSTUME RESEARCH IN ATLANTA, GA. SAMPLE COSTUMES RESEARCHED AND CREATED TO REPRESENT TYPICAL FASHION WORN BY UPLAND GEORGIANS RESIDING IN TULLIE SMITH HOUSE FROM 1840 TO 1860. DOCENTS TO EXHIBIT COSTUMES IN CELEBRATION OF AMER BICENT '76. (LOCAL). SALLY WHITE, COORDINATOR, TULLIE SMITH PROJECT; THE FASHION GROUP, INC, ATLANTA REGIONAL CHAPTER; 6410 COLEWOOD CT, NW; ATLANTA, GA 30328. (#12237). **ARBA GRANTEE.**

CULTURAL EXCHANGE VISIT WITH GERMANY. AN EXPRESSION OF INTEREST FROM THE CONSUL GENERAL OF THE FEDERAL REPUBLIC FOR GERMAN PARTICIPATION IN ATLANTA'S CELEBRATION OF THE BICENTENNIAL. (INT'L). DR ERNST INGENDAAY, PROJ COORDINATOR; CONSUL GENERAL OF THE FEDERAL REPUBLIC OF GERMANY; 229 PEACHTREE ST, NE, SUITE 1000; ATLANTA, GA 30303. (#22495).

DEVELOPMENT OF WILDLIFE MANAGEMENT AREAS IN GA. DEVELOPMENT OF NEW WILDLIFE MANAGEMENT AREAS FOR SMALL AND BIG GAME ACCESSIBLE FOR PUBLIC HUNTING. (ST-WIDE). JIM OATES, CHIEF, RECREATION & PLANNING SECTION; GEORGIA DEPT OF NATURAL RESOURCES; 270 WASHINGTON ST SW; ATLANTA, GA 30334. (#640).

DISCOVERY '76, ATLANTA, GEORGIA. A PROGRAM OF TEACHER WORKSHOPS AND MINI-GRANTS SPONSORED BY THE GCNBC TO ENCOURAGE EDUCATORS AND STUDENTS TO DESIGN & IMPLEMENT STUDY COURSES INVOLVING ORAL HISTORY ON THE LOCAL LEVEL. (ST-WIDE). A K JOHNSON, JR, DIRECTOR; GEORGIA COMMISSION FOR THE NATIONAL BICENTENNIAL CELEBRATION; SUITE 520, 1776 PEACHTREE ST NW; ATLANTA, GA 30309. (#32706).

EARLY AMERICAN CRAFTS REVIVAL IN ATLANTA. 5000 ELEMENTARY SCHOOL CHILDREN & 160 TEACHERS WILL CREATE OBJECTS BASED ON OUR HERITAGE FROM GEORGIA'S INDIGENOUS MATERIALS SUCH AS CLAY, FIBERS, METALS & WOOD. (ST-WIDE). MRS SARA JO SIRMANS, PRESIDENT; GEORGIA ART EDUCATION ASSOCIATION; 2860 GUINIVERE DR, NE; ATLANTA, GA 30345. (#12002). **ARBA GRANTEE.**

ENGLISH AS A SECOND LANGUAGE PROGRAM, ATLANTA, GA. PROVIDES INSTRUCTION IN IMPROVING ENGLISH USAGE BY FOREIGN STUDENTS. (LOCAL). DAVID HEMPLEMAN, COORDINATOR OF ESL; GSU SCHOOL OF GENERAL STUDIES; UNIVERSITY PLAZA; ATLANTA, GA 30303. (#22490).

EXHIBITION, ARTISTS IN THE SOUTHEAST, ATLANTA, GA. 100 REPRESENTATIVE WORKS BY NO MORE THAN 30 REGIONAL & PROMINENT SOUTHERN ARTISTS; WORKS WILL INCLUDE: PAINTINGS, PHOTOGRAPHS, SCULPTURE, CRAFTS AND PRINT MEDIUMS. (REGN'L). GUDMUND VIGTEL, DIRECTOR; THE HIGH MUSEUM OF ART; 1280 PEACHTREE ST, NE; ATLANTA, GA 30309. (#13639).

'FAMOUS GEORGIANS' BIOGRAPHICAL SKETCHES. COMPILATION OF BIOGRAPHICAL SKETCHES OF 29 'FAMOUS GEORGIANS' FOR DISTRIBUTION TO SCHOOLS AND INTERESTED CITIZENS. (ST-WIDE). JACKIE ERNEY, BICENTENNIAL COORDINATOR; GEORGIA DEPT OF ARCHIVES & HISTORY; 330 CAPITOL AVE SE; ATLANTA, GA 30334. (#619).

'FERNBANK CONSERVATION COVENANT' - ATLANTA, GA. COMMIT CONTEMPORARY PUBLIC OFFICIALS AND PRIVATE GROUPS TO THE IDENTIFICATION AND PRESERVATION OF THE NATURAL BEAUTY OF THE FERNBANK FOREST, THE CHILDREN'S REHABILITATION CENTER, ETC. (LOCAL). JIM CHERRY, DIRECTOR; GEORGIA CONSERVANCY LAND USE COMMITTEE, INC; 3376 PEACHTREE RD, NE; ATLANTA, GA 30326. (#24157).

FLAGS WITH THE BICENTENNIAL SYMBOL. BICENTENNIAL FLAG; BICENTENNIAL LICENSE NO 76-19-0593. (NAT'L). DURWARD GERSON, PRESIDENT; SOUTHERN TAILORS INC - THE FLODING CO; 684 SPRING ST NW; ATLANTA, GA 30308. (#17827).

FOLK ART EXHIBIT OF ATLANTA, GEORGIA. A TOURING EXHIBIT OF 200 YEARS OF FOLK ART PRODUCED IN GEORGIA. THIS WILL HELP DISCOVER AND PRESERVE THE BEST OF OUR SOUTHERN FOLK ART HERITAGE. (ST-WIDE). JANE FERRISS, ACTING DIR; GEORGIA COUNCIL FOR THE ARTS; 225 PEACHTREE ST, NE; ATLANTA, GA 30303. (#9420).

'FOOTLIGHTS AND FANFARE!' - ATLANTA, GA. A SALUTE TO THE HISTORY OF THE AMERICAN MUSICAL THEATRE: FROM THE DAYS OF THE TRAVELING MEDICINE SHOW TO THE PRESENT; TO BE PRESENTED FOR AMERICAN SERVICEMEN & THEIR FAMILIES ON MILITARY BASES ABROAD. (INT'L). BILLY G DENSONS, DIRECTOR; NORTHSIDE SCHOOL OF PERFORMING ARTS & U S DEPT OF DEFENSE; 2875 NORTHSIDE DR; ATLANTA, GA 30305. (#26105). **ARBA GRANTEE.**

FORT STANDING PEACHTREE - ATLANTA, GA. REBUILD A VERSION OF THE FORT, SITE OF THE FIRST SETTLERS IN ATLANTA. (LOCAL). W F BROWN, DIRECETOR; ATLANTA BUREAU OF WATER; 68 MITCHELL ST; ATLANTA, GA 30303. (#24170).

FOUNTAIN HALL - HISTORIC LANDMARK - ATLANTA, GA. FOUNTAIN HALL WILL BE RESTORED AND DESIGNATED AS A HISTORIC LANDMARK. (LOCAL). BLANTON E BLACK, CHAIRPERSON; MORRIS BROWN COLLEGE; 643 HUNTER ST; ATLANTA, GA 30314. (#25462).

'FOUR CHEERS FOR ATLANTA' FILM - ATLANTA, GA. PRODUCTION OF THE FILM 'FOUR CHEERS FOR ATLANTA' FROM A MULTI-MEDIA HISTORY EXHIBIT OF ATLANTA. (LOCAL). MRS CATHERINE FRANGIAMORE, DIRECTOR; THE ATLANTA HISTORICAL SOCIETY; PO BOX 12423; ATLANTA, GA 30305. (#24154).

FUTURE SOLAR ENERGY SOURCES - GEORGIA TECH. AN EXHIBITION OF WORKING MODELS SHOWING THE PRINCIPLES OF SCIENTIFIC AND TECHNOLOGICAL SOURCES OF SOLAR ENERGY. (LOCAL). FRANK J CLARKE, ASSOCIATE PROFESSOR; GEORGIA TECH BICENTENNIAL COMMITTEE; 325 NORTH AVE; ATLANTA, GA 30332. (#17000).

'GEORGIA AND THE WORLD COMMUNITY' TV DOCUMENTARY. PRODUCTION OF A ONE HOUR DOCUMENTARY 'GEORGIA & THE WORLD COMMUNITY' IDENTIFYING 2 OR 3 GEORGIANS WHO HAVE HAD AN OUTSTANDING IMPACT ON THE WORLD COMMUNITY. (ST-WIDE). DR HOWARD JORDAN, VICE CHANCELLOR FOR SERVICES; GEORGIA UNIVERSITY SYSTEM CENTER FOR CONTINUING EDUCATION; 244 WASHINGTON ST SW; ATLANTA, GA 30334. (#612).

GEORGIA ARCHIVES TRAVELING EXHIBIT, ATLANTA, GA. PRODUCTION & DISTRIBUTION OF STATEWIDE TRAVELING EXHIBITS ON LITTLE KNOWN ASPECTS OF GEORGIA'S COLONIAL & AMERICAN REVOLUTION PERIODS. TWO EXHIBITS UNDERWAY; 6 TO BE COMPLETED BY 1976. (ST-WIDE). JACKIE ERNEY, BICENT COORDINATOR; GEORGIA DEPT OF ARCHIVES AND HISTORY; 330 CAPITOL AVE, SE; ATLANTA, GA 30334. (#10607). **ARBA GRANTEE.**

GEORGIA BICENTENNIAL RADIO NETWORK. SERIES OF VIGNETTE TYPE RADIO SPOTS TO TELL THE STORY OF THE REVOLUTIONARY WAR, USING RADIO STATIONS STATEWIDE. (ST-WIDE). A K JOHNSON, EXEC DIRECTOR; GEORGIA COMMISSION FOR THE NATIONAL BICENTENNIAL CELEBRATION; 1776 PEACHTREE, SOUTH WING; ATLANTA, GA 30309. (#591).

GEORGIA BICENTENNIAL POSTERS - ATLANTA. REPRODUCTIONS OF AWARD-WINNING GEORGIA BICENTENNIAL POSTERS IN 3 NATIONWIDE THEMES HAVE BEEN MADE AVAILABLE TO THE GENERAL PUBLIC BY THE GCNBC. (ST-WIDE). A K JOHNSON, JR, DIRECTOR; GEORGIA COMMISSION FOR THE NATIONAL BICENTENNIAL CELEBRATION; SUITE 520, 1776 PEACHTREE ST NW; ATLANTA, GA 30309. (#32704).

GEORGIA HERITAGE PORTFOLIO. A PORTFOLIO OF DOCUMENTS REFLECTING COLONIAL GEORGIA AND HER ROLE IN THE REVOLUTION DISTRIBUTED FREE TO PUBLIC SCHOOLS & LIBRARIES IN GA. AVAILABLE FOR $5.00 EACH, INCL. POSTAGE. (ST-WIDE). A K JOHNSON, EXEC DIRECTOR; GEORGIA COMMISSION FOR THE NATIONAL BICENTENNIAL CELEBRATION; 1776 PEACHTREE 520 SOUTH WING; ATLANTA, GA 30309. (#514).

GEORGIA HERITAGE SPECIAL. A TRAVELLING RAIL EXHIBIT TELLING THE STORY OF GEORGIA'S COLONIAL HERITAGE ON VISITS TO 27 CITIES IN THE STATE. (ST-WIDE). RON HENRY, PROJECT MANAGER; GEORGIA HERITAGE SPECIAL; PO BOX Q; TIFTON, GA 31794. (#20221). **ARBA GRANTEE.**

GEORGIA HIGH SCHOOL BAND COMPETITION. COMPETITION SPONSORED BY THE GCNBC TO SELECT THE OUTSTANDING GEORGIA HIGH SCHOOL BAND TO REPRESENT STATE AT 'FESTIVAL OF COLONIES' IN ALLENTOWN, PA. HARDWAY HS OF COLUMBUS WON & WAS SENT TO PA. (LOCAL). A K JOHNSON, JR, CHAIRMAN; GEORGIA COMMISSION FOR THE NATIONAL BICENTENNIAL CELEBRATION; SUITE 520, 1776 PEACHTREE ST, NW; ATLANTA, GA 30309. (#109526-3).

GEORGIA INTERNATIONALE - ATLANTA. A MULTI-ETHNIC CELEBRATION FEATURING FINNISH, TURKISH, HELLENIC, HUNGARIAN AND SWISS CELEBRATIONS. (ST-WIDE). A K JOHNSON, EXEC DIRECTOR; GEORGIA COMMISSION FOR THE NATIONAL BICENTENNIAL CELEBRATION; 1776 PEACHTREE ST; ATLANTA, GA 30309. (#26429). **ARBA GRANTEE.**

GEORGIA NATIONAL GUARD FIFE & DRUM CORPS. FORMATION OF FIFE AND DRUM SECTIONS WITHIN THE TWO NATIONAL GUARD BANDS TO PARTICIPATE IN PARADES AND COMMEMORATIVE CEREMONIES. (ST-WIDE). COL DOUGLAS EMBRY, INFORMATION DIRECTOR; GEORGIA DEPT OF DEFENSE; PO BOX 18055; ATLANTA, GA 30316. (#656).

GEORGIA REDCOAT BAND. DEVELOPMENT OF SPECIAL MUSIC FOR HALF-TIME SHOWS FOR USE OF GEORGIA HIGH SCHOOLS AND COLLEGES DURING THE BICENTENNIAL ERA. (ST-WIDE). DR HOWARD JORDAN, JR, VICE CHANCELLOR FOR SERVICES; GEORGIA UNIVERSITY SYSTEM-CENTER FOR CONTINUING EDUCATION; 244 WASHINGTON ST SW; ATLANTA, GA 30334. (#662).

GEORGIA STATE UNIV CONTINENTAL BATTALION: ATLANTA. A REPLICATION OF GEORGIA'S REVOLUTIONARY ERA FORCES, INCLUDING FIFE & DRUM CORPS, COLOR GUARD & INFANTRY UNITS WILL PARTICIPATE IN CEREMONIAL BICENTENNIAL EVENTS. (ST-WIDE). CPT JOHN C HEDLEY, ASST PROF; GEORGIA STATE UNIV ROTC; UNIV PLAZA; ATLANTA, GA 30303. (#8746). **ARBA GRANTEE.**

GEORGIA WOMEN: A BICENTENNIAL CELEBRATION. PUBLICATION OF BOOKLET ON GEORGIA WOMEN FROM ALL HISTORICAL PERIODS, CELEBRATING THEIR CONTRIBUTIONS TO SOCIETY; WOMEN'S HISTORY, STATE AND LOCAL. (ST-WIDE). BARBARA B REITT, PROJECT DIRECTOR; AMERICAN ASSOCIATION OF UNIVERSITY WOMEN; 3505 HAMPTON HALL WAY; ATLANTA, GA 30319. (#20442). **ARBA GRANTEE.**

GEORGIAN FURNITURE EXHIBIT, 1750-1850 IN ATLANTA. THE FIRST MAJOR EXHIBITION OF EARLY GA FURNITURE INCLUDING, 100 PIECES ILLUSTRATING REGIONAL DESIGN, DECORATIVE DETAIL, CONSTRUCTION & WOOD PREFERENCES. (REGN'L). GUDMUND VIGTEL, DIRECTOR; THE HIGH MUSEUM OF ART; 1280 PEACHTREE ST, NE; ATLANTA, GA 30309. (#13641).

THE GEORGIANS CREATING A CULTURE - EXHIBIT. SHOWS CONTRIBUTIONS OF BLACKS, JEWS, SCOTCH, IRISH AND OTHER ETHNIC GROUPS TO GEORGIA HISTORY. (LOCAL). JOEL SARRETT, COORD; ATLANTA COUNCIL FOR INTERNATIONAL VISITORS; 1000 CUMBERLAND ST; ATLANTA, GA 30339. (#107363-2).

'GEORGIA: LAND OF OUR DELIGHT' - ATLANTA. A JOINT PUBLICATION BY THE OFFICE OF THE GOVERNOR & THE GCNBC WHICH FOCUSES ON THE REVOLUTIONARY HISTORY OF GEORGIA, HISTORIC SITES & FACTS & FIGURES ON GEORGIA & HER GOVERNMENT. (ST-WIDE). A K JOHNSON, JR, DIRECTOR; GEORGIA COMMISSION FOR THE NATIONAL BICENTENNIAL CELEBRATION; SUITE 520, 1776 PEACHTREE ST NW; ATLANTA, GA 30309. (#32701).

GEORGIA'S BOOKLET ON HISTORIC REVOLUTIONARY SITES. BOOKLET ON GEORGIA'S REVOLUTIONARY SITES, WITH A ROUTING GUIDE. (ST-WIDE). A K JOHNSON, EXEC DIRECTOR; GEORGIA COMMISSION FOR THE NATIONAL BICENTENNIAL CELEBRATION; 1776 PEACHTREE, SOUTH WING; ATLANTA, GA 30309. (#589).

GOVERNOR'S BICENT INTERN PROGRAM, ATLANTA, GA. COLLEGE STUDENTS ARE BEING INVOLVED IN THE IMPLEMENTATION OF SPECIFIC TASK PROJECTS IDENTIFIED BY LOCAL AMERICAN BICENT COMMISSIONS AS BICENTENNIAL INTERNS. (ST-WIDE). T STEPHEN JOHNSON, COORDINATOR OF PROGRAMS; GOVERNOR'S OFFICE OF SPECIAL AFFAIRS; RM 104, STATE CAPITOL; ATLANTA, GA 30334. (#10606). **ARBA GRANTEE.**

GSU REVOLUTIONARY ERA FIFE AND DRUM CORPS - GA. AUTHENTICALLY TRAINED AND DRILLED IN MUSIC AND MARCHING ROUTINES OF GEORGIA 3RD BATTALION OF THE CONTINENTAL LINE; PERFORMANCES LOCALLY AND NATIONALLY. (REGN'L). CAPT JOHN C HEDLEY, ADVISOR; GEORGIA STATE UNIVERSITY ROTC; UNIVERSITY PLAZA; ATLANTA, GA 30303. (#22491).

HIGH SCHOOL CHORAL COMPETITION, ATLANTA, GA. ALL-STATE CHORUS PERFORMANCE OF SONGS SELECTED FROM PIECES SUBMITTED BE GIVEN $200.00. WINNING COMPOSITION WILL BE PERFORMED. (LOCAL). MRS NANCY HARPER, PRESIDENT; ATLANTA ALUMNAE CHAPTER OF SIGMA ALPHA IOTA; 2616 D OAK SHADOW LANE; ATLANTA, GA 30345. (#23767). **ARBA GRANTEE.**

ATLANTA — CONTINUED

HIGHPOINTS LITTLE RED SCHOOLHOUSE - ATLANTA, GA. A REPLICA OF A TYPICAL LITTLE RED SCHOOLHOUSE WILL BE PLACED WITHIN HIGHPOINT ELEMENTARY SCHOOL; REGULAR CLASSES WILL BE HELD ALONG WITH INSTRUCTIONS OF CRAFTS OF THE COLONIAL PERIOD. (LOCAL). JOYCE HOGE, PROJ COORDINATOR; HIGHPOINT ELEMENTARY SCHOOL PTA; 520 GREENLAND RD NE; ATLANTA, GA 30342. (#17954). **ARBA GRANTEE.**

HIGHWAY & ROADSIDE BEAUTIFICATION IN GEORGIA. ENCOURAGEMENT OF THE GROWTH OF WILD FLOWERS ALONG THE STATE'S HIGHWAYS WITH THE COOPERATION OF THE GARDEN CLUB OF GEORGIA. (ST-WIDE). BOB KIRK, TRANSPORTATION PLANNING ENGINEER; GEORGIA DEPT OF TRANSPORTATION; 2 CAPITOL SQUARE; ATLANTA, GA 30334. (#629). **(??).**

HILLSDALE NEIGHBORHOOD ASSOCIATION - ATLANTA, GA. ORGANIZATION OF A NEW RESIDENTIAL NEIGHBORHOOD ASSOCIATION WITH A CHARTER AND BYLAWS. (LOCAL). CARLETON ERICKSON, PRESIDENT; HILLSDALE NEIGHBORHOOD ASSOC; 2184 FAIRWAY CIRCLE NE; ATLANTA, GA 30319. (#24151).

HISTORIC MARKER FOR FIRST SETTLERS IN ATLANTA. CONSTRUCTION OF FORT STANDING PEACH TREE ON THE SITE OF FIRST SETTLEMENT IN ATLANTA. (LOCAL). BILL BUSH, COORDINATOR; CITY OF ATLANTA WATER WORKS; CITY HALL; ATLANTA, GA 30303. (#8938).

HISTORY OF GEORGIA EDUCATION. PUBLICATION OF A HISTORY OF EDUCATION IN GEORGIA. (ST-WIDE). ANNE RAYMOND, DIRECTOR, PUBLICATION SERVICES; GEORGIA DEPT OF EDUCATION; 103 STATE OFFICE BLDG; ATLANTA, GA 30334. (#573).

THE HISTORY OF GEORGIA TECH. THE BOOK WILL EMPHASIZE THE ROLE OF GEORGIA TECH IN THE DEVELOPMENT OF SCIENCE AND TECHNOLOGY IN THE STATE AND THE NATION. (LOCAL). DR ROBERT C MCMATH, ASSOCIATE PROFESSOR; GEORGIA TECH BICENTENNIAL COMMITTEE; 325 NORTH AVE; ATLANTA, GA 30332. (#17001).

HISTORY OF MORRIS BROWN COLLEGE - ATLANTA, GA. THE HISTORY OF THE COLLEGE, FROM 1881 TO 1976, WILL BE PUBLISHED, EMPHASIZING THE VALUES OF EDUCATION FOR CITIZENSHIP AND SERVICE TO SOCIETY. (LOCAL). BLANTON E BLACK, CHAIRPERSON; MORRIS BROWN COLLEGE; 643 HUNTER ST; ATLANTA, GA 30314. (#25463).

HISTORY & OUTLINE OF GEORGIA COUNTY GOVERNMENT. AN OUTLINE OF GEORGIA COUNTY GOVERNMENT OVER THE PAST 200 YEARS. (ST-WIDE). JOHN LANGSFELD, ASSOC DIRECTOR; ASSOC OF COUNTY COMMISSIONERS OF GEORGIA; 133 CARNEGIE WAY; ATLANTA, GA 30303. (#17956). **ARBA GRANTEE.**

HOSPITALITY PATROL, ATLANTA, GA. A GROUP OF PEOPLE WHO PATROL ATLANTA'S HOTELS AND DOWNTOWN DISTRICT GIVING INFORMATION TO OUT-OF-TOWN VISITORS AS WELL AS INFORMATION ABOUT BICENTENNIAL EVENTS. (LOCAL). BOB MANNS, COORDINATOR; BUREAU OF CULTURAL AND INTERNATIONAL AFFAIRS, CITY OF ATLANTA; OMNI INTERNATIONAL, 520 NORTH; ATLANTA, GA 30303. (#24206).

IDENTIFICATION OF NATURAL & HISTORICAL TRAILS; GA. IDENTIFICATION OF TRAILS WITH NATURAL & HISTORICAL SIGNIFICANCE IN GEORGIA. (ST-WIDE). JIM OATES, CHIEF RECREATION & PLANNING SECTION; GEORGIA DEPT OF NATURAL RESOURCES; 270 WASHINGTON ST SW; ATLANTA, GA 30334. (#596). **(??).**

IMMUNIZATION AGAINST COMMUNICABLE DISEASES IN GA. FULL IMMUNIZATION AGAINST COMMUNICABLE DISEASES FOR ALL BEGINNING STUDENTS IN GEORGIA SCHOOLS. (ST-WIDE). BOB PARDUE, INFORMATION SPECIALIST; GEORGIA DEPT OF HUMAN RESOURCES; HEALTH BLDG, 47 TRINITY AVE, SW; ATLANTA, GA 30334. (#638).

IMPROVING SALTWATER FISHING OPPORTUNITIES IN GA. ESTABLISHMENT OF TWO OFFSHORE FISHING REEFS TO IMPROVE SALTWATERFISHING OPPORTUNITIES. (ST-WIDE). JIM OATES, CHIEF RECREATION & PLANNING SECTION; GEORGIA DEPT OF NATURAL RESOURCES; 270 WASHINGTON ST SW; ATLANTA, GA 30334. (#631).

INTERFAITH COUNCIL OF CHURCHES BICENT MESSAGE, GA. LEADERS OF FAITH WILL USE THE THEME 'UNITY NOT CONFORMITY' AS THE MESSAGE TO THEIR CONGREGATIONS THROUGHOUT METRO ATLANTA. (LOCAL). MRS VIVIAN BEAVERS, PROJ COORDINATOR; INTERFAITH COUNCIL OF CHURCHES; 1206 FOUNTAIN DR, SW; ATLANTA, GA 30314. (#23017).

INVENTORY OF 18TH CENTURY HOLDINGS IN GEORGIA. PUBLICATION OF AN INVENTORY OF 18TH CENT. HOLDINGS OF THE DEPT. OF ARCHIVES & THE GEORGIA HISTORICAL SOCIETY AS AN AID FOR TEACHERS & SCHOLARS. (ST-WIDE). JACKIE M ERNEY, BICENTENNIAL COORDINATOR; GEORGIA DEPT OF ARCHIVES & HISTORY; 330 CAPITOL AVE; ATLANTA, GA 30334. (#614). **(??).**

'LEGACY OF LEADERSHIP' PROJECT, GA NATIONAL GUARD. AUDIO VISUAL PRESENTATION ABOUT THE HISTORY OF THE GEORGIA NATIONAL GUARD. (ST-WIDE). COL DOUGLAS EMBRY, INFORMATION DIRECTOR; GEORGIA DEPT OF DEFENSE; PO BOX 18055; ATLANTA, GA 30316. (#576).

'LET THERE BE PEACE ON EARTH' - ATLANTA, GA. LONG BEACH INTERNATIONAL CHILDREN'S CHOIR RECORDING OF 'LET THERE BE PEACE ON EARTH' CHOSEN BY THE GEORGIA CHAMBER OF COMMERCE AS ITS OFFICIAL BICENTENNIAL SONG. (NAT'L). MS EASTER N BEEKLEY, DIRECTOR; INTERNATIONAL CHILDREN'S CHOIR; PO BOX 5656; LONG BEACH, CA 90805. (#17478).

LITERACY ACTION VOLUNTEERS - ATLANTA, GA. PROGRAM DESIGNED TO PROVIDE HIGH QUALITY READING ASSISTANCE AND INSTRUCTION FOR FUNCTIONALLY ILLITERATE YOUTHS AND ADULTS. TAILORS INSTRUCTION TO MEET THE INDIVIDUAL INTERESTS AND NEEDS OF STUDENTS. (LOCAL). JIM RADFORD, DIRECTOR; LITERACY ACTION, INC; 201 WASHINGTON ST, SW; ATLANTA, GA 30303. (#24165).

'MARCH OF ATLANTA', ATLANTA, GA. PROMOTION OF MUSICAL ARRANGEMENT AS THE OFFICIAL MARCH OF ATLANTA, A BAND ARRANGEMENT FROM THE ORIGINAL SCORE FOR PIANO, PRINTED IN ATLANTA MAGAZINE, DEC 1972. (LOCAL). JOHN CHAGY, COORDINATOR; 77 E ANDREWS DR NW; ATLANTA, GA 30305. (#24194).

MARTA BICENTENNIAL BUS - ATLANTA, GA. A REGULAR METROPOLITAN ATLANTA RAPID TRANSIT AUTHORITY BUS PAINTED TO REFLECT THE BICENTENNIAL MOOD ON THE EXTERIOR AND HISTORICAL THEMES ON THE INTERIOR DISPLAY PANELS. (LOCAL). DENNIS MOLLENKAMP, DIRECTOR; METROPOLITAN ATLANTA RAPID TRANSIT AUTHORITY; 100 PEACHTREE ST; ATLANTA, GA 30303. (#24166).

MISS BRONZE ATLANTA PAGEANT. PAGEANT OF 40-50 WOMEN, EACH TO PORTRAY A FAMOUS BLACK PERSON AND THEIR CONTRIBUTION TO AMERICAN HISTORY. (LOCAL). MRS IRMA WILLIAMS, COORD; MRS IRMA WILLIAMS; 1050 TUCKAWANA DR, SW; ATLANTA, GA 30311. (#106703-1).

MOBILE EXHIBIT PROGRAM OF GEORGIA. DEVELOPMENT OF A MOBILE EXHIBIT PROGRAM TO BRING THE STORY OF THE AMERICAN REVOLUTION AND GEORGIA'S HERITAGE TO ALL AREAS OF THE STATE. (ST-WIDE). JACKIE ERNEY, BICENTENNIAL COORDINATOR; GEORGIA DEPT OF ARCHIVES & HISTORY; 330 CAPITOL AVE SE; ATLANTA, GA 30334. (#615). **ARBA GRANTEE.**

MULTI-MEDIA HISTORY EXHIBIT OF ATLANTA. EXHIBIT. (LOCAL). WILLIAM PRESSLY, PRES; THE ATLANTA HISTORICAL SOCIETY; 3099 ANDREW DR; ATLANTA, GA 30305. (#107363-1).

MY BICENTENNIAL STORYBOOK, ATLANTA, GA. AN ILLUSTRATED 13 CHAPTER STORY BOOK WITH LEARNING CENTER ACTIVITIES 23 PAGES OF BICENTENNIAL REFERENCE MATERIALS APPROVED AS EARLY CHILDHOOD & ELEMENTARY TEXT; $1.92. (NAT'L). W WESLEY DEVOTO, PRESIDENT; HISTORICAL CHILDREN'S PUBLICATIONS, INC; 3422 FIRST NATIONAL BANK TWR; ATLANTA, GA 30303. (#16382).

NATL BICENTENNIAL INTERNSHIP PGM -SOUTHEAST AREA. STUDENT INTERNSHIP ASSISTANCE IN DEVELOPING THE SOCIAL AND ECONOMIC RESOURCES TO SUPPORT LOCALLY INITIATED, STATE AGENCY, AND COMMUNITY BICENTENNIAL PROGRAMMING. (REGN'L). HARLAN T COOPER, DIRECTOR; SOUTHERN REGIONAL EDUCATION BOARD; 130 6TH ST, NW; ATLANTA, GA 30313. (#24). **ARBA RECOGNIZED. ARBA GRANTEE.**

OAKLAND CEMETERY WATCHHOUSE/ENTRY RESTORATION - GA. RESTORATION & PRESERVATION OF THE WATCHHOUSE FOR A VISITOR/TOUR CENTER; RESTORATION INCLUDES LANDSCAPE, GATE & ROAD WORK. GUIDED TOURS WILL BE AVAILABLE. (LOCAL). THEODORE MASTROIANNI, DIRECTOR; CITY OF ATLANTA BUREAU OF PARKS & RECREATION; 260 CENTRAL AVE S W; ATLANTA, GA 30303. (#23599). **ARBA GRANTEE.**

'THE OLD IN NEW ATLANTA' - ATLANTA, GA. 134-PAGE PUBLICATION-200 ENTRIES & 150 ILLUSTRATIONS DESCRIBING HOMES, BUILDINGS & CHURCHES BUILT PRIOR TO 1914 IN ATLANTA, DECATUR, STONE MOUNTAIN, ROSWELL & VININGS. BUILDINGS STILL STANDING. (LOCAL). MS ELIZABETH SAWYER, PROJ DIRECTOR; 598 CHESTNUT OAK COURT NW; ATLANTA, GA 30327. (#24159).

ORGANIZING FOR ACTION - ATLANTA, GA. A NARRATIVE SURVEY OF ATLANTA'S NEIGHBORHOOD ORGANIZATIONS, EMPHASIZING THE RIGHT FOR CITIZENS TO WORK TOGETHER FOR THE IMPROVEMENT OF SOCIETY. (LOCAL). JOE PARKO, DIRECTOR; URBAN LIFE ASSOCIATES; 33 GILMER ST SW; ATLANTA, GA 30303. (#24153).

PAMPHLETS ON GEORGIA DURING THE REVOLUTION. PREPARATION AND DISTRIBUTION TO GEORGIA SCHOOLS OF 15 DIFFERENT PAMPHLETS ABOUT GEORGIA'S ROLE DURING THE REVOLUTIONARY WAR. (ST-WIDE). ANNE RAYMOND, DIRECTOR, PUBLICATION SERVICES; GEORGIA DEPT OF EDUCATION; 103 STATE OFFICE BLDG; ATLANTA, GA 30334. (#574).

PAST IS PROLOGUE - FUTURE WE DETERMINE - GEORGIA. TO INSTILL IN STUDENTS, EMPLOYEES, AND PATRONS A COMPREHENSIVE KNOWLEDGE AND APPRECIATION OF THE RICHNESS OF OUR NATIONAL HERITAGE; AN AWARENESS AND UNDERSTANDING OF OUR NATION'S ACHIEVEMENTS & FAILURES. (LOCAL). BARBARA WITTAKER, DIRECTOR; ATLANTA PUBLIC SCHOOL SYSTEM; 224 CENTRAL AVE SW; ATLANTA, GA 30311. (#8933).

PHOENIX-ATLANTA SPIRIT, GA. AN ATLANTA BICENTENNIAL SONG IS WRITTEN IN TWO VERSIONS. (LOCAL). CHARLES K HOWARD, MD, PROJ DIRECTOR; FULTON COUNTY HEALTH DEPT; 99 BUTLER ST SE; ATLANTA, GA 30303. (#26644).

PINES OF ATLANTA: HISTORICAL POEM - ATLANTA, GA. POEM TO ENCOURAGE HISTORICAL AWARENESS OF & PRIDE IN CITY OF ATLANTA ATLANTA. (LOCAL). ROBERT MANNS, PROJ DIRECTOR; 11-5 E JAMESTOWN RD; ATLANTA, GA 30333. (#24163).

PLAQUE & BEAUTIFICATION PROJ - ATLANTA, GA. TWO ISLANDS IN THE MIDDLE OF LANIER DRIVE, ADJOINING HISTORIC OGLETHORPE UNIV AND FACING PEACHTREE RD, WILL BE BEAUTIFIED; COMMEMORATIVE PLAQUE WILL THEN BE PLACED. (LOCAL). MRS BARBARA G SMITH, PRESIDENT; SILVER LAKE GARDEN CLUB; 3262 WOODROW WAY NE; ATLANTA, GA 30319. (#26963). **ARBA GRANTEE.**

PRESERVATION OF WILDLIFE RESOURCES IN GEORGIA. RESTORATION OF GA'S WILD TURKEY POPULATION,OYSTER BEDS & STRIPED BASS RUNS IN ORDER TO REPLENISH & PRESERVE GEORGIA'S WILDLIFE RESOURCES. (ST-WIDE). JIM OATES, CHIEF, RECREATION & PLANNING SECTION; GEORGIA DEPT OF NATURAL RESOURCES; 270 WASHINGTON ST SW; ATLANTA, GA 30334. (#641).

PRESERVATION & RESTORATION OF COVERED BRIDGES--GA. PRESERVATION & RESTORATION OF COVERED BRIDGES IN GEORGIA. (ST-WIDE). BOB KIRK, TRANSPORTATION PLANNING ENGINEER; GEORGIA DEPT OF TRANSPORTATION; 2 CAPITOL SQUARE; ATLANTA, GA 30334. (#611). **(??).**

REGIONAL MEETING OF BOARD OF FOREIGN SCHOLARSHIPS. SEMINAR. (REGN'L). DR RICHARD WIEGAND, DIR; CONTINUING EDUCATION OF GA TECH; 325 NORTH AVE; ATLANTA, GA 30332. (#103095-1).

RELANDSCAPING HISTORIC SITE IN ATLANTA. RESTORATION AND ADAPTATION OF 12 ACRE HISTORICAL SITE, FOR PRESENT DAY USE. (LOCAL). MRS JAMES H LOFTIS, BEAUTIFICATION CIVIC CHAIRMAN; ATLANTA BEAUTIFICATION COMMITTEE; 952 LULLWATER RD, NE; ATLANTA, GA 30307. (#9745). **ARBA GRANTEE.**

RENOVATION, CLIMATE CONTROL IN ATLANTA, GA. PROVIDE AIR CONDITIONING SYSTEM FOR AREA OF ATLANTA MEMORIAL ARTS CENTER WHICH IS BEING DEVELOPED FOR 2690 ADDITIONAL EXHIBITION SPACE FOR THE HIGH MUSEUM OF ART. (LOCAL). GUDMUND VIGTEL, DIRECTOR; THE HIGH MUSEUM OF ART; 1280 PEACHTREE ST; ATLANTA, GA 30309. (#13640).

RESTORATION OF CYCLORAMA, ATLANTA, GA. EDUCATE THE PUBLIC ABOUT THE CYCLORAMA AS A HISTORICAL SITE, PUBLICIZE THE PLIGHT OF THE CYCLORAMA AND RAISE FUNDS NECESSARY FOR ITS RESTORATION. (LOCAL). JACK STEPHENS, CHAIRPERSON; CYCLORAMA RESTORATION, INC; PO BOX 1561; ATLANTA, GA 30301. (#24195).

RESTORATION OF OAKLAND CEMETERY - ATLANTA, GA. RESTORATION OF MUSEUM OFFICES, LANDSCAPING OF 88 ACRES OF CEMETERY AND GUIDED TOURS OF THE CEMETERY 3 TIMES A WEEK. (LOCAL). ED WALTERS, COORDINATOR; OAKLAND CEMETERY & ATLANTA BUREAU OF PARKS & RECREATION; 248 OAKLAND AVE SE; ATLANTA, GA 30312. (#24161).

'THE RIGHT TO PRIVACY' - SEMINAR. SEMINAR ON THE CONSTITUTIONAL RIGHT TO PRIVACY OF AMERICANS. (LOCAL). MS BETSY BAKER, COORD; THE ATLANTA SECTION NATIONAL COUNCIL OF JEWISH WOMEN; 3224 PEACHTREE RD, NE; ATLANTA, GA 30305. (#106704-7).

SEMINAR ON THE BARTRAM TRAIL. GROUPS ARE RESEARCHING & RESTORING PARTS OF BARTRAM'S TRAIL, WHICH COVERED 7 STATES. WORK IS STATE-ORIENTED; ALL GROUPS WANT TO COORDINATE & SHARE INFORMATION. THIS SEMINAR WILL FILL THE NEED. (REGN'L). MRS CHARLES YARN, BARTRAM TRAIL CHRMN; DEEP SOUTH REGION OF NATIONAL COUNCIL OF STATE GARDEN CLUBS; 881 W CONWAY RD N W; ATLANTA, GA 30327. (#7942). **ARBA RECOGNIZED. ARBA GRANTEE.**

STATE PARKS - BICENTENNIAL FLAGS & PATCHES, GA. ALL STATE PARKS ARE FLYING THE GEORGIA BICENTENNIAL FLAG AND ALL STATE PARK PERSONNEL ARE WEARING GEORGIA BICENTENNIAL PATCHES AS PART OF THEIR OFFICIAL UNIFORMS. (ST-WIDE). HENRY STRUBLE, DIRECTOR; GEORGIA PARKS & HISTORIC SITES DIV, DEPT NATURAL RESOURCES; 270 WASHINGTON ST SW; ATLANTA, GA 30334. (#32707).

STOP DRUGS AT THE SOURCE LTD, ATLANTA, GA. NATIONWIDE PETITION CAMPAIGN DEMANDING THAT DRUGS ABUSE BE ELIMINATED. (NAT'L). KEN KRAUHTER, DIRECTOR; STOP DRUGS AT THE SOURCE LTD; PO BOX 29185; ATLANTA, GA 30329. (#16365).

STUDY OF STATE & LOCAL GOV'T - ATLANTA, GA. A YEARBOOK WILL BE PUBLISHED WHICH INCLUDES TEACHER PROVEN IDEAS FOR TEACHING STATE AND LOCAL GOVERNMENT AND HISTORY. (ST-WIDE). DR TERRY NORTHUP, EXEC SECRETARY; GEORGIA COUNCIL FOR THE SOCIAL SCIENCES; BOX 124, GEORGIA STATE UNIV; ATLANTA, GA 30303. (#17957). **ARBA GRANTEE.**

TEACHER'S PACKET ON THE REVOLUTIONARY PERIOD - GA. PACKET OF INFORMATION FOR TEACHERS IN GEORGIA FOR USE IN TEACHING THE AMERICAN REVOLUTION AND GEORGIA'S SPECIFIC ROLE THEREIN. (ST-WIDE). A K JOHNSON, EXEC DIRECTOR; GEORGIA COMMISSION FOR THE NATIONAL BICENTENNIAL CELEBRATION; 1776 PEACHTREE, SOUTH WING; ATLANTA, GA 30309. (#590).

THIRTEEN ORIGINAL STATES BICENTENNIAL INTERN PROJ. STUDENT INTERNS WORK ON EXPERIMENTAL PROJECTS IN ENERGY, HEALTH, HISTORY & BICENT PLANNING FOR GROUPS & INDIVIDUALS AT THE REGIONAL, STATE & LOCAL LEVELS. FUNDS PROVIDED THRU MATCHING GRANT TO NBIP. (REGN'L). CLARK CLIFFORD, EXEC DIRECTOR; BICENTENNIAL COUNCIL OF THE THIRTEEN ORIGINAL STATES; 400 COLONY SQUARE, SUITE 2001; ATLANTA, GA 30361. (#1523). **ARBA RECOGNIZED.**

'TOCANTA' - MUSICAL. PERFORMANCE OF AN UNRECORDED MUSICAL COMPOSITION BY HENRY COWELL. (LOCAL). DONNA ANGEL, COORD; MASTER ARTS; 235 BRIGHTON RD, NE; ATLANTA, GA 30309. (#108913-13).

TOLL-FREE TELEPHONE INFORMATION SERVICE OF GEORGIA. TOLL-FREE TELEPHONE INFORMATION & REFERRAL SERVICE WITHIN THE STATE. WILL PROVIDE RELIABLE INFORMATION TO CITIZENS OF THE STATE ABOUT ANY HUMAN RESOURCES PROGRAM. (ST-WIDE). BOB PARDUE, INFORMATION SPECIALIST; GEORGIA DEPT OF HUMAN RESOURCES; HEALTH BLDG, 47 TRINITY AVE, SW; ATLANTA, GA 30334. (#639).

TOURING DRAMA IN GEORGIA. TWO PLAYS TO BE SHOWN THROUGHOUT THE STATE ON THE AMERICAN REVOL AND THE GOLD RUSH IN GEORGIA. (ST-WIDE). LONICE BARRETT, PROJ DIRECTOR; DEPARTMENT OF NATURAL RESOURCES; 270 WASHINGTON ST, SW; ATLANTA, GA 30144. (#11005). **ARBA GRANTEE.**

TRIBUTE TO MINORITY BUSINESS & INDUSTRY, GA. ICBO TO SEND AWARDS TO THOSE MINORITY AND MAJORITY BUSINESS PEOPLE & ENTERPRISES WHICH HAVE MADE VALUABLE CONTRIBUTIONS TO THE EFFORT OF MINORITY BUSINESSES DURING THE PAST YEAR. (LOCAL). JOE HUDSON, CHAIRMAN; INTERRACIAL

ATLANTA — CONTINUED

COUNCIL FOR BUSINESS OPPORTUNITIES; 40 MARIETTA ST NW; ATLANTA, GA 30303. (#29941).

THE U S FLAG IN DOWNTOWN ATLANTA. AN OLD FLAG POLE LOCATED IN CENTRAL ATLANTA WILL BE RESTORED SO THAT THE U S FLAG MAY FLY 24 HOURS A DAY. (LOCAL). BILL PUGH, COORDINATOR; HAMILTON BANK AND TRUST CO; 74 PEACHTREE ST NW; ATLANTA, GA 30301. (#8935).

VENEREAL DISEASE TREATMENT PROJECT OF GEORGIA. TREATMENT FOR VENEREAL DISEASE VICTIMS TO BE MADE MORE ACCESSIBLE TO THE CITIZENS OF GEORGIA. (ST-WIDE). BOB PARDUE, INFORMATION SPECIALIST; GEORGIA DEPT OF HUMAN RESOURCES; HEALTH BLDG, 47 TRINITY AVE, SW; ATLANTA, GA 30334. (#624). **(??).**

VIRGINIA-HIGHLAND SIGN, ATLANTA, GA. REFURBISH AND PAINT A BILL BOARD WITH THE ATLANTA BICENTENNIAL COMMISSION'S LOGO, AT THE VIRGINIA-HIGHLAND INTERSECTION. (LOCAL). CHARLES LONGLEY, JR; VA HIGHLAND CIVIC ASSOC; 946 RUPLEY DR; ATLANTA, GA 30306. (#24193).

VOTER REGISTRATION DRIVE OF ATLANTA, GEORGIA. MODEL PROJECT DESIGNED TO REGISTER 20 MILLION NEW VOTERS BY 1976. V-O-T-E IS SPONSORED BY 5 CIVIC GROUPS: OPTIMISTS, JAYCEES, KIWANIS, LEAGUE OF WOMEN VOTERS, & AMER ASSOC OF RETIRED PERSON. (ST-WIDE). ROBERT STANLEY, COORDINATOR; VOICE OF THE ELECTOR; PO BOX 77046; ATLANTA, GA 30309. (#8971).

WALTER MCELREATH HALL - ATLANTA, GA. A TRIBUTE TO THE CITY AT THE TIME OF THE NATION'S BICENTENNIAL. A BUILDING WHICH WILL HOLD IMPORTANT RECORDS & HAVE EXHIBIT SPACE FOR DISPLAY OF ARTIFACTS AND MATERIAL RELATED TO ATLANTA'S HISTORY. (LOCAL). DR WILLIAM L PRESSLY, CHAIRMAN; ATLANTA HISTORICAL SOCIETY; 3099 ANDREWS DR, NW; ATLANTA, GA 30305. (#24156).

WELL-BABY CLINICS OF GEORGIA. WELL-BABY CLINICS ESTABLISHED THROUGHOUT GEORGIA. (ST-WIDE). BOB PARDUE, INFORMATION SPEIALIST; GEORGIA DEPT OF HUMAN RESOURCES; HEALTH BLDG, 47 TRINITY AVE, SW; ATLANTA, GA 30334. (#643). **(??).**

WESTBROOK, HOME OF GEN JAMES EDWARD OGLETHORPE, GA. BOOK AND SCALE MODELS DESCRIBING WESTBROOK, THE COUNTRY HOME OF GEN JAMES OGLETHORPE, AND ITS HISTORY. SCALE MODELS WILL BE PERMANENTLY MAINTAINED IN SAVANNAH, ATLANTA & GODALMING, ENGLAND. (ST-WIDE). DOROTHY SPENCE, EXEC DIRECTOR; ATLANTA CHAPTER, AMERICAN INSTITUTE OF ARCHITECTS; 230 PEACHTREE ST, NW; ATLANTA, GA 30303. (#24726). **ARBA GRANTEE.**

WILLIAMSBURG DEBATE REPRESENTATIVES, ATLANTA, GA. TWO OUTSTANDING DEBATE TEAMS REPRESENTING THE STATE OF GEORGIA HAVE BEEN SPONSORED EACH YEAR BY THE GCNBC TO COMPETE IN THE NATIONAL BICENTENNIAL DEBATES IN WILLIAMSBURG, VA. (LOCAL). A K JOHNSON, JR, DIRECTOR; GEORGIA COMMISSION FOR THE NATIONAL BICENTENNIAL CELEBRATION; SUITE 520, 1776 PEACHTREE ST NW; ATLANTA, GA 30309. (#32702).

WSB AM-FM 2-HR DEBATES ON THE REVOLUTION - NBMRP. IN COOP W/ EMORY & OXFORD COLLEGES, STUDENTS DEBATE ASPECTS OF AMER REV. ALSO DAILY 2-MIN ORIGINAL REENACTMENTS OF REV EVENT & MONTHLY PGMS ON MEANINGS OF SUCH EVENTS; COVERAGE OF SPECIAL BICENT PGM/EVNT. (ST-WIDE). AUBREY R MORRIS, BICENTENNIAL COORDINATOR; WSB AM-FM RADIO; 1601 PEACHTREE ST; ATLANTA, GA 30309. (#23266).

'75 IN '76-THE ATLANTA YWCA' - ATLANTA, GA. PORTABLE SLIDE SHOW OF HISTORY OF THE ATLANTA YWCA, CELEBRATING ITS 75TH BIRTHDAY IN 1976. SLIDES DEPICT GROWTH OF YWCA IN RELATION TO COMMUNITY AND ESP HIGHLIGHT RELATIONSHIP OF YWCA LEADERS TO OTHERS. (LOCAL). HAVILAND H MILLIGAN, CHAIRMAN; THE ATLANTA YWCA; 1027 COLUMBIA AVE, NE; ATLANTA, GA 30309. (#24155).

SEPT 5 - 8, '73. GEORGE V. ALLEN ESSAY CONTEST FOR YOUNG PEOPLE IN SISTER CITIES. SISTER CITIES PROJECT. A PRIVATE NONPROFIT NATIONAL ORGANIZATION COORDINATING 420 US CITIES & THEIR AFFILIATED SISTER CITIES IN 61 OTHER COUNTRIES. PROGRAM AIMS TO ENCOURAGE INVOLVEMENT OF WORLD COMMUNITY IN BICENTENNIAL. (INT'L). THOMAS GITTINS, EXEC; THE TOWN AFFILIATION ASSOCIATION, INC; 1625 K ST, NW; WASHINGTON, DC 20006. (#187-902).

FEB 15, '74. OGLETHORPE BALL SPONSORED BY THE BRITISH AMERICAN ASSOCIATION. BRITISH-AMERICAN ASSOC BICENTENNIAL BALLS. SERIES OF BALLS EMPHASIZING BRITISH AMERICAN HERITAGE LEADING TO A BICENTENNIAL BALL IN 1976. (ST-WIDE). REGINALD MITCHELL, PRES; BRITISH-AMERICAN ASSOCIATION OF THE SOUTHEAST; PO BOX 24; AVONDALE ESTS, GA 30002. (#900-901).

MAR 29, '74. NEW WORK BY JOHN ADAMS PERFORMED AT GA STATE UNIVERSITY. NEW AMERICAN MUSIC BY COMPOSER JOHN ADAMS. GRANT/FELLOWSHIP SPONSORED BY NATL ENDOWMENT FOR THE ARTS TO AID IN PERFORMANCES OF NEW MUSIC BY JOHN ADAMS IN LOS ANGELES, ATLANTA, & OTHER AREAS. (ST-WIDE). JOHN ADAMS, DIRECTOR; JOHN ADAMS; ROUTE 1, BOX 44; STOCKBRIDGE, GA 30281. (#1221-902).

NOV 1, '74 - CONTINUING . 'GREAT GEORGIANS' TV SERIES. PRODUCTION OF A 12-PART SERIES ENTITLED 'GREAT GEORGIANS' FOR AIRING STATEWIDE ON EDUCATIONAL TV. AT GEORGIA UNIV AT ATHENS, GA. (ST-WIDE). DR HOWARD JORDAN; GEORGIA UNIVERSITY SYSTEM CENTER FOR CONTINUING EDUCATION; 244 WASHINGTON ST SW; ATLANTA, GA 30334. (#578-1).

NOV 19, '74. DEDICATION OF COMMEMORATIVE PLAQUES. DEDICATION OF TWO COMMEMORATIVE PLAQUES TO BE MOUNTED ON STONE ON FOUNTAIN DRIVE AND MORRIS BROWN DRIVE. ONE OF THE PLAQUES HONORS MARTIN LUTHER KING, JR. (LOCAL). VIVIAN BEAVERS, COORD; ATLANTA BICENT COMMISSION; 1206 FOUNTAIN DR, NW; ATLANTA, GA 30314. (#8932-1).

JAN 15, '75 - FEB 1, '76. THE INTERFAITH PROJECT FOR 1976. LIVE PERFORMANCE AT ATLANTA CIVIC CENTER. (LOCAL). VIVIAN BEAVERS, COORD; CHRISTIAN COUNCIL OF CHURCHES AND OTHER RELIGIOUS LEADERS; 1206 FOUNTAIN DR SW; ATLANTA, GA 30318. (#103258-2).

FEB 1 - 28, '75. WATERCOLOR DEMONSTRATIONS. EXHIBIT. (LOCAL). GERRY POWELL, PRESIDENT; ATLANTA ARTISTS CLUB; 3099 PEACHTREE RD; ATLANTA, GA 30305. (#22622-1).

MAR 10, '75 - JULY 10, '76. PAST IS PROLOGUE FUTURE WE DETERMINE. COMPETITION, EXHIBIT, LIVE PERFORMANCE AT SCHOOL AUDITORIUMS THROUGHOUT ATLANTA AREA. (LOCAL). BARBARA WHITTAKER; ATLANTA PUBLIC SCHOOL SYSTEM; 820 PEACHTREE CTR, SOUTH TOWER; ATLANTA, GA 30303. (#103773-5).

APR 7, '75. PERFORMANCE OF 'SONGBIRDSONGS' BY JOHN ADAMS AT GA STATE UNIV. NEW AMERICAN MUSIC BY COMPOSER JOHN ADAMS. GRANT/FELLOWSHIP SPONSORED BY NATL ENDOWMENT FOR THE ARTS TO AID IN PERFORMANCES OF NEW MUSIC BY JOHN ADAMS IN LOS ANGELES, ATLANTA, & OTHER AREAS. (ST-WIDE). JOHN ADAMS, DIRECTOR; JOHN ADAMS; ROUTE 1, BOX 44; STOCKBRIDGE, GA 30281. (#1221-501).

JUNE 3, '75. STAR SPANGLED BONANZA. MILITARY DISPLAY, BAND, BOOK STORES, BAKE SHOP AND CHILDREN'S SHOW. AT 805 MT VERNON HIGHWAY NW. (LOCAL). MS NANCY CADOVA, COORD; HOLY INNOCENTS EPISCOPAL SCHOOL; 805 MT VERNON HWY NW; ATLANTA, GA 30327. (#200012-1).

JUNE 12 - AUG 31, '75. 'GOLD', DRAMA OF THE GOLD RUSH IN GA. TWO PLAYS TO BE SHOWN THROUGHOUT THE STATE ON THE AMERICAN REVOL AND THE GOLD RUSH IN GEORGIA. (ST-WIDE). LONICE BARRETT; DEPARTMENT OF NATURAL RESOURCES; 270 WASHINGTON ST, SW; ATLANTA, GA 30144. (#11005-502).

JUNE 12 - AUG 31, '75. 'THE VIGIL', REVOL WAR DRAMA IN GA. TWO PLAYS TO BE SHOWN THROUGHOUT THE STATE ON THE AMERICAN REVOL AND THE GOLD RUSH IN GEORGIA. (ST-WIDE). LONICE BARRETT; DEPARTMENT OF NATURAL RESOURCES; 270 WASHINGTON ST, SW; ATLANTA, GA 30144. (#11005-501).

JULY 4, '75. 4TH OF JULY PARADE. PARADE. (LOCAL). WILLARD E WRIGHT, CO-CHMN; GA TECH BICENTENNIAL COMMITTEE & RAMBLING RECK CLUB; 325 NORTH AVE; ATLANTA, GA 30332. (#200012-38).

AUG 4 - 9, '75. BICENTENNIAL EXPOSITION IN ATLANTA, GA. IN AUGUST 1975, A BICENTENNIAL EXPOSITION WILL BE HELD IN LENNOX SQUARE; EXHIBIT INCLUDES CRAFT DEMONSTRATIONS, LIVE PERFORMANCES BY BANDS, CHORAL & DANCE GROUPS AND EXHIBITS. (LOCAL). MINA WHITE; GEORGIA COMMISSION FOR THE NATIONAL BICENTENNIAL CELEBRATION; 1776 PEACHTREE, 520 SOUTH WING; ATLANTA, GA 30309. (#13446-1).

SEPT 20 - DEC 30, '75. DISPLAY OF CRAFTWORK. 5000 ELEMENTARY SCHOOL CHILDREN & 160 TEACHERS WILL CREATE OBJECTS BASED ON OUR HERITAGE FROM GEORGIA'S INDIGENOUS MATERIALS SUCH AS CLAY, FIBERS, METALS & WOOD. (ST-WIDE). MRS SARA JO SIRMANS; GEORGIA ART EDUCATION ASSOCIATION; 2860 GUINIVERE DR, NE; ATLANTA, GA 30345. (#12002-501).

SEPT 25 - OCT 5, '75. SOUTHEASTERN FAIR BICENT EXHIBIT IN ATLANTA. THE GROWTH OF THE U S IS FEATURED THROUGH THE ARTS & INDUSTRY. EACH DECADE IS COVERED. (LOCAL). BILL PUGH, PROJ DIRECTOR; SOUTHEASTERN STATE FAIR; PO BOX 6826; ATLANTA, GA 30315. (#8937-1).

SEPT '75 - APR '76. SEMINAR: 'CHAIR OF PRIVATE ENTERPRISE. PROGRAM DESIGNED TO ENCOURAGE BETTER UNDERSTANDING OF AMERICAN PRIVATE ENTERPRISE. (LOCAL). HENRY T MALONE, CHMN; GEORGIA STATE UNIV - SCHOOL OF BUSINESS ADMINISTRATION/THE SPONSORS; UNIVERSITY PLAZA, GA STATE UNIV; ATLANTA, GA 30303. (#106122-1).

OCT 1 - 31, '75. FINNISH MUSIC & HANDICRAFTS. FESTIVAL, EXHIBIT. (ST-WIDE). A K JOHNSON, EXEC DIR; GEORGIA COMMISSION FOR THE NATIONAL BICENTENNIAL CELEBRATION; 1776 PEACHTREE ST; ATLANTA, GA 30309. (#26429-1).

OCT 1 - 31, '75. WOMEN IN THE ARTS. A FESTIVAL OF WOMEN IN THE ARTS TO COMMEMORATE INTERNATIONAL WOMEN'S YEAR AND TO HEIGHTEN AWARENESS OF WOMEN'S PARTICIPATION IN THE ARTS BY EXHIBITING ART CREATED BY WOMEN. AT THE ATLANTA CIVIC CENTER, 395 PIEDMONT AVE NE. (LOCAL). MS SUZANNE DONNER, COORD; FEMINIST ACTION ALLIANCE, INC; BOX 54717 CIVIC CENTER STATION; ATLANTA, GA 30308. (#200012-7).

OCT 21 - NOV 1, '75. ART AMERICAN - THEN & NOW. ART FESTIVAL FOR ARTISTS & CRAFTSMEN TO DISPLAY & SELL THEIR WORKS; VARIOUS ENTERTAINMENT GROUPS WILL PERFORM. AT PHIPPS PLAZA MALL, 3500 PEACHTREE RD. (LOCAL). MS FAYE HALFORD, CHAIRMAN; SANDY SPRINGS JUNIOR WOMEN'S CLUB; 1100 MARTIN RIDGE RD; ROSWELL, GA 30075. (#200012-8).

OCT 23, '75. MULTI-CAMPUS VOTER REGISTRATION DRIVE. EXHIBIT AT DEKALB & FULTON COUNTY CAMPUSES. (LOCAL). ED MARSHALL, COORDINATOR; ATLANTA BICENTENNIAL STUDENT COMMITTEE; 225 PEACHTREE ST NE; ATLANTA, GA 30303. (#200012-9).

OCT 29 - NOV 1, '75. GEORGIA TECH CELEBRATES AMERICA'S BICENTENNIAL. CELEBRATION WILL INCLUDE FIREWORKS DISPLAY, A CABARET, THE MUSICAL '1776' & THE RAMBLING WRECK PARADE - THEME, 200 YRS OF ENGINEERING. (LOCAL). DON NELSON, PROGRAM DIR; GA TECH STUDENT CENTER & BICENTENNIAL COMMITTEE; 325 NORTH AVE; ATLANTA, GA 30332. (#103095-6).

NOV 1, '75. TURKISH CELEBRATION. FESTIVAL. (ST-WIDE). A K JOHNSON, EXEC DIR; GEORGIA COMMISSION FOR THE NATIONAL BICENTENNIAL CELEBRATION; 1776 PEACHTREE ST; ATLANTA, GA 30309. (#26429-2).

NOV 15, '75. HELLENIC FESTIVAL. FESTIVAL. (ST-WIDE). A K JOHNSON, EXEC DIR; GEORGIA COMMISSION FOR THE NATIONAL BICENTENNIAL CELEBRATION; 1776 PEACHTREE ST; ATLANTA, GA 30309. (#26429-3).

NOV 15 - DEC 13, '75. POSITIVE ACTION FOR WOMEN IN MANAGEMENT. WORKSHOPS COVERING THE FOLLOWING TOPICS: COMMUNICATION SKILLS DEVELOPMENT, MOTIVATION DECISION-MAKING SKILLS, ASSERTIVE TRAINING, ETC. AT GEORGIA STATE UNIV, URBAN LIFE SCHOOL. (LOCAL). MS NANCY LYDECKEN, COORD; THE J C SINGLES; BOX 52883; ATLANTA, GA 30305. (#200012-3).

NOV 20 - 22, '75. BICENTENNIAL PROGRAM ON GOVERNMENT: 200 YEARS OF CHANGE. CONFERENCE AT GEORGIA STATE CAPITAL AND OLD DEKALB COUNTY COURTHOUSE. (LOCAL). PHILIP SWATEK, COORD; EMORY UNIV CENTER FOR RESEARCH IN SOCIAL CHANGE; ATLANTA, GA 30322. (#200012-4).

NOV 23, '75. INTERDENOMINATIONAL THANKSGIVING SERVICE. CEREMONY AT FIRST PRESBYTERIAN CHURCH, 1328 PEACHTREE ST NE. (LOCAL). DR HARRY FIFIELD, COORD; CHURCHES & TEMPLES IN ATLANTA; 1328 PEACHTREE ST NE; ATLANTA, GA 30309. (#200012-5).

NOV 27, '75. BICENTENNIAL HALF-TIME SHOW AT GA TECH HOMECOMING. FESTIVAL. (LOCAL). EDWARD S BRIDGES, DIR; GA TECH BICENTENNIAL COMMITTEE & MUSIC DEPT; 325 NORTH AVE; ATLANTA, GA 30332. (#103095-5).

DEC 1, '75 - DEC 31, '76. TOURS OF TULLIE SMITH HOUSE. SAMPLE COSTUMES RESEARCHED AND CREATED TO REPRESENT TYPICAL FASHION WORN BY UPLAND GEORGIANS RESIDING IN TULLIE SMITH HOUSE FROM 1840 TO 1860. DOCENTS TO EXHIBIT COSTUMES IN CELEBRATION OF AMER BICENT '76. SUNDAYS 2-4:30. CLOSED HOLIDAYS & THE MONTH OF JANUARY. AT ATLANTA HISTORICAL SOCIETY GROUNDS, 3099 ANDREWS DR, NW. (ST-WIDE). SALLY WHITE; THE FASHION GROUP, INC, ATLANTA REGIONAL CHAPTER; 6410 COLEWOOD CT, NW; ATLANTA, GA 30328. (#12237-1).

DEC 9, '75. BOND REFERENDUM. SUPPORT OF BOND REFERENDUM THAT WOULD PROVIDE $41 MILLION FOR A NEW LIBRARY, ZOO, PARK, CYCLORAMA IMPROVEMENTS AND SEWER & TRAFFIC IMPROVEMENTS. AT ATLANTA CITY VOTER AREA. (LOCAL). MS ESTELLE FORD GREENE; ATLANTA BICENTENNIAL COMMISSION & THE CITY OF ATLANTA; 225 PEACHTREE ST NE; ATLANTA, GA 30303. (#200012-10).

JAN 2 - DEC 31, '76. BICENTENNIAL FLAG RAISING. GEORGIA BICENTENNIAL & ARBA FLAGS WERE RAISED & WILL REMAIN THROUGH 1976 IN RECOGNITION OF THE BICENTENNIAL OBSERVANCE IN GEORGIA. AT GEORGIA STATE CAPITAL BLDG. (ST-WIDE). MINA WHITE, PGM DIR; GEORGIA COMMISSION FOR THE NATIONAL BICENTENNIAL CELEBRATION; 1776 PEACHTREE ST, #520; ATLANTA, GA 30309. (#200012-47).

JAN 2, '76 - CONTINUING . MUSEUM OF GA FOLK CULTURE. COLLECTION OF GA FOLK ARTIFACTS AT GA STATE UNIVERSITY. AT ROOM 218-G BUILDING. (ST-WIDE). JOHN BURRISON, MUSEUM DIR; GA STATE UNIV SCHOOL OF ARTS & SCIENCES; UNIVERSITY PLAZA; ATLANTA, GA 30303. (#106097-1).

JAN 12, '76. OPENING DAY OF GEORGIA LEGISLATURE - 1976. BICENTENNIAL SKIT AND CEREMONIES INCLUDING SPECIAL ADDRESS BY JOHN WARNER OPENED THE 1976 EDITION OF THE GEORGIA LEGISLATURE. (ST-WIDE). MINA WHITE, PGM DIR; GEORGIA COMMISSION FOR THE NATIONAL BICENTENNIAL CELEBRATION; 1776 PEACHTREE, #520; ATLANTA, GA 30309. (#200012-48).

JAN 14 - 17, '76. INDUSTRIAL HERITAGE USA. A HISTORICAL EXHIBIT OF THE GREENFIELD VILLAGE AND THE HENRY FORD MUSEUM. AT LENOX SQUARE, 3393 PEACHTREE RD NE. (LOCAL). MS ESTELLE FORD GREENE; ATLANTA BICENTENNIAL COMMISSION & THE COCA-COLA COMPANY; 225 PEACHTREE ST NE; ATLANTA, GA 30303. (#200012-11).

JAN 15 - JUNE 13, '76. THE INTERFAITH PROJECT FOR 1976. PRESENTATION OF RELIGIOUS HERITAGE AND A LOOK AT RELIGION AND MORES OF THE FUTURE. AT ATLANTIC CIVIC CENTER. (LOCAL). VIVIAN BEAVERS; CHRISTIAN COUNCIL OF CHURCHES & OTHER RELIGIOUS LEADERS; 1206 FOUNTAIN DR, SW; ATLANTA, GA 30314. (#8936-1).

JAN 18, '76. 'THE REVOLUTIONARY BOWL'. A PLAY ABOUT HAYM SOLOMON, REVOLUTIONARY PATRIOT. AT THE TEMPLE, 1589 PEACHTREE ST NE. (LOCAL). MS ROSALYN BAUER, COORD; TEMPLE SISTERHOOD; 2559 RIDGEWOOD RD NW; ATLANTA, GA 30318. (#200012-12).

JAN 23 - 25, '76. BLACKS IN COMMUNICATION. FILM FESTIVAL, EXHIBIT, CONFERENCE AND BANQUET DEMONSTRATING BLACK CONTRIBUTIONS TO THE MEDIA. (ST-WIDE). GLORIA PRYOR WALKER, DIR; CLARK COLLEGE; 3168 CANDLEWOOD DR; EAST POINT, GA 30344. (#10875-1).

JAN 29 - 31, '76. 'INTERNATIONAL FESTIVAL'. PAYS TRIBUTE TO VARIOUS ETHNIC GROUPS WITH UNIQUE DEMONSTRATIONS CHINESE ACROBATICS, HUNGARIAN COSTUMES, GREEK COOKING, ETC. (ST-WIDE). CAROL BAKER, COORD; GEORGIA COMMISSION FOR THE BICENTENNIAL CELEBRATION; 1776 PEACHTREE NW, SUITE 520; ATLANTA, GA 30309. (#103416-122).

ATLANTA — CONTINUED

JAN 29 - 31, '76. 'A SALUTE TO THE PEOPLES OF AMERICA'. AN INTERNATIONAL FESTIVAL OF EXHIBITS & ENTERTAINMENT SPONSORED BY THE GCNBC AS A CELEBRATION OF THE CULTURAL INFLUENCES THAT HAVE CONTRIBUTED TO THE AMERICAN WAY OF LIFE. AT SHOPPING MALL. (INT'L). MINA WHITE, DIRECTOR; GEORGIA COMMISSION FOR THE NATIONAL BICENTENNIAL CELEBRATION; SUITE 520, 1776 PEACHTREE ST, NW; ATLANTA, GA 30309. (#109526-2).

FEB 1 - JUNE 1, '76. ARTIST IN ACTION. EXHIBIT AT PARK AREA BUCKHEAD ATLANTA. (LOCAL). ADAIR L WILLIAM; ATLANTA ARTIST CLUB; 820 PEACHTREE CTR, SOUTH TOWER; ATLANTA, GA 30303. (#103773-1).

FEB 4 - APR 21, '76. OCCUPATIONAL AWARENESS & LIFE PLANNING WORKSHOP. PURPOSE OF WORKSHOP IS TO IMPRESS WOMEN W/ THE VARIETY OF AVENUES OPEN TO THEM IN PLANNING THE FUTURE. (LOCAL). MS SUZANNE DONNER, COORD; FEMINIST ACTION ALLAINCE, INC; PO BOX 54717, CIVIC CENTER STA; ATLANTA, GA 30308. (#106704-10).

FEB 9, '76. 'THE BRITISH ARE COMING!' - BRITISH MILITARY BAND PERFORMANCE. TOUR OF MAJOR U S CITIES BY BRITISH MILITARY UNITS AS REPRESENTATIVE OF UNITS INVOLVED IN REVOLUTIONARY WAR CAMPAIGN. AT THE OMNI. (INT'L). CHARLES K JONES, PRES; COLUMBIA ARTISTS FESTIVALS CORP; 165 W 57TH ST; NEW YORK, NY 10088. (#6532-15).

FEB 9, '76. MOHAWK INDIANS VISIT GEORGIA TECH CAMPUS. MOHAWK INDIANS WILL BRING TO THE CAMPUS VARIOUS EXHIBITS AND DEMONSTRATIONS OF THEIR CULTURE; LECTURES AND SEMINARS WILL ALSO BE CONDUCTED DURING THE THREE DAY EVENT. (ST-WIDE). WILLARD E WRIGHT, CO-CHMN; GEORGIA TECH PROGRAMS BOARD OF STUDENT CENTER; 325 NORTH AVE; ATLANTA, GA 30332. (#103095-2).

FEB 14, '76. 'PROCLAIM LIBERTY' - MUSICAL PAGEANT. MULTIMEDIA MUSICAL PAGEANT STRESSING THE PARALLEL BETWEEN AMERICAN JEWRY, ATLANTA JEWRY AND THE INDEPENDENT STATE OF ISRAEL WELFARE FEDERATION. AT ATLANTA CIVIC CENTER AUDITORIUM, 395 PIEDMONT AVE, NE. (REGN'L). MARVIN SCHPEISER, COORD; ATLANTA JEWISH WELFARE FEDERATION; 1753 PEACHTREE RD, NE; ATLANTA, GA 30309. (#106704-3).

FEB 19 - 22, '76. VISIT BY THE U S MILITARY ACADEMY GLEE CLUB. GLEE CLUB IS ALSO VISITING THE ATLANTA CIVIC AUDITORIUM. AT STATE CAPITAL, GEORGIA TECH & WESTMINSTER SCHOOLS. (LOCAL). IRVING SCHOENBERG, COORD; GA STATE LEGIS, UNITED WAY & WESTMINSTER SCHOOLS; ATLANTA BOY SCOUTS; PO BX 1969; ATLANTA, GA 30304. (#200012-13).

FEB 21 - DEC 31, '76. GRAPHIC EXHIBIT OF ETHNIC CONTRIBUTIONS - COLONIAL GA. PUBLIC EXHIBIT OF GRAPHICS, DOCUMENTS AND AUDIO-VISUALS SHOWING THE CONTRIBUTIONS OF A VARIETY OF ETHNIC GROUPS TO THE LIFE AND CULTURE OF COLONIAL GEORGIA. (LOCAL). FAYE P MCKAY, EXEC DIR; ATLANTA COUNCIL FOR INTERNATIONAL VISITORS; 235 PEACHTREE ST; ATLANTA, GA 30319. (#22306-1).

FEB '76. BRITISH-AMERICAN ASSOCIATION BICENTENNIAL BALLS. SERIES OF BALLS EMPHASIZING BRITISH AMERICAN HERITAGE LEADING TO A BICENTENNIAL BALL IN 1976. (ST-WIDE). REGINALD MITCHELL, PRES; BRITISH-AMERICAN ASSOCIATION OF THE SOUTHEAST; PO BOX 24; AVONDALE ESTS, GA 30002. (#900-1).

MAR 1 - 31, '76. DRAWING DEMONSTRATIONS. EXHIBIT. (LOCAL). GERRY POWELL, PRESIDENT; ATLANTA ARTISTS CLUB; 3099 PEACHTREE RD; ATLANTA, GA 30305. (#22622-2).

MAR 15, '76. FORUMS & LECTURES ON INTERPRETING THE BLACK EXPERIENCE IN AMERICA. SEMINAR. (ST-WIDE). CASPER JORDON, LIBRARIAN; ATLANTA UNIV BICENTENNIAL COMMITTEE; 223 CHESTNUT ST SW; ATLANTA, GA 30314. (#108128-1).

MAR 16 - 29, '76. THE ARTIST & THE ANIMAL. A DISPLAY OF ANIMAL ART HONORING AMERICA'S WILDLIFE ARTIST. AT THE GALLERIA OF THE ATLANTA MEMORIAL ARTS CENTER. (LOCAL). FRANCES BREED, DIRECTOR; NATIONAL AUDUBON SOCIETY; 950 3RD AVE; NEW YORK, NY 10022. (#19976-9).

MAR 18 - APR 16, '76. 'USA '76: THE FIRST 200 YEARS' EXHIBIT VISITS ATLANTA, GEORGIA. THIS TRAVELING EXHIBIT PREPARED BY THE ARBA WILL TOUR 10 CITIES DURING THE BICENTENNIAL. IT EXPLORES THE CULTURAL AND SCIENTIFIC HERITAGE OF THE USA. (REGN'L). JACK MASEY; AMERICAN REVOLUTION BICENTENNIAL ADMINISTRATION; 2401 E STREET, NW; WASHINGTON, DC 20276. (#5661-507).

MAR 28, '76. 'HAPPY BIRTHDAY AMERICA'. A CHILDREN'S BIRTHDAY PARTY AND CONCERT PERFORMED BY THE ATLANTA COMMUNITY ORCHESTRA. AT FIRST PRESBYTERIAN CHURCH AUDITORIUM, PEACHTREE & 16TH ST. (LOCAL). COORDINATOR; JUNIOR ASSOCIATES OF THE ATLANTA MUSIC CLUB; 2646 PIEDMONT RD, NE; ATLANTA, GA 30324. (#200012-14).

APR 1 - 30, '76. POTTERY DEMONSTRATIONS. EXHIBIT. (LOCAL). GERRY POWELL, DIRECTOR; ATLANTA ARTISTS CLUB; 3099 PEACHTREE RD; ATLANTA, GA 30305. (#22622-3).

APR 1 - DEC 31, '76. 'TOBASCO, OREGANO & THE FREEING OF FAPOOSTA' -PUPPET SHOW. CHILDREN'S PUPPET SHOW CONCERNING DEMOCRACY. (LOCAL). MS CAROL DANIEL, COORD; THE PICCADILLY PUPPET; 1249 STILLWOOD DR NE; ATLANTA, GA 30306. (#106704-8).

APR 2 - 4, '76. BICENTENNIAL YOUTH DEBATES REGIONAL COMPETITION. PROGRAM DESIGNED TO INVOLVE HIGH SCHOOL & COLLEGE STUDENTS IN A SERIOUS EXAMINATION OF AMERICA'S PAST THROUGH PUBLIC SPEAKING. AT PEACHTREE PLAZA HOTEL, 210 PEACHTREE ST NW. (REGN'L). JOHN BLOODWORTH, COORD; UNIV OF GEORGIA, DEPT OF MANAGEMENT; ATHENS, GA 30602. (#200012-15).

APR 3 - 4, '76. 'PRIDE OF MORNINGSIDE' A TOUR OF 8 HOMES. A TOUR OF HOMES INCLUDING BOTH 2 STORY GEORGIAN & COTSWOLD COTTAGES. INTERIORS VARY FROM TRADITIONAL TO CONTEMPORARY. AT MORNINGSIDE-LENOX PARK AREA. (LOCAL). MRS E B BROWN, COORD; MORNINGSIDE-LENOX PARK ASSOCIATION; PO BOX 14072; ATLANTA, GA 30324. (#200012-18).

APR 3 - 10, '76. EMBROIDERY EXHIBIT - BICENTENNIAL EMBROIDERY. OPEN FROM 10:00 AM - 9:30 PM ON MONDAY, THURSDAY & FRIDAY. AT KALEIDOSCOPE ROOM, NEIMAN MARCUS/LENOX SQUARE 3393 PEACHTREE RD, NE. (LOCAL). MRS VICTOR P SUTT, COORD; NEIMAN MARCUS; 105 WILLOWICK DR; DECATUR, GA 30034. (#200012-17).

APR 3 - 11, '76. DOGWOOD FESTIVAL. A REFLEXTION OF ATLANTA'S DOGWOOD-FILLED SPRINGTIME, FEATURING BICENTENNIAL GRADE PARADE DOWN PEACHTREE STREET. (ST-WIDE). LOIS HANEVOLD, DIRECTOR; DOGWOOD FESTIVAL COMMITTEE & GEORGIA COMMISSION FOR THE NATL BICENT; SUITE 520, S TOWER-1776 PEACH; ATLANTA, GA 30309. (#103558-1).

APR 3 - 18, '76. DOGWOOD ART SHOW. EXHIBIT AT GEORGIA TECH STUDENT CENTER GALLERY. (LOCAL). DIRECTOR; GEORGIA TECH STUDENT CENTER & ATLANTA PLAYHOUSE THEATRE, LTD; 225 NORTH AVE NW; ATLANTA, GA 30330. (#200012-16).

APR 4 - 9, '76. BICENTENNIAL FESTIVAL - WEEK OF ART EXHIBITS AND ENTERTAINMENT. FESTIVAL, EXHIBIT. (LOCAL). CASPER JORDON, LIBRARIAN; ATLANTA UNIV BICENTENNIAL COMMISSION; 223 CHESTNUT ST SW; ATLANTA, GA 30314. (#108175-1).

APR 5 - 11, '76. TULLIE SMITH HOUSE TOUR & CRAFTS DEMONSTRATIONS. 1840 PLANTATION RESTORED BY ATLANTA HISTORICAL SOCIETY. RESERVATIONS REQUIRED FOR LARGE GROUPS. SUNDAY HOURS 1:30 - 4:30 PM. AT TULLIE SMITH HOUSE RESTORATION, 3136 SLATON DR, NW. (LOCAL). VERNON PAINE, COORD; ATLANTA HISTORICAL SOCIETY; PO BOX 12423; ATLANTA, GA 30305. (#200012-19).

APR 7, '76. BICENTENNIAL CELEBRATION TO COMMEMORATE PONCE DE LEON PARKS. 12 PM COVENANT SIGNING TO PROTECT & PRESERVE THE PONCE DE LEON PARKS AND PARKWAYS. UNVEILING OF HISTORIC MARKERS, STREET SIGNS, COMMEMORATIVE FLAG. AT CATOR WOOLFORD GARDENS, ATLANTA, GA. (LOCAL). DEAN GARY R SMITH; EMORY LAW SCHOOL & DRUID HILLS CIVIC ASSOC; PO BOX 33222; DECATUR, GA 30333. (#106752-2).

APR 8 - 10, '76. COUNTRY FAIR GOES UNDERGROUND. COUNTRY FAIR AND BICENTENNIAL EXPOSITION WITH EXHIBITORS FROM 38 STATES. FEATURES FOOD, ARTS, CRAFTS, FLOWERS & FAMILY ENTERTAINMENT. AT UNDERGROUND ATLANTA. (ST-WIDE). TOM POWERS, COORD; ATLANTA DOGWOOD FESTIVAL; ROUTE 1 - BOX 700; NEWNAN, GA 30263. (#104473-1).

APR 11, '76. DEDICATION OF COMMEMORATIVE PLAQUES. CEREMONY, LIVE PERFORMANCE, RADIO/TV AT TRIANGLE FLOWER PLOT AT CONVERGING POINT OF MORRIS BROWN/FOUNTAIN DR. (LOCAL). VIVIAN BEAVERS, COORD; JUNS JUST US NEIGHBORS COMMUNITY GROUP; 1206 FOUNTAIN DR SW; ATLANTA, GA 30314. (#103258-1).

APR 19 - 23, '76. BICENTENNIAL MULTI-MEDIA SHOW. 300 SLIDES & 16MM FILM PROGRAMMED TO A 35 MINUTE TAPED NARRATION & MUSIC COVERING 200 YEARS OF AMERICAN HISTORY, PROJECTED ONTO THREE SCREENS SIMULTANEOUSLY; PROGRAM WILL BE PRESENTED SEVERAL TIMES FOR A VARIETY OF GROUPS. (ST-WIDE). JEANNETTE ABI-NADER, DIR; ST PIUS X HIGH SCHOOL; 2674 JOHNSON RD NE; ATLANTA, GA 30345. (#22305-1).

APR 24 - 25, '76. INMAN PARK SPRING FESTIVAL & HISTORIC HOMES TOUR. ARTS & CRAFTS FAIR, ANTIQUE FLEA MARKET, PARADE & FOOD; TOURS OF VICTORIAN HOMES AT 1, 6, 7 & 9 PM. AT 192 HURT ST, NE. (LOCAL). MS PATTI MANN, PROJ COORD; INMAN PARK RESTORATION, INC; 100 WAVERLY WAY, NE; ATLANTA, GA 30307. (#106703-4).

APR 25, '76. 'MASSING OF COLORS' - 27TH ANNUAL MEMORIAL SERVICE. THE 27TH ANNUAL MEMORIAL SERVICE TO HONOR THE ARMED FORCES, THE DESCENDANTS OF THOSE WHO HAVE SERVED IN THE PAST & THE GOLD STAR MOTHERS OF AMERICA. THERE WILL BE A PARADE, CONCERT & OTHER EVENTS. AT PEACHTREE PRESBYTARIAN CHURCH, 3834 ROSWELL RD, NW. (LOCAL). JOHN A SCHUPP; ATLANTA CHAPTER, MILITARY ORDER OF WORLD WARS; 60 BRANDON RIDGE DR, NW; ATLANTA, GA 30328. (#106704-1).

APR '76. BICENTENNIAL YOUTH DEBATED - REGIONAL EVENT. A $1500 SCHOLARSHIP AWARD WAS GIVEN BY THE GCNBC ALONG WITH STAFF SUPPORT IN JUDGING FOR THE SOUTHEAST REGIONAL EVENT OF THE BICENTENNIAL YOUTH DEBATES. AT GEORGIA STATE CAPITOL BLDG. (REGN'L). A K JOHNSON, JR, EXEC DIR; GEORGIA COMMISSION FOR THE NATIONAL BICENTENNIAL CELEBRATION; 1776 PEACHTREE, #520; ATLANTA, GA 30309. (#200012-51).

MAY 1 - 31, '76. PAINTING DEMONSTRATIONS. EXHIBIT. (LOCAL). GERRY POWELL, PRESIDENT; ATLANTA ARTISTS CLUB; 3099 PEACHTREE RD; ATLANTA, GA 30305. (#22622-4).

MAY 19 - 25, '76. AMERICAN FREEDOM TRAIN DISPLAY DAYS AT ATLANTA. THE AMERICAN FREEDOM TRAIN WILL INCLUDE 10 EXHIBIT CARS AND 2 SHOWCASE CARS DEPICTING DIFFERENT PHASES OF THE AMERICAN EXPERIENCE. ITS ARRIVAL WILL SERVE AS A CATALYST FOR LOCAL BICENTENNIAL CELEBRATIONS BY PEOPLE THROUGHOUT THIS NATION. (ST-WIDE). SY FREEDMAN, DIR OF P R; THE AMERICAN FREEDOM TRAIN FOUNDATION, INC.; 5205 LEESBURG PKE, SUITE 800; BAILEY'S XRDS, VA 22041. (#1776-74).

MAY 25, '76. AUSTRALIAN YOUTH ORCHESTRA CONCERT. LIVE PERFORMANCE AT ATLANTA SYMPHONY HALL. (INT'L). JOHN MAUNDER, DIRECTOR; AUSTRALIAN GOVERNMENT; AUSTRALIAN CG, 636 FIFTH AVENUE; NEW YORK, NY 10020. (#108021-4).

MAY 30 - JUNE ??, '76. WATERCOLOR EXHIBIT AND DEMONSTRATION. WATERCOLOR EXHIBIT AND DEMONSTRATION BY 12 ARTISTS. THIS WILL BE FOLLOWED IN JUNE BY SEVERAL WATERCOLOR WORKSHOPS ON SUCCEEDING WEEKENDS. AT THE APARK IN BUCKHEAD SUBURB, NORTH ATLANTA. (LOCAL). CORINNE WORKMASTER, DIR; ATLANTA ARTISTS CLUB; 3099 PEACHTREE RD NE; ATLANTA, GA 30305. (#22622-6).

JUNE 1 - 30, '76. SCULPTURE DEMONSTRATIONS. EXHIBIT. (LOCAL). GERRY POWELL, PRESIDENT; ATLANTA ARTISTS CLUB; 3099 PEACHTREE RD; ATLANTA, GA 30305. (#22622-5).

JUNE 4, '76. THE TODAY SHOW FEATURES THE STATE OF GEORGIA. A CONTINUING WEEKLY SERIES OF PROGRAMS COMMEMORATING EACH STATE. GEORGIA WAS ADMITTED INTO THE UNION IN JANUARY, 1788. (NAT'L). STUART SCHULBERG, EX PROD; NATIONAL BROADCASTING CO; 30 ROCKEFELLER PLAZA; NEW YORK, NY 10020. (#7981-28).

JUNE 5, '76. TOWN MEETING '76. A PROPOSED RELIGIOUS CELEBRATION TO GIVE THANKS FOR OUR HERITAGE, CONFESS OUR SHORTCOMINGS AS A PEOPLE AND SEEK GUIDANCE AND STRENGTH AS WE BEGIN A NEW CENTURY; TO BE CONDUCTED IN THE NEIGHBORHOODS. (LOCAL). WARREN TOLLMAN, COORD; INSTITUTE OF CULTURAL AFFAIRS; 820 PEACHTREE CNTR, S TOWER; ATLANTA, GA 30303. (#8941-1).

JUNE 11 - 12, '76. COLLECTION '76: A BICENTENNIAL ART REVUE. AN ART EXHIBITION SPONSORED BY THE GCNBC TO FAMILIARIZE THE PUBLIC WITH THE THREE BICENTENNIAL THEMES & VARIOUS WAYS THAT THEY ARE EXPRESSED THROUGH THE ARTS. HRS: 2-8P ON 6/11; 10-5P ON 6/12. AT ANDREWS SQUARE. (LOCAL). CAROLYN LEVIN, COORD; GEORGIA COMMISSION FOR NATIONAL BICENTENNIAL CELEBRATION; SUITE 520, 1776 PEACHTREE ST NW; ATLANTA, GA 30309. (#109526-1).

JUNE 14 - AUG 20, '76. HERITAGE ART PARK. AMERICAN FOLKLORE WILL BE PRESENTED THROUGH ARTS, MUSIC & CRAFTS BY COORDINATING THE RESOURCES OF GOVERNMENT, BUSINESSES & CULTURAL GROUPS. AT PONCE DE LEON PARK. (LOCAL). MADELYN SUMMERS, COORD; DEPT OF PARKS, LIBRARIES & CULTURAL AFFAIRS; 135 W WIEUCA RD NW; ATLANTA, GA 30342. (#108913-1).

JUNE 27 - JULY ??, '76. 'POTPOURRI' OF VARIOUS DISCIPLINES; WORKSHOPS. SUNDAY, JUNE 27TH, A 'POTPOURRI' OF VARIOUS DISCIPLINES, FOLLOWED BY WORKSHOPS IN JULY. AT PARK IN BUCKHEAD, NORTH ATLANTA. (LOCAL). CORINNE WORKMASTER, DIR; ATLANTA ARTISTS CLUB; 3099 PEACHTREE ST NE; ATLANTA, GA 30305. (#22622-7).

JUNE '76. ARMED FORCES WEEK LUNCHEON. REPRESENTATIVES OF ALL ARMED SERVICES & 20 MILITARY AFFILIATED ORGANIZATIONS WILL ATTEND LUNCHEON. AT PEACHTREE PLAZA HOTEL. (LOCAL). AURELIA FUNDI, PUBLICITY; ATLANTA CHAMBER OF COMMERCE; COMMERCE BLDG; ATLANTA, GA 30303. (#106703-2).

JULY 1 - 4, '76. LONGHORN WORLD CHAMPIONSHIP RODEO. TOP AMERICAN, CANADIAN AND AUSTRALIAN COWBOYS AND COWGIRLS COMPETE FOR WORLD CHAMPIONSHIP POINTS IN 6 COMPETITIVE EVENTS; INCLUDES BICENTENNIAL OPENING PAGEANT, RODEO CLOWNS AND SPECIALITY PERFORMERS. AT LAKELAND PARK. (ST-WIDE). BRUCE LEHRKE, DIRECTOR; LONGHORN RODEO COMPANY; PO BOX 8280; NASHVILLE, TN 37207. (#104573-1).

JULY 3, '76. VIRGINIA HIGHLAND CIVIC ASSOCIATION ANNUAL 4TH OF JULY PICNIC. ACTIVITIES WILL INCLUDE OLD-FASHIONED BAR-B-QUE LUNCH, FLEA MARKET, PARADE, BLUE-GRASS BAND AND SOFTBALL. AT VIRGINIA AVENUE AT BARNETT ST. (LOCAL). STARLING SUTTON; VIRGINIA HIGHLAND CIVIC ASSOC; 561 PARK DR NE; ATLANTA, GA 30306. (#108913-8).

JULY 3, '76. '200 YEARS OF READINESS' - CONCERT BY 24TH ARMY BAND. LIVE PERFORMANCE AT ATLANTA CIVIC CENTER, AT FOREST & PIEDMONT. (LOCAL). MS ESTELLE GREENE, COORD; ATLANTA BICENTENNIAL COMMISSION; 225 PEACHTREE ST, NE; ATLANTA, GA 30303. (#106703-5).

JULY 3 - 4, '76. BICENTENNIAL BALL. THE BALL WILL FEATURE A MINI-PAGEANT INCLUDING RE-ENACTMENT GROUPS FROM THE 2ND GEORGIA BATTALION OF THE CONTINENTAL LINE. AT OMNI INTERNATIONAL HOTEL. (LOCAL). BETH HERZOG, COORD; BRITISH AMERICAN ASSOC; BOX 24; AVONDALE EST, GA 30002. (#108913-7).

JULY 4, '76. A BICENTENNIAL CELEBRATION IN THE PARK. ATLANTA POPS CONCERT OF AMERICAN MUSIC, FOLLOWED BY FIEWORKS. AT CHASTAIN PARK. (LOCAL). JANE BROWN, COORDINATOR; J C PENNEY, INC; 715 PEACHTREE ST NE; ATLANTA, GA 30308. (#108913-3).

JULY 4, '76. CONCERT IN CENTRAL CITY PARK. POPULAR BANDS TO PERFORM IN CENTRAL CITY PARK AFTER THE PARADE ON JULY 4TH. AT CENTRAL CITY PARK. (LOCAL). ROBERT RIVERS, COORD; BUREAU OF CULTURAL & INTERNATIONAL AFFAIRS; 520 N OMNI INTERNATIONAL; ATLANTA, GA 30303. (#108913-11).

JULY 4, '76. ETHNIC FESTIVAL. 2 HOURS OF ENTERTAINMENT WILL FEATURE A DOZEN COUNTRIES FROM LATIN AMERICA, EUROPE AND AFRICA. AT CENTRAL CITY PARK. (LOCAL). FAYE MCKAYE, DIRECTOR; ATLANTA COUNCIL FOR INTERNATIONAL VISITORS; 235 PEACHTREE ST NE, SUITE 1809; ATLANTA, GA 30303. (#108913-2).

JULY 4, '76. FOURTH OF JULY FIREWORKS SPECTACULAR. FESTIVAL AT EAST PACES FERRY. (LOCAL). ROSALENE CRIMM, COORD; LENOX SQUARE MERCHANT ASSOC; 3393 PEACHTREE RD NE; ATLANTA, GA 30326. (#108913-5).

ATLANTA — CONTINUED

JULY 4, '76. 'LITTERBUG NO' - PARADE. CLEAN-UP DOWNTOWN ATLANTA ON JULY 3RD, PAINTING AND PLACING 200 RED, WHITE AND BLUE LITTER BARRELS DOWNTOWN ON THE 4TH. TO WORK TOWARDS MAKING ATLANTA THE CLEANEST CITY IN THE NATION IN 1976. (LOCAL). ELMER RUSH; SAMUEL L JONES BOYS CLUB & METRO ATLANTA BOYS' CLUB; 450 E LAKE DR; DECATUR, GA 30030. (#108913-12).

JULY 4, '76. WSB SALUTE TO AMERICA PARADE. ONE OF THE USA'S LARGEST 4TH OF JULY PARADES, DOWN PEACHTREE ST. (ST-WIDE). JEAN HENDRIX, DIRECTOR; WSB-TV; 1601 W PEACH TREE ST; ATLANTA, GA 30309. (#103557-1).

JULY 4, '76. 1976 PEACHTREE ROAD RACE. A ROAD RACE FOR AMATEUR RUNNERS, FROM BUCKHEAD TO CENTRAL CITY PARK. AT THE END OF THE 10,000 METER COURSE, PRIZES WILL BE AWARDED TO THE WINNERS & THOSE WHO FINISH. AT BEGIN AT SEARS PARKING LOT AT BUCKHEAD, PROCEED TO CENTRAL CITY PARK. (LOCAL). SUE PETERS, COORD; THE ATLANTA JOURNAL & ATLANTA CONSTITUTION; GA STATE UNIV, UNIV PLAZA; ATLANTA, GA 30303. (#108913-4).

JULY 4, '76. '76 BELLS' - COMMEMORATION OF THE U S BICENTENNIAL. STATE-WIDE NOON TIME RINGING OF BELLS IN COMMEMORATION OF THE BICENTENNIAL. AT STATEWIDE. (ST-WIDE). MOZELLE CHRISTIAN, MGR; CHAMBER OF COMMERCE; 1200 COMMERCE BUILDING; ATLANTA, GA 30303. (#106703-7).

JULY 17, '76. A FESTIVAL IN AMERICAN THEATER. SHOW HONORS BICENTENNIAL YEAR WITH DISPLAY OF STATE FLAGS, U S FLAG AND U N FLAG. AT ALLIANCE THEATRE. (LOCAL). GEORGE BELL; CONTINENTAL COMPANY OF BEAUTIFUL PEOPLE, GALAXEE CULTURAL PRODUCTION; 1000 HARWELL ROAD #114D; ATLANTA, GA 30318. (#108913-9).

JULY 27, '76. PHILADELPHIA DANCE CO PERFORMANCE FOR ZETA PHI BETA SORORITY. WILL MARK FIRST TIME THIS TROUPE HAS PERFORMED SOUTH OF THE MASONDIXON LINE & WILL GIVE PORTIONS OF ITS BICENTENNIAL PROGRAM, 'ROOTS/ REFLECTIONS' TO THE NATIONAL CONCLAVE OF ONE OF THE NATION'S LARGEST BLACK SORORITIES. AT ATLANTA'S CITY AUDITORIUM. (REGN'L). MARILYN SUITER, PUBL REL; THE PHILADELPHIA DANCE COMPANY; 6249 MARKET ST; PHILADELPHIA, PA 19139. (#200012-42).

AUG 3, '76. DRUMS ACROSS AMERICA. A MUSICAL MARCHING SALUTE TO THE BICENTENNIAL FEATURING 8 OF THE NATION'S TOP DRUM & BUGLE CORPS. AT GEORGIA TECH'S GRANT FIELD. (LOCAL). JON BEACHER, DIRECTOR; WXIA-TV; 1611 W PEACHTREE ST NE; ATLANTA, GA 30309. (#108913-10).

AUG 20 - 24, '76. CONFERENCE ON YOUTH NEEDS AND YOUTH EXHIBITION. CONFERENCE, EXHIBIT AT HILTON AIRPORT INN, ATLANTA AIRPORT. (REGN'L). STUART RADO, EXEC DIR; NATIONAL NETWORK OF YOUTH ADVISORY BOARDS; PO BOX 402036, OCEAN VIEW BRANCH; MIAMI BEACH, FL 33140. (#1536-8).

SEPT 11 - OCT 31, '76. 'GEORGIA PIEDMONT FURNITURE BEFORE 1830' - A BICENTENNIAL EXHIBITION. THE FIRST MAJOR EXHIBITION OF EARLY GEORGIA FURNITURE, INCLUDING 100 PIECES ILLUSTRATING REGIONAL DESIGN, DECORATIVE DETAIL & CONSTRUCTION. AT THE HIGH MUSEUM OF ART: NEW GALLERY. (REGN'L). THE HIGH MUSEUM OF ART; 1280 PEACHTREE ST, NE; ATLANTA, GA 30309. (#13641-501).

SEPT 23 - 25, '76. ATLANTA GREEK FESTIVAL. FESTIVAL AT GROUNDS OF GREEK ORTHODOX CHURCH OF THE ANNUNCIATION. (LOCAL). TASSIE PORTULAS, COORD; GREEK ORTHODOX CHURCH OF THE ANNUNCIATION; 2500 CLAIRMONT RD NE; ATLANTA, GA 30329. (#103416-605).

SEPT 25 - 26, '76. GRANT PARK FESTIVAL & TOUR OF HISTORIC HOMES. ARTS & CRAFTS BOOTH & EXHBITS BY CRAFTSPEOPLE ALL OVER GEORGIA. SUNDAY 10 AM - 10 PM. AT GRANT PARK. (LOCAL). MS DEBBY HARDY; THE ASSOCIATION TO REVIVE GRANT PARK; PO BOX 54245; ATLANTA, GA 30308. (#106703-8).

OCT 5, '76. REPUBLIC OF CHINA YOUTH SYMPHONY ORCHESTRA. 60 PIECE YOUTH ORCHESTRA SPONSORED BY THE REPUBLIC OF CHINA TO PERFORM. AT FOX THEATRE. (LOCAL). TOM DEAN, CHAIRMAN; ATLANTA LANDMARKS; 660 PEACHTREE ST, NW; ATLANTA, GA 30308. (#200012-55).

OCT 15 - DEC 1, '76. DOCULANTA - PHOTOGRAPHY EXHIBITION. PHOTOGRAPHERS THROUGHOUT ATLANTA WILL BE RECRUITED TO PARTICIPATE IN A PHOTOGRAPHY EXHIBITION FEATURING PRINTS WHICH EXPRESS THE NATURE OF ATLANTA IN FLUX, AS IT EXISTS IN 1976. AT ATLANTA CIVIC CENTER. (LOCAL). JACK BAGRIANSKY, COORD; BUREAU OF CULTURAL & INTERNATIONAL AFFAIRS; 260 CENTRAL AVE, SW; ATLANTA, GA 30303. (#106704-4).

OCT 16 - NOV 14, '76. 'REMEMBER THE LADIES' WOMEN IN AMERICA 1750-1815 -EXHIBIT. ART EXHIBITION OF ART & ARTIFACTS ON THE ROLE & STATUS OF WOMEN DURING THE REVOLUTIONARY PERIOD INCLUDING SECTIONS ON CHILDHOOD, MARRIAGE, DEATH, FASHION & CREATIVE WOMEN. AT HIGH MUSEUM OF ART, 1280 PEACHTREE ST, NE. (LOCAL). GUDMUND VIGTEL; PHILIP MORRIS, INC; CLAIROL, INC; THE HIGH MUSEUM OF ART; 1280 PEACHTREE ST, NE; ATLANTA, GA 30309. (#107840-2).

NOV 13 - DEC 26, '76. RELATED LECTURES AND TOURS OF THE EXHIBITION. 100 REPRESENTATIVE WORKS BY NO MORE THAN 30 REGIONAL ARTISTS OF HIGH QUALITY, LITTLE KNOWN OUTSIDE THE SOUTH; WILL INCLUDE PAINTINGS, PHOTOS, SCULPTURE, CRAFTS AND PRINT MEDIUMS SUNDAY HOURS: 12 NOON - 5 PM. AT HIGH MUSEUM OF ART: NEW GALLERY. (REGN'L). GUDMUND VIGTEL, DIRECTOR; THE HIGH MUSEUM OF ART; 1280 PEACHTREE ST, NE; ATLANTA, GA 30309. (#13641-502).

NOV 13, '76 - DEC 26, '77. EXHIBITION, ARTISTS IN THE SOUTHEAST. 100 REPRESENTATIVE WORKS BY NO MORE THAN 30 REGIONAL & PROMINENT SOUTHERN ARTISTS; WORKS WILL INCLUDE: PAINTINGS, PHOTOGRAPHS, SCULPTURE, CRAFTS AND PRINT MEDIUMS. HOURS ON SUNDAY ARE 12-5PM. AT THE HIGH MUSEUM OF ART. (REGN'L). GUDMUND VIGTEL, DIRECTOR; THE HIGH MUSEUM OF ART; 1280 PEACHTREE ST, NE; ATLANTA, GA 30309. (#13639-501).

DEC 2, '76 - CONTINUING . GEORGIA FOLK ART EXHIBIT. SHOW OPENS AT ATLANTA HISTORIC SOCIETY IN DEC 1976; TOURS TO COLUMBUS MUSEUM OF ARTS & CRAFTS IN COLUMBUS, GA THEN TO TELFAIR ACADEMY IN SAVANNAH. EXHIBIT OF 19TH & 20TH CENTURY GEORGIA FOLK ART INCLUDING PAINTINGS, SCULPTURE AND TRADITIONAL CRAFTS. AT ATLANTA/COLUMBUS/SAVANNAH. (LOCAL). ANNA WADSWORTH, COORD; GEORGIA COUNCIL FOR THE ARTS; 225 PEACHTREE ST NE; ATLANTA, GA 30303. (#103497-1).

DEC 5, '76 - FEB 28, '77. THE MISSING PIECES: GEORGIA'S FOLK TRADITION (1793-1976). 19TH & 20TH CENTURY GEORGIA-MADE FOLK ART EXHIBIT WILL TOUR TO ATLANTA HISTORICAL SOCIETY, TELAIR ACADEMY(SAVANNAH), COLUMBUS(GEORGIA) MUSEUM OF ARTS & CRAFTS, FOLK MUSIC PERFORMANCES AT EACH OPENING. GEORGIA FOLK ARTISTS FILM & ILLUSTRATED CATALOGS WILL ACCOMPANY. AT 3099 ANDREWS DR NW, ATLANTA. (ST-WIDE). ANNA WADSWORTH; GEORGIA COUNCIL FOR THE ARTS & ATLANTA HISTORICAL SOCIETY; SUITE 1610, 225 PEACHTREE ST NE; ATLANTA, GA 30303. (#107774-1).

JAN 8 - FEB 20, '77. 'TWO CENTURIES OF BLACK AMERICAN ART' - EXHIBIT. EXHIBIT OF 200 WORKS BY 62 ARTISTS FEATURING PAINTING, SCULPTURE, GRAPHS, DRAWINGS, CRAFTS, DECORATIVE ARTS & PHOTOGRAPHS. SUNDAY HOURS: 12 - 5 PM. AT THE HIGH MUSEUM OF ART, 1280 PEACHTREE ST, NE. (LOCAL). MARY JO SAUNDERS, SEC; THE HIGH MUSEUM OF ART; 1280 PEACHTREE ST, NE; ATLANTA, GA 30309. (#106703-9).

JAN '77 - CONTINUING . PLANNING AMERICA'S GREAT CITIES, AN EXHIBITION. EXHIBIT, RADIO/TV AT FERNVANK SCIENCE CENTER. (REGN'L). MS LEE KIMCHE; ASSOC OF SCIENCE & TECHNOLOGY; 2100 PENNSYLVANIA AVE, NW; WASHINGTON, DC 20037. (#8615-5).

MAR 18 - APR 8, '77. STAR-SPANGLED HISTORY: DRAWINGS BY J B BEALE - MAGIC LANTERN ARTIST. NATIONAL TRAVELLING EXHIBITION OF 65 ORIGINAL WASH DRAWINGS BY JOSEPH BOGGS BEALE, A 19TH CENTURY ILLUSTRATOR. SLIDE PRESENTATION. AT ATLANTA HISTORICAL SOCIETY, PO BOX 12423. (REGN'L). KAREN HUGHES, PROJ MGR; AMER NATL INSURANCE CO, AMER NATL TOWER OF GALVESTON, TX; RUDER & FINN, 110 E 59TH ST; NEW YORK, NY 10022. (#9820-12).

APR 27 - 30, '77. HIGH SCHOOL CHORAL COMPETITION. ALL-STATE CHORUS PERFORMANCE OF SONG SELECTED FROM PIECES SUBMITTED BY COMPOSERS TO SAI. CONTEST TO BE JUDGED AND WINNING COMPOSER WILL BE GIVEN $200.00. WINNING COMPOSITION WILL BE PERFORMED. (LOCAL). NANCY HARPER, PRES; ATLANTA ALUMNAE CHAPTER OF SIGMA ALPHA IOTA; 6177 WOODLANDS DR; NORCROSS, GA 30071. (#23767-1).

OCT 1, '77. GROUND BREAKING CEREMONY FOR NEW ATLANTA PUBLIC LIBRARY. THIS WILL BE THE CENTRAL LIBRARY BUILDING FOR ATLANTA. AT CARNEGIE WAY & FORSYTH ST. (LOCAL). LIBRARY DIRECTOR; THE ATLANTA PUBLIC LIBRARY; 10 PRYOR ST; ATLANTA, GA 30303. (#106618-1).

DEC 10, '77 - FEB 5, '78. BICENTENNIAL ART PROGRAM OF DEPT OF THE INTERIOR. PAINTINGS BY MODERN ARTISTS DEPICTING THE NATURAL & HISTORIC PROPERTIES ADMINISTERED BY THE DEPT OF INTERIOR. AT THE HIGH MUSEUM OF ART. (REGN'L). MRS JEAN HAWKINS; DEPT OF THE INTERIOR; WASHINGTON, DC 20240. (#1239-8).

AUGUSTA

BARTRAM MEMORIAL TRAIL - AUGUSTA, GA. 14 MILES OF THE WILLIAM BARTRAM TRAIL WILL BE MARKED; THE TRAIL RUNS THROUGH TOWN, ALONG THE AUGUSTA CANAL AND THE SAVANNAH RIVER PARK. (LOCAL). MRS MORTON WITTENBERG, COORDINATOR; AUGUSTA-RICHMOND COUNTY BICENTENNIAL COMMISSION; 1822 BROAD; AUGUSTA, GA 30903. (#19357). **ARBA GRANTEE.**

BICENTENNIAL INTERN PROGRAM IN AUGUSTA, GA. TWO BICENTENNIAL INTERNS HAVE BEEN WORKING ON A BICENT INTEREST SURVEY, HISTORIC MAP AND BROCHURE OF HISTORIC SITES. (LOCAL). TRAVIS BARNES, CHAIRMAN; AUGUSTA-RICHMOND COUNTY BICENTENNIAL COMMITTEE; PO BOX 1776; AUGUSTA, GA 30903. (#11295).

BICENTENNIAL SYMPHONY IN AUGUSTA, GEORGIA. NEW MAJOR WORK FOR CHORUS & ORCHESTRA ON PRE-REVOLUTIONARY WAR TEXTS COMPOSED BY WAYNE BARLOW TO PREMIER ON FEB 28, 1976. WORK WILL THEN BE MADE AVAILABLE TO OTHER ORCHESTRAS & CHORUSES AT NO CHARGE. (LOCAL). HARRY JACOBS, MUSICAL DIRECTOR; AUGUSTA SYMPHONY ORCHESTRA; AUGUSTA COLLEGE; AUGUSTA, GA 30904. (#16124). **ARBA GRANTEE.**

THE CENTRAL SAVANNAH RIVER AREA IN THE AMER REV. A BOOKLET ON THE PARTICIPATION OF THE CENTRAL SAVANNAH AREA IN THE AMERICAN REVOLUTION, INCLUDING NARRATIVES, PHOTOGRAPHS & MAPS OF PLACES OF HISTORICAL INTEREST. (REGN'L). WILLIAM E DREW, DIRECTOR OF PLANNING; CSRA PLANNING & DEVELOPMENT COMMISSION; 2123 WRIGHTSBORO RD; AUGUSTA, GA 30904. (#8377). **ARBA GRANTEE.**

CONCEPT '76 -REGIONAL PARK OF AUGUSTA, GEORGIA. DEVELOPMENT OF AUGUSTA CANAL, 8 MILE STRETCH INTO HISTORICAL AND RECREATIONAL AREA-CAMPING, BOATS, CHILDREN'S DEMONSTRATION FARM ONLY 2 MILES FROM DOWNTOWN AUGUSTA. (LOCAL). CHUCK PARRISH, DIRECTOR; DEPT OF NATURAL RESOURCES; 270 WASHINGTON ST SW; ATLANTA, GA 30334. (#2627). **(??).**

COURTHOUSE SQUARE RESTORATION IN AUGUSTA, GA. THE CITY BLOCK THAT COMPOSES THE COURTHOUSE SQUARE WILL BE RECONSTRUCTED & RESTORED. (LOCAL). TRAVIS BARNES, CHAIRMAN; AUGUSTA-RICHMOND COUNTY BICENTENNIAL COMMITTEE; PO BOX 1776; AUGUSTA, GA 30903. (#10628).

HISTORICAL BOOKLET - AUGUSTA, GA. BIOGRAPHICAL BOOKLETS WILL BE WRITTEN ABOUT GEORGIANS WHO WERE BURIED IN ST PAUL'S CHURCHYARD FROM 1750 TO 1820. (LOCAL). DR EDWARD CASHIN, PRESIDENT; RICHMOND COUNTY HISTORICAL SOCIETY; AUGUSTA COLLEGE LIBRARY; AUGUSTA, GA 30904. (#17952). **ARBA GRANTEE.**

MACKAY HOUSE EXHIBITS PROJECT OF GEORGIA. COMPLETION OF EXHIBITS & INTERPRETATIVE PROGRAM FOR THE MACKAY HOUSE IN AUGUSTA, GA, INCLUDING LIVING HISTORY DISPLAYS & COSTUNED INTERPRETERS. (ST-WIDE). JIM OATES, CHIEF RECREATION & PLANNING SECTION; GEORGIA DEPT OF NATURAL RESOURCES; 270 WASHINGTON ST SW; ATLANTA, GA 30334. (#584). **(??).**

PUBLICATION OF HISTORY OF AUGUSTA, GA. THE HISTORY OF AUGUSTA, FROM 1773-1783, WILL BE PUBLISHED & PLACED IN SCHOOLS; IT WILL ALSO BE AVAILABLE FOR GENERAL SALES. (LOCAL). TRAVIS BARNES, CHAIRMAN; AUGUSTA-RICHMOND COUNTY BICENTENNIAL COMMITTEE; PO BOX 1776; AUGUSTA, GA 30903. (#10627).

'PURSUIT OF HAPPINESS' - AUGUSTA, GA. DISTINGUISHED SPEAKERS AND SERIES OF ACTIVITIES ON THE AMERICA EXPERIENCE STRESSING THE THEME 'THE PURSUIT OF HAPPINESS.'. (ST-WIDE). A K JOHNSON, EXEC DIRECTOR; GEORGIA COMMISSION FOR THE NATIONAL BICENTENNIAL CELEBRATION; 1776 PEACHTREE ST; ATLANTA, GA 30909. (#15790). **ARBA GRANTEE.**

REINTERMENT OF WILLIAM FEW, SIGNER OF CONSTITUTION. REINTERMENT OF WILLIAM FEW (1748-1828) A GEORGIA SIGNER OF THE UNITED STATES CONSTITUTION, AT ST PAUL'S CHURCH IN AUGUSTA, GEORGIA. (NAT'L). A K JOHNSON, EXEC DIRECTOR; GEORGIA COMMISSION FOR THE NATIONAL BICENTENNIAL CELEBRATION; 1776 PEACHTREE, SOUTH WING; ATLANTA, GA 30309. (#597).

RESTORATION PROJECT IN AUGUSTA, GA. THE GEORGIA SOCIETY'S BICENTENNIAL PROJECT IS THE RESTORATION OF THE MEADOW GARDEN HOME OF GEORGE WALTON. (LOCAL). MRS ARTHUR H WAITE, HONORARY STATE REGENT; GEORGIA STATE SOCIETY, NSDAR; 5555 ROSWELL RD NE, APT V-3; ATLANTA, GA 30342. (#12554).

WGAC'S GREAT AMERICAN CONTEST - NBMRP. STUDENTS IN GA & SC INVITED TO WRITE SHORT PAPER ON THE AMERICAN WHO CONTRIBUTED MOST IN PAST 200 YRS. ALSO AIRS BICENT TRIVIA QUESTIONS & BICENT HERITAGE REMINDERS THROUGHOUT EACH DAY, & SYNDICATED PGMS. (LOCAL). BOB YOUNG, BICENTENNIAL COORDINATOR; WGAC-RADIO; PO BOX 1131; AUGUSTA, GA 30903. (#23267). **ARBA GRANTEE.**

APR 1, '75 - DEC 30, '76. BICENTENNIAL ACTIVITIES. EVENTS INCLUDE FLAG RAISING AT ONE LIBRARY EVERY & MONTHS, SEWING DRESSES OF REVOLUTIONARY WAR PERIOD, FILMS ON AMERICANISM EACH CLUB MEETING THRU 1976, BOOTHS IN THE WOODRUFF COUNTY FAIR AND PLACING A MARKER OF HISTORICAL INTEREST. AT MORTON BAPTIST COMMUNITY CENTER, FAKES CAHPPEL, FAIR GROUNDS. (LOCAL). MRS CRYSTAL DAWSON, PRES; EXTENSION HOMEMAKERS OF WOODRUFF COUNTY; 420 SPRUCE; AUGUSTA, AR 72006. (#103799-10).

FEB 22, '76. WASHINGTON DAY PARADE. 150 COMMUNITY GROUPS WILL COMMEMORATE WASHINGTON'S VISIT TO AUGUSTA. BALL WILL BE HELD AT RICHMOND ACADEMY, WHERE WASHINGTON REVIEWED THE TROOPS IN 1791. (LOCAL). TRAVIS BARNES, CHAIRMAN; AUGUSTA-RICHMOND COUNTY BICENT COMMITTEE; PO BOX 1776; AUGUSTA, GA 30903. (#100302-1).

FEB 28, '76. BICENTENNIAL SYMPHONY. NEW MAJOR WORK FOR CHORUS & ORCHESTRA ON PRE-REVOLUTIONARY WAR TEXTS COMPOSED BY WAYNE BARLOW TO PREMIER ON FEB 28, 1976. WORK WILL THEN BE MADE AVAILABLE TO OTHER ORCHESTRAS & CHORUSES AT NO CHARGE. AT AUGUSTA COLLEGE. (LOCAL). HARRY JACOBS; AUGUSTA-RICHMOND COUNTY BICENT COMMITTEE & AUGUSTA SYMPHONY; AUGUSTA COLLEGE; AUGUSTA, GA 30904. (#16124-1).

MAR 30 - MAY 31, '76. WORKSHOP IN AMERICAN PAINTING. SEMINAR. (LOCAL). A K JOHNSON, EXEC DIR; GEORGIA COMMISSION FOR THE NATIONAL BICENTENNIAL CELEBRATION; 1776 PEACHTREE ST; ATLANTA, GA 30909. (#15790-4).

APR 1 - MAY 31, '76. 'PURSUIT OF HAPPINESS' - LECTURE SERIES. SEMINAR. (LOCAL). A K JOHNSON, EXEC DIR; GEORGIA COMMISSION FOR THE NATIONAL BICENTENNIAL CELEBRATION; 1776 PEACHTREE ST; ATLANTA, GA 30909. (#15790-1).

APR 8, '76. KENTUCKY BLUEGRASS MUSIC FESTIVAL. SEMINAR. (LOCAL). A K JOHNSON, EXEC DIR; GEORGIA COMMISSION FOR THE NATIONAL BICENTENNIAL CELEBRATION; 1776 PEACHTREE ST; ATLANTA, GA 30909. (#15790-2).

APR 15, '76. PERFORMANCE OF AMERICAN FOLK DANCE. SEMINAR. (LOCAL). A K JOHNSON, EXEC DIR; GEORGIA COMMISSION FOR THE NATIONAL BICENTENNIAL CELEBRATION; 1776 PEACHTREE ST; ATLANTA, GA 30909. (#15790-3).

APR 22, '76. PERFORMANCE OF AUGUSTA SYMPHONY. SEMINAR. (LOCAL). A K JOHNSON, EXEC DIR; GEORGIA COMMISSION FOR THE NATIONAL BICENTENNIAL CELEBRATION; 1776 PEACHTREE ST; ATLANTA, GA 30909. (#15790-5).

AUGUSTA — CONTINUED

MAY 12 - 16, '76. HERITAGE SPECIAL - TRAIN TOUR. TRAVELING RAIL EXHIBIT EMPHASIZING COLONIAL & REVOLUTIONARY GEORGIA HISTORY, CRAFTS & LIFESTYLE OF GEORGIA COLONISTS. EXHIBITS WILL BE DISPLAYED WITH COMBINATION OF SIGHT & SOUND ACTIVITY. (LOCAL). RON HENRY, COORDINATOR; GEORGIA AGRIRAMA DEVELOPMENT AUTHORITY/GEORGIA BICENTENNIAL; 8TH ST A I 75; TIFTON, GA 31794. (#7999-5).

AUSTELL

COMMUNITY IMPROVEMENT IN AUSTELL, GA. UNSIGHTLY SOUTHERN RAILROAD BUILDING DEMOLISHED AND PARKING AREA BUILT FOR ADJACENT MUNICIPAL BUILDINGS. (LOCAL). MARTHA BATES, PRESIDENT; AUSTELL WOMAN'S CLUB; 116 ANNETTE LANE; AUSTELL, GA 30001. (#31122).

EXPANSION OF RECREATION FACILITIES IN AUSTELL, GA. APPLICATION FOR FEDERAL GRANT TO BUILD NATURE TRAILS, PICNIC AREAS & BOY AND GIRL SCOUT CABINS. (LOCAL). BOBBY CAUSEY, CITY MANAGER; CITY OF AUSTELL; BROAD ST; AUSTELL, GA 30001. (#31121).

LOG CABIN RAISING IN AUSTELL, GA. LOG CABIN TO BE RAISED BY COMMUNITY EFFORT, FURNISHED WITH COLONIAL ERA FURNITURE TO BE BUILT BY SCHOOL CHILDREN AND OPEN TO COMMUNITY FOR USE. (LOCAL). DR FRANK CROKER, PRINCIPAL; AUSTELL BICENTENNIAL COMMITTEE/GARRETT MIDDLE SCHOOL; POWDER SPRINGS RD; AUSTELL, GA 30001. (#31120).

MAR 6, '76. BICENTENNIAL TREE PLANTING CEREMONY. CEREMONY AT PUBLIC GROUNDS. (LOCAL). JACKIE HEADLEY, CHMN; AUSTELL PARKS & RECREATION DEPT; AUSTELL, GA 30001. (#200012-63).

MAR 26, '76. FEDERATION OF WOMENS' CLUBS 7TH DISTRICT SPRING LUNCHEON. FESTIVAL AT GARRETT MIDDLE SCHOOL. (LOCAL). MARTHA BATES, CHMN; AUSTELL WOMAN'S CLUB; 116 ANNETTE LN; AUSTELL, GA 30001. (#200012-62).

MAY 22, '76. CLEANUP AUSTELL DAY CONTEST. COMPETITION, AWARD. (LOCAL). DELORE LOCKRIDGE, CHMN; CITIZENS & SOUTHERN BANK; AUSTELL, GA 30001. (#200012-64).

MAY 29, '76. BICENTENNIAL DAY FESTIVITIES. FESTIVAL AT PUBLIC GROUNDS. (LOCAL). DELORES LOCKRIDGE, CHMN; CITY OF AUSTELL; AUSTELL, GA 30001. (#200012-61).

MAY 29, '76. OPENING OF MARSHALS OFFICE & MUSEUM. CEREMONY, EXHIBIT AT BROAD ST. (LOCAL). BOBBY CAUSEY, CHMN; CITY OF AUSTELL; AUSTELL, GA 30001. (#200012-60).

BARNESVILLE

DEC 11, '75. 'HAIL TO THE CHIEF', BICENTENNIAL MUSICAL PLAY. THE PLAY IS BOTH A SERIOUS & HUMOROUS LOOK AT THE PRESIDENTS. THE SCRIPT WAS WRITTEN BY GORDON FACULTY. THE PLAY WILL BE PERFORMED BY GORDON STUDENTS. AMATEUR & PROFESSIONAL MUSICIANS COMPOSE THE ORCHESTRA. THE COLLEGE 4 YEARS OF EXPERIENCE IN PLAY PRODUCTION. AT ALUMNI MEMORIAL HALL, GYMNASIUM, COLLEGE DR. (LOCAL). DR JIM RICHARDS, PROJ DIR; GORDON JUNIOR COLLEGE; BARNESVILLE, GA 30204. (#103476-1).

SEPT 17 - 25, '76. BUGGY DAYS. THE 150TH ANNIVERSARY OF BARNESVILLE, COMMEMORATING AMERICA'S BICENTENNIAL; AND HIGHLIGHTING BARNESVILLE'S HISTORY AS A BUGGY MANUFACTURING CENTER OF THE SOUTHEASTERN UNITED STATES. WILL ALSO CELEBRATE BARNESVILLE'S SESQUICENTENNIAL. (LOCAL). BILL KITCHING, PRESIDENT; LAMAR HISTORY SOC/BARNESVILLE CHAMBER OF COMMERCE/GORDON JR COLLEGE; 406 HOLMES ST; BARNESVILLE, GA 30204. (#106739-1).

BAXLEY

CITY PARK OF BAXLEY, GEORGIA. PROPERTY PURCHASED BY CITY IN CENTER OF BUSINESS DISTRICT BEING MADE INTO PARK; WILL BE DEDICATED JULY 4, 1976 WITH COMMUNITY PICNIC. SIGN TO BE ERECTED COMMEMORATING BICENT & BAXLEY'S CENTENNIAL. (LOCAL). MRS H L HARBIN AND JACK FROST, PROJ COORDINATORS; CITY OF BAXLEY AND APPLING BICENT COMMITTEE; PO BOX 479; BAXLEY, GA 31513. (#9065).

FOOTPRINTS OF APPLING HISTORY PROJ OF GEORGIA. HISTORY OF APPLING COUNTY BEING WRITTEN BY MEMBER OF BICENTENNIAL COMMITTEE; TO BE PUBLISHED, PROMOTED AND SOLD BY COMMITTEE. (LOCAL). MRS H L HARBIN, PROJ DIRECTOR; APPLING COUNTY BICENT COMMITTEE; PO BOX 479; BAXLEY, GA 31513. (#9063).

NEW APPLING COUNTY LIBRARY IN BAXLEY, GEORGIA. NEW LIBRARY TO BE BUILT ON SITE DONATED BY CITY & LOCAL LEVEL FUNDS GUARANTEED BY COUNTY BICENT COMMITTEE; THE COMMITTEE IS ASSISTING WITH PLANNING AND FURNISHING. THE DEDICATION WILL BE IN 1976. (LOCAL). MRS H L HARBIN, CHAIRMAN; APPLING COUNTY BICENT COMMITTEE; PO BOX 479; BAXLEY, GA 31513. (#9067).

JUNE 13, '74. 'RECALLING OUR PAST' - BAXLEY, GEORGIA. PROGRAM ON LOCAL HISTORY INCLUDING LIBERTY TREE PLANTING CEREMONY, GROUP SONGFEST AND FLAG CEREMONY. THE PUBLIC IS INVITED TO THIS AFFAIR SPONSORED BY GOVERNMENT AND CIVIC CLUB PERSONNEL. (LOCAL). MRS H L HARBIN, CHAIRMAN; APPLING COUNTY BICENT COMMITTEE; PO BOX 479; BAXLEY, GA 31513. (#9062-1).

MAY 9, '75. AMERICA THE BEAUTIFUL - BAXLEY, GEORGIA. OUTDOOR PAGEANT OF MUSIC AND DRAMA PORTRAYING AMERICA'S HISTORY; TO PRESENT CHALLENGE BY SPIRIT OF FREEDOM; SCHOOL BANDS, ROTC, & FHA TO PARTICIPATE; CEREMONY FOR RECOGNITION AS BICENT COMMUNITY. (LOCAL). MRS H L HARBIN & MRS CHAR; APPLING COUNTY HIGH SCHOOL AND APPLING COUNTY BICENT COMMISSIONS; PO BOX 479; BAXLEY, GA 31513. (#9064-1).

MAR 2, '76. UNITED STATES ARMED FORCES BICENTENNIAL CARAVAN. CARAVAN IS COMPOSED OF EXHIBIT VANS FOR EACH MILITARY SERVICE. PROJECT THEME IS 'HISTORY OF THE ARMED FORCES AND THEIR CONTRIBUTIONS TO THE NATION'. (LOCAL). MRS H L HARBIN; US ARMED FORCES BICENTENNIAL EXHIBIT VANS PROJECT; PO BOX 479; BAXLEY, GA 31513. (#1775-438).

BETWEEN

FLAG PLACEMENT, BETWEEN, GA. THE AMERICAN FLAG & A CHRISTIAN FLAG WILL BE PLACED IN THE NEW HOPE UNITED METHODIST CHURCH, IN HONOR OF LEWIS B SMITH. (LOCAL). MRS LEWIS B SMITH, PROJ COORDINATOR; NEW HOPE UNITED METHODIST CHURCH; ROUTE 3; MONROE, GA 30655. (#24386).

TREE PLANTING - BETWEEN, GA. A CREPE MYRTLE WILL BE PLANTED IN EVERY YARD IN THE TOWN. (LOCAL). MRS BENNIE QUEEN, CHAIRPERSON; BETWEEN HOMEMAKERS CLUB; ROUTE 3; MONROE, GA 30655. (#22719).

ZIP CODE BOOK UNITED METHODIST WOMEN, BETWEEN, GA. NATIONAL ZIP CODE BOOK, 1600 WORDS OF WALTON COUNTY HISTORY AND CURRENT STATISTICS INCLUDED. (LOCAL). MRS BENNIE QUEEN, CHAIRPERSON; NEW HOPE UNITED METHODIST WOMEN; ROUTE 3; MONROE, GA 30655. (#24387).

JULY 4, '76. WALL HANGING. BICENTENNIAL EMBLEM IS BEING DONE IN NEEDLEPOINT, APPROXIMATELY 2 1/2 FT SQUARE, TO BE HUNG PERMANENTLY IN THE COURT HOUSE. AT COURT HOUSE. (LOCAL). MRS L F SMITH, COORD; BETWEEN HOMEMAKERS' CLUB; RT #1; LOGANVILLE, GA 30249. (#106615-1).

BLAIRSVILLE

COUNTY HISTORY BOOK - BLAIRSVILLE, GA. ESTABLISH A UNION COUNTY HISTORIC SOCIETY, GATHER MATERIALS ON COUNTY HISTORY AND PUBLISH BOOK. SOCIETY TO ATTEMPT TO PRESERVE OLD BUILDINGS OF LOCAL, HISTORIC IMPORTANCE. (LOCAL). BRYAN WEBB, CHAIRMAN; CITY OF BLAIRSVILLE-UNION COUNTY BICENTENNIAL COMMITTEE; RT 2, BOX 125-AA; BLAIRSVILLE, GA 30512. (#29395).

JULY 1 - 4, '76. GEORGIA MT, OLD-FASHIONED BICENTENNIAL JUBILEE. A FOUR DAY JUBILEE FOR ALL AGES & INTERESTS FEATURING ARTS & CRAFTS SALES, RIVER CANOE RACES, PARADE, MUSIC & DANCING EACH NIGHT, BLACK POWDER RIFLE SHOOTING, QUILTING, GOSPEL SINGING, BLUE GRASS BANDS, YOUTH FISHING, TENNIS & SWIMMING CONTESTS AND FIREWORKS. AT COUNTY COURTHOUSE, CIVIC CENTER AND FORT SORGHUM. (REGN'L). BRYAN WEBB; CITY OF BLAIRSVILLE-UNION COUNTY BICENTENNIAL COMMITTEE; RT 2, BOX 125-AA; BLAIRSVILLE, GA 30512. (#200012-44).

BLAKELY

CAPTAIN BLAKELY MEMORIAL MARKER - BLAKELY, GA. A MARBLE & BRONZE MARKER WAS PLACED IN FRONT OF CITY HALL WITH THE APPROPRIATE INSCRIPTION AS A MEMORIAL TO CAPTAIN BLAKELY, NAVAL HERO OF WAR OF 1812, FOR WHOM THE CITY WAS NAMED. (LOCAL). MRS GEORGE NELSON, CHAIRMAN; BLAKELY SESQUICENTENNIAL COMM OF THE BLAKE-EARLY BICENT COMM; BLAKELY, GA 31723. (#21346).

COHELEE CREEK COVERED BRIDGE - BLAKELY, GA. COHELEE CREEK BRIDGE IS THE ONLY REMAINING COVERED BRIDGE IN EARLY COUNTY. IT IS BEING PRESERVED AND RESTORED. IT IS THE SOUTHERNMOST COVERED BRIDGE IN THE NATION. (LOCAL). MRS WM BARKSDALE, CHAIRMAN; BLAKELY-EARLY BICENTENNIAL COMMISSION; BLAKELY, GA 31723. (#21347).

COMMUNITY BEAUTIFICATION BY TREE PLANTING - GA. 1,000 DOGWOODS WILL BE PLANTED BY VOLUNTEERS. (LOCAL). MRS ROBERT E TINER, PRESIDENT; COMMUNITY SERVICE LEAGUE; BLAKELY, GA 31723. (#21348).

TOMB INDEX OF BLACK CITIZENS OF EARLY COUNTY, GA. A SURVEY AND RECORDING OF MARKERS FROM 22 CEMETERIES. (LOCAL). MRS FLOYE MAE R EZELL, CHAIRMAN; PRESERVATION COMMITTEE, BLAKELY-EARLY BICENTENNIAL COMMISSION; 108 S BLVD; BLAKELY, GA 31723. (#25197).

SEPT 21, '75. HERITAGE DAY CELEBRATION. PARADE, EXHIBITS, CONTESTS, GAMES & CONCERT; JUDGING OF BEARDS, COOKING & COSTUMES. AT EARLY CO HIGH SCHOOL FOOTBALL STADIUM AND AUDITORIUM. (LOCAL). MRS FRANK PICKLE, CHMN; COMMUNITY SERVICE & COMBINED ART COMMITTEE OF BICENTENNIAL COMM; BLAKELY, GA 31723. (#105289-1).

APR 1, '76 - CONTINUING . KOLOMOKI STATE MUSEUM REOPENING. THE MUSEUM WILL REOPEN - EXHIBIT WILL FEATURE RELICS FROM INDIAN SOCIETIES DATING BACK 2000 YEARS. AT NEAR TEMPLE MOUND, 5 MILES OFF US HWY 27. (LOCAL). MRS W M BARKSDALE, CHMN; PRESERVATION COMMITTEE OF BLAKELY-EARLY BICENTENNIAL COMMITTEE; BLAKELY, GA 31723. (#105029-1).

APR 26, '76. CONFEDERATE MEMORIAL DAY PROGRAM. NAMES OF ALL MEN FROM EARLY COUNTY WHO DIED FOR 'THE LOST CAUSE' WILL BE READ AND AN APPROPRIATE PROGRAM WILL BE HELD ON APR 26TH, THE CONFEDERATE MEMORIAL DAY. THE SITE OF THE LAST REMAINING CONFEDERATE FLAGPOLE IN THE SOUTH. AT COURT SQUARE, BLAKELY, GA. (LOCAL). MRS GEORGE NELSON, CHMN; BLAKELY SESQUICENT COMM OF BLAKELY-EARLY BICENT COMM; BLAKELY-EARLY BICENT COMM; BLAKELY, GA 31723. (#21344-1).

BLUE RIDGE

REVIVAL OF WEAVING, SPINNING & BLACKSMITHING, GA. CRAFTS WILL BE TAUGHT TO HIGH SCHOOL STUDENTS & ADULT MEMBERS OF THE COMMUNITY; LOOMS, SPINNING WHEELS & A FORGE WILL BE AVAILABLE FOR USE TO PARTICIPANTS AFTER THE INSTRUCTION. (LOCAL). KATHLEEN THOMPSON, PROJ DIRECTOR; FANNIN COUNTY BICENTENNIAL COMMITTEE; BLUE RIDGE, GA 30513. (#17955). **ARBA GRANTEE.**

JAN 2 - OCT 30, '76. CRAFT TEACHING SESSIONS. JAN 2 - FEB 1, QUILTING BEE; FEB 1 - MAR 1, RUG HOOKING & BRAIDING; MAR 1 - APR 1, NEEDLECRAFT; APR 1 - MAY 1, POTTERY MAKING; MAY 1 JUN 1, CORN SHUCK CRAFT; JUN 1 - JUL 1, CHAIR CANING; JUL 1 - AUG 1, BASKET WEAVING; AUG 1, WEAVING & SPINNING; SEPT 1, LYE SOAP. (LOCAL). IMOGENE STEWART, CHMN; FANNIN COUNTY HOMEMAKERS COUNCIL; BLUERIDGE, GA 30513. (#103491-3).

JULY 2, '76. STREET DANCE & FIREWORKS. FESTIVAL. (LOCAL). MARTY GODFREY, MGR; JOYETTES OF BLUE RIDGE & HOME FEDERAL SAVINGS AND LOAN ASSOC; HOME FEDERAL SAVINGS & LOAN; BLUE RIDGE, GA 30513. (#103747-6).

JULY 4, '76. FESTIVAL OF FAITH. CEREMONY AT WEST FANNIN HIGH SCHOOL, 6 MI NORTH OF BLUE RIDGE ON HWY #5. (LOCAL). GROVER D JONES, COORD; MORGANTON BAPTIST ASSOC; MAIN ST; BLUE RIDGE, GA 30513. (#103747-5).

OCT 1 - DEC 15, '76. HARVEST SALE, QUILT SHOW & OLD FASHIONED CHRISTMAS DECORATIONS. HARVEST SALE WITH VARIOUS DEMONSTRATIONS, OCT 1 '76 TO OCT 26 '76; QUILT SHOW NOV 1 '76 TO NOV 15 '76; OLD FASHIONED CHRISTMAS DECORATIONS EXHIBITION, DEC 1 '76 TO DEC 15 '76. (LOCAL). IMOGENE STEWART, CHMN; FANNIN COUNTY HOMEMAKERS COUNCIL; BLUERIDGE, GA 30513. (#103491-4).

BRUNSWICK

AMERICAN WIND SYMPHONY FLOATING ARTS CENTER - GA. 65-MEMBER GROUP PERFORMS ON INTRACOASTAL WATERWAY. THERE WILL BE 60 SMALL GROUP INSTRUCTIONAL SESSIONS AND SYMPOSIA THROUGHOUT COMMUNITY IN ALL AREAS OF THE FINE AND PERFORMING ARTS. (LOCAL). JOHN E JOHNSON, CHAIRMAN; GLYNN COUNTY BICENTENNIAL COMMITTEE; 1053 SHERMAN AVE; ST SIMONS IS, GA 31522. (#11004). **ARBA GRANTEE.**

THE GLYNN REPORTER VOTER REGISTRATION DRIVE -NBMRP. PAPER'S BIG PROJECT WAS VOTER REGISTRATION DRIVE AIMED TO GET OUT THE VOTE AS TRIBUTE TO BICENT. ALSO RAISED FUNDS FOR 'AMERICAN WIND SYMPHONY'; HEAVY COVERAGE OF BICENT PROJECTS. (LOCAL). MRS CHERRY D L TAYLOR, BICENT COORDINATOR; THE GLYNN REPORTER; PO BOX 1694; BRUNSWICK, GA 31520. (#23647).

REFERENCE GUIDE TO HISTORIC GEORGIA COASTAL SITES. PUBLICATION AND SLIDE PRODUCTION OF COLLECTED RESOURCE MATERIALS ON HISTORIC SITES, TOURS AND TRAILS IN COASTAL GEORGIA. (ST-WIDE). VERNON MARTIN, EXEC DIRECTOR; COASTAL AREA PLANNING & DEVELOPMENT COMMISSION; PO BOX 1316; BRUNSWICK, GA 31520. (#515). **ARBA GRANTEE.**

JUNE 15 - AUG 30, '75. TOURS & TALKS ON GEORGIA'S COASTAL HISTORY. ALSO SUMMER 1976. FT FREDERICA, BUILT DURING ANGLO-SPANISH STRUGGLE FOR SE SECTION OF US, IS OFFERING PGMS ENCOMPASSING THE DEVELOPMENT OF GEORGIAN CULTURE, COLONIAL GEORGIAN LIFE, AND THE EFFECTS OF THE REVOLUTION UPON GEORGIA. AT VISITOR CENTER AT PARK. (REGN'L). SUPT, FT FREDERICA NM; NATIONAL PARK SERVICE; P.O. BOX 816, ST SIMON'S ISLAND; BRUNSWICK, GA 31522. (#6730-8).

FEB 25 - 26, '76. UNITED STATES ARMED FORCES BICENTENNIAL CARAVAN. CARAVAN IS COMPOSED OF EXHIBIT VANS FOR EACH MILITARY SERVICE. PROJECT THEME IS 'HISTORY OF THE ARMED FORCES AND THEIR CONTRIBUTIONS TO THE NATION'. (LOCAL). DR J E JOHNSON; GLYNN COUNTY BICENTENNIAL COMMITTEE; GLYNN COUNTY BICENTENNIAL COMMIT; BRUNSWICK, GA 31520. (#1775-436).

MAY 19, '76. SYMPHONIC PRESENTATION OF THE AMERICAN WIND SYMPHONY. 65-MEMBER GROUP PERFORMS ON INTRACOASTAL WATERWAY. THERE WILL BE 60 SMALL GROUP INSTRUCTIONAL SESSIONS AND SYMPOSIA THROUGHOUT COMMUNITY IN ALL AREAS OF THE FINE AND PERFORMING ARTS. (LOCAL). JOHN E JOHNSON, CHAIRMAN; GLYNN COUNTY BICENTENNIAL COMMITTEE; 1053 SHERMAN AVE; ST SIMONS IS, GA 31522. (#11004-501).

MAY 20, '76. AMERICAN WIND SYMPHONY'S FLOATING ARTS CENTER VISITS BRUNSWICK. EMBARKING UPON A BICENTENNIAL CULTURAL TOUR, THE WIND SYMPHONY WILL VISIT 76 CITIES BRINGING MUSIC, DANCE, SYMPOSIA, AND CHILDREN'S THEATER TO THE WATERWAYS OF AMERICA DURING ITS 6-MONTH TOUR. (LOCAL). PAULA BERN, COORDINATOR; AMERICAN WIND SYMPHONY ORCHESTRA OF WESTERN PENNSYLVANIA; GATEWAY TOWERS 18G; PITTSBURGH, PA 15222. (#2800-9).

JUNE 15 - AUG 30, '76. FT FREDERICA NM PRESENTS TOURS & TALKS ON GEORGIA'S COASTAL HIST. FORT FREDERICA, BUILT DURING ANGLO-SPANISH STRUGGLE FOR SOUTHEAST SECTION OF U.S., IS OFFERING PGMS ENCOMPASSING THE DEVELOPMENT OF GEORGIAN CULTURE, COLONIAL GEORGIAN LIFE, AND

BRUNSWICK — CONTINUED

THE EFFECTS OF THE REVOLUTION UPON GEORGIA. AT VISITOR CENTER AT PARK. (REGN'L). FT FREDERICA NATL MON; NATIONAL PARK SERVICE; ROUTE 4, BOX 286-C; BRUNSWICK, GA 31522. (#6730-508).

JUNE 30, '76. NATL PK SVC '...A LITTLE LOOK AROUND' VISITS FT FREDERICA NM. THIS SHORT PROGRAM FEATURES ACTORS PORTRAYING FAMOUS AMERICANS OF THE PAST WHO'VE RETURNED TO SEE AMERICA'S GROWTH. (REGN'L). FT FREDERICA N M; NATIONAL PARK SERVICE; P.O. BOX 816; ST SIMONS ISL, GA 31522. (#5653-87).

JULY 28 - AUG 1, '76. HERITAGE SPECIAL - TRAIN TOUR. TRAVELING RAIL EXHIBIT EMPHASIZING COLONIAL & REVOLUTIONARY GEORGIA HISTORY, CRAFTS & LIFESTYLE OF GEORGIA COLONISTS. EXHIBITS WILL BE DISPLAYED WITH COMBINATION OF SIGHT & SOUND ACTIVITY. (ST-WIDE). RON HENRY, COORDINATOR; GEORGIA AGRIRAMA DEVELOPMENT AUTHORITY/ GEORGIA BICENTENNIAL; 8TH ST A I 75; TIFTON, GA 31794. (#7999-4).

BUCHANAN

'ATTIC ARCHAEOLOGY' PROJ OF BUCHANAN, GA. THE ATTIC ARCHAEOLOGY PEOPLE WILL BE LOCATING AND OBTAINING RELICS FROM THE PAST FOR VIEWING. (LOCAL). SHIRLEY PATTERSON, COORDINATOR; BUCHANAN AREA BICENTENNIAL COMMITTEE & ATTIC ARCHAEOLOGY; BOX 246; BUCHANAN, GA 30113. (#18288).

CEMETERY RESEARCH - BUCHANAN, GA. THE OLDEST GRAVE SITES IN HARALSON WILL BE INDENTIFIED. (LOCAL). HARVIE PERRY, CHAIRMAN; BUCHANAN AREA BICENTENNIAL COMMITTEE; BOX 246; BUCHANAN, GA 30113. (#18282).

DOWNTOWN FACELIFT - BUCHANON, GA. STOREFRONTS WILL BE PAINTED AND WALKWAYS COVERED. (LOCAL). ANN HUGHES, SECRETARY; BUCHANAN AREA BICENTENNIAL COMMITTEE & MERCHANTS ASSOC; BOX 246; BUCHANAN, GA 30113. (#18273).

DRUG ABUSE INFORMATION PROJ, BUCHANAN, GA. POLICE PROVIDE PROGRAMS AND INFORMATION ABOUT DRUGS AND DRUG ABUSE TO THE PUBLIC AND TO SCHOOLS. (LOCAL). ANN HUGHES, SECRETARY; BUCHANAN AREA BICENTENNIAL COMMITTEE; BOX 246; BUCHANAN, GA 30113. (#18272).

FALL ARTS AND CRAFTS FESTIVAL - HANDICRAFTS, FOOD & ARTWORK. FESTIVAL. (LOCAL). RUTH WOODS, CHAIRMAN; BUCHANAN AREA BICENTENNIAL COMMITTEE & BUCHANAN HISTORICAL SOCIETY; BOX 246; BUCHANAN, GA 30113. (#103747-4).

HARALSON COUNTY SUPERSTITIONS & FOLKLORE - GA. BUCHANAN JUNIOR HIGH SCHOOL STUDENTS WILL BE COLLECTING FOLKLORE AND STORIES OF CENTRAL GEORGIA. (LOCAL). ETHEL SCOTT, SCIENCE DEPT CHAIRPERSON; BUCHANAN AREA BICENTENNIAL COMMITTEE & BUCHANAN JR HIGH; BOX 246; BUCHANAN, GA 30113. (#18289).

HISTORICAL ESSAYS - BUCHANAN, GA. HIGH SCHOOL STUDENTS WILL RESEARCH AND PREPARE ESSAYS RELATED TO THE AMERICAN REVOLUTION, GEORGIA AND HARALSON COUNTY HISTORY. (LOCAL). ANN HUGHES, COORDINATOR; BUCHANAN AREA BICENTENNIAL COMMITTEE & WOMAN'S CLUB; BOX 246; BUCHANAN, GA 30113. (#18286).

HISTORICAL SITES IN BUCHANAN, GA. AN INVENTORY OF HISTORICAL SITES SHOWING THE DEVELOPMENT OF HARALSON COUNTY SINCE THE AREA WAS INHABITED BY THE INDIANS. (LOCAL). FRANK SCOTT, COORDINATOR; BUCHANAN AREA BICENTENNIAL COMMITTEE; BOX 246; BUCHANAN, GA 30113. (#18290).

HISTORICAL SITES MAP - BUCHANAN, GA. SITES OF HISTORICAL INTEREST ARE BEING MARKED ON A MAP TO FACILITATE TRAVELING IN CENTRAL GEORGIA. THE MAPS WILL BE PUBLISHED AND MADE AVAILABLE TO TOURISTS. (LOCAL). FRANK SCOTT, MAP CHAIRMAN; BUCHANAN AREA BICENTENNIAL COMMITTEE; BOX 246; BUCHANAN, GA 30113. (#18291).

INFORMATION CENTER - BUCHANAN, GA. VISITOR CENTER PROVIDED FOR INFORMATIONAL SERVICES AT CITY HALL. (LOCAL). ANN HUGHES, SECRETARY; BUCHANAN AREA BICENTENNIAL COMMITTEE; BOX 246; BUCHANAN, GA 30113. (#18274).

PARADE OF STUDENTS & BANDS IN SPECIAL DAYS RELATED TO HISTORY. PARADE. (LOCAL). WARD MABRY, CHAIRMAN; BUCHANAN AREA BICENTENNIAL COMMITTEE; BOX 246; BUCHANAN, GA 30113. (#103747-3).

PRESERVATION OF OLD COURTHOUSE - BUCHANAN, GA. THE COURTHOUSE WILL BE RESTORED TO USE AS A MUSEUM. (LOCAL). MARY KNIGHT, PRES OF HISTORICAL SOCIETY; BUCHANAN AREA BICENTENNIAL COMMITTEE; BOX 246; BUCHANAN, GA 30113. (#18287).

SPIRIT OF '76 POSTER - BUCHANAN, GA. HIGH SCHOOL STUDENTS WILL DEVELOP A POSTER TO REPRESENT THE GROWTH OF HARALSON COUNTY. (LOCAL). ANN HUGHES, RESOURCE TEACHER; BUCHANAN AREA BICENTENNIAL COMMITTEE; BOX 246; BUCHANAN, GA 30113. (#18284).

STORE FRONT MUSEUM - BUCHANAN, GA. ARTICLES OF CLOTHING, TOOLS, HANDWORK AND OTHER ITEMS REFLECTING THE DEVELOPMENT OF THE BUCHANAN AREA WILL BE DISPLAYED. (LOCAL). HARVIE PERRY, COORDINATOR; BUCHANAN AREA BICENTENNIAL COMMITTEE & MERCHANTS CLUB; BOX 246; BUCHANAN, GA 30113. (#18285).

BUDAPEST

OCT 20 - 22, '75. HUNGARIAN GRAPE FESTIVAL. FESTIVAL. (ST-WIDE). A K JOHNSON, EXEC DIR; GEORGIA COMMISSION FOR THE NATIONAL BICENTENNIAL CELEBRATION; 1776 PEACHTREE ST; ATLANTA, GA 30309. (#26429-4).

BUENA VISTA

BEAUTIFY DOWNTOWN BUENA VISTA, GA. THE BEAUTIFICATION PROJECT WILL INCLUDE COURTHOUSE SQUARE. (LOCAL). LOUISE A LOWE, CHAIRMAN; MARION COUNTY BICENTENNIAL COMMITTEE; BUENA VISTA, GA 31803. (#14338).

BICENTENNIAL COSTUMES - PROJ OF BUENA VISTA, GA. THE COMMUNITY WILL BE ENCOURAGED TO MAKE AND WEAR BICENTENNIAL COSTUMES. (LOCAL). LOUISE A LOWE, CHAIRMAN; MARION COUNTY BICENTENNIAL COMMITTEE; BUENA VISTA, GA 31803. (#14333).

BICENTENNIAL QUILT - PROJ OF BUENA VISTA, GA. A QUILT TELLING THE HISTORY OF MARION COUNTY TO BE HUNG AS A TAPESTRY IN THE COURTHOUSE. (LOCAL). LOUISE LOWE, CHAIRMAN; MARION COUNTY BICENTENNIAL COMMITTEE; BUENA VISTA, GA 31803. (#14334).

FOLKLORE OF MARION COUNTY, GA. FOLKLORE WILL BE GATHERED BY SCHOOL PUPILS TO BE USED IN NEWSPAPER ARTICLES. (LOCAL). LOUISE A LOWE, CHAIRMAN; MARION COUNTY BICENTENNIAL COMMITTEE; BUENA VISTA, GA 31803. (#14335).

HISTORIC BICENTENNIAL FLAGS - BUENA VISTA, GA. HISTORIC BICENTENNIAL FLAGS WILL BE DISPLAYED ON COURTHOUSE SQUARE. (LOCAL). MRS LOUISE A LOWE, CHAIRMAN; MARION COUNTY BICENTENNIAL COMMITTEE; BUENA VISTA, GA 31803. (#14326).

LIBERTY TREE IN BUENA VISTA, GA. A LIBERTY TREE IS TO BE PLANTED ON LAWN OF NEW TRI-COUNTY SCHOOL. (LOCAL). LOUISE LOWE, CHAIRMAN; MARION COUNTY BICENTENNIAL COMMITTEE; BUENA VISTA, GA 31803. (#14339).

MARION COUNTY HISTORY, BUENA VISTA, GA. THE HISTORY OF MARION COUNTY WILL BE REPRINTED BY NETTIE POWELL. (LOCAL). LOUISE A LOWE, CHAIRMAN; MARION COUNTY BICENTENNIAL COMMITTEE; BUENA VISTA, GA 31803. (#14340).

NEWSPAPER ARTICLES ON GEORGIA - BUENA VISTA. NEWSPAPER ARTICLES WILL BE PRINTED ON GEORGIA IN THE REVOLUTION. (ST-WIDE). LOUISE A LOWE, CHAIRMAN; MARION COUNTY BICENTENNIAL COMMITTEE; BUENA VISTA, GA 31803. (#14337).

NEWSPAPER INTERVIEWS - BUENA VISTA, GA. SCHOOL PUPILS WILL INTERVIEW CITIZENS OVER 80 FOR THE LOCAL NEWSPAPER. (LOCAL). LOUISE A LOWE, CHAIRMAN; MARION COUNTY BICENTENNIAL COMMITTEE; BUENA VISTA, GA 31803. (#14336).

OCT 25, '75. PRESENTATION OF FIFE & DRUM CORPS FROM FORT BENNING. LIVE PERFORMANCE. (LOCAL). LOUISE A LOWE, CHMN; MARION COUNTY BICENTENNIAL COMMITTEE; BUENA VISTA, GA 31803. (#101741-1).

JULY 4, '76. JULY 4TH FESTIVAL. FESTIVITIES WILL INCLUDE MUSIC, PARADE AND BARBEQUE. (LOCAL). LOUISE LOWE, CHMN; MARION COUNTY BICENTENNIAL COMMITTEE; BUENA VISTA, GA 31803. (#101742-1).

BUTLER

BEAUTIFICATION OF COURTHOUSE SQUARE, GA. PLANTING OF TREES ON COURTHOUSE SQUARE AS LIBERTY TREES FOR FUTURE GENERATIONS TO REMEMBER CELEBRATION. (LOCAL). JAMES L RUSSELL, COMMITTEE CHAIRMAN; TAYLOR COUNTY BICENTENNIAL COMMITTEE; RT 2, BOX 170; BUTLER, GA 31006. (#24048).

MAR 9 - 10, '76. TEXAS BICENTENNIAL MULE TRAIN. EXHIBIT AT BUTLER SQUARE. (LOCAL). JIM RUSSELL, CHAIRMAN; TAYLOR COUNTY BICENTENNIAL COMMITTEE; RT 2 BOX 170; BUTLER, GA 31006. (#200012-21).

APR 9 - MAY 22, '76. KIWANIS CLUB BEARD GROWING CONTEST. COMPETITION AT ON THE SQUARE. (LOCAL). JIM RUSSELL, CHMN; KIWANIS CLUB, REYNOLDS GA; RT 2 BOX 170; BUTLER, GA 31006. (#107273-6).

APR 10, '76. TAYLOR COUNTY SHRINE CLUB BAR-B-QUE. FESTIVAL AT BUTLER SQUARE. (LOCAL). JIM RUSSELL, COORD; TAYLOR COUNTY SHRINE CLUB; RT 2, BOX 170; BUTLER, GA 31006. (#200012-23).

APR 10, '76. WOMANLESS WEDDING & FASHION SHOW. CEREMONY, EXHIBIT AT GIRLS' SCHOOL. (LOCAL). JIM RUSSELL, CHAIRMAN; TAYLOR COUNTY BICENTENNIAL COMMITTEE; RT 2, BOX 170; BUTLER, GA 31006. (#200012-22).

MAY 21, '76. BEAUTY PAGEANT. COMPETITION AT TAYLOR COUNTY GIRLS SCHOOL. (LOCAL). JIM RUSSELL, CHMN; TAYLOR COUNTY BICENTENNIAL COMMITTEE; RT 2 BOX 170; BUTLER, GA 31006. (#107273-5).

MAY 21, '76. HISTORICAL PAGEANT. LIVE PERFORMANCE AT TAYLOR COUNTY GIRLS SCHOOL. (LOCAL). JIM RUSSELL, CHMN; TAYLOR COUNTY BICENTENNIAL COMMITTEE; RT 2 BOX 170; BUTLER, GA 31006. (#107273-13).

MAY 21, '76. SALUTE TO TAYLOR COUNTY & USA. LIVE PERFORMANCE AT TAYLOR COUNTY GIRLS SCHOOL. (LOCAL). JIM RUSSELL, CHMN; ELANCO PRODUCTS COMPANY; RT 2 BOX 170; BUTLER, GA 31006. (#107273-12).

MAY 21, '76. STREET DANCE. FESTIVAL AT ON SQUARE. (LOCAL) JIM RUSSELL, CHMN; TAYLOR COUNTY BICENTENNIAL COMMITTEE; RT 2 BOX 170; BUTLER, GA 31006. (#107273-4).

MAY 22, '76. AIRPORT ACTIVITIES. FESTIVAL, LIVE PERFORMANCE AT AIRPORT. (ST-WIDE). JIM RUSSELL, CHMN TAYLOR COUNTY BICENTENNIAL COMMITTEE; RT 2 BOX 170 BUTLER, GA 31006. (#107273-7).

MAY 22, '76. ANTIQUE DISPLAY AND ARTS & CRAFTS EXHIBITS. EXHIBIT AT ON THE SQUARE. (LOCAL). JIM RUSSELL, CHMN TAYLOR COUNTY BICENTENNIAL COMMITTEE; RT 2 BOX 170 BUTLER, GA 31006. (#107273-11).

MAY 22, '76. ARTS & CRAFTS FAIR. FAIR, EXHIBIT AT ON THE SQUARE. (LOCAL). JIM RUSSELL, CHAIRMAN; TAYLOR COUNTY BICENTENNIAL COMMITTEE; RT 2 BOX 170; BUTLER, GA 31006 (#107273-2).

MAY 22, '76. COSTUME CONTEST. COMPETITION, LIVE PERFORMANCE AT ON THE SQUARE. (LOCAL). JIM RUSSELL, CHAIRMAN; TAYLOR COUNTY BICENTENNIAL COMMITTEE & WESLEY COMMUNITY; RT 2 BOX 170; BUTLER, GA 31006. (#107273-1).

MAY 22, '76. FLAG RAISING AND RETREAT. CEREMONY AT ON THE SQUARE. (LOCAL). JIM RUSSELL, CHMN; TAYLOR COUNTY BICENTENNIAL COMMITTEE; RT 2 BOX 170; BUTLER, GA 31006 (#107273-10).

MAY 22, '76. HISTORICAL FLAG PRESENTATION-DRUM & FIFE CORPS. CEREMONY AT AIRPORT. (LOCAL). JIM RUSSELL, CHMN, TAYLOR COUNTY BICENTENNIAL COMMITTEE; RT 2 BOX 170, BUTLER, GA 31006. (#107273-9).

MAY 22, '76. REV JIMMY WATERS INSPIRATIONAL & RELIGIOUS SPEAKER. CEREMONY AT ON THE SQUARE. (LOCAL). JIM RUSSELL, CHAIRMAN; TAYLOR COUNTY BICENTENNIAL COMMITTEE; RT 2 BOX 170; BUTLER, GA 31006. (#107273-3).

MAY 22, '76. TAYLOR CO SHRINE CLUB BAR-B-Q. FESTIVAL AT ON THE SQUARE. (LOCAL). JIM RUSSELL, CHMN; TAYLOR COUNTY SHRINE CLUB; RT 2 BOX 170; BUTLER, GA 31006. (#107273-8).

CAIRO

BICENTENNIAL FLAG, CAIRO, GA. HALF-SIZE REPLICA OF THE STAR SPANGLED BANNER WILL BE PLANTED ON THE COURTHOUSE LAWN. (LOCAL). MRS HELEN WHITFIELD, DIRECTOR; COUNTY BOARD OF ROADS AND REVENUE; COURTHOUSE; CAIRO, GA 31728. (#14120).

BLACK HERITAGE COOKBOOK - CAIRO, GA. COLLECTION AND COMPILATION OF UNWRITTEN RECIPES OF THIS COMMUNITY. (LOCAL). MRS WILLETTE MCCORD, PROJ DIRECTOR; BLACK MINISTERIAL ASSOC; PO BOX 74; CAIRO, GA 31728. (#14119).

CANDELIGHT CONCERT. A CONCERT REMINISCENT OF WILLIAMSBURG DAYS WITH HARPSICHORD AND RECORDERS. (LOCAL). JIMMY MITCHELL, CHMN; GRADY COUNTY HISTORICAL SOCIETY; PO BOX 254; CAIRO, GA 31728. (#101716-1).

CHARTING THE PAST - PROJ OF CAIRO, GA. RECORDING 33 CEMETERIES BY HIGH SCHOOL STUDENTS AND THE HISTORICAL SOCIETY. (LOCAL). MRS CAROLYN BROWN, CHAIRMAN; GRADY COUNTY HISTORICAL SOCIETY; RT 1; CAIRO, GA 31728. (#14104).

CRACKER BARREL - PROJ OF CAIRO, GA. AMERICAN ISSUES FORUM TO BE HELD AT VARIED SPOTS IN COUNTY; TOPICS ARE LAND USE; FREEDOM OF SPEECH; ASSEMBLY AND RELIGION; FREEDOM OF THE PRESS AND EQUAL PROTECTION UNDER THE LAW. (LOCAL). WILLIAM BARRINEAU, CHAIRMAN; CAIRO KIWANIS CLUB; RT 2; CAIRO, GA 31728. (#14103).

FARM WIVES COOKBOOK OF CAIRO, GA. FARM WIVES WILL COLLECT RECIPES INDIGENOUS TO THE CAIRO AREA. (LOCAL). MRS DOUGLAS HARRELL, PRESIDENT; GRADY CO WOMEN'S FARM BUREAU; RT 1 BOX 416; CAIRO, GA 31728. (#14101).

FIFE AND DRUM CLUB - PROJ OF CAIRO, GA. PINPOINTING AMERICAN HERITAGE THRU BOOKS, FILMS AND RECORDS; ACTIVITIES FOR YOUTH. (LOCAL). MRS BARBARA WILLIAMS, PROJ DIRECTOR; RODDENBERY MEMORIAL LIBRARY; N BROAD ST; CAIRO, GA 31728. (#14102).

'FLY WITH THE SCOUTS', CAIRO, GA. SCOUTS EMPHASIZING DISPLAYS FOR STORES & HOMES ON PATRIOTIC OCCASIONS. (LOCAL). SKEET MILLER, PROJ DIRECTOR; SUWANNEE RIVER BOY SCOUT COUNCIL; 508 CULPEPPER DR; CAIRO, GA 31728. (#14115).

HERITAGE TEAS. OPEN HOUSE WITH EMPHASIS ON RESTORED AND PERIOD HOUSES. (LOCAL). MRS RICHARD PORTER, CHMN; BICENTENNIAL STEERING COMMITTEE; LULLWATER CIR; CAIRO, GA 31728. (#101707-1).

'HIDDEN HEROINES', CAIRO, GA. A SEARCH FOR THE HISTORIES OF LOCAL WOMEN WHO HELPED DEVELOP THE COMMUNITY. (LOCAL). MRS JULIEN RODDENBERY, JR, PROJ DIRECTOR; GIRL SCOUT COUNCIL; BAINBRIDGE RD; CAIRO, GA 31728. (#14114).

A HISTORY OF DUNCANVILLE, GA. RESEARCH, PREPARATION AND PRESENTATION OF HISTORY OF THE DESERTED VILLAGE OF DUNCANVILLE, THE OLDEST COMMUNITY IN THE COUNTY. (LOCAL). MRS L R WELLS, PROJ DIRECTOR; GRADY COUNTY HISTORICAL SOCIETY; RT 13, BOX 152; THOMASVILLE, GA 31792. (#14113).

KEEP IT STRAIGHT - PROJ OF CAIRO, GA. SCHOOL CHILDREN WILL ENLIST INFORMATION FROM GRANDPARENTS FOR FAMILY CHARTS; RECORDS TO BE FILED. (LOCAL). MRS JUDSON MAYFIELD, PROJ DIRECTOR; GRADY CO HISTORICAL SOCIETY; 203 4TH AVE SE; CAIRO, GA 31728. (#14109).

LET'S RECORD IT - PROJ OF CAIRO, GA. SMALL GROUPS MET WEEKLY TO TAPE TOPICS ON LOCAL HISTORY OF A BY-GONE

CAIRO — CONTINUED

ERA; TAPES ON FILE AT THE LIBRARY. (LOCAL). J E FORSYTH, PROJ DIRECTOR; ORAL HISTORY FORUM, RODDENBERY MEMORIAL LIBRARY; 39 6TH AVE SW; CAIRO, GA 31728. (#14110).

'LET'S VISIT OUR NEIGHBORS', BROCHURE, CAIRO, GA. A BROCHURE LISTING HISTORICAL, RECREATIONAL AND GARDEN SPOTS WITHIN A 100 MILE RADIUS OF CAIRO. THE PUBLICATION ALSO GIVES A PARALLEL LISTING OF BOOKS & PAMPHLETS. (LOCAL). MISS ANN WHITE, PROJ DIRECTOR; CAIRO-GRADY CHAMBER OF COMMERCE; N BROAD ST; CAIRO, GA 31728. (#14112).

LIBERTY TREES AS LIVING MEMORIALS - CAIRO, GA. PLANTING TREES ON ARBOR DAY HONORING LOCAL LEADERS. (LOCAL). MRS WILLARD CHASON, PROJ DIRECTOR; CAIRO-GRADY CO BICENTENNIAL COMMITTEE; 1208 6TH ST NW; CAIRO, GA 31728. (#14105).

MAPPING THE PAST FOR PRESENT HISTORIANS - GA. PREPARATION OF A GRADY CO MAP LOCATING EXTINCT PUBLIC BUILDINGS. (LOCAL). DR FRANCES SILVERMAN, PROJ DIRECTOR; GRADY CO HISTORICAL SOCIETY; RT 2; CAIRO, GA 31728. (#14111).

MUSIC IN THE PARK, CAIRO, GA. PROJECT TO BUILD A REPLICA OF THE BANDSTAND IN CITY PARK AT TURN OF CENTURY, CULMINATING IN ORGANIZATION OF A COMMUNITY BAND OPENING WIT A FESTIVAL OF MUSIC AND REGULAR PLANNED CONCERTS. (LOCAL). MRS RICHARD MOSES, CHAIRPERSON; GRADY CO HISTORICAL SOCIETY; 645 11TH AVE NW; CAIRO, GA 31728. (#14100).

MUSIC TO REMEMBER - CAIRO, GA. BAND DIRECTORS OF THE SCHOOLS PLAN TO HIGHLIGHT PATRIOTIC THEMES AT ALL PUBLIC AND SPORTS EVENTS. (LOCAL). JOE DAVID, CHAIRMAN; CAIRO HIGH SCHOOL MUSIC DEPT; PO BOX 593; CAIRO, GA 31728. (#14117).

OUR NATION'S CALLING CARD - PROJ OF CAIRO, GA. STAMP CLUB FOCUSING ATTENTION ON HISTORICAL STAMPS. (LOCAL). DON NICKERSON, PROJ DIRECTOR; RODDENBERY MEMORIAL LIBRARY; N BROAD ST; CAIRO, GA 31728. (#14108).

PRIDE IN US - PROJ OF CAIRO, GA. PREPARATION OF UNITS OF STUDY WITH BIBLIOGRAPHIC LISTINGS FOR EVERY GRADE, KINDERGARTEN THRU HIGH SCHOOL. LISTS BEING PREPARED BY PROFESSIONAL STAFF AT RODDENBERY MEMORIAL LIBRARY. (LOCAL). WESSIE CONNELL, DIRECTOR; RODDENBERY MEMORIAL LIBRARY; N BROAD ST; CAIRO, GA 31728. (#14107).

REACH FOR BEAUTY PROJECT IN CAIRO, GA. HANGING BASKETS OR DOORYARD GARDENS PLANTED IN RED, WHITE AND BLUE COLORS IN A HOUSING PROJECT. (LOCAL). MRS FEROL PERKINS, PRESIDENT; CAIRO FEDERATED GARDEN CLUB; 319 1ST ST SW; CAIRO, GA 31728. (#14118).

OCT 2, '75. PATRIOTS' HORSE SHOW. COUNTY AFFAIR HONORING A COLONIAL SPORT. (LOCAL). EARL HARRISON, DIRECTOR; CAIRO ROTARY CLUB; LAKEVIEW DR; CAIRO, GA 31728. (#101701-1).

OCT 27, '75. 'LEST WE FORGET'. PATRIOTIC PROGRAM FOR VETERAN'S DAY, 1975. (LOCAL). FRED PEARCE, DIRECTOR; AMERICAN LEGION; 585 10TH AVE NW; CAIRO, GA 31728. (#101714-1).

DEC 2, '75. CHRISTMAS PARADE. PUBLIC AFFAIR HONORING ST NICKOLAS WITH FLOATS AND BANDS FOLLOWING A BICENTENNIAL THEME. (LOCAL). TIM MORAN, CHMN; CAIRO MERCHANTS ASSOC; 7TH AVE SW; CAIRO, GA 31728. (#101709-1).

DEC 17, '75. CAROLING ON THE LAWN. COMMUNITY CAROLING INVOLVING STUDENTS, CHOIRS AND COMMUNITY SINGERS NEAR OUTDOOR CRECHE WITH COLONIAL INFLUENCE. (LOCAL). ED TIMMERMAN, DIRECTOR; CAIRO HIGH SCHOOL CHOIR; ROUTE 1, BOX 146; CAIRO, GA 31728. (#101702-1).

JAN '76. OLD BEN'S DAY. KITE CONTEST; A FUN FESTIVAL FOR YOUNG AND OLD ALIKE; PLANNED AS A TRIBUTE TO BENJAMIN FRANKLIN. (LOCAL). CHARLES GOFFE, CHMN; CAIRO RECREATION DEPT; FIRST ST; CAIRO, GA 31728. (#101717-1).

APR 30 - MAY 1, '76. RED, WHITE AND BLUE FOLLIES. DANCE GROUPS PRESENT AN EVENING OF MUSIC CENTERING ON A PATRIOTIC THEME. (LOCAL). MARIE JOINER, CHMN; CAIRO-GRADY COUNTY BICENTENNIAL COMMITTEE; 596 6TH AVE SE; CAIRO, GA 31728. (#101713-1).

JUNE 14, '76. PATRIOTS' CHESS TOURNAMENT. FLAG DAY CELEBRATED BY CHESS TOURNAMENT PRESERVING A SPORT POPULAR IN COLONIAL TIMES. (LOCAL). FRANK VEALE JR, CHMN; CAIRO CHESS CLUB; 1120 4TH ST NE; CAIRO, GA 31728. (#101715-1).

JULY 2 - 4, '76. 'GETTING TOGETHER FOR A BIRTHDAY PARTY'. FESTIVITIES WILL INCLUDE TENNIS MATCHES, SWIM MEETS AND GOLF TOURNAMENTS. (LOCAL). MRS J SLATER WIGHT, DIR; GRADY COUNTY HISTORICAL SOCIETY; 204 4TH AVE SE; CAIRO, GA 31728. (#101703-1).

JULY 3, '76. PICNICS IN THE PARKS. FRIENDS AND FAMILY REUNIONS COMPLETE WITH COMPETITIVE GAMES. (LOCAL). MISS CONNELL, CHMN; BICENTENNIAL STEERING COMMITTEE; 1575 LULLWATER CIR; CAIRO, GA 31728. (#101705-1).

JULY 4, '76. BICENTENNIAL PRAYER LIFT. CEREMONY. (LOCAL). REV CHARLES WOLFE, CHMN; GRADY CO BAPTIST ASSOC; 311 5TH ST NE; CAIRO, GA 31728. (#14099-1).

JULY 4, '76. CREEK TRIBE POW-WOW. ANNUAL CELEBRATION OF INDIANS OF CREEK TRIBE CLAIMING THEIR HERITAGE. (ST-WIDE). NEAL MCCORMICK, CHMN; LOWER CREEK INDIANS; 594 5TH ST NE; CAIRO, GA 31728. (#101712-1).

JULY 4, '76. 'FAITH OF OUR FATHERS'. COMMUNITY THANKSGIVING DAY CELEBRATION. AT CAIRO HIGH SCHOOL STADIUM. (LOCAL). REV LESTER PARKS; GRADY COUNTY MINISTERIAL ASSOC; PO BOX 311; CAIRO, GA 31728. (#14106-1).

JULY 4, '76. 'OUR RICH YEARS'. A PAGEANT OF EARLY HISTORY OF THIS AREA. (LOCAL). JACK WILLIS, DIR; GRADY COUNTY SCHOOLS; N BROAD ST; CAIRO, GA 31728. (#101704-1).

CALVARY

NOV 1, '75. MULE DAY. FOCUS ON EARLY HISTORY OF SOUTHWEST GEORGIA FARM COMMUNITY; A COUNTY FAIR. (LOCAL). DAN JONES, CHMN; CALVARY LIONS CLUB; ROUTE 2; WHIGHAM, GA 31797. (#101706-1).

CANTON

CITIZENSHIP EDUCATION IN CHEROKEE COUNTY, GA. VOTER INFORMATION WILL BE MADE PUBLIC AND VOTER REGISTRATION WILL BE ENCOURAGED; FORUM AND DISCUSSION GROUPS WILL BE ORGANIZED. (LOCAL). MRS LELAND BAGWELL, PROJ DIRECTOR; CHEROKEE COUNTY BICENTENNIAL COMMITTEE; BOX 192; CANTON, GA 30114. (#12558).

CLEANUP & BEAUTIFICATION PROGRAM, CHEROKEE CO, GA. ALL CIVIC-MINDED COUNTY GROUPS WILL WORK TOGETHER TO BEAUTIFY, PRESERVE AND PROTECT THE ENVIRONMENT. (LOCAL). U G MOORE, PROJ DIRECTOR; COMMUNITY AND GARDEN CLUBS; CHEROKEE COURTHOUSE; CANTON, GA 30114. (#12562).

COMMUNITY VEGETABLE GARDENS IN CANTON, GA. PLOTS WILL BE SPONSORED & SUPERVISED BY LOCAL GARDEN CLUB FOR THOSE UNABLE TO GARDEN AT HOME. (LOCAL). LESTER MORRIS, PROJ DIRECTOR; CHEROKEE MENS' GARDEN CLUB; HEMBRIDGE HILLS; CANTON, GA 30114. (#12560).

DRAMA PRESENTED IN CANTON, GA. PLAY BASED UPON EARLY HISTORY OF THE AREA TO BE PRESENTED IN 1976. (LOCAL). NEELY YOUNG, PROJ DIRECTOR; SPECIAL DRAMA COMMITTEE OF CHEROKEE CO BICENTENNIAL COMMITTEE; BOX 966; CANTON, GA 30114. (#12563).

FILM SERIES IN CANTON, GA. A FILM SERIES BASED ON ALISTAIR COOKE'S AMERICA. (LOCAL). MRS CHARLES HALES, PROJ DIRECTOR; JONES MEMORIAL LIBRARY; MAIN ST; CANTON, GA 30114. (#12566).

HIKING AND NATURE TRAIL - PROJ OF CANTON, GA. DESIGNATION, PLANNING AND ESTABLISHMENT OF A 10-MILE HIKING TRAIL. (LOCAL). DAN OWEN, PROJ DIRECTOR; BOY SCOUT TROOP 240; 640 LONGVIEW RD; CANTON, GA 30114. (#12650).

HISTORICAL SOCIETY IN CANTON, GA. A COUNTY HISTORICAL SOCIETY WILL BE ORGANIZED. (LOCAL). MRS CHARLES MALONE, PROJ DIRECTOR; CHEROKEE COUNTY BICENTENNIAL COMMITTEE; BALL GROUND, GA 30107. (#12569).

HISTORY OF CHEROKEE COUNTY SCHOOLS, GA. RESEARCHING AND WRITING HISTORY OF COMMUNITY SCHOOLS IN COUNTY'S PAST. (LOCAL). H A BELL, PROJ DIRECTOR; COUNTY SCHOOL PERSONNEL; BOX 429; CANTON, GA 30114. (#12568).

READING PROGRAM IN CANTON, GA. REVOLUTIONARY ERA READING PROGRAM WITH STORY HOURS; HISTORY BOOKS WILL BE MADE AVAILABLE TO GENERAL PUBLIC. (LOCAL). MRS CHARLES HALES, PROJ DIRECTOR; JONES MEMORIAL LIBRARY; MAIN ST; CANTON, GA 30114. (#12564).

RECREATIONAL PROGRAM IN CHEROKEE COUNTY, GA. THE DEVELOPMENT OF EXISTING PROGRAMS AND PARKS AND THE EXTENSION OF SERVICES TO OTHER AREAS. (LOCAL). TRAMMELL CARMICHAEL, PROJ DIRECTOR; COUNTY RECREATION COMMITTEE; COUNTY COURT; CANTON, GA 30114. (#12557).

TREE PLANTING IN CANTON, GA. SPECIAL LIBERTY TREES PLANTED AND DEDICATED AT DESIGNATED AREAS IN CHEROKEE COUNTY. (LOCAL). U G MOORE, PROJ DIRECTOR; 4-H CLUBS & SCOUT TROOPS; CHEROKEE COURT HOUSE; CANTON, GA 30114. (#12561).

VISUAL HISTORY OF CANTON AREA, GA. OLD PICTURE, DOCUMENT AND ARTIFACTS DISPLAY. (LOCAL). MRS EVELYN CARMICHAEL, PROJ DIRECTOR; CHEROKEE COUNTY BICENTENNIAL COMMITTEE; ROUTE 5; CANTON, GA 30114. (#12567).

JUNE 28 - JULY 4, '76. CHEROKEE ARTS & CRAFTS FESTIVAL. FESTIVAL. (LOCAL). NEELY YOUNG, DIRECTOR; CHEROKEE COUNTY BICENTENNIAL FESTIVAL COMMITTEE; PO BOX 124M; CANTON, GA 30114. (#102434-1).

AUG 18 - 21, '76. HERITAGE SPECIAL - TRAIN TOUR. TRAVELING RAIL EXHIBIT EMPHASIZING COLONIAL & REVOLUTIONARY GEORGIA HISTORY, CRAFTS & LIFESTYLE OF GEORGIA COLONISTS. EXHIBITS WILL BE DISPLAYED WITH COMBINATION OF SIGHT & SOUND ACTIVITY. (LOCAL). RON HENRY, COORDINATOR; GEORGIA AGRIRAMA DEVELOPMENT AUTHORITY/GEORGIA BICENTENNIAL; 8TH ST A I 75; TIFTON, GA 31794. (#7999-12).

SEPT 16 - 17, '76. FLOWER SHOW. FLOWER ARRANGEMENTS DEPICTING CHEROKEE COUNTY HISTORY. AT FIRST BAPTIST CHURCH, CHURCH ST. (LOCAL). MRS RALPH ALLISON; CHEROKEE GARDEN CLUB COUNCIL; PO BOX 329; CANTON, GA 30114. (#12565-1).

CARNESVILLE

FRANKLIN COUNTY: OUR COMMON HERITAGE, GA. HISTORY, SLIDE/TAPE PRESENTATION, MAPS, TOUR GUIDE, ALBUM, LISTING OF HISTORIC ITEMS, TOURIST INFORMATION, HISTORIC PICTURES & HISTORIC DOCUMENTS. (LOCAL). RICHARD T MILLER, CO-CHAIRMAN; FRANKLIN COUNTY BICENTENNIAL COMMISSION; ROUTE 2, BOX 155; CARNESVILLE, GA 30521. (#27238). **ARBA GRANTEE.**

CARROLLTON

BICENTENNIAL MEMORIAL PARK - CARROLLTON, GA. IN HONOR OF THE BICENTENNIAL, A PARK WILL BE BUILT ON CAMPUS. (LOCAL). TROY HOLCOMBE, DIRECTOR OF LANDSCAPE & GROUNDS; WEST GEORGIA COLLEGE; CARROLLTON, GA 30117. (#15993).

EDUCATION IN CARROLL COUNTY, GA. THE FILMSTRIP WILL DEPICT THE HISTORY OF EDUCATION IN CARROLL COUNTY. (LOCAL). WILTON KEY, PROFESSOR OF EDUCATION; WEST GEORGIA COLLEGE; CARROLLTON, GA 30117. (#15994).

FURNISHING SHARPE GUNN BONNER HOUSE, GA. FURNISH A MID-19TH CENTURY HOUSE LOCATED ON THE WEST GEORGIA COLLEGE CAMPUS WITH ANTIQUE PERIOD PIECE FURNITURE; THE HOUSE WILL BE USED AS A RECEPTION CENTER & MUSEUM OF WEST GEORGIAN HISTORY. (LOCAL). GENE HUTSELL, DIRECTOR OF ALUMNI AFFAIRS; WEST GEORGIA COLLEGE; CARROLLTON, GA 30117. (#15992). **ARBA GRANTEE.**

MUSEUM IN CARROLLTON, GA. A MUSEUM TO HOUSE ANTIQUE BUSINESS MACHINES. (LOCAL). DORA PETE, PROFESSOR OF BUSINESS; WEST GEORGIA COLLEGE; CARROLLTON, GA 30117. (#15995).

OCT 22, '75. KEYNOTE ADDRESS. AN ADDRESS BY PROFESSOR JAMES HENRETTA OF HARVARD ON A HISTORY OF THE HOME FRONT DURING THE AMERICAN REVOLUTION. (LOCAL). JOHN FERLING, ASST PROF; WEST GEORGIA COLLEGE; CARROLLTON, GA 30117. (#102665-1).

MAY 5 - 19, '76. BICENTENNIAL FINE ARTS FESTIVAL. WEST GEORGIA COLLEGE'S ANNUAL FINE ARTS FESTIVAL WILL FEATURE A BICENTENNIAL THEME ON HISTORIC AND CLASSIC AMERICAN DRAMA & MUSIC. AT CASHEN HALL; FIELD HOUSE; COLLEGE THEATER. (LOCAL). ROBERT COE, CHMN; WEST GEORGIA COLLEGE; CARROLLTON, GA 30117. (#102664-1).

CARTERSVILLE

BICENTENNIAL FOUNTAIN, CARTERSVILLE, GA. BICENTENNIAL FOUNTAIN WILL BE ERECTED IN PUBLIC PARK AREA. (LOCAL). DON QUILLIAN, EXEC SECRETARY; CARTERSVILLE BICENTENNIAL COMMITTEE; 251 S TENN, PO BOX 70; CARTERSVILLE, GA 30120. (#26958). **ARBA GRANTEE.**

JUNE 1, '76. ETOWAH VALLEY TOUR OF HISTORIC HOMES. TOUR. (LOCAL). DOT QUILLIAN, CHAIRPERSON; CARTERSVILLE WOMANS CLUB; BOX 70; CARTERSVILLE, GA 30120. (#102073-1).

AUG 12 - 15, '76. HERITAGE SPECIAL - TRAIN TOUR. TRAVELING RAIL EXHIBIT EMPHASIZING COLONIAL & REVOLUTIONARY GEORGIA HISTORY, CRAFTS & LIFESTYLE OF GEORGIA COLONISTS. EXHIBITS WILL BE DISPLAYED WITH COMBINATION OF SIGHT & SOUND ACTIVITY. (ST-WIDE). RON HENRY, COORDINATOR; GEORGIA AGRIRAMA DEVELOPMENT AUTHORITY/GEORGIA BICENTENNIAL; 8TH ST A I 75; TIFTON, GA 31794. (#7999-17).

CENTERVILLE

PARK PROJ - CENTERVILLE, GA. A VACANT LOT WAS LANDSCAPED AND TURNED INTO A MIN-PARK; A MARKER WAS ERECTED. (LOCAL). IRENE REYNOLDS, CO-CHAIRMAN; CENTERVILLE BICENTENNIAL COMMITTEE; 103 HAROLD DR; CENTERVILLE, GA 31028. (#28674).

CHATSWORTH

BEAUTIFICATION OF MURRAY COUNTY COURTHOUSE, GA. LANDSCAPE COURTHOUSE GROUNDS, ERECT FOUNTAIN AND REPLACE TREES TO REVITALIZE THE AREA FOR THE BICENTENNIAL. (LOCAL). ROBBIE COWART, CHAIRMAN; CHATSWORTH-MURRAY COUNTY BICENTENNIAL COMMITTEE; COURTHOUSE; CHATSWORTH, GA 30705. (#23778). **ARBA GRANTEE.**

MAY 22 - 23, '76. FRONTIER DAYS - ACTIVITIES, CRAFTS, FOODS OF WAYBACK WHEN. STREET DANCE, FRIDAY, MAY 21, SQUARE DANCING FOR ALL; TOBACCO SPITTING, ARM WRESTLING, SACK RACES, TUG O' WAR ETC. AT MURRAY COUNTY COURTHOUSE. (LOCAL). ROBBIE COWART; CHATSWORTH CITY COUNCIL, MURRAY COUNTY COMMISSION; MURRAY COUNTY COURTHOUSE; CHATSWORTH, GA 30705. (#103465-1).

MAY 29 - 30, '76. FRONTIER DAYS - EXHIBITS AND EVENTS. EXHIBIT, FESTIVAL. (LOCAL). ROBBIE COWART, CHAIRMAN; CHATSWORTH-MURRAY COUNTY BICENTENNIAL COMMITTEE; COUTHOUSE; CHATSWORTH, GA 30705. (#23778-1).

JULY 4, '76. COUNTY-WIDE CRUSADE. FESTIVAL. (LOCAL). ROBBIE COWART, CHAIRMAN; CHATSWORTH-MURRAY COUNTY BICENTENNIAL COMMITTEE/COUNTY BAPTIST ASSOC; COURTHOUSE; CHATSWORTH, GA 30705. (#23778-2).

CHICKAMAUGA

CHICKAMAUGA BICENTENNIAL COOKBOOK - GA. A COMMUNITY COOKBOOK OF OLD FAMILY RECIPES; GRAPHICALLY ILLUSTRATED LANDMARK SKETCHES INCLUDED. (LOCAL). MRS ROBERT M HOWARD, VICE PRESIDENT; CHICKAMAUGA HOMEMAKERS CLUB; BOX 274; CHICKAMAUGA, GA 30707. (#12651).

CHICKAMAUGA — CONTINUED

COMMUNITY PARK & AMPHITHEATRE IN CHICKAMAUGA, GA. A COMMUNITY PARK AND AN AMPHITHEATRE TO BE BUILT AT LOCAL SPRINGS AREA; AMPHITHEATRE TO BE USED FOR BAND CONCERTS, COMMUNITY CHURCH SERVICES AND CULTURAL PROGRAMS. (LOCAL). DR FRANK GREENE & MRS G MCMILLIAN, CO-DIRECTORS; CHICKAMAUGA BICENTENNIAL COMMITTEE; CHICKAMAUGA, GA 30707. (#12594).

RESTORATION OF BUSINESS DISTRICT, CHICKAMAUGA, GA. PRESERVATION AND RESTORATION OF LOCAL BUSINESS AND CIVIC AREA, THROUGH A PROJECT OF COMMUNITY DEVELOPMENT; LOCAL HISTORIC ARTIFACTS WILL BE PUT ON DISPLAY. (LOCAL). W H EDWARDS, PRESIDENT; LUMPKIN AREA BICENTENNIAL COMMITTEE; GORDON ST; CHICKAMAUGA, GA 30707. (#12590).

TRAIN DEPOT RESTORATION IN CHICKAMAUGA, GA. LOCAL TRAIN DEPOT IS BEING RESTORED & PRESERVED FOR USE AS A CULTURAL EXHIBIT FOR THE COMMUNITY. (LOCAL). MRS ROY POPE, JR, PRESIDENT; TSIKAMAGI GARDEN CLUB; GORDON ST; CHICKAMAUGA, GA 30707. (#12591).

TREE PLANTING - CHICKAMAUGA, GA. PROVIDE DOGWOOD AND PINE TREES AND INSTRUCTION TO ELEMENTARY STUDENTS TO PLANT BICENTENNIAL TREES. (LOCAL). MILDRED CROWDER, CHAIRPERSON; CHICKAMAUGA AREA PTA; RT 2; CHICKAMAUGA, GA 30707. (#17857).

SEPT 8, '75 - MAR 31, '76. ART WORKSHOPS & EXHIBITS. PHOTO TEXTILE POTTERY DRAWING PAINTING WORKSHOPS; EXHIBITS AS AVAILABLE OR ARRANGED. AT CITY DEPOT. (LOCAL). DAVID BOOZE; CHICKAMAUGA RECREATION DEPT; PO BOX 125; CHICKAMAUGA, GA 30707. (#12593-1).

SEPT 6, '76. GORDON LEE HOME TOURS. AN 1847 HOUSE TO BE RESTORED AND OPENED FOR TOURS IN THE SPRING '76. ALSO: BUILDING/FACILITY/MONUMENT. AT GORDON-LEE HOUSE. (LOCAL). DR FRANK GREEN; GORDON-LEE HOUSE RESTORATION; 217 COVE RD; CHICKAMAUGA, GA 30707. (#12592-1).

CLARKESVILLE

MAY 24, '75. 12TH ANNUAL MOUNTAIN LAUREL FESTIVAL W/ THEME SOUNDS OF AMER MUSIC. MOUNTAIN LAUREL FESTIVAL OF CLARKESVILLE, GEORGIA. 12TH ANNUAL MOUNTAIN LAUREL FESTIVAL IN MAY, 1975, WITH THEME OF 'SOUNDS OF AMERICAN MUSIC'. (ST-WIDE). JACK S REEVES; 12TH ANNUAL MOUNTAIN LAUREL FESTIVAL; CLARKESVILLE, GA 30523. (#6228-501).

COCHRAN

ADOPT-A-GRANDPARENT PROGRAM IN COCHRAN, GEORGIA. ADOPTION OF ELDERLY COUPLES AS GRANDPARENTS BY LOCAL COLLEGE CIVITAN CLUB, WITH FREQUENT VISITS PLANNED. (LOCAL). FRETWELL G CRIDER, PROJ DIRECTOR; MIDDLE GEORGIA COLLEGE BICENTENNIAL COMMITTEE; MIDDLE GEORGIA COLLEGE; COCHRAN, GA 31014. (#13474).

BICENTENNIAL PUBLICATION IN COCHRAN, GA. THE ENGLISH DEPT WILL PREPARE A PUBLICATION CONTAINING WRITINGS OF AUTHORS OF THE AMERICAN REVOLUTIONARY PERIOD. (LOCAL). FRETWELL G CRIDER, CHAIRMAN; MIDDLE GEORGIA COLLEGE BICENTENNIAL COMMITTEE; MIDDLE GEORGIA COLLEGE; COCHRAN, GA 31014. (#13465).

BICENTENNIAL TOUR PROJECT - COCHRAN, GEORGIA. STUDENT STUDY TOUR TO PHILADELPHIA & VALLEY FORGE. (LOCAL). FRETWELL G CRIDER, PROJ DIRECTOR; MIDDLE GEORGIA COLLEGE BICENTENNIAL COMMITTEE; MIDDLE GEORGIA COLLEGE; COCHRAN, GA 31014. (#13479).

CLEANUP WEEK IN COCHRAN, GA. CLEANUP WEEK WILL BE HELD IN PREPARATION FOR THE BICENTENNIAL. (LOCAL). HON CHAS KILLEBREW, MAYOR; CITY OF COCHRAN; 110 E DYKES ST; COCHRAN, GA 31014. (#13674).

COLONIAL HERB GARDEN - COCHRAN, GA. PLANTING OF COLONIAL HERB 'KITCHEN' GARDEN IN REAR OF EBENEZER HALL, WITH TYPICAL PLANTS OF THE PERIOD APPROPRIATELY MARKED. (LOCAL). FRETWELL G CRIDER, CHAIRMAN; MIDDLE GEORGIA COLLEGE BICENTENNIAL COMMITTEE; MIDDLE GEORGIA COLLEGE; COCHRAN, GA 31014. (#13470).

COUNTY HISTORY - PROJ OF COCHRAN, GA. PUBLICATION OF HISTORY OF THE COUNTY FROM ITS BEGINNING. (LOCAL). LOUIS ALDERMAN, CHAIRMAN; BICENTENNIAL COMMITTEE OF COCHRAN; COCHRAN, GA 31014. (#13667).

FACSIMILE OF GEORGIA GAZETTE, COCHRAN, GA. A NEWSPAPER DESIGNED IN THE FORMAT OF THE GEORGIA GAZETTE WILL BE RELEASED ON SIGNIFICANT DATES DURING THE BICENTENNIAL PERIOD. (LOCAL). FRETWELL G CRIDER, CHAIRMAN; MIDDLE GEORGIA COLLEGE BICENTENNIAL COMMITTEE; MIDDLE GEORGIA COLLEGE; COCHRAN, GA 31014. (#13460).

HERITAGE TRAIL - PROJ OF COCHRAN, GA. DEVELOPMENT OF HERITAGE TRAIL OF HISTORIC SITES IN AREA WITH MARKERS AND ACCOMPANYING BROCHURE. (LOCAL). LOUIS ALDERMAN, CHAIRMAN; BICENTENNIAL COMMITTEE OF COCHRAN; COCHRAN, GA 31014. (#13662). **ARBA GRANTEE.**

HISTORICAL FILMS IN COCHRAN, GA. THE HISTORY DEPT WILL SCHEDULE A SERIES OF HISTORICAL FILMS BASED ON THE AMERICAN REVOLUTION. (LOCAL). FRETWELL G CRIDER, CHAIRMAN; MIDDLE GEORGIA COLLEGE BICENTENNIAL COMMITTEE; MIDDLE GEORGIA COLLEGE; COCHRAN, GA 31014. (#13461).

INVENTORY OF OLD HOUSES - PROJ OF COCHRAN, GA. PUBLISHING INVENTORY OF STRUCTURES BUILT IN COMMUNITY BEFORE 1900. (LOCAL). LOUIS ALDERMAN, CHAIRMAN; BICENTENNIAL COMMITTEE OF COCHRAN; COCHRAN, GA 31014. (#13665).

MEETING IN SIGNERS' MEMORIAL - COCHRAN, GA. A MEETING WILL BE HELD IN THE NEWLY RENOVATED SIGNERS' MEMORIAL. (LOCAL). LOUIS ALDERMAN, CHAIRMAN; COCHRAN-BLECKLEY BICENTENNIAL COMMITTEE; COCHRAN, GA 31014. (#13673-1).

NATURE TRAIL PROJECT IN COCHRAN, GEORGIA. DEVELOPMENT OF NATURE TRAIL ON WOODED AREA OF CAMPUS WITH SIGNS GIVING BOTANNICAL NAMES OF TREES & PLANTS. (LOCAL). FRETWELL G CRIDER, PROJ DIRECTOR; MIDDLE GEORGIA COLLEGE BICENTENNIAL COMMITTEE; MIDDLE GEORGIA COLLEGE; COCHRAN, GA 31014. (#13473).

OLD DINING HALL 'SIGNERS' MEMORIAL' - COCHRAN, GA. CONVERSION OF OLD DINING HALL TO A CHAPEL AS A MEMORIAL TO SIGNERS OF DECLARATION OF INDEPENDENCE, WITH SIGNATURE OF EACH SIGNER MOUNTED ON A PEW AS A PERMANENT MEMORIAL TO HIM. (LOCAL). FRETWELL G CRIDER, PROJ DIRECTOR; MIDDLE GEORGIA COLLEGE BICENTENNIAL COMMITTEE; MIDDLE GEORGIA COLLEGE; COCHRAN, GA 31014. (#13471).

PATRIOTS INDEX - PROJ OF COCHRAN, GA. PUBLICATION OF INDEX OF ALL PATRIOTS WHO WERE ANCESTORS OF LOCAL CITIZENS THAT SERVED IN THE AMERICAN REVOLUTION. (LOCAL). LOUIS ALDERMAN, CHAIRMAN; BICENTENNIAL COMMITTEE OF COCHRAN; COCHRAN, GA 31014. (#13666).

PLAZA OF PATRIOTS - PROJ OF COCHRAN, GA. PLAZA OF FLAGPOLES OF 13 ORIGINAL STATES WITH MEMORIALS AT BASE LISTING NAMES OF ANCESTORS OF THE PEOPLE IN THE COMMUNITY WHO SERVED IN THE REVOLUTION. (LOCAL). LOUIS ALDERMAN, CHAIRMAN; BICENTENNIAL COMMITTEE OF COCHRAN; COCHRAN, GA 31014. (#13669).

RESTORATION OF OLD CITY HALL - PROJ OF COCHRAN, GA. RESTORATION OF THE ORIGINAL TOWN HALL. (LOCAL). LOUIS ALDERMAN, CHAIRMAN; BICENTENNIAL COMMITTEE OF COCHRAN; COCHRAN, GA 31014. (#13671).

RESTORATION OF PACE HOUSE IN COCHRAN, GEORGIA. RESTORATION OF 100 YR OLD PACE HOUSE, HOME OF FIRST PRESIDENT OF NEW EBENEZER COLLEGE, FORERUNNER OF MIDDLE GEORGIA COLLEGE. (LOCAL). FRETWELL G CRIDER, PROJ DIRECTOR; MIDDLE GEORGIA COLLEGE BICENTENNIAL COMMITTEE; MIDDLE GEORGIA COLLEGE; COCHRAN, GA 31014. (#13472). **ARBA GRANTEE.**

REVOLUTIONARY DRILL CORPS - COCHRAN, GA. THE ROTC PROGRAM WILL ARRANGE DRILL TEAMS IN COSTUME TO EXECUTE MILITARY DRILLS OF THE REVOLUTIONARY PERIOD. (LOCAL). FRETWELL G CRIDER, CHAIRMAN; MIDDLE GEORGIA COLLEGE BICENTENNIAL COMMITTEE; MIDDLE GEORGIA COLLEGE; COCHRAN, GA 31014. (#13469).

TREE PLANTING PROJECT IN COCHRAN, GEORGIA. PLANTING OF BAY TREE ON CAMPUS OF MIDDLE GEORGIA COLLEGE BY JOHN ALDEN CHAPTER OF COLONIAL DAMES OF AMERICA AS REENACTMENT OF COLONIAL TREE PLANTINGS. (LOCAL). FRETWELL G CRIDER, PROJ DIRECTOR; MIDDLE GEORGIA COLLEGE BICENTENNIAL COMMITTEE; MIDDLE GEORGIA COLLEGE; COCHRAN, GA 31014. (#13475).

JUNE 5, '75. TONDEE'S TAVERN ALUMNI BANQUET. REENACTMENT OF 200TH ANNIVERSARY OF ERECTION OF LIBERTY POLE BY LIBERTY BOYS IN FRONT OF TANDEE'S TAVERN; BANQUET WITH COLONIAL MENU TO FOLLOW. AT GEORGIA HALL, DESOTO ROOM. (LOCAL). FRETWELL G CRIDER; MIDDLE GEORGIA COLLEGE BICENTENNIAL COMMITTEE; MIDDLE GEORGIA COLLEGE; COCHRAN, GA 31014. (#13476-1).

SEPT 20 - 25, '75. ANNUAL FAIR. ANNUAL FAIR - PROJ OF COCHRAN, GA. BICENTENNIAL THEME FOR THE ANNUAL FAIR. (LOCAL). ROGER ALLEN, PRESIDENT; JAYCEES; COCHRAN, GA 31014. (#13664-501).

SEPT 30, '75 - CONTINUING . ESSAY CONTESTS IN AREA HIGH SCHOOLS. ESSAY CONTESTS WILL BE HELD IN AREA HIGH SCHOOLS ON TOPICS RELATED TO THE AMERICAN REVOLUTION & GEORGIA HISTORY; AWARDS WILL BE GIVEN. (LOCAL). FRETWELL G CRIDER; MIDDLE GEORGIA COLLEGE BICENTENNIAL COMMITTEE; MIDDLE GEORGIA COLLEGE; COCHRAN, GA 31014. (#13466-1).

FEB 12, '76. GEORGIA DAY. OFFICIAL OPENING OF BICENTENNIAL ON MIDDLE GEORGIA COLLEGE CAMPUS BANQUET FOR ALL STUDENT PRESIDENTS. AT MIDDLE GEORGIA COLLEGE CAMPUS. (LOCAL). FRETWELL G CRIDER; MIDDLE GEORGIA COLLEGE BICENTENNIAL COMMITTEE; MIDDLE GEORGIA COLLEGE; COCHRAN, GA 31014. (#13480-1).

MAR 1 - 6, '76. '1776' - MUSICAL PRODUCTION. THE MUSICAL WILL BE PRESENTED IN MARCH 1976 AS A COLLEGE AND COMMUNITY PRODUCTION; IT WILL GO FOR A WEEK TOUR IN CENTRAL GEORGIA. AT RUSSELL HALL AUDITORIUM. (LOCAL). FRETWELL G CRIDER; MIDDLE GEORGIA COLLEGE BICENTENNIAL COMMITTEE; MIDDLE GEORGIA COLLEGE; COCHRAN, GA 31014. (#13459-1).

MAR 17 - 22, '76. HISTORY STUDYCADES. VARIOUS STUDYCADES IN AMERICAN HISTORY ARE BEING PLANNED FOR TRIPS TO SIGNIFICANT REVOLUTIONARY SITES IN GEORGIA & IN OTHER STATES. (LOCAL). FRETWELL G CRIDER; MIDDLE GEORGIA COLLEGE BICENTENNIAL COMMITTEE; MIDDLE GEORGIA COLLEGE; COCHRAN, GA 31014. (#13467-1).

MAY 1 - 31, '76. MUSEUM EXHIBIT. ARTIFACTS OF THE REVOLUTIONARY PERIOD WILL BE COLLECTED & EXHIBITED IN THE LIBRARY MUSEUM ROOM. AT ROBERTS MEMORIAL LIBRARY MUSEUM. (LOCAL). FRETWELL G CRIDER; MIDDLE GEORGIA COLLEGE BICENTENNIAL COMMITTEE; MIDDLE GEORGIA COLLEGE; COCHRAN, GA 31014. (#13464-1).

MAY 2 - 8, '76. BICENTENNIAL CELEBRATION. THE BICENTENNIAL WILL BE HIGHLIGHTED IN 1976 WITH A WEEK OF CELEBRATION TO BE OBSERVED BY THE COLLEGE & COMMUNITY. (LOCAL). FRETWELL G CRIDER; MIDDLE GEORGIA COLLEGE BICENTENNIAL COMMITTEE; MIDDLE GEORGIA COLLEGE; COCHRAN, GA 31014. (#13468-1).

MAY 3 - 7, '76. ART EXHIBITS. ART DEPT WILL ARRANGE ART EXHIBITS ON ART & ARTISTS OF THE REVOLUTIONARY PERIOD. AT RUSSELL HALL, SARAH ST. (LOCAL). FRETWELL G CRIDER; MIDDLE GEORGIA COLLEGE BICENTENNIAL COMMITTEE; MIDDLE GEORGIA COLLEGE; COCHRAN, GA 31014. (#13462-1).

MAY 6, '76. OLD-FASHIONED MAY DAY. HONORS DAY WITH PATRIOTIC SPEECHES, DANCES & MUSIC BY MIDDLE GEORGIA COLLEGE VOCAL ENSEMBLE IN BICENTENNIAL COSTUME. (LOCAL). FRETWELL G CRIDER; MIDDLE GEORGIA COLLEGE BICENTENNIAL COMMITTEE; MIDDLE GEORGIA COLLEGE; COCHRAN, GA 31014. (#13478-1).

MAY 18, '76. DANCE RECITAL. THE PHYSICAL EDUCATION DEPT IS PLANNING RECITALS BY DANCE ENSEMBLE DEPICTING DANCE OF THE REVOLUTIONARY PERIOD. AT RUSSELL HALL AUDITORIUM. (LOCAL). FRETWELL G CRIDER; MIDDLE GEORGIA COLLEGE BICENTENNIAL COMMITTEE; MIDDLE GEORGIA COLLEGE; COCHRAN, GA 31014. (#13463-1).

COLBERT

CEMETERY PRESERVATION, COLBERT, GA. DRIVEWAYS CLEANED, GRAVEL SPREAD, SHRUBBERY PLANTED, GENERAL MAINTENANCE. (LOCAL). MILDRED C PORTERFIELD, BICENTENNIAL CHAIRMAN; COLBERT IMPROVEMENT CLUB AND CITY OF COLBERT; COLBERT, GA 30628. (#19747).

HISTORY OF COLBERT, GA. THE HISTORY OF THE COLBERT AREA IS BEING RESEARCHED AND MADE AVAILABLE TO CITIZENS TO FACILITATE THEIR UNDERSTANDING OF THE PAST AND THE BICENTENNIAL ANNIVERSARY. (LOCAL). MILDRED C PORTERFIELD, BICENTENNIAL CHAIRMAN; COLBERT IMPROVEMENT CLUB; 5TH ST; COLBERT, GA 30628. (#19748).

MAR 7, '75. JOINT CHURCH SERVICE TO VIEW FILM 'GOD BLESS AMERICA'. EXHIBIT, CEREMONY AT COLBERT BAPTIST CHURCH. (LOCAL). MRS T W PORTERFIELD; COLBERT IMPROVEMENT CLUB, COLBERT LIONS CLUB & FIRE DEPARTMENT; COLBERT, GA 30628. (#200012-30).

JAN 1 - DEC 31, '76. MUSEUM EXHIBIT. COLLECTION OF MEMORABILIA DATES BACK TO EARLY DAYS; ITEMS DISPLAYED IN VINTAGE CASES IN RESTORED DEPOT. INFORMATION & MATERIAL SENT BY FORMER & PRESENT RESIDENTS. (LOCAL). MRS JOHN ROUSH, CHAIRMAN; COLBERT IMPROVEMENT CLUB; 200 ROBIN RD; ATHENS, GA 30601. (#104358-3).

FEB 8, '76. JOINT CHURCH SERVICE & BICENTENNIAL FLAG RAISING. GUEST SPEAKER: JUDGE JOHN W WILLFORD. PATRIOTIC MUSIC & PRESENTATION OF BICENTENNIAL FLAG. AT COLBERT BAPTIST CHURCH. (LOCAL). HON JOHN WAGGONER, MAYOR; COLBERT IMPROVEMENT CLUB, COLBERT LIONS CLUB & COLBERT FIRE DEPT; COLBERT, GA 30628. (#200012-28).

FEB 18, '76. TVA CARAVAN & CHICKEN BARBECUE - OFFICIAL GA COVERED WAGON DISPLAY. FESTIVAL, EXHIBIT AT 4TH ST. (LOCAL). MRS T W PORTERFIELD; COLBERT LIONS CLUB, COLBERT FIRE DEPT & COLBERT IMPROVEMENT CLUB; COLBERT, GA 30628. (#200012-29).

JULY 3, '76. RESTORED COURT HOUSE. RESTORED COURT HOUSE WILL BE USED AS A LIBRARY; RESTORED UNDER THE DIRECTION OF NE GA AREA PLANNING COMMISSION; FINANCED BY THE COLBERT LIONS CLUB & THE COLBERT IMPROVEMENT CLUB; PROJECT OF THE COLBERT IMPROVEMENT CLUB. (LOCAL). JOHN WAGGONER, MAYOR; CITY OF COLBERT; COLBERT, GA 31740. (#104528-1).

JULY 3 - 4, '76. JULY 4TH CELEBRATION. PARADE, BEAUTY PAGEANT, PATRIOTIC MUSIC, SPEECHES BY NATIONAL FIGURES, BICENTENNIAL DISPLAYS, BARBECUE, GAMES & BANDS. (LOCAL). HON JOHN WAGONER, MAYOR; CITY OF COLBERT; COLBERT, GA 30628. (#104358-2).

NOV 9 - 10, '76. UNITED STATES ARMED FORCES BICENTENNIAL CARAVAN. CARAVAN IS COMPOSED OF EXHIBIT VANS FOR EACH MILITARY SERVICE. PROJECT THEME IS 'HISTORY OF THE ARMED FORCES & THEIR CONTRIBUTIONS TO THE NATION'. (LOCAL). MAYOR JOHN A WAGGONER; UNITED STATES ARMED FORCES BICENTENNIAL CARAVAN; PO BOX 215; COLBERT, GA 30628. (#1775-774).

COLLEGE PARK

ASSOCIATION OF CHILDHOOD EDUCATION INTERNATIONAL CONFERENCE. CONFERENCE. (LOCAL). JOHN NUNNALLY, CHMN; ASSOCIATION OF CHILDHOOD EDUCATION INTERNATIONAL CONFERENCE; 3971 PINE VLY DR; COLLEGE PARK, GA 30337. (#200012-54).

DEC 5 - 7, '75. UNITED STATES ARMED FORCES BICENTENNIAL CARAVAN. THE CARAVAN IS COMPOSED OF EXHIBIT VANS FOR EACH BRANCH OF THE MILITARY SERVICE. THE THEME OF THE EXHIBITION IS 'HISTORY OF THE ARMED FORCES AND THEIR CONTRIBUTION TO THE NATION'. (LOCAL). MRS JUDI ROGERS, CHMN; COLLEGE PARK BICENTENNIAL COMMITTEE; 4734 WINTHROP DR; COLLEGE PARK, GA 30337. (#1775-206).

COLQUITT

AVENUE OF FLAGS, COLQUITT, GA. NATIONAL AND HISTORICAL FLAGS WILL BE ON DISPLAY DOWNTOWN. (LOCAL). MRS

OLQUITT — CONTINUED

AVON COOK, CHAIRPERSON; MILLER COUNTY BICENTENNIAL OMMITTEE; MAIN ST; COLQUITT, GA 31737. (#25543).

EAUTIFY COLQUITT, GA. LOCAL GARDEN CLUB MEMBERS ARE PONSORING A COMMUNITY BEAUTIFICATION PROJECT. .OCAL). MRS LAVON COOK, CHAIRPERSON; MILLER COUNTY ICENTENNIAL COMMITTEE; MAIN ST; COLQUITT, GA 31737. #25544).

OMMUNITY CLEANUP, COLQUITT, GA. PAINT TRASH CANS AND IRE HYDRANTS IN PATRIOTIC FIGURES; GENERAL MAIN- ENANCE OF ENTIRE COMMUNITY. (LOCAL). MRS LAVON COOK, HAIRPERSON; MILLER COUNTY BICENTENNIAL COMMITTEE; AIN ST; COLQUITT, GA 31737. (#25542).

ISTORY OF MILLER COUNTY, GEORGIA. HISTORICAL ACCOUNT OF OUNTY WILL BE WRITTEN. (LOCAL). MRS TOM J DAVIS, PROJ OORDINATOR; MILLER COUNTY BICENTENNIAL COMMITTEE; ORNER FIRST & PINE STS; COLQUITT, GA 31737. (#25541).

ULY 3 - 4, '76. BICENTENNIAL CELEBRATION. THE CELEBRATION VILL FEATURE CONTESTS, BAR-B-CUE, BAZAAR, AMERICANA XHIBIT, WORSHIP SERVICE AND LOCAL ENTERTAINMENT. LOCAL). MRS LAVON COOK, CHAIRMAN; MILLER COUNTY ICENTENNIAL COMMITTEE; MAIN ST; COLQUITT, GA 31737. #108187-1).

ULY 23 - 24, '76. 'SPIRIT OF '76' ALL AMERICAN FIELD DAY. FESTIVAL, COMPETITION AT JOSULI FARMS INC, 15 MILES NORTHWEST OF COLQUITT, GEORGIA. (LOCAL). GARY B BISHOP, DIRECTOR; AMERICAN JUNIOR HEREFORD ASSOCIATION; 715 HEREFORD DR; KANSAS CITY, MO 64105. (#104989-1).

COLUMBUS

AMERICAN CHORAL MUSIC FESTIVAL IN COLUMBUS, GA. CHORAL MUSIC BY AMERICAN COMPOSERS PERFORMED BY GUEST ARTISTS, AREA COLLEGE CHOIRS AND MUSIC DEPARTMENTS FROM THOSE COLLEGES. THIS FESTIVAL WILL BE HELD AN- NUALLY. (REGN'L). DR KATHERINE MAHAN, CHAIRPERSON; COLUMBUS COLLEGE BICENTENNIAL COMMITTEE; ALGONQUIN DR; COLUMBUS, GA 31907. (#6616).

AMERICA'S BIRTHDAY, 200 YEARS OF FREEDOM, GA. MUSICAL PRESENTATION OF THE AMERICAN SPIRIT, HISTORICAL HIGHLIGHTS, OUR HERITAGE & THE GROWTH OF AMERICA, ALL PRESENTED IN MUSICAL NARRATION FORM. (LOCAL). D H SHARPE, CHAIRMAN; CHATTAHOOCHEE CHATTERS CITIZEN BAND, INC; 701 4TH ST; COLUMBUS, GA 31904. (#27233). **ARBA GRANTEE.**

ARCHIVES & GENEALOGICAL LIBRARY OF COLUMBUS, GA. AN ARCHIVES & GENEALOGICAL SECTION WILL BE ADDED TO THE BRADLEY LIBRARY. IT WILL BE HOUSED IN A NEW WING CON- STRUCTED IN 1974. (LOCAL). MRS JAMES J W BIGGERS, JR, CHAIRMAN; COLUMBUS AREA BICENTENNIAL COMMITTEE; PO BOX 5312; COLUMBUS, GA 31906. (#4990).

CHATTOHOOCHEE RIVER-SHOWBOAT PROJECT OF GEORGIA. A VIC- TORIAN STEAM-POWERED RIVERBOAT AND SHOWBOAT WILL GIVE TOURS ON THE CHATTAHOOCHEE RIVER AS A PERMANENT TOURIST ATTRACTION. IT WILL STOP AT PLACES OF HISTORIC SIGNIFICANCE. (ST-WIDE). MRS JAMES J W BIGGERS, JR, CHAIRMAN; COLUMBUS AREA BICENTENNIAL COMMITTEE; PO BOX 5312; COLUMBUS, GA 31906. (#4992).

COLUMBUS, GEORGIA, PROMENADE PROJECT. BUILD OUTDOOR GENERAL HISTORY MUSEUM, PARK, CHATTAHOOCHEE RIVER PROMANADE. SITE ASSOCIATED WITH GEN. OGLETHORPE, CREEK NATION, FOUNDING OF COLUMBUS, CIVIL WAR BATTLE AND EARLY MANUFACTURING OF IRONWARE. (LOCAL). MRS JAMES J W BIGGERS JR, CHAIRWOMAN; COLUMBUS AREA BICENTENNIAL COMMITTEE; 1344 13TH AVE, PO BOX 1200; COLUMBUS, GA 31902. (#4700).

COLUMBUS, GEORGIA OF THE FUTURE, VISUAL DISPLAY. A DISPLAY OF THE PROJECTED CITY OF COLUMBUS IN 2000 A D TO BE SHOWN IN THE NEW LIBRARY BUILDING. PROJECT INCLUDES A MODEL CITY, PLANS & BUILDINGS DONE TO SCALE. (ST-WIDE). DR KATHERINE MAHAN, CHAIRPERSON; COLUMBUS COLLEGE BICENTENNIAL COMMITTEE; ALGONQUIN DR; COLUMBUS, GA 31907. (#6619).

DOWNTOWN REVITALIZATION IN COLUMBUS, GEORGIA. A MAJOR PORTION OF THE COLUMBUS CENTRAL BUSINESS DISTRICT WILL BE REVITALIZED TO COMPLETE THE RESTORATION NOW BEING ACCOMPLISHED BY THE COLUMBUS FOUNDATION INC. (LOCAL). MRS JAMES J W BIGGERS, JR, CHAIRMAN; COLUM- BUS AREA BICENTENNIAL COMMITTEE; PO BOX 5312; COLUM- BUS, GA 31906. (#4987).

FLAG PROJECT IN COLUMBUS, GEORGIA. COLUMBUS JAYCEES & DAR WILL DISTRIBUTE & ENCOURAGE THE FLYING OF THE AMERICAN FLAG AT HOMES & BUSINESSES THROUGHOUT THE REGION. (LOCAL). MRS JAMES J W BIGGERS, JR, CHAIRMAN; COLUMBUS AREA BICENTENNIAL COMMITTEE; PO BOX 5312; COLUMBUS, GA 31906. (#4989).

'LET'S NOT FORGET OUR HERITAGE' - COLUMBUS, GA. A PUBLICA- TION ON OUTSTANDING HISTORIC BUILDINGS AND SITES IN COLUMBUS; THE OBJECTIVE IS TO PROMOTE AWARENESS & AP- PRECIATION OF ARCHITECTURAL & HISTORIC HERITAGE AND STIMULATE PRESERVATION ACTIVITIES. (LOCAL). MRS JANICE BIGGERS, CHAIRMAN; COLUMBUS AREA BICENTENNIAL COM- MITTEE; 1334 13TH AVE; COLUMBUS, GA 31902. (#12261). **ARBA GRANTEE.**

LOCAL ARCHIVES PROJ AT NEW LIBRARY IN COLUMBUS, GA. A SPE- CIAL COLLECTION OF DOCUMENTS CONCERNING LOCAL FAMI- LIES IN COLUMBUS IS BEING ASSEMBLED FOR RESEARCH & DIS- PLAY IN AN ARCHIVES OF THE NEW LIBRARY. (LOCAL). DR KATHERINE H MAHAN, CHAIRPERSON; COLUMBUS COLLEGE BICENTENNIAL COMMITTEE; ALGONQUIN DR; COLUMBUS, GA 31907. (#6615).

SPRINGER OPERA HOUSE RESTORATION PROJ OF GEORGIA. THE SPRINGER OPERA HOUSE, AN OUTSTANDING EXAMPLE OF 19TH CENTURY ARCHITECTURE WILL BE RESTORED TO BROADEN THEATRICAL & CULTURAL PROGRAMS IN THE CITY. (LOCAL). MRS JAMES J W BIGGERS, JR, CHAIRMAN; COLUMBUS AREA BICENTENNIAL COMMITTEE; PO BOX 5312; COLUMBUS, GA 31906. (#4988).

MAY 25, '75. NEW COLLECTION OF LOCAL ARCHIVES FORMAL OPEN- ING AT LIBRARY. EXHIBIT, OPENING. (LOCAL). DR KATHERINE H MAHAN; COLUMBUS COLLEGE BICENTENNIAL COMMITTEE; AL- GONQUIN DR; COLUMBUS, GA 31907. (#6615-501).

APR 7 - 11, '76. HERITAGE SPECIAL - TRAIN TOUR. TRAVELING RAIL EXHIBIT EMPHASIZING COLONIAL & REVOLUTIONARY GEORGIA HISTORY, CRAFTS & LIFESTYLE OF GEORGIA COLONISTS. EXHIBITS WILL BE DISPLAYED WITH COMBINATION OF SIGHT & SOUND ACTIVITY. (ST-WIDE). RON HENRY, COOR- DINATOR; GEORGIA AGRIRAMA DEVELOPMENT AUTHORITY/ GEORGIA BICENTENNIAL; 8TH ST A I 75; TIFTON, GA 31794. (#7999-25).

MAY 15 - 17, '76. AMERICAN FREEDOM TRAIN DISPLAY DAYS AT COLUMBUS. THE AMERICAN FREEDOM TRAIN INCLUDES 10 EX- HIBIT CARS & 2 SHOW CASE CARS DEPICTING DIFFERENT PHASES OF THE AMERICAN EXPERIENCE. ITS ARRIVAL WILL SERVE AS A CATALYST FOR LOCAL BICENTENNIAL CELEBRA- TIONS BY PEOPLE THROUGHOUT THIS NATION. (ST-WIDE). SY FREEDMAN, DIR OF P/R; THE AMERICAN FREEDOM TRAIN FOUN- DATION; 5205 LEESBURG PIKE, SUITE 800; BAILEY'S XRDS, VA 22041. (#1776-93).

JUNE 1 - 30, '76. 'NO SONG NO SUPPER' - MUSICAL FARCE. ORIGINALLY PLAYED IN THE CITY IN 1829. (LOCAL). MRS JAMES J W BIGGERS JR; COLUMBUS AREA BICENTENNIAL COMMITTEE; 1344 13TH AVE, PO BOX 1200; COLUMBUS, GA 31902. (#4700- 501).

JUNE 14 - 25, '76. CARL HAVERLIN/BROADCAST MUSIC, INC, ARCHIVES BICENTENNIAL EXHIBIT. OFFERS A VERSATILE PICTURE OF HISTORY, REGIONAL LIFE & MUSIC FOR OVER 200 YEARS. CONTAINS PRESIDENTIAL LETTERS, LETTERS OF FAMOUS AMER- ICANS, OLD BOOKS, MANUSCRIPTS, HISTORY OF 'THE STAR SPANGLED BANNER' & COMPOSER AUTOGRAPHS, PLUS SHEET MUSIC OF THE PAST. AT COLUMBUS COLLEGE LIBRARY. (ST- WIDE). JOEL H HOLMES, COORD; COLUMBUS COLLEGE; COLUM- BUS COLLEGE; COLUMBUS, GA 31907. (#20784-14).

JUNE 25 - SEPT ??, '76. AMERICA'S BIRTHDAY-200 YEARS OF FREEDOM: MUSICAL PRESENTATION. LIVE PERFORMANCE. (LOCAL). D H THARPE, CHAIRMAN; CHATAHOOCHEE CHATTERS CITIZEN BAND, INC; 701 4TH ST; COLUMBUS, GA 31904. (#27233-1).

SEPT 25 - 29, '76. HERITAGE SPECIAL - TRAIN TOUR. TRAVELING RAIL EXHIBIT EMPHASIZING COLONIAL AND REVOLUTIONARY GEORGIA HISTORY, CRAFTS & LIFESTYLE OF GEORGIA COLONISTS. EXHIBITS WILL BE DISPLAYED WITH COMBINATION OF SIGHT & SOUND ACTIVITY. AT DEPOT. (LOCAL). RON HENRY, DIRECTOR; GEORGIA BICENTENNIAL COMMISSION; 1776 PEACHTREE NW, ROOM 520 S; ATLANTA, GA 30309. (#7999- 31).

OCT 11 - 16, '76. CHATTAHOOCHEE VALLEY FAIR. ANNUAL AGRICULTURAL FAIR WITH EXHIBITS AND ENTRIES FROM 23 GA COUNTIES AND 9 ALABAMA COUNTIES; GRANDSTAND SHOWS AT 7 & 8:30 PM NIGHTLY WITH DIFFERENT STARS EACH NIGHT; FIREWORKS, CARNIVAL, EXHIBITS, LIVESTOCK JUDGING, DOG OBEDIENCE AND SQUARE DANCE CONTESTS. AT FAIRGROUNDS, 4TH ST AND 4TH AVE. (REGN'L). ARTHUR G SPRINGER JR, MGR; CHATTAHOOCHEE VALLEY EXPOSITION, INC; PO BOX 1358; COLUMBUS, GA 31902. (#106095-10).

CONCORD

OCT 18 - 19, '75. CONCORD COUNTRY JUBILEE. VARIETY OF COUNTRY FOODS COOKED AT FESTIVAL; SQUARE DANCE SATURDAY NIGHT; 100 BOOTHS OF ARTS & CRAFTS; LOCAL AR- TIFACT MUSEUM & LOCAL PAINTING GALLERY. (LOCAL). C H DAYHUFF, DIRECTOR; CITY OF CONCORD; PO BO X 6; CON- CORD, GA 30206. (#101827-1).

CONYERS

AVENUE OF FLAGS - CONYERS, GEORGIA. THE DISPLAY OF THE NA- TIONAL AND STATE FLAGS ALONG CITY STREETS ON AP- PROPRIATE DAYS. FLAGS WILL REPRESENT ORIGINAL AND VARIOUS STAGES OF DEVELOPMENT OF THE NATIONAL FLAG. (LOCAL). A SILVERMAN, COMMITTEE CHAIRMAN; CHAMBER OF COMMERCE, VFW; 2469 LAKE CAPRI DR; LITHONIA, GA 30058. (#8951).

BICENTENNIAL BEAUTIFICATION OF CONYERS, GEORGIA. THIS PRO- JECT INVOLVES THE DRESSING UP OF AREAS AROUND GAR- BAGE CONTAINERS, LITTER PICK-UPS, AND THE PLANTING AND CARE OF FLOWERS AND SHRUBS ALONG STREETS. (LOCAL). MARGARET TOWSE, SUB-COMMITTEE CHAIRPERSON; GARDEN CLUB AND NEIGHBORHOOD ASSOC; 120K MAPLE ST; CONYERS, GA 30207. (#8949).

CAMPAIGN FOR VOTER REGISTRATION IN CONYERS, GA. INFORMA- TION ON VOTER REGISTRATION WILL BE DISSEMINATED BY THE KIWANIS CLUB WITH THE AID OF YOUTH IN THE COMMUNITY. (LOCAL). JAMES P CULPEPPER JR, COMMITTEE CHAIRMAN; KIWANIS CLUB; 1354 NORTHSIDE DR; CONYERS, GA 30207. (#8956).

HISTORICAL MARKERS FOR CONYERS, GEORGIA. PLACING OF HISTORICAL MARKERS AT HIGHTOWER TRAIL, A PRE REVOLU- TIONARY INDIAN TRAIL AND AT DIAL'S MILL. (LOCAL). GLEN L HODGES, COMMITTEE CHAIRMAN; HISTORICAL SOCIETY; 1550 NORTHSIDE DR; CONYERS, GA 30207. (#8948).

HISTORICAL PUBLICATIONS OF CONYERS, GEORGIA. ESTABLISHING A SYSTEM OF COLLECTING INFORMATION CONCERNING THE HISTORIES OF CHURCHES, SCHOOLS, AND THE COUNTY WITH PUBLICATION AS THE OUTCOME. (LOCAL). MRS A R BARKS, DALE SUB-COMMITTEE CHAIRPERSON; HISTORICAL SOCIETY, CIVIC LEAGUE; N MAIN ST; CONYERS, GA 30207. (#8950).

MARKING OF BICYCLE ROUTE IN CONYERS, GEORGIA. THIS PROJECT INVOLVES THE MARKING OF A SAFE BIKE ROUTE THROUGH THE OLD AND SCENIC PARTS OF THE COMMUNITY. (LOCAL). JAMES P CULPEPPER JR, PROJ COORDINATOR; GIRL SCOUTS, CUB SCOUTS & BOY SCOUTS; 1354 NORTHSIDE DR; CONYERS, GA 30207. (#8954).

MEMORIAL FOREST OF CONYERS, GEORGIA. THE PLANTING OF THIRTEEN TREES IN THE COUNTY PARK ALONG WITH THE CON- STRUCTION OF A MEMORIAL CONTAINING A TIME CAPSULE CONTAINING ITEMS SUGGESTED BY COMMUNITY MEMBERS. (LOCAL). DAVID W MESSER, CHAIRMAN; ROCKDALE COUNTY BICENT COMMITTEE; 1500 C PINE LOG RD; CONYERS, GA 30207. (#8957).

OLD ROCKDALE COUNTY JAIL RESTORATION - CONYERS, GA. RESTORATION OF OLD JAILHOUSE TO PROVIDE SPACE FOR MUSEUM OF LOCAL HISTORY AS WELL AS MEETING FACILITIES FOR CIVIC ORGANIZATIONS & OFFICES FOR HISTORICAL SOCIETY. (LOCAL). DAVID W MESSNER, CHAIRMAN; ROCKDALE COUNTY BICENTENNIAL COMMITTEE; 1500 C PINE LOG RD; CONYERS, GA 30207. (#8958). **ARBA GRANTEE.**

'SUGGESTIONS '76', BICENT NEWS IN CONYERS, GEORGIA. THE WEEKLY PUBLICATION OF A BICENTENNIAL COLUMN WITH FORMS WHICH MAKE IT POSSIBLE FOR READERS TO CON- TINUALLY SUGGEST PROGRAMS AND ACTIVITIES. (LOCAL). DAVID W MESSER, CHAIRMAN; ROCKDALE COUNTY BICENT COMMITTEE; 1500 S PINE LOG RD; CONYERS, GA 30207. (#8952).

SUNDAYS IN THE PARK PROJ OF CONYERS, GEORGIA. BAND CON- CERTS, PICNICS AND DISPLAYS BY LOCAL PERFORMERS WILL BE HELD MONTHLY ON SUNDAYS IN THE PARKS OF CONYERS. (LOCAL). A SILVERMAN, COMMITTEE CHAIRMAN; CHAMBER OF COMMERCE; 2469 LAKE CAPRI DR; LITHONIA, GA 30058. (#8953).

MAY 26 - 29, '76. HERITAGE SPECIAL - TRAIN TOUR. TRAVELING RAIL EXHIBIT EMPHASIZING COLONIAL & REVOLUTIONARY GEORGIA HISTORY, CRAFTS & LIFESTYLE OF GEORGIA COLONISTS. EXHIBITS WILL BE DISPLAYED WITH COMBINATION OF SIGHT & SOUND ACTIVITY. (LOCAL). RON HENRY, COOR- DINATOR; GEORGIA AGRIRAMA DEVELOPMENT AUTHORITY/ GEORGIA BICENTENNIAL; 8TH ST A I 75; TIFTON, GA 31794. (#7999-26).

CORDELE

MAY 5, '76. PARADE. PARADE AT 7TH ST HWY 41. (LOCAL). M F CARTER, JR; CORDELE-CRISP COUNTY BICENTENNIAL CELEBRA- TION; BOX 1776; CORDELE, GA 31015. (#103116-1).

JULY 2 - 4, '76. BICENTENNIAL PAGEANT. LIVE PERFORMANCE. (LOCAL). M F CARTER, JR, CHAIRMAN; CORDELE-CRISP COUNTY BICENTENNIAL CELEBRATION; BOX 1776; CORDELE, GA 31015. (#103116-2).

COVINGTON

COVINGTON NEWS BICENTENNIAL PARTICIPATION - NBMRP. PRE- SIDENT-EDITOR IS CHAIRMAN OF NEWTON COUNTY BICENTEN- NIAL COMMITTEE & IS ALSO PUBLISHING 2 SERIES-'HISTORY CORNER' ABOUT THE REVOLUTIONARY PERIOD & 'BUILDERS OF A NATION' ON GREAT MEN IN USA HISTORY. (LOCAL). LEO S MALLARD, PRESIDENT-EDITOR; THE COVINGTON NEWS, INC; BOX 431, 4132 HIGHWAY 278; COVINGTON, GA 30209. (#22106).

FURNISHINGS FOR THE BRICK STORE - COVINGTON, GA. PLANS FOR MUSEUM WITH ARTIFACTS AND FURNISHINGS FOR HISTORIC BRICK STORE, NEWTON COUNTY'S FIRST COURTHOUSE WHERE THE FIRST SESSION OF THE SUPERIOR COURT CONVENED ON APRIL 15, 1822. (LOCAL). S M HAY, PRESIDENT; NEWTON COUNTY HISTORICAL SOCIETY, INC; PO BOX 552; COVINGTON, GA 30209. (#28046). **ARBA GRANTEE.**

CUTHBERT

OLD FREIGHT DEPOT - CUTHBERT, GA. PROJECT INCLUDES COMPLETE RENOVATION OF THE CUTHBERT FREIGHT DEPOT, BUILT IN 1860. RENOVATION WOULD PRESERVE HISTORICAL SIGNIFICANCE OF DEPOT & SERVE AS A REMINDER OF THE COMMUNITY'S HERITAGE. (LOCAL). MRS T N STAPLETON, PRE- SIDENT; RANDOLPH HISTORICAL SOCIETY; BOX 456; CUTHBERT, GA 31740. (#19367).

PAINTING OF CITY FIREPLUGS, CUTHBERT, GA. CITY FIREPLUGS WILL BE PAINTED RED, WHITE & BLUE & A ''76' PLAQUE WILL BE HUNG ON EACH FIREPLUG. (LOCAL). MRS R T HARRIS, PRE- SIDENT; CUTHBERT GARDEN CLUB; CUTHBERT, GA 31740. (#19370).

RADIO BROADCAST OF HISTORICAL FACT, CUTHBERT, GA. HISTORI- CAL FACTS WILL BE RESEARCHED & PROVIDED FOR BROAD- CAST BY LOCAL RADIO STATIONS. (LOCAL). MISS SARAH STA- PLES, PROJ DIRECTOR; THETA LAMDA CHAPTER, KAPPA HONOR SOCIETY - ANDREW COLLEGE; COLLEGE ST; CUTHBERT, GA 31740. (#19369).

CUTHBERT — CONTINUED

RESTORATION OF CONFEDERATE MONUMENT; CUTHBERT, GA. THE CONFEDERATE MONUMENT WHICH CONSISTS OF A STATUE OF A CONFEDERATE SOLDIER WILL BE CLEANED & RESTORED. (LOCAL). MRS J C BURGIN, CHAIRMAN; RANDOLPH COUNTY HISTORICAL SOCIETY; CUTHBERT, GA 31740. (#19368).

RESTORATION & BEAUTIFICATION OF CEMETERY, GA. GREENWOOD CEMETERY WILL BE CLEANED, SHRUBBERY WILL BE PRUNED, HISTORIC MONUMENTS, MARKERS & IRON FENCES & GATES WILL BE RESTORED. (LOCAL). MRS NORMAN LUMPKIN, PRESIDENT; PILOT CLUB OF CUTHBERT; CUTHBERT, GA 31740. (#19371).

MAR 12, '76. FASHION SHOW. FASHION SHOW OF HISTORICAL FASHIONS AND SPRING FASHIONS. AT ANDREW COLLEGE. (LOCAL). MRS T N STAPLETON, PRES; RANDOLPH HISTORICAL SOCIETY & RANDOLPH CHAMBER OF COMMERCE; BOX 456; CUTHBERT, GA 31740. (#104266-3).

APR 10 - 11, '76. FLEA MARKET AND INDIAN ARTIFACTS DISPLAY. EXHIBIT, FESTIVAL AT OLD FREIGHT DEPOT, RANDOLPH COUNTY COURTHOUSE GROUNDS. (LOCAL). MRS T N STAPLETON, PRES; RANDOLPH HISTORICAL SOCIETY; BOX 456; CUTHBERT, GA 31740. (#19367-1).

APR 10 - 11, '76. HISTORIC HOMES TOUR & FESTIVAL. APRIL 10 & 11: FLEA MARKET; APRIL 10: ARTS & CRAFTS FESTIVAL, DISPLAY OF LOCAL ART & HANDCRAFT; APRIL 11 & 12: ANTIQUE AUTO SHOW, PARADE 04/09. FLOATS, BANDS, HORSES & BUGGIES; HOME COMING EVENTS AT ANDREW COLLEGE; PRIVATE HOMES DISPLAYED ADM. $5. AT ANDREW COLL. OLD FREIGHT DEPOT RANDOLPH COUNTY COCOURTHOUSE. (LOCAL). MRS T N STAPLETON, PRES; RANDOLPH HISTORICAL SOCIETY & RANDOLPH CHAMBER OF COMMERCE; BOX 456; CUTHBERT, GA 31740. (#104266-2).

DAHLONEGA

BASEBALL FIELD PROJECT IN DAHLONEGA, GEORGIA. LIGHTING WILL BE PROVIDED FOR A BASEBALL FIELD BUILT FOR YOUTH BY THE DAHLONEGA AMERICAN LEGION POST. (LOCAL). MRS NEWTON OAKES, CHAIRMAN; DAHLONEGA-LUMPKIN COUNTY BICENT COMMITTEE; BOX 141; DAHLONEGA, GA 30533. (#6749).

'CHEROKEE GOLD', DRAMA AT N GEORGIA COLLEGE. AN ORIGINAL HISTORICAL DRAMA BY GENE WIGGINS CONCERNING THE NATION'S FIRST MAJOR GOLD RUSH. (LOCAL). RAY C RENSI, ASSOC PROFESSOR; NORTH GEORGIA COLLEGE; DAHLONEGA, GA 30533. (#6661).

CLEANUP CAMPAIGNS IN DAHLONEGA, GEORGIA. ELEMENTARY & HIGH SCHOOL STUDENTS, 'FRIENDS OF THE EARTH' ECOLOGY GROUP, CIVIC & RELIGIOUS ORGANIZATIONS WILL PARTICIPATE IN CLEANUP CAMPAIGNS COUNTY-WIDE. (LOCAL). MRS NEWTON OAKES, CHAIRMAN; DAHLONEGA-LUMPKIN COUNTY BICENT COMMITTEE; BOX 141; DAHLONEGA, GA 30533. (#6752).

GEORGIA HISTORICAL MINUTES PROJ OF N GEORGIA COL. THIRTY ONE-MINUTE SPOT RADIO PROGRAMS ON GEORGIA'S HISTORY. (ST-WIDE). RAY C RENSI, ASSOC PROFESSOR; NORTH GEORGIA COLLEGE BICENTENNIAL COMMITTEE; NORTH GEORGIA COLLEGE; DAHLONEGA, GA 30533. (#6659).

HISTORIC SITES REFERENCE GUIDE: DAHLONEGA, GEORGIA. A GUIDE TO HISTORIC MARKERS IN LUMPKIN COUNTY & A BRIEF HISTORY OF EACH WILL BE DEVELOPED. (LOCAL). MRS NEWTON OAKES, CHAIRMAN; DAHLONEGA-LUMPKIN COUNTY BICENT COMMITTEE; BOX 141; DAHLONEGA, GA 30533. (#6753). **(??).**

LUMPKIN COUNTY BICENTENNIAL WELCOME CENTER-GEORGIA. CONSTRUCT STATE WELCOME CENTER AT ENTRANCE OF OR NEAR DOWNTOWN SQUARE OF DAHLONEGA. (LOCAL). MORRISON MOORE, DIRECTOR; DAHLONEGA LUMPKIN COUNTY CHAMBER OF COMMERCE; PARK ST; DAHLONEGA, GA 30533. (#2806). **(??).**

LUMPKIN COUNTY HOSPITAL, GA. A 50 BED HOSPITAL WILL BE COMPLETED IN FEBRUARY 1976. IT WILL BE THE ONLY HOSPITAL IN LUMPKIN COUNTY. (LOCAL). DR MAC CALLAHAM, CHAIRMAN; LUMPKIN COUNTY HOSPITAL AUTHORITY; HELEN DR; DAHLONEGA, GA 30533. (#15470).

LUMPKIN COUNTY VOTER REGISTRATION DRIVES -GEORGIA. DRIVES TO INCREASE VOTER REGISTRATION & TO REGISTER 18 YEAR OLDS VOTERS FOR LOCAL, STATE, & NATL ELECTIONS. (LOCAL). MRS FRANCES MOORE, DIRECTOR; LUMPKIN COUNTY VOTERS REGISTRATION OFFICE; HILL ST; DAHLONEGA, GA 30533. (#2807).

MUSEUM PROJECT IN DAHLONEGA, GEORGIA. A PERMANENT MUSEUM FOR LUMPKIN COUNTY/DAHLONEGA & N GEORGIA COLLEGE WILL PORTRAY THE STORY OF THE COUNTY, CITY & COLLEGE FROM THE GOLD RUSH OF THE 1850'S TO THE PRESENT. (LOCAL). MRS NEWTON OAKES, CHAIRMAN; DAHLONEGA-LUMPKIN COUNTY BICENT COMMITTEE; BOX 141; DAHLONEGA, GA 30533. (#6754).

RESTORATION OF VICKERY HOUSE - DAHLONEGA, GA. PROJECT WILL INCLUDE THE RESTORATION OF VICKERY HOUSE & FURNISHING THE DOWNSTAIRS WITH ANTIQUES. (LOCAL). MRS NEWTON OAKES, CHAIRMAN; DAHLONEGA-LUMPKIN COUNTY BICENT COMMITTEE; BOX 141; DAHLONEGA, GA 30533. (#10684). **ARBA GRANTEE.**

SPRING AND SUMMER CELEBRATION AT N GEORGIA COLLEGE. A PRESENTATION OF HISTORICAL MUSIC AND VISITING ARTISTS AND CRAFTSMEN AT NORTH GEORGIA COLLEGE AND NEIGHBORING HIGH SCHOOLS. (LOCAL). RAY C RENSI, ASSOC PROFESSOR; NORTH GEORGIA COLLEGE FINE ARTS DEPARTMENT; NORTH GEORGIA COLLEGE; DAHLONEGA, GA 30533. (#6662).

TOWN SQUARE HOUSE RESTORATION: DAHLONEGA, GEORGIA. THE RESTORATION OF THE OLDEST HOUSE ON DAHLONEGA'S TOWN SQUARE WILL COMPLETE THE 1828 GOLD RUSH ERA ATMOSPHERE OF THE RENOVATED TOWN SQUARE. (LOCAL). MRS NEWTON OAKES, CHAIRMAN; DAHLONEGA-LUMPKIN COUNTY BICENT COMMITTEE; BOX 141; DAHLONEGA, GA 30533. (#6751).

WELCOME SIGNS IN DAHLONEGA, GORGIA. FOUR SIGNS WELCOMING VISITORS TO DAHLONEGA WILL BE ERECTED TO EXTEND A HOSPITABLE WELCOME TO VISITORS DURING THE BICENTENNIAL YEAR. (LOCAL). MRS NEWTON OAKES, CHAIRMAN; DAHLONEGA-LUMPKIN COUNTY BICENT COMMITTEE; BOX 141; DAHLONEGA, GA 30533. (#6750).

JUNE 14, '75. MOONSHINE DAY. FESTIVAL AT GOLD HILLS. (LOCAL). MR DON DALTON; GOLD HILLS OF DAHLONEGA; DAHLONEGA, GA 30533. (#50305-2).

JUNE 28 - 29, '75. ARTS & CRAFTS FESTIVAL. FESTIVAL AT GOLD HILLS DAHLONEGA GA. (LOCAL). STELLA IVIE; GOLD HILLS OF DAHLONEGA; NORTH HALL; DAHLONEGA, GA 30533. (#50305-3).

JULY 4, '75. WORLD'S LARGEST GOLD PANNING CONTEST. COMPETITION AT GOLD HILLS. (ST-WIDE). STELLA IVIE; GOLD HILLS OF DAHLONEGA; NORTH HALL; DAHLONEGA, GA 30533. (#50305-4).

AUG 16, '75. FIDDLERS & PICKERS DAY. MOUNTAIN FIDDLERS & PICKERS WILL PARTICIPATE IN THE MANY FESTIVITIES OF THE DAY. (ST-WIDE). DAN DALTON, CHMN; GOLD HILLS OF DAHLONEGA; HIGHWAY 60 S; DAHLONEGA, GA 30533. (#100128-1).

OCT 17, '75. 'MULE DAY' - A TRIBUTE TO THE MULE. MULE DAY CELEBRATION WILL INCLUDE A MULE BEAUTY CONTEST AND A MULE RACE. (LOCAL). DAN DALTON, CHAIRMAN; GOLD HILLS OF DAHLONEGA; HWY 60 S; DAHLONEGA, GA 30533. (#100125-1).

OCT 18 - 19, '75. GOLD RUSH DAYS. IN HONOR OF THE BICENTENNIAL, A GOLD RUSH FESTIVAL WILL BE HELD THAT IS TYPICAL OF THE GOLD RUSH ERA OF 1828; ACTIVITIES WILL INCLUDE A PARADE, CRAFTS, GOLD PANNING, ETC. AT TOWN SQUARE. (ST-WIDE). DAHLONEGA-LUMPKIN JAYCEES; DAHLONEGA-LUMPKIN CO JAYCEES; PO BOX 774; DAHLONEGA, GA 30533. (#9826-1).

OCT 25 - 26, '75. SORGHUM SYRUP FESTIVAL - MAKING OF SORGHUM SYRUP & OTHER ACTIVITIES. FESTIVAL. (LOCAL). DAN DALTON, CHAIRMAN; GOLD HILLS OF DAHLONEGA; HWY 60 S; DAHLONEGA, GA 30533. (#100126-1).

NOV 29, '75. UNITED STATES ARMED FORCES BICENTENNIAL CARAVAN. THE CARAVAN IS COMPOSED OF EXHIBIT VANS FOR EACH BRANCH OF THE MILITARY SERVICE. THE THEME OF THE EXHIBITION IS 'HISTORY OF THE ARMED FORCES AND THEIR CONTRIBUTION TO THE NATION'. (LOCAL). MISS NEWTON OAKES, CHMN; U S ARMED FORCES BICENTENNIAL EXHIBIT VANS PROJECT; BOX 141; DAHLONEGA, GA 30533. (#1775-203).

FEB 24, '76. TVA BICENTENNIAL CARAVAN, DAHLONEGA, GA. EXHIBIT AT LUMPKIN COUNTY HIGH SCHOOL GROUNDS. (LOCAL). MRS NEWTON OAKES, CHMN; DAHLONEGA-LUMPKIN COUNTY BICENTENNIAL; 1615 N GROVE, BOX 141; DAHLONEGA, GA 30533. (#102407-1).

APR 20, '76. HERITAGE FASHION SHOW. LIVE PERFORMANCE AT LUMPKIN COUNTY SCHOOL AUDITORIUM. (LOCAL). ELIZ CORNELIUS, DIRECTOR; HOME DEMONSTRATION AGENCY; CANE CREEK VALLEY; DAHLONEGA, GA 30533. (#105305-4).

APR 30 - MAY 2, '76. PARENTS ALUMNI WEEKEND. INCLUDES: FIELD EVENTS, PARADE, ART DISPLAYS AND BAND CONCERT. (LOCAL). TOM DALTON, DIRECTOR; NORTH GEORGIA COLLEGE; HWY 60 SOUTH; DAHLONEGA, GA 30533. (#105305-5).

JULY 3 - 4, '76. BICENTENNIAL PARADE AND CELEBRATION. EVENTS INCLUDE DINNER AND WATERMELON CUTTING, OLD-FASHIONED FAMILY DAY, 'HOLLIES FOLLIES' AND FASHION SHOW; BELL RINGING SUNDAY AT 2. AT DOWNTOWN SQUARE. (LOCAL). MRS NEWTON OAKES, CHMN; DAHLONEGA-LUMPKIN COUNTY BICENTENNIAL COMMITTEE; 1615 N GROVE, BOX 141; DAHLONEGA, GA 30533. (#102407-2).

JULY 4, '76. INTER-DENOMINATIONAL DAY OF PRAYER. ALL TOWN CHURCH BELLS WILL RING AT A DESIGNATED TIME. (LOCAL). MRS NEWTON OAKES, CHMN; DAHLONEGA-LUMPKIN COUNTY BICENTENNIAL COMMISSION; 1615 N GROVE; DAHLONEGA, GA 30533. (#105305-2).

OCT 15 - 17, '76. GOLD RUSH DAYS. FESTIVITIES WILL INCLUDE A BICENTENNIAL PARADE. AT DOWNTOWN SQUARE. (LOCAL). DR GORDON PARKS, CHMN; DAHLONEGA JAYCEES; KENIMER DR; DAHLONEGA, GA 30533. (#105305-3).

DALTON

DALTON-WHITFIELD COUNTY HERITAGE TRAIL AND MAP, GA. RESEARCH, ESTABLISH AND MAINTAIN HERITAGE TRAIL THROUGHOUT CITY AND COUNTY WHICH HIGHLIGHTS HISTORICAL SITES OF COMMUNITY. IS SUITABLE FOR HIKING AND CYCLING AND PROVIDES RESOURCE MATERIAL FOR EDUCATION. (LOCAL). CHARLES E BOWEN, CHAIRMAN; DALTON-WHITFIELD COUNTY BICENTENNIAL COMMISSION; PO BOX 1408; DALTON, GA 30720. (#12597).

GENEAOLOGY WORKSHOP IN DALTON, GA. EDUCATIONAL COURSE, RESEARCH AND SEMINAR TO AID CITIZENRY IN SEARCHING FOR REVOLUTIONARY ANCESTORS AND TYPES OF PEOPLE WHO MAKE UP THE HERITAGE OF THE REGION. (LOCAL). DR THOMAS DEATON, CHAIRMAN SOCIAL SCIENCE DIV; DALTON JUNIOR COLLEGE; PO BOX 1740; DALTON, GA 30720. (#12595).

SEPT 27 - 28, '75. OLD FIREHOUSE FESTIVAL. TWO DAY ARTS & CRAFTS FESTIVAL WITH EXHIBITIONS AND ACTIVITIES WHICH EMPHASIZE THE BICENTENNIAL THEME. (LOCAL). BERNICE SPIGEL, DIRECTOR; CREATIVE ARTS GUILD; 210 N PENTZ ST; DALTON, GA 30720. (#101344-1).

MAR 10 - 14, '76. HERITAGE SPECIAL - TRAIN TOUR. TRAVELING RAIL EXHIBIT EMPHASIZING COLONIAL & REVOLUTIONARY GEORGIA HISTORY, CRAFTS & LIFESTYLE OF GEORGIA COLONISTS. EXHIBITS WILL BE DISPLAYED WITH COMBINATION OF SIGHT & SOUND ACTIVITY. (ST-WIDE). RON HENRY, COORDINATOR; GEORGIA AGRIRAMA DEVELOPMENT AUTHORITY; GEORGIA BICENTENNIAL; 8TH ST A I 75; TIFTON, GA 31794. (#7999-8).

MAY 8 - 9, '76. PRATER'S MILL COUNTRY FAIR. CRAFTS WHICH WERE PRACTICED IN 1776 ARE EXHIBITED AT THE 1859 GRIST MILL. ALSO 150 EXHIBITS OF OTHER HANDICRAFTS AND ART. MILL IS IN OPERATION AND OPEN TO THE PUBLIC. AT HISTORIC PRATER'S MILL, GA HWY 2, 10 MI NE OF DALTON, GA. (ST-WIDE). JANE HARRELL; THE PRATER'S MILL COUNTRY FAIR, INC; 101 TIMBERLAND DR; DALTON, GA 30720. (#103416-89).

MAY 15 - 22, '76. DALTON-WHITFIELD COUNTY BICENTENNIAL CELEBRATION AND PAGEANT. VARIED ACTIVITIES INCLUDING A PAGEANT, SPORTS TOURNAMENTS & TASTING SPREES COMPOSE THIS WEEK-LONG FESTIVAL; PARADE, PIONEER DAYS PARADE ON MAY 15TH; BALL ON MAY 22ND. DESCENDANTS OF EARLY PIONEERS WELCOMED ESPECIALLY ON MAY 18TH. AT DALTON HIGH STADIUM 'HARMON FIELD'. (ST-WIDE). MARY GENE DYKES, COORD; DALTON-WHITFIELD COUNTY BICENTENNIAL COMM; 623 EMMONS DR; DALTON, GA 30720. (#103416-287).

SEPT 10 - 14, '76. HERITAGE SPECIAL - TRAIN TOUR. TRAVELING RAIL EXHIBIT EMPHASIZING COLONIAL AND REVOLUTIONARY GEORGIA HISTORY, CRAFTS & LIFESTYLE OF GEORGIA COLONISTS. EXHIBITS WILL BE DISPLAYED WITH COMBINATION OF SIGHT & SOUND ACTIVITY. AT DEPOT. (LOCAL). RON HENRY, DIRECTOR; GEORGIA BICENTENNIAL COMMISSION; 1776 PEACHTREE NW, ROOM 520 S; ATLANTA, GA 30309. (#7999-34).

OCT 9 - 10, '76. PRATER'S MILL COUNTRY FAIR. CRAFTS WHICH WERE PRACTICED IN 1776 ARE EXHIBITED AT THE 1859 GRIST MILL. ALSO 150 EXHIBITS OF OTHER HANDICRAFTS AND ART. MILL IS IN OPERATION AND OPEN TO THE PUBLIC. AT HISTORIC PRATER'S MILL, GA HWY 2, 10 MI NE OF DALTON, GA. (ST-WIDE). JUDY ALDERMEN, CHMN; THE PRATER'S MILL COUNTRY FAIR, INC; 101 TIMBERLAND DR; DALTON, GA 30720. (#104879-1).

DARIEN

MAN IN THE LANDSCAPE CONFERENCE - DARIEN, GA. FOCUS ON NATURAL, HISTORIC AND CULTURAL HERITAGE OF THE COUNTY WITH A PURPOSE OF EDUCATING CITIZENS IN THE COASTAL REGION, ON THE AREA'S IMPORTANT RESOURCES. (ST-WIDE). DONALD THOMPSON, PROJ DIRECTOR; DARIEN-MCINTOSH COUNTY BICENTENNIAL COMMITTEE; PO BOX 766; DARIEN, GA 31305. (#27853). **ARBA GRANTEE.**

NOV 13 - 14, '76. MAN IN LANDSCAPE CONFERENCE. FOCUS ON NATURAL, HISTORIC AND CULTURAL HERITAGE OF THE COUNTY WITH THE INTENTION OF EDUCATING CITIZENS IN THE COASTAL REGION ON THE AREA'S IMPORTANT RESOURCES. AT VILLAGE INN MOTEL, SAPLO ISLAND, LEWIS CREEK. (LOCAL). DONALD THOMPSON, PROJ DIR; DARIEN-MCINTOSH COUNTY BICENTENNIAL COMMITTEE; PO BOX 766; DARIEN, GA 31305. (#27853-1).

DAWSON

AVENUE OF FLAGS, DAWSON, GA. A COLLECTION OF FLAGS WILL BE DISPLAYED ON MAIN STREET. (LOCAL). MS EDWARD J YOUNG, CHAIRMAN; TERRELL COUNTY CHAMBER OF COMMERCE & DAWSON ROTARY CLUB; 109 E LEE ST; DAWSON, GA 31742. (#31661).

HISTORIC MOMENTS & POSTER CONTEST; DAWSON, GA. A POSTER CONTEST AND HISTORIC MOMENTS USED DAILY BY RADIO; POSTERS 'NOSTALGIA 1856-1906'. (LOCAL). MS EDWARD J YOUNG, CHAIRMAN; TERRELL COUNTY CHAMBER OF COMMERCE; 109 E LEE ST; DAWSON, GA 31742. (#31657).

RESTORATION OF COURTHOUSE, DAWSON, GA. NEW ROOF, CLEAN EXTERIOR MARBLE, PAINT EXTERIOR & INTERIOR, PAINT SURFACES, REPAIR & REPLACE WINDOWS AND ADD AIR CONDITIONING. (LOCAL). MRS EDWARD J YOUNG, CO-CHAIRMAN; TERRELL COUNTY CHAMBER OF COMMERCE; 109 E LEE ST; DAWSON, GA 31742. (#31660).

JULY 1 - 3, '75. NOSTALGIA, 1856-1906. FESTIVAL AT DOMESTIC LOAN BLDG. (LOCAL). MS EDWARD J YOUNG, CHMN; TERRELL COUNTY CHAMBER OF COMMERCE; 109 E LEE ST; DAWSON, GA 31742. (#200012-57).

JUNE 19, '76. HORSE SHOW. LIVE PERFORMANCE AT DAWSON AIRPORT, U S HWY 82 SOUTH. (LOCAL). MS EDWARD J YOUNG, CHMN; TERRELL COUNTY CHAMBER OF COMMERCE; 109 E LEE S; DAWSON, GA 31742. (#200012-58).

DAWSONVILLE

CONSTRUCTION OF LIBRARY IN DAWSONVILLE, GA. CONSTRUCTION OF LIBRARY IN DAWSONVILLE. (LOCAL). HERBERT H HARBEN, COMMISSIONER; DAWSON COUNTY; COURTHOUSE; DAWSONVILLE, GA 30534. (#22840). **ARBA GRANTEE.**

DAWSONVILLE — CONTINUED

LIBRARY EQUIPMENT, DAWSON COUNTY, GA. SHELVING FOR APPROXIMATELY 1400 VOLUMES OF BOOKS IN THE NEW LIBRARY. (LOCAL). H H HARBEN, COMMISIONER; CITY OF DAWSONVILLE; PO BOX 192; DAWSONVILLE, GA 30534. (#25545). **ARBA GRANTEE.**

DECATUR

ASSOCIATION OF MENTAL HEALTH ADMINISTRATORS CONVENTION. ASSOCIATION'S PURPOSE IS TO GATHER VITAL INFORMATION & IMPROVE HUMAN SERVICES FOR OUR CITY & COUNTRY. (LOCAL). HELEN GORDON, COORD; ASSOCIATION OF MENTAL HEALTH ADMINISTRATORS; 2192 STERLING RIDGE RD; DECATUR, GA 30032. (#200012-56).

BICENTENNIAL FIRE HYDRANTS, DECATUR, GA. DEKALB COUNTY JAYCEES WILL PAINT ALL FIRE HYDRANTS IN THE BICENTENNIAL COLORS OF RED, WHITE AND BLUE. (LOCAL). TOMMY CLACK, PRESIDENT; DEKALB JAYCEES; 81 RUE FONTAINE; DECATUR, GA 30034. (#16725).

CAMPUS BEAUTIFICATION, DECATUR, GA. PURCHASING TREES FROM U S FORESTRY SERVICE AND LANDSCAPING THE CAMPUS; OTHER CLUBS ARE PLANTING FLOWERS AND SHRUBS. (LOCAL). DR HARTWELL QUINN, CHAIRMAN; DEKALB COLLEGE BICENTENNIAL COMMITTEE; 3251 PANTERSVILLE RD; DECATUR, GA 30034. (#24851).

EDUCATION MONUMENT, DECATUR, GA. A PERMANENT MONUMENT WILL BE ERECTED ON THE CAMPUS WITH INSCRIPTION EMPHASIZING EDUCATION AND DEKALB COLLEGE PHILOSOPHY. (LOCAL). DR HARTWELL QUINN, CHAIRMAN BICENT COMMITTEE; HISTORY DEPARTMENT DEKALB COLLEGE SOUTH; 3251 PANTHERSVILLE RD; DECATUR, GA 30034. (#24859).

NATURAL AREA - DECATUR, GA. 300 ACRES OF FORESTS, NATURAL AREAS, GARDENS AND PARKS DESIGNATED BY THE SIGNERS OF THE COVENANT. (LOCAL). LJIM HURLEY, COORDINATOR; DEKALB COUNTY BICENTENNIAL COMMITTEE; COURTHOUSE SQUARE; DECATUR, GA 30030. (#20764).

SEPT 22 - DEC 18, '75. BICENTENNIAL SYMBOL CONTEST. COMPETITION. (LOCAL). JAMES A HURLEY, COORD; DEKALB PARKS & RECREATION LIBRARY SYSTEM; 556 NORTH MCDONOUGH ST; DECATUR, GA 30030. (#103023-2).

DEC 8, '75. DECATUR/DEKALB BICENTENNIAL CHRISTMAS FESTIVAL. CEREMONY, FESTIVAL, PARADE AT TOWN SQUARE. (LOCAL). ALISA HARRIS, CHMN; DECATUR BICENTENNIAL COMMISSION; BOX 220; DECATUR, GA 30031. (#103454-1).

MAR 3 - 7, '76. HERITAGE SPECIAL - TRAIN TOUR. TRAVELING RAIL EXHIBIT EMPHASIZING COLONIAL & REVOLUTIONARY GEORGIA HISTORY, CRAFTS & LIFESTYLE OF GEORGIA COLONISTS. EXHIBITS WILL BE DISPLAYED WITH COMBINATION OF SIGHT & SOUND ACTIVITY. (ST-WIDE). RON HENRY, COORDINATOR; GEORGIA AGRIRAMA DEVELOPMENT AUTHORITY/GEORGIA BICENTENNIAL; 8TH ST A I 75; TIFTON, GA 31794. (#7999-3).

MAY 5, '76. AMERICA ARTS & CRAFTS FESTIVAL. A LARGE EXHIBIT OF AMERICAN ARTS & CRAFTS SUCH AS QUILTING, POTTERY AND BLACKSMITHING. (LOCAL). DR HARTWELL QUINN, CHMN; DEKALB COLLEGE SOUTH ENGLISH DEPT; 3251 PANTHERSVILLE RD; DECATUR, GA 30034. (#108156-1).

MAY 8, '76. SPRING '76. FESTIVAL, PARADE AT TOWN SQUARE. (LOCAL). IRENE SANDERS, CHMN; DECATUR BICENTENNIAL COMMISSION; 206 UPLAND PL; DECATUR, GA 30030. (#103454-2).

MAY 27, '76. LAW DAY 1976 - GA REPRESENTATIVE LECTURES ON LAW & AMER TRADITION. SEMINAR. (LOCAL). DR HARTWELL QUINN, CHMN; DEKALB COLLEGE BICENTENNIAL COMMITTEE; 3251 PANTHERSVILLE RD; DECATUR, GA 30034. (#108127-2).

JULY 2, '76. 'HAPPY BIRTHDAY AMERICA'. A GIGANTIC CAKE WILL BE CUT IN THE COURTYARD WITH STUDENTS AND THE COMMUNITY PARTICIPATING. AT CAMPUS COURTYARD. (LOCAL). DR HARTWELL QUINN, CHMN; DEKALB COLLEGE SOUTH STUDENT GOVERNMENT ASSOC; 3251 PANTHERSVILLE RD; DECATUR, GA 30034. (#108156-2).

JULY 4, '76. METRO ATLANTA BAPTIST BICENTENNIAL RALLY. A RALLY COMPOSED OF THE COMBINED CHURCHES OF THE ATLANTA BAPTIST ASSOC. SPECIAL MUSIC AND A FLAG DISPLAY WILL BE INCLUDED. AT DEKALB MEMORIAL STADIUM. (LOCAL). H EARL PEACOCK, COORD; EVANGELISM COMMITTEE, ATLANTA BAPTIST ASSOC; 1995 CLAIRMONT RD; DECATUR, GA 30033. (#108914-1).

AUG 28 - 29, '76. 'TOKALITTA' AND 'THE VIGIL'. HISTORICAL DRAMAS DEPICT GEORGIA'S FIRST SETTLERS WITH INDIANS; AND GEORGIA IN THE AMERICAN REVOLUTION. AT FRANKLIN D ROOSEVELT STATE PARK, 14 MILES SOUTH OF WARM SPRINGS. (ST-WIDE). JOHN DOWN, COORDINATOR; DEKALB COMMUNITY COLLEGE; DECATUR, GA 30030. (#103416-504).

DOBBINS AFB

JUNE 12, '76. ARMED FORCES-COMMUNITY OPEN HOUSE. OPEN HOUSE, ANTIQUE CARS & AIRCRAFT, BANDS, HISTORICAL EXHIBITS, SQUARE DANCING, HOT AIR BALLOON RIDES. (LOCAL). LT COL J A PEERY; 94 TACTICAL AIRLIFT WING, DOBBINS AFB; MARIETTA, GA 30060. (#200012-45).

DOUGLAS

BICENTENNIAL MARKER IN DOUGLAS, GA. A PERMANENT BICENTENNIAL COMMEMORATIVE MARKER WILL BE ERECTED. (LOCAL). GEORGE SCHLEGEL, CHAIRMAN; DOUGLAS-COFFEE COUNTY BICENTENNIAL COMMITTEE; 1248 W BRYAN ST; DOUGLAS, GA 31533. (#11304).

COMMUNITY FESTIVALS IN DOUGLAS, GA. ANNUAL FESTIVALS WILL BE INITIATED TO STIMULATE CIVIC PRIDE & INTEREST IN LOCAL HERITAGE; PLANS INCLUDE BICENTENNIAL PARADES, ART & AUTO SHOWS, COOKING CONTESTS, FILM FESTIVAL & STREET DANCES. (LOCAL). GEORGE SCHLEGEL, CHAIRMAN; DOUGLAS-COFFEE COUNTY BICENTENNIAL COMMITTEE; 1249 W BRYAN ST; DOUGLAS, GA 31533. (#11307).

DOUGLAS - COFFEE COUNTY HERITAGE '76 CABIN - GA. AUTHENTICALLY RENOVATE AND FURNISH AN EARLY 1800 LOG CABIN WITH APPROPRIATE LANDSCAPING AND MOVE IT TO GENERAL COFFEE STATE PARK ON JULY 4TH 1976. (ST-WIDE). MRS B CARLYLE RAMSEY, EXEC DIRECTOR; DOUGLAS - COFFEE COUNTY BICENTENNIAL COMMITTEE; PO BOX 1776, 101 W PETERSON ST; DOUGLAS, GA 31533. (#8721). **(??). ARBA GRANTEE.**

ENVIRONMENTAL INVENTORY IN DOUGLAS, GA. THE PROJECT IS AN INVENTORY; WILL DETERMINE THE ENDANGERED TREES, PLANTS AND WILDLIFE IN COFFEE COUNTY. (LOCAL). GEORGE SCHLEGEL, CHAIRMAN; DOUGLAS-COFFEE COUNTY BICENTENNIAL COMMITTEE; 1248 W BRYAN ST; DOUGLAS, GA 31533. (#11311).

FLAG DISPLAYS IN DOUGLAS, GA. CITIZENS WILL BE ENCOURAGED TO DISPLAY AMERICAN FLAG, GEORGIA FLAG AND APPROPRIATE BICENTENNIAL FLAGS DURING BICENTENNIAL ERA. (LOCAL). GEORGE SCHLEGEL, CHAIRMAN; DOUGLAS-COFFEE COUNTY BICENTENNIAL COMMITTEE; 1248 W BRYAN ST; DOUGLAS, GA 31533. (#11308).

HERITAGE '76 PARK IN DOUGLAS, GA. COFFEE COUNTY PARK WILL BE DEVELOPED & IMPROVED AND RENAMED HERITAGE '76 PARK. (LOCAL). GEORGE SCHLEGEL, CHAIRMAN; DOUGLAS-COFFEE COUNTY BICENTENNIAL COMMITTEE; 1248 W BRYAN ST; DOUGLAS, GA 31533. (#11309).

HISTORIC SITES IN DOUGLAS, GA. HISTORIC SITES AND SIGNIFICANT LANDMARKS IN THE DOUGLAS-COFFEE COUNTY AREA WILL BE IDENTIFIED AND MARKED. (LOCAL). GEORGE SCHLEGEL, CHAIRMAN; DOUGLAS-COFFEE COUNTY BICENTENNIAL COMMITTEE; 1248 W BRYAN ST; DOUGLAS, GA 31533. (#11305).

HISTORY OF COFFEE COUNTY, DOUGLAS, GA. RESEARCH WILL BE UNDERTAKEN & INFORMATION COLLECTED FOR PUBLICATION OF THE HISTORY OF THE COFFEE COUNTY AREA. (LOCAL). GEORGE SCHLEGEL, CHAIRMAN; DOUGLAS-COFFEE COUNTY BICENTENNIAL COMMITTEE; 1248 W BRYAN ST; DOUGLAS, GA 31533. (#11302).

RECORDS & PHOTOGRAPHS COLLECTION IN DOUGLAS, GA. RESEARCH & DOCUMENTATION OF RECORDS & PHOTOS WILL BE INITIATED FOR USE BY SATILLA REGIONAL LIBRARY AND THE PUBLIC SCHOOLS. (LOCAL). GEORGE SCHLEGEL, CHAIRMAN; DOUGLAS-COFFEE COUNTY BICENTENNIAL COMMITTEE; 1248 W BRYAN ST; DOUGLAS, GA 31533. (#11303).

RECREATION CENTER IN DOUGLAS, GA. THE COMMUNITY RECREATION CENTER & RECREATIONAL FACILITIES WILL BE RENOVATED FOR USE BY CITIZENS OF ALL AGES. (LOCAL). GEORGE SCHLEGEL, CHAIRMAN; DOUGLAS-COFFEE COUNTY BICENTENNIAL COMMITTEE; 1248 W BRYAN ST; DOUGLAS, GA 31533. (#11310).

REVITALIZATION OF DOWNTOWN AREA IN DOUGLAS, GA. DOWNTOWN AREA WILL BE REVITALIZED; CITY STREETS AND STOREFRONTS WILL BE BEAUTIFIED. (LOCAL). GEORGE SCHLEGEL, CHAIRMAN; DOUGLAS-COFFEE COUNTY BICENTENNIAL COMMITTEE; 1248 W BRYAN ST; DOUGLAS, GA 31533. (#11312).

SOUTH GEORGIA COLLEGE HISTORY, DOUGLAS, GA. THE HISTORY OF SOUTH GEORGIA WILL BE WRITTEN. (LOCAL). GEORGE SCHLEGEL, CHAIRMAN; DOUGLAS-COFFEE COUNTY BICENTENNIAL COMMITTEE; 1248 W BRYAN ST; DOUGLAS, GA 31533. (#11306).

FEB 28 - 29, '76. UNITED STATES ARMED FORCES BICENTENNIAL CARAVAN. CARAVAN IS COMPOSED OF EXHIBIT VANS FOR EACH MILITARY SERVICE. PROJECT THEME IS 'HISTORY OF THE ARMED FORCES AND THEIR CONTRIBUTIONS TO THE NATION'. (LOCAL). MAYOR GEORGE SCHLEGAL; US ARMED FORCES BICENTENNIAL EXHIBIT VANS PROJECT; 1248 W BRYAN ST; DOUGLAS, GA 31533. (#1775-437).

JUNE 14, '76. OPENING CEREMONY OF 1840 RESTORED CABIN. EXHIBIT, FESTIVAL AT PETERSON AVE. (LOCAL). GEORGE M SCHLEGEL, CHRMN; DOUGLAS-COFFEE COUNTY BICENT COMMITTEE; NORTH PATERSON AVE; DOUGLAS, GA 31533. (#4049-1).

DUBLIN

MAR 12 - 28, '76. DUBLIN-LAURENS ST PATRICK'S FESTIVAL. CELEBRATION OF THE SPIRIT OF '76 INCLUDES PARADE, ARTS & CRAFTS, MAGIC SHOW, CONCERTS, TOURNAMENTS, BEAUTY PAGEANT, SQUARE DANCE, GOLF TOURNAMENTS, HORSE SHOW, BOAT SHOW, IRISH STEW DINNER, WORSHIP SERVICES AND MANY OTHER EVENTS AT VARYING TIMES DURING FESTIVAL. AT MANY EVENTS AT VARYING LOCATIONS AROUND DUBLIN-LAURENS. (REGN'L). JAMES F NELSON JR, DIR; DUBLIN-LAURENS ST PATRICK'S FESTIVAL, INC; PO BOX 336; DUBLIN, GA 31021. (#103416-91).

DULUTH

JUNE 14 - 20, '76. 76TH US OPEN GOLF CHAMPIONSHIP. FIELD OF 150 OF WORLD'S FOREMOST PROFESSIONAL AND AMATEUR GOLFERS COMPETE AT HOME CLUB OF THE LATE BOB JONES. AT ATLANTA ATHLETIC CLUB. (NAT'L). GENE BRANCH, DIRECTOR; U S GOLF ASSOCIATION; PO BOX 1976; DULUTH, GA 30136. (#103416-90).

DUNWOODY

NOV 22, '75. BICENTENNIAL PSALM CONCERT. SECOND PERFORMANCE IN ATLANTA AT GLEN MEMORIAL CHURCH ON 11/23/75. AT DUNWOODY METHODIST CHURCH. (LOCAL). THOMAS L SCHWARTZ, DIR; CHORAL GUILD OF ATLANTA; 124 PEACHTREE MEMORIAL DR #4; ATLANTA, GA 30309. (#20496-1).

EAST POINT

DICK LANE VELODROME, EAST POINT, GA. A HIGH BANKED COMPETITION BIKE TRACK WITH A FLAT INNER MULTIPLE USE TRACK WILL BE BUILT. IT WILL BE 1/5 MILE LONG. (LOCAL). DICK LANE, DIRECTOR OF RECREATION; CITY OF EAST POINT; 1431 NORMAN BERRY DR; EAST POINT, GA 30344. (#20015).

EASTMAN

DODGE COUNTY BICENTENNIAL PARK - EASTMAN, GA. A SMALL CITY PARK WILL BE LOCATED AT THE DODGE COUNTY COURTHOUSE; THE PARK WILL INCLUDE BENCHES, LIGHTS, DRINKING FOUNTAIN, TREES, FLOWERS AND SHRUBS. (LOCAL). S C CADWELL, COUNTY COMMISSIONER; DODGE COUNTY; EASTMAN, GA 31023. (#23780). **ARBA GRANTEE.**

EATONTON

BICENTENNIAL CAMP WEEKEND, EATONTON, GA. CAMP WEEKEND TO PROVIDE OPPORTUNITY FOR HANDICAPPED CHILDREN & THEIR FAMILIES TO PARTICIPATE IN BICENTENNIAL CELEBRATION; FOCUS ON FOREFATHERS AND INDIAN HERITAGE. (ST-WIDE). BETTY O NICHOLS, PROGRAM DIRECTOR; GEORGIA EASTER SEAL SOCIETY FOR CRIPPLED CHILDREN AND ADULTS; 1211 SPRING ST NW; ATLANTA, GA 30309. (#21855). **ARBA GRANTEE.**

SEPT 15, '75 - DEC 31, '76. PUTNAM COUNTY SCHOOL'S BICENTENNIAL HERITAGE FESTIVAL. EVENTS WILL INCLUDE A HISTORY FAIR, ARTS & CRAFTS SHOW, PAGEANTS, TAPE & SLIDE SHOW, CAMPUS BEAUTIFICATION, 'BICENT BITS' NEWS COLUMN, AND MUCH MORE. (LOCAL). KATHERINE WALTERS, DIR; PUTNAM COUNTY BOARD OF EDUCATION; 304 W MARION ST; EATONTON, GA 31024. (#103497-2).

MAY 28 - 30, '76. BICENTENNIAL CAMP WEEKEND. CAMP WEEKEND TO PROVIDE OPPORTUNITY FOR HANDICAPPED CHILDREN & THEIR FAMILIES TO PARTICIPATE IN BICENTENNIAL CELEBRATION; FOCUS ON FOREFATHERS AND INDIAN HERITAGE. (ST-WIDE). BETTY O NICHOLS, PROJ DIR; GEORGIA EASTER SEAL SOCIETY FOR CRIPPLED CHILDREN AND ADULTS; 1211 SPRING ST NW; ATLANTA, GA 30309. (#21855-1).

ELBERTON

GRANITE BICENTENNIAL MEMORIALS. BICENTENNIAL GRANITE MEMORIALS; ARBA LICENSE NO 76-19-0609. (NAT'L). THOMAS A ROBINSON, VICE PRESIDENT; CENTURY GRANITE COMPANY, INC; PO BOX 370; ELBERTON, GA 30635. (#22149).

ELLAVILLE

BICENTENNIAL HORIZONS HYDRANTS - ELLAVILLE, GA. THE CITY FIRE HYDRANTS WILL BE PAINTED RED, WHITE & BLUE. (LOCAL). NANCY M YOUNG, CHAIRMAN; SCHLEY COUNTY BICENTENNIAL COMMITTEE; BOX 175; ELLAVILLE, GA 31806. (#18407).

BICENTENNIAL PROJECTS & COMMUNITY DEVELOPMENT - GA. FUND RAISING EVENTS ARE UNDERWAY TO RAISE MONEY FOR A LIBRARY, COURTHOUSE EXPANSION & RENOVATION, PROVISION OF ADDITIONAL EQUIPMENT & TRAINING FOR EMERGENCY MEDICAL FACILITIES. (LOCAL). NANCY M YOUNG, CHAIRMAN; SCHLEY COUNTY BICENTENNIAL COMMITTEE; BOX 175; ELLAVILLE, GA 31806. (#18409).

COMMUNITY WELCOME SIGNS - SCHLEY COUNTY, GA. WELCOME SIGNS WILL BE ERECTED ON MAJOR HIGHWAYS ENTERING SCHLEY COUNTY. (LOCAL). NANCY M YOUNG, CHAIRMAN; SCHLEY COUNTY BICENTENNIAL COMMITTEE; BOX 175; ELLAVILLE, GA 31806. (#18410).

DOWNTOWN PAINT-UP - CLEANUP IN ELLAVILLE, GA. THE DOWNTOWN AREA WILL BE CLEANED. PAINTERS WILL DESIGN COLOR SCHEME COORDINATES FOR BUILDING STOREFRONTS IN DOWNTOWN AREA. STORE OWNERS ARE TO PROVIDE PAINT AND MANPOWER. (LOCAL). NANCY M YOUNG, CHAIRMAN; SCHLEY COUNTY BICENTENNIAL COMMITTEE; BOX 175; ELLAVILLE, GA 31806. (#18408).

FOLK HISTORY OF SCHLEY COUNTY - ELLAVILLE, GA. A COLLECTION OF BITS OF HISTORY OF SCHLEY COUNTY; THE BOOK WILL BE AVAILABLE TO SCHLEY COUNTY CITIZENS. (LOCAL). NANCY M YOUNG, CHAIRMAN; SCHLEY COUNTY BICENTENNIAL COMMITTEE; BOX 175; ELLAVILLE, GA 31806. (#18405).

RECREATION FACILITIES - ELLAVILLE, GA. PLANS ARE UNDERWAY TO BUILD TENNIS COURTS AND TO IMPROVE RECREATION FACILITIES AT THE OLD HIGH SCHOOL GYM. (LOCAL). NANCY M YOUNG, CHAIRMAN; SCHLEY COUNTY BICENTENNIAL COMMITTEE; BOX 175; ELLAVILLE, GA 31806. (#18411).

ELLAVILLE — CONTINUED

ZONING PROJECT - ELLAVILLE, GA. COMMITTEE WILL WORK WITH CITY OFFICIALS ON FUTURE PLANS FOR ZONING IN ELLAVILLE. (LOCAL). NANCY M YOUNG, COMMITTEE CHAIRMAN; CITY OF ELLAVILLE; ELLAVILLE, GA 31806. (#18412).

APR 3, '76. BICENTENNIAL FESTIVAL - ARTS, CRAFTS, PARADE, BAR B QUE & SPEAKERS. FESTIVAL, PARADE AT CITY SQUARE. (LOCAL). NANCY M YOUNG, CHAIRMAN; SCHLEY COUNTY BICENTENNIAL COMMITTEE; ELLAVILLE, GA 31806. (#103747-8).

EPWORTH

JULY 3, '76. JULY 4TH CELEBRATION ON JULY 3RD. FESTIVAL. (LOCAL). RICHARD JABALEY, COORD; EPWORTH RURITAN CLUB; EPWORTH, GA 30541. (#103747-7).

FAYETTEVILLE

HISTORIC DRIVING TOUR OF FAYETTEVILLE, GEORGIA. PLANS ARE TO INITIATE A DRIVING TOUR SO THAT VISITORS MAY ENJOY THE HISTORIC SITES OF THE COUNTY. (ST-WIDE). ROBERT K PRICE, CHAIRMAN; FAYETTE COUNTY BICENT COMMISSION; 110 CEDAR PT; PEACHTREE CTY, GA 30269. (#8963).

HISTORY OF FAYETTE COUNTY, GEORGIA. A BOOK TO BE PUBLISHED DURING 1976 ON THE FOUNDING AND HISTORY OF FAYETTE COUNTY. (LOCAL). MRS CAROLYN CARY, PRESIDENT; FAYETTE COUNTY HISTORICAL SOCIETY; PO BOX 495; FAYETTEVILLE, GA 30214. (#8967).

RESTORATION OF TANDY KING HOUSE - FAYETTEVILLE, GA. RESTORATION OF FAYETTE COUNTY'S OLDEST DWELLING, THE TANDY KING HOUSE. (LOCAL). MRS CAROLYN CARY, PRESIDENT; FAYETTE COUNTY HISTORICAL SOCIETY; PO BOX 495; FAYETTEVILLE, GA 30214. (#8966).

SPEAKERS BUREAU OF FAYETTEVILLE, GEORGIA. ESTABLISH A SPEAKERS BUREAU TO PROVIDE BICENTENNIAL RELATED PROGRAMS TO ORGANIZATIONS AND CLUBS. (LOCAL). ROBERT K PRICE, CHAIRMAN; FAYETTE COUNTY BICENT COMMISSION; 110 CEDAR PT; PEACHTREE CTY, GA 30269. (#8960).

SPECIAL ART PROGRAM OF FAYETTEVILLE, GEORGIA. TO INITIATE AN ARTIST-IN-RESIDENCE PROGRAM IN FAYETTE CO SCHOOLS. (LOCAL). ROBERT K PRICE, CHAIRMAN; FAYETTE COUNTY BICENT COMMISSION; 110 CEDAR PT; PEACHTREE CTY, GA 30269. (#8965).

YATES APPLE ORCHARD MARKER, FAYETTEVILLE, GA. THE SITE OF ORIGINAL YATES APPLE ORCHARD WILL BE MARKED. (ST-WIDE). ROBERT K PRICE, CHAIRMAN; FAYETTE COUNTY BICENT COMMISSION; 110 CEDAR PT; PEACHTREE CY, GA 30269. (#8959).

FITZGERALD

FITZGERALD BICENTENNIAL FAIR IN GEORGIA. BICENTENNIAL FAIR WILL PROMOTE TOTAL SCHOOL INVOLVEMENT BY COORDINATING A SCHOOL & COMMUNITY PROJECT RELATED TO THE ANNUAL COMMUNITY PAGEANT. (LOCAL). PAUL D HUGHES, PRINCIPAL; FITZGERALD ELEMENTARY SCHOOL; FITZGERALD, GA 31750. (#16093). **ARBA GRANTEE.**

OCT 20 - 24, '76. FITZGERALD BICENTENNIAL FAIR. BICENTENNIAL FAIR WILL PROMOTE TOTAL SCHOOL INVOLVEMENT BY COORDINATING A SCHOOL & COMMUNITY PROJECT RELATED TO THE ANNUAL COMMUNITY PAGEANT. AT FITZGERALD ELEMENTARY SCHOOL, ALTAMAHA ST. (LOCAL). PAUL D HUGHES, PRINCIPAL; FITZGERALD ELEMENTARY SCHOOL; FITZGERALD, GA 31750. (#16093-1).

FLOVILLA

BICENTENNIAL MINI-PARK IN FLOVILLA, GEORGIA. FLOVILLA CITY PARK WILL CONSIST OF VARIOUS PIECES OF PLAY & PICNIC EQUIPMENT ON A NEWLY CLEARED & LANDSCAPED PLOT OF PROPERTY ALREADY OWNED BY THE CITY. (LOCAL). HON CHARLES T HUGGINS, JR, MAYOR; CITY OF FLOVILLA; BOX 578; FLOVILLA, GA 30216. (#16092). **ARBA GRANTEE.**

FOLKSTON

CHARLTON COUNTY/ST MARY'S RIVER CENTER IN GEORGIA. AN OLD STATION HOUSE WILL BE RELOCATED & RENOVATED AS A MUSEUM FACILITY WITH EXHIBITS DEPICTING EARLY HISTORY OF CHARLTON COUNTY & THE ST MARY'S RIVER. (LOCAL). VIRGINIA ALTMAN, EXEC DIRECTOR; CHARLTON COUNTY BICENTENNIAL COMMISSION; BOX 98; FOLKSTON, GA 31537. (#16099). **ARBA GRANTEE.**

CHARLTON MEMORIAL HOSPITAL, FOLKSTON, GA. THE OPENING CELEBRATION FOR A NEW HOSPITAL IN CHARLTON COUNTY. (LOCAL). THEO DINKINS, CHAIRMAN; CHARLTON COUNTY HOSPITAL AUTHORITY; 512 W MAIN ST; FOLKSTON, GA 31537. (#12556).

FUND RAISING CAMPAIGN IN FOLKSTON, GA. THE FUND RAISING PROJECT IS FOR THE BENEFIT OF THE NEW HOSPITAL. (LOCAL). THEO DINKINS, CHAIRMAN; CHARLTON COUNTY HOSPITAL AUTHORITY - CHARLTON MEMORIAL HOSPITAL; 512 MAIN ST; FOLKSTON, GA 31537. (#12555).

OKEFENOKEE FESTIVAL 1975 - FOLKSTON, GA. A YEARLY EVENT TO ACCENT THE OKEFENOKEE SWAMP NATIONAL WILDLIFE REFUGE AT FOLKSTON, GA. (LOCAL). MRS JOAN AYERS, CHAIRMAN; FOLKSTON-CHARLTON COUNTY CHAMBER OF COMMERCE; 100 3RD ST; FOLKSTON, GA 31537. (#11329).

RESTORATION PLAN FOR DOWNTOWN FOLKSTON, GA. RENOVATION AND OVERALL BEAUTIFICATION OF DOWNTOWN FOLKSTON WILL REFLECT THE MIDDLE AND LATE 1800'S. (LOCAL). VIRGINIA ALTMAN, EXEC DIRECTOR; STAY AND SEE AMERICA IN GEORGIA; 100 3RD ST; FOLKSTON, GA 31537. (#11333).

SELF-GUIDED TOUR BOOKLET - PROJ OF FOLKSTON, GA. A HISTORY OF CHARLTON COUNTY INCLUDING MAP, POINTS OF INTEREST AND RECREATIONAL FACILITIES. (LOCAL). VIRGINIA ALTMAN, EXEC DIRECTOR; CHARLTON COUNTY BICENTENNIAL COMMISSION; 100 3RD ST; FOLKSTON, GA 31537. (#11331).

FEB 14, '76. FREEDOM PARK OPENING. PROJECT WILL BE A PERMANENT OUTDOOR FLAG DISPLAY ON SITE OF CHARLTON-ST MARYS RIVER CENTER. AT FREEDOM PARK. (LOCAL). VIRGINIA ALTMAN; CHARLTON COUNTY BICENTENNIAL COMMISSION; 100 3RD ST; FOLKSTON, GA 31537. (#11334-1).

FEB 21, '76. CHARLTON-ST MARYS RIVER CENTER OPENING FESTIVAL. OPENING OF CENTER WILL BE MARKED BY AN EXHIBIT OF POINTS OF INTEREST IN CHARLTON COUNTY INCLUDING: OLE KINGS ROAD, TRADERS HILL AND OKEFENOKEE. AT CHARLTON-ST MARYS RIVER CENTER. (LOCAL). VIRGINIA ALTMAN; CHARLTON COUNTY BICENTENNIAL COMMISSION; 100 3RD ST; FOLKSTON, GA 31537. (#11330-1).

FEB 22, '76. OPENING CELEBRATION OF TRADERS HILL. A CELEBRATION IN HONOR OF THE OPENING OF TRADERS HILL RECREATION AREA AND HISTORIC SITE. AT TRADERS HILL. (LOCAL). VIRGINIA ALTMAN; CHARLTON COUNTY BICENTENNIAL COMMISSION; 100 3RD ST; FOLKSTON, GA 31537. (#11332-1).

JULY 4 - 5, '76. HERITAGE DAY. FESTIVAL. (LOCAL). VIRGINIA ALTMAN, DIR; CHARLTON COUNTY BICENTENNIAL COMMISSION; BOX 98; FOLKSTON, GA 31537. (#16099-1).

JULY 4 - 5, '77. JULY FESTIVAL. FESTIVAL. (LOCAL). VIRGINIA ALTMAN, DIR; CHARLTON COUNTY BICENTENNIAL COMMISSION; BOX 98; FOLKSTON, GA 31537. (#16099-2).

SEPT 2 - 3, '77. FERRYBOAT PICNIC & FUND-RAISING FESTIVAL. FESTIVAL. (LOCAL). VIRGINIA ALTMAN, DIR; CHARLTON COUNTY BICENTENNIAL COMMISSION; BOX 98; FOLKSTON, GA 31537. (#16099-3).

FOREST PARK

BICENTENNIAL MINI PARKS - PROJ OF FOREST PARK, GA. LANDSCAPING AREAS OWNED BY CITY AND ASSIGNING BICENTENNIAL NAMES, PREPARING SOME AREAS AS NATURE STUDY AREAS WHICH WILL BE AVAILABLE TO STUDENTS IN NEAR-BY SCHOOLS. (LOCAL). ANGELA COLE, CHAIRWOMAN; FOREST PARK BICENT COMMITTEE; 745 FOREST PARKWAY; FOREST PARK, GA 30050. (#9815).

FLAG ETIQUETTE WORKSHOPS - PROJ OF FOREST PARK, GA. WORKSHOP FOR RESIDENTS AND MERCHANTS ON HISTORY AND PROPER DISPLAY OF U S FLAG TO ENCOURAGE DISPLAY OF FLAG. WILL INCLUDE DEMONSTRATION AND FILMS. (LOCAL). ANGELA COLE, CHAIRWOMAN; FOREST PARK BICENT COMMITTEE; 745 FOREST PARKWAY; FOREST PARK, GA 30050. (#9819).

FOREST PARK COLONIAL BAND PROJ OF FOREST PARK, GA. BAND COMPOSED OF FOREST PARK RESIDENTS, WITH UNIFORMS APPROPRIATE TO REVOLUTIONARY ERA, PLANNED AS CONTINUING COMMUNITY ACTIVITY. (LOCAL). TOM GUARDALA, DIRECTOR; JAYCEES; 803 MIDDLEBROOK DR; FOREST PARK, GA 30050. (#9817).

HISTORIC MURALS - PROJ OF FOREST PARK, GA. MURALS DEPICTING LOCAL HISTORY TO BE PAINTED ON OLDER BUSINESS BUILDINGS TO EMPHASIZE THE CITY'S PAST AND ENHANCE THE BEAUTY OF THE AREA. (LOCAL). ANGELA COLE, CHAIRWOMAN; FOREST PARK BICENT COMMITTEE; 702 BROOKWOOD DR; FOREST PARK, GA 30050. (#9814).

HISTORY OF FOREST PARK, GA. A WRITTEN HISTORY IN BOOK FORM AS A RESULT OF COURSES INCLUDED IN CURRICULUM OF FOREST PARK SENIOR HIGH SCHOOL. STUDENTS WILL RESEARCH MATERIALS UNDER THE DIRECTION OF QUALIFIED ADULTS. (LOCAL). ANGELA COLE, CHAIRWOMAN; FOREST PARK BICENT COMMITTEE; 745 FOREST PARKWAY; FOREST PARK, GA 30050. (#9818).

QUICK STATION MUSEUM IN FOREST PARK, GEORGIA. COLLECTING PICTURES AND DOCUMENTS OF FOREST PARK HISTORY TO BE DISPLAYED IN RESTORED RAILROAD VEHICLE; THIS MATERIAL WILL FORM THE BASIS OF A PERMANENT CITY ARCHIVES. (LOCAL). ANGELA COLE, CHAIRWOMAN; FOREST PARK BICENTENNIAL COMMITTEE; 702 BROOKWOOD DR; FOREST PARK, GA 30050. (#9812).

APR 11 - 25, '76. FREEDOM OF RELIGION ESSAYS. ESSAY CONTEST CONDUCTED THROUGH THE CHURCHES IN THE AREA, INCLUDES ENTRANTS FROM GRADE FOUR THROUGH ADULTS. THEME OF ESSAYS CENTERED AROUND ROLE OF RELIGION IN SHAPING THE CHARACTER OF OUR NATION. (LOCAL). ANGELA COLE; FOREST PARK BICENTENNIAL COMMITTEE; 702 BROOKWOOD DR; FOREST PARK, GA 30050. (#9813-1).

FORT BENNING

'ACTION 75' - A CHALLENGE TO IMPROVE OURSELVES NOW. A VOLUNTARY PROGRAM OF ACTION INVOLVING SMALL GROUP PARTICIPATION IN ACTIVITIES STRESSING INDIVIDUAL IMPROVEMENT IN ONE OF FOUR AREAS OF INTEREST: PHYSICAL, MENTAL, SPIRITUAL & SOCIAL. (LOCAL). MAJOR CHARLES D WOODSON, COORDINATOR; FORT BENNING BICENTENNIAL PROJECT AGENCY; US ARMY INFANTRY CENTER; FORT BENNING, GA 31905. (#5625).

JULY 4, '75. AWARDS CEREMONY FOR SELF-IMPROVEMENT PROJ BY US ARMY. AWARD. (LOCAL). MAJOR CHARLES D WOODSON; FORT BENNING BICENTENNIAL PROJECT AGENCY; US ARMY INFANTRY CENTER; FORT BENNING, GA 31905. (#5625-501).

JAN 15, '76. AWARDS CEREMONY FOR SELF-IMPROVEMENT PROJ BY US ARMY. AWARD. (LOCAL). MAJOR CHARLES D WOODSON; FORT BENNING BICENTENNIAL PROJECT AGENCY; US ARMY INFANTRY CENTER; FORT BENNING, GA 31905. (#5625-502).

JULY 4, '76. AWARDS CEREMONY FOR SELF-IMPROVEMENT PROJ BY US ARMY. AWARD. (LOCAL). MAJOR CHARLES D WOODSON; FORT BENNING BICENTENNIAL PROJECT AGENCY; US ARMY INFANTRY CENTER; FORT BENNING, GA 31905. (#5625-503).

FORT GAINES

DILL HOUSE RESTORATION - FT GAINES, GA. THE DILL HOUSE IS IN THE NATIONAL REGISTER. PLANS ARE TO MAKE IT INTO A SHOW PLACE AND INN. (LOCAL). MRS H I MCKISSACK, CHAIRMAN; CLAY COUNTY BICENTENNIAL COMMISSION; 309 E HARTFORD RD; FT GAINES, GA 31751. (#17855).

LIGHTED FOUNTAIN PARK - FT GAINES, GA. THE PARK IS AT THE ENTRANCE TO THE BUSINESS DISTRICT AND IT CAN BE ENJOYED BY NURSING HOME RESIDENTS AND HOSPITAL PATIENTS. (LOCAL). MRS HERB MCKISSACK, CHAIRPERSON; CLAY COUNTY BICENTENNIAL COMMISSION; 309 E HARTFORD RD; FT GAINES GA 31751. (#17856). **ARBA GRANTEE.**

JULY 4, '75. FIRECRACKER FESTIVAL. ANNUAL EVENT INCLUDING FISHING RODEO, CHICKEN-Q, BASEBALL, HISTORICAL TOUR, ARTS-CRAFTS SHOW, STREET DANCE, FIREWORKS DISPLAY. AT DIRECTIONAL SIGNS-WITH TIME. (LOCAL). JANE M MCKISSACK; CLAY COUNTY BICENT COMMISSION & LIONS CLUB; 309 E HARTFORD RD; FT GAINES, GA 31751. (#4496-2).

NOV 22, '75. ARTS & CRAFTS CHRISTMAS FAIR. FAIR AT CORNELIA CLUB HOUSE BLUFF ST, SCOUT HSE & PIONEER SETTLEMENT. (LOCAL). MRS D T SMITH; FT GAINES HOME & GARDEN CLUB; FORT GAINES, GA 31751. (#50015-1).

JULY 4 - 5, '76. 2-DAY FIRECRACKER FESTIVAL. FESTIVAL. (LOCAL). RUSTY COOPER, PRES; LIONS CLUB & CLAY COUNTY BICENTENNIAL COMMITTEE; FORT GAINES, GA 31751. (#103463-1).

FORT GORDON

U S ARMY SIGNAL SCHOOL MOBILE DISPLAY IN GA. EXHIBIT OF U S ARMY SIGNAL CENTER. (LOCAL). ROBERT E SMITH, DIRECTOR; U S ARMY SIGNAL CENTER; FT GORDON, GA 30905. (#30979).

U S ARMY SIGNAL SCHOOL MOBILE DISPLAY IN GA. A MODULAR TRANSPORTABLE MUSEUM EXHIBIT TRACING THE DEVELOPMENT OF U S ARMY SIGNAL CORPS AND ITS CONTRIBUTIONS TO THE NATION. (REGN'L). SSG ROBERT E SMITH, PROJECT OFFICER; US ARMY SIGNAL CENTER AND FORT GORDON, ATZHDPT-P; FORT GORDON, GA 30905. (#31033).

FORT VALLEY

ANNUAL COMMUNITY CALENDAR - FORT VALLEY, GA. ANNUAL CALENDAR FEATURES SKETCHES OF HISTORICAL HOUSES IN THE AREA. (LOCAL). JACK EVANS, PRESIDENT; JAILHOUSE ALLEY ART CENTER; 143 OAK ST; FORT VALLEY, GA 31030. (#24400).

BICENTENNIAL MUSICAL PROGRAM. MEDLEY OF TUNES BY LYCOMING CHOIR OF LYCOMING COLLEGE, PA. (LOCAL). JANE BUSSEY, DIRECTOR; PEACH COUNTY BICENTENNIAL COMMITTEE; CENTRAL AVE; FORT VALLEY, GA 31030. (#107290-4).

BICENTENNIAL PLANTING - FORT VALLEY, GA. PLANTING OF RED, WHITE AND BLUE FLOWERS IN LOCAL GARDENS. (LOCAL). MRS ALTMAN, PRESIDENT; PEACHLAND GARDEN COUNCIL; HARDEMAN AVE; FORT VALLEY, GA 31030. (#24403).

BICENTENNIAL TREES - FORT VALLEY, GA. PLANT BICENTENNIAL TREES AROUND THE COUNTY. (LOCAL). MRS L W SMITH, CHAIRMAN; PEACH COUNTY BICENTENNIAL COMMITTEE; TROUTMAN AVE; FORT VALLEY, GA 31030. (#24402).

BLACK COLLEGE HALL OF FAME, FORT VALLEY, GA. A PARK & MUSEUM COMMEMORATING ACHIEVEMENTS OF BLACK COLLEGES & UNIVERSITIES IN AMERICA. (REGN'L). ROBERT W GREEN, PROFESSOR OF EDUCATION; FORT VALLEY STATE COLLEGE; FORT VALLEY, GA 31030. (#17145). **ARBA GRANTEE.**

FOX VALLEY HORSE TRIALS & DRESSAGE SHOW. ANNUAL NATIONAL EVENT WITH OLYMPIC COMPETITORS. (REGN'L). ADAIR DUKE, COORDINATOR; KAY COMMUNITY TRAINING CENTER; 210 ALLEN ST; FORT VALLEY, GA 31030. (#107290-2).

LOG CABIN SCHOOL PROJ OF FT VALLEY STATE COLLEGE. RECONSTRUCTION OF A ONE ROOM LOG CABIN SCHOOLHOUSE WITH AN EXHIBITION OF DOCUMENTS DEPICTING BLACK EDUCATION PAST & PRESENT. (LOCAL). ROBERT W GREEN, CHAIRMAN; FT VALLEY STATE COLLEGE BICENTENNIAL PLANNING COMMITTEE; PO BOX 155; FT VALLEY, GA 31030. (#6648).

LYCEUM FEATURES 1976, ARTS AT FT VALLEY COL, GA. A CULTURAL PROGRAM OF MUSIC, DRAMA AND DANCE BY NATIONALLY FAMOUS ARTISTS PRESENTED QUARTERLY. (LOCAL). ROBERT W GREEN, CHAIRMAN; FT VALLEY STATE COLLEGE BICENTENNIAL PLANNING COMMITTEE; PO BOX 155; FT VALLEY, GA 31030. (#6653).

OUR INDIANS AND INDIAN TRIBES - FORT VALLEY, GA. COMPILE HISTORY OF THE CREEKS IN THIS AREA AND RETRACE MAJOR

FORT VALLEY — CONTINUED

TRADING PATH. (LOCAL). FLORENCE BALES, COORDINATOR; PEACH COUNTY BICENTENNIAL COMMITTEE; 324 PERSONS ST; FORT VALLEY, GA 31030. (#24399).

PARKS & GARDENS PROJ OF FT VALLEY ST COLLEGE, GA. GENERAL CAMPUS FACE LIFTING, INSTALLATION OF SMALL GARDENS AND SPOTS OF BEAUTY TO CELEBRATE THE BICENTENNIAL. (LOCAL). ROBERT W GREEN, CHAIRMAN; FT VALLEY STATE COLLEGE BICENTENNIAL PLANNING COMMITTEE; PO BOX 155; FT VALLEY, GA 31030. (#6647). **(??).**

RESTORATION OF JAMES EVERETTE HOME - GA. THE 19TH CENTURY HOME OF THE FOUNDER OF FORT VALLEY, JAMES EVERETTE, WILL BE RESTORED AND USED A COMMUNITY CENTER. (LOCAL). FLORENCE BALES, COORDINATOR; PEACH COUNTY BICENTENNIAL COMMITTEE; 324 PERSONS ST; FORT VALLEY, GA 31030. (#24398).

SPECIAL BICENTENNIAL DRILL TEAM AT FT VALLEY COL. ROTC COLOR GUARD AND DRILL TEAM IN REVOLUTIONARY COSTUMES TO OPEN ALL MAJOR EVENTS IN 1976. (LOCAL). ROBERT W GREEN, CHAIRMAN; FT VALLEY STATE COLLEGE BICENTENNIAL PLANNING COMMITTEE; PO BOX 155; FT VALLEY, GA 31030. (#6657).

1776 HOME GUARD - FORT VALLEY, GA. AUTHENTIC COSTUMED GROUP FOR FLAG RAISINGS AND OTHER EVENTS. (LOCAL). H E BRYANT, LEADER; BOY SCOUTS; 813 S MACON ST; FORT VALLEY, GA 31030. (#24401).

MAY 1, '75. BICENTENNIAL FESTIVAL DAYS AT FT VALLEY COLLEGE. A DAY OF RACES, PARADES, BAND CONTESTS, ARTS & CRAFTS AND DISPLAYS TO CELEBRATE THE BICENTENNIAL. (LOCAL). ROBERT W GREEN, CHAIRMAN; FT VALLEY STATE COLLEGE BICENTENNIAL PLANNING COMMITTEE; PO BOX 155; FT VALLEY, GA 31030. (#6646-1).

NOV 5 - 8, '75. HOMECOMING ACTIVITIES '76 AT FT VALLEY COLLEGE. PARADE, FOOTBALL GAME, ASSEMBLY & DANCE DEDICATED TO THE BICENTENNIAL CELEBRATION. (LOCAL). ROBERT W GREEN, CHMN; FT VALLEY STATE COLLEGE BICENTENNIAL PLANNING COMMITTEE; PO BOX 155; FT VALLEY, GA 31030. (#6655-1).

DEC 12 - 19, '75. EBONY TREE & THE SPIRIT OF CHRISTMAS. SLIDE AND SOUND PRODUCTION FOR CHILDREN PRESENTING THE BLACK EXPERIENCE THROUGH THE STORY OF A BLACK TREE. ALSO: FILM/SLIDES. AT COLLEGE AUDITORIUM. (LOCAL). ROBERT W GREEN, CHAIRMAN; FT VALLEY STATE COLLEGE BICENTENNIAL PLANNING COMMITTEE; PO BOX 155; FT VALLEY, GA 31030. (#6654-1).

FEB 1 - 7, '76. BICENTENNIAL BLACK HISTORY WEEK. ONE WEEK OF PROGRAMS AND ACTIVITIES HIGHLIGHTING THE ACHIEVEMENTS OF BLACKS IN AMERICA. AT COLLEGE AUDITORIUM. (LOCAL). ROBERT W GREEN, CHAIRMAN; FT VALLEY STATE COLLEGE BICENTENNIAL PLANNING COMMITTEE; PO BOX 155; FT VALLEY, GA 31030. (#6652-1).

FEB 28 - MAR 3, '76. CREEK INDIAN EXHIBIT & AMERICAN HERITAGE EXHIBIT. ARTIFACTS, DIAGRAMS & PROJECTS OF INDIANS IN THIS AREA. AT THOMAS PUBLIC LIBRARY, PERSONS ST, FT VALLEY, GA. (LOCAL). JEAN MCKENZIE, LIBRARIAN; FORT VALLEY MIDDLE SCHOOL; CHAMLEE DR; FORT VALLEY, GA 31030. (#107290-1).

MAR 3 - 4, '76. STUDENT ESSAY CONTEST. HIGH SCHOOL AND COLLEGE STUDENTS WILL COMPETE IN AN ESSAY CONTEST ON EDUCATION WITH A BLACK FOCUS. AT ACADEMIC AUDITORIUM. (LOCAL). ROBERT W GREEN, CHAIRMAN; FT VALLEY STATE COLLEGE BICENTENNIAL PLANNING COMMITTEE; PO BOX 155; FT VALLEY, GA 31030. (#6649-1).

APR 28 - 30, '76. MUSIC & DRAMA PRODUCTION. AN ORIGINAL DRAMATIC PRODUCTION HIGHLIGHTING THE BLACK EXPERIENCE WITH AN EPILOGUE ON THE FUTURE. AT ACADEMIC AUDITORIUM. (LOCAL). ROBERT W GREEN, CHAIRMAN; FT VALLEY STATE COLLEGE BICENTENNIAL PLANNING COMMITTEE; PO BOX 155; FT VALLEY, GA 31030. (#6651-1).

MAY 2 - 5, '76. FINE ARTS FESTIVAL. AN EXHIBITION OF PAINTINGS & SCULPTURE WILL COMPLEMENT THE MUSIC & DRAMA FESTIVAL IN CELEBRATION OF THE BICENTENNIAL. AT COLLEGE AUDITORIUM. (LOCAL). ROBERT W GREEN, CHAIRMAN; FT VALLEY STATE COLLEGE BICENTENNIAL PLANNING COMMITTEE; PO BOX 155; FT VALLEY, GA 31030. (#6656-1).

JUNE 23 - 25, '76. CONGRESS ON EDUCATION. ANNUAL CONGRESS ON BLACK EDUCATION PAST, PRESENT AND FUTURE. AT COLLEGE AUDITORIUM. (LOCAL). ROBERT W GREEN, CHAIRMAN; FT VALLEY STATE COLLEGE BICENTENNIAL PLANNING COMMITTEE; PO BOX 155; FT VALLEY, GA 31030. (#6650-1).

JUNE 24, '76. BARBER SHOP MUSICAL. LIVE PERFORMANCE. (LOCAL). FLETCHER BARNES, COORD; SOCIETY FOR PRESERVATION OF BARBERSHOP QUARTETS; FORREST DR; FORT VALLEY, GA 31030. (#107290-3).

JULY 4, '76. JULY 4TH FIELD DAY. OLD-TIME FIELD TRIALS, PARADE, BARBECUE, FIREWORKS, ETC. (LOCAL). FLORENCE BALES, COORD; PEACH COUNTY BICENTENNIAL COMMITTEE; 324 PERSONS ST; FORT VALLEY, GA 31030. (#107290-6).

JULY 5, '76. THE RED, WHITE & BLUE: HISTORICAL DRESS REVIEW. COMPETITION, EXHIBIT. (LOCAL). ROSE LATIMER, COORD; 4-H CLUB; EVERETT SQUARE; FORT VALLEY, GA 31030. (#107290-5).

JULY 5, '76. 1776 BAKE-OFF: RECIPE CONTEST USING OLD RECIPES. COMPETITION. (LOCAL). ROSE LATIMER, COORD; FORT VALLEY 4-H CLUB; EVERETT SQ; FORT VALLEY, GA 31030. (#107290-7).

NOV 13 - 14, '76. ANNUAL CAMELLIA SHOW WITH BICENTENNIAL THEME. COMPETITION, EXHIBIT AT NO PICNIC FACILITIES. (REGN'L). MILTON BROWN, PRESIDENT; AMERICAN CAMELLIA SOCIETY; HWY 49S, BOX 212; FORT VALLEY, GA 31030. (#107290-8).

FRANKLIN

HEARD COUNTY BICENTENNIAL OBSERVANCE, GA. A COUNTY WIDE OBSERVANCE DESIGNED FOR THE COUNTY'S ENTIRE POPULATION, INCLUDED IN THE OBSERVANCE WILL BE THE DEVELOPMENT OF TOWN & COMMUNITY HISTORIES. (LOCAL). LOUIS E LONG, PRESIDENT; HEARD COUNTY LIONS CLUB; FRANKLIN, GA 30217. (#22300). **ARBA GRANTEE.**

NOV 11, '75 - JULY 4, '76. 4 FLAG DAYS. EXHIBIT. (LOCAL). LOUIS E LONG, PRESIDENT; HEARD COUNTY LIONS CLUB; FRANKLIN, GA 30217. (#22300-2).

NOV '75 - MAY '76. ESSAY CONTEST IN THE SCHOOLS. COMPETITION. (LOCAL). LOUIS E LONG, PRESIDENT; HEARD COUNTY LIONS CLUB; FRANKLIN, GA 30217. (#22300-1).

MAR '76. BICENTENNIAL OBSERVANCES IN COUNTY CHURCHES. CEREMONY. (LOCAL). LOUIS E LONG, PRESIDENT; HEARD COUNTY LIONS CLUB; FRANKLIN, GA 30217. (#22300-3).

JULY 3, '76. COUNTY-WIDE CELEBRATION OF NATION'S BIRTHDAY. FESTIVAL. (LOCAL). LOUIS E LONG, PRESIDENT; HEARD COUNTY LIONS CLUB; FRANKLIN, GA 30217. (#22300-4).

FT GILLEN

MAY 14 - 16, '76. BOY SCOUT BICENTENNIAL ENCAMPMENT (ATLANTA AREA COUNCIL). LIVE PERFORMANCE AT FT GILLEN AIRFIELD. (LOCAL). COL WILLIAM W LEWIS; ATLANTA AREA BOY SCOUT COUNCIL; HQ FT MCPHERSON; ATLANTA, GA 30330. (#200012-68).

FT MC PHERSON

BICENTENNIAL EXHIBIT - FT MC PHERSON, GA. A PORTABLE EXHIBIT WITH 3 SLIDE/SOUND PROGRAMS. (LOCAL). CAPT DONALD P KIRCHOFFNER; FORT MC PHERSON AFKZ-10; FT MC PHERSON, GA 30330. (#31716).

HISTORICAL PROPERTIES RECORDS - MC PHERSON, GA. DEVELOPMENT OF 2 FT MC PHERSON REAL PROPERTY BOOKS CONSISTING OF MATERIAL DATING BACK TO 1885 WHEN LAND WAS FIRST PURCHASED FOR MILITARY RESERVATION. (LOCAL). CAPT DONALD P KIRCHOFFNER; FORT MC PHERSON AFZK-10; FT MC PHERSON, GA 30330. (#31714).

PRESERVATION & DESIGNATION OF HISTORICAL SITES-GA. PRESERVATION OF SITES ON POST AS NATIONAL HISTORIC SITES. (LOCAL). CAPT DONALD P KIRCHOFFNER; FORT MC PHERSON AFZK-10; FT MC PHERSON, GA 30330. (#31717).

'200 YEARS OF READINESS' PAGEANT - GA. NOSTALGIC MUSIC PRESENTATION IN SONGS OF SUCCESSIVE GENERATIONS OF SOLDIERS OVER THE ARMY'S 200 YEARS. (LOCAL). CAPT DONALD P KIROHOFFNER; FORT MC PHERSON AFZK-10; FT MC PHERSON, GA 30330. (#31715).

JUNE 13, '75. FORT MCPHERSON/HDQ/FORSCOM ARMY'S 200TH BIRTHDAY OPEN HOUSE. MILITARY FAIR, FAMILY PICNIC, DISPLAYS AND ATHLETIC EVENTS. AT FORT MCPHERSON. (LOCAL). LTC JOHN HOLECEK, COORD; FORT MCPHERSON - U S ARMY; ATLANTA, GA 30330. (#200012-2).

JUNE 14, '76. ARMY BICENTENNIAL BIRTHDAY. CEREMONY, LIVE PERFORMANCE AT FT MCPHERSON; HEDEKIN FIELD; POST THEATER; OFFICER CLUB. (LOCAL). CPT ROY W TURGEON; HQ FT MCPHERSON, GA; POST PUB AFFAIRS OFFICE; ATLANTA, GA 30330. (#200012-69).

FT OGLETHORPE

BANDSTAND RESTORATION IN FT OGLETHORPE, GA. RESTORE & PRESERVE THE BANDSTAND ON THE PARADE GROUND TO THE PERIOD WHEN THE MILITARY POST OF FT OGLETHORPE WAS ACTIVE. (LOCAL). BECKY MCGREGOR, CHAIRPERSON; FT OGLETHORPE PRESERVATION SOCIETY; 205 BARNHARDT CIRCLE; FT OGLETHORPE, GA 30742. (#14096). **ARBA GRANTEE.**

BICENTENNIAL SPARKLE DAYS OF FT OGLETHORPE, GA. CLEANUP OF ROADSIDES AND VACANT LOTS THROUGHOUT THE CITY. (LOCAL). W G GUTHRIE, CHAIRMAN; FT OGLETHORPE BICENTENNIAL COMMITTEE; PO BOX 5377; FT OGLETHORPE, GA 30741. (#14097).

FT OGLETHORPE PRESERVATION SOCIETY, GA. FORMATION OF LOCAL SOCIETY DEDICATED TO PRESERVATION OF THE UNIQUE HISTORY OF FORT OGLETHORPE. (LOCAL). DOYLE CAMP, DIRECTOR; FT OGLETHORPE CHAMBER OF COMMERCE; PO BOX 2026; FT OGLETHORPE, GA 30742. (#14098).

MAY 31, '75. CHATTANOOGA SYMPHONY SUMMER CONCERT SERIES. FREE OUTDOOR EVENING CONCERTS TO CELEBRATE THE BICENTENNIAL. AT CHICKAMAUGA PARK, ROUTE 2; FREE PARKING. (LOCAL). JANET MCENERNY, COORD; NATIONAL PARK SERVICE OF THE DEPARTMENT OF INTERIOR; 730 CHERRY ST; CHATTANOOGA, TN 37402. (#200045-213).

JUNE 29 - AUG 30, '75. HISTORICAL LECTURES BY DR. R. GOVAN. ALSO IN 1976. AS PART OF ITS BICENTENNIAL PROGRAM, CHICKAMAGUACHATTANOOGA NHP HAS ASKED DR GOVAN TO LECTURE ON VARIOUS ASPECTS OF AMERICAN HISTORY IN THIS AREA. AT POINT PARK LOOKOUT MT. (REGN'L). SUPT, CHICK-CHATT NMP; NATIONAL PARK SERVICE; P.O. BOX 2126; FT OGELTHORPE, GA 30742. (#6730-7).

JULY 5, '75. CHATTANOOGA SYMPHONY SUMMER CONCERT SERIES. FREE OUTDOOR EVENING CONCERTS TO CELEBRATE THE NATION'S BICENTENNIAL. AT CHICKAMAUGA PARK, ROUTE 2 FREE PARKING. (REGN'L). JANET MCENERNY, COORD; NATIONAL PARK SERVICE OF THE DEPARTMENT OF INTERIOR; 730 CHERRY ST; CHATTANOOGA, TN 37402. (#200045-215).

JULY 18 - 19, '75. NATL PK SVC 'A LITTLE LOOK AROUND' VISITS CHICKAMAGUA-CHATTANOOGA. THIS SHORT PROGRAM FEATURES ACTORS PORTRAYING FAMOUS AMERICANS OF THE PAST WHO'VE RETURNED TO SEE AMERICA'S GROWTH. (LOCAL). SUPT, CHICK-CHATT; NATIONAL PARK SERVICE; PO BOX 2126; FT OGELTHORPE, GA 30742. (#5653-220).

SEPT 6, '75. CHATTANOOGA SYMPHONY SUMMER CONCERT SERIES. FREE OUTDOOR EVENING CONCERTS TO CELEBRATE THE NATION'S BICENTENNIAL. AT CHICKAMAUGA PARK, ROUTE 2, FREE PARKING. (REGN'L). JANET MCENERNY, COORD; NATIONAL PARK SERVICE OF THE DEPARTMENT OF INTERIOR; 730 CHERRY ST; CHATTANOOGA, TN 37402. (#200045-219).

OCT 1 - 30, '75. BICENTENNIAL CONCERTS. LIVE PERFORMANCE AT WILDER TOWER IN CHICKAMAUGA NATL MILITARY PARK. (LOCAL). W G GUTHRIE, CHAIRMAN; FT OGLETHORPE BICENTENNIAL COMMITTEE; PO BOX 5377; FT OGLETHORPE, GA 30742. (#101699-1).

MAR 28, '76. EAST RIDGE CHORUS AND BAND AT CHICKAMAUGA-CHATTANOOGA NMP. LIVE PERFORMANCE AT WILDER TOWER, OUTDOORS. (REGN'L). CHICK-CHATT NMP; NATIONAL PARK SERVICE; P O BOX 2126; FT OGLETHORPE, GA 30742. (#6728-318).

MAY 29, '76. CHATTANOOGA SYMPHONY SUMMER CONCERT SERIES. FREE OUTDOOR EVENING CONCERTS TO CELEBRATE THE NATION'S BICENTENNIAL. AT CHICKAMAUGA PARK, ROUTE 2. (LOCAL). JANET MCENERNY, COORD; NATIONAL PARK SERVICE OF THE DEPARTMENT OF INTERIOR; 730 CHERRY ST; CHATTANOOGA, TN 37402. (#200045-253).

MAY 30 - SEPT 4, '76. SUMMER SYMPHONY IN THE PARK SERIES. PUBLIC IS INVITED TO BRING FOOD AND REFRESHMENTS FOR A COMMUNITYWIDE PICNIC; MUSIC WILL BE PERFORMED BY THE CHATTANOOGA SYMPHONY ORCHESTRA. SCHEDULED FOR MAY 29, JULY 2, AUG 14, AND SEPTEMBER 4. AT CHATTANOOGA-CHICKAMAUGA NATIONAL MILITARY PARK, FORT OGLETHORPE, GA. (REGN'L). ROBERT HENNING, DIRECTOR; CHATTANOOGA SYMPHONY ASSOCIATION; 819 BROAD ST; CHATTANOOGA, TN 37402. (#102028-1).

JUNE 29 - AUG 30, '76. HISTORICAL LECTURES BY DR. R. GOVAN. ALSO IN 1976. AS PART OF ITS BICENTENNIAL PROGRAM, CHICKAMAGUACHATTANOOGA NHP HAS ASKED DR GOVAN TO LECTURE ON VARIOUS ASPECTS OF AMERICAN HISTORY IN THIS AREA. AT POINT PARK LOOKOUT MT. (REGN'L). SUPT, CHICK-CHATT NMP; NATIONAL PARK SERVICE; P.O. BOX 2126; FT OGELTHORPE, GA 30742. (#6730-507).

JULY 2, '76. CHATTANOOGA SYMPHONY SUMMER CONCERT SERIES. FREE OUTDOOR EVENING CONCERTS TO CELEBRATE THE NATION'S BICENTENNIAL. AT CHICKAMAUGA PARK, ROUTE 2; FREE PARKING. (LOCAL). JANET MCENERNY, COORD; NATIONAL PARK SERVICE OF THE DEPARTMENT OF INTERIOR; 730 CHERRY ST; CHATTANOOGA, TN 37402. (#200045-249).

JULY 8, '76. NATL PK SVC 'PEOPLE OF 1776' PLAYS AT CHICKAMAUGA-CHATTANOOGA NMP. TRAVELING TROUPE WILL BRING VARIOUS ASPECTS OF COLONIAL LIFE (MILITARY LIFE, MUSIC, CRAFTS) TO VISITORS TO THIS NATIONAL PARK SERVICE AREA. (REGN'L). CHICKAMAGUA-CHATT NMP; NATIONAL PARK SERVICE; P. O. BOX 2126; FT OGELTHORPE, GA 30742. (#1469-6).

AUG 14, '76. CHATTANOOGA SYMPHONY SUMMER CONCERT SERIES. FREE OUTDOOR EVENING CONCERTS TO CELEBRATE THE BICENTENNIAL. AT CHICKAMAUGA PARK, ROUTE 2. (LOCAL). JANET MCENERNY, COORD; NATIONAL PARK SERVICE OF THE DEPARTMENT OF THE INTERIOR; 730 CHERRY ST; CHATTANOOGA, TN 37402. (#109048-7).

GAINESVILLE

BICENTENNIAL MINI PARKS - GAINESVILLE, GA. SELECTED AREAS IN THE CITY WILL BE SET APART FOR BEAUTIFICATION PROJECTS. (LOCAL). SYBIL MCRAY, CHAIRMAN; GAINESVILLE-HALL COUNTY BICENTENNIAL COMMITTEE; CITY HALL; GAINESVILLE, GA 30501. (#17375).

GAINESVILLE CULTURE AND RECREATION CENTER - GA. THIS CENTER WILL BE CONSTRUCTED FOR THE PERFORMING ARTS AND RECREATION. (LOCAL). JEAN MOONEY, EXECUTIVE SECRETARY; GAINESVILLE-HALL COUNTY BICENTENNIAL COMMITTEE; CITY HALL; GAINESVILLE, GA 30501. (#17377).

THE HERITAGE SPECIAL TRAIN - GAINESVILLE, GA. THIS TRAIN WILL EXHIBIT GEORGIA'S PIONEER LIFE, AGRICULTURE, FREEDOM STRUGGLE, FOLK ARTS & CRAFTS. (LOCAL). JEAN MOONEY, EXECUTIVE SECRETARY; GAINESVILLE-HALL COUNTY BICENTENNIAL COMMITTEE; CITY HALL; GAINESVILLE, GA 30501. (#17376).

MULE CAMP SPRINGS PARK, GAINESVILLE, GA. A BICENTENNIAL PARK DEPICTING THE HERITAGE & BEGINNING OF MULE CAMP SPRINGS, KNOWN NOW AS GAINESVILLE, WILL BE DEVELOPED. (LOCAL). JEAN MOONEY, PROJ COORDINATOR; CITY OF GAINESVILLE COMMUNITY DEVELOPMENT DEPARTMENT; CITY HALL, BROAD ST; GAINESVILLE, GA 30501. (#26961). **ARBA GRANTEE.**

RESTORATION OF BOWMAN-PIRKLE HOME, GAINESVILLE, GA. BOWMAN-PIRKLE HOME THAT CHEROKEE INDIANS HELPED BUILD WILL BE RELOCATED ON HERITAGE CORNER & RESTORED AS A MUSEUM. A BLACKSMITH AND TOURIST INFORMATION CENTER WILL ALSO BE INCLUDED IN THE COMPLEX. (LOCAL). CARLYLE COX, COORDINATOR; GAINESVILLE-HALL COUNTY BICENTENNIAL COMMITTEE; CITY HALL; GAINESVILLE, GA 30501. (#5064).

GAINESVILLE — CONTINUED

FEB 1, '75 - SEPT 1, '76. HISTORICAL MUSICALS, FEATURING GLEE CLUBS, BANDS & CHURCH CHOIRS. LIVE PERFORMANCE. (LOCAL). CARLYLE COX, COORDINATOR; GAINESVILLE-HALL COUNTY BICENTENNIAL COMMITTEE; CITY HALL; GAINESVILLE, GA 30501. (#5064-503).

MAR 22 - 30, '75. EGG ART SHOW OF HISTORICAL INTEREST AT POULTRY CAPITAL OF THE WORLD. EXHIBIT. (LOCAL). CARLYLE COX, COORDINATOR; GAINESVILLE-HALL COUNTY BICENTENNIAL COMMITTEE; CITY HALL; GAINESVILLE, GA 30501. (#5064-506).

MAR 30 - APR 1, '75. BICENTENNIAL FLOWER SHOW FEATURING FLOWERS AND BOOKS. EXHIBIT. (LOCAL). CARLYLE COX, COORDINATOR; GAINESVILLE-HALL COUNTY BICENTENNIAL COMMITTEE; CITY HALL; GAINESVILLE, GA 30501. (#5064-504).

JULY 4, '75. CHILDREN'S BICENTENNIAL PARADE, ALL SCHOOL CHILDREN INVOLVED. PARADE. (LOCAL). CARLYLE COX, COORDINATOR; GAINESVILLE-HALL COUNTY BICENTENNIAL COMMITTEE; CITY HALL; GAINESVILLE, GA 30501. (#5064-507).

NOV 28, '75. UNITED STATES ARMED FORCES BICENTENNIAL CARAVAN. THE CARAVAN IS COMPOSED OF EXHIBIT VANS FOR EACH BRANCH OF THE MILITARY SERVICE. THE THEME OF THE EXHIBITION IS 'HISTORY OF THE ARMED FORCES AND THEIR CONTRIBUTION TO THE NATION'. (LOCAL). MRS SUBIL MCRAY, CHMN; U S ARMED FORCES BICENTENNIAL EXHIBIT VANS PROJECT; CHESTATEE REGIONAL LIBRARY; GAINESVILLE, GA 30501. (#1775-202).

NOV 29, '75. SACRED HARP SONG FESTIVAL. LIVE PERFORMANCE. (LOCAL). SYBIL MCRAY, CHAIRMAN; GAINESVILLE-HALL COUNTY BICENTENNIAL COMMITTEE; CITY HALL; GAINESVILLE, GA 30501. (#103298-3).

JAN '76. GOSPEL SONG FESTIVAL. LIVE PERFORMANCE. (LOCAL). SYBIL MCRAY, CHAIRMAN; GAINESVILLE-HALL COUNTY BICENTENNIAL COMMITTEE; CITY HALL; GAINESVILLE, GA 30501. (#103298-8).

FEB '76. YOUTH CHORUS SONG FESTIVAL. LIVE PERFORMANCE. (LOCAL). SYBIL MCRAY, CHAIRMAN; GAINESVILLE-HALL COUNTY BICENTENNIAL COMMITTEE; CITY HALL; GAINESVILLE, GA 30501. (#103298-4).

MAR '76. 'QUEEN OF THE MOUNTAINS' HISTORICAL PAGEANT. HISTORY OF GAINESVILLE WITH CAST OF 100 PEOPLE. (LOCAL). SYBIL MCRAY, CHAIRMAN; GAINESVILLE-HALL COUNTY BICENTENNIAL COMMITTEE; CITY HALL; GAINESVILLE, GA 30501. (#103298-2).

JUNE 11 - 14, '76. HERITAGE SPECIAL - TRAIN TOUR. TRAVELING RAIL EXHIBIT EMPHASIZING COLONIAL & REVOLUTIONARY GEORGIA HISTORY, CRAFTS & LIFESTYLE OF GEORGIA COLONISTS. EXHIBITS WILL BE DISPLAYED WITH COMBINATION OF SIGHT & SOUND ACTIVITY. (ST-WIDE). RON HENRY, COORDINATOR; GEORGIA AGRIRAMA DEVELOPMENT AUTHORITY/ GEORGIA BICENTENNIAL; 8TH ST A I 75; TIFTON, GA 31794. (#7999-9).

JUNE 21 - SEPT 20, '76. HISTORICAL DRAMAS. PERFORMANCES BY TRAVELING CAST OF HIGH SCHOOL & COLLEGE STUDENTS. (LOCAL). SYBIL MCRAY, CHAIRMAN; GAINESVILLE-HALL COUNTY HISTORICAL SOCIETY; CITY HALL; GAINESVILLE, GA 30501. (#103298-7).

JULY 6, '76. 4TH OF JULY PARADE. HISTORICAL FLOATS, OLD CARS, HORSES, BANDS, BAR-B-QUE, FIREWORKS & FAMILY GAMES. (LOCAL). SYBIL MCRAY, CHAIRMAN; GAINESVILLE-HALL COUNTY BICENTENNIAL COMMITTEE; CITY HALL; GAINESVILLE, GA 30501. (#103298-5).

OCT '76. HARVEST FESTIVAL. BOOTHS & DISPLAYS SHOWING THE OLD WAYS OF MARKETING & LIVING. ALSO: CONESTOGA WAGON DISPLAY. (LOCAL). SYBIL MCRAY, CHAIRMAN; GAINESVILLE-HALL COUNTY BICENTENNIAL COMMITTEE; CITY HALL; GAINESVILLE, GA 30501. (#103298-1).

GAY

REGISTRY OF CEMETERIES IN MERIWETHER COUNTY, GA. LOCATION, IDENTIFICATION AND REGISTRATION OF PERSONS BURIED IN MERIWETHER COUNTY. (LOCAL). LUCY CLARK, CHAIRMAN; MERIWETHER HISTORICAL SOCIETY; 1776 OAKLAND RD; GAY, GA 30218. (#23343).

SEPT 27 - 28, '75. THE COTTON PICKIN' ANTIQUE & CRAFT FAIR. FAIR FEATURING LOCAL CRAFTSMEN & ORGANIZATIONS. (LOCAL). W F GAY, DIRECTOR; MR & MRS W F GAY; 1776 OAKLAND RD; GAY, GA 30218. (#200012-27).

GREENSBORO

COUNTY-WIDE CLEANUP, GREENE COUNTY, GA. SPRING CLEANUP PRIOR TO WAGON TRAIN ENCAMPMENT WITH BEFORE & AFTER PICTURES TO BE DISPLAYED IN LOCAL BANKS. PLANS WILL BE MADE TO DEVELOP AN ANNUAL COUNTY-WIDE SPRING CLEANUP. (LOCAL). W S ASHLEY, CHAIRMAN; GREENE COUNTY BICENTENNIAL ORGANIZATION; 204 E SOUTH ST; GREENSBORO, GA 30642. (#18730).

COURTHOUSE RENOVATION PROJECT, GREENSBORO, GA. RENOVATION OF THE GREENE COUNTY COURTHOUSE. (LOCAL). W S ASHLEY, COMMISSIONER; GREENE COUNTY BOARD OF COMMISSIONERS; GREENSBORO, GA 30642. (#18727).

GREENE COUNTY HISTORY BOOKS - GREENSBORO, GA. GREENE COUNTY HISTORY BOOKS WILL BE PROMOTED AND SOLD. THE BOOK WILL BE ENTITLED 'PRIDE IN OUR PAST'. (LOCAL). W S ASHLEY, CHAIRMAN; GREENE COUNTY BICENTENNIAL COMMITTEE; 206 E SOUTH ST; GREENSBORO, GA 30642. (#17379).

GREENSBORO CLEANUP PROJECT, GA. FORMATION OF GREENSBORO MERCHANTS COMMITTEE TO WORK ON BEAUTIFICATION OF THE CITY STREETS. (LOCAL). LY KENIMER, SUPERINTENDENT; GREENSBORO CITY COUNCIL; GREENSBORO, GA 30642. (#18729).

GREENSBORO HISTORICAL SOCIETY - GREENSBORO, GA. COLLECTION OF OLD PHOTOGRAPHS OF PLACES AND PEOPLE AND OTHER ARTIFACTS FOR THE GREENE COUNTY HISTORICAL MUSEUM. (LOCAL). CATHERINE CORNWELL, HISTORIAN; GREENE COUNTY HISTORICAL SOCIETY; PO BOX 6; GREENSBORO, GA 30642. (#19207).

LOOKING BACKWARD: DECORATIONS FOR COMMUNITIES - GA. RECALLING YULETIDE TRADITIONS ASSOCIATED WITH THE REVOLUTIONARY PERIOD; EMPHASIS IS ON PERIOD DECORATIONS & A COMMUNITY TREE ON THE COURTHOUSE LAWN. (LOCAL). W S ASHLEY, CHAIRMAN; GREENE COUNTY BICENTENNIAL COMMITTEE; GREENBORO, GA 30642. (#18406).

LOOKING FORWARD READING PROGRAM - GREENSBORO, GA. A SCHOOL READING DEVELOPMENT PROGRAM MANNED BY VOLUNTEERS. (LOCAL). FORD BOSTON, SUPERINTENDENT; GREENE COUNTY BOARD OF EDUCATION; 206 E SOUTH ST; GREENSBORO, GA 30642. (#19206).

REGISTRATION OF HISTORIC SITES - GREENSBORO, GA. THE GREENE COUNTY HISTORICAL SOCIETY WILL BE ORGANIZED TO DISCOVER HISTORIC SITES AND BUILDINGS AND REGISTER THEM WITH THE NATIONAL REGISTER OF HISTORIC PRESERVATION. (LOCAL). W S ASHLEY, CHAIRMAN; GREENE COUNTY BICENTENNIAL COMMITTEE; 206 E SOUTH ST; GREENSBORO, GA 30642. (#17378).

SUMMER READING PROGRAM, GREENSBORO, GA. SUMMER READING PROGRAM FOR CHILDREN WITH EMPHASIS ON STATE & COUNTY FACTS. (LOCAL). LUCILLE MASSEY, LIBRARIAN; GREENE COUNTY LIBRARY; GREENSBORO, GA 30642. (#18728).

APR 16, '76. 'PRIDE IN OUR PAST' ART CONTEST. ART CONTEST, DEALING WITH REVOLUTIONARY PERIOD THEMES, TO BE HELD FOR STUDENTS IN GREENE COUNTY SCHOOLS. (LOCAL). FORD BOSTON, SCHOOL SUPT; GREENE COUNTY BOARD OF EDUCATION; GREENSBORO, GA 30642. (#104019-4).

APR 18 - 19, '76. GREENE COUNTY PARTICIPATION IN NATIONAL WAGON TRAIN. FESTIVAL, TOUR. (LOCAL). W S ASHLEY, CHAIRMAN; GREENE COUNTY BICENTENNIAL COMMITTEE; 206 E SOUTH ST; GREENSBORO, GA 30642. (#103298-9).

GREENVILLE

HISTORICAL ACCOUNT OF MERIWETHER COUNTY, GA. BOOK DESCRIBING HISTORY OF MERIWETHER COUNTY. (LOCAL). MRS ROS ATKINSON, PRESIDENT; MERIWETHER HISTORICAL SOCIETY; 1776 OAKLAND RD; GAY, GA 30218. (#23345).

MERIWETHER COUNTY HIST SITES GUIDES - GA. BROCHURE, MAP AND MARKERS ON SEVEN HISTORICAL SITES IN COUNTY. (LOCAL). RICHARD R MCINTYRE, CHAIRMAN; MERIWETHER COUNTY BICENTENNIAL COMMITTEE; BOX 1776; MANCHESTER, GA 31816. (#23344).

RESTORATION OF HISTORICAL SITES, GA. RESTORATION OF TWO COVERED BRIDGES, COUNTY COURTHOUSE AND JAILHOUSE. (LOCAL). MRS W F GAY, PRESIDENT; MERIWETHER HISTORICAL SOCIETY; 1776 OAKLAND RD; GAY, GA 30218. (#23346).

GRIFFIN

AMERICAN FLAG PROGRAM OF GRIFFIN, GA. ENCOURAGE FLYING OF AMERICAN FLAG EVERY DAY AT ALL STORES, BUSINESSES, FACTORIES, HOMES,& SCHOOLS FROM NOW UNTIL JULY 30,1976. (LOCAL). DOUGLASS HOLLBERG, CHAIRMAN; GRIFFIN-SPALDING CO COMMUNITY BICENTENNIAL PLANNING COMMITTEE; 123 N HILL ST; GRIFFIN, GA 30223. (#4232).

BICENTENNIAL AWARENESS PROJECT OF GRIFFIN, GA. HIGH SCHOOL SOPHOMORES WILL ELECT BOY & GIRL FROM CLASS OF '76 TO SERVE ON LOCAL BICENTENNIAL COMMITTEE AND ADVISE ON PROJECTS. (LOCAL). DOUGLASS HOLLBERG, CHAIRMAN; GRIFFIN-SPALDING CO COMMUNITY BICENTENNIAL PLANNING COMMITTEE; 123 N HILL ST; GRIFFIN, GA 30223. (#4229).

BICENTENNIAL FIRE HYDRANT PROJECT -GRIFFIN, GA. CITY & COUNTY FIRE HYDRANTS TO BE PAINTED RED, WHITE & BLUE TO AROUSE CITIZEN AWARENESS OF THE BICENTENNIAL. (LOCAL). DOUGLASS HOLLBERG, CHAIRMAN; GRIFFIN-SPALDING COMMUNITY BICENTENNIAL PLANNING COMMITTEE; 123 N HILL ST; GRIFFIN, GA 30223. (#4240).

FOURTH OF JULY PROGRAMS OF GRIFFIN, GA. A CELEBRATION ENCOMPASSING ALL PHASES OF AMERICA'S HISTORY WILL BE ARRANGED BY THE COMMITTEE & THE JR CHAMBER OF COMMERCE. (LOCAL). DOUGLASS HOLLBERG, CHAIRMAN; GRIFFIN-SPALDING CO COMMUNITY BICENTENNIAL PLANNING COMMITTEE; 123 N HILL ST; GRIFFIN, GA 30223. (#4237).

GRIFFIN, GA, CITY HISTORY PROJECT. COMPLETION OF A HISTORY OF THE CITY OF GRIFFIN BY QUIMBY MELTON,JR & QUIMBY MELTON III. (LOCAL). DOUGLASS HOLLBERG, CHAIRMAN; GRIFFIN-SPALDING CO COMMUNITY BICENTENNIAL PLANNING COMMITTEE; 123 N HILL ST; GRIFFIN, GA 30223. (#4231).

HISTORICAL LIBRARY PROJECT - GRIFFIN, GA. A HISTORICAL LIBRARY IS PLANNED FOR THE RESTORED LEWIS-MILLS HOUSE WHICH WILL CONTAIN INFO. ABOUT THE BEGINNING OF THE NATION, STATE, CITY & COUNTY & WILL HELP ADVANCE STUDIES OF LOCAL HISTORY. (LOCAL). DOUGLASS HOLLBERG, CHAIRMAN; GRIFFIN-SPALDING CO COMMUNITY BICENTENNIAL PLANNING COMMITTEE; 123 N HILL ST; GRIFFIN, GA 30223. (#4238).

LAW & ORDER AWARENESS PROGRAM OF GRIFFIN, GA. PROVIDE SPECIAL SHOULDER & SLEEVE INSIGNIA FOR UNIFORMS OF ALL LAW ENFORCEMENT OFFICIALS TO MAKE CITIZENS AWARE OF THE IMPORTANCE OF LAW AND ORDER. (LOCAL). DOUGLASS HOLLBERG, CHAIRMAN; GRIFFIN-SPALDING CO COMMUNITY BICENTENNIAL PLANNING COMMITTEE; 123 N HILL ST; GRIFFIN, GA 30223. (#4230).

MARKING OF HISTORIC SITES IN GRIFFIN, GA. 10 HISTORICAL SITES IN THE AREA NOW LISTED IN THE NATIONAL REGISTER WILL BE MARKED & A PAMPHLET DESCRIBING THEM WILL BE PUBLISHED. (LOCAL). DOUGLASS HOLLBERG, CHAIRMAN; GRIFFIN-SPALDING CO COMMUNITY BICENTENNIAL PLANNING COMMITTEE; 123 N HILL ST; GRIFFIN, GA 30223. (#4239). **(??).**

RESTORATION OF LEWIS-MILLS HOUSE IN GRIFFIN, GA. RESTORATION OF HOME WHICH LINKS PAST & PRESENT. PRESERVATION OF HOUSE IN ITS NATURAL STATE IS OF THE ESSENCE. HOME WILL BE A MONUMENT FOR ALL GENERATIONS TO ENJOY. (ST-WIDE). M DOUGLAS HOLLBERG, PRESIDENT; GRIFFIN HISTORICAL AND PRESERVATION SOCIETY; 123 N HILL ST; GRIFFIN, GA 30223. (#729). **ARBA GRANTEE.**

MAR 17 - 21, '76. HERITAGE SPECIAL - TRAIN TOUR. TRAVELING RAIL EXHIBIT EMPHASIZING COLONIAL & REVOLUTIONARY GEORGIA HISTORY, CRAFTS & LIFESTYLE OF GEORGIA COLONISTS. EXHIBITS WILL BE DISPLAYED WITH COMBINATION OF SIGHT & SOUND ACTIVITY. (LOCAL). RON HENRY, COORDINATOR; GEORGIA AGRIRAMA DEVELOPMENT AUTHORITY/ GEORGIA BICENTENNIAL; 8TH ST A I 75; TIFTON, GA 31794. (#7999-14).

MAY 8, '76. CRIMSON CLOVER ART FESTIVAL USA - BICENTENNIAL. EXHIBITS ON BICENTENNIAL THEME, CONTEMPORARY VISUAL ARTS, COLONIAL CRAFTS, PHOTOGRAPHY-THEN & NOW, & SCULPTURE. AT COMMERCIAL BANK & TRUST CO, 110 S HILL ST. (LOCAL). MRS HELEN S BRYANT, PRES; GRIFFIN-SPALDING ART ASSOC; 904 MOCKINGBIRD LN; GRIFFIN, GA 30223. (#104006-1).

SEPT 16 - 22, '76. HERITAGE SPECIAL - TRAIN TOUR. TRAVELING RAIL EXHIBIT EMPHASIZING COLONIAL AND REVOLUTIONARY GEORGIA HISTORY, CRAFTS & LIFESTYLE OF GEORGIA COLONISTS. EXHIBITS WILL BE DISPLAYED WITH COMBINATION OF SIGHT & SOUND ACTIVITY. AT DEPOT. (LOCAL). RON HENRY, DIRECTOR; GEORGIA BICENTENNIAL COMMISSION; 1776 PEACHTREE NW, ROOM 520 S; ATLANTA, GA 30309. (#7999-33).

OCT 8, '76. STUDIO BAND OF THE UNITED STATES ARMY FIELD BAND. LIVE PERFORMANCE AT GRIFFIN-SPALDING HIGH SCHOOL AUDITORIUM. (LOCAL). M DOUGLAS HOLLBERG, COORD; GRIFFIN-SPALDING COMMUNITY BICENTENNIAL PLANNING COMMITTEE; 123 N HILL ST; GRIFFIN, GA 30223. (#109032-2).

NOV 13 - 16, '76. UNITED STATES ARMED FORCES BICENTENNIAL CARAVAN. CARAVAN IS COMPOSED OF EXHIBIT VANS FOR EACH MILITARY SERVICE. PROJECT THEME IS 'HISTORY OF THE ARMED FORCES & THEIR CONTRIBUTIONS TO THE NATION'. (LOCAL). DOUGLAS HOLLBERG; UNITED STATES ARMED FORCES BICENTENNIAL CARAVAN; PO BOX 255; GRIFFIN, GA 30223. (#1775-776).

HAMILTON

BEAUTIFICATION OF HAMILTON-ON-THE-SQUARE, GA. THE AREA WILL BE CLEARED OF TRASH AND WEEDS; FIRE HYDRANTS WILL BE PAINTED AND FLOWERS WILL BE PLANTED. (LOCAL). JAMES MCMICHAEL, PROJ CHAIRMAN; HARRIS COUNTY BICENTENNIAL COMMITTEE; PO BOX 283; HAMILTON, GA 31811. (#26962).

HISTORIC EDITION OF HARRIS COUNTY JOURNAL, GA. A SPECIAL EDITION OF THE HARRIS COUNTY JOURNAL, FEATURING HISTORICAL EVENTS & FACTS ABOUT HARRIS COUNTY & THE USA. (LOCAL). MICHAEL HICKERSON, PRESIDENT; HARRIS COUNTY JAYCEES; PO BOX 101; PING MOUNTAIN, GA 31822. (#25143).

OPERATION BEAUTIFICATION, HAMILTON, GA. COMMUNITY BEAUTIFICATION TO INCLUDE: TRASH & LITTER CLEANUP, REMOVAL OF OVERGROWN WEEDS & SHRUBBERY, FIRE HYDRANT DECORATION, PLANTING OF FLOWERS, COMMUNITY PAINT-UP-FIX-UP & RESTORATION OF TOWN HALL. (LOCAL). JAMES MCMICHAEL, COORDINATOR; HARRIS COUNTY BICENTENNIAL COMMISSION; PO BOX 283; HAMILTON, GA 31811. (#25141).

'PATRIOTISM '76', HAMILTON, GA. PROJECT IS DESIGNED TO ENCOURAGE A DISPLAY OF FLAGS ON SPECIAL OCCASIONS AT RESIDENTIAL HOMES AND COMMERICAL AREAS IN THE COMMUNITY. (LOCAL). W B STEIS, PROJ CHAIRMAN; AMERICAN LEGION; HAMILTON, GA 31811. (#25144).

MAR 1 - MAY 1, '76. THE HISTORY OF HAMILTON ESSAY CONTEST FOR HIGH SCHOOL STUDENTS. WINNER TO RECEIVE A $25 U S SAVINGS BOND. BOND PRESENTED TO MISS ALYSON HOOK OF HAMILTON, GA ON MAY 28TH, 1976. (LOCAL). CHARLES CARSON, COUNCILMN; HARRIS CO SCHOOLS AND HAMILTON CITY COUNCIL; HAMILTON, GA 31811. (#107934-2).

JULY 17, '76. FESTIVAL '76. PARADE WITH BANDS, FLOATS, COSTUMES, ANTIQUE CARS, HORSE AND BUGGY, BICYCLE ORGANIZATIONS; ARTS & CRAFTS FESTIVAL WITH NATIVE CRAFTS; MR & MISS BICENTENNIAL CONTEST, GAMES, AWARDS AND HO-DOWN. (LOCAL). JULIA K ROBINSON; HAMILTON CIVIC LEAGUE; PO BOX 282; HAMILTON, GA 31811. (#107773-1).

JULY 18, '76. RELIGIOUS CAMPGROUND MEETING - COMMUNITY WORSHIP SERVICE. CEREMONY. (LOCAL). MRS JULIA THOMPSON, DIR; CHURCHES OF THE HAMILTON COMMUNITY; RT 1, BOX 63; HAMILTON, GA 31811. (#107934-1).

HAWKINSVILLE

PULASKI HISTORICAL MUSEUM - HAWKINSVILLE, GA. A COUNTY-WIDE EFFORT WILL BE MADE TO DEVELOP A PERMANENT MUSEUM TO DISPLAY HISTORICAL ITEMS. (LOCAL). MRS CARL KIMBERLY, PRESIDENT; PULASKI CO BICENTENNIAL COMMITTEE; BOX 245; HAWKINSVILLE, GA 31036. (#28268). **ARBA GRANTEE.**

MAR 12 - 14, '76. HAWKINSVILLE HARNESS FESTIVAL. BICENTENNIAL PARADE STARTS FESTIVAL FOLLOWED BY BEAUTY PAGEANT, HORSE RACES, FLEA MARKET & ARTS & CRAFTS. (LOCAL). BOBBY SHEPARD, COORD; PINE LEVEL ESTATES; PINE LEVEL ESTATES; HAWKINSVILLE, GA 31036. (#104482-1).

HAZLEHURST

BICENTENNIAL LIBRARY - HAZLEHURST, GA. PROCEEDS FROM FUND RAISING ACTIVITIES WILL BE USED FOR THE LIBRARY BUILDING FUND. (LOCAL). MARY ALLEN, COORDINATOR; BICENTENNIAL LIBRARY BUILDING COMMITTEE; GILL ST; HAZLEHURST, GA 31539. (#27383).

JUNE 26, '76. RAFT CANOE RACE. COMPETITION. (LOCAL). VERLE THIGPEN, COORD; CHAMBER OF COMMERCE; 6 JEFFERSON DAVIS OFFICE COURTS; HAZLEHURST, GA 31539. (#200012-40).

JULY 3, '76. BICENTENNIAL FUN DAY. BALL GAMES, CONTESTS, SPECIAL OLYMPICS, RACES, PIE-THROWING, BAR-B-Q SUPPER AND FIREWORKS. (LOCAL). GLEN DIXON, PRES; JEFF DAVIS BOOSTER CLUB; 202 OAK ST; HAZLEHURST, GA 31539. (#200012-41).

JULY 4, '76. BICENTENNIAL SUNDAY. COUNTY-WIDE RELIGIOUS BICENTENNIAL COMMEMORATIVE SERVICE. (LOCAL). REV MARION EDWARDS, COORD; MINISTERIAL ASSOC; 307 S TALLAHASSEE; HAZLEHURST, GA 31539. (#200012-53).

HELEN

UNICOI FARM IN HELEN, GEORGIA. THE ESTABLISHING OF A LIVING FARM OF LATE 19TH-EARLY 20TH CENTURY ERA TYPICAL TO NORTHERN GEORGIA. (LOCAL). BARBARA WYATT, PROJECT COORDINATOR; UNICOI OUTDOOR RECREATION EXPERIMENT STATION; BOX 256; HELEN, GA 30545. (#11046). **ARBA GRANTEE.**

SEPT 10 - OCT 10, '76. BAVARIAN OKTOBERFEST. FESTIVAL. (ST-WIDE). BUZZ LEE, COORD; THE GREATER HELEN CHAMBER OF COMMERCE; BOX 157; HELEN, GA 30545. (#103416-539).

HINESVILLE

RESTORATION, HINESVILLE JAIL - GA. A PROJECT TO RESTORE A HISTORICAL STRUCTURE IN THE CENTER OF THE CITY. BUILT IN 1880 AND CURRENTLY OWNED BY THE LIBERTY COUNTY HISTORICAL SOCIETY; WILL BE USED AS A MUSEUM AND STORAGE OF ARTIFACTS. (LOCAL). MRS WILLIAM H ROSIER, PRESIDENT; LIBERTY COUNTY HISTORICAL SOCIETY; RFD; MIDWAY, GA 31313. (#27895). **ARBA GRANTEE.**

HIRAM

RESTORATION OF SCHOOL - HIRAM, GA. RE-LOCATION OF OLD BUILDING FROM PRIVATE LAND TO LAND OWNED BY CITIZENS OF HIRAM. EXTENSIVE RESTORATION WILL BE DONE. (LOCAL). SARAH DOKEY, PRESIDENT; COUNTRYSIDE GARDEN CLUB; RT 2, NORTH AVE; HIRAM, GA 30141. (#25198).

SEPT '76. FALL FESTIVAL '76. CELEBRATION TO ENCOMPASS PAST PRESENT FUTURE LIFESTYLES OF NATIVE N GA INCLUDES BOOTHS & PARADE HELD IN ORIGINAL DOWNTOWN AREA. WILL HAVE HIRAM HERITAGE BOOTH WITH MAPS DIORAMAS, CHARTS ETC. (LOCAL). SARAH DOKEY PRES; COUNTRYSIDE GARDEN CLUB; RT 2 NORTH AVE; HIRAM, GA 30141. (#107848-1).

HOMERVILLE

CLINCH COUNTY SPIRIT OF '76 RECREATION PARK, GA. DEVELOPMENT OF RECREATION FACILITIES IN LENOX. INCLUDES A BALLFIELD, MULTI-PURPOSE COURT, FISHING POND AND PICNIC FACILITIES. (LOCAL). MRS MARY ALICE LEE, EXEC DIRECTOR; CLINCH COUNTY BICENTENNIAL COMMISSION; COURTHOUSE SQUARE; HOMERVILLE, GA 31634. (#23673). **ARBA GRANTEE.**

JULY 4, '76. SPIRIT OF '76 DAY AND PARADE. THE CELEBRATION WILL INCLUDE A BICENTENNIAL PAGEANT AND PARADE. (LOCAL). MARY ALICE LEE, DIRECTOR; CLINCH COUNTY BICENTENNIAL COMMISSION; COURTHOUSE SQUARE; HOMERVILLE, GA 31634. (#23673-1).

IRWINTON

ARTS AND CRAFTS FAIR - LOCAL CRAFTSMEN DISPLAY GOODS. FAIR. (LOCAL). REV BILLY ANGLIN, CHMN; WILKINSON COUNTY BICENTENNIAL COMMISSION; RT 2; GORDON, GA 31031. (#106004-2).

BICENTENNIAL FESTIVAL PARADE. PARADE. (LOCAL). REV BILLY ANGLIN, CHMN; WILKINSON COUNTY BICENTENNIAL COMMISSION; RT 2; GORDON, GA 31031. (#106004-3).

COUNTY-WIDE CHURCH SERVICES. THERE WILL ALSO BE A COUNTRY DRESS PAGEANT. (LOCAL). REV BILLY ANGLIN, CHMN; WILKINSON COUNTY BICENTENNIAL COMMITTEE; RT 2; GORDON, GA 31031. (#106004-1).

HISTORICAL PAPERS - IRWINTON, GA. THE 4-H CLUB WILL COLLECT AND DISPLAY HISTORICAL PAPERS. (LOCAL). MRS MARY D REECE, CHAIRMAN; IRWINTON 4-H CLUB; PO BOX 197; IRWINTON, GA 31042. (#22452).

HISTORICAL POSTER CONTEST. COMPETITION. (LOCAL). ROBERT L JAMES, CHMN; WILKINSON COUNTY SCHOOLS; IRWINTON, GA 31042. (#105829-1).

ROADSIDE CLEANUP PROJECT - IRWINTON, GA. THE FOUR COUNTY BANK WILL SPONSOR A COUNTY-WIDE ROADSIDE CLEANUP. (LOCAL). MISS OPAL CHANCE, CHAIRMAN; FOUR COUNTY BANK; ALLENTOWN, GA 31003. (#22453).

TOURS OF HISTORICAL SITES. DRIVING TOURS OF HISTORICAL SITES IN WILKINSON COUNTY. (LOCAL). ROBERT L JAMES, CHMN; WILKINSON COUNTY SCHOOLS; IRWINTON, GA 31042. (#105828-1).

WILKINSON COUNTY SCHOOLS OPEN HOUSE - IRWINTON, GA. VISIT TO HISTORY & GOVERNMENT CLASSES TO SHOW WHAT IS BEING TAUGHT. (LOCAL). ROBERT L JAMES, CHAIRMAN; WILKINSON COUNTY SCHOOLS; IRWINTON, GA 31042. (#22454).

JEFFERSON

ESSAY COMPETITION. ESSAY MUST BE ON AMERICA. (LOCAL). JIMMIE JACOBS, CHMN; JEFFERSON BICENTENNIAL COMMITTEE; JEFFERSON, GA 30549. (#108915-1).

FESTIVAL. FESTIVAL WILL INCLUDE HISTORICAL SLIDE SHOW, MUSIC, DANCING & FIREWORKS. AT STADIUM. (LOCAL). JIMMIE JACOBS, CHMN; JEFFERSON BICENTENNIAL COMMITTEE; JEFFERSON, GA 30549. (#108915-3).

FIRE PLUGS PROJ - JEFFERSON, GA. FIRE PLUGS WILL BE PAINTED RED, WHITE & BLUE. (LOCAL). JIMMIE JACOBS, CHAIRMAN; JEFFERSON BICENTENNIAL COMMITTEE; JEFFERSON, GA 30549. (#26648).

PARADE AND BAZAAR. FESTIVAL, PARADE. (LOCAL). JIMMIE JACOBS, CHMN; JEFFERSON BICENTENNIAL COMMITTEE; JEFFERSON, GA 30549. (#108915-2).

JESUP

JULY 5, '75 - JULY 4, '76. HERITAGE HAPPENINGS. THESE HERITAGE HAPPENINGS WILL BE HELD THE FIRST SATURDAY IN EACH MONTH FROM NOW ON UNTIL JULY 4, 1976. EVENTS WILL VARY; RAFT RACE, BICYCLE RACE, FESTIVALS, STREET DANCES, ETC. AT JESUP-WAYNE COUNTY CHAMBER OF COMMERCE BUILDING. (LOCAL). MARTHA JEAN BURNS, DIR; JESUP-WAYNE COUNTY BICENTENNIAL COMMITTEE; 261 W ORANGE ST; JESUP, GA 31545. (#102430-8).

JONESBORO

AMERICAN FLAG PROGRAM - JONESBORO, GA. PROGRAM WILL ENCOURAGE DAILY FLYING OF THE AMERICAN FLAG AT ALL GOVERNMENT BUILDINGS, STORES, HOMES AND BUSINESSES. (LOCAL). MRS C E LAMB, CHAIRMAN; JONESBORO BICENTENNIAL COMMISSION; 146 HUIE ST; JONESBORO, GA 30236. (#18325).

BOY SCOUT BICENTENNIAL GUARD OF HONOR - GA. AUTHENTIC COLONIAL MILITIA UNIFORMS WITH MUSKETS, DRUMS AND FIFES WILL PERFORM AT PUBLIC CEREMONIES AND OFFICIALLY REPRESENT COUNTY, STATE AND LOCAL COMMUNITIES AT VARIOUS FUNCTIONS. (ST-WIDE). HAROLD KRAU, CHAIRMAN; CLAYTON COUNTY BICENTENNIAL COMMITTEE; 124 SMITH ST; JONESBORO, GA 30236. (#23600). **ARBA GRANTEE.**

CITY SEAL CONTEST - JONESBORO, GA. CONTEST IN HIGH SCHOOL ART DEPARTMENT TO DESIGN A CITY SEAL. (LOCAL). MRS C E LAMB, CHAIRMAN; JONESBORO BICENTENNIAL COMMITTEE; 146 HUIE ST; JONESBORO, GA 30236. (#18281).

COMMEMORATIVE GAS LIGHT - JONESBORO, GA. THE ERECTION AND DEDICATION OF A GAS LIGHT TO TWO JONESBORO MEN FOR OUTSTANDING CONTRIBUTIONS TO COMMUNITY, STATE & NATION. (LOCAL). MRS C E LAMB, CHAIRMAN; JONESBORO BICENTENNIAL COMMISSION; 146 HUIE ST; JONESBORO, GA 30236. (#18327).

DISPLAYS AND EXHIBITS - JONESBORO, GA. DOCUMENTS, POSTERS, PICTURES AND FLAGS WILL BE DISPLAYED. THE HISTORY OF THE U S ARMY WILL BE THE SUBJECT OF THE EXHIBIT. (LOCAL). MRS C E LAMB, CHAIRMAN; JONESBORO BICENTENNIAL COMMITTEE; 146 HUIE ST; JONESBORO, GA 30236. (#18275).

HISTORICAL PRESENTATION, JONESBORO, GA. MAYOR PROCLAIMED SEPTEMBER 9, 1975 SAMUEL GOOD JONES DAY. A SUBSEQUENT ARTICLE WAS PUBLISHED ON HIS LIFE AND ACCOMPLISHMENTS. (LOCAL). MRS C E LAMB, CHAIRMAN; JONESBORO BICENTENNIAL COMMITTEE; 146 HUIE ST; JONESBORO, GA 30236. (#18278).

HISTORY OF JONESBORO, GA. PROJECT TO PUBLISH THE HISTORY OF JONESBORO. (LOCAL). MRS A B SMITH, PROJ DIRECTOR; JONESBORO BICENTENNIAL COMMITTEE; 146 HUIE ST; JONESBORO, GA 30236. (#18277).

MEMORIAL FLAG AVENUE - JONESBORO, GA. THE FLAGS OF THE THIRTEEN ORIGINAL COLONIES WILL BE DISPLAYED AROUND THE SQUARE. (LOCAL). MRS C E LAMB, CHAIRMAN; JONESBORO BICENTENNIAL COMMISSION; 146 HUIE ST; JONESBORO, GA 30236. (#18326).

MIAMI TO INDIANA RELAY OF FLAGS. A RELAY OF FLAGS FROM MIAMI TO INDIANA. (LOCAL). MRS C E LAMB, CHAIRMAN; JONESBORO BICENTENNIAL COMMISSION; 146 HUIE ST; JONESBORO, GA 30236. (#18324).

REVITALIZATION OF DOWNTOWN JONESBORO, GA. INVOLVE BUSINESSMEN IN IMPROVING APPEARANCE OF STORES & STREETS. (LOCAL). MRS C E LAMB, CHAIRMAN; JONESBORO BICENTENNIAL COMMITTEE; 146 HUIE ST; JONESBORO, GA 30236. (#18280).

SEPT 9, '75. SAMUEL GOODE JONES DAY CELEBRATION. THE MAYOR PROCLAIMED 9/9/75 AS SAMUEL GOODE JONES DAY. A NEWSPAPER ARTICLE WAS WRITTEN ON HIS LIFE AND ACCOMPLISHMENTS. (LOCAL). MRS C E LAMB, CHAIRMAN; JONESBORO BICENTENNIAL COMMITTEE; 146 HUIE ST; JONESBORO, GA 30236. (#200012-24).

JAN 1 - APR 1, '76. ESSAY CONTEST ON PHASES OF THE AMERICAN REVOLUTION. COMPETITION. (LOCAL). MRS A B SMITH, PRES; UNITED DAUGHTERS OF CONFEDERACY; 139 COLLEGE ST; JONESBORO, GA 30236. (#103594-1).

JUNE 1 - 5, '76. COMMUNITY CELEBRATION AND PARADE. FESTIVAL, PARADE. (LOCAL). MRS C E LAMB, CHAIRMAN; JONESBORO BICENTENNIAL COMMISSION; 146 HUE ST; JONESBORO, GA 30236. (#103747-2).

JUNE 1 - 5, '76. DISPLAY OF EARLY AMERICAN FLAGS. EXHIBIT AT MAIN ST. (LOCAL). MRS C E LAMB, CHWMN; JONESBORO BICENTENNIAL COMMITTEE; 146 HULE ST; JONESBORO, GA 30236. (#107364-1).

JUNE 1 - 5, '76. HERITAGE SPECIAL - TRAIN TOUR. TRAVELING RAIL EXHIBIT EMPHASIZING COLONIAL & REVOLUTIONARY GEORGIA HISTORY, CRAFTS & LIFESTYLE OF GEORGIA COLONISTS. EXHIBITS WILL BE DISPLAYED WITH COMBINATION OF SIGHT & SOUND ACTIVITY. (LOCAL). RON HENRY, COORDINATOR; GEORGIA AGRIRAMA DEVELOPMENT AUTHORITY/GEORGIA BICENTENNIAL; 8TH ST A I 75; TIFTON, GA 31794. (#7999-16).

JUNE 5, '76. MARINE DRUM AND BUGLE CORPS, LIVE APPEARANCE. LIVE PERFORMANCE. (LOCAL). MRS C E LAMB, CHAIRMAN; JONESBORO BICENTENNIAL COMMISSION; 146 HUIE ST; JONESBORO, GA 30236. (#103747-1).

KENNESAW

KENNESAW HISTORIC SPRING PARK, GA. RESTORATION OF HISTORIC SPRING AND LANDSCAPING OF PARK. (ST-WIDE). MIMI JO BUTLER, CHAIRPERSON; KENNESAW BICENTENNIAL COMMITTEE; PO BOX 386; KENNESAW, GA 30144. (#23745). **ARBA GRANTEE.**

KEYSVILLE

BEAUTIFICATION OF KEYSVILLE, GA. LIBERTY MAGNOLIA TREE PLANTED IN CEMETERY, GRANITE MARKER WITH DATES PLACED NEAR A LARGE CYPRESS SIGN SAYING 'WELCOME TO KEYSVILLE, GA' HAS BEEN ERECTED. RECEIVED ARBA EMBLEM FOR THE PROJECT. (LOCAL). MRS DEWEY L DAVIS, CHAIRMAN; BEAUTIFICATION COMMITTEE; KEYSVILLE, GA 30833. (#24404).

'ECHOES OF A DREAM' - KEYSVILLE, GA. A 45 MINUTE DRAMATIC EXPERIENCE IN BLACK PRIDE AND BLACK HISTORY IN SONG, POETRY AND DANCE; THE PROGRAM TELLS WHAT BLACKS CELEBRATE AT THE BICENTENNIAL AND WHY; THE PROGRAM WILL ALSO BE ON FILM. (ST-WIDE). WILMAGENE BROWN, STAGE DIRECTOR; BOGGS ACADEMY; KEYSVILLE, GA 30816. (#23618). **ARBA GRANTEE.**

LAFAYETTE

AREA SCHOOL PROJECTS - LAFAYETTE, GA. SCHOOL PROJECTS WILL INCLUDE ESSAYS, TOURS OF HISTORICAL SITES, SPEAKERS AND FILMS. (LOCAL). JOHNNE WILLIAMS, COORDINATOR; LAFAYETTE AREA SCHOOLS; 602 S CHEROKEE ST; LAFAYETTE, GA 30728. (#12619).

BEAUTIFICATION OF SCHOOL LAWNS - LAFAYETTE, GA. BEAUTIFICATION OF SCHOOL GROUNDS WILL INCLUDE LANDSCAPING AND REPLACEMENT OF SHRUBBERY. (LOCAL). HENRY BROWN, PROJ DIRECTOR; FORTUNE SCHOOL PTA; WALKER COUNTY BANK; LAFAYETTE, GA 30728. (#12617).

BEAUTIFICATION OF CITY SQUARE - LAFAYETTE, GA. RESTORATION OF SQUARE WITH PLANTING OF TREES AND SHRUBS AND LANDSCAPING TO RESTORE THE SQUARE TO RESEMBLE THE FORMER VILLAGE GREEN OF THE 1800'S. (LOCAL). MRS FRED HENRY, PROJ DIRECTOR; WOMAN'S CLUB/CHAMBER OF COMMERCE; N MAIN ST; LAFAYETTE, GA 30728. (#12621). **ARBA GRANTEE.**

CITY BEAUTIFICATION PROJECT, LAFAYETTE, GA. DEBRIS WILL BE CLEANED UP, RED, BLUE AND WHITE FLOWERS WILL BE PLANTED AND SOME CITIZENS WILL FLY FLAG EVERY DAY DURING 76 AT THEIR HOMES. (LOCAL). JOHNNE WILLIAMS, PROJ DIRECTOR; LAFAYETTE BICENTENNIAL COMMITTEE; CITY HALL; LAFAYETTE, GA 30728. (#12612).

CLUB LUNCHEONS IN LAFAYETTE, GA. ALL CLUBS WILL HAVE LUNCHEONS WITH BICENTENNIAL THEMES. (LOCAL). J F COBB, PRESIDENT; CHAMBER OF COMMERCE; DUKE ST; LAFAYETTE, GA 30728. (#12611).

FOLKWAYS STUDY IN LAFAYETTE, GA. STUDY OF OLD FOLKWAYS, GAMES AND DANCES. (LOCAL). BILL KRAUSE, RECREATION

LAFAYETTE — CONTINUED

DIRECTOR; LAFAYETTE SQUARE DANCE GROUP; RECREATION DEPT; LAFAYETTE, GA 30728. (#12603).

FORT CUMMINS MARKER, LAFAYETTE, GA. PROJECT ENTAILS MAKING THE MARKER FOR FT CUMMINS, AN OLD CHEROKEE CAMP, MORE VISIBLE. (LOCAL). GRADY MCCALLOMN, CITY MANAGER; LAFAYETTE DAUGHTERS OF AMERICAN REVOLUTION; CITY HALL; LAFAYETTE, GA 30728. (#12607).

GEORGIA WEEK IN FEBRUARY '76 - LAFAYETTE, GA. SCHOOL PROJECTS, RADIO PROGRAMS, RESEARCH, PROGRAMS BY CIVIC GROUPS AND ARTICLES FOR LOCAL PAPER. (LOCAL). JENNIFER ALLGOOD, PROJ DIRECTOR; LAFAYETTE AREA SCHOOLS; CULBERSON AVE; LAFAYETTE, GA 30728. (#12615).

HISTORY OF FLAG IN LAFAYETTE, GA. THE HISTORY OF THE FLAG WILL BE PRESENTED THROUGH FILMS, ART AND MUSIC. (LOCAL). JOHNNE WILLIAMS, PROJ DIRECTOR; LAFAYETTE AREA SCHOOLS; 602 S CHEROKEE ST; LAFAYETTE, GA 30728. (#12614).

MINI-PARK - PROJ OF LAFAYETTE, GA. MINI-PARK WILL INCLUDE PICNIC AREA, BENCHES, FOUNTAIN; IT WILL BE LOCATED NEAR THE CHAMBER OF COMMERCE BUILDING. (LOCAL). J F COBB, PROJ DIRECTOR; WOMAN'S CLUB/CHAMBER OF COMMERCE; LAFAYETTE, GA 30728. (#12620).

NEWS MEDIA PARTICIPATION IN LAFAYETTE, GA. COMMUNITY PARTICIPATION IN SPECIAL RADIO & TELEVISION NEWS SPOTS. (LOCAL). JOHNNIE WILLIAMS, PROGRAM COORDINATOR; STATION WLAFA--WALKER COUNTY MESSENGER; LAFAYETTE, GA 30728. (#12598).

OLD FASHIONED COOKING CONTEST IN LAFAYETTE, GA. FOOD TASTING PARTY WITH EMPHASIS ON EARLY AMERICAN DISHES WILL BE HELD AT THE LAFAYETTE RECREATION CENTER FESTIVAL CELEBRATION. (LOCAL). HELEN PEGUES, PROJECT DIRECTOR; 4-H CLUBS AND ECONOMIST; PO BOX 827, FEDERAL BLDG; LAFAYETTE, GA 30728. (#12605).

PRESERVATION OF 'MESSENGERS', LAFAYETTE, GA. OLD ISSUES OF THE COUNTY NEWSPAPER, 'THE MESSENGER', WILL BE MICROFILMED FOR PRESERVATION PURPOSES. (LOCAL). MRS D A SHOW, REGENT; DAUGHTERS OF THE AMERICAN REVOLUTION; 1103 N MAIN ST; LAFAYETTE, GA 30728. (#12606).

PTA PROGRAMS - PROJ OF LAFAYETTE, GA. SCHOOL CLASS PROGRAMS, SPEAKERS AND FILMS. (LOCAL). HENRY BROWN, PROJ DIRECTOR; LAFAYETTE AREA PTA; 11 SUNSET DR; LAFAYETTE, GA 30728. (#12616).

TREE PLANTING IN LAFAYETTE, GA. TREES WILL BE PLANTED ON LIBRARY LAWN. (LOCAL). MRS D A SHOW, REGENT; DAUGHTERS OF AMERICAN REVOLUTION; 1103 N MAIN ST; LAFAYETTE, GA 30728. (#12609).

SEPT 10, '75 - MAY 21, '76. SCHOOL ESSAY CONTEST. COMPETITION. (LOCAL). JOHNNE WILLIAMS, CHMN; LAFAYETTE BICENTENNIAL COMMITTEE; BOX 307; LAFAYETTE, GA 30728. (#102430-3).

OCT 17, '75. HIGH SCHOOL HOMECOMING IN LAFAYETTE, GA. HOMECOMING PARADE FLOATS WITH BICENTENNIAL THEME. (LOCAL). GLEN JONES, PROJ DIRECTOR; LAFAYETTE HIGH SCHOOL; CORINTH RD; LAFAYETTE, GA 30728. (#12613-1).

NOV 25, '75. OUTDOOR CHRISTMAS TREE LIGHTING & COMMUNITY SING. THIS EVENT IS THE BEGINNING OF CHRISTMAS PROMOTION FOR LOCAL MERCHANTS. AT CHAMBER OF COMMERCE LAWN. (LOCAL). DONNA MORGAN, DIRECTOR; LAFAYETTE CHAMBER OF COMMERCE/BETA SIGMA PHI SORORITY; CHEROKEE ST; LAFAYETTE, GA 30728. (#102430-2).

DEC 3, '75. MILITARY VANS DINNER MEETING. FESTIVITIES WILL INCLUDE PERFORMANCES BY THE RAMBLER BAND AND THE CROWNING OF MISS 1776 AND MR 1976. AT EAST SIDE PUBLIC SQUARE. (LOCAL). GRADY MCCALMON, DIRECTOR; CITY OF LAFAYETTE; CITY HALL; LAFAYETTE, GA 30728. (#102430-1).

DEC 3, '75. UNITED STATES ARMED FORCES BICENTENNIAL CARAVAN. THE CARAVAN IS COMPOSED OF EXHIBIT VANS FOR EACH BRANCH OF THE MILITARY SERVICE. THE THEME OF THE EXHIBITION IS 'HISTORY OF THE ARMED FORCES AND THEIR CONTRIBUTION TO THE NATION'. (LOCAL). MISS JOHNNE WILLIAMS, DIR; U S ARMED FORCES BICENTENNIAL EXHIBIT VANS PROJECT; PO BOX 307; LAFAYETTE, GA 30728. (#1775-205).

APR 24 - 25, '76. HISTORY THROUGH THE THEATRE. COMMUNITY WIDE DRAMA, FEATURING THE LOCAL HIGH SCHOOL BAND & THE SENIOR CLASS, PORTRAYING COMMUNITY HERITAGE, INCLUDING BLACK AND INDIAN HISTORY. AT FORTUNE GRAMMAR SCHOOL AUDITORIUM. (ST-WIDE). DONNA MORGAN, CHAIRWOMAN; LITTLE THEATRE GROUP; 201 S CHEROKEE; LAFAYETTE, GA 30728. (#12599-1).

JUNE 25 - JULY 5, '76. MERCHANT PARTICIPATION IN LAFAYETTE, GA. IN HONOR OF THE BICENTENNIAL, LOCAL MERCHANTS ARE HAVING SPECIAL SALES, PUTTING UP SPECIAL WINDOW DISPLAYS AND STORE CLERKS ARE DRESSING UP IN BICENTENNIAL COSTUMES. (LOCAL). JOE STOCK, PROJ DIRECTOR; MERCHANTS ASSOC; BOSTON STORE; LAFAYETTE, GA 30728. (#12600-1).

JUNE '76. LOCAL FIELD DAY. HOOP ROLE, 3-LEGGED RACE, GREASED POLE, GREASED PIG, LOG CUT, SEED SPITTING CONTEST, WATERMELON CUT, PICKLE & PERSERVE CONTEST, BEST COSTUME AWARD, SQUARE DANCING, SMALL CRAFTS & FIREWORKS DISPLAY, ARE THE ACTIVITIES PLANNED. AT MAX STOKER CENTER. (LOCAL). BILL KRAUSE, DIRECTOR; LAFAYETTE RECREATION & PARKS DEPT; PO BOX 189; LAFAYETTE, GA 30728. (#103107-1).

JULY 3, '76. BARBECUE IN LAFAYETTE, GA. A CITY WIDE BARBECUE WILL BE HELD. (LOCAL). DAVID CUNNINGHAM; JAYCEES; 201 N CIRCLE DR; LAFAYETTE, GA 30728. (#12610-1).

JULY 3, '76. JULY '76 PARADE IN LAFAYETTE, GA. IN HONOR OF THE BICENTENNIAL, A JULY 4TH PARADE WILL BE HELD. (LOCAL). DON STULTZ, PROJ DIRECTOR; ROTARY CLUB, LIONS CLUB AND JAYCEES; LAFAYETTE, GA 30728. (#12608-1).

JULY 3, '76. OLD-FASHIONED FIELD DAY IN LAFAYETTE, GA. FAIR. (LOCAL). BILL KRAUSE; RECREATION DEPARTMENT; 638 S MAIN STREET; LAFAYETTE, GA 30728. (#12604-1).

JULY 4, '76. CHRISTIAN HERITAGE SUNDAY. CHRISTIAN CITIZENSHIP SERMON IN EVERY CHURCH IN AREA ON JULY 4TH, 1976; CHURCH DINNERS, FELLOWSHIPS AND OLD FASHIONED SONG 'FEST'. (LOCAL). REV HOWARD KILLINGSWORTH; MINISTERIAL ASSOC; PRESBYTERIAN CHURCH; LAFAYETTE, GA 30728. (#12601-1).

NOV 23, '76. CHRISTMAS TREE LIGHTING. PROJECT IS THE CITY CHRISTMAS TREE LIGHTING, FEATURING CHRISTMAS CAROLLING & A SENIOR CITIZEN'S PARTY. LOCAL RESIDENTS WILL DRESS IN BICENTENNIAL COSTUMES. AT LAFAYETTE CHAMBER OF COMMERCE LAWN. (LOCAL). MRS MARY HARMON; LAFAYETTE AREA CHAMBER OF COMMERCE; 201 S CIRCLE DR; LAFAYETTE, GA 30728. (#12602-1).

LAGRANGE

BICENTENNIAL CAMPUS PUBLICATIONS, LAGRANGE, GA. QUADRANGE, THE COLLEGE YEARBOOK WILL FEATURE A NOSTALGIC LOOK AT LAGRANGE COLLEGE. THE HILLTOP NEWS WILL CONTAIN ARTICLES COMPARING THE PAST & PRESENT. (LOCAL). JULIE CLIFTON, SGA PRESIDENT; SGA-LAGRANGE COLLEGE; BROAD ST; LAGRANGE, GA 30240. (#22662).

CELEBRATION OF AMERICA'S FREEDOM, LAGRANGE, GA. SCULPTURE OF LAFAYETTE TO BE FOCAL POINT FOR MUSIC, FIREWORKS, ADDRESSES & DRAMA. (LOCAL). W G HENRY, CHAIRMAN; LAGRANGE BICENTENNIAL COMMITTEE; LAGRANGE, GA 30240. (#16135). **ARBA GRANTEE.**

CITY OF LAGRANGE CELEBRATION. PARADES, DEDICATION OF STATUE OF GENERAL LAFAYETTE, PERFORMANCE OF PERIOD MUSIC BY ATLANTA SYMPHONY. (LOCAL). WAIGHTS G HENRY, CHMN; BICENTENNIAL COMMITTEE - LAGRANGE COLLEGE; BROAD ST; LAGRANGE, GA 30240. (#106213-5). **(??).**

FESTIVAL USA. HOMECOMING WITH FLOATS AND DANCE COURT PRESENTATION. (LOCAL). JULIE CLIFTON, PRES; LAGRANGE COLLEGE STUDENT GOVERNMENT ASSOC; BROAD ST; LAGRANGE, GA 30240. (#106213-8). **(??).**

LAGRANGE COLLEGE CHOIR. SEVERAL BICENTENNIAL WORKS WILL BE PERFORMED. (LOCAL). DAVID BLALOCK, DIR; LAGRANGE COLLEGE CHOIR; BROAD ST; LAGRANGE, GA 30240. (#106213-3). **(??).**

PRESIDENTS' EXHIBIT. EXHIBIT OF PRESIDENTIAL MEMORABILIA. (LOCAL). CHUCK KELLY, DIR; LAGRANGE COLLEGE - ARA FOOD SERVICE; BROAD ST; LAGRANGE, GA 30240. (#106213-2). **(??).**

STATUE OF LAFAYETTE - LA GRANGE, GA. A REPLICA OF THE STATUE OF LAFAYETTE WHICH STANDS IN LE PUY, FRANCE, HAS BEEN ERECTED ON THE CAMPUS OF LA GRANGE COLLEGE. IT WAS DEDICATED ON FEBRUARY 21, 1976. (INT'L). CULTURAL ATTACHE; EMBASSY OF FRANCE; 2535 BELMONT RD; WASHINGTON, DC 20008. (#31924).

OCT 21 - NOV 18, '75. SEMINAR: LAND USE IN TROUP COUNTY. TO BE OFFERED ON 4 SEPARATE OCCASIONS IN: LAGRANGE, HOGANSVILLE, MOUNTVILLE & WEST POINT. (LOCAL). DR FRED B MILLS, PROJ DIR; LA GRANGE COLLEGE; LA GRANGE, GA 30240. (#103169-1).

DEC 8 - 9, '75. UNITED STATES ARMED FORCES BICENTENNIAL CARAVAN. THE CARAVAN IS COMPOSED OF EXHIBIT VANS FOR EACH BRANCH OF THE MILITARY SERVICE. THE THEME OF THE EXHIBITION IS 'HISTORY OF THE ARMED FORCES AND THEIR CONTRIBUTION TO THE NATION'. (LOCAL). WAIGHTS G HENRY JR, CHMN; U S ARMED FORCES BICENTENNIAL EXHIBIT VANS PROJECT; LAGRANGE COLLEGE; LAGRANGE, GA 30240. (#1775-207).

JAN 2, '76 - JAN 31, '77. ART EXHIBIT OF LIFE OF LAFAYETTE. SEVEN PICTORAL SCENES FROM THE LIFE OF GENERAL LAFAYETTE, BY CHARLES HARGENS OF DOYLESTOWN, PA. (LOCAL). JOHN LAWRENCE, HEAD; LAGRANGE COLLEGE - ART DEPT; BROAD ST; LAGRANGE, GA 30240. (#22549-1).

JAN 16, '76. WINTER CONVOCATION. COUNT RENE DE CHAMBRUM, GREAT-GREAT GRANDSON OF LAFAYETTE, RECEIVES HONORARY DOCTOR OF HUMANE LETTERS & LAYS WREATH OF FLOWERS AT THE BRONZE STATUE OF LAFAYETTE. (INT'L). DR WAIGHTS G HENRY, CHMN; BICENTENNIAL COMMISSION OF LAGRANGE COLLEGE; BROAD ST; LAGRANGE, GA 30240. (#106213-7).

FEB 14 - 15, '76. 'AND THEY CALL IT MACARONI'. ORIGINAL WORK PERFORMED BY LAGRANGE COLLEGE STUDENTS. (LOCAL). MAX ESTES, CHMN; LA GRANGE COLLEGE - SPEECH & DRAMA DEPT; BROAD ST; LAGRANGE, GA 30240. (#106213-1).

FEB 20 - 21, '76. DEDICATION OF STATUE OF LAFAYETTE; FIREWORKS, PARADE & SPEECHES. CEREMONY, PARADE. (LOCAL). W G HENRY, CHAIRMAN; LAGRANGE BICENTENNIAL COMMISSION; LAGRANGE COLLEGE; LAGRANGE, GA 30240. (#16135-1).

FEB 21, '76. ATLANTA SYMPHONY ORCHESTRA IN CONCERT. LIVE PERFORMANCE. (LOCAL). W G HENRY, CHAIRMAN; LAGRANGE BICENTENNIAL COMMISSION; LAGRANGE COLLEGE; LAGRANGE, GA 30240. (#16135-2).

APR 22, '76. JACK BRINKLEY, U S CONGRESSMAN - FORUM. SEMINAR AT PRICE DRAMA THEATRE. (LOCAL). JACK ANDERSON, PROFESSOR; LAGRANGE COLLEGE - HISTORY DEPT - FORUM COMMITTEE; BROAD ST; LAGRANGE, GA 30240. (#106213-4).

AUG 25 - 27, '76. HERITAGE SPECIAL - TRAIN TOUR. TRAVELING RAIL EXHIBIT EMPHASIZING COLONIAL & REVOLUTIONARY GEORGIA HISTORY, CRAFTS & LIFESTYLE OF GEORGIA COLONISTS. EXHIBITS WILL BE DISPLAYED WITH COMBINATION OF SIGHT & SOUND ACTIVITY. (LOCAL). RON HENRY, COORDINATOR; GEORGIA AGRIRAMA DEVELOPMENT AUTHORITY/GEORGIA BICENTENNIAL; 8TH ST A I 75; TIFTON, GA 31794. (#7999-27).

LAKELAND

A BROCHURE TO PROMOTE LANIER COUNTY, GEORGIA. THE BROCHURE WILL EXPLAIN THE SERVICES & ATTRIBUTES OF LANIER COUNTY TO SHOW THAT IT IS A FINE PLACE TO LIVE. (LOCAL). ROBERT PATTEN, CHAIRMAN; LANIER COUNTY-LAKELAND BICENT COMMITTEE; N LAKESHORE DR; LAKELAND, GA 31635. (#9070).

200 YEARS OF HISTORY IN LANIER COUNTY, GEORGIA. A LANIER COUNTY NEWSPAPER WILL PRINT THE HISTORY OF THE COUNTY COMPLETE WITH MAPS AND PICTURES IN SERIAL FORM. BOUND COPIES WILL BE PRINTED & SOLD. (LOCAL). BILLY GIDDENS, COMMITTEE CHAIRMAN; LANIER COUNTY - LAKELAND BICENT COMMITTEE; 190 N LAKESHORE DR; LAKELAND, GA 31635. (#9068).

SEPT 4, '76. PAGEANT 'MEMOIRS OF LANIER COUNTY PEOPLE'. LIVE PERFORMANCE. (LOCAL). HELEN STRICKLAND; LANIER COUNTY-LAKELAND BICENT COMMITTEE; RT 1; LAKELAND, GA 31635. (#9069-1).

SEPT 4 - 6, '76. ARTS AND CRAFT SHOW. EXHIBIT. (LOCAL). HELEN STRICKLAND; LANIER COUNTY-LAKELAND BICENT COMMITTEE; RT 1; LAKELAND, GA 31635. (#9071-1).

LAVONIA

BICENTENNIAL READING LIST - LAVONIA, GA. BOOKS WILL BE LISTED AND PUBLISHED IN LOCAL PAPER. THEY WILL BE ON DISPLAY AT THE LIBRARY. (LOCAL). MRS JOHN CORAM, LIBRARIAN; LAVONIA LIBRARY COMMITTEE; HARTWELL RD; LAVONIA, GA 30553. (#25201).

HISTORY OF LAVONIA, GA. HISTORY BEING BROUGHT UP TO DATE BY LOCAL CITIZEN USING OLD NEWSPAPERS AND PERSONAL FACTS FROM OLDER CITIZENS. (LOCAL). MRS MORGAN WILLIAMS, JR, CHAIRMAN; LAVONIA BICENTENNIAL COMMITTEE; 106 JONES ST; LAVONIA, GA 30553. (#25202).

RESTORATION OF OLDEST BUILDING IN LAVONIA, GA. ORIGINAL LOG CABIN IS BEING RESTORED AND MOVED TO PERMANENT LOCATION IN CITY PARK. MEMBERS MADE LOG CABIN QUILT TO BE AUCTIONED OFF. BANK DONATED BUILDING AND FINANCIAL AID. (LOCAL). MRS ROBERT EBERHARDT, COORDINATOR; LAVONIA WOMEN'S CLUB; 18 MASON ST; LAVONIA, GA 30553. (#25203).

SAVE LAVONIA-CARNEGIE LIBRARY - LAVONIA, GA. CITY IS 2ND SMALLEST CITY TO HAVE CARNEGIE LIBRARY; ONE OF 17 ORIGINAL IN THE STATE OF GA. BUILDING WAS COMPLETE IN 1911 & NEEDS RENOVATION. (LOCAL). MRS ERNEST VANDIVER, CHAIRMAN; LAVONIA LIBRARY COMMITTEE, LAVONIA BICENTENNIAL COMMITTEE; 109 HARTWELL RD; LAVONIA, GA 30553. (#25199).

MAR 22 - APR 9, '76. ESSAY CONTEST-AMERICA-A 200 YEAR ODYSSEY. COMPETITION AT LAVONIA ELEMENTARY SCHOOL. (LOCAL). BOYD OUTZ, COORD; LAVONIA BICENTENNIAL COMMITTEE; LAVONIA, GA 30553. (#200012-20).

MAR 23, '76. FLAG RAISING AND TREE PLANTING. OFFICIAL BICENTENNIAL FLAG WILL BE RAISED AND TREES WILL BE PRESENTED TO THE CITY. AT LAVONIA CITY HALL & CITY PARK. (LOCAL). MRS FRED WELDON, COORD; LAVONIA BICENTENNIAL COMMITTEE; WELDONS FUNERAL HOME; LAVONIA, GA 30553. (#107948-1).

JULY '76. ANCESTORS ATTIC KITCHEN SHOW. OLD KITCHEN ARTICLES COLLECTED FROM MEMBERS' HOMES AND PUT ON DISPLAY. SKIT WILL BE PRESENTED BY MEMBERS WEARING BICENTENNIAL COSTUMES. (LOCAL). MRS JOE AGNEW; LAUONIA EASTERN STAR; GILMER ST; LAUONIA, GA 30553. (#107850-1).

LAWRENCEVILLE

GWINNETT COUNTY MUSEUM - LAWRENCEVILLE, GA. THE MUSEUM WILL HOUSE ARTIFACTS AND DATA PERTINENT TO GWINNETT COUNTY & GEORGIA HISTORY. (LOCAL). MS ANNIE FRANCES FLANIGAN, PROJ COORDINATOR; GWINNETT COUNTY BICENTENNIAL COMMITTEE; 370 PIKE ST NW; LAWRENCEVILLE, GA 30245. (#16305).

LANDSCAPING OF GWINNETT COUNTY MUSEUM GROUNDS, GA. THE LAWRENCEVILLE FEMALE SEMINARY, BUILT IN 1853 & RESTORED IN 1974 HOUSES THE GWINNETT COUNTY MUSEUM; ITS GROUNDS WILL BE LANDSCAPED. (ST-WIDE). MRS HUBERT E TUCKER, PROJ DIRECTOR; GWINNETT COUNTY BOARD OF COMMISSIONERS; 240 OAK ST NW; LAWRENCEVILLE, GA 30245. (#16136). **ARBA GRANTEE.**

LANDSCAPING OF LAWRENCEVILLE, GA, FEMALE SEMINARY. LANDSCAPING OF THE GROUNDS OF THE FEMALE SEMINARY WITH PLANTINGS FROM THE 1850 PERIOD. (LOCAL). MRS HUBERT TUCKER, CHAIRMAN; GWINNETT COUNTY BICENTENNIAL COMMITTEE; 115 DOGWOOD DR NW; LAWRENCEVILLE, GA 30245. (#16303).

LAWRENCEVILLE, GA, FEMALE SEMINARY BUILDING. RESTORATION OF THE 1850 SEMINARY BUILDING FOR USE AS A CULTURAL AND CIVIC CENTER. (LOCAL). MRS HUBERT TUCKER, CHAIR-

LAWRENCEVILLE — CONTINUED

MAN; GWINNETTE COUNTY BICENTENNIAL COMMITTEE; 115 DOGWOOD DR NW; LAWRENCEVILLE, GA 30245. (#16304).

OCT 4, '75. BICENTENNIAL FESTIVAL & BEAUTY PAGEANT. FESTIVAL WILL FEATURE FLEA MARKET, ARTS & CRAFTS, WITH PAGEANT TO SELECT MISS GWINNETT HIGH SCHOOL. AT CROGAN ST. (LOCAL). MS JANE MCDANAL; CENTRAL GWINNETT HIGH SCHOOL & PTA; LAWRENCEVILLE, GA 30245. (#102885-1).

LILBURN

BROCHURE ON HISTORY OF LILBURN, GA. HANDOUT FOR AREA RESIDENTS COVERING ARRIVAL OF FIRST SETTLER AND THE COMING OF THE RAILROAD, TO LAND DEVELOPMENT OF SIXTIES. (LOCAL). MRS JOHN MARTIN, CHAIRMAN; GWINNETT HISTORICAL SOCIETY; 341 ROCKBRIDGE RD; LILBURN, GA 30247. (#24045).

HISTORY OF GWINNETT COUNTY, VOL III - LILBURN, GA. A CONTINUATION OF THE HISTORY OF GWINNETT COUNTY; THE 3RD IN A SERIES. (LOCAL). MARVIN WORTHY, PROJ DIRECTOR; GWINNETT COUNTY HISTORIAN; PO BOX 333; LILBURN, GA 30247. (#16302).

THOMAS WYNNE HOUSE AS NATIONAL HISTORIC SITE, GA. APPLICATION MADE TO ENTER THOMAS WYNNE HOUSE ON NATIONAL REGISTER OF HISTORIC PLACES. (LOCAL). JANIS K SAWYER, CO-CHAIRMAN; LILBURN WOMEN'S CLUB; 4304 LAWRENCEVILLE HWY; LILBURN, GA 30247. (#24044).

MAR 15, '76. 6TH GRADE ESSAY CONTEST. CONTEST THEME: 'A PAST TO REMEMBER, A FUTURE TO MOLD.'. (LOCAL). MRS FELICIA TANZOSCH; LILBURN BICENTENNIAL COMMITTEE; 669 SOUTHWIND DR; LILBURN, GA 30247. (#107365-7).

MAY 16, '76. TOUR OF LOCAL HOMES OF INTEREST. TOUR AT IN HOMES. (LOCAL). MRS JUDY BUFORD, DIRECTOR; PATRONS OF LILBURN LIBRARY; 4243 THERESA WAY; LILBURN, GA 30247. (#107365-1).

JULY 4, '76. INDEPENDENCE DAY PARADE. PARADE THEME - 'A PAST TO REMEMBER, A FUTURE TO MOLD. (LOCAL). MRS BETTY PASEK, COORD; LILBURN WOMEN'S CLUB; 903 BRADFORD COURT; LILBURN, GA 30247. (#107365-5).

JULY 5, '76. ART CONTEST WITH THEME - 'A PAST TO REMEMBER, A FUTURE TO MOLD'. 5 AREA ELEMENTARY SCHOOLS PARTICIPATED, GRADES ONE THRU FIVE. A RIBBON AWARD WAS AWARDED WINNING ENTRIES FROM ROCKBRIDGE, LILBURN, CAMP CREEK, KNIGHT AND BETHESDA ELEMENTARY SCHOOLS. AT LILBURN CITY HALL, MAIN STREET, LILBURN, GA. (LOCAL). MRS FAYE MOORE, COORD; LILBURN WOMEN'S CLUB; 907 BRADFORD COURT; LILBURN, GA 30247. (#107365-6).

JULY 5, '76. DEDICATION CEREMONY AT CITY HALL. CEREMONY. (LOCAL). HON JOHN F SAWYER, MAYOR; CITY OF LILBURN; 4304 LAWRENCEVILLE HWY; LILBURN, GA 30247. (#107365-4).

JULY 5, '76. DISPLAYS OF OLD PICTURES AND DOCUMENTS OF LOCAL AREA. EXHIBIT AT NEW CITY MUNICIPAL BBLDG & ADJACENT AREA. (LOCAL). MRS NELLIE MCCOY, COORD; BOY SCOUTS OF AMERICA; 4814 CHURCH ST; LILBURN, GA 30247. (#107365-3).

JULY 5, '76. PRESENTATION OF PORTRAIT OF ORIGINAL SETTLER. CEREMONY. (LOCAL). MRS LUCILLE BALDWIN, DIR; DESCENDENTS OF MCDANIEL & LILBURN BICENTENNIAL COMMITTEE; 1764 FULTON WAY; NORCROSS, GA 30071. (#107365-2).

LINCOLNTON

AUDIO-VISUAL PRESENTATION ON ELIJAH CLARKE-GA HERO. PREPARATION OF AN AUDIO-VISUAL ABOUT ELIJAH CLARKE, ONE OF GEORGIA'S REVOLUTIONARY HEROES. PLANNING OTHER COMMEMORATIONS HONORING CLARKE AT ELIJAH CLARKE STATE PARK. (ST-WIDE). JIM OATES, CHIEF RECREATION & PLANNING SECTION; GEORGIA DEPT OF NATURAL RESOURCES; 270 WASHINGTON ST SW; ATLANTA, GA 30334. (#579). **(??).**

LITHIA SPRING

TRAIL MARKING PROJECT, LITHIA SPRING, GA. THE TRAILS TRAVELLED BY WILLIAM BARTRAM, IN THE COLONY OF GEORGIA FROM 1773 TO 1776 WILL BE CLEARED & MARKED. (LOCAL). GRADY BELL, PRESIDENT; BARTRAM TRAIL SOCIETY; 6688 MARSH AVE; LITHIA SPRING, GA 30057. (#19353). **ARBA GRANTEE.**

LITHONIA

OCT 2, '76. FALL FESTIVAL. FESTIVAL INCLUDES ARTS & CRAFTS EXHIBITS, A CARNIVAL & POLITICAL DEBATES. AT LITHONIA PLAZA. (LOCAL). LINDA BRYANT, CHMN; POSITIVE ACTION FOR LITHONIA; 2586 REAGIN ST; LITHONIA, GA 30058. (#200012-59).

LOGANVILLE

LOGANVILLE BICENTENNIAL MESSAGE BOARD - GA. A MESSAGE BOARD FOR THE PUBLIC TO DRIVE BY AND READ. (LOCAL). DEWEY MOODY, CHAIRMAN; LOGANVILLE BICENTENNIAL COMMITTEE; ROUTE 1; LOGANVILLE, GA 30249. (#24167). **ARBA GRANTEE.**

LOGANVILLE BICENTENNIAL PARK - LOGANVILLE, CA. A PARK FOR PUBLIC USE WITH PICNIC TABLES AND GRILLS. (LOCAL). DEWEY MOODY, CHAIRMAN; LOGANVILLE BICENTENNIAL COMMITTEE; ROUTE 1; LOGANVILLE, GA 30249. (#24168).

STUDY - SEARCH FOR NEW NEGRO LEADERSHIP 1915-1925. STUDIES RISE OF NEW NEGRO LEADERS LIKE MARCUS GARVEY AND THE STRUGGLES OF OLD LEADERS LIKE EMMETT J SCOTT AND ROBERT R MOTON. ALSO DEALS WITH THE RISE OF A MULATTO MIDDLE CLASS ESTABLISHMENT. (NAT'L). PROF CARL S MATTHEWS; ROUTE #3; LOGANVILLE, GA 30249. (#4228).

JAN 1 - DEC 31, '76. PERFORMANCES BY LOGANVILLE AREA BICENTENNIAL CHORUS. 50 SINGERS DRESSED IN RED, WHITE & BLUE WILL PERFORM PATRIOTIC & RELIGIOUS MUSIC. THIS GROUP IS AVAILABLE FOR PERFORMANCES ANYWHERE IN GEORGIA. (LOCAL). DEWEY MOODY, CHAIRMAN; LOGANVILLE BICENTENNIAL COMMITTEE; RT 1; LOGANVILLE, GA 30249. (#106753-1).

LOUISVILLE

COMMUNITY MAINTENANCE PROJECT OF LOUISVILLE, GA. PROJECT WILL BE TO CLEANUP STREETS AND PUBLIC PLACES; YOUTH GROUPS WILL SUPERVISE REMOVAL OF LITTER; AN AWARD WILL BE GIVEN FOR BEST KEPT YARDS. (LOCAL). NELL IRWIN, CHAIRMAN; LOUISVILLE BICENTENNIAL COMMITTEE; 609 MULBERRY ST; LOUISVILLE, GA 30434. (#11327).

HISTORICAL DOCUMENTS EXHIBITION IN LOUISVILLE, GA. PROJECT IS AN EXHIBIT OF HISTORIC MAPS, LEAFLETS, NEWSPAPERS AND BOOKS FROM AND ABOUT JEFFERSON COUNTY AND ITS PRIMARY CITY, LOUISVILLE. (LOCAL). NELL IRWIN, CO-CHAIRMAN; LOUISVILLE BICENTENNIAL COMMITTEE; 609 MULBERRY ST; LOUISVILLE, GA 30434. (#11324).

PRESERVATION OF OLD MARKET HOUSE - LOUISVILLE, GA. PROJECT WILL BE TO PRESERVE ORIGINAL MARKET HOUSE BY MAINTAINING SHRUBBERY & GROUNDS; PLACING PLAQUES STATING HISTORY OF STRUCTURE & MAINTENANCE OF ADJOINING PARKWAY GROUNDS. (LOCAL). NELL IRWIN, CHAIRMAN; LOUISVILLE BICENTENNIAL COMMITTEE; 609 MULBERRY ST; LOUISVILLE, GA 30434. (#11328).

RESTORATION OF HISTORIC CEMETERY IN LOUISVILLE, GA. PROJECT ENTAILS CLEARING DEBRIS, CLEANING HEADSTONES, REPAINTING SIGNS & REBUILDING ROADS AT A PRE-REVOLUTIONARY CEMETERY. (LOCAL). NELL IRWIN, CO-CHAIRMAN; LOUISVILLE BICENTENNIAL COMMITTEE; 609 MULBERRY ST; LOUISVILLE, GA 30434. (#11323).

JULY 1 - 5, '76. ANNUAL COMMUNITY FESTIVAL. FESTIVAL, EXHIBIT. (LOCAL). NELL IRWIN; 609 MULBERRY ST; LOUISVILLE, GA 30434. (#11326-1).

JULY 4, '76. FESTIVAL OF FAITHS. CEREMONY, EXHIBIT. (LOCAL). NELL IRWON; LOUISVILLE BICENTENNIAL COMMITTEE; 609 MULBERRY ST; LOUISVILLE, GA 30434. (#11325-1).

LUDOWICI

MAR 3, '76. UNITED STATES ARMED FORCES BICENTENNIAL CARAVAN. CARAVAN IS COMPOSED OF EXHIBIT VANS FOR EACH MILITARY SERVICE. PROJECT THEME IS 'HISTORY OF THE ARMED FORCES AND THEIR CONTRIBUTIONS TO THE NATION'. AT MCQUEEN ST, ADJ TO DEPOT BAND ON DEPOT PLATFORM.. (LOCAL). MRS J W JACKSON; US ARMED FORCES BICENTENNIAL EXHIBIT VANS PROJECT; PO BOX 306; LUDOWICI, GA 31316. (#1775-439).

MAR 3 - 4, '76. FORT STEWART ARMY BAND CONCERT. LIVE PERFORMANCE AT LODOWICI DEPOT. (LOCAL). MRS J W JACKSON, DIR; LONG COUNTY BICENTENNIAL COMMITTEE; GILL & ACADEMY; LUDOWICI, GA 31316. (#104162-1).

LULA

CHILDREN'S ART CONTEST: 'NEW LOOK FOR MY TOWN'. SCHOOL AGE CHILDREN TO COMPETE BY DEPICTING FUTURE LOOK OF THE TOWN. (LOCAL). TOM TERRELL, PRESIDENT; LULA AREA BUSINESS ASSOC; PO BOX 505; LULA, GA 30554. (#108036-6).

COMMUNITY DEVELOPMENT CONCEPT, LULA, GA. REVITILIZATION OF DOWNTOWN BUSINESS AREA. (LOCAL). HONORABLE I J WHITWORTH, MAYOR; CITY OF LULA; LULA, GA 30554. (#25394).

'HAPPY BIRTHDAY AMERICA'-PATRIOTIC MUSIC BY LOCAL HS CHORUS. LIVE PERFORMANCE. (LOCAL). CAROL FRANKYM, COORD; EAST HALL HIGH SCHOOL; ROUTE 10; GAINESVILLE, GA 30554. (#108036-5).

HERITAGE DEVELOPMENT PROJECT, LULA, GA. RECONSTRUCT BELTON BRIDGE, ONLY COVERED BRIDGE IN HALL CO. (LOCAL). TOM TERRELL, PROJ COORDINATOR; LULA BUSINESS ASSOC; PO BOX 505; LULA, GA 30554. (#25392).

HERITAGE FESTIVAL WITH DISPLAYS, CONTEST & COMMUNITY ACTIVITIES. FESTIVAL. (LOCAL). TOM TERRELL, PRESIDENT; LULA AREA BUSINESS ASSOC; PO BOX 505; LULA, GA 30554. (#108036-4).

HERITAGE OF COMMUNITY, LULA, GA. SERIES OF DISPLAYS, PICTURES AND ARTICLES ON LOCAL HISTORY FOR THE PUBLIC. (LOCAL). TOM TERRELL, PROJ COORDINATOR; LULA AREA BUSINESS ASSOC; PO BOX 505; LULA, GA 30554. (#25391).

'HURRAY FOR THE RED, WHITE & BLUE' - PERFORMANCE ON AMER HERITAGE. PERFORMANCE BY GROUP OF SCHOOL CHILDREN. (LOCAL). STEVE BRINSON, PRESIDENT; LULA ELEMENTARY PARENT-TEACHER ASSOC; LULA, GA 30554. (#108036-3).

OPEN AIR WORSHIP SERVICE WITH FOCUS ON NATL RELIGIOUS HERITAGE. CEREMONY. (LOCAL). R S PRESSLEY, CO-CHAIRMAN; LULA AREA CHURCHES; LULA, GA 30554. (#108036-2).

OPERATION CLEANUP, LULA, GA. INDIVIDUAL & COMMUNITY PARTICIPATION IN CLEANUP CAMPAIGN; CLEARING DEBRIS, PLANTING SHRUBBERY, PLANTS AND FLOWERS IN PUBLIC AND PRIVATE SECTORS. (LOCAL). HONORABLE I J WHITWORTH, MAYOR; CITY OF LULA; LULA, GA 30554. (#25393).

PARADE WITH SALUTE TO THE OLDEN DAYS THEME. PARADE. (LOCAL). TOM TERRELL, PRESIDENT; LULA AREA BUSINESS ASSOC; PO BOX 505; LULA, GA 30554. (#108036-1).

SEPT 6, '76. NEIGHBORHOOD ENHANCEMENT CONTEST. COMPETITION. (LOCAL). HON I J WHITWORTH, MAYOR; CITY OF LULA & LULA AREA BUSINESS ASSOC; LULA, GA 30554. (#107960-1).

LUMBER CITY

BICENTENNIAL DECOR FOR DOWNTOWN, LUMBER CITY, GA. DECORATE DOWNTOWN AREA AND INDOOR AREAS WITH PATRIOTIC THEME. (LOCAL). JILL BOWEN, PROJ DIRECTOR; DECORATION COMMITTEE OF LUMBER CITY BICENTENNIAL COMMITTEE; EAST RIVER ST; LUMBER CITY, GA 31549. (#25359).

BICENTENNIAL UPDATE, LUMBER CITY, GA. KEEPING CITIZENS ABREAST OF PROGRESS MADE TOWARDS GOALS OF THE OVERALL BICENTENNIAL COMMITTEE. (LOCAL). KATHLEEN BREWER, COORDINATOR; PUBLICITY COMMITTEE OF THE LUMBER CITY BICENTENNIAL COMMITTEE; RT 1; LUMBER CITY, GA 31549. (#25361).

CITY PARADE LED BY U S ARMY BAND & INCLUDING HIGH SCHOOL BANDS. PARADE. (LOCAL). JAMES RIGSHY, CHMN; LUMBER CITY BICENTENNIAL COMMITTEE; OLD SAND PIT RD; LUMBER CITY, GA 31549. (#107954-2).

DRILL LESSONS, LUMBER CITY, GA. LONG RANGE PROGRAM TEACHING CHILDREN MARCHES AND DRILLS. THIS WILL HELP REVIVE PATRIOTISM IN THE COMMUNITY. (LOCAL). BILL YEOMANS, CHAIRMAN; DRILL COMMITTEE OF LUMBER CITY BICENTENNIAL COMMITTEE; RT 1; LUMBER CITY, GA 31549. (#25357).

LANDSCAPE AND COMMUNITY CLEAN-UP, LUMBER CITY, GA. BEAUTIFICATION OF COMMUNITY BY CLEANING UP AND LANDSCAPING. (LOCAL). MRS LEAH THOMPSON, COORDINATOR; LANDSCAPE COMMITTEE OF LUMBER CITY BICENTENNIAL COMMITTEE; BOYD; LUMBER CITY, GA 31549. (#25364).

MOVIE DISTRIBUTION, LUMBER CITY, GA. THE FINANCE COMMITTEE WILL RECEIVE AND DISTRIBUTE MONIES. (LOCAL). RANDALL HAND, COORDINATOR; FINANCE COMMITTEE OF LUMBER CITY BICENTENNIAL COMMITTEE; CENTRAL AVE; LUMBER CITY, GA 31549. (#25354).

MUSEUM PROJECT, LUMBER CITY, GA. OLD JAIL HOUSE WILL BE RENOVATED & CONVERTED INTO A MUSEUM FOR THE PRESERVATION OF LOCAL HISTORY. THE INDUSTRIAL COMMITTEE WILL DONATE MATERIALS & FUNDS. (LOCAL). MRS LAURA BRAMBLET, CHAIRMAN; INDUSTRIAL COMMITTEE & LUMBER CITY BICENTENNIAL COMMITTEE; INDUSTRIAL PARK; LUMBER CITY, GA 31549. (#25365).

PATRIOTIC CONCERT BY CHURCH CHOIRS FROM THE COMMUNITY. LIVE PERFORMANCE. (LOCAL). MARGARET HULETTE, CHWMN; LUMBER CITY BICENTENNIAL COMMITTEE; OLD RIVER RD; LUMBER CITY, GA 31549. (#107954-3).

PERIOD COSTUMES, LUMBER CITY,GA. DESIGN AND MAKE PERIOD COSTUMES FOR COSTUME BALL. (LOCAL). MARTHA T BROWN, PROJ COORDINATOR; COSTUME COMMITTEE OF LUMBER CITY BICENTENNIAL COMMITTEE; EAST RIVER ST; LUMBER CITY, GA 31549. (#25358).

PUBLIC SAFETY, LUMBER CITY, GA. PUBLIC SAFETY WILL BE EMPHASIZED BY SIGNS, POSTERS, NEWSPAPER ARTICLES, RADIO PROGRAMS AND BY STRICT ENFORCEMENT OF THE SAFETY LAWS. (LOCAL). HUGH HARRIS, PROJ CHAIRMAN; PUBLIC SAFETY DEPT; ERIC ST; LUMBER CITY, GA 31549. (#25356).

RESTORATION AND CONVERSION PROJ, LUMBER CITY, GA. RESTORATION OF OLD BUILDING WHICH WILL BE CONVERTED INTO THE PUBLIC LIBRARY. (LOCAL). MRS LUCILLE MOORE, PROJ DIRECTOR; LIBRARY COMMITTEE OF LUMBER CITY BICENTENNIAL COMMITTEE; CHURCH ST; LUMBER CITY, GA 31549. (#25355).

RESTORATION OF OLD JAIL, LUMBER CITY, GA. RESTORE THE OLD JAIL AS A PERMANENT BUILDING TO HOUSE AND DISPLAY ARTICLES USED BY CITIZENS OF THIS AREA FROM 1800'S TO PRESENT TIME. (LOCAL). MONTERIE C BREWER, CHAIRMAN; MUSEUM COMMITTEE OF THE LUMBER CITY BICENTENNIAL COMMITTEE; CHURCH ST; LUMBER CITY, GA 31549. (#25372).

SHOPPING DISTRICT IMPROVEMENTS, LUMBER CITY, GA. MERCHANTS WILL IMPROVE APPEARANCE OF SHOPPING DISTRICT BY PAINTING AND REMODELING STORE FRONTS; AMERICAN FLAGS WILL ALSO BE DISPLAYED. (LOCAL). KITTY DARBY, CHAIRPERSON; MERCHANTS COMMITTEE OF LUMBER CITY BICENTENNIAL COMMITTEE; CHURCH ST; LUMBER CITY, GA 31549. (#25366).

JULY 2 - 3, '76. ARTS AND CRAFTS EXHIBIT FEATURING HANDWORK OF LOCAL CITIZENS. EXHIBIT. (LOCAL). BETTY BROWN, CHMN; LUMBER CITY BICENTENNIAL COMMITTEE; GLENWOOD HWY; LUMBER CITY, GA 31549. (#107954-1).

JULY 3, '76. AGRICULTURAL EXHIBITS: DISPLAYS OF FARM PRODUCE & TOOLS OF THE PAST. EXHIBIT. (LOCAL). JEANETTE BAN, CHAIRMAN; LUMBER CITY BICENTENNIAL COMMITTEE; RT 1; LUMBER CITY, GA 31549. (#107973-1).

LUMBER CITY — CONTINUED

JULY 3, '76. STREET DANCE AND FESTIVAL. DOWNTOWN STREETS WILL BE BLOCKED OFF AND USED AS A GROUNDS FOR A FESTIVAL WHICH WILL INCLUDE GAMES, EXHIBITS, CRAFTS SHOW, DANCING AND MANY OTHER ACTIVITIES. (LOCAL). HARRIETT BROWN, COORD; LUMBER CITY BICENTENNIAL COMMITTEE; CENTRAL AVE; LUMBER CITY, GA 31549. (#107955-1).

LUMPKIN

BICENTENNIAL CELEBRATION IN SCHOOLS, LUMPKIN, GA. STUDENTS WILL BE ENCOURAGED TO TAKE PART IN LOCAL, STATE & NATIONAL BICENTENNIAL EVENTS, SUCH AS ART SHOWS, ESSAY CONTESTS AND OTHER PROJECTS DEALING WITH THE BICENTENNIAL. (LOCAL). MRS T M FORT, PROJ DIRECTOR; LUMPKIN AREA BICENTENNIAL COMMITTEE; MAIN ST; LUMPKIN, GA 31815. (#12578).

BICYCLE SAFETY PROGRAM IN LUMPKIN, GA. PROGRAM IN CONJUNCTION WITH CITY AND COUNTY PERSONNEL TO EDUCATE BICYCLERS IN SAFETY PROCEDURES. (LOCAL). JIM RAULSTON, PROJ DIRECTOR; LUMPKIN AREA BICENTENNIAL COMMITTEE; PROVIDENCE CANYON RD; LUMPKIN, GA 31815. (#12574).

CIVIC UNDERSTANDING AND PUBLIC AFFAIRS SEMINARS. COMMUNITY DISCUSSIONS ON PROBLEM IDENTIFICATION, ECONOMIC DEVELOPMENT, HUMAN RESOURCES PLANNING & PHYSICAL PLANNING FOR THE COMMUNITY. (LOCAL). HON PERRY USHER, COORD; STEWART COUNTY; STEWART COUNTY COURTHOUSE; LUMPKIN, GA 31815. (#108354-1).

DOWNTOWN BEAUTIFICATION IN LUMPKIN, GA. A JOINT PROJECT OF AREA BICENTENNIAL COMMITTEE, GARDEN CLUB, SCOUTS, 4-H, HISTORICAL COMMISSION, DOWNTOWN MERCHANTS & GOVERNMENT, TO GIVE DOWNTOWN A FACE LIFT. (LOCAL). MRS T E MILLER, CHAIRMAN; LUMPKIN AREA BICENTENNIAL COMMITTEE; LONGVIEW FARMS, RTE 1 BOX 98; LUMPKIN, GA 31815. (#12576).

EARLY AMERICAN FOOD & HOSPITALITY IN LUMPKIN, GA. PROJECT IS A BOOKLET DESCRIBING OLD TABLE CUSTOMS, MENUS, HISTORY OF FOOD ORIGINS, INFORMATION ON EARLY STAGE COACH INNS AND HISTORICAL ANECDOTE. (LOCAL). MRS T E MILLER, CHAIRWOMAN; LUMPKIN AREA BICENTENNIAL COMMITTEE; LONGVIEW FARMS, RT 1, BOX 98; LUMPKIN, GA 31815. (#12589).

EDUCATION CENTER IN LUMPKIN, GA. CHATTAHOOCHEE COUNTY COURTHOUSE, BUILT IN 1800'S, IS BEING PRESERVED AND RELOCATED IN WESTVILLE; BUILDING WILL BE USED AS A CONTINUING EDUCATION HISTORY CENTER. (LOCAL). DR JOSEPH MAHAN, DIRECTOR; WESTVILLE HANDICRAFTS, INC; LUMPKIN, GA 31815. (#12587).

GARDEN CLUB PARK & BIRD SANCTUARY, LUMPKIN, GA. ESTABLISHMENT AND MAINTENANCE OF PARK AND BIRD SACTUARY AT HISTORIC WESTVILLEVILLAGE. (LOCAL). MRS RICHARD MORRISON, CHAIRMAN; LUMPKIN AREA BICENTENNIAL COMMITTEE; COUNTY LINE RD; LUMPKIN, GA 31815. (#12582).

HERITAGE HALL, LUMPKIN, GA. ESTABLISHING PERMANENT DISPLAY OF DOCUMENTS RELATING TO THE FOUNDING OF THE NATION, STATE AND COMMUNITY, WHICH WILL BE PLACED IN CENTER DOWNSTAIRS HALL OF STEWART COUNTY COURTHOUSE. (LOCAL). JACK HARRIS, CHAIRMAN; LUMPKIN AREA BICENTENNIAL COMMITTEE; MAIN ST; LUMPKIN, GA 31815. (#12585).

A HERITAGE OF MUSIC IN LUMPKIN, GA. SINGING ENGAGEMENTS THROUGHOUT SEVERAL COMMUNITIES WILL SPECIALIZE IN APPROPRIATE BICENTENNIAL SELECTIONS; GROUP PLANS TO MAKE BICENTENNIAL COSTUMES. (LOCAL). JIMMY BABB, CO-DIRECTOR; LUMPKIN YOUTH CHOIR; BROAD ST; LUMPKIN, GA 31815. (#12586).

INDIAN RESEARCH IN LUMPKIN, GA. RESEARCH OF AREA INDIAN TRIBES, DESCRIBING IMPACT & EFFECT ON AREA. TRIBAL LOCATIONS WILL BE DEPICTED ON LARGE COUNTY MAP FOR DISPLAY. (LOCAL). MRS BOB GILMAN, CUB SCOUT TASK FORCE; LUMPKIN AREA BICENTENNIAL COMMITTEE; LUMPKIN, GA 31815. (#12572).

'JUNK THE JUNKS' - CLEANUP PROJ OF LUMPKIN, GA. THE LOCAL 4-H WILL CLEANUP ABANDONED CARS. (LOCAL). MRS IRENE DUBOSE, CHAIRMAN; LUMPKIN AREA BICENTENNIAL COMMITTEE; HOUSE AVE; LUMPKIN, GA 31815. (#15246).

MASONIC LODGE RESTORATION, LUMPKIN, GA. RESTORATION AND DEDICATION OF LODGE HALL AT WESTVILLE; BUILDING DATES BACK TO EARLY 1800'S. (LOCAL). HENRY LYNCH, SR, GRAND MASON; CROSS LODGE #173, F & A M; PLEASANT VALLEY RD; LUMPKIN, GA 31815. (#12580).

NATURE TRAIL IN LUMPKIN, GA. ESTABLISHMENT & MAINTENANCE OF NATURE TRAIL AT HISTORIC WESTVILLE. PLANT LIFE WILL BE LABELED. (LOCAL). MRS RICHARD MORRISON, PROJ DIRECTOR; LUMPKIN AREA BICENTENNIAL COMMITTEE; COUNTY LINE RD; LUMPKIN, GA 31815. (#12575).

NEW LUMPKIN LIBRARY AND CULTURAL CENTER - GA. THE LIBRARY IS BEING RELOCATED AND EXPANDED TO ADD A PERMANENT RESEARCH SECTION, A MINI ART GALLERY, FILM & VISUAL AIDS CENTER, DISPLAY AND EXHIBITION AREA AND A CENTER FOR THE COMMUNITY. (LOCAL). MRS T E MILLER, CHMN; LUMPKIN AREA COMMISSION FOR THE NATL BICENTENNIAL CELEBRATION; LONGVIEW FARMS, RT 1, BOX 98; LUMPKIN, GA 31815. (#16126). **ARBA GRANTEE.**

ORAL HISTORY OF STEWART COUNTY, LUMPKIN, GA. STUDENTS WILL INTERVIEW OLDER RESIDENTS OF THE AREA; TAPES OF THESE INTERVIEWS WILL BE MADE AVAILABLE TO THE PUBLIC THROUGH THE LUMPKIN LIBRARY. (LOCAL). MRS T E MILLER, CHAIRMAN; LUMPKIN AREA BICENTENNIAL COMMITTEE; LONGVIEW FARMS, RTE 1, BOX 98; LUMPKIN, GA 31815. (#12584).

RECREATION CENTER IN LUMPKIN, GA. PERMANENT RECREATION CENTER FOR COMMUNITY, CONTAINING FACILITIES FOR TENNIS AND OTHER SPORTS, WITH A PLAYGROUND AREA. (LOCAL). HON THOMAS S KEMP, MAYOR; CITY OF LUMPKIN; CITY HALL; LUMPKIN, GA 31815. (#12579).

RESTORATION OF ELAM CEMETERIES - LUMPKIN, GA. CLEAN-UP, RESTORATION, MARKER IDENTIFICATION & LANDSCAPING OF CEMETERY; PRE-CIVIL WAR HISTORY WILL BE RESEARCHED. (LOCAL). MRS LYDIA CATCHINGS, PROJ COORDINATOR; MILL BETHEL BAPTIST CHURCH; EUFAULA HWY; LUMPKIN, GA 31815. (#26640).

SALUTE TO WOMEN - WHITE HOUSE HOSTESSES, GA. SLIDE PRESENTATION OBTAINED FROM SMITHSONIAN DEPICTING GOWNS WORN BY FIRST LADIES & WHITE HOUSE HOSTESSES FROM MARTHA WASHINGTON TO PRESENT. AVAILABLE TO CLUBS, GROUPS, HISTORICAL SOCIETIES, ETC. (ST-WIDE). MRS T E MILLER, CHAIRMAN; LUMPKIN AREA BICENTENNIAL COMMITTEE; LONGVIEW FARMS, ROUTE 1 BOX 98; LUMPKIN, GA 31815. (#12571).

STEWART COUNTY HISTORY UPDATE, LUMPKIN, GA. ADDITIONS TO STEWART COUNTY'S PUBLISHED HISTORY WILL BE MADE. (ST-WIDE). MRS T E MILLER, CHAIRMAN; LUMPKIN AREA BICENTENNIAL COMMITTEE; LONGVIEW FARMS, RTE 1 BOX 98; LUMPKIN, GA 31815. (#12577).

STEWART COUNTY HISTORICAL INVENTORY, LUMPKIN, GA. EXTENSIVE RESEARCH & CATALOGUING OF ITEMS FROM EARLY STEWART COUNTY, TO PROVIDE A PHOTOGRAPHIC RECORD OF HANDMADE DOMESTIC ITEMS CREATED IN STEWART COUNTY. (ST-WIDE). MRS L M MOYE, PUBLICATIONS CHAIRMAN; LUMPKIN AREA BICENTENNIAL COMMITTEE; CUTHBERT HWY; LUMPKIN, GA 31815. (#12583).

STEWART COUNTY HISTORY ARTICLES - LUMPKIN, GA. WEEKLY PUBLICATION IN COUNTY NEWSPAPER OF IMPORTANT EVENTS AND DATES IN STEWART COUNTY HISTORY, TO MAKE COMMUNITY AWARE OF ITS HERITAGE. (LOCAL). MRS L M MOYE, PUBLICATION TASK FORCE; LUMPKIN AREA BICENTENNIAL COMMITTEE; CUTHBERT HWY; LUMPKIN, GA 31815. (#12588).

YOUNG COMMUNITY VOLUNTEERS, LUMPKIN, GA. PLANNED PROGRAM OF CONTINUING VOLUNTEERISM AT STEWART-WEBSTER HOSPITAL, HISTORIC WESTVILLE AND BEDINGFIELD INN. (LOCAL). MRS IRENE DUBOSE, PROJ DIRECTOR; LUMPKIN AREA BICENTENNIAL COMMITTEE; HOUSE AVE; LUMPKIN, GA 31815. (#12581).

YOUTH CORPS TRAINING PROGRAM IN LUMPKIN, GA. PROGRAM FOR YOUTH PROVIDING TRAINING, EMPLOYMENT & MEANINGFUL ACTIVITY FOR MINORITY & UNDERPRIVILEGDED YOUNG PEOPLE. (LOCAL). MRS LEON BUTTS, CHAIRMAN; STEWART COUNTY HISTORICAL COMMITTEE; CHESTNUT ST; LUMPKIN, GA 31815. (#12573).

SEPT 25, '75. SALUTE TO WOMEN - VOLUNTEER APPRECIATION, GA. RECEPTION FOR VOLUNTEERS TO BE HELD AT BEDINGFIELD INN, WITH A CHORAL PROGRAM BY LUMPKIN YOUTH CHOIR. (LOCAL). MRS W B SINGER; LUMPKIN AREA BICENTENNIAL COMMITTEE; MAIN ST; LUMPKIN, GA 31815. (#12570-1).

MAR 19 - 21, '76. BICENTENNIAL SADDLE RIDE THROUGH HISTORIC SITES OF STEWART COUNTY. TOUR. (LOCAL). T M FORT, JR, COORD; ROANOKE SADDLE CLUB; MAIN ST; LUMPKIN, GA 31815. (#200012-25).

MAY 8, '76. SALUTE TO WOMEN FASHION PAGEANT - FIRST LADIES' GOWNS, 1825-1853. FASHION SHOW FEATURING REPRODUCTIONS OF WHITE HOUSE HOSTESS GOWNS WORN BY FIRST LADIES IN 2ND QUARTER OF 19TH CENTURY. AT WESTVILLE VILLAGE, RECONSTRUCTED 1850'S TOWN. (REGN'L). MRS T E MILLER, COORD; LUMPKIN AREA BICENTENNIAL COMMITTEE & ROANOKE CHAPTER DAR; LONGVIEW FARMS; LUMPKIN, GA 31815. (#200012-26).

JULY 4, '76. WESTVILLE VILLAGE INDEPENDENCE DAY CELEBRATION. OLD-FASHIONED INDEPENDENCE DAY FEATURING EARLY AMERICAN CRAFTS, EVENTS, BARBEQUE & POLITICAL STUMP ACTIVITIES. AT 2:30PM, ROLL CALL & RECOGNITION OF SOUTHERN INDIAN TRIBES. DEDICATION OF CHATTAHOOCHEE COURTHOUSE. (LOCAL). LEE MILLER, DIRECTOR; LUMPKIN BICENTENNIAL COMMISSION; LUMPKIN, GA 31815. (#103556-1).

MACON

AFRO-AMERICAN LIFE & HERITAGE CENTER OF MACON, GA. PROJECT IS DESIGNED TO PRODUCE & DISSEMINATE MATERIALS OF CONTRIBUTIONS MADE BY OUTSTANDING AFRO-AMERICANS IN THE MIDDLE GEORGIA AREA TO THE TOTAL HISTORY OF GEORGIA & THE NATION. (ST-WIDE). JOHN D MATTOX, CHAIRMAN; BOOKER T WASHINGTON COMMUNITY CENTER, INC; 509 COTTON AVE; MACON, GA 31201. (#28289). **ARBA GRANTEE.**

GEORGIA'S WILDLIFE HERITAGE 1776-1976, MACON. GEORGIA'S WILDLIFE HERITAGE INCLUDES 6 OF AMERICA'S BEST WILDLIFE ARTISTS EXHIBITING 48 ORIGINAL PAINTINGS AND LIMITED EDITION PRINTS AND VISITING MIDDLE AMERICA. (LOCAL). DOUGLAS R NOBLE, DIRECTOR; MUSEUM OF ARTS & SCIENCES; 4182 FORSYTH RD; MACON, GA 31204. (#23512). **ARBA GRANTEE.**

THE SPIRIT OF '76 - AMERICA IN REVIEW, MACON, GA. LIVE THEATER PERFORMANCE TRACING THE HISTORY OF THE U S FOR 6TH GRADE STUDENTS IN BIBB COUNTY SCHOOLS. (LOCAL). MRS ALFRED LOWE, JR, PLACEMENT CHAIRMAN; JUNIOR LEAGUE OF MACON, INC; 345 SPRING ST; MACON, GA 31201. (#22691). **ARBA GRANTEE.**

JUNE 6 - SEPT 6, '75. CREEK INDIAN VILLAGE AT OCMULGEE NATL MON. LIVE PERFORMANCE, EXHIBIT. (REGN'L). SUPT, OCMULGEE NATL MON; NATIONAL PARK SERVICE; P.O. BOX 4186; MACON, GA 31208. (#6729-61).

FEB 9 - 10, '76. THE SPIRIT OF '76 AMERICA IN REVIEW. A LIVE THEATER PERFORMANCE TRACING HISTORY OF THE U S. (LOCAL). MRS ALFRED LOWE, CHMN; JUNIOR LEAGUE OF MACON, INC; 345 SPRING ST; MACON, GA 31201. (#22691-1).

APR 1, '76 - CONTINUING . EXHIBITION OF N AMERICAN WILDLIFE PAINTINGS BY 6 NOTED AMER ARTISTS. INCLUDES 6 OF AMERICA'S BEST WILDLIFE ARTISTS EXHIBITING 48 ORIGINALS AND PRINTS TO MAKE MIDDLE GEORGIANS MORE AWARE OF THEIR GREAT NATURAL HERITAGE; THE HOURS GIVEN APPLY TO MON-DAY-FRIDAY. SATURDAY HOURS ARE 11-5; SUNDAY, IT IS OPEN FROM 2-5 PM. AT MUSEUM OF ARTS & SCIENCES. (REGN'L). DOUGLAS R NOBLE, DIRECTOR; MUSEUM OF ARTS & SCIENCES; 4182 FORSYTH RD; MACON, GA 31204. (#23512-1).

APR 4, '76. GOD BLESS AMERICA DAY. BICENTENNIAL THEME WILL BE CARRIED OUT IN A PATRIOTIC CELEBRATION INCLUDING DEMONSTRATIONS, CONTESTS & MUSIC. AT CENTRAL CITY PARK. (LOCAL). TOM STEVENS, CHMN; MACON JAYCEES; 4919 KATHRYN DR; MACON, GA 31204. (#103416-93).

APR 24, '76. LOST ARTS OF AMERICA FAIR. EACH TROOP IS RESPONSIBLE FOR MASTERING A COLONIAL ART SUCH AS QUILTING, CANDLEMAKING, SOAPMAKING AND DEMONSTRATING IT AT THE FAIR; THERE WILL ALSO BE COLONIAL GAMES, SKITS AND MUSICAL PERFORMANCES; FOOD WILL ALSO BE AVAILABLE. AT CENTRAL CITY PARK. (LOCAL). SUE CHIPMAN, DIRECTOR; MIDDLE GEORGIA GIRL SCOUT COUNCIL; 262 RILEY AVE; MACON, GA 31204. (#104278-3).

MAY 1 - 2, '76. GEORGIA JUBILEE. ARTS FESTIVAL FEATURES TWO DAYS OF ENTERTAINMENT, SPECIAL EXHIBITS, AND ACTIVITIES SALUTING THE BICENTENNIAL. AT CENTRAL CITY PARK. (ST-WIDE). JOSEPHINE BLAMB; GEORGIA JUBILEE, INC; 4182 FORSYTH RD; MACON, GA 31204. (#104464-1).

JUNE 19 - SEPT 6, '76. 1976 VISITING CRAFTSMEN LIVING INTERPRETATION PROGRAM. DEMONSTRATIONS OF CREEK INDIAN ARTS AND CRAFTS, AS WELL AS PRESENTATIONS ON CREEK INDIAN FOLKWAYS, WILL BE GIVEN BY CRAFTSMEN FROM CREEK NATION IN OKLAHOMA. INCLUDES SUCH AS BASKETWEAVING, DANCING, POTTERY DECORATION, PAINTING, WOOD CARVING. AT VISITOR CENTER. (REGN'L). OCMULGEE NATL MON; NATIONAL PARK SERVICE; P.O. BOX 4186; MACON, GA 31208. (#6729-561).

AUG 4 - 8, '76. HERITAGE SPECIAL - TRAIN TOUR. TRAVELING RAIL EXHIBIT EMPHASIZING COLONIAL AND REVOLUTIONARY GEORGIA HISTORY, CRAFTS & LIFESTYLE OF GEORGIA COLONISTS. EXHIBITS WILL BE DISPLAYED WITH COMBINATION OF SIGHT & SOUND ACTIVITY. AT DEPOT. (LOCAL). RON HENRY, DIRECTOR; GEORGIA BICENTENNIAL COMMISSION; 1776 PEACHTREE NW, ROOM 520 S; ATLANTA, GA 30309. (#7999-37).

OCT 18 - 23, '76. 121ST ANNUAL GEORGIA STATE FAIR. FAIR AT GEORGIA STATE FAIRGROUNDS. (REGN'L). CHARLES INMAN, CHMN; GEORGIA STATE FAIR; PO BOX 5260; MACON, GA 31208. (#103416-651).

NOV 18 - 19, '76. UNITED STATES ARMED FORCES BICENTENNIAL CARAVAN. CARAVAN IS COMPOSED OF EXHIBIT VANS FOR EACH MILITARY SERVICE. PROJECT THEME IS 'HISTORY OF THE ARMED FORCES & THEIR CONTRIBUTIONS TO THE NATION'. (LOCAL). MS BETTY JORDAN; UNITED STATES ARMED FORCES BICENTENNIAL CARAVAN; PO BOX 169; MACON, GA 31202. (#1775-777).

MADISON

CALVARY BAPTIST CHURCH - MADISON, GA. RESTORATION AND PRESERVATION OF THE CALVARY BAPTIST CHURCH, THE TOWN'S OLDEST CHURCH. (LOCAL). HENRY VEASLEY, CHAIRMAN; CALVARY BAPTIST CHURCH; 184 ACADEMY ST; MADISON, GA 30650. (#27888). **ARBA GRANTEE.**

RESTORATION OF OLD BLDG FOR CULTURAL CENTER, GA. AN AUDITORIUM FOR PERFORMING & CREATIVE ARTS, WITH MUSEUM ROOMS, TOURIST INFORMATION CENTER & HEADQUARTERS FOR TOURS OF OLD MADISON. MEETING ROOMS & ART, MUSIC & BALLET STUDIOS AVAILABLE. (LOCAL). PAUL W REID, CHAIRMAN; MORGAN COUNTY FOUNDATION, INC; PO BOX 643; MADISON, GA 30650. (#20219). **ARBA GRANTEE.**

RESTORATION OF RICHTER COTTAGE - MADISON, GA. THE RICHTER COTTAGE, BUILT IN 1820, IS BEING RESTORED. A GARDEN OF PLANTS AND SHRUBS FOUND IN MADISON IS PLANNED FOR THE GROUNDS. (LOCAL). W J ATKINSON, CHAIRMAN; MADISON-MORGAN BICENTENNIAL COMMITTEE; 1093 COLLEGE DR; MADISON, GA 30650. (#17920).

MAY 13, '76. MADISON BICENTENNIAL TOUR OF HOMES. MADISON'S BICENTENNIAL TOUR OFFERS BEAUTY, HISTORY AND OLD HOMES. AT MADISON METHODIST CHURCH. (ST-WIDE). MRS JACKIE PENNINGTON; RUTLEDGE ACADEMY; PO BOX 83; MADISON, GA 30650. (#103416-286).

NOV 11 - 12, '76. UNITED STATES ARMED FORCES BICENTENNIAL CARAVAN. CARAVAN IS COMPOSED OF EXHIBIT VANS FOR EACH MILITARY SERVICE. PROJECT THEME IS 'HISTORY OF THE ARMED FORCES & THEIR CONTRIBUTIONS TO THE NATION'. (LOCAL). WILLIAM ATKINSON; UNITED STATES ARMED FORCES BICENTENNIAL CARAVAN; ROUTE 2 BOX 4; MADISON, GA 30650. (#1775-775).

MANCHESTER

HISTORIC MERIWETHER COUNTY FILMSTRIP - GA. FILMSTRIP WITH SOUND DEPICTING HISTORIC SITES AND HAPPENINGS IN MERIWETHER COUNTY. (LOCAL). RICHARD R MCINTYRE, II, CHAIRMAN; MERIWETHER COUNTY BICENTENNIAL COMMITTEE; PO BOX 1776; MANCHESTER, GA 31816. (#27361). **ARBA GRANTEE.**

MAR 20, '76. MISS BICENTENNIAL BEAUTY PAGEANT. COMPETITION. (LOCAL). LYNNE C CARLISLE, PRES; MANCHESTER JUNIOR WOMEN'S CLUB; 5 CALLAWAY ST; MANCHESTER, GA 31816. (#200012-35).

MAR 24, '76. BICENTENNIAL DAY AT MANCHESTER ELEMENTARY SCHOOL. SPECIAL LUNCH MENU, ASSEMBLY PROGRAM, BICENTENNIAL FLAG TO BE RAISED. AT MANCHESTER ELEMENTARY SCHOOL, PERRY ST. (LOCAL). CAROLYN G KILBY, COORD; MANCHESTER ELEMENTARY SCHOOL; PERRY ST; MANCHESTER, GA 31816. (#200012-34).

MAY 1 - 2, '76. MAY FESTIVAL DAYS HONORING THE BICENTENNIAL. ACTIVITIES INCLUDE: HOMEMADE FOOD CONTEST, SPORTS EVENTS, ARTIFACTS EXHIBITS, ARTS & CRAFTS EXHIBITS, STREET DANCE, COUNTY ARTISTS EXHIBITS, HIGH SCHOOL BAND, GLEE CLUB AND FLAG DRILL TEAM PRESENTATION AND SQUARE DANCE DEMONSTRATION. (LOCAL). E BAKER, CO-CHAIRMAN; MANCHESTER-WARM SPRINGS PILOT & ROTARY CLUB; BOX 73, RFD #1; MANCHESTER, GA 31816. (#106544-1).

MARIETTA

AMERICA THROUGH LITERATURE, MARIETTA, GA. AN APPRAISAL OF AMERICA TO DATE THROUGH LITERATURE & HISTORY CLASSES TAUGHT BY ENGLISH AND SOCIAL STUDIES DEPARTMENT. (LOCAL). ROBERT FISCHER, CHAIRMAN; SOUTHERN TECH BICENTENNIAL COMMITTEEE; CLAY ST; MARIETTA, GA 30060. (#19010).

AMERICAN DOMESTIC ARCHITECTURE, MARIETTA, GA. BIBLIOGRAPHIES FROM 1900 COMPILED BY THE LIBRARY AS A SERVICE FOR RESEARCHERS. (LOCAL). ROBERT FISCHER, CHAIRMAN; SOUTHERN TECH BICENTENNIAL COMMITTEE; CLAY ST; MARIETTA, GA 30060. (#19011).

AMERICAN FILM FESTIVAL - MARIETTA, GA. FILMS CELEBRATING THE DIVERSITY OF AMERICAN CULTURE WILL BE SHOWN. (LOCAL). FRANK WILSON, COORDINATOR; OFFICE OF STUDENT AFFAIRS; KENNESAW JR COLLEGE; MARIETTA, GA 30061. (#20301).

BLACK HISTORY, LOST, STOLEN, OR STRAYED?, GA. BLACK HISTORY WILL BE DEPICTED IN A FILM PRESENTATION. (LOCAL). KENNETH SAGOES, PRESIDENT; BLACK STUDENTS ALLIANCE; KENNESAW JUNIOR COLLEGE; MARIETTA, GA 30061. (#20302).

BRIDGES TO THE PAST - BRIDGES TO THE FUTURE - GA. A YEAR-LONG PROGRAM TO INCULCATE PUPILS WITH APPRECIATION OF EARLY AMERICAN MORES; FOLKWAYS, CRAFTS FINALE AND COLONIAL FAIR INVOLVING STUDENTS AND PARENTS. (LOCAL). JACQUELINE GOLDEN, DIRECTOR; BRIDGES-COBB COUNTY, INC; 2568 HOLLY LANE, NE; MARIETTA, GA 30062. (#16191). **ARBA GRANTEE.**

CAMPUS ARBORETUM - MARIETTA, GA. DESIGN AND PLANTING OF ARBORETUM ON KJC CAMPUS TO CREATE INTEREST AMONG STUDENTS AND AREA RESIDENTS IN NATIVE TREES AND SHRUBS AS WELL AS 'INTRODUCED' VARIETIES. (LOCAL). DR MARY LANCE, ASSOC PROF OF BIOLOGY; DIVISION OF NATURAL SCIENCE; KENNESAW JR COLLEGE; MARIETTA, GA 30061. (#20300).

CAMPUS DISPLAYS, MARIETTA, GA. COMMEMORATIONS OF AMERICAN HISTORY: TRAIL OF TEARS, BLACK HISTORY, NURSING IN AMERICA, AMERICAN FLAGS. (LOCAL). MS MARTY GILES, ASSOCIATE LIBRARIAN; KENNESAW JUNIOR COLLEGE LIBRARY; KENNESAW JR COLLEGE; MARIETTA, GA 30061. (#20299).

CONCERT OF AMERICAN MUSIC. RECITAL BY A SOPRANO, ACCOMPANIED BY A PIANIST. (LOCAL). JOSEPH MEEKS, PROJ COORD; DIVISION OF HUMANITIES, KENNESAW JR COLLEGE; MARIETTA, GA 30061. (#104730-4).

GEORGIA STATE UNIVERSITY ORCHESTRA CONCERT. CONCERT FEATURING AMERICAN MUSIC WITH SOLOIST, JOSEPH MEEKS, KENNESAW JR COLLEGE FACULTY MEMBER. (LOCAL). JOSEPH MEEKS, PROJ COORD; DIVISION OF HUMANITIES, KENNESAW JR COLLEGE; MARIETTA, GA 30061. (#104730-1).

'HORIZONS '76' PLAQUE - MARIETTA, GA. RETIREES FROM AFPRO LOCKHEED GEORGIA CO WILL HAVE THEIR NAMES ENGRAVED ON A PLAQUE; THE PLAQUE WILL BE PRESENTED TO AFPRO ON RETIREMENT OF THE DEPUTY COMMANDER. (LOCAL). LAURA J WALLACE, CHAIRPERSON; AFPRO LOCKHEED GEORGIA COMPANY; S COBB DR; MARIETTA, GA 30063. (#28673).

STATE TREE PROJ, MARIETTA, GA. TREES WILL BE SOLICITED FROM EACH STATE AND PLANTED ON THE SOUTHERN TECH CAMPUS; THESE STATE TREES WILL PROVIDE A LASTING COMMEMORATION OF THE NATION'S BICENTENNIAL. (LOCAL). ROBERT FISCHER, CHAIRMAN; SOUTHERN TECH BICENTENNIAL COMMITTEE; CLAY ST; MARIETTA, GA 30060. (#19009).

SUMMER BICENTENNIAL PLAYGROUND & ARTS PROGRAM, GA. BICENTENNIAL ARTS & CRAFTS PLAYGROUND PROGRAMS CONDUCTED AT VARIOUS PARKS IN COBB COUNTY IN ROTATING FASHION THROUGH USE OF MOBILE UNITS IN ORDER TO REACH YOUTHS & ADULTS IN ALL AREAS IN COBB COUNTY. (LOCAL). ROBERT L ASH, JR, ASST DIRECTOR; COBB COUNTY PARKS AND RECREATION DEPARTMENT; PO BOX 649; MARIETTA, GA 30061. (#21949). **ARBA GRANTEE.**

NOV 20, '75. DIALOGUE II LECTURE: THE CONSTITUTION IN A TECHNOLOGICAL AGE. LECTURE ON TRADITIONAL CONSTITUTIONAL FREEDOMS IN A TECHNOLOGICAL SOCIETY. TO BE GIVEN BY LARRY MCDONALD. PART OF COMMUNITY DIALOGUE II. (LOCAL). ROBERT FISCHER, CHAIRMAN; STUDENT GOVERNMENT ASSOC OF SOUTHERN TECH; CLAY ST; MARIETTA, GA 30060. (#200012-32).

JAN 15, '76. LECTURE: TECHNOLOGY & THE FUTURE OF FREE ENTERPRISE. PART OF SOUTHERN TECH'S COMMUNITY DIALOGUE II, THIS LECTURE WILL BE GIVEN BY PROFESSOR MICHAEL MESCON. AT SOUTHERN TECH. (LOCAL). ROBERT FISCHER; STUDENT GOVERNMENT ASSOC, SOUTHERN TECH; CLAY ST, SOUTHERN TECH; MARIETTA, GA 30060. (#104117-11).

JAN 30, '76. THE AMERICAN REVOLUTION: ENGLAND'S VIETNAM?. PRESENTATION OF A PAPER BY PROFESSOR GIRD ROMER; GROUP DISCUSSION. AT JAMES V CARMICHAEL STUDENT CENTER, ACTIVITIES ROOM. (LOCAL). DR BARBARA KARCHER, CHMN; KENNESAW JR COLLEGE BICENTENNIAL COMMITTEE; MARIETTA, GA 30061. (#104730-11).

JAN '76. BLACK HISTORY WEEK. SERIES OF EVENTS: SPEAKERS, FILMS AND VARIETY SHOW RELATING THE BLACK EXPERIENCE TO THE BICENTENNIAL AND OF THE FUTURE. (LOCAL). KENNETH SAGOES, PRES; BLACK STUDENTS ALLIANCE, KENNESAW JR COLLEGE; MARIETTA, GA 30061. (#104730-9).

FEB 2 - 29, '76. EXHIBITION OF AMERICAN ART. EXHIBITION OF AMERICAN PAINTING FROM THE BENTLEY-SELLARS COLLECTION. THE EXHIBITION PRESENTS WORK BY AMERICAN ARTISTS OF THE LATE 19TH & EARLY 20TH CENTURIES. PAINTINGS ARE LARGELY LANDSCAPES. WORK BY SUCH PAINTERS AS BIERSTADT, CASILEAR, DOUGHTY, FISHER & SHINN INCL. AT SEMINAR ROOM, LIBRARY, KENNESAW JUNIOR COLLEGE. (LOCAL). TOM SALTER, PROJ COORD; DIVISION OF HUMANITIES, KENNESAW JR COLLEGE; MARIETTA, GA 30061. (#104730-6).

FEB 13, '76. KENNESAW JR COLLEGE COLLOQUIUM ON THE AMERICAN REVOLUTION. PAPERS AND PANEL DISCUSSION BY THREE HISTORIANS; PERFORMANCE BY THE KENNESAW JR COLLEGE CHORALE, US ARMY FORSCOM BAND SHOW, '200 YEARS OF READINESS'. AT GYMNASIUM ON CAMPUS. (LOCAL). DR FRED ROACH, PROJ COORD; DIVISION OF SOCIAL SCIENCE, KENNESAW JR COLLEGE; MARIETTA, GA 30061. (#104730-8).

MAY 28, '76. KENNESAW JR COLLEGE DAY AND FOLK FAIR. CRAFTS FAIR, EARLY AMERICAN GAMES, BLUEGRASS AND FOLK MUSIC, FOCUS ON KENNESAW JR COLLEGE AS PART OF THE COMMUNITY; ALL OF COMMUNITY IS INVITED. (LOCAL). MS BECK RENTZ, CHMN; STUDENT GOVERNMENT ASSOCIATION, KENNESAW JR COLLEGE; MARIETTA, GA 30061. (#104730-7).

MAY 30, '76. LITERATURE OF THE AMERICAN SOUTH. PAPERS AND PANEL DISCUSSIONS BY THREE KENNESAW JUNIOR COLLEGE FACULTY MEMBERS; SOUTHERN LITERATURE AS PART OF THE US HERITAGE. (LOCAL). GARY FOX, PROJ COORD; DIVISION OF HUMANITIES, KENNESAW JR COLLEGE; MARIETTA, GA 30061. (#104730-10).

JUNE 1 - AUG 31, '76. SUMMER ARTS FESTIVAL. BICENTENNIAL ARTS & CRAFTS PLAYGROUND PROGRAMS CONDUCTED AT VARIOUS PARKS IN COBB COUNTY IN ROTATING FASHION THROUGH USE OF MOBILE UNITS IN ORDER TO REACH YOUTHS & ADULTS IN ALL AREAS IN COBB COUNTY. (LOCAL). ROBERT ASH, JR, ASST DIR; COBB COUNTY PARKS AND RECREATION DEPARTMENT; PO BOX 649; MARIETTA, GA 30061. (#22561-1).

JUNE 1 - SEPT 6, '76. DRUM AND FIFE PRESENTATION AT KENNESAW MTN. COSTUMED HIGH SCHOOL STUDENTS WILL GIVE WEEKLY CONCERTS STRESSING OUR MUSICAL HERITAGE AT THE SITE OF TWO ENGAGEMENTS DURING THE ATLANTA CAMPAIGN OF THE CIVIL WAR. AT ADJACENT TO VISITOR CENTER. (REGN'L). KENNESAW MTN N B P; NATIONAL PARK SERVICE; P.O. BOX 1167; MARIETTA, GA 30061. (#6728-54).

JUNE 10, '76. FLAG PRESENTATION TO LOCKHEED & COBB COUNTY. PHOTO ENCLOSED OF CEREMONY, RECEPTION FOLLOWED. AT ADMIN BUILDING. (LOCAL). LAURA WALLACE; AIR FORCE PLANT #6 REPRESENTATIVE OFFICE; 2848 POWDER SPRINGS RD; MARIETTA, GA 30064. (#200012-46).

JUNE 26, '76. AMERICAN FOLK MUSIC CONCERT. PERFORMANCE BY FOLK SINGER, CELEBRATING OUR NATIONAL MUSICAL HERITAGE. BETTY SMITH & JOHN MCCUTCHEON. (LOCAL). FRANK WILSON, COORD; OFFICE OF STUDENT AFFAIRS, KENNESAW JR COLLEGE; MARIETTA, GA 30061. (#104730-3).

JUNE 26 - 27, '76. NATL PK SVC '...A LITTLE LOOK AROUND' VISITS KENNESAW MOUNTAIN NBP. THIS SHORT PROGRAM FEATURES ACTORS PORTRAYING FAMOUS AMERICANS OF THE PAST WHO'VE RETURNED TO SEE AMERICA'S PROGRESS. (REGN'L). KENNESAW MOUNTAIN NBP; NATIONAL PARK SERVICE; P.O. BOX 1167; MARIETTA, GA 30061. (#5653-85).

METTER

BICENTENNIAL COMMUNITY CENTER PROJECT - METTER, GA. PROJECT TO IMPROVE COMMUNITY CENTER AS A FOCAL POINT FOR FESTIVAL ACTIVITIES STRESSING OUR HERITAGE AND PROVIDING A LASTING CONTRIBUTION TO OUR YOUTH AND ADULTS. (LOCAL). VIRGINIA B SNELL, COMMUNITY DEVELOPMENT SPECIALIST; CITY OF METTER; PO BOX 74; METTER, GA 30439. (#26764). **ARBA GRANTEE.**

MIDWAY

ARCHAEOLOGICAL DIG-SITE OF LYMAN HALL'S HOME IN GA. INITIATION OF ARCHAEOLOGICAL EXPLORATION AT THE SITE OF LYMAN HALL'S HOME IN MIDWAY, GEORGIA. (ST-WIDE). JIM OATES, CHIEF RECREATION & PLANNING SECTION; GEORGIA DEPT OF NATURAL RESOURCES; 270 WASHINGTON ST SW; ATLANTA, GA 30334. (#585). **(??).**

FORT MORRIS MIDWAY INTERPRETATION PROGRAM OF GA. INTERPRETATION PROGRAM AT FORT MORRIS INCLUDING MUSEUM EXHIBITS, AND COSTUMED INTERPRETERS, LIVING HISTORY DISPLAYS & AIDS TO BRING THIS REVOLUTIONARY FORT & COLONIAL TOWN OF MIDWAY TO LIFE. (ST-WIDE). JIM OATES, CHIEF RECREATION & PLANNING SECTION; GEORGIA DEPT OF NATURAL RESOURCES; 270 WASHINGTON ST SW; ATLANTA, GA 30334. (#583).

LYMAN HALL HISTORICAL MARKER, MIDWAY, GA. A METAL HISTORICAL MARKER WILL BE ERECTED AT MIDWAY CONGREGATIONAL CHURCH HONORING LYMAN HALL, ONE OF THE SIGNERS OF THE DECLARATION OF INDEPENDENCE. (LOCAL). MRS ELIZABETH STEVENS AMASON, REGENT; ST JOHN'S PARISH CHAPTER; MIDWAY, GA 31320. (#16132). **ARBA GRANTEE.**

RESTORATION OF THE MIDWAY COLONIAL CEMETERY, GA. COLONIAL GRAVE HEADSTONES WILL BE REPAIRED, BANK VAULTS REBUILT, GRAVES REMARKED AND THE GROUNDS LANDSCAPED. TOURIST PARKING WILL BE AVAILABLE & A HISTORICAL SUMMARY WILL BE DISTRIBUTED. (LOCAL). OLIN S FRASER, SELECTMAN OF THE CHURCH; MIDWAY CHURCH & SOCIETY; PINE HOPE; HINESVILLE, GA 31313. (#20467). **ARBA GRANTEE.**

MILLEDGEVILLE

GEORGIA CRAFTS FESTIVAL IN MILLEDGEVILLE. THE CAMPUS OF GEORGIA COLLEGE WILL SERVE AS THE SITE OF A STATE-WIDE FESTIVAL WHICH RECOGNIZES THE WORTH OF THE ARTS AND PRODUCTS OF GA'S CRAFTSMEN. (ST-WIDE). J WHITNEY BUNTING, PRESIDENT; GEORGIA COLLEGE; 231 W HANCOCK ST; MILLEDGEVILLE, GA 31061. (#10669). **ARBA GRANTEE.**

'HISTORY OF MILLEDGEVILLE' - BOOK, GA. A HISTORY OF MILLEDGEVILLE, WRITTEN BY DR J C BONNER WILL BE PUBLISHED & COPIES WILL BE PLACED IN ALL SCHOOLS. (LOCAL). PAUL KING, CHAIRMAN; MILLEDGEVILLE BICENTENNIAL COMMISSION; 120 S JEFFERSON ST; MILLEDGEVILLE, GA 31061. (#19971).

MUSEUM AND ARCHIVES OF GEORGIA EDUCATION. GEORGIA COLLEGE WILL OPEN TO THE PUBLIC A COLLECTION OF MATERIALS & ARTIFACTS ON THE HISTORY OF PUBLIC EDUCATION IN GEORGIA ON APRIL 15, 1976. THIS WILL BE A PERMANENT COLLECTION. (ST-WIDE). J WHITNEY BUNTING, PRESIDENT; GEORGIA COLLEGE; 231 W HANCOCK ST; MILLEDGEVILLE, GA 31061. (#14560).

MAR 26 - 27, '76. GENERAL LAFAYETTE DAYS (1776). RE-ENACTMENT OF GENERAL LAFAYETTE'S VISIT TO TOWN IN 1776 INCLUDES PARADE, BARBEQUE, ETC. (LOCAL). PAUL KING, DIRECTOR; GEORGIA POWER COMPANY/MILLEDGEVILLE & BALDWIN CO CHAMBER OF COMMERCE; 120 S JEFFERSON ST; MILLEDGEVILLE, GA 31061. (#103416-195).

APR 12, '76. AN EVENING OF AMERICAN MUSIC. A PUBLIC CONCERT OF AMERICAN MUSICAL FORMS FROM THE COLONIAL PERIOD TO THE PRESENT. (LOCAL). J WHITNEY BUNTING, PRES; GEORGIA COLLEGE; 231 W HANCOCK ST; MILLEDGEVILLE, GA 31061. (#101847-1).

APR 12 - 14, '76. GEORGIA CRAFTS FESTIVAL, 'THE USEFULNESS OF THE PAST'. FESTIVAL AT ON COLLEGE CAMPUS. (LOCAL). J WHITNEY BUNTING, PRES; GEORGIA COLLEGE; 231 W HANCOCK ST; MILLEDGEVILLE, GA 31061. (#101848-1).

APR 13, '76. AN EVENING OF AMERICAN FOLK DANCING. FESTIVAL AT GEORGIA COLLEGE CAMPUS. (LOCAL). J WHITNEY BUNTING, PRES; GEORGIA COLLEGE; 231 N HANCOCK ST; MILLEDGEVILLE, GA 31061. (#101845-1).

APR 15, '76. OPENING OF MUSEUM & ARCHIVES OF GEORGIA EDUCATION. OPENING. (LOCAL). J WHITNEY BUNTING, PRES; GEORGIA COLLEGE; 231 W HANCOCK ST; MILLEDGEVILLE, GA 31061. (#14560-1).

APR 15, '76. SEMINAR & DEBATE - THE LIBERAL & CONSERVATIVE POINTS OF VIEW. A LIBERAL AND A CONSERVATIVE SPOKESMAN WILL DEBATE PRESENT AND FUTURE PROSPECTS OF THE U S; THE MEANING OF THE AMER REVOLUTION WILL ALSO BE DISCUSSED. THE PARTICIPANTS ARE FRANK MANKIEWICZ AND RUSSEL KIRK. (LOCAL). J WHITNEY BUNTING, PRES; GEORGIA COLLEGE; 231 W HANCOCK ST; MILLEDGEVILLE, GA 31061. (#101846-1).

JUNE 14, '76. OUTDOOR HISTORICAL PAGEANT. A DRAMATIC PRESENTATION BASED UPON GEORGIA'S HISTORICAL PAST. (LOCAL). J WHITNEY BUNTING, PRES; GEORGIA COLLEGE; 231 W HANCOCK; MILLEDGEVILLE, GA 31061. (#101844-1).

JUNE 24 - 27, '76. HERITAGE SPECIAL - TRAIN TOUR. TRAVELING RAIL EXHIBIT EMPHASIZING COLONIAL & REVOLUTIONARY GEORGIA HISTORY, CRAFTS & LIFESTYLE OF GEORGIA COLONISTS. EXHIBITS WILL BE DISPLAYED WITH COMBINATION OF SIGHT & SOUND ACTIVITY. (LOCAL). RON HENRY, COORDINATOR; GEORGIA AGRIRAMA DEVELOPMENT AUTHORITY/GEORGIA BICENTENNIAL; 8TH ST A I 75; TIFTON, GA 31794. (#7999-2).

MONROE

COLONIAL DECORATION FOR COUNTYWIDE CELEBRATION, GA. DECORATION OF LAWNS & TREES FOR COMMUNITY FESTIVAL. (LOCAL). MRS EVELYN COOK, PRESIDENT; EVERGREEN GARDEN CLUB; 317 WOODLAND RD; MONROE, GA 30655. (#24394).

MONROE—CONTINUED

COURTHOUSE TREE, MONROE, GA. A TREE COMMEMORATING THE 13 ORIGINAL COLONIES WILL BE PLANTED AT THE COURTHOUSE. (LOCAL). FRANK WHITLEY, CHAIRMAN; MONROE MERCHANTS ASSOC; 316 EDWARDS ST; MONROE, GA 30655. (#24395).

LANDSCAPING OF GROUNDS, GEORGE WALTON ACADEMY, GA. RED, WHITE & BLUE FLOWERS WILL BE PLANTED. (LOCAL). MRS LUCY MORRIS, COORDINATOR; GEORGE WALTON ACADEMY; BOLD SPRINGS RD; MONROE, GA 30655. (#24391).

PARK-IMPROVEMENT, MONROE, GA. BEAUTIFICATION OF PARK AREA. (LOCAL). MRS HELEN STONE, COORDINATOR; MONROE GARDEN CLUB; 119-GLEN IRIS DR; MONROE, GA 30655. (#24389).

PARK-RENOVATION, MONROE, GA. BEAUTIFICATION OF PILOT PARK. (LOCAL). EULA MAE QUEEN, PROJ COORDINATOR; PILOT CLUB OF MONROE, INC; ROUTE 1; MONROE, GA 30655. (#24390).

STREET PLANTERS, MONROE, GA. RED, WHITE & BLUE FLOWERS WILL BE PLANTED IN RED, WHITE & BLUE PLANTERS. (LOCAL). MRS RANDALL PUGH, CHAIRMAN; MONROE JUNIOR WOMEN'S CLUB & CIVINETTES; 740 WALTON RD; MONROE, GA 30655. (#24396).

THEATRE BUILDING, MONROE, GA. RESTORATION OF BUILDING TO BE USED FOR PLAYHOUSE. (LOCAL). W G ARMSTRONG, CITY ADMINISTRATOR; CITY OF MONROE; S BROAD ST; MONROE, GA 30655. (#24388).

WALTON COUNTY BICENTENNIAL CENTER - MONROE, GA. THE CENTER WILL PROVIDE A COUNTY FOCAL POINT FOR THE BICENTENNIAL FOR THE ENTIRE COMMUNITY. (LOCAL). ROBERT W HAWK, CHAIRMAN; WALTON COUNTY COMMISSIONERS; COURT HOUSE; MONROE, GA 30655. (#23617). **ARBA GRANTEE.**

JUNE 25, '75. PAGEANT ON BLACK HISTORY. LIVE PERFORMANCE AT CARVER JR HIGH SCHOOL GYM. (LOCAL). CATHERINE THOMPSON, COORD; PEACHETTES & COTILLIONS OF MONROE; GRATIS RD; MONROE, GA 30655. (#107899-1).

MAY 23, '76. MUSICAL PRESENTATION 'THE SOUND OF AMERICA' BY TERRY KIRKLAND. PRESENTED BY THE YOUNG MUSICIANS' CHOIR. AT MCDANIEL & WAYNE STREETS, MONROE, GA. (LOCAL). MRS HELEN ARNOLD, CHMN; MONROE FIRST BAPTIST CHURCH; 217 JACKSON ST; MONROE, GA 30655. (#107225-2).

DEC '76. CHRISTMAS TREE DECORATION. SCHOOL CHILDREN WILL MAKE DECORATIONS FOR CHRISTMAS TREE. AT COURTHOUSE. (LOCAL). MARY RUTH WATSON, CHMN; MONROE GARDEN CLUB; 114 PINE CIRCLE; MONROE, GA 30655. (#107225-1).

MONTEZUMA

APR 1 - 3, '76. HERITAGE SPECIAL - TRAIN TOUR. TRAVELING RAIL EXHIBIT EMPHASIZING COLONIAL & REVOLUTIONARY GEORGIA HISTORY, CRAFTS & LIFESTYLE OF GEORGIA COLONISTS. EXHIBITS WILL BE DISPLAYED WITH COMBINATION OF SIGHT & SOUND ACTIVITY. (LOCAL). RON HENRY, COORDINATOR; GEORGIA AGRIRAMA DEVELOPMENT AUTHORITY/GEORGIA BICENTENNIAL; 8TH ST A I 75; TIFTON, GA 31794. (#7999-19).

AUG 30 - SEPT 1, '76. HERITAGE SPECIAL - TRAIN TOUR. TRAVELING RAIL EXHIBIT EMPHASIZING COLONIAL AND REVOLUTIONARY GEORGIA HISTORY, CRAFTS & LIFESTYLE OF GEORGIA COLONISTS. EXHIBITS WILL BE DISPLAYED WITH COMBINATION OF SIGHT & SOUND ACTIVITY. AT DEPOT. (LOCAL). RON HENRY, DIRECTOR; GEORGIA BICENTENNIAL COMMISSION; 1776 PEACHTREE NW, ROOM 520 S; ATLANTA, GA 30309. (#7999-36).

MOODY AFB

BOOKS ON HISTORIC HEROES - MOODY AFB, GA. THE BASE LIBRARY MAINTAINS A LIST OF BOOKS ON KEY HISTORICAL HEROES FOR USE BY BASE PERSONNEL. (LOCAL). N M GUENTHER, CHIEF OF INFORMATION; 347 TFW OI; MOODY AFB, GA 31601. (#32446).

NOV 28, '75. CHANGE OF COMMAND DINING OUT. FESTIVAL AT OFFICERS OPEN MESS. (LOCAL). MAJOR N M GUENTHER; 347TH TACTICAL FIGHTER WING; OFFICE OF INFORMATION; MOODY AFB, GA 31601. (#200012-65).

SEPT 29, '76. WING ANNIVERSARY. FESTIVAL AT OFFICERS OPEN MESS. (LOCAL). MAJOR N M GUENTHER; 347TH TACTICAL FIGHTER WING; OFFICE OF INFORMATION; MOODY AFB, GA 31601. (#200012-66).

MORELAND

COMMUNITY IMPROVEMENT PROJECTS OF MORELAND, GA. PROJECTS WILL INCLUDE: COMMUNITY BEAUTIFICATION, A WATER SYSTEM, BICYCLE TRAIL, TENNIS COURTS AND CIVIC CENTER MUSEUM. (LOCAL). HON WILLIAM R MILLER, MAYOR; MORELAND TOWN COUNCIL; MORELAND, GA 30259. (#14909).

HISTORY OF MORELAND, GA. TAPED INTERVIEWS WITH OLDER RESIDENTS & WRITTEN REPORTS BY VARIOUS CITIZENS WILL BE COMPILED INTO A BOOKLET. (LOCAL). BOB ENTREKIN, HISTORY CHAIRMAN; MORELAND COMMUNITY BICENTENNIAL COMMISSION; MORELAND, GA 30259. (#14910).

LASTING REMINDER COMMEMORATIVE STONE - GA. STONE WEIGHING 1000 LBS WITH METAL MARKER TELLING ABOUT MORELAND AND THE CHURCH BELL WILL BE ERECTED AS A MEMORIAL. (LOCAL). MIRIAM MILLER, CHAIRMAN; MORELAND BICENTENNIAL COMMITTEE; MORELAND, GA 30259. (#14908).

JAN 2, '76. HISTORICAL PAGEANT, A LIGHTHEARTED APPROACH TO HISTORY. LIVE PERFORMANCE. (LOCAL). LAMAR HAYNES, CHAIRMAN; MORELAND BICENTENNIAL COMMISSION; MORELAND, GA 30259. (#102076-1).

JAN 2 - 31, '76. BAR B QUE, FESTIVAL & EXHIBIT. A TRADITIONAL SOUTHERN BAR B QUE WILL BE FOLLOWED BY A BOY SCOUT FLAG CEREMONY. LOCAL ARTS, CRAFTS & HISTORICAL ITEMS WILL BE ON EXHIBIT AND FOR SALE. (LOCAL). RAY PARKS, CHAIRMAN; MORELAND CHURCHES & BICENTENNIAL COMMISSION; MORELAND, GA 30259. (#102075-1).

MORROW

MAY 1 - 2, '76. AN 18TH CENTURY WEEKEND. LIVING HISTORY EXHIBITS, MUSIC &/OR DANCING, PARADE & A RE-CREATION OF THE BATTLE OF BRIAR CREEK, COMPLETE WITH REVOLUTIONARY ERA DRESS. (LOCAL). DR HARVEY H JACKSON; CLAYTON JR COLLEGE; BOX 285; MORROW, GA 30260. (#8747-1).

MOULTRIE

ADOPTION OF CITY FLAG - MOULTRIE, GA. RESEARCH OF MOULTRIE FLAG FLOWN AT CHARLESTOWN DURING REVOLUTION. FLAG WILL BE SEWN BY SCHOOL GIRLS AND AN OFFICIAL CEREMONY WILL BE HELD TO ADOPT NEW CITY FLAG. (LOCAL). MRS MITCHELL SMITH, CHAIRMAN; MOULTRIE-COLQUITT COUNTY BICENTENNIAL COMMITTEE; PO BOX 1362; MOULTRIE, GA 31768. (#16720).

AUDIO VISUAL AIDS FOR AREA SCHOOLS - MOULTRIE, GA. SLIDES OF LOCAL AND STATE HISTORICAL SITES & FIGURES WILL BE MADE AVAILABLE TO LOCAL SCHOOLS AND CLUBS. (LOCAL). MRS J M ODOM, CHAIRMAN-HIST-COMM; MOULTRIE BICENTENNIAL COMMISSION; PO BOX 1362; MOULTRIE, GA 31768. (#16715).

CLEAN UP AND BEAUTIFICATION - MOULTRIE, GA. PROJECT INCLUDES: FLOWER & SHRUB PLANTING AND SPRING CLEANUP WEEK CALLED PRIDE WEEK. (LOCAL). AL JONES, CHAIRMAN; BICENTENNIAL COMMITTEE OF MOULTRIE; PO BOX 1362; MOULTRIE, GA 31768. (#16717).

COMMUNITY IMPROVEMENT PROJ - MOULTRIE, GA. PRIVATE ORGANIZATIONS AND CITIZENS OF THE COMMUNITY WILL BE ENCOURAGED TO MAKE IMPROVEMENTS THROUGHOUT THE CITY. (LOCAL). MRS MITCHELL SMITH, CHAIRMAN; MOULTRIE BICENTENNIAL COMMITTEE; PO BOX 1362; MOULTRIE, GA 31768. (#16716).

FLAG DISPLAY AND PROMOTION, MOULTRIE, GA. FLAGS FLOWN AT THE SQUARE & HOMES AND BUSINESSES WILL BE ENCOURAGED TO BUY AND DISPLAY FLAGS. (LOCAL). JULIEN BOWLES, FLAG CHAIRMAN; BICENTENNIAL COMMITTEE OF MOULTRIE; PO BOX 1362; MOULTRIE, GA 31768. (#16718).

HISTORICAL RECORDS PRESERVED, MOULTRIE, GA. LOCAL AND STATE HISTORICAL RECORDS AND ARTIFACTS WILL BE EXHIBITED. (ST-WIDE). MS MERLE BAKER, HISTORY CHAIRMAN; MOULTRIE-COLQUITT COUNTY BICENTENNIAL COMMISSION; PO BOX 1362; MOULTRIE, GA 31768. (#16723).

HISTORICAL SOCIETY ORGANIZED, MOULTRIE, GA. COLGUITT COUNTY CITIZENS WILL ORGANIZE A HISTORICAL SOCIETY. (LOCAL). MRS A BAKER, CHAIRMAN; MOULTRIE-COLGUITT COUNTY BICENTENNIAL COMMISSION; PO BOX 1362; MOULTRIE, GA 31768. (#16722).

HISTORY OF MOULTRIE AND COLQUITT COUNTY - GA. RESEARCH AND COMPILATION OF A CITY AND COUNTRY HISTORY. (LOCAL). MRS A B BAKER, CHMN HISTORY COMMITTEE; MOULTRIE COLQUITT COUNTY BICENTENNIAL COMMITTEE; PO BOX 1362; MOULTRIE, GA 31768. (#16721).

MONUMENT TO VETERANS, MOULTRIE, GA. MONUMENT BUILT NAMING VETERANS KILLED IN WARS FROM 1914 TO PRESENT. (LOCAL). ED AOUFF, ASST COUNTY ADMINISTRATOR; COLQUITT COUNTY BICENTENNIAL COMMITTEE; COURT HOUSE; MOULTRIE, GA 31768. (#16719).

MUSIC PROGRAM. LIVE PERFORMANCE. (LOCAL). BILL CALDWELL, DIRECTOR; A CAPELLA CHOIR; MOULTRIE HIGH SCHOOL; MOULTRIE, GA 31768. (#103021-4). **(??).**

MAY 1, '76 - JULY 3, '77. ESSAYS AND POSTER CONTEST. AWARDS WILL BE GIVEN TO THE BEST ESSAY AND POSTER ON CLEANUP AND ECOLOGY. POSTERS USED TO PROMOTE GOOD ENVIRONMENT AND PREVENT LITTER. CLEAN-UP EFFORT WAS DESIGNATED 'PRIDE WEEK'. (LOCAL). MRS MITCHELL SMITH, CHMN; MOULTRIE BICENTENNIAL COMMITTEE; PO BOX 1362; MOULTRIE, GA 31768. (#103021-5).

JULY 2, '76. ADDRESS BY PAUL HARVEY & 'MOULTRIE FLAG' DEDICATION. SPEECH PRECEDED BY BLUEGRASS MUSIC AND DEDICATION OF 'MOULTRIE FLAG' AS OFFICIAL FLAG OF THE CITY OF MOULTRIE. AT STADIUM. (LOCAL). JIMMY JETER, EVENTS COORD; MOULTRIE BICENTENNIAL COMMITTEE; PO BOX 1362; MOULTRIE, GA 31768. (#103021-3).

JULY 3, '76. PATRIOT'S DAY - COLONIAL FAIR AND PARADE. EXHIBITS SUCH AS QUILTS, OLD KITCHEN & FARM EQUIPMENT, HISTORICAL DOCUMENTS AND ARTIFACTS, POLE CLIMBING, LOG ROLLING, PIE EATING, COSTUME & BEARD CONTESTS. THE PARADE HAD 45 FLOATS, 4 BANDS, HORSES, OLD CARS. MARCHING UNITS ALSO PARTICIPATED AT 3 PM. AT COURT HOUSE SQUARE. (LOCAL). JACK HUNNICUTT, COORD; MOULTRIE BICENTENNIAL COMMITTEE; PO BOX 1362; MOULTRIE, GA 31768. (#103021-2).

JULY 4, '76. GOD AND COUNTRY RALLY. THIS WILL BE A COUNTY-WIDE ASSEMBLY IN THE STADIUM. RAIN DROVE THE EVENT TO THE FIRST BABTIST CHURCH. AT STADIUM. (LOCAL). WM HURDLE, MINISTER; MOULTRIE BICENTENNIAL COMMITTEE; PO BOX 1362; MOULTRIE, GA 31768. (#103021-1).

MOUNT VERNON

EXHIBITS ON DECORATIVE ARTS & EARLY TOOLS - GA. 2 EXHIBITS WITH MUSICAL PEVIEWS; ONE IS ON THE AMERICAN DECORATIVE ARTS DURING THE VICTORIAN PERIOD AND THE OTHER DEVOTED TO AMERICAN TRADE WITH THE ORIENT; ALSO, EXHIBIT ON EARLY AMERICAN TOOLS. (LOCAL). FRED HAMILTON, CHAIRMAN; MONTGOMERY COUNTY/BREWTON PARKER BICENTENNIAL COMMITTEE; BREWTON PARKER COLLEGE; MOUNT VERNON, GA 30445. (#22620). **ARBA GRANTEE.**

FEB 7 - 21, '76. EXHIBIT ON DECORATIVE ARTS IN VICTORIAN AMERICA & MUSICAL PREVIEW. EXHIBIT. (LOCAL). FRED HAMILTON, CHAIRMAN; MONTGOMERY COUNTY/BREWTON PARKER BICENTENNIAL COMMITTEE; BREWTON PARKER COLLEGE; MOUNT VERNON, GA 30445. (#22620-1).

MAY 3 - 21, '76. EXHIBIT ON EARLY AMERICAN WORK TOOLS & HOUSEHOLD UTENSILS. EXHIBIT. (LOCAL). FRED HAMILTON, CHAIRMAN; MONTGOMERY COUNTY/BREWTON PARKER BICENTENNIAL COMMITTEE; BREWTON PARKER COLLEGE; MOUNT VERNON, GA 30445. (#22620-2).

NOV 2 - 19, '76. EXHIBIT ON AMERICAN TRADE WITH THE ORIENT WITH MUSICAL PREVIEW. EXHIBIT. (LOCAL). FRED HAMILTON, CHAIRMAN; MONTGOMERY COUNTY/BREWTON PARKER BICENTENNIAL COMMITTEE; BREWTON PARKER COLLEGE; MOUNT VERNON, GA 30445. (#22620-3).

MT BERRY

AMERICAN ISSUES FORUM OF MT BERRY, GEORGIA. AMERICAN ISSUES FORUM IS A NATIONWIDE OBSERVANCE DEVELOPED BY NATL ENDOWMENT FOR THE HUMANITIES. (LOCAL). WILLIAM C MORAN, ACADEMIC DEAN; BERRY COLLEGE; MT BERRY, GA 30149. (#6471).

AMERICAN MUSIC: EVOL OF JAZZ & HISTORICAL CAPSULES. MUSICAL SERIES WILL STRESS THE BROAD EUROPEAN HERITAGE & DEVELOPMENT OF AMERICAN MUSIC OF ALL TYPES. (ST-WIDE). OUIDA W DICKEY, ASSOC DEAN & CHRMN; BICENTENNIAL STEERING COMMITTEE; BERRY COLLEGE; MT BERRY, GA 30149. (#7888). **ARBA RECOGNIZED. ARBA GRANTEE.**

BICENTENNIAL TRAIL AT BERRY ACADEMY IN GEORGIA. BICENTENNIAL TRAIL - DEVELOPMENT OF EXTENSIVE HIKING TRAIL EMPHASIZING FLORA AND FAUNA AT BERRY ACADEMY. (LOCAL). CHARLES JOHNSTON, HEADMASTER; BERRY ACADEMY; MT BERRY, GA 30149. (#8700). **(??).**

BLACK SYMPOSIUM AT BERRY COLLEGE, GEORGIA. FIFTH ANNUAL SYMPOSIUM ON BLACK CULTURE - A FILM AND DISCUSSION SERIES EXAMINING WEEKLY THE OPPORTUNITIES & DILEMMAS FACING THE BLACK MAN IN CONTEMPORARY SOCIETY. (LOCAL). DR N GORDON CARPER, CHAIRMAN, SOCIAL SCIENCE DEPT; ETHNIC STUDIES COMMITTEE OF BERRY COLLEGE; MT BERRY, GA 30149. (#8704).

COMMUNITY PLANNING PROGRAM AT BERRY COLLEGE, GA. LEADERSHIP IN THE '70'S COMMUNITY PLANNING PROGRAM TO DEVELOP RIVERFRONT PARK IN ROME, GEORGIA. (LOCAL). GENE B CLARK, DIRECTOR; CONTINUING EDUCATION DEPT OF BERRY COLLEGE; BERRY COLLEGE; MT BERRY, GA 30149. (#6472).

GOLDEN YEARS OF MOVIES AT BERRY COLLEGE, GEORGIA. THE GOLDEN YEARS OF MOTION PICTURES WILL BE EXPLORED IN SPECIAL WEEKLY SHOWINGS OF MOVIES FROM THE THIRTIES AND FORTIES. (LOCAL). DR D CANTRELL, CHAIRMAN; BERRY COLLEGE DEPT OF ENGLISH; MT BERRY, GA 30149. (#6733).

'HISTORIC CAPSULES' PROJ AT BERRY COLLEGE, GEORGIA. 'HISTORIC CAPSULES' FOR RADIO BROADCAST EMPHASIZING DRAMATIC MOMENTS IN NATION'S HISTORY. (LOCAL). DR D DEAN CANTRELL, CHAIRMAN; BERRY COLLEGE, DEPT OF ENGLISH & SPEECH; MT BERRY, GA 30149. (#8702).

HISTORICAL MOMENTS RADIO SPOTS, MT BERRY, GA. ONE-MINUTE HISTORICAL ACCOUNTS ON TAPE TO BE AIRED ON LOCAL RADIO. (LOCAL). QUIDA W DICKEY, ASSOCIATE ACADEMIC DEAN; BERRY COLLEGE; BOX 328; MT BERRY, GA 30149. (#16447).

LECTURES ON CULTURE & FREEDOM AT BERRY COL, GA. A SERIES OF LECTURES & SYMPOSIA DISCUSSING THE VARIOUS ASPECTS OF FREEDOM. (LOCAL). DR N GORDAN CARPER, CHAIRMAN; BERRY COLLEGE DEPT OF SOCIAL SCIENCES; BERRY COLLEGE; MT BERRY, GA 30149. (#8708).

MEDIA SHOW AT BERRY COLLEGE, GEORGIA. HISTORICAL SLIDES OF COLONIAL TIMES EMPHASIZING COLONIAL LIFESTYLE IN AMERICA PRESENTED BY THE MARTHA BERRY MUSEUM. (LOCAL). JAMES BURDETTE, DIRECTOR; MARTHA BERRY MUSEUM OF BERRY COLLEGE; MT BERRY, GA 30149. (#6732). **(??).**

THE RIGHT TO CHOOSE, LECTURES AT BERRY COL, GA. A CONFERENCE BASED ON WOMAN'S ROLES IN THE LATER PART OF THE 20TH CENTURY. (LOCAL). DR D CANTRELL, PROJ COORDINATOR; BERRY COLLEGE BICENT COMMITTEE; MT BERRY, GA 30149. (#8698).

SOCIAL ISSUES FILMS IN MT BERRY, GA. PROJECT INVOLVES 6 ISSUE FILMS THAT CONCENTRATE ON ECOLOGY, WOMEN'S STATUS, CULTURAL CONDITIONING OF YOUTH, VIOLENCE & GUN CONTROL, SOCIAL MINORITIES AND THE ROLE OF EXISTENTIAL MAN IN SOCIETY. (LOCAL). QUIDA W DICKEY, ASSOC ACADEMIC DEAN; BERRY COLLEGE & STATE COMMITTEE FOR HUMANITIES; BOX 328; MT BERRY, GA 30149. (#16449).

MT BERRY — CONTINUED

MAR 4, '75. 'GIVE ME LIBERTY', MUSIC AT BERRY COLLEGE. PREMIERE PRESENTATION COMPOSED BY BERRY COLLEGE INSTRUCTOR WITH TEXT FROM SPEECH BY PATRICK HENRY AND PERFORMED BY BERRY COLLEGE CONCERT CHOIR; PUBLISHED BY DALMAR PUBLISHING COMPANY. ALSO: RECORDING. AT BERRY COLLEGE CHAPEL. (LOCAL). DR DARWIN G WHITE; BERRY COLLEGE, DEPT OF MUSIC; MT BERRY, GA 30149. (#8701-1).

APR 17, '75. ADDRESS BY DEAN RUSK AT BERRY STATE COLLEGE. THE FORMER SECRETARY OF STATE, DEAN RUSK, WILL ADDRESS THE BERRY COLLEGE COMMUNITY. (REGN'L). JOHN R BERTRAND; BERRY COLLEGE; MT BERRY, GA 30149. (#6473-1).

MAY 10, '75. FRONTIER FESTIVAL. FRONTIER FESTIVAL & BICENT SHOWCASE AT POSSUM TROT. AN ALL DAY EVENT WITH ARTS & CRAFTS EXHIBITS, SERMON IN POSSUM TROT CHURCH AND A PERFORMANCE BY THE BERRY SINGERS. (LOCAL). DAN V BIGGERS; BERRY BICENT COMMITTEE; BERRY COLLEGE; MT BERRY, GA 30149. (#8699-1).

SEPT 8 - OCT 13, '75. 'HOW FREE IS FREE'. SERIES OF 5 SYMPOSIA ON INDIVIDUAL FREEDOMS & THEIR EROSION. AT KRAMER CENTER, BERRY COLLEGE. (LOCAL). GENE CLARK, DIRECTOR; BERRY COLLEGE; MOUNT BERRY, GA 30149. (#200012-33).

SEPT 12, '75. A NATION OF NATIONS FORUM. RADIO/TV, SEMINAR AT KRENNERT CNTR BALLROOM. (LOCAL). OUIDA W DICKEY; BERRY COLLEGE; BOX 328; MT BERRY, GA 30149. (#6471-501).

OCT 15, '75. THE LAND OF PLENTY FORUM. RADIO/TV, SEMINAR AT KRENNERT CNTR BALLROOM. (LOCAL). OUIDA W DICKEY; BERRY COLLEGE; BOX 328; MT BERRY, GA 30149. (#6471-502).

NOV 10, '75. CERTAIN UNALIENABLE RIGHTS FORUM. RADIO/TV, SEMINAR AT KRENNERT CNTR BALLROOM. (LOCAL). OUIDA W DICKEY; BERRY COLLEGE; BOX 328; MT BERRY, GA 30149. (#6471-503).

DEC 8, '75. A MORE PERFECT UNION FORUM. RADIO/TV, SEMINAR AT KRENNERT CNTR BALLROOM. (LOCAL). OUIDA W DICKEY; BERRY COLLEGE; BOX 328; MT BERRY, GA 30149. (#6471-504).

JAN 6, '76. WORKING IN AMERICA. RADIO/TV, SEMINAR AT KRENNERT CNTR BALLROOM. (LOCAL). OUIDA W DICKEY; BERRY COLLEGE; BOX 328; MT BERRY, GA 30149. (#6471-505).

FEB 9, '76. THE BUSINESS OF AMERICA. RADIO/TV, SEMINAR AT KRENNERT CNTR BALLROOM. (LOCAL). OUIDA W DICKEY; BERRY COLLEGE; BOX 328; MT BERRY, GA 30149. (#6471-506).

MAR 9, '76. AMERICA IN THE WORLD. RADIO/TV, SEMINAR AT KRENNERT CNTR BALLROOM. (LOCAL). OUIDA W DICKEY; BERRY COLLEGE; BOX 328; MT BERRY, GA 30149. (#6471-507).

APR 1 - 30, '76. PRESIDENTIAL POSTER SHOWING. GALLERY SHOWING OF PRESIDENTIAL POSTERS. AT MOON ART GALLERY. (LOCAL). THOMAS MEW, CHMN; BERRY COLLEGE; BOX 580; MT BERRY, GA 30149. (#102933-2).

APR 5, '76. GROWING UP IN AMERICA. RADIO/TV, SEMINAR AT KRENNERT CNTR BALLROOM. (LOCAL). OUIDA W DICKEY; BERRY COLLEGE; BOX 328; MT BERRY, GA 30149. (#6471-508).

MAY 1 - 31, '76. FINE ARTS MONTH. FINE ARTS MONTH - AMERICA CELEBRATES: THE MONTH OF MAY 1976 WILL BE SET ASIDE TO CELEBRATE THE FINE ARTS AT BERRY COLLEGE. AT BERRY COLLEGE CAMPUS. (LOCAL). OUIDA W DICKEY; FINE ARTS COMMITTEE OF BERRY COLLEGE; MT BERRY, GA 30149. (#8705-1).

MAY 3, '76. LIFE, LIBERTY AND THE PURSUIT OF HAPPINESS. RADIO/TV, SEMINAR AT KRENNERT CNTR BALLROOM. (LOCAL). OUIDA W DICKEY; BERRY COLLEGE; BOX 328; MT BERRY, GA 30149. (#6471-509).

NASHVILLE

RESTORATION OF SWEAT'S OPERA HOUSE, GA. RESTORATION OF HISTORIC OPERA HOUSE TO BE USED AS A CIVIC AUDITORIUM. (LOCAL). HON BOBBY CARROLL, MAYOR; CITY OF NASHVILLE; CITY HALL; NASHVILLE, GA 31639. (#24725). **ARBA GRANTEE.**

NEWNAN

BICENTENNIAL PARK - NEWNAN, GA. REMOVAL OF OLD HIGH SCHOOL BUILDING & USE OF THE LAND FOR A PARK. (LOCAL). DR CHARLES M BARROW, CHAIRMAN; NEWNAN-COWETA BICETNENNIAL COMMITTEE; PO BOX 1776; NEWNAN, GA 30264. (#24152).

SEPT 4 - 6, '76. POWERS' CROSSROADS COUNTRY FAIR & ART FESTIVAL. GEORGIA'S COLONIAL & INDIAN HERITAGE IS REFLECTED THROUGHOUT THIS FAIR, WITH ARTS, CRAFTS, MUSIC, AND FOOD. AT POWERS CROSSROADS PLANTATION. (LOCAL). JIM HARDIN; POWERS CROSSROADS FAIR; POWERS XROADS, BOX 899; NEWNAN, GA 30263. (#103416-501).

PEACHTREE

AMPHITHEATER COMPLEX IN PEACHTREE, GA. RELATED BUILDINGS FOR AN OUTDOOR HISTORICAL DRAMA. (LOCAL). ROBERT K PRICE, CHAIRMAN; MCINTOSH TRAIL ARTS COUNCIL, INC; PO BOX 2336; PEACHTREE, GA 30269. (#22839). **ARBA GRANTEE.**

BICENTENNIAL ESSAY CONTEST. AN ESSAY CONTEST ON BICENTENNIAL TOPICS WILL BE SPONSORED FOR STUDENTS FROM LOCAL ELEMENTARY, JUNIOR AND SENIOR HIGH SCHOOLS. (LOCAL). ROBERT K PRICE, CHAIRMAN; FAYETTE COUNTY BICENT COMMISSION; 110 CEDAR PT; PEACHTREE CY, GA 30263. (#8961-1). (??).

CLASS OF '76 REPRESENTATIVES OF FAYETTE COUNTY. ONE BOY AND GIRL FROM THE CLASS OF '76 WILL REPRESENT THAT AGE GROUP ON THE BICENTENNIAL COMMISSION. (LOCAL). ROBERT K PRICE, CHAIRMAN; FAYETTE COUNTY BICENT COMMISSION; 110 CEDAR PT; PEACHTREE CTY, GA 30269. (#8962).

FLAG DISPLAY OF PEACHTREE CITY, GEORGIA. ENCOURAGE ALL FAMILIES AND BUSINESSES TO DISPLAY THE FLAG THROUGHOUT 1976. (LOCAL). ROBERT K PRICE, CHAIRMAN; FAYETTE COUNTY BICENT COMMISSION; 110 CEDAR PT; PEACHTREE CTY, GA 30269. (#8969).

LIBERTY TREES OF PEACHTREE CITY, GEORGIA. PLANTING OF LIBERTY TREES IN EVERY COMMUNITY IN THE COUNTY. (LOCAL). ROBERT K PRICE, CHAIRMAN; FAYETTE COUNTY BICENT COMMISSION; 110 CEDAR PT; PEACHTREE CTY, GA 30269. (#8970).

MCINTOSH TRACE OF FAYETTE COUNTY. THE PROJECT INCLUDES THE MARKING OF THE HISTORIC MCINTOSH TRACE THROUGH FAYETTE COUNTY AND MAKING THIS TRAIL SUITABLE FOR HIKING. (ST-WIDE). ROBERT K PRICE, CHAIRMAN; FAYETTE COUNTY BICENT COMMISSION; 110 CEDAR PT; PEACHTREE CTY, GA 30263. (#8964).

SHAKERAG SETTLEMENT, PEACHTREE, GA. SHAKERAG SETTLEMENT, AN INTEGRAL PART OF THE MCINTOSH TRAIL COMPLEX AND THE KEY TO YEAR-ROUND OPERATION, BRINGS TOGETHER ACCOMPLISHED CRAFTSMEN TO WORK, DEMONSTRATE AND SELL THEIR CRAFTS. (ST-WIDE). J LEWIS HAMRICK, EXEC ASSISTANT; MCINTOSH TRAIL ARTS COUNCIL, INC; PO BOX 2336; PEACHTREE, GA 30269. (#22304). **ARBA GRANTEE.**

JAN 1 - DEC 31, '76. SHAKERAG SETTLEMENT - EXHIBIT. SHAKERAG SETTLEMENT, AN INTEGRAL PART OF THE MCINTOSH TRAIL COMPLEX AND THE KEY TO YEAR-ROUND OPERATION, BRINGS TOGETHER ACCOMPLISHED CRAFTSMEN TO WORK, DEMONSTRATE AND SELL THEIR CRAFTS. AT GLENLOCK VILLAGE, PEACH TREE CITY,. (ST-WIDE). J LEWIS HAMRICK, COORD; MCINTOSH TRAIL ARTS COUNCIL, INC; PO BOX 2336; PEACHTREE, GA 30269. (#22304-1).

JUNE 18 - SEPT 5, '76. OUTDOOR DRAMA- PEACHTREE CITY, GEORGIA. AN HISTORICAL DRAMA BASED ON THE LIFE OF CHIEF WM MCINTOSH, HALF CREEK, HALF-SCOT INDIAN CHIEF. AT 25MI SOUTH OF ATLANTA; OFF I-85,PEACHTREE. (ST-WIDE). ROBERT K PRICE, CHAIRMAN; MCINTOSH TRAIL ARTS COUNCIL, INC; 110 CEDAR PT; PEACHTREE CTY, GA 30269. (#8968-1).

JUNE 18 - SEPT 7, '76. OPENING OF 'THE MCINTOSH TRAIL'. DRAMA BY PLAYWRIGHT KERMIT HUNTER DEPICTS TURBULENT TIMES OF GEORGIA DURING THE PERIOD 1800-1825. AT PEACHTREE PARKWAY, PEACHTREE CITY, GA. (ST-WIDE). ROBERT K PRICE, DIRECTOR; MCINTOSH TRAIL ARTS COUNCIL, INC; PO BOX 2336; PEACHTREE CY, GA 30269. (#103416-95).

PELHAM

'DAYS OF YESTERYEAR' FESTIVAL IN PELHAM, GEORGIA. INAUGURATION OF AN ANNUAL FESTIVAL 'THE DAYS OF YESTERYEAR' TO STIMULATE CIVIC PRIDE AND INTEREST IN LOCAL HERITAGE AS PART OF THE LOCAL BICENT CELEBRATION. (LOCAL). MRS J ALTON WHALEY, CO-CHAIRMAN; PELHAM-MITCHELL COUNTY BICENT COMMITTEE; BOX 125; PELHAM, GA 31779. (#6756). **ARBA GRANTEE.**

FREEDOM PLAZA PARK OF PELHAM, GA. CREATION OF DOWNTOWN PARK TO EMPHASIZE AMERICAN AND GA HISTORY, WITH FLAGS FOUNTAIN & MONUMENT TO AMERICAN DOCUMENTS OF FREEDOM. (LOCAL). MRS J ALTON WHALEY, CO-CHAIRMAN; PELHAM-MITCHELL CO BICENTENNIAL COMMITTEE; PO BOX 125; PELHAM, GA 31779. (#1577).

HISTORIC MARKERS FOR PELHAM, GEORGIA. MARKERS WILL BE ERECTED TO DESIGNATE 25 HISTORICALLY SIGNIFICANT SITES IN THE PELHAM AREA AND A MARKER GUIDE BROCHURE WILL BE MADE AVAILABLE TO THE PUBLIC. (LOCAL). MRS J ALTON WHALEY, CO-CHAIRMAN; PELHAM-MITCHELL COUNTY BICENTENNIAL COMMITTEE; PO BOX 125; PELHAM, GA 31779. (#6470).

LOCAL HISTORY OF PELHAM, GEORGIA. A HISTORY OF THE PELHAM AREA WILL BE PREPARED FOR PUBLICATION AND A FILM & SLIDES PRESENTED. (LOCAL). MRS J ALTON WHALEY, CO-CHAIRMAN; PELHAM-MITCHELL COUNTY BICENTENNIAL COMMITTEE; PO BOX 125; PELHAM, GA 31779. (#6468).

PELHAM-MITCHELL COUNTY, GA, ACTIVITIES CENTER. CIVIC CENTER FOR CULTURAL ACTIVITIES TO BE CONSTRUCTED IN PELHAM FOR RESIDENTS OF THE REGION. (LOCAL). MRS J ALTON WHALEY, CO-CHAIRMAN; PELHAM-MITCHELL CO BICENTENNIAL COMMITTEE; PO BOX 125; PELHAM, GA 31779. (#1579). (??).

'TOWN LIFT' PROJECT OF PELHAM, GA. DOWNTOWN FACELIFT INCLUDING A MALL, PARK AND MUSEUM. (LOCAL). MRS J ALTON WHALEY, CO-CHAIRMAN; PELHAM-MITCHELL CO BICENTENNIAL COMMITTEE; PO BOX 125; PELHAM, GA 31779. (#1578).

URBAN DEVELOPMENT IN PELHAM, GEORGIA. A CENTRAL BUSINESS DISTRICT PLAN WILL BE DEVELOPED FOR THE RENOVATION OR ELIMINATION OF OLD BUILDINGS AND THE OVER ALL BEAUTIFICATION OF THE DOWNTOWN SHOPPING AREA. (LOCAL). MRS J ALTON WHALEY, CO-CHAIRMAN; PELHAM-MITCHELL COUNTY BICENTENNIAL COMMITTEE; PO BOX 125; PELHAM, GA 31779. (#6469).

MAY 2 - 9, '76. 'DAYS OF YESTERYEAR' FESTIVAL. INAUGURATION OF AN ANNUAL FESTIVAL 'THE DAYS OF YESTERYEAR' TO STIMULATE CIVIC PRIDE AND INTEREST IN LOCAL HERITAGE AS PART OF THE LOCAL BICENT CELEBRATION. AT DOWNTOWN PELHAM AT RAILROAD DEPOT,CHAMBER OF COMM PARK. (LOCAL). MRS J ALTON WHALEY; PELHAM-MITCHELL COUNTY BICENT COMMITTEE; BOX 125; PELHAM, GA 31779. (#6756-1).

PERRY

PERRY BICENTENNIAL TIME CAPSULE, GA. PURCHASE AND INSTALL A TIME CAPSULE ON CITY HALL LAWN. CONTENTS OF CAPSULE TO CONSIST OF WIDE RANGE OF ITEMS REPRESENTATIVE OF CONTEMPORARY CULTURE AND TECHNOLOGY. CAPSULE TO BE OPENED JULY 4, 2076. (LOCAL). HON JAMES O MCKINLEY, MAYOR; CITY OF PERRY; PO DRAWER A; PERRY, GA 31069. (#26960).

PINE MOUNTAIN

TIDY THE TOWN, PINE MOUNTAIN, GA. CLEAN, PAINT AND DO GENERAL MAINTENANCE TO IMPROVE THE TOWN'S APPEARANCE. (LOCAL). KEN ASKEW, COORDINATOR; PINE MOUNTAIN CHAMBER OF COMMERCE; PINE MOUNTAIN, GA 31822. (#25145).

PRESTON

DEC 10, '75. UNITED STATES ARMED FORCES BICENTENNIAL CARAVAN. THE CARAVAN IS COMPOSED OF EXHIBIT VANS FOR EACH BRANCH OF THE MILITARY SERVICE. THE THEME OF THE EXHIBITION IS 'HISTORY OF THE ARMED FORCES AND THEIR CONTRIBUTION TO THE NATION'. (LOCAL). MRS JERRIE WALKER, CHMN; U S ARMED FORCES BICENTENNIAL EXHIBIT VANS PROJECT; BOX 32; PRESTON, GA 31824. (#1775-208).

DEC 11, '76. UNITED STATES ARMED FORCES BICENTENNIAL CARAVAN. CARAVAN IS COMPOSED OF EXHIBIT VANS FOR EACH MILITARY SERVICE. PROJECT THEME IS 'HISTORY OF THE ARMED FORCES & THEIR CONTRIBUTIONS TO THE NATION'. (LOCAL). MRS THOMAS WALKER; UNITED STATES ARMED FORCES BICENTENNIAL CARAVAN; PO BOX 32; PRESTON, GA 31824. (#1775-785).

RAY CITY

DEVELOPMENT OF A PARK IN RAY CITY, GA. DEVELOPMENT OF A TENNIS COURT, MULTI-PURPOSE COURT, BALL FIELD AND PICNIC AREA IN RAY CITY. (LOCAL). MRS JUANELLE WILSON, SECRETARY; RAY CITY BICENTENNIAL COMMITTEE; CITY HALL; RAY CITY, GA 31645. (#26967). **ARBA GRANTEE.**

REYNOLDS

BEAUTIFICATION OF CITY HALL, REYNOLDS, GA. PLANTING OF TREES ON CITY HALL GROUNDS AS LIBERTY TREES FOR FUTURE GENERATIONS TO REMEMBER CELEBRATION. (LOCAL). JAMES L RUSSELL, COMMITTEE CHAIRMAN; TAYLOR COUNTY BICENTENNIAL COMMITTEE; RT 2, BOX 170; BUTLER, GA 31006. (#24046).

RICEBORO

PAPER MILL WASTE TREATMENT-INTERSTATE PAPER CORP. A PAPER MILL BROUGHT NEEDED JOBS TO AN AREA OF HIGH UNEMPLOYMENT WHILE MEETING STRINGENT WATER QUALITY STANDARDS. THE TREATMENT PROCESS UTILIZED HAS WON NATIONAL AND INTERNATIONAL RECOGNITION. (LOCAL). WILLIAM M BATES, PUBLIC RELATIONS REPRESENTATIVE; INTERSTATE PAPER CORPORATION; 133 CARNEGIE WAY, NW; ATLANTA, GA 30303. (#20105).

RICHLAND

BOY SCOUT BEAUTIFICATION PROGRAM, RICHLAND, GA. PROJECT TO REMOVE THE TRASH AND LITTER WITHIN THE BUSINESS DISTRICT AND CLEAR VACANT LOTS. SHRUBS AND FLOWERS WILL ALSO BE PLANTED IN ROADSIDE PARK. (LOCAL). JOHN PARKS, CITY CLERK; CUB AND BOY SCOUTS OF RICHLAND; CITY HALL; RICHLAND, GA 31825. (#16250).

DOWNTOWN IMPROVEMENTS IN RICHLAND, GA. THE COMPLETE REVITALIZATION OF THE CENTRAL BUSINESS DISTRICT OF RICHLAND INCLUDING: STOREFRONT RENOVATION, SIDEWALK IMPROVEMENTS, BEAUTIFICATION OF VACANT LOTS, INSTALLING PLANTERS & BENCHES. (LOCAL). MRS RUBY TURNER, CHAIRPERSON; RICHLAND GARDEN CLUB; PO BOX 91; RICHLAND, GA 31825. (#23782). **ARBA GRANTEE.**

FLAG DISPLAYS IN RICHLAND, GA. FLAG DISPLAYS WILL BE ENCOURAGED ON SPECIAL OCCASIONS AT HOMES AND COMMERCIAL AREAS IN THE COMMUNITY. (LOCAL). MRS BILL MAYO, DAR REGENT; DAUGHTERS OF THE AMERICAN REVOLUTION; 912 CHARLEVOIX ST; RICHLAND, GA 31825. (#16251).

STOREFRONT IMPROVEMENTS FOR THE CBD - RICHLAND, GA. COMPLETE REVITALIZATION OF THE DOWNTOWN BUSINESS DISTRICT INCLUDING FACELIFTING OF STOREFRONTS, CLEANING AND PAINTING STOREFACADES AND BEAUTIFICATION IMPROVEMENTS. (LOCAL). RUBY W TURNER, CHAIRPERSON; RICHLAND BICENTENNIAL COMMITTEE; PO BOX 91; RICHLAND, GA 31825. (#15320).

RICHLAND — CONTINUED

JUNE 19 - AUG 21, '76. SUMMER FILM FESTIVAL. A FREE FILM PROGRAM FOR ELEMENTARY SCHOOL CHILDREN PRESENTED BY FINE ARTS DEPARTMENT OF CHATTAHOOCHEE REGIONAL LIBRARY. (LOCAL). BILL MAYO, CHMN; STEWART COUNTY LIBRARY BOARD; 912 CHARLEVOIX ST; RICHLAND, GA 31825. (#102313-1).

JULY 4, '76. RELIGIOUS FREEDOM RALLY-RELIGIOUS SPEAKER, DINNER & EVENTS. OPENING. (LOCAL). RUBY W TURNER; RICHLAND BICENTENNIAL COMMITTEE; PO BOX 91; RICHLAND, GA 31825. (#15320-501).

RICHMOND HILL

PRESERVATION OF LOCAL HERITAGE AND CULTURE - GA. BUILDING A REPLICA OF AN EARLY RURAL HOUSE AND RESTORING A FORD HOME TO REPRESENT TWO ERAS OF LOCAL HISTORY AND CULTURE; TO HOUSE MEMORABILIA AND ARTIFACTS FOR EDUCATION AND INFORMATION. (LOCAL). KAY SPEIR, CO-CHAIRMAN; RICHMOND HILL BICENTENNIAL COMMITTEE; PO BOX 200; RICHMOND HILL, GA 31324. (#25920). **ARBA GRANTEE.**

RIVERDALE

JAN '76. TIME CAPSULE PLACEMENT - 33 YEARS HENCE. THE TIME CAPSULE WILL BE OPENED JULY 4, 2008; IT WILL CONTAIN PROPHECY & ODYSSEY CONCERNING THE CITY AS SUBMITTED BY CONTEST WINNERS FROM GRADES 7, 8 & 9, MAPS, PICTURES, SEAL, FLAG AND VARIOUS OTHER MEMORABILIA. AT RIVERDALE RECREATION PARK, BETHSAIDA RD. (LOCAL). DON LANDGREBE, CHAIRMAN; CITY OF RIVERDALE CITIZENS PARTICIPATION & BICENTENNIAL COMMITTEE; 6690 CHURCH ST, CITY HALL; RIVERDALE, GA 30274. (#103335-1).

JULY 4, '76. 4TH OF JULY CELBRATION. PARADE, FIREWORKS, CRAFTS, FLEA MARKET, AWARDS AND A DANCE. AT RIVERDALE RECREATION PARK, BETHSAIDA RD. (LOCAL). DON LANDGREBE, CHMN; RIVERDALE BICENTENNIAL COMMITTEE; 6690 CHURCH ST; RIVERDALE, GA 30274. (#103375-1).

ROCHELLE

BICENTENNIAL SCRAPBOOK - PROJ OF ROCHELLE. THE COMMITTEE WILL PREPARE A BICENTENNIAL SCRAPBOOK CONTAINING ALL ARTICLES AND MEMORABILIA OF ROCHELLE'S BICENTENNIAL ACTIVITIES. (LOCAL). MARY LOU MCDONALD, EXEC DIRECTOR; ROCHELLE COMMUNITY BICENTENNIAL COMMITTEE; PO BOX 78; ROCHELLE, GA 31079. (#11341).

BICYCLE MARATHON - PROJ OF ROCHELLE, GA. A BICYCLE MARATHON SIMILAR TO ONES HELD IN FRANCE IS PLANNED BY THE BICENTENNIAL COMMITTEE'S YOUTH GROUP. (LOCAL). MARY LOU MCDONALD; ROCHELLE COMMUNITY BICENTENNIAL COMMITTEE; PO BOX 78; ROCHELLE, GA 31079. (#11343-1).

COMMUNITY MUSEUM - PROJ OF ROCHELLE, GA. A COMMUNITY MUSEUM OF LOCAL HISTORY WILL BE DEVELOPED. (LOCAL). MARY LOU MCDONALD, EXEC DIRECTOR; ROCHELLE COMMUNITY BICENTENNIAL COMMITTEE; PO BOX 78; ROCHELLE, GA 31079. (#11337).

CRAFTS PROJECT OF ROCHELLE, GA. THE BICENTENNIAL COMMITTEE PLANS TO DEVELOP A PROGRAM TO PROMOTE THE MANUFACTURE AND SALE OF LOCAL CRAFTS. (LOCAL). MARY LOU MCDONALD, EXEC DIRECTOR; ROCHELLE COMMUNITY BICENTENNIAL COMMITTEE; PO BOX 78; ROCHELLE, GA 31079. (#11338).

EIFFEL TOWER REPLICA, ROCHELLE, GA. THE BICENTENNIAL COMMITTEE IS STUDYING THE POSSIBILITY OF ERECTING A REPLICA OF THE EIFFEL TOWER IN ROCHELLE. (LOCAL). MARY LOU MCDONALD, EXEC DIRECTOR; ROCHELLE BICENTENNIAL COMMITTEE; PO BOX 78; ROCHELLE, GA 31079. (#11345).

FLAG MEMORIAL AVENUE - PROJ OF ROCHELLE, GA. FLAG MEMORIAL AVENUE WILL BE DEDICATED ON JULY 4, 1976; THE AMERICAN FLAG, THE BICENTENNIAL FLAG, THE FRENCH FLAG & FLAGS OF ALL THE STATES WILL BE DISPLAYED. (LOCAL). MARY LOU MCDONALD, EXEC DIRECTOR; ROCHELLE COMMUNITY BICENTENNIAL COMMITTEE; PO BOX 78; ROCHELLE, GA 31079. (#11336).

'HERITAGE' COOKBOOK - PROJ OF ROCHELLE, GA. THE ROCHELLE BICENTENNIAL COMMITTEE WILL PUBLISH A 'HERITAGE' COOKBOOK CONTAINING SOUTHERN AND FRENCH RECIPES. (LOCAL). MARY LOU MCDONALD, EXEC DIRECTOR; ROCHELLE COMMUNITY BICENTENNIAL COMMITTEE; PO BOX 78; ROCHELLE, GA 31079. (#11340).

LANDSCAPING AND PUBLICATION - ROCHELLE, GA. IMPROVEMENT & LANDSCAPING OF BUSINESS DISTRICT & SURROUNDING AREAS OF MAJOR THOROUGHFARE. ALSO, PAMPHLETS TO PUBLICIZE THE COMMUNITY. (LOCAL). RALPH SUTTON, CHAIRMAN; ROCHELLE BICENTENNIAL COMMISSION; PO BOX 473; ROCHELLE, GA 31079. (#12003). **ARBA GRANTEE.**

LOCAL HISTORY PROJECT OF ROCHELLE, GA. A HISTORY OF THE TOWN OF ROCHELLE WILL BE PUBLISHED BY JULY 4, 1976. (LOCAL). MARY LOU MCDONALD, EXEC DIRECTOR; ROCHELLE COMMUNITY BICENTENNIAL COMMITTEE; PO BOX 78; ROCHELLE, GA 31079. (#11335).

PRAYER AND HYMN - PROJ OF ROCHELLE, GA. THE COMMITTEE WILL SPONSOR THE WRITING OF A BICENTENNIAL HYMN AND PRAYER FOR USE IN THE COMMUNITY DURING THE BICENTENNIAL ERA. (LOCAL). MARY LOU MCDONALD, EXEC DIRECTOR; ROCHELLE COMMUNITY BICENTENNIAL COMMITTEE; PO BOX 78; ROCHELLE, GA 31079. (#11342).

TEACHER'S GUIDE - PROJ OF ROCHELLE, GA. A TEACHER'S GUIDE WILL BE PUBLISHED TO PROMOTE APPRECIATION AND LOVE IN AMERICA. (LOCAL). MARY LOU MCDONALD, EXEC DIRECTOR; ROCHELLE COMMUNITY BICENTENNIAL COMMITTEE; PO BOX 78; ROCHELLE, GA 31079. (#11339).

APR 1 - 3, '76. HERITAGE SPECIAL - TRAIN TOUR. TRAVELING RAIL EXHIBIT EMPHASIZING COLONIAL & REVOLUTIONARY GEORGIA HISTORY, CRAFTS & LIFESTYLE OF GEORGIA COLONISTS. EXHIBITS WILL BE DISPLAYED WITH COMBINATION OF SIGHT & SOUND ACTIVITY. (LOCAL). RON HENRY, COORDINATOR; GEORGIA AGRIRAMA DEVELOPMENT AUTHORITY/GEORGIA BICENTENNIAL; 8TH ST A I 75; TIFTON, GA 31794. (#7999-20).

ROCKMART

BICENTENNIAL COOKBOOK - ROCKMART, GA. THE BOOK INCLUDES GRANDMA'S FAVORITE RECIPES. (LOCAL). MRS LINDA KING, SECRETARY; ROCKMART BICENTENNIAL PLANNING COMMITTEE; PO BOX 231; ROCKMART, GA 30153. (#25460).

CHILDREN'S ZOO - ROCKMART, GA. A CHILDREN'S ZOO WILL BE DEVELOPED WITH A BARNYARD WITH COWS, CHICKENS AND MANY OTHER ANIMALS. (LOCAL). MRS LINDA KING, SECRETARY; ROCKMART BICENTENNIAL PLANNING COMMITTEE; PO BOX 231; ROCKMART, GA 30153. (#25459).

FAMILY STREET DANCE & SQUARE & ROUND DANCE FESTIVAL. FESTIVAL AT CITY SQUARE. (LOCAL). MRS LYNDA KING, SECRETARY; ROCKMART BICENTENNIAL PLANNING COMMITTEE; PO BOX 231; ROCKMART, GA 30153. (#108257-1).

HISTORICAL MUSEUM - ROCKMART, GA. A MUSEUM WILL BE BUILT TO HOUSE HISTORICAL DISPLAYS. (LOCAL). MRS LINDA KING, SECRETARY; ROCKMART BICENTENNIAL PLANNING COMMITTEE; PO BOX 231; ROCKMART, GA 30153. (#25461).

MAY 3 - 5, '76. '1776' MOVIE - THE STORY OF THE DECLARATION OF INDEPENDENCE. EXHIBIT AT ROCKMART THEATRE. (LOCAL). MRS LYNDA KING, SECRETARY; ROCKMART BICENTENNIAL PLANNING COMMITTEE; PO BOX 231; ROCKMART, GA 30153. (#108257-5).

JUNE 26, '76. BICENTENNIAL BALL. DRESS WILL BE FROM 1776 - 1976. THERE WILL BE A LIVE BAND. AT ROCKMART HIGH SCHOOL LUNCHROOM. (LOCAL). LYNDA KING, SECRETARY; PLANNING COMMITTEE OF ROCKMART; PO BOX 231; ROCKMART, GA 30153. (#108071-2).

JUNE 26, '76. PARADE. CARS, BANDS, ANTIQUE CARS, WALKING PARTICIPANTS & FLOATS. (LOCAL). LYNDA KING, SECRETARY; PLANNING COMMITTEE OF ROCKMART; PO BOX 231; ROCKMART, GA 30153. (#108071-1).

JUNE 27, '76. COMMUNITY CHOIR PERFORMANCE. ALL PEOPLE IN THE COMMUNITY WILL PARTICIPATE WITH THE 'FA SO LA' SINGERS OF BREMAN, GA. DAVID HENDRIX WILL DIRECT. (LOCAL). LYNDA KING, SECRETARY; PLANNING COMMITTEE OF ROCKMART; PO BOX 231; ROCKMART, GA 30153. (#108071-3).

JUNE 28, '76. OLD TIMERS' DAY. SCHEDULED EVENTS ARE QUILTING, GOLFING, CARD GAMES, CHECKERS, HORSESHOES AND REMINISCING. AT WAYSIDE PARK. (LOCAL). LYNDA KING, SECRETARY; PLANNING COMMITTEE OF ROCKMART; PO BOX 231; ROCKMART, GA 30153. (#108071-4).

JUNE 29, '76. EXHIBIT OF ARTS & CRAFTS BY SENIOR CITIZENS. EXHIBIT AT LIBRARY & STREET BEHIND LIBRARY. (LOCAL). LYNDA KING, SECRETARY; PLANNING COMMITTEE OF ROCKMART; PO BOX 231; ROCKMART, GA 30153. (#108071-5).

JUNE 30, '76. FIELD DAY AND PICNIC. BASEBALL GAMES, 3-LEGGED RACES, TUG-OF-WAR, BAKING & BEARD GROWING CONTESTS AND COMMUNITY PICNIC AT CITY HALL. AT WAYSIDE PARK, AND RECREATION CENTER. (LOCAL). LYNDA KING, SECRETARY; PLANNING COMMITTEE OF ROCKMART; PO BOX 231; ROCKMART, GA 30153. (#108071-6).

JULY 1, '76. REFLECTIONS OF TIME - SEMINAR. THERE WILL BE DISCUSSIONS & SLIDE PRESENTATIONS ON NATIONAL, STATE, LOCAL & BLACK HISTORY. AT ROCKMART LIBRARY. (LOCAL). MRS LYNDA KING, SECRETARY; ROCKMART BICENTENNIAL PLANNING COMMITTEE; PO BOX 231; ROCKMART, GA 30153. (#108257-3).

JULY 1, '76. TEEN DANCE WITH MUSIC BY 'REASONS WHY'. FESTIVAL AT CITY SQUARE. (LOCAL). MRS LYNDA KING, SECRETARY; ROCKMART BICENTENNIAL PLANNING COMMITTEE; PO BOX 231; ROCKMART, GA 30153. (#108257-2).

JULY 3, '76. 'SALUTE TO AMERICA' & FIREWORKS DISPLAY. STAGE PRODUCTION OF MUSIC & ARTS DEPICTING 200 YEARS OF U S GROWTH. SLIDES, COMMUNITY PARTICIPATION, BAND & VOCALISTS. AT HILLBURN FIELD (FOOTBALL STADIUM). (LOCAL). MRS LYNDA KING, SECRETARY; ROCKMART BICENTENNIAL PLANNING COMMITTEE; PO BOX 231; ROCKMART, GA 30153. (#108257-4).

ROME

NOV 30 - DEC 1, '75. UNITED STATES ARMED FORCES BICENTENNIAL CARAVAN. THE CARAVAN IS COMPOSED OF EXHIBIT VANS FOR EACH BRANCH OF THE MILITARY SERVICE. THE THEME OF THE EXHIBITION IS 'HISTORY OF THE ARMED FORCES AND THEIR CONTRIBUTION TO THE NATION'. (LOCAL). CAPT G L BARLOW USMC, DIR; U S ARMED FORCES BICENTENNIAL EXHIBIT VANS PROJECT; 1 SHORTER AVE; ROME, GA 30161. (#1775-204).

MAY 28 - 29, '76. THE COOSA VALLEY CLASSIC RODEO. COMPETITION AT FAIRGROUNDS. (ST-WIDE). JAY JORDAN, COORD; ROME JAYCEES, INC; PO BOX 643; ROME, GA 30161. (#103416-302).

SEPT 15 - NOV 17, '76. WROM RADIO SERIES - AMERICAN MUSIC. WROM ALSO RUNS A PUBLIC SERVICE CULTURAL PROGRAM THROUGH THE MIDDLE OF JULY. (REGN'L). WILLIAM C MORAN, DEAN; BERRY COLLEGE; MOUNT BERRY, GA 30149. (#7888-1).

SEPT 15 - NOV 17, '76. WROM RADIO SERIES - EVOLUTION OF JAZZ. COURSE MAY BE TAKEN FOR 3 HRS CREDIT, SUPPLEMENTED BY AN ON-CAMPUS LECTURE EACH THURSDAY AT 4 PM. AT RADIO STATION WROM, ROME, GA. (REGN'L). WILLIAM C MORAN, DEAN; BERRY COLLEGE; MOUNT BERRY, GA 30149. (#7888-2).

ROSSVILLE

RESTORATION OF CHIEF JOHN ROSS HOUSE - GA. RESTORE, PRESERVE AND REFURBISH THE HOME OF JOHN ROSS, PRINCIPAL CHIEF OF THE CHEROKEE NATION. (LOCAL). JAMES E MCDANIEL, CHAIRMAN; ROSSVILLE BICENTENNIAL COMMITTEE; PO BOX 159; ROSSVILLE, GA 30741. (#25797). **ARBA GRANTEE.**

ROSWELL

HISTORIC ROSWELL SQUARE BICENT RESTORATION - GA. RENOVATION OF BAND STAND FROM WHICH THEODORE ROOSEVELT SPOKE, ACTIVATION OF FOUNDERS FOUNTAIN, REMOVAL OF UNSIGHTLY WIRING, IMPROVED LIGHTING & SEATING, SIDEWALKS ON TWO SIDES, CLEANUP & LANDSCAPE. (LOCAL). ROSE JACKSON POLATTY, CHAIRMAN; ROSWELL BICENTENNIAL COMMITTEE; PO BOX 1776; ROSWELL, GA 30075. (#17865). **ARBA GRANTEE.**

HISTORY OF ROSWELL CHURCHES, GA. A BOOKLET WILL BE PREPARED CONTAINING THE HISTORY OF CHURCHES IN ROSWELL. (LOCAL). EDWARD C WASHINGTON, PROJ CHAIRMAN; ROSWELL BICENTENNIAL COMMITTEE; PO BOX 1776; ROSWELL, GA 30077. (#24821).

N FULTON BICENTENNIAL COMMEMORATIVE COIN SALE, GA. BRONZE, SILVER & GOLD COINS AVAILABLE WITH INSCRIPTION 'NORTH FULTON BICENTENNIAL - ALPHARETTA, MTN PARK, ROSWELL' & ENGRAVING OF ROSWELL MILLS ON ONE SIDE & GEORGIA STATE SEAL ON OTHER SIDE. (LOCAL). HERBERT ENGEL, PROJ CHAIRMAN; ROSWELL BICENTENNIAL COMMITTEE; PO BOX 1776; ROSWELL, GA 30077. (#24822).

RESTORATION OF GATE AT HISTORIC BARRINGTON HALL-GA. RECONSTRUCTION OF ORIGINAL WOODEN SUNBURST GATE AT THE ENTRANCE TO BARRINGTON HALL BY STUDENT CHAPTERS OF THE AMERICAN SOCIETY OF INTERIOR DESIGN AT GA STATE UNIV AND THE ART INSTITUTE OF ATLANTA. (LOCAL). DAVID HATTER, BICENTENNIAL CHAIRMAN; AMER SOC OF INTERIOR DESIGN - GA STATE UNIV, ART INST OF ATLANTA; 1294 FAIRHILL LANE, NE; ATLANTA, GA 30319. (#25659).

ROSWELL ORAL HISTORY PROJECT, GA. CITIZENS OF COMMUNITY ARE BEING TAPED TO BRING HISTORY OF ROSWELL UP TO DATE; TRANSCRIPTIONS OF THE TAPES WILL BE THE BASIS OF A BOOK BY THE ROSWELL HISTORICAL SOCIETY. (LOCAL). MRS DOLLE REEVES, PROJ CHAIRMAN; ROSWELL HISTORICAL SOCIETY; RT 3, BOX 199; ALPHARETTA, GA 30201. (#24820).

JULY 2, '76. UNITED FAITH BICENT CHURCH SERVICE. TO REDISCOVER OUR COMMON HERITAGE OF RELIGIOUS FREEDOM, 21 AREA CHURCHES PLAN TO UNITE & HONOR OUR 'ONE NATION, UNDER GOD' BY SHARING A UNITED FAITH SERVICE. AT UNITED METHODIST CHURCH, MIMOSA BLVD. (LOCAL). JANET W RUSSELL; ROSWELL BICENTENNIAL COMMITTEE; BOX 1776; ROSWELL, GA 30077. (#107232-1).

JULY 3, '76. GRAND BICENTENNIAL COSTUME BALL. FESTIVAL AT ROSWELL SQUARE. (LOCAL). M RUSSELL, GEN CHMN; THE ROSWELL HISTORICAL SOCIETY, INC; PO BOX 274; ROSWELL, GA 30075. (#106571-1).

JULY 3, '76. 'HAPPY BIRTHDAY, UNCLE SAM'. TRADITIONAL JULY 4TH FAMILY-ORIENTED DAY: PARADE FEATURES MANY BANDS & FLOATS; BARBECUE ON TOWN SQUARE; BAND CONCERT, TRADITIONAL GAMES, RACES & SWIMMING AT PARK; AERIAL FIREWORKS AT DARK. (LOCAL). RONALD F LE ROY; GREATER ROSWELL JAYCEES; BOX 122; ROSWELL, GA 30075. (#107232-2).

JULY 3 - 4, '76. OPEN HOUSE AT HISTORIC BARRINGTON HALL WITH TOURS OF HOUSE AND YARD. NORTH FULTON COUNCIL OF GARDEN CLUBS AND NONFEDERATED GARDEN CLUBS IN ROSWELL ARE DEDCORATING AND STAFFING HOUSE WHILE EASTERN ROSWELL CIVIC ASSOCIATION AND ROCK LILY GARDEN CLUB ARE WORKING ON THE GROUNDS. RESTORED GATE WILL BE DEDICATED JULY 4 AT 2:00 PM. AT INTERSECTION OF HWY 19 & HWY 120 FACING ROSWELL SQUARE WITH PARKING. (LOCAL). MRS MARGARET HARRIS; NORTH FULTON COUNCIL OF GARDEN CLUBS AND NONFEDERATED GARDEN CLUBS; 705 LAKE CHARLES WAY; ROSWELL, GA 30075. (#107232-4).

JULY 4, '76. DEDICATION OF HISTORIC ROSWELL SQUARE RESTORATION PROJECT. CEREMONY. (LOCAL). ROSE JACKSON POLATTY-CHMN; ROSWELL BICENTENNIAL COMMITTEE; PO BOX 1776; ROSWELL, GA 30075. (#17865-1).

JULY 4, '76. OLD-FASHIONED ICE CREAM SOCIAL. AFTER DEDICATION OF ROSWELL BICENT PROJECT ON TOWN SQUARE, OLD-FASHIONED ICE CREAM TOP BE SERVED BY COSTUMED LADIES IN CONJUNCTION WITH DEDICATION & HERITAGE OPEN HOUSE. AT TOWN SQUARE. (LOCAL). POLLY CUTLIP, CHMN; ROSWELL NEWCOMERS & ALUMNI; 1180 FALSTAFF DR; ROSWELL, GA 30076. (#107232-3).

SANDERSVILLE

AID FOR MENTALLY RETARDED - SANDERSVILLE, GA. FINANCIAL CONTRIBUTION TOWARD SUMMER CAMP PROGRAM AT WASHINGTON COUNTY TRAINING CENTER FOR THE MENTALLY RETARDED. (LOCAL). MRS TOMMY WALKER, CHAIRMAN; THE GUILD; 505 WOODLAND TERR; SANDERSVILLE, GA 31082. (#12625).

BEAUTIFICATION AND CLEANUP CAMPAIGN - GA. ENCOURAGE TOWNS AND COMMUNITIES IN COUNTY TO SPONSOR BEAUTIFICATION AND CLEANUP CAMPAIGNS. (LOCAL). LEWIS WEST, CHAIRMAN; WASHINGTON COUNTY BICENTENNIAL STEERING COMMITTEE; 307 MIAMOLA AVE; SANDERSVILLE, GA 31082. (#12628).

COUNTY HISTORY PROJECTS - SANDERSVILLE, GA. RESEARCH TOWARD PUBLICATION OF HISTORY OF WASHINGTON COUNTY BY SEVERAL GROUPS AND INDIVIDUALS. (LOCAL). LEWIS WEST, CHAIRMAN; WASHINGTON COUNTY BICENTENNIAL STEERING COMMITTEE; 307 MIAMOLA AVE; SANDERSVILLE, GA 31082. (#12635).

'DISCOVERIES' PROJECT - SANDERSVILLE, GA. WASHINGTON CO HIGH SCHOOL HAS RECEIVED A 'DISCOVERIES' GRANT TO RESEARCH COUNTY HISTORY FOR 3 HUMANITIES COURSES; TENNILLE ELEMENTARY SCHOOL PRESENTED PAGEANT ON ESSAYS, POSTERS, MUSIC & DEBATES. (LOCAL). BUDDY OUZTS, SUPERINTENDENT; WASHINGTON COUNTY PUBLIC SCHOOL SYSTEM; 210 N HARRIS ST; SANDERSVILLE, GA 31082. (#12622).

DOWNTOWN SANDERSVILLE REVITALIZATION PROJECT - GA. REMOVE OLD COMMERCIAL BUILDINGS AND CONVERT INTO LANDSCAPED, LIGHTED PARKING AREAS. (LOCAL). LARRY MATHIS, CHAIRMAN; WASHINGTON COUNTY CHAMBER OF COMMERCE/CITY OF SANDERSVILLE; 650 W CHURCH ST; SANDERSVILLE, GA 31082. (#12629).

FIGHT DRUG ABUSE - PROJ OF SANDERSVILLE, GA. BICENTENNIAL COMMITTEE ENDORSES AND WILL SUPPORT THE LOCAL ORGANIZATION TO FIGHT DRUG ABUSE IN THE COUNTY. (LOCAL). JOE GIDDENS, CHAIRMAN; WASHINGTON COUNTY DRUG ABUSE COUNCIL, INC; 435 MOYE DR; SANDERSVILLE, GA 31082. (#12627).

FLAGS, WELCOME CENTER & POLICE STATION - GA. AVENUE OF FLAGS IN DOWNTOWN SANDERSVILLE. POLICE STATION WILL BE REDESIGNED IN COLONIAL ARCHITECTURE AND DOUBLE AS WELCOME CENTER IN DOWNTOWN SANDERSVILLE. (LOCAL). DAVID GINN, CHAIRMAN; CITY OF SANDERSVILLE/AMERICAN LEGION; 805 W CHURCH ST; SANDERSVILLE, GA 31082. (#12631).

HISTORICAL SOCIETY - PROJ OF SANDERSVILLE, GA. A WASHINGTON COUNTY HISTORICAL SOCIETY WILL BE ORGANIZED. (LOCAL). LEWIS WEST, CHAIRMAN; WASHINGTON COUNTY BICENTENNIAL STEERING COMMITTEE; 307 MIAMOLA AVE; SANDERSVILLE, GA 31082. (#12636).

KAOLIN INDUSTRY TRIBUTE, SANDERSVILLE, GA. BICENTENNIAL SOUVENIR CERAMIC ITEM, MADE OF WASHINGTON COUNTY CLAY, FEATURING COUNTY'S NEW MAP WILL BE INTRODUCED FOR SALE. (LOCAL). RAY AVIRETT, CHAIRMAN; SANDERSVILLE LION'S CLUB; 206 RICHMOND ST; SANDERSVILLE, GA 31082. (#12626).

NEW MAP OF WASHINGTON COUNTY, GA. NEW MAP NAMES ALL COUNTY ROADS, CREEKS & BRIDGES. (LOCAL). CECIL HODGES JR, CHAIRMAN; SANDERSVILLE ROTARY CLUB; 609 KINNEY ST; SANDERSVILLE, GA 31082. (#12633).

PUBLICATIONS AND PROGRAMS - SANDERSVILLE, GA. SYMPOSIUM OF TRIBUTES TO AMERICA, HERITAGE COOKBOOK, RECORDINGS FOR RADIO ON RELIGIOUS FREEDOM AND HISTORY OF COUNTY & GUIDE TO HISTORIC SITES; PUBLISHING OF COUNTY HISTORY TENATIVE. (LOCAL). LEWIS WEST, CHAIRMAN; WASHINGTON COUNTY BICENTENNIAL COMMITTEE; 307 MIAMOLA AVE; SANDERSVILLE, GA 31082. (#12624).

SANDERSVILLE, GA, DISPLAY OF PLATES. OFFICIAL GEORGIA HISTORICAL PLATES WILL BE ON PERMANENT DISPLAY AT THE SANDERSVILLE PUBLIC LIBRARY. (LOCAL). MRS WARREN NEWMAN, EXEC DIRECTOR; SANDERSVILLE PUBLIC LIBRARY; 113 FIRST AVE; SANDERSVILLE, GA 31082. (#16329).

APR - AUG '75. SCHOOL PROJECTS - SANDERSVILLE, GA. FLAG DISPLAYS, FACSIMILES OF FAMOUS DOCUMENTS ON DISPLAY, COMMEMORATIVE BULLETIN BOARDS, PROJECTS REPRESENTING COLONIAL AND REVOLUTIONARY PERIODS WERE MADE BY U S HISTORY CLASS. (LOCAL). MRS ISABEL SNYDER; WASHINGTON COUNTY INDEPENDENT SCHOOL; LINTON RD; SANDERSVILLE, GA 31082. (#12623-1).

NOV 9, '75. FLAG RAISING CEREMONY. PATRIOTIC ADDRESS BY SENATOR SAM NUNN, PATRIOTIC BAND MUSIC AND DEDICATION OF NEW COMBINATION POLICE STATION AND INFORMATION CENTER IN DOWNTOWN SANDERSVILLE WHICH IS TO BE BUILT IN COLONIAL ARCHITECTURAL DESIGN AS LASTING REMINDER OF BICENTENNIAL. AT WASHINGTON COUNTY COURT HOUSE SQUARE. (ST-WIDE). LEWIS WEST, PROJ CHMN; WASHINGTON COUNTY BICENTENNIAL STEERING COMMITTEE; 307 MIAMOLA AVE; SANDERSVILLE, GA 31082. (#102873-2).

APR 5 - 6, '76. 'HATS OFF TO AMERICA' BICENTENNIAL MUSICAL. LIVE PERFORMANCE. (LOCAL). MRS MAURICE FRIEDMAN; SANDERSVILLE MUSIC CLUB; 442 ORCHARD LN; SANDERSVILLE, GA 31082. (#102873-5).

MAY 1, '76. 'THIS IS MY COUNTRY' FLOWER SHOW & TOUR OF CLIFFORD BELL HOME. EXHIBIT AT CLIFFORD BELL HOME, 249 NORTH HARRIS STREET. (LOCAL). MRS HERDERT MCCASKILL, JR; SPADE & TROWEL GARDEN CLUB & TOWN & COUNTRY GARDEN CLUB; 702 LAUREL DR; SANDERSVILLE, GA 31082. (#102873-4).

JULY 4, '76. JULY 4, 1976: CELEBRATION. A SPECIAL SERVICE HIGHLIGHTING RELIGIOUS FREEDOM THROUGH WORSHIP AND FIREWORKS AFTER SERVICE AT WASHINGTON COUNTY HIGH SCHOOL STADIUM SPONSORED BY LOCAL NATIONAL GUARD. AT COURT HOUSE SQUARE. (LOCAL). REV BURNS WILLIS, CHMN; WASHINGTON COUNTY MINISTERIAL ASSOC; UNITED METHODIST CHURCH; SANDERSVILLE, GA 31082. (#102873-3).

OCT 9 - 10, '76. ARTS & CRAFTS FAIR. ARTS AND CRAFTS COUNTY WIDE FAIR WILL HIGHLIGHT HISTORY OF FARMING IN WASHINGTON COUNTY. NEEDLEWORK SUCH AS QUILTS AND SAMPLERS WILL BE FEATURED. ALSO OLD FARMING TOOLS, CANE GRINDING & BASKET WEAVING. (LOCAL). GERALD ANDREWS; COMMUNITY CLUB; 205 MIAMOLA AVE; SANDERSVILLE, GA 31082. (#12630-1).

SAVANNAH

ARMSTRONG STATE COLLEGE BICENT LIBRARY PROJ - GA. THE COLLEGE WILL PLACE EXHIBITS IN THE LIBRARY ON THE THREE THEMES OF THE BICENTENNIAL, HERITAGE, FESTIVAL AND HORIZONS. (LOCAL). DONALD D ANDERSON, DEAN OF COMMUNITY SERVICES; ARMSTRONG STATE COLLEGE; 11935 ABERCORN ST; SAVANNAH, GA 31406. (#17004).

BICENT PARK FOR SAVANNAH, GEORGIA. RESTORATION OF REVOLUTIONARY BATTLEFIELD SITE ASSOCIATED WITH THE SIEGE OF SAVANNAH AND PRESERVATION OF EXISTING RAILROAD STRUCTURES ON NATIONAL REGISTER AS PARK & EDUCATIONAL CENTER. (LOCAL). LEOPOLD ADLER, II, CHAIRMAN; CHATHAM' COUNTY - SAVANNAH HISTORIC SITES & MONUMENT COMMISSION; CITY HALL; SAVANNAH, GA 31401. (#10811).

BICENTENNIAL SHORT COURSES - ARMSTRONG COL, GA. COURSES WILL INCLUDE A HISTORY OF SAVANNAH, SAVANNAH ARCHITECTURE, THE U S & THE USSR, THE FAR EAST, THE ERA OF DETENTE. THE COURSES ARE DEGREE FREE, OPEN TO STUDENTS AND THE PUBLIC. (LOCAL). DONALD D ANDERSON, DEAN OF COMMUNITY SERVICES; ARMSTRONG STATE COLLEGE; 11935 ABERCORN ST; SAVANNAH, GA 31401. (#17003).

BICENTENNIAL TOUR OF SAVANNAH, GEORGIA. BICENTENNIAL TOUR OF HISTORIC SAVANNAH & THE GEORGIA HISTORICAL SOCIETY HEADQUARTERS. (LOCAL). FRETWELL G CRIDER, PROJ DIRECTOR; MIDDLE GEORGIA COLLEGE BICENTENNIAL COMMITTEE; MIDDLE GEORGIA COLLEGE; COCHRAN, GA 31014. (#13477).

BROCHURE ON BICENTENNIAL ACTIVITIES - SAVANNAH, GA. BROCHURE WITH MAP OF CITY AND HISTORICAL AREA, SPECIAL EVENTS, HISTORICAL LANDMARKS, HOTELS, RESTAURANTS AND PERTINANT TOURIST INFORMATION. TO BE DISTRIBUTED THRU CHAMBER OF COMMERCE. (ST-WIDE). BETH GLASS, DIR VISITOR PROGRAMS; SAVANNAH AREA CONVENTION & VISITORS BUREAU; P O BOX 530, 301 WEST BROAD; SAVANNAH, GA 31402. (#8207). **ARBA GRANTEE.**

BROUGHTON STREET REVITALIZATION IN SAVANNAH, GA. BROUGHTON STREET IN SAVANNAH'S CENTRAL BUSINESS DISTRICT WILL BE REVITALIZED TO CREATE AN ATMOSPHERE CONDUCIVE TO RETAIL, FINANCIAL AND PROFESSIONAL ACTIVITIES AS WELL AS TOURIST ATTRACTIONS. (LOCAL). BOB LYNN, EXEC DIRECTOR; SAVANNAH '76 COMMITTEE; PO BOX 1027; SAVANNAH, GA 31402. (#11296).

DAVENPORT HOUSE BICENTENNIAL COURTYARD, GA. THE PARKING AREA OF DAVENPORT HOUSE MUSEUM-GARDEN WILL BE CONVERTED INTO A BICENTENNIAL COURTYARD FOR MEETINGS AND ENTERTAINMENT. (LOCAL). JAMES R LIENTZ, CHAIRMAN, DISTRIBUTION COMMITTEE; FORWARD SAVANNAH TRUST INC; PO BOX 9119; SAVANNAH, GA 31402. (#13839). **ARBA GRANTEE.**

FIRST AFRICAN BAPTIST CHURCH RECOGNIZED - GA. THE FIRST BLACK RELIGIOUS CONGREGATION IN AMERICA, ESTABLISHED IN SAVANNAH IN 1788, WILL BE COMMEMORATED AND RECOGNIZED. (LOCAL). BOB LYNN, EXEC DIRECTOR; SAVANNAH '76 COMMITTEE; PO BOX 1027; SAVANNAH, GA 31402. (#11300).

FIRST AFRICAN BAPTIST CHURCH MUSEUM & ARCHIVES, GA. THE ESTABLISHMENT OF A PERMANENT MUSEUM & ARCHIVES TO PRESERVE & DISPLAY ARTIFACTS & RECORDS OF THE OLDEST BLACK CHURCH IN NORTH AMERICA. (LOCAL). REV LAWRENCE MCKINNEY, PASTOR; FIRST AFRICAN BAPTIST CHURCH; 23 MONTGOMERY ST; SAVANNAH, GA 31401. (#16134). **ARBA GRANTEE.**

GOVERNOR'S BICENTENNIAL YOUTH CONGRESS, GA. DELEGATES WILL BE SELECTED BY COMMITTEES TO ATTEND THE CONFERENCE. (ST-WIDE). DAVID POWERS, CHAIRMAN; GOVERNORS BICENTENNIAL YOUTH CONGRESS; PO BOX 1027; SAVANNAH, GA 31402. (#21202). **ARBA GRANTEE.**

HISTORIC SAVANNAH, GA. H U D 'HORIZONS ON DISPLAY' DESIGNATION PRESENTED TO SAVANNAH, GA. TROOP WARD PROJECT: TWELVE BLOCK INNERCITY URBAN RENEWAL HISTORIC RENOVATION PROGRAM INITIATED IN 1961. (LOCAL). ROBERT J LYNN, DIRECTOR; CHATHAM COUNTY SAVANNAH METROPOLITAN PLANNING COMMISSION; PO BOX 1027; SAVANNAH, GA 31402. (#20048).

N S SAVANNAH AND EISENHOWER PEACE CENTER, GA. TITLE TO N S SAVANNAH WILL BE ACQUIRED FROM FEDERAL GOVERNMENT AND SHIP WILL CONVERTED INTO EISENHOWER PEACE CENTER & MARITIME MUSEUM. (ST-WIDE). BOB LYNN, EXEC DIRECTOR; SAVANNAH '76 COMMITTEE; PO BOX 1027; SAVANNAH, GA 31402. (#11299).

A NIGHT IN OLD SAVANNAH - SAVANNAH, GA. COMMUNITY CELEBRATION DESIGNED TO PAY TRIBUTE TO ETHNIC GROUPS IN SAVANNAH THAT HAVE HELPED TO SHAPE OUR HERITAGE. THE MAIN ATTRACTION WILL BE ETHNIC FOODS ALONG WITH MUSIC, GAMES & GOOD ENTERTAINMENT. (LOCAL). ANN N JONES, EXEC DIRECTOR; GIRL SCOUT COUNCIL OF SAVANNAH, GA, INC; 330 DRAYTON ST; SAVANNAH, GA 31402. (#21857). **ARBA GRANTEE.**

POLAND'S GIFT TO SAVANNAH. THE 'DAR POMORZA' WILL BRING AN URN OF EARTH FROM THE ESTATE OF COUNT KAZIMIERZ PUL?ASKI, FAMOUS POLISH PATRIOT & AMER REV WAR GENERAL, AS A GIFT TO SAVANNAH WHERE PULASKI WAS MORTALLY WOUNDED. (INT'L). INFORMATION ATTACHE; EMBASSY OF POLAND; 2640 16TH ST; WASHINGTON, DC 20009. (#31913).

RESTORATION OF MASSIE, SAVANNAH'S OLDEST SCHOOL. MASSIE COMMON SCHOOL HOUSE IS CRADLE OF PUBLIC EDUC IN SAVANNAH. PROJECT INVOLVES BOTH PROGRAM AND RESTORATION FOR NATIONAL LANDMARK. FIRST PHASE: REPLICATION OF ORIGINAL ENTRY DOORS AND STONE LINTEL. (ST-WIDE). FLOYD E MORRIS, ASST SUPERINTENDENT; SAVANNAH SCHOOLS; 208 BULL ST; SAVANNAH, GA 31401. (#27743). **ARBA GRANTEE.**

RESTORATION OF SCARBROUGH HOUSE IN SAVANNAH, GA. RESTORATION OF SCARBROUGH HOUSE FOR A PUBLIC MUSEUM, FOUNDATION HEADQUARTERS AND CONSERVATION CENTER. (LOCAL). DECOURCY E MCINTOSH, EXEC DIRECTOR; HISTORIC SAVANNAH FOUNDATION, INC; PO BOX 1733; SAVANNAH, GA 31402. (#14561). **ARBA GRANTEE.**

REVOLUTIONARY BATTLEFIELD PARK IN SAVANNAH, GA. PLANS ARE BEING DEVELOPED TO CREATE A RECREATIONAL & CULTURAL FACILITY OF NATIONAL SIGNIFICANCE, AT THE SITE OF A HISTORIC REVOLUTIONARY BATTLE. (REGN'L). BOB LYNN, EXEC DIRECTOR; SAVANNAH '76 COMMITTEE; PO BOX 1027; SAVANNAH, GA 31402. (#11292).

RIVER STREET URBAN RENEWAL PLAN, SAVANNAH, GA. PRESERVATION & MAINTENANCE OF THE OLD, HISTORICALLY & ARCHITECTURALLY SIGNIFICANT STRUCTURES, SITES, MONUMENTS AND OTHER ELEMENTS CREATING THE UNIQUE CHARACTER OF HISTORIC SAVANNAH. (LOCAL). BOB LYNN, EXEC DIRECTOR; SAVANNAH '76 COMMITTEE; PO BOX 1027; SAVANNAH, GA 31402. (#11297).

SAVANNAH RELIGIOUS HERITAGE PROJECT. ESTABLISH A HISTORIC AND A TOURIST ORIENTED ARCHIVES IN EACH OF SAVANNAH'S REVOLUTIONARY ERA CHURCHESF BROCHURE ON RELIGIOUS FREEDOM IN EARLY GEORGIA INCLUDING RESEARCH ON EACH OF THE CHURCHES. (LOCAL). ALAN GAYNOR, CHAIRMAN; SAVANNAH '76 COMMITTEE; PO BOX 8608; SAVANNAH, GA 31402. (#910). **ARBA GRANTEE.**

SAVANNAH, GA, VISITORS' CENTER. THE SAVANNAH AREA CHAMBER OF COMMERCE IS RESTORING THE OLD CENTRAL GEORGIA RAILWAY PASSENGER STATION, FOR USE AS A TOURISTS INFORMATION CENTER AND CHAMBER HEADQUARTERS. (ST-WIDE). BOB LYNN, EXEC DIRECTOR; SAVANNAH '76 COMMITTEE; PO BOX 1027; SAVANNAH, GA 31402. (#11301).

OCT 1, '75 - MAY 1, '76. HERITAGE OF AMERICAN CINEMA. FESTIVAL AT AUDITORIUM - JENKINS HALL. (LOCAL). DONALD D ANDERSON; ARMSTRONG STATE COLLEGE; 11935 ABERCORN ST; SAVANNAH, GA 31406. (#103331-1).

OCT 9, '75 - MAR 13, '76. AMERICAN HERITAGE LECTURE SERIES. SERIES INCLUDES 6 LECTURES BY ASC FACULTY AND OTHERS; OPEN TO ALL FREE OF CHARGE. AT LECTURE HALL, FINE ARTS BLDG. (LOCAL). DONALD D ANDERSON, DEAN; ARMSTRONG STATE COLLEGE BICENTENNIAL COMMITTEE; 11935 ABERCORN ST; SAVANNAH, GA 31206. (#103095-7).

DEC 12 - 13, '75. 'GEORGE M'. LIVE PERFORMANCE AT AUDITORIUM; NEW FINE ARTS BLDG. (LOCAL). DONALD D ANDERSON, DEAN; ARMSTRONG STATE COLLEGE BICENTENNIAL COMMITTEE; 11935 ABERCORN ST; SAVANNAH, GA 31206. (#103095-9).

JAN 17, '76. SAVANNAH SYMPHONY PERFORMANCE. LIVE PERFORMANCE AT AUDITORIUM; NEW FINE ARTS BLDG. (LOCAL). DONALD D ANDERSON, DEAN; ARMSTRONG STATE COLLEGE BICENTENNIAL COMMITTEE; 11935 ABERCORN ST; SAVANNAH, GA 31206. (#103095-8).

FEB 8 - 15, '76. GEORGIA WEEK CELEBRATION. PAGEANTS, ART EXHIBITS, CONCERTS, OPEN HOUSES, LECTURES, CRAFT SHOWS & SUPPORTING EVENTS TO COMMEMORATE FOUNDING OF GEORGIA, FEB 12, 1733 & WILL EMBRACE BICENTENNIAL THEME. (ST-WIDE). MARY S HAM CHM; HISTORIC SAVANNAH FOUNDATION, INC.; 119 HABERSHAM ST. PO BOX 1733; SAVANNAH, GA 31402. (#100303-1).

FEB 19 - 21, '76. GOVERNOR'S BICENTENNIAL YOUTH CONGRESS. DELEGATES WILL BE SELECTED BY COMMITTEES TO ATTEND THE CONFERENCE. PURPOSE OF CONGRESS IS TO LET STUDENT DELEGATES DRAFT & SIGN A DECLARATION FOR THE FUTURE. DECLARATION IS THEN PRINTED AND DISTRIBUTED. AT DESOTO HILTON HOTEL, SAVANNAH, GA. (ST-WIDE). DAVID POWERS, CHAIRMAN; SAVANNAH JAYCEES; GA COMMISSION - NATIONAL BICENTENNIAL CELEBRATION; PO BOX 1027; SAVANNAH, GA 31402. (#21202-1).

MAR 5 - 7, '76. UNITED STATES ARMED FORCES BICENTENNIAL CARAVAN. CARAVAN IS COMPOSED OF EXHIBIT VANS FOR EACH MILITARY SERVICE. PROJECT THEME IS 'HISTORY OF THE ARMED FORCES AND THEIR CONTRIBUTIONS TO THE NATION'. (LOCAL). ROBERT J LYNN; METROPOLITAN PLANNING COMMISSION; 2E BAY ST, BOX 1027; SAVANNAH, GA 31402. (#1775-440).

MAR 17, '76. ST PATRICK'S DAY PARADE. 2ND LARGEST ST PATRICK'S DAY PARADE IN U S WILL PAY TRIBUTE TO THE 200TH BIRTHDAY WITH A THEME OF HERITAGE, HORIZON AND FESTIVAL. (LOCAL). MS BETTY PLATT, CHMN; SAVANNAH VISITOR CENTER SAVANNAH AREA CHAMBER OF COMMERCE; PO BOX 530; SAVANNAH, GA 31401. (#103416-94).

SAVANNAH — CONTINUED

APR 17 - 19, '76. OPERATION SAIL IN SAVANNAH. TALL SHIPS VISIT SAVANNAH HARBOR OVER THE WEEKEND. AT SAVANNAH HARBOR. (INT'L). DAVID POWERS, COORD; SAVANNAH '76 COMMITTEE; PO BOX 1027; SAVANNAH, GA 31402. (#200012-49).

APR 30 - MAY 2, '76. SAVANNAH ARTS FESTIVAL. OUTDOOR ART FESTIVAL FEATURES PAINTINGS FROM THROUGHOUT THE SOUTHEAST: ARTS, CRAFTS, PUPPET SHOWS, BALLET ARE FEATURED. (REGN'L). FRANK BRYSON, DIRECTOR; SAVANNAH ART ASSOC; 119 JEFFERSON; SAVANNAH, GA 31401. (#103416-173).

MAY 6 - 8, '76. A NIGHT IN OLD SAVANNAH. COMMUNITY CELEBRATION DESIGNED TO PAY TRIBUTE TO ETHNIC GROUPS IN SAVANNAH THAT HAVE HELPED TO SHAPE OUR HERITAGE. THE MAIN ATTRACTION WILL BE ETHNIC FOODS ALONG WITH MUSIC, GAMES & GOOD ENTERTAINMENT. AT JOHNSON SQUARE. (ST-WIDE). BOB LYNN; SAVANNAH BICENTENNIAL; PO BOX 9389; SAVANNAH, GA 31402. (#21857-1).

JUNE 20, '76. BLESSING OF THE FLEET. BLESSING OF SHRIMP FLEET INCLUDES FESTIVAL FEATURING STREET DANCING, BAND CONCERTS, FLEA MARKETS AND BEAUTY PAGEANT. (LOCAL). HAL C LANE, PGM MANAGER; TOWN OF THUNDERBOLT; THUNDERBOLT, GA 31404. (#103416-187).

JULY 1, '76. UNIVERSITY OF CALIFORNIA MARCHING BAND PRESENTS 'SPIRIT OF AMERICA'. THIS IS PART OF A 6-WEEK PERFORMANCE TOUR OF THE U S; 'SPIRIT OF AMERICA' IS A COLLEGIATE MUSICAL REVIEW CELEBRATING OUR NATION'S BICENTENNIAL; WILL INCLUDE FOLK MUSIC, MARCHING, VAUDEVILLE, ROCK, DIXIELAND, JAZZ, BARBERSHOP & SOLOS. AT RIVERFRONT. (ST-WIDE). ROBERT LYNN, DIRECTOR; SAVANNAH BICENTENNIAL COMMISSION; PO BOX 1027; SAVANNAH, GA 31402. (#10515-10).

JULY 1 - 6, '76. HERITAGE SPECIAL - TRAIN TOUR. TRAVELING RAIL EXHIBIT EMPHASIZING COLONIAL & REVOLUTIONARY GEORGIA HISTORY, CRAFTS & LIFESTYLE OF GEORGIA COLONISTS. EXHIBITS WILL BE DISPLAYED WITH COMBINATION OF SIGHT & SOUND ACTIVITY. (ST-WIDE). RON HENRY, COORDINATOR; GEORGIA AGRIRAMA DEVELOPMENT AUTHORITY/GEORGIA BICENTENNIAL; 8TH ST A I 75; TIFTON, GA 31794. (#7999-6).

JULY 4, '76. JULY 4TH CELEBRATION. PATRIOTIC PROGRAM IS AT 8PM AND A GIANT FIREWORKS DIPLAY IS AT 9PM. AT MEMORIAL STADIUM. (LOCAL). ROBERT S PORTER, CHMN; SAVANNAH CHAMBER OF COMMERCE; PO BOX 530; SAVANNAH, GA 31402. (#103416-189).

JULY 19, '76. OPERATION SAIL POLISH COMMEMORATIVE CEREMONY. POLISH AMBASSADOR PRESENTS URN FROM BIRTHPLACE OF GENERAL PULASKI TO CITY OF SAVANNAH & RECEIVES URN CONTAINING EARTH OF SAVANNAH FOR POLAND IN CEREMONIES CENTERED AROUND THE VISIT OF OPERATION SAIL. (INT'L). DAVID POWERS, COORD; SAVANNAH '76 COMMITTEE; PO BOX 1027; SAVANNAH, GA 31402. (#200012-50).

OCT 1 - 31, '76. 'AMERICAN NAVAL PRINTS' EXHIBITION OF 65 HISTORIC NAVAL SCENES. EXHIBIT AT TELFAIR ACADEMY OF ARTS AND SCIENCES, INC. (ST-WIDE). MRS JOHN A POPE, PRES; INTERNATIONAL EXHIBITIONS FOUNDATION; 1729 H ST - SUITE 310; WASHINGTON, DC 20006. (#109108-1).

OCT 8, '76. BICENTENNIAL CELEBRATION. ALSO: BOOK/GUIDE/OTHER PUBLICATION, RESEARCH. (LOCAL). JESSIE LEGRAND CELESTIN; INTL SOCIETY FOR APPLIED STUDIES TRANSCULTURAL ADAPTATION, INC; 9315 W PARKHILL DR; BETHESDA, MD 20014. (#10365-1).

OCT 9, '76. COMMEMORATION OF THE SEIGE OF SAVANNAH. CEREMONY & MAYOR'S LUNCHEON TO COMMEMORATE THE SEIGE OF SAVANNAH DURING THE AMERICAN REVOLUTION. UNVEILING & DEDICATION OF BUST OF COUNT D'ESTAING & SALUTE TO THE REPUBLIC OF FRANCE. (INT'L). JOHN D ROUSAKIS, MAYOR; CITY OF SAVANNAH; CITY HALL, BAY ST; SAVANNAH, GA 31402. (#200012-52).

OCT 9, '76. YORKTOWN IRISH REGIMENT CEREMONY. HONOR REGIMENTS OF IRISH BRIGADE OF FRENCH ARMY UNDER ROCHAMBEAU AT BATTLE OF YORKTOWN BY CEREMONY AND PROVIDE LASTING MEMORIAL TO THE AMERICAN PEOPLE BY THE AMERICAN IRISH BICENTENNAL COMMITTEE. AT BATTLE SITE VICINITY, OLD RAILROAD STATION. (INT'L). JOSEPH F O'CONNOR; AMERICAN IRISH BICENTENNIAL COMMITTEE/CITY OF SAVANNAH; 1629 K ST NW; WASHINGTON, DC 20006. (#2193-3).

NOV 1 - 7, '76. COASTAL EMPIRE FAIR. ANNUAL FAIR FEATURES MIDWAY, LOCAL COMMERCE EXHIBITS AND LIVESTOCK JUDGING. AT MONTGOMERY ST. (ST-WIDE). DON FERGUSON, DIRECTOR; EXCHANGE CLUB OF SAVANNAH; 7 N FAHM ST; SAVANNAH, GA 31401. (#103416-188).

NOV 16 - 18, '76. AMERICAN FREEDOM TRAIN DISPLAY DAYS AT SAVANNAH. THE AMERICAN FREEDOM TRAIN WILL INCLUDE 10 EXHIBIT CARS AND 2 SHOWCASE CARS DEPICTING DIFFERENT PHASES OF THE AMERICAN EXPERIENCE. ITS ARRIVAL WILL SERVE AS A CATALYST FOR LOCAL BICENTENNIAL CELEBRATIONS BY PEOPLE THROUGHOUT THIS NATION. (ST-WIDE). SY FREEDMAN, DIR OF P/R; THE AMERICAN FREEDOM TRAIN FOUNDATION, INC.; 5205 LEESBURG PKE, SUITE 800; BAILEY'S XRDS, VA 22041. (#1776-76).

SAVANNAH BCH

MAR 22, '76. 'BICENTENNIAL SAIL' OF HISTORIC SHIP VISITS FORT PULASKI NATL MON. HISTORIC FISHING SCHOONER 'MARY E', SAILING THE ATLANTIC COAST, WILL STOP AT THIS NATIONAL PARK SERVICE AREA, PROVIDING SHIPBOARD PROGRAMS TO VISITORS TO THIS AREA. (REGN'L). FT PULASKI NATL MONUMENT; SEA VENTURES, INC. & NATIONAL PARK SERVICE; P.O. BOX 98; SAVANNAH BCH, GA 31328. (#7960-6).

SILOAM

LOOKING FORWARD DEBATE. PARTICIPATION IN THE NATIONAL BICENTENNIAL YOUTH DEBATE USING LINCOLN-DOUGLAS DEBATE. (LOCAL). CLYDE DUNN, HEADMASTER; NATHANAEL GREENE ACADEMY; SILOAM, GA 30665. (#104019-1).

SMYRNA

BOY SCOUT TROOP 244 EXHIBITION AND CELEBRATION. THE EXHIBIT WILL INCLUDE A TOWER, ROPE BRIDGE AND FIRE TABLE, ALL HANDMADE BY SCOUTS FROM TREES; FLYING OF FLAGS FROM HOMEMADE POLES; SELLING OF BICENTENNIAL TAGS; DINNER ON THE GROUNDS AND GAMES. (LOCAL). PAUL SMITH, SCOUT MASTER; BOY SCOUT TROOP 244; PO BOX 40; SMYRNA, GA 30080. (#102909-1). **(??).**

SEPT 20, '75. HANDCRAFTS FAIR. HOMEMADE CRAFTS, BICENTENNIAL TAGS & PINS TO BE SOLD. AT FIRST METHODIST CHURCH, PARKING LOT. (LOCAL). MRS NOREEN WHITE, COORD; DEERWOOD NEIGHBORS GARDEN CLUB; SMYRNA, GA 30080. (#200012-31).

NOV 8, '75. BEAUTY PAGEANT: BICENTENNIAL QUEEN. JUDGES TO COME FROM OUTSIDE COBB COUNTY FOR THE BEAUTY PAGEANT. THE QUEEN TO REIGN THRU JULY 4, 1976 AND MAKE PUBLIC APPEARANCES AT ALL THE SMYRNA FESTIVITIES. AT GRIFFIN MIDDLE SCHOOL - ON KING SPRINGS RD (3 MI NO OF 285). (LOCAL). MRS JUANITA TOLBERT; SMYRNA FEDERATED WOMAN'S CLUB; MARIETTA, GA 30060. (#102893-1).

SOCIAL CIRCLE

BICENTENNIAL PUBLIC LIBRARY IN SOCIAL CIRCLE, GA. RESTORE BUILDING AND CONVERT TO A PUBLIC LIBRARY, IN HONOR OF THE BICENTENNIAL. (LOCAL). GLENN PELHAM, CHAIRMAN; COMMITTEE FOR THE SOCIAL CIRCLE PUBLIC LIBRARY; 104 CHEROKEE RD; SOCIAL CIRCLE, GA 30279. (#21809). **ARBA GRANTEE.**

ST MARYS

LANDSCAPING OF ORANGE HALL, ST MARYS GA. GROUNDS OF ORANGE HALL WILL BE LANDSCAPED WITH FLOWERS, SHRUBS & PLANTS COMPATIBLE WITH THOSE USED APPROXIMATELY 150 YEARS AGO WHEN IT WAS BUILT. (LOCAL). MRS G W BARKER, CHAIRPERSON; SAINT MARYS BICENTENNIAL COMMISSION; 900 CONYERS ST; SAINT MARYS, GA 31558. (#23725). **ARBA GRANTEE.**

FEB 1, '75 - CONTINUING . PERMANENT DISPLAY & TOUR OF ORANGE HALL. EXHIBIT, TOUR AT ORANGE HALL. (LOCAL). MRS G W BARKER, CHMN; SAINT MARYS BICENTENNIAL COMMISSION; 900 CONYERS ST; SAINT MARYS, GA 31558. (#23725-1).

MAR 16, '76. 'BICENTENNIAL SAIL' OF HISTORIC SHIP VISITS CUMBERLAND ISLAND NS. HISTORIC FISHING SCHOONER 'MARY E', SAILING THE ATLANTIC COAST, WILL STOP AT THIS NATIONAL PARK SERVICE AREA, PROVIDING SHIPBOARD PROGRAMS TO VISITORS TO THIS AREA. (REGN'L). CUMBERLAND ISLAND NS; SEA VENTURES, INC. & NATIONAL PARK SERVICE; P.O. BOX 806; ST MARY'S, GA 31558. (#7960-4).

ST SIMONS ISL

MAR 18, '76. 'BICENTENNIAL SAIL' OF HISTORIC SHIP VISITS FORT FREDERICA. HISTORIC FISHING SCHOONER 'MARY E', SAILING THE ATLANTIC COAST, WILL STOP AT THIS NATIONAL PARK SERVICE AREA, PROVIDING SHIPBOARD PROGRAMS TO VISITORS TO THIS AREA. (REGN'L). FT FREDERICA NATL MON; SEA VENTURES, INC. & NATIONAL PARK SERVICE; P.O. BOX 816; ST SIMONS ISL, GA 31522. (#7960-5).

STATESBORO

BOOK ON COASTAL GEORGIA CULTURE (NEH FELLOWSHIP). STUDY OF CULTURE & FOLKLORE OF RIVER VALLEYS OF SOUTHEAST GEORGIA, PERIOD 1800-1890, INCLUDING A FULL LENGTH PLAY ON HOW CONSERVATIVE PEOPLES INTERPRET AMERICAN CULTURE. (ST-WIDE). PROF D E PRESLEY; DEPT OF ENGLISH; GEORGIA SOUTHERN COLLEGE; STATESBORO, GA 30458. (#4235). **(??).**

BULLOCH COUNTY HISTORICAL MUSEUM - GA. LOCAL HISTORICAL MUSEUM FOR SIGNIFICANT ARTIFACTS AND RECORDS. (LOCAL). FRED BROGDON, CHAIRMAN; STATESBORO-BULLOCH COUNTY BICENTENNIAL COMMITTEE; PO BOX 42; STATESBORO, GA 30458. (#27287). **ARBA GRANTEE.**

STOCKBRIDGE

NEW AMERICAN MUSIC BY COMPOSER JOHN ADAMS. GRANT/FELLOWSHIP SPONSORED BY NATL ENDOWMENT FOR THE ARTS TO AID IN PERFORMANCES OF NEW MUSIC BY JOHN ADAMS IN LOS ANGELES, ATLANTA, & OTHER AREAS. (REGN'L). JOHN ADAMS, DIRECTOR; ROUTE 1, BOX 44; STOCKBRIDGE, GA 30281. (#1221).

JAN 1, '74 - DEC 31, '76. NEW AMERICAN MUSIC BY JOHN ADAMS-SONGBIRD SONGS & MUSIC OF THE EARTH. COMPOSER AVAILABLE FOR LECTURE/RECITALS TO VARIOUS GROUPS, COLLEGES, & OTHER ORGANIZATIONS. (LOCAL). JOHN ADAMS; COMPOSER; ROUTE 1 BOX 44; STOCKBRIDGE, GA 30281. (#1221-1).

STOCKTON

STOCKTON, GA, RECREATION CENTER. DEVELOPMENT OF A PARK TO CONTAIN MULTI-PURPOSE COURT, PLAYGROUND EQUIPMENT, BALL FIELD AND PICNIC FACILITIES. (LOCAL). M KELL, CHAIRMAN; STOCKTON BICENTENNIAL COMMISSION; LAKELAND, GA 31649. (#22882). **ARBA GRANTEE.**

JULY 4 - 5, '76. JULY FOURTH CEREMONIES. INCLUDES PARK DEDICATION, CHURCH SERVICES & DINNER AT THE PARK. (LOCAL). EDWARD C CULPEPPER, CHMN; STOCKTON BICENTENNIAL COMMISSION; LAKELAND, GA 31649. (#22882-1).

STONE MTN

DE KALB COUNTY BICENTENNIAL FESTIVAL. EXHIBITS, DEMONSTRATIONS, MUSIC PERFORMANCES, ARTS & CRAFTS AND CONTRIBUTIONS OF THE COUNTY GOVERNMENT WILL BE HIGHLIGHTED DURING THE FESTIVAL. (LOCAL). JAMES A HURLEY, COORD; DE KALB COUNTY BICENTENNIAL COMMITTEE; 556 N MCDONOUGH ST; DECATUR, GA 30030. (#103023-1). **(??).**

A SCOTTISH HIGHLAND GATHERING IN GEORGIA. A RE-ENACTMENT OF AN 18TH CENTURY GATHERING OF HIGHLAND SCOTS WITH A CELEBRATION OF THE CLOSE RELATIONSHIP OF THE SCOTS & CREEK INDIANS. (LOCAL). GEORGE L NEWBERRY, JR, DIRECTOR; STONE MOUNTAIN HIGHLAND GAMES, INC; 1090 LANIER BLVD; ATLANTA, GA 30306. (#11896). **ARBA GRANTEE.**

OCT 18 - 19, '75. SCOTTISH HIGHLAND GAMES AND FESTIVAL. A RE-ENACTMENT OF AN 18TH CENTURY GATHERING OF HIGHLAND SCOTS WITH A CELEBRATION OF THE CLOSE RELATIONSHIP OF THE SCOTS & CREEK INDIANS. (LOCAL). GEORGE L NEWBERRY; STONE MOUNTAIN HIGHLAND GAMES, INC; 1090 LANIER BLVD; ATLANTA, GA 30306. (#11896-501).

MAR 27, '76. KITE DAY. KITE FLYING COMPETITION FOR ADULTS AND CHILDREN. AT STONE MOUNTAIN PARK. (LOCAL). BETTY ROSSER, DIRECTOR; STONE MOUNTAIN PARK; PO BOX 778; STONE MTN, GA 30083. (#103416-159).

APR 10 - 26, '76. BICENTENNIAL WAGON TRAIN PILGRIMAGE IN GEORGIA. A RE-ENACTMENT OF THE WESTWARD MOVEMENT BACKWARDS THROUGHOUT THE STATE. PILGRIMAGE CONTINUES ALL DAY; EVENING CEREMONIES USUALLY AT 7:30 OR 8:00 PM. AT STONE MOUNTAIN, FOREST PARK, PEACHTREE CITY, GRIFFIN, ETC. (ST-WIDE). CAROLYN LEVIN, COORD; GEORGIA COMMISSION FOR THE NATIONAL BICENTENNIAL CELEBRATION; SUITE 520 S TOWER 1776 PEACH TR; ATLANTA, GA 30309. (#103559-1).

APR 18, '76. EASTER SUNRISE SERVICES-EASTER EGG HUNT. SUNRISE SERVICES PRECEED AFTERNOON HUNT FOR 20,000 EGGS; 200 PRIZE EGGS HIDDEN FOR CHILDREN 3-9 YEARS OLD. AT STONE MOUNTAIN PARK. (LOCAL). BETTY ROSSER, DIRECTOR; STONE MOUNTAIN PARK; PO BOX 778; STONE MTN, GA 30083. (#103416-192).

APR 24, '76. SOUTHERN INTERCOLLEGIATE ROWING ASSOCIATION REGATTA. ASSOCIATION MEMBERS COMPETE FOR ASSOCIATION CHAMPIONSHIP. 300 COMPETITORS ARE EXPECTED. AT STONE MOUNTAIN PARK, PARK LAKE. (REGN'L). BETTY ROSSER, DIRECTOR; STONE MOUNTAIN PARK; PO BOX 778; STONE MTN, GA 30083. (#103416-194).

MAY 22, '76. WPLO FISHING DERBY. PRIZES IN MANY CATEGORIES. AT STONE MOUNTAIN PARK. (LOCAL). BETTY ROSSER, DIRECTOR; STONE MOUNTAIN PARK; PO BOX 778; STONE MTN, GA 30083. (#103416-193).

JUNE 27 - JULY 4, '76. STAR SPANGLED WEEK. FIREWORKS, CONCERTS AND CHILDREN'S ACTIVITIES CELEBRATE THE NATION'S BICENTENNIAL WITH THE THEME 'THE RIGHT TO ASSEMBLE.'. AT STONE MOUNTAIN PARK. (LOCAL). BETTY ROSSER, DIRECTOR; STONE MOUNTAIN PARK; PO BOX 778; STONE MOUNTN, GA 30083. (#103416-88).

SEPT 10 - 12, '76. YELLOW DAISEY FESTIVAL. FEATURES ARTS, CRAFTS, FLOWER SHOWS, LIVE ENTERTAINMENT FROM THROUGHOUT SOUTHEAST. AT STONE MOUNTAIN PARK. (REGN'L). BETTY ROSSER, DIRECTOR; STONE MOUNTAIN PARK/FIELD EVENTS BY GEORGIA FORESTRY COMMISSION; PO BOX 778; STONE MTN, GA 30083. (#103416-191).

OCT 16 - 17, '76. STONE MOUNTAIN SCOTTISH FESTIVAL & HIGHLAND GAMES. FESTIVAL. (LOCAL). DONALD L BONEY, COORD; CLAN DONALD; 3800 GRANGER DR; CHAMBLEE, GA 30341. (#103416-570).

SUGAR HILL

MAY 1 - JULY 5, '76. COSTUME & BEARD CONTEST. THERE WILL BE A PRIZE FOR THE BEST. (LOCAL). PHYLLIS GRIZZLE; SUGAR HILL BICENTENNIAL; SUGAR HILL, GA 30518. (#107849-4).

JULY 2, '76. MISS BICENTENNIAL BEAUTY CONTEST. ENTRANTS MUST BE NINE TO TWENTY YEARS OLD. (LOCAL). MARY ANN MURPHY, CHRMN; SUGAR HILL BICENTENNIAL; BROAD ST; SUGAR HILL, GA 30518. (#107849-2).

JULY 2, '76. SQUARE DANCE. THERE WILL BE A STREET DANCE WITH A LOCAL BAND. (LOCAL). MARY WHIDBY; SUGAR HILL BICENTENNIAL; BROAD ST; SUGAR HILL, GA 30518. (#107849-7).

SUGAR HILL — CONTINUED

JULY 3, '76. CRAFT SHOW, ANTIQUES & NOVELTIES. EXHIBIT. (LOCAL). MARY WHIDBY; SUGAR HILL BICENTENNIAL; BROAD ST; SUGAR HILL, GA 30518. (#107849-3).

JULY 3, '76. FIREWORKS SHOW & FIELD DAY ACTIVITIES. FESTIVAL, COMPETITION. (LOCAL). EDWIN WHIDBY; SUGAR HILL BICENTENNIAL; BROAD ST; SUGAR HILL, GA 30518. (#107849-1).

JULY 4, '76. COMMUNITY-WIDE CHURCH SERVICES & PICNIC LUNCH. MORNING SERVICE IN LARGEST CHURCH, EVENING FEST & VESPERS OUTSIDE. EARLY AMERICAN COSTUMES WILL BE WORN. (LOCAL). REV JERRY JOHNSON; SUGAR HILL BICENTENNIAL; BROAD ST; SUGAR HILL, GA 30518. (#107849-6).

JULY 5, '76. BICENTENNIAL PARADE & BARBEQUE. PARADE. (LOCAL). LOIS CRONIC; SUGAR HILL BICENTENNIAL; BROAD ST; SUGAR HILL, GA 30518. (#107849-5).

SUMMERVILLE

CHATTOOGA COUNTY HISTORY, GA. A HISTORY OF CHATTOOGA COUNTY WILL BE PUBLISHED IN BOOK FORM. (LOCAL). EMILY N FARRAR, PROJ DIRECTOR; CHATTOOGA COUNTY BICENTENNIAL COMMITTEE; PO BOX 171; SUMMERVILLE, GA 30747. (#13709).

DISPLAY OF DOCUMENTS, SUMMERVILLE, GA. A DISPLAY OF OLD DEEDS AND POLICIES IN SUMMERVILLE, GA. (LOCAL). EMILY N FARRAR, PROJ DIRECTOR; CHATTOOGA COUNTY BICENTENNIAL COMMITTEE; PO BOX 171; SUMMERVILLE, GA 30747. (#13710).

HISTORY PROGRAMS IN CHATTOOGA COUNTY SCHOOLS, GA. DISPLAYS OF CRAFTS AND RELICS, DRAMATIC RE-CREATIONS OF HISTORICAL EVENTS AND AN EMPHASIS ON LITERARY WORKS OF EARLIER DAYS. (LOCAL). MRS SARAH MYERS, PROJ DIRECTOR; LIBRARIANS OF CHATTOOGA COUNTY SCHOOLS; SUMMERVILLE, GA 30747. (#13707).

MUSIC FESTIVAL IN SUMMERVILLE, GA. HALF TIME SHOWS, CONCERTS AND PERFORMANCES OF ORIGINAL MUSIC BEFORE CIVIC GROUPS. (LOCAL). MRS ANNAJANE GREESON, PROJ DIRECTOR; TRION HIGH BAND BOOSTERS; TRION, GA 30753. (#13708).

NEW COUNTY MUSEUM IN SUMMERVILLE, GA. THE OPENING OF A COUNTY MUSEUM FILLED WITH LOCAL ARTIFACTS. (LOCAL). WOODROW W ESPY, CO-CHAIRMAN; CHATTOOGA COUNTY BICENTENNIAL COMMITTEE; PO BOX 400; SUMMERVILLE, GA 30747. (#13714).

OLD FASHIONED FOURTH OF JULY. AN OLD-FASHIONED 4TH OF JULY CELEBRATION WITH PARADE, SPEECHES & OTHER ACTIVITIES. (LOCAL). WOODROW W ESPY, CO-CHAIRMAN; CHATTOOGA COUNTY BICENTENNIAL COMMITTEE; PO BOX 400; SUMMERVILLE, GA 30747. (#13715).

'OLDEST' CONTEST, CHATTOOGA COUNTY, GA. CONTEST TO CHOOSE THE OLDEST HOME, CHURCH & CITIZEN IN CHATTOOGA COUNTY. (LOCAL). EMILY FARRAR, PROJ DIRECTOR; CHATTOOGA COUNTY BICENTENNIAL COMMITTEE; PO BOX 171; SUMMERVILLE, GA 30747. (#13720).

SEQUOYAH MEMORIAL IN SUMMERVILLE, GA. A MEMORIAL TO SEQUOYAH WILL BE ERECTED. (LOCAL). WOODROW W ESPY, CO-CHAIRMAN; CHATTOOGA COUNTY BICENTENNIAL COMMITTEE; PO BOX 400; SUMMERVILLE, GA 30747. (#13716).

OCT 11, '75. 'SUM NELLY', ARTS & CRAFTS SHOW. OLD FASHIONED ARTS AND CRAFT DISPLAY. AT SUMMERVILLE RECREATION CENTER GROUNDS. (REGN'L). PAM TAWZER; COOPERATIVE EXTENSION SERVICE; PO BOX 398; SUMMERVILLE, GA 30747. (#13719-1).

NOV 1 - 30, '75. WINDOW DISPLAY IN SUMMERVILLE, GA. A DISPLAY OF NEEDLEWORK ITEMS OF PATRIOTIC THEMES IN RED, WHITE & BLUE. AT DOWNTOWN, ACROSS FROM COUNTY COURTHOUSE. (LOCAL). SUE SPIVEY, INSTRUCTOR; SUMMERVILLE RECREATION CENTER NEEDLEWORK CLASS; BOX 429; SUMMERVILLE, GA 30747. (#13711-1).

NOV 10 - 13, '75. SPIRIT OF '76 FOLLIES. A VARIETY SHOW WITH PATRIOTIC THEMES. AT SUMMERVILLE JUNIOR HIGH SCHOOL AUDITORIUM. (LOCAL). PAM TAWZER, PROJ DIRECTOR; CHATTOOGA COUNTY BICENTENNIAL COMMITTEE; PO BOX 398; SUMMERVILLE, GA 30747. (#13717-1).

APR 1 - 30, '76. BICENTENNIAL CANTATA. A CELEBRATION AND PERFORMANCE OF THE MUSIC OF AMERICA. AT CHATTOOGA HIGH SCHOOL GYMNASIUM. (LOCAL). W E THORNTON; CHATTOOGA COUNTY BICENTENNIAL COMMITTEE; PO BOX 400; SUMMERVILLE, GA 30747. (#13718-1).

NOV 1 - DEC 20, '76. HIGH SCHOOL DEBATE IN CHATTOOGA COUNTY. HIGH SCHOOL STUDENTS WILL HOLD A DEBATE ON IMPROVING THE QUALITY OF LIFE IN CHATTOOGA COUNTY. (LOCAL). W E THORNTON; CHATTOOGA COUNTY CIVIC ORGANIZATION; PO BOX 400; SUMMERVILLE, GA 30747. (#13712-1).

DEC 5 - 10, '76. CHRISTMAS PARADE. A CHRISTMAS PARADE WITH AN OLD-FASHIONED THEME: LIFE IN CHATTOOGA COUNTY. (LOCAL). W E THORNTON; CHATTOOGA COUNTY CIVIC ORGANIZATION; PO BOX 400; SUMMERVILLE, GA 30747. (#13713-1).

SYLVANIA

HISTORICAL BOOKLET: THE BETHANY COLONY, GA. HISTORY OF GERMAN COLONY ON SAVANNAH RIVER ESTABLISHED BY WILLIAM GERALD DE BRAHM IN 1751; COLONY ORGINALLY CONSISTED OF 320 PEOPLE. (LOCAL). C D HOLLINGSWORTH, JR, PROJECT COORDINATOR; 103 PEACHTREE CIRCLE; SYLVANIA, GA 30467. (#18213).

PIONEER DAYS, SYLVANIA, GA. PROJECT IS PUBLICATION OF BOOK ON HISTORY OF THE SCREVEN COUNTY AREA. (LOCAL). C D HOLLINGSWORTH, JR, PROJ COORDINATOR; 103 PEACHTREE CIRCLE; SYLVANIA, GA 30467. (#18215).

RESTORATION OF DELL-GOODALL HOUSE, SYLVANIA, GA. RESTORATION OF INTERIOR & EXTERIOR OF HISTORIC DELL-GOODALL HOUSE & REPLACEMENT OF FURNITURE IN HOUSE. (ST-WIDE). MRS ALEX S BOYER, JR, BICENTENNIAL CHAIRMAN; BRIER CREEK CHAPTER DAR; PO BOX 378; SYLVANIA, GA 30467. (#730). **ARBA GRANTEE.**

APR 5 - 7, '76. SCREVEN COUNTY LIVESTOCK FESTIVAL. COMPETITION, EXHIBIT, FESTIVAL AT AGRICULTURAL CENTER, ROCKYFORD ROAD, PARKING AVAILABLE. (LOCAL). W E PACE III, COORD; SCREVEN COUNTY LIVESTOCK ASSOC; 314 MOCK ST; SYLVANIA, GA 30467. (#105641-1).

JULY 8 - 11, '76. HERITAGE SPECIAL - TRAIN TOUR. TRAVELING RAIL EXHIBIT EMPHASIZING COLONIAL & REVOLUTIONARY GEORGIA HISTORY, CRAFTS & LIFESTYLE OF GEORGIA COLONISTS. EXHIBITS WILL BE DISPLAYED WITH COMBINATION OF SIGHT & SOUND ACTIVITY. (LOCAL). RON HENRY, COORDINATOR; GEORGIA AGRIRAMA DEVELOPMENT AUTHORITY/GEORGIA BICENTENNIAL; 8TH ST A I 75; TIFTON, GA 31794. (#7999-10).

SYLVESTER

INDOOR RECREATION CENTER FOR SYLVESTER, GEORGIA. PLANS ARE BEING MADE FOR AN INDOOR RECREATION CENTER. ACTIVITIES WILL INCLUDE ARTS & CRAFTS, ORAL HISTORY PROJECTS AND A COMMUNITY INFORMATION CENTER. (LOCAL). WAYNE CALLAWAY, CHAIRMAN; SYLVESTER - WORTH COUNTY BICENT COMMITTEE; PO BOX 368; SYLVESTER, GA 31791. (#9060).

ORAL HISTORY PROJECT OF SYLVESTER, GEORGIA. A SECTION WILL BE ADDED TO THE DESOTA TRAIL LIBRARY FOR A HISTORY OF WORTH COUNTY DATING BACK 200 YRS. (LOCAL). WAYNE CALLAWAY, CHAIRMAN; SYLVESTER-WORTH COUNTY BICENT COMMITTEE; PO BOX 368; SYLVESTER, GA 31791. (#9061).

PEANUT FESTIVAL IN SYLVESTER, GEORGIA. THE WORTH COUNTY PEANUT FESTIVAL WILL PRESENT ARTS & CRAFTS DISPLAYS AT THE PEANUT FESTIVAL. (LOCAL). WILLIAM DAVIS, CHAIRMAN; SYLVESTER-WORTH COUNTY BICENT COMMITTEE; PO BOX 368; SYLVESTER, GA 31791. (#9059).

'1776' PERFORMED IN SYLVESTER, GEORGIA. THE WORTH PLAYERS WILL PERFORM THE PLAY '1776'. (LOCAL). WILLIAM DAVIS, CHAIRMAN; SYLVESTER WORTH COUNTY BICENT COMMITTEE; PO BOX 368; SYLVESTER, GA 31791. (#8972).

TALBOTTON

FLAG PROJECT, TALBOTTON, GA. A NEW FLAG POLE WILL BE ERECTED ON COURTHOUSE SQUARE & DEDICATED AS THE BEGINNING OF A CAMPAIGN TO SELL & ENCOURAGE THE DISPLAY OF THE U S FLAG THROUGHOUT THE COUNTRY DURING '76. (LOCAL). MARY BASSETT, CHAIRMAN; TALBOT COUNTY BICENTENNIAL COMMITTEE; PO BOX 188; TALBOTTON, GA 31827. (#17073).

GAZEBO PROJECT, TALBOTTON, GA. A REPLICA OF THE GAZEBO WHICH ONCE STOOD ON THE TALBOT COUNTY COURTHOUSE GROUNDS WILL BE CONSTRUCTED. (LOCAL). EDDIE B BASSET, JR, COUNTY COMMISSIONER; TALBOT COUNTY COMMISSIONERS & TALBOT COUNTY BICENTENNIAL COMM; TALBOTTON, GA 31827. (#17072).

HISTORY OF TALBOT COUNTY, GA. LOCAL HIGH SCHOOL HISTORY CLASSES WILL COMPILE A HISTORY OF TALBOT COUNTY. (LOCAL). MRS E D ROWE, SUPERINTENDENT; TALBOT COUNTY BOARD OF EDUCATION; TALBOTTON, GA 31827. (#17074).

TALLAPOOSA

JULY 2 - 4, '76. HISTORICAL PAGEANT, HOME TOUR, PARADE & CHURCH SERVICES. JULY 2, PAGEANT; TOUR OF HOMES ON JULY 3, ALONG WITH BICENTENNIAL PARADE & BARBEQUE SUPPER; SERVICES AT UNION CHURCH ON JULY 4TH. (LOCAL). S T SKAGGS, CHAIRMAN; TALLA; TALLAPOOSA, GA 30176. (#108027-1).

THOMASVILLE

LIVING FARM MUSEUM OF THOMAS COUNTY, GEORGIA. A LIVING FARM OF THE 1850'S WILL BE ESTABLISHED AS AN EDUCATIONAL LIVING HISTORY MUSEUM TELLING ABOUT THE ROLE AGRICULTURE HAS PLAYED IN THE COUNTY'S DEVELOPMENT. (LOCAL). WILLIAM H FLOWERS, CHAIRMAN; THOMAS COUNTY BICENTENNIAL-SESQUICENTENNIAL COMMISSION; PO BOX 1338; THOMASVILLE, GA 31792. (#4984). **ARBA GRANTEE.**

NATURE CENTER AND HISTORICAL MUSEUM, GA. 30 ACRES OF COUNTY-OWNED LAND WILL BE DEVELOPED AS A NATURE CENTER & HISTORICAL MUSEUM; THE COMPLEX WILL INCLUDE TRAILS, WEATHER STATION, BIRD FEEDER AND ONE ROOM COMPLEX. (LOCAL). NORMAN C LARSON, EXEC DIRECTOR; THOMAS COUNTY BICENTENNIAL/SESQUICENTENNIAL COMMISSION; PO BOX 1285; THOMASVILLE, GA 31792. (#13852). **ARBA GRANTEE.**

STOREFRONT EXHIBITS IN THOMASVILLE, GEORGIA. BICENTENNIAL EXHIBITS FOR LOCAL STOREFRONTS WILL BE CREATED ALONG WITH SPECIAL EXHIBITS BY THE THOMAS COUNTY HISTORICAL SOCIETY. (LOCAL). MR WILLIAM FLOWERS, CHAIRMAN; THOMAS COUNTY BICENT SESQUICENTENNIAL COMMISSION; PO BOX 1338; THOMASVILLE, GA 31792. (#6755).

THOMAS COUNTY, GEORGIA, CIVIC CENTER. A CIVIC CENTER WILL BE ESTABLISHED AS A PERMANENT MEMORIAL TO COMMEMORATE THE BICENTENNIAL & THOMAS COUNTY'S SESQUICENTENNIAL. (LOCAL). WILLIAM H FLOWERS, CHAIRMAN; THOMAS COUNTY BICENTENNIAL SESQUICENTENNIAL COMMISSION; PO BOX 1338; THOMASVILLE, GA 31792. (#4985). **(??).**

DEC 7 - 13, '75. THOMAS COUNTY BICENTENNIAL/SESQUICENTENNIAL 'KICK-OFF'. INTERDENOMINATIONAL RELIGIOUS SERVICE, EXHIBITS, US ARMED FORCES BICENTENNIAL CARAVAN. AT CITYWIDE. (LOCAL). NORMAN C LARSON; THOMAS COUNTY BICENTENNIAL/SESQUICENTENNIAL COMMISSION; BOX 1285; THOMASVILLE, GA 31792. (#50716-1).

DEC 12 - 13, '75. UNITED STATES ARMED FORCES BICENTENNIAL CARAVAN. THE CARAVAN IS COMPOSED OF EXHIBIT VANS FOR EACH BRANCH OF THE MILITARY SERVICE. THE THEME OF THE EXHIBITION IS 'HISTORY OF THE ARMED FORCES AND THEIR CONTRIBUTION TO THE NATION'. (LOCAL). NORMAN L LARSON, CHMN; U S ARMED FORCES BICENTENNIAL EXHIBIT VANS PROJECT; BOX 1285; THOMASVILLE, GA 31792. (#1775-209).

APR 19 - 25, '76. 55TH ANNUAL ROSE FESTIVAL. 'THE CITY OF ROSES' CELEBRATES AMERICA'S 200TH BIRTHDAY WITH THEMES OF 'STAY & SEE AMERICA IN THOMASVILLE' AND 'GEORGIA-A BICENTENNIAL OF BEAUTY.'. (ST-WIDE). LLOYD E ECKBERG, DIRECTOR; THOMAS-THOMASVILLE CHAMBER OF COMMERCE; PO BOX 560; THOMASVILLE, GA 31792. (#103416-92).

APR 21 - 25, '76. HERITAGE SPECIAL - TRAIN TOUR. TRAVELING RAIL EXHIBIT EMPHASIZING COLONIAL & REVOLUTIONARY GEORGIA HISTORY, CRAFTS & LIFESTYLE OF GEORGIA COLONISTS. EXHIBITS WILL BE DISPLAYED WITH COMBINATION OF SIGHT & SOUND ACTIVITY. (LOCAL). RON HENRY, COORDINATOR; GEORGIA AGRIRAMA DEVELOPMENT AUTHORITY/GEORGIA BICENTENNIAL; 8TH ST A I 75; TIFTON, GA 31794. (#7999-24).

OCT 8 - 12, '76. HERITAGE SPECIAL - TRAIN TOUR. TRAVELING RAIL EXHIBIT EMPHASIZING COLONIAL AND REVOLUTIONARY GEORGIA HISTORY, CRAFTS & LIFESTYLE OF GEORGIA COLONISTS. EXHIBITS WILL BE DISPLAYED WITH COMBINATION OF SIGHT & SOUND ACTIVITY. AT DEPOT. (LOCAL). RON HENRY, DIRECTOR; GEORGIA BICENTENNIAL COMMISSION; 1776 PEACHTREE NW, ROOM 520 S; ATLANTA, GA 30309. (#7999-29).

TIFTON

AGRIRANA ENTRANCE GARDEN - PROJ OF TIFTON, GA. CREATION OF ATTRACTIVE ENTRANCEWAY INTO GEORGIA'S FOREMOST BICENTENNIAL PROJECT. (ST-WIDE). MRS FORD SPINKS, PRESIDENT; TIFTON COUNCIL OF GARDEN CLUBS; RT 6; TIFTON, GA 31794. (#13859).

BICENT LECTURE SERIES AT COLLEGE IN TIFTON, GA. A LECTURE SERIES ON THE PAST, PRESENT & FUTURE OF AMERICAN SOCIETY TO BE HELD AT ABRAHAM BALDWIN AGRICULTURAL COLLEGE IN 1976. (LOCAL). MRS MARY EMMA HENDERSON, CHAIRMAN; BICENTENNIAL COMMITTEE, ABRAHAM BALDWIN AGRICULTURAL COLLEGE; ABAC STATION; TIFTON, GA 31794. (#8672).

BIOGRAPHY OF ABRAHAM BALDWIN - GEORGIA. UPDATED BIOGRAPHY OF ABRAHAM BALDWIN, SIGNER OF U S CONSTITUTION, FOR WHOM THE COLLEGE IS NAMED. (ST-WIDE). MRS MARY EMMA HENDERSON, CHAIRMAN; ABRAHAM BALDWIN AGRICULTURAL COLLEGE BICENTENNIAL; ABAC STATION; TIFTON, GA 31794. (#8669).

'BURY MY HEART AT WOUNDED KNEE' - PLAY, TIFTON, GA. PLAY DEPICTING WHITE MAN'S INVASION OF INDIAN LAND BETWEEN 1860-90. PORTRAYS MINORITY PREYED UPON BY AGGRESSOR AND VIOLATION OF HUMAN RIGHTS AND DIGNITY. (LOCAL). MRS MARY EMMA HENDERSON; ABRAHAM BALDWIN AGRICULTURAL COLLEGE BICENTENNIAL; ABAC STATION; TIFTON, GA 31794. (#8667-1).

CITY SPIRIT - ARTS PGM PROPOSED FOR TIFTON, GA. BICENTENNIAL PROGRAM OF N E A DESIGNED TO DEVELOP PROGRAMS IN THE ARTS FOR ALL CITIZENS OF THE COMMUNITY. THE PROPOSAL INVOLVES A SEVEN-COUNTY AREA. (LOCAL). MRS MARY EMMA HENDERSON, CHAIRMAN; ABRAHAM BALDWIN AGRICULTURAL COLLEGE BICENTENNIAL; ABAC STATION; TIFTON, GA 31794. (#8670).

EXPERIMENTAL ARTS CENTER, TIFTON, GA. A LONG RANGE PROGRAM FOR CONTEMPORARY RURAL SOCIETY, INVOLVING CITIZEN PLANNING & PARTICIPATION IN THE ARTS. (LOCAL). MRS MARY EMMA HENDERSON, CHAIRMAN; ABRAHAM BALDWIN AGRICULTURAL COLLEGE; ABAC STATION; TIFTON, GA 31794. (#13863).

FAMILY HISTORIES IN TIFTON, GA. FAMILY HISTORIES, COMPILED BY STUDENTS, IN ANECDOTAL OR SCRAPBOOK FORM, USING INTERVIEWS WITH PARENTS, GRANDPARENTS & OTHER RELATIVES. (LOCAL). MRS MARY EMMA HENDERSON, CHAIRMAN; ABRAHAM BALDWIN AGRICULTURAL COLLEGE BICENTENNIAL; ABAC STATION; TIFTON, GA 31794. (#8673). **(??).**

GEORGIA HERITAGE SPECIAL TRAIN TOUR. TRAVELING RAIL EXHIBIT EMPHASIZING COLONIAL & REVOLUTIONARY GEORGIA HISTORY, CRAFTS & LIFESTYLE OF GEORGIA COLONISTS. EXHIBITS WILL BE DISPLAYED WITH COMBINATION OF SIGHT & SOUND ACTIVITY. (ST-WIDE). RON HENRY, COORDINATOR; GEORGIA AGRIRAMA DEVELOPMENT AUTHORITY/GEORGIA BICENTENNIAL; 1776 PEACHTREE NW, SUITE 520; ATLANTA, GA 30309. (#7999). **ARBA GRANTEE.**

HIST OF ABRAHAM BALDWIN AGRICULTURAL COLLEGE, GA. HISTORY OF ABAC, INCLUDING DEVELOPMENT OF EDUCATION IN GEORGIA, HOW REGION INFLUENCED COLLEGE, INFLUENCE OF

TIFTON — CONTINUED

COLLEGE ON REGION & IMPACT OF ECONOMIC, SOCIAL & POLITICAL EVENTS ON DEVELOPMENT OF EDUCATION. (LOCAL). MRS MARY EMMA HENDERSON, CHAIRMAN; ABRAHAM BALDWIN AGRICULTURAL COLLEGE BICENTENNIAL; ABAC STATION; TIFTON, GA 31794. (#8668).

LANDSCAPING AND SITE RENOVATION IN TIFTON, GA. LANDSCAPING FOR MUSEUM SITE; COMPLETE FARM AND THE RESTORATION OF CLARK CABIN. (LOCAL). FRANK P KING, DIRECTOR; GEORGIA AGRIRAMA DEVELOPMENT AUTHORITY; PO BOX Q; TEMPLETON, GA 31794. (#22841). **ARBA GRANTEE.**

LIFE IN GEORGIA. A WEEKLY SERIES OF SHORT NEWS RELEASES TO DAILY AND WEEKLY NEWSPAPERS; REPORTING ON LIFE IN GEORGIA 'THEN' AND 'NOW'. (ST-WIDE). BARRY JONES, EXTENSION EDITOR; GEORGIA AGRIRAMA AND COOPERATIVE EXTENSION SERVICE; PO BOX Q; TIFTON, GA 31794. (#20443).

'PITCH IN' - PROJ OF TIFTON, GA. PEOPLE WILL BE INVOLVED IN LITTER REDUCATION & CLEANUP; EDUCATIONAL FILM STRIP, WORKSHOPS, LECTURES TO STIMULATE INTEREST IN LITTER REDUCTION AND BEAUTIFICATION. (LOCAL). ALFRED R PURSELL, CHAIRMAN; 'PITCH IN'; TIFTON, GA 31794. (#14012).

RENOVATION OF CHAMBER OF COMMERCE BLDG, TIFTON, GA. THE TIFT COUNTY CHAMBER OF COMMERCE RENOVATED A 60 YEAR OLD RAILROAD DEPOT TO HOUSE OFFICES FOR LOCAL NON-PROFIT ORGANIZATIONS. (LOCAL). DOUGLAS M EVERETT, EXEC VICE-PRESIDENT; TIFT COUNTY CHAMBER OF COMMERCE; 1 CENTRAL AVE; TIFTON, GA 31794. (#19662).

TIFTAREA MAGNOLIA GARDEN, TIFTON, GA. PRESERVATION OF NATION'S 2ND LARGEST MAGNOLIA GRANDIFLORA & ESTABLISHMENT AND MAINTENANCE OF A MINI-PARK SURROUNDING IT, TO BE KNOWN AS TIFTAREA MAGNOLIA GARDEN. (LOCAL). MRS J L STEPHENS, CHAIRMAN; COUNCIL OF GARDEN CLUBS OF TIFTON; RT 4; TIFTON, GA 31794. (#13861). **ARBA GRANTEE.**

'1776' - PLAY PRESENTATION IN TIFTON, GA. HISTORICAL COMEDY-DRAMA ABOUT THE MEMBERS OF THE CONTINENTAL CONGRESS WHICH RESULTED IN THE DECLARATION OF INDEPENDENCE AND THE BIRTH OF THE NATION. (LOCAL). MRS MARY EMMA HENDERSON; ABRAHAM BALDWIN AGRICULTURAL COLLEGE BICENTENNIAL; ABAC STATION; TIFTON, GA 31794. (#8666-1).

NOV 7, '75. ART DISPLAYS AT FALL FESTIVAL. SPONSORED BY THE BANK FOR CIVIC, GARDEN, CHURCH & SCHOOL GROUPS. AT THE MALL OF THE TOWN & COUNTRY PLAZA. (ST-WIDE). MRS VIRGINIA FLEMMING; FARMERS BANK OF TIFTON; 218 LOVE AVE; TIFTON, GA 31794. (#13860-501).

NOV 8 - 9, '75. ANNUAL WIREGRASS ARTS AND CRAFTS SHOW '75. EXHIBIT. (LOCAL). HELEN STRICKLAND, DIR; EXCHANGE CLUB OF TIFTON AND THE TIFTON ART ASSOCIATION; PO BOX 1492; TIFTON, GA 31794. (#101700-1).

NOV 20, '75. BICENTENNIAL BALL. COSTUME BALL THEME: 200 YEARS OF DANCING, WITH FLOORSHOW DEMONSTRATING DIFFERENT DANCES POPULAR THROUGH THE LAST 200 YEARS. (LOCAL). MRS MARY EMMA HENDERSON; ABRAHAM BALDWIN AGRICULTURAL COLLEGE BICENTENNIAL; ABAC STATION; TIFTON, GA 31794. (#8671-1).

MAY '76. TIFTON ANNUAL ARTS & CRAFTS FESTIVAL. OUTDOOR EXHIBITION BY REGIONAL ARTISTS AND CRAFTSMEN INCLUDING POTTERY, NEEDLECRAFT, PAINTING, LEATHERCRAFT, JEWELRY & SCULPTURE. (LOCAL). VINCENT A KEESEE, PRES; TIFTON ART ASSOC; 1425 MARY ANN AVE; TIFTON, GA 31794. (#7998-1).

JULY 1 - 31, '76. GRAND OPENING FOR THE GEORGIA AGRIRAMA. RE-CREATION OF FARM & VILLAGE ACTIVITIES IN THE WIREGRASS SECTION OF GEORGIA DURING 1870-1899. WILL SHOW FARMSTEAD, FUNCTIONING SAWMILL, TURPENTINE STILL, COTTON GIN, ETC. AT CORNER OF INTERSTATE 75 AND 8TH STREET IN TIFTON GEORGIA. (ST-WIDE). GEORGIA AGRIRAMA; GEORGIA AGRIRAMA DEVELOPMENT AUTHORITY; PO BOX Q; TIFTON, GA 31794. (#3100-1).

JULY 21 - 25, '76. HERITAGE SPECIAL - TRAIN TOUR. TRAVELING RAIL EXHIBIT EMPHASIZING COLONIAL & REVOLUTIONARY GEORGIA HISTORY, CRAFTS & LIFESTYLE OF GEORGIA COLONISTS. EXHIBITS WILL BE DISPLAYED WITH COMBINATION OF SIGHT & SOUND ACTIVITY. (LOCAL). RON HENRY, COORDINATOR; GEORGIA AGRIRAMA DEVELOPMENT AUTHORITY/ GEORGIA BICENTENNIAL; 8TH ST A I 75; TIFTON, GA 31794. (#7999-1).

OCT '76 - CONTINUING . RURAL LIFE EXPO. EXHIBIT. (LOCAL). J E BURNSIDE, DIRECTOR; RURAL DEVELOPMENT CENTER; TIFTON, GA 31794. (#7997-1).

NOV 12 - 13, '76. ANNUAL WIREGRASS ARTS AND CRAFTS SHOW '76. EXHIBIT. (LOCAL). HELEN STRICKLAND, DIR; EXCHANGE CLUB OF TIFTON AND THE TIFTON ART ASSOCIATION; PO BOX 1492; TIFTON, GA 31794. (#101700-2).

TOCCOA

NOV 27, '75. UNITED STATES ARMED FORCES BICENTENNIAL CARAVAN. THE CARAVAN IS COMPOSED OF EXHIBIT VANS FOR EACH BRANCH OF THE MILITARY SERVICE. THE THEME OF THE EXHIBITION IS 'HISTORY OF THE ARMED FORCES AND THEIR CONTRIBUTION TO THE NATION'. (LOCAL). JAMES M GRANT, CHMN; U S ARMED FORCES BICENTENNIAL EXHIBIT VANS PROJECT; BOX 146, TOCCOA FALLS; TOCCOA, GA 30577. (#1775-201).

JUNE 7 - 9, '76. HERITAGE SPECIAL - TRAIN TOUR. TRAVELING RAIL EXHIBIT EMPHASIZING COLONIAL & REVOLUTIONARY GEORGIA HISTORY, CRAFTS & LIFESTYLE OF GEORGIA COLONISTS. EXHIBITS WILL BE DISPLAYED WITH COMBINATION OF SIGHT & SOUND ACTIVITY. (LOCAL). RON HENRY, COORDINATOR; GEORGIA AGRIRAMA DEVELOPMENT AUTHORITY/ GEORGIA BICENTENNIAL; 8TH ST A I 75; TIFTON, GA 31794. (#7999-22).

TOCCOA FALLS

AVENUE OF FLAGS & INTERNATIONAL PLAZA, GA. A DISPLAY OF FLAGS WILL BE ESTABLISHED FROM EVERY COUNTRY WHERE ALUMNI HAVE SERVED, HOME COUNTRIES OF STUDENTS AND EACH STATE IN THE UNION. OVER 100 FLAGS WILL BE FEATURED. (LOCAL). JAMES M GRANT, CHAIRMAN; TOCCOA FALLS INSTITUTE; TOCCOA FALLS, GA 30577. (#18321).

CLEAN-UP DAYS - TOCCOA FALLS, GA. A DAY WILL BE SET ASIDE EACH SEMESTER TO CLEAN-UP THE CAMPUS. (LOCAL). JAMES M GRANT, CHAIRMAN; TOCCOA FALLS INSTITUTE; TOCCOA FALLS, GA 30577. (#18320).

ORAL HISTORY PROJECT, TOCCOA FALLS, GA. STUDENTS WILL INTERVIEW ELDERLY CITIZENS CONCERNING THEIR LIVES; THE INTERVIEWS WILL BE TAPED AND HOUSED IN THE COUNTY LIBRARY. (LOCAL). JAMES M GRANT, CHAIRMAN; TOCCOA FALLS INSTITUTE; TOCCOA FALLS, GA 30577. (#18319).

TREE PLANTING - TOCCOA FALLS, GA. TREES WILL BE PLANTED AND DEDICATED IN HONOR OF THE BICENTENNIAL. (LOCAL). JAMES M GRANT, CHAIRMAN; TOCCOA FALLS INSTITUTE; TOCCOA FALLS, GA 30577. (#18318).

NOV 28 - 30, '75. FOUNDER'S WEEKEND. THIS WILL BE HELD THANKSGIVING WEEKEND WITH BICENTENNIAL THEMES; A HIGH POINT WILL BE WORLD DAY ON FRIDAY, WITH SEMINARS AND CULTURAL EVENTS. (LOCAL). JAMES M GRANT, CHAIRMAN; TOCCOA FALLS INSTITUTE; TOCCOA FALLS, GA 30577. (#103658-2).

APR 1, '76. PATRIOTS BANQUET. FESTIVAL. (LOCAL). JAMES M GRANT, CHAIRMAN; TOCCOA FALLS INSTITUTE; TOCCOA FALLS, GA 30577. (#103658-4).

VALDOSTA

AMERICANA - ART EXHIBIT IN VALDOSTA, GA. EXHIBIT OF TRADITIONAL AND CONTEMPORARY ART OWNED BY VALDOSTANS AND REGIONAL CITIZENS. (LOCAL). MS JANE T SHELTON, CHAIRMAN; VALDOSTA STATE COLLEGE BICENT COMMITTEE; BOX 114; VALDOSTA, GA 31601. (#8689).

BICENT MUSIC COMPOSED AT VALDOSTA STATE COLLEGE. A FACULTY MEMBER OF THE COLLEGE WILL COMPOSE A MUSICAL WORK FOR THE BICENTENNIAL. (LOCAL). JANE T SHELTON, CHAIRMAN; BICENTENNIAL COMMITTEE, VALDOSTA STATE COLLEGE; BOX 114; VALDOSTA, GA 31601. (#8696).

BICENTENNIAL BAND CONCERT AT VALDOSTA, GA. TOURING UNIVERSITY OF CALIFORNIA BAND TO PRESENT CONCERT. (LOCAL). MS JANE T SHELTON, CHAIRMAN; VALDOSTA STATE COLLEGE BICENT COMMITTEE; BOX 114; VALDOSTA, GA 31601. (#8694).

CAMP ADVENTURE - VALDOSTA, GA. DEVELOPMENT OF RECREATIONAL FACILITIES FOR THE MENTALLY AND PHYSICALLY HANDICAPPED. (LOCAL). DAVID CHRISTIAN, RECREATIN DIRECTOR; VALDOSTA PARK AND RECREATION DEPT; CITY HALL; VALDOSTA, GA 31601. (#23601). **ARBA GRANTEE.**

EXHIBIT OF GRAPHICS, 1975 - VALDOSTA STATE COL, GA. DISPLAY OF STUDENT GRAPHICS, SKETCHES & DRAWINGS INSPIRED BY AMERICANA. CONTINUOUS SHOWING FROM JANUARY 1975. (LOCAL). MS JANE T SHELTON, CHAIRMAN; VALDOSTA STATE COLLEGE BICENT COMMITTEE; BOX 114; VALDOSTA, GA 31601. (#8692).

HIST LECTURE SERIES, VALDOSTA STATE COLLEGE, GA. PROGRAM OF LECTURES WITH BICENTENNIAL AND AMERICAN REVOLUTIONARY THEME BY VISITING SPEAKER AND MEMBERS OF VSC HISTORY DEPARTMENT. (LOCAL). MS JANE T SHELTON, CHAIRMAN; VALDOSTA STATE COLLEGE BICENT COMMITTEE; BOX 114; VALDOSTA, GA 31601. (#8693).

HISTORIC DIRECTORY OF GEORGIA'S COASTAL PLAIN. AN INVENTORY OF PLACES AND EVENTS OF HISTORIC INTEREST IN TEN COUNTY AREA OF GEORGIA; DATA COLLECTION COMPILED IN DIRECTORY FORM PROVIDING INSIGHT INTO THE PAST HISTORY AND PRESENT ACTIVITIES OF THE AREA. (ST-WIDE). JAMES H RAINWATER, JR, ASST EXEC DIRECTOR; COASTAL PLAIN AREA PLANNING & DEVELOPMENT COMM; PO BOX 1223; VALDOSTA, GA 31601. (#518). **ARBA GRANTEE.**

'PINES & PIONEERS: A HISTORY OF LOWNDES COUNTY'. RESEARCH, WRITING, PUBLICATION OF BOOK ON HISTORY OF LOWNDES & ADJACENT SUCCESSOR COUNTIES; COMPLETION OF WORK IN PROGRESS BY JANE T SHELTON, VSC BICENTENNIAL CHAIRMAN & HISTORY INSTRUCTOR. (LOCAL). DR WILLIAM M GABARD, CHAIRMAN; VALDOSTA STATE COLLEGE & LOWNDES COUNTY BICENT COMMITTEE; BOX 123; VALDOSTA, GA 31601. (#8695).

TOM PAINE - A PLAY AT VALDOSTA STATE COLLEGE, GA. PLAY WITH REVOLUTIONARY PERIOD THEME. (LOCAL). MS BETH MCRAE, ASST PROFESSOR, SPEECH DEPT; VALDOSTA STATE COLLEGE SPEECH DEPT; VALDOSTA, GA 31601. (#8690).

VALDOSTA STATE COLLEGE SPEAKERS BUREAU, GEORGIA. LECTURES AVAILABLE TO COMMUNITY GROUPS ON BICENTENNIAL THEMES FROM ARTS AND SCIENCE, EDUCATION, BUSINESS ADMINISTRATION AND FINE ARTS SCHOOLS. (LOCAL). MR JAMES L BLACK, ADMIN ASSISTANT; VALDOSTA STATE COLLEGE BICENT COMMITTEE; BOX 114; VALDOSTA, GA 31601. (#8691).

APR 29 - MAY 2, '76. HERITAGE SPECIAL - TRAIN TOUR. TRAVELING RAIL EXHIBIT EMPHASIZING COLONIAL & REVOLUTIONARY GEORGIA HISTORY, CRAFTS & LIFESTYLE OF GEORGIA COLONISTS. EXHIBITS WILL BE DISPLAYED WITH COMBINATION OF SIGHT & SOUND ACTIVITY. (LOCAL). RON HENRY, COORDINATOR; GEORGIA AGRIRAMA DEVELOPMENT AUTHORITY/ GEORGIA BICENTENNIAL; 8TH ST A I 75; TIFTON, GA 31794. (#7999-7).

JUNE '76. DEDICATION CEREMONY FOR CAMP ADVENTURE. DEDICATION OF RECREATIONAL FACILITIES FOR THE MENTALLY AND PHYSICALLY HANDICAPPED. (LOCAL). DAVID CHRISTIAN, DIR; VALDOSTA PARK AND RECREATION DEPT; CITY HALL; VALDOSTA, GA 31601. (#23601-1).

OCT 15 - 18, '76. HERITAGE SPECIAL - TRAIN TOUR. TRAVELING RAIL EXHIBIT EMPHASIZING COLONIAL AND REVOLUTIONARY GEORGIA HISTORY, CRAFTS & LIFESTYLE OF GEORGIA COLONISTS. EXHIBITS WILL BE DISPLAYED WITH COMBINATION OF SIGHT & SOUND ACTIVITY. AT DEPOT. (LOCAL). RON HENRY, DIRECTOR; GEORGIA BICENTENNIAL COMMISSION; 1776 PEACHTREE NW, ROOM 520 S; ATLANTA, GA 30309. (#7999-30).

NOV 26 - 27, '76. UNITED STATES ARMED FORCES BICENTENNIAL CARAVAN. CARAVAN IS COMPOSED OF EXHIBIT VANS FOR EACH MILITARY SERVICE. PROJECT THEME IS 'HISTORY OF THE ARMED FORCES & THEIR CONTRIBUTIONS TO THE NATION'. (LOCAL). TYSON MCLANE; UNITED STATES ARMED FORCES BICENTENNIAL CARAVAN; PO BOX 1976; VALDOSTA, GA 31601. (#1775-780).

VIDALIA

ARTS & CULTURAL PROGRAMS - PROJ OF VIDALIA, GA. A PAGEANT INVOLVING ALL PERFORMING ARTS, FILM FESTIVAL, THE COMPOSITION OF NEW MUSICAL WORKS & THE STUDY OF GA PERSONS PROMINENT IN THE PERFORMING ARTS WILL BE SPONSORED BY THE BICENT COMMITTEE. (LOCAL). MRS LEIGH B HUMPHREY, CHAIRMAN; VIDALIA BICENTENNIAL COMMITTEE; 308 W MAIN ST; VIDALIA, GA 30474. (#12644).

CIVIC CENTER & AUDITORIUM - VIDALIA, GA. A CIVIC CENTER AND/OR AUDITORIUM WILL BE BUILT & DEDICATED TO THOSE WHO GAVE THEIR LIVES IN DEFENSE OF AMERICA. (LOCAL). MRS LEIGH B HUMPHREY, CHAIRMAN; VIDALIA BICENTENNIAL COMMITTEE; 308 W MAIN ST; VIDALIA, GA 30474. (#12637).

ENVIRONMENTAL PROGRAMS IN VIDALIA, GA. VIDALIA BEAUTIFICATION COMMITTEE AND BICENTENNIAL COMMITTEE WILL PROMOTE CLEANUP & BEAUTIFICATION PROJECTS WITH TREE PLANTINGS & DISTRIBUTION OF INFORMATION ON FUEL CONSERVATION & POLLUTION CONTROL. (LOCAL). MRS LEIGH B HUMPHREY, CHAIRMAN; VIDALIA BICENTENNIAL COMMITTEE; 308 W MAIN ST; VIDALIA, GA 30474. (#12646).

ESSAYS & SUMPOSIA ON AMERICAN REVOLUTION, GA. ESSAY CONTESTS ON TOPICS RELATED TO THE AMERICAN REVOLUTION WILL BE SPONSORED FOR STUDENTS. IN-SCHOOL SYMPOSIA ARE PLANNED ON GA'S COLONIAL, REVOL & EARLY FEDERAL HISTORY AND ON GA'S INDIAN CULTURES. (LOCAL). MRS LEIGH B HUMPHREY, CHAIRMAN; VIDALIA BICENTENNIAL COMMITTEE; 308 W MAIN ST; VIDALIA, GA 30474. (#13835).

EXHIBITS - PROJ OF VIDALIA, GA. HISTORICAL ARTIFACTS & DOCUMENTS WILL BE DISPLAYED IN SCHOOLS, LIBRARIES & STORE WINDOWS. A SPECIAL DISPLAY WILL RELATE THE HISTORICAL DEVELOPMENT OF LOCAL PRODUCTS & INDUSTRIES. (LOCAL). MRS LEIGH B HUMPHREY, CHAIRMAN; VIDALIA BICENTENNIAL COMMITTEE; 308 W MAIN ST; VIDALIA, GA 30474. (#12643).

INVITATION TO THE WORLD - PROJ OF VIDALIA, GA. A COMMUNITY HOSPITALITY PROGRAM TO WELCOME VISITORS TO THE AREA IS BEING DEVELOPED. A BICENTENNIAL MAP SHOWING SITES OF HISTORIC INTEREST WILL BE PREPARED & DISTRIBUTED. (LOCAL). MRS LEIGH B HUMPHREY, CHAIRMAN; VIDALIA BICENTENNIAL COMMITTEE; 308 W MAIN ST; VIDALIA, GA 30474. (#12645).

PRESERVATION & RESTORATION - PROJ OF VIDALIA, GA. IMPORTANT STRUCTURES IN VIDALIA WILL BE IDENTIFIED & RESTORED; BI CENTENNIAL MARKERS WILL BE PLACED AT LOCAL POINTS OF HISTORICAL INTEREST. (LOCAL). MRS LEIGH B HUMPHREY, CHAIRMAN; VIDALIA BICENTENNIAL COMMITTEE; 308 W MAIN ST; VIDALIA, GA 30474. (#12640).

PUBLICATIONS & RESEARCH - PROJ OF VIDALIA, GA. LOCAL HISTORIES ON TOPICAL THEMES; BUSINESS & INDUSTRY; ETHNIC GROUPS; FAMOUS PERSONALITIES; LANDMARKS & ARCHITECTURAL FEATURES; AND A STUDY OF THE GA CONSTITUTION & PLACE NAMES WILL BE PUBLISHED. (LOCAL). MRS LEIGH B HUMPHREY, CHAIRMAN; VIDALIA BICENTENNIAL COMMITTEE; 308 W MAIN ST; VIDALIA, GA 30474. (#12638).

RECREATIONAL FACILITIES - PROJ OF VIDALIA, GA. THE BICENT COMMITTEE WILL SPONSOR THE CREATION OF MINI-PARKS, NATURE TRAILS, BICYCLE TRAILS & GREEN AREAS. (LOCAL). MRS LEIGH B HUMPHREY, CHAIRMAN; VIDALIA BICENTENNIAL COMMITTEE; 308 W MAIN ST; VIDALIA, GA 30474. (#12648).

RE-ENACTMENTS - PROJ OF VIDALIA, GA. A RE-ENACTMENT GROUP WILL PRESENT LIVING HISTORY DEMONSTRATIONS OF THE COLONIAL ERA & WILL PARTICIPATE IN COMMEMORATIVE EVENTS & CEREMONIES. (LOCAL). MRS LEIGH B HUMPHREY, CHAIRMAN; VIDALIA BICENTENNIAL COMMITTEE; 308 W MAIN ST; VIDALIA, GA 30474. (#12642).

SPEAKERS BUREAU - PROJ OF VIDALIA, GA. A SPEAKERS BUREAU HAS BEEN ESTABLISHED TO PROVIDE PROGRAMS THAT WILL CREATE INTEREST IN VIDALIA'S HERITAGE & STIMULATE DISCUSSIONS ON THE GOALS & PURPOSES OF THE BICENTENNIAL CELEBRATION. (LOCAL). MRS LEIGH B HUMPHREY, CHAIRMAN; VIDALIA BICENTENNIAL COMMITTEE; 308 W MAIN ST; VIDALIA, GA 30474. (#12639).

VIDALIA — CONTINUED

JULY 15 - 18, '76. HERITAGE SPECIAL - TRAIN TOUR. TRAVELING RAIL EXHIBIT EMPHASIZING COLONIAL & REVOLUTIONARY GEORGIA HISTORY, CRAFTS & LIFESTYLE OF GEORGIA COLONISTS. EXHIBITS WILL BE DISPLAYED WITH COMBINATION OF SIGHT & SOUND ACTIVITY. (LOCAL). RON HENRY, COORDINATOR; GEORGIA AGRIRAMA DEVELOPMENT AUTHORITY/ GEORGIA BICENTENNIAL; 8TH ST A I 75; TIFTON, GA 31794. (#7999-15).

NOV 20 - 22, '76. UNITED STATES ARMED FORCES BICENTENNIAL CARAVAN. CARAVAN IS COMPOSED OF EXHIBIT VANS FOR EACH MILITARY SERVICE. PROJECT THEME IS 'HISTORY OF THE ARMED FORCES & THEIR CONTRIBUTIONS TO THE NATION'. (LOCAL). BILL LEDFORD; UNITED STATES ARMED FORCES BICENTENNIAL CARAVAN; PO BOX 669; VIDALIA, GA 30474. (#1775-778).

VILLA RICA

DOWNTOWN PARK - VILLA RICA, GA. DOWNTOWN PARK WITH BENCHES, BAND PLATFORM, GOLD MINING EQUIPMENT, PARKING AREA AND FOUNTAIN. (LOCAL). DOROTHEA DYER, CHAIRMAN; VILLA RICA BICENTENNIAL COMMITTEE; CITY HALL; VILLA RICA, GA 30180. (#27626). **ARBA GRANTEE.**

WALESKA

BICENTENNIAL PROJECTS OF REINHARDT COLLEGE IN GA. ACTIVITIES WILL INCLUDE A TOUR OF BOTANICAL GARDENS, A COUNTY-WIDE CELEBRATION ON THE 4TH OF JULY, SEMINARS & LECTURES ON PREPARATION OF LIFE FOR THE FUTURE AND THEATRICAL PRODUCTIONS. (LOCAL). MARGARET S LEE, LIBRARIAN; REINHARDT COLLEGE; BOX 68; WALESKA, GA 30183. (#8062).

SPIRIT OF '76, MUSICAL IN WALESKA, GA. A MUSICAL, THE SPIRIT OF '76, AND DRAMATIC PRODUCTIONS. (LOCAL). MARGARET S LEE, LIBRARIAN; REINHARDT COLLEGE; BOX 68; WALESKA, GA 30183. (#7799).

OCT 11, '75. HERITAGE OF THE PAST CRAFTS SHOW. DISPLAY AND DEMONSTRATION OF VARIOUS CRAFTS AND ART FORMS. AT REINHARDT COLLEGE CAMPUS. (LOCAL). MARGARET S LEE, LIBRARIAN; REINHARDT COLLEGE; BOX 68; WALESKA, GA 30183. (#8061-1).

WARNER ROBINS

AVENUE OF FLAGS IN WARNER ROBINS, GEORGIA. TO ENCOURAGE LOCAL BUSINESSES AND RESIDENTS TO FLY THE AMERICAN FLAG DURING 1976, AND ASSIST THEM IN ORDERING FLAGS FOR THEIR PERSONAL USE. (LOCAL). B G HARLESS, CHAIRMAN; WARNER ROBINS BICENT COMMITTEE; 412 TODD CIR; WARNER ROBINS, GA 31093. (#10673).

BICENTENNIAL COOKBOOK PROJ OF WARNER ROBINS, GA. THE SENIOR CITIZENS CLUB WILL COMPILE A COOKBOOK CONSISTING OF SOUTHERN RECIPES THAT HAVE BEEN FAMILIAR TO THE AREA FOR THE LAST 200 YEARS. (LOCAL). B-G HARLESS, PROJ CHAIRMAN; WARNER ROBINS BICENT COMMITTEE; 412 TODD CR; WARNER ROBINS, GA 31093. (#10146).

COUNTRY DAY. SPONSOR PLANS INCOMPLETE AS OF 04/28/75. AT BIZZELS VILLAGE SHOPPING AREA WATSON BLVD. (LOCAL). B-G HARLESS; BIZZELS INTERNATIONAL VILLAGE; 412 TODD CR; WARNER ROBINS, GA 31093. (#50769-1).

DEPOT RESTORATION, WARNER ROBBINS, GA. RESTORATION OF RAILROAD DEPOT, ONE OF THE OLDEST BUILDINGS IN THE CITY. THE BUILDING WILL BE USED BY COMMUNITY MEMBERS TO CONDUCT MEETINGS & SPECIAL PROJECTS, AND AS BICENT COMMITTEE HEADQUARTERS. (LOCAL). MRS B G HARRIS, CHAIRWOMAN; WARNER ROBINS BICENTENNIAL COMMITTEE; PO BOX 1776-1976; WARNER ROBINS, GA 31093. (#19354). **ARBA GRANTEE.**

MINI PARK TO BE BUILT IN WARNER ROBINS, GA. MINI PARK IN WARNER ROBINS, GA WILL BOAST AN INTL THEME, EMPHASIZING AMERICA'S BEING FOUNDED BY MANY NATIONALITIES. (LOCAL). B HARLESS, CHAIRMAN; WARNER ROBINS BICENT COMMISSION; 412 TODD CR; WARNER ROBINS, GA 31093. (#10130).

RECREATIONAL PAVILION IN WARNER ROBINS, GA. CONSTRUCTION OF PAVILION AT LOCAL RECREATION PARK. (LOCAL). B G HARLESS, PROJ CHAIRMAN; WARNER ROBINS BICENT COMMUNITY; 412 TODD CIR; WARNER ROBINS, GA 31093. (#8884).

'SEWING FOR THE BICENT' IN WARNER ROBINS, GEORGIA. THE WARNER ROBINS LANTANNA CLUB & ROBINETTES HOMEMAKERS ARE PREPARING & MAKING AVAILABLE, PATTERNS & 1776 DRESS FOR THOSE WHO REQUEST COSTUMES FOR THE BICENT CELEBRATION. (LOCAL). B G HARLESS, PROJ CHAIRMAN; WARNER ROBINS BICENT COMMITTEE; 412 TODD CIR; WARNER ROBINS, GA 31093. (#10148).

VOICES FOR POSTERITY WARNER ROBINS, GEORGIA. TAPE RECORDINGS OF SOME OF THE OLDEST RESIDENTS OF WARNER ROBINS, TO BE PRESENTED TO THE CITY'S HISTORICAL SOCIETY. (LOCAL). B G HARLESS, CHAIRMAN; WARNER ROBINS BICENT COMMITTEE; 412 TODD CIR; WARNER ROBINS, GA 31093. (#8885).

VOTER REGISTRATION PROJECT IN WARNER ROBINS, GA. THIS PROJECT IS TO ENCOURAGE CITIZENS TO BECOME REGISTERED VOTERS. (LOCAL). B G HARLESS, CHAIRMAN; WARNER ROBINS BICENT COMMITTEE; 412 TODD CIR; WARNER ROBINS, GA 31093. (#10137).

WARNER ROBINS, GEORGIA 'CLEANS UP'. THE WARNER ROBINS BEAUTIFICATION COMMITTEE WILL CONDUCT CLEANUP CAMPAIGNS, FIVE TIMES EACH YEAR; CITY WILL BE DIVIDED INTO FIVE SECTIONS. THE ENTIRE CITY WILL BE COVERED IN ONE YEAR. (LOCAL). B G HARLESS, PROJ CHAIRMAN; WARNER ROBINS BICENT COMMITTEE; 412 TODD CIR; WARNER ROBINS, GA 31093. (#10126).

JUNE 4, '75. CHORAL SOCIETY CONCERT. ALL SELECTIONS WILL BE OF A PATRIOTIC NATURE. AT WARNER ROBINS CIVIC CENTER. (LOCAL). B-G HARLESS; WARNER ROBINS CHORAL SOCIETY; 412 TODD CR; WARNER ROBINS, GA 31093. (#50761-1).

JULY 4, '75. BAR B QUE. FESTIVAL AT RECREATION DEPT WATSON BLVD. (LOCAL). B-G HARLESS; EXCHANGE CLUB; 412 TODD CR; WARNER ROBINS, GA 31093. (#50764-1).

JULY 4, '75. BICENT SONG & LOGO CONTESTS AT WARNER ROBINS, GA. A CONTEST TO CHOOSE AN ORIGINAL SONG TO COMMEMORATE THE BICENT; ALSO A LOGO CONTEST WILL BE HELD IN ORDER TO FIND AN OFFICIAL LOGO FOR LETTERS AND DOCUMENTS. (LOCAL). B G HARLESS; WARNER ROBINS BICENT COMMITTEE; 412 TODD CIR; WARNER ROBINS, GA 31093. (#10147-1).

JULY 4, '75. FIREWORKS. FESTIVAL AT RECREATION DEPT. WATSON BLVD. (LOCAL). B-G HARLESS; CITY OF WARNER ROBINS; 412 TODD CR; WARNER ROBINS, GA 31093. (#50766-1).

JULY 4, '75. PARADE. ALL ENTRIES WILL DEPICT SPECIAL EVENTS IN OUR NATIONS FIRST 300 YRS. A PROGRESSIVE SEQUENCE WILL BE USED BEGINNING WITH EVENTS FROM 1776 AND ENDING WITH ENTRIES DEPICTING MOST CURRENT HAPPENINGS WHICH HAVE MADE HISTORY. AT WATSON BLVD. (LOCAL). B-G HARLESS; CHAMBER OF COMMERCE; 412 TODD CR; WARNER ROBINS, GA 31093. (#50763-1).

JULY 4, '75. ROCK CONCERT. LIVE PERFORMANCE AT RECREATION DEPT. WATSON BLVD. (LOCAL). B-G HARLESS; WARNER ROBINS BICENTENNIAL COMMITTEE; 412 TODD CR; WARNER ROBINS, GA 31093. (#50762-1).

JULY 4, '75. WATERMELON CUTTING. WATERMELON WILL BE SOLD WARM OR CHILLED, WHOLE OR SLICED. AT RECREATION DEPT WATSON BLVD. (LOCAL). B-G HARLESS; CIVITAN CLUB; 412 TODD CR; WARNER ROBINS, GA 31093. (#50765-1).

JULY 5, '75. MISS BICENTENNIAL PAGEANT. A MISS BICENTENNIAL WILL BE CHOSEN TO REIGHN FROM JULY 4 1975 TO JULY 4 1976. AT CIVIC CENTER WATSON BLVD. (LOCAL). B-G HARLESS; BICENTENNIAL COMMITTEE; 412 TODD CR; WARNER ROBINS, GA 31093. (#50762-2).

JULY 6, '75. INTER-DEMONINATIONAL DAY OF PRAYER. CEREMONY AT EACH INDIVIDUAL CHURCH. (LOCAL). B-G HARLESS; ALL LOCAL CHURCHES; 412 TODD CR; WARNER ROBINS, GA 31093. (#50767-1).

OCT 24 - 26, '75. ANTIQUE AUTO SHOW. THE CARS WILL DRIVE ON A PARADE AROUND & OWN BEFORE GOING TO WALKERS LAKE FOR THE EXHIBITION. AT WALKERS LAKE. (ST-WIDE). B-G HARLESS; MIDDLE GEORGIA REGION ANTIQUE AUTO CLUB OF AMERICA; 412 TODD CR; WARNER ROBINS, GA 31093. (#50768-1).

JAN 24, '76. INTERNATIONAL BALL. REFRESHMENTS MADE AND SERVED BY MEMBERS OF ALL NATIONALITIES TO STRESS IMPORTANCE OF REMEMBERING THAT AMERICA WAS FOUNDED BY PERSONS FROM ALL NATIONS. AT CITY HALL COMPLEX, 700 WATSON BLVD.. (LOCAL). B G HARLESS; BICENTENNIAL COMMITTEE; 412 TODD CR; WARNER ROBINS, GA 31093. (#50762-3).

MAR 24 - 28, '76. HERITAGE SPECIAL - TRAIN TOUR. TRAVELING RAIL EXHIBIT EMPHASIZING COLONIAL & REVOLUTIONARY GEORGIA HISTORY, CRAFTS & LIFESTYLE OF GEORGIA COLONISTS. EXHIBITS WILL BE DISPLAYED WITH COMBINATION OF SIGHT & SOUND ACTIVITY. (LOCAL). RON HENRY, COORDINATOR; GEORGIA AGRIRAMA DEVELOPMENT AUTHORITY/ GEORGIA BICENTENNIAL; 8TH ST A I 75; TIFTON, GA 31794. (#7999-21).

APR 24, '76. FLOWER SHOW. ALL ARRANGEMENTS WILL BE BASED ON THE BICENTENNIAL THEME. AT HOUSTON MALL N. HOUSTON RD. WARNER ROBINS, GA.. (LOCAL). B-G HARLESS; WARNER ROBINS GARDEN CLUB COUNCIL; 412 TODD CR; WARNER ROBINS, GA 31093. (#50770-1).

MAY 7 - 8, '76. ART SHOW. ALL ENTREES WILL BE BASED ON THE BICENTENNIAL THEME. AT HOUSTON MALL N. HOUSTON RD WARNER ROBINS, GA. (ST-WIDE). B-G HARLESS; WARNER ROBINS ART ASSOC ART SHOW COMM; 412 TODD CR; WARNER ROBINS, GA 31093. (#50771-1).

JULY 3, '76. PAGEANT, LITTLE THEATRE - PLAY '1776'. PAGEANT WILL CONSIST OF SONG, DANCE, & THEATRE ALL PORTRAYING BICENTENNIAL THEME. AT INTERNATIONAL CITY STADIUM. (LOCAL). B-G HARLESS; BICENTENNIAL COMM; 412 TODD CR; WARNER ROBINS, GA 31093. (#50762-4).

JULY 4, '76. INTER-DENOMINATIONAL DAY OF PRAYER. EMPHASIS WILL BE PLACED ON THE BICENTENNIAL COMMEMORATION. AT AT EACH PARTICIPATING CHURCH. (LOCAL). B-G HARLESS; ALL LOCAL CHURCHES; 412 TODD CR; WARNER ROBINS, GA 31093. (#50767-2).

JULY 4, '76. WARNER ROBINS, GA SPONSORS BICENT LITERARY CONTEST. CONTEST WILL FEATURE ORIGINAL POEMS AND ESSAYS COMMEMORATING THE BICENTENNIAL. WINNERS WILL BE ANNOUNCED & WINNING ENTRIES READ DURING JULY 4TH ACTIVITIES. (LOCAL). B G HARLESS; WARNER ROBINS BICENT COMMITTEE; 412 TODD CIR; WARNER ROBINS, GA 31093. (#10672-1).

SEPT 3 - 7, '76. HERITAGE SPECIAL - TRAIN TOUR. TRAVELING RAIL EXHIBIT EMPHASIZING COLONIAL AND REVOLUTIONARY GEORGIA HISTORY, CRAFTS & LIFESTYLE OF GEORGIA COLONISTS. EXHIBITS WILL BE DISPLAYED WITH COMBINATION OF SIGHT & SOUND ACTIVITY. AT DEPOT. (LOCAL). RON HENRY, DIRECTOR; GEORGIA BICENTENNIAL COMMISSION; 1776 PEACHTREE NW, ROOM 520 S; ATLANTA, GA 30309. (#7999-35).

WARTHEN

AARON BURR JAIL - PROJ OF WARTHEN, GA. OLD LOG JAIL WHERE BURR WAS INCARCERATED WILL BE MADE INTO A TOURIST ATTRACTION. (LOCAL). LEWIS WEST, CHAIRMAN; WASHINGTON COUNTY BICENTENNIAL STEERING COMMITTEE; 307 MIAMOLA AVE; SANDERSVILLE, GA 31082. (#12632).

WASHINGTON

CARPENTER SHOP RESTORATION IN WASHINGTON, GEORGIA. RELOCATION & RESTORATION OF A UNIQUE CARPENTER SHOP BUILDING AT CALLOWAY PLANTATION. (LOCAL). DR J T BRYSON, PRESIDENT; WASHINGTON-WILKES BICENT COMMISSION, INC; RT 1, BOX 55; WASHINGTON, GA 30673. (#8745).

INTERPRETIVE TRAIL AT KETTLE CREEK BATTLE SITE, GA. MARKING AN INTERPRETIVE TRAIL AT KETTLE CREEK BATTLE SITE USING OUTDOOR EXHIBITS & A RECORDED NARRATIVE BROADCAST BY SPEAKERS STRATEGICALLY LOCATED ALONG THE TRAIL. (ST-WIDE). JIM OATES, CHIEF RECREATION & PLANNING SECTION; GEORGIA DEPT OF NATURAL RESOURCES; 270 WASHINGTON ST SW; ATLANTA, GA 30334. (#586).

JUNE 11, '74. FLEA MARKET - TRADING DAY - BICENTENNIAL SUMMER FESTIVAL. SUMMER FESTIVAL ARTS, CRAFTS, DANCING & COMPETITIONS WHICH IS TO BECOME AN ANNUAL EVENT. (LOCAL). DR J TURNER BRYSON, CHMN; WASHINGTON-WILKES BICENTENNIAL COMMISSION; PO BOX 661; WASHINGTON, GA 30673. (#1582-901).

JUNE 12, '74. LADIES QUILTING BEE-BICENTENNIAL SUMMER FESTIVAL. FESTIVAL. (LOCAL). DR J TURNER BRYSON, CHMN; WASHINGTON-WILKES BICENTENNIAL COMMISSION; PO BOX 661; WASHINGTON, GA 30673. (#1582-902).

JUNE 13 - 14, '74. BICENTENNIAL SUMMER FESTIVAL ARTS AND CRAFT SHOW. FESTIVAL. (LOCAL). DR J TURNER BRYSON, CHMN; WASHINGTON-WILKES BICENTENNIAL COMMISSION; PO BOX 661; WASHINGTON, GA 30673. (#1582-903).

JUNE 14 - 15, '74. BICENTENNIAL SUMMER FESTIVAL MARKSMANSHIP & ATHLETIC CONTESTS. FESTIVAL. (LOCAL). DR J TURNER BRYSON, CHMN; WASHINGTON-WILKES BICENTENNIAL COMMISSION; PO BOX 661; WASHINGTON, GA 30673. (#1582-904).

JUNE 15, '74. BICENTENNIAL SUMMER FESTIVAL STREET DANCE. FESTIVAL. (LOCAL). DR J TURNER BRYSON, CHMN; WASHINGTON-WILKES BICENTENNIAL COMMISSION; PO BOX 661; WASHINGTON, GA 30673. (#1582-905).

MAY 20 - 23, '76. HERITAGE SPECIAL - TRAIN TOUR. TRAVELING RAIL EXHIBIT EMPHASIZING COLONIAL & REVOLUTIONARY GEORGIA HISTORY, CRAFTS & LIFESTYLE OF GEORGIA COLONISTS. EXHIBITS WILL BE DISPLAYED WITH COMBINATION OF SIGHT & SOUND ACTIVITY. (LOCAL). RON HENRY, COORDINATOR; GEORGIA AGRIRAMA DEVELOPMENT AUTHORITY/ GEORGIA BICENTENNIAL; 8TH ST A I 75; TIFTON, GA 31794. (#7999-13).

WATKINSVILLE

FALL FESTIVAL IN WATKINSVILLE, GA. WEEKEND, PUBLIC DISPLAY OF ARTS AND CRAFTS OF COUNTY CITIZENS WITH ATMOSPHERE OF COUNTY FAIR. (LOCAL). MRS J SWANTON IVY, JR, CHAIRPERSON; OCONEE COUNTY LIBRARY COMMITTEE & BICENTENNIAL COMMITTEE; 860 ROCKINWOOD DR; ATHENS, GA 30601. (#10626).

FLOWER & SHRUB PROJECT IN WATKINSVILLE, GA. PROJECT ENTAILS THE NAMING OF A PERMANENT COUNTY FLOWER AND SHRUB; ALL COUNTY CITIZENS ARE BEING ENCOURAGED TO PLANT GREENERY. (LOCAL). MRS ARTHUR BUTLER, CHAIRPERSON; WOMEN'S GARDEN CLUB; RT 2 BOX 67; WATKINSVILLE, GA 30677. (#11318).

HARRIS SHOALS PARK IMPROVEMENT, WATKINSVILLE, GA. INCREASE OF RECREATIONAL FACILITIES AT HARRIS SHOALS PARK AND PRESERVING OF NATURAL HABITAT OF SIX ACRES RECENTLY GIVEN TO WATKINSVILLE BY THE FEDERAL GOVERNMENT. (LOCAL). PAUL WOODWORTH, PRESIDENT; CIVITAN CLUB; RT 1, BOX 47-B; FARMINGTON, GA 30638. (#11321).

HISTORY OF ALL CHURCHES IN OCONEE COUNTY, GA. COUNTY CHURCHES ARE TO RESEARCH AND WRITE THEIR OWN HISTORY AND DO AN INVENTORY ON COUNTY CEMETERIES. (LOCAL). JOE L COLLIER, CHAIRMAN; OCONEE COUNTY BICENTENNIAL COMMITTEE; RT 1 BOX 216; WATKINSVILLE, GA 30677. (#11316).

HISTORY OF OCONEE COUNTY, GA. THE HISTORY OF THE AREA WILL BE RESEARCHED, RECORDED AND DOCUMENTED BY SENIOR CITIZENS. (LOCAL). MRS DAISY B HARRELL, PRESIDENT; OCONEE COUNTY HERITAGE FOUNDATION, INC; PO BOX 24; WATKINSVILLE, GA 30677. (#11313).

HISTORY OF WATKINSVILLE, GA CHRISTIAN CHURCH. RESEARCH AND PUBLISH HISTORY OF WATKINSVILLE, GEORGIA CHRISTIAN CHURCH AND EARLY MEMBERS AND PASTORS. (LOCAL). MRS Z S NORVILLE, PRESIDENT; FLAT ROCK WOMAN'S CLUB; RT 1, BOX 10; WATKINSVILLE, GA 30677. (#11315).

NEW LIBRARY IN WATKINSVILLE, GA. A NEW COUNTY LIBRARY IS BEING BUILT AND EQUIPPED. (LOCAL). MRS J SWANTON IVY, JR, CHAIRPERSON; OCONEE COUNTY LIBRARY COMMITTEE; 860 ROCKINWOOD DR; ATHENS, GA 30601. (#11319).

WATKINSVILLE — CONTINUED

NEW SEWAGE SYSTEM IN OCONEE COUNTY, GA. A NEW WATER AND SEWAGE SYSTEM IS BEING OBTAINED FOR THE COUNTY. (LOCAL). ROY E BERRY, CHAIRMAN; BOARD OF COMMISSIONERS, OCONEE COUNTY, GA; PO BOX 145; WATKINSVILLE, GA 30677. (#11320).

NEW STREET & ROAD SIGNS IN OCONEE COUNTY, GEORGIA. INSTALLATION OF STREET AND ROAD SIGNS AT EVERY INTERSECTION IN THE COUNTY AND THE INSTALLATION OF SPEED LIMIT SIGNS WHERE SAFETY IS A GRAVE CONCERN. (LOCAL). ROY E BERRY, CHAIRMAN; BOARD OF COMMISSIONERS, OCONEE COUNTY; PO BOX 145; WATKINSVILLE, GA 30677. (#10625).

OCONEE COUNTY, GA, ROADSIDE BEAUTIFICATION. PROJECT ENTAILS THE CLEANING UP OF ALL ROADSIDES, CLEARING OF UNDESIRABLE GROWTH AND INSTALLATION OF BINS FOR LITTER, THROUGHOUT THE COUNTY BY COUNTY GOVERNMENT AND RESIDENTS. (LOCAL). ROY E BERRY, CHAIRMAN; BOARD OF COMMISSIONERS; PO BOX 145; WATKINSVILLE, GA 30677. (#11322).

PRESERVE HISTORICAL SITES IN OCONEE COUNTY, GA. PRESERVATION OF COVERED BRIDGE, METHODIST PARSONAGE AND EAGLE TAVERN. (LOCAL). MRS DAISY B HARRELL, PRESIDENT; OCONEE COUNTY HERITAGE FOUNDATION, INC; PO BOX 24; WATKINSVILLE, GA 30677. (#11314).

OCT 11, '75. OCONEE COUNTY CENTENNIAL FALL FESTIVAL. DISPLAY OF ARTS & CRAFTS OF COUNTY CITIZENS, HISTORICAL EXHIBIT OF CRAFTS AT EAGLE TAVERN MUSEUM, AUCTION, BOOTHS, BBQ AT NOON, FREE ENTERTAINMENT. AT COURTHOUSE SQUARE. (LOCAL). MRS J SWANTON IVY; OCONEE CO LIBRARY COMMITTEE & BICENTENNIAL COMM; 860 ROCKINWOOD DR; ATHENS, GA 30601. (#11317-1).

OCT 9, '76. OCONEE COUNTY BICENTENNIAL FESTIVAL. DISPLAY OF ARTS & CRAFTS BY COUNTY CITIZENS, HISTORIC EXHIBIT OF CRAFTS AT EAGLE TAVERN MUSEUM, AUCTION, BOOTHS, NOON BBQ, FREE ENTERTAINMENT. ONE DAY ONLY, SATURDAY, OCT 9, 1976. PROCEEDS GO TO OCONEE LIBRARY FUND. AT COURTHOUSE SQUARE, HIGHWAY 441. (ST-WIDE). MRS J S IVY, JR, COORD; OCONEE CO LIBRARY COMMITTEE; 860 ROCKINWOOD DR; ATHENS, GA 30601. (#108916-1).

WAYCROSS

OKEFENOKEE HERITAGE CENTER RAILROAD EXHIBIT - GA. A COMPLETE RAILROAD EXHIBIT AS A PART OF THE OKEFENOKEE HERITAGE CENTER. ALSO, RELOCATION & RENOVATION OF A LATE 1800 STATION HOUSE & EXHIBITS IN THE STATION HOUSE & TRAIN MAIL CAR. (LOCAL). MRS S WILLIAM CLARK, CHAIRWOMAN; WAYCROSS/WARE COUNTY CENTENNIAL CORPORATION; RT 5, BOX 406; WAYCROSS, GA 31501. (#12011). **ARBA GRANTEE.**

SLASH PINE AREA HISTORICAL INVENTORY OF GEORGIA. HISTORICAL INVENTORY OF PLACES AND EVENTS IN THE EIGHT COUNTY SLASH PINE AREA IN GEORGIA. (ST-WIDE). MAX W HARRAL, EXEC DIRECTOR; SLASH PINE AREA PLANNING AND DEVELOPMENT COMMISSION; PO BOX 1276; WAYCROSS, GA 31501. (#728). **ARBA GRANTEE.**

NOV 1, '75. OKEFENOKEE HARVEST FESTIVAL. FESTIVAL AT OKEFENOKEE HERITAGE CENTER, N AUGUSTA AVE. (LOCAL). MRS S WILLIAM CLARK, CHMN; WAYCROSS/WARE COUNTY BICENTENNIAL COMMISSION; RT 5, BOX 406; WAYCROSS, GA 31501. (#102755-1).

MAR 12 - 14, '76. OKEFENOKEE FUNFARE WEEKEND. BICENTENNIAL EXHIBITS, ARTS & CRAFTS, ANTIQUE SHOW & MUCH MORE; FRIDAY THERE WILL BE A PARADE & ROCK CONCERT; SATURDAY THERE WILL BE A HISTORICAL PAGEANT; SUNDAY AFTERNOON THERE WILL BE A TOUR OF HOMES OF FEDERATED GARDEN CLUBS. AT OKEFENOKEE HERITAGE CENTER, N AUGUSTA AVE. (LOCAL). MRS S WILLIAM CLARK, CHMN; WAYCROSS/WARE COUNTY BICENTENNIAL COMMITTEE; RT 5, BOX 406; WAYCROSS, GA 31501. (#102755-2).

APR 2 - 4, '76. OKEFENOKEE CHAPTER AACA FIRST ANNUAL ANTIQUE CAR SHOW & FLEA MARKET. FLEA MARKET - CAR PARTS, CRAFTS, ANTIQUES, 'JUNK'; ANTIQUE CAR SHOW OPEN TO ANTIQUES, STREET RODS, SPECIAL INTEREST AUTOS, BARBECUE & OKEFENOKEE SWAMP STOMP ONE NIGHT, PARADE TO OKEFENOKEE SWAMP PARK AND TOUR, OPPORTUNITY TO ENJOY OTHER LOCAL SIGHTS AND ATTRACTIONS. AT PARKING LOT OF SATILLA SQUARE SHOPPING CENTER. (ST-WIDE). PERRY SWANSON, CHMN; OKEFENOKEE CHAPTER, ANTIQUE AUTOMOBILE CLUB OF AMERICA; 104 DEWEY ST; WAYCROSS, GA 31501. (#105290-1).

MAY 6 - 9, '76. HERITAGE SPECIAL - TRAIN TOUR. TRAVELING RAIL EXHIBIT EMPHASIZING COLONIAL & REVOLUTIONARY GEORGIA HISTORY, CRAFTS & LIFESTYLE OF GEORGIA COLONISTS. EXHIBITS WILL BE DISPLAYED WITH COMBINATION OF SIGHT & SOUND ACTIVITY. (LOCAL). RON HENRY, COORDINATOR; GEORGIA AGRIRAMA DEVELOPMENT AUTHORITY/GEORGIA BICENTENNIAL; 8TH ST A I 75; TIFTON, GA 31794. (#7999-11).

JULY 3 - 4, '76. OKEFENOKEE HERITAGE CELEBRATION. SAT NIGHT: PATRIOTIC PROGRAM; SUNDAY NIGHT: CITY-WIDE RELIGIOUS CEREMONY, BOTH AT MUNICIPAL STADIUM; SPECIAL PROGRAMS AT OKEFENOKEE SWAMP ON US 1 & AT OKEFENOKEE HERITAGE CENTER & THROUGHOUT COUNTY BOTH DAYS. AT OKEFENOKEE HERITAGE CENTER, N AUGUSTA AVE. (LOCAL). MRS S WILLIAM CLARK; WAYCROSS/WARE COUNTY CENTENNIAL CORPORATION; RT 5, BOX 406; WAYCROSS, GA 31501. (#12011-501).

OCT 22 - 25, '76. HERITAGE SPECIAL - TRAIN TOUR. TRAVELING RAIL EXHIBIT EMPHASIZING COLONIAL & REVOLUTIONARY GEORGIA HISTORY, CRAFTS & LIFESTYLE OF GEORGIA COLONISTS. EXHIBITS WILL BE DISPLAYED WITH COMBINATION OF SIGHT & SOUND ACTIVITY. AT DEPOT. (LOCAL). RON HENRY, DIRECTOR; GEORGIA BICENTENNIAL COMMISSION; 1776 PEACHTREE NW, ROOM 520 S; ATLANTA, GA 30309. (#7999-28).

WAYNESBORO

BEAUTIFICATION PROGRAM - WAYNESBORO, GA. OVER 200 TREES WILL BE PLANTED THIS YEAR THROUGHOUT THE CITY AND PARK ALONG WITH LIBERTY TREES & FLOWERS AS A BEAUTIFICATION PROGRAM. (LOCAL). MRS MARION WALKER, CHAIRMAN; CITY BEAUTIFICATION COMMISSION; PO BOX 471; WAYNESBORO, GA 30830. (#24397).

SHELL BLUFF AREA RESTORATION - WAYNESBORO, GA. RESTORATION TO INCLUDE WALKING TRAIL FOR SECTION OF BERTRAM TRAIL, LYMAN HALL GRAVESITE, BOTSFORD CHURCH AND CEMETERY. (LOCAL). EDWIN FULCHER, PRESIDENT; WAYNESBORO-BURKE HISTORICAL ASSOC; 213 E 8TH ST; WAYNESBORO, GA 30830. (#24405).

JULY 1 - 4, '76. BURKE 200 CELEBRATION. HISTORICAL RE-ENACTMENT, FISHING RODEO, PARADE, BARBECUE, SAILBOAT RACE, FREEDOM TREE PLANTING, STREET DANCE, FLAG CEREMONY, BELL RINGING, MUSEUM OPEN HOUSE, ATHLETIC & COSTUME CONTESTS. RELIGIOUS RALLY. LT GOV ZELL MILLER AT OPENING CEREMONIES, MAIN SPEAKER. (LOCAL). LOUISE KNIGHT; BURKE JUNIOR WOMENS CLUB/BURKE CO BICENTENNIAL COMMITTEE; KEYSVILLE, GA 30833. (#107287-1).

WEST POINT

AVENUE OF FLAGS, WEST POINT, GA. 105 FLAGS WERE PURCHASED TO FORM AN AVENUE OF FLAGS DOWN MAIN STREET. (LOCAL). MRS G P BARNWELL, CHAIRMAN; WEST POINT BICENTENNIAL COMMITTEE; 124 HILLCREST RD; WEST POINT, GA 31833. (#25378).

BICENTENNIAL EVENTS CALENDAR, WEST POINT, GA. A CALENDAR OF BICENTENNIAL EVENTS IS PUBLISHED IN LOCAL NEWSPAPER. A BICENTENNIAL EDITION IS ALSO PLANNED. (REGN'L). MAE THOMPSON, PROJ COORDINATOR; VALLEY TIMES NEWS; N 4TH AVE & 12TH; LANETT, AL 36863. (#25386).

BICENTENNIAL POSTER CONTEST, WEST POINT, GA. THE FIRST NATIOAL BANK OF WEST POINT SPONSORED A BICENTENNIAL POSTER CONTEST, WITH SCHOOL CHILDREN COMPETING FOR MOST APPROPRIATE AND BEST POSTER & THE WINNERS RECEIVING AWARDS. (LOCAL). JACK KEITH, CHAIRMAN; FIRST NATIONAL BANK; 10TH ST; WEST POINT, GA 31833. (#29988).

BICENTENNIAL PUBLICATION, WEST POINT, GA. PUBLICATION, WRITTEN BY LOCAL AUTHOR, IS A TRIBUTE OF THE CHATTAHOOCHEE VALLEY HISTORICAL SOCIETY; PUBLICATION IS ENTITLED 'PROUDEST INHERITANCE'; LISTS REVOL SOLDIERS OF THE AREA. (REGN'L). WILLIAM H DAVIDSON, AUTHOR; CHATTAHOOCHEE VALLEY HISTORICAL SOCIETY; 309 E 9TH ST; WEST POINT, GA 31833. (#25387).

CEMETERY CENSUS, WEST POINT, GA. SURVEY OF 2000 GRAVES IN OLD PINEWOOD CEMETERY. (LOCAL). EARL EDWARDS, COORDINATOR; CHATTAHOOCHEE VALLEY HISTORICAL SOCIETY; 1401 ROPER AVE; WEST POINT, GA 31833. (#25385).

CERTIFIED CITIES PROJ, WEST POINT, GA. THE CITY OF WEST POINT, IN HOPES OF BECOMING 'A CERTIFIED CITY,' HAS INSTALLED NEW STREET SIGNS, PROVIDED ADDITIONAL PARKING SPACES AND NEW PLAYGROUNDS, PURCHASED GARBAGE RECEPTACLES & BUILT CITY BARN. (LOCAL). WILLIAM SCOTT, JR, COORDINATOR; CITY COUNCIL OF WEST POINT; 118 TEEL RD; WEST POINT, GA 31833. (#25376).

CITY PLANNING FOR URBAN IMPROVEMENTS, W POINT, GA. COMPREHENSIVE PLAN FOR DEVELOPING CENTRAL BUSINESS DISTRICT, WHICH INCLUDES LITTER CONTROL PLANS AND BEAUTIFICATION PROGRAMS. (LOCAL). CLIFF GLOVER, CHAIRMAN; MUNICIPAL PLANNING BOARD; HILLCREST RD; WEST POINT, GA 31835. (#25375).

HISTORY PUBLICATION, WEST POINT, GA. REPRODUCTION OF PUBLICATION ENTITLED 'JOURNEY OF BENJAMIN HAWKINS THROUGH THE VALLEY' BY MARK FRETWELL, FORMER AREA RESIDENT. (REGN'L). BILL GILBERT, DIRECTOR; VALLEY BICENTENNIAL COMMITTEE; BROAD AVE; LANETT, AL 36863. (#25389).

LANDSCAPING & PARKS PROJ, WEST POINT, GA. MANY COMMUNITY AREAS HAVE BEEN LANDSCAPED AND PLANTED WITH TREES AND SHRUBS; APPROXIMATELY 200 DOGWOOD TREES HAVE BEEN PLANTED & 15 NEW MINI-PARKS DEVELOPED THROUGH FUNDS PROVIDED BY LOCAL BUSINESSES. (LOCAL). MRS G P BARNWELL, CHAIRMAN; WEST POINT BICENTENNIAL COMMITTEE; 124 HILLCREST RD; WEST POINT, GA 31833. (#25377).

LIBRARY GROUNDS PROJ, WEST POINT, GA. PROJECT IS THE MAINTENANCE OF THE HAWKS LIBRARY GROUNDS. RED AND WHITE AZALEAS, DAYLILIES, DOGWOOD TREES, CLEYERAS AND YAUPON HOLLIES HAVE BEEN PLANTED THIS YEAR. (LOCAL). MRS JOHN CURLEE, JR, PRESIDENT; GARDEN STUDY CLUB; TYLER TERRACE; WEST POINT, GA 31833. (#25370).

NATL BICENTENNIAL COMMUNITY RD SIGN, W POINT, GA. CITY OF WEST POINT HAS PURCHASED 5 ROAD SIGNS TO BE PLACED AT CITY LIMITS TO PROUDLY INFORM TRAVELERS THAT IT IS A BICENTENNIAL COMMUNITY. (LOCAL). FLOYD MEADORS, CITY MANAGER; CITY OF WEST POINT; 9TH ST; WEST POINT, GA 31833. (#25368).

PATRIOTIC MURAL, WEST POINT, GA. PATRIOTIC MURAL ON SIDE OF BUILDING IN DOWNTOWN WEST POINT, DEPICTING SCENES OF LOCAL INTEREST. (LOCAL). MRS G P BARNWELL, CHAIRMAN; BICENTENNIAL AND COMMUNITY PLANNING OF WEST POINT; 124 HILLCREST RD; WEST POINT, GA 31833. (#25380).

PERMANENT FLAG POLE, WEST POINT, GA. PERMANENT FLAG POLE TO FLY U S 50-STAR FLAG & SPECIAL VALLEY BICENTENNIAL FLAG DURING BICENTENNIAL AND ON SPECIAL OCCASIONS, IN DOWNTOWN AREA. (LOCAL). H E STEEL, PRESIDENT; VALLEY NATIONAL BANK; FRAN COLYN TERRACE; WEST POINT, GA 31833. (#25381).

RED, WHITE AND BLUE FLOWERS PLANTED, W POINT, GA. A $100.00 DONATION TO CITY BY CHARTER GARDEN CLUB HAS RESULTED IN RED, WHITE & BLUE FLOWERS BEING PLANTED IN MINI-PARKS AND AROUND HISTORICAL MARKERS. (LOCAL). MRS W B LANE, COORDINATOR; CHARTER GARDEN CLUB OF WEST POINT; WEST POINT, GA 31833. (#25373).

RESTORATION OF HISTORICAL MARKERS, WEST POINT, GA. RESTORATION OF HISTORICAL MARKERS IN AREA AND ERECTION OF NEW MARKER AT BURNT VILLAGE PARK, SITE OF INDIAN VILLAGE VISITED BY BENJAMIN HAWKINS, INDIAN AGENT. (REGN'L). BILL GILBERT, DIRECTOR; VALLEY BICENTENNIAL COMMITTEE; BROAD AVE; LANETT, AL 36863. (#25390).

SLOGAN CONTEST, WEST POINT, GA. RADIO STATION WRLD SPONSORED A BICENTENNIAL SLOGAN CONTEST. THE VALLEY BICENTENNIAL'S SLOGAN IS, 'ONE GOD, ONE NATION, ONE VALLEY'. (LOCAL). MILES FERGUSON, CHAIRMAN; RADIO STATION WRLD; FRAN COLYN TERR; WEST POINT, GA 31833. (#29987).

VALLEY BEAUTIFICATION PROGRAM, WEST POINT, GA. VALLEY-WIDE CLEAN-UP AND BEAUTIFICATION PROGRAMS ARE BEING DEVELOPED AND A VALLEY BICENTENNIAL GROUP HAS BEEN FORMED WITH REPRESENTATIVE PERSONS FROM ALL VALLEY TOWNS PARTICIPATING. (LOCAL). VINCE MCDONALD, MANAGER; CHAMBER OF COMMERCE; 400 AVE E; WEST POINT, GA 31833. (#25369).

WELCOMING SIGN, WEST POINT, GA. LARGE 'WELCOME TO WEST POINT' SIGN, PAINTED IN RED, WHITE AND BLUE, WITH 4 FLAGS FLYING OVER IT. (LOCAL). MRS G P BARNWELL, CHAIRMAN; WEST POINT BICENTENNIAL COMMITTEE; 124 HILLCREST RD; WEST POINT, GA 31833. (#25374).

DEC 1 - 13, '75. FIREPLUG DECORATING CONTEST. CONTEST WITH FIREPLUGS PAINTED TO RESEMBLE REVOLUTIONARY FIGURES; CASH PRIZES AWARDED TO THREE BEST. (LOCAL). MRS GEORGE SAPP, MEMBER; WEST POINT BICENTENNIAL COMMITTEE; 4TH AVE; WEST POINT, GA 31833. (#107959-3).

JAN 2 - DEC 31, '76. 'AMERICA, WHAT SHE WORE'; FASHION SHOW PRODUCTION. HAS BEEN PRESENTED 36 TIMES THROUGHOUT UNITED STATES. IT REVEALS AMERICA'S HISTORY AS FASHIONS THAT BEGIN WITH THE PILGRIMS AND CONTINUE TO THE PRESENT DAY ARE MODELED. IT'S A FASHION SHOW FOR BOTH LADIES & MEN WITH THE EMPHASIS ON HISTORY RATHER THAN FASHION. (LOCAL). SARA JEAN PONDER, DIR; WEST POINT PEPPERELL AND BICENTENNIAL COMMITTEE; 10TH ST; WEST POINT, GA 31833. (#107959-2).

FEB 20, '76. ARBOR DAY PLANTING OF 9 DOGWOOD TREES. THE GARDEN CLUB WAS ASSISTED BY MAYOR BARROW. AT DOWNTOWN WEST POINT. (LOCAL). MRS LOUIS KIRBY JR, COORD; KALUSKA GARDEN CLUB; HILLCREST RD; WEST POINT, GA 31833. (#200012-36).

FEB 22, '76. COMMEMORATIVE CHERRY TREE PLANTING. CHERRY TREE WAS PLANTED ON GEORGE WASHINGTON'S BIRTHDAY AT THE GIRL SCOUT HUT. CHURCH CHOIR, MAYOR AND GIRL SCOUTS PARTICIPATED. (LOCAL). MRS BRUCE SMITH, COORD; WEDGEWOOD GARDEN CLUB; FRAN-COLYN TER; WEST POINT, GA 31833. (#200012-43).

APR 16, '76. MEMORIAL SERVICE ON ANNIVERSARY OF BATTLE OF FORT TYLER. WREATH WILL BE PLACED ON THE GRAVE OF BRIG GENERAL ROBERT C TYLER WHO LOST HIS LIFE IN THE CAST CIVIL WAR BATTLE. (LOCAL). EARL EDWARDS, COORD; CHATTAHOOCHEE VALLEY HISTORICAL SOCIETY; 1401 ROPER AVE; WEST POINT, GA 31833. (#200012-37).

APR 26, '76. COMMEMORATIVE WREATH CEREMONY - SOUTHERN MEMORIAL DAY. PATRIOTIC WREATH OF RED, WHITE & BLUE CARNATIONS WAS PLACED ON CONFEDERATE MONUMENT. (LOCAL). MRS W B LANE, PRES; CHARTER GARDEN CLUB; 3011 20TH AVE; SHAWMUT, AL 36876. (#107960-2).

JUNE 3 - 5, '76. FIREWORKS EXTRAVAGANZA & BAND CONCERT. A BICENTENNIAL OPEN AIR CONCERT BY MAXWELL AF BAND & COLOR GUARD & FIREWORKS EXTRAVAGANZA AT WEST POINT DAM ON 6/3 TO KICK OFF 3-DAY FESTIVAL. (LOCAL). BILL GILBERT, COORDINATOR; VALLEY BICENTENNIAL COMMITTEE; BROAD AVE; LANETT, AL 36863. (#108032-6).

JUNE 4, '76. PARADE & FUN FESTIVAL. A GIANT, COLORFUL PARADE, FEATURING LOCAL & PROFESSIONAL FLOATS, MARCHING BANDS, DRUM & BUGLE CORPS, CLOWNS & ANTIQUE AUTOMOBILES ENDING AT SHAWMUT CIRCLE FOR A FUN FESTIVAL. (LOCAL). BILL GILBERT, COORDINATOR; VALLEY BICENTENNIAL COMMITTEE; BROAD AVE; LANETT, AL 36863. (#108032-5).

JUNE 14, '76. FLAG DAY CEREMONY FEATURING VALLEY HS BAND & SCOUT TROOP 13. THE MAYOR WILL PRESIDE OVER CEREMONIES. AT FLAG PARK. (LOCAL). MRS LILLIAN CUMBEE, CHMN; WEST POINT WOMEN'S CLUB; 1309 5TH AVE; WEST POINT, GA 31833. (#108032-4).

JULY 2, '76. 'THE 2ND SIGNING OF THE DECLARATION OF INDEPENDENCE' - PROGRAM. LIVE PERFORMANCE AT BANK LOBBY, FIRST NATIONAL BANK, WEST POINT, GA. (LOCAL). JACK KEITH, PRESIDENT; FIRST NATIONAL BANK; W 10TH ST; WEST POINT, GA 31833. (#108032-3).

JULY 4, '76. PATRIOTIC COMMEMORATION CEREMONY. A COMMEMORATIVE WREATH WILL BE PLACED ON HISTORIC MONUMENT AT THE SAME TIME THE BELLS, INDICATING 200 YRS OF

WEST POINT — CONTINUED

INDEPENDENCE, RING. (LOCAL). GEORGE NADER, COORDINATOR; KALUSKA GARDEN CLUB & WEST POINT BICENTENNIAL COMMITTEE; 1011 5TH AVE; WEST POINT, GA 31833. (#107959-1).

DEC '76. ANNUAL CHRISTMAS PARADE. CHRISTMAS PARADE SPONSORED BY WEST POINT MERCHANTS' ASSOCIATION WHICH WILL BRING SANTA CLAUS TO THE VALLEY AREA & WIND UP EVENTS IN WEST POINT & VICINITY THIS BICENTENNIAL YEAR. (LOCAL). GARY W HOBBS, COORDINATOR; MERCHANTS' ASSOCIATION; 130 TEEL RD; WEST POINT, GA 31833. (#108032-1).

WHIGHAM

A LIBERTY BELL ON WHIGHAM SCHOOL CAMPUS, GA. A LIBERTY BELL ON WHIGHAM SCHOOL CAMPUS, PLANNED BY COMMUNITY LEADERS & DESIGNED BY SCHOOL FACULTY. THE PLOT WHERE IT WILL STAND TO BE PREPARED BY THE AGRICULTURAL CLASS. (LOCAL). MRS ELIZABETH GROSE, CLERK; CITY OF WHIGHAN; RT 2; WHIGHAM, GA 31797. (#14116).

JAN 31, '76. RATTLESNAKE ROUNDUP. SMALL COMMUNITY'S OCCASSION TO RID THE AREA OF RATTLESNAKES AND TO CELEBRATE THE ONENESS OF THE COMMUNITY. (LOCAL). SONNY COX, DIRECTOR; WHIGHAM COMMUNITY CLUB; RT 1; WHIGHAM, GA 31797. (#101710-1).

WINTERVILLE

JUNE 14 - 20, '76. THE MARIGOLD FESTIVAL. SATURDAY FEATURES LOTS OF FOOD, LIVE ENTERTAINMENT, A PARADE & FIREWORKS. A CAMP MEETING OF 100 YRS AGO WILL BE RE-CREATED SUNDAY, WITH GOSPEL SINGING & SUPPER ON THE GROUND. THE HERITAGE SPECIAL WILL BE IN TOWN MONDAY-SATURDAY. ARTS & CRAFTS ON DISPLAY ALL WEEK. (ST-WIDE). MRS JOAN BILES; THE CITY OF WINTERVILLE; 1045 ATHENS RD; WINTERVILLE, GA 30683. (#104384-6).

JUNE 16 - 20, '76. HERITAGE SPECIAL - TRAIN TOUR. TRAVELING RAIL EXHIBIT EMPHASIZING COLONIAL & REVOLUTIONARY GEORGIA HISTORY, CRAFTS & LIFESTYLE OF GEORGIA COLONISTS. EXHIBITS WILL BE DISPLAYED WITH COMBINATION OF SIGHT & SOUND ACTIVITY. (LOCAL). RON HENRY, COORDINATOR; GEORGIA AGRIRAMA DEVELOPMENT AUTHORITY/ GEORGIA BICENTENNIAL; 8TH ST A I 75; TIFTON, GA 31794. (#7999-18).

JULY 9, '76. RURAL LIFE DAY. A REAL GERMAN VILLAGE WILL BE RE-CREATED, COMPLETE WITH OOMPAH BAND & GERMAN FOOD, IN HONOR OF WINTERVILLE'S GERMAN FOUNDERS. TANDEM BICYCLES, SURREYS & HORSES WILL BE AVAILABLE FOR RENT. 4 MUSICAL PRODUCTION BASED ON THE FOUNDING OF WINTERVILLE WILL BE PRESENTED FRI. (LOCAL). MRS JOAN BILES, CHAIRMAN; ATHENS-CLARKE COUNTY BICENTENNIAL COMMISSION; 1045 ATHENS RD; WINTERVILLE, GA 30683. (#104384-14).

WOODBINE

CAMDEN'S CHALLENGE, WOODBINE, GA. WRITE AND PUBLISH COUNTY HISTORY. (LOCAL). MRS L B PROCTOR, PROJ DIRECTOR; CAMDEN COUNTY HISTORICAL SOCIETY; RT 1; WOODBINE, GA 31569. (#25532).

COUNTY MUSEUM, WOODBINE, GA. DEVELOPMENT OF LOCAL MUSEUM. (LOCAL). MRS LIBBY BASS, CHAIRPERSON; WOODBINE IMPROVEMENT COMMITTEE; WOODBINE, GA 31569. (#25531).

LIBERTY TREE, WOODBINE, GA. AN OAK TREE WILL BE PLANTED IN AREA BEING DEVELOPED AS A PARK. (LOCAL). MRS J D PROCTOR, VICE-PRESIDENT; WOODBINE WOMEN'S CLUB; WOODBINE, GA 31569. (#25533).

SATILLA RIVER FISHING TOURNAMENT. WEEK-LONG CONTEST - FISH TO BE USED FOR COMMUNITY FISH FRY. (LOCAL). LIBBY BASS, CHAIRPERSON; WOODBINE IMPROVEMENT COMMITTEE; WOODBINE, GA 31569. (#108181-3). **(??).**

JAN 2 - DEC 31, '76. ARTS & CRAFTS FAIRS. BI-MONTHLY DISPLAYS AND SALES OF HANDMADE ITEMS BY AREA RESIDENTS. (LOCAL). LIBBY BASS, CHAIRPERSON; WOODBINE IMPROVEMENT COMMITTEE; WOODBINE, GA 31569. (#108181-1).

JUNE 12, '76. PHOTO CONTEST. PICTURES SHOULD BE TAKEN WITHIN CAMDEN COMMUNITY TO SHOW HISTORIC SITES, ECOLOGICAL PROBLEMS, ENVIRONMENTAL DEVELOPMENT AND CONSERVATION PROJECTS. (LOCAL). CHARLES PERRY, CHAIRMAN; WOODBINE IMPROVEMENT COMMITTEE; HOLLY HILL; WOODBINE, GA 31569. (#108181-4).

JULY 3, '76. ANYTHING GOES DAY - INTERCOMMUNITY COMPETITION. FESTIVAL, COMPETITION. (LOCAL). R J BRIESE, ASST CHIEF; WOODBINE VOLUNTEER FIRE DEPT; BEDELL AVE; WOODBINE, GA 31569. (#108181-2).

WOODSTOCK

BETTER HEALTH PROGRAMS IN WOODSTOCK, GA. CITIZENS INFORMED AND URGED TO TAKE ADVANTAGE OF COUNTY HEALTH FACILITIES; A SCHOOL ROUNDUP WILL BE PUBLICIZED. (LOCAL). MRS S L JOHNSTON, JR, COORDINATOR; CHEROKEE COUNTY BICENTENNIAL COMMITTEE & COUNTY HEALTH DEPT; HANEY RD; WOODSTOCK, GA 30188. (#12559).

Territory of Guam

Guam American Revolution Bicentennial Commission

Commissioned December 26, 1969

ARBA Statistics

Officially Recognized
Military Installations—4
BINET Projects—23
Events—6
1973 Population—100,000

Bicentennial Archives

Latte of Freedom Museum
Agana, Guam 96910

Membership

Madeleine Bordallo, *chairperson* (1976-)
Professor Paul Carano, *former vice-chairman*
Delfina T. Aguigui, *former executive director*
Lágrimas F. Aflague
Hugh C. Barton
Edward G. Camacho
Robert E. León Guerrero
Mal A. Linthwaite
Monsignor Vicente Martinez
Gloria B. Nelson
Honorable Antonio M. Palomo
Commissioner Ramón L. G. Quinata
Dr. Pedro C. Sanchez
Honorable Frank R. Santos
Captain Raymond W. Volkwine
Lieutenant Dale R. Wilkison
Colonel Lester Zielinski

Guam

Geographically, the American day begins on Guam, and Guamanians were quick to say: "Guam, where America's Bicentennial begins. Where better to begin the Bicentennial celebration than on Guam?" With that in mind, the Guam American Revolution Bicentennial Commission planned the first official celebration that would kick off the American Bicentennial on the morning of March 1, 1975, the date specified in Public Law 93-179 as the beginning of the Bicentennial era.

Shortly after midnight on March 1 (still February 28 elsewhere in the United States), Guam's Bicentennial child, 10 year old Patrick Guzman, waved goodbye to hundreds of Guamanians who had gathered at the airport to see him off on a trip that included Honolulu, San Francisco, Washington, D.C. and Los Angeles. He carried a message to fellow Americans which encouraged them to use the Bicentennial celebration as a time for renewed dedication to the ideals of a democratic nation and to chart the nation's course of action for a brighter future enriched by our past.

Thus, Saturday, March 1, 1975 was the official beginning of the Bicentennial on Guam, as it was for all America, and all residents were encouraged to participate and involve themselves in Bicentennial activities. The Guam ARBC extended an invitation to Guamanians living on the United States mainland to visit the territory during 1976 and to participate in the year-long festival.

Guests found much to enhance their stay. Both the historic old palaces, which are considered to be the oldest buildings on Guam, and their surrounding grounds were restored and provided attractive sites for natives and tourists alike. The 4,000 acre Bolands Conservation Reserve was developed into a wildlife and outdoor recreation area that includes an artificial lake. Visitors found, too, that the outdoor recreation facilities on Cosos Island had been renovated, restored and further developed.

The people of Guam are strongly patriotic and have a long adherence to American ideals. Many of their Bicentennial activities were directed toward the democratic principles of their ancestors, the Chamorros, and that of all Americans. Even before official American policy allowed Vietnamese refugees into the United States, Guam's Governor Ricardo J. Bordallo, cognizant of the impending collapse of the South Vietnamese government, invited the South Vietnamese to "look to Guam as a haven."

His invitation triggered *Operation New Life.* As part of that program, the Guam Bicentennial commission sponsored a "Fiesta Hospitality" for nearly 400 refugees on May 1, 1975. Since refugees were not allowed to leave their compounds, native foods were prepared in the village of Nerizo and transported via a Bicentennial Caravan to the site. Interpretors assisted the Guamanians in spreading the Bicentennial word throughout the camp.

Early in 1976, Governor Bordallo looked for a Bicentennial project that would show the proud heritage of the Guamanian people and at the same time depict the freedom that all Americans enjoy. Thus the "Latte of Freedom" was born.

"Latte" is a symbol of the long cultural history of the Chamorro people. It was first described by Spanish explorers, who, in recording their travels to the Pacific, noted that most of the buildings were "made of wood and are erected on long column-like stones" in the shape of pyramids.

The "Latte of Freedom" will look a great deal like the torch in the hand of the Statue of Liberty. There will be an eternal flame which will rise from the top, acting as a kind of beacon of freedom. This symbol, equivalent to the torch of the Statue of Liberty, will stand as a "Pacific doorway" to the United States in the same way that the Statue of Liberty is the "Atlantic doorway" for foreign visitors.

Other Bicentennial projects also were undertaken. At the University of Guam, resources and courses relating to the history of Guam were developed, as were teaching and reference materials for other schools on the island. A book was published depicting the growth of democracy in Guam through the development of the Guam legislature. And because Guam's architectural history spans centuries—from prehistoric structures, Spanish forts and bridges to recent, modern structures—a guidebook was published and depicts, through photographs, plans and narrative, this evolution.

The first American flag to greet Independence Day, 1976, when the day dawned on Guam, has been placed in the official time capsule at the National Archives in Washington, D.C. The flag, which had flown on the Seventh Fleet Flagship *U.S.S. Fox,* was raised on Guam at 12:01 a.m. to welcome the nation's 200th birthday. It was delivered to the United States with a special message: ". . . it [the flag] is presented to the people in perpetuity as the Bicentennial flag which launched the nation's third century. This salute from the people of Guam is sent with love to all other Americans 'from sea to shining sea. . . .' "

Guam's enthusiastic participation gave special meaning to the Bicentennial of our nation.

AGANA

BICENTENNIAL CAMPOUT IN GUAM. THERE WILL BE A TERRITORY-WIDE, SIMULTANEOUS CAMPOUT FOR ALL BOY SCOUT TROOPS ON GUAM; ALL TROOPS WILL COMPLETE SERVICE PROJECTS BY IMPROVING, MARKING, IDENTIFYING & PUBLICIZING HISTORICAL SITES. (ST-WIDE). JOHN W SEIGAL, DISTRICT COMMISSIONER; BOY SCOUTS OF AMERICA, ALOHA COUNCIL, CHAMORRO DISTRICT; 3RD 1291 MANGO DR, APO SAN FRAN; AGANA, GU 96910. (#12016). **ARBA GRANTEE.**

BICENTENNIAL CONCERTS OF AMERICAN MUSIC - GUAM. LARGE AND SMALL WORKS FOR ORCHESTRA AND CHORUS WILL BE SELECTED, REHEARSED AND PERFORMED IN GUAM. (ST-WIDE). DR PATRICK LEDDY, COORDINATOR; GUAM AMERICAN REVOLUTION BICENTENNIAL COMMISSION; BOX 2950; AGANA, GU 96910. (#27363). **ARBA GRANTEE.**

BICENTENNIAL LIBERATION DAYS CELEBRATION - GUAM. IN OBSERVANCE OF JULY 4 CELEBRATION AND GUAM'S LIBERATION DAY, A 21DAY FESTIVAL WILL BE HELD. (ST-WIDE). FRANCISCA V S QUINTANILLA, ADMIN OFFICER; GUAM AMERICAN REVOLUTION BICENTENNIAL COMMISSION; PO BOX 2950; AGANA, GU 96910. (#26543). **ARBA GRANTEE.**

COCONUT - THE TREE OF HERITAGE IN AGANA, GU. THIS PROJECT SHOWS THE VALUE OF THE COCONUT TREE AS A SOURCE OF LIFE TO THE PEOPLE OF THE PACIFIC ISLANDS. THE COCONUT IS USED FOR FOOD, SHELTER, HOUSEHOLD UTENSILS & BEAUTY OBJECTS. (ST-WIDE). MADELEINE BORDALLO, COORDINATOR; GUAM AREA BICENTENNIAL COMMITTEE; PO BOX 2950; AGANA, GU 96910. (#33308). **ARBA GRANTEE.**

CULTURAL REVIVAL PROJECT OF GUAM. FESTIVAL FEATURING FROM CULTURAL RENDITIONS OF THE PACIFIC ISLANDS, TO 20TH CENTURY MUSIC OF OUR TIME WILL BE HOSTED IN THE SUMMER OF 74 & ANNUALLY THEREAFTER. THEME: 'GUAM - AN ISLAND IN HARMONY'. (ST-WIDE). RAYMOND QUINTANILLA, DIRECTOR; YOUTH INC, C/O UNIV OF GUAM; PO BOX 1993; AGANA, GU 96910. (#1003). **(??). ARBA GRANTEE.**

THE FLYING PROA - AGANA, GUAM. THE CARVING OF A REPLICA OF THE ANCIENT CHAMORRDS MODEL OF SEA TRANSPORTATION. (ST-WIDE). OFFICE OF THE GOVERNOR; GUAM AMERICAN REVOLUTION BICENTENNIAL COMMISSION; PO BOX 2950; AGANA, GU 96910. (#27362). **ARBA GRANTEE.**

GUAM BICENTENNIAL LATTE STONE MEMORIAL - AGANA, GU. MEMORIAL PROJECT DEPICTING CULTURAL HISTORY OF THE CHAMORRO PEOPLE AND ROLE OF UNITED STATES ARMED FORCES TOWARD GROWTH AND DEVELOPMENT OF GUAM. (ST-WIDE). CHAIRMAN; GUAM AMERICAN REVOLUTION BICENTENNIAL COMMISSION; PO BOX 2950; AGANA, GU 96910. (#22623). **ARBA GRANTEE.**

GUAM CULTURAL CENTER - AGANA. DRAWINGS, RESEARCH, PRELIMINARY ENGINEERING, SURVEY AND CONSTRUCTION SPECS WILL BE PREPARED, SUFFICIENT TO PRESENT TO LEGISLATURE FOR APPROVAL, DEVELOPMENT OF FUNDS AND INVITING CONSTRUCTION BIDS. (LOCAL). DR PATRICK LEDDY, COORDINATOR; GUAM BICENTENNIAL COMMISSION; OFFICE OF GOVERNOR, BOX 96910; AGANA, GU 96910. (#28546). **ARBA GRANTEE.**

GUAMERICAN HERITAGE - SCENES TO COLOR - AGANA, GU. A 48-PAGE COLORING BOOK DEPICTING GUAM'S HERITAGE. (ST-WIDE). DR DONALD KENNETH MAAS, CHAIRMAN; INTERNATIONAL READING ASSOCIATION - GUAM COUNCIL; PO BOX EK; AGANA, GU 96910. (#25909). **ARBA GRANTEE.**

GUAM'S BICENTENNIAL PARK. DEVELOP 4000 ACRE AREA CALLED BOLANDS CONSERVATION RESERVE INTO A WILDLIFE AND OUTDOOR RECREATION AREA INCLUDING AN ARTIFICIAL LAKE. (ST-WIDE). MRS DELFINA AGUIGUI, EXEC DIRECTOR; GUAM ARBC; C/O UNIV OF GUAM, PO BOX EK; AGANA, GU 96910. (#365). **(??).**

GUAM'S YANKEE DOODLE BICENTENNIAL ROCK CONCERTS. ROCK CONCERTS BY THREE BANDS ON GUAM. MUSIC FROM REVOLUTIONARY TIMES THROUGH CONTEMPORARY PERFORMED BY MUSICIANS IN REVOLUTIONARY WAR COSTUMES. (LOCAL). ROBERT CRUZ, DIRECTOR; PARKS AND RECREATION DEPT; C/O GOVERNMENT HOUSE; AGANA, GU 96910. (#23497). **ARBA GRANTEE.**

GUAM/MICRONESIA YOUTH WEEK CONVENTION. ONE YOUTH REPRESENTATIVE FROM EACH OF THE MICRONESIAN ISLANDS AND ONE FROM NATION'S CAPITAL TO MEET WITH GUAMANIAN YOUNG PEOPLE TO REFLECT UPON AMERICAN HERITAGE AND FUTURE. (INT'L). DELFINA AGUIGUI, EXEC DIRECTOR; GUAM AMERICAN REVOLUTION BICENTENNIAL COMMITTEE; OFFICE OF THE GOVERNOR; AGANA, GU 96910. (#23667). **ARBA GRANTEE.**

GUIDEBOOK TO THE EVOLUTION OF ARCHITECTURE ON GUAM. GUAM'S HISTORY SPANS CENTURIES INCLUDING PREHISTORIC STRUCTURES, SPANISH FORTS & BRIDGES, PRE & POST WAR CONSTRUCTION & RECENT, MODERN STRUCTURES; EVOLUTION IS DEPICTED IN PHOTOS, PLANS & COMMENT. (LOCAL). JACK B JONES, CHAIRMAN; GUAM & TRUST TERRITORY CHAP OF AMERICAN INSTITUTE OF ARCHITECTS; PO BOX 283; AGANA, GU 96910. (#19201). **ARBA GRANTEE.**

'HISTORY AND CULTURE OF GUAM' PROJECT. THE DEVELOPMENT OF RESOURCES AND COURSES RELATING TO THE HISTORY AND CULTURE OF GUAM AT THE UNIVERSITY OF GUAM. (ST-WIDE). PEDRO C SANCHEZ, CHAIRMAN; GUAM ARBC; UNIVERSITY OF GUAM-BOX EK; AGANA, GU 96910. (#1195). **ARBA GRANTEE.**

HISTORY OF THE GUAM LEGISLATURE (1950-1975). BOOK DEPICTING THE GROWTH OF DEMOCRACY IN GUAM THROUGH THE DEVELOPMENT OF THE GUAM LEGISLATURE. (ST-WIDE). MADELEINE BORDALLO, COORDINATOR; GUAM AMERICAN REVOLUTION BICENTENNIAL COMMISSION; PO BOX 2950; AGANA, GU 96910. (#27364). **ARBA GRANTEE.**

A PHOTO HISTORY OF VIETNAMESE REFUGEES ON GUAM. A PHOTO HISTORY OF REFUGEES & REPATRIATES ON GUAM SHOWING PATRIOTIC ACTIONS OF THE PEOPLE OF GUAM RENDERING SERVICE TO THE THOUSANDS OF HOMELESS; DOCUMENTATION OF RECENT AMERICAN HISTORY. (INT'L). DOREEN MINSINGER BAST, ASSOC EDITOR; PACIFIC ASIAN STUDIES ASSOCIATION, UNIV OF GUAM; BX EK; AGANA, GU 96910. (#23748). **ARBA GRANTEE.**

PRODUCTION OF 5 TV SPECIALS & DOCUMENTARY, GUAM. PRODUCTION OF 5 TV SPECIALS & DOCUMENTARY ON GUAM, INCLUDING HISTORICAL ASPECTS, ISLAND CRAFTS, BICENTENNIAL ACTIVITIES & CHAMORRO LEGENDS. (LOCAL). FRANCES BAUMANN, DEVELOPMENT DIRECTOR; KGTF-TV, GUAM EDUCATIONAL TELECOMMUNICATIONS CORP; AGANA, GU 96910. (#24891). **ARBA GRANTEE.**

RENOVATION AND RESTORATION AT COCOS ISLAND. RENOVATION, RESTORATION, DEVELOPMENT AND ESTABLISHMENT OF OUTDOOR RECREATIONAL FACILITIES AT COCOS ISLAND. (LOCAL). FELIPE G BORJA, PRESIDENT; MERIZO CIVIC IMPROVEMENT CLUB; PO STATION MERIZO; AGANA, GU 96910. (#11651). **ARBA GRANTEE.**

RESTORATION OF OLD PALACE GROUNDS - AGANA, GU. THE OLD PALACE GROUNDS ARE AN ATTRACTIVE PLACE FOR TOURISTS & THE PEOPLE OF GUAM TO VISIT; THE BUILDINGS ARE CONSIDERED THE OLDEST ON GUAM; BOTH THE GROUNDS AND THE BUILDINGS WILL BE RESTORED. (ST-WIDE). SENATOR FRANK SANTOS, PROJ CHAIRMAN; GUAM BICENTENNIAL COMMISSION; BOX 2950; AGANA, GU 96910. (#25316). **ARBA GRANTEE.**

RETURN TO GUAM PROJECT FOR GUAMANIANS. GUAMANIANS LIVING ON THE U.S. MAINLAND WILL BE ENCOURAGED TO VISIT GUAM DURING 1976 TO PARTICIPATE IN THE YEAR LONG FESTIVAL. (NAT'L). DELFINA T AQUIQUI, EXEC DIRECTOR; GUAM ARBC; UNIV OF GUAM, PO BOX ER; AGANA, GU 96910. (#297). **(??).**

STARS AND STRIPES FLAG DISPLAY IN GUAM. INSTALL FACILITIES AND PURCHASE NEEDS TO PROVIDE FOR PLAZA DISPLAY OF NATIONAL, BICENTENNIAL AND ALL STATE AND TERRITORIAL FLAGS AND HISTORICAL FLAGS AT SPECIAL AND HOLIDAY EVENTS. (ST-WIDE). ROBERT CRUZ, DIRECTOR; PARKS AND GROUNDS DEPARTMENT; C/O GOVERNMENT HOUSE; AGANA, GU 96910. (#22693). **ARBA GRANTEE.**

TEACHING CULTURE & HISTORY OF GUAM REF MATERIAL. THE DEVELOPMENT OF TEACHING AND REFERENCE MATERIALS RELATING TO THE HISTORY AND CULTURE OF GUAM AT THE VARIOUS SCHOOLS ON GUAM. (LOCAL). GLORIA B NELSON, DEPUTY DIRECTOR OF EDUCATION; DEPARTMENT OF EDUCATION; PO BOX DE; AGANA, GU 96910. (#11891).

MAY 1, '74. MUSIC PRESENTATION ON GUAM. ART DISPLAY. CULTURAL REVIVAL PROJECT OF GUAM. FESTIVAL FEATURING FROM CULTURAL RENDITIONS OF THE PACIFIC ISLANDS, TO 20TH CENTURY MUSIC OF OUR TIME WILL BE HOSTED IN THE SUMMER OF 74 & ANNUALLY THEREAFTER. THEME: 'GUAM - AN ISLAND IN HARMONY'. (ST-WIDE). RAYMOND QUINTANILLA, DIR; YOUTH INC, C/O UNIV OF GUAM; PO BOX 1993; AGANA, GU 96910. (#1003-901).

DEC 26 - 30, '75. CHAMORRO DISTRICT BICENTENNIAL CONSERVATION CAMP. EXHIBIT, TOUR AT VARIOUS HISTORICAL SITES AND PARKS ISLANDWIDE IN TERRITORY OF GUAM. (LOCAL). JOHN W SEIGAL, PROJ DIR; CHAMORRO DISTRICT ALOHA COUNCIL BOY SCOUTS OF AMERICA; 1291 MANGO DR; APO SAN FRAN, CA 96334. (#100708-1).

JULY 1, '76. RIBBON CUTTING CEREMONY ON OLD PALACE GROUNDS. CEREMONY AT PLAZA DE ESPANA. (ST-WIDE). MS DELFINA T AGUIGUI, DIR; GUAM BICENTENNIAL COMMISSION; BOX 2950; AGANA, GU 96910. (#25316-1).

JULY 2 - 21, '76. BICENTENNIAL LIBERATION DAYS CELEBRATION. JULY 4 PARADE; MUSIC ENTERTAINMENTS DURING 21 DAYS OF CELEBRATION, FIREWORKS, CONCESSION, RIDES, ARTS AND CRAFTS DISPLAY, AGRICULTURAL EXHIBIT, GAME FOR ALL SPORTS COMPETITION, QUEEN'S CORONATION BALL. AT CAMP ASAN. (ST-WIDE). FRANCISCA V QUINTANILLA; BICENTENNIAL LIBERATION DAY COMMITTEE; OFFICE OF THE GOVERNOR, BOX 2950; AGANA, GU 96910. (#26543-1).

BARRIGADA

BICENTENNIAL OPEN HOUSE - BARRIGADA, GU. STUDENTS ARE COMPETING IN BICENT PROJECTS IN ART, COMPOSITION, MUSIC & DRAMA WITH THEMES OF HERITAGE, FESTIVAL & HORIZON; PROJECTS WILL BE JUDGED & AWARDS GIVEN AT THE BICENTENNIAL OPEN HOUSE. (LOCAL). LINDA HOLLINGSWORTH, ADVISOR; BARRIGADA JUNIOR HIGH SCHOOL NATIONAL HONOR SOCIETY; BARRIGADA, GU 96910. (#25221). **ARBA GRANTEE.**

MAY 30, '76. BICENTENNIAL OPEN HOUSE. STUDENT PROJECTS IN ART, COMPOSITION, MUSIC & DRAMA BASED ON BICENTENNIAL THEMES OF HERITAGE, FESTIVAL & HORIZONS WILL BE JUDGED; THE AWARDS WILL BE GIVEN AT THE OPEN HOUSE. AT BARRIGADA JUNIOR HIGH SCHOOL. (LOCAL). LINDA HOLLINGSWORTH; BARRIGADA JUNIOR HIGH SCHOOL NATIONAL HONOR SOCIETY; BARRIGADA, GU 96910. (#25221-1).

MARIANA IS

JULY 4 - 5, '76. 4TH OF JULY PARADE WITH INTERNATIONAL PARTICIPATION. PARADE. (INT'L). CAPT W Z DEMENT; MARINE BARRACKS GUAM; FPO; SAN FRANCISCO, CA 96630. (#200013-1).

Hawaii

Hawaii Bicentennial Commission

Commissioned by Act 98 of the 1970 Legislature

Theme: Hawaii's People Celebrate—America's Bicentennial

ARBA Statistics

Officially Recognized
Communities—4
Colleges/Universities—1
Military Installations—11
BINET Projects—97
Events—103
1976 Population—887,000

Bicentennial Archives

Hawaii State Archives
Iolani Palace Grounds
Honolulu, Hawaii 96813

Membership

Nine members appointed by the governor with Senate approval.

Thurston Twigg-Smith, *chairman* (1972-76)
Sam Okinaga, *vice-chairman* (1972-76)
James D. Evans (1972-76)
John G. Simpson (1972-76)
Hideto Kono (1975-76)
Paul W. Goudsmit (1975-76)
Sandy Young (1974-76)
Gabriel I (1975-76)
Monsignor Charles Kekumanu (1973-76)
Shelly Mark (1972-75)
(Mrs.) B. Howell Bond (1972-73)
Lowell S. Dillingham (1972-75)
(Mrs.) Piilani Ramler (1973-74)
Donald K. Tokunaga (1972-73)
Kenneth Harding (1974-75)
Turk Tokita (1972-74)

Staff

John Pincetich, *executive director* (1972-July 1974; 1975-)
(Mrs.) Piilani Ramler, *executive director* (July 1974-January 1975)

Hawaii

Hawaii's Bicentennial program during the past year can be best described with the state's colorful colloquial phrase: "Chop Suey."

In it was a bit of everything—for everybody.

It came together after three years of all-island efforts by many hundreds of people meeting, conferring, arguing, imploring. And then, doing things. Often, their own things.

The program ranged from the evanescence of a sand-building contest at Waikiki Beach to the sturdy uprightness of a restored church steeple at Kaupo, Maui; from the melodic unity of a world-wide ukulele contest to the complex harmony of a special symphonic work; from a backward reach of hundreds of years to retrace canoe voyages of early Polynesians in their discovery of Hawaii to an architectural exhibit showing how Hawaiians might be living in the quadricentennial year of 2176.

For 1976, it began the morning of January 1 with a statewide "gathering in prayer," a five minute spiritual offering simultaneously telecast/ broadcast throughout Hawaii—a brief time when all Hawaii was united in a common spirit of thankfulness.

And it continued from January through December with hundreds of other events extolling patriotic themes and examining Hawaii's unique cultural and ethnic contributions to our 200 year old nation.

There were cultural events ranging from artistic displays to festivals featuring the many different peoples of Hawaii: Hawaiian, Japanese, Chinese, Portuguese, Filipino, Samoan and Tahitian.

A Hawaiian pageant, *The Golden Gift,* opened the year and highlighted the Captain Cook era of Hawaiian history. Held in the rotunda of the new State Capitol building, which represents a volcano, the program brought to life a sense of cohesion between the old and the new Hawaii. A similar program, *The First Aloha,* ended the year in the same unique setting.

Both the Japanese and Chinese communities staged numerous activities that brought into focus the contributions of the Orient to historical and present day Hawaii.

But the Bicentennial was also books, ranging from a translation of political commentary in various old Hawaiian newspapers to the state's very first *Encyclopedia of Hawaii* and a series of pamphlets which covered the major books about Hawaii in more than a dozen categories.

Several movies and slide shows were produced: one depicting the impact of Hawaii's artists on its culture, another capturing the wildlife—the sea and land birds—of Hawaii's remote Leeward Islands.

Many Bicentennial projects were helped with grant money from the American Revolution Bicentennial Administration, state appropriations and funds raised by the commission from the public. All projects generally fell within the three national themes: *Heritage '76,* calling to mind the fundamental precepts of the past; *Festival USA,* engaging the realities and opportunities of the present; and *Horizons '76,* embracing the challenge of the future.

It all sort of came together on the weekend of July 4th, with dozens of public events, including the largest parade in Hawaii's history. The Bicentennial year, long cuffed about by critics, suddenly got rave reviews.

For a fleeting moment, in Hawaii and elsewhere, 1976 seemed the best of the 200 years since America's revolutionaries stood fast for justice, freedom and the fundamental rights of man.

EWA BEACH

EWA, THE PEOPLES' HISTORY - BOOK, HI. A HISTORICAL RECORD DURING THE LAST 25 YEARS OF THE LIFESTYLE OF SUGAR PLANTATION WORKERS AND THEIR CULTURAL CONTRIBUTIONS TO THE STATE. (LOCAL). MRS EMOGENE MARTIN, GENERAL CHAIRMAN; LEEWARD HAWAII BICENTENNIAL STEERING COMMITTEE; 91-840 HANAKAHI ST; EWA BEACH, HI 96706. (#22673). **ARBA GRANTEE.**

'PRIDE IN EWA' FLOAT FOR PACIFICA '76 PARADE. A FLORAL FLOAT IS PLANNED WHICH WILL DEPICT EWA'S CONTRIBUTION TO THE ECONOMIC & CULTURAL GROWTH OF HAWAII & WILL BE IN KEEPING WITH THE THEME OF THE PARADE TO SALUTE ETHNIC GROUPS. (LOCAL). MRS EMOGENE MARTIN, GENERAL CHAIRMAN; LEEWARD HAWAII BICENTENNIAL STEERING COMMITTEE; 91-840 HUNAKAHI ST; EWA BEACH, HI 96706. (#22672).

HI VOLCAN NP

JAN 1 - DEC 31, '76. ARTISTS IN RESIDENCE AT HAWAII VOLCANOES NP. ON DISPLAY AT THE VOLCANO HOUSE ARE PAINTINGS OF HAWAIIAN LIFE ON THE LAND. THERE ARE ON-GOING DEMONSTATIONS, PERFORMANCES, AND CLASSES AT THE VOLCANO HOUSE IN HULA, PHOTOGRAPHY, WOODCARVING, WEAVING, PUPPETRY, AND INSTRUMENTAL MUSIC. AT 1877 VOLCANO HOUSE, HAWAII VOLCANOES NATIONAL PARK. (REGN'L). HAWAII VOLCANOES NP; VOLCANO ARTS CENTER AND NATIONAL PARK SERVCIE; HAWAII VOLCAN, HI 96718. (#6729-157).

JAN 1 - DEC 31, '76. LIVING HISTORY DEMONSTRATIONS AT HAWAII VOLCANOES NATL PK. LIVING HISTORY PROGRAM ON THE PEOPLE OF ANCIENT KALAPANA. INCLUDES DEMONSTRATIONS OF AND INSTRUCTION ON LAUHALA WEAVING, HAWAIIAN FOOD PREPARATION, HAWAIIAN MUSIC, AND HAWAIIAN LANGUAGE. AT WAHAULA VISITOR CENTER WITHIN THE PARK. (REGN'L). HAWAII VOLCANOES NP; NATIONAL PARK SERVICE; HAWAII VOLCAN, HI 96718. (#6727-66).

JUNE 1 - DEC 31, '76. MURAL EXHIBITS OF HAWAIIAN & EARLY WESTERN HISTORY HAWAII VOLCANOES. PHOTOGRAPHIC MURALS OF THE HAWAIIAN AND EARLY WESTERN HISTORY OF HAWAII VOLCANOES NATIONAL PARK AND LOCAL AREA. AT AT 1877 VOLCANO HOUSE WITHIN THE PARK. (REGN'L). HAWAII VOLCANOES NP; NATIONAL PARK SERVICE; HAWAII VOLC, HI 96718. (#6729-31).

JULY 1 - DEC 31, '76. MURAL OF WAHAULA HEIAU AT HAWAII VOLCANOES NP. THIS PAINTING CREATES A SCENE AT THE WAHAULA HEIAU, WHICH WAS THE LAST MAJOR HAWAIIAN TEMPLE OF PUNA, AS IT MIGHT HAVE APPEARED BEFORE EXPLORERS LANDED IN HAWAII. AT WAHAULA VISITOR CENTER, HAWAII VOLCANOES NATIONAL PARK. (REGN'L). HAWAII VOLCANOES NP; NATIONAL PARK SERVICE; HILO, HI 96718. (#6729-160).

AUG 8 - 21, '76. ARTISTS-IN-THE-PARKS EXHIBIT VISITS HAWAII VOLCANOES NP. THIS ART EXHIBIT CONSISTS OF 21 ORIGINAL PAINTINGS, EACH OF WHICH IS IDENTIFIED WITH PERSONS, PLACES, OR EVENTS OF THE AMER REVOLUTION. AT WAILOA CENTER. (REGN'L). SUPERINTENDENT; NATIONAL PARK SERVICE; WAILOA CENTER; HILO, HI 96720. (#1474-21).

HILO

BICENTENNIAL FOOTPATH IN HILO, HI. RECONSTRUCTION AND DEVELOPMENT OF ANCIENT HAWAIIAN FOOT TRAIL AND ENVIRONS. (LOCAL). RICHARD A MORTEMORE, DIRECTOR; HAWAII 2000 OUTDOOR EDUCATION CENTER; STAINBACK HIGHWAY; HILO, HI 96720. (#10605). **ARBA GRANTEE.**

BIG ISLAND 4TH OF JULY FESTIVAL, HILO, HI. TRADITIONAL 4TH OF JULY CELEBRATION-FIREWORKS, PARADES, PAGEANTRY, ETHNIC SONGS & DANCES, GAMES, CONTESTS, CANOE RACING, ARTS & CRAFTS AND ENTERTAINMENT. (LOCAL). ED CHEPLIC, PROJ CHAIRMAN; HAWAII COUNTY BICENTENNIAL COMMITTEE; 25 AUPUNI ST; HILO, HI 96720. (#25279). **ARBA GRANTEE.**

KOHALA TONG WO SOCIETY EXHIBIT, HI. DEVELOPMENT OF UNDERSTANDING AND APPRECIATION OF CULTURAL DIVERSITY AND DISSEMINATION OF KNOWLEDGE TO THIS END THROUGH EDUCATIONAL EXHIBITS, PERFORMANCES, AND PERSONAL INTERACTION. (LOCAL). CLYDE D G WONG, MUSEUM CONSULTANT; KOHALA TONG WO SOCIETY; 112 KALO ST; HILO, HI 96720. (#23723). **ARBA GRANTEE.**

PORTABLE HISTORIC DISPLAY - HILO, HAWAII. PORTABLE EXHIBITS OF HILO, HAWAII 100 YEARS AGO. (LOCAL). EDWARD CHEPLIC, COORDINATOR; 368 TASK FORCE; 25 AUPUNI ST; HILO, HI 96720. (#11009). **ARBA GRANTEE.**

PRESERVATION OF HISTORIC DOCUMENTS IN HAWAII. PRESERVING VALUABLE DOCUMENTS WILL BE A BICENTENNIAL PROJECT. (LOCAL). ORLANDO H LYMAN, DIRECTOR; LYMAN MUSEUM; HILO, HI 96720. (#12148). **ARBA GRANTEE.**

SUGAR PLANTATION HISTORY EXHIBIT, HI. AUDIO-VISUAL DOCUMENTARY OF LIFE IN SUGAR PLANTATION CAMPS, USING PHOTOGRAPHS AND TAPE RECORDINGS OF INTERVIEWS STRESSING CONTRIBUTION OF IMMIGRANT GROUPS. (LOCAL). DR JOHN T BOWEN, ASSOCIATE PROFESSOR; UNIVERSITY OF HAWAII, HILO; 461 W LANIKAULA ST; HILO, HI 96720. (#23724). **ARBA GRANTEE.**

JULY 4 - 5, '74. COUNTY OF HAWAII JULY 4, 1974, FESTIVAL. JULY 4TH FESTIVITIES INCLUDING MUSIC, GAMES, COMMUNITY PICNICS, & CHURCHES' RECOGNITION BY RINGING BELLS. (REGN'L). THURSTON TWIGG-SMITH; HAWAII BICENTENNIAL COMMISSION; PO BOX 2359; HONOLULU, HI 96804. (#358-903).

AUG 14, '75. NATL PK SVC '...A LITTLE LOOK AROUND' VISITS HILO. THIS SHORT PROGRAM FEATURES ACTORS PORTRAYING FAMOUS AMERICANS OF THE PAST WHO'VE RETURNED TO SEE AMERICA'S GROWTH. (REGN'L). SUPERINTENDENT; NATIONAL PARK SERVICE - HAWAII VOLCANOES NATIONAL PARK; HI VOLCANOES, HI 96718. (#5653-205).

JULY 4, '76. BIG ISLAND 4TH OF JULY FESTIVAL. CELEBRATION TO INCLUDE FIREWORKS, PARADES, PAGEANTRY, ETHNIC SONGS AND DANCES, GAMES AND MANY OTHER ACTIVITIES. (LOCAL). ED CHEPLIC, CHAIRMAN; HAWAII COUNTY BICENTENNIAL COMMITTEE; 25 AUPUNI ST; HILO, HI 96270. (#25279-1).

JULY 20 - AUG 5, '76. SUGAR PLANTATION HISTORY EXHIBIT. AUDIO-VISUAL DOCUMENTARY OF LIFE IN SUGAR PLANTATION CAMPS, USING PHOTOGRAPHS AND TAPE RECORDINGS OF INTERVIEWS, STRESSING CONTRIBUTIONS OF IMMIGRANT GROUPS. WILL BE SHOWN IN HONOLULU SEPTEMBER 1 TO 30, 1976. (LOCAL). DR JOHN BOWEN, ASSOC PROF; UNIVERSITY OF HAWAII, HILO; 461 W LANIKAULA ST; HILO, HI 96720. (#23724-1).

HONAUNAU

JUNE 29 - JULY 4, '75. BICENT COMMEMORATION - THE CITY OF REFUGE CELEBRATES ANCIENT WAYS. FESTIVAL. (ST-WIDE). JOHN TYLER, PROJ MGR; HONAUNAU - CITY OF REFUGE; CITY OF REFUGE; HONAUNAU KONA, HI 96726. (#100123-1).

AUG 15, '75. NATL PK SVC '...A LITTLE LOOK AROUND' VISITS CITY OF REFUGE NHP. THIS SHORT PROGRAM FEATURES ACTORS PORTRAYING FAMOUS AMERICANS OF THE PAST WHO'VE RETURNED TO SEE AMERICA'S GROWTH. (REGN'L). SUPERINTENDENT; NATIONAL PARK SERVICE - CITY OF REFUGE NATL HISTORIC PARK; HONAUNAU, HI 96726. (#5653-204).

JULY 1 - 4, '76. HAWAIIAN CULTURAL FESTIVAL. PRESENTATION OF SKILLS AND CRAFTS ASSOCIATED WITH CANOES, TRAVEL GAMES, SPORTS, METHODS USED TO OBTAIN FOOD FROM THE SEA, HOMEARTS, MUSIC AND FOOD PREPARATION IN ANCIENT HAWAII. AT CITY OF REFUGE PALACE GROUND AREA. (REGN'L). CITY OF REFUGE NHS; NATIONAL PARK SERVICE; PO BOX 128; HONAUNAU, HI 96726. (#6727-233).

HONOLULU

AMERICAN CIVIL LIBERTIES UNION FILM PROJECT, HI. HAWAII'S LEGAL CASES SHOWING THAT THE BILL OF RIGHTS IS A LIVING DOCUMENT, PRODUCED ON FILM AND TV. (ST-WIDE). EVAN SHIRLEY, LIASON; AMERICAN CIVIL LIBERTIES UNION OF HAWAII; SUITE 200, 888 MILILANI ST; HONOLULU, HI 96813. (#16977). **ARBA GRANTEE.**

AMERICAN MUSIC CONCERT SERIES, HONOLULU, HI. CONCERTS WILL INCLUDE JAZZ ENSEMBLE, ORCHESTRA, SOLOISTS, BAND AND DANCE MUSIC. (LOCAL). DR ALLEN R TRUBITT, CHAIRMAN; UNIV OF HAWAII, MUSIC DEPT; 2411 DOYLE ST; HONOLULU, HI 96822. (#15296). **ARBA GRANTEE.**

BIBLIOGRAPHY OF PUBLICATIONS ABOUT HAWAII. GUIDE TO BOOKS ABOUT HAWAII. PUBLICATION IN 16 PAMPHLETS BY SUBJECT. (ST-WIDE). ROBERT BOOM, SUB-COMM CHAIRMAN; HAWAII BICENTENNIAL COMMISSION; PO BOX 4349; HONOLULU, HI 96813. (#852). **ARBA GRANTEE.**

BICENTENNIAL CONCERT - HONOLULU SYMPHONY. ALL-AMERICAN COMPOSERS WILL BE FEATURED IN WAIKIKI SHELL CONCERTS AS SPECIAL MUSICAL SALUTE TO THE BICENTENNIAL. (LOCAL). CATHARINE HITE, CHAIRMAN; HONOLULU SYMPHONY SOCIETY; 1000 BISHOP ST; HONOLULU, HI 96713. (#10680). **ARBA GRANTEE.**

BICENTENNIAL FLAG PAGEANT - HONOLULU, HI. SUNSET PARADE AND BICENTENNIAL FLAG PAGEANT DEPICTING HISTORICAL FLAGS TO FLY OVER HAWAII - CONDUCTED BY MARINES OF MARINE BARRACKS, HAWAII. (ST-WIDE). 1/LT GL SILLER, JR, TRAINING OFFICER; MARINE BARRACKS H&S CO OPERATIONS AND TRAINING; FDO; SAN FRANCISCO, CA 96610. (#31077).

BICENTENNIAL GYMNASTICS MEET FOR WOMEN, HI. A WEEK-LONG COMPETITION OF GYMNASTIC EVENTS INVOLVING INTERNATIONAL PARTICIPANTS. (INT'L). MITCHELL BAROSH, DIRECTOR; HAWAII SCHOOL OF GYMNASTICS; BOX 746; KAILUA, HI 96734. (#26965). **ARBA GRANTEE.**

BICENTENNIAL SEEDLING PLANTING IN HONOLULU, HI. THREE GEORGE WASHINGTON TULIP POPLAR TREES AT WHEELER AFB, FIRST OF ITS KIND IN STATE. DONATED TO AIR FORCE HAWAII BY MOUNT VERNON LADIES ASSOCIATION OF UNION, VA. (LOCAL). COL RICHARD THOMPSON, BICENTENNIAL COORDINATOR; 15TH AIR BASE WING, HICKAM AIR FORCE BASE; HONOLULU, HI 96553. (#32280).

BICENTENNIAL SERIES SCRIPTOGRAPHIC BOOKLETS - HI. DISTRIBUTE EDUCATIONAL MATERIAL RELATING TO OUR DEMOCRATIC HERITAGE AND OUR GOVERNMENT INSTITUTIONS TO SHIPYARDERS. (LOCAL). ALFRED WONG, CHAIRMAN; PEARL HARBOR NAVAL SHIPYARD, CODE 140; BOX 400, FPO; SAN FRANCISCO, CA 96610. (#29575).

CABLE TV FOR CITIZEN PARTICIPATION, HONOLULU, HI. DEMONSTRATION MODELS OF TWO-WAY AUDIOVISUAL EQUIPMENT & TECHNOLOGY WHICH WOULD AID IN INCREASING CITIZEN PARTICIPATION & ACCOUNTABILITY OF OFFICIALS IN THE DEMOCRATIC PROCESS. (ST-WIDE). JOHN PINCETICH, EXEC DIRECTOR; HAWAII BICENTENNIAL COMMISSION; PO BOX 2359; HONOLULU, HI 96804. (#12263). **ARBA GRANTEE.**

CAPTAIN COOK PORTFOLIO - PROJ OF HONOLULU, HI. DRAWINGS, PRINTS AND PAINTINGS ON THE LAST DAYS OF NAVIGATOR JAMES COOK WITH A TEXT BY EDWARD A STASACK; TO BE ON EXHIBIT IN HONOLULU. (ST-WIDE). JOHN PINCETICH, EXEC DIRECTOR; HAWAII BICENTENNIAL COMMITTEE; 250 S KING ST; HONOLULU, HI 96813. (#10196). **ARBA GRANTEE.**

A CHILD'S HISTORY OF AMERICA, HONOLULU, HI. GLIMPSES OF AMERICA'S HISTORY AS TOLD BY OVER 400 OF AMERICA'S CHILDREN IN THEIR OWN STORIES & ILLUSTRATIONS. PUBLICATION IS 96 PAGES, IN FULL COLOR. (REGN'L). EDWARD J MCGRATH, JR, DIRECTOR; ISLAND HERITAGE LTD; 556 KAMANI ST; HONOLULU, HI 96813. (#19987).

CHINESE FOLK ART EXHIBIT - HONOLULU, HI. CHINESE FOLK ART ASSEMBLED FROM MUSEUMS IN NEW YORK, CHICAGO, SAN FRANCISCO AND HONOLULU WILL BE ON EXHIBIT. (ST-WIDE). MRS GUSTAV ECKE, PROFESSOR OF ART; UNIV OF HAWAII; 129 GEORGE HALL, 2560 CAMPUS RD; HONOLULU, HI 96822. (#16184). **ARBA GRANTEE.**

CITY & COUNTY OF HONOLULU, FESTIVAL FOR THE FOURTH. 'COUNTDOWN' CONCEPT WHICH EXPRESSES ITSELF AS '200 MINUS 3' IN 1973, '200 MINUS 2 IN '74' ETC. AN EFFORT TO GENERATE INTEREST & STIMULATE PLANNING & ACTIVITY IN CONNECTION WITH THE BICENTENNIAL. (ST-WIDE). THURSTON TWIGG-SMITH, CHAIRMAN; HAWAII BICENTENNIAL COMMISSION; PO BOX 2359; HONOLULU, HI 96804. (#1200). **ARBA GRANTEE.**

COOK COLLECTION PUBLISHED IN HONOLULU, HI. DESCRIPTIONS OF THE CAPTAIN COOK COLLECTIONS, ON DISPLAY IN EUROPEAN MUSEUMS, WILL BE TRANSLATED AND PUBLISHED. (ST-WIDE). THOMAS NICKERSON, PROJ COORDINATOR; HAWAII BICENTENNIAL COMMISSION; 250 S KING ST; HONOLULU, HI 96813. (#11383). **ARBA GRANTEE.**

COUNTDOWN TO '76 FESTIVAL IN HONOLULU, HI. ART, AQUATICS, GAMES & MUSIC ARE ALL PART OF THE FESTIVITIES. (LOCAL). MORONI MEDEIROS, CHAIRMAN; CITY BICENTENNIAL COUNTDOWN COMMITTEE; KAPIOLANI BANDSTAND; HONOLULU, HI 96815. (#11382). **ARBA GRANTEE.**

EAST/WEST CENTER SEMINAR ON THE BICENTENNIAL. THEME 'THE AMERICAN REVOLUTION: ITS MEANING TO ASIANS & AMERICANS'. PARTICIPANTS FROM JAPAN, KOREA, PAKISTAN, INDONESIA, MALAYSIA, PHILIPPINES, THAILAND & REPUBLIC OF CHINA. KEY SPEAKER-RICHARD B MORRIS. (INT'L). DR JOHN BROWNELL, VICE PRESIDENT; THE EAST/WEST CENTER OF THE UNIV OF HAWAII; 1777 EAST/WEST CENTER; HONOLULU, HI 96822. (#33267). **ARBA RECOGNIZED.**

THE EDMUND WILSON PAPERS. AN EDITION OF THE UNPUBLISHED NOTEBOOKS, DIARIES, LETTERS OF THE LATE CRITIC EDMUND WILSON IN A SERIES OF VOLUMES. (NAT'L). ARTHUR N L CHIU, ASSOCIATE DEAN; OFFICE OF RESEARH ADMINISTRATION, UNIV OF HAWAII; 2540 MAILE WAY; HONOLULU, HI 96822. (#3807).

ENSEMBLE PLAYERS GUILD PRESENTATIONS - HI. STATE-WIDE CHAMBER, ORCHESTRAL AND OPERATIC PRESENTATIONS FEATURING AMERICAN COMPOSERS AND HAWAIIAN THEMES. (ST-WIDE). RICHARD CORNWELL, MANAGER; ENSEMBLE PLAYERS GUILD OF HAWAII; 4754 KAHALA AVE; HONOLULU, HI 96816. (#20823). **ARBA GRANTEE.**

ESSAY CONTESTS AT PEARL HARBOR NAVAL SHIPYARD - HI. ONE CONTEST FOR DEPENDENT CHILDREN ON 'WHAT THE SPIRIT OF '76 MEANS TO ME'; THE OTHER ESSAY CONTEST, OPEN TO ALL AT THE SHIPYARD, IS ON 'WHAT AMERICA MEANS TO ME'. (LOCAL). ALFRED WONG, CHAIRMAN; PEARL HARBOR NAVAL SHIPYARD, CODE 140; BOX 400, FPO; SAN FRANCISCO, CA 96610. (#29581).

FESTIVAL - HONOLULU COUNTY, HI. THE FESTIVAL WILL INCLUDE ART, MUSIC, AQUATICS, PHYSICAL FITNESS AND MARTIAL ARTS. (LOCAL). MORONI MEDEIROS, CHAIRMAN; HONOLULU BICENTENNIAL COMMITTEE; KAPIOLANI BANDSTAND; HONOLULU, HI 96815. (#12546).

FUTURES DEVELOPMENT PROJECT OF HAWAII. TO PROVIDE HAWAII'S DECISIONMAKERS WITH A CONCEPTION OF THE FUTURE OF THE STATE DECIDE TO TAKE. SEEKS TO ENCOURAGE CITIZENS TO INCREASE PARTICIPATION IN FORMULATING FUTURE POLICIES. (ST-WIDE). RICHARD BARBER, PROJ DIRECTOR; HAWAII BICENTENNIAL COMMISSION; PO BOX 2359; HONOLULU, HI 96804. (#1202). **ARBA GRANTEE.**

GENERAL INTRODUCTION TO PACIFIC CULTURES - HI. AN ANNOTATED BIBLIOGRAPHY ON MUSIC, DANCE, CRAFTS, ART FORMS AND GENERAL CULTURE OF HAWAII, TAHITI, SAMOA, FIJI, AND NEW ZEALAND. (LOCAL). VICKY L MCGRATH, DIRECTOR; 1634 MAKIKI ST; HONOLULU, HI 96822. (#24723). **ARBA GRANTEE.**

HAWAII BICENTENNIAL WATER CARNIVAL, HONOLULU. WATER SPORTS DISPLAY AND PERFORMANCES; COMPETITION IN SKIING, JUMPING, FLAG CARRYING, KITE FLYING AND RACES. (ST-WIDE). KENNETH BROCKMAN, TREASURER; HAWAII POWER BOAT ASSOC; 531 WAIKAMILO RD; HONOLULU, HI 96817. (#26947). **ARBA GRANTEE.**

HAWAII COUNTY FESTIVAL FOR THE FOURTH PROJECT. 'COUNTDOWN'CONCEPT, '200 MINUS 2 PROJECT' AN EFFORT TO GENERATE INTEREST AND STIMULATE PLANNING & ACTIVITY IN CONNECTION WITH THE BICENTENNIAL. (THE 1974 CELEBRATION). (ST-WIDE). THURSTON TWIGG-SMITH, CHAIRMAN; HAWAII BICENTENNIAL COMMISSION C/O GOVERNOR'S OFFICE; BOX 2359; HONOLULU, HI 96804. (#1199). **ARBA GRANTEE.**

HAWAII ENCYCLOPEDIA. AN ENCYCLOPEDIA WHICH WILL OFFER CONCISE COMPREHENSIVE INFORMATION ABOUT HAWAII; ITS SCIENCE, LITERATURE,HISTORY, PEOPLE, & ECONOMICS. (ST-WIDE). ROBERT BOOM, CHRMN PUBLICATIONS COMM; HAWAII BICENTENNIAL COMMISSION; PO BOX 4349; HONOLULU, HI 96813. (#355). **ARBA GRANTEE.**

HAWAII WATER RESOURCES REGIONAL STUDY AND PLAN. THE STUDY WILL RESULT IN A COMPREHENSIVE PLAN FOR THE CONSERVATION, DEVELOPMENT AND USE OF HAWAII'S WATER AND RELATED LAND RESOURCES INVOLVING FEDERAL, STATE AND COUNTY GOVERNMENTS & PRIVATE INTERESTS. (ST-WIDE). MANABU TAGOMORI, STUDY MANAGER; HAWAII WATER

HONOLULU – CONTINUED

RESOURCES REGIONAL STUDY; 190 S KING ST; HONOLULU, HI 96813. (#20090).

HAWAII 2176 - QUADRICENTENNIAL CITY. A CEREMONIAL EXPOSITION WITH EXHIBITS AND DISPLAYS OF CITIES PAST, PRESENT AND TWO HUNDRED YEARS INTO THE FUTURE. (ST-WIDE). JOHN PINCETICH, EXECUTIVE DIRECTOR; HAWAII BICENTENNIAL COMMISSION; 250 S KING ST; HONOLULU, HI 96813. (#15290). **ARBA GRANTEE.**

HAWAIIAN RAILWAY RESTORATION. TO RESTORE & OPERATE EXISTING 12-MI. R.R. AND HISTORICALLY SIGNIFICANT R.R. EQUIPMENT FOR EDUCATIONAL & RECREATIONAL PURPOSES. PROVIDE LIVING HISTORY EXPERIENCE OF SUGAR PLANTATION ERA IN HAWAII. (ST-WIDE). NICHOLAS A CARTER, VICE PRESIDENT; HAWAIIAN RAILWAY SOCIETY; BOX 11126; HONOLULU, HI 96814. (#1148). **ARBA GRANTEE.**

HAWAII-POLYNESIAN VOYAGAGE PHILATELIC COVERS, HI. A SERIES OF CACHETED COVERS MARKING VARIOUS EVENTS OF THE PREPARATIONS & ACTUAL VOYAGE; FINAL LIMITED EDITION OF 1000 COVERS WILL BE CARRIED ON THE 1976 TRIP BETWEEN HAWAII & TAHITI. (LOCAL). KAY H HOKE, PROJ DIRECTOR; HAWAIIAN PHILATELIC SOCIETY; PO BOX 10115; HONOLULU, HI 96816. (#12020).

HAWAII-TAHITI CANOE VOYAGE. CREW OF 24 WILL RECREATE PREHISTORIC CONDITIONS OF ORIGINAL POLYNESIAN VOYAGE IN DOUBLE HULL CANOE DESIGNED & BUILT BY POLYNESIAN EXPERTS & NAUTICAL AUTHORITIES. (INT'L). DR BEN FINNEY, DIRECTOR; POLYNESIAN VOYAGING SOCIETY; PO BOX 2359; HONOLULU, HI 96804. (#354). **ARBA GRANTEE.**

HEALTHING HAWAII CONVOCATION, HONOLULU, HI. PURPOSE IS THE IDENTIFICATION OF MAJOR HEALTH DETERMINANTS, EVALUATION OF EFFECTIVENESS OF LOCAL HEALTH CARE & FAMILIARIZATION OF THE COMMUNITY WITH HEALTH ASSISTANCE AVAILABLE TO INCREASE WELL-BEING. (ST-WIDE). WALLY MIYAZONO, COORDINATOR; PACIFIC HEALTH RESEARCH INSTITUTE; 1000 WARD AVE; HONOLULU, HI 96814. (#21159). **ARBA GRANTEE.**

HISTORY MOBILE FOR STATE TOUR OF HAWAII. REDESIGNING OF ARTMOBILE FOR TRAVEL THROUGHOUT THE STATE AS AID TO TEACHING AMERICAN HISTORY. (ST-WIDE). STANLEY YAMAMOTO, SPECIALIST; STATE OF HAWAII DEPARTMENT OF EDUCATION; 1390 MILLER ST; HONOLULU, HI 96813. (#15788). **ARBA GRANTEE.**

HONOLULU BICENTENNIAL MARATHON. FOURTH ANNUAL HONOLULU MARATHON WITH ROYAL RUNNER THEME. (LOCAL). DR JACK H SCAFF, JR, DIRECTOR; HONOLULU MARATHON ASSOC; 550 S BERETANIA ST; HONOLULU, HI 96813. (#17926). **ARBA GRANTEE.**

HONOLULU'S HO'OLAULEA MAKAHIKI CRATER FESTIVAL. 3-DAY EVENT, BEGINNING WITH BLOWING OF TRADITIONAL CONCH SHELL & HAWAIIAN CHANTERS; WILL HAVE AUTHENTIC VILLAGES, CRAFTS, DANCING, MUSIC & DISPLAYS. (ST-WIDE). MORONI MEDEIROS, CRATER FESTIVAL DIRECTOR; CITY & COUNTY OF HONOLULU BICENTENNIAL COMMITTEE; KAPIOLANI BANDSTAND; HONOLULU, HI 96815. (#14395). **ARBA GRANTEE.**

HUMAN RESOURCES DEVELOPMENT, HONOLULU, HI. RESTORATION AND PRESERVATION OF CLOTHING AND HOUSING OF HAWAII'S ETHNIC GROUPS FOR NEWLY FORMED MUSEUM. (LOCAL). MARY ELLEN DES JARLAIS, PROFESSOR; HUMAN RESOURCES DEVELOPMENT, UNIV OF HAWAII, MANOA; 2515 CAMPUS RD; HONOLULU, HI 96822. (#20690). **ARBA GRANTEE.**

IN PURSUIT OF DEMOCRACY: A FILM SERIES IN HAWAII. A SERIES OF FILMS THAT WILL PRESENT EVERYDAY PEOPLE IN PURSUIT OF DEMOCRACY WILL BE PRODUCED. (LOCAL). DR GARY KRANE, CONSULTANT; PEOPLE'S FUND; CHURCH OF THE CROSSROADS; HONOLULU, HI 96822. (#16123). **ARBA GRANTEE.**

INVOLVEMENT OF KEY SHIPYARD LEADERS - HONOLULU, HI. INVOLVEMENT OF KEY SHIPYARD LEADERS IN DEVELOPING THE REAFFIRMATION OF THE SPIRIT OF '76 PROGRAMS. (LOCAL). ALFRED WONG, CHAIRMAN; PEARL HARBOR NAVAL SHIPYARD, CODE 140; BOX 400, FPO; SAN FRANCISCO, CA 96610. (#29580).

JAPANESE CULTURAL CELEBRATION IN HONOLULU. JAPANESE CULTURAL SOCIETY CELEBRATION TO INCLUDE CULTURAL EXHIBITS, DANCES, MUSIC, SPORTS & LANTERN PARADE. (ST-WIDE). RAYMOND H INAFUKU, CHAIRMAN; UNITED JAPANESE SOCIETY OF HAWAII BICENTENNIAL CELEBRATION; 1149 BETHEL ST; HONOLULU, HI 96813. (#19973). **ARBA GRANTEE.**

KA LEI NO KANE - HAWAIIAN OPERA. ONE ACT HAWAIIAN OPERA BASED ON TWO WARRING CHIEFS WHO MEET TO SETTLE THEIR DIFFERENCES ON THE PLAIN BETWEEN MAUNA KEA AND MAUNA LOA. (ST-WIDE). RICHARD CORNWELL; ENSEMBLE PLAYERS GUILD; 4744 KAHALA AVE; HONOLULU, HI 96818. (#25762). **ARBA GRANTEE.**

KAMEHAMEHA POST OFFICE GROUNDS PROJECT, HI. LANDSCAPING AND BEAUTIFICATION OF KAMEHAMEHAV POST OFFICE GROUNDS. (LOCAL). MRS ALAN S DAVIS, PRESIDENT; THE OUTDOOR CIRCLE GARDEN CLUB OF HONOLULU; 200 N VINEYARD BLVD; HONOLULU, HI 96817. (#11959). **ARBA GRANTEE.**

KAUAI HISTORICAL BUILDING GUIDE, HI. PHOTOGRAPHIC AND TEXTUAL DOCUMENTATION OF HISTORIC BUILDINGS ON THE ISLAND OF KAUAI. (LOCAL). ROBERT SCHLECK, PRESIDENT; KAUAI HISTORICAL SOCIETY; BOX 248; LIHUE, HI 96766. (#20220). **ARBA GRANTEE.**

LEEWARD ISLAND FILM, HONOLULU, HI. A FILM DEPICTING BIRD AND ANIMAL LIFE ON THE LEEWARD ISLANDS, A REMOTE AND UNOCCUPIED SECTION SET ASIDE BY PRESIDENT THEODORE ROOSEVELT IN 1904 AS AN ORIGINAL WILD LIFE REFUGE. (LOCAL). J PINCETICH, COORDINATOR; HAWAII FILM BOARD & HAWAII BICENTENNIAL COMMISSION; 714 PROSPECT ST; HONOLULU, HI 96813. (#25631). **ARBA GRANTEE.**

LEGAL HISTORY OF LAND TENURE IN HAWAII. PRODUCTION OF SLIDE PRESENTATION REFLECTING THE LEGAL HISTORY OF LAND TENURE IN HAWAII. (ST-WIDE). MS KAIPO PREJEAN, ASSISTANT; HAWAII COALITION OF NATIVE CLAIMS; 116 S KING ST; HONOLULU, HI 96813. (#22674). **ARBA GRANTEE.**

MAKING A CONSTITUTIONAL REVOLUTION: HONOLULU. RADIO/CASSETTE COLLEGE LEVEL COURSE ON AMERICAN GOVERNMENTAL VALUES. (ST-WIDE). THEODORE BECKER, PROJECT DIRECTOR; UNIV LAW SCHOOL AT UNIV OF HAWAII; BOX 2359; HONOLULU, HI 96804. (#16097). **ARBA GRANTEE.**

MULTI-CULTURAL EXHIBITS - HONOLULU, HI. INTERPRETIVE EXHIBIT COMMEMORATING HAWAII'S MULTI-CULTURAL HERITAGE AND STIMULATE AWARENESS OF SUCH CONTRIBUTIONS TO THE STATE AND THE NATION. (ST-WIDE). MRS KAREN MOTOSU, PROJ DIRECTOR; MULTI-CULTURAL CENTER PROJECT; ROOM 303, 100 N BERETANIA ST; HONOLULU, HI 96817. (#20807). **ARBA GRANTEE.**

NA MELE O MAUI MUSIC FESTIVAL, HONOLULU, HI. MUSIC PROGRAMS AND ART EXHIBITS TO PRESERVE, ENHANCE AND PROMOTE HAWAIIAN CULTURE. (LOCAL). AMES C HAYNES, TREASURER; NA MELE O HAWAII; PO BOX 778; WAILUKU, MAUI, HI 96793. (#23749). **ARBA GRANTEE.**

NATURAL HISTORY EXHIBIT - HONOLULU, HI. A NATURAL HISTORY HALL AT THE BISHOP MUSEUM, PRESENTING THE MICROCOSM OF HAWAII AS AN INSULAR LIVING LABORATORY OF UNIQUE SCIENTIFIC AND CULTURAL SIGNIFICANCE. (LOCAL). FRANK J RADOVSKY, CHAIRMAN DEPT OF ENTOMOLOGY; BISHOP MUSEUM; PO BOX 6037; HONOLULU, HI 96818. (#19355). **ARBA GRANTEE.**

'ONE ON ONE' VOTER PROGRAM - PEARL HARBOR, HI. ENCOURAGE EACH REGISTERED VOTER TO PLEDGE TO VOTE IN THE FALL ELECTION AND IN ADDITION, OBTAIN PLEDGE FROM ANOTHER QUALIFIED VOTER. (LOCAL). ALFRED WONG, CHAIRMAN; PEARL HARBOR NAVAL SHIPYARD, CODE 140; BOX 400, FPO; SAN FRANCISCO, CA 96610. (#29577).

PACIFIC REGIONAL CONSERVATION CENTER IN HAWAII. REGIONAL CENTER FOR CONSERVATION OF ETHNOLOGY, ARCHAEOLOGY, NATURAL HISTORY SPECIMENS, LIBRARY/ARCHIVE MATERIALS FOR PACIFIC REGION INCLUDING HAWAII, GUAM, AM. SAMOA, FIJI, TRUST TERRITORIES. (REGN'L). MARY WOOD LEE, LIBRARY COSERVATOR; BERNICE PAUAHI BISHOP MUSEUM; 1355 KALIHI ST, PO BOX 6037; HONOLULU, HI 96818. (#908). **ARBA GRANTEE.**

PARTICIPATION IN THE POLITICAL PROCESS - HI. ENCOURAGE STUDY AND PARTICIPATION IN THE POLITICAL PROCESS; 'MEET' THROUGH A NEWSLETTER, CANDIDATES RUNNING FOR HAWAII'S CONGRESSIONAL SEATS IN THE COMING ELECTION. (LOCAL). ALFRED WONG, CHAIRMAN; PEARL HARBOR NAVAL SHIPYARD, CODE 140; BOX 400, FPO; SAN FRANCISCO, CA 96610. (#29573).

PERPETUATION OF THE SPIRIT OF '76 - HONOLULU, HI. LEAVE DOCUMENTS AND OTHER RECORDS OF PEARL HARBOR NAVAL SHIPYARD'S PARTICIPATION IN THE BICENTENNIAL FOR SHIPYARDERS OF 2076. (LOCAL). ALFRED WONG, CHAIRMAN; PEARL HARBOR NAVAL SHIPYARD, CODE 140; BOX 400, FPO; SAN FRANCISCO, CA 96610. (#29578).

POLITICAL AND SOCIAL ESSAYS IN NEWSPAPER, HI. TRANSLATION FROM HAWAIIAN NEWSPAPERS OF POLITICAL AND SOCIAL ESSAYS. (ST-WIDE). DR RUBELITE JOHNSON, SUPERVISOR; HAWAII RESEARCH FOUNDATION; 845 MISSION LN; HONOLULU, HI 96813. (#19083). **ARBA GRANTEE.**

POLYNESIAN VOYAGING SOCIETY CHILDREN'S BOOKS - HI. SERIES OF FOUR BOOKS FOR CHILDREN ON ASPECTS OF VOYAGE OF DOUBLEHULLED CANOE TO TAHITI. (ST-WIDE). NANCY MOWER, EDITOR-COORDINATOR; POLYNESIAN VOYAGING SOCIETY CHILDREN'S BOOK PROJECT; 1536 KAMOLE ST; HONOLULU, HI 96821. (#19285). **ARBA GRANTEE.**

'POTPOURRI' - AMERICA'S MENU - HONOLULU, HI. FEATURE AT PEARL HARBOR NAVAL SHIPYARD RESTAURANT AMERICA'S FAVORITE DISHES. (LOCAL). ALFRED WONG, CHAIRMAN; PEARL HARBOR NAVAL SHIPYARD, CODE 140; BOX 400, FPO; SAN FRANCISCO, CA 96610. (#29579).

'PRIDE IN HAWAII'-RET'D TEACHERS ASSOC BOOK. STATE-WIDE PROJECT INVOLVING CLEANUP, ANCIENT GAMES, YOUTH FREE ENTERPRISE SEMINARS, BICYCLE AND FIREARMS SAFETY, INDEPENDENCE DAY AND MISS HAWAII OBSERVANCES. (ST-WIDE). PAUL M GOUDSMIT, PROGRAM MANAGER; HAWAII STATE JAYCEES; 611 MIDDLE ST; HONOLULU, HI 96819. (#14991). **ARBA GRANTEE.**

'REAFFIRMATION OF THE SPIRIT OF 1776' SEMINARS-HI. DEVELOP A REVIEW PROGRAM TO ENLIGHTEN SHIPYARD WORKERS ON THE BASIC FOUNDATIONS OF OUR DEMOCRACY: THE CONSTITUTION, THE 'BILL OF RIGHTS' AND THE CONGRESS. (LOCAL). ALFRED WONG, CHAIRMAN; PEARL HARBOR NAVAL SHIPYARD, CODE 140; BOX 400, FPO; SAN FRANCISCO, CA 96610. (#29574).

REDISCOVERY OF OUR NATURAL HERITAGE, HAWAII. SLIDE PRESENTATION OF EDUCATIONAL DOCUMENTARY ON HAWAII AS MICROCOSM OF MAN'S RELATIONSHIP TO HIS ENVIRONMENT. (ST-WIDE). WAYNE GAGNE, PRESIDENT; HAWAII AUDUBON SOCIETY; PO BOX 5032; HONOLULU, HI 96814. (#9577). **ARBA GRANTEE.**

RESTORATION OF HISTORIC STEAM RR OF HAWAII-PHASE I. OPERATING 36-INCH-GAUGE STEAM RAILROAD UTILIZING APPROX.12 MILES OF EXISTING RAILROAD TRACK BETWEEN NANAKULI & THE WEST LOCH OF PEARL HARBOR ON OAHU. (ST-WIDE). NICHOLAS A CARTER, PRESIDENT; HAWAIIAN RAILWAY SOCIETY, INC.; P. O. BOX 11126 MOILIILI STATION; HONOLULU, HI 96814. (#1198). **ARBA GRANTEE.**

ROOSEVELT HIGH BAND - ROSE FESTIVAL. ROOSEVELT HIGH BAND PARTICIPATED IN REKNOWNED ROSE FESTIVAL IN PORTLAND, OREGON. (REGN'L). CLIFFORD YOUNG; ROOSEVELT HIGH BAND BOOSTER CLUB; 1120 NEHOR ST; HONOLULU, HI 96822. (#24409). **ARBA GRANTEE.**

SERIES OF YOUTH WORKSHOPS IN HAWAII. DISCUSSIONS OF FUTURE ALTERNATIVES AND REPORTS OF YOUTH ANALYSIS OF TRENDS IN SOCIETY. (ST-WIDE). CHARLES BROCKMAN; YOUTH ACTION, INC C/O HAWAII BICENTENNIAL COMMISSION; PO BOX 2359; HONOLULU, HI 96804. (#370). **ARBA GRANTEE.**

SHIPYARD LOG PUBLICITY - HONOLULU, HI. ENCOURAGE SHIPYARD-WIDE PARTICIPATION IN THE BICENTENNIAL PROGRAM THROUGH THE SHIPYARD LOG (SHIPYARD NEWSPAPER). (LOCAL). ALFRED WONG, CHAIRMAN; PEARL HARBOR NAVAL SHIPYARD, CODE 140; BOX 400, FPO; SAN FRANCISCO, CA 96610. (#29599).

STATE BICENTENNIAL COMMEMORATION PROGRAM, HAWAII. MUSICAL PANORAMA OF AMERICAN HISTORY. (LOCAL). CORNELIUS DOWNES,INFO DIR; DEPARTMENT OF PLANNING AND ECONOMIC DEVELOPMENT; 250 S KING ST; HONOLULU, HI 96813. (#25278). **ARBA GRANTEE.**

STATUE OF LIBERTY PROGRAM - HONOLULU, HI. EXTEND THE SHIPYARD REAFFIRMATION OF THE SPIRIT OF '76 SEMINAR TO THE COMMUNITY THROUGH VOLUNTEER LEADERS. (LOCAL). ALFRED WONG, CHAIRMAN; PEARL HARBOR NAVAL SHIPYARD, CODE 140; BOX 400, FPO; SAN FRANCISCO, CA 96610. (#29576).

STRENGTHEN EQUAL EMPLOYMENT OPPORTUNITY PROGRAM-HI. STRENGTHEN THE EEO PROGRAM THROUGH INITIATION OF NEW OPPORTUNITIES THROUGH: THE MANAGEMENT ASSOCIATE PROGRAM (TRNG PROGRAM IN MGMT & ADMIN) & UPWARD MOBILITY FOR THOSE WITH LIMITED FORMAL EDUCATION. (LOCAL). ALFRED WONG, CHAIRMAN; PEARL HARBOR NAVAL SHIPYARD, CODE 140; BOX 400, FPO; SAN FRANCISCO, CA 96610. (#29582).

SURVEY OF PORTRAITS IN IOLANI PALACE IN HAWAII. SURVEY OF REPAIR REQUIRED TO RESTORE PORTRAITS IN IOLANI PALACE. (ST-WIDE). SUNAO KIDO, CHAIRMAN; HAWAII DEPT OF LAND & NATURAL RESOURCES; BOX 621; HONOLULU, HI 96809. (#841). **ARBA GRANTEE.**

SURVEY TO STIMULATE SCHOOL PARTICIPATION IN HAWAII. QUESTIONAIRE INQUIRING WHAT IDEAS & SUGGESTIONS TEACHERS MIGHT HAVE TO INCREASE PARTICIPATION IN THE BICENTENNIAL. MAIN OBJECTIVE IS TO INVOLVE THE YOUNG MINORITIES OF EVERY ETHNIC PERSUASION. (ST-WIDE). BROTHER ROBERT C MAGUIRE, PROJ DIRECTOR; HAWAII BICENTENNIAL COMMISSION; BOX 2359; HONOLULU, HI 96804. (#1196). **ARBA GRANTEE.**

TIME-LINE POSTER OF HAWAII. POSTER OF CONCURRENT EVENTS IN HAWAII, THE US MAINLAND & THE WORLD. (ST-WIDE). ROBERT BOOM, CHAIRMAN, PUBL SUBCOMMITTEE; HAWAII BICENTENNIAL COMMISSION; PO BOX 4349; HONOLULU, HI 96813. (#859). **ARBA GRANTEE.**

TOOLS FOR TEACHING AMERICAN HISTORY PROJECT OF HI. HIRE PERSON TO PREPARE INVENTORY OF MATERIALS AVAILABLE FOR TEACHING AMERICAN HISTORY. (ST-WIDE). DR ROBERT MAGUIRE, CHAIRMAN; HAWAII BICENTENNIAL COMMISSION EDUCATION SUBCOMMITTEE; PO BOX 2359; HONOLULU, HI 96816. (#854). **ARBA GRANTEE.**

VOTER AWARENESS PROGRAM OF HAWAII. THE HAWAII BICENTENNIAL COMMISSION IS PLANNING FOR A VOTER AWARENESS PROGRAM AIMED AT ESTABLISHING 100% VOTER PARTICIPATION IN THE STATE. (ST-WIDE). JOHN PINCETECH, EXEC DIRECTOR; HAWAII BICENTENNIAL COMMISSION; PO BOX 2359; HONOLULU, HI 96804. (#364).

'WHAT THE BICENTENNIAL MEANS TO ME'-ART PROGRAM-HI. PROGRAM TO ENCOURAGE COMPETITION IN ART IN GRADES K TO 12 ON THEME 'WHAT THE BICENTENNIAL MEANS TO ME'. (ST-WIDE). STANLEY YAMAMOTO, PROGRAM SPECIALIST; STATE DEPARTMENT OF EDUCATION; PO BOX 2360; HONOLULU, HI 96804. (#19485). **ARBA GRANTEE.**

WORLD BICENT CANOE CHAMPIONSHIP, HONOLULU, HI. A WORLD'S OUTRIGGER CANOE CHAMPIONSHIP COMPETITION, COMBINED WITH SWIMMING, DIVING, SAILING & OTHER WATER SPORTS. (INT'L). MORONI MEDEIROS, WATER FESTIVAL DIRECTOR; CITY & COUNTY OF HONOLULU BICENTENNIAL COMMITTEE; KAPIOLANI BANDSTAND; HONOLULU, HI 96815. (#14394). **ARBA GRANTEE.**

WORLD EDUCATORS CONFERENCE - HONOLULU, HI. TO BRING TOGETHER EDUCATORS FROM ALL PARTS OF THE WORLD TO EXCHANGE IDEAS, DISCUSS ISSUES RELATED TO EDUCATION AND BROADEN COMMUNICATION LINES BETWEEN ALL SCHOOL LEVELS. (INT'L). LORETTA KRAUSE, EXEC DIRECTOR; CURRICULUM RESEARCH AND DEVELOPMENT GROUP; 1776 UNIVERSITY AVE; HONOLULU, HI 96822. (#15881). **ARBA GRANTEE.**

1976 INTL CONVENTION PACIFIC AREA TRAVEL ASSOC. PACIFIC AREA TRAVEL ASSOCIATION'S 1976 CONVENTION IN HAWAII TO SPOTLIGHT HAWAII'S DIVERSE CULTURAL COMPOSITION AND INTER-RELATIONSHIPS OF PACIFIC AREA CULTURAL GROUPS. (INT'L). THURSTON TWIGG-SMITH, CHAIRMAN; HAWAII BICENTENNIAL COMMISSION; 605 KAPIOLANI BLVD; HONOLULU, HI 96813. (#2842). **ARBA RECOGNIZED.**

200 YEARS OF HAWAIIAN AGRICULTURE RECORDS SURVEY. PREPARE GRANT APPLICATION FOR FUNDS WITH WHICH TO SURVEY RECORDS OF AGRICULTURAL ACTIVITIES IN HAWAII. (ST-WIDE). BARBARA DUNN, SECRETARY; HAWAIIAN HISTORICAL SOCIETY; 560 KAWAIAHAO ST; HAWAII, HI 96813. (#829). **ARBA GRANTEE.**

JAN 1 - JUNE 1, '74. CITY & COUNTY OF HONOLULU FESTIVAL FOR THE FOURTH. 'COUNTDOWN' CONCEPT WHICH EXPRESSES ITSELF

HONOLULU — CONTINUED

AS '200 MINUS 3' IN 1973, '200 MINUS 2 IN '74' ETC. AN EFFORT TO GENERATE INTEREST & STIMULATE PLANNING & ACTIVITY IN CONNECTION WITH THE BICENTENNIAL. (ST-WIDE). THURSTON TWIGG-SMITH; HAWAII BICENTENNIAL COMMISSION; PO BOX 2359; HONOLULU, HI 96804. (#1200-901).

JAN 1 - JULY 1, '74. HAWAII COUNTY FESTIVAL FOR THE FOURTH. 'COUNTDOWN'CONCEPT, '200 MINUS 2 PROJECT' AN EFFORT TO GENERATE INTEREST AND STIMULATE PLANNING & ACTIVITY IN CONNECTION WITH THE BICENTENNIAL. (THE 1974 CELEBRATION). (ST-WIDE). THURSTON TWIGG-SMITH; HAWAII BICENTENNIAL COMMISSION C/O GOVERNOR'S OFFICE; BOX 2359; HONOLULU, HI 96804. (#1199-901).

JAN 31 - JULY 31, '74. YOUTH WORKSHOPS ON THE BICENTENNIAL. DISCUSSIONS OF FUTURE ALTERNATIVES AND REPORTS OF YOUTH ANALYSIS OF TRENDS IN SOCIETY. (ST-WIDE). ANSON CHONG, HORIZONS; YOUTH ACTION, INC C/O HAWAII BICENTENNIAL COMMISSION; PO BOX 2359; HONOLULU, HI 96804. (#370-901).

MAR 2, '74. HAWAII 200 CONGRESS II CONVENES. WORKSHOPS TO DETERMINE NATURE OF BICENTENNIAL IDEAS AND PROJECTS. FIRST MET IN 1971 FOR PRIMING IDEAS FOR THE BICENTENNIAL. (ST-WIDE). THOMAS NICKERSON, CONSULT; HAWAII BICENTENNIAL COMMISSION; PO BOX 2359; HONOLULU, HI 96804. (#371-902).

JULY 4 - 5, '74. FESTIVAL FOR THE FOURTH. JULY 4TH FESTIVITIES INCLUDING MUSIC, GAMES, COMMUNITY PICNICS, & CHURCHES' RECOGNITION BY RINGING BELLS. (REGN'L). THURSTON TWIGG-SMITH; HAWAII BICENTENNIAL COMMISSION; PO BOX 2359; HONOLULU, HI 96804. (#358-901).

FEB 17, '75. QUEEN KAPIOLANI ROSE GARDEN FESTIVAL, MUSIC AND DANCE. FESTIVAL, LIVE PERFORMANCE. (ST-WIDE). MRS PIILANI A RAMLER; HAWAII BICENTENNIAL COMMISSION; BOX 2359; HONOLULU, HI 96804. (#5649-902).

APR 1 - OCT 1, '75. EXHIBITION OF PANTINGS ON CAPTAIN JAMES COOK. DRAWINGS, PRINTS AND PAINTINGS ON THE LAST DAYS OF NAVIGATOR JAMES COOK WITH A TEXT BY EDWARD A STASACK; TO BE ON EXHIBIT IN HONOLULU. (ST-WIDE). JOHN PINCETICH; HAWAII BICENTENNIAL COMMITTEE; 250 S KING ST; HONOLULU, HI 96813. (#10196-501).

APR 6, '75. OPENING PAGEANT FOR HAWAII'S BICENTENNIAL IN CAPITOL SQUARE. BICENTENNIAL CELEBRATIONS IN THE HAWAIIAN ISLANDS. VARIOUS FESTIVITIES ARE PLANNED THROUGHOUT HAWAII TO BRING BICENTENNIAL MEANING TO THE PEOPLE AND VISITORS OF THE FIFTIETH STATE. (ST-WIDE). MS PIILANI A RAMLER; HAWAII BICENTENNIAL COMMISSION; BOX 2359; HONOLULU, HI 96804. (#5649-501).

JULY 1, '75 - DEC 31, '76. HAWAII 2176 - QUADRICENTENNIAL CITY. EXHIBIT. (ST-WIDE). JOHN PINCETICH, EXEC DIR; HAWAII BICENTENNIAL COMMISSION; 250 S KING ST; HONOLULU, HI 96813. (#15290-1).

JULY 4, '75. PHYSICAL FITNESS FESTIVAL. FESTIVAL. (ST-WIDE). MS PIILANI A RAMLER; HAWAII BICENTENNIAL COMMISSION; BOX 2359; HONOLULU, HI 96804. (#5649-504).

JULY 4 - 13, '75. AQUATIC FESTIVAL ON WAIKIKI BEACH. FESTIVAL. (ST-WIDE). MS PIILANI A RAMLER; HAWAII BICENTENNIAL COMMISSION; BOX 2359; HONOLULU, HI 96804. (#5649-505).

AUG 19, '75. WAIKIKI BICENTENNIAL CONCERT. ALL-AMERICAN COMPOSERS WILL BE FEATURED IN WAIKIKI SHELL CONCERTS AS SPECIAL MUSICAL SALUTE TO THE BICENTENNIAL. (LOCAL). CATHARINE HITE, CHAIRMAN; HONOLULU SYMPHONY SOCIETY; 1000 BISHOP ST; HONOLULU, HI 96713. (#10680-501).

SEPT 17, '75. JAZZ CONCERT, AMERICAN MUSIC CONCERT SERIES, UNIV OF HAWAII. LIVE PERFORMANCE AT ORVIS AUDITORIUM, 2411 DOLE ST. (LOCAL). ALLEN R TRUBITT, CHAIRMAN; UNIV OF HAWAII MUSIC DEPARTMENT; 2411 DOLE ST; HONOLULU, HI 96822. (#200014-1).

OCT 1, '75 - JUNE 1, '76. YOUTH CONGRESS ACTIVITY EXHIBIT III. EXHIBIT. (LOCAL). GIFFORD JOHNSON, CHMN; YOUTH ACTION; CHURCH OF THE CROSSROADS; HONOLULU, HI 96822. (#102743-1).

NOV 2, '75. YOUTH CONGRESS NOVEMBER CONFERENCE. CONFERENCE, SEMINAR. (ST-WIDE). GIFFORD JOHNSON, CHMN; YOUTH ACTION; CHURCH OF THE CROSSROADS; HONOLULU, HI 96822. (#102743-2).

NOV 3, '75. AMERICAN ENSEMBLE MUSIC, AMERICAN MUSIC CONCERT SERIES. LIVE PERFORMANCE AT ORVIS AUDITORIUM, 2411 DOLE ST. (LOCAL). ALLEN R TRUBITT, CHAIRMAN; UNIV OF HAWAII MUSIC DEPARTMENT; 2411 DOLE ST; HONOLULU, HI 96822. (#15296-2).

NOV 24, '75. ORCHESTRAL CONCERT, AMERICAN MUSIC CONCERT SERIES. LIVE PERFORMANCE AT BALL ROOM, CAMPUS CENTER BUILDING, 2465 CAMPUS RD. (LOCAL). ALLEN R TRUBITT, CHAIRMAN; UNIV OF HAWAII MUSIC DEPARTMENT; 2411 DOLE ST; HONOLULU, HI 96822. (#15296-3).

JAN 1 - DEC 31, '76. PRIDE IN HAWAII. A SERIES OF EVENTS INCLUDING ANCIENT GAMES, YOUTH FREE ENTERPRISE SEMINARS, INDEPENDENCE DAY PARADE AND MISS HAWAII COMPETITION. (ST-WIDE). PAUL M GOUDSMIT, PGM MGR; HAWAII STATE JAYCEES; 838 S BERETANIA ST, SUITE 207; HONOLULU, HI 96813. (#14991-1).

JAN 2, '76. HONOLULU SYMPHONY BICENTENNIAL CONCERT. LIVE PERFORMANCE. (ST-WIDE). THOMAS NICKERSON; HAWAII BICENTENNIAL COMMISSION; PO BOX 2359; HONOLULU, HI 96804. (#5649-2).

JAN 2 - JUNE 30, '76. MULTI-CULTURAL EXHIBITS. INTERPRETIVE EXHIBITS COMMEMORATING HAWAII'S MULTI-CULTURAL HERITAGE AND STIMULATE AWARENESS OF SUCH CONTRIBUTIONS TO THE STATE AND THE NATION. (LOCAL). MRS KAREN MOTOSUE, DIR; MULTI-CULTURAL CENTER; ROOM 303, 100 N BERETHNIA ST; HONOLULU, HI 96817. (#20807-1).

FEB 1 - JUNE 4, '76. SAILING OF AUTHENTIC CANOE FROM HONOLULU TO TAHITI. CREW OF 24 WILL RECREATE PREHISTORIC CONDITIONS OF ORIGINAL POLYNESIAN VOYAGE IN DOUBLE HULL CANOE DESIGNED & BUILT BY POLYNESIAN EXPERTS & NAUTICAL AUTHORITIES. (INT'L). DR BEN FINNEY, DIRECTOR; POLYNESIAN VOYAGING SOCIETY; PO BOX 2359; HONOLULU, HI 96804. (#354-501).

FEB 9, '76. AMERICA SOLO SONG, AMERICAN MUSIC CONCERT SERIES. LIVE PERFORMANCE AT ORVIS AUDITORIUM, 2411 DOLE ST. (LOCAL). ALLEN R TRUBITT, CHMN; UNIV OF HAWAII MUSIC DEPARTMENT; 2411 DOLE ST; HONOLULU, HI 96822. (#15296-4).

FEB 12 - 22, '76. 'OKLAHOMA', AMERICAN MUSIC CONCERT SERIES. LIVE PERFORMANCE AT J F KENNEDY THEATRE, 1770 EAST-WEST RD. (LOCAL). GLENN CANNON, CHMN; UNIV OF HAWAII THEATRE AND DRAMA DEPARTMENT; 1770 EAST-WEST RD; HONOLULU, HI 96822. (#15296-5).

FEB 17, '76. COMMEMORATIVE ROSE FESTIVAL & HORTICULTURAL WORKSHOP. HORTICULTURAL WORKSHOPS MUSIC & ENTERTAINMENT. AT KAPIOLANI ROSE GARDENS. (LOCAL). MORONI MEDEIROS, CHAIRMAN; HONOLULU CITY & COUNTY BICENTENNIAL COMMITTEE; KAPIOLANI PARK BANDSTAND; HONOLULU, HI 96815. (#102325-1).

FEB 23, '76. MUSIC OF HAWAII'S IMMIGRANTS, AMERICAN MUSIC CONCERT SERIES. LIVE PERFORMANCE AT ORVIS AUDITORIUM, 2411 DOLE ST. (LOCAL). ALLEN R TRUBITT, CHMN; UNIV OF HAWAII MUSIC DEPARTMENT; 2411 DOLE ST; HONOLULU, HI 96822. (#15296-6).

MAR 2 - 9, '76. MAKAHIKI KAI; FESTIVAL OF THE SEA, MARINE EDUCATIONAL EXPERIENCE. A MARINE EDUCATIONAL EXPOSITION WILL BE BARGED TO NEIGHBOR ISLAND COUNTIES DURING 1976 AND MADE AVAILABLE TO ALL PEOPLE IN THE STATE SEPARATED FROM THE CAPITOL CITY BY MILES OF OCEAN. AT HIC EXHIBITION, ASSEMBLY HALLS & MEETING ROOMS, 777 WARD AVE. (ST-WIDE). ROSE PFUND, COORDINATOR; SEA GRANT COLLEGE PROGRAM, UNIV OF HAWAII; 2540 MAILE WAY, SPALDING 253; HONOLULU, HI 96822. (#12411-1).

MAR 14, '76. 24TH CHERRY BLOSSOM FESTIVAL RED & WHITE SONG FESTIVAL. LIVE PERFORMANCE, RADIO/TV, COMPETITION AT HIC CONCERT HALL; 777 WARD AVE; PAID PARKING. (LOCAL). MORONI L MEDEIROS, COORD; HONOLULU JAPANESE JUNIOR CHAMBER OF COMMERCE; 2454 S BERETANIA ST; HONOLULU, HI 96814. (#102132-1).

MAR 14 - APR 3, '76. 24TH CHERRY BLOSSOM FILM FESTIVAL. EXHIBIT. (LOCAL). MORONI L MEDEIROS, COORD; HONOLULU JAPANESE JUNIOR CHAMBER OF COMMERCE; 2454 S BERETANIA ST; HONOLULU, HI 96814. (#102132-8).

MAR 17, '76. NAVY BICENTENNIAL COMMAND DESIGNATION CEREMONY. IN CONNECTION WITH OPENING CEREMONY, PRESENT BICENTENNIAL FLAG AND CERTIFICATE TO THE SHIPYARD COMMANDER BY UNCLE SAM. AT PEARL HARBOR NAVAL SHIPYARD. (LOCAL). ALFRED WONG, PHNSYD; PEARL HARBOR NAVAL SHIPYARD/PEARL HARBOR ASSOC; FPO, BOX 400; SAN FRANCISCO, CA 96610. (#200014-5).

MAR 17, '76. OPENING CEREMONY FOR SHIPYARD BICENTENNIAL PROGRAMS. SHIPYARD ANNOUNCED THE 'REAFFIRMATION OF THE SPIRIT OF '76' ACTIVITIES TO SHIPYARDERS. THE CEREMONY INCLUDED UNCLE SAM, BICENTENNIAL COLOR GUARD, NAVY BAND & SINGING GROUP. AT PEARL HARBOR NAVAL SHIPYARD. (LOCAL). ALFRED WONG, PHNSYD; PEARL HARBOR NAVAL SHIPYARD/PEARL HARBOR ASSOC; FPO, BOX 400; SAN FRANCISCO, CA 96610. (#200014-4).

MAR 20, '76. 24TH CHERRY BLOSSOM FASHION SHOW. LIVE PERFORMANCE AT WAIKIKI SHERATON HOTEL MEETING ROOM. (LOCAL). MORONI L MEDEIROS, COORD; HONOLULU JAPANESE JUNIOR CHAMBER OF COMMERCE; 2454 S BERETANIA ST; HONOLULU, HI 96814. (#102132-2).

MAR 22 - 23, '76. 24TH CHERRY BLOSSOM EAST SHOW. LIVE PERFORMANCE AT HIC ARENA; 777 WARD AVE. (LOCAL). MORONI L MEDEIROS, COORD; HONOLULU JAPANESE JUNIOR CHAMBER OF COMMERCE; 2454 S BERETANIA ST; HONOLULU, HI 96814. (#102132-3).

MAR 25 - 27, '76. 24TH CHERRY BLOSSOM FESTIVAL JAPANESE CULTURE & ARTS SHOW. EXHIBIT, LIVE PERFORMANCE AT HIC EXHIBTION HALL; 777 WARD AVE; PAID PARKING. (LOCAL). MORONI L MEDEIROS, COORD; HONOLULU JAPANESE JUNIOR CHAMBER OF COMMERCE; 2454 S BERETANIA ST; HONOLULU, HI 96814. (#102132-4).

MAR 26, '76. 24TH CHERRY BLOSSOM QUEEN PAGEANT. COMPETITION, LIVE PERFORMANCE AT HIC CONCERT HALL; 777 WARD AVE. (LOCAL). MORONI L MEDEIROS, COORD; HONOLULU JAPANESE JUNIOR CHAMBER OF COMMERCE; 2454 S BERETANIA ST; HONOLULU, HI 96814. (#102132-5).

MAR 27 - 28, '76. 24TH CHERRY BLOSSOM WEST SHOW. LIVE PERFORMANCE AT HIC ARENA; 777 WARD AVE. (LOCAL). MORONI L MEDEIROS, COORD; HONOLULU JAPANESE JUNIOR CHAMBER OF COMMERCE; 2454 S BERETANIA ST; HONOLULU, HI 96814. (#102132-6).

APR 2 - 3, '76. ODORI FESTIVAL OF JAPAN VISITS HONOLULU. LIVE PERFORMANCE. (INT'L). DIRECTOR; MEL HOWARD PRESENTS; 143 E 27TH ST; NEW YORK, NY 10016. (#108965-1).

APR 3, '76. 24TH CHERRY BLOSSOM FESTIVAL CORONATION BALL. FESTIVAL AT WAIKIKI SHERATON HOTEL. (LOCAL). MORONI L MEDEIROS, COORD; HONOLULU JAPANESE JUNIOR CHAMBER OF COMMERCE; 2454 S BERETANIA ST; HONOLULU, HI 96814. (#102132-7).

APR 5, '76. ORATORIO - AMERICAN MUSIC CONCERT SERIES. ARMAND RUSSELL'S 'AMERICA' BASED ON JOHN DONNE'S 'AMERICA : A PROPHESY.'. AT CAMPUS CENTER BALLROOM. (LOCAL). ALLEN R TRUBITT, CHMN; UNIV OF HAWAII MUSIC DEPARTMENT; 2411 DOLE ST; HONOLULU, HI 96822. (#15296-7).

APR 9, '76. BAND CONCERT - AMERICAN MUSIC CONCERT SERIES. LIVE PERFORMANCE AT 1039 S KING ST. (LOCAL). ALLEN R TRUBITT, CHMN; MCKINLEY HIGH SCHOOL AUDITORIUM; 2411 DOLE ST; HONOLULU, HI 96822. (#15296-9).

APR 12, '76. CLASSES OF '76 REVOLUTIONARY ERA BALL. INVOLVES STUDENTS GRADUATING IN '76 FROM THROUGHOUT THE STATE. AT ROYAL HAWAIIAN HOTEL, MONARCH RM. (ST-WIDE). SANDY YOUNG, CHMN; HAWAII BICENTENNIAL COMMISSION & THE CLASSES OF '76 PROJECT; HONOLULU, HI 96817. (#102142-1).

APR 17, '76. STATE PHYSICAL EXCELLENCE CHAMPIONSHIPS. WEIGHTLIFTING, JOGGING & GYMNASTIC COMPETITION. AT WAIALUA RECREATION CENTER, 67-180 GOODALE AVE. (ST-WIDE). MORONI MEDEIROS, CHAIRMAN; HONOLULU CITY & COUNTY BICENTENNIAL COMMITTEE; KAPIOLANI PARK BANDSTAND; HONOLULU, HI 96815. (#102325-2).

APR 22 - 29, '76. PATA ETHNIC ENTERTAINMENT. TALENT REPRESENTING THE CULTURES OF COUNTRIES SUCH AS JAPAN, KOREA, REPUBLIC OF CHINA, SAMOA AND TAHITI. VISITING ONE OR MORE OF THE NEIGHBOR ISLANDS-HAWAII, MAUI, MOLOKA, LANAI & KAUAI. AT SHERITAN WAIKIKI CONVENTION CENTER. (INT'L). JOHN PINCETICH; PACIFIC AREA TRAVEL ASSOC; PO BOX 2359; HONOLULU, HI 96804. (#7858-1).

APR 23 - 28, '76. 1976 INTL CONVENTION, PACIFIC AREA TRAVEL ASSOC-HI. PACIFIC AREA TRAVEL ASSOCIATION'S 1976 CONVENTION IN HAWAII TO SPOTLIGHT HAWAII'S DIVERSE CULTURAL COMPOSITION AND INTER-RELATIONSHIPS OF PACIFIC AREA CULTURAL GROUPS. AT WORKSHOPS- HAWAII, MAUI & KAUAI 4/23,24; CONFERENCE- OAHU 4/25-28. (INT'L). THURSTON TWIGG-SMITH; HAWAII BICENTENNIAL COMMISSION; 605 KAPIOLANI BLVD; HONOLULU, HI 96813. (#2842-1).

MAY 1, '76. MAY DAY & LEI DAY BICENTENNIAL CELEBRATION. MUSIC & PAGEANTRY SURROUND HAWAII'S FESTIVE CELEBRATION OF 'MAY DAY IS LEI DAY'. AT WAIKIKI SHELL. (ST-WIDE). HAWAII VISITORS BUREAU; 2270 KALAKAUA AVE; HONOLULU, HI 96815. (#102325-3).

MAY 6 - 8, '76. DANCE CONCERT - AMERICAN MUSIC CONCERT SERIES. LIVE PERFORMANCE AT JOHN F KENNEDY THEATRE, 1770 EAST-WEST RD. (LOCAL). CARL WOLZ, CHMN; UNIV OF HAWAII DRAMA AND THEATRE DEPARTMENT; 1770 EAST-WEST RD; HONOLULU, HI 96822. (#15296-8).

MAY 15 - JUNE ??, '76. FIESTA FILIPINA. AN ADAPTATION OF A TRADITIONAL TOWN FESTIVAL OF THE PHILIPPINES. (LOCAL). JOSE SANIDAD, DIRECTOR; UNITED FILIPINO COUNCIL OF HAWAII; FIESTA FILIPINA; HONOLULU, HI 96813. (#103416-108).

JUNE 7, '76. AUSTRALIAN YOUTH ORCHESTRA CONCERT. LIVE PERFORMANCE. (INT'L). JOHN MAUNDER, DIRECTOR; AUSTRALIAN GOVERNMENT; AUSTRALIAN CG, 636 FIFTH AVENUE; NEW YORK, NY 10020. (#108021-9).

JUNE 11 - 13, '76. KING KAMEHAMEHA CELEBRATION. CELEBRATION HONORS THE LIFE & DEEDS OF KING KAMEHAMEHA, MAN CREDITED WITH FIRST UNITING THE ISLANDS. (ST-WIDE). R-M. KEAHI ALLEN (MRS); STATE OF HAWAII, KING KAMEHAMEHA CELEBRATION COMMISSION; 355 N KING ST; HONOLULU, HI 96817. (#103416-353).

JUNE 23 - JULY 21, '76. VOTER REGISTRATION PROGRAM. CEREMONY, LIVE PERFORMANCE, EXHIBIT AT PEARL HARBOR NAVAL SHIPYARD. (LOCAL). ALFRED WONG, PHNSYD; PEARL HARBOR NAVAL SHIPYARD/PEARL HARBOR ASSOC; FPO, BOX 400; SAN FRANCISCO, CA 96610. (#200014-6).

JUNE 28 - JULY 1, '76. EAST/WEST CONFERENCE ON THE BICENTENNIAL. THEME: THE AMERICAN REVOLUTION: ITS MEANING TO ASIANS & AMERICANS. PARTICIPANTS FROM JAPAN, KOREA, PAKISTAN, INDONESIA, MALAYSIA, PHILIPPINES, THAILAND & REPUBLIC OF CHINA. RICHARD B MORRIS OF COLUMBIA UNIV WILL DELIVER THE KEYNOTE ADDRESS. AT THE EAST-WEST CENTER. (INT'L). DR JOHN BROWNELL, V/PRES; THE EAST-WEST CENTER/UNIVERSITY OF HAWAII; 1777 EAST/WEST CTR; HONOLULU, HI 96822. (#104882-1).

JUNE 29 - JULY 6, '76. HAWAIIAN FESTIVAL OF MUSIC. FESTIVAL, LIVE PERFORMANCE AT WAIKIKI SHELL. (LOCAL). AUDREY DE BOER; INTERNATIONAL FESTIVALS, INC; 202 E MICHIGAN AVE; KALAMAZOO, MI 49006. (#107233-4).

JULY 2, '76. HAWAII'S BICENTENNIAL COMMEMORATION PROGRAM-MUSICAL HISTORY PANORAMA. LIVE PERFORMANCE AT ALOHA STADIUM, HALAWA. (LOCAL). CORNELIUS DOWNES,INFO DIR; STATE OF HAWAII DEPT OF PLANNING & ECONOMIC DEVELOPMENT; 250 S KING ST; HONOLULU, HI 96813. (#25278-1).

JULY 2 - 4, '76. HONOLULU'S HO'OLAULEA MAKAHIKI CRATER FESTIVAL. A 3 DAY EVENT BEGINNING ON JULY 2, 1976 WITH THE BLOWING OF THE TRADITIONAL CONCH SHELL, ALONG WITH HAWAIIAN CHANTERS. AUTHENTIC VILLLAGES, CRAFTS, DISPLAYS, DANCING & MUSIC WILL BE PART OF THE CONTINUOS PROGRAM. AT DIAMOND HEAD CRATER. (ST-WIDE). MORONI MEDEIROS, CHAIRMAN; HONOLULU BICENTENNIAL COMMITTEE; KAPIOLANI BANDSTAND; HONOLULU, HI 96815. (#14395-1).

JULY 3 - 5, '76. DIAMOND HEAD CRATER FESTIVAL. THE 50TH STATE AND ITS ETHNIC COMMUNITIES ARE HONORED DURING THIS FESTIVAL OF MUSIC, FOOD & FIREWORKS. AT DIAMOND HEAD CRATER. (ST-WIDE). DIRECTOR; FRIENDS OF THE BICENTENNIAL, INC; 850 KAPIOLANI BLVD, SUITE 205; HONOLULU, HI 96813. (#103416-410).

HONOLULU — CONTINUED

JULY 4, '76. CHARLES E KING BICENTENNIAL MEMORIAL CONCERT. ROYAL HAWAIIAN BAND SALUTE TO CHARLES E KING. AT KAPIOLANI PARK BANDSTAND. (ST-WIDE). MORONI MEDEIROS, CHAIRMAN; HONOLULU CITY & COUNTY BICENTENNIAL COMMITTEE; KAPIOLANI PARK BANDSTAND; HONOLULU, HI 96815. (#102325-4).

JULY 4, '76. HAWAIIAN RAILWAY DEMONSTRATION. TO RESTORE & OPERATE EXISTING 12-MI. R.R. AND HISTORICALLY SIGNIFICANT R.R. EQUIPMENT FOR EDUCATIONAL & RECREATIONAL PURPOSES. PROVIDE LIVING HISTORY EXPERIENCE OF SUGAR PLANTATION ERA IN HAWAII. AT LEEWARD O'AHU OCEANFRONT BETWEEN NANAKULI AND KAHE POINT. (ST-WIDE). NICHOLAS A CARTER; HAWAIIAN RAILWAY SOCIETY; BOX 11126; HONOLULU, HI 96814. (#1148-1).

JULY 4, '76. PACIFICA '76 BICENTENNIAL PARADE. PARADE'S THEME IS A SALUTE TO THE ETHNIC GROUPS WHO HAVE PLAYED IMPORTANT PARTS IN HAWAII'S HISTORICAL DEVELOPMENT. AT KAPIOLANI BLVD TO THE OLD STADIUM. (ST-WIDE). JOHN PINCETICH, EXEC DIR; HAWAII BICENTENNIAL COMMISSION; PO BOX 2359; HONOLULU, HI 96804. (#107864-1).

JULY 4, '76. 4TH OF JULY PICNIC. FESTIVAL AT PEARL HARBOR NAVAL SHIPYARD. (LOCAL). ALFRED WONG, PHNSYD; PEARL HARBOR NAVAL SHIPYARD/PEARL HARBOR ASSOC; FPO, BOX 400; SAN FRANCISCO, CA 96610. (#200014-3).

JULY 5 - 6, '76. ART IN THE PARK, CITY AND COUNTY OF HONOLULU. EXHIBIT. (ST-WIDE). MORONI L MEDEIRAS; HAWAII BICENTENNIAL COMMISSION; 650 S KING ST; HONOLULU, HI 96813. (#5649-506).

JULY 12 - 18, '76. WORLD'S BICENTENNIAL CANOE CHAMPIONSHIP & WATER FESTIVAL. WORLD'S OUTRIGGER CANOE CHAMPIONSHIP ALONG WITH COMPETITION IN SWIMMING, DIVING, SAILING AND OTHER WATER SPORTS. AT FORD ISLAND, PEARL HARBOR. (INT'L). MORONI MEDEIROS, CHAIRMAN; HONOLULU BICENTENNIAL COMMITTEE; KAPIOLANI BANDSTAND; HONOLULU, HI 96815. (#14394-1).

JULY 13, '76. TIME CAPSULE SEALING. CEREMONY AT FRONT OF 15TH AIR BASE WING HEADQUARTERS BUILDING, SCOTT CIRCLE. (LOCAL). COL RICHARD L THOMPSON; 1KTH AIR BASE WING/01 - HICKAM AIR FORCE BASE; FPO; SAN FRANCISCO, CA 96553. (#200014-8).

JULY 15 - 20, '76. YOUTH BICENTENNIAL CONGRESS 1976. CONFERENCE AT GATEWAY DORM - UNIVERSITY OF HAWAII - DOLE ST. (ST-WIDE). GIFFORD JOHNSON, CHMN; YOUTH ACTION; CHURCH OF THE CROSSROADS; HONOLULU, HI 96822. (#102743-4).

JULY 27 - 28, '76. JAPANESE YOUTH GOODWILL CRUISE VISITS HONOLULU. HOURS ON TUESDAY 6 PM TO 8 PM; WEDNESDAY 4 PM TO 6 PM. (INT'L). MITAKE KATSUBE, COORD; JAPANESE PRIME MINISTER'S OFFICE; OCHANOMIZU WOMEN'S UNIV; TOKYO/JAPAN. (#109014-3).

AUG 10, '76. 3RD DUKE KAHANAMOKU MEMORIAL CANOE REGATTA. HAWAII CANOE CLUBS' SALUTE TO THEIR BELOVED DUKE. TIVITIES. AT WAIKIKI BEACH FACING MOANA HOTEL. (ST-WIDE). MORONI MEDEIROS, CHAIRMAN; HONOLULU CITY & COUNTY BICENTENNIAL COMMITTEE; KAPIOLANI PARK BANDSTAND; HONOLULU, HI 96815. (#102325-6).

AUG 23 - 28, '76. JAPANESE SOCIETY BICENTENNIAL CELEBRATION. CULTURAL EXHIBITS, DANCES, MUSIC, SPORTS & LANTERN PARADE. AT NEAL BLAISDELL CENTER, HONOLULU. (ST-WIDE). RAYMOND H INAFUKU, CHMN; UNITED JAPANESE SOCIETY OF HAWAII BICENTENNIAL CELEBRATION; 1149 BETHEL ST; HONOLULU, HI 96813. (#19973-1).

SEPT 1 - NOV 30, '76. 'VIGNETTES OF AMERICAN ART AND LIFE'. EXHIBIT AT HONOLULU ACADEMY OF ARTS. (ST-WIDE). THOMAS NICKERSON; HAWAII BICENTENNIAL COMMISSION; PO BOX 2359; HONOLULU, HI 96804. (#5649-1).

SEPT 18, '76. HAWAII MARTIAL ARTS FESTIVAL. MANY DIFFERENT SYSTEMS WILL PARTICIPATE WITH DEMONSTRATIONS & EXHIBIT. AT KAPIOLANI PARK BANDSTAND. (ST-WIDE). MORONI MEDEIROS, CHAIRMAN; HONOLULU CITY & COUNTY BICENTENNIAL COMMITTEE; KAPIOLANI PARK BANDSTAND; HONOLULU, HI 96815. (#102325-7).

SEPT 19 - OCT 23, '76. ALOHA FESTIVAL. FESTIVAL. (ST-WIDE). SUSAN SUNDERLAND, COORD; HAWAII VISITORS BUREAU; 2270 KALAKAUA AVE; HONOLULU, HI 96815. (#103416-569).

OCT 1 - 3, '76. BICENTENNIAL WATER CARNIVAL, A TWO-DAY COMPETITION-WATER SPORTS. COMPETITION, LIVE PERFORMANCE, FESTIVAL AT HONOLULU HARBOR, KEEHI LAGOON. (LOCAL). KENNETH BROCKMAN, COORD; HAWAII POWER BOAT ASSOC; 531 WAIKAMILO RD; HONOLULU, HI 96817. (#26947-1).

NOV 12, '76. SENIOR CITIZENS' BICENTENNIAL CULTURAL FAIR. EXHIBIT, FAIR AT HONOLULU INTERNATIONAL CENTER. (LOCAL). MORONI MEDEIROS, CHAIRMAN; HONOLULU CITY & COUNTY BICENTENNIAL COMMITTEE; KAPIOLANI PARK BANDSTAND; HONOLULU, HI 96815. (#102325-8).

NOV 27, '76. BICENTENNIAL THANKSGIVING MUSIC FESTIVAL. LIVE PERFORMANCE AT KAPIOLANI PARK BANDSTAND. (LOCAL). MORONI MEDEIROS, CHAIRMAN; HONOLULU CITY & COUNTY BICENTENNIAL COMMITTEE; KAPIOLANI PARK BANDSTAND; HONOLULU, HI 96815. (#102325-9).

DEC 12, '76. HONOLULU BICENTENNIAL MARATHON. COMPETITION AT ISLAND OF OAHU. (ST-WIDE). DR JACK H SOAFF, JR, CHMN; HONOLULU MARATHON ASSOC; 550 S BERETANIA ST; HONOLULU, HI 96813. (#17926-1).

DEC 24 - 30, '76. GYMNASTIC MEET FOR WOMEN - INTERNATIONAL PARTICIPATION. COMPETITION, LIVE PERFORMANCE AT BLAISDELL MEMORIAL CENTER, KAPIOLANI BLVD. (INT'L). MITCHELL BAROSH, DIRECTOR; HAWAII SCHOOL OF GYMNASTICS; BOX 746; KAILUA, HI 96734. (#26965-1).

DEC '76 - MAY '77. KA LEI NO KANE - HAWAIIAN OPERA. LIVE PERFORMANCE. (ST-WIDE). RICHARD CORNWELL; ENSEMBLE PLAYERS GUILD; 4744 KAHALA AVE; HONOLULU, HI 96818. (#25762-1).

MAR 1 - 31, '77. CHINESE FOLK ART EXHIBIT. CHINESE FOLK ART ASSEMBLED FROM MUSEUMS IN NEW YORK, CHICAGO, SAN FRANCISCO AND HONOLULU WILL BE ON EXHIBIT. (ST-WIDE). BETTY TSENG YU-HO ECKE; UNIVERSITY OF HAWAII, DEPT OF ART; 3460 KAOHINANI DR; HONOLULU, HI 96817. (#16184-1).

HUIALOHA

CHURCH STEEPLE RESTORATION OF HUIALOHA CHURCH - HI. RESTORATION OF STEEPLE, BELL TO RING JULY 4TH 1976. (LOCAL). CARL LINDQUIST, CONSULTANT; HAWAII BICENTENNIAL COMMISSION; 250 S KING ST; HONOLULU, HI 96813. (#18242). **ARBA GRANTEE.**

HUIALOHA CHURCH RESTORATION PROJECT, HI. RESTORATION OF CHURCH BUILDING FOR COMMUNITY PURPOSES. (LOCAL). T TWEGG SMITH, PROJ DIRECTOR; HAWAII BICENTENNIAL COMMITTEE; PO BOX 2359; HONOLULU, HI 96804. (#18612). **ARBA GRANTEE.**

KAHULUI

SEPT 15 - 21, '75. SERIES OF PRODUCTIONS OF MUSICAL EVENTS WITH CULTURAL EXHIBITS. SERIES OF PRODUCTIONS OF MUSICAL EVENTS WITH CULTURAL EXHIBITS THAT SEEK TO PRESERVE AND PERPETUATE THE AUTHENTIC HAWAIIAN CULTURE. (LOCAL). JAMES C HAYNES, TREASURER; HAWAIIAN BICENTENNIAL COMMISSION; BOX 2359; HONOLULU, HI 96793. (#12273-502).

KAILUH-KONA

HULIHEE PALACE RESTORATION, KAILUA-KONA, HI. RESTORATION OF MUSEUM WHICH WAS FORMERLY THE RESIDENCE OF HAWAIIAN ROYALTY. (LOCAL). MRS FRED W KOCH, REGENT; DAUGHTERS OF HAWAII; 2913 PALI HIGHWAY; HONOLULU, HI 96817. (#23765). **ARBA GRANTEE.**

KAPAA

TAHITI FETE, KAPAA, HI. DAY-LONG FESTIVAL OF TAHITIAN MUSIC, DANCE, COSTUMES & FIELD EVENTS. (LOCAL). MRS LYNN SMITH, PROJ MANAGER; MARKET PLACE, COCONUT PLANTATION; 484 KUHIO HWY; KAPAA, HI 96746. (#23674). **ARBA GRANTEE.**

JULY 4, '76. TAHITI FETE. FESTIVAL AT GREEN AREA, COCONUT PLANTATION. (LOCAL). MRS LYNN SMITH, PROJ MGR; KAUAI ETHNIC EDUCATION ASSOC; 484 KUHIO HWY; KAPAA, HI 96746. (#23674-1).

KAUAI

MAR 20 - 28, '76. PRINCE KUHIO FESTIVAL. CELEBRATION HONORS THE LIFE OF PRINCE KUHIO, HAWAIIAN STATESMAN. AT ISLAND OF KAUAI. (ST-WIDE). MAILE SEMIPEHOL, COORD; HAWAII VISITORS BUREAU; BOX 507; LUHUE, HI 96766. (#103416-236).

KAWAIHAE

JULY 31 - AUG 28, '76. THE CULTURE OF ANCIENT HAWAII. TWO CULTURAL DEMONSTRATORS AND ASSISTANTS WILL INSTRUCT VISITORS IN CRAFTS AND SKILLS SUCH AS LAUHALA WEAVING MUSICAL IMPLEMENT MAKING, FEATHER LEI MAKING, LANGUAGE, DANCES, TI LEAF ARTICLES, FLOWER LEI MAKING, GAMES, COCONUT ITEMS AND HAWAIIAN DYES. AT INFORMATION CENTER. (REGN'L). PUUKOHOLA HEIAU NHS; NATIONAL PARK SERVICE; P O BOX 128; HONAUNAU, HI 96726. (#6728-317).

KEKAHA

FOURTH OF JULY CELEBRATION - KEKAHA, HI. THIS WILL BE A 2-DAY CELEBRATION FROM JULY 3-4. (LOCAL). ALLAN A SMITH, PROJ CHAIRMAN; KEKAHA COMMUNITY ASSOC; BOX 121; LIHUE, HI 96766. (#24422). **ARBA GRANTEE.**

JULY 3 - 4, '76. FOURTH OF JULY CELEBRATION. FESTIVAL, PARADE. (LOCAL). ALLAN A SMITH, PROJ CHMN; KEKAHA COMMUNITY ASSOC; BOX 121; LIHUE, HI 96766. (#24422-1).

LAHAINA

SEPT 15 - 21, '75. SERIES OF PRODUCTIONS OF MUSICAL EVENTS WITH CULTURAL EXHIBITS. LIVE PERFORMANCE, EXHIBIT, FESTIVAL. (LOCAL). JAMES C HAYNES, TREASURER; HAWAIIAN BICENTENNIAL COMMISSION; BOX 2359; HONOLULU, HI 96793. (#12273-501).

LANAI

LANAI PHOTOGRAPHY PROJECT OF HAWAII. PHOTOGRAPHS OF PEOPLE AND ECOLOGY ON SMALL ISLAND IN TRANSITION. (LOCAL). BARBARA DUNN, SECRETARY; HAWAIIAN HISTORICAL SOCIETY; 560 KAWAIAHAO ST; HONOLULU, HI 96813. (#5713). **ARBA GRANTEE.**

MAY - JUNE '76. YOUTH CONGRESS SPRING WORKSHOPS. DATES AND TIMES NOT YET EXACT. (LOCAL). GIFFORD JOHNSON, CHMN; YOUTH ACTION; CHURCH OF THE CROSSROADS; HONOLULU, HI 96822. (#102743-3).

LIHUE

HISTORICAL EXHIBIT IN LIHUE, HAWAII. EXHIBIT ILLUSTRATING ATTEMPTED RUSSIAN EXPANSION ON KAUAI AGAINST BACKGROUND OF NORTHWEST MARITIME FUR TRADE. (LOCAL). ROBERT A GAHRAN, DIRECTOR; KAUAI MUSEUM; BOX 248; LIHU, HI 96766. (#10604). **ARBA GRANTEE.**

KEKAHA COMMUNITY ASSOCIATION - LIHUE, HI. TRADITIONAL 4TH OF JULY CELEBRATION WITH PARADES, SPEECHES, FLAG CEREMONIES, GAMES, HORSE RACING & FIREWORKS. (LOCAL). ALLAN A SMITH, PROJ COORDINATOR; KEKAHA COMMUNITY ASSOCIATION; BOX 121; LIHUE, HI 96766. (#25483). **ARBA GRANTEE.**

SPIRIT OF '76' - LIHUE, HI. LIGHT-ROCK MUSICAL PRESENTATION EXTOLLING AMERICA'S GREATNESS. (LOCAL). WILLIAM WOODALL, PRODUCER-DIRECTOR; WAIMEA HIGH SCHOOL; WAIMEA; WAIMEA, KAUA, HI 96796. (#20555). **ARBA GRANTEE.**

FEB 6 - 7, '76. SPIRIT OF '76, A LIGHT-ROCK MUSICAL EXTOLLING AMERICA'S GREATNESS. LIVE PERFORMANCE. (LOCAL). WILLIAM WOODALL, DIR; WAIMEA HIGH SCHOOL; WAIMEA, HI 96796. (#20555-1).

MAY 15 - DEC 31, '76. THE ATTEMPTED RUSSIAN EXPANSION ON KAUAI, 1815 - 1817. EXHIBIT ILLUSTRATING ATTEMPTED RUSSIAN EXPANSION ON KAUAI AGAINST BAXKGROUND OF NORTHWEST MARITIME FUR TRADE. INCLUDES PHOTOGRAPHS, DRAWINGS, MAPS & ARTIFACTS. AT WILCOX BLDG OF KAUAI MUSEUM COMPLEX. (LOCAL). ROBERT A GAHRAN, DIRECTOR; KAUAI MUSEUM; BOX 248; LIHUE, HI 96766. (#10604-1).

MAKAWAO

MAY 1 - SEPT 30, '76. KIPAHULU HAWAIIAN FARM. ONE MILE, 1 1/2 HOUR RANGER-CONDUCTED WALK TO HAWAIIAN FARM SITE. VISITORS WILL HAVE OPPORTUNITY TO SEE JUST WHAT PLANTS WERE GROWN & HOW THEY WERE CULTIVATED, AND TO DEVELOP EXPANDED APPRECIATION OF THE HAWAIIAN CULTURE. AT 9 MILES SW OF HANA (HWY 31) IN KIPAHULU DISTRICT OF PARK. (REGN'L). HALEAKALA NATL PK; NATIONAL PARK SRVICE; P.O. BOX 537; MAKAWAO, MAUI, HI 96768. (#6727-62).

MAY 15 - SEPT 15, '76. HALEAKALA ARTIST-IN-RESIDENCE PROGRAM. A RESIDENT ARTIST WILL BE PRODUCING WORKS IN HIS OR HER SPECIAL ART FORM AND INTERPRETING THE NATURAL FEATURES OF THE PARK. THE PROGRAM HOPES TO BRING INTO FOCUS A KEENER UNDERSTANDING OF THE NATURAL SCENE THROUGH THE TALENT AND SKILL OF AN ARTIST. AT HALEAKALA NATIONAL PARK. (REGN'L). HALEAKALA NP; NATIONAL PARK SERVICE; PO BOX 537; MAKAWAO, HI 96768. (#6729-158).

MAUI

MAUI COUNTY FESTIVAL FOR THE FOURTH PROJECT. 'COUNTDOWN' CONCEPT, WHICH EXPRESSES ITSELF AS '200 MINUS 3' IN 1973 '200 MINUS 2 IN '74' ETC. AN EFFORT TO GENERATE INTEREST & STIMULATE PLANNING & ACTIVITY IN CONNECTION WITH THE BICENTENNIAL. (ST-WIDE). THURSTON TWIGG-SMITH, CHAIRMAN; HAWAII BICENTENNIAL COMMISSION; PO BOX 2359; HONOLULU, HI 96804. (#1201). **ARBA GRANTEE.**

NA MELE O MAUI - FESTIVAL IN MAUI COUNTY, HI. SERIES OF PRODUCTIONS OF MUSICAL EVENTS WITH CULTURAL EXHIBITS THAT SEEK TO PRESERVE AND PERPETUATE THE AUTHENTIC HAWAIIAN CULTURE. (LOCAL). JAMES C HAYNES, TREASURER; HAWAIIAN BICENTENNIAL COMMISSION; BOX 2359; HONOLULU, HI 96793. (#12273). **ARBA GRANTEE.**

JAN 1 - JUNE 1, '74. MAUI COUNTY FESTIVAL FOR THE 4TH. 'COUNTDOWN' CONCEPT, WHICH EXPRESSES ITSELF AS '200 MINUS 3' IN 1973 '200 MINUS 2 IN '74' ETC. AN EFFORT TO GENERATE INTEREST & STIMULATE PLANNING & ACTIVITY IN CONNECTION WITH THE BICENTENNIAL. (ST-WIDE). THURSTON TWIGG-SMITH; HAWAII BICENTENNIAL COMMISSION; PO BOX 2359; HONOLULU, HI 96804. (#1201-901).

MIDWAY ISLAND

NAVAL HISTORY PROJECT IN MIDWAY ISLAND, HI. SHORT READING ON EVENTS AND SAYINGS WHICH WERE AND ARE IMPORTANT IN THE DEVELOPMENT OF THE NAVY. (LOCAL). BETTY JO BRUNER, ENSIGN; U S NAVAL FACILITY, MIDWAY ISLAND; BOX 100, FPO; SAN FRANCISCO, CA 96614. (#29911).

JULY 4, '76. FESTIVAL DAY. PARADES, FOOD & GAMES, CRAFTS & BOOTHS ARE ALL A PART OF THIS TRADITIONAL FESTIVAL. AT HARTLEY FIELD. (LOCAL). BETTYJO BRUNER, CHMN; U S NAVAL FACILITY, MIDWAY ISLAND; BOX 100, FPO; SAN FRANCISCO, CA 96614. (#200014-9).

MOLOKAI

YOUTH CONGRESS, MOLOKAI, HI. A CONFERENCE ON THE CONCERNS OF YOUTH. (LOCAL). T TWEGG SMITH, PROJ DIR; HAWAII BICENTENNIAL COMMITTEE; PO BOX 2359; HONOLULU, HI 96804. (#18613). **ARBA GRANTEE.**

PEARL HARBOR

NOV 6, '75. BICENTENNIAL SUNSET PARADE & HISTORICAL PAGEANT. PARADE INCLUDED DRILL EXHIBITION BY 1ST MARINE BRIGADE DRUM & BUGLE CORPS. MARINE RIFLE COMPANIES FROM MARINE BARRACKS PEARL HARBOR AND THE FLEET MARINE FORCE PACIFIC BAND. PAGEANT INCLUDED HISTORICAL PERIOD UNIFORMS AND NARRATIVE HISTORY OF U S MARINE CORPS. AT MARINE BARRACKS. (LOCAL). MAJOR WALTER S DEFOREST; UNITED STATES MARINE CORPS; FPO; SAN FRANCISCO, CA 96610. (#200014-2).

DEC 17, '76. DEDICATION, OPEN HOUSE, STATIC & ECOLOGICAL DISPLAY. OPERATE FIRE FIGHTING SCHOOL TO SHOW ECOLOGICAL PROGRESS OF SMOKE ABATEMENT EQUIPMENT. FEATURE SIGNIFICANT REDUCTION IN AIR POLLUTION WHILE TRAINING NAVY FIREFIGHTERS. DEMONSTRATE BY STATIC DISPLAY ADVANCEMENTS IN FIREFIGHTING CAPABILITY & LIFE SAVING EQUIPMENT. AT SOUTH AVE & SIXTH ST, PEARL HARBOR NAVAL STATION. (LOCAL). LCDR R G GODBEHERE, CHMN; FLEET TRAINING GROUP; 59-530 MAKANA RD; HALEIWA, HI 96712. (#200014-10).

WAILUKU

EXCHANGE CLUB/FREEDOM SHRINE - WAILUKU, HI. INSTALLATION OF FREEDOM SHRINE IN EACH PUBLIC HIGH SCHOOL IN HAWAII. SHRINES CONSIST OF 28 OF THE MOST IMPORTANT AND HISTORIC DOCUMENTS DEALING WITH AMERICAN FREEDOMS. (ST-WIDE). JAMES K ANDERSON, COORDINATOR; EXCHANGE CLUB OF HONOLULU; 190 S KING ST, SUITE 900; HONOLULU, HI 96813. (#25484). **ARBA GRANTEE.**

FESTIVAL FOR THE FOURTH-HAWAII COUNTY. 4TH OF JULY FESTIVITIES ON THE BIG ISLAND-COMMUNITY PICNICS, MUSIC, GAMES ETHNIC FESTIVAL PROGRAMS. (ST-WIDE). MSGR CHARLES KEKUMANO, MAUI COMMISSIONER; MAUI COUNTY BICENTENNIAL COMMISSION; 1627 MILL ST; WAILUKU, HI 96813. (#826). **ARBA GRANTEE.**

SEPT 15 - 19, '76. NA MELE O MAUI MUSIC FESTIVAL. MUSIC PROGRAMS AND ART EXHIBITS TO PRESERVE, ENHANCE AND PROMOTE HAWAIIAN CULTURE. SEPT 15 WAILUKU, MAUI, HI, 3 HRS; SEPT 17 LAHAINA HI, 3 HRS; SEPT 19 LAHAINA, HI, 4 HRS; SEPT 20 MAKAWAO, HI, 3 HRS. (INT'L). JAMES C HAYNES, TREAS; NA MELE O MAUI; PO BOX 778; WAILUKU, MAUI, HI 96793. (#23749-1).

HA3689A

Idaho

Idaho Bicentennial Commission

Commissioned March 16, 1973 by a legislative act

ARBA Statistics

Officially Recognized
Communities—28
Colleges/Universities—4
Military Installations—1
BINET Projects—67
Events—85
1976 Population—831,000

Bicentennial Archives

Idaho State Historical Society
610 North Julia Davis Drive
Boise, Idaho 83706

Membership

W. Anthony Park, *chairman*
J. Meredith Neil, *executive director*
Richard Bieber
Steven W. Bly
John Caylor
Becky Fanning
Senator Richard High
Representative Dorothy McCann
Ann Rydalch
Hillary Skanen
Suzanne D. Taylor
Marcus Ware
Merle W. Wells
Clifford Allen

Idaho

Idaho planned an extensive array of events and activities for its Bicentennial celebration. They ranged from the restoration of an historic Indian mission to the dedication of a new science museum. The preservation of the Indian mission was a cooperative effort by the Idaho Bicentennial Commission, the Catholic Diocese of Boise and the Coeur d'Alene Indian tribe. The Mission of the Sacred Heart at Cataldo (sometimes known as the "Cataldo Mission") is the state's oldest building still standing. It was begun in 1848 and completed in 1853, and is a unique tribute to the Coeur d'Alene Indians and the Jesuit missionaries who helped the tribe.

The Intermountain Science Experience Center was constructed in Idaho Falls. It is the largest and most elaborate science museum in the interior northwest and will serve as an aid to visitors of all ages in acquiring a basic understanding of scientific contributions in many areas, among them nuclear science and agriculture.

There were other impressive projects. The Veterans Memorial State Park in Boise was dedicated on July 4, 1976. It is truly unique, for it provides, within the city limits of the state's largest urban area, a lovely green park and environmental interpretive center. Also dedicated was the Malad Gorge State Park in south central Idaho, a rugged but beautiful setting only a few miles off Interstate Highway 80. Both are designated as Bicentennial parks.

Idaho had two impressive "firsts" in its Bicentennial program. Its Bicentennial commission was the first to mount a large-scale effort to develop an oral history project; and it was the first state to plan a statewide language bank where non-English speaking visitors can talk to interpreters.

Locally, Cassia County and the town of Rigby worked on a history of the area; Benneville mounted a clean-up campaign; Lewiston developed a walking tour; Marsing created a city park and made improvements to its river banks; Pocatello restored a magnificent old historic home and conducted tours of historic sites; and Twin Falls developed a museum which depicts the American Indian and his history in the western part of the U.S., from Alaska to Mexico.

All in all, there were some 43 local, city and county Bicentennial commissions, and each made valuable contributions.

Two local performing arts companies, the Ballet Folk of Moscow and the Antique Festival Theater, focused their efforts on serving the needs of the many small and widely scattered towns in Idaho and helped them in staging Bicentennial activities and festivities. Both troupes were assisted by IBC grants.

Idaho planned a major involvement in the *Bicentennial Parade of American Music.* A band, orchestra and choir were selected competitively by audition; these groups, together with the Ballet Folk of Moscow, performed throughout the state and later gave performances on "Idaho Day" at Independence Square in Philadelphia and at the Kennedy Center in Washington, D.C. And in cooperation with the Idaho Association of Broadcasters, a statewide committee organized a series of 13 one-half hour radio programs featuring the music of Idaho.

Throughout the state, citizens worked to make the Bicentennial something special, and with the present memories and future-oriented projects, the many contributions of Idaho will last for years to come.

ABERDEEN

ABERDEEN CITY PARK SHELTER, ID. BUILDING OF A PICNIC SHELTER BY THE ABERDEEN ROTARY CLUB. (LOCAL). KENNETH WESTFALL, PROJ DIRECTOR; ABERDEEN ROTARY CLUB; RR #1; ABERDEEN, ID 83210. (#27254). **ARBA GRANTEE.**

ARCO

EBR-1 -ATOMIC ENERGY GENERATOR EXHIBIT - IDAHO. EXHIBITION OF 1ST EXPERIMENTAL BREEDER REACTOR TO GENERATE ELECTRICITY WITH HEAT FROM NUCLEAR REACTOR. NOW A REGISTERED NATIONAL LANDMARK. ALSO OTHER NUCLEAR ENERGY DISPLAYS. (NAT'L). CHARLES W PELZER, ASST DIR FOR EDUC SERVICES; ENERGY RESEARCH AND DEVELOPMENT ADMINISTRATION; WASHINGTON, DC 20545. (#1182).

JUNE 10, '75 - CONTINUING . EXPERIMENTAL BREEDER REACTOR I, NAT'L HISTORIC LANDMARK EXHIBIT. EXHIBITION OF 1ST EXPERIMENTAL BREEDER REACTOR TO GENERATE ELECTRICITY WITH HEAT FROM NUCLEAR REACTOR & OTHER DISPLAYS A REGISTERED NATL LANDMARK GROUP TOUR RESERVATIONS CONTACT R BLACKLEDGE ERBA IDAHO FALLS IDAHO NO RESERV MID JUNE-SEPT. (REGN'L). CHARLES PELZER; ENERGY RESEARCH & DEVELOPMENT ADMINISTRATION; OFFICE OF PUBLIC AFFAIRS; WASHINGTON, DC 20545. (#1182-1).

JUNE 1 - SEPT 6, '76. BICENTENNIAL QUILTING BEE AT CRATERS OF THE MOON NATL MONUMENT. ADMISSION FEE TO PARK. EMPLOYEES' WIVES WILL HOLD AN OLD-FASHIONED QUILTING BEE SATURDAYS & SUNDAYS EVERY OTHER WEEK JULY TO AUGUST END; THEY WILL WORK ON A BICENTENNIAL QUILT. AT VISITORS CENTER LOBBY. (REGN'L). SUPT CRATERS OF THE MOON; NATIONAL PARK SERVICE; P.O. BOX 29; ARCO, ID 83213. (#6728-8).

BLACKFOOT

SEPT 3, '74. JOHNNY HORIZON CLEANUP -- EASTERN IDAHO STATE FAIR PARADE ROUTE. BONNEVILLE COUNTY, ID, CLEANUP PROGRAM JOHNNY HORIZON '76 CAMPAIGN TO CLEAN BONNEVILLE FOR BICENTENNIAL. (LOCAL). RUSSELL HOLM; BONNEVILLE BICENTENNIAL COMMISSION; PO BOX 339; IDAHO FALLS, ID 83401. (#2694-903).

AUG 23, '75. UNITED STATES ARMED FORCES BICENTENNIAL CARAVAN. CARAVAN NUMBER FOUR-COMPOSED OF EXHIBIT VANS FOR EACH MILITARY SERVICE. PROJECT THEME IS 'HISTORY OF THE ARMED FORCES & THEIR CONTRIBUTIONS TO THE NATION.'. (LOCAL). MRS MARGE VON DER LIETH; US ARMED FORCES BICENT EXHIBIT VAN PROJECT; 11 NW MAIN ST; BLACKFOOT, ID 83221. (#1775-163).

BOISE

IDAHO BICENTENNIAL MEETING HOUSE. LEASING OF WAITING ROOM OF BOISE UNION PACIFIC RAILROAD DEPOT FOR PUBLIC USE. (ST-WIDE). J MEREDITH NEIL, EXEC DIRECTOR; IDAHO ARBC; 210 MAIN ST; BOISE, ID 83702. (#1038). **(??).**

IDAHO BICENTENNIAL REVIEW - MAGAZINE PROJECT. ANNUAL MAGAZINE CONTAINING STORIES REGARDING BICENTENNIAL PROJECTS AROUND IDAHO TO APPEAR ON JULY 4 OF 1974, 1975,AND 1976. PUBLISHED BY MCGINNIS PUBLISHING COMPANY OF BOISE. (ST-WIDE). J MEREDITH NEIL EXECUTIVE DIRECTOR; IDAHO ARBC; 210 MAIN ST; BOISE, ID 83702. (#1708). **(??).**

IDAHO ORAL HISTORY PROJECT. DEVELOPMENT OF A MASTER TAPE FILE OF 1000 HOURS PLAYING TIME AND A FINAL TRANSCRIPT READY IN 1976 DUE TO COORDINATED STATEWIDE EFFORTS AT RECORDING REMINISCENCES. (ST-WIDE). A W DAWSON, PROJ COORDINATOR; IDAHO ARBC; 210 MAIN ST; BOISE, ID 83702. (#381). **ARBA GRANTEE.**

IDAHO TERRITORIAL PAPERS PROJECT. THE IDAHO HISTORICAL SOCIETY IS GATHERING AND MICROFILMING THE MANY DOCUMENTS RELATING TO IDAHO'S TERRITORIAL HISTORY; SERVING TO AID SCHOLARS AND EXPIDITE A NATIONAL ARCHIVES PROJECT. (ST-WIDE). DR MERLE WELLO, DIRECTOR; IDAHO HISTORICAL SOCIETY; 610 N JULIA DAVIS DR; BOISE, ID 83707. (#360). **ARBA GRANTEE.**

LAND RESOURCE DEMONSTRATION PROJECT - BOISE, ID. INVESTIGATION AND APPLICATION OF REMOTE SENSED (ESPECIALLY LANDSAT SATELLITE) NATURAL RESOURCE INFORMATION IN THE PLANNING, MANAGEMENT AND DECISION MAKING PROCESS. (REGN'L). WALLACE E HEDRICK, PROJ DIRECTOR; PACIFIC NORTHWEST REGIONAL COMMISSION; STATEHOUSE; BOISE, ID 83704. (#20086).

PAINTING EXHIBIT: NEZ PERCE INDIAN HISTORY - ID. THE NEZ PERCE TRIBE WILL EXHIBIT PAINTINGS OF THEIR INDIAN HISTORY AT THE STATE CAPITOL. (ST-WIDE). RICHARD HALFMOON, CHAIRMAN; NEZ PERCE TRIBE; BOX 305; LAPWAI, ID 83540. (#27089). **ARBA GRANTEE.**

'SAINTS & ODDFELLOWS' - BOOK ON IDAHO ARCHITECTURE. WRITTEN BY DIRECTOR OF THE IDAHO BICENTENNIAL COMMISSION & SUBTITLED 'A BICENTENNIAL SAMPLER OF IDAHO ARCHITECTURE', FUNDS FROM BOOK SALE ARE BEING USED FOR FUTURE PUBLICATIONS ON THE ARTS IN IDAHO. (ST-WIDE). THE DIRECTOR; BOISE GALLERY OF ART; PO BOX 1505; BOISE, ID 83701. (#28711).

SCAGLIOLA REFURBISHING OF IDAHO'S STATEHOUSE. SCAGLIOLA PLASTERING IN STATEHOUSE HAS BEEN EXTENSIVELY REFINISHED. THE PLASTERING IS A SPECIAL MATERIAL VERY CLOSELY RESEMBLING MARBLE, & WAS ORIGINATED IN THE 16TH CENTURY IN ITALY. (ST-WIDE). J MERIDITH NEIL, EXEC DIRECTOR; IDAHO ARBC; 210 MAIN ST; BOISE, ID 83702. (#28712).

VETERANS MEMORIAL STATE PARK, BOISE, IDAHO. CONSTRUCTION OF A RIVERSIDE PARK TO CLIMAX THE DEVELOPMENT OF A GREENBELT ALONG THE BOISE RIVER IN THE CITY OF BOISE. (ST-WIDE). STEVEN W BLY, DIRECTOR; IDAHO DEPT OF PARKS & RECREATION; 2263 WARM SPRINGS AVE; BOISE, ID 83707. (#351).

WAGON TRAIN PILGRIMAGE - BOISE, ID. ASSIST THE IDAHO TEAMSTERS WITH A GRANT TO PAY THE COSTS OF MOVING THE IDAHO TEAM OF HORSES FROM ST JOSEPH, MO TO PITTSBURGH, PA AND FROM VALLEY FORGE TO IDAHO. (ST-WIDE). J MEREDITH NEIL, EXEC DIRECTOR; IDAHO ARBC; 210 MAIN ST; BOISE, ID 83702. (#24890). **ARBA GRANTEE.**

AUG 1, '75 - JULY 4, '76. IDAHO'S WAGON TRAIN PILGRIMAGE. TOUR. (REGN'L). J MEREDITH NEIL, EXEC DIR; IDAHO ARBC; 210 MAIN ST; BOISE, ID 83702. (#24890-1).

AUG 17 - 19, '75. UNITED STATES ARMED FORCES BICENTENNIAL CARAVAN. CARAVAN NUMBER FOUR-COMPOSED OF EXHIBIT VANS FOR EACH MILITARY SERVICE. PROJECT THEME IS 'HISTORY OF THE ARMED FORCES & THEIR CONTRIBUTIONS TO THE NATION.'. (LOCAL). KEITH GABRIEL; US ARMED FORCES BICENT EXHIBIT VAN PROJECT; 7421 COLEHAVEN; BOISE, ID 83702. (#1775-161).

OCT 22 - 24, '75. AMERICAN FREEDOM TRAIN DISPLAY DAYS AT BOISE. THE AMERICAN FREEDOM TRAIN WILL INCLUDE 10 EXHIBIT CARS & 2 SHOWCASE CARS DEPICTING DIFFERENT PHASES OF THE AMERICAN EXPERIENCE. ITS ARRIVAL WILL SERVE AS A CATALYST FOR LOCAL BICENTENNIAL CELEBRATIONS BY PEOPLE THROUGHOUT THIS NATION. AT UP TRAIN DEPOT, CAPITOL BLVD. (ST-WIDE). DON MALLICOAT, EDIT SVCS; THE AMERICAN FREEDOM TRAIN FOUNDATION, INC.; 5205 LEESBURG PIKE, SUITE 800; BAILEY'S XRDS, VA 22041. (#1776-29).

APR 6, '76. RE-ENACTMENT OF 1ST COMMERCIAL AIRLINE FLIGHT IN USA. RE-ENACT HISTORIC FLIGHT W/RESTORED ANTIQUE 'SWALLOW' BIPLANE WHICH MADE FLIGHT FROM PASCO, WA, TO BOISE IN 1926. TO MARK 50TH ANNIVERSARY OF COMMERCIAL AVIATION, PARADE, LUNCHEON & OTHER ACTIVITIES. BOISE WILL BREAK GROUND FOR NEW AIR MUSEUM. AT PLANE LEAVES PASCO, WA, 6:30AM(PST) & ARRIVES AT BOISE AIRPORT 10AM. (NAT'L). JAMES A KENNEDY, P/R DIR; UNITED AIRLINES; PO BOX 66100; CHICAGO, IL 60666. (#103785-1).

APR 30 - MAY 8, '76. MUSICAL '1776' PERFORMED LIVE, PARADE, CHURCH NIGHT, SCHOOL NIGHT. MUSIC WEEK WILL PRESENT 9 DAYS OF FREE ENTERTAINMENT SHOW '1776' PERFORMING PARADE SCHOOL NIGHT CHURCH NIGHT. AT CAPITOL HIGH SCHOOL. (LOCAL). DOROTHY MOUSETIS; BOISE MUSIC WEEK; 430 HILLVIEW DR.; BOISE, ID 83702. (#1041-1).

JUNE 17 - 20, '76. IDAHO STATE SQUARE DANCE FESTIVAL. LIVE PERFORMANCE AT WESTERN IDAHO FAIRGROUNDS, 5610 GLENWOOD. (ST-WIDE). DOUG HYSLOP, PROJ DIR; IDAHO FEDERATION OF SQUARE AND ROUND DANCE CLUBS; RT 4; NAMPA, ID 83651. (#101031-1).

JULY 1 - 31, '76. EXHIBITION OF CAPT FERGUSON'S COMMEMORATIVE PAINTINGS. CAPT BEN F FERGUSON BICENT PAINTING IN BOISE, ID. BICENTENNIAL SERIES OF HISTORICAL EVENTS PAINTED AT THE SITES AND ON THE ANNIVERSARY OF THE EVENTS. PAINTINGS ARE DEPICT WESTERN HISTORY. AT FIRST SECURITY BANK. (LOCAL). GLENN LUNGREN; FIRST SECURITY BANK OF IDAHO; 9TH & IDAHO; BOISE, ID 83730. (#2401-501).

AUG 1, '76 - FEB 28, '77. PAINTING EXHIBIT: NEZ PERCE INDIAN HISTORY. EXHIBIT AT IDAHO CAPITOL, NORTH END OF CAPITOL BLVD. (ST-WIDE). RICHARD HALFMOON, CHMN; NEZ PERCE TRIBE; BOX 305; LAPWAI, ID 83540. (#27089-1).

AUG 28 - SEPT 4, '76. WESTERN IDAHO STATE FAIR. FAIR AT WESTERN IDAHO FAIRGROUNDS. (ST-WIDE). SCOTT ANDERSON; WESTERN IDAHO FAIR; 5610 GLENWOOD; BOISE, ID 83702. (#103416-491).

BUHL

ANTIQUE FESTIVAL THEATER TOUR - BUHL, ID. STATEWIDE TOURS OF A PROFESSIONAL REPERTOIRE COMPANY WITH SPECIAL EMPHASIS ON RELEVANT HISTORICAL DRAMA WITH THEATER IN THE SCHOOLS. (ST-WIDE). ALDRICH BOWLER, PRODUCER-DIRECTOR; ANTIQUE FESTIVAL THEATER; PO BOX 26; BUHL, ID 83316. (#13395). **ARBA GRANTEE.**

BICENTENNIAL FESTIVAL OF THE ARTS OF BUHL, IDAHO. PREPARATION FOR A WEEK-LONG ARTS FESTIVAL IN 1976 BY STAGING A STATE WIDE THEATRE-IN-THE-SCHOOLS PROGRAM DURING THE 1973-1974 SCHOOL YEAR AND BY GATHERING NEEDED MATERIALS. (ST-WIDE). GRAY WRIGHT, CHAIRMAN, BOARD OF TRUSTEES; ANTIQUE FESTIVAL THEATER; PO BOX 26; BUHL, ID 83316. (#651). **ARBA GRANTEE.**

JULY 2 - 4, '76. JULY 4TH CELEBRATION. HISTORICAL PLAY ON JULY 2. RODEO, BARBEQUE, SIDEWALK SALE, DANCE ON JULY 3. PARADE WITH 103 ENTRIES, GAMES AND FIREWORKS ON JULY 4. (LOCAL). CECIL C CHILDS; WEST END BICENTENNIAL COMMITTEE; 918 SPRAGUE AVE; BUHL, ID 83316. (#200015-4).

JULY 3 - 5, '76. SAGE BRUSH DAYS. THE DAYS OF FRONTIER DESPERADOS AND PIONEER FESTIVITIES COMPRISE THIS COUNTYWIDE 4TH OF JULY CELEBRATION. (LOCAL). DORIS RUTHERFORD, CHMN; BUHL CHAMBER OF COMMERCE; PO BOX 28; BUHL, ID 83316. (#103416-411).

BURLEY

GUIDE BOOK OF HISTORIC SITES IN CASSIA COUNTY, ID. A SOFT-COVERED BOOK WITH MANY ILLUSTRATIONS RECOUNTING THE HISTORY AND DESCRIBING THE HISTORIC SITES OF CASSIA COUNTY, IDAHO. (NAT'L). MIKE FEILER, PRESIDENT; CASSIA COUNTY HISTORICAL SOCIETY; PO BOX 331; BURLEY, ID 83318. (#359). **(??). ARBA GRANTEE.**

AUG 2 - 31, '75. HISTORICAL TOUR OF PIONEER HOMES. TOUR AT CASSIA COUNTY MUSEUM. (LOCAL). RUTH LARSON MILLERD, CHMN; CASSIA COUNTY HISTORICAL SOCIETY; HILAND AND MAIN ST; BURLEY, ID 83318. (#100224-1).

CALDWELL

SNAKE RIVER STORY THROUGH SIGHT AND SOUND. PREPARATION OF SEVERAL MAPS, PHOTO EXHIBIT, & PUBLICATION OF 3 15 MINUTE SLIDE-TAPE SHOWS & A PAMPHLET TO TELL STORY OF USES, HISTORY, PROBLEMS & FUTURE OF RIVER. (ST-WIDE). MRS DONNA PARSONS, DIRECTOR; COLLEGE OF IDAHO, REGIONAL STUDIES CENTER; CLEVELAND BLVD, US HIGHWAY 30; CALDWELL, ID 83605. (#362). **ARBA GRANTEE.**

SEPT 2, '75. UNITED STATES ARMED FORCES BICENTENNIAL CARAVAN. CARAVAN NUMBER FOUR-COMPOSED OF EXHIBIT VANS FOR EACH MILITARY SERVICE. PROJECT THEME IS 'HISTORY OF THE ARMED FORCES & THEIR CONTRIBUTIONS TO THE NATION.'. (LOCAL). MS HELEN MCKINNEY; US ARMED FORCES BICENT EXHIBIT VAN PROJECT; 404 S 10TH AVE; CALDWELL, ID 83605. (#1775-169).

DEC 8, '75. BICENTENNIAL PROGRAM OF AMERICAN MUSIC. LIVE PERFORMANCE AT JEWETT AUDITORIUM. (LOCAL). D L PARSONS; COLLEGE OF IDAHO; CALDWELL, ID 83605. (#200015-5).

CASCADE

CITY PARK, CASCADE, ID. DEVELOPMENT OF CITY PARK. (LOCAL). JIM HAAS, CHAIRMAN; JAYCEES; CASCADE, ID 83611. (#22716).

JULY 3 - 5, '76. THUNDER MT DAYS. PARADES, BASQUE DANCERS, GAMES, DANCES, BARBEQUE. AT DOWNTOWN CASCADE. (REGN'L). PAULINE BISOM, COORD; CASCADE CHAMBER OF COMMERCE; BOX 490; CASCADE, ID 83611. (#106199-3).

AUG 13 - 14, '76. CASCADE HIGH SCHOOL CLASS REUNION. REUNION OF CLASSES 1921 THRU 1956. AT CASCADE HIGH SCHOOL AUDITORIUM & SCHOOL GROUNDS. (LOCAL). MARILYN CALLENDER, CHMN; CASCADE HIGH SCHOOL; CASCADE, ID 83611. (#106199-1).

AUG 17 - 21, '76. VALLEY COUNTY FAIR. EXHIBIT, FAIR, FESTIVAL, OPENING AT FAIRGROUNDS CASCADE. (ST-WIDE). ADOLPH HEINRICH, COORD; VALLEY COUNTY FAIR BOARD; LAKEFORK, ID 83635. (#106199-2).

AUG 18 - 22, '76. LITTLE BRITCHES RODEO AND QUEEN CONTEST. QUEEN CONTEST WILL BE HELD THE EVENING OF WEDNESDAY, AUGUST 18. AT COUNTY FAIR GROUNDS. (LOCAL). PAULINE BISOM, COORD; COUNTY FAIR BOARD & CASCADE CHAMBER OF COMMERCE; BOX 490; CASCADE, ID 83611. (#106199-4).

CATALDO

OLD CATALDO MISSION OF IDAHO. COOPERATIVE EFFORT AT PRESERVATION AND RESTORATION BY THE CATHOLIC DIOCESE OF BOISE AND THE COEUR D'ALENE INDIAN TRIBE OF THE MISSION OF THE SACRED HEART, OLDEST BUILDING IN IDAHO, BUILT IN 1848. (ST-WIDE). J MEREDITH NEIL, EXEC DIRECTOR; IDAHO ARBC; 210 MAIN ST; BOISE, ID 83702. (#382). **(??). ARBA GRANTEE.**

COEUR D'ALENE

COEUR D'ALENE PLAYLAND PIER, ID. EXPANSION OF THE CITY PARK WITH A LANDSCAPED PIER ON LAKE COEUR D'ALENE. (LOCAL). JOHN C SIATH, ASSISTANT CITY ENGINEER; CITY OF COEUR D'ALENE; 5TH & SHERMAN; COEUR D'ALENE, ID 83814. (#27223). **ARBA GRANTEE.**

AUG 15 - 16, '76. UNITED STATES ARMED FORCES BICENTENNIAL CARAVAN. CARAVAN IS COMPOSED OF EXHIBIT VANS FOR EACH MILITARY SERVICE. PROJECT THEME IS 'HISTORY OF THE ARMED FORCES & THEIR CONTRIBUTIONS TO THE NATION.'. (LOCAL). ROBERT NOBIS, CHMN; UNITED STATES ARMED FORCES BICENTENNIAL CARAVAN; 105 N 4TH ST, PO BOX 244; COUER D'ALENE, ID 83814. (#1775-704).

DONNELLY

JR HIGH BICENTENNIAL HISTORY CLASS, DONNELLY, ID. PIONEER HISTORY OF AREA WILL BE TAUGHT. (LOCAL). BEVERLY BRADFORD, PRINCIPAL; MCCALL-DONNELLY JR HIGH SCHOOL; DONNELLY, ID 83615. (#22711).

TENNIS COURTS IN CITY PARK, DONNELLY, ID. CONSTRUCTION OF TENNIS COURTS. (LOCAL). ROSAMOND BURGESS, CHAIRMAN; EXTENSION CLUB; DONNELLY, ID 83615. (#22708).

JULY 24, '76. CHUCK WAGON DAYS BARBECUE. COMMUNITY BARBECUE-DONATIONS ACCEPTED. AT 4-H CAMP LAKE CASCADE. (LOCAL). MRS TED BURGESS, CHMN; DONNELLY EXTENSION CLUB; PO BOX 662; DONNELLY, ID 83615. (#106200-1).

EMMETT

IMPROVEMENTS OF GEM COUNTY, ID, HISTORICAL MUSEUM. PURCHASE AND SUBSEQUENT RENOVATION OF THE FORMER EMMETT PUBLIC LIBRARY TO BE USED AS THE MUSEUM FOR THE NEWLY FORMED GEM COUNTY HISTORICAL ASSN AND ITS NEW ACQUISITIONS. (ST-WIDE). MRS HARRY LYON, PRESIDENT; GEM COUNTY HISTORICAL SOCIETY; 600 EVERGREEN DR; EMMETT, ID 83617. (#361). **ARBA GRANTEE.**

FAIRFIELD

CAMAS COUNTY NEWSPAPER - FAIRFIELD, ID. CREATION OF A WEEKLY NEWSPAPER FOR A RURAL AREA EDITED AND PRODUCED BY HIGH SCHOOL STUDENTS. (LOCAL). HAROLD STROUD, SUPERINTENDENT; SCHOOL DISTRICT NO 121; FAIRFIELD, ID 83327. (#27251). **ARBA GRANTEE.**

FRANKLIN

HATCH HOME ACQUISITION AND RESTORATION, ID. CREATION OF A PERIOD MUSEUM IN AN 1870 GREER REVIVAL RESIDENCE. (LOCAL). MARLOWE WOODWARD, PRESIDENT; IDAHO PIONEER ASSOC; FRANKLIN, ID 83237. (#27722). **ARBA GRANTEE.**

GOODING

BICENTENNIAL FESTIVAL OF ARTS IN IDAHO. STATEWIDE TOURS OF A PROFESSIONAL REPERTOIRE COMPANY WITH SPECIAL EMPHASIS ON HISTORICAL DRAMA. (ST-WIDE). ALDRICH BOWLER, PRODUCER; ANTIQUE FESTIVAL THEATER; US-20 AT STATE HWY 46; GOODING, ID 83330. (#8366). **ARBA GRANTEE.**

NEW PERFORMING ARTS CENTER - GOODING, ID. THE NEW PERFORMANCE ARTS CENTER IS IN FULL OPERATION. (LOCAL). ALDRICH BOWLER, PRODUCER; ANTIQUE FESTIVAL THEATER; US-20 AT STATE HWY 46; GOODING, ID 83330. (#30138).

GRANDVIEW

TIME CAPSULE AND PARK - GRANDVIEW, ID. THE PARK WILL BEAUTIFY GRANDVIEW AND THE TIME CAPSULE WILL BE BURIED THERE. CAPSULE CONTAINS CITY PAPERS, MAPS AND SIGNATURES OF ALL THE LOCAL STUDENTS AND TEACHERS, FROM ELEMENTARY TO HIGH SCHOOL. (LOCAL). DIANE OSBORNE, CHAIRMAN; GRANDVIEW BICENTENNIAL COMMITTEE; PO BOX 165; GRANDVIEW, ID 83624. (#28659).

JULY 4, '76. PARADE - A SHOWING OF OUR COUNTRY'S HERITAGE. PARADE AT MAIN STREET PAST ELEM SCHOOL AND POST OFFICE. (LOCAL). DIANE OSBORNE, CHMN; GRANDVIEW BICENTENNIAL COMMITTEE; PO BOX 165; GRANDVIEW, ID 83624. (#200015-6).

GRANGEVILLE

BICENTENNIAL MUSEUM FOR IDAHO COUNTY - ID. FUND RAISING IS BEING DONE FOR A NEW MUSEUM. (LOCAL). CAROL SPENCER, CHAIRMAN; BICENTENNIAL MUSEUM COMMITTEE, INC; GRANGEVILLE, ID 83530. (#29017).

AUG 25, '76. BICENTENNIAL DAY WITH BARBECUE, FESTIVAL, KIDDIE PARADE & RODEO. FESTIVAL AT GRANGEVILLE ELEMENTARY SCHOOL. (LOCAL). LONALEE HOOGLAND, CHMN; GRANGEVILLE BICENTENNIAL COMMITTEE; 910 CROOK; GRANGEVILLE, ID 83530. (#200015-7).

IDAHO CITY

HISTORIC AMERICAN BUILDING SURVEY TEAM PROJ -IDAHO. HISTORIC AMERICAN BUILDING SURVEY IS SENDING A TEAM TO DOCUMENT IDAHO CITY. WILL GREATLY STIMULATE LOCAL EFFORTS, & INCREASE AWARENESS OF THE HISTORY. (LOCAL). J MEREDITH NEIL, EXECUTIVE DIRECTOR; IDAHO ARBC; 210 MAIN ST; BOISE, ID 83702. (#1223). **ARBA GRANTEE.**

IDAHO FALLS

INTERMOUNTAIN SCIENCE EXPERIENCE CENTER- IDAHO. SCIENCE EXPERIENCE CENTER FOR ENERGY ENVIRONMENT AND EDUCATION WILL AID VISITORS OF ALL AGES TO ACQUIRE A BASIC UNDERSTANDING OF SCIENTIFIC CONTRIBUTIONS TO A PAST TO REMEMBER--A FUTURE TO MOLD. (REGN'L). JOE HUNTER, PRESIDENT; INTERMOUNTAIN SCIENCE EXPERIENCE CENTER, INC; 1776 SCIENCE CENTER DRIVE; IDAHO FALLS, ID 83401. (#2695). **ARBA GRANTEE.**

KID-RADIO BICENTENNIAL PROMOTION PROGRAM - NBMRP. BROADCASTING HUMAN INTEREST STORIES ON LOCAL LISTENING AREA. DEVELOPED TV VIGNETTES FOR SISTER TV STATIONS & A HISTORY BOOK FOR LIBRARIES & THE STATE HISTORICAL SOCIETY. (LOCAL). JANET THOMAS, BICENTENNIAL COORDINATOR; KID BROADCASTING; 1255 E 17TH ST; IDAHO FALLS, ID 83401. (#22104).

POST-REGISTER & INTERMOUNTAIN SCIENCE CENTER-NBMRP. PAPER WAS PROME MOVER IN SUPPORT OF DEVELOPMENT OF THE AREA'S PRIME BICENTENNIAL PROJECT, THE INTERMOUNTAIN SCIENCE EXPERIENCE CENTER. ALSO HAD HISTORICAL SPECIAL EDITION ON JULY 3, 1976. (REGN'L). JOE MARKER, BICENTENNIAL COORDINATOR; THE POST-REGISTER; 333 NORTHGATE MILE; IDAHO FALLS, ID 83401. (#29122).

APR 27, '74. BONNEVILLE COUNTY KEEP AMERICA BEAUTIFUL DAY. BONNEVILLE COUNTY, ID, CLEANUP PROGRAM JOHNNY HORIZON '76 CAMPAIGN TO CLEAN BONNEVILLE FOR BICENTENNIAL. (LOCAL). RUSSELL HOLM, CHMN; BONNEVILLE BICENTENNIAL COMMISSION; PO BOX 339; IDAHO FALLS, ID 83401. (#2694-901).

JULY 4, '74. JOHNNY HORIZON CLEANUP--JULY 4TH PARADE ROUTE. BONNEVILLE COUNTY, ID, CLEANUP PROGRAM JOHNNY HORIZON '76 CAMPAIGN TO CLEAN BONNEVILLE FOR BICENTENNIAL. (LOCAL). RUSSELL HOLM; BONNEVILLE BICENTENNIAL COMMISSION; PO BOX 339; IDAHO FALLS, ID 83401. (#2694-902).

AUG 24 - 25, '75. UNITED STATES ARMED FORCES BICENTENNIAL CARAVAN. CARAVAN NUMBER FOUR-COMPOSED OF EXHIBIT VANS FOR EACH MILITARY SERVICE. PROJECT THEME IS 'HISTORY OF THE ARMED FORCES & THEIR CONTRIBUTIONS TO THE NATION.'. (LOCAL). CAPT THOMAS J WADSWORTH; US ARMED FORCES BICENT EXHIBIT VAN PROJECT; BOX 339; IDAHO FALLS, ID 83401. (#1775-164).

JUNE 25 - JULY 24, '76. FESTIVAL MONTH - JULY 1976 - OF IDAHO FALLS, ID. INVITATIONAL SOFTBALL TOURNAMENT, SHRINE CIRCUS, RODEO, COLONIAL BALL, CHUCK WAGON BREAKFAST, 10TH ANNUAL NATIONAL PARADE, FAMILY GAMES, WATER SKIING AND RINGING OF LIBERTY BELL AT CIVIC AUDITORIUM. VARYING TIMES AND PLACES DURING MONTH'S FESTIVITIES. (ST-WIDE). JERRY WADSWORTH, EXEC DIR; BONNEVILLE COUNTY ARBC; PO BOX 339; IDAHO FALLS, ID 83401. (#1037-501).

JULY 4, '76 - CONTINUING . INTERMOUNTAIN SCIENCE EXPERIENCE CENTER OPENS. EXHIBIT & INFORMATION CENTER FOR PUBLIC, A TRAINING & DEMONSTRATION CENTER FOR STUDENTS. (REGN'L). JOHN BRADBURNE; ENERGY RESEARCH & DEVELOPMENT ADMINISTRATION; OFFICE OF PUBLIC AFFAIRS; WASHINGTON, DC 20545. (#2695-1).

KETCHUM

RESTORATION OF ORE WAGONS, KETCHUM, ID. RESTORATION OF ORE WAGONS FORMERLY USED IN LOCAL MINES AND NOW A MAJOR PART OF THE ANNUAL WAGON DAYS CELEBRATION. (LOCAL). HON GERALD N SEIFFERT, MAYOR; CITY OF KETCHUM; PO BOX 567; KETCHUM, ID 83340. (#27255). **ARBA GRANTEE.**

LAPWAI

NEZ PERCE HISTORY AND LANGUAGE DEVELOPMENT -BOOK. THE BOOK IS ABOUT THE MODERN HISTORY OF THE NEZ PERCE INDIANS. THE GRANT FOR THIS BOOK IS PRESENTLY BEING TIED INTO THE NEZ PERCE LANGUAGE DICTIONARY. (NAT'L). ALLEN P SLICKPOO, SR, DIRECTOR; NEZ PERCE TRIBE; PO BOX 305; LAPWAI, ID 83540. (#3794).

LEWISTON

PIONEER PARK FOUNTAIN, LEWISTON, ID. RESTORATION OF A HISTORIC FOUNTAIN IN THE CITY'S OLDEST PARK, BY LOCAL YOUTH. (LOCAL). ROGER FULTON, ASSISTANT CITY MANAGER; CITY OF LEWISTON; PO BOX 617; LEWISTON, ID 83501. (#27253). **ARBA GRANTEE.**

WALKING TOUR OF DOWNTOWN LEWISTON, IDAHO. ILLUSTRATED BROCHURE BRIEFLY DESCRIBING 21 BUILDINGS IN A SIX BLOCK AREA OF THE OLDEST PART OF LEWISTON, ID. (LOCAL). MRS TONI EARLE, PROJECT DIRECTOR; LUNA HOUSE HISTORICAL MUSEUM; 0310 3RD ST; LEWISTON, ID 83501. (#1710).

MARSING

BEAUTIFICATION OF PARKS - PROJ OF MARSING, ID. DEVELOPMENT OF CITY PARK: PLANTINGS, PLAYGROUND, BOAT DOCKS, TABLES AND TREES ON THE ISLAND PARK; RIVER BANK BEAUTIFICATION AND STREET IMPROVEMENT. (LOCAL). BEA LARSON, SECRETARY; CITY OF MARSING; BOX 459; MARSING, ID 83439. (#17012).

MAY 22, '76. BICENTENNIAL CELEBRATION. FESTIVAL, PARADE, LIVE PERFORMANCE AT STREETS, PARKS & HIGH SCHOOL GYM. (ST-WIDE). BEATRICE LARSEN, SEC; MARSING BICENTENNIAL COMMITTEE; BOX 459; MARSING, ID 83639. (#103274-1).

MCCALL

BICENTENNIAL COOKBOOK, MCCALL, ID. HISTORICAL COOKBOOK; FAVORITE RECIPES WITH HISTORICAL SIGNIFICANCE TO AREA. (LOCAL). MARJ EVANS, COORDINATOR; PROGRESSIVE CLUB; PO BOX; MCCALL, ID 83638. (#22706).

BICENTENNIAL INFORMATION CENTER, MCCALL, ID. BICENTENNIAL INFORMATION ON NATIONWIDE EVENTS IN CATALOGUES AND CLIPPINGS. (LOCAL). VELMA L SHOEMAKER, SECRETARY; MCCALL AREA CHAMBER OF COMMERCE; PO BOX D; MCCALL, ID 83638. (#22715).

CITY PARK ON OLD DUMPSITE, MCCALL, ID. DEVELOPMENT OF NEIGHBORHOOD PARK. (LOCAL). LEE MCDOUGAL, COUNCILMAN; PARKS AND BEACHES DEPT; BOX 374; MCCALL, ID 83638. (#22707).

FLAG POLE IN ART ROBERTS PARK, MCCALL, ID. LODGEPOLE PINE FLAGPOLE IN PARK. (LOCAL). LEONARD ZBOROWSKI, CHAIRMAN; MCCALL CHAMBER OF COMMERCE; PO BOX D; MCCALL, ID 83638. (#22705).

HISTORICAL FILE-MCCALL LIBRARY, ID. CATALOGUED FILE OF HISTORICAL PAPERS AND PICTURES. (ST-WIDE). MARY THURSTON, CHAIRMAN; PHYETTE LAKES PROGRESSIVE CLUB; PARK AVE; MCCALL, ID 83638. (#22710).

ORAL HISTORY OF VALLEY COUNTY, MCCALL, ID. TAPING OF OLD TIMERS' EXPERIENCES. (ST-WIDE). JAYNE BROWN COORDINATOR; LONG VALLEY PRESERVATION SOCIETY, INC; PO BOX 444; DONNELLY, ID 83615. (#22712).

APR 18 - 20, '75. PAUL REVERE DAYS. PARADE, EXHIBIT, FESTIVAL AT LAKE ST MCCALL, MAIN ST, DONNELLY, ROSEBERRY TOWNSITE. (LOCAL). CHAIRMAN; MCCALL CHAMBER OF COMMERCE; PO BOX D; MCCALL, ID 83638. (#200015-1).

NOV 22, '75. MCCALL HOSPITAL BENEFIT 'BLESS THE AMERICAN HOME 1776-1976'. LUNCHEON, FASHION SHOW AND BOUTIQUE SALE. AT SHORE LODGE. (LOCAL). GLENDA MULLER, COORD; MCCALL HOSPITAL AUXILIARY; PO BOX 685; MCCALL, ID 83638. (#200015-2).

DEC 14, '75. CROSS COUNTRY SKI PARTY TO REMEMBER VALLEY FORGE. X-C SKI TOUR IN PARK FOLLOWING SIGNS DESIGNATING A MAKE BELIEVE VALLEY FORGE AREA; MEAGER RATIONS PROVIDED FOR LUNCH, COLONIAL COSTUME & PRIZES AWARDED. AT PONDEROSA STATE PARK. (LOCAL). VELMA SHOEMAKER, CHAIRMAN; VALLEY COUNTY BICENTENNIAL COMMISSION; PO BOX D; MCCALL, ID 83638. (#200015-3).

FEB 6 - 8, '76. MCCALL WINTER CARNIVAL. HERITAGE '76 IS THEME OF SNOW SPORTS CARNIVAL FEATURING EXOTIC ICE SCULPTURES. (ST-WIDE). VELMA SHOEMAKER, COORD; MCCALL AREA CHAMBER OF COMMERCE; MCCALL AREA CHAMBER OF COMMERCE; MCCALL, ID 83638. (#103416-114).

FEB 12 - 26, '76. AMERICAN HISTORY DISCUSSION/SEMINAR. HISTORY DISCUSSION AND VIDEOTAPES OF AMERICAN REVOLUTION, BILL OF RIGHTS, DECLARATION OF INDEPENDENCE & CONSTITUTION. AT MCCALL-DONNELLY HIGH SCHOOL. (LOCAL). TED THORNTON, COORDINATOR; VALLEY COUNTY BICENTENNIAL COMMISSION; BOX 967; MCCALL, ID 83638. (#106201-5).

APR 15, '76. RED, WHITE & BLUE CONCERT. CONCERT FEATURING BICENTENNIAL MUSIC FROM J C PENNEY. AT HIGH SCHOOL GYM. (LOCAL). CUB LYON, COORD; MCCALL DONNELLY SCHOOLS; BOX 967; MCCALL, ID 83638. (#106201-3).

MAY 21 - 23, '76. ALPINE PLAYHOUSE CHILDREN'S THEATRE PLAY. ORIGINAL WESTERN HISTORY DRAMA. AT ALPINE THEATRE GOLF COURSE RD. (ST-WIDE). HELEN M MILLER, COORD; ALPINE PLAYHOUSE; ROUTE 1, BOX 109; MCCALL, ID 83638. (#106201-2).

JULY 4, '76. FLAG RAISING CEREMONY. FLAG RAISING IN COOPERATION WITH BOY SCOUTS, FIRST RAISING OF FLAG ON A NEW POLE. AT ART ROBERTS PARK. (LOCAL). LEONARD ZBOROWSKI; MCCALL CHAMBER OF COMMERCE; BOX K; MCCALL, ID 83638. (#106201-1).

JULY 4, '76. FOURTH OF JULY FIREWORKS. EXHIBIT, FESTIVAL AT PAYETTE LAKE, LAKE ST. (LOCAL). PAT HAYES, COORD; MCCALL AREA CHAMBER OF COMMERCE; PO BOX D; MCCALL, ID 83638. (#106201-4).

MELBA

BEAUTIFICATION OF MELBA, IDAHO. CONVERSION OF SMALL AREA OF LAND AT ENTRANCE TO TOWN INTO A SHOWCASE OF FLOWERS TO BEAUTIFY ENTRANCE. (LOCAL). PAM WRIGHT, COORDINATOR; MELBA COMMUNITY BICENTENNIAL COMMISSION; PO BOX 220; MELBA, ID 83641. (#23437).

COMMUNITY RECREATION PARK IN MELBA, IDAHO. LONG RANGE PROJECT, INVOLVING MANY LOCAL GROUPS IN SURROUNDING AREA IN DEVELOPMENT OF PARK. (LOCAL). CHARLOTTE NELSON, COORDINATOR; MELBA CITY COUNCIL; PO BOX 132; MELBA, ID 83641. (#23436). **ARBA GRANTEE.**

HISTORY OF MELBA, IDAHO BY MADGE WYLIE. BOOK BEING SPONSORED BY MELBA BICENTENNIAL COMMISSION ON MELBA & NEARBY AREAS; TO BE PUBLISHED BY JUNE 1, 1976. (LOCAL). MS MADGE WYLIE, COORDINATOR; MELBA COMMUNITY BICENTENNIAL COMMISSION; PO BOX 220; MELBA, ID 83641. (#23435).

APR 18, '76. EASTER SUNRISE SERVICES. SUNRISE SERVICE IN WHICH ALL LOCAL CHURCHES WILL PARTICIPATE. THE BICENTENNIAL CHOIR WILL SING. A BREAKFAST SERVICE WILL BE HELD AFTER IT. AT SCHOOL AUDITORIUM. (LOCAL). MS FRANCES SMITH, COORD; MELBA COMMUNITY BICENTENNIAL COMMISSION; 206 N RANDOLPH; MELBA, ID 83641. (#106581-1).

MAY 1, '76. LADIES BICENTENNIAL FASHION SHOW AND LUNCHEON. BICENTENNIAL FASHION SHOW. ALL WOMEN ORGANIZATIONS ARE PARTICIPATING. CLOTHES FROM YESTERDAY AND A DISPLAY OF ANTIQUES WILL BE INCLUDED. AT MELBA AMERICAN LEGION HALL. (LOCAL). BETTY PECK, COORD; MELBA COMMUNITY BICENTENNIAL COMMITTEE; MELBA, ID 83641. (#106586-2).

JUNE 28 - JULY 4, '76. OLD-FASHIONED COUNTRY STYLE CELEBRATION. FESTIVAL. (LOCAL). ELIZABETH SUCKY, COORD; MELBA BICENTENNIAL COMMISSION; PO BOX 220; MELBA, ID 83641. (#106128-1).

JULY 1 - 4, '76. OLD-TIME COMMUNITY 4TH OF JULY CELEBRATION. WEEK LONG EVENT INCLUDING DANCES, ART SHOWS, COMPETITIONS, PICNICS, BANQUETS, FIREWORKS, SPEECHES, OLD MACHINERY SHOW, PARADE AMERICA WITH NAMPA, IDAHO. AT CITY OF MELBA. (LOCAL). BART PITMAN, COORD; MELBA COMMUNITY BICENTENNIAL COMMISSION; 215 BROADWAY; MELBA, ID 83641. (#106586-1).

MELBA — CONTINUED

SEPT 12, '76. HARVEST BARBECUE. OLD-FASHIONED BARBECUE BY SNAKE RIVER WITH A RAFT RACE. AT WALTER'S FERRY ALONG SNAKE RIVER. (LOCAL). ELIZABETH SUCHY, COORD; MELBA BICENTENNIAL COMMISSION; PO BOX 220; MELBA, ID 83641. (#106587-1).

MOSCOW

BALLET FOLK OF MOSCOW, IDAHO, BICENTENNIAL TOUR. PERFORMANCE AT KENNEDY CENTER, PLUS PHILADELPHIA & IN FOUR CITIES IN IDAHO AS PART OF IDAHO'S BICENTENNIAL PARADE OF MUSIC. (REGN'L). MRS JOAN MUNETA, BOARD OF DIRECTORS; BALLET FOLK OF MOSCOW, INC; BOX 146; MOSCOW, ID 83843. (#796). **ARBA GRANTEE.**

BARNARD-STOCKBRIDGE PHOTOGRAPHIC COLLECTION - ID. PRINTING OF 5000 HISTORIC PHOTOS RELATING TO THE COEUR D'ALENE MINING DISTRICT. (REGN'L). JAN SCHAUMBERG, ACTING COORDINATOR; UNIV OF IDAHO FOUNDATION; 104 ADMINISTRATION BLDG; MOSCOW, ID 83843. (#27271). **ARBA GRANTEE.**

LATAH MUSEUM SOCIETY ORAL HISTORY PROJECT IN IDAHO. A THOROUGH DOCUMENTATION OF AN IDAHO COUNTY'S HISTORY BY USE OF ORAL HISTORY TECHNIQUES. (ST-WIDE). KENNETH B PLATT, PRESIDENT; LATAH MUSUEM SOCIETY; 110 SOUTH ADAMS; MOSCOW, ID 83843. (#462). **(??). ARBA GRANTEE.**

AUG 25, '76. UNITED STATES ARMED FORCES BICENTENNIAL CARAVAN. CARAVAN IS COMPOSED OF EXHIBIT VANS FOR EACH MILITARY SERVICE. PROJECT THEME IS 'HISTORY OF THE ARMED FORCES & THEIR CONTRIBUTIONS TO THE NATION.'. (LOCAL). JOAN MUNETA, CHMN; UNITED STATES ARMED FORCES BICENTENNIAL CARAVAN; 203 S HOWARD ST; MOSCOW, ID 83843. (#1775-708).

MT HOME

AUG 30, '75. UNITED STATES ARMED FORCES BICENTENNIAL CARAVAN. CARAVAN NUMBER FOUR-COMPOSED OF EXHIBIT VANS FOR EACH MILITARY SERVICE. PROJECT THEME IS 'HISTORY OF THE ARMED FORCES & THEIR CONTRIBUTIONS TO THE NATION.'. (LOCAL). DERWARD PEDERSON; US ARMED FORCES BICENT EXHIBIT VAN PROJECT; BOX 890; MT HOME, ID 83647. (#1775-167).

MTN HOME AFB

MAY 17, '76. OPEN HOUSE ARMED FORCES DAY. STATIC DISPLAYS OF USAF AIRCRAFT - USAF AERIAL DEMONSTRATION SQDN, THUNDERBIRDS, FIRE FIGHTING, RESCUE DEMONSTRATION, MODEL FLYING DEMO, FOOD & GAMES BOOTHS WERE INCLUDED IN THIS EVENT. AT MOUNTAIN HOME AIR FORCE BASE. (ST-WIDE). KEITH LARNER, 2LT, USAF; 366 TACTICAL FIGHTER WING; MTN HOME AFB, ID 83648. (#200015-24).

NAMPA

AUG 31 - SEPT 1, '75. UNITED STATES ARMED FORCES BICENTENNIAL CARAVAN. CARAVAN NUMBER FOUR-COMPOSED OF EXHIBIT VANS FOR EACH MILITARY SERVICE. PROJECT THEME IS 'HISTORY OF THE ARMED FORCES & THEIR CONTRIBUTIONS TO THE NATION.'. (LOCAL). LARRY MCSHANE; US ARMED FORCES BICENT EXHIBIT VAN PROJECT; RT 1, BOX 1249A; NAMPA, ID 83651. (#1775-168).

OAKLEY

SILENT CITY OF ROCKS IN IDAHO. GEOLOGICAL FORMATION IN SOUTHERN CHSSIA COUNTY, IDAHO. PROJECT INVOLVES PLACING THE AREA WITHIN THE NATIONAL PARK SERVICE SYSTEM AS A MONUMENT OR PARK. (NAT'L). MIKE FEILER, PRESIDENT; CASSIA COUNTY HISTORICAL SOCIETY; PO BOX 331; BURLEY, ID 83318. (#384). **(??).**

PARMA

PARMA, ID, HERITAGE. A BOOK ON THE HISTORY OF PARMA. (LOCAL). ELMO PETERSON, COORDINATOR; PARMA BICENTENNIAL COMMITTEE; 604 6TH ST, BOX 576; PARMA, ID 83660. (#23901).

RECONSTRUCTION OF OLD FORT BOISE, IDAHO. ACCURATE RECONSTRUCTION FOR CONVENIENCE OF TOURISTS OF OLD FORT BOISE BUILT 1850 AS A FUR TRADING FORT AT THE CONFLUENCE OF THE SNAKE AND BOISE RIVERS. (ST-WIDE). MRS ARTHUR YENSEN, CO-CHAIRMAN; OLD FORT BOISE HISTORICAL SOCIETY; BOX 369; PARMA, ID 83660. (#380). **(??).**

MAY 7 - 8, '76. HISTORICAL PLAY: PROLOGUE TO PARMA. LIVE PERFORMANCE AT PARMA HIGH SCHOOL GYM. (LOCAL). ELMO PETERSON, COORD; PARMA BICENTENNIAL COMMITTEE; 604 6TH ST; PARMA, ID 83660. (#106355-1).

MAY 8, '76. OLD FORT BOISE BICENTENNIAL DAYS. BEGINS WITH PLAY ABOUT EARLY HISTORY OF AREA- 'PROLOGUE TO PARMA' WHICH IS GIVEN TWO NIGHTS. CELEBRATION ENDS WITH A BICENTENNIAL MUSICAL PROGRAM NO CHARGE EXCEPT FOR PLAY. AT IN TOWN. (LOCAL). ELMO PETERSON; PARMA BICENTENNIAL COMMITTEE; BOX 576; PARMA, ID 83660. (#50313-1).

MAY 9, '76. SUNDAY BI-CENTENNIAL MUSIC PROGRAM. CONCERT GIVEN BY LOCAL MUSICIANS - RELIGIOUS AND PATRIOTIC MUSIC. AT OLD FORT BOISE CITY PARK. (LOCAL). MRS MYRTLE STARK, COORD; PARMA MUSICALE; RR 3; PARMA, ID 83660. (#106355-2).

PAYETTE

SEPT 4, '75. UNITED STATES ARMED FORCES BICENTENNIAL CARAVAN. CARAVAN NUMBER FOUR-COMPOSED OF EXHIBIT VANS FOR EACH MILITARY SERVICE. PROJECT THEME IS 'HISTORY OF THE ARMED FORCES & THEIR CONTRIBUTIONS TO THE NATION.'. (LOCAL). HON WESLEY ROSHER, MAYOR; US ARMED FORCES BICENT EXHIBIT VAN PROJECT; 700 CENTER AVE; PAYETTE, ID 83661. (#1775-171).

PIERCE

PIERCE BATEAU RESTORATION, ID. RESTORATION AND PERMANENT DISPLAY OF A BATEAU USED IN LOG DRIVES ON THE CLEARWATER RIVER. (LOCAL). HON X E DURANT, MAYOR; CITY OF PIERCE; PO BOX 356; PIERCE, ID 83546. (#27252). **ARBA GRANTEE.**

POCATELLO

BICENTENNIAL TV DOCUMENTARY SERIES, POCATELLO, ID. A 5 PROGRAM SERIES OF HAL HOUR DOCUMENTARY VIDEO-TAPES ON SIGNIFICANT BICENTENNIAL PROJECTS THROUGHOUT THE STATE OF IDAHO: CATALDO MISSION RESTORATION, BICENTENNIAL WAGON TRAIN & FORT HALL. (ST-WIDE). DEAN DAVIES, COORDINATOR; PBS AFFILIATE STATION - KBGL; IDAHO STATE UNIV, PO BOX 8111; POCATELLO, ID 83209. (#31788).

ORAL HISTORY PROJECT IN POCATELLO, ID. COLLECTING TAPED INTERVIEWS WITH SENIOR CITIZENS & OTHERS ON HISTORY OF POCATELLO AREA. TAPE TRANSFERRED TO ARCHIVAL TAPES FOR IDAHO MUSEUM & TRANSCRIBED IN LOCAL PUBLIC LIBRARY FOR USE BY PUBLIC. (LOCAL). MABLE PARRISH, COORDINATOR; POCATELLO-BANNOCK BICENTENNIAL COMMISSION; 160 PARRISH DR; POCATELLO, ID 83201. (#30029).

PAINT-A-PLUG PROJECT IN POCATELLO, ID. PAINT CITY FIREPLUGS CHARACTERIZING IMPORTANT HISTORICAL PEOPLE, BOTH LOCAL & NATIONAL. (LOCAL). F W ROSKELLEY, PROJECT DIRECTOR; POCATELLO LENDING INSTITUTIONS; 1623 SYRINGA; POCATELLO, ID 83201. (#30028).

STANDROD MANSION PROJECT OF POCATELLO, ID. ACQUISITION BY CITY OF POCATELLO & OPEN FOR PUBLIC USE AFTER RESTORATION WORK IS COMPLETED. (LOCAL). PEGGY NOORDA, CHAIRMAN; POCATELLO-BANNOCK BICENTENNIAL COMMISSION; PO BOX 1776; POCATELLO, ID 83201. (#1040). **ARBA GRANTEE.**

OCT 19, '74. BICENTENNIAL COMMUNITY PRESENTATION CEREMONY. PRESENTATION OF BICENTENNIAL FLAG & CERTIFICATE DESIGNATING POCATELLO AN OFFICIAL BICENTENNIAL COMMUNITY. AT POCATELLO HIGH SCHOOL GROUNDS. (LOCAL). JIM MARTIN, COORD; POCATELLO-BANNOCK BICENTENNIAL COMMISSION; 931 GRAY; POCATELLO, ID 83201. (#200015-8).

OCT 19, '74. BICENTENNIAL FAIR. TOUR OF STANDROD HOUSE & FUND RAISING FAIR. FUND RAISING FOR RESTORATION OF STANDROD & TO ACQUAINT LOCAL CITIZENS WITH POCATELLO'S BICENTENNIAL PROJECT. AT STANDROD HOUSE & GROUNDS. (LOCAL). JERRY SQUIRES, COORD; POCATELLO-BANNOCK BICENTENNIAL COMMISSION; JOHNNY CREEK RD; POCATELLO, ID 83201. (#200015-9).

OCT 19, '74. STANDROD BICENTENNIAL BALL & STANDROD PATRONS RECEPTION. DANCE HELD IN 3 MAJOR AREAS OF BANNOCK HOTEL, FEATURING 3 ORCHESTRA'S. MAJOR PURPOSE TO RAISE FUNDS FOR RESTORATION OF THE STANDROD HOUSE, THE POCATELLO BICENTENNIAL PROJECT. AT BANNOCK HOTEL. (LOCAL). JERRY SQUIRES, COORD; POCATELLO-BANNOCK BICENTENNIAL COMMISSION; JOHNNY CREEK RD; POCATELLO, ID 83201. (#200015-10).

FEB 24, '75. BALLET FOLK PERFORMANCE. FUND RAISING EVENT FOR POCATELLO BICENTENNIAL PROJECT, STANDROD RESTORATION PROJECT. AT POCATELLO HIGH SCHOOL AUDITORIUM. (LOCAL). PEGGY NORDA, CO-CHMN; POCATELLO KIWANIS CLUB; 104 VALLEYVIEW DR; POCATELLO, ID 83201. (#200015-19).

MAY 11 - 17, '75. BICENTENNIAL SCHOOL ARTS FAIR. ART WORK BY STUDENTS GRADE 1 THRU 12 EXHIBITED AT STANDROD HOUSE. EMPHASIS TO STIMULATE INTEREST IN THE BICENTENNIAL & POCATELLO BICENTENNIAL PROJECT: STANDROD HOUSE RESTORATION. AT STANDROD HOUSE. (LOCAL). BETTY HOWARD, COORD; POCATELLO-BANNOCK BICENTENNIAL COMMISSION; 401 1/2 N MAIN; POCATELLO, ID 83201. (#200015-11).

AUG 21 - 22, '75. DOWNTOWN BICENTENNIAL CELEBRATION. FOLK MUSIC & DANCE PERFORMANCES, COMMUNITY BAR-B-QUE, STREET DANCE HELD IN BLOCKED OFF DOWNTOWN STS NEAR LOCATION OF ARMED FORCES EXHIBIT VANS. AT DOWNTOWN POCATELLO STS & RAILROAD PARKING AREA. (LOCAL). HELEN HUMPHREYS, COORD; POCATELLO-BANNOCK BICENTENNIAL COMMISSION; JOHNNY CREEK RD; POCATELLO, ID 83201. (#200015-17).

AUG 21 - 22, '75. UNITED STATES ARMED FORCES BICENTENNIAL CARAVAN. CARAVAN NUMBER FOUR-COMPOSED OF EXHIBIT VANS FOR EACH MILITARY SERVICE. PROJECT THEME IS 'HISTORY OF THE ARMED FORCES & THEIR CONTRIBUTIONS TO THE NATION.'. (LOCAL). MRS RUSSELL HUMPHERYS; US ARMED FORCES BICENT EXHIBIT VAN PROJECT; JOHNNY CREEK RD; POCATELLO, ID 83201. (#1775-162).

SEPT 20, '75. BICENTENNIAL BAND PERFORMANCE. UNITED STATES ARMED FORCES BICENTENNIAL BAND IN OPEN AIR BANDSHELL. AT POSS PARK BANDSHELL. (LOCAL). PEGGY NORDA, CO-CHMN; POCATELLO-BANNOCK BICENTENNIAL COMMISSION; 104 VALLEYVIEW DR; POCATELLO, ID 83201. (#200015-20).

JAN 1 - JUNE 25, '76. BICENTENNIAL QUILT EXHIBITION. ALL LOCAL LADIES ORGANIZATIONS INVITED TO MAKE QUILT FOR AUCTION FOR BENEFIT OF STANDROD HOUSE RESTORATION PROJECT. THE 36 QUILTS WILL BE OPEN TO THE PUBLIC FOR VIEWING UNTIL THE AUCTION. AT STANDROD HOUSE. (LOCAL). PEGGY NOORDA, CO-CHMN; POCATELLO-BANNOCK BICENTENNIAL COMMISSION; 104 VALLEYVIEW DR; POCATELLO, ID 83201. (#200015-22).

MAY 1, '76. BICENTENNIAL DECAL DAY. ALL LOCAL YOUTH GROUPS STAGED DOOR-TO-DOOR CAMPAIGN TO SELL BICENTENNIAL LOGO WINDOW DECALS. EMPHASIS WAS TO ENCOURAGE CITIZENS TO BE A BICENTENNIAL HOME BY DISPLAYING OFFICIAL LOGO & PARTICIPATING IN THE STANDROD RESTORATION BY CONTRIBUTING TO THE PROJECT. (LOCAL). MAXINE TRAUGHBER, COORD; POCATELLO-BANNOCK BICENTENNIAL COMMISSION; KRAFT RD; POCATELLO, ID 83201. (#200015-12).

JUNE 28, '76. PONY EXPRESS PICNIC. PONY EXPRESS RIDERS FROM SKAGITT COUNTY, WASHINGTON CONVERGED WITH RIDERS FROM MONTANA AT FORT HALL REPLICA. PUBLIC INVITED TO ATTEND CEREMONY & OBSERVE RIDERS & ENTOURAGE, THEN STAY FOR PICNIC LUNCH WITH MEMBERS OF THE PONY EXPRESS GROUP. AT FORT HALL REPLICA AT ROSS PARK. (REGN'L). PERRY SWISHER, COORD; POCATELLO-BANNOCK BICENTENNIAL COMMISSION; 355 S 11TH; POCATELLO, ID 83201. (#200015-16).

JUNE 30, '76. BICENTENNIAL QUILT AUCTION. 36 QUILTS MADE BY WOMENS GROUPS & DONATED TO STANDROD RESTORATION PROJECT WERE AUCTIONED. PROCEEDS WENT TOWARD FURTHER RESTORATION OF HISTORIC STANDROD HOUSE, POCATELLO'S BICENTENNIAL PROJECT. AT POCATELLO HIGH SCHOOL AUDITORIUM. (LOCAL). ELLEN MCCASHLAND; POCATELLO-BANNOCK BICENTENNIAL COMMISSION; 969 HIGHLAND BLVD; POCATELLO, ID 83201. (#200015-14).

JULY 3, '76. BICENTENNIAL PARADE. PARADE THEME 'A PAST TO REMEMBER, A FUTURE TO MOLD'. AT DOWNTOWN POCATELLO. (LOCAL). LUUERN JOHNSON, COORD; POCATELLO-BANNOCK BICENTENNIAL COMMISSION; 356 S EIGHTH; POCATELLO, ID 83201. (#200015-15).

JULY 3, '76. BICENTENNIAL '76 BALL. HAPPY BIRTHDAY AMERICA DANCE: PART OF JULY 4TH WEEKEND CELEBRATION. AT HOTEL BANNOCK. (LOCAL). MAXINE TRAUGHBER, COORD; POCATELLO-BANNOCK BICENTENNIAL COMMISSION; RT 1, BOX 129A; POCATELLO, ID 83201. (#200015-13).

JULY 4, '76. BICENTENNIAL SUNRISE SERVICE & FIREWORKS DISPLAY AT DUSK. MULTI-DENOMINATION PATRIOTIC OBSERVANCE OF NATIONAL BIRTHDAY. AT OPEN AIR BANDSHELL, ROSS PARK. (LOCAL). PEGGY NOORDA, CO-CHMN; POCATELLO MINISTERIAL ASSOC FOR THE BICENTENNIAL COMMISSION; 104 VALLEYVIEW DR; POCATELLO, ID 83201. (#200015-21).

JULY 4, '76. POCATELLO'S FIESTA HONORING ETHNIC GROUPS. FESTIVAL. (LOCAL). PEGGY NOORDA, CO-CHMN; POCATELLO-BANNOCK BICENTENNIAL COMMISSION; 104 VALLEYVIEW; POCATELLO, ID 83201. (#108938-1).

JULY 5, '76. FESTIVAL OF PEOPLE. ETHNIC GROUPS SET UP FOOD & GAME BOOTHS FEATURING NATIVE FOODS & GAMES. LIVE PROGRAMS FEATURING NATIVE DANCES & MUSIC CLIMAX DAY. PARTICIPATION BY ITALIAN, MEXICAN, GREEK, JAPANESE, DANISH, BLACKS & COMMUNITY CENTER. (PARACHUTE JUMP, PUPPET SHOWS, ETC). AT ROSS PARK. (LOCAL). HELEN HUMPHREYS, COORD; POCATELLO-BANNOCK BICENTENNIAL COMMISSION; JOHNNY CREEK RD; POCATELLO, ID 83201. (#200015-18).

DEC '76. GRAND OPENING OF STANDROD HOUSE. RIBBON CUTTING CEREMONY BY CITY, COUNTY OFFICIALS, CHAMBER OF COMMERCE TOURS OF HOUSE - OPEN TO PUBLIC TO CELEBRATE THE BICENTENNIAL. AT STANDROD HOUSE, 648 N GARFIELD. (LOCAL). PEGGY NOORDA, CHM; POCATELLO-BANNOCK BICENTENNIAL COMMISSION; 104 VALLEYVIEW DR; POCATELLO, ID 83201. (#1040-1).

RIGBY

HISTORY OF RIGBY, ID. RESEARCH, WRITING & PUBLICATION OF A BOOK-LENGTH HISTORY OF RIGBY BY PATRICIA LYNN SCOTT. (LOCAL). HON G K MADSEN, MAYOR; CITY OF RIGBY; 158 W FREMONT; RIGBY, ID 83442. (#13381).

'HUB OF EASTERN IDAHO: A HISTORY OF RIGBY' - BOOK. THE BOOK, BY PATRICIA LYN SCOTT, IS A 230 PAGE THOROUGHLY RESEARCHED HISTORY OF THE AREA. PROCEEDS FROM ITS SALE WILL BE USED FOR IMPROVEMENTS TO THE RIGBY CITY LIBRARY. (ST-WIDE). THE DIRECTOR; RIGBY BICENTENNIAL PROJECT; CITY HALL; RIGBY, ID 83442. (#28710).

ROCKLAND

ROCKLAND CITY PARK SHELTER - ID. A PICNIC SHELTER WILL BE BUILT IN ROCKLAND CITY PARK. (LOCAL). HON WAYNE HARTLEY, MAYOR; CITY OF ROCKLAND; ROCKLAND, ID 83271. (#27090). **ARBA GRANTEE.**

ROSEBERRY

LONG VALLEY MUSEUM, ROSEBERRY, ID. BUILDING IS BEING RESTORED AS A MUSEUM TO HOUSE HISTORICAL EXHIBITS. (LOCAL). VELMA SHOEMAKER, SECRETARY; LONG VALLEY PRESERVATION SOCIETY, INC; BOX 444; DONNELLY, ID 83615. (#22714).

JUNE 13, '76. LONG VALLEY MUSEUM DEDICATION. RECEPTION & RIBBON CUTTING. AT MUSEUM BUILDING 1-1/2 MILE E OF DONNELLY. (ST-WIDE). VELMA L SHOEMAKER, CHMN; LONG VALLEY PRESERVATION SOCIETY, INC; PO BOX 444; DONNELLY, ID 83615. (#106198-1).

JUNE 14, '76 - CONTINUING . LONG VALLEY MUSEUM EXHIBITS. EXHIBIT AT MUSEUM BUILDING, 1-1/2 MILE E OF DONNELLY. (LOCAL). VELMA L SHOEMAKER, COORD; LONG VALLEY PRESERVATION SOCIETY, INC; PO BOX 444; DONNELLY, ID 83615. (#106198-2).

RUPERT

MINIDOKA COUNTY HISTORICAL MUSEUM, RUPERT, ID. ESTABLISHMENT OF A MUSEUM IN MINIDOKA COUNTY. (LOCAL). H MARTIN O'DONNELL, PRESIDENT; MINIDOKA COUNTY HISTORICAL SOCIETY; 324 SCOTT AVE; RUPERT, ID 83350. (#23250). **ARBA GRANTEE.**

AUG 27, '75. UNITED STATES ARMED FORCES BICENTENNIAL CARAVAN. CARAVAN NUMBER FOUR-COMPOSED OF EXHIBIT VANS FOR EACH MILITARY SERVICE. PROJECT THEME IS 'HISTORY OF THE ARMED FORCES & THEIR CONTRIBUTIONS TO THE NATION.'. (LOCAL). JOHN CAMERON; US ARMED FORCES BICENT EXHIBIT VAN PROJECT; BOX 452; RUPPERT, ID 83350. (#1775-165).

JULY 1 - 5, '76. RUPERT ANNUAL JULY 4TH CELEBRATION. 50TH ANNUAL RODEO WITH A HUGE CELEBRATION. AT MINIDOKA COUNTY FAIRGROUNDS. (LOCAL). LAVONNE COLBERT, SEC; RUPERT CHAMBER OF COMMERCE RODEO COMMITTEE; 324 SCOTT AVE; RUPERT, ID 83350. (#106479-1).

SPALDING

MAY 13 - SEPT 15, '75. BEADWORK, CORNHUSK WEAVING, & LEATHERWORK DEMONSTRATION SESSIONS. A DRAMATIC & POPULAR ASPECT OF NPS' INTERPRETATION OF THE HISTORIC FEATURES OF A PARK. THESE LIVE PGMS, SUPPLEMENTING OTHER INTERPRETIVE PGMS, DEAL WITH CRAFTS, MILITARY LIFE, OR AMERICAN LIFESTYLES. AT THE NEZ PERCE NHP, 15 MI. EAST OF LEWISTON ON US 95. (REGN'L). SUPT, NEZ PERCE NHP; NATIONAL PARK SERVICE; PO BOX 93; SPALDING, ID 83551. (#6727-47).

JUNE 1 - SEPT 5, '75. MOUNTAIN MAN DEMONSTRATIONS: TRAPPING SKILLS. THERE WILL BE A MAN DEMONSTRATING TRAPPING SKILLS USED BY INDIANS & EARLY PIONEERS. AT THE NEZ PERCE NHP, 15 MILES EAST OF LEWISTON ON US 95.. (REGN'L). SUPT, NEZ PERCE NHP; NATIONAL PARK SERVICE; PO BOX 93; SPALDING, ID 83551. (#6727-46).

JUNE 1 - SEPT 15, '75. 'FOLK FEST' DAY PROGRAMS AT NEZ PERCE NHP. A DRAMATIC & POPULAR ASPECT OF NPS' INTERPRETATION OF THE HISTORIC FEATURES OF A PARK. THESE LIVE PGMS, SUPPLEMENTING OTHER INTERPRETIVE PGMS, DEAL WITH CRAFTS, MILITARY LIFE, OR AMERICAN LIFESTYLES. THERE WILL BE GAMES, DANCING, MUSIC, SINGING, FOODS & ARTS & CRAFTS. AT NEZ PERCE NHP 15 MILES EAST OF LEWISTON ON US 95. (REGN'L). SUPT, NEZ PERCE NHP; NATIONAL PARK SERVICE; PO BOX 93; SPALDING, ID 83551. (#6727-51).

MAY 9 - SEPT 11, '76. INDIAN ARTS & CRAFTS CULTURAL DEMONSTRATION. A DRAMATIC & POPULAR ASPECT OF NPS' INTERPRETATION OF THE HISTORIC FEATURES OF A PARK. THESE LIVE PGMS, SUPPLEMENTING OTHER INTERPRETIVE PGMS, DEAL WITH CRAFTS, MILITARY LIFE, OR AMERICAN LIFESTYLES. AT THE NEZ PERCE NHP, 15 MI. EAST OF LEWISTON ON US 95.. (REGN'L). SUPT, NEZ PERCE; NATIONAL PARK SERVICE; PO BOX; SPALDING, ID 83551. (#6727-48).

JUNE 1 - SEPT 6, '76. MOUNTAIN MAN DEMONSTRATIONS OF EARLY TRAPPERS' SKILLS. THERE WILL BE A MAN DEMONSTRATING TRAPPING SKILLS USED BY INDIANS & EARLY PIONEERS. AT THE NEZ PERCE NHP, 15 MILES E OF LEWISTON. (REGN'L). SUPT, NEZ PERCE NHP; NATIONAL PARK SERVICE; PO BOX 93; SPALDING, ID 83551. (#6737-49).

JUNE 3 - SEPT 5, '76. PIONEER SPINNING & WEAVING DEMONSTRATIONS. A DRAMATIC & POPULAR ASPECT OF NPS' INTERPRETATION OF THE HISTORIC FEATURES OF A PARK. THESE LIVE PGMS, SUPPLEMENTING OTHER INTERPRETIVE PGMS, DEAL WITH CRAFTS, MILITARY LIFE, OR AMERICAN LIFESTYLES. AT THE NEZ PERCE NHP. (REGN'L). NEZ PERCE N H P; NATIONAL PARK SERVICE; PO BOX 93; SPALDING, ID 83551. (#6727-45).

TUTTLE

MALAD CANYON STATE PARK OF IDAHO. CONSTRUCTION OF A PARK OF 700 ACRES ADJOINING I80 IN SOUTH CENTRAL IDAHO AS A MAJOR FOCUS FOR TRAVLERS ON THE INTERSTATE HIGHWAY THROUGH IDAHO. INCLUDES GEOLOGICAL DISPLAYS. (ST-WIDE). STEVEN W BLY, DIRECTOR; IDAHO DEPT OF PARKS & RECREATION; 2263 WARM SPRINGS AVE; BOISE, ID 83202. (#352). **ARBA GRANTEE.**

TWIN FALLS

WORKING MUSEUM IN TWIN FALLS, IDAHO. MUSEUM DEPICTS THE AMERICAN INDIAN AND HIS HISTORY IN THE WESTERN PART OF THE U S, EXTENDING FROM ALASKA TO MEXICO. (LOCAL). DR JAMES L TAYLOR, PRESIDENT; HISTORICAL ARTS, INC; 315 FALLS AVE; TWIN FALLS, ID 83301. (#10935).

AUG 28 - 29, '75. UNITED STATES ARMED FORCES BICENTENNIAL CARAVAN. CARAVAN NUMBER FOUR-COMPOSED OF EXHIBIT VANS FOR EACH MILITARY SERVICE. PROJECT THEME IS 'HISTORY OF THE ARMED FORCES & THEIR CONTRIBUTIONS TO THE NATION.'. (LOCAL). ARLAN CALL; US ARMED FORCES BICENT EXHIBIT VAN PROJECT; 434 2ND ST E; TWIN FALLS, ID 83301. (#1775-166).

WEISER

OLDTIME FIDDLERS FESTIVAL AND CONTEST OF IDAHO. GAINING NATIONWIDE MEDIA COVERAGE OF WEEKLONG FOLK FESTIVAL FOR 1976 BY DEVELOPING NATIONWIDE MARKETING ARRANGEMENT FOR THEIR RECORDS & PLANS FOR A TV SPECIAL AND/OR FEATURE LENGTH FILM. (ST-WIDE). DAVID CORNWELL, PRESIDENT; WEISER CHAMBER OF COMMERCE; WEISER, ID 83672. (#1184). **ARBA GRANTEE.**

SEPT 3, '75. UNITED STATES ARMED FORCES BICENTENNIAL CARAVAN. CARAVAN NUMBER FOUR-COMPOSED OF EXHIBIT VANS FOR EACH MILITARY SERVICE. PROJECT THEME IS 'HISTORY OF THE ARMED FORCES & THEIR CONTRIBUTIONS TO THE NATION.'. (LOCAL). MRS MARGARET WHITTINGTON; US ARMED FORCES BICENT EXHIBIT VAN PROJECT; 16 E IDAHO ST; WEISER, ID 83672. (#1775-170).

JUNE 21 - 26, '76. OLDTIME FIDDLERS' FESTIVAL & CONTEST WITH SMALL TIME ATMOSPHERE. GAINING NATIONWIDE MEDIA COVERAGE OF WEEKLONG FOLK FESTIVAL FOR 1976 BY DEVELOPING NATIONWIDE MARKETING ARRANGEMENT FOR THEIR RECORDS & PLANS FOR A TV SPECIAL AND/OR FEATURE LENGTH FILM. FULL PRICE FOR ALL FRI & SAT NITES CHILDREN HALF PRICE OTHER TIMES. AT WEISER HIGH SCHOOL GYM. (ST-WIDE). MR HARRY NELSON; WEISER CHAMBER OF COMMERCE; WEISER CHAMBER OF COMMERCE; WEISER, ID 83672. (#1184-1).

YELLOW PINE

BIOGRAPHIES OF OLD TIMERS, YELLOW PINE, ID. LIFE STORIES AND REMEMBRANCES OF EARLY SETTLERS IN THE AREA. (LOCAL). JERRI MONTGOMERY, CHAIRMAN; CIVIC CLUB; YELLOW PINE, ID 83677. (#22709).

FLAG POLE AT PIONEER CEMETERY, YELLOW PINE, ID. POLE AND FLAG AT HISTORIC PIONEER CEMETERY. (LOCAL). PAUL MONTGOMERY, COMMANDER; VFW POST 10324; YELLOW PINE, ID 83677. (#22717).

Illinois'
Celebration
'76

Illinois

Illinois Bicentennial Commission

Established by the Illinois General Assembly in 1972

ARBA Statistics

Officially Recognized
Communities—453
Colleges/Universities—40
Military Installations—8
BINET Projects—876
Events—1,522
1976 Population—11,229,000

Bicentennial Archives

Illinois State Historical Library
Old State Capitol
Springfield, Illinois 62701

Membership

Andrew McNally, III (1972-77), *chairman* (1972-75)
Howard Fricke (1972-74), *chairman* (1975-76)
A. D. VanMeter, Jr., *chairman* (1976-77)
Senator Sam M. Vadalabene, *vice-chairman* (1972-77)
Representative J. David Jones, *secretary* (1972-77)
Dr. Edward C. Rozanski, *treasurer* (1972-77)
William K. Alderfer (1972-77)
Representative Victor A. Arrigo (1972-73)
Dr. Michael J. Bakalis (1972-73)
Representative W. Robert Blair (1972-74)
Representative Gerald Bradley (1972-77)
Senator Terrel E. Clarke (1972-75)
Dr. John Hope Franklin (1972-75)
Earl W. Henderson (1972-77)
(Mrs.) William C. Limacher (1972-77)
Senator Cecil A. Partee (1972-77)
Representative Paul J. Randolph (1972-77)
Senator Sam Romano (1972-76)
J. Robert Smith (1972-74)
Milton D. Thompson (1972-77)
Reverend Monsignor John Michael Whelan (1972-75)
Lillian Williams (1972-75)
Representative Clyde Choate (1973-75)
Representative John D'Arco (1973-75)
Senator William C. Harris (1973-77)
Dr. Joseph Cronin (1974-77)
Representative Lawrence DiPrima (1975-77)
Senator Thomas Merritt (1975-77)
Senator Howard R. Mohr (1975)
Representative William Redmond (1974-77)
Joseph P. Pisciotte (1974-77)
Representative James R. Washburn (1974-77)
Eugene Sage (1975-77)
Robert V. Guelich (1975-77)
Stuart Miller (1975-77)
Senator James "Pate" Philip (1975-77)
Senator Hudson R. Sours (1972-75)

Staff

Michael J. Linderman, *executive director* (1975-77)
Samuel A. Lilly, *executive director* (1972-75)

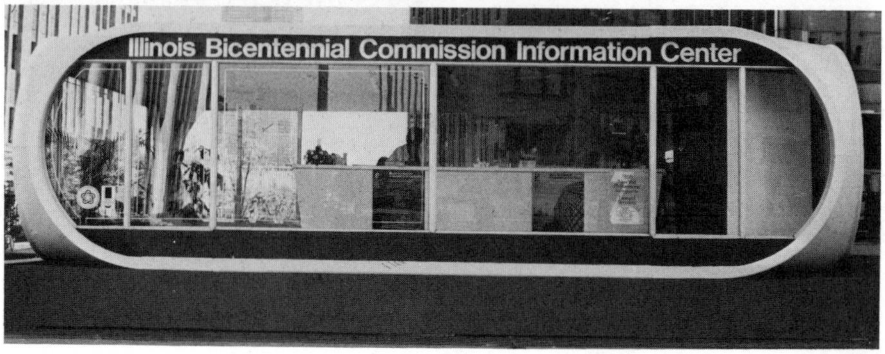

Illinois

From the confluence of the Mississippi and Ohio Rivers, across the rolling plains, down the crowded boulevards of Chicago to the precipitous heights around Galena, the people of Illinois poured forth their hopes and dreams in a variety of Bicentennial projects and events.

While they are visible evidence of many activities, the archived records, newspaper clippings, awards, banners, buttons and medallions in no way indicate the hours of work by millions of people: people who contributed a part of their lives to celebrate 200 years of the American way of life and their future.

Among the more visible projects throughout the state was the official Illinois Bicentennial Commission medallion design contest. Sponsored each year for four years, the subsequent sale of the medallions provided mementos for the future.

The Illinois Bicentennial Commission displayed continuing interest in the school Bicentennial program by funding a week-long workshop for teachers to prepare a *Teachers Bicentennial Resource Guide.* The guide was produced in sufficient quantity by the commission, with a private donation, to allow free distribution of a copy to each public library in the state and multiple copies to all Illinois elementary and secondary schools.

Many institutions prepared extensive Bicentennial programs. Few were more extensive than the three phase exhibit, *America's Inventive Genius,* at the Chicago Museum of Science and Industry. The exhibit traced America's scientific and technical heritage and showed how such technical know-how was applied to meet the nation's social, economic, industrial and defense needs.

In cooperation with the Illinois Arts Council, a multifaceted statewide project, *Illinois Architecture: A Revolution on the Prairie,* featured tours, exhibits, films and pamphlets detailing the contributions of the Chicago School of Architecture. During the Bicentennial, emphasis on Illinois' unique architectural heritage was enhanced by ArchiCenter, an architectural information and tour center in downtown Chicago.

A special Illinois Bicentennial Commission concern was that Bicentennial programs and events be available to as many people as wished to participate. In conjunction with the *American Issues Forum,* the commission urged Bicentennial planners to see that events could be enjoyed by handicapped citizens and held several meetings and conferences to accomplish that end.

As a truly lasting reminder of the Bicentennial, the commission funded a sound and light presentation at the Old State Capitol. Operated by the Illinois State Historical Library, the program is a highly sophisticated electronic recreation of the story of Abraham Lincoln and the building that served for 24 years as the center of his public life. The drama of those years is recreated each summer night in Springfield, a city rich with Lincoln-related historical sites.

The Illinois Labor History Society, in conjunction with the AFL–CIO and the Illinois Bicentennial Commission, prepared a well-received photographic display, *On the Job in Illinois: Then and Now.* Recent photographs were interspersed with older prints which highlighted the changes in our ways of working in modern times. Crafts unknown to many people today were recreated by means of the exhibit.

Always a major Illinois attraction during August, the 1976 Illinois State Fair was particularly important because of "Heritage Square." During the fair, special ethnic exhibits, dances, crafts, music and foods were featured. Ethnic groups who contributed to the founding, settling and building of Illinois proudly displayed their heritage.

As grand as many projects were, none held more importance than a local school Bicentennial festival, a county fair Bicentennial contest or the erection of a flagpole. By such activities, each resident signified pride in the United States and faith in the future.

ADDISON

MUSICAL PRODUCTIONS IN ADDISON, ILLINOIS. A MUSICALE, BASED ON ACTUAL INCIDENTS RESEARCHED FROM LOCAL HISTORY, WILL BE STAGED. (LOCAL). EUNICE SCOTT, BICENT PROJ CHAIRMAN; ADDISON VILLAGE; ADDISON, IL 60101. (#8807).

ALBANY

ALBANY/GARDEN PLAIN HISTORICAL BOOKLET - IL. A COMPILATION OF HISTORICAL INFORMATION AND BICENTENNIAL EVENTS OF THE ALBANY/GARDEN PLAIN AREA. (LOCAL). HELEN HANSON, PROJECT CHAIRPERSON; ALBANY-GARDEN PLAIN BICENTENNIAL COMMISSION; RURAL RTE; ALBANY, IL 61230. (#29841).

ALBANY/GARDEN PLAIN COMMUNITY FLAGS - IL. PAPER REPLICAS OF OFFICIAL ALBANY AND GARDEN PLAIN COMMUNITY FLAGS WERE PRINTED AND ARE ON SALE. (LOCAL). FRANK FALEY, CHAIRMAN; ALBANY-GARDEN PLAIN BICENTENNIAL COMMISSION; PO BOX 453; ALBANY, IL 61230. (#29845).

ALBANY/GARDEN PLAIN FLAG DESIGN CONTESTS - IL. ALL CITIZENS OF BOTH COMMUNITIES WERE INVITED TO SUBMIT DESIGNS FOR FOR A COMMUNITY FLAG FOR EACH COMMUNITY. (LOCAL). FRANK FALEY, CHAIRMAN; ALBANY-GARDEN PLAIN BICENTENNIAL COMMISSION; PO BOX 453; ALBANY, IL 61230. (#29846).

FLAGPOLE CONSTRUCTION AND PRESENTATION - IL. THE FLAGPOLE WAS ERECTED BY THE ALBANY LIONS CLUB TO ACCOMMODATE THE OFFICIAL ALBANY COMMUNITY FLAG. (LOCAL). RAY BRANDT, PRESIDENT; ALBANY LIONS CLUB; RIVERVIEW HGTS; ALBANY, IL 61230. (#29844).

LOCAL ARTIFACT ROOM IN ALBANY, IL, LIBRARY. AN HISTORIC ARTIFACT ROOM WILL BE MAINTAINED IN ALBANY'S NEWEST LIBRARY. DISPLAYS WILL BE PROVIDED BY LOCAL CITIZENS. (LOCAL). HELEN HANSON, COMMITTEE CHAIRMAN; ALBANY GARDEN PLAIN BICENTENNIAL COMMISSION; PO BOX 453; ALBANY, IL 61230. (#29842).

PARADE FLOAT IN ALBANY, IL. BUILT BICENTENNIAL FLOAT FOR ANNUAL MISS FLAME PARADE. (LOCAL). FRANK FALEY, CHAIRMAN; ALBANY-GARDEN PLAIN BICENTENNIAL COMMISSION; PO BOX 453; ALBANY, IL 61230. (#29843).

OCT 13, '75. ALBANY-GARDEN PLAIN BICENTENNIAL KICK OFF HISTORICAL VARIETY SHOW. TROPHIES WERE AWARDED TO THE WINNERS OF THE ALBANY GARDEN PLAIN FLAG DESIGN CONTEST ON THIS DATE. HISTORICAL NARRATION OF EVENTS FROM 1492 UNTIL PRESENT WITH PERIOD VARIETY ACTS INSERTED. AT ALBANY GRADE SCHOOL. (LOCAL). FRANK FALEY, CHAIRMAN; ALBANY GARDEN PLAIN BICENTENNIAL COMMISSION; PO BOX 453; ALBANY, IL 61230. (#200016-423).

FEB 22, '76. ARBA FLAG PRESENTATION TO ALBANY MAYOR ON WASHINGTON'S BIRTHDAY. THE FLAG WAS PRESENTED WITH PATRIOTIC SPEECH AND MUSICAL PROGRAM. A FLAG RAISING CEREMONY FOLLOWED THE PRESENTATION. AT ALBANY GRADE SCHOOL. (LOCAL). FRANK FALEY, CHAIRMAN; ALBANY-GARDEN PLAIN BICENTENNIAL COMMISSION; PO BOX 453; ALBANY, IL 61230. (#200016-422).

APR 4, '76. ALBANY TOWNSHIP BIRTHDAY CELEBRATION. AN ANTIQUE CAR PARADE ENDED AT THE ALBANY GRADE SCHOOL WHERE THE 'SALUTE TO GREAT AMERICANS' HISTORICAL PRESENTATION WAS PERFORMED BY MASONIC MEMBERS. A HUGE BIRTHDAY CAKE WAS SERVED. AT ALBANY GRADE SCHOOL. (LOCAL). FRANK FALEY, CHAIRMAN; ALBANY/GARDEN PLAIN BICENTENNIAL COMMISSION; PO BOX 453; ALBANY, IL 61230. (#200016-419).

MAY 30, '76. MEMORIAL DAY CEREMONY. ALBANY CITIZENS MET IN THE PARK AND MARCHED TO THE ALBANY CEMETERY FOR AN INSPIRING MEMORIAL DAY CEREMONY. AT ALBANY PARK & ALBANY CEMETERY. (LOCAL). FRANK FALEY, CHAIRMAN; ALBANY-GARDEN PLAIN BICENTENNIAL COMMISSION & AMERICAN LEGION; PO BOX 453; ALBANY, IL 61230. (#200016-418).

JUNE 13, '76. ALBANY COMMUNITY FLAG PRESENTATION. THE OFFICIAL ALBANY COMMUNITY FLAG WAS TAKEN BY STAGE COACH FROM THE ALBANY GRADE SCHOOL BY THE FLAG DESIGN CONTEST WINNERS TO THE ALBANY PARK WHERE IT WAS PRESENTED TO THE MAYOR OF ALBANY FROM ALBANY. STAGECOACH PROCEEDED TO GARDEN PLAIN. AT ALBANY GRADE SCHOOL TO ALBANY PARK. (LOCAL). FRANK FALEY, CHAIRMAN; ALBANY GARDEN PLAIN BICENTENNIAL COMMISSION; PO BOX 453; ALBANY, IL 61230. (#200016-417).

JULY 26 - AUG 1, '76. HISTORICAL DOCUMENT DISPLAY. EXHIBIT AT FIRST TRUST & SAVINGS BANK, MAIN STREET. (LOCAL). FRANK FALEY, CHAIRMAN; FIRST TRUST & SAVINGS BANK; PO BOX 453; ALBANY, IL 61230. (#200016-415).

JULY 27, '76. ALBANY, IL FLAG PRESENTATION TO MAYOR OF ALBANY, NEW YORK. CEREMONY. (LOCAL). CAROL GIAGNONI, CHAIRMAN; ALBANY-GARDEN PLAIN BICENTENNIAL COMMISSION; PO BOX 484; ALBANY, IL 61230. (#200016-414).

AUG 29, '76. RELIGIOUS UNITY SERVICE. ALBANY-GARDEN PLAIN'S THREE CHURCHES PARTICIPATED IN THIS UNITY SERVICE. THE BICENTENNIAL COMMISSION CHAIRMAN REVIEWED THE HISTORY OF ORGANIZED CHRISTIAN RELIGIONS AND URGED RELIGIOUS UNITY THROUGHOUT THE WORLD. AT ALBANY METHODIST CHURCH. (LOCAL). FRANK FALEY, CHAIRMAN; ALBANY BICENTENNIAL COMMISSION & ALBANY METHODIST CHURCH; PO BOX 453; ALBANY, IL 61230. (#200016-413).

ALEDO

MARK TWAIN WILDLIFE REFUGE - IL. RECREATIONAL 2.1 MILE TRAIL WILL BE BUILT. (LOCAL). NORMAN BROWN, COORDINATOR; MERCER COUNTY BICENTENNIAL COMMISSION; ROOM 23, COURTHOUSE; ALEDO, IL 61231. (#28552). **ARBA GRANTEE.**

MERCER COUNTY HISTORY PROJ OF ILLINOIS. WRITE AND PUBLISH HISTORY OF MERCER COUNTY FROM 1882 TO 1976. (LOCAL). HAROLD SEIVERS, CHAIRMAN HERITAGE COMMITTEE; MERCER COUNTY BICENTENNIAL COMMISSION; COUNTY COURTHOUSE; ALEDO, IL 61231. (#8225). **(??).**

MAR 20, '76. MERCER COUNTY BICENTENNIAL COSTUME BALL. FESTIVAL. (LOCAL). MRS GLENN APPLETON, CHMN; ALEDO BICENTENNIAL COMMISSION; 403 N W FOURTH AVE; ALEDO, IL 61231. (#200016-128).

ALGONQUIN

DEDICATION OF RIVERSIDE PARK, ALGONQUIN, IL. PLANTINGS, BENCHES, LIGHTS, FLAG MONUMENT AND WALKWAYS. (LOCAL). ED LAMB, BICENTENNIAL CHAIRMAN; ALGONQUIN BICENTENNIAL COMMISSION; 2 SOUTH MAIN ST; ALGONQUIN, IL 60102. (#21620).

JULY 29, '76. FLEA MARKET. RESERVATIONS REQUIRED FOR EXHIBITORS ONLY. AT MAIN STREET. (LOCAL). EVELYN VOJIK, PRES; FOUNDERS COMMITTEE; PO 101; ALGONQUIN, IL 60102. (#105494-2).

JULY 29 - 31, '76. CHICKEN FRY, FISH FRY & STEER ROAST. RESERVATIONS ARE REQUIRED FOR THE STEER ROAST ONLY. THE CHICKEN FRY WILL BE ON 7/29; THE FISH FRY WILL BE ON 7/30; AND THE STEER ROAST WILL BE ON 7/31. AT VILLAGE PARK MAIN STREET. (LOCAL). EVELYN VOJIK, PRES; FOUNDERS DAY COMMITTEE; PO 101; ALGONQUIN, IL 60102. (#105494-4).

JULY 31, '76. FOUNDERS DAY BICENTENNIAL PARADE. PARADE AT MAIN STREET. (LOCAL). EVELYN VOJIK, PRES; FOUNDERS DAY COMMITTEE; PO 101; ALGONQUIN, IL 60102. (#105494-1).

AUG 1, '76. ART AND ANTIQUE SHOW. RESERVATIONS REQUIRED FOR EXHIBITORS ONLY. AT VILLAGE PARK, TURN RIGHT OFF WASHINGTON STREET. (LOCAL). EVELYN VOJIK, PRES; FOUNDERS DAY COMMITTEE; PO 101; ALGONQUIN, IL 60102. (#105494-3).

ALSIP

BICENTENNIAL MEMORIAL IN ALSIP, IL. A STEEL SCULPTURE OF 'THE FLAME OF FREEDOM.'. (LOCAL). KENNETH DORIAN, CHAIRMAN; ALSIP BICENTENNIAL COMMISSION; 4500 W 123RD ST; ALSIP, IL 60658. (#15309).

OCT 25, '75. HOW TO WORKSHOPS-TO TRAIN BICENTENNIAL PROGRAM LEADERS. SEMINAR. (LOCAL). DR GLEN GABERT, CHMN; MORAINE VALLEY COMMUNITY COLLEGE BICENTENNIAL COMMISSION; 10900 S 88TH AVE / MVCC; PALOS HILLS, IL 60415. (#102378-2).

JULY 3, '76. FESTIVAL USA. MRS ANDREWS WILL HANG MODEL OF LIBERTY BELL. AT 119TH E KEELER, 119TH E KOSTNER, 119TH PL, CONTROLLED PARKING. (LOCAL). MRS ANDREWS, DIRECTOR; ALSIP BICENTENNIAL COMMISSION; 12460 S TRIPP AVE; ALSIP, IL 60658. (#102281-1).

ALTON

CIVIC MEMORIAL PROJECT IN ALTON, ILLINOIS. CIRCULAR MEMORIAL HAS 3 LEVELS, EACH WITH MURALS: THE BOTTOM MURAL TO SHOW HERITAGE THEME, MIDDLE TO SHOW FESTIVAL & TOP ONE HORIZON. AREA LANDSCAPED WITH FOUR ENTRY WALKS, SYMBOLIC OF THE 4 FREEDOMS. (LOCAL). B L POWLES, CHAIRMAN; ALTON BICENTENNIAL COMMISSION; BOX 1776; ALTON, IL 62002. (#8757). **(??).**

SEPT 24 - 28, '75. INDUSTRIAL AND HISTORIC EXHIBITS, ALTON, ILLINOIS. EXHIBITION TO INCLUDE ALL INDUSTRIES AND CIVIC GROUPS TO GENERATE AN AWARENESS OF PARTICIPATING GROUP ACTIVITIES, LOCAL HISTORY & BICENT EVENTS PLANNED FOR ALTON & SURROUNDING AREA. FIVE DAYS. AT RIVER FRONT PARK, ALTON, ILL. (LOCAL). B L POWLES; ALTON BICENTENNIAL COMMISSION; 200 MERCURY DR; GODFREY, IL 62002. (#8758-1).

FEB 8 - 9, '77. LA SALLE EXPEDITION II, A HISTORIC RE-ENACTMENT. THIS IS AN AUTHENTIC RE-ENACTMENT OF THE 1681 LASALLE EXPEDITION FROM MONTREAL, CANADA TO NEW ORLEANS, LA WHICH WILL BEGIN TOURING ON AUGUST 11, 1976 AND END ON APRIL 9, 1977. (LOCAL). REID H LEWIS, DIRECTOR; LA SALLE EXPEDITION II; 135 S LA SALLE ST, RM 411; CHICAGO, IL 60690. (#102805-53).

AMBOY

AMBOY, ILL, COMMUNITY CULTURAL CENTER & MUSEUM. ACQUISITION & RENOVATION OF 3 STORY, 22 ROOM, 1876 RAILROAD DEPOT. BUILDING WILL BE USED AS A COMMUNITY CULTURAL CENTER & HISTORIC MUSEUM. (LOCAL). CLINTON C CONWAY, CHAIRMAN; AMBOY BICENTENNIAL COMMISSION; AMBOY, IL 61310. (#873). **ARBA GRANTEE.**

JULY 16 - 18, '76. AMBOY BICENTENNIAL WEEKEND - OLD-TIME COMMUNITY CELEBRATION. COMPETITION, EXHIBIT, FESTIVAL. (LOCAL). MIKE HECKMAN, CO-CHAIRMAN; LEE COUNTY BICENTENNIAL COMMISSION; PO BOX 348; DIXON, IL 61021. (#104268-7).

ANDOVER

JENNY LIND CHAPEL RESTORATION, ANDOVER, IL. RESTORATION OF ORIGINAL CHURCH BUILDING OF THE AUGUSTANA LUTHERAN CHURCH, MOTHER CHURCH OF THE LUTHERAN CHURCH IN AMERICA. (LOCAL). DR CONRAD BERGENDOFF, PRESIDENT; ILLINOIS SYNOD, LUTHERAN CHURCH IN AMERICA, JENNY LIND CHAPEL FU; 10 HAWTHORNE RD; ROCK ISLAND, IL 61201. (#9594).

MAR 18 - DEC 25, '75. 125TH ANNIVERSARY OF AUGUSTANA LUTHERAN CHURCH. FESTIVAL. (LOCAL). PASTOR ALBERT LESTER; ILLINOIS SYNOD, LUTHERAN CHURCH IN AMERICA, JENNY LIND CHAPEL FUND; ROCK ISLAND, IL 61201. (#9594-1).

MAY 4 - OCT 2, '75. VESPERS SERVICES AT JENNY LIND CHAPEL (1850). SERVICES TO BE PERFORMED WEEKLY BY PASTORS OF THE ROCK ISLAND DISTRICT, ILLINOIS SYNOD. AT JENNY LIND CHAPEL, ANDOVER. (ST-WIDE). REV. ALBERT LESTOR; ILLINOIS SYNOD OF THE LUTHERAN CHURCH OF AMERICA; JENNY LIND CHAPEL; ANDOVER, IL 61233. (#50317-1).

SEPT 11 - 14, '75. ANDOVER FOUNDER'S DAY. CARNIVAL, PARADE, ETC. TO COMMEMORATE 140TH ANNIVERSARY OF ANDOVER, HOME OF JENNY LIND CHAPEL, FIRST POST OFFICE IN HENRY COUNTY, ANDOVER HISTORICAL SOCIETY. SWEDISH COMMUNITY. AT CITYWIDE. (LOCAL). VILLAGE OF ANDOVER; VILLAGE HALL; ANDOVER, IL 61233. (#50330-1).

SEPT 28, '75. SWEDISH PIONEER NATIONAL CENTENNIAL SOCIETY EXEC COMMITTEE MEETING. CONFERENCE. (NAT'L). DR CONRAD BERGENDOFF; ILLINOIS SYNOD, LUTHERAN CHURCH IN AMERICA, JENNY LIND CHAPEL FUND; 10 HAWTHORNE RD; ROCK ISLAND, IL 61201. (#9594-2).

OCT 4, '75. W PORTER WARE, COLLECTOR OF MEMORABILIA - EXHIBITION. EXHIBIT. (LOCAL). PASTOR ALBERT LESTER; ILLINOIS SYNOD, LUTHERAN CHURCH IN AMERICA, JENNY LIND CHAPEL FUND; ANDOVER, IL 61201. (#9594-4).

APR 20, '76. KING OF SWEDEN VISITS JENNY LIND CHAPEL. KING CARL GUSTAV XVI VISITS ANDOVER. (INT'L). RONNIE PETERSON, COORD; HENRY COUNTY BICENTENNIAL COMMISSION; ANDOVER, IL 61233. (#9594-5).

APR 20, '76. VISIT BY THE KING OF SWEDEN AND OTHER DIGNITARIES. CEREMONY. (INT'L). DR CONRAD BEGENDOFF, CHMN; ILLINOIS SYNOD, LUTHERAN CHURCH IN AMERICA, JENNY LIND CHAPEL FUND; 10 HAWTHORNE RD; ROCK ISLAND, IL 61201. (#200016-72).

JUNE 13, '76. DEDICATION OF JENNY LIND CHAPEL. CEREMONY. (LOCAL). RONNIE PETERSON, COORD; HENRY COUNTY BICENTENNIAL COMMISSION; ANDOVER, IL 61233. (#9594-6).

JULY 23, '76. SWEDISH CONCERT AT JENNY LIND CHAPEL. LIVE PERFORMANCE AT JENNY LIND CHAPEL. (INT'L). RONNIE PETERSON, CHMN; HENRY COUNTY BICENTENNIAL COMMISSION; ANDOVER, IL 61233. (#200016-157).

ANTIOCH

HISTORICAL BUILDING AND MUSEUM, ANTIOCH, IL. PRESERVATION OF 1892 SCHOOL BUILDING TO HOUSE LOCAL HISTORICAL ARTIFACTS AND DOCUMENTS AND PROVIDE CIVIC MEETING ROOM FACILITIES. (LOCAL). WILLIAM E BROOK, CHAIRMAN; ANTIOCH BICENTENNIAL COMMISSION; PO BOX 369; ANTIOCH, IL 60002. (#17277).

SEQUOIT CREEK SAW MILL - ANTIOCH, IL. RESTORATION OF HISTORICAL SITE ON SEQUOIT CREEK WHERE FIRST SAW MILL WAS CONSTRUCTED IN 1839 BY THE GAGE BROS; ERECTION OF REPLICA MILL. (LOCAL). MR WALTER SHEPARD, PROJECT DIRECTOR; VILLAGE OF ANTIOCH; 874 MAIN STREET; ANTIOCH, IL 60002. (#17276). **ARBA GRANTEE.**

MAR 27, '76. ST PETERS BICENTENNIAL VIP DINNER AND DANCE. SELECTION OF ANTIOCH AREA RESIDENT BY CITIZEN NOMINATIONS TO HONOR THIS VIP FOR HIS-HER CONTRIBUTION TO THE ANTIOCH COMMUNITY: VILLAGE PLAQUE WILL BE PRESENTED AT CEREMONY DINNER AND DANCE WILL FOLLOW PRESENTATIONS. AT ST PETERS SOCIAL CENTER - STS PETER & ELIZABETH STS. (LOCAL). BETTY HOPE, DIRECTOR; ST PETERS CATHOLIC CHURCH; PO BOX 396; ANTIOCH, IL 60002. (#105408-5).

APR 1 - 3, '76. BICENTENNIAL VARIETY SHOW. ORIGINAL MUSICAL VARIETY SHOW. AT A C H S AUDITORIUM. (LOCAL). JOHN OLISAR, COORDINATOR; ANTIOCH COMMUNITY HIGH SCHOOL; 1133 S MAIN ST; ANTIOCH, IL 60002. (#105408-6).

APR 7, '76. HISTORICAL ARTS AND CRAFTS FAIR. COLONIAL CRAFTS DEMONSTRATIONS - CHURN BUTTER, BLACKSMITHING, QUILT MAKING & SHEEP SHEARING, RAIL SPLITTING, GLASS BLOWING & CANDLE AND CIDER MAKING. INDIAN CULTURE & ANTIQUES, GUN & FLAG DISPLAYS. FILM ON LOCAL REVOL HISTORY. CHOIR AND BAND MUSIC OF COLONIAL ERA. AT ANTIOCH COMMUNITY HIGH SCHOOL/1133 S MAIN ST (SCHOOL PARKING LOT). (LOCAL). GARY ALLEN; ANTIOCH COMMUNITY HIGH SCHOOL; 565 ORCHARD ST; ANTIOCH, IL 60002. (#103268-1).

APR 10, '76. BICENTENNIAL LAS VEGAS NIGHT. FESTIVAL AT ST PETERS SOCIAL CENTER, ST PETER AND ELIZABETH STS. (LOCAL). PAUL A KINAS, COORDINATOR; ANTIOCH JAYCEES & VIKINGS FOOTBALL TEAM; PO BOX 254; ANTIOCH, IL 60002. (#105408-2).

APR 10 - 24, '76. THE EDUCATION OF HYMAN KAPLAN - A PLAY. A POIGNANT PLAY PORTRAYING THE STRUGGLES OF NEW CITIZENS - AUTHOR, LEO ROSTEN - PERFORMANCES ON APRIL 10 - 16, 17 - 23 - 24, 1976. AT P M & L THEATRE/877 MAIN ST; VILLAGE PARKING - FREE. (LOCAL). AILEEN BIEL; PALETTE MASQUE AND LYRE COMMUNITY THEATRE, INC; PO BOX 23; ANTIOCH, IL 60002. (#103268-2).

ANTIOCH — CONTINUED

APR 24, '76. JOHNNY APPLESEED DAY - JOHNNY APPLESEED & CREWS TO PLANT APPLETREES. 6'-7' TREES - VOLUNTEER CREWS COSTUMED AS JOHNNY APPLESEED TO PLANT OVER 100 APPLE TREES THROUGHOUT ANTIOCH TOWNSHIP ON PROPERTY OF CITIZENS WHOSE NAMES WILL BE DRAWN BY CHANCE. AT TREE PLANTING THROUGHOUT ANTIOCH TOWNSHIP. (LOCAL). DAVE BUSHING, COORD; NORTHERN ILLINOIS CONSERVATION CLUB; COUNTY CLUB RD; ANTIOCH, IL 60002. (#105408-3).

MAY 15, '76. BICENTENNIAL FAIR 1776-1976. OLD FASHIONED FAIR FEATURING ARTS AND CRAFTS EXHIBIT, GAMES, BAKE SALE AND SING-A-LONG; REFRESHMENTS SERVED. AT OAKLAND GRADE SCHOOL AUDITORIUM - DEEP LAKE RD & GRASS LAKE RD. (LOCAL). SHIRLEY MORRIS, DIRECTOR; ANTIOCH GIRL SCOUTS; 644 HILLSIDE AVE; ANTIOCH, IL 60002. (#105408-1).

JULY 4, '76. FOURTH OF JULY VILLAGE OF ANTIOCH BICENTENNIAL CELEBRATION. MAIN ST PARADE WITH MARCHING BANDS, FLOATS, FIRE DEPT & RESCUE SQUAD EQUIP; CIVIC, SOCIAL, FRATERNAL & RELIGIOUS ORGANIZATIONS ASKED TO PARTICIPATE; FIREWORKS DISPLAY IN EVENING HOURS. AT ANTIOCH HIGH SCHOOL FOOTBALL FIELD & MAIN STREET. (LOCAL). HON ROBERT WILTON, MAYOR; VILLAGE OF ANTIOCH-ANTIOCH FIRE DEPT-ANTIOCH BICENT COMMISSION; 874 MAIN ST; ANTIOCH, IL 60002. (#105408-4).

ARCOLA

MEMORIAL ENTRANCE TO MOORE PARK - ARCOLA, IL. CONSTRUCTION OF MEMORIAL ENTRANCE TO MOORE PARK AT ARCOLA. (LOCAL). SALLY HEUERMAN, CHAIRMAN; ARCOLA BICENTENNIAL COMMISSION; 617 E MAIN; ARCOLA, IL 61910. (#30397).

MAY 8 - 30, '76. RAILSPLITTING DAYS. COMPETITION, LIVE PERFORMANCE AT ROCKOME GARDENS. (LOCAL). SALLY HEUERMAN, CHMN; ROCKOME GARDENS; 617 E MAIN ST; ARCOLA, IL 61910. (#200016-164).

JUNE 20, '76. ANTIQUE AUTO SHOW. EXHIBIT AT ROCKOME GARDENS. (LOCAL). SALLY HEUERMAN, CHMN; ROCKOME GARDENS; 617 E MAIN ST; ARCOLA, IL 61910. (#200016-165).

JULY 7 - 10, '76. DOUGLAS COUNTY CHAUTAUQUA IN ARCOLA. FESTIVITIES INCLUDE FARMER DAYS, AIR FORCE DRUM & BUGLE CORPS, DANCES & PARADES. (LOCAL). SALLY HEURRMMANN, CHMN; DOUGLAS COUNTY BICENTENNIAL COMMITTEE; 617 E MAIN; ARCOLA, IL 61910. (#106546-1).

JULY 11, '76. GERMAN MUSIC FESTIVAL. FESTIVAL AT ROCKOME GARDENS. (LOCAL). SALLY HEUERMAN, CHMN; ROCKOME GARDENS; 617 E MAIN ST; ARCOLA, IL 61910. (#200016-166).

JULY 25, '76. BLUEGRASS FESTIVAL. FESTIVAL AT ROCKOME GARDENS. (LOCAL). SALLY HEUERMAN, CHMN; ROCKOME GARDENS; 617 E MAIN ST; ARCOLA, IL 61910. (#200016-158).

AUG 14 - 15, '76. CHILDREN'S DAYS. FESTIVAL AT ROCKOME GARDENS. (LOCAL). SALLY HEUERMAN, CHMN; ROCKOME GARDENS; 617 E MAIN ST; ARCOLA, IL 61910. (#200016-159).

SEPT 24 - OCT 10, '76. HORSEFARMING DAYS. COMPETITION, LIVE PERFORMANCE AT ROCKOME GARDENS. (LOCAL). SALLY HEUERMAN, CHMN; ROCKOME GARDENS; 617 E MAIN ST; ARCOLA, IL 61910. (#200016-160).

ARLINGTON HTS

JUNE 30 - JULY 5, '76. FESTIVAL '76, A COMMUNITY-WIDE 5 DAY BICENT CELEBRATION. FESTIVAL AT RECREATION PARK, 500 E MINER ST. (LOCAL). GEORGE L WEINAND, COORD; ARLINGTON HEIGHTS BICENTENNIAL - FESTIVAL COMMISSION; 33 S ARLINGTON HTS RD; ARLINGTON HTS, IL 60005. (#200016-231).

ARTHUR

JULY 7 - 10, '76. DOUGLAS COUNTY CHAUTAUQUA IN ARTHUR. FESTIVITIES INCLUDE FARMER DAYS, AIR FORCE DRUM & BUGLE CORPS, DANCES & PARADES. (LOCAL). MARVIN JONES, COORD; DOUGLAS COUNTY BICENTENNIAL COMMITTEE; PO BOX; ARTHUR, IL 61911. (#106550-1).

AUG 20 - 21, '76. CENTURY PLUS THREE DAYS. FESTIVAL. (LOCAL). GARY V CONLIN, CHMN; ARTHUR BICENTENNIAL COMMISSION; 718 COLUMBIA; ARTHUR, IL 61911. (#200016-163).

ASHTON

JUNE 18 - 20, '76. ASHTON BICENTENNIAL CELEBRATION. FESTIVAL, PARADE. (LOCAL). MIKE HECKMAN, CO-CHAIRMAN; LEE COUNTY BICENTENNIAL COMMISSION; PO BOX 348; DIXON, IL 61021. (#104268-4).

ATKINSON

SIX-ACRE FLAG OF FLOWERS - ATKINSON, IL. PLANTING OF SIX-ACRE FLAG OF PETUNIAS BY VERN MOENS, A FARMER, NEAR ATKINSON. (LOCAL). VERN MOENS, COORDINATOR; HENRY COUNTY BICENTENNIAL COMMISSION; RR; ATKINSON, IL 61235. (#30387).

ATWOOD

JULY 4 - 10, '76. BICENTENNIAL 4TH OF JULY CELEBRATION - WEEK LONG FESTIVAL. EVENTS INCLUDE CRAFTS, SINGING, THRESHING, A TRACTOR PULL, GAMES AND FOOD. (LOCAL). MRS LORETTA HOFSAS, CHMN; ATWOOD BICENTENNIAL COMMISSION; 124 N MAIN; ATWOOD, IL 61913. (#104000-1).

JULY 7 - 10, '76. DOUGLAS COUNTY CHAUTAUQUA IN ATWOOD. FESTIVITIES INCLUDE FARMER DAYS, AIR FORCE DRUM & BUGLE CORPS, DANCES & PARADES. (LOCAL). ALBERTA FOMBELL, COORD; DOUGLAS COUNTY BICENTENNIAL COMMITTEE; PO BOX; ATWOOD, IL 61913. (#106549-1).

AUGUSTA

JULY 28, '76. HANCOCK COUNTY FAIR-PARADE ARTS CRAFTS HISTORY. FAIR. (ST-WIDE). DONNA L CLAMPITT; HANCOCK COUNTY BICENTENNIAL COMMITTEE; RR; AUGUSTA, IL 62311. (#107279-1).

AURORA

AURORA CITY OPTIONS PROGRAM - ILLINOIS. PRESERVATION OF CBD PHYSICAL URBAN DESIGN ATTRIBUTES EMPHASIZING THE RELATION OF ISLAND TO RIVER. FORMULATION OF CIVIC AND CULTURAL PROGRAMS TO COINCIDE WITH PHYSICAL IMPROVEMENTS AND BICENTENNIAL. (LOCAL). EDMOND BROWNE, ADMIN ASST TO MAYOR; CITY OF AURORA; 44 E DOWNER PL; AURORA, IL 60504. (#2375).

BICENTENNIAL THEME IN PUBLICATIONS - AURORA, IL. COLLEGE AND STUDENT PUBLICATIONS TO USE A BICENTENNIAL THEME. TO HELP IN THIS, AN OFFICIAL LOGO HAS BEEN DEVELOPED. (LOCAL). SCOTT B PALMER, REGISTRAR; AURORA COLLEGE BICENTENNIAL COMMITTEE; AURORA, IL 60507. (#13570).

COLOR MOVIE WITH SOUND CASSETTE - AURORA, IL. A PERMANENT RECORD OF THE HIGHLIGHTS OF THE COLLEGE BICENTENNIAL CELEBRATION FOR LOCAL SHOWING AND PERMANENT DEPOSIT IN THE LIBRARY. (LOCAL). CLYDE E HEWITT, CHAIRMAN; AURORA COLLEGE BICENTENNIAL COMMITTEE; AURORA, IL 60507. (#13572).

CURRICULAR OFFERINGS - AURORA COLLEGE, IL. ACADEMIC COURSES SPECIFICALLY DESIGNED TO FURTHUR THE BICENTENNIAL OBSERVANCE, 'TOPICS IN THE HISTORY OF THE AMERICAN REVOLUTION' BEING OFFERED THIS SUMMER; OTHERS WILL FOLLOW. (LOCAL). DAVID T ARTHUR, DEAN; AURORA COLLEGE BICENTENNIAL COMMITTEE; AURORA, IL 60507. (#13573).

DEPARTMENTAL AND DIVISIONAL DISPLAYS - AURORA, IL. STRESS HISTORY OF VARIOUS DEPARTMENTS AND DIVISIONS ON AURORA COLLEGE CAMPUS. (LOCAL). C E HEWITT, CHAIRMAN; AURORA COLLEGE BICENTENNIAL COMMITTEE; AURORA, IL 60507. (#13562).

FACULTY LECTURE SERIES - AURORA COLLEGE, IL. LECTURES FROM VARIOUS DISCIPLINES FEATURING OUR HERITAGE VIEWED IN LIGHT OF ONGOING IDEALS AND FUTURE PROSPECTS. (LOCAL). DR DAVID ARTHUR, DEAN; AURORA COLLEGE BICENTENNIAL COMMITTEE; AURORA, IL 60507. (#13565).

HISTORICAL FILM SERIES - AURORA COLLEGE, IL. STRESSING GREAT MOMENTS IN OUR HISTORY AND GREAT ONGOING THEMES IN OUR NATION'S DEVELOPMENT. (LOCAL). MS DOROTHY CROUSE, CHAIRMAN; AURORA COLLEGE PROGRAM BOARD; AURORA, IL 62507. (#13569).

HOSTING COMMUNITY BAND CONCERTS - AURORA, IL. SUMMER BAND CONCERTS TO BE HELD ON AURORA COLLEGE CAMPUS. BANDS WILL FEATURE MUSIC OF HISTORIC AND CULTURAL INTEREST. (LOCAL). ROBERT F RICHARDSON, PROJ DIRECTOR; AURORA COLLEGE BICENTENNIAL COMMITTEE; AURORA, IL 60507. (#13568).

LASTING REMINDER - AURORA COLLEGE, IL. COLLEGE SEAL AND PLAQUE IN BRONZE COMMEMORATING THE AURORA COLLEGE OBSERVANCE. OTHER LASTING REMINDERS IN PLANNING STAGE. (LOCAL). MARK H TRUMBO, EXEC VICE PRESIDENT; AURORA COLLEGE BICENTENNIAL COMMITTEE; AURORA, IL 60507. (#13571).

LIBRARY DISPLAYS AND TRAVELLING EXHIBITS - IL. COLLEGE-OWNED MATERIALS AND TRAVELLING EXHIBITS WITH BICENTENNIAL THEMES. (LOCAL). RICHARD WASSUM, ASSISTANT; AURORA COLLEGE BICENTENNIAL COMMITTEE; AURORA, IL 60507. (#13561).

MARMION ACADEMY BICENTENNIAL HERITAGE SEMINARS. SERIES OF BIOGRAPHICAL SEMINARS ON SELECTED RESIDENTS OF EARLY ILL. FIVE SEMINARS BY UNIVERSITY SCHOLARS FOR PUBLIC & OTHER SEMINARS BY MARMION ACADEMY, AURORA, ILL., STUDENTS FOR PRIMARY SCHOOL CLASSES. (LOCAL). REV PETER ENDERLIN, OSB, DEAN OF STUDIES; MARMION MILITARY ACADEMY; BUTTERFIELD RD; AURORA, IL 60504. (#884). **ARBA GRANTEE.**

MUSIC, ART, DRAMA DEPT PERFORMANCES - AURORA, IL. ORIGINAL AND OTHER WORKS ALL STRESSING BICENTENNIAL THEMES IN ART, MUSIC AND DRAMA. (LOCAL). J L DUNHAM, PROJ DIRECTOR; AURORA COLLEGE BICENTENNIAL COMMITTEE; AURORA, IL 60507. (#13563).

'OLD TIME' SOCIAL EVENTS - AURORA COLLEGE, IL. MAJOR SOCIAL EVENTS BY AND FOR FACULTY/STAFF AND STUDENTS (JOINTLY OR SEPARATELY) CAST IN A HISTORICAL SETTING. (LOCAL). ROBERT ZBONSKI, PRESIDENT; AURORA COLLEGE STUDENTS' ASSOC; AURORA, IL 60507. (#13566).

VISITING LECTURERS - AURORA COLLEGE, IL. COLLEGE HAS AT LEAST TWO ON-GOING LECTURE SERIES. AMERICAN HISTORICAL THEMES WILL BE FEATURED DURING BICENTENNIAL. OTHER LECTURES MAY BE SCHEDULED. (LOCAL). MRS DORIS K COLBY, LIBRARIAN; AURORA COLLEGE BICENTENNIAL COMMITTEE; AURORA, IL 60507. (#13564).

JULY 1 - 31, '75. AURORAFEST. PRESERVATION OF CBD PHYSICAL URBAN DESIGN ATTRIBUTES EMPHASIZING THE RELATION OF ISLAND TO RIVER. FORMULATION OF CIVIC AND CULTURAL PROGRAMS TO COINCIDE WITH PHYSICAL IMPROVEMENTS AND BICENTENNIAL. ARTS AND CRAFTS EXHIBITS PARADES AND FIREWORKS LOCAL PERFORMANCES. AT CITYWIDE. (LOCAL). EDMOND BROWNE, ASST MAYOR; CITY OF AURORA; 44 E DOWNER PL; AURORA, IL 60504. (#2375-1).

AUG 12 - 13, '75. AMERICAN FREEDOM TRAIN DISPLAY DAYS AT AURORA, ILLINOIS. THE AMERICAN FREEDOM TRAIN WILL INCLUDE 10 EXHIBIT CARS & 2 SHOWCASE CARS DEPICTING DIFFERENT PHASES OF THE AMERICAN EXPERIENCE. ITS ARRIVAL WILL SERVE AS A CATALYST FOR LOCAL BICENTENNIAL CELEBRATIONS BY PEOPLE THROUGHOUT THIS NATION. (ST-WIDE). SY FREEDMAN, DIR OF P/R; THE AMERICAN FREEDOM TRAIN FOUNDATION; 5205 LEESBURG PIKE, SUITE 800; BAILEY'S XRDS, VA 22041. (#1776-141).

NOV 16, '75 - MAY 16, '76. MARMION ACADEMY BICENTENNIAL HERITAGE SEMINARS. SERIES OF BIOGRAPHICAL SEMINARS ON SELECTED RESIDENTS OF EARLY ILL. FIVE SEMINARS BY UNIVERSITY SCHOLARS FOR PUBLIC & OTHER SEMINARS BY MARMION ACADEMY, AURORA, ILL., STUDENTS FOR PRIMARY SCHOOL CLASSES. AT MARMION MILITARY ACADEMY. (LOCAL). REV PETER ENDERLIN DEAN; MARMION MILITARY ACADEMY; MARMION MILITARY ACDBUTTERFLD RD; AURORA, IL 60504. (#884-1).

SEPT 30 - DEC 10, '76. A BICENTENNIAL FAREWELL: AURORA COLLEGE FACULTY AND GUEST LECTURES. SEMINAR AT ECKHART HALL, AURORA COLLEGE. (LOCAL). DR CLYDE E HEWITT, COORD; AURORA COLLEGE; AURORA, IL 60507. (#109342-1).

OCT 15 - 17, '76. HOMECOMING '76. PROGRAM WILL BE BUILT AROUND A BICENTENNIAL THEME. AT HOTEL BAKER. (LOCAL). ROBERT ZBONSKI, PRESIDENT; AURORA COLLEGE STUDENTS' ASSOC; AURORA, IL 60507. (#13567-1).

AVISTON

JULY 4, '76. JULY 4TH CELEBRATION. FESTIVAL, PARADE AT AVISTON CITY PARK. (LOCAL). JAMES C QUAID, CHAIRMAN; CLINTON COUNTY BICENTENNIAL COMMISSION; 206 E HANOVER; NEW BADEN, IL 62265. (#104059-1).

AVON

ILLINOIS PLANNING GUIDE FOR LOCAL BICENT PROJECTS. HANDBOOK TO GUIDE LOCAL GROUPS TO PLAN & IMPLEMENT BICENTENNIAL PROJECTS. WILL BE DISTRIBUTED FREE TO ORGANIZATIONS. (ST-WIDE). MRS E H DAVIS, BICENTENNIAL CHAIRMAN; ILLINOIS FEDERATION OF WOMEN; 30 W WASHINGTON ST; CHICAGO, IL 61415. (#721).

BARTLETT

HIKERS OF AMERICA LIBERTY TOUR IN BARTLETT, IL. A SELF-GUIDED WALKING TOUR OF HISTORICAL SITES IN BARTLETT, IL. (LOCAL). JAMES BENTZ, PROJ PRESIDENT; HIKERS OF AMERICA, INC; RT 1 BOX 68; OSWEGO, IL 60543. (#10161).

MAR 22, '75. BARTLETT DAY - 63RD ANNIVERSARY COMMEMORATION OF INCORPORATION. ANNIVERSARY OF TOWN INCORPORATION -BARTLETT, ILL. BARTLETT DAY PLANNED TO CELEBRATE 63RD YEAR OF INCORPORATION. (LOCAL). JUDITH SZAJEK; BARTLETT BICENTENNIAL COMMISSION; 228 SO MAIN ST; BARTLETT, IL 60103. (#4531-501).

MAY 24 - 25, '75. MEMORIAL DAY COMMEMORATION CIVIL WAR DAYS ORIGIN OF MEMORIAL DAY. ORIGINAL CIVIL WAR BAND FIRST BRIGADE; MUSKET COMPETITION; BLUE GRAY BALL; COSTUME JUDGING; LIVE ENTERTAINMENT FREE. AT BARTLETT PARK NORTH & EASTERN. (REGN'L). JUDITH SZAJEK; BARTLETT BICENTENNIAL COMMISSION; 228 SO MAIN ST; BARTLETT, IL 60103. (#4532-1).

NOV 1, '75 - MAR 1, '76. FLAG DESIGN CONTEST. CONTEST TO DESIGN FIRST VILLAGE FLAG. DEADLINE 3/01/76. (LOCAL). JUDY SZAJEK, CHAIRMAN; BARTLETT BICENTENNIAL COMMISSION; 228 S MAIN ST; BARTLETT, IL 60103. (#104219-3).

MAR 13, '76. 2ND ANNUAL DINNER DANCE. FESTIVAL. (LOCAL). JUDY SZAJEK, CHAIRMAN; BARTLETT BICENTENNIAL COMMISSION; 228 S MAIN ST; BARTLETT, IL 60103. (#104219-2).

MAY 9 - DEC 31, '76. DISPLAY OF RESTORED 1897 HAND PUMPER. EXHIBIT AT MEMORIAL PARK. (LOCAL). JUDY SZAJEK, CHAIRMAN; BARTLETT BICENTENNIAL COMMISSION; 228 S MAIN ST; BARTLETT, IL 60103. (#104219-4).

MAY 29 - 30, '76. 2ND ANNUAL MEMORIAL DAY COMMEMORATION OF CIVIL WAR DAYS. THERE WILL BE A CANNON DEMONSTRATION BY CONFEDERATE & UNION TROOPS, A MUSKET COMPETITION, TEAM & INDIVIDUAL TOMAHAWK COMPETITION. THERE WILL BE FREE ENTERTAINMENT, FOOD AVAILABLE, & A MILITARY BALL. ALSO A CIVIL WAR RE-ENACTMENT; HOT AIR BALLOON, CRAFT DEMO'S. AT BARTLETT PARK, OAK ST & NORTH AVE, SO OF RT 20. (REGN'L). JUDY SZAJEK, CO-CHMN; BARTLETT BICENTENNIAL COMMITTEE; 228 S MAIN ST; BARTLETT, IL 60103. (#103071-1).

BARTONVILLE

COVERED PICNIC SHELTER IN BARTONVILLE, IL. BUILDING OF MAIN LASTING MEMORIAL: A 2000 SQ FT PICNIC SHELTER IN ALPHA PARK. (LOCAL). MRS DONALD STEWART, CHAIRMAN; BARTONVILLE BICENTENNIAL COMMISSION; 15 ALEXANDER LN; BARTONVILLE, IL 61607. (#33669).

BARTONVILLE — CONTINUED

OCT 31, '76. TIME CAPSULE BURIAL. CEREMONY AT VILLAGE HALL. (LOCAL). ESTALINE R STEWART; BARTONVILLE BICENTENNIAL COMMISSION; 15 ALEXANDER LN; BARTONVILLE, IL 61607. (#200016-493).

BATAVIA

BICENTENNIAL FLAGS - BATAVIA, IL. BICENTENNIAL FLAGS FOR ALL SCHOOLS IN THE COMMUNITY. (LOCAL). COORDINATOR; AMERICAN LEGION WOMEN'S AUXILIARY; BATAVIA, IL 60510. (#28655).

BICENTENNIAL PARK - BATAVIA, IL. LEISURE & RECREATION WILL BE ENHANCED BY THE ADDITION OF THIS PARK. (LOCAL). TOM TAGGART, CHAIRMAN; BATAVIA PARK DISTRICT; 327 W WILSON; BATAVIA, IL 60510. (#28658).

BICENTENNIAL TREES - BATAVIA, IL. PLANTING OF HARDWOOD TREES IN THE COMMUNITY. (LOCAL). VIC KESSLER, PROJECT CHAIRMAN; ROTARY CLUB OF BATAVIA; PO BOX 125; BATAVIA, IL 60510. (#28656).

DEPOT MUSEUM - BATAVIA, IL. HISTORICAL MUSEUM WILL BE MADE FROM THE LOCAL DEPOT. (ST-WIDE). TOM TAGGART, CHAIRMAN; BATAVIA HISTORICAL SOCIETY; PO BOX 15; BATAVIA, IL 60510. (#28657).

APR 19, '75. PAUL REVERE'S RIDE. LIVE PERFORMANCE AT CONGREGATIONAL CHURCH OF BATAVIA. (LOCAL). TOM TAGGART, CHMN; PLAYMAKERS; 15 E WILSON; BATAVIA, IL 60510. (#200016-232).

MAY 1, '76. BICENTENNIAL LAW DAY PARADE. PARADE AT CITY OF BATAVIA. (LOCAL). TOM TAGGART, CHMN; BATAVIA V F W POST; 15 E WILSON; BATAVIA, IL 60510. (#200016-233).

MAY 2, '76. BICENTENNIAL CHURCH WALK. TOUR AT CITY OF BATAVIA, ALL CHURCHES. (LOCAL). TOM TAGGART, CHMN; BATAVIA MINISTERIAL ASSOC; 15 E WILSON; BATAVIA, IL 60510. (#200016-235).

JULY 4, '76. BICENTENNIAL FIREWORKS. FESTIVAL AT BATAVIA HIGH SCHOOL FIELD. (LOCAL). TOM TAGGART, CHMN; BATAVIA FIRE DEPARTMENT; 15 E WILSON; BATAVIA, IL 60510. (#200016-236).

JULY 30 - 31, '76. BICENTENNIAL SALE DAYS. FESTIVAL AT CITY OF BATAVIA. (LOCAL). TOM TAGGART, CHMN; BATAVIA CHAMBER OF COMMERCE; 15 E WILSON; BATAVIA, IL 60510. (#200016-234).

OCT 10, '76. LANDMARK HIKE. TOUR. (LOCAL). TOM TAGGART, CHAIRMAN; BATAVIA HISTORICAL SOCIETY; PO BOX 15; BATAVIA, IL 60510. (#109336-1).

BEARDSTOWN

CASS COUNTY COURTHOUSE MUSEUM - BEARDSTOWN, IL. RESTORATION OF FORMER CASS COUNTY COURTHOUSE, WHERE ABRAHAM LINCOLN SUCCESSFULLY DEFENDED DUFF ARMSTRONG, INTO A MUSEUM OF STATE HISTORY. (ST-WIDE). GLENN HERZBERGER, CHAIRMAN; CASS COUNTY BICENTENNIAL COMMISSION; 210 WASHINGTON; BEARDSTOWN, IL 62618. (#30406).

JULY 4, '76. BICENTENNIAL WORSHIP SERVICE. CEREMONY. (LOCAL). GLENN HERZBERGER, CHMN; CASS COUNTY BICENTENNIAL COMMISSION; 210 WASHINGTON; BEARDSTOWN, IL 62618. (#200016-162).

JULY 4 - 11, '76. BICENTENNIAL TOUR OF CHURCHES. TOUR. (LOCAL). GLENN HERZBERGER, CHMN; CASS COUNTY BICENTENNIAL COMMISSION; 210 WASHINGTON; BEARDSTOWN, IL 62618. (#200016-161).

JAN 31 - FEB 2, '77. LA SALLE EXPEDITION II, A HISTORIC RE-ENACTMENT. THIS IS AN AUTHENTIC RE-ENACTMENT OF THE 1681 LASALLE EXPEDITION FROM MONTREAL, CANADA TO NEW ORLEANS, LA WHICH WILL BEGIN TOURING ON AUGUST 11, 1976 AND END ON APRIL 9, 1977. (LOCAL). REID H LEWIS, DIRECTOR; LA SALLE EXPEDITION II; 135 S LA SALLE ST, RM 411; CHICAGO, IL 60690. (#102805-47).

BELLEVILLE

BICENTENNIAL BANDANA QUILTS, BELLEVILLE, IL. LOCAL WOMEN'S CLUB QUILTED 3 BANDANA QUILTS OF RED, WHITE AND BLUE. (LOCAL). MRS CARL GRUINLEY, BICENTENNIAL CHAIRMAN; CIVIC LEAGUE OF BELLEVILLE; 43 CARNATION DR; BELLEVILLE, IL 62221. (#14396). **ARBA GRANTEE.**

BICENTENNIAL COMMEMORATIVE QUILT - BELLEVILLE, IL. A RED, WHITE & BLUE GINGHAM & CALICO EMBROIDERED QUILT DEPICTS 200 YEARS OF AMERICAN SYMBOLS & MIGRATION TO ILLINOIS. (LOCAL). MRS DONALD WORLEY, REGENT; BELLEVILLE CHAPTER OF THE DAR; 27 CLOVER DR; BELLEVILLE, IL 62221. (#14799).

COVENANTER PROJECT - ILLINOIS PSALM-SINGING RECORD. RECORDED DOCUMENTATION OF PSALM-SINGING IN SOUTHERN ILLINOIS FOCUSING ON SMALL CONGREGATIONS & INDIVIDUAL SINGERS. LP ALBUM AND BOOK LET TO BE PRODUCED. (REGN'L). PETER LIPPINCOTT & WAYNE LANTER, CO-SPONSORS; BELLEVILLE AREA COLLEGE; 2500 CARLYLE RD; BELLEVILLE, IL 62221. (#26137).

EMBROIDERED BICENTENNIAL SAMPLER, BELLEVILLE, IL. AN EMBROIDER SAMPLER BEARING THE NAMES OF 45 REVOLUTIONARY SOLDIERS AND PATRIOTS BURIED IN LOCAL ST CLAIR COUNTY; TO BE PRESENTED AS A GIFT TO LOCAL HISTORICAL SOCIETY. (LOCAL). MRS DONALD WORLEY, CHAIRMAN; BELLEVILLE CHAPTER DAR; 27 CLOVER DR; BELLEVILLE, IL 62221. (#14313).

HANDICAPPED VISITOR TRAIL - BELLEVILLE, IL. SPECIAL FACILITIES WILL BE CREATED FOR THE HANDICAPPED IN FRANCIS FOLEY COUNTY PARK; IT WILL INCLUDE SPECIAL TRAILS, PARKING AREAS & OTHER SUPPORTIVE FACILITIES. (LOCAL). JOANNE R KURTZ, CHAIRPERSON; ST CLAIR COUNTY BICENTENNIAL COMMISSION; 56 RUGBY DR; BELLEVILLE, IL 62223. (#18095).

HISTORICAL ART DISPLAYS PROJECT - BELLEVILLE, IL. A SCHOOL-ORIENTED PROGRAM WILL BE DEVELOPED FEATURING CHILDREN'S HISTORICAL ART PROJECTS AT THE NEW COUNTY COURTHOUSE; ALL SCHOOL DISTRICTS IN THE COUNTY ARE INVITED TO PARTICIPATE. (LOCAL). JOANNE R KURTZ, CHAIRPERSON; ST CLAIR COUNTY BICENTENNIAL COMMISSION; 56 RUGBY DR; BELLEVILLE, IL 62223. (#18096).

LOCAL HISTORY TOURS OF ST CLAIR COUNTY, IL. LOCAL HISTORY TOURS WILL BE CONDUCTED DESCRIBING EVENTS AND PLACES SIGNIFICANT IN THE COUNTY HISTORY. (LOCAL). JOANNE R KURTZ, CHAIRPERSON; ST CLAIR COUNTY BICENTENNIAL COMMISSION; 56 RUGBY DR; BELLEVILLE, IL 62223. (#18098).

LOG FORT CONSTRUCTION - BELLEVILLE, IL. A SMALL SCALE LOG FORT WILL BE RECONSTRUCTED WITHIN THE RECREATIONAL AREA AT FRANCIS FOLEY COUNTY PARK. (LOCAL). JOANNE R KURTZ, CHAIRPERSON; ST CLAIR COUNTY BICENTENNIAL COMMISSION; 56 RUGBY DR; BELLEVILLE, IL 62223. (#18097).

'OLD BELLEVILLE TODAY' - IL. INSTALLATION OF 16 ANTIQUE GASLIGHTS AND 48 PAIRS OF WINDOW SHUTTERS IN HISTORIC DISTRICT OF BELLEVILLE TO HELP RECREATE ORIGINAL FEELING OF THE NEIGHBORHOOD. (LOCAL). JAMES D YOUNG, CHAIRMAN; CITIZENS' COURT HOUSE COMMITTEE; 19 WOODLAND COURT; BELLEVILLE, IL 62220. (#25910). **ARBA GRANTEE.**

OLD CEMETERY CLEANUP, ST CLAIR COUNTY, IL. GENERAL CLEANUP OF POTTERS' FIELDS WITH MARKING OF HISTORICAL GRAVES INCLUDING THOSE OF REVOLUTIONARY WAR SOLDIERS & PLANTING OF FLOWERS. (LOCAL). JOANNE R KURTZ, CHAIRPERSON; ST CLAIR COUNTY BICENTENNIAL COMMISSION; 56 RUGBY DR; BELLEVILLE, IL 62223. (#17715).

JULY '76. SHRINERS' PARADE - SPIRIT OF 76. PARTICIPANTS ARE CHILDREN & 'ALL AGES' DRESSED IN BEAUTIFUL COLONIAL COSTUMES. ALL ARE DESCENDENTS OF 1776 SOLDIERS OR PATRIOTS. AT MAIN STREET. (LOCAL). MRS DONALD WORLEY, REGENT; SHRINERS; 27 CLOVER DR; BELLEVILLE, IL 62221. (#102064-1).

BELLFLOWER

MUSEUM & COMMUNITY HALL, BELLFLOWER, IL. CONSTRUCTION OF MUSEUM AND COMMUNITY HALL. (LOCAL). WILSON MEARS, COORDINATOR; MCLEAN BICENTENNIAL COMMISSION; BELLFLOWER, IL 61724. (#33668).

BELLWOOD

BELLWOOD COMMEMORATIVE COIN - BELLWOOD, IL. STRIKING OF BRONZE COMMEMORATIVE COIN CELEBRATING THE BICENTENNIAL AND BELLWOOD'S HISTORY. (LOCAL). AL KORBEL, PUBLICITY; BELLWOOD BICENTENNIAL COMMISSION; BOX 176; BELLWOOD, IL 60104. (#18187).

LASTING MONUMENT - BELLWOOD, IL. THE ENCASING OF A BELL FROM THE FIRST CHURCH BUILT IN TOWN TO COMMEMORATE BELLWOOD'S HERITAGE AND THE BICENTENNIAL. (LOCAL). AL KORBEL, PUBLICITY DIRECTOR; BELLWOOD BICENTENNIAL COMMISSION; BOX 176; BELLWOOD, IL 60104. (#18186).

APR 3, '76. BICENTENNIAL BALL. FESTIVAL AT NORTHLAKE HOTEL, 401 W LAKE ST. (LOCAL). JEAN KEATING, CHMN; BELLWOOD BICENTENNIAL COMMISSION; 3708 BUTTERFIELD; BELLWOOD, IL 60104. (#103701-1).

BELVIDERE

DAILY REPUBLICAN BICENT SPECIAL EDITION - NBMRP. PRIMARY BICENTENNIAL PROJECT IS SPECIAL EDITION COVERING OFFICIAL BICENTENNIAL ACTIVITIES. WILL HAVE SOUVENIR/HISTORICAL VALUE. ---. (LOCAL). PATRICK B MATTISON, PRESIDENT, ASSOC PUBLISHER; BELVIDERE DAILY REPUBLICAN; 401 WHITNEY BLVD; BELVIDERE, IL 61008. (#26601).

HERITAGE TRAIL '76, BELVIDERE JAYCEES - IL. CONSTRUCTION OF BICENTENNIAL PATHWAY WITH LANDSCAPING, NATURE TRAILS AND BIKE TRAILS. (ST-WIDE). DAVE RODEN, PRESIDENT; BELVIDERE JAYCEES; 530 S STATE; BELVIDERE, IL 61008. (#27793). **ARBA GRANTEE.**

RESTORATION OF ONE ROOM SCHOOLHOUSE - IL. REFURBISHING OF 100 YEAR OLD, ONE ROOM PRAIRIE SCHOOLHOUSE. (LOCAL). HAROLD LUHMAN, CHAIRMAN; BOONE COUNTY BICENTENNIAL COMMISSION; PO BOX 444; BELVIDERE, IL 61008. (#27878). **ARBA GRANTEE.**

BENTON

CRUSADE FOR WORLD PEACE - STUDY GROUP, BENTON, IL. GROUPS WILL BE FORMED TO STUDY & ACT ON THE BOOK, 'MACHINERY FOR WORLD PEACE IN THE SEVENTIES', A PROGRAM FOR ACHIEVING WORLD PEACE BY MEANS OF INFORMED PUBLIC OPINION. (LOCAL). ROY A KALE, CONSULTANT; WESTMINSTER PRESBYTERIAN CHURCH OF FRANKLIN COUNTY; 900 N DU QUOIN ST, PO BOX 572; BENTON, IL 62812. (#6433).

BERWYN

JULY 1 - 4, '76. BICENTENNIAL DAYS. A MOSAIC PROGRAM TO IDENTIFY THE RICH HERITAGE AND EXCITING FUTURE OF A SUBURBAN COMMUNITY WHOSE MOTTO IS 'A CITY OF HOMES & PROGRESS'. EXHIBITS, RE-ENACTMENTS, PARADE, FIREWORKS AND ARTS & CRAFTS PROGRAM WILL BE VIDEOTAPED FOR LATER PRESENTATIONS. AT MORTON WEST HIGH SCHOOL WITH SECONDARY ACTIVITY SITES. (LOCAL). ROBERT C PECHOUS, DIR; BERWYN BICENTENNIAL COMMISSION; 6700 W 26TH ST; BERWYN, IL 60402. (#104197-1).

BETHALTO

LIGHTING & BUILDING IN BETHALTO, IL. RAISED 1000 DOLLARS BY VOLUNTEERS, GIVING OF CIVIC ORGANIZATIONS, AUCTION; SOLD COMMEMORATIVE COINS, JAM; HAVE LANDSCAPED 3-ACRE PARK; BOUGHT PLAYGROUND EQUIPMENT & LIGHTS FOR TENNIS COURTS. (LOCAL). LES DREHN, CHAIRMAN; BETHALTO BICENTENNIAL COMMISSION; 215 BUTCHER; BETHALTO, IL 62010. (#33667).

SEPT 4 - 6, '76. HISTORICAL PLAY-CONTINENTAL CAMP SITE. HISTORICAL PLAY BY DRAMA DEPT AT HIGH SCHOOL-HISTORY OF VILLAGE SINCE 1820 AS WRITTEN BY LOCAL HISTORIANS. FIRING & DRILL TEAM OF FRENCH, BRITISH & CONTINENTAL SOLDIERS IN ENCAMPMENT DURING VILLAGE HOMECOMING ANNUALLY LABOR DAY WEEKEND. AT CITY HALL PRAIRIE AT CENTRAL. (LOCAL). LES PREHN; BETHALTO BICENTENNIAL COMM; 215 BUTCHER; BETHALTO, IL 62010. (#200016-281).

BISHOP HILL

KRUSBO COLONY BARN - BISHOP HILL, IL. RELOCATION OF KRUSBO COLONY BARN INTO BISHOP HILL, A SWEDISH COMMUNAL SETTLEMENT, TO CREATE A LIVING AGRICULTURAL DEMONSTRATION. (LOCAL). BETTY GUYER, CHAIRMAN; BISHOP HILL BICENTENNIAL COMMISSION; BOX B; BISHOP HILL, IL 61419. (#30420).

OCT 4 - 5, '75. JORDBRUKDAGARNA-SWEDISH COMMUNAL. AGRARIAN DEMONSTRATION OF 1840'S. (ST-WIDE). MS JANET PICKETT; ILL DEPT OF CONSERVATION; 901 SOUTH SPRING; SPRINGFIELD, IL 62704. (#50272-5).

NOV 29 - 30, '75. BISHOP HILL JULEMARKNAD. THIS IS A MARKET FEATURING THE FOOD, CRAFTS, AND GOODS OF THE TRADIT IONAL SWEDISH CHRISTMAS CELEBRATION IN THE MID-19TH CENTURY. THE ENT IRE COMMUNITY OF BISHOP HILL IS INVOLVED. AT BISHOP HILL. (ST-WIDE). MS JANET PICKETT; ILLINOIS DEPARTMENT OF CONSERVATION; 901 SOUTH SPRING; SPRINGFIELD, IL 62704. (#50272-1).

DEC 25, '75. BISHOP HILL JULOTTA. THE EVENT IS A 6:00 A.M. TRADITIONAL 19TH CENTURY SWEDISH SERVICE AT THE COLONY CHURCH. AT BISHOP HILL. (ST-WIDE). MS JANET PICKETT; ILLINOIS DEPARTMENT OF CONSERVATION; 901 SOUTH SPRING; SPRINGFIELD, IL 62704. (#50272-2).

APR 20, '76. RECEPTION HONORING KING CARL XVI GUSTAV OF SWEDEN. CEREMONY. (INT'L). ELIZABETH GUYER, CHMN; HENRY COUNTY BICENTENNIAL COMMISSION; BOX B; BISHOP HILL, IL 61419. (#200016-172).

MAY 2, '76. SWEDISH ROYALTY VISITS BISHOP HILL. PRINCESS DESIREE AND HER HUSBAND, BARON NICLAS SILFVERSCHIOLD VISIT BISHOP HILL'S EXHIBITS AND HISTORIC BUILDINGS. (INT'L). ELIZABETH GUYER, CHMN; HENRY COUNTY BICENTENNIAL COMMISSION; BOX B; BISHOP HILL, IL 61419. (#200016-173).

JULY 4, '76. BICENTENNIAL PARADE AND FESTIVAL. FESTIVAL, PARADE. (LOCAL). ELIZABETH GUYER, CHMN; BISHOP HILL BICENTENNIAL COMMISSION; BOX B; BISHOP HILL, IL 61419. (#200016-167).

JULY 27, '76. RILLEN, FOLK-DANCE GROUP FROM GAVLE, SWEDEN PERFORMS. LIVE PERFORMANCE. (LOCAL). ELIZABETH GUYER, CHMN; HENRY COUNTY BICENTENNIAL COMMISSION; BOX B; BISHOP HILL, IL 61419. (#200016-168).

OCT 2 - 3, '76. JORDBRUKDAGARNA-SWEDISH COMMUNAL. AGRARIAN DEMONSTRATION OF 1840'S. (ST-WIDE). MS JANET PICKETT; ILL DEPT OF CONSERVATION; 901 SOUTH SPRING; SPRINGFIELD, IL 62704. (#50272-6).

NOV 26 - 28, '76. BISHOP HILL JULEMARKNAD. THIS IS A MARKET FEATURING THE FOOD CRAFTS AND GOODS OF THE TRADITIO NAL SWEDISH CHRISTMAS CELEBRATION IN THE MID-19TH CENTURY THE ENTRE COMMUNITY OF BISHOP HILL IS INVOLVED. AT BISHOP HILL. (ST-WIDE). MS JANET PICKETT; ILLINOIS DEPARTMENT OF CONSERVATION; 901 SOUTH SPRING; SPRINGFIELD, IL 62704. (#50272-3).

DEC 25, '76. BISHOP HILL JULOTTA. THE EVENT IS A 6:00 A.M. TRADITIONAL 19TH CENTURY SWEDISH SERVICE AT THE COLONY CHURCH. AT BISHOP HILL. (ST-WIDE). MS JANET PICKETT; ILLINOIS DEPARTMENT OF CONSERVATION; 901 SOUTH SPRING; SPRINGFIELD, IL 62740. (#50272-4).

BLOOMINGTON

DAILY PANTAGRAPH'S AMER HISTORICAL VANS - NBMRP. VAN, PAINTED WITH AMER HIST MURALS & EQUIPPED WITH PA SYSTEM TO PLAY MARCHING MUSIC & FOR LOGISTICAL SUPPORT, TRAVELS THRU CENTRAL ILLINOIS TO AID WITH COMMUNITY BICENTENNIAL EVENTS. (LOCAL). DALE LASKOWSKI, BICENTENNIAL COORDINATOR; THE DAILY PANTAGRAPH; 301 W WASHINGTON ST; BLOOMINGTON, IL 61701. (#23289).

BLOOMINGTON — CONTINUED

IMPROVEMENTS: COLFAX PARK IN BLOOMINGTON, IL. BUILDING OF A COMMUNITY BUILDING, RESTROOM AND A STAGE FOR COLFAX PARK. (LOCAL). GUY FRAKER, COORDINATOR; MCLEAN COUNTY BICENTENNIAL COMMISSION; 308 E WASHINGTON; BLOOMINGTON, IL 61701. (#33666).

MCLEAN COUNTY ARTS FESTIVAL IN BLOOMINGTON, IL. THREE-YEAR PROJECT TO IDENTIFY HISTORIC SITES IN THE COUNTY, TEACH ART FORMS IN LOCAL COMMUNITIES & HOLD AN ARTS FESTIVAL. (LOCAL). GUY FRAKER, COORDINATOR; MCLEAN COUNTY BICENTENNIAL COMMISSION; 308 E WASHINGTON; BLOOMINGTON, IL 61701. (#33665).

RADIO WJBC HERITAGE/FESTIVAL PROGRAMS -NBMRP. INCLUDES PAUL 'REVERE' DUNN'S RIDE AROUND MCLEAN COUNTY FOR THE WALK OF MANKIND IN 1975 TO LAUNCH BICENT PROGRAMMING & 'THE SOUND OF AMERICA' 2 HOUR MUSICAL TRIBUTE. (LOCAL). MS JAN DRAGIN, BICENTENNIAL COORDINATOR; RADIO STATION WJBC; 236 GREENWOOD AVE; BLOOMINGTON, IL 61701. (#24680).

OCT 25 - 26, '75. CORNPEX '75 STAMP EXHIBIT. STAMP SHOW FEATURING EXHIBITS, SHOW CACHETS, & AWARDS CACHET WILL FEATURE GEORGE ROGERS CLARK KASKASKIA - VINCENNES TRIP. AT SCOTTISH RITE TEMPLE. (REGN'L). CORN BELT PHILATELIC SOC; CORN BELT PHILATELIC SOCIETY; BOX 625; BLOOMINGTON, IL 61701. (#3693-1).

MAR 11, '76. 'OUR COUNTRY 'TIS OF THEE' PAGEANT OF WASHINGTON SCHOOL. A CHORAL PAGEANT OF THE HISTORY OF AMERICA, WITH 570 CHILDREN FROM KINDERGARTEN THROUGH 6TH GRADE. AT 1201 E WASHINGTON ST. (LOCAL). DR ROBERT BARNARD; WASHINGTON SCHOOL; 1201 E WASHINGTON ST; BLOOMINGTON, IL 61701. (#7919-1).

MAY 11 - 14, '76. BICENTENNIAL EXHIBITS AND ACTIVITIES. ILLINOIS TRAVELING BICENTENNIAL EXHIBIT, HERITAGE DANCERS & SQUARE DANCERS. AT EASTLAND MALL. (LOCAL). GUY FRANKER, CHMN; MCLEAN COUNTY BICENTENNIAL COMMISSION; 308 E WASHINGTON ST; BLOOMINGTON, IL 61701. (#200016-142).

JUNE 5, '76. GIRL SCOUTS HERITAGE FAIR. FAIR. (LOCAL). GUY FRAKER, CHMN; GIRL SCOUTS OF AMERICA; 308 E WASHINGTON ST; BLOOMINGTON, IL 61701. (#200016-140).

AUG 19 - 20, '76. UNITED STATES ARMED FORCES BICENTENNIAL CARAVAN. CARAVAN IS COMPOSED OF EXHIBIT VANS FOR EACH MILITARY SERVICE. PROJECT THEME IS 'HISTORY OF THE ARMED FORCES & THEIR CONTRIBUTIONS TO THE NATION.'. (LOCAL). DR ROBERT BARNARD, CHMN; UNITED STATES ARMED FORCES BICENTENNIAL CARAVAN; 1201 E WASHINGTON ST; BLOOMINGTON, IL 61701. (#1775-635).

SEPT 8, '76. EIGHTH JUDICIAL CIRCUIT RIDE. PARADE, LIVE PERFORMANCE. (ST-WIDE). PHYLLIS EUBANKS, CHMN; ILLINOIS DEPARTMENT OF CONSERVATION; 901 S SPRING ST; SPRINGFIELD, IL 62706. (#200016-136).

OCT 11, '76. AMATEUR MUSIC CLUB BICENTENNIAL CONCERT. LIVE PERFORMANCE AT SCOTTISH RITE TEMPLE. (LOCAL). GUY FRAKER, COORD; MCLEAN COUNTY BICENTENNIAL COMMISSION; 308 E WASHINGTON ST; BLOOMINGTON, IL 61701. (#200016-134).

BLUFORD

JULY 12 - 13, '75. ILLINOIS ANTIQUE ENGINE SHOW. ILLINOIS ANTIQUE ENGINE & MACHINERY SHOW, BLUFORD. A DISPLAY AND DEMONSTRATION OF THE FIRST TOOLS AND MACHINES USED IN THE EVOLUTION OF THE INTERNAL COMBUSTION ENGINE WILL BE PART OF A FESTIVAL CELEBRATION. (REGN'L). CORNELIUS BERGBOWER; BLUFORD COMMUNITY RURITAN CLUB; LOUIE AVE; BLUFORD, IL 62814. (#6741-501).

JULY 10 - 11, '76. ILLINOIS ENGINE SHOW. ILLINOIS ENGINE SHOW FEATURING THE EVOLUTION OF MECHANICAL POWER. AT LEE DONOHO'S WOODSE, NORTH EDGE OF BLUFORD. (REGN'L). CORNELIUS BERGBOWER, CHMN; BLUFORD BICENTENNIAL COMMISSION AND BLUFORD PURITAN CLUB; LOVIE AVE; BLUFORD, IL 62814. (#104980-1).

BOLINGBROOK

BOLINGBROOK, IL, TIME CAPSULE. A TIME CAPSULE WILL BE FILLED WITH LOCAL ARTIFACTS & BURIED. (LOCAL). JUDITH BREDEWEG, CHAIRMAN; BOLINGBROOK BICENTENNIAL COMMISSION; 529 CONCORD LN; BOLINGBROOK, IL 60439. (#33661).

DECORATING CONTEST IN BOLINGBROOK, IL. GARAGE DOOR, MAILBOX, FIRE HYDRANT DECORATING CONTEST. (LOCAL). JUDITH BREDEWEG, CHAIRMAN; BOLINGBROOK BICENTENNIAL COMMISSION; 529 CONCORD LN; BOLINGBROOK, IL 60439. (#33662).

RESTORATION OF BOARDMAN CEMETERY, BOLINGBROOK, IL. PRESERVATION & RESTORATION OF WILL COUNTY'S OLDEST CEMETERY: REPAIRING STONES, CATALOGUING GRAVES, & MAKING CEMETERY PRESENTABLE AGAIN; PRESENTING FINDINGS IN SLIDE LECTURE AVAILABLE TO THE PUBLIC. (LOCAL). JIM BINGLE, CHAIRMAN; BOLINGBROOK HISTORICAL SOCIETY; 128 TAMARACK; BOLINGBROOK, IL 60439. (#33663).

USED BOOK DRIVE IN BOLINGBROOK, IL. USED BOOK DRIVE FOR FOUNTAINDALE LIBRARY. (LOCAL). VIRGIL BANKER, COORDINATOR; AMERICAN LEGION POST 1288; 489 ROCKHURST; BOLINGBROOK, IL 60439. (#33664).

JAN 24 - MAY 1, '76. BICENTENNIAL EVENTS OF BOLINGBROOK, ILL JAN-MAY '76. 1/24 STUDENT GOVT DAY; 2/21 BOLINGBROOK BICENT PRESIDENTIAL BALL; 4/24 TOWN MEETING; 5/1 'DANDELION WINE' A PLAY WRITTEN BY RAY BRADBURY, AN ILLINOIS AUTHOR; 5/1 JOHNNY HORIZONS PITCH-IN FOR PATHWAYS CAMPAIGN. (LOCAL). JUDITH BREDEWEG; BOLINGBROOK BICENTENNIAL COMMISSION; 529 CONCORD LN; BOLINGBROOK, IL 60439. (#200016-352).

JUNE 7 - SEPT 12, '76. BICENTENNIAL EVENTS OF BOLINGBROOK, ILL JUN-SEPT '76. 6/7 VALLEYVIEW SCHOOL DISTRICT CELEBRATES THE BICENTENNIAL; 6/3 BICENTENNIAL HERITAGE CONCERT; 9/9 PATHWAYS DAY CELEBRATION. (LOCAL). JUDITH BREDEWEG; BOLINGBROOK BICENTENNIAL COMMITTEE; 529 CONCORD LN; BOLINGBROOK, IL 60439. (#200016-353).

BOULDER HILL

JUNE 26, '76. MISS BICENTENNIAL BOULDER HILL BEAUTY CONTEST. BEAUTY PAGEANT FOR ALL GIRLS BETWEEN AGES 14-18 THAT ARE RESIDENTS OF BOULDER HILL. AT OSWEGOLAND CIVIC CENTER, ASHLAWN ST. (LOCAL). PAUL E TUREK, COORD; BOULDER HILL CIVIC ASSOC; 16 PICKFORD RD; BOULDER HILL, IL 60538. (#107270-1).

BOWEN

LIONS CLUB ATHLETIC AND RECREATION POOL - ILLINOIS. BUILDING OF OLYMPIC SIZED POOL WITH BATHHOUSE IN 3 ACRE PARK. (LOCAL). H DAVID MYERS, PRESIDENT; LIONS CLUB ATHLETIC AND RECREATION FUND; BOWEN, IL 62316. (#8117).

AUG 21, '76. BOWEN FALL FESTIVAL. FESTIVAL. (LOCAL). HAROLD SHERRICK, CHAIRMAN; LIONS CLUB; RFD; BOWEN, IL 62316. (#105194-1).

BRADFORD

BEAUTIFICATION OF BRADFORD, IL. OVERALL BEAUTIFICATION OF THE CITY OF BRADFORD. (LOCAL). MAGGIE SULLIVAN, CHAIRPERSON; CONCERNED CITIZENS FOR BETTERMENT OF BRADFORD BICENTENNIAL COMM; 522 S PEORIA; BRADFORD, IL 61421. (#15568).

A HISTORY OF BRADFORD, IL. A PAPERBACK BOOK ON THE HISTORY OF BRADFORD, IL. (LOCAL). MAGGIE SULLIVAN, CHAIRPERSON; CONCERNED CITIZENS FOR BETTERMENT OF BRADFORD BICENTENNIAL COMM; 522 S PEORIA; BRADFORD, IL 61421. (#15569).

MAY 30, '76. DEDICATION OF VETERANS MEMORIAL & PARK. NEWLY ERECTED MEMORIAL MADE POSSIBLE BY DONATIONS & FUND-RAISING PROJECTS. AT CITY PARK. (LOCAL). MARGARET SULLIVAN, CHMN; BRADFORD BICENTENNIAL COMMISSION; BRADFORD, IL 61421. (#200016-506).

SEPT 6, '76. LABOR DAY FESTIVAL. PATRIOTIC PARADE, ART DISPLAYS, SENIOR KING & QUEEN CONTEST, COLONIAL CRAFT DEMONSTRATIONS, FROG & BICYCLE RACES, & MUSICAL PROGRAM IN THE EVENING USING HIGH SCHOOL TALENT. (LOCAL). MARGARET SULLIVAN, CHMN; BRADFORD BICENTENNIAL COMMISSION; BRADFORD, IL 61421. (#200016-91).

BREESE

APR 30, '76. BICENTENNIAL PAGEANT & ART SHOW. THEME: 'OUR COUNTRY 'TIS OF THEE'; ENTIRE SCHOOL PARTICIPATED IN SINGING, ACTING, BUILDING PROPS, MAKING COSTUMES. AT ST DOMINIC GYM. (LOCAL). MRS BEA GRAPPERHAUS, CHMN; ST DOMINIC SCHOOL & BREESE BICENTENNIAL COMMITTEE; 290 NORTH CHERRY ST; BREESE, IL 62230. (#200016-426).

JUNE 5 - 7, '76. BREESE SOMMERFEST. CHICKEN DINNER, BASEBALL GAME & TWO HIGH SCHOOL BAND CONCERTS, DRILL TEAMS, RIDES & CONCESSION STANDS, 4 DANCE BANDS. MONEY RAISED WILL BE USED TO BUILD A DOUBLE TENNIS COURT AS OUR BICENTENNIAL PROJECT. AT CITY PARK, N 10TH & WALNUT ST. (LOCAL). MRS BEA GRAPPERHAUS, CHMN; BREESE BICENTENNIAL COMMITTEE & CIVIC & FRATERNAL ORGANIZATIONS; 645 NORTH SIXTH ST; BREESE, IL 62230. (#200016-425).

BRIDGEPORT

ONE-ROOM SCHOOLHOUSE PRESERVATION - BRIDGEPORT, IL. MOVING AND REFURBISHING OF HISTORIC SCHOOLHOUSE TO SERVE AS MUSEUM. (LOCAL). RALEIGH BAKER, CHAIRMAN; LAWRENCE COUNTY BICENTENNIAL COMMISSION; BRIDGEPORT, IL 62417. (#27805). **ARBA GRANTEE.**

BRIGHTON

JUNE 25 - 27, '76. THREE DAY BICENTENNIAL CELEBRATION. TRESHING, SOAP-MAKING, PARADE, BURGOO SOUP PROGRAMS, ENTERTAINMENT, ARTS AND CRAFTS EXHIBITS. AT BETSEY ANN PARK. (LOCAL). RAY HEIDEMAN, COORD; BRIGHTON BICENTENNIAL COMMISSION; 408 W CENTER; BRIGHTON, IL 62012. (#106370-1).

BRIMFIELD

JUNE 21 - 22, '75. OLDE ENGLISH FAIRE. ENGLISH MUSIC; MEDIEVAL TOURNAMENTS-COUNTRY FAIRE. (LOCAL). MS JANET PICKETT; ILL DEPT OF CONSERVATION; 901 SOUTH SPRING; SPRINGFIELD, IL 62704. (#50272-7).

JUNE 12 - 13, '76. OLDE ENGLISH FAIRE. ENGLISH MUSIC-MEDIEVAL TOURNAMENTS-COUNTRY FAIRE. (LOCAL). MS JANET PICKETT; ILL DEPT OF CONSERVATION; 901 SOUTH SPRING; SPRINGFIELD, IL 62704. (#50272-8).

JUNE 17 - 27, '76. 'O PHILANDER' - PAGEANT. LIVE PERFORMANCE AT JUBILEE COLLEGE. (LOCAL). DON BRIDE, CHMN; BRIMFIELD BICENTENNIAL COMMISSION; PO BOX 98; BRIMFIELD, IL 61614. (#200016-109).

BROADVIEW

THE ARCHIVES OF BROADVIEW, IL. A COLLECTION OF PHOTOGRAPHS, TAPE RECORDINGS, OLD SOUVENIERS FROM THE POLICE & FIRE DEPARTMENT AND OTHER MEMORABILIA TO BE ON DISPLAY IN THE NEW LIBRARY. (LOCAL). EDWARD J MCGORRY, CO-CHAIRMAN; BICENTENNIAL COMMISSION OF BROADVIEW; 1600 ROOSEVELT RD; BROADVIEW, IL 60153. (#21539).

FLAGS FOR VILLAGE, BROADVIEW, IL. FLAGS FOR ROOSEVELT RD FROM 17TH AVE TO 25TH AVE. AMER & 50 STATE FLAGS, 3 NEW FLAG POLES WILL BE INSTALLED IN FRONT OF VILLAGE HALL, FLYING AN AMERICAN FLAG, A STATE FLAG & A BICENTENNIAL LOGO FLAG. (LOCAL). EDWARD J MCGORRY, CO-CHAIRMAN; BROADVIEW BICENTENNIAL COMMISSION; 1600 ROOSEVELT RD; BROADVIEW, IL 60153. (#21538).

DEC 1, '75 - FEB 1, '76. BICENTENNIAL ESSAY CONTEST. AWARD, COMPETITION. (LOCAL). EDWARD J MCGRORY, CO-CHMN; BROADVIEW PUBLIC LIBRARY; 2226 S 16TH AVE; BROADVIEW, IL 60153. (#200016-69).

JAN 7 - FEB 10, '76. BICENTENNIAL QUEEN CONTEST. AWARD, CEREMONY, COMPETITION, PARADE. (LOCAL). EDWARD J MCGRORY, CO-CHMN; BROADVIEW UNIT 626, AMERICAN LEGION AUXILIARY; 1607 ROOSEVELT RD; BROADVIEW, IL 60153. (#200016-71).

FEB 21, '76. FREEDOM SHRINE PRESENTATION. CEREMONY, EXHIBIT AT BROADVIEW VILLAGE HALL, 1600 ROOSEVELT RD. (LOCAL). EDWARD J MCGRORY, CO-CHMN; EXCHANGE CLUB; 2250 S 13TH AVE; BROADVIEW, IL 60153. (#200016-70).

MAR 26, '76. BICENTENNIAL FASHION SHOW. EXHIBIT, LIVE PERFORMANCE. (LOCAL). EDWARD J MCGORRY, CHMN; BROADVIEW BUSINESS & PROFESSIONAL WOMEN'S CLUB; 2235 S 12TH AVE; BROADVIEW, IL 60153. (#105417-3).

APR 3, '76. ARMY STATIC DISPLAY. EXHIBIT AT 16TH AVE & ROOSEVELT RD. (LOCAL). FRANK ROSATO, DIRECTOR; BOY SCOUTS, LINDOP SCHOOL; 2344 S 17TH AVE; BROADVIEW, IL 60153. (#105417-12).

APR 3, '76. CIVIL WAR DISPLAY. EXHIBIT AT COURT ROOM VILLAGE HALL, 1600 ROOSEVELT RD. (LOCAL). COL HAROLD BROWN, DIR; 55TH INFANTRY REGIMENT ILLINOIS VOLUNTEERS; 2501 S 16TH AVE; BROADVIEW, IL 60153. (#105417-17).

APR 4, '76. LINDOP SCHOOL SPRING CONCERT. LIVE PERFORMANCE AT 2400 S 18TH AVE. (LOCAL). EDWARD J MCGORRY, CHMN; LINDOP SCHOOL; 2400 S 18TH AVE; BROADVIEW, IL 60153. (#105417-5).

APR 10, '76. BROADVIEW POLICE DEPARTMENT OPEN HOUSE. EXHIBIT AT 1600 ROOSEVELT RD. (LOCAL). EDWARD J MCGORRY; BROADVIEW POLICE DEPARTMENT; 1600 ROOSEVELT RD; BROADVIEW, IL 60153. (#105417-6).

APR 24, '76. PIONEER VILLAGE AND FRYING PANS WEST. LIVE PERFORMANCE, EXHIBIT AT PARKING LOT, 16TH AVE & ROOSEVELT RD. (LOCAL). COL HAROLD BROWN, DIR; GIRL & BOY SCOUTS OF LINDOP SCHOOL; 2501 S 10TH ST; BROADVIEW, IL 60153. (#105417-7).

APR 26 - 28, '76. HISTORICAL MOBILE. EXHIBIT AT 1600 ROOSEVELT RD. (LOCAL). MRS CAROLINE O'GARA; HISTORICAL COMMITTEE OF THE BROADVIEW BICENTENNIAL COMMISSION; 2232 S 17TH AVE; BROADVIEW, IL 60153. (#105417-9).

APR 29, '76. BICENTENNIAL ART SHOW. EXHIBIT AT 2600 13TH AVE. (LOCAL). MRS CHARLOTTE OLESEN, DIR; BROADVIEW PARK DISTRICT; 2600 S 13TH AVE; BROADVIEW, IL 60153. (#105417-8).

MAY 1, '76. NAVY STATIC DISPLAY. EXHIBIT AT PARKING LOT, 16TH AVE & ROOSEVELT RD. (LOCAL). DELORAS VALEK, DIRECTOR; BOY SCOUT TROOP, LINDROP SCHOOL; VILLAGE HALL, 1600 ROOSEVELT RD; BROADVIEW, IL 60153. (#105417-2).

MAY 8, '76. REVOLUTIONARY SKITS. LIVE PERFORMANCE AT 2400 S 18TH AVE. (LOCAL). EDW J MCGORRY, CO-CHMN; CUB SCOUT PACK LINDOP SCHOOL; 2400 S 18TH AVE; BROADVIEW, IL 60153. (#105417-16).

MAY 22 - 23, '76. BOOK SALE AND FLEA MARKET. FAIR AT 1600 ROOSEVELT RD. (LOCAL). MRS VIRGINIA HRUBY, COORD; BROADVIEW BICENTENNIAL COMMISSION; 2624 S 10TH AVE; BROADVIEW, IL 60153. (#105417-20).

JUNE 6, '76. CIVIL WAR BATTLE SKIRMISH. LIVE PERFORMANCE, EXHIBIT AT 17TH & 1C RAILROAD TRACKS. (LOCAL). COL HAROLD BROWN, DIR; 55TH INFANTRY REGIMENT ILLINOIS VOLUNTEERS; 2501 S 10TH AVE; BROADVIEW, IL 60153. (#105417-13).

JUNE 12, '76. MARINE STATIC DISPLAY. EXHIBIT AT PARKING LOT, 16TH AVE & ROOSEVELT RD. (LOCAL). DELORAS VALEK, DIRECTOR; BOY SCOUT TROOP, LINDOP SCHOOL; VILLAGE HALL, 1600 ROOSEVELT RD; BROADVIEW, IL 60153. (#105417-1).

BROADVIEW — CONTINUED

JUNE 12 - 13, '76. MUSIC RECITAL. LIVE PERFORMANCE AT SCHROEDER PARK, 2600 S 13TH AVE. (LOCAL). CLINTON JONES, DIRECTOR; MELODY MUSIC SCHOOL; 2118 S 17TH AVE; BROADVIEW, IL 60153. (#105417-10).

JUNE 19, '76. BROADVIEW FIRE DEPARTMENT OPEN HOUSE. EXHIBIT AT BROADVIEW FIRE DEPT. (LOCAL). CAPT JAS WROSEH, DIR; BROADVIEW FIRE DEPT; 25TH AVE & 14TH ST; BROADVIEW, IL 60153. (#105417-19).

JULY 17, '76. COAST GUARD STATIC DISPLAY. EXHIBIT AT 16TH AVE & ROOSEVELT RD. (LOCAL). FRANK ROSATO, DIRECTOR; BOY SCOUT TROOP, LINDOP SCHOOL; 2400 S 18TH AVE; BROADVIEW, IL 60153. (#105417-14).

AUG 7, '76. AIR FORCE STATIC DISPLAY. EXHIBIT AT LINDOP SCHOOL, 2400 S 18TH AVE. (LOCAL). FRANK ROSATO, DIRECTOR; BOY SCOUT TROOP, LINDOP SCHOOL; 2400 S 18TH AVE; BROADVIEW, IL 60153. (#105417-15).

SEPT 4, '76. ORDER OF ARROW INDIAN DANCE AND INDIAN VILLAGE DEMONSTRATION. LIVE PERFORMANCE, CEREMONY AT 16TH AVENUE AND ROOSEVELT ROAD PARKING. (LOCAL). EDW J MCGORRY, CO-CHMN; LINDOP SCHOOL BOY SCOUT TROOP; 2400 S 18TH AVE; BROADVIEW, IL 60153. (#105417-18).

SEPT 19, '76. BICENTENNIAL PARADE & FESTIVITIES. PARADE, FESTIVAL AT 1607 ROOSEVELT RD. (LOCAL). GLEN WILLIAMS, CHMN; BROADVIEW POST 626, THE AMERICAN LEGION DEPT OF ILLINOIS; 2101 S 22ND AVE; BROADVIEW, IL 60153. (#105417-11).

BROUGHTON

JUNE 19 - 20, '76. BROUGHTON FREEDOM FESTIVAL. EXHIBIT, FESTIVAL, PARADE AT VILLAGE PARK. (LOCAL). CHARLOTTE JONES, CHAIRMAN; BROUGHTON BICENTENNIAL COMMITTEE; RT 1; BROUGHTON, IL 62817. (#108418-1).

BROWNFIELD

JULY 27, '75. MACEDONIA CHURCH BARBECUE IN BROWNFIELD, IL. THE BARBEQUE IS A MONEY-MAKING PROJECT FOR THE MACEDONIA FREE BAPTIST CHURCH; THE 100 YEAR OLD EVENT WILL INCLUDE SINGING, GAMES & CONTESTS AND PATRIOTIC PRESENTATIONS. (LOCAL). JAMES CRIM; MACEDONIA FREE BAPTIST CHURCH; BROWNFIELD, IL 62911. (#12349-1).

BROWNING

'THE SUN GAVE MAN THE POWER', BROWNING, ILLINOIS. THE FILM WILL UTILIZE ORAL HISTORIES GIVEN BY ELDER MEMBERS OF THE PIKUNI-BLACKFEET TRIBE OF MONTANA, AND WILL PRESENT THE HISTORICAL AND RELIGIOUS HERITAGE OF THE BLACKFEET TRIBAL LIFE. (ST-WIDE). BOB ERICKSEN, PROJ DIRECTOR; THE SUN FOUNDATION; BOX 156E; WASHBURN, IL 61570. (#10279). **ARBA GRANTEE.**

BRUSSELS

RESTORATION OF 1850 BRUSSELS JAIL - BRUSSELS, IL. RESTORATION OF 10'X10' JAIL DATING BACK TO 1850 IN BRUSSELS. (LOCAL). PAUL HANKS, CHAIRMAN; CALHOUN COUNTY BICENTENNIAL COMMISSION; HARDIN, IL 62047. (#30407).

BURBANK

BICENT PROJECTS - MCCORD SCHOOL IN BURBANK, IL. STUDENTS KEPT A BICENTENNIAL BULLETIN BOARD, & MADE & WORE BICENTENNIAL OUTFITS. (LOCAL). J BOKENKAMP, SUPERINTENDENT; MCCORD SCHOOL; 85TH & NASHVILLE; BURBANK, IL 60459. (#33653).

BICENT PROJECTS - TOBIN SCHOOL IN BURBANK, IL. EXHIBIT ON CIVIL WAR BATTLES; LETTER SENT TO PRESIDENT FORD; EXHIBIT OF QUILTS AND STAMPS; MADE MAPS SHOWING HISTORICAL BATTLES; RAISED BENNINGTON FLAG DAILY; & TAPED 'AMERICA THE BEAUTIFUL'. (LOCAL). J BOKENKAMP, SUPERINTENDENT; TOBIN SCHOOL; 85 & NARRAGANSETT; BURBANK, IL 60459. (#33654).

BICENT PROJECTS - BYRD SCHOOL IN BURBANK, IL. ACTIVITIES INCLUDED ACTING OUT EVENTS FROM AMERICA'S PAST, MAINTAINING A BOOK DISPLAY, KEEPING BICENT BULLETIN BOARDS, AND CONSTRUCTING FARMS/PLANTATIONS TO LEARN ABOUT LIVING CONDITIONS 200 YEARS AGO. (LOCAL). J BOKENKAMP, SUPERINTENDENT; BYRD SCHOOL; 83 & LAVERGNE AVE; BURBANK, IL 60459. (#33657).

BICENT PROJECTS: KENNEDY SCHOOL IN BURBANK, IL. ACTIVITIES INCLUDED A BICENT BULLETIN BOARD, MURAL, BOOK DISPLAY, RELATED THE CONSTITUTION TO THE BICENTENNIAL, BICENT COOKBOOK AND LEARNED THE MINUET. (LOCAL). J BOKENKAMP, SUPERINTENDENT; KENNEDY SCHOOL; 77TH & CENTRAL AVE; BURBANK, IL 60459. (#33655).

BICENTENNIAL BULLETIN BOARD - BURBANK, IL. BULLETIN BOARD AT NOTTINGHAM SCHOOL WITH BICENTENNIAL THEME. (LOCAL). J BOKENKAMP, SUPERINTENDENT; NOTTINGHAM SCHOOL; 77 L NOTTINGHAM; BURBANK, IL 60459. (#33166).

FLAG RAISING CEREMONY IN BURBANK, IL. DAILY BICENTENNIAL FLAG RAISING CEREMONY. (LOCAL). MR KIPNIS, PRINCIPAL; FRY SCHOOL; 9805 S MOBILE; BURBANK, IL 60459. (#33660).

ROTC BICENTENNIAL FLAG UNIT IN BURBANK, IL. PERFORMANCE GIVING THE HISTORY OF 21 FLAGS USED IN AMERICA. (LOCAL). COL G R GRUBBS, COORDINATOR; REAVIS HIGH SCHOOL; 77 & AUSTIN AVE; BURBANK, IL 60459. (#33658).

SOUTH STICKNEY PUBLIC LIBRARY, BURBANK, IL. BIBLIOGRAPHY OF BICENT-RELATED BOOKS PREPARED; CHILDREN'S PUZZLE USING FAMOUS NAMES, DATES, EVENTS; ORAL HISTORY TAPE MADE OF MEMOIRS OF THE BURBANK AREA. (LOCAL). HEAD LIBRARIAN; SOUTH STICKNEY PUBLIC LIBRARY; 5627 W 79TH ST; BURBANK, IL 60459. (#33656).

TIME CAPSULE IN BURBANK, IL. A TIME CAPSULE WILL BE FILLED WITH LOCAL MEMORABILIA AND BURIED. (LOCAL). F LOJAS, CHAIRMAN; BURBANK BICENTENNIAL COMMISSION; 6530 W 79TH ST; BURBANK, IL 60459. (#33659).

JUNE 6, '75. BURBANK BICENTENNIAL CELEBRATION. PERFORMANCE 'AMERICA, THE BEAUTIFUL'; FIFE & DRUM FOR CHICAGO CAMERA CHANNEL 5. (LOCAL). DON MELKA & R POSTORE; TOBIN SCHOOL; 85TH & NARRAGANSETT; BURBANK, IL 60459. (#200016-333).

JUNE 6 - OCT 31, '75. BICENT ACTIVITIES AT TOBIN SCHOOL - 1975. 6/6 MUSICAL PERFORMANCE FOR TV; SEPT- CAREER DAY SEMINAR; OCTOBERSEMINARS ON THE ENVIRONMENT DIFFICULTIES FACING POINEERS & NATL POPCORN WEEK. (LOCAL). J BOKENKAMP. SUPT; TOBIN SCHOOL; 85 & NARRAGANSETT; BURBANK, IL 60459. (#200016-321).

OCT 7, '75 - SEPT 17, '76. BICENT ACTIVITIES AT KENNEDY SCHOOL DURING 1976 SCHOOL YEAR. 10/7/75 BENNINGTON FLAG RAISING CEREMONY; 11/24 PUPPET SHOW; SPRING 1976-FAMOUS PEOPLE & EVENTS SYMPOSIUM & PERFORMANCE; 5/7 'LISTEN AMERICA' PROGRAM; 5/27 CHORUS PERFORMANCE; 6/5 PARADE; 9/13-17 THE MAGNA CARTA ON DISPLAY. (LOCAL). J BOKENKAMP, SUPT; KENNEDY SCHOOL; 77 & CENTRAL AVE; BURBANK, IL 60459. (#200016-324).

OCT 21, '75 - JUNE 8, '76. BICENTENNIAL EVENTS SPONSORED BY REAVIS HIGH SCHOOL. 10/21/75 HOMECOMING PARADE; 5/10/76 BICENTENNIAL DANCE; 6/8/76 BICENTENNIAL CONCERT. (LOCAL). BERNARD HAYTON, SUPT; REAVIS HIGH SCHOOL; AUSTIN & 77TH ST; BURBANK, IL 60459. (#200016-345).

OCT 27, '75 - MAY 14, '76. BICENT ACTIVITIES AT MCCORD SCHOOL. 10/27/75 BENNINGTON FLAG RAISING CEREMONY; 3/4/76 BICENT ASSEMBLY; 3/16 BICENT PLAY; 4/15 BICENT PLAY; 5/7 PARADE; 5/14 TALENT CLUB PERFORMANCE. (LOCAL). J BOKENKAMP, SUPT; MCCORD SCHOOL; 85 & NASHVILLE; BURBANK, IL 60459. (#200016-322).

OCT 27, '75 - JUNE 6, '76. BICENT ACTIVITIES AT OWENS SCHOOL. 10/27 BENNINGTON FLAG RAISING CEREMONY;03/04 SCHOOL ASSEMBLY; 05/26 'OUR COUNTRY IN SONG' CHORAL PROGRAM; MAY-JUNE, STAMP EXHIBIT. (LOCAL). J BOKENKAMP, SUPT; OWENS SCHOOL; 7730 S LECLAIRE; BURBANK, IL 60459. (#200016-317).

OCT 27, '75 - OCT 28, '76. BICENTENNIAL EVENTS AT SOUTH STICKNEY PUBLIC LIBRARY. OCT 1975 - HISTORY MOBILE VISITED, LIBERTY BELL EXHIBIT, & FILM ON NORMAN ROCKWELL; NOV 1975 - DISPLAY OF COLONIAL COSTUMES & RELATED BOOKS; JULY 1976 - BICENTENNIAL READING CLUB & CHILDREN'S ESSAY CONTEST; AND OCT 1976 - FILMS ON LINCOLN & AMERICAN FLAG. AT THE LIBRARY. (LOCAL). ELIZA BIEBER, CHAIRPERSON; SOUTH STICKNEY PUBLIC LIBRARY; 5627 W 79TH ST; BURBANK, IL 60459. (#200016-344).

NOV 18, '75 - MAR 9, '76. BICENT ACTIVITIES AT BURBANK SCHOOL. NOV 18, BICENT ASSEMBLY; MAR 3, 1776 DAY. (LOCAL). J BOKENKAMP, SUPT; BURBANK SCHOOL; 83 & LINDEN; BURBANK, IL 60459. (#200016-319).

NOV 22, '75. DINNER THEATRE. PERFORMANCE OF HISTORY OF AMERICA; PREREVOLUTION THROUGH CIVIL WAR. (LOCAL). AL MATUG, DIRECTOR; STICKNEY YOUTH COMMISSION; 5635 STATE RD; BURBANK, IL 60459. (#200016-337).

NOV 28, '75. HERITAGE EXHIBIT. RESEARCHED HISTORY, MODELS OF HISTORIC BATTLES & PLACES, & DUPLICATED WEAPONS. (LOCAL). STAN ABBOTT, CUB MASTER; CUB SCOUT PACK 3481; 5555 STATE RD; BURBANK, IL 60459. (#200016-339).

JAN 21 - APR 14, '76. BICENT ACTIVITIES AT NOTTINGHAM SCHOOL. 1/21 COLE MARIONETTES PRESENT 'FLAG FOR THE BRAVE'; 4/14 BICENT SHOW PREPARED BY THE SCHOOL. (LOCAL). J BOKENKAMP, SUPT; NOTTINGHAM SCHOOL; 77 & NOTTINGHAM; BURBANK, IL 60459. (#200016-323).

JAN 24, '76. BICENTENNIAL DANCE. FESTIVAL. (LOCAL). JIM BARNHART, PRES-ELECT; BURBANK CHAMBER OF COMMERCE; 7754 S CICERO AVE; BURBANK, IL 60459. (#200016-340).

JAN 25, '76. ARBA CHARTER PRESENTATION. EXHIBIT, LIVE PERFORMANCE. (LOCAL). FRANK LOJAS, CHAIRMAN; BURBANK BICENTENNIAL COMMISSION; 6530 W 79TH ST; BURBANK, IL 60459. (#200016-335).

MAR 1 - MAY 31, '76. BICENT ACTIVITIES AT TOBIN SCHOOL - 1976. MARCH-NATIONAL MUSIC DAY, SPRING TEA, COIN EXHIBIT; 3/10 BICENT ASSEMBLY; MAY-COLONIAL COSTUME EXHIBIT, BICENT PAGEANT; 5/6 BICENT BAND CONCERT; 5/13 BEGINNER'S BAND CONCERT. (LOCAL). J BOKENKAMP SUPT; TOBIN SCHOOL; 85 & NARRAGANSETT; BURBANK, IL 60459. (#200016-320).

MAR 10 - MAY 31, '76. BICENT ACTIVITIES AT MADDOCK SCHOOL. 3/10 BICENT MUSICAL AWARENESS PROGRAM; MAY- A BICENT TRILOGY SEMINAR ON COLONIAL, FRONTIER & CONTEMPORARY LIFE; 'MUSICAL AMERICANA'. (LOCAL). J BOKENKAMP, SUPT; MADDOCK SCHOOL; 83 & SAYRE AVE; BURBANK, IL 60459. (#200016-318).

MAR 10 - JUNE 11, '76. BICENT ACTIVITIES AT BYRD SCHOOL - SPRING 1976. 3/10 SPIRIT OF 76 ASSEMBLY; 4/8 BIRTHDAY SEMINAR; 4/14 BICENT PLAY; 5/18 AMERICAN HISTORY PLAY; 5/4 AMERICAN HISTORY PLAY; 5/20 BICENT PAGEANT; 5/27 SPECIAL BICENT PERFORMANCE; 6/7 'WE SING TOGETHER' PRESENTATION; 6/11 GRADUATION CEREMONIES. (LOCAL). J BOKENKAMP, SUPT; BYRD SCHOOL; 83 & LAVERGNE; BURBANK, IL 60459. (#200016-348).

MAR 13, '76. BICENTENNIAL LIBERTY BALL. THERE WAS COSTUME JUDGING. (LOCAL). ELLEN MAREK, CHAIRMAN; ST ALBERT LADIES GUILD; 5555 STATE RD; BURBANK, IL 60459. (#200016-338).

MAR 27, '76. BICENTENNIAL LIBERTY BALL. FESTIVAL. (LOCAL). HERB EBBENS, CHAIRMAN; BURBANK ORGANIZATION OF UNITED TAX PAYERS; 8231 S MEADE AVE; BURBANK, IL 60459. (#200016-343).

APR - SEPT '76. BICENT ACTIVITIES AT FRY SCHOOL - SPRING 1976. BICENT MUSIC FESTIVAL IN APRIL; BICENT ART EXHIBIT IN MAY; BICENT TRIBUTE JUNE 13; BICENT ESSAY CONTEST IN SEPTEMBER. (LOCAL). J BOKENKAMP, SUPT; FRY SCHOOL; 7805 MOBILE; BURBANK, IL 60459. (#200016-347).

MAY 26, '76. BICENTENNIAL GYM SHOW & MUSICAL AT DULLES SCHOOL. LIVE PERFORMANCE AT 80TH & MASON. (LOCAL). J BAKENKAMP SUPT; DULLES SCHOOL; 80TH & MASON; BURBANK, IL 60459. (#200016-325).

JUNE 6, '76. BICENTENNIAL PARADE. PARADE, WITH CIVIL WAR BATTLE, & INTERVIEW WITH A LINCOLN PRESIDENT. (LOCAL). DAN SUKEL, DIRECTOR; BURBANK CIVIL DEFENSE; 6530 W 79TH ST; BURBANK, IL 60459. (#200016-336).

JUNE 26, '76. BICENTENNIAL SCROLL. RE-AFFIRM COMMUNITY BELIEF & TRUST IN OUR FORM OF GOVERNMENT. (LOCAL). JEAN O'CONNOR, PRESIDENT; BURBANK ORGANIZATION OF UNITED TAX PAYERS; 8231 S MEADE ST; BURBANK, IL 60459. (#200016-342).

JULY 3 - 4, '76. OLD FASHIONED 4TH OF JULY. SAT: CONCERT; SUN: PICNIC, GAMES, FIREWORKS, FLAG RAISING CEREMONY & BICENTENNIAL MASS. (LOCAL). BOB SKOWRONSKI, DIRECTOR; S STICKNEY PARK DISTRICT; 8050 S NEWCASTLE; BURBANK, IL 60459. (#200016-341).

SEPT 18 - 19, '76. BICENTENNIAL COUNTRY FAIR. FAIR, EXHIBIT, LIVE PERFORMANCE. (LOCAL). RAY TIERE, COORD; BURBANK BICENTENNIAL; 6530 W 79TH ST; BURBANK, IL 60459. (#200016-334).

BUSHNELL

APR 4, '76. DEDICATION OF CULTURAL CENTER. CEREMONY. (LOCAL). EUGENE MCGREW, CHMN; MCDONOUGH COUNTY BICENTENNIAL COMMISSION; E TYMAN ST; BUSHNELL, IL 61422. (#200016-145).

AUG 26 - 28, '76. BUSHNELL TOWN AND COUNTRY FESTIVAL. CARNIVAL, PARADE, CONTESTS AND PAGEANTS ARE THE PLANNED ENTERTAINMENT. AT EAST PARK. (LOCAL). EUGENE MCGREW, CHMN; TOWN AND COUNTRY FESTIVAL COMMITTEE; E TWYMAN; BUSHNELL, IL 61422. (#106216-1).

BYRON

JULY 12, '75. BICENTENNIAL COSTUME BALL. A DANCE FEATURING COSTUMES FROM EARLY AMERICAN TIMES TO THE PRESENT. (LOCAL). REV ARMIN G WENG; OGLE COUNTY AMERICAN REVOLUTION BICENTENNIAL COMMITTEE; 114 55TH ST; OREGON, IL 61061. (#8187-501).

CAHOKIA

MAY 22 - 23, '76. THE NATIVE ILLINOISAN. THE PRE-HISTORIC MISSISSIPPIAN CULTURE IS PORTRAYED IN THIS CRAFT AND ARCHAEOLOGY EXHIBIT. AT CAHOKIA MOUNDS STATE PARK. (REGN'L). JAN PICKETT; ILLINOIS DEPARTMENT OF CONSERVATION; 60 I ST; SPRINGFIELD, IL 62706. (#103416-326).

JUNE 28 - JULY 17, '76. GEORGE ROGERS CLARK TREK. RE-ENACTMENT OF JOURNEY. (REGN'L). MS JANET PICKETT; ILL DEPT OF CONSERVATION; 901 SOUTH SPRING; SPRINGFIELD, IL 62704. (#50272-9).

JULY 5 - 6, '76. 13 STAR DAY. THIS EVENT COMMENORATES THE ENTRY OF ILLINOIS INTO THE UNITED STATES AS A TERRITORY OF THE STATE OF VIRGINIA CRAFTS DEMONSTRATIONS, SHOOTING, TOMAHAWK AND KNIFE THROWING CONTESTS ARE PERFORMED BY COSTUMED PERSONNEL. AT 112 M STREET. (LOCAL). MS JANET PICKETT; ILLINOIS DEPARTMENT OF CONSERVATION; 901 SOUTH SPRING; SPRINGFIELD, IL 62704. (#50272-11).

JULY 17, '76. CAHOKIA COURT HOUSE CELEBRATION. GREETING GEORGE ROGERS CLARK. (LOCAL). MS JANET PICKETT; ILL DEPT OF CONSERVATION; 901 SOUTH SPRING; SPRINGFIELD, IL 62704. (#50272-12).

CAIRO

CAIRO CUSTOMS HOUSE HISTORIC PLACE-CITY MUSEUM -IL. ALFRED MULLET DESIGNER OF BUILDING FEDERAL COURT ROOM WEATHER BUREAU MODEL OF CAIRO TO HOUSE RIVER-RAIL MEMORABILIA JULY4 DEDICATION '75. HORSESHOW, BOAT RACE, ANTIQUE CARS. (ST-WIDE). GUYLA WALLIS MORELAND, PROJECT DIRECTOR; ALEXANDER PULASKI U S BICENTENNIAL COMMISSION; 228 8TH ST; CAIRO, IL 62914. (#4596).

CAIRO — CONTINUED

CAIRO, IL WOMEN'S CLUB & LIBRARY ASSOC CENTENNIAL. MONTHLY PROGRAMS TO OBSERVE HISTORICAL AND CULTURAL SIGNIFICANCE OF OLDEST WOMEN'S ASSOC IN ILLINOIS. TEAS, COSTUMED TABLEAUS & BOOK RECOUNTING MEMBERS' ROLE IN GROWTH OF CITY. ASSOC FOUNDED IN 1875. (LOCAL). MRS HALLEY N THISTLEWOOD, PRESIDENT; CAIRO WOMENS' CLUB AND LIBRARY ASSOC; 1600 WASHINGTON AVE; CAIRO, IL 62914. (#5747).

MAR 6, '75 - JULY 4, '76. 100TH ANNIVERSARY WOMAN'S CLUB & LIBRARY ASSOC OF CAIRO, IL. HISTORICAL BACK GROUND, FOUNDING OF LIBRARY, ART AND MUSIC LITERATURE HOME HEALTH & GARDENS CULTURAL TIES IN THE TOWN-HOW IT HAS ENCOURAGED THE GROWTH OF WOMEN MEETING DAY IS FIRST WEDNESDAY OF MONTH EXCEPT JUNE-SEPT. AT 1600 WASHINGTON AVE, SAFFORD MEMORIAL BLDG, CAIRO PUBLIC LIBRARY. (LOCAL). MRS HALLEY N THISTLEWOOD; WOMAN'S CLUB & LIBRARY ASSOCIATION OF CAIRO INC.; 1600 WASHINGTON AVE; CAIRO, IL 62914. (#50176-1).

MAR 15, '75. ART EXHIBIT AT CAIRO, ILLINOIS NATIONAL ARMORY. EXHIBIT OPEN TO ALL ARTISTS IN 150 MILE AREA AND FORMER RESIDENTS W/ HISTORY THEME. COLOR SLIDE PRESENTATION OF SCENIC AND HISTORIC SITES BY GRAPHIC ARTS DEPARTMENT OF SOUTHERN ILLINOIS UNIVERSITY. ALSO: FILM/SLIDES. (LOCAL). CURTIS E PROFILET; PULASKI-ALEXANDER BICENTENNIAL COMMISSION; 228 8TH ST; CAIRO, IL 62914. (#5746-1).

MAR 16, '75. ARTS-CRAFTS SHOW NATIVE SKILLS AT MASONIC TEMPLE. EXHIBIT, CEREMONY. (ST-WIDE). GUYLA WALLIS MORELAND; ALEXANDER PULASKI U S BICENTENNIAL COMMISSION; 228 8TH ST; CAIRO, IL 62914. (#4596-903).

JUNE 26, '75. OTRABANDA COMPANY'S THIRD ANNUAL MISSISSIPPI RIVER TOUR. LIVE PERFORMANCE, PARADE AT OFF CEDAR ST., ACROSS FROM THE HOSPITAL. (LOCAL). JERRY NURENBERG; OPERATION OUTREACH (CHIRO ARTS CENTER); 903 CEDAR ST.; CAIRO, IL 62914. (#50550-4).

JULY 4, '75. DEDICATE BUILDING BOAT RACES OLD AUTO PARADE HORSESHOW. PARADE, OPENING, LIVE PERFORMANCE. (ST-WIDE). GUYLA WALLIS MORELAND; ALEXANDER PULASKI U S BICENTENNIAL COMMISSION; 228 8TH ST; CAIRO, IL 62914. (#4596-501).

SEPT 28, '75. 'OUR COUNTRY 'TIS OF THEE'. CHORAL PAGEANT INVOLVING CHURCH MEMBERSHIPS AND CHURCH SCHOOL STUDENTS. SCRIPT WON FREEDOM FOUNDATION MEDAL. AT BONDURANT GYM OF CAMELOT SCHOOL 421-30TH ST CAIRO ON STREET PARKING. (LOCAL). MRS. LARRY POTTS; CAIRO BAPTIST CHURCH; 227-11TH ST; CAIRO,, IL 62914. (#50506-1).

OCT 1, '75. DEDICATE ROOSEVELT PAVILLION IN ST MARY'S PARK. FESTIVAL. (LOCAL). MRS HALLEY N THISTLEWOOD; CAIRO WOMENS' CLUB AND LIBRARY ASSOC; 1600 WASHINGTON AVE; CAIRO, IL 62914. (#5747-501).

MAR 5, '76. ILLINOIS FEDERAL WOMEN'S CLUB SCROLL PRESENTATION. SCROLL PRESENTED TO CLUB FOUNDED 100 YEARS AGO ON MARCH 6, 1875. (LOCAL). MRS H N THISTLEWOOD, DIR; WOMEN'S CLUB & LIBRARY ASSOC OF CAIRO, INC; 27 EDGEWOOD PARK; CAIRO, IL 62914. (#200016-61).

APR 30, '76. ARBOR DAY PLANTING. 18 TREES PLANTED IN MEMORY OF DECEASED MEMBERS OF THE WOMEN'S CLUB. AT LIBRARY GARDEN. (LOCAL). MRS H N THISTLEWOOD, DIR; WOMEN'S CLUB & LIBRARY; 27 EDGEWOOD PARK; CAIRO, IL 62914. (#200016-507).

APR 30, '76. BICENTENNIAL ARBOR DAY TREE PLANTING. HONORING DECEASED MEMBERS OF THE WOMEN'S CLUB. AT LIBRARY GARDEN. (LOCAL). MRS H N THISTLEWOOD, CHMN; WOMEN'S CLUB & LIBRARY ASSOC OF CAIRO, INC; 27 EDGEWOOD PARK; CAIRO, IL 62914. (#200016-64).

MAY 17, '76. WAGON TRAIN STOPS IN CAIRO, IL ENROUTE FROM SAN FRANCISCO. LIVE PERFORMANCE, TOUR. (LOCAL). MRS H N THISTLEWOOD, DIR; WOMEN'S CLUB & LIBRARY ASSOCIATION OF CAIRO, INC; 27 EDGEWOOD PARK; CAIRO, IL 62914. (#102805-67).

MAY 30, '76. DEDICATION OF MONUMENT TO VETERANS OF VIETNAM WAR. MONUMENT WILL JOIN ONES FOR WWII & KOREAN WAR VETERANS. AT CANDEE PARK. (LOCAL). MRS H N THISTLEWOOD, DIR; JR WOMEN'S CLUB; 27 EDGEWOOD PARK; CAIRO, IL 62914. (#102805-69).

JULY 2, '76. JUNIOR ASSOCIATION OF COMMERCE'S BICENTENNIAL PARADE. PARADE. (LOCAL). MRS H N THISTLEWOOD, DIR; JR ASSOC OF COMMERCE; 27 EDGEWOOD PARK; CAIRO, IL 62914. (#102805-70).

JULY 4, '76. BICENTENNIAL RACES ON THE OHIO RIVER. COMPETITION AT CANDEE PARK. (LOCAL). MRS H N THISTLEWOOD, DIR; WOMEN'S CLUB & LIBRARY ASSOCIATION OF CAIRO, INC; 27 EDGEWOOD PARK; CAIRO, IL 62914. (#102805-71).

FEB 18 - 19, '77. LA SALLE EXPEDITION II, A HISTORIC RE-ENACTMENT. THIS IS AN AUTHENTIC RE-ENACTMENT OF THE 1681 LASALLE EXPEDITION FROM MONTREAL, CANADA TO NEW ORLEANS, LA WHICH WILL BEGIN TOURING ON AUGUST 11, 1976 AND END ON APRIL 9, 1977. (LOCAL). REID H LEWIS, DIRECTOR; LA SALLE EXPEDITION II; 135 S LA SALLE ST, RM 411; CHICAGO, IL 60690. (#102805-56).

CALUMET CITY

NOV 23, '75. FENWICK PLACE, A LOOK TO THE PAST. THIS ANNUAL EVENT INCLUDES A PIONEER THANKSGIVING & CRAFTS EXHIBIT. AT SANDRIDGE NATURE CENTER. (LOCAL). MARY MULCAHY, CO-CHMN; COOKE COUNTY FOREST PRESERVE DISTRICT; 267 LEONARD AVE; CHICAGO HTS, IL 60411. (#100963-1).

FEB 1, '76 - DEC 30, '77. FENWICK LOG CABIN TOURS & CRAFT DEMONSTRATIONS. TOURS OF LOG CABIN AND DEMONSTRATION OF CRAFTS TYPICAL OF THE ILLNOIS FRONTIER AROUND 1818. (LOCAL). MARY MULCAHY; SENIOR GIRL SCOUT TROOP 654; 267 LEONARD AVE; CHICAGO HTS, IL 60411. (#6496-501).

CAMBRIDGE

COLLEGE SQUARE MEMORIAL PARK IN CAMBRIDGE, IL. REDEVELOPED CITY PARK: PLAYGROUND EQUIPMENT, VOLLEYBALL, BASEBALL, BASKETBALL, TENNIS COURT, PICNIC AREA, LANDSCAPED AREAS, & MEMORIAL TIME CAPSULE BURIED AT SITE. (LOCAL). MARY ALICE LINDBURG, VILLAGE TRUSTEE; VILLAGE OF CAMBRIDGE; 211 E COURT ST; CAMBRIDGE, IL 61238. (#33652).

JULY 4, '76. JOINT CHURCH SERVICE FOR THE BICENTENNIAL. CEREMONY AT COURTHOUSE LAWN. (LOCAL). JACK CLIFFORD, CHMN; CAMBRIDGE BICENTENNIAL COMMITTEE; 306 N EAST ST; CAMBRIDGE, IL 61238. (#200016-508).

CANTON

MAY 17, '75. FORMAL BICENTENNIAL TEA AND TOUR OF REDCREST MANSION. TOUR, FESTIVAL. (LOCAL). MARJORIE BORDNER; FULTON COUNTY BICENTENNIAL COMMISSION; 430 E OAK; CANTON, IL 61520. (#5323-501).

JUNE 14, '75. PAGEANT AND AUDIENCE INVOLVEMENT - CANTON, IL. PAGEANT WRITTEN TO PORTRAY EVENTS WHICH LED TO THE BOSTON TEA PARTY AND REVOLUTIONARY WAR; 60 CHARACTERS PLUS AUDIENCE PARTICIPATION. A MUSICAL DRAMA. (LOCAL). MRS LAWRENCE I BORDNER; FULTON COUNTY BICENTENNIAL COMMISSION; 45 N PARK DR; CANTON, IL 61520. (#11012-1).

JAN 1 - JULY 31, '76. FULTON COUNTY ART GALLERY DISPLAYS. ART BY MARIAN DENSHANE OF ST DAVID, IL; ROBERT TANQUERY OF CANTON, IL; LORRAINE CUDDINGTON OF FARMINGTON, IL; GRACE CORRELL OF PEORIA, IL; MIKE RUSSELL & MARGARET COMFORT OF BLOOMINGTON, IL; IL STATE. AT GRAHAM HOSPITAL ART GALLERY. (LOCAL). NANCY ELSON, DIRECTOR; FULTON COUNTY ARTS COUNCIL; 639 N 2ND ST; CANTON, IL 61520. (#105195-3).

MAY 1 - 31, '76. '200 YEARS WITH A FUTURE'. FAIR AT SPOON RIVER COLLEGE. (LOCAL). MARJORIE BORDNER, CHMN; SPOON RIVER COLLEGE; PO BOX 492; CANTON, IL 61520. (#200016-171).

JUNE 10 - 12, '76. THEATER PRODUCTION OF '1776'. HUGE EXPERIENCED CAST OF TOP TALENT. AT CANTON SENIOR HIGH SCHOOL AUDITORIUM. (LOCAL). DONALD E ENGLISH, CHMN; FULTON COUNTY PLAYHOUSE; 602 N 2ND ST; CANTON, IL 61520. (#105195-2).

JULY 4, '76. CANTON BICENTENNIAL FESTIVAL. GIANT FIREWORKS DISPLAY. AT CANTON ARMORY, ATHLETIC PARK & PUBLIC SQUARE. (LOCAL). MRS LAWRENCE I BORDNER; CANTON FESTIVAL ASSOC; 45 N PARK DR; CANTON, IL 61520. (#105195-1).

OCT 2 - 10, '76. SPOON RIVER VALLEY FALL FESTIVAL WITH BICENTENNIAL THEME. ENORMOUS FESTIVAL BASED ON THE FAMOUS BOOK 'SPOON RIVER ANTHOLOGY' BY EDGAR LEE MASTERS; EXHIBITS, DISPLAYS, ARTS, MUSIC, THEATRE, ANTIQUE SALES, FLEA MARKETS & RECREATION. (LOCAL). MRS LAWRENCE I BORDNER; SPOON RIVER DRIVE ASSOCIATES; 45 N PARK DR; CANTON, IL 61520. (#105198-1).

CARBON CLIFF

AUG 13 - 15, '76. 'ARGILLO DAYS' - A THREE DAY CELEBRATION. 'ARGILLO DAYS' WAS NAMED AFTER THE BRICKYARD (ARGILLO) WHICH FATHERED THE VILLAGE OF CARBON CLIFF. THE DAYS INCLUDED AN OPENING CEREMONY, PARADE, TWO STREET DANCES, ARTS AND CRAFT FAIR, HISTORY EXHIBIT, SPECIAL POSTAGE CANCELLATION STAMP & BALLOON ASCENSION. AT CARBON CLIFF VILLAGE PARK, VILLAGE HALL AND APOLLO SCHOOL. (LOCAL). KENNETH A WILLIAMS, CHMN; CARBON CLIFF BICENTENNIAL COMMISSION; 116 6TH ST; CARBON CLIFF, IL 61239. (#200016-403).

CARBONDALE

BICENTENNIAL TREE PLANTINGS IN CARBONDALE, IL. PLANTINGS OF WHITE PINE & GUM TREES ALONG THE MAIN DOWNTOWN INTERSECTION. (LOCAL). MRS LINCOLN CANFIELD, CHAIRMAN; CARBONDALE FOUNDATION FOR A BETTER ENVIRONMENT; 1609 TAYLOR DR; CARBONDALE, IL 62901. (#33650).

'CARBONDALE REMEMBERED', BOOKLET, ILLINOIS. A BOOKLET THAT DESCRIBES CARBONDALE NEIGHBORHOOD STREETS, WRITTEN BY LONG TIME RESIDENTS. (LOCAL). AGNES WRIGHT, PROJ DIRECTOR; CARBONDALE WOMEN'S CLUB; HERITAGE HILLS, BOX 25C, RT 1; CARBONDALE, IL 62901. (#13053).

COMPREHENSIVE PLAN UPDATE: GREATER EGYPT REGION-IL. LAND USE SURVEY AND COMPREHENSIVE PLAN UPDATE FOR A FIVE-COUNTY PLANNING REGION IN SOUTHERN ILLINOIS; FRANKLIN, JACKSON, JEFFERSON, PERRY & WILLIAMSON COUNTIES. (LOCAL). FRANKLYN H MORENO, DIRECTOR; GREATER EGYPT REGIONAL PLANNING AND DEVELOPMENT COMMISSION; BOX 3160; CARBONDALE, IL 62901. (#29937).

GROWING HORIZONS/INT'L COMMUNITY: CARBONDALE, IL. EXHIBIT OF CONTRIBUTIONS OF VARIOUS ETHNIC & RACIAL GROUPS TO OUR AREA; PERFORMANCES, NATIVE DRESS; POSTER CONTEST IN SCHOOL DEPICTING WORK OF UNITED NATIONS. (LOCAL). NANCY BAUMAN, CHAIRMAN; UNITED NATIONS ASSOC/USA SO IL CHAPTER; PO BOX 3067; CARBONDALE, IL 62901. (#33648).

HISTORIC INVENTORY OF CARBONDALE, IL. AN INVENTORY OF THE HISTORICAL ARCHITECTURE. RESULTS WILL BE PUBLISHED. (LOCAL). DR CARROLL RILEY, PROJ COORDINATOR; DEPTS OF HISTORY AND ANTHROPOLOGY AND UNIVERSITY MUSEUM; SOUTHERN ILLINOIS UNIVERSITY; CARBONDALE, IL 62901. (#22338).

ILLINOIS COMPOSERS: PAST & PRESENT, CARBONDALE. A SERIES OF THIRTEEN HALF-HOUR RADIO TAPES OF THE MUSIC OF ILLINOIS COMPOSERS, DEVOTED TO SERIOUS MUSIC AND TO FOCUSING ATTENTION ON THE HERITAGE AND FUTURE OF MUSIC IN ILLINOIS. (LOCAL). DR WILL GAY BOTTJE, PROJ DIRECTOR; SOUTHERN ILLINOIS UNIV; CARBONDALE, IL 62901. (#26594). **ARBA GRANTEE.**

LANGUAGE IN AMERICA, CARBONDALE, IL. A COURSE WITH TWO AUDIO VISUAL PRESENTATIONS, CONCERNED WITH ENGLISH AND OTHER LANGUAGES AS USED IN NORTH AMERICA. (LOCAL). R KARNES, CHAIRMAN; SOUTHERN ILLINOIS UNIV AT CARBONDALE BICENTENNIAL COMMITTEE; CARBONDALE, IL 62901. (#22339).

MIDDLE WORKS OF JOHN DEWEY VOLUMES 1-3. EDITING THREE VOLUMES OF DEWEY'S WORKS. TRAINING TWO SCHOLARS IN THE TECHNIQUES OF MODERN TEXTUAL EDITING AS THESE APPLY TO PHILOSOPHICAL WRITINGS. (NAT'L). DR JO ANN BOYDSTON; CENTER FOR DEWEY STUDIES; 803 S OAKLAND; CARBONDALE, IL 62901. (#3692).

MURAL FOR CARBONDALE, IL. A COLLAGE OF PSORTS FIGURES DRAWN BY HIGH SCHOOL STUDENTS FOR A MURAL ON A SPORT SHOP IN DOWNTOWN AREA. (LOCAL). MARGIE PARKER, COORDINATOR; INTER-CHURCH COUNCIL BICENTENNIAL COMMISSION; 1702 TAYLOR DR; CARBONDALE, IL 62901. (#33651).

SELF-PORTRAIT OF THE AMERICAN ARTIST, IL. A SERIES OF EIGHT ONE-HALF HOUR TELEVISION PROGRAMS ON THE AMERICAN ARTIST. (ST-WIDE). GEORGE MAUGLIANO, CHAIRMAN; DEPT OF ART-SOUTHERN ILLINOIS UNIV AT CARBONDALE; CARBONDALE, IL 62901. (#22340).

SPOTLIGHT: HERITAGE '76 - CARBONDALE, IL. WEEKLY TV SHOW CARRIED ON SOUTHERN ILLINOIS UNIVERSITY'S PBS STATION HIGHLIGHTING STATE HISTORICAL SITES AND EVENTS. PAST HISTORY IS CONTRASTED WITH PRESENT CONDITIONS IN THIS FILM/VTR PRESENTATION. (ST-WIDE). EDWARD HAUER-PRODUCER/DIRECTOR; BROADCASTING SERVICE; SOUTHERN ILLINOIS UNIVERSITY; CARBONDALE, IL 62901. (#17685).

WOODLAWN CEMETERY RESTORATION IN CARBONDALE, ILL. RESTORATION OF HISTORIC WOODLAWN CEMETERY IN CARBONDALE, ILLINOIS. A HISTORY OF CEMETERY WILL ALSO BE COMPILED & PUBLISHED. (LOCAL). NANCY BAUMANN, PROJ DIRECTOR; CARBONDALE BICENTENNIAL COMMISSION; 609 E COLLEGE ST; CARBONDALE, IL 62901. (#892). **ARBA GRANTEE.**

JULY 4, '75. CARBONDALE, IL, COMMUNITY FREEDOM FESTIVAL. COMMUNITY FESTIVAL INCLUDING BLUEGRASS MUSIC, ARTS & CRAFTS SALE, COMMUNITY PICNIC, CHILDREN'S GAME AREA, SPEAKERS AND OPEN FORUM. (LOCAL). NANCY BAUMANN; CITY OF CARBONDALE; CITY HALL; CARBONDALE, IL 62901. (#13056-1).

OCT 30, '75. BICENTENNIAL YOUTH DEBATE. COMPETITION AT SHRYOCK AUDITORIUM. (ST-WIDE). MARVIN KLEINAU, COORD; DEPT OF SPEECH, SOUTHERN ILLINOIS UNIVERSITY AT CARBONDALE; CARBONDALE, IL 62901. (#200016-63).

MAR 1 - MAY 1, '76. SOUTHERN ILLINOIS HISTORY OF GEOLOGY. EXHIBIT AT PARKINSON BUILDING. (ST-WIDE). REX D KARNES, CHMN; DEPT OF GEOLOGY-SOUTHERN ILLINOIS UNIVERSITY AT CARBONDALE; 6 FRAUNFELTER; CARBONDALE, IL 62901. (#106031-7).

MAR 27, '76. TOWN MEETING '76. ONE DAY COMMUNITY FORUM, AM AND PM WORKSHOPS, FESTIVE BUFFET LUNCH, ENTERTAINMENT, FORMULATE TOWN MEETING REPORT ON COMMUNITY'S CHALLENGES AND PROPOSAWLS. AT CITY HALL COMPLEX, 607 E COLLEGE. (LOCAL). NANCY BAUMANN, EXEC SEC; TOWN MEETING SPONSORSHIP COMMITTEE; CITY HALL; CARBONDALE, IL 62901. (#104640-2).

APR 4 - 30, '76. EXHIBITS OF CRAFTS OF APPALACHIA & SOUTHERN ILLINOIS. THERE WILL BE AN OPEN CRAFTS COMPETITION. AT UNIVERSITY MUSEUM IN FANER HALL. (REGN'L). BONNIE KRAUSE, COORD; SOUTHERN ILLINOIS UNIV AT CARBONDALE; ILLINOIS OZARKS CRAFT GUILD; CARBONDALE, IL 62901. (#106031-6).

APR 21 - 23, '76. A CLUB OF ROME SYMPOSIUM ON SYSTEMS SCIENCE. A SYMPOSIUM ON SYSTEMS SCIENCE AND AMERICA'S NEXT 100 YEARS; THE PREDICAMENT OF MANKIND WILL BE DISCUSSED. AT STUDENT CENTER - ADMINISTRATIVE SCIENCES. (INT'L). T H MATTHEISS, COORD; SOUTHERN ILLINOIS UNIVERSITY AT CARBONDALE; CARBONDALE, IL 62901. (#106031-1).

APR 25 - 28, '76. BICENTENNIAL FESTIVAL OF EXHIBITS. TOURING SMITHSONIAN INSTITUTE EXHIBITS, ILLINOIS ARTS COUNCIL ARCHITECTURAL EXHIBITS, AREA CLUBS AND ORGANIZATIONS WILL CONTRIBUTE DISPLAYS DEALING WITH BICENTENNIAL THEME; HOSTESSES IN BICENTENNIAL ERA CLOTHING. AT STUDENT CENTER, SOUTHERN ILLINOIS UNIVERSITY, BALLROOMS A,B,C,D. (LOCAL). NANCY A BAUMANN, EXEC SEC; CARBONDALE BICENTENNIAL COMMISSION & STUDENT ACTIVITIES OFFICE, SIU; CITY HALL; CARBONDALE, IL 62901. (#104640-1).

MAY 11 - 12, '76. ACROSS THE CHICHIMEC SEA, A CONFERENCE ON ARCHAEOLOGY. EMPHASIS ON THE CONTACTS OF NATIVE, CIVILIZED PEOPLE OF MEXICO WHICH INFLUENCED PARTS OF THE U S BEFORE COLUMBUS. AT CAMPUS. (REGN'L). CARROLL RILEY, COORD; SOUTHERN ILLINOIS UNIVERSITY AT CARBONDALE; CARBONDALE, IL 62901. (#106031-5).

CARBONDALE — CONTINUED

MAY 30, '76. MEMORIAL DAY SERVICES AT HISTORIC WOODLAWN CEMETERY. CEREMONIES HONORING VETERANS, SPEAKERS; FLAG CEREMONY FESTIVITIES FOLLOWING. AT WOODLAWN CEMETERY, MAIN AND LOGAN ST. (LOCAL). NANCY BAUMANN, EXEC SEC; CARBONDALE BICENTENNIAL COMMISSION; CITY HALL; CARBONDALE, IL 62901. (#104640-3).

JUNE - SEPT '76. SUMMER FESTIVAL OF AMERICANA. FESTIVAL OF MUSICAL, THEATRICAL & MOTION PICTURE PRESENTATIONS THAT WILL FURTHER RECOGNIZE THE HISTORICAL PLACE OF THE PERFORMING ARTS IN THE EVOLUTION OF LEGEND AND FACT ABOUT THE UNITED STATES. AT COMMUNICATIONS BUILDING. (ST-WIDE). REX D KARNES, CHMN; SOUTHERN ILLINOIS UNIVERSITY AT CARBONDALE; CARBONDALE, IL 62901. (#106031-3).

AUG '76. FOUR HUNDRED YEARS OF BLACK AMERICAN MUSIC. FIVE DAY FESTIVAL, PLANNED FOR AUGUST 1976, THAT WILL FEATURE MUSICAL PROGRAMS AND LECTURES BASED ON AND CENTERED AROUND SIGNIFICANT MUSICAL EVENTS INVOLVING BLACK AMERICANS FROM 1776 TO THE PRESENT. (REGN'L). REX D KARNES, CHMN; SOUTHERN ILLINOIS UNIVERSITY AT CARBONDALE; CARBONDALE, IL 62901. (#106031-2).

OCT 11 - 12, '76. BICENTENNIAL FLOWER SHOW. 'AMERICAN HERITAGE' TO INCLUDE: ARTISTIC ARRANGEMENTS; HORTICULTURE EXHIBITS; EDUCATIONAL EXHIBITS; COMMERICAL DISPLAYS. AT UNIVERSITY MALL. (ST-WIDE). MURIEL CANFIELD; CARBONDALE COUNCIL OF GARDEN CLUBS; 1609 TAYLOR DR; CARBONDALE, IL 62901. (#105640-1).

NOV 22 - 25, '76. 200 YEARS & BEYOND IN FAMILY & CHILDCARE. A THANKSGIVING FESTIVAL HIGHLIGHTING THE STRENGTHS OF THE FAMILY UNIT AS A BASIS IN OUR SYSTEM OF GOVERNMENT WITH EXHIBITS, DISPLAYS & AUDIO-VISUAL EXPERIENCES. (LOCAL). JENNY JONES, CHAIRMAN; SOUTHERN ILLINOIS UNIV, DEPT OF CHILD & FAMILY; CARBONDALE, IL 62901. (#200016-504).

CARLINVILLE

COUNTY HISTORICAL MUSEUM IN CARLINVILLE, IL. ACQUISITION OF ANDERSON PLACE IN CARLINVILLE AS MACOUPIN COUNTY HISTORICAL MUSEUM. (LOCAL). DORRELL KILDUFF, COORDINATOR; MACOUPIN COUNTY HISTORICAL SOCIETY BICENTENNIAL COMMITTEE; 646 E MACOUPIN; STAUNTON, IL 62088. (#33649).

MAY 25, '75 - CONTINUING . MEMORABILIA OF MACOUPIN COUNTY EXHIBIT & OPEN HOUSE. A COLLECTION OF MATERIALS FROM ALL PARTS OF COUNTY, CARPET LOOM, PICTURES OF PEOPLE & PLACES, FAMILY HISTORIES, DIARIES. CENTENNIAL BOOKLETS OF TOWNS, CHURCHES, ORGANIZATIONS, ETC. (LOCAL). MS DORRELL KILDUFF, CHMN; MACOUPIN COUNTY HISTORICAL SOCIETY; BRECKENRIDGE ST; CARLINVILLE, IL 62626. (#50351-1).

APR 24, '76. TWO HUNDRED YEARS OF AMERICA. STREET FAIR WITH BOOTHS PUT UP BY LOCAL GROUPS TO SHOW HOW AMERICA HAS BEEN AFFECTED BY ALL WHO HAVE COME TO LIVE HERE; LOCAL HISTORY WILL BE SHOWN WITH PLAYS AND DISPLAYS. (LOCAL). MICHAEL LUPPINO, CHAIRMAN; BLACKBURN COLLEGE BICENTENNIAL COMMITTEE; CARLINVILLE, IL 62626. (#103767-1).

JULY 3 - 4, '76. BICENTENNIAL FESTIVAL. FESTIVAL. (LOCAL). ROY SKEEN, CHMN; CARLINVILLE JAYCEES; CARLINVILLE, IL 62626. (#200016-150).

JULY 13 - 18, '76. EXHIBITS & COMPETITION FOR PRIZES - MACOUPIN COUNTY FAIR. COUNTY FAIR: LIVESTOCK & ART HALL JUDGING, HARNESS RACING, PARADE AND EXHIBITS FOR THE BICENTENNIAL. (LOCAL). ALICE TOSTBERG, SECRETARY; MACOUPIN COUNTY FAIR & AGRICULTURAL ASSOC; RR 3; CARLINVILLE, IL 62626. (#105196-1).

CARLOCK

HISTORIC SITES BOOK IN CARLOCK, IL. BOOK DESCRIBING HISTORIC SITES OF WOODFORD COUNTY. (LOCAL). ELAINE ROMERSBERGER, DIRECTOR; WOODFORD COUNTY BICENTENNIAL COMMISSION; RR 1; CARLOCK, IL 61725. (#33526).

CARLYLE

JULY 4TH BICENTENNIAL FESTIVAL IN CARLYLE, IL. FESTIVAL WILL SERVE AS A KICK-OFF FOR BICENTENNIAL ACTIVITIES IN CLINTON COUNTY. (LOCAL). SANDY TILKENS, CHAIRMAN; CLINTON COUNTY BICENTENNIAL COMMISSION; 1491 ABBOTT; CARLYLE, IL 62231. (#10621).

RENOVATION OF THE CARLYLE COMMUNITY CENTER, IL. RENOVATION OF A COMMUNITY CENTER TO PROVIDE MEETING FACILITIES, MEANINGFUL COMMUNITY AND EDUCATIONAL ACTIVITIES. (LOCAL). MRS CATHERINE DOMINGUEZ, PROJ DIRECTOR; CARLYLE BICENTENNIAL COMMISSION; 1071 ST CLAIR; CARLYLE, IL 62231. (#27769). **ARBA GRANTEE.**

CAROL STREAM

JULY 4, '76. GRETNA RAILROAD STATION MUSEUM DEDICATION. OPENING AT ARMSTRONG PARK/391 ILLINI DR, ADJACENT PARKING LOT. (LOCAL). JEAN MOORE, CHAIRMAN; CAROL STREAM BICENTENNIAL COMMISSION - CAROL STREAM PARK DISTRICT; 245 W SHAWNEE DR; CAROL STREAM, IL 60187. (#106065-1).

CARPNTERSVLLE

JUNE 25 - 29, '75. JAMBOREE CARNIVAL & PARADE. PARADE, FESTIVAL AT CARNIVAL IN CARPENTER PARK; PARADE ON ROUTE 25. (LOCAL). JEANNE M MCFADDEN; CARPENTERSVILLE BICENTENNIAL COMMISSION; 89 HICKORY COURT; CARPENTERSVIL, IL 60110. (#50051-1).

CARROLLTON

EMERGENCY NUMBERING SYSTEM - CARROLLTON, IL. IDENTIFICATION OF 2,000 RURAL HOMES WITH NUMBERS FOR EMERGENCY PURPOSES. (LOCAL). CHARLES BARNETT, CHAIRMAN; GREENE COUNTY BICENTENNIAL COMMISSION; GREENE COUNTY COURTHOUSE; CARROLLTON, IL 62016. (#30415).

CARTERVILLE

'ALONG THE GEORGE ROGERS CLARK TRAIL', IL. SHAWNEE LIBRARY SYSTEM'S MINI-WORKSHOP ON THE AMERICAN BICENTENNIAL, RELATING TO MATERIALS AND ACTIVITIES FOR PUBLIC LIBRARIES AND READING CENTERS IN SOUTHERN ILLINOIS. (LOCAL). RONALD D REED, ADULT SERVICES LIBRARIAN; SHAWNEE LIBRARY SYSTEM; RR #2, BOX 136A; CARTERVILLE, IL 62918. (#12255).

CARTERVILLE HISTORICAL SOCIETY - CARTERVILLE, IL. HERITAGE HOUSE, CARTERVILLE FAIR, TOUR OF HOMES AT CHRISTMAS '75 & RESTORATION OF THE OLD JAIL HOUSE WILL BE SPONSORED BY THE HISTORICAL SOCIETY. (LOCAL). MARGARET CAMNESS, CHAIRMAN; CARTERVILLE HISTORICAL SOCIETY; 214 WASHINGTON ST, BOX C; CARTERVILLE, IL 62918. (#14182).

A LEGACY OF STATESMANSHIP: CARTERVILLE, IL. SCHEDULED PRESENTATIONS OF THE COLLEGE HISTORICAL COLLECTION TO ANY GROUP IN THE COLLEGE COMMUNITY. (ST-WIDE). RACHEL KLEIN, CHAIRMAN, LOGAN COLLEGE BICENTENNIAL; JOHN A LOGAN COLLEGE; CARTERVILLE, IL 62901. (#13495).

RESTORATION OF HERITAGE HOUSE, CARTERVILLE, IL. RESTORE 85 YEAR OLD HOME, 'HERITAGE HOUSE' WITH AUTHENTIC FURNITURE OF THAT ERA. (LOCAL). MARGARET CHAMMESS, CHAIRMAN; CARTERVILLE HISTORICAL SOCIETY; 214 WASHINGTON ST; CARTERVILLE, IL 62918. (#16059).

RESTORATION OF OLD JU WALKER HOME - IL. AN 85 YEAR OLD HOME WITH CARTERVILLE'S FIRST BATHROOM WILL BE RESTORED AND TURNED INTO A HOME OF HISTORIC PERSONALITIES CALLED 'HERITAGE HOUSE.'. (LOCAL). MARGARET CHAMNESS, CHAIRMAN; CARTERVILLE HISTORICAL SOCIETY; N DIVISION ST; CARTERVILLE, IL 62918. (#14371).

RE-PRINT OF 4 COUNTY HISTORIES - CARTERVILLE, IL. 4 COUNTY HISTORIES WILL BE RE-PRINTED, THESE WILL INCLUDE JOHNSON, MASSAC, POPE AND HARDIN COUNTIES, THE FIRST COUNTIES IN ILLINOIS TO BE SETTLED. (LOCAL). RACHEL KLEIN, CHAIRMAN; GENEAOLOGY SOCIETY OF SOUTHWESTERN ILLINOIS; JOHN A LOGAN COLLEGE; CARTERVILLE, IL 62918. (#15325).

SOUTHERN ILLINOIS UNDERGROUND: THE NEXT 100 YEARS. ASSEMBLING ORAL AND WRITTEN MATERIALS, PHOTOGRAPHS, UTILITARIAN OBJECTS, MUSIC, TAPED INTERVIEWS AND MODELS ON THE HISTORY AND ECONOMIC FUTURE OF THE SOUTHERN ILLINOIS COAL INDUSTRY. (ST-WIDE). RACHEL KLEIN, CHAIRMAN, LOGAN COLLEGE BICENTENNIAL; JOHN A LOGAN COLLEGE; CARTERVILLE, IL 62901. (#13494).

SEPT 11 - 13, '75. FAIR AND TALENT SHOW. FAIR, PARADE AT MAIN ST & EASTERN STAR AUDITORIUM. (LOCAL). RODGER HUME, PRESIDENT; LIONS CLUB; TEXAS AVE; CARTERVILLE, IL 62918. (#101892-1).

APR 9 - 11, '76. BICENTENNIAL FAIR. A FAIR INVOLVING DIVERSE COMMUNITY GROUPS IN SIMULTANEOUS AND SEQUENTIAL HISTORICAL, CULTURAL, CRAFT AND MUSICAL EVENTS CELEBRATING OUR BICENTENNIAL AND OUR AMERICAN FREEDOM. (LOCAL). RACHEL KLEIN; JOHN A LOGAN COLLEGE; JOHN A LOGAN COLLEGE; CARTERVILLE, IL 62901. (#101117-1).

MAY 1 - 2, '76. JOHN A LOGAN COLLEGE BICENTENNIAL FAIR. FAIR AT COLLEGE CAMPUS. (LOCAL). PRISCILLA WINKLER, CHMN; JOHN A LOGAN COLLEGE; CARTERVILLE, IL 62918. (#104248-3).

CARTHAGE

CARTHAGE TOURIST INFORMATION CENTER AND MUSEUM, IL. TOURIST INFORMATION CENTER AND MUSEUM TO PROVIDE INFORMATION ABOUT LOCAL HISTORIC AND RECREATIONAL SITES AND TO HOUSE COLLECTION OF HISTORIC ITEMS AND PROVIDE SPACE FOR THEIR DISPLAY TO THE PUBLIC. (LOCAL). VERLYN BETHARD, CO-CHARIMAN; CARTHAGE ILLINOIS BICENTENNIAL COMMISSION; 50 S ADAMS; CARTHAGE, IL 62321. (#24100). **ARBA GRANTEE.**

CASEYVILLE

AMERICAN HERITAGE FESTIVAL IN CASEYVILLE, ILLINOIS. FESTIVAL, OCCURING JUNE 28 & 29, 1975, TO HAVE PARADE WITH FLOATS ON AMERICAN HERITAGE THEME, BANDS, CARNIVAL RIDES AND WILL CULMINATE IN CROWNING OF HERITAGE QUEEN AND COURT. (LOCAL). RAY STEPHENS SR, PRESIDENT; CASEYVILLE VOLUNTEER FIREMEN; 10 W MORRIS; CASEYVILLE, IL 62232. (#8185).

JOHNNY HORIZON '76 PGM FOR YOUTH IN CASEYVILLE, IL. YOUTH OF THE VILLAGE WILL PARTICIPATE IN AN ECOLOGY PROGRAM. SCOUTS AND 4-H GROUP TO PLANT SEEDLINGS & CLEAN-UP VILLAGE PROPERTY. LOCAL JOHNNY HORIZON TO ENROLL STUDENTS IN PROGRAM ON SCHOOLYARD IN 1975. (LOCAL). ADA KNUSSMANN, CHAIRPERSON; CASEYVILLE BICENTENNIAL COMMISSION; PO BOX 1776; CASEYVILLE, IL 62232. (#8184). **(??).**

APR 1 - MAY 15, '75. SCOUTS & 4-H GROUP PLANT SEEDLINGS & CLEAN-UP VILLAGE PROPERTY. YOUTH OF THE VILLAGE WILL PARTICIPATE IN AN ECOLOGY PROGRAM. SCOUTS AND 4-H GROUP TO PLANT SEEDLINGS & CLEAN-UP VILLAGE PROPERTY. LOCAL JOHNNY HORIZON TO ENROLL STUDENTS IN PROGRAM ON SCHOOLYARD IN 1975. (LOCAL). ADA KNUSSMANN; CASEYVILLE BICENTENNIAL COMMISSION; PO BOX 1776; CASEYVILLE, IL 62232. (#8184-502).

MAY 26, '75. OLD FASHIONED CAKE WALK AND OTHER SOCIAL ACTIVITIES OF YESTERYEAR. CEREMONY, PARADE, FESTIVAL. (LOCAL). ADA KNUSSMANN; CASEYVILLE BICENTENNIAL COMMISSION; PO BOX 1776; CASEYVILLE, IL 62232. (#8186-506).

MAY 26, '75. OLD FASHIONED COMMUNITY GET TOGETHER AND DINNER. CEREMONY, PARADE, FESTIVAL. (LOCAL). ADA KNUSSMANN; CASEYVILLE BICENTENNIAL COMMISSION; PO BOX 1776; CASEYVILLE, IL 62232. (#8186-502).

MAY 26, '75. OLD TIMERS GALLERY - DISPLAY PHOTOS OF PEOPLE & EVENTS IN LOCAL HIST. CEREMONY, PARADE, FESTIVAL. (LOCAL). ADA KNUSSMANN; CASEYVILLE BICENTENNIAL COMMISSION; PO BOX 1776; CASEYVILLE, IL 62232. (#8186-503).

MAY 26, '75. PATRIOTIC SKITS AND LOCAL THEME SKITS. CEREMONY, PARADE, FESTIVAL. (LOCAL). ADA KNUSSMANN; CASEYVILLE BICENTENNIAL COMMISSION; PO BOX 1776; CASEYVILLE, IL 62232. (#8186-507).

MAY 26, '75. ROTC DRILL-HISTORIC WEAPON DISPLAY & COMPETITION. CEREMONY, PARADE, FESTIVAL. (LOCAL). ADA KNUSSMANN; CASEYVILLE BICENTENNIAL COMMISSION; PO BOX 1776; CASEYVILLE, IL 62232. (#8186-505).

MAY 26, '75. VIEWING THE VILLAGE VIA HELICOPTER RIDES. CEREMONY, PARADE, FESTIVAL. (LOCAL). ADA KNUSSMANN; CASEYVILLE BICENTENNIAL COMMISSION; PO BOX 1776; CASEYVILLE, IL 62232. (#8186-504).

MAY 26, '75. YOUTH ENROLL IN JOHNNY HORIZONS PROGRAM, JOHNNY ARRIVES BY COPTER. YOUTH OF THE VILLAGE WILL PARTICIPATE IN AN ECOLOGY PROGRAM. SCOUTS AND 4-H GROUP TO PLANT SEEDLINGS & CLEAN-UP VILLAGE PROPERTY. LOCAL JOHNNY HORIZON TO ENROLL STUDENTS IN PROGRAM ON SCHOOLYARD IN 1975. (LOCAL). ADA KNUSSMANN; CASEYVILLE BICENTENNIAL COMMISSION; PO BOX 1776; CASEYVILLE, IL 62232. (#8184-501).

JUNE 28, '75. PARADE - FLOATS ON OLD HIGH SCHOOL BANDS & OLD FIRE EQUIPMENT. FESTIVAL, OCCURING JUNE 28 & 29, 1975, TO HAVE PARADE WITH FLOATS ON AMERICAN HERITAGE THEME, BANDS, CARNIVAL RIDES AND WILL CULMINATE IN CROWNING OF HERITAGE QUEEN AND COURT. (LOCAL). RAY STEPHENS SR; CASEYVILLE VOLUNTEER FIREMEN; 10 W MORRIS; CASEYVILLE, IL 62232. (#8185-501).

JUNE 28 - 29, '75. TWO DAY FESTIVAL-REFRESHMENTS-CARNIVAL RIDES-BOOTHS. FESTIVAL, PARADE. (LOCAL). RAY STEPHENS SR; CASEYVILLE VOLUNTEER FIREMEN; 10 W MORRIS; CASEYVILLE, IL 62232. (#8185-502).

JUNE 29, '75. CROWNING OF HERITAGE QUEEN AND COURT. FESTIVAL, PARADE. (LOCAL). RAY STEPHENS SR; CASEYVILLE VOLUNTEER FIREMEN; 10 W MORRIS; CASEYVILLE, IL 62232. (#8185-503).

MAY 30, '76. VFW COMMUNITY MEMORIAL DAY SERV & PARADE TO CEMETERY W/FESTIVITIES. OLD FASHIONED MEMORIAL DAY WITH VETERANS' SERVICES, PROCESSION TO CEMETERY, COMMUNITY DINNER & OLD-TIME GET TOGETHER, PHOTO GALLERY DISPLAY OLD TIMERS, HELICOPTER VIEW OF VILLAGE ETC. (LOCAL). ADA KNUSSMANN; CASEYVILLE BICENTENNIAL COMMISSION; PO BOX 1776; CASEYVILLE, IL 62232. (#8186-501).

CEDARVILLE

AUG 7 - 8, '76. OLD SETTLERS REUNION & PICNIC. AN ANNUAL EVENT FOR EARLY SETTLERS OF STEPHENSON COUNTY, IL, FROM 1850'S TO 1950'S. THE REUNION IS BEING REVIVED TO CELEBRATE THE BICENTENNIAL & PROMOTE THE LOCAL HISTORY OF THE CEDARVILLE AREA. FOOD, GAMES, SPEAKERS, STREET DANCE & SCHOOL CHILDREN'S PAGEANT. (LOCAL). MRS R F GOODSPEED; CEDARVILLE BICENTENNIAL COMMISSION; CEDARVILLE, IL 61013. (#11839-501).

CENTRALIA

CENTRALIA SENTINEL'S BICENT INVOLVEMENT - NBMRP. PAPER HAS URGED COMMUNITY INVOLVEMENT IN CONSTRUCTING BICENT PARK IN CITY WITH DONATIONS, PLANS GIANT JUNE ISSUE, HAS ASSISTED A.P. IN RESEARCH, & HAS LENT ONE OF ITS EDITORS AS CITY BICENT CHAIRWOMAN. (LOCAL). MARIETTA BROUGHTON, BICENTENNIAL COORDINATOR; CENTRALIA EVENING & SUNDAY SENTINEL; 232 E BROADWAY; CENTRALIA, IL 62801. (#25418).

CHAMPAIGN

ARCHIVAN ILLINOIS ARCHITECTURE MOBILE VAN MUSEUM. LARGE MOBILE MUSEUM TRAVELING TO 60 SITES IN STATE DURING 1976 WITH ARCHITECTURAL EXHIBIT DESIGNED FOR GENERAL VIEWING EMPHASIZING CONTRIBUTIONS ILLINOIS HAS MADE TO WORLD'S ARCHITECTURAL HERITAGE. (ST-WIDE). GARY L OLSEN, PROJ DIRECTOR; CHAMPAIGN COUNTY HISTORICAL

CHAMPAIGN — CONTINUED

MUSEUM; 709 W UNIVERSITY AVE; CHAMPAIGN, IL 61820. (#25683). **ARBA GRANTEE.**

BICENTENNIAL EFFORTS OF THE NEWS GAZETTE -NBMRP. PAPER HAS SUPPORTED LOCAL EFFORTS, INCL TURNING LOCAL CREEK INTO A PARKLAND, PROMOTION OF FUND RAISING & ASSISTED DRIVE FOR A LOCAL TIME CAPSULE. (LOCAL). CHARLES E FLYNN, GENERAL MANAGER; CHAMPAIGN-URBANA NEWS GAZETTE; 48 MAIN ST; CHAMPAIGN, IL 61820. (#24693).

BICENTENNIAL SHORT TRACK SPEEDING COMPETITIONS, IL. SHORT TRACK SPEEDING COMPETITIONS WILL BE HELD AT VARIOUS LOCATIONS ACROSS THE COUNTRY. (NAT'L). BILL MARKLAND, COORDINATOR; AMATEUR SKATING UNION OF THE U S; CHAMPAIGN, IL 61820. (#27948).

BONEYARD CREEK PROJECT IN CHAMPAIGN, ILLINOIS. HISTORIC BONEYARD CREEK WHICH RUNS ALL THROUGH CHAMPAIGN AND URBANA WILL BE THE SITE FOR A HYDROLOGICALLY BEAUTIFUL PARK WITH A BIKEWAY AND WALKING PATH AS BEAUTIFUL AS IT WAS IN 1776. (LOCAL). BILL HELMS, PROJECT DIRECTOR; CHAMPAIGN COUNTY BICENT COMMISSION; 1103 HARRINGTON DR; CHAMPAIGN, IL 61820. (#8760). **ARBA GRANTEE.**

CHAMPAIGN COUNTY HISTORY BIBLIOGRAPHY IN ILLINOIS. RESOURCE LIST TO BE COMPILED & DISSEMINATED TO ALL SCHOOLS IN THE COUNTY. (LOCAL). JANET CORNELIUS, PROJECT DIRECTOR; CHAMPAIGN COUNTY BICENT COMMISSION; 1103 HARRINGTON DR; CHAMPAIGN, IL 61820. (#8764).

CHAMPAIGN COUNTY, IL, UPDATED HISTORICAL CALENDAR. A HISTORICAL CALENDAR OF THE COMMUNITY, PAST AND PRESENT, WITH HISTORICAL FACTS BESIDE EACH DATE TO BE PRINTED AS A 1976 CALENDAR. (LOCAL). JEANNE ROCKFORD, CHAIRMAN; CHAMPAIGN COUNTY BICENT COMMISSION; 1103 HARRINGTON DR; CHAMPAIGN, IL 61820. (#9415).

CHAMPAIGN COUNTY HISTORICAL MUSEUM IN ILLINOIS. THE WILBER MANSION HAS BEEN RESTORED & IS THE NEW COUNTY MUSEUM; THE 1ST FLOOR TO BE FURNISHED IN EARLY 20TH CENTURY DECOR. PROGRAMS INCLUDE CRAFT CLASSES & SPECIAL EXHIBITS ON COUNTY HISTORY. (LOCAL). PATRICIA L MILLER, DIRECTOR; CHAMPAIGN COUNTY HISTORICAL MUSEUM; 709 W UNIVERSITY; CHAMPAIGN, IL 61820. (#9416).

CHAMPAIGN, ILLINOIS, HERITAGE PARK AND TRAIL. DEVELOPING PARK AS NATURAL PRAIRIE TO PROVIDE VIEW OF ILLINOIS AS IT WAS IN 1776. ALSO CONSTRUCT BIKING AND HIKING TRAILS TO ENCOURAGE CITIZEN PARTICIPATION AND APPRECIATION. (LOCAL). PATRICIA A NORRIS, PROJ DIRECTOR; CHAMPAIGN PARK DISTRICT; 706 HOLIDAY PARK DR; CHAMPAIGN, IL 61820. (#6482). **ARBA GRANTEE.**

COURTHOUSE CLOCK AND BELL RESTORATION, IL. FLYING COURTHOUSE TOWER CLOCK AND RESTORING BELL TO TOWER; TOWER WAS STRUCK BY LIGHTENING TWICE AND BELL IS NOW ON THE GROUND; BELL WILL RING EVERY HOUR ON THE HOUR. (LOCAL). BRUCE KANNOV, COORDINATOR; CHAMPAIGN COUNTY BICENTENNIAL COMMISSION; 1208 W UNION; CHAMPAIGN, IL 61820. (#21227).

'FROM THE HEARTS OF MEN' - CHAMPAIGN, IL. VIDEOTAPE SHOWING DEVELOPMENT OF BANDS AND BAND MUSIC IN UNITED STATES. (LOCAL). HARRY BEGIAN, DIRECTOR; UNIVERSITY OF ILLINOIS BANDS AT CHAMPAIGN-URBANA; 1103 S SIXTH ST; CHAMPAIGN, IL 61820. (#33646).

'GATEWAYS TO THE CITIES' IN CHAMPAIGN, ILLINOIS. BEAUTIFICATION OF THE ENTRANCES TO CHAMPAIGN & URBANA, WITH LANDSCAPING & CONSTRUCTION OF AN INFORMATION KIOSK IN URBANA. (LOCAL). EARL PORTER, CHAIRMAN; CCDC FOUNDATION; 1016 W HEALEY, IL 61820. (#8767).

HERITAGE SHRINES IN CHAMPAIGN CO, ILLINOIS. DOCUMENTS FROM THE BIRTH AND GROWTH OF OUR NATION HAVE BEEN PLACED ON EXHIBIT AT PERMANENT DISPLAYS AT AIRPORTS, LINCOLN SQUARE MALL, SCHOOLS AND A NEW DISPLAY CASE AT PARKLAND COLLEGE. (LOCAL). DON KRUSE, CLUB PRESIDENT; EXCHANGE CLUB; 612 VENTURA; CHAMPAIGN, IL 61820. (#9414).

HISTORIC MODEL TRAIN DIORAMA, CHAMPAIGN CO, IL. MODEL OF FIRST TRAIN IN CHAMPAIGN AND FIRST INTERURBAN TRAIN TO BE BUILT AND PLACED IN CHAMPAIGN HISTORICAL MUSEUM. (LOCAL). GEOFFREY HAINES, PROJ DIRECTOR; CHAMPAIGN COUNTY BICENT COMMISSION; 1103 HARRINGTON DR; CHAMPAIGN, IL 61820. (#9412).

'ILLINOIS PRAIRIE - OUR GRASS ROOTS', IL. LIMITED EDITION PRINT OF 'ILLINOIS PRAIRIE', BY HARRY BREEN. (LOCAL). VIRGINIA RETTBERG, CHAIRMAN; CHAMPAIGN COUNTY BICENTENNIAL COMMISSION; 1424 MAYFAIR; CHAMPAIGN, IL 61820. (#21225).

LANDMARK PRESERVATION IN CHAMPAIGN, ILLINOIS. MARKING & PRESERVATION OF ARCHAEOLOGICAL & ARCHITECTURAL LANDMARKS, SUCH AS SITE OF LINCOLN'S LAST FORMAL ADDRESS TO AN AUDIENCE IN THE STATE, THE STAGE COACH STOP & THE STONE ARCH BRIDGE. (LOCAL). WILLIS C BAKER, PROJECT DIRECTOR; CHAMPAIGN COUNTY BICENT COMMISSION; 1103 HARRINGTON DR; CHAMPAIGN, IL 61820. (#8763).

LANDSCAPING OF RAILROAD DEPOT: CHAMPAIGN, IL. PLANS ARE TO BEAUTIFY THE TRAIN DEPOT IN COMMEMORATION OF THE SIGNIFICANT ROLE THE RAILROAD PLAYED IN THE DEVELOPMENT OF THE TWIN CITIES OF CHAMPAIGN-URBANA. (LOCAL). JEANNE ROCHFORD, CHAIRMAN; CHAMPAIGN COUNTY BICENT COMMISSION; 1103 HARRINGTON DR; CHAMPAIGN, IL 61820. (#8761). **ARBA GRANTEE.**

NEEDLEPOINT TAPESTRY OF CHAMPAIGN COUNTY, ILLINOIS. PROJECT ENTAILS THE MAKING OF A HUGE TAPESTRY WORKED ON BY WOMEN OF THE COUNTY; ONCE COMPLETED, IT WILL BE HUNG IN THE COURTHOUSE OR THE MUSEUM. (LOCAL). MICHAEL ALISANDRELLI, PROJECT DIRECTOR; CHAMPAIGN COUNTY BICENT COMMISSION; 1103 HARRINGTON DR; CHAMPAIGN, IL 61820. (#9411).

PAINTING OF FIRE HYDRANTS, CHAMPAIGN, IL. PAINTING OF KEY FIRE HYDRANTS TO RESEMBLE REVOLUTIONARY SOLDIERS. (LOCAL). NONA LEEPER, COORDINATOR; CHAMPAIGN COUNTY BICENTENNIAL COMMISSION; 3006 MEADOWBROOK DR; CHAMPAIGN, IL 61820. (#21226).

TOURISTS INFORMATION BOOKLET FROM CHAMPAIGN, ILL. PROJECT ENTAILS THE DEVISING OF INFORMATION BOOKLETS ON WALKING, BICYCLING AND DRIVING FOR TOURISTS VISITING CHAMPAIGN COUNTY POINTS OF INTEREST. (LOCAL). PAT MILNER, MUSEUM DIRECTOR; CHAMPION COMMUNITY HISTORICAL MUSEUM; 709 W UNIVERSITY; CHAMPAIGN, IL 61820. (#9413).

WORLD SHORT TRACK SPEED SKATING EVENT, IL. COMPETITION WILL TAKE PLACE IN CHAMPAIGN, IL AT THE UNIV OF ILLINOIS ICE ARENA AND WYANDOTTE, MICHIGAN AT BENJAMIN YALK ARENA; AND IN ST FOY, QUEBEC, CANADA. (INT'L). BILL MARKLAND, COORDINATOR; ILLINOIS OLYMPIC PARK NORTHBROOK & USA AMATEUR SKATING UNION; 803 WILLIAM ST; CHAMPAIGN, IL 61820. (#23318). **ARBA GRANTEE.**

76 SHOPPE - CHAMPAIGN, IL. THE SHOP SELLS RED, WHITE & BLUE ITEMS FOR EVERY AGE GROUP, COMMEMORATIVE GLASS ITEMS, ARTS & CRAFTS BY LOCAL ARTISANS AND TOYS & GAMES; STORE IS STAFFED BY VOLUNTEERS. (LOCAL). MARGI HAHN, PROJ COORDINATOR; CHAMPAIGN COUNTY BICENTENNIAL COMMISSION; 1012 S FIRST ST .; CHAMPAIGN, IL 61820. (#21163).

JUNE 20, '75. OUR GRASS ROOTS KICK-OFF DINNER. CEREMONY AT RAMADA INN CONVENTION CENTER. (LOCAL). RAY DICKERSON; CHAMPAIGN COUNTY BICENTENNIAL COMMISSION; 916 W CLARK; CHAMPAIGN, IL 61820. (#50422-1).

JUNE 28 - JULY 6, '75. HEARTLAND HERITAGE DAYS OF CHAMPAIGN COUNTY FESTIVAL. DAY-LONG FESTIVAL OF EVENTS DEDICATED TO HERITAGE, FELLOWSHIP & FUN. AT CITYWIDE. (LOCAL). G T HARDWICK, EXEC SEC; CHAMPAIGN-URBANA AMERICAN BUSINESS CLUB; CHAMPAIGN, IL 61820. (#50690-1).

SEPT 1, '75 - JUNE 1, '76. HISTORICAL MUSEUM PRESENTS HERITAGE & HORIZONS OF CHAMPAIGN COUNTY. AN ALL-DAY PROGRAM FOR FOURTH GRADE CLASSES, ONCE A WEEK AT THE MUSEUM. EDUCATIONAL DISPLAYS OF FOOD PREPARATION, CRAFTS, DRAMA. AT CHAMPAIGN COUNTY HISTORICAL MUSEUM, 709 W UNIVERSITY. (LOCAL). PATRICIA L MILLER, DIR; CHAMPAIGN COUNTY HISTORICAL MUSEUM; 709 WEST UNIVERSITY; CHAMPAIGN, IL 61820. (#50689-1).

FEB 22 - MAR 21, '76. PAINTING AND SCULPTURE BY MID-WEST FACULTY ARTISTS. EXHIBIT AT KRANNERT ART MUSEUM. (REGN'L). MURIEL B CHRISTISON; KRANNERT ART MUSEUM; INDIANA UNIV ART MUSEUM; UNIV OF ILLINOIS; CHAMPAIGN, IL 61820. (#200016-378).

MAR 8, '76. 'THE BRITISH ARE COMING!' - BRITISH MILITARY BAND PERFORMANCE. TOUR OF MAJOR U S CITIES BY BRITISH MILITARY UNITS AS REPRESENTATIVE OF UNITS INVOLVED IN REVOLUTIONARY WAR CAMPAIGN. AT U OF ILL ASSEMBLY HALL. (INT'L). CHARLES K JONES, PRES; COLUMBIA ARTISTS FESTIVALS CORP; 165 W 57TH ST; NEW YORK, NY 10019. (#6532-33).

APR 2 - 13, '76. WORLD SHORT TRACK SPEED SKATING EVENT. COMPETITION WILL TAKE PLACE IN 2 U S CITIES, CHAMPAIGN, IL AT THE UNIV OF IL ICE ARENA AND WYANDOTTE, MI AT BENJAMIN YALK ARENA; AND IN ST FOY, QUEBEC, CANADA. AT U OF ILLINOIS ICE ARENA, 3RD & GREEN STS; PARKING FREE. (INT'L). BILL MARKLAND, COORD; ILLINOIS OLYMPIC PARK NORTHBROOK & USA AMATEUR SKATING UNION; 803 WILLIAM ST; CHAMPAIGN, IL 61820. (#23318-1).

APR 4 - MAY 2, '76. NATIONAL INVITATIONAL CRAFTS EXHIBITION, '76. EXHIBIT AT KRANNERT ART MUSEUM. (NAT'L). MURIEL B CHRISTISON; UNIV OF ILLINOIS; KRANNERT ART MUSEUM; CHAMPAIGN, IL 61820. (#200016-379).

JUNE 1 - SEPT 30, '76. BICENT MAILBOX COMPETITION IN CHAMPAIGN, ILLINOIS. DESIGN & PAINTING OF RURAL MAILBOXES TO FIT IN WITH BICENT THEMES PRIZES WILL BE AWARDED FOR BEST ENTRIES. (LOCAL). MRS MICHAEL THOMPSON; CHAMPAIGN COUNTY BICENT COMMISSION; 1103 HARRINGTON DR; CHAMPAIGN, IL 61820. (#8762-1).

JUNE 26, '76. DEDICATION OF BELL CLOCK. CEREMONY. (LOCAL). JEANNE ROCHFORD, CHMN; CHAMPAIGN COUNTY BICENTENNIAL COMMISSION; 1103 HARRINGTON DR; CHAMPAIGN, IL 61820. (#200016-180).

JULY 1 - 3, '76. 'JUST OUTSIDE CHICAGO THERE'S A PLACE CALLED ILLINOIS'. LIVE PERFORMANCE AT KRANNERT CENTER. (LOCAL). JEANNE ROCHFORD, CHMN; CHAMPAIGN COUNTY BICENTENNIAL COMMISSION; 1103 HARRINGTON DR; CHAMPAIGN, IL 61820. (#200016-170).

JULY 1 - 5, '76. GARDEN COMPETITION IN CHAMPAIGN, ILLINOIS. A GARDEN COMPETITION WILL BE HELD, WITH PRIZES GIVEN FOR THE BEST COLONIAL AND RED/WHITE/BLUE GARDENS. ALSO: NATURAL AREA/PARK/PLANTING. (LOCAL). JEANNE ROCHFORD, CHAIRMAN; CHAMPAIGN COUNTY BICENT COMMISSION; 1103 HARRINGTON DR; CHAMPAIGN, IL 61820. (#8766-1).

JULY 4, '76. AMERICA'S BIRTHDAY PARTY WITH EVERYONE BRINGING A BIRTHDAY CAKE. FESTIVAL AT SCOTT PARK. (LOCAL). JEANNE ROCHFORD, CHAIRMAN; CHAMPAIGN COUNTY BICENTENNIAL COMMISSION; 1103 HARRINGTON DR; CHAMPAIGN, IL 61820. (#105207-1).

JULY 4, '76. MASS FREEDOM RING AT BEGINNING OF 4TH OF JULY PARADE. PARADE AT CITYWIDE. (LOCAL). JEANNE ROCHFORD; BICENT COMMISSION OF CHAMPAIGN COUNTY; 1103 HARRINGTON DR; CHAMPAIGN, IL 61820. (#50412-1).

JULY 24 - 31, '76. MINI EXPOSITION AT COUNTY FAIR. EXHIBIT AT CHAMPAIGN COUNTY FAIRGROUNDS. (LOCAL). NELLIE HAYS, CHAIRMAN; GREATER CHAMPAIGN CO FAIR; CHAMPAIGN COUNTY BICENT COMMISSION; 1408 W SPRINGFIELD; CHAMPAIGN, IL 61820. (#105207-3).

JULY '76. POPCORN FESTIVAL, BRING TOGETHER POPCORN WAGONS. BRING TOGETHER POPCORN WAGONS FROM ALL OVER US. (ST-WIDE). JEANNE ROCHFORD, CHMN; CHAMPAIGN COUNTY BICENT COMMISSION; 1103 HARRINGTON; CHAMPAIGN, IL 61820. (#50688-1).

SEPT 1 - 30, '76. ILLINOIS BICENTENNIAL COMMISSION TRAVELING EXHIBIT ON LABOR. EXHIBIT, TOUR. (LOCAL). JEANNE ROCHFORD, CHMN; CHAMPAIGN COUNTY BICENTENNIAL COMMISSION; 1103 HARRINGTON DR; CHAMPAIGN, IL 61820. (#200016-169).

SEPT 1, '76 - MAY 31, '77. HISTORICAL MUSEUM PRESENTS HERITAGE & HORIZONS OF CHAMPAIGN COUNTY. ALL-DAY PROGRAM FOR FOURTH GRADE CLASSES, ONCE A WEEK AT THE MUSEUM. EDUCATIONAL DISPLAYS OF FOOD PREPARATION, CRAFTS, DRAMA. AT CHAMPAIGN COUNTY HISTORICAL MUSEUM, 709 W UNIVERSITY. (LOCAL). PATRICIA L MILLER; CHAMPAIGN COUNTY HISTORICAL MUSEUM; 709 WEST UNIVERSITY; CHAMPAIGN, IL 61820. (#108856-1).

NOV 11, '76. DEDICATION OF BONEYARD SCULPTURE. CEREMONY. (LOCAL). JEANNE ROCHFORD, CHMN; CHAMPAIGN BICENTENNIAL COMMISSION; 1103 HARRINGTON DR; CHAMPAIGN, IL 61820. (#109479-1).

NOV 11, '76. LONDON PHILHARMONIC ORCHESTRA VISITS CHAMPAIGN, IL. LIVE PERFORMANCE AT KRANNERT CITY. (INT'L). CULTURAL AFFAIRS OFFICE; BRITISH EMBASSY; 3100 MASSACHUSETTS AVE, NW; WASHINGTON, DC 20008. (#108958-4).

NOV 25, '76. TIME CAPSULE IN CHAMPAIGN, ILLINOIS. A TIME CAPSULE, TO BE OPENED IN 100 YEARS, WILL BE BURIED WITH ITEMS CHARACTERISTIC OF THE LAST 200 YEARS IN AMERICA. ALSO: PROGRAM FACILITATION. (LOCAL). SARA ANDREWS; CHAMPAIGN COUNTY BICENT COMMISSION; 408 WEST FLORIDA; URBANA, IL 61801. (#8765-1).

NOV '76. TRUNK TALES: A MUSICAL REVUE WITH ORIGINAL SCRIPT. LIVE PERFORMANCE AT THE VIRGINIA THEATRE. (LOCAL). HARRIET BROWN, CHAIRMAN; CHAMPAIGN COUNTY BICENTENNIAL COMMISSION; 1701 GOLF VIEW; URBANA, IL 61801. (#105207-5).

CHANUTE AFB

JOHNNY HORIZON '76 - CHANUTE AFB, IL. 'LETS CLEAN UP AMERICA FOR OUR 200TH BIRTHDAY' CHANUTE WILL BECOME A JOHNNY HORIZON SPONSOR. VOLUNTEER STUDENTS WILL ASSIST IN CLEANUP PROGRAMS; DECALS, BUMPTER STICKERS, ETC WILL BE BOUGHT AND SOLD. (LOCAL). MARIAN RHORA, DIRECTOR; 3345TH AIR BASE GROUP; SSRS/STOP 96; CHANUTE AFB, IL 61866. (#21100).

MAY 15, '76. 'PACESETTER' MALL DEDICATION. PREVIOUSLY UNUSED AREA IS BEING TURNED INTO A LARGE MALL AREA FOR USE OF ALL BASE PEOPLE; WILL CONTAIN A LARGE SCULPTURE, TREES AND FLAGS OF ALL STATES. (LOCAL). MAJOR DOUGLAS K RHODES; CHANUTE TECHNICAL TRAINING CENTER; OI STOP 7; CHANUTE AFB, IL 61868. (#21101-1).

JUNE 5 - 27, '76. 'FAREWELL CENTURY 2'. THE MONTH-LONG FESTIVAL WILL FEATURE MUSIC, A PARADE AND CRAFTS. (LOCAL). MARIAN RHORA, PROJ CHMN; CHANUTE AIR FORCE BASE; SSRS STOP 96; CHANUTE AFB, IL 61866. (#20881-1).

CHARLESTON

FOLK ARTS PROJECT - CHARLESTON, IL. FIELD INVESTIGATION OF FOLK ARTISTS, MUSICIANS, VISUAL ARTISTS AND TRADITIONAL CRAFTSMEN. TAPE RECORDINGS AND PHOTOGRAPHS UTILIZED TO PRESERVE ARTIST'S WORKS. (LOCAL). VAUGHN JAENIKE, DEAN; EASTERN ILLINOIS UNIV, SCHOOL OF FINE ARTS; CHARLESTON, IL 61920. (#28535).

GREENWOOD SCHOOL MUSEUM RESTORATION, IL. RESTORATION OF GREENWOOD SCHOOL EDUCATIONAL HISTORICAL MUSEUM. (LOCAL). DANIEL THORNBURGH, DIRECTOR; JOURNALISM STUDIES, EASTERN ILLINOIS UNIVERSITY; CHARLESTON, IL 61920. (#27527). **ARBA GRANTEE.**

LIBERTY BELL REPLICA - CHARLESTON, IL. PURCHASE OF REPRODUCTION OF THE LIBERTY BELL FOR THE CHARLESTON CITY PARK. (LOCAL). BETTY BOYER, CHAIRMAN; CHARLESTON BICENTENNIAL COMMISSION; BOX 250; CHARLESTON, IL 61920. (#30403).

RENOVATION OF GREENWOOD SCHOOL, CHARLESTON, IL. RENOVATION OF GREENWOOD SCHOOL, BUILT IN THE 1800'S ON EASTERN ILLINOIS UNIVERSITY LAND. (LOCAL). VAUGH JOENIKE, DEAN SCHOOL OF FINE ARTS; EASTERN ILLINOIS UNIV & COLES COUNTY HISTORICAL SOCIETY; CHARLESTON, IL 61920. (#22482).

FEB 27 - MAR 8, '76. '1776'. LIVE PERFORMANCE AT FINE ARTS THEATRE. (LOCAL). E G GABBARD, CHAIRMAN; EASTERN ILLINOIS UNIVERSITY - THEATRE ARTS DEPARTMENT; CHARLESTON, IL 61920. (#106019-3).

APR 25, '76. SYMPHONIC WINDS CONCERTS. LIVE PERFORMANCE. (LOCAL). RHODERICK KEY, CHAIRMAN; MUSIC DEPARTMENT - EASTERN ILLINOIS UNIVERSITY; CHARLESTON, IL 61920. (#106019-2).

CHARLESTON — CONTINUED

AUG 1 - 8, '76. CRAFT MULTIPLES. EXHIBIT. (LOCAL). BETTY BOYER, CHMN; EASTERN ILLINOIS UNIV; BOX 250; CHARLESTON, IL 61920. (#200016-90).

SEPT 5 - OCT 16, '76. BICENTENNIAL REGIONAL EXHIBITION. EXHIBITION OF PAINTINGS, DRAWINGS, PRINTS, CERAMICS & SCULPTURE. SUNDAY HOURS: 1-4 PM. AT PAUL SARGENT GALLERY, EASTERN ILLINOIS UNIV. (LOCAL). JOHN LINN, CHAIRMAN; SCHOOL OF FINE ARTS, EASTERN ILLINOIS UNIVERSITY; CHARLESTON, IL 61920. (#106019-1).

OCT 22 - 31, '76. 'TOM PAINE' BY PAUL FOSTER. LIVE PERFORMANCE AT FINE ARTS THEATRE. (LOCAL). E G GABBARD, CHAIRMAN; EASTERN ILLINOIS UNIVERSITY - THEATRE ARTS DEPT; CHARLESTON, IL 61920. (#106019-4).

APR 21 - 24, '77. ART FESTIVAL FEATURING FOLK MUSIC, CRAFTS AND VISUAL ARTS. EXHIBIT, FESTIVAL. (LOCAL). VAUGHN JAENIKE; EASTERN ILLINOIS UNIV; CHARLESTON, IL 61920. (#28535-1).

CHEBANSE

BICENTENNIAL PROJECTS - CHEBANSE, IL. ARBOR DAY TREE PLANTINGF FLAG CONTEST; HISTORY FO THE VILLAGE COMPILED; FIRE HYDRANT PAINTING CONTEST. (LOCAL). LINDA SADLER, CHAIRMAN; VILLAGE OF CHEBANSE; CHEBANSE, IL 60922. (#33703).

SEPT 17 - 19, '76. BICENTENNIAL & HOMECOMING CELEBRATION. AMONG THE ACTIVITIES WERE A PARADE, HISTORICAL DISPLAY, FLAG DEDICATION AND FARM MACHINERY DISPLAY. (LOCAL). LINDA SADLER; CHEBANSE BICENT COMMITTEE; CHEBANSE, IL 60922. (#200016-349).

CHESTER

CATALOGING SOURCE MATERIAL OF RANDOLPH COUNTY, IL. RECORDS CONCERNING MATERIAL DATING BACK TO 1703 INCLUDING: TERRITORIAL, PRE-REVOLUTION, REVOLUTIONARY, LOUISIANA PURCHASE, INDENTURED PAPERS & MANY OTHERS WILL BE CATALOGUED. (LOCAL). GENEVIEVE J RAINEY, COORDINATOR; RANDOLPH COUNTY BICENTENNIAL COMMISSION; CHESTER, IL 62233. (#19496). **ARBA GRANTEE.**

HIGHWAY SIGN - CHESTER, IL. A HIGHWAY SIGN WILL TELL OF HISTORIC LOCATIONS IN RANDOLPH COUNTY. (LOCAL). THEDA RIPPERDAN, CHAIRMAN; XI UPSILON CHAPTER OF BETA SIGMA PHI; RR 1; CHESTER, IL 62233. (#25114).

STATUE OF POPEYE IN CHESTER, IL. ELZIE SEGAR, THE CREATOR OF POPEYE, WAS BORN & GREW TO ADULTHOOD IN CHESTER. THE POPEYE & OLIVE OIL CHARACTERS ARE BASED ON ACTUAL PEOPLE OF CHESTER. A 5' BRONZE STATUE OF POPEYE WILL BE BUILT. (NAT'L). THEDA RIPPERDAN, CHAIRMAN OF POPEYE; XI UPSILON CHAPTER OF BETA SIGMA PHI; 1405 COURT; CHESTER, IL 62233. (#23215).

CHICAGO

AFRICAN CULTURAL EXCHANGE IN CHICAGO, IL. ARTIST IN RESIDENCE FROM WEST AFRICA TO WORK WITH AMERICANS IN CULTURAL LEARNING AND SHARING IN AREAS OF ART, MUSIC, DANCE & WRITING. (ST-WIDE). JOHN P BROWN, ADMINISTRATOR; EBONY TALENT CREATIVE ARTS FOUNDATION; 8949 S STONY ISLAND AVE; CHICAGO, IL 60617. (#10835).

AMERICA & THE ENVIRONMENTAL CHALLENGE, CHICAGO, IL. A RESEARCH AND PUBLIC EDUCATION PROJECT, CALLING FOR PROFESSIONALLY CONDUCTED SYMPOSIA TO PROBE AMERICA'S ROLE IN THE CHANGING INTERNATIONAL ENVIRONMENT. (REGN'L). FRANK BAILEN, DIRECTOR; DE PAUL UNIVERSITY; 2323 N SEMINARY AVE; CHICAGO, IL 60614. (#11798).

THE AMERICAN PROMISE - CHICAGO, IL. FOLDER WITH REPRODUCTIONS OF DECLARATION OF INDEPENDENCE AND OTHER DOCUMENTS AS WELL AS A BOOKLET ABOUT THEM. (NAT'L). RICHARD E KOZITKA, EMPLOYEE COMMUNICATIONS DIR; QUAKER OATS COMPANY; MERCHANDISE MART; CHICAGO, IL 60654. (#23411).

THE AMERICAN REPUBLIC: 1776-1976 - CHICAGO, IL. POLITICAL SCIENCE COURSE ON THE AMERICAN SEARCH FOR POLITICAL IDENTITY; 3 CREDIT HOURS. (LOCAL). SAM C SARKESIAN, CHAIRMAN; LOYOLA UNIV; 6525 N SHERIDAN RD; CHICAGO, IL 60626. (#19242).

AMERICAN SPIRITUALITY, PAST AND PRESENT - IL. A THREE CREDIT HOUR COURSE THAT WILL BEGIN IN FEB OF 1976. GIVEN BY PROFESSORS: RICHARD WOODS, ROBERT BARRY & JON ALEXANDER. (LOCAL). JEROME O'LEARY, INSTITUTE OF PASTORAL; LOYOLA UNIVERSITY; 6525 N SHERIDAN RD; CHICAGO, IL 60626. (#19240).

'AMERICA'S INVENTIVE GENIUS'. THREE-PART EXHIBIT AND PROGRAM ON HISTORY AND CONTRIBUTIONS OF AMERICAN SCIENCE, TECHNOLOGY & INDUSTRY DURING NATION'S FIRST 200 YEARS. THE PROJECT WILL CONSIST OF 2 EXHIBIT SECTIONS & A THEATER PROGRAM. (NAT'L). DR VICTOR J DANILOV, MUSEUM DIRECTOR; MUSEUM OF SCIENCE AND INDUSTRY; 57TH ST & LAKE SHORE DR; CHICAGO, IL 60637. (#5). **ARBA RECOGNIZED. ARBA GRANTEE.**

APPEARANCE OF FLOATING MUSEUM, CHICAGO, IL. SCHEDULED APPEARANCE OF SGT FLOYD IM 14 CITIES ALONG ILLINOIS RIVER: JULY 16, 1976, THRU AUGUST 20, 1976. (ST-WIDE). FERD STAUCH, PUBLIC AFFAIRS OFFICER; CHICAGO DISTRICT U S A CORPS OF ENGINEERS; 219 S DEARBORN; CHICAGO, IL 60604. (#29718).

ARCHICENTER - CHICAGO, IL. ARCHITECTURAL TOUR & INFORMATION CENTER WILL FEATURE EXHIBITS, TOURS, FILM & SLIDE PRESENTATIONS AND SPECIAL EVENTS TO CELEBRATE THE ARCHITECTURAL HERITAGE OF CHICAGO & ILLINOIS. (LOCAL). VICTORIA MATRANGA, ARCHICENTER DIRECTOR; CHICAGO SCHOOL OF ARCHITECTURE FOUNDATION; 111 S DEARBORN ST; CHICAGO, IL 60603. (#25690). **ARBA GRANTEE.**

ARCHITECTURE OF DEMOCRACY - CHICAGO, IL. TWO MEDIATED SHOWS ON THE HISTORY OF CHICAGO ARCHITECTURE WITH OUTSTANDING EXAMPLES OF MASTERPIECES OF THE CHICAGO SCHOOL OF ARCHITECTURE BY CROMBIE TAYLOR, FAIA. (ST-WIDE). ALEXIA LALLI, DIRECTOR; ILLINOIS ARTS COUNCIL; 111 N WABASH AVE; CHICAGO, IL 60602. (#25739). **ARBA GRANTEE.**

ARTISTIC EXPRESSIONS OF CONTRIBUTIONS TO AMERICA. A 28 DAY PANORAMIC DISPLAY OF ARTISTIC WORKS SHOWING THE ROLE OF BLACKS, LATINOS & NATIVE AMERICANS IN ESTABLISHING THE NATION'S BEGINNINGS. (ST-WIDE). GLENICE B PEARSON, DEAN OF UNIVERSITY SERVICES; DANIEL HALE WILLIAMS UNIV; 5414 W MADISON ST; CHICAGO, IL 60644. (#8421).

ATLAS OF THE AMERICAN REVOLUTION PROJECT OF IL. ONE VOLUME ATLAS OF AMERICAN REVOLUTION. WILL PORTRAY GRAPHICALLY MAJOR MILITARY, POLITICAL, ECONOMIC, INTELLECTUAL, & SOCIAL DEVELOPMENTS. FIRST OF PROJECTED SERIES OF ENTIRE EARLY AMERICAN HISTORY. (NAT'L). DR LESTER J CAPPON, PROJECT DIRECTOR; NEWBERRY LIBRARY; 60 W WALTON; CHICAGO, IL 60610. (#536).

AYER INDIAN ART PROJECT OF CHICAGO. PRESERVATION OF COLLECTION OF PRINTS AND DRAWINGS OF OR BY INDIANS OF THE AMERICAS. (NAT'L). PAUL N BANKS, CONSERVATOR; THE NEWBERRY LIBRARY; 60 W WALTON ST; CHICAGO, IL 60610. (#2257).

BEVERLY HILLS/MORGAN PARK, ILL, COMMUNITY CENTER. RENOVATION & EQUIPPING OF DRISCOLL HOUSE-A MANSION DONATED TO BEVERLEY HILLS/MORGAN PARK COMMUNITY, IN CHICAGO, ILL.,--FOR USE AS COMMUNITY, CULTURAL, AND SOCIAL CENTER. (LOCAL). ROBERT J WHITE, PRESIDENT; RIDGE HISTORICAL SOCIETY; 10621 S SEELEY AVE; CHICAGO, IL 60643. (#879). **ARBA GRANTEE.**

BIBLIOGRAPHY OF FRENCH IN OLD NORTHWEST. COMPUTERIZED CRITICAL BIBLIOGRAPHY OF FRENCH SOURCES THAT CONTAIN INFORMATION ON FRENCH IN EARLY AMERICA, PARTICULARLY THE OLD NORTHWEST, WHICH INCLUDED PRESENT-DAY ILLINOIS. (INT'L). DR ANDREW J TORRIELLI, DEPT OF MODERN LANGUAGES; LOYOLA UNIV, CHICAGO; 6525 N SHERIDAN RD; CHICAGO, IL 60626. (#885). **ARBA GRANTEE.**

BICENTENNIAL BROCHURE IN BRAILLE, CHICAGO, IL. THE IL BICENT COMMISSION, IN COOPERATION WITH THE NATL FEDERATION OF THE BLIND & BLIND SERVICES ASSOC HAS PUBLISHED 'AMER REVOL BICENT' IN BRAILLE, WHICH CONTAINS INFORMATION ON BICENT CELEBRATION IN IL. (ST-WIDE). CAROL L SILVERMAN, PGM COORDINATOR; ILLINOIS BICENTENNIAL COMMISSION; 410 N MICHIGAN AVE, SUITE 1044; CHICAGO, IL 60611. (#16714).

BICENTENNIAL GARDEN AT CHICAGO STATE UNIV. THE GARDEN WILL CONTAIN FLORA FROM AROUND THE WORLD AS A TRIBUTE TO THE DIVERSE ETHNIC COMPOSITION OF THE SCHOOL. (LOCAL). DR ROBERT J KOVARIK, EXEC OFFICER; CHICAGO STATE UNIV BICENTENNIAL COMMISSION; 95 AT RING DR; CHICAGO, IL 60628. (#13600).

BICENTENNIAL ORIENTATION CENTER IN CHICAGO, ILL. A MULTILINGUAL, MULTI-MEDIA ORIENTATION GALLERY DESCRIBING THE MUSEUM'S BICENTENNIAL PROGRAM ON 'AMERICA'S INVENTIVE GENIUS' AND OTHER MUSEUM ATTRACTIONS FOR FOREIGN VISITORS. (REGN'L). VICTOR J DANILOV, DIRECTOR; MUSEUM OF SCIENCE AND INDUSTRY; 57TH ST AND LAKE SHORE DR; CHICAGO, IL 60637. (#4804).

BICENTENNIAL PAMPHLETS, MAPS, CHARTS & BROCHURES. EDUCATIONAL PAMPHLETS, MAPS, CHARTS, BROCHURES. ARBA LICENSE NO. 76-19-0526. (NAT'L). BERNARD SLEPAK, PROJ DIRECTOR; CREATIVE MERCHANDISERS, INC; 61 W SUPERIOR ST; CHICAGO, IL 60610. (#6871).

BICENTENNIAL PLAQUES. PLAQUES BEARING THE BICENTENNIAL SYMBOL ARBA LICENSE NO 76-19-0613. (LOCAL). EDWARD ZIMBROFF, PRESIDENT; FULCRUM MARKETING ENTERPRISES, INC; 6 W RANDOLPH; CHICAGO, IL 60601. (#22785).

BICENTENNIAL THEOLOGIES, CHICAGO, IL. GRADUATE SEMINAR EXAMINING ENDURING ASPECTS OF EARLY U S THEOLOGIES AND THEIR INFLUENCE ON THE AMERICAN ETHOS. (LOCAL). EARL WEISS, CHAIRMAN; LOYOLA UNIV; 6525 N SHERIDAN RD; CHICAGO, IL 60626. (#19241).

BLACK AND OTHER MINORITY SCIENTISTS' CONTRIBUTIONS TO AMERICA. SPONSOR PLANS INCOMPLETE AS OF 04/28/75. AT 5414 WEST MADISON STREET. (REGN'L). GLENICE B PEARSON; DANIEL HALE WILLIAMS UNIVERSITY; 5414 WEST MADISON STREET; CHICAGO, IL 60644. (#50733-5). **(??).**

BLACK BICENTENNIAL CELEBRATION IN CHICAGO. FESTIVAL IN CHICAGO. (LOCAL). ALDEN LAWSON; THE WOODLAWN ORGANIZATION; 1180 E 83RD ST; CHICAGO, IL 60637. (#27668). **ARBA GRANTEE.**

BLACK EXPERIENCE IN AMERICA ESSAY SERIES. SIX SCHOLARLY ESSAYS ON BLACK EXPERIENCE IN AMERICA. 2 ON RELIGION, & TWO ON INFLUENCE OF BLACK EXPERIENCE ON AMERICA. ESSAYS WILL BE DISTRIBUTED TO NEWSPAPERS AND PUBLISHED AS A BOOK. (NAT'L). WILLIAM L TIBBS, CHAIRMAN/TREASURER; ROUNDTABLE FOR AFRICAN-AMERICAN HISTORY; 7700 S CHAPPEL AVE; CHICAGO, IL 60649. (#877). **(??). ARBA GRANTEE.**

BOOK 'UNCLE SAM: THE MAN AND THE LEGEND', IL. STORY BEHIND THE UNCLE SAM SYMBOL. BIOGRAPHY OF UNCLE SAM WILSON AND IMPACT ON OUR NATION. AUTHOR - ALTON KETCHUM. (NAT'L). HARRY G BROHEN, STAFF VICE PRESIDENT; NATIONAL ASSOCIATION OF REALTORS; 155 E SUPERIOR ST; CHICAGO, IL 60611. (#23199).

BROCHURE ON ILLINOIS HISTORICAL SITES - IL. A 24-PAGE HISTORICAL SITES BROCHURE WITH MAPS AND PHOTOGRAPHS OF HISTORICAL SITES THROUGHOUT THE STATE. (ST-WIDE). JOSEPH PISCIOTTE, DIRECTOR; ILLINOIS DEPT OF BUSINESS AND ECONOMIC DEVELOPMENT; 205 WACKER DR; CHICAGO, IL 60606. (#17866). **ARBA GRANTEE.**

CATHOLIC SCHOOLS WEEK & BICENTENNIAL CONVENTION. A CELEBRATION OF THE BICENTENNIAL THROUGH A SPECIAL WEEK-LONG OBSERVANCE OF OUR AMERICAN CATHOLIC HERITAGE, CULMINATING IN A 4-DAY CONVENTION AND EXPOSITION. (NAT'L). JOSEPH O'DONNELL, VICE PRESIDENT, BUSINESS AFFAIRS; NATIONAL CATHOLIC EDUCATIONAL ASSOC; SUITE 350, ONE DUPONT CIR; WASHINGTON, DC 20036. (#13686).

CHEYENNE INDIAN WARRIORS & ARTISTS BOOK. A HISTORY OF THE ROLE OF THE CHIEFS AND MILITARY SOCIETIES IN NORTHERN CHEYENNE LIFE AND ART, 1830-1970. (NAT'L). FR PETER J POWELL, PROF DIRECTOR; ST AUGUSTINE'S CENTER FOR AMERICAN INDIANS, INC; 4512 N SHERIDAN RD; CHICAGO, IL 60640. (#4935).

CHICAGO HISTORICAL SOCIETY FIFE & DRUM CORPS. THIRTY PERSON FIFE & DRUM CORPS TO PERFORM AUTHENTIC PERIOD MUSIC AT LOCAL, STATE, & NATIONAL CEREMONIAL FUNCTIONS, PARADES, SPECIAL EVENTS, ETC. (REGN'L). CHRISTINE ROSE, DIRECTOR; CHICAGO HISTORICAL SOCIETY; NORTH AVE & CLARK ST; CHICAGO, IL 60614. (#891). **ARBA GRANTEE.**

CHICAGO INTERNATIONAL TRADE EXPOSITION, IL. THE PROJECT WILL PORTRAY HISTORY AND IMPORTANCE OF WORLD TRADE TO THE NATION & CHICAGO'S ROLE IN WORLD TRADE; THERE WILL BE EXHIBITS FROM U S AND FOREIGN COMPANIES ON TRADE AND ECONOMIC DEVELOPMENT. (INT'L). THOMAS COULTER, CHIEF EXECUTIVE OFFICER; CHICAGO ASSOC OF COMMERCE AND INDUSTRY; 130 S MICHIGAN AVE; CHICAGO, IL 60603. (#18314). **ARBA RECOGNIZED.**

CHICAGO SCHOOL OF ARCHITECTURE STUDY. PROJECT OF MANY DISCIPLINES DESIGNED TO CELEBRATE AND PROMOTE THE PRESERVATION OF FINE EXAMPLES OF THE CHICAGO SCHOOL OF ARCHITECTURE IN CHICAGO AND THROUGHOUT ILLINOIS. (ST-WIDE). PAULA PROKIPOFF, PROJECT COORDINATOR; ILLINOIS ARTS COUNCIL; 111 N WABASH; CHICAGO, IL 60602. (#5183).

COAL MINING & PROCESSING MAGAZINE JULY ISSUE-NBMRP. FOR JULY, 1976 THE MAGAZINE PUBLISHED SPECIAL BICENTENNIAL EDITION WITH AN EDUCATIONAL, HISTORICAL & COMMEMORATIVE THEME. (NAT'L). PERRY KING, BICENTENNIAL COORDINATOR; COAL MINING & PROCESSING MAGAZINE; 300 W ADAMS ST; CHICAGO, IL 60606. (#28522).

CONTEST - UNCLE SAM: THE MAN AND THE LEGEND. ESSAY, DRAWING OR PAINTING, OR MUSIC ON UNCLE SAM, TO REAWAKEN INTEREST IN UNCLE SAM AS A TRUE AND LASTING SYMBOL OF THE LAND. (LOCAL). HARRY G BROHEN, V PRES; NATIONAL ASSOC OF REALTORS; 155 E SUPERIOR ST; CHICAGO, IL 60611. (#106419-1). **(??).**

CONTRIBUTIONS OF MINORITY SCIENTISTS TO AMER - EXH. SCIENCE DISPLAYS TO BE SET UP IN VARIOUS LOW INCOME AREAS DURING A THIRTY DAY PERIOD OF EMPHASIS. VOLUNTEERS WILL BE USED TO MAN THE EXHIBITS SO THAT QUESTIONS CAN BE RESPONDED TO FORTHRIGHTLY. (LOCAL). GLENICE B PEARSON, DEAN, UNIVERSITY SERVICES; DANIEL HALE WILLIAMS UNIV; 5414 W MADISON ST; CHICAGO, IL 60644. (#8427).

CULTURAL & RECREATIONAL FACILITIES PROGRAM IN IL. COMMUNITY CULTURAL AND RECREATIONAL FACILITIES DEVELOPMENT PROGRAM OF ILLINOIS - A STATEWIDE PROGRAM. (ST-WIDE). MICHAEL LINDERMAN, EXEC DIRECTOR; ILLINOIS BICENTENNIAL COMMISSION; 410 N MICHIGAN (1044); CHICAGO, IL 60611. (#22842). **ARBA GRANTEE.**

DEDICATION OF DANIEL HALE WILLIAMS UNIV IN CHICAGO. THE FIRST CONVOCATION AND DEDICATION OF THE DANIEL HALE WILLIAMS UNIVERSITY, MARKING ANOTHER SIGNIFICANT ACHIEVEMENT OF BLACK AMERICANS TO THIS NATION. (ST-WIDE). GLENICE B PEARSON, DEAN UNIVERSITY SERVICES; DANIEL HALE WILLIAMS UNIV; 5414 W MADISON ST; CHICAGO, IL 60644. (#8422).

DOCUMENTARY FILM ON ENVIRONMENTAL ISSUES. EXHIBIT AT FIELD MUSEUM OF NATURAL HISTORY. (LOCAL). MS JORY GRAHAM; FIELD MUSEUM OF NATURAL HISTORY; E ROOSEVELT RD; CHICAGO, IL 60605. (#7979-4).

ECUMENICAL SERVICES FOR NATL SPIRITUAL RENEWAL, IL. SERVICES BASED ON A DETERMINATION TO BEGIN THE NEXT 100 YEARS OF U S HISTORY IN A WAY THAT WILL GUARANTEE GROWTH AS A NATION DEVOTED TO GOD AND JUSTICE. (ST-WIDE). GLENICE B PEARSON, DEAN UNIVERSITY SERVICES; DANIEL HALE WILLIAMS UNIV; 5414 W MADISON ST; CHICAGO, IL 60644. (#8420).

EXHIBIT ON MEDICAL CENTER AT UNIV OF ILLINOIS. THREE PART EXHIBIT TRACING PAST DEVELOPMENT, PRESENT STATUS & FUTURE GROWTH OF THE UNIVERSITY OF ILLINOIS MEDICAL CENTER. (ST-WIDE). IRWIN PIZER, UNIVERSITY LIBRARIAN; UNIV OF ILLINOIS AT THE MEDICAL CENTER; 1750 W POLK ST; CHICAGO, IL 60612. (#8431).

FAITH AND FORM: SYNAGOGUE ARCHITECTURE - IL. PHOTOGRAPHIC EXHIBITION ON HISTORY OF SYNAGOGUE ARCHITECTURE. (ST-WIDE). ARTHUR FELDMAN, DIRECTOR; SPERTUS MUSEUM; 618 S MICHIGAN; CHICAGO, IL 60605. (#27737). **ARBA GRANTEE.**

CHICAGO — CONTINUED

FEDERAL ART PROJECT - FILM IN CHICAGO, ILLINOIS. A DOCUMENTARY FILM WILL BE MADE ON THE MURALS AND OTHER WORKS DONE BY ARTISTS OF THE ILLINOIS ART PROJECT OF THE W P A DURING THE DEPRESSION OF THE 1930'S. (NAT'L). BARBARA BERNSTEIN, PROJECT DIRECTOR; PUBLIC ART WORKSHOP; 5623 W MADISON ST; CHICAGO, IL 60644. (#6588).

FIFTH CITY COMMUNITY REFORMULATION PROJECT, IL. COMMUNITY REDEVELOPMENT IN ALL AREAS OF COMMUNITY ACTIVITIES; ECONOMIC AND SOCIAL EMPHASIS ON HUMAN VALUE AND UNDERSTANDING. (LOCAL). MRS LELA MOSLEY, COORDINATOR; FIFTH CITY CHICAGO COMMUNITY REFORMULATION CORPORATION; 3444 W CONGRESS PKWY; CHICAGO, IL 60624. (#20111).

FILM ON UNCLE SAM: THE MAN AND THE LEGEND - IL. 16MM FILM ON STORY BEHIND UNCLE SAM SYMBOL AND THE MAN WHO INSPIRED IT SAMUEL WILSON; TREASURE OF HISTORIC AMERICAN SCENES; NARRATED BY E G MARSHALL. (ST-WIDE). HARRY G BROHEN, PROJ DIRECTOR; NATIONAL ASSOCIATION OF REALTORS; 155 E SUPERIOR ST; CHICAGO, IL 60611. (#23200).

FILM SERIES AT THE UNIV OF ILLINOIS MEDICAL CENTER. FEATURE FILMS WITH HISTORICAL THEMES. (LOCAL). IRWIN PIZER, UNIVERSITY LIBRARIAN; UNIV OF ILLINOIS AT THE MEDICAL CENTER; 1750 W POLK ST; CHICAGO, IL 60612. (#8434).

FILM SHOWINGS & BOOK PRESENTATIONS, CHICAGO, IL. THIS IS A CONTINUIOUS PROJECT INCLUDING, FILM SHOWINGS, BOOK PRESENTATIONS AND UNCLE SAM CONTESTS. (LOCAL). HARRY G BROHEN, CHAIRMAN; NATIONAL ASSOCIATION OF REALTORS; 155 E SUPERIOR ST; CHICAGO, IL 60611. (#29990).

FILM: 'A CALL TO ACTION', CHICAGO, IL. OFFICIAL STORY OF AMERICA'S BICENTENNIAL CELEBRATION AVAILABLE ON A MONTH'S NOTICE. (LOCAL). COORDINATOR; ARBA REGIONAL OFFICE; 219 S DEARBORN AVE; CHICAGO, IL 60604. (#28100).

FILM: 'ILLINOIS '76' IN CHICAGO. 13 1/2 MIN COLOR FILM DESIGNED TO ENCOURAGE INDIVIDUAL PARTICIPATION IN BICENTENNIAL. PRESENTS BICENTENNIAL PROJECT IDEAS THROUGH USE OF ANIMATION AND GRAPHICS. (ST-WIDE). PATRICIA INGRAHAM, PUBLIC INFORMATION OFFICER; ILLINOIS BICENTENNIAL COMMISSION; 410 N MICHIGAN, RM 1044; CHICAGO, IL 60611. (#12103).

FOLK SONG CONTEST IN CHICAGO. CONTEST INVOLVES ONE OR MORE ORIGINAL FOLK SONGS CONCERNING ANY ASPECT OF THE HISTORICAL, POLITICAL, SOCIAL OR RELIGIOUS DEVELOPMENT OF AMERICA AS IT RELATES TO ILLINOIS IN THE PAST 300 YEARS. (ST-WIDE). V SCATES, SECRETARY, FINE ARTS DEPT; LOYOLA UNIV; 820 N MICHIGAN; CHICAGO, IL 60611. (#12107).

FREE STREET PROGRAMS - CELEBRATING CREATIVE SPIRIT. VARIETY OF FREE PERF ARTS PROG REACHING APPROX 250 LOCATIONS IN 80 CITIES YEARLY-ACTS AS CATALYST TO CREATIVE LIFE IN THOSE COMMUNITIES STRENGTHENING EXISTING AVENUES OF EXPRESSION & PROMOTING NEW ONES. (NAT'L). PATRICK HENRY, ARTISTIC DIRECTOR; FREE STREET THEATER; 59 W HUBBARD ST; CHICAGO, IL 60610. (#6875). **ARBA RECOGNIZED. ARBA GRANTEE.**

GRAPHICS ARTS MONTHLY JULY 1976 ISSUE - NBMRP. IN-DEPTH TREATMENT BICENT THEME ARTICLES, INCL 'AMERICA'S PATRIOT PRINTERS: CATALYST FOR FREEDOM'; '200 YEARS OF PAPERMAKING PROGRESS' & SIMILAR ARTICLES ON PRINTING INDUSTRY'S ROLE IN HISTORY OF THE US. (NAT'L). B D CHAPMAN, EDITOR; GRAPHIC ARTS MONTHLY; 222 S RIVERSIDE PLAZA; CHICAGO, IL 60606. (#32945).

GROWING OF INDEPENDENCE TREE - CHICAGO, IL. PLANTING OF SAPLING TAKEN FROM GEORGE WASHINGTON'S ESTATE IN MT VERNON, VA & SEEDS PICKED FROM THE INDEPENDENCE TREE, A TREE THAT WAS TRANSPLANTED TO WASHINGTON'S ESTATE BY GEORGE WASHINGTON IN 1785. (LOCAL). JEROMIA H TROFIMUK, PROJ DIRECTOR; COR-WOOD, CHICAGO BICENTENNIAL COMMITTEE; 1850 N WOOD ST; CHICAGO, IL 60622. (#28386).

HIST OF HULL-HOUSE NEIGHBORHOOD ETHNIC GROUPS-IL. AN EXHIBIT TELLING THE HISTORY OF THE OLD HULL-HOUSE NEIGHBORHOOD ON THE NEAR WEST SIDE OF CHICAGO INCLUDING A MODEL OF HULL HOUSE, AN EXHIBIT OF HISTORIC MATERIALS & SLIDE-TAPE PRESENTATIONS. (LOCAL). MARY ANN JOHNSON, ADMINISTRATOR; JANE ADDAMS HULL-HOUSE AT THE UNIV OF ILLINOIS-CHICAGO CIR; BOX 4348; CHICAGO, IL 60680. (#24290). **ARBA GRANTEE.**

HISTORIC CHICAGO RIVER WALK. LANDSCAPED PATH COMMEMORATING SITES OF FOURTEEN HISTORIC STRUCTURES AND EVENTS RELATING TO CHICAGO'S GROWTH AND DEVELOPMENT ALONG THE CHICAGO RIVER FROM 1779 THRU 1915. (ST-WIDE). MARTIN R MURPHY, ASSISTANT COMMISSIONER; CITY OF CHICAGO, DEPT OF DEVELOPMENT & PLANNING; 121 N LASALLE ST ROOM 1000; CHICAGO, IL 60602. (#2161).

HISTORY OF PUBLIC WORKS IN UNITED STATES 1776-1976. PUBLIC WORKS' ROLE IN GROWTH AND DEVELOPMENT OF AMERICAN SOCIETY; AND CONTRIBUTIONS MADE TO NATION'S SOCIAL AND ECONOMIC PROGRESS. (NAT'L). ROBERT D BUGHER, EXEC DIRECTOR; AMERICAN PUBLIC WORKS ASSOC; 1313 W 16TH ST; CHICAGO, IL 60637. (#8614).

HOSPITALITY '76 IN CHICAGO, ILLINOIS. LODGING FOR FOREIGN TOURISTS WITH AMERICAN FAMILIES, CHICAGO AREA ONLY. HOSTS ARE VOLUNTEERS, LODGING IS FREE, ADMINISTRATIVE FEE $15, MAXIMUM LENGTH OF VISIT, 2 DAYS, 2 NIGHTS. (INT'L). ANN K HEALY, PRESIDENT; HOSPITALITY '76; 1173 TOWER RD; WINNETKA, IL 60093. (#8514).

ILLINOIS BICENT COMMISSION COMMEMORATIVE BOOK. A BOOK DISCUSSING THE BICENTENNIAL CELEBRATION IN ILLINOIS. (ST-WIDE). MICHAEL LINDERMAN, EXEC DIRECTOR; ILLINOIS BICENTENNIAL COMMISSION; 410 N MICHIGAN AVE; CHICAGO, IL 60611. (#27795). **ARBA GRANTEE.**

ILLINOIS CELEBRATION '76 IN CHICAGO. TOURIST-RELATED MASS COMMUNICATIONS PROGRAM. (ST-WIDE). MICHAEL LINDERMAN, ASST DIRECTOR; ILL DEPT OF BUSINESS AND ECONOMIC DEVELOPMENT; 205 W WACKER; CHICAGO, IL 60606. (#8181).

ILLINOIS MINORITY BICENTENNIAL SYMPOSIUM FILM. FILM ON ILLINOIS MINORITY BICENTENNIAL SYMPOSIUM IS BEING PRODUCED. PROCEEDINGS OF SYMPOSIUM ARE BEING EDITED FOR PUBLICATION. (ST-WIDE). MRS BEVERLY HURST, COORDINATOR; CHICAGO URBAN LEAGUE; 4500 S MICHIGAN AVE; CHICAGO, IL 60657. (#26880). **ARBA GRANTEE.**

ILLINOIS TEACHER'S RESOURCE GUIDE - CHICAGO. GUIDE WITH IDEAS FOR TEACHING THE BICENTENNIAL IN ILLINOIS. CREATED BY A 38 TEACHER WORKSHOP AND EDITED BY TWO ILLINOIS TEACHERS. (ST-WIDE). PATRICIA INGRAHAM, PUBLIC INFORMATION OFFICER; ILLINOIS BICENTENNIAL COMMISSION; 410 N MICHIGAN, RM 1044; CHICAGO, IL 60611. (#12104).

INFORMATION CENTER IN CHICAGO, IL. MODULAR BUILDING PROVIDING BROCHURES, POSTERS, BINET COMPUTER TERMINAL. JOINT EFFORT: FED GOVT & PRIVATE SECTOR. BLDG FACILITIES & LOCATION DONATED SERVED AS TRAVEL CENTER ALSO. (LOCAL). MICHAEL J LINDERMAN, EXEC DIRECTOR; ILLINOIS BICENTENNIAL COMMISSION; 410 N MICHIGAN AVE; CHICAGO, IL 60611. (#33645).

KENNEDY-KING & BICENT, BLACK ARTS & CULTURAL FAIR. FURTHER INFORMATION MAY BE OBTAINED FROM THE GENERAL CONTACT. (LOCAL). DR H ADRIAN REHNER; KENNEDY-KING COLLEGE; 6800 WENTWORTH; CHICAGO, IL 60621. (#24411). **ARBA GRANTEE.**

LA SALLE EXPEDITION II. AUTHENTIC RE-ENACTMENT OF LA SALLE 1681 EXPEDITION FROM MONTREAL, CANADA TO NEW ORLEANS, LA. (REGN'L). REID H LEWIS, PROJ DIRECTOR; LA SALLE: EXPEDITION II; 135 S LA SALLE ST; CHICAGO, IL 60690. (#8598). **ARBA RECOGNIZED. ARBA GRANTEE.**

LEADING AMERICA INTO THE 20TH CENTURY: CHICAGO. EXHIBIT ON CHICAGE (1876-1926) ARCHITECTURE, CITY PLANNING, LITERATURE, MUSIC, CULTURAL PHILANTHROPY, RETAIL TRADE & COMMERCE & SOCIAL REFORM; & THEIR DISTINCTIVE CONTRIBUTION TO MODERN U S LIFE. (LOCAL). HAROLD SKRAMSTAD, JR, DIRECTOR; THE CHICAGO HISTORICAL SOCIETY; CLARK ST AT NORTH AVE; CHICAGO, IL 60614. (#6238).

'THE MALCOLM X DEBATE', PROJ IN CHICAGO. A DISCUSSION OF MORAL LEADERSHIP FOR KEY NATIONAL INSTITUTIONS THAT WILL COVER A BROAD SPECTRUM OF THE COMMUNITY INCLUDING SCHOOL GROUPS, CHURCHES & CIVIC GROUPS. (LOCAL). GLENICE B PEARSON, DEAN, UNIVERSITY SERVICES; DANIEL HALE WILLIAMS UNIV; 5414 W MADISON ST; CHICAGO, IL 60644. (#8429).

'MAN IN HIS ENVIRONMENT'. ENVIRONMENTAL EDUCATIONAL PROGRAM CONSISTING OF PERMANENT EXHIBIT, TRAVELING EXHIBITS, EDUCATIONAL KITS, LECTURE/FILM SERIES, AIMED AT EDUCATING PEOPLE ON ENVIRONMENTAL PROBLEMS. (NAT'L). ROBERT F INGER, ASST DIRECTOR, SCIENCE & EDUCATION; FIELD MUSEUM OF NATURAL HISTORY; ROOSEVELT RD AT LAKE SHORE DR; CHICAGO, IL 60605. (#7979). **ARBA RECOGNIZED.**

MEMORABILIA FOR THE BICENTENNIAL. LABELS, DECALS, PLACARDS & SIGNS. ARBA LICENSE #76-19-0548. (NAT'L). HARRY FUND, PROJ DIRECTOR; GRAPHIC DIRECTIONS; PO BOX 60105; CHICAGO, IL 60660. (#11469).

MONTGOMERY WARD BICENTENNIAL TOUR & EVENT GUIDES. GUIDE FEATURING HISTORICAL POINTS OF INTEREST, LOCATION OF HOTELS, MOTELS, RESTAURANTS & LOCATION OF MONTGOMERY WARD AUTO CLUB STORES; BICENTENNIAL LICENSE NO 76-19-0575. (NAT'L). RICHARD CREMER, PROJ DIRECTOR; MONTGOMERY WARD AUTO CLUB; 535 W CHICAGO AVE; CHICAGO, IL 60610. (#15339).

MULTI-MEDIA EXHIBIT ON BLACK WOMEN IN CHICAGO, IL. THE EXHIBIT'S FOCUS IN ON VISUAL IMAGES THAT SERVE TO ALLEVIATE & RECTIFY THE MISCONCEPTIONS AND DISTORTIONS IN HISTORY ABOUT BLACK PEOPLE, SPECIFICALLY BLACK WOMEN. (ST-WIDE). VALENCIA HOLLINS COAR, PROJ DIRECTOR; BLACKWOMAN COLLABORATIVE; 5050 LAKE SHORE DR, NO 2701; CHICAGO, IL 60615. (#10878).

'MY BROTHERS' KEEPER' - EXHIBITION IN CHICAGO. EXHIBIT ON JEWISH COMMUNAL CONTRIBUTIONS. (REGN'L). MARCIA JOSEPHY; AMERICAN JEWISH CONGRESS & JEWISH FEDERATION OF METRO CHICAGO; 22 W MONROE ST, SUITE 2102; CHICAGO, IL 60603. (#27666). **ARBA GRANTEE.**

NAMED LECTURE SERIES AT UNIV OF ILLINOIS. BICENTENNIAL THEMES FOR NAMED LECTURES IN ALL COLLEGES OF THE MEDICAL CENTER. (LOCAL). IRWIN PIZER UNIVERSITY LIBRARIAN; UNIV OF ILLINOIS AT THE MEDICAL CENTER; 1750 W POLK ST; CHICAGO, IL 60612. (#8435).

NATL SYMPOSIUM-THE GREEK EXPERIENCE IN AMERICA, IL. SYMPOSIUM WILL PRESENT 24 PAPERS ON ASPECTS OF THE GREEK DIASPORA AND CONTRIBUTION TO THE UNITED STATES BY EXPERTS ON GREEK ETHNICITY. AFTERWARDS, THE PAPERS WILL BE PUBLISHED IN BOOK FORM. (NAT'L). ANDREW T KOPAN, SYMPOSIUM CHAIRMAN; MODERN GREEK STUDIES ASSOC; 1228 ASHLAND AVE; RIVER FOREST, IL 60605. (#24722). **ARBA GRANTEE.**

NEW MODELS OF EDUCATION FOR THE '80'S - CHICAGO. A NATIONAL SYMPOSIUM TO PROPOSE EDUCATIONAL MODELS AT ALL LEVELS FOR THE 1980'S IN THE BELIEF THAT A SOUND & EFFECTIVE EDUCATION IS ONE OF THE PRINCIPLE RIGHTS OF CITIZENSHIP IN A DEMOCRACY. (NAT'L). GLENICE B PEARSON, DEAN, UNIVERSITY SERVICES; DANIEL HALE WILLIAMS UNIV; 5414 W MADISON ST; CHICAGO, IL 60644. (#8426).

ORAL-VIDEO HISTORY OF PULLMAN DISTRICT OF CHICAGO. DOCUMENTARY FILM OF HISTORIC PULLMAN DISTRICT IN CHICAGO, ILL. FILM WILL UTILIZE INTERVIEWS WITH LONG-TIME RESIDENTS, HISTORICAL PHOTOS & DOCUMENTS. WILL BE AVAILABLE FOR NATIONAL DISTRIBUTION. (LOCAL). MICHAEL SHYMANSKI, SECRETARY; HISTORIC PULLMAN FOUNDATION; 614 E 113TH ST; CHICAGO, IL 60628. (#883). **(??). ARBA GRANTEE.**

'OVER A CENTURY OF SERVICE' - CHICAGO STATE UNIV. OBTAIN PARTS OF OLD COLLEGE BUILDING; DISCOVER AND TAPE THE 10 OLDEST ALUMNI AND FACULTY; PHOTOGRAPHIC & GRAPHICS EXHIBIT. (LOCAL). DR ROBERT J KOVARIK, EXEC OFFICER; CHICAGO STATE UNIV BICENTENNIAL COMMITTEE; 95 AT KING DR; CHICAGO, IL 60678. (#13602).

PACKAGE ENGINEERING MAGAZINE'S BICENT SPEECH-NBMRP. JULY, 1976, ISSUE FEATURES AN INSERT ENTITLED 'THIS SPEECH COULD HAVE PREVENTED THE AMERICAN REVOLUTION', EXTRACTED FROM EDMUND BURKE'S ORATION TO THE PARLIAMENT. (NAT'L). R BRUCE HOLMGREW, BICENTENNIAL COORDINATOR; PACKAGE ENGINEERING MAGAZINE; 5 S WABASH; CHICAGO, IL 60603. (#30422).

A PART OF U S. NISEI VETERANS REUNION; WEEK-LONG CELEBRATION WITH FOCUS ON JAPANESE AND AMERICAN HERITAGE. (LOCAL). HOSEN OSHITA, BICENT CHMN; AMERICAN LEGION NISEI POST 1183; 628 CHARLEMAGNE DR; NORTHBROOK, IL 60062. (#105346-1).

'A PART OF U S'-JAPANESE-AMERICAN PROJ, CHICAGO. ACTIVITIES AIMED AT JAPANESE-AMERICANS, INCLUDING A REUNION OF JAPANESE-AMERICAN VETERANS. (NAT'L). HOSEN OSHITA, PROJ COORDINATOR; AMERICAN LEGION, NISEI POST 1183; 628 CHARLEMAGNE DR; NORTHBROOK, IL 60062. (#19556).

PASSION FOR SOLO, CHORUS & ORCHESTRA, CHICAGO, IL. PROJECT IS A VOCAL WORK ON BIBLICAL PASSION STORY, SCORED FOR SIX SOLOISTS, CHORUS AND FULL ORCHESTRA. (LOCAL). MARGARET HILLIS, DIRECTOR; CHICAGO SYMPHONY CHORUS; 220 S MICHIGAN AVE; CHICAGO, IL 60604. (#19670).

PAWNEE EARTH LODGE ENVIRONMENT EXHIBITION, CHICAGO. LIFE SIZED PAWNEE EARTH LODGE, IROQUOIS FALSE-FACE SOCIETY WORKSHOP SET UP AS ENVIRONMENT-TYPE EXHIBITIONS IN CONTEXT OF AMERICAN INDIAN EXHIBITS. (LOCAL). PHILLIP LEWIS, ACTING CHMN, DEPT OF ANTHROPOLOGY; FEILD MUSEUM OF NATURAL HISTORY; ROOSEVELT RD & LAKE SHORE DR; CHICAGO, IL 60605. (#16137).

REFLECTIVE BICENTENNIAL SAFETY BUMPER STICKER. PRESSURE SENSITIVE BUMPER STICKER WITH REFLECTIVE SAFETY BACKGROUND. ARBA LICENSE NO 76-19-0538. (NAT'L). MICHAEL MILLER, PROJ MGR; COACH HOUSE GAME AND PROMOTIONS, INC; 741 BUENA AVE; CHICAGO, IL 60613. (#9040).

RESTORATION OF PRAIRIE AVENUE - CHICAGO, ILLINOIS. RESTORATION & PRESERVATION OF OLD HOMES & BUILDINGS IN THIS HISTORIC DISTRICT OF THE CITY. (LOCAL). MARIAN DESPRES, CHAIRMAN OF THE BOARD; CHICAGO SCHOOL OF ARCHITECTURE FOUNDATION; 1800 S PRAIRIE AVE; CHICAGO, IL 60616. (#5267).

REVOLUTIONARY WAR BOARD GAMES. BICENTENNIAL BOARD GAME SERIES OF REVOLUTIONARY WAR YEARS. EXCELLENT FOR FUND RAISING, EDUCATIONAL, INFORMATIVE. FOR AGES 8 AND UP. ARBA LICENSE NO 76-19-0519. (NAT'L). MICHAEL MILLER, PROJECT MANAGER; COACH HOUSE GAME SALES & PROMOTIONS, INC; 741 BUENA; CHICAGO, IL 60613. (#6282).

ROCK PRODUCTS MAGAZINE BICENTENNIAL EDITION -NBMRP. THE JULY 1976 ISSUE OF THE MAGAZINE IS A SALUTE TO 200 YEARS OF TECHNICAL PROGRESS IN THE NATION'S MINERAL INDUSTRY. (NAT'L). PERRY KING, BICENTENNIAL COORDINATOR; ROCK PRODUCTS MAGAZINE; 300 W ADAMS ST; CHICAGO, IL 60606. (#28521).

'SALUTE & TRIBUTE TO THE APPLIANCE INDUSTRY'-NBMRP. A SPECIAL 4-COLOR, 12 PAGE INSERT ON THE HISTORICAL SIGNIFICANCE & PROGRESS OF THE APPLIANCE INDUSTRY, AS WELL AS BICENTENNIAL AWARDS TO THE LEADING TRADE ASSOC'S & THEIR MEMBERS. (NAT'L). F WARREN DICKSON, BICENTENNIAL COORDINATOR; APPLIANCE MANUFACTURER MAGAZINE - CAHNERS PUBLISHING CO; 5 S WABASH AVE; CHICAGO, IL 60603. (#25549).

'SCULPTURE FOR A NEW ERA'. SCULPTURE SELECTED FROM REGIONAL COMPETITION TO BE DISPLAYED IN FEDERAL BUILDINGS IN CHICAGO. DESIGNED TO PROMOTE THE TALENTS OF ESTABLISHED & LITTLE KNOWN SCULPTORS FROM MIDWEST. (REGN'L). ANN FARMER, PRESIDENT; ART IN PUBLIC PLACES; 1682 N ADA ST; CHICAGO, IL 60622. (#7937). **ARBA RECOGNIZED.**

SEMINAR ON EARLY AMERICAN MUSIC. RESEARCH STUDIES IN EARLY CHORAL SOCIETIES, ORCHESTRAS, OPERA GROUPS, PIANO & ORGAN BUILDERS. AT AMERICAN CONSERVATORY OF MUSIC. (ST-WIDE). HELENE QUIRMBACH, PROF; AMERICAN CONSERVATORY OF MUSIC; 410 S MICHIGAN; CHICAGO, IL 60605. (#104012-1).

'SMILE AMERICA' - NATIONAL DENTAL HEALTH WEEK. 28TH NATIONAL CHILDREN'S DENTAL HEALTH WEEK, OBSERVED NATION-WIDE BY STATE & LOCAL DENTAL SOCIETIES; ITS PURPOSE IS TO IMPROVE DENTAL HEALTH THROUGH CONCENTRATED HEALTH EDUCATION ACTIVITIES FOR YOUTH. (NAT'L). C GORDON WATSON, DDS, EXEC DIRECTOR; AMERICAN DENTAL ASSOC; 211 E CHICAGO AVE; CHICAGO, IL 60611. (#13055).

CHICAGO — CONTINUED

'SPIRIT OF 76', CHURCH CELEBRATION PROJ OF CHICAGO. THE EVAN COVENANT CHURCH IS SPONSORING A TRAVELING RELIGIOUS SHOW WITH AN AMERICAN REVOLUTIONARY THEME. THE PROGRAM WILL INCLUDE VISUAL AIDS, MARIONETTES, SONGS & BIBLE STORIES. (REGN'L). REV WILLARD E GRANT, MINISTER; EVAN COVENANT CHURCH OF AMERICA; 6355 N SPOKANE; CHICAGO, IL 60646. (#9250).

STAND-UP DISPLAY IN CHICAGO, ILLINOIS. PROMOTIONAL AND INFORMATIONAL FREE-STANDING DISPLAY CONCERNING BOTH ILLINOIS AND THE BICENTENNIAL. (ST-WIDE). PATRICIA INGRAHAM, PUBLIC INFORMATION OFFICER; ILLINOIS BICENTENNIAL COMMISSION; 410 N MICHIGAN, RM 1044; CHICAGO, IL 60611. (#12105).

'A TIME OF THANKSGIVING', FESTIVAL IN CHICAGO. A CHICAGO AREA PROGRAM FEATURING CHOIRS IN MUSICAL THANKSGIVING FOR THE CONTINUING OPPORTUNITY TO WORK TOWARD A BETTER QUALITY OF LIFE. (LOCAL). GLENICE B PEARSON, DEAN, UNIVERSITY SERVICES; DANIEL HALE WILLIAMS UNIV; 5414 W MADISON ST; CHICAGO, IL 60644. (#8424).

TOWN MEETING '76 PROGRAM. NATIONAL CITIZEN PARTICIPATION PROGRAM OF 5,000 LOCALLY SPONSORED ONE-DAY TOWN MEETINGS ANALYZING PRESENT CHALLENGES & CREATING PRACTICAL PROPOSALS FOR THE FUTURE OF THE COMMUNITY & THE NATION. (NAT'L). MARSHALL JONES, PROJECT DIRECTOR; THE INSTITUTE OF CULTURAL AFFAIRS; 4750 N SHERIDAN RD; CHICAGO, IL 60640. (#7897). **ARBA RECOGNIZED.**

TREE PLANTING PROJECT, CHICAGO, IL. SEEDS TAKEN FROM THE INDEPENDENCE TREE IN MT VERNON, VA WILL BE GROWN BY THE CHILDREN OF ST MARY OF THE ANGELS SCHOOL AT THE BURIAL SITE OF THE COR-WOOD, CHICAGO BICENTENNIAL TIME CAPSULE. (LOCAL). JEROMIA TROFIMUK, PROJ COORDINATOR; COR-WOOD, CHICAGO BICENTENNIAL COMMITTEE; 1850 N WOOD ST; CHICAGO, IL 60622. (#22618).

'TUTANKHAMEN TREASURES' EXHIBIT. EXHIBIT. (INT'L). CULTURAL ATTACHE; ARAB REPUBLIC OF EGYPT; 2310 DECATUR PL; WASHINGTON, DC 20008. (#31906-6). **(??).**

UKRAINIANS IN ILLINOIS: AN ORAL HISTORY. STUDENTS RESEARCH AND RECORD ORAL HISTORY AS RELATED BY UKRAINIAN PIONEERS. STATEWIDE CANVAS WITH IN-DEPTH STUDY OF CHICAGO'S UKRAINIAN POPULATION TO BE PUBLISHED. (ST-WIDE). MS LUBA TOLOCZKO/MARKEWYCZ, CHAIRPERSON; UKRAINIAN CONGRESS COMMITTEE; 762 N OAKLEY; CHICAGO, IL 60612. (#27794). **ARBA GRANTEE.**

'USA BICENTENNIAL-TIME ITALIAN CONTRIBUTION'-NBMRP. 'LA PAROLA DEL POPLO' - A COLLECTION OF ARTICLES DOCUMENTING THE MULTIFOLD ACTIVITY OF ITALIAN IMMIGRANTS, NOTING IN THE INTRODUCTION THE PUBLICATION IS A COMPENDIUM OF 'AN ACT OF FAITH & A LEGACY'. (NAT'L). CHARLES CAROSELLA, BICENTENNIAL COORDINATOR; LA PAROLA DEL POPLO; 6740 W DIVERSITY AVE; CHICAGO, IL 60635. (#33451).

USART. 28 MINUTE FILM ON 200 YEARS OF AMERICAN ART & AN ACCOMPANYING BOOK WILL BE DISTRIBUTED & LOANED FREE TO SCHOOLS & OTHER INSTITUTIONS & GROUPS THROUGHOUT THE USA. (NAT'L). ED QUINN, EXEC DIRECTOR; SEARS ROEBUCK FOUNDATION; SEARS TOWER; CHICAGO, IL 60606. (#17741). **ARBA RECOGNIZED.**

VISIT BY PRIME MINISTER LIAM COSGRAVE OF IRELAND. CEREMONY. (INT'L). CULTURAL ATTACHE; EMBASSY OF IRELAND; 2234 MASSACHUSETTS AVE, NW; WASHINGTON, DC 20008. (#200016-278).

WALL & DESK PLAQUES WITH BICENTENNIAL SYMBOL. WALL AND DESK PLAQUES BEARING THE OFFICIAL BICENTENNIAL SYMBOL ARBA LICENSE NO 76-19-0598. (NAT'L). EDWARD BALASKO, PRESIDENT; CREATIVE ACCENTS, INC; 3550 W PETERSON AVE, SUITE 303; CHICAGO, IL 60659. (#21176).

WBEZ-FM BICENTENNIAL EDUCATION PROGRAMMING-NBMRP. OPERATED BY THE PUBLIC SCHOOLS & AFFILIATED WITH NATL PUBLIC RADIO, STATION HAS VERY EXTENSIVE BICENTENNIAL COVERAGE, FROM AMERICAN ISSUES FORUM THRU 'SALUTE TO THE STATES', HISTORICAL & ETHNIC WORKS. (LOCAL). CAROLE R NOLAN, BICENTENNIAL COORDINATOR; RADIO STATION WBEZ; 228 N LA SALLE ST -ROOM 701; CHICAGO, IL 60601. (#27141).

WILLIAMS UNIV AS A CREATION OF THE SPIRIT OF '76. A SPECIAL ALL DAY PROGRAM ON THE ROLE OF DANIEL HALE WILLIAMS UNIV AND ITS COMMITMENT TO BECOMING A VEHICLE FOR AIDING IN THE RECONCILIATION OF THE DIVISIVENESS IN THE NATION. (LOCAL). GLENICE B PEARSON, DEAN, UNIVERSITY SERVICES; DANIEL HALE WILLIAMS UNIV; 5414 W MADISON ST; CHICAGO, IL 60644. (#8430).

WRITING COMPETITION ON HERITAGE 76 PROJ OF CHICAGO. HIGH SCHOOL AND COLLEGE STUDENTS WILL ENGAGE IN A WRITING COMPETITION ON THE TOPIC, HERITAGE 76. ONE THOUSAND DOLLAR PRIZE WILL BE GIVEN TO THE WINNER OF EACH DIVISION. (LOCAL). GLENICE B PEARSON, DEAN, UNIVERSITY SERVICES; DANIEL HALE WILLIAMS UNIV; 5414 W MADISON ST; CHICAGO, IL 60644. (#8423).

'YES WE CAN!' - CLEANUP IN CHICAGO. A CITYWIDE EFFORT TO BEGIN A MOVEMENT TO CLEAN UP THE COMMUNITIES WE LIVE IN WITH EMPHASIS ON ECOLOGICAL FACTS THAT SHOULD BE OF CONCERN TO ALL CITIZENS. (LOCAL). GLENICE B PEARSON, DEAN, UNIVERSITY SERVICES; DANIEL HALE WILLIAMS UNIV; 5414 W MADISON ST; CHICAGO, IL 60644. (#8428). **(??).**

YOUNG ARTIST STUDIOS CONCERT SERIES, CHICAGO, IL. A CONCERT SERIES OF NEW MUSIC FROM YOUNG ARTISTS IN CHICAGO. (LOCAL). JAMES GRIGSBY, ART INSTRUCTOR; THE ART INSTITUTE OF CHICAGO; CHICAGO, IL 60603. (#24286). **ARBA GRANTEE.**

YOUTH RECOGNITION IN THE SPIRIT OF 76 - CHICAGO. A MULTIRACIAL PROGRAM FOR YOUNG ACHIEVERS WITH THE ANNOUNCEMENTS OF THE WRITING COMPETITION WINNERS. EACH YOUTH WILL BE ACCOMPANIED BY A DISTINGUISHED ADULT ACHIEVER FROM THE WORLD OF AMER BUSINESS. (LOCAL). GLENICE B PEARSON, DEAN, UNIVERSITY SERVICES; DANIEL HALE WILLIAMS UNIV; 5414 W MADISON ST; CHICAGO, IL 60644. (#8425).

17 ARTISTS HISPANO/MEXICAN-AMERICAN/CHICANO. AN EXHIBITION OF WORK BY ARTISTS OF MEXICAN-AMERICAN HERITAGE WILL TRAVEL TO 5 MUSEUMS ACROSS THE COUNTRY. (NAT'L). ROBERT H GLAUBER, CURATOR; ILLINOIS BELL TELEPHONE; 225 W RANDOLPH ST; CHICAGO, IL 60606. (#21921). **ARBA RECOGNIZED.**

60-SECOND BICENTENNIAL FILM COMPETITION. ASKING FILMAKERS AROUND THE WORLD TO MAKE A 60-SECOND FILM ON THE BICENTENNIAL & ENTER IT IN A COMPETITION. (INT'L). JUDY GAYNOR, ADMIN DIRECTOR; CHICAGO FILM BOARD, INC; 415 N DEARBORN ST; CHICAGO, IL 60610. (#15976). **ARBA RECOGNIZED.**

NOV 9, '71 - CONTINUING . 'THE CHICAGO ODYSSEY'. SPECTACULAR MULTI-MEDIA SHOW ABOUT CHICAGO'S PAST, PRESENT & FUTURE; SHOW IS PRESENTED ON A 70 FOOT SCREEN USING 30 PROJECTORS AND MANY SPECIAL EFFECTS; IT WILL INCLUDE A DRAMATIC SIMULATION OF THE CHICAGO FIRE. AT CHICAGO ODYSSEY THEATRE; 1608 NORTH WELLS ST, PIPER'S ALLEY. (ST-WIDE). PAUL CONDYLIS, DIRECTOR; POLYMEDIA CORP; 1608 N WELLS-PIPER'S ALLEY; CHICAGO, IL 60614. (#103022-1).

MAR 20, '74. LECT, EDW. BANFIELD, INQUIRY NATURE, CAUSES WEALTH-POVERTY AM CITIES. DISTINGUISHED LECTURE SERIES ON BICENTENNIAL. 18 DISTINGUISHED SCHOLARS DISCUSS NATURE, FUTURE OF AM REVOLUTION AT NATION'S HISTORIC SITES---TAPED FOR BROADCAST ON PBS IN SPRING 1974. TOPICS COVER REV & SOCIETY, RELIGION, PRESS, LAW, CULTURE, GOV'T. (NAT'L). EARL H VOSS; AMERICAN ENTERPRISE INSTITUTE FOR PUBLIC POLICY RESEARCH; 1150 17TH STREET, N.W.; WASHINGTON, DC 20036. (#1297-911).

APR 1 - 30, '74. DEDICATION OF CHICAGO RIVER HISTORIC WALK DISTRICT. LANDSCAPED PATH COMMEMORATING SITES OF FOURTEEN HISTORIC STRUCTURES AND EVENTS RELATING TO CHICAGO'S GROWTH AND DEVELOPMENT ALONG THE CHICAGO RIVER FROM 1779 THRU 1915. (ST-WIDE). MARTIN R MURPHY; CITY OF CHICAGO, DEPT OF DEVELOPMENT & PLANNING; 121 N LASALLE ST ROOM 1000; CHICAGO, IL 60602. (#2161-501).

OCT 9 - 10, '74. BICENTENNIAL FORUM FOR PR/MARKETING EXECUTIVES - CHICAGO. BICENTENNIAL FORUM PLANNING PR/MARKETING PROGRAMS. TWO-DAY SEMINAR FOR PUBLIC RELATIONS & MARKETING EXECUTIVES TO STIMULATE PARTICIPATION IN BICENTENNIAL ACTIVITIES, SPONSORED BY NYU & PUBLIC RELATIONS SOCIETY OF AMERICA. (NAT'L). RICHARD M NEWMAN, COORD; NEW YORK UNIV BUSINESS & MANAGEMENT PGMS; 310 MADISON AVE; NEW YORK, NY 10017. (#2343-901).

NOV 1, '74 - DEC 31, '76. CHICAGO ARCHITECTURE: REVOLUTION ON THE PRAIRIE. CONFERENCE, EXHIBIT, FESTIVAL, RADIO/TV, TOUR AT 111 N WABASH, CHICAGO, IL, 60602. (ST-WIDE). PAULA PROKOPOFF; ILLINOIS ARTS COUNCIL; 111 N WABASH; CHICAGO, IL 60602. (#50026-1).

JAN 1, '75 - DEC 31, '77. 'AMERICA'S INVENTIVE GENIUS'. EXHIBIT & PROGRAM ON AMERICAN SCIENCE, TECHNOLOGY & INDUSTRY DURING NATION'S FIRST 200 YEARS. THE PROJECT WILL CONSIST OF TWO EXHIBIT SECTIONS & A THEATER PROGRAM. CLOSED CHRISTMAS DAY ONLY. (REGN'L). DR VICTOR J DANILOV; MUSEUM OF SCIENCE AND INDUSTRY; 57TH ST & LAKE SHORE DR; CHICAGO, IL 60637. (#5-1).

JAN 20 - DEC 18, '75. BICENTENNIAL PREVIEW, MONTHLY SUPPER. OUR LADY OF MERCY IS A HOME & SCHOOL FOR HOMELESS BOYS. IN ORDER TO MAKE THEM AWARE OF THE BICENTENNIAL, A MONTHLY SUPPER WITH ENTERTAINMENT IS BEING PLANNED. EACH MONTH A PARTICULAR REGION OF THE COUNTRY WILL BE HIGHLIGHTED. AT 1140 W JACKSON BLVD. (LOCAL). ALBERT L PAQUETTE, CHEF; OUR LADY OF MERCY MISSION; 1140 W JACKSON BLVD; CHICAGO, IL 60607. (#100697-1).

FEB 18, '75 - DEC 31, '76. BICENTENNIAL SCIENCE PLAYHOUSE. SERIES OF FREE SCIENCE ORIENTED HISTORIC PLAYS PRESENTED IN COOPERATION WITH GOODMAN THEATRE AS PART OF MUSEUM'S BICENTENNIAL PROGRAM CLOSED CHRISTMAS DAY ONLY. AT AUDITORIUM OF MUSEUM OF SCIENCE & INDUSTRY. (REGN'L). DR VICTOR J DANILOV, DIR; MUSEUM OF SCIENCE & INDUSTRY; 57TH ST & LAKE SHORE DR; CHICAGO, IL 60637. (#5-4).

FEB 19 - APR 13, '75. SHOWING OF 'USA '76: THE FIRST TWO HUNDRED YEARS' EXHIBIT IN CHICAGO. THIS TRAVELING EXHIBIT PREPARED BY THE ARBA WILL TOUR 10 CITIES DURING THE BICENTENNIAL. IT EXPLORES THE CULTURAL AND SCIENTIFIC HERITAGE OF THE USA. (REGN'L). JACK MASEY; AMERICAN REVOLUTION BICENTENNIAL ADMINISTRATION; 2401 E STREET, NW; WASHINGTON, DC 20276. (#5661-501).

MAR 19 - 21, '75. MEAT INDUSTRY RESEARCH CONFERENCE. AMER MEAT SCIENCE ASSOC, A PROFESSIONAL SCIENTIFIC SOCIETY, WILL HOLD EDUCATIONAL AND RESEARCH CONFERENCES IN 1975. (NAT'L). DR WILLIAM C SHERMAN, SEC; AMERICAN MEAT SCIENCE ASSOCIATION; 36 S WABASH AVE; CHICAGO, IL 60603. (#5563-901).

MAY 10, '75. DANIEL HALE WILLIAMS FIRST CONVOCATION AND DEDICATION. CEREMONY, OPENING, RADIO/TV AT 930 EAST 50TH STREET CHICAGO ILLINOIS 60644. (NAT'L). GLENICE B PEARSON; DANIEL HALE WILLIAMS UNIVERSITY; 5414 WEST MADISON STREET; CHICAGO, IL 60644. (#50733-1).

MAY 28, '75. BOYS' CLUBS OF AMERICA 'A GIFT OF SERVICE TO AMERICA' MINI SEMINAR. THIS BICENTENNIAL PROGRAM CAUROSEL IS A PART OF THE BOYS CLUBS OF AMERICA 69TH ANNUAL CONFERENCE. MUCH OF THE PROGRAM IDEAS WILL RELATE TO WORKING IN BOYS' CLUB SITUATION. AT PALMER HOUSE, STATE & MONROE STS. (REGN'L). HERBERT A LOWE; BOYS' CLUBS OF AMERICA; BCA, 771 FIRST AVE; NEW YORK, NY 10017. (#3795-2).

MAY 30, '75 - SEPT 1, '76. STEAMSHIP MILWAUKEE CLIPPER EXCURSION BOAT OPENING. OPERATES MEMORIAL DAY-LABOR DAY. THREE 4-HOUR TRIPS DAILY. ORIGINALLY BUILT IN 1905 AND REBUILT IN 1941, 361FT, 900 PASSENGER EXCURSION SHIP OFFERS FULL MEAL SERVICE AND ENTERTAINMENT. AT NAVY PIER FOOT OF GRAND AVENUE AT LAKE MICHIGAN. (REGN'L). GREAT LAKES TRANSIT CO.; GREAT LAKES CRUISES INC.; 224 S MICHIGAN AVE.; CHICAGO, IL 60604. (#50186-1).

JULY 11 - OCT 31, '75. SCULPTURE FOR A NEW ERA, EXHIBIT OF OUTDOOR WORKS OF ART. 27 PROMINENT MIDWESTERN SCULPTORS PRESENT A WIDE RANGE OF UNIQUE PUBLIC WORKS EXHIBITED BOTH OUTSIDE & INSIDE PUBLIC PLAZAS & BLDGS; SPONSORED BY 4 FEDERAL AGENCIES & ART IN PUBLIC PLACES, A NON-FORPROFIT CORPORATION. AT FEDERAL BUILDING PLAZA, 200 BLOCK OF DEARBORN. (LOCAL). MRS ANN FARMER, CHMN; ART IN PUBLIC PLACES; 777 ROSEWOOD DR; WINNETCA, IL 60093. (#101192-1).

JULY 28 - AUG 3, '75. AMERICAN FREEDOM TRAIN DISPLAY DAYS AT CHICAGO. THE AMERICAN FREEDOM TRAIN WILL INCLUDE 10 EXHIBIT CARS & 2 SHOWCASE CARS DEPICTING DIFFERENT PHASES OF THE AMERICAN EXPERIENCE. ITS ARRIVAL WILL SERVE AS A CATALYST FOR LOCAL BICENTENNIAL CELEBRATIONS BY PEOPLE THROUGHOUT THIS NATION. (ST-WIDE). DON MALLICOAT, EDIT SVCS; THE AMERICAN FREEDOM TRAIN FOUNDATION, INC; 5205 LEESBURG PIKE, SUITE 800; BAILEY'S XRDS, VA 22041. (#1776-18).

AUG 8 - 10, '75. GOLD COAST ART FAIR. EXHIBIT AT CHICAGO'S RUSH ST AREA. (LOCAL). SYLVIA ZAPPA; NEAR NORTH NEWS & GOLD COAST ASSOC; 26 E HURON ST; CHICAGO, IL 60611. (#50004-1).

OCT 3, '75 - MAY 16, '76. A BICENTENNIAL SEASON OF AMERICAN PLAYS. LIVE PERFORMANCE AT MULLADY MEMORIAL THEATER (ON CAMPUS). (LOCAL). ARTHUR BLOOM, CHAIRMAN; LOYOLA UNIVERSITY OF CHICAGO THEATRE DEPARTMENT; 6525 N SHERIDAN RD; CHICAGO, IL 60626. (#104236-3).

OCT 3, '75 - MAR 1, '77. ECOLOGY EDUCATION PROGRAMS. ALL EDUCATION PROGRAMS AIMED AT EDUCATING PEOPLE ON ENVIRONMENTAL PROBLEMS, INCLUDING LECTURES, FILMS, EDUCATIONAL COURSES, AND FIELD TRIPS. RESERVATIONS ARE REQUIRED FOR SOME PROGRAMS. AT FIELD MUSEUM OF NATURAL HISTORY. (LOCAL). MS JORY GRAHAM; FIELD MUSEUM OF NATURAL HISTORY; E ROOSEVELT RD; CHICAGO, IL 60605. (#7979-3).

OCT 9, '75 - APR 11, '76. A SALUTE TO BLACK THEATRE. 'RAISIN IN THE SUN' - OCT 9,10,11. 'SIMPLY HEAVEN' - NOV 20,21,22. 'TAMBOURINES TO GLORY' - MAR 4,5,6. 'RIVER NIGER' - APR 9,10,11. AT KENNEDY-KING COLLEGE THEATRE. (LOCAL). DR H ADRIAN REHNER; KENNEDY-KING COLLEGE; 6800 S WENTWORTH AVE; CHICAGO, IL 60621. (#11795-1).

OCT 16 - 18, '75. AMERICA AND THE CONTEMPORARY INTERNATIONAL MILIEU - CONFERENCE. CONFERENCE AT SCHMITT ACADEMIC CENTER, 2323 N SEMINARY AVE. (REGN'L). RICHARD FARKAS, PROJ DIR; DEPAUL UNIV; 2323 N SEMINARY AVE; CHICAGO, IL 60614. (#100428-3).

OCT 27, '75. RELIGIOUS HERITAGE CELEBRATION. CENTRAL CHURCH OF CHICAGO CENTENNIAL CELEBRATION WITH DR NORMAN VINCENT PEALE AS GUEST SPEAKER. 'A LOOK AT THE NATION'S RELIGIOUS/ CULTURAL HERITAGE' IN HONOR OF THE BICENTENNIAL. AT DINNER AT HYATT REGENCY. (LOCAL). CHARLIE SOO, CO-CHAIRMAN; CENTRAL CHURCH OF CHICAGO; 1250 N STONE; CHICAGO, IL 60610. (#101199-1).

OCT 29, '75 - DEC 31, '77. ILLINOIS LAND OF INNOVATION. AN EXHIBITION ON THE CONTRIBUTIONS OF ILLINOIS ENGINEERS, INVENTORS, SCIENTISTS AND INDUSTRIAL INNOVATORS TO THE DEVELOPMENT OF THE NATION. (REGN'L). VICTOR J DANILOV; MUSEUM OF SCIENCE AND INDUSTRY; 57TH ST AND LAKE SHORE DR; CHICAGO, IL 60637. (#6345-1).

NOV 1, '75 - CONTINUING . WRITTEN WORD OF THE REVOLUTION. A COLLECTION OF BOOKS, COSTUMES, PAPERS, ARTIFACTS AND MATERIALS WILL BE DISPLAYED FOR STUDENTS AND THE PUBLIC; IT WILL BE A PERMANENT COLLECTION. AT LOCATED IN COLLEGE LIBRARY. (LOCAL). DR H ADRIAN REHNER; KENNEDY-KING COLLEGE; 6800 S WENTWORTH AVE; CHICAGO, IL 60621. (#11778-1).

NOV 3, '75 - JAN 13, '76. ANNUNCIATION SCHOOL ESSAY CONTEST. COMPETITION. (LOCAL). EMILY KLOC, PROJ DIR; COR-WOOD-CHICAGO-BICENTENNIAL COMMITTEE; 1850 N WOOD ST; CHICAGO, IL 60622. (#103510-1).

NOV 3, '75 - JAN 13, '76. ESSAY CONTEST: 'WHAT AMERICA MEANS TO ME'. COMPETITION AT ST MARY OF THE ANGELS SCHOOL. (LOCAL). EMILY KLOC, PROJ DIRECTOR; COR-WOOD-CHICAGO BICENTENNIAL COMMITTEE; 1850 NORTHWOOD ST; CHICAGO, IL 60622. (#103402-1).

NOV 9, '75 - CONTINUING . 'MAN IN HIS ENVIRONMENT'. EXHIBIT DESCRIBING ECCOSYSTEMS AND MAN'S IMPACT ON THE ENVIRONMENT. CLOSED CHRISTMAS AND NEW YEAR'S DAY ONLY. AT FIELD MUSEUM OF NATURAL HISTORY. (REGN'L). MS JORY GRAHAM; FIELD MUSEUM OF NATURAL HISTORY; E ROOSEVELT RD; CHICAGO, IL 60605. (#7979-1).

NOV 11, '75. HONOR VETERANS DAY. CEREMONY AT FLAG POLE (ON CAMPUS). (LOCAL). DONALD FISCH, COORD; LOYOLA UNIVERSITY OF CHICAGO; 6525 N SHERIDAN RD; CHICAGO, IL 60626. (#200016-67).

CHICAGO — CONTINUED

DEC 6 - 31, '75. LARRY RIVERS ART EXHIBIT. EXHIBIT AT CUDAHY LIBRARY, 6525 N SHERIDAN RD. (LOCAL). RALPH ARNOLD, FINE ARTS; LOYOLA UNIVERSITY OF CHICAGO; 820 N MICHIGAN AVE; CHICAGO, IL 60611. (#200016-65).

DEC 15, '75 - JAN 16, '76. STAR-SPANGLED HISTORY: DRAWINGS BY J B BEALE - MAGIC LANTERN ARTIST. 'STAR-SPANGLED HISTORY', A PROJ OF AMERICAN NATL INSURANCE CO: NATIONAL TRAVELING EXHIBITION OF SIXTY-FIVE ORIGINAL WASH DRAWINGS BY JOSEPH BOGGS BEALE, A 19TH CENTURY ILLUSTRATOR. CLOSED MAJOR HOLIDAYS. AT CHICAGO PUBLIC LIBRARY SATURDAY HRS: 9AM - 5PM. (REGN'L). SUE PEARLMAN; AMERICAN NATIONAL INSURANCE CO OF GALVESTON, TX; C/O RUDER & FINN, 110 E 59TH ST; NEW YORK, NY 10022. (#9820-503).

JAN 1 - MAR 31, '76. BICENTENNIAL FOLK SONG CONTEST. CONTEST OPEN TO ALL RESIDENTS OF ILLINOIS. ENTRIES MUST BE SENT IN ON CASSETTES WITH $2.00 HANDLING FEE. PRIZES OF $500, $250 AND $100. CONTEST CLOSES ON DEC 31, 1975. WINNERS WILL BE ANNOUNCED IN MARCH, 1976. (LOCAL). RALPH ARNOLD, CHMN; LOYOLA UNIV OF CHICAGO; 820 N MICHIGAN AVE; CHICAGO, IL 60611. (#200016-66).

JAN 1 - JULY 3, '76. TIME CAPSULE DEDICATION. TIME CAPSULE DEDICATION AND CLOSING CEREMONIES INCLUDE: SOCIAL ACTIVITIES, AWARD PRESENTATION AND OTHER FESTIVITIES. (LOCAL). GEORGE S TROFIMUK, CHMN; COR-WOOD & CHICAGO BICENTENNIAL COMMITTEE; 1850 N WOOD ST; CHICAGO, IL 60622. (#104893-1).

JAN 1 - DEC 30, '76. ARCHITECTURAL TOURS OF CHICAGO. DISCOVER AND EXPLORE CHICAGOS FAMOUS BUILDINGS WITH SPECIALLY TRAINED GUIDES. ONE HOUR WALK DAILY OF DOWNTOWN. 4 HOUR HIGHLIGHTS BUS TOUR OF THE CITY. (REGN'L). JEANETTE FIELDS; CHICAGO SCHOOL OF ARCHITECTURE FOUNDATION; 1800 SOUTH PRAIRIE AVENUE; CHICAGO, IL 60616. (#50393-1).

JAN 15, '76. RELIGIOUS SERVICES IN HONOR OF THE MEMORY OF DR MARTIN L KING. CEREMONY AT 5414 WEST MADISON STREET. (REGN'L). GLENICE B PEARSON; DANIEL HALE WILLIAMS UNIVERSITY; 5414 WEST MADISON STREET; CHICAGO, IL 60644. (#50733-2).

JAN 15 - 18, '76. NATIONAL STRATEGIES SYMPOSIUM ON VIOLENCE AND CRIME IN AMERICA. CONFERENCE, SEMINAR AT 5414 WEST MADISON STREET. (ST-WIDE). GLENICE B PEARSON; DANIEL HALE WILLIAMS UNIVERSITY; 5414 WEST MADISON STREET; CHICAGO, IL 60644. (#50890-1).

JAN 23 - APR 29, '76. BICENTENNIAL LECTURE SERIES. 6 OPEN LECTURES ON HISTORY & DEVELOPMENT OF VARIOUS ASPECTS OF U S BUSINESS BY EXPERTS IN THE FIELD. (LOCAL). TASSIO MILLIARIS, CHMN; LOYOLA UNIVERSITY, ECONOMIC DEPT; 820 N MICHIGAN; CHICAGO, IL 60611. (#104236-5).

FEB 1 - 29, '76. ARTISTIC DISPLAYS BY BLACKS, LATINOS, & NATIVE AMERICANS. EXHIBIT AT 5247 WEST MADISON CHICAGO ILLINOIS 60644. (REGN'L). GLENICE B PEARSON; DANIEL HALE WILLIAMS UNIVERSITY; 5414 WEST MADISON; CHICAGO, IL 60644. (#50733-3).

FEB 1 - MAR 31, '76. HORIZONS '76 AND THE COLLEGE - CHICAGO, IL. THE ENGLISH AND HUMANITIES DEPARTMENTS WILL HOLD PUBLIC SEMINARS TO DEFINE THE PLACE OF THE COLLEGE IN TERMS OF THE PAST, PRESENT AND FUTURE. WILL BE HELD TWICE EACH MONTH. AT MEETING ROOM IN THE COLLEGE. (LOCAL). DR H ADRIAN REHNER; KENNEDY-KING COLLEGE; 6800 S WENTWORTH AVE; CHICAGO, IL 60621. (#11779-1).

FEB 2 - 7, '76. WORLD FAIR FOR TECHNOLOGY EXCHANGE. WORLD FAIR FOR TECHNOLOGY, UTILIZATION BY INDUSTRY. FORUM FOR TECHNOLOGY TRANSFER, COOPERATION AMONG UNIVERSITIES, INDUSTRIES & GOVERNMENTS FOR INVENTION & KNOW-HOW LICENSING. AT HOLIDAY INN - O'HARE/KENNEDY CONVENTION COMLEX, ROSEMONT, IL. (INT'L). DAVID S DEVOR; DR DVORKOVITZ & ASSOC; 216 ATLANTIC AVE POB 1748; ORMOND BEACH, FL 32074. (#7950-1).

FEB 10, '76. BICENTENNIAL LADIES NIGHT PARTY. FESTIVAL, LIVE PERFORMANCE AT BEVERLY WOODS RESTAURANT, 11532 S WESTERN AVE. (LOCAL). JOHN W GILLULY, COORD; KIWANIS CLUB OF SOUTHWEST CHICAGO; 9730 S WESTERN AVE; EVERGREEN PK, IL 60642. (#200016-62).

FEB 19 - 21, '76. THE BILATERAL APPROACH TO GLOBAL PROBLEMS - CONFERENCE. CONFERENCE AT SCHMITT ACADEMIC CENTER, 2323 N SEMINARY AVE. (REGN'L). RICHARD FARKAS, PROJ DIR; DEPAUL UNIV; 2323 N SEMINARY AVE; CHICAGO, IL 60614. (#100428-2).

FEB 21 - 29, '76. CHICAGO AUTO SHOW. AMERICA'S LARGEST DISPLAY OF AUTOMOBILES FEATURES EXHIBITS AND DECORATIONS WITH BICENTENNIAL THEMES. AT MCCORMICK PLACE, 23RD ST AT LAKE SHORE DRIVE. (NAT'L). ROSS KELSEY, COORDINATOR; CHICAGO AUTO TRADE ASSOC; O'HARE PLAZA, 5725 E RIVER RD; CHICAGO, IL 60631. (#103416-163).

MAR 1 - APR 29, '76. US INDUSTRIAL FILM FESTIVAL, 9TH ANNUAL INT'L AWARDS COMPETITION. INTERNATIONAL AWARDS COMPETITION FOR INDUSTRIAL MOTION PICTURES, FILMSTRIPS AND SLIDE PROGRAMS FEATURING A CATEGORY FOR THOSE PRODUCT IONS WHICH EMBRACE THE U.S. BICENTENNIAL CELEBRATION. TWENTY FIVE OTHER SUBJECT CATEGORIES INCLUDING HISTORY, BIOGRAPHY, POLITICS,. (INT'L). U.S. INDUSTRIAL FILM FEST; U.S. INDUSTRIAL FILM FESTIVAL; 1008 BELLWOOD AVENUE; BELLWOOD, IL 60104. (#50254-1).

MAR 3 - MAY 9, '76. 72ND AMERICAN EXHIBITION. IN HONOR OF BICENTENNIAL, EXHIBITION WILL SURVEY ACCOMPLISHMENTS AND DIVERSITY OF CONTEMPORARY ART. AT MORTON WING OF THE ART INSTITUTE OF CHICAGO. (REGN'L). HELEN M LETHERT,; ART INSTITUTE OF CHICAGO; MICHIGAN AVE AT ADAMS STREET; CHICAGO, IL 60603. (#103416-167).

MAR 5 - 7, '76. 'THE BRITISH ARE COMING!' - BRITISH MILITARY BAND PERFORMANCE. TOUR OF MAJOR U S CITIES BY BRITISH MILITARY UNITS AS REPRESENTATIVE OF UNITS INVOLVED IN REVOLUTIONARY WAR CAMPAIGN. AT INTERNATIONAL AMPHITHEATRE. (INT'L). CHARLES K JONES, PRES; COLUMBIA ARTISTS FESTIVALS CORP; 165 W 57TH ST; NEW YORK, NY 10019. (#6532-32).

MAR 11, '76 - FEB 19, '77. 17 ARTIST--HISPANO, MEXICAN-AMERICAN & CHICANO EXHIBIT. EXHIBIT AT LOBBY GALLERY, 225 W RANDOLPH ST. (REGN'L). ROBERT H GLAUBER, COORD; ILLINOIS BELL TELEPHONE COMPANY; ILLINOIS BELL, 225 W RANDOLPH ST; CHICAGO, IL 60606. (#21921-1).

MAR 15, '76 - JUNE 30, '78. NATIONAL TRAVELING 'SITES' EXHIBIT: MAN & HIS ENVIRONMENT. AN EXHIBIT, TRAVELING THROUGHOUT THE USA AS PART OF THE SMITHSONIAN INSTITUTION TRAVELING EXHIBITION SERVICE (SITES), AIMED AT EDUCATING PEOPLE ON ENVIRONMENTAL PROBLEMS. WILL BE SHOWN AT VARIOUS MUSEUMS ACROSS COUNTRY. TIMES AND ADMISSION PRICES WILL VARY. AT 12 MUSEUMS IN USA. (LOCAL). ELAINE HARAKAL, COORD; SMITHSONIAN INSTITUTION - SITES; 1000 JEFFERSON DR, SW; WASHINGTON, DC 20560. (#7979-2).

MAR 17, '76. ST PATRICK'S DAY PARADE. 70,000 MARCHERS AND 50 FLOATS DEPICT IRISH HERITAGE & CONTRIBUTIONS TO AMERICA. AT STATE STREET TO WACKER DR. (LOCAL). DAN LYDON, CHAIRMAN; ST PATRICK'S DAY COMMITTEE; 1340 W WASHINGTON BLVD; CHICAGO, IL 60607. (#103416-201).

MAR 19 - 21, '76. POLPEX 76 - NATIONAL STAMP & COIN EXHIBITION HONORING BICENTENNIAL. EXHIBIT AT LA SALLE HOTEL, 10 N LA SALLE ST. (NAT'L). ALFRED SZEBEL, EXEC CHMN; POLONUS PHILATELIC SOCIETY; 9041 EMERSON ST; DES PLAINES, IL 60016. (#104670-1).

MAR 20 - JUNE 3, '76. FREE WEEKLY 'DINNER-FOR-TWO' DRAWINGS. COMPETITION. (LOCAL). LILLIAN DEMSKI, PROJ DIR; COR-WOOD-CHICAGO BICENTENNIAL COMMITTEE; 1850 N WOOD ST; CHICAGO, IL 60622. (#106100-1).

MAR 22 - 26, '76. ART & THE REVOLUTION - PROJ OF CHICAGO, ILL. STUDENTS WILL PRODUCE ART WORK SHOWING BLACKS IN THE REVOLUTION; SOME OF THE ART WORK WILL REMAIN AT THE COLLEGE. AT LIBRARY-ART AREA, ADMINISTRATION AREA. (LOCAL). DR H ADRIAN REHNER; KENNEDY-KING COLLEGE; 6800 S WENTWORTH AVE; CHICAGO, IL 60621. (#11777-1).

MAR 24, '76. MUSIC OF THE REVOLUTION IN CHICAGO. THE PROJECT INVOLVES THE COLLECTION, REHEARSAL AND PRESENTATION OF SOLO CHORUS AND INSTRUMENTAL MATERIAL ABOUT THE REVOLUTION, FOR THE COLLEGE & SURROUNDING COMMUNITY; PERMANENT RECORD WILL BE KEPT. AT JACKIE ROBINSON MEMORIAL HALL; KENNEDY-KING COLLEGE,CHICAGO. (LOCAL). DR H ADRIAN REHNER; KENNEDY-KING COLLEGE; 6800 S WENTWORTH AVE; CHICAGO, IL 60621. (#11796-1).

APR 1 - MAY 2, '76. AMERICAN POSTER EXHIBITION, 'IMAGES OF AN ERA, 1945 TO 1975'. A COLLECTION OF 200 POSTERS THAT ARE REPRESENTATIVE OF THE LAST 30 YEARS IN POSTER ART. SHOWN WILL BE POSTERS FROM POLITICS, THE ENTERTAINMENT & ROCK FIELD, PROTEST, ECOLOGY AND CULTURAL EVENTS. AT MUSEUM OF SCIENCE & INDUSTRY. (REGN'L). DR VICTOR J DANILOV, DIR; MUSEUM OF SCIENCE AND INDUSTRY AND MOBIL OIL COMPANY; 57TH AND LAKE SHORE DR; CHICAGO, IL 60637. (#103416-242).

APR 4 - 10, '76. NATIONAL RURAL HEALTH WEEK. COMMEMORATIVE WEEK CELEBRATED NATIONWIDE ON COMMUNITY LEVEL IN CONJUNCTION WITH NATIONAL CONFERENCE ON RURAL HEALTH '76; PURPOSE: TO IMPROVE QUALITY OF LIFE THROUGH LOCAL INITIATIVE IN HEALTH PLANNING. AT NATIONWIDE. (NAT'L). KAREN ZUPKO; AMERICAN MEDICAL ASSOC; 535 N DEARBORN ST; CHICAGO, IL 60610. (#10950-1).

APR 5 - 6, '76. 26TH NATIONAL DENTAL HEALTH CONFERENCE. CONFERENCE FOR DENTISTS, HEALTH PROFESSIONALS, GOVERNMENT REPRESENTATIVES & CONSUMERS TO EXPLORE DEVELOPMENTS IN DENTAL HEALTH & DELIVERY SYSTEMS. AT ADA BLDG, 211 E CHICAGO AVE. (NAT'L). MARY BERNHARDT, PROJ DIR; AMER DENTAL ASSOC; 211 E CHICAGO AVE; CHICAGO, IL 60611. (#100941-1).

APR 7 - 8, '76. NATIONAL SENEGALESE DANCE COMPANY VISITS CHICAGO. LIVE PERFORMANCE AT AUDITORIUM THEATRE. (INT'L). PRESIDENT; MEL HOWARD PRESENTS; 143 E 27TH ST; NEW YORK, NY 10016. (#108968-2).

APR 7 - DEC 31, '76. 'CREATING A NEW NATION: 1763 - 1803'. EXHIBIT EXPLORES 40 TURBULENT YEARS FOLLOWING THE FRENCH AND INDIAN WARS. EXHIBIT HOURS SUNDAYS 12PM-5PM; GROUP RESERVATIONS ARE REQUIRED; EXHIBIT WILL BE CLOSED THANKSGIVING, CHRISTMAS, NEW YEAR'S. AT AMERICAN HISTORY GALLERY OF THE CHICAGO HISTORICAL SOCIETY. (ST-WIDE). CHRISTINE ROSE, COORD; CHICAGO HISTORICAL SOCIETY; CLARK ST AT NORTH AVE; CHICAGO, IL 60614. (#103416-365).

APR 9 - 10, '76. BICENT CONFERENCE ON A MODEL UNITED NATIONS. THE 20TH CENTURY PERSPECTIVE OF THE UNITED NATION WILL BE USED TO RE-EXAMINE THE ISSUES OF THE AMERICAN REVOLUTION, THE SLAVERY QUESTION AND THE CONDITION OF NATIVE AMERICANS. AT DOUGLAS LIBRARY, CHICAGO STATE UNIV. (LOCAL). DR ROBERT J KOVARIK; CHICAGO STATE UNIV BICENTENNIAL COMMISSION; 95 AT KING DR; CHICAGO, IL 60628. (#13601-1).

APR 11, '76. AMERICANA, AN ORIGINAL ORATORIO. LIVE PERFORMANCE AT MADONNA DELLA STRADA CHAPEL, ON CAMPUS, 6525 N SHERIDAN RD. (LOCAL). B G GROSS, PROF FINE ARTS; LOYOLA UNIVERSITY OF CHICAGO; 820 N MICHIGAN AVE; CHICAGO, IL 60611. (#104236-4).

APR 19 - 22, '76. NATIONAL CATHOLIC EDUCATIONAL ASSOCIATION CONVENTION & EXPOSITION. CONVENTION WILL BE DEVOTED TO SPECIAL 5-PART BICENTENNIAL THEME: LIFE, LIBERTY, HAPPINESS, EQUALITY AND PARTICIPATORY GOVERNMENT; EXHIBITS ON SCHOOL PRODUCTS, AMERICAN RELIGIOUS HERITAGE AND FAMOUS AMERICAN CATHOLICS. AT MCCORMICK PLACE, 23RD & S LAKE SHORE DR. (NAT'L). JOSEPH O'DONNELL, V-PRES; NATIONAL CATHOLIC EDUCATIONAL ASSOC; ONE DUPONT CIR, SUITE 350; WASHINGTON, DC 20036. (#101427-1).

APR 26 - 30, '76. KENNEDY-KING AND THE BICENTENNIAL, A BLACK ARTS AND CULTURAL FAIR. EXHIBIT, FESTIVAL, LIVE PERFORMANCE AT CAMPUS OF THE KENNEDY-KING COLLEGE, 6800 S WENTWORTH. (LOCAL). DR H ADRIAN REHNER; KENNEDY-KING COLLEGE; KENNEDY-KING COL, 6800 WENTWORTH; CHICAGO, IL 60621. (#24411-1).

APR 30 - MAY 2, '76. MIDWEST POSTAGE STAMP & COIN SHOW. EXHIBIT AT PALMER HOUSE HOTEL - STATE & MONROE STS. (REGN'L). RAY J WEST, CHAIRPERSON; MIDWEST STAMP AND COIN DEALERS; 3938 N PULASKI RD; CHICAGO, IL 60641. (#105707-1).

APR '76. KING GUSTAF OF SWEDEN OPENS EXHIBIT ON SWEDISH TECHNOLOGY & RESEARCH. EXHIBIT, OPENING AT MUSEUM OF SCIENCE & TECHNOLOGY. (INT'L). INFORMATION ATTACHE; EMBASSY OF SWEDEN; 600 NEW HAMPSHIRE AVE, NW; WASHINGTON, DC 20037. (#200016-279).

MAY 1, '76. BICENTENNIAL BENEFIT AND BRUNCH. AWARD, CEREMONY, FESTIVAL. (LOCAL). MARVA N LAND, CHMN; YPWW, DEPARTMENT #8; 9949 S WINSTON AVE; CHICAGO, IL 60643. (#200016-68).

MAY 17 - 23, '76. MARQUETTE FILM - SHOWING. COLOR FILM OF REID LEWIS'S 1973 RE-ENACTMENT OF MARQUETTE-JOLLIET CANOE VOYAGE OF DISCOVERY IN 17TH CENTURY. SHOWN ON WTTW-TV, CH 11 - CHICAGO EDUCATIONAL TV. (LOCAL). MICHAEL J WARD, PUB REL; LOYOLA UNIVERSITY OF CHICAGO & MARQUETTE NATIONAL BANK OF CHICAGO; 2160 S FIRST AVE, MEDICAL CNTR; MAYWOOD, IL 60153. (#104236-2).

MAY 17 - 31, '76. YOUNG ARTIST STUDIOS CONCERT SERIES-NEW MUSIC FROM CHICAGO. LIVE PERFORMANCE AT GOODMAN THEATER OF THE ART INSTITUTE OF CHICAGO. (LOCAL). JAMES GRIGSBY, ART INST; THE ART INSTITUTE OF CHICAGO; CHICAGO, IL 60603. (#24286-1).

MAY 19 - 21, '76. SYMPOSIUM ON HEALTH CARE DELIVERY AND RESEARCH 1976-2000. A SYMPOSIUM ON HEALTH CARE DELIVERY WILL FOCUS ON LOCAL, STATE AND NATIONAL NEEDS, POLICY, SERVICES AND RESEARCH TRENDS. AT PALMER HOUSE HOTEL. (ST-WIDE). DR C ASKEW, JR, COORD; UNIV OF ILLINOIS AT THE MEDICAL CENTER; 1750 W POLK ST; CHICAGO, IL 60612. (#8432-1).

MAY 19 - 22, '76. THE CASE FOR A UNITED NATIONS SYSTEM OF BICAMERAL WORLD FEDERATION. SEMINAR AT PRUDENTIAL BLDG, PRUDENTIAL PLAZA. (REGN'L). RICHARD FARKAS, PROJ DIR; DEPAUL UNIV; 2323 N SEMINARY AVE; CHICAGO, IL 60614. (#100428-1).

MAY 22 - 24, '76. ODORI FESTIVAL OF JAPAN VISITS CHICAGO. LIVE PERFORMANCE AT AUDITORIUM THEATRE. (INT'L). DIRECTOR; MEL HOWARD PRESENTS; 143 E 27TH ST; NEW YORK, NY 10016. (#108965-20).

MAY 23, '76. BICENTENNIAL CONCERT - CHICAGO CHAMBER CHOIR. LIVE PERFORMANCE AT CHURCH OF OUR SAVIOUR, 530 FULLERTON. (LOCAL). GEORGE ESTEVEZ, DIRECTOR; CHICAGO CHAMBER CHOIR; 2153 N SEDGWICK ST; CHICAGO, IL 60614. (#105208-1).

MAY '76. UNIV OF ILLINOIS CAMPUS DECORATION. WINDOW PAINTINGS AND WALL POSTERS, ETC WITH BICENTENNIAL THEMES IN HOSPITAL AND OTHER PUBLIC AND PATIENT CARE BUILDINGS. (LOCAL). IRWIN PIZER; UNIV OF ILLINOIS AT THE MEDICAL CENTER; 1750 W POLK ST; CHICAGO, IL 60612. (#8433-1).

MAY '76. VISIT BY QUEEN MARGRETHE II AND PRINCE HENRICK OF DENMARK. TOUR. (INT'L). BENT SKOU, PRESS OFFICE; DANISH EMBASSY; 3200 WHITEHAVEN PKY, NW; WASHINGTON, DC 20008. (#104972-11).

MAY - JUNE '76. 'A PROSPECT OF SCOTLAND' EXHIBIT. AN EXHIBITION PORTRAYING THE CLOSE LINKS BETWEEN SCOTLAND AND THE UNITED STATES. (INT'L). DIRECTOR; SCOTTISH COUNCIL, DEVELOPMENT & INDUSTRY; 1 CASTLE ST, EH2 3AJ; EDINBURGH/UNITED KINGDOM. (#109003-1).

JUNE 12, '76. CHICAGO CUP. COMPETITION. (LOCAL). CHRISTOPHER HIGHAM; US OF A RUGBY FOOTBALL UNION; 1 FIRST NATIONAL PLAZA; CHICAGO, IL 60603. (#200016-282).

JUNE 16 - SEPT 1, '76. ARCHITECTURE OF DEMOCRACY. TWO MEDIATED SHOWS ON THE HISTORY OF CHICAGO ARCHITECTURE WITH OUTSTANDING EXAMPLES OF MASTERPIECES OF THE CHICAGO SCHOOL OF ARCHITECTURE BY CROMBIE TAYLOR, FAIA. AT MUSEUM OF SCIENCE & INDUSTRY. (ST-WIDE). ALEXIA LALLI, DIRECTOR; ILLINOIS ARTS COUNCIL; 111 N WABASH AVE; CHICAGO, IL 60602. (#25739-1).

JUNE 21 - AUG 8, '76. EXHIBITION OF CONTEMPORARY YUGOSLAV PRINTS. EXHIBIT OF 99 PIECES OF GRAPHIC ARTS; INCL LITHOGRAPHS, SEROGRAPHS, ETCHINGS, ENGRAVINGS & AQUATINTS FROM THE BIENNAL GRAPHIC ARTS EXHIBIT HELD IN YUGOSLAVIA LAST YEAR. AT MUSEUM OF SCIENCE & INDUSTRY. (INT'L). DR VICTOR DANILOV, DIR; MUSEUM OF SCIENCE & INDUSTRY; MUSEUM OF SCIENCE & INDUST; CHICAGO, IL 60607. (#107162-1).

JUNE 23 - 26, '76. TRUCK WEEK '76 TRUCK AND EQUIPMENT EXHIBITION AND CONFERENCES. DISPLAY OF TRUCKING EQUIPMENT AND SERVICES FOR COMMERCIAL VEHICLES; CONFERENCES COVERING ENERGY CRISIS, MAINTENANCE LEGISLATION AND

CHICAGO — CONTINUED

REGULATIONS; AND SPECIAL DISPLAY OF ANTIQUE VEHICLES AND HISTORY OF TRUCKING INDUSTRY. AT MCCORMICK PLACE. (REGN'L). HENRY MARTIN, COORDINATOR; MOTOR & EQUIPMENT MANUFACTURERS ASSOC & SOCIETY OF AUTOMOTIVE ENG; PO BOX 439, 222 CEDAR LN; TEANECK, NJ 07666. (#15974-1).

JUNE 27 - JULY 4, '76. MULTI-RACIAL FESTIVAL OF THE AMERICAN REVOLUTION. MINORITIES FROM THE CITY'S WEST SIDE ARE HONORED DURING THIS CELEBRATION OF ETHNIC HERITAGE. AT DANIEL HAIL WILLIAMS UNIV. (LOCAL). DOROTHY FOSTER, COORD; DANIEL HAIL WILLIAMS UNIV; HURST MEM BLDG, 5247 W MADISON; CHICAGO, IL 60644. (#103416-432).

JUNE '76. 'BETWEEN FRIENDS/ENTRE AMIS'. AN EXHIBIT FROM CANADA, FEATURING PHOTOGRAPHS ON SHARED TOPOGRAPHY ALONG OUR COMMON BORDER. (INT'L). CULTURAL ATTACHE; CANADIAN EMBASSY; 1746 MASSACHUSETTS AVE; WASHINGTON, DC 20036. (#200016-453).

JULY 1 - 7, '76. STREET CELEBRATIONS THROUGHOUT THE CITY FOCUSING ON HISTORICAL EVENT. FESTIVAL AT DANIEL HALE WILLIAMS UNIVERSITY 5247 WEST MADISON CHICAGO ILLINOIS. (LOCAL). GLENICE B PEARSON; DANIEL HALE WILLIAMS UNIVERSITY; 5414 WEST MADISON; CHICAGO, IL 60644. (#50733-4).

JULY 1 - 18, '76. CANADIAN PARTICIPATION IN THE CHICAGO INTERNATIONAL FAIR. FAIR. (INT'L). K DE B PERCY, COORD; GOVERNMENT OF CANADA; 1746 MASSACHUSETTS AVE, NW; WASHINGTON, DC 20036. (#105111-12).

JULY 1 - 18, '76. CHICAGO INTERNATIONAL TRADE EXPOSITION. THE PROJECT WILL PORTRAY HISTORY AND IMPORTANCE OF WORLD TRADE TO THE NATION & CHICAGO'S ROLE IN WORLD TRADE; THERE WILL BE EXHIBITS FROM U S AND FOREIGN COMPANIES ON TRADE AND ECONOMIC DEVELOPMENT. AT NAVY PIER LAKE FRONT IN DOWNTOWN CHICAGO. (INT'L). THOMAS COULTER, EXEC DIR; CHICAGO ASSOC OF COMMERCE AND INDUSTRY; 130 S MICHIGAN AVE; CHICAGO, IL 60603. (#18314-1).

JULY 1 - SEPT 1, '76. WORLD OF FRANKLIN JEFFERSON EXHIBIT AT THE ART INSTITUTE. AN EXHIBIT OF HISTORICAL MEMORABILIA SPANNING 120 YEARS IN THE LIVES OF FRANKLIN AND JEFFERSON. DESIGNED BY CHARLES EAMES & SHOWN BY USIA OVERSEAS, IT WILL BE GIVEN A U.S. SHOWING BY ARBA IN 1976. (REGN'L). JACK MASEY; AMERICAN REVOLUTION BICENTENNIAL ADMINISTRATION; 2401 E STREET, NW; WASHINGTON, DC 20276. (#112-505).

JULY 1 - DEC 31, '76. EMPLOYEE SPIRIT OF '76 PERSONAL ACHIEVEMENT PROJECTS. PROJECTS TO ENCOURAGE PARTICIPANTS TO RECOGNIZE, RELATE, ASSIMILATE AND ACT ON THE PRINCIPLES OF BENJAMIN FRANKLIN SUCH AS SELF-MOTIVATORS AND A POSITIVE MENTAL ATTITUDE (PMA). (INT'L). ROBINSON P RIGG, V-PRES; COMBINED INSURANCE COMPANY OF AMERICA; 5050 BROADWAY; CHICAGO, IL 60640. (#18501-1).

JULY 1, '76 - CONTINUING . PAWNEE EARTH-LODGE ENVIRONMENT EXHIBITION. EXHIBIT AT ROOSEVELT RD & LAKE SHORE DR. (LOCAL). PHILLIP LEWIS, CHAIRMAN; FIELD MUSEUM OF NATURAL HISTORY; CHICAGO, IL 60605. (#16137-1).

JULY 3, '76. TIME CAPSULE BURIAL. CEREMONY. (LOCAL). LILLIAN DEMSKI, PROJ DIR; COR-WOOD-CHICAGO BICENTENNIAL COMMITTEE; 1850 N WOOD ST; CHICAGO, IL 60622. (#106100-2).

JULY 24, '76. SCOTTISH NATIONAL ORCHESTRA CHORUS. LIVE PERFORMANCE AT RAVINIA THEATER. (INT'L). CULTURAL AFFAIRS OFFICE; BRITISH EMBASSY; 3100 MASSACHUSETTS AVE, NW; WASHINGTON, DC 20008. (#108960-6).

JULY 27 - 29, '76. BATH SILVER RING CHOIR. LIVE PERFORMANCE. (INT'L). CULTURAL AFFAIRS OFFICE; BRITISH EMBASSY; 3100 MASSACHUSETTS AVE, NW; WASHINGTON, DC 20008. (#108959-3).

AUG 20, '76 - OCT 1, '77. HISTORICAL EXHIBITION TOUR. EXHIBIT WILL ILLUSTRATE PARALLELS BETWEEN AUSTRALIAN & AMERICAN HISTORICAL DEVELOPMENT. AT MUSEUM OF SCIENCE & INDUSTRY. (INT'L). JOHN MAUNDER, DIRECTOR; AUSTRALIAN CONSULATE GENERAL; 636 5TH AVE; NEW YORK, NY 10020. (#108143-1).

SEPT 4 - 5, '76. THE FIFTH LITHUANIAN FOLK DANCE FESTIVAL IN THE UNITED STATES. OVER 2,000 DANCERS FROM THE USA, CANADA, VENEZUELA, BRAZIL & EUROPE WILL PERFORM FESTIVAL'S PROGRAM WHICH IS DEDICATED TO AMERICA'S BICENTENNIAL. THE FESTIVAL'S ACTIVITIES WILL START SEPT 4, 1976 BUT DANCE PROGRAM AT INTERNATL AMPHITHEATRE ON SEPT 5 WILL START 2PM. AT INTERNATIONAL AMPHITHEATRE, CHICAGO, ILLINOIS. (INT'L). BRUNO P JUODELIS, COORD; LITHUANIAN AMERICAN COMMUNITY & LITHUANIAN FOLK DANCE FESTIVALS, INC; 912 PLAINFIELD ROAD; DOWNERS GROVE, IL 60515. (#106671-1).

SEPT 6 - 24, '76. CARL HAVERLIN/BROADCAST MUSIC, INC, ARCHIVES BICENTENNIAL EXHIBIT. OFFERS A VERSATILE PICTURE OF HISTORY, REGIONAL LIFE & MUSIC FOR OVER 200 YEARS. CONTAINS PRESIDENTIAL LETTERS, LETTERS OF FAMOUS AMERICANS, OLD BOOKS, MANUSCRIPTS, HISTORY OF 'THE STAR SPANGLED BANNER' & COMPOSER AUTOGRAPHS, PLUS SHEET MUSIC OF THE PAST. AT CHICAGO PUBLIC LIBRARY, CULTURAL CENTER, 78 E WASHINGTON ST. (ST-WIDE). JUDY WEISMAN, COORD; CHICAGO PUBLIC LIBRARY; 78 E WASHINGTON ST; CHICAGO, IL 60602. (#20784-17).

SEPT 7 - 9, '76. UNITED STATES ARMED FORCES BICENTENNIAL CARAVAN. CARAVAN IS COMPOSED OF EXHIBIT VANS FOR EACH MILITARY SERVICE. PROJECT THEME IS 'HISTORY OF THE ARMED FORCES & THEIR CONTRIBUTIONS TO THE NATION.'. (LOCAL). JACK REILLY, MAYOR'S OFC; UNITED STATES ARMED FORCES BICENTENNIAL CARAVAN; 121 N. LASALLE ST; CHICAGO, IL 60670. (#1775-643).

SEPT 12, '76. DEDICATION OF ETERNAL FLAME AND BRONZE PLAQUE WITH VETERANS NAMES. DEDICATION OF ETERNAL FLAME & BRONZE PLAQUE WITH 244 NAMES OF VETERANS INTERRED IN CEDAR PARK. U S CONGRESSMAN MARTIN RUSSO WAS SPEAKER OF THE DAY. AT CEDAR PARK CEMETERY. (ST-WIDE). LAWRENCE C ANSPACH, CHMN; CEDAR PARK CEMETERY ASSOCIATION, INC; 12540 S HALSTED ST; CHICAGO, IL 60643. (#200016-375).

SEPT 15 - NOV 30, '76. 'MY BROTHERS' KEEPER' EXHIBIT. EXHIBIT OF JEWISH COMMUNAL CONTRIBUTIONS. AT MUSEUM OF SCIENCE & INDUSTRY, 57TH & LAKESHORE DR. (LOCAL). MARCIA JOSEPHY; AMERICAN JEWISH CONGRESS & JEWISH FEDERATION OF METRO CHICAGO; 22 W MONROE ST, SUITE 2102; CHICAGO, IL 60603. (#27666-1).

SEPT 19 - ??, '76. ISRAELI PHILHARMONIC ORCHESTRA VISITS CHICAGO. LIVE PERFORMANCE. (INT'L). URI AHARON BAR-NEV; ISRAELI GOVERNMENT; 1621 21ST ST, NW; WASHINGTON, DC 20008. (#109015-17).

SEPT 26, '76. LONDON SCHOOLS SYMPHONY ORCHESTRA. LIVE PERFORMANCE AT ORCHESTRA HALL. (INT'L). CULTURAL AFFAIRS OFFICE; BRITISH EMBASSY; 3100 MASSACHUSETTS AVE, NW; WASHINGTON, DC 20008. (#108963-4).

SEPT 27 - OCT 8, '76. CARL HAVERLIN/BROADCAST MUSIC, INC, ARCHIVES BICENTENNIAL EXHIBIT. OFFERS A VERSATILE PICTURE OF HISTORY, REGIONAL LIFE & MUSIC FOR OVER 200 YEARS. CONTAINS PRESIDENTIAL LETTERS, LETTERS OF FAMOUS AMERICANS, OLD BOOKS, MANUSCRIPTS, HISTORY OF 'THE STAR SPANGLED BANNER' & COMPOSER AUTOGRAPHS, PLUS SHEET MUSIC OF THE PAST. AT DE PAUL UNIV LIBRARIES. (ST-WIDE). GLENN RSCHARFENORTH; DE PAUL UNIVERSITY; 25 E JACKSON BLVD; CHICAGO, IL 60604. (#20784-19).

SEPT 30, '76 - CONTINUING . 'GRAPHIC WORKS OF JAMES ENSOR' EXHIBIT. EXHIBIT AT ART INSTITUTE OF CHICAGO. (REGN'L). CULTURAL ATTACHE; EMBASSY OF BELGIUM; 3330 GARFIELD ST; WASHINGTON, DC 20008. (#200016-503).

OCT 1 - NOV 18, '76. U S TELEVISION COMMERCIALS FESTIVAL. AWARDS COMPETITION FOR U S & CANADIAN TELEVISION COMMERCIALS WITH SPECIAL CATEGORY FOR THOSE RELATING TO U S BICENTENNIAL CELEBRATION; THIS WILL BE FOLLOWED BY SCREENING OF WINNING COMMERCIALS & AWARDS PRESENTATIONS; THIS IS THE 6TH ANNUAL EVENT. (INT'L). J W ANDERSON, CHAIRMAN; U S TELEVISION COMMERCIALS FESTIVAL; 1008 BELLWOOD AVE; BELLWOOD, IL 60104. (#100190-1).

OCT 1 - DEC 31, '76. ILLINOIS PIONEER LIFE GALLERY. LIVE DEMONSTRATIONS OF DOMESTIC ACTIVITIES INCLUDING SPINNING, WEAVING, NATURAL DYEING, CANDLE DIPPING, CORN MEAL PREPARATION, QUILTING, AND FLAX PROCESSING. CLOSED DEC 5. AT CLARK ST AT NORTH AVE. (REGN'L). NANCY LACE, COORD; CHICAGO HISTORICAL SOCIETY; CHICAGO, IL 60614. (#103416-653).

OCT 5, '76 - MAR 1, '77. FAITH & FORM - PHOTOGRAPHIC EXHIBIT. AN EXHIBIT ON THE HISTORY OF SYNAGOGUE ARCHITECTURE. AT 618 S MICHIGAN AVE, CHICAGO, IL 60605. (LOCAL). ARTHUR FELDMAN, DIRECTOR; SPERTUS MUSEUM; 618 S MICHIGAN; CHICAGO, IL 60605. (#27737-1).

OCT 11 - DEC 26, '76. 'ITALIAN EXPLORERS OF AMERICA'. AN EXHIBIT ON THE CONTRIBUTIONS OF EARLY ITALIAN EXPLORERS TO THE DISCOVERY & DEVELOPMENT OF THE NEW WORLD. CLOSED CHRISTMAS DAY ONLY. (REGN'L). DR VICTOR J DANILOV, DIR; MUSEUM OF SCIENCE & INDUSTRY; 57TH ST & LAKE SHORE DR; CHICAGO, IL 60637. (#5-3).

OCT 29 - 31, '76. NATIONAL SYMPOSIUM: 'THE GREEK EXPERIENCE IN AMERICA'. SYMPOSIUM WILL PRESENT 24 PAPERS ON ASPECTS OF THE GREEK DIASPORA AND CONTRIBUTION TO THE UNITED STATES BY EXPERTS ON GREEK ETHNICITY. AFTERWARDS, THE PAPERS WILL BE PUBLISHED IN BOOK FORM. AT CENTER FOR CONTINUING EDUCATION, 1307 E 60TH. (REGN'L). ANDREW T KOPAN, DIRECTOR; MODERN GREEK STUDIES ASSOC; 1228 ASHLAND AVE; RIVER FOREST, IL 60605. (#24722-1).

OCT 30, '76. SOKOL USA 80TH ANNIVERSARY BANQUET. CEREMONY. (NAT'L). A VENGLARCHIK, JR,PRES; SOKOL USA; 276 PROSPECT ST; EAST ORANGE, NJ 07019. (#109113-1).

NOV 1, '76. HISTORY OF HULL HOUSE NEIGHBORHOOD ETHNIC GROUPS - EXHIBIT. AN EXHIBIT TELLING THE HISTORY OF THE OLD HULL-HOUSE NEIGHBORHOOD ON THE NEAR WEST SIDE OF CHICAGO INCLUDING A MODEL OF HULL-HOUSE, AN EXHIBIT OF HISTORIC MATERIALS & SLIDE-TAPE PRESENTATIONS. (LOCAL). MARY ANN JOHNSON, ADMIN; JANE ADDAMS HULL-HOUSE AT THE UNIV OF ILLINOIS-CHICAGO CIR; BOX 4348; CHICAGO, IL 60680. (#24290-1).

NOV 7, '76. LONDON PHILHARMONIC ORCHESTRA VISITS CHICAGO. LIVE PERFORMANCE AT ORCHESTRA HALL. (INT'L). CULTURAL AFFAIRS OFFICE; BRITISH EMBASSY; 3100 MASSACHUSETTS AVE, NW; WASHINGTON, DC 20008. (#108958-1).

NOV 8 - 11, '76. 'INFO 76' EXPOSITION & CONFERENCE. EMPHASIS IS ON APPLICATIONS-HOW TO USE THE COMPUTER & OTHER INFORMATION SYSTEMS TO INCREASE PRODUCTIVITY & PROFITABILITY. MORE THAN 150 EXHIBITORS, 2,000 APPLICATION ENGINEERS, 10,000 APPLICATION PACKAGES FOR INFO MANAGEMENT EXECUTIVES, CORPORATE EXECUTIVES & OTHERS. AT MCCORMICK PLACE. (NAT'L). DIRECTOR, INFO 76; CLAPP & POLIAK, INC; 245 PARK AVE; NEW YORK, NY 10017. (#109317-1).

NOV 19 - 21, '76. BLACK BICENTENNIAL CELEBRATION. FESTIVAL AT HARRIS YWCA, 6200 S DREXEL. (LOCAL). ALDEN LAWSON; THE WOODLAWN ORGANIZATION; 1180 E 83RD ST; CHICAGO, IL 60637. (#27668-1).

DEC 8 - 11, '76. LA SALLE EXPEDITION II, A HISTORIC RE-ENACTMENT. THIS IS AN AUTHENTIC RE-ENACTMENT OF THE 1681 LASALLE EXPEDITION FROM MONTREAL, CANADA TO NEW ORLEANS, LA WHICH WILL BEGIN TOURING ON AUGUST 11, 1976 AND END ON APRIL 9, 1977. (LOCAL). REID H LEWIS, DIRECTOR; LA SALLE EXPEDITION II; 135 S LA SALLE ST, RM 411; CHICAGO, IL 60690. (#102805-28).

JAN 17 - FEB 20, '77. 'REMEMBER THE LADIES' WOMEN IN AMERICA 1750-1815 EXHIBIT. ART EXHIBITION OF ART & ARTIFACTS ON THE ROLE & STATUS OF WOMEN, IN CLUDING SECTIONS ON CHILDHOOD, MARRIAGE, DEATH, FASHION, & CREATIVE WOMEN. AT CHICAGO HIST SOCIETY, NORTH AVE & CLARK ST. (REGN'L). MRS SKRAMSTAD; THE PILGRIM SOCIETY; CHICAGO HISTORICAL SOCIETY; CHICAGO, IL 60614. (#107840-4).

JAN '77 - CONTINUING . PLANNING AMERICA'S GREAT CITIES, AN EXHIBITION. EXHIBIT, RADIO/TV AT MUSEUM OF SCIENCE & INDUSTRY. (REGN'L). MS LEE KIMCHE; ASSOC OF SCIENCE & TECHNOLOGY; 2100 PENNSYLVANIA AVE, NW; WASHINGTON, DC 20037. (#8615-8).

MAR 18 - APR 24, '77. 'THE DUTCH REPUBLIC IN THE DAYS OF JOHN ADAMS' - SITES EXHIBIT. THIS EXHIBIT DEPICTS THE HISTORY, ART, SCIENCE AND SOCIETY OF 18TH CENTURY HOLLAND. AT THE ART INSTITUTE. (INT'L). CONSUL GENERAL; SITES & ROYAL NETHERLANDS EMBASSY; 410 N MICHIGAN AVE, SUITE 642; CHICAGO, IL 60611. (#26670-3).

MAR 28 - 31, '77. INTERNATIONAL ELECTRIC VEHICLE EXPOSITION & CONFERENCE. EXHIBIT WILL FEATURE URBAN MASS TRANSIT SYSTEMS, ELECTRIC BUSES AND VANS, AUTOS, GOLF CARTS, PEOPLE MOVER SYSTEMS, FORKLIFT TRUCKS AND SUBMARINES; IT IS THE FIRST INTERNATIONAL FORUM & EXPOSITION DEVOTED TO ALL FORMS OF ELECTRICALLY POWERED VEHICLES. AT MCCORMICK PL. (INT'L). JERRY VAN DYK, MANAGER; THE ELECTRIC VEHICLE COUNCIL; 331 MADISON AVE; NEW YORK, NY 10017. (#104551-1).

CHICAGO HGTS

AMERICAN BUSINESS, EXHIBITS & SPEAKERS - CHICAGO. AMERICAN BUSINESS WILL BE EXPLORED THROUGH EXHIBITS & SPEAKERS. (LOCAL). N. FRANKLIN HURT, CHAIRMAN; PRAIRIE STATE COLLEGE BICENTENNIAL COMM; 197TH AND HALSTED; CHICAGO HGTS, IL 60411. (#13513).

AMERICAN EDUCATION, ITS PAST & FUTURE. A SERIES OF SEMINARS & PROJECTS ON THE PHILOSOPHY OF AMERICAN EDUCATION. (LOCAL). N. FRANKLIN HURT, CHRMN; PRAIRIE STATE COLLEGE BICENTENNIAL COMM; 197TH AND HALSTED; CHICAGO HGTS, IL 60411. (#13510).

AMERICAN LABOR, LECTURES & EXHIBITS IN CHICAGO. THE HISTORY OF AMERICAN LABOR & THE PROTESTANT WORK ETHIC WILL BE EXAMINED THROUGH LECTURES & EXHIBITS. (LOCAL). N. FRANKLIN HURT, CHAIRMAN; PRAIRIE STATE COLLEGE BICENTENNIAL COMM; 197TH AND HALSTED; CHICAGO HGTS, IL 60411. (#13512).

AMERICAN MOVIES, HISTORY IN ART - CHICAGO, IL. A FILM SERIES & HISTORY STARTING WITH D W GRIFFITH'S 'BIRTH OF A NATION.'. (LOCAL). N. FRANKLIN HURT, CHAIRMAN; PRAIRIE STATE COLLEGE BICENTENNIAL COMM; 197TH AND HALSTED; CHICAGO HGTS, IL 60411. (#13511).

AMERICAN SCULPTURING, A SERIES OF LECTURES - IL. THE PROJECT CONSIST OF LECTURES AND EXHIBITS ON AMERICAN SCULPTURE. (LOCAL). N FRANKLIN HURT, CHAIRMAN, BICENT COMMITTEE; PRAIRIE STATE COLLEGE; 197TH AND HALSTED; CHICAGO HGTS, IL 60411. (#13509).

A CALENDAR OF HISTORIC EVENTS - CHICAGO, IL. A CALENDAR OF NOTABLE HISTORIC EVENTS WILL BE DEVISED BY THE PRAIRIE STATE HISTORY DEPT AND PUBLISHED IN A LOCAL NEWSPAPER. 2. (LOCAL). N. FRANKLIN HURT, CHAIRMAN; PRAIRIE STATE COLLEGE BICENTENNIAL COMM; 197TH AND HALSTED; CHICAGO HGTS, IL 60411. (#13517).

DRAMATIC PRESENTATIONS BASED IN AMERICANA - IL. PLAYS AND READINGS WILL BE PRESENTED WITH EMPHASIS ON ALL THE FINE ARTS. (LOCAL). N. FRANKLIN HURT, CHAIRMAN; PRAIRIE STATE COLLEGE BICENTENNIAL COMM; 197TH AND HALSTED; CHICAGO HGTS, IL 60411. (#13516).

HISTORY OF THE MEXICAN AMERICANS IN CHICAGO HGTS. A RESEARCHED & WRITTEN HISTORY OF THE MEXICAN AMERICANS IN THE CHICAGO HEIGHTS AREA. THE BOOK TRACES THE ORIGINS, PROBLEMS & COMMUNITY DEVELOPMENT OF THIS ETHNIC GROUP. (LOCAL). N FRANKLIN HURT, CHAIRMAN; PRAIRIE STATE COLLEGE BICENTENNIAL COMMITTEE; 197TH & HALSTED; CHICAGO HGTS, IL 60411. (#13507).

A METRIC SYSTEM BROCHURE PROJ OF PRAIRIE ST, IL. THIS BROCHURE WILL GIVE THE METRIC EQUIVALENTS TO THE PRESENT ENGLISH DERIVED SYSTEM TO AID THE GENERAL PUBLIC WITH THE FORTHCOMING CONVERSION TO THE METRIC SYSTEM. (LOCAL). N FRANKLIN HURT, CHAIRMAN; PRAIRIE STATE COLLEGE BICENTENNIAL COMMITTEE; 197TH & HALSTED; CHICAGO HGTS, IL 60411. (#13508).

ORAL HISTORY PROJECT AT PRAIRIE STATE COLLEGE, IL. TAPES WILL BE MADE OF VIGNETTES & ANECDOTES TOLD BY THE AGED IN THE COMMUNITY SO THAT ALL MAY BETTER UNDERSTAND OUR HISTORY. (LOCAL). N. FRANKLIN HURT, CHAIRMAN; PRAIRIE STATE COLLEGE BICENTENNIAL COMM; 197TH AND HALSTED; CHICAGO HGTS, IL 60411. (#13515).

REVOLUTIONARY WAR PROJECT FOR PRAIRIE ST COL - IL. THE COLLEGE WILL DEVELOPE A REVOLUTIONARY WAR CALENDAR DIORAMAS DIORAMAS. (LOCAL). N. FRANKLIN HURT, CHAIRMAN; PRAIRIE STATE COLLEGE BICENTENNIAL COMM; 197TH AND HALSTED; CHICAGO HGTS, IL 60411. (#13506).

CHICAGO HGTS — CONTINUED

THE ROLE OF WOMEN IN AMERICAN HISTORY - CHICAGO. A SERIES OF SEMINARS AND SPEAKERS ON WOMEN. (LOCAL). N. FRANKLIN HURT, CHAIRMAN; PRAIRIE STATE COLLEGE BICENTENNIAL COMM; 197TH AND HALSTED; CHICAGO HGTS, IL 60411. (#13514).

FEB 10 - DEC 23, '76. LATIN AMERICAN FORUM. BI-WEEKLY FORUMS TO BRING INFORMATION TO LATIN AMERICAN COMMUNITY ABOUT THE VARIOUS SOCIAL SERVICES AVAILABLE. WRITE FOR MORE INFORMATION. NO PHONE CALLS. AT PRAIRIE STATE COLLEGE, 197TH & HALSTED. (LOCAL). FRANCISCO RODRIGUEZ, DIR; COUNCIL OF LATIN AMERICAN AGENCIES, INC; 2709 CHICAGO RD; CHICAGO HTS, IL 60411. (#107759-1).

MAY 14 - 16, '76. AWARD MUSICAL: '1776'. AWARD-WINNING MUSICAL '1776' TO BE PRESENTED LIVE. RELIVE THE SIGNING OF THE DECLARATION OF INDEPENDENCE AND ITS IMPACT UPON ALL PEOPLE. SUNDAY PERFORMANCE - 7:30 PM. AT BLOOM HIGH SCHOOL AUDITORIUM, 210 & DIXIE. (LOCAL). PAUL MANDEL, PRESIDENT; CHICAGO HEIGHTS DRAMA GROUP; 330 W 202ND ST; CHICAGO HGTS, IL 60411. (#100957-1).

CHILICOTHE

RENOVATION OF SHORE ACRES IN CHILICOTHE, IL. SHORE ACRES WILL BE RENOVATED. (LOCAL). RICHARD SMITH, COORDINATOR; PEORIA COUNTY BICENTENNIAL COMMISSION; 8075 SANTA FE; CHILICOTHE, IL 61523. (#33644).

CICERO

MAR 28, '76. SPIRIT OF CLOVERLEAF SCOUTS IN '76'. ARTS AND CRAFTS AND FOOD. AT CICERO COMMUNITY CHEST BUILDDING, 5341 W. CERMAK RD. (LOCAL). MRS HARDING; CLOVERLEAF GIRL SCOUT COUNCIL; 3507 S 53RD AVE; CICERO, IL 60650. (#104434-1).

CLAYTON

SEPT 13 - 14, '75. TURN OF CENTURY 1890-1910. GAY NINETIES LIFESTYLE ENTERTAINMENT. (ST-WIDE). MS JANET PICKETT; ILL DEPT OF CONSERVATION; 901 SOUTH SPRING; SPRINGFIELD, IL 62704. (#50272-13).

JUNE 13, '76. DEDICATION OF THE AVENUE OF FLAGS. CEREMONY AT CLAYTON TOWNSHIP LIBRARY. (LOCAL). ISABEL BAPTIST, CHMN; EASTERN ADAMS COUNTY BICENTENNIAL COMMISSION; CLAYTON, IL 62324. (#200016-179).

SEPT 11 - 12, '76. TURN OF CENTURY 1890-1910. GAY NINETIES LIFESTYLE ENTERTAINMENT. (ST-WIDE). MS JANET PICKETT; ILL DEPT OF CONSERVATION; 901 SOUTH SPRING; SPRINGFIELD, IL 62704. (#50272-14).

CLINTON

A GIFT TO DEWITT COUNTY - CLINTON, IL. THE HISTORIC HERITAGE OF DEWITT COUNTY, INCLUDING VALUABLE DOCUMENTS AND ARTIFACTS, WILL BE PRESERVED IN A FACILITY PROVIDED BY THE DEWITT COUNTY BICENT COMMISSION; IT WILL SERVE AS A REFERENCE SOURCE. (LOCAL). MRS JAMES THORP, PROJ DIRECTOR; DEWITT COUNTY BICENTENNIAL COMMISSION; RR 3; CLINTON, IL 61727. (#10653).

OCT 1, '75 - DEC 3, '76. DEDICATION OF HISTORY EXHIBIT. EXHIBIT CONTAINS MEMORABILIA FROM CLINTON, IL. DEWITT COUNTY. AT DEWITT COUNTY MUSEUM, 'HOMESTEAD', 217 E WOODLAWN. (LOCAL). MRS JAMES THORP; DEWITT COUNTY BICENTENNIAL COMMISSION; RR 3; CLINTON, IL 61727. (#10622-1).

SEPT 10, '76. LINCOLN'S EIGHTH JUDICIAL CIRCUIT COURT RIDE. LIVE PERFORMANCE. (ST-WIDE). PHYLLIS EUBANKS, CHMN; ILLINOIS DEPARTMENT OF CONSERVATION; 901 S SPRING ST; SPRINGFIELD, IL 62706. (#200016-178).

CNTRY CLB HLS

INDEPENDENCE PARK - COUNTRY CLUB HILLS, IL. DEVELOP EXISTING SITE INTO PARK WITH BALL FIELDS, PAVILION, PLAYGROUND EQUIPMENT & MONUMENT. (LOCAL). DONALD RICHTER, CHAIRMAN; BICENTENNIAL COMMISSION OF COUNTRY CLUB HILLS; 3701 W 175TH PL; CNTRY CLB HLS, IL 60477. (#28649).

JULY 4, '76. PARADE & COMMUNITY UNITY DAY - 4TH OF JULY. PARADE, FESTIVAL AT MAX ATKINS PARK - 179TH ST & MAPLE AVE. (LOCAL). ADRIENNE HARDT, COORD; BICENTENNIAL COMMISSION OF COUNTRY CLUB HILLS & PARK DISTRICT; 3701 W 175TH PL; CNTRY CLB HLS, IL 60477. (#200016-228).

COLCHESTER

SEPT 2 - 6, '76. MCDONOUGH COUNTY SESQUICENTENNIAL & BICENTENNIAL CELEBRATION. FESTIVAL AT FRIENDWAY PARK & ARGYLE LAKE STATE PARK. (LOCAL). LARRY CARSON; COLCHESTER LIONS CLUB; COLCHESTER, IL 62326. (#103391-6).

COLFAX

SEPT 23, '75. BICENTENNIAL KICK-OFF PROGRAM. KICK-OFF FOR BICENTENNIAL ACTIVITIES WILL INCLUDE PRESENTATION OF BICENTENNIAL COMMUNITY FLAG, THE HONORABLE LES AREND AS KEYNOTE SPEAKER; JOE DOWELL AS EMCEE PRESENTING MUSIC WITH A BICENTENNIAL THEME. (LOCAL). JOAN POOL, CHMN; COLFAX ANCHOR BICENTENNIAL COMMISSION; 311 W NORTH ST; COLFAX, IL 61728. (#102098-1).

JUNE 18 - 20, '76. BICENTENNIAL FESTIVAL. PARK DEDICATION, PAGEANT, DANCE, PARADE, CRAFT DEMONSTRATIONS, EXHIBITS, FOOD AND HORSE SHOW. AT COLFAX PARK. (LOCAL). JOAN POOL, CHAIRMAN; COLFAX ANCHOR BICENTENNIAL COMMITTEE; COLFAX, IL 61728. (#50485-1).

COLLINSVILLE

MAY 22 - 23, '76. THE NATIVE ILLINOISAN-CAHOKIA MOUNDS. ILLINOIS' INDIAN CULTURES. (ST-WIDE). MS JANET PICKETT; ILL DEPT OF CONSERVATION; 901 SOUTH STREET; SPRINGFIELD, IL 62704. (#50272-15).

COLONA

MAY 29, '76 - CONTINUING . ANNUAL MEMORIAL DAY PARADE. VARIOUS THEMES, FLOATS, BANDS & MARCHING GROUPS. (LOCAL). PATRICIA PERKINS, CHMN; COLONA-GREEN ROCK AMERICAN LEGION; BROADWAY AVE; COLONA, IL 61241. (#109291-1).

COMPTON

BICENTENNIAL PROJECTS IN COMPTON, IL. MUCH-NEEDED NEW PROJECTS INVOLVING ENTIRE COMMUNITY WERE BEGUN, SUCH AS FREE LENDING LIBRARY & WEEKLY CARD SOCIALS. (LOCAL). MRS DONALD SWOPE, CHAIRMAN; COMPTON BICENTENNIAL COMMISSION; BOX 148; COMPTON, IL 61318. (#29524).

JUNE 25 - 27, '76. COMPTON BICENTENNIAL HOMECOMING & PARADE. STRAWBERRY ICE CREAM SOCIAL, DEDICATION OF TIME CAPSULE MONUMENT & FLAGPOLE. CHORUS, STAGE SHOW, 'LITTLE SUSIE', DANCING AND TOURS. AT BICENTENNIAL HEADQUARTERS AND CITY PARK. (REGN'L). MRS DONALD SWOPE, CHMN; BICENTENNIAL COMMISSION OF COMPTON; BOX 148; COMPTON, IL 61318. (#200016-219).

COOKSVILLE

BICENTENNIAL EMBLEM - COOKSVILLE, IL. A CONTEST WAS HELD TO DESIGN A TOWN EMBLEM; THE WINNING EMBLEM WAS IMPRINTED ON PLATES AND PINS. (LOCAL). LAUREL QUAID, CHAIRMAN; COOKSVILLE-BLUE MOUND TWP BICENTENNIAL COMMISSION; BOX 41; COOKSVILLE, IL 61730. (#29335).

BICENTENNIAL NEWSPAPER - COOKSVILLE, IL. A CONTEST WAS HELD FOR STORIES OF THE AREA'S PAST; ENTRIES WERE PUBLISHED IN A NEWSPAPER FORMAT. (LOCAL). LAUREL QUAID, CHAIRMAN; COOKSVILLE-BLUE MOUND TWP BICENTENNIAL COMMISSION; BOX 41; COOKSVILLE, IL 61730. (#29334).

HISTORICAL MARKERS - COOKSVILLE, IL. 4 INSCRIBED BOULDERS WERE PLACED AT HISTORIC SITES IN THE TOWNSHIP. (LOCAL). LAUREL QUAID, CHAIRMAN; COOKSVILLE-BLUE MOUND TWP BICENTENNIAL COMMISSION; BOX 41; COOKSVILLE, IL 61730. (#29332).

PLAYGROUND EQUIPMENT - COOKSVILLE, IL. A SWING SET, SLIDE, MERRY-GO-ROUND, VOLLEYBALL NET AND TETHER BALL WILL BE SET UP ON THE SCHOOL GROUNDS. (LOCAL). LAUREL QUAID, CHAIRMAN; COOKSVILLE-BLUE MOUND TWP BICENTENNIAL COMMISSION; BOX 41; COOKSVILLE, IL 61730. (#29333).

APR 28, '75. PAUL REVERE RECEPTION. RECEPTION FOR LOCAL RADIO PERSONALITY WHO WAS TOURING COUNTY FOR BICENTENNIAL KICKOFF AND TAKING PLEDGES FOR WALK FOR MANKIND. TAPED INTERVIEW & REFRESHMENTS. AT VILLAGE HALL. (LOCAL). LAUREL QUAID, CHMN; COOKSVILLE-BLUE MOUND TOWNSHIP BICENTENNIAL COMMISSION; BOX 41; COOKSVILLE, IL 61730. (#200016-216).

JULY 4, '75. 4TH OF JULY CELEBRATION. COMPETITION, FESTIVAL, PARADE AT DOWNTOWN AREA. (LOCAL). LAUREL QUAID, CHMN; COOKSVILLE-BLUE MOUND TOWNSHIP BICENTENNIAL COMMISSION; BOX 41; COOKSVILLE, IL 61730. (#200016-214).

DEC 14, '75. BICENTENNIAL FLAG PRESENTATION PROGRAM. BAND CONCERT, CHORUS, PATRIOTIC READING, PRESENTATION OF ARBA FLAG BY STATE REPRESENTATIVE GERALD BRADLEY, REFRESHMENTS. AT SCHOOL GYM. (LOCAL). LAUREL QUAID, CHMN; COOKSVILLE-BLUE MOUND TOWNSHIP BICENTENNIAL COMMISSION; BOX 41; COOKSVILLE, IL 61730. (#200016-217).

JULY 4, '76. 4TH OF JULY CELEBRATION. FLAG PRESENTED TO BOY SCOUTS BY AMVETS AND LEGION. COMMUNITY CHURCH SERVICE, PARADE, GAMES, CONTESTS, CAKE WALK, PIG ROAST AND FIREWORKS. AT DOWNTOWN AREA. (LOCAL). LAUREL QUAID, CHMN; COOKSVILLE-BLUE MOUND TOWNSHIP BICENTENNIAL COMMISSION; BOX 41; COOKSVILLE, IL 61730. (#200016-215).

COUNTRYSIDE

BICENTENNIAL FESTIVAL. FESTIVAL. (LOCAL). WALTER KLIMCKE; BICENTENNIAL COMMITTEE; 5426 7 AVE; COUNTRYSIDE, IL 60525. (#200016-283).

COUNTRYSIDE, IL BICENTENNIAL PROJECTS. PROJECTS INCLUDE A COMMEMORATIVE PLAQUE & A TIME CAPSULE. (LOCAL). M TLAPA, CO-CHAIRMAN; COUNTRYSIDE BICENTENNIAL COMMITTEE; 5550 EAST AVE; COUNTRYSIDE, IL 60525. (#33643).

COWDEN

COVERED BRIDGE MARKING, COWDEN, IL. THE THOMPSON MILL COVERED BRIDGE WAS MARKED AND DEDICATED. (LOCAL). GRACE MOYER, PROJ COORDINATOR; SHELBY COUNTY BICENTENNIAL COMMISSION; BOX 387, HICKORY RIDGE LA; SHELBYVILLE, IL 62565. (#33642).

PIONEER VILLAGE OF COWDEN, ILLINOIS. RECREATE LIFESTYLE & ACTIVITIES OF PIONEERS. VILLAGE WILL COVER AREAS SUCH AS CRAFTS, ENTERTAINMENT, ETC. (LOCAL). T A MOORE, PRESIDENT; COWDEN PIONEER DAYS; COWDEN, IL 62422. (#2587).

TWO LOG CABINS FOR PIONEER VILLAGE - COWDEN, IL. RELOCATION AND RECONSTRUCTION OF TWO LOG CABINS FOR COWDEN'S PIONEER VILLAGE. (LOCAL). HON MOORE, MAYOR; VILLAGE OF COWDEN; COWDEN, IL 62422. (#27877). **ARBA GRANTEE.**

AUG 26 - 29, '76. PIONEER VILLAGE ARTS & CRAFTS AND RODEO. FESTIVAL AT VILLAGE PARK. (LOCAL). T A MOORE, CHMN; COWDEN PIONEER DAYS; STATE BANK BLDG; COWDEN, IL 62422. (#103503-1).

CRESCENT CITY

JULY 4, '76. COUNTYWIDE PRAYER SERVICE & FIREWORKS DISPLAY. CEREMONY, FESTIVAL AT COUNTY 4-H FAIRGROUNDS RTE 49. (LOCAL). ROBERT CLINKSCALES, COORD; IROQUOIS COUNTY BICENTENNIAL COMMISSION; 407 S 2ND; WATSEKA, IL 60970. (#105653-2).

JULY 9 - 11, '76. IROQUOIS COUNTY HISTORICAL PAGEANT. LIVE PERFORMANCE AT IROQUOIS CO, 4-H FAIRGROUNDS, RT 49. (LOCAL). ROBERT CLINKSCALES, COORD; IROQUOIS COUNTY BICENTENNIAL COMMISSION; 407 S 2ND; WATSEKA, IL 60970. (#105653-1).

CRESTWOOD

HISTORICAL BOOK - CRESTWOOD, IL. BOOK ON HISTORY OF CRESTWOOD IS BEING PRINTED. (LOCAL). COORDINATOR; CRESTWOOD BICENTENNIAL COMMITTEE; 13840 S CICERO; CRESTWOOD, IL 60445. (#29441).

SEPT 24 - 26, '76. CHAMPIONSHIP RODEO AND PARADE. COMPETITION, LIVE PERFORMANCE AT PARADE 127TH AND CENTRAL; RODEO 141ST AND KENTON. (LOCAL). DOROTHY KUBASAK, COORD; CRESTWOOD BICENTENNIAL COMMISSION; 5249 ARBOR LANE; CRESTWOOD, IL 60445. (#200016-218).

CREVE COEUR

FORT CREVE COEUR ENTRANCE & PUBLIC USE AREA, IL. FORT CREVE COEUR ENTRANCE & PUBLIC USE AREA TO BE IMPROVED. (LOCAL). FOREST A PHILLIPS, PROJ DIRECTOR; CREVE COEUR BICENTENNIAL COMMISSION; 125 SHERWOOD CT; CREVE COEUR, IL 61611. (#27792). **ARBA GRANTEE.**

MAY 16 - 25, '75. BICENTENNIAL CARNIVAL. PROCEEDS TO BE USED FOR RECONSTRUCTION OF FORT CREVE COEUR FIRST PERMANENT WHITE SETTLEMENT IN ILLINOIS, BUILT BY LASALLE IN 1680. AT MAIN STREET. (LOCAL). ROY BOCKLER; CREVE COEUR BICENTENNIAL COMMISSION; 117 VIRGINIA; CREVE COEUR, IL 61611. (#50415-1).

JULY 4, '75. FORT CREVE COEUR ECUMENICAL RELIGIOUS SERVICE. ECUMENICAL RELIGIOUS SERVICE TO BE PERFORMED AT FORT CREVE COEUR, SITE OF FIRST PERMANENT WHITE SETTLEMENT IN ILLINOIS, ESTABLISHED BY LASALLE IN 1680. AT FORT CREVE COEUR, CREVE COEUR,ILL.. (LOCAL). MARGARET MILLER; CREVE COEUR BICENTENNIAL COMMISSION; 125 SHERWOOD COURT; CREVE COEUR, IL 61611. (#50415-2).

MAY 14 - 23, '76. CARNIVAL AND FESTIVAL. BOOTHS, DANCING, ART SHOW, PARADE, PHOTO CONTEST, BBQ, FISH FRY AND AN OVER 65 KING & QUEEN CONTEST. AT RT 29 AT N HIGHLAND ST. (LOCAL). MARGARET MILLER, CHMN; CREVE COEUR BICENTENNIAL COMMISSION; 125 SHERWOOD CT; CREVE COEUR, IL 61611. (#102173-1).

JULY 4, '76. ECUMENICAL PRAYER SERVICE. RELIGION IN ILLINOIS FROM 1679 - 1976; MUSIC & CEREMONY. (LOCAL). MARGARET MILLER, CHMN; CREVE COEUR BICENTENNIAL COMMISSION; 125 SHERWOOD CT; CREVE COEUR, IL 61611. (#105706-1).

SEPT 18, '76. BICENTENNIAL DOG SHOW. COMPETITION, EXHIBIT. (LOCAL). MARGARET MILLER, CHMN; CREVE COEUR BICENTENNIAL COMMISSION; 125 SHERWOOD CT; CREVE COEUR, IL 61611. (#200016-98).

SEPT 19, '76. AUCTION AND FLEA MARKET. FESTIVAL. (LOCAL). MARGARET MILLER, CHMN; CREVE COEUR BICENTENNIAL COMMISSION; 125 SHERWOOD CT; CREVE COEUR, IL 61611. (#200016-97).

SEPT 24, '76. ECUMENICAL PRAYER SERVICE. CANDLELIGHT ECUMENICAL PRAYER SERVICE OPENING FOR DEDICATION OF FORT CREVE COEUR. AT FORT CREVE COEUR STATE PARK. (LOCAL). MARGARET MILLER, CHMN; CREVE COEUR BICENTENNIAL COMMISSION & FORT CREVE COEUR, IN; 125 SHERWOOD CT; CREVE COEUR, IL 61611. (#105451-3).

CREVE COEUR — CONTINUED

SEPT 24 - 26, '76. FORT CREVE COEUR DEDICATION. CEREMONY AT FORT CREVE COEUR STATE PARK, ONE BLOCK WEST OFF STATE RT 29. (LOCAL). MARGARET MILLER, CHMN; FORT CREVE COEUR INC & CREVE COEUR BICENTENNIAL COMMISSION; 125 SHERWOOD CT; CREVE COEUR, IL 61611. (#105451-2).

SEPT 25, '76. CREVE COEUR BICENTENNIAL ARTS AND CRAFTS SHOW. CEREMONY, LIVE PERFORMANCE, FESTIVAL, RADIO/TV AT FORT CREVE COEUR STATE PARK. (LOCAL). MARGARET MILLER, CHMN; CREVE COEUR BICENTENNIAL COMMISSION; 125 SHERWOOD CT; CREVE COEUR, IL 61611. (#105451-1).

CRYSTAL LAKE

AUG 5 - 6, '75. AMERICAN FREEDOM TRAIN DISPLAY DAYS AT CRYSTAL LAKE, ILLINOIS. THE AMERICAN FREEDOM TRAIN WILL INCLUDE 10 EXHIBIT CARS & 2 SHOWCASE CARS DEPICTING DIFFERENT PHASES OF THE AMERICAN EXPERIENCE. ITS ARRIVAL WILL SERVE AS A CATALYST FOR LOCAL BICENTENNIAL CELEBRATIONS BY PEOPLE THROUGHOUT THIS NATION. (ST-WIDE). SY FREEDMAN, DIR OF P/R; THE AMERICAN FREEDOM TRAIN FOUNDATION; 5205 LEESBURG PIKE, SUITE 800; BAILEY'S XRDS, VA 22041. (#1776-139).

CUBA

BIG BLUESTEM PRAIRIE - CUBA, IL. RECONSTRUCTION OF ILLINOIS PRAIRIE WITH PRAIRIE PLANTINGS, BUFFALO AND INDIAN VILLAGE BETWEEN CANTON AND CUBA. (LOCAL). TOM EDWARDS, COORDINATOR; METROPOLITAN SANITARY DISTRICT; BIG BLUESTEM PRAIRIE; CUBA, IL 61427. (#30393).

DALZELL

MISS BICENTENNIAL CONTEST, JR MISS. COMPETITION. (LOCAL). MRS RONALD LEONATTI, CHMN; DALZELL JR WOMEN'S CLUB; LUCE ST; DALZELL, IL 61320. (#200016-229).

DANVERS

SENIOR CITIZENS CLUB, DANVERS, IL. ORGANIZATION PLANS ACTIVITIES FOR SENIOR CITIZENS. MEETS EACH MONTH. (LOCAL). FRIEDA FERRENBURG, CHAIRWOMAN; SENIOR CITIZEN'S CLUB; 100 E COLUMBIA; DANVERS, IL 61732. (#33641).

JULY 2 - 4, '76. PARADE & PAGEANT. FESTIVAL AT VILLAGE PARK. (LOCAL). ADA FRANZ; VILLAGE OF DANVERS; 209 W COLUMBIA; DANVERS, IL 61732. (#200016-284).

DANVILLE

BICENTENNIAL BIKE & HIKE TRAIL OF DANVILLE, IL. THE LAYING OF A PERMANENT MARKED TRAIL FOR BICYCLISTS AND HIKERS. IT WILL BE 25-MILES LONG. (LOCAL). LEWIS D LEVITE, PLANNER; SCOUT TROOP 307, PIANKESHAW COUNCIL; 26 W 16TH ST; DANVILLE, IL 61832. (#9588).

CHAPEL RENOVATION PROJ OF DANVILLE, ILLINOIS. AN OLD CHAPEL HAS BEEN RENOVATED AND MOVED TO A PIONEER VILLAGE. (LOCAL). NINA PAYNE, CHAIRPERSON; ALTRUSA CLUB; 401 W WINTER; DANVILLE, IL 61832. (#9587).

FILMSTRIP ON HISTORICAL LANDMARKS & HOMES - IL. FILMSTRIPS & SLIDES ON VERMILION COUNTY LANDMARKS AS IDENTIFIED BY THE ILLINOIS HISTORIC LANDMARKS SURVEY FOR ALL COUNTY SCHOOLS AND FOR SERVICE CLUBS OR OTHER ORGANIZATIONS. (LOCAL). JAMES H ELLIS, CHAIRMAN; VERMILION COUNTY BICENTENNIAL COMMISSION; 7 N VERMILION ST; DANVILLE, IL 61832. (#27320).

FORMER RESIDENTS BIOGRAPHIES OF VERMILION CO, IL. ONE HUNDRED ILLUSTRATED BIOGRAPHIES WILL BE DONE ON FORMER VERMILION COUNTY RESIDENTS. (LOCAL). JAMES H ELLIS, CHAIRMAN; VERMILION COUNTY BICENT COMMISSION; 408 N VERMILION ST; DANVILLE, IL 61832. (#9589).

LANDMARKER - DANVILLE, IL. IDENTIFY BEGINNING POINT SURVEYOR USED TO ESTABLISH LAND PLOTS OF THE CITY OF DANVILLE. (LOCAL). JAMES H ELLIS, CHAIRMAN; VERMILION COUNTY BICENTENNIAL COMMISSION; 7 N VERMILION ST; DANVILLE, IL 61832. (#27321).

RESTORATION OF CARRIAGE HOUSE AND MUSEUM - IL. RESTORATION OF WILLIAM FITHIAN CARRIAGE HOUSE TO ADD SPACE TO THE VERMILLION COUNTY MUSEUM. (LOCAL). JAMES H SPRINGER, PGM DIRECTOR; VERMILLION COUNTY MUSEUM SOCIETY; 211 SWISHER ST; DANVILLE, IL 61832. (#26097). **ARBA GRANTEE.**

TIME CAPSULE - DANVILLE, IL. A TIME CAPSULE WITH INFORMATION OF BICENTENNIAL PROJECTS AND EVENTS WILL BE BURIED AT THE MUSEUM. (LOCAL). JAMES H ELLIS, CHAIRMAN; VERMILION BICENTENNIAL COMMISSION; 7 N VERMILION ST; DANVILLE, IL 61832. (#27319).

OCT 3 - 5, '75. FESTIVAL OF THE ARTS & FESTIVAL PARADE. THE FESTIVAL WILL FEATURE: ART EXHIBITS, RECITALS, GALLERY DEMONSTRATIONS, FESTIVAL THEATRE, COFFEE HOUSE, DANCING AND AN INVITATIONAL MARCHING BAND FESTIVAL. AT DANVILLE JUNIOR COLLEGE, 2002 E MAIN ST. (LOCAL). JEANETTE WESTFALL, COORD; VERMILON COUNTY BICENTENNIAL COMMITTEE & DANVILLE AREA ARTS COUNCIL; 1 MAYWOOD DR; DANVILLE, IL 61832. (#101409-1).

AUG 21 - OCT 3, '76. HISTORIC PAINTING DISPLAY. EXHIBIT AT VARIOUS LOCATIONS THROUGHOUT THE COUNTY. (LOCAL). JAMES H ELLIS, CHAIRMAN; VERMILION COUNTY BICENTENNIAL COMMISSION; 7 N VERMILION ST; DANVILLE, IL 61832. (#108845-1).

SEPT 6 - 8, '76. BICENTENNIAL WEEK-END. FESTIVAL. (LOCAL). JAMES H ELLIS, CHMN; VERMILION COUNTY BICENTENNIAL COMMISSION; 408 VERMILION; DANVILLE, IL 61832. (#200016-78).

SEPT 13, '76. LINCOLN'S EIGHTH JUDICIAL CURCUIT RIDE. DICUSSION OF LINCOLN'S FAMOUS COURT CASES AN LIFE ON THE CURCUIT. AT MASONIC TEMPLE. (LOCAL). JAMES H ELLIS; VERMILION COUNTY BICENTENNIAL COMMISSION; 7N VERMILION; DANVILLE, IL 61832. (#109142-1).

SEPT 13, '76. UNITED STATES ARMED FORCES BICENTENNIAL CARAVAN. CARAVAN IS COMPOSED OF EXHIBIT VANS FOR EACH MILITARY SERVICE. PROJECT THEME IS 'HISTORY OF THE ARMED FORCES & THEIR CONTRIBUTIONS TO THE NATION.'. (LOCAL). JEANETTE WESTFALL, CHMN; UNITED STATES ARMED FORCES BICENTENNIAL CARAVAN; 1 MAYWOOD DR; DANVILLE, IL 61832. (#1775-646).

DARIEN

RENOVATION OF THE OLD LACE SCHOOL - DARIEN, IL. RENOVATION OF OLD LACE SCHOOL, A ONE-ROOM SCHOOLHOUSE. (LOCAL). GEORGE J TIKALSKY, PROJ DIRECTOR; DARIEN HISTORICAL SOCIETY; 1702 PLAINFIELD RD; DARIEN, IL 60559. (#28047). **ARBA GRANTEE.**

JAN 24 - MAR 8, '75. A CONTEST TO DESIGN A CITY SEAL FOR DARIEN, IL. CITY SEAL DESIGN CONTEST IN DARIEN, ILLINOIS CONTEST FOR ALL AGES TO DESIGN A CITY SEAL. (LOCAL). NANCY TEMPLEMAN, CHAIRPER; DARIEN BICENTENNIAL COMMISSION; 1702 PLAINFIELD RD; DARIEN, IL 60559. (#5754-901).

MAR 11, '76. ETHNIC FOOD TASTING AND PROGRAM ON PSYCHIC 'FUNOMENA'. FESTIVAL AT HINSBROOK REC CLUBHOUSE, 1101 HINSBROOK. (LOCAL). BETTY RYBERG, COORD; DARIEN NEWCOMERS CLUB; 546 MAPLE LN; DARIEN, IL 60559. (#200016-24).

MAR 11 - 20, '76. 'ANNIE GET YOUR GUN' - MUSICAL. LIVE PERFORMANCE AT HINSDALE S HIGH SCHOOL, 7401 CLARENDON HILLS RD. (LOCAL). CAROL JIRIK, COORD; 75TH ST PLAYERS AND HINSDALE SOUTH HIGH SCHOOL; 425 69TH ST; DARIEN, IL 60559. (#200016-23).

DAVIS JCT

JUNE 20 - 22, '75. CENTENNIAL CELEBRATION. INCLUDES ARTS & CRAFTS SHOW,PAGEANT & BOOKLET OF LOCAL HISTORY, PARADE,RECOGNITION OF OLDEST RESIDENTS,PRAYER & FLAG RAISING DAY. PROPERTY FOR CHURCH,SCHOOL & RAILROAD RIGHT OF WAY DONATED BY JEREMIAH DAVIS,FOUNDER.DESCENDANTS ACTIVE IN CENTENNIAL CELEBRATION. AT CITYWIDE. (LOCAL). BERNICE I DUHIGG; DAVIS JUNCTION CENTENNIAL ORGANISATION; CITY HALL; DAVIS JCT, IL 61020. (#50324-1).

DECATUR

CENTENNIAL FILM DOCUMENTARY IN DECATUR, IL. A DOCUMENTARY FILM FOR SCHOOLS & LOCAL PUBLIC TV; CONSISTS OF INTERVIEWS WITH OWNER-OPERATORS OF MACON COUNTY FARMS THAT HAVE ORIGINS BEFORE 1876. (LOCAL). JOHN CORDULAC, PROJ DIRECTOR; RICHLAND COMMUNITY COLLEGE; 100 N WATER ST; DECATUR, IL 62525. (#12313).

JAMES MILLIKIN HOMESTEAD RESTORATION - IL. RESTORATION OF THE HOME OF JAMES MILLIKIN, AN IMPORTANT PERSON FROM DECATUR, ILLINOIS. (LOCAL). MRS ROBERT C SCHAUB, CHAIRMAN; JUNIOR WELFARE ASSOCIATION OF DECATUR; PO BOX 602; DECATUR, IL 62521. (#27883). **ARBA GRANTEE.**

LINCOLN'S LOG CABIN, DECATUR, IL. CONSTRUCTION AND DEDICATION OF A REPLICA OF LINCOLN'S LOG CABIN AT LINCOLN'S HOMESTEAD PARK. (LOCAL). ROBERT KING, CHAIRMAN; MACON COUNTY BICENTENNIAL COMMISSION; CITIZEN'S NATIONAL BANK; DECATUR, IL 62523. (#33638).

MACON COUNTY HISTORY, DECATUR, IL. PUBLICATION OF 600-PAGE HISTORY OF MACON COUNTY. (LOCAL). ROBERT KING, CHAIRMAN; MACON COUNTY BICENTENNIAL COMMISSION; CITIZEN'S NATIONAL BANK; DECATUR, IL 62523. (#33637).

NORTH FORK CHILDREN'S MUSEUM, DECATUR, IL. ACQUISITION OF PROPERTY AND DEVELOPMENT OF NORTH FORK CHILDREN'S MUSEUM. (LOCAL). ROBERT KING, CHAIRMAN; MACON COUNTY BICENTENNIAL COMMISSION; CITIZEN'S NATIONAL BANK; DECATUR, IL 62523. (#33639).

ROCK SPG CENTER FOR ENVIRONMENTAL DISCOVERY, IL. OPENING AND DEDICATION OF ROCK SPRINGS CENTER FOR ENVIRONMENTAL DISCOVERY. (LOCAL). ROBERT KING, CHAIRMAN; MACON COUNTY BICENTENNIAL COMMISSION; CITIZEN'S NATIONAL BANK; DECATUR, IL 62523. (#33640).

MAY 16 - 17, '76. BICENTENNIAL YESTERYEAR ANTIQUE SHOW. EXHIBIT. (LOCAL). ROBERT KING, CHMN; MACON COUNTY BICENTENNIAL COMMISSION; CITIZENS NATIONAL BANK; DECATUR, IL 62523. (#200016-155).

MAY 29 - 31, '76. NATIONAL BICENT SUMMER POWER BOAT RACES IN IL. AMERICAN POWER BOAT ASSOC NATIONAL CHAMPIONSHIP RACES ON LAKE DECATUR, ILLINOIS WILL BE HELD MAY 25-26 1975 AND MAY 29-31 1976. AT BASIN LAKE 2, DECATUR, ILL. (NAT'L). EDWARD WOARE, JR; DECATUR WATER FESTIVAL CORP; 1595 N CALHOUN; DECATUR, IL 62521. (#5750-3).

JUNE 14, '76. BICENTENNIAL FLAG DAY. CEREMONY, PARADE. (LOCAL). ROBERT KING, CHMN; DECATUR ELKS CLUB; CITIZENS NATIONAL BANK; DECATUR, IL 62523. (#200016-154).

JULY 4, '76. DEDICATION OF BAND SHELL. CEREMONY. (LOCAL). ROBERT KING, CHMN; MACON COUNTY BICENTENNIAL COMMISSION; CITIZENS NATIONAL BANK; DECATUR, IL 62523. (#200016-156).

AUG 16 - 26, '76. CARL HAVERLIN/BROADCAST MUSIC, INC, ARCHIVES BICENTENNIAL EXHIBIT. OFFERS A VERSATILE PICTURE OF HISTORY, REGIONAL LIFE & MUSIC FOR OVER 200 YEARS. CONTAINS PRESIDENTIAL LETTERS, LETTERS OF FAMOUS AMERICANS, OLD BOOKS, MANUSCRIPTS, HISTORY OF 'THE STAR SPANGLED BANNER' & COMPOSER AUTOGRAPHS, PLUS SHEET MUSIC OF THE PAST. AT SCHOOL OF MUSIC. (ST-WIDE). CLAYTON W HENDERSON; MILLIKIN UNIVERSITY; 1184 W MAIN ST; DECATUR, IL 62522. (#20784-16).

AUG 17 - 18, '76. UNITED STATES ARMED FORCES BICENTENNIAL CARAVAN. CARAVAN IS COMPOSED OF EXHIBIT VANS FOR EACH MILITARY SERVICE. PROJECT THEME IS 'HISTORY OF THE ARMED FORCES & THEIR CONTRIBUTIONS TO THE NATION.'. (LOCAL). NANCY MUIRHEAD, CHMN; UNITED STATES ARMED FORCES BICENTENNIAL CARAVAN; 250 N WATER; DECATUR, IL 62525. (#1775-634).

SEPT 4 - 6, '76. YESTERYEAR FAIR. FESTIVAL AT NORTH FORK MUSEUM. (LOCAL). ROBERT KING, CHMN; MACON COUNTY HISTORICAL SOCIETY; DECATUR, IL 62523. (#200016-86).

SEPT 6, '76. BICENTENNIAL LABOR DAY PARADE. PARADE. (LOCAL). ROBERT KING, CHMN; MACON COUNTY BICENTENNIAL COMMISSION; CITIZENS NATIONAL BANK; DECATUR, IL 62523. (#200016-153).

SEPT 17, '76. EIGHTH JUDICIAL CIRCUIT RIDE. TOUR, LIVE PERFORMANCE. (ST-WIDE). PHYLLIS EUBANKS, CHMN; ILLINOIS DEPARTMENT OF CONSERVATION; 901 SPRING ST; SPRINGFIELD, IL 62706. (#200016-152).

OCT 3, '76. DEDICATION OF MILLIKIN HOUSE. CEREMONY. (LOCAL). ROBERT KING, CHMN; MACON COUNTY BICENTENNIAL COMMISSION; CITIZENS NATIONAL BANK; DECATUR, IL 62523. (#200016-151).

DEERFIELD

DEERFIELD BICENTENNIAL PROJECTS, IL. PROJECTS INCLUDE: A FOUNTAIN & SCULPTURE GARDEN IN THE CENTER OF VILLAGE. (LOCAL). N GAVIN, CHAIRMAN; DEERFIELD BICENTENNIAL COMMITTEE; WAUKEGAN RD; DEERFIELD, IL 60015. (#33636).

JULY 3 - 5, '76. '76 TREES IN CBD' - ORIGINAL MUSICAL HISTORY OF THE VILLAGE. LIVE PERFORMANCE AT HIGH SCHOOL. (LOCAL). NORMA GAVIN, CHAIRMAN; BICENTENNIAL COMMISSION OF DEERFIELD; 209 PINE; DEERFIELD, IL 60015. (#200016-424).

DEKALB

AMERICAN REVOLUTION SPECIAL COURSE: DEKALB, IL. GUEST LECTURES, MULTI-MEDIA, SPECIAL STUDENT PROJECTS: CREDIT & NONCREDIT FOR UNDERGRADS AND GRADUATES; SPECIAL TEACHER WORKSHOPS. (LOCAL). ALFRED A YOUNG, PROF OF HISTORY; NORTHERN ILLINOIS UNIV; DEKALB, IL 60115. (#13498).

CENTER FOR REGIONAL HISTORY IN DEKALB, IL. ESTABLISH A CENTER TO COLLECT AND HOUSE HISTORICAL SOURCE MATERIALS FOR RESEARCH IN HISTORY OF NORTHERN ILLINOIS. (ST-WIDE). J CARROLL MOODY, CHAIRMAN, HISTORY DEPT; NORTHERN ILLINOIS UNIV; DEKALB, IL 60115. (#13497).

CONCERTO FOR PIANO AND ORCHESTRA IN DEKALB, IL. A MUSICAL WORK FOR LARGE ORCHESTRA & PIANO SOLOIST LASTING APPROXIMATELY ONE HALF HOUR. (NAT'L). DONALD WALKER, PIANIST; 132 PARK AVE; DEKALB, IL 60115. (#8639). **(??).**

SEPT 26, '75 - APR 24, '76. 14 PLAYS BY AMERICAN PLAYWRIGHTS - BICENTENNIAL SEASON. PLAYS BY SAROYAN, ZINDEL, TAYLEURE, O'NEILL; MUSICAL BY BACHARACH AND DAVID; BLACK THEATRE WORKSHOP; OPERA WORKSHOP. AT OCONNELL THEATRE & STUDIO THEATRE. (LOCAL). RICHARD L ARNOLD; NORTHERN ILLINOIS UNIV; DEKALB, IL 60115. (#13496-1).

NOV 12, '76. LONDON PHILHARMONIC ORCHESTRA VISITS DEKALB, IL. LIVE PERFORMANCE AT UNIVERSITY CENTER BALLROOM. (INT'L). CULTURAL AFFAIRS OFFICE; BRITISH EMBASSY; 3100 MASSACHUSETTS AVE, NW; WASHINGTON, DC 20008. (#108958-5).

DELAVAN

MAR 27, '76. BICENTENNIAL BALL. FESTIVAL AT DELAVAN ARMORY. (LOCAL). JERRY HOWARD, DIRECTOR; DELAVAN BICENTENNIAL COMMISSION; DELAVAN, IL 61734. (#105201-2).

JULY 4, '76. BICENTENNIAL CELEBRATION. ECUMENICAL SERVICE, RINGING OF BELLS, ICE CREAM SOCIAL ARE THE SCHEDULED EVENTS. (LOCAL). JERRY HOWARD, COORD; DELAVAN BICENTENNIAL COMMISSION; RR3, BOX 2; DELAVAN, IL 61734. (#200016-210).

SEPT 4 - 6, '76. DELAVAN FALL FESTIVAL. SATURDAY EVENING STREET SQUARE DANCE; SUNDAY EVENING CONCERT BY COMMUNITY CHORUS; MONDAY PARADE, ENTERTAINMENT BARBECUE & FIREWORKS. AT DELAVAN LAKE PARK. (LOCAL). MS SANDY DEWMAN, CHMN; DELAVAN JR WOMENS CLUB/ DELAVAN BICENTENNIAL COMMISSION; DELAVAN, IL 61734. (#105201-1).

DEPUE

OCT 4 - 5, '75. OKTOBERFEST. FLEA MARKET, ETHNIC FOODS, BAND CONCERT, GAMES & STREET DANCE. AT LAKESHORE PARK. (LOCAL). JOHN WIDMAR, CHAIRMAN; DEPUE BICENTENNIAL COMMISSION; BOX 695; DEPUE, IL 61322. (#102285-1).

JULY 30 - AUG 1, '76. BICENTENNIAL FESTIVAL. FESTIVAL. (LOCAL). JOHN WIDMAR, CHMN; DEPUE BICENTENNIAL COMMISSION; DEPUE, IL 61322. (#200016-177).

DES PLAINES

COMMUNITY CENTER PRESERVATION IN DES PLAINES. PRESERVATION OF OLD CITY HALL FOR BENEFIT OF COMMUNITY AND LOCAL ORGANIZATIONS IN PARTICULAR. (LOCAL). DAVID R WOLF, CHAIRMAN; DES PLAINESBICENTENNIAL COMMISSION; MUNICIPAL BLDG; DES PLAINES, IL 60016. (#4477). **(??).**

DES PLAINES HISTORICAL LANDMARK PROJ. IDENTIFICATION AND DESIGNATION OF WORTHWHILE LOCAL LANDMARKS. (LOCAL). RICHARD WELCH, DIRECTOR; DES PLAINES HISTORICAL SOCIETY; 777 LEE ST; DES PLAINES, IL 60016. (#4478).

DES PLAINES, ILL, BICENTENNIAL CELEBRATION. COSTUME BALLS, DANCES & MANY OTHER SOCIAL EVENTS ARE SCHEDULED FOR '76 CELEBRATION. (LOCAL). DAVID R WOLF, CHAIRMAN; DES PLAINES BICENTENNIAL COMMISSION; MUNICIPAL BLDG; DES PLAINES, IL 60016. (#4479).

LOCKSMITH LEDGER MAGAZINE'S HIST MANUSCRIPT -NBMRP. THIS TRADE PUBL ACQUIRED HISTORICAL MANUSCRIPT ON THE SECURITY INDUSTRY TO BE PUBLISHED IN LIMITED EDITION. A SOFT-BACK VERSION WILL BENEFIT THE LOCK MUSEUM OF AMERICA IN TERRYVILLE, CT. (NAT'L). J S ROBINSON, BICENTENNIAL COORDINATOR; NICKERSON & COLLINS CO; 2720 DES PLAINES AVE; DES PLAINES, IL 60018. (#23652).

SHEEP-SHEARING TO TAPESTRY PROJ IN DES PLAINES, IL. 500 CUMBERLAND ELEMENTARY SCHOOL STUDENTS WILL CARD, CLEAN, DYE AND SPIN THE WOOL OF SHEARED SHEEP. STUDENTS WILL THEN WEAVE A TAPESTRY OF THEIR OWN DESIGN; PROJECT WILL TAKE TWO YEARS. (LOCAL). MRS JULIA JORDAN, PROJ DIRECTOR; CUMBERLAND SCHOOL; 700 GOLF RD; DES PLAINES, IL 60016. (#10139).

JULY 5, '75. DINNER AND DANCE. COSTUME BALLS, DANCES & MANY OTHER SOCIAL EVENTS ARE SCHEDULED FOR '76 CELEBRATION. (LOCAL). DAVID R WOLF, CHAIRMAN; DES PLAINES BICENTENNIAL COMMISSION; MUNICIPAL BLDG; DES PLAINES, IL 60016. (#4479-501).

SEPT 7, '75. LIBERTY MARCH. THE MARCH IS A SELF-GUIDED WALKING TOUR OF DES PLAINES. AT DES PLAINES HISTORICAL SOCIETY MUSEUM, 777 LEE ST. (LOCAL). JAMES BENTZ, PRESIDENT; DES PLAINES HISTORICAL SOCIETY; RT 1, BOX 68; OSWEGO, IL 60543. (#101990-1).

JULY 9, '76. BICENTENNIAL BALL & DINNER. FESTIVAL AT CASA ROYALE/783 LEE ST. (LOCAL). DAVID R WOLF; DES PLAINES BICENTENNIAL COMMISSION; 1420 MINER ST; DES PLAINES, IL 60016. (#104244-1).

DIXON

SPECIAL EDITION OF DIXON EVENING TELEGRAPH - NBMRP. A GIANT 128-PAGE SPECIAL BICENTENNIAL EDITION ON LOCAL HISTORY OF AREA HAS BEEN COMPILED. THERE ARE SPECIAL ARTICLES ON EACH LOCAL TOWN & AREA OF COUNTIES IN THE CIRCULATION AREA. (LOCAL). THOMAS D SHAW, GENERAL MANAGER; DIXON EVENING TELEGRAPH; 113 PEORIA AVE; DIXON, IL 61021. (#25555).

APR 29, '76. CLOTHES OF YESTERYEAR - FASHION SHOW. THERE WILL BE 2 SHOWS: 1-3 AND 7-9. (LOCAL). MIKE HECKMAN, CO-CHAIRMAN; LEE COUNTY BICENTENNIAL COMMISSION; PO BOX 348; DIXON, IL 61021. (#104268-2).

JULY 3 - 5, '76. DIXON PETUNIA FESTIVAL. ACTIVITIES INCLUDE A PARADE ON THE 4TH BEGINNING AT 2; CARNIVAL AND BEER GARDEN; DRUM & BUGLE COMPETITION; FIREWORKS. (LOCAL). MIKE HECKMAN, CO-CHAIRMAN; LEE COUNTY BICENTENNIAL COMMISSION; PO BOX 348; DIXON, IL 61021. (#104268-6).

DIXON SPRINGS

DIXON SPRINGS, IL, FESTIVAL. FESTIVAL ACTIVITIES INCLUDE AN ANTIQUE & CRAFTS SHOW, FREE FILMS, CONTESTS, HAYRIDES AND GUIDED TOURS. (LOCAL). BETTIE DAVIS, COMMITTEE CHAIRPERSON; HOMEMAKER UNITS DIXON SPRINGS, BRUNFIELD, ROBBS; GRANTSBURG, IL 62943. (#12063).

AUG 29 - 30, '75. COUNTY PICNIC: ANTIQUE/CRAFT SHOW, DANCE, TALENT SHOW, ETC. COUNTY HISTORY FILMS, HIKES, CRAFTS & ANTIQUE DISPLAYS, CONTESTS, HAY RIDES & GAMES WILL BE INCLUDED AT THIS OLD FASHIONED COUNTY PICNIC. (LOCAL). BETTIE DAVIS, COORDINATOR; ROBBS/DIXON SPRINGS/ BROWNFIELD HOMEMAKER UNITS; GRANTSBURG, IL 62943. (#7682-501).

DOLTON

MAY 1, '76. BICENTENNIAL COSTUME BALL. COSTUME BALL FEATURING THE NORM KRONE EMPIRE ROOM ORCHESTRA $500 ADMISSION. ANY TYPE OF AMERICAN OR ETHNIC COSTUMES MAY BE WORN, COSTUMES ARE NOT MANDATORY; PRIZES WILL BE AWAREDED; CASH BAR. AT RAMADA INN MUSIC HALL. (LOCAL). HAROLD JOHNSON, CHAIRMAN; DOLTON BICENTENNIAL COMMISSION; 14014 PARK AVE; DOLTON, IL 60419. (#105157-1).

DOWNERS GROVE

BICENTENNIAL DRAMA IN DOWNERS GROVE, IL. TOURING DRAMA GROUP IMPROVISATIONS WILL RELATE TO AMERICAN IDEALS, DEMOCRACY, REVOLUTION, LITERATURE & REENACTMENTS OF HISTORIC EVENTS. (LOCAL). KAREN L ERICKSON, PROJECT DIRECTOR; DOWNERS GROVE NORTH HIGH SCHOOL; 4436 MAIN ST; DOWNERS GROVE, IL 60515. (#5327).

JAN 10 - MAY 20, '76. A CRITICAL LOOK AT THE PROGRESS OF THE PILGRIMS; AN IMPROVISATION. COMEDY SKETCHES, SONGS, READINGS, SERIOUS SKETCHES SHOWING THE DEVELOPMENT OF THE U.S. AND IT'S PEOPLE. WE THINK ONE OF THE AMERICAN PEOPLE'S MOST ENDEARING QUALITIES IS THAT OF LAUGHING AT MISTAKES AS WELL AS APPLAUDING SUCCESS. WE WANT TO SHOW BOTH SIDES. AT WE TRAVEL TO YOUR THEATER, AUDITORIUM, CAFETERIA, GYMNASIUM, ETC.. (ST-WIDE). KAREN L ERICKSON; ILLINOIS BICENTENNIAL COMMISSION AND DOWNERS GROVE NORTH HIGH SCHOOL; 1007 FRONT ST APT 204; LISLE, IL 60532. (#50494-1).

MAY 31, '76. DEDICATION OF VETERANS MEMORIAL. DEDICATION OF 8 ACRE PARK AND 30 FOOT OBELISK TO THE MEMORY OF ALL DECEASED VETERANS OF OUR NATION'S CONFLICTS. AT 4000 SARATOGA. (LOCAL). CHESTER KOTOWSKI, CMDR; ALEXANDER BRADLEY BURNS POST 80 - AMERICAN LEGION; 4000 SARATOGA; DOWNERS GROVE, IL 60515. (#21309-1).

DU QUOIN

MAR 1, '75. ANNOUNCE WINNERS OF CHILDREN'S BICENT POSTER CONTEST IN ALL SCHOOLS. CONTEST OPEN TO ALL SCHOOL CHILDREN IN PERRY COUNTY. BICENT THEMES WILL BE USED. PRIZES TO BE GIVEN TO WINNERS OF 4 GRADE LEVEL GROUPS: 1-3, 4-6, 7-9, & 10-12. (LOCAL). FRED HUFF, COORDINATOR; DU QUOIN STATE FAIR INC; RTE 2; DU QUOIN, IL 62832. (#5748-901).

AUG 30, '75. 50TH HAMBLETONIAN--MOST PRESTIGIOUS TROTTING RACE IN WORLD. THE HAMBLETONIAN IS MOST PRESTIGIOUS AND IMPORTANT EVENT IN HARNESS RACING, ONE OF THE FEW MAJOR SPORTS OF U.S. ORIGIN. HELD IN DU QUOIN, ILL. IT IS PRAISED FOR ITS TRUE RURAL FLAVOR. AT DU QUOIN STATE FAIRGROUNDS. (NAT'L). FRED HUFF; DU QUOIN STATE FAIR; P.O. BOX 182; DU QUOIN, IL 62832. (#4208-1).

JULY 2 - 4, '76. DU QUOIN STATE FAIR & AGRICULTURAL EXPOSITION 'AGPO'. THE FAIR WILL HAVE A BICENTENNIAL EMPHASIS; EVENTS WILL INCLUDE THE ROY ROGERS-DALE EVANS SHOW, TRACTOR PULL AND QUARTER HORSE SHOW. AT FAIRGROUNDS, HIGHWAY 51 SOUTH. (LOCAL). FRED HUFF, PROJ CHAIRMAN; DU QUOIN STATE FAIR; BOX 182; DU QUOIN, IL 62832. (#106095-39).

AUG 28 - SEPT 6, '76. DU QUOIN STATE FAIR. USAC STOCK AND DIRT CAR RACES, HARNESS HORSE RACES & GRANDSTAND ENTERTAINMENT. AT DU QUOIN STATE FAIRGROUNDS, HIGHWAY 51-SOUTH. (REGN'L). FRED HUFF, COORD; DU QUOIN STATE FAIR; BOX 182; DU QUOIN, IL 62832. (#106095-38).

SEPT 4, '76. HAMBLETONIAN RACE. HAMBLETONIAN RACE IS ONE OF THE WORLD'S MOST PRESTIGIOUS TROTTING HORSE RACES. AT FAIRGROUNDS. (REGN'L). FRED HUFF, PROJ CHAIRMAN; DU QUOIN STATE FAIR; BOX 182; DU QUOIN, IL 62832. (#106095-40).

OCT 1 - 3, '76. 5TH ANNUAL SOUTHERN ILLINOIS FOLK FESTIVAL. FESTIVAL, EXHIBIT AT DUQUOIN STATE FAIRGROUNDS. (ST-WIDE). MRS M R PRUSACKI, COORD; SOUTHERN ILLINOIS FOLK FESTIVAL; PO BOX 303; DUQUOIN, IL 62832. (#103416-568).

DUPAGE

ILLINOIS PRAIRIE PATH - DUPAGE, IL. HIKING, BIKING & EQUESTRIAN NATURE TRAIL IS 40 MILES LONG; IT OCCUPIES THE FORMER RIGHT-OF-WAY OF CHICAGO, AURORA & ELGIN RAILROAD. OPEN ALL YEAR TO PUBLIC FREE OF CHARGE. NO MOTOR VEHICLES ALLOWED. (LOCAL). LOUISE HEADEN, V-PRESIDENT; ILLINOIS PRAIRIE PATH; 616 DELLES; WHEATON, IL 60187. (#20092).

E HAZEL CREST

COMFORT STATION - E HAZEL CREST, IL. WASHROOM FACILITIES IN FRIENDSHIP PARK. (LOCAL). ANN P PRATER, CHAIRWOMAN; EAST HAZELCREST BICENTENNIAL COMMISSION; 17223 S THROOP ST; E HAZEL CREST, IL 60429. (#29839).

JUNE 26 - 27, '76. BICENTENNIAL PARADE & 200TH BIRTHDAY CELEBRATION. FESTIVITIES BEGAN WITH A PARADE FOLLOWED BY A DEDICATION OF THE NEW COMFORT STATION, CONTEST AWARDS, STREET DANCE. SUNDAY SAW A FAMILY PICNIC. (LOCAL). ANN P PORTER; EAST HAZEL CREST BICENTENNIAL COMMISSION; 1519 W 179 ST; E HAZEL CREST, IL 60429. (#200016-350).

EAST ALTON

EAST ALTON PUBLIC LIBRARY, IL. NEW PUBLIC LIBRARY TO BE OPENED. ALL FUND RAISING ACTIVITIES TO BE GEARED TOWARD FURNISHING IN GENERAL & THE HISTORY ROOM IN PARTICULAR. (LOCAL). DAVID HOPKINS, CO-CHAIRMAN; VILLAGE EAST ALTON BICENTENNIAL; BOX 270; EAST ALTON, IL 62024. (#29767).

MAY 18 - 23, '76. E ALTON BICENTENNIAL CELEBRATION. FOOD, GAMES, RIDES, LOCAL ACTS & PARADE. AT VANPRETEN PARK. (LOCAL). DAVID HOPKINS; E ALTON BICENTENNIAL COMMISSION & VILLAGE OF EAST ALTON; BOX 270; E ALTON, IL 62024. (#200016-285).

EAST DUNDEE

TOWNSHIP LIBRARY CHILDREN'S ROOM DECORATION, IL. FURNITURE; HISTORIC FILMS, FILMSTRIPS & SLIDES; VIDEO TAPE INTERVIEWS WITH SENIOR CITIZENS ON HISTORY OF THE TOWNSHIP; & MURAL DEPICTING HISTORY OF TOWNSHIP WILL BE PROVIDED FOR THE BICENTENNIAL. (LOCAL). CHERYL ARMENTROUT, PROJ DIRECTOR; DUNDEE TOWNSHIP BICENTENNIAL COMMISSION; 200 EDWARDS; WEST DUNDEE, IL 60118. (#13017).

EAST PEORIA

HISTORY OF EAST PEORIA, ILLINOIS. A YOUTH PRODUCED FILM ON THE HISTORY OF EAST PEORIA USING INTERVIEWS WITH SENIOR CITIZENS, ANECDOTES FROM PREVIOUS HISTORIES & HISTORIC RE-ENACTMENTS; TO BE PRODUCED ON VIDEOTAPE FOR TV & CLASSROOMS. (LOCAL). ROBERT MOSS, VICE CHAIRMAN; EAST PEORIA BICENTENNIAL COMMISSION; 500 N STEWART; CREVE COEUR, IL 61611. (#8118).

MARKING OF TRAIL, EAST PEORIA, IL. IDENTIFICATION OF HISTORIC SITES & TRAILS IN COUNTY. (LOCAL). K RUSSELL CRAWFORD, CHAIRMAN; TAZEWELL COUNTY BICENTENNIAL COMMISSION; 3541/2 COLE; EAST PEORIA, IL 61611. (#33635).

JUNE 1 - JULY 3, '76. FLOAT CONTEST. COMPETITION. (LOCAL). ROSE CHAPMAN, CHMN; EAST PEORIA BICENTENNIAL COMMISSION; 551 BLOOMINGTON RD; EAST PEORIA, IL 61611. (#200016-92).

EAST ST LOUIS

AMERICANA PERFORMING ARTS TRAINING CTR-SO ILL UNIV. BLACK AMERICAN DANCE, SONG, AND MUSIC FROM SLAVERY THROUGH TO THE CONTEMPORARY TIMES. (REGN'L). KATHERINE DUNHAM, DIR, PERF ARTS TRAINING CNTR; S ILLINOIS UNIV, PERFORMING ARTS TRAINING CNTR; 530 N 10TH ST; E ST LOUIS, IL 62201. (#1709).

AMERICANA - BLACK AMERICA MUSIC PRESENTATION IN IL. HISTORICAL & CONTEMPORARY DANCE, MUSIC & SONG. TOURING PRODUCTION BY PERFORMING ARTS TRAINING CENTER OF SOUTHERRN ILLINOIS UNIV AT EDWARDSVILLE/EAST ST LOUIS. (ST-WIDE). KATHERINE DUNHAM, DIRECTOR; PERFORMING ARTS TRAINING CENTER, SO. ILL. UNIV., EDWARDSVILLE/ES; 530 N. 10TH ST.; EAST ST LOUIS, IL 62201. (#1511).

COURSES BY NEWSPAPER, E ST LOUIS, IL. A SERIES ON AMERICAN ISSUES IN NEWSPAPER FORM OFFERED AS A COLLEGE COURSE. (LOCAL). DR R D WHEADON, DEAN OF INSTRUCTION; STATE COMMUNITY COLLEGE OF EAST ST LOUIS; 417 MISSOURI AVE; E ST LOUIS, IL 62201. (#16370).

TREE PLANTING & GROUNDBREAKING, E ST LOUIS, IL. PLANTING OF TWO STATE TREES AT GROUNDBREAKING FOR NEW CAMPUS - ONE FOR EACH 100 YEARS. (LOCAL). JEFFERSON H WARE, PRESIDENT; STATE COMMUNITY COLLEGE OF EAST ST LOUIS; 417 MISSOURI AVE; E ST LOUIS, IL 62201. (#16371).

SEPT 1, '75 - MAY 30, '76. BICENTENNIAL ESSAY & ORATORICAL CONTEST. COMPETITION. (LOCAL). DR R D WHEAD, DEAN; STATE COMMUNITY COLLEGE OF EAST ST LOUIS; 417 MISSOURI AVE; EAST ST LOUIS, IL 62201. (#102922-1).

SEPT 1, '75 - DEC 31, '76. BICENTENNIAL HAPPENINGS AT STATE COMMUNITY COLLEGE OF EAST ST LOUIS. FESTIVAL, SEMINAR, LIVE PERFORMANCE. (LOCAL). CHARLES L TURNER; STATE COMMUNITY COLLEGE OF EAST ST LOUIS; 417 MISSOURI AVE; EAST ST LOUIS, IL 62201. (#102922-2).

EDDYVILLE

JULY 3 - 4, '75. 4TH OF JULY CELEBRATION. FIREWORKS, DANCING, MUSIC & A HOMECOMING REUNION WILL BE PART OF THIS INDEPENDENCE DAY CELEBRATION. (LOCAL). HON RALPH ALY, MAYOR; TOWN OF EDDYVILLE; EDDYVILLE, IL 62928. (#7679-501).

EDWARDSVILLE

AMERICAN FOLKLORE ARCHIVE IN EDWARDSVILLE, IL. OVER 60,000 FOLKLORE ITEMS ON EXHIBIT. (LOCAL). JOHN OLDANI, COORDINATOR; SOUTHERN ILLINOIS UNIV BICENTENNIAL COMMITTEE; UNIV INFORMATION CENTER; EDWARDSVILLE, IL 62026. (#23407).

BICENTENNIAL COMPOSITION: EDWARDSVILLE, IL. 'DREAM SONGS OF STEPHEN FOSTER' COMPOSED BY JAMES WOODARD; COMPOSITION FOR SOPRANO, SOLO VIOLIN, HARP & STRING ORCHESTRA. (ST-WIDE). UNIVERSITY INFORMATION CENTER; UNIV BICENTENNIAL COMMITTEE & MUSIC DEPT, SOUTHERN ILL UNIV; SIU AT EDWARDSVILLE; EDWARDSVILLE, IL 62026. (#23410).

EDWARDSVILLE — CONTINUED

BICENTENNIAL SCULPTURE PROJECTS AT S ILLINOIS UNIV. THREE ARTISTS HAVE BEEN COMMISSIONED BY THE ILLINOIS BICENTENNIAL COMMISSION TO CREATE SCULPTURE THAT WILL STAND AS A LASTING MEMORIAL TO OUR NATION'S 200TH BIRTHDAY. (ST-WIDE). ANNETTE GRAEBE, CHAIRMAN; SOUTHERN ILLINOIS UNIV AT EDWARDSVILLE; BOX 15A; EDWARDSVILLE, IL 62026. (#15402).

DENTAL EXHIBIT: THEN, NOW AND HERE - ILLINOIS. HISTORICAL EXHIBIT BY THE SCHOOL OF DENTAL MEDICINE WHICH WILL BE AVAILABLE FOR OFF-CAMPUS BOOKINGS. (REGN'L). ANNETTE GRAEBE, CHAIRMAN; SOUTHERN ILLINOIS UNIV BICENT COMM & SCHOOL OF DENTAL MEDICINE; UNIV INFORMATION CENTER; EDWARDSVILLE, IL 62026. (#23408).

HERITAGE '76 SCHOOL DIRECTORY PROJ OF S ILL UNIV. THE DIRECTORY WILL LIST SIGNIFICANT HISTORICAL SITES IN MADISON COUNTY. IT WILL BE DISTRIBUTED TO SCHOOLS, CLUBS AND CIVIC GROUPS. (LOCAL). ANNETTE GRAEBE, CHAIRMAN; SOUTHERN ILLINOIS UNIV AT EDWARDSVILLE; BOX 15A; EDWARDSVILLE, IL 62026. (#15401).

'IT'S BEEN A LONG TIME COMING' - BOOKLET, IL. TWO-VOLUME HISTORICAL BOOKLET IN SHORT STORY FORM EMPHASIZING THE STRUGGLES OF BLACK AMERICANS FROM 1776 UNTIL THE PRESENT. (LOCAL). ANNETTE M GRAEBE, CHAIRMAN; UNIVERSITY BICENTENNIAL COMMITTEE, SIU AT EDWARDSVILLE; EDWARDSVILLE, IL 62026. (#25875).

LOG CABIN RESTORATION - EDWARDSVILLE, IL. 1840 LOG CABIN RE-CONSTRUCTED ON CAMPUS. (LOCAL). ANNETTE M GRAEBE, CHAIRMAN; UNIVERSITY BICENTENNIAL COMMITTEE, SIU AT EDWARDSVILLE; EDWARDSVILLE, IL 62026. (#25876).

LOG CABIN TOUR. TOUR. (LOCAL). ANNETTE GRAEBE, CHMN; ANTHROPOLOGY DEPT, SOUTHERN ILLINOIS UNIV; BOX 15A, SIU; EDWARDSVILLE, IL 62026. (#102395-7). **(??).**

MADISON COUNTY BICENTENNIAL LOBBY - IL. A RENOVATION OF THE LOBBY OF THE COUNTY COURTHOUSE TO INCLUDE A LIFE SIZE STATUE OF JAMES MADISON, PLANTINGS & SEATING, AS WELL AS ROTATING DISPLAYS ON VARIOUS ASPECTS OF THE COUNTY. (LOCAL). LOUIS WHITSELL, COORDINATOR; NAMEOKI TOWNSHIP; 4250 HIGHWAY 162; GRANITE CITY, IL 62040. (#26871).

MUSEUM ARCHEOLOGY TOUR. MUSEUM OPEN THROUGHOUT YEAR. AT CAMPUS. (LOCAL). ANNETTE GRAEBE, CHMN; ANTHROPOLOGY DEPT, SOUTHERN ILLINOIS UNIV; BOX 15A, SIU; EDWARDSVILLE, IL 62026. (#102395-6). **(??).**

'SMORGASBORD OF TALENT' BROCHURE - IL. FREE BOOKLET AVAILABLE TO AREA SCHOOLS, COMMUNITIES, CHURCHES AND CLUBS. INCLUDES EXTENSIVE SPEAKERS' BUREAU AND SPECIAL PROGRAMS AND SERVICES. WRITE FOR FREE COPY. (LOCAL). ANNETTE M GRAEBE, CHAIRMAN; UNIVERSITY BICENTENNIAL COMMITTEE, SIU AT EDWARDSVILLE; EDWARDSVILLE, IL 62026. (#25874).

UNIVERSITY CLUB BICENTENNIAL MENU IN ILLINOIS. SPECIAL COMMEMORATIVE MENU FEATURING DAILY FOOD SPECIALS HONORING U S PRESIDENTS. (LOCAL). ANNETTE GRAEBE, CHAIRMAN; SOUTHERN ILLINOIS UNIV BICENT COMM & UNIV FOOD SERVICE; UNIV INFORMATION CENTER; EDWARDSVILLE, IL 62026. (#23409).

APR 15 - 30, '75. MUSIC OF WILLIAM BILLINGS & OTHER COLONIAL COMPOSERS PERFORMANCE. PERFORMING EDITIONS OF AMERICAS FIRST IMPORTANT COMPOSER. 13 SACRED, ANTHEMS, CHRISTMAS CANTATA, LENT & EASTER CANTATA (CONCORDIA PUB HS) PATRIOTIC WORKS (SOMERSET) & SECULAR CANTATA (MARK FOSTER) & OTHERS. AT COMMUNICATIONS BLDG, SO ILLINOIS UNIV, EDWARDSVILLE CAMPUS. (ST-WIDE). LEONARD W VAN CAMP, DIR; SOUTHERN ILLINOIS UNIVERSITY; 50 ILLINOIS UNIV, CHORAL ACTIVT; EDWARDSVILLE, IL 62025. (#2096-1).

SEPT 28, '75. BICENTENNIAL HOUSE TOUR. TOUR AT 6 PRIVATE HOMES IN EDWARDSVILLE. (LOCAL). PATRICIA G BLYTHE, CHMN; JUNIOR SERVICE CLUB OF EDWARDSVILLE; 1817 STANFORD PL; EDWARDSVILLE, IL 62025. (#200016-1).

OCT 3, '75. FACULTY RECITAL BY SARAH TURNER. LIVE PERFORMANCE AT CB THEATER. (LOCAL). ANNETTE GRAEBE, CHMN; MUSIC DEPT, SOUTHERN ILLINOIS UNIV; BOX 15A, SIU; EDWARDSVILLE, IL 62026. (#102394-13).

OCT 6 - 31, '75. ART & PHOTOGRAPHY SHOW, 'THE UNITED NATIONS AT WORK'. EXHIBIT AT FIRST FLOOR - UNIVERSITY CENTER. (LOCAL). ANNETTE GRAEBE, CHMN; UNIVERSITY CENTER BOARD; BOX 15A, SIU; EDWARDSVILLE, IL 62026. (#102396-14).

OCT 7, '75. 'FOUR BLACK WOMEN' - PLAY. LIVE PERFORMANCE AT BALLROOM - UNIVERSITY CENTER. (LOCAL). ANNETTE GRAEBE, CHMN; BLACK STUDENTS ASSOC/SOUTHERN ILLINOIS UNIV; BOX 15A, SIU; EDWARDSVILLE, IL 62026. (#102396-1).

OCT 8, '75. SYMPOSIUM - BLACK PROFESSIONALS. SEMINAR AT GOSHEN LOUNGE - UNIVERSITY CENTER. (LOCAL). ANNETTE GRAEBE, CHMN; BLACK STUDENTS ASSOC/SOUTHERN ILLINOIS UNIV; BOX 15A, SIU; EDWARDSVILLE, IL 62234. (#102396-4).

OCT 9, '75. 'A RETURN TO OLD EAST ST LOUIS'. HISTORY OF EAST ST LOUIS AS TOLD BY OLDER RESIDENTS. AT BALLROOM - UNIVERSITY CENTER. (LOCAL). ANNETTE GRAEBE, CHMN; BLACK STUDENTS ASSOC/SOUTHERN ILLINOIS UNIV; BOX 15A, SIU; EDWARDSVILLE, IL 62234. (#102396-2).

OCT 10, '75. CAMPUS COMPOSERS CONCERT. LIVE PERFORMANCE AT THEATER, COMMUNICATIONS BLDG. (LOCAL). ANNETTE GRAEBE, CHMN; SOUTHERN ILLINOIS UNIV BICENTENNIAL COMMITTEE, MUSIC DEPT; BOX 15A, SIU; EDWARDSVILLE, IL 62026. (#102396-12).

OCT 10, '75. GOSPEL: THE HAYNES MIRACLE TEMPLE CHOIR. LIVE PERFORMANCE AT GOSHEN LOUNGE - UNIVERSITY CENTER. (LOCAL). ANNETTE GRAEBE, CHMN; SOUTHERN ILLINOIS UNIV BICENTENNIAL COMMITTEE; BOX 15A, SIU; EDWARDSVILLE, IL 62234. (#102396-22).

OCT 11 - NOV 5, '75. CHRISTO POPOFF ART SHOW. EXHIBIT AT UNIVERSITY CENTER, OPAPI LOUNGE. (LOCAL). ANNETTE M GRAEBE, CHMN; SOUTHERN ILLINOIS UNIV BICENTENNIAL COMMITTEE; EDWARDSVILLE, IL 62026. (#109345-1).

OCT 13 - 17, '75. UNIVERSITY 10TH ANNIVERSARY KICKOFF WEEK. CAMPUS CELEBRATING BOTH BICENTENNIAL AND ANNIVERSARY ALL YEAR; MULTITUDE OF EVENTS PLANNED. (LOCAL). ANNETTE GRAEBE, CHMN; 10TH ANNIVERSARY COMMITTEE/ SOUTHERN ILLINOIS UNIV; BOX 15A, SIU; EDWARDSVILLE, IL 62026. (#102396-3).

OCT 16, '75. GREGG SMITH SINGERS - CHORAL CLINIC AND PERFORMANCE. LIVE PERFORMANCE AT BALLROOM - UNIVERSITY CENTER. (LOCAL). ANNETTE GRAEBE, CHMN; SOUTHERN ILLINOIS UNIV; BOX 15A, SIU; EDWARDSVILLE, IL 62026. (#102395-3).

OCT 20, '75. SOUTHERN ILLINOIS UNIV BICENTENNIAL KICK-OFF CEREMONY. ASCENSION OF HOT AIR BALLOON, RAISING OF BICENTENNIAL FLAG, MUSIC & PROMINENT SPEAKER. AT CAMPUS. (LOCAL). ANNETTE GRAEBE, CHMN; SOUTHERN ILLINOIS UNIV; BOX 15A, SIU; EDWARDSVILLE, IL 62026. (#102395-4).

OCT 23, '75. 'LOST, STOLEN OR STRAYED', FILM NARRATED BY BILL COSBY. 2 SHOWINGS: 11:30 AM & 3:30 PM. AT BALLROOM - UNIVERSITY CENTER. (LOCAL). ANNETTE GRAEBE, CHMN; BLACK STUDENTS ASSOCIATION, SOUTHERN ILLINOIS UNIVERSITY; BOX 15A, SIU; EDWARDSVILLE, IL 62026. (#102395-1).

NOV 3 - 28, '75. 'NEXT DOOR, DOWN THE ROAD & AROUND THE CORNER', ART EXHIBIT. EXHIBIT AT OPAPI LOUNGE, UNIVERSITY CENTER. (LOCAL). ANNETTE GRAEBE, CHMN; UNIVERSITY CENTER BOARD, SOUTHERN ILLINOIS UNIVERSITY; BOX 15A, SIU; EDWARDSVILLE, IL 62026. (#102395-2).

NOV 3 - DEC 1, '75. EXHIBIT - HATS & HEADDRESSES. EXHIBIT AT COMMUNICATIONS BUILDING LOBBY. (LOCAL). ANNETTE M GRAEBE, CHMN; THEATRE/DANCE DEPARTMENT, SOUTHERN ILLINOIS UNIV; EDWARDSVILLE, IL 62026. (#200016-3).

NOV 11, '75. SCIENCE LECTURE BY DR R J SEEGER. SEMINAR AT COMMUNICATIONS BUILDING LOBBY. (LOCAL). ANNETTE M GRAEBE, CHMN; SIGMA XI, SOUTHERN ILLINOIS UNIV; EDWARDSVILLE, IL 62026. (#200016-4).

NOV 14, '75. UNIVERSITY ORCHESTRA CONCERT / GUEST COMPOSER - J BODA. LIVE PERFORMANCE AT THEATER, COMMUNICATIONS BLDG. (LOCAL). ANNETTE GRAEBE, CHMN; SOUTHERN ILLINOIS UNIV BICENTENNIAL COMMITTEE, MUSIC DEPT; BOX 15A, SIU; EDWARDSVILLE, IL 62026. (#102396-13).

DEC 1 - 26, '75. ART EXHIBIT: PHOTOGRAPHY-DORTHEA LANGE, 'AN AMERICAN EXODUS'. EXHIBIT AT OPAPI LOUNGE - UNIVERSITY CENTER. (LOCAL). ANNETTE GRAEBE, CHMN; UNIVERSITY CENTER BOARD; BOX 15A, SIU; EDWARDSVILLE, IL 62026. (#102396-15).

DEC 4, '75. MINNESOTA SYMPHONIC ORCHESTRA PERFORMANCE. LIVE PERFORMANCE AT BALLROOM - UNIVERSITY CENTER. (LOCAL). ANNETTE GRAEBE, CHMN; CULTURAL ARTS COUNCIL - ILL ARTS COUNCIL SIUE STUDENT ORGAN; BOX 15A, SIU; EDWARDSVILLE, IL 62234. (#102396-16).

JAN 5 - 30, '76. ART EXHIBIT: PRINTMAKERS OF ILLINOIS. EXHIBIT AT UNIV CENTER, 2ND FL. (LOCAL). ANNETTE GRAEBE, CHMN; SOUTHERN ILLINOIS UNIV BICENTENNIAL COMMITTEE; BOX 15A, SIU; EDWARDSVILLE, IL 62026. (#102396-17).

JAN 13, '76. SIUE HISTORY FORUM - SPEAKERS: A MCCURRY AND R MILLETT. 'WASHINGTON AS REVOLUTIONARY LEADER' AND 'MILITARY CAMPAIGNS OF THE REVOLUTION' ARE THE SELECTED TOPICS. AT UNIV CENTER, ILLINOIS ROOM. (LOCAL). ANNETTE M GRAEBE, CHMN; HISTORY DEPT, SOUTHERN ILLINOIS UNIV; EDWARDSVILLE, IL 62026. (#200016-16).

JAN 13, '76. '1776', CONTINENTAL THEATER CO PERFORMANCE. LIVE PERFORMANCE AT UNIV CENTER BALLROOM. (LOCAL). ANNETTE GRAEBE, CHMN; SOUTHERN ILLINOIS UNIV BICENTENNIAL COMMITTEE; CULTURAL ARTS COUNCIL; BOX 15A, SIU; EDWARDSVILLE, IL 62234. (#102396-18).

JAN 14 - 16, '76. RAYMOND JOHNSON DANCE CO; PERFORMANCE. MASTER CLASSES: LECTURE/DEMONSTRATION; PUBLIC PERFORMANCE JAN 16, 1975, 8:15 PM COMMUNICATIONS THEATER. AT CAMPUS. (LOCAL). ANNETTE GRAEBE, CHMN; SOUTHERN ILLINOIS UNIV BICENTENNIAL COMMITTEE; BOX 15A, SIU; EDWARDSVILLE, IL 62234. (#102396-19).

JAN 15, '76. 'I HAVE A DREAM', A FILM ABOUT DR MARTIN LUTHER KING, JR. WILL ALSO BE SHOWN AT 2:00 PM AND 7:00 PM. AT UNIV CENTER BALLROOM. (LOCAL). ANNETTE GRAEBE, CHMN; SOUTHERN ILLINOIS UNIV BICENTENNIAL COMMITTEE; BOX 15A, SIU; EDWARDSVILLE, IL 62234. (#102396-20).

JAN 18, '76. FESTIVAL AND PERFORMANCE. FESTIVAL INCLUDES DINNER AT 5 PM, AN ADDRESS BY MRS KING AND 8 PM - 10 PM A PERFORMANCE BY THE EDWIN HAWKINS SINGERS. AT MERIDIAN, UNIVERSITY CENTER. (LOCAL). ANNETTE GRAEBE, CHMN; SOUTHERN ILLINOIS UNIV BICENTENNIAL COMMITTEE; BOX 15A, SIU; EDWARDSVILLE, IL 62234. (#102396-21).

JAN 23, '76. CAMPUS COMPOSERS CONCERT. LIVE PERFORMANCE AT COMMUNICATIONS BUILDING THEATER. (LOCAL). ANNETTE M GRAEBE, CHMN; MUSIC DEPARTMENT, SOUTHERN ILLINOIS UNIV; EDWARDSVILLE, IL 62026. (#200016-17).

JAN 23, '76. FACULTY PIANO RECITAL BY LAMPE & KOZLOWSKI. LIVE PERFORMANCE AT THEATER IN COMMUNICATIONS BLDG. (LOCAL). ANNETTE GRAEBE, CHMN; MUSIC DEPARTMENT, SOUTHERN ILLINOIS UNIV; BOX 15A, SIU; EDWARDSVILLE, IL 62026. (#102394-2).

FEB 1, '76. 'MUSIC OF AMERICA' - BICENTENNIAL CONCERT. LIVE PERFORMANCE AT COMMUNICATIONS BUILDING. (LOCAL). ANNETTE M GRAEBE, CHMN; MUSIC DEPT, SOUTHERN ILLINOIS UNIVERSITY; EDWARDSVILLE, IL 62026. (#200016-6).

FEB 2, '76. C A M PHOTOGRAPHY EXHIBIT. EXHIBIT AT UNIV CENTER, 2ND FLR. (LOCAL). ANNETTE GRAEBE, CHMN; SOUTHERN ILLINOIS UNIV; BOX 15A, SIU; EDWARDSVILLE, IL 62026. (#102394-3).

FEB 3, '76. NATIONAL MARIONETTE THEATER. LIVE PERFORMANCE AT BALLROOM, UNIV CENTER. (LOCAL). ANNETTE GRAEBE, CHMN; SOUTHERN ILLINOIS UNIV; BOX 15A, SIU; EDWARDSVILLE, IL 62234. (#102394-4).

FEB 4, '76. OLYMPIA JAZZ BRASS BAND FROM NEW ORLEANS. LIVE PERFORMANCE AT BALLROOM - UNIVERSITY CENTER. (LOCAL). ANNETTE GRAEBE, CHMN; SOUTHERN ILLINOIS UNIV; BOX 15A, SIU; EDWARDSVILLE, IL 62234. (#102394-5).

FEB 4, '76. SIUE HISTORY FORUM - SPEAKERS J HAAS AND N NORDHAUSER. 'BRITISH VIEW OF THE REVOLUTION' AND 'ECONOMIC FACTORS IN THE COMING OF THE REVOLUTION' ARE THE TOPICS OF DISCUSSION. AT UNIV CENTER, DEJA VU ROOM. (LOCAL). ANNETTE M GRAEBE, CHMN; HISTORY DEPT; SOUTHERN ILLINOIS UNIV; EDWARDSVILLE, IL 62026. (#200016-7).

FEB 6, '76. FACULTY RECITAL: DAVID FERGUSON - PIANO & DARWIN APPLE - VIOLIN. LIVE PERFORMANCE AT THEATER, COMMUNICATIONS BLDG. (LOCAL). ANNETTE GRAEBE, CHMN; MUSIC DEPT, SOUTHERN ILLINOIS UNIV; BOX 15A, SIU; EDWARDSVILLE, IL 62026. (#102394-6).

FEB 9 - 13, '76. BLACK HISTORY WEEK. LIVE PERFORMANCE. (LOCAL). ANNETTE GRAEBE, CHMN; BLACK STUDENT ASSOC, SOUTHERN ILLINOIS UNIV; BOX 15A, SIU; EDWARDSVILLE, IL 62026. (#102394-7).

FEB 12 - 13, '76. CONCERT CHORALE BICENTENNIAL TOUR. SPECIAL MUSICAL TRIBUTE TO LINCOLN. AT CONCERT TOURS SEVERAL ILLINOIS CITIES. (ST-WIDE). ANNETTE M GRAEBE, CHMN; MUSIC DEPT; SOUTHERN ILLINOIS UNIV; EDWARDSVILLE, IL 62026. (#200016-8).

FEB 18 - 20, '76. WINTERFEST. FESTIVAL AT UNIVERSITY CENTER. (LOCAL). ANNETTE M GRAEBE, CHMN; SOUTHERN ILLINOIS UNIVERSITY; SOUTHERN ILLINOIS UNIV; EDWARDSVILLE, IL 62026. (#200016-9).

FEB 19, '76. LECTURE BY MUSLIM MINISTER FARENKAN. LIVE PERFORMANCE AT UNIV CENTER BALLROOM. (LOCAL). ANNETTE GRAEBE, CHMN; BLACK STUDENTS ASSOC, SOUTHERN ILLINOIS UNIV; BOX 15A, SIU; EDWARDSVILLE, IL 62234. (#102394-8).

FEB 20, '76. FACULTY RECITAL - GEORGE MELLOTT, CLARINET. LIVE PERFORMANCE AT LIBRARY AUDITORIUM. (LOCAL). ANNETTE GRAEBE, CHMN; MUSIC DEPARTMENT, SOUTHERN ILLINOIS UNIV; EDWARDSVILLE, IL 62026. (#200016-21).

FEB 25, '76. SIUE HISTORY FORUM - SPEAKERS J GALLAHER AND W FARRAR. SPEECHES ON 'THE IMPACT OF THE REVOLUTION IN EUROPE' AND 'THE IMPACT OF THE REVOLUTION IN LATIN AMERICA'. AT UNIV CENTER-MISSOURI ROOM. (LOCAL). ANNETTE M GRAEBE, CHMN; HISTORY DEPT; SOUTHERN ILLINOIS UNIVERSITY; EDWARDSVILLE, IL 62026. (#200016-11).

FEB 26, '76. LECTURE - CHURCH HISTORIAN REV DR WESLEY SCHLATZHAUER. TITLE OF THE LECTURE IS 'THE STATE OF RELIGION IN THE COLONIES IN 1776'. AT UNIV CENTER. (LOCAL). ANNETTE M GRAEBE, CHMN; CAMPUS MINISTRY; SOUTHERN ILLINOIS UNIVERSITY; EDWARDSVILLE, IL 62026. (#200016-10).

FEB 27, '76. UNIVERSITY SYMPHONY ORCHESTRA PERFORMANCE. LIVE PERFORMANCE AT THEATER, COMMUNICATIONS BLDG. (LOCAL). ANNETTE GRAEBE, CHMN; MUSIC DEPT, SOUTHERN ILLINOIS UNIV; BOX 15A, SIU; EDWARDSVILLE, IL 62026. (#102394-9).

MAR 1, '76. CHORAL CONCERT. LIVE PERFORMANCE AT THEATER - COMMUNICATIONS BLDG. (LOCAL). ANNETTE GRAEBE, CHMN; MUSIC DEPT, SOUTHERN ILLINOIS UNIV; BOX 15A, SIU; EDWARDSVILLE, IL 62026. (#102394-10).

MAR 3, '76. 'FEELIN' GOOD', A PLAY RECOGNIZING BLACK HISTORY. THE PLAY WILL BE PERFORMED BY THE NATIONAL THEATER COMPANY. AT BALLROOM - UNIV CENTER. (LOCAL). ANNETTE GRAEBE, CHMN; CULTURAL ARTS COUNCIL, SOUTHERN ILLINOIS UNIV; BOX 15A, SIU; EDWARDSVILLE, IL 62026. (#102394-11).

MAR 4, '76. FACULTY RECITAL - JOSEPH PIVAL, VIOLINCELLO. LIVE PERFORMANCE AT LIBRARY AUDITORIUM. (LOCAL). ANNETTE M GRAEBE, CHMN; MUSIC DEPARTMENT, SOUTHERN ILLINOIS UNIV; EDWARDSVILLE, IL 62026. (#200016-15).

MAR 5, '76. SYMPHONIC BAND CONCERT. LIVE PERFORMANCE AT AUDITORIUM - LOVEJOY LIBRARY. (LOCAL). ANNETTE GRAEBE, CHMN; MUSIC DEPT, SOUTHERN ILLINOIS UNIV; BOX 15A, SIU; EDWARDSVILLE, IL 62026. (#102394-12).

MAR 7, '76. FACULTY CHAMBER MUSIC. LIVE PERFORMANCE AT THEATER-COMMUNICATIONS BLDG. (LOCAL). ANNETTE GRAEBE, CHMN; MUSIC DEPT, SOUTHERN ILLINOIS UNIV; BOX 15A, SIU; EDWARDSVILLE, IL 62026. (#102394-14).

MAR 8, '76. FACULTY RECITAL - RUTH SLENCYNSKA, PIANIST. LIVE PERFORMANCE AT THEATER - COMMUNICATIONS BLDG. (LOCAL). ANNETTE GRAEBE, CHMN; MUSIC DEPT, SOUTHERN ILLINOIS UNIV; BOX 15A, SIU; EDWARDSVILLE, IL 62026. (#102394-15).

MAR 9, '76. UNIVERSITY BAND CONCERT. LIVE PERFORMANCE AT THEATER-COMMUNICATIONS BLDG. (LOCAL). ANNETTE GRAEBE, CHMN; MUSIC DEPT, SOUTHERN ILLINOIS UNIV; BOX 15A, SIU; EDWARDSVILLE, IL 62026. (#102394-16).

EDWARDSVILLE — CONTINUED

MAR 10 - 11, '76. PROGRAM ON INDIAN CULTURE. LIVE PERFORMANCE AT UNIV CENTER. (LOCAL). ANNETTE GRAEBE, CHMN; SOUTHERN ILLINOIS UNIV; BOX 15A, SIU; EDWARDSVILLE, IL 62234. (#102394-1).

MAR 13 - 14, '76. SIUE FRIENDS OF LOVEJOY LIBRARY, ANTIQUES SHOW AND SALE. FAIR AT UNIVERSITY CENTER. (LOCAL). ANNETTE M GRAEBE, CHMN; FRIENDS OF LOVEJOY LIBRARY; SOUTHERN ILLINOIS UNIVERSITY; EDWARDSVILLE, IL 62026. (#200016-14).

MAR 15 - 18, '76. VISITING LECTURER - PROF DANIEL ROYOT. SEMINAR. (LOCAL). ANNETTE M GRAEBE, CHMN; SCHOOL OF HUMANITIES, SOUTHERN ILLINOIS UNIV; EDWARDSVILLE, IL 62026. (#200016-19).

MAR 18, '76. SCHOOL BOARD CONFERENCE - 'A BICENTENNIAL VIEW OF EDUCATION'. CONFERENCE AT UNIVERSITY CENTER - MERIDIAN HALL. (LOCAL). ANNETTE M GRAEBE, CHMN; SCHOOL OF EDUCATION - EDUCATIONAL ADMINISTRATION DEPT; SOUTHERN ILLINOIS UNIVERSITY; EDWARDSVILLE, IL 62026. (#200016-13).

MAR 24, '76. SPRING SENIOR FAIR - 'THE WAY WE WERE'. FAIR AT UNIV CENTER. (LOCAL). ANNETTE GRAEBE, CHMN; STUDENT ACTIVITIES, SOUTHERN ILLINOIS UNIV; EDWARDSVILLE, IL 62026. (#200016-20).

APR 5, '76. 'I'VE BEEN TO THE MOUNTAIN TOP', A FILM ABOUT DR MARTIN LUTHER KING. SEMINAR AT BALLROOM, UNIVERSITY CENTER. (LOCAL). ANNETTE GRAEBE, CHMN; BLACK STUDENTS ASSOC/SOUTHERN ILLINOIS UNIV; BOX 15A, SIU; EDWARDSVILLE, IL 62234. (#102395-12).

APR 6, '76. SIVE HISTORY FORUM FEATURING W MCAFFE & E NORDHAUSER. LECTURES ON ROLE OF BLACKS IN THE REVOLUTION & THE ROLE OF WOMEN IN THE REVOLUTION. AT UNIV CENTER, MISSISSIPPI-ILLINOIS ROOM. (LOCAL). ANNETTE M GRAEBE, CHMN; SOUTHERN ILLINOIS UNIV BICENT COMM & THE HISTORY DEPT; UNIV INFORMATION CENTER; EDWARDSVILLE, IL 62026. (#106572-1).

APR 7, '76. FINE ARTS SERIES: WILLIAM HEILES, PIANO. LIVE PERFORMANCE AT COMMUNICATIONS BUILDING THEATER. (LOCAL). ANNETTE M GRAEBE, CHMN; FINE ARTS SCHOOL; SOUTHERN ILLINOIS UNIVERSITY; EDWARDSVILLE, IL 62026. (#200016-12).

APR 9, '76. CAMPUS COMPOSERS. LIVE PERFORMANCE AT THEATER, COMMUNICATIONS BLDG. (LOCAL). ANNETTE GRAEBE, CHMN; MUSIC DEPT, SOUTHERN ILLINOIS UNIV; BOX 15A, SIU; EDWARDSVILLE, IL 62026. (#102396-5).

APR 20, '76. MUSIC OF THE OZARKS. LIVE PERFORMANCE, EXHIBIT AT BALLROOM, UNIVERSITY CENTER. (LOCAL). ANNETTE GRAEBE, CHMN; CULTURAL ARTS COUNCIL/GILL ARTS COUNCIL/SOUTHERN ILLINOIS UNIV; BOX 15A, SIU; EDWARDSVILLE, IL 62234. (#102396-6).

APR 20, '76. SIVE HISTORY FORUM WITH W SANTONI/REVOLUTIONS IN THE U S & RUSSIA. SEMINAR. (LOCAL). ANNETTE M GRAEBE, CHMN; SOUTHERN ILLINOIS UNIV BICENT COMM; UNIV INFORMATION CENTER; EDWARDSVILLE, IL 62026. (#106572-2).

APR 26, '76. 'CELEBRATE NURSING'; SPEAKER, MARY KELLY MULLANE, PHD. SEMINAR AT UNIV CENTER, MERIDIAN BALLROOM. (LOCAL). ANNETTE M GRAEBE, CHMN; SOUTHERN ILLINOIS UNIV BICENT COMM; UNIV INFORMATION CENTER; EDWARDSVILLE, IL 62026. (#106572-4).

APR 26, '76. HYPERTENSION SCREENING CLINIC AT SIU'S OHIO ROOM. SEMINAR AT UNIV CENTER, OHIO ROOM. (LOCAL). ANNETTE M GRAEBE, CHMN; SOUTHERN ILLINOIS UNIV BICENT COMM; UNIV INFORMATION CENTER; EDWARDSVILLE, IL 62026. (#106572-5).

APR 26 - 30, '76. THE SCHOOL OF NURSING CELEBRATES NURSING. CONFERENCE AT ON CAMPUS. (LOCAL). ANNETTE M GRAEBE, CHMN; SOUTHERN ILLINOIS UNIV BICENT COMM & THE SCHOOL OF NUR; UNIV INFORMATION CENTER; EDWARDSVILLE, IL 62026. (#106572-3).

APR 27, '76. CAREER DAY AT NURSING SCHOOL. FAIR AT UNIV CENTER, GOSHEN LOUNGE. (LOCAL). ANNETTE M GRAEBE, CHMN; SOUTHERN ILLINOIS UNIV BICENT COMM; UNIV INFORMATION CENTER; EDWARDSVILLE, IL 62026. (#106572-6).

APR 29, '76. HYPERTENSION SCREENING CLINIC AT SIU'S SCIENCE BLDG. SEMINAR AT SCIENCE BLDG. (LOCAL). ANNETTE M GRAEBE, CHMN; SOUTHERN ILLINOIS UNIV BICENT COMM & THE SCHOOL OF NURSING; UNIV INFORMATION CENTER; EDWARDSVILLE, IL 62026. (#106572-7).

APR 30, '76. NURSING EXHIBIT - STUDENT PROJECTS. EXHIBIT AT UNIV CENTER. (LOCAL). ANNETTE M GRAEBE, CHMN; SOUTHERN ILLINOIS UNIV BICENT COMM; UNIV INFORMATION CENTER; EDWARDSVILLE, IL 62026. (#106572-8).

MAY 3, '76. BICENTENNIAL FESTIVAL - OLD GUYS CONCERT, CHORALE MUSIC PROGRAM. LIVE PERFORMANCE AT UNIV CENTER. (LOCAL). ANNETTE M GRAEBE, CHMN; SOUTHERN ILL UNIV BICENT COMM, OLD GUYS, MUSIC DEPT & UNIV WOMEN; UNIV INFORMATION CENTER; EDWARDSVILLE, IL 62026. (#106572-11).

MAY 3 - 9, '76. BICENTENNIAL FESTIVAL - SCHOOL OF DENTAL MEDICINE EXHIBIT. EXHIBIT AT SIVE CAMPUS. (ST-WIDE). ANNETTE M GRAEBE, CHMN; SOUTHERN ILLINOIS UNIV BICENT COMM; UNIV INFORMATION CENTER; EDWARDSVILLE, IL 62026. (#106572-10).

MAY 3 - 9, '76. BICENTENNIAL FESTIVAL - DAILY CAMPUS TOURS. TOUR AT UNIVERSITY CAMPUS. (LOCAL). ANNETTE M GRAEBE, CHMN; UNIVERSITY AMBASSADORS - SOUTHERN ILLINOIS UNIV; EDWARDSVILLE, IL 62026. (#107227-8).

MAY 3 - 9, '76. WEEK LONG UNIVERSITY BICENTENNIAL FESTIVAL. FESTIVAL. (LOCAL). ANNETTE GRAEBE, CHMN; SOUTHERN ILLINOIS UNIV; BOX 15A, SIU; EDWARDSVILLE, IL 62026. (#102395-5).

MAY 4, '76. AMERICAN FOLKLORE PRESENTATION BY DR JOHN OLDANI. LIVE PERFORMANCE, EXHIBIT AT UNIV CENTER, MERIDIAN BALLROOM. (ST-WIDE). ANNETTE M GRAEBE, CHMN; SOUTHERN ILLINOIS UNIV BICENT COMM; UNIV INFORMATION CENTER; EDWARDSVILLE, IL 62026. (#106572-14).

MAY 4, '76. BICENTENNIAL FESTIVAL - SCULPTURE UNVEILING. CEREMONY, OPENING AT UNIV CENTER, GOSHEN LOUNGE. (ST-WIDE). ANNETTE M GRAEBE, CHMN; SOUTHERN ILLINOIS UNIV BICENT COMM & DEPT OF ART AND DESIGN; UNIV INFORMATION CENTER; EDWARDSVILLE, IL 62026. (#106572-12).

MAY 4, '76. 'COMPLIANT REBELLION: THE AMERICAN AVANTE-GARDE AS SOCIAL NARCOTIC'. LECTURE GIVEN BY JOHN ADKINS RICHARDSON. AT LOVEJOY LIBRARY AUDITORIUM. (LOCAL). ANNETTE M GRAEBE, CHMN; SOUTHERN ILLINOIS UNIV BICENT COMM; UNIV INFORMATION CENTER; EDWARDSVILLE, IL 62026. (#106572-13).

MAY 5, '76. LECTURE/SLIDE PRESENTATION BY JOHN CELUCH. LECTURE WILL BE ENTITLED 'LOUIS H SULLIVAN, AMERICAN ARCHITECTURAL PIONEER'. AT UNIV CENTER, MISSISSIPPI-ILLINOIS ROOM. (LOCAL). ANNETTE M GRAEBE, CHMN; SOUTHERN ILLINOIS UNIV BICENT COMM; UNIV INFORMATION CENTER; EDWARDSVILLE, IL 62026. (#106572-15).

MAY 5, '76. RIVERBOAT RAGTIME REVIEW. LIVE PERFORMANCE AT BALLROOM, UNIVERSITY CENTER. (LOCAL). ANNETTE GRAEBE, CHMN; CULTURAL ARTS COUNCIL/ILL ARTS COUNCIL/ SOUTHERN ILLINOIS UNIV; BOX 15A, SIU; EDWARDSVILLE, IL 62026. (#102396-7).

MAY 6, '76. BICENTENNIAL FESTIVAL - INTERNATIONAL PROGRAM. CEREMONY, LIVE PERFORMANCE AT UNIV CENTER, GOSHEN LOUNGE. (ST-WIDE). ANNETTE M GRAEBE, CHMN; SOUTHERN ILLINOIS UNIV BICENT COMM; UNIV INFORMATION CENTER; EDWARDSVILLE, IL 62026. (#106572-17).

MAY 6, '76. AN EVENING OF ILLINOIS POETRY & MUSIC W/ SIMPSON, ROBBINS & OTHERS. LIVE PERFORMANCE AT LOVEJOY LIBRARY AUDITORIUM. (ST-WIDE). ANNETTE M GRAEBE, CHMN; SOUTHERN ILLINOIS UNIV BICENT COMM; UNIV INFORMATION CENTER; EDWARDSVILLE, IL 62026. (#106572-19).

MAY 6, '76. HISTORY FORUM, SPEAKER: S WEISSIR ERICKSON. LECTURES ENTITLED: 'AMERICAN DIPLOMACY, FROM WEAKNESS AND STRENGTH', 'THE REVOLUTION AND THE COLD WAR', 'IMPLICATIONS OF THE AMERICAN REVOLUTION FOR PUBLIC POLICY, 1976'. AT UNIV CENTER, MISSISSIPPI-ILLINOIS ROOM. (LOCAL). ANNETTE M GRAEBE, CHMN; SOUTHERN ILLINOIS UNIV BICENT COMM; UNIV INFORMATION CENTER; EDWARDSVILLE, IL 62026. (#106572-18).

MAY 7, '76. 'AFTER HOURS' - JAM SESSION. LIVE PERFORMANCE AT KNIGHTS OF COLUMBUS HALL. (LOCAL). ANNETTE M GRAEBE, CHMN; SOUTHERN ILLINOIS UNIV AT EDWARDSVILLE BICENTENNIAL COMMITTEE; EDWARDSVILLE, IL 62026. (#108338-3).

MAY 7, '76. BICENTENNIAL FESTIVAL - JAZZ ARCHIVE DEDICATION CEREMONY. CEREMONY AT LOVEJOY LIBRARY, FIRST FLOOR. (LOCAL). ANNETTE M GRAEBE, CHMN; SOUTHERN ILLINOIS UNIV BICENT COMM; UNIV INFORMATION CENTER; EDWARDSVILLE, IL 62026. (#106572-24).

MAY 7, '76. BICENTENNIAL FESTIVAL AND LECTURE. THE LECTURE WILL BE GIVEN BY PROF CHRISTOPHER HILL. (LOCAL). ANNETTE M GRAEBE, CHMN; SOUTHERN ILLINOIS UNIVERSITY, SOCIAL SCIENCES & HISTORY DEPARTMENTS; EDWARDSVILLE, IL 62026. (#107227-1).

MAY 7, '76. JAZZ ARCHIVE DEDICATION, CONCERT BY BILLY BUTTERFIELD. CEREMONY, LIVE PERFORMANCE AT LOVEJOY LIBRARY MALL. (LOCAL). ANNETTE M GRAEBE, CHMN; SOUTHERN ILLINOIS UNIV BICENT COMM; UNIV INFORMATION CENTER; EDWARDSVILLE, IL 62026. (#106572-20).

MAY 7, '76. JAZZ ARCHIVE DEDICATION, CONCERT BY THE OLD GUYS JAZZ ENSEMBLE. CEREMONY, LIVE PERFORMANCE AT LOVEJOY LIBRARY MALL. (LOCAL). ANNETTE M GRAEBE, CHMN; SOUTHERN ILLINOIS UNIV BICENT COMM; UNIV INFORMATION CENTER; EDWARDSVILLE, IL 62026. (#106572-21).

MAY 7, '76. JAZZ ARCHIVE OPEN HOUSE. CEREMONY AT LOVEJOY LIBRARY, 1ST FLOOR. (LOCAL). ANNETTE M GRAEBE, CHMN; SOUTHERN ILLINOIS UNIV BICENT COMM; UNIV INFORMATION CENTER; EDWARDSVILLE, IL 62026. (#106572-23).

MAY 7, '76. LECTURE BY CHRISTOPHER HILL. SEMINAR AT UNIV CENTER, MISSISSIPPI-ILLINOIS ROOM. (LOCAL). ANNETTE M GRAEBE, CHMN; SOUTHERN ILLINOIS UNIV BICENT COMM; UNIV INFORMATION CENTER; EDWARDSVILLE, IL 62026. (#106572-22).

MAY 8, '76. BICENTENNIAL FESTIVAL - JAZZ 'JAM' BRUNCH. LIVE PERFORMANCE AT SUNSET HILLS COUNTRY CLUB. (LOCAL). ANNETTE M GRAEBE, CHMN; SOUTHERN ILLINOIS UNIV BICENT COMM/OLD GUYS BAND; UNIV INFORMATION CENTER; EDWARDSVILLE, IL 62026. (#106572-26).

MAY 8, '76. SIVE BICENTENNIAL GOVERNORS BALL. LIVE PERFORMANCE AT SUNSET HILLS COUNTRY CLUB. (LOCAL). ANNETTE M GRAEBE, CHMN; SOUTHERN ILLINOIS UNIV BICENT COMM; UNIV INFORMATION CENTER; EDWARDSVILLE, IL 62026. (#106572-27).

MAY 9, '76. LINCOLN QUARTET. LIVE PERFORMANCE AT LOVEJOY LIBRARY AUDITORIUM. (LOCAL). ANNETTE GRAEBE, CHMN; MUSIC DEPT, SOUTHERN ILLINOIS UNIV; BOX 15A, SIU; EDWARDSVILLE, IL 62026. (#102396-8).

MAY 10 - 15, '76. BICENTENNIAL JAZZ FESTIVAL. COMMEMORATION OF THE HISTORY OF JAZZ. AT MISSISSIPPI RIVER FESTIVAL SITE (ON CAMPUS). (LOCAL). ANNETTE GRAEBE, CHMN; CULTURAL ARTS COUNCIL/SOUTHERN ILLINOIS UNIV; BOX 15A, SIU; EDWARDSVILLE, IL 62234. (#102396-9).

MAY 17 - 22, '76. SPRINGFEST. FAIR, FESTIVAL AT CAMPUS. (LOCAL). ANNETTE GRAEBE, CHMN; BOX 15A, SIU; EDWARDSVILLE, IL 62026. (#102396-10).

MAY 19, '76. DAVID FRYE SHOW (COMEDIAN). LIVE PERFORMANCE AT UNIVERSITY CENTER, MERIDIAN HALL. (LOCAL). ANNETTE M GRAEBE, CHMN; SOUTHERN ILLINOIS UNIVERSITY, MAJOR EVENTS COUNCIL; EDWARDSVILLE, IL 62026. (#107227-2).

MAY 21, '76. FOLKLORE ARCHIVE - QUILT SHOW. EXHIBIT, FAIR AT MERIDIAN BALLROOM, UNIVERSITY CENTER. (LOCAL). ANNETTE M GRAEBE, CHMN; SOUTHERN ILLINOIS UNIV AT EDWARDSVILLE BICENTENNIAL COMMITTEE; EDWARDSVILLE, IL 62026. (#108338-2).

MAY 23, '76. SYMPHONIC BAND CONCERT. LIVE PERFORMANCE AT THEATER - COMMUNICATIONS BLDG. (LOCAL). ANNETTE GRAEBE, CHMN; MUSIC DEPT, SOUTHERN ILLINOIS UNIV; BOX 15A, SIU; EDWARDSVILLE, IL 62026. (#102395-8).

MAY 26, '76. SENIOR FAIR '76. FESTIVAL AT ARENA EXHIBITION HALL, 5700 OAKLAND ST, ST LOUIS, MO 63110. (LOCAL). TIM TIGHE, CHAIRMAN; ST LOUIS SPIRIT OF '76; PO BOX 244; EDWARDSVILLE, IL 62025. (#102396-23).

MAY 28 - 29, '76. CHORUS AND ORCHESTRA CONCERT. LIVE PERFORMANCE AT THEATER - COMMUNICATIONS BLDG. (LOCAL). ANNETTE GRAEBE, CHMN; MUSIC DEPT, SOUTHERN ILLINOIS UNIV; BOX 15A, SIU; EDWARDSVILLE, IL 62026. (#102395-9).

JUNE 5, '76. COLLEGIUM MUSICUM. LIVE PERFORMANCE AT RELIGIOUS CENTER. (LOCAL). ANNETTE GRAEBE, CHMN; SOUTHERN ILLINOIS UNIV; BOX 15A, SIU; EDWARDSVILLE, IL 62026. (#102395-11).

JUNE 12 - 25, '76. 12-DAY BICENTENNIAL CONCERT TOUR TO EAST COAST. LIVE PERFORMANCE, TOUR. (LOCAL). ANNETTE M GRAEBE, CHMN; SOUTHERN ILLINOIS UNIV AT EDWARDSVILLE BICENTENNIAL COMMITTEE; EDWARDSVILLE, IL 62026. (#108338-4).

JUNE 13, '76. BICENTENNIAL MARATHON. LIVE PERFORMANCE AT SIVE CAMPUS. (LOCAL). ANNETTE M GRAEBE, CHMN; SOUTHERN ILLINOIS UNIV BICENT COMM; UNIV INFORMATION CENTER; EDWARDSVILLE, IL 62026. (#106572-30).

JUNE 21, '76. CHICAGO SYMPHONY ORCHESTRA. LIVE PERFORMANCE AT MISSISSIPPI RIVER FESTIVAL TENT SITE. (ST-WIDE). ANNETTE M GRAEBE, CHMN; SOUTHERN ILLINOIS UNIV BICENT COMM & MISSISSIPPI RIVER FESTIVAL; UNIV INFORMATION CENTER; EDWARDSVILLE, IL 62026. (#106572-31).

JUNE 21 - 25, '76. BHAM-SYMPOSIUM ON 'WHAT IS AMERICAN IN AMERICAN MUSIC'. HUMANITIES AND THE PERFORMING ARTS. AT SOUTHERN ILLINOIS UNIVERSITY AT EDWARDSVILLE, IL. (LOCAL). ELIZABETH G SAYAD, CHRMAN; ST LOUIS SPIRIT OF 76; 115 N UNION BLVD; ST LOUIS, MO 63108. (#2314-7).

JUNE 23, '76. PRESERVATION HALL JAZZ BAND PERFORMANCE. LIVE PERFORMANCE AT MISSISSIPPI RIVER FESTIVAL TENT SITE. (ST-WIDE). ANNETTE M GRAEBE, CHMN; SOUTHERN ILLINOIS UNIV BICENT COMM; UNIV INFORMATION CENTER; EDWARDSVILLE, IL 62026. (#106572-33).

JUNE 24, '76. BENNY GOODMAN SEXTET. LIVE PERFORMANCE. (ST-WIDE). ANNETTE M GRAEBE, CHMN; SOUTHERN ILLINOIS UNIV BICENT COMM; UNIV INFORMATION CENTER; EDWARDSVILLE, IL 62026. (#106572-34).

JUNE 25, '76. THE CHUCK MANGIONE QUARTET, JAZZ AT ITS BEST. LIVE PERFORMANCE AT MISSISSIPPI RIVER FESTIVAL TENT SITE. (ST-WIDE). ANNETTE M GRAEBE, CHMN; SOUTHERN ILLINOIS UNIV BICENT COMM; UNIV INFORMATION CENTER; EDWARDSVILLE, IL 62026. (#106572-35).

JUNE 26, '76. AMERICAN BARBERSHOP HARMONY, PART OF JAZZ SERIES. LIVE PERFORMANCE AT MISSISSIPPI RIVER FESTIVAL TENT SITE. (ST-WIDE). ANNETTE M GRAEBE, CHMN; SOUTHERN ILLINOIS UNIV BICENT COMM; UNIV INFORMATION CENTER; EDWARDSVILLE, IL 62026. (#106572-36).

JUNE 26 - JULY 1, '76. BHAM - MISSISSIPPI RIVER FESTIVAL. 6/26 SALUTE TO AMERICAN BARBERSHOP QUARTETS 6/28 HAL HOLBROOK PRESENTS 'MARK TWAIN TONITE' 6/30 'EAGLES' 7/1 'JULLIARD STRING QUARTETS'. AT NATURAL AMPHITHEATRE ON CAMPUS OF SOUTHERN ILLINOIS UNIV. (REGN'L). ELIZABETH G SAYAD, CHMN; ST LOUIS SPIRIT OF 76; 115 N UNION BLVD; ST LOUIS, MO 63108. (#107858-1).

JUNE 28, '76. MISSISSIPPI RIVER FESTIVAL BICENTENNIAL PERFORMANCE. HAL HOLBROOK WILL PRESENT 'MARK TWAIN TONIGHT'. AT MISSISSIPPI RIVER FESTIVAL TENT SITE. (LOCAL). ANNETTE M GRAEBE, CHMN; MISSISSIPPI RIVER FESTIVAL COMMITTEE - SOUTHERN ILLINOIS UNIVERSITY; EDWARDSVILLE, IL 62026. (#107227-4).

JULY 1, '76. MISSISSIPPI RIVER FESTIVAL BICENTENNIAL CONCERT. THE JUILLIARD STRING QUARTET WILL PERFORM. AT UNIVERSITY CENTER MERIDIAN HALL. (LOCAL). ANNETTE M GRAEBE, CHMN; MISSISSIPPI RIVER FESTIVAL COMMITTEE - SOUTHERN ILLINOIS UNIVERSITY; EDWARDSVILLE, IL 62026. (#107227-5).

JULY 9 - 11, '76. ARCHIVAN EXHIBIT. PART OF UNIVERSITY EXHIBIT ENTITLED 'ILLINOIS ARCHITECTURE: REVOLUTION ON THE PRAIRIE.'. (LOCAL). ANNETTE M GRAEBE, CHMN; SOUTHERN ILLINOIS UNIV AT EDWARDSVILLE BICENTENNIAL COMMITTEE; EDWARDSVILLE, IL 62026. (#108338-1).

OCT 3, '76. BICENTENNIAL OPEN HOUSE IN THE SCHOOL OF BUSINESS. FESTIVAL. (LOCAL). ANNETTE M GRAEBE, CHMN;

EDWARDSVILLE — CONTINUED

SOUTHERN ILLINOIS UNIVERSITY SCHOOL OF BUSINESS; EDWARDSVILLE, IL 62026. (#107227-6).

OCT 10 - NOV 7, '76. ART EXHIBIT: GRAPHICS '75 WATERGATE - THE UNMAKING OF A PRESIDENT. THE EXHIBIT WILL CONSIST OF EDITORIAL AND POLITICAL CARTOONS. AT UNIVERSITY CENTER OPAPI LOUNGE. (LOCAL). ANNETTEM GRAEBE,CHMN; SOUTHERN ILLINOIS UNIVERSITY CENTER BOARD; EDWARDSVILLE, IL 62026. (#107227-3).

NOV 16, '76. FACULTY RECITAL FEATURING JANET SCOTT ON THE FLUTE. LIVE PERFORMANCE AT COMMUNICATIONS BUILDING THEATRE. (LOCAL). ANNETTE M GRAEBE, CHMN; SOUTHERN ILLINOIS UNIVERSITY MUSIC DEPARTMENT; EDWARDSVILLE, IL 62026. (#107227-7).

EFFINGHAM

HISTORICAL BOOKLETS - EFFINGHAM, IL. PUBLICATION OF SET OF HISTORIC BOOKLETS ON EFFINGHAM COUNTY HISTORY. (LOCAL). PEGGY PULLIAM, CHAIRMAN; EFFINGHAM BICENTENNIAL COMMISSION; 210 W WABASH; EFFINGHAM, IL 62401. (#30394).

APR 11, '76. DEDICATION OF LORD EFFINGHAM MARKER. CEREMONY. (LOCAL). MS ZONA DAVIS, CHMN; EFFINGHAM COUNTY BICENTENNIAL COMMISSION; 701 S FIRST, BOX 563; EFFINGHAM, IL 62401. (#200016-174).

JULY 13 - 24, '76. EFFINGHAM'S BICENTENNIAL FESTIVAL. FESTIVAL, PARADE. (LOCAL). PEGGY PULLIUM, CHMN; EFFINGHAM BICENTENNIAL COMMISSION; 210 W WABASH; EFFINGHAM, IL 62401. (#200016-175).

AUG 1, '76. LORD AND LADY EFFINGHAM VISIT EFFINGHAM. CEREMONY. (INT'L). MS ZONA DAVIS, CHMN; EFFINGHAM COUNTY BICENTENNIAL COMMISSION; 701 S FIRST, BOX 563; EFFINGHAM, IL 62401. (#200016-176).

AUG 12 - 13, '76. UNITED STATES ARMED FORCES BICENTENNIAL CARAVAN. CARAVAN IS COMPOSED OF EXHIBIT VANS FOR EACH MILITARY SERVICE. PROJECT THEME IS 'HISTORY OF THE ARMED FORCES & THEIR CONTRIBUTIONS TO THE NATION.'. (LOCAL). ZONA B DAVIS, CHMN; UNITED STATES ARMED FORCES BICENTENNIAL CARAVAN; EFFINGHAM CITY HALL; EFFINGHAM, IL 62401. (#1775-632).

EL PASO

COMMUNITY FESTIVAL IN EL PASO, IL. OLDER FESTIVAL, CRAFTS, MUSICAL, DEDICATION OF MEMORIAL BANDSHELL & FLAGPOLE. (LOCAL). RITA PIERCE/REBA ROTH, CO-CHAIRMEN; EL PASO BICENTENNIAL COMMISSION; EL PASO, IL 61738. (#33631).

ELBURN

AUG 23 - 24, '75. LIBERTY MARCH - ELBURN DAYS. LIBERTY MARCH TO RAISE FUNDS FOR NEW CITY PARK IN ELBURN. AT 132 MAIN ST. (LOCAL). JAMES BENTZ, PRES; HIKERS OF AMERICA, INC; RT 1, BOX 68; OSWEGO, IL 60543. (#200016-5).

ELGIN

BICENTENNIAL ART COMPETITION IN ELGIN, IL. AN ART CONTEST, THE WINNERS TO BE AWARDED PRIZES AND THEIR WORK WILL BECOME A PERMANENT PART OF THE COLLECTION OF THE COLLEGE. (LOCAL). CAROLE ACKEMANN, CHAIRMAN; ELGIN COMMUNITY COLLEGE BICENT COMMISSION; 1700 SPARTAN DR; ELGIN, IL 60120. (#14344).

BIOGRAPHICAL STUDIES IN ELGIN, IL. A BIOGRAPHICAL STUDY OF PARTICIPANTS OF THE AMERICAN REVOLUTIONARY WAR; STUDIES WILL BE DONE IN TEAMS OF 2. (LOCAL). CAROLE ACKEMANN, CHAIRPERSON; ELGIN COMMUNITY COLLEGE BICENTENNIAL COMMISSION; 1700 SPARTAN DR; ELGIN, IL 60120. (#14074).

COMPARATIVE STUDY IN ELGIN, IL. A COMPARATIVE STUDY ON THE MODERN DAY METHODS OF THE MEDIA AND THOSE USED IN COLONIAL TIMES BY SAMUEL ADAMS. (LOCAL). CAROLE ACKEMANN, CHAIRPERSON; ELGIN COMMUNITY COLLEGE BICENTENNIAL COMMISSION; 1700 SPARTAN DR; ELGIN, IL 60120. (#14075).

HIGH SCHOOL ATHLETIC EVENTS, ELGIN, IL. A SERIES OF COMPETITIVE ATHLETIC EVENTS AT THE HIGH SCHOOL LEVEL. (NAT'L). CLIFFORD B FAGEN, COORDINATOR; NATIONAL FEDERATION OF STATE HIGH SCHOOL ASSOC; 400 LESLIE ST, PO BOX 98; ELGIN, IL 60120. (#27926).

INDIVIDUAL EXPRESSION PROGRAM, ELGIN, IL. A PROGRAM DESIGNED TO AWARD THE EFFORTS BY INDIVIDUALS IN ACTIVITIES RELATED TO THE BICENTENNIAL; PATCHES, PINS AND CERTIFICATED WILL BE GIVEN. (LOCAL). CAROLE ACKEMANN, CHAIRPERSON; ELGIN COMMUNITY COLLEGE BICENTENNIAL COMMISSION; 1700 SPARTAN DR; ELGIN, IL 60120. (#14078).

LANDMARK PROJECT IN ELGIN, IL. PROJECT IS THE DESIGNATION OF LANDMARKS BY CITIES THROUGHOUT THE DISTRICT, IN COOPERATION WITH SCHOOL. (LOCAL). CAROLE ACKEMANN, CHAIRPERSON; ELGIN COMMUNITY COLLEGE BICENTENNIAL COMMISSION; 1700 SPARTAN DR; ELGIN, IL 60120. (#14077).

LEGISLATION - JEFFERSON'S BIRTHDATE, ELGIN, IL. ENACTMENT OF LEGISLATION TO IMPLEMENT NATIONAL DAY OF OBSERVANCE OF JEFFERSON'S BIRTHDATE, APRIL 13, ON A CONTINUING BASIS. (ST-WIDE). DENNIS SIENKO, CO-CHAIRMAN; ELGIN COMMUNITY COLLEGE BICENTENNIAL COMMISSION; 1700 SPARTAN DR; ELGIN, IL 60120. (#14029).

TIME LINE: TRAVELING EXHIBIT, ELGIN, IL. SIGNIFICANT EVENTS OF REVOLUTIONARY ERA THROUGH 1791, ARE DEPICTED IN GRAPHIC & PRINTED FORM. (LOCAL). CAROLE ACKEMANN, CHAIRPERSON; ELGIN COMMUNITY COLLEGE BICENTENNIAL COMMISSION; 1700 SPARTAN DR; ELGIN, IL 60120. (#14076).

JULY 31 - SEPT 26, '75. PLAYWRITING COMPETITION ON HISTORICAL THEME. COMPETITION, LIVE PERFORMANCE. (LOCAL). DORIS L DETTMAN, CHMN; ELGIN COMMUNITY THEATRE; PO BOX 208; ELGIN, IL 60120. (#101852-1).

DEC 5, '75 - DEC 31, '76. TOUR OF WINNING HISTORICAL PLAY IN LOCAL AREA. TOUR. (LOCAL). DENNIS M LEOPOLD, CHMN; ELGIN COMMUNITY THEATRE; PO BOX 208; ELGIN, IL 60120. (#101852-2).

JUNE 10 - 19, '76. SONG OF HIAWATHA INDIAN PAGEANTS; 50TH CELEBRATION. AUTHENTIC AMERICAN DANCE WITH AUTHENTIC COSTUMING; PAGEANT DONE IN PANTOMIME WITH NARRATION & MUSIC IN THE BACKGROUND; STORY LINE FROM POEM SONG OF HIAWATHA; SEATING FOR 2000 AROUND HALF ACRE LAKE; FACILITIES FOR PICNIC LUNCH ON GROUNDS. AT CAMP BIG TIMBER, BIG TIMBER RD. (ST-WIDE). CLAYTON WOOD, ASST; HIAWATHA PRODUCTION; 5 DOUGLAS AVE; ELGIN, IL 60120. (#103114-1).

JUNE '76. FESTIVAL OF AMERICAN MUSIC. INCLUDED IN BICENTENNIAL PROG BEGINNING NOV 5, 1975 THRU MAY 1, 1976 IN-SCHOOL WORKSHOPS, TEACHERS & STUDENTS REENACTMENTS OF EVENTS IN RI HIST - FEE $35; 2 SESSIONS; $50 & $75 3 SESSIONS;ALSO A PLAY BASED ON THE GASPEE AFFAIR, MAR THRU JUNE 4, 1976 TOURS SCHOOLS. (LOCAL). CAROLE ACKEMANN, PROJ DIR; ELGIN COMMUNITY COLLEGE BICENTENNIAL COMMISSION; 1700 SPARTAN DR; ELGIN, IL 60120. (#101687-1).

ELLIS GROVE

JUNE 6 - 8, '75. THE FRENCH IN ILLINOIS- MENARD'S HOME. THIS EVENT COINCIDES WITH THE ANNUAL RENDERVOUS AT FORT DE CHARTRES AND INTERPRETS THE IMPACT OF THE EARLY 19TH CENTURY FRENCH CULTURE IN ILLINOIS. AT MENARD'S HOME. (LOCAL). MS JANET PICKETT; ILLINOIS DEPARTMENT OF CONSERVATION; 901 SOUTH SPRING; SPRINGFIELD, IL 62704. (#50272-16).

JULY 4, '75. RINGING OF KASKASKIA BELL. THIS EVENT OCCURS EACH YEAR TO CELEBRATE GEORGE RODGERS CLARK'S CAPT URE OF FORT KASKASKIA FROM THE BRITISH. ON JULY 4, 1778 HE CAPTURED THE FORT AND RUNG THE BELL SYMBOLIZING THE ESTABLISHMENT OF AMERICAN INDEPENDENCE IN THE WEST. AT KASKASKIA BELL. (LOCAL). MS JANET PICKETT; ILLINOIS DEPARTMENT OF CONSERVATION; 901 SOUTH SPRING; SPRINGFIELD, IL 62704. (#50272-19).

JAN 4, '76. 12TH NIGHT. THIS EVENT CAPTURES THE SPIRIT OF THE 19TH CENTURY, TRADITIONAL FREN CH CHRISTMAS CELEBRATION. AT MENARD'S HOME. (LOCAL). MS JANET PICKETT; ILLINOIS DEPARTMENT OF CONSERVATION; 901 SOUTH SPRING; SPRINGFIELD, IL 62704. (#50272-17).

JUNE 26 - JULY 17, '76. GEORGE ROGERS CLARK TREK-REENACTMENT OF JOURNEY. ILLINOIS CONSERVATION SERVICE SPECIAL EVENTS. TWO DAY HISTORICAL RECREATIONS OF ILL HISTORY AT HISTORICAL PARKS OR MEMORIALS, WILL GO FROM FROM METROPOLIS TO CAHOKIA, ILL. (ST-WIDE). JANET L PICKETT; IL DEPT OF CONSERVATION, PROGRAM SERVICES DIVISION; 605 STATE OFFICE BLDG; SPRINGFIELD, IL 62706. (#4400-522).

JULY 4, '76. MENARD'S HOME CELEBRATION. OPEN HOUSE. (LOCAL). MS JANET PICKETT; ILL DEPT OF CONSERVATION; 901 SOUTH SPRING; SPRINGFIELD, IL 62704. (#50272-18).

JULY 4, '76. RINGING OF KASKASKIA BELL. THIS EVENT OCCURS EACH YEAR TO CELEBRATE GEORGE RODGERS CLARK'S CAPT URE OF FORT KASKASKIA FROM THE BRITISH ON JULY 4, 1778 HE CAPTURED T HE FORT AND RUNG THE BELL SYMBOLIZING THE ESTABLISHMENT OF AMERICAN INDEPENDENCE IN THE WEST. AT KASKASKIA BELL. (LOCAL). MS JANET PICKETT; ILLINOIS DEPARTMENT OF CONSERVATION; 901 SOUTH SPRING; SPRINGFIELD, IL 62704. (#50272-20).

JULY 9 - 11, '76. THE FRENCH IN ILLINOIS-MENARD'S HOME. THIS EVENT COINCIDES WITH THE ANNUAL RENDEZNOUS AT FORT DE CHARTRES AND INTERPRETS THE IMPACT OF THE EARLY 19TH CENTURY FRENCH CULTURE IN ILLINOIS. AT MENARD'S HOME. (LOCAL). MS JANET PICKETT; ILLINOIS DEPARTMENT OF CONSERVATION; 901 SOUTH SPRING; SPRINGFIELD, IL 62704. (#50272-21).

ELMHURST

HISTORIC MARKERS - ELMHURST, IL. MARKERS WILL BE PLACED ON ALL BUILDINGS & SITES OF HISTORIC OR ARCHITECTURAL SIGNIFICANCE AS DESIGNATED BY THE STATE OF ILLINOIS DEPT OF CONSERVATION. (LOCAL). MRS MARGARET COOPER, PRESIDENT; DAUGHTERS OF AMERICAN REVOLUTION; 489 FAIR ST; ELMHURST, IL 60126. (#25115).

RESTORATION OF A PASSENGER & FREIGHT DEPOT - IL. THE ELMHURST PARK DISTRICT WILL RESTORE THE PASSENGER & FREIGHT DEPOT CIRCA 1890. (LOCAL). DAN SCHOUREK, CHAIRMAN; ELMHURST PARK DISTRICT; ELMHURST, IL 60126. (#22701).

'SO PROUDLY WE HAIL' - ELMHURST, IL. ONE STATE WILL BE FEATURED EACH WEEK. BOOK, BROCHURES & FACTS ON THE STATES TO BE AVAILABLE TO LIBRARY PATRONS. ALSO A REGISTER OF PATRONS AND THEIR BIRTH STATES. (LOCAL). LARRY KNUDSEN, LIBRARIAN; ELMHURST PUBLIC LIBRARY; WILDER PARK; ELMHURST, IL 60126. (#17730).

JULY 5, '76. DEDICATION OF HORIZONS-HERITAGE PROJECTS WITH BAND & SING-A-LONG. DEDICATION OF NEW BICENTENNIAL FOUNTAIN, RESTORED RAIL DEPOT & TOUR OF THE NEW ELMHURST BIKE ROUTE SYSTEM. AT WILD MEADOWS TRACE PARK, YORK ROAD & THE ILLINOIS PRARIE PATH. (LOCAL). NORMAN P SMALLEY, CHMN; ELMHURST BICENTENNIAL COMMISSION; 429 AVERY ST; ELMHURST, IL 60126. (#106203-1).

ELMWOOD

CONSTRUCTION OF BANDSHELL IN ELMWOOD, IL. CONSTRUCTION OF A BANDSHELL FOR PUBLIC USE. (LOCAL). KENNETH MATSON, CHAIRMAN; PEORIA COUNTY BICENTENNIAL COMMISSION; 307 N KNOX ST; ELMWOOD, IL 61529. (#33632).

ELWOOD

BICENTENNIAL DAYS CHURCH SCHOOL, ELWOOD, ILLINOIS. PAGEANT WITH COMPLETE SCHOOL PARTICIPATION IN GRADES 1-8. COMMUNITY CHURCH WITH 18TH CENTURY SERMONS, HYMNS & DRESS ON SUNDAYS. ALSO A HOMECOMING WITH BICENTENNIAL THEME & PAINTINGS ON HISTORY. (LOCAL). ROGER SWEETWOOD, CHAIRMAN; ELWOOD BICENTENNIAL TOWNSHIP COMMITTEE; 117 GARDNER; ELWOOD, IL 60421. (#6324).

JUNE 18 - 22, '75. ELWOOD BICENTENNIAL DAYS. ELWOOD PAGEANT, COMPLETE SCHOOL PARTICIPATION GRADES ONE THRU EIGHT; ELWOOD COMMUNITY CHURCH TO PRESENT 18TH CENTURY SERMONS, HYMNS & DRESS ON SUNDAYS; HOMECOMING; BICENTENNIAL THEME PAINTINGS OF HISTORICAL EVENTS. AT CITYWIDE, SCHOOLS & CHURCHES. (LOCAL). ROGER SWEETWOOD, CHAIRMAN; ELWOOD BICENT TOWNSHIP COMMITTEE; 117 GARDNER; ELWOOD, IL 60421. (#50606-1).

EUREKA

COURTHOUSE BELL & CLOCK RESTORATION IN EUREKA, IL. RESTORATION OF PART OF COUNTY COURTHOUSE. (LOCAL). WILLIAM MAJORS, COORDINATOR; WOODFORD COUNTY BICENTENNIAL COMMISSION; ROUTE 1; EUREKA, IL 61530. (#33630).

JULY 19, '75. ILLINOIS ODDFELLOWS STATE FAIR. PLANNING AN OLD FASHIONED CARNIVAL & BARBECUE TO CELEBRATE THE BICENTENNIAL. (ST-WIDE). DALE A LIGGETT, COORD; ILLINOIS ODDFELLOW AND REBEKAH GRAND LODGES; 629 S 12TH ST; PEKIN, IL 61554. (#6495-501).

MAY 13, '76. BICENTENNIAL CHOIR CONCERT. LIVE PERFORMANCE. (LOCAL). WILLIAM MAJORS, CHMN; WOODFORD COUNTY BICENTENNIAL COMMISSION; ROUTE 1; EUREKA, IL 61530. (#200016-83).

EVANSTON

AN AMERICAN PROSPECTUS, EVANSTON, ILLINOIS. A FULL ACCOUNT OF THE DESIGN & MEANING OF THE GREAT SEAL OF THE UNITED STATES WILL BE GIVEN. (NAT'L). KEVIN LYNCH, DIRECTOR; ONAR, INC; BOX 302; EVANSTON, IL 60204. (#8578).

DEVELOPMENT IN FOUNTAIN SQUARE, EVANSTON, ILLINOIS. IN 1876 A FOUNTAIN WAS PLACED IN FOUNTAIN SQUARE. PLANS ARE TO PLACE A NEW FOUNTAIN IN THE SQUARE IN 1976 & MAKE IT AN ASSEMBLY PLACE. (LOCAL). JOHN O WYANDT, CHAIRMAN; EVANSTON BICENTENNIAL COMMISSION; 1501 OAK ST; EVANSTON, IL 60201. (#5845).

EVANSTON BLACK ORAL HISTORY - IL. STUDENT ORAL HISTORY ON BLACKS IN EVANSTON. (LOCAL). MRS A SNOW, CHAIRMAN; EVANSTON ARTS COUNCIL; MARYWOOD CIVIC CENTER; EVANSTON, IL 60201. (#27764). **ARBA GRANTEE.**

RESEARCH OF FREE SPEECH IN EVANSTON, IL. RESEARCH AND WRITING OF A BOOK OR ARTICLE ON CASES OF CAMPUS DISSENT , FREEDOM OF PRESS, ACADEMIC FREEDOMS & PHILOSOPHICAL ISSUES. (NAT'L). JEROME A STONE, CHRMN HUMANITIES; KENDALL COLLEGE; EVANSTON, DC 20506. (#3813).

'YANKEE DOODLE WAS A TRAVELING MAN'-PLAY. THEATER PRODUCTION DEPICTING MOBILITY OF EARLY AMERICANS. USE OF AUTHENTIC DOCUMENTS & MUSIC FOR SCRIPT. CAST OF TEN NORTHWESTERN STUDENTS WILL TOUR IN 1973-1976 TO PERFORM BEFORE STUDENTS & OTHERS. (REGN'L). JANE DINSMOOR TRIPLETT, EXEC DIRECTOR; CHILDREN'S THEATRE OF EVANSTON (THEATER 65); 1316 OAKTON; EVANSTON, IL 60202. (#657).

APR 18, '76. BICENTENNIAL FASHION SHOW. FASHION SHOW OF HISTORIC COSTUMES OF FAMOUS LOCAL WOMEN AND COMMENTARY ON COSTUMES OF NATIONALLY FAMOUS PEOPLE. AT 1702 CHICAGO AVE. (LOCAL). MRS BETH WRIGHT, CHMN; EVANSTON WOMENS CLUB & EVANSTON HISTORICAL SOCIETY; 1310 JUDSON; EVANSTON, IL 60201. (#103665-1).

JULY 4, '76. FOUNTAIN SQUARE PARK DEDICATION. PARK WILL CONTAIN 3 ILLUMINATED FOUNTAINS, A PLAZA, MEMORIAL COLUMNS HONORING THE CITY'S WAR DEAD, & THE FLAG POLE DEDICATED BY GENERAL DOUGLAS MACARTHUR IN 1951. TREES, FLOWERS, PLANTS & BENCHES WILL COMPLETE THE PARK. FUNDED BY PUBLIC DONATIONS ONLY. AT INTERSECTION OF SHERMAN & ORRINGTON AVES WITH DAVIS ST. (LOCAL). DONALD YABUSH, COMM CHRMN; EVANSTON BICENTENNIAL COMMISSION; 2655 ASBURY AVE; EVANSTON, IL 60201. (#106781-1).

EVANSTON — CONTINUED

DEC 6 - 8, '76. LA SALLE EXPEDITION II, A HISTORIC RE-ENACTMENT. THIS IS AN AUTHENTIC RE-ENACTMENT OF THE 1681 LASALLE EXPEDITION FROM MONTREAL, CANADA TO NEW ORLEANS, LA WHICH WILL BEGIN TOURING ON AUGUST 11, 1976 AND END ON APRIL 9, 1977. (LOCAL). REID H LEWIS, DIRECTOR; LA SALLE EXPEDITION II; 135 S LA SALLE ST, RM 411; CHICAGO, IL 60690. (#102805-25).

JAN 1 - 31, '77. CARL HAVERLIN/BROADCAST MUSIC, INC, ARCHIVES BICENTENNIAL EXHIBIT. OFFERS A VERSATILE PICTURE OF HISTORY, REGIONAL LIFE & MUSIC FOR OVER 200 YEARS. CONTAINS PRESIDENTIAL LETTERS, LETTERS OF FAMOUS AMERICANS, OLD BOOKS, MANUSCRIPTS, HISTORY OF 'THE STAR SPANGLED BANNER' & COMPOSER AUTOGRAPHS, PLUS SHEET MUSIC OF THE PAST. AT NORTHWESTERN UNIV MUSIC LIBRARY. (ST-WIDE). DON L ROBERTS, LIBRARIAN; NORTHWESTERN UNIVERSITY; 1810 HINMAN AVE; EVANSTON, IL 60201. (#20784-18).

EVANSVILLE

BICENTENNIAL CREATIVE WRITING PROJ, EVANSVILLE, IL. THE 2 EVANSVILLE UNIVERSITIES ARE SPONSORING A HIGH SCHOOL - COLLEGE STUDENT WRITING CONTEST ON THE THEME, 'THE FUTURE OF THE AMERICAN DREAM '; AWARDS CEREMONY AT OLD COUNTY COURTHOUSE FEBRUARY 21, 1976. (LOCAL). TOM BOHN, PROJ CHAIRMAN; UNIV OF EVANSVILLE; EVANSVILLE, IN 47702. (#17901).

HISTORY OF VILLAGE OF EVANSVILLE, IL. THE DEVELOPMENT & GROWTH OF TOWN TO BE PORTRAYED IN A BOOK. (LOCAL). REV EDWARD FRESEN, CHAIRMAN; EVANSVILLE BICENTENNIAL PLANNING GROUP; EVANSVILLE, IL 62242. (#20589).

A PHOTOGRAPHIC HISTORY OF EVANSVILLE, IL. PHOTOGRAPHS DEALING WITH THE HISTORY OF EVANSVILLE WILL BE COMPILED AND PRINTED IN A MAGAZINE. (LOCAL). TONY M PAUTLER, CO-CHAIRMAN; EVANSVILLE BICENTENNIAL COMMITTEE; EVANSVILLE, IL 62242. (#24845).

RIVER DOCK PROJECT - EVANSVILLE, IL. RIVER FRONT WILL BE CLEANED AND A LOADING DOCK AND MARINA BUILT IN COMMEMORATION OF THE BICENTENNIAL. (LOCAL). HON JIM BIETHMAN, MAYOR; CITY OF EVANSVILLE; EVANSVILLE, IL 62242. (#24844).

MAR 27, '76. EVANSVILLE BICENTENNIAL BALL. MUSIC BY THE SUNSETS. AT AMERICAN LEGION HALL. (LOCAL). JIM ROBERT, COORD; EVANSVILLE BICENTENNIAL COMMITTEE; EVANSVILLE, IL 62242. (#200016-18).

MAY 2, '76. CELEBRATION. CEREMONY, FESTIVAL, LIVE PERFORMANCE. (LOCAL). EDWARD H FRESEN, COORD; EVANSVILLE BICENTENNIAL COMMITTEE; BOX 87; EVANSVILLE, IL 62242. (#200016-2).

AUG 14 - 15, '76. ARTS & CRAFTS FESTIVAL & PARADE. ARTS, CRAFTS & PARADE. AT CITY PARK. (LOCAL). JIM ROBERT, CHAIRMAN; EVANSVILLE BICENTENNIAL COMMITTEE; EVANSVILLE, IL 62242. (#107280-1).

EVERGREEN PK

CONSTRUCTION OF GAZEBO - EVERGREEN PARK, ILLINOIS. CONSTRUCTION OF AN ENCLOSED BANDSHELL IN PARK FOR USE IN ALL OUTDOOR EVENTS DURING BICENTENNIAL & AFTERWARDS; ALSO FOR CONCERTS, AWARDS, CEREMONIES, PLAYS & RELIGIOUS SERVICES. (LOCAL). MELANIE BALDERMANN, PROGRAM COORDINATOR; EVERGREEN PARK BICENT COMMISSION; 9720 S MILLARD AVE; EVERGREEN PRK, IL 60642. (#9100).

JULY 2, '75. COSTUME DINNER DANCE. THIS IS A FUND RAISING EVENT ALSO THE 1ST SOCIAL EVENT OF OUR BICI. SUMMER ACTIVITIES, THERE WILL BE PATRIOTIC ENTERTAINMENT, BICI MOMENTOS AVAILABLE & STATEWIDE DIGNITERIES PRESENT. AT GRAND BALLROOM MARTINQUE 2500 W 94 ST. LARGE PRIVATE PARKING LOT. (LOCAL). MELANIE BAIDERMANN; EVERGREEN PARK BICENTENNIAL COMMISSION; 9720 S MILLARD AVE; EVERGREEN PK, IL 60642. (#50442-2).

JULY 2 - 6, '75. 4TH OF JULY CELEBRATION. 5-DAY CELEBRATION INCLUDES DINNER, DANCE, PARADE, FIREWORKS, SPORTING EVENTS, OPENING OF GAZEBO IN PARK, MUSICAL ENTERTAINMENT, AWARDS, FESTIVAL. AT E.P. HS 99TH KEDZIE, HOMAN PARK 97TH E HOMAN MARTINQUE,2500 W 94ST. (LOCAL). MELANIE BAIDERMANN; EVERGREEN PARK BICENTENNIAL COM. AND CHAMBER OF COMMERCE; 9720 S MILLARD AVE; EVERGREEN PK, IL 60642. (#50442-1).

SEPT 10, '76. UNITED STATES ARMED FORCES BICENTENNIAL CARAVAN. CARAVAN IS COMPOSED OF EXHIBIT VANS FOR EACH MILITARY SERVICE. PROJECT THEME IS 'HISTORY OF THE ARMED FORCES & THEIR CONTRIBUTIONS TO THE NATION.'. (LOCAL). MELANIE BALDERHANN, CHMN; UNITED STATES ARMED FORCES BICENTENNIAL CARAVAN; 9730 S WESTERN, ROOM G-38; EVERGREEN PK, IL 60642. (#1775-644).

EXETER

RECYCLING CENTER FOR SCOTT COUNTY IN EXETER, IL. PERMANENT CENTER ESTABLISHED WITH CLEAN-UP DAYS IN SPRING AND FALL. (LOCAL). AUDREY PEAK, COORDINATOR; SCOTT COUNTY BICENTENNIAL COMMISSION; 360 W CHERRY; WINCHESTER, IL 62694. (#33629).

FAIRVIEW

MAY 15, '76. BICENTENNIAL TEA AND OPENHOUSE. BICENTENNIAL TEA AND OPEN HOUSE LIMITED TO FIRST 200 RESERVATIONS. AT OLD INN FARM. (LOCAL). MRS LAWRENCE BORDNER, DIR; FARMINGTON CHAPTER NSDAR; 45 N PARK DR; CANTON, IL 61520. (#105202-2).

JULY 8 - 10, '76. HOMECOMING AND FAT STOCK SHOW. VILLAGE HOMECOMING WITH STAGE ENTERTAINMENT, COUNTRY FOODS AND LIVESTOCK SHOW. AT FAIRVIEW PARK. (LOCAL). MRS LYMAN ROBERTS, COORD; FAIRVIEW COMMUNITY AND AMERICAN LEGION; BOX 66; FAIRVIEW, IL 61432. (#105202-1).

FAIRVIEW HTS

REPAIR AND RESTORATION OF KINSELLA LOG CABIN - IL. REPAIR AND RESTORATION OF LOG CABIN IN PLEASANT RIDGE PARK FOR USE AS A MUSEUM. (LOCAL). WILLIAM KEMP, PROJ DIRECTOR; FAIRVIEW HEIGHTS BICENTENNIAL COMMISSION; CITY HALL, 10218 LINCOLN TRAIL; FAIRVIEW HTS, IL 62208. (#26111). **ARBA GRANTEE.**

FLORA

CLAY COUNTY, ILL 4-H AND COMMUNITY CENTER PROJECT. CONSTRUCTION OF A BUILDING FOR USE BY THE 4-H CLUB AND COMMUNITY ORGANIZATIONS BEING CONSTRUCTED BY THE 4-H FEDERATION. (LOCAL). LARRY CAMP, U OF ILL COOP EXTENSION SERV ADVISOR; CLAY COUNTY, ILL 4-H FEDERATION; PO BOX F; LOUISVILLE, IL 62858. (#4884). **(??). ARBA GRANTEE.**

FLORENCE

FEB 3 - 4, '77. LA SALLE EXPEDITION II, A HISTORIC RE-ENACTMENT. THIS IS AN AUTHENTIC RE-ENACTMENT OF THE 1681 LASALLE EXPEDITION FROM MONTREAL, CANADA TO NEW ORLEANS, LA WHICH WILL BEGIN TOURING ON AUGUST 11, 1976 AND END ON APRIL 9, 1977. (LOCAL). REID H LEWIS, DIRECTOR; LA SALLE EXPEDITION II; 135 S LA SALLE ST, RM 411; CHICAGO, IL 60690. (#102805-50).

FORREST

BICENTENNIAL PROJECTS - FORREST, IL. PLANTED FLOWERS ALONG RT 47; SOLD FLAGS; COMPILED TOWN'S HISTORY; A PLAQUE MARKING THE WAGON TRAIL THROUGH FORREST. (LOCAL). MARGE MORINE, CHAIRMAN; FORREST BICENTENNIAL COMMITTEE; 115 PARKVIEW DR; FORREST, IL 61741. (#33705).

PLAQUE MARKING WAGON TRAIL - FORREST, IL. MARKING WAGON TRAIL THROUGH LOCAL PARK. (LOCAL). MARGE HORIHE, PRESIDENT; BICENTENNIAL COMMITTEE; 115 PARKVIEW DR; FORREST, IL 61741. (#29818).

DEC '76. CENTENNIAL BALL. FESTIVAL AT LEGION BLDG. (LOCAL). MARGE HORINE, CHMN; FORREST BICENTENNIAL COMMITTEE; PARKVIEW DR; FORREST, IL 61741. (#200016-407).

FORT SHERIDAN

MAY 22, '76. HIGHLAND PARK HISTORICAL SOCIETY MEETING - JUNIOR DIVISION. CONFERENCE, EXHIBIT, TOUR AT FORT SHERIDAN, IL, MUSEUM. (LOCAL). HENRY X ARENBERG, CHMN; HIGHLAND PARK HISTORICAL SOCIETY; 1171 LINDEN AVE; HIGHLAND PARK, IL 60035. (#200016-253).

FRANKFORT

RESTORATION OF HERITAGE HALL IN FRANKFORT, IL. OLD LIVERY STABLE AND GARAGE ARE BEING RESTORED, REFURBISHED & CONVERTED INTO A COMMUNITY CENTER WITH A HOMEY MEETING ROOM - THE LOFT, A LARGE ALL-PURPOSE ROOM; THE LIVERY KITCHENETTE & A MUSEUM. (LOCAL). ALLAN MAGER, TRUSTEE; FRANKFORT BICENTENNIAL COMMISSION; 123 KANSAS ST; FRANKFORT, IL 60423. (#33628).

AUG 23 - 25, '75. HERITAGE HOLIDAYS. EVENTS WERE: TENTED COSTUME BALL, DEDICATION OF HERITAGE HALL, ARTS AND CRAFTS EXHIBITS, VILLAGE THEATER, HISTORICAL SKITS, CHILDREN'S THEATER AND TEEN-AGE DANCE. AT FRANKFORT VILLAGE HALL, 123 KANSAS ST. (LOCAL). MRS FRANCES BREIDERT; FRANKFORT BICENTENNIAL COMMISSION; 241 OAK ST; FRANKFORT, IL 60423. (#200016-436).

AUG 30 - SEPT 1, '75. FRANKFORT FALL FESTIVAL '75. 1890'S FESTIVAL: STREET ARTS & CRAFTS FAIR; TENTED BEER GARDEN; CORN ROAST; COUNTRY STORE; CARNIVAL RIDES; FOOD CONCESSIONS; GAMES; BICENTENNIAL PARADE; COMMUNITY CHURCH SERVICE, HISTORICAL WAGON TOURS, CHICKEN DINNERS & OUTDOOR ENTERTAINMENT. AT HISTORICAL DISTRICT OF VILLAGE. (LOCAL). CHAIRMAN; FRANKFORT CHAMBER OF COMMERCE & BICENTENNIAL COMMISSION; 20 S RT 45; FRANKFORT, IL 60423. (#200016-439).

JULY 5, '76. FIFTH OF JULY FAMILY PICNIC. FLAG CEREMONY, SOFT BALL, VOLLEYBALL, HORSESHOES, ETC. BICENTENNIAL ART CONTEST, BAND CONCERT, BICENTENNIAL ADDRESS, HISTORICAL SKITS, BOY SCOUT CEREMONY & BONFIRE; FAMILY BASKET MEALS. AT FRANKFORT PARK, LOCUST ST. (LOCAL). FRANCES BREIDERT, CHMN; FRANKFORT BICENTENNIAL COMMISSION; 241 OAK ST; FRANKFORT, IL 60423. (#200016-437).

SEPT 4 - 6, '76. FRANKFORT FALL FESTIVAL. FESTIVAL. (LOCAL). FRANCES BREIDERT, CHMN; FRANKFORT CHAMBER OF COMMERCE; 241 OAK ST; FRANKFORT, IL 60423. (#200016-438).

FREEPORT

AUG 28 - 29, '76. UNITED STATES ARMED FORCES BICENTENNIAL CARAVAN. CARAVAN IS COMPOSED OF EXHIBIT VANS FOR EACH MILITARY SERVICE. PROJECT THEME IS 'HISTORY OF THE ARMED FORCES & THEIR CONTRIBUTIONS TO THE NATION.'. (LOCAL). WILLIAM GERLOFF, CHMN; UNITED STATES ARMED FORCES BICENTENNIAL CARAVAN; 230 W STEPHENSON ST; FREEPORT, IL 61032. (#1775-639).

GALENA

RECOGNITION PLAQUES FOR HISTORIC BUILDINGS, IL. 175 METAL IDENTIFICATION PLAQUES TO BE MOUNTED ON DESIGNATED BUILDINGS OF HISTORIC INTEREST IN DOWNTOWN GALENA, TO GIVE INFORMATION ON EACH STRUCTURE. (LOCAL). EDWARD J GANSHIRT, CHAIRMAN; GALENA BICENTENNIAL COMMISSION; 810 PARK AVE; GALENA, IL 61036. (#25682). **ARBA GRANTEE.**

APR 26 - 27, '75. U S GRANT SCOUT PILGRIMAGE. ANNUAL BOY SCOUT PILGRAMAGE TO GALENA, PARTICULARLY GRANT'S HOME. HE RE THE BOYS ARE EXPOSED TO NUMEROUS FACTS ON GALENA AND THE LIFE STY LES OF THE MID-EIGHTEEN HUNDREDS. AT GRANT'S HOME. (LOCAL). MS JANET PICKETT; ILLINOIS DEPARTMENT OF CONSERVATION; 901 SOUTH SPRING; SPRINGFIELD, IL 62704. (#50272-24).

MAY 16 - 18, '75. U S GRANT CANTONMENT (CIVIL WAR). REENACTMENT OF THE CIVIL WAR PERIOD BY VOLUNTEER RE-ACTIVATED CIVIL WAR GROUPS BRING THE EXCITEMENT AND COLOR OF PERIOD COSTUMES AND THE BOOM OF THE CANON TO HISTORIC OLD GALENA. AT GALENA. (REGN'L). MS JANET PICKETT; ILLINOIS DEPARTMENT OF CONSERVATION; 901 SOUTH SPRING; SPRINGFIELD, IL 62704. (#50272-22).

JUNE 14 - 15, '75. SPRING SKILLS FROM THE HILLS. VOLUNTEERS FROM THE GALENA AREA DRESS IN APPROPRIATE COSTUME AND DEM ONSTRATE AND EXPLAIN CRAFTS COMMON IN THE 19TH CENTURY. AT GALENA. (LOCAL). MS JANET PICKETT; ILLINOIS DEPARTMENT OF CONSERVATION; 901 SOUTH SPRING; SPRINGFIELD, IL 62704. (#50272-26).

SEPT 27 - 28, '75. MARKET DAYS. MARKET DAY STRIVES TO RECREATE THE ATMOSPHERE AND TIMES SURROUNDING THIS HISTORIC BUILDING. AT GALENA MARKET SQUARE MEMORIAL. (LOCAL). MS JANET PICKETT; ILLINOIS DEPT OF CONSERVATION; 901 SOUTH SPRING; SPRINGFIELD, IL 62704. (#50272-23).

DEC 6 - 7, '75. CHRISTMAS WALK. A SPECIAL CHRISTMAS OPEN HOUSE GRANT'S HOME AND MARKET SQUARE ARE DE CKED OUT IN THEIR CHRISTMAS FINERY AND INVITE THE GENERAL PUBLIC TO BECOME PART OF THIS OLD FASHIONED CHRISTMAS. AT GRANT'S HOME AND THE MARKET SQUARE. (LOCAL). MS JANET PICKETT; ILLINOIS DEPARTMENT OF CONSERVATION; 901 SOUTH SPRING; SPRINGFIELD, IL 62704. (#50272-29).

APR 23 - 25, '76. U S GRANT SCOUT PILGRIMAGE. BOY SCOUT PILGRIMAGE CELEBRATING GENERAL GRANT'S BIRTHDAY; MERIT AWARDS EARNED. AT ENTIRE CITY. (LOCAL). JUSTIN KNEELAND, DIR; BLACKHAWK AREA COUNCIL BOY SCOUTS OF AMERICA; PO BOX 4085; ROCKFORD, IL 61110. (#104088-5).

MAY 14 - 16, '76. CIVIL WAR COMEMORATION ACTIVITIES. ACTIVITIES WILL INCLUDE AUTHENTIC CIVIL WAR CAMPS, CIVIL WAR PARADE, A BATTLE REENACTMENT WITH 1,000 SOLIDERS, A MUSKET & CANNON SHOOTING CONTEST AND A MILITARY BALL. (LOCAL). ROBERT HANSEN, DIR; 45TH LEADMINE REGIMENT; 211 S HIGH ST; GALENA, IL 61036. (#104088-3).

JUNE 12, '76. GALENA HISTORICAL SOCIETY'S TOUR OF HOMES. TOUR OF HOMES OVER 100 YEARS WHICH HAVE BEEN RESTORED FOR MODERN LIVING. AT ENTIRE CITY. (LOCAL). CHARLES F PRIMROSE, DIR; GALENA HISTORICAL SOCIETY; 301 HIGH ST; GALENA, IL 61036. (#104088-1).

JUNE 12 - 13, '76. SPRING SKILLS IN THE HILLS. VOLUNTEERS FROM THE GALENA AREA DRESS IN APPROPRIATE COSTUME AND DEM ONSTRATE AND EXPLAIN CRAFTS COMMON IN THE 19TH CENTURY. AT GALENA. (LOCAL). MS JANET PICKETT; ILLINOIS DEPARTMENT OF CONSERVATION; 901 SOUTH SPRING; SPRINGFIELD, IL 62704. (#50272-27).

JULY 2 - 5, '76. EARLY AMERICAN CRAFT SHOW. DEMONSTRATION OF EARLY AMER CRAFTS: SPINNING, WEAVING, CANDLEMAKING, QUILTING, ETC. AT GALENA HISTORICAL MUSEUM, 211 BENCH ST. (LOCAL). E J GANSHIRT, CHMN; GALENA HISTORICAL SOCIETY; 211 S BENCH ST; GALENA, IL 61036. (#105659-1).

JULY 2 - 5, '76. GALENA SESQUICENTENNIAL CELEBRATION. CELEBRATION OF SESQUICENTENNIAL OF GALENA WITH A PAGEANT, BALL AND PARADE. AT RECREATION PARK, TURNER HALL, MAIN ST. (LOCAL). VERA HELLER, DIR; GALENA BICENTENNIAL COMMISSION; RR 2; GALENA, IL 61036. (#104088-4).

SEPT 25 - 26, '76. MARKET DAYS. MARKET DAY STRIVES TO RECREATE THE ATMOSPHERE & TIMES SURROUNDING THIS HISTORICAL BUILDING. AT MARKET SQUARE, GALENA MARKET SQUARE MEMORIAL. (LOCAL). MS JANET PICKETT; ILLINOIS DEPARTMENT OF CONSERVATION; 901 SOUTH SPRING; SPRINGFIELD, IL 62704. (#50272-28).

SEPT 25 - 26, '76. TOUR OF 5 RESTORED PRE-CIVIL WAR GALENA HOMES. OTHER ACTIVITIES WILL INCLUDE MARKET DAYS, MILITARY BAND CONCERT AND A MELODRAMA PERFORMANCE. (LOCAL). MRS WALTER EHRLER, DIR; FIRST PRESBYTERIAN CHURCH; 1009 3RD ST; GALENA, IL 61036. (#104088-2).

GALENA — CONTINUED

DEC 4 - 5, '76. CHRISTMAS WALK. A SPECIAL CHRISTMAS OPEN HOUSE GRANT'S HOME AND MARKET SQUARE ARE DE CKED OUT IN THEIR CHRISTMAS FINERY AND INVITE THE GENERAL PUBLIC TO BECOME PART OF THIS OLD FASHIONED CHRISTMAS. AT GRANT'S HOME AND THE MARKET SQUARE. (LOCAL). MS JANETT PICKETT; ILLINOIS DEPARTMENT OF CONSERVATION; 901 SOUTH SPRING; SPRINGFIELD, IL 62704. (#50272-30).

GALESBURG

BICENTENNIAL INTERCULTURAL FESTIVAL OF ILLNOIS. A TWO DAY AFFAIR SHOWING CULTURAL EXHIBITS OF ETHNIC GROUPS AND HISTORICAL EXHIBITS OF TOWNS IN THE COUNTY; PROGRAMS BY TALENT OF THE COUNTY; AND A TASTING TABLE OF FOREIGN FOODS & PIONEER FOODS. (LOCAL). VIRGINIA HINCHLIFF, CHAIRMAN; KNOX COUNTY BICENT COMMISSION; 125 S CHERRY ST; GALESBURG, IL 61401. (#6067).

BSA TROOP 206, AMERICAN FLAG AND CLEANUP PROJ, IL. TROOP 206 WILL RAISE AND RETIRE THE FLAG ON 10 HOLIDAYS EACH YEAR. THEY WILL ALSO CLEANUP THE DOWNTOWN AREA OF GALESBURG WEEKLY. (LOCAL). E W HOLLER, SCOUTMASTER; BOY SCOUT TROOP 206; 1572 WEBSTER ST; GALESBURG, IL 61401. (#10641).

PHOTO EXHIBITS OF KNOX COUNTY IN GALESBURG, IL. TEN TOURING PHOTO EXHIBITS OF KNOX COUNTY. (LOCAL). MARGARET WAINER, COORDINATOR; CARL SANDBURG COLLEGE; GALESBURG, IL 61401. (#33627).

PUBLIC LIBRARY MEDIA PROGRAM, GALESBURG, ILLINOIS. SLIDE, AUDIO & TAPE PROGRAM DEPICTING BUILDINGS, SCENES & PEOPLE OF HISTORIC VALUE IN GALESBURG & KNOX COUNTY, ILL. (LOCAL). EDYTHE SQUIRES, PROJECT DIRECTOR; GALESBURG PUBLIC LIBRARY; 40 E SIMMONS ST; GALESBURG, IL 61401. (#5328).

PUBLIC SAFETY BUILDING IN GALESBURG, ILLINOIS. COMBINED CITY-COUNTY LAW ENFORCEMENT BUILDING AND CENTRAL FIRE STATION SERVING THE CITY OF GALESBURG AND KNOX COUNTY WILL BE BUILT. (LOCAL). THOMAS B HERRING, CITY MANAGER; CITY OF GALESBURG; 161 S CHERRY ST; GALESBURG, IL 61401. (#6241). **(??).**

REHABILITATION OF DOWNTOWN GALESBURG, ILLINOIS. RENEWAL OF CENTRAL BUSINESS DISTRICT INCLUDING REVAMPING THE CENTRAL SQUARE, A DOWNTOWN PARK, ORNAMENTAL PLANTING AND LIGHTING, DISTINCTIVE STREET AND SIDEWALK TREATMENT AND A SENIOR CITIZENS CENTER. (LOCAL). THOMAS B HERRING, CITY MANAGER; CITY OF GALESBURG; 161 S CHERRY ST; GALESBURG, IL 61401. (#6240).

RETRACING SETTLERS' MIGRATION ROUTE, GALESBURG, IL. TWO MEN, PHILLIP WATKINS AND MICHAEL BRIGGS, TO RIDE CROSS-COUNTRY ON BIKES, RETRACING THE ROUTE TAKEN IN 1837 BY GALESBURG FOUNDERS FROM WHITEBORO, NY, TO KNOX COUNTY, ILLINOIS, SOME 950 MILES. (REGN'L). RONALD HARMS, CHMN; KNOX COUNTY BICENT COMMISSION; 125 S CHERRY ST; GALESBURG, IL 61401. (#10525).

SLIDE-TAPE PROGRAMS ON HISTORY OF GALESBURG, ILL. OLD GALESBURG HOUSES-CARL SANDBURG IN GALESBURG; WALKING TOUR OF OLD GALESBURG; GALESBURG INVENTORS & INVENTIONS; A HISTORY OF RAILROADING IN GALESBURG. (LOCAL). MS E SQUIRES; GALESBURG PUBLIC LIBRARY; 14 E SIMMONS; GALESBURG, IL 61401. (#3778).

VETERAN'S MONUMENT IN GALESBURG, IL. VETERAN'S MONUMENT AT KNOX CO COURTHOUSE. (LOCAL). RONALD HARMS, COORDINATOR; KNOX COUNTY BICENTENNIAL COMMISSION; 125 SOUTH CHERRY; GALESBURG, IL 61401. (#33625).

WORKSHOPS ON COLONIAL WEAVING IN GALESBURG, IL. WORKSHOPS ON COLONIAL WEAVING AT GALESBURG CIVIC ART CENTER. (LOCAL). BARBARA FACTOR, COORDINATOR; GALESBURG CIVIC ART CENTER; GALESBURG, IL 61401. (#33626).

SEPT 5 - 7, '75. 4TH NATIONAL STEARMAN FLY-IN. NAVY REUNION OF WORLD WAR II FIGHTER PLANES. AT GALESBURG AIRPORT. (NAT'L). JIM LEAHY; NATIONAL STEARMAN; 241 SOUTH KELLOGG; GALESBURG, IL 61401. (#50413-1).

SEPT 20 - 21, '75. EXHIBITS OF ETHNIC CULTURE & HISTORY OF TOWNS IN THE COUNTY. A TWO DAY AFFAIR SHOWING CULTURAL EXHIBITS OF ETHNIC GROUPS AND HISTORICAL EXHIBITS OF TOWNS IN THE COUNTY; PROGRAMS BY TALENT OF THE COUNTY; AND A TASTING TABLE OF FOREIGN FOODS & PIONEER FOODS. (LOCAL). VIRGINIA HINCHLIFF; KNOX COUNTY BICENT COMMISSION; 125 S CHERRY ST; GALESBURG, IL 61401. (#6067-501).

SEPT 20 - 21, '75. PROGRAM BY SPECIAL TALENT OF THE COUNTY. EXHIBIT, FESTIVAL, LIVE PERFORMANCE. (LOCAL). VIRGINIA HINCHLIFF; KNOX COUNTY BICENT COMMISSION; 125 S CHERRY ST; GALESBURG, IL 61401. (#6067-502).

NOV 11, '75. BICENTENNIAL-VETERANS DAY FESTIVITIES. PARADE, UNVEILING AND DEDICATION OF MONUMENT HONORING VETERANS OF 200 YEARS OF WARS; INDUCTION OF VIETNAM POWS INTO KNOX COUNTY COURT OF PATRIOTS, DINNER DANCE FEATURING HIGH MILITARY OFFICIALS AS SPEAKERS AND EXHIBITIONS OF MILITARY BRANCHES THROUGHOUT THE DAY. AT DOWNTOWN GALESBURG (PARADE) & KNOX COUNTY COURTHOUSE (CEREMONIES). (ST-WIDE). MICHAEL PECK, PROJ DIR; AMERICAN LEGION POST 285; 870 N CEDAR; GALESBURG, IL 61401. (#103206-1).

JUNE 30, '76. OPENING OF NEW CITY/COUNTY PUBLIC SAFETY BUILDING - IL. THE CITY/COUNTY PUBLIC SAFETY BUILDING IS COMPLETE AND IS IN USE. AT CITY/COUNTY PUBLIC SAFETY BUILDING. (LOCAL). THOMAS B HERRING, CTY MGR; CITY OF GALESBURG; 161 S CHERRY ST; GALESBURG, IL 61401. (#6240-1).

JULY 4, '76. ECUMENICAL SERVICE. CEREMONY. (LOCAL). RONALD HARMS, CHMN; KNOX COUNTY BICENTENNIAL COMMISSION; 125 S CHERRY ST; GALESBURG, IL 61401. (#200016-187).

AUG 24 - 25, '76. UNITED STATES ARMED FORCES BICENTENNIAL CARAVAN. CARAVAN IS COMPOSED OF EXHIBIT VANS FOR EACH MILITARY SERVICE. PROJECT THEME IS 'HISTORY OF THE ARMED FORCES & THEIR CONTRIBUTIONS TO THE NATION.'. (LOCAL). MICHAEL PARK, CHMN; UNITED STATES ARMED FORCES BICENTENNIAL CARAVAN; 870 N CEDAR ST; GALESBURG, IL 61401. (#1775-637).

SEPT 3 - 5, '76. LABOR DAY CELEBRATION. FESTIVAL AT GALESBURG MALL. (LOCAL). RON HARMS, CHMN; KNOX COUNTY BICENTENNIAL COMMISSION; 125 S CHERRY; GALESBURG, IL 61401. (#200016-84).

SEPT 10 - 12, '76. '5TH NATIONAL STEARMAN FLY-IN'. LIVE PERFORMANCE AT GALESBURG AIRPORT. (LOCAL). RONALD HARMS, CHMN; KNOX COUNTY BICENTENNIAL COMMISSION; 125 S CHERRY ST; GALESBURG, IL 61401. (#200016-188).

SEPT 18, '76. STATE SHRINE PARADE WITH BICENTENNIAL THEME. PARADE. (ST-WIDE). RONALD HARMS, CHMN; KNOX COUNTY BICENTENNIAL COMMISSION; 125 S CHERRY ST; GALESBURG, IL 61401. (#200016-189).

OCT 2 - 10, '76. KNOX COUNTY SCENIC DRIVE. TOUR. (LOCAL). RON HARMS, CHMN; KNOX COUNTY BICENTENNIAL COMMISSION; 125 S CHERRY; GALESBURG, IL 61401. (#200016-85).

GALVA

MAY 21, '76. BICENTENNIAL SCHOOL FESTIVAL. FESTIVAL AT HIGH SCHOOL FOOTBALL FIELD. (LOCAL). MARY LOU HOLDING, COORD; GALVA BICENTENNIAL COMMISSION; 515 NW 11TH; GALVA, IL 61434. (#200016-190).

JULY 5, '76. INDEPENDENCE DAY WEEKEND PARADE. ATTENDED BY THOUSANDS, FOLLOWING THE PARADE WERE FIREWORKS & A DANCE ON THE TENNIS COURTS. AT DOWNTOWN GALVA & THE WILEY PARK DISTRICT. (LOCAL). MARY LOU HOLDING, CHMN; GALVA BICENTENNIAL COMMITTEE; 515 NW 11TH; GALVA, IL 61434. (#200016-443).

NOV 9, '76. PHILADELPHIA '76. FESTIVAL AT GALVA HOTEL. (LOCAL). THEODORE COBERLEY; BLACK HAWK COLLEGE, EAST CAMPUS; PO BOX 489; KEWANEE, IL 61443. (#105192-1).

NOV 11, '76. DEDICATION OF CITY FOUNDER MONUMENT & TIME CAPSULE BURIAL. MONUMENT IS IN MEMORY OF THE WILEY FAMILY WHO FOUNDED THE CITY IN 1854. TIME CAPSULE IS BURIED BEHIND MONUMENT. AT WILEY PARK. (LOCAL). MARY LOU HOLDING, CHMN; GALVA BICENTENNIAL COMMITTEE; 515 NW 11TH; GALVA, IL 61434. (#200016-444).

GARDEN PLAIN

FEB 22, '76. ARBA FLAG PRESENTATION TO GARDEN PLAIN TOWNSHIP SUPERVISOR. THE FLAG WAS PRESENTED WITH PATRIOTIC SPEECH AND MUSICAL PROGRAM; FREE REFRESHMENTS WERE SERVED FOLLOWING FLAG RAISING CEREMONY. AT GARDEN PLAIN GRADE SCHOOL. (LOCAL). FRANK FALEY, CHAIRMAN; ALBANY-GARDEN PLAIN BICENTENNIAL COMMISSION; PO BOX 453; ALBANY, IL 61230. (#200016-421).

APR 3, '76. GARDEN PLAIN TOWNSHIP BIRTHDAY CELEBRATION. A FLEA MARKET AND SQUARE DANCE WAS HELD TO CELEBRATE THE BIRTHDAY OF GARDEN PLAIN TOWNSHIP. A HUGE BIRTHDAY CAKE WAS SERVED & ENJOYED BY ALL. AT GARDEN PLAIN GRADE SCHOOL. (LOCAL). FRANK FALEY, CHAIRMAN; ALBANY/GARDEN PLAIN BICENTENNIAL COMMISSION; PO BOX 453; ALBANY, IL 61230. (#200016-420).

JUNE 13, '76. HISTORIC STAGE COACH RUN AND GARDEN PLAIN COM FLAG PRESENTATION. THE OFFICIAL GARDEN PLAIN COMMUNITY FLAG WAS TAKEN BY STAGE COACH OVER THE OLD STAGE COACH ROUTE BY THE FLAG DESIGN CONTEST WINNER AND THE FLAG WAS PRESENTED TO THE GARDEN PLAIN TWP COMMISSIONER AT FLAG RAISING CEREMONY, AN ICE CREAM SOCIAL FOLLOWED. AT ALBANY PARK TO GARDEN PLAIN GRADE SCHOOL. (LOCAL). FRANK FALEY, CHAIRMAN; ALBANY-GARDEN PLAIN BICENTENNIAL COMMISSION; PO BOX 453; ALBANY, IL 61230. (#200016-416).

GARDNER

VILLAGE LIFE, AMERICAN STYLE - GARDNER, IL. PARADE WITH A BICENTENNIAL THEME, ANTIQUE DISPLAYS, HOME TALENT SHOWS AND OTHER HISTORICAL EVENTS ARE BEING HELD IN GARDNER. (LOCAL). ELDA M SORENSON, SECRETARY; VILLAGE OF GARDNER & BICENTENNIAL; VILLAGE HALL, PO BOX 545; GARDNER, IL 60424. (#29440).

GENESEO

HISTORICAL DIRECTORY OF ONE-ROOM SCHOOLS - IL. PUBLICATION AND SALE OF HISTORICAL DIRECTORY OF ONE-ROOM SCHOOLS IN STARK AND HENRY COUNTIES. (LOCAL). CLYDE WALTER, CHAIRMAN; HENRY COUNTY BICENTENNIAL COMMISSION; 205 S STATE; GENESEO, IL 61254. (#30388).

INDEX OF HENRY COUNTY GRAVES - GENESEO, IL. INDEXING AND PUBLICATION OF GRAVES IN ALL CEMETERIES IN HENRY CO. (LOCAL). CLYDE WALTER, CHAIRMAN; HENRY COUNTY BICENTENNIAL COMMISSION; 205 STATE ST; GENESEO, IL 61254. (#30390).

GENEVA

FLAG DESIGN CONTEST IN GENEVA, IL. CONTEST TO DEVELOP IDEAS FOR FLAG DESIGN TO BE DONE BY PROFESSIONAL ARTIST & DESIGNER. (LOCAL). RONALD ANDERSON, CO-CHAIRMAN; CITY OF GENEVA BICENTENNIAL COMMISSION; 22 S FIRST ST; GENEVA, IL 60134. (#33110).

GENEVA LANDMARK DIRECTORY IN IL. METAL KOSK WITH BRONZE PLATES; MAP OF CITY HISTORICAL BUILDINGS & LOCATIONS. (LOCAL). HELEN JANE HAMLIN, COORDINATOR; BICENTENNIAL COMMISSION OF GENEVA & HISTORICAL SOCIETY; STEVENS ST; GENEVA, IL 60134. (#33108).

HISTORY OF GENEVA, IL. HISTORICAL DATES, HAPPENINGS, PROGRESS & GROWTH OF CITY. (LOCAL). JULIA EHRESMANN, COORDINATOR; GENEVA PUBLIC LIBRARY; 27 S SECOND ST; GENEVA, IL 60134. (#33109).

GENOA

GENOA-KINGSTON'S BICENT PROJECTS, IL. HISTORY BOOK, BICENT BOOKLET, FLOWER BEDS IN BOTH TOWNS, HANGING FLOWER BASKETS, GENOA GARDEN CLUB BEAUTIFIED PARADE ROUTE; CHAMBER OF COMMERCE SPONSORED SCHOOL MURAL. (LOCAL). W A SKINNER, CHAIRMAN; G-K BICENT COMMISSION; GENOA, IL 60135. (#28216).

JUNE 16 - 19, '76. G-K COMMUNITY DAYS. FESTIVAL. (LOCAL). W A SKINNER, CHMN; G-K BICENT COMMISSION & G-K FIRE DEPT; GENOA, IL 60135. (#200016-211).

GIBSON CITY

JULY 1 - 4, '76. BICENTENNIAL WEEK AT GIBSON CITY. 7/1 YOUTH GROUPS HAD VARIOUS GAMES GOING; 7/2 SAW CRAFT DEMONSTRATIONS ADDED TO THE ACTIVITIES; 7/3 WAS HIGHLIGHTED BY A BICENT BALL; 7/4 THE DAY ENDED WITH A FIREWORKS DISPLAY. OTHER GROUPS PARTICIPATED & THERE WERE MANY OTHER ACTIVITIES. AT THROUGHOUT THE TOWN. (LOCAL). LAUREL PING; GIBSON CITY BICENTENNIAL COMMITTEE; RT 9 EAST; GIBSON CITY, IL 60936. (#200016-354).

GILLESPIE

JULY 1 - 4, '76. FESTIVAL OF NATIONALITIES. 22 NATIONALITIES WILL CELEBRATE THE FOUNDING OF THE COMMUNITY. (LOCAL). KATHRYN A BLANCHARD; CANNA AMBASSADOR CORPORATION, GILLESPIE, ILL; 112 W CHESTNUT ST; GILLESPIE, IL 62033. (#103020-1).

GILMAN

FLOWING WELL REPLICA, GILMAN, IL. A REPLICA OF AN OLD LANDMARK, A FLOWING WELL WILL BE DUG IN RAILROAD PARK. (LOCAL). MRS OTTO SCHRIEFER, CHAIRMAN; CITY OF GILMAN; GILMAN, IL 60938. (#28976).

NOV 6, '76. 'A YEAR TO REMEMBER'. A COMBINATION OF HISTORY, MUSIC & ACTING. AT GILMAN HIGH SCHOOL GYM. (LOCAL). MRS OTTO F SCHRIEFER; CITY OF GILMAN; 110 N THOMAS; GILMAN, IL 60938. (#109420-1).

GILSON

BICENT CAMPOREE & DEDICATION OF HIST TRAIL, IL. CAMPOREE FOR ADULTS & YOUTHS TO FOSTER APPRECIATION FOR HISTORIC PRESERVATION; AND DEDICATION OF HISTORIC INDIAN TRAIL. (LOCAL). JIM ENLOE, EXPLORING EXEC; PRAIRIE COUNCIL BOY SCOUTS OF AMERICA; 520 BANK OF GALESBURG; GILSON, IL 61401. (#10643).

GLASFORD

JUNE 25 - 27, '76. GLASFORD BICENTENNIAL CELEBRATION. LOCAL PAGEANT, FESTIVAL, MISS SPIRIT OF '76 BEAUTY PAGEANT, TALENT SHOW, ETC. AT GLASFORD. (LOCAL). MRS. MARLA SCARCLIFF; GLASFORD BICENTENNIAL COMMISSION; GLASFORD, IL 61533. (#50327-1).

GLEN ELLYN

AMERICAN COMPOSER IN RESIDENCE, GLEN ELLYN, IL. ILLINOIS BICENTENNIAL COMMISSION GRANT TO FUND AMERICAN COMPOSER IN RESIDENCE SPRING QUARTER 1976. COMPOSER RANDALL THOMPSON. (LOCAL). C LAMBERT, PROJ COORDINATOR; COLLEGE OF DUPAGE; GLEN ELLYN, IL 60137. (#19586).

AMERICAN HERITAGE AND LIFESTYLE OF 18TH CENT, IL. STUDY OF AMERICAN LIFESTYLE THROUGH LITERATURE AND TRAVEL TO HISTORICAL PLACES. CLASSES WILL TOUR BOSTON, WILLIAMSBURG AND CHARLESTON. TOURS AVAILABLE SEPARATELY FOR MEMBERS OF COMMUNITY. (LOCAL). D J WILKES, INSTRUCTOR; COLLEGE OF DUPAGE; GLEN ELLYN, IL 60137. (#19587).

BICENTENNIAL EVENTS CALENDAR, GLEN ELLYN, IL. AS PART OF QUARTERLY CLASS SCHEDULE MAILED TO ALL HOMES IN COLLEGE AREA, LIST BICENTENNIAL EVENTS SUBMITTED BY CHAIRPERSONS IN COLLEGE AREA. (LOCAL). MICHAEL POTTS, DIRECTOR, COLLEGE RELATIONS; COLLEGE OF DUPAGE; GLEN ELLYN, IL 60137. (#19583).

GLEN ELLYN — CONTINUED

BICENTENNIAL FANFARE IN GLEN ELLYN, IL. COLLEGE OF DUPAGE FOUNDATION GRANT WILL ALLOW COMMISSIONING A BICENTENNIAL FANFARE FOR USE IN CONCERTS. TO BE COMPOSED BY DANIEL PINKHAM AND PUBLISHED BY E C SHIRMER OF BOSTON. (LOCAL). C LAMBERT, PROJ DIRECTOR; COLLEGE OF DUPAGE; GLEN ELLYN, IL 60137. (#19446).

BICENTENNIAL VARIETY SHOW. LIVE PERFORMANCE. (LOCAL). TERRY WINN, DIRECTOR; COLLEGE OF DUPAGE; GLEN ELLYN, IL 60137. (#104316-6). **(??).**

BOOK ON DUPAGE COUNTY, GLEN ELLYN, IL. STUDENT WRITING COMPREHENSIVE GUIDE TO DUPAGE COUNTY FOR NEWCOMERS; HISTORICAL POLITICAL, SOCIAL SERVICES, SITES OF INTEREST. (LOCAL). MIKE CHEMEL, STUDENT; COLLEGE OF DUPAGE; GLEN ELLYN, IL 60137. (#19585).

HISTORIC ILLINOIS - GLEN ELLYN, IL. ON EACH OF FIVE WEEKENDS, CLASS TRAVELS TO A DIFFERENT PART OF ILLINOIS THAT HAS A HISTORICAL BACKGROUND, SOME AREAS RELATING TO THE AMERICAN REVOLUTION. (ST-WIDE). DR WM LEPPERT, DEAN OF ALPHA CLUSTER; COLLEGE OF DUPAGE; GLEN ELLYN, IL 60137. (#19584).

RESTORATION-STACY'S TAVERN, NATL HISTORIC SITE- IL. RESTORATION OF STACY'S TAVERN BUILT IN 1846 AND DESIGNATED AS A NATIONAL HISTORIC SITE. (LOCAL). LEE MARKS, PRESIDENT; GLEN ELLYN HISTORICAL SOCIETY; 475 HAWTHORN; GLEN ELLYN, IL 60137. (#12170).

SEPT 27 - OCT 26, '75. MANUSCRIPTS OF THE AMERICAN REVOLUTION. 33 DOCUMENTS AND LETTERS SELECTED BY MANUSCRIPT SOCIETY PROVIDING PANORAMA OF HISTORY-1765 TO 1794 ON LOAN FROM SMITHSONIAN INSTITUTE. AT LEARNING RESOURCE CENTER - J BUILDING. (LOCAL). R L DUCOTE, DEAN; COLLEGE OF DUPAGE; GLEN ELLYN, IL 60137. (#200016-26).

FEB 29, '76. SPRING CONCERT - CONCERT CHOIR. FEATURING DOWN IN THE VALLEY BY WEIL (IN CONCERT) AND FROSTIANA BY FROST-THOMPSON. AT CONVOCATION CENTER - M BUILDING. (LOCAL). DR CARL LAMBERT, COORD; COLLEGE OF DUPAGE; GLEN ELLYN, IL 60137. (#104316-4).

MAR 12 - 13, '76. NJCAA MEN'S CHAMPIONSHIP GYMNASTICS MEET. COMPETITION. (REGN'L). DAVE WEBSTER, COORD; COLLEGE OF DUPAGE; GLEN ELLYN, IL 60137. (#28033-21).

MAR 14, '76. SPRING CONCERT - COMMUNITY CHORUS. FEATURING 'PORGY AND BESS' (IN CONCERT) & VARIATIONS ON AMERICA BY IVES. AT CONVOCATION CENTER - M BUILDING. (LOCAL). DR CARL LAMBERT, CHMN; COLLEGE OF DUPAGE; COLLEGE OF DUPAGE; GLEN ELLYN, IL 60137. (#104316-1).

MAY 30, '76. BICENTENNIAL CONCERT. CHORAL PIECES BY AMERICAN COMPOSERS ON AMERICAN THEMES. AT CONVOCATION CENTER - M BUILDING. (LOCAL). DR CARL LAMBERT, COORD; COLLEGE OF DUPAGE; GLEN ELLYN, IL 60137. (#104316-2).

JUNE 6, '76. COMMENCEMENT CONCERT. FEATURING TESTAMENT OF FREEDOM AND A CONCORD HYMN BY RANDALL THOMPSON. DANIEL PINKHAM HAS BEEN COMMISSIONED TO COMPOSE A BICENTENNIAL FANFARE FOR THE COLLEGE. AT CONVOCATION CENTER - M BUILDING. (LOCAL). DR CARL LAMBERT, COORD; COLLEGE OF DUPAGE; GLEN ELLYN, IL 60137. (#104316-3).

GLENCOE

MUSICAL COMPOSITION. EXTENDED WORK FOR SOLO TENOR VOICE WITH ELECTRONIC ACCOMPANIMENT TO BE USED WITH A PLANETARIUM PROGRAM. (LOCAL). JAMES DASHOW, COORDINATOR; NATIONAL ENDOWMENT FOR THE ARTS; 272 RANDOLPH ST; GLENCOE, IL 60022. (#33360).

DEC 2 - 4, '76. LA SALLE EXPEDITION II, A HISTORIC RE-ENACTMENT. THIS IS AN AUTHENTIC RE-ENACTMENT OF THE 1681 LASALLE EXPEDITION FROM MONTREAL, CANADA TO NEW ORLEANS, LA WHICH WILL BEGIN TOURING ON AUGUST 11, 1976 AND END ON APRIL 9, 1977. (LOCAL). REID H LEWIS, DIRECTOR; LA SALLE EXPEDITION II; 135 S LA SALLE ST, RM 411; CHICAGO, IL 60690. (#102805-22).

GLENDALE HTS

AMERICA SALUTES YOU. THE ETHNIC FESTIVAL: GREEK, NORWEGIAN, MEXICAN, POLISH, UKRAINIAN, SPANISH, IRISH & LITHUANIAN. (LOCAL). HENRY F THIELE; GLENDALE HEIGHTS BICENTENNIAL COMMISSION; 1611 BLOOMINGDALE RD; GLENDALE HTS, IL 60137. (#200016-332).

JULY 10 - 11, '76. CIVIC CENTER DEDICATION & VILLAGE INCORPORATION DAY. CEREMONY, FAIR AT 1611 BLOOMINGDALE RD. (LOCAL). HENRY F THIELE; GLENDALE HEIGHTS BICENTENNIAL COMMISSION; 1611 BLOOMINGDALE RD; GLENDALE HTS, IL 60137. (#200016-286).

GLENVIEW

HISTORY OF NORTHFIELD TOWNSHIP, IL. BROCHURE DETAILING THE EVENTS IN THE DEVELOPMENT OF THE TOWNSHIP FROM 1850 TO PRESENT DAY. (LOCAL). GRACE LEE, CHAIRPERSON; NORTHFIELD TOWNSHIP OF COOK COUNTY; 1607 WAUKEGAN RD; GLENVIEW, IL 60025. (#18178).

PRESERVATION GARDEN AT THE HISTORICAL SOCIETY, IL. A GARDEN IN WHICH HISTORICAL CORNERSTONES AND MARKERS WILL BE PRESERVED & DISPLAYED. (LOCAL). JOHN C MENG, VICE PRESIDENT; GLENVIEW HISTORICAL SOCIETY; 1121 WAUKEGAN RD; GLENVIEW, IL 60025. (#18177).

PRESERVATION OF 94 ACRES OF WOODLAND - IL. THE AREA IS KNOWN AS THE KENNICOTT GROVE & INCLUDES THE 1855 HOME OF DR JOHN KENNICOTT. HOUSE WILL BE RESTORED & THE WOODLAND ALLOWED TO RETURN TO ITS NATURAL STATE; A NATURE APPRECIATION STUDY CENTER. (LOCAL). RICHARD JOHNS, SUPERINTENDENT; GLENVIEW PARK DISTRICT; 2320 GLENVIEW RD; GLENVIEW, IL 60025. (#18001).

RIVER BANK CLEANUP, CONSTRUCTION OF A PARK - IL. CLEANUP, WEED OUT, TRIM TREES & ESTABLISH PATH WITH REST AREAS ALONG WEST FORK OF THE NORTH BRANCH OF THE CHICAGO RIVER. (LOCAL). MRS ALLAN BRODIE, CHAIRPERSON; COMMUNITY OF GLENVIEW GARDEN CLUBS; 1143 SEQUOIA; GLENVIEW, IL 60025. (#18023).

WINDOW DISPLAYS, GLENVIEW, IL. WINDOWS IN THE BUSINESS DISTRICT WILL BE DECORATED IN SCENES REMINISCENT OF YESTERYEAR. (LOCAL). JANE HIBBARD, PROJ DIRECTOR; GLENVIEW LAMPLIGHTERS; 1403 ESTATE LA; GLENVIEW, IL 60025. (#18176).

JULY 5, '75. RECOGNITION OF GLENVIEW AS A BICENTENNIAL COMMUNITY. PRESENTATION OF ARBA FLAG TO MAYOR OF VILLAGE, EDWARD K PATTON BY RICHARD L HIBBARD, CHAIRMAN, GLENVIEW BICENTENNIAL COMMISSION. PATRIOTIC FLAG PAGEANT, 2ND MARINE DIVISION BAND FROM CAMP LEGUENE, NC. AT MEMORIAL SQUARE. (LOCAL). RICHARD L HIBBARD, CHMN; GLENVIEW BICENTENNIAL COMMISSION; 1403 ESTATE LN; GLENVIEW, IL 60025. (#200016-263).

NOV 10, '75. GLENBROOK SOUTH HIGH SCHOOL VETERANS DAY. ADDRESS BY ROBERT ADAMS, DIRECTOR, SOCIAL STUDIES DEPT. AT GYMNASIUM. (LOCAL). RICHARD L HIBBARD, CHMN; GLENBROOK SOUTH HIGH SCHOOL; 1403 ESTATE LN; GLENVIEW, IL 60025. (#200016-275).

NOV 23, '75. FREE CONCERT BY GLENBROOK SOUTH HIGH SCHOOL. PRIOR TO THEIR PARTICIPATION IN THE ORANGE BOWL IN MIAMI, FL. PRESENTATION OF A PLAQUE OF RECOGINATION TO THE BAND DIRECTOR, BY RICHARD L HIBBARD, CHAIRMAN OF GLENVIEW BICENTENNIAL COMMISSION. AT AUDITORIUM. (LOCAL). RICHARD L HIBBARD, CHMN; GLENBROOK SOUTH HIGH SCHOOL BAND; 1403 ESTATE LN; GLENVIEW, IL 60025. (#200016-274).

JAN 15, '76. IN MEMORY OF MARTIN LUTHER KING ASSEMBLY. TO HONOR THE CONTRIBUTION OF BLACK AMERICANS TO THIS AMERICAN EXPERIENCE. AT WATSON AUDITORIUM, GLENBROOK SOUTH HIGH SCHOOL. (LOCAL). RICHARD L HIBBARD, CHMN; GLENBROOK SOUTH HIGH SCHOOL, SOCIAL STUDIES DEPT; 1403 ESTATE LN; GLENVIEW, IL 60025. (#200016-264).

MAR 1 - AUG 31, '76. A BICENTENNIAL DISPLAY WITH AUDIO TAPES. STREET LEVEL - TWELVE DISPLAY ITEMS WITH COMPANION AUDIO TAPES; LOWER LEVEL DISPLAY OF TWELVE HISTORICAL FLAGS WITH DESCRIPTIVE M LITERATURE. AT STREET LEVEL AND LOWER LEVEL. (LOCAL). LYNN WELDON, CHMN; GLENVIEW STATE BANK; 800 WAUKEGAN; GLENVIEW, IL 60025. (#105004-2).

MAR 9, '76. SPECIAL STUDENTS INSTITUTE DAY. A REVIEW OF THE CANOE VOYAGE BY MARQUETTE AND JOLIET BY REID LEWIS WHO IN 1973 WITH 7 MEN AND 13 YEAR OLD BOY RETRACED THE HISTORIC 3000 MILE JOURNEY. AT GYMNASIUM. (LOCAL). RICHARD L HIBBARD, CHMN; SPRINGMAN JR HIGH SCHOOL; 1403 ESTATE LN; GLENVIEW, IL 60025. (#200016-273).

MAR 16, '76. EQUAL PROTECTION UNDER THE LAW. AN AMERICAN ISSUES FORUM PROGRAM, THE EQUAL RIGHTS OF WOMEN. AT GLENVIEW PUBLIC. (LOCAL). RICHARD L HIBBARD, CHMN; GLENVIEW JR WOMEN'S CLUB; 1403 ESTATE LN; GLENVIEW, IL 60025. (#200016-272).

MAR 21, '76. CONCERT GLENVIEW COMMUNITY CHURCH YOUTH CHOIR. PRE-TOUR CONCERT WHICH WILL INCLUDE, ST LOUIS, NATCHEZ, NEW ORLEANS, NASHVILLE & LOUISVILLE DIRECTOR, RONALD CLONTS. AT COMMUNITY CHURCH 1000 ELM ST. (LOCAL). RICHARD L HIBBARD, CHMN; GLENVIEW COMMUNITY CHURCH YOUTH CHOIR; 1403 ESTATE LN; GLENVIEW, IL 60025. (#200016-271).

MAR 31, '76. 'YOU'VE COME A LONG WAY BABY' FASHION SHOW. FEATURING FASHIONS OF YESTERYEAR, AN EARLY AMERICAN MEAL & A DOOR PRIZE OF A HAND MADE QUILT. AT SEVEN EAGLES RESTAURANT 1050 E OAKTON, DESPLAINES, IL. (LOCAL). RICHARD L HIBBARD, CHMN; GLENVIEW WOMEN'S CLUB; 1403 ESTATE LN; GLENVIEW, IL 60025. (#200016-270).

MAY 9, '76. DEDICATION OF THE CORNER STONE GARDEN. THERE WILL BE AN OLD SCHOOL WALK WITH RELATED ACTIVITIES. AT GROUNDS OF THE GLENVIEW HISTORICAL SOCIETY. (LOCAL). JOHN MENG, V PRES; GLENVIEW HISTORICAL SOCIETY; 1121 WAUKEGAN RD; GLENVIEW, IL 60025. (#105004-1).

MAY 14, '76. SPRING THING '76 - A BICENTENNIAL CELEBRATION. 'UP WITH PEOPLE'; A SPECIAL BICENTENNIAL PRODUCTION OF MUSIC & DANCE PERFORMED BY THE INTERNATIONALLY FAMOUS GROUP OF YOUNG PEOPLE FROM ARIZONA. AT GLENBROOK SOUTH HIGH SCHOOL, 4000 W LAKE AVE. (LOCAL). DAVID H SMITH, COORD; GLENBROOK SOUTH HIGH SCHOOL DISTRICT 225; 4000 W LAKE AVE; GLENVIEW, IL 60025. (#105004-4).

JUNE 2 - 5, '76. FILM FESTIVAL. 18 CENTURY LIFE IN WILLIAMSBURG, BASKET WEAVING IN COLONIAL VIRGINIA, PLYMOUTH COLONY-THE FIRST YEAR GUNSMITH OF WILLIAMSBURG AND WILLIAMSBURG, STORY OF A PATRIOT. AT MAYNARD ROOM. (LOCAL). RICHARD L HIBBARD, CHMN; GLENVIEW PUBLIC LIBRARY; 1403 ESTATE LN; GLENVIEW, IL 60025. (#200016-269).

JUNE 24 - 27, '76. 'RED, WHITE AND BLUE' - A BROADWAY REVUE. SPECIAL BICENTENNIAL PRODUCTION WRITTEN AND PRODUCED BY THE GLENVIEW THEATER GUILD. AT WATSON AUDITORIUM, GLENBROOK SOUTH HIGH SCHOOL. (LOCAL). RICHARD L HIBBARD, CHMN; THE GLENVIEW THEATER GUILD; 1403 ESTATE LN; GLENVIEW, IL 60025. (#200016-268).

JULY 1 - OCT 31, '76. QUESTER WINDOW DISPLAY. DECORATE WINDOWS IN MANNER OF YESTERYEARS IN THE VILLAGE OF GLENVIEW, IL. AT BUSINESS DISPLAY ON GLENVIEW AND WAUKEGAN RDS. (LOCAL). JANE HIBBARD, CHMN; GLENVIEW LAMPLIGHTERS AND LITTLE FORT TRAILS CHAPTERS OF QUESTERS; 1403 ESTATE LN; GLENVIEW, IL 60025. (#105004-3).

JULY 2, '76. 'FAITH OF AMERICA' MUSICAL PRESENTATION. SPECIAL PARTICIPATION BY THE NORTH SHORE CONCERT BAND. AT NEW HANGER, GLENVIEW NAVAL AIR STATION. (LOCAL). RICHARD L HIBBARD, CHMN; GLENVIEW FEDERATION OF CHURCHES; 1403 ESTATE LN; GLENVIEW, IL 60025. (#200016-262).

JULY 4, '76. THE GLENVIEW PARK DISTRICT'S 11TH ANNUAL JULY 4TH CELEBRATION. PARADE, PARADE PRIZE AWARDS, JR TENNIS TOURNAMENT, SWIM MEET, MODEL AIRPLANE SHOW, FIREWORKS DISPLAY, WNDER THE DIRECTION OF TOM RICHARDSON. (LOCAL). RICHARD L HIBBARD, CHMN; GLENVIEW PARK DISTRICT; 1403 ESTATE LN; GLENVIEW, IL 60025. (#200016-267).

JULY 5, '76. ETHNIC GROUPS EXHIBITS & DEMONSTRATIONS. DISPLAYED THEIR NATIVE DRESS, CULTER CUSTOMS, WARES, FOOD, INCLUDING AMERICAN DAUGTHERS OF SWEDEN, AMERICAN COMMUNITY OF GLENVIEW, CHINESE COOKING, BIELARUSIAN SOCIETY OF CHICAGO, BRITISH CULTURE CLUB, GERMAN AMERICAN, DANK, ITALIAN, POLISH, HOLLAND IMPORTS, ETC. AT GLENVIEW NAVAL AIR STATION. (LOCAL). RICHARD L HIBBARD, CHMN; LOCAL ETHNIC GROUPS; 1403 ESTATE LN; GLENVIEW, IL 60025. (#200016-276).

JULY 5, '76. VOTERS REGISTRATION DRIVE. CEREMONY AT PICNIC AREA, GLENVIEW NAVAL AIR STATION. (LOCAL). RICHARD L HIBBARD, CHMN; LEAGUE OF WOMEN VOTERS OF GLENVIEW; 1403 ESTATE LN; GLENVIEW, IL 60025. (#200016-277).

SEPT 4 - 5, '76. UNITED STATES ARMED FORCES BICENTENNIAL CARAVAN. CARAVAN IS COMPOSED OF EXHIBIT VANS FOR EACH MILITARY SERVICE. PROJECT THEME IS 'HISTORY OF THE ARMED FORCES & THEIR CONTRIBUTIONS TO THE NATION.'. (LOCAL). RICHARD L HIBBARD, CHMN; UNITED STATES ARMED FORCES BICENTENNIAL CARAVAN; 1403 ESTATE LN; GLENVIEW, IL 60025. (#1775-642).

OCT 20, '76. HISTORICAL TOUR OF GLENVIEW. INCLUDING GLENVIEW AREA HISTORICAL SOCIETY HOUSE BUILT 1890 BY HENRY APPLEYARD AND GLENVIEW HOUSE TAVERN. (LOCAL). RICHARD L HIBBARD, CHMN; GLENVIEW LAMPLIGHTERS, AND LITTLE FORT TRAILS, CHAPTERS OF QUESTERS; 1403 ESTATE LN; GLENVIEW, IL 60025. (#200016-265).

GOLCONDA

ABBOTT HOUSE RENOVATION IN GOLCONDA, ILLINOIS. THIS OLD HOUSE WILL BE RESTORED FOR USE BY SENIOR CITIZENS USING TITLE SEVEN FUNDS. THE COUNTY WILL MAKE BUS SERVICE AVAILABLE. (LOCAL). ROBERT KRAMER, PRESIDENT; POPE COUNTY SENIOR CITIZENS COMMITTEE; RR 2; GOLCONDA, IL 62938. (#7683).

BRIDAL REVUE IN GOLCONDA, IL. A PAGEANT EXHIBITING TRADITIONAL BRIDAL GOWNS OF 1893 ERA WILL BE FEATURED ALONG WITH ORIGINAL SETTINGS & MUSIC OF PERIOD. (LOCAL). SHIRLEY WEBB, COMMITTEE CHAIRMAN; POPE CO HOMEMAKERS EXTENSION ASSOC; SIMPSON, IL 62985. (#12061).

DEER FESTIVAL IN GOLCONDA, IL. A QUEEN CONTEST & PARADE WILL HIGHLIGHT ANNUAL DEER FESTIVAL. (LOCAL). ED TURNER, PROJ COORDINATOR; GOLCANDA ROTARY CLUB; GOLCANDA, IL 62938. (#12062).

JUNE 14, '75. BRIDAL REVIEW FASHIN SHOW. WILL BE STAGED IN CONJUNCTION WITH THE PUBLICATION OF A COOKBOOK FEATURING OLD RECIPES, UNDER THE SPONSORSHIP OF THE POPE COUNTY HOMEMAKERS EXTENSION ASSOCIATION. (LOCAL). MARY LEWIS, ADVISOR; POPE COUNTY HOMEMAKERS ASSOC; SIMPSON, IL 62985. (#7680-501).

OCT 12, '75. FALL FESTIVAL: CRAFT SHOWS, TOURS, OLD-TIME FARM INSTITUTE, ETC. SPECIAL FEATURES AT THE LIBRARY, MUSEUM DEMONSTRATIONS OF VARIOUS CRAFTS, CHILDRENS' GAMES, FLEA MARKET & ARTS SHOW & SALE. AT POPE COUNTY COURTHOUSE LAWN. (LOCAL). HELEN GARD, PRESIDENT; POPE COUNTY CHAPTER/SHAWNEE HILLS RECREATION; RR 2; BROWNFIELD, IL 62911. (#7684-501).

GOOD HOPE

JULY 9 - 11, '76. BICENTENNIAL CELEBRATION OF GOOD HOPE. PARADE, FISH FRY, ENTERTAINMENT, CHURCH SERVICES, ICE CRAM FESTIVAL & CHILDREN'S GAMES. (LOCAL). MARTHA ROBBINS, CHMN; GOOD HOPE BICENTENNIAL COMMITTEE; GOOD HOPE, IL 61438. (#103378-5).

GOREVILLE

APR 26 - 27, '75. SOUTHERN ILL COUNTRY DAYS. PORTRAY UNIQUE HERITAGE OF SO. ILL. (LOCAL). MS JANET PICKETT; ILL DEPT. OF CONSERVATION; 901 SOUTH SPRING; SPRINGFIELD, IL 62704. (#50272-31).

APR 24 - 25, '76. SOUTHERN ILL COUNTRY DAYS. PORTRAY UNIQUE HERITAGE OF SO. ILL. (ST-WIDE). MS JANET PICKETT; ILL DEPT OF CONSERVATION; 901 SOUTH SPRING; SPRINGFIELD, IL 62704. (#50272-32).

GRAFTON

MAY 3, '75. FRONTIER DAY. CRAFT DEMONSTRATIONS, EDIBLE WILD FOODS AND NATURE TOURS. AT PERE MARQUETTE STATE PARK INTERPRETIVE CENTER. (ST-WIDE). MS JANET PICKETT; ILLINOIS DEPARTMENT OF CONSERVATION; 901 SOUTH SPRING; SPRINGFIELD, IL 62704. (#50272-34).

JULY 27, '75. SUNDAY IN THE PARK. OLD FASHIONED TURN OF THE CENTURY ATMOSPHERE, GAMES, MUSIC, CRAFTS. AT PERE MARQUETTE STATE PARK INTERPRETIVE CENTER. (LOCAL). MS JANET PICKETT; ILLINOIS STATE DEPARTMENT OF CONSERVATION; 901 SOUTH SPRING; SPRINGFIELD, IL 62704. (#50272-36).

OCT 18, '75. FALL FESTIVAL. EMPHASIS ON FALL EDIBLE WILD FOODS WITH NATURE TOURS AND GAMES. AT PERE MARQUETTE STATE PARK INTERPRETIVE CENTER. (LOCAL). MS JANET PICKETT; ILLINOIS DEPARTMENT OF CONSERVATION; 901 SOUTH SPRING; SPRINGFIELD, IL 62704. (#50272-33).

MAY 8, '76. FRONTIER DAY. CRAFT DEMONSTRATIONS, EDIBLE WILD FOODS AND NATURE TOURS. AT PERE MARQUETTE STATE PARK INTERPRETIVE CENTER. (LOCAL). MS JANET PICKETT; ILLINOIS DEPARTMENT OF CONSERVATION; 901 SOUTH SPRING; SPRINGFIELD, IL 62704. (#50272-35).

JULY 2 - 4, '76. BICENTENNIAL FESTIVAL. FESTIVAL, PARADE. (LOCAL). LARRY BURTON, CHMN; JERSEY COUNTY BICENTENNIAL COMMISSION; PO BOX 61; GRAFTON, IL 62037. (#200016-186).

JULY 25, '76. SUNDAY IN THE PARK. OLD FASHIONED TURN OF THE CENTURY ATMOSPHERE, GAMES, MUSIC, CRAFTS. AT PERE MARQUETTE STATE PARK INTERPRETIVE CENTER. (LOCAL). MS JANET PICKETT; ILLINOIS DEPARTMENT OF CONSERVATION; 901 SOUTH SPRING; SPRINGFIELD, IL 62704. (#50272-37).

AUG 21, '76. INDIAN POTS AND CRAFTS. EXHIBIT, FESTIVAL AT PERE MARQUETTE STATE PARK. (LOCAL). PHYLLIS EUBANK, COORD; ILLINOIS DEPARTMENT OF CONSERVATION; 901 S. SPRING ST; SPRINGFIELD, IL 62706. (#200016-247).

OCT 16 - 17, '76. WILD FOODS & FRONTIER CRAFTS FALL FESTIVAL. EMPHASIS ON FALL EDIBLE WILD FOODS WITH NATURE TOURS AND GAMES. AT PERE MARQUETTE STATE PARK. (ST-WIDE). DIRECTOR; ILLINOIS DEPARTMENT OF CONSERVATION; 222 S COLLEGE ST; SPRINGFIELD, IL 62706. (#50272-38).

FEB 6 - 8, '77. LA SALLE EXPEDITION II, A HISTORIC RE-ENACTMENT. THIS IS AN AUTHENTIC RE-ENACTMENT OF THE 1681 LASALLE EXPEDITION FROM MONTREAL, CANADA TO NEW ORLEANS, LA WHICH WILL BEGIN TOURING ON AUGUST 11, 1976 AND END ON APRIL 9, 1977. (LOCAL). REID H LEWIS, DIRECTOR; LA SALLE EXPEDITION II; 135 S LA SALLE ST, RM 411; CHICAGO, IL 60690. (#102805-52).

GRAND TOWER

CREATIVE PRESERVATION PROJECT - GRAND TOWER, IL. RENOVATE AND RELOCATE TWO LOG CABINS IN A PARK TO SERVE AS A COMMUNITY CENTER. (LOCAL). MS BARBARA TRENT, PROJ DIRECTOR; GRAND TOWER BICENTENNIAL COMMISSION; PO BOX 253; GRAND TOWER, IL 62942. (#26870). **ARBA GRANTEE.**

FOLK ARTS, CRAFTS & CULTURAL PROGRAM, ILLINOIS. DISPLAYS DEMONSTRATIONS AND CULTURAL PROGRAMS OF NINETEENTH CENTURY PRESENTED IN HUTHMACHER HOUSE BUILT IN 1870, INVOLVES CHILDREN, YOUTH AND SENIOR CITIZENS. (LOCAL). MIKE JONES, PRESIDENT; HUTHMACHER HOUSE ASSOC; GRAND TOWER, IL 62942. (#6452).

HUTHMACHER CULTURAL CENTER - GRAND TOWER, ILLINOIS. RESTORATION OF HISTORIC BUILDING LOCATED ON ESTATE DONATED TO GRAND TOWER, ILL. BY CHARLES HUTMACHER. FIRST PHASE OF PROJECT TO CONVERT ENTIRE ESTATE INTO COMMUNITY CULTURAL CENTER & MUSEUM. (LOCAL). TOM HALE, CHAIRMAN; GRAND TOWER BICENTENNIAL COMMITTEE; BOX 272; GRAND TOWER, IL 62942. (#882). **ARBA GRANTEE.**

JAN 1, '75 - DEC 31, '77. COMMUNITY ACTIVITIES; PIONEER ARTS & CRAFTS. REENACTMENT OF TRADING BOAT ARRIVAL MAY 5; RAFT SHOWBOAT JUNE 20; OCTOBER WEEKENDS CIDER & APPLE BUTTER MAKING; CANDLE MAKING; JUNE, MUSIC. AT HUTHMACHER HOUSE. (LOCAL). THOMAS F HALE; HUTHMACHER HOUSE ASSOICATION; PO BOX 272; GRAND TOWER, IL 62942. (#882-1).

MAR 2 - 30, '75. PATCHWORK QUILTING SHOW AND DEMONSTRATIONS. DISPLAYS DEMONSTRATIONS AND CULTURAL PROGRAMS OF NINETEENTH CENTURY PRESENTED IN HUTHMACHER HOUSE BUILT IN 1870, INVOLVES CHILDREN, YOUTH AND SENIOR CITIZENS. (LOCAL). MIKE JONES, PRESIDENT; HUTHMACHER HOUSE ASSOC; GRAND TOWER, IL 62942. (#6452-501).

APR 5, '75 - DEC 31, '76. ART SHOW AND ART DEMONSTRATIONS. DISPLAYS, DEMONSTRATIONS & CULTURAL PROGRAMS OF NINETEENTH CENTURY PRESENTED IN HUTHMACHER HOUSE BUILT IN 1870, INVOLVES CHILDREN, $ .25 SUGGESTED DONATION; RESERVE FOR TOURS MON-SAT. (LOCAL). MIKE JONES, PRESIDENT; HUTHMACHER HOUSE ASSOC; GRAND TOWER, IL 62942. (#6452-502).

MAY 4 - 26, '75. HOBBY DISPLAY, BAKING DEMONSTRATIONS. EXHIBIT, TOUR. (LOCAL). MIKE JONES, PRESIDENT; HUTHMACHER HOUSE ASSOC; GRAND TOWER, IL 62942. (#6452-503).

JUNE 1 - 30, '75. FOLK MUSIC, ARTS & CRAFTS FAIR. EXHIBIT, TOUR. (LOCAL). MIKE JONES, PRESIDENT; HUTHMACHER HOUSE ASSOC; GRAND TOWER, IL 62942. (#6452-504).

JULY 6 - 28, '75. FLOWER SHOW & GARDEN TOUR. EXHIBIT, TOUR. (LOCAL). MIKE JONES, PRESIDENT; HUTHMACHER HOUSE ASSOC; GRAND TOWER, IL 62942. (#6452-505).

AUG 3 - 31, '75. ANTIQUE SHOW FLEA MARKET & FURNITURE REFINISHING. EXHIBIT, TOUR. (LOCAL). MIKE JONES, PRESIDENT; HUTHMACHER HOUSE ASSOC; GRAND TOWER, IL 62942. (#6452-506).

SEPT 1 - 29, '75. YOUTH MONTH, SCHOOL WORK DISPLAY W/STORY HOURS & GAMES. EXHIBIT, TOUR. (LOCAL). MIKE JONES, PRESIDENT; HUTHMACHER HOUSE ASSOC; GRAND TOWER, IL 62942. (#6452-507).

OCT 5 - 27, '75. FOLK WAYS & CUSTOMS. EXHIBIT, TOUR. (LOCAL). MIKE JONES, PRESIDENT; HUTHMACHER HOUSE ASSOC; GRAND TOWER, IL 62942. (#6452-508).

NOV 2 - 30, '75. NEEDLEWORK INDOOR PASTIMES. EXHIBIT, TOUR. (LOCAL). MIKE JONES, PRESIDENT; HUTHMACHER HOUSE ASSOC; GRAND TOWER, IL 62942. (#6452-509).

DEC 1 - 29, '75. CHRISTMAS CELEBRATION W/CAROLS, TOYS, COOKIES AND CANDY. EXHIBIT, TOUR. (LOCAL). MIKE JONES, PRESIDENT; HUTHMACHER HOUSE ASSOC; GRAND TOWER, IL 62942. (#6452-510).

MAR 17 - 21, '76. OTRABANDA COMPANY'S THIRD ANNUAL MISSISSIPPI RIVER TOUR. HOURS: 17 & 18 - 3:30 PM - 11:30 PM. 19 - 3:30 PM - 12:01 AM. 20 - 8:00 AM - 12:01 AM. 21 - 12 :01 PM - 12:01 AM. AT DEVIL'S BACKBONE PARK, NORTH OF GRAND TOWER BY THE MISSISSIPPI RIVER. (LOCAL). HELEN LINSENMEYER; GRAND TOWER BICENTENNIAL COMMITTEE; P.O. BOX 272; GRAND TOWER, IL 62694. (#50550-1).

GRANITE CITY

ETHNIC CELEBRATION PROJ OF GRANITE CITY, IL. A VARIETY OF CULTURAL EVENTS AND CELEBRATIONS TO EMPHASIZE AND RECOGNIZE VARIOUS ETHNIC CONTRIBUTIONS TO COMMUNITY AND NATIONAL HERITAGE. (LOCAL). RICHARD CHOSICH, BICENT COORDINATOR; CITY OF GRANITE CITY BICENTENNIAL COMMISSION; CITY HALL, 2000 EDISON AVE; GRANITE CITY, IL 62040. (#26878). **ARBA GRANTEE.**

AUG 10 - 11, '76. UNITED STATES ARMED FORCES BICENTENNIAL CARAVAN. CARAVAN IS COMPOSED OF EXHIBIT VANS FOR EACH MILITARY SERVICE. PROJECT THEME IS 'HISTORY OF THE ARMED FORCES & THEIR CONTRIBUTIONS TO THE NATION.'. (LOCAL). EDWARD F REISKE, CHMN; UNITED STATES ARMED FORCES BICENTENNIAL CARAVAN; 1831 DEMAR AVE; GRANITE CITY, IL 62040. (#1775-631).

OCT 24 - NOV 7, '76. NATIONS WITHIN THE COMMUNITY - ETHNIC CELEBRATION. A SERIES OF DANCES REPRESENTING THE CITY'S VARIOUS ETHNIC GROUPS; AN ETHNIC-CULTURAL FESTIVAL IN OCTOBER. AT GRANITE CITY HIGH SCHOOL, SOUTH AUDITORIUM, 3101 MADISON AVE. (LOCAL). RICHARD CHOSICH, COORD; CITY OF GRANITE CITY BICENTENNIAL COMMISSION; CITY HALL, 2000 EDISON AVE; GRANITE CITY, IL 62040. (#26878-1).

GRANVILLE

APR 26, '75. BICENTENNIAL DANCE, 'GET IN THE MOOD'. PUTNAM COUNTY HIGH SCHOOL BAND COMBO. 'VENTURA EXPRESS' TO PLAY. PROCEEDS GO TO 9-DAY CONCERT TOUR TO EASTERN STATES IN AUGUST, 1976. AT PUTNAM COUNTY HIGH SCHOOL. (LOCAL). BETTY BOUXSEIN; PUTNAM COUNTY HIGH SCHOOL BAND PARENTS; BOX 995; GRANVILLE, IL 61326. (#50331-1).

APR 24, '76. WAGON TRAIN STOPOVER. CEREMONY AT OLD STATE CAPITOL PLAZA. (LOCAL). JULIE WILLIAMS, CHMN; ILLINOIS BICENTENNIAL COMMISSION; SPRINGFIELD, IL 62706. (#200016-108).

GRAYSLAKE

NOV 15, '75. FREEDOM SHRINE DEDICATION. SET OF HISTORICAL FREEDOM SHRINE BICENTENNIAL DOCUMENTS PRESENTED TO LIBRARY FOR DISPLAY. CONGRESSMAN PHILLIP CRANE, 13TH DIST, GUEST SPEAKER. (LOCAL). JEANN B FRANK, CHAIRMAN; GRAYSLAKE BICENT COMMITTEE; GRAYSLAKE EXCHANGE CLUB; 232 E BELVIDERE; GRAYSLAKE, IL 60030. (#105217-4).

APR 4, '76. LIBERTY BELL CELEBRATION. AN AUTHENTIC REPRODUCTION OF THE LIBERTY BELL ON DISPLAY; CONCERT BAND FROM THE COLLEGE OF LAKE COUNTY. CLC SINGERS & COMMUNITY CHORUS; 'SPIRIT' GROUP FROM GRAYSLAKE HIGH SCHOOL. AT GRAYSLAKE NATIONAL BANK, 33 S WHITNEY ST. (LOCAL). JEANN B FRANK, CHAIRMAN; GRAYSLAKE NATIONAL BANK/GRAYSLAKE BICENTENNIAL COMMISSION; 232 E BELVIDERE RD; GRAYSLAKE, IL 60030. (#105217-1).

MAY 4 - 8, '76. LAKE COUNTY FAIR BOOTH. BOOTHS FROM LAKE COUNTY SHOWING & SELLING CRAFTS AND OTHER ITEMS; INFORMATION BOOTH, QUILT MAKING AND WAGON TRAIN. AT LAKE COUNTY FAIRGROUNDS. (LOCAL). JEANN B FRANK, CHAIRMAN; GRAYSLAKE BICENTENNIAL COMMITTEE; 232 E BELVIDERE RD; GRAYSLAKE, IL 60030. (#105217-3).

JUNE 13, '76. BICENTENNIAL COMMUNITY SING - 'I LOVE AMERICA'. MUSICAL IS DIVIDED INTO THREE SECTIONS: 'PATRIOTISM FOR AMERICA OUR HISTORY'; 'PRAISE FOR AMERICA OUR TRIBUTE' AND 'PRAYER FOR AMERICA OUR PLEA.' GUEST CONDUCTOR, WARREN SIMPKINS. LIBERTY BELL ON DISPLAY FROM 12-5 PM, FREE PUBLIC SHOWING. AT GRAYSLAKE HIGH SCHOOL, 400 N. LAKE ST, GRAYSLAKE, ILL. (LOCAL). JEANN B FRANK, CHAIRMAN; GRAYSLAKE BICENTENNIAL CHORUS COMMITTEE; 232 E BELVIDERE RD; GRAYSLAKE, IL 60030. (#105217-2).

GREENFIELD

GREENFIELD BICENTENNIAL SHELTER, IL. A HEATED SHELTER IN COMMUNITY PARK FOR MEETINGS. (LOCAL). ROBERT A NARMONT, COORDINATOR; GREENFIELD BICENTENNIAL COMMITTEE; PO BOX 328; GREENFIELD, IL 62044. (#27744). **ARBA GRANTEE.**

GREENUP

RESTORATION OF RAILROAD DEPOT - GREENUP, IL. RESTORATION OF TWO-STORY VANDALIA DEPOT AS A MUSEUM. (LOCAL). ELLEN DECKER, CHAIRMAN; CUMBERLAND COUNTY HISTORICAL SOCIETY; GREENUP, IL 62468. (#30399).

MAY 26 - 29, '76. BICENTENNIAL DAYS. PARADE, DEDICATION, PAGEANT, ARTS & CRAFTS. AT MUNICIPAL BLDG, TOWN SQUARE, HAUGHTON PARK. (LOCAL). ROSEMARY BARZ; GREENUP BICENTENNIAL COMMITTEE; 412 E CINCINNATI; GREENUP, IL 62428. (#200016-296).

GREENVILLE

DEC 3, '75. DEDICATION OF HISTORICAL PLAQUE. PLAQUE GIVES HISTORICAL FACTS ABOUT THE AREA. AT WEST COURT HOUSE LAWN, CORNER OF 3RD ST & COLLEGE AVE, RT 127. (LOCAL). MRS FRANK V DAVIS, COORD; GREENVILLE & BOND COUNTY BICENTENNIAL COMMISSION; RR 2, BOX 49A; GREENVILLE, IL 62246. (#200016-25).

GURNEE

BICENTENNIAL GRAND AVENUE ENHANCEMENT OF ILLINOIS. TO PREPARE IMPLEMENT AND MAINTAIN A PLAN FOR THE MAIN STREET IN GURNEE WHICH INCLUDES LANDSCAPING, LIGHTING, ARCHITECTURAL PERSPECTIVES WHILE MAINTAINING THE INDIVIDUAL INTEGRITY OF PROPERTIES INVOLVED. (LOCAL). PAULETTE WHITE, CHAIRMAN; GURNEE BICENTENNIAL COMMISSON; 4573 GRAND AVE; GURNEE, IL 60031. (#4277).

GURNEE DAYS-A BICENTENNIAL FESTIVAL IN ILLINOIS. COMMUNITY WIDE CELEBRATION, INCLUDING FAIR, EXHIBITS, DANCES, BIKE RACES, PAGEANT, JUNIOR OLYMPICS & OTHER ACTIVITIES. (LOCAL). PAULETTE WHITE, CHAIRMAN; GURNEE BICENTENNIAL COMMISSION; 926 NORTH ESTES; GURNEE, IL 60031. (#4276).

AUG 22, '75. BIKE RACES CHILDREN 11 YEARS AND UP. GURNEE DAYS-A BICENTENNIAL FESTIVAL IN ILLINOIS. COMMUNITY WIDE CELEBRATION, INCLUDING FAIR, EXHIBITS, DANCES, BIKE RACES, PAGEANT, JUNIOR OLYMPICS & OTHER ACTIVITIES. (LOCAL). PAULETTE WHITE, CHAIRMAN; GURNEE BICENTENNIAL COMMISSION; 926 NORTH ESTES; GURNEE, IL 60031. (#4276-504).

AUG 23, '75. GURNEE FESTIVAL WITH DISPLAYS, FAIR, JR OLYMPICS. COMMUNITY WIDE CELEBRATION, INCLUDING FAIR, EXHIBITS, DANCES, BIKE RACES, PAGEANT, JUNIOR OLYMPICS & OTHER ACTIVITIES. (LOCAL). PAULETTE WHITE, CHAIRMAN; GURNEE BICENTENNIAL COMMISSION; 926 NORTH ESTES; GURNEE, IL 60031. (#4276-501).

AUG 24, '75. BAND CONCERTS. GURNEE DAYS-A BICENTENNIAL FESTIVAL IN ILLINOIS. COMMUNITY WIDE CELEBRATION, INCLUDING FAIR, EXHIBITS, DANCES, BIKE RACES, PAGEANT, JUNIOR OLYMPICS & OTHER ACTIVITIES. (LOCAL). PAULETTE WHITE, CHAIRMAN; GURNEE BICENTENNIAL COMMISSION; 926 NORTH ESTES; GURNEE, IL 60031. (#4276-503).

AUG 24, '75. BICENTENNIAL PARADE. GURNEE DAYS-A BICENTENNIAL FESTIVAL IN ILLINOIS. COMMUNITY WIDE CELEBRATION, INCLUDING FAIR, EXHIBITS, DANCES, BIKE RACES, PAGEANT, JUNIOR OLYMPICS & OTHER ACTIVITIES. (LOCAL). PAULETTE WHITE, CHAIRMAN; GURNEE BICENTENNIAL COMMISSION; 926 NORTH ESTES; GURNEE, IL 60031. (#4276-502).

MAY 29 - OCT 3, '76. MARRIOTT'S GREAT AMERICA FAMILY ENTERTAINMENT PARK OPENS. 31 THRILL RIDES, PARADES, GIFT AND CRAFT SHOPS, LIVE MUSICAL AND VARIETY ENTERTAINMENT, LIVE CHIMPANZEE & DOLPHIN SHOW, WORLD'S ONLY TRIPLE FERRIS WHEEL, LARGEST LOOPING ROLLER COASTER, TWO GIANT WATER FLUME RIDES, SPECTACULAR ENTERTAINMENT THROUGHOUT 100-ACRE PARK. AT NEAR TRI-STATE TOLLWAY, I-95, JUST OFF GRAND AVE, ROUTE 132 EXIT. (REGN'L). ARTHUR A LARSON, COORD; MARRIOTT CORPORATION; ONE GREAT AMERICA PKY; GURNEE, IL 60031. (#104845-1).

HAMPSHIRE

JULY 21 - 24, '76. CENTENNIAL-BICENTENNIAL SPECTACLE, A NARRATED PRESENTATION. LOCAL RESIDENTS BRINGING TO LIFE THE HISTORY OF HAMPSHIRE OVER THE PAST 100 YEARS. AT HAMPSHIRE HIGH SCHOOL FOOTBALL FIELD. (LOCAL). ROBERT G WILCOX; HAMPSHIRE CENTENNIAL-BICENTENNIAL 1976 CORP; 199 S STATE ST; HAMPSHIRE, IL 60140. (#103889-1).

HANOVER PARK

COMMUNITY CENTER OF HANOVER PARK, ILLINOIS. DEVELOPMENT OF 140,000 SQ FT COMMUNITY CENTER FOR THE USE OF ALL RESIDENTS ON THE LAST 40 ACRES OF OPEN SPACE CENTRALLY LOCATED IN HANOVER PARK. (LOCAL). MRS PHILL , KESLER, CHAIRMAN; HANOVER PARK BICENTINEL COMMISSION; 6641 DEERPATH; HANOVER PARK, IL 60103. (#2605). **(??).**

HANOVER PARK — CONTINUED

'FROM CAMELOT TO METROPOLIS' HISTORY, HANOVER, ILL. AN IN-DEPTH HISTORY OF THE HANOVER PARK-ONTARIOVILLE AREA DESCRIBING THE DEVELOPMENT FROM FARM COMMUNITY TO MODERN SUBURBIA. (LOCAL). BEVERLY KESLER, CHAIRMAN; HANOVER PARK BICENTENNIAL COMMISSION; 6641 DEERPATH LANE; HANOVER PARK, IL 60103. (#2609).

MUNICIPAL CNTR OF HANOVER PARK, ILLINOIS. A NEW CIVIC CNTR WILL BE COMP BY 1976, INCL A VILLAGE HALL, PUBLIC WORKS BLDG AND OFFICES, A POLICE FACILITY, AND A COURTROOM. (LOCAL). LOUIS F BARONE, VILLAGE PRESIDENT; HANOVER PARK VILLAGE HALL; 2121 LAKE ST; HANOVER PARK, IL 60103. (#2610).

RELOCATION & RESTORATION - CHAMBERLIN HOUSE, IL. VILLAGE-OWNED HOUSE HAS BEEN NOTED AS EXAMPLE OF CIVIL WAR ARCHITECTURE. BUILDING WILL BE MOVED TO PARK DISTRICT SITE & RESTORED TO BECOME PART OF A HISTORIC PARK SITE MUSEUM AREA. (LOCAL). SONYA A CRAWSHAW, CHMN; HANOVER PARK BICENTENNIAL COMMISSION; 2121 W LAKE ST; HANOVER PARK, IL 60103. (#20580).

JULY 11, '76. ANNUAL VILLAGE 'I AM AN AMERICAN' DAY PARADE. FUTURE PLANS OF HANOVER PARK, ILLINOIS. JULY JUBILEE MONTH-LONG FESTIVAL SCHEDULED FOR 1976 INCL COMMUNITY PICNIC, COLONIAL FAIR, PARADE, PAGEANT, ART & MUSICS PGMS & VARIOUS TYPES OF COMPETITIONS. (LOCAL). CHARLES H SOBLE; AMERICAN LEGION, STANLEY C SOBLE POST 1272; 1836 EVERGREEN ST; HANOVER PARK, IL 60103. (#2611-502).

JULY 17 - 18, '76. 'I LOVE AMERICA' CANTATA. LIVE PERFORMANCE AT TEFFT JUNIOR HIGH SCHOOL, IRVING PARK RD, STREAMWOOD. (LOCAL). SONYA A CRAWSHAW, CHMN; HANOVER PARK BICENTENNIAL COMMISSION; 2121 W LAKE ST; HANOVER PARK, IL 60103. (#104824-1).

AUG 14, '76. PRESIDENT'S BALL. COSTUME BALL AND DINNER TO COMMEMORATE BICENTENNIAL & 18TH ANNIVERSARY OF THE INCORPORATION OF THE VILLAGE. AT APPLE ORCHARD COUNTRY CLUB, BARTLETT. (LOCAL). SONYA A CRAWSHAW, CHMN; HANOVER PARK BICENTENNIAL COMMISSION; 2121 W LAKE ST; HANOVER PARK, IL 60103. (#104824-2).

SEPT 4 - 5, '76. HARVEST FESTIVAL. SUNDAY HOURS: 12 NOON - 10 PM. AT COMMUNITY PARK, CHURCH & WALNUT STS. (LOCAL). SONYA A CRAWSHAW; HANOVER PARK BICENTENNIAL COMMISSION; 2121 W LAKE ST; HANOVER PARK, IL 60103. (#2611-501).

HARDIN

CALHOUN COUNTY MUSEUM - HARDIN, IL. ORGANIZATION OF CALHOUN COUNTY MUSEUM IN HARDIN. (LOCAL). PAUL HANKS, CHAIRMAN; CALHOUN COUNTY HISTORICAL SOCIETY; HARDIN, IL 62047. (#30408).

HISTORY OF CALHOUN COUNTY, ILLINOIS. CALHOUN COUNTY WILL ESTABLISH A MUSEUM OF HISTORY, PUBLISH A HISTORY WRITTEN BY LOCAL GRADE STUDENTS, REPRODUCE 1891 BIOGRAPPHY OF CALHOUN CO, & CELE 150TH BIRTH OF CALHOUN 0& BICENT IN JULY L1975. (LOCAL). GEORGE W CARPENTER, COORDINATOR; CALHOUN HISTORICAL SOCIETY; HARDIN, IL 62047. (#9592).

JULY 3 - 4, '76. BICENTENNIAL CELEBRATION. FESTIVAL. (LOCAL). PAUL HANKS, CHMN; CALHOUN COUNTY BICENTENNIAL COMMISSION; HARDIN, IL 62047. (#200016-185).

FEB 5 - 6, '77. LA SALLE EXPEDITION II, A HISTORIC RE-ENACTMENT. THIS IS AN AUTHENTIC RE-ENACTMENT OF THE 1681 LASALLE EXPEDITION FROM MONTREAL, CANADA TO NEW ORLEANS, LA WHICH WILL BEGIN TOURING ON AUGUST 11, 1976 AND END ON APRIL 9, 1977. (LOCAL). REID H LEWIS, DIRECTOR; LA SALLE EXPEDITION II; 135 S LA SALLE ST, RM 411; CHICAGO, IL 60690. (#102805-51).

HARRISBURG

SOUTHEASTERN'S HERITAGE FESTIVAL. DISPLAYS & EXHIBITIONS OF HISTORICAL CRAFTS, TRADES, DANCES, ART WORK, COOKERY - PUT ON JOINTLY WITH COMMUNITY & HISTORY STUDENTS. (LOCAL). EUGENIA PLATER, COORD; SOUTHEASTERN ILLINOIS COLLEGE; RR #4 COLLEGE DR; HARRISBURG, IL 62946. (#107341-1).

JAN 21 - APR 12, '76. HISTORY OF SOUTHERN ILLINOIS - GENERAL STUDIES OPEN TO ADULT PUBLIC. GUEST SPEAKERS ON INDIAN LORE, AREA HISTORIC WRITERS, ROCK COLLECTORS, AREA CULTURE AND LANDMARK EXPERTS. INSTRUCTOR IS LOCAL AUTHOR AND CULTURE PRESERVER, GARY DENEAL. AT INTERIM BUILDING. (LOCAL). GARY WILSON, DIRECTOR; SOUTHERN ILLINOIS COLLEGE; RT 4, COLLEGE DR; HARRISBURG, IL 62946. (#200016-30).

MAR 2 - APR 15, '76. HISTORY OF BLACK AMERICA SINCE 1865 - GEN STUDIES CLASS FOR ADULTS. THIS CLASS MAY BE EXPANDED TO ACCOMODATE ANY NUMBER OF INTERESTED PERSONS. AT INTERIM BUILDING. (LOCAL). GARY WILSON, DIRECTOR; SOUTHEASTERN ILLINOIS COLLEGE; RT 4, COLLEGE DR; HARRISBURG, IL 62946. (#200016-31).

HARVARD

APR 19, '75. PATRIOTS DAY OBSERVANCE. FESTIVAL. (LOCAL). ROBERTA HORN, SECRETARY; HARVARD BICENTENNIAL COMMITTEE; 407 DEWEY ST; HARVARD, IL 60033. (#200016-27).

SEPT 14, '75. HARVARD BICENTENNIAL FREEDOM MARCH. MARCH LED BY DRUMS, FLUTE & FLAGS. (LOCAL). MRS FRANK HORN, CHMN; HARVARD BICENTENNIAL COMMITTEE; 407 DEWEY ST; HARVARD, IL 60033. (#102097-1).

NOV 1, '75 - FEB 28, '76. FIRST LADY OF HARVARD. RESIDENTS WILL CHOOSE MOST POPULAR LADY IN HARVARD OVER AGE 35 TO BE THE HOSTESS AT ALL BICENTENNIAL FESTIVITIES FOR THE REST OF THE TOWN'S CELEBRATION. (LOCAL). DR NORBERT PATTERSON, DIR; HARVARD ROTARY CLUB; 75 N AYER ST; HARVARD, IL 60033. (#103828-1).

NOV 21 - 22, '75. FESTIVAL OF QUILTS WITH HERITAGE. A QUILT OF NATIONAL HISTORIC EVENTS DEPICTED AS THE SEAMSTRESS PLEASED AND QUILTED BY OTHER LADIES WILL BE AWARDED. RESIDENTS ARE INVITED TO DISPLAY THEIR OWN HEIRLOOM QUILTS TOO. AT HARVARD CIVIC CENTER. (LOCAL). ROBERTA HORN, SECRETARY; HARVARD BICENTENNIAL COMMITTEE; 407 DEWEY ST; HARVARD, IL 60033. (#200016-28).

JUNE 14, '76. FLAG DAY & HUMAN KINDESS DAY. AWARD, CEREMONY AT CENTRAL SCHOOL LAWN. (LOCAL). MRS FRANK HORN, CHMN; HARVARD VFW; 407 DEWEY ST; HARVARD, IL 60033. (#102097-3).

JULY 4, '76. 4TH OF JULY CELEBRATION. FESTIVITIES WILL INCLUDE A POTLUCK PICNIC & BAND CONCERT. AT LIONS PARK. (LOCAL). MRS FRANK HORN, CHMN; HARVARD VFW; 407 DEWEY ST; HARVARD, IL 60033. (#102097-2).

HARVEY

MAR 26, '76. BICENTENNIAL HERITAGE LUNCHEON. FESTIVAL, LIVE PERFORMANCE AT REGENCY ROOM, HOLIDAY INN, 17100 SHALSTED. (LOCAL). MRS LEE SHELTON, CHMN; THIRD DISTRICT, ILLINOIS FEDERATION WOMEN'S CLUBS; 629 CARROLL PARKWAY; GLENWOOD, IL 60425. (#200016-32).

MAY 2, '76. ALL AMERICAN CONCERT, INCLUDING BERNSTEIN'S CHICHESTER PSALMS. WITH PAUL NEEDHAM, ALTO SOLOIST, THE THORNTON CHORAL ORGANIZATIONS & THE CHICAGO CHAMBER ORCHESTRA. (LOCAL). DR ROBERT L JACK, DEAN; DIVISION OF ARTS & HUMANITIES, THORNTON COMMUNITY COLLEGE; OFFICE OF COMMUNITY SERVICES; HARVEY, IL 60426. (#200016-73).

HAVANA

AUG 27, '76. AMERICAN WIND SYMPHONY'S FLOATING ARTS CENTER VISITS HAVANA. EMBARKING UPON A BICENTENNIAL CULTURAL TOUR, THE WIND SYMPHONY WILL VISIT 76 CITIES BRINGING MUSIC, DANCE, SYMPOSIA & CHILDREN'S THEATER TO THE WATERWAYS OF AMERICA DURING ITS 6 MONTH TOUR. (NAT'L). PAULA BERN, COORD; AMERICAN WIND SYMPHONY ORCHESTRA OF WESTERN PENNSYLVANIA; GATEWAY TOWERS 18G; PITTSBURGH, PA 15222. (#2800-32).

HAZEL CREST

BICENTENNIAL PARK IN HAZEL CREST, IL. A HERITAGE PARK WITH A MEMORIAL CANNON AND A FLAG FROM THE CAPITAL WILL BE DEVELOPED. (LOCAL). JEFF BOUBELIK, SUPERINTENDENT; BICENTENNIAL COMMISSION OF HAZEL CREST & AMERICAN LEGION; HAZEL CREST, IL 60429. (#33623).

BICENTENNIAL RECYCLE CENTER IN HAZEL CREST, IL. CENTER FOR COLLECTION OF RECYCLE MATERIALS: PAPER, TIN, GLASS, ALUMINUM. FUNDS TO BE USED FOR BEAUTIFICATION AND YOUTH ACTIVITIES. (LOCAL). ARTHUR W CROWLEY, CHAIRMAN; BICENTENNIAL COMMISSION OF HAZEL CREST, RECYCLE COMMITTEE; HAZEL CREST, IL 60429. (#33624).

STUDENT GOVERNMENT DAY. DURING YOUTH APPRECIATION WEEK STUDENTS PARTICIPATED IN VILLAGE & PARK DISTRICT GOVERNMENT. (LOCAL). KEN GRANETH, CHAIRMAN; OPTIMIST CLUB & BICENTENNIAL COMMISSION; HAZEL CREST, IL 60429. (#200016-397).

TOWN MEETING '76. THE TOWN MEETING DISCUSSED IDENTIFYING BASIC CHALLENGES TO COMMUNITY FUTURE, DEVELOP PROPOSAL FOR MEETING CHALLENGES, CELEBRATE ACCOMPLISHMENTS, VILLAGE SYMBOL, MOTTO & SONG. (LOCAL). ARTHUR W CROWLEY, CHMN; HAZEL CREST BICENTENNIAL COMMISSION; 17109 LOCUST DR; HAZEL CREST, IL 60429. (#200016-396).

OCT 23, '74. HISTORICAL TRIP TO GALENA, IL. TOUR. (LOCAL). ARTHUR W CROWLEY, CHMN; BICENTENNIAL COMMISSION OF HAZEL CREST; 17109 LOCUST DR; HAZEL CREST, IL 60429. (#200016-391).

JUNE 22, '75. PARADE, PICNIC, AND CONCERT. FESTIVAL, PARADE AT OAK HILL PARK. (LOCAL). ARTHUR W CROWLEY, CHMN; HAZEL CREST BICENTENNIAL COMMISSION; 17109 LOCUST DR; HAZEL CREST, IL 60429. (#200016-393).

JUNE 27, '76. BICENTENNIAL PARADE. PARADE AT 170TH ST. (LOCAL). ARTHUR W CROWLEY, CHMN; HAZEL CREST BICENTENNIAL COMMISSION; 17109 LOCUST DR; HAZEL CREST, IL 60429. (#200016-395).

JULY 4, '76. 'HANDS ACROSS THE VILLAGE'. FESTIVAL AT BRIDGE OVER TOLLROAD. (LOCAL). JOYCE BAUC, CHAIRMAN; 4H CLUB & HAZEL CREST BICENTENNIAL COMMISSION; 3512 CHESTNUT DR; HAZEL CREST, IL 60429. (#200016-392).

JULY 4, '76. 4TH OF JULY CELEBRATION. FESTIVAL AT OAK HILL PARK. (LOCAL). ARTHUR W CROWLEY, CHMN; HAZEL CREST BICENTENNIAL COMMISSION; 17109 LOCUST DR; HAZEL CREST, IL 60429. (#200016-394).

HEBRON

HEBRON RENOVATION & BEAUTIFICATION, IL. EVERGREENS HAVE BEEN PLANTED, VILLAGE MARKERS & WELCOME SIGNS HAVE BEEN ERECTED, STORE FRONTS HAVE BEEN RENOVATED. PURPOSE OF PROJECT WAS TO STRESS LOCAL PRIDE, INVOLVEMENT & COOPERATION. (LOCAL). STEVEN E AAVANGE, CHAIRMAN; HEBRON BICENTENNIAL COMMISSION; 9703 ILLINOIS ST; HEBRON, IL 60034. (#28785).

HENNEPIN

PUTNAM COUNTY HISTORICAL SOCIETY MUSEUM, IL. MUSEUM CONTAINING LOCAL HISTORICAL & CULTURAL ARTIFACTS. (LOCAL). MRS JOHN WILSON, PRESIDENT; PUTNAM COUNTY HISTORICAL SOCIETY; HENNEPIN, IL 61327. (#17084).

JAN 20 - 21, '77. LA SALLE EXPEDITION II, A HISTORIC RE-ENACTMENT. THIS IS AN AUTHENTIC RE-ENACTMENT OF THE 1681 LASALLE EXPEDITION FROM MONTREAL, CANADA TO NEW ORLEANS, LA WHICH WILL BEGIN TOURING ON AUGUST 11, 1976 AND END ON APRIL 9, 1977. (LOCAL). REID H LEWIS, DIRECTOR; LA SALLE EXPEDITION II; 135 S LA SALLE ST, RM 411; CHICAGO, IL 60690. (#102805-42).

HENRY

BANDSHELL RESTORATION IN HENRY, IL. RESTORATION OF BANDSHELL IN HENRY CITY PARK FOR MUSICAL AND THEATRICAL PERFORMANCES. (LOCAL). MARY JANE MATTINGLY, CHAIRMAN; HENRY BICENTENNIAL COMMISSION; RR; LACON, IL 61540. (#33622).

JULY 4, '76. BICENTENNIAL FESTIVAL. SUNRISE SERVICE, CANOE AND RAFT RACES. (LOCAL). BECKY BRANT, CHMN; MARSHALL COUNTY BICENTENNIAL COMMISSION; BOX 196; HENRY, IL 61537. (#200016-149).

JULY 24, '76. MARSHALL COUNTY BICENTENNIAL SHOW. EXHIBIT, FAIR AT PUTNAM-MARSHALL COUNTY FAIRGROUNDS. (LOCAL). MRS RALPH WIER, CHMN; MARSHALL COUNTY BICENTENNIAL COMMISSION; RR; LACON, IL 61540. (#200016-148).

JAN 21 - 22, '77. LA SALLE EXPEDITION II, A HISTORIC RE-ENACTMENT. THIS IS AN AUTHENTIC RE-ENACTMENT OF THE 1681 LASALLE EXPEDITION FROM MONTREAL, CANADA TO NEW ORLEANS, LA WHICH WILL BEGIN TOURING ON AUGUST 11, 1976 AND END ON APRIL 9, 1977. (LOCAL). REID H LEWIS, DIRECTOR; LA SALLE EXPEDITION II; 135 S LA SALLE ST, RM 411; CHICAGO, IL 60690. (#102805-43).

HERRIN

JULY 4, '76. HERRIN DIAMOND JUBILEE, JULY 4TH CELEBRATION. BASEBALL GAME, CHICKEN BARBECUE, COUNTRY BAND, FIREWORKS, GIANT DIAMOND IN HONOR OF JUBILEE & THE AMERICAN FLAG IN HONOR OF THE BICENTENNIAL. AT HERRIN CITY PARK. (LOCAL). JACK BALIN, CHAIRMAN; HERRIN KIWANIS CLUB; 1108 E POPLAR; HERRIN, IL 62948. (#102175-1).

HICKORY HILLS

PARK AREA FOR ADULTS & SENIOR CITIZENS - IL. PAVILLION AND GAME SIT DOWN AREA IN NATURAL PARK SETTING. (LOCAL). BEVERLY STURTEVANT, CHAIRMAN; HICKORY HILLS BICENTENNIAL COMMITTEE; 8652 W 95TH ST; HICKORY HILLS, IL 60457. (#29209).

JULY 2 - 5, '76. HICKORY HILLS BICENTENNIAL ACTIVITIES. INCLUDED: SCOUT JAMBOREE, ECUMENICAL OUTDOOR SERVICE, PARADE, FIREWORKS AND STREET FAIR. (LOCAL). BEVERLY STURTEVANT, CHMN; HICKORY HILLS BICENTENNIAL COMMISSION; 8652 W 95TH ST; HICKORY HILLS, IL 60457. (#200016-212).

HIGHLAND

BICENTENNIAL HISTORICAL CALENDAR 1976, IL. 1400 DATES OF LOCAL, STATE, NATIONAL & INTERNATIONAL IMPORTANCE WHICH HAVE HAD AN EFFECT ON POLITICAL, SOCIAL AND CULTURAL HISTORY OF THIS AREA ARE INCLUDED IN THE CALENDAR. (LOCAL). ELAINE STRATTON, COMMITTEE CHAIRMAN; HISTORICAL RESEARCH & DISSEMINATION COMMITTEE, HIGHLAND ARBC; 1800 LINDENTHAL; HIGHLAND, IL 62249. (#20346).

HIGHLAND BICENTENNIAL COOKBOOK, IL. RECIPES OF COLONIAL & PIONEER TIMES AND LOCAL SPECIALTIES WILL BE FEATURED IN THE COOKBOOK. (LOCAL). ELAINE STRATTON, COMMITTEE CHAIRMAN; HISTORICAL RESEARCH & DISSEMINATION COMMITTEE, HIGHLAND ARBC; 1800 LINDENTHAL; HIGHLAND, IL 62249. (#20345).

JAN 2, '75 - FEB 29, '76. SUNDAY AFTERNOON EVENTS. LIVE PERFORMANCE, SEMINAR AT LOUIS LATZER MEMORIAL LIBRARY. (LOCAL). ELAINE STRATTON, CHMN; HISTORICAL RESEARCH COMMITTEE OF HIGHLAND BICENTENNIAL COMMISSION; 1800 LINDENTHAL AVE; HIGHLAND, IL 62249. (#200016-29).

AUG 9, '75 - JULY 19, '76. HISTORICAL DISPLAYS AT THE LIBRARY. ALSO DISPLAYED FROM 6:30 PM TO 8:00 PM, TUES, THURS, & FRIDAY. AT LOUIS LATZER MEMORIAL LIBRARY, WASHINGTON & 9TH ST. (LOCAL). ELAINE STRATTON, PROJ DIR; HISTORICAL RESEARCH COMMITTEE OF BICENTENNIAL COMMISSION; 1800 LINDENTHAL AVE; HIGHLAND, IL 62249. (#103653-2).

HIGHLAND — CONTINUED

OCT 23, '75 - JUNE 1, '76. BICENTENNIAL QUILTING AT THE LIBRARY. RAFFLE TICKETS ARE BEING SOLD ON THESE QUILTS FOR $.50 EACH, THE DRAWING WILL BE JULY 4, 1976, PROCEEDS WILL GO TO SUPPORT BICENTENNIAL ACTIVITIES; SIX QUILTS HAVE ALREADY BEEN COMPLETED; THIS IS A SEQUEL TO A BETSY ROSS JR SEWING CLUB PROJECT OF THE SUMMER OF 1975. AT LOUIS LATZER MEMORIAL LIBRARY. (LOCAL). ELAINE STRATTON, CHMN; HISTORICAL RESEARCH & DISSEMINATION COMMITTEE OF BICENT COMMISSION; 1800 LINDENTHAL AVE; HIGHLAND, IL 62249. (#104742-2).

DEC 7, '75. WILLIAMSBURG DINNER - A LIBRARY BENEFIT. FESTIVAL, CEREMONY AT LOUIS LATZER MEMORIAL LIBRARY, WASHINGTON & 9TH. (LOCAL). ELAINE STRATTON, PROJ DIR; HISTORICAL RESEARCH COMMITTEE OF BICENTENNIAL COMMISSION; 1800 LINDENTHAL AVE; HIGHLAND, IL 62249. (#103653-1).

JULY 2 - 4, '76. VISIT OF BRITISH SILVER WINGS OVERSEAS AIRWAY BAND. RETURN VISIT TO THE ONE PAID THEM IN SUMMER OF 1975, WHEN HIGHLAND COMMUNITY HIGH SCHOOL BAND VISITED ENGLAND; PART OF THE LARGE 4TH OF JULY WEEKEND PLANNED. THEY WILL PLAY AT A FRI NITE OUTDOOR BAND CONCERT AT THE PLAZA SQUARE & SAT & SUN NITE AT LINDENDALE PARK. (INT'L). KENNETH KRAUSE, DIR; HIGHLAND COMMUNITY SCHOOLS; 1800 LINDENTHAL AVE; HIGHLAND, IL 62249. (#104809-1).

OCT 10, '76. A VISIT TO A RESTORED COUNTRY SCHOOLHOUSE, II. THIS IS A SEQUEL TO A HIGHLY SUCCESSFUL BICENTENNIAL EVENT HELD IN OCTOBER, 19759. AT GIGER SCHOOL HOUSE - 1 MILE NORTH OF HIGHLAND. (LOCAL). ELAINE STRATTON, CHMN; HISTORICAL RESEARCH COMMITTEE OF BICENTENNIAL COMMISSION; 1800 LINDENTHAL AVE; HIGHLAND, IL 62249. (#104742-3).

DEC 5, '76. WILLIAMSBURG DINNER II, A LIBRARY BENEFIT. THIS IS A SEQUEL TO A HIGHLY SUCCESSFUL WILLIAMSBURG CHRISTMAS DINNER. THE FIRST LIBRARY BENEFIT WAS HELD ON DECEMBER 7, 1975. AT LOUIS LATZER MEMORIAL LIBRARY, WASHINGTON AND 9TH. (LOCAL). ELAINE STRATTON, CHMN; BICENTENNIAL COMMISSION, HISTORICAL RESEARCH & DISSEMINATION; 1800 LINDENTHAL AVE; HIGHLAND, IL 62249. (#104742-1).

HIGHLAND PARK

BICENTENNIAL CALENDARS OF EVENTS IN HIGHLAND, IL. SIX CALENDARS ISSUED TO KEEP PUBLIC INFORMED OF SOME 50 DIFFERENT BICENTENNIAL EVENTS/PROJECTS THAT TOOK PLACE IN HIGHLAND PARK, IL IN 1975-1976. (LOCAL). HENRY X ARENBERG, CHAIRMAN; HIGHLAND PARK BICENTENNIAL COMMISSION; 1707 ST JOHNS AVE; HIGHLAND PARK, IL 60035. (#33615).

BOOK ON LOCAL HISTORY OF HIGHLAND PARK, IL. REPRINT OF TWO OUT-OF-PRINT BOOKS ON HIGHLAND PARK HISTORY WITH MORE THAN 50 PICTURES, CHARTS, TIMETABLES & STATISTICS, 144 PAGES. PUBLICATION DATE: NOV 22, 1976. (LOCAL). HENRY X ARENBERG, CHAIRMAN; HIGHLAND PARK BICENTENNIAL COMMISSION; CITY HALL, 1707 ST JOHN AVE; HIGHLAND PARK, IL 60035. (#33621).

CITY VEHICLE LICENSE DESIGN CONTEST - IL. CITY-WIDE CONTEST FOR DESIGN OF VEHICLE STICKER OPEN TO RESIDENTS; $1400 IN SAVINGS BONDS FOR PRIZES. (LOCAL). HENRY X ARENBERG, CHAIRMAN; HIGHLAND PARK BICENTENNIAL COMMISSION; 1707 ST JOHNS AVE; HIGHLAND PARK, IL 60035. (#33617).

COMMEMORATIVE POSTER FOR HIGHLAND PARK, IL. HISTORICAL POSTER BY LOCAL ARTIST JOHN ASQUITH; 2000 PRINTED IN COLOR & SOLD FOR ONE DOLLAR; COMMISSIONED BY 'FOCUS ON ARTS' AT HIGHLAND PARK HIGH SCHOOL, MAY, 1975. (LOCAL). HENRY X ARENBERG, CHAIRMAN; HIGHLAND PARK BICENTENNIAL COMMISSION; CITY HALL, 1707 ST JOHN AVE; HIGHLAND PARK, IL 60035. (#33620).

CONSTRUCTION OF ANALEMMATIC SUN DIAL - IL. CONSTRUCTION OF ANALEMMATIC OR 'LIVING' SUN DIAL IN DOWNTOWN HIGHLAND PARK; ONLY DIAL LIKE THIS IN THE WORLD. DIAL IS 26FT WIDE. HOUR MARKERS ARE FIR TREES. VISITOR LOOKS AT HIS SHADOW TO TELL THE TIME. (LOCAL). JEROME V MAN, DESIGNER; HIGHLAND PARK YOUTH COMMITTEE; 1811 ST JOHNS AVE; HIGHLAND PARK, IL 60035. (#33612).

FLAGPOLE AND BRONZE PLAQUE, IN HIGHLAND PARK, IL. 40 FOOT FLAGPOLE AND BRONZE PLAQUE BEING PLACED IN FRONT OF CITY HALL BY BICENTENNIAL COMMISSION. PLAQUE WILL HAVE THE PLEDGE OF ALLEGIANCE AND ALSO MARK BICENTENNIAL OBSERVANCE. (LOCAL). HENRY X ARENBERG, CHAIRMAN; HIGHLAND PARK BICENTENNIAL COMMISSION; 1707 ST JOHNS AVE; HIGHLAND PARK, IL 60035. (#33616).

HAND-MADE 13 STAR FLAGS - HIGHLAND PARK, IL. THIRTY 13 STAR 'BETSY ROSS' FLAGS, 3 FEET BY FIVE FEET WERE HAND SEWN BY HIGHLAND PARK WOMEN. 30 FLAGS WERE THEN GIVEN TO ALL SCHOOLS, LIBRARIES, ETC. (LOCAL). HENRY X ARENBERG, CHAIRMAN; HIGHLAND PARK BICENTENNIAL COMMISSION; 1707 ST JOHNS AVE; HIGHLAND PARK, IL 60035. (#33613).

LIBRARY REMODELING/REFURBISHING IN HIGHLAND, IL. ROBERT G ROBINSON LIBRARY OF HIGHLAND PARK HISTORICAL SOCIETY, BOOKS ON LOCAL, STATE & NATIONAL HISTORY; PLUS OFFICE, RECEPTION, & SALES AREAS OPENED. (LOCAL). HENRY X ARENBERG, CHAIRMAN; HIGHLAND PARK HISTORICAL SOCIETY; PO BOX 56, 326 CENTRAL AVE; HIGHLAND PARK, IL 60035. (#33619).

MUSEUM ADDITION IN HIGHLAND PARK, IL. RAVINIA FESTIVAL MINI-MUSEUM OF HIGHLAND PARK HISTORICAL SOCIETY, DEVOTED TO HISTORY OF RAVINIA PARK FESTIVAL SINCE 1904; ROOM OPENED 10-24-76. (LOCAL). HENRY X ARENBERG, CHAIRMAN; HIGHLAND PARK HISTORICAL SOCIETY; PO BOX 56, 326 CENTRAL AVE; HIGHLAND PARK, IL 60035. (#33618).

RESTORATION OF BRICK WATER TOWER IN HIGHLAND, IL. 125 FOOT HIGH BRICK WATER TOWER BUILT IN 1930 WAS RESTORED; CAPACITY OF 500,000 GALLONS. (LOCAL). HENRY X ARENBERG, CHAIRMAN; HIGHLAND PARK BICENTENNIAL COMMISSION; 1707 ST JOHNS AVE; HIGHLAND PARK, IL 60035. (#33614).

'UNCLE SAM: THE MAN & THE LEGEND'-FILM OF ILLINOIS. A 16MM SOUND FILM AVAILABLE FREE TO ANY SCHOOL OR GROUP REQUESTING IT IN NORTHERN ILLINOIS. PRODUCED BY THE HIGHLAND PARKS BICENTENNIAL COMMISSION. (ST-WIDE). HENRY X ARENBERG, CHMN; HIGHLAND PARKS BICENTENNIAL COMMISSION; 1171 LINDEN AVE; HIGHLAND PARK, IL 60035. (#32948).

APR 10, '75. AMERICAN REVOLUTION BICENTENNIAL OBSERVANCE. CEREMONY AT RECREATION CENTER, 1850 GREEN BAY RD. (LOCAL). HENRY X ARENBERG; HIGHLAND PARK BICENTENNIAL COMMISSION; CITY HALL; HIGHLAND PARK, IL 60035. (#50416-1).

MAY 4, '75. DEDICATION OF BRONZE PLAQUE AT WALT DURBAHN TOOL MUSEUM. CEREMONY, EXHIBIT AT 326 CENTRAL AVE. (ST-WIDE). HENRY X ARENBERG, CHMN; HIGHLAND PARK HISTORICAL SOCIETY; 1171 LINDEN AVE; HIGHLAND PARK, IL 60035. (#200016-250).

MAY 20, '75. 'MY COUNTRY TIS O' THEE' MUSICAL PAGEANT WITH SLIDES. LIVE PERFORMANCE AT RAVINA SCHOOL AUDITORIUM, 763 DEAN AVE. (LOCAL). HENRY X ARENBERG, CHMN; RAVINA SCHOOL & HIGHLAND PARK BICENTENNIAL COMMISSION; 1171 LINDEN AVE; HIGHLAND PARK, IL 60035. (#200016-258).

OCT 1, '75 - DEC 31, '76. DISPLAYS OF LOCAL HISTORY. EXHIBIT AT MUSEUM, 326 CENTRAL AVE. (LOCAL). HENRY X ARENBERG, CHMN; HIGHLAND PARK HISTORICAL SOCIETY; 1171 LINDEN AVE; HIGHLAND PARK, IL 60035. (#200016-259).

NOV 6 - 8, '75. 'MUSIC MAN' BROADWAY MUSICAL BY LOCAL TALENT. LIVE PERFORMANCE AT HIGHLAND PARK HIGH SCHOOL AUDITORIUM, ST JOHNS & VINE AVES. (LOCAL). HENRY X ARENBERG, CHMN; HIGHLAND PARK HISTORICAL SOCIETY, PARK DISTRICT & BICENT COMMISSION; 1171 LINDEN AVE; HIGHLAND PARK, IL 60035. (#200016-249).

NOV 13 - 14, '75. COLONIAL DINNER & CRAFTS SHOW WITH BICENTENNIAL THEME. EXHIBIT, RADIO/TV AT CHURCH HALL, 425 LAUREL AVE. (LOCAL). REV DOUGLAS SPENCE; TRINITY EPISCOPAL CHURCH; 425 LAUREL AVE; HIGHLAND PARK, IL 60035. (#200016-257).

FEB 12, '76. 'ELISHA GRAY: THE MAN & THE PHONE' A MEMORIAL LECTURE. LIVE PERFORMANCE AT RECREATION CENTER, 1850 GREENBAY. (LOCAL). HENRY X ARENBERG, CHMN; HIGHLAND PARK HISTORICAL SOCIETY & BICENTENNIAL COMMISSION; 1171 LINDEN AVE; HIGHLAND PARK, IL 60035. (#200016-260).

MAR 11, '76. BICENTENNIAL FOLK MUSIC CONCERT. LIVE PERFORMANCE AT RECREATION CENTER, 1850 GREENBAY RD. (LOCAL). HENRY X ARENBERG, CHMN; HIGHLAND PARK HISTORICAL SOCIETY & BICENTENNIAL COMMISSION; 1171 LINDEN AVE; HIGHLAND PARK, IL 60035. (#200016-255).

MAY 1, '76. RE-DEDICATION YERKES FOUNTAIN ORIGINALLY BUILT IN 1896. CEREMONY AT SHERIDAN RD & FOREST AVE. (LOCAL). HENRY X ARENBERG, CHMN; HIGHLAND PARK BICENTENNIAL COMMISSION & CITY OF HIGHLAND PARK; 1171 LINDEN AVE; HIGHLAND PARK, IL 60035. (#200016-251).

MAY 2, '76. BICENTENNIAL CONCERT BY FLUTE & FIDDLE CLUB. LIVE PERFORMANCE AT EPISCOPAL CHURCH HALL, 425 LAUREL AVE. (LOCAL). HENRY X ARENBERG, CHMN; HIGHLAND PARK BICENTENNIAL COMMISSION; 1171 LINDEN AVE; HIGHLAND PARK, IL 60035. (#200016-248).

MAY 15 - JUNE 10, '76. ART EXHIBIT IN STORES BY STUDENTS OF LOCAL PUBLIC SCHOOLS. EXHIBIT AT ALL STORE WINDOWS THROUGHOUT HIGHLAND PARK. (LOCAL). HENRY X ARENBERG, CHMN; HIGHLAND PARK BICENTENNIAL COMMISSION; 1171 LINDEN AVE; HIGHLAND PARK, IL 60035. (#200016-256).

MAY 20, '76. HISTORICAL SOCIETY MEETING 'WHAT IS AN ANTIQUE?' BY R ROBINSON. LIVE PERFORMANCE, EXHIBIT AT RECREATION CENTER, 1850 GREENBAY. (LOCAL). HENRY X ARENBERG, CHMN; HIGHLAND PARK HISTORICAL SOCIETY; 1171 LINDEN AVE; HIGHLAND PARK, IL 60035. (#200016-254).

JULY 4 - 5, '76. 4TH OF JULY CELEBRATION. ACTIVITIES INCLUDE PARADE, CARNIVAL, DRUM & BUGLE CORPS COMPETITION, GAMES, RACES, PICNIC, FIREWORKS, ETC. AT BUSINESS DISTRICT, WOLTERS FIELD & SUNSET PARK. (LOCAL). HENRY X ARENBERG, CHMN; HIGHLAND PARK BICENTENNIAL COMMISSION, CITY, PARK DISTRICT & JAYCEES; 1171 LINDEN AVE; HIGHLAND PARK, IL 60035. (#200016-252).

DEC 1 - 2, '76. LA SALLE EXPEDITION II, A HISTORIC RE-ENACTMENT. THIS IS AN AUTHENTIC RE-ENACTMENT OF THE 1681 LASALLE EXPEDITION FROM MONTREAL, CANADA TO NEW ORLEANS, LA WHICH WILL BEGIN TOURING ON AUGUST 11, 1976 AND END ON APRIL 9, 1977. (LOCAL). REID H LEWIS, DIRECTOR; LA SALLE EXPEDITION II; 135 S LA SALLE ST, RM 411; CHICAGO, IL 60690. (#102805-21).

HILLSIDE

MAY 17, '76. AREA SCHOOL BANDS CONCERT. LIVE PERFORMANCE AT PROVISO WEST SCHOOL MALL, WOLF & HARRISON. (LOCAL). EDWARD J MCGORRY, CHMN; LINDOP SCHOOL; 2400 S 18TH AVE; BROADVIEW, IL 60153. (#105416-1).

MAY 20, '76. ECUMENICAL CHURCH CHOIR CONCERT. MINISTERS AND CHOIRS FROM COMMUNTIY COMBINE TO PRESENT PROGRAM OF RELIGIOUS AND PATRIOTIC SONGS INDIVIDUALLY AND COLLECTIVELY. ALSO: INSPIRATIONAL COMMENTS BY MINISTERS. AUDIENCE WILL PARTICIPATE IN SEVERAL NUMBERS. AT ST DOMITILLA CATHOLIC CHURCH, 4940 WASHINGTON ST. (LOCAL). MRS HELEN GRECO, CHAIRMAN; HILLSIDE BICENTENNIAL COMMISSION AND CHURCHES OF HILLSIDE; 4856 WASHINGTON ST; HILLSIDE, IL 60162. (#107121-1).

HINSDALE

MAR 24, '76. HINSDALE BICENTENNIAL MUSIC FESTIVAL. LIVE PERFORMANCE AT HINSDALE CENTRAL HIGH SCHOOL AUDITORIUM. (LOCAL). DAVID L GOSSARD, DIR; HINSDALE BICENTENNIAL COMMISSION; 19 E CHICAGO AVE; HINSDALE, IL 60521. (#200016-238).

HOFFMAN ESTS

BICENTENNIAL BIKEWAYS PROJECT. INITIAL EDUCATION IN THE LAWFUL OPERATION OF BICYCLES, MARKING OF STREETS & CONSTRUCTION OF BIKEWAYS ALONG HIGHWAYS TO CONNECT WITH A COUNTY-WIDE PROGRAM. (LOCAL). RICHARD REGAN, CHAIRMAN; PLANS COMMISSION, VILLAGE OF HOFFMAN ESTATES; 1200 N GANNON DR; HOFFMAN ESTS, IL 60194. (#32332).

BICENTENNIAL COMMEMORATIVE MEDALLION - IL. DESIGN CONTEST WAS OPEN TO JR AND SR HIGH SCHOOL STUDENTS. 1,000 MEDALLIONS WERE CAST. ALL PROFITS FROM MEDALLION SALES WILL BENEFIT THE FARMHOUSE RESTORATION PROJECT. (LOCAL). MARILYN R LIND, CHAIRMAN; HOFFMAN ESTATES BICENTENNIAL COMMITTEE; 172 HARPER LANE; HOFFMAN EST, IL 60195. (#33611).

BICENTENNIAL FILM FESTIVAL IN HOFFMAN ESTATES, IL. ONCE A MONTH SHOWING OF AMERICAN FILMS INCLUDING SILENTS, CARTOONS, COMEDY, DRAMA, MUSICALS & HORROR; EACH FILM REPRESENTS A CLASSIC IN DIRECTION OR CONTENT. (LOCAL). MARILYN R LIND, CHAIRMAN; HOFFMAN ESTATES BICENTENNIAL COMMITTEE; HOFFMAN EST, IL 60195. (#33167).

HOFFMAN-SCHAUMBURG TOWN MEETING '76. A ONE DAY COMMUNITY FORUM HELD WITH COMMUNITY LEADERS & ICA TRAINING --HOFFMAN ESTATES & SCHAUMBURG RESIDENTS OF ALL AGES MET TO DISCUSS MUTUAL COMMUNITY PROBLEMS & OFFERED POSSIBLE WAYS OF OVERCOMING THEM. AT HOFFMAN ESTATES HIGH SCHOOL 1100 HIGGINS RD. (LOCAL). TERRY PARKE; HOFFMAN ESTS-SCHAUMBURG BICENT COMM & ROTARY & LWV; 1990 N HOLBROOK; HOFFMAN ESTS, IL 60195. (#200016-359).

RESTORATION OF 120 YEAR OLD FARMHOUSE & GROUNDS. SUPPORT FROM VOLUNTEERS, CIVIC ORGANIZATIONS & LOCAL GOVERNMENT WILL AID IN THE ESTABLISHMENT OF A SOURCE OF HISTORIC PRESERVATION & EDUCATION NOW LACKING IN THE COMMUNITY. (LOCAL). MARILYN R LINO, PRES; POPULAR CREEK HISTORICAL SOCIETY OF HOFFMAN ESTATES; 172 HARPER LANE; HOFFMAN ESTS, IL 60195. (#32331).

SEPT 6 - 7, '75. 'THE DRUNKARD' A 19TH CENTURY MELODRAMA SET TO MUSIC. LIVE PERFORMANCE AT VOGELEI BARN PLAYHOUSE 605 W HIGGINS RD. (LOCAL). MARILYN R LIND; THE COUNTRY PLAYERS & HOFFMAN ESTATES BICENTENNIAL COMMITTEE; 172 HARPER LN; HOFFMAN ESTS, IL 60195. (#200016-361).

JAN 16 - 17, '76. HOFFMAN HALLMARK CHORUS: BICENTENNIAL CONCERT. LIVE PERFORMANCE AT HOFFMAN ESTATES HIGH SCHOOL AUDITORIUM 1200 W HIGGINS RD H E. (LOCAL). MARILYN R LIND; HOFFMAN HALLMARK CHORUS & HOFFMAN ESTATES BICENTENNIAL COMMITTEE; 172 HARPER LN; HOFFMAN ESTS, IL 60195. (#200016-360).

JULY 3 - 5, '76. OLD FASHIONED FOURTH OF JULY. SAT EVE-A BICENTENNIAL 'BIRTHDAY PARTY' DINNER DANCE. SUNDAY EVE-A DRUM CORPS COMPETITION & FIREWORKS DISPLAY. MONDAY MORN-A PARADE FOLLOWED BY DAY LONG EVENTS INCL A HORSE SHOW, RACES, GAMES, SQUARE DANCING, BINGO, MUSIC & REFRESHMENTS. AT MOON LAKE REC HALL, CONANT HS STADIUM, OLD VILLAGE HALL. (LOCAL). MARILYN R LIND; HOFFMAN ESTATES 4TH OF JULY & BICENTENNIAL COMMITTEES; 172 HARPER LANE; HOFFMAN ESTS, IL 60195. (#200016-297).

HOMER

HISTORICAL SOCIETY MUSEUM - HOMER, IL. MUSEUM TO HOUSE ITEMS PERTAINING TO HOMER HISTORY. (LOCAL). BOBBIE NEWLIN, CO-CHAIRMAN; HOMER BICENTENNIAL COMMITTEE; 208 W 2ND ST; HOMER, IL 61849. (#31740).

JAN 11 - 14, '76. ANTIQUE PARLOR & KITCHEN. ANTIQUES DATING 100 YR & LOANED BY AREA RESIDENTS WERE ON DISPLAY. AT VILLAGE HALL, 1ST & MAIN. (LOCAL). BOBBIE NEWLIN, CO-CHMN; HOMER BICENTENNIAL COMMITTEE; 208 N 2ND ST; HOMER, IL 61849. (#200016-386).

APR 4 - 11, '76. BICENTENNIAL CRAFTS, OLD & NEW. 32 OLD & NEW CRAFTS WERE DEMONSTRATED ON APRIL 4TH; ALSO THERE WERE FREE REFRESHMENTS AND A GREAT DEAL OF FELLOWSHIP. AT VILLAGE HALL. (LOCAL). NONOUS WAKEFIELD, COORD; HOMER BICENTENNIAL COMMITTEE; ELLEN ST; HOMER, IL 61849. (#200016-387).

JULY 4, '76. ANNUAL FREEDOM DAY CELEBRATION. ALL DAY CELEBRATION - UNION CHURCH SERVICES WITH A CHOIR, FIREWORKS, FLAG-RAISING CEREMONY, FOOD & GAMES & DANCE.

HOMER — CONTINUED

AT HOMER VILLAGE PARK. (LOCAL). EVERETT WALTERS, COORD; HOMER RECREATION BOARD; 2ND ST; HOMER, IL 61849. (#200016-383).

SEPT 11 - 18, '76. INDIAN ARTIFACTS. INDIAN ARTIFACTS FOUND BY LOCAL RESIDENTS IN HOMER CITY WERE PLACED ON EXHIBIT. AT VILLAGE HALL, 1ST & MAIN STS. (LOCAL). BOBBIE NEWLIN, CO-CHMN; HOMER BICENTENNIAL COMMITTEE; 208 W 2ND ST; HOMER, IL 61849. (#200016-384).

OCT 17 - 30, '76. ANTIQUE DINING ROOM & BEDROOM EXHIBIT. ANTIQUE FURNITURE LOANED BY AREA RESIDENTS FOR THIS SPECIAL EXHIBIT. SLIDES OF HOMER CITY CENTENNIAL IN 1955 SHOWN, 10/17. AT VILLAGE HALL, 1ST & MAIN ST. (LOCAL). BOBBIE NEWLIN, CO-CHMN; HOMER BICENTENNIAL COMMITTEE; 208 W 2ND ST; HOMER, IL 61849. (#200016-385).

HOMEWOOD

EXHIBIT ON THE HISTORY OF HOMEWOOD, IL. THE PROJECT INCLUDES A PHOTOGRAPHIC EXHIBITION, A BOOK ABOUT THE HISTORIC SITES OF THE AREA AND A BUILDING FOR USE AS A MUSEUM. (LOCAL). MS PEGGY BOIVIN, COORDINATOR; HOMEWOOD CITIZENS BICENTENNIAL COMMISSION; 2020 CHESTNUT RD; HOMEWOOD, IL 60430. (#9525).

HOMEWOOD, ILLINOIS, BICENTENNIAL COMMISSION WEEK. A WEEK OF FESTIVITIES LEADING UP TO PRESENTATION OF THE ARBA CHARTER AND ARBA FLAG. (LOCAL). LUCILLE SALVATO, SECRETARY; HOMEWOOD BICENTENNIAL COMMISSION; VILLAGE HALL, 2020 CHESNUT RD; HOMEWOOD, IL 60430. (#6498).

FEB 17, '75. CHERRY PIE BAKING AND EATING CONTEST. HOMEWOOD, ILLINOIS, BICENTENNIAL COMMISSION WEEK. A WEEK OF FESTIVITIES LEADING UP TO PRESENTATION OF THE ARBA CHARTER AND ARBA FLAG. (LOCAL). LUCILLE SALVATO; HOMEWOOD BICENTENNIAL COMMISSION; VILLAGE HALL, 2020 CHESNUT RD; HOMEWOOD, IL 60430. (#6498-501).

FEB 18, '75. SCHOOL DISTRICT'S CIRCUS CLUB PRESENTATION. HOMEWOOD, ILLINOIS, BICENTENNIAL COMMISSION WEEK. A WEEK OF FESTIVITIES LEADING UP TO PRESENTATION OF THE ARBA CHARTER AND ARBA FLAG. (LOCAL). LUCILLE SALVATO; HOMEWOOD BICENTENNIAL COMMISSION; VILLAGE HALL, 2020 CHESNUT RD; HOMEWOOD, IL 60430. (#6498-502).

FEB 19, '75. HOMEWOOD-FLOSSMOOR HIGH SCHOOL'S VIKING ENSEMBLE. HOMEWOOD, ILLINOIS, BICENTENNIAL COMMISSION WEEK. A WEEK OF FESTIVITIES LEADING UP TO PRESENTATION OF THE ARBA CHARTER AND ARBA FLAG. (LOCAL). LUCILLE SALVATO; HOMEWOOD BICENTENNIAL COMMISSION; VILLAGE HALL, 2020 CHESNUT RD; HOMEWOOD, IL 60430. (#6498-503).

FEB 20, '75. A MUSICAL PROGRAM AND A CHILDREN'S PUPPET SHOW. HOMEWOOD, ILLINOIS, BICENTENNIAL COMMISSION WEEK. A WEEK OF FESTIVITIES LEADING UP TO PRESENTATION OF THE ARBA CHARTER AND ARBA FLAG. (LOCAL). LUCILLE SALVATO; HOMEWOOD BICENTENNIAL COMMISSION; VILLAGE HALL, 2020 CHESNUT RD; HOMEWOOD, IL 60430. (#6498-504).

FEB 21, '75. BARBERSHOP SINGING. HOMEWOOD, ILLINOIS, BICENTENNIAL COMMISSION WEEK. A WEEK OF FESTIVITIES LEADING UP TO PRESENTATION OF THE ARBA CHARTER AND ARBA FLAG. (LOCAL). LUCILLE SALVATO; HOMEWOOD BICENTENNIAL COMMISSION; VILLAGE HALL, 2020 CHESNUT RD; HOMEWOOD, IL 60430. (#6498-505).

FEB 22, '75. NAVY BAND, CHOIR & CONCERT WITH HENRY MANCINI. HOMEWOOD, ILLINOIS, BICENTENNIAL COMMISSION WEEK. A WEEK OF FESTIVITIES LEADING UP TO PRESENTATION OF THE ARBA CHARTER AND ARBA FLAG. (LOCAL). LUCILLE SALVATO; HOMEWOOD BICENTENNIAL COMMISSION; VILLAGE HALL, 2020 CHESNUT RD; HOMEWOOD, IL 60430. (#6498-506).

MAR 8 - 9, '75. ORIGINAL ARTS AND CRAFTS SHOW. BICENTENNIAL ARTS & CRAFTS SHOW IN ILLINOIS. AN ORIGINAL ARTS & CRAFTS SHOW WILL BE HELD IN HOMEWOOD TO CELEBRATE THE BICENTENNIAL. (LOCAL). LUCILLE SALVATO; HOMEWOOD BICENTENNIAL COMMISSION; 2020 CHESTNUT RD; HOMEWOOD, IL 60430. (#6499-501).

HUDSON

JULY 4, '76. HUDSON COLONY DAY. EXHIBIT, FESTIVAL, PARADE, LIVE PERFORMANCE AT HUDSON GRADE SCHOOL. (LOCAL). JAMES J HAMM, CHAIRMAN; HUDSON BICENTENNIAL COMMISSION; 101 S BROADWAY; HUDSON, IL 61748. (#104063-1).

HULL

COMMUNITY CENTER PROJECT IN HULL, IL. HULL BUILT A COMMUNITY CENTER. (LOCAL). IVAN WHARTON, DIRECTOR; PIKE COUNTY BICENTENNIAL COMMISSION; HULL, IL 62343. (#33610).

HUME

MAY 10 - 14, '76. SHILOH SCHOOL BICENTENNIAL ACTIVITIES WEEK. SPECIAL ACTIVITIES WILL BE FEATURED EACH DAY: FIELD DAY, MAY 11TH, SKITS, MAY 12TH & FESTIVAL, MAY 14TH. (LOCAL). DR WILLIAM J BACH, SUPT; SHILOH SCHOOL; RR #1; HUME, IL 61932. (#105116-1).

JULY 4, '76. BICENTENNIAL FESTIVAL. FESTIVAL. (LOCAL). RUSSELL GRAFTON, CHMN; HUME BICENTENNIAL COMMISSION; HUME, IL 61932. (#200016-89).

HUNTLEY

HISTORY OF HUNTLEY, IL, 1830 - 1976. THE HISTORY OF HUNTLEY, IL, 1830 TO 1976, WILL BE RESEARCHED & PUBLISHED. (STWIDE). LOUISE KREUTZER, CHAIRMAN; HUNTLEY 125TH ANNIVERSARY COMMITTEE & HUNTLEY BICENTENNIAL; 203 E MAIN ST, PO BOX 53; HUNTLEY, IL 60142. (#16335).

AUG 14 - 15, '76. HUNTLEY, ILLINOIS: 125TH ANNIVERSARY. 2-DAY CELEBRATION BEGINNING WITH PARADE-BAND CONTEST-DANCE ON SATURDAY, 8-14-76 & THE HOMECOMING PICNIC ENTERTAINMENT AND SPEAKERS ON SUNDAY. THERE WILL BE DEDICATION OF NEW GYM AT HIGH SCHOOL ANTIQUE SHOW AND OTHER PUBLIC DISPLAYS DURING BOTH DAYS. (LOCAL). LOUISE KREUTZER; HUNTLEY 125TH ANNIVERSARY AND BICENTENNIAL COMMITTEES; 203 E MAIN, PO BOX 53; HUNTLEY, IL 60142. (#16335-1).

INA

SEPT 26, '75. SQUARE DANCE & ICE CREAM SOCIAL. AMERICAN SQUARE DANCING & OLD FASHIONED ICE CREAM SOCIAL. (LOCAL). DR RICHARD DOHERTY, CHMN; REND LAKE COLLEGE BICENTENNIAL ORGANIZATION; REND LAKE COLLEGE; INA, IL 62846. (#102018-1).

SEPT 27, '75. FUN FAIR. ANTIQUE SHOW, GAMES & ACTIVITIES; LUNCH SERVED BY 4H CLUB, DOUBLEHEADER BASEBALL GAME WITH COLLEGE TEAM PLAYING SOUTHWESTERN. (LOCAL). RICHARD DOHERTY, CHAIRMAN; REND LAKE COLLEGE BICENTENNIAL; REND LAKE COLLEGE; INA, IL 62846. (#102019-1).

FEB 7, '76. RURITAN BICENTENNIAL PANCAKE & SAUSAGE DAY. FESTIVAL AT JEFFERSON COUNTY RURAL FIRE DEPARTMENT, RURITAN CLUBROOM. (LOCAL). MRS ED STEVENS, CHMN; INA RURITAN CLUB; BOX 112; INA, IL 62846. (#200016-35).

JULY 4, '76. BICENTENNIAL CONCERT. LIVE PERFORMANCE AT LITTLE THEATER. (LOCAL). RICHARD DOHERTY, CHAIRMAN; REND LAKE COLLEGE BICENTENNIAL COMMITTEE; REND LAKE COLLEGE; INA, IL 62846. (#102016-1).

INDUSTRY

JULY 16 - 18, '76. INDUSTRY BICENTENNIAL CELEBRATION. CEREMONY, COMPETITION, FESTIVAL AT MAIN STREET. (LOCAL). JAMIE TROTTER, CHMN; INDUSTRY BICENTENNIAL COMMITTEE; INDUSTRY, IL 61440. (#106217-1).

ITASCA

AMERICAN FLAG FLOWER GARDEN IN ITASCA, IL. RED, WHITE & BLUE FLOWERS PLANTED IN A FLAG MOTIF. (LOCAL). LORRAINE KRASINSKI, PROJECT CHAIRMAN; ITASCA GARDEN CLUB; 451 S MAPLE; ITASCA, IL 60143. (#33000).

BICENTENNIAL QUILT IN ITASCA, IL. QUILT W/BUILDINGS AND OBJECTS IMPORTANT TO THE TOWN. (LOCAL). MRS GERALD DANZER, COORDINATOR; BICENTENNIAL COMMITTEE OF ITASCA; 200 S WALNUT; ITASCA, IL 60143. (#33609).

BOOK OF ITASCA HISTORY, IL. A BOOK ON LOCAL HISTORY HAS BEEN COMPILED. (LOCAL). GLENN MENSCHING, DIRECTOR; ITASCA STATE BANK; 308 W IRVING PK RD; ITASCA, IL 60143. (#33358).

PAINTING OF HYDRANTS IN ITASCA, IL. FIRE HYDRANTS WILL BE PAINTED RED, WHITE & BLUE. (LOCAL). MARIE BURTON, ART COMMITTEE CHAIRMAN; BICENTENNIAL COMMITTEE OF ITASCA; 428 BONNIE BRAE; ITASCA, IL 60143. (#33001).

SAVING THE 100-YEAR-OLD TRAIN STATION: ITASCA, IL. RE-LOCATION & PRESERVATION OF THE STATION FOR USE AS A MUSEUM. (LOCAL). HAROLD OLLMANN, PRESIDENT; ITASCA AREA HISTORICAL SOCIETY; 525 W DIVISION; ITASCA, IL 60143. (#33002).

SLIDE PRESENTATION AND SCRIPT IN ITASCA, IL. ITASCA HISTORY IS THE SUBJECT OF A SLIDE PRESENTATION W/SCRIPT. (LOCAL). BARBARA F SMITH, COORDINATOR; ITASCA AREA HISTORICAL SOCIETY; 345 S CHERRY; ITASCA, IL 60143. (#33359).

FEB 12, '76. BICENTENNIAL DANCE. PRESENTATION OF QUILT; JUDGING OF BEARD CONTEST & COSTUMES. AT ITASCA COUNTRY CLUB, WALNUT AND ORCHARD. (LOCAL). BARBARA F SMITH, CHMN; ITASCA BICENTENNIAL COMMITTEE; 345 S CHERRY; ITASCA, IL 60143. (#200016-427).

APR 8 - 9, '76. PAGEANT ON NATIONAL & LOCAL HISTORY. LIVE PERFORMANCE AT F E PEACOCK JUNIOR HIGH, 301 E NORTH. (LOCAL). MRS ANN LESHER, CHMN; ITASCA PUBLIC SCHOOL DISTRICT; 6 N 450 NEVA; ITASCA, IL 60143. (#200016-428).

MAY 1, '76. TOWN MEETING OF '76. CONFERENCE AT ITASCA HOLIDAY INN, 860 W IRVING PARK RD. (LOCAL). BILL ELSBERG, CHMN; ITASCA JAYCEES; 464 S MAPLE; ITASCA, IL 60143. (#200016-429).

MAY 29, '76. MEMORIAL DAY PARADE. PARADE AT WALNUT STREET. (LOCAL). ED SCHUBLE, COORDINATOR; LYONS CLUB; 343 S HOME; ITASCA, IL 60143. (#200016-430).

JUNE 4, '76. JUNIOR HIGH SCHOOL OUT-DOOR BAND CONCERT & ICE CREAM SOCIAL. LIVE PERFORMANCE, FESTIVAL AT VILLAGE GREEN. (LOCAL). BARBARA F SMITH, CHMN; PUBLIC SCHOOLS, MARINERS, BICENTENNIAL COMMITTEE OF ITASCA; 345 S CHERRY; ITASCA, IL 60143. (#200016-431).

JULY 4, '76. JULY 4TH BIRTHDAY PARTY. DEDICATION OF ITASCA ROOM IN LIBRARY, RINGING OF BELLS, FIREWORKS, COMMUNITY WORSHIP SERVICE, GAMES, CONTESTS. AT WASHINGTON PARK. (LOCAL). BARBARA F SMITH, CHMN; VILLAGE BOARD, LYONS CLUB & BICENTENNIAL COMMITTEE OF ITASCA; 345 S CHERRY; ITASCA, IL 60143. (#200016-432).

AUG 15, '76. ART FAIR. FAIR AT VILLAGE GREEN, 100 W IRVING PARK RD. (LOCAL). BETH ZWOLFER, COORD; JUNIOR WOMEN'S CLUB; 613 IRMAN DR; WOOD DALE, IL 60191. (#200016-433).

SEPT 5, '76. PORK ROAST & SWEET CORN DINNER WITH STREET DANCE. FESTIVAL AT BEN'S TAVERN, LINE ST & IRVING PARK RD. (LOCAL). RED BENHART, COORD; LIONS CLUB & BUSINESS ASSOCIATION; 518 N WALNUT; ITASCA, IL 60143. (#200016-434).

JACKSONVILLE

BICENTENNIAL GROVE OF TREES - JACKSONVILLE, IL. LANDSCAPING OF NEW EDUCATIONAL COMPLEX AND PLANTING OF A BICENTENNIAL GROVE OF TREES. (LOCAL). DR R BURNETTE, CHAIRPERSON; EDUCATION COMPLEX DEDICATION COMMITTEE, MACMURRAY COLLEGE; JACKSONVILLE, IL 62650. (#23403).

NATIONAL & INTERNATIONAL BASKETBALL GAMES - IL. THE AMATEUR BASKETBALL ASSOC OF THE USA IS SPONSORING NATIONAL P INTERNATIONAL BASKETBALL GAMES. (INT'L). WILLIAM WALL, CHAIRMAN; AMATEUR BASKETBALL ASSOC OF THE USA; PO BOX 297; JACKSONVILLE, IL 62651. (#27939).

PERMANENT MUSEUM OF JACKSONVILLE, ILL. THE ESTABLISHMENT OF A MUSEUM IN OUR CITY OF ALL ITS HISTORY. HOPEFULLY ESTABLISHED IN THE DOWNTOWN AREA. (LOCAL). BOB CHIPMAN, SECRETARY; COMMITTEE FOR THE BICENTENNIAL & JACKSONVILLE SESQUICENTENNIAL; 200 W DOUGLAS; JACKSONVILLE, IL 62650. (#2577).

RESTORATION OF GOVERNOR DUNCAN'S HOME IN IL. HOME, OWNED BY DAR, RESTORED FOR BICENTENNIAL TO PERIOD DECOR. (LOCAL). DON ROBINSON, CHAIRMAN; MORGAN COUNTY BICENTENNIAL COMMISSION; 834 N CHURCH ST; JACKSONVILLE, IL 62650. (#32999).

RESTORATION OF JACKSONVILLE, ILL CITY RECORDS. REPAIR, RESTORATION, BINDING, INDEXING & MICROFILMING OF CITY RECORDS WHICH HAVE BEEN MAINTAINED SINCE 1834. ABOUT 11,000 PAGES WILL BE BOUND & AVAILABLE TO THE PUBLIC. (LOCAL). VERNON R Q FERNANDES, CHAIRMAN; COMMITTEE FOR THE BICENTENNIAL & THE JACKSONVILLE SESQUICENTENNI; MUNICIPAL BLDG, 200 DOUGLAS; JACKSONVILLE, IL 62650. (#4883). **ARBA GRANTEE.**

JULY 5, '75. 200TH YEAR OPENING. FESTIVAL AT JACKSONVILLE CENTRAL PARK PLAZA. (LOCAL). R E CHIPMAN; COMMITTEE FOR THE BICENTENNIAL AND JACKSONVILLE SESQUICENTENNIAL; 200 W STATE; JACKSONVILLE, IL 62650. (#50056-1).

SEPT 12 - 14, '75. PORTUGUESE ETHNIC CELEBRATION. FESTIVAL, EXHIBIT AT CITYWIDE. (LOCAL). MRS GEORGE W DAVIS; PORTUGUESE SESQUICENTENNIAL COMMITTEE; 928 NORTH WEST; JACKSONVILLE, IL 62650. (#50546-1).

MAR 7, '76. BICENTENNIAL CONCERT. LIVE PERFORMANCE AT EDUCATION COMPLEX. (LOCAL). DR HENRY BUSCHE, COORD; MACMURRAY CONCERT BAND, MACMURRAY COLLEGE; JACKSONVILLE, IL 62650. (#200016-34).

MAR 12 - 14, '76. THEATRICAL PRODUCTION. LIVE PERFORMANCE AT COLLEGE THEATRE. (LOCAL). DR EUGENE LAURENT, COORD; MACMURRAY COLLEGE THEATRE; JACKSONVILLE, IL 62650. (#200016-33).

MAR 16, '76. BICENTENNIAL PROGRAM OF AMERICAN ART SONGS. LIVE PERFORMANCE AT MERNER CHAPEL. (LOCAL). DON ROBINSON, CHMN; MORGAN COUNTY BICENTENNIAL COMMISSION; 834 N CHURCH; JACKSONVILLE, IL 62650. (#200016-125).

APR 10 - 11, '76. ANNUAL ART FAIR DEDICATED TO THE BICENTENNIAL. FAIR. (LOCAL). DON ROBINSON, CHMN; MORGAN COUNTY BICENTENNIAL COMMISSION; 834 N CHURCH; JACKSONVILLE, IL 62650. (#200016-121).

APR 28 - JULY 28, '76. BICENTENNIAL TRAVELOGUE - AMERICA ON PARADE, 1776-1976. EXHIBIT. (LOCAL). DON ROBINSON, CHMN; JACKSONVILLE KIWANIS CLUB; 834 N CHURCH; JACKSONVILLE, IL 62650. (#200016-124).

APR 30 - MAY 2, '76. 'THE DEVIL AND DANIEL WEBSTER' PLAY. LIVE PERFORMANCE. (LOCAL). DON ROBINSON, CHMN; MORGAN COUNTY BICENTENNIAL COMMISSION; 834 N CHURCH; JACKSONVILLE, IL 62650. (#200016-123).

JULY 3 - 4, '76. INDEPENDENCE DAY CELEBRATION. FESTIVAL. (LOCAL). DON ROBINSON, CHMN; MORGAN COUNTY BICENTENNIAL COMMISSION; 834 N CHURCH; JACKSONVILLE, IL 62650. (#200016-122).

JULY 24 - 29, '76. NATIONAL 2-MAN RAILROAD HANDCAR CHAMPIONSHIPS. COMPETITION AT MORGAN COUNTY ILLINOIS CITY HALL JACKSONVILLE ILL. (REGN'L). DANIEL FOTH; BICENTENNIAL & JACKSONVILLE SESQUICENTENNIAL COMMITTEE; MUNICIPAL BUILDING 200 W DOUGLAS; JACKSONVILLE, IL 62650. (#50227-1).

OCT 30, '76. SALUTE TO AMERICA. LIVE PERFORMANCE AT MERNER CHAPEL. (LOCAL). DON ROBINSON, CHMN; MACMURRAY COLLEGE; 834 N CHURCH; JACKSONVILLE, IL 62650. (#200016-120).

NOV 11, '76. WW II MEMORIAL DEDICATION. CEREMONY. (LOCAL). DON ROBINSON, CHMN; JACKSONVILLE BICENTENNIAL COMMISSION; 834 N CHURCH; JACKSONVILLE, IL 62650. (#109478-1).

JERSEYVILLE

'FIRSTS OF AMERICA' - JERSEYVILLE, IL. PAGEANT WITH CAST OF 300 FEATURING FAMOUS FIRSTS IN AMER HISTORY GIVEN AT JERSEY COUNTY FAIRGROUNDS. (LOCAL). PAUL MILLER, CHAIRMAN; JERSEY COUNTY BICENTENNIAL COMMISSION; 105 N WASHINGTON; JERSEYVILLE, IL 62052. (#30391).

JOHNSTON CITY

JULY 1 - 4, '76. JOHNSTON CITY HOMECOMING CELEBRATION. PIONEER DAY, SQUARE DANCING, FOLK MUSIC, DAYLIGHT FIREWORKS, BICENTENNIAL QUEEN CONTEST; AWARD $1200 U S SAVINGS BONDS, NIGHT FIREWORKS. AT CITY PARK. (LOCAL). ETHEL ASHBY, CHAIRMAN; JOHNSTON CITY LIONS CLUB; 214 WASHINGTON ST; JOHNSTON CITY, IL 62918. (#102174-1).

JOLIET

'BRINGING THE BICENTENNIAL INTO YOUR CLASSROOM'. SEMINAR. (LOCAL). DR ARNOLD GOOD, DIRECTOR; COLLEGE OF ST FRANCIS; 500 N WILCOX ST; JOLIET, IL 60435. (#101180-1). **(??).**

FILM 'HAPPY BIRTHDAY USA' OF WILL COUNTY, ILLINOIS. 22-MINUTE FILM OF 65 SLIDES TAPED WITH NARRATION AND MUSIC DEPICTING HISTORY FROM 1776 TO PRESENT DAY IN WILL COUNTY. SIX SETS AVAILABLE FREE TO SCHOOLS & GROUPS. (LOCAL). MRS WILLIAM C LIMACHER, CHAIRMAN; WILL COUNTY BICENTENNIAL COMMITTEE; 14 W JEFFERSON - ROOM 300; JOLIET, IL 60431. (#6323).

GROWTH OF COLLEGE OF ST FRANCIS IN 50 YEARS - IL. 3-YEAR AND 4-YEAR DEGREE PROGRAMS, REORGANIZATION OF ACADEMIC PROGRAMS AND A NEW GOVERNANCE STRUCTURE. (LOCAL). TOM BRUNICK, PROJ DIRECTOR; COLLEGE OF ST FRANCIS; 500 N WILCOX; JOLIET, IL 60435. (#13585).

PLAY COMMEMORATING 50TH ANNIVERSARY OF COLLEGE. LIVE PERFORMANCE AT TOWER HALL. (LOCAL). DAN MCCARTER, DIRECTOR; COLLEGE OF ST FRANCIS; 500 N WILCOX ST; JOLIET, IL 60435. (#101179-1). **(??).**

TEACHING STRATEGIES: HISTORY OF WILL COUNTY, ILL. TEACHING STRATEGY FOR SOCIAL STUDIES TEACHERS INCLUDING LESSON PLANS & PICTURES, MAINLY FOR JUNIOR & SENIOR HIGH TEACHERS' USE DURING MARCH, 1975, DESIGNATED AS WILL COUNTY MONTH. (LOCAL). MRS WILLIAM C LIMACHER, CHAIRMAN; WILL COUNTY BICENTENNIAL COMMITTEE; 14 W JEFFERSON - ROOM 300; JOLIET, IL 60431. (#6322).

WILL-JOLIET BICENTENNIAL MEMORIAL & CULTURAL PARK. CREATION OF AN OUTDOOR RECREATION AREA WITH A BICENTENNIAL THEME. (LOCAL). MRS WILLIAM C LIMACHER, PRESIDENT; WILL-JOLIET BICENTENNIAL PARK, INC; 14 W JEFFERSON ST, ROOM 300; JOLIET, IL 60431. (#8625). **ARBA RECOGNIZED. ARBA GRANTEE.**

1878 HISTORY OF WILL COUNTY, ILLINOIS. REPRINT OF 1878 HISTORY OF WILL COUNTY, ILLINOIS. INDEX ADDED. (LOCAL). MRS WILLIAM LIMACHER, CHAIRMAN; WILL COUNTY BICENTENNIAL COMMISSION; 14 W JEFFERSON ST; JOLIET, IL 60431. (#537).

OCT 5, '75. OPEN HOUSE HISTORICAL ART AND DRAMA - WITH PATRIOTIC MUSIC PROGRAM. EXHIBIT, LIVE PERFORMANCE AT TOWER HALL, 500 N WILCOX ST. (LOCAL). TOM BRUNICK, DIRECTOR; COLLEGE OF ST FRANCIS; 500 N WILCOX ST; JOLIET, IL 60436. (#101177-1).

NOV 11, '75. WILL COUNTY BICENTENNIAL MARATHON. COMPETITION. (LOCAL). TOM BRUNICK, DIRECTOR; COLLEGE OF ST FRANCIS; 500 N WILCOX ST; JOLIET, IL 60436. (#101178-1).

NOV 11, '75. WORLD RUNNING MARATHON, 26 MILES, THROUGH JOLIET TO NEW PARK. LONG DISTANCE MARATHON ON 26 MILE COURSE THRU JOLIET TO THE NEW BICENTENNIAL PARK. COURSE TO BE CERTIFIED BY THE WORLD MARATON ASSOC, AMATEUR UNION & US TRACK & FIELD ASSOC. AWARDS FOR EACH FINISHER. AT AT THE WILL JOLIET BICENTENNIAL PARK. (ST-WIDE). MRS WILLIAM C LIMACHER; WILL COUNTY BICENTENNIAL COMMISSION; 14 W JEFFERSON STREET; JOLIET, IL 60431. (#1716-1).

SEPT 11 - 12, '76. UNITED STATES ARMED FORCES BICENTENNIAL CARAVAN. CARAVAN IS COMPOSED OF EXHIBIT VANS FOR EACH MILITARY SERVICE. PROJECT THEME IS 'HISTORY OF THE ARMED FORCES & THEIR CONTRIBUTIONS TO THE NATION.'. (LOCAL). MRS WILLIAM LIMACHER, DIR; UNITED STATES ARMED FORCES BICENTENNIAL CARAVAN; WILL COUNTY COURTHOUSE; JOLIET, IL 60431. (#1775-645).

JUBILEE

JUNE 12 - 13, '76. 'OLD ENGLISH FAIRE'. A MEDIEVAL FAIR CELEBRATES THE ENGLISH HERITAGE BEHIND AN EARLY ILLINOIS EDUCATIONAL INSTITUTION. AT JUBILEE COLLEGE STATE PARK. (LOCAL). PHYLLIS EUBANKS, COORD; ILLINOIS DEPARTMENT OF CONSERVATION; 605 STATE OFFICE BLDG; SPRINGFIELD, IL 62706. (#103416-364).

KANKAKEE

'AMERICA SOUNDS GREAT', DRAMA AT NAZARENE COL, IL. AN ORIGINAL DRAMA TO BE TITLED 'AMERICA SOUNDS GREAT' ON THE SOUNDS OF AMERICA. TO BE CREATED BY MEMBERS OF OLIVET NAZARENE COLLEGE SPEECH & DRAMA DEPTS. THE DRAMA WILL BE VIDEO TAPED. (ST-WIDE). DR JOSEPH NIELSON, CHAIRMAN; OLIVET NAZARENE COLLEGE BICENTENNIAL COMMITTEE; KANKAKEE, IL 60901. (#6684).

HISTORY OF OLIVET NAZARENE COLLEGE, PROJECT IN IL. DOCUMENTARY FILM OF HISTORY OF OLIVET NAZARENE COLLEGE DESIGNED TO EMPHASIZE ROLE OF PRIVATE CHURCH RELATED EDUCATION IN AMERICA. (ST-WIDE). DR JOSEPH NIELSON, CHAIRMAN; OLIVET NAZARENE COLLEGE BICENTENNIAL COMMITTEE; KANKAKEE, IL 60901. (#6681). **(??).**

FEB 1 - 7, '76. PUBLIC LECTURES ON REVOLUTIONARY & CIVIL WARS. PUBLIC LECTURES ON REVOLUTIONARY & CIVIL WARS, IL. OLIVET NAZARENE COLLEGE PROFESSORS WILL PRESENT LECTURES, SUPPLEMENTED BY SLIDES, TO COMMUNITY SERVICE GROUPS AND SCHOOLS ON REVOLUTIONARY & CIVIL WARS. VIDEO-TAPES FOR LOCAL TV. (LOCAL). DR JOSEPH NIELSON; OLIVET NAZARENE COLLEGE BICENTENNIAL COMMITTEE; KANKAKEE, IL 60901. (#6685-501).

FEB 4, '76. OLIVET NAZARENE COLLEGE BUSINESSMEN'S CONFERENCE. BUSINESSMEN'S BICENTENNIAL CONFERENCE IN ILLINOIS. LEADERS IN BUSINESS, GOVERNMENT & LABOR WILL PARTICIPATE IN CONFERENCE ON BUSINESS IN AMERICAN SOCIETY. (LOCAL). DR JOSEPH NIELSON; OLIVET NAZARENE COLLEGE BICENTENNIAL COMMITTEE; KANKAKEE, IL 60901. (#6682-501).

MAR 1 - 7, '76. WERNHER VON BRAUN LECTURES ON SPACE EXPLORATION. WERNHER VON BRAUN ON SPACE EXPLORATION, ILLINOIS. PUBLIC LECTURES WITH SLIDES & FILMS BY DR WERNHER VON BRAUN ON SPACE EXPLORATION & RELATED SCIENTIFIC TOPICS. WILL INCLUDE SESSIONS WITH SCIENCE TEACHERS OF OLIVET NAZARENE COLLEGE, KANKAKEE, ILL. (ST-WIDE). DR JOSEPH NIELSON; OLIVET NAZARENE COLLEGE BICENTENNIAL COMMITTEE; KANKAKEE, IL 60901. (#6686-501).

JULY 4, '76. FESTIVAL OF RELIGIOUS FREEDOM. COMMUNITY WIDE RELIGIOUS SERVICE FOR MEMBERS OF ALL FAITHS TO BE HELD IN OUTDOOR ARENA ON JULY 4, 1976. (LOCAL). DR JOSEPH NIELSON; OLIVET NAZARENE COLLEGE BICENTENNIAL COMMITTEE; KANKAKEE, IL 60901. (#6683-501).

JAN 12 - 13, '77. LA SALLE EXPEDITION II, A HISTORIC RE-ENACTMENT. THIS IS AN AUTHENTIC RE-ENACTMENT OF THE 1681 LASALLE EXPEDITION FROM MONTREAL, CANADA TO NEW ORLEANS, LA WHICH WILL BEGIN TOURING ON AUGUST 11, 1976 AND END ON APRIL 9, 1977. (LOCAL). REID H LEWIS, DIRECTOR; LA SALLE EXPEDITION II; 135 S LA SALLES, ST, RM 411; CHICAGO, IL 60690. (#102805-36).

KASKASKIA

DEDICATION OF BELL IN KASKASKIA, ILLINOIS. MUSIC, SPEAKERS & DEDICATION OF PLAQUE COMMEMORATING BELL OF OLD KASKASKIA & RANDOLPH COUNTY INCLUDING REPRINT OF 1859 MONTEGUE COUNTY HISTORY TO BE SOLD FOR THE FIRST TIME. (LOCAL). DON C WILEY, CHAIRMAN; RANDOLPH COUNTY BICENTENNIAL COMMISSION; RR#1; SPARTA, IL 62286. (#5752).

AUG 31, '75. BARBECUE PORK SAUSAGE CARNIVAL & RECIPES OF OLD KASKASKIA. ALSO FEATURES HISTORICAL BOOKLET RECIPES OF OLD KASKASKIA. (LOCAL). FATHER CARL PIMESKERN; IMMACULATE CONCEPTION CHURCH OF KASKASKIA; R#1 PO ST MARYS MO 63673; KASKASKIA, IL 63673. (#5751-501).

KEITHSBURG

MARK TWAIN WILDLIFE REFUGE NATURE TRAIL - IL. DEVELOPMENT OF NATURE AND CANOE TRAIL THROUGH MARK TWAIN WILDLIFE REFUGE AT KEITHSBURG, ON THE MISSISSIPPI RIVER. (LOCAL). NORMAN BROWN, CHAIRMAN; MERCER COUNTY BICENTENNIAL COMMISSION; ROOM 23, COURTHOUSE; ALEDO, IL 61231. (#30414).

KEWANEE

FRANCIS PARK NATURE TRAILS - KEWANEE, IL. CONSTRUCTION OF NATURE TRAILS IN FRANCIS PARK NEAR KEWANEE. (LOCAL). ROSEMARY KUSTER, COORDINATOR; HENRY COUNTY BICENTENNIAL COMMISSION; RR; KEWANEE, IL 61443. (#30386).

GROUND BREAKING 2000. CEREMONY. (LOCAL). F E STAHL, DEAN; BLACK HAWK COLLEGE, EAST CAMPUS; PO BOX 489; KEWANEE, IL 61443. (#105192-4). **(??).**

HISTORY OF BLACK HAWK EAST AND CAMPUS - IL. A DEVELOPMENTAL HISTORY OF THE CAMPUS AND A HISTORY OF THE SITE ON WHICH CAMPUS IS LOCATED. (LOCAL). F E STAHL, DEAN; BLACK HAWK COLLEGE EAST CAMPUS; PO BOX 489; KEWANEE, IL 61443. (#21131).

THE STATE OF AGRICULTURE IN HENRY COUNTY, IL. A SPECIAL SOCIOLOGICAL, ECONOMIC AND HISTORICAL EXAMINATION OF FARM LIFE IN HENRY COUNTY FOCUSING ON METHODS OF SWINE PRODUCTION. (LOCAL). ELDON AUPPERLE, COORDINATOR; BLACK HAWK EAST AGRICULTURAL CLUB; PO BOX 489; KEWANEE, IL 61443. (#21129).

VETERAN'S MEMORIAL PARK - KEWANEE, IL. CONSTRUCTION OF VETERAN'S MEMORIAL PARK IN KEWANEE. (LOCAL). FRED STAHL, CHAIRMAN; KEWANEE BICENTENNIAL COMMISSION; BOX 489; KEWANEE, IL 61443. (#30389).

JAN 5 - DEC 15, '76. BICENTENNIAL THEMATIC MOVIE SERIES. EXHIBIT AT ADULT LEARNING CENTER, #9 BRACKEN'S CENTER. (LOCAL). F E STAHL, DEAN; BLACK HAWK COLLEGE, EAST CAMPUS; 518 ROOSEVELT; KEWANEE, IL 61443. (#105192-6).

JAN 17, '76. TOWN MEETING '76. CONFERENCE. (LOCAL). F E STAHL, DEAN; BLACK HAWK COLLEGE, EAST CAMPUS; 518 ROOSEVELT; KEWANEE, IL 61443. (#105192-2).

APR 20, '76. PAUL REVERE RIDE REENACTMENT. LIVE PERFORMANCE. (LOCAL). F E STAHL, DEAN; BLACK HAWK COLLEGE, EAST CAMPUS; PO BOX 489; KEWANEE, IL 61443. (#105192-5).

MAY 9 - 15, '76. SENIOR CITIZENS FESTIVAL. FESTIVAL. (LOCAL). FRED STAHL, CHMN; HENRY COUNTY BICENTENNIAL COMMISSION; BOX 489; KEWANEE, IL 61443. (#200016-184).

KIRKWOOD

LOG CABIN IN KIRKWOOD, IL. CONSTRUCTION OF A LOG CABIN IN KIRKWOOD PARK. (LOCAL). ED FRANK, COORDINATOR; WARREN COUNTY BICENTENNIAL COMMISSION; KIRKWOOD, IL 61447. (#32998).

MEETING HALL IN KIRKWOOD, IL. KIRKWOOD'S SCOUTS CONSTRUCTED A MEETING HALL. (LOCAL). ED FRANK, COORDINATOR; WARREN COUNTY BICENTENNIAL COMMISSION; KIRKWOOD, IL 61447. (#32997).

KNOXVILLE

NEWMAN SCHOOL RESTORATION IN KNOXVILLE, IL. RESTORATION AND RELOCATION OF NEWMAN SCHOOL AS PART OF KNOXVILLE HISTORIC SITES DISTRICT. (LOCAL). WILLIAM GOODWIN, COORDINATOR; KNOX COUNTY RETIRED TEACHERS ASSOCIATION; KNOXVILLE, IL 61488. (#32996).

JULY 29 - AUG 3, '75. VISIT OF HISTORY-MOBILE 'ETHNIC HISTORY IN ILLINOIS'. EXHIBIT AT KNOX COUNTY FAIR. (LOCAL). CLIFFORD HAKA, FIELD REP; ILLINOIS STATE HISTORICAL SOCIETY; OLD STATE CAPITOL; SPRINGFIELD, IL 62706. (#200016-514).

SEPT 12 - 14, '75. KNOXVILLE CIVIL WAR DAYS: BATTLE OF STONY HOLLOW. LIVE PERFORMANCE AT STONY HOLLOW BATTLE FIELD. (LOCAL). JERRY CARLTON, COORD; KNOXVILLE BUSINESS ASSOC; 223 E MAIN; KNOXVILLE, IL 61448. (#200016-36).

AUG 3 - 8, '76. KNOX COUNTY FAIR. FAIR. (ST-WIDE). RICHARD SHOVER, SECRETARY; KNOX COUNTY FAIR BOARD; BOX 204; KNOXVILLE, IL 61445. (#106293-1).

SEPT 18 - 19, '76. KNOXVILLE CANTONMENT. LIVE PERFORMANCE. (LOCAL). RONALD HARMS, CHMN; KNOX COUNTY BICENTENNIAL COMMISSION; 125 S CHERRY ST; GALESBURG, IL 61401. (#200016-183).

LA CROSSE

RESTORATION OF HIXON ROSE GARDENS IN LA CROSSE, IL. THE ROSE GARDENS AT THE HISTORIC HIXON HOUSE WILL BE RESTORED TO THEIR ORIGINAL CONDITION. (LOCAL). RENA STUHR, PRESIDENT; MEDARY WOMEN'S GARDEN CLUB; 9262 U S HWY 16; LA CROSSE, WI 54601. (#12355).

LA GRANGE

MAY 30, '75. SENIOR CITIZEN PARTICIPATION IN PARADE IN COLONIAL COSTUME. PARADE. (LOCAL). NINA L EDWARDS; SOUTHWEST SUBURBAN CENTER ON AGING; 111 W HARRIS AVENUE; LA GRANGE, IL 60525. (#50350-2).

JUNE 7, '75. SENIOR CITIZEN PARTICIPATION IN PARADE IN COSTUME. PARADE. (LOCAL). NINA L EDWARDS; SOUTHWEST SUBURBAN CENTER ON AGING; 111 HARRIS AVENUE; LA GRANGE, IL 60525. (#50350-1).

AUG 13, '75. BICENTENNIAL EVENTS FOR SENIOR CITIZENS. ONE SPECIAL BICENTENNIAL EVENT PER MONTH; COLONIAL TEAS FOR LOCAL ORGANIZATIONS, BICENTENNIAL FILMS AND SQUARE DANCING. (LOCAL). NINA L EDWARDS, CHAIRMAN; SOUTHWEST SUBURBAN CENTER ON AGING; 111 W HARRIS AVE; LA GRANGE, IL 60525. (#10153-1).

LA SALLE

CONSTRUCTION OF A BANDSHELL IN PULASKI PARK, IL. CONSTRUCTION OF A BANDSHELL IN PULASKI PARK FOR COMMUNITY USE. (LOCAL). BETTY KASAP, PROJ DIRECTOR; LA SALLE BICENTENNIAL COMMISSION; 745 2ND ST; LA SALLE, IL 61301. (#27790). **ARBA GRANTEE.**

RESTORED RURAL SCHOOLHOUSE & PICNIC AREA, IL. RURAL SCHOOLHOUSE & PICNIC AREA, PART OF TURN OF THE CENTURY FARMSTEAD, WAS RESTORED. (LOCAL). JAMES F AITKEN, OWNER; COFFEE TREE FARM; 2812 5TH ST; PERU, IL 61354. (#25097).

VISIT A FARM DAY IN LASALLE COUNTY, ILLINOIS. TOUR OF LARGE FARMS IN LASALLE COUNTY TO SEE HOW THEY ARE OPERATED. (ST-WIDE). ROBERT BURNS, COORDINATOR; LASALLE COUNTY COOPERATIVE EXTENSION SERVICE; 125 SWANSON ST; OTTAWA, IL 61350. (#5722).

AUG 1 - 10, '75. HERITAGE DAY CELEBRATION. TEN DAY COOPERATIVE CELEBRATION OF THE SEVEN COMMUNITIES SURROUNDING LA SALLE, INCLUDING A FESTIVAL & PARADE. (LOCAL). JOHN M SCHOEPH, MANAGER; ILLINOIS VALLEY AREA CHAMBER OF COMMERCE; 535 THIRD ST; LA SALLE, IL 61301. (#5325-501).

DEC 14, '75. THE CHRISTMAS STORY, EARLY AMERICAN SETTING & MUSIC. LIVE PERFORMANCE. (LOCAL). JOE TERRANDO; LASALLE-PERU TOWNSHIP HIGH SCHOOL; 541 CHARTRES ST; LASALLE, IL 61301. (#8183-501).

LA SALLE — CONTINUED

JAN 27, '76. TESTAMENT OF FREEDOM, WORDS BY THOMAS JEFFERSON. LIVE PERFORMANCE. (LOCAL). JOE TERRANDO; LASALLE-PERU TOWNSHIP HIGH SCHOOL; 541 CHARTRES ST; LASALLE, IL 61301. (#8183-502).

APR 1 - 3, '76. 'TAKE ME ALONG' MUSICAL, LASALLE-PERU HIGH SCHOOL. LIVE PERFORMANCE. (LOCAL). JOE TERRANDO; LASALLE-PERU TOWNSHIP HIGH SCHOOL; 541 CHARTRES ST; LASALLE, IL 61301. (#8183-503).

MAY 12, '76. BALLAD FOR AMERICANS EVENING ON BROADWAY, LASALLE-PERU HIGH SCHOOL. LIVE PERFORMANCE. (LOCAL). JOE TERRANDO; LASALLE-PERU TOWNSHIP HIGH SCHOOL; 541 CHARTRES ST; LASALLE, IL 61301. (#8183-504).

MAY 22 - 23, '76. PULASKI PARK PICNIC, ETHNIC FOOD, GAMES & ENTERTAINMENT. IRISH, POLISH, GERMAN, ITALIAN, MEXICAN, SLAVIC AND ENGLISH FOODS; ENTERTAINMENT BY LOCAL ETHNIC GROUPS & SCHOOLS. AT PULASKI PARK, 5TH CROSAT ON RT 6, ON EAST SIDE OF LASALLE. (LOCAL). BETTY KASAP, CHMN; LASALLE BICENTENNIAL COMMITTEE; 905 CHARTRES; LASALLE, IL 61301. (#105881-1).

JAN 18 - 20, '77. LA SALLE EXPEDITION II, A HISTORIC RE-ENACTMENT. THIS IS AN AUTHENTIC RE-ENACTMENT OF THE 1681 LASALLE EXPEDITION FROM MONTREAL, CANADA TO NEW ORLEANS, LA WHICH WILL BEGIN TOURING ON AUGUST 11, 1976 AND END ON APRIL 9, 1977. (LOCAL). REID H LEWIS, DIRECTOR; LA SALLE EXPEDITION II; 135 S LA SALLE ST, RM 411; CHICAGO, IL 60690. (#102805-41).

LACON

BIKE AND HIKING TRAILS IN LACON, IL. BICYCLE & HIKING TRAILS THROUGH MARSHALL COUNTY. (LOCAL). RALPH WIER, DIRECTOR; MARSHALL COUNTY BICENTENNIAL COMMISSION; RR; LACON, IL 61540. (#32995).

BOOK PUBLICATION IN LACON, IL. PUBLICATION OF TWO HISTORIES OF MARSHALL COUNTY: 'MARSHALL COUNTY SKETCHES' & 'DEEP ARE THE ROOTS'. (LOCAL). RALPH WIER, DIRECTOR; MARSHALL COUNTY BICENTENNIAL COMMISSION; RR; LACON, IL 61540. (#32994).

FILM ON BLACKFOOT INDIANS IN LACON, IL. FILM OF BLACKFOOT INDIANS ENTITLED 'SUN GAVE MAN THE POWER'. (LOCAL). BOB ERICKSON, CHAIRMAN; SUN FOUNDATION; RR; WASHBURN, IL 61570. (#33596).

MARSHALL-PUTNAM COUNTY ART GUILD IN LACON, IL. FORMATION OF MARSHALL-PUTNAM COUNTY ART GUILD, INCLUDING THEATRE GROUP AND COUNTY-WIDE CHORUS. (LOCAL). MARY JANE MATTINGLY, COORDINATOR; HENRY BICENTENNIAL COMMISSION; RR; LACON, IL 61540. (#33008).

AUG 20 - 22, '76. ARTS & CRAFTS FESTIVAL. FESTIVAL, EXHIBIT. (LOCAL). MRS RALPH WIER, CHMN; MARSHALL COUNTY BICENTENNIAL COMMISSION; RR; LACON, IL 61540. (#200016-147).

JAN 22 - 23, '77. LA SALLE EXPEDITION II, A HISTORIC RE-ENACTMENT. THIS IS AN AUTHENTIC RE-ENACTMENT OF THE 1681 LASALLE EXPEDITION FROM MONTREAL, CANADA TO NEW ORLEANS, LA WHICH WILL BEGIN TOURING ON AUGUST 11, 1976 AND END ON APRIL 9, 1977. (LOCAL). REID H LEWIS, DIRECTOR; LA SALLE EXPEDITION II; 135 S LA SALLE ST, RM 411; CHICAGO, IL 60690. (#102805-44).

LADD

LADD BICENTENNIAL PREPAREDNESS RAFFLE IN LADD, IL. PROFITS WERE DONATED TO THE LADD FIRE DEPT AND LADD EMERGENCY SERVICES. (LOCAL). JAMES WLASH, CHAIRMAN; LADD BICENTENNIAL COMMISSION; LADD, IL 61312. (#33396).

APR 24 - 25, '76. WAGON TRAIN PROGRAM. HAD PARADE DOWN MAIN ST WITH BAND, WAGON TRAIN, LOCAL BICENTENNIAL CHAIRMAN, SCOUTS, SADDLE CLUB. HAD FLAG RAISING CEREMONY IN PARK. HOSTED DINNER FOR WAGON TRAIN. AT CITY HALL, WAR MEMORIAL PARK. (LOCAL). ROSE M CASOLARI, CHMN; LADD BICENTENNIAL COMMISSION; RR 1; ARLINGTON, IL 61312. (#200016-440).

LAKE FOREST

NOV 29 - DEC 1, '76. LA SALLE EXPEDITION II, A HISTORIC RE-ENACTMENT. THIS IS AN AUTHENTIC RE-ENACTMENT OF THE 1681 LASALLE EXPEDITION FROM MONTREAL, CANADA TO NEW ORLEANS, LA WHICH WILL BEGIN TOURING ON AUGUST 11, 1976 AND END ON APRIL 9, 1977. (LOCAL). REID H LEWIS, DIRECTOR; LA SALLE EXPEDITION II; 135 S LA SALLE ST, RM 411; CHICAGO, IL 60690. (#102805-20).

LANARK

AMERICAN REVOLUTION LIBRARY COLLECTION, ILLINOIS. COLLECTION OF MATERIALS: FILM STRIPS, BOOKS & SLIDES, ABOUT THE FOUNDING OF OUR COUNTRY, DEVELOPED IN LANARK, ILLINOIS. AVAILABLE TO ANY ORGANIZATION OR INDIVIDUAL & CIRCULATED BY PUBLIC LIBRARIES. (LOCAL). MARJORIE SMITH, CHAIRMAN; CARROLL COUNTY BICENTENNIAL COMMISSION; BOX 76; MT CARROLL, IL 61053. (#5180). **(??).**

LANSING

CHILDREN'S SECTION OF NEW LANSING LIBRARY, IL. FURNISHINGS OF ART WORKS WILL BE PURCHASED WITH PROFITS FROM BICENTENNIAL ACTIVITIES. (LOCAL). JUDI MAGLIO, HORIZONS CHAIRMAN; LANSING BICENTENNIAL COMMISSION; 3263 LOUISE CT; LANSING, IL 60438. (#33006).

FILM ON LANSING'S BICENTENNIAL CELEBRATION: IL. ALL BICENTENNIAL PROJECTS AND EVENTS TO BE FILMED STARTING WITH OFFICIAL OPENING JULY 4, '75 THROUGH OUR FINAL EVENT IN DECEMBER OF 1976. (LOCAL). BARRY BERGSTROM, CHAMBER PRESIDENT; LANSING CHAMBER OF COMMERCE & BICENTENNIAL COMMITTEE; 18835 WILLIAM ST; LANSING, IL 60438. (#33007).

HISTORIC BUSINESS WINDOW DISPLAYS IN LANSING, IL. DISPLAYS OF HISTORIC ITEMS IN WINDOWS OF DOWNTOWN BUSINESSES. ITEMS DISPLAYED RELATED TO HISTORY OF THE BUSINESS. (LOCAL). JO FENNEMA, CHAIRMAN; LANSING CHAMBER OF COMMERCE & BICENTENNIAL COMMITTEE; 18200 BURNHAM AVE; LANSING, IL 60438. (#33593).

LANSING HISTORICAL SOCIETY AND MUSEUM - IL. MUSEUM NOW HOUSED IN TWO VACANT ROOMS OF LOCAL BANK UNTIL AN OLD BUILDING CAN BE SECURED. (LOCAL). JULIA GAULT, PRESIDENT; LANSING BICENTENNIAL COMMISSION & HISTORICAL SOCIETY; 2300-1 E HOLIDAY COURT; LANSING, IL 60438. (#33594).

LANSING, IL, BICENTENNIAL HISTORY BOOK. A HISTORY OF LANSING, PLUS PICTURES AND STORIES OF OUR BICENTENNIAL CELEBRATION. (LOCAL). BARRY BERGSTROM, PRESIDENT; LANSING CHAMBER OF COMMERCE & BICENTENNIAL COMMITTEE; 18835 WILLIAM ST; LANSING, IL 60438. (#33589).

LIVE TREE PRESENTATION IN LANSING, IL. PRESENTED LIVE TREE FOR ATRIUM OF NEW LANSING PUBLIC LIBRARY. (LOCAL). JACKOLINE ZUKLEY, CHAIRMAN; LANSING BICENTENNIAL COMMISSION; 18257 WILDWOOD ST; LANSING, IL 60438. (#33592).

THREE NEW FLAGPOLES IN PARK AREA OF LANSING, IL. 3 NEW FLAGPOLES ERECTED ON SMALL TRIANGLE OF LAND DOWNTOWN. ALSO: AREA WAS LANDSCAPED AND GRADED. (LOCAL). JACKOLINE ZUKLEY, CHAIRMAN; LANSING BICENTENNIAL COMMISSION; 18257 WILDWOOD ST; LANSING, IL 60438. (#33005).

JULY 4, '75. FLAGPOLE DEDICATION & 199TH BIRTHDAY OF AMERICA. AFTER FLAG CEREMONY, WALK TO SCHULTZ PARK FOR BIRTHDAY PARTY-FREE CAKE & DRINK, LIVE ENTERTAINMENT, BALLOON LAUNCH FOR $125 SAVINGS BOND. AT CORNER RIDGE RD & HENRY ST SCHULTZ PARK-SCHULTZ AVE. (LOCAL). JACKOLINE ZUKLEY; LANSING BICENTENNIAL COMMISSION; 18257 WILDWOOD; LANSING, IL 60438. (#200016-367).

NOV 15, '75. HARVEST FESTIVAL-ANTIQUE SHOW & OLDTIME CRAFT DEMONSTRATION. FESTIVAL AT NATHAN HALE SCHOOL GYM. (LOCAL). JACKOLINE ZUKLEY; LANSING BICENTENNIAL COMMISSION; 18257 WILDWOOD; LANSING, IL 60438. (#200016-368).

FEB 7 - MAY 22, '76. BICENTENNIAL EVENTS OF LANSING, ILL FEB-MAY '76. 2/7 BICENT QUEEN CONTEST; 2/21 BICENT BALL; 3/1 GOOD NEIGHBOR BICENT PARADE; 3/26 'UNCLE SAM'S BIRTHDAY' AN OPERETTA; 5/12 LIBERTY MARCH; 5/22 THORNTON FRACTIONAL SOUTH PAGEANT. (LOCAL). JACKOLINE ZUKLEY; LANSING BICENTENNIAL COMMITTEE; 18257 WILDWOOD; LANSING, IL 60438. (#200016-369).

JULY 3 - 12, '76. BICENTENNIAL EVENTS OF LANSING, ILL JULY '76. 7/3-7/5 JULY 4TH FESTIVAL-HOT AIR BALLOON LAUNCH, OLD TIME CRAFTS, SPORTS TOURNAMENTS, BEARD CONTEST, HANDMADE COSTUME CONTEST, DANCE, FIREWORKS; 7/12 BARBERSHOP QUARTET & CHOIR CONTEST 8PM; 7/12 CIVIL WAR ENCAMPMENT & BATTLE RE-ENACTMENT 9:30-3:00PM. (LOCAL). JACKOLINE ZUKLEY; LANSING BICENTENNIAL COMMITTEE; 18257 WILDWOOD; LANSING, IL 60438. (#200016-370).

LAWRENCEVILLE

ART DISPLAY AT LAWRENCE COUNTY, ILLINOIS FAIR. AN EXHIBITION OF ART WORKS BASED ON THE AMERICAN REVOLUTION THEME. DONE BY STUDENTS OF THE SCHOOLS IN LAWRENCE COUNTY. (LOCAL). SUPERINTENDENT OF EDUCATIONAL SERVICE; 4-H CLUBS OF LAWRENCE COUNTY; RICHLAW BLDG; LAWRENCEVILLE, IL 62439. (#5921).

AUG 13 - 19, '75. LAWRENCE COUNTY JR FAIR W/ BICENT POSTER, DISPLAY, MURAL CONTEST. ANNUAL FAIR WITH 4-H CLUBS & LOCAL STUDENTS PARTICIPATING, 1975 FAIR WILL OFFER PRIZES FOR POSTERS, MURALS & DISPLAYS ON BICENTENNIAL & AMERICAN REVOLUTION. (LOCAL). HUGH LIVESAY; LAWRENCE COUNTY EDUCATIONAL SERVICE REGION; COUNTY COURTHOUSE; LAWRENCEVILLE, IL 62439. (#5744-501).

LE ROY

'HERITAGE ON THE PRAIRIE' - LE ROY, IL. HISTORY OF EMPIRE & WEST TOWNSHIPS AND THE CITY OF LE ROY, MCLEAN COUNTY, IN TWO VOLUMES. (LOCAL). MARIAN SPRATT, HISTORY BOOK COMMITTEE CHAIRMAN; LE ROY BICENTENNIAL COMMISSION; 204 E ELM ST; LE ROY, IL 61752. (#33580).

INDIAN STATUE IN LE ROY, IL. RESTORATION OF KICKAPOO INDIAN CHIEF, 'OSAKETA', WITH A MONUMENT. (LOCAL). HONORABLE O J LERE, MAYOR; CITY OF LE ROY; CITY HALL; LE ROY, IL 61752. (#33013).

LE ROY HISTORICAL SOCIETY IN IL. ORGANIZATION IN ORGANIZATIONAL STAGE IS AN OUTGROWTH OF THE LE ROY BICENTENNIAL COMMISSION. (LOCAL). MARIAN SPRATT, TEMPORARY PRESIDENT; LE ROY HISTORICAL SOCIETY; 204 E ELM; LE ROY, IL 61752. (#33577).

NEW STREET SIGNS IN LE ROY, IL. NEW SIGNS MARKING STREETS. (LOCAL). HON O J LERE, MAYOR; LEROY CITY; CITY HALL; LE ROY, IL 61752. (#33579).

REVOLUTIONARY WAR SOLDIER'S MONUMENT IN LE ROY, IL. GRAVE MARKER FOR REVOL WAR SOLDIER. (LOCAL). HAROLD DICKSON, CHAIRMAN; LE ROY BICENTENNIAL COMMISSION; 410 N HEMLOCK ST; LE ROY, IL 61752. (#33578).

JUNE 20 - 30, '76. BICENTENNIAL DISPLAYS IN WINDOW. EXHIBIT AT MANY STORES AND STORE WINDOWS. (LOCAL). JAMES CROUCH, COORDINATOR; LE ROY BICENTENNIAL COMMISSION AND BOY SCOUTS OF LE ROY; 120 E CENTER; LE ROY, IL 61752. (#200016-388).

JUNE 25, '76. LE ROY'S BICENTENNIAL CELEBRATION - JUNE 25 ACTIVITIES. OPEN HOUSE AT THE CRUMBAUGH LIBRARY (THRU SUNDAY), QUEEN CONTEST, CORN SHOW, CIRCUS (THRU SAT), PAGEANT (THRU SAT), AND 'ANYTHING GOES, PRACTICALLY'. (LOCAL). HAROLD DICKSON, CHAIRMAN; LE ROY BICENTENNIAL COMMITTEE; BOX 128; LE ROY, IL 61752. (#200016-409).

JUNE 25 - 27, '76. LE ROY'S BICENTENNIAL CELEBRATION - CONTINUOUS ACTIVITIES. THE FOLLOWING ACTIVITIES WILL BE AVAILABLE DURING ALL 3 DAYS OF THE CELEBRATION: OPEN HOUSE AT THE LIBRARY, DUNK THE CLOWN, ENTERTAINMENT BY THE HAROLD JONES FAMILY; AND OPEN HOUSE AT THE CRUMBAUGH MANSION. AT LE ROY CITY PARK. (LOCAL). HAROLD DICKSON, COORD; LE ROY BICENTENNIAL COMMITTEE; PO BOX 128; LE ROY, IL 61752. (#200016-380).

JUNE 26, '76. LE ROY'S BICENTENNIAL CELEBRATION - JUNE 26 ACTIVITIES. ANTIQUE FARM MACHINERY EXHIBIT, FARM ANIMALS BROUGHT TO PET, MOCK OLD-TIME BANK ROBBERY, PARADE, FIREMEN'S WATER CONTESTS, PAGEANT, & BALL (ADMISSION FEE TO THE BALL). (LOCAL). HAROLD DICKSON, CHAIRMAN; LE ROY BICENTENNIAL COMMITTEE; BOX 128; LE ROY, IL 61752. (#200016-410).

JUNE 27, '76. LE ROY'S BICENTENNIAL CELEBRATION - LAST DAY'S ACTIVITIES. SOAP BOX DERBY, SQUARE DANCE, BEARD CONTEST, PIE EATING CONTEST, COSTUME JUDGING, AND AN HISTORICAL BUS TOUR. (LOCAL). HAROLD DICKSON, CHAIRMAN; LE ROY BICENTENNIAL COMMITTEE; BOX 128; LE ROY, IL 61752. (#200016-411).

LEAF RIVER

SEPT 27 - 28, '75. LEAF RIVER BICENTENNIAL CELEBRATION. FESTIVAL AT BERTOLET MEMORIAL BLDG MAIN ST. (LOCAL). DORIS KUNTZELMAN; LEAF RIVER BICENTENNIAL COMMITTEE; BOX 143; LEAF RIVER, IL 61047. (#200016-298).

LEBANON

BICENTENNIAL HERITAGE & FESTIVAL PAGEANT, IL. PRODUCTION OF PAGEANT TO CELEBRATE HERITAGE OF SOUTHERN ILLINOIS. (LOCAL). MRS SHIRLEY SCHAEFER, COORDINATOR; LEBANON BICENTENNIAL COMMISSION; C/O HARDIN, 1001 COLLEGE ST; LEBANON, IL 62254. (#27730). **ARBA GRANTEE.**

HISTORY IN A NUTSHELL: LEBANON, ILLINOIS. WRITTEN HISTORY OF LEBANON AND ITS ENVIRONS WILL BE DONE. (ST-WIDE). WILLIAM H BEST, CHAIRMAN; LEBANON CENTENNIAL COMMISSION; 105 FLORENCE ST; LEBANON, IL 62254. (#10223).

LEBANON, ILL, WRITTEN HISTORY & MUSICAL PAGEANT. ILLUSTRATED BROCHURE & MUSICAL PAGEANT DEPICTING LEBANON'S HISTORY. (LOCAL). BRIG GEN W H BEST (RETD), CHAIRMAN; LEBANON CENTENNIAL COMMISSION; 105 FLORENCE ST; LEBANON, IL 62254. (#888). **ARBA GRANTEE.**

AUG 1 - 30, '75. HISTORICAL PAGEANT: 'YEARS, YEARS, AGO'. ILLUSTRATED BROCHURE & MUSICAL PAGEANT DEPICTING LEBANON'S HISTORY. (LOCAL). BRIG GEN W H BEST CHRMN; LEBANON CENTENNIAL COMMISSION; 105 FLORENCE ST; LEBANON, IL 62254. (#888-1).

AUG 13 - 14, '76. BICENTENNIAL HERITAGE & FESTIVAL PAGEANT. PAGEANT TO CELEBRATE HERITAGE OF SOUTHERN ILLINOIS. (LOCAL). MRS SHIRLEY SCHAEFFER; LEBANON BICENTENNIAL COMMISSION; C/O HARDIN, 1001 COLLEGE ST; LEBANON, IL 62254. (#27730-1).

LEMONT

HISTORICAL WALKING TOURS IN LEMONT, IL. WALKING TOURS OF THE COMMUNITY TO SEE HISTORIC SITES, SIGNIFICANT BUILDINGS & ATTRACTIVE SCENERY. (LOCAL). DONALD A URICK, CHAIRMAN; LEMONT BICENTENNIAL COMMISSION; 505 WARNER AVE; LEMONT, IL 60439. (#33365).

LEMONT BICENTENNIAL AWARD OF DISTINCTION - IL. MONTHLY AWARD TO DESERVING CITIZEN, NOMINATED BY GENERAL PUBLIC, WHO HAS MADE A CONTRIBUTION TO THE BETTERMENT OF THE COMMUNITY. (LOCAL). DONALD A URICK, CHAIRMAN; LEMONT BICENTENNIAL COMMISSION; 505 WARNER AVE; LEMONT, IL 60439. (#33010).

LIVING HISTORY PROGRAM IN LEMONT, IL. DEVELOP A 1900 ONE-ROOM SCHOOL FOR STUDENT AND TEACHER PARTICIPATION. (LOCAL). DONALD A URICK, CHAIRMAN; LEMONT BICENTENNIAL COMMISSION; 505 WARNER AVE; LEMONT, IL 60439. (#33014).

OUTDOOR BICENTENNIAL MURAL IN LEMONT, IL. PUBLIC WORK OF ART DEPICTING THE HISTORICAL AND CULTURAL HERITAGE OF OUR COMMUNITY. (LOCAL). DONALD A URICK, CHAIRMAN; LEMONT BICENTENNIAL COMMISSION; 505 WARNER AVE; LEMONT, IL 60439. (#33588).

LEMONT — CONTINUED

PRESERVATION OF HISTORIC LANDMARK IN LEMONT, IL. OLDEST CONTINUOUSLY-OPERATING SCHOOL IN ILLINOIS PLACED ON NATIONAL REGISTER OF HISTORIC PLACES. (NAT'L). DONALD A URICK, CHAIRMAN; LEMONT BICENTENNIAL COMMISSION; 505 WARNER AVE; LEMONT, IL 60439. (#33011).

SCULPTURE IN LEMONT, IL. A PERMANENT MEMORIAL TO THE BICENTENNIAL OF THE UNITED STATES AND THE HERITAGE OF THE COMMUNITY - TITLED 'SPIRIT OF LEMONT'. (LOCAL). DONALD A URICK, CHAIRMAN; LEMONT BICENTENNIAL COMMISSION; 505 WARNER AVE; LEMONT, IL 60439. (#33004).

APR 25, '76. BICENTENNIAL CONCERT. MUSIC INSPIRED BY AMERICAN FOLKLORE & HISTORY BY SOUTHWEST SYMPHONY ORCHESTRA. AT LEMONT HIGH SCHOOL AUDITORIUM. (LOCAL). DONALD A URICK, CHMN; LEMONT BICENTENNIAL COMMISSION; 505 WARNER AVE; LEMONT, IL 60439. (#200016-454).

LERNA

SEPT 20 - 21, '75. WANDER'S WEEKEND. ECOLOGY-BASED, SHOWING RESPONSIBLE RECREATION. (LOCAL). MS JANET PICKETT; ILL DEPT OF CONSERVATION; 901 SOUTH SPRING; SPRINGFIELD, IL 62704. (#50272-39).

OCT '75. HARVEST FROLIC. THE CONCENTRATION OF THIS EVENT IS THE AGRICULTURAL BASE OF CENTRAL ILL. IN THE 1850'S. TAKES PLACE AT THE RECONSTRUCTED FARM OF THOMAS LINCOLN WHICH IS DUALLY INTERPRETED AS THE RESIDENCE OF THE LINCOLN FAMILY & AS A TYPICAL 1850'S FARM. SPONSOR PLANS INCOMPLETE 04/10/75. AT LINCOLN LOG CABIN STATE PARK RR#2 LERNA. (LOCAL). MS JANET PICKETT; ILLINOIS DEPARTMENT OF CONSERVATION; 901 SOUTH SPRING; SPRINGFIELD, IL 62704. (#50272-40).

OCT 9 - 10, '76. HARVEST FROLIC. THE CONCENTRATION OF THIS EVENT IS THE AGRICULTURAL BASE OF CENTRAL ILLINOIS IN THE 1850'S. THIS TAKES PLACE AT THE RECONSTRUCTED FARM OF THOMAS LINCOLN, RESIDENCE OF THE LINCOLN FAMILY & TYPICAL 1850'S FARM. AT LINCOLN LOG CABIN STATE PARK RR#2 LERNA. (LOCAL). MS JANET PICKETT; ILLINOIS DEPARTMENT OF CONSERVATION; 901 SOUTH SPRING; SPRINGFIELD, IL 62704. (#50272-41).

LEWISTOWN

FULTON COUNTY, ILL, BICENTENNIAL COURTYARD. CONSTRUCTION OF BICENTENNIAL COMMEMORATIVE COURTYARD ADJACENT TO FULTON COUNTY, ILL. COURTHOUSE IN LEWISTOWN, ILL. ALSO DEDICATE STATE MARKER OF LEWISTON TRAIL WHICH LED TO GALENA. (LOCAL). ROBERT R WOLFORD, CHAIRMAN, COUNTY BOARD; FULTON COUNTY; 430 OAK ST, PO BOX 492; CANTON, IL 61520. (#889). **ARBA GRANTEE.**

JULY 27, '75. DEDICATION OF MARKER FOR HISTORIC TRAIL LEADING TO GALENA LEAD MINES. PLACEMENT OF MARKER AT FULTON COUNTY COURTHOUSE TO DESIGNATE THE LEWISTOWN TRAIL LEADING TO THE GALENA LEAD MINES. (LOCAL). MARJORIE BORDNER; FULTON COUNTY BICENTENNIAL COMMISSION; 430 E OAK; CANTON, IL 61520. (#5322-501).

JULY 27, '75. DEDICATION OF THE COURTHOUSE COURTYARD. CONSTRUCTION OF BICENTENNIAL COMMEMORATIVE COURTYARD ADJACENT TO FULTON COUNTY, ILL. COURTHOUSE IN LEWISTOWN, ILL. (LOCAL). ROBERT R WOLFORD; FULTON COUNTY; 430 OAK ST, PO BOX 492; CANTON, IL 61520. (#889-501).

JULY 3 - 4, '76. BICENTENNIAL CELEBRATION. FESTIVAL, PARADE. (LOCAL). MARJORIE BORDNER, CHMN; FULTON COUNTY BICENTENNIAL COMMISSION; PO BOX 492; CANTON, IL 61520. (#200016-182).

JULY 25 - 31, '76. SENIOR QUEEN CONTEST - FULTON COUNTY FAIR. A COUNTY FAIR WITH A BICENTENNIAL THEME TO INCLUDE A YOUNG LADIES BEAUTY QUEEN CONTEST. AT FULTON COUNTY FAIRGROUNDS. (LOCAL). MRS DOTTIE JACKSON, PRES; LEWISTOWN SENIOR WOMENS CLUB; 307 W EUCLID; LEWISTOWN, IL 61542. (#105199-1).

LIBERTYVILLE

'CRAFTSPIRIT '76' BICENTENNIAL COVERAGE - NBMRP. A 3-ISSUE MAGAZINE/NEWSLETTER FOR SUBSCRIBERS OF 'ARTISAN CRAFT MAGAZINE' & ALL OTHER INTERESTED PERSONS. TELLS HOW PEOPLE ARE RELATING & REACTING TO THE BICENTENNIAL CELEBRATION. (NAT'L). BARBARA BRABEC, BICENTENNIAL COORDINATOR; ARTISAN CRAFTS; P O BOX 398; LIBERTYVILLE, IL 60048. (#26070).

JULY 4, '76. PAGEANT-FOURTH OF JULY. LIVE PERFORMANCE AT LIBERTYVILLE HIGH SCHOOL FOOTBALL FIELD. (LOCAL). PHYLLIS EGGERT, DIRECTOR; LIBERTYVILLE BICENTENNIAL COMMISSION; 112 HOMEWOOD; LIBERTYVILLE, IL 60048. (#104782-1).

LINCOLN

DISPLAYS ON MINORITY GROUPS IN LINCOLN, ILLINOIS. DISPLAYS FOR PUBLIC BUILDINGS CONCERNING THE HERITAGE OF THE MINORITY GROUPS IN AMERICA & LOGAN COUNTY. ORGANIZED BY YOUTH COMMITTEE. (LOCAL). JOHN DAVIDSON, CHAIRMAN OF YOUTH COMMITTEE; LOGAN COUNTY BICENTENNIAL COMMISSION; PO BOX 291; LINCOLN, IL 62656. (#1972).

GUIDE TO HISTORIC SITES: LINCOLN, IL. PUBLICATION OF GUIDE TO HISTORIC SITES IN LOGAN COUNTY. (LOCAL). PAUL GLEASON, COORDINATOR; LOGAN COUNTY BICENTENNIAL COMMISSION; 621 RUTLEDGE DR; LINCOLN, IL 62656. (#33576).

SPIRIT OF AMERICAN INDEPENDENCE WEEK, LINCOLN, IL. THE CLERGY WILL DEVOTE A SERMON TO GROWTH AND DEVELOPMENT OF THE SPIRITUAL HERITAGE. THERE WILL ALSO BE PICNICS, BAND CONCERTS AND SACK RACES. (LOCAL). PAUL GLEASON, CHAIRMAN; LOGAN CO BICENTENNIAL COMMISSION; PO BOX 291; LINCOLN, IL 62656. (#6347).

YOUNG COLONIALS & SPIRIT OF CHESTNUT: LINCOLN, IL. COLOR GUARDS FORMED FOR THE BICENTENNIAL CELEBRATION. (NAT'L). PAUL GLEASON, DIRECTOR; LOGAN COUNTY BICENTENNIAL COMMISSION; 621 RUTLEDGE DR; LINCOLN, IL 62656. (#33575).

APR 1 - 30, '75. PUBLIC DISCUSSIONS AMONG BUSINESS, CHURCHES & CIVIC ORGANIZATIONS. PROGRAM TO PROVIDE 15 MONTHS OF STUDY WITH PUBLIC DISCUSSION FOR THE PURPOSE OF TAKING COMMUNITY ACTION TO IMPROVE CONDITIONS IN LINCOLN COUNTY. (LOCAL). PAUL GLEASON, CHAIRMAN; LOGAN CO BICENTENNIAL COMMISSION; PO BOX 291; LINCOLN, IL 62656. (#6349-501).

APR 17 - 18, '75. '1776 AND ALL THAT', PREMIER PERFORMANCE. STUDENTS OF LINCOLN JR HIGH SCHOOL ARE PERFORMING THIS PLAY AS PART OF THEIR AWARENESS OF THE BICENTENNIAL & THRIER COMMUNITY. (LOCAL). PAUL E GLEASON, CHAIRMAN; LOGAN CO BICENTENNIAL COMMISSION; LINCOLN, IL 62656. (#6348-501).

JUNE 29, '75. SPIRITUAL HERITAGE SUNDAY, SERMONS OF CLERGY KEYED TO THEME. FESTIVAL, CEREMONY. (LOCAL). PAUL GLEASON, CHAIRMAN; LOGAN CO BICENTENNIAL COMMISSION; PO BOX 291; LINCOLN, IL 62656. (#6347-501).

JUNE 29 - JULY 5, '75. SPIRIT OF AMERICAN INDEPENDENCE WEEK. SPIRIT OF AMERICAN INDEPENDENCE WEEK, LINCOLN, IL. THE CLERGY WILL DEVOTE A SERMON TO GROWTH AND DEVELOPMENT OF THE SPIRITUAL HERITAGE. THERE WILL ALSO BE PICNICS, BAND CONCERTS AND SACK RACES. (LOCAL). PAUL GLEASON, CHAIRMAN; LOGAN CO BICENTENNIAL COMMISSION; PO BOX 291; LINCOLN, IL 62656. (#6347-505).

JULY 4, '75. FOURTH OF JULY PICNIC IN THE PARK. FESTIVAL, CEREMONY. (LOCAL). PAUL GLEASON, CHAIRMAN; LOGAN CO BICENTENNIAL COMMISSION; PO BOX 291; LINCOLN, IL 62656. (#6347-502).

JULY 5, '75. J C PENNY BICENTENNIAL MUSIC CONCERT. FESTIVAL, CEREMONY. (LOCAL). PAUL GLEASON, CHAIRMAN; LOGAN CO BICENTENNIAL COMMISSION; PO BOX 291; LINCOLN, IL 62656. (#6347-504).

SEPT 13 - 14, '75. ABRAHAM LINCOLN NATL RAILSPLITTING CONTEST & FESTIVAL. RAILSPLITTING CONTEST AND CRAFT FESTIVAL TO CELEBRATE THE BICENT. (REGN'L). PAUL GLEASON, CHAIRMAN; LOGAN CO BICENTENNIAL COMMISSION; PO BOX 291; LINCOLN, IL 62656. (#6350-501).

NOV 25, '75. PARADE FOR THE SPIRIT OF AMERICAN CHRISTMAS. WILL CONSIST OF FLOATS, BANDS, MARCHERS & REPRESENTATIVES OF CIVIC GROUPS. THE THEME WILL BE HERITAGE & RELIGION. (LOCAL). PAUL GLEASON, CHAIRMAN; LOGAN CO BICENTENNIAL COMMISSION; PO BOX 291; LINCOLN, IL 62656. (#6346-501).

LISLE

AMERICAN CHARACTER IN SOCIAL INSTITUTIONS, IL. SERIES OF LECTURES ON THE CONTRIBUTIONS OF ETHNIC GROUPS TO THE AMERICAN SOCIAL CHARACTER; SECONDARY THEME IS TO OFFER SOLUTIONS TO AMERICA'S MAJOR PROBLEMS. (LOCAL). PHILIP BEAN, CHAIRPERSON; ILLINOIS BENEDICTINE COLLEGE BICENTENNIAL COMMITTEE; 5700 COLLEGE RD; LISLE, IL 60532. (#15356).

BICENTENNIAL FOUNTAIN - LISLE, IL. AN ILLUMINATED FOUNTAIN WILL BE DISPLAYED AT THE COLLEGE ENTRANCE; THERE WILL BE SHRUBS, PLANTS AND PARK BENCHES IN THE AREA. (LOCAL). PHILIP BEAN, CHAIRPERSON; ILLINOIS BENEDICTINE COLLEGE BICENTENNIAL COMMITTEE; 5700 COLLEGE RD; LISLE, IL 60532. (#15355).

CZECH IMMIGRANT CULTURE IN LISLE, IL. THE COLLEGE SLAV-CENTER WILL PRESENT LITERATURE AND ARTIFACTS DEPICTING THE CONTRIBUTIONS OF ETHNIC GROUPS IN DEVELOPING AMERICA. (LOCAL). PHILIP BEAN, CHAIRPERSON; ILLINOIS BENEDICTINE COLLEGE BICENTENNIAL COMMITTEE; 5700 COLLEGE RD; LISLE, IL 60532. (#15357).

LINCOLN HOME REPLICA - EXHIBIT. ACCURATE REPRODUCTION OF LINCOLN'S HOME ON EXHIBIT IN COLLEGE LIBRARY ACCOMPAINED BY SLIDE PRESENTATION. (LOCAL). PHILIP BEAN, CHAIRPERSON; ILLINOIS BENEDICTINE COLLEGE; 5700 COLLEGE RD; LISLE, IL 60532. (#102377-1). **(??).**

LIVING NEWSPAPER. READERS THEATER WILL SPONSOR 2 HISTORICAL PRODUCTIONS AND A REENACTMENT OF LINCOLN-DOUGLAS DEBATES. (LOCAL). PHILIP BEAN, CHAIRMAN; ILLINOIS BENEDICTINE COLLEGE BICENTENNIAL COMMITTEE; 5700 COLLEGE RD; LISLE, IL 60532. (#102376-1). **(??).**

ORIGINAL SYMPHONY. COLLEGE ORCHESTRA & CHORUS WILL PERFORM ORIGINAL SYMPHONY; FOLK SINGERS & DANCE WILL HAVE AMERICAN THEME. (LOCAL). PHILIP BEAN, CHAIRMAN; ILLINOIS BENEDICTINE COLLEGE BICENTENNIAL COMMITTEE; 5700 COLLEGE RD; LISLE, IL 60532. (#102375-1). **(??).**

LITCHFIELD

BICENTENNIAL MEMORIAL PARK IN LITCHFIELD, ILLINOIS. THE CONSTRUCTION OF A BICENTENNIAL MEMORIAL WITH FLAGPOLE, PLAQUE, CAMPGROUND, AND RECREATION FACILITIES AT LITCHFIELD LAKE. (LOCAL). GORHAM PIGG, PRESIDENT; LITCHFIELD BICENT COMMISSION; PO BOX 1776; LITCHFIELD, IL 62056. (#9593).

COMMUNITY CIVIC CENTER IN LITCHFIELD, IL. CIVIC CENTER BUILDING WILL HAVE A BICENTENNIAL ROOM FURNISHED WITH RESTORED PHOTOGRAPHS OF EARLY LITCHFIELD, FOR COMMUNITY USE. (LOCAL). GORHAM PIGG, CHAIRMAN; LITCHFIELD BICENTENNIAL COMMISSION; BOX 1776; LITCHFIELD, IL 62056. (#33574).

LITCHFIELD, ILL, BICENTENNIAL CAMPSITE. ESTABLISHMENT OF PUBLIC CAMPING AND RECREATION AREA AT LAKE LOU YAEGER NEAR LITCHFIELD, ILLINOIS. (LOCAL). GORHAM PIGG, CHAIRMAN; LITCHFIELD BICENTENNIAL COMMISSION; PO BOX 1776; LITCHFIELD, IL 62056. (#887). **ARBA GRANTEE.**

MAR 27, '76. BICENTENNIAL BALL. FESTIVAL. (LOCAL). GORHAM PIGG, CHMN; LITCHFIELD BICENTENNIAL COMMISSION; PO BOX 1776; LITCHFIELD, IL 62056. (#200016-127).

JULY 3 - 4, '76. DEDICATION OF LAKE LOU YAEGAR PARK. BICENTENNIAL POOL TOURNAMENT WILL BE INCLUDED. (LOCAL). GORHAM PIGG, CHMN; LITCHFIELD BICENTENNIAL COMMISSION; PO BOX 1776; LITCHFIELD, IL 62056. (#200016-126).

LOCKPORT

BICENTENNIAL MUSIC COMPOSITION, LOCKPORT, IL. A MUSICAL COMPOSITION WILL BE COMPOSED IN HONOR OF THE BICENTENNIAL'. (LOCAL). DANIEL BINDER, PROJECT DIRECTOR; LEWIS UNIVERSITY DEPT OF MUSIC; RT 53; LOCKPORT, IL 60441. (#23227).

BICENTENNIAL PUBLICATIONS - LOCKPORT, IL. ARTICLES PERTAINING TO LEWIS UNIVERSITY'S HISTORY WILL BE PUBLISHED IN THE SCHOOL NEWSPAPER. (LOCAL). DEBORAH JO KUCER, CHAIRPERSON; LEWIS UNIV BICENTENNIAL COMMITTEE; RT 53; LOCKPORT, IL 60441. (#23228).

CURRICULAR OFFERINGS - LOCKPORT, IL. COURSES IN HONOR OF THE BICENTENNIAL WILL BE GIVEN THROUGHOUT 1976. (LOCAL). LEO GILSKEY, ACADEMIC DEAN; LEWIS UNIVERSITY; RT 53; LOCKPORT, IL 60441. (#23226).

LIBRARY DISPLAYS AND TRAVELING EXHIBITS - IL. DISPLAYS OF HISTORICAL ITEMS BELONGING TO PRIVATE INDIVIDUALS IN THE SURROUNDING COMMUNITIES PLUS DISPLAYS OF LEWIS LIBRARY WILL BE PRESENTED THROUGHOUT THE YEAR. (LOCAL). CHERYL DOWNER, PROJECT COORDINATOR; LEWIS LIBRARY AND LEWIS BICENTENNIAL COMMISSION; RT 53; LOCKPORT, IL 60441. (#23229).

MUSIC AND DRAMA PERFORMANCES. LIVE PERFORMANCE. (LOCAL). DEBORAH JO KUCER, CHMN; LEWIS UNIV MUSIC & DRAMA DEPARTMENTS; RT 53; LOCKPORT, IL 60441. (#106460-2). **(??).**

TIME CAPSULE BURIAL. THE CAPSULE WILL CONTAIN SUCH THINGS AS PHOTOS, NEWSPAPERS AND CHRISTMAS ORNAMENTS. (LOCAL). DEBORAH JO KUCER, CHMN; LEWIS UNIVERSITY BICENTENNIAL COMMISSION; RT 53; LOCKPORT, IL 60441. (#106460-1). **(??).**

NOV 13 - DEC 23, '75. BICENTENNIAL CHRISTMAS ORNAMENTS EXHIBIT. ORNAMENTS WILL HAVE MAKER'S NAME ON IT. THESE ORNAMENTS SHALL BE BURIED IN A TIME CAPSULE SOMETIME IN 1976 ALONG W/OTHER KEEPSAKES. AT LIBRARY, LEWIS UNIVERSITY, RT 53. (LOCAL). DEBORAH KUCER, CHMN; LEWIS UNIVERSITY BICENTENNIAL COMMISSION; RR 2, BOX 13; LOCKPORT, IL 60441. (#200016-37).

APR 30 - MAY 2, '76. SPRING FESTIVAL. INCLUDED IN THIS WEEKEND WILL BE A COOKOUT, FOLKSINGING, MOVIES, A CONCERT WITH VARIOUS TYPES OF BANDS, BICENTENNIAL DISPLAYS WITH A CONTEST AND A PLAY. AT CAMPUSWIDE. (LOCAL). TOM FRACARO, COORDINATOR; STUDENT GOVERNMENT; RT 53; LOCKPORT, IL 60441. (#106460-3).

MAY 2, '76. LEWIS UNIVERSITY OPEN HOUSE. TOUR, EXHIBIT AT OVER ENTIRE CAMPUS. (LOCAL). JAMES TUFO, COORD; ADMISSION OFFICE; RT 53; LOCKPORT, IL 60441. (#106460-4).

MAY 30, '76. GRADUATION SERMON ON BICENTENNIAL THEME. HOURS ALSO: 7 - 9 PM. AT ST ALBERTA CHAPEL. (LOCAL). FATHER FOGARTY; CAMPUS MINISTRY; RT 53; LOCKPORT, IL 60441. (#106460-5).

LODA

ARTS AND CRAFTS SHOW IN LODA, IL. DISPLAY OF LOCAL ARTISTS' WORK, OIL & WATER COLOR. DISPLAY OF WORKS OF LOCAL ARTISTS OF YESTERDAY YEARS; UNUSUAL & UNIQUE COLLECTIONS & HOBBIES. (LOCAL). JOHN W NORDSTROM LT COL USAF RETIRED, CHAIRMAN; LODA BICENTENNIAL COMMITTEE; LODA, IL 60948. (#4666).

BOOK - HISTORY OF LODA, ILLINOIS. THE WRITING OF 'THE STORY OF LODA, ILLINOIS' BY MARNA PETERSON WILL BE A BICENTENNIAL PROJECT. (LOCAL). JOHN W NORDSTROM, CHAIRMAN; LODA BICENT COMMITTEE; LODA, IL 60948. (#9453).

LODA — CONTINUED

FAMILY HISTORIES PROJ OF LODA, ILL. HAVE HIGH AND JUNIOR HIGH SCHOOL STUDENTS WRITE THEIR FAMILY HISTORY COMPLETED PROJ WILL BE GIVEN TO IROQUOIS COUNTY GENERAL GROUP OF THE IROQUOIS COUNTY HISTORICAL SOCIETY FOR PERMANENT RECORD. (LOCAL). JOHN W NORDSTROM LT COL USAF RETIRED, CHAIRMAN; LODA BICENTENNIAL COMMITTEE; LODA, IL 60948. (#4667). **(??).**

HOMECOMING CELEBRATION IN LODA, IL. BARBECUE AND PICNIC FOR FORMER CITIZENS OF THE TOWN. (LOCAL). JOHN W NORDSTROM, LT COL USAF RET, CHAIRMAN; LODA BICENTENNIAL COMMITTEE; LODA, IL 60940. (#4641).

JUNE 1, '75. ARTS AND CRAFT SHOW. DISPLAY OF LOCAL ARTISTS' WORK, OIL & WATER COLOR. DISPLAY OF WORKS OF LOCAL ARTISTS OF YESTERDAY YEARS; UNUSUAL & UNIQUE COLLECTIONS & HOBBIES. AT AMERICAN LEGION HALL, LODA, ILLINOIS. (LOCAL). JOHN W NORDSTROM; LODA BICENTENNIAL COMMITTEE; BOX 216; LODA, IL 60948. (#4666-1).

JUNE 1, '75. PRESENTATION BICENTENNIAL FLAG. DISPLAY OF LOCAL ARTISTS' WORK, OIL & WATER COLOR. DISPLAY OF WORKS OF LOCAL ARTISTS OF YESTERDAY YEARS; UNUSUAL & UNIQUE COLLECTIONS & HOBBIES. AT FLAG POLE, MAIN STREET, LODA, %LLINOIS. (LOCAL). JOHN W NORDSTROM; LODA BICENTENNIAL COMMITTEE; BOX 216; LODA, IL 60948. (#4666-2).

LOMBARD

HISTORY OF LOMBARD, ILLINOIS. PUBLICATION OF 300 PAGE, ILLUSTRATED HISTORY OF LOMBARD, ILLINOIS & SURROUNDING AREA. (LOCAL). RONALD A FIPPINGER, CHAIRMAN; LOMBARD HISTORICAL SOCIETY; 23 W MAPLE; LOMBARD, IL 60148. (#886). **ARBA GRANTEE.**

OCT 19, '75. ANTIQUE AND COLLECTORS' SHOW. EXHIBIT AT GLENBARD EAST HIGH SCHOOL, 1014 S MAIN ST. (LOCAL). RONALD A FIPPINGER; LOMBARD HISTORICAL SOCIETY; 25 W MAPLE ST; LOMBARD, IL 60148. (#886-1).

MAR 5 - 7, '76. PROUD HERITAGE - PROMISING FUTURE. GIRL SCOUT PROGRAM DISPLAY WILL INCLUDE STUDY PROJECTS IN AREAS OF THE ARTS, THE HOME & OUT-DOORS. A STAGE PRESENTATION WILL BE GIVEN THREE TIMES TO AUDIENCES SHOPPING AT THE MALL, 7 TO 9 PM 9:30 AM TO 5 PM AND 12 TO 5 PM. AT YORKTOWN SHOPPING CENTER MALL BUTTERFIELD & HIGHLAND. (LOCAL). KATHLEEN SULLIVAN, COORD; GIRL SCOUTS OF DUPAGE COUNTY COUNCIL; 20 S PARK; GLEN ELLYN, IL 60137. (#103743-1).

LONDON MILLS

RESTORATION PROJECT IN LONDON MILLS, ILLINOIS. A PROJECT TO UNEARTH & RESTORE HISTORIC BRICK SIDEWALKS. (LOCAL). ROBERT C BODEN, DIRECTOR; VILLAGE OF LONDON MILLS, BOARD OF TRUSTEES; LONDON MILLS, IL 61544. (#8822).

JULY 11, '76. CANOE RACES ON SPOON RIVER. COMPETITION. (LOCAL). MARJORIE BORDNER, CHMN; FULTON COUNTY BICENTENNIAL COMMISSION; PO BOX 492; CANTON, IL 61520. (#200016-181).

LONG GROVE

RESTORATION OF THE DREXLER INN IN LONG GROVE, IL. RESTORATION OF 1859 INN FOR USE AS MUNICIPAL BUILDING. (LOCAL). MRS DENNIS CHAUDRUC, COORDINATOR; LONG GROVE HISTORICAL SOCIETY & BICENTENNIAL COMMISSION; PO BOX 573; LONG GROVE, IL 60047. (#33309). **ARBA GRANTEE.**

LOVINGTON

LOVINGTON BICENTENNIAL PROJECTS, IL. PROJECTS INCLUDE: SENIOR CITIZENS APARTMENTS, REMODELING OF STORE FRONTS & ESTABLISHMENT OF HISTORIC MUSEUM. (LOCAL). MRS GLORIA FOLEY, CHAIRPERSON; LOVINGTON BICENTENNIAL & HERITAGE COMMITTEE; 617 S MCMULLEN CT; LOVINGTON, IL 61937. (#28978).

JUNE 24 - 27, '76. LOVINGTON BICENTENNIAL CELEBRATION. CEREMONY, EXHIBIT, PARADE, COMPETITION AT LOVINGTON GRADE SCHOOL & CITY PARK & BICENTENNIAL APTS. (LOCAL). MRS GLORIA FOLEY; LOVINGTON BICENTENNIAL AND HERITAGE COMMITTEE; 617 S MCMULLEN CT; LOVINGTON, IL 61937. (#200016-245).

MACOMB

BLACK NEWSPAPERS IN ILLINOIS: MACOMB. MICROFILMING OF BLACK NEWSPAPERS IN ILLINOIS. (ST-WIDE). GILBERT BELLES, COORDINATOR; WESTERN ILLINOIS UNIVERSITY; MACOMB, IL 61455. (#33573).

'EARLY MACOMB': MACOMB, IL. SLIDE/TAPE PROGRAM ON EARLY MACOMB, USING HISTORIC PHOTOS. (LOCAL). MARGARET LEWIS, DIRECTOR; MCDONOUGH COUNTY BICENTENNIAL COMMISSION; RR; TENNESSEE, IL 62374. (#33572).

RESTORATION & CONVERSION OF OLD SCHOOLHOUSE, IL. HISTORICAL SCHOOLHOUSE WILL BE CONVERTED TO MUSEUM OF LOCAL HISTORY; PROGRAMS FOR LOCAL YOUTH WILL BE CONDUCTED IN MUSEUM. (LOCAL). JAMES B SCHISLER, PRESIDENT; MACOMB AREA CHAMBER OF COMMERCE; 301 W CALHOUN ST; MACOMB, IL 61435. (#17729).

JULY 4, '75. 4TH OF JULY CELEBRATION. FESTIVAL, PARADE, CEREMONY, COMPETITION AT MACOMB CITY SQ & CHANDLER PARK. (LOCAL). JOHN P SAPPINGTON; MACOMB CITY COUNCIL; 718 N MADISON; MACOMB, IL 61455. (#7929-1).

NOV 22, '75. BICENTENNIAL TURKEY SHOOT. CONTEST FOR 36 TO 58 CALIBER MUZZEL-LOADERS ONLY. AT STATE POLICE HEADQUARTERS, HIGHWAY 67 N. (LOCAL). JOHN SAPPINGTON, CHAIRMAN; MACOMB BICENTENNIAL COMMITTEE; 7 N MADISON; MACOMB, IL 61455. (#103378-4).

MAR 20, '76. VALLEY FORGE SQUARE DANCE. FESTIVAL AT MACOMB ARMORY. (LOCAL). JOHN SAPPINGTON, CHMN; MCDONOUGH COUNTY BICENTENNIAL COMMISSION; 718 N MADISON ST; MACOMB, IL 61455. (#200016-144).

MAY 7 - SEPT ??, '76. FRONTIER LIFE IN THE MILITARY TRACT (1750-1850). EXHIBIT. (LOCAL). JOHN SAPPINGTON, CHMN; WESTERN ILLINOIS UNIV STUDENT MUSEUM; 718 N MADISON ST; MACOMB, IL 61455. (#200016-143).

JULY 3 - 5, '76. MACOMB BICENTENNIAL CELEBRATION. PARADE, DINNERS, DANCES, TALENT CONTESTS, EXHIBITS, RELIGIOUS FESTIVAL, CIVIL WAR RE-ENACTMENTS, GAMES, COSTUME CONTESTS AND A PAGEANT ARE THE SCHEDULED ACTIVITIES. AT CHANDLER PARK. (LOCAL). JOHN SAPPINGTON, CHMN; MACOMB BICENTENNIAL COMMITTEE; 718 N MADISON; MACOMB, IL 61455. (#106215-1).

MADISON

JULY 2 - 4, '76. MADISON ETHNIC FESTIVAL. ETHNIC FOODS, MUSIC & DANCING. SENIOR CITIZENS AND COMMUNITY ORGANIZATIONS TO SELL PRODUCTS. AT ST MARYS CATHOLIC CHURCH, 12TH & ALTON AVE. (LOCAL). WILLIAM L GUSHLEFF, COORD; MADISON BICENTENNIAL COMMITTEE; 1671 4TH ST; MADISON, IL 62060. (#200016-230).

MAKANDA

JUNE 21, '75. COUNTRY CRAFT DAY. ACTIVITIES INCLUDE CRAFT DEMONSTRATIONS, NATURE TOURS AND BLUEGRASS MUSIC. AT GIANT CITY STATE PARK INTERPRETIVE CENTER. (LOCAL). MS JANET PICKETT; ILLINOIS DEPARTMENT OF CONSERVATION; 901 SOUTH SPRING; SPRINGFIELD, IL 62704. (#50272-45).

JULY 19, '75. COUNTRY CRAFT DAY. ACTIVITIES INCLUDE, CRAFT DEMONSTRATIONS, NATURE TOURS AND BLUEGRASS MUSIC. AT GIANT CITY STATE PARK INTERPRETIVE CENTER. (LOCAL). MS JANET PICKETT; ILLINOIS DEPARTMENT OF CONSERVATION; 901 SOUTH SPRING; SPRINGFIELD, IL 62704. (#50272-44).

AUG 16, '75. COUNTRY CRAFT DAY. ACTIVITIES INCLUDE, CRAFT DEMONSTRATIONS, NATURE TOURS AND BLUE GRASS MUSIC. AT GIANT CITY STATE PARK INTERPRETIVE CENTER. (LOCAL). MS JANET PICKETT; ILLINOIS DEPARTMENT OF CONSERVATION; 901 SOUTH SPRING; SPRINGFIELD, IL 62704. (#50272-43).

JULY 17, '76. COUNTRY CRAFT DAY. ACTIVITIES INCLUDE CRAFT DEMONSTRATIONS, NATURE TOURS AND BLUEGRASS MUSIC. AT GIANT CITY STATE PARK INTERPRETIVE CENTER. (LOCAL). MS JANET PICKETT; ILLINOIS DEPARTMENT OF CONSERVATION; 901 SOUTH SPRING; SPRINGFIELD, IL 62704. (#50272-42).

AUG 14, '76. COUNTRY CRAFT DAY. ACTIVITIES INCLUDE, CRAFT DEMONSTRATIONS, NATURE TOURS AND BLUEGRASS MUSIC. AT GIANT CITY STATE PARK INTERPRETIVE CENTER. (LOCAL). MS JANET PICKETT; ILLINOIS DEPARTMENT OF CONSERVATION; 901 SOUTH SPRING; SPRINGFIELD, IL 62704. (#50272-46).

MALTA

AMERICAN REVOLUTION - MALTA, IL. PROGRAM FOR COMMUNITY CLUBS & SCHOOL CHILDREN ON LIFE DURING THE REVOLUTIONARY WAR TIMES. (LOCAL). T JAN WISEMAN, DEAN; KISHWAUKEE COLLEGE; MALTA, IL 60150. (#23232).

COBBLESTONES, CORNBREAD AND CANDLESTICKS - IL. PROGRAM FOR SCHOOL CHILDREN & COMMUNITY CLUBS ON ROLE OF WOMEN IN EARLY AMERICA & TODAY. (LOCAL). T JAN WISEMAN, DEAN; KISHWAUKEE COLLEGE; MALTA, IL 60150. (#23231).

COFFEE BEANS & GOOBER PEAS - MALTA, IL. PROGRAM FOR COMMUNITY CLUBS & SCHOOL CHILDREN ON EVERY DAY LIFE OF THE CIVIL WAR AND PERIOD VALUES. (LOCAL). T JAN WISEMAN, DEAN; KISHWAUKEE COLLEGE; MALTA, IL 60150. (#23230).

COMMUNITY LEADERSHIP HALL OF FAME - MALTA, IL. A PERMANENT HALL OF FAME FOR COMMUNITY PERSONS WHO WORK TO IMPROVE THE QUALITY OF LIFE IN THEIR OWN COMMUNITY AND WHO EXEMPLIFY THE IDEALS OF THE AMERICAN EXPERIENCE. (LOCAL). T JAN WISEMAN, DEAN; KISHWAUKEE COLLEGE; MALTA, IL 60150. (#23233).

JULY 12 - 13, '75. BICENTENNIAL ARTS AND CRAFTS. EXHIBIT. (LOCAL). T JAN WISEMAN, DEAN; KISHWAUKEE COLLEGE; MALTA, IL 60150. (#106461-1).

MANLIUS

RESTORATION OF BERRY-SULLIVAN BANK BUILDING - IL. RESTORATION OF BANK BUILDING DESIGNED BY THE ARCHITECTS, BERRY AND SULLIVAN. (LOCAL). GRANT ANDRESEN, CHAIRMAN; MANLIUS BICENTENNIAL COMMISSION; BOX 192; MANLIUS, IL 61338. (#30410).

MARENGO

SEPT 26, '76. FIRST ANNUAL ARTS & CRAFTS FAIR. EXHIBIT AT GRADE SCHOOL GYM, ZION LUTHERAN SCHOOL. (LOCAL). CHRISTA MILLER; MARENGO BICENTENNIAL COMMISSION; MARENGO, IL 60152. (#200016-299).

MARION

HISTORY OF WILLIAMSON COUNTY - MARION, IL. THE HISTORY OF WILLIAMSON COUNTY WILL BE REPRINTED; THE AUTHOR IS MILO ERWIN. (LOCAL). ETHEL ASHBY, CHAIRMAN; WILLIAMSON COUNTY HISTORICAL SOCIETY; 105 S VAN BUREN ST; MARION, IL 62959. (#15326).

PIONEERS OF WILLIAMSON COUNTY, IL. MICROFILMING OF RECORDS OF 500 PIONEERS OF WILLIAMSON COUNTY BY THE MORMON CHURCH OF SALT LAKE CITY, UTAH. (LOCAL). ETHEL ASHBY, CHAIRMAN; WILLIAMSON COUNTY HISTORICAL SOCIETY; 105 S VAN BUREN; MARION, IL 62959. (#15327).

WILLIAMSON COUNTY, IL, HISTORICAL MUSEUM. RESTORATION OF THE OLD COUNTY JAIL AND SHERIFF'S HOME AS A MUSEUM. (LOCAL). ETHEL ASHBY, CHAIRMAN; WILLIAMSON COUNTY HISTORICAL SOCIETY; 105 S VAN BUREN; MARION, IL 62959. (#15328).

AUG 30 - SEPT 6, '75. WILLIAMSON COUNTY FAIR BICENTENNIAL FESTIVAL. THIS IS THE OLDEST FAIR IN ILLINOIS. IN 1976 IT WILL BE 120 YEARS OLD. AT WILLIAMSON COUNTY FAIR GROUNDS ON E MAIN ST. (LOCAL). ETHEL ASHBY, CHAIRMAN; WILLIAMSON COUNTY BICENTENNIAL COMMISSION; 301 E ALLEN, BOX 41; MARION, IL 62959. (#100958-1).

MARISSA

RENOVATION OF CITY PARK - MARISSA, ILLINOIS. RESTORATION OF CENTURY-OLD ACADEMY IN EXISTING PARK. EXPANSION TO INCLUDE ERECTION OF MINI-PLANETARIUM & COAL MUSEUM; RECONSTRUCTION OF 2 LOG CABINS & BANDSHELL; LANDSCAPING & GUEST PARKING. (LOCAL). JULIETTA BOTTIAUX, PRES; MARISSA NATIONAL BICENT COMMISSION; 212 N MAIN; MARISSA, IL 62257. (#10444).

JUNE 26, '76. HERITAGE FESTIVAL II. CITYWIDE HERITAGE FESTIVAL TO DEDICATE RESTORED CENTURY-OLD ACADEMY AT ALL DAY PICNIC WITH CRAFTSMEN FROM SOUTHERN ILLINOIS TO FINANCE COMPLETION OF CITY PARK. AT MARISSA CITY PARK. (LOCAL). MRS JULIETTA BOTTIAUX; MARISSA NATIONAL BICENTENNIAL COMMISSION; 212 N MAIN ST; MARISSA, IL 62257. (#103662-1).

MARSHALL

CLARK COUNTY, ILL, MUSEUM & LIBRARY PROJECT. MUSEUM WILL DISPLAY ITEMS SUCH AS CUT GLASS, OLD DOCUMENTS, COINS & STAMP COLLECTION. THERE WILL BE WORKSHOPS ON GENEALOGY & EXPANSION OF GENEALOGICAL LIBRARY. (LOCAL). JOY L MILLER, SECRETARY & TREASURER; CLARK COUNTY HISTORICAL SOCIETY; 502 S FOURTH; MARSHALL, IL 62441. (#2826).

RESTORATION AND RELOCATION OF LOG CABIN - IL. RESTORATION OF 1850 LOG CABIN AS MUSEUM AT BAPTIST CHURCH IN ORANGE TOWNSHIP. (LOCAL). DREW CASTEEL, CHAIRMAN; CLARK COUNTY BICENTENNIAL COMMISSION; 207 ARCHER AVE; MARSHALL, IL 62441. (#30404).

MAY 17 - 18, '75. ENVIRONMENTAL WEEK-END. ECOLOGY TOURS; SEMINARS; WILD FOODS. (LOCAL). MS JANET PICKETT; ILL DEPT OF CONSERVATION; 901 SOUTH SPRING; SPRINGFIELD, IL 62704. (#50272-47).

JUNE 6 - 8, '75. BICENTENNIAL SPRING FESTIVAL. BAND CONCERT, ART SHOW, SQUARE DANCING, ARTS & CRAFTS, EXHIBITS, PARADE. AT CLARK COUNTY COURTHOUSE SQUARE. (LOCAL). JOY L MILLER; CLARK COUNTY HISTORICAL SOCIETY & MARSHALL CHAMBER OF COMMERCE; 415 NORTH SEVENTH; MARSHALL, IL 62441. (#50723-1).

JULY 3 - 10, '76. BICENTENNIAL CARNIVAL. FESTIVAL. (LOCAL). R DREW CASTEEL; CLARK COUNTY BICENTENNIAL COMMISSION; 207 ARCHER AVE; MARSHALL, IL 62441. (#200016-208).

MASCOUTAH

RESTORATION OF THE L & N RAILROAD STATION - IL. RESTORATION OF RR STATION FOR USE AS A COMMUNITY CENTER. (LOCAL). ROBERT FRITZ, CHAIRMAN; MASCOUTAH BICENTENNIAL COMMISSION; 55 W CHURCH ST; MASCOUTAH, IL 62258. (#27881). **ARBA GRANTEE.**

MATTESON

MATTESON HISTORICAL SOCIETY - IL. CREATION OF GROUP TO PRESERVE AND DOCUMENT HISTORY OF VILLAGE, PLATTED IN 1855. (LOCAL). HENRY W LEHMANN, PRESIDENT; MATTESON HISTORICAL SOCIETY; 3624 W 216TH ST; MATTESON, IL 60443. (#28650).

OCT 12 - 25, '75. MATTESON HISTORICAL SOCIETY EXHIBIT. EXHIBIT AT LINCOLN MALL SHOPPING CENTER. (LOCAL). ELIZABETH F GOYAK, CHMN; BICENTENNIAL COMMISSION & MATTESON HISTORICAL SOCIETY; 21310 BUTTERFIELD PKY; MATTESON, IL 60443. (#200016-242).

MATTESON — CONTINUED

OCT 25, '75. BICENTENNIAL BALL. FESTIVAL AT LINCOLN MALL SHOPPING CENTER. (LOCAL). ELIZABETH F GOYAK; MATTESON BICENTENNIAL COMMISSION & MATTESON FIREMEN'S ASSOC; 21310 BUTTERFIELD PKY; MATTESON, IL 60443. (#200016-243).

MAY 31, '76. BICENTENNIAL PARADE. PARADE. (LOCAL). ELIZABETH F GOYAK, CHMN; BICENTENNIAL COMMISSION & AMERICAN LEGION POST NO 474; 21310 BUTTERFIELD PKY; MATTESON, IL 60443. (#200016-225).

JULY 31, '76. BLOCK PARTY. FESTIVAL AT 216TH ST HISTORICAL AREA. (LOCAL). ELIZABETH F GOYAK, CHMN; BICENTENNIAL COMMISSION & MATTESON LIONS CLUB; 21310 BUTTERFIELD PKY; MATTESON, IL 60443. (#200016-226).

MATTOON

BICENTENNIAL GARDEN - MATTOON, IL. CONSTRUCTION OF BICENTENNIAL GARDEN AT SARAH BUSH LINCOLN HEALTH CENTER. (LOCAL). ROBERT KORACK, CHAIRMAN; MATTOON BICENTENNIAL COMMISSION; MATTOON, IL 61938. (#30400).

HISTORY OF COLES COUNTY - MATTOON, IL. PUBLICATION OF 'HISTORY OF COLES COUNTY', A 900-PAGE BOOK. (LOCAL). ROBERT KOVACK, COORDINATOR; MATTOON AND CHARLESTON BICENTENNIAL COMMISSIONS; MATTOON, IL 61938. (#30402).

REPAIR OF SHILOH CHURCH - MATTOON, IL. RESTORATION OF INTERIOR AND EXTERIOR OF SHILOH CHURCH. (LOCAL). BURNHAM NEAL, COORDINATOR; LAKE LAND COLLEGE; MATTOON, IL 61938. (#30401).

MAYWOOD

MAYWOOD BANDSTAND RECONSTRUCTION - MAYWOOD, IL. CONSTRUCTION OF A TURN-OF-THE-CENTURY REPLICA BANDSTAND TO SERVE AS A FOCAL POINT OF COMMUNITY ACTIVITIES. (LOCAL). PATRICIA WHITE, CO-CHAIRMAN; MAYWOOD BICENTENNIAL COMMISSION; 115 S 5TH AVE; MAYWOOD, IL 60153. (#24889). **ARBA GRANTEE.**

JUNE 5, '76. DANCE RECITAL. LIVE PERFORMANCE AT ROVISO EAST AUDITORIUM, 807 S 1ST AVE. (LOCAL). EDWARD J MCCORRY, CHMN; BROADVIEW PARK DISTRICT DANCE CLASSES; 2600 S 13TH AVE; BROADVIEW, IL 60153. (#105415-1).

MCLEANSBORO

FEB 28, '76. PIE & BOX SUPPER. FESTIVAL AT EASTSIDE GRADE SCHOOL. (LOCAL). JOSEPHINE TRAPP, CHMN; HAMILTON COUNTY BICENTENNIAL COMMITTEE; MCLEANSBORO, IL 62859. (#200016-43).

MAY 16, '76. HISTORICAL HOMES TOUR AND MUSEUM TOUR. TOUR AT MCCOY LIBRARY. (LOCAL). FRANK BONAN, DIRECTOR; HAMILTON COUNTY HISTORICAL SOCIETY; MCLEANSBORO, IL 62859. (#108342-3).

MEDIA

HENDERSON COUNTY HISTORY BOOKS - MEDIA, IL. PUBLICATION OF NEW COUNTY HISTORY AND REPRINTING OF 1882 AND 1911 HISTORIES OF HENDERSON COUNTY. (LOCAL). ART KANE, CHAIRMAN; HENDERSON COUNTY BICENTENNIAL COMMISSION; RR; MEDIA, IL 61460. (#30419).

MELVIN

DEC 22, '75. COMMUNITY CHRISTMAS CAROLLING. FESTIVAL AT LUTHERAN CHURCH. (LOCAL). JOY THOMPSON; BICENTENNIAL COMM OF MELVIN; 211 N HUNT ST; MELVIN, IL 60952. (#200016-287).

JAN 24, '76. FAMILY GAME NIGHT. FESTIVAL AT METHODIST CHURCH. (LOCAL). JOY THOMPSON; MELVIN BICENTENNIAL COMMISSION; 211 N HUNT ST; MELVIN, IL 60952. (#200016-288).

FEB 21, '76. BOX SOCIAL & ENTERTAINMENT. LIVE PERFORMANCE AT HS GYM. (LOCAL). MYRON BOYD; MELVIN BICENTENNIAL COMMITTEE; MELVIN, IL 60952. (#200016-290).

MAR 20, '76. QUILT & CRAFT SHOW. EXHIBIT AT ST PETER'S LUTHERAN PARISH HALL. (LOCAL). GENEVA BRINKMAN; ST PETER'S LUTHERAN CHURCH; MELVIN, IL 60952. (#200016-295).

APR 3, '76. KITE FLYING CONTEST. FESTIVAL AT ATHLETIC FIELD. (LOCAL). GERALD LACKEY, CUBMASTER; MELVIN CUB SCOUT PACK 34; RR 1; MELVIN, IL 60952. (#200016-442).

APR 24, '76. VILLAGE FLAG PRESENTATION, TREE PLANTING, ARBA FLAG PRESENTATION. CEREMONY, PARADE AT MAIN ST. (LOCAL). JOY THOMPSON; MELVIN BICENTENNIAL COMMISSION; 211 N HUNT ST; MELVIN, IL 60952. (#200016-289).

MAY 10, '76. AMERICAN ISSUES FORUM DEBATE. TOPIC:'RESOLVED-EXTREMISM IN THE DEFENSE OF LIBERTY IS NO VICE' FROM AMERICAN ISSUES FORUM. AT MELVIN HS. (LOCAL). WILLIAM WALKER; MELVIN BICENTENNIAL COMMISSION; MELVIN, IL 60952. (#200016-291).

JUNE 19, '76. PROMENADE & STREET DANCE. FESTIVAL AT MAIN ST. (LOCAL). RAY BRINKMAN; MELVIN BICENTENNIAL COMMITTEE; MELVIN, IL 60952. (#200016-294).

AUG 28, '76. OUTDOOR MOVIE. EXHIBIT AT CENTER ST. (LOCAL). JOHN CLARK; LIONS CLUB; MELVIN, IL 60952. (#200016-292).

SEPT 4 - 5, '76. COMMUNITY CELEBRATION. CEREMONY, COMPETITION, AWARDS, EXHIBIT, FESTIVAL & PARADE. AT MELVIN SCHOOL GROUNDS. (LOCAL). JOY THOMPSON; MELVIN BICENTENNIAL COMMITTEE; 211 N HUNT ST; MELVIN, IL 60952. (#200016-300).

MENDOTA

AUG 8 - 10, '75. MENDOTA SWEET CORN FESTIVAL. ANNUAL SWEET CORN FESTIVAL TO HAVE BICENTENNIAL THEME IN 1975 AND 1976. (LOCAL). MIKE O'CONNOR; MENDOTA AREA CHAMBER OF COMMERCE; MENDOTA, IL 61342. (#5720-501).

APR 24 - 25, '76. WAGON TRAIN STOPOVER. CEREMONY. (ST-WIDE). JULIE WILLIAMS, COORD; ILLINOIS BICENTENNIAL COMMISSION; 1 W OLD STATE CAPITOL PLAZA; SPRINGFIELD, IL 62706. (#200016-209).

AUG 13 - 15, '76. MENDOTA SWEET CORN FESTIVAL. ANNUAL SWEET CORN FESTIVAL TO HAVE BICENTENNIAL THEME IN 1975 AND 1976. (LOCAL). MIKE O'CONNOR; MENDOTA AREA CHAMBER OF COMMERCE; MENDOTA, IL 61342. (#5720-502).

MEREDOSIA

MAY 29, '76. BICENTENNIAL FESTIVAL. FESTIVAL. (LOCAL). DON ROBINSON, CHMN; MORGAN COUNTY BICENTENNIAL COMMISSION; 834 N CHURCH; JACKSONVILLE, IL 62650. (#200016-119).

JUNE 25, '76. THEATRE PRODUCTION - 1776. LIVE PERFORMANCE. (LOCAL). DON ROBINSON, CHMN; JACKSONVILLE SUMMER THEATRE; 834 N CHURCH; JACKSONVILLE, IL 62650. (#200016-118).

FEB 2 - 3, '77. LA SALLE EXPEDITION II, A HISTORIC RE-ENACTMENT. THIS IS AN AUTHENTIC RE-ENACTMENT OF THE 1681 LASALLE EXPEDITION FROM MONTREAL, CANADA TO NEW ORLEANS, LA WHICH WILL BEGIN TOURING ON AUGUST 11, 1976 AND END ON APRIL 9, 1977. (LOCAL). REID H LEWIS, DIRECTOR; LA SALLE EXPEDITION II; 135 S LA SALLE ST, RM 411; CHICAGO, IL 60690. (#102805-49).

METAMORA

REENACTMENT OF HISTORICAL EVENT - METAMORA, IL. ACTUAL CASE TRIED IN METAMORE WITH LINCOLN AS DEFENSE ATTORNEY. A LOCAL CASE: MELISSA GOINGS STRUCK HER HUSBAND ON THE HEAD WITH A PIECE OF FIRE WOOD AND KILLED HIM. (LOCAL). JEAN TANTON/ALVERDA GARBER, CO-CHAIRMEN; METAMORA BICENTENNIAL COMMISSION; 815 EASTMORE DR; METAMORA, IL 61548. (#33512).

RE-ENACTMENT OF MELISSA GOINGS TRIAL OF 1857. RE-ENACTMENT OF MELISSA GOINGS TRIAL OF 1857 IN METAMORA COURTHOUSE. (ST-WIDE). ROBERT ELBERT; METAMORA BICENTENNIAL COMMISSION; BOX 1776; METAMORA, IL 61548. (#27665). **ARBA GRANTEE.**

APR 23, '76. WAGON TRAIN STOP. EXHIBIT AT OLD STATE CAPITOL PLAZA. (LOCAL). JULIE WILLIAMS, CHMN; ILLINOIS BICENTENNIAL COMMISSION; SPRINGFIELD, IL 62706. (#200016-79).

JUNE 23 - 26, '76. OLD SETTLER'S DAYS. FESTIVAL AT VILLAGE SQUARE. (LOCAL). ALVERDA GARBER, CHMN; METAMORA & WOODFORD COUNTY BICENT COMM & OLD SETTLERS' ASSN; 815 EASTMOOR DR; METAMORA, IL 61548. (#200016-81).

JULY 4, '76. ECUMENICAL SERVICE. SERVICE HELD IN A LOVELY SHADED PARK IN THE CENTER OF THE TOWN SQUARE. (LOCAL). ALVERDA GARBER, CHMN; METAMORA & WOODFORD COUNTY BICENT COMMISSIONS; 815 EASTMOOR DR; METAMORA, IL 61548. (#200016-80).

SEPT 7, '76. EIGHTH JUDICIAL CIRCUIT RIDE. PARADE. (LOCAL). PHYLLIS EUBANKS, CHMN; ILLINOIS DEPARTMENT OF CONSERVATION; 901 S SPRING ST; SPRINGFIELD, IL 62706. (#200016-82).

SEPT 19, '76. RE-ENACTMENT OF MELISSA GOINGS TRIAL OF 1857 IN METAMORA COURTHOUSE. LIVE PERFORMANCE AT METAMORA COURTHOUSE. (ST-WIDE). ROBERT ELBERT; METAMORA BICENTENNIAL COMMISSION; BOX 1776; METAMORA, IL 61548. (#27665-1).

METROPOLIS

MASSAC COUNTY HORIZONS PROJECT, IL. IN HONOR OF THE BICENT, THE ENTIRE COURTHOUSE BLOCK OF METROPOLIS WILL UNDERGO A FACELIFT WHICH WILL INCLUDE: ANTIQUE DRINKING FOUNTAINS, A WATERING SYSTEM, NEW SIDEWALKS & PLANTS. (LOCAL). BETTY E GRACE, CHAIRMAN; MASSAC COUNTY BICENTENNIAL COMMITTEE; PO BOX 378; METROPOLIS, IL 62960. (#10651).

APR 19, '75. HISTORIC FILM FESTIVAL. FILMS ON EARLY AMERICAN HISTORY ESPECIALLY THOSE PERTAINING TO CULTU RES WHICH HELPED TO SETTLE THE ILLINOIS COUNTRY. AT FORT MASSAC STATE PARK INTERPRETIVE CENTER. (LOCAL). MS JANET PICKETT; ILLINOIS DEPARTMENT OF CONSERVATION; 901 SOUTH SPRING; SPRINGFIELD, IL 62704. (#50272-50).

JULY 5, '75. FRONTIER DAYS. CRAFTS, FLINTLOCK RIFLE DEMONSTRATION AND FRENCH VOYAGEURS. AT FORT MASSAC STATE PARK INTERPRETIVE CENTER. (LOCAL). MS JANET PICKETT; ILLINOIS DEPARTMENT OF CONSERVATION; 901 SOUTH SPRING; SPRINGFIELD, IL 62704. (#50272-52).

SEPT 13, '75. HARVEST CRAFT FESTIVAL. CRAFTS AND MUSIC ABOUND AS THE FORT ONCE AGAIN RETURNS TO THE EARLY EIGHTEEN HUNDREDS. AT FORT MASSAC STATE PARK INTERPRETIVE CENTER. (LOCAL). MS JANET PICKETT; ILLINOIS DEPARTMENT OF CONSERVATION; 901 SOUTH SPRING; SPRINGFIELD, IL 62704. (#50272-54).

NOV 1 - 2, '75. FT MASSAC-1776. DEPICTS AMERICAN FRONTIER LIFE AT FORT IN 1770'S. (LOCAL). MS JANET PICKETT; ILL DEPT OF CONSERVATION; 901 SOUTH SPRING; SPRINGFIELD, IL 62704. (#50272-48).

MAR 6, '76. HISTORIC FILM FESTIVAL. FILMS ON EARLY AMERICAN HISTORY ESPECIALLY THOSE PERTAINING TO CULTURES WHICH HELPED TO SETTLE THE ILLINOIS COUNTRY. AT FORT MASSAC STATE PARK INTERPRETIVE CENTER. (LOCAL). MS JANET PICKETT; ILLINOIS DEPARTMENT OF CONSERVATION; 901 SOUTH SPRING; SPRINGFIELD, IL 62704. (#50272-51).

JUNE 26 - 27, '76. FT MASSAC-1776. DEPICTS AMERICAN FRONTIER LIFE AT FORT IN 1770'S. (LOCAL). MS JANET PICKETT; ILL DEPT OF CONSERVATION; 901 SOUTH SPRING; SPRINGFIELD, IL 62704. (#50272-49).

AUG 14, '76. FRONTIER DAYS. CRAFTS, FLINTLOCK RIFLE DEMONSTRATION, AND FRENCH VOYAGEURS. AT ILLINOIS DEPARTMENT OF CONSERVATION. (LOCAL). MS JANET PICKETT; ILLINOIS DEPT OF CONSERVATION; 901 SOUTH SPRING; SPRINGFIELD, IL 62704. (#50272-53).

OCT 2, '76. HARVEST CRAFT FESTIVAL. CRAFTS AND MUSIC ABOUND AS THE FORT ONCE AGAIN RETURNS TO THE EARLY EIGHTEEN HUNDREDS. AT FORT MASSAC STATE PARK INTERPRETIVE CENTER. (LOCAL). MS JANET PICKETT; ILLINOIS DEPARTMENT OF CONSERVATION; 901 SOUTH SPRING; SPRINGFIELD, IL 62704. (#50272-55).

MIDDLETOWN

FEB 1, '75. 'BICENTENNIAL COMEDY REVUE'. FIRST BICENTENNIAL EVENT IN LOGAN COUNTY, ILLINOIS. AT NEW HOLLAND-MIDDLETOWN MIDDLE SCHOOL GYMNASIUM. (LOCAL). WINIFRED GOLDEN, COORD; MIDDLETOWN BICENTENNIAL COMMISSION; PO BOX 225; MIDDLETOWN, IL 62666. (#200016-446).

MAR 27, '76. 'MEMORIES WITH MUSIC' - A HISTORICAL MUSICAL. LIVE PERFORMANCE AT NEW HOLLAND-MIDDLETOWN MIDDLE SCHOOL GYMNASIUM. (LOCAL). WINIFRED GOLDEN, V-PRES; MIDDLETOWN BICENTENNIAL COMMISSION; PO BOX 225; MIDDLETOWN, IL 62666. (#200016-41).

JUNE 11 - 13, '76. BICENTENNIAL FESTIVAL '76. SOME OF THE SCHEDULED ACTIVITIES ARE CRAFTS SHOWS, DANCING, RAILSPLITTING CONTESTS AND A PARADE. ALSO, MUSKET SHOOT, TOMAHAWK THROW, TRACTOR PULL AND MANY OTHER OLD-FASHIONED GAMES; CHURCH SERVICE AND A HISTORICAL TOUR. AT MIDDLETOWN PUBLIC SQUARE AND PARK. (LOCAL). TERRY STEINHOUR, COORD; MIDDLETOWN BICENTENNIAL COMMITTEE; RR #1; GREENVIEW, IL 62642. (#106219-1).

MILAN

ADOPTION OF INDIAN GIRL IN MILAN, ILLINOIS. SPONSORSHIP & SUPPORT OF AN INDIAN CHILD ON A RESERVATION IN ARIZONA BECAUSE OF LOCAL INDIAN HISTORY & PAGEANTRY & TO COMMEMORATE THE BICENTENNIAL. (LOCAL). MRS DWAIN WYANT, CHAIRMAN BICENTENNIAL COMMISSION; MILAN WOMENS CLUB; 452 4TH ST EAST; MILAN, IL 61264. (#2678).

PARK PROJECT FOR MILAN, ILLINOIS. HORIZONS PROJECT OF MILAN. PARK TO BE EQUIPPED, COMPLETED, NAMED, AND DEDICATED IN JULY, 1976 FOR THE CITIZENRY OF MILAN AND SURROUNDING ROCK ISLAND COUNTY. (LOCAL). MRS DWAIN WYANT, PROJECT DIRECTOR; MILAN BICENTENNIAL COMMISSION; 452 4TH ST E; MILAN, IL 61264. (#4881). **ARBA GRANTEE.**

JUNE 8, '75. COUNTRY FAIR FLEA MARKET. PROJECT FUND RAISING EVENT PROCEEDS TO CAMDEN PARK MILAN BICENTENNIAL COMMISSIONS BIG EFFORT TO HELP DEVELOPE NEW PARK. AT BOB ERIKSON CHEVY CENTER. (LOCAL). CONNIE WYANT; MILAN IMPROVEMENT PROJECTS; 452 4TH EAST; MILAN, IL 61264. (#50500-1).

JULY 4, '75. LANTERN PARADE. GRADE SCHOOL CHILDREN MAKING PATRIOTIC LANTERNS FOR COMPETETION IN CONJUNCTION WITH PARK PROGRAM SEVERAL LOCAL ORGANIZATIONS DONATING MONEY FOR MATERIALS PLUS AWARDS THREE LOCAL CHURCH YOUTH GROUPS WILL MERGE TOGETHER TO PRESENT CHORAL PROGRAM WITH PATRIOTIC THEME. AT DICKSON BALL PARK. (LOCAL). CONNIE WYANT; MILAN BICENTENNIAL COMMISSION; 452 4TH EAST; MILAN, IL 61264. (#50499-1).

JUNE 13, '76. DEDICATION OF PARK FACILITIES IN MILAN, ILLINOIS. DEDICATED TO THE CITIZENRY OF MILAN AND SURROUNDING ROCK ISLAND COUNTY. (LOCAL). MRS DWAIN WYANT, CHAIRMAN; MILAN BICENTENNIAL COMMISSION; 452 4TH ST E; MILAN, IL 61264. (#4881-1).

MILLEDGEVILLE

JUNE 19, '76. PIONEER DAY FESTIVAL. ENTERTAINMENT, EXHIBITS, CRAFTS, MOVIES, DANCES, DEMONSTRATIONS SPEAKERS, & REFRESHMENTS, HORSE PULLS, & ANTIQUE VEHICLE DISPLAY. AT CARROLL COUNTY FAIRGROUNDS, 1 MILE OFF

MILLEDGEVILLE — CONTINUED

STATE ROUTE 88. (LOCAL). MS JERRY ASHBY, FIELD DIR; GREEN HILLS GIRL SCOUT COUNCIL; 4 E STEPHENSON ST; FREEPORT, IL 61032. (#105725-1).

MINOOKA

BOOKS FOR MANKIND, A USED BOOK DRIVE IN IL. COLLECTION OF USED AND NEW BOOKS FOR NEW LIBRARY. (LOCAL). LORETTA MCLAUGHLIN, CHAIRMAN; MINOOKA BICENTENNIAL COMMISSION; 103 ILLINI DR; MINOOKA, IL 60447. (#33571).

JULY 2, '76. THE 4TH OF JULY FOLLIES. FESTIVAL AT MINOOKA JR HIGH GYM. (LOCAL). LORETTA MCLAUGHLIN, CHMN; MINOOKA BICENTENNIAL COMMISSION; 103 ILLINI DR; MINOOKA, IL 60447. (#200016-408).

MOKENA

RESTORATION OF OLD ST MARY'S CHURCH - IL. RESTORING 1864 CHURCH TO ORIGINAL APPEARANCE. (LOCAL). JAMES COOPER, CHAIRMAN; MOKENA BICENTENNIAL COMMISSION; 10940 FRONT ST; MOKENA, IL 60448. (#27887). **ARBA GRANTEE.**

MOLINE

BICENTENNIAL GEMS FROM MOLINE, ILLINOIS. AUDIO-VISUAL TV-TAPED DISCUSSION WITH SENIORS ON THE ART OF LOST CRAFTS AND ORAL HISTORY. (LOCAL). ROBERT FLETCHER, DIR OF TELEVISION; BLACK HAWK COLLEGE BICENTENNIAL COMMISSION; 6600-34TH AVE; MOLINE, IL 61265. (#10238).

BILLBOARDS - PROJ OF MOLINE, IL. ORIGINAL DESIGN FOR 5 BILLBOARDS TO BE PLACED IN THE AREA; THEY WILL PROVIDE INFORMATION ON THE CITY OF MOLINE. (LOCAL). SANDY BELLINGER, CHAIRPERSON; MOLINE BICENTENNIAL COMMISSION; 619 19TH ST; MOLINE, IL 61265. (#14865).

BLACK HAWK COLLEGE CATALOG DEDICATED TO BICENT, IL. COLLEGE CATALOG FOR 1976 WILL BE DEDICATED TO THE BICENTENNIAL WITH PICTURES DEPICTING HISTORY OF THE COLLEGE DISTRICT AND PROGRAMS. (ST-WIDE). WILLIAM HANNAN, ASST PROFESSOR; BLACK HAWK COLLEGE BICENT COMMISSION; 6600 34TH AVE; MOLINE, IL 61265. (#9926).

BROCHURES - PROJ OF MOLINE, IL. AN ORIGINAL, DESCRIPTIVE PAMPHLET CONTAINING INFORMATION ON THE CITY OF MOLINE WILL BE DISTRIBUTED. (LOCAL). SANDY BELLINGER, CHAIRPERSON; MOLINE BICENTENNIAL COMMISSION; 619 19TH ST; MOLINE, IL 61265. (#14867).

COUNTY HISTORICAL BOOKLET - PROJ OF MOLINE, IL. A BOOKLET ON THE HISTORY OF THE COUNTY WILL BE COMPILED BY THE COUNTY COMMITTEE. (LOCAL). SANDY BELLINGER, CHAIRPERSON; MOLINE BICENTENNIAL COMMISSION; 619 19TH ST; MOLINE, IL 61265. (#14868).

GUIDE TO HISTORIC SITES IN ROCK ISLAND CO, IL. A COMPILATION OF HISTORIC SITES IN ROCK ISLAND COUNTY TO BE PUBLISHED AS TOUR GUIDE. OWNERS OF SUCH SITES WILL BE PRESENTED WITH CERTIFICATES OF RECOGNITION. (LOCAL). OTTO W SCHWEINBERGER, CHAIRMAN; ROCK ISLAND COUNTY BICENTENNIAL COMMISSION; 6600 34TH AVE; MOLINE, IL 61265. (#7738).

HISTORY OF COLLEGE IN MOLINE, IL TO BE PUBLISHED. UPDATE AND PUBLISH HISTORY OF BLACK HAWK COLLEGE FOR PAST 30 YEARS. (LOCAL). MARY MORRISSEY, ASSOC PROFESSOR; BLACK HAWK COLLEGE BICEN COMMISSION; 6600 34TH AVE; MOLINE, IL 61265. (#9722).

A HISTORY OF TERRITORIAL MONTANA. RESEARCH INTO THE SOCIAL, CULTURAL, AND POLITICAL HISTORY OF THE TERRITORY OF MONTANA, 1862-1889. (NAT'L). CHAIRMAN; DEPT OF HISTORY; BLACK HAWK COLLEGE; MOLINE, IL 61265. (#3814). **(??).**

MINI-PARK - PROJ OF MOLINE, IL. A MINI-PARK WILL BE DEVELOPED IN THE AREA OF I-74 IN COOPERATION WITH THE PARK DEPT AND THE ILLINOIS DEPT OF TRANSPORTATION. (LOCAL). SANDY BELLINGER, CHAIRPERSON; MOLINE BICENTENNIAL COMMISSION; 619 19TH ST; MOLINE, IL 61265. (#14864).

PARK DEPARTMENT FLOWER BEDS - PROJ OF MOLINE, IL. RED, WHITE AND BLUE FLOWERS WILL BE PLACED IN THE CITY'S PARKS. (LOCAL). SANDY BELLINGER, CHAIRPERSON; MOLINE BICENTENNIAL COMMISSION; 619 19TH ST; MOLINE, IL 61265. (#14866).

PIONEER HOMES OF ROCK ISLAND COUNTY, ILLINOIS. ON JULY 4TH '76, ROCK ISLAND COUNTY BICENT COMM WILL RECOGNIZE & PREPARE MARKERS FOR CERTIFIED PIONEER HOMES IN THE COUNTY. A TOUR GUIDE WITH A HISTORY OF EACH HOME WILL BE PUBLISHED. (LOCAL). OTTO W SCHWEINBERGER, CHAIRMAN; ROCK ISLAND COUNTY BICENTENNIAL COMMISSION; 6600 34TH AVE; MOLINE, IL 61265. (#8653).

PLACEMATS - PROJ OF MOLINE, IL. AN ORIGINAL, PATRIOTIC DESIGN FOR BICENTENNIAL PLACEMATS. (LOCAL). SANDY BELLINGER, CHAIRPERSON; MOLINE BICENTENNIAL COMMISSION; 619 19TH ST; MOLINE, IL 61265. (#14863).

ROCK ISLAND COUNTY CLEANUP - ILLINOIS. PROMOTION OF JOHNNY HORIZONS THROUGHOUT COUNTY PARKS AND RECREATION AREAS. (LOCAL). OTTO W SCHWEINBERGER, CHAIRMAN; ROCK ISLAND COUNTY BICENTENNIAL COMMISSION; 6600 34TH AVE; MOLINE, IL 61265. (#7737).

ROCK ISLAND & SCOTT COUNTY, ILL, HISTORY PROJ. A COMPREHENSIVE HISTORY OF ROCK ISL CO, ILL AND SCOTT CO, IOWA TO BE PRODUCED AND PUBLISHED FOR DISTRIBUTION TO AREA SCHOOLS TO AID IN TEACHING LOCAL HISTORY. (ST-WIDE). OTTO W SCHWEINBERGER, PROJECT DIRECTOR; ROCK ISLAND BICENTENNIAL COMMISSION; BLACK HAWK COLLEGE; MOLINE, IL 61265. (#5329).

SPEAKER'S BUREAU - PROJ OF MOLINE, IL. A COMMISSION AND A FEW COMMITTEE MEMBERS WERE TRAINED TO SHARE TALKS, FILM AND SLIDE PRESENTATIONS TO GROUPS UPON REQUEST. IN 19741975 THIS GROUP GAVE 14 TALKS TO 950 PERSONS. (LOCAL). SANDY BELLINGER, CHAIRPERSON; MOLINE BICENTENNIAL COMMISSION; 619 19TH ST; MOLINE, IL 61265. (#14861).

TRIVETS - PROJ OF MOLINE, IL. USE OF MOLINE'S BICENTENNIAL LOGO FOR PERMANENT SOUVENIRS. (LOCAL). SANDY BELLINGER, CHAIRPERSON; MOLINE BICENTENNIAL COEMISSION; 619 19TH ST; MOLINE, IL 61265. (#14862).

WHEEL TAX STICKERS - MOLINE, IL. THE STICKERS CONTAIN THE FIRST USAGE OF MOLINE'S BICENTENNIAL SYMBOL. (LOCAL). SANDY BELLINGER, CHAIRPERSON; MOLINE BICENTENNIAL COMMISSION; 619 19TH ST; MOLINE, IL 61265. (#14860).

JUNE 13, '75. RESEARCHING LOCAL HISTORY CONFERENCE IN MOLINE, IL. CONFERENCE PROVIDING PROPER PROCEDURES AND TECHNIQUES FOR RESEARCHING LOCAL HISTORY. ALSO: RESEARCH. (LOCAL). MS MARY MORRISSEY & OTTO; BLACK HAWK COLLEGE BICENT COMMISSION; 6600 34TH AVE; MOLINE, IL 61265. (#9720-1).

NOV '75. AMERICAN EDUCATION WEEK DISPLAY BY AREA SCHOOLS. EXHIBIT, TOUR. (LOCAL). SANDY BELLINGEE; MOLINE BICENTENNIAL COMMISSION; 619 16TH ST; MOLINE, IL 61265. (#14845-502).

FEB 22, '76. HAIR FAIR '76. FAIR AT MOLINE YWCA. (LOCAL). SANDRA BELLINGER, COORD; NORTHWESTERN HAIRDRESSERS & COSMETOLOGY ASSOC; 619 16TH ST; MOLINE, IL 61265. (#200016-42).

APR 17 - MAY 9, '76. BICENTENNIAL FINE ARTS FAIR. PRESENTATION OF A PLAY, ART, RECITALS & CONCERTS BY THE FINE ARTS DIVISION OF BLACK HAWK COLLEGE. AT BLACK HAWK COLLEGE STUDENT CNTR & LECTURE HALL 1-306. (LOCAL). RALPH DREXLER; BLACK HAWK COLLEGE BICENT COMMISSION; 6600 34TH AVE; MOLINE, IL 61265. (#9721-1).

APR '76. TOUR OF HISTORIC HOMES. EXHIBIT, TOUR. (LOCAL). SANDY BELLINGEE; MOLINE BICENTENNIAL COMMISSION; 619 16TH ST; MOLINE, IL 61265. (#14845-503).

MAY 13, '76. BICENTENNIAL CONCERT. IN HONOR OF THE BICENTENNIAL, THERE WILL BE A CONCERT BY THE COLLEGE BAND OF PATRIOTIC SONGS. AT STUDENT CENTER BLDG. (LOCAL). OTTO W SCHWEINBERGER; BLACK HAWK COLLEGE BICENTENNIAL COMMISSION; 6600 34TH AVE; MOLINE, IL 61265. (#10254-1).

MAY 21, '76. JOINT BLACK HAWK DISTRICT GRADUATION. CEREMONY. (LOCAL). F E STAHL, DEAN; BLACK HAWK COLLEGE; PO BOX 489; KEWANEE, IL 61443. (#105192-3).

MAY 22, '76. BICENTENNIAL PARADE. PARADE AT OPENING CEREMONY AT PARKING LOT 20TH STREET AND 5TH AVENUE. (LOCAL). SANDRA BELLINGER, COORD; MOLINE AMERICAN LEGION POST 246 AND MOLINE BICENTENNIAL COMMISSION; 619 16TH ST; MOLINE, IL 61265. (#107753-1).

MAY 29 - 30, '76. COLONIAL CRAFT FAIR. FAIR. (LOCAL). SANDY BELLINGER, CHMN; MOLINE BICENTENNIAL COMMISSION; 619 16TH ST; MOLINE, IL 61265. (#102091-4).

MAY 31, '76. ANNUAL BICYCLE RACES. COMPETITION AT 7TH STREET BUSINESS AREA. (LOCAL). SANDRA BELLINGER; SW BLUFF BUSINESSMEN'S ASSOC; 619 16TH ST; MOLINE, IL 61265. (#107753-2).

JUNE 1 - SEPT 1, '76. WINDOW DISPLAYS BY MERCHANTS. VARIOUS WINDOW DISPLAYS WILL BE SET UP IN HONOR OF THE BICENTENNIAL AND THERE WILL BE A TOUR OF HISTORIC HOMES. (LOCAL). SANDY BELLINGEE; MOLINE BICENTENNIAL COMMISSION; 619 16TH ST; MOLINE, IL 61265. (#14845-501).

JUNE 13, '76. PROSPECT PARK FESTIVAL. LOG ROLLING OPEN TO PUBLIC; CANOE RACE LIMITED TO MEMBERS OF CITY COUNCIL, MAYOR, CITY ADMINISTRATOR OR A DESIGNATED REPRESENTATIVE; MUSKET SHOOTING DEMONSTRATION. AT PROSPECT PARK, 16TH STREET PLACE, 32ND AVENUE AND PARK LAGOON. (LOCAL). SANDRA BELLINGER, COORD; MOLINE BICENTENNIAL COMMISSION; 619 16TH ST; MOLINE, IL 61265. (#107402-5).

JUNE 19 - 20, '76. MOLINE EVENING OPTIMIST CLUB HORSESHOW. APPROVED EVENT OF THE ILLINOIS STOCKHORSE ASSOCIATION. CASH PRIZES; 13 EVENTS. AT GREEN VALLEY PARK, MOLINE. (LOCAL). SANDRA BELLINGER, COORD; MOLINE EVENING OPTIMIST CLUB AND MOLINE BICENTENNIAL COMMISSION; 619 16TH ST; MOLINE, IL 61265. (#107402-4).

JUNE 26, '76. AMERICAN MIDSUMMER FESTIVAL. BOOTHS SET UP BY LOCAL ETHNIC GROUPS DISPLAYING ARTS, CRAFTS & FOODS & FEATURING ENTERTAINMENT BY LOUIE BELSON AT 2 PM & 8 PM. AT WHARTON FIELD HOUSE, 1800 20TH AVE. (LOCAL). SANDRA BELLINGER, COORD; MOLINE BICENTENNIAL COMMISSION; 619 16TH ST; MOLINE, IL 61265. (#107402-3).

JUNE 27, '76. ETHNIC FESTIVAL. DISPLAYING CRAFTS & FOODS OF LOCAL ETHNIC GROUPS THAT CONTRIBUTED TO GROWTH OF THE AREA; BELGIANS, SWEDES, MEXICANS, GREEKS & AFRICANS. THERE WILL BE A PAGEANT & LOUIS BELLSON & A 20 PIECE ORCHESTRA WILL PLAY AT 2:15PM & 8PM. AT WHARTON FIELDHOUSE. (LOCAL). SANDY BELLINGER, CHMN; MOLINE BICENTENNIAL COMMISSION; 2447 28TH ST; MOLINE, IL 61265. (#102091-3).

JULY 3, '76. BICENTENNIAL STREET DANCE. FESTIVAL. (LOCAL). SANDY BELLINGER, CHMN; MOLINE BICENTENNIAL COMMISSION; 619 16TH ST; MOLINE, IL 61265. (#102091-1).

JULY 3, '76. CANOE RACE AND WATERMELON FESTIVAL. FESTIVAL. (LOCAL). SANDY BELLINGER, CHMN; MOLINE BICENTENNIAL COMMISSION; 619 16TH ST; MOLINE, IL 61265. (#102091-2).

JULY 4, '76. JULY 4TH FESTIVAL. FESTIVITIES WILL INCLUDE: PICNIC, PARADE, GAMES, FIREWORKS AND HORIZON DEDICATION. (LOCAL). SANDY BELLINGER, CHMN; MOLINE BICENTENNIAL COMMISSION; 619 16TH ST; MOLINE, IL 61265. (#102091-5).

AUG 20 - 21, '76. PERFORMANCE BY 'DIE ROOSELAER' A FLEMISH FOLK DANCE GROUP. 45 MEMBER GROUP WILL PROVIDE FOLK DANCING & SINGING. AT JOHN DEERE ADMINISTRATION BUILDING - JOHN DEERE ROAD. (INT'L). SANDRA BELLINGER, COORD; CENTER FOR BELGIAN CULTURE & MOLINE BICENTENNIAL COMMISSION; 619 16TH ST; MOLINE, IL 61265. (#107402-2).

AUG 26 - 27, '76. UNITED STATES ARMED FORCES BICENTENNIAL CARAVAN. CARAVAN IS COMPOSED OF EXHIBIT VANS FOR EACH MILITARY SERVICE. PROJECT THEME IS 'HISTORY OF THE ARMED FORCES & THEIR CONTRIBUTIONS TO THE NATION.'. (LOCAL). OTTO W SCHWEINBERGER, DIR; UNITED STATES ARMED FORCES BICENTENNIAL CARAVAN; BLACK HAWK COLLEGE; MOLINE, IL 61265. (#1775-638).

OCT 5, '76. BELGIAN FESTIVAL. FLEA MARKET, LACE MAKING DEMONSTRATION, BELGIAN SINGERS, STREET DANCE & ROLLE BOLLE GAMES. AT STEPHENS PARK, 19TH ST & 6TH AVE. (LOCAL). SANDRA BELLINGER, COORD; CENTER FOR BELGIAN CULTURE & MOLINE BICENTENNIAL COMMISSION; 619 16TH ST; MOLINE, IL 61265. (#107402-1).

OCT 15, '76. DEDICATION OF INDIAN SCULPTURE AND THIRTIETH ANNIVERSARY OF COLLEGE. OPENING, CEREMONY, EXHIBIT. (ST-WIDE). OTTO W SCHWEINBERGER; ROCK ISLAND COUNTY BICENTENNIAL COMMITTEE; 6600 34TH AVE; MOLINE, IL 61265. (#6351-501).

OCT 15 - 20, '76. BLACK HAWK COLLEGE BICENTENNIAL FOUNDERS DAY CELEBRATION. CELEBRATION OF THIRTEENTH ANNIVERSARY WITH BICENTENNIAL DINNER PLAY, UNVEILING OF INDIAN SCULPTURE; AND OTHER FESTIVAL ACTIVITIES. (LOCAL). OTTO W SCHWEINBERGER; BLACK HAWK COLLEGE BICENTENNIAL COMMISSION; 6600-34TH AVE; MOLINE, IL 61265. (#10237-501).

MOMENCE

JAN 11 - 12, '77. LA SALLE EXPEDITION II, A HISTORIC RE-ENACTMENT. THIS IS AN AUTHENTIC RE-ENACTMENT OF THE 1681 LASALLE EXPEDITION FROM MONTREAL, CANADA TO NEW ORLEANS, LA WHICH WILL BEGIN TOURING ON AUGUST 11, 1976 AND END ON APRIL 9, 1977. (LOCAL). REID H LEWIS, DIRECTOR; LA SALLE EXPEDITION II; 135 S LA SALLE ST, RM 411; CHICAGO, IL 60690. (#102805-35).

MONMOUTH

RESTORATION OF WYATT EARP HOME IN MONMOUTH, IL. RESTORATION OF HOME OF HISTORIC PERSONALITY OF THE WILD WEST. (LOCAL). ROBERT MATSON, COORDINATOR; WARREN COUNTY BICENTENNIAL COMMISSION; 1020 E DETROIT AVE; MONMOUTH, IL 61462. (#33570).

WARREN COUNTY HISTORY: MONMOUTH, IL. SLIDE-TAPE PRESENTATION ON COUNTY HISTORY DEVELOPED BY WARREN COUNTY LIBRARY. (LOCAL). ROBERT MATSON, COORDINATOR; WARREN COUNTY BICENTENNIAL COMMISSION; 1020 E DETROIT AVE; MONMOUTH, IL 61462. (#33569).

MONTICELLO

COUNTY ARCHIVES ROOM IN MONTICELLO, IL. LOCATED AT PIATT COUNTY COURTHOUSE. (LOCAL). JESSIE MORGAN, DIRECTOR; PIATT COUNTY BICENTENNIAL COMMISSION; 907 LONGVIEW RD; MONTICELLO, IL 61856. (#33565).

DEDICATION OF REVOLUTIONARY SOLDIER PLAQUE IN IL. PLAQUE PLACED IN PLATT COUNTY COURTHOUSE BY THE DAR TO HONOR ONLY REVOLUTIONARY SOLDIER, LT SAMUEL OLNEY, WHO IS BURIED IN PLATT CO. (LOCAL). JUDY GREENE, CITIZENSHIP CHAIRMAN; ALLERTON CHAPTER, DAUGHTERS OF THE AMERICAN REVOLUTION; 708 N CHARTER ST; MONTICELLO, IL 61856. (#33568).

HISTORIC PRESERVATION: PRIDE AND PROGRESS IN IL. PROGRAM TO PRESERVE BUILDINGS WORTHY OF BEING SAVED TO BE MARKED WITH MEDALLIONS; ALSO PLAN WALKING TOURS & EDUCATIONAL PROGRAMS IN SCHOOLS. (LOCAL). JESSIE B MORGAN, CHAIRMAN; MONTICELLO BICENTENNIAL COMMISSION; 907 LONGVIEW RD; MONTICELLO, IL 61856. (#33567).

MINI-PARK AND A REST AREA IN MONTICELLO, IL. BEAUTIFICATION PROGRAM OF A REST AREA FOR SENIOR CITIZENS IN COOPERATION WITH THE MONTICELLO GARDEN CLUB. (LOCAL). JESSIE B MORGAN, CHAIRMAN; MONTICELLO BICENTENNIAL COMMISSION; 907 LONGVIEW RD; MONTICELLO, IL 61856. (#33566).

MOOSEHEART

JULY 4, '76. ECUMENICAL SERVICE. SERVICE WILL INCLUDE 4 AREA MINISTERS, COMMUNITY CHORUS, MOOSEHEART BAND, MOOSEHEART CHORUS, BOY SCOUT FLAG CEREMONY; THEME IS 'REDEDICATION OF AMERICAN SPIRIT'. AT MOOSEHEART FOOTBALL STADIUM. (LOCAL). VERNAL D LAYTON, SEC; NORTH AURORA BICENTENNIAL COMMITTEE; N AURORA VILLAGE HALL; N AURORA, IL 60542. (#107278-1).

MORRIS

JAN 15 - 16, '77. LA SALLE EXPEDITION II, A HISTORIC RE-ENACTMENT. THIS IS AN AUTHENTIC RE-ENACTMENT OF THE 1681 LASALLE EXPEDITION FROM MONTREAL, CANADA TO NEW ORLEANS, LA WHICH WILL BEGIN TOURING ON AUGUST 11, 1976 AND END ON APRIL 9, 1977. (LOCAL). REID H LEWIS, DIRECTOR; LA SALLE EXPEDITION II; 135 S LA SALLES, ST, RM 411; CHICAGO, IL 60690. (#102805-38).

MORRISON

HERITAGE, HORIZONS & YOU PROJ OF MORRISON, IL. HISTORICAL SLIDE PRESENTATION ON THE HISTORY OF WHITESIDE COUNTY & A HERITAGE POSTER & ESSAY CONTEST FOR STUDENTS. (LOCAL). DR GLEN WATERLOO, VICE CHAIRMAN; WHITESIDE COUNTY BICENTENNIAL COMMISSION; 209 W MAIN ST; MORRISON, IL 61270. (#7767).

INDUSTRY & FARM PRODUCTS DISPLAY IN MORRISON, IL. FARM MACHINERY & PRODUCTS WILL BE DISPLAYED IN PORTABLE CASES TO ILLUSTRATE TODAYS TECHNOLOGY. A PAMPHLET WILL ACCOMPANY THESE DISPLAYS TO LEAVE A WRITTEN RECORD OF AGRICULTURAL ACCOMPLISHMENTS. (LOCAL). K O MILLER, PROJECT COORDINATOR; WHITESIDE COUNTY BICENTENNIAL COMMISSION; 207 W MAIN ST; MORRISON, IL 61270. (#7766).

WHITESIDE COUNTY, ILL, BICENTENNIAL HERITAGE PGM. EDUCATION PROGRAM TO INCLUDE SLIDE SHOW DEPICTING LOCAL, STATE, AND NATIONAL HISTORY; COUNTY HISTORY BOOKS IN ALL COUNTY SCHOOLS; AND BICENTENNIAL HERITAGE ESSAY CONTEST FOR STUDENTS. (LOCAL). RONALD KOSTER, CHAIRMAN; WHITESIDE COUNTY BICENTENNIAL COMMISSION; PO BOX 169; MORRISON, IL 61270. (#881). **ARBA GRANTEE.**

AUG 12 - 16, '75. DISPLAY AT COUNTY FAIR - FARM MACHINERY & PRODUCTS. FARM MACHINERY & PRODUCTS WILL BE DISPLAYED IN PORTABLE CASES TO ILLUSTRATE TODAYS TECHNOLOGY. A PAMPHLET WILL ACCOMPANY THESE DISPLAYS TO LEAVE A WRITTEN RECORD OF AGRICULTURAL ACCOMPLISHMENTS. (LOCAL). K O MILLER; WHITESIDE COUNTY BICENTENNIAL COMMISSION; 207 W MAIN ST; MORRISON, IL 61270. (#7766-501).

MORTON

CONTEST TO SELECT CITY BICENTENNIAL SLOGAN IN IL. LOGO TO BE DESIGNED & CITY SLOGAN WILL BE SELECTED. (LOCAL). WILLIAM LYMAN, CHAIRMAN; MORTON BICENTENNIAL COMMISSION; TAZEWELL NEWS/DETROIT ST; MORTON, IL 61550. (#33563).

FREEDOM HALL '76 IN MORTON, IL. COLONIAL COMMUNITY BUILDING FOR PUBLIC USE. (LOCAL). AL REBHOLZ, CHAIRMAN; HORIZON COMMITTEE OF MORTON BICENTENNIAL COMMITTEE; 200 E KAY ST; MORTON, IL 61550. (#33564).

NAMING OF THE OLDEST HOME & BUSINESS IN MORTON, IL. OLDEST HOME & BUSINESS IN MORTON TO BE AWARDED. (LOCAL). ROBERT CONIBEAR, COORDINATOR; MORTON BICENTENNIAL COMMISSION AND HISTORICAL HISTORY; 408 N MAIN; MORTON, IL 61550. (#33562).

MAY 17, '75. BIKE RODEO. BIKES SAFETY CHECKED & TAGGED WITH US FLAG DECALS. AT BLESSED SACRAMENT SCHOOL PLAYGROUND, GREENWOOD ST. (LOCAL). JAMES COMBS; MORTON KIWANIS; 110 E EDGEWOOD; MORTON, IL 61550. (#200016-301).

JUNE '75. OLD FASHIONED DAYS: MERCHANTS SALES PROMOTION ARTS & CRAFTS DISPLAYS. FESTIVAL, EXHIBIT AT MAIN ST, DOWNTOWN, FREE CITY PARKING. (LOCAL). EXECUTIVE DIRECTOR; CHAMBER OF COMMERCE; 134 W ADAMS; MORTON, IL 61550. (#200016-463).

JULY 5, '75. COMMUNITY WORSHIP SERVICE & BICENTENNIAL FLAG PRESENTATION. CEREMONY AT IDLEWOOD PARK, GREENWOOD ST, LIMITED SEATING: BRING CHAIR OR BLANKET. (LOCAL). WILLIAM LYMAN, COORD; MORTON BICENTENNIAL COMMISSION & TAZEWELL PUP CO; DETROIT ST; MORTON, IL 61550. (#200016-464).

SEPT 10 - 12, '75. MORTON PUMPKIN FESTIVAL. PAGEANT, PARADE, FAIR, CARNIVAL & ARTS & CRAFTS EXHIBITS. AT JEFFERSON GRADE SCHOOL GROUNDS, JEFFERSON ST, FREE PARKING DOWNTOWN. (LOCAL). EXECUTIVE DIRECTOR; CHAMBER OF COMMERCE; 134 W ADAMS; MORTON, IL 61550. (#200016-466).

OCT 3 - 4, '75. MORTON HIGH SCHOOL HOMECOMING. COMPETITION, FESTIVAL AT HIGH SCHOOL ATHLETIC FIELD, JACKSON ST, FREE PARKING. (LOCAL). STUDY COUNCIL PRESIDENT; MORTON HIGH SCHOOL STUDENT COUNCIL; W JACKSON ST; MORTON, IL 61550. (#200016-468).

OCT 30, '75. MOONLIGHT MADNESS SALES PROMOTION & BICENT MEMORABILIA SALE. FESTIVAL AT CITY WIDE, FREE PARKING DOWNTOWN & AT FIELD SHOPPING CENTER. (LOCAL). EXECUTIVE DIRECTOR; CHAMBER OF COMMERCE; 134 W ADAMS; MORTON, IL 61550. (#200016-469).

NOV 1 - DEC 1, '75. BICENTENNIAL POSTER & ESSAY CONTEST & AWARD CEREMONY. COMPETITION, AWARD, CEREMONY. (LOCAL). BURDELL HALL, COORDINATOR; MORTON BICENTENNIAL COMMISSION; 200 N ILLINOIS ST; MORTON, IL 61550. (#200016-470).

DEC 22, '75. COMMUNITY CHRISTMAS SING. LIVE PERFORMANCE, FESTIVAL AT FIELD SHOPPING CENTER, MAIN ST. (LOCAL). SARAH DAWDY, COORDINATOR; MORTON BICENTENNIAL COMMISSION; 600 COLUMBUS ST; MORTON, IL 61550. (#200016-471).

JAN 9, '76. STUDENT PANEL DISCUSSION - THE MEANING OF THE BICENTENNIAL. SEMINAR AT UNITED METHODIST CHURCH, CHICAGO ST, FREE PARKING. (LOCAL). ARAMINTA BIGELOW, COORD; MORTON WOMAN'S CLUB; 207 MAYWOOD; MORTON, IL 61550. (#200016-472).

FEB 3, '76. CHAMBER OF COMMERCE ANNUAL DINNER W/BICENTENNIAL THEME. FESTIVAL AT PEPPERMILL RESTAURANT, N MORTON AVE, FREE PARKING AT RESTAURANT. (LOCAL). EXECUTIVE DIRECTOR; CHAMBER OF COMMERCE; 134 W ADAMS; MORTON, IL 61550. (#200016-473).

FEB 15, '76. BICENTENNIAL FLAG PRESENTATION BY R MICHEL TO BOY SCOUT TROOP. FLAG PRESENTED BY CONGRESSMAN MICHEL HAD BEEN FLOWN OVER INDEPENDENCE HALL, PHILADELPHIA. AT KNIGHTS OF COLUMBUS HALL, W DAVID ST, FREE PARKING. (LOCAL). SARAH DAWDY, COORDINATOR; MORTON KNIGHTS OF COLUMBUS; 600 COLUMBUS; MORTON, IL 61550. (#200016-475).

FEB 19 - 21, '76. WASHINGTON'S BIRTHDAY SALES PROMOTION. FESTIVAL AT CITY WIDE, FREE PARKING DOWNTOWN & AT FIELD SHOPPING CENTER. (LOCAL). EXECUTIVE DIRECTOR; CHAMBER OF COMMERCE; 134 W ADAMS; MORTON, IL 61550. (#200016-474).

MAR 1 - 31, '76. 'A STAR FOR OLD GLORY' & 'YANKEE DOODLE', READER'S THEATER. LIVE PERFORMANCE AT DISTRICT GRADE SCHOOLS, FREE PARKING, SEATING PROVIDED. (LOCAL). MRS PHILIP KUHL, COORD; MORTON JR WOMEN'S CLUB; 934 E MADISON; MORTON, IL 61550. (#200016-476).

APR 9 - 10, '76. 'GEORGE WASHINGTON SLEPT HERE', HIGH SCHOOL PLAY. LIVE PERFORMANCE AT MORTON HIGH SCHOOL GYM, FREE PARKING. (LOCAL). DRAMA COACH; MORTON UNIT SCHOOL DISTRICT 709, HIGH SCHOOL DRAMA DEPT; ILLINOIS AVE; MORTON, IL 61550. (#200016-477).

APR 22, '76. BICENTENNIAL WAGON TRAIN STOP, ILLINOIS CONTINGENT. PARADE, EXHIBIT AT MAIN ST PARADE; VISIT WAGON TRAIN AT JEFFERSON SCHOOL GROUNDS. (LOCAL). WILLIAM LYMAN, CHMN; MORTON BICENTENNIAL COMMISSION; TAZEWELL NEWS, DETROIT ST; MORTON, IL 61550. (#200016-479).

APR '76. SPRING FLING SALES PROMOTION. FESTIVAL, EXHIBIT AT CITY WIDE, FREE PARKING - AT FIELD SHOPPING CENTER & DOWNTOWN. (LOCAL). EXECUTIVE DIRECTOR; CHAMBER OF COMMERCE; 134 W ADAMS; MORTON, IL 61550. (#200016-478).

MAY 1, '76. 'TOWNE MEETING '76'. CONFERENCE AT MORTON JR HIGH SCHOOL GYM, JACKSON ST; FREE PARKING & CHILD CARE. (LOCAL). GEORGE BURRIER, CHMN; MORTON JAYCEES; 401 E EDGEWOOD; MORTON, IL 61550. (#200016-480).

MAY 7 - 8, '76. 'MY COUNTRY 'TIS OF THEE', GRADE SCHOOL PRODUCTION. LIVE PERFORMANCE AT MORTON HIGH SCHOOL GYM, ILLINOIS ST; FREE PARKING. (LOCAL). MRS JOHN SWANSTROM, CHMN; MORTON UNIT SCHOOL DISTRICT 709, WARD GRUNDY GRADE SCHOOL; 432 N ILLINOIS; MORTON, IL 61550. (#200016-481).

MAY 14 - 15, '76. 'WHAT A COUNTRY', MUSICAL REVUE, KIDNEY FOUNDATION BENEFIT. LIVE PERFORMANCE AT MORTON HIGH SCHOOL GYM, ILLINOIS ST; FREE PARKING. (LOCAL). MRS FRANK HAINES, CHMN; MORTON WOMAN'S CLUB & JR WOMAN'S CLUB; 456 S MISSISSIPPI; MORTON, IL 61550. (#200016-482).

MAY 22 - 23, '76. BIKE RODEO & 'PEDAL IN', BIKES SAFETY CHECKED. FESTIVAL AT BLESSED SACRAMENT SCHOOL PLAYGROUND, GREENWOOD ST. (LOCAL). JAMES COMBS, CHMN; MORTON KIWANIS; 110 E EDGEWOOD; MORTON, IL 61550. (#200016-483).

JULY 1 - 8, '76. 'MEET YOUR CANDIDATES' NIGHTS - POLITICAL FORUMS. CONFERENCE AT JEFFERSON GRADE SCHOOL GYM, JEFFERSON ST; FREE PARKING. (LOCAL). MRS GERALD WAPPELHORST; MORTON NEWCOMER'S CLUB & BICENTENNIAL COMMISSION; 111 LAKEWOOD; MORTON, IL 61550. (#200016-484).

JULY 2 - 3, '76. OLD-FASHIONED DAYS & SALUTE TO CRAFTS. EXHIBIT, FESTIVAL AT MAIN ST, DOWNTOWN, FIELD SHOPPING CENTER; FREE PARKING. (LOCAL). CHAIRMAN; MORTON CHAMBER OF COMMERCE; 134 W ADAMS; MORTON, IL 61550. (#200016-485).

JULY 3 - 6, '76. SPORTS JUBILEE. COMPETITION, FESTIVAL AT HIGH SCHOOL TENNIS COURTS, LIONSFIELD, CITY POOL, HORSESHOE PARK. (LOCAL). JOHN WOODWORTH, COORD; MORTON PARK DISTRICT; 120 N MAIN; MORTON, IL 61550. (#200016-486).

JULY 4, '76. RE-DEDICATION CEREMONY & TOWN BIRTHDAY PARTY. CEREMONY, FESTIVAL AT LION'S FIELD. (LOCAL). DONALD F ROTH, CHMN; MORTON BICENTENNIAL COMMISSION; 249 BALTIMORE; MORTON, IL 61550. (#200016-487).

JULY 12 - 13, '76. RED, WHITE & BLUE FLOWER GARDEN CONTEST. COMPETITION. (LOCAL). MRS CHALMER ARNETT, CHMN; MORTON GARDEN CLUB; 475 E GREENWOOD; MORTON, IL 61550. (#200016-488).

AUG 15 - 16, '76. FREEDOM FESTIVAL: SALES PROMOTION & ARTS & CRAFTS DISPLAYS. EXHIBIT, FESTIVAL AT FIELD SHOPPING CENTER, FREE ON SITE PARKING. (LOCAL). TODD HATTERMAN, COORD; FIELD MERCHANTS ASSOCIATION; MAIN ST; MORTON, IL 61550. (#200016-465).

SEPT 15 - 18, '76. MORTON PUMPKIN FESTIVAL, PAGEANT, PARADE, CARNIVAL, ARTS & CRAFTS. PAGEANT, PARADE, CARNIVAL & ARTS & CRAFTS EXHIBITS. AT JEFFERSON GRADE SCHOOL GROUNDS, JEFFERSON ST, FREE PARKING. (LOCAL). EXECUTIVE DIRECTOR; CHAMBER OF COMMERCE; 134 W ADAMS; MORTON, IL 61550. (#200016-467).

SEPT 15 - 18, '76. VOTER REGISTRATION DRIVE. FESTIVAL AT PUMPKIN FESTIVAL MAIN TENT. (LOCAL). DONALD F ROTH; MORTON BICENTENNIAL COMMISSION, MORTON AAUW, MORTON BPW; 249 BALTIMORE; MORTON, IL 61550. (#200016-489).

OCT 28 - 30, '76. MOONLIGHT MADNESS SALES PROMOTION, BICENTENNIAL BOOTH. EXHIBIT, FESTIVAL. (LOCAL). CHAIRMAN; MORTON CHAMBER OF COMMERCE; 134 W ADAMS; MORTON, IL 61550. (#200016-490).

NOV 21, '76. COMMUNITY THANKSGIVING SERVICES. CEREMONY AT MORTON CHRISTIAN & MENNONITE CHURCHES. (LOCAL). REV PHILLIP ICENOGLE; MORTON BICENTENNIAL COMMISSION & MINISTERIAL ASSOCIATION; 311 W CHICAGO; MORTON, IL 61550. (#200016-491).

DEC 4, '76. CHRISTMAS FINALE. FESTIVAL AT PEPPERMILL RESTAURANT, N MORTON AVE. (LOCAL). DONALD F ROTH, CHMN; MORTON BICENTENNIAL COMMISSION; 249 BALTIMORE; MORTON, IL 61550. (#200016-492).

MOWEAQUA

MOWEAQUA, IL, BICENTENNIAL PROJECTS. PLANNING TO RESTORE 8 BLOCK AREA, COMPILED 288 PAGE LOCAL HISTORY & COMPILED 500 PAGE COOKBOOK. (LOCAL). NORMA SCHORFHEIDE, CHAIRMAN; MOWEAQUA BICENTENNIAL COMMITTEE; 220 SOUTH EAST; MOWEAQUA, IL 62550. (#29838).

JULY 2 - 5, '76. GIANT JOLLIFICATION DAYS. FESTIVAL AT VILLAGE PARK, SCHOOL PARK WEST. (LOCAL). NORMA SCHORFHEIDE, CHMN; MOWEAQUA BICENTENNIAL COMMITTEE; 220 SOUTH EAST ST; MOWEAQUA, IL 62550. (#200016-402).

MT CARMEL

LITTLE RED SCHOOLHOUSE PROJECT - MT CARMEL, IL. ACQUISITION OF COUNTRY SCHOOLHOUSE FOR PRESERVATION OF A PART OF LOCAL HISTORY AND FOLK TRADITION. (LOCAL). C DEAN HIGGINBOTHAM, CHAIRMAN; WABASH VALLEY COLLEGE; 2200 COLLEGE DR; MT CARMEL, IL 62863. (#24521).

JAN 3 - AUG 10, '76. CULTURAL EVENTS PROGRAM. A SERIES OF EVENTS INCLUDING MUSICAL PRODUCTIONS DRAMATIC PRESENTATIONS AND ART DISPLAYS WITH HISTORICAL AND BICENTENNIAL THEMES. AT BRUBECK ARTS CENTER. (LOCAL). TONY KRUG, COORDINATOR; WABASH VALLEY COLLEGE; 2200 COLLEGE DR; MT CARMEL, IL 62863. (#107178-2).

MAR 10 - JUNE 2, '76. BICENTENNIAL TOWN MEETING. A SERIES OF MEETINGS DEVOTED TO CURRENT EVENTS. AT WABASH AUDITORIUM. (LOCAL). JAMES GILLESPIE, CHAIRMAN; WABASH VALLEY COLLEGE; 2200 COLLEGE DR; MT CARMEL, IL 62863. (#107178-4).

JULY 3, '76. WABASH COUNTY BICENTENNIAL PARADE. A PARADE DEDICATED TO A LOCAL CELEBRATION OF THE BICENTENNIAL. AT MAIN ST. (LOCAL). GENE BLAIR, COORDINATOR; BICENTENNIAL PARADE COMMITTEE, WABASH VALLEY COLLEGE; 2200 COLLEGE DR; MT CARMEL, IL 62863. (#107178-3).

OCT 15 - 16, '76. CHILD ABUSE: AN AMERICAN PERSPECTIVE. SEMINAR TO FOCUS ON THE AMERICAN EXPERIENCE WITH CHILD ABUSE. A TV DOCUMENTARY IS SCHEDULED TO BE MADE FROM THE SEMINAR. AT WABASH AUDITORIUM. (REGN'L). BARBARA WALLACE, CHMN; WABASH VALLEY COLLEGE; 2200 COLLEGE DR; MT CARMEL, IL 62863. (#107178-1).

MT CARROLL

BICENT RESOURCES COLLECTION OF CARROLL COUNTY, ILL. FILMS, BOOKS, DOCUMENTS, ETC, DEPICTING HERITAGE OF COUNTY, THE STATE & THE U.S. WILL BE DISTRIBUTED FREE TO SCHOOLS, LIBRARIES, ETC IN THE COUNTY. (LOCAL). JAY MCCALL, CHAIRMAN; CARROLL COUNTY BICENTENNIAL COMMISION; PO BOX 76; MT CARROLL, IL 61270. (#890). **(??). ARBA GRANTEE.**

MT MORRIS

JULY 2 - 4, '76. 'LET FREEDOM RING', 4TH OF JULY CELEBRATION. JULY 2, CARNIVAL ALL DAY, QUEEN CORONATION, CONCERT & DANCE; JULY 3, CARNIVAL, KIDDIE PARADE, GRAND PARADE, PATRIOTIC PROGRAM; JULY 4, CARNIVAL, NATIONAL BELL-RINGING, PATRIOTIC PROGRAM AND FIREWORKS. OFFICIAL ILLINOIS FREEDOM BELL CONNECTED TO INDEP HALL IN PHILA, PA. AT VILLAGE SQUARE. (LOCAL). MRS HARRY VESTED, CHMN; CITY OF MT MORRIS; MT MORRIS, IL 61054. (#102172-1).

MT PROSPECT

RESTORATION OF A 1902 SCHOOL & HISTORIC ROUTE - IL. RESTORATION OF A 1902 SCHOOLHOUSE TO BE USED AS A HISTORIC MUSEUM OF ELK GROVE AND WHEELING TOWNSHIPS; ALSO PLACING OF PLAQUES AT TEN HISTORIC SITES AND MAP OF ROUTE LINKING THESE SITES AND MUSEUM. (LOCAL). DOROTHY HAUGH, PRESIDENT; MT PROSPECT HISTORICAL SOCIETY; 1100 S LINNEMANN RD; MT PROSPECT, IL 60056. (#26110). **ARBA GRANTEE.**

MT STERLING

CEMETERY RECORDINGS & FAMILY HISTORIES, ILLINOIS. RECORDING OF THE BURIALS IN BROWN COUNTY AND TRACING GENEOLOGIES OF COMMUNITY RESIDENTS. BOOK OF 668 PAGES PUBLISHED IN DEC, 1975. (LOCAL). MERIBETH CLARK, PROJECT CHAIRMAN; BROWN COUNTY HISTORICAL SOCIETY; MT STERLING, IL 62353. (#8190).

HISTORY OF BROWN COUNTY (1880 - 1970) - BOOK. BOOK WAS PUBLISHED IN 1972 AND IS 772 PAGES LONG. (LOCAL). MERIBETH CLARK, PROJECT CHAIRMAN; BROWN COUNTY HISTORICAL SOCIETY; MT STERLING, IL 62353. (#30139).

OPERATION WHISTLESTOP - MT STERLING, IL. RESTORATION OF WABASH RAILROAD DEPOT AS A MUSEUM ON THE BROWN CO FAIRGROUNDS. (LOCAL). MARJORIE CLEAVES, CHAIRMAN; BROWN COUNTY BICENTENNIAL COMMISSION; RR 1; TIMEWELL, IL 62375. (#30411).

RESTORE BROWN COUNTY COURTHOUSE IN ILLINOIS. REFURBISHING OF THE COURTHOUSE WILL ENTAIL PAINTING THE EXTERIOR, MENDING BROKEN BRICK WORK AND RESTORING DOME THAT WAS REMOVED IN 1939, WHEN THE COURTHOUSE WAS GUTTED BY FIRE. (LOCAL). MARJORIE LEAVES, CHAIRMAN; BROWN COUNTY BOARD & BICENTENNIAL COMMISSION; MT STERLING, IL 62353. (#8189).

JULY 28 - 29, '75. BROWN COUNTY FAIR SPECIAL BICENTENNIAL PROGRAM IN 1975 AND 1976. OPENING, FESTIVAL. (LOCAL). MARJORIE LEAVES, CHAIRMAN; BROWN COUNTY BOARD & BICENTENNIAL COMMISSION; MT STERLING, IL 62353. (#8189-502).

MT VERNON

HISTORICAL BOOKLET IN MT VERNON, IL. A BOOKLET DEPICTING THE HISTORY OF MT VERNON AND JEFFERSON COUNTY, ILLINOIS, RECALLING PROMINENT CITIZENS, EVENTS AND STRUCTURES; MAPS PHOTOS AND DRAWINGS WILL BE EMPLOYED. (LOCAL). STEVEN J KORRIS, EDITOR, BICENTENNIAL BOOK; MT VERNON BICENTENNIAL COMMISSION; MT VERNON REGISTER-NEWS, 112 N 9; MT VERNON, IL 62864. (#12259).

'A PAST TO REMEMBER, A FUTURE TO MOLD', IL. A BOOKLET DEPICTING THE HISTORY OF MT VERNON & JEFFERSON COUNTY, IL, RECALLING PROMINENT CITIZENS, EVENTS & STRUCTURES THROUGH PHOTOS, DRAWINGS & MAPS. (LOCAL). STEVEN J KORRIS, PROJ DIRECTOR; MT VERNON BICENTENNIAL COMMITTEE; 112 N 9TH; MT VERNON, IL 62864. (#13054).

SPIRIT OF '76 BUMPER STICKERS, MT VERNON, IL. SALE OF BUMPER STICKERS TO PROMOTE THE BICENTENNIAL AND RAISE MONEY FOR COMMISSION PROJECTS. (LOCAL). MARY B WARD, CHAIRMAN; MT VERNON BICENTENNIAL COMMITTEE; 112 N 9TH; MT VERNON, IL 62864. (#13050).

JULY 4, '75 - JULY 4, '76. SPIRIT OF '76 BICENTENNIAL BEARD-GROWING CONTEST. COMPETITION AT TIMES SQUARE MALL, 42ND & BROADWAY STS. (LOCAL). MARY B WARD, CHAIRMAN; MT VERNON BICENTENNIAL COMMISSION; C/O REGISTER-NEWS, 112 N 9TH; MT VERNON, IL 62864. (#100956-1).

AUG 21 - 23, '75. SOUTHERN ILLINOIS SWEETCORN-WATERMELON FESTIVAL. THREE-DAY FESTIVAL HIGHLIGHTED BY SERVING FREE CORN AND MELON ON THE PUBLIC SQUARE ON SATURDAY; ALSO, 100 UNIT PARADE, STAGE SHOW, BIKE RACES AND DANCES. (LOCAL). BILL STEFFY, PRESIDENT; SOUTHERN ILLINOIS SWEETCORN-WATERMELON FESTIVAL ASSOC; 8 WILDWOOD DR; MT VERNON, IL 62864. (#200016-40).

OCT 8 - 18, '75. BICENTENNIAL SONGFEST. LIVE PERFORMANCE AT MT VERNON TOWNSHIP HIGH SCHOOL AUDITORIUM. (LOCAL). VERNON FRENCH, PRINCIPAL; EDISON HOME & SCHOOL ASSOC; 521 PERKINS AVE; MT VERNON, IL 62864. (#200016-38).

OCT 27, '75. HISTORIC HOME TOURS. THERE WILL BE AN OPEN HOUSE AT EVERY HISTORIC HOME. (LOCAL). MS MARY B WARD, CHMN; MT VERNON BICENT COMMISSION AND GALLERY OF HOMES; 112 N 9TH ST; MT VERNON, IL 62864. (#100263-1).

MURPHYSBORO

BICENTENNIAL CLASS PROJECTS, MURPHYSBORO, IL. EACH MONTH ONE CLASS WILL BE IN CHARGE OF BICENTENNIAL PROJECTS COVERING ALL THEMATIC AREAS. OBJECTIVES ARE TO UNDERSTAND SIMILARITIES AND DIFFERENCES OF LIFE TODAY AND DURING THE REVOLUTION. (LOCAL). RON THOMAS, PRINCIPAL; LONGFELLOW ELEMENTARY SCHOOL, UNIT DISTRICT 186; 2002 LOGAN; MURPHYSBORO, IL 62966. (#18093).

RESTORATION OF MURPHYSBORO RIVERSIDE PARK SHELL-IL. RESTORE AND PRESERVE BY PAINTING IN FESTIVE COLORS THE PARK SHELL WHICH IS USED FOR RECREATIONAL PURPOSES. (LOCAL). ELIZABETH TAYLOR, CO-CHAIRPERSON; MURPHYSBORO BICENTENNIAL COMMISSION; 1012 WALNUT ST; MURPHYSBORO, IL 62966. (#14871).

RESTORATION OF MURPHYSBORO CITY CEMETERY - IL. RESTORATION CONSISTS OF REPAIRING, STRAIGHTENING, AND RESETTING PRIVATE AND MILITARY GRAVE MARKERS. (LOCAL). ELIZABETH TAYLOR, CO-CHAIRPERSON; MURPHYSBORO BICENTENNIAL COMMISSION; 1012 WALNUT ST; MURPHYSBORO, IL 62966. (#14872). **ARBA GRANTEE.**

SEPT 10, '75. NATIONAL APPLE PEELING CONTEST. CONTEST OPEN TO ANY AGE OR SEX. BRING OWN PARING KNIFE. WINNERS DETERMINED ON THE GREATEST AMOUNT OF APPLE PEELINGS, PEELED IN 3 MINUTES. A SPECIAL PEEL OFF BETWEEN THE MILITARY SERVICES. NO ENTRY FEE. AT JACKSON COUNTY COURT HOUSE. (REGN'L). MARION NASH, CHMN; MURPHYSBORO CHAMBER OF COMMERCE; 21 N 11TH ST; MURPHYSBORO, IL 62966. (#102096-1).

SEPT 10 - 13, '75. MURPHYSBORO MERCHANTS WINDOW DISPLAYS. WINDOW THEME: THE WORLD AND ITS PEOPLE. WINDOWS MAY BE VIEWED DURING THE FOUR-DAY APPLE FESTIVAL. AT MURPHYSBORO BUSINESS DISTRICT. (LOCAL). MARION NASH, CHAIRMAN; MURPHYSBORO CHAMBER OF COMMERCE; 21 N 11TH ST; MURPHYSBORO, IL 62966. (#102096-2).

SEPT 10, '75 - DEC 30, '76. EXHIBITS OF EARLY MURPHYSBORO. SUBJECT OF EXHIBIT CHANGED MONTHLY. AT INSURANCE CONSULTANTS BUILDING, 1110 WALNUT ST. (LOCAL). ELIZABETH TAYLOR, CHMN; MURPHYSBORO CHAMBER OF COMMERCE; 1012 WALNUT ST; MURPHYSBORO, IL 62966. (#102096-3).

SEPT 13, '75. MURPHYSBORO APPLE FESTIVAL GRAND PARADE. PARADE THEME: THE WORLD AND IT'S PEOPLE. AT JACKSON COUNTY COURT HOUSE SQUARE, WALNUT ST. (LOCAL). MARION NASH, CHAIRMAN; MURPHYSBORO CHAMBER OF COMMERCE; 21 N 11TH ST; MURPHYSBORO, IL 62966. (#102096-4).

OCT 13, '75. PLANTING AND DEDICATION OF APPLE TREE. MURPHYSBORO GIRL SCOUT ASSOCIATION WILL PRESENT TREE TO CITY ON BEHALF OF THE MURPHYSBORO BICENTENNIAL COMMISSION. DEDICATION SPEECH BY MAYOR MICHAEL BOWERS. AT JACKSON COUNTY COURT HOUSE LAWN, WALNUT ST. (LOCAL). ELIZABETH TAYLOR, CHMN; MURPHYSBORO BICENTENNIAL COMMISSION; 1012 WALNUT ST; MURPHYSBORO, IL 62966. (#102096-5).

NOV 30, '75. OPEN HOUSE: ILLINOIS HISTORY WEEK. GUEST SPEAKER-JOHN W D WRIGHT. TOPIC: LITTLE KNOWN NOTABLES OF JACKSON COUNTY. REFRESHMENTS AND TOUR OF HOME FOLLOW SPEAKER. AT ROBERT'S HOME, CORNER OF 10TH AND MULBERRY. (LOCAL). ELIZABETH TAYLOR, SEC; JACKSON COUNTY HISTORICAL SOCIETY; 1012 WALNUT; MURPHYSBORO, IL 62966. (#200016-39).

FEB 14, '76. GEORGE WASHINGTON BIRTHDAY BALL. PARKING ON GROUNDS. AT CARRUTHERS JR HIGH SCHOOL, CANDY LANE. (LOCAL). ELIZABETH TAYLOR, CHMN; MURPHYSBORO BICENTENNIAL COMMISSION; 1012 WALNUT; MURPHYSBORO, IL 62966. (#103626-1).

MAR 6, '76. MOUNTAIN MUSIC FESTIVAL. ADVANCE TICKETS ARE REQUIRED. ENTERTAINMENT WILL INCLUDE LIVE COMEDY, FOLK, MODERN & MOUNTAIN MUSIC. AT MURPHYSBORO TOWNSHIP HIGH SCHOOL, 2125 SPRUCE ST. (LOCAL). BOB HALL, CHMN; MURPHYSBORO KEY CLUB; 2135 EDITH ST; MURPHYSBORO, IL 62966. (#102096-6).

JULY 1 - 4, '76. OLD-FASHIONED 4TH OF JULY CELEBRATION. GEORGE ROGERS CLARK TREK CAMPING AT LAKE MURPHYSBORO ON JULY 1 & 2. COMMUNITY COORDINATION OF BICENT ACTIVITIES IN MURPHYSBORO. ENCOURAGEMENT OF ORGANIZATIONS TO PRESENT PROGRAMS AND EXHIBITS HAVING MEANING TO THEIR INDIVIDUAL HERITAGE. AT LAKE MURPHYSBORO, RR#4, PARKING IN BOAT DOCK AREA, MAIN ENTRANCE. (LOCAL). ELIZABETH TAYLOR, CHMN; MURPHYSBORO BICENTENNIAL COMMISSION; 1012 WALNUT; MURPHYSBORO, IL 62966. (#103609-1).

SEPT 15 - 18, '76. 25TH ANNUAL MURPHYSBORO APPLE FESTIVAL. THEME-OUR PROUD HERITAGE, EVENTS INCLUDE NATIONAL APPLE PEELING CONTEST, WINDOW DISPLAYS, ARTS & CRAFT SHOW, GOLF TOURNAMENT, DRUM CORPS COMPETITION, THEATRE, QUEEN CONTEST, PARADES, HIGH SCHOOL BAND COMPETITION. SO. ILL. FINEST APPLES, FREE APPLE CIDER. AT JACKSON COUUNTY COURT HOUSE SQUARE, WALNUT ST. (ST-WIDE). MARION NASH, CHAIRMAN; MURPHYSBORO CHAMBER OF COMMERCE; 21 N 11TH ST; MURPHYSBORO, IL 62966. (#105158-1).

NAPERVILLE

BICENTENNIAL PARK IN NAPERVILLE, IL. NAPERVILLE WILL SELECT AND ACQUIRE A PARK SITE ON THE DUPAGE RIVER FOR DEVELOPMENT OF EDUCATIONAL, RECREATIONAL AND HISTORICAL FACILITIES. (LOCAL). C WILLIAM NORMAN, CITY MANAGER; CITY OF NAPERVILLE; NAPERVILLE, IL 60540. (#10465).

CITY VECHICLE STICKER DESIGN CONTEST, ILLINOIS. ELEMENTRY SCHOOL CHILDREN WILL DESIGN THE NAPERVILLE'S 1976 VEHICLE STICKER IN COMMEMORATION OF THE BICENTENNIAL. (LOCAL). MRS SHIRLEY PACE; NAPERVILLE BICENTENNIAL COMMISSION; PO BOX 1976; NAPERVILLE, IL 60540. (#10463-1).

'DISPLAY THE FLAG' - NAPERVILLE, IL. THE NAPERVILLE BICENT COMMITTEE WILL PURCHASE AND SELL 50-STAR, BETSY ROSS AND COLONIAL AMERICAN FLAGS, TO PROMOTE FLYING THE U S FLAG; THE SALE WILL BEGIN ON FLAG DAY 1975. (LOCAL). MRS SHIRLEY PACE, FESTIVAL CHAIRMAN; NAPERVILLE BICENT COMMITTEE; PO BOX 1976; NAPERVILLE, IL 60540. (#10464).

DOWNTOWN REVITALIZATION PROJECT: NAPERVILLE, IL. REDEVELOPMENT AND RENOVATION OF DOWNTOWN AREA, PRESERVING HISTORICAL NATURE OF STRUCTURES. (LOCAL). MRS A T SINDT, MEMBER OF BOARD; C A N D O; 1021 W JACKSON; NAPERVILLE, IL 60540. (#10459).

HISTORIC MARKERS - PROJ OF NAPERVILLE, ILLINOIS. MARKERS WILL BE PLACED ON ALL BUILDINGS & SITES OF HISTORIC OR ARCHITECTURAL SIGNIFICANCE AS DESIGNATED BY THE STATE OF ILLINOIS DEPARTMENT OF CONSERVATION. A BOOKLET WILL BE PUBLISHED. (LOCAL). MRS A T SINDT, PRES; NAPERVILLE HERITAGE SOCIETY; PO BOX 1776; NAPERVILLE, IL 60540. (#10461).

HISTORIC VILLAGE PROJECT - NAPERVILLE, ILLINOIS. RECREATION OF VILLAGE DEPICTING HISTORY OF NORTHERN ILLINOIS DURING THE PERIOD 1831-1870. ALL BUILDINGS WILL BE ORIGINAL STRUCTURES OR AUTHENTIC REPRODUCTIONS CONSISTENT WITH THE PERIOD. (LOCAL). MRS A T SINDT, PRES; NAPERVILLE HERITAGE SOCIETY; PO BOX 1776; NAPERVILLE, IL 60540. (#10458).

MUSICAL COMPOSITION FOR CONCERT BAND - IL. A MUSICAL COMPOSITION OF AMERICAN FOLK MELODIES WILL BE DONE FOR THE CONCERT BAND. (LOCAL). RONALD KELLER, MUSICAL DIRECTOR; NAPERVILLE MUNICIPAL CONCERT BAND; 25 W 623 BURLINGTON; NAPERVILLE, IL 60540. (#21381).

PARKS BEAUTIFICATION - PROJ OF NAPERVILLE, IL. PROJECT WILL BE TO DEVELOP PROFESSIONAL LANDSCAPE PLANS FOR TWO EXISTING PARKS. THIS WILL INCLUDE THE PURCHASE OF PLANTS & NECESSARY AMENITIES AND INSTALLATION. (LOCAL). STEVEN HYETT, COMMUNITY SERVICES DIR; CITY OF NAPERVILLE; NAPERVILLE, IL 60540. (#10462).

RESTORATION OF THE MEETING HOUSE, NAPERVILLE, IL. RESTORATION OF THE MEETING HOUSE TO BE USED AS A WELCOMING CENTER FOR THE NAPER SETTLEMENT. (LOCAL). JANE SINDT, PROJ DIRECTOR; NAPERVILLE HERITAGE SOCIETY; PO BOX 1776; NAPERVILLE, IL 60540. (#27250). **ARBA GRANTEE.**

RIVERFRONT BEAUTIFICATION - PROJ OF NAPERVILLE, IL. COMMUNITY-WIDE EFFORT TO CLEAN AND BEAUTIFY THE DUPAGE RIVERFRONT. (LOCAL). WALTER SCHALL, HORIZONS '76 CHMN; NAPERVILLE BICENT COMMISSION; PO BOX 1976; NAPERVILLE, IL 60540. (#10460).

JUNE 14 - 16, '75. JOE NAPER DAYS, THREE DAY CELEBRATION OF FOUNDING. CRAFTS, FOOD, DANCE,. AT NAPER SETTLEMENT, AURORA & WEBSTER, NAPERVILLE. (LOCAL). MRS A. T. SINDT; NAPERVILLE HERITAGE SOCIETY; 1021 W JACKSON; NAPERVILLE, IL 60540. (#50824-1).

OCT 31 - NOV 2, '75. ANNUAL ANTIQUE SHOW & SALE. FOOD AVAILABLE. AT MERNER FIELDHOUSE, NC COLLEGE, BRAINARD & HIGHLAND AVES. (LOCAL). JANE SINOT, CHAIRMAN; NAPERVILLE HERITAGE SOCIETY; 1021 W JACKSON AVE; NAPERVILLE, IL 60540. (#103064-1).

JUNE 24 - 27, '76. CENTRAL PARK FINE ARTS FESTIVAL. 6/24, 8PM-MUNICIPAL BAND CIRCUS MUSIC; 6/25, 7:30PM, CHICAGO WOODWIND QUINTET; 8:30PM, GIES GIORDANO DANCE COMPANY; 6/26, 1PM, DINGLEFEST THEATER CO; 2:30PM, BLUEGRASS BAND; 4:00PM, US NAVY JAZZ BAND; 8PM, LES ELGART ORCHEST; 6/27,2PM, CHILDRENS' CHORUS. AT CENTRAL PARK BAND SHELL BENTON AND CENTRAL PARK PL. (LOCAL). STEVEN P HYETT; NAPERVILLE BICENTENNIAL COMMISSION; MUNICIPAL CENTER-175 W JACKSON; NAPERVILLE, IL 60540. (#104949-2).

JULY 1 - 4, '76. FOURTH OF JULY FESTIVAL. BAND CONCERTS, PARADE WITH US MARINE DRILL TEAM, BAND ENTERTAINMENT AND FIREWORKS. AT DOWNTOWN PARADE ROUTE, NAPERVILLE CENTRAL HIGH SCHOOL FIELD. (LOCAL). STEVEN P HYETT, COORD; NAPERVILLE PARK DISTRICT; MUNICIPAL CENTER, 175 W JACKSON; NAPERVILLE, IL 60540. (#104949-1).

NASHVILLE

SCHOOLHOUSE RESTORATION - NASHVILLE, IL. RESTORATION OF MCKELVEY ONE-ROOM SCHOOLHOUSE. (LOCAL). MRS WANDA GOODNER, CHAIRMAN; NASHVILLE BICENTENNIAL COMMISSION; BOX 309; NASHVILLE, IL 62263. (#27894). **ARBA GRANTEE.**

'1776 TO 1976', HIST OF FLAGS IN AMERICA, ILLINOIS. EVERY FLAG EVER FLOWN OVER THE UNITED STATES FROM 1776 TO 1976 WILL BE DISPLAYED AT AS MANY BICENTENNIAL CELEBRATIONS AS POSSIBLE. (LOCAL). BOB SCHALTENBRAND, SCOUTMASTER; KNIGHTS OF COLUMBUS BOY SCOUT TROOP 4384; S KASKASKIA ST; NASHVILLE, IL 62263. (#6503).

NAUVOO

CITY OF JOSEPH, A HISTORY OF NAUVOO, IL. A HISTORY OF NAUVOO, IL WILL BE PRESENTED. (LOCAL). DON OSCARSON, CHAIRMAN; NAUVOO RESTORATION, INC; 6905 LAKESIDE HILLS DR; FLORISSANT, MO 63033. (#28551). **ARBA GRANTEE.**

SURVEY OF HISTORIC SITES - NAUVOO, IL. SURVEY AND PUBLICATION OF HISTORIC SITES IN HANCOCK COUNTY. (LOCAL). PAXON LEWIS, CHAIRMAN; HANCOCK COUNTY BICENTENNIAL COMMISSION; RR; NAUVOO, IL 62354. (#30417).

AUG 18 - 21, '76. 'CITY OF JOSEPH' - HISTORICAL MUSICAL. NAUVOO WAS BUILT BY MORMONS FROM 1839 TO 1845; AFTER THEIR LEADER WAS KILLED, BRIGHAM YOUNG LED THEM TO UTAH & CITY WAS DESERTED. IT IS NOW BEING RESTORED & HAS BEEN CALLED WILLIAMSBURG OF THE WEST. AT VISITORS CENTER. (REGN'L). DON OSCARSON, CHMN; NAUVOO RESTORATION, INC; 6905 LAKESIDE HILLS DR; FLORISSANT, MO 63033. (#28551-1).

NEOGA

COMMUNITY BUILDING AND LIBRARY - NEOGA, IL. CONSTRUCTION OF A MUNICIPAL BUILDING, INCLUDING A MEETING ROOM & LIBRARY, AS THE COMMUNITY'S BICENTENNIAL PROJECT. (LOCAL). MAYOR; VILLAGE OF NEOGA; NEOGA, IL 62447. (#30398).

NEW BERLIN

JULY 23 - 27, '75. VISIT OF HISTORY-MOBILE 'ETHNIC HISTORY IN ILLINOIS'. EXHIBIT AT SANGAMON COUNTY FAIR. (LOCAL). CLIFFORD HAKA, FIELD REP; ILLINOIS STATE HISTORICAL SOCIETY; OLD STATE CAPITOL; SPRINGFIELD, IL 62706. (#200016-513).

NEW SALEM

APR 20 - OCT 19, '75. LINCOLN'S NEW SALEM VILLAGE OPENED. THIRD SUNDAY OF THE MONTH, APRIL-OCT, VILLAGE WILL BE OPENED TO THE PUBLIC AND, THROUGH CONTACT WITH STAFF DRESSED IN HISTORIC COSTUME, WILL GAIN A BETTER UNDERSTANDING OF LIFE IN THE 1800'S. AT NEW SALEM STATE PARK. (REGN'L). MS JANET PICKETT; ILLINOIS DEPT OF CONSERVATION; 901 SOUTH SPRING; SPRINGFIELD, IL 62704. (#50138-1).

OCT 7 - 16, '75. SCHOOL TOURS AT NEW SALEM. THE FEDERATED JUNIOR WOMEN'S CLUB OF SPRINGFIELD SUPPLIES COSTUMED PERSONNEL TO OPEN & STAFF BLDGS ON TUES & THURS TO PROVIDE SCHOOL GROUPS WITH A BETTER UNDERSTANDING OF THE ILLINOIS FRONTIER. AT LINCOLN'S NEW SALEM STATE PARK. (LOCAL). MS JANET PICKETT; ILL DEPT OF CONSERVATION; 901 SOUTH SPRING; SPRINGFIELD, IL 62704. (#50272-56).

DEC 6 - 7, '75. A NEW SALEM CHRISTMAS. CELEBRATES TRADITIONAL PRAIRIE CHRISTMAS-1830'S. (LOCAL). MS JANET PICKETT; ILL DEPT OF CONSERVATION; 901 SOUTH STREET; SPRINGFIELD, IL 62704. (#50272-57).

FEB 12, '76. LINCOLN POST ROAD DEDICATION. CEREMONIES AT NEW SALEM STATE PARK TO FORMALLY OPEN LINCOLN POST ROAD WILL MOVE BY 7TH ILLINOIS CAVALRY (RE-ENACTED); BIKES, VANS, CARS TO OLD STATE CAPITOL IN SPRINGFIELD ON THAT ROAD. AT NEW SALEM STATE PARK TO SPRINGFIELD ON THE POST ROAD ROUTE. (LOCAL). ALVIN MAVIS, CHAIRMAN; CENTRAL ILLINOIS TOURISM; OAK HILLS RD; ROCHESTER, IL 62563. (#104827-1).

FEB 12, '76. LINCOLN'S BIRTHDAY. LINCOLN'S NEW SALEM VILLAGE CELEBRATES THIS DATE IN A SPECIAL WAY. SPECIAL ACTIVITIES COUPLED WITH A BIRTHDAY PARTY FOR 'OLD ABE' HIGHLIGHT THE DAY FESTIVITIES. AT NEW SALEM VILLAGE. (LOCAL). MS JANET PICKETT; ILLINOIS DEPARTMENT OF CONSERVATION; 901 SOUTH SPRING; SPRINGFIELD, IL 62704. (#50272-59).

APR 17, '76. WAGON TRAIN STOPOVER. TO JOIN WITH NATIONAL WAGON TRAIN IN CHICAGO AND GO ON TO PHILADELPHIA. (REGN'L). JULIE WILLIAMS, CHMN; ILLINOIS BICENTENNIAL COMMISSION; 1 W OLD STATE CAPITOL PLAZA; SPRINGFIELD, IL 62706. (#200016-129).

APR 18 - OCT 17, '76. LINCOLN'S NEW SALEM VILLAGE OPENED. THIRD SUNDAY OF THE MONTH, APRIL-OCT, VILLAGE WILL BE OPENED TO THE PUBLIC AND, THROUGH CONTACT WITH STAFF DRESSED IN HISTORIC COSTUME, WILL GAIN A BETTER UNDERSTANDING OF LIFE IN THE 1800'S. AT NEW SALEM STATE PARK. (REGN'L). MS JANET PICKETT; ILLINOIS DEPT OF CONSERVATION; 901 SOUTH SPRING; SPRINGFIELD, IL 62704. (#50138-2).

OCT 5 - 14, '76. SCHOOL TOURS AT NEW SALEM. THE FEDERATED JR WOMENS CLUB SUPPLIES COSTUMED PERSONNEL TO OPEN & STAFF BLDGS ON TUES & THURS OF 2 WEEKS TO PROVIDE SPRINGFIELD AREA SCHOOL GROUPS WITH A BETTER UNDERSTANDING OF THE ILLINOIS FRONTIER. AT LINCOLN'S NEW SALEM STATE PARK. (LOCAL). MS JANET PICKETT; ILLINOIS DEPARTMENT OF CONSERVATION; 901 SOUTH SPRING; SPRINGFIELD, IL 62704. (#50272-60).

DEC 4 - 5, '76. A NEW SALEM CHRISTMAS. CELEBRATES TRADITIONAL PRAIRIE CHRISTMAS-1830. (LOCAL). MS JANET PICKETT; ILL DEPT OF CONSERVATION; 901 SOUTH STREET; SPRINGFIELD, IL 62704. (#50272-58).

NEWARK

MAY 16, '76. FORT BEGGS TREK. SPECIAL PRESENTATION BY ARBA RECOGNIZING HIKERS OF AMERICA, INC AS A MEMBER ORGANIZATION IN THE NATIONAL BICENTENNIAL SERVICE ALLIANCE. AT MAIN STREET. (ST-WIDE). JAMES BENTZ, CHMN; HIKERS OF AMERICA, INC; RT 1 BOX 68; OSWEGO, IL 60543. (#104945-1).

DEC 31, '76. KENDALL COUNTY BICENTENNIAL COMMISSION GOING OUT OF BUSINESS PARTY. A FUN PARTY FOR THE KENDALL COUNTY BICENTENNIAL COMMISSION MEMBERS MEMBERS CONCLUDING TWO AND A HALF YEARS OF HARD WORK. AT TOM'S HOUSE. (LOCAL). TOM FLETCHER, COORD; KENDALL COUNTY BICENTENNIAL COMMISSION; BOX 175; NEWARK, IL 60541. (#104945-2).

NEWMAN

JULY 7 - 10, '76. DOUGLAS COUNTY CHAUTAUQUA IN NEWMAN. FESTIVITIES INCLUDE FARMER DAYS, AIR FORCE DRUM & BUGLE CORPS, DANCES & PARADES. (LOCAL). PALMER HALES, CHAIRMAN; DOUGLAS COUNTY BICENTENNIAL COMMITTEE; YATES ST; NEWMAN, IL 61942. (#106548-1).

NILES

HISTORICAL MARKER: DUTCHMEN POINT, NILES, IL. LANDSCAPING AT MILWAUKEE AND TOUHY AVES (DUTCHMEN POINT) AROUND THE HISTORICAL MARKER. (LOCAL). CAROL PANCK, CHAIRMAN; NILES BICENTENNIAL COMMISSION; 7601 MILWAUKEE AVE; NILES, IL 60648. (#33561).

JULY 5, '75. OFFICIAL OPENING NILES BICENTENNIAL CELEBRATION. CEREMONY AT NOTRE DAME HIGH SCHOOL, 7655 DEMPSTER. (LOCAL). CAROL PANEK, CHMN; NILES BICENTENNIAL COMMISSION; 7601 MILWAUKEE AVE; NILES, IL 60648. (#200016-495).

APR 22 - 25, '76. 'AMERICA WE LOVE YOU'. LIVE PERFORMANCE AT JEFFERSON SCHOOL. (LOCAL). CAROL PANEK, CHMN; NILES BICENTENNIAL COMMISSION AND WOMEN'S CLUB OF NILES; 7601 MILWAUKEE AVE; NILES, IL 60648. (#200016-496).

MAY 16, '76. ECUMENICAL SERVICES. CEREMONY AT ST JOHN BREBEUF CHURCH. (LOCAL). CAROL PANEK, CHMN; ST JOHN BREBEUF CHURCH; 7601 MILWAUKEE AVE; NILES, IL 60648. (#200016-497).

JULY 3, '76. NILES BICENTENNIAL DAYS. FESTIVAL AT NOTRE DAME HIGH SCHOOL. (LOCAL). CAROL PANEK, CHMN; NILES BICENTENNIAL COMMISSION; 7601 MILWAUKEE AVE; NILES, IL 60648. (#200016-498).

JULY 4, '76. NILES BICENTENNIAL DAYS PARADE. PARADE AT MILWAUKEE AVE FROM MAIN ST TO HOWARD ST. (LOCAL). CAROL PANEK, CHMN; NILES BICENTENNIAL COMMISSION & NILES JAYCEES; 7601 MILWAUKEE AVE; NILES, IL 60648. (#200016-499).

JULY 4, '76. NILES BICENTENNIAL DAYS FIREWORKS SPECTACULAR. FESTIVAL AT TAM OSHANTER GOLF COURSE. (LOCAL). CAROL PANEK, CHMN; NILES BICENTENNIAL COMMISSION; 7601 MILWAUKEE AVE; NILES, IL 60648. (#200016-500).

AUG 14, '76. RED, WHITE AND BLUE GARDEN CONTEST. COMPETITION. (LOCAL). CAROL PANEK, CHMN; NILES BICENTENNIAL COMMISSION AND GARDEN CLUB OF NILES; 7601 MILWAUKEE AVE; NILES, IL 60648. (#200016-501).

SEPT 18, '76. 'NILES LOOKS AT THE YEAR 2000'. SEMINAR AT NILES RECREATION CENTER. (LOCAL). CAROL PANEK, CHMN; NILES BICENTENNIAL COMMISSION AND LEAGUE OF WOMEN VOTERS; 7601 MILWAUKEE AVE; NILES, IL 60648. (#200016-502).

NORMAL

AMERICAN FOLK DANCE FESTIVAL TOUR - IL STATE UNIV. PROGRAM OF AMERICAN FOLK DANCES PERFORMED IN 5 EUROPEAN DANCE FESTIVALS. (INT'L). DUANE GOODWIN, PROJ DIRECTOR; ILLINOIS STATE UNIV; NORMAL, IL 61761. (#13579).

AMERICAN STUDIES PROGRAM AT ILLINOIS STATE UNIV. A 54-HOUR MAJOR WITH CONCENTRATION IN ENGLISH OR HISTORY, INCLUDING FIELD COURSES AT HISTORIC AREAS. (LOCAL). STEVEN KAGLE, ASSOC PROFESSOR; ENGLISH DEPARTMENT, ILLINOIS STATE UNIV; NORMAL, IL 61761. (#14919).

ANTHOLOGY OF BICENTENNIAL AMERICAN POETRY, IL. THIS BOOK WILL BE AN ANTHOLOGY OF CONTEMPORARY AMERICAN POEMS DEALING WITH LIFE IN AMERICA (PAST, PRESENT AND FUTURE) AND WILL BE PUBLISHED IN CONJUNCTION WITH THE 1976 ISU BICENTENNIAL ARTS FESTIVAL. (ST-WIDE). JAMES R SCRIMGEOUR, PROF OF ENGLISH; ILLINOIS STATE UNIVERSITY; NORMAL, IL 61761. (#21950).

BICENTENNIAL COURSES - NORMAL, IL. 8 NEW COURSES RELATING TO THE BICENTENNIAL WILL BE ADDED IN 6 DEPARTMENTS. (LOCAL). STANLEY RIVES, DEAN; ILLINOIS STATE UNIV; NORMAL, IL 61761. (#18577).

BOOK ON REVOLUTIONARY WAR VETERANS BURIED IN ILL. PUBLICATION & DISTRIBUTION BY ILL STATE GENEALOGICAL SOCIETY OF A BOOK CONTAINING INFORMATION - BURIAL PLACE, SPOUSES, DESCENDANTS & SERVICE RECORDS - ON REVOLUTIONARY WAR VETS BURIED IN ILL. (ST-WIDE). LESLIE A BRYAN, PROJECT DIRECTOR; ILLINOIS STATE GENEALOGICAL SOCIETY; PO BOX 2225; SPRINGFIELD, IL 62705. (#4882). **ARBA GRANTEE.**

CANTATA FOR PEACE, MUSIC PROJ IN NORMAL, ILLINOIS. CHORUS AND ORCHESTRA WITH TEXT BY LINCOLN, GANDHI, J F KENNEDY AND M L KING, JR. (NAT'L). ROQUE CORDERO, COMPOSER; DEPT OF MUSIC, ILLINOIS STATE UNIV; CENTENNIAL BLDG; NORMAL, IL 61761. (#7060). **(??).**

CATALOG OF CIRCUS - NORMAL, IL. AN EXTENSIVE LIBRARY COLLECTION WILL BE COMPILED ON THE AMERICAN CIRCUS. (LOCAL). ROBERT SOKAN, DIRECTOR OF SPECIAL COLLECTIONS; ILLINOIS STATE UNIV; NORMAL, IL 61761. (#18575).

CONTROVERSIAL IMAGES OF AMER REVOL GENERATIONS- IL. DISCUSSION OF BOOKS AVAILABLE IN LOCAL LIBRARIES WITH ADULT EDUCATION PROGRAM. (LOCAL). MARK PLUMMER, CHAIRMAN; ILLINOIS STATE UNIV; NORMAL, IL 61761. (#13580).

DIARY LITERATURE OF THE AMER REVOLUTION RESEARCH. A STUDY OF DIARIES OF INTRINSIC VALUE RELATED TO THE AMERICAN REVOLUTION. THIS STUDY WILL BE PART OF A BOOK ON AMERICAN DIARIES AND OF A COLLEGE COURSE ON THE LITERATURE OF THE AMERICAN REVOLUTION. (NAT'L). PROF STEVEN E KAGLE; 513 S VALE ST; BLOOMINGTON, IL 61701. (#4791).

HISTORIC PRESERVATION OF HOVEY HOME - NORMAL, IL. THE HOME OF GENERAL CHARLES E HOVEY & HIS SON, POET RICHARD HOVEY, WILL BE MOVED FOR HISTORIC & EDUCATIONAL PURPOSES TO THE CAMPUS. THE HOME WILL BE RESTORED AND MADE AVAILABLE TO THE PUBLIC. (ST-WIDE). LEO EASTMAN, ASSOCIATE SECRETARY; ILLINOIS STATE UNIV; NORMAL, IL 61761. (#18578).

ILLINOIS STATE UNIV MEN'S GLEE CLUB BICENT PROJECT. A PROGRAM WILL BE MADE AVAILABLE TO ANY GROUP OR ORGANIZATION WISHING TO CELEBRATE THE NATION'S 200TH BIRTHDAY IN A SPECIAL WAY. (ST-WIDE). CARL F MUSSON, PROFESSOR; ISU DEPT OF MUSIC; NORMAL, IL 61761. (#16444).

INTERNATIONAL EXCHANGE SCHOLARSHIP, NORMAL, IL. FREE TUITION & FEES PLUS A $1,000 STIPEND FOR ONE YEAR FOR FOREIGN STUDENT INTERESTED IN AMERICAN HISTORY, POLITICAL SCIENCE OR ARTS. (LOCAL). THEODORE SANDS, DIRECTOR; DEPT OF INTERNATIONAL STUDIES, ILLINOIS STATE UNIV; NORMAL, IL 61761. (#14918).

PLAYHOUSE SERIES - ILLINOIS STATE UNIV. PERFORMANCE OF THE MUSICAL '1776.'. (LOCAL). BRUCE KAISER, PROJ DIRECTOR; ILLINOIS STATE UNIV; NORMAL, IL 61761. (#13582).

'TREES OF ILLINOIS', BOOK, NORMAL, IL. A BOOK WITH DRAWINGS & DESCRIPTIONS OF 55 TREES COMMON TO ILLINOIS. (LOCAL). GENE BUDIG, PRESIDENT; ILLINOIS STATE UNIV; NORMAL, IL 61761. (#14967).

200 YEARS OF ILLINOIS ART - ILLINOIS STATE UNIV. GALLERY I PRESENTS 5 EXHIBITS ON ILLINOIS ART. EXHIBITS WILL TRAVEL TO 4 LOCATIONS AND WILL BE AVAILABLE FOR LATER DISPLAYS. (ST-WIDE). TOM TOPERZER, PROJ DIRECTOR; ILLINOIS STATE UNIV; NORMAL, IL 61761. (#13584).

FEB 16, '75. BICENTENNIAL YOUTH DEBATES. COMPETITION. (LOCAL). WILLIAM SEMLAK, SPONSOR; ILLINOIS STATE UNIV; NORMAL, IL 61761. (#103224-1).

AUG 31 - SEPT 25, '75. AMISTAD II EXHIBITION. 11,000 PAINTINGS & SCULPTURES FROM 1790-1975. AT GALLERY I, CVA BLDG. (LOCAL). TOM TOPERZER, CHAIRMAN; BLACK AFFAIRS COUNCIL, ILLINOIS STATE UNIV; NORMAL, IL 61761. (#10712-2).

SEPT 1, '75 - MAY 1, '76. ART, ESSAY, MUSIC, POETRY, NATIONAL COMPETITION. COMPETITION AT ILLINOIS STATE UNIV. (NAT'L). BETTY BROWN, PROJ DIR; KAPPA DELTA PI SOCIETY; NORMAL, IL 61761. (#102170-1).

SEPT 2 - DEC 2, '75. 'PAST IS PROLOGUE'. RADIO/TV AT RADIO STATION WGLT. (LOCAL). WILLIAM HADDAD, COORD; DEPT OF HISTORY, ILLINOIS STATE UNIV; NORMAL, IL 61761. (#200016-48).

OCT 5 - 13, '75. BICENTENNIAL HOMECOMING CELEBRATION. CARNIVAL, MOTION PICTURES, TALENT SHOW, STREET DANCING, FOOTBALL GAME, BALL & THEATRE PRESENTATION. THEME IS 'ISU CHANGES WITH OUR NATION. AT UNION BALLROOM, AUDITORIUM, HANCOCK STADIUM. (LOCAL). RICHARD DIDIER, COORD; HOMECOMING BOARD, ILLINOIS STATE UNIV; NORMAL, IL 61761. (#200016-45).

OCT 10, '75 - FEB 6, '76. 'SHOWCASE '76'. PROGRAMS ON AMERICAN MUSIC. AT UNIVERSITY UNION AUDITORIUM. (LOCAL). CARL F MUSSON, PROJ DIR; ILLINOIS STATE UNIV; NORMAL, IL 61761. (#13583-1).

OCT 10, '75 - MAY 1, '76. GREAT AMERICAN PLAYS - ILLINOIS STATE UNIV. 'THE MUSIC MAN' ON OCT 10-12. 12TH IS MATINEE AT 2:00PM. 'A STREETCAR NAMED DESIRE' ON NOV 13-16 & 19-22. 'DEATH OF A SALESMAN' ON FEB 19-22 & 26-28. 'THE MAN WHO CAME TO DINNER' ON APRIL 22-25 & APRIL 28-MAY 1. AT 'MUSIC MAN' AT UNIV UNION AUDITORIUM. WESTHOFF THEATRE OTHERS.. (LOCAL). CALVIN PRITNER; ILLINOIS STATE UNIV; NORMAL, IL 61761. (#13581-1).

OCT 31 - NOV 1, '75. BICENTENNIAL BAND PROGRAM. LIVE PERFORMANCE AT HIGH SCHOOL FIELD, 7TH ST AND MCCORMACK FIELD. (LOCAL). GEORGE FOELLER, CHAIRMAN; ILLINOIS STATE UNIV MARCHING BAND; NORMAL, IL 61761. (#200016-46).

NOV 5, '75. BICENTENNIAL INAUGURAL PROGRAM. BICENTENNIAL FLAG PRESENTATION TO PRESIDENT; ADDRESS BY SENATOR ERVIN; EXHIBITS BY STUDENTS AND COMMUNITY ORGANIZATIONS. AT UNION-AUDITORIUM, CIRCUS ROOM. (LOCAL). ANDREW MONTELEONE, CHMN; FORUM COMMITTEE, ILLINOIS STATE UNIV; NORMAL, IL 61761. (#200016-47).

NOV 20, '75 - APR 22, '76. AMERICA IN LITERATURE - LECTURE SERIES. MARCH 25, 1976-MARK TWAIN'S AMERICA; APRIL 22, 1976-DICKEN'S VIEW OF AMERICA. AT STEVENSON HALL, UNIV UNION, CENTER FOR VISUAL ARTS. (LOCAL). CHARLES HARRIS, CHMN; DEPT OF ENGLISH ILLINOIS STATE UNIV; NORMAL, IL 61761. (#105755-1).

FEB 12, '76. BICENTENNIAL AGRICULTURE SYMPOSIUM. SEMINAR AT HAYDEN AUDITORIUM & HUDELSON MUSEUM. (LOCAL). FREDERICK W FUESS, COORD; DEPT OF AGRICULTURE, ILLINOIS STATE UNIV; NORMAL, IL 61761. (#200016-49).

FEB 17 - APR 6, '76. AMERICAN FILM SERIES. FILMS INCLUDE: 'BIRTH OF A NATION', 'JAZZ SINGER', 'CITY LIGHTS', 'GOLDDIGGERS OF 1933', 'CITIZEN KANE', 'SINGIN' IN THE RAIN' AND 'SOME LIKE IT HOT.'. AT UNIVERSITY UNION, BALLROOM, PRAIRIE ROOM, CIRCUS ROOM. (LOCAL). ERIC BICKLEY, CHAIRMAN; UNION BOARD/FILM SOCIETY; NORMAL, IL 61761. (#102171-1).

MAY 15, '76. BICENTENNIAL COMPOSITION, BICENTENNIAL COMMENCEMENT. COMPOSITION FOR CONCERT BAND & NARRATOR. WORDS FROM SPEECHES OF AMBASSADOR ADLAI E STEVENSON II, IRWIN SPECTOR, COMPOSER FOR BICENTENNIAL COMMENCEMENT OF ISU. AT HORTON FIELDHOUSE. (ST-WIDE). IRWIN SPECTOR; ILLINOIS STATE UNIV COMMENCEMENT COMMITTEE; ILLINOIS STATE UNIVERSITY; NORMAL, IL 61761. (#106790-1).

MAY 16, '76. WJBC FESTIVAL OF AMERICAN MUSIC. RADIO/TV AT ISU UNION. (LOCAL). DR ALICE EBEL, CHMN; ILLINOIS STATE UNIV; NORMAL, IL 61761. (#200016-141).

JUNE 16 - 23, '76. 'NAIVE ILLINOIS' - ART EXHIBIT. EXHIBIT AT ISU CENTER FOR THE VISUAL ARTS, GALLERY I. (LOCAL). DR ALICE EBEL, CHMN; ILLINOIS STATE UNIV; NORMAL, IL 61761. (#200016-139).

JULY 4, '76. BICENTENNIAL FESTIVAL AND CITY HALL DEDICATION. CEREMONY, FESTIVAL. (LOCAL). GUY FRAKER, CHMN; MCLEAN COUNTY BICENTENNIAL COMMISSION; 308 E WASHINGTON ST; BLOOMINGTON, IL 61701. (#200016-133).

AUG 8 - SEPT 26, '76. ILLINOIS LANDSCAPES - ILLINOIS ART. EXHIBIT AT ISU CENTER FOR THE VISUAL ARTS, GALLERY I. (LOCAL). DR ALICE EBEL, CHMN; ILLINOIS STATE UNIV; NORMAL, IL 61761. (#200016-138).

NORMAL — CONTINUED

AUG 15 - OCT 3, '76. 200 YEARS OF QUILTS IN ILLINOIS - PRIVATE COLLECTIONS. EXHIBIT AT ISU CENTER FOR THE VISUAL ARTS. (LOCAL). DR ALICE EBEL, CHMN; ILLINOIS STATE UNIV; NORMAL, IL 61761. (#200016-137).

SEPT 18, '76. ISRAELI PHILHARMONIC ORCHESTRA VISITS NORMAL. LIVE PERFORMANCE. (INT'L). URI AHARON BAR-NEV; ISRAELI GOVERNMENT; 1621 21ST ST, NW; WASHINGTON, DC 20008. (#109015-16).

OCT 6 - 11, '76. EMERGENCE OF MODERNISM IN ILLINOIS. EXHIBIT AT ISU CENTER FOR THE VISUAL ARTS - GALLERY I. (LOCAL). DR ALICE EBEL, CHMN; ILLINOIS STATE UNIV; NORMAL, IL 61761. (#200016-135).

NORRIDGE

NORRIDGE BOOK DRAWING - IL. PROCEEDS TO PURCHASE HERITAGE BELL TO BE PRESENTED AT A LATER DATE. (LOCAL). JOSEPH G MICEK; NORRIDGE BICENTENNIAL COMMISSION; 4935 N FRANK PARKWAY; NORRIDGE, IL 60656. (#32169).

NORRIDGE FLAG PRESENTATION & CEREMONY. CEREMONY PRESENTATION OF FLAG & BICENTENNIAL CERTIFICATE BY CONGRESSMAN HENRY HYDE. (LOCAL). MICHAEL MIELA, CHMN; NORRIDGE BICENTENNIAL COMMISSION; 4020 N OLCOTT; NORRIDGE, IL 60634. (#200016-364).

OLD-FASHIONED PICNIC & CEREMONY. FESTIVAL. (LOCAL). LUCILLE GUTOWSKI, CHMN; DIVINE SAVIOR CHURCH & NORRIDGE BICENTENNIAL COMMITTEE; 7750 W MONTROSE; NORRIDGE, IL 60634. (#200016-365).

PROFILE '76 - NORRIDGE, IL. FILM ON AMERICAN LIFE OR LIVING PRESENTED BY EASTMAN KODAK. (LOCAL). MS F COVEY, CHAIRMAN; EASTMAN KODAK & THE NORRIDGE BICENTENNIAL COMMISSION; 4020 N OLCOTT; NORRIDGE, IL 60634. (#32167).

SCROLL SIGNING - NORRIDGE, IL. OFFICIAL SCROLL SIGNING AFFIRMING FAITH IN THE PRINCIPLES OF OUR BILL OF RIGHTS & CONSTITUTION. (LOCAL). HELEN R HOGAN; HARLEM IRVING PLAZA & NORRIDGE BICENTENNIAL COMM; 4104 N HARLEM; NORRIDGE, IL 60634. (#32166).

TREE PLANTING - NORRIDGE, IL. FIFTY CRIMSON KING MAPLES PLANTED ON SCHOOL, CHURCH & PUBLIC BUILDINGS. (LOCAL). MICHAEL W MIELA, CHIARMAN; NORRIDGE BICENTENNIAL COMMISSION; 5196 MISSION DR; NORRIDGE, IL 60656. (#32168).

MAY 7 - 15, '76. SHOWTIME USA. HISTORIC OR PATRIOTIC MUSICAL ADULT & STUDENT COMBINED. AT NORRIDGE PARK DISTRICT 4631 N OVERHILL AVE. (LOCAL). ANITA STEELE; NORRIDGE PARK DISTRICT BICENTENNIAL COMMISSION; 4139 N OZARK; NORRIDGE, IL 60634. (#200016-366).

JULY 4, '76. JULY 4TH PARADE. PARADE INCLUDED PARTICIPATION BY ADJACENT COMMUNITY GROUPS. (LOCAL). WILLIAM DAMMELER, CHMN; NORRIDGE BICENTENNIAL COMMITTEE; 7700 W STRONG ST; NORRIDGE, IL 60656. (#200016-363).

JULY 4 - NOV 21, '76. LIBERTY BELL PRESENTATION. PROCEEDS FROM NORRIDGE DRAWING TO PURCHASE HERITAGE SYMBOL, THE LIBERTY BELL-CEREMONY AT BICENTENNIAL BALL 11/21/76. AT STARLIGHT ROOM AT LAWRENCE & MANHEIM O'HARE OFFICE BLDG SCHILLER PK. (LOCAL). JO ANNE WHEELER; NORRIDGE BICENTENNIAL COMMISSION; 4837 N ORANGE; NORRIDGE, IL 60656. (#200016-362).

NORTH AURORA

SPIRIT OF '76 PARK - NORTH AURORA, IL. RENOVATION OF RAILROAD RIGHT-OF-WAY TO FORM A RECREATION AREA. (LOCAL). VERNAL LAYTON, SECRETARY; NORTH AURORA BICENTENNIAL COMMITTEE & LIONS CLUB; NORTH AURORA VILLAGE HALL; NORTH AURORA, IL 60542. (#24846).

JUNE 6, '76. ARTS & CRAFTS SHOW. EXHIBIT AT NORTH AURORA ISLAND PARK. (LOCAL). VERNAL D LAYTON, SEC; NORTH AURORA BICENTENNIAL COMMITTEE; N AURORA VILLAGE HALL; N AURORA, IL 60542. (#107277-1).

NORTHBROOK

RESTORATION OF THE NORTHFIELD INN - NORTHBROOK, IL. RESTORATION OF THE NORTHFIELD INN FOR COMMUNITY USE. (LOCAL). LAWRENCE SOMMERS, CHAIRMAN; NORTHBROOK HISTORICAL SOCIETY; PO BOX 1776; NORTHBROOK, IL 60062. (#27897). **ARBA GRANTEE.**

NORTHFIELD

JUNE 12 - 27, '76. FIRST RUGBY MATCH BETWEEN USA & FRANCE. COMPETITION AT NEW TRIER TWP HS WEST NORTHFIELD. (INT'L). RICHARD W SMITH; USA RUGBY FOOTBALL UNION; 1 FIRST NATIONAL PLAZA; CHICAGO, IL 60603. (#200016-302).

NORTHLAKE

BICENTENNIAL SYMBOL FLAGS. BICENTENNIAL FLAG; LICENSE NO 76-19-0579. (NAT'L). JOHN CHRISTIANSEN, PROJ DIRECTOR; J C SCHULTZ ENTERPRISES, INC; 48 S WOLF RD; NORTHLAKE, IL 60164. (#15410).

NORWAY

CLENG PEERSON MEMORIAL HIGHWAY AND DUG-OUT IN IL. CONSTRUCTION AND DEDICATION OF CLENG PEERSON MEMORIAL HIGHWAY AND DUG-OUT. DEDICATION BY KING OLAV OF NORWAY. (LOCAL). WAYNE BORCHSENIUS, COORDINATOR; SONS OF NORWAY; RR; SHERIDAN, IL 60551. (#33560).

RURAL COMMUNITY PARK IN NORWAY, ILLINOIS. RURAL PARK WITH MUSEUM, PLAYGROUND, COMMUNITY BUILDING & HISTORICAL MONUMENT WILL BE BUILT. DEDICATED BY KING OLAF OF NORWAY. (INT'L). WAYNE BORCHSENIUS, PARK CHAIRMAN; NORWAY IMPROVEMENT LEAGUE; RFD 2 BOX 68; SHERIDAN, IL 60551. (#8557).

OCT 17, '75. VISIT BY KING OLAF OF NORWAY. CEREMONY. (INT'L). DON PERISHO, COORD; LASALLE COUNTY BICENTENNIAL COMMISSION; 317 LASALLE ST; STREATOR, IL 61364. (#200016-207).

OAK BROOK

MCDONALD'S 'TREES FOR AMERICA' - OAKBROOK, IL. MCDONALD'S CORPORATION DONATING 1,776 TREES TO EACH OF 50 STATES AND THE DISTRICT OF COLUMBIA. (NAT'L). MATTHEW J LAMBERT, DIRECTOR OF PUBLIC RELATIONS; MCDONALD'S CORPORATION; MCDONALD'S PLAZA; OAK BROOK, IL 60521. (#26064).

SEPT 1, '75 - DEC 31, '77. SEMINAR '76 SESSIONS. HELP UNITE NATION BY PROVIDING FORUMS TO CLARIFY PERSONAL & NATIONAL VALUES, GOALS, AND PRIORITIES WHAT DO CITIZENS REALLY THINK AFTER LOGICAL REFLECTION? ESTABLISH CENTERS FOR THE STUDY OF HUMAN VALUES. (ST-WIDE). ARTHUR I MELVIN, EXEC DIR; CENTURY III FOUNDATION; 1 FREEWAY, BOX C; OAK BROOK, IL 60521. (#2132-1).

OAK GROVE

JULY 4, '76. BICENTENNIAL PICNIC AND FIREWORKS. FESTIVAL. (LOCAL). MORRIS BUSKE, CHMN; OAK PARK BICENTENNIAL COMMISSION; 831 N GROVE AVE; OAK PARK, IL 60302. (#107867-1).

OAK PARK

ANALYSIS OF HISTORIC DISTRICT RESOURCES PROJECT. METHODS, TECHNIQUES AND TIME STUDIES FOR MAKING VERBAL AND VISUAL ANALYSES AND DESCRIPTIONS OF VISUAL RESOURCES IN HISTORIC DISTRICTS FOR PRESERVATION PLANNING. NEA GRANT. (NAT'L). PAUL E SPRAGUE, PROJECT DIRECTOR; PAUL E SPRAGUE, PROJECT DIRECTOR; 1810 W 103RD ST; CHICAGO, IL 60643. (#2198).

BICENTENNIAL ISSUE OF THE JOURNAL OF GEOGRAPHY-IL. THE AMERICAN EXPERIENCE: PAST, PRESENT & FUTURE; 4 ARTICLES ON THE THEME BY DISTINGUISHED SCHOLARS. (LOCAL). DR RONALD E NELSON, EDITOR; DEPT OF GEOGRAPHY, WESTERN ILLINOIS UNIV; MACOMB, IL 61455. (#24875).

BOOK, F L WRIGHT & PRAIRIE SCHOOL ARCHITECTURE-IL. 24 BUILDINGS DESIGNED BY WRIGHT IN OAK PARK PLUS 40 SIGNIFICANT HOMES WILL BE USED AS A LIVING MUSEUM OF MODERN ARCHITECTURE TO SHOW DEVELOPMENT OVER PERIOD OF 1889-1926. (LOCAL). ROY G HLAVACEK, CHAIRMAN; OAK PARK BICENTENNIAL COMMISSION; PO BOX 1976; OAK PARK, IL 60303. (#10831).

CHICAGO AREA EXPRESSWAY SURVEILLANCE PROJECT, IL. TRAFFIC SURVEILLANCE CENTER HOUSES THE WORLD'S FIRST AND LARGEST COMPUTERIZED FREEWAY SURVEILLANCE AND CONTROL NETWORK; OPERATED BY THE ILLINOIS DEPARTMENT OF TRANSPORTATION, DIVISION OF HIGHWAYS. (LOCAL). JOSEPH M MCDERMOTT, PROJ DIRECTOR; CHICAGO AREA EXPRESSWAY SURVEILLANCE PROJECT, I D O T; 230 MADISON ST; OAK PARK, IL 60302. (#20006).

HISTORY OF REVOL PERIOD, LECTURE SERIES IN IL. A SERIES OF SEVEN LECTURES TO BE GIVEN AT THE PUBLIC LIBRARIES OF OAK PARK AND RIVER FOREST, ILLINOIS. (LOCAL). M R BUSKE, CHAIRMAN; OAK PARK ARBA; BOX 1976; OAK PARK, IL 60303. (#6214).

MAR 18, '75. REENACTMENT OF PAUL REVERE'S RIDE. LIVE PERFORMANCE. (LOCAL). M R BUSKE, CHAIRMAN; OAK PARK ARBA; BOX 1976; OAK PARK, IL 60301. (#6214-501).

JULY 4 - 5, '75. PRESENTATION OF THE PLAY '1776'. LIVE PERFORMANCE. (LOCAL). M R BUSKE, CHAIRMAN; OAK PARK ARBA; BOX 1976; OAK PARK, IL 60301. (#6214-503).

JULY 4, '76. JULY FOURTH FESTIVITIES IN OAK PARK. PARADE, FIREWORKS & PICNIC FOR OAK PARK & RIVER FOREST. (LOCAL). MORRIS BUSKE; OAK PARK BICENTENNIALOMMISSION; 831 N GROVE AVE; OAK PARK, IL 60302. (#6214-504).

JULY 4 - 5, '76. PRODUCTION OF PLAY '1776'. LIVE PERFORMANCE AT OAK PARK HIGH SCHOOL AUDITORIUM. (LOCAL). MORRIS BUSKE; OAK PARK BICENTENNIAL COMMISSION; 831 N GROVE AVE; OAK PARK, IL 60302. (#7912-1).

OAKBROOK TERR

BICENTENNIAL BIKEWAY - OAKBROOK TERRACE, IL. TWO MILE BIKEWAY LINKING MAJOR PARKS AND PUBLIC BUILDINGS, ONE AND ONE HALF MILES ALONG CREEK THROUGH RESIDENTIAL AREA. (LOCAL). BEVERLY E DRZKA, CHAIRPERSON; OAKBROOK TERRACE COMMUNITY BICENTENNIAL COMMISSION; 1 S 325 ARDMORE; VILLA PARK, IL 60181. (#28654).

JUNE 27 - JULY 4, '76. FESTIVAL WEEK. FAIR, LIVE PERFORMANCE, COMPETITION AT ANDERSON CENTER, HERITAGE PARK, SWARTZ PARK, VILLA-ROOSEVELT PARK. (LOCAL). BEVERLY E DRZKA, COORD; OAKBROOK TERRACE COMMUNITY BICENTENNIAL COMMISSION; 1 S 325 ARDMORE; VILLA PARK, IL 60181. (#200016-237).

OAKLAND

HISTORIC BARN FOR LANDMARKS, INC COMPOUND - IL. A BARN WILL BE RELOCATED IN COMPOUND AND RENOVATED TO HOUSE ANTIQUE FARM IMPLEMENTS AS MUSEUM. THIS WILL BE PART OF HISTORIC COMPOUND ALREADY OPEN TO VISITORS. (LOCAL). HELEN E PARKES, PROJ DIRECTOR; OAKLAND BICENTENNIAL COMMISSION; OAKLAND, IL 61943. (#26876). **ARBA GRANTEE.**

ODELL

PUPPET SHOW ON AMERICAN HISTORY IN ODELL, IL. PUPPET SHOW PERFORMANCES BY ODELL HIGH SCHOOL STUDENTS. (LOCAL). ROBERT HAUSE, COORDINATOR; ODELL HIGH SCHOOL; ODELL, IL 60460. (#33559).

OGLESBY

A TIME TO REMEMBER, OGLESBY, IL. A 2-DAY CULTURAL AND HISTORICAL OPEN HOUSE. (LOCAL). JAMES HUFFSTODT, ASST DIRECTOR; ILLINOIS VALLEY COMMUNITY COLLEGE & LA SALLE CO HISTORICAL SOC; RFD #1; OGELSBY, IL 61348. (#24277). **ARBA GRANTEE.**

APR 26 - MAY 2, '76. A TIME TO REMEMBER. 2-DAY CULTURAL & HISTORICAL OPEN-HOUSE. AT CAMPUS OF ILLINOIS VALLEY COMMUNITY COLLEGE. (LOCAL). JAMES HUFFSTODT, ASST DIR; ILLINOIS VALLEY COMMUNITY COLLEGE AND LASALLE CO HISTORICAL SOCIETY; PUBLIC INFO SERV, IVCC, RFD #1; OGLESBY, IL 61348. (#24277-1).

MAY 30, '76. CIVIL WAR BATTLE RE-ENACTMENT & TOWN CELEBRATION. A MOCK CIVIL WAR BATTLE WILL BE RE-ENACTED BY A UNION & CONFEDERATE REGIMENT WEARING AUTHENTIC UNIFORMS & CARRYING AUTHENTIC EQUIPMENT; REFRESHMENTS WILL BE SERVED. AT LEHIGH CITY PARK. (LOCAL). KENNETH J FICEK, CO-CHMN; OGLESBY BICENTENNIAL COMMISSION; 109 JORDAN ST; OGLESBY, IL 61348. (#107120-1).

OHIO

NOV 22, '75. BICENTENNIAL FUN NIGHT. FESTIVAL AT THE HIT 'N' WRECK (YOUTH RESTAURANT IN OHIO). (LOCAL). PATRICIA DENNEY, CO-CHMN; BICENTENNIAL COMMITTEE; 203 CHURCH ST; OHIO, IL 61349. (#200016-75).

DEC 10, '75. BAKE SALE. EXHIBIT, FESTIVAL AT GOY'S HARDWARE STORE, MAIN ST. (LOCAL). PATRICIA DENNEY, CO-CHMN; BICENTENNIAL COMMITTEE OF OHIO; 203 CHURCH ST; OHIO, IL 61349. (#200016-74).

JULY 23 - 25, '76. OHIO '76 REUNION. FESTIVAL. (LOCAL). PATRICIA DENNEY, CO-CHMN; BICENTENNIAL COMMITTEE OF OHIO; 203 CHURCH ST; OHIO, IL 61349. (#200016-76).

OKAWVILLE

READING CENTER IN OKAWVILLE, IL. PROJECT INVOLVES THE INITIAL STEP IN ESTABLISHING A PUBLIC LIBRARY; BOOKS, PICTURES AND FILMS WILL BE AVAILABLE. (LOCAL). ROGER SUNNQUIST, PRESIDENT; OKAWVILLE EDUCATION ASSOC; PO BOX 101; OKAWVILLE, IL 62271. (#12258).

RECREATIONAL LAND DEVELOPMENT - OKAWVILLE, IL. PLANNED PROJECT REQUIRES MANPOWER TO CLEAR & DEVELOP AREA TO BE A RECREATIONAL AREA. (LOCAL). WILLIAM KOETTING, CHAIRMAN; OKAWVILLE LIONS CLUB; OKAWVILLE, IL 62271. (#15319).

JUNE 28, '75. KICK-OFF DINNER. KICK-OFF DINNER WILL INCLUDE FESTIVAL COSTUMES & SKITS; COMMUNITYWIDE PARTICIPATION. (LOCAL). POLLY D KOETTING, DIR; OKAWVILLE BICENTENNIAL COMMITTEE; OKAWVILLE, IL 62271. (#101379-1).

OLYMPIA FLDS

FEB 29, '76. GOOD GOVERNMENT CELEBRATION. FESTIVAL, AWARD, CEREMONY AT OLYMPIA FIELDS COUNTRY CLUB. (LOCAL). ELIZABETH F GOYAK, CHMN; MATTESON BICENTENNIAL COMMISSION; 21310 BUTTERFIELD PKY; MATTESON, IL 60443. (#200016-227).

OMAHA

FIRST TERRITORIAL BANK REFURBISHING - OMAHA, IL. FURNISHING AND EQUIPPING FIRST TERRITORIAL BANK. (LOCAL). MRS HAROLD WEST, CHAIRMAN; GALLATIN COUNTY BICENTENNIAL COMMISSION; OMAHA, IL 62871. (#27803). **ARBA GRANTEE.**

MAR 30, '76. COUNTY BICENTENNIAL DAY. 300 PEOPLE ARE EXPECTED AT EACH LOCATION. AT SHAWNEETOWN, RIDGWAY, EQUALITY AND OLD SHAWNEETOWN PARKS. (LOCAL). MARY WEST, CHAIRMAN; GALLATIN COUNTY HISTORICAL SOCIETY; OMAHA, IL 62871. (#104546-5).

OMAHA — CONTINUED

APR 30, '76. PLANT TREES AND PIONEER DAYS. LOCAL COUNTY SCHOOL STUDENTS WILL PLANT TREES & PIONEER GARDENS AT 4 PARK LOCATIONS. 300 PEOPLE ARE EXPECTED AT EACH LOCATION. AT SHAWNEETOWN, RIDGWAY, EQUALITY AND OLD SHAWNEETOWN PARKS. (LOCAL). MARY WEST, CHAIRMAN; GALLATIN COUNTY HISTORICAL SOCIETY; OMAHA, IL 62871. (#104546-4).

SEPT 25, '76. EQUALITY SALT DAY. CEREMONY, FESTIVAL AT EQUALITY, IL ON ROUTE 13, GALLATIN COUNTY. (LOCAL). MARY WEST, CHAIRMAN; GALLATIN COUNTY HISTORICAL SOCIETY & EQUALITY SALT DAY ASSOC; OMAHA, IL 62871. (#104546-3).

ONARGA

PRESERVATION OF ONARGA GRADE SCHOOL BUILDING IN IL. BUILDING BUILT IN 1867; OLDEST SCHOOL BUILDING STILL IN USE IN THE STATE ILLINOISE. (LOCAL). MRS LESLIE BORK, SR, CHAIRMAN; BICENTENNIAL COMMISSION OF ONARGA; 436 E SEMINARY; ONARGA, IL 60955. (#33558).

JUNE 12, '76. PRINCESS ONARGA FESTIVAL AND QUESTER'S HISTORICAL STYLE SHOW. EXHIBIT AT ONARGA HIGH SCHOOL NORTH EVERGREEN ST. (LOCAL). MRS LESLIE BORK, SR; FINE ARTS CLUB AND QUESTERS OF ONARGA; 436 E SEMINARY; ONARGA, IL 60955. (#200016-455).

OQUAWKA

JUNE 11 - 13, '76. BICENTENNIAL CELEBRATION. FESTIVAL. (LOCAL). VERA WEBB, COORD; HENDERSON COUNTY BICENTENNIAL COMMISSION; BOX 352; OQUAWKA, IL 61469. (#200016-204).

JUNE 20, '76. HENDERSON COUNTY INTERFAITH COMMUNITY SERVICE. COUNTY WIDE WORSHIP SERVICE WITH MUSIC WILL BE HELD. AT DELABAR STATE PARK. (LOCAL). REV R J ONGNA, COORD; HENDERSON COUNTY BICENTENNIAL COMMISSION; BOX 1776; RARITAN, IL 61471. (#108216-1).

ORANGEVILLE

BAKE SALE. EXHIBIT AT ORANGEVILLE COMMUNITY BANK; HIGH STREET. (LOCAL). MRS EARL DITTMAR, COORD; AMERICAN LEGION AUXILLARY OF THE KLINE POST; ORANGEVILLE, IL 61060. (#102939-1).

BICENTENNIAL PARKING LOT - PROJ OF ORANGEVILLE, IL. A 48-SPACE LOT IS IN THE IMPLEMENTATION STAGE; LAND AQUISITION BEING FORMALIZED; SURVEY COMPLETED; TARGET COMPLETION DATE IS THE SUMMER OF '76. (LOCAL). J MILTON, PRESIDENT; VILLAGE BOARD; CITY HALL; ORANGEVILLE, IL 61060. (#12451).

FUND RAISING FOR BICENTENNIAL ACTIVITIES. LOCAL LOGO BOOSTER BUTTONS AND WOODEN NICKELS WILL BE SOLD AT LOCAL EVENTS; ALSO, CHANCES ON HOMEMADE BICENTENNIAL QUILT AND TREASURE CHEST FILLED WITH HANDMADE ITEMS WILL BE SOLD. (LOCAL). DORIS LENKER, CHAIRMAN; ORANGEVILLE BICENTENNIAL COMMISSION; RFD #1; ORANGEVILLE, IL 61060. (#12453).

PLAYGROUND BEAUTIFICATION PROJ - ORANGEVILLE, IL. A FAMILY PROJECT; ALL PLAYGROUND EQUIPMENT TO BE PAINTED WITH STARS AND STRIPES. PAINT DONATED BY STEPHENSON SERVICE CO. THREE TRASH CANS FOR VILLAGE ALSO PAINTED. (LOCAL). SUSAN WICHMAN, PROJ DIRECTOR; ORANGEVILLE CUB SCOUTS & WEBELOS PACK 23, CEDARVILLE; RFD 1; ORANGEVILLE, IL 61060. (#16409).

RESTORATION-RENOVATION OF IOOF LODGE BLDG - IL. EXTERIOR IMPROVEMENTS OF LODGE SUCH AS SIDING, ROOFING AND INTERIOR FACELIFTING; COMPLETION TARGET DATE IS MID '76. (LOCAL). LLOYD KOEHNER, PROJ DIRECTOR; IOOF LODGE; HIGH ST; ORANGEVILLE, IL 61060. (#12452).

AUG 25, '75. TEACHER ORIENTATION. A SEMINAR FOR TEACHERS ON TEACHER PARTICIPATION IN COMMEMORATIVE EVENTS. AT HIGH SCHOOL BUILDING. (LOCAL). DORIS E LENKER, CHMN; ORANGEVILLE BICENTENNIAL COMMISSION; RFD 1; ORANGEVILLE, IL 61060. (#100780-1).

SEPT 16 - OCT 5, '75. ORANGEVILLE HISTORICAL EXHIBIT. LOCAL HERITAGE ITEMS WILL BE ON DISPLAY AT THE ORANGEVILLE MUSEUM; CITIZENS WILL DONATE ITEMS TO BE ON EXHIBIT; FIELD TRIPS AVAILABLE FOR STUDENTS. AT IOOF BLDG, HIGH ST. (LOCAL). DEAN RICHTENMEIER, CHMN; IOOF LODGE & REBEKAH LODGE; RFD 1; ORANGEVILLE, IL 61060. (#100778-1).

SEPT 20, '75. COUNTRY SWINGERS BICENTENNIAL BENEFIT DANCE. FESTIVAL AT GS MULTI-PURPOSE ROOM. (LOCAL). DORIS E LENKER, CHMN; COUNTRY SWINGERS; RFD #1; ORANGEVILLE, IL 61060. (#200016-44).

NOV 17, '75. PTO BICENTENNIAL COMMEMORATION NITE. ONE HOUR BICENTENNIAL FILMS AND QUESTION & ANSWER PERIOD. AT HIGH SCHOOL GYM. (LOCAL). MRS ALBERT BILGRI, CHMN; PARENT TEACHER ORGANIZATION; RFD #1; DAKOTA, IL 61060. (#102283-1).

NOV 22, '75. ORANGEVILLE BICENTENNIAL BOX LUNCH AUCTION. BOXES DECORATED WITH PATRIOTIC THEME FILLED WITH DINNER FOR 2 TO BE AUCTIONED OFF TO HIGHEST MALE BIDDER; BOXES NOT PREVIOUSLY IDENTIFIED; BUYER EATS WITH LADY WHO MADE BOX. PRIZES FOR BOXES, A FUND RAISING EVENT. MUSICAL SAW 'FIDDLER' & LOCAL ENTERTAINMENT. AT HIGH SCHOOL GYM. (LOCAL). DORIS E LENKER, CHRWMN; HOME EXTENSION CLUB; RFD #1; ORANGEVILLE, IL 61060. (#100777-1).

APR 25, '76. DOWN MEMORY LANE: STYLE SHOW & TEA. A PERIOD STYLE SHOW WITH COMMUNITY PARTICIPATION OF FAMILY HERITAGE ATTIRE; SHOW WILL BE FOLLOWED BY A TEA. AT HIGH SCHOOL GYM. (LOCAL). MARGARET SCHEIDER, DIR; ORANGEVILLE BICENTENNIAL COMMISSION; RFD 5; FREEPORT, IL 61032. (#100776-1).

MAY 16, '76. BICENTENNIAL FAMILY FUN DAY. GAMES WILL INCLUDE CATCH THE GREASED PIG, PIE EATING, FLAPJACK FLIPPING, ROLLING PIN THROWING, EGG TOSSING TEAMS AND MANY OTHER OLD FASHIONED GAMES FOR THE WHOLE FAMILY. AT HS ATHLETIC FIELD & ADJOINING SCHOOL PROPERTY. (LOCAL). LELIA VINCENT, DIRECTOR; ORANGEVILLE BICENTENNIAL COMMISSION; RR #1; ORANGEVILLE, IL 61060. (#102282-1).

JULY 15 - 17, '76. BICENTENNIAL MID-SUMMER STREET CARNIVAL. STREET CARNIVAL WITH RIDES, PET SHOW, DOG DRILL TEAM DEMO, MUSKET TEAM DEMO, PAGEANT, TALENT SHOW, PARADE AND PRIZES ON FARMER RECOGNITION DAY, G S HISTORY OF FLAGS DEMO, CRAFT FAIR & DEMO. (LOCAL). DORIS LENKER, CHMN; ORANGEVILLE BICENTENNIAL COMMISSION; RFD 1; ORANGEVILLE, IL 61060. (#100775-1).

OREGON

LUTHERAN OUTDOOR MINISTRIES CENTER IN ILLINOIS. WEEK-LONG SUMMER CAMPING EXPERIENCES FOR GRADES 4-8, HIGH SCHOOL AND FAMILIES USING BICENTENNIAL THEME IN AREAS OF MUSIC, ART, RELIGION, NATURE, CRAFTS, AND RECREATION. (LOCAL). NORMAN MANDEHR, EXEC DIRECTOR; ILLINOIS SYNOD OUTDOOR MINISTRIES CENTER; BOX 239; OREGON, IL 61061. (#6599).

MANAGEMENT OF SELECTED PRAIRIE REMNANTS, IL. MANAGEMENT OF PRAIRIE REMNANT TRACTS IN ORDER TO RESTORE THEM TO BETTER CONDITION AND MAINTAIN THEM AS EDUCATIONAL AND HISTORICAL AREAS. SIGNS WILL BE POSTED & BROCHURES WILL BE MADE AVAILABLE. (LOCAL). DOUGLAS E WADE, PROJECT DIRECTOR; OGLE COUNTY AMERICAN REVOLUTION BICENT CELEBRATION COMMISSION; 112 S 5TH; OREGON, IL 61061. (#25684). **ARBA GRANTEE.**

JUNE 22 - AUG 9, '75. PIONEER CAMPING FOR GRADES 4-8. OPENING, TOUR. (LOCAL). NORMAN MANDEHR; ILLINOIS SYNOD OUTDOOR MINISTRIES CENTER; BOX 239; OREGON, IL 61061. (#6599-503).

JUNE 29 - AUG 9, '75. JUNIOR CHOIR WEEKS FOR GRADES 4-8. OPENING, TOUR. (LOCAL). NORMAN MANDEHR; ILLINOIS SYNOD OUTDOOR MINISTRIES CENTER; BOX 239; OREGON, IL 61061. (#6599-501).

JULY 6 - 26, '75. EQUESTRIAN CAMPS FOR GRADES 6-9. OPENING, TOUR. (LOCAL). NORMAN MANDEHR; ILLINOIS SYNOD OUTDOOR MINISTRIES CENTER; BOX 239; OREGON, IL 61061. (#6599-504).

JULY 13 - 19, '75. SPIRIT OF '76 FAMILY CAMPING PROGRAM. OPENING, TOUR. (LOCAL). NORMAN MANDEHR; ILLINOIS SYNOD OUTDOOR MINISTRIES CENTER; BOX 239; OREGON, IL 61061. (#6599-502).

AUG 10 - 16, '75. HIGH SCHOOL CAMPING. OPENING, TOUR. (LOCAL). NORMAN MANDEHR; ILLINOIS SYNOD OUTDOOR MINISTRIES CENTER; BOX 239; OREGON, IL 61061. (#6599-505).

AUG 29 - SEPT 1, '75. VISIT OF HISTORY-MOBILE 'ETHNIC HISTORY IN ILLINOIS'. EXHIBIT AT OGLE COUNTY FAIR. (LOCAL). CLIFFORD HAKA, FIELD REP; ILLINOIS STATE HISTORICAL SOCIETY; OLD STATE CAPITOL; SPRINGFIELD, IL 62706. (#200016-517).

SEPT 19 - 21, '75. ROCK & HOBBY SHOW. DEMONSTRATIONS: CUTTING & POLISHING GEMS, FACETING, ARROWHEAD MAKING. BLACK LIGHT DISPLAY, GEMS, CRYSTALS, INDIAN ARTIFACTS, MINERALS, ROCK DISPLAYS. SILENT AUCTION. AT COLISEUM BLDG CLOSES 9PM SAT & 5PM SUN.. (LOCAL). CARL DACH; BLACKHAWK ROCK CLUB; 6150 SOUTH MERIDIAN; ROCKFORD, IL 61102. (#50325-1).

ORION

ORION, IL, BICENTENNIAL PROJECTS. PROJECTS INCLUDE A WRITTEN HISTORY OF THE VILLAGE, HISTORICAL DISPLAYS, FIRE HYDRANT PAINTING AND FLOWER PLANTING. (LOCAL). MRS WILLARD ANDERSON, CHAIRMAN; ORION BICENTENNIAL COMMISSION; 1417 5TH ST, BOX 702; ORION, IL 61273. (#29207).

JULY 5, '76. LEISURE AND RECREATION - JULY 4TH CELEBRATION. FESTIVAL, PARADE, TOUR, LIVE PERFORMANCE. (LOCAL). MRS WILLARD ANDERSON; ORION BICENTENNIAL COMMISSION; 1417 5TH ST, BOX 702; ORION, IL 61273. (#200016-213).

OSWEGO

HIKERS OF AMERICA, INC - OSWEGO, IL. A NATIONAL PROJECT, A LIBERTY MARCH WHICH IS A SELF GUIDED TOUR OF THE HISTORIC SITES OF THE LOCAL COMMUNITY OR AREA. EACH PARTICIPANT RECEIVES A PATCH OR PEWTER MEDALLION. (ST-WIDE). JAMES BENTZ, PRESIDENT; HIKERS OF AMERICA, INC; ROUTE 1, BOX 68; OSWEGO, IL 60543. (#19048).

LIBERTY MARCH - OSWEGO, IL. THE LIBERTY MARCH IS A SELF-GUIDED TOUR OF THE HISTORIC SITES OF THE LOCAL COMMUNITY; EACH PARTICIPANT WILL RECEIVE A PATCH OR PEWTER MEDALLION; REGISTRATION IS $2.00 OR $2.50. (LOCAL). JAMES BENTZ, PRESIDENT; HIKERS OF AMERICA, INC; ROUTE 1 BOX 68; OSWEGO, IL 60543. (#19572).

OSWEGO JAYCEES BICENTENNIAL PARK - OSWEGO, IL. PARK IS BEING DEVELOPED BY THE OSWEGOLAND JAYCEES AS A TRIBUTE TO THE BICENTENNIAL. (LOCAL). MIKE ZWIJAC, CHAIRMAN; OSWEGOLAND JAYCEES & KENDALL COUNTY BICENTENNIAL COMMISSION; 17 HAMPTON; BOULDER HILL, IL 60538. (#23641).

APR 27, '76. JEWEL BICENTENNIAL CONCERT. A BICENTENNIAL TRIBUTE BY JEWEL COMPANIES, INC EMPLOYEES. AT OSWEGO HIGH SCHOOL AUDITORIUM. (LOCAL). JAMES BENTZ, CHMN; KENDALL COUNTY BICENTENNIAL COMMISSION; RT 1 BOX 68; OSWEGO, IL 60543. (#104943-1).

OTTAWA

BICENT ORAL HISTORY PROJ OF OTTAWA, ILLINOIS. TAPED INTERVIEWS WITH OLDER RESIDENTS LIVING IN THE SIX COUNTY STARVED ROCK AREA. TAPES WILL BE AVAILABLE THRU LOCAL LIBRARIES. (ST-WIDE). MARY T HOWE, DIRECTOR; STARVED ROCK LIBRARY SYSTEM; HITT & SWANSON STS; OTTAWA, IL 61350. (#5724).

KNOW YOUR COUNTY GOVERNMENT: OTTAWA, IL. PUBLICATION OF BOOKLET ON LASALLE COUNTY GOVERNMENT. (LOCAL). COORDINATOR; LEAGUE OF WOMEN VOTERS; OTTAWA, IL 61350. (#33556).

REDDICK'S MANSION IN OTTAWA, IL. RESTORATION OF REDDICK'S MANSION. (LOCAL). CONNIE FETZER, COORDINATOR; LASALLE COUNTY HISTORICAL SOCIETY; BOX 577; OTTAWA, IL 61350. (#33557).

STARVED ROCK LIBRARY SYSTEM OF OTTAWA, ILLINOIS. DEVELOP A BASIC COLLECTION OF ORAL HISTORY TO MEET THE REFERENCE NEEDS OF LOCAL RESIDENTS AND TO CONTRIBUTE TO THE DEVELOPMENT OF STATE HISTORY RESOURCES. (ST-WIDE). MRS MARY T HOWE, DIRECTOR; STARVED ROCK LIBRARY SYSTEM; HITT & SWANSON STS; OTTAWA, IL 61350. (#6352).

WASHINGTON SQUARE NATIONAL HISTORIC PLACE OF IL. PRESERVATION OF SITE OF FIRST LINCOLN-DOUGLASS DEBATE ON AUGUST 21, 1858. WASHINGTON SQUARE INCLUDES REDDICK MANSION, APPELLATE COURT, CONGREGATIONAL CHURCH, CHRIST EPISCOPAL CHURCH, LASALLE COUNTY JAIL. (ST-WIDE). LEONARD LOCK, CHAIRMAN; OTTAWA BICENTENNIAL COMMISSION; 301 W MADISON ST; OTTAWA, IL 61350. (#5717).

MAR 13 - APR 3, '75. WORKSHOP ON GENERAL OVERVIEW OF ORAL HISTORY; 8 TRAINING SESSIONS. SEMINAR. (ST-WIDE). MRS MARY T HOWE, DIRECTOR; STARVED ROCK LIBRARY SYSTEM; HITT & SWANSON STS; OTTAWA, IL 61350. (#6352-501).

JULY 19 - 20, '75. ARTS AND CRAFT SHOW. ARTISTS AND CRAFTSMEN DISPLAYING SCENES & CRAFTS OF LA SALLE COUNTY. REGIONAL AND NATIONAL CRAFT WORK WILL ALSO BE REPRESENTED. AT WASHINGTON PARK IN DOWNTOWN OTTAWA. (LOCAL). FRANK LANGLEY; OTTAWA ART LEAGUE PO BOX 88 OTTAWA IL 61350; 1113 4H ROAD; OTTAWA, IL 61350. (#5182-1).

AUG 24, '75. LINCOLN-DOUGLAS DEBATE REENACTMENT. CONFERENCE. (LOCAL). LEONARD E LOCK JR, CHMN; OTTAWA BICENTENNIAL COMMITTEE; 301 W MADISON ST; OTTAWA, IL 61350. (#5717-1).

JULY 4, '76. STARVED ROCK KENNEL CLUB DOG SHOW. DOGS COMPETE INDIVIDUALLY WITHIN THEIR OWN BREED & ALSO IN GROUPS. ALL PUREBRED DOGS WILL BE SHOWN. AT LASALLE COUNTY 4-H GROUNDS. (ST-WIDE). MRS FRANK GEORGE JR; STARVED ROCK KENNEL CLUB; 617 FIFTH; OTTAWA, IL 61350. (#5718-1).

JULY 17 - 18, '76. ARTS & CRAFTS SHOW. ARTISTS AND CRAFTSMEN DISPLAYING SCENES & CRAFTS OF LA SALLE COUNTY. REGIONAL AND NATIONAL CRAFT WORK WILL ALSO BE REPRESENTED. AT WASHINGTON PARK, DOWNTOWN OTTAWA. (LOCAL). FRANK LANGLEY; OTTAWA ART LEAGUE, PO BOX 88, OTTAWA, IL 61350; 1113 4H RD; OTTAWA, IL 61350. (#5182-2).

JULY 24, '76. KANTOREI CHOIR. LIVE PERFORMANCE AT OTTAWA CENTRAL SCHOOL. (LOCAL). JOE HEIMAN, COORD; LASALLE COUNTY BICENTENNIAL COMMISSION; 202 PRAIRIE; OTTAWA, IL 61350. (#200016-206).

AUG 22, '76. LINCOLN & DOUGLAS: FIRST DEBATE RE-ENACTMENT. CONFERENCE. (LOCAL). LEONARD E LOCK JR, CHMN; OTTAWA BICENTENNIAL COMMITTEE; 301 W MADISON ST; OTTAWA, IL 61350. (#5717-3).

AUG 27 - 29, '76. ARTS AND CRAFTS FAIR. ARTS & CRAFTS GUILD DEMONSTRATION AND DISPLAY OF RURAL AMERICAN LIFE, EARLY HOME LIFE AND EARLY AMERICAN CRAFTS PERFORMED BY MEMBERS OF THE GUILD AND LOCAL ARTISTS. (LOCAL). MRS HELEN HAYNER; LASALLE COUNTY BICENTENNIAL ORGANIZATION; 620 E VAN BUREN; OTTAWA, IL 61350. (#6057-502).

SEPT 12 - 14, '76. ARTS, CRAFTS & FOLK FESTIVAL. DEMONSTRATION AND DISPLAY OF EARLY AMERICAN CRAFTS PERFORMED BY THE MEMBERS OF LASALLE COUNTY COOPERATIVE EXTENSION. AT 4 H CLUB GROUNDS. (LOCAL). ARVENA PEARSON; LASALLE COUNTY COOPERATIVE EXTENSION; 125 SWANSON ST; OTTAWA, IL 61350. (#6057-501).

JAN 17 - 18, '77. LA SALLE EXPEDITION II, A HISTORIC RE-ENACTMENT. THIS IS AN AUTHENTIC RE-ENACTMENT OF THE 1681 LASALLE EXPEDITION FROM MONTREAL, CANADA TO NEW ORLEANS, LA WHICH WILL BEGIN TOURING ON AUGUST 11, 1976 AND END ON APRIL 9, 1977. (LOCAL). REID H LEWIS, DIRECTOR; LA SALLE EXPEDITION II; 135 S LA SALLES, ST, RM 411; CHICAGO, IL 60690. (#102805-40).

OTTERVILLE

RESTORATION OF DR SILAS HAMILTON SCHOOL - IL. RESTORATION OF DR SILAS HAMILTON SCHOOL AT OTTERVILLE. (LOCAL). PAUL MILLER, CHAIRMAN; JERSEY COUNTY BICENTENNIAL COMMISSION; 105 N WASHINGTON; JERSEYVILLE, IL 62052. (#30392).

PALATINE

CANTATA CONTEST. A BICENTENNIAL CANTATA WILL BE PRESENTED. (LOCAL). URBAN A THOBE, CHMN; WILLIAM RAINEY HARPER COLLEGE; ROSELLE & ALGONQUIN RD; PALATINE, IL 60067. (#102382-3). **(??).**

CRAFTS EXHIBIT. CRAFT/INDUSTRY REVIVAL EXHIBIT. (LOCAL). URBAN A THOBE, CHMN; WILLIAM RAINEY HARPER COLLEGE; ROSELLE & ALGONQUIN RD; PALATINE, IL 60067. (#102382-1). **(??).**

DEDICATION OF MUSIC BUILDING. DEDICATION OF THE NEW MUSIC BUILDING AND KICK-OFF OF THE BICENTENNIAL. (LOCAL). URBAN A THOBE, CHMN; WILLIAM RAINEY HARPER COLLEGE; ROSELLE & ALGONQUIN RD; PALATINE, IL 60067. (#102382-2). **(??).**

DOCUMENTARY, PALATINE, IL. A FILM DOCUMENTARY OF BICENTENNIAL EVENTS IN DISTRICT 512. (LOCAL). URBAN A THOBE, CHAIRMAN, FINE ARTS & DESIGN; WILLIAM RAINEY HARPER COLLEGE; ROSELLE & ALGONQUIN RDS; PALATINE, IL 60067. (#15376).

FABRIC REVOLUTION - TEXTILE EXHIBIT. EXHIBIT. (LOCAL). URBAN A THOBE, CHMN; WILLIAM RAINEY HARPER COLLEGE; ROSELLE & ALGONQUIN RD; PALATINE, IL 60067. (#102383-11).

HALL OF FAME - EIGHT EXHIBITS WITH GUEST SPEAKERS. RADIO/TV. (LOCAL). URBAN A THOBE, CHMN; WILLIAM RAINEY HARPER COLLEGE; ROSELLE & ALGONQUIN RD; PALATINE, IL 60067. (#102381-1). **(??).**

HARPER AREA HABITAT 2076 PROJECT - PALATINE, IL. FOUR-PHASE PROGRAM TO EDUCATE PEOPLE ON RELATIONSHIP OF ENVIRONMENTAL DESIGN AND ENERGY CONSUMPTION. INCLUDES DESIGN & DEVELOPMENT OF FULL-SCALE, LIVE-IN, FUTURISTIC HABITAT. (LOCAL). DR MICHAEL CARROLL, CHAIRMAN; WILLIAM RAINEY HARPER COLLEGE; ALGONQUIN AND ROSELLE RD; PALATINE, IL 60067. (#15975).

ICE AGE TRAIL BROCHURE, PALATINE, IL. A BROCHURE DESCRIBING ICE AGE BIKE TRAIL IN WISCONSIN, TO INCLUDE: A MAP, ACCOMODATIONS INFORMATION, HISTORICAL, ARCHEOLOGICAL AND GEOGRAPHICAL SITES. TO BE DISTRIBUTED TO BIKE CLUBS AND STATE AGENCIES. (LOCAL). MORGAN P GROVES, EXEC DIRECTOR; LEAGUE OF AMERICAN WHEELMAN; 19 S BOTHWELL; PALATINE, IL 60067. (#12236). **ARBA GRANTEE.**

QUALITY OF LIFE EXPOSITION. A HEALTH CARE DELIVERY EXPOSITION; DEMONSTRATION OF STRESS TESTING, CARDIAC PROBLEMS AND REHABILITATION; PANEL DISCUSSION ON THE EFFECTS OF SPORTS ON SOCIETY. (LOCAL). URBAN A THOBE, CHMN; WILLIAM RAINEY HARPER COLLEGE; ROSELLE & ALGONQUIN RD; PALATINE, IL 60067. (#102383-10).

SURVEY OF HISTORICAL SITES IN PALATINE, IL. SURVEY OF HISTORICAL SITES WITH PHOTOGRAPHS & COMMENTARY. (LOCAL). URBAN A THOBE, CHAIRMAN, FINE ARTS & DESIGN; WILLIAM RAINEY HARPER COLLEGE; ROSELLE & ALGONQUIN RDS; PALATINE, IL 60067. (#15375).

200 YEARS OF FASHION. AN EXHIBIT OF DOLLS DRESSED IN PERIOD COSTUMES. (LOCAL). URBAN A THOBE, CHMN; WILLIAM RAINEY HARPER COLLEGE; ROSELLE & ALGONQUIN RD; PALATINE, IL 60067. (#102380-1).

AUG 25 - DEC 15, '75. DOCUMENTING SOCIAL HISTORY. SEMINAR AT BUILDING F, ROOM 313. (LOCAL). URBAN A THOBE, CHMN; WILLIAM RAINEY HARPER COLLEGE; ROSELLE & ALGONQUIN RD; PALATINE, IL 60067. (#102383-9).

SEPT 12, '75. THE MAGNIFICENT AMBERSONS - AMERICAN FILM CLASSIC. EXHIBIT AT BUILDING E, ROOM 106. (LOCAL). URBAN A THOBE, CHMN; WILLIAM RAINEY HARPER COLLEGE; ROSELLE & ALGONQUIN RD; PALATINE, IL 60067. (#101193-1).

SEPT 30, '75. UNDERSTANDING LOCAL GOVERNMENT-WHERE THE ACTION IS. SEMINAR AT BUILDING A, BOARD ROOM. (LOCAL). URBAN A THOBE, CHMN; WILLIAM RAINEY HARPER COLLEGE; ROSELLE & ALGONQUIN RD; PALATINE, IL 60067. (#102383-1).

OCT 2, '75. MOTHERHOOD - AMERICAN STYLE. SEMINAR AT BUILDING A, BOARD ROOM. (LOCAL). URBAN A THOBE, CHMN; WILLIAM RAINEY HARPER COLLEGE; ROSELLE & ALGONQUIN RD; PALATINE, IL 60067. (#102383-2).

OCT 15, '75. PUBLIC INFORMATION LAWS-WHAT THE PUBLIC HAS A RIGHT TO KNOW. SEMINAR AT BUILDING A, BOARD ROOM. (LOCAL). URBAN A THOBE, CHMN; WILLIAM RAINEY HARPER COLLEGE; ROSELLE & ALGONQUIN RD; PALATINE, IL 60067. (#102383-3).

OCT 16, '75. WHO IS JANE DOE?. SEMINAR AT BUILDING A, BOARD ROOM. (LOCAL). URBAN A THOBE, CHMN; WILLIAM RAINEY HARPER COLLEGE; ROSELLE & ALGONQUIN RD; PALATINE, IL 60067. (#102383-4).

OCT 18 - DEC 13, '75. PRESERVING AND RESTORING OLD PLACES. SEMINAR AT BUILDING F, ROOM 313. (LOCAL). URBAN A THOBE, CHMN; WILLIAM RAINEY HARPER COLLEGE; ROSELLE & ALGONQUIN RD; PALATINE, IL 60067. (#102383-5).

NOV 5, '75. ORDINANCES & STATUTES SIMPLIFIED-RULES & REGULATIONS OF GVERNMENT. SEMINAR AT BUILDING A, BOARD ROOM. (LOCAL). URBAN A THOBE, CHMN; WILLIAM RAINEY HARPER COLLEGE; ROSELLE & ALGONQUIN RD; PALATINE, IL 60067. (#102383-6).

NOV 25, '75. GOVERNMENTAL FINANCES-UNDERSTANDING LOCAL FISCAL POLICIES. SEMINAR AT BUILDING A, BOARD ROOM. (LOCAL). URBAN A THOBE, CHMN; WILLIAM RAINEY HARPER COLLEGE; ROSELLE & ALGONQUIN RD; PALATINE, IL 60067. (#102383-7).

DEC 10, '75. ZONING & ANNEXATION PROCESS-PROCEDURES FOR CHANGE. SEMINAR AT BUILDING A, BOARD ROOM. (LOCAL). URBAN A THOBE, CHMN; WILLIAM RAINEY HARPER COLLEGE; ROSELLE & ALGONQUIN RD; PALATINE, IL 60067. (#102383-8).

PALOS HILLS

AMERICAN HERITAGE COURSE, PALOS HILLS, IL. A COURSE OFFERED FOR CREDIT ON AMERICAN HERITAGE. (LOCAL). DR GLEN GABERT, CHAIRMAN; MORAINE VALLEY COMMUNITY COLLEGE BICENTENNIAL COMMISSION; 10900 S 88TH AVE; PALOS HILLS, IL 60465. (#15366).

AMERICAN ISSUES FORUM IN PALOS HILLS, IL. ACTIVITIES DESIGNED TO ENHANCE COMMUNITY INVOLVEMENT IN THE AMERICAN ISSUES FORUM. (LOCAL). DR GLEN GABERT, CHAIRMAN; MORAINE VALLEY COMMUNITY COLLEGE BICENTENNIAL COMMISSION; 10900 S 88TH AVE; PALOS HILLS, IL 60465. (#15361).

BICENTENNIAL BIBLIOGRAPHY, PALOS HILLS, IL. A LISTING OF BICENTENNIAL RELATED MATERIALS AVAILABLE IN THE MORAINE VALLEY COMMUNITY COLLEGE LEARNING RESOURCES CENTER COLLECTIONS. (LOCAL). DR GLEN GABERT, CHAIRMAN; MORAINE VALLEY COMMUNITY COLLEGE BICENTENNIAL COMMISSION; 10900 S 88TH AVE; PALOS HILLS, IL 60465. (#15371).

BICENTENNIAL NEWSLETTER - PALOS HILLS, IL. A MONTHLY PUBLICATION WILL BE PRINTED FOR AREA BICENTENNIAL COMMISSIONS AND CIVIC GROUPS, A CLEARINGHOUSE FOR LOCAL BICENTENNIAL PROGRAMS. (LOCAL). DR GLEN GABERT, CHAIRMAN; MORAINE VALLEY COMMUNITY COLLEGE BICENTENNIAL COMMISSION; 10900 S 88TH AVE; PALOS HILLS, IL 60465. (#15358).

FILM FESTIVAL IN PALOS HILLS, IL. MONTHLY SHOWING OF FILMS ON BICENTENNIAL RELATED TOPICS IN COOPERATION WITH LOCAL LIBRARIES WITH ACCOMPANYING LECTURES. (LOCAL). DR GLEN GABERT, CHAIRMAN; MORAINE VALLEY COMMUNITY COLLEGE BICENTENNIAL COMMISSION; 10900 S 88TH AVE; PALOS HILLS, IL 60465. (#15368).

GARDEN ACTIVITIES IN PALOS HILLS, IL. A SERIES OF GARDEN ACTIVITIES DESIGNED TO BEAUTIFY THE CAMPUS AND NEIGHBORING COMMUNITY. (LOCAL). DR GLEN GABERT, CHAIRMAN; MORAINE VALLEY COMMUNITY COLLEGE BICENTENNIAL COMMISSION; 10900 S 88TH AVE; PALOS HILLS, IL 60465. (#15369).

HERITAGE & FESTIVAL TOURS, PALOS HILLS, IL. TOURS TO PLACES OF HISTORICAL SIGNIFICANCE. (LOCAL). DR GLEN GABERT, CHAIRMAN; MORAINE VALLEY COMMUNITY COLLEGE BICENTENNIAL COMMISSION; 10900 S 88TH AVE; PALOS HILLS, IL 60465. (#15370).

HISTORY PROJECTS IN PALOS HILLS, IL. ACTIVITIES DESIGNED TO ENCOURAGE LOCAL GROUPS TO BECOME ACTIVE IN SEMINARS, WORKSHOPS AND CONSULTANT SERVICES. (LOCAL). DR GLEN GABERT, CHAIRMAN; MORAINE VALLEY COMMUNITY COLLEGE BICENTENNIAL COMMITTEE; 10900 S 88TH AVE; PALOS HILLS, IL 60465. (#15360).

MORAINE GOES METRIC - PALOS HILLS, IL. ACTIVITIES DESIGNED TO PREPARE THE COMMUNITY FOR THE METRIC SYSTEM-MEDIATED INSTRUCTIONAL UNITS AND WORKSHOPS. (LOCAL). DR GLEN GABERT, CHAIRMAN; MORAINE VALLEY COMMUNITY COLLEGE BICENTENNIAL COMMISSION; 10900 S 88TH AVE; PALOS HILLS, IL 60465. (#15364).

MORAINE VALLEY MUSEUM, PALOS HILLS, IL. A MUSEUM TO PRESERVE AND RESTORE ARTIFACTS OF LOCAL HISTORICAL SIGNIFICANCE; WILL SECURE CHARTER, BOARD OF GOVERNORS, BYLAWS, PLANT & STAFF. (LOCAL). DR GLEN GABERT, CHAIRMAN; MORAINE VALLEY COMMUNITY COLLEGE BICENTENNIAL COMMISSION; 10900 S 88TH AVE; PALOS HILLS, IL 60465. (#15359).

NEWSPAPER COLUMN - PALOS HILLS, IL. A REGULAR COLUMN WILL APPEAR IN LOCAL NEWSPAPERS ON THE AMERICAN HERITAGE. (LOCAL). DR GLEN GABERT, CHAIRMAN; MORAINE VALLEY COMMUNITY COLLEGE BICENTENNIAL COMMISSION; 10900 S 88TH AVE; PALOS HILLS, IL 60465. (#15365).

OUR ETHNIC HERITAGE - PALOS HILLS, IL. THE CULTURES OF VARIOUS ETHNIC GROUPS IN THE AREA WILL BE PRESENTED THROUGH FOOD, COSTUMES, MUSIC, DANCE AND HISTORY. (LOCAL). DR GLEN GABERT, CHAIRMAN; MORAINE VALLEY COMMUNITY COLLEGE BICENTENNIAL COMMISSION; 10900 S 88TH AVE; PALOS HILLS, IL 60465. (#15362).

PROGRAM LISTING OF BICENTENNIAL SPEAKERS - IL. A CATALOGUE WILL BE COMPILED WITH A LIST OF SPEAKERS AVAILABLE TO MAKE PRESENTATIONS TO LOCAL GROUPS ON BICENTENNIAL-RELATED TOPICS. (LOCAL). DR GLEN GABERT, CHAIRMAN; MORAINE VALLEY COMMUNITY COLLEGE BICENTENNIAL COMMISSION; 10900 S 88TH AVE; PALOS HILLS, IL 60465. (#15363).

200 YEARS OF AMERICAN DRESS, DISPLAY, IL. A MUSEUM DISPLAY OF COSTUMES BASED ON RESEARCH OF 200 YEARS OF AMERICAN DRESS. (LOCAL). DR GLEN GABERT, CHAIRMAN; MORAINE VALLEY COMMUNITY COLLEGE BICENTENNIAL COMMISSION; 10900 S 88TH AVE; PALOS HILLS, IL 60465. (#15367).

MAR 20, '76. GENEOLOGY WORKSHOPS. SHORT COURSE IN HOW TO TRACE PERSONAL AND FAMILY HISTORIES. (LOCAL). DR GLEN GABERT, CHMN; MORAINE VALLEY COMMUNITY COLLEGE BICENTENNIAL COMMISSION; 10900 SOUTH 88TH AVE / MVCC; PALOS HILLS, IL 60465. (#102378-1).

APR 23 - MAY 1, '76. 'THE DEVIL'S DISCIPLE' A PLAY BY GEORGE BERNARD SHAW. REVOLUTIONARY WAR PLAY BY GEORGE BERNARD SHAW, JOYCE KLOWDEN, DIRECTOR. FREE PARKING. AT 600 BUILDING. (LOCAL). DR GLEN GABERT, CHMN; MORAINE VALLEY COMMUNITY COLLEGE BICENTENNIAL COMMISSION; 10900 S 88TH AVE / MVCC; PALOS HILLS, IL 60465. (#102378-5).

APR 24 - 25, '76. INVITATIONAL JURIED ART SHOW. SHOW WILL CONSIST OF PAINTINGS, SCULPTURES, CERAMICS, TEXTILES, PASTELS, AND WATERCOLORS; APPLICATION WITH SLIDES AND FEE; AWARDS WILL BE GIVEN. (LOCAL). DR GLEN GABERT, CHMN; MORAINE VALLEY COMMUNITY COLLEGE BICENTENNIAL COMMISSION; 10900 S 88TH AVE / MVCC; PALOS HILLS, IL 60465. (#102378-3).

AUG 13 - 14, '76. 18TH CENTURY MILITARY EXHIBITION. MILITARY EXHIBIT, UNIFORM DISPLAY, COLONIAL CRAFTS DISPLAY, COLONIAL MUSIC. (ST-WIDE). DR GLEN GABERT, CHMN; MORAINE VALLEY COMMUNITY COLLEGE BICENTENNIAL COMMISSION; 10900 S 88TH AVE / MVCC; PALOS HILLS, IL 60465. (#102378-4).

PARIS

BICENTENNIAL ART CENTER AND MUSEUM - PARIS, IL. ESTABLISHMENT OF BICENTENNIAL ART CENTER AND MUSEUM, FEATURING ARTS AND CRAFTS OF PROFESSIONAL AND AMATEUR ARTISTS. (LOCAL). MRS WILLIAM DENNIS; EDGAR COUNTY ART CENTER AND MUSEUM; PARIS, IL 61944. (#30396).

PRAIRIE PROGRESS - PARIS, IL. PUBLICATION OF 595-PAGE HISTORY OF EDGAR COUNTY FROM 1880. (LOCAL). WALTER KIMBLE, CHAIRMAN; EDGAR COUNTY HISTORICAL SOCIETY; PARIS, IL 61944. (#30395).

MAR 26, '76. 'UP WITH PEOPLE' - SINGING GROUP. BICENTENNIAL CONTRIBUTION OF PARIS YOUTH CENTER, INC. AT PARIS HIGH SCHOOL GYM. (LOCAL). MRS JANE BONALDI, COORD; PARIS YOUTH CENTER, INC (HANGAR); 307 E WOOD; PARIS, IL 61944. (#105708-3).

MAY 21, '76. EDGAR COUNTY SCHOOLS' SALUTE TO AMERICA'S BICENTENNIAL. PARADE OF 4400 SCHOOL CHILDREN OF EDGAR COUNTY; CONTEST FOR FLOATS & COSTUMES; BAND CONCERT AFTER PARADE; BURIAL OF TIME CAPSULE FILLED WITH STUDENTS' LETTERS. (LOCAL). HAROLD MEANS, COORD; EDGAR COUNTY PUBLIC SCHOOLS SYSTEM; COURT HOUSE; PARIS, IL 61944. (#105708-4).

JULY 4, '76. OLD-FASHIONED 4TH OF JULY: AMERICAN LEGION BICENTENNIAL SALUTE. PARADE, BARBECUE, HELICOPTER RIDES, LOCAL BANDS, FIREWORKS, AUCTION, FLEA MARKET, BINGO, CONTESTS, LITTLE LEAGUE BALL GAMES, GOD & COUNTRY COMMUNITY SERVICE & RAFFLE OF BONDS VALUED AT $25, $50 & $100 WITH LARGEST SHARE OF PROCEEDS DONATED TO THE CANCER CAUSE. (LOCAL). JACK KERRICK, COORD; AMERICAN LEGION POST 211; RR 6; PARIS, IL 61944. (#105708-2).

JULY 23 - 26, '76. EDGAR COUNTY BICENTENNIAL PAGEANT. PAGEANT WITH CAST OF 250 PRESENTED BY THE JOHN RODGERS COMPANY. AT EDGAR COUNTY FAIRGROUNDS. (ST-WIDE). CHESTER SUTTON, COORD; EDGAR COUNTY BICENTENNIAL COMMISSION - FESTIVAL COMMITTEE; 114 E WASHINGTON; PARIS, IL 61944. (#105708-5).

SEPT 10 - 12, '76. HOMEMAKERS HERITAGE FESTIVAL OF EDGAR COUNTY. AWARD, CEREMONY, EXHIBIT, FESTIVAL, LIVE PERFORMANCE AT 4-H GROUNDS. (LOCAL). MRS JUNE VANCE, COORD; EDGAR COUNTY HOMEMAKERS EXTENSION ASSOCIATION; RR 2; PARIS, IL 61944. (#105708-1).

SEPT 14, '76. LINCOLN'S EIGHTH JUDICIAL CIRCUIT RIDE. LIVE PERFORMANCE. (ST-WIDE). PHYLLIS EUBANKS, COORD; ILLINOIS DEPARTMENT OF CONSERVATION; 901 S SPRING ST; SPRINGFIELD, IL 62706. (#200016-203).

PARK FOREST

JUNE 14, '76. DEDICATION OF NEW COMMUNITY AMPHITHEATER. OUTDOOR AMPHITHEATER TO BE ERECTED BY NEW COMMUNITY CENTER IN '76 FOR SHOWS, MEETINGS & CONCERTS. DEDICATION IS SCHEDULED FOR JUNE 14. AT FREEDOM HALL,1776 CENTRAL PARK. (LOCAL). J RON MCLEOD, CHRMN; US BICENT COMMISSION OF THE VILLAGE OF PARK FOREST,IL; 200 FOREST BLVD; PARK FOREST, IL 60466. (#3548-1).

PAW PAW

JUNE 25 - 27, '76. PAW PAW BICENTENNIAL CELEBRATION - OLD-TIME FESTIVAL OF EVENTS. CEREMONY, COMPETITION, EXHIBIT, FESTIVAL. (LOCAL). MIKE HECKMAN, CO-CHAIRMAN; LEE COUNTY BICENTENNIAL COMMISSION; PO BOX 348; DIXON, IL 61021. (#104268-5).

PEKIN

COUNTY FARM BUREAU BICENTENNIAL EXHIBITS, IL. THE COUNTY FARM BUREAU WILL SPONSOR A SERIES OF BICENTENNIAL EXHIBITS. (LOCAL). K RUSSELL CRAWFORD, CHAIRMAN; TAZEWELL COUNTY BICENTENNIAL COMMISSION; 354-1/2 COLE; EAST PEORIA, IL 61611. (#33634).

COUNTY MUSEUM IN PEKIN, IL. ESTABLISHMENT OF COUNTY MUSEUM IN CONJUNCTION WITH TAZEWELL COUNTY HISTORICAL SOCIETY. (LOCAL). K RUSSELL CRAWFORD, COORDINATOR;

PEKIN — CONTINUED

TAZEWELL COUNTY BICENTENNIAL COMMISSION; 354 1/2 COLE; EAST PEORIA, IL 61611. (#33633).

JULY 4, '76. BICENTENNIAL CELEBRATION. FESTIVAL. (LOCAL). LYNDELL HOWARD, CHMN; PEKIN BICENTENNIAL COMMISSION; 1613 CRESCENT; PEKIN, IL 61554. (#200016-96).

AUG 31 - SEPT 1, '76. MARIGOLD FESTIVAL. FESTIVAL. (LOCAL). LYNDELL HOWARD, CHMN; PEKIN BICENTENNIAL COMMISSION; 1613 CRESCENT; PEKIN, IL 61554. (#200016-94).

SEPT 1, '76. TRIBUTE TO THE AMERICAN CONVOY - 25 TRUCKS. EXHIBIT. (LOCAL). LYNDELL HOWARD, CHMN; PEKIN BICENTENNIAL COMMISSION; 1613 CRESCENT; PEKIN, IL 61554. (#200016-93).

SEPT 5, '76. BICENTENNIAL PAGEANT. LIVE PERFORMANCE. (INT'L). LYNDELL HOWARD, CHMN; PEKIN BICENTENNIAL COMMISSION; 1613 CRESCENT; PEKIN, IL 61554. (#200016-95).

NOV 20, '76. BICENTENNIAL BALL. FESTIVAL. (LOCAL). LYNDELL HOWARD, CHMN; PEKIN BICENTENNIAL COMMISSION; 1613 CRESCENT; PEKIN, IL 61554. (#109476-1).

JAN 27 - 28, '77. LA SALLE EXPEDITION II, A HISTORIC RE-ENACTMENT. THIS IS AN AUTHENTIC RE-ENACTMENT OF THE 1681 LASALLE EXPEDITION FROM MONTREAL, CANADA TO NEW ORLEANS, LA WHICH WILL BEGIN TOURING ON AUGUST 11, 1976 AND END ON APRIL 9, 1977. (LOCAL). REID H LEWIS, DIRECTOR; LA SALLE EXPEDITION II; 135 S LA SALLE ST, RM 411; CHICAGO, IL 60690. (#102805-46).

PEORIA

BICENTENNIAL MINUTES IN PEORIA, IL. TELEVISION SCHEDULE OF BICENTENNIAL MINUTES IN PEORIA COUNTY. (LOCAL). GARY GRESHAM, COORDINATOR; PEORIA COUNTY BICENTENNIAL COMMISSION; 5909 N ROSEMEAD; PEORIA, IL 61614. (#33555).

HISTORY OF PEORIA, ILLINOIS. HISTORICAL AND INFORMATIVE BOOK DESIGNED TO TELL THE STORY OF STEAMBOAT DAYS IN PEORIA, TO INCLUDE FREEDOM TRAIN INFORMATION. ARTICLES TO BE WRITTEN BY OUTSTANDING LOCAL AUTHORS. (LOCAL). JOE KAUFMAN, VICE-PRESIDENT; PEORIA AREA JAYCEES; BOX 2; PEORIA, IL 61601. (#12102).

ORAL HISTORY PROJECT IN PEORIA, IL. PROJECT INVOLVED ALL TOWNSHIPS IN PEORIA COUNTY. (LOCAL). GARY GRESHAM, DIRECTOR; PEORIA COUNTY BICENTENNIAL COMMISSION; 5909 N ROSEMEAD; PEORIA, IL 61614. (#33553).

RESEARCH PROJ ON BAIL IN COURTS OF COLONIAL PHILA. ARCHIVAL AND BEHAVIORAL RESEARCH TO DISCOVER, ANALYZE AND DESCRIBE PATTERNS OF ADMIN OF BAIL IN CRIMINAL COURT CASES IN COLONIAL PHILADELPHIA, 1760-1780. (NAT'L). PAUL LERMACK, ASSISTANT PROFESSOR; DEPT OF POLITICAL SCIENCE, BRADLEY UNIV; PEORIA, IL 61606. (#3789).

RESTORATION OF GAR HALL IN PEORIA, IL. PRESERVATION & RESTORATION OF THE GRAND ARMY OF THE REPUBLIC HALL. (LOCAL). GARY GRESHAM, COORDINATOR; PEORIA COUNTY BICENTENNIAL COMMISSION; 5909 N ROSEMEAD DR; PEORIA, IL 61614. (#33554).

MAR 2 - 23, '75. PARADE FROM THE PAST-BICENTENNIAL STYLE SHOW. STUDENTS FROM PEORIA HIGH SCHOOLS MODELLING 81 HISTORICAL COSTUMES AT FLANAGAN HOUSE, OWNED BY THE PEORIA HISTORICAL SOCIETY. EVENT INCLUDES TOUR OF FLANAGAN HOUSE AND GROUNDS. AT FLANAGAN HOUSE, 942 N.E. GLEN OAK, PEORIA. (LOCAL). FLANAGAN HOUSE; PEORIA HISTORICAL SOCIETY; 942 N.E. GLEN OAK AVENUE; PEORIA, IL 61603. (#50326-1).

APR 19, '75. GRAND MILITARY BALL: FULL-DRESS UNIFORM OR PERIOD DRESS. MUSIC TO BE FURNISHED BY FIRST BRIGADE BAND PLAYING CIVIL WAR BAND INSTRUMENTS. AT NORTHWOODS MALL, ROUTE 150 (WAR MEMORIAL) AND GLEN, OFF I-74. (ST-WIDE). MRS FRED SOADY; CAMP LYON ASSOCIATION; 1116 SOUTH FIFTH; PEKIN, IL 61554. (#50329-1).

JULY 5, '75. SALUTE TO 200 YEARS OF TRANSPORTATION. PRESENTATION OF ARBA FLAGS TO MAYORS AND BICENTENNIAL COMMISSION REPRESENTATIVES WHO WILL ARRIVE AND DEPART VIA DIFFERENT HISTORIC FORMS OF TRANSPORTATION. ENTERTAINMENT, PARADE, ART SHOW AND CEREMON IES AT PLAZA. AT COURTHOUSE PLAZA, PEORIA (CORNER OF MAIN AND ADAMS STREETS). (LOCAL). MARGARET MILLER; TRI-COUNTY BICENTENNIAL COMMITTEE; 125 SHERWOOD COURT; CREVE COEUR, IL 61611. (#50323-1).

JULY 5, '75 - JULY 5, '76. OPERA IN THE GARDEN. PRESENTATION OF 'THE MASKED BALL' BY VERDI ON LAWN OF MORRON HOUSE, BICENTENNIAL DECOR; HOSTS AND HOSTESSES IN REVOLUTIONARY COSTUMES. AT MORRON HOUSE AT 1212 WEST MOSS AVENUE. (LOCAL). MR AND MRS ROBERT G DAY; AMATEUR MUSICAL CLUB AND PEORIA CIVIC OPERA COMPANY; 2601 N KINGSTON DR; PEORIA, IL 61604. (#6600-1).

JULY 11 - 19, '75. HEART OF ILLINOIS FAIR-BICENTENNIAL CRAFTS AND FOLK ART EXHIBIT. FOLK ARTS AND CRAFTS DEMONSTRATIONS IN BICENTENNIAL BUILDING. ITEMS PRODUCED MAY BE SOLD, WITH PROCEEDS GOING TO BICENTENNIAL PROJECTS. AT OPERA HOUSE, EXPOSITION GARDENS. UNIVERSITY & NORTHMOOR STREETS. (ST-WIDE). GARY GRESHAM; PEORIA COUNTY BICENTENNIAL COMMISSION; 300 LIBERTY STREET; PEORIA, IL 61602. (#50315-1).

JULY 11 - 19, '75. VISIT OF HISTORY-MOBILE 'ETHNIC HISTORY IN ILLINOIS'. EXHIBIT AT HEART OF ILLINOIS FAIR. (LOCAL). CLIFFORD HAKA, FIELD REP; ILLINOIS STATE HISTORICAL SOCIETY; OLD STATE CAPITOL; SPRINGFIELD, IL 62706. (#200016-512).

JULY 18 - 21, '75. AMERICAN FREEDOM TRAIN DISPLAY DAYS AT PEORIA. THE AMERICAN FREEDOM TRAIN WILL INCLUDE 10 EXHIBIT CARS & 2 SHOWCASE CARS DEPICTING DIFFERENT PHASES OF THE AMERICAN EXPERIENCE. ITS ARRIVAL WILL SERVE AS A CATALYST FOR LOCAL BICENTENNIAL CELEBRATIONS BY PEOPLE THROUGHOUT THIS NATION. (ST-WIDE). DON MALLICOAT, EDIT SVCS; THE AMERICAN FREEDOM TRAIN FOUNDATION, INC; 5205 LEESBURG PIKE, SUITE 800; BAILEY'S XRDS, VA 22041. (#1776-17).

JULY 29 - 31, '75. PERFORMANCES OF GHARIAN DANCE TROUPE. DURING THESE 3 DAYS, THE GROUP PERFORMED AT VARIOUS PLACES THROUGHOUT THE CITY. (LOCAL). GARY GRESHAM; PEORIA COUNTY BICENTENNIAL COMMISSION; PO BOX 1776; PEORIA, IL 61601. (#200016-326).

APR 8, '76. 'WHAT IS AMERICAN FOLK ART'. EXHIBIT AT LAKEVIEW CENTER FOR THE ARTS. (LOCAL). GARY GRESHAM, CHMN; PEORIA BICENTENNIAL COMMISSION; PO BOX 1776; PEORIA, IL 61601. (#200016-246).

JUNE 5, '76. PEORIA JUNIOR SPORTS JAMBOREE BICENTENNIAL FESTIVAL. FESTIVAL, COMPETITION AT PEORIA STADIUM. (LOCAL). GARY GRESHAM, CHMN; PEORIA BICENTENNIAL COMMISSION; PO BOX 1776; PEORIA, IL 61601. (#200016-113).

JULY 4, '76. BICENTENNIAL CELEBRATION. ICE CREAM SOCIAL & COMMUNITY SING. AT ECKWOOD PARK. (LOCAL). GARY GRESHAM, CHMN; PEORIA BICENTENNIAL COMMISSION; PO BOX 1776; PEORIA, IL 61601. (#200016-112).

JULY 16 - 24, '76. HEART OF ILLINOIS FAIR. FAIR AT FAIRGROUNDS, 1601 NORTHMOOR RD. (REGN'L). JAMES D TAYLOR, GEN MGR; EXPOSITION GARDENS, INC; PO BOX 3334; PEORIA, IL 61614. (#106095-46).

JULY 25, '76. 'AMERICANS ARE COMING'. LIVE PERFORMANCE AT ALPHA PARK. (LOCAL). GARY GRESHAM, CHMN; PEORIA BICENTENNIAL COMMISSION; PO BOX 1776; PEORIA, IL 61601. (#200016-111).

AUG 21 - 22, '76. UNITED STATES ARMED FORCES BICENTENNIAL CARAVAN. CARAVAN IS COMPOSED OF EXHIBIT VANS FOR EACH MILITARY SERVICE. PROJECT THEME IS 'HISTORY OF THE ARMED FORCES & THEIR CONTRIBUTIONS TO THE NATION.'. (LOCAL). ROBERT G DAY, CHMN; UNITED STATES ARMED FORCES BICENTENNIAL CARAVAN; 2601 N KINGSTON DR; PEORIA, IL 61604. (#1775-636).

AUG 22, '76. OLD-FASHIONED SING. FESTIVAL AT PEORIA COURTHOUSE. (LOCAL). GARY GRESHAM, CHMN; PEORIA BICENTENNIAL COMMISSION; PO BOX 1776; PEORIA, IL 61601. (#200016-110).

AUG 28, '76. AMERICAN WIND SYMPHONY'S FLOATING ARTS CENTER VISITS PEORIA. EMBARKING UPON A BICENTENNIAL CULTURAL TOUR, THE WIND SYMPHONY WILL VISIT 76 CITIES BRINGING MUSIC, DANCE, SYMPOSIA & CHILDREN'S THEATER TO THE WATERWAYS OF AMERICA DURING ITS 6 MONTH TOUR. (ST-WIDE). PAULA BERN, COORD; AMERICAN WIND SYMPHONY ORCHESTRA OF WESTERN PENNSYLVANIA; GATEWAY TOWERS 18G; PITTSBURGH, PA 15222. (#2800-33).

OCT 1 - 4, '76. WORKING IN AMERICA: A BICENTENNIAL LABOR FAIR. A WORKING DEMONSTRATION OF SKILLED AMERICAN LABOR, UTILIZING LOCAL UNIONS AND COMPANIES. AT GLEN OAK PARK PAVILION. (LOCAL). DR BRUCE BOYER, DIRECTOR; ILLINOIS BICENTENNIAL COMMISSION; 410 N MICHIGAN AVE, ROOM 1044; CHICAGO, IL 60611. (#108419-1).

JAN 25 - 27, '77. LA SALLE EXPEDITION II, A HISTORIC RE-ENACTMENT. THIS IS AN AUTHENTIC RE-ENACTMENT OF THE 1681 LASALLE EXPEDITION FROM MONTREAL, CANADA TO NEW ORLEANS, LA WHICH WILL BEGIN TOURING ON AUGUST 11, 1976 AND END ON APRIL 9, 1977. (LOCAL). REID H LEWIS, DIRECTOR; LA SALLE EXPEDITION II; 135 S LA SALLE ST, RM 411; CHICAGO, IL 60690. (#102805-45).

PEOTONE

JUNE 18 - 20, '76. 'ONE NATION UNDER GOD'. THE PAGEANT TRACES SOME OF THE MAJOR EVENTS IN AMERICAN HISTORY FROM THE LANDING OF THE PILGRIMS TO THE CIVIL RIGHTS MARCHES; IT WILL DRAMATIZE THE INFLUENCE OF CHRISTIANS & CHRISTIANITY UPON THE COURSE OF AMERICAN HISTORY. AT WILL COUNTY FAIRGROUNDS, WILMINGTON RD AT WEST ST. (LOCAL). HON H SCRIVENS, MAYOR; PEOTONE BICENTENNIAL COMMISSION; VILLAGE HALL, 208 E MAIN ST; PEOTONE, IL 60468. (#103834-1).

PESOTUM

PESOTUM RESTORATION PROJECT - IL. RESTORATION OF A JAIL, GENERAL STORE AND DEPOT TO THEIR ORIGINAL STATES AS REMINDERS OF THE HERITAGE OF PESOTUM. (LOCAL). M L MENELEY; PESOTUM BICENTENNIAL COMMISSION; PO BOX 197; PESOTUM, IL 61863. (#28051). **ARBA GRANTEE.**

JUNE 19, '76. BICENTENNIAL FESTIVAL. FESTIVAL. (LOCAL). DARWIN HURSEY, CHMN; PESOTUM BICENTENNIAL COMMISSION; PESOTUM, IL 61863. (#200016-88).

PETERSBURG

BOOK PROJECT IN PETERSBURG, ILLINOIS. REPRINTING OF SIX TO EIGHT OLD MENARD COUNTY HISTORY BOOKS. (LOCAL). LUANN BECKER, CO-CHAIRMAN; PETERSBURG BICENT COMMISSION; C/O LUANN BECKER, RR #1; PETERSBURG, IL 62675. (#8756).

MARKING OF LINCOLN POST ROAD IN PETERSBURG, IL. MARKING OF REGULAR POSTAL ROUTE OF ABE LINCOLN FROM NEW SALEM TO ATHENS TO SPRINGFIELD, SO THAT ROUTE MAY BE FOLLOWED BY CAR. (LOCAL). PAT WHEELER, CHAIRMAN; MENARD COUNTY BICENTENNIAL COMMISSION; RR 3; PETERSBURG, IL 62950. (#33552).

RESTORATION OF FRACKELTON BANK BUILDING IN IL. RESTORATION OF OLD BANK FOR USE AS A COUNTY MUSEUM. (LOCAL). LUANN BECKER, CHAIRPERSON; MENARD COUNTY BICENTENNIAL COMMISSION; RR 1; PETERSBURG, IL 62950. (#33551).

OCT 4 - 5, '75. LAND OF LINCOLN CRAFT FESTIVAL. OVER 70 WORKING CRAFTS AS PRACTISED BY OUR FOREFATHERS. IS 9TH ANNUAL FESTIVAL. FOOD ON GROUNDS, FLEA MARKET & PRODUCTS BY THE CRAFTSMEN FOR SALE. AT NEW SALEM CARRIAGE MUSEUM. (LOCAL). KAREN J ALLEN, CHAIRMAN; TOWN AND COUNTRY WOMAN'S CLUB; BOX 405; PETERSBURG, IL 62675. (#8227-501).

APR 18, '76. PANORAMIC CHATAUQUA. FESTIVAL. (LOCAL). PAT WHEELER, CHMN; MENARD COUNTY BICENTENNIAL COMMISSION; RR 3; PETERSBURG, IL 62950. (#200016-131).

APR 18, '76. WAGON TRAIN STOP. TOUR, CEREMONY. (LOCAL). JULIE WILLIAMS, CHMN; ILLINOIS BICENTENNIAL COMMISSION; 1 W OLD STATE CAPITOL PLAZA; SPRINGFIELD, IL 62706. (#200016-130).

APR 18 - 20, '76. 1776 PLUS, FAMILY FESTIVAL. FAMILY FESTIVAL W/CONTESTS, GAMES, COMMUNITY CHURCH SERVICE, MUSICAL PGMS, FOOD, PARADE, FLEA MARKET. HRS: 4/19 10AM-10PM; 4/20 9AM-NOON. AT AT MENARD COUNTY FAIRGROUNDS, PETERSBURG. (LOCAL). LUANN BECKER, CO-CHAIRMAN; PETERSBURG BICENT COMMISSION; 109 ALMOND LN, RR 1; PETERSBURG, IL 62675. (#8228-501).

PINCKNEYVILLE

PERRY CO, ILLINOIS LANDFILL RECLAMATION MINI-PARK. PROJECT TO RECLAIM LAND USED FOR LANDFILL BY LEVELING, ADDING TOP SOIL AND LANDSCAPING WITH SHADE TREES. EVENTUALLY PICNIC TABLES AND A BICENTENNIAL DEDICATION PLAQUE WILL BE ADDED. (LOCAL). GLEN SEEBER, ADVISOR; UNIV OF ILLINOIS EXTENSION SERVICE; 113 E SOUTH ST; PINCKNEYVILLE, IL 62274. (#5923).

PIOSA

ORAL HISTORY PROJECT IN PIOSA, IL. SOUTHWESTERN SCHOOL DISTRICT ORAL HISTORY PROJ, FOCUSING ON ETHNIC AND MINORITY GROUPS IN MACAUPIN COUNTY. (LOCAL). DONALD STUCKEY, CHAIRMAN; SOUTHWESTERN SCHOOL DISTRICT; PIASA, IL 62079. (#33039).

PITTSFIELD

RESTORATION OF EAST SCHOOL IN PITTSFIELD, IL. HISTORIC EAST SCHOOL TO BE MADE INTO PERFORMING ARTS CENTER. (LOCAL). MIKE BOREN, CHAIRMAN; PIKE COUNTY BICENTENNIAL COMMISSION & HISTORICAL SOCIETY; BOREN'S GROCERY; NEBO, IL 62355. (#33550).

PLAINFIELD

HISTORY OF PLAINFIELD THEN AND NOW - IL. A HISTORY OF PLAINFIELD TOWNSHIP FROM 1823 - 1976, ALL ARTICLES WRITTEN BY LOCAL CITIZENS. (LOCAL). IONE MUELLER, CHAIRMAN; PLAINFIELD BICENTENNIAL COMMITTEE; PLAINFIELD, IL 60544. (#32132).

JULY 3 - 4, '76. FOURTH OF JULY CELEBRATION. FESTIVAL AT VILLAGE GREEN FOX RIVER CHICAGO OTTAWA DESPLAINES. (LOCAL). IONE MUELLER; PLAINFIELD BICENTENNIAL COMMISSION; RR #4; PLAINFIELD, IL 60544. (#200016-356).

PLANO

AUG 23, '75. BICENTENNIAL FAMILY FUN DAYS. FESTIVAL AT LATHROP PARK. (LOCAL). SANDY HOFFMAN, CHMN; PLANO JUNIOR WOMEN'S CLUB; 210 S BEN ST; PLANO, IL 60545. (#200016-51).

AUG 23, '75. LIBERTY MARCH - PLANO JUNIOR WOMEN'S CLUB WALKING TOUR OF PLANO. TOUR AT PLANO CITY PARK. (LOCAL). JAMES BENTZ, COORD; HIKERS OF AMERICA, INC; RT 1, BOX 68; OSWEGO, IL 60543. (#200016-50).

FEB 23, '76. WASHINGTON'S BIRTHDAY PARTY. FESTIVAL AT METHODIST CHURCH PALORS. (LOCAL). PARKIE EMMONS, COORD; GOLDEN HARVESTERS SENIOR CITIZENS CLUB; HALE ST RD; PLANO, IL 60545. (#104942-1).

OCT 10 - 17, '76. OUR CHURCH'S CENTENNIAL CELEBRATION. CHURCH CENTENNIAL CELEBRATION ENDORSED BY THE KENDALL COUNTY BICENTENNIAL COMMISSION. AT FIRST BAPTIST CHURCH OF PLANO, 502 E CHURCH ST. (LOCAL). JERRY JILES, COORDINATOR; FIRST BAPTIST CHURCH OF PLANO; 502 E CHURCH ST; PLANO, IL 60545. (#106478-1).

PLATTVILLE

APR 24, '76. EXHIBITION OF MARKSMANSHIP. EXHIBITION OF MARKSMANSHIP; MILITIA DRESSED IN REVOLUTIONARY WAR COSTUMES AND USING WEAPONS OF THE ERA; SHERIFF'S DEPARTMENT DRESSED IN MODERN DAY UNIFORMS AND FIRING MODERN DAY WEAPONS. AT CLYDE HOWELL FARM - NORTH OF

PLATTVILLE — CONTINUED

PLATTVILLE ON CHURCH RD. (LOCAL). ROGER MATILE, COORD; KENDALL COUNTY BICENTENNIAL COMMISSION - KENDALL COUNTY MILITIA; 266 N ADAMS; OSWEGO, IL 60543. (#104944-1).

PLEASANT PLNS

JUNE 17 - 19, '76. 'THE EPIC OF RICHLAND CREEK'. A PAGEANT DEPICTING 200 YEARS OF LOCAL HISTORY. AT PLEASANT PLAINS CEMETERY, HALF MILE SOUTH OF TOWN. (LOCAL). HOWARD BAIRD, PRESIDENT; PLEASANT PLAINS BICENTENNIAL COMMITTEE; BOX 18; PLEASANT PLNS, IL 62677. (#200016-441).

PLEASANTDALE

LOCAL HISTORY BOOK - PLEASANTDALE, IL. RESEARCH AND COMPILE AREA HISTORY, REPRODUCE OLD MAPS, PHOTOS AND DOCUMENTS. (LOCAL). MRS LARRY JINES, CO-CHAIRMAN; PLEASANTDALE CIVIC ASSOC; 7400 S WOLF RD; LA GRANGE, IL 60525. (#23300).

LOG CABIN SCHOOLHOUSE - PLEASANTDALE, IL. PERMANENT STRUCTURE, SMALL REPLICA OF ORIGINAL SCHOOL DATED 1851 TO BE DONATED TO DISTRICT 107 SCHOOL FOR USE ON PLAYGROUND. (LOCAL). MRS LOREN STEPHENSON, PRESIDENT; PLEASANTDALE PARENT-TEACHERS ASSOC; 7450 S WOLF RD; LA GRANGE, IL 60525. (#23299).

JUNE 19, '76. ARTS AND CRAFTS EXHIBIT. INDIAN LEATHERWORK AND PLANTS WILL ALSO BE ON EXHIBIT. AT PLEASANTDALE PARK DISTRICT, 7425 S WOLF RD. (LOCAL). MRS DONALD PAULEY, DIR; PLEASANTDALE CIVIC ASSOC; 10715 MAPLEWOOD; COUNTRYSIDE, IL 60525. (#106509-3).

JUNE 19, '76. DEDICATION OF PINE OAK. A STATE TREE AS A LIVING MEMORIAL AND GIFT OF BICENTENNIAL PARTICIPANTS; IT WILL BE MARKED WITH A BRONZE PLAQUE ENCLOSED WITHIN A CONCRETE SEATING AREA. (LOCAL). JACK SCHAUS, PRESIDENT; PLEASANTDALE CIVIC ASSOC; 7400 S WOLF RD; LA GRANGE, IL 60525. (#106510-1).

JUNE 19, '76. FIREMEN'S WATER BALL FIGHT. COMPETITION AT PLEASANTDALE PARK, 7425 S WOLF RD. (LOCAL). LT JACOB ULTHUIS, CHMN; PLEASANTVIEW FIRE DEPARTMENT; 11035 W 80TH ST; LA GRANGE, IL 60525. (#106509-2).

JUNE 19, '76. FLAG CEREMONY FOR SCOUTS, VETERANS, BROWNIES & CADETS. CEREMONY AT PLEASANTDALE PARK, 7425 S WOLF RD. (LOCAL). BASIL MROZ, CHAIRMAN; PLEASANTDALE CIVIC ASSOC; 9 DEERCREST SQUARE; INDIANHEAD PK, IL 60525. (#106509-4).

JUNE 19, '76. GAY 90'S BATHING BEAUTY CONTEST. COMPETITION AT PLEASANTDALE PARK, 7425 S WOLF RD. (LOCAL). LARRY PASS, COORDINATOR; PLEASANTDALE CIVIC ASSOC; 8404 PLEASANTVIEW DR; WILLOW SPG, IL 60480. (#106509-6).

JUNE 19, '76. JAIL FOR BEARDLESS. FESTIVAL AT PLEASANTDALE PARK, 7425 S WOLF RD. (LOCAL). ANTHONY BUSHEMI, CHMN; PLEASANTDALE CIVIC ASSOC; 11216 W 73RD PL; LA GRANGE, IL 60525. (#106509-1).

JUNE 19, '76. MUSICAL WITH BICENTENNIAL THEME. LIVE PERFORMANCE AT PLEASANTDALE SCHOOL, 7450 S WOLF RD. (LOCAL). RICK ALLEN, DIRECTOR; TDAPASS THEATER GROUP; 902 COUNTRY CLUB DR; LA GRANGE, IL 60525. (#106509-5).

JUNE 19, '76. SPIRIT OF '76 PARADE. PARADE AT BEGINS 7900 S WILLOW SPRINGS RD TO 7400 S WOLF, PLEASANTDALE PARK. (LOCAL). MRS JAMES SUCHA, DIR; PLEASANTDALE CIVIC ASSOC; 7870 CIRCLE DR; LA GRANGE, IL 60525. (#106509-7).

JUNE 19, '76. TRICENTENNIAL SCROLL AND TIME CAPSULE BURIAL. PARTICIPANTS AND GUESTS' AUTOGRAPHS ON SCROLL TO BE BURIED IN THE TIME CAPSULE. (LOCAL). SOL GIAMPA, COORDINATOR; PLEASANTDALE CIVIC ASSOC; 7400 S WOLF RD; LE GRANGE, IL 60525. (#106510-2).

PONTIAC

LIBERTY BELL REPLICA IN PONTIAC, IL. PURCHASE OF LIBERTY BELL REPLICA FOR LIVINGSTON COUNTY COURTHOUSE BY COUNTY SCHOOL CHILDREN. (LOCAL). DOROTHEA GREEN, CHAIRMAN; LIVINGSTON COUNTY BICENTENNIAL COMMISSION; WPOK, RR2; PONTIAC, IL 61764. (#33549).

JUNE 16 - 20, '76. PONTIAC'S CHATAUQUA. LIVE PERFORMANCE. (LOCAL). DOROTHY GREEN; LIVINGSTON COUNTY BICENTENNIAL COMMISSION; WPOK-RRZ; PONTIAC, IL 61764. (#200016-327).

PORT BYRON

WORKING MUSEUM WITH PRINTING PRESS IN IL. OLD NEWS PAPER PRESS ROOM TO BE RESTORED FOR MUSEUM PRESS & STILL WORKS. (LOCAL). FRANCES M LEFFER, CHAIRPERSON; PORT BYRON BICENTENNIAL COMMITTEE; 23119 115 AVE N; PORT BYRON, IL 61275. (#33548).

DEC 23, '76. TIME CAPSULE DEDICATION & CHRISTMAS CELEBRATION. CEREMONY, FESTIVAL AT MEMORIAL SQUARE & LEGION HALL. (LOCAL). WILLIAM PETERSON; PORT BYRON BICENTENNIAL COMMISSION; 301 BENTON; PORT BYRON, IL 61275. (#200016-303).

PRAIRIE CITY

JULY 31 - AUG 1, '76. PRAIRIE CITY BICENTENNIAL CELEBRATION. CEREMONY, COMPETITION, FESTIVAL AT CITY PARK. (LOCAL). KATE SCHURMAN, COORD; PRAIRIE CITY BICENTENNIAL COMMITTEE; PRAIRIE CITY, IL 61470. (#106218-1).

PRARIE ROCHER

DOCUMENT COPIES, FORT DE CHARTRES, IL. GIFT OF DOCUMENT COPIES RELATING TO FRENCH FORT DE CHARTRES IN RANDOLPH COUNTY, IL, TO CONTRIBUTE TO ITS RESTORATION. (INT'L). AMBASSADOR HERVE ALPHAND, PRESIDENT; COMITE FRANCAIS DU BICENTENAIRE DE L'INDEPENDANCE DES ETATS-UNIS; 9, AVE FRANKLIN D ROOSEVELT; PARIS/FRANCE. (#22270).

JUNE 7 - 8, '75. FT DE CHARTRES RENDEZVOUS. FRENCH-INDIAN TRADER'S MEETING. (LOCAL). MS JANET PICKETT; ILL DEPT OF CONSERVATION; 901 SOUTH SPRING; SPRINGFIELD, IL 62704. (#50272-62).

JAN 3, '76. TWELFTH NIGHT KING AND QUEEN BALL. SINCE 1722 THE KING AND QUEEN BALL HAS MARKED THE END OF THE CHRISTMAS SEASON. SELECTION OF KING THRU CAKE WITH BEAN BAKED IN IT, FIRST MAN TO GET BEAN BECOMES KING AND SELECTS QUEEN; TRADITIONAL FRENCH CEREMONY. AT AMERICAN LEGION HALL, RT 155 PARKING AVAILABLE. (LOCAL). MARGARET BROWN, COORD; LA COMPAGNIE DES AMIS DE FORT DE CHARTRES; 937 SWANWICK; CHESTER, IL 62233. (#103391-7).

JULY 10 - 11, '76. FT DE CHARTRES RENDEZVOUS. FRENCH-INDIAN TRADERS MEETING. (LOCAL). MS JANET PICKETT; ILL DEPT OF CONSERVATION; 901 SOUTH SPRING; SPRINGFIELD, IL 62704. (#50272-61).

PRINCETON

BUREAU COUNTY BICENTENNIAL MEDALLION - IL. DESIGN, MINTING AND SALE OF BUREAU COUNTY BICENTENNIAL MEDALLIONS. (LOCAL). LOU BROWN, CHAIRMAN; BUREAU COUNTY BICENTENNIAL COMMISSION; BOX 373; PRINCETON, IL 61356. (#30409).

TOWN ENTRANCE REDEVELOPMENT PROJ, PRINCETON, IL. THE PROJECT INVOLVES RENOVATION OF EXISTING PARK FACILITIES AT ENTRANCE TO PRINCETON; FACILITIES WILL BE USED BY LOCAL RESIDENTS AND TRAVELLERS ON INTERSTATE 80. (LOCAL). DUNCAN L BRYANT, PRESIDENT; ROTARY CLUB OF PRINCETON; 654 PARK AVE, E; PRINCETON, IL 61356. (#10830).

AUG 20 - 24, '75. VISIT OF HISTORY-MOBILE 'ETHNIC HISTORY IN ILLINOIS'. EXHIBIT AT BUREAU COUNTY FAIR. (LOCAL). CLIFFORD HAKA, FIELD REP; ILLINOIS STATE HISTORICAL SOCIETY; OLD STATE CAPITOL; SPRINGFIELD, IL 62706. (#200016-516).

JULY 2 - 3, '76. BICENTENNIAL CELEBRATION. LIVE PERFORMANCE AT PRINCETON HIGH SCHOOL. (LOCAL). MRS LOU BROWN, COORD; BUREAU COUNTY BICENTENNIAL CELEBRATION COMMITTEE; BOX 373; PRINCETON, IL 61356. (#200016-202).

SEPT 10 - 12, '76. HOMESTEAD FESTIVAL. PARADE, PORK BAR-B-QUE, ICE CREAM SOCIAL, BEER GARDEN. AT COURT HOUSE SQUARE. (LOCAL). MR & MRS PETER ECKDAHL; PRINCETON CHAMBER OF COMMERCE; 931 S FIFTH; PRINCETON, IL 61356. (#50408-1).

PROPHETSTOWN

WINNING WHEELS, INC, PROPHETSTOWN, IL. THE ONLY US CENTER DEDICATED TO THE CARE AND REHABILITATION OF YOUTHFUL SPINAL CORD INJURY VICTIMS. (ST-WIDE). DORIS HERALD, PRESIDENT; PROPHETSTOWN WOMEN'S CLUB & BICENTENNIAL COMMITTEE; 109 LOCUST ST; PROPHETSTOWN, IL 61277. (#18163).

PROSPECT HTS

INDIAN ART PROJECT - PROSPECT HEIGHTS, IL. INDIAN ART PROJECT BY LOCAL ARTIST WM NELSON WHO WAS OFFICIAL ARTIST FOR 1976 OLYMPICS. LITHOGRAPHS OF HIS ORIGINAL SERIES OF INDIAN CUSTOMS WILL BE A ROTATING EXHIBIT. (LOCAL). KENT KRAUTSTRUNK, DIRECTOR; PROSPECT HEIGHTS PARK DISTRICT; CAMP MC DONALD & ELM ST; PROSPECT HTS, IL 60070. (#33547).

JUNE 4 - 6, '76. PROSPECT HEIGHTS BICENTENNIAL WEEKEND. OTHER EVENTS: 5/14 INCORPORATION BALL TO CELEBRATE OUR NEW & BICENTENNIAL CITY; 10/24 1876 WAR RE-ENACTMENT & SIGNATURES OF A COMMUNITY SCROLL. AT PROSPECT HEIGHTS PARK DISTRICT-CAMP MCDONALD. (LOCAL). LYNN KLOTZ; PROSPECT HEIGHTS PARK DISTRICT; 204 N PINE; PROSPECT HTS, IL 60070. (#200016-445).

PUTNAM

RESTORATION OF CONDIT HOUSE IN PUTNAM, IL. COMPLETE RESTORTION OF CONDIT HOUSE FOR USE AS A LIBRARY. (LOCAL). JANE DONNEY, CHAIRMAN; PUTNAM COUNTY BICENTENNIAL COMMISSION; PUTNAM, IL 61327. (#33546).

QUAD CITIES

SEPT 1, '75. ARTS SHOWCASE FILM DOCUMENTARY. RADIO/TV. (ST-WIDE). QUAD CITIES ARTS COUNCIL; 639 38TH ST; ROCK ISLAND, IL 61201. (#50359-1).

QUINCY

BICENTENNIAL PARK - QUINCY, IL. RIVERFRONT BICENTENNIAL PARK CONSTRUCTED WITH FUNDS RAISED BY YOUTH. (LOCAL). CHARLES RADEL, CHAIRMAN; ADAMS COUNTY BICENTENNIAL COMMISSION; COUNTY COURTHOUSE; QUINCY, IL 62301. (#30412).

CERTIFICATES FOR ILLINOIS PIONEER ANCESTORS. CERTIFICATES WILL BE AWARDED TO DESCENDANTS OF PIONEERS OF ADAMS COUNTY, WHO SETTLED BEFORE 1875; SUCH DESCENDANTS MUST COMPLETE PROOF OF ANCESTRY FORMS. DONATION ALSO REQUIRED. (LOCAL). MARK CLAMPITT, CHAIRMAN; GREAT RIVER GENEALOGICAL SOCIETY; 526 JERSEY; QUINCY, IL 62301. (#11889).

FAMOUS QUINCYANS IN THE ARTS AND HUMANITIES, IL. SEMINARS, CONCERTS, THEATER EVENTS, LECTURES, EXHIBITS & TELEVISION PRESENTATIONS ON THIRTEEN LOCAL NOTABLES FROM ILLINOIS HISTORY. (LOCAL). SAM GRABARSKI, COORDINATOR; QUINCY SOCIETY OF FINE ARTS; 1624 MAINE ST; QUINCY, IL 62301. (#27731). **ARBA GRANTEE.**

HISTORICAL MARKER PROJECT IN QUINCY, IL. ERECTION OF HISTORICAL MARKERS ACKNOWLEDGING IMPORTANT LOCAL & STATE SITES. (ST-WIDE). REV LANDRY GENOSKY, OFM, COMMISSIONER; IL STATE HISTORICAL SOCIETY & ADAMS COUNTY BICENT COMMISSION; 2727 TAMALA; QUINCY, IL 62301. (#12353).

ILLINOIS ART TASK FORCE. A PILOT PROGRAM WITH A 5 ARTIST TASK FORCE--ARCHITECTURAL HISTORIAN, DECORATIVE ARTS HISTORIAN, GRAPHIC ARTIST, PHOTOGRAPHER, COORDINATOR --HELPING THE COMMUNITY IDENTIFY ITS CULTURAL HERITAGE & RESOURCES. (NAT'L). SENIOR PROGRAM OFFICER, FESTIVAL USA; AMERICAN REVOLUTION BICENTENNIAL ADMINISTRATION; 2401 E STREET, NW; WASHINGTON, DC 20276. (#91).

37TH BICENTENNIAL REGIMENT - QUINCY, IL. FORMATION OF CONTINENTAL ARMY ARTILLERY UNIT;RE-ENACTMENTS OF REVOLUTIONARY WAR BATTLES AND MUSTER; MANUFACTURE AND DISPLAY OF CANNON. (LOCAL). CHARLES RADEL, COORDINATOR; QUINCY AMERICAN LEGION POST #37; QUINCY, IL 62301. (#30413).

'76 BICENTENNIAL YEARBOOK, QUINCY, IL. A RECORD OF SCHOOL AND COMMUNITY EVENTS DURING THE BICENTENNIAL YEAR. (LOCAL). FATHER DONALD WELL, OFM; QUINCY COLLEGE BICENTENNIAL COMMISSION; 1831 COLLEGE AVE; QUINCY, IL 62301. (#14323).

APR 12, '75. OFFICIAL CEREMONIES FOR BICENTENNIAL FOLLOWED BY RECEPTION. CEREMONY AT ADAMS COUNTY COURT HOUSE, 521 VERMONT ST. (LOCAL). CHARLES E RADEL, CHMN; ADAMS COUNTY BICENTENNIAL COMMISSION; 2727 TAMALA TERRACE; QUINCY, IL 62301. (#50339-1).

JUNE 29, '75. NATION UNDER GOD, PERFORMANCE. LIVE PERFORMANCE AT 215 NORTH TWENTYFIFTH STREET. (LOCAL). F FREDDIE GRIFFITH, MIN; MADISON PARK CHRISTIAN CHURCH; 215 NORTH TWENTYFIFTH STREET; QUINCY, IL 62301. (#50337-1).

JULY 11 - 13, '75. GIRL SCOUT ENCAMPMENT AT ADAMS LANDING ON QUINSIPPY ISLAND. SUNDAY HOURS 01:00PM-05:00PM. AT ADAMS LANDING QUINSIPPY ISLAND A RESTORED PIONEER VILLAGE. (LOCAL). TWO RIVERS GIRL SCOUTS; TWO RIVERS GIRL SCOUT COUNCIL; 2002 MAINE STREET; QUINCY, IL 62301. (#50338-1).

JULY 30 - SEPT 17, '75. GREAT RIVER RIDE ITINERARY THROUGH IOWA, ILLINOIS & MISSOURI. GREAT RIVER MISSISSIPPI HORSEBACK RIDE-QUINCY, IL. THE GREAT MISSISSIPPI HORSEBACK RIDE WILL PRESERVE THE ECOLOGY OF THE GREAT RIVER ROAD FOR TRAVEL ENJOYMENT; IT WILL BE MADE BY M E ECKELBERG FROM ST PAUL, MN TO HANNIBAL, MO; IT WILL STOP IN QUINCY. (LOCAL). RICHARD WATERKOTTE; QUINSIPPI HORSE AND PONY CLUB; 2441 N 12TH; QUINCY, IL 62301. (#11984-501).

MAY 18, '76. BICENTENNIAL KODAK ROAD SHOW. EXHIBIT. (NAT'L). CHARLES RADEL, COORD; ADAMS COUNTY BICENTENNIAL COMMISSION; 2727 TAMALA TER; QUINCY, IL 62301. (#200016-200).

JULY 3 - 4, '76. INDEPENDENCE 200 FESTIVAL. FESTIVAL. (LOCAL). CHARLES RADEL, COORD; ADAMS COUNTY BICENTENNIAL COMMISSION; 2727 TAMALA TER; QUINCY, IL 62301. (#200016-201).

RANKIN

COMMUNITY DEVELOPMENT IN RANKIN, IL. LANDSCAPING, STREETS REPAIRED, NEW ROOF, FURNACE, PLUMBING & PARKING FOR LIBRARY. SHELVES FOR ARTIFACTS ADDED & A MEETING ROOM FOR COMMUNITY GROUPS. (LOCAL). HON FRANK KARLOCK, MAYOR; RANKIN BICENTENNIAL COMMISSION; 515 S JOHNSON; RANKIN, IL 60960. (#33545).

RESTORATION OF COMMUNITY DEPOT IN RANKIN, IL. RESTORATION OF OLD TRAIN DEPOT. (LOCAL). MRS RON OVERBY, CHAIRMAN; VERMILION COUNTY BICENTENNIAL COMMISSION; 213 N MAIN ST; RANKIN, IL 60690. (#33544).

JULY 4, '76. 4TH OF JULY CELEBRATION. FESTIVAL. (LOCAL). SOPHIA F LUTZ, CHMN; BICENTENNIAL COMMISSION OF RANKIN; 129 S GROVE ST; RANKIN, IL 60960. (#200016-401).

RANSOM

AUG 1 - 3, '75. BICENTENNIAL/CENTENNIAL DAYS. HOURS 8/2 - 8AM-12AM, 8/3 - 9AM-10:30PM. GAMES, PET PARADE, ARTS & CRAFTS DISPLAY, BAKED & CANNED GOODS SALE, BALL GAME, SQUARE DANCE FRIDAY NIGHT, DANCES FOR YOUTH & ADULT ON SATURDAY NIGHT. (ST-WIDE). DAL ESTES, CHAIRMAN; RANSOM BICENTENNIAL COMM & LIONS-AMERICAN LEGION; WALNUT HILL; RANSOM, IL 60470. (#8182-501).

RANTOUL

DOWNTOWN REDEVELOPMENT, RANTOUL, IL. REDEVELOPMENT OF RANTOUL DOWNTOWN. CONSTRUCTING MALL REPAIRING BUILD ING, PLANTING 200 TREES, UPGRADING BUSINESS AREA, INITIATING SIGN CONTROL, GENERALIZED BEAUTIFICATION. (LOCAL). KATHY PODAGROSI, TRUSTEE; RAUTOUL-CHANUTE BICENTENNIAL COMMITTEE; 319 E CONGRESS; RANTOUL, IL 61866. (#29768).

OCT 21, '76. AWARDS NIGHT. AWARD, CEREMONY, EXHIBIT AT BICENTENNIAL ROOM, FIRST NATIONAL BANK. (LOCAL). ERNESTO G PODAGROSI; RANTOUL-CHANUTE BICENTENNIAL COMM & RANTOUL CHAMBER OF COMMERCE; 319 E CONGRESS AVE; RANTOUL, IL 61866. (#200016-304).

RARITAN

HENDERSON COUNTY MUSEUM - RARITAN, IL. ESTABLISHMENT OF HENDERSON COUNTY MUSEUM IN RARITAN OPERA HOUSE. (LOCAL). ART KANE, CHAIRMAN; HENDERSON COUNTY BICENTENNIAL COMMISSION; RR; MEDIA, IL 61460. (#30418).

OCT 25, '75. FLEA MARKET. FESTIVAL AT ST PATRICK COMMUNITY CENTER. (LOCAL). MILDRED MELVIN, CO-CHMN; BICENTENNIAL COMMISSION FESTIVAL COMMITTEE; STRONG HURST, IL 61480. (#200016-52).

MAY 31, '76. RE-ENACTMENT OF DECORATION DAY SERVICES. CEREMONY AT OPERA HOUSE. (LOCAL). KENNETH DIERS, COORD; CITIZEN'S COMMITTEE; BOX 1776; RARITAN, IL 61471. (#200016-199).

JULY 4, '76. RARITAN COMMUNITY SPIRIT OF '76 CELEBRATION. COMMUNITY WIDE RELIGIOUS SERVICE, OPEN AIR MARKET, SPIRIT OF '76 PARADE, DINNER, MUSIC, FIREWORKS. AT MAIN & TRENTON ST. (LOCAL). KENNETH DIERS, CHAIRMAN; RARITAN COMMUNITY SPIRIT OF '76 ORGANIZATION; BOX 1776; RARITAN, IL 61471. (#108217-1).

RIDGEFARM

WEANING CABIN RESTORED IN RIDGEFARM, ILLINOIS. AN OLD WEANING CABIN WILL BE PLACED IN A CITY PARK. (LOCAL). MARILYN BUSOY, CO-CHAIRMAN; RIDGEFARM/ELWOOD & LOVE TOWNSHIP; RIDGEFARM, IL 61870. (#9586). **ARBA GRANTEE.**

RIDGWAY

SEPT 11, '76. RIDGWAY POPCORN DAY. FESTIVAL. (LOCAL). MARY WEST, CHAIRPERSON; GALLATIN COUNTY HISTORICAL SOCIETY; OMAHA, IL 62871. (#104546-1).

RIPLEY

SEPT 1 - 2, '75. LABOR DAY CELEBRATION. OPENING, FESTIVAL. (LOCAL). MARJORIE LEAVES, CHAIRMAN; BROWN COUNTY BOARD & BICENTENNIAL COMMISSION; MT STERLING, IL 62353. (#8189-503).

SEPT 6, '76. RIPLEY BICENTENNIAL FESTIVAL. FESTIVAL. (LOCAL). MARJORIE CLEAVES, COORD; BROWN COUNTY BICENTENNIAL COMMISSION; RR 1; TIMEWELL, IL 62375. (#200016-198).

RIVER FOREST

BICENTENNIAL ACTIVITIES OF RIVER FOREST, IL. CELEBRATION OF ALL MAJOR REVOLUTIONARY EVENTS; LIBERTY TREE PLANTING & FLAG DISPLAY; LIBRARY REFURBISHMENT & SPECIAL EXHIBITS; BICENT QUILT & WALL TAPESTRY; ADULT HISTORY CLASSES; & SCHOLARSHIP FUND. (LOCAL). MRS JOHN R ORNDORFF, CHAIRMAN; RIVER FOREST BICENTENNIAL COMMISSION; 1009 BONNIEBRAE - 3B; RIVER FOREST, IL 60305. (#33489).

BICENTENNIAL PROJECTS OF RIVER FOREST, ILLINOIS. INCL COMMEMORATION OF REVOLUTIONARY EVENTS; PRESENTATION OF PLAY '1776'; PATRIOT'S BALL; KEPT BICENT SCRAPBOOK; MADE BICENT QUILT; EXTENSIVE SCHOOL PROGRAM; HISTORY & POEMS ABOUT VILLAGE; ETC. (LOCAL). MRS JOHN R ORNDORFF, CO-CHAIRMAN; RIVER FOREST BICENTENNIAL COMMITTEE; 1009 BONNIEBRAE, 3B; RIVER FOREST, IL 60305. (#33170).

HISTORY LECTURES - RIVER FOREST, IL. A 3-YR SERIES OF LECTURES WITH AUDIOVISUAL AIDS ON A VARIETY OF TOPICS RELATED TO THE DEVELOPMENT OF THE UNITED STATES FROM THE REVOLUTION TO THE PRESENT. (LOCAL). MRS JOHN ORNDORF, CHAIRMAN; RIVER FOREST BICENTENNIAL COMMISSION; 1009 BONNIE BRAE; RIVER FOREST, IL 60305. (#33436).

DEC 16, '73. BOSTON TEA PARTY. LIVE PERFORMANCE. (LOCAL). MRS JOHN R ORNDORFF, CHMN; RIVER FOREST BICENTENNIAL COMMITTEE; 1009 BONNIEBRAE - 3B; RIVER FOREST, IL 60305. (#200016-452).

MAR 1, '75 - APR 30, '76. AMERICAN HISTORY SEMINARS FOR THE VILLAGE. GIVEN IN THE EVENINGS, A FOUR WEEK LECTURE SERIES ON THE HISTORY OF RIVER FOREST & ONE ON AMERICAN RESIDENTIAL ARCHITECTURE. (LOCAL). MRS JOHN R ORNDORFF; RIVER FOREST BICENTENNIAL COMMITTEE; 1009 BONNIEBRAE - 3B; RIVER FOREST, IL 60305. (#200016-450).

JULY 4, '75. FOURTH OF JULY CELEBRATION & FIREWORKS. FESTIVAL, PARADE AT IN THE VILLAGE. (LOCAL). MRS JOHN R ORNDORFF, CHMN; RIVER FOREST BICENTENNIAL COMMITTEE; 1009 BONNIEBRAE - 3B; RIVER FOREST, IL 60305. (#200016-449).

NOV 22, '75. RIVER FOREST BICENTENNIAL COMMISSION PATRIOTS' BALL. LIVE PERFORMANCE AT LEWIS HALL, GREAT HALL & DINING ROOM, ROSARY COLLEGE. (LOCAL). MRS JOHN R ORNDORFF; RIVER FOREST BICENTENNIAL COMMISSION; 1009 BONNIE BRAE; RIVER FOREST, IL 60305. (#200016-505).

JULY 4, '76. BURIAL OF THE BICENTENNIAL TIME CAPSULE. TO BE OPENED JULY 4, 2076. AT IN THE VILLAGE HALL. (LOCAL). MRS JOHN R ORNDORFF, CHMN; RIVER FOREST BICENTENNIAL COMMITTEE; 1009 BONNIEBRAE - 3B; RIVER FOREST, IL 60305. (#200016-451).

JULY 4, '76. JULY 4TH CELEBRATION. BICENTENNIAL PARADE, VILLAGE PICNIC & BURIAL OF TIME CAPSULE. (LOCAL). MRS JOHN R ORNDORFF, CHMN; RIVER FOREST BICENTENNIAL COMMISSION; 1009 BONNIEBRAE - 3B; RIVER FOREST, IL 60305. (#200016-510).

RIVER GROVE

BICENTENNIAL TAPES, RIVER GROVE, IL. TAPES OF INTERVIEWS WITH SENIOR CITIZENS HAVE BEEN MADE & DISTRIBUTED TO 4 ELEMENTARY SCHOOLS & THE LIBRARY. (LOCAL). DOROTHEA LEDER, CHAIRPERSON; RIVER GROVE BICENTENNIAL COMMISSION; 2719 MARWOOD ST; RIVER GROVE, IL 60171. (#32202).

JAN 25 - JULY 4, '76. BICENTENNIAL EVENTS OF RIVER GROVE, ILL JAN-JULY '76. 1/25 BICENT WINTER CARNIVAL; 4/17 EASTER EGG HUNT; 5/1 HISTORY ESSAY CONTEST; 5/22 BICENT WALK-AROUND; 6/26 BICENT COSTUME BALL; 7/4 4TH OF JULY PARADE & PICNIC. (LOCAL). DOROTHEA LEDER, CHMN; RIVER GROVE BICENTENNIAL COMMISSION; 2719 MARWOOD ST; RIVER GROVE, IL 60171. (#200016-357).

DEC 26, '76. BICENTENNIAL HOLIDAY BALL. FESTIVAL AT AMERICAN LEGION HALL 8664 GRAND AVE. (LOCAL). DOROTHEA LEDER, CHMN; BICENTENNIAL COMMISSION; 2719 MARWOOD ST; RIVER GROVE, IL 60171. (#200016-328).

RIVERDALE

FLAG FESTIVAL IN RIVERDALE, IL. THE VILLAGE WILL FLY BICENTENNIAL, AMERICAN AND VILLAGE FLAGS ON EVERY HOLIDAY FOR THE NEXT 18 MONTHS. (LOCAL). RONALD RETT, PROJ CHAIRMAN; RIVERDALE BICENTENNIAL COMMISSION; 142 N STEWART; RIVERDALE, IL 60627. (#12060).

PHOTOGRAPHS OF EARLY RIVERDALE, IL. CITIZENS OF RIVERDALE HAVE CONTRIBUTED TO A DISPLAY OF EARLY PHOTOS TO BE SET UP IN THE NEW RIVERDALE LIBRARY. (LOCAL). LAURA KRUSE, HERITAGE CHAIRMAN; RIVERDALE BICENTENNIAL COMMISSION; 131 W 141ST ST; RIVERDALE, IL 60627. (#13057).

SPIRIT OF '76 PASSENGER BUS - RIVERDALE, IL. A BUS WILL BE PURCHASED FOR SENIOR CITIZENS AND THE HANDICAPPED TO RIDE ANYWHERE IN THE VILLAGE FREE OF CHARGE. (LOCAL). FRED ZAWADA, CHAIRMAN; RIVERDALE BICENTENNIAL COMMISSION; 14305 S WALLACE; RIVERDALE, IL 60627. (#18348).

STUDENTS PARTICIPATE IN COLORING BOOK CONTEST. ELEMENTARY STUDENTS IN GRADES 1 THRU 6 WILL PARTICIPATE IN A HERITAGE COLORING BOOK CONTEST WITH THEIR TEACHERS AS PRELIMINARY JUDGES. THE PRIZES WILL BE AWARDED ON JAN 1 THRU JAN 15. (LOCAL). FRED ZAWADA, CHAIRMAN; RIVERDALE BICENTENNIAL COMMISSION; 14305 S WALLACE AVE; RIVERDALE, IL 60627. (#18584).

VILLAGE LIBRARY DISPLAYS - RIVERDALE, IL. ALL AREA ORGANIZATIONS WILL PUT UP DISPLAYS IN THE LIBRARY; EACH WEEK A NEW DISPLAY WILL BE PUT OFF. (LOCAL). FRED ZAWADA, CHAIRMAN; RIVERDALE BICENTENNIAL COMMISSION; RIVERDALE, IL 60627. (#18354).

NOV 21 - DEC 20, '75. MOVIES & BAND CONCERT. LIVE PERFORMANCE AT VILLAGE HALL, 142 STEWART AVE. (LOCAL). FRED ZAWADA, CHAIRMAN; RIVERDALE BICENTENNIAL COMMISSION; 14305 S WALLACE AVE; RIVERDALE, IL 60627. (#200016-53).

JAN 7 - JUNE 27, '76. BEARD GROWING CONTEST. ALL CONTESTANTS WILL START ON JANUARY 7 WITH A CLEAR FACE; PARADE AND PICNIC. THE LONGEST AND NEATEST BEARD WILL RECEIVE A PRIZE. AT RIVERDALE PARK, 137 STEWART ST. (LOCAL). FRED ZAWADA, CHMN; RIVERDALE BICENTENNIAL COMMISSION; 14305 S WALLACE AVE; RIVERDALE, IL 60627. (#103903-1).

JUNE 27, '76. BICENTENNIAL PARADE & PICNIC. A PARADE AND PICNIC WILL BE HELD TO KICK OFF THE BICENTENNIAL CELEBRATION. (LOCAL). FRED ZAWADA, CHMN; RIVERDALE BICENTENNIAL COMMISSION; 14305 S WALLACE; RIVERDALE, IL 60627. (#103903-2).

ROANOKE

RENOVATION OF DEPOT IN ROANOKE, IL. THE OLD DEPOT WAS RESTORED FOR USE AS AN ARTS CENTER. (LOCAL). JOANN ARMSTRONG, DIRECTOR; WOODFORD COUNTY BICENTENNIAL COMMISSION; BOX 57; ROANOKE, IL 61561. (#33543).

ROCHELLE

THIRD ANNUAL ART FAIR IN ROCHELLE, IL. PROFESSIONAL AND AMATEUR ARTISTS AND CRAFTS PEOPLE WILL EXHIBIT WORK. ENTRY FEE IS CHARGED, PROCEEDS PAY FOR ART SCHOLARSHIP. (LOCAL). MRS KAY DRAPER, PRESIDENT; WOMEN'S CLUBS OF ROCHELLE; ROCHELLE, IL 61068. (#11013).

JUNE 13, '76. FOURTH ANNUAL ART FAIR. FAIR AT MAY MART SHOPPING CENTER AT ROUTE 38, EAST OF ROUTE 51. (LOCAL). CATHERINE M DRAPER, PRES; ROCHELLE FEDERATED WOMEN'S CLUBS; 523 N 11TH ST; ROCHELLE, IL 61068. (#105637-1).

ROCK FALLS

BICENTENNIAL SCHOLARSHIP - ROCK FALLS, IL. SCHOLARSHIP TO BE AWARDED TO 1976 HIGH SCHOOL GRADUATE TO FURTHER HIS EDUCATION; DONATIONS FROM ENTIRE COMMUNITY. (LOCAL). FLOYD TOMPKINS, CHAIRMAN; ROCK FALLS BICENTENNIAL COMMISSION; 608 E 2ND ST; ROCK FALLS, IL 61071. (#19259).

DIRECTIONAL SIGNS TO PARKS FOR ROCK FALLS, IL. DIRECTIONAL SIGNS WILL BE PLACED AROUND THE CITY TO FACILITATE THE CITIZEN USE OF THE COMMUNITY'S EIGHT PARKS. (LOCAL). LOUIS PIGNATELLI, MAYOR; ROCK FALLS CITY COUNCIL; 1007 7TH AVE; ROCK FALLS, IL 61071. (#19257).

LIBERTY BELL MONUMENT - ROCK FALLS, IL. ERECTION OF SUITABLE ENCLOSURE FOR REPLICA OF THE LIBERTY BELL AT A PROMINENT INTERSECTION. (LOCAL). FLOYD C TOMPKINS, CHAIRMAN; ROCK FALLS BICENTENNIAL COMMISSION; 608 E 2ND ST; ROCK FALLS, IL 61071. (#19258).

JUNE 18, '76. ROCK FALLS DAY. COMPETITION, PARADE AT PARADE 1ST AVE & W 2ND ST ALSO COMPETITION AT HIGH SCHOOL FIELD. (LOCAL). LEE WOLF, DIRECTOR; ROCK FALLS CHAMBER OF COMMERCE; 601 W 10TH ST; ROCK FALLS, IL 61091. (#104248-5).

JULY 29 - 31, '76. AGRICULTURE DAYS. FESTIVAL AT ROUTE 88 & 30 SOUTH EDGE OF CITY. (LOCAL). FLOYD C TOMPKINS, DIR; ROCK FALLS BICENTENNIAL COMMITTEE; 608 E 2ND ST; ROCK FALLS, IL 61071. (#104248-4).

ROCK ISLAND

CORPS OF ENGINEERS TOWBOAT & BARGE. THIS TOWBOAT & BARGE TRAVELED DOWN THE MISSISSIPPI RIVER TO 12 CITIES, INDIANA. (LOCAL). RICHARD S GUSTAFSON PUBLIC AFFAIRS OFFICER; ROCK ISLAND DISTRICT US ARMY CORPS OF ENGINEERS; CLOCK TOWER BUILDING; ROCK ISLAND, IL 61201. (#32256).

NATIVE AMERICAN HERITAGE FESTIVAL - IL. A CELEBRATION OF NATIVE AMERICAN HERITAGE. (LOCAL). VINCENT G THOMAS, COORDINATOR; PROJECT NOW; 1823 2ND AVE; ROCK ISLAND, IL 61201. (#27750). **ARBA GRANTEE.**

RESTORATION OF HISTORIC MURAL. HISTORIC MURAL ON CORPS OF ENGINEERS ACTIVITIES PAINTED IN 1943 WAS RESTORED, FRAMED & HUNG ON FIRST FLOOR CORRIDOR AT CLOCK TOWER BLDG, ROCK ISLAND DISTRICT HEADQUARTERS ON ARSENAL ISLAND, QUAD CITIES. (LOCAL). RICHARD S GUSTAFSON PUBLIC AFFAIRS OFFICER; ROCK ISLAND DISTRICT US ARMY CORPS OF ENGINEERS; CLOCK TOWER BUILDING; ROCK ISLAND, IL 61201. (#32255).

WORKING IN AMERICA: A BICENTENNIAL LABOR FAIR. A WORKING DEMONSTRATION OF SKILLED AMERICAN LABOR, UTILIZING LOCAL UNIONS & COMPANIES. (LOCAL). DR BRUCE BOYER, DIRECTOR; ILLINOIS BICENTENNIAL COMMISSION; 410 N MICHIGAN, ROOM 1044; CHICAGO, IL 60611. (#107990-1).

JULY 3, '75. 'TIME & RIVER' -THEATRICAL PRODUCTION OF ILLINOIS. PRODUCTION & PERFORMANCE OF 'TIME & RIVER' AN ORIGINAL DRAMATIZATION OF ROLE OF MISSISSIPPI RIVER IN SOCIAL, CULTURAL, & ECONOMIC DEVELOPMENT OF QUAD CITIES IN NORTHWEST ILLINOIS. (REGN'L). HARRIETTE FREEMAN; QUAD CITIES ARTS COUNCIL; 639 38TH ST; ROCK ISLAND, IL 61201. (#876-1).

JULY 4, '76. CERTIFICATE PRESENTATION TO PIONEER SETTLERS' DESCENDENTS. BICENTENNIAL COMMISSION WILL PRESENT A CERTIFICATE OF HONOR TO DESCENDENTS OF EARLY SETTLERS OF ROCK ISLAND COUNTY. (LOCAL). OTTO W SCHWEINBERGER, CHM; ROCK ISLAND COUNTY BICENTENNIAL COMMITTEE; 6600 34TH AVE; MOLINE, IL 61265. (#50604-1).

SEPT 25, '76. NATIVE AMERICAN HERITAGE FESTIVAL. FESTIVAL AT BLACK HAWK STATE PARK. (LOCAL). VINCENT G THOMAS, COORD; PROJECT NOW; 1823 2ND AVE; ROCK ISLAND, IL 61201. (#27750-1).

ROCKFORD

BIBLIOGRAPHY OF HISTORICAL WORKS, ROCKFORD, IL. 100 KEY WORKS ON THE REVOLUTION AND OUR HERITAGE TO BE CATEGORIZED FOR A BIBLIOGRAPHY. (LOCAL). DAIN TRAFTON, ASSOC PROFESSOR; ROCKFORD COLLEGE; 5050 E STATE ST; ROCKFORD, IL 61101. (#9719).

BICENTENNIAL COUNTY CALENDAR OF WINNEBAGO, ILL. WILL LIST ALL COUNTY DATES FOR BICENTENNIAL CELEBRATIONS DURING A 13 MONTH PERIOD. FULL COLOR, INCLUDES 5 PIECES OF STUDENT ART WORK. SIZE: 16' X '33. COST: $2.00 + $.75 POSTAGE. (LOCAL). GEORGE WHINNA, PROJ DIRECTOR; WINNEBAGO COUNTY BICENTENNIAL STUDENT COMMITTEE; WEST HIGH 1940 N ROCKTON; ROCKFORD, IL 61103. (#6863).

ROCKFORD — CONTINUED

BICENTENNIAL HIGH SCHOOL STUDENT EXCHANGE-ILLINOIS. 13 COUNTY HIGH SCHOOLS WILL EXCHANGE WITH HIGH SCHOOLS IN ORIGINAL 13 STATES. EACH COUNTY HIGH WILL PICK ONE OF THE ORIGINAL STATES, SEEK A SCHOOL AND INITIATE AN EXCHANGE FOR ONE SCHOOL WEEK IN 1976. (REGN'L). GEORGE W WHINNA, ADVISOR; WINNEBAGO COUNTY BICENTENNIAL STUDENT COMMITTEE; WEST HIGH 1940 N ROCKTON AVE; ROCKFORD, IL 61103. (#6865).

BOOK, WE THE PEOPLE, ROCKFORD & WINNEBAGO CO'S, IL. THE STORY OF ROCKFORD AND WINNEBAGO COUNTY THRU THE EYES OF THE MANY ETHNIC GROUPS WHICH MAKE UP THE COMMUNITY'S POPULATION TOLD THROUGH INTERVIEWS WITH CITIZENS CLOSELY ASSOCIATED WITH EVENTS. (LOCAL). HAL NELSON, EDITOR; WINNEBAGO COUNTY BICENTENNIAL COMMISSION; 415 W STATE ST; ROCKFORD, IL 61101. (#2821).

ETHNIC FESTIVAL OF WINNEBAGO COUNTY, IL. A WEEK LONG FESTIVAL OBSERVANCE OF OUR ETHNIC HERITAGE WITH WORLDWIDE, NATION-WIDE AND LOCAL EMPHASIS. (LOCAL). FRANK PARNINO, CHAIRMAN, ETHNIC HERITAGE COMMITTEE; WINNEBAGO COUNTY BICENTENNIAL COMMISSION; 415 W STATE ST; ROCKFORD, IL 61101. (#2822).

FOUNDERS' BICENTENNIAL PARK MEMORIAL, ROCKFORD, IL. A METAL SCULPTURE DEPICTING THE THREE FOUNDERS OF ROCKFORD WORKING TOGETHER TO SURVIVE WILL BE PLACED IN THE NEW FOUNDERS' BICENTENNIAL PARK IN ROCKFORD, IL. (LOCAL). CLARK GALLOWAY, PROJ DIRECTOR; WINNEBAGO COUNTY BICENTENNIAL COMMISSION; ROOM 310, OLD COURTHOUSE BLDG; ROCKFORD, IL 61101. (#26877). **ARBA GRANTEE.**

THEATER ARTS SERIES IN ROCKFORD, IL. SERIES CENTERS ON AMERICAN MUSICALS. (LOCAL). NEIL THACKABERRY INSTRUCTOR; ROCKFORD COLLEGE; 5050 EAST STATE ST; ROCKFORD, IL 61101. (#9717).

WINNEBAGO CO BICENTENNIAL STUDENT SCHOLARSHIP, ILL. $500 SCHOLARSHIP WILL BE GIVEN EACH YEAR STARTING IN 1976 TO A GRADUATING SENIOR FROM ONE OF THE THIRTEEN COUNTY HIGH SCHOOLS IN COMMEMORATION OF THE 200TH ANNIVERSARY OF THE U S. (LOCAL). GEORGE W WHINNA, ADVISOR; WINNEBAGO COUNTY BICENTENNIAL STUDENT COMMITTEE; WEST HIGH 1940 N ROCKTON AVE; ROCKFORD, IL 61103. (#6864).

WREX -TV BICENTENNIAL PROGRAMMING - NBMRP. ORIENTED TOWARDS HISTORICAL & EDUCATIONAL ASPECTS OF THE BICENTEN NIAL & HAS ORIGINATED A LONG SERIES OF PROGRAMS & FEATURES INCLUDING 'LOOKING BACK'; 'AFRO-AMERICAN HISTORY'; 'WE THE PEOPLE'; ETC. (LOCAL). JOHN T MAZZIE, BICENTENNIAL COORDINATOR; WREX-TELEVISION; AUBURN & WINNEBAGO ROADS; ROCKFORD, IL 61105. (#25885).

FEB 15 - 16, '75. ROCK CUT WINTER CARNIVAL. WINTER RECREATIONAL ACTIVITIES. (LOCAL). MS JANET PICKETT; ILL. DEPT. OF CONSERVATION; 901 SOUTH SPRING; SPRINGFIELD, IL 62704. (#50272-63).

MAY 17 - 18, '75. SECOND SEASON: AN AWAKENING OF SPRING. WILDFLOWERS, PHOTOGRAPHY, TOURS, ORGANIC GARDENING, WILDFLOWER VIEWI NG, BIRD MIGRATION, AND KITE MAKING. AT ROCK CUT STATE PARK INTERPRETIVE CENTER. (LOCAL). MS JANET PICKETT; ILLINOIS DEPARTMENT OF CONSERVATION; 901 SOUTH SPRING; SPRINGFIELD, IL 62704. (#50272-65).

JUNE 28 - 30, '75. PERFORMANCES BY NATIONAL AND INTERNATIONAL GROUPS. ETHNIC FESTIVAL OF WINNEBAGO COUNTY, IL. A WEEK LONG FESTIVAL OBSERVANCE OF OUR ETHNIC HERITAGE WITH WORLDWIDE, NATION-WIDE AND LOCAL EMPHASIS. (LOCAL). FRANK PARNINO; WINNEBAGO COUNTY BICENTENNIAL COMMISSION; 415 W STATE ST; ROCKFORD, IL 61101. (#2822-501).

JUNE 28 - JULY 5, '75. BUS AND BOAT TOURS WITH EMPHASISM ON HISTORIC BACKGROUNDS. ETHNIC FESTIVAL OF WINNEBAGO COUNTY, IL. A WEEK LONG FESTIVAL OBSERVANCE OF OUR ETHNIC HERITAGE WITH WORLDWIDE, NATION-WIDE AND LOCAL EMPHASIS. (LOCAL). FRANK PARNINO; WINNEBAGO COUNTY BICENTENNIAL COMMISSION; 415 W STATE ST; ROCKFORD, IL 61101. (#2822-504).

JUNE 28 - JULY 5, '75. MAJOR EXHIBITS OF ARTS AND CRAFTS FROM ETHNIC CULTURES. ETHNIC FESTIVAL OF WINNEBAGO COUNTY, IL. A WEEK LONG FESTIVAL OBSERVANCE OF OUR ETHNIC HERITAGE WITH WORLDWIDE, NATION-WIDE AND LOCAL EMPHASIS. (LOCAL). FRANK PARNINO; WINNEBAGO COUNTY BICENTENNIAL COMMISSION; 415 W STATE ST; ROCKFORD, IL 61101. (#2822-503).

JULY 1 - 5, '75. PERFORMANCES BY LOCAL GROUPS. ETHNIC FESTIVAL OF WINNEBAGO COUNTY, IL. A WEEK LONG FESTIVAL OBSERVANCE OF OUR ETHNIC HERITAGE WITH WORLDWIDE, NATION-WIDE AND LOCAL EMPHASIS. (LOCAL). FRANK PARNINO; WINNEBAGO COUNTY BICENTENNIAL COMMISSION; 415 W STATE ST; ROCKFORD, IL 61101. (#2822-502).

JULY 5, '75. WHAT ON EARTH? AN EXERCISE ON ENVIRONMENTAL LIVING. EXPLORES ENERGY USES, ALTERNATIVE CONSERVATION MEASURES AND RESOURCE CONCEPTS. AT ROCK CUT STATE PARK INTERPRETIVE CENTER. (LOCAL). MS JANET PICKETT; ILLINOIS DEPARTMENT OF CONSERVATION; 901 SOUTH SPRING; SPRINGFIELD, IL 62704. (#50272-67).

AUG 8 - 10, '75. AMERICAN FREEDOM TRAIN DISPLAY DAYS AT ROCKFORD, ILLINOIS. THE AMERICAN FREEDOM TRAIN WILL INCLUDE 10 EXHIBIT CARS & 2 SHOWCASE CARS DEPICTING DIFFERENT PHASES OF THE AMERICAN EXPERIENCE. ITS ARRIVAL WILL SERVE AS A CATALYST FOR LOCAL BICENTENNIAL CELEBRATIONS BY PEOPLE THROUGHOUT THIS NATION. (ST-WIDE). SY FREEDMAN, DIR OF P/R; THE AMERICAN FREEDOM TRAIN FOUNDATION; 5205 LEESBURG PIKE, SUITE 800; BAILEY'S XRDS, VA 22041. (#1776-140).

SEPT 10, '75 - APR 7, '76. HERITAGE FORUM SERIES. THE PROJECT INVOLVES 8 LECTURES ON THE REVOLUTION AND OUR HERITAGE. LECTURES: 09/10, 10/08, 11/05, 12/03, 02/04, 02/27, 03/10 & 04/07. AT MADDOX THEATRE, SEAVER GYM. (LOCAL). THOMAS GIDDENS; ROCKFORD COLLEGE; 5050 EAST STATE ST; ROCKFORD, IL 61101. (#9718-1).

SEPT 13 - 14, '75. FORGOTTEN TIMES. LIFE STYLES AND CRAFTS OF THE POST I.E, CANNING, SMOKING PRESERVING FOOD, SOURDOUGH BREAD, SQUARE DANCING AND PERIOD GAMES. AT ROCK CUT STATE PARK INTERPRETIVE CENTER. (ST-WIDE). MS JANET PICKETT; ILLINOIS DEPARTMENT OF CONSERVATION; 901 SOUTH SPRING; SPRINGFIELD, IL 62704. (#50272-69).

OCT 10 - 18, '75. THEATRE, USA: 3 AMERICAN PLAYS & AN EVENING OF DANCE. 'THE CRUCIBLE': NOV 13-15, 20-22; 'THE GLASS MENAGERIE': FEB 27-28; 'DANCE AMERICA': APRIL 22-24, 29-30; 'OKLAHOMA': MAY 1. AT CLARK ARTS CENTER (ROCKFORD COLLEGE CAMPUS). (LOCAL). NEIL THACKABERRY; ROCKFORD COLLEGE; 5050 E STATE ST; ROCKFORD, IL 61101. (#102860-1).

FEB 7 - 8, '76. ROCK CUT WINTER CARNIVAL. WINTER RECREATIONAL ACTIVITIES. (LOCAL). MS JANET PICKETT; ILL. DEPT. OF CONSERVATION; 901 SOUTH SPRING; SPRINGFIELD, IL 62704. (#50272-64).

MAR 26 - 28, '76. IFPEX-ROCKFORD '76 - PHILATELIC EXHIBITION & BOURSE. ANNUAL CONVENTION OF ILLINOIS FED OF STAMP CLUBS, BELGIUM PHILATELIC SOCIETY & ILLINOIS POSTAL HISTORY SOCIETY; AUCTION BY DR ARNOUIST. AT CLOCK TOWER INN, I-90 & US 20. (ST-WIDE). ROBERT G WAIT, CONSULTANT; ROCKFORD STAMP CLUB; BOX 512; BELVIDERE, IL 61008. (#103397-1).

APR 7 - 10, '76. SPRING BICENTENNIAL FESTIVAL. TALKS, ART EXHIBITS, THEATER, DANCE, AND MUSIC COMPRISE ROCKFORD, ILLINOIS' SPRING BICENTENNIAL FESTIVAL. AT ROCKFORD COLLEGE CAMPUS. (LOCAL). DAIN TRAFTON; ROCKFORD COLLEGE; 5050 E STATE ST; ROCKFORD, IL 61101. (#9716-1).

MAY 3, '76. WHAT ON EARTH? AN EXERCISE ON ENVIRONMENTAL LIVING. EXPLORES ENERGY USES, ALTERNATIVE CONSERVATION MEASURES AND RESOURCE CONCEPTS. AT ROCK CUT STATE PARK INTERPRETIVE CENTER. (LOCAL). MS JANET PICKETT; ILLINOIS DEPARTMENT OF CONSERVATION; 901 SOUTH SPRING; SPRINGFIELD, IL 62704. (#50272-68).

MAY 15 - 16, '76. SECOND SEASON: AN AWAKENING OF SPRING. WILDFLOWERS, PHOTOGRAPHY, TOURS, ORGANIC GARDENING, BIRD MIGRATION, AND KITE MAKING. AT ROCK CUT STATE PARK INTERPRETIVE CENTER. (LOCAL). MS JANETT PICKETT; ILLINOIS DEPARTMENT OF CONSERVATION; 901 SOUTH SPRING; SPRINGFIELD, IL 62704. (#50272-66).

AUG 31 - SEPT 1, '76. UNITED STATES ARMED FORCES BICENTENNIAL CARAVAN. CARAVAN IS COMPOSED OF EXHIBIT VANS FOR EACH MILITARY SERVICE. PROJECT THEME IS 'HISTORY OF THE ARMED FORCES & THEIR CONTRIBUTIONS TO THE NATION.'. (LOCAL). DENNIS W JOHNSON, COORD; UNITED STATES ARMED FORCES BICENTENNIAL CARAVAN; ROCKFORD CITY HALL; ROCKFORD, IL 61111. (#1775-640).

SEPT 4 - 6, '76. WORKING IN AMERICA: A BICENTENNIAL LABOR FAIR. A WORKING DEMONSTRATION OF SKILLED AMERICAN LABOR, UTILIZING LOCAL UNIONS AND COMPANIES. AT ROCKFORD ARMORY, 605 N MAIN ST. (ST-WIDE). DR BRUCE BOYER, DIRECTOR; ILLINOIS BICENTENNIAL COMMISSION; 410 N MICHIGAN AVE, ROOM 1044; CHICAGO, IL 60611. (#108420-1).

SEPT 11 - 12, '76. FORGOTTEN TIMES. LIFE STYLES AND CRAFTS OF THE PAST I.E. CANNING, SMOKING PRESERVING FOOD, SOURDOUGH BREAD, SQUARE DANCING AND PERIOD GAMES. AT ROCK CUT STATE PARK INTERPRETIVE CENTER. (LOCAL). MS JANET PICKETT; ILLINOIS DEPARTMENT OF CONSERVATION; 901 SOUTH SPRING; SPRINGFIELD, IL 62704. (#50272-70).

ROODHOUSE

ROODHOUSE MUSEUM - IL. ESTABLISHMENT OF ROODHOUSE MUSEUM. (LOCAL). BETTY BENNER, COORDINATOR; ROODHOUSE RECORD; ROODHOUSE, IL 62082. (#30416).

ROSEMONT

HANDS ACROSS AMERICA - ROSEMONT, IL. A LINE OF PEOPLE FROM COAST TO COAST CLASPING HANDS AT A DESIGNATED TIME JULY 4, 1976. (NAT'L). MARVIN J ROSENBLUM, PROJ DIRECTOR; O'HARE INTERNATIONAL TRADE AND EXPOSITION CENTER; ROSEMONT, IL 60018. (#19791).

RUSHVILLE

THE RECOLLECTIONS OF ABRAHAM LINCOLN IN IL. THIS PUBLICATION HAS BEEN REPRINTED. (LOCAL). MARGARET WALKER, DIRECTOR; SCHUYLER COUNTY BICENTENNIAL COMMISSION; 507 W CLINTON; RUSHVILLE, IL 62681. (#33541).

RENOVATION OF SCRIPPS PARK IN RUSHVILLE, IL. FORMERLY THE ESTATE OF THE SCRIPPS NEWSPAPER FAMILY, RENOVATED FOR PARK. (LOCAL). MARGARET WALKER, CHAIRMAN; SCHUYLER COUNTY BICENTENNIAL COMMISSION; 507 W CLINTON; RUSHVILLE, IL 62681. (#33542).

MAY 10, '75 - OCT '76. MONTHLY SQUARE DANCES THROUGHOUT SCHUYLER COUNTY. TOUR, FESTIVAL, EXHIBIT. (LOCAL). GARY CRUM, CHAIRMAN; COUNTY BOARD; COUNTY COURTHOUSE; RUSHVILLE, IL 62681. (#12254-501).

JULY 1 - 6, '75. VISIT OF HISTORY-MOBILE 'ETHNIC HISTORY IN ILLINOIS'. EXHIBIT AT SCHUYLER COUNTY FAIR. (LOCAL). CLIFFORD HAKA, FIELD REP; ILLINOIS STATE HISTORICAL SOCIETY; OLD STATE CAPITOL; SPRINGFIELD, IL 62706. (#200016-511).

OCT 10, '75. SMILES DAY - SCHUYLER COUNTY HOMECOMING CELEBRATION. TOUR, FESTIVAL, EXHIBIT. (LOCAL). GARY CRUM, CHAIRMAN; COUNTY BOARD; COUNTY COURTHOUSE; RUSHVILLE, IL 62681. (#12254-503).

OCT 11, '75 - OCT 12, '76. WESTWARD TRAIL - MAPPED TOUR OF SCHUYLER COUNTY. TOUR, FESTIVAL, EXHIBIT. (LOCAL). GARY CRUM, CHAIRMAN; COUNTY BOARD; COUNTY COURTHOUSE; RUSHVILLE, IL 62681. (#12254-502).

JUNE 13, '76. HOUSE AND GARDEN TOUR OF HOMES. TOUR. (LOCAL). MARGARET WALKER, CHMN; SCHUYLER COUNTY BICENTENNIAL COMMISSION; 507 W CLINTON; RUSHVILLE, IL 62681. (#200016-104).

SEPT 5, '76. DEDICATION AND FESTIVAL. FESTIVAL, CEREMONY. (LOCAL). MARGARET WALKER, CHMN; SCHUYLER COUNTY BICENTENNIAL COMMISSION; 507 W CLINTON; RUSHVILLE, IL 62681. (#200016-105).

SALEM

HYMNS OF THE COLONIAL ERA PROJ OF MARION, ILLINOIS. CHURCHES IN THE MARION COUNTY AREA ARE PLANNING TO INCLUDE ONE OR MORE HYMNS THAT WERE USED IN COLONIAL TIMES. (LOCAL). CLYDE D SMITH, CHAIRMAN; MARION COUNTY BICENTENNIAL COMMISSION; TONTI RD, RD4; SALEM, IL 62881. (#6497).

LINCOLN PLAQUE PROJECT IN SALEM, ILLINOIS. A PLAQUE WILL BE PLACED COMMEMORATING ABRAHAM LINCOLN'S FAMOUS PHRASE: 'TIPPECANOE AND TYLER TOO.'. (LOCAL). JASON W FELL, COMMITTEE CHAIRMAN; CITY OF SALEM BICENT COMMISSION; 101 S BROADWAY; MARION, IL 62881. (#9591).

JULY 4 - AUG 4, '75. PLAYING OF OLD TIME GAMES. CLAY COUNTY REGULATORS FIRE ARMS DEMOSTRATION OF MUSKET RIFLES JULY 4,1975. (LOCAL). JASON W FELL, CHAIRMAN; CITY OF SALEM BICENT COMMISSION; 101 S BROADWAY; MARION, IL 62881. (#9591-2).

AUG '75. CONCERT OF OLD TIME MUSIC. FESTIVAL. (LOCAL). JASON W FELL, CHAIRMAN; CITY OF SALEM BICENTENNIAL COMMISSION; 101 S BROADWAY; MARION, IL 62881. (#9591-3).

AUG '75. STAGE COACH RUN. FESTIVAL. (LOCAL). JASON W FELL, CHAIRMAN; CITY OF SALEM BICENT COMMISSION; 101 S BROADWAY; MARION, IL 62881. (#9591-1).

OCT '75. CITY OF SALEM PARADE. PARADE. (LOCAL). JASON W FELL, CHAIRMAN; CITY OF SALEM BICENT COMMISSION; 101 S BROADWAY; MARION, IL 62881. (#9591-4).

SAN JOSE

SAN JOSE BICENT COMM ACTIVITIES. PLANTED FREEDOM TREE, 12 ANGEL FLOWERING CRAB TREES, ENTERTAINED WAGON TRAIN ON ITS TRIP TO VALLEY FORGE, HAD COMMUNITY MEMORIAL SERVICE, STUNT SHOW, PAID FOR & ERECTED STREET SIGNS. (LOCAL). SAN JOSE BICENTENNIAL COMMITTEE; SAN JOSE BICENTENNIAL COMMITTEE; SAN JOSE, IL 62682. (#32243).

MAY 31, '76. BICENTENNIAL MEMORIAL DAY VESPER SERVICE. CEREMONY AT HIGH SCHOOL GYM. (LOCAL). MS MILTON FROEBE; SAN JOSE BICENTENNIAL COMMITTEE; SAN JOSE, IL 62682. (#200016-355).

SANDWICH

SEPT 3 - 6, '75. VISIT OF HISTORY-MOBILE 'ETHNIC HISTORY IN ILLINOIS'. EXHIBIT AT DEKALB COUNTY FAIR. (LOCAL). CLIFFORD HAKA, FIELD REP; ILLINOIS STATE HISTORICAL SOCIETY; OLD STATE CAPITOL; SPRINGFIELD, IL 62706. (#200016-518).

SAVANA

JUNE 14, '75. REPTILES AND MAN. ONE DAY INTERPRETIVE PROGRAM ON MAN AND HIS RELATIONSHIP TO SNAKES ACTIVITIES INCLUDE SPEAKERS, DEMONSTRATION ON HANDLING SNAKES AND VI EWING OF POISNOUS SNAKES. AT MISSISSIPPI PALISADES STATE PARK INTERPRETIVE CENTER. (LOCAL). MS JANET PICKETT; ILLINOIS DEPARTMENT OF CONSERVATION; 901 SOUTH SPRING; SPRINGFIELD, IL 62704. (#50272-71).

JULY 5, '75. CENTURY CRAFT DAYS. OLD TIME CRAFTS, HANDICRAFTS AND HOUSEHOLD ITEMS PLAY UP LIFE STYLES PRIOR TO PRESENT REFINED METHODS. AT MISSISSIPPI PALISADES STATE PARK INTERPRETIVE CENTER. (LOCAL). MR JANET PICKETT; ILLINOIS DEPARTMENT OF CONSERVATION; 901 SOUTH SPRING; SPRINGFIELD, IL 62704. (#50272-73).

AUG 16, '75. PALISADES OUTDOOR BAND CONCERTS. OUTDOOR BAND CONCERT WHICH EXPLORES MUSIC FROM THE TURN OF THE CENTU RY TO THE PRESENT DAY. DANCE CONTEST. AT MISSISSIPPI PALISADES STATE PARK INTERPRETIVE CENTER. (LOCAL). MS JANET PICKETT; ILLINOIS DEPARTMENT OF CONSERVATION; 901 SOUTH SPRING; SPRINGFIELD, IL 62704. (#50272-76).

AUG 31, '75. CIVIL WAR CAMPGROUND. AN EXAMPLE OF LIVING AMERICAN HISTORY DURING THE CIVIL WAR COMPLETE WITH COSTUMES AND EQUIPMENT FOR THE PUBLIC TO OBSERVE. AT MISSISSIPPI PALISADES STATE PARK INTERPRETIVE CENTER. (LOCAL). MS JANET PICKETT; ILLINOIS DEPARTMENT OF CONSERVATION; 901 SOUTH SPRING; SPRINGFIELD, IL 62704. (#50272-77).

SAVANA — CONTINUED

JAN 24, '76. PALISADES WINTER CARNIVAL. WINTER SPORTS WITH AN EMPHASIS ON PARTICIPANT ACTIVITY, I.E., SKATIN G, ICE FISHING, BOBSLEDDING, SNOWMOBILING, CROSS COUNTRY SKIING. AT MISSISSIPPI PALISADES STATE PARK INTERPRETIVE CENTER. (LOCAL). MS JANET PICKETT; ILLINOIS DEPARTMENT OF CONSERVATION; 901 SOUTH SPRING; SPRINGFIELD, IL 62704. (#50272-72).

JULY 10, '76. CENTURY CRAFT DAYS. OLD TIME CRAFTS, HANDICRAFTS AND HOUSEHOLD ITEMS PLAY UP LIFE STYLES PRIOR TO PRESENT REFINED METHOD. AT MISSISSIPPI PALISADES STATE PARK. (LOCAL). MS JANET PICKETT; ILLINOIS DEPARTMENT OF CONSERVATION; 901 SOUTH SPRING; SPRINGFIELD, IL 62704. (#50272-74).

AUG 21, '76. NATURAL FOODS AND PRESERVATION DAY. EXAMINATION OF HISTORICAL USAGE OF NATURAL PLANTS FOR FOOD AND MEDIC INE IN CONJUNCTION WITH PRESENT USAGE OF NATURAL FOODS. AT MISSISSIPPI PALISADES STATE PARK INTERPRETIVE CENTER. (LOCAL). MS JANET PICKETT; ILLINOIS DEPARTMENT OF CONSERVATION; 901 SOUTH SPRING; SPRINGFIELD, IL 62704. (#50272-75).

SEPT 5, '76. CIVIL WAR CAMPGROUND. AN EXAMPLE OF LIVING AMERICAN HISTORY DURING THE CIVIL WAR COMPLETE WITH COSTUMES AND EQUIPMENT FOR THE PUBLIC TO OBSERVE. AT MISSISSIPPI PALISADES STATE PARK INTERPRETIVE CENTER. (LOCAL). MS JANET PICKETT; ILLINOIS DEPARTMENT OF CONSERVATION; 901 SOUTH SPRING; SPRINGFIELD, IL 62704. (#50272-78).

OCT 15, '76. FALL FESTIVAL. FALL FOLIGE AND GEOLOGY OF PALISADES ARE VIEWED AND EXPLAINED VIA VA RIOUS VISITOR ACTIVITIES. AT MISSISSIPPI PALISADES STATE PARK INTERPRETIVE CENTER. (LOCAL). MS JANET PICKETT; ILLINOIS DEPARTMENT OF CONSERVATION; 901 SOUTH SPRING; SPRINGFIELD, IL 62704. (#50272-79).

SAYBROOK

'SHADE & WATER' - SESQUICENTENNIAL OF SAYBROOK, IL. SESQUICENTENNIAL CELEBRATION & KICK-OFF FOR BICENTENNIAL TO INCLUDE PAGEANTS, PARADES, HISTORIC TOURS, HISTORY BOOKS & COMMEMORATIVE ITEMS. (LOCAL). DON GIBBONS, PRESIDENT; SHADE & WATER, INC; BOX 206; SAYBROOK, IL 61770. (#8226).

JULY 4, '75. STYLE SHOW, BEARD JUDGING, FIREWORKS & CHICKEN BAR-B-QUE. FESTIVAL, PARADE. (LOCAL). DON GIBBONS, PRESIDENT; SHADE & WATER, INC; BOX 206; SAYBROOK, IL 61770. (#8226-502).

JULY 5, '75. PAGEANT, 'PROGRESS IS ONWARD', PARADE, TEEN DANCE & HISTORIC TOURS. SESQUICENTENNIAL CELEBRATION & KICK-OFF FOR BICENTENNIAL TO INCLUDE PAGEANTS, PARADES, HISTORIC TOURS, HISTORY BOOKS & COMMEMORATIVE ITEMS. (LOCAL). DON GIBBONS, PRESIDENT; SHADE & WATER, INC; BOX 206; SAYBROOK, IL 61770. (#8226-501).

JULY 6, '75. ECUMENICAL OUTDOOR CHURCH SERVICE, GOSPEL SINGING QUARTET. FESTIVAL, PARADE. (LOCAL). DON GIBBONS, PRESIDENT; SHADE & WATER, INC; BOX 206; SAYBROOK, IL 61770. (#8226-503).

JULY 4 - 6, '76. SUSQUICENTENNIAL AND BICENTENNIAL CELEBRATION. FESTIVAL. (LOCAL). DONALD GIBBONS, CHMN; SAYBROOK BICENTENNIAL COMMISSION; BOX 206; SAYBROOK, IL 61770. (#200016-132).

SCHAUMBURG

OPERATION SCHOOLHOUSE PROJECT OF SCHAUMBURG, IL. RESTORE THE TOWN'S LAST ONE-ROOM SCHOOLHOUSE & MOVE IT TO AN APPROPRIATE SITE. (LOCAL). MRS ROBERT ATCHER, PRESIDENT; SCHAUMBURG HISTORICAL SOCIETY; 101 S SCHAUMBURG CT; SCHAUMBURG, IL 60172. (#5218).

SCHAUMBURG CENTRE PROJECT OF ILLINOIS. PROJECT TO RESTRICT BY ORDINANCE THE TYPE OF BUILDINGS PLANNED IN AN AREA OF 1/4 MILE RADIUS OF THE MAIN INTERSECTION OF TOWN. BLDGS ARE TO BE OLD STYLE ARCHITECTURE AS IN SCHAUMBURG FARM DAYS. (LOCAL). JOHN E COSTE, VILLAGE ADMINISTRATOR; SCHAUMBURG PLANS COMMISSION; 101 SCHAUMBURG CRT; SCHAUMBURG, IL 60172. (#5909).

SPRING VALLEY NATURE SANCTUARY, SCHAUMBURG, IL. PRESERVATION OF APPROX 250 ACRES OF PRAIRIE & WOODS. INCLUDES RESTORATION OF OLD FARM BUILDINGS, NEW STUDY CENTER & PLAN FOR CONSTRUCTIVE USE OF FLOOD PLAIN & WILDLIFE PRESERVE. (LOCAL). ELLSWORTH A MEINKE, PROJECT DIRECTOR; SCHAUMBURG PARK DISTRICT; 220 E WEATHERSFIELD WAY; SCHAUMBURG, IL 60172. (#5221). **ARBA GRANTEE.**

SEPT 1, '75. LIBERTY MARCH. LIBERTY MARCH ALONG SEPTEMBERFEST PARADE ROUTE. (LOCAL). JAMES BENTZ, PRES; HIKERS OF AMERICA, INC; ROUTE 1, BOX 68; OSWEGO, IL 60543. (#101987-1).

SEPT 1, '75. SEPTEMBERFEST. SCHAUMBURG'S OFFICAL LABOR DAY CELEBRATION INCLUDING: PARADE WITH 'SPIRIT OF '76' THEME, FAIR, RIDES, CORN ROASTS, WATERMELON EATING CONTEST, MUSIC, CLOWNS, PICNIC, FIREWORKS & WATER COMPETITION. AT BETWEEN SCHAUMBURG HIGH & CAMPANELLILAKE ON SCHAUMBERG RD. (LOCAL). ALAN L LARSON, PROJ DIR; SEPTEMBERFEST COMMITTEE; 608 ANDREW CT; SCHAUMBURG, IL 60172. (#100355-1).

SEPT 1, '76. PARADE AT NOON FOLLOWED BY FESTIVAL LASTING TILL MIDNIGHT. SEPTEMBERFEST '76 IN SCHAUMBURG, ILLINOIS. GALA PARADE & FESTIVAL TO COMMEMORATE THE EARLY SETTLERS OF SCHAUMBURG & OUR AMERICAN HERITAGE, AND FLOATS DEPICTING OUR FUTURE; INCLUDES OLD-TIME CONTESTS & EVENTS. (LOCAL). RON BROCK; SEPTEMBERFEST COMMITTEE; 1806 CRANDON LANE; SCHAUMBURG, IL 60193. (#5222-501).

SCOTT AFB

CPL FRANK S SCOTT MEMORIAL, SCOTT AFB. MEMORIAL TO CPL FRANK S SCOTT, FIRST ENLISTED MAN TO LOSE HIS LIFE IN AN AIRCRAFT ACCIDENT & THE ONLY ENLISTED MAN TO HAVE AN AIR FORCE BASE NAMED AFTER HIM. (LOCAL). COL DALTON W MCCULLAR, JR, CHAIRMAN; SCOTT AFB BICENTENNIAL COMMITTEE; 375 ABG/DD; SCOTT AFB, IL 62225. (#28977).

JULY 4, '76. FUN DAY, USA FOURTH OF JULY CELEBRATION. COMMEMORATION DAY INCLUDED FOOD, GAMES, RIDES, PATRIOTIC PROGRAMS, BAND CONCERTS AND FIREWORKS OPEN TO BASE RESIDENTS AND LOCAL COMMUNITY CITIZENS. (LOCAL). COL DALTON W MCCULLAR, JR; SCOTT AFB; 375ABGIOP; SCOTT AFB, IL 62225. (#200016-244).

SENECA

JAN 16 - 17, '77. LA SALLE EXPEDITION II, A HISTORIC RE-ENACTMENT. THIS IS AN AUTHENTIC RE-ENACTMENT OF THE 1681 LASALLE EXPEDITION FROM MONTREAL, CANADA TO NEW ORLEANS, LA WHICH WILL BEGIN TOURING ON AUGUST 11, 1976 AND END ON APRIL 9, 1977. (LOCAL). REID H LEWIS, DIRECTOR; LA SALLE EXPEDITION II; 135 S LA SALLES, ST, RM 411; CHICAGO, IL 60690. (#102805-39).

SEPO

MAY 29 - 31, '76. MEMORIAL DAY WEEKEND. OLD-TIME CRAFTS, DEMONSTRATIONS, DISPLAYS, ANTIQUE SALE, FLEA MARKET AND TOUR OF RESTORED BUILDINGS. (LOCAL). MRS LAWRENCE I BORDNER; WATERFORD PROMOTION GROUP; 45 N PARK DR; CANTON, IL 61520. (#105200-3).

JULY 2 - 5, '76. 4TH OF JULY WEEKEND. OLD-TIME CRAFT DEMONSTRATIONS, DISPLAYS, ANTIQUE SALE, FLEA MARKET & TOUR OF RESTORED BUILDINGS. ON THE AFTERNOON OF JULY 4, THERE WILL BE COUNTRY MUSIC ON THE COUNTY FAIRGROUNDS, A FISH FRY AT 3:00PM & CHILD GAMES. PARADE, BABY CONTEST (0-2 YRS) & MUSICAL REVUE EVE. (LOCAL). DON CATES; LEWISTON PROMOTION GROUP; 45 N PARK DR; CANTON, IL 61520. (#105200-2).

SEPT 4 - 6, '76. LABOR DAY WEEKEND FESTIVAL WITH BICENTENNIAL THEME. OLD-TIME CRAFTS & DEMONSTRATIONS, DISPLAYS, ANTIQUE SALE, FLEA MARKET & TOUR OF RESTORED BUILDINGS. (LOCAL). MRS LAWRENCE I BORDNER; WATERFORD PROMOTION GROUP; 45 N PARK DR; CANTON, IL 61520. (#105200-1).

SESSER

SESSER OPERA HOUSE PRESERVATION - SESSER, IL. RESTORATION OF HISTORIC OPERA HOUSE FOR USE AS COMMUNITY CENTER. (LOCAL). EDITH B MILLER; SESSER BICENTENNIAL COMMISSION; SESSER, IL 62884. (#27880). **ARBA GRANTEE.**

SHANNON

BICENTENNIAL MINI-PARK IN SHANNON, ILLINOIS. CONSTRUCTION OF MINI-PARK FEATURING FLORAL AREAS, TREES, WALKWAYS, ROUGH HEWN STONE MONUMENT & PLAQUE. (LOCAL). LAURA WIRTJES, CHAIRMAN; SHANNON BICENTENNIAL COMMISSION; 605 S HICKORY; SHANNON, IL 61078. (#5324).

SHAWNEETOWN

METHODIST CHURCH MUSEUM - SHAWNEETOWN, IL. RESTORATION OF THE METHODIST CHURCH (CIRCA 1842) BY PAINTING THE INTERIOR, PLASTERING WALLS AND RE-FINISHING WALNUT FURNISHINGS. (LOCAL). MARY WEST, PRESIDENT; GALLATIN COUNTY HISTORICAL SOCIETY; SHAWNEETOWN, IL 62984. (#19802).

SEPT 5 - 6, '76. OLD SHAWNEETOWN CHIPOLA DAY. CHIPOLA (INDIAN NAME FOR FESTIVAL) WILL HAVE INDIAN EXHIBITS, TOURS OF HISTORIC BUILDINGS, DANCES & ARTS & CRAFT DEMONSTRATIONS. AT FIRST BANK MUSEUM, OLD SHAWNEETOWN, S MAIN ST. (LOCAL). MARY WEST, PRESIDENT; GALLATIN COUNTY HISTORICAL SOCIETY & VILLAGE OF OLD SHAWNEETOWN; OMAHA, IL 62871. (#104546-6).

SHEFFIELD

RESTORATION OF LUTHERAN EVANGELICAL CHURCH IN IL. ST PETER'S IS OLDEST DANISH LUTHERAN CHURCH IN AMERICA, ESTABLISHED IN 1869. BUILT IN 1880 IT WILL BE RESTORED TO THE LOOK OF THE 18801890 PERIOD. (LOCAL). MARGARET SCHMITT, CHAIRMAN; SHEFFIELD HISTORICAL SOCIETY; SHEFFIELD, IL 61361. (#5753).

RESTORATION OF ST PETERS CHURCH - SHEFFIELD, IL. ST PETERS DANISH EVANGELICAL LUTHERAN CHURCH, THE OLDEST DANISH CHURCH IN THE U S BUILT IN 1880 BY DANISH IMMIGRANTS, WILL BE RESTORED AND RECONSECRATED. (INT'L). NIELS TOFT, PROJ DIRECTOR; DANISH EMBASSY; 3200 WHITEHAVEN PKY, NW; WASHINGTON, DC 20007. (#20780).

AUG 14 - 16, '75. SHEFFIELD HOMECOMING. OPENING. (LOCAL). MARGARET SCHMITT; SHEFFIELD HISTORICAL SOCIETY; SHEFFIELD, IL 61361. (#5753-502).

DEC 14, '75. ANNUAL DANISH CHRISTMAS SERVICE. OPENING. (LOCAL). MARGARET SCHMITT; SHEFFIELD HISTORICAL SOCIETY; SHEFFIELD, IL 61361. (#5753-501).

MAY 15, '76. DEDICATION OF ST PETER'S CHURCH BY QUEEN MARGRETHE OF DENMARK. PRESENTATION OF DENMARKS BICENTENNIAL GIFT TO THE UNITED STATES. (ST-WIDE). OLLIE STIER, COORD; SHEFFIELD BICENTENNIAL COMMISSION; SHEFFIELD, IL 61361. (#200016-196).

JUNE 6, '76. BICENTENNIAL FUN DAY. FAIR. (INT'L). OLLIE STIER, COORD; SHEFFIELD BICENTENNIAL COMMISSION; SHEFFIELD, IL 61361. (#200016-197).

SHELBYVILLE

LAST BRIDGE CROSSING. CEREMONY AT OLD IRON BRIDGE ON RT #16, SHELBYVILLE. (LOCAL). JAMES A WARD; SHELBYVILLE BICENTENNIAL COMM; 316 E WALNUT; SHELBYVILLE, IL 62565. (#200016-306).

RESTORATION OF CHATAUQUA BUILDING - IL. THE CHATAUQUA BUILDING WILL BE RESTORED. (LOCAL). GRACE MOYER, DIRECTOR; SHELBY COUNTY BICENTENNIAL COMMISSION; BOX 387, HICKORY RIDGE LN; SHELBYVILLE, IL 62565. (#33537).

RESTORE COURTHOUSE & PUBLISH BOOKLET IN IL. ONE OF A KIND COURTHOUSE RESTORED & LOCAL HISTORY BOOKLET PUBLISHED. (LOCAL). JAMES A WARD, CHAIRMAN; SHELBYVILLE BICENTENNIAL COMMISSION; 143 N MORGAN ST; SHELBYVILLE, IL 62565. (#33539).

SHELBYVILLE, IL, COUNTY HISTORY. COUNTY HISTORY REPRINTED AND HISTORIC MAP OF COUNTY COMPILED. (LOCAL). GRACE MOYER, DIRECTOR; SHELBY COUNTY BICENTENNIAL COMMISSION; BOX 387, HICKORY RIDGE LN; SHELBYVILLE, IL 62565. (#33538).

TOWER HILL PARK IN SHELBYVILLE, IL. A CITY PARK WAS DEVELOPED. (LOCAL). GRACE MOYER, DIRECTOR; SHELBY COUNTY BICENTENNIAL COMMISSION; BOX 387, HICKORY; SHELBYVILLE, IL 62565. (#33531).

JULY 1 - 4, '76. WEEK OF 4TH OF JULY '76 FESTIVAL & PAGEANT. COMPETITION, EXHIBIT, FESTIVAL AT FOREST PARK. (LOCAL). JAMES A WARD; SHELBYVILLE BICENTENNIAL COMMITTEE; 316 N WALNUT; SHELBYVILLE, IL 62565. (#200016-305).

SEPT 5, '76. FALL FESTIVAL. AWARD, EXHIBIT, FESTIVAL AT 100 BLOCK SOUTH BROADWAY & ADJ PARKING LOT. (LOCAL). JAMES A WARD; SHELBYVILLE BICENTENNIAL COMM; 316 E WALNUT; SHELBYVILLE, IL 62565. (#200016-307).

SHELDON

ARTS & CRAFTS - PAST, PRESENT AND FUTURE. DEMONSTRATIONS OF QUILTING, YARN SPINNING, CERAMICS AND RUG MAKING. (LOCAL). MRS JOE HELLER, COORD; WOMEN'S CLUB; 275 W CONCORD; SHELDON, IL 60966. (#200016-241).

'HAPPY BIRTHDAY AMERICA' - RECORDS, SHELDON, IL. RECORDS TELLING THE HISTORY OF U S. ALSO: DISPLAY OF PICTURES OF ALL THE PRESIDENTS. (LOCAL). MARGARET M MARSH, PRESIDENT; SHELDON GRANDMOTHERS; 12050 2ND; SHELDON, IL 60966. (#28634).

SHELDON BICENTENNIAL TEA - HONORING MOTHERS IN IROQUOIS COUNTY. FESTIVAL. (LOCAL). MARIE HUSS, COORD; BICENTENNIAL COMMITTEE OF SHELDON; 120 S 2ND; SHELDON, IL 60966. (#200016-240).

SHELDON TOWN HALL - IL. THE TOWN BUILDING IN SHELDON IS BEING RESTORED. (LOCAL). MARGARET M MARSH, CHAIRMAN; SHELDON TOWNSHIP; CENTER ST; SHELDON, IL 60966. (#28653).

TREE AND SHRUBBERY PLANTING IN SHELDON, IL. THE TOWN WILL BE MADE A MORE BEAUTIFUL PLACE TO LIVE THROUGH THE PLANTING OF TREES AND SHRUBBERY. (LOCAL). MARGARET M MARSH, CHAIRMAN; SHELDON TOWN BOARD; CENTER ST; SHELDON, IL 60966. (#28652).

JULY 9 - 12, '76. SHELDON FUN DAYS, BICENTENNIAL 1976 PARADE, HONORED OLDEST CITIZENS. FESTIVAL, PARADE AT SHELDON HIGH SCHOOL, SHELDON PARK, MAIN ST. (LOCAL). MARGARET M MARSH, CHMN; SHELDON BOOSTER; 120 S 2ND; SHELDON, IL 60966. (#200016-239).

SHERMAN

AUG 30 - SEPT 1, '75. SHERMAN ETHNIC FESTIVAL. CEREMONY, EXHIBIT, FESTIVAL, LIVE PERFORMANCE AT ST JOHN VIANNEY CHURCH. (LOCAL). FATHER PETER MASCARI, DIR; ST JOHN VIANNEY CHURCH; SHERMAN, IL 62684. (#101891-1).

SEPT 4 - 6, '76. ETHNIC FESTIVAL - BICENTENNIAL CELEBRATION. FESTIVAL AT ST JOHN VIANNY CHURCH. (LOCAL). SALLY SCHANBACHER, CHMN; CAPITOL BICENTENNIAL COMMISSION; 500 E CAPITOL; SPRINGFIELD, IL 62701. (#200016-106).

SHIPMAN

RESTORATION OF LITTLE RED SCHOOLHOUSE. RESTORATION OF LITTLE RED SCHOOL IN SHIPMAN PARK FOR YOUTH AND ADULT GROUP MEETINGS. DISPLAYS OF PROJECTS AND ANTIQUES. (LOCAL). MRS LESTER ALWARD, CHAIRPERSON; SHIPMAN BICENTENNIAL COMMITTEE; SHIPMAN, IL 62685. (#33536).

SHIPMAN — CONTINUED

JULY 20 - 21, '76. SHIPMAN BICENTENNIAL HOMECOMING & PARADE. BICENTENNIAL COMM-KITCHEN BAND & ALL TOWN GROUPS-CHURCHES WILL HAVE RECORDS, PICTURES, HISTORIES BURIED IN SOUTHWESTERN TIME CAPSULE; PRESENTATION CEREMONY-LIVE RADIO-SHIPMAN BICENT PICNIC-BICENT COSTUMES CONTEST-ANTIQUE CARS. AT SHIPMAN COMMUNITY PARK. (LOCAL). MS LESTER ALWARD; SHIPMAN BICENTENNIAL COMMITTEE; SHIPMAN, IL 62685. (#200016-308).

SHIRLAND

AVENUE OF FLAGS IN SHIRLAND, IL. FLAGS & FLAG STANDS BOUGHT TO BE PLACED IN STREETS AS PERMANENT MARKERS. (LOCAL). PRENTICE GILLETT, DIRECTOR; SHIRLAND FIRE DEPARTMENT; SHIRLAND, IL 61079. (#33533).

PLANTING FLOWERS IN SHIRLAND, IL. PLANTED RED, WHITE & BLUE PETUNIAS ALONG STREETS TO PREPARE FOR PARADE. (LOCAL). HELEN WEAVER, CHAIRMAN; SHIRLAND BROWNIE TROOP; SHIRLAND, IL 61079. (#33535).

TOWNSHIP FLAG CONTEST IN SHIRLAND, IL. CONTEST BY SHIRLAND GRADE SCHOOL CHILDREN TO DESIGN A FLAG FOR TOWNSHIP USE. (LOCAL). FRANK L BOLIN, CHAIRMAN; SHIRLAND TOWNSHIP BOARD; BOX 65; SHIRLAND, IL 61079. (#33534).

JUNE 14, '75. FATHER-SON BANQUET WITH CEREMONY BY CIVIL WAR BUFFS. CEREMONY AT SHIRLAND UNITED METHODIST CHURCH. (LOCAL). FRANK L BOLIN; UNITED METHODIST WOMEN & UNITED METHODIST CHURCH OF SHIRLAND; BOX 65; SHIRLAND, IL 61079. (#200016-371).

SEPT 7, '75. ICE CREAM SOCIAL. FESTIVAL AT UNITED METHODIST CHURCHYARD. (LOCAL). FRANK L BOLIN; UNITED METHODIST WOMEN & CHURCH; BOX 65; SHIRLAND, IL 61079. (#200016-372).

JAN 24 - JUNE 19, '76. BICENTENNIAL EVENTS OF SHIRLAND, ILL JAN-JUN '76. 1/24 PICTORIAL HISTORY OF SHIRLAND TWP; 2/24 ICE CUTTING EVENT; 2/28 SENIOR CITIZENS' RECOGNITION DAY; 4/30 SHIRLAND FESTIVAL SINGERS & TRI-RIVER TRYERS 4-H SKIT; 5/7 HAPPY BIRTHDAY AMERICA; 6/19 CRAFTS & ITEMS OF YESTERYEAR. (LOCAL). FRANK L BOLIN; SHIRLAND BICENTENNIAL COMMITTEE; BOX 65; SHIRLAND, IL 61079. (#200016-373).

JULY 4 - 5, '76. JULY 4TH IN SHIRLAND, ILL. 7/4 UNITED METHODIST CHURCH SUN SERVICE & OPEN HOUSE AT 8AM; PARADE AT 10:30 FOLLOWED BY SHIRLAND CONGREGATIONAL OPEN HOUSE & AT 2:30PM FT TICONDEROGA BATTLE RE-ENACTED SEVERAL TIMES THROUGHOUT THE DAY. (LOCAL). FRANK L BOLIN; SHIRLAND BICENTENNIAL COMMITTEE; BOX 65; SHIRLAND, IL 61079. (#200016-374).

SILVIS

COMMUNITY IMPROVEMENT IN SILVIS, ILLINOIS. NEW PARK AND BALL DIAMOND, 2 NEW MUNICIPAL PARKING LOTS, AND AN ADDITION TO SCHOOL. (LOCAL). JAMES A GOODRICH, CHAIRMAN; SILVIS BICENTENNIAL COMMITTEE; 420 14TH ST; SILVIS, IL 61282. (#5067).

SKOKIE

ESSAY CONTEST IN SKOKIE, IL. SUBJECT WAS NILES TOWNSHIP HISTORY & WAS OPEN TO ALL HIGH SCHOOLS IN AREA. THREE WINNERS SPENT WEEK WORKING WITH SENATOR IN SPRINGFIELD. (LOCAL). HAROLD J FEDER, CHAIRMAN; NILES TOWNSHIP BICENTENNIAL COMMISSION; 5255 MAIN; SKOKIE, IL 60076. (#33532).

FILM ON HISTORICAL NILES TOWNSHIP, SKOKIE, IL. COLOR-AUDIO FILM ON THE HISTORY OF NILES TOWNSHIP: 'THE REMEMBERING EYE: A RETROSPECTION OF NILES TOWNSHIP'. REQUEST FOR SHOWING BY ALL EDUCATIONAL, CIVIC, CHURCH, SYNOGOGUE GROUPS. (LOCAL). DR HAROLD J FEDER, PROJ DIRECTOR; NILES TOWNSHIP BICENTENNIAL COMMISSION; 8528 CENTRAL PARK; SKOKIE, IL 60076. (#19459).

SKOKIE, IL, MEMORABILIA COLLECTION. TAPING CITIZENS' RECALL OF LOCAL HISTORY. COLLECTING PHOTOS & MEMORABILIA, LOCATING LANDMARKS, DISPLAY IN LIBRARY, PRINTING BROCHURE, POSTING BRONZE LANDMARK PLAQUES & COLLECTION TENDED BY HIST SOC. (LOCAL). MARIAN V HERSHENSON, ASSOC PLANNER; SKOKIE BICENT COMMITTE; 5127 OAKTON ST; SKOKIE, IL 60076. (#9367).

200 YEARS OF AMERICAN HISTORY. A PARADE WITH DIFFERENT COMMUNITY GROUPS REPRESENTING DIFFERENT EVENTS OR ERAS IN AMERICAN HISTORY. ENTERTAINMENT RELATED TO BICENTENNIAL. (LOCAL). MARIA V HERSHENSON; SKOKIE BICENT COMMITTEE; 5127 OAK ST; SKOKIE, IL 60022. (#9368-1).

AUG 3, '75. BICENTENNIAL PARADE. PARADE. (LOCAL). DR HAROLD J FEDER, COORD; NILES TOWNSHIP BICENTENNIAL COMMISSION; 8528 CENTRAL PARK; SKOKIE, IL 60076. (#200016-57).

AUG 3, '75. DRUM AND BUGLE CORPS COMPETITION. CORPS FROM FIVE STATES COMPETED. AT NILES WEST HIGH SCHOOL. (REGN'L). DR HAROLD J FEDER, COORD; NILES TOWNSHIP BICENTENNIAL COMMISSION; 8528 CENTRAL PARK; SKOKIE, IL 60076. (#200016-56).

OCT 17, '76. DEDICATION OF LANDSCAPED DEVELOPMENT. LANDSCAPING OF CANAL BANKS AND BIKEWAY, MEMORIAL GARDEN; 15 1/2 ACRES. (LOCAL). MARIAN V HERSHENSON; SKOKIE BICENT COMMITTEE; 5127 OAKTON ST; SKOKIE, IL 60076. (#9369-501).

SOUTH ELGIN

A FLAG FOR OUR VILLAGE IN FOUR COLORS, S ELGIN, IL. DESIGNED A FLAG FOR OUR VILLAGE IN A CONTEST WITH ALL VILLAGE RESIDENTS PARTICIPATING. A UNITED STATES SAVINGS BOND WAS GIVEN TO THE BEST DESIGN. WE NOW HAVE A VILLAGE FLAG FLYING AT OUR VILLAGE HALL. (LOCAL). MS WANDA L BOHNE, CHAIRMAN; SOUTH ELGIN BICENTENNIAL COMMISSION; 165 BEACH COURT; SOUTH ELGIN, IL 60177. (#29840).

JULY 4 - 5, '76. 4TH OF JULY CELEBRATION. A MOON WALK & TRACKLESS TRAIN WERE PROVIDED FOR AMUSEMENT, PLUS A PIE EATING CONTEST, HOT DOGS & ICE CREAM, MANY COVERED DISHES, COLD DRINKS, ANTIQUE CARS, CEREMONY WITH ALL OFFICIALS PRESENT, DISPLAY OF OLD PICTURES & A TIME CAPSULE BURIED FOR 2076. AT LIONS PARK, 500 FULTON ST. (LOCAL). MS WANDA L BOHNE, CHMN; SOUTH ELGIN BICENTENNIAL COMMISSION; 165 BEACH CT; SOUTH ELGIN, IL 60177. (#200016-406).

SOUTH HOLLAND

BICENTENNIAL PRAYER - S HOLLAND, IL. A PRAYER, BIBLE STUDY & EVANGELISM PROGRAM FOR THE BICENTENNIAL OF THE U S. AN INREACH AND OUTREACH PROGRAM FOR THE CHURCH. CAN BE USED ON AN INTERDENOMINATIONAL, COMMUNITY-WIDE BASIS. (NAT'L). REV JOHN F DE VRIES, DIRECTOR; WORLD HOME BIBLE LEAGUE; 16801 VAN DAM RD; SOUTH HOLLAND, IL 60473. (#6566). **ARBA GRANTEE.**

ETHNIC MURAL, SOUTH HOLLAND, IL. A LARGE MURAL FOR THE NEW BUILDING AT THORNTON COMMUNITY COLLEGE. THIS WILL DEPICT THE VARIOUS ETHNIC GROUPS OF THE COMMUNITY AND THEIR HISTORICAL ROLE IN AMERICAN HISTORY. (LOCAL). DR ROBERT L JACK, DEAN COMMUNITY SERVICES; THORNTON COMMUNITY COLLEGE; 50 W 162ND ST; SOUTH HOLLAND, IL 60433. (#19588).

MAR 8, '76. A BICENTENNIAL COMMEMORATIVE PROGRAM. A BICENTENNIAL FLAG WILL BE RAISED IN A CEREMONY TO BEGIN TCC BICENTENNIAL ACTIVITIES. AT MAIN CAMPUS - U LEVEL. (LOCAL). DR ROBERT L JACK, DEAN; THORNTON COMMUNITY COLLEGE; 50 W 162ND ST; SOUTH HOLLAND, IL 60473. (#104317-2).

MAR 18 - APR 15, '76. SERIES OF GUEST LECTURES ON LOCAL HISTORY. SEMINAR. (LOCAL). DR ROBERT L JACK, DEAN; THORNTON COMMUNITY COLLEGE; 50 W 162ND ST; SOUTH HOLLAND, IL 60473. (#104317-5).

APR 13 - 14, '76. SHOWING OF '1776' - MOVIE. EXHIBIT. (LOCAL). DR ROBERT L JACK, DEAN; THORNTON COMMUNITY COLLEGE; 50 W 162ND ST; SOUTH HOLLAND, IL 60473. (#104317-4).

MAY 20 - 21, '76. ETHNIC HERITAGE DAYS. A ONE DAY FESTIVAL OF PRESENTATIONS TO EMPHASIZE THE VARIED CULTURAL BACKGROUNDS OF THE COMMUNITY. (LOCAL). DR ROBERT L JACK, DEAN; THORNTON COMMUNITY COLLEGE; 50 W 162ND ST; SOUTH HOLLAND, IL 60473. (#104317-6).

JUNE 21 - 25, '76. POLITICAL MOVIE WEEK. COMPETITION. (LOCAL). DR ROBERT L JACK, DEAN; THORNTON COMMUNITY COLLEGE; 50 W 162ND ST; SOUTH HOLLAND, IL 60473. (#104317-3).

AUG 2, '76. DEDICATION OF PHASE II OF THORNTON COMMUNITY COLLEGE. DEDICATION OF NEW ADDITION TO TCC CAMPUS. ACENT ON ILLINOIS HISTORY. (LOCAL). DR ROBERT L JACK, DEAN; THORNTON COMMUNITY COLLEGE; 50 W 162ND ST; SOUTH HOLLAND, IL 60473. (#104317-1).

SPARTA

MR & MRS ALFRED A BROWN MEMORIAL MUSEUM. CATALOGING & PUTTING ON DISPLAY MUSEUM ITEMS. (LOCAL). HAROLD FRAZIER, CHAIRMAN OF BOARD; SPARTA MUSEUM BOARD; 126 W MAIN; SPARTA, IL 62286. (#33460).

OCT 31, '75. SPARTA HALLOWEEN MARDI GRAS. CROWNING OF MARDI GRAS QUEEN AND FULL DRESS BALL WILL BE INCLUDED IN THE FESTIVAL. (LOCAL). DON C WILEY, CHAIRMAN; RANDOLPH COUNTY BICENTENNIAL COMMISSION; RR 1; SPARTA, IL 62286. (#102705-1).

SPRING VALLEY

BICENTENNIAL WINDOW DISPLAYS, SPRING VALLEY, IL. DISPLAY OF ANTIQUES IN WINDOWS OF BUSINESS DISTRICT. (LOCAL). BEVERLY WEST, SECRETARY; SPRING VALLEY BICENTENNIAL COMMITTEE; 215 W GREENWOOD ST; SPRING VALLEY, IL 61362. (#29544).

CITY ENTRANCE SIGNS, SPRING VALLEY, IL. SIGNS WILL BE ERECTED AT ALL ENTRANCES TO THE CITY. (LOCAL). BEVERLY WEST, SECRETARY; SPRING VALLEY BICENTENNIAL COMMITTEE; 215 N GREENWOOD ST; SPRING VALLEY, IL 61362. (#29545).

HISTORICAL TOUR BY BUS - SPRING VALLEY, IL. A GUIDED TOUR OF ALL HISTORICAL PLACES. FLAGS TO BE PLACED ON THE GRAVES OF DECEASED VETERANS AND TWO REVOLUTIONARY SOLDIERS. (LOCAL). BEVERLY WEST, SECRETARY; SPRING VALLEY WOMENS CLUB; 215 N GREENWOOD ST; SPRING VALLEY, IL 61362. (#29534).

PAINTING OF FIRE HYDRANTS IN SPRING VALLEY, IL. ALL CITY HYDRANTS PAINTED AS REVOLUTIONARY CHARACTERS. (LOCAL). BEVERLY WEST, SECRETARY; BICENTENNIAL COMMITTEE OF SPRING VALLEY; 215 N GREENWOOD ST; SPRING VALLEY, IL 61362. (#29519).

AUG 3, '75. FLAG RAISING CEREMONY W/BAND SELECTION & SPEECHES. CEREMONY AT CITY PARK. (LOCAL). BEVERLY WEST, SECY; SPRING VALLEY BICENTENNIAL COMMITTEE; 215 N GREENWOOD ST; SPRING VALLEY, IL 61362. (#200016-221).

APR 5, '76. ETHNIC DINNER. FESTIVAL. (LOCAL). BEVERLY WEST, SECY; SPRING VALLEY BICENTENNIAL COMMITTEE; 215 N GREENWOOD ST; SPRING VALLEY, IL 61362. (#200016-223).

JULY 3, '76. BICENTENNIAL COSTUME BALL. FESTIVAL. (LOCAL). BEVERLY WEST, SECY; SPRING VALLEY BICENTENNIAL COMMITTEE; 215 N GREENWOOD ST; SPRING VALLEY, IL 61362. (#200016-220).

JULY 3, '76. COMMUNITY PARADE. PARADE. (LOCAL). BEVERLY WEST, SECY; SPRING VALLEY BICENTENNIAL COMMITTEE; 215 N GREENWOOD ST; SPRING VALLEY, IL 61362. (#200016-222).

SPRINGFIELD

ARTIST IN RESIDENCE; GWENDOLYN BROOKS - IL. THE POET-LAUREAT OF ILLINOIS WILL BE AVAILABLE TO SCHOOLS & COMMUNITY GROUPS TO READ AND DISCUSS HER POETRY AND ITS BACKGROUND. (ST-WIDE). JOSEPHINE K OBLINGER, PROJ DIRECTOR; LINCOLN AND COMMUNITY COLLEGE; SHEPHERD ROAD CAMPUS; SPRINGFIELD, IL 62708. (#16986).

ARTS, CRAFTS & ARCHITECTURE IN EARLY ILLINOIS. STUDY OF ART, CRAFTS & ARCHITECTURE IN ILLINOIS BEFORE 1860. EMPHASIS ON ARTISANS & THEIR RELATION TO NATIONAL TRENDS & LIFE IN ILL. AUTHOR IS BETTY MADDEN, CURATOR OF ART AT ILLINOIS STATE MUSEUM. (ST-WIDE). BETTY I MADDEN, CURATOR; ILLINOIS STATE MUSEUM; SPRING & EDWARDS STS; SPRINGFIELD, IL 62706. (#933).

BIBLIOGRAPHY OF ILLINOIS HISTORY 1763-1787. BIBLIOGRAPHY OF PUBLICATIONS ISSUED BY ILLINOIS STATE HISTORICAL LIBRARY & SOCIETY ON ILLINOIS HISTORY 1763-1787. ANNOTATION FOR EACH ITEM. DISTRIBUTED FREE TO SOCIETY MEMBERS, SCHOOLS, LIBRARIES, ETC. (ST-WIDE). OLIVE S FOSTER, SUPERVISOR SCHOOL SERVICES; ILLINOIS STATE HISTORICAL LIBRARY AND SOCIETY; OLD STATE CAPITOL; SPRINGFIELD, IL 62706. (#564).

BICENTENNIAL BITS BY CHILDREN IN SPRINGFIELD, IL. RADIO SPOTS PRODUCED WEEKLY ON WTAX BY 4TH GRADE CHILDREN OF WANDA COLLINS AT ENOS SCHOOL; MS COLLINS WAS GIVEN THE SCHOLASTIC TEACHER'S AWARD IN 1975. (LOCAL). WANDA COLLINS, 4TH GRADE TEACHER; ENOS SCHOOL; SPRINGFIELD, IL 62702. (#10152).

BICENTENNIAL TEACHER'S WORKSHOP - SPRINGFIELD, IL. 40 CHOSEN TEACHERS PREPARED A TEACHER'S RESOURCE GUIDE TO THE BICENTENNIAL. (LOCAL). DR JOHN KEISER, VICE PRESIDENT; SANGAMON STATE UNIV; SHEPHERD RD; SPRINGFIELD, IL 62708. (#11780).

CONFERENCE ON THE LIBRARY IN THE BICENTENNIAL, IL. CONFERENCE TO INFORM LIBRARIES OF THEIR ROLE AS INFORMATION RESOURCES FOR BICENTENNIAL ACTIVITIES; PROVIDE BACKGROUND OF ILLINOIS DURING AMERICAN REVOLUTION; & INITIATE BICENTENNIAL ACTIVITY. (ST-WIDE). CLYDE WALTON, PROJ DIRECTOR; ILLINOIS LIBRARY ASSOC; 716 N RUSH; CHICAGO, IL 60611. (#6481). **ARBA GRANTEE.**

COURSE ON THE AMERICAN REVOLUTION, SPRINGFIELD, IL. A GENERAL STUDIES, NON-TRANSFER COURSE ON THE ORIGINS, DEVELOPMENT & IMPACT OF THE AMERICAN REVOLUTION. (LOCAL). JOHN SQUIBB, SOCIAL SCIENCE DIVISION CHAIRMAN; LINCOLN LAND COMMUNITY COLLEGE; SHEPHERD RD; SPRINGFIELD, IL 62708. (#16753).

FILMS ON THE AMERICAN REVOLUTION - SPRINGFIELD, IL. 8 FILMS PRODUCED BY ENCYCLOPEDIA BRITANNICA WILL BE AVAILABLE TO SCHOOLS FREE OF CHARGE, SUPPORTED BY LLCC RESOURCES AS NEEDED; CLUBS & ORGANIZATIONS WILL BE INCLUDED AFTER CHRISTMAS. (LOCAL). JOSEPHINE K OBLINGER, ASST TO PRESIDENT; LINCOLN LAND COMMUNITY COLLEGE; SHEPHERD RD CAMPUS; SPRINGFIELD, IL 62708. (#16754).

FOLK DANCE WORKSHOP - SPRINGFIELD, IL. THE COMMUNITY EDUCATION WORKSHOP WILL TEACH ETHNIC DANCES OF THE 18TH CENTURY TO LEADERS OF VARIOUS ORGANIZATIONS, WHO WILL THEN TEACH THEIR GROUPS. (LOCAL). JOSEPHINE K OBLINGER, ASST TO PRESIDENT; LINCOLN LAND COMMUNITY COLLEGE; SHEPHERD RD CAMPUS; SPRINGFIELD, IL 62708. (#16756).

GRAVE RESTORATION PROJECT IN SPRINGFIELD, IL. LOCATE, RESTORE & MARK GRAVES OF ALL REVOLUTIONARY WAR SOLDIERS BURIED IN CEMETERIES WITHIN THE COLLEGE DISTRICT. (LOCAL). JOSEPHINE K OBLINGER, ASST TO PRESIDENT; LINCOLN LAND COMMUNITY COLLEGE; SHEPHERD RD CAMPUS; SPRINGFIELD, IL 62708. (#16755).

HONORARY FIFE AND DRUM CORPS - SPRINGFIELD, IL. CONSISTS OF 20 CHILDREN IN REVOLUTIONARY UNIFORM WITH FIFE AND DRUM. THIS GROUP IS PART OF EVERY BICENTENNIAL EVENT (BY REQUEST). HONOR GUARD IN UNIFORM IS ALSO PART OF THIS GROUP. (LOCAL). LOU HUEBNER, CHAIRMAN; CAPITAL BICENTENNIAL COMMISSION; 500 E CAPITOL; SPRINGFIELD, IL 62701. (#14369).

ILLINOIS BICENTENNIAL COMMEMORATIVE SCULPTURE. MONUMENTAL SCULPTURE COMMISSIONED TO COMMEMORATE ILLINOIS BICENTENNIAL CELEBRATION, TO BE ON PERMANENT DISPLAY IN CAPITOL COMPLEX. (ST-WIDE). MICHAEL J LINDERMAN, EXEC DIRECTOR; ILLINOIS BICENTENNIAL COMMISSION; 410 N MICHIGAN AVE; CHICAGO, IL 60611. (#27753). **ARBA GRANTEE.**

SPRINGFIELD — CONTINUED

ILLINOIS HISTORIC SITES BROCHURE. 24-PAGE HISTORICAL SITE BROCHURE FEATURING MAPS AND PHOTOGRAPHS TO STIMULATE INTEREST IN HISTORICAL SITES AND TRAVEL IN ILLINOIS. (ST-WIDE). MS SANDY GUETTLER, MANAGING DIRECTOR; ILLINOIS OFFICE OF TOURISM; 205 W WACKER DR; CHICAGO, IL 60606. (#16357).

LANDSCAPING OF EAST GARDEN OF EXEC MANSION, IL. LANDSCAPING AND REPLANTING OF THE EAST GARDEN OF THE GOVERNOR'S MANSION IN SPRINGFIELD. (ST-WIDE). CONSTANCE SMITH, SECRETARY; ILLINOIS EXECUTIVE MANSION ASSOC; OLD STATE CAPITOL; SPRINGFIELD, IL 62706. (#27766). **ARBA GRANTEE.**

LECTURE SERIES, SPRINGFIELD, IL. LECTURE SERIES ON HISTORY, ART, LITERATURE AND SCIENCE BY LEADING SPECIALISTS IN THESE FIELDS. (LOCAL). VIRGINIA MASCUNANA, CHAIRPERSON; SPRINGFIELD COLLEGE BICENT COMMITTEE; 1500 N 5TH ST; SPRINGFIELD, IL 62702. (#9998).

LITERARY PUBLICATION - SPRINGFIELD, IL. A LITERARY PUBLICATION WILL BE COMPILED ON THE HISTORY OF LITERATURE AND THE ARTS DURING THE AMERICAN REVOLUTION. (LOCAL). VIRGINIA MASCUNANA, CHAIRMAN; SPRINGFIELD COLLEGE BICENTENNIAL COMMITTEE; 1500 N 5TH; SPRINGFIELD, IL 62702. (#18529).

'THE LUCKY AMERICAN' :SPRINGFIELD, IL. PRODUCTION PRESENTS AN INSPIRING LOOK AT AMERICAN HERITAGE & LIFE THROUGH SUBTLE BUT IDENTIFIABLE SCENES; INSPIRES THE VIEWER FOR THE FUTURE OF AMRICANISM. A MULTI-MEDIA PRESENTATION. (LOCAL). S R POE, MGR P/R; CENTRAL ILLINOIS PUBLIC SERVICE COMPANY; 607 E ADAMS STREET; SPRINGFIELD, IL 62761. (#24523).

A MUSICAL CANTATA, SPRINGFIELD, IL. DEPICT AMERICA'S TRADITION THROUGH THE MEDIUM OF SONGS AND WORDS. (LOCAL). VIRGINIA MASCUNANA, CHAIRPERSON; SPRINGFIELD COLLEGE BICENT COMMITTEE; 1500 N 5TH ST; SPRINGFIELD, IL 62702. (#9997).

ORAL HISTORY: 'WE WERE THERE' - SPRINGFIELD, IL. 20 MINI-BIOGRAPHIES OF ILLINOISANS CLOSELY ASSOCIATED WITH SOUTHERN BAPTIST WORK IN ILLINOIS FROM 1906 TO 1976 WILL BE WRITTEN. THE MATERIAL WILL STRESS HUMAN INTEREST & INCLUDE LOCAL CULTURE & LIFE. (ST-WIDE). ROBERT J HASTINGS, COORDINATOR; ILLINOIS BAPTIST STATE ASSOC; BOX 3486; SPRINGFIELD, IL 62708. (#12106).

SANGAMON COUNTY BICENTENNIAL COOKBOOK - IL. RECIPES OF OLD FAMILIES AND CONTEMPORARY FAMILIES. FUNDS DERIVED FROM THIS SALE WILL BE USED TO FURNISH A CONFERENCE ROOM IN THE LINCOLN LIBRARY. (LOCAL). EILEEN MCCUNE, CHAIRMAN; ALTRUSA CLUB OF SPRINGFIELD; 80 BOB-O-LINK DR; SPRINGFIELD, IL 62704. (#14370).

'SANGAMON SAGA' - SPRINGFIELD, IL. A BOOK ON THE HISTORY OF THE AREA WAS WRITTEN & PUBLISHED. (LOCAL). EARL HENDERSON, DIRECTOR; CAPITOL BICENTENNIAL COMMISSION; 500 E CAPITOL; SPRINGFIELD, IL 62701. (#33540).

SANGAMON STATE UNIV'S ORAL HISTORY PROJECT. ORAL HISTORY OF CENTRAL ILL. CONDUCTED BY HISTORY DEPT. OF SANGAMON STATE UNIV. EMPHASIS ON SANGAMON CO., ILL. BUSINESS, INDUSTRY, LABOR & MINORITES. TRANSCRIPTS TO BE PLACED IN SELECTED ILLINOIS LIBRATIES. (ST-WIDE). CULLOM DAVIS, PROFESSOR, HISTORY DEPT; SANGAMON STATE UNIV; SPRINGFIELD, IL 62708. (#878). **ARBA GRANTEE.**

SPRINGFIELD, IL, STUDENT ARTS PUBLICATION. STUDENTS ARE PUTTING TOGETHER A PUBLICATION CONSISTING OF POETRY, ESSAYS, HISTORICAL AND CONTEMPORARY ART FORMS. (LOCAL). VIRGINIA MASCUNANA, CHAIRPERSON; SPRINGFIELD COLLEGE BICENT COMMITTEE; 1500 N 5TH ST; SPRINGFIELD, IL 62702. (#9999).

APR 9 - 10, '75. CONFERENCE ON THE LIBRARY IN THE BICENTENNIAL. CONFERENCE TO INFORM LIBRARIES OF THEIR ROLE AS INFORMATION RESOURCES FOR BICENTENNIAL ACTIVITIES; PROVIDE BACKGROUND OF ILLINOIS DURING AMERICAN REVOLUTION; & INITIATE BICENTENNIAL ACTIVITY. (ST-WIDE). CLYDE WALTON; ILLINOIS LIBRARY ASSOC; 716 N RUSH; CHICAGO, IL 60611. (#6481-501).

JUNE 21 - 22, '75. JUBILEE OLDE ENGLISH FAIRE. OLDE ENGLISH MARKET PLACE, STROLLING TROUBADOURS, PAGEANTS, KNIGHTS IN COMBAT, OTHER OLDE ENGLISH ACTIVITIES. PICNICKING AND CAMPING FACILITIES. LOCATION OF JUBILEE COLLEGE, ESTABLISHED IN 1835 BY BISHOP PHILANDER CHASE. JUBILEE COLLEGE BEING RESTORED FOR 1976. AT 15 MILES NORTHWEST OF PEORIA ON ROUTE 150 AT JUBILEE COLLEGE PARK. (ST-WIDE). DEPT OF CONSERVATION; DEPARTMENT OF CONSERVATION, DIVISION OF PARKS AND MEMORIALS; STATE OFFICE BUILDING; SPRINGFIELD, IL 62706. (#50322-1).

JUNE - AUG '75. CIVIL WAR RETREAT CEREMONY AT LINCOLN HOME NHS. REACTIVATED 114TH ILLINOIS INFANTRY REGIMENT PERFORMS THE RETREAT CEREMONY ONCE A WEEK THROUGHOUT THE SUMMER. (REGN'L). SUPT, LINCOLN HOME NHS; NATIONAL PARK SERVICE; 413 SOUTH EIGHTH STREET; SPRINGFIELD, IL 62701. (#6728-100).

JULY 4, '75 - JULY 6, '76. 'THREE PAGES PAST'. FESTIVAL. (LOCAL). EARL HENDERSON; CAPITOL BICENTENNIAL COMMISSION; 500 E CAPITOL; SPRINGFIELD, IL 62701. (#200016-329).

JULY 23 - 26, '75. AMERICAN FREEDOM TRAIN DISPLAY DAYS AT SPRINGFIELD, ILLINOIS. THE AMERICAN FREEDOM TRAIN WILL INCLUDE 10 EXHIBIT CARS & 2 SHOWCASE CARS DEPICTING DIFFERENT PHASES OF THE AMERICAN EXPERIENCE. ITS ARRIVAL WILL SERVE AS A CATALYST FOR LOCAL BICENTENNIAL CELEBRATIONS BY PEOPLE THROUGHOUT THIS NATION. (ST-WIDE). SY FREEDMAN, DIR OF P/R; THE AMERICAN FREEDOM TRAIN FOUNDATION; 5205 LEESBURG PIKE, SUITE 800; BAILEY'S XRDS, VA 22041. (#1776-138).

JULY 27, '75. NATL PK SVC '...A LITTLE LOOK AROUND' VISITS LINCOLN HOME NHS. THIS SHORT PROGRAM FEATURES ACTORS PORTRAYING FAMOUS AMERICANS OF THE PAST WHO'VE RETURNED TO SEE AMERICA'S GROWTH. (REGN'L). SUPERINTENDENT; NATIONAL PARK SERVICE - LINCOLN HOME NATL HISTORIC SITE; 413 S EIGHTH ST; SPRINGFIELD, IL 62701. (#5653-215).

AUG 8 - 17, '75. ILLINOIS STATE FAIR. CONSERVATION EXHIBITS. (REGN'L). MS JANET PICKETT; ILL DEPT OF CONSERVATION; 901 SOUTH SPRING; SPRINGFIELD, IL 62704. (#50272-80).

AUG 8 - 17, '75. VISIT OF HISTORY-MOBILE 'ETHNIC HISTORY IN ILLINOIS'. EXHIBIT AT ILLINOIS STATE FAIR. (LOCAL). CLIFFORD HAKA, FIELD REP; ILLINOIS STATE HISTORICAL SOCIETY; OLD STATE CAPITOL; SPRINGFIELD, IL 62706. (#200016-515).

OCT 10 - 12, '75. HISTORICAL CONFERENCE ON THE NORTHWEST TERRITORIES. STATE HISTORICAL SOCIETY WILL HOLD A CONFERENCE ON THE NORTHWEST TERRITORIES AFTER THE ANERICAN REVOLUTION, EMPHASIZING ASPECTS OF TRANSISTION FROM COLONIAL TO THE EARLY NATIONAL PERIODS. (REGN'L). DAN HOLT; ILLINOIS STATE HISTORICAL SOCIETY; OLD STATE CAPITOL; SPRINGFIELD, IL 62706. (#6590-501).

OCT 25, '75. AMERICAN ISSUES FORUM. AMERICAN ISSUES FORUM WITH VIDEO-TAPES, DISCUSSION LEADERS, INSTRUCTORS AND SUPPORTIVE SERVICES TO GROUPS EXPRESSING A DESIRE TO ENGAGE IN A STUDY OF THE ISSUES OF THE AIF. (LOCAL). CAROL GOODE, ASSISTANT; LINCOLNLAND COMMUNITY COLLEGE; SHEPHERD RD; SPRINGFIELD, IL 62708. (#103046-2).

DEC 5, '75. THE TODAY SHOW FEATURES THE STATE OF ILLINOIS. A CONTINUING WEEKLY SERIES OF PROGRAMS COMMEMORATING EACH STATE. ILLINOIS WAS ADMITTED INTO THE UNION IN DECEMBER, 1818. (NAT'L). STUART SCHULBERG, EX PROD; NATIONAL BROADCASTING CO; 30 ROCKEFELLER PLAZA; NEW YORK, NY 10020. (#7981-2).

DEC 13, '75. WORKSHOP FOR COLLEGE TEACHERS OF ILLINOIS HISTORY. WORKSHOP OF SPEAKERS & PANEL DISCUSSIONS FOR COLLEGE TEACHERS OF ILLINOIS STATE & LOCAL HISTORY. WILL PROVIDE FORUM FOR EXCHANGE OF IDEAS, MATERIALS & METHODS. AT OLD STATE CAPITAL. (ST-WIDE). RODGER BRIDGES; ILLINOIS STATE HISTORICAL SOCIETY; OLD STATE CAPITOL; SPRINGFIELD, IL 62706. (#4937-1).

DEC 24, '75 - JAN 10, '76. ARTISTS-IN-THE-PARKS PAINT THE BICENTENNIAL EXHIBIT. ORIGINAL ART EXHIBIT DEPICTING REVOLUTIONARY WAR-RELATED NPS SITES IN VARIOUS MEDIUMS. (REGN'L). DIRECTOR; NATIONAL PARK SERVICE & LINCOLN HOME; 413 S EIGHTH ST; SPRINGFIELD, IL 62701. (#200016-55).

FEB 12, '76. LINCOLN'S NEW SALEM-SPRINGFIELD POST ROAD. FORMAL DEDICATION SCHEDULES FOR LINCOLN'S BIRTHDAY, A 22-MILE PILGRIMAGE. OVER 1000 HORSEMEN IN CIVIL WAR & 19TH CENTURY CLOTHING RIDE ENTIRE ROUTE. ANTIQUE WAGONS, COACHES, SURREYS ALSO ENTERED. DEDICATION CEREMONIES AT NEW SALEM, SPRINGFIELD & OTHER POINTS. (ST-WIDE). AL MAVIS, DIRECTOR; SPRINGFIELD CONVENTION & TOURISM COMMISSION; ROCHESTER, IL 62563. (#103416-105).

FEB 26, '76. LECTURE SERIES: 'WOMEN IN THE REVOLUTION'. SEMINAR AT BECKER LIBRARY, 1500 N 5TH. (LOCAL). VIRGINIA MASCUNANA, CHMN; SPRINGFIELD COLLEGE BICENTENNIAL COMMITTEE; 1500 N 5TH; SPRINGFIELD, IL 62702. (#103875-3).

MAR 3 - APR 1, '76. LECTURE SERIES: 1776 ERA HISTORY. 5 LECTURES IN A 10-WEEK TIME PERIOD; LECTURERS WILL SPEAK ON A SUBJECT PERTINENT TO ILLINOIS DURING THE REVOLUTIONARY WAR PERIOD. (LOCAL). JOSEPHINE K OBLINGER, DIR; LINCOLNLAND COMMUNITY COLLEGE; SHEPHERD RD; SPRINGFIELD, IL 62708. (#103046-3).

MAR 11 - 13, '76. ILLINOIS STATE DAR CONFERENCE. ILLINOIS DAR BICENTENNIAL STATE CONFERENCE-ALSO HOSTING NATIONAL OFFICERS AND DIGNITARIES. AT FORUM 30 CONVENTION CENTER. (ST-WIDE). MRS LAWRENCE I BORDNER; ILLINOIS STATE DAR; 45 N PARK DR; CANTON, IL 61520. (#105197-1).

APR 4 - 12, '76. ART EXHIBITS. PROJECT ENTAILS EXHIBITS OF OIL PAINTINGS AND OTHER MEDIA OF FOREIGN PAINTERS IN THE FAR EAST. AT PRESENT BEING SHOWN ARE THE WORKS OF PHILIPPINE PAINTERS. AT CHARLES E BECKER LIBRARY. (LOCAL). VIRGINIA MASCUNANA; SPRINGFIELD COLLEGE BICENTENNIAL COMMITTEE; 1500 N 5TH ST; SPRINGFIELD, IL 62702. (#10000-1).

APR 15, '76. NATIONAL HIGH SCHOOL ORATORICAL CONTEST. THERE WILL BE A BICENTENNIAL DINNER ON APRIL 14TH AT 6PM. DINNER AND CONTEST WILL BE BY INVITATION. ALL HIGH SCHOOLS IN SPRINGFIELD AREA WILL BE PARTICIPATING - APPROX 250-300 PEOPLE. AT OLD STATE CAPITOL, HALL OF REPRESENTATIVES. (LOCAL). JEROME IRWIN, VICE-CHMN; THE AMERICAN LEGION, DEPT OF ILLINOIS; 126 W JEFFERSON ST; SPRINGFIELD, IL 61701. (#104892-1).

APR 16 - 18, '76. WAGON TRAIN FESTIVAL. ILLINOIS WAGON TRAIN (FROM CAIRO TO WISCONSIN LINE) IS ENTERTAINED, AND HOSTED BY 7TH ILLINOIS CAVALRY (RE-ENACTED) FOR THREE DAYS IN SPRINGFIELD, ILLINOIS AT THE STATE FAIRGROUNDS. AT ILLINOIS STATE FAIR GROUNDS. (ST-WIDE). ALVIN MAVIS, CHAIRMAN; ILLINOIS BICENTENNIAL COMMISSION; OAK HILLS ROAD; ROCHESTER, IL 62563. (#104826-1).

JUNE 1 - SEPT 30, '76. CIVIL WAR RETREAT CEREMONY AT LINCOLN HOME NHS. REACTIVATED 114TH ILLINOIS INFANTRY REGIMENT PERFORMS THE RETREAT CEREMONY TUESDAY EVENINGS THROUGHOUT THE SUMMER. AT 7 & JACKSON STS, SPRINGFIELD, IL. (REGN'L). SUPT, LINCOLN HOME NHS; NATIONAL PARK SERVICE; 413 SOUTH EIGHTH STREET; SPRINGFIELD, IL 62701. (#6728-600).

JUNE 7 - 12, '76. LINCOLN INTERSESSION. SIX DAY CONFERENCE BRINGING LEADING HISTORIANS TO DISCUSS THEMES OF 6 LINCOLN SITES. ALSO: BOOK/GUIDE/OTHER PUBLICATION, EDUCATIONAL COURSE. AT BROOKENS LIBRARY & HISTORIC LINCOLN SITES IN SPRINGFIELD AREA. (LOCAL). CHARLES B STROZIER; SANGAMON STATE UNIV; SHEPARD RD; SPRINGFIELD, IL 62708. (#11782-1).

JUNE 25 - JULY 4, '76. '1776' MUSICAL. HISTORIC OPERA ABOUT THE SIGNERS OF THE DECLARATION OF INDEPENDENCE STARRING A WELL-KNOWN PROFESSIONAL ACTOR IN THE ROLE OF BENJAMIN FRANKLIN. (LOCAL). MOLLY BECKER, DIRECTOR; ILLINOIS STATE HISTORICAL SOCIETY; SPRINGFIELD, IL 62706. (#104891-2).

JULY 4 - SEPT 11, '76. SOUND AND LIGHT AT THE OLD STATE CAPITOL. SOPHISTICATED OUTDOOR ELECTRONIC PRESENTATION USING MUSIC, SOUND EFFECTS, ETC, TO RE-CREATE THE STORY OF ABRAHAM LINCOLN'S RELATIONSHIP WITH THE HISTORIC OLD STATE CAPITOL. PRODUCED BY GUGGENHEIM PRODUCTIONS, INC, OF WASHINGTON, DC. AT OLD STATE CAPITOL. (REGN'L). WILLIAM K ALDERFER; ILLINOIS BICENTENNIAL COMMISSION & ABRAHAM LINCOLN ASSOCIATION; OLD STATE CAPITOL; SPRINGFIELD, IL 62706. (#103416-161).

JULY 5, '76. FREEDOM RALLY FOR THE BAPTISTS OF ILLINOIS. FOR THE GENERAL PUBLIC, FEATURING CONCERT BY ANDRE CROUCH & THE DISCIPLES. AT STATE FAIRGROUNDS. (ST-WIDE). ROBERT J HASTINGS, DIR; ILLINOIS BAPTIST STATE ASSOC; BOX 3486; SPRINGFIELD, IL 62708. (#101422-1).

JULY 10, '76. NATL PK SVC '...A LITTLE LOOK AROUND' COMES TO LINCOLN HOME NHS. THIS SHORT PROGRAM FEATURES ACTORS PLAYING THE ROLES OF FAMOUS AMERICANS OF THE PAST WHO'VE RETURNED TO SEE AMERICA'S GROWTH. RIIS PARK; AND 6/27 AT FLOYD BENNETT FIEL. AT IN THE PARK. (REGN'L). LINCOLN HOME NHS; NATIONAL ARK SERVICE; 413 SOUTH EIGHTH STREET; SPRINGFIELD, IL 62701. (#5653-15).

JULY 30 - 31, '76. BICENTENNIAL AIR SHOW. LIVE PERFORMANCE. (ST-WIDE). SALLY SCHANBACHER, CHMN; CAPITOL BICENTENNIAL COMMISSION; 500 E CAPITOL; SPRINGFIELD, IL 62701. (#200016-107).

AUG 12 - 22, '76. ILLINOIS STATE FAIR. NATIONS LARGEST LIVESTOCK SHOW, 12 ENTERTAINMENT STAGES, RICHEST HARNESS RACING MEETS, USAC DIRT CHAMPIONSHIPS & STOCK AUTO RACES. AT ILLINOIS STATE FAIRGROUNDS. (REGN'L). PAUL H KING, MANAGER; ILLINOIS STATE FAIR AGENCY; PO BOX 576; SPRINGFIELD, IL 62705. (#106292-1).

AUG 14 - 15, '76. UNITED STATES ARMED FORCES BICENTENNIAL CARAVAN. CARAVAN IS COMPOSED OF EXHIBIT VANS FOR EACH MILITARY SERVICE. PROJECT THEME IS 'HISTORY OF THE ARMED FORCES & THEIR CONTRIBUTIONS TO THE NATION.'. (LOCAL). JANET L PICKETT, CHMN; UNITED STATES ARMED FORCES BICENTENNIAL CARAVAN; 901 S SPRING ST; SPRINGFIELD, IL 62704. (#1775-633).

SEPT 5 - 18, '76. LINCOLN'S EIGHTH JUDICIAL CIRCUIT RIDE - HISTORIC RE-ENACTMENT. 'LINCOLN' WILL GREET AND TALK WITH THE PEOPLE AT VARIOUS SITES BETWEEN DANVILLE AND METAMORA. AT LOCAL HISTORIC SITES. (ST-WIDE). JANET L PICKETT, CHMN; ILLINOIS DEPARTMENT OF CONSERVATION - PROGRAM SERVICES SECTION; 901 S SPRING ST; SPRINGFIELD, IL 62704. (#100985-1).

SEPT 24, '76. LECTURE SERIES: 'SCIENCE & TECHNOLOGY IN THE REVOLUTION'. SEMINAR AT BECKER LIBRARY, 1500 N 5TH. (LOCAL). VIRGINIA MASCUNANA, CHMN; SPRINGFIELD COLLEGE BICENTENNIAL COMMITTEE; 1500 N 5TH; SPRINGFIELD, IL 62702. (#103875-2).

NOV 12, '76. LECTURE SERIES: 'ART IN THE AMERICAN REVOLUTION'. SEMINAR AT BECKER LIBRARY, 1500 N 5TH. (LOCAL). VIRGINIA MASCUNANA, CHMN; SPRINGFIELD COLLEGE BICENTENNIAL COMMITTEE; 1500 N 5TH; SPRINGFIELD, IL 62702. (#103875-1).

NOV 17 - 19, '76. A CANTATA, MUSICAL PROGRAM ABOUT AMERICA'S PAST. LIVE PERFORMANCE. (LOCAL). VIRGINIA MASCUNANA, CHMN; SPRINGFIELD COLLEGE BICENTENNIAL COMMITTEE; 1500 N 5TH; SPRINGFIELD, IL 62702. (#103875-4).

DEC 1 - 31, '76. DISPLAY OF ETHNIC CHRISTMAS TREES. EXHIBIT. (LOCAL). SALLY SCHANBACHER, CHMN; CAPITOL BICENTENNIAL COMMISSION; 500 E CAPITOL; SPRINGFIELD, IL 62701. (#109477-1).

FEB 1, '77. LA SALLE EXPEDITION II, A HISTORIC RE-ENACTMENT. THIS IS AN AUTHENTIC RE-ENACTMENT OF THE 1681 LASALLE EXPEDITION FROM MONTREAL, CANADA TO NEW ORLEANS, LA WHICH WILL BEGIN TOURING ON AUGUST 11, 1976 AND END ON APRIL 9, 1977. (LOCAL). REID H LEWIS, DIRECTOR; LA SALLE EXPEDITION II; 135 S LA SALLE ST, RM 411; CHICAGO, IL 60690. (#102805-48).

FEB 13, '77. DEDICATION OF VISITOR CENTER AT LINCOLN HOME NATIONAL HISTORIC SITE. EARLY IN THE FALL OF 1976, THE NEW VISITOR CENTER WILL BE DEDICATE. AT 7 & JACKSON STS, SPRINGFIELD, IL. (NAT'L). LINCOLN HOME NHS; NATIONAL PARK SERVICE; 413 S 8TH ST; SPRINGFIELD, IL 62701. (#6728-233).

STEELEVILLE

AVENUE OF FLAGS - STEELEVILLE, IL. FLAGS WILL BE PLACED ALONG BROADWAY TO FLY ON ALL HOLIDAYS. (LOCAL). DORIS SALGER, SECRETARY; AMERICAN LEGION AUXILIARY BBK POST #480; CHESTER ST; STEELEVILLE, IL 62288. (#25870).

BUILDING FOR SPORTS STADIUM - STEELEVILLE, IL. SPORTS FIELD BUILDING WILL BE BUILT WITH BASEBALL FIELD AND BLEACHERS. (LOCAL). HAROLD HARMSEN, COORDINATOR; AMERICAN LEGION POST #480; CHESTER ST; STEELEVILLE, IL 62288. (#25869).

STEELEVILLE — CONTINUED

PAINTING OF FIREPLUGS - STEELEVILLE, IL. FIREPLUGS WILL BE PAINTED AS REVOLUTIONARY WAR SOLDIERS. (LOCAL). PATRICIA FALKENHAIN, COORDINATOR; FUTURE BUSINESS LEADERS OF AMERICA; 512 N OAK; STEELEVILLE, IL 62288. (#26728).

PAINTING OF MURAL - STEELEVILLE, IL. 12 X 32' MURAL DEPICTING THE HISTORY OF STEELEVILLE WILL BE PAINTED BY HIGH SCHOOL STUDENTS. (LOCAL). PATRICIA FALKENHEIN, CHAIRMAN; MURAL COMMITTEE; 512 N OAK ST; STEELEVILLE, IL 62288. (#25867).

SPOON FOR 1976 BABIES - STEELEVILLE, IL. BICENTENNIAL COMMEMORATIVE SPOON FOR EACH BABY BORN IN STEELEVILLE IN 1976. (LOCAL). MRS ARTHUR BURNS, CHAIRMAN; STEELEVILLE BICENTENNIAL COMMITTEE; 506B S JAMES; STEELEVILLE, IL 62288. (#25868).

JULY 3, '76. DEDICATION OF FOUNDERS' MARKER. CEREMONY AT CIVIC CENTER, BROADWAY. (LOCAL). HON GERALD ZACHEIS, MAYOR; VILLAGE OF STEELEVILLE; VILLAGE HALL, 107 W BROADWAY; STEELEVILLE, IL 62288. (#108328-1).

JULY 5, '76. INDEPENDENCE DAY PARADE. PARADE. (LOCAL). FELIX A WILLIAMS; AMERICAN LEGION POST 480/STEELEVILLE LIONS CLUB; 104 W JASPER; STEELEVILLE, IL 62288. (#104399-1).

STERLING

HISTORY MULTI-MEDIA RESOURCE PROJ OF STERLING, ILL. REPOSITORY OF ALL MEDIA MATERIALS OF AMERICAN HISTORY. WILL CONTAIN BOOKS, PUBLICATIONS, MOVIES, VIDEO TAPES, SLIDES, FILMSTRIPS, TAPES, RECORDS, MAPS, PICTURES, CHARTS, MICROFILM, LOCALLY-PRODUCED ITEMS. (LOCAL). GUNNAR A BENSON, CHAIRMAN; AMERICAN REVOLUTION BICENTENNIAL COMMITTEE FOR STERLING, ILLINOI; 1513 4TH AVE; STERLING, IL 61081. (#5886).

'WHITESIDE COUNTY: ITS ORIGINS & HISTORY' BOOK. A REPRINT FROM THE BENT-WILSON HISTORY OF WHITESIDE COUNTY. (LOCAL). GUNNAR BENSON, PRESIDENT; STERLING-ROCK FALLS HISTORICAL SOCIETY; 213 3RD AVE, COLISIEUM BLDG; STERLING, IL 61081. (#1974).

JAN 1 - JULY 4, '75. 'I REMEMBER WHEN' CREATIVE WRITING CONTEST. FOR CITIZENS OF AGE 50 & OVER WHO ARE NOW HAVE BEEN RESIDENTS OF WHITESIDE COUNTY - 500 TO 1000 WORDS REQUIRED. (LOCAL). JEANNETTE ERICKSON; WHITESIDE COUNTY GENEALOGISTS; 613 W 13TH ST; STERLING, IL 61081. (#6068-501).

APR 19, '75 - DEC 4, '76. MUSEUM OPEN HOUSE. REVOLUTION EXHIBIT, GUNS, DOCUMENTS, FLAGS, SLIDE PROJECTIONS. AT STERLING MUNICIPAL COLISEUM THIRD AVE AT E THIRD ST NO PARKING PROB. (LOCAL). GUNNAR BENSON; STERLING-ROCK FALLS HISTORICAL SOCIETY; 1513 FOURTH AVE; STERLING, IL 61081. (#50435-1).

AUG 18 - SEPT 2, '75. DISPLAY OF FARM MACHINERY AND PRODUCTS AT MORRISON MALL. FARM MACHINERY & PRODUCTS WILL BE DISPLAYED IN PORTABLE CASES TO ILLUSTRATE TODAYS TECHNOLOGY. A PAMPHLET WILL ACCOMPANY THESE DISPLAYS TO LEAVE A WRITTEN RECORD OF AGRICULTURAL ACCOMPLISHMENTS. (LOCAL). K O MILLER; WHITESIDE COUNTY BICENTENNIAL COMMISSION; 207 W MAIN ST; MORRISON, IL 61270. (#7766-502).

SEPT 3 - 9, '75. DISPLAY AT COLISEUM OF FARM MACHINERY AND PRODUCTS. FARM MACHINERY & PRODUCTS WILL BE DISPLAYED IN PORTABLE CASES TO ILLUSTRATE TODAYS TECHNOLOGY. A PAMPHLET WILL ACCOMPANY THESE DISPLAYS TO LEAVE A WRITTEN RECORD OF AGRICULTURAL ACCOMPLISHMENTS. (LOCAL). K O MILLER; WHITESIDE COUNTY BICENTENNIAL COMMISSION; 207 W MAIN ST; MORRISON, IL 61270. (#7766-503).

OCT 1, '75 - MAY 1, '76. ART CONTEST IN SCHOOLS. HISTORY MULTI-MEDIA RESOURCE PROJ OF STERLING, ILL. REPOSITORY OF ALL MEDIA MATERIALS OF AMERICAN HISTORY. WILL CONTAIN BOOKS, PUBLICATIONS, MOVIES, VIDEO TAPES, SLIDES, FILMSTRIPS, TAPES, RECORDS, MAPS, PICTURES, CHARTS, MICROFILM, LOCALLY-PRODUCED ITEMS. (LOCAL). GUNNAR A BENSON, CHAIRMAN; AMERICAN REVOLUTION BICENTENNIAL COMMITTEE FOR STERLING, ILLINOIS; 1513 4TH AVE; STERLING, IL 61081. (#5886-502).

JULY 3, '76. GALA FOURTH OF JULY CELEBRATION. EXHIBIT, PARADE. (LOCAL). GUNNAR A BENSON, CHAIRMAN; AMERICAN REVOLUTION BICENTENNIAL COMMITTEE FOR STERLING, ILLINOIS; 1513 4TH AVE; STERLING, IL 61081. (#5886-501).

STONE PARK

MAY 28 - JULY 4, '76. ITALIAN AMERICAN BICENTENNIAL CELEBRATION. FESTIVAL AT ICC BUILDING & GROUNDS. (LOCAL). REV AUGUST FECCIA, DIR; ITALIAN CULTURAL CENTER; 1621 N 39TH AVE; STONE PARK, IL 60165. (#103193-1).

STREATOR

JULY 4, '76. 4TH OF JULY CELEBRATION. STREATOR, ILLINOIS, 4TH OF JULY CELEBRATION. 4TH OF JULY CELEBRATION TO INCLUDE DRUM AND BUGLE CORPS AND OTHER REVOLUTIONARY WAR PERIOD EVENTS. (LOCAL). DALE CHIAVENE, CHAIRMAN; STREATOR BICENTENNIAL COMMISSION; 625 W BLUFF; STREATOR, IL 61364. (#5721-501).

SUBLETTE

FEB 28, '76. BICENTENNIAL DANCE. FESTIVAL AT GREEN RIVER SADDLE CLUB. (LOCAL). FLOYD PRY, DIRECTOR; SUBLETTE BICENTENNIAL COMMISSION; SUBLETTE, IL 61367. (#104248-6).

APR 30, '76. GERMAN FOLK FESTIVAL. FESTIVAL AT SUBLETTE COMMUNITY BUILDING. (LOCAL). DON J DINGES, CHAIRMAN; SUBLETTE BICENTENNIAL COMMISSION; 208 W 3RD ST; SUBLETTE, IL 61367. (#104546-8).

JUNE 18 - 20, '76. PROGRESS DAYS IN SUBLETTE. THE WEEKEND WILL INCLUDE VARIOUS COMPETITIONS, DANCES AND AN ICE CREAM SOCIAL. (LOCAL). MIKE HECKMAN, CO-CHAIRMAN; LEE COUNTY BICENTENNIAL COMMISSION; PO BOX 348; DIXON, IL 61021. (#104268-3).

SUGAR GROVE

BICENTENNIAL COURSE OFFERING, SUGAR GROVE, IL. DAY AND NIGHT CLASSES IN ADULT EDUCATION AND BACCALAUREATE PROGRAMS IN HISTORY; SUBJECT MATTER WILL BE MODIFIED TO A BICENTENNIAL THEME. (LOCAL). J WILLIAM HOBAN, ASST DEAN OF INSTRUCTION; WAUBONSEE COMMUNITY COLLEGE; RTE 47 & HARTER RD; SUGAR GROVE, IL 60554. (#14426).

BICENTENNIAL DISPLAYS IN SUGAR GROVE, IL. PROJECT CONSISTS OF DISPLAYS ON EVENTS, LEADERS, ARTIFACTS OF NATIONAL, STATE & LOCAL HISTORY. (LOCAL). ADAH NEUBAUER, DIRECTOR OF LIBRARY; WAUBONSEE COMMUNITY COLLEGE; RTE 47 & HARPER RD; SUGAR GROVE, IL 60554. (#14424).

BICENTENNIAL PRAIRIE, SUGAR GROVE, IL. PROJECT IS THE REPLANTING OF A ONE ACRE PLOT OF GROUND ON CAMPUS; PLANTS WILL BE TYPICAL OF ILLINOIS PRAIRIES. (LOCAL). RAY HAUSER, HISTORY INSTRUCTOR; WAUBONSEE COMMUNITY COLLEGE; RTE 47 & HARTER RD; SUGAR GROVE, IL 60554. (#14423).

COMMEMORATIVE SCULPTURE, SUGAR GROVE, IL. A SCULPTURE IN HONOR OF THE BICENTENNIAL WILL BE PLACED ON MAIN CAMPUS. (LOCAL). DEE RYNESS, COORDINATOR OF INSTRUCTION; WAUBONSEE COMMUNITY COLLEGE; RT 47 & HARTER RD; SUGAR GROVE, IL 60554. (#14422).

REPOSITORY FOR LOCAL HISTORY OF SUGAR GROVE, IL. A CARD CATALOG OF ALL MATERIALS, ARTIFACTS AND RELICS FROM THE COMMUNITIES IN THE COLLEGE DISTRICT. (LOCAL). ADAH NEUBAUER, LIBRARY DIRECTOR; WAUBONSEE COMMUNITY COLLEGE; RT 47 & HARTER RD; SUGAR GROVE, IL 60554. (#14421).

SPEAKERS BUREAU IN SUGAR GROVE, IL. TALKS TO LOCAL GROUPS ON SELECTED TOPICS PERTINENT TO THE BICENTENNIAL THEME. (LOCAL). DAVE ROBINSON, PUBLIC RELATIONS DIRECTOR; WAUBONSEE COMMUNITY COLLEGE; RTE 47 & HARTER RD; SUGAR GROVE, IL 60554. (#14427).

TV PRODUCTION PROJECT IN SUGAR GROVE, IL. A CREDIT COURSE INVOLVING WRITING, PRODUCING, DIRECTING AND RECORDING OF A TAPE WHICH IS AIRED ON LOCAL CABLE TV. (LOCAL). ROBERT GREGORY, CHAIRMAN; WAUBONSEE COMMUNITY COLLEGE; RTE 47 & HARPER RD; SUGAR GROVE, IL 60554. (#14425).

'1776' - A MUSICAL PRODUCTION. LIVE PERFORMANCE. (LOCAL). LUCILLE HALFVARSON, CHMN; WAUBONSEE COMMUNITY COLLEGE; RTE 47 AT HARTER RD; SUGAR GROVE, IL 60554. (#101830-3). **(??).**

DEC '75. AMERICAN CHORAL MUSIC. LIVE PERFORMANCE. (LOCAL). LUCILLE HALFVARSON, CHMN; WAUBONSEE COMMUNITY COLLEGE; RTE 47 AT HARTER RD; SUGAR GROVE, IL 60554. (#101830-2).

SULLIVAN

ADOPTION OF A COUNTY FLAG - SULLIVAN, ILLINOIS. ADOPT ONE OF TWO MOULTRIE FLAGS WHICH FLEW DURING REVOLUTION, NAMED FOR GENERAL WILLIAM MOULTRIE FROM WHOM OUR COUNTY GOT ITS NAME. (LOCAL). MARY L STORM, CHAIRMAN; MOULTRIE COUNTY BICENT COMMISSION; BOX 2; LOVINGTON, IL 61937. (#8230).

FILMSTRIP ON HISTORY OF MOULTRIE COUNTY, ILLINOIS. A 20 MINUTE SILENT FILMSTRIP ILLUSTRATING THE HISTORY & HERITAGE OF MOULTRIE COUNTY. A NARRATIVE WILL ACCOMPANY THE FILM. (LOCAL). JANET RONEY, CHAIRMAN; MOULTRIE CO BICENTENNIAL COMMISSION; RR 1; SULLIVAN, IL 61951. (#8229).

JUNE 11 - 13, '76. SULLIVAN LAKE FESTIVAL. FESTIVAL. (LOCAL). MARY STORM; MOULTRIE COUNTY BICENTENNIAL COMMISSION; 21 COTTONTAIL LANE; SULLIVAN, IL 61951. (#200016-115).

JULY 1 - 3, '76. BICENTENNIAL QUILT DISPLAY. EXHIBIT. (LOCAL). MARY STORM, CHMN; MOULTRIE COUNTY BICENTENNIAL COMMISSION; 21 COTTONTAIL LANE; SULLIVAN, IL 61951. (#200016-117).

SEPT 16, '76. EIGHTH JUDICIAL CIRCUIT RIDE. REENACTMENT OF THE 8TH JUDICIAL COURT RIDE. (ST-WIDE). PHYLLIS EUBANKS, CHMN; ILLINOIS DEPARTMENT OF CONSERVATION; 901 S SPRING ST; SPRINGFIELD, IL 62706. (#200016-116).

SUMMIT

JULY 4 - 23, '76. BICENTENNIAL DEMONSTRATION OF WATERBORNE MASS TRANSPORTATION. EXHIBIT AT PORT OF SUMMIT BOAT CLUB DOCK, ILLINOIS WATERWAY. (ST-WIDE). MORRIS FELDMAN, CHAIRMAN; VILLAGE OF SUMMIT, ILLINOIS BICENTENNIAL COMMISSION; 631 N SHAW CT; SCHAUMBURG, IL 60172. (#19977-1).

TAMAROA

ROOTS SCHOOL MUSEUM PROJECT IN TAMAROA, ILLINOIS. RESTORED ONE-ROOM SCHOOL SHOWING 19TH CENTURY FURNITURE, CLOTHING & ARTIFACTS WILL BE THE SUBJECT OF HISTORIC TOUR. TOURS BY APPOINTMENT. (LOCAL). CALVIN IBENDAHL, PROJ DIRECTOR; ROUTE 1; TAMAROA, IL 62888. (#6742).

TAYLORVILLE

CHRISTIAN COUNTY LOG CABIN RESTORATION - IL. RESTORATION AND RELOCATION OF TWO-STORY LOG CABIN ON GROUNDS OF CHRISTIAN COUNTY HISTORICAL SOCIETY MUSEUM IN TAYLORVILLE. (LOCAL). DON WAREHAM, CHAIRMAN; CHRISTIAN COUNTY BICENTENNIAL COMMISSION; 400 E MAIN; TAYLORVILLE, IL 62568. (#30405).

JUNE 13, '76. DRUM AND BUGLE CORPS FIELD DEMONSTRATION. COMPETITION, FESTIVAL. (LOCAL). DON WAREHAM; CHRISTIAN COUNTY BICENTENNIAL COMMISSION; 400 EAST MAIN; TAYLORVILLE, IL 62568. (#200016-195).

JULY 4, '76. LOG CABIN DEDICATION. FESTIVITIES INCLUDE: ENTERTAINMENT, EXHIBITS, MUSEUM TOUR, REFRESHMENTS & SPEAKERS. AT CHRISTIAN CO MUSEUM, RT 29 & 48, AT INTERSECTION. (LOCAL). ROSELLA BROOKENS, SEC; CHRISTIAN COUNTY BICENTENNIAL COMMISSION; R R 1; OWANECO, IL 62555. (#106214-1).

SEPT 18, '76. LINCOLN'S EIGHTH JUDICIAL CIRCUIT RIDE. LIVE PERFORMANCE. (ST-WIDE). PHYLLIS EUBANKS, COORD; ILLINOIS DEPARTMENT OF CONSERVATION; 901 S SPRING ST; SPRINGFIELD, IL 62706. (#200016-194).

TEUTOPOLIS

REPRINT OF 1926 HISTORY OF TEUTOPOLIS, IL. TEUTOPOLIS AREA BICENTENNIAL FOUNDATION IS REPRINTING '1926 HISTORICAL SKETCH OF TEUTOPOLIS & ST FRANCIS CHURCH' IN LIMITED EDITION OF 500 COPIES. (ST-WIDE). MRS ALPHONSE HARTKE, SECRETARY; TEUTOPOLIS AREA BICENTENNIAL FOUNDATION; BOX 341; TEUTOPOLIS, IL 62467. (#33726).

TEUTOPOLIS BICENTENNIAL PARK PROJECT - IL. TEUTOPOLIS BICENTENNIAL PARK PROJECT WILL IMPROVE A COMMUNITY PARK. (LOCAL). EDWARD JANSEN, COORDINATOR; RECREATION BOARD OF THE VILLAGE OF TEUTOPOLIS; TEUTOPOLIS, IL 62467. (#27804). **ARBA GRANTEE.**

TEUTOPOLIS, IL, BICENTENNIAL FOUNDATION PROJECTS. PROJECTS WILL INCLUDE: OLD BUILDING RESTORATION, PARADE & FESTIVAL; AND REPRINTING 500 COPIES OF 'HISTORICAL SKETCH OF TEUTOPOLIS AND ST FRANCIS CHURCH'. (LOCAL). MRS ALPHONSE HARTKE, SECRETARY; TEUTOPOLIS AREA BICENT FOUNDATION; 210 N JOHN ST; TEUTOPOLIS, IL 62467. (#10492).

OCT 12, '75. ZWEI-HUNDERT-JAHR-DEUTSCHES-FEST. FESTIVAL AT ST FRANCIS MONASTERY. (LOCAL). MRS MARYELLEN RAUCH, CHMN; TEUTOPOLIS AREA BICENTENNIAL FOUNDATION; WEST MAIN ST; TEUTOPOLIS, IL 62467. (#200016-58).

FEB 22 - NOV 7, '76. TEUTOPOLIS MONASTERY MUSEUM TOUR. THE MUSEUM, BUILT IN 1800, WAS THE FIRST HOME OF THE FRANCISCANS IN CENTRAL U S; 20 ROOMS ARE ON DISPLAY, SOME WITH ORIGINAL FURNISHINGS; THE TOUR WILL BE OFFERED ON THE FIRST SUNDAY OF THE MONTH AND TAKES AT LEAST ONE HOUR. AT FORMER NOVITIATE BLDG, S GARRETT ST. (LOCAL). MARY ELLEN RAUCH, CHMN; TEUTOPOLIS AREA BICENTENNIAL FOUNDATION; 303 W MAIN ST, BOX 624; TEUTOPOLIS, IL 62467. (#105118-1).

JULY 3, '76. DEDICATION OF MONASTERY PARK. CEREMONY. (LOCAL). LUCILLE HOEDEBECKE, CHMN; TEUTOPOLIS BICENTENNIAL COMMISSION; PO BOX 201; TEUTOPOLIS, IL 62467. (#200016-87).

TIMEWELL

JULY 4, '75. AMERICAN LEGION CHICKEN DINNER & SPECIAL BICENTENNIAL PROGRAM. OPENING, FESTIVAL. (LOCAL). MARJORIE LEAVES, CHAIRMAN; BROWN COUNTY BOARD & BICENTENNIAL COMMISSION; MT STERLING, IL 62353. (#8189-501).

JULY 4, '76. TIMEWELL LEGION FESTIVAL. CHICKEN DINNER, CHURCH SERVICE. (LOCAL). MARJORIE CLEAVES, COORD; BROWN COUNTY BICENTENNIAL COMMISSION; RR 1; TIMEWELL, IL 62375. (#200016-193).

TINLEY PARK

BICENTENNIAL HORSE TROOP PARADE IN TINLEY PARK, IL. PART OF TINLEY PARK'S MOUNTED POLICE FORCE WILL PARTICIPATE IN THE BICENT FESTIVAL PARADE. (LOCAL). DR ROBERT J KOVARIK; TINLEY PARK BICENT COMMISSION; 17355 S 68TH COURT; TINLEY PARK, IL 60477. (#6058-1).

BICENTENNIAL PARK & RECREATIONAL AREA-TINLEY PK IL. COMBINATION OF ACTIVE & LEISURE RECREATION. DESIGN EMPHASIS ON ESTHETICS & USE OF NATURAL OBJECTS. OVER 300 TREES PROMISED FROM AROUND THE WORLD. PARK WILL

TINLEY PARK — CONTINUED

REFLECT DIVERSE ORIGINS OF AMERICANS. (LOCAL). DR ROBERT J KOVARIK, CHAIRPERSON; TINLEY PARK BICENTENNIAL COMMISSION; 17355 SO 68 COURT; TINLEY PARK, IL 60477. (#3912).

HISTORIC PRESERVATION PGM OF TINLEY PARK, ILL. PRESERVATION OF COMMUNITY ARTIFACTS, DOCUMENTS, RECORDS, PHOTOS, ORAL HISTORY, ETC. CRIATION OF THE BREMEN HISTORICAL SOCIETY. TEMPORARY OFFICE IN THE TINLEY PARK LIBRARY. (LOCAL). DR ROBERT KOVARIK, CHAIRPERSON; TINLEY PARK BICENTENNIAL COMMISSION; 17355 S 68TH COURT; TINLEY PARK, IL 60477. (#875). **ARBA GRANTEE.**

OLD ZION LUTHERAN CHURCH PRESERVATION, ILLINOIS. ACQUISITION, PRESERVATION & DEVELOPMENT OF CHURCH AS A LIVING, HISTORICAL MONUMENT. ADJOINING STRUCTURE AS COMMUNITY CENTER, COMMUNITY MUSEUM, FINAL HEADQUARTERS FOR BREMEN HISTORICAL SOCIETY. (LOCAL). DR ROBERT J KOVARIK, CHAIRPERSON; TINLEY PARK BICENTENNIAL COMMISSION; 17355 SO 68 COURT; TINLEY PARK, IL 60477. (#3910).

AUG 26 - SEPT 1, '75. FALL FESTIVAL: AMERICA'S HERITAGE. PARADE ON 8/31/75 4:00P.M. FLOATS: BIC THEMES EACH EVENING: CARNIVAL AND ENTERTAINMENT: GERMAN ETHNIC AT 159TH & HARLEM. 7:30 P.M. TO 12:00 A.M. (LOCAL). MARCIA WISE; COMMUNITY FALL FESTIVAL ASSOC.; 6880 W 173RD PLACE; TINLEY PARK, IL 60477. (#50102-1).

OCT 10 - 18, '75. LET US ENTERTAIN YOU: BICENTENNIAL PRODUCTION. FIVE LIVE PLAYS: AM REVOL; OLD WEST; TURN OF CENTURY; THIRTIES; CONTEMPORARY ONLY ON OCT. 10 & 11, 17 & 18. AT 6707 175TH. (LOCAL). DOLORES FITTANTO; ST GEORGE CHURCH; 16317 65TH AVE; TINLEY PARK, IL 60477. (#50103-1).

NOV 15, '75. HERITAGE BALL: 1975 DINNER PROGRAM DANCE FUND RAISING. RAISE FUNDS FOR BIC PROJECTS. AWARDS TO CONTRIBUTORS IN ENERGY OR FUNDS, DINNER, ENTERTAINMENT, PROGRAM, DANCE. AT BREMENHOUSE RESTAURANT, 159TH & OAK PARK AVE. (LOCAL). WALT JAGIELLO; TINLEY PARK BICENTENNIAL COMMISSION; 16842 GAYNELLE; TINLEY PARK, IL 60477. (#50101-1).

MAY 9, '76. WAGON TRAIN & PROCLAMATION REVIEW. CEREMONY AT STONEBRIDGE SHOPPING CENTER, 175TH & KETHOFUE. (LOCAL). MARTIN KAUCHAK, CHAIRMAN; VILLAGE & BICENTENNIAL COMMISSION OF HAZEL CREST; HAZEL CREST, IL 60429. (#200016-390).

NOV 13, '76. BICENTENNIAL HERITAGE BALL. COCKTAILS & DINNER; PROGRAM HONORING COMMUNITY MEMBERS & BICENT COMM MEMBERS. AT BREMENHOUSE RESTAURANT. (LOCAL). DR ROBERT KOVARIK; TINLEY PARK BICENT COMM; 6819 KINGSTON RD; TINLEY PARK, IL 60477. (#200016-309).

TISKILWA

JULY 30 - AUG 1, '76. BICENTENNIAL FESTIVAL. FESTIVAL INCLUDES BAR-B-QUE, A DANCE AND MANY OTHER EVENTS. AT WEST PARK ON MAIN ST. (LOCAL). LEONARD MCMACAULEY, DIR; TISKILWA LIONS CLUB; TISKILWA, IL 61368. (#104546-2).

TUSCOLA

BEAUTIFICATION OF TUSCOLA, ILLINOIS. THE MAIN STREET OF TUSCOLA IS TO BE WIDENED & LANDSCAPED. (LOCAL). JUNEY A ROWE, CHAIRPERSON; TUSCOLA BICENT COMMISSION; 100-1/2 W MAIN ST; TUSCOLA, IL 61953. (#9398).

JULY 7 - 10, '76. DOUGLAS COUNTY CHAUTAUQUA IN TUSCOLA. FESTIVITIES INCLUDE FARMER DAYS, AIR FORCE DRUM & BUGLE CORPS, DANCES & PARADES. (LOCAL). JUNEY ROWE, CHAIRMAN; DOUGLAS COUNTY BICENTENNIAL COMMISSION; BOX 55; TUSCOLA, IL 61953. (#106545-1).

ULLIN

SHAWNEE MUSEUM FOR SOUTHERN ILLINOIS ARTIFACTS. SHAWNEE COLLEGE WILL PROVIDE A BUILDING THAT WILL BE DESIGNATED THE SHAWNEE COLLEGE BICENTENNIAL MUSEUM SO THAT AREA HISTORY CAN BE PRESENTED AND PRESERVED. (LOCAL). DALE BISHOP, EVENING COLLEGE DEAN; SHAWNEE COLLEGE; SHAWNEE COLLEGE RD; ULLIN, IL 62992. (#16521).

THE SHAWNEE NATURE TRAIL - ULLIN, IL. A NATURE TRAIL WILL BE CREATED ON CAMPUS TO PRESERVE THE CONDITIONS OF EARLY AMERICAN FLORA IN THE SHAWNEE NATIONAL FOREST. (ST-WIDE). DALE BISHOP, EVENING COLLEGE DEAN; SHAWNEE COLLEGE; SHAWNEE COLLEGE RD; ULLIN, IL 62992. (#16520).

SEPT 19, '75. FIVE COUNTY AREA BICENTENNIAL CONFERENCE. A DINNER CONFERENCE WILL BE HELD AT SHAWNEE COLLEGE, SO THAT AREA GROUPS CAN PRESENT THEIR BICENTENNIAL PLANS. (LOCAL). DALE BISHOP, EVENING DEAN; SHAWNEE COLLEGE; SHAWNEE COLLEGE RD; ULLIN, IL 62992. (#102986-2).

SEPT 12, '76. PROFESSIONAL & AMATEUR CRAFTS SHOW. EXHIBIT. (LOCAL). DALE BISHOP, EVENING DEAN; SHAWNEE COLLEGE; SHAWNEE COLLEGE RD; ULLIN, IL 62992. (#102986-1).

URBANA

FREE BLACK RESPONSE TO AMERICAN RACISM - BOOK. RESEARCH & REVISION PROJECT TO WRITE A BOOK ON THE REACTION OF FREE BLACK PEOPLE TO RACISM THRU 1865. (NAT'L). ROBERT L HARRIS, JR, PROJ DIRECTOR; UNIVERSITY OF ILLINOIS; URBANA, IL 61801. (#4936).

'FROM THE HEARTS OF MEN', TV PROGRAM, URBANA, IL. A 30 MINUTE TELEVISION PROGRAM OF PATRIOTIC BAND MUSIC ON TAPE. (LOCAL). CHARLES E FLYNN, ASST TO PRESIDENT; UNIV OF ILLINOIS; URBANA, IL 61801. (#14322).

ILLINOIS IN AMERICAN REVOLUTION, 1770-1780, BOOK. A VOLUME OF DOCUMENTS AND INTERPRETATION OF ILLINOIS'S ROLE IN THE AMERICAN REVOLUTION. (ST-WIDE). ROBERT M SUTTON, PROFESSOR OF HISTORY; UNIV OF ILLINOIS; URBANA, IL 61801. (#14320).

MCCULLOUGH FARM MUSEUM - URBANA, IL. RESTORATION OF FARM COMPLEX FOR USE AS A MUSEUM. (LOCAL). ROBIN HALL, CHAIRMAN; URBANA PARK DISTRICT; 901 N BROADWAY; URBANA, IL 61801. (#27882). **ARBA GRANTEE.**

THEORY & AMERICAN SOCIETY RSRCH PROJ, URBANA, ILL. HISTORICAL RESEARCH ON HOW CHANGES IN BIOLOGICAL THEORY, SOCIAL THEORY, & AMERICAN SOCIETY HAVE AFFECTED VIEWS OF HUMAN NATURE. (NAT'L). PROF RICHARD BURKHARDT; DEPT OF HISTORY; UNIV OF ILLINOIS; URBANA, IL 61801. (#4029).

JULY 1, '75 - DEC 31, '76. A 200 YEAR INTROSPECTION. FORUM, HELD THIRD WEDNESDAY OF EACH MONTH, FOLLOWING A SPECIFIC THEME, SUCH AS AMERICA & AFRO-AMERICAN CULTURE, AMERICA & RELIGION AND AMERICA & AGRICULTURE. AT URBANA LIBRARY AUDITORIUM. (LOCAL). KATHLEEN WISSMILLER, DIR; CHAMPAIGN COUNTY BICENTENNIAL COMMISSION; 113 S DODSON DR; URBANA, IL 61801. (#21165-1).

JULY 1, '75 - CONTINUING . BICENTENNIAL HISTORY SERIES - 18 FOUR MINUTE RADIO SHOWS. HISTORIANS INCLUDE: NATALIE BOLTING - COLONIAL HISTORY; JOHN PRUETT - ANGLICAN CLERGY; ROBERT MCCOLLEY - COLONIAL SLAVERY, AND ROBERT SUTTON, PRESIDENT OF IL STATE HIST SOCIETY. (ST-WIDE). MAXINE C ENGERT; OFFICE OF PUBLIC INFORMATION,UNIV OF ILLINOIS; 142 DAVENPORT HOUSE; CHAMPAIGN, IL 61820. (#100001-2).

JULY 1, '75 - CONTINUING . 'FROM THE HEARTS OF MEN' - A BAND SHOW FOR RADIO. BICENTENNIAL SALUTE TO PATRIOTIC BAND MUSIC & ITS COMPOSERS (DR HARRY BEGIAN, CONDUCTOR). (LOCAL). C E FLYNN, ASST TO PRES; UNIV OF ILLINOIS/ILLINOIS BICENTENNIAL COMMISSION; PUBLIC INFORMATION OFFICE; CHAMPAIGN, IL 61820. (#100589-1).

JULY 1, '75 - CONTINUING . HISTORICAL OUTLOOKS & BOOK REVIEWS BY ROBERT B DOWNS - RADIO SERIES. ROBERT B DOWNS, NOTED AUTHOR & LIBRARIAN, IS FEATURED IN A SERIES OF 5 MINUTE TAPED RADIO BROADCASTS. HE WILL DISCUSS NEW BOOKS, SCIENTIFIC CONCEPTS & HISTORICAL REPUTATIONS, EXAMINE THE AMERICAN SUCCESS STORY AND REVIEW BENJAMIN FRANKLIN'S AUTOBIOGRAPHY. (ST-WIDE). MAXINE C ENGERT; UNIV OF ILLINOIS OFFICE OF PUBLIC INFORMATION; 142 DAVENPORT HOUSE; CHAMPAIGN, IL 61820. (#100001-1).

SEPT 4 - 6, '75. HISTORIC PRESERVATION INSTITUTE IN URBANA, IL. ESTABLISHMENT OF HISTORIC PRESERVATION INSTITUTE TO OFFER TRAINING & EXPERIENCE IN HISTORIC PRESERVATION. ALSO: EDUCATIONAL COURSE. (REGN'L). LACHLAN F BLAIR, CHAIRMAN; HISTORIC PRESERVATION INSTITUTE, DEPT OF URBAN/REGIONAL PLANNING; UNIV OF ILLINOIS; URBANA, IL 61801. (#10825-1).

OCT 1 - NOV 1, '75. 'ARCHIVES AND THE REVOLUTION'. EXHIBIT AT UNIVERSITY LIBRARY ROOM 19. (LOCAL). MAYNARD BRICHFORD, CHMN; UNIV OF ILLINOIS; UNIVERSITY LIBRARY ROOM 19; URBANA, IL 61801. (#200016-400).

DEC 1 - 25, '75. THE HISTORY OF AMERICAN CHRISTMAS THROUGH MUSIC - 30 MIN VIDEOTAPE. AN OUTSTANDING SERIES OF MUSICAL PRESENTATIONS BY CHORAL GROUPS OF THE URBANA CAMPUS OF THE UNIV OF ILLINOIS, DIRECTED BY PROF HAROLD DECKER. THE PROGRAMS WILL BE VIDEO TAPED FOR TV STATIONS. (REGN'L). MAXINE C ENGERT; UNIV OF ILLINOIS OFFICE OF PUBLIC INFORMATION; 142 DAVENPORT HOUSE; CHAMPAIGN, IL 61820. (#100001-3).

DEC 1, '75 - CONTINUING . CHORAL AMERICAN CHRISTMAS MUSIC - 30 MINUTE TAPED RADIO PGMS. RECORDED IN KRANNERT CENTER, UNIV OF ILLINOIS CHORAL GROUPS PERFORM CHRISTMAS MUSIC STARTING WITH EARLY CAROLS TO PRESENT. RADIO STATIONS SUPPLY OWN TAPES - OUT OF STATE PAY MINIMUM DUBBING CHARGES. (ST-WIDE). MAXINE C ENGERT; SCHOOL OF MUSIC, UNIV OF ILLINOIS; 142 DAVENPORT HOUSE; CHAMPAIGN, IL 61820. (#100001-4).

APR 1 - 30, '76. ILL INDUSTRIAL UNIV & PHILADELPHIA EXHIBITION. EXHIBIT AT ROOM 19 LIBR?ARY. (LOCAL). UNIV OF ILLINOIS; UNIVERSITY ARCHIVES; UNIV LIBRARY RM 19; URBANA, IL 61801. (#200016-330).

APR 8 - 9, '76. THE HUMAN PROSPECT: THE UNITED STATES AND THE GLOBAL COMMUNITY. CONFERENCE AT UNIVERSITY AUDITORIUM. (LOCAL). J TERRY IVERSON, CHAIRMAN; UNIV OF ILLINOIS; 205 ARCADE BLDG; CHAMPAIGN, IL 61820. (#200016-398).

JUNE 13 - 18, '76. HISTORIC PRESERVATION INSTITUTE SEMINAR. INSTITUTE WILL CONSIST OF CONFERENCE, SEMINARS AND SHORT COURSES; IT WILL BE OPEN TO STUDENTS, PROFESSIONALS AND PERSONS INTERESTED IN HISTORIC PRESERVATION. AT FLORIDA AVE RESIDENCE HALLS, UNIV OF IL. (ST-WIDE). L F BLAIR, CHAIRMAN; UNIV OF IL, HISTORY, ARCHITECTURE, GEOGRAPHY & URBAN PLANNING DEPTS; 909 W NEVADA; URBANA, IL 61820. (#10776-1).

JUNE 14 - 25, '76. CARL HAVERLIN/BROADCAST MUSIC, INC, ARCHIVES BICENTENNIAL EXHIBIT. OFFERS A VERSATILE PICTURE OF HISTORY, REGIONAL LIFE & MUSIC FOR OVER 200 YEARS. CONTAINS PRESIDENTIAL LETTERS, LETTERS OF FAMOUS AMERICANS, OLD BOOKS, MANUSCRIPTS, HISTORY OF 'THE STAR SPANGLED BANNER' & COMPOSER AUTOGRAPHS, PLUS SHEET MUSIC OF THE PAST. AT UNIV OF ILLINOIS LIBRARY. (ST-WIDE). ROBERT ORAM, LIBRARIAN; UNIVERSITY OF ILLINOIS AT URBANA-CHAMPAIGN; UNIVERSITY OF ILLINOIS; URBANA, IL 61801. (#20784-15).

SEPT 12, '76. LINCOLN'S EIGHTH JUDICIAL CIRCUIT RIDE. LIVE PERFORMANCE. (ST-WIDE). PHYLLIS EUBANKS, COORD; ILLINOIS DEPARTMENT OF CONSERVATION; 901 S SPRING ST; SPRINGFIELD, IL 62706. (#200016-192).

OCT 7 - 9, '76. SYMPOSIUM TOPIC TRANSFORMATIONS OF THE AMERICAN HERO. NINE SPEAKERS IN THE FIELDS OF AFRO-AMERICAN HISTORY, CINEMA, FEMINISM AND LITERATURE, LANGUAGE, RELIGION, POLITICS, ADVERTISING, ART, BUSINESS. AT UNION BLDG, 1301 W GREEN ST. (LOCAL). HENRY KAHANE, CHAIRMAN; COLLEGE OF LAS HUMANITIES DIVISION MILLER COMMITTEE; 4088 FLB UIUC; URBANA, IL 61801. (#200016-399).

DEC 12, '76. CHORAL MUSIC CONCERT. FIRST LOCAL PERFORMANCE OF 'AMERICAN CANTATA' BY LUKAS FOSS. AT GREAT HALL KRANNERT CENTER, UNIVERSITY OF IL. (LOCAL). HAROLD A DECKER, DIRECTOR; UNIVERSITY OF ILLINOIS SCHOOL OF MUSIC; 1204 SO VINE ST; URBANA, IL 61801. (#200016-376).

UTICA

MAY 3 - 10, '75. WILD FLOWER PILGRIMAGE. WILDFLOWER/ PHOTOGRAPHY TOURS CONTINUE THROUGHOUT THE DAY TRAVELLING INTO MANY BEAUTIFUL AREAS OF THE PARK. AT STARVED ROCK STATE PARK INTERPRETIVE CENTER. (LOCAL). MS JANET PICKETT; ILLINOIS DEPARTMENT OF CONSERVATION; 901 SOUTH SPRING; SPRINGFIELD, IL 62704. (#50272-82).

AUG 2, '75. NATURAL NOURISHMENT BOUNTY DAYS. HIGHLIGHTS TECHNIQUES AND MATERIALS NECESSARY FOR GATHERING AND PREP ARING WILD EDIBLE FOODS. AT STARVED ROCK STATE PARK INTERPRETIVE CENTER. (LOCAL). MS JANET PICKETT; ILLINOIS DEPARTMENT OF CONSERVATION; 901 SOUTH SPRING; SPRINGFIELD, IL 62704. (#50272-84).

SEPT 13, '75. ALTERNATIVE ENERGY SYMPOSIUM. ALTERNATIVE APPROACHES TO THE ENERGY CRISIS WILL BE EXPLORED THROUGH A SERIES OF DEMONSTRATIONS, LECTURES AND DISCUSSIONS. AT STARVED ROCK STATE PARK INTERPRETIVE CENTER. (LOCAL). MS JANET PICKETT; ILLINOIS DEPARTMENT OF CONSERVATION; 901 SOUTH SPRING; SPRINGFIELD, IL 62704. (#50272-86).

MAY 1 - 8, '76. WILDFLOWER PILGRIMAGE. WILDFLOWER/ PHOTOGRAPHY TOURS CONTINUE THROUGHOUT THE DAY TRAVELLING INTO MANY BEAUTIFUL AREAS OF THE PARK. AT STARVED ROCK STATE PARK INTERPRETIVE CENTER. (LOCAL). MS JANET PICKETT; ILLINOIS DEPARTMENT OF CONSERVATION; 901 SOUTH SPRING; SPRINGFIELD, IL 62704. (#50272-83).

AUG 7, '76. NATURAL NOURISHMENT BOUNTY DAY. HIGHLIGHTS TECHNIQUES AND MATERIALS NECESSARY FOR GATHERING AND PREP ARING WILD EDIBLE FOODS. AT STARVED ROCK STATE PARK INTERPRETIVE CENTER. (LOCAL). MS JANET PICKETT; ILLINOIS DEPARTMENT OF CONSERVATION; 901 SOUTH SPRING; SPRINGFIELD, IL 62704. (#50272-85).

AUG 25, '76. AMERICAN WIND SYMPHONY'S FLOATING ARTS CENTER VISITS UTICA. EMBARKING UPON A BICENTENNIAL CULTURAL TOUR, THE WIND SYMPHONY WILL VISIT 76 CITIES BRINGING MUSIC, DANCE, SYMPOSIA & CHILDREN'S THEATER TO THE WATERWAYS OF AMERICA DURING ITS 6 MONTH TOUR. (ST-WIDE). PAULA BERN, COORD; AMERICAN WIND SYMPHONY ORCHESTRA OF WESTERN PENNSYLVANIA; GATEWAY TOWERS 18G; PITTSBURGH, PA 15222. (#2800-31).

SEPT 11, '76. ALTERNATIVE ENERGY SYMPOSIUM. ALTERNATIVE APPROACH TO THE ENERGY CRISIS WILL BE EXPLORED THROUGH A SERIES OF DEMONSTRATIONS, LECTURES AND DISCUSSIONS. AT STARVED ROCK STATE PARK INTERPRETIVE CENTER. (LOCAL). MS JANET PICKETT; ILLINOIS DEPARTMENT OF CONSERVATION; 901 SOUTH SPRING; SPRINGFIELD, IL 62704. (#50272-87).

VANDALIA

'SEVEN STORIES' - A BOOK IN VANDALIA, ILLINOIS. COLLECTION OF STORIES BY JAMES HALL, THE FIRST MAN OF LETTERS FROM ILLINOIS WHO HAS RECEIVED NATIONAL RECOGNITION AS AN AUTHOR, TO BE REPRINTED. BOOK COVERS ERA 1750-1833 & IS BASED ON HISTORICAL FACT. (NAT'L). MARY BURTSCHI, CHAIRMAN; FAYETTE COUNTY AMER REVOL BICENT COMMISSION; 307 N 6TH ST; VANDALIA, IL 62471. (#9595).

JUNE 21, '75. GRAND LEVEE. THIS EVENT CAPTURES THE SPIRIT OF 19TH CENTURY GRAND LEVEES (IN EFFE CT, AN OPEN HOUSE). THERE ARE CRAFT DEMONSTRATIONS ON THE LAWN IN TH E AFTERNOON AND COSTUMED GUIDES FOR AN EVENING CANDLELIGHT TOWN OF T HE STATE HOUSE WITH REFRESHMENTS FOR VISITORS. AT 315 GALLATIN. (LOCAL). MS JANET PICKETT; ILLINOIS DEPARTMENT OF CONSERVATION; 901 SOUTH SPRING; SPRINGFIELD, IL 62704. (#50272-88).

DEC 13 - 19, '75. VANDALIA CHRISTMAS CAROLING. CHRISTMAS CAROLING OCCURS AT VANDALIA STATE HOUSE WITH THE BUILDING DECORATED WITH NATURAL MATERIALS. AT VANDALIA STATE HOUSE 315 GALLATIN. (LOCAL). MS JANET PICKETT; ILLINOIS DEPARTMENT OF CONSERVATION; 901 SOUTH SPRING; SPRINGFIELD, IL 62704. (#50272-90).

JUNE 19, '76. GRAND LEVEE. THIS EVENT CAPTURES THE SPIRIT OF 19TH CENTURY GRAND LEVEE (IN EFFEC T, AN OPEN HOUSE) THERE ARE CRAFTS DEMONSTRATIONS ON THE LAWN IN THE AFTERNOON AND COSTUMED GUIDES FOR AN EVENING CANDLELIGHT TOUR OF THE STATE HOVER WITH REFRESHMENTS FOR VISITORS. AT 315 GALLATIN. (LOCAL). MS JANET PICKETT;

VANDALIA — CONTINUED

ILLINOIS DEPARTMENT OF CONSERVATION; 901 SOUTH SPRING; SPRINGFIELD, IL 62704. (#50272-89).

DEC 11 - 17, '76. VANDALIA CHRISTMAS CAROLING. CHRISTMAS CAROLING OCCURS AT VANDALIA STATE HOUSE WITH THE BUILDING DECORATED WITH NATURAL MATERIALS. AT VANDALIA STATE HOUSE 315 GALLATIN. (LOCAL). MS JANET PICKETT; ILLINOIS DEPARTMENT OF CONSERVATION; 901 SOUTH SPRING; SPRINGFIELD, IL 62704. (#50272-91).

VERONA

RESTORATION OF COMMUNITY HALL IN VERONA, IL. RESTORATION OF OLD COMMUNITY HALL. (REGN'L). VERONA KINSMAN, DIRECTOR; VERONA KINSMAN FIREMEN'S ASSOC; BOX 27; VERONA, IL 60479. (#33530).

JUNE 11 - 13, '76. HISTORICAL MUSEUM & COMBINED ARTS. BALL GAMES, CHURCH CHOIR, LOG SAWING, TRACTOR PULL, TREE PLANTING, FLAG RAISING CEREMONIES, ECOLOGY POEM CONTEST & DEDICATION OF VERONA COMMUNITY HALL. AT COMMUNITY HALLS IN VERONA & KINSMAN. (LOCAL). DOROTHY WHITTEMORE; VERONA KINSMAN FIREMEN'S ASSOCIATION; BOX 95; VERONA, IL 60479. (#200016-310).

VERSAILLES

SEPT 15 - 16, '75. VERSAILLES SESQUICENTENNIAL. OPENING, FESTIVAL. (LOCAL). MARJORIE LEAVES, CHAIRMAN; BROWN COUNTY BOARD & BICENTENNIAL COMMISSION; MT STERLING, IL 62353. (#8189-504).

SEPT 18, '76. VERSAILLES BICENTENNIAL FESTIVAL. DINNER, HORSE SHOW. (LOCAL). MARJORIE CLEAVES, COORD; BROWN COUNTY BICENTENNIAL COMMISSION; RR 1; TIMEWELL, IL 62375. (#200016-191).

VIENNA

PRESERVATION OF HISTORIC JOHNSON COUNTY JAIL - IL. PRESERVATION OF OLD COUNTY JAIL AS AN HISTORIC LANDMARK, TOURIST ATTRACTION, AND A CENTER FOR SENIOR CITIZENS. (LOCAL). RON ROGERS, CHAIRPERSON; JOHNSON COUNTY BICENTENNIAL COMMISSION; VIENNA, IL 62995. (#19256).

PURCHASE MICROFILM READER, VIENNA, IL. PURCHASE MICROFILM READER FOR 16 & 25 MM ROLL FILM TO READ PERICALS, NEWSPAPERS, OUT OF PRINT BOOKS, FEDERAL POPULATION CENSUS AND SCHEDULES FOR RESEARCH OF AMERICA; WILL BE PUT IN VIENNA LIBRARY. (LOCAL). MARJORIE BELLAMY, CHAIRPERSON; VIENNA WOMAN'S CLUB & HORIZONS '76; VIENNA, IL 62995. (#18530).

MAR 17, '76. DEDICATION OF HISTORIC JAIL AND SENIOR CITIZENS CENTER. DEDICATION OF OLD JAIL & AN ARTS & CRAFTS FAIR. AT OLD JOHNSON COUNTY JAIL, VIENNA COURTHOUSE SQUARE. (LOCAL). ANNA BENSON, DIRECTOR; JOHNSON COUNTY BICENTENNIAL COMMISSION; ROUTE 3; VIENNA, IL 62995. (#104248-1).

VILLA GROVE

JULY 7 - 10, '76. DOUGLAS COUNTY CHAUTAUQUA IN VILLA GROVE. FESTIVITIES INCLUDE FARMER DAYS, AIR FORCE DRUM & BUGLE CORPS, DANCES & PARADES. AT COMMUNITY BLDG. (LOCAL). LOUISE SHERRICK, COORD; DOUGLAS COUNTY BICENTENNIAL COMMITTEE; 104 VINE; VILLA GROVE, IL 61956. (#106547-1).

VILLA PARK

COMMUNITY ATTITUDES SURVEY, VILLA PARK, ILLINOIS. SURVEY DESIGNED TO ENCOURAGE VILLAGE CITIZENS TO EXPRESS FEELINGS ABOUT VARIOUS PHASES OF VILLAGE LIFE & THEIR DESIRES FOR THE BICENTENNIAL CELEBRATION. (LOCAL). DICK SELOOVER, CHAIRMAN; VILLA PARK BICENTENNIAL COMMISSION; 20 S ARDMORE AVE; VILLA PARK, IL 60181. (#5081). **(??).**

VIRDEN

JUNE 26, '76. ACTIVITIES IN VIRDEN, IL. ACTIVITIES INCLUDE PARADE, ARTS AND CRAFTS FESTIVAL, COMMUNITY DANCE, AND OLD TIME GAMES. (LOCAL). DANIEL MCKENNEDY, COORD; TOWN OF VIRDEN BICENT COMMITTEE & AMERICAN LEGION; 129 E STODDARD; VIRDEN, IL 62690. (#200016-77).

W FRANKFORT

FRANKFORT AREA HISTORICAL MUSEUM & PROJECTS, IL. PRESERVATION OF HISTORIC (1806) MUSEUM W/EXHIBITS, ANTIQUES, DEMONSTRATIONS AND CITY-WIDE PROJECTS. THESE INCLUDE LECTURES, BICENT MURAL, RESEARCH BY GENEOLOGY DEPT. (ST-WIDE). MAVIS L WRIGHT, DIRECTOR; FRANKFORT AREA HISTORICAL SOCIETY; 2000 E ST LOUIS ST; W FRANKFORT, IL 62896. (#33528).

AUG 7, '75. 'HERITAGE '76' - HISTORICAL PAGEANT. A PAGEANT FILLED WITH BEAUTY & PATRIOTISM ON THE HERITAGE OF OUR COUNTRY FROM THE 13 COLONIES THROUGH THE CIVIL WAR PERIOD; NARRATION AND MUSIC BY 35 VOICE COSTUMED CHORUS. AT FRANKFORT AREA HIST MUSEUM, 2000 E ST LOUIS ST, WEST FRANKFORT. (LOCAL). MRS WAYNE B WRIGHT, PRES; FRANKFORT AREA HISTORICAL SOCIETY; 2000 E ST LOUIS ST; FRANKFORT, IL 62896. (#103114-2).

FEB 10 - MAY 5, '76. 'FIRST LADIES OF AMERICA'S FIRST 200 YEARS' - PAGEANT. LIVE PERFORMANCE. (LOCAL). MRS WAYNE R WRIGHT, PRES; FRANKFORT AREA HISTORICAL SOCIETY 'HERITAGE PLAYERS'; 2000 E ST LOUIS; W FRANKFORT, IL 62896. (#200016-59).

SEPT 1 - DEC 15, '76. FALL ACTIVITIES. EXHIBIT, FESTIVAL, TOUR. (LOCAL). MARVIS WRIGHT, PRESIDENT; FRANKFORT HISTORICAL SOCIETY; 2000 E ST LOUIS ST; W FRANKFORT, IL 62896. (#200016-377).

WALNUT

BICENTENNIAL PROJECTS - WALNUT, IL. PLANTING OF TREES & FLOWERS; LIGHTING FOR FLAGS; 4TH GRADE CRAFT PROJECTS; TOWN HISTORY SUPPLEMENT; PURCHASE OF BOOKS BY LOCAL AUTHOR; PUBL COOKBOOK; FILMS SHOWN TO SR CITIZENS. (LOCAL). MRS O C BAIRD, SECRETARY; WALNUT BICENT COMMITTEE; WALNUT, IL 61378. (#32993).

MAY 31, '76. MEMORIAL DAY CELEBRATION. FLAG CEREMONY; BICENTENNIAL FLAG PRESENTED TO MAYOR ALVIN JOHNSON BY DAVID SHAPIRO; CERTIFICATE & LETTER PRESENTED TO DOROTHY SWANSON & TO WALNUT MEMORIAL LIBRARY. (LOCAL). DICK WHITVER, CHMN; AMERICAN LEGION; 204 E WALNUT; WALNUT, IL 61376. (#200016-331).

JULY 4, '76. FOURTH OF JULY WEEKEND EVENTS. AMONG THE EVENTS: JAYCEES SPONSORED PICNIC, BELL RINGING, SHOWING OF FILMS, MOTHER-DAUGHTER TEA, CHURCH PICNICS, MUSICAL PROGRAMS, & SPECIAL COMMEMORATIVE SERVICES. (LOCAL). MRS O C BAIRD, SECRETARY; WALNUT BICENTENNIAL COMMITTEE; WALNUT, IL 61376. (#200016-346).

WALTONVILLE

AUG 2 - 3, '75. HISTORIC FUN FOLK FESTIVAL. FEATURING HISTORIC FOLK CUSTOMS: FLINTLOCK RIFLE SHOOTING, TOURS IN HORSEDRAWN VEHICLES, OLD AUTOS, RUG WEAVING, SOAP MAKING, BLACKSMITHING, GOOSE PLUCKING, ARTS, CRAFTS & STAGE SHOWS. (LOCAL). JERRY ELLISTON, EDITOR; THE PRAIRIE HISTORIANS; COLE & ELM STS; WALTONVILLE, IL 62894. (#6740-501).

WAPELLA

OCT 18, '75. SALUTE TO THE PAST TWO CENTURIES. EXHIBIT, FAIR AT HIGH SCHOOL. (LOCAL). CHARLES L SCHETTLER, CHMN; WAPELLA BICENTENNIAL COMMITTEE; WAPELLA, IL 61777. (#200016-435).

WARSAW

AUG 7 - 8, '76. WARSAW BICENTENNIAL FUN DAYS, 1975-76. EVENTS INCLUDE A CARNIVAL, CHARITY AUCTION, PARADE, FIRE DEPT WATER FIGHT, MUSIC, LOCAL TALENT & A STREET DANCE. AT STREET DANCE FROM 3RD & MAINE TO 6TH & MAINE. (LOCAL). C JENKINS, PRES; WARSAW CHAMBER OF COMMERCE; 602 MAINE ST; WARSAW, IL 62379. (#102741-1).

WASHBURN

TRADITIONAL BLACKFEET CRAFTS BICENTENNIAL PROJECT. PRODUCTION, IN COOPERATION WITH BLACKFEET CRAFTS ASSOC, OF 25-MINUTE SLIDE SHOW ILLUSTRATING TRADITIONAL ARTS & CRAFTS: MOCASSIN & BEAD WORK, HIDE TANNING & SINEW MAKING, DOLL MAKING & STORY TELLING. (NAT'L). DIRECTOR; SUN FOUNDATION; PO BOX 156E; WASHBURN, IL 61570. (#33282). **ARBA RECOGNIZED.**

WATERLOO

MAY 26, '75. PRESENTATION REVOL WAR VETERANS COMMEMORATIVE PLAQUE. PLAQUE PRESENTED IN MEMORY OF REVOLUTIONARY WAR SOLDIERS. AT COURT HOUSE. (LOCAL). ALFRED B MUELLER, CHMN; MONROE COUNTY AMER REVOL BICENT CELEBRATION COMMISSION; 301 SO MAIN ST; WATERLOO, IL 62298. (#50603-2).

JULY 4, '75. FOURTH OF JULY CELEBRATION. INTERFAITH CHURCH SERVICE, ARCHAEOLOGY SCHOOL, CONCERTS, INDIAN DANCING, STYLE SHOW, BARBER SHOP SING ALONG, FRENCH SINGERS, GRIST MILL MUZZLE LOADING GUNS, SOUVENIRS, FIREWORKS. AT MONROE COUNTY FAIRGROUNDS. (LOCAL). ALFRED B MUELLER, CHMN; MONROE COUNTY AMER REVOL BICENT CELEBRATION COMMISSION; 301 SO MAIN ST; WATERLOO, IL 62298. (#50603-1).

WATSEKA

HUBBARD'S LANDING SITE MARKER IN WATSEKA, IL. MARK LANDING SITE OF FIRST WHITE SETTLER IN IROQUOIS COUNTY. (LOCAL). AVERY D SHEPHERD, CHAIRMAN; IROQUOIS COUNTY BICENTENNIAL COMMISSION; 520 S CRESCENT ST; GILMAN, IL 60938. (#8512).

INTERSECTION MARKERS - IROQUOIS COUNTY, IL. PROJECT CONSISTS OF NUMBERING & ERECTING INTERSECTION MARKERS ON ALL ROADS IN COUNTY. (LOCAL). AVERY D SHEPHERD, CHAIRMAN; IROQUOIS COUNTY BICENTENNIAL COMMISSION; 520 S CRESCENT; GILMAN, IL 60938. (#33732).

RECORDING BICENTENNIAL ACTIVITIES IN WATSEKA, IL. RECORD AND PRESERVE COUNTYWIDE BICENT ACTIVITIES FOR POSTERITY. (LOCAL). AVERY D SHEPHERD, CHAIRMAN; IROQUOIS COUNTY BICENTENNIAL COMMISSION; 520 S CRESCENT ST; GILMAN, IL 60938. (#8493).

JULY 8 - 10, '76. IROQUOIS COUNTY BICENTENNIAL PAGEANT. LIVE PERFORMANCE AT IROQUOIS COUNTY FAIRGROUNDS. (LOCAL). AVERY D SHEPERD, CHMN; IROQUOIS COUNTY BICENTENNIAL COMMISSION; 520 S CRESCENT; GILMAN, IL 60938. (#200016-519).

WAUCONDA

BICENTENNIAL PROJECTS - WAUCONDA, IL. FLAG DESIGN CONTEST; BICENT EMPORIUM HELD TO RAISE MONEY FOR THE MUSEUM; BICENT BIRTH CERTIFICATES; RENAMING OF STREETS AFTER THE ORIGINAL COLONIES; ACQUIRED OLD BLDG FOR A MUSEUM. (LOCAL). R HARRIS, CHMN; WAUCONDA BICENT COMMITTEE; RR 1, BOX 204A; WAUCONDA, IL 60084. (#33003).

SPECIAL SCHOOL CLASSES IN WAUCONDA, IL. SPEECHES TO 6TH GRADE ON LOCAL HISTORY, CRAFTS & GENEOLOGY. (LOCAL). R HARRIS, DIRECTOR; WAUCONDA HISTORICAL SOCIETY; WAUCONDA, IL 60084. (#33529).

APR 30, '76. ARBOR DAY. EACH GRADE PLANTED A TREE AT ELEMENTARY SCHOOL. TREES ALSO PLANTED IN PARK. ALL TREES MARKED WITH PLAQUE STATING BICENTENNIAL TREE. AT ELEMENTARY SCHOOL AND LAGOON PARK. (LOCAL). R HARRIS, CHAIRMAN; ELEMENTARY SCHOOL, PARK DISTRICT AND WOMENS CLUB OF WAUCONDA; RR 1, BOX 204A; WAUCONDA, IL 60084. (#200016-457).

APR 30, '76. HISTORICAL FASHION SHOW. EACH MODEL REPRESENTED A SPECIFIC WOMAN PROMINENT IN U S HISTORY. AT HIGH SCHOOL. (LOCAL). R HARRIS, CHAIRMAN; REPUBLICAN WOMEN'S CLUB; RR 1, BOX 204A; WAUCONDA, IL 60084. (#200016-456).

JULY 3 - 11, '76. BICENTENNIAL WEEK - JULY 4 CELEBRATION AND RODEO. FESTIVAL, PARADE. (LOCAL). R HARRIS; CHAMBER OF COMMERCE; RR 1, BOX 204A; WAUCONDA, IL 60084. (#200016-494).

AUG 21, '76. ART FAIR. FAIR, EXHIBIT AT SHOPPING CENTER. (LOCAL). R HARRIS, CHAIRMAN; ARTS COUNCIL OF THE CHAMBER OF COMMERCE OF WAUCONDA; RR 1, BOX 204A; WAUCONDA, IL 60084. (#200016-447).

NOV 21, '76. ECUMENICAL SERVICE OF THANKSGIVING. CEREMONY. (LOCAL). R HARRIS, CHMN; WAUCONDA BICENTENNIAL COMMITTEE; RR 1, BOX 204A; WAUCONDA, IL 60084. (#109483-1).

WAUKEGAN

BICENTENNIAL TREE PLANTING - WAUKEGAN, IL. TREES WILL BE PLANTED THROUGHOUT WAUKEGAN. (LOCAL). DIRECTOR; UNITED STATES MARINE CORPS; 1721 MCAREE RD; WAUKEGAN, IL 60085. (#29142).

AUG 10 - 14, '76. NATL FINNISH AMERICAN BICENTENNIAL MEETING & FESTIVAL. BICENT FESTIVALS WILL BE HELD IN FINNISH-AMERICAN CENTERS LOCATED IN SEVERAL CITIES DURING 1976. (REGN'L). RALPH J JALKANEN, PRES; SUOMI COLLEGE; QUINCY ST; HANCOCK, MI 49930. (#8628-8).

SEPT 2 - 3, '76. UNITED STATES ARMED FORCES BICENTENNIAL CARAVAN. CARAVAN IS COMPOSED OF EXHIBIT VANS FOR EACH MILITARY SERVICE. PROJECT THEME IS 'HISTORY OF THE ARMED FORCES & THEIR CONTRIBUTIONS TO THE NATION.'. (LOCAL). MRS SARA GRIFFIN, CHMN; UNITED STATES ARMED FORCES BICENTENNIAL CARAVAN; WAUKEGAN, IL 60085. (#1775-641).

NOV 28 - 29, '76. LA SALLE EXPEDITION II, A HISTORIC RE-ENACTMENT. THIS IS AN AUTHENTIC RE-ENACTMENT OF THE 1681 LASALLE EXPEDITION FROM MONTREAL, CANADA TO NEW ORLEANS, LA WHICH WILL BEGIN TOURING ON AUGUST 11, 1976 AND END ON APRIL 9, 1977. (LOCAL). REID H LEWIS, DIRECTOR; LA SALLE EXPEDITION II; 135 S LA SALLE ST, RM 411; CHICAGO, IL 60690. (#102805-19).

WENONA

APR 18, '75. 'A NIGHT TO REMEMBER', A FESTIVAL IN WENONA, IL. A ONE NIGHT NOSTALGIC REVIEW OF WENONA'S 100TH ANNIVERSARY IN 1953 INCLUDING FILMS, SLIDES & MUSIC. ALSO: FILM/SLIDES. AT WENONA COMMUNITY SCHOOL AUDITORIUM. (LOCAL). ALYCE REINMANN, CHAIRMAN; WOMAN'S LITERARY CLUB; WENONA, IL 61377. (#6063-1).

JULY 3 - 4, '76. BICENTENNIAL CELEBRATION. FESTIVAL. (LOCAL). REV PAUL BENGSTON; MARSHALL COUNTY BICENTENNIAL CELEBRATION; BOX 176; WENONA, IL 61377. (#200016-146).

WEST CHICAGO

TURNER JUNCTION HISTORICAL PARK. LOCATED NEXT TO CITY HALL, PARK WILL HAVE ORIGINAL RAILROAD STATION MOVED TO THE SITE AND A MONUMENT. PRESENTLY, A DONATED CB&Q CABOOSE IS AT THE SITE. (LOCAL). JOHN WHENNAN, CHAIRMAN; WEST CHICAGO BICENTENNIAL COMMISSION; PO BOX 447; W CHICAGO, IL 60185. (#32155).

WEST CHICAGO — CONTINUED

JULY 4, '76. 4TH OF JULY CELEBRATION. PARADE WITH OLD FASHIONED PICNIC IN THE PARK AFTERWARDS. (LOCAL). JOHN WHENNEN, CHAIRMAN; WEST CHICAGO BICENTENNIAL COMMISSION; PO BOX 447; WEST CHICAGO, IL 60185. (#200016-261).

AUG 19 - 22, '76. BICENTENNIAL RAILROAD DAYS PARADE & CARNIVAL. PROCEEDS FROM THIS CARNIVAL GO TOWARDS TURNER JUNCTION HISTORICAL PARK. (LOCAL). JOHN WHENNEN; WEST CHICAGO BICENTENNIAL COMMISSION; PO BOX 447; W CHICAGO, IL 60185. (#200016-351).

WEST DUNDEE

REMODELING OF TOWNSHIP HISTORICAL MUSEUM, IL. ONE ROOM OF THE TOWNSHIP HISTORICAL MUSEUM WILL BE REMODELED; THE ROOM WILL SERVE AS A SITE TO PRESERVE THE HISTORY OF THE TOWNSHIP BICENTENNIAL COMMITTEE. (LOCAL). VIVIAN OSTH, HERITAGE CHAIRPERSON; DUNDEE TOWNSHIP BICENTENNIAL COMMISSION; 5 SUMMIT AVE; EAST DUNDEE, IL 60118. (#13016).

SEPT 27, '75. BICENTENNIAL BALL. FESTIVAL AT CHATEAU LOUISE, RT 31, WEST DUNDEE. (LOCAL). ROBERT BUHROW, PROJ MGR; DUNDEE TOWNSHIP BICENTENNIAL COMMISSION; 8 SUMMIT AVE; EAST DUNDEE, IL 60118. (#100877-1).

WESTERN SPG

ARTS & CRAFTS SHOW FEATURING LOCAL ARTISTS. FAIR. (LOCAL). K L MEANS, CO-CHMN; WESTERN SPRINGS BICENTENNIAL COMMISSION; 5029 WOODLAND AVE; WESTERN SPG, IL 60558. (#200016-461).

BICENTENNIAL PROJECTS - WESTERN SPRINGS, IL. TREE PLANTING THROUGHOUT THE TOWN; GET OUT THE VOTE DRIVE; WRITING CONTEST; SHOWING OF FILMS ON AMERICANA; VEHICLE STICKER CONTEST; COMMEMORATIVE QUILT; 2 HIGH SCHOOL SCHOLARSHIPS. (LOCAL). KENNETH L MEANS, CHMN; WESTERN SPRINGS BICENT COMMISSION; 5029 WOODLAND AVE; WESTERN SPG, IL 60558. (#33009).

FILM SERIES ON AMERICA - WESTERN SPRINGS, IL. THE 20 FILM ALISTAIR COOKE, AMERICA SERIES WAS SHOWN IN COOPERATION WITH THE HISTORICAL SOCIETY. (LOCAL). KENNETH L MEANS, CO-CHAIRMAN; WESTERN SPRINGS BICENTENNIAL COMMISSION; 5029 WOODLAND AVE; WESTERN SPG, IL 60558. (#33205).

FLOWER PLANTINGS FOR WESTERN SPRINGS, IL. RED, WHITE, BLUE PLANTS FOR SALE FOR THE BICENTENNIAL THEME. (LOCAL). MRS MEANS, CHAIRMAN; WESTERN SPRINGS BICENTENNIAL COMMISSION; 5029 WOODLAND; WESTERN SPG, IL 60558. (#29930).

LITERARY CONTEST - WESTERN SPRINGS, IL. THE CONTEST INCLUDED POETRY, PROSE AND DRAMA. (LOCAL). MRS KENNETH L MEANS, CO-CHAIRMAN; WESTERN SPRINGS BICENTENNIAL COMMISSION; 5029 WOODLAND AVE; WESTERN SPG, IL 60558. (#33206).

ORAL HISTORIES OF WESTERN SPRINGS, IL. SLIDES AND VOICE PREPARED BY WESTERN SPRINGS HISTORICAL SOCIETY. (LOCAL). MRS R L MEANS, CHAIRMAN; WESTERN SPRINGS BICENTENNIAL COMMISSION; 5029 WOODLAND; WESTERN SPG, IL 60558. (#32672).

TREE PLANTING 1976 - WESTERN SPRINGS, IL. THE HOUSEHOLDERS PURCHASED MAPLE, ASH AND CHESTNUT TREES TO REPLACE LOST ELMS. (LOCAL). MRS KENNETH L MEANS, CO-CHAIRMAN; WESTERN SPRINGS BICENTENNIAL COMMISSION; 5029 WOODLAND AVE; WESTERN SPG, IL 60558. (#33203).

TREE-PLANTING PROJECT-1975 - WESTERN SPRINGS, IL. HOMEOWNERS PURCHASED RED, SUGAR, AND NORWAY MAPLES AND HORSE CHESTNUTS FOR PLANTING IN PARKWAYS AND ON PRIVATE PROPERTY. (LOCAL). MRS KENNETH MEANS, CO-CHAIRMAN; WESTERN SPRINGS BICENTENNIAL COMMISSION; 5029 WOODLAND AVE; WESTERN SPG, IL 60558. (#33208).

VEHICLE STICKER CONTEST - WESTERN SPRINGS, IL. THE CONTEST WAS OPEN TO ALL SCHOOL STUDENTS AND WAS HELD TO ESTABLISH THE DESIGN FOR THE VILLAGE VEHICLE STICKER. (LOCAL). KENNETH L MEANS, CO-CHAIRMAN; WESTERN SPRINGS BICENTENNIAL COMMISSION; 5029 WOODLAND AVE; WESTERN SPG, IL 60559. (#33204).

VILLAGE FLAG DESIGN CONTEST, WESTERN SPRING, IL. A CONTEST TO SELECT A VILLAGE FLAG. (LOCAL). KENNETH L MEANS, CO-CHAIRMAN; WESTERN SPRINGS BICENTENNIAL COMMISSION; 5029 WOODLAND AV; WESTERN SPG, IL 60558. (#30980).

VOTER REGISTRATION/PARTICIPATION - IL. VOTER PARTICIPATION ACTIVITIES INCLUDED GETTING OUT THE VOTE, CALING AND CANVASSING. (LOCAL). KENNETH MEANS, CO-CHAIRMAN; WESTERN SPRINGS BICENTENNIAL COMMISSION; 5029 WOODLAND; WESTERN SPG, IL 60558. (#33207).

NOV 10, '74. 'JOLLIET & MARQUETTE EXPLORATION'. LIVE PERFORMANCE AT MCCLURE JUNIOR HS. (LOCAL). KENNETH L MEANS; WESTERN SPRINGS BICENTENNIAL COMMISSION; 5029 WOODLAWN AVE; WESTERN SPGS, IL 61558. (#200016-311).

MAY 24, '75. COLONIAL COSTUME BALL. FESTIVAL. (LOCAL). K L MEANS, CO-CHMN; WESTERN SPRINGS BICENTENNIAL COMMISSION; 5029 WOODLAND AVE; WESTERN SPG, IL 60558. (#200016-460).

MAY 24 - 25, '75. COLONIAL WEEK-END 1775. BATTLES, SKIRMISHES & COLONIAL LIFE EXHIBITS. AT SPRING ROCK PARK. (LOCAL). K L MEANS, CO-CHMN; WESTERN SPRINGS BICENTENNIAL COMMISSION; 5029 WOODLAND; WESTERN SPG, IL 60558. (#200016-462).

JULY 4, '75. BICENTENNIAL CELEBRATION. CEREMONY AT SPRING ROCK PARK TO VILLAGE GREEN. (LOCAL). KENNETH L MEANS; WESTERN SPRINGS BICENTENNIAL COMMISSION; 5029 WOODLAND AV; WESTERN SPGS, IL 60558. (#200016-312).

SEPT 6, '75. FALL FESTIVAL OF THE 1860'S. INCLUDES GARDEN SHOW, SQUARE DANCE, ANTIQUE SHOW WITH ROOM SETTINGS AS THEY WOULD HAVE BEEN IN THE COMMUNITY IN THE 1860'S BY THE QUESTER GROUPS, ETC. AT SPRING ROCK PARK. (LOCAL). MS K L MEANS, CO-CHMN; WESTERN SPRINGS BICENTENNIAL COMMISSION; 5029 WOODLAWN AVE; WESTERN SPGS, IL 60558. (#200016-358).

NOV 25, '75. RELIGIOUS HERITAGE SERVICE. CEREMONY AT ST JOHN OF THE CROSS SCHOOL. (LOCAL). K L MEANS, CO-CHMN; WESTERN SPRINGS BICENTENNIAL COMMISSION; 5029 WOODLAND AVE; WESTERN SPG, IL 60558. (#200016-459).

JAN 11, '76. SALUTE TO THE FOUNDING OF OUR COUNTRY. MUSIC PERFORMED BY MILLIKIN UNIV STUDENTS. AT MCCLURE JR HS. (LOCAL). KENNETH L MEANS; WESTERN SPRINGS BICENTENNIAL COMMISSION; 5029 WOODLAND AVE; WESTERN SPGS, IL 60558. (#200016-313).

FEB 22, '76. MUSICAL PROGRAM-THE SINGING BOYS OF ROCKFORD. LIVE PERFORMANCE AT MCCLURE JR HS. (LOCAL). K L MEANS; WESTERN SPRINGS BICENTENNIAL COMMISSION; 5029 WOODLAND AVE; WESTERN SPGS, IL 60558. (#200016-314).

MAR 1, '76. BILL OF RIGHTS DAY. SEMINAR AT CYPRESS RESTAURANT. (LOCAL). K L MEANS; LEAGUE OF WOMEN VOTERS & WESTERN SPRINGS BICENTENNIAL COMMISSION; 5029 WOODLAND AVE; WESTERN SPGS, IL 60558. (#200016-315).

JULY 3 - 4, '76. 4TH OF JULY WEEKEND CELEBRATION. JULY 3-LOCAL AREA ARTS & CRAFT SHOW, W/EMPHASIS ON LOCAL SKILLS & FREEDOM BALL W/INTL GUEST, ROWENA HARVEY OF RUGELEY, ENGLAND. JULY 4 -ECUMENICAL WORSHIP AT 10:00AM, SINGING PLUS READING OF DECLARATION, 'JULY 76 PHILADELPHIA' DRAMA & LARGE PARADE W/MANY FLOATS, ETC. AT WESTERN SPRINGS AREA. (LOCAL). MRS R L MEANS, CHMN; WESTERN SPRINGS BICENTENNIAL COMMISSION; 5029 WOODLAND; WESTERN SPG, IL 60558. (#200016-412).

SEPT 13 - 15, '76. ARCHITECTURAL HISTORY, ILLINOIS-ARCHIVAN. EXHIBIT AT VILLAGE GREEN. (LOCAL). K L MEANS; WESTERN SPRINGS BICENTENNIAL COMMISSION & ILLINOIS ARTS COUNCIL; 5029 WOODLAND AVE; WESTERN SPGS, IL 60558. (#200016-316).

WESTVILLE

THE ILLINOIS PRAIRIE PROJ OF WESTVILLE, ILLINOIS. SEEDS COLLECTED FROM REMNANT PRAIRIE AREAS FOR RESTORATION OF OLD PRAIRIE AREAS. (LOCAL). DORIS L WESTFALL, CHAIRMAN; VERMILION COUNTY AUDUBON SOCIETY; 604 N BEARD; DANVILLE, IL 61832. (#9590).

WHEATON

MAY 3, '75. FESTIVAL OF AMERICAN MUSIC. HONORING OUR NATION'S BICENT WITH MUSIC BY AMERICAN COMPOSERS, DIRECTED BY CLAYTON HALVORSEN, REX HICKS & ARTHUR KATTERJOHN. FEATURING WHEATON'S FIVE MUSIC ORGANIZATIONS, CONCERT CHOIR, MENS & WOMENS GLEE CLUBS, CONCERT BAND & SYMPHONY ORCHESTRA. AT ORCHESTRA HALL, 220 S MICHIGAN AVE, CHICAGO. (LOCAL). RICHARD E GERIG; WHEATON COLLEGE CONSERVATORY OF MUSIC; PUBL RELA OFFICE, WHEATON COLL; WHEATON, IL 60187. (#50309-1).

JULY 29 - AUG 1, '76. DUPAGE COUNTY FAIR. ANNUAL DUPAGE COUNTY FAIR, 4-H SHOW & JUNIOR FAIR. AT COUNTY FAIRGROUNDS. (LOCAL). DON C MILLER, ADMIN; DUPAGE COUNTY FAIR; 2015 W MANCHESTER RD; WHEATON, IL 60187. (#106095-19).

WILLOW SPG

STORY - SONG OF WILLOW SPRINGS, IL. A NARRATIVE AND PICTORIAL HISTORY OF WILLOW SPRINGS AREA AND ITS PEOPLE FROM EARLIEST TIME TO PRESENT AND A RECORDING OF ORIGINAL SONG OF WILLOW SPRINGS. (LOCAL). EDWARD J KUBAITIS, AUTHOR; WILLOW SPRINGS BICENTENNIAL COMMISSION; ARCHER E PEARL ST; WILLOW SPG, IL 60480. (#33527).

WILMETTE

INTERCULTURAL COMMUNICATIONS CENTER - WILMETTE, IL. CENTER WITH LECTURE FACILITIES, LANGUAGE LAB, AUDIO-VISUAL FACILITIES & LIBRARY FOR ENGLISH AS A SECOND LANGUAGE & FOREIGN LANGUAGES. (LOCAL). SISTER CECILE KUHN, PROJ DIRECTOR; MALLINCKRODT COLLEGE; 1041 RIDGE RD; WILMETTE, IL 60091. (#13577).

NORTHSHORE CONCERT BAND - MUSIC FOR AMERICA, IL. THROUGH REGIONAL AND NATIONAL TOURS, WORKSHOPS AND CLINCS, THE BAND WILL STIMULATE PUBLIC INTEREST IN THE CREATION OF COMMUNITY BANDS THROUGHOUT THE COUNTRY. (REGN'L). BERNARD DOBROSKI, PROJECT COORDINATOR; NORTHSHORE CONCERT BAND - MUSIC FOR AMERICA; 1133 GREENWOOD AVE; DEERFIELD, IL 60015. (#14708).

SEPT 29 - NOV 17, '75. BILL OF RIGHTS TODAY: FORUM APPLYING BILL OF RIGHTS TO TODAY. SEMINAR AT MALLINCKRODT COLLEGE, ROOM 128; FREE PARKING IN FRONT. (LOCAL). SISTER CECILE KUHN, DIR; MALLINCKRODT COLLEGE; 1041 RIDGE RD; WILMETTE, IL 60091. (#101183-1).

OCT 3 - NOV 28, '75. LIBERTY & JUSTICE FOR ALL: LECTURE-DISCUSSION SERIES. THERE WILL ALSO BE AFTERNOON LECTURES FROM 1:00 - 3:00. (LOCAL). SISTER CECILE KUHN, DIR; MALLINCKRODT COLLEGE; 1041 RIDGE RD; WILMETTE, IL 60091. (#101184-1).

OCT 6 - DEC 10, '75. DISPLAY & EXHIBITS AMERICANA. DISPLAYS & EXHIBITS OF BOOKS, DOCUMENTS & INTERESTING AMERICANA RELATING TO OUR HISTORY & CULTURE; LIBRARY PROJECT. AT MALLINCKRODT COLLEGE. (LOCAL). SISTER CECILE KUHN; MALLINCKRODT COLLEGE; 1041 RIDGE RD; WILMETTE, IL 60091. (#13576-1).

JAN 19 - MAR 16, '76. OUR HERITAGE OF FOLK MUSIC-LECTURES WITH AUDIENCE PARTICIPATION. SEMINAR. (LOCAL). SISTER CECILE KUHN, DIR; MALLINCKRODT COLLEGE; 1041 RIDGE RD; WILMETTE, IL 60091. (#101181-1).

FEB 4 - MAR 24, '76. AMERICAN ART & ARTISTS: ILLUSTRATED LECTURE SERIES. THERE WILL ALSO BE AFTERNOON LECTURES FROM 1:00 - 3:00. (LOCAL). SISTER CECILE KUHN, DIR; MALLINCKRODT COLLEGE; 1041 RIDGE RD; WILMETTE, IL 60091. (#101182-1).

DEC 5 - 6, '76. LA SALLE EXPEDITION II, A HISTORIC RE-ENACTMENT. THIS IS AN AUTHENTIC RE-ENACTMENT OF THE 1681 LASALLE EXPEDITION FROM MONTREAL, CANADA TO NEW ORLEANS, LA WHICH WILL BEGIN TOURING ON AUGUST 11, 1976 AND END ON APRIL 9, 1977. (LOCAL). REID H LEWIS, DIRECTOR; LA SALLE EXPEDITION II; 135 S LA SALLE ST, RM 411; CHICAGO, IL 60690. (#102805-24).

WILMINGTON

JUNE 27, '76. WILMINGTON RECREATION CLUB LIBERTY MARCH. TOUR THROUGH RECREATION AREA GROUNDS & PICNIC, SANCTIONED BY HIKERS OF AMERICA, INC. AT WILMINGTON RECREATION AREA. (LOCAL). AUDREY KORENIK, COORD; WILMINGTON RECREATION CLUB; 737 E END AVE; HILLSIDE, IL 60162. (#108284-1).

JAN 13 - 14, '77. LA SALLE EXPEDITION II, A HISTORIC RE-ENACTMENT. THIS IS AN AUTHENTIC RE-ENACTMENT OF THE 1681 LASALLE EXPEDITION FROM MONTREAL, CANADA TO NEW ORLEANS, LA WHICH WILL BEGIN TOURING ON AUGUST 11, 1976 AND END ON APRIL 9, 1977. (LOCAL). REID H LEWIS, DIRECTOR; LA SALLE EXPEDITION II; 135 S LA SALLES, ST, RM 411; CHICAGO, IL 60690. (#102805-37).

WINCHESTER

SCOTT CO VETERANS' MEMORIAL MONUMENT, IL. MONUMENT TO SERVE AS A LASTING MEMORIAL TO HONOR THE VETERANS OF SCOTT COUNTY. (LOCAL). MRS WINNIE BAIRD, PROJ DIRECTOR; SCOTT CO BICENTENNIAL COMMISSION; CHERRY ST; WINCHESTER, IL 62694. (#24083). **ARBA GRANTEE.**

APR 25, '76. TREE PLANTING DEDICATION. TREE PLANTING IS FOR POW'S AND MIA'S OF ALL WARS. (LOCAL). AUDREY PEAK, CHMN; SCOTT COUNTY BICENTENNIAL COMMISSION; 360 W CHERRY; WINCHESTER, IL 62694. (#200016-103).

JUNE 6 - JULY 4, '76. COUNTY-WIDE TOUR OF CHURCHES. TOUR. (LOCAL). AUDREY PEAK, CHMN; SCOTT COUNTY BICENTENNIAL COMMISSION; 360 W CHERRY; WINCHESTER, IL 62694. (#200016-102).

JULY 3, '76. PATRIOT'S BALL. FESTIVAL. (LOCAL). AUDREY PEAK, CHMN; SCOTT COUNTY BICENTENNIAL COMMISSION; 360 W CHERRY; WINCHESTER, IL 62694. (#200016-101).

SEPT 26, '76. FRONTIER DAYS - DEDICATION OF VETERAN'S MONUMENT. FESTIVAL, CEREMONY AT SCOTT COUNTY FAIRGROUNDS. (LOCAL). AUDREY PEAK, CHMN; SCOTT COUNTY BICENTENNIAL COMMISSION; 360 W CHERRY; WINCHESTER, IL 62694. (#200016-100).

OCT 3, '76. SENIOR CITIZEN'S RECOGNITION DAY. CEREMONY. (LOCAL). AUDREY PEAK, CHMN; SCOTT COUNTY BICENTENNIAL COMMISSION; 360 W CHERRY; WINCHESTER, IL 62694. (#200016-99).

WINFIELD

SEPT 12, '76. VON PARADE FOR ANNUAL LOCAL CELEBRATION. THIS WAS THE 9TH YEAR FOR OUR VILLAGE TO CELEBRATE GOOD OLE DAYS. IT IS A WEEKEND WHEN ALL LOCAL ORGANIZATIONS WORK TOGETHER FOR A FINE LOCAL FESTIVAL. THIS IS THE FIRST YEAR WE HAVE HAD A BIG PARADE. AT BEECHER ST; CHURCH ST & SUNNYSIDE ST. (LOCAL). MARTHA C INGRAM; GOOD OLE DAYS BICENTENNIAL COMMISSION OF WINFIELD; 27W466 MANCHESTER RD; WINFIELD, IL 60190. (#200016-389).

WINNETKA

HOSPITALITY '76, WINNETKA, IL. HOME STAY PROGRAM FOR FOREIGN TOURISTS WHO WISH TO MEET & VISIT WITH AMERICAN FAMILIES FOR ONE OR TWO DAYS. (LOCAL). ANN K HEALY, PRESIDENT; WINNETKA BICENTENNIAL COMMITTEE; GREEN BAY RD; WINNETKA, IL 60093. (#19552).

NAME INDEX OF ILLINOIS COUNTY HISTORIES. NAME INDEX OF PUBLISHED HISTORIES OF 102 ILLINOIS COUNTY HISTORIES AND MASTER NAME INDEX OF THOSE HISTORIES. (ST-WIDE). MS JOAN S HARRIS, LIBRARIAN; WINNETKA LIBRARY DISTRICT; 768 OAK ST; WINNETKA, IL 60093. (#880). **ARBA GRANTEE.**

WINNETKA — CONTINUED

DEC 4 - 5, '76. LA SALLE EXPEDITION II, A HISTORIC RE-ENACTMENT. THIS IS AN AUTHENTIC RE-ENACTMENT OF THE 1681 LASALLE EXPEDITION FROM MONTREAL, CANADA TO NEW ORLEANS, LA WHICH WILL BEGIN TOURING ON AUGUST 11, 1976 AND END ON APRIL 9, 1977. (LOCAL). REID H LEWIS, DIRECTOR; LA SALLE EXPEDITION II; 135 S LA SALLE ST, RM 411; CHICAGO, IL 60690. (#102805-23).

WOLF LAKE

PINE HILLS GATEWAYS PROJECT - IL. CONSTRUCTION OF TWO 18TH CENTURY REPLICA BUILDINGS. (LOCAL). LEE ROY RENDLEMAN, PROJ DIRECTOR; PINE HILLS BICENTENNIAL COMMISSION; BOX 133; WOLF LAKE, IL 62998. (#27789). **ARBA GRANTEE.**

WOOD RIVER

CITY HALL LANDSCAPING IN WOOD RIVER, ILLINOIS. THE CITY HALL AREA WILL BE LANDSCAPED; A WATERFALL AND BENCHES TO BE PROVIDED. (LOCAL). RALPH K YEMM, CHAIRMAN; WOOD RIVER BICENTENNIAL COMMISSION; 235 E LORENA AVE, PO BOX 201; WOOD RIVER, IL 62095. (#8004).

WOODRIDGE

HERITAGE LANDSCAPE - WOODRIDGE, IL. TWO SCULPTURES FOR OUTDOOR DISPLAY AT THE ENTRANCES TO WOODRIDGE, ILLINOIS AS PART OF A PROJECT TO IMPROVE THE VILLAGE AND ESTABLISH A PRAIRIE LANDSCAPE. (LOCAL). ALICE PETERSON, PROJ DIRECTOR; WOODRIDGE BICENTENNIAL COMMISSION; 2900 W 83RD ST; WOODRIDGE, IL 60515. (#24099). **ARBA GRANTEE.**

WORTH

BICENTENNIAL LITERATURE AND CRAFT CONTEST, IL. STUDENTS WILL BE INVITED TO SUBMIT LITERATURE, ART, MUSIC, PHOTOGRAPHY AND PRACTICAL ARTS ARTIFACTS WHICH THEY THINK ARE MOST APPROPRIATE GIFTS TO THE NATION FOR ITS 200TH BIRTHDAY. (LOCAL). DR JAMES SPIVEY, AREA CHAIRMAN FOR SOCIAL STUDIES; COMMUNITY HIGH SCHOOL DISTRICT #218 BICENTENNIAL COMMITTEE; 5933 W 115TH ST; WORTH, IL 60482. (#12543).

FILMS ON THE BICENTENNIAL THEME - WORTH, IL. THE FOLLOWING FILMS WILL BE SHOWN: 'HOW THE WEST WAS WON', 'CITIZEN KANE', 'THE GRAPES OF WRATH', 'TO KILL A MOCKINGBIRD' AND 'PATTON.'. (LOCAL). DR JAMES SPIVEY, AREA CHAIRMAN FOR SOCIAL STUDIES; COMMUNITY HIGH SCHOOL DISTRICT #218 BICENTENNIAL COMMITTEE; 5933 W 115TH ST; WORTH, IL 60482. (#12544).

SEPT 1, '75 - JUNE 1, '76. BICENTENNIAL DAYS. PLANS INCLUDE TWO DAYS FOR SPECIAL EVENTS; THE FIRST FOR CRAFTS FROM THE SCHOOLS AND COMMUNITY WHICH WILL BE DISPLAYED IN THE EVENINGS; THE SECOND FOR MINI-LESSONS TO BE CONDUCTED DURING THE SCHOOL DAY. THESE WILL ALL BE ON THE BICENTENNIAL THEMES. AT RICHARDS HS IN OAKLAWN AND EISENHOWER HS IN BLUE ISLAND. (LOCAL). DR JAMES SPIVEY, PROJ DIR; COMMUNITY HIGH SCHOOL DISTRICT 218, BICENTENNIAL COMMITTEE; 5933 W 115TH ST; WORTH, IL 60482. (#100801-1).

WYANET

TENNIS COURT & ICE SKATING RINK IN WYANET IL. DOUBLE TENNIS COURT, SKATING RINK, HORSE SHOE AREA, WITH FENCE & LIGHTS. (LOCAL). MAXINE TROTTER, DIRECTOR; WYANET BICENTENNIAL COMMISSION; WYANET, IL 61379. (#33525).

JUNE 20 - 21, '75. ALUMNI WEEKEND. HISTORICAL PLAY, DISPLAY & BANQUET. PROCEEDS DONATED TO BAND BOOSTERS FOR UNIFORMS. HOURS ON FRI 7:30 TO 9:00PM; SAT 4:00 TO 10:00PM. AT WYANET HIGH SCHOOL & GRADE SCHOOL CAFETERIA. (LOCAL). MAXINE TROTTER, COORD; WYANET BICENTENNIAL COMMISSION; 210 S KING; WYANET, IL 61379. (#200016-224).

JULY 15, '76. DEDICATION OF LIFT BRIDGE ON THE HENNEPIN CANAL. COMPLETION OF RESTORATION OF THE LIFT BRIDGE. (LOCAL). DOROTHY ILL, COORD; SPORTSMAN CLUB; WEST ST; WYANET, IL 61379. (#28651-1).

WYOMING

ORAL HISTORY PROGRAM IN WYOMING, IL. COUNTY-WIDE PROGRAM ON ORAL HISTORY. (LOCAL). MEL STAHL, DIRECTOR; STARK COUNTY BICENTENNIAL COMMISSION; WYOMING, IL 61491. (#33523).

STARK COUNTY HISTORICAL MARKERS - WYOMING, IL. MARKERS WERE PLACED AT HISTORICAL SITES. (LOCAL). MEL STAHL, COORDINATOR; STARK COUNTY BICENTENNIAL COMMISSION; WYOMING, IL 61491. (#33202).

TABLEAUX OF CITIES IN WYOMING, IL. TABLEAUX OF FIVE CITIES OF COUNTY INCLUDING SLIDE PRESENTATION. (LOCAL). MEL STAHL, DIRECTOR; STARK COUNTY BICENTENNIAL COMMISSION; WYOMING, IL 61491. (#33524).

YATES

AUG 7 - 9, '75. HARVEST HOME FESTIVAL. A COMMUNITY PROJECT INCL A PARADE, PRODUCE EXHIBIT, CARNIVAL, RIDES, FOOD STAND, SQUARE DANCE & OTHER LOCAL ACTIVITIES. (LOCAL). J W BURROWS, PRES; HARVEST HOME PARK ASSOC; BOX 14; YATES, IL 61572. (#11011-501).

YORKVILLE

ADULT EDUCATION PROJECT - YORKVILLE, IL. A SERIES OF ADULT LECTURES ON ASPECTS OF KENDALL COUNTY HISTORY AND GOVERNMENT GIVEN BY LOCAL AUTHORITIES. (LOCAL). RICHARD KRASE, SUPERINTENDANT; KENDALL COUNTY EDUCATIONAL REGION; 108 RIDGE ST; YORKVILLE, IL 60560. (#23246).

FOX & ILLINOIS UNION ELECTRIC RAILWAY TRAIL, IL. A 20 MI TRAIL WILL BE DEVELOPED ALONG FOX & ILLINOIS UNION ELECTRIC RAILWAY. (LOCAL). JAMES BENTZ, TRAIL CHAIRMAN; KENDALL COUNTY BICENTENNIAL COMMITTEE; RT 1, BOX 68; OSWEGO, IL 60543. (#23247).

MONOGRAPHS ON KENDALL COUNTY: YORKVILLE, ILLINOIS. THIS PROJECT CONSISTS OF A SERIES OF AT LEAST SIX MONOGRAPHS ON ASPECTS OF COUNTY HISTORY; INCLUDING INDIANS, THE COURTHOUSE AND POLITICS, AND THE MILLS AND MILLERS. (LOCAL). ROGER MATILE, EDUCATION CHAIRMAN; KENDALL COUNTY BICENT COMMISSION; BOX 1976; YORKVILLE, IL 60560. (#6244). **(??).**

PHOTOGRAPHS OF KENDALL COUNTY, IL. 3 BOOKS OF PHOTOGRAPHS REFLECTING AMERICAN LIFE IN 1976 WILL BE MADE; ONE WILL BE PLACED IN A TIME CAPSULE, ONE IN A PUBLIC LIBRARY AND ONE TO THE KENDALL COUNTY HISTORICAL SOCIETY. (LOCAL). LEE HILL, CHAIRMAN; KENDALL COUNTY BICENTENNIAL COMMISSION; PO BOX 1976; YORKVILLE, IL 60560. (#17399).

12 TRAILS OF PATRIOTISM & GIRL SCOUTS IN 1776, IL. A PROGRAM DESIGNED TO TEACH GIRLS ABOUT THEIR HERITAGE. (LOCAL). BARBARA JOHNSON, COORDINATOR; YORKVILLE BRISTOL GIRL SCOUTS; 609 HEUSTIS ST; YORKVILLE, IL 60560. (#23248).

SEPT 27, '75. BICENTENNIAL HARVEST FESTIVAL. FESTIVAL, PARADE, TOUR AT YORKVILLE CITY PARK. (LOCAL). JAMES BENTZ, PROJ DIR; KENDALL COUNTY BICENTENNIAL COMMISSION; RT #1, BOX 68; OSWEGO, IL 60543. (#101410-1).

JUNE 14 - JULY 26, '76. KENDALL COUNTY AMERICAN GOVERNMENT COURSE. SEMINAR. (LOCAL). TOM FLETCHER, INSTRUCTOR; KENDALL COUNTY EDUCATIONAL SERVICE REGION; BOX 175; NEWARK, IL 60541. (#27070-1).

JULY 3, '76. BICENTENNIAL FOURTH OF JULY CELEBRATION. FESTIVAL, PARADE AT CITY PARK, RT 47. (LOCAL). BLAINE HARKER, CHAIRMAN; BRISTOL KENDALL FIRE DEPT; 209 FRANKLIN; YORKVILLE, IL 60560. (#106477-1).

JULY 4, '76. COLONIAL WORSHIP 1776. COLONIAL 1776 WORSHIP SERVICE IN THE STYLE OF THE CONGREGATIONAL CHURCH. PEOPLE WILL BE SEATED AS IN COLONIAL DAYS AND FOLLOW A SIMILAR ORDER OF WORSHIP. PEOPLE ARE REQUESTED TO WEAR APPROPRIATE DRESS IF AVAILABLE. AT YORKVILLE CONGREGATIONAL CHURCH, 105 W CENTER. (LOCAL). REV LAWRENCE J REZASH; YORKVILLE CONGREGATIONAL CHURCH; PO BOX 486; YORKVILLE, IL 60560. (#107269-1).

JULY 25, '76. OLD-FASHIONED ICE CREAM SOCIAL. HOMEMADE CAKES, PIES AND ICE CREAM; HOSTS WILL BE IN COSTUME; 17.76% OF THE PROCEEDS WILL BE DONATED TO THE KENDALL COUNTY BICENTENNIAL COMMISSION. AT YORKVILLE CITY PARK. (LOCAL). MRS ROBERT MITCHLER, DIR; KENDALL COUNTY REPUBLICAN WOMEN'S CLUB & CENTRAL COMMITTEE; HILL SPRINGS OAKS; OSWEGO, IL 60543. (#106477-2).

SEPT 9, '76. KENDALL COUNTY BICENTENNIAL HISTORIC TOUR. TOUR AT KENDALL COUNTY COURT HOUSE. (LOCAL). MRS LINDA GATES, COORD; KENDALL HOME ECONOMICS EXTENSION COUNCIL; 4 BRIARCLIFF RD; OSWEGO, IL 60543. (#109045-1).

SEPT 19, '76. KENDALL COUNTY HORSE ASSOCIATION OPEN HORSE SHOW. OPEN HORSE SHOW BEING HELD IN CONJUNCTION WITH KENDALL COUNTY BICENTENNIAL COMMISSION BICENTENNIAL HARVEST FESTIVAL. THE KCBC WILL PRESENT THE GRAND CHAMPION AND RESERVE GRAND CHAMPION TROPHIES. AT HARRIS FOREST PRESERVE HORSE ARENA. (LOCAL). ALICIA HOLSTEIN, CHMN; KENDALL COUNTY HORSE ASSOCIATION; RT 2, BOX 32; PLANO, IL 60545. (#200016-114).

SEPT 25 - 26, '76. BICENTENNIAL HARVEST FESTIVAL. PARADE, BANDSTAND, ARTS AND CRAFTS, FUN FOR EVERYONE. AT YORKVILLE CITY PARK, RT 47. (LOCAL). JAMES BENTZ, CHMN; KENDALL COUNTY BICENTENNIAL COMMISSION; RT 1 BOX 68; OSWEGO, IL 60543. (#104946-2).

NOV 5, '76. GUY FAWKES PARTY. THE KENDALL COUNTY BICENTENNIAL COMMISSION IS HOSTING A GUY FAWKES PARTY AS A REMINDER OF OUR ENGLISH HERITAGE. AT YORKVILLE CONGREGATIONAL CHURCH, 105 W CENTER. (LOCAL). TOM FLETCHER, COORD; KENDALL COUNTY BICENTENNIAL COMMISSION; BOX 175; NEWARK, IL 60541. (#104946-1).

ZION

NOV 26 - 28, '76. LA SALLE EXPEDITION II, A HISTORIC RE-ENACTMENT. THIS IS AN AUTHENTIC RE-ENACTMENT OF THE 1681 LASALLE EXPEDITION FROM MONTREAL, CANADA TO NEW ORLEANS, LA WHICH WILL BEGIN TOURING ON AUGUST 11, 1976 AND END ON APRIL 9, 1977. (LOCAL). REID H LEWIS, DIRECTOR; LA SALLE EXPEDITION II; 135 S LA SALLE ST, RM 411; CHICAGO, IL 60690. (#102805-18).

Indiana

Indiana American Revolution Bicentennial Commission

Established by the Indiana General Assembly (I.C. 4-23-7.5-1) in 1971

ARBA Statistics

Officially Recognized
- Communities—200
- Colleges/Universities—21
- Military installations—5

BINET Projects—463
- Events—661

1976 Population—5,302,000

Bicentennial Archives

State Archives
Indiana State Library
140 North Senate Street
Indianapolis, Indiana 46204

Membership

Roger D. Branigin, *chairman* (1971-75)
Robert D. Orr, *interim chairman* (1975)
Walter P. Helmke, *chairman* (1975-)
James M. Guthrie, *executive director* (1972-75)
Dale Fruchtnicht, *acting director* (1975)
Michele A. White, *executive director* (1975-)

District Members

(Mrs.) Robert Kieswetter
(Mrs.) James B. Dean
Dr. Jack J. Detzler
Walter Helmke
Elizabeth Kurtz
(Mrs.) Herbert R. Hill
Dr. Donald F. Carmony
Rita Eykamp
Dr. James A. Joseph
Richard A. Greene
Dr. George M. Waller

Legislative Members

Senator John F. Shawley
Senator Earl Wilson
Senator Frank L. O'Bannon
Representative Lindel O. Hume
Representative Kenneth Snider
Representative Richard M. Delliger

Ex Officio Members

Lieutenant Governor Robert D. Orr
Secretary of State Larry A. Conrad
Carl H. Armstrong, *director,* Indiana State Museum
Marcelle Foote, *director,* Indiana State Library
Pamela J. Bennett, *director,* Indiana Historical Bureau
Joseph D. Cloud, *director,* Department of Natural Resources
Dr. John J. Pruis, *president,* Ball State University
Dr. John W. Ryan, *president,* Indiana University
Dr. Richard Landini, *president,* Indiana State University
Dr. Arthur G. Hansen, *president,* Purdue University
Dr. Isaac K. Beckes, *president,* Vincennes University
Gayle Thornbrough, *executive secretary,* Indiana Historical Society

Honorary Members

Reverend Charles Banet
John V. Barnett
Dr. Walter Beardsley
Peter Beczkiewicz
John Brooks
(Mrs.) Thomas Egan
Thomas S. Emison
Jack Carmichael
(Mrs.) Robert I. Clark
Galen Colclesser
Honorable George N. Craig
Leo Craig
John W. Hillenbrand, Sr.
Dr. Maynard Hine
General Robert G. Moorhead
Jimmy Ross
Dr. Thaddeus Seymour
Dr. John F. Stover
Beth Hardwick Walters
Fred Reynolds
Honorable Matthew E. Welsh
Siegfried Weng
Doris Werner
(Mrs.) Evans Woolen, III
Willis Zagrovich
Honorable Ralph F. Gates
William A. Gumberts
Frederic M. Hadley
Marshall F. Kizer
Eli Lilly
H. Roll McLaughlin
Marshall Miller
Murray Holliday
Hazel Hopper
Clyde Kassens
Sanford Peterson
Wendel Phillipi
H. J. Post
(Mrs.) H. W. Ramsey
Janice Crimmins
Charles D. Wise
Arthur C. Hayes

Indiana

The Bicentennial celebration in Indiana was as diverse as the citizenry that populates the state. In many cases, months—even years—of organized preparation climaxed in the "biggest and best" Independence Day seen by Hoosiers.

The statehouse belonged to the people on the 4th of July, as over 15,000 came to join the festivities sponsored by the IARBC. For many, it was their first visit to the seat of Indiana's government. The day's events centered around history-making—the signing of documents which reaffirmed the principles of the Declaration of Independence. They will be preserved for future generations.

Elsewhere in the state, the spirit ran just as high. Vincennes, the city that boasts of Indiana's most direct link with the Revolutionary era, celebrated with the month long *Conquest of the Old Northwest Festival.* Vincennes was one of the few places west of the Appalachian Mountains to play an active part in the colonial liberation. George Rogers Clark led his band of volunteers into Vincennes and captured Fort Sackville from the British in February of 1779, thus establishing America's claim to the Northwest Territory.

The Indiana State Museum in Indianapolis has developed a major walk-through exhibit on the life and career of George Rogers Clark. The highlight of the exhibit is an environmental theater depicting the march and attack on the British at Vincennes. An outreach component including film and curriculum units brings the program to all of Indiana's citizens.

Communities across the state celebrated with a range of parades, games, picnics, talent contests and fireworks—a multitude of variations of old-fashioned fun. Pekin, Indiana celebrated the Bicentennial in much the same way as other small communities across the land. But it had a special distinction: this year's observance was the 146th such event in Pekin, the oldest without-a-miss 4th of July celebration in the nation.

July 5 marked the dedication of Bedford's Bicentennial gift to the nation—a lifesize limestone sculpture of Washington crossing the Delaware. The sculpture, weighing 30 tons, consists of 26 separate pieces of stone expertly fitted to appear as a single piece. The community of Bedford and the area limestone industry raised an estimated $100,000 to complete the project to reflect their patriotism and their pride in the rich limestone resource. The sculpture was donated to the Washington Crossing Foundation in Pennsylvania, and is now situated on the banks of the Delaware River where Washington made his famous crossing.

National attention has also been directed to the Indiana State Prison (ISP) Bicentennial project. ISP was the nation's only prison declared an official Bicentennial Community. The inmates' projects included art exhibits, Red Cross training programs, audio-visual programming and special activities undertaken by special interest clubs. Specially bound braille transcriptions of historic American documents were presented by the ISP community to the Library of Congress.

Another project unique to the nation was undertaken by the Indiana Department of Mental Health/Central State Hospital, which was designated a Bicentennial Community. A series of public forums, a traveling exhibit and a festival program at the state hospital were designed to chip away at the myths, embarrassment and fear that surround mental illness and to promote citizen contact with the patients.

In many communities, Bicentennial planners have left lasting civic improvements or monuments—such as the Emanual Hatfield Museum in Newburgh and the newly renovated Obelisk Square, located in downtown Indianapolis. For future generations, Evansville developed a monument to the ideals of individual freedom—the *Evansville Bicentennial Tribute.* Others have developed a stronger sense of local history and of the ethnic heritage of the citizenry. In community after community, previously untapped talents came to light, and a cooperative spirit developed among community organizations which will provide a positive force for the next century.

AKRON

JULY 4, '76. FOURTH OF JULY CELEBRATION. CELEBRATE INDEPENDENCE DAY ON THE GROUNDS OF AKRON GRADE SCHOOL WITH A BIG PARADE; THEN WATCH FIREWORKS LIGHT UP THE EVENING SKY AT THE FREE FESTIVITIES WHICH RUN ALL DAY. AT AKRON GRADE SCHOOL. (LOCAL). DALE SHEETZ, PROJ DIR; AKRON CHAMBER OF COMMERCE; 316 W ROCHESTER ST; AKRON, IN 46910. (#100342-1).

ALBION

HISTORY OF ALBION, 1908-1976, IN. SENIOR CITIZENS WILL WRITE & PUBLISH A HISTORY BOOK, A CONTINUATION OF ONE PRINTED IN 1908 & REPRINTED IN 1975. INCLUDES PICTURES & ADS, IN SAME FORMAT AS EARLIER ONE. (LOCAL). MRS LINDA J SHULTZ, SECRETARY; ALBION AREA BICENTENNIAL COMMITTEE; 109 N YORK; ALBION, IN 46701. (#23066).

PUBLIC PARK AND SWIMMING POOL, ALBION, IN. A COMMUNITY PARK AND SWIMMING POOL WILL BE BUILT. (LOCAL). MRS LINDA J SHULTZ, SECRETARY; ALBION AREA BICENTENNIAL COMMITTEE; 109 N YORK; ALBION, IN 46701. (#23065).

AUG 2 - 3, '75. BICENTENNIAL - CENTENNIAL CELEBRATION. CELEBRATE THE 100TH BIRTHDAY OF THE 'OLD JAIL' BY TAKING A TOUR OF THIS MUSEUM. IF YOU ESCAPE UNSHACKLED, ENJOY THE BROOM MAKING, MUZZLE LOADING, TOMAHAWK THROWING, BUGGY RIDES, BANDS, FIDDLER, ON W MAIN STREET. (LOCAL). GENEVA ZINK; NOBLE COUNTY HISTORICAL SOCIETY; 207 S ORANGE ST; ALBION, IN 46701. (#100323-1).

NOV 2, '75 - NOV 28, '76. AMERICAN ISSUES FORUM DISCUSSION PROGRAMS. PROGRAMS ON LAST SUNDAY AFTERNOON OF FEBRUARY, MARCH, APRIL, SEPTEMBER, OCTOBER AND NOVEMBER; ALBION CLUBS SERVE REFRESHMENTS. AT COURTHOUSE SQUARE, 109 N YORK. (LOCAL). MRS LINDA J SHULTZ, SEC; NOBLE COUNTY PUBLIC LIBRARY; 109 N YORK ST; ALBION, IN 46701. (#106327-3).

JUNE 13 - 19, '76. CHAIN-O-LAKES DAYS FESTIVAL. TOUR OF HISTORIC HOMES, TALENT CONTEST, FISH FREY, PANCAKE SUPPER, CHICKEN BARBEQUE, SQUARE & ROUND DANCING, KIDS CONTESTS AND PARADE; GRAND PARADE ON FINAL DAY. AT AROUND COURTHOUSE SQUARE. (LOCAL). MRS LINDA J SHULTZ, SEC; ALBION CHAMBER OF COMMERCE; 109 N YORK; ALBION, IN 46701. (#106327-2).

JULY 4, '76. 100 YEAR FOURTH OF JULY FESTIVAL. DAY FESTIVITIES SIMILIAR TO 1876: SUNRISE SALUTE, COMMUNITY LUNCH, PROGRAM, RACES, GAMES, CONTESTS, PARADE, BALLOON ASCENSION, FIREWORKS, COTILLION BALL, ICE CREAM SOCIAL. AT COURTHOUSE SQUARE AND CENTRAL NOBEL SCHOOL, E MAIN ST. (LOCAL). MRS LINDA J SHULTZ, SEC; ALBION AREA BICENTENNIAL COMMITTEE; 109 N YORK; ALBION, IN 46701. (#106327-1).

OCT 17, '76. ALBION PARK DEDICATION & FUND PRESENTATION TO ALBION PARK BOARD. ALBION BICENTENNIAL COMMITTEE & OTHER ALBION ORGANIZATIONS PRESENTED FUNDS & GIFTS TO PARK BOARD. EVERY ONE PRESENT HAD A PIECE OF BIRTHDAY CAKE. AT ALBION COMMUNITY PARK, E MAIN ST. (LOCAL). MRS LINDA J SHULTZ, SECY; ALBION AREA BICENTENNIAL COMMITTEE & ALBION PARK BOARD; 109 N YORK; ALBION, IN 46701. (#200017-87).

ANDERSON

CAMPUS BEAUTIFICATION - ANDERSON, IN. TREE PLANTING AND OTHER PERMANENT LANDSCAPING WILL BE DONE. (LOCAL). W SHIRELL FOX, ASST TO PRESIDENT; ANDERSON COLLEGE; 1100 E 5TH ST; ANDERSON, IN 46011. (#24508).

HISTORICAL FILMS - ANDERSON, IN. FILMS ON OUR AMERICAN HERITAGE WILL BE MADE. (LOCAL). W SHIRELL FOX, ASSISTANT; ANDERSON COLLEGE; 1100 E 5TH ST; ANDERSON, IN 46011. (#24509).

MADISON COUNTY HISTORICAL HOME RESTORATION - IN. THE MARTIN GRUENWALD HOME WILL BE RESTORED. (LOCAL). RONALD ACTIS, DIRECTOR; MADISON COUNTY HISTORIC HOME COMMISSION; 2401 COLUMBUS AVE; ANDERSON, IN 46011. (#26872). **ARBA GRANTEE.**

JUNE 17, '75. HISTORIC BUILDING DEDICATION. CEREMONY. (LOCAL). W SHIRELL FOX; ANDERSON COLLEGE; ANDERSON, IN 46011. (#200017-3).

OCT 25, '75. HOMECOMING. PARADE, FESTIVAL. (LOCAL). W SHIRELL FOX; ANDERSON COLLEGE; ANDERSON, IN 46011. (#200017-2).

NOV 13, '75. 'THE CONCERT OF DISCOVERY' - SPAIN'S CONTRIBUTIONS. SEMINAR. (LOCAL). W SHIRELL FOX, COORD; ANDERSON COLLEGE; 1100 E 5TH ST; ANDERSON, IN 46011. (#200017-53).

NOV 18, '75. 'NEGRO HISTORY'. SEMINAR. (LOCAL). W SHIRELL FOX, COORD; ANDERSON COLLEGE; 1100 E 5TH ST; ANDERSON, IN 46011. (#200017-52).

FEB 10, '76. 'LIFE OF WASHINGTON'. SEMINAR. (LOCAL). W SHIRELL FOX, COORD; ANDERSON COLLEGE; 1100 E 5TH ST; ANDERSON, IN 46011. (#200017-54).

JUNE 14, '76. DEDICATION OF HISTORICAL MARKER. CEREMONY. (LOCAL). W SHIRELL FOX, COORD; ANDERSON COLLEGE; 1100 E 5TH ST; ANDERSON, IN 46011. (#107175-1).

SEPT '76. DEDICATION OF EXCHANGE CLUB FREEDOM SHRINE. CEREMONY. (LOCAL). W SHIRELL FOX, ADM ASST; ANDERSON COLLEGE; 1100 E 5TH ST; ANDERSON, IN 46011. (#107354-1).

SEPT '76 - MAY '77. ART EXHIBITS. EXHIBITS OF HERITAGE & CONTEMPORARY ART, INCLUDING PAINTING & SCULPTURE. (LOCAL). W SHIRELL FOX, ASST; ANDERSON COLLEGE; 1100 E 5TH ST; ANDERSON, IN 46011. (#107175-2).

SEPT '76 - MAY '77. LECTURE SERIES: ALL FACETS OF THE AMERICAN HERITAGE. NEGRO HISTORY; LIFE OF WASHINGTON; RELIGIOUS HISTORY; OLD WORLD CONTRIBUTIONS TO AMERICA. (LOCAL). W SHIRELL FOX, ADM ASST; ANDERSON COLLEGE; 1100 E 5TH ST; ANDERSON, IN 46011. (#107354-2).

ANGOLA

FOLIOS ON STEUBEN COUNTY, IN. 2 FOLIOS CONTAINING SKETCHES OF COUNTY LANDMARKS. (LOCAL). MILDRED FOSTER, CHAIRMAN; FREMONT BICENTENNIAL COMMITTEE & HISTORICAL SOCIETY; FREMONT, IN 46737. (#17571).

HISTORICAL BLDGS LISTED ON NATIONAL REGISTRY, IN. COUNTY COURTHOUSE AND STEUBEN COUNTY JAIL WILL BE LISTED IN THE NATIONAL REGISTRY. (LOCAL). MRS RALPH LAYMAN, REGENT; POKAGON CHAPTER, DAUGHTERS OF THE AMERICAN REVOLUTION; STEINMONT; HAMILTON, IN 46742. (#17569).

MARKING OF LOCAL LANDMARKS - ANGOLA, IN. ALL LANDMARKS OVER 100 YEARS WILL BE COMMEMORATED WITH MARKERS. (LOCAL). MRS GAYLORD C CRAIN, CHAIRPERSON; STEUBEN COUNTY AMERICAN REVOLUTION BICENTENNIAL COMMISSION; HAMILTON, IN 46742. (#17572).

SURVEY OF STEUBEN COUNTY BUILDINGS, ANGOLA, IN. GRANT TO TRI-STATE COLLEGE FOR STUDY OF LOCAL COUNTY BUILDINGS. (LOCAL). DR DON ZIMMER, PROJ DIRECTOR; TRI STATE COLLEGE; 1000 SPRINGHILL DR; ANGOLA, IN 46703. (#17570).

TIME CAPSULE PROJECT - ANGOLA, IN. SEALED MESSAGES TO DESCENDANTS, KEPT IN BANK VAULT, TO BE OPENED IN 50 YEARS. (LOCAL). ERVIN BLAIR, COORDINATOR; LIONS CLUB AND BICENTENNIAL COMMITTEE; 18 BROOKSIDE PARK; HAMILTON, IN 46742. (#17568).

JULY 4, '75. STEUBEN COUNTY 4TH OF JULY CELEBRATION. FESTIVAL AT ANGOLA MONUMENT. (LOCAL). MRS RALPH E LAYMAN, CHMN; STEUBEN COUNTY AMERICAN REVOLUTION BICENTENNIAL COMMISSION; STEINMONT; HAMILTON, IN 46742. (#200017-1).

OCT 1, '75 - JULY 30, '76. GENERAL LEWIS B HERSHEY HISTORICAL EXHIBIT. EXHIBIT AT TRI-STATE COLLEGE, HERSHEY HALL MUSEUM. (REGN'L). GERALD MOORE, CHAIRMAN; PERFORMING ARTS AND LECTURE SERIES COMMITTEE; TRI-STATE COLLEGE; ANGOLA, IN 46703. (#100332-1).

MAY 16, '76. DEDICATION OF STEUBEN COUNTY COURTHOUSE. CEREMONY AT PUBLIC SQUARE. (LOCAL). MRS RALPH E LAYMAN, CHMN; POKAGON CHAPTER OF THE DAR; HAMILTON, IN 46742. (#103337-1).

MAY 16, '76. FOUR SCHOOL BAND CONCERT. LIVE PERFORMANCE AT ANGOLA HIGH SCHOOL GYM. (LOCAL). MRS RALPH E LAYMAN, CHMN; POKAGON CHAPTER OF THE DAR; HAMILTON, IN 46742. (#103367-1).

ATTICA

OCT 1 - 3, '76. POTAWATOMI BICENTENNIAL FESTIVAL AND RIVERFRONT DAYS. OLD-FASHIONED CHAUTAUQUA AND TIME CAPSULE BURIAL. AT RAVINE PARK, WABASH RIVER FRONT. (LOCAL). MARGUERITE NORMAN, CHMN; POTAWATOMI ORGANIZATION & BICENTENNIAL COMMITTEE; 305 S BRADY ST; ATTICA, IN 47918. (#109369-1).

AUBURN

COURTYARD PARK - AUBURN, IN. BEAUTIFICATION OF COURTYARD PARK. (LOCAL). DENNIS K KEUSE, COORDINATOR; AUBURN AUTO HERITAGE; 360 S UNION; AUBURN, IN 46706. (#27784). **ARBA GRANTEE.**

DEKALB HISTORIC DISPLAY, IN. PROVIDE AN AREA FOR A HISTORIC DISPLAY OF COUNTY ARTIFACTS. (LOCAL). SKIP MARKETTI, COORDINATOR; AUBURN AUTOMOTIVE HERITAGE, INC; 1600 S WAYNE; AUBURN, IN 46706. (#24270). **ARBA GRANTEE.**

SEPT 3, '76 - CONTINUING . DEKALB HISTORICAL DISPLAY. COUNTY ARTIFACTS WILL BE ON DISPLAY. AT AUBURN-CORD-DUESENBERG MUSEUM, 1600 S WAYNE ST. (LOCAL). SKIP MARKETTI; AUBURN AUTOMOTIVE HERITAGE, INC; 1600 S WAYNE; AUBURN, IN 46706. (#24270-1).

AVILLA

RESTORATION OF ONE-ROOM SCHOOL, AVILLA, IN. SCHOOLHOUSE TO BE MOVED TO TOWN PARK, RESTORED & USED AS A BRANCH LIBRARY. THE SCHOOLHOUSE IS THE OLDEST ONE-ROOM SCHOOL IN NOBLE COUNTY. (LOCAL). KATHRYN DELUCENAY, COORDINATOR; TOWN OF AVILLA; BOX 137; AVILLA, IN 46710. (#24716). **ARBA GRANTEE.**

BATTLE GROUND

BATTLE OF TIPPECANOE IN BATTLE GROUND, IN. CONSTRUCTION OF MAJOR EXHIBITS AT TIPPECANOE BATTLEFIELD, A NATIONAL HISTORIC LANDMARK; OPEN TO PUBLIC IN 1976 IN HONOR OF BICENTENNIAL. (NAT'L). WILLIAM BAUGH, DIRECTOR; BATTLE GROUND HISTORICAL CORP; BOX 225; BATTLE GROUND, IN 47920. (#10918).

MAY 31 - JUNE 1, '75. RALLY FOR OLD TIPPECANOE. 'TIPPECANOE AND TYLER TOO' SHOUTED THE WHIGS AT THEIR RALLY IN 1840 AND EACH YEAR THE PATRIOTIC FERVOR OF WILLIAM HENRY HARRISON'S SUCCESSFUL PRESIDENTIAL CAMPAIGN IS RECREATED WITH MILITARY MUSKETS IN PERIOD COSTUME, EARLY AMERICAN MUSIC, FIFES AND DRUMS. AT TIPPECANOE BATTLEFIELD, 7 MILES NORTH OF LAFAYETTE ON S-R 43. (NAT'L). DAVE SAMUELSON, CHMN; BATTLEGROUND HISTORICAL CORPORATION; BOX 225; BATTLEGROUND, IN 47920. (#100320-1).

MAY 29 - 30, '76. RALLY FOR OLD TIPPECANOE; HISTORICAL CEREMONY. RECREATION OF TTE FAMOUS 1840 WHIG RALLY THAT SENT GEN WILLIAM HENRY HARRISON TO THE WHITE HOUSE & GAVE BIRTH TO MODERN POLITICAL CAMPAIGNS.FIFE & DRUM CORPS,GRASS ROOTS THEATRE,COVERED WAGONS,BUFFALO STEW,STUMP SPEAKERS & 1840 DECOR RECREATE ATMOSPHERE OF EARLY 1800'S. AT TIPPECANOE BATTLEFIELD,7 MI N OF LAFAYETTE,OFF S-R 43,EXIT OF I-65. (ST-WIDE). DAVID SAMUELSON; BATTLEGROUND HISTORICAL CORP; BOX 225; BATTLEGROUND, IN 47920. (#100316-1).

BEAN BLOSSOM

JUNE 16 - 20, '76. BEAN BLOSSOM BLUEGRASS FESTIVAL. BLUEGRASS PERFORMERS FROM AROUND THE NATION PERFORM IN THIS SMALL RURAL COMMUNITY IN TRIBUTE TO ONE OF AMERICA'S NATIVE MUSICAL FORMS. AT BROWN COUNTY JAMBOREE BARN. (LOCAL). JAMES MONROE, COORDINATOR; BEAN BLOSSOM BLUEGRASS FESTIVAL; BEAN BLOSSOM, IN 47501. (#103416-380).

BEDFORD

STATUARY OF 'WASHINGTON CROSSING THE DELAWARE'. USE OF INDIANA LIMESTONE IN MANY BLDGS IN NATION'S CAPITAL WILL BE COMMEMORATED BY CARVING LIFE-SIZE STONE STATUE OF 'WASHINGTON CROSSING THE DELAWARE'. DEDICATE AT WASHINGTON CROSSING IN JULY, 1976. (NAT'L). MERLE EDINGTON, CHAIRMAN; BEDFORD BICENTENNIAL COMMITTEE; 2999 W 16TH ST; BEDFORD, IN 47421. (#3315). **ARBA GRANTEE.**

MAY 30 - JUNE 5, '76. BICENTENNIAL FESTIVAL WEEK. A FULL WEEK CELEBRATION INCLUDING SPECIAL CHURCH SERVICE, A PARADE, GOLF TOURNAMENT, CARNIVAL, EXHIBIT, LIMESTONE STATUE, WASHINGTON CROSSING THE DELAWARE, BANQUET AND TOURS OF INDIANA LIMESTONE QUARRIES. AT THROUGHOUT CITY. (LOCAL). MERLE E EDINGTON, DIR; BEDFORD BICENTENNIAL COMMITTEE; 2999 W 16TH ST; BEDFORD, IN 47421. (#104778-1).

BEECH GROVE

'REVOLUTION EVOLUTION', BEECH GROVE, IN. HEIGHTEN AWARENESS OF REVOLUTIONARY ERA THROUGH THEATER PRODUCTION. (LOCAL). RICHARD L BROWN, MANAGER; BUCK CREEK PLAYERS; 156 E MARKET ST, 4TH FLOOR; INDIANAPOLIS, IN 46204. (#25223). **ARBA GRANTEE.**

OCT 1 - 10, '76. 'REVOLUTION EVOLUTION' THEATER PRODUCTION. LIVE PERFORMANCE. (LOCAL). RICHARD L BROWN, MANAGER; BUCK CREEK PLAYERS; 156 E MARKET ST, 4TH FLOOR; INDIANAPOLIS, IN 46204. (#25223-1).

BEVERLY SHRS

HISTORICAL MUSEUM, BEVERLY SHORES, IN. USING A NATIONAL HISTORICAL LANDMARK HOUSE, COLLECT & DISPLAY FOR LOCAL AND NATIONAL PARK SERVICE VISITOR THE HISTORY OF AREA FROM INDIAN DAYS TO PRESENT. (LOCAL). NORMA SCHAEFFER, CHAIRMAN; BEVERLY SHORES BICENTENNIAL COMMITTEE; BOX 371; BEVERLY SHRS, IN 46301. (#29769).

JUNE 17, '76. LITHUANIAN DAY. ART, FOLK MUSIC, FOLK DANCING, FOLK COSTUMES & LITERATURE OF LITHUANIA TOPPED BY NATIVE FOOD. (REGN'L). NORMA SCHAEFFER, CHMN; LITHUANIAN-AMERICAN CLUB OF BEVERLY SHORES; BOX 371; BEVERLY SHRS, IN 46301. (#200017-79).

BLOOMFIELD

JUNE 7, '76. RE-CREATION OF CHAUTAUQUA PERFORMANCE. FOLK MUSIC, READING OF JEFFERSON-HAMILTON LETTERS, SPEECH BY CARL WINTERS, INTERNATIONALLY KNOWN SPEAKER. ALSO ANTIQUE SHOW & OLD FASHIONED STYLE SHOW. AT LOCAL HIGH SCHOOL BUILDING. (LOCAL). NANCY DOWDEN, CHAIRMAN; BLOOMFIELD BICENTENNIAL COMMITTEE; 743 SUNSET DR; BLOOMFIELD, IN 47424. (#200017-119).

JULY 4, '76. 4TH OF JULY BICENTENNIAL CELEBRATION. SERVING OF HUGE BICENTENNIAL BIRTHDAY CAKE, BICENTENNIAL MUSICAL IN AFTERNOON & EXTRAVAGANT FIREWORKS AT NIGHT. AT CITY PARK. (LOCAL). NANCY DOWDEN; BLOOMFIELD BICENTENNIAL COMMITTEE; 743 SUNSET DR; BLOOMFIELD, IN 47424. (#200017-56).

OCT 3, '76. BICENTENNIAL PARADE ON OCTOBER 3, 1976. PARADE AT IN BLOOMFIELD APPROXIMATELY 3 MILES. (LOCAL). NANCY DOWDEN, CHAIRMAN; BLOOMFIELD BICENTENNIAL COMMITTEE AND LIONS CLUB; 743 SUNSET DR; BLOOMFIELD, IN 47424. (#109385-1).

NOV 11, '76. BURIAL OF 1976 BLOOMFIELD TIME CAPSULE. PRAYER, SALUTE BY LOCAL AMERICAN LEGION COLOR GUARD & RAISING OF THE AMERICAN FLAG. TIME CAPSULE HAS STONE

BLOOMFIELD — CONTINUED

MARKER ON TOP & IS TO BE OPENED ON NOVEMBER 11, 2001. AT LOCAL TOWN PARK, NEXT TO FLAG POLE. (LOCAL). NANCY DOWDEN, CHAIRMAN; BLOOMFIELD BICENTENNIAL COMMITTEE; 743 SUNSET DR; BLOOMFIELD, IN 47424. (#200017-118).

BLOOMINGTON

AMERICAN CRAFTS EXHIBITION, BLOOMINGTON, IN. EXHIBITION DEDICATED TO CONTRIBUTIONS OF AMERICAN CRAFTSMEN TO CURRENT 'RENAISSANCE' OF CRAFTS. (ST-WIDE). JOHN W RYAN, CHAIRMAN; INDIANA UNIV FOUNDATION/ART MUSEUM; PO BOX F; BLOOMINGTON, IN 47401. (#10905).

BICENTENNIAL TRAVELING EXHIBITION, IN. BICENTENNIAL TRAVELING EXHIBITION OF HISTORIC INDIANA COSTUMES. (ST-WIDE). NELDA CHRIST, PROJ DIRECTOR; HOME ECONOMICS DEPT, INDIANA UNIV; WYLIE 100 IU; BLOOMINGTON, IN 47401. (#24098). **ARBA GRANTEE.**

CONCERTO FOR TUBA & ORCHESTRA, BLOOMINGTON, IN. SYMPHONIC WORK FOR SOLOIST & ORCHESTRA. (LOCAL). BERNHARD HEIDEN, PROFESSOR OF MUSIC; 915 E UNIVERSITY; BLOOMINGTON, IN 47401. (#23187).

CONFERENCE ON LOCAL GOVERNMENTS IN INDIANA. THE BLOOMINGTON BICENTENNIAL COMMITTEE IS SPONSORING A CONFERENCE ON LOCAL GOVERNMENT IN INDIANA. (ST-WIDE). MARY ALICE GRAY, DIRECTOR; BLOOMINGTON BICENTENNIAL COMMISSION; BOX 100, MUNICIPAL BLDG; BLOOMINGTON, IN 47401. (#25798). **ARBA GRANTEE.**

FREEDOM FESTIVAL - BLOOMINGTON, IN. BLOOMINGTON-MONROE COUNTY BICENTENNIAL COMMITTEE WILL SPONSOR A 3MONTH FREEDOM FESTIVAL. (LOCAL). MARY ALICE GRAY, COORDINATOR; BLOOMINGTON-MONROE COUNTY BICENTENNIAL COMMITTEE; BOX 100, MUNICIPAL BLDG; BLOOMINGTON, IN 47401. (#25580). **ARBA GRANTEE.**

HONEY CREEK SCHOOL PROJECTS, BLOOMINGTON, IN. COMMUNITY PARTICIPATION IN GUIDANCE STEERING COMMITTEE FOR PRESERVATION OF HOOSIER HERITAGE IN LOCAL CURRICULUM. (LOCAL). STELLA ALEXANDER, COORDINATOR; MONROE COUNTY SCHOOL & ASSOC FOR CHILDHOOD EDUCATION; 315 NORTH DR; BLOOMINGTON, IN 47401. (#26857). **ARBA GRANTEE.**

NATL BICENTENNIAL INTERNSHIP PGM -MIDWEST AREA. STUDENT INTERNSHIP ASSISTANCE IN DEVELOPING THE SOCIAL AND ECONOMIC RESOURCES TO SUPPORT LOCALLY INITIATED, STATE AGENCY, AND COMMUNITY BICENTENNIAL PROGRAMMING. (REGN'L). DR JEANNE PATTERSON, PRESIDENT; MIDWESTERN RESOURCE DEVELOPMENT CORP; POPLARS BLDG, 400 E7TH ST; BLOOMINGTON, IN 47401. (#25). **ARBA RECOGNIZED. ARBA GRANTEE.**

PROJECT '76 INFORM - BICENTENNIAL INFORMATION. EDUCATION DISTRIBUTION OF A SPECIAL BICENTENNIAL ISSUE OF THE PHI DELTA KAPPAN & A SPECIAL MINI-BOOK TO DECISION MAKERS, NEWS MEDIA AND LAY CITIZENS. (NAT'L). LOWELL C ROSE, EXEC SECRETARY; PHI DELTA KAPPA; 8TH & UNION; BLOOMINGTON, IN 47401. (#6895).

PROJECT '76: EDUCATION - THEN & NOW. THE PROGRAM DEPICTS TO THE GENERAL PUBLIC THE PROGRESS MADE IN EDUCATION AND SERVES TO OPEN PUBLIC DEBATE ON THE FUTURE OF EDUCATION. (NAT'L). KENNETH G LOVELESS, ADMINISTRATIVE ASSISTANT; PHI DELTA KAPPA; PO BOX 789; BLOOMINGTON, IN 47401. (#3845). **ARBA RECOGNIZED.**

JAN 1 - DEC 31, '76. THE EARLY INDIANA FARMER - EXHIBIT. HOURS ARE 8 AM - 12 NOON AND 1 PM - 5 PM MON-SAT. AT INDIANA UNIV MUSEUM, BLOOMINGTON, INDIANA. (LOCAL). DR WESLEY HURT, CHAIRMAN; INDIANA UNIVERSITY MUSEUM; BLOOMINGTON, IN 47401. (#103812-1).

APR 1 - JULY 1, '76. FREEDOM FESTIVAL. FESTIVAL. (LOCAL). MARY ALICE GRAY, COORD; BLOOMINGTON-MONROE COUNTY BICENTENNIAL COMMISSION; BOX 100, MUNICIPAL BLDG; BLOOMINGTON, IN 47401. (#25580-1).

APR 13, '76. NATIONAL SENEGALESE DANCE COMPANY VISITS BLOOMINGTON. LIVE PERFORMANCE AT UNIVERSITY AUDITORIUM. (INT'L). PRESIDENT; MEL HOWARD PRESENTS; 143 E 27TH ST; NEW YORK, NY 10016. (#108968-6).

JULY 26 - AUG 6, '76. CARL HAVERLIN/BROADCAST MUSIC, INC, ARCHIVES BICENTENNIAL EXHIBIT. OFFERS A VERSATILE PICTURE OF HISTORY, REGIONAL LIFE & MUSIC FOR OVER 200 YEARS. CONTAINS PRESIDENTIAL LETTERS, LETTERS OF FAMOUS AMERICANS, OLD BOOKS, MANUSCRIPTS, HISTORY OF 'THE STAR SPANGLED BANNER' & COMPOSER AUTOGRAPHS, PLUS SHEET MUSIC OF THE PAST. AT INDIANA UNIV SCHOOL OF MUSIC LIBRARY. (ST-WIDE). DR DAVID FENSKE; INDIANA UNIVERSITY; INDIANA UNIV SCHOOL OF MUSIC; BLOOMINGTON, IN 47401. (#20784-20).

OCT 8 - 15, '76. CONFERENCE ON LOCAL GOVERNMENTS IN INDIANA. CONFERENCE. (ST-WIDE). MARY ALICE GRAY, DIRECTOR; BLOOMINGTON BICENTENNIAL COMMITTEE; BOX 100, MUNICIPAL BLDG; BLOOMINGTON, IN 47401. (#25798-1).

NOV '76. PERFORMANCE OF TUBA & ORCHESTRA CONCERTO. LIVE PERFORMANCE. (LOCAL). BERNARD HEIDEN, PROFESSOR; BERNARD HEIDEN; 915 E UNIVERSITY; BLOOMINGTON, IN 47401. (#23187-1).

BLUFFTON

DAY IN THE PARK IN BLUFFTON, IN. A DAY IN THE PARK SPONSORED BY THE WELLS COUNTY BICENT COMMITTEE. (LOCAL). BEVERLY RICH, EXEC DIR; WELLS COUNTY BICENTENNIAL COMMITTEE; R R 3; BLUFFTON, IN 46714. (#27667). **ARBA GRANTEE.**

NEWS-BANNER BICENTENNIAL PROMOTION PROGRAM - NBMRP. PAPER DONATED ALL OF ITS SERVICES TO PROMOTE LOCAL ACTIVITY, INCL COLOR PRINTING OF SYMBOLS, PROMOTED 232 PAGE HISTORY OF COUNTY, PUBLICIZED EVENTS & HAD 184 PAGE BICENTENNIAL EDITION. (LOCAL). JAMES BARBIERI, BICENTENNIAL COORDINATOR; THE NEWS-BANNER; 125 N JOHNSON ST; BLUFFTON, IN 46714. (#30427).

BOONVILLE

HISTORY OF WARRICK COUNTY, IN. REPRINT OF FOUR WARRICK COUNTY HISTORIES IN ONE BOOK. (LOCAL). ZELLA DAVIDSON, COORDINATOR; JACOB WARRICK CHAPTER OF THE DAR; 206 GOUGH AVE; BOONVILLE, IN 47601. (#19634).

WARRICK COUNTY MUSEUM - BOONVILLE, INDIANA. ESTABLISH A COUNTYWIDE MUSEUM. (LOCAL). CAROL BAKER; WARRICK COUNTY MUSEUM COMMITTEE; RT 2; BOONVILLE, IN 47601. (#19515).

WARRICK COUNTY REVOLUTIONARY WAR SOLDIERS - IN. THE DAR IS RESEARCHING AND WRITING ABOUT THE 'REVOLUTIONARY WAR SOLDIERS AND PATRIOTS BURIED IN WARRICK COUNTY AND SOME OF THEIR DESCENDENTS'. 20 SOLDIERS BURIED HERE WITH OVER 8,000 DESCENDENTS. (LOCAL). OPAL B PHILLIPS, BICENT COORD - MABEL MILLER, SEC; JACOB WARRICK CHAPTER OF THE DAR & WARRICK CO BICENT COMM; 424 E LOCUST; BOONVILLE, IN 47601. (#19636).

JAN 3, '76. PRESENTATION OF OFFICIAL BICENTENNIAL COMMUNITY FLAG. CEREMONY AT COURTHOUSE LAWN. (LOCAL). MARY RACHEL FORSYTHE; WARRICK COUNTY AMERICAN REVOLUTION BICENTENNIAL COMMITTEE; 115 E JENNINGS ST; NEWBURGH, IN 47630. (#200017-50).

MAY 16, '76. HISTORICAL TOUR OF WARRICK COUNTY. BUSES TO TRAVEL AROUND THE COUNTY TO VARIOUS HISTORICAL SPOTS. AT BOONVILLE HIGH SCHOOL PARKING LOT, N THIRD ST. (LOCAL). HAROLD MCCLARY, COORD; WARRICK COUNTY BICENTENNIAL COMMITTEE; 509 N THIRD ST; BOONVILLE, IN 47601. (#104468-4).

JULY 4, '76. HISTORICAL MARKER DEDICATION. PLAQUE WITH NAMES OF REVOLUTIONARY WAR SOLDIERS BURIED IN WARRICK COUNTY TO BE DEDICATED; DESCENDANTS INVITED. AT WARRICK COUNTY COURTHOUSE LAWN. (LOCAL). JANE CRENSHAW, COORD; WARRICK COUNTY BICENTENNIAL COMMISSION; 12 E WATER; NEWBURGH, IN 47630. (#104468-5).

BOURBON

JUNE 18 - 19, '76. RE-CREATION OF OLD BOURBON FAIR AND MUSKET SHOOT. INCLUDES EXHIBITS, RIDES, ENTERTAINMENT, MUSKET SHOOT AND MEMORIAL SERVICES. AT BOURBON PARK & SCHOOLGROUNDS. (LOCAL). TONY WOOD, CHAIRMAN; BOURBON BICENTENNIAL COMMITTEE; 112 N MAIN ST; BOURBON, IN 46504. (#103598-1).

BRANDYWINE

AUG 28, '76. BICENTENNIAL FESTIVAL. FESTIVAL AT BRANDYWINE SCHOOL. (LOCAL). MRS FLOYD TUCKER, CHMN; BRANDYWINE BICENTENNIAL COMMITTEE; RR 4; GREENFIELD, IN 46140. (#104770-1).

BRAZIL

HOOSIER HERITAGE '76 - BRAZIL, IN. THE BRAZIL ROTARY CLUB WILL SPONSOR THE FESTIVAL HOOSIER HERITAGE '76. (LOCAL). FRED ADAMSON, PROJ CHAIRMAN; BRAZIL ROTARY CLUB; 608 W NATIONAL AVE; BRAZIL, IN 47834. (#26805). **ARBA GRANTEE.**

BREMEN

BICENTENNIAL ROOM IN BREMEN, IN. A ROOM AT THE HOSPITAL WILL BE DEDICATED AS A BICENTENNIAL ROOM. (LOCAL). CHARLES LAFREE & JIM TRICE, CO-CHAIRMEN; BICENTENNIAL '76 & HOSPITAL FUND DRIVE; BREMEN, IN 46506. (#12995).

FIRE HYDRANTS PAINTING IN BREMEN, IN. REVOLUTIONARY FIGURES HAVE BEEN PAINTED ON ALL FIRE HYDRANTS. (LOCAL). JIM TRICE, PROJ CHAIRMAN; BREMEN BICENTENNIAL COMMITTEE; PO BOX 203; BREMEN, IN 46506. (#12994).

STATE TREE WALK IN BREMEN, IN. A TREE WILL BE PLANTED FOR EACH OF THE ORIGINAL 13 STATES, AS WELL AS THE INDIANA STATE TREE. (LOCAL). JIM TRICE, PROJ CHAIRMAN; BREMEN BICENTENNIAL COMMITTEE; BREMEN, IN 46506. (#12993). **ARBA GRANTEE.**

DEC 6, '75. COLONIAL DINNER. FESTIVAL AT MASONIC LODGE. (LOCAL). JIM TRICE, BICENT CHMN; EASTERN STAR; BREMEN, IN 46506. (#100895-1).

FEB 7, '76. BICENTENNIAL COSTUME BALL. FESTIVAL AT BREMEN ELEMENTARY SCHOOL 700 W SOUTH ST. (LOCAL). JAMES E TRICE, CHMN; TRI KAPPA SORORITY; PO BOX 203; BREMEN, IN 46506. (#100896-1).

BROWNSBURG

BICENTENNIAL COMMUNITY SIGNS - BROWNSBURG, IN. TWENTY FIVE BICENTENNIAL SIGNS WERE DESIGNED USING OUR OFFICIAL LOGO AND HUNG ON STREET CORNERS ALONG THE MAIN STREETS. THE TOTAL COST WAS APPROXIMATELY $1,700 WHICH WAS RAISED THRU DONATIONS. (LOCAL). RICHARD H ISENHOUR, CHAIRMAN; BROWNSBURG BICENTENNIAL COMMITTEE; 312 SCHOOL ST; BROWNSBURG, IN 46112. (#32379).

FESTIVAL USA PROJECTS - BROWNSBURG, IN. 3000 CITIZENS REAFFIRMED THEIR BELIEFS IN THE BASIC FREEDOMS; DECLARATION OF INDEPENDENCE DISPLAYED; BICENT SCRAPBOOK; AMERICAN & BENNINGTON FLAGS FOR PURCHASE; BICENT LICENSE PLATES & DECALS. (LOCAL). RICHARD H ISENHOUR, CHAIRMAN; BROWNSBURG BICENTENNIAL COMMITTEE; 312 SCHOOL ST; BROWNSBURG, IN 46112. (#32129).

HERITAGE '76 PROJECTS - BROWNSBURG, IN. BICENT YOUTH ESSAY CONTEST; LOGO CONTEST; COMMUNITY PRIDE; HIGH SCHOOL HALL OF FAME PROJECT. (LOCAL). RICHARD H ISENHOUR, CHAIRMAN; BROWNSBURG BICENTENNIAL COMMITTEE; 312 SCHOOL ST; BROWNSBURG, IN 46112. (#28252).

HORIZONS '76 PROJECTS FOR BROWNSBURG, IN. ROADWAYS IN BROWN & LINCOLN TOWNSHIPS CLEANED UP; ARBUCKLE ACRES PARK DEVELOPED; TREES PLANTED IN LOCAL PARKS ON ARBOR DAY. (LOCAL). RICHARD H ISENHOUR, CHAIRMAN; BROWNSBURG BICENTENNIAL COMMITTEE; 312 SCHOOL ST; BROWNSBURG, IN 46112. (#32130).

OFFICIAL ARBA BICENTENNIAL COMMUNITY SIGNS - IN. TWO ARBA BICENTENNIAL SIGNS WERE DONATED TO THE BICENTENNIAL COMMITTEE BY TWO FAMILIES. THESE SIGNS WERE ERECTED AT CITY LIMITS. (LOCAL). SUZANNE BOWLING, CHAIRMAN; BROWNSBURG BICENTENNIAL COMMITTEE; 5 ROBINWOOD DR; BROWNSBURG, IN 46112. (#32378).

SHE'S A GRAND OLE FLAG - BROWNSBURG, IN. DISPLAY OF 50 STAR AMERICAN FLAGS ON MAIN STREETS IN TOWN DURING EACH HOLIDAY PERIOD. (LOCAL). W KENT HUBER, PRESIDENT; BROWNSBURG JAYCEES; 20 ROSELAWN AVE; BROWNSBURG, IN 46112. (#32380).

MAR 2, '76. BICENTENNIAL SALUTE TO OUR TOWN. THE MUSICAL DRAMA 'GOD'S COUNTRY', WHICH DEPICTS 300 YEARS OF INTERNAL, SOCIAL AND ENVIRONMENTAL CONFLICTS IN THE UNITED STATES. AT 636 E MAIN ST. (LOCAL). BEA SCHIER, CHAIRMAN; BROWNSBURG AMERICAN LEGION AUXILIARY; 426 RODNEY; BROWNSBURG, IN 46112. (#200017-100).

APR 9, '76. 'THIS IS YOUR LIFE' - DR A N SCUDDER. DR SCUDDER HAS BEEN A PHYSICIAN IN BROWNSBURG FOR 43 YEARS AND HIS CONTRIBUTIONS ARE MANY. AT 1000 S ODELL, HIGH SCHOOL AUDITORIUM. (LOCAL). RICHARD H ISENHOUR, CHMN; BROWNSBURG HIGH SCHOOL; 312 SCHOOL ST; BROWNSBURG, IN 46112. (#200017-102).

APR 30, '76. 'OUR FREEDOM'. AN AMERICAN HERITAGE PROGRAM CONSISTING OF MUSIC AND DIRECT READINGS COMMEMORATING THE EVENTS FROM 1776 TO 1976. AT 1000 S ODELL, HIGH SCHOOL AUDITORIUM. (LOCAL). RICHARD H ISENHOUR, CHMN; BROWNSBURG HIGH SCHOOL; 312 SCHOOL ST; BROWNSBURG, IN 46112. (#200017-101).

MAY 8, '76. 'MARCH FOR AMERICA'. STUDENTS AND RESIDENTS PARTICIPATED IN A PARADE IN HONOR OF AMERICAN BICENTENNIAL. THE PARADE CONSISTED OF BANDS, FLOATS AND STUDENTS PORTRAYING THE 'SPIRIT OF 1776' TO THE 'SPIRIT OF 1976.'. AT 1000 S ODELL STREET. (LOCAL). PAUL ACTON, CHAIRMAN; BROWNSBURG HIGH SCHOOL; 1000 S ODELL ST; BROWNSBURG, IN 46112. (#200017-99).

JUNE 30 - JULY 5, '76. LIONS BICENTENNIAL EXTRAVAGANZA. FISH FRY, MERCHANTS DISPLAY TENT, CARNIVAL RIDES AND FIREWORKS DISPLAY. AT ARBUCKLE ACRES PARK. (LOCAL). RICHARD H ISENHOUR, CHMN; BROWNSBURG LIONS CLUB; 312 SCHOOL ST; BROWNSBURG, IN 46112. (#200017-103).

JULY 3, '76. BICENTENNIAL STYLE SHOW. THIS WAS A STYLE SHOW SPONSORED IN AN EFFORT TO ENCOURAGE CITIZENS TO MAKE & WEAR BICENTENNIAL CLOTHING DURING OUR BICENTENNIAL YEAR. VARIOUS PRIZES WERE AWARDED IN SEVERAL CATEGORIES. AT STAGE AT ONE END OF EXHIBITION TENT. (LOCAL). DOROTHY KELLEY, CHAIRMAN; BROWNSBURG BICENTENNIAL COMMITTEE; RR, PREBSTER RD; BROWNSBURG, IN 46112. (#200017-104).

SEPT 11 - 12, '76. BROWNSBURG OLD-FASHION FESTIVAL. ARBUCKLE ACRES PARK IS TURNED INTO A QUAINT OLD FASHIONED VILLAGE WITH VARIOUS BOOTHS & EXHIBITS. A PARADE AND VARIOUS CONTESTS ARE FEATURED. AT ARBUCKLE ACRES PARK. (LOCAL). SUZANNE BOWLING, CHMN; BROWNSBURG JAYNCEES; 5 ROBINWOOD DR; BROWNSBURG, IN 46112. (#200017-98).

NOV 21, '76. BICENTENNIAL THANKSGIVING SMORGASBORD. THIS PROJECT IS INTENDED AS A WAYS AND MEANS TO HELP DEFRAY THE BICENTENNIAL'S EXPENSES. A FULL HOME COOKED SMORGASBORD DINNER WILL BE SERVED. FREE ENTERTAINMENT WILL BE PROVIDED. AT BROWNSBURG HIGH SCHOOL CAFETERIA. (LOCAL). RICHARD H ISENHOUR, CHMN; BROWNSBURG BICENTENNIAL COMMITTEE; 312 SCHOOL ST; BROWNSBURG, IN 46112. (#200017-90).

BROWNSTOWN

JULY 4, '76. BURIAL OF TIME CAPSULE. CEREMONY AT JACKSON COUNTY COURTHOUSE, MAIN ST. (LOCAL). C C MAY, CHMN; JACKSON COUNTY BICENTENNIAL COMMITTEE; 809 W 8TH ST; SEYMOUR, IN 47274. (#104471-1).

JULY 27 - 30, '76. JACKSON COUNTY HISTORICAL PAGEANT. WILL INVOLVE 300 LOCAL PEOPLE IN AUTHENTIC COSTUMES DOING SKITS ON JACKSON COUNTY HISTORY. AT JACKSON CO FAIR GRANDSTAND. (LOCAL). MRS JOSEPH ERP, COORD; JACKSON CO FAIR BOARD; 1313 STADIUM DR; SEYMOUR, IN 47274. (#104302-5).

BROWNSTOWN — CONTINUED

SEPT 3 - 5, '76. WATERMELON FESTIVAL. FESTIVAL WILL INCLUDE STAGE PERFORMANCES; ART EXHIBITS, ANTIQUE CAR DISPLAYS, CONTESTS AND CRAFT DEMONSTRATIONS. AT CITY SQUARE. (ST-WIDE). BETTY SMALL WOOD, COORD; JACKSON COUNTY BICENTENNIAL COMMUNITY; 206 S MAIN; BROWNSTOWN, IN 47220. (#104302-6).

BUCK CREEK

PRINTING & DISTRIBUTION OF DEDICATORY SPEECH, IN. THE SPEECH DELIVERED BY REV VICTOR STONER AT THE SITE OF HANCOCK COUNTY'S FIRST 4TH OF JULY PICNIC, WILL BE PRINTED & DISTRIBUTED IN BUCK CREEK TOWNSHIP. SPEECH RECALLS EARLY DAYS IN THE TOWNSHIP. (LOCAL). ROBERT L BELL, CHAIRMAN; BUCK CREEK TOWNSHIP BICENTENNIAL COMMITTEE; RR #2, PO BOX 313; GREENFIELD, IN 46140. (#20365).

CAMBRIDGE CY

SEPT 18 - 19, '76. WHITEWATER CANAL DAYS. HISTORICAL TOURS DEPICT IMPORTANCE OF WHITEWATER CANAL TO GROWTH OF MIDWEST AND EASTERN INDIANA. (LOCAL). RICK RICHARDS, CHAIRMAN; CAMBRIDGE CITY CHAMBER OF COMMERCE; PO BOX 245; CAMBRIDGE CY, IN 47327. (#105159-1).

CANAAN

SEPT 10 - 12, '76. CANAAN FALL FESTIVAL. UNUSUAL COMPETITIONS INCLUDING CONTESTS FOR THE INDIAN PRINCESS,THE LARGEST FROG,FROG JUMPING,FREASED POLE CLIMBING & TALENT SELECTIONS. OLD FASHIONED PARADE,FLEA MARKET,FARM DISPLAYS,ARTS & CRAFTS,ONLY ANNUAL US PONY EXPRESS MAIL RUN. AT CANAAN. (LOCAL). GALE H FERRIS, PROJ DIR; CANAAN RESTORATION COUNCIL, INC; RT 1; CANAAN, IN 47224. (#100344-1).

CARMEL

HISTORIC HOME RESTORATION - CARMEL, IN. RESTORATION OF 100 YEAR OLD HOME OF LOCAL HISTORICAL SIGNIFICANCE. (LOCAL). HARLAN TUDOR, CHAIRMAN; CARMEL BICENTENNIAL COMMISSION; CARMEL, IN 46032. (#27247). **ARBA GRANTEE.**

JULY 4, '75. BICENTENNIAL HORSE & BUGGY PARADE & FIREWORKS. FESTIVAL, PARADE AT CARMEL. (LOCAL). DOROTHY SMITH; CARMEL-CLAY CHAMBER OF COMMERCE; PO BOX 1; CARMEL, IN 46032. (#7925-1).

CASTLE HIGH

APR 8, '76. BAND AND CHORAL MUSICAL AND CONTEST AWARDS. AWARDS FOR COUNTY POSTER AND ESSAY CONTEST. AT CASTLE HIGH SCHOOL, HWY 261. (LOCAL). KATHY EWING, COORDINATOR; WARRICK COUNTY BICENTENNIAL COMMISSION; 76 LARCH PL W; NEWBURGH, IN 47630. (#104468-6).

JUNE 7, '76. RELIGIOUS CELEBRATION OF BICENTENNIAL. LIVE PERFORMANCE AT CASTLE HIGH SCHOOL, HWY 261. (LOCAL). REV RAY LEY, COORDINATOR; WARRICK COUNTY MINISTERIAL ASSOCIATION; 323 E SYCAMORE ST; BOONVILLE, IN 47601. (#104468-3).

CASTLETON

JUNE 11 - 13, '76. INDIANA ROSE FESTIVAL: FLORAL ARRANGEMENTS AND EXHIBITS. ROSES BEND, FOR A MOMENT, TO THE FREE-SPIRITED WILL OF THE BICENTENNIAL DURING AN IMPRESSIVE CEREMONY BY THE GOVERNOR'S HONOR GUARD; HISTORIC AMERICAN FLAGS ARE PRESENTED & FLOWERS REIGN SUPREME OVER THE ROSE FESTIVAL QUEEN. AT NORTH EASTERN IND.. (ST-WIDE). TED TUSCHINSKY, CHAIRMAN; CASTLETON VOL FIRE DEPT; 7845 JOHNSON RD; INDIANAPOLIS, IN 46250. (#100337-1).

CEDAR LAKE

BRAILLE TRAIL TOUCHSTONE OF CEDAR LAKE, INDIANA. NATURE TRAIL EASILY ACCESSIBLE TO THE BLIND AND HANDICAPPED. (LOCAL). MRS WILLIAM LANDSKE, PRESIDENT; CEDAR LAKE JUNIOR WOMENS CLUB; 7325 W 143RD AVE; CEDAR LAKE, IN 46303. (#4581).

SENIOR CITIZENS PARK, CEDAR LAKE, INDIANA. OPEN NATURAL 200 X 200 SQUARE FOOT PARK WHICH IS PARTIALLY SHADED. (LOCAL). DR JAMES NOWLAN, PRESIDENT; SENIOR CITIZEN'S CLUB; 7308 145TH ST; CEDAR LAKE, IN 46303. (#4533). **(??).**

JULY 7, '74. DEDICATION CEREMONY OF REVOLUTIONARY WAR MEMORIAL. WILLIAM VAN GORDER MEMORIAL LOCATED IN AN OLD INDIAN MOUND WHICH SERVES AS A CEMETERY. (LOCAL). MRS BEATRICE HORNER, TOWN; CEDAR LAKE HISTORY CENTER; 9201 W 133RD AVE; CEDAR LAKE, IN 46303. (#4582-901).

SEPT 20, '75. NIKE GUIDED MISSILE MONUMENT DEDICATION. ACQUIRED FROM THE US ARMY MISSILE COMMAND. THE TINO NIKE ANTI-AIRCRAFT GUIDED MISSILES WILL BE A PART OF THE COMMUNITY'S BICENTENNIAL HERITAGE CEREMONY & SPEECHES, FOLLOWED BY A BANQUET. AT AMERICAN LEGION POST 261 NEW BUILDING. (LOCAL). NICK TAYLOR, COMMANDER; CEDAR LAKE AMERICAN LEGION POST 261; 13050 WASHINGTON ST; CEDAR LAKE, IN 46303. (#200017-89).

JULY 10, '76. LAROSE TAYLOR SURPRISE MEMORIAL PLAQUE DEDICATION. GIRL SCOUTS DRESSED IN RED, WHITE & BLUE, IN PLAQUE MOUNTING CEREMONY ON GRAVE OF ONLY KNOWN INDIAN BURIED IN LAKE COUNTY, ON 100TH ANNIVERSARY OF HER BIRTH. WAS MOTHER OF OLD AREA PIONEER FAMILY. DESCENDENTS & NEIGHBORS IN ATTENDANCE. AT CRESTTON CEMETERY. (LOCAL). MS WALLACE WEIERT, COORD; GIRL SCOUT TROOP 454 & CEDAR LAKE BICENTENNIAL COMMITTEE; 11525 W 143 AVE; CEDAR LAKE, IN 46303. (#200017-88).

CENTERVILLE

FARM CERTIFICATES OF CENTERVILLE, INDIANA. FRAMED CERTIFICATES WERE PRESENTED TO OWNERS OF ALL FARMS IN FAMILES SINCE 1816. (LOCAL). DONALD MCKINNEY, CHAIRMAN; CENTERVILLE-ABINGTON BICENTENNIAL COMMISSION; CENTERVILLE, IN 47330. (#29828).

JULY 3 - 4, '76. CENTERVILLE SALUTES AMERICA. ACTIVITIES INCLUDED A COSTUMED BREAKFAST, FLEA MARKET, DISPLAYS, CONTESTS, DANCING, PARADE, RELIGIOUS SERVICES, TOURS, DEDICATIONS, AND FIREWORKS. (LOCAL). DONALD MCKINNEY; CENTERVILLE-ABINGDON BICENTENNIAL COMMISSION; NOLANSFORK RD; RICHMOND, IN 47374. (#200017-108).

CHESTERTON

AVENUE OF FLAGS - PROJ OF CHESTERTON, IN. AMERICAN FLAGS FROM PRE-REVOLUTION TO PRESENT DAY WILL FLY ALONG BROADWAY. (LOCAL). WILLIAM H KING, CHAIRMAN; NORTH PORTER COUNTY BICENTENNIAL COORDINATING COMMITTEE; PO BOX 1776; CHESTERTON, IN 46304. (#14901).

BEAUTIFICATION OF THOMAS CENTENNIAL PARK, IN. BEAUTIFICATION TO INCLUDE THE PLANTING OF TREES & THE INSTALLATION OF WALKS. (LOCAL). WILLIAM H KING, CHAIRMAN; NORTH PORTER COUNTY BICENTENNIAL COORDINATING COMMITTEE; PO BOX 1776; CHESTERTON, IN 46304. (#14899).

DECORATION OF FIRE PLUGS, CHESTERTON, IN. STUDENTS WILL PAINT CHESTERTON & PORTER FIRE PLUGS IN A REVOLUTIONARY MOTIF. (LOCAL). WILLIAM H KING, CHAIRMAN; NORTH PORTER COUNTY BICENTENNIAL COORDINATING COMMITTEE; PO BOX 1776; CHESTERTON, IN 46304. (#14900).

HISTORY OF NORTHERN INDIANA. MULTI-MEDIA SHOW ON HISTORY OF NORTHWEST INDIANA & AMERICA, ITS PEOPLE, TRADITIONS AND LEGACY; SHOW WILL BE MULTI-PROJECTOR & PANORAMIC SCREENS. (ST-WIDE). CONRAD KOMINAREK, CHAIRMAN; MICHIGAN CITY BICENTENNIAL COMMISSION; PO BOX 11; MICHIGAN CITY, IN 46360. (#10841).

NOV 15, '75. BICENTENNIAL CONCERT. CONCERT OF AMERICAN MUSIC WILL BE PRESENTED BY VALPARAISO UNIV CHOIR AND CONCERT ORCHESTRA. AT CHESTERTON HIGH SCHOOL. (LOCAL). WILLIAM H KING, CHAIRMAN; N PORTER COUNTY BICENTENNIAL COORDINATING COMMITTEE; PO BOX 1776; CHESTERTON, IN 46304. (#102155-1).

MAY 23 - JUNE 11, '76. FILM FESTIVAL AT INDIANA DUNES NATIONAL LAKESHORE. FILM FESTIVAL USING NATIONAL PARK SERVICE PRODUCED FILMS UPON THE COMPLETION OF THE RENOVATION OF THE VISITOR CENTER. AT INDIANA DUNES NL VISITOR CENTER, U.S. 12 AND KEMIL ROAD. (REGN'L). INDIANA DUNES NL; NATIONAL PARK SERVICE; ROUTE 2-BOX 135 A; CHESTERTON, IN 46304. (#6728-210).

JUNE 5 - 6, '76. VISITOR CENTER DEDICATION AT INDIANA DUNES NATL LAKESHORE. OPEN HOUSE CEREMONIES TO DEDICATE THE RENOVATED VISITOR CENTER. AT VISITOR CENTER, US 12 AND KEMIL ROAD. (REGN'L). INDIANA DUNES NL; NATIONAL PARK SERVICE; ROUTE 2 BOX 135 A; CHESTERTON, IN 46304. (#6728-208).

JULY 11, '76. BAILLY HOMESTEAD DEDICATION. BICENTENNIALLY-THEMED DEDICATION ACTIVITIES DURING RESTORATION PROJECT AT BAILLY HISTORIC SITE. (REGN'L). INDIANA DUNES NL; NATIONAL PARK SERVICE; ROUTE 2 BOX 135 A; CHESTERTON, IN 46304. (#6728-214).

JULY 11, '76. NATL PK SVC '...A LITTLE LOOK AROUND' VISITS INDIANA DUNES NL. THIS SHORT PROGRAM FEATURES ACTORS PLAYING THE ROLES OF FAMOUS AMERICANS OF THE PAST WHO'VE RETURNED TO SEE AMERICA'S GROWTH. RIIS PARK; AND 6/27 AT FLOYD BENNETT FIEL. AT CHELLBURG FARM. (REGN'L). INDIANA DUNES NL; NATIONAL PARK SERVICE; ROUTE 2, BOX 139A; CHESTERTON, IN 46304. (#5653-16).

JULY 25 - AUG 5, '76. NPS AUDIO CHAIR EXHIBIT VISITS INDIANA DUNES NL. TAPES DISCUSS THE ROLE OF WOMEN, NATIVE AMERICANS AND BLACKS IN THE REVOLUTIONARY WAR. (REGN'L). INDIANA DUNES NL; NATIONAL PARK SERVICE; ROUTE 2, BOX 135A; CHESTERTON, IN 46304. (#5581-9).

AUG 8 - 14, '76. FESTIVAL WEEK. FESTIVAL AT CHESTERTON & PORTER CITY PARKS. (LOCAL). WILLIAM H KING, CHAIRMAN; N PORTER COUNTY BICENTENNIAL COORDINATING COMMITTEE; PO BOX 1776; CHESTERTON, IN 46304. (#102154-1).

DEC 19 - 24, '76. LA SALLE EXPEDITION II. IN COOPERATION WITH THE LOCAL COMMUNITY ORGANIZATIONS, A RE-ENACTMENT OF THE LASALLE EXPEDITION WILL OCCUR. (LOCAL). INDIANA DUNES NL; NATIONAL PARK SERVICE; ROUTE 2, BOX 135 A; CHESTERTON, IN 46304. (#6729-129).

CHRISNEY

APR 24 - 25, '76. ARTS AND CRAFTS SPRING SHOW. EXHIBITS AND DEMONSTRATIONS OF PAINTING, CERAMICS, CANDLE MAKING, WOODWORKING AND OTHER CRAFTS. AT 4-H YOUTH AND COMMUNITY CENTER. (LOCAL). MRS HUGH BARCLAY, CHMN; LINCOLN HILLS ARTS AND CRAFTS ASSOC; 211 N LINCOLN AVE; ROCKPORT, IN 47635. (#104721-6).

JUNE 26 - 27, '76. SPENCER COUNTY REACT JAMBOREE. PATRIOTIC PROGRAM, MUSIC, DISPLAYS & EQUIPMENT. AT YOUTH AND COMMUNITY CENTER. (LOCAL). LESTER PURVIANCE, COORD; SPENCER COUNTY REACT; CHRISNEY, IN 47611. (#104721-5).

JULY 3 - 4, '76. PATCHWORK PATRIOTS QUILT AND COMFORTER SHOW. FROM BETSY ROSS TO MODERN COVERLET-NEEDLECRAFTERS SHOW OF QUILTS AND COMFORTERS OF HISTORICAL SIGNIFICANCE; MUSIC AND FOOD WILL AVAILABLE. AT 4-H YOUTH & COMMUNITY CENTER. (LOCAL). MRS EDWIN CONEN, COORD; LINCOLN HILLS ARTS AND CRAFTS ASSOC; HARVEST HILL FARM; GRANDVIEW, IN 47615. (#106024-1).

JULY 10, '76. ICE CREAM FESTIVAL. HOMEMADE ICE CREAM, CAKE, PIES, SHORT ORDERS FOR SALE; FREE ENTERTAINMENT. (LOCAL). MRS FRANK WETHERILL, CHMN; ZION UNITED CHURCH OF CHRIST; CHRISNEY, IN 47611. (#104721-4).

AUG 20 - 22, '76. CHRISNEY FALL FESTIVAL. PATRIOTIC PARADE, GAMES, FOOD, MUSIC. AT CITY PARK. (LOCAL). HARRY YEARBY, COORD; CHRISNEY CIVIC ASSOC; CHRISNEY, IN 47611. (#104721-3).

OCT 2 - 3, '76. ARTS AND CRAFTS COMBINED 4 COUNTY SHOW. SPINNING, WEAVING, CANDLEMAKING, POTTERY, LEATHER WORK, PAINTING, BLOCK PRINTING, CERAMICS, QUILTING, WOODWORKING EXHIBITS AND DEMONSTRATIONS. AT 4-H YOUTH & COMMUNITY CENTER. (LOCAL). MRS HUGH BARCLAY, COORD; 4 COUNTY LINCOLN HILLS ARTS AND CRAFTS; 211 N LINCOLN AVE; ROCKPORT, IN 47635. (#104721-2).

NOV 20 - 21, '76. HOLIDAY HARVEST FESTIVAL. CRAFT DEMONSTRATION AND SALE OF CERAMICS, WOOD CRAFTS, LEATHERWORK, PAINTINGS, CERAMICS, NEEDLEWORK, QUILTS, CORNSHUCK DOLLS & FLOWERS. AT YOUTH AND COMMUNITY CENTER. (LOCAL). MRS HUGH BARCLAY, COORD; SPENCER COUNTY, LINCOLN HILLS ARTS AND CRAFTS ASSOC; 211 N LINCOLN AVE; ROCKPORT, IN 47635. (#104721-1).

CICERO

JULY 1 - 5, '76. CICERO BICENTENNIAL CELEBRATION. FLEA MARKET, FISH FRY, BIRTHDAY PARTY, BELL RINGING, CHILDREN'S GAMES, STYLE SHOW, CHILDREN'S PARADE, VESPERS SERVICE, FIREWORKS AND TALENT SHOW. AT TRI-TOWN PARK. (LOCAL). SANDRA CASTOR, CHAIRMAN; CICERO BICENTENNIAL COMMITTEE; RR1, BOX 13; CICERO, IN 46034. (#108323-1).

CLARKSVILLE

BICENTENNIAL YOUTH FESTIVAL, CLARKSVILLE, IN. WEEK-LONG BICENTENNIAL YOUTH FESTIVAL. ACTIVITIES INCLUDE: BATON TWIRLING CONTEST, RELIGIOUS DAY, HISTORY DAY, NATURE ACTIVITIES, BIKE HIKE, BICENTENNIAL PARADE & DANCE. (LOCAL). EDWARD C COOPER, COORDINATOR; CLARKSVILLE BICENTENNIAL COMMISSION; 1776 ROY COLE DR; CLARKSVILLE, IN 47130. (#25242). **ARBA GRANTEE.**

JUNE 5 - 13, '76. BICENTENNIAL YOUTH FESTIVAL & PARADE. BICENTENNIAL YOUTH WEEK, ACTIVITIES INCLUDE: BATON TWIRLING CONTEST, RELIGIOUS DAY, HISTORICAL DAY, NATURE ACTIVITIES, BIKE HIKE, PARADE & DANCE. (LOCAL). EDWARD C COOPER, COORD; CLARKSVILLE BICENTENNIAL COMMITTEE; 1776 ROY COLE DR; CLARKSVILLE, IN 47130. (#25242-1).

CLOVERDALE

JULY 3 - 4, '76. 4TH OF JULY CELEBRATION. TALENT SHOW, ARTS & CRAFTS DISPLAY, BALLOON ASCENSION, SKY DIVING, COUNTRY MUSIC, AEROBATICS & PARADE. AT CLOVERDALE HIGH SCHOOL. (LOCAL). MARY HILL; SPIRIT OF CLOVERDALE '76; R 1; QUINCY, IN 47456. (#200017-120).

COLUMBIA CITY

THE POST & MAIL BICENTENNIAL SUPPORT - NBMRP. COLUMBIA CITY POST & THE COMMERCIAL MAIL CARRYING EDUCATIONAL & HISTORICAL MATERIAL TO STIMULATE BICENT INTEREST & PARTICIPATION. WILL FEATURE SCHOOL TRIP TO WASHINGTON, DC, IN OCTOBER 1976. (LOCAL). MRS HESTER ADAMS, PUBLISHER; THE POST & MAIL PUBLISHING CO, INC; 116 N CHAUNCEY ST; COLUMBIA CITY, IN 46725. (#30429).

COLUMBUS

BLACK HISTORY WEEK CELEBRATION, COLUMBUS, IN. CELEBRATION OF BLACK HISTORY WEEK (FEB 8-14) THROUGH PUBLIC DISCUSSION & DEBATE. (LOCAL). DARLENE HUNTER, COORDINATOR; MONTSHO SUHUBA; 1005 5TH ST; COLUMBUS, IN 40519. (#23542). **ARBA GRANTEE.**

CLAIMING THE PROMISE - COLUMBUS, IN. A MAJOR VOTER EDUCATION CAMPAIGN ATTEMPTING TO HAVE 76% OF REGISTERED VOTERS PARTICIPATE IN 1976; A SPEAKERS BUREAU AVAILABLE TO ALL GROUPS WILL PLAY A MAJOR ROLE. (LOCAL). SUSAN PAPP, PRESIDENT; LEAGUE OF WOMEN VOTERS; 4260 KENNEDY; COLUMBUS, IN 47201. (#21560).

THE COLUMBUS JAZZ FESTIVAL - COLUMBUS, IN. A JAZZ FESTIVAL WILL BE HELD IN HONOR OF THE BICENTENNIAL. (LOCAL). DANIEL EBLING, DIRECTOR; IUPUI COLUMBUS; 2080 BAKALAR DR; COLUMBUS, IN 47201. (#23595). **ARBA GRANTEE.**

COLUMBUS — CONTINUED

COLUMBUS REPUBLIC'S BICENTENNIAL PROJECTS - NBMRP. HAS CO-SPONSORED FREE CONCERTS BY US ARMED FORCES BICENTENNIAL BAND, US AIR FORCE BAND & SINGING SERGEANTS. PLANS SPECIAL EDITION ON JULY 4. EXTENSIVE COVERAGE OF LOCAL BICENTENNIAL ACTIVITIES. (LOCAL). ROBERT N BROWN, PUBLISHER; THE COLUMBUS REPUBLIC; 333 2ND STREET; COLUMBUS, IN 47201. (#26067).

THE COMMONS, COLUMBUS, IN. THE COMMONS IS A YEAR-ROUND, MULTI-USE PUBLIC SPACE ENTIRELY ENCASED IN GLASS. IT HAS A STAGE, EXHIBIT SPACES, INDOOR PLAYGROUND, MEETING ROOMS AND CHAOS I, A LARGE KINETIC SCULPTURE BY JEAN TINGUELY. (ST-WIDE). G JAMES OLSEN, EXEC DIRECTOR; THE COMMONS; 302 WASHINGTON ST; COLUMBUS, IN 47201. (#20115).

COURTHOUSE PARK - COLUMBUS, IN. A PARK WITH PERMANENT SEATING, GARDENS AND THE ONLY FOUNTAIN IN THE COUNTY AS A MEMORIAL TO THE BICENTENNIAL. (LOCAL). JOANNE PEARCY, PRESIDENT; MUDLARK GARDEN CLUB; 1311 CRESCENT DR; COLUMBUS, IN 47201. (#21558).

HISTORY PROJ - COLUMBUS, IN. THE HISTORY OF 3 INDIANA CITIES WILL BE RECORDED. (ST-WIDE). VIRGINIA J ROUSE, DIRECTOR; VIDEO ACCESS CENTER; BOX 146; COLUMBUS, IN 47201. (#26639). **ARBA GRANTEE.**

NEW & OLD BARTHOLOMEW CO HISTORY PUBLICATION - IN. A REPRINT OF THE COUNTY HISTORY WITH NEW ADDITIONS. (LOCAL). ROBERT MARSHALL, CHAIRMAN; BARTHOLOMEW COUNTY HISTORICAL SOCIETY; 500 WASHINGTON RD; COLUMBUS, IN 46622. (#27210). **ARBA GRANTEE.**

STATE ROAD 46 ENTRANCE BEAUTIFICATION - IN. A COMMUNITY-WIDE FUND RAISING OF $30,000 TO PURCHASE WILLOW, CRABAPPLE, SUGAR MAPLE & TULIP TREES TO LANDSCAPE THE MAJOR ENTRANCE TO COLUMBUS. (LOCAL). DENNIS KING, FUND DRIVE CHAIRMAN; COLUMBUS-BARTHOLOMEW BICENTENNIAL COMMISSION; 500 FRANKLIN; COLUMBUS, IN 47201. (#21559).

TWO DAY FESTIVAL - COLUMBUS, IN. THE COLUMBUS-BARTHOLOMEW CO BICENTENNIAL COMMITTEE IS SPONSORING A TWO DAY FESTIVAL. (LOCAL). PEG CHARIPAR, CHAIRMAN; COLUMBUS-BARTHOLOMEW COUNTY BICENTENNIAL COMMITTEE; 5001 FRANKLIN ST; COLUMBUS, OH 42701. (#27781). **ARBA GRANTEE.**

MAR 19 - 20, '76. THE COLUMBUS JAZZ FESTIVAL. LIVE PERFORMANCE. (LOCAL). DANIEL EBLING, DIRECTOR; IUPUI COLUMBUS; 2080 BAKALAR DR; COLUMBUS, IN 47201. (#23595-1).

MAY 1 - 2, '76. 'FREEDOM IS' - FLOWER SHOW. EXHIBIT AT THE COMMONS, 302 WASHINGTON. (LOCAL). JOANNE SPROUSE, COORD; 5 FEDERATED GARDEN CLUBS; SHOSHONEE DR; COLUMBUS, IN 47201. (#105429-1).

MAY 27, '76. BICENTENNIAL BAND CONCERT. LIVE PERFORMANCE AT EAST COLUMBUS HIGH SCHOOL GYMNASIUM, 230 MAR. (LOCAL). RICHARD COACHYS, COORD; PRO MUSICA, THE PREPUBLIC NEWSPAPER; 1000 5TH; COLUMBUS, IN 47201. (#105429-2).

JUNE 12, '76. OFFICIAL PARADE. PARADE. (LOCAL). DUANE MOTTIER, COORD; COLUMBUS/BARTHOLOMEW COUNTY BICENTENNIAL COMMISSION; 1000 5TH ST; COLUMBUS, IN 47201. (#105429-4).

JUNE 27 - JULY 5, '76. FREEDOM FESTIVAL. FESTIVAL. (LOCAL). PEG TIBBETTS, COORD; DRIFTWOOD VALLEY ARTS COUNCIL; 427 3RD; COLUMBUS, IN 47201. (#105429-3).

JULY 21, '76. HAMPSHIRE COUNTY YOUTH ORCHESTRA. LIVE PERFORMANCE AT HIGH SCHOOL. (INT'L). CULTURAL AFFAIRS OFFICE; BRITISH EMBASSY; 3100 MASSACHUSETTS AVE, NW; WASHINGTON, DC 20008. (#108957-2).

OCT 25 - 26, '76. UNITED STATES ARMED FORCES BICENTENNIAL CARAVAN. CARAVAN IS COMPOSED OF EXHIBIT VANS FOR EACH MILITARY SERVICE. PROJECT THEME IS 'HISTORY OF THE ARMED FORCES & THEIR CONTRIBUTIONS TO THE NATION'. (LOCAL). MRS LINDA BELL; UNITED STATES ARMED FORCES BICENTENNIAL CARAVAN; 500 FRANKLIN ST; COLUMBUS, IN 47201. (#1775-737).

NOV 6, '76. ONE DAY SYMPOSIUM: 'THIRD CENTURY TOWN MEETING'. SEMINAR AT COLUMBUS EAST HIGH SCHOOL. (LOCAL). PEG CHARIPAR, CHAIRMAN; COLUMBUS-BARTHOLOMEW CO BICENT COMM/COLUMBUS AREA CHAMBER OF COMM; 5001 FRANKLIN ST; COLUMBUS, IN 47201. (#27781-1).

CONNERSVILLE

HERITAGE PRESERVATION BOOK - CONNERSVILLE, IN. PRINT COPIES OF A BOOK ON CRAFTSMEN & INDIVIDUALS WISHING TO PRESERVE OUR HERITAGE. (LOCAL). MIKE HOWARD, PROJ COORDINATOR; PUBLICATIONS DEPT, CONNERSVILLE HIGH SCHOOL; 1000 RANCH RD; CONNERSVILLE, IN 47331. (#27009). **ARBA GRANTEE.**

CORTLAND

OCT 20, '75 - MAY 7, '76. SPIRIT OF '76 ART EXHIBIT. CHILDREN'S ART DEPICTING HISTORIC SCENES. AT CORTLAND ELEMENTARY SCHOOL. (LOCAL). EARL SEWELL, DIR; CORTLAND ELEMENTARY SCHOOL; CORTLAND, IN 47228. (#104471-8).

APR 9, '76. TREE PLANTING. CEREMONY. (LOCAL). EARL SEWELL, PRINCIPAL; CORTLAND ELEMENTARY SCHOOL; CORTLAND, IN 47228. (#104471-23).

CORYDON

BATTLE OF CORYDON MEMORIAL PARK - CORYDON, IN. THE BATTLEGROUND OF CORYDON IS TO BE ADDED TO PARK. (LOCAL). ARVILLE L FUNK, COORDINATOR; HARRISON COUNTY BICENTENNIAL COMMITTEE; 303 N CAPITOL AVE; CORYDON, IN 47112. (#26614). **ARBA GRANTEE.**

COVINGTON

MAY 1, '76. SESQUICENTENNIAL BIRTHDAY CELEBRATION. FESTIVAL AT TOWN SQUARE. (LOCAL). WILLARD WILLIAMS, CHMN; COVINGTON CIVIL DEFENSE; 601 8TH ST; COVINGTON, IN 47939. (#106364-2).

JUNE 29 - JULY 4, '76. BICENTENNIAL & SESQUICENTENNIAL CELEBRATION & PARADE. FAIR, FESTIVAL, PARADE AT COVINGTON CITY STREETS & CITY PARK. (LOCAL). WILLARD WILLIAMS, COORD; COVINGTON CIVIL DEFENSE; 601 8TH ST; COVINGTON, IN 47932. (#106364-1).

CRANE

MAY 8, '76. DEDICATION OF USS CONSTITUTION OAK GROVE. CEREMONY AT AT THE BASE. (LOCAL). LT S T NYLEN; NAVAL WEAPONS SUPPORT CENTER; NAVAL WEAPONS SUPPORT CENTER; CRANE, IN 47522. (#200017-116).

CRAWFORDSVL

GEORGE ROGERS CLARK REGIMENT - CRAWFORDSVILLE, IN. OBJECTIVE RE-ENACTMENT GROUP MOLDED AFTER EXPEDITION OF CLARK TO VINCENNES. (LOCAL). ROBERT BURGESS, COORDINATOR; CRAWFORDSVILLE SENIOR HIGH SCHOOL; E JEFFERSON ST; CRAWFORDSVL, IN 47933. (#27787). **ARBA GRANTEE.**

HIGH SCHOOL NEWSPAPER ARTICLES ON REVOL WAR, IN. ARTICLES BY LOCAL HIGH SCHOOL STUDENTS ON EVENTS OF REVOLUTIONARY WAR. (LOCAL). WILLIAM SIKES, CHAIRMAN; CRAWFORDSVILLE COMMUNITY BICENTENNIAL COMMITTEE; 1111 S GRANT AVE; CRAWFORDSVL, IN 47933. (#23047).

MONTGOMERY COUNTY JAIL RESTORATION - IN. THE CULTURAL FOUNDATION IS RESTORING THE MONTGOMERY COUNTY JAIL. (LOCAL). PATRICIA SOMMER, CHAIRMAN; MONTGOMERY COUNTY CULTURAL FOUNDATION, INC; 1209 DURHAM ST; CRAWFORDSVL, IN 47932. (#28045). **ARBA GRANTEE.**

NEWSPAPER ARTICLES ON LOCAL HISTORY, IN. ARTICLES ON LOCAL PERSONALITIES AND EVENTS OF HISTORICAL SIGNIFICANCE. (LOCAL). WILLIAM SIKES, CHAIRMAN; CRAWFORDSVILLE COMMUNITY BICENTENNIAL COMMITTEE; 1111 S GRANT AVE; CRAWFORDSVL, IN 47933. (#23044).

JAN 1 - DEC 31, '76. DISPLAY OF HISTORIC FLAGS AND BICENTENNIAL SYMBOL. TRAVELLING DISPLAY OF HISTORIC FLAGS AND TOWNWIDE DISPLAY OF BICENTENNIAL FLAGS, POSTERS AND LOGO. EXHIBITS HAVE BEEN USED SINCE JAN '76 AND HAVE ADDED COLOR AND ZEAL TO MANY PROGRAMS. (LOCAL). D BURNS, COMMITTEEMAN; CRAWFORDSVILLE COMMUNITY BICENTENNIAL COMMITTEE; 614 S WATER ST; CRAWFORDSVL, IN 47933. (#106223-1).

JAN 15, '76 - CONTINUING . HISTORIC MUSEUM. EXHIBIT AT MONTGOMERY COUNTY HISTORICAL MUSEUM, N WASHINGTON. (REGN'L). PATTI SOMMER, COORD; CRAWFORDSVILLE COMMUNITY BICENTENNIAL COMMITTEE; 1209 DURHAM DR; CRAWFORDSVL, IN 47933. (#200017-17).

JAN 26 - 30, '76. FILM FESTIVAL ON AMERICAN REVOLUTION. SERIES OF FILMS ON PERSONALITIES AND EVENTS OF HISTORICAL SIGNIFICANCE. (LOCAL). D GOLLIHER, PRINCIPAL; CRAWFORDSVILLE HIGH SCHOOL; 1101 DURHAM DR; CRAWFORDSVL, IN 47933. (#106182-1).

JUNE 16 - 18, '76. BICENTENNIAL FAIR. FAIR, FESTIVAL AT 4-H FAIRGROUNDS. (LOCAL). WILLIAM SIKES, CHMN; CRAWFORDSVILLE COMMUNITY BICENTENNIAL COMMITTEE; 1111 S GRANT AVE; CRAWFORDSVLE, IN 47933. (#106358-1).

CROMWELL

CROMWELL COMMUNITY PLAYGROUND & PARK - IN. PURCHASE AVAILABLE LAND, CLEAN & ERECT PARK & PLAYGROUND FACILITIES. (LOCAL). KENNETH CRIPE, CHAIRMAN; CROMWELL BUSINESS ASSOC; CROMWELL, IN 46732. (#27786). **ARBA GRANTEE.**

CROWN POINT

AUG 16 - 23, '75. LAKE COUNTY FAIR. FAIR AT LAKE COUNTY FAIRGROUNDS. (LOCAL). J H PATTERSON; LAKE COUNTY AGRICULTURAL SOCIETY; 150 N. EAST; CROWN POINT, IN 46307. (#50333-1).

AUG 21 - 28, '76. COUNTY FAIR. 4-H AND HORSE SHOWS, GRANDSTAND ENTERTAINMENT, CIRCUS, CARNIVAL, FLOWER SHOW, CATTLE SHOW, COMMERCIAL AND INDUSTRIAL EXHIBITS AND A PLANT COMPETITION. AT LAKE COUNTY FAIRGROUNDS. (ST-WIDE). J H PATTERSON, COORD; LAKE COUNTY AGRICULTURAL SOCIETY; PO BOX 327; CROWN POINT, IN 46307. (#106095-17).

DEC 12 - 17, '76. LA SALLE EXPEDITION II, A HISTORIC RE-ENACTMENT. THIS IS AN AUTHENTIC RE-ENACTMENT OF THE 1681 LASALLE EXPEDITION FROM MONTREAL, CANADA TO NEW ORLEANS, LA WHICH WILL BEGIN TOURING ON AUGUST 11, 1976 AND END ON APRIL 9, 1977. (LOCAL). REID H LEWIS, DIRECTOR; LA SALLE EXPEDITION II; 135 S LA SALLE ST, RM 411; CHICAGO, IL 60690. (#102805-33).

CULVER

HISTORY OF UNION TOWNSHIP, IN. THE CULVER CITY CLUB REPUBLISHED THIS OUT-OF-PRINT BOOK. (LOCAL). LATHAM L LAWSON, COORDINATOR; CULVER - UNION TOWNSHIP BICENT COMMITTEE; CULVER, IN 46511. (#32158).

JUNE 11, '76. VFW LOYALTY DAY PARADE. PARADE AT DOWN SCHOOL STREET & LAKE SHORE DRIVE. (LOCAL). LATHAM L LAWSON; VETERANS OF FOREIGN WARS & CULVER-UNION TOWNSHIP BICENT COMMITTEE; BOX 109; CULVER, IN 46511. (#200017-113).

DALE

MAY 23, '76. ANNIVERSARY CELEBRATION OF CHRISTIAN GENERATION SINGERS. SPECIAL BICENTENNIAL PROGRAM OF RELIGIOUS MUSIC WITH POPULAR APPEAL. AT DALE UNITED METHODIST CHURCH. (LOCAL). MRS LEO HEICHELBECH, CHMN; DALE UNITED METHODIST CHURCH; DALE, IN 47523. (#104720-1).

SEPT 10 - 12, '76. DALE FALL FESTIVAL. PATRIOTIC PARADE, PRIZES, BOOTHS, FOOD, RIDES, GAMES, BEER GARDEN & BAND. AT DALE CITY PARK. (LOCAL). JEAN WITTE, CHRPSN; DALE FALL FESTIVAL COMMITTEE; PO BOX 275; DALE, IN 47523. (#104716-1).

DALEVILLE

JULY 10 - 11, '76. COMMUNITY PARADE AND FESTIVAL. HELD IN CONJUNCTION WITH ANNUAL 4-H FAIR, THE CELEBRATION INCLUDES A BARN DANCE; A PARADE OF LOCAL AND GUEST UNITS ENDING AT THE NEW BICENTENNIAL PARK AND OLD-FASHIONED GAMES AT THE PARK. COMMUNITY VESPER SERVICES ARE PLANNED TO CONCLUDE THE EVENING'S PROGRAM. AT DALEVILLE HIGH SCHOOL, ALONG WALNUT ST TO BICENTENNIAL PARK. (LOCAL). ANNETTE ERNSTING, CHMN; SALEM TOWNSHIP BICENTENNIAL COMMUNITY; RR 8, BOX 349; MUNCIE, IN 47302. (#200017-51).

DECATUR

BICENTENNIAL HALLOWEEN PARADE OF DECATUR, IN. HALLOWEEN PARADE IN DECATUR, IN. (LOCAL). LARRY ISCH; DECATUR CHAMBER OF COMMERCE; 223 LIMBERLOST TRAIL; DECATUR, IN 46733. (#27664). **ARBA GRANTEE.**

ST MARY'S RIVER BICENTENNIAL PARK - IN. 2 ACRES OF GROUND TO BE MADE INTO PARK AND CANOE LAUNCH TO COMMEMORATE THE BICENTENNIAL YEAR. (LOCAL). REV HAROLD LEININGER, COORDINATOR; ADAMS COUNTY BICENTENNIAL COMMITTEE; 512 LIMBERLOST TRAIL; DECATUR, IN 46733. (#25785). **ARBA GRANTEE.**

OCT 30, '76. BICENTENNIAL HALLOWEEN PARADE. PARADE. (LOCAL). LARRY ISCH; DECATUR CHAMBER OF COMMERCE; 223 LIMBERLOST TRAIL; DECATUR, IN 46733. (#27664-1).

DEMOTTE

ARTS & CRAFTS FAIR. LOCAL ARTISTS AND CRAFTSMEN WILL DISPLAY AND SELL THEIR WARES. PROFIT TO BE USED FOR EXPANSION AND/OR UPDATE OF PUBLIC LIBRARY IN TOWN OF DEMOTTE. (LOCAL). PRESIDENT; FRIENDS OF THE LIBRARY; DEMOTTE PUBLIC LIBRARY; DEMOTTE, IN 45310. (#14605-1).

DILLSBORO

DILLSBORO CIVIC CLUB BICENTENNIAL PARK, IN. A PLAYGROUND WILL BE BUILT ON DILLSBORO CIVIC GROUNDS. (LOCAL). MICHAEL FORTNER, COORDINATOR; DILLSBORO CIVIC CLUB; DILLSBORO, IN 47018. (#26795). **ARBA GRANTEE.**

DUNKIRK

JULY 21 - 24, '76. DUNKIRK GLASS DAYS FESTIVAL; MODERN ARTS & CRAFTS. TOUR THE KERR GLASS FACILITIES WHERE CONTAINERS ARE MADE; THEN VIEW THE CRAFTING OF TABLEWARE AT THE INDIANA GLASS PLANT DURING THIS FESTIVAL WHICH INCLUDES THE QUEEN OF GLASS, AMUSEMENT RIDES AND REFRESHMENTS. AT DUNKIRK, INDIANA GLASS PLANT. (LOCAL). LOU WATSON, PROJ CHMN; GLASS DAYS FESTIVAL COMMITTEE; 121 E WASHINGTON ST; DUNKIRK, IN 47336. (#100318-1).

DUNLAPSVILLE

JULY 4 - 6, '75. HOOSIER HERITAGE HANDICRAFT FESTIVAL. LISTEN TO THE THUD OF BUTTER CHURNING, SMELL CRUSTY LOAVES OF FRESH BAKED BREAD AND WATCH SPARKS FLY FROM THE BLACKSMITH'S ANVIL; WHILE YOUNGSTERS PET ANIMALS, JUMP FROM THE HAY LOFT, AND DELIGHT AT ANIMATED PUPPETS. AT TREATY-LINE MUSEUM, 5 MILES S W OF LIBERTY AT NORTHGATE. (ST-WIDE). PHYLLIS HOWARD, PROJ DIR; TREATY-LINE MUSEUM, INC; RR 4; LIBERTY, IN 47353. (#100346-1).

EAST CHICAGO

EAST CHICAGO BICENTENNIAL CELEBRATION, IN. BICENTENNIAL CELEBRATION BY PUERTO RICAN COMMUNITY. (LOCAL). FRANCISCO GONZALES, COORDINATOR; PUERTO RICAN COMMUNITY BICENTENNIAL COMMITTEE; 3406 ELM ST; EAST CHICAGO, IN 46312. (#26592). **ARBA GRANTEE.**

EAST CHICAGO EXCHANGE CLUB, IN. CONVENTION DEDICATED TO FREEDOM SHRINES TO EAST CHICAGO'S HERITAGE HALL. (ST-WIDE). WILLIAM A PASSMORE, COORDINATOR; EAST CHICAGO EXCHANGE CLUB; 3522 1/2 MAIN ST; EAST CHICAGO, IN 46312. (#27013). **ARBA GRANTEE.**

EAST CHICAGO WOMEN IN HISTORY - IN. AN EXHIBIT ON EAST CHICAGO WOMEN IN HISTORY. (LOCAL). GAIL H PUGH, DIRECTOR; CITY OF EAST CHICAGO PLANNING DEPT; 4525 INDIANAPOLIS BLVD; E CHICAGO, IN 46312. (#26873). **ARBA GRANTEE.**

FOLK DANCE FESTIVAL, EAST CHICAGO, IN. FOLK DANCE & SONG FESTIVAL. (LOCAL). PETER ANTON, COORDINATOR; RILEY CULTURAL & ART ASSOC; 210 E COLUMBUS DR; EAST CHICAGO, IN 46312. (#26593). **ARBA GRANTEE.**

JULY 1 - 31, '76. EAST CHICAGO FOLK DANCE & SONG FESTIVAL. FESTIVAL AT EAST CHICAGO PUBLIC SCHOOLS. (LOCAL). PETER ANTON, COORD; RILEY CULTURAL AND ART ASSOC; 210 EAST COLUMBUS DR; EAST CHICAGO, IN 46312. (#26593-1).

JULY 21 - 27, '76. EAST CHICAGO PUERTO RICAN COMMUNITY BICENTENNIAL CELEBRATION. FESTIVAL. (LOCAL). FRANCISCO GONZALES, COORD; PUERTO RICAN COMMUNITY BICENTENNIAL COMMITTEE; 3406 ELM ST; EAST CHICAGO, IN 46312. (#26592-1).

ELKHART

BICENTENNIAL CONCERTS - ELKHART, IN. THE CONCERTS WILL BE HELD THE FIRST WEEK IN AUGUST '76 AT THE FAIRGROUNDS. (LOCAL). ROBERT J PICKRELL, COORDINATOR; ELKHART SYMPHONY SOCIETY; PO BOX 144; ELKHART, IN 46514. (#26638). **ARBA GRANTEE.**

HERITAGE PARK, ELKHART, IN. LANDSCAPING OF AN AREA OF LAND IN PARK FOR THE BICENTENNIAL CELEBRATION. (LOCAL). KENNETH W CANTSLER, COORDINATOR; ELKHART DEPT OF PARKS & RECREATION; 229 S 2ND ST; ELKHART, IN 46514. (#26794). **ARBA GRANTEE.**

RECREATION STUDY OF URBAN RIVER CORRIDORS, INDIANA. IMPLEMENTATION OF BIKE/WALKWAYS ALONG RIVERS, CANOEING PROGRAMS AND DEVELOPMENT OF LINEAR RIVER PARKS INTERCONNECTING PARKS ALONG WATERWAYS OF ELKHART, INDIANA. (LOCAL). NANCY HANKS, CHAIRMAN; NATIONAL ENDOWMENT FOR THE ARTS; WASHINGTON, DC 20506. (#4977). **(??).**

AUG 1 - 7, '76. BICENTENNIAL CONCERTS. LIVE PERFORMANCE AT FAIRGROUNDS. (LOCAL). ROBERT J PICKRELL, COORD; ELKHART SYMPHONY SOCIETY; PO BOX 144; ELKHART, IN 46514. (#26638-1).

ELLETTSVILLE

PRESERVATION OF MONON RAILROAD STATION - IN. THE MONON STATION WILL BE RESTORED TO SERVE AS A MEETING PLACE AND A MUSEUM. (LOCAL). BERTHA BOSTWICK; MONON BICENTENNIAL COMMISSION; MAIN STREET; MONON, IN 47959. (#27091). **ARBA GRANTEE.**

EVANSVILLE

ACROSS THE GENERATIONS - EVANSVILLE, IN. DEVELOPMENT OF AN EDUCATIONAL PROGRAM FOR ALL GENERATIONS. (LOCAL). FRANCIS KING, CHAIRMAN; SOUTHWEST INDIANA REGIONAL COUNCIL ON AGING, INC; 528 MAIN ST, R-307; EVANSVILLE, IN 47708. (#24086). **ARBA GRANTEE.**

AMER ISSUES FORUM COURSES AT INDIANA STATE UNIV. LOCAL USE OF THIS NATIONAL PROGRAM INCLUDES A TWO-SEMESTER COURSE ON AMERICAN ISSUES AT THE STATE UNIV AT EVANSVILLE. SEVERAL CLUBS ALSO PLAN TO USE THE FORUM'S SCHEDULE OF DISCUSSION. (LOCAL). DARREL E BIGHAM, CHAIRMAN; EVANSVILLE BICENTENNIAL COUNCIL; 1101 N FULTON AVE; EVANSVILLE, IN 47710. (#8341).

ARTISTS PERFORM IN NEIGHBORHOODS OF EVANSVILLE, IN. THE ARTS COUNCIL AND THE CITY PARKS DEPARTMENT WILL BRING ARTISTS IN RESIDENCE TO CITY PARKS AND SENIOR CITIZEN NEIGHBORHOOD CENTERS. 150,000 PERSONS TO BE REACHED. (LOCAL). MS PEGGY JACK, DIRECTOR; EVANSVILLE ARTS COUNCIL; 10600 OLD STATE RD; EVANSVILLE, IN 47711. (#8329).

BENT TWIG OUTDOOR EDUCATION CENTER - IN. RELOCATION AND RENOVATION OF EARLY 1800 2 STORY LOG HOUSE FOR USE AS AN OUTDOOR EDUCATION CENTER. (LOCAL). DORIS EICHER, CHAIRMAN; WESTWOOD GARDEN CLUB & INDIANA STATE UNIV; 1900 SHULTE RD; EVANSVILLE, IN 47112. (#27248). **ARBA GRANTEE.**

BICENTENNIAL HANDBOOK FOR TEACHERS, IN. TEACHERS GUIDE TO INITIATE BICENTENNIAL ACTIVITIES AND PROJECTS IN THE CLASSROOM AND SCHOOL. (LOCAL). WILLIAM LYLES, CHAIRMAN; EVANSVILLE-VANDERBURGH SCHOOL CORP BICENT COMMITTEE; EVANSVILLE, IN 47112. (#16410).

BICENTENNIAL MARKER - EVANSVILLE, IN. 15 X 30 FT REPLICA OF THE INDIANA BICENTENNIAL COMMITTEE LOGO WILL BE RAISED ON CAMPUS. THE MARKER IS MADE OF CONCRETE AND WILL BE PART OF A SPECIAL LANDSCAPE PROJECT. (LOCAL). MARY LOU RUSSLER, CHAIRMAN; INDIANA STATE UNIV, CLERICAL AND SUPPORT STAFF; 8600 UNIVERSITY BLVD; EVANSVILLE, IN 47712. (#24500).

BICENTENNIAL READING & MUSIC CAROUSEL, IN. A BICENTENNIAL READING & MUSIC CAROUSEL WILL BE PRESENTED TO THE EVANSVILLE LIBRARY. (LOCAL). MRS JOSEPH B HENNINGFORD, CHAIRMAN; EVANSVILLE PHILHARMONIC GUILD; 665 S BEEKS RD; EVANSVILLE, IN 47714. (#24284). **ARBA GRANTEE.**

BICENTENNIAL SPEAKER'S BUREAU FOR EVANSVILLE, IN. INDIANA STATE UNIVERSITY AT EVANSVILLE WILL RE-ISSUE DURING THE FALL OF 1976, A BOOKLET LISTING FACULTY AVAILABLE TO ADDRESS LOCAL CLUBS ON TOPICS RELATED TO AMERICA'S PAST AND PRESENT. (LOCAL). KATHY WILL, ASST TO PRESIDENT; INDIANA STATE UNIV AT EVANSVILLE; 8600 UNIVERSITY BLVD; EVANSVILLE, IN 47712. (#8331).

BICENTENNIAL TRIBUTE - EVANSVILLE, IN. THE 4 COLUMNS SAVED FROM THE ENTRANCE OF THE NOW DEMOLISHED C & EI RWY STATION WILL BE USED AS THE FOCAL POINT OF A TRIBUTE TO THE 4 FREEDOMS; A $100,000 MONUMENT WILL BE LOCATED ALONG OHIO RIVER. (ST-WIDE). C THOMAS AKIN, CHAIRMAN; EVANSVILLE BICENTENNIAL TRIBUTE, INC; BOX 1976; EVANSVILLE, IN 47701. (#17900).

BUSINESS AND ECONOMIC HISTORY OF EVANSVILLE, IN. A STUDY OF THE EVOLUTION OF EVANSVILLE BUSINESS AND INDUSTRY. ADDS PERSPECTIVE TO EVANSVILLE'S BUSINESS AND TRANSPORTATION GROWTH AND PLACES IT IN THE MAINSTREAM OF AMERICAN ECONOMIC DEVELOPMENT. (LOCAL). DR DALE N SHOOK, ASSISTANT PROFESSOR OF BUSINESS; INDIANA STATE UNIV - EVANSVILLE; 8600 UNIVERSITY BLVD; EVANSVILLE, IN 47712. (#24501).

CALL FOR ACHIEVEMENT - PROJ IN EVANSVILLE, IN. LOCAL ADAPTATION OF ARBA PROGRAM -TO COMMENCE IN SEPT '75. NOV,DEC OF '76 ARE SET ASIDE ON OUR CALENDAR AS CALL FOR ACHIEVEMENT MONTHS IN WHICH PART OF LOCAL CFA PROJECT RESULTS WILL BE REVEALED. (LOCAL). MRS RITA EYKAMP, ASST CHAIRMAN; EVANSVILLE BICENTENNIAL COUNCIL; 1101 N FULTON AVE; EVANSVILLE, IN 47710. (#3429).

CHICAGO FREE STREET THEATER - EVANSVILLE, IN. THE POLICE RECREATION PROGRAM SPONSORED THE 2-DAY PERFORMANCE. (LOCAL). BOBBY GOLD, COORDINATOR; POLICE RECREATION PROGRAM; 502 S ELLIOTT; EVANSVILLE, IN 47713. (#25764). **ARBA GRANTEE.**

CHRISTIAN DECKER BICENT LINEN SAMPLER IN INDIANA. THE DESIGN IS COMPOSED OF 17 PATTERNS FROM PRE-1870 STAMPING BLOCKS MADE BY CHRISTIAN DECKER OF EVANSVILLE; THE BLOCKS ARE FORERUNNERS OF TODAY'S IRON-ON EMBROIDERY DESIGN. (LOCAL). BERNICE BRILL, MANAGER; CHRISTIAN DECKER HANDSTAMPING SHOP-CONRAD BAKER FOUNDATION; 4TH & COURT ST; EVANSVILLE, IN 47708. (#12138).

COMMEMORATIVE PLAQUE IN EVANSVILLE, INDIANA. THE TWO LOCAL CHAPTERS OF THE DAR WILL PLACE A MARKER IN A PROMINENT PLACE IN 1976 TO HONOR THE NINE VETERANS OF THE REVOLUTIONARY WAR BURIED IN VANDERBURGH COUNTY. (LOCAL). MRS MARVIN HUFF, SR/MRS CARL HOTTENSTEIN, CO-CHWM; MCEARY AND VANDERBURGH CHAPTERS OF THE DAR; 417 OLMSTEAD AVE; EVANSVILLE, IN 47711. (#12140).

COMMISSION PARK SCULPTURE FOR EVANSVILLE, INDIANA. THE CITY PLANS TO COMMISSION AN ENVIRONMENTAL SCULPTURE WITH RIVER AND LIBERTY THEMES FOR A CITY PARK. (LOCAL). MRS RITA EYKAMP, ASST CHAIRMAN; EVANSVILLE BICENTENNIAL COMMITTEE; 1101 N FULTON AVE; EVANSVILLE, IN 47710. (#8325).

CONGRESSIONAL COOKBOOK IN EVANSVILLE, IN. AS ITS BICENTENNIAL PROJECT, TO STRESS THE NATION'S DIVERSITY, THE LEAGUE OF WOMEN VOTERS IN EVANSVILLE WILL PUBLISH A COOKBOOK WITH FAVORITE RECIPES OF 160 CONGRESSMEN AND SENATORS OF THE USA. (LOCAL). BARBARA MCKENNA, PRESIDENT; LEAGUE OF WOMEN VOTERS OF SOUTHWEST INDIANA; 416 RUNNYMEADE; EVANSVILLE, IN 47714. (#12136).

ERECT LOG CABINS ON 4-H GROUNDS IN EVANSVILLE, IN. OLD LOG BARNS IN AREA TO BE TORN DOWN AND MATERIALS USED TO ERECT A FEW LOG CABINS ON VANDERBURGH COUNTY'S 4-H GROUNDS. (LOCAL). W A GUMBERTS, CO-CHAIRMAN; EVANSVILLE BICENTENNIAL COUNCIL; 1101 N FULTON AVE; EVANSVILLE, IN 47710. (#8334). **(??).**

ERECT REPLICA OF BLACKSMITH SHOP IN EVANSVILLE, IN. ART DEPT OF INDIANA STATE UNIVERSITY AT EVANSVILLE WILL BUILD A REPLICA OF A BLACKSMITH SHOP ON CAMPUS. CLASSES & DEMONSTRATIONS ON IRON-WORKING WILL BE HELD IN THE SHOP DURING 1975. (LOCAL). DAN ENGELKE, ASST PROFESSOR OF ART; INDIANA STATE UNIV AT EVANSVILLE; 8600 UNIVERSITY BLVD; EVANSVILLE, IN 47712. (#8342). **(??).**

EVANSVILLE BICENTENNIAL MONUMENT - EVANSVILLE, IN. CONSTRUCTION OF BICENTENNIAL MEMORIAL MONUMENT, 'CIRCLE OF UNITY', FOR FREEDOM & PEACE. (ST-WIDE). MICHILE WHITE, EXEC DIRECTOR; INDIANA ARBC; 100 STATE OFFICE BLDG; INDIANAPOLIS, IN 46204. (#23178). **ARBA GRANTEE.**

EVANSVILLE COURIER'S BICENTENNIAL EDITION - NBMRP. PAPER GAVE MAJOR FUND RAISING SUPPORT FOR THE EVANSVILLE BICENTENNIAL COMMITTEE & PUBLISHED A SPECIAL SECTION FOR THE JULY 4TH, 1976, WEEKEND. (LOCAL). LENORD U KREUGER, EDITOR; THE EVANSVILLE COURIER; 201 NW 2ND ST; EVANSVILLE, IN 47714. (#31869).

EVANSVILLE HIGH SCHOOL REGIONAL HIST PROJECTS, IN. LOCAL HIGH SCHOOL STUDENTS, WITH AID OF INDIANA STATE UNIV AT EVANSVILLE, WILL CONDUCT HISTORY PROJECTS: STUDENTS WILL WRITE THEIR OWN FAMILY HISTORIES & RECORD NEIGHBORHOOD HIST THRU TAPED INTERVIEWS. (LOCAL). WILLIAM LYLES, DIRECTOR OF SOCIAL STUDIES; EVANSVILLE-VANDERBURGH SCHOOL CORP; 1 SE 9TH ST; EVANSVILLE, IN 47708. (#8339).

EVANSVILLE, IN, CHAPTER RED CROSS PROJECT. AS ITS BICENTENNIAL PROJECT, THE RED CROSS HAS OFFERED TO PROVIDE FIRST AID STATIONS FOR ALL LARGE GATHERINGS HERE. (LOCAL). THOMAS LAMBERT, COORDINATOR; AMERICAN RED CROSS, EVANSVILLE CHAPTER; 1008 FIRST AVE; EVANSVILLE, IN 47710. (#18700).

FIRE HYDRANT PAINTING IN EVANSVILLE, IN. CITY FIRE HYDRANTS TO BE PAINTED TO RESEMBLE REVOL WAR FIGURES. (LOCAL). CAROLYN SCRUGGS, DIRECTOR, OPER CITY BEAUTIFUL; CHAMBER OF COMMERCE; SOUTHERN SECURITIES BLDG; EVANSVILLE, IN 47708. (#8345).

FREEDOM VAN - PROJ OF EVANSVILLE, IN. TWO LOCAL CLUBS ARE PREPARING A VAN WITH EXHIBITS OF LOCAL HISTORY; FEATURES LIKE STEAMBOATING ON THE OHIO AND LINCOLN'S BOYHOOD HOME. THE VAN IS TO BE COMPLETED IN APRIL '76 & WILL VISIT LOCAL SCHOOLS. (LOCAL). EDWARD HARRISON, CHAIRMAN; DOWNTOWN OPTIMIST CLUB/ARMY RESERVE; 2256 E WALNUT ST; EVANSVILLE, IN 47714. (#13117).

THE FUTURE OF AMERICAN DREAM ESSAY CONTEST - IN. AN ESSAY CONTEST FOR STUDENTS WAS HELD. (LOCAL). DR THOMAS BOHN, CHAIRMAN; UNIVERSITY OF EVANSVILLE; EVANSVILLE, IN 47702. (#26860). **ARBA GRANTEE.**

GREEN SURVIVAL PROGRAM, EVANSVILLE, IN. COUNTYWIDE LANDSCAPING PROGRAM INVOLVING PUBLIC & PRIVATE SECTORS DURING 1976, SALE OF 1000 TREES, ORGANIZE COMMUNITY GARDENING PROJECTS, LANDSCAPE PUBLIC AREAS AND EDUCATE PUBLIC ON PLANTS. (LOCAL). CAROLYN J SCRUGGS, DIRECTOR; OPERATION CITY BEAUTIFUL; 329 MAIN ST; EVANSVILLE, IN 47708. (#21901).

A GUIDE TO ARCHITECTURE FOUND IN EVANSVILLE, IN. A GUIDE TO SIXTY ARCHITECTURALLY SIGNIFICANT HOMES IN EVANSVILLE WILL BE COMPILED AND PRINTED FOR THE FIRST TIME. (LOCAL). MRS STAN TILLMAN, PROJECT CHAIRMAN; JUNIOR LEAGUE OF EVANSVILLE; ELM DR; NEWBURGH, IN 47630. (#8330).

HISTORICAL EXHIBIT, EVANSVILLE, IN. EXHIBIT: OLD WAYS IN THE NEW WORLD ON TOUR. (LOCAL). DONALD MCNARY, COORDINATOR; EVANSVILLE HUMAN RELATIONS COMMISSION; EVANSVILLE, IN 47708. (#26591). **ARBA GRANTEE.**

HISTORICAL STUDIES BY EVANSVILLE, INDIANA MUSEUM. IN 1976, THE MUSEUM WILL BEGIN TO PUBLISH SHORT STUDIES ON VARIED ASPECTS OF AREA HISTORY. THIS WILL INCREASE THE AVAILABILITY OF HISTORICAL WORKS TO STUDENTS & OTHERS AND RAISE FUNDS FOR THE MUSEUM. (LOCAL). DARREL E BIGHAM, EDITOR; EVANSVILLE MUSEUM; 411 SE RIVERSIDE DR; EVANSVILLE, IN 47713. (#8328). **(??).**

INTERNATIONAL CENTER TO BE LOCATED IN INDIANA. THE EVANSVILLE BICENTENNIAL COUNCIL IS STUDYING THE FEASIBILITY OF SECURING A BUILDING FOR FOREIGN RESIDENTS OF THE AREA & OTHER COMMUNITY MEMBERS FOR SOCIAL ACTIVITIES, LECTURES ETC. (LOCAL). DON MCNARY, PROJECT COORDINATOR; EVANSVILLE BICENTENNIAL COUNCIL; 1101 N FULTON AVE; EVANSVILLE, IN 47710. (#8327). **(??).**

INVENTORY OF PUBLIC RECORDS IN EVANSVILLE, IN. THE ARCHIVES COMMITTEE OF THE CONRAD BAKER FOUNDATION AND THE VANDERBURGH CHAPTER OF DAR HAVE COMPLETED, AS BICENTENNIAL CONTRIBUTION, INVENTORY OF THOUSANDS OF PUBLIC RECORDS; GUIDE PUBLISHED IN '75. (LOCAL). RICHARD BRENNAN, ADMINISTRATOR; CONRAD BAKER FOUNDATION; 4TH & COURT; EVANSVILLE, IN 47708. (#12135).

LOCAL TV SHOWS ON NEIGHBORHOODS IN EVANSVILLE, IN. A PRESENTATION ON LOCAL PUBLIC TV OF EIGHT HALF-HOUR SHOWS ON THE DEVELOPMENT OF EVANSVILLE NEIGHBORHOODS. MODERATOR IS L D SEITS OF THE EVANSVILLE PRESS. INTERVIEWS WITH OLDER RESIDENTS TO BE FOCUS. (LOCAL). DARREL E BIGHAM, CHAIRMAN; EVANSVILLE BICENTENNIAL COUNCIL; 1101 N FULTON AVE; EVANSVILLE, IN 47710. (#8338).

OHIO RIVER LECTURE SERIES - EVANSVILLE, IN. THE EVANSVILLE-VANDERBURGH COUNTY COMMITTEE OF LIBRARIANS WILL SPONSOR THE LECTURE SERIES THROUGHOUT THE SUMMER OF '76. (LOCAL). MARGARET J KYLE, CHAIRMAN; EVANSVILLE-VANDERBURGH COUNTY COMMITTEE OF LIBRARIANS; 22 SOUTHEAST 5TH ST; EVANSVILLE, IN 47708. (#26637). **ARBA GRANTEE.**

OHIO RIVER VALLEY UNION BIBLIOGRAPHY - IN. IN FEB, 1976, THE EVANSVILLE PUBLIC LIBRARY WILL ISSUE AN ANNOTATED GUIDE TO PRIMARY AND SECONDARY SOURCES ON THE OHIO RIVER. THE BOOK WILL BE USED IN RELATION TO THE LECTURE SERIES BEGINNING IN FEB. (REGN'L). MARGARET KYLE, ASST DIRECTOR; EVANSVILLE PUBLIC LIBRARY AND VANDERBURGH PUBLIC LIBRARY; 22 S E 5TH ST; EVANSVILLE, IN 47708. (#18699).

OPERATION RECOGNITION IN EVANSVILLE, INDIANA. THE SOUTHWEST INDIANA STATUS OF WOMEN ASSOC IS COMPILING A LIST OF PROMINENT PROFESSIONAL WOMEN IN AREA HISTORY AND WILL PREPARE A SET OF PLAQUES AS PERMANENT REMINDERS. (LOCAL). DR BARBARA J MARTING, DIRECTOR; SOUTHWEST INDIANA STATUS OF WOMEN ASSOC; INDIANA STATE UNIV; EVANSVILLE, IN 47712. (#12141).

OUR AMERICAN HERITAGE, BICENTENNIAL SALUTE, IN. THE BOY SCOUTS WILL PRESENT A BICENTENNIAL SALUTE TO AMERICA'S HERITAGE AT VARIOUS LOCATIONS IN EVANSVILLE; THESE INCLUDE: STATE HOSPITAL GROUNDS, WESSELMAN PARK ARMY RESERVE CENTER & ROBERTS STADIUM. (LOCAL). GEORGE W SPICE, COORDINATOR; BUFFALO TRACE COUNCIL, INC - BOY

EVANSVILLE — CONTINUED

SCOUTS OF AMERICA; 1050 BAYARD PARK, BOX 3245; EVANSVILLE, IN 47714. (#25245). **ARBA GRANTEE.**

PRESERVATION OF THE F J REITZ HOME: EVANSVILLE, IN. THE REITZ HOME PRESERVATION SOCIETY, FORMED IN 1974 TO MAINTAIN THE HISTORIC HOME OF FRANCIS J REITZ, PLANS TO OPEN HOME TO VISITORS BY JULY 4, 1976 AFTER INTERIOR WORK IS COMPLETED. (LOCAL). ALEXANDER L LEICH, PRESIDENT; REITZ HOME PRESERVATION SOCIETY; 1107 HARRELTON CT; EVANSVILLE, IN 47714. (#12139).

PUBLISH TOURIST MAP OF HISTORIC EVANSVILLE, IN. A COLORFUL ILLUSTRATED MAP HIGHLIGHTING HISTORIC SITES IN 3 SOUTHWESTERN COUNTIES IN INDIANA WILL BE PUBLISHED. (LOCAL). MRS JOSEPH BEGLEY, PROJECT COORDINATOR; EVANSVILLE MUSEUM; 411 SE RIVERSIDE DR; EVANSVILLE, IN 47713. (#8335). **(??).**

READING GUIDES ON THE AMER REVOLUTION, INDIANA. BOOK LISTS ON THE AMERICAN REVOLUTION FOR YOUNG READERS AND GENERAL READERS WILL BE AVAILABLE TO THE PUBLIC FREE OF CHARGE IN EVANSVILLE. (LOCAL). EDWARD A HOWARD, DIRECTOR; EVANSVILLE-VANDERBURGH PUBLIC LIBRARY; 22 SE 5TH; EVANSVILLE, IN 47708. (#8343).

REGIONAL ARCHIVES - INDIANA STATE UNIV, IN. BEGUN IN 1972 IN ANTICIPATION OF THE BICENTENNIAL, THE REGIONAL ARCHIVES HAS DEVELOPED A LIST OF REGIONAL MANUSCRIPT COLLECTIONS, AN ORAL HISTORY PROGRAM & A UNIVERSITY HISTORICAL RECORDS COLLECTION. (LOCAL). JOSEPHINE ELLIOTT, UNIV ARCHIVIST; INDIANA STATE UNIV - EVANSVILLE; 8600 UNIVERSITY BLVD; EVANSVILLE, IN 47712. (#24502).

REPRINT 1880 COUNTY ATLAS IN EVANSVILLE, INDIANA. WILLARD LIBRARY HAS REPRINTED AN 1880 VANDERBURGH COUNTY ATLAS AND 1889 PLAT BOOKS TO AID RESEARCH AND RAISE FUNDS FOR THE LIBRARY. (LOCAL). BETTYE MILLER, PROJECT COORDINATOR; WILLARD LIBRARY; EVANSVILLE, IN 47710. (#8332).

RESTORATION OF A CITY PARK IN EVANSVILLE, INDIANA. A SMALL NEIGHBORHOOD PARK ON THE CITY'S WEST SIDE WILL BE RESTORED BY INTERESTED PERSONS AND GROUPS, INCLUDING OPERATION CITY BEAUTIFUL, THE EVANSVILLE AUDUBON SOCIETY AND INDIANA STATE UNIV JAYCEES. (LOCAL). MARY LUE RUSSLER, COMMITTEE CHAIRMAN; INDIANA STATE UNIV AT EVANSVILLE; EVANSVILLE, IN 47712. (#8336). **(??).**

SPACE MODIFICATION '76 - EVANSVILLE, INDIANA. CONSTRUCTION OF A SOLAR ENERGY BUILDING IS BEING EXPLORED. (LOCAL). DR BENNY RILEY, PROJ DIR; UNIVERSITY OF EVANSVILLE; EVANSVILLE, IN 47702. (#19620).

STUDENT RESEARCH PROJ - EVANSVILLE, IN. HIGH SCHOOL AND COLLEGE STUDENTS WILL DO RESEARCH ON INDIANA'S GERMAN CULTURAL HERITAGE. (LOCAL). DR JOHN E SHELL, PROJ CHAIRMAN; INDIANA STATE UNIV - EVANSVILLE; EVANSVILLE, IN 47712. (#25353). **ARBA GRANTEE.**

'UNITY THROUGH FREEDOM' - EVANSVILLE, IN. THE LANDMARK TRIBUTE IS ENTITLED 'UNITY THROUGH FREEDOM'. (LOCAL). C THOMAS AKIN, PRESIDENT; EVANSVILLE BICENTENNIAL TRIBUTE, INC.; PO BOX 1976; EVANSVILLE, IN 47701. (#26808). **ARBA GRANTEE.**

'WAKE UP, AMERICA' - EVANSVILLE, IN. A GIRL SCOUT CAMPING WEEKEND WHERE PATRIOTISM WILL BE STRESSED. (LOCAL). SUSAN C HUCK, COORDINATOR; RAINTREE GIRL SCOUT COUNCIL, INC; 14 1/2 SE 2ND ST; EVANSVILLE, IN 47708. (#26613). **ARBA GRANTEE.**

WEHT-TV AWARENESS PROGRAM - NBMRP. BLACK HISTORY RECOGNITION PGM, HIGH SCHOOL STUDENTS DELIVER 1 MINUTE MESSAGES; ALMANAC PGM ON TRI-STATE HERITAGE; ON-GOING HALF-HOUR SERIES ON COMMUNITIES WITHIN STATION'S AREA; BICENT PSA'S AND ID'S. (LOCAL). HAL WOLFORD, BICENT COORDINATOR; TELEVISION STATION WEHT-TV; PO BOX 395; EVANSVILLE, IN 47703. (#25305).

1976 RAINTREE GIRL SCOUT PROJECTS, EVANSVILLE, IN. EACH TROOP IS INVOLVED IN SEARCH FOR 'HIDDEN HEROINE' AND ALSO HAS A SPECIAL CIVIC PROJECT. (LOCAL). MARLYN TREBERG, PROJECT COORDINATOR; RAINTREE BICENTENNIAL COUNCIL; 14 SE 2ND; EVANSVILLE, IN 47708. (#8333).

SEPT 1 - 30, '74. REVOLUTIONARY WAR PORTRAITS EXHIBIT IN EVANSVILLE. REVOLUTIONARY WAR PORTRAITS PROJECT OF INDIANA. GALLERY OF COLOR PHOTOS OF 65 PERSONS ASSOCIATED WITH INDIANA & THE AMERICAN REVOLUTION IS BEING EXHIBITED IN PUBLIC BUILDINGS THROUGHOUT STATE. BOOK OF SHORT BIOGRAPHIES OF SUBJECTS AVAILABLE. (ST-WIDE). DALE FRUCHTNICHT; INDIANA STATE BICENTENNIAL COMMISSION; 504 STATE OFFICE BLDG; INDIANAPOLIS, IN 46204. (#1635-906).

APR 17, '75 - CONTINUING . AMERICAN REVOLUTION ROUNDTABLE MEETINGS. DINNER-DISCUSSION MEETINGS ON EVENTS, LEADERS AND MEANING OF REVOLUTION TO BE HELD QUARTERLY BEGINNING APRIL 17, 1975, IN CELEBRATION OF THE 200TH ANNIVERSARY OF LEXINGTON & CONCORD. PUBLIC INVITED. AT EXECUTIVE INN. (LOCAL). DARREL E BIGHAM, CHAIRMAN; EVANSVILLE BICENTENNIAL COUNCIL; 1101 N FULTON AVE; EVANSVILLE, IN 47710. (#8344-1).

APR 26 - 27, '75. OHIO RIVER HERITAGE - A TWO DAY GIRL SCOUT STUDY. RIVER CRUISE INCLUDED. AT OHIO RIVER, EVANSVILLE AREA. (LOCAL). MARLYN TREBERG; RAINTREE GIRL SCOUT COUNCIL; 2050 ADAMS AVE; EVANSVILLE, IN 47714. (#50387-2).

APR 30 - MAY 10, '75. BICENTENNIAL SKILL AND CRAFT FESTIVAL. DURING 1976 OHIO RIVER ARTS FESTIVAL, THIS PROJECT INCLUDES DEEMON STRATION OF LOST SKILLS LIKE HORSE-SHOEING & GLASS BLOWING. ANN EFFORT IS BEING MADE TO LOCATE ALL FOLK CRAFTSMEN OF AREA TO PARTICIPATE. AT ONE OF CITY'S PARKS. (LOCAL). KARLI WINK; EVANSVILLE JR WOMEN'S CLUB; 8000 LAUDERDALE; EVANSVILLE, IN 47715. (#50388-1).

JUNE 2 - JULY 7, '75. FREEDOM FESTIVAL. PAGEANTS, TOURNAMENTS AND CEREMONIES HERALD THE FREEDOM FESTIVAL'S ACTIVITIES IN JUNE WITH MOST EVENTS SCHEDULED ON THE WEEKENDS; PRELIMINARIES INCLUDE A HORSE SHOW, CHESS TOURNAMENT, DRUM AND BUGLE CORPS DRILL, BEAUTY PAGEANTS, BOAT RACES AND BANQUETS. (LOCAL). J HENRY BALLMAN, CHAIRMAN; FREEDOM FESTIVAL FOUNDATION OF EVANSVILLE INC; EXECUTIVE INN, 600 WALNUT ST; EVANSVILLE, IN 47708. (#100338-1).

JUNE 7, '75. RIVER DINNER DANCE AND ART AUCTION. ANNUAL DANCE OF MUSEUM GUILD-TO BE BICENTENNIAL EVENT IN 1975. AT EVANSVILLE MUSEUM OF ARTS AND SCIENCE. (LOCAL). MRS JANE ANNAKIN; EVANSVILLE MUSEUM GUILD; 1355 BAYARD PARK DR; EVANSVILLE, IN 47714. (#50397-1).

JUNE 15, '75. OLD-FASHIONED ICE CREAM SOCIAL. AN AFTERNOON OF GAY NINETIES FUN IN CITY'S DOWNTOWN. PLANS INCLUDE NICKEL ICE CREAM CONES, BICYCLE RACE WITH OLD-FASHIONED BICYCLES, AN ANTIQUE AUTO PARADE, HOT-AIR BALLOON ASCENSION, AND MANY GAMES AND SINGING GROUPS. AT DOWNTOWN WALKWAY. (LOCAL). MRS RUTH LEVI; EVANSVILLE BICENTENNIAL COUNCIL; 7208 E CHERRY ST; EVANSVILLE, IN 47715. (#50394-2).

JUNE 28 - JULY 6, '75. FREEDOM FESTIVAL. A 10 DAY FESTIVAL WITH PARADES, BEAUTY CONTEST, FOLK EVENTS, FIREWORKS, ETC. RESERVATIONS REQUIRED FOR SOME EVENTS. AT CITYWIDE. (LOCAL). J HENRY BALLMAN; EVANSVILLE FREEDOM FESTIVAL INC; 216 S FAIRLAWN; EVANSVILLE, IN 47714. (#50400-1).

JULY 20 - AUG 17, '75. AMERICAN SAMPLER EXHIBIT. THE EXHIBIT CONTAINS SAMPLES OF 19TH CENTURY AMERICANA AND COMES VIA THE LIBRARY OF CONGRESS. AT 411 SE RIVERSIDE DR. (LOCAL). W A GUMBERTS, PROJ DIR; EVANSVILLE MUSEUM OF ARTS AND SCIENCE; 22 CHANDLER AVE; EVANSVILLE, IN 47713. (#100619-1).

AUG 19, '75. CHICAGO FREE STREET THEATRE PERFORMANCES. THE CHICAGO GROUP IS TO GIVE TWO TWO-AND-ONE-HALF HOUR PERFORMANCES OF THEIR BICENTENNIAL SHOW, 'TOMORROW, ETC', ON THE GROUNDS OF THE COMMUNITY CENTER. IT IS ONE OF ONLY 25 PERFORMING ARTS GROUPS TO HAVE ARBA RECOGNITION. AT EVANSVILLE COMMUNITY CENTER. (LOCAL). PEGGY D JACK, DIRECTOR; ARTS AND EDUCATION COUNCIL; 10600 OLD STATE RD; EVANSVILLE, IN 47711. (#100946-1).

SEPT 1, '75 - JAN 1, '77. INFORMAL LEARNING SEQUENCE/THEATRE/MUSIC RECITALS. ONGOING LECTURE AND RECITAL SERIES; & SCHEDULED THEATRE PRODUCTIONS FOCUS ON AMERICA'S HERITAGE AND FUTURE. AT WHEELER CONCERT HALL/SHANKLIN THEATRE/STUDENT UNION. (LOCAL). JOHN DAVID LUTZ/L LAND; UNIV OF EVANSVILLE; UNIV OF EVANSVILLE; EVANSVILLE, IN 47702. (#104441-2).

SEPT 20, '75 - APR 10, '76. EVANSVILLE PHILHARMONIC ORCHESTRA'S BICENTENNIAL YEAR. THE ORCHESTRA'S 8 PERFORMANCES WILL FEATURE OUTSTANDING AMERICAN COMPOSERS IN HONOR OF THE BICENTENNIAL: SEPT 20/OCT 18/NOV 8/NOV 22/JAN 17/FEB 14/MAR 13/APR 10. AT VANDERBURGH COUNTY AUDITORIUM, SEVENTH AND WALNUT STS. (LOCAL). KAREN GENETT LIPTON; EVANSVILLE PHILHARMONIC ORCHESTRA; BOX 84; EVANSVILLE, IN 47701. (#100944-1).

NOV 1 - 30, '75. RELIGIOUS FREEDOM IN AMERICA MONTH. THE EVENTS ARE DESIGNED TO FOCUS, IN SERMONS AND CHURCH SCHOOLS, ON AMERICA'S RELIGIOUS HERITAGE. THE COUNCIL OF CHURCHES PLANS TO INVOLVE SYNAGOGUES AND CATHOLIC CHURCHES. TO BE HELD IN VARIOUS CHURCHES OF EVANSVILLE. AT CITYWIDE. (LOCAL). REV FRANCIS FRELLICK; EVANSVILLE COUNCIL OF CHURCHES; 203 NW FIFTH; EVANSVILLE, IN 47708. (#50399-1).

NOV 5 - 25, '75. CRIME CONTROL-LIMITATIONS ON CIVIL LIBERTIES?. CONFERENCE. (LOCAL). WALTER HOPKINS, COORD; INDIANA STATE UNIV AT EVANSVILLE; EVANSVILLE, IN 47712. (#200017-6).

NOV 23, '75. AFRO-AMERICAN HERITAGE MUSICAL. THE CONCERT WILL FEATURE BRUCE HUBBARD, BARITONE SOLOIST FROM INDIANA UNIV; HE WILL PRESENT AFRO-AMER LYRICS OF SELECTED COMPOSERS. AT EVANSVILLE COMMUNITY CENTER. (LOCAL). VERNA COOPER, PROJ DIR; CARVER COMMUNITY ORGANIZATION; 300 S HEIDELBACH; EVANSVILLE, IN 47713. (#200017-5).

DEC 5 - 6, '75. ST NIKOLAUS DAY GRANDFEST. ONE OF THE SALUTES TO EVANSVILLE'S RICH GERMAN HERITAGE; THIS GERMAN CHRISTMAS MADRIGAL IS OFFERED IN COOPERATION WITH REITZ HIGH SCHOOL GLEE CLUB. AT 916 N FULTON AVE. (LOCAL). WILLIAM C GREER, DIRECTOR; GERMANIA MAENNERCHOR; RR 4, BOX 365; EVANSVILLE, IN 47712. (#103472-1).

DEC 9, '75. CHRISTMAS IN COLONIAL WILLIAMSBURG. A LOOK AT COLONIAL COOKERY WITH EMPHASIS ON COLONIAL WILLIAMSBURG; COOKING METHODS AND TYPICAL FOODS DEMONSTRATED. AT 7525 SYLS DR. (LOCAL). MRS KENNETH SETTLE, CHMN; EVANSVILLE HOME ECONOMISTS; 71 PARK RIDGE DR; MT VERNON, IN 47620. (#103472-6).

JAN 1 - DEC 31, '76. WOMEN IN EVANSVILLE HISTORY EXHIBIT. TWELVE MONTH-LONG EXHIBITS ON PROMINENT LOCAL WOMEN, AND PREPARED BY TWELVE LOCAL WOMEN'S CLUBS. AT EVANSVILLE MUSEUM. (LOCAL). JAYNE BRYANT; EVANSVILLE MUSEUM OF ARTS AND SCIENCE; 5615 TULANE RD; EVANSVILLE, IN 47711. (#50398-1).

JAN 12 - FEB 15, '76. BICENTENNIAL BLACK HISTORY CELEBRATION. 1/15 - NIKKI GIOVANNI/BLACK POETRY; 1/20-22, EARTH PRODUCTIONS, LTD PRESENTS 'TREASURE ISLAND'; 1/27-28, LORGO PLAYERS, LTD PRESENTS 'PASSING THROUGH'; 1/26-21, A BLACK MUSIC HISTORY WORKSHOP; 2/3 - A TALENT SHOW; 2/14, KO THI DANCE COMPANY. ALSO A SPECIAL NEWSPAPER. AT MANY LOCATIONS THROUGHOUT CITY. (ST-WIDE). IRA T NEAL; EVANSVILLE-VANDERBURGH SCHOOL CORP/HUMAN RELATIONS COMMISSION ET AL; 1 SE 9TH ST; EVANSVILLE, IN 47708. (#104394-2).

JAN 13 - NOV 9, '76. EVANSVILLE PUBLIC LIBRARY BICENTENNIAL LECTURES. ON THE SECOND TUESDAY OF EACH MONTH IN 1976, THE PUBLIC LIBRARIES OF THE CITY WILL SPONSOR A FREE PUBLIC LECTURE ON LOCAL HISTORY & CULTURE. THE SERIES WILL INCLUDE SUCH TOPICS AS GERMAN CONTRIBUTIONS AND NEW HARMONY HISTORY. (LOCAL). MARGARET KYLE, ASST DIR; EVANSVILLE PUBLIC LIBRARY AND VANDERBURGH COUNTY PUBLIC LIBRARY; 22 SE 5TH ST; EVANSVILLE, IN 47708. (#103472-7).

JAN 19 - 20, '76. CHICAGO FREE STREET THEATER. LIVE PERFORMANCE AT FREE STREET THEATER. (LOCAL). BOBBY GOLD, COORD; POLICE RECREATION PROGRAM; 502 S ELLIOTT; EVANSVILLE, IN 47713. (#25764-1).

JAN 21 - 25, '76. DISCOVER AMERICA EXHIBIT. DISCOVER AMERICA EXHIBIT IS DESIGNED TO ENCOURAGE TRAVEL IN 1976. THE EXHIBIT CONSISTS OF PHOTOS, FILMS AND SLIDES. AT WASHINGTON SQUARE MALL, GREENRIVER & WASHINGTON AVE. (REGN'L). PATTIE DAVIS, DIRECTOR; WASHINGTON SQUARE MALL; 1220 WASHINGTON SQ; EVANSVILLE, IN 47715. (#103472-4).

FEB 1 - 29, '76. BLACK HISTORY MONTH. ONE FEATURE IS AN EXHIBIT, THE BLACK PRESENCE IN THE AMERICAN REVOLUTION, FROM THE SMITHSONIAN, TO BE AT EVANSVILLE MUSEUM. VARIOUS CULTURAL EVENTS PLANNED. AT CITYWIDE. (LOCAL). DON MCNARY; EVANSVILLE BICENTENNIAL COUNCIL; 826 BAYARD PARK DR; EVANSVILLE, IN 47713. (#50394-1).

FEB 12 - OCT 14, '76. LECTURE SERIES ON THE OHIO RIVER. APRIL 1 LECTURER: MISKEL WOLFINGER; FOODS OF THE OHIO RIVER AND THE VALLEY. MAY 4 LECTURER: WALTER HAVIGHURST, AUTHOR HISTORIAN OF OXFORD, OHIO. TOPIC OF ALL LECTURES IS THE OHIO RIVER. FOUR ADDITIONAL LECTURES & THEIR LOCATIONS TO BE ANNOUNCED. AT MEADOW PARK BRANCH LIBRARY, 750 NORTH PARK DRIVE. (LOCAL). MARGARET KYLE, CHAIRMAN; EVANSVILLE-VANDERBURGH COUNTY COMMITTEE OF LIBRARIANS; 22 SE 5TH ST; EVANSVILLE, IN 47708. (#103320-1).

FEB 19, '76. SOUR DOUGH: THE TRAVELLING BREAD. EVENING WILL STRESS IMPORTANCE OF SOUR-DOUGH COOKERY IN U S HISTORY; SAMPLES OF STARTER AND FINISHED PRODUCT AVAILABLE. AT SIGECO, 4TH AND SYCAMORE. (LOCAL). MRS KENNETH SETTLE, CHMN; EVANSVILLE HOME ECONOMISTS; 71 PARK RIDGE; MT VERNON, IN 47620. (#103472-8).

FEB 21, '76. BICENTENNIAL CREATIVE WRITING CONTEST & AWARDS CEREMONY. THE 2 EVANSVILLE UNIVERSITIES SPONSOR A HIGH-SCHOOL & COLLEGE STUDENT WRITING CONTEST; THEME IS 'THE FUTURE OF THE AMERICAN DREAM.'. AT OLD COUNTY COURTHOUSE. (LOCAL). TOM BOHN, CHAIRMAN; UNIV OF EVANSVILLE; EVANSVILLE, IN 47702. (#108252-1).

FEB 21, '76. OLD COURTHOUSE BICENTENNIAL COSTUME BALL: 1776-1976. FESTIVAL AT OLD COURTHOUSE, (FOURTH AND COURT STS). (LOCAL). IRMA REDGRAVE; OLD COURTHOUSE AUXILIARY; 3908 VISTA DR; EVANSVILLE, IN 47710. (#104394-1).

FEB 24, '76. DEDICATION OF MARKER DENOTING THE FIRST LAND SURVEY IN EVANSVILLE. INSTALLATION OF 2X3 FT MARKER SHOWING OUTLINE OF ORIGINAL SURVEY PLAT, YEAR AND NAME OF CHIEF SURVEYOR. AT FIRST AND MAIN STS-FLOOD WALL. (LOCAL). ALBERT C ROSENCRANE; SW CHAPTER INDIANA SOCIETY OF PROFESSIONAL ENGINEERS; C/O SIGECO 20-24 NW 4TH ST; EVANSVILLE, IN 47708. (#104010-1).

FEB 26, '76. BICENTENNIAL CHORAL FESTIVAL. ELEMENTARY AND SECONDARY STUDENTS WILL PRESENT CONCERT IN HONOR OF BICENTENNIAL. AT VANDERBURGH CIVIC AUDITORIUM. (LOCAL). WM LYLES, CHAIRMAN; EVANSVILLE-VANDERBURGH SCHOOL CORP; SCHOOL CORP, 1 SE 9TH ST; EVANSVILLE, IN 47708. (#104010-3).

MAR 4, '76. OHIO RIVER LECTURE SERIES - COLONEL JAMES ELLIS. MARCH 4 LECTURER: COLONEL JAMES ELLIS, USA CORPS OF ENGINEERS: SLIDE LECTURE ON OHIO RIVER ENGINEERING, PAST, PRESENT & FUTURE. AT ROOM A 126, ADMINISTRATION BLDG, INDIANA STATE UNIV AT EVANSVILLE. (ST-WIDE). MARGARET KYLE, CHAIRMAN; EVANSVILLE-VANDERBURGH COUNTY COMMITTEE OF LIBRARIANS; 22 SE 5TH ST; EVANSVILLE, IN 47708. (#12137-2).

MAR 6, '76. SALUTE TO AMERICA. THE ANNUAL SPEBQSA CHAPTER SHOW TO FEATURE GUEST AND LOCAL QUARTETS; SONGS WILL BE NOSTALGIC AND PATRIOTIC. AT VANDERBURGH CIVIC AUDITORIUM, 7TH AND WALNUT ST. (LOCAL). MIKE CANNON, DIRECTOR; SOC FOR PRESERVATION AND ENCOURAGEMENT OF BARBER SHOP SINGING IN AM; 708 WINDSOR AVE; EVANSVILLE, IN 47710. (#103472-5).

MAR 14, '76. MANY HAPPY RETURNS USA-THE CATHOLIC SCHOOLS' ALL-CITY CONCERT. LIVE PERFORMANCE AT REITZ MEMORIAL H S AUDITORIUM. (LOCAL). SISTER MARY INEZ MITCHELL; EVANSVILLE CATHOLIC SCHOOLS; 1300 HARMONY WAY; EVANSVILLE, IN 47712. (#104010-5).

APR 1 - 30, '76. CUSTIS-LEE PORTRAIT EXHIBIT. EXHIBIT OF PORTRAITS VIA WASHINGTON AND LEE UNIV. AT 411 SE RIVERSIDE DR. (ST-WIDE). W A GUMBERTS; EVANSVILLE MUSEUM; 22 CHANDLER AV; EVANSVILLE, IN 47713. (#50389-1).

APR 1 - 30, '76. SAVE OUR AMERICAN RESOURCES MONTH. RADIO/TV, EXHIBIT AT CITYWIDE. (LOCAL). CAROLYN SCRUGGS;

EVANSVILLE — CONTINUED

OPERATION CITY BEAUTIFUL; CHAMBER OF COMMERCE; EVANSVILLE, IN 47708. (#50483-1).

APR 1 - OCT 1, '76. CAVALCADE OF HISTORIC TRAILS. THE EVENTS ARE TOURS OF 3 AREA TRAILS IN WEST KY - CHICKASAW TRAIL, TRAIL OF TEARS & FORD'S FERRY TRAIL. OF GREAT HISTORIC VALUE. AT TOURS WILL COMMENCE AT WILLARD LIBRARY OR PRINCETON, KY. (LOCAL). W D SNIVELY; WILLARD LIBRARY; WILLARD LIBRARY; EVANSVILLE, IN 47710. (#50395-1).

APR 5 - 9, '76. CLEANUP FOR AMERICA'S BIRTHDAY. ENCOURAGE ALL CLASSES TO DO LITTER PROJECTS, CERTIFICATES TO TEACHERS, BUTTONS TO STUDENTS & PLAQUES TO PRINCIPALS HAVING 100,. (LOCAL). C J SCRUGGS, COORD; OPERATION CITY BEAUTIFUL, PTA & THE CATHOLIC FEDERATION; 329 MAIN ST; EVANSVILLE, IN 47708. (#105147-1).

APR 19 - 23, '76. BICENTENNIAL OAK TREE PLANTING. CEREMONY. (LOCAL). PAT BELL, COORDINATOR; EVANSVILLE AREA COUNCIL OF PTA'S; 5010 CUNNINGHAM DR; EVANSVILLE, IN 47715. (#102558-1).

APR 22 - MAY 10, '76. FORUM: 5 PART SERIES ON EVANSVILLE'S DEVELOPMENT AND FUTURE. SEMINAR. (LOCAL). DR GEORGE ABSHIER, PROF; INDIAN STATE UNIV; 8600 UNIV BLVD; EVANSVILLE, IN 47712. (#107352-1).

APR 27, '76. AMERICA IN SONG, ELEMENTARY BAND CONCERT. LIVE PERFORMANCE AT EVANSVILLE LUTHERAN SCHOOL, 1000 W ILLINOIS. (LOCAL). MRS ROBERT DICK, DIRECTOR; EVANSVILLE LUTHERAN SCHOOL; 13131 WOODLAND LANE; EVANSVILLE, IN 47711. (#200017-4).

APR 28, '76. MUSIC ANTIQUES OF THE TEMPERANCE MOVEMENT - LIVE PERFORMANCE. A PERFORMANCE OF 19TH CENTURY TEMPERANCE SONGS BY ISUE MID-AMERICA SINGERS. PROGRAM IS PART OF ISUE HUMANITIES FORUM. AT ADMINISTRATION BLDG, RM 28. (LOCAL). JON O CARLSON, COORD; INDIANA STATE UNIV-EVANSVILLE; INDIANA STATE UNIV EVANSVILLE; EVANSVILLE, IN 47712. (#107173-1).

APR 30 - MAY 2, '76. WAKE UP AMERICA. A CAMPING WEEKEND FOR GIRL SCOUTS WHICH WILL STRESS PATRIOTISM. AT LINCOLN CITY STATE PARK. (REGN'L). SUSAN C HUCK, COORD; RAINTREE GIRL SCOUT COUNCIL INC; 14 1/2 SE 2ND ST; EVANSVILLE, IN 47708. (#26613-1).

APR 30 - MAY 16, '76. OHIO RIVER ARTS FESTIVAL. A THREE WEEK FESTIVAL OF ARTS-CRAFTS. MOST EVENTS FREE. THIRTY LOCAL ORGANIZATIONS INVOLVED. BICENTENNIAL THEME IN 1976. AT CITYWIDE. (REGN'L). MRS MEL WELBORN, JR.; EVANSVILLE ARTS AND EDUCATION COUNCIL; 514 S ROOSEVELT DR; EVANSVILLE, IN 47715. (#50386-1).

MAY 1, '76. BICENTENNIAL READING & MUSIC CAROUSEL PRESENTATION. THIS RED, WHITE AND BLUE CAROUSEL IS THE CENTER OF ATTRACTION IN OUR CHILDREN'S LIBRARY. IT CONTAINS RECORDS & BOOKS, IS WIRED FOR SOUND AND PROVIDES A WONDERFUL PLACE FOR CHILDREN TO READ & LISTEN TO GOOD MUSIC. AT EVANSVILLE LIBRARY, MCCULLOUGH BRANCH. (REGN'L). MRS JOSEPHINE HENNINGFORD; EVANSVILLE PHILHARMONIC GUILD; 665 S BOEKE RD; EVANSVILLE, IN 47714. (#24284-1).

MAY 8, '76. BICENTENNIAL CRAFT & SKILL DEMONSTRATION FESTIVAL. EXHIBIT, FESTIVAL AT MESKER PARK ZOO - ST JOSEPH AVE. (LOCAL). PATRICIA O'LEARY, V-PRES; EVANSVILLE JUNIOR WOMENS CLUB; 4019 JENNINGS; EVANSVILLE, IN 47712. (#106453-1).

MAY 20, '76. THIS IS OUR STORY - MUSICAL CONCERT. BICENTENNIAL CONCERT BY INSTRUMENTAL MUSIC STUDENTS OF EVANSVILLE SCHOOLS. AT ROBERTS MUNICIPAL STADIUM. (LOCAL). WM LYLES, CHAIRMAN; EVANSVILLE-VANDERBURGH SCHOOL CORP; SCHOOL CORP, 1 SE 9TH ST; EVANSVILLE, IN 47708. (#104010-2).

MAY 22, '76. ARMED FORCES BICENTENNIAL BAND CONCERT. LIVE PERFORMANCE AT ROBERTS MUNICIPAL STADIUM, 2600 DIVISION ST, FREE PARKING. (ST-WIDE). JUDY CLABES, PUB SER DIR; THE EVANSVILLE PRESS; EVANSVILLE, IN 47703. (#104976-3).

JUNE 1 - 30, '76. GERMAN HERITAGE MONTH. MONTH-LONG CELEBRATION, VIA MANY FORMS, OF THE CONTRIBUTIONS OF THE CITY'S LARGEST ETHNIC GROUP. AT VARY. (LOCAL). WM GREER, CITY EDITOR; EVANSVILLE BICENTENNIAL CL; SUNDAY COURIER AND PRESS; EVANSVILLE, IN 47701. (#3346-1).

JUNE 7 - AUG 13, '76. BICENTENNIAL CERTIFICATE PROGRAM. CERTIFICATES ARE AWARDED TO STUDENTS ENROLLED IN 3 OR MORE COURSES WHICH FOCUS ON AMERICAN HERITAGE. (LOCAL). LARRAINE MATUSAK, DEAN; COLLEGE OF ALTERNATIVE PROGRAMS; UNIV OF EVANSVILLE; EVANSVILLE, IN 47702. (#104441-3).

JUNE 9, '76. FREEDOM FESTIVAL HORSE SHOW. THE SHOW WILL ALSO BE HELD FROM 7:00 PM - 9:00 PM. AT 4-H CTR, HWY 41, NORTH COUNTY FAIRGROUNDS; PLENTY OF PARKING. (REGN'L). WALTER REINE, COORD; ENGLISH HORSEMAN SOCIETY; 7400 NEWBURGH RD; EVANSVILLE, IN 47715. (#104835-15).

JUNE 13, '76. FREEDOM FESTIVAL SCHOLARSHIP PAGEANT. PAGEANT IS MISS AMERICA PRELIMINARY. AT CENTRAL HIGH SCHOOL, 5400 FIRST AVE N. (LOCAL). CHAS KROENER, DIRECTOR; FREEDOM FESTIVAL FOUNDATION, INC; 3873 BELLEMEADE AVE; EVANSVILLE, IN 47714. (#104835-4).

JUNE 15 - 17, '76. AMERICAN FREEDOM TRAIN DISPLAY DAYS AT EVANSVILLE. THE AMERICAN FREEDOM TRAIN WILL INCLUDE 10 EXHIBIT CARS AND 2 SHOWCASE CARS DEPICTING DIFFERENT PHASES OF THE AMERICAN EXPERIENCE. ITS ARRIVAL WILL SERVE AS A CATALYST FOR LOCAL BICENTENNIAL CELEBRATIONS BY PEOPLE THROUGHOUT THIS NATION. (ST-WIDE). SY FREEDMAN, DIR OF P/R; THE AMERICAN FREEDOM TRAIN FOUNDATION, INC; 5205 LEESBURG PKE, SUITE 800; BAILEY'S XRD, VA 22041. (#1776-117).

JUNE 16 - 19, '76. OLD WAYS IN THE NEW WORLD ON TOUR - EXHIBIT. EXHIBIT AT CIVIC CENTER. (LOCAL). DONALD MCNARY, COORD; EVANSVILLE HUMAN RELATIONS COMMISSION; CIVIC CENTER; EVANSVILLE, IN 47708. (#26591-1).

JUNE 17, '76. RIVER CRUISE ON OHIO RIVER. RIVER MUSIC ON THE OHIO RIVER WITH DENNIS SHEPPARD AND FOLK SINGERS, DURING A RIVER CRUISE, ON JUNE 17, 1976. AT ABOARD JULIA BELLE SWAIN, PADDLEWHEELER DRESS PLAZA. (ST-WIDE). MARGARET KYLE, CHMN; EVANSVILLE-VANDERBURGH COUNTY COMMITTEE OF LIBRARIANS; 22 SE 5TH ST; EVANSVILLE, IN 47708. (#104835-18).

JUNE 19 - 20, '76. FREEDOM FESTIVAL FOUNDATION CHESS TOURNAMENT. COMPETITION. (LOCAL). CRAIG HINES, CHAIRMAN; EVANSVILLE BICENTENNIAL COUNCIL; 680 COVERT AVE; EVANSVILLE, IN 47714. (#104835-3).

JUNE 21, '76. LITTLE MISS FREEDOM FESTIVAL PAGEANT. COMPETITION AT WASHINGTON SQUARE SHOPPING MALL; PARKING AT THE DOOR. (LOCAL). PATTIE DAVIS, COORD; FREEDOM FESTIVAL FOUNDATION, INC; 1220 WASHINGTON AVE; EVANSVILLE, IN 47715. (#104835-14).

JUNE 21, '76. VESPER SERVICE. CEREMONY. (LOCAL). REV GENE TON, DIRECTOR; INTER-FAITH RELIGIOUS COUNCIL; 320 CHERRY ST; EVANSVILLE, IN 47708. (#104835-9).

JUNE 23 - 26, '76. INTERNATIONAL BROTHERHOOD OF MAGICIANS 48TH ANNUAL CONVENTION. 3 BIG PUBLIC SHOWS THUR, FRI & SAT NIGHT WITH INTERNATIONALLY KNOWN MAGICIANS; THURSDAY NIGHT SHOW WILL FEATURE ALL BRITISH MAGICIANS, BILLED AS AN 'ALL BRITISH NIGHT'. AT VANDERBURGH AUDITORIUM, 715 LOCUST ST, FREE PARKING. (INT'L). SCOTT R BRITT, COORD; INTERNATIONAL BROTHERHOOD OF MAGICIANS; 10519 MERRIHILL DR; EVANSVILLE, IN 47712. (#104976-1).

JUNE 24 - 28, '76. 'GEORGE M' - MUSICAL. LIVE PERFORMANCE AT MESKER MUSIC THEATER, MESKER PARK DR. (LOCAL). DICK ENGBERS, PRESIDENT; EVANSVILLE CIVIC THEATRE INC; 411 WASHINGTON AVE; EVANSVILLE, IN 47713. (#108005-2).

JUNE 25 - 28, '76. AMERICANA FESTIVAL. A WEEK-LONG FILM AND FINE ARTS/CRAFTS EXHIBITS. AT UNIV GROUNDS. (REGN'L). RICHARD HANSEN; UNIV OF EVANSVILLE; UNIV OF EVANSVILLE; EVANSVILLE, IN 47702. (#104441-1).

JUNE 26, '76. AMERICANA FESTIVAL DRUM & BUGLE COMPETITION. COMPETITION AT CENTRAL HIGH SCHOOL STADIUM. (LOCAL). BILL MONTRASTELLE, CHMN; FREEDOM FESTIVAL FOUNDATION; 412 S E 4TH ST; EVANSVILLE, IN 47708. (#104835-11).

JUNE 26, '76. AMERICANA FESTIVAL PARADE. PARADE AT STREETS OF DOWNTOWN EVANSVILLE. (LOCAL). BILL MONTRASTELLE, CHMN; FREEDOM FESTIVAL FOUNDATION; 412 S E 4TH ST; EVANSVILLE, IN 47708. (#104835-12).

JUNE 26, '76. AMERICANA FESTIVAL OPENING CEREMONIES. CEREMONY AT 7TH AND MAIN ST, IN FRONT OF CIVIC CENTER. (REGN'L). GEN ROBT M LEICH, COORD; FREEDOM FESTIVAL FOUNDATION; PO BOX 869; EVANSVILLE, IN 47708. (#104835-13).

JUNE 27, '76. AMERICANA FESTIVAL CHAMPIONSHIP BOAT RACES. COMPETITION AT OHIO RIVER AT DRESS PLAZA, DOWNTOWN EVANSVILLE. (LOCAL). JACK KIRWER; EVANSVILLE OUTBOARD BOAT CLUB; PO BOX 3728; EVANSVILLE, IN 47736. (#104835-7).

JUNE 27, '76. SPECIAL BICENTENNIAL POPS CONCERT. LIVE PERFORMANCE AT VANDERBURGH CIVIC AUDITORIUM, 715 LOCUST ST. (LOCAL). KAREN G LIPTON, GEN MGR; EVANSVILLE PHILHARMONIC ORCHESTRA; PO BOX 84, 14-1/2 SE 2ND ST; EVANSVILLE, IN 47701. (#104976-2).

JUNE 30 - JULY 6, '76. FREEDOM FESTIVAL. ANNUAL EVENT WILL HAVE LARGEST NUMBER OF EVENTS EVER IN 1976. RESERVATIONS REQUIRED FOR SOME EVENTS. AT CITYWIDE. (LOCAL). J HENRY RALLMAN; FREEDOM FESTIVAL INC; 216 S FAIRLAWN; EVANSVILLE, IN 47714. (#50400-2).

JULY 3, '76. FREEDOM FESTIVAL DANCE. FESTIVAL AT DOWNTOWN WALKWAY. (LOCAL). DARREL BIGHAM, CHMN; EVANSVILLE BICENTENNIAL COUNCIL; KUEBLER RD; EVANSVILLE, IN 47712. (#104835-10).

JULY 3 - 4, '76. FREEDOM FESTIVAL RUGBY TOURNAMENT. COMPETITION. (REGN'L). BRANDY MELTON, COORD; EVANSVILLE BICENTENNIAL COUNCIL; 1421 LINCOLN AVE; EVANSVILLE, IN 47715. (#104835-16).

JULY 3 - 5, '76. FREEDOM FESTIVAL OPEN TENNIS TOURNAMENT. COMPETITION. (LOCAL). CHICKIE FRIEBERG, CHMN; EVANSVILLE BICENTENNIAL COUNCIL; 1320 S E FIRST ST; EVANSVILLE, IN 47713. (#104835-6).

JULY 3 - AUG 29, '76. AMERICANA EXHIBIT OF ART AND MEMORABILIA (ESP. 18TH CENT). ART-CRAFTS-DOCUMENTS FROM MUSEUM'S COLLECTION, ESPECIALLY 18TH CENTURY IN MAIN GALLERY; CONTEMPORARY ART IN RIVER ROOM. SUNDAY HOURS: 12-5 PM. AT 411 SE RIVERSIDE DR; EVANSVILLE IN. (LOCAL). JOHN W STREETMAN III; EVANSVILLE MUSEUM OF ARTS AND SCIENCE; 411 SE RIVERSIDE DR; EVANSVILLE, IN 47713. (#50396-1).

JULY 4, '76. FREEDOM FESTIVAL FIREWORKS DISPLAY. LIVE PERFORMANCE AT OHIO RIVERFRONT. (LOCAL). ROBT LEAHY, DIRECTOR; STERLING BREWERY/WASHINGTON SQUARE MERCHANTS; 1301 PENNSYLVANIA ST; EVANSVILLE, IN 47710. (#104835-8).

JULY 4, '76. FREEDOM SABBATH. CEREMONY AT ALL CHURCHES THROUGHOUT THE CITY. (LOCAL). REV BILL SCHWEIN, CHMN; INTER-FAITH RELIGIOUS COUNCIL; 5130 LINCOLN AVE; EVANSVILLE, IN 47715. (#104835-2).

JULY 6, '76. CAVALCADE OF MUSIC. THIS WILL BE A PERFORMANCE OF A CONTATA WRITTEN BY RABBI TOPEL WITH A BICENTENNIAL THEME. (LOCAL). DR JOSEPH BAUS, DIRECTOR; INTER-FAITH RELIGIOUS COUNCIL; 634 COLLEGE HWY; EVANSVILLE, IN 47714. (#104835-1).

JULY 8 - 10, '76. OHIO RIVER WRITERS' WORKSHOP. 3 DAY WRITERS' WORKSHOP WITH 5 VISITING INSTRUCTORS. OBJECT IS TO IMPROVE WRITING SKILLS AND ENCOURAGE WRITING ON SOUTHERN INDIANA CULTURE. AT SARTO CENTER. (REGN'L). W A GUMBERTS, COORD; EVANSVILLE ARTS AND EDUCATION COUNCIL; 22 CHANDLER AVE; EVANSVILLE, IN 47713. (#108285-1).

JULY 11, '76. NATIONAL RELIGIOUS SPEAKER. SEMINAR. (LOCAL). REV JOSEPH ZILIAK, CHMN; INTER-FAITH RELIGIOUS COUNCIL; 208 N W 3RD ST; EVANSVILLE, IN 47708. (#104835-5).

OCT 1 - 31, '76. THE AMERICAN FARM EXHIBIT FROM CALIF HISTORICAL SOC. AN INTERPRETIVE TRAVELING EXHIBITION ON THE HISTORY OF AMERICAN AGRICULTURE. AT CITY-COUNTY BLDG. (ST-WIDE). D E BIGHAM; EVANSVILLE BICENT COUNCIL; INDIANA ST U EVANSVILLE; EVANSVILLE, IN 47712. (#2846-1).

OCT 2, '76. HARVEST BALL. LARGE COMMUNITY 'GET-TOGETHER' PLANNED. AS OF DATE OF APPLICATION, PETER DUCHIN AND BAND WILL PROVIDE MUSIC. AT ROBERTS MUNICIPAL STADIUM. (LOCAL). MRS BETTY MC CUTCHAN; EVANSVILLE BICENTENNIAL CL; 2411 BAYARD PARK DR; EVANSVILLE, IN 47714. (#3347-1).

OCT 14, '76. OHIO RIVER LECTURE. OCTOBER 14, LECTURER: DR VICTOR JOHNSON, SLIDE LECTURE ON PORT OF EVANSVILLE: TRADE AND TRANSPORTATION. AT WEST BRANCH LIBRARY, 2000 WEST FRANKLIN ST. (ST-WIDE). MARGARET KYLE, CHMN; EVANSVILLE-VANDERBURGH COUNTY COMMITTEE OF LIBRARIANS; 22 SE 5TH ST; EVANSVILLE, IN 47708. (#104835-17).

OCT 15 - 17, '76. BUFFALO TRACE COUNCIL, BOY SCOUTS BICENTENNIAL OBSERVANCE. AREA SCOUTS WILL HAVE 3-DAY FESTIVAL FEATURING: CUB SCOUT DISPLAYS 10/16 OF CRAFTS 200 YRS AGO; SCOUT CAMPOREE 10/15-17 SHOWING SKILLS OF 200 YRS AGO; EXPLORERS SHOW 10/16; BARBECUE AND PAGEANT THE EVENING OF 10/16 AT ROBERTS STADIUM. AT SEVERAL LOCATIONS IN CITY OVER THIS 3-DAY FESTIVAL. (LOCAL). G W SPICE, DIRECTOR; BUFFALO TRACE COUNCIL NO 156, BOY SCOUTS OF AMERICA-AREA 4, E CENT; PO BOX 3245; EVANSVILLE, IN 47731. (#104010-4).

OCT 30 - 31, '76. UNITED STATES ARMED FORCES BICENTENNIAL CARAVAN. CARAVAN IS COMPOSED OF EXHIBIT VANS FOR EACH MILITARY SERVICE. PROJECT THEME IS 'HISTORY OF THE ARMED FORCES & THEIR CONTRIBUTIONS TO THE NATION'. (LOCAL). DR DARREL E BIGHAM; UNITED STATES ARMED FORCES BICENTENNIAL CARAVAN; 1101 N FULTON AVE; EVANSVILLE, IN 47710. (#1775-740).

NOV 9 - 10, '76. COUNCIL OF GARDEN CLUBS HOLIDAY FLOWER SHOW. THIS SHOW WILL FEATURE FLOWER ARRANGEMENTS TYPICAL OF VARIOUS PERIODS OF AMER HISTORY AND EXHIBITS OF NATIVE PLANTS. AT VANDERBURGH COUNTY AUDITORIUM, GOLD RM. (LOCAL). MS KENNETH CAMPBELL; COUNCIL OF GARDEN CLUBS; 8216 PETERSBURG RD; EVANSVILLE, IN 47711. (#100945-1).

FERDINAND

JULY 2 - 3, '76. JULY 2 & 3 IN FERDINAND. ACTIVITIES INCLUDE PICNIC, PARADE, GENERAL ATTRACTIONS, FIREWORKS, AND A BALL GAME. (LOCAL). JAMES L VAAL, CHMN; PO BOX 81; FERDINAND, IN 47532. (#200017-59).

FORT WAYNE

ALLEN COUNTY 4-H FAIR, FORT WAYNE, IN. ALLEN COUNTY AGRICULTURAL HERITAGE IS A STIMULUS FOR THE 4-H CLUBS OF FUTURE, AND WILL BE SEEN AT THE FAIR. (LOCAL). CATHERINE A SEYMOURE, COORDINATOR; ALLEN COUNTY 4-H CLUBS, INC; 4001 CRESCENT AVE; FORT WAYNE, IN 46805. (#23665). **ARBA GRANTEE.**

ALLEN COUNTY, INDIANA, HISTORY PUBLICATION. A NEW PUBLICATION OF ALLEN CO. HISTORY BY FORT WAYNE HISTORIAN AND AUTHOR, JOHN ANKENBRUCK. (LOCAL). CURATOR; ALLEN COUNTY HISTORICAL MUSEUM; 1424 W. JEFFERSON; FORT WAYNE, IN 46804. (#4441).

AMER REVOL: A UNION LIST OF SELECTED MATERIALS, FL. A LIST OF NON-FICTION AND FICTION BOOKS, CHILDREN'S BOOKS, MUSIC & RECORDS IN 3 FORT WAYNE, IN LIBRARIES; 560 ITEMS ARE LISTED. (LOCAL). RICHARD MCKEE, LIBRARIAN; CONCORDIA SENIOR COLLEGE LIBRARY; 6600 N CLINTON ST; FORT WAYNE, IN 46825. (#21872).

AMERICAN FILM RETROSPECTIVE: FORT WAYNE, INDIANA. 10-20 FILMS OF HISTORICAL IMPORTANCE TO THE U S PRESENTED IN A PROGRAM. (LOCAL). CHARLES CALLERY, COORDINATOR; FORT WAYNE BICENT COMMITTEE; ONE MAIN ST, CITY-CO BLDG, RM 83; FORT WAYNE, IN 46802. (#8829). **(??).**

AMERICAN MUSICAL CONCERTS IN FORT WAYNE, INDIANA. A SERIES OF POP CONCERTS DEDICATED TO THE MUSIC OF THE AMERICAN MUSICAL THEATRE WILL BE HELD. (LOCAL). DONNA JEAN DARBY, CHAIRWOMAN; FT WAYNE PHILHARMONIC WOMEN'S COMMITTEE; 927 S HARRISON; FORT WAYNE, IN 46802. (#8257).

FORT WAYNE — CONTINUED

BICENT ICE SHOW IN FORT WAYNE, INDIANA. A BICENTENNIAL THEME ICE SHOW: A BRIEF HISTORY OF THE COUNTRY PERFORMED ON ICE. NATIONAL SKATERS AND LOCAL ICE SKATING CLUB WILL MAKE UP THE CAST. (LOCAL). JOHN VAUGHN, PROJ COORDINATOR; THE FORT WAYNE ICE SKATING CLUB; FORT WAYNE, IN 46802. (#8826).

BICENT TAPES FOR THE SIGHTLESS PROJ OF FT WAYNE. A PROJECT TO PROVIDE CASSETTE TAPE RECORDINGS OF HISTORIC EVENTS AND THE HERITAGE OF THE FT WAYNE, ALLEN COUNTY AREA. (LOCAL). MONABELLE VOSMEIER, CHAIRMAN; HISTORICAL COMM OF THE FT WAYNE BICENTENNIAL COMMISSION; ONE MAIN ST, RM 830 CITY-COUNTY; FORT WAYNE, IN 46802. (#6466). **(??).**

BICENTENNIAL AMERICA: EVALUATIONS. THERE WILL BE A SERIES OF PANELS ON THE STATE OF AMERICAN FREEDOMS & DEMOCRATIC GOALS AFTER 200 YEARS AND PROPOSALS FOR THE FUTURE. (LOCAL). J R KIRBY, EDUCATION PROF; INDIANA UNIV & PURDUE UNIV; 2101 COLISEUM BLVD E; FORT WAYNE, IN 46805. (#103101-6). **(??).**

BICENTENNIAL CONCERTS IN FORT WAYNE, INDIANA. SPECIAL BICENTENNIAL PROGRAMMING ON FIRST TWO PHILHARMONIC SUBSCRIPTION CONCERTS OF NEGLECTED AMERICAN MUSIC FROM THE 18TH, 19TH, AND 20TH CENTURIES. (LOCAL). R P EISENSTEIN, MANAGER; FORT WAYNE PHILHARMONIC, INC; 927 S HARRISON; FORT WAYNE, IN 46802. (#8259).

BICENTENNIAL FUNMOBILE, FT WAYNE, IN. THE ROLE OF LEISURE ACTIVITIES & INTEREST IN EARLY AMER LIFE WILL BE DEMONSTRATED THROUGH THE FUNMOBILE. (LOCAL). PHIL BENNETT, COORDINATOR; DEPARTMENT OF PUBLIC PARKS; CITY COUNTY BLDG, 1 MAIN; FT WAYNE, IN 46802. (#26791). **ARBA GRANTEE.**

BICENTENNIAL INVITATIONAL EXHIBITION - FORT WAYNE. REGIONAL INVITATIONAL EXHIBITION RELATING TO USA, PAST, PRESENT AND FUTURE, THRU PAINTINGS. (REGN'L). PATTY GRIEST, CHAIRMAN; FORT WAYNE MUSEUM OF ART-VISUAL ARTS; 1202 W WAYNE ST; FORT WAYNE, IN 46804. (#4444).

BICENTENNIAL MEDAL FOR FORT WAYNE, INDIANA. FORT WAYNE'S BICENT MEDAL, DESIGNED BY HECTOR GARCIA, MADE OF SILVER, BRONZE AND GOLD WILL BE STRUCK AT A LEADING MINT. (LOCAL). RUSSELL OETTEL, CHAIRMAN; FORT WAYNE BICENT COMMISSION, DESIGN COMMITTEE; ONE MAIN ST, CITY-CO BLDG, RM 83; FORT WAYNE, IN 46802. (#8839).

CANAL HOUSE RESTORATION, FT WAYNE,IN. RESTORATION OF CANAL HOUSE LANDMARK, TESTIFYING TO 125 YEARS OF GROWTH OF FORT WAYNE. (LOCAL). MS ROBERT ANDERSON; FORT WAYNE BICENTENNIAL COMMISSION; 1115 W BERRY ST; FORT WAYNE, IN 46802. (#27235). **ARBA GRANTEE.**

CANAL WAREHOUSE RESTORATION OF FORT WAYNE, INDIANA. RESTORE TO EXTERIOR APPEARANCE AND TO USEFUL INTERIOR USAGE THE CANAL WAREHOUSE ON SUPERIOR ST. THIS BLDG IS THE OLDEST STRUCTURE STILL STANDING IN FORT WAYNE. (LOCAL). DAVID DRURY, CHAIRMAN; FORT WAYNE BICENT COMMISSION-HISTORICAL COMMITTEE; CITY--COUNTY BLDG; FORT WAYNE, IN 46802. (#4440). **(??).**

'CELEBRATION OF INDIVIDUAL' - FORT WAYNE, IN. THEATRE FOR IDEAS PRESENTS 'CELEBRATION OF INDIVIDUAL'. (LOCAL). TERRY DORAN, CHAIRMAN; FORT WAYNE ART SCHOOL; BOX 681; FORT WAYNE, IN 46801. (#27890). **ARBA GRANTEE.**

CHOIR DIRECTION BY JESTER HAIRSTON, FORT WAYNE, IN. CHORAL DIRECTOR WHO HAS BEEN U S GOODWILL AMBASSADOR WILL DIRECT 1,000 PERSON CHOIR AT THE MEMORIAL STADIUM. (LOCAL). DONNA JEAN DARBY, CHAIRWOMAN; FORT WAYNE BICENT COMMITTEE - FINE ARTS COMMITTEE; ONE MAIN ST, CITY-CO BLDG, RM 83; FORT WAYNE, IN 46802. (#8837).

CITY SPIRIT PROJECT - FT WAYNE, IN. IDENTIFICATION AND USE OF LOCAL CULTURAL RESOURCES AND CULTURAL FACILITIES. (LOCAL). LADONNA HUNTLEY, CHAIRMAN; FT WAYNE BICENTENNIAL COMMITTEE; FT WAYNE, IN 46802. (#18878).

CULTURAL ENRICHMENT AND TRANSPORTATION - IN. PROVIDE AN OPPORTUNITY FOR SENIOR CITIZENS TO ENJOY THE BICENTENNIAL. (LOCAL). YVONNE STEWART, COORDINATOR; CATHOLIC CHARITIES OF THE DIOCESE OF FORT WAYNE; 919 S FAIRFIELD; FORT WAYNE, IN 46802. (#24087). **ARBA GRANTEE.**

DOCK STREET EXPLORATION - PROJ OF FT WAYNE, IN. A MUSEUM FOR CHILDREN; CONTINUOUS MOVIES; COLLECTIONS OF 18TH CENTURY; 2 BOX CARS, ONE CONTAINING MUSICAL INSTRUMENTS AND ONE A WORKSHOP; A ROCKETSHIP AND DAILY EVENTS. (LOCAL). GREGORY JACOBS, PROJ; 4316 COVINGTON RD; FORT WAYNE, IN 46802. (#13857).

ESSAY ON AMERICANISM PROJ OF FORT WAYNE, INDIANA. JR HIGH SCHOOL STUDENTS WILL BE ELIGIBLE TO WRITE AN ESSAY ON ASPECT OF AMERICANISM FOR BICENTENNIAL YEAR 1976. (LOCAL). WILLIAM WHETSEL, PATRIOT COMMITTEE; DISABLED AMER VETERANS ASSOC; 1833 KINSMORE; FORT WAYNE, IN 46806. (#3706).

ETHNIC FACETS OF FORT WAYNE. ETHNIC PROGRAM. (LOCAL). HAROLD H VISINO; INTERNATIONAL COUNCIL, INC; 1230 S CLINTON; FORT WAYNE, IN 46802. (#27576). **ARBA GRANTEE.**

FACES OF FORT WAYNE - PHOTO DISPLAY, INDIANA. ARRAY OF OLD AND NEW PHOTOS WHICH RELATE TO FT WAYNE, ITS HERITAGE, CULTURE AND PEOPLE. (LOCAL). GABRIEL DELOBBE, CHAIRMAN; FORT WAYNE BICENT COMMITTEE - VISUAL ARTS COMMITTEE; ONE MAIN ST, CITY-CO BLDG, RM 83; FORT WAYNE, IN 46802. (#8835).

FIRST SUB LEGION FIFE & DRUM CORPS OF FT WAYNE, IN. ANCIENT FIFE AND DRUM CORPS PATTERNED AND UNIFORMED AFTER A UNIT IN THE LEGION OF GENERAL ANTHONY WAYNE. (LOCAL). RICHARD FRIEDRICH, CHAIRMAN; HISTORICAL COMMITTEE, FWBC; ONE MAIN ST, RM 830 CITY-COUNTY; FORT WAYNE, IN 46802. (#6465).

FORT WAYNE BICENTENNIAL ART EXHIBIT IN INDIANA. COMPETITIVE EXHIBITION OF ARTWORK WHICH DEPICTS FORT WAYNE IN 1976. (LOCAL). PATTY GRIEST, CHAIRWOMAN; VISUAL ARTS COMMITTEE, FORT WAYNE BICENT COMMITTEE; RM 830 CITY-COUNTY BLDG, ONE MAI; FORT WAYNE, IN 46802. (#8255).

FRED PINKARD CONCERT IN FORT WAYNE, IN. PROJECT INVOLVES RELATING HISTORY OF BLACK PEOPLE AS SEEN THROUGH THEIR HUMOR, FOLKLORE, PROSE, POETRY AND SONGS. (LOCAL). HAL VIZINO, PROJ DIRECTOR; ETHNIC HERITAGE; FORT WAYNE, IN 46802. (#16333).

GENEOLOGY STUDY OF GAYINGS FAMILY, FORT WAYNE, IN. HISTORY OF THE GAYINGS FAMILY AND THEIR MIGRATION FROM VIRGINIA TO FT WAYNE, FROM 1792 TO 1920 WILL BE RESEARCHED AND PUBLISHED. (LOCAL). BARBARA BELOTE, DIRECTOR; HISTORICAL COMMITTEE; 1308 PARK AVE; FORT WAYNE, IN 46807. (#16331).

INDIAN-AMERICAN '76, FORT WAYNE, IN. INDIAN DANCE PERFORMANCE SPONSORED BY THE DEPT OF PUBLIC PARKS. (LOCAL). ANN RANCK, COORDINATOR; FORT WAYNE DEPT OF PUBLIC PARKS; ONE MAIN ST; FORT WAYNE, IN 46802. (#27232). **ARBA GRANTEE.**

INTERCOLLEGIATE BICENT LECTURE SERIES - FT WAYNE. SIX PUBLIC LECTURES, EACH APPROACHING THE REVOLUTION & THE DEVELOPMENT OF AMERICA. (LOCAL). JAMES HAW, CHAIRMAN; INTERCOLLEGIAL BICENT COMMITTEE; CITY-COUNTY BLDG; FORT WAYNE, IN 46802. (#4448).

INTERNATIONAL CABARET NIGHT: FORT WAYNE, INDIANA. DINNER AND ENTERTAINMENT OF AN INTERNATIONAL NATURE: POSSIBLY 20 DIFFERENT ETHNIC FOODS IN BUFFET STYLE, LOCAL ETHNIC ENTERTAINMENT; $15 PER COUPLE. (LOCAL). CHARLIE CUNNINGHAM, CHAIRMAN; FORT WAYNE BICENT COMMITTEE; ONE MAIN ST, RM 830; FORT WAYNE, IN 46802. (#8825).

INTERNATIONAL CENTER AT FORT WAYNE, INDIANA. THE ESTABLISHMENT OF A FACILITY THAT WILL BRING A VAST PROGRAM OF CULTURAL, LANGUAGE & ETHNIC EXPERIENCES TO THE COMMUNITY. (LOCAL). DOUGLAS BAUGH, PRESIDENT; NEW HORIZON COMMITTEE, FWBC; ONE MAIN ST, RM 830 CITY-COUNTY; FORT WAYNE, IN 46802. (#6464). **(??).**

THE J C DOME GREENHOUSE PROJ OF FORT WAYNE, IN. A CLIMATE CONTROLLED STRUCTURE CAPABLE OF FEEDING 40 PEOPLE, UTILIZING CURRENT TECHNOLOGIES OF SOLAR POWER AND AGRICULTURE. INNER CITY YOUTHS WILL ASSIST IN CONSTRUCTION AND OPERATION. (LOCAL). JERRY DYBEN, PROJ MANAGER; FORT WAYNE BICENT COMMISSION - NEW HORIZONS COMMITTEE; ONE MAIN ST, CITY-CO BLDG, RM 83; FORT WAYNE, IN 46802. (#8841). **(??).**

JOHNNY APPLESEED GRAVESITE INTERPRETATION. UNMANNED INTERPRETATIVE EXHIBIT AT JOHNNY APPLESEED'S GRAVESITE IN ARCHER PARK. (REGN'L). DAVID DRURY AND PHYLLIS FLOREA, HISTORICAL COMM; FORT WAYNE BICENTENNIAL COMMITTEE; ROOM 830, CITY-COUNTY BLDG; FORT WAYNE, IN 46802. (#3713).

JOHNNY APPLESEED ORCHARD IN FORT WAYNE, INDIANA. TREES DONATED BY PUBLIC TO BE PLANTED AROUND JOHNNY APPLESEED GRAVESITE. (LOCAL). ANDREA MCFADDEN, PROJ COORDINATOR; FORT WAYNE BICENT COMMITTEE; ONE MAIN ST, CITY-CO BLDG, RM 83; FORT WAYNE, IN 46802. (#8831). **(??).**

A LABOR HISTORY OF ALLEN COUNTY, FT WAYNE, IN. A COMPREHENSIVE HISTORY OF LABOR IN FT WAYNE AND ALLEN COUNTY WILL BE RESEARCHED AND WRITTEN BY A PROFESSIONAL HISTORIAN. (LOCAL). RICHARD KRESHER, PROJ DIRECTOR; LABOR EDUCATION PROJECT OF THE UNITED WAY; FORT WAYNE, IN 46802. (#16332).

LATIN WEEK IN FORT WAYNE, INDIANA. A CELEBRATION OF THE ANCIENT ROMAN CULTURE WITH A FESTIVAL, A NATL CATAPULT CONTEST & A COUNTY WIDE 'LATIN IN AMERICA' POSTER CONTEST. (LOCAL). NANCY MACK, PROJ COORDINATOR; WAYNE HIGH SCHOOL LATIN CLUB; 9100 WINCHESTER RD; FORT WAYNE, IN 46819. (#8633).

MODEL CONGRESS IN FORT WAYNE, IN. 4-DAY SIMULATION OF U S CONGRESS. (LOCAL). CHARLIE HALL, PROJ DIRECTOR; NEW HORIZONS; FORT WAYNE, IN 46802. (#16334). **ARBA GRANTEE.**

THE OFFICIAL FT WAYNE, INDIANA BICENT COOKBOOK. THE COOKBOOK WILL BE A HISTORICAL COLLECTION OF 200 YEARS OF COOKERY IN THE INDIANA AREA. (LOCAL). MARCIA ADAMS, MEMBERSHIP COUNCIL; FT WAYNE MUSEUM OF ART; 1202 W WAYNE; FORT WAYNE, IN 46804. (#8630).

A PATRIOTIC SALUTE TO AMERICA, FORT WAYNE, IN. A SERIES OF 17 BICENTENNIAL MUSICAL & DRAMATIC PERFORMANCES, PUT ON FOR THE INSTITUTIONALIZED & DISABLED IN FT WAYNE & ALLEN COUNTY, BY INDIANA UNIV, PURDUE & ST FRANCIS COLLEGE STUDENTS. (LOCAL). MS LILLIAN C EMBICK, COORDINATOR; HOSPITAL AUDIENCES, INC; 1501 CALIFORNIA; FORT WAYNE, IN 46805. (#25241). **ARBA GRANTEE.**

PHOTO & MEMORABILIA DISPLAY IN FORT WAYNE, INDIANA. THE 50TH ANNIVERSARY OF WOWO RADIO STATION; PHOTOS AND MEMORABILIA WILL BE BROUGHT TO SHOPPING MALLS FOR DISPLAY. (LOCAL). DAVID DRURY, CHAIRMAN; FORT WAYNE BICENT COMMISSION, HISTORICAL COMMITTEE; 1 MAIN ST, CITY-CTY BLDG, RM 830; FORT WAYNE, IN 46802. (#8634).

PROJECT CELEBRATION, FORT WAYNE, IND. CELEBRITIES WILL ARRIVE AT EMBASSY THEATER IN ANTIQUE CARS, GREET PATRONS IN WHITE-GLOVE RECEIVING LINE, DRESSED IN ANTIQUE COSTUMES AS HISTORY IS VERBALLY RECOUNTED IN MUSIC & SLIDES. (LOCAL). DONNA JEAN DARBY, CHAIRMAN FWBC; TRI KAPPA SORORITY/FORT WAYNE BICENT COMMITTEE; ONE MAIN ST, RM 830; FORT WAYNE, IN 46802. (#8827).

PUBLICATION 'COLUMBIA STREET STORY' OF FORT WAYNE. 140-150 PAGE PAMPHLET BY ROY BATES ABOUT FAMOUS LOCAL STREET. (LOCAL). FRED REYNOLDS, LIBRARIAN; FORT WAYNE PUBLIC LIBRARY; 900 WEBSTER; FORT WAYNE, IN 46802. (#3707).

PUBLICATION 'HISTORY OF FORT WAYNE 1714-1828'. 200 PG THESIS OF PROF CHARLES POINSETTE. IT IS DESCRIPTION OF THE EARLY HISTORY OF FORT WAYNE. (LOCAL). FRED REYNOLDS, LIBRARIAN; FORT WAYNE PUBLIC LIBRARY; 900 WEBSTER; FORT WAYNE, IN 46802. (#3708).

THE RECONSTRUCTION OF OLD FORT WAYNE. REBUILDING THE FORT FROM WHICH FORT WAYNE GOT ITS NAME. (REGN'L). KEITH R. BARKER, PRESIDENT; HISTORIC FORT WAYNE, INC; 107 S QUENTIN; FORT WAYNE, IN 46802. (#4443). **ARBA GRANTEE.**

RELIGIOUS FESTIVAL IN FORT WAYNE, INDIANA. RELIGIOUS FILM FESTIVAL & ORIGINAL PLAY, BUSINESS/CLERGY ETHICAL DIALOGUE, MASS RALLY & CHOIR SINGING SACRED MUSIC FROM THE REVOLUTIONARY ERA. (LOCAL). REV JOHN WOLF/REV MELVIN PHILLIPS, COORDINATORS; FORT WAYNE BICENT COMMITTEE; ONE MAIN ST, RM 830; FORT WAYNE, IN 46802. (#8830).

RELIGIOUS HERITAGE PROJECT OF FORT WAYNE, INDIANA. COLLECTING MATERIALS FROM THE 338 CHURCHES AND OTHER RELIGIOUS INST. AND 42 DENOM'S IN FORT WAYNE. PLANNED THAT A PERMANENT COLLECTION BE TURNED OVER TO THE PUBLIC LIBRARY. (LOCAL). JOSEPH LEVINE, PROJECT DIRECTOR; FORT WAYNE BICENTENNIAL COMMISSION; CITY--COUNTY BLDG; FORT WAYNE, IN 46802. (#4449).

STAR SPANGLED SPECIALS IN FORT WAYNE, INDIANA. TWO GMC 4512 MODEL COACHES MADE IN 1957 PAINTED W/RED AND WHITE STRIPES AND STARS ON FIELD OF BLUE. NATIONAL, STATE & LOCAL BICENTENNIAL LOGOS WILL BE PAINTED ON THE EXTERIORS. (LOCAL). JOHN VAUGHN, CONTROLLER; FT WAYNE PUBLIC TRANSPORTATION CORPORATION; 801 LEESBURG RD; FORT WAYNE, IN 46808. (#8256).

SWEATSHOP REVISITED, A PROJ OF FORT WAYNE, INDIANA. THE WOMEN'S HERITAGE COMMITTEE OF THE FWBC IS ORGANIZING A PROJECT TO SEW, CUT & FIT COSTUMES FOR THE BICENT. VOLUNTEER SEWERS WILL SPOTLIGHT LOCAL GARMENT INDUSTRY & WOMEN'S GARMENT WORKERS. (LOCAL). BARBARA LAKE, CHAIRMAN; FORT WAYNE BICENT COMMISSION - WOMEN'S HERITAGE COMMITTEE; ONE MAIN ST, CITY-CO BLDG, RM 83; FORT WAYNE, IN 46802. (#8833). **(??).**

U S ARMY FIELD BAND APPEARANCE IN FORT WAYNE, IN. THE U S ARMY BAND WILL PLAY MUSIC OF GENERAL INTEREST AT MEMORIAL COLISEUM. (LOCAL). EARL KLINBERGER, CHAIRMAN; FORT WAYNE BICENT COMMISSION, PATRIOTIC COMMITTEE; 1 MAIN ST, CITY-CTY BLDG, RM 830; FORT WAYNE, IN 46802. (#8635).

'THE VOICE OF FORT WAYNE BICENTENNIAL'. PROVIDE SPEAKERS AT NO CHARGE FOR PROGRAMS TO SCHOOLS, CIVIC GROUPS, CHURCHES, ETC. (LOCAL). SHARON EBERHARD, CHAIRMAN; TOAST MISTRESS & TOASTMASTERS CLUB; 3220 E WASHINGTON; FORT WAYNE, IN 46802. (#3709).

'WOMEN IN HISTORY' PLAY OF FORT WAYNE, INDIANA. PLAY THAT WILL BE PERFORMED FOR SCHOOLS AND COMMUNITY GROUPS. (LOCAL). HARRIET MILLER, CHAIRMAN; WOMENS HERITAGE COMMITTEE; ROOM 830, CITY-COUNTY BLDG; FORT WAYNE, IN 46802. (#3710).

WOMEN'S ART SHOW IN FORT WAYNE, IN. INVITATIONAL WOMEN'S ART SHOW HELD IN HONOR OF THE BICENTENNIAL. (LOCAL). PEG WHONSETLER, CHAIRMAN; FORT WAYNE BICENT COMMITTEE - WOMEN'S HERITAGE COMMITTEE; ONE MAIN ST, CITY-CO BLDG, RM 83; FORT WAYNE, IN 46802. (#8834).

WOMEN'S HERITAGE MONTH - FORT WAYNE, IN. THE MONTH OF MARCH IS WOMEN'S HERITAGE MONTH; THERE WILL BE CONFERENCES & SEMINARS. (LOCAL). VIRGINIA PETIT, CHAIRMAN; WOMEN'S HERITAGE COMMITTEE; CITY-COUNTY BLDG; FORT WAYNE, IN 46802. (#24279). **ARBA GRANTEE.**

WRITING CONTEST IN FORT WAYNE, INDIANA. BIOGRAPHIES OF LOCALLY SIGNIFICANT WOMEN, PAST AND PRESENT, THE WINNING ENTRIES TO BE PUBLISHED IN BOOK FORM. (LOCAL). HARRIET MILLER, CHAIRMAN; WOMEN'S HERITAGE, FWBC; ONE MAIN ST, RM 830 CITY-COUNTY; FORT WAYNE, IN 46802. (#6462).

4TH OF JULY PARADE IN FORT WAYNE, INDIANA. PARADE WILL CHRONOLOGICALLY PORTRAY THE HISTORY OF FORT WAYNE. (LOCAL). LEONARD VOSMEIER, CHAIRMAN; PATRIOTISM COMMITTEE OF THE FWBC; ONE MAIN ST, RM 830 CITY-COUNTY; FORT WAYNE, IN 46802. (#6463).

APR 1 - 30, '74. REVOLUTIONARY WAR PORTRAITS EXHIBIT IN FORT WAYNE. GALLERY OF COLOR PHOTOS OF 65 PERSONS ASSOCIATED WITH INDIANA & THE AMERICAN REVOLUTION IS BEING EXHIBITED IN PUBLIC BUILDINGS THROUGHOUT STATE. BOOK OF SHORT BIOGRAPHIES OF SUBJECTS AVAILABLE. (ST-WIDE). DALE FRUCHTNICHT; INDIANA STATE BICENTENNIAL COMMISSION; 504 STATE OFFICE BLDG; INDIANAPOLIS, IN 46204. (#1635-901).

JAN 25, '75. WORKSHOP ON THE REVOLUTION AND THE BICENTENNIAL. SEMINAR AT STUDENT UNION, INDIANA UNIVERSITY-PURDUE UNIVERSITY AT FT WAYNE. (LOCAL). JAMES HAW, CHAIRMAN; INDIANA UNIV & PURDUE UNIV, FT WAYNE BICENTENNIAL COMMISSION; FORT WAYNE, IN 46805. (#200017-8).

APR 18, '75. PAUL REVERE RIDES AGAIN. THE SHRINE HORSE PATROL MEMBERS WILL RE-CREATE THIS FAMOUS RIDE. A FLARE DROP BY A NAVAL RESERVE PLANE WILL START THE PROGRAM. (LOCAL). JOHN A BLEICH, CHAIRMAN; SHRINE CLUB; 407 W BERRY ST; FORT WAYNE, IN 46802. (#6467-501).

FORT WAYNE — CONTINUED

MAY 30, '75. 1975 MEMORIAL DAY PARADE. THERE WILL BE A PARADE THEN CEREMONY COMMEMORATING MEMORIAL DAY, WITH SPEECHES. AT MEMORIAL COLISEUM. (LOCAL). HENRY RADKE, COORDINATOR; WAYNE TNSHIP & ALLEN COUNTY VETERAN ORG COMMISSIONERS; ROOM 830 CITY COUNTY BLDG; FORT WAYNE, IN 46802. (#3703-1).

JUNE 17 - 19, '75. AMERICAN FREEDOM TRAIN DISPLAY DAYS AT FORT WAYNE. THE AMERICAN FREEDOM TRAIN WILL INCLUDE 10 EXHIBIT CARS & 2 SHOWCASE CARS DEPICTING DIFFERENT PHASES OF THE AMERICAN EXPERIENCE. ITS ARRIVAL WILL SERVE AS A CATALYST FOR LOCAL BICENTENNIAL CELEBRATIONS BY PEOPLE THROUGHOUT THIS NATION. (ST-WIDE). DON MALLICOAT, EDIT SVCS; THE AMERICAN FREEDOM TRAIN FOUNDATION, INC; 5205 LEESBURG PIKE, SUITE 800; BAILEY'S XRDS, VA 22041. (#1776-13).

JULY 4, '75. RADIO STATION WOWO-CITY BICENTENNIAL SOFTBALL GAME. MAYOR WILL CAPTAIN TEAM OF CITY MANAGERS VS WOWO-RADIO PERSONALITIES & STAFFERS IN THE GAME. AT MCMILLAN PARK. (LOCAL). BILL FONG, COORDINATOR; WOWO RADIO STATION; 128 W WASHINGTON; FORT WAYNE, IN 46802. (#8838-501).

JULY 5 - 13, '75. THREE RIVERS FESTIVAL. OVER 120 EVENTS PROCLAIM FORT WAYNE'S DIVERSE ETHNIC HERITAGE WITH PAGEANTS, PARADES, AN INTERNATIONAL VILLAGE & ACTIVITIES WHICH ENCOMPASS THE ENTIRE TOWN; BOAT RIDES, A RAFT RACE, ART AND HOBBY SHOWS ARE A SAMPLING OF THE MANY FESTIVE EVENTS. AT FORT WAYNE. (REGN'L). WILLIAM H HAUSMAN, CHMN; THREE RIVERS FESTIVAL; 309 CENTRAL BUILDING; FORT WAYNE, IN 46802. (#100322-1).

JULY 11 - 18, '75. FRIDAY ENTERTAINMENT PGM FOR CHILDREN IN FT WAYNE'S FREIMANN SQUARE. AN ENTERTAINMENT PROJECT FOR CHILDREN ON FRIDAYS TO INCLUDE GYMNAST, MUSICIANS, CIRCUS ACTS, PUPPETS, DANCE GROUPS & ART DISPLAYS IN FIREMAN SQUARE. (LOCAL). KATHY CHOKA, CHAIRWOMAN; DAY-IN-THE-PARK COMMITTEE, FORT WAYNE BICENT COMMISSION; ONE MAIN ST, RM 830; FORT WAYNE, IN 46802. (#8636-1).

AUG 2 - SEPT 2, '75. BOX CAR EXHIBITS. DOCK STREET EXPLORATION - PROJ OF FT WAYNE, IN. (LOCAL). GREGORY JACOBS, PROJ; GREGORY JACOBS; 4316 COVINGTON RD; FORT WAYNE, IN 46802. (#13857-503).

AUG 2 - SEPT 2, '75. CONTINUOUS MOVIES FOR CHILDREN IN SPECTATOR THEATER. DOCK STREET EXPLORATION - PROJ OF FT WAYNE, IN. A MUSEUM FOR CHILDREN; CONTINUOUS MOVIES; COLLECTIONS OF 18TH CENTURY; 2 BOX CARS, ONE CONTAINING MUSICAL INSTRUMENTS AND ONE A WORKSHOP; A ROCKETSHIP AND DAILY EVENTS. (LOCAL). GREGORY JACOBS, PROJ; GREGORY JACOBS; 4316 COVINGTON RD; FORT WAYNE, IN 46802. (#13857-501).

AUG 2 - SEPT 2, '75. DOCK STREET EXPLORATORIUM. HANDS-ON MUSEUM FOR CHILDREN; CONTINUOUS MOVIES; COLLECTION OF 19TH CENTURY TOOLS & APPLIANCES; 2 RR BOXCARS, ONE CONTAINING MUSICAL INSTRUMENTS FOR CHILDREN TO USE & ONE A CRAFT WORKSHOP; A ROCKET SIMULATOR BUILT BY LOCAL KIDS, PLUS DAILY EVENTS. (LOCAL). G G JACOBS, DIR; EUREKA RAILROAD CORP; 4316 COVINGTON RD; FORT WAYNE, IN 46802. (#13587-1).

AUG 2 - SEPT 2, '75. EXHIBITS OF GIZMOS, UTENSILS & APPLIANCES FROM THE 18TH CENTURY. DOCK STREET EXPLORATION - PROJ OF FT WAYNE, IN. (LOCAL). GREGORY JACOBS, PROJ; GREGORY JACOBS; 4316 COVINGTON RD; FORT WAYNE, IN 46802. (#13857-502).

AUG 2 - SEPT 2, '75. MUSICIAN PERFORMANCES. DOCK STREET EXPLORATION - PROJ OF FT WAYNE, IN. (LOCAL). GREGORY JACOBS, PROJ; GREGORY JACOBS; 4316 COVINGTON RD; FORT WAYNE, IN 46802. (#13857-505).

AUG 2 - SEPT 2, '75. ROCKETSHIP SIMULATOR EXHIBIT. DOCK STREET EXPLORATION - PROJ OF FT WAYNE, IN. (LOCAL). GREGORY JACOBS, PROJ; GREGORY JACOBS; 4316 COVINGTON RD; FORT WAYNE, IN 46802. (#13857-504).

SEPT 11 - NOV 20, '75. PERSPECTIVES ON THE AMERICAN REVOLUTION. PUBLIC LECTURE SERIES/COLLEGE CREDIT COURSE ON THE SIGNIFICANCE OF AMERICAN REVOLUTION FOR THE U S & WORLD; LECTURES TO BE PUBLISHED AS A BOOK. AT KETTLER HALL, ROOM 146. (LOCAL). JAMES HAW, BICENT CHMN; HISTORY DEPT, INDIANA UNIV - PURDUE UNIV; FORT WAYNE, IN 46805. (#103101-4).

SEPT 20, '75. SPIRIT OF '76 UNIT FOR FORT WAYNE, IND, PARADES. UNIT TO MARCH IN PARADE. WOULD INCLUDE FLAGBEARER WITH THIRTEEN STAR FLAG, DRUMMER, FIFE PLAYER. AT 130 W. TILLMAN RD. (LOCAL). JOHN J O'LEARY, COMMANDER; AMERICAN LEGION POST 296; 130 W TILLMAN ROAD; FORT WAYNE, IN 46802. (#3701-1).

SEPT 23, '75 - APR '76. INTERCOLLEGIATE BICENTENNIAL LECTURE SERIES. 6 LECTURES WILL BE GIVEN BY NOTED AUTHORITIES ON THE SIGNIFICANCE OF THE AMERICAN REVOLUTION IN AMERICA FROM THE VIEWPOINT OF THEIR SPECIALTIES. (LOCAL). JAMES HAW, BICENT CHMN; INTERCOLLEGIATE BICENTENNIAL COMMITTEE (INDIANA UNIV & PURDUE UNIV); INDIANA UNIV; FORT WAYNE, IN 46805. (#103101-7).

SEPT 26 - 28, '75. JOHNNY APPLESEED FESTIVAL. AN OLD TIME FESTIVAL WITH EMPHASIS ON JOHNNY APPLESEED & APPLE-BASED FOOD, AN ANTIQUE FLEA MARKET, CARNIVAL, GAMES, ART SALE, OLD CRAFTS, PATRIOTIC CEREMONY, THEATRE & HISTORICAL PAGEANTS. (LOCAL). SHARI DODD, CHAIRWOMAN; FORT WAYNE BICENT COMMITTEE; ONE MAIN ST, RM 830; FORT WAYNE, IN 46802. (#8637-1).

OCT 1, '75 - JUNE 1, '76. AMERICAN ISSUES FORUM. SEMINAR, CONFERENCE. (LOCAL). CHARLIE HALL, PRES; NEW HORIZONS; FORT WAYNE, IN 46802. (#102842-2).

OCT 23, '75. BICENTENNIAL CRAFTS SYMPOSIUM FOR ELEMENTARY TEACHERS. SEMINAR AT PLYMOUTH CONGREGATIONAL CHURCH, 501 W BERRY ST. (ST-WIDE). ROSALIE GINGERICK, COCHMN; OLD FORT SETTLER SERIES & INDIANA STATE TEACHERS ASSOC; 290 MORSE ST; MARKLE, IN 46770. (#102365-1).

FEB 2 - MAR 14, '76. IMAGE OF AMERICA IN CARICATURE & CARTOON. PICTORIAL SURVEY OF 200 YEARS OF AMERICAN HISTORY AS RECORDED BY THE ARTISTS OF THE DAY, BOTH FOREIGN & DOMESTIC. OUR SOCIETY, POLITICS, MORES, HABITS WHICH REFLECT AMERICA TODAY & IN OUR 200 YEAR HISTORY. AT FORT WAYNE PUBLIC LIBRARY. (REGN'L). DR RON C TYLER, CURATOR; AMON CARTER MUSEUM OF WESTERN ART; 3501 CAMP BOWIE BLVD; FORT WORTH, TX 76101. (#2063-2).

FEB 7 - MAR 20, '76. BICENTENNIAL FILM SERIES. FILMS OF COLONIAL WILLIAMSBURG ON 18TH CENTURY AMERICAN ARTS, CRAFTS AND LIFE; ALTERNATE SATURDAYS. AT NEFF, ROOM 101. (LOCAL). PAULINE FLYNN; INDIANA UNIV - PURDUE UNIV AT FORT WAYNE; FORT WAYNE, IN 46805. (#103083-1).

FEB 20 - MAR 27, '76. PHOTOGRAPHY OF ABIGAIL HEYMAN. PHOTOGRAPHS BY ABIGAIL HEYMAN, 'GROWING UP FEMALE', DISPLAYED WITH PHOTOS THAT ARE ALL EITHER OF WOMEN OR TAKEN BY WOMEN PHOTOGRAPHERS. AT INDIANA UNIVERSITY BALLROOM AT FORT WAYNE. (LOCAL). CAROL SOWLE, COORD; FORT WAYNE BICENT COMM - WOMENS HERITAGE COMM; ONE MAIN ST, RM 83; FORT WAYNE, IN 46802. (#8836-1).

MAR 1 - 31, '76. WOMEN'S HERITAGE MONTH. SPOTLIGHT, THROUGHOUT MARCH 1976, CONTRIBUTIONS THAT WOMEN HAVE MADE TO OUR HISTORY; VIA FILMS, TV, PROGRAMS, & DISPLAYS. (LOCAL). HARRIET MILLER; FORT WAYNE BICENT COMMISSION WOMEN'S HERITAGE; CITY-COUNTY BLDG; FORT WAYNE, IN 46802. (#4445-1).

MAR 6 - 14, '76. OPERA WORKSHOP--'THE TELEPHONE' & 'CAPTAIN LOVELOCK'. SIX PERFORMANCES INCL 2 FOR GIRL SCOUTS FINE ARTS DAY, 1 ON CAMPUS (FREE TO STUDENTS; $1.50 FOR OTHERS), 1 FOR SR CITIZENS AND 2 PERFORMANCES IN LOCAL HIGH SCHOOLS. AT NORTHSIDE HS, SOUTHSIDE HS, HARDING HS, IND PURDUE STUDENT UNION. (LOCAL). ANDREW HARPER, PROFESSOR; INDIANA UNIV & PURDUE UNIV; FORT WAYNE, IN 46805. (#103101-8).

MAR 11 - 14, '76. THE MODEL CONGRESS - FORT WAYNE, INDIANA. 4-DAY SIMULATION OF U S CONGRESS. (ST-WIDE). MARKANGEL; FORT WAYNE BICENTENNIAL COMMISSION; 2611 INWOOD DR; FORT WAYNE, IN 46802. (#16334-1).

MAR 26 - APR 11, '76. '1776' STAGE PLAY. LIVE PERFORMANCE AT KETTLER HALL, ROOM G-32. (LOCAL). O F KENWORTHY, PROJ DIR; PURDUE-INDIANA THEATER, INDIANA UNIV-PURDUE UNIV; FORT WAYNE, IN 46805. (#103101-5).

APR 1 - 30, '76. VARIOUS USES OF WOOD. EXHIBIT. (LOCAL). PATTY GRIEST, CHAIRMAN; DESIGNER/CRAFTSMAN GUILD, INC-BICENTENNIAL COMMISSION; CITY-COUNTY BLDG; FORT WAYNE, IN 46802. (#4446-501).

APR 10 - 11, '76. UNIVERSITY SINGERS PRESENT 'A SALUTE TO COLE PORTER'. IN CONJUNCTION WITH THE FORT WAYNE PHILHARMONIC. AT EMBASSY THEATER. (LOCAL). ANDREW HARPER, PROFESSOR; INDIANA UNIV & PURDUE UNIV; FORT WAYNE, IN 46805. (#200017-7).

APR 24, '76. DAVID HAGY RECITAL FEATURING THE BARBER VIOLIN CONCERTO. LIVE PERFORMANCE AT NEFF HALL 101. (LOCAL). ANDREW HARPER, PROFESSOR; INDIANA UNIV & PURDUE UNIV; FORT WAYNE, IN 46805. (#103101-11).

APR 24, '76. LOYALTY DAY PARADE OF FORT WAYNE. PARADE CONSISTING OF 18 DISTRICT POSTS, BANDS, COLORS, FLOATS, AND SPECIAL GUESTS. AT LOCATION UNDECIDED. (LOCAL). ED GRIDER; VFW DISTRICT POSTS; ROOM 830 CITY COUNTY BLDG; FORT WAYNE, IN 46802. (#3702-1).

APR 24 - MAY 2, '76. AMERICAN MUSIC SERIES. LIVE PERFORMANCE AT NEFF HALL 101. (LOCAL). ANDREW HARPER, PROFESSOR; INDIANA UNIV & PURDUE UNIV; FORT WAYNE, IN 46805. (#103101-1).

APR 30, '76. THE DUQUESNE UNIV 'TAMBURITZANS' PERFORM IN FORT WAYNE, INDIANA. THE 'TAMBURITZANS' PORTRAY THE MUSIC OF THE SLAVIC PEOPLE OF THE WORLD IN MUSIC AND DANCE. AT THE SCOTTISH RITE AUDITORIUM. (LOCAL). KATHY CHOKA, CHAIRWOMAN; FORT WAYNE BICENT COMMISSION; ONE MAIN ST, CTY-CO BLDG, RM 830; FORT WAYNE, IN 46802. (#8632-1).

MAY 1, '76. JOHNNY APPLESEED GRAVESITE EXHIBIT DEDICATION. UNMANNED INTERPRETATIVE EXHIBIT AT JOHNNY APPLESEED'S GRAVESITE IN ARCHER PARK. (ST-WIDE). DAVID DRURY AND PHYLLIS F; FORT WAYNE BICENTENNIAL COMMITTEE; ROOM 830, CITY-COUNTY BLDG; FORT WAYNE, IN 46802. (#3713-501).

MAY 1 - 6, '76. FINE ARTS FESTIVAL. EXHIBIT AT COMMUNITY CENTER FOR PERFORMING ARTS & FRIEMAN PARK. (LOCAL). JOHN V MCKENNA, DIR; FORT WAYNE FINE ARTS FOUNDATION; 000000000000000 14; FORT WAYNE, IN 46802. (#102842-1).

MAY 2 - 30, '76. TOURS OF THE HISTORIC BASS MANSION AT ST FRANCIS COLLEGE. PUBLIC TOURS ARE BEING OFFERED OF THIS HISTORICAL HOUSE WHICH IS NOW A LIBRARY ON THE CAMPUS OF ST FRANCES COLLEGE. (LOCAL). PHYLLIS FLOREA, CHMN; FORT WAYNE BICENT COMMISSION; ONE MAIN ST, RM 830; FORT WAYNE, IN 46802. (#8629-1).

MAY 29 - 30, '76. INDIAN POW WOW CEREMONIES, PARADES, INDIAN VILLAGE. A 2-DAY INDIAN POW-WOW WITH INDIAN VILLAGE, CEREMONIES, PARADES, ETC INDIAN TRADERS, TIPI VILLAGE, INDIAN ART, MOVIES OF INDIANS OF TODAY. AT NORTHSIDE HIGH SCHOOL 475 E STATE BLVD FORT WAYNE IN. (ST-WIDE). MRS JOSEPH F RANCK, CHMN; INDIAN AMERICAN AND KEKIONGA B&PW CLUB; 3101 W TILL ROAD; FORT WAYNE, IN 46808. (#3711-1).

MAY '76. INDIAN-AMERICAN '76 - DANCE PERFORMANCE. LIVE PERFORMANCE. (LOCAL). ANN RANCK, COORD; FORT WAYNE DEPT OF PUBLIC PARKS; 1 MAIN ST; FORT WAYNE, IN 46802. (#27232-1).

JUNE 5, '76. DEDICATION AND OPENING OF HISTORIC FORT WAYNE. CEREMONY, OPENING AT HISTORIC FORT WAYNE ACCESS AND PARKING IN 200 BLOCK OF S CLINTON ST. (REGN'L). BRIAN DUNNIGAN; HISTORIC FORT WAYNE, INC; 1130 SPY RUN AVENUE; FORT WAYNE, IN 46805. (#50521-1).

JULY 2 - 5, '76. FOURTH OF JULY CELEBRATION. FESTIVAL AT FRANKE PARK. (LOCAL). MARY BALL BRANT, CHMN; FORT WAYNE BICENTENNIAL COMMISSION; 303 E MAIN ST; FORT WAYNE, IN 46802. (#102948-1).

JULY 4, '76. JULY 4, 1976 PATRIOTIC FLOAT & MARCHING GROUP PERFORMANCE. BICENTENNIAL PARADE COMMEMORATING THE LAST 2 HUNDRED YEARS OF OUR AMERICAN HISTORY. AT MAIN STREET. (LOCAL). SGT JOHN R NELSON; POLICE ATHLETIC LEAGUE; 2121 OLLADALE DR; FORT WAYNE, IN 46802. (#3704-1).

JULY 10 - 18, '76. THREE RIVERS FESTIVAL. 9-DAY PAGEANT PROCLAIMING FORT WAYNE'S DIVERSE ETHNIC ORIGINS; SPECIAL EVENTS FOR CHILDREN, CONCERTS, RAFT RACES, ART DISPLAYS & PA RADES. (REGN'L). WILLIAM H HAUSMAN, CHMN; THREE RIVERS FESTIVAL; 309 CENTRAL BLDG; FORT WAYNE, IN 46802. (#100311-1).

JULY 30 - AUG 2, '76. ALLEN COUNTY 4-H FAIR. FAIR AT ALLEN COUNTY MEMORIAL COLISEUM, FORT WAYNE, IN. (LOCAL). CATHERINE A SEYMOUR; ALLEN COUNTY 4-H CLUBS; 4001 CRESCENT AVE; FORT WAYNE, IN 46805. (#23665-1).

SEPT 25 - 26, '76. JOHNNY APPLESEED FESTIVAL. FESTIVAL AT ARCHER PARK. (LOCAL). COORDINATOR; FORT WAYNE BICENTENNIAL COMMITTEE; ONE MAIN ST; FORT WAYNE IN, IN 46802. (#103416-565).

OCT 2, '76. ETHNIC FACETS OF FORT WAYNE. LIVE PERFORMANCE AT MEMORIAL COLISEUM, FORT WAYNE. (REGN'L). HAROLD H VISINO; INTERNATIONAL COUNCIL, INC; 1230 S CLINTON; FORT WAYNE, IN 46802. (#27576-1).

OCT 5 - 6, '76. UNITED STATES ARMED FORCES BICENTENNIAL CARAVAN. CARAVAN IS COMPOSED OF EXHIBIT VANS FOR EACH MILITARY SERVICE. PROJECT THEME IS 'HISTORY OF THE ARMED FORCES & THEIR CONTRIBUTIONS TO THE NATION'. (LOCAL). MARK REEZON; UNITED STATES ARMED FORCES BICENTENNIAL CARAVAN; ONE MAIN ST; FORT WAYNE, IN 46802. (#1775-728).

OCT - NOV '76. A PATRIOTIC SALUTE TO AMERICA. SERIES OF 17 BICENTENNIAL MUSICAL & DRAMATIC PERFORMANCES, PUT ON FOR THE INSTITUTIONALIZED & DISABLED IN FT WAYNE & ALLEN COUNTY BY INDIANA UNIV, PURDUE & ST FRANCIS COLLEGE STUDENTS. AT LUTHERAN HOME, BYRON HEALTH CTR, FT WAYNE ST HOSPITAL & OTHERS. (LOCAL). MS LILLIAN C EMBICK, CHMN; HOSPITAL AUDIENCES, INC; 1501 CALIFORNIA AVE; FORT WAYNE, IN 46805. (#25241-1).

NOV 6 - 13, '76. SMITHSONIAN EXHIBITION AND STUDY, 'REVIVAL'. EXHIBITION AT FIRST PRESBYTERIAN GALLERY. STUDY TO FOLLOW BOOK, 'REVIVAL' BY DICKINSON AND BENZIGER. (LOCAL). PATTY GRIEST; FORT WAYNE BICENTENNIAL COMMITTEE; ONE MAIN ST, RM 830 CITY-COUNTY; FORT WAYNE, IN 46802. (#8260-501).

NOV 11, '76. VETERANS DAY PARADE. EVENING PARADE IN DOWNTOWN FORT WAYNE TO SHOW PATRIOTISM. AT CALHOUN STREET. (LOCAL). HENRY RADKE, COMMANDER; AMERICAN LEGION POST 47; 2730 HOLTON; FORT WAYNE, IN 46802. (#3705-1).

FORTVILLE

JULY 1 - 4, '76. FOURTH OF JULY CELEBRATION. BICENTENNIAL THEME THROUGHOUT FOUR DAY FESTIVAL AND FAIR; FIREWORKS DISPLAY IS FINALE. AT FORTVILLE CITY PARK. (LOCAL). FORREST FISHER, COORD; VERNON TOWNSHIP BICENTENNIAL COMMITTEE; 124 E STAAT ST; FORTVILLE, IN 46040. (#104741-1).

FOUNTAIN CITY

'HISTORY OF NORTHEASTERN WAYNE COUNTY, INDIANA'. BOOK IS FIRST PUBLISHED FOR 90 YEARS & BRINGS TOGETHER THE ENTIRE HISTORY OF THE AREA FROM ITS BEGINNINGS TO 1976. IT IS DEDICATED IN THE FRONT TO THE USA BICENTENNIAL. (LOCAL). MARY L WILLIAMS, EXEC DIRECTOR; OLD NEWPORT AREA BICENTENNIAL COMMISSION; BOX 197; FOUNTAIN CITY, IN 47341. (#25551).

MAY 1 - OCT 31, '76. GRAND CENTRAL STATION OF THE UNDERGROUND RAILROAD-LEVI COFFIN HOUSE. HOUSE HAS GUIDED COSTUMED TOURS OF THIS REGISTERED HISTORIC LANDMARK. AT LEVI COFFIN HOUSE. (REGN'L). MARY WILLIAMS, EXEC DIR; OLD NEWPORT AREA BICENTENNIAL COMMISSION; BOX 197; FOUNTAIN CITY, IN 47341. (#104709-2).

JULY 3, '76. EASTERN INDIANA BICENTENNIAL PARADE & TOURS. HOME OF THE GRAND CENTRAL STATION OF THE UN-

FOUNTAIN CITY — CONTINUED

DERGROUND RAILROAD, FOUNTAIN CITY WILL HAVE A PARADE OF OVER 100 MARCHING BANDS & FLOATS FOR A COMBINED PARADE OF 8 EASTERN INDIANA TOWNS. ALSO TOUR OF PATRIOTIC FLOWER GARDEN & TOURS OF UNDERGROUND RAILROAD SYSTEM. (REGN'L). MARY WILLIAMS, EXEC DIR; OLD NEWPORT AREA BICENTENNIAL COMMISSION; BOX 197; FOUNTAIN CITY, IN 47341. (#104709-1).

OCT 1 - 2, '76. UNITED STATES ARMED FORCES BICENTENNIAL CARAVAN. CARAVAN IS COMPOSED OF EXHIBIT VANS FOR EACH MILITARY SERVICE. PROJECT THEME IS 'HISTORY OF THE ARMED FORCES & THEIR CONTRIBUTIONS TO THE NATION'. (LOCAL). MRS MARY L WILLIAMS; UNITED STATES ARMED FORCES BICENTENNIAL CARAVAN; BOX 197; FOUNTAIN CITY, IN 47341. (#1775-726).

OCT 1 - 3, '76. 'LEVI COFFIN DAYS'. FIRST STOP OF THE US ARMED FORCES CARAVAN IN INDIANA. WILL INCLUDE TOURS OF THE LEVI COFFIN HOUSE (GRAND CENTRAL STATION OF THE UNDERGROUND RAILROAD), ARTS & CRAFTS SHOWS ON THE STREET, RIDES IN HORSEDRAWN VEHICLE, AND TOURS OF OTHER HISTORIC HOUSES IN THE AREA. (ST-WIDE). MARY WILLIAMS, EXEC DIR; OLD NEWPORT AREA BICENTENNIAL COMMISSION; BOX 197; FOUNTAIN CITY, IN 47341. (#104709-3).

FRANKFORT

BEAUTIFICATION & RENOVATION OF COURTHOUSE LAWN; IN. THE PROJECT INCLUDES PLANTING TREES, BUSHES AND FLOWERS, ERECTING FLAGPOLES AND BUILDING PARK BENCHES. (LOCAL). SUSAN DAVIS, SECRETARY; CLINTON COUNTY BICENTENNIAL COMMITTEE; 659 RICKER DR; FRANKFORT, IN 46041. (#18589).

CLINTON COUNTY HISTORICAL BOOK PUBLISHED - IN. THE BOOK CONTAINS HISTORY, FOLKLORE AND MAPS OF ALL TOWNS IN THE COUNTY SINCE ITS EARLY SETTLEMENT. THE BOOK IS BEING PREPARED BY LOCAL RESIDENTS AND WILL BE RELEASED FEB 1, 1976. (LOCAL). SUSAN DAVIS, SECRETARY; CLINTON COUNTY BICENTENNIAL COMMITTEE; 659 RICKER DR; FRANKFORT, IN 46041. (#18588).

ESSAY CONTEST - FRANKFORT, IN. JUNIOR AND SENIOR HIGH STUDENTS WILL PARTICIPATE IN AN ESSAY CONTEST ON THE HISTORY OF CLINTON COUNTY WITH FIRST PLACE AWARDED IN BOTH CATEGORIES; THE ESSAYS WILL BE PUBLISHED IN A LEGACY. (LOCAL). RITA TROXEL, SECRETARY; EPSILON ETA-BETA SIGMA PHI; 304 E GREEN ST; FRANKFORT, IN 46041. (#18591).

FIREPLUG PAINTING - FRANKFORT, IN. A STUDENT CONTEST WILL BE HELD TO PAINT FIREPLUGS. (LOCAL). SUSAN DAVIS, SECRETARY; CLINTON COUNTY BICENTENNIAL COMMITTEE; 659 RICKER DR; FRANKFORT, IN 46041. (#18592).

MAY 1, '76. 200 YEARS OF FASHION. FASHION SHOW WILL FEATURE COSTUMES FROM ALL ERAS AND TURN OF THE CENTURY WEDDING; PRIZES WILL BE AWARDED FOR ESSAY CONTEST. AT FRANKFORT SENIOR HIGH AUDITORIUM, MAISH ROAD & 28E. (LOCAL). MRS JACK HARSHBARGER, DIR; EPSILON ETA-BETA SIGMA PHI; 1456 CENTRAL AVE; FRANKFORT, IN 46041. (#103826-1).

JULY 4, '76. FRANKFORT FOURTH OF JULY CELEBRATION. THE CELEBRATION INCLUDES CHILDREN'S GAMES, A SOFTBALL TOURNEY, TURTLE RACE, BINGO, FIREWORKS AND AN EVENING TEEN DANCE. AT TPA PARK, E GREEN ST. (LOCAL). DON RUSK, CHAIRMAN; CLINTON COUNTY JAYCEES; 358 E ARMSTRONG; FRANKFORT, IN 46041. (#103905-1).

FRANKTON

JUNE 11 - 13, '76. FRANKTON HERITAGE DAYS. PARADE, EXHIBIT, FESTIVAL. (LOCAL). J J GALBREATH; FRANKTON BICENTENNIAL COMMITTEE; BOX 111; FRANKTON, IN 46044. (#200017-63).

FREETOWN

JULY 1 - 4, '76. FREETOWN FOURTH OF JULY CELEBRATION. FESTIVAL AT CITY PARK. (LOCAL). DARRELL RUCKER, DIRECTOR; FREETOWN COMMUNITY; RT 5; SEYMOUR, IN 47274. (#104302-2).

FREMONT

BICENTENNIAL MEMORIAL PLAQUE, FREMONT, IN. MEMORIAL PLAQUE PRESENTED DEPICTING HISTORICAL EVENTS OF LOCAL AREA. (LOCAL). KENNETH N CRANDALL, CHAIRMAN; FREMONT AREA BICENTENNIAL COMMITTEE; PO BOX 00; FREMONT, IN 46737. (#24713). **ARBA GRANTEE.**

FRIENDSHIP

MAY 30 - JUNE 5, '76. MUZZLE LOADING RIFLE SHOOT. BUCKSKIN-CLAD MUZZLE LOADERS CELEBRATE THE BICENT WITH A SPECIAL SPRING SHOOT AT THE HOME OF THE NATIONAL MUZZLE LOADING RIFLE ASSOC; THERE WILL ALSO BE KNIFE & TOMAHAWK THROWS, ANTIQUE FLEA MARKETS AND THE ECHOING REPORTS OF PIONEER FIREARMS TO RECREATE AMERICAN SPIRIT. AT FRIENDSHIP. (ST-WIDE). MERRILL P DEER, CHAIRMAN; NATIONAL MUZZLE LOADING RIFLE ASSOC; RT 1; BARGERSVILLE, IN 46106. (#100339-1).

OCT 29 - 31, '76. NATIONAL MUZZLELOADING TURKEY SHOOT. COMPETITION AT WALTER CLINE RANGE. (REGN'L). MAXINE MOSS, COORD; NATIONAL MUZZLELOADERS ASSOC; FRIENDSHIP, IN 47021. (#103416-652).

FT BEN HARSN

JUNE '75 - CONTINUING . BICENTENNIAL PLAY-'GOD'S COUNTRY'. LIVE PERFORMANCE. (REGN'L). SALLY L SPRIGGS, INFO DIR; FORT BENJAMIN HARRISON; PUBLIC AFFAIRS OFFICE; FT BEN HARSN, IN 46216. (#200017-83).

MAY 8, '76. ARMED FORCES DAY. EXHIBIT, PARADE, COMPETITION, LIVE PERFORMANCE AT PARADE GROUND-FORT HARRISON. (ST-WIDE). SALLY L SPRIGGS, INFO DIR; FORT BENJAMIN HARRISON; PUBLIC AFFAIRS OFFICE; FT BEN HARSN, IN 46216. (#200017-86).

FULDA

APR 19, '75 - NOV 6, '76. DEDICATION & PLANTING OF HERITAGE PARK. HERITAGE PARK DEDICATED ON APRIL 19, 1975. GIRL SCOUTS OF SPENCER COUNTY PLANTED THE ENTRANCE ON NOV 1, 1975. ON JULY 4, 1976, A PLAQUE WITH NAMES OF REVOLUTIONARY ANCESTORS OF PEOPLE IN SPENCER COUNTY WILL BE INSTALLED IN ENTRANCE AREA. (LOCAL). CHARLOTTE N BAIRD; SPENCER COUNTY BICENTENNIAL COMMITTEE & MEMORIAL FOREST ASSN; PO BOX 186; LINCOLN CITY, IN 47552. (#2814-501).

GARY

ARCHIVES, POLISH AMERICAN CONGRESS (INDIANA DIV). THE POLISH AMERICAN CONGRESS (INDIANA DIV) IS PLANNING AN ARCHIVAL COLLECTION OF ARB PRINT & NON-PRINT MATERIALS. PROJECT WILL CENTER AROUND THE IND & CHICAGO METRO AREA. (REGN'L). FRANK B ROMAN, ARCHIVIST; POLISH AMERICAN CONGRESS; 561 TAFT ST; GARY, IN 46404. (#6422). **ARBA GRANTEE.**

ASALH FREEDOM COACH, GARY, IN. A COACH TO TRAVEL THE MIDWEST AND DISTRIBUTE MATERIALS. (ST-WIDE). OHARATHULA MILLENDER, COORDINATOR; ASALH FREEDOM COACH; 2409 W 5TH ST; GARY, IN 46404. (#27772). **ARBA GRANTEE.**

BICENTENNIAL ISSUE OF REVISTA CHICANO-PEQUENO, IN. A BILINGUAL MAGAZINE OF CHICANO & PUERTO RICAN LITERATURE. (LOCAL). DR NICHOLAS KANELLOS, DIRECTOR; INDIANA UNIV NORTHWEST; 3400 BROADWAY; GARY, IN 46408. (#25243). **ARBA GRANTEE.**

CONTRIBUTIONS FOR MEDICAL CENTER, GARY, IN. PAINTING FOR RECEPTION AREA OR OTHER MEDICAL FACILITY OF NEWLY PROPOSED MEDICAL CENTER. (ST-WIDE). JILL M KEETON, BICENT REPRESENTATIVE; HORIZONS '76 BICENTENNIAL SUBCOMMITTEE; 900 MADISON ST; GARY, IN 46402. (#21497).

GARY'S BICENTENNIAL PANORAMA OF ARTISTS, IN. 43 ELEMENTARY SCHOOLS PARTICIPATING IN JAZZ, ETHNIC & CLASSICAL MUSIC. (LOCAL). JOHN H CLEVELAND, COORDINATOR; GARY PUBLIC SCHOOLS; 504 BROADWAY; GARY, IN 46402. (#27770). **ARBA GRANTEE.**

LATINO HORISONS - GARY, IN. 10 THEATRICAL PROGRAMS FEATURE THE CONTRIBUTIONS OF MEXICAN-AMERICANS & PUERTO-RICANS TO THE U S. (LOCAL). NICHOLAS KANELLOS, COORDINATOR; TEATRO DESENGANO DEL PUEBLO; 3400 BROADWAY; GARY, IN 46408. (#26636). **ARBA GRANTEE.**

RENOVATION OF A MAJOR LOCAL PARK, GARY, IN. INSTALLATION OF MORE RECREATIONAL FACILITIES AND CONSTRUCTION OF A BOATING HARBOR. (LOCAL). JILL M KEETON, BICENT REPRESENTATIVE; HORIZONS '76 COMMITTEE & PARK DEPT; 900 MADISON ST; GARY, IN 46402. (#21498).

U S STEEL MUSEUM & RESEARCH FACILITY - GARY, IN. FACILITY REFLECTING THE HISTORY OF THE STEEL MILL IN GARY AND ALSO HOUSING EQUIPMENT FOR FURTHER RESEARCH IN STEEL PRODUCTION. (ST-WIDE). JILL M KEETON, PROJ DIRECTOR; HORIZONS '76 COMMITTEE & U S STEEL COMMUNITY AFFAIRS; 900 MADISON ST; GARY, IN 46402. (#21499).

WGVE-FM IN-SCHOOL BICENTENNIAL PROGRAMS - NBMRP. COMPREHENSIVE/IMAGINATIVE PGMS INCL ONE ON CONSTITUTION DONE IN COOP LOCAL AAUW CHAPTER FOR SCHOOL NETWORK; COOPS W/ LOCAL BICENT COMM FOR RADIO SPOTS & DRAMATIC BICENTENNIAL PRESENTATIONS. (LOCAL). LAWRENCE VENTURA, BICENTENNIAL COORDINATOR; WGVE-FM; 1800 E 35TH AVE; GARY, IN 46409. (#23253).

JAN 30, '76. FELLOWSHIP BREAKFAST WITH SPEAKERS AND ROTC GUARD. CEREMONY AT HOLY TRINITY HALL, 1226 MADISON ST. (LOCAL). JILL MARIE KEETON, REP; INTERFAITH CLERGY COUNCIL OF GARY & VICINITY, HERITAGE '76 COMMITTEE; 900 MADISON ST; GARY, IN 46407. (#200017-18).

JULY 3 - 14, '76. 'FESTIVAL WEEK' PARADE. THE PARADE IS THE FIRST IN A SERIES OF EVENTS: FIREWORKS, RODEOS, PICNICS, DANCES & SPORT COMPETITION FROM JULY 3 THRU JULY 14, '76. PARADE TO FEATURE ETHNIC GROUPS, FLOATS & BAND. AT 47TH BROADWAY TO DOWNTOWN GARY. (LOCAL). IVAN SILVERMAN, COORD; GARY BICENTENNIAL COMMISSION & GARY FOUNDERS DAY COMMITTEE; 11 E 4TH AVE; GARY, IN 46402. (#105389-2).

JULY 14, '76. GARY FOUNDERS DAY CELEBRATION. FILM SHOW, CELEBRITIES & CROWNING OF BICENTENNIAL QUEEN. AT WEST SIDE HIGH SCHOOL, 9TH GERRY ST. (LOCAL). RAY FORSYTH, COORD; GARY FOUNDERS DAY COMMITTEE & GARY BICENT FESTIVAL '76 COMMITTEE; 11 E 4TH AVE; GARY, IN 46402. (#105389-3).

AUG 1 - 31, '76. LIBRARY DISPLAYS. EXHIBIT AT 220 WEST 5TH AVE. (LOCAL). JILL MARIE KEETON, REP; GARY PUBLIC LIBRARY & HERITAGE '76 COMMITTEE; 900 MADISON ST; GARY, IN 46402. (#105389-1).

DEC 12 - 14, '76. LA SALLE EXPEDITION II, A HISTORIC RE-ENACTMENT. THIS IS AN AUTHENTIC RE-ENACTMENT OF THE 1681 LASALLE EXPEDITION FROM MONTREAL, CANADA TO NEW ORLEANS, LA WHICH WILL BEGIN TOURING ON AUGUST 11, 1976 AND END ON APRIL 9, 1977. (LOCAL). REID H LEWIS, DIRECTOR; LA SALLE EXPEDITION II; 135 S LA SALLE ST, RM 411; CHICAGO, IL 60690. (#102805-26).

GEORGETOWN

GERMAN-AMERICAN ETHNIC WEEKEND - GEORGETOWN, IN. A WEEKEND CELEBRATION OF TWO HERITAGES, GERMAN AND AMERICAN. (LOCAL). JOHN R RICHERT, PROJ DIRECTOR; COMMUNITY OF GEORGETOWN; GEORGETOWN, IN 47122. (#27902). **ARBA GRANTEE.**

JULY 17 - 18, '76. GERMAN-AMERICAN ETHNIC WEEKEND. A WEEKEND CELEBRATION OF TWO HERITAGES, GERMAN AND AMERICAN. (LOCAL). JOHN R RICHERT, PROJ DIR; COMMUNITY OF GEORGETOWN; GEORGETOWN, IN 47122. (#27902-1).

GRABILL

SEPT 9 - 11, '76. GRABILL 'OLD TIME' COUNTRY FAIR. OLD TIME COUNTRY FAIR INCLUDED DEMONSTRATIONS, PRIZES FOR HOMEGROWN VEGETABLES, BUGGY RIDES, HAYRIDES, HOMEMADE APPLE BUTTER & APPLE DUMPLINGS, AND THREE DAYS OF ENTERTAINMENT. AT COMMUNITY CENTER, TOWN SQUARE, BUSINESS AREA. (LOCAL). DIANE DELAGRANGE; GRABILL CHAMBER OF COMMERCE; 2ND ST; GRABILL, IN 46741. (#200017-115).

GRANDVIEW

SEPT 4, '76. GRANDVIEW FALL FESTIVAL. OLD FASHIONED FUN DAY, 2 FREE SHOWS, CONTESTS, NASHVILLE MUSIC, RIDES, BOOTHS, BEER GARDEN AND BAND. AT COMMUNITY CENTER GROUNDS. (LOCAL). MARION RUST, CHAIRMAN; GRANDVIEW CIVIC ASSOC; GRANDVIEW, IN 47615. (#104717-1).

GREEN

GREEN TOWNSHIP FOLK LORE, IN. INFORMATION REGARDING EARLY FAMILIES, BUSINESSES & SCHOOLS WILL BE COLLECTED & PRINTED IN THE FORM OF A BOOKLET. (LOCAL). THOMAS BUTCHER, CHAIRMAN; GREEN TOWNSHIP BICENTENNIAL COMMITTEE; RR #2; PENDLETON, IN 46064. (#20366).

GREENCASTLE

CHAPLINS LIVING UNIT COUNCIL, GREENCASTLE, IN. A PROGRAM WHERE STUDENTS LIVE IN AN URBAN ENVIRONMENT & HELP REBUILD THE AREA PHYSICALLY & MENTALLY. (LOCAL). DR W F LAMAR, COORDINATOR; DEPAUW UNIVERSITY; GREENCASTLE, IN 46135. (#27229). **ARBA GRANTEE.**

THE PRACTICAL IDEALISM OF VICENTE ROCAFUERTE-BOOK. A BOOK ON THE INFLUENCE OF THE FOUNDING FATHERS ON EARLY 19TH CENTURY SPANISH AMERICA. (INT'L). DR KENT MECUM, COORD; DE PAUW UNIV ROMANCE LANGUAGE DEPARTMENT; GREENCASTLE, IN 46135. (#22336).

STUDENT INVOLVEMENT IN SOCIAL SERVICES, IN. THE DEVELOPMENT, THROUGH USE OF STUDENT WORK TEAMS, OF A PROGRAM OF URBAN COMMUNITY DEVELOPMENT CENTERING ON THE PRESERVATION & REHABILITATION OF HOMES & FACILITIES USED BY URBAN BLACKS & AGING PERSONS. (LOCAL). DR FRED LAMAR, CHAPLAN; DE PAUW UNIVERSITY; UNIVERSITY CHRISTIAN CENTER; GREENCASTLE, IN 46135. (#22337).

WGRE-FM RADIO'S BICENTENNIAL SUPPORT - NBMRP. EXTENSIVE BICENTENNIAL COVERAGE INCL DAILY 5-MIN LOCAL HISTORY VIGNETTES, LOCAL & STATE BICENTENNIAL ACTIVITIES COVERAGE & WIDE VARIETY OF PRE-PACKAGED PROGRAMMING ON THE BICENTENNIAL. (LOCAL). DENISE BITTNER, BICENTENNIAL COORDINATOR; WGRE-FM RADIO STATION; DEPAUW UNIV; GREENCASTLE, IN 46135. (#30421).

THE 13 COLONIES ADOPT THE DECLARATION OF INDEPENDENCE. LIVE PERFORMANCE AT MEHARRY HALL EAST COLLEGE. (LOCAL). MARGARET CHASE, SEC; DE PAUW UNIVERSITY ENCOUNTER SERIES; GREENCASTLE, IN 46135. (#106030-1).

FEB 2 - MAY 12, '75. RHETORIC OF THE AMERICAN REVOLUTION. SEMINAR AT SPEECH HALL. (LOCAL). WALTER KIRKPATRICK, COORD; DEPAUW UNIVERSITY; GREENCASTLE, IN 46135. (#200017-11).

MAY 7, '75. 25TH ANNIVERSARY OF ARCHIVES OF INDIANA UNITED METHODISM. CEREMONY, EXHIBIT AT ROY O WEST LIBRARY ON CAMPUS. (ST-WIDE). DAVID HORN, PROJ COORD; DEPAUW UNIV; GREENCASTLE, IN 46135. (#200017-9).

JAN 5, '76. 'LET'S SET THE RECORD STRAIGHT'. LIVE PERFORMANCE AT MEHARRY HALL IN EAST COLLEGE. (LOCAL). JOHN BAUGHMAN, PROJ DIR; DEPAUW UNIV ENCOUNTER SERIES; GREENCASTLE, IN 46135. (#200017-10).

GREENFIELD

BICENTENNIAL FESTIVAL OF HANCOCK COUNTY, INDIANA. DEDICATION OF ALL REGULAR PUBLIC AFFAIRS OF HANCOCK COUNTY FROM JANUARY 1976 TO THE COMMEMORATION OF NATIONS 200TH BIRTHDAY. TO INCLUDE A JAMES WHITCOMB RILEY FESTIVAL IN OCTOBER 1976. (LOCAL). TOM WILLIAMS, CHAIR-

GREENFIELD — CONTINUED

MAN; HANCOCK COUNTY BICENTENNIAL COMMISSION; 216 WEST 5TH STREET; GREENFIELD, IN 46140. (#2827).

BICENTENNIAL GROVE - GREENFIELD, IN. 200 TREES & 20 FLOWER BEDS WILL BE PLANTED AS PART OF THE PARK PROJ. (LOCAL). STEVEN SMIDLEY, COORDINATOR; GREENFIELD PARK & RECREATION DEPT; 110 S STATE ST; GREENFIELD, IN 46140. (#26881). **ARBA GRANTEE.**

JUNE 6, '76. BLUE RIVER HOMECOMING. FESTIVAL AT HANCOCK COUNTY 4-H BUILDING. (LOCAL). ANN MCDANIELS, CHAIRMAN; BLUE RIVER BICENTENNIAL COMMITTEE; RR 3; GREENFIELD, IN 46140. (#104771-1).

HAGERSTOWN

HISTORIC HAGERSTOWN MUSEUM, INDIANA. HISTORICAL EXHIBITS OF THE SURROUNDING AREA, INCLUDING ARCHITECTURE, CRAFTS & ARTS, HISTORY, ETC. (LOCAL). HELEN R HUDSON, SECRETARY; HISTORIC HAGERSTOWN, INC; PO BOX 126; HAGERSTOWN, IN 47346. (#2607).

HAMLET

OCT 29 - 30, '76. HAMLET'S BICENTENNIAL FESTIVAL. ACTIVITIES INCLUDED A DANCE. AT TOWN HALL. (LOCAL). DONNA M TOTH; HAMLET BICENTENNIAL COMMITTEE; RR 1, BOX 105; HAMLET, IN 46532. (#200017-114).

HAMMOND

BICENTENNIAL ART GALLERY - HAMMOND, IN. CREATION OF A PERMANENT ART EXHIBITION AREA IN THE CAMPUS LIBRARY. (LOCAL). N L TRUSTY, CHAIRMAN; PURDUE UNIV BICENTENNIAL COMMITTEE; HAMMOND, IN 40323. (#24510).

BICENTENNIAL BOOK COLLECTION - HAMMOND, IN. PURCHASE OF SEVERAL HUNDRED BOOKS DEALING WITH OUR HERITAGE FOR THE CAMPUS LIBRARY. (LOCAL). N L TRUSTY, CHAIRMAN; PURDUE UNIV BICENTENNIAL COMMITTEE; HAMMOND, IN 46323. (#24511).

BICENTENNIAL UNIVERSITY LECTURES - HAMMOND, IN. A SERIES OF LECTURES ON SUBJECTS OF BICENTENNIAL RELEVANCE BY PROMINANT INDIVIDUALS. (LOCAL). N L TRUSTY, CHAIRMAN; PURDUE UNIV BICENTENNIAL COMMITTEE; HAMMOND, IN 46323. (#24512). **ARBA GRANTEE.**

SCHOLARSHIPS FOR YOUNG & OLD OF HAMMOND, INDIANA. THE LITTLE RED SCHOOLHOUSE RESTORATION-THIS 105 YR OLD SCHOOL WILL BE USED DAILY BY STUDENTS KINDERGARDEN THRU COLLEGE-RAMPS FOR HANDICAPPED ARE PROVIDED. (ST-WIDE). JOHN W BOWLBY, CHAIRMAN; HAMMOND COMMUNITY AMERICAN BICENTENNIAL COMMITTEE; 566 STATE ST; HAMMOND, IN 46320. (#3146).

JUNE 1 - 30, '74. REVOLUTIONARY WAR PORTRAITS EXHIBIT IN HAMMOND. REVOLUTIONARY WAR PORTRAITS PROJECT OF INDIANA. GALLERY OF COLOR PHOTOS OF 65 PERSONS ASSOCIATED WITH INDIANA & THE AMERICAN REVOLUTION IS BEING EXHIBITED IN PUBLIC BUILDINGS THROUGHOUT STATE. BOOK OF SHORT BIOGRAPHIES OF SUBJECTS AVAILABLE. (ST-WIDE). DALE FRUCHTNICHT; INDIANA STATE BICENTENNIAL COMMISSION; 504 STATE OFFICE BLDG; INDIANAPOLIS, IN 46204. (#1635-903).

SEPT 1, '75 - MAR 31, '76. SERIES OF BICENTENNIAL FILMS BASED ON GREAT AMERICAN NOVELS. FILMS SHOWN MONTHLY. (LOCAL). N L TRUSTY, CHMN; PURDUE CALUMET BICENTENNIAL COMMITTEE; HAMMOND, IN 46323. (#107351-1).

SEPT 6 - 7, '75. INTERNATIONAL CULTURE FESTIVAL. INTERNATIONAL CULTURE FESTIVAL OF HAMMOND, INDIANA. FESTIVAL WITH THEME OF 'PEACE THROUGH UNDERSTANDING', WITH ETHNIC BOOTHS, ARTS & CRAFTS, & ENTERTAINMENT BY ETHNIC GROUPS. (LOCAL). JOHN W BOLBY, CHAIRMAN; HAMMOND COMMUNITY BICENTENNIAL COMMITTEE; 566 STATE ST; HAMMOND, IN 46320. (#6505-501).

MAR 29, '76. BICENTENNIAL ESSAY COMPETITION. COMPETITION. (LOCAL). NORMAN L TRUSTY, CHMN; PURDUE UNIV BICENTENNIAL COMMITTEE, CALUMET CAMPUS; HAMMOND, IN 46323. (#200017-15).

APR 1, '76. COLONIAL FESTIVAL. FESTIVAL. (LOCAL). NORMAN L TRUSTY, CHMN; PURDUE UNIV BICENTENNIAL COMMITTEE, CALUMET CAMPUS; HAMMOND, IN 46323. (#200017-16).

SEPT 11 - 12, '76. INTERNATIONAL CULTURE FESTIVAL AND ARTS AND CRAFTS FAIR. BOOTHS MARKETING & DISPLAYING ETHNIC FOOD & CRAFTS FROM 15 DIFFERENT CULTURES. CONTINUOUS ENTERTAINMENT OF ETHNIC MUSIC & DANCE; OVER 100 BOOTHS SELLING ITEMS FOR THE ART & CRAFTS FAIR. AT HOWARD BRANCH LIBRARY-7047 GRAND; OFF INTERSTATE 80. (LOCAL). HARRIETT E PINKERTON, DIR; HAMMOND PUBLIC LIBRARY, LACARE ART LEAGUE HAMMOND BICENT COMM; HOWARD BRANCH LIBRARY-7047 GRAND; HAMMOND, IN 46323. (#103938-1).

HARTFORD CITY

'ADOPT A HYDRANT' - HARTFORD CITY, IN. FIRE HYDRANTS IN THE TOWN WILL BE PAINTED. (LOCAL). JESSIE GARINGER, PRESIDENT; LAMPLIGHTERS HOME DEMONSTRATION CLUB; RT 4 BOX 81A; HARTFORD CITY, IN 47348. (#27066).

HISTORICAL MUSEUM AND LIBRARY - HARTFORD CITY, IN. HISTORICAL MUSEUM & LIBRARY ESTABLISHED TO HOUSE CECIL BEESONS COLLECTION. (LOCAL). DWIGHT MIKKELSON, PRESIDENT; BLACKFORD COUNTY HISTORICAL SOCIETY; 1421 N MULBERRY; HARTFORD CITY, IN 47348. (#26540).

TIME CAPSULE - HARTFORD CITY, IN. TIME CAPSULE TO BE BURIED ON THE BLACKFORD COUNTY COURTHOUSE GROUNDS; TO BE OPENED JULY 4, 2038, THE BICENTENNIAL YEAR OF BLACKFORD COUNTY. (LOCAL). KAREN HENDERSON, SECRETARY; BLACKFORD COUNTY BICENTENNIAL COMMITTEE; 622 W ELM; HARTFORD CITY, IN 47348. (#26541).

MAR 15 - 16, '76. OLD TIME KNOW-HOW. VARIOUS GROUPS WILL DEMONSTRATE OLD TIME KNOW-HOW TECHNIQUES, SUCH AS QUILTING/CHURNING/BUTTER-MAKING/BRAID RUGS/MAKING BREAD AND SOAP. AT 4-H BLDG, E PARK AVE. (LOCAL). MARIE DAVIS, COORD; EXTENSION HOMEMAKERS; MOON RD; HARTFORD CITY, IN 47348. (#105721-3).

MAY 4, '76. ALL BLACKFORD COUNTY SCHOOLS BICENTENNIAL DAY. FAMOUS AMERICAN DAY: CHILDREN TO DRESS IN COSTUME & PARADE DOWNTOWN. AT SOUTH SIDE SCHOOL/1315 S MONROE. (LOCAL). MISS SONIA COE, COORD; SOUTH SIDE SCHOOL TEACHERS; 1315 S MONROE; HARTFORD CITY, IN 47348. (#105721-1).

JULY 3, '76. BICENTENNIAL BALL. FESTIVAL AT ELKS CLUB STATE RD, 3 NORTH. (LOCAL). MRS LARRY DOXSEE, COORD; TRI KAPPA SORORITY; 402 N HICH; HARTFORD CITY, IN 47348. (#108941-3).

JULY 4, '76. BICENTENNIAL BABY CONTEST. FIRST BABY BORN ON JULY 4TH TO PARENTS WHO RESIDE IN BLACKFORD CO WILL WIN THE CONTEST. (LOCAL). KAREN HENDERSON, SEC; BLACKFORD COUNTY BICENTENNIAL COMMITTEE; 622 W ELM; HARTFORD CITY, IN 47348. (#108941-5).

JULY 4, '76. 'THE CROSS IS MY STATUE OF LIBERTY'. RELIGIOUS PAGEANT COMBINED WITH FIREWORKS. AT 4-H BLDG, E PARK AVE. (LOCAL). REV ROBERT NEEL, COORD; MINISTERIAL ASSOC; 401 W WASHINGTON; HARTFORD CITY, IN 47348. (#108941-4).

JULY 4, '76. 200 AND COUNTING. FAMILY-ORIENTED DAY OF GAMES & BASKET PICNIC - FOLLOWED BY VESPER SERVICE BY LOCAL MINISTERS AND FIREWORKS. AT SIGMA PHI GAMMA PARK/W ELM ST. (LOCAL). MAXIE MALOTT, COORD; SIGMA PHI GAMMA SORORITY; 629 E CONGER; HARTFORD CITY, IN 47348. (#105721-4).

AUG 7, '76. HAPPY BIRTHDAY AMERICA, 4-H FAIR & PARADE. FAIR, PARADE AT 4-H BUILDING, E PARK AVE. (LOCAL). KAREN HENDERSON, SEC; 4-H FAIR BOARD; 622 W ELM; HARTFORD CITY, IN 47348. (#108941-1).

NOV 12, '76. FALL CHORAL CONCERT. FALL CHORAL CONCERT FEATURING ALL FOUR CHOIRS PRESENTING A FULL CONCERT OF MUSIC BY AMERICAN COMPOSERS, INCLUDING SOME WORKS COMMISSIONED BY J C PENNEY. AT BLACKFORD COUNTY HIGH SCHOOL/STATE RD - 3 NORTH. (LOCAL). PHILIP TURLEY, COORD; BLACKFORD COUNTY HIGH SCHOOL CHORAL DEPT; 107 FAIRWAY CT; HARTFORD CITY, IN 47348. (#105721-2).

HIGHLAND

JAN 1 - JULY 3, '76. SPIRIT OF 1776-1976, AMERICAN UNITY PROJECT 41. 2 AMERICAN FLAGS WILL BE HAND CARRIED BY CITIZENS THE ENTIRE LENGTH OF RT 41 TO ARRIVE AT HIGHLAND ON JULY 3, 1976. THEY WILL BE PERMANENTLY HOUSED AT THE HIGHWAY OF FLAGS SERVICEMEN'S MEMORIAL. (REGN'L). MARY LOU KIESWETTER, CHMN; NATIONAL COUNCIL FOR THE ENCOURAGEMENT OF PATRIOTISM; 1502 JANICE LANE; MUNSTER, IN 46321. (#15967-1).

HOBART

BALLANTYNE MEMORIAL GALLERY - HOBART, IN. RECONSTRUCTION OF WAINWRIGHT SHOP, BLACKSMITH SHOP, AGRICULTURAL IMPLEMENTS, OTHER CRAFTS OF PIONEER DAYS. (LOCAL). PHILIP STAFFORD, CURATOR; HOBART HISTORICAL SOCIETY; 141 BEVERLY BLVD; HOBART, IN 46342. (#19102).

FLAGS OF THE AMERICAN REVOLUTION - HOBART, IN. AREA WOMEN HAVE HANDMADE REPLICAS OF 25 NATIONAL AND REGIMENTAL FLAGS OF THE REVOLUTIONARY PERIOD FOR EXHIBITS AND PROGRAMS. (LOCAL). MRS E CHRISTIANSON, CHAIRMAN; HOBART BICENTENNIAL COMMISSION; 141 BEVERLY BLVD; HOBART, IN 46342. (#19100).

FOOTBRIDGE AND NATURE TRAIL - HOBART, IN. FOOTBRIDGE WILL BE CONSTRUCTED ACROSS A BAYOU IN FRED ROSE PARK; NATURE TRAIL WILL BE MARKED. (LOCAL). MRS PEGGY ADDISON, PRESIDENT; HOBART HERITAGE CLUB; 250 W 8TH PLACE; HOBART, IN 46342. (#24239).

FOREMAN SCHOOL BICENTENNIAL PROJECTS - HOBART, IN. OUTDOOR DISPLAY OF 'THE SPIRIT OF '76'; PLANTING OF BICENTENNIAL GROVE; DECORATING GUARDRAIL RED, WHITE & BLUE AND PERFORMANCE OF THE FOREMAN BICENTENNIAL SINGERS. (LOCAL). DR NEIL VAN DER KOLK, CHAIRMAN; FOREMAN SCHOOL; E 10TH ST; HOBART, IN 46342. (#20961).

GEORGE EARLE BICENTENNIAL PROJECTS - HOBART, IN. PROJECTS INCLUDE: FLOWER PLANTINGS; LIBERTY TREE PLANTINGS; WRITING TO OTHER U S SCHOOLS; EARLY AMERICAN CRAFTS; COLONIAL DRESS DAYS. (LOCAL). MRS ALICE PANDORF, CHAIRMAN; GEORGE EARLE SCHOOL; 400 N WILSON; HOBART, IN 46342. (#21007).

HISTORY OF EDUCATION IN HOBART, IN. RESEARCH, COLLECT ARTIFACTS AND PREPARE EXHIBITS ON THE HISTORY OF HOBART SCHOOLS. (LOCAL). MRS LORETTA CHRISTOFFERSEN, PRESIDENT; PTA COUNCIL; 641 S WISCONSIN ST; HOBART, IN 46342. (#22158).

HISTORY OF HOBART CHURCHES, IN. RESEARCH AND PUBLISH HISTORY OF LOCAL CHURCHES, 1847 TO DATE. (LOCAL). MRS D BALLANTYNE, MUSEUM DIRECTOR; HOBART HISTORICAL SOCIETY; PO BOX 24; HOBART, IN 46342. (#19097).

HOBART JR HIGH SCHOOL BICENTENNIAL PROJECTS - IN. A BICENTENNIAL WEEK STUDY OF COLONIAL ARTS, CRAFTS & COSTUMES; ENGLISH CLASSES WILL WRITE BICENTENNIAL PLAYS; STUDENTS WILL RESEARCH & PHOTOGRAPH OLD HOBART BUILDINGS. (LOCAL). MRS MARY COLLINS, CHAIRMAN; HOBART JR HIGH SCHOOL; 705 E 4TH ST; HOBART, IN 46342. (#22159).

HOBART, IN, HISTORICAL MUSEUM. RENOVATION AND RESTORATION OF MUSEUM BUILDING, A FORMER CARNEGIE LIBRARY, BUILT 1915. (LOCAL). MRS D BALLANTYNE, DIRECTOR; HOBART HISTORICAL SOCIETY; PO BOX 24; HOBART, IN 46342. (#19099).

LANDFILL PARK DEVELOPMENT, HOBART, IN. RECLAMATION & LANDSCAPING OF LANDFILL OVER AN 8 YEAR PERIOD. PROJECT INCLUDES SOIL BALANCE & FERTILIZATION, GROUND COVER & LANDSCAPING. (LOCAL). T D FERKINHOFF, EXEC DIRECTOR; HOBART CHAMBER OF COMMERCE; 18 E RIDGE RD; HOBART, IN 46342. (#23515).

LIBERTY SCHOOL BICENTENNIAL PROJECTS - HOBART, IN. A BICENTENNIAL TOTEM POLE WILL BE PAINTED RED, WHITE & BLUE; DRESS DAYS AND A QUILT OF STATE FLOWERS WILL BE MADE. (LOCAL). MRS THERESA DURKLE, CHAIRMAN; LIBERTY SCHOOL; 130 N LIBERTY; HOBART, IN 46342. (#22157).

A MASTER PLAN FOR HOBART, IN. A LOCAL GROUP STUDIED & PREPARED A SUMMARY BOOK & SPOKE ON THE PROCESS OF ADOPTING A MASTER PLAN FOR LAND USE FOR THE CITY THUS PROVIDING CITIZEN INPUT & PARTICIPATION IN PLANNING FOR THE CITY. (LOCAL). MRS NANCY MCAFEE, CHAIRMAN; HOBART BRANCH AAUW; 440 N COUNTY LINE RD; HOBART, IN 46342. (#24240).

MUNDELL SCHOOL BICENTENNIAL PROJECTS - HOBART, IN. THE STUDENTS WILL MAKE A BICENTENNIAL TULIP GARDEN, NAME CLASSROOMS AS COLONIAL SHOPS AND THROW A BICENTENNIAL BIRTHDAY PARTY. (LOCAL). MRS C MATTIX, CHAIRMAN; MUNDELL SCHOOL; 52 N WISCONSIN ST; HOBART, IN 46342. (#21186).

OLD SETTLERS CEMETERY - HOBART, IN. RESTORATION OF OLD (1837-1860) BURIAL GROUND AND MONUMENT FOR KNOWN GRAVES. (LOCAL). MRS E CHRISTIANSON, CHAIRMAN; HOBART BICENTENNIAL COMMISSION; 141 BEVERLY BLVD; HOBART, IN 46342. (#19101).

RIDGEVIEW SCHOOL BICENTENNIAL PROJECTS - IN. IMPROVEMENT OF SWAMP AND DEVELOPMENT OF NATURE TRAIL; QUILTS WILL BE MADE; A U S MAP WILL BE PAINTED ON THE BASKETBALL COURT; THERE WILL BE COLONIAL DRESS DAYS AND EARLY AMERICAN FLAGS WILL BE MADE. (LOCAL). MS BECKY CARTER, CHAIRMAN; RIDGEVIEW SCHOOL; 3333 W RIDGE RD; HOBART, IN 46342. (#20996).

TIME CAPSULE 2076, HOBART, IN. LETTERS & PHOTOS, DEPOSITED IN CAPSULE TO BE OPENED JULY 4, 2076 AND DELIVERED TO DESCENDANTS OF WRITERS. (LOCAL). MRS E CHRISTOFFERSEN, PRESIDENT; HOBART PTA COUNCIL; 641 S WISCONSIN ST; HOBART, IN 46342. (#19098).

MAR 29, '75. AMERICAN FOREIGN POLICY & THE RIGHTS OF MAN. SEMINAR AT HOBART HIGH SCHOOL. (LOCAL). MRS J HALLER, COORD; HOBART BICENTENNIAL COMMISSION; 648 LIBERTY ST; HOBART, IN 46342. (#200017-20).

JUNE 28 - JULY 4, '75. FESTIVAL USA, 4TH OF JULY CELEBRATION. FESTIVAL INCLUDES: WATERMELON AND PIE EATING CONTESTS, MUSIC, GAMES, CARNIVAL RIDES, AN AIR SHOW, PARADE, FLEA MARKETS AND FIRE WORKS. AT HOBART. (LOCAL). T O FERKINHOFF, CHAIRMAN; HOBART CHAMBER OF COMMERCE; 18 E RIDGE RD; HOBART, IN 46342. (#100347-1).

JULY 26, '75. OLD TIMERS' STREET SALE. MERCHANTS AND CRAFTSMEN DISPLAY ALL TYPES OF ANTIQUES, BAKED GOODS, CRAFTS AND ART OBJECTS IN DOWNTOWN HOBART. AT HOBART - DOWNTOWN. (LOCAL). T O FERKINHOFF, CHAIRMAN; HOBART CHAMBER OF COMMERCE; 18 E RIDGE RD; HOBART, IN 46342. (#100348-1).

DEC 5, '75. ARE THE STATES OBSOLETE? HOBART COMMUNITY FORUM. SEMINAR AT WEST HOBART CIVIC CLUB. (LOCAL). MRS J HALLER, PROJ DIR; HOBART BICENTENNIAL COMMISSION; 648 LIBERTY ST; HOBART, IN 46342. (#200017-19).

JAN 29, '76. THE NEW AMERICAN WORK ETHIC -- HOBART COMMUNITY FORUM. SEMINAR AT HOBART HIGH SCHOOL. (LOCAL). MRS J HALLER, COORD; HOBART BICENTENNIAL COMMISSION; 648 LIBERTY ST; HOBART, IN 46342. (#104204-3).

FEB 29, '76. MUTTERINGS IN THE MARKETPLACE, HOBART COMMUNITY FORUM. SEMINAR AT HOBART HIGH SCHOOL. (LOCAL). MRS J HALLER, COORD; HOBART BICENTENNIAL COMMISSION; 648 LIBERTY ST; HOBART, IN 46342. (#104204-4).

APR 29, '76. GROWING UP IN AMERICA - THE CHALLENGE OF CHANGE. SEMINAR AT WEST HOBART CIVIC CLUB. (LOCAL). MRS J HALLER, COORD; HOBART BICENTENNIAL COMMISSION; 648 LIBERTY ST; HOBART, IN 46342. (#104204-5).

JUNE 26 - 27, '76. ARTS AND CRAFTS FAIR. EXHIBIT, FAIR AT HOBART HIGH SCHOOL. (LOCAL). MRS JEAN WOLVERTON, DIR; KAPPA KAPPA KAPPA SORORITY; 2106 E CLEVELAND AVE; HOBART, IN 46342. (#105851-5).

SEPT 4, '76. BICENTENNIAL FLOWER SHOW. EXHIBIT AT HOBART HISTORICAL SOCIETY, 706 E 4TH ST. (LOCAL). MRS ROSE BRAUN, COORD; HOBART GARDEN CLUB; 408 N OHIO ST; HOBART, IN 46342. (#106806-1).

HOMER

JUNE 19 - 20, '76. HOMER FESTIVAL OF ARTS AND CRAFTS. 'MOSEY' ON INTO THE QUIET TOWN OF HOMER FOR A TASTE OF ROASTED CORN, SALT-RISING BREAD, HOMEMADE CANDY AND COUNTRY CURED MEATS; WHILE YOUR EYES FEAST ON BROOMSTICK LACE, CORNHUSK DOLLS, BAKED BREAD BASKETS AND DRIED FLOWER ARRANGEMENTS. AT HOMER. (LOCAL). BOB WAGGENER, CHAIRMAN; HOMER FESTIVAL OF ARTS AND CRAFTS; PO BOX 68; HOMER, IN 46146. (#100333-1).

HUNTINGBURG

BICENTENNIAL FILM SERIES - HUNTINGBURG, IN. THE FILM SERIES IS ON THE HISTORY OF THE UNITED STATES. (LOCAL). LEE AYRES, CHAIRMAN; SOUTHERN INDIANA EDUCATION CENTER; 511 4TH ST; HUNTINGBURG, IN 47542. (#25222). **ARBA GRANTEE.**

HUNTINGTON

HUNTINGTON HERITAGE MAPS - IN. 18 LIGHTED MAPS TO SHOW LOCAL HISTORICAL SITES. THESE ARE TO BE PREPARED FOR SCHOOL SYSTEMS. (LOCAL). DR DANIEL HENDERSHOTT, COORDINATOR; HUNTINGTON COUNTY COMMUNITY SCHOOL CORP; 959 GUILFORD ST; HUNTINGTON, IN 46750. (#26615). **ARBA GRANTEE.**

'OUR AMERICAN CATHOLIC HERITAGE' - BOOK. 1-VOLUME COLOR ILLUSTRATED ENCYCLOPEDIA OF GREAT AMER CATHOLICS. PORTRAYS THE LIVES OF MODERN HEROES, GREAT EXPLORERS AND PIONEERS. (NAT'L). JOSEPH J ISCA, SALES PROMOTION COORDINATOR; OUR SUNDAY VISITOR, INC; NOLL PLAZA; HUNTINGTON, IN 46750. (#2449).

THE WAY WE WERE, HUNTINGTON, IN. A MULTIFACETED ATTEMPT TO REVITALIZE HUNTINGTON COMMUNITY'S AWARENESS OF ITS HERITAGE. (LOCAL). JACK BARLOW, SR, DIRECTOR; HUNTINGTON COMMUNITY BICENTENNIAL; RR 8, BOX 28-A; HUNTINGTON, IN 46750. (#26787). **ARBA GRANTEE.**

OCT 4, '76. UNITED STATES ARMED FORCES BICENTENNIAL CARAVAN. CARAVAN IS COMPOSED OF EXHIBIT VANS FOR EACH MILITARY SERVICE. PROJECT THEME IS 'HISTORY OF THE ARMED FORCES & THEIR CONTRIBUTIONS TO THE NATION'. (LOCAL). MYRON J SMITH, JR; UNITED STATES ARMED FORCES BICENTENNIAL CARAVAN; 20 E PARK DR; HUNTINGTON, IN 46750. (#1775-727).

INDIANAPOLIS

'THE AGING SPIRIT OF REVOLUTION' - IN. IMITATION OF INDIANA'S CENTURY CLUB DEVELOPMENT OF ORAL HISTORY PROJECTS. (LOCAL). MAURICE E ENDWRIGHT, CHAIRMAN; INDIANA COMMISSION ON AGING; 215 N SENATE AVE; INDIANAPOLIS, IN 46204. (#27779). **ARBA GRANTEE.**

'ALL THINGS MOVE' - A MOBILE MUSEUM, IN. A MOBILE EXTENSION OF THE INDIANA CHILDREN'S MUSEUM SPONSORED BY AMERICAN RED BALL TRANSIT CO, INC, WHICH WILL TOUR THE U S DURING THE BICENTENNIAL YEAR WITH ARTIFACT DISPLAYS AND ILLUSTRATIONS. (REGN'L). DAN S HINER, PRESIDENT; AMERICAN RED BALL TRANSIT CO, INC; 1335 SADLIER CIR, E DR; INDIANAPOLIS, IN 46239. (#22274).

'THE AMERICAN REVOLUTION IN THE WEST', IN. COPIES OF 'THE AMERICAN REVOLUTION IN THE WEST' WILL BE DISTRIBUTED TO ALL HIGH SCHOOLS, PUBLIC LIBRARIES & MUSEUMS IN THE STATE. (ST-WIDE). MICHELE WHITE, EXEC DIRECTOR; INDIANA BICENTENNIAL ADMINISTRATION; 100 STATE OFFICE BLDG; INDIANAPOLIS, IN 46204. (#28274). **ARBA GRANTEE.**

ANNUAL COMMUNITY FESTIVAL - INDIANAPOLIS, IN. THE NEAR EASTSIDE COMMUNITY ORGANIZATION IS SPONSORING THE ANNUAL COMMUNITY FESTIVAL. (LOCAL). SHARON L PUTNAM, COORDINATOR; THE NEAR EAST SIDE COMMUNITY ORGANIZATION, INC.; 2236 E 10TH ST; INDIANAPOLIS, IN 46201. (#26862). **ARBA GRANTEE.**

BICENTENNIAL COLOR GUARD - INDIANAPOLIS, IN. CREATION OF A BICENTENNIAL COLOR GUARD AND HONOR GUARD. (LOCAL). DIRECTOR; SONS OF THE AMERICAN REVOLUTION; 9465 LAFAYETTE RD; INDIANAPOLIS, IN 46278. (#27777). **ARBA GRANTEE.**

BICENTENNIAL CONSTITUTIONS BOOKLET - IN. BOOKLET WITH DECLARATION OF INDEPENDENCE, CONSTITUTION OF U S AND CONSTITUTION OF INDIANA WILL BE PUBLISHED. (ST-WIDE). THEODORE L SENDAK, ATTORNEY GENERAL OF INDIANA; OFFICE OF ATTORNEY GENERAL; 219 STATE HOUSE; INDIANAPOLIS, IN 46204. (#27761). **ARBA GRANTEE.**

BICENTENNIAL POETS CORNER - INDIANAPOLIS, IN. A POETRY CONTEST WILL BE HELD FOR HIGH SCHOOL STUDENTS. (LOCAL). MARY L CONNER, DIRECTOR; THE POETS CORNER, INC; 3440 E KESSLER BLVD; INDIANAPOLIS, IN 46220. (#25799). **ARBA GRANTEE.**

BOOK, GENTLEMEN FROM INDIANA - INDIANAPOLIS, IN. WRITTEN BY IUPUI FACULTY MEMBERS FROM HISTORY DEPT ABOUT HOOSIERS WHO RAN FOR PRESIDENCY OR VICE PRESIDENCY FROM 1840-1940. (LOCAL). DR RALPH GRAY, CHAIRMAN; INDIANA UNIV-PURDUE UNIV AT INDIANAPOLIS; 925 W MICHIGAN AVE; INDIANAPOLIS, IN 46202. (#24183).

BUTLER'S FESTIVAL '76: AMERICAN MUSIC & DANCE. A 6 DAY FESTIVAL OF AMERICAN MUSIC & DANCE. (LOCAL). LOUIS C HENETTE, PROJ DIRECTOR; BUTLER UNIV; 4600 SUNSET; INDIANAPOLIS, IN 46208. (#24718). **ARBA GRANTEE.**

CALLIOPE CIRCUS WAGON - INDIANAPOLIS, IN. INDIANA UNIV & PURDUE UNIV WILL BUILD A FLOAT FOR THE '500' PARADE. (LOCAL). NICK KESTNER, DIRECTOR; IUPUI BICENTENNIAL COMMITTEE & ALUMNI ASSOC; ALUMNI OFFICE; INDIANAPOLIS, IN 46202. (#24073).

EXHIBIT ON ETHNIC MINORITIES - INDIANAPOLIS, IN. EXHIBIT WILL FEATURE THE CONTINUING CONTRIBUTIONS OF ETHNIC MINORITIES IN THE U S. (ST-WIDE). JANET BELL, PROJ DIRECTOR; DEPT OF PUBLIC INSTRUCTION; 120 W MARKET ST; INDIANAPOLIS, IN 46204. (#26538). **ARBA GRANTEE.**

FALL CREEK CLEANUP - INDIANAPOLIS, IN. TROOPS UTILIZED IN CLEANUP AT THE REQUEST OF THE MAYOR'S OFFICE. (LOCAL). SALLY SPRIGGS, INFORMATION SPECIALIST; FORT BENJAMIN HARRISON; FT BEN HARSN, IN 46216. (#29827).

FESTIVAL OF AMERICAN MUSIC - IN. THE FESTIVAL WILL BE HELD AT THE MARKET SQUARE ARENA, WITH 5,000 STUDENT PERFORMERS. (LOCAL). HARRY R MAMLIN, COORDINATOR; INDIANAPOLIS PUBLIC SCHOOLS; 120 E WALNUT ST; INDIANAPOLIS, IN 46204. (#26626). **ARBA GRANTEE.**

FOUNTAIN RENOVATION - IN. RESTORATION OF 3 CENTURY-OLD FOUNTAINS. (LOCAL). RODGER BENSON, CHAIRMAN; INDIANAPOLIS PARKS DEPT; CITY BUILDING; INDIANAPOLIS, IN 46204. (#27762). **ARBA GRANTEE.**

FREDERICK DOUGLAS: A ONE MAN CONCERT, IN. 5 CONCERTS OF CLASSICAL MUSIC IN INDIANAPOLIS, ANDERSON, FT WAYNE, MARION & SOUTH BEND, INDIANA. (LOCAL). WALTER BELL, COORDINATOR; INDIANAPOLIS URBAN LEAGUE; 445 N PENNSYLVANIA, #406; INDIANAPOLIS, IN 46204. (#24721). **ARBA GRANTEE.**

GENESIS BICENTENNIAL, INDIANAPOLIS, IN. ESSAY COMPETITION INVOLVING COLLEGE STUDENTS; BICENTENNIAL THEME. (LOCAL). JEFF PURVIS, PROJ DIRECTOR; GENESIS LITERARY JOURNAL, INDIANA UNIV & PURDUE UNIV; 925 W MICHIGAN ST; INDIANAPOLIS, IN 46202. (#24714). **ARBA GRANTEE.**

GEOGRAPHIC BASE FILE SYSTEM, INDIANAPOLIS, IN. A GEOGRAPHIC BASE FILE SYSTEM THAT ALLOWS FOR THE ANALYSIS OF SELECTED STUDY AREAS. (LOCAL). BERNIE WILCOX, PRINCIPAL PLANNER; DEPT OF METROPOLITAN DEVELOPMENT; 2041 CITY-COUNTY BLDG; INDIAPOLIS, IN 46204. (#20017).

GEORGE ROGERS CLARK BICENT EXHIBIT IN INDIANA. EXHIBIT AT STATE MUSEUM IN INDIANAPOLIS TO DEPICT CLARK'S EXPEDITION WHICH WAS THE MOST REVOLUTIONARY ACTION WEST OF THE ALLEGHENY MOUNTAINS. OUTREACH PROG TO SEND EXHIBITS, FILMS & SLIDES AROUND STATE. (ST-WIDE). JACK KAMMINS, PRESIDENT; INDIANA STATE MUSEUM SOCIETY, INC; 202 N ALABAMA ST; INDIANAPOLIS, IN 46204. (#7350). **ARBA GRANTEE.**

GEORGE ROGERS CLARK - FILM. FILM DEPICTING THE REVOLUTIONARY WAR CAREER OF GEORGE ROGERS CLARK WHO LED THE EXPEDITION WHICH ESTABLISHED THE AMERICAN CLAIM TO THE OLD NORTHWEST TERRITORY. (NAT'L). HUBERT H HAWKINS, EXEC SECRETARY; INDIANA HISTORICAL SOCIETY; 140 N SENATE AVE; INDIANAPOLIS, IN 46204. (#7849). **(??).**

GIRL SCOUTS BICENTENNIAL CELEBRATION - IN. THE GIRL SCOUTS WILL HAVE A SPECIAL CELEBRATION FOR THE BICENTENNIAL. (LOCAL). NORM WILKENS, CHAIRMAN; HOOSIER CAPITAL GIRL SCOUT COUNCIL; 615 N ALABAMA; INDIANAPOLIS, IN 46204. (#27783). **ARBA GRANTEE.**

HISTORIC OHIO RIVER VALLEY PAINTINGS, IN. PAINTINGS OF HARRY A DAVIS. HISTORIC BUILDINGS ARE THE SUBJECT. (ST-WIDE). HARRY A DAVIS, PROJ COORDINATOR; HERRON ART SCHOOL INDIANA U-PURDUE U AT INDIANAPOLIS; 1701 N PENNSYLVANIA ST; INDIANAPOLIS, IN 46205. (#18666).

HISTORY OF WARREN TOWNSHIP, IN. THE COMMUNITY'S HISTORY WILL BE RESEARCHED & WRITTEN BY STUDENTS OF NATIONAL HONOR SOCIETY. (LOCAL). HERB KORRA, PROJ DIRECTOR; NATL HONOR SOCIETY, WCHS & WARREN TOWNSHIP BICENT COMMUNITY; 9500 E 16TH ST; INDIANAPOLIS, IN 46229. (#18171).

IMPROVING THE CITIZENSHIP OF CHILDREN, IN. GOOD CITIZENSHIP & PROPER ATTITUDE TOWARDS INDIVIDUAL RESPONSIBILITY WILL BE ENCOURAGED FOR COMMUNITY YOUTH. (LOCAL). ELMO CONEY, PRESIDENT; CITIZENS' FORUM, INC; 2735 N ILLINOIS ST; INDIANAPOLIS, IN 46208. (#25680). **ARBA GRANTEE.**

INDIANA MICROFILMING PROJECT - INDIANAPOLIS. MICROFILMING NEWSPAPERS TO PRESERVE THE INFORMATION FOR YEARS TO COME. (ST-WIDE). JOHN J NEWMAN, COORDINATOR; INDIANA STATE LIBRARY; 140 N SENATE AVE; INDIANAPOLIS, IN 46204. (#27394). **ARBA GRANTEE.**

INDIANA MUSEUMS INVENTORY. TO INVENTORY AND PREPARE FOR COMPUTER TAPES THE ART, ETHNOLOGY, AND HISTORY COLLECTIONS HOUSED IN THE MUSEUMS OF THE STATE OF INDIANA. A PART OF INDIANA'S BICENTENNIAL CELEBRATION. (ST-WIDE). MRS ALEX J BLACK, PROJECT COORDINATOR; ASSOCIATION OF INDIANA MUSEUMS, C/O CHILDRENS MUSEUM; 3000 N MERIDIAN ST; INDIANAPOLIS, IN 46208. (#2384).

INDIANAPOLIS-SCARBOROUGH PEACE GAMES, IN. A PROGRAM WITH SPORTS AS THE MEDIUM FOR CULTURAL EXCHANGE, LEARNING AND PARTICIPATION DESIGNED TO BRING AMERICANS INTO A MORE PERSONAL RELATIONSHIP WITH RESIDENTS OF ANOTHER COUNTRY. (INT'L). SARAH MEEKER - EXECUTIVE SECRETARY; INDIANAPOLIS-SCARBOROUGH PEACE GAMES; 2916 N HARDING ST; INDIAPOLIS, IN 46208. (#20025).

INTERNATIONAL BICENTENNIAL FESTIVAL WEEK - IN. THE WEEK FROM OCTOBER 4TH TO OCTOBER 10TH HAS BEEN DECLARED INTERNATIONAL BICENTENNIAL FESTIVAL WEEK; MANY ACTIVITIES HAVE BEEN PLANNED. (ST-WIDE). JOSEPH BRIGAND, CHAIRMAN; INTERNATIONAL CENTER OF INDIANAPOLIS, INC; 1050 W 42ND ST; INDIANAPOLIS, IN 46208. (#24280). **ARBA GRANTEE.**

LITERARY MAGAZINE-STUDENT SPECIAL ISSUE - IN. FEATURING WINNING ESSAYS ON THE THEME 'AMERICAN HORIZONS', SPRING ISSUE OF GENESIS. (LOCAL). DR PHYLLIS I DANIELSON, CHAIRMAN; INDIANA UNIV-PURDUE UNIV AT INDIANAPOLIS; 355 N LANSING ST; INDIANAPOLIS, IN 46202. (#24175).

LOCKERBIE SQUARE REVITALIZATION, INDIANAPOLIS, IN. THE RENOVATION & RESTORATION OF THE AREA SURROUNDING THE HOME OF JAMES WHITCOMB RILEY, THE HOOSIER POET, IN DOWNTOWN INDIANAPOLIS. (LOCAL). JOHN L KRAUSS, EXEC DIRECTOR; INDIANAPOLIS BICENTENNIAL COMMITTEE; 1842 CITY-COUNTY BLDG; INDIANAPOLIS, IN 46204. (#5954).

MULTI-SPORT ATHLETIC PROGRAM - INDIANAPOLIS, IN. THE AMATEUR ATHLETIC UNION OF THE UNITED STATES, INC IS SPONSORING A MULTI-SPORT ATHLETIC PROGRAM. (INT'L). OLLAN C CASSELL, COORDINATOR; AMATEUR ATHLETIC UNION OF THE UNITED STATES, INC; 3400 W 86TH ST; INDIANAPOLIS, IN 46268. (#27934).

MUSEUM OF INDIAN HERITAGE PICTORIAL PANORAMA - IN. MURALS DEPICTING SCENES IN THE OLD NORTHWEST TERRITORY AND EVENTS FROM THE AMERICAN REVOLUTION TO THE WAR OF 1812 WILL BE DISPLAYED. (LOCAL). JAMES H LAWTON, COORDINATOR; MUSEUM OF INDIAN HERITAGE; 6040 DELONG RD; INDIANAPOLIS, IN 46254. (#25918). **ARBA GRANTEE.**

PIANO-ORCHESTRA FESTIVAL - INDIANAPOLIS, IN. THE FESTIVAL IS IN HONOR OF LOUIS COTTSCHALK. (LOCAL). GIANNINA HOFMEISTER, DIRECTOR; METROPOLITAN ARTS COUNCIL; 143 W MERIDIAN ST; INDIANAPOLIS, IN 46204. (#25765). **ARBA GRANTEE.**

'READMORE HISTORY & YOU', INDIANAPOLIS, IN. THE INDIANA DEPT OF PUBL INSTRUCTION, DIV OF READING EFFECTIVENESS, WILL PRESENT AUDIO VISUAL BICENT PRESENTATIONS TO CITIZENS OF IND. PRESENTATIONS MADE VIA PUBLIC SERVICE TV. (LOCAL). GAIL TISSIER, COORDINATOR; DEPARTMENT OF PUBLIC INSTRUCTION; 120 W MARKET ST; INDIANAPOLIS, IN 46204. (#26792). **ARBA GRANTEE.**

RESTORATION OF OLD MOORE SCHOOL - IN. RESTORATION OF 1850-1855 WOOD FRAME, ONE ROOM SCHOOL BUILDING. (LOCAL). CHARLOTTE DIAL, COORDINATOR; COMMUNITY HISTORICAL ORGANIZATION; 1500 E STOP 10 RD; INDIANAPOLIS, IN 46227. (#26112). **ARBA GRANTEE.**

ROOTS OF OUR FREEDOM, INDIANAPOLIS, IN. A 10-PART, TELEVISED EDUCATIONAL PROGRAM ON PRINCIPLES OF LAW AS GROUNDED IN AMERICA'S BILL OF RIGHTS. VIDEOTAPED RECREATION OF 1789 CONGRESSSIONAL DEBATES WHICH PRODUCED THE BILL OF RIGHTS. (LOCAL). KARL J STIPHER, COORDINATOR; INDIANA CONTINUING LEGAL EDUCATION FORUM; 810 FLETCHER TRUST BLDG; INDIANAPOLIS, IN 46204. (#26793). **ARBA GRANTEE.**

SPIRIT OF FREEDOM - MENTAL HEALTH AWARENESS PGM. PROGRAM TO PROMOTE AWARENESS OF MENTAL ILLNESS: 10 MURALS DEPICTING PROGRESS OF MENTAL HEALTH CARE SINCE 1776. PROVIDED TOPICS FOR 3 PUBLIC FORUMS & TAPED FORUM HIGHLIGHTS FOR FURTHER DISTRIBUTION. (ST-WIDE). LOUIS A REALE, BICENTENNIAL CHAIRPERSON; INDIANA DEPT OF MENTAL HEALTH, CENTRAL STATE HOSPITAL; 3000 W WASHINGTON ST; INDIANAPOLIS, IN 46222. (#32990). **ARBA RECOGNIZED.**

SUMMER OF '76 FILM SERIES, INDIANAPOLIS, IN. FILM TOPICS ARE: 'THE SECRET OF SURVIVAL' AND 'MAN AND NATURE'. (LOCAL). KAREN BOWER, COORDINATOR; INDIANAPOLIS DEPT PARKS & RECREATION; 5901 DELONG RD; INDIANAPOLIS, IN 46254. (#25634). **ARBA GRANTEE.**

TREE PLANTING - INDIANAPOLIS, IN. CAMPUS-WIDE PLANTING OF ARBORETUM ON NEWLY DEVELOPED URBAN CAMPUS IN ACCORD WITH MASTER PLAN. (LOCAL). DR PHYLLIS I DANIELSON, CHAIRMAN; INDIANA UNIV-PURDUE UNIV AT INDIANAPOLIS; 355 N LANSING ST; INDIANAPOLIS, IN 46202. (#24177).

UNIFIED PROJ FOR URBAN PROGRESS IN INDIANAPOLIS. A COMMUNITY SELF-HELP PROJECT TO IMPROVE THE DELIVERY OF HUMAN SERVICES AND THE QUALITY OF LIFE THROUGH BETTER PROCESSES OF COMMUNICATION, PLANNING, AND DECISION-MAKING. (LOCAL). ROBERT R HAWKINS, EXEC DIRECTOR; BOARD FOR FUNDAMENTAL EDUCATION; 333 N PENNSYLVANIA; INDIANAPOLIS, IN 46204. (#4838).

THE WINGS OF FREEDOM, INDIANAPOLIS, IN. A DANCE SPONSORED BY THE PHILIPPINE-AMERICAN NATIONAL ASSOCIATION ENTITLED 'THE WINGS OF FREEDOM'. (LOCAL). JULIO U NASIS, COORDINATOR; PHILIPPINE AMERICAN NATIONAL ASSOC; 3514 PIXLEY COURT; INDIANAPOLIS, IN 46236. (#25633). **ARBA GRANTEE.**

'WOMEN MAKING AMERICA WORK' - INDIANAPOLIS, IN. A WORKSHOP DEALING WITH THE CONTRIBUTIONS WOMEN HAVE MADE TO AMERICA. (LOCAL). PAT TEHAN, CHAIRMAN; YWCA; 822 FT WAYNE AVE; INDIANAPOLIS, IN 46204. (#23616). **ARBA GRANTEE.**

'YOUTH FOR UNDERSTANDING' - INDIANAPOLIS, IN. A YOUTH EXCHANGE PROGRAM IN INDIANAPOLIS. (LOCAL). STEPHEN MOORE, CHAIRMAN; YOUTH FOR UNDERSTANDING; 3442 SHERBURNE CIRCLE; INDIANAPOLIS, IN 46222. (#27901). **ARBA GRANTEE.**

'200 & AWAY WE GO' - FAIR, INDIANAPOLIS, IN. A COMMUNITY FAIR TO BE HELD AT CENTRAL STATE HOSPITAL GROUNDS. (LOCAL). LAMAR PETERSON, JR, COORDINATOR; CENTRAL STATE HOSPITAL; 3000 W WASHINGTON ST; INDIANAPOLIS, IN 46204. (#24717). **ARBA GRANTEE.**

3-D DIORAMA OF INDIANS MEETING LASALLE - IN. A 3-D DIORAMA OF INDIANS MEETING LASALLE WILL BE A PER-

INDIANAPOLIS — CONTINUED

MANENT EXHIBIT AT THE MUSEUM OF INDIAN HERITAGE. (LOCAL). JAMES H LAWTON, COORDINATOR; MUSEUM OF INDIAN HERITAGE; 6040 DELONG RD; INDIANAPOLIS, IN 46254. (#24285). **ARBA GRANTEE.**

APR 18, '75. 200TH ANNIVERSARY CELEBRATION OF PAUL REVERE'S RIDE. THIS EVENT IS DESIDNED TO RECOGNIZE THE ON SET OF THE AMERICAN REVOLUTION AND TO ENCOURAGE PARTICIPATION IN FUTURE BICENTENNIAL EVENTS. AT INDIANA STATE CAPITOL BUILDING. (LOCAL). TIM KENNEDY; INDIANA AMERICAN REVOLUTION BICENTENNIAL COMMISSION; STATE CAPITOL ROOM 201; INDIANAPOLIS, IN 46204. (#50410-1).

NOV 1, '75 - OCT 30, '76. AMERICAN NEGRO UNITED STATEWIDE MINORITY EVENTS PROGRAM. A SERIES OF EVENTS AND ACTIVITIES HAVE BEEN AND ARE IN THE PROCESS OF BEING PLANNED TO FOCUS PUBLIC ATTENTION, UNDERSTANDING AND APPRECIATION FOR THE AMERICAN WAY OF LIFE, ITS PROBLEMS AND PROGRESS THROUGH THE UNITED EFFORTS OF MANY DIVERSE GROUPS AND BACKGROUNDS. AT HEADQUARTERS AT 414 W VERMONT ST, OTHER FACILITIES AS NEGOTIATED. (LOCAL). J SOLOMON BENN III, DIR; AMERICAN NEGRO BICENTENNIAL ASSOC OF INDIANA; 414 W VERMONT ST; INDIANAPOLIS, IN 46202. (#15579-1).

NOV 1, '75 - MAY 31, '77. GRAPHIC DISPLAY OF MINERAL RESOURCES OF ORIGINAL 13 COLONIES. EXHIBIT AT 4TH FLR LOBBY OF CAVANAUGH BLDG; 925 W MICHIGAN ST. (LOCAL). DR ARTHUR MIRSKY, COORD; BICENTENNIAL COMMITTEE & GEOLOGY DEPT; 925 W MICHIGAN, CAVANAUGH HALL; INDIANAPOLIS, IN 42602. (#107350-1).

NOV 7, '75. BICENTENNIAL VETERANS DAY PROGRAM. FESTIVAL AT WCHS, 9500 E 16TH ST. (LOCAL). CLIFFORD GATES, CHMN; WARREN TWP BICENTENNIAL COMMUNITY; 9500 E 16TH ST; INDIANAPOLIS, IN 46229. (#200017-13).

DEC 19, '75. THE TODAY SHOW FEATURES THE STATE OF INDIANA. A CONTINUING WEEKLY SERIES OF PROGRAMS COMMEMORATING EACH STATE. INDIANA WAS ADMITTED INTO THE UNION IN DECEMBER, 1816. (NAT'L). STUART SCHULBERG, EX PROD; NATIONAL BROADCASTING CO; 30 ROCKEFELLER PLAZA; NEW YORK, NY 10020. (#7981-4).

JAN 2 - JULY 31, '76. 'WISEST MAN IN THE VALLEY' - FILM ON EARLY MEDICAL EDUCATION. RADIO/TV. (ST-WIDE). DR GEORGE LUKEMEYER, DEAN; INDIANA UNIV SCHOOL OF MEDICINE; 1100 W MICHIGAN ST; INDIANAPOLIS, IN 46202. (#103811-1).

JAN 2 - DEC 31, '76. REVOLUTIONARY WAR PORTRAITS PROJECT. GALLERY OF COLOR PHOTOS OF 52 PERSONS ASSOCIATED WITH INDIANA & THE AMERICAN REVOLUTION IS BEING EXHIBITED IN PUBLIC BUILDINGS THROUGHOUT STATE. (ST-WIDE). DALE FRUCHTNICT, ASST DIR; INDIANA STATE BICENTENNIAL COMMISSION; 504 STATE OFFICE BLDG; INDIANAPOLIS, IN 46204. (#1635-1).

JAN 12 - APR 24, '76. PIANO-ORCHESTRA FESTIVAL HONORING LOUIS COTTSCHALK. LIVE PERFORMANCE, FESTIVAL AT CLOWES HALL. (LOCAL). GIANNINO HOFMEISTER, DIR; METROPOLITAN ARTS COUNCIL; 143 W MERIDIAN ST; INDIANAPOLIS, IN 46204. (#25765-1).

FEB 16 - 22, '76. FESTIVAL 1976: THE MUSIC OF LEONARD BERNSTEIN. A WEEK LONG CELEBRATION OF AMERICAN MUSIC, IN PARTICULAR, THAT OF LEONARD BERNSTEIN; CONCERTS WILL INCLUDE PERFORMANCES BY HIGH SCHOOL BANDS AND ORCHESTRAS AND THE BUTLER ORCHESTRA AND BALLET; THE FESTIVAL FINALE WILL BE BERNSTEIN'S 'MASS'. AT CLOWES HALL. (REGN'L). LOUIS F CHENETTE, CHMN; BUTLER UNIVERSITY - JORDAN COLLEGE OF MUSIC; 4600 SUNSET AVE; INDIANAPOLIS, IN 46208. (#104334-10).

FEB 20, '76. ARCHIVES-OFFICIAL OPENING CEREMONY. OPENING AT 3RD FLOOR ARCHIVES. (LOCAL). JEANETTE MATTHEW, COORD; IUPUI, BLAKE ST LIBRARY; 420 BLAKE ST; INDIANAPOLIS, IN 46202. (#200017-14).

FEB 24 - MAR 28, '76. 'BETWEEN TRADITIONS: NAVAJO WEAVING TOWARD THE END OF 19TH CENTURY'. KRANNERT PAVILION: TUES 11-9; WED-SUN 11-5, NO CHARGE; STOUT LIBRARY: TUES-SAT 11-5, NO CHARGE; LILLY PAVILION OF DECORATIVE ARTS: TUES-SUN 1-4, ADULTS $1, STUDENTS & CHILDREN UNDER 16, .50, MEMBERS NO CHARGE, CLOSED MONDAYS. (REGN'L). ROBERT YASSIN, DIRECTOR; UNIV OF IOWA, MUSEUM OF ART & INDIANAPOLIS MUSEUM OF ART; INDIANAPOLIS, IN 46208. (#6548-504).

FEB 25 - NOV 28, '76. EXHIBIT OF PAINTINGS. 30 PAINTINGS OF HISTORICAL SITES IN SOUTHERN INDIANA BY HARRY A DAVIS WILL BE EXHIBITED THROUGHOUT INDIANA. (ST-WIDE). DR PHULLIS I DANIELSON; INDIANA UNIV-PURDUE UNIV AT INDIANAPOLIS; 355 N LANING ST; INDIANAPOLIS, IN 46202. (#107836-1).

FEB 27, '76 - JUNE 30, '79. GEORGE ROGERS CLARK AMERICAN REVOLUTION BICENTENNIAL EXHIBIT. EXHIBIT AT STATE MUSEUM IN INDIANAPOLIS TO DEPICT CLARK'S EXPEDITION WHICH WAS THE MOST REVOLUTIONARY ACTION WEST OF THE ALLEGHENY MOUNTAINS. OUTREACH PROG TO SEND EXHIBITS, FILMS & SLIDES AROUND STATE. AT INDIANA STATE MUSEUM, 202 N ALA ST. (REGN'L). JACK KAMMINS, PRESIDENT; INDIANA STATE MUSEUM SOCIETY, INC; 202 N ALABAMA ST; INDIANAPOLIS, IN 46204. (#7350-1).

MAR 9, '76. 'THE BRITISH ARE COMING' - BRITISH MILITARY BAND PERFORMANCE. TOUR OF MAJOR U S CITIES BY BRITISH MILITARY UNITS AS REPRESENTATIVE OF UNITS INVOLVED IN REVOLUTIONARY WAR CAMPAIGN. AT HINKLE FIELD HOUSE (BUTLER U). (INT'L). CHARLES K JONES, PRES; COULMBIA ARTISTS FESTIVALS CORP; 165 W 57TH ST; NEW YORK, NY 10019. (#6532-34).

MAR 23 - 28, '76. BUTLER UNIVERSITY'S FESTIVAL '76: AMERICAN MUSIC & DANCE. LIVE PERFORMANCE, FESTIVAL AT CLOWES HALL. (LOCAL). LOUIS CHENETTE, PROJ DIR; BUTLER UNIV; 4600 SUNSET; INDIANAPOLIS, IN 46208. (#24718-1).

MAR 23 - DEC 31, '76. 'ALL THINGS MOVE' - A MUSEUM ON WHEELS. MOBILE MUSEUM VISITING 150 COMMUNITIES AROUND THE NATION; STOPS ARE SCHEDULED AT MUSEUMS, SCHOOLS, SHOPPING CENTERS, ETC; FOR INFORMATION ON STOPS IN SPECIFIC AREAS, CONTACT THE NEAREST AMERICAN RED BALL (ARB) AGENT. (REGN'L). A G WOYTINEK; THE CHILDREN'S MUSEUM, AMERICAN RED BALL & GENERAL MOTORS CORP; 3000 N MERIDIAN ST; INDIANAPOLIS, IN 46208. (#107903-7).

MAR 26 - APR 10, '76. FREDERICK DOUGLAS: A ONE MAN CONCERT. LIVE PERFORMANCE AT 8 CONCERTS: INDIANAPOLIS, MICHIGAN CITY, INDIANA WOMEN'S PRISON. (LOCAL). WALTER BELL, COORD; INDIANAPOLIS URBAN LEAGUE; 445 N PENNSYLVANIA, #406; INDIANAPOLIS, IN 46204. (#24721-1).

APR 20 - 25, '76. ROMANTIC MUSIC FESTIVAL. ROMANTIC MUSIC COVERS THE FULL SPECTRUM OF EMOTIONS DURING BALLET, INSTRUMENTAL AND CHORAL PRESENTATIONS OF SCORES BY AMER COMPOSERS FROM THIS ERA; THIS FESTIVAL IS INTERNATIONALLY ACCLAIMED AND HAS BEEN COPIED IN THE NETHERLANDS AT ARNHEM. AT CLOWES MEMORIAL HALL, 4600 SUNSET AVE. (ST-WIDE). FRANK COOPER, CHAIRMAN; BUTLER UNIV - JORDAN COLLEGE OF MUSIC; 4600 CLARENDON RD; INDIANAPOLIS, IN 46208. (#100308-1).

APR 23, '76. GIRL SCOUTS BICENTENNIAL CELEBRATION. FESTIVAL. (LOCAL). NORMA WILKENS, CHAIRMAN; HOOSIER CAPITAL GIRL SCOUT COUNCIL; 615 N ALABAMA; INDIANAPOLIS, IN 46204. (#27783-1).

APR 24, '76. SPIRIT OF '76. DISPLAYS WILL BE PREPARED BY INDIVIDUAL TROOPS FROM THEIR RESEARCH INTO AMERICAN HISTORY; A ONE HOUR MUSICAL WILL BE PRESENTED WITH 7,000 GIRLS; OPEN SQUARE DANCING WILL BE FEATURED. THIS IS A NON-PROFIT EVENT. AT MARKET SQUARE ARENA. (LOCAL). MRS GEORGE HAERLE, PR DIR; HOOSIER CAPITOL GIRL SCOUT COUNCIL; 615 N ALABAMA; INDIANAPOLIS, IN 46204. (#104334-8).

APR 26 - 27, '76. SYMPHONY ORCHESTRA & BALLET PERFORMANCE. THEME DEALS WITH LIFE OF ARTIST IN AMERICA TODAY AND HIS ALONENESS, WHICH IS NECESSARY FOR FREEDOM OF CREATION BY COMPOSER KAREL HUSA. OTHER PREMIERES ALSO OF BALLETS BY VITTORIO RIETI AND NIKOLAI LOPATNIKOFF. (ST-WIDE). DR LOUIS CHENETTE, DEAN; BUTLER UNIV-JORDON COLLEGE OF MUSIC; INDIANAPOLIS, IN 46208. (#104788-1).

MAY 1, '76. BICENTENNIAL POETS CORNER. COMPETITION AT PRAPYLAEUM. (LOCAL). MARY L CONNER, DIRECTOR; THE POETRY CORNER, INC; 3440 E KESSLER BLVD; INDIANAPOLIS, IN 46220. (#25799-1).

MAY 1, '76. WARREN TOWNSHIP FAIR. FAIR AT WASHINGTON SQUARE MALL. (LOCAL). J CLIFFORD GATES; BICENTENNIAL COMMUNITY OF WARREN TWP; 9500 E 16TH ST; INDIANAPOLIS, IN 46229. (#200017-68).

MAY 7, '76. FESTIVAL OF AMERICAN MUSIC. 5,000 STUDENTS FROM 5TH GRADE THROUGH HIGH SCHOOL WILL PARTICIPATE, PROGRAM DIVIDED INTO FOUR 50-YEAR TIME PERIODS; SELECTIONS WILL CONSIST OF MUSIC WRITTEN DURING THE PERIOD OR CURRENT COMPOSITIONS THAT REFLECT THE TIME; SCORE WILL BE TIED TOGETHER WITH NARRATION. AT MARKET SQUARE ARENA. (LOCAL). HARRY R MAMLIN, COORD; INDIANAPOLIS PUBLIC SCHOOLS; 120 E WALNUT ST; INDIANAPOLIS, IN 46204. (#26626-1).

MAY 8, '76. '200 AND AWAY WE GO'. FAIR AT CENTRAL STATE HOSPITAL. (LOCAL). LAMAR PETERSON, JR, COORD; CENTRAL STATE HOSPITAL; 3000 W WASHINGTON ST; INDIANAPOLIS, IN 46204. (#24717-1).

MAY 11, '76. PRESENTATION OF HISTORICAL MARKER PLAQUE. THE MILITARY ORDER OF THE WORLD WARS WILL PRESENT OFFICIAL MARKER. THE SCHOOL WAS BUILT AS A U S ARSENAL AND SERVED AS ONE FOR OVER 40 YEARS; 6 OF THE 9 ORIGINAL BLDGS DATE FROM 1862 AND HAVE BEEN ADAPTED FOR USE AS A SCHOOL; CEREMONY WILL EMPHASIZE THE HISTORY. AT GATE GUARD HOUSE, TECHNICAL HIGH SCHOOL. (LOCAL). JAMES SCHELLER, CHMN; MILITARY ORDER OF THE WORLD WARS; 7015 NORTH PENNSYLVANIA STREET; INDIANAPOLIS, IN 46220. (#104334-6).

MAY 29, '76. '500' FESTIVAL MEMORIAL PARADE. FESTIVAL, PARADE. (NAT'L). JOSEPHINE HAUCK, EXEC DIR; '500' FESTIVAL ASSOCIATES, INC; ONE INDIANA SQUARE-SUITE 2260; INDIANAPOLIS, IN 46204. (#105010-2).

MAY 29, '76. 74TH ARMY BAND-3D INFANTRY OLD GUARD-FLOAT '500' FESTIVAL PARADE. PARADE AT PARADE ROUTE-DOWNTOWN INDIANAPOLIS. (REGN'L). SALLY L SPRIGGS, INFO DIR; FORT BENJAMIN HARRISON-INDIANAPOLIS RECRUITING COMMAND; PUBLIC AFFAIRS OFFICE; FT BEN HARSN, IN 46216. (#200017-85).

MAY 30, '76. 500 MILE RACE (AUTO RACE - 60TH ANNUAL RENEWAL). COMPETITION, LIVE PERFORMANCE AT 16TH & GEORGETOWN RD. (NAT'L). JUNE SWANGO, SEC; INDIANAPOLIS MOTOR SPEEDWAY; INDIANAPOLIS, IN 46224. (#105010-1).

JUNE 11 - 20, '76. MUSICAL PRODUCTION. SHERMAN EDWARDS' AND PETER STONE'S FULL LENGTH MUSICAL PLAY BRINGS THE SIGNERS OF THE DECLARATION OF INDEPENDENCE TO THE STAGE FOR A HILARIOUS PORTRAYAL OF THE HOT WEEKS OF DEBATE THAT LED TO THE APPROVAL OF OUR COUNTRY'S HISTORIC DOCUMENT. AT SHOWALTER PAVILION, 1200 W 38 ST. (LOCAL). MS HARRIET GLAZIER, CHMN; BOOTH TARKINGTON CIVIC THEATRE; 1200 W 38TH ST; INDIANAPOLIS, IN 46208. (#100310-1).

JUNE 12, '76. BICENTENNIAL FIREMEN'S PARADE. PARADE ENTRIES WILL INCLUDE: ANTIQUE FIRE EQUIPMENT AND CARS, BANDS, FLOATS AND HORSE UNITS; TROPHIES WILL BE GIVEN FOR FIRST, SECOND AND THIRD PLACE IN EACH OF THE TEN CATEGORIES; THE GOVERNOR'S TROPHY WILL BE PRESENTED TO THE BEST BICENTENNIAL ENTRY. AT ALONG SHADELAND AVE FROM 21ST ST TO EASTGATE. (LOCAL). GENE BATTALY, CHMN; INDIANA VOLUNTEER FIREMEN'S ASSOC; PO BOX 19036; INDIANAPOLIS, IN 46219. (#104334-5).

JUNE 18 - 20, '76. NEIGHBORHOOD AMERICA BICENTENNIAL CELEBRATION. FESTIVITIES TO INCLUDE A PARADE AND FESTIVAL WITH BOOTHS & DISPLAYS FROM LOCAL GROUPS IN AN EFFORT TO CHANNEL INFO ABOUT COMMUNITY RESOURCES TO RESIDENTS. AT BROOKSIDE PARK, 3500 BROOKSIDE PKWY S. (LOCAL). JOANNE LINN; NEAR EAST SIDE COMMUNITY ORGANIZATION; 958 N BEVILLE AVE; INDIANAPOLIS, IN 46201. (#10854-1).

JUNE 21 - 24, '76. 1976 UNITED STATES JAYCEES ANNUAL MEETING. SEPARATE SHEETS FOR PUBLIC EVENTS WILL BE ISSUED; GENERAL CHAIRMAN, ROBERT H SPRINGER, JR; 6060 N COLLEGE, PO BOX 20395 (317)255-6673. AT INDIANA CONVENTION EXPOSITION CENTER. (NAT'L). JOHN W GUY, PAST PRES; INDIANAPOLIS JAYCEES; 6115 HAZELWOOD AVE; INDIANAPOLIS, IN 46208. (#104334-4).

JUNE 22 - AUG 17, '76. SUMMER OF '76 FILM SERIES. FILM TOPICS ARE: 'THE SECRET OF SURVIVAL' AND 'MAN AND NATURE'. RAIN DATES ARE WEDNESDAYS. AT EAGLE CREEK PARK. (LOCAL). KAREN BOWER, COORDINATOR; INDIANAPOLIS DEPT OF PARKS & RECREATION; 5901 DELONG RD; INDIANAPOLIS, IN 46254. (#25634-1).

JUNE 24, '76. THE PARADE OF STATES OF THE UNITED STATES JAYCEES. EACH STATE WILL MARCH IN A DISTINCTIVE, HISTORICALLY RELATED COSTUME. AT MERIDIAN & PENNSYLVANIA ST. (NAT'L). ART BROWN, LOCAL CHMN; THE UNITED STATES JAYCEES + INDIANAPOLIS JAYCEES; ONE INDIANA SQUARE; INDIANAPOLIS, IN 46204. (#104334-2).

JUNE 24, '76. 'UP, UP AND AWAY', JAYCEE NATIONAL CONVENTION SHOW. TWO BIG NAME ACTS WILL PERFORM. AT MARNET SQUARE ARENA. (NAT'L). JOHN GUY, PAST PRES; THE INDIANAPOLIS JAYCEES; ONE INDIANA SQUARE; INDIANAPOLIS, IN 46204. (#104334-3).

JULY 1, '76. 'PEARL OF THE ORIENT CULTURAL GALLERY' - EXHIBIT OPENING. PRESS RELEASE CEREMONY OF SPECIAL EXHIBITION OF PHILIPPINE ARTS AND CRAFTS BY SPECIAL INVITATION; ARRANGED BY THE MUSEUM. EXHIBITS TO REMAIN INDEFINITELY AT THE MUSEUM. AT INDIANAPOLIS MUSEUM OF ART. (LOCAL). JULIO VILLAMOR NASIS; PHILIPPINE AMERICAN NATIONAL ASSOC; 3514 PIXLEY CT; INDIANAPOLIS, IN 46236. (#25633-2).

JULY 1 - 31, '76. MUSEUM OF INDIAN HERITAGE PICTORAL PANORAMA. MURALS DEPICTING SCENES IN THE OLD NORTHWEST TERRITORY AND EVENTS FROM THE AMERICAN REVOLUTION TO THE WAR OF 1812 WILL BE DISPLAYED. (ST-WIDE). JAMES H LAWTON, COORD; MUSEUM OF INDIAN HERITAGE; 6040 DELONG RD; INDIANAPOLIS, IN 46254. (#25918-1).

JULY 1, '76 - CONTINUING . 'PEARL OF THE ORIENT CULTURAL GALLERY' - CONTINUING EXHIBIT. SPECIAL EXHIBITION OF PHILIPPINE ARTS AND CRAFTS, ARRANGED BY THE MUSEUM. EXHIBIT TO REMAIN INDEFINITELY AT THE MUSEUM. AT INDIANAPOLIS MUSEUM OF ART. (LOCAL). JULIO VILLAMOR NASIS; PHILIPPINE AMERICAN NATIONAL ASSOC; 3514 PIXLEY CT; INDIANAPOLIS, IN 46236. (#25633-3).

JULY 4, '76. DANCE: THE WINGS OF FREEDOM. FESTIVAL AT SPECIAL BOOTH ON MERIDIAN ST IN DOWNTOWN INDIANAPOLIS. (LOCAL). JULIO V NASIS, COORD; PHILIPPINE-AMERICAN NATIONAL ASSOC; 3514 PIXLEY COURT; INDIANAPOLIS, IN 46236. (#25633-1).

JULY 4, '76. HAPPY BIRTHDAY AMERICA. 8 HOURS OF CONTINUAL FREE ENTERTAINMENT IN DOWNTOWN INDIANAPOLIS, EMPHASIZING AMERICAN FOODS, DANCES, MUSIC; SOLICITING SUPPORT FROM ALL GROUPS IN THE CITY. AT AREA BOUNDED BY MERIDAN AND CITY LIBRARY. (LOCAL). JAMES WHITFIELD, CHMN; INDIANAPOLIS BICENTENNIAL COMMITTEE; 700 N PENNSYLVANIA ST; INDIANAPOLIS, IN 46204. (#104334-1).

JULY 23, '76. HAMPSHIRE COUNTY YOUTH ORCHESTRA. LIVE PERFORMANCE AT MONUMENT CIRCLE. (INT'L). CULTURAL AFFAIRS OFFICE; BRITISH EMBASSY; 3100 MASSACHUSETTS AVE, NW; WASHINGTON, DC 20008. (#108957-3).

JULY 31 - AUG 4, '76. CONFERENCE ON YOUTH NEEDS AND YOUTH EXHIBITION. CONFERENCE, EXHIBIT AT MARRIOTT INN, 7202 E 21ST ST. (REGN'L). STUART RADO, EXEC DIR; NATIONAL NETWORK OF YOUTH ADVISORY BOARD; PO BOX 402036, OCEAN VIEW BRANCH; MIAMI BEACH, FL 33140. (#1536-9).

AUG 6 - 8, '76. ANNUAL COMMUNITY FESTIVAL. FESTIVAL AT BROOKSIDE PARK. (LOCAL). SHARON L PUTNAM, COORD; THE NEAR EAST SIDE COMMUNITY ORGANIZATION, INC.; 2236 E 10TH ST; INDIANAPOLIS, IN 46201. (#26862-1).

AUG 19 - 29, '76. EXHIBIT ON NATIONAL PARK SERVICE AT INDIANA STATE FAIR. EXHIBIT. (REGN'L). INDIANA DUNES NL; NATIONAL PARK SERVICE; ROUTE 2 BOX 135 A; CHESTERTON, IN 46304. (#6728-249).

AUG 19 - 29, '76. INDIANA STATE FAIR. BICENTENNIAL FEATURE PROGRAM, AUG 19; GRANDSTAND WITH FREE ADMISSION. AT STATE FAIRGROUNDS. (REGN'L). ESTEL CALLAHAN, SEC-MGR; INDIANA STATE FAIR BOARD; INDIANAPOLIS, IN 46205. (#106095-54).

OCT 2 - NOV 21, '76. FLYING COLORS COLLECTION AIRCRAFT MODELS EXHIBIT. FOUR SIX-FOOT AIRCRAFT MODELS DESIGNED AND PAINTED BY ALEXANDER CALDER FOR BRANIFF INTERNA-

INDIANAPOLIS — CONTINUED

TIONAL AIRLINES. MUSEUM HOURS TUESDAY THROUGH SATURDAY 10 AM TO 5 PM; SUNDAY 1 TO 5 PM; CLOSED MONDAYS AND MAJOR HOLIDAYS. AT CORNER 30TH AND MERIDIAN, U S 31. (ST-WIDE). A G WOYTINEK; THE CHILDREN'S MUSEUM; 3000 N MERIDIAN ST; INDIANAPOLIS, IN 46208. (#107903-5).

OCT 2, '76 - JAN 2, '77. INDIANA COVERLETS OF THE 19TH CENTURY. EXHIBIT INCLUDES 60 COVERLETS SELECTED FROM THE MONTGOMERY COLLECTION REPRESENTING ALL 19TH CENTURY INDIANA WEAVERS; MUSEUM HOURS TUES THROUGH SATURDAY 10 AM TO 5 PM; SUNDAY 1 TO 5 PM; CLOSED MONDAYS AND MAJOR HOLIDAYS. AT CORNER 30TH AND MERIDIAN, U S 31. (ST-WIDE). A G WOYTINEK; THE CHILDREN'S MUSEUM; 3000 N MERIDIAN ST; INDIANAPOLIS, IN 46208. (#107903-4).

OCT 2, '76 - MAR 13, '77. AMERICAN FOLK ART OF THE 18TH, 19TH AND 20TH CENTURIES. EXHIBIT INCLUDES OVER 200 WORKS SELECTED FROM THE PRIVATE COLLECTION OF HERBERT WAIDE HEMPHILL, JR, RELATED TO THE SUBJECTS OF PATRIOTISM, RELIGION & BUSINESS. MUSEUM OPEN TUESDAY THROUGH SATURDAY 10 AM TO 5 PM; SUNDAY 1 TO 5 PM; CLOSED MONDAYS & MAJOR HOLIDAYS. AT CORNER 30TH AND MERIDIAN, U S 31. (ST-WIDE). A G WOYTINEK; THE CHILDREN'S MUSEUM; 3000 N MERIDIAN ST; INDIANAPOLIS, IN 46208. (#107903-6).

OCT 2, '76 - CONTINUING . GRAND OPENING OF THE CHILDREN'S MUSEUM. PUBLIC OPENING OF ENTIRELY NEW 215,000 SQUARE FOOT FACILITY, THE LARGEST CHILDREN'S MUSEUM IN THE WORLD. MUSEUM HOURS TUESDAY THRU SATURDAY 10:00AM TO 5:00PM, SUNDAY 1:00 TO 5:00PM. CLOSED MAJOR HOLIDAYS. AT CORNER 30TH & MERIDIAN STS (US 31). (REGN'L). PUBLIC RELATIONS DEPT; THE CHILDREN'S MUSEUM; 3000 N MERIDIAN ST; INDIANAPOLIS, IN 46208. (#107851-1).

OCT 4 - 10, '76. INTERNATIONAL BICENTENNIAL FESTIVAL WEEK. FESTIVAL AT AUDITORIUM. (ST-WIDE). JOSEPH BRIGANDI, CHAIRMAN; INTERNATIONAL CENTER OF INDIANAPOLIS, INC; 1050 W 42ND ST; INDIANAPOLIS, IN 46208. (#24280-1).

OCT 19 - 21, '76. UNITED STATES ARMED FORCES BICENTENNIAL CARAVAN. CARAVAN IS COMPOSED OF EXHIBIT VANS FOR EACH MILITARY SERVICE. PROJECT THEME IS 'HISTORY OF THE ARMED FORCES & THEIR CONTRIBUTIONS TO THE NATION'. (LOCAL). JOHN L KRAUSS; UNITED STATES ARMED FORCES BICENTENNIAL CARAVAN; 1842 CITY-COUNTY BLDG; INDIANAPOLIS, IN 46204. (#1775-735).

NOV 1 - 30, '76. 3-D DIORAMA OF INDIANS MEETING LASALLE. EXHIBIT AT MUSEUM OF INDIAN HERITAGE. (LOCAL). JAMES H LAWTON, COORD; MUSEUM OF INDIAN HERITAGE; 6040 DELONG RD; INDIANAPOLIS, IN 46254. (#24285-1).

DEC 10, '76 - CONTINUING . THE CONTINUING CONTRIBUTIONS OF ETHNIC MINORITIES TO U S. EXHIBIT AT NORTH CENTRAL HIGH SCHOOL. (ST-WIDE). JANET BELL, PROJ DIR; IND DEPT OF PUBLIC INSTRUCTION; 120 W MARKET ST; INDIANAPOLIS, IN 46204. (#26538-1).

FEB 18, '77 - MAR 20, '78. SPIRIT OF INNOVATION. EXHIBIT IS A CELEBRATION OF SCIENTIFIC CONTRIBUTIONS TO OUR NATION'S HISTORY; MUSEUM HOURS TUESDAY THROUGH SATURDAY 10 AM TO 5 PM; INFORMATION ON STOPS IN SPECIFIC AREAS, CONTACT THE NEAREST AMERICAN RED BALL (ARB) AGENT. AT CORNER 30TH AND MERIDIAN, U S 31. (REGN'L). A G WOYTINEK; THE CHILDREN'S MUSEUM; 3000 N MERIDIAN ST; INDIANAPOLIS, IN 46208. (#107903-2).

APR 16 - MAY 28, '77. AUSTRALIA EXHIBIT. MUSEUM HOURS TUESDAY THROUGH SATURDAY 10 AM TO 5 PM; SUNDAY 1 TO 5 PM; CLOSED MONDAYS AND MAJOR HOLIDAYS. AT CORNER 30TH AND MERIDIAN, U S 31. (INT'L). JOHN MAUNDER, DIRECTOR; AUSTRALIAN CONSULATE GENERAL; 636 5TH AVE; NEW YORK, NY 10020. (#108143-3).

JAN 7 - FEB 12, '78. EXHIBITION OF YUGOSLAV NAIVE ART - SITES. EXHIBIT ILLUSTRATES CURRENT DIRECTIONS & EVOLUTION OF NAIVE YUGOSLAV ART. INCLUDES ART BY VECENAJ, RABUZIN, SKURJENI, KOVACIC & LACKOVIC. WOOD SCULPTURES, PAINTINGS; MAPS, FILMS; TAPES ON TRADITIONAL YUGOSLAV FOLK MUSIC. HOURS ON SUNDAY ARE 1-5PM. AT CORNER 30TH & MERIDIAN (U S 31) STS. (ST-WIDE). PUBLIC RELATIONS DEPT; THE CHILDREN'S MUSEUM; 30TH & MERIDIAN; INDIANAPOLIS, IN 46208. (#106778-1).

JAMESTOWN

THEATRE PROJECT: JAMESTOWN, IN. SEVERAL ACTS AND PARTICIPANTS ON OUTDOOR STAGE FEATURING OLD-TIME MEDICINE MAN. (LOCAL). M L HILA, CHAIRMAN; JAMESTOWN BICENTENNIAL COMMITTEE; JAMESTOWN, IN 46147. (#31002).

JASONVILLE

SEPT 25, '76. HIGH SCHOOL HOMECOMING AND BICENTENNIAL PARADE. MILITARY UNITS, NATIONAL GUARD, JET FLYING OVER, HIGH SCHOOL BAND HELPED CELEBRATE THIS EVENT. AT EAST TO WEST MAIN ST PARADE ROUTE. (LOCAL). FRANK W HASTINGS, CHMN; JHS-SHS ALUMNI ASSOCIATION AND JASONVILLE BICENTENNIAL COMMITTEE; RR 2, BOX 219 D; JASONVILLE, IN 47438. (#200017-91).

JASPER

'WELCOME WORLD TO COLONIAL AMERICA' - JASPER, IN. A DRAMA PORTRAYING THE REVOLUTIONARY WAR ERA; PERFORMED BY INDIANA UNIVERSITY ACTORS. (LOCAL). JACK RUMBACK, CHAIRMAN; DUBOIS COUNTY BICENTENNIAL COMMITTEE; PO BOX 1776; JASPER, IN 47546. (#27209). **ARBA GRANTEE.**

APR 5 - 8, '76. 'WELCOME WORLD TO COLONIAL AMERICA' - REVOLUTIONARY WAR DRAMA. BEN FRANKLIN & 3 OTHER COLONIALS VISITED CLUBS, ORGANIZATIONS AND SCHOOLS; CLIMAX WAS DINNER APRIL 8 FEATURING COLONIAL FOODS AND COLONIAL MUSIC, WITH FRANKLIN, CHARLES CARROLL, MARY WASHINGTON, AND PIERRE TOUSSAINT. AT COLONIAL BANQUET: HERITAGE INN, US 231 N. (LOCAL). JACK RUMBACK, CHAIRMAN; DUBOIS COUNTY BICENTENNIAL COMMITTEE; PO BOX 1776; JASPER, IN 47546. (#27209-1).

KENDALLVILLE

JULY 4, '75. KENDALLVILLE BICENTENNIAL 4TH OF JULY. FESTIVAL. (LOCAL). FRED A MANAHAN; KENDALLVILLE BICENTENNIAL COMMISSION; PO BOX 1776; KENDALLVILLE, IN 46755. (#7928-1).

JUNE 27 - JULY 4, '76. KENDALLVILLE BICENTENNIAL WEEK-LONG CELEBRATION. EXHIBIT, FESTIVAL, PARADE AT NOBLE COUNTY FAIR GROUNDS ON NORTH SIDE OF KENDALLVILLE. (LOCAL). JOHN B HUTCHINS, CHAIRMAN; KENDALLVILLE ROTARY CLUB; 103 W DIAMOND ST; KENDALLVILLE, IN 46755. (#103835-1).

KNIGHTSTOWN

KNIGHTSTOWN RESTORATION PROJECT, IN. RESTORATION & BEAUTIFICATION OF THE AREA OF TOWN KNOWN AS PUBLIC SQUARE. (LOCAL). KENNETH FERGUSON, CHAIRMAN; KNIGHTSTOWN BICENTENNIAL COMMITTEE; 236 N JEFFERSON; KNIGHTSTOWN, IN 46148. (#25240). **ARBA GRANTEE.**

KOKOMO

BICENTENNIAL PARK, KOKOMO, IN. DEVELOPMENT OF NEW TOWNSHIP PARK W/FACILITIES FOR PICNICS, SPORTING EVENTS, FISHING, HOCKEY & AN AREA FOR THE STUDY OF NATURE BY GROUPS & SCHOOLS. (LOCAL). DR RONALD P ANJARD, CHAIRMAN; CLAY TOWNSHIP BICENTENNIAL COMMITTEE; 906 BELLEVUE PL; KOKOMO, IN 46901. (#28636).

HISTORICAL MARKERS - KOKOMO, IN. 12 HISTORICAL MARKERS FOR HISTORICAL SITES FOR FUTURE GENERATIONS WILL BE PLACED IN KOKOMO. (LOCAL). RAY BAKEHORN, CHAIRMAN; MIAMI COUNTY BICENTENNIAL COMMITTEE; RR #3; KOKOMO, IN 46901. (#26930). **ARBA GRANTEE.**

KOKOMO TRIBUNE SPECIAL BICENTENNIAL EDITION -NBMRP. A GIANT SPECIAL (BOUND) EDITION OF 128 PAGES ON JULY 4, 1976, COVERING HISTORY OF COUNTY, STATE & NATION. (LOCAL). GLEN BANNER, BICENTENNIAL COORDINATOR; THE KOKOMO TRIBUNE; 300 N UNION ST; KOKOMO, IN 46901. (#30426).

PATHS OF PROGRESS - KOKOMO, IN. CONSTRUCTION OF A SMALL MONUMENT, ROCK GARDEN & FLOWER GARDEN ON THE EAST PARK AREA OF WILDCAT CREEK RESERVOIR. (LOCAL). SARA VIVEIROS, COORDINATOR; HOWARD COUNTY BICENTENNIAL COMMITTEE; HOWARD CO COURTHOUSE, ROOM 200; KOKOMO, IN 46901. (#26616). **ARBA GRANTEE.**

APR 2 - 3, '76. EARLY AMERICAN JAZZ FESTIVAL (QUEEN CITY & ROSIE O'GRADY JAZZ BANDS). FESTIVAL, LIVE PERFORMANCE AT USW HALL & HAY, HAYWORTH AUDITORIUM. (LOCAL). JAMES B SWARTZ, COORD; CREATIVE ARTS COUNCIL, INC; 1719 W ZARTMAN RD; KOKOMO, IN 46901. (#200017-12).

KOONTZ LAKE

HISTORICAL MARKER - KOONTZ LAKE, IN. A HISTORICAL MARKER WILL BE PLACED AT THE SITE OF THE GRAIN MILL. (LOCAL). ALLEN Q SEAHOLM, DIRECTOR; GREATER WALKERTON AREA BICENTENNIAL COMMITTEE; WALKERTON, IN 46574. (#22943). **ARBA GRANTEE.**

KOUTS

MAY 21, '76. ARTS & CRAFTS FESTIVAL. FESTIVAL, EXHIBIT AT SCHOOL BUILDING & STREETS. (LOCAL). JIM ROSE, CHAIRMAN; PLEASANT TOWNSHIP BICENTENNIAL COMMITTEE; BOX 348, COLLEGE AVE; KOUTS, IN 46347. (#200017-78).

SEPT 4 - 6, '76. THREE DAY LABOR PROGRAM WITH TIME CAPSULE & VETERAN'S DAY PROGRAM. CEREMONY, PARADE, FESTIVAL AT IN THE TOWNSHIP & AT THE CEMETERY. (LOCAL). JIM ROSE, CHAIRMAN; PLEASANT TOWNSHIP BICENTENNIAL COMMITTEE; BOX 348, COLLEGE AVE; KOUTS, IN 46347. (#200017-76).

LA PORTE

MARKING HISTORICAL SITES - LA PORTE, IN. IDENTIFING AN MARKING, WITH METALIC PLAQUES, TWENTY HISTORICAL SITES IN THE COMMUNITY. (LOCAL). JOHN C HARGRAVE, CHAIRMAN; LAPORTE AMERICAN REVOLUTION BICENTENNIAL COMMITTEE; 1200 MICHIGAN AVE; LA PORTE, IN 46350. (#29824).

SCULPTURE PROJ - LA PORTE, IN. RAISED FUNDS BY PUBLIC SUBSCRIPTION. COMMISSIONED ARTIST TO CREATE A HISTORICAL SCULPTURE FOR ERECTION IN PUBLIC PLAZA. STATUE OF POTAWATOMI INDIAN. (LOCAL). JOHN C HARGRAVE, CHAIRMAN; LA PORTE AMERICAN REVOLUTION BICENTENIAL COMMITTEE; 1200 MICHIGAN AVE; LA PORTE, IN 46350. (#29826).

SPACE CAPSULE - LA PORTE, IN. FABRICATING AND PLACING A SPACE CAPSULE IN INDEPENDENCE PLAZA. TO BE OPENED IN THE YEAR 2076. (LOCAL). KENDALL I VAIL, PRESIDENT; LAPORTE KIWANIS CLUB; 1412 SPRUCE ST; LA PORTE, IN 46350. (#29825).

APR 18, '75. REENACTMENT-PAUL REVERE'S RIDE. 'PAUL REVERE' VISITED ALL GRADE SCHOOLS IN THE COMMUNITY; CALLING ALL PATRIOTS TO ARMS; TWO LIGHTED LANTERNS DISPLAYED FROM BELL TOWER IN COUNTY COURT HOUSE. AT LA PORTE COMMUNITY GRADE SCHOOLS. (LOCAL). JOHN C HARGRAVE; LA PORTE AMERICAN REVOLUTION BICENTENNIAL COMMITTEE; 1200 MICHIGAN AVE; LA PORTE, IN 46350. (#200017-81).

APR 20, '75. BICENTENNIAL CELEBRATION KICK-OFF. MUSIC, FOLK DANCING, ETC. PARTICIPANTS WERE: LA PORTE HIGH SCHOOL ORCHESTRA, SWEET ADELINE CHORUS, HIGH SCHOOL A CAPELLA CHOIR, LA PORTE CHANTEURS CHORUS, THE WEINSTOCK DANCERS AND THE DRUM & BUGLE CORP. AT CIVIC AUDITORIUM. (LOCAL). JOHN C HARGRAVE; LAPORTE AMERICAN REVOLUTION BICENTENNIAL COMMITTEE; 1200 MICHIGAN AVE; LA PORTE, IN 46350. (#200017-82).

JULY 3, '76. PRESENTATION OF HISTORICAL SCULPTURE. PRESENTATION BY ARTIST TO LA PORTE ARBC & OFFICIAL WELCOME TO VISITORS FROM GRANGEMOUTH, SCOTLAND (30 GUESTS) LA PORT'S SISTER CITY. AT STEPS OF CITY HALL. (LOCAL). JOHN C HARGRAVE, CHMN; LA PORTE AMERICAN REVOLUTION BICENTENNIAL COMMITTEE; 1200 MICHIGAN AVE; LA PORTE, IN 46350. (#200017-80).

AUG 5 - 10, '76. SENIOR CITIZEN FAIR BOOTH. EXHIBIT AT LAPORTE COUNTY FAIR GROUNDS, STATE RD 2. (LOCAL). MRS J CYRUS LLOYD; COMMUNITY ENDEAVOR FOR SENIOR CITIZENS OF SE LAPORTE COUNTY; 9908 S 300 WEST; LAPORTE, IN 46382. (#200017-69).

LAFAYETTE

ORAL HIST OF BLACKS IN MID-NORTH CENTRAL INDIANA. LOCAL ORAL HISTORY CONFERENCES WILL BE HELD THROUGHOUT THIS PART OF INDIANA FROM SEPT - NOV 1976. (LOCAL). SAMUEL A HAY, PROJ COORDINATOR; PURDUE UNIV; LAFAYETTE, IN 47907. (#23541). **ARBA GRANTEE.**

MAY 29 - JUNE 6, '76. BICENTENNIAL VOYAGE. 9 DAY TRIP BY GROUP OF MEN & HIGH SCHOOL BOYS FROM FT WAYNE TO VINCENNES IN A FIBERGLASS REPLICA OF NORTH CANGE. GROUP WORE 18TH CENTURY CLOTHING & ATE 18TH CENTURY FOODS THEN PERFORMED AT 3 FRENCH COMMUNITIES: TERRE HAUTE, ATTICA & MIAMIS. AT LAFAYETTE. (ST-WIDE). JOHN M HARRIS, COORD; OUIATENON BRIGADE; 909 SOUTH ST; LAFAYETTE, IN 47901. (#27000-1).

JULY 25, '76. HAMPSHIRE COUNTY YOUTH ORCHESTRA. LIVE PERFORMANCE AT PURDUE UNIVERSITY. (INT'L). CULTURAL AFFAIRS OFFICE; BRITISH EMBASSY; 3100 MASSACHUSETTS AVE, NW; WASHINGTON, DC 20008. (#108957-4).

OCT 15 - 16, '76. UNITED STATES ARMED FORCES BICENTENNIAL CARAVAN. CARAVAN IS COMPOSED OF EXHIBIT VANS FOR EACH MILITARY SERVICE. PROJECT THEME IS 'HISTORY OF THE ARMED FORCES & THEIR CONTRIBUTIONS TO THE NATION'. (LOCAL). ALBERT P STEWART; UNITED STATES ARMED FORCES BICENTENNIAL CARAVAN; 336 MAIN ST, BOX 1776; LAFAYETTE, IN 47901. (#1775-733).

LAKEVILLE

LAKEVILLE BEAUTIFICATION PROJECT, IN. LANDSCAPING AND PLANTING OF TREES, FLOWERS & SHRUBS THROUGHOUT THE TOWN, PROJECTING TO A SPRING FESTIVAL IN FUTURE YEARS. (LOCAL). MRS BEVERLY A STANLEY, CHAIRMAN; TOWN BOARD OF LAKEVILLE BICENTENNIAL COMMITTEE; 301 N MICHIGAN ST; LAKEVILLE, IN 46536. (#31625).

MAY 11 - 12, '76. WAGON TRAIN ENCAMPMENT. CEREMONY, PARADE AT LAKEVILLE ELEMENTARY SCHOOL. (LOCAL). MRS BEVERLY STANLEY, CHMN; LAKEVILLE POLICE DEPT; 301 N MICH ST; LAKEVILLE, IN 46536. (#200017-105).

LAWRENCE

JUNE 11 - 12, '76. FT HARRISON-LAWRENCE, IN JOINT ACTIVITY - BICENTENNIAL WEEKEND. CEREMONY, EXHIBIT, COMPETITION AT LAWRENCE CENTRAL HIGH SCHOOL. (LOCAL). SALLY L SPRIGGS, INFO DIR; LAWRENCE-FORT BENJAMIN HARRISON; PUBLIC AFFAIRS OFFICE; FT BEN HARSN, IN 46216. (#200017-84).

LEBANON

JULY 4TH EDITION OF THE LEBANON REPORTER - NBMRP. JULY 4TH, 1976, EDITION WAS LARGEST IN PAPER'S HISTORY, GIVING AN HISTORICAL ACCOUNT OF THE AREA & INFO ON AREA'S FUTURE & GROWTH. ALSO SPONSORED A BICENTENNIAL POETRY & ESSAY CONTEST. (LOCAL). JAMES MOSSMAN, GENERAL MANAGER; THE LEBANON REPORTER; 117 E WASHINGTON ST; LEBANON, IN 46052. (#30431).

JULY 3, '76. BICENTENNIAL BALL & COSTUME DANCE. WEAR YOUR COSTUME TO THE GRAND BALL AT THE BOONE COUNTY COURTHOUSE. AT BOONE COUNTY COURTHOUSE. (LOCAL). MRS JOE GAROFFOLO, CHMN; PSI IOTA XI SORORITY; LEBANON, ZIONSVILLE AND THORNTOWN CHAPTERS; 216 N WEST ST; LEBANON, IN 46052. (#100334-1).

OCT 18, '76. UNITED STATES ARMED FORCES BICENTENNIAL CARAVAN. CARAVAN IS COMPOSED OF EXHIBIT VANS FOR EACH MILITARY SERVICE. PROJECT THEME IS 'HISTORY OF THE ARMED FORCES & THEIR CONTRIBUTIONS TO THE NATION'.

LEBANON — CONTINUED

(LOCAL). JAMES V MASON; UNITED STATES ARMED FORCES BICENTENNIAL CARAVAN; PO BOX 70; LEBANON, IN 46052. (#1775-734).

LEWISVILLE

RESTORATION OF GUYER OPERA HOUSE, LEWISVILLE, IN. THE OLD OPERA HOUSE WILL BE RESTORED AND USED FOR PLAYS & OTHER COMMUNITY AFFAIRS. (LOCAL). T SAUNDERS, PROJ DIRECTOR; RAINTREE OPERA HOUSE GUILD; LEWISVILLE, IN 47352. (#22944).

JUNE 6 - 12, '76. LEWISVILLE FAIR. EXHIBIT, FAIR, FESTIVAL AT LEWISVILLE PARK. (LOCAL). JUNE WILLIAMSON, COORD; LEWISVILLE LIONS CLUB, FIRE DEPT & BICENTENNIAL COMMITTEE; LEWISVILLE, IN 47352. (#106255-1).

LINCOLN CITY

APR 15 - OCT 30, '75. DEMONSTRATIONS OF FARMING DEVELOPMENTS--LINCOLN BOYHOOD NMEM. LIVE PERFORMANCE. (REGN'L). SUPERINTENDENT; NATIONAL PARK SERVICE; LINCOLN BOYHOOD NATL MEMORIAL; LINCOLN CITY, IN 47552. (#6727-64).

JULY 24, '75. NATL PK SVC '...A LITTLE LOOK AROUND' VISITS LINCOLN BOYHOOD MEM. THIS SHORT PROGRAM FEATURES ACTORS PORTRAYING FAMOUS AMERICANS OF THE PAST WHO'VE RETURNED TO SEE AMERICA'S GROWTH. (REGN'L). SUPERINTENDENT; NATIONAL PARK SERVICE - LINCOLN BOYHOOD NATIONAL MEMORIAL; LINCOLN CITY, IN 47552. (#5653-217).

FEB 15 - 28, '76. ARTISTS-IN-THE-PARKS PAINT THE BICENTENNIAL EXHIBIT. ORIGINAL ART EXHIBIT DEPICTING REVOLUTIONARY WAR; RELATED NATIONAL PARK SERVICE SITES IN VARIOUS MEDIUMS. AT MEMORIAL VISITOR CENTER. (REGN'L). LINCOLN BOYHOOD NM; NATIONAL PARK SERVICE; LINCOLN CITY, IN 47552. (#1474-6).

MAY 7, '76. COMPLETE SALUTE TO THE BICENTENNIAL-CONCERT. CELEBRATED MARCHING PATRIOTS BAND COMPOSED OF SYMPHONIC BAND (GRADES 10-12) AND CONCERT BAND (FRESHMAN); WILL ALSO TAKE PART IN CHERRY BLOSSOM FESTIVAL IN WASH, DC IN APRIL AND PARADES IN FERDINAND, IN, JULY 2, IN ROCKPORT, IN-JULY 10; BOTH AT 1:00 PM. AT AUDITORIUM OF HERITAGE HILLS HIGH SCHOOL. (LOCAL). CHARLES MALLORY, COORD; HERITAGE HIGH SCHOOL MUSIC DEPARTMENT; MARIAH HILL RD; DALE, IN 47523. (#106025-1).

MAY 30 - SEPT 30, '76. DEMONSTRATIONS OF FARMING DEVELOPMENTS--LINCOLN BOYHOOD NMEM. EXHIBIT, LIVE PERFORMANCE. (REGN'L). LINCOLN BOYHOOD NATL MEM; NATIONAL PARK SERVICE; LINCOLN CITY, IN 47552. (#6727-564).

JULY 7, '76. NATL PK SVC '...A LITTLE LOOK AROUND' COMES TO LINCOLN BOYHOOD NMEM. THIS SHORT PROGRAM FEATURES ACTORS PLAYING THE PARTS OF FAMOUS AMERICANS OF THE PAST WHO'VE RETURNED TO SEE AMERICA'S GROWTH. AT AT THE PARK'S VISITOR CENTER. (REGN'L). LINCOLN BOYHOOD NMEM; NAATIONAL PARK SERVICE; LINCOLN CITY, IN 47552. (#5653-13).

LINCOLN ST PK

APR 30 - MAY 2, '76. ALL-COUNCIL CELEBRATION OF RAINTREE GIRL SCOUTS. 7500 GIRL SCOUTS OF EVANSVILLE AREA TO GATHER AT STATE PARK FOR 3 DAY BICENTENNIAL CELEBRATION. AT LINCOLN STATE PARK INDIANA. (LOCAL). MARLYN TREBERG; RAINTREE GIRL SCOUT COUNCIL OF EVANSVILLE IN; 2050 ADAMS AV; EVANSVILLE, IN 47714. (#50387-1).

LINTON

BICENTENNIAL MUSIC & DANCE PROGRAM - LINTON, IN. THE ALPHA CHAPTER TRIAD WILL PRESENT A BICENTENNIAL MUSIC AND DANCE PROGRAM. (LOCAL). MRS RICHARD JERRELS, CHAIRMAN; ALPHA CHAPTER TRIAD; LINTON, IN 47441. (#27891). **ARBA GRANTEE.**

LOGANSPORT

CASS COUNTY LOG CABIN RENOVATION - LOGANSPORT, IN. THE LOG CABIN WILL BE MOVED TO THE PARK AND RESTORED. (LOCAL). KEN BENNETT, COORDINATOR; CASS COUNTY PARKS & RECREATION DEPT; PO BOX 1976; LOGANSPORT, IN 46947. (#27246). **ARBA GRANTEE.**

CASS COUNTY ORAL HISTORY PROJECT, LOGANSPORT, IN. AN ORAL HISTORY PROJECT TO BE PRESENTED ON RADIO BY CASS COUNTY SENIOR CITIZENS. (LOCAL). KATHLEEN WILLIAMS, COORDINATOR; SENIOR CITIZENS INFORMATION PROGRAM; PO BOX 1776; LOGANSPORT, IN 46974. (#26856). **ARBA GRANTEE.**

JUNE 25 - 27, '76. YESTERYEAR FAIR, PIONEER CRAFTS. CRAFTSMEN ARE BUSY SPINNING POTS OR YARN, WEAVING, QUILTING, DIPPING CANDLES AND BREWING UP SOME OLD-FASHIONED SOAP CAKES IN THEIR BILLOWY PIONEER ATTIRE; APPLE BUTTER SIMMERS OVER A FIRE, WHILE MUZZLE LOADERS COMPETE, HOOSIER ARTISTS DISPLAY CONTEMPORARY WORKS. AT CASS COUNTY HISTORICAL SOCIETY MUSEUM GROUNDS, 10TH AND MARKET ST. (ST-WIDE). JULIAN L RIDLEN, PROJ DIR; CASS COUNTY BICENT COMMITTEE; 417 NORTH ST; LOGANSPORT, IN 46947. (#100306-1).

LONG BEACH

HISTORICAL SKETCH BOOK OF MICHIGAN CITY, INDIANA. BRIEF CHAPTERS ON HISTORICAL HOMES, EVENTS AND PERSONALITIES OF THE LONG BEACH AND MICHIGAN CITY AREA. (LOCAL). R S KUNKEL, CHAIRMAN; TOWN OF LONG BEACH; TOWN HALL; MICHIGAN CITY, IN 46360. (#5840). **(??).**

LOWELL

'THE BEGINNINGS'-HISTORY OF CEDAR CREEK TWP, IN. A HISTORY OF THE LOWELL, IN, AREA, RESEARCHED & COMPILED BY CHRISTINE ANGLIS. (LOCAL). EDWARD ROSS CANFIELD, TRUSTEE; CEDAR CREEK TOWNSHIP BICENTENNIAL COMMITTEE; 725 E COMMERCIAL AVE; LOWELL, IN 46356. (#33510).

HERITAGE ASSOCIATION & MUSEUM, LOWELL, IN. A HISTORICAL ASSOCIATION HAS BEEN FORMED TO PRESERVE AND RESTORE THE HERITAGE OF THREE CREEK TOWNSHIP; MAJOR EMPHASIS WILL BE ON LOCAL HERITAGE MUSEUM. (LOCAL). ROBERT L HEIN, CHAIRPERSON; THREE CREEK HISTORICAL ASSOC; 427 E COMMERICAL AVE; LOWELL, IN 46356. (#19147).

OCT 14, '76. UNITED STATES ARMED FORCES BICENTENNIAL CARAVAN. CARAVAN IS COMPOSED OF EXHIBIT VANS FOR EACH MILITARY SERVICE. PROJECT THEME IS 'HISTORY OF THE ARMED FORCES & THEIR CONTRIBUTIONS TO THE NATION'. (LOCAL). ROBERT L HEIN; UNITED STATES ARMED FORCES BICENTENNIAL CARAVAN; 427 E COMMERCIAL AVE; LOWELL, IN 46356. (#1775-732).

LYONS

MINI-MALL, LYONS, IN. SMALL OUTDOOR AREA FOR FRIENDS AND NEIGHBORS TO GATHER AND TALK; LOCATED IN CENTER OF TOWN BETWEEN BANK AND DRUGSTORE; CONSISTS OF SHRUBS, TREES, BENCHES AND WINDING PATHWAYS. (LOCAL). GORDON GROUNDS, CO-CHAIRMAN; LYONS BICENTENNIAL COMMITTEE; LYONS, IN 47443. (#22939). **ARBA GRANTEE.**

MADISON

ESTABLISHMENT OF A REVOLVING FUND IN MADISON, IN. GRANT WILL BE MATCHED & USED BY HISTORIC MADISON INC TO STOP DESTRUCTION OF ENDANGERED STRUCTURES WITHIN ITS HISTORIC DISTRICT. REVOLVING FUND PURCHASES WILL THEN BE RESOLD WITH DEED RESTRICTIONS. (ST-WIDE). THOMAS MORIARITY, DIRECTOR; HISTORIC MADISON, INC; 301 W FIRST ST; MADISON, IN 47250. (#7879). **(??).**

MUSICAL HORIZONS '76 - MADISON, IN. A SERIES OF MUSICAL PERFORMANCES DURING THE BICENTENNIAL YEAR. (LOCAL). CLIFFORD TAYLOR, CHAIRMAN; MADISON SCHOOLS, MADISON-OHIO VALLEY ARTS COUNCIL; 743 CLIFFTY DR; MADISON, IN 47250. (#24282). **ARBA GRANTEE.**

MAY 23 - 26, '75. SPRING FESTIVAL - ANTIQUES, ARTS & CRAFTS. EXHIBITOR FEE -$5.00 DAILY; FARMERS MARKET; HOME BAKED FOOD; HISTORI C HOMES. AT AROUND JEFF COUNTY COURT HOUSE AREA & RIVER FRONT, MAIN & JEFFERSON. (LOCAL). HELEN COURLEY; HISTORIC HOOSIER HILLS GUILD OF COLLECTORS & CRAFTSMEN; 2242 CRAGMONT ST; MADISON, IN 47250. (#50040-1).

JULY 5 - 6, '75. MADISON REGATTA. COMPETITION, FESTIVAL. (LOCAL). A NEIL YORK; MADISON REGATTA; 201 E VAUGHAN; MADISON, IN 47250. (#10383-1).

SEPT 26 - 28, '75. ANTIQUES, ARTS & CRAFTS FALL FESTIVAL. FESTIVAL AT AROUND JEFFERSON CO COURTHOUSE, MAIN ST DOWN TO RIVER FRONT. (LOCAL). HELEN GOURLEY, PROJ CHMN; HISTORIC HOOSIER HILLS GUILD OF COLLECTORS & CRAFTSMEN; 2242 CRAGMONT; MADISON, IN 47250. (#100625-1).

MAY 28 - 31, '76. 8TH ANNUAL HANDCRAFT & ANTIQUE FESTIVAL. MADISON HAS 130 BLOCKS OF HISTORICAL ARCHITECTURE REGISTERED ON NATIONAL REGISTER OF HISTORIC PLACES. WILL INCLUDE HOME-BAKED FOOD & FISHFRY. AT COURT HOUSE AREA TO RIVERFRONT. (ST-WIDE). HELEN COURLEY; HISTORIC HOOSIER HILLS GUILD; 2242 CRAGMONT; MADISON, IN 47250. (#103277-1).

JULY 2 - 5, '76. MADISON REGATTA. THERE WILL BE A REGATTA, PARADE, HYDROPLANE RACING, BEAUTY PAGEANT, FIREWORKS, GOVERNOR'S BALL & AIR SHOW. GOVERNOR'S CUP HYDROPLANE RACE PARADE JULY 2ND. AIR SHOW ON JULY 3-4 BETWEEN RACES. AT VAUGHN DRIVE ON RIVERFRONT. (LOCAL). MADISON REGATTA, INC; BOX 341; MADISON, IN 47250. (#105093-1).

SEPT 24 - 26, '76. HISTORIC HOOSIER HILLS GUILD 9TH ANNUAL FALL FESTIVAL. HOME BAKED FOODS, FIREMEN'S FISH FRY, CRAFTSMEN & ANTIQUE DEALERS, HOUSE TOURS, ART DISPLAY & SALE. AT COURTHOUSE AREA TO RIVER FRONT. (LOCAL). HELEN GOURLEY, CHAIRMAN; HISTORIC HOOSIER HILLS GUILD; 2242 CRAGMONT; MADISON, IN 47250. (#106553-1).

OCT 27, '76. UNITED STATES ARMED FORCES BICENTENNIAL CARAVAN. CARAVAN IS COMPOSED OF EXHIBIT VANS FOR EACH MILITARY SERVICE. PROJECT THEME IS 'HISTORY OF THE ARMED FORCES & THEIR CONTRIBUTIONS TO THE NATION'. AT JAYCEE PARK AREA ON RIVER FRONT. (LOCAL). MRS HELEN GOURLEY; UNITED STATES ARMED FORCES BICENTENNIAL CARAVAN; 2242 GRAGMONT ST; MADISON, IN 47250. (#1775-738).

MARIAH HILL

AUG 8, '76. HOMECOMING CELEBRATION. BICENTENNIAL THEME FOR HOMECOMING WITH EXHIBITS FEATURING HANDMADE QUILTS, GAMES, RAFFLE, CHICKEN DINNER AND TURTLE SOUP. AT PICNIC GROUNDS. (LOCAL). MRS HAROLD PUND, CHMN; MARIAH HILL FOUNDATION; MARIAH HILL, IN 47556. (#104718-1).

MARION

BICENTENNIAL PAGEANT - MARION, IN. GRANT COUNTY BICENTENNIAL COMMITTEE WILL SPONSOR A BICENTENNIAL PAGEANT. (LOCAL). BERTHA O'DELL, COORDINATOR; GRANT COUNTY BICENTENNIAL COMMITTEE; 405 E BRADFORD ST; MARION, IN 46952. (#26786). **ARBA GRANTEE.**

BLACK HISTORY WEEK - MARION, IN. A BLACK HISTORY WEEK TO INCLUDE CEREMONIES, FESTIVALS & EXHIBITS. (LOCAL). ALVIN R SMITH, DIRECTOR; MARION URBAN LEAGUE; 1221 W 12TH ST; MARION, IN 46952. (#24281). **ARBA GRANTEE.**

JULY 3, '76. HISTORICAL EXHIBITIONS WITHIN BICENTENNIAL FESTIVAL. FESTIVAL, EXHIBIT AT MARION URBAN LEAGUE CENTER. (LOCAL). ALVIN R SMITH, DIRECTOR; MARION URBAN LEAGUE; 1221 W 12TH ST; MARION, IN 46952. (#24282-1).

JULY 4, '76. TRIBUTE TO AMERICAN REVOLUTIONARY WAR SOLDIERS. BRONZE MARKERS WILL BE PLACE ON GRAVES OF TWO REVOLUTIONARY WAR SOLDIERS. AT MAPLE GROVE CEMETERY - 1/2 MI NORTH SWEETSER. (LOCAL). MRS LLOYD C COOK, PRES; SWEETSER BICENTENNIAL ORGANIZATION; 2648 N 500 W; MARION, IN 46952. (#105440-1).

MARTINSVILLE

RESTORATION OF THE CROSS SCHOOL, MARTINSVILLE, IN. RESTORATION OF ONE ROOM BRICK SCHOOL BUILT 1854. (LOCAL). HOMER TERRELL, COORDINATOR; RETIRED TEACHERS ASSOCIATION; 49 JUDY DR; MARTINSVILLE, IN 46151. (#27366). **ARBA GRANTEE.**

JULY 4, '76. NATIONAL BICENTENNIAL ACA CAMPFIRE. SIMULTANEOUS LIGHTING OF CAMPFIRES IN ALL YOUTH CAMPS IN USA ON JULY 4TH, 1976. (NAT'L). ARMAND BALL, EXEC V PRES; AMERICAN CAMPING ASSOCIATION; BRADFORD WOODS; MARTINSVILLE, IN 46151. (#105902-1).

MATTHEWS

JULY 4, '76. COMMUNITY PARK DEDICATION, HAPPY BIRTHDAY AMERICA PARTY. ALL DAY COMMUNITY PARTY, PICNIC, AWARDS, MAN'S BEARD CONTEST, LADIES GARTERS, ADULT AND CHILDRENS GAMES AND CONTESTS AND OLD TIME MOVIES. AT MINNESOTA AVE, FREE PARKING. (LOCAL). PEGGY GARDNER, CHMN; MATTHEWS BICENTENNIAL COMMITTEE; BOX 222; MATTHEWS, IN 46957. (#108015-1).

OCT 1 - 3, '76. ANNUAL COVERED BRIDGE & ANTIQUE ENGINE FESTIVAL. QUEEN CHOSEN, BAKING CONTEST, 200 YR FASHION SHOW PLUS LIVE ENTERTAINMENT. AT COVERED BRIDGE FESTIVAL SITE, AMPLE PARKING. (ST-WIDE). PEGGY GARDNER, CHMN; MATTHEWS LIONS CLUB; BOX 222; MATTHEWS, IN 46957. (#108015-2).

MELLOTT

JUNE 11 - 13, '76. AMERICAN FLAG APPRECIATION DAY. PROMOTION OF PATRIOTISM; MOTTO - 'SERVE GOD AND COUNTRY'; PARADE BY EARLY AMERICAN UNITS AND SCOUTS ORGANIZATIONAL UNITS. AT MELLOTT PARK AND TOWN STREETS. (LOCAL). RUBY D HELGERS, COORD; AMERICAN FLAG APPRECIATION DAY, INC; BOX 7; NELLOTT, IN 47958. (#104299-1).

MENTONE

LAWRENCE D BELL AIRCRAFT MUSEUM, METONE, IN. AIRCRAFT MUSEUM ON LAWRENCE D BELL, A PIONEER IN AIR CRAFT. (LOCAL). MRS FRANK D SMITH, COORDINATOR; MENTONE BICENTENNIAL COMMISSION; BOX 267; MENTONE, IN 46539. (#26854). **ARBA GRANTEE.**

MERRILLVILLE

JULY 2 - 4, '76. ETHNIC FAIR WITH CHOIR & DANCERS. FAIR, LIVE PERFORMANCE AT MERRILLVILLE HIGH SCHOOL AUDITORIUM & STADIUM. (LOCAL). BOSWELL OSCAR; MERRILLVILLE-ROSS BICENTENNIAL COMMISSION; 38 DEERPATH RD; MERRILLVILLE, IN 46410. (#200017-72).

METAMORA

OCT 2 - 3, '76. CANAL DAYS TRADERS' RENDEZVOUS. ARTS, CRAFTS & ANTIQUES; SCARECROW CONTEST SAT MORNING; OLD-TIME BANJO & FIDDLE CONTEST SAT NIGHT; MOZZLE LOADING CONTEST. AT THROUGHOUT METAMORA AT WHITEWATER CANAL STATE MEMORIAL. (ST-WIDE). AL ROGERS, PROJ DIRECTOR; METAMORA SHOPKEEPERS ASSOC, INC; PO BOX 106; METAMORA, IN 47030. (#103850-1).

MICHIGAN CITY

AMERICAN FILM FESTIVAL - MICHIGAN CITY, IN. THE FESTIVAL DEPICTS THE DEVELOPMENT OF FILMS FROM SILENT MOVIES TO THE PRESENT. (LOCAL). BARBARA BOHLEY, COORDINATOR; MICHIGAN CITY PUBLIC LIBRARY; 8TH & SPRING ST; MICHIGAN CITY, IN 46360. (#26634). **ARBA GRANTEE.**

INDIANA STATE PRISON CLOCKWORK ORANGE - IN. THIS PROJECT IS THE INSTITUTION'S CONTRIBUTION TO THE NATION'S BICENTENNIAL CELEBRATION. (ST-WIDE). LEO JENKINS, PROJ COORDINATOR; INDIANA STATE PRISON; PO BOX 41; MICHIGAN CITY, IN 46360. (#27791). **ARBA GRANTEE.**

WASHINGTON PARK BANDSTAND - MICHIGAN CITY, IN. THE BANDSTAND IN WASHINGTON PARK WILL BE RESTORED. (LOCAL). MS GERALD S LEWIS, PRESIDENT; MARQUETTE CHAPTER OF THE QUESTERS; 2113 AVONDALE DR, LONG BEACH; MICHIGAN CITY, IN 46360. (#26635). **ARBA GRANTEE.**

OCT 12 - 13, '76. UNITED STATES ARMED FORCES BICENTENNIAL CARAVAN. CARAVAN IS COMPOSED OF EXHIBIT VANS FOR EACH MILITARY SERVICE. PROJECT THEME IS 'HISTORY OF THE ARMED FORCES & THEIR CONTRIBUTIONS TO THE NATION'. (LOCAL). ROBERT S KUNKEL; UNITED STATES ARMED FORCES BICENTENNIAL CARAVAN; 2408 S LAWRENCE AVE; MICHIGAN CITY, IN 46360. (#1775-731).

DEC 17 - 18, '76. LA SALLE EXPEDITION II, A HISTORIC RE-ENACTMENT. THIS IS AN AUTHENTIC RE-ENACTMENT OF THE 1681 LASALLE EXPEDITION FROM MONTREAL, CANADA TO NEW ORLEANS, LA WHICH WILL BEGIN TOURING ON AUGUST 11, 1976 AND END ON APRIL 9, 1977. (LOCAL). REID H LEWIS, DIRECTOR; LA SALLE EXPEDITION II; 135 S LA SALLE ST, RM 411; CHICAGO, IL 60690. (#102805-27).

MIDDLETOWN

JUNE 14 - 19, '76. ANNUAL LIONS CLUB FAIR & BICENTENNIAL PARADE. PARADE ON TUESDAY, JUNE 15 AT 6:30PM. (LOCAL). DOROTHY N BRUCE, CHMN; LIONS CLUB & AMERICAN REVOLUTION BICENTENNIAL COMMITTEE; 102 N 5TH ST; MIDDLETOWN, IN 47356. (#200017-125).

JULY 4, '76. ANNUAL HORSE SHOW. LIVE PERFORMANCE. (LOCAL). DOROTHY N BRUCE, CHMN; CHAMBER OF COMMERCE & AMERICAN REVOLUTION BICENTENNIAL COMMISSION; 102 N 5TH ST; MIDDLETOWN, IN 47356. (#200017-124).

JULY 23 - 25, '76. CIVIL WAR RE-ENACTMENT. SATURDAY-ENCAMPMENT, CANON DEMONSTRATIONS, DRILL & CAVALRY COMPETITIONS, COSTUME & UNIFORMS CONTESTS & BLUE & GREY BALL. SUNDAY-9:00AM CHURCH SERVICES & WAR MEMORIAL DEDICATION; 1:30 PM-BATTLE OF RICH MOUNTAIN, VA; 3:00PM ICE CREAM SOCIAL & SHENANDOAH HIGH SCHOOL BAND. (LOCAL). DOROTHY N BRUCE, CHMN; ARBC & TOWN COUNCIL; 102 N 5TH ST; MIDDLETOWN, IN 47356. (#200017-123).

AUG 7 - 15, '76. MIDDLETOWN COMMUNITY DAYS. 7TH-HORSESHOE PITCHING, SQUARE DANCE; 8TH-TURKEY SHOOT, PIONEER GAMES, VESPER SERVICES; 9TH & 10TH-SOFTBALL TOURNAMENT; 11TH-WEINER ROAST; 12TH & 13TH-RADIO CONTROL AIRPLANE SHOW, SKYDIVERS & DANCE; 14TH-OX ROAST, TRUCK, JEEP & TRACTOR PULL; 15TH-TRACTOR PULL. (LOCAL). DOROTHY D BRUCE, CHMN; MIDDLETOWN BICENTENNIAL COMMITTEE, JAYC'S & CONSERVATION CLUB; 102 N 5TH ST; MIDDLETOWN, IN 47356. (#200017-67).

MILLERSBURG

JUNE 24 - 26, '76. MILLERSBURG BICENTENNIAL DRESS REVUE & PAGEANT. PARADE, LIVE PERFORMANCE. (LOCAL). MAX AUST; MILLERSBURG BICENTENNIAL COMMITTEE; PO BOX 235; MILLERSBURG, IN 46543. (#200017-70).

MISHAWAKA

LEGACY OF INDUSTRIAL GROWTH IN MISHAWAKA, IN. THE BEIGER MANSION WILL BE USED AS A FOCAL POINT FOR EXHIBITS ON THE MISHAWKA AREA. (LOCAL). TERRY SPRISER, COORDINATOR; BEIGER HERITAGE CORPORATION; PO BOX 651; MISHAWAKA, IN 46544. (#26861). **ARBA GRANTEE.**

MODOC

MODOC MEMORIAL PARK, IN. 4-ACRE PARK AND RECREATIONAL AREA WILL BE IMPROVED. (LOCAL). RICHARD M MYERS, COORDINATOR; TOWN OF MODOC; BOX 18; MODOC, IN 47358. (#27010). **ARBA GRANTEE.**

MONON

BANK RESTORATION & LIBRARY FACILITY FOR MONON, IN. RESTORATION OF ABANDONED BANK BUILDING TO BE USED FOR CULTURAL AND EDUCATIONAL PURPOSES AS AN ANNEX TO THE PUBLIC LIBRARY. (LOCAL). BERTHA J BOSTICK, CHAIRMAN; MONON BICENTENNIAL COMMISSION; MONON, IN 47959. (#13034).

BICENTENNIAL PUBLICATIONS IN MONON, IN. COOKBOOKS, CALENDARS & PLACEMATS WILL BE PRINTED WITH THE BICENTENNIAL SYMBOL ON THEM. (LOCAL). BERTHA J BOSTICK, CHAIRMAN; MONON BICENTENNIAL COMMISSION; MONON, IN 47959. (#13033).

LANDSCAPING CREEK BANKS OF MONON, IN. CLEAR AND LANDSCAPE BANKS OF HISTORICAL CREEK AT THE EDGE OF MONON. (LOCAL). BERTHA J BOSTICK, CHAIRMAN; MONON BICENTENNIAL COMMISSION; MONON, IN 47959. (#13032). **ARBA GRANTEE.**

JUNE 14, '76. PRAYER BREAKFAST. CEREMONY. (LOCAL). BERTHA S BOSTICK, CHMN; MONON CENTENNIAL - BICENTENNIAL COMMISSION; MONON, IN 47959. (#100862-1).

SEPT 1 - 30, '76. CENTENNIAL - BICENTENNIAL FESTIVAL. FESTIVAL AT CITY PARK. (LOCAL). BERTHA S BOSTICK, CHMN; MONON CENTENNIAL - BICENTENNIAL COMMISSION; MONON, IN 47959. (#100861-1).

MONTGOMERY

SEPT 16 - 18, '76. DAVIESS TURKEY TROT FESTIVAL. FESTIVAL AT RURITAN PARK. (LOCAL). EVELYN R HANSON, CHMN; CHAMBER OF COMMERCE; PO BOX 430; WASHINGTON, IN 47501. (#103416-563).

MONTICELLO

AMERICAN HERITAGE ALL SCHOOL ESSAY CONTEST - IN. EACH CHILD CHOSE AN HISTORICAL CHARACTER TO WRITE ABOUT. (LOCAL). ROBERT CROUSE, CHAIRMAN; MONTICELLO BICENTENNIAL COMMITTEE; 226 N RAILROAD; MONTICELLO, IN 47960. (#31444).

FEB 21, '76. BICENTENNIAL COLONIAL COSTUME BALL. PATRIOTIC MUSIC PROVIDED BY HIGH SCHOOL GOLDEN THROAT CHOIR. ALSO, OTHER ACTIVITIES INCLUDED COSTUME AWARDS, DANCING, GRAND MARCH, DECORATIONS HONORING GEORGE WASHINGTON & THE REVOLUTIONARY PERIOD. AT TIPPECANOE COUNTRY CLUB, N OF MONTICELLO ON RR 1. (LOCAL). ROBERT CROUSE, PM; MONTICELLO BICENTENNIAL COMMITTEE; 125 WEST BROADWAY; MONTICELLO, IN 47960. (#200017-117).

MONTPELIER

MONTPELIER CIVIC AND YOUTH BICENT MEMORIAL, IN. TWO TENNIS COURTS WILL BE BUILT, A FLAG POLE ERECTED AND STONE MARKERS PROVIDED IN REMEMBRANCE OF THE BICENTENNIAL. (LOCAL). VADA SCHWARZKOPF, CHAIRWOMAN; MONTPELIER HISTORICAL BICENTENNIAL SOCIETY; 116 W HUNTINGTON ST; MONTPELIER, IN 47359. (#24097). **ARBA GRANTEE.**

SEPT 12 - 14, '75. AMERICAN LEGION JAMBOREE. FESTIVAL, PARADE AT AMERICAN LEGION HOME. (LOCAL). VADA SCHWARZKOPF, CHMN; AMERICAN LEGION; 128 W HUNTINGTON; MONTPELIER, IN 47359. (#101936-1).

JULY 1 - 3, '76. 'FOOTLIGHT FOLLIES'. LIVE PERFORMANCE. (LOCAL). KENNETH D NEFF, ADVISOR; MONTPELIER BICENTENNIAL COMMITTEE; 128 W HUNTINGTON; MONTPELIER, IN 47359. (#14600-1).

MOORESVILLE

BICENTENNIAL COOKBOOK OF MOORESVILLE, IN. HISTORY OF THE CITY IS PREFACE TO THE FAVORITE RECIPES OF THE CITY'S RESIDENTS. (REGN'L). REBECCA S HARDIN, SECRETARY; MOORESVILLE BICENTENNIAL COMMITTEE; 133 CARTER ST; MOORESVILLE, IN 46158. (#32327).

BICENTENNIAL PROJECTS OF MOORESVILLE, INDIANA. INCLUDES EXTENSIVE BICENT NEWSPAPER COVERAGE BY TIMES & DAILY REPORTER; EVENT BROADCAST BY WCBK & WART; MATERIAL FOR MORGAN COUNTY TIME CAPSULE; OLD TIMERS BOOKLET; TREE PLANTINGS BY JAYCEES; QUILT; ETC. (LOCAL). REBECCA S HARDIN, SECRETARY; MOORESVILLE BICENTENNIAL COMMITTEE; 133 CARTER ST; MOORESVILLE, IN 46158. (#31965).

'THE INDIANA STATE FLAG: ITS DESIGNER' - BOOK. BOOK IS HONORING PAUL HADLEY, AN ARTIST OF MOORESVILLE, WHO DESIGNED THE FLAG, & MADE MANY WATERCOLOR PAINTINGS OF THE AREA. ALSO HAS ANTHOLOGY OF HADLEY'S PAINTINGS, 40 PAGES & 70 PICTURES & PAINTINGS. (REGN'L). REBECCA S HARDIN, SECRETARY; MOORESVILLE BICENTENNIAL COMMITTEE; 133 CARTER ST; MOORESVILLE, IN 46158. (#32328).

VETERANS MEMORIAL OF MOORESVILLE, IN. A GRANITE MARKER ON MEMORIAL DRIVE, ORIGINALLY WITH NAMES OF WWII VETERANS. NAMES OF KOREAN CONFLICT & VIETNAM GOLD STAR VETERANS ADDED & AREA RELANDSCAPED WITH LIGHTS, SHRUBS & FLOWERS. (LOCAL). REBECCA S HARDIN, SECRETARY; MOORESVILLE BICENTENNIAL COMMITTEE; 133 CARTER ST; MOORESVILLE, IN 46158. (#32326).

50 YEAR MEMBERS HONORED, MOORESVILLE, IN. EACH 50 YEAR MEMBER IN CHURCH WAS GIVEN A 50 YEAR CERTIFICATE & BOOKLET ABOUT THE CHURCH. (LOCAL). DR ROBERT HOLDEW; UNITED METHODIST CHURCH; HARRISON & INDIANA ST; MOORESVILLE, IN 46158. (#28227).

MAY 31, '76. MEMORIAL DAY PARADE & PROGRAM. PARADE. (LOCAL). REBECCA S HARDIN, SECY; MOORESVILLE BICENTENNIAL COMMITTEE; 133 CARTER ST; MOORESVILLE, IN 46158. (#200017-111).

JUNE 7, '76. WHITE LICK ART LEAGUE'S BIRTHDAY PARTY. FAIR. (LOCAL). REBECCA S HARDIN, SECY; WHITE LICK ART LEAGUE & MOORESVILLE BICENTENNIAL COMMITTEE; 133 CARTER ST; MOORESVILLE, IN 46158. (#200017-110).

JUNE 13, '76. 'I LOVE AMERICA' MUSICAL. LIVE PERFORMANCE. (LOCAL). REBECCA S HARDIN, SECY; NEIL ARMSTRONG SCHOOL, CHURCH OF GOD, METHODIST & CHRISTIAN CHURCHES; 133 CARTER ST; MOORESVILLE, IN 46158. (#200017-107).

JULY 11, '76. 'IN GOD WE TRUST' MOVIE SHOWN. EXHIBIT AT GRACE MISSIONARY CHURCH. (LOCAL). REBECCA S HARDIN, SECY; GRACE MISSIONARY CHURCH & MOORESVILLE BICENTENNIAL COMMITTEE; 133 CARTER ST; MOORESVILLE, IN 46158. (#200017-112).

JULY 25, '76. BELL CHOIR PERFORMANCE. LIVE PERFORMANCE AT FRIENDS MEETING HOUSE. (LOCAL). REBECCA S HARDIN, SECY; FRIENDS MEETING & MOORESVILLE BICENTENNIAL COMMITTEE; 133 CARTER ST; MOORESVILLE, IN 46158. (#200017-106).

AUG 8, '76. OLD SETTLERS PARADE & CARNIVAL. PARADE, FAIR AT DOWNTOWN MOORESVILLE. (LOCAL). REBECCA S HARDIN, SECY; MOORESVILLE BICENTENNIAL COMMITTEE; 133 CARTER ST; MOORESVILLE, IN 46158. (#200017-109).

MULBERRY

HISTORICAL MARKERS & DIRECTORY, MULBERRY, IN. MARKERS WILL BE ERECTED AT 10 HISTORIC SITES. (LOCAL). SHERRY KALEY, COORDINATOR; MULBERRY BICENTENNIAL COMMITTEE; 264 E 2ND ST; MULBERRY, IN 46058. (#26590). **ARBA GRANTEE.**

MUNCIE

AMERICAN INDEPENDENCE & THE BICENTENNIAL, IN. THIS IS A SPECIAL ISSUE OF THE INDIANA SOCIAL STUDIES QUARTERLY, VOL XXVIII NO 1. (ST-WIDE). DR ALTHEA STOECKEL, GUEST EDITOR; BALL STATE UNIV; DEPT OF HISTORY; MUNCIE, IN 47306. (#16765).

'THE AMERICAN REVOLUTION' - MUNCIE, IN. A SPECIAL ISSUE OF THE INDIANA SOCIAL STUDIES QUARTERLY, VOL XXVII NO 3, DEALS WITH THE AMERICAN REVOLUTION. (ST-WIDE). DR ALTHEA STOECKEL, GUEST EDITOR; BALL STATE UNIV; DEPT OF HISTORY; MUNCIE, IN 47306. (#16764).

BICENTENNIAL PARK - MUNCIE, IN. FIVE-ACRE COMMUNITY PARK ON GROUND DONATED BY ROBERT TAYLOR, LOCAL CONTRACTOR. PLAYGROUND, PICNIC, BOATING FACILITIES & MULTI-PURPOSE COURT PLANNED. MANY LOCAL DONATIONS OF MATERIAL AND LABOR. (LOCAL). ANNETTE K ERNSTING, CHAIRPERSON; SALEM TOWNSHIP BICENTENNIAL COMMITTEE; RR 8, BOX 349; MUNCIE, IN 47302. (#27594).

HAPPY BIRTHDAY, AMERICA - MUNCIE, IN. A SLIDE PRESENTATION APPROXIMATELY 45 MINUTES IN LENGTH ILLUSTRATING AMERICA'S PROGRESS AS REFLECTED IN FASHION. (LOCAL). PROFESSOR SHIRLEY ADAMS, PROJ DIRECTOR; BALL STATE UNIV; DEPT OF HOME ECONOMICS; MUNCIE, IN 47306. (#16758).

HISTORY OF PHYSICAL EDUCATION IN U S, MUNCIE, IN. SEVERAL 35MM COLORED FILMSTRIPS ENCOMPASSING A BRIEF HISTORY OF VARIOUS SPORTS AND THE DEVELOPMENT OF PHYSICAL EDUCATION IN THE SCHOOLS OF THE UNITED STATES WILL BE FEATURED. (LOCAL). DAVID FIELD, CHAIRMAN; BALL STATE UNIV; DEPT OF MEN'S PHYSICAL EDUCATION; MUNCIE, IN 47306. (#16761).

INDIANA HEIRLOOMS - MUNCIE, IN. A SERIES OF 200 SLIDES WILL PORTRAY THE HISTORY OF INDIANA THROUGH A STUDY OF COSTUMES, HOMES AND HOUSEHOLD ITEMS. (LOCAL). ESTHER BRUNER, PROFESSOR; BALL STATE UNIV; DEPT OF HOME ECONOMICS; MUNCIE, IN 47306. (#16759).

'LET'S REDISCOVER INDIANA' - BOOK, MUNCIE, IN. A BOOK ON INDIANA'S HISTORY COMPILED BY YOUNG HISTORIANS, KNOWN AS LITTLE HOOSIERS. (ST-WIDE). PATRICIA M DENKER, COORDINATOR; LITTLE HOOSIER HISTORIANS; 1708 N COLSON DRIVE; MUNCIE, IN 47304. (#25244). **ARBA GRANTEE.**

MEMORY OF A NATION - MUNCIE, IN. AN ADAPTABLE PRESENTATION OF HISTORICAL AMERICANA IN THE FORM OF HOLOGRAPHIC, AUTOGRAPHIC MANUSCRIPTS FROM THE SPEAKER'S COLLECTION. (REGN'L). D N DIEDRICH, ASSISTANT TO DEAN; BALL STATE UNIV; COLLEGE OF SCIENCE & HUMANITIES; MUNCIE, IN 47306. (#16757).

MUNCIE - PAST, PRESENT & FUTURE, IN. PROGRAM TO GENERATE INTEREST IN HERITAGE AND FUTURE OF MUNCIE. (LOCAL). ANTHONY J COSTELLO, COORDINATOR; BALL STATE UNIV; MUNCIE, IN 47306. (#25781). **ARBA GRANTEE.**

'ON THE BICENTENNIAL' - MUNCIE, IN. A QUARTERLY NEWSLETTER WILL BE CIRCULATED FREE OF CHARGE AMONG CIVIC & SOCIAL GROUPS, SCHOOLS AND HISTORICAL SOCIETIES IN EASTERN INDIANA. (ST-WIDE). NORMA J FULTZ, EDITOR; BALL STATE UNIV; UNIV LIBRARY; MUNCIE, IN 47306. (#16760).

TEACHING UNITS ON THE BICENTENNIAL - MUNCIE, IN. 3 BICENTENNIAL RESOURCE UNITS WILL BE DESIGNED FOR PRIMARY, INTERMEDIATE AND UPPER GRADES IN THE MUNCIE COMMUNITY SCHOOLS FOR USE BY THE TEACHERS IN THE SYSTEM. (LOCAL). DR ROSANNE MAREK, ASST PROFESSOR; BALL STATE UNIV; DEPT OF HISTORY; MUNCIE, IN 47306. (#16763).

TREE PLANTING BY BURRIS SCHOOL - MUNCIE, IN. THE STUDENTS ACTIVE IN BURRIS SCHOOL'S LITTLE HOOSIER CLUB PLANTED 1776 PINE SEEDLINGS AT A NEARBY FARM. (LOCAL). CHARLES V BRANCH, PRINCIPAL; BALL STATE UNIV; BURRIS LABORATORY SCHOOL; MUNCIE, IN 47306. (#16762).

OCT 8, '75. 'LIMITED WAR & POLITICAL ORDER' - SIR NORMAN ANGELL MEM LECTURE. THE HONORABLE CHRISTOPHER M WOODHOUSE, WHO WILL DELIVER THE LECTURE, IS A MEMBER OF THE BRITISH PARLIAMENT. AT BALLROOM, STUDENT CENTER. (LOCAL). DR RICHARD WIRES, CHMN; BALL STATE UNIV; MUNCIE, IN 47306. (#200017-21).

NOV 12, '75. HISTORY LECTURE ON THE AMERICAN REVOLUTION. PROFESSOR RICHARD MORRIS IS EMERSON PROFESSOR OF HIS-

MUNCIE — CONTINUED

TORY AT COLUMBIA UNIVERSITY. THE TITLE OF HIS LECTURE WILL BE 'THE AMERICAN REVOLUTION AS AN ANTI-COLONIAL WAR'. AT BALLROOM, STUDENT CENTER. (LOCAL). DR RICHARD WIRES, CHMN; DEPT OF HISTORY, BALL STATE UNIV; BALL STATE UNIV; MUNCIE, IN 47306. (#103047-8).

DEC 7, '75 - JAN 25, '76. INDIANA ARTISTS-THEN AND NOW, AN EXHIBITION. A SERIES OF SIX EXHIBITIONS COMBINING THE ART OF AN ARTIST'S OF AN EARLIER PERIOD WITH THE ART OF AN ARTIST'S OF THE PRESENT. THE BOND BETWEEN THESE TWO WILL BE THE MEDIUM. THESE EXHIBITIONS ARE BEING SPONSORED BY THE ART DEPARTMENT AND ART GALLERY. AT ART GALLERY, ARTS BLDG. (LOCAL). ROSANNE MAREK, SECRETARY; BALL STATE UNIV; BALL STATE UNIV; MUNCIE, IN 47306. (#103047-1).

JAN 15, '76. THE RADICAL RIGHT AND THE REVOLUTION, A HISTORY LECTURE. PROFESSOR DAVID W KAMENS, AN ASSOCIATE PROFESSOR OF HISTORY AT BALL STATE UNIVERSITY, SPECIALIZES IN EARLY AMERICAN HISTORY. THE TITLE OF HIS LECTURE WILL BE 'THROUGH A GLASS DARKLY'. AT TEACHERS COLLEGE BUILDING, ROOM M-1. (LOCAL). DR RICHARD WIRES, CHMN; DEPT OF HISTORY, BALL STATE UNIV; BALL STATE UNIV; MUNCIE, IN 47306. (#103047-4).

MAR 18, '76. HISTORY LECTURE ON THE COLONIAL COLLEGES AND THE AMERICAN REVOLUTION. DR ALTHEA STOECKEL IS A MEMBER OF THE HISTORY DEPT AT BALL STATE UNIV. SHE IS ALSO THE GUEST EDITOR OF TWO SPECIAL ISSUES OF THE INDIANA SOCIAL STUDIES QUARTERLY. THE TITLE OF HER LECTURE WILL BE 'PRESIDENTS, PROFESSORS AND POLITICS'. AT BALLROOM, STUDENT CENTER. (LOCAL). DR RICHARD WIRES, CHMN; DEPT OF HISTORY, BALL STATE UNIV; BALL STATE UNIV; MUNCIE, IN 47306. (#103047-5).

APR 6, '76. DR SAMUEL JOHNSON AND THE AMERICAN REVOLUTION. ALEXANDER D MACGIBBON, PROFESSOR OF ENGLISH AT BALL STATE UNIV, SPECIALIZES IN EIGHTEENTH CENTURY BRITISH LITERATURE. AT FORUM ROOM, STUDENT CENTER. (LOCAL). DR RICHARD WIRES, CHMN; DEPT OF HISTORY, BALL STATE UNIV; BALL STATE UNIV; MUNCIE, IN 47306. (#103047-3).

MAY 6, '76. AMERICAN REVOLUTIONARY INFLUENCES ON THE FRENCH REVOLUTION. THE LECTURE WILL BE GIVEN BY RICHARD MACKEY WHO IS AN ASSOCIATE PROFESSOR OF HISTORY AT BALL STATE UNIV. HIS INTERESTS ARE THE SOCIAL AND INTELLECTUAL HISTORY OF FRANCE AND GERMANY. AT TEACHERS COLLEGE BLDG, RM M-1. (LOCAL). DR RICHARD WIRES, CHMN; DEPT OF HISTORY, BALL STATE UNIV; BALL STATE UNIV; MUNCIE, IN 47306. (#103047-2).

MAY 7 - 8, '76. AMERICAN SUITE - A FOLK DANCE REPERTORY. THE BANEVOLKS, DIRECTED BY MR EDEN, WILL PRESENT THE AMERICAN SUITE. THIS DANCE REPERTORY IS BEING GIVEN BY THE WOMEN'S PHYSICAL EDUCATION DEPARTMENT. AT EMENS AUDITORIUM. (LOCAL). YAAKOV EDEN, DIRECTOR; DEPT OF PHYSICAL EDUCATION, BALL STATE UNIV; BALL STATE UNIV; MUNCIE, IN 47306. (#103047-7).

JUNE 21 - 26, '76. INTERNATIONAL THEATRE ARTS CONFERENCE; THEME: 'SALUTE TO FREEDOM'. INTENSIVE WORKSHOPS, DISCUSSIONS, THEATRE PRODUCTIONS; EXHIBIT SPACE AVAILABLE FOR RENT; GUEST ARTISTS, SUPERB HIGH SCHOOL THEATRE PERFORMANCES. AT BALL STATE UNIV. (REGN'L). DIANE J COLONEL, DIR; INTERNATIONAL THESPIAN SOCIETY; COLLEGE HILL STATION, BOX E; CINCINNATI, OH 45224. (#105092-1).

JULY 22 - 31, '76. LIONS DELAWARE COUNTY FAIR. 2 NIGHTS HARNESS AND AUTO RACING DEMOLITION DERBY, BAND CONTEST, DRILL TEAM CONTEST, LIVESTOCK SHOW, BEAUTY PAGEANT, SQUARE DANCING, SENIOR CITIZEN & CHILDRENS' DAY ARE THE SCHEDULED ACTIVITIES. (ST-WIDE). CHARLES O RUSSELL, PRES; LIONS DELAWARE CO FAIR; 410 W HIGHLAND; MUNCIE, IN 47303. (#106095-21).

MUNSTER

MUNSTER COMMUNITY HERITAGE & MEMORIAL, MUNSTER, IN. A HERITAGE MEMORIAL, 24' IN LIMESTONE, 4' BASE SQUARE TAPERING STRUCTURE & 5 POINT STAR FLAG, BASE 19' WITH 3 FLAG POLES; USA, IN & BICENTENNIAL FLAGS, ALL DEDICATED TO THE CITIZENS OF MUNSTER. (LOCAL). WILLIAM T HENSEY, JR, COORDINATOR; MUNSTER BICENTENNIAL COMMISSION; 8144 SCHREIBER DR; MUNSTER, IN 46321. (#32619).

JULY 5, '76. MUNSTER INDEPENDENCE DAY. FESTIVAL AT MUNSTER MUSTANG FIELD. (LOCAL). WILLIAM T HENSEY, CHMN; MUNSTER AMERICAN REVOLUTION BICENTENNIAL COMMISSION; 8144 SCHREFER DR; MUNSTER, IN 46321. (#200017-93).

N MANCHESTER

MARKING HOLDERMAN CEMETERY - N MANCHESTER, IN. MARK AN OLD CEMETERY WITH BOLDERS & BRONZE PLAQUES. (LOCAL). MRS F R BURNS, CHAIRMAN; DOCTOR MANASSEH CULTER CHAPTER, NSDAR; N MANCHESTER, IN 46962. (#27788). **ARBA GRANTEE.**

'A SENSE OF PLACE', FILM ON NORTH MANCHESTER, IN. DOCUMENTARY FILM ON NORTH MANCHESTER, INDIANA WITH DIALOGUE & INTERVIEWS; PURPOSE: TO INSTILL PRIDE IN COMMUNITY AND CONCERN FOR PAST & FUTURE BY SHOWING HISTORIC ROOTS, CHANGES & ARCHITECTURAL LANDMARKS. (LOCAL). ROBERT KNECHEL, PRESIDENT; NORTH MANCHESTER HUMANITIES COUNCIL; 718 BOND ST; N MANCHESTER, IN 46962. (#9403).

AUG 8 - 17, '75. FUN FEST, COUNTY FESTIVAL. SUN SHINES BRIGHT OVER THE FIFTH ANNUAL FREE FUN FEST WITH A SQUARE DANCE AUGUST 8. COLORFUL PARADE AUGUST 9; ANTIQUE SHOW AUGUST 9 AND 10; HISTORIC HOME AND EXHIBITS AUGUST 10 TRACTOR PULLS AUGUST 13 AND 16; AND A MARCHING BAND SHOW AUGUST 16; ALL EVENTS ARE FREE. (LOCAL). GEORGE W SCHEERER, CHMN; NORTH MANCHESTER CHAMBER OF COMMERCE; 114 W MAIN ST; N MANCHESTER, IN 46962. (#100324-1).

NAPOLEON

BICENTENNIAL FESTIVAL - NAPOLEON, IN. THE 3-DAY FESTIVAL WILL FEATURE CRAFTS & VARIOUS ACTIVITIES. (LOCAL). DONALD BULTMAN, COORDINATOR; CATHOLIC CHURCH, LUTHERAN CHURCH & METHODIST CHURCH; RR 1; BATESVILLE, IN 47006. (#25219). **ARBA GRANTEE.**

JULY 2 - 4, '76. NAPOLEON BICENTENNIAL FESTIVAL. FESTIVAL. (LOCAL). DONALD BULTMAN, COORD; CATHOLIC CHURCH, LUTHERN CHURCH & METHODIST CHURCH; RR 1; BATESVILLE, IN 47006. (#25219-1).

NASHVILLE

HEMLOCK BLUFF GARDEN CLUB OF INDIANA. PRESERVATION OF HEMLOCK TREES. (LOCAL). DENNIS WOLKOFF, COORDINATOR; THE GARDEN CLUB OF INDIANA; RR 1, BOX 115; NASHVILLE, IN 47448. (#26589). **ARBA GRANTEE.**

JULY 4, '76. CELEBRATION 'FOR GOD AND COUNTRY'. THERE WILL BE A DIALOGUE BY THE ARMY NATIONAL GUARD RECRUITER, JAMES FULK, AND PRESENTATION OF FLAGS BY THE ARMY NATIONAL GUARD. AT E GOULD ST AND LOCUST LN. (LOCAL). REV RICHARD FISHER; FIRST CHURCH OF THE NAZARENE; RR #2, BOX 28F; NASHVILLE, IN 47448. (#108234-1).

NEW ALBANY

BICENTENNIAL BUS TRIP. EXHIBIT AT UNIVERSITY CAMPUS. (LOCAL). A PETER RICH, CHRMAN; INDIANA UNIV SOUTHEAST BICENTENNIAL COMMITTEE; 4201 GRANTLNE RD; NEW ALBANY, IN 47150. (#100326-3).

DEDICATION OF HILLSIDE HALL. CEREMONIES WILL FEATURE INDIANAPOLIS SYMPHONY CONCERT BICENTENNIAL THEME. AT UNIVERSITY CAMPUS. (LOCAL). A PETER RICH, CHRMN; INDIANA UNIV SOUTHEAST BICENTENNIAL COMMITTEE; 4201 GRANTLINE RD; NEW ALBANY, IN 47150. (#100326-5).

HERITAGE DAY. EXHIBIT AT UNIVERSITY CAMPUS. (LOCAL). A PETER RICH, CHRMAN; INDIANA UNIV SOUTHEAST BICENTENNIAL COMMITTEE; 4201 GRANTLNE RD; NEW ALBANY, IN 47150. (#100326-2).

HERITAGE '76 FESTIVAL USA - NEW ALBANY, IN. THE NEW ALBANY FLOYD COUNTY SCHOOLS PRESENT A CRAFT EXHIBIT. (LOCAL). MS ANN MAHAN; NATHANIEL SCRIBNER JUNIOR HIGH SCHOOL; 910 OLD VINCENNES RD; NEW ALBANY, IN 47150. (#26920). **ARBA GRANTEE.**

INDIANA UNIVERSITY SOUTHEAST THEATER - IN. CHILDREN'S THEATRE WILL BE PRESENTED BY INDIANA UNIV SOUTHEAST. (LOCAL). DAVID K LONGEST, CHAIRMAN; INDIANA UNIV SOUTHEAST; 1US GRANT LINE RD; NEW ALBANY, IN 47150. (#27763). **ARBA GRANTEE.**

TOM SAWYER - A CHILDREN'S PLAY. LIVE PERFORMANCE AT UNIVERSITY CAMPUS. (LOCAL). A PETER RICH, CHRMN; INDIANA UNIV SOUTHEAST BICENTENNIAL COMMITTEE; 4201 GRANTLINE RD; NEW ALBANY, IN 47150. (#100326-6).

UNCLE REMUS STORIES. A CHILDREN'S PLAY. AT UNIVERSITY CAMPUS. (LOCAL). A PETER RICH, CHRMN; INDIANA UNIV SOUTHEAST BICENTENNIAL COMMITTEE; 4201 GRANTLINE RD; NEW ALBANY, IN 47150. (#100326-4).

JULY 4, '76. FOURTH OF JULY ARTS FESTIVAL. TWO BLOCKS ARE CLOSED OFF DOWNTOWN, AS ARTS AND CRAFTS BOOTHS LINE THE AVENUES AND ENTERTAINMENT HERALDS A FUN, FOOD-FILLED DAY. (LOCAL). MELVIN FRANCIS, CHMN; NEW ALBANY JAYCEES; 4433 PAYNE KOEHLER RD; NEW ALBANY, IN 47150. (#100326-1).

SEPT 21, '76. HERITAGE '76 CRAFT EXHIBIT. EXHIBIT AT NEW ALBANY FLOYD COUNTY SCHOOLS. (LOCAL). MS ANN MAHAN, TEACHER; NATHANIEL SCRIBNER JUNIOR HIGH SCHOOL; 910 OLD VINCENNES RD; NEW ALBANY, IN 47150. (#26920-1).

OCT 2 - 10, '76. HARVEST HOMECOMING FESTIVAL. TOUR MANSION ROW ON THE ROBERT E LEE STEAMBOAT BUS; TREAD CAREFULLY THROUGH THE HAUNTED HOUSE AND STROLL PAST HISTORIC EXHIBITS, ANTIQUE DISPLAYS, FARM MARKETS & DECORATED WINDOWS DURING THIS 9TH ANNUAL CELEBRATION; PUMPKINS ARE AWARDED PRIZES. (LOCAL). FRANK C MILLER JR; SOUTHERN INDIANA HARVEST HOMECOMING INC; P O BOX 290; NEW ALBANY, IN 47150. (#100314-1).

NEW CARLISLE

NEW CARLISLE HISTORICAL PROJECT - IN. THE RESTORATION OF HOMES; PRESERVATION OF FLAG, BOOKS & COLLECTERS' PLATES; PLANTING OF TREES AND ELEMENTARY SCHOOL PROGRAM COMPRISED LOCAL BICENTENNIAL PROJECT. (LOCAL). PAUL GAROUTTE, TOWNSHIP TRUSTEE; NEW CARLISLE BUSINESS AND PROFESSIONAL MENS' ASSOC; NEW CARLISLE, IN 46552. (#31364).

JULY 29 - AUG 1, '76. 4TH ANNUAL NEW CARLISLE HISTORICAL DAYS. INCLUDED HOME TOURS, HORSE PULL AND HORSE SHOW, GAMES AND SUNDAY WORSHIP SERVICE FOR THE COMMUNITY. AT ENTIRE TOWN AREA INCLUDING LOCAL TOWN PARK. (REGN'L). MARGARET L CALHOUN; NEW CARLISLE BUSINESS AND PROFESSIONAL MENS' ASSOC; 56150 TIMOTHY RD; NEW CARLISLE, IN 46552. (#200017-75).

NEW CASTLE

EXPANSION OF THE HENRY COUNTY HISTORICAL SOC, IN. EXPANSION OF HISTORICAL SOCIETY TO 15 ROOM GENERAL WILLIAM GROSE HOME. (LOCAL). JOHN M JORDAN, COORDINATOR; HENRY COUNTY HISTORICAL SOCIETY, INC; 614 S 104TH ST; NEW CASTLE, IN 47362. (#26991). **ARBA GRANTEE.**

FIREPLUG PAINTING - PROJ OF NEW CASTLE, IN. FIREPLUGS WILL BE PAINTED RED, WHITE AND BLUE. (LOCAL). JUDI MURRAY, CHAIRMAN; NEW CASTLE BICENTENNIAL COMMITTEE; NEW CASTLE, IN 47362. (#15539).

REVOLUTIONARY SOLDIERS IN HENRY COUNTY, IN. REVOLUTIONARY SOLDIERS WHO LIVED IN HENRY COUNTY WILL BE LISTED IN A BOOK. (LOCAL). RICHARD RATCLIFF, CHAIRMAN; 303 S PEARL ST; SPICELAND, IN 47385. (#15540).

SEPT 25 - 26, '76. WILBUR WRIGHT BICENTENNIAL AVIATION FESTIVAL. FESTIVAL AT CHRYSLER HIGH SCHOOL, BAKER PARK, MUNICIPAL AIRPORT. (NAT'L). BETTIE EADE, COORD; WILBUR WRIGHT BICENTENNIAL AVIATION FESTIVAL; 516 REDBUD LN; NEW CASTLE, IN 47362. (#103416-566).

NEW HARMONY

MAY 16 - 17, '75. INDIANA AMERICAN REVOLUTION BICENTENNIAL SYMPOSIUM. CONTEST FOR EMPIRE IN THE OHIO VALLEY AND THE OLD NORTHWEST 15001775. AN AMERICAN BICENTENNIAL SYMPOSIUM. AT THRALL'S OPERA HOUSE NEW HARMONY IN. (ST-WIDE). JOHN ELLIOTT; INDIANA AMERICAN REVOLUTION BICENTENNIAL COMMISSION; ROUTE 1; NEW HARMONY, IN 47631. (#50411-1).

MAR 11 - JUNE 10, '76. AMERICAN EXPERIENCE THROUGH FILM. A SERIES OF 10 AMERICAN FILMS ON 10 THURS EVENINGS FROM MAR 11 TO JUNE 10. EACH WILL BE FOLLOWED BY DISCUSSION OF AMERICAN ISSUES RAISED. AT MURPHY AUDITORIUM. (LOCAL). JAMES R BLEVINS, COORD; INDIANA STATE UNIV-EVANSVILLE & HISTORIC NEW HARMONY, INC; EVANSVILLE, IN 47712. (#107172-1).

NEWBURGH

'A BICENTENNIAL LOOK AT NEWBURGH' - IN. THE TEXT WILL BE A HISTORY OF OLD HOMES, FAMILIES, CULTURE & TIMES IN NEWBURGH. (LOCAL). BETTY WELLS, COORDINATOR; NEWBURGH LIBRARY BOARD; 110 W WATER ST; NEWBURGH, IN 47630. (#19633).

HISTORICAL MARKERS - NEWBURGH, IN. HISTORIC HOMES IN NEWBURGH WILL BE MARKED WITH DATES & INFORMATION. (LOCAL). JANE CRENSHAW, COORDINATOR; NEWBURG WOMEN'S CLUB; 12 E WATER ST; NEWBURGH, IN 47630. (#19635).

OCT 14, '76. TOUR OF HISTORIC OLD HOMES. TOUR AT BEGIN AT TOWN HALL, STATE & MAIN ST. (LOCAL). MRS RICHARD DENNIS, COORD; WOMEN'S CLUB OF NEWBURGH; RR 2, BOX 278; NEWBURGH, IN 47630. (#104468-2).

NEWPORT

'LET FREEDOM RING' - NEWPORT, IN. A FESTIVAL HONORING HISTORIC PERSONALITIES WHO HAVE CONTRIBUTED TO THE AMERICAN IDEAL OF FREEDOM. (LOCAL). BILL KILGORE, COORDINATOR; NORTH VERMILLION COMMUNITY SCHOOL CORP; BOX 6; KILGORE, IN 47966. (#33053). **ARBA GRANTEE.**

OCT 2 - 3, '76. ANTIQUE AUTO HILL CLIMB & FESTIVE AUTO PARADE. ANTIQUE AUTOS GEAR UP FOR THE ASCENT OF AN 1800 FOOT PAVED HILL; WHILE A HORSESHOE CONTEST. FLEA MARKET, PARADE, QUEEN CONTEST, GAMES AND A STREET FAIR SPICE UP ACTIVITIES IN THE VALLEY. (LOCAL). REN BROWNFIELD, CHMN; NEWPORT LIONS CLUB; PO BOX 392; NEWPORT, IN 47966. (#100327-1).

NEWTOWN

JUNE 26 - 27, '76. NEWTOWN BICENT & SESQUICENT CELEBRATION. HOMEMADE FOOD, SPELLING BEE, GAMES, TALENT SHOW, MOVIES OF 1935, CORNHUSKING, ANTIQUE DISPLAYS AND GUEST SPEAKERS. AT NEWTOWN PARK. (LOCAL). SANDRA TAYLOR, CHMN; NEWTOWN TOWN BOARD; RR 3, BOX 201; VEEDERSBURG, IN 47987. (#200017-64).

NOBLESVILLE

RESTORATION OF UNION TRACTION INTERURBAN #429 - IN. RESTORATION OF VINTAGE 1926 ELECTRIC INTERURBAN COMBINE CAR, NOBLESVILLE UNION TRACTION #429. (LOCAL). THOMAS H BADER, PROJ COORDINATOR; INDIANA MUSEUM OF TRANSPORTATION & COMMUNICATION, INC; PO BOX 83; NOBLESVILLE, IN 46060. (#27011).

NORTH JUDSON

NORTH JUDSON COMMUNITY PARK, IN. PARK FOR AREA RESIDENTS WILL BE BUILT. (LOCAL). CARL HENNING, COORDINATOR; NORTH JUDSON BICENTENNIAL COMMITTEE; RR 2, BOX 326; N JUDSON, IN 46366. (#24085). **ARBA GRANTEE.**

NOTRE DAME

'AN ALMOST CHOSEN PEOPLE', NOTRE DAME, IN. THE CONFERENCE DEALS WITH THE MORAL ASPIRATIONS OF AMERICA. (ST-WIDE). DR THOMAS BERGIN, CHAIRMAN; UNIV OF NOTRE DAME & ST MARYS COLLEGE; BOX 72; NOTRE DAME, IN 46556. (#25352). **ARBA GRANTEE.**

MICROFILM RECORDS OF HOLY CROSS SISTERS, IN. MICROFILM RECORD OF CSC SISTERS & A HISTORY OF THE CONGREGATION. (LOCAL). J DETZLER, PROF OF HISTORY; ST MARY'S COLLEGE; NOTRE DAME, IN 46556. (#15372).

'A NIGHT IN WILLIAMSBURG' - NOTRE DAME, IN. THE PLAY 'A NIGHT IN WILLIAMSBURG' WILL BE PERFORMED BY THE STUDENTS. (LOCAL). MARY GERBER, DIRECTOR OF PROGRAMMING; SAINT MARY'S COLLEGE; NOTRE DAME, IN 46556. (#26929). **ARBA GRANTEE.**

ST MARY'S COLLEGE HISTORY, NOTRE DAME, IN. A HISTORY OF ST MARY'S COLLEGE. (LOCAL). J DETZLER, PROF OF HISTORY; ST MARY'S COLLEGE; NOTRE DAME, IN 46556. (#15373).

OCT 29, '75 - APR 21, '76. HUMANISTIC LECTURES. SEMINAR. (LOCAL). DR JACK DETZLER, CHMN; ST MARYS COLLEGE; NOTRE DAME, IN 46556. (#102379-1).

MAR 7 - 11, '76. 'AN ALMOST CHOSEN PEOPLE' - THE MORAL ASPIRATIONS OF AMERICA. CONFERENCE. (ST-WIDE). DR THOMAS BERGIN, CHMN; UNIV OF NOTRE DAME & ST MARYS COLLEGE; BOX 72; NOTRE DAME, IN 46556. (#25352-1).

MAR 7 - 11, '76. BICENTENNIAL FESTIVAL OF NOTRE DAME UNIVERSITY. ENTITLED 'AN ALMOST CHOSEN PEOPLE: THE MORAL ASPIRATIONS OF AMERICANS.' THE FESTIVAL WILL COMBINE A MAJOR NATIONAL CONFERENCE OF VERY DISTINGUISHED AMERICAN SCHOLARS AND PUBLIC FIGURES WITH A WIDE VARIETY OF CULTURAL EVENTS. AT CENTER FOR CONTINUING EDUCATION. (NAT'L). DEAN THOMAS P BERGIN; UNIV OF NOTRE DAME AND ST MARY'S COLLEGE; CENTER FOR CONTINUING EDUCATION; NOTRE DAME, IN 46556. (#100016-1).

MAR 7 - 12, '76. MURAL ASPIRATIONS OF AMERICANS. SEMINAR. (LOCAL). DR JACK DETZLER, CHMN; ST MARYS COLLEGE; NOTRE DAME, IN 46556. (#102379-3).

APR 2 - 4, '76. WILLIAMSBURG DINNER. FESTIVAL, LIVE PERFORMANCE. (LOCAL). DR JACK DETZLER, CHMN; ST MARYS COLLEGE; NOTRE DAME, IN 46556. (#102379-2).

APR 9 - 11, '76. 'A NIGHT IN WILLIAMSBURG'. LIVE PERFORMANCE. (LOCAL). MARY GERBER, COORD; ST MARY'S COLLEGE; NOTRE DAME, IN 46556. (#26929-1).

OLDENBURG

JULY 3, '76. FIREMEN FESTIVAL AND PARADE. PARADE AT 2 PM; CHICKEN SUPPER AT 4 PM; RIDES, REFRESHMENTS AND ENTERTAINMENT UNTIL 1 AM. (LOCAL). VIRGIL GIESTING, CHMN; EAGLE FIRE COMPANY; PERLEN ST; OLDENBURG, IN 47036. (#107353-1).

JULY 31, '76. OLDENBURG BICENTENNIAL HOMECOMING DAY. FESTIVAL AT TOWN PARK. (LOCAL). GILBERT MUNCHEL, DIRECTOR; OLDENBURG BICENTENNIAL COMMISSION; MAIN ST; OLDENBURG, IN 47036. (#107109-1).

ORLEANS

HISTORIC MOMENTS CONTEST. CONTEST OPEN TO ORLEANS JUNIOR-SENIOR HIGH SCHOOL STUDENTS. ESSAYS 150 TO 300 WORDS ON AMERICAN HISTORIC EVENTS. PRIZE WINNERS TO READ ESSAYS AT LOCAL DOGWOOD FESTIVAL DURING APRIL, 1976. (LOCAL). MRS JOHN R STRANGE, REP; ETA CHAPTER, KAPPA KAPPA KAPPA; 401 HARDING ST; ORLEANS, IN 47452. (#105056-1).

ORLEANS FIFE AND DRUM CORPS, IN. OUTFIT AND TRAIN A GROUP OF YOUTH TO BE AVAILABLE TO PLAY WHENEVER A FIFE AND DRUM CORPS WOULD BE APPROPRIATE DURING YEAR. (LOCAL). GARY SMITH, DIRECTOR; ORLEANS BICENTENNIAL COMMISSION; OLD 37 SOUTH; BEDFORD, IN 47421. (#21468).

PAINTING FIRE HYDRANTS, ORLEANS, IN. DECORATE FIRE HYDRANTS TO REPRESENT FAMOUS PEOPLE IN AMERICAN HISTORY. (LOCAL). CAROL CHASE, DIRECTOR; ORLEANS BICENTENNIAL COMMISSION; EISENHOWER ST; ORLEANS, IN 47452. (#21465).

RECORDING MEMORIES, ORLEANS, IN. STUDENTS WILL RECORD INTERVIEWS WITH SENIOR CITIZENS ON LIFE DURING EARLY PART OF THE CENTURY IN ORLEANS. (LOCAL). JERROLD FINLEY, DIRECTOR; ORLEANS BICENTENNIAL COMMISSION; 365 N 2ND ST; ORLEANS, IN 47452. (#21472).

STETSON HOUSE PAINTING, ORLEANS, IN. COMMISSIONED PAINTING OF HOUSE BUILT BY JOHN B STETSON OF ORLEANS, FOR HIS IN-LAWS; TO BE HUNG IN LOCAL LIBRARY. (LOCAL). CATHERINE CARTWRIGHT, COORDINATOR; BUSINESS AND PROFESSIONAL WOMEN; S MAPLE ST; ORLEANS, IN 47452. (#21467).

SULFUR WELL PARK, ORLEANS, IN. RENOVATION OF NEIGHBORHOOD PARK (SITE OF EARLY SULFUR WELL - UNIQUE FEATURE OF COUNTY) BY VOLUNTEERS; PARK TO INCLUDE PLAY EQUIPMENT FOR CHILDREN AND YOUTH. (LOCAL). EDWARD KING, DIRECTOR; ORLEANS BICENTENNIAL COMMISSION; 672 HAWTHORNE ST; ORLEANS, IN 47452. (#21469). **ARBA GRANTEE.**

TOWN HISTORY, ORLEANS, IN. HISTORY OF ORLEANS PUBLISHED IN INSTALLMENTS IN LOCAL NEWSPAPER. (LOCAL). BECKY FINLEY, EDITOR; ORLEANS BICENTENNIAL COMMISSION; 365 N SECOND ST; ORLEANS, IN 47452. (#21470).

TRASH BARREL PAINTING, ORLEANS, IN. DECORATING OF TRASH BARRELS FOR BEAUTIFICATION AND ANTI-LITTER. (LOCAL). CAROL CHASE, DIRECTOR; ORLEANS BICENTENNIAL COMMISSION; EISENHOWER ST; ORLEANS, IN 47452. (#21466).

APR 24 - MAY 2, '76. DOGWOOD FESTIVAL WITH ARTS & CRAFTS SHOW. DRESSED IN PALE DOGWOOD BLOSSOMS, THE HOMES AND COUNTRYSIDE OF ORLEANS INVITE EXPLORERS TO JOIN A DAY-LONG TOUR; ARTS AND CRAFTS SHOWS, EXHIBITS OF ANTIQUES, COLLECTIBLES AND FLOWERS, A FESTIVAL QUEEN, TOURNAMENTS AND ENTERTAINING BAND CONCERTS. AT ORLEANS, TOWN SQUARE PARK. (LOCAL). MRS DONALD MAHAN, CHMN; ORLEANS DOGWOOD FESTIVAL COMMITTEE; 247 E VINCENNES RD; ORLEANS, IN 47452. (#100328-1).

OWENSBURG

EMMANUEL HATFIELD MUSEUM & LIBRARY, OWENSBURG, TN. CONSTRUCTION OF NEW BUILDING OF RUSTIC DESIGN TO HOUSE LOCAL MEMORABILIA & EFFICIENCY LIBRARY. FUNDS FOR BUILDING WERE RAISED BY COMMUNITY PROJECTS. (LOCAL). LUCILE THOMASSON, COORDINATOR; OWENSBURG IMPROVEMENT GROUP; BOX #1; OWENSBURG, IN 47453. (#28547). **ARBA GRANTEE.**

AUG 7 - 8, '76. FOUNDERS DAY DEDICATION OF HATFIELD MUSEUM & LIBRARY. ARTS & CRAFTS, ANTIQUES, FLEA BOOTHS, PARADE, ENTERTAINMENT, FOOD & OLD OWENSBURG MOVIES FROM 1930-40. AT SOUTHEASTERN GREEN CO, 1 MLE EAST OF HWY 45; 1/4 MLE NORTH HWY 58. (LOCAL). LUCILE THOMASSON, PRES; OWENSBURG COMMUNITY IMPROVEMENT ASSOC; RR #1; SPRINGVILLE, IN 47462. (#106710-1).

PEKIN

JULY 3 - 5, '76. PEKIN COMMUNITY BICENTENNIAL CELEBRATION. 146TH CONSECUTIVE JULY 4TH CELEBRATION. LONGEST WITHOUT-A-MISS CELEBRATION OF ITS KIND, STARTED IN 1830. LINCOLN'S VICE PRES, HANNIBAL HAMLIN, SENATORS & GOVERNORS HAVE SPOKEN IN THE GROVE. AT PEKIN COMMUNITY PARK. (LOCAL). WILLIAM L ELROD, CHMN; PEKIN COMMUNITY BETTERMENT BICENTENNIAL COMM & BANNER PUBLICATIONS; PEKIN, IN 47165. (#106251-1).

PERU

DOWNTOWN BICENT DECORATIONS - PERU, IN. THE CHAMBER MAIDS WILL ERECT STREET SIGNS TO DEPICT THE BICENTENNIAL YEAR. (LOCAL). LARRY KINDLES PARKER, COORDINATOR; PERU CHAMBER OF COMMERCE & CHAMBER MAIDS; PERU, IN 46970. (#26796). **ARBA GRANTEE.**

JULY 16 - 24, '76. CIRCUS CITY FESTIVAL: YOUTH CIRCUS (AGES 6 THRU TEENS). PARADE IS JULY 24TH; PERFORMANCES AT DIFFERENT SCHEDULED TIMES. AT 7TH & BROADWAY. (REGN'L). BETTY BLACK; CIRCUS CITY FESTIVAL, INC; 154 N BROADWAY; PERU, IN 46970. (#100321-1).

PETERSBURG

A HISTORY OF PIKE COUNTY, IN. A HISTORY OF PIKE COUNTY TO BE PUBLISHED IN BOOK FORM. (LOCAL). LOIS WILSON, COORDINATOR; PIKE COUNTY BICENTENNIAL COMMITTEE; RR 3, HICKORY LA; PETERSBURG, IN 47567. (#26855). **ARBA GRANTEE.**

PLAINFIELD

'THE MESSENGER' BICENTENNIAL PROGRAM - NBMRP. IS CARRYING SERIES OF ARTICLES ON GROWTH OF USA. ENCOURAGING & DEVELOPING COMMUNITY BICENTENNIAL PROGRAMS & HAS SPONSORED ESSAY CONTEST ON HOW TOWN SHOULD COMMEMORATE THE BICENTENNIAL. (LOCAL). WILLIAM A BROOKS, EDITOR; THE MESSENGER; BOX 157; PLAINFIELD, IN 46168. (#21754).

PLYMOUTH

ARCHITECTURAL SURVEY - PLYMOUTH, IN. AN ARCHITECTURAL SURVEY WILL BE DONE IN THE COUNTY. (LOCAL). MRS MARY DURNAN, DIRECTOR; MARSHALL CO HISTORICAL SOCIETY, INC; 317 W MONROE; PLYMOUTH, IN 46563. (#29408).

HISTORY OF MARSHALL COUNTY - PLYMOUTH, IN. REPRINT LOCAL HISTORY WITH PLATS 1880-1908-1922. (LOCAL). MRS MARY DURNAN, DIRECTOR; MARSHALL CO HISTORICAL SOCIETY, INC; 317 W MONROE; PLYMOUTH, IN 46563. (#29410).

ITS RED WHITE AND BLUEBERRY TIME. PARADE, EXHIBIT, FESTIVAL. (LOCAL). MRS KAREN METZKER; MARSHALL COUNTY BLUEBERRY FESTIVAL COMMITTEE; RT 5; PLYMOUTH, IN 46563. (#200017-61).

PLYMOUTH, IN, BICENTENNIAL PROJECTS. ANNUAL OF 100 YRS OF PLYMOUTH HIGH SCHOOL; CONSTRUCTION OF A NEW LIBRARY FACILITY; PAINTING OF FIRE HYDRANTS IN THE CITY; A HISTORY OF CHURCHES IN MARSHALL COUNTY; A TIME CAPSULE FOR 2076; FLOAT. (LOCAL). MRS MARY DURNAN, COORDINATOR; PLYMOUTH AREA BICENTENNIAL COMMISSION; 317 W MONROE; PLYMOUTH, IN 46563. (#29409).

JUNE 27, '76. OUR TOWN - 1976, TOWN WALK. TOUR. (LOCAL). MARY DURNAN, MUSEUM DIR; MARSHALL COUNTY HISTORICAL SOCIETY; 317 W MONROE; PLYMOUTH, IN 46563. (#200017-62).

JULY 4, '76. THE GLORIOUS FOURTH, 1976. COMMUNITY PICNIC, CEREMONY, MUSIC, PATRIOTIC ORATORY, GAMES & FOOD. AT PLYMOUTH CENTENNIAL PARK. (LOCAL). KENNETH KOERBER; PLYMOUTH AREA BICENTENNIAL COMMITTEE; 317 W MONROE; PLYMOUTH, IN 46563. (#200017-60).

PORTAGE

PORTAGE CENTURY 3 COMMUNITY SHELTER - IN. A COMMUNITY SHELTER WILL BE BUILT. (LOCAL). THOMAS ROGERS, CHAIRMAN; BICENTENNIAL COMMISSION OF PORTAGE, INC; 5624 FITS AVE; PORTAGE, IN 46368. (#27778). **ARBA GRANTEE.**

JULY 4 - 6, '75. FESTIVAL USA CELEBRATION. FESTIVAL INCLUDES: SOFTBALL TOURNAMENT, SQUARE DANCE AND PICNIC. (LOCAL). MARY ANN ROCKHILL, CHMN; PORTAGE BICENT COMMITTEE; 2541 PATRICIA ST; PORTAGE, IN 46368. (#100349-1).

PORTLAND

RESTORATION OF CONCRETE SPAN BRIDGE, PORTLAND, WI. REPAIR OF CONCRETE STRUCTURE AND REPLACEMENT OF PERIOD LAMPS TO RETURN BRIDGE TO ORIGINAL SHAPE. (LOCAL). CONSTANCE F RONALD, CO-CHAIRMAN; PORTLAND BICENTENNIAL COMMITTEE; 709 W NORTH ST; PORTLAND, IN 47371. (#31093).

PRINCETON

SEPT 18 - 19, '76. AGRICULTURAL AND ART FESTIVAL. THE COUNTY COURT HOUSE LAWN IS BRIMMING WITH ARTS, ANTIQUES AND ARGRICULTURAL DISPLAYS FROM THE SURROUNDING COUNTRYSIDE, WHILE FOOD CONCESSIONS, CONTESTS AND CHURCH EXHIBITS ADD TO THE MERRIMENT. THE FESTIVAL IS OPEN TO THE PUBLIC FREE OF CHARGE. AT COUNTY COURT HOUSE LAWN. (LOCAL). BEN BROWNFIELD, PROJ DIR; PRINCETON CHAMBER OF COMMERCE; 204 E BROADWAY; PRINCETON, IN 47670. (#100343-1).

REMINGTON

SALE OF COOKBOOK - PROJ OF REMINGTON, IN. THE DORCAS CLUB WILL SPONSOR A SALE OF COOKBOOKS. (LOCAL). IRMA BOWMAN, CHAIRMAN; DORCAS CLUB; 8 S OHIO; REMINGTON, IN 47977. (#14627).

JUNE 13, '76. JORDAN/CARPENTER TOWNSHIP PIONEER DAYS. FESTIVAL AT FOUNTAIN PARK CHATAQUA SITE. (LOCAL). EVELYN STANLEY, DIRECTOR; JORDAN/CARPENTER COMMUNITY CLUBS; 520 PARK AVE; RENSSELAER, IN 47978. (#101924-1).

RENSSELAER

DECORATION OF CITY FIRE HYDRANTS, RENSSELAER, IN. PAINTING OF HYDRANTS IN AMERICAN REVOLUTIONARY MOTIF. (LOCAL). IRA HUNTINGTON, PROJ DIRECTOR; SIGMA PHI GAMMA SOCIETY; JACKSON ST; RENSSELAER, IN 47978. (#14626).

FIFE AND DRUM CORPS IN RENSSELAER, IN. THE CORPS WILL APPEAR AT MANY EVENTS THROUGHOUT THE COUNTY. (LOCAL). IRA HUNTINGTON, CHAIRMAN; JASPER COUNTY BICENTENNIAL COMMITTEE; RR 4; RENSSELAER, IN 47978. (#14623). **ARBA GRANTEE.**

HERITAGE ART SHOW. HISTORICAL ARTWORK WILL BE SUBMITTED AND JUDGED. WINNING ART WILL TRAVEL THROUGHOUT THE COUNTRY AND BE ON PUBLIC DISPLAY. (LOCAL). IRA HUNTINGTON, CO-CHMN; JASPER COUNTY ART LEAGUE; 603 E ANGELICA ST; RENSSELAER, IN 47978. (#14604-1). **(??).**

PUBLICATION OF COUNTY'S HISTORY, RENSSELAER, IN. PUBLICATION OF BOOK FROM RECORDS COMPILED BY RESEARCH COMMITTEE. (LOCAL). MRS G DOREMEIRE, CHAIRMAN RESEARCH COMMITTEE; JASPER COUNTY BICENTENNIAL; 624 CLARK ST; RENSSELAER, IN 47978. (#14624).

SALE OF COMMEMORATIVE PLATES, RENSSELAER, IN. PLATES WITH PICTURE OF COUNTY COURTHOUSE; PROCEEDS TO BE USED TO HELP FINANCE BICENTENNIAL PROJECTS AND EVENTS. (LOCAL). IRA HUNTINGTON, PROJ DIRECTOR; JASPER COUNTY HISTORICAL SOCIETY; MILROY AVE; RENSSELAER, IN 47978. (#14625).

WJCK-FM RADIO BICENTENNIAL SUPPORT-NGMRP. BROADCAST OF WIDE RANGE OF BICENTENNIAL PROGRAMMING, INCL PUBLIC SERVICE ANNOUNCEMENTS, INTERVIEWS WITH BICENTENNIAL OFFICIALS & EXTENSIVE LOCAL COVERAGE OF BICENTENNIAL ACTIVITIES. (LOCAL). ANTHONY J CAPPUCCILLI, NEWS DIRECTOR; RADIO STATION WJCK-FM; RURAL RT 6 BOX 3; RENSSELAER, IN 47978. (#32955).

1776-1976: TWO HUNDRED YEARS IN AMERICA. FESTIVAL AT SCHOOL. (LOCAL). BEULAR ARNOTT, COORD; RENSSELAER SCHOOL CORP; AUGUSTA ST; RENSSELAER, IN 47978. (#27012-1).

RENSSELAER — CONTINUED

'1776-1976: TWO HUNDRED YEARS IN AMERICA' - IN. THE RENSSELAER SCHOOL CORPORATION PUT ON A FESTIVAL TO CELEBRATE THE BICENTENNIAL. (LOCAL). BEULAH ARNOTT, COORDINATOR; RENSSELAER SCHOOL CORP; AUGUSTA ST; RENSSELAER, IN 47978. (#33052). **ARBA GRANTEE.**

AUG 9, '75. BICENTENNIAL VARIETY SHOW. LIVE PERFORMANCE AT JASPER COUNTY FAIRGROUNDS. (LOCAL). MRS LARRY JENKINS, COORD; PROGRAM COMMITTEE OF JASPER COUNTY AMERICAN BICENT COMMITTEE; RR 4; RENSSELAER, IN 47978. (#200017-24).

MAY 10 - 14, '76. RENSSELAER CENTRAL SCHOOLS BICENTENNIAL PAGEANT. HISTORY-BASED PAGEANT, STARTING WITH ELEMENTARY SCHOOLS AND ENDING WITH HIGH SCHOOL, DEPICTING DIFFERENT EVENTS IN US HISTORY; WRITTEN AND PERFORMED BY THE GROUPS THEMSELVES. AT SCHOOL BUILDINGS IN RENESSELAER. (LOCAL). MISS BEULAH ARNOTT, COORD; SCHOOL CORPORATION; AUGUSTA ST; RENESSELAER, IN 47978. (#102002-1).

JUNE 20, '76. HANGING GROVE - MCCOYSBURG RURAL CELEBRATION. FESTIVAL AT OLD HANGING GROVE SCHOOL BLDG. (LOCAL). MRS LAVERN MEYERS, COORD; COMMUNITY CLUBS; RR #5; RENSSELAER, IN 47978. (#102001-1).

JULY 3 - 4, '76. JASPER COUNTY BICENTENNIAL CELEBRATION. JULY 3, PARADE & EVENTS AT FAIRGROUNDS; JULY 4, ALL DAY WITH EXHIBITS, CRAFTSMEN, MEALS, FOOD BOOTHS, CONTESTS & GAMES, ANTIQUES, AUTO RACES, MUSIC, DANCING, PARACHUTE JUMPING, TURKEY SHOOT AND ENDING WITH A SPECTACULAR FIREWORKS DISPLAY. HOT AIR BALLOONIST. AT JASPER COUNTY FAIRGROUNDS. (LOCAL). IRA HUNTINGTON, CO-CHMN; JASPER COUNTY BICENTENNIAL COMMISSION; 309 W WASHINGTON ST; RENSSELAER, IN 42978. (#102010-10).

RICHMOND

JOHN TOWNSEND CABIN RESTORATION - IN. RESTORATION OF JOHN TOWNSEND CABIN FOR EDUCATIONAL PURPOSES. (LOCAL). GEORGE T BLAKELY, CHAIRMAN; RICHMOND BICENTENNIAL COMMITTEE; MAYOR'S OFFICE-MUNICIPAL BLDG; RICHMOND, IN 47374. (#27679). **ARBA GRANTEE.**

RICHVALLEY

SEPT 11 - 12, '76. RICHVALLEY HARVEST DAYS BICENTENNIAL CELEBRATION. INCLUDES BIKE RODEO, PET RACES, TRACTOR PULLS, GREASED PIG CONTEST, ICE CREAM SOCIAL, ANTIQUE FLEA MARKET & HOBBY SHOW, HORSE SHOW ON SATURDAY, & OLD FASHIONED SINGING & PREACHING SERVICE ON SUNDAY, PLUS CHURCH CARRY-IN DINNER & THE NEW LIFE QUARTET. (LOCAL). RONALD THRUSH, CHMN; RICHVALLEY BICENTENNIAL COMMITTEE; RR 2; RICHVALLEY, IN 46922. (#200017-66).

RISING SUN

FEB 28, '76. OLD FASHIONED PANCAKE DINNER AND HISTORICAL AWARENESS DAY. EXHIBIT AT OHIO CO HISTORICAL SOCIETY BLDG, S WALNUT ST. (LOCAL). R E ROBERTS, CHMN; ROTARY; 717 4TH ST; RISING SUN, IN 47040. (#105060-1).

APR 29, '76. GOD AND COUNTRY PATRIOTIC CONCERT. CONCERT PRESENTED BY 'REGENERATION', FROM NASHVILLE, TN. AT RISING SUN HIGH SCHOOL AUDITORIUM HENRIETTA ST. (LOCAL). RAYMOND E ROBERTS, CHMN; RISING SUN OHIO COUNTY BICENTENNIAL COMMITTEE; 717 4TH ST; RISING SUN, IN 47040. (#105060-2).

MAY 7, '76. TREE PLANTING CEREMONY. 13 TREES WILL BE PLANTED & A BICENTENNIAL MARKER WILL BE SET UP. (LOCAL). MARY STAPLETON, COORD; 4H JR LEADERS; R 1; RISING SUN, IN 47040. (#20848-1).

MAY 30, '76. MEMORIAL DAY OBSERVANCE. PARADE. (LOCAL). ROBERT WADSWORTH, COORD; AMERICAN LEGION AND BICENTENNIAL COMMITTEE; US POST OFFICE BLDG; RISING SUN, IN 47040. (#105060-3).

JUNE 16 - 19, '76. BLUE JEANS FESTIVAL AND PARADE. FESTIVAL, PARADE, LIVE PERFORMANCE AT MAIN ST. (LOCAL). RAYMOND E ROBERTS, CHMN; OHIO CO BLUE JEANS COMMITTEE & BICENTENNIAL COMMITTEE; 717 4TH ST; RISING SUN, IN 47040. (#105060-4).

JULY 3 - 5, '76. INDEPENDENCE DAY WEEKEND CELEBRATION. CEREMONY, FESTIVAL AT OHIO COUNTY FAIRGROUNDS. (LOCAL). BARBARA SCRANTON, COORD; LIONS CLUB, HOME ECONOMICS CLUB & BICENTENNIAL COMMITTEE; 601 MAIN ST; RISING SUN, IN 47040. (#105060-5).

SEPT 12, '76. MARKER PLACING ON PIONEER GRAVE SITE. A MARKER TO BE PLACED ON FULTON FAMILY GRAVE SITE COMMEMORATING THE FIRST SETTLERS OF RISING SUN. ALSO GOV. STONES DEDICATED ON 2 FULTON REVOLUTIONARY SOLDIERS, FATHER & SON, JOHN & SAMUEL FULTON; JOHN, UNCLE TO ROBERT FULTON, STEAMBOAT INVENTOR. AT STATE RT 56, MARKED 'LEWIS & CLARK TRAIL' & BELLVIEW LANE. (LOCAL). HAZEL STEWART, COORD; COL ARCHIBALD LOCHRY CHAP, #66, DAR; N HIGH ST; RISING SUN, IN 47040. (#105060-6).

ROCHESTER

PIONEER PARK - ROCHESTER, IN. PIONEER PARK, TRIANGULAR 3 ACRE PLOT ON MONTICELLO RD & MILL CREEK, FORMERLY OCCUPIED BY HOMES DESTROYED BY TORNADO, WILL BE MARKED BY A BOULDER WITH BRONZE PLAQUE, PICNIC TABLES & TULIP TREES. (LOCAL). GEORGE JANICEK, CHAIRMAN; ROCHESTER CITY PARK & RECREATION BOARD; 317 W 9TH ST; ROCHESTER, IN 46975. (#22166).

PIONEER WOMAN'S LOG CABIN MUSEUM - ROCHESTER, IN. LOG CABIN RECONSTRUCTED OF LOGS FROM 2 LOG CABINS BUILT IN 1865 FURNISHED WITH 100 YEAR OLD FURNITURE & UTENSILS & TOOLS USED BY PIONEER WOMEN IN FULTON COUNTY & AREA. (LOCAL). SHIRLEY WILLARD, PRESIDENT; FULTON COUNTY HISTORICAL SOCIETY; RR 1; ROCHESTER, IN 46975. (#22167). **ARBA GRANTEE.**

SLIDE PROGRAM OF FULTON COUNTY HISTORY - IN. SLIDES & TAPED PROGRAM OF FULTON COUNTY HISTORY & DEVELOPMENT WITH SLIDES OF BUILDINGS, FAMOUS LOCAL PEOPLE, TOWN CENTENNIALS, FARM EQUIPMENT, DISASTERS, SPORTS, TOWN BANDS AND BICENTENNIAL EVENTS. (LOCAL). FRANKLIN HEISLER, CHAIRMAN; FULTON COUNTY BICENTENNIAL COMMITTEE; RR 2; ROCHESTER, IN 46975. (#22168).

TRAIL OF DEATH HISTORICAL MARKER - ROCHESTER, IN. TRAIL OF DEATH HISTORICAL MARKER TO COMMEMORATE THE FIRST DEATH ON FORCED REMOVAL OF POTTAWATTOMI INDIANS IN 1838, LOCATED AT MUD CREEK ON STATE ROAD 25 THREE MILES NORTH OF FULTON. (ST-WIDE). RICHARD FAUGHT, SCOUTMASTER; BOY SCOUT TROOP 285, SAGAMORE COUNCIL; 302 W 4TH ST; ROCHESTER, IN 46975. (#22165).

MAR 26, '76. FULTON COUNTY BICENTENNIAL COMMUNITY BANQUET. BANQUET FEATURING AUNT FRAN'S CHICKEN & DUMPLINGS. PATRIOTIC PROGRAM OF MUSIC, SLIDES, DANCE, PATRIOTIC & HISTORICAL SPEECHES, PRESENTATION OF OFFICIAL BICENTENNIAL COMMUNITY CERTIFICATE TO FULTON COUNTY. AT ST JOSEPH CATHOLIC PARISH HALL, 13TH & JEFFERSON ST. (LOCAL). LEE JENNINGS, COORD; FULTON COUNTY BICENTENNIAL COMMITTEE; RR 6; ROCHESTER, IN 46975. (#105857-1).

MAY 7 - 8, '76. PIONEER DAY. MAYOR WILL PROCLAIM PIONEER DAY. MERCHANTS TO DECORATE STORE WINDOW WITH PIONEER ARTIFACTS. SCHOOLS WILL HAVE SPECIAL STUDIES & PROGRAMS & DRESS IN PIONEER COSTUMES; CEREMONY TO WELCOME BICENT WAGON TRAIN, ESPECIALLY WAGONMASTER, TOM SMITH & HIS TEAM OF MINI-MULES. AT AMERICAN LEGION HOME, 611 MAIN ST. (LOCAL). JEAN HURD, CHAIRMAN; FULTON COUNTY BICENTENNIAL COMMITTEE; RR 1; ROCHESTER, IN 46975. (#105857-5).

JULY 4, '76. BICENTENNIAL AWARD CEREMONY. WOODEN HAND-PAINTED PLAQUES WILL BE AWARDED TO OWNERS OF BUILDINGS OVER 100 YEARS OLD & LAND WHICH HAS BEEN IN THE SAME FAMILY FOR OVER A CENTURY, THE OLDEST BUSINESS IN THE COUNTY AND THE OLDEST PIONEER PROFESSION IN THE SAME FAMILY. AT 12TH STREET TO THE CITY PARK. (LOCAL). JANE HEISLER, SEC; FULTON COUNTY BICENTENNIAL COMMITTEE; RR 2; ROCHESTER, IN 46975. (#105857-6).

JULY 4, '76. OLD-FASHIONED 4TH OF JULY PICNIC. OLD-TIME HYMN SING, OUTDOOR CHURCH SERVICE, HUCK FINN FISHING CONTEST FOR KIDS, BICENTENNIAL BAND CONTEST, PICNIC LUNCH, PIE-EATING, CONTEST, 4 LEGGED & SACK RACES; PRIZES FOR CONTEST WINNERS. AT ROCHESTER CITY PARK, 12TH & PARK STS. (LOCAL). LEE JENNINGS, CHAIRMAN; FULTON COUNTY BICENTENNIAL COMMITTEE; RR 6; ROCHESTER, IN 46975. (#105857-4).

JULY 9 - 11, '76. ROUND BARN FESTIVAL OF FULTON COUNTY. TOURS OF 12 ROUND BARNS, PARADE SATURDAY AT 10 AM, ARTS & CRAFTS EXHIBIT ON COURTHOUSE SQUARE & BLOCKED OFF MAIN STREET; PARADE, MUZZLE LOADING CONTEST; DEDICATION OF PIONEER PARK, WATER SKI SHOW AND BEARD GROWING CONTEST. AT COURTHOUSE SQUARE & LAKE VIEW PARK ON 9TH & RACE ST. (LOCAL). FRANCES PFEIFFER, CHMN; ROUND BARN FESTIVAL & FULTON COUNTY BICENTENNIAL COMMITTEE; RR 3; ROCHESTER, IN 46975. (#105857-3).

SEPT 4 - 5, '76. TRAIL OF DEATH RENDEZVOUS AND RE-ENACTMENT OF INDIAN REMOVAL. 9 MILE HIKE ON ORIGINAL TRAIL OF DEATH WHEN POTTAWATTOMIES FORCED TO LEAVE IN 1838, BUCKSKINNER TEPEE VILLAGE & BLANKET TRADING, SHOOTING & TOMAHAWK & SPITTING CONTESTS, PIONEER FOOD & CRAFT BOOTHS, INDIAN CEREMONIES & DANCES BY BOY SCOUTS, DEDICATION OF HISTORICAL MARKER. AT RENDEZVOUS SITE, 5 MILES S OF ROCHESTER ON SR 25. (LOCAL). SHIRLEY WILLARD, PRES; FULTON COUNTY HISTORICAL SOCIETY, BICENTENNIAL COMMITTEE & SCOUTS; RR 1; ROCHESTER, IN 46975. (#105857-2).

ROCKPORT

JULY 3 - 10, '76. SPENCER COUNTY FAIR AND FESTIVAL. OLD FASHIONED COUNTY FAIR FOR BICENTENNIAL WITH CRAFTS, COMMUNITY EXHIBITS, AGRICULTURAL PRODUCTS, ENTERTAINMENT, RIDES, BEER GARDEN. AT COUNTY FAIR GROUNDS. (ST-WIDE). FERMAN YEARBY, COORD; SPENCER COUNTY FAIR ASSOC; ELM ST; ROCKPORT, IN 47635. (#104723-2).

JULY 23, '76. COLONIAL TEA. COSTUMED HOSTESSES POUR TEA AND PARTICIPATE WITH OFFICIALS IN RE-DED ICATION OF COURTHOUSE, TOUR OF COURTHOUSE AND HISTORICAL DISPLAYS. AT ROCKPORT COURTHOUSE. (LOCAL). MRS FRANK WETHERILL, CHMN; COUNTY COMMISSIONERS; CHRISNEY, IN 47611. (#104723-3).

NOV 22, '76. VARIETY SHOW. VARIED PATRIOTIC PROGRAM OF MUSIC, DRAMATIC READINGS, SINGING GROUPS AND OTHER LOCAL TALENT. AT ROCKPORT CITY SCHOOL. (LOCAL). MRS DAVID BURNS, COORD; ROCKPORT CIVIC IMPROVEMENT ASSOCIATION; HATFIELD, IN 47617. (#104723-1).

ROCKVILLE

INDIANA FOLK MUSIC FOR SCHOOL DAYS, ROCKVILLE. LIVE MUSICAL PERFORMANCE FOR SCHOOL CHILDREN WILL BE HELD IN MAY. (LOCAL). MICHAEL ALLEN, COORDINATOR; BILLIE CREEK VILLAGE, INC; PO BOX 165; ROCKVILLE, IN 47872. (#24283). **ARBA GRANTEE.**

PARKE COUNTY LONG-TIME PLANNING COMMITTEE - IN. COMMUNITY LEADERS WORKING TOGETHER ON A VOLUNTEER BASIS TO ALLEVIATE LOCAL PROBLEMS; STUDY GROUP MAKES REFERRALS TO APPROPRIATE GROUP FOR ACTION TO BE TAKEN. (LOCAL). CHARLES T FELKNER, COORDINATOR; PARKE COUNTY LONG-TIME PLANNING COMMITTEE; E OHIO, BOX 165; ROCKVILLE, IN 47872. (#20071).

TORCH NEWSPAPERS BICENTENNIAL SUPPORT - NBMRP. CONTINUAL PROMOTION OF COUNTY BICENTENNIAL ACTIVITIES ON PAGE ONE. ENCOURAGEMENT OF FLAG-FLYING, FEATURES ON LOCAL HISTORY & PROMOTION OF DOWNTOWN RESTORATION TO TURN-OF-THE-CENTURY ARCHITECTURE. (LOCAL). RICHARD E HARNEY, PUBLISHER; TORCH NEWSPAPERS; 125 W HIGH ST; ROCKVILLE, IN 47872. (#30428).

MAY 3 - 27, '76. INDIANA FOLK MUSIC FOR SCHOOL DAYS. LIVE PERFORMANCE AT BILLIE CREEK VILLAGE. (LOCAL). MICHAEL ALLEN, COORD; BILLIE CREEK VILLAGE, INC; PO BOX 165; ROCKVILLE, IN 47872. (#24283-1).

OCT 8 - 17, '76. 20TH ANNUAL PARKE COUNTY COVERED BRIDGE FESTIVAL 1976. FESTIVAL, PARADE. (REGN'L). CHARLES FELKNER, COORD; PARKE COUNTY, INC; BOX 165; ROCKVILLE, IN 47872. (#103416-645).

OCT 14 - 23, '77. 21ST ANNUAL PARKE COUNTY COVERED BRIDGE FESTIVAL 1977. FESTIVAL. (REGN'L). CHARLES FELKNER, COORD; PARKE COUNTY, INC; BOX 165; ROCKVILLE, IN 47872. (#109517-1).

ROLLING PR

JULY 13 - AUG 10, '76. CHILDREN'S INTERNATIONAL SUMMER VILLAGE A PROGRAM FOR 11-YEAR OLDS. A PROGRAM DEDICATED TO THE CONCEPT OF INTERNATIONAL UNDERSTANDING AND PEACE THROUGH THE CLOSE FRIENDSHIPS FORMED AMONG 11-YEAR OLDS, FROM COUNTRIES AROUND THE WORLD, LIVING TOGETHER FOR ONE MONTH. AT LE MANS ACADEMY. (LOCAL). JOHN J FABINA, DIRECTOR; CHILDREN'S INTERNATIONAL SUMMER VILLAGES, INC; 2130 RED OAK DR; MICHIGAN CITY, IN 46360. (#104338-5).

ROME CITY

PEAL PEOPLE ENJOY A LEGACY - ROME CITY, IN. SCHOOL BELL WILL BE RESTORED AND PLACED IN AN APPROPRIATE SETTING. (LOCAL). EDWARD KEIL, COORDINATOR; ROME CITY SCHOOL; ROME CITY, IN 46784. (#26928). **ARBA GRANTEE.**

ROSSVILLE

JULY 10 - 11, '76. OLD-FASHIONED THRASHING FESTIVAL. FESTIVAL AT ROSSVILLE HIGH SCHOOL. (ST-WIDE). RICHARD HAMILTON, CHMN; ROSSVILLE BUSINESS AND PROFESSIONAL ORGANIZATION; ROSSVILLE, IN 46065. (#103905-2).

RUSHVILLE

RESTORATION OF WOLFE HOUSE - RUSHVILLE, IN. THE HOME OF COL E H WOLFE, WHO SERVED IN THE CIVIL WAR, WILL BE RESTORED. (LOCAL). JOSEPH PIKE, COORDINATOR; RUSH COUNTY BICENTENNIAL COMMITTEE; 614 N JACKSON ST; RUSHVILLE, IN 46173. (#27688). **ARBA GRANTEE.**

RUSH COUNTY HISTORY - RUSHVILLE, IN. PUBLICATION OF THE COUNTY'S HISTORY. (LOCAL). JOHN WORTH, CHAIRMAN; RUSH COUNTY BICENTENNIAL COMMISSION; 127 W 3RD ST; RUSHVILLE, IN 46173. (#27780). **ARBA GRANTEE.**

OCT 22 - 23, '76. UNITED STATES ARMED FORCES BICENTENNIAL CARAVAN. CARAVAN IS COMPOSED OF EXHIBIT VANS FOR EACH MILITARY SERVICE. PROJECT THEME IS 'HISTORY OF THE ARMED FORCES & THEIR CONTRIBUTIONS TO THE NATION'. (LOCAL). ALBERT HODGE; UNITED STATES ARMED FORCES BICENTENNIAL CARAVAN; 223 N PERKINS; RUSHVILLE, IN 46173. (#1775-736).

SALEM

BICENTENNIAL PARK - SALEM, IN. SALEM PARK & RECREATION DEPT GUILDING BICENTENNIAL PARK FOR AREA RESIDENTS. (LOCAL). JAMES HORNER, COORDINATOR; SALEM PARKS & RECREATION AREA; 105 E MARKET ST; SALEM, IN 47167. (#26918). **ARBA GRANTEE.**

SEPT 10 - 11, '76. OLD SETTLERS DAYS. CRAFTSMEN DEMONSTRATE THEIR SKILLS IN THE STEVENS MEMORIAL MUSEUM. AT STEVENS MEMORIAL MUSEUM, 107 E MARKET ST. (LOCAL). MISS LULIE DAVIS, CHMN; WASHINGTON COUNTY HISTORICAL SOCIETY INC; 307 E MARKET ST; SALEM, IN 47167. (#100330-1).

SCOTLAND

RESTORATION OF OLD HOTEL IN SCOTLAND, IN. REPAIR & RESTORATION OF OLD HOTEL IN SCOTLAND, GREENE COUNTY. (LOCAL). MRS ALBERT FREELAND, COORDINATOR; SCOTLAND HISTORICAL SOCIETY; RR 9; BLOOMINGTON, IN 47401. (#26858). **ARBA GRANTEE.**

SCOTTSBURG

FIRE HYDRANT PAINTING, SCOTTSBURG, IN. PAINT FIRE HYDRANTS RED, WHITE & BLUE THROUGHOUT THE COUNTY, AUSTIN,. (LOCAL). WILLIAM SANDERS, CHAIRMAN; SCOTT COUNTY BICENTENNIAL COMMISSION; 2 E MCCLAIN ST OR RR 6; SCOTTSBURG, IN 47170. (#21168).

HERITAGE '76 SMALL FARM SETTLEMENT, SCOTTSBURG, IN. LOG CABINS TO PORTRAY AN EARLY FARM SETTLEMENT, HOUSE, BARN & SMOKEHOUSE USED AS MUSEUM FURNISHED WITH RELICS FROM COUNTY. TOURS GIVEN ON HOLIDAYS & THROUGHOUT SPRING, SUMMER & FALL. (LOCAL). WILLIAM SANDERS, CHAIRMAN; SCOTT COUNTY BICENTENNIAL COMMISSION; 2 E MCLAIN ST OR RR 6; SCOTTSBURG, IN 47170. (#21169). **ARBA GRANTEE.**

JUNE 18 - 26, '76. BICENTENNIAL CELEBRATION. MARKETS, CUSTOM CAR SHOW, ANTIQUE CAR SHOW, ARTS & CRAFTS, GO CART RACES, CYCLE RACES, MIDGET RACES, BLUE GRASS MUSIC, ROCK MUSIC, FIREWORKS, LOG SAWING CONTEST, BICENTENNIAL QUEEN PAGEANT, AND MUCH MORE. AT SCOTT COUNTY FAIRGROUNDS, HWY 31. (LOCAL). WILLIAM SANDERS, CHAIRMAN; SCOTT COUNTY BICENTENNIAL COMMISSION; 2 E MCCLAIN ST, RR 6; SCOTTSBURG, IN 47170. (#105209-1).

SEYMOUR

BICENTENNIAL EDITION OF SCHOOL PAPER; SEYMOUR, IN. AN ISSUE OF THE SHIELDS JR HIGH SCHOOL PAPER WILL BE DEDICATED TO THE BICENTENNIAL. (LOCAL). JOE PITMAN, PRINCIPAL; SHIELDS JR HIGH; SEYMOUR, IN 47274. (#19514).

COVERED BRIDGES PROJ - SEYMOUR, IN. THE COVERED BRIDGES IN JACKSON COUNTY WILL BE RE-ROOFED. (LOCAL). CHRISTOPHER MAY, PROJ COORDINATOR; JACKSON COUNTY BICENTENNIAL COMMISSION; 809 W 8TH ST; SEYMOUR, IN 47274. (#26633). **ARBA GRANTEE.**

YEARBOOK PUBLICATION OF BICENTENNIAL DISPLAYS - IN. YEARBOOK OF PICTURES OF BICENTENNIAL DISPLAYS. (LOCAL). PAUL RUCKER, PRINCIPAL; WASHINGTON ELEMENTARY SCHOOL; SEYMOUR, IN 47274. (#19513).

SEPT '75 - MAY '76. BICENTENNIAL THEME: CHILDREN'S ARTWORK EXHIBIT. EXHIBIT AT RILEY ELEMENTARY SCHOOL. (LOCAL). TOM JOHNSON, DIR; RILEY ELEMENTARY SCHOOL; SEYMOUR, IN 47274. (#104471-10).

OCT 1, '75 - DEC 31, '76. CHILD NUTRITION BICENTENNIAL PROGRAM. SPECIAL HERITAGE SCHOOL LUNCH MENUS. AT SCHOOL CAFETERIAS. (LOCAL). JEAN AUFFENBERG, DIR; SEYMOUR COMMUNITY SCHOOLS; 1638 S WALNUT ST; SEYMOUR, IN 47274. (#104471-9).

NOV 26, '75. PILGRIMS MEAL. FESTIVAL. (LOCAL). CECIL MOORE, COORDINATOR; REDDING ELEMENTARY SCHOOL; SEYMOUR, IN 47274. (#200017-26).

DEC 11, '75. WINTER BAND CONCERT. LIVE PERFORMANCE. (LOCAL). EDWIN LYSKOWINSKI, COORD; SEYMOUR HIGH SCHOOL; SEYMOUR, IN 47274. (#200017-27).

JAN 5 - 30, '76. SPIRIT OF '76 ART EXHIBIT. DISPLAY OF PUPILS' ARTWORK DEPICTING HISTORICAL EVENTS AND PIONEER LIFE IN HALLWAYS OF SCHOOL. AT LINCOLN ELEMENTARY SCHOOL. (LOCAL). DARRELL BARNETT, DIR; LINCOLN ELEMENTARY SCHOOL; SEYMOUR, IN 47274. (#104471-6).

JAN 12 - APR 30, '76. DISPLAY OF U S HISTORICAL SCENES. DISPLAY OF HISTORICAL SCENES ON DISHES. AT EMERSON ELEMENTARY SCHOOL. (LOCAL). WILLIAM ESTELL; EMERSON ELEMENTARY SCHOOL; SEYMOUR, IN 47274. (#104471-5).

JAN 12 - MAY 14, '76. COLONIAL LIFE. SEVERAL CLASSES WILL DEPICT CERTAIN PHASES OF COLONIAL LIFE. (LOCAL). ROBERT DEMSKE, PRINCIPAL; IMMANUEL LUTHERAN SCHOOL; 520 S CHESTNUT ST; SEYMOUR, IN 47274. (#104471-13).

JAN 12 - DEC ??, '76. MEDIA CENTER COLONIAL DISPLAYS AT VARIOUS TIMES THROUGHOUT 1976. EXHIBIT AT IMMANUEL LUTHERAN SCHOOL, INDIVIDUAL CLASSROOMS. (LOCAL). ROBERT DEMSKE, PRINCIPAL; IMMANUEL LUTHERAN SCHOOL; 520 S CHESTNUT ST; SEYMOUR, IN 47274. (#104471-14).

FEB 1 - 29, '76. SERTOMA FREEDOM PROGRAM. ESSAY CONTEST OF 300 WORDS ON 'WHAT FREEDOM MEANS TO ME'; EACH 5TH GRADE STUDENT RECEIVES A COPY OF THE DECLARATION OF INDEPENDENCE. THE DISTRICT, CITY & STATE WINNERS AND THEIR PARENTS & TEACHERS WILL ATTEND A BANQUET. (LOCAL). RALPH P MICHAEL, PRES; THE SERTOMA CLUB OF SEYMOUR IN/SERTOMA INTERNATIONAL; 314 W 7TH ST; SEYMOUR, IN 47274. (#105210-1).

FEB 6, '76 - CONTINUING . MINI-COURSES ON PIONEER ACTIVITIES. LIVE PERFORMANCE. (LOCAL). RAYMOND CORYELL, DIR; JACKSON ELEMENTARY SCHOOL; SEYMOUR, IN 47274. (#104471-4).

FEB 12, '76 - CONTINUING . PROGRAM ON AMERICAN PRESIDENTS. BIOGRAPHIES OF AMERICAN PRESIDENTS PRESENTED LIVE THROUGH SCHOOL PUBLIC ADDRESS SYSTEM. (LOCAL). RAYMOND CORYELL, DIR; JACKSON ELEMENTARY SCHOOL; SEYMOUR, IN 47274. (#104471-2).

FEB 13, '76 - CONTINUING . PRE-BASKETBALL GAME BAND AND CHOIR BICENTENNIAL PROGRAM. PRESENTATION BY HIGH SCHOOL BAND AND CHOIR BEFORE SCHEDULED VARSITY BASKETBALL GAME. AT JACKSON ELEMENTARY SCHOOL. (LOCAL). EDWIN LYSKOWINSKI, DIR; SEYMOUR HIGH SCHOOL; SEYMOUR, IN 47274. (#104471-3).

FEB 23, '76. FLAG PROGRAM. LIVE PERFORMANCE. (LOCAL). TOM JOHNSON, PRINCIPAL; RILEY ELEMENTARY SCHOOL; SEYMOUR, IN 47274. (#104471-22).

FEB 23 - 27, '76. JUNIOR HIGH BICENTENNIAL ART EXHIBIT. EXHIBIT. (LOCAL). JOE PITMAN, PRINCIPAL; SHIELDS JR HIGH SCHOOL; SEYMOUR, IN 47274. (#104471-21).

FEB 27, '76. U S HISTORIC PLAY. LIVE PERFORMANCE. (LOCAL). PAUL RUCKER; WASHINGTON ELEMENTARY SCHOOL; SEYMOUR, IN 47274. (#104471-20).

MAR 1, '76. PRIMARY GRADES BICENTENNIAL PROGRAM. LIVE PERFORMANCE AT IMMANUEL GYM, 520 S CHESTNUT ST. (LOCAL). ROBERT DEMSKE, PRINCIPAL; IMMANUEL LUTHERAN SCHOOL; 520 S CHESTNUT ST; SEYMOUR, IN 47274. (#104471-12).

MAR 19, '76. CONVOCATION OF PATRIOTIC SONGS. LIVE PERFORMANCE AT LINCOLN ELEMENTARY SCHOOL. (LOCAL). DARRELL BARNETT, DIR; LINCOLN ELEMENTARY SCHOOL; SEYMOUR, IN 47274. (#104471-19).

APR 5 - 30, '76. CURRIER-IVES DISPLAY. EXHIBIT AT JACKSON ELEMENTARY SCHOOL. (LOCAL). RAYMOND CORYELL, DIR; JACKSON ELEMENTARY SCHOOL; SEYMOUR, IN 47274. (#104471-18).

APR 6, '76. CURRICULUM BICENTENNIAL FAIR BY CHILDREN OF GRADES 1-8. FAIR AT IMMANUEL GYM, 520 S CHESTNUT ST. (LOCAL). ROBERT DEMSKE, PRINCIPAL; IMMANUEL LUTHERAN SCHOOL; 520 S CHESTNUT ST; SEYMOUR, IN 47274. (#104471-11).

APR 9, '76. TREE PLANTING. THIS EVENT WILL TAKE PLACE AT THE FOLLOWING SCHOOLS WITH THEIR RESPECTIVE CONTACTS: LINCOLN ELEMENTARY, DARRELL BARNETT; WASHINGTON ELEMENTARY, PAUL RUCKER; RILEY ELEMENTARY, TOM JOHNSON. AT JACKSON, LINCOLN, RILEY & WASHINGTON ELEMENTARY SCHOOLS. (LOCAL). RAYMOND CORYELL, COORD; SEYMOUR COMMUNITY SCHOOLS; LINCOLN ELEMENTARY SCHOOL; SEYMOUR, IN 47274. (#104479-21).

APR 20, '76. YOUNG BEN FRANKLIN - AMERICAN HERITAGE IN ACTION. LIVE PERFORMANCE AT SEYMOUR HIGH SCHOOL AUDITORIUM. (LOCAL). DR CONRAD GALLOWAY, DIR; SEYMOUR COMMUNITY SCHOOLS; 1638 S WALNUT ST; SEYMOUR, IN 47274. (#104471-24).

APR 24, '76. HERITAGE BALL. FESTIVAL AT NATIONAL GUARD ARMORY. (ST-WIDE). MRS JON ROBERTSON DIR; JACKSON COUNTY BICENTENNIAL COMMITTEE; LAKE & FOREST STS; BROWNSTOWN, IN 47220. (#104302-1).

APR 25 - 29, '76. GRADE EIGHT WASHINGTON, DC TRIP. TOUR. (LOCAL). ROBERT DEMSKE, PRINCIPAL; IMMANUEL LUTHERAN SCHOOL; 520 S CHESTNUT ST; SEYMOUR, IN 47274. (#104471-16).

APR 26, '76. 'LET GEORGE DO IT'; OPERETTA WITH A BICENTENNIAL THEME. LIVE PERFORMANCE AT IMMANUEL GYM, 520 CHESTNUT ST. (LOCAL). ROBERT DEMSKE, PRINCIPAL; IMMANUEL LUTHERAN SCHOOL; 520 S CHESTNUT ST; SEYMOUR, IN 47274. (#104471-15).

APR 30, '76. BICENTENNIAL CONVOCATION. CEREMONY. (LOCAL). JOE PITMAN, PRINCIPAL; SHIELDS JR HIGH SCHOOL; SEYMOUR, IN 47274. (#104471-28).

MAY 6, '76 - CONTINUING . SPRING HIGH SCHOOL CHOIR CONCERT. LIVE PERFORMANCE. (LOCAL). EDWIN LYSKOWINSKI, DIR; SEYMOUR HIGH SCHOOL; SEYMOUR, IN 47274. (#104471-27).

MAY 25, '76. SCHOOL PICNIC WITH GAMES OF PIONEER CHILDREN. GRADES 1-6 WILL PLAY GAMES PIONEER CHILDREN PLAYED. AT LOCAL PARK. (LOCAL). DARRELL BARNETT, DIR; LINCOLN ELEMENTARY SCHOOL; SEYMOUR, IN 47274. (#104471-26).

AUG 15, '76. VJ DAY PARADE. OUR CITY IS THE ONLY CITY IN THE US THAT HAS CONTINUOUSLY CELEBRATED VJ DAY. THIS YEAR IS OUR 30TH YEAR FOR THIS CELEBRATION. IT WILL BE THE BIGGEST AND BEST EVER. AT 311 JACKSON PARK DRIVE, SEYMOUR, IN. (LOCAL). WALFRED KLEIMDLA, DIR; VETERANS OF FOREIGN WARS, POST 1925; 418 CARTER BLVD; SEYMOUR, IN 47274. (#104302-4).

SEPT 29 - OCT 2, '76. OKTOBERFEST, FALL ARTS AND CRAFTS FESTIVAL. FESTIVAL WILL ALSO INCLUDE FOOD AND LIVE ENTERTAINMENT. AT DOWNTOWN SEYMOUR 2ND & CHESTNUT STS. (LOCAL). LARRY KRUKEWITT, DIR; SEYMOUR CHAMBER OF COMMERCE; 2212 MARK TWAIN AVE; SEYMOUR, IN 47274. (#104302-3).

DEC 8 - 12, '76. DECORATION OF PIONEER CHRISTMAS TREE. CHILDREN WILL DECORATE CHRISTMAS TREE AS PIONEER CHILDREN DID. AT JACKSON ELEMENTARY SCHOOL. (LOCAL). RAYMOND CORYELL, DIR; JACKSON ELEMENTARY SCHOOL; SEYMOUR, IN 47274. (#104471-7).

SHELBY

DEC 27, '76 - JAN 11, '77. LA SALLE EXPEDITION II - PORTAGE & FROZEN RIVER 15 DAYS. THIS IS AN AUTHENTIC RE-ENACTMENT OF THE 1681 LASALLE EXPEDITION FROM MONTREAL, CANADA TO NEW ORLEANS, LA WHICH WILL BEGIN TOURING ON AUGUST 11, 1976 AND END ON APRIL 9, 1977. (LOCAL). REID H LEWIS, DIRECTOR; LA SALLE EXPEDITION II; 135 S LA SALLE ST, RM 411; CHICAGO, IL 60690. (#102805-34).

SOUTH BEND

BICENTENNIAL NATURE PRESERVE - SOUTH BEND, IN. PRESERVE AND EXPAND NATURE AREA ON A CROWDED URBAN CAMPUS; EMPHASIS ON FLORA NATIVE TO AREA. (LOCAL). V L RIEMENSCHNEIDER, PROJ DIRECTOR; INDIANA UNIV AT SOUTH BEND; SOUTH BEND, IN 46615. (#20684).

CEREMONIAL FIFE & DRUM CORPS OF SOUTH BEND, IN. 30 HIGH SCHOOL STUDENTS IN REVOLUTIONARY ERA UNIFORM. (LOCAL). GWEN STIVER, EXEC CHAIRMAN; SOUTH BEND BICENTENNIAL COMMITTEE; 1127 E WAYNE N; SOUTH BEND, IN 46615. (#12092).

COMPOSITION OF IDENTITY - SOUTH BEND, IN. AN ENVIRONMENTAL AND AUDIENCE INTERACTION WORK WITH ELECTRONIC MUSIC. (LOCAL). BARTON K MCLEAN, DIRECTOR; 58412 LOCUST RD; SOUTH BEND, IN 46614. (#21228).

EXHIBITION OF LANDSCAPES BY THOMAS MORAN -INDIANA. ORGANIZE 59 UNPUBLISHED MORAN DRAWINGS OF WESTERN LANDSCAPE AND RELEVANT PAINTINGS FOR EXHIBIT. DETERMINE THEIR STYLISTIC ORIGINS AND INFLUENCE ON SUBSEQUENT PAINTING & PUBLISH FINDINGS IN CATALOG. (REGN'L). THOMAS S FERN, PRINCIPAL INVESTIGATOR; UNIV OF NOTRE DAME; NOTRE DAME, IN 46556. (#2542).

SOUTH BEND BICENTENNIAL PAGEANT, IN. A PAGEANT DEPICTING LOCAL HISTORY INCLUDING THE LASALLE EXPLORATION, WOMEN OF THE REVOLUTION & OTHER ASPECTS OF LOCAL HISTORY AS RELATED TO THE AMERICAN REVOLUTION. (LOCAL). NEAL I FISHER, COORDINATOR; SOUTH BEND BICENTENNIAL COMMITTEE; 2920 KETTERING DR; SOUTH BEND, IN 46635. (#26807). **ARBA GRANTEE.**

SOUTH BEND, IND, BICENTENNIAL COMMEMORATIVE PARK. THE SOUTH BEND COMMUNITY BICENTENNIAL PROJECT IS A PARK ON THE WEST SIDE OF THE ST JOSEPH RIVER. TIERED AMPHITHEATER WILL SERVE AS PUBLIC FORUM NEAR THE CIVIC CENTER COMPLEX AND DOWNTOWN MALL. (LOCAL). JAMES SEITZ, SOUTH BEND PARK SUPERINTENDENT; CITY OF SOUTH BEND; CITY-COUNTY BLDG; SOUTH BEND, IN 46601. (#1241). **ARBA GRANTEE.**

MAY 1 - 31, '74. REVOLUTIONARY WAR PORTRAITS EXHIBIT IN SOUTH BEND. GALLERY OF COLOR PHOTOS OF 65 PERSONS ASSOCIATED WITH INDIANA & THE AMERICAN REVOLUTION IS BEING EXHIBITED IN PUBLIC BUILDINGS THROUGHOUT STATE. BOOK OF SHORT BIOGRAPHIES OF SUBJECTS AVAILABLE. (ST-WIDE). DALE FRUCHTNICHT; INDIANA STATE BICENTENNIAL COMMISSION; 504 STATE OFFICE BLDG; INDIANAPOLIS, IN 46204. (#1635-902).

JULY 4 - 6, '75. ETHNIC FESTIVAL 1975. COMMUNITY FIREWORKS-ETHNIC, CRAFTS, FOOD, DANCING INVOLUMENT OF MANY COMMUNITY ORGANIZATIONS AND INDIVIDUALS, INVOLVMENT OF COMMUNITY GOVERNMENTAL DEPARTMENTS DEDICATION OF BICENTENNIAL PARK. AT CITY PARKING GARAGES RIVER BEND PLAZA. (LOCAL). MRS GWEN STIVER; SOUTH BEND BICENTENNIAL COMMITTEE; 1127 EAST WAYNE ST NORTH; SOUTH BEND, IN 46615. (#50530-1).

JULY 14 - 16, '75. AMERICAN FREEDOM TRAIN DISPLAY DAYS AT SOUTH BEND. THE AMERICAN FREEDOM TRAIN WILL INCLUDE 10 EXHIBIT CARS & 2 SHOWCASE CARS DEPICTING DIFFERENT PHASES OF THE AMERICAN EXPERIENCE. ITS ARRIVAL WILL SERVE AS A CATALYST FOR LOCAL BICENTENNIAL CELEBRATIONS BY PEOPLE THROUGHOUT THIS NATION. (ST-WIDE). SY FREEDMAN, DIR OF P/R; THE AMERICAN FREEDOM TRAIN FOUNDATION; 5205 LEESBURG PIKE, SUITE 800; BAILEY'S XRDS, VA 22041. (#1776-137).

APR 1 - OCT 1, '76. AN ENVIRONMENTAL AND AUDIENCE INTERACTION, ELECTRONIC MUSIC. EXHIBIT, LIVE PERFORMANCE. (LOCAL). BARTON MCLEAN, PROJ DIR; BARTON MCLEAN; 58412 LOCUST RD; SOUTH BEND, IN 46614. (#22146-1).

APR 4 - MAY 30, '76. AN EXHIBITION OF LANDSCAPES BY THOMAS MORAN. A CATALOG WITH ESSAYS AND INFORMATION ON MORAN'S LIFE AND WORK WILL ACCOMPANY. PAINTINGS MOSTLY OF ROCKY MTS W/ SOME ITALIAN LANDSCAPES. AT UNIV ART GALLERY, O'SHAUGHNESSY HALL, NOTRE DAME CAMPUS. (REGN'L). THOMAS S FERN; NATIONAL ENDOWMENT FOR THE ARTS, UNIVERSITY OF NOTRE DAME; DEPT OF ART, UNIV OF NOTRE DAME; NOTRE DAME, IN 46556. (#2542-1).

JUNE 1, '76. NORTHFIELD BOYS CHORUS. LIVE PERFORMANCE, TOUR. (LOCAL). ROBERT SWANSON; NORTHFIELD BOYS CHORUS AND NORTHFIELD BICENTENNIAL COMMITTEE; 1117 COLLEGE ST; NORTHFIELD, MN 55057. (#104457-1).

JUNE 1 - 30, '76. 'THE ARTS AMID AMERICA'. FOCUS ON WOMEN'S ART CONTRIBUTIONS; 4 WEEK WORKSHOP FOR MEN AND WOMEN WITH VISITING ARTISTS; THERE WILL BE REGIONAL PARTICIPATING ARTISTS, DOCUMENTATION AND TRAVELING EXHIBITIONS. AT OLD FIELDHOUSE, UNIV OF NOTRE DAME. (LOCAL). MOIRA GEOFFRION; NOTRE DAME UNIV; O'SHAUGHNESSY HALL; NOTRE DAME, IN 46556. (#10919-1).

JULY 3 - 5, '76. ETHNIC FESTIVAL. INVOLVES MANY ETHNIC CRAFTS, FOOD AND DANCING, CRAFTS, ACTIVITIES AND FIREWORKS. AT RIVER BEND PLAZA - DOWNTOWN SOUTH BEND. (LOCAL). GWEN STIVER, CHAIRMAN; SOUTH BEND BICENTENNIAL COMMITTEE; 1127 E WAYNE ST; SOUTH BEND, IN 46615. (#103920-2).

JULY 4 - 5, '76. SOUTH BEND BICENTENNIAL PAGEANT. HISTORIC OUTDOOR PAGEANT INVOLVING 3000 PEOPLE WITH ORIGINAL SCRIPT & MUSIC; HAD 8 SEGMENTS; RELIGION, EDUCATION, COMMUNICATION, INDUSTRY, SPORTS, ETC. AT PINHOOK PARK - SOUTH BEND PARK DEPT. (LOCAL). NEAL I FISHER, COORD; SOUTH BEND BICENTENNIAL COMMITTEE; 2920 KETTERING DR; SOUTH BEND, IN 46635. (#26807-1).

SOUTH BEND — CONTINUED

OCT 7 - 8, '76. UNITED STATES ARMED FORCES BICENTENNIAL CARAVAN. CARAVAN IS COMPOSED OF EXHIBIT VANS FOR EACH MILITARY SERVICE. PROJECT THEME IS 'HISTORY OF THE ARMED FORCES & THEIR CONTRIBUTIONS TO THE NATION'. (LOCAL). MRS GWEN STIVER; UNITED STATES ARMED FORCES BICENTENNIAL CARAVAN; 1127 E WAYNE NORTH; SOUTH BEND, IN 46615. (#1775-729).

DEC 23 - 26, '76. LA SALLE EXPEDITION II, A HISTORIC RE-ENACTMENT. THIS IS AN AUTHENTIC RE-ENACTMENT OF THE 1681 LASALLE EXPEDITION FROM MONTREAL, CANADA TO NEW ORLEANS, LA WHICH WILL BEGIN TOURING ON AUGUST 11, 1976 AND END ON APRIL 9, 1977. (LOCAL). REID H LEWIS, DIRECTOR; LA SALLE EXPEDITION II; 135 S LA SALLE ST, RM 411; CHICAGO, IL 60690. (#102805-32).

NOV '77. COMPOSITION OF IDENTITY. AN ENVIRONMENTAL & AUDIENCE INTERACTION WORK WITH ELECTRONIC MUSIC. (LOCAL). BARTON K MCLEAN, DIRECTOR; BARTON K MCLEAN; 58412 LCOUST RD; SOUTH BEND, IN 46614. (#21228-1).

SPEEDWAY

SPEEDWAY GOLDEN ANNIVERSARY CELEBRATION. THIS EVENT WAS TO CELEBRATE THE CHARTERING OF THE TOWN IN 1926 AS WELL AS THE NATION'S BICENTENNIAL. (LOCAL). R P MCCLAMROCH, CHMN; SPEEDWAY GOLDEN JUBILEE, INC; PO BOX 24-1926; SPEEDWAY, IN 46224. (#200017-97).

JULY 4, '76. PATRIOTIC CELEBRATION. A PICNIC, PATRIOTIC PARADE, BAND CONCERT & FIREWORKS WERE INCLUDED IN THIS EVENT. AT SPEEDWAY STREETS AND LEONARD PARK. (LOCAL). R P MCCLAMROCH, COORD; SPEEDWAY GOLDEN JUBILEE, INC; 5741 W 18TH ST; SPEEDWAY, IN 46224. (#200017-95).

JULY 7 - 10, '76. HISTORIC PAGEANT. PAGEANT DEPICTS SPEEDWAY'S GROWTH FROM INDIAN TERRITORY TO PRESENT. AT SPEEDWAY HIGH SCHOOL ATHLETIC FIELD ON WEST 25TH ST. (LOCAL). R P MCCLAMROCH, CHMN; SPEEDWAY GOLDEN JUBILEE, INC; 5741 W 18TH ST; SPEEDWAY, IN 46224. (#200017-94).

JULY 11, '76. CLASSIC CAR PARADE. PARADE AT SPEEDWAY STREETS. (LOCAL). R P MCCLAMROCH, CHAIRMAN; SPEEDWAY GOLDEN JUBILEE, INC; 5741 W 18TH ST; SPEEDWAY, IN 46224. (#200017-96).

SPENCER

HISTORY OF LOCAL AMER REVOL VETERANS; SPENCER, IA. WAR RECORDS & GENEALOGY DATA ON 40 VETERANS OF AMER REVOL & DATA ON INDIAN POPULATIONS WHO SETTLED IN OWEN COUNTY IS BEING COLLECTED FOR A SERIES IN LOCAL PAPER & LIBRARY LOCAL HISTORY COLLECTION. (ST-WIDE). DIXIE KLINE, CHAIRMAN; SPENCER BICENTENNIAL COMMITTEE; PO BOX 226; SPENCER, IN 47460. (#19383).

PIONEER DAYS, SPENCER, IN. A PIONEER DAYS FESTIVAL THROUGHOUT OWEN COUNTY. (LOCAL). DIXIE KLINE, COORDINATOR; OWEN COUNTY BICENTENNIAL COMMITTEE; PO BOX 226; SPENCER, IN 47460. (#27365). **ARBA GRANTEE.**

RESTORATION OF 1820 COURTHOUSE, SPENCER, IN. RESTORE THE HAND-HEWED LOG COURTHOUSE BUILT IN 1820. (ST-WIDE). DIXIE KLINE, CHAIRMAN; OWEN COUNTY BICENTENNIAL COMMITTEE; SPENCER, IN 47460. (#20385).

SPENCER EVENING WORLD BICENTENNIAL COVERAGE -NBMRP. REPORTS REGULARLY ON COMMUNITY BICENTENNIAL ACTIVITIES, IS RUNNING A SERIES ON OWEN COUNTY FACT & FOLKLORE, A 'OWEN COUNTY ANCESTORS' COLUMN, & ASSISTANCE IN GENEALOGICAL RESEARCH. (LOCAL). THOMAS L DOUGLAS, ASST GENERAL MANAGER; SPENCER EVENING WORLD; 114 E FRANKLIN ST; SPENCER, IN 47460. (#20605).

THEATRE IN THE WOODS, SPENCER, IN. PLAYS FROM EARLY AMERICAN THEATRE. (LOCAL). PENELOPE KOOB, COORDINATOR; OWEN COUNTY COMMITTEE FOR PERFORMING ARTS; 216 N MAIN ST; SPENCER, IN 47460. (#27771). **ARBA GRANTEE.**

JUNE 5 - 20, '76. PIONEER DAYS. FESTIVAL. (LOCAL). DIXIE KLINE, COORD; OWEN COUNTY BICENTENNIAL COMMITTEE; PO BOX 226; SPENCER, IN 47460. (#27365-1).

ST HENRY

MAY 28 - 29, '76. HEINRICHSDORF FEST, A GERMAN ETHNIC CELEBRATION. GERMAN FESTIVITIES BEGIN IN THE BEER GARDENS ON FRIDAY, WITH MUSIC, COUNTRY SAUSAGES AND FAMOUS SAINT HENRY STYLE BARBEQUE RIBS, CHICKEN AND BEER. THE FREE ACTIVITIES CONTINUE UNTIL SATURDAY MIDNIGHT. (LOCAL). DENNIS L DURCHOLZ, CHMN; SAINT HENRY COMMUNITY CLUB; RR #1, BOX 42-A; FERDINAND, IN 47532. (#100341-1).

ST MEINRAD

APR 16, '76. THE PASSION ACCORDING TO SAINT JOHN. ORIGINAL COMPOSITION FOR BICENTENNIAL BY FATHER COLUMBA KELLY, OSB, FOR CHORUS; TWO PERFORMANCES, NOON AND 3:00 PM. AT ARCHABBEY CHURCH. (LOCAL). BROTHER LAMBERT ZINK, DIR; ST MEINRAD ARCHABBEY; ST MEINRAD, IN 47577. (#104722-1).

OCT 10, '76. VOLUNTEER FIREMAN PARADE. BICENTENNIAL THEME PARADE WITH 100 ENTRIES INCLUDING THREE HIGH SCHOOL BANDS AND QUEEN CONTEST. AT MAIN STREET. (LOCAL). TERRY UEBELHOR, CHMN; DISTRICT 18 VOLUNTEER FIREMEN; ST MEINRAD, IN 47577. (#104722-2).

SULLIVAN

HISTORICAL MARKER & TREE PLANTING IN SULLIVAN, IN. PERMANENT IDENTIFICATION OF INTER-URBAN STOP #25 & PLANTING OF TREE. (LOCAL). LEE FRENCH, CHAIRMAN; SULLIVAN BICENTENNIAL COMMITTEE/AMERICAN LEGION/CENTRAL SCHOOL; 219 E JACKSON ST; SULLIVAN, IN 47882. (#28635).

SEPT 18, '76. CORN FESTIVAL & BICENTENNIAL PARADE. FESTIVAL, PARADE AT SULLIVAN PUBLIC SQUARE, DOWNTOWN, STATE RD 41. (LOCAL). LEE FRENCH, CHAIRMAN; BUSINESS WOMEN BICENTENNIAL COMMITTEE; 219 E JACKSON ST; SULLIVAN, IN 47882. (#200017-65).

SWAYZEE

MONUMENT, SWAYZEE, IN. DEDICATION OF MONUMENT FOR ALL THOSE WHO MADE THE SUPREME SACRIFICE IN ALL WARS. (LOCAL). JERRY D SMITH, CO-CHAIRMAN; SWAYZEE BICENTENNIAL COMMITTEE; BOX 247; SWAYZEE, IN 46986. (#31295).

JUNE 28 - JULY 4, '76. FULL WEEK OF BICENTENNIAL ACTIVITIES. FESTIVAL AT 101 N WASHINGTON, BANK PROPERTY AND SWAYZEE SCHOOL PARKING LOT. (LOCAL). JERRY D SMITH, CHAIRMAN; SWAYZEE BICENTENNIAL COMMITTEE; BOX 247; SWAYZEE, IN 46986. (#200017-92).

SWEETSER

SWEETSER MUSEUM, IN. ESTABLISHMENT OF LOCAL MUSEUM TO HOUSE LOCAL HISTORICAL ITEMS. (LOCAL). KENNETH JACKSON; SWEETSER BICENTENNIAL COMMITTEE; 2648N 500W; MARION, IN 46952. (#21576). **ARBA GRANTEE.**

JULY 4, '76. FOURTH OF JULY MEMORIAL CELEBRATION. ALL AREA CHURCH SERVICE 9:30 AM GRAVESIDE MEMORIAL CEREMONY FOR REV WAR SOLDIERS 11:00 AM COMMUNITY PICNIC ON SCHOOLGROUND 12:00 SPEAKER BUD HILLIS 2PM; PARADE 2:30 PM; CHICKEN BARBEQUE & LIONS FISH FRY 4:30 PM; HIGH SCHOOL BAND CONCERT 6:30; FIREWORKS DISPLAY AT DUSK. AT SWEETSER ELEMENTARY SCHOOL GROUNDS ON HIGHWAY 18. (LOCAL). MRS LLOYD C COOK, PRES; SWEETSER BICENTENNIAL ORGANIZATION; 2648N 500W; MARION, IN 46952. (#105441-1).

SYRACUSE

JULY 4 - 6, '76. 3RD ANNUAL 1976 FOURTH OF JULY FARM HELLER. FEATURING 76 KEGS OF OLD CROWN BEER; LIVE PERFORMANCES OF LOCAL TALENT. AT FARM HOUSE. (ST-WIDE). D DAVID BUTLER, CHMN; THE FARM; RR 3, BOX 240; SYRACUSE, IN 46567. (#103872-1).

TELL CITY

LAFAYETTE SPRING MARKER, TELL CITY, IN. A MARKER WILL BE PLACED AT THE SITE WHERE GEN MARQUIS DE LAFAYETTE SPENT THE NIGHT IN 1825. (LOCAL). CLYDE WALTERS, COORDINATOR; PERRY COUNTY BICENTENNIAL COMMISSION & DAR; 1004 FRANKLIN; TELL CITY, IN 47520. (#24720). **ARBA GRANTEE.**

JULY 4, '76. RE-ENACTMENT OF SIGNING OF THE DECLARATION OF INDEPENDENCE. AS THE DEBATING OVER THE DECLARATION OF INDEPENDENCE BEGINS, OUR NATION'S FOREFATHERS PRESENT HEATED ARGUMENTS FOR VARIOUS CAUSES ON THE EAST GROUNDS OF CITY HALL FROM 7-8PM. AT GROUNDS OF CITY HALL. (LOCAL). CLYDE WALTERS, CHAIRMAN; TELL CITY; 1004 FRANKLIN ST; TELL CITY, IN 47586. (#100331-1).

OCT 29, '76. UNITED STATES ARMED FORCES BICENTENNIAL CARAVAN. CARAVAN IS COMPOSED OF EXHIBIT VANS FOR EACH MILITARY SERVICE. PROJECT THEME IS 'HISTORY OF THE ARMED FORCES & THEIR CONTRIBUTIONS TO THE NATION'. (LOCAL). CLYDE WALTERS; UNITED STATES ARMED FORCES BICENTENNIAL CARAVAN; 1004 FRANKLIN ST; TELL CITY, IN 47586. (#1775-739).

TERRE HAUTE

ALLEN CHAPEL A M E CHURCH RESTORATION IN INDIANA. RESTORATION OF OLDEST BLACK CHURCH & SCHOOL IN VIGO COUNTY. THE CHURCH WAS ORGANIZED IN 1837 & WHEN RESTORED WILL ILLUSTRATE THE RICH CULTURAL AND ARCHITECTURAL HISTORY OF BLACKS IN INDIANA. (LOCAL). GLENN GRAHAM, PRESIDENT; ALLEN CHAPEL RESTORATION COMMITTEE; RURAL ROUTE 1; MEROM, IN 47861. (#5646). **ARBA GRANTEE.**

BICENTENNIAL HISTORY LECTURES - TERRE HAUTE, IN. THE ROSE HULMAN INSTITUTE OF TECHNOLOGY IS SPONSORING HISTORY LECTURES. (LOCAL). DR WILLIAM PICKETT, CHAIRMAN; ROSE HULMAN INSTITUTE OF TECHNOLOGY; 5500 WABASH AVE; TERRE HAUTE, IN 47803. (#27782). **ARBA GRANTEE.**

BICENTENNIAL WEEK. COSTUME BALL, FILM SERIES, DEBATES, ARTS AND CRAFTS, PLANNED AND CARRIED OUT BY STUDENTS; MUSICAL THEATRE. AT TIREY MEMORIAL UNION. (LOCAL). LINDA ELDRED, DIR; INDIANA STATE UNIV; TERRE HAUTE, IN 47809. (#104992-1). **(??).**

HOOSIERS SHARE AFRO-AMERICAN CULTURE - IN. EXHIBIT ON AFRO-AMERICAN CULTURE AND HISTORY. (LOCAL). DR TIMOTHY S KNOWLES, DIRECTOR; AFRO-AMERICAN STUDIES PROGRAM - INDIANA STATE UNIV; 214 ALUMNI CENTER; TERRE HAUTE, IN 47809. (#26919). **ARBA GRANTEE.**

PERMANENT PATRIOTIC SALUTE, TERRE HAUTE, IN. A STATUE OF ETHAN ALLEN WILL BE ERECTED, 50 FLAGS WILL BE DISPLAYED, FLOWERS WILL BE PLANTED, PLAYS PRESENTED & AN EDITION OF THE HIGH SCHOOL NEWSPAPER WILL BE DEDICATED TO THE BICENTENNIAL. (LOCAL). REX MAGNER, COORDINATOR; TERRE HAUTE NORTH OIGO HIGH SCHOOL; 3434 MAPLE AVE; TERRE HAUTE, IN 47804. (#26859). **ARBA GRANTEE.**

SEMINAR ON INDIANA'S CONSTITUTION, TERRE HAUTE. A SEMINAR WILL BE HELD ON THE CONSTITUTION OF INDIANA IN THE 20TH CENTURY. (ST-WIDE). DR PAUL C FOWLER, PROJ CHAIRMAN; DEPT OF POLITICAL SCIENCE, INDIANA STATE UNIV; TERRE HAUTE, IN 47809. (#26806). **ARBA GRANTEE.**

UNIVERSITY BEAUTIFICATION - TERRE HAUTE, IN. PLANNING AND SUPERVISING CAMPUS PARKS, PLANTING AND LABELING PLANTS, TREES, SHRUBS & BUSHES FOR STUDENT STUDY AND A VOCATIONAL STUDY. (LOCAL). MARION JACKSON, CHAIRMAN; INDIANA STATE UNIV PLANTING AND DEVELOPMENT COMMITTEE; TERRE HAUTE, IN 47809. (#20759).

JULY 1 - 31, '74. REVOLUTIONARY WAR PORTRAITS EXHIBIT IN TERRE HAUTE. REVOLUTIONARY WAR PORTRAITS PROJECT OF INDIANA. GALLERY OF COLOR PHOTOS OF 65 PERSONS ASSOCIATED WITH INDIANA & THE AMERICAN REVOLUTION IS BEING EXHIBITED IN PUBLIC BUILDINGS THROUGHOUT STATE. BOOK OF SHORT BIOGRAPHIES OF SUBJECTS AVAILABLE. (ST-WIDE). DALE FRUCHTNICHT; INDIANA STATE BICENTENNIAL COMMISSION; 504 STATE OFFICE BLDG; INDIANAPOLIS, IN 46204. (#1635-904).

JULY 4 - OCT 10, '75. AUSTIN LOWREY'S AMERICAN ARTS. GRAPHIC DESIGNER AUSTIN LOWREY USES MANY MEDIA TO EXPLORE VARIOUS BICENTENNIAL VISIONS IN THIS EXHIBIT AT TURMAN GALLERY. AT FINE ARTS BUILDING, 7TH & CHESTNUT STS. (LOCAL). BEN BROWNFIELD, CHAIRMAN; INDIANA STATE UNIV; 117 ALUMNI CENTER; TERRE HAUTE, IN 47809. (#100313-1).

AUG 1, '75 - DEC 31, '76. HOOSIERS SHARE AFRO-AMERICAN CULTURE & HISTORY. INCLUDES: A 'BLACK EXPERIENCE' CAMP-OUT AT LOST CREEK FOR 15 YOUTH, AGES 8-14 IN AUGUST & A PANEL DISCUSSION ON BLACKS IN EDUCATION SINCE 1776, TO BE LED BY DR LYDA & DR JOE RUSSELL IN SEPTEMBER & A VARIETY OF PROGRAMS THROUGHOUT 1976. (LOCAL). DR TIMOTHY S KNOWLES, DIR; AFRO-AMERICAN STUDIES PROGRAM, INDIANA STATE UNIV; 214 ALUMNI CENTER; TERRE HAUTE, IN 47809. (#26919-1).

JAN 1 - MAY 30, '76. FROM BETSY ROSS TO WOMAN BOSS. DRAMATIC READINGS ON WOMEN'S PERSPECTIVES ON AMERICAN HISTORY; PERFORMED FOR SELECTED ORGANIZATIONS IN INDIANA BY UNIVERSITY STUDENTS. STUDENTS. AT DREISER HALL. (ST-WIDE). SHERON PATTISON, DIR; INDIANA STATE UNIV; TERRE HAUTE, IN 47809. (#104992-2).

MAR 22 - 26, '76. THE AMERICAN REVOLUTION AND THE TRADITION OF DISSENT. FIVE LECTURES, A FILM SERIES AND DRAMATIC READINGS. AT HOLMSTEDT HALL. (LOCAL). GARY DAILY, COORD; HISTORY DEPARTMENT, INDIANA STATE UNIV; TERRE HAUTE, IN 47809. (#104992-4).

APR 1 - 3, '76. TECHNOLOGY AT THE TURNING POINT: CONFERENCE ON TECHNOLOGY & SOCIETY. TALKS BY MELVIN KRANSBERG, VICTOR FERKISS, HENRY CAULFIELD, THOMAS HUGHES AND OTHERS ON HISTORY AND FUTURE OF AMERICAN TECHNOLOGY. EXHIBITS AND FILMS ON MEANING OF TECHNOLOGY IN AMERICAN SOCIETY. DISCUSSIONS WITH THE AUDIENCE WILL FOLLOW EACH CONFERENCE ADDRESS. AT ROSE-HULMAN INSTITUTE OF TECHNOLOGY, 5500 WABASH AVE. (LOCAL). WILLIAM B PICKETT, CHMN; ROSE-HULMAN BICENTENNIAL COMMITTEE/INDIANA COMMITTEE FOR HUMANITIES; TERRE HAUTE, IN 47803. (#104032-1).

APR 9 - 10, '76. IN THE AMERICAN GRAIN: A BICENTENNIAL CELEBRATION. PAPERS, PANELS & PERFORMANCES ON AMERICAN FOLK CULTURE, MUSIC AND LITERATURE. AT DREISER HALL-TIREY MEMORIAL UNION. (ST-WIDE). CHARLES BLANEY, CHMN; INDIANA STATE UNIV ENGLISH DEPARTMENT; TERRE HAUTE, IN 47809. (#104992-6).

APR 9 - MAY 7, '76. BICENTENNIAL STUDENT ART SHOW. PURCHASE PRIZE OFFERED BY UNIVERSITY BICENTENNIAL COMMITTEE. AT TURMAN ART GALLERY. (LOCAL). CHARLES REDDINGTON, CHMN; INDIANA STATE UNIV, ART DEPARTMENT; TERRE HAUTE, IN 47809. (#104992-5).

MAY 30, '76. DEDICATION OF A M E RESTORES CHURCH. OPENING, EXHIBIT. (LOCAL). GLENN GRAHAM, PRESIDENT; ALLEN CHAPEL RESTORATION COMMITTEE; RURAL ROUTE 1; MEROM, IN 47861. (#5646-501).

SEPT 24 - 26, '76. OKTOBERFEST. GAY GERMAN BANDS ECHO THROUGHOUT THE BIERGARTEN WHILE SONGSTERS AND DANCERS PROVIDE ENTERTAINMENT AT THE FEST HALL. SCHUHPLATTLERS DEMONSTRATE FOLK DANCES WHILE GERMAN BEER AND FOOD REFRESH THE BUSY FESTIVAL-GOERS FROM 5 PM - 2 AM FRIDAY 10-2 AM SATURDAY. (LOCAL). LEE PHIFER, CHAIRMAN; TERRE HAUTE GERMAN OBERLANDER CLUB, INC; 1937 CLAY AVE; TERRE HAUTE, IN 47805. (#100345-1).

OCT 13 - 15, '76. 'FICTIONS & FACTS: DRAMATIC LICENSE AND THE AMERICAN PAST'. SYMPOSIUM ON DRAMATIZING REAL EVENTS IN LITERATURE, FILMS, TELEVISION AND STAGE WITH PROMINENT WRITERS, PRODUCERS AND SCHOLARS. SESSIONS AT: 9 AM, 1 PM, AND 8 PM. (LOCAL). RICHARD CLOKEY, COORD; INDIANA STATE UNIVERSITY BICENTENNIAL COMMITTEE; HISTORY DEPARTMENT; TERRE HAUTE, IN 47809. (#104992-3).

THORNTOWN

SEPT 25 - 26, '76. THE FESTIVAL OF THE TURNING LEAVES. INDIAN TRADERS AND DANCE SPECTACLES MIX WITH FRIENDLY PIONEER CRAFT DEMONSTRATIONS AND DISPLAYS IN A TRIBUTE TO HOOSIER LIFESTYLES OF THE 1800'S; FOOD AND REFRESHMENTS ADD TO THE FESTIVE FLAIR AT OLD MILL RUN PARK. AT OLD MILL RUN PARK - ONE MILE WEST OF THORNTOWN ON STATE ROAD 47. (LOCAL). MRS MARTHA BOWEN, CHMN; SOCIETY FOR THE PRESERVATION OF OUR INDIAN HERITAGE; RR #1; COLFAX, IN 46035. (#100315-1).

TIPTON

SEPT 9 - 11, '76. 8TH ANNUAL TIPTON COUNTY PORK FESTIVAL. FESTIVAL. (ST-WIDE). RANDY BYAL, COORD; CHAMBER OF COMMERCE; PO BOX 26; TIPTON, IN 46072. (#103416-564).

TWELVE MILE

JUNE 30, '76. '500' RIDING LAWN MOWER RACE. THIS RUN FOR THE FASTEST RIDING LAWN MOWER RIVALS THE INDIANAPOLIS 500. THE FESTIVITIES INCLUDE: PRELIMINARY, GAMES, DINNER AND A GALA PARADE. PARADE BEGINS 1:00, RACE BEGINS 3:00 PM. AT PLANK HILL PARK, ON SR-16, BETWEEN US-31 AND SR-25. (LOCAL). NED GRABLE, PROJ DIRECTOR; TWELVE MILE LIONS CLUB; BOX 34; TWELVE MILE, IN 46988. (#100350-1).

UNION CITY

CHOOSING OF BIRD FOR UNION CITY, IN. THE 6TH GRADE CHOSE THE DOVE TO BE THE UNION CITY BIRD. (LOCAL). ROBERT STEBLETON, CHAIRMAN; UNION CITY SCHOOL; RT 2, BOX 332; UNION CITY, IN 47390. (#28947).

CHOOSING OF FLOWER FOR UNION CITY, IN. THE 6TH GRADE CHOSE THE ROSE TO BE THE UNION CITY FLOWER. (LOCAL). ROBERT STEBLETON, CHAIRMAN; UNION CITY SCHOOL; RT 2, BOX 332; UNION CITY, IN 47390. (#28946).

FIRE PLUG PAINTING - UNION CITY, IN. FIRE PLUGS IN UNION CITY WERE PAINTED WITH A BICENTENNIAL THEME. (LOCAL). ROBERT STEBLETON, CHAIRMAN; TRI KAPPA; RT 2, BOX 332; UNION CITY, IN 47390. (#28944).

FORMATION OF HISTORICAL SOCIETY - UNION CITY, OH. A HISTORICAL SOCIETY IS BEING FORMED TO SERVE UNION CITY. (LOCAL). ROBERT STEBLETON, CHAIRMAN; UNION CITY HISTORICAL SOCIETY; R2, BOX 332; UNION CITY, IN 47390. (#28943).

HISTORIC PLAQUE - UNION CITY, IN. A PLAQUE WILL BE HUNG, DESIGNATING THE GREENVILLE TREATY LINE OF AUGUST 3, 1795. (LOCAL). EUGENE FOSNIGHT, COORDINATOR; BICENTENNIAL COMMITTEE; W DIVISION; UNION CITY, IN 47390. (#28942).

PLAQUE - UNION CITY, IN. A PLAQUE WILL BE PLACED WHERE GEN ISAAC P GRAY LIVED FROM 1870-1940, AND ONE FOR THE GOVERNOR FROM 1880-1881 AND 1885-1889. (LOCAL). BETTY CORBIN, COORDINATOR; ZETA CHAPTER; 701 HOWARD ST; UNION CITY, IN 47390. (#28945).

TREATY LINE MUSEUM - UNION CITY, IN. RELOCATION AND RENOVATION OF TEMPLETON CABIN MUSEUM. (LOCAL). PHYLLIS HOWARD, DIRECTOR; TREATY LINE MUSEUM, INC; UNION CITY, IN 47353. (#27249). **ARBA GRANTEE.**

50 STATE FLAGS PLACED AROUND POST OFFICE - IN. UNION CITY BOUGHT A SET OF ALL STATE FLAGS IN 1975 AND PLACED THEM ON 20 FT POLES AROUND THE POST OFFICE. (LOCAL). ROBERT STEBLETON, CHAIRMAN; HISTORICAL SOCIETY; RT 2, BOX 332; UNION CITY, IN 47390. (#28948).

JUNE 14, '75. FLAG DAY CEREMONY & PLAQUE PRESENTATION. 24' PLAQUE PRESENTED TO MAYORS OF UNION CITY, OH AND UNION CITY, IN. TO BE MOUNTED ON POST OFFICE WHICH IS AT THE STATE LINE. (REGN'L). ROBERT STEBLETON; BICENTENNIAL COMMITTEE OF UNION CITY; RT 2, BOX 332; UNION CITY, IN 47390. (#200017-58).

JUNE 14, '75. UNION CITY COVERED WAGON DISPLAY. EXHIBIT. (LOCAL). ROBERT STEBLETON; BICENTENNIAL COMMITTEE OF UNION CITY; RT 2, BOX 332; UNION CITY, IN 47390. (#200017-57).

UNION MILLS

UNION MILLS BICENTENNIAL PROJECTS, IN. PROJECTS INCLUDE: A COMMUNITY-MADE QUILT, FREE BLUEBERRY PICKING, FREE ORANGES FOR CESC AREA, APPLE PICKING, A FAIR & SPONSORSHIP OF BIC CLUB AT LOCAL PRISON. (LOCAL). MRS J CYRUS LLOYD, PRESIDENT; COMMUNITY ENDEAVOR FOR SENIOR CITIZENS OF SE LAPORTE COUNTY; 9908 S 300 W; UNION MILLS, IN 46382. (#28639).

UPLAND

COVERED BRIDGE PROJECT, UPLAND, IN. A COVERED BRIDGE WILL BE BUILT ON CAMPUS. (LOCAL). RANDALL GERMANN, ASSISTANT DIRECTOR OF ADMISSIONS; TAYLOR UNIVERSITY; UPLAND, IN 46989. (#19582).

FILM SERIES ON COLONIAL WILLIAMSBURG - UPLAND, TN. A SERIES OF FILMS ON COLONIAL WILLIAMSBURG WILL BE SHOWN. (LOCAL). WILLIAM C RINGENBERG, ASSISTANT DEAN; TAYLOR UNIVERSITY; UPLAND, IN 46989. (#19581).

'PROFESSORS IN THE COMMUNITY', UPLAND, IN. SPEAKERS (COLLEGE PROFESSORS) AVAILABLE TO AREA RELIGIOUS, CIVIC, AND COMMUNITY ORGANIZATIONS ON A VARIETY OF TOPICS FOR LECTURE AND DISCUSSION. (LOCAL). W C RINGENBERG, ASSISTANT DEAN; TAYLOR UNIV; UPLAND, IN 46989. (#19443).

SEPT 9 - DEC 10, '75. 'JEFFERSON AND THE FOUNDING OF AMERICAN DEMOCRACY'. SEMINAR AT LIBERAL ARTS BUILDING. (LOCAL). PROF PHILIP LOY; TAYLOR UNIV; UPLAND, IN 46989. (#200017-29).

OCT 6, '75. FORMER CONGRESSMAN DAVID DENNIS LECTURE/CONVOCATION. MR DENNIS, MEMBER OF THE HOUSE JUDICIARY COMMITTEE HEARING THE NIXON IMPEACHMENT CASE, SPOKE ON THE SUBJECT 'ETHICS AND GOVERNMENT.'. AT TAYLOR UNIV PHYSICAL EDUCATION BUILDING. (LOCAL). WILLIAM C RINGENBERG; TAYLOR UNIV; UPLAND, IN 46989. (#200017-30).

OCT 11, '75. INDIANA UNIVERSITY SCHOOL OF MUSIC RAGTIME ENSEMBLE CONCERT. LIVE PERFORMANCE AT EASTBROOK MIDDLE SCHOOL. (LOCAL). W C RINGENBERG; TAYLOR UNIV; UPLAND, IN 46989. (#200017-31).

JAN 5 - 28, '76. 'THE AMERICAN INDIANS'. SEMINAR AT LIBERAL ARTS BUILDING. (LOCAL). PROF DWIGHT MIKKELSON; TAYLOR UNIVERSITY; UPLAND, IN 46989. (#104315-5).

JAN 5 - 28, '76. 'LINCOLN AND HIS TIMES'. SEMINAR AT LIBERAL ARTS BUILDING. (LOCAL). PROF DAVID NEUHUUSER; TAYLOR UNIVERSITY; UPLAND, IN 46989. (#104315-6).

JAN 5 - 28, '76. 'THE LITERATURE OF FREEDOM'. SEMINAR AT LIBERAL ARTS BUILDING. (LOCAL). PROF EDWARD DINZIE; TAYLOR UNIVERSITY; UPLAND, IN 46989. (#104315-8).

JAN 14, '76. 'THE LAST KING OF AMERICA' - FILM. EXHIBIT AT PHYSICAL EDUCATION BUILDING. (LOCAL). W C RINGENBERG, ASST DEAN; TAYLOR UNIVERSITY; UPLAND, IN 46989. (#104315-3).

FEB 2 - MAY 7, '76. 'THE UNITED STATES AS THE FIRST NEW NATION'. SEMINAR AT LIBERAL ARTS BUILDING. (LOCAL). PROF SUNKI CHOE; TAYLOR UNIVERSITY; UPLAND, IN 46989. (#104315-7).

FEB 9, '76. JAN LEIGHTON AS GEORGE WASHINGTON - LIVE PERFORMANCE. THIS PROGRAM ON GEORGE WASHINGTON IS SIMILAR TO HAL HOLBROOK'S MARK TWAIN. AT GYMNASIUM. (LOCAL). W C RINGENBERG, ASST DEAN; TAYLOR UNIVERSITY; UPLAND, IN 46989. (#104315-4).

MAR 31, '76. NEW YORK THEATER COMPANY'S ADAPTATION OF 'SPOON RIVER ANTHOLOGY'. LIVE PERFORMANCE AT REDIGER AUDITORIUM. (LOCAL). W C RINGENBERG, ASST DEAN; TAYLOR UNIVERSITY; UPLAND, IN 46989. (#104315-9).

APR 12 - 27, '76. LELAND BOREN AMERICAN INDIAN ART EXHIBIT. EXHIBIT AT ART GALLERY, ART BUILDING. (LOCAL). W C RINGENBERG, ASST DEAN; TAYLOR UNIVERSITY; UPLAND, IN 46989. (#104315-10).

VALLONIA

OCT 15 - 17, '75. FORT VALLONIA DAYS. FESTIVAL. (LOCAL). MRS NOBLE SMITH, SEC; FORT VALLONIA DAYS; BOX 104; VALLONIA, IN 47281. (#200017-32).

DEC 31, '75 - JAN 1, '76. BICENTENNIAL BICYCLE TRAIL RIDE. TOUR. (LOCAL). DALLAS MUNTER, CHAIRMAN; JACKSON CO BICENTENNIAL COMMITTEE; RR 1; VALLONIA, IN 47281. (#200017-33).

VALPARAISO

BICENT EDITION OF THE SENITORIAN, VALPARAISO, TN. THIS YEAR'S ANNUAL WILL BE DEDICATED TO BICENTENNIAL; WILL HAVE SPECIAL SECTION ON COMMUNITY BICENTENNIAL EVENTS. (LOCAL). JUDY LARSON, PROJ CHAIRMAN; WASHINGTON TWP SCHOOL; RR 1; VAIPARISO, IN 46306. (#24712). **ARBA GRANTEE.**

BICENTENNIAL FOUNTAIN - VALPARAISO, IN. A BICENTENNIAL FOUNTAIN WILL BE BUILT ON HERITAGE SQUARE. (LOCAL). DELORES DEAN, CHAIRMAN; BICENTENNIAL COMMITTEE OF PORTER COUNTY; BOX 1776; VALPARAISO, IN 46383. (#27773). **ARBA GRANTEE.**

VALPARAISO UNIV BICENTENNIAL EXHIBITIONS, IN. TRAVELING EXHIBITIONS: AMERICAN AGRICULTURE, WORKERS & ALLIES, BLACKS IN WESTWARD MOVEMENT, CURRIER & IVES, ARTERY BICENTENNIAL. (LOCAL). PROFESSOR RICHARD BRAUER, COORDINATOR; CULTURAL ARTS COMMISSION & UNIV BICENTENNIAL COMMITTEE; MOELLING LIBRARY; VALPARAISO, IN 46383. (#26809). **ARBA GRANTEE.**

JAN 16, '76. BICENTENNIAL CONVOCATION. GOV OTIS BOWEN - GUEST SPEAKER. AT CHAPEL OF RESURRECTION, VALPARAISO UNIV. (LOCAL). DANIEL R GAHL, CHAIRMAN; VALPARAISO UNIV; MOELLERING LIBRARY; VALPARAISO, IN 46383. (#104315-1).

OCT 20 - 23, '76. ECOLOGY & CHRISTIAN RESPONSIBILITY - LECTURE & SEMINAR. LECTURES & SEMINARS ON CHRISTIAN RESPONSIBILITY TOWARD CONSERVATION OF PHYSICAL & HUMAN ENVIRONMENT. AT CHAPEL, STUDENT UNION & CHRIST COLLEGE ON VALPARAISO UNIV CAMPUS. (LOCAL). DANIEL R GAHL, CHAIRMAN; AID ASSOC FOR LUTHERANS & VALPARAISO UNIV; MOELLERING LIBRARY; VALPARAISO, IN 46383. (#104315-2).

VAN BUREN

BICENTENNIAL PARK - VAN BUREN, IN. A DOWNTOWN LOT WAS CLEANED AND A PLAYGROUND AND PICNIC AREA WAS ESTABLISHED. (LOCAL). RUTH M BOLE, CO-CHAIRMAN; VAN BUREN POPCORN FESTIVAL COMMITTEE; 108 E PARK; VAN BUREN, IN 46991. (#29106).

BICENTENNIAL PROJECTS OF VAN BUREN, IN. ATTACH PLAQUE TO 1901 OPERA HOUSE, PAINTING OF BENNINGTON FLAG ON A DOWNTOWN BLDG, FIRE PLUG PAINTING, PLANTING OF STATE TULIP TREE AT LIBRARY, & CREATION OF A MINI-WALK IN PARK IN CENTER OF TOWN. (LOCAL). RUTH M BOLE, CHAIRMAN; VAN BUREN BICENTENNIAL COMMITTEE; 108 E PARK; VAN BUREN, IN 46991. (#33497).

OCT 11, '75. 1975 STATE STUDENT COUNCIL CONVENTION - BICENTENNIAL THEME. ART & SOCIAL STUDIES DEPTS DECORATED HALLWAYS WITH REVOLUTIONARY WAR SCENES & RE-NAMED HALLWAYS 'PAUL REVERE AVENUE', 'BETSY ROSS BOULEVARD', ETC. SO SUCCESSFUL THAT IT HAS BECOME PERMANENT PART OF THE SCHOOL. AT EASTBROOK HIGH SCHOOL. (ST-WIDE). RUTH M BOLE, CHMN; VAN BUREN BICENTENNIAL COMMITTEE/ EASTBROOK STUDENT COUNCIL; 108 E PARK; VAN BUREN, IN 46991. (#200017-121).

AUG 12 - 14, '76. FESTIVAL '76 PARADE. FESTIVAL, PARADE. (LOCAL). RUTH M BOLE; VAN BUREN POPCORN COMMITTEE; 108 E PARK; VAN BUREN, IN 46991. (#200017-55).

AUG 12 - 14, '76. POPCORN FESTIVAL. PARADES, BOOTHS, RIDES, ENTERTAINMENT, RACES & PARACHUTE JUMPS. (ST-WIDE). RUTH M BOLE, CHMN; VAN BUREN POPCORN COMMITTEE & BICENTENNIAL COMMITTEE; 108 E PARK; VAN BUREN, IN 46991. (#200017-122).

VANDERBURGH

OCT 9 - 23, '75. IMMUNIZATION ACTION MONTH. OPENING AT CIVIC CENTER PUBLIC HEALTH DEPT. (LOCAL). MRS LARRY SIMS, CHMN; VANDERBURGH-SOUTHWESTERN MEDICAL AUXILARY; F521 KIRKWOOD DR; EVANSVILLE, IN 47715. (#102559-1).

VEEDERSBURG

FOUNTAIN COUNTY BICENTENNIAL CELEBRATION, IN. HISTORICAL MARKER PLAQUES WILL BE PLACED IN EACH OF THE 11 TOWNSHIPS IN THE COUNTY. (LOCAL). WISHER MYERS, PRESIDENT; FOUNTAIN COUNTY HISTORICAL SOCIETY; 200 N MAIN ST; VEEDERSBURG, IN 47987. (#26632). **ARBA GRANTEE.**

VINCENNES

COMMEMORATIVE PLATE - VINCENNES UNIV, IN. AN OLD ENGLISH STAFFORDSHIRE PLATE WILL BE ISSUED TO COMMEMORATE THE 175 YEARS OF VINCENNES UNIV. THE PLATE WILL PICTURE THE BANKS OF THE WABASH, FORT SACKVILLE AND THE UNIVERSITY SEAL. (REGN'L). MS CLAUDIA HUTCHISON, ASST DIRECTOR; VINCENNES UNIV ALUMNI ASSOC; N 1ST ST AND COLLEGE; VINCENNES, IN 47591. (#14088).

'CONTRIBUTIONS IN BLACK & RED'-BOOK, VINCENNES,IN. EDUCATE COMMUNITY; PARTICULARLY STUDENTS, ON THE CONTRIBUTIONS OF AFRO-AMERICANS AND AMERICAN INDIANS TO AMERICAN SOCIETY. (LOCAL). JACQUELINE CORTEZ, COORDINATOR; VINCENNES UNIV; 1002 N 1ST ST; VINCENNES, IN 47591. (#23766). **ARBA GRANTEE.**

GEORGE ROGERS CLARK NATL HIST PARK IMPROVEMENTS. INCLUDES REHABILITATING EXISTING STRUCTURES & BUILDING NEW VISITOR FACILITIES. PARK HONORS CLARK'S ACHIEVEMENTS IN WINNING THE OLD NORTHWEST DURING THE REVOLUTION. (NAT'L). SUPERINTENDENT, GEORGE ROGERS CLARK NHP; NATIONAL PARK SERVICE; 401 S SECOND ST; VINCENNES, IN 47591. (#32). **ARBA RECOGNIZED.**

HISTORIC PERSONALITIES PROJ OF VINCENNES UNIV - IN. THE HOME ECONOMICS DEPT OF VINCENNES UNIV IS MAKING AND OUTFITTING IN HISTORIC COSTUME, A ROGERS CLARK DOLL AND AN ALICE OF OLD VINCENNES DOLL. (LOCAL). CARROLL DEEM, PROF OF HOME ECONOMICS; VINCENNES UNIV HOME ECONOMICS CLUB; N 1ST ST AND COLLEGE; VINCENNES, IN 47591. (#14089).

HISTORICAL DOCUMENTS PROJECT IN VINCENNES, INDIANA. PROJECT DESIGNED TO COLLECT AND PRESERVE HISTORICAL MATERIALS OF SOUTHWESTERN INDIANA. BICENTENNIAL MEDALLION OFFERED AS MONTHLY PRIZE FOR MOST IMPORTANT DONATION EACH MONTH. (ST-WIDE). THOMAS KRASEAN, DIRECTOR LEWIS LIBRARY; OLD NORTHWEST BICENTENNIAL CORP; LEWIS LIBRARY VINCENNES UNIV; VINCENNES, IN 47591. (#4636).

INDIAN CULTURE VILLAGE - VINCENNES, IN. CREATION OF INDIAN CULTURE EXHIBIT & ADJACENT PREHISTORIC INDIAN TEMPLE MOUND. (REGN'L). JOHN A WARD, DIRECTOR; OLD NORTHWEST BICENTENNIAL CORPORATION; BOX 1979; VINCENNES, IN 47591. (#26631). **ARBA GRANTEE.**

PRODUCTS FOR PATRIOTISM-GOODWILL OF VINCENNES, IN. TO SUPPLY VARIOUS KINDS OF PLAQUES, HAVING MEANINFUL OR SYMBOLIC EMPHASIS ON OUR HERITAGE, FOR CITIES AND TOWNS, USING THEIR SUGGESTIONS WHENEVER POSSIBLE. (NAT'L). WILLIAM D CULLISON, MANAGER; VINCENNES BRANCH GOODWILL INDUSTRIES; PO BOX 733, 602 N 1ST ST; VINCENNES, IN 47591. (#2406). **(??).**

VINCENNES — CONTINUED

SUN-COMMERCIAL BICENTENNIAL FEATURES - NBMRP. PUBLISHED 2 HISTORICAL & BICENTENNIAL FEATURES APPEARING DAILY & 1 LOCAL HISTORY FEATURE ON SUNDAY. ALSO HISTORICAL EDITION ON AREA & GEORGE ROGERS CLARK'S CAMPAIGN. (LOCAL). ADDIE MCELFRESH, BICENTENNIAL COORDINATOR; THE SUN-COMMERCIAL; 702 MAIN ST; VINCENNES, IN 47591. (#28519).

VINCENNES FRENCH TOWN LOT RESTORATION, INDIANA. RESTORATION OF 18TH CENTURY FRENCH HOUSE & LOT TO ITS APPEARANCE AT THE TIME OF CLARK'S CAPTURE OF VINCENNES IN 1779. IT WILL BE A REAL LIVING MUSEUM, CONVEYING SIGHTS, SOUNDS, ETC OF THAT ERA. (LOCAL). THOMAS KRASEAN; OLD NORTHWEST BICENTENNIAL CORPORATION; BYRON LEWIS LIBRARY,VINCENNES U; VINCENNES, IN 47591. (#8232). **ARBA GRANTEE.**

VINCENNES UNIVERSITY AMERICAN ISSUES FORUM, IN. A SERIES OF PUBLIC MEETINGS ENABLING AREA RESIDENTS TO ACTIVELY PARTICIPATE IN DISCUSSION OF THEIR HERITAGE, ROLE IN DEMOCRATIC PROCESS AND OTHER RELATED ISSUES. (LOCAL). CONSTANCE SMITH, SECRETARY; VINCENNES UNIVERSITY JUNIOR COLLEGE; 1002 N 1ST; VINCENNES, IN 47591. (#26996). **ARBA GRANTEE.**

JAN 1, '74 - DEC 31, '77. GEORGE ROGERS CLARK NHP-EXHIBITS DEPICTING STORY. SEVEN MURALS DEPICTINGIMPORTANT EVENTS OF CLARK'S ILLINOIS COUNTRY CAMPAIGN, FT SACKVILLE ASSAULT, & DEVELOPMENT OF THE NORTHWEST TERRITORY. AT CLARK MEMORIAL. (REGN'L). G ROGERS CLARK NHP; NATIONAL PARK SERVICE; 115 DUBOIS ST; VINCENNES, IN 47591. (#6729-27).

AUG 1 - 31, '74. REVOLUTIONARY WAR PORTRAITS EXHIBIT IN VINCENNES. REVOLUTIONARY WAR PORTRAITS PROJECT OF INDIANA. GALLERY OF COLOR PHOTOS OF 65 PERSONS ASSOCIATED WITH INDIANA & THE AMERICAN REVOLUTION IS BEING EXHIBITED IN PUBLIC BUILDINGS THROUGHOUT STATE. BOOK OF SHORT BIOGRAPHIES OF SUBJECTS AVAILABLE. (ST-WIDE). DALE FRUCHTNICHT; INDIANA STATE BICENTENNIAL COMMISSION; 504 STATE OFFICE BLDG; INDIANAPOLIS, IN 46204. (#1635-905).

APR 1 - OCT 30, '75. GEORGE ROGERS CLARK NHP--LIVING INTERPRETATION. THREE PERFORMANCES EACH SUNDAY APRIL THROUGH OCTOBER AT 1, 2, & 3 PM. COSTUMED HISTORIANS PORTRAY BRITISH REDCOAT & OCASSIONALLY KY FRONTIERSMAN IN THE BATTLE FOR THE OLD NORTHWEST TERRITORY. AT ON GROUNDS BEHIND THE CLARK MEMORIAL. (REGN'L). PK MGR, G ROGERS CLARK; NATIONAL PARK SERVICE; 115 DUBOIS ST; VINCENNES, IN 47591. (#6727-14).

JULY 22 - 23, '75. NATL PK SVC '...A LITTLE LOOK AROUND' VISITS G ROGERS CLARK NHP. THIS SHORT PROGRAM FEATURES ACTORS PORTRAYING FAMOUS AMERICANS OF THE PAST WHO'VE RETURNED TO SEE AMERICA'S GROWTH. (REGN'L). SUPERINTENDENT; NATIONAL PARK SERVICE - G ROGERS CLARK NATIONAL HISTORIC PARK; 115 DUBOIS ST; VINCENNES, IN 47591. (#5653-218).

AUG 17, '75. NATL PK SVC 'PEOPLE OF 1776' (PILOT) VISITS GEORGE ROGERS CLARK NHP. TRAVELING TROUPE WILL BRING VARIOUS ASPECTS OF COLONIAL LIFE (MILITARY LIFE, MUSIC, CRAFTS) TO VISITORS TO THIS NATIONAL PARK SERVICE AREA. (REGN'L). SUPERINTENDENT; NATIONAL PARK SERVICE - GEORGE ROGERS CLARK NATL HISTORIC PARK; 115 DUBOIS ST; VINCENNES, IN 47591. (#1469-213).

FEB 10 - 23, '76. RE-ENACTMENT OF THE TRIP TAKEN BY GEO CLARK TO CAPTURE FT SACKVILLE. THE ROUTE TAKEN BY GEORGE ROGERS CLARK TO CAPTURE FORT SACKVILLE IN VINCENNES, IN, WILL BE RE-ENACTED. (REGN'L). DON C WILEY, DIRECTOR; RANDOLPH COUNTY LONG KNIVES; RR #1; SPARTA, IL 62286. (#102967-1).

FEB 29 - MAR 13, '76. ARTISTS-IN-THE-PARKS PAINT THE BICENTENNIAL EXHIBIT. ORIGINAL ART EXHIBIT IN VARIOUS MEDIUMS DEPICTING REVOLUTIONARY WAR RELATED NATIONAL PARK SERVICE SITES. (REGN'L). GEORGE ROGERS CLARK NHP; NATIONAL PARK SERVICE; 115 DUBOIS ST; VINCENNES, IN 47591. (#1474-1).

APR 1 - OCT 30, '76. GEORGE ROGERS CLARK NHP--LIVING INTERPRETATION. THREE PERFORMANCES EACH SUNDAY APRIL THROUGH OCTOBER AT 1, 2, & 3 PM. COSTUMED HISTORIANS PORTRAY BRITISH REDCOAT & OCASSIONALLY KY FRONTIERSMAN IN THE BATTLE FOR THE OLD NORTHWEST TERRITORY. AT ON GROUNDS BEHIND THE CLARK MEMORIAL. (REGN'L). G ROGERS CLARK NHP; NATIONAL PARK SERVICE; 115 DUBOIS ST; VINCENNES, IN 47591. (#6727-514).

APR 6, '76. 'UP WITH PEOPLE'. LIVE PERFORMANCE AT PHYSICAL EDUCATION COMPLEX. (LOCAL). CLAUDIA HUTCHISON, DIR; VINCENNES UNIV; VINCENNES, IN 47591. (#101691-1).

MAY 14 - 15, '76. GEORGE ROGERS CLARK HISTORY SYMPOSIUM. SEMINAR, TOUR AT VINCENNES UNIVERSITY. (REGN'L). TOM KRASEAN, COORDINATOR; VINCENNES UNIV BICENTENNIAL COMMISSION & INDIANA HISTORICAL SOCIETY; VINCENNES, IN 47591. (#103948-1).

MAY 28 - 31, '76. OLD NORTHWEST BICENTENNIAL SQUARE DANCE FESTIVAL. FLIP YOUR SKIRTS, WAX UP YOUR MUSTACHE AND PICK UP YOUR HEELS FOR THE FIRST ANNUAL SQUARE DANCE FESTIVAL ON THE CAMPUS OF VINCENNES; HOOTIN' AND HOLLERIN' IN THE CALLER'S CORNER ARE COLONEL F BEDELL & MEL ROBERTS, WHILE ROUNDS ARE PROVIDED BY BETTY & CLANCY MUELLER. AT VINCENNES UNIV. (ST-WIDE). JOSEPH C LACKEY, CHAIRMAN; KNOX COUNTY CHAMBER OF COMMERCE; PO BOX 553; VINCENNES, IN 47591. (#100317-1).

MAY 28 - JULY 4, '76. CONQUEST OF THE OLD NORTHWEST FESTIVAL. THE FESTIVAL WILL FEATURE MANY EVENTS INCLUDING THE DEDICATION OF VISITORS CENTER AT CLARK MEMORIAL. (LOCAL). THELMA LAWRENCE, PROJ DIR; OLD NORTHWEST BICENTENNIAL CORP; 1219 BURNEL LANE; VINCENNES, IN 47591. (#103948-3).

JUNE 1 - OCT 31, '76. PREHISTORIC INDIAN MOUND AND MUSEUM EXHIBITS. EXHIBIT, TOUR AT STATE ROAD 61 & WABASH AVENUE-TURN RIGHT 500 FEET. (LOCAL). JACK WARD, COORD; OLD NORTHWEST BICENTENNIAL CORP; BOX 1979; VINCENNES, IN 47591. (#103948-2).

JUNE 5 - 6, '76. BRIGADE OF THE AMERICAN REVOLUTION AT GEORGE ROGERS CLARK NHP. LIVING HISTORY ENCAMPMENT BY THE BRIGADE OF AMERICAN REVOLUTION, A GROUP WHICH IS TRAVELING TO MANY PLACES DURING THE BICENTENNIAL TO DEMONSTRATE MILITARY LIFE DURING THE REVOLUTIONARY WAR. (REGN'L). GEOGE ROGERS CLARK NHP; NATIONAL PARK SERVICE; 115 DUBOIS ST; VINCENNES, IN 47591. (#6727-211).

JUNE 13, '76. FIELD MASS AND CONCERT AT GEORGE ROGERS CLARK NHP. OPEN AIR CONCERT OF PATRIOTIC SELECTIONS BY THE MUNICIPAL BAND, ON CLARK MEMORIAL PLAZA FOLLOWED BY FIELD MASS IN OLD CATHEDRAL CEMETERY ADJACENT TO MEMORIAL PLAZA. (REGN'L). GEORGE ROGERS CLARK NHP; NATIONAL PARK SERVICE; 115 DUBOIS ST; VINCENNES, IN 47591. (#6728-218).

JUNE 13 - 14, '76. BOY SCOUT MARCH OVER GEORGE ROGERS CLARK ROUTE. BOY SCOUTS WILL MARCH FROM ST FRANCISVILLE TO THE CLARK MEMORIAL FOLLOWING CLARK'S ROUTE DURING THE REVOLUTIONARY WAR AND THE WINNING OF THE NORTHWEST TERRITORY FROM THE BRITISH. (REGN'L). GEORGE ROGERS CLARK NHP; NATIONAL PARK SERVICE; 115 DUBOIS ST; VINCENNES, IN 47591. (#6728-238).

JUNE 24 - 27, '76. HISTORICAL THEATRICAL PRODUCTION. LIVE PERFORMANCE AT SHIRCLIFF CENTER THEATER; PARKING LOT ADJACENT TO CENTER. (LOCAL). HARRIETTE G KLINKER, CHMN; VINCENNES UNIV; VINCENNES, IN 45791. (#101690-1).

JUNE 26 - 27, '76. VINCENNES UNIVERSITY BICENTENNIAL FESTIVAL. FESTIVAL. (LOCAL). DALE E DOWDEN, DIR; VINCENNES UNIV; VINCENNES, IN 47591. (#101692-1).

JULY 8, '76. NATL PK SVC '...A LITTLE LOOK AROUND' COMES TO G. ROGERS CLARK NHP. THIS SHORT PROGRAM FEATURES ACTORS PLAYING THE PARTS OF FAMOUS AMERICANS OF THE PAST WHO'VE RETURNED TO SEE AMERICA'S GROWTH. RIIS PARK; AND 6/27 AT FLOYD BENNETT FIEL. AT BEHIND THE MEMORIAL BLDG. (REGN'L). G. ROGERS CLARK NHP; NATIONAL PARK SERVICE; 115 DUBOIS STREET; VINCINNES, IN 47591. (#5653-14).

AUG 1 - 30, '76. CONTRIBUTIONS IN BLACK & RED - SEMINARS. EDUCATE COMMUNITY, PARTICULARY STUDENTS, ON THE CONTRIBUTIONS OF AFRO-AMERICANS AND AMERICAN INDIANS TO AMERICAN SOCIETY. (LOCAL). JACQUELINE CORTEZ, COORD; VINCENNES UNIV; 1002 N 1ST ST; VINCENNES, IN 47591. (#23766-1).

AUG 17, '76. DEDICATION OF VISITOR CENTER AT GEORGE ROGERS CLARK NHP. CEREMONY. (REGN'L). GEORGE ROGERS CLARK NHP; NATIONAL PARK SERVICE; 115 DUBOIS ST; VINCENNES, IN 47591. (#6728-239).

W LAFAYETTE

AMERICA:A PERSONAL HISTORY OF THE UNITED STATES-IN. A FILM SERIES ON AMERICAN HISTORY. (LOCAL). GORMAN PIERCE, COORDINATOR; W LAFAYETTE SCHOOL CORP; 600 CUMBERLAND AVE; W LAFAYETTE, IN 47906. (#24715). **ARBA GRANTEE.**

BICENTENNIAL RECORD ALBUM, W LAFAYETTE, IN. PREPARATION & RECORDING OF AN ALBUM OF PURDUE BICENTENNIAL MUSIC. (LOCAL). CAROLYN SCHILLING, CHAIRPERSON; BICENTENNIAL COMMITTEE PURDUE UNIVERSITY; HOUDE HALL; W LAFAYETTE, IN 47906. (#22333).

A BICENTENNIAL SALUTE FROM PURDUE, W LAFAYETTE, IN. A PACKET OF 13 FEATURES, 'ANECDOTES OF THE AMERICAN REVOLUTION', BY PROFESSOR MAURICE M ROSS. (REGN'L). KEN KAISER, ACTING DIRECTOR UNIV NEWS SERVICE; PURDUE UNIVERSITY; W LAFAYETTE, IN 47907. (#22332).

BICENTENNIAL TREE GROVES, W LAFAYETTE, IN. PLANTING OF TREES ON THE PURDUE CAMPUS-WEST LAFAYETTE. (LOCAL). CAROLYN SCHILLING, CHAIRPERSON; PURDUE UNIVERSITY BICENTENNIAL COMMITTEE; HOUDE HALL; W LAFAYETTE, IN 47907. (#22328).

BOOK ON SCHOOL OF PHARMACY, PURDUE UNIVERSITY, IN. HISTORY OF THE SCHOOL OF PHARMACY AND PHARMACAL SCIENCE WILL BE PUBLISHED. (REGN'L). DEAN VARRO TYLER; PURDUE UNIVERSITY SCHOOL OF PHARMACY; W LAFAYETTE, IN 47907. (#22331).

FLOWER BEDS ON CAMPUS, W LAFAYETTE, IN. FLOWER BEDS IN DESIGNS OF THE BICENTENNIAL STAR, U S FLAG, STATE FLAG & PERDUE UNIVERSITY FLAG TO BE PLANTED ON CAMPUS. (LOCAL). CAROLYN SHILLING, CHAIRPERSON; PURDUE UNIVERSITY; W LAFAYETTE, IN 47907. (#22335).

FRANCE'S ROLE IN THE DEVELOPMENT OF AMERICA, IN. PACKAGE OF MATERIALS FOR USE BY TEACHERS OF FRENCH ON FRANCES ROLE IN THE DEVELOPMENT OF AMERICA. (ST-WIDE). MAURICE ROSS, COORD; PURDUE UNIVERSITY DEPARTMENT OF MODERN LANGUAGE; STANLEY COULTER; W LAFAYETTE, IN 47907. (#22329).

NEWSREEL ON PURDUE UNIVERSITY, W LAFAYETTE, IN. NEWSREEL OF THE YEAR'S EVENTS AT THE UNIVERSITY WITH AN EMPHASIS ON A PATRIOTIC THEME. (LOCAL). JOSEPH RUDOLPH, EXEC DIRECTOR; PURDUE ALUMNI ASSOCIATION; PURDUE MEMORIAL UNION; W LAFAYETTE, IN 47907. (#22334).

SLIDE PRESENTATION: HISTORY OF PURDUE UNIV, IN. PUBLIC RELATIONS STUDENT SOCIETY OF AMERICA CHAPTER AT PURDUE IS PREPARING AN HISTORICAL SLIDE SHOW OF PURDUE UNIVERSITY. (LOCAL). CAROLYN SCHILLING, CHAIRPERSON; PURDUE UNIVERSITY BICENTENNIAL COMMITTEE; HOUDE HALL; W LAFAYETTE, IN 47907. (#22330).

THIS IS YOUR COMMUNITY, W LAFAYETTE, IN. A PROGRAM TO EDUCATE YOUTH ON THE WAY GOVERNMENT WORKS. (LOCAL). CATHY POTTER, COORDINATOR; LEAGUE OF WOMEN VOTERS; 817 N CHANCERY; W LAFAYETTE, IN 47906. (#24022). **ARBA GRANTEE.**

'A VISION OF THE PAST 1975-1976' - BOOK, IN. A BOOK TO COMMEMORATE SUSQUITENNIAL OF TIPPECANOE COUNTY & 200TH BIRTHDAY OF THE U S. (LOCAL). WILLIAM FLOYD, COORDINATOR; WEST LAFAYETTE SCHOOL CORP; 920 N GRANT ST; W LAFAYETTE, IN 47906. (#24719). **ARBA GRANTEE.**

JULY 6, '75. OLD FASHIONED FOURTH OF JULY. GAMES, LEMONADE, ANTIQUE CARS AND PATRIOTIC SPEECHES ADD UP TO A TRADITIONAL INDEPENDENCE DAY CELEBRATION. AT FORT QUIATENON, 4 MILES S OF W LAFAYETTE ON S RIVER RD. (LOCAL). PAULA WOODS, PROJ CHMN; TIPPECANOE COUNTY HISTORICAL ASSOC, TIPPECANOE CO PARK BOARD; COUNTY MUSEUM-10TH AND S ST; LAFAYETTE, IN 47901. (#100319-1).

SEPT 22, '75. A BLACK VIEW OF THE BICENTENNIAL. SEMINAR. (LOCAL). CAROLYN SCHILLING, CHMN; CHRISTIAN MINISTRY CENTER, PURDUE UNIV; W LAFAYETTE, IN 47907. (#200017-36).

FEB 4 - APR 27, '76. SEARS LECTURE PROGRAM. AMERICA CONFRONTS A REVOLUTIONARY WORLD-2/4, FUTURE WORLD AND AMERICAN POLITICS-3/1, TO BE ANNOUNCED-3/25, WORLD POLITICS AND THEORIES OF RATIONAL DECISION-4/12, TWO FUTURES FOR THE ARMS RACE4/21, AMERICAN ROLE IN FUTURE WORLD POLITICS-4/27. (LOCAL). CAROLYN SCHILLING, CHMN; DEPARTMENT OF POLITICAL SCIENCE; HOVDE HALL-PURDUE UNIV; W LAFAYETTE, IN 47907. (#106029-2).

FEB 29, '76. UNIVERSITY SYMPHONY CONCERT. LIVE PERFORMANCE AT ELLIOTT HALL OF MUSIC. (LOCAL). CAROLYN SCHILLING, CHMN; UNIVERSITY BANDS, PURDUE UNIV; W LAFAYETTE, IN 47907. (#200017-35).

APR 1 - 3, '76. THREE DAY FESTIVAL, PLANNED AND IMPLEMENTED BY PURDUE STUDENTS. RE-ENACTMENT OF PAUL REVERE'S RIDE, SIGNING OF DECLARATION OF INDEPENDENCE; PHOTOGRAPHY CONTEST; CRAFT EXHIBITS; FOLK MUSIC; RED, WHITE AND BLUE DAY; FOODS OF AMERICA SERVED IN HOUSING UNITS. AT PURDUE MEMORIAL UNION AND UNIVERSITY MALL. (LOCAL). CAROLYN SCHILLING, CHMN; PURDUE BICENTENNIAL COMMITTEE; PURDUE UNIV; W LAFAYETTE, IN 47907. (#106029-4).

APR 8, '76. RED, WHITE AND YOU - PURDUE ALUMNI ASSOCIATION WOMEN'S DAY. SPEAKER, MRS EARL BUTZ, WILL DISCUSS 'WHAT AMERICAN WOMEN HAVE CONTRIBUTED AND CAN CONTRIBUTE'. 'WOMEN IN WASHINGTON'. AT PURDUE MEMORIAL UNION. (ST-WIDE). MARY RUTH SNYDER, COORD; PURDUE ALUMNI ASSOC; PURDUE MEMORIAL UNION; W LAFAYETTE, IN 47907. (#106029-1).

APR 12, '76. UNIVERSITY SING. LIVE PERFORMANCE AT ELLIOTT HALL OF MUSIC. (LOCAL). CAROLYN SCHILLING, CHMN; STUDENT UNION BOARD; HOVDE HALL-PURDUE UNIV; W LAFAYETTE, IN 47907. (#106029-5).

APR 21 - 24, '76. PRESENTATION OF '1776'. PERFORMANCES: APRIL 22 & 23 - 8:00 PM, APRIL 24 - 8:30 PM, APRIL 25 - 2:30 PM. AT ELLIOTT HALL OF MUSIC. (LOCAL). CAROLYN SCHILLING, CHMN; PURDUE BICENTENNIAL COMMITTEE; PURDUE UNIV; W LAFAYETTE, IN 47907. (#106029-3).

WABASH

RICH VALLEY BICENTENNIAL PROJECTS, IN. PROJECTS INCLUDE: A BICENTENNIAL BOOK, BICENTENNIAL CEREMONIES, A REPLICA OF A WATER POWERED GRIST MILL BUILT BY RICH VALLEY LIONS CLUB. (LOCAL). RONALD THRUSH, CHAIRMAN; RICH VALLEY BICENTENNIAL COMMITTEE; RURAL ROUTE 2; WABASH, IN 46992. (#28638).

WALDRON

WALDRON BICENTENNIAL AND RETROSPECT, IN. HISTORY OF WALDRON TO BE PUBLISHED AND SOLD IN 1976. (LOCAL). SCOTT POPE, PRESIDENT; WALDRON COMMUNITY CLUB; RR 1; WALDRON, IN 46182. (#25681). **ARBA GRANTEE.**

WALKERTON

JUNE 12, '76. COMBINED COMMUNITY CHURCH CHOIRS 'I LOVE AMERICA'. ONE OF COMPOSERS, DON WYRTZEN, IS COMING TO DIRECT PERFORMANCE. TO BE PERFORMED WITH PRE-RECORDED INSTRUMENTAL TAPE TRACK. AT JOHN GLENN HIGH SCHOOL GYMNASIUM, GEORGIA ST. (LOCAL). SHARON KLINEDINST, DIR; GREATER WALKERTON AREA BICENTENNIAL COMMITTEE; R 2, BOX 825; WALKERTON, IN 46574. (#200017-39).

JUNE 27, '76. WALKERTON BICENTENNIAL RELIGIOUS CELEBRATION. THEME: THE ROLE OF RELIGION IN AMERICA; WORSHIP SERVICE, GUEST SPEAKER, CHOIR, MINISTERS & MINUTE MEN FOR 'THE COLORS'. AT JOHN GLENN HS STADIUM OR AUDITORIUM GEORGIA ST. (LOCAL). REV ROBERT C BOWMAN; WALKERTON MINISTERIAL; 104 CLARK ST; WALKERTON, IN 46574. (#106250-1).

WANATAH

MAR 1, '75. PAGEANT AND HISTORICAL EXHIBITS OF LOCAL CULTURE. LOCAL TALENT WILL BE USED TO MAKE THE COMMUNITY AWARE OF ITS HERITAGE AND LOCAL CULTURE. (LOCAL). GENE RICE, CHAIRMAN; BICENTENNIAL COMMITTEE OF WANATAH; WANATAH, IN 46390. (#5243-901).

APR 12, '75. OLD FASHION DINNER, PHOTO EXHIBIT, ANTIQUE DISPLAYS, SQUARE DANCE. PHOTO EXHIBIT; ANTIQUE DISPLAYS; SQUARE DANCE. AT WANATAH ELEMENTARY SCHOOL. (LOCAL). GENE L RICE; WANATAH BICENTENNIAL COMMITTEE; BOX 304; WANATAH, IN 46390. (#50372-1).

WARREN

JULY 3 - 6, '75. SALAMONIE SUMMER FESTIVAL. FESTIVAL, FAIR. (LOCAL). BARBARA SHUTTLEWORTH; SALAMONIE SUMMER FESTIVAL COMMITTEE; RR 1; WARREN, IN 46792. (#7926-1).

MAY 1, '76. BICENTENNIAL FAIR. FESTIVAL. (LOCAL). J CLIFFORD GATES, CHMN; WARREN TWP BICENTENNIAL COMMITTEE; 9500 E 16TH; INDIANAPOLIS, IN 46229. (#103690-2).

JULY 2 - 3, '76. LOCAL HISTORICAL PLAY WRITTEN & DIRECTED BY LOCAL COUPLE. LIVE PERFORMANCE AT WARREN ELEMENTARY SCHOOL GROUNDS NANCY ST WARREN. (ST-WIDE). JANICE RAMP; SALAMONIE SUMMER FESTIVAL COMMITTEE; BOX 116; WARREN, IN 46792. (#107806-2).

JULY 2 - 5, '76. SALAMONIE SUMMER FESTIVAL. A 4-DAY FESTIVAL WITH ACTIVITIES FOR ALL AGES, INCLUDES A FLEA MARKET, RIVER EVENTS, ARTS AND CRAFTS DISPLAY, YOUTH ACTIVITIES, A LIVE HISTORICAL PLAY AND NUMEROUS OTHER EVENTS. (ST-WIDE). JANICE RAMP, PRES; SALAMONIE SUMMER FESTIVAL COMMITTEE; BOX 116; WARREN, IN 46792. (#107806-1).

WARSAW

BICENTENNIAL PARK 1976 - WARSAW, IN. 1 ACRE OF LAND WILL BE DEVELOPED FOR A PARK AND PLAYGROUND. (LOCAL). CAROL HARTMAN, COORDINATOR; CITY OF WARSAW; CITY BLDG; WARSAW, IN 46580. (#27776). **ARBA GRANTEE.**

SEPT 16, '75. AN EVENING WITH MARK TWAIN. LIVE PERFORMANCE AT WARSAW HIGH SCHOOL AUDITORIUM, SMITH ST. (LOCAL). STEVE YOUNG, COORDINATOR; GRACE COLLEGE; WINONA LAKE, IN 46590. (#200017-38).

DEC 19, '75. AMERICAN ISSUES FORUM 1975-76. SEMINAR AT COUNTING HOUSE COMMUNITY ROOM. (LOCAL). R WAYNE SNIDER, CHAIRMAN; KOSCINCKO COUNTY HUMANITIES COUNCIL; PO BOX 691; WINONA LAKE, IN 46590. (#200017-37).

OCT 9 - 10, '76. UNITED STATES ARMED FORCES BICENTENNIAL CARAVAN. CARAVAN IS COMPOSED OF EXHIBIT VANS FOR EACH MILITARY SERVICE. PROJECT THEME IS 'HISTORY OF THE ARMED FORCES & THEIR CONTRIBUTIONS TO THE NATION'. AT COUNTY FAIR GROUNDS. (LOCAL). COL VICTOR J REAFSNYDER; UNITED STATES ARMED FORCES BICENTENNIAL CARAVAN; CREST LANE DR; WARSAW, IN 46580. (#1775-730).

WESTVILLE

HISTORIC SITES MARKING PROJ IN WESTVILLE, IN. HISTORIC SITES IN THE COUNTY WILL BE MARKED. (LOCAL). DR HOWARD JABLON, PROFESSOR OF HISTORY; PURDUE NORTH CENTRAL CAMPUS; HWY 421, WESTVILLE, IN 46391. (#19238).

SEPT 4, '75. COUNTY BICENTENNIAL HOST. CONFERENCE. (LOCAL). DR HOWARD JABLON, CHMN; PURDUE NORTH CENTRAL; HWY 421; WESTVILLE, IN 46391. (#200017-34).

OCT 31, '75. BICENTENNIAL YOUTH DEBATE. COMPETITION AT PURDUE NORTH CENTRAL, HWY 421. (LOCAL). DR HOWARD JABLON, COORD; PURDUE NORTH CENTRAL; WESTVILLE, IN 46391. (#200017-40).

MAR 1 - 31, '76. AMERICAN ISSUES FORUM. CONFERENCE, LIVE PERFORMANCE AT PURDUE NORTH CENTRAL. (LOCAL). DR HOWARD JABLON, CHMN; PURDUE NORTH CENTRAL AND SINAI FORUM; HWY 421; WESTVILLE, IN 46391. (#104235-1).

MAR 1 - 31, '76. CRAFTY AMERICANS - CRAFTS COMPETITION. COMPETITION AT PURDUE NORTH CENTRAL CAMPUS. (ST-WIDE). DR HOWARD JABLON, CHMN; PURDUE NORTH CENTRAL & LAPORTE COUNTY BICENTENNIAL COMMISSION; HWY 421; WESTVILLE, IN 46391. (#104235-2).

APR 1 - MAY 1, '76. THE CONSTITUTION AND AMERICAN LIFE FORUM - PURDUE, NC. SEMINAR AT PURDUE NORTH CENTRAL. (LOCAL). DR HOWARD JABLON, CHMN; PURDUE NORTH CENTRAL; HWY 421; WESTVILLE, IN 46391. (#104235-3).

WHEATFIELD

SEPT 12 - 13, '75. KANKAKEE VALLEY FINE ARTS COUNCIL VARIETY SHOW. LIVE PERFORMANCE AT KANKAKEE VALLEY HIGH SCHOOL, STATE RD. (LOCAL). MRS RICHARD MYERS, CHMN; KANKAKEE VALLEY FINE ARTS COUNCIL; RR 1, BOX 267; WHEATFIELD, IN 46392. (#101923-1).

MAY 28 - 29, '76. KANKAKEE VALLEY SCHOOL COMMUNITY HERITAGE FESTIVAL. EACH ORGANIZATION IN AREA IS RESPONSIBLE FOR AN EVENT INVOLVING THE ENTIRE SCHOOL COMMUNITY; INCLUDING ANTIQUES, DEMONSTRATIONS, GAMES THEATRE OF THE PAST, ETC. AT KANKAKEE VALLEY JR SR HIGH SCHOOL. (LOCAL). MRS RICHARD MYERS, CO-CHM; KANKAKEE VALLEY SCHOOL COMMUNITY; NRR1 BOX 267; WHEATFIELD, IN 46392. (#102009-1).

WHITESTOWN

SEPT 16 - 18, '77. WHITESTOWN PIONEER DAYS; RUSTIC SETTLER EXHIBITS. PIONEER LASSIE REIGNS OVER AN ARRAY OF RIDES, GAMES, BOOTHS, FOOD, ENTERTAINMENT & PARADE. ANTIQUE & HISTORICAL DISPLAYS. QUARTER MIDGET RACES HOURS ON: 11:30AM-7:00PM. 9/16 5PM-12AM; 9/17 9AM-1AM 9/18 11:30-7:00PM. AT WHITESTOWN LIONS CLUB PARK. (LOCAL). MARY FRANCES HARDIN, CHMN; WHITESTOWN COMMUNITY CENTER; PO BOX 62; WHITESTOWN, IN 46075. (#100325-1).

WINCHESTER

APR 1 - JULY 4, '76. ESSAY CONTEST FOR RANDOLPH COUNTY STUDENTS. THEME OF THE ESSAY IS 'WHAT FREEDOM MEANS TO ME'. WINNERS WILL BE ANNOUNCED ON JULY 4TH. (LOCAL). GENE FOUST, COORDINATOR; FESTIVAL COMMITTEE; 603 E NORTH; WINCHESTER, IN 47394. (#108344-1).

JULY 4, '76. FOURTH OF JULY PARADE AND FESTIVAL. PARADE, FESTIVAL AT STARTING LOCATION - RT 32 AND MERIDIAN ST. (LOCAL). JOHN SEGRAVES, JR, COORD; AMERICAN LEGION; 622 N EAST ST; WINCHESTER, IN 47394. (#108327-1).

WINGATE

GILKEY MEMORIAL PARK, WINGATE, IN. LANDSCAPING, PLAY AREAS, SMALL TRAILER PARK, SMALL MUSEUM, AND GENERAL REFURBISHING. (LOCAL). ROY MEHARRY, PRESIDENT; WINGATE BICENTENNIAL COMMISSION; WINGATE, IN 47994. (#31001).

JUNE 27, '76. BICENTENNIAL DAY IN WINGATE. LIVE PERFORMANCE, FESTIVAL AT WINGATE GILKY PARK ON GARFIELD ST & ST RD 25. (LOCAL). R H MEHARRY; WINGATE BICENTENNIAL COMMITTEE; RR 1, BOX 110; NEW RICHMOND, IN 47967. (#200017-74).

WINONA LAKE

MICROFICHE LIBRARY - WINONA LAKE, IN. LIBRARY OF CONGRESS CARDS FOR GRACE COLLEGE LIBRARY OF AMERICAN CIVILIZATION MICROFICHE TO BE INSERTED IN TEH CARD CATALOGUE. THERE ARE OVER 120,000 LIBRARY OF CONGRESS CARDS. (LOCAL). R WAYNE SNIDER, PROFESSOR; GRACE COLLEGE; WOOSTER RD; WINONA LAKE, IN 46590. (#24505).

NOV 19, '75. MARQUIS DE LAFAYETTE - STEVE GRILL IMPERSONATING. LIVE PERFORMANCE AT MCCLAIN HALL AUDITORIUM. (LOCAL). R WAYNE SNIDER, CHAIRMAN; GRACE COLLEGE; PO BOX 691; WINONA LAKE, IN 46590. (#200017-41).

DEC 5, '75. 'CHARLES PLUMB RETURNED-POW'. LIVE PERFORMANCE AT MCCLAIN HALL AUDITORIUM. (LOCAL). ROBERT MATHISEN, COORD; GRACE COLLEGE; WINONA LAKE, IN 46590. (#200017-42).

DEC 10, '75. 'JOHN BURNS: THE CIVILIAN HERO AT GETTYSBURG, 1863'. LIVE PERFORMANCE AT MCCLAIN HALL AUDITORIUM. (LOCAL). R WAYNE SNIDER, CHAIRMAN; GRACE COLLEGE; PO BOX 691; WINONA LAKE, IN 46590. (#200017-43).

FEB 18, '76. PATRICK HENRY 'GIVE ME LIBERTY OR GIVE ME DEATH' SPEECH. LIVE PERFORMANCE AT MCCLAIN HALL AUDITORIUM. (LOCAL). R WAYNE SNIDER, CHAIRMAN; GRACE COLLEGE; PO BOX 691; WINONA LAKE, IN 46590. (#200017-44).

FEB 27, '76. 'THE KANTORE: THE SINGING BOYS OF ROCKFORD'. LIVE PERFORMANCE AT RODEHEAVER AUDITORIUM. (LOCAL). R WAYNE SNIDER, CHAIRMAN; GRACE SCHOOLS; PO BOX 691; WINONA LAKE, IN 46590. (#200017-45).

MAR 5, '76. 'COL HEATH BOTTOMLY'. LIVE PERFORMANCE AT MCCLAIN HALL AUDITORIUM. (LOCAL). R WAYNE SNIDER, CHAIRMAN; GRACE COLLEGE; PO BOX 691; WINONA LAKE, IN 46590. (#200017-46).

MAR 16, '76. MERCY OTIS WARREN 'WOMEN IN THE AMERICAN REVOLUTION'. LIVE PERFORMANCE AT MCCLAIN HALL AUDITORIUM. (LOCAL). R WAYNE SNIDER, CHAIRMAN; GRACE COLLEGE; PO BOX 691; WINONA LAKE, IN 46590. (#200017-47).

MAR 24, '76. 'AMERICA ON PARADE' BY ROBERT BROUWER. EXHIBIT AT RODEHEAVER AUDITORIUM. (LOCAL). R WAYNE SNIDER, CHAIRMAN; GRACE SCHOOLS; PO BOX 691; WINONA LAKE, IN 46590. (#200017-48).

APR 12 - MAY 17, '76. SECOND ANNUAL JURIED SHOW OF STUDENTS ART WORK. EXHIBIT, COMPETITION AT NORTH HALL. (LOCAL). MRS JEAN COVERSTONE, CHMN; GRACE COLLEGE ART DEPARTMENT; WINONA LAKE, IN 46590. (#107174-3).

APR 14, '76. 'ABRAHAM LINCOLN'. LIVE PERFORMANCE AT MCCLAIN HALL AUDITORIUM. (LOCAL). R WAYNE SNIDER, CHAIRMAN; GRACE COLLEGE; PO BOX 691; WINONA LAKE, IN 46590. (#200017-49).

APR 30, '76. 'SONG OF AMERICA' & 'TESTAMENT OF FREEDOM'. LIVE PERFORMANCE AT RODEHEAVER AUDITORIUM. (LOCAL). R WAYNE SNIDER, CHMN; GRACE SCHOOLS & GRACE COLLEGE BICENTENNIAL COMMITTEE; PO BOX 691; WINONA LAKE, IN 46590. (#107174-1).

MAY 1, '76. 'FROM COLONY TO COUNTRY'. LIVE PERFORMANCE AT RODEHEAVER AUDITORIUM. (LOCAL). R WAYNE SNIDER, CHMN; GRACE SCHOOLS & GRACE COLLEGE BICENTENNIAL COMMITTEE; PO BOX 691; WINONA LAKE, IN 46590. (#107174-2).

WOLCOTT

COMMUNITY PARK DEVELOPMENT, WOLCOTT, INDIANA. DEVELOPMENT OF A WOLCOTT TOWN RECREATIONAL PARK AREA ADJACENT TO THE GROUNDS OF THE WOLCOTT HOUSE HISTORICAL PROJECT. (LOCAL). MAC DISMORE CLERK-TREASURER; WOLCOTT TOWN PARK BOARD; WOLCOTT, IN 47995. (#4520).

JULY 4, '75. WOLCOTT SUMMER FESTIVAL. FESTIVAL, PARADE AT TWO RIVERS CENTRAL PARK, WASHINGTON ST. (LOCAL). REV JIM MILLER; WOLCOTT BICENTENNIAL COMMITTEE; WOLCOTT, IN 47995. (#7927-1).

JULY 3 - 4, '76. WOLCOTT HOUSE DEDICATION DURING WOLCOTT SUMMER FESTIVAL. THE WOLCOTT HOUSE AN OLD MANSION OF LOCAL HISTORIC AND ARCHITECTURAL INTEREST TO BE RESTORED AS A PERIOD REPRESENTATION OF THE LATE 1800S WITH PROVISIONS FOR PARTICULAR COMMUNITY SOCIAL USES. (LOCAL). RICHARD NAGEL, PRESIDENT; ANSON WOLCOTT HISTORICAL SOCIETY; BOX 294; WOLCOTT, IN 47995. (#4577-501).

JULY 4, '76. PRAIRIE PAGEANT FESTIVAL-ARTS, CRAFTS, ENTERTAINMENT. AN ANNUAL PATRIOTIC FESTIVAL HELD ON JULY 4. FEATURING PARADE, FIREWORKS, ARTS, CRAFTS, FLEA MARKET, FISH FRY, EXHIBITS, ENTERTAINMENT, SPECIAL EVENTS, ETC. AT HISTORIC WOLCOTT HOUSE GROUNDS; US #24 IN WOLCOTT, 4 MI OFF I-65. (LOCAL). JIM MILLER; SUMMER FESTIVAL COMMITTEE; BOX 396; WOLCOTT, IN 47995. (#4578-1).

JULY 3 - 4, '77. ANNUAL PATRIOTIC COMMUNITY FESTIVAL. WOLCOTT, INDIANA, SUMMER FESTIVAL. AN ANNUAL PATRIOTIC FESTIVAL HELD ON JULY 4. FEATURING PARADE, FIREWORKS, ARTS, CRAFTS, FLEA MARKET, FISH FRY, EXHIBITS, ENTERTAINMENT, SPECIAL EVENTS, ETC. (LOCAL). JAMES W MILLER, CHAIRMAN; WOLCOTT SUMMER FESTIVAL COMMITTEE; WOLCOTT, IN 47995. (#4578-503).

WORTHINGTON

REPLACEMENT OF FOUNTAIN IN PLAZA - WORTHINGTON, IN. REPLACE THE PRESENT NONOPERATING FOUNTAIN IN THE PLAZA. (LOCAL). KECK MYERS, COORDINATOR; WORTHINGTON CHAMBER OF COMMERCE; 23 S JEFFERSON ST; WORTHINGTON, IN 47471. (#27774). **ARBA GRANTEE.**

YORKTOWN

YORKTOWN, IN, BICENTENNIAL PARK. A SMALL PARK WILL BE DEVELOPED WITHIN THE CITY. (LOCAL). FRANK SCHUER, CHAIRMAN; YORKTOWN JAYCEES; TOWN HALL; YORKTOWN, IN 47396. (#27785). **ARBA GRANTEE.**

ZIONSVILLE

JULY 4, '76. FIREWORKS SHOW. FIREWORKS SOAR INTO THE AIR, AS THE VOLUNTEER FIREMEN HAVE A BLAST CREATING THIS SPARKLING CONFLAGRATION TO TOP OFF A FUN-FILLED DAY OF GAMES & FOOD AT LION'S PARK. AT ZIONSVILLE LIONS PARK, 2 MILES WEST OF U S 421 ON SR 334. (LOCAL). REN BROWNFIELD, CHAIRMAN; ZIONSVILLE VOLUNTEER FIREMEN; ZIONSVILLE TOWN HALL; ZIONSVILLE, IN 46077. (#100335-1).

SEPT 11 - 12, '76. COLONIAL VILLAGE FALL FESTIVAL. COBBLESTONE STREETS AND COLONIAL-STYLED STRUCTURES INVITE THE PUBLIC TO ZIONSVILLE, WHERE ENTERTAINMENT, GAMES AND FOODS MINGLE WITH THE CROWDS AT LION'S PARK; HANDMADE CRAFTS AND ART EXHIBITS DECORATE THIS COMMUNITY WITH THE GALA PARADE SCHEDULED FOR SATURDAY. AT LIONS PARK, TWO MILES WEST OF US 421 ON SR 334. (LOCAL). JERRY ABBOT, PROJ CHMN; ZIONSVILLE LIONS CLUB; FARMERS STATE BANK; ZIONSVILLE, IN 46077. (#100336-1).

OCT 9 - 10, '76. THE VILLAGE TOUR, A COLONIAL STYLE TOWN WITH STORES & HOUSES. COLONIAL-STYLED ZIONSVILLE OPENS ITS DOORS FOR TOURS OF HOMES THAT REFLECT OUR AMERICAN HERITAGE IN THEIR FURNISHINGS AND DESIGN; MEANDER DOWN THE COBBLESTONE STREETS OF THE VILLAGE AND EXPLORE INTERESTING BOUTIQUES ALONG THE WAY. AT ZIONSVILLE. (LOCAL). MRS HELEN KOGAN, CHMN; ZIONSVILLE CHAMBER OF COMMERCE; PO BOX 148; ZIONSVILLE, IN 46077. (#100312-1).

IOWA

BICENTENNIAL USA

Iowa

Theme: Iowa '76

Iowa American Revolution Bicentennial Commission

Commissioned by the State Legislature in January 1971

ARBA Statistics

Officially Recognized
Communities—811
Colleges/Universities—36
Military Installations—2
BINET Projects—1,922
Events—1,808
1976 Population—2,870,000

Bicentennial Archives

Iowa State Archives
East 7th and Court Streets
Des Moines, Iowa 50319

Membership

Two members of the Senate appointed by the president of the Senate, each of whom shall be a member of a different political party; two members of the House of Representatives, appointed by the speaker of the House of Representatives, each of whom shall be a member of a different political party; the secretary of state, superintendent of the State Historical Society, curator of the Iowa State Department of History and Archives, director of the State Conservation Commission, president of the State University of Iowa, president of the Iowa State University of Science and Technology, president of the University of Northern Iowa, director of the Iowa Development Commission, chairman of the Iowa State Fair and World Food Exposition Study Committee, secretary of the Iowa State Fair Board, and seven citizens of the state appointed by the governor, one of whom shall be designated by the governor as chairman of the commission.

Robert W. Dillon, *chairman* (1971-76)
Don N. Kersten, *vice-chairman* (1971-76)
Senator Charles O. Laverty (1971-73)
Representative Ed Skinner (1971-72)
Senator Forrest V. Schwengels (1973-76)
Representative Quentin Anderson (1973-74)
Representative Don Alt (1972-73)
Representative Charles Knoblauch (1971-73)
Representative Richard Byerly (1973-76)
Senator Lee Gaudineer (1971-73)
Senator Norman Rodgers (1973-76)
Senator C. Joseph Coleman (1971-76)
Representative Lillian McElroy (1975-76)
Don Muhm (1971-75)
C. Robert Brenton (1971-75)
Evelyn Birkby (1975-76)
William J. Peterson (1971-72)
Peter J. Harstad (1972-76)
Chad Wymer (1971-73)
Del Van Horn (1973-76)
(Mrs.) Edwin W. Bruere (1971-76)
William G. Murray (1971-76)
Robert M. Stone (1971-76)
Melvin Synhorst (1971-76)
Jack W. Musgrove (1971-76)
Fred A. Priewert (1971-76)
Willard L. Boyd (1971-76)
John J. Kamerick (1971-76)
W. Robert Parks (1971-76)
Kenneth R. Fulk (1971-76)
Jerry Coughlon (1976-)

Staff

Murray Goodman, *executive director* (1972-76)
R. Edwin Redfern, *executive director* (July 9, 1976-September 9, 1976)
Kathy Cashman, *executive director* (September 9, 1976-)

Iowa

The Bicentennial in the state of Iowa was a grassroots celebration involving thousands of Iowans. Activities of every size and nature were carried on. On July 4, 1976, Iowa was first on the BINET system for the number of projects and events Iowans planned and were carrying out for the Bicentennial.

Restoration was the major focus. Homes, rural schoolhouses, log cabins and museums were restored to their original state.

Next, Iowans looked to the future with the construction of museums, libraries, senior citizen homes, tennis courts and new parks. All 811 of Iowa's Bicentennial Communities planned at least one project for a better Iowa.

Celebrations were evident all over the state during 1975 and 1976. The 4th of July proved to be a festive occasion beyond expectations. Parades, old-fashioned games and church services showed the pride Iowans have in our history and the importance the past plays in our future.

The Iowa American Revolution Bicentennial Commission endorsed several statewide projects, putting an emphasis on youth.

Iowa had a school recognition program which acknowledged the efforts of elementary and high schools in the Bicentennial. An Iowa history kit for fifth graders was funded by the commission from the sale of our state Bicentennial medallion. Kits were distributed to schools throughout the State of Iowa.

Another statewide project stressing the importance of agriculture was supported by the Iowa American Revolution Bicentennial Commission. The *World Food Conference* held at the Iowa State University at Ames was attended by people from throughout the world. Ways to improve agriculture in all countries was the main theme of the conference.

The continuing Living History Farms, a commission-endorsed project, stress agriculture. The farms depict farming in the 1800's, 1900's and the future. They are living museums, showing all phases of farm life.

A final report will be published by the Iowa American Revolution Bicentennial Commission. It will show the next generation what Iowans accomplished for the Bicentennial. A copy will be put in a time capsule, to be opened in 2075.

When future Iowans study the Bicentennial years, they will see a period of history when fellow Iowans not only looked back with pride, but ahead with hope.

ACKLEY

JULY 25 - 27, '76. ACKLEY BICENTENNIAL SAUERKRAUT DAYS. ATHLETIC EVENTS, PICNIC, FESTIVAL, PARADE, HISTORIC DISPLAY & BICENT BOOKLET, 'PIONEER ACKLEY'. (LOCAL). ED WALDORF, COORD; ACKLEY CHAMBER OF COMMERCE; 526 MAIN; ACKLEY, IA 50601. (#109024-1).

ADEL

DALLIS COUNTY FOXFIRE PROGRAM - IA. HISTORICAL RECOLLECTIONS OF TOWN'S SENIOR CITIZENS WILL BE RECORDED. (LOCAL). LOWEL OWEN, PROJECT DIRECTOR; DALLIS COUNTY BICENTENNIAL COMMITTEE; 609 S 9TH; ADEL, IA 50003. (#18546).

DALLIS COUNTY HISTORY - IA. THE HISTORY OF DALLIS COUNTY IS BEING WRITTEN FOR PUBLICATION. (LOCAL). LOWEL OWEN, PROJECT DIRECTOR; DALLIS COUNTY BICENTENNIAL COMMITTEE; 609 S 9TH; ADEL, IA 50003. (#18548).

DOCUMENTATION OF CEMETERY RECORDS - ADEL, IA. CEMETERY RECORDS WILL BE LISTED AND UPDATED FOR THE STATE BICENTENNIAL PROJECT. (ST-WIDE). LOWEL OWEN, PROJECT DIRECTOR; DALLIS COUNTY BICENTENNIAL COMMITTEE; 609 S 9TH; ADEL, IA 50003. (#18549).

TREE PLANTING - DALLIS COUNTY, IA. TOWN CITIZENS WILL PLANT TREES TO REPLACE ELM TREES LOST BY DUTCH ELM DISEASE. (LOCAL). LOWEL OWEN, PROJECT DIRECTOR; DALLIS COUNTY BICENTENNIAL COMMITTEE; 609 S 9TH; ADEL, IA 50003. (#18547).

JUNE 19 - 20, '76. CITY FESTIVAL. ARTS & CRAFTS EXHIBIT, ANTIQUE SHOW, MUSIC & TALENT CONTEST. PARADE, BARBEQUE, 2 DANCES, SHOOTING CONTEST BETWEEN MUZZLE LOADERS & MODERN RIFLES. WAGON TRAIN FROM DALLAS CENTER TO ADEL, MUSICAL PAGEANT, TREE SALE, PRESENTATION OF BICENTENNIAL FLAGS. AT COURTHOUSE SQUARE & CITY PARK. (LOCAL). VERN DANILSON, CHMN; AMERICAN BICENTENNIAL CORPORATION OF ADEL; 434 N 10TH; ADEL, IA 50003. (#101763-1).

AFTON

HISTORICAL PERSONALITIES - AFTON, IA. BRONZE PLAQUE TO BE DISPLAYED IN CITY HALL COMMEMORATING PAST AND PRESENT PROMINENT CITIZENS. (LOCAL). RONALD FLAM, CHAIRMAN; AFTON BICENTENNIAL COMMITTEE; AFTON, IA 50830. (#20331).

TREE PLANTING PROJ - AFTON, IA. TREES WILL BE PLANTED IN THE CITY PARK. (LOCAL). RONALD FLAM, BICENT CO-CHAIRMAN; AFTON CUB SCOUTS; AFTON, IA 50830. (#20330).

JUNE 26, '76. TIME CAPSULE. BURY TIME CAPSULE AT THE SITE OF MONUMENT, ORIGINAL COUNTY COURTHOUSE. (LOCAL). RONALD FLAM, CHMN; AFTON BICENTENNIAL; AFTON, IA 50830. (#104734-2).

JUNE 26 - 27, '76. AFTON TEA PARTY. THE PARADE WILL BE ON 6/26 AT 2:30PM. (LOCAL). RONALD N FLAM, CHMN; AFTON BICENTENNIAL COMMITTEE; AFTON, IA 50830. (#104734-1).

AGENCY

FLAG DISPLAY - AGENCY, IA. AMERICAN FLAGS DISPLAYED ALONG MAIN STREET IN PAINTED OIL DRUMS WITH FLOWERED PLANTERS. (LOCAL). VERNON MILLER, PROJECTS CHAIRPERSON; AGENCY LIONS CLUB; RR #1; AGENCY, IA 52530. (#17495).

HISTORICAL BOOTHS AT BICENTENNIAL CELEBRATIONS, IA. HISTORICAL BOOTHS AT AGENCY FOURTH OF JULY CELEBRATION AND WAPELLO COUNTY FAIR TO PROMOTE CHIEF WAPELLO'S PARK. (LOCAL). W C TREMBLY, PRESIDENT; CHIEF WAPELLO'S MEMORIAL PARK ASSOCIATION; BOX 115; AGENCY, IA 52530. (#17351).

HISTORICAL SITE PRESERVATION & RESTORATION, IA. CHIEF WAPELLO'S MEMORIAL PARK TO RECEIVE EXTENSIVE RESTORATION AND SPECIAL ATTENTION WILL BE GIVEN TO ITS UPKEEP. (ST-WIDE). W C TREMBLY, PRESIDENT; CHIEF WAPELLO'S MEMORIAL PARK ASSOCIATION; BOX 115; AGENCY, IA 52530. (#17465). **ARBA GRANTEE.**

NEW HISTORICAL SITE ASSOCIATION - AGENCY, IA. ORGANIZATION OF AN ASSOCIATION FOR THE CHIEF WAPELLO MEMORIAL PARK, DEDICATED TO MAKING THE PARK ONE OF IOWA'S OUTSTANDING HISTORICAL SITES. (ST-WIDE). W C TREMBLY, PRESIDENT; CHIEF WAPELLO'S MEMORIAL PARK ASSOC; BOX 115; AGENCY, IA 52530. (#17479).

WAPELLO COUNTY CELEBRATION, AGENCY, IA. WAPELLO COUNTY BICENTENNIAL CELEBRATION, WEEK OF JUNE 8, 1976, WILL FEATURE TOURS TO CHIEF WAPELLO'S MEMORIAL PARK. (LOCAL). W C TREMBLY, PRESIDENT; CHIEF WAPELLO'S MEMORIAL PARK ASSOC; BOX 115; AGENCY, IA 52530. (#17480).

FEB 15 - MAR 31, '76. ESSAY CONTEST RELATED TO CHIEF WAPELLO PARK. PARTICIPATION BY CHILDREN IN SCHOOL DISTRICTS OF TEN COUNTIES, SURROUNDING AND INCLUDING WAPELLO COUNTY. AT SCHOOLS OF TEN COUNTY AREA (INDIAN HILLS REGION). (LOCAL). W C TREMBLY, PRESIDENT; CHIEF WAPELLO'S MEMORIAL PARK ASSOCIATION; BOX 115; AGENCY, IA 52530. (#103342-4).

JUNE 28 - JULY 5, '76. HISTORIC WINDOW DISPLAY CONTEST. COMPETITION, EXHIBIT AT MAIN ST BUSINESS WINDOWS. (LOCAL). VERNON MILLER, PROJ DIR; AGENCY LIONS CLUB; RR 1; AGENCY, IA 52530. (#103342-1).

JULY 3 - 5, '76. FOURTH OF JULY CELEBRATION. PARADE & FLOATS, RECOUNTING OF HISTORY OF AGENCY CITY, CELEBRATION ACTIVITIES, BALL GAMES, CONTESTS & BARBECUE. (LOCAL). HON DONALD KROUSE, MAYOR; AGENCY FOURTH OF JULY COMMITTEE; 401 N COLLEGE; AGENCY, IA 52530. (#103342-2).

JULY 4, '76. OLD FASHIONED CAMP MEETING. COMMEMORATING THE FIRST CHRISTIAN SERVICE IN CHIEF WAPELLO'S WICKIUP IN 1838. OTHER CHURCHES INVITED. (LOCAL). W C TREMBLY, PASTOR; AGENCY UNITED METHODIST CHURCH; 119 N COLLEGE; AGENCY, IA 52530. (#103342-3).

OCT 9, '76. CELEBRATION OF 1842 TREATY & DEDICATION OF PARK. COMMEMORATION OF SIGNING OF TREATY OF 1842 FOR THE PURCHASE OF MUCH OF IOWA FROM SAC & FOX INDIANS; DEDICATION OF PARK IMPROVEMENTS TO DATE; JOHN KYL, KEY NOTE SPEAKER. AT ON PARK SITE. (LOCAL). W C TREMBLY, PRESIDENT; CHIEF WAPELLO'S MEMORIAL PARK ASSOCIATION; BOX 115; AGENCY, IA 52530. (#103342-12).

OCT 9, '76. INDIAN ART AND ARTIFACTS FESTIVAL. FESTIVAL IN CONJUNCTION WITH ANOTHER COMMEMORATIVE MEETING FEATURING ART BY AND ABOUT INDIANS; INDIAN AFTIFACT DISPLAYS. AT OPEN AIR AT PARK SITE IN TENT BOOTHS. (LOCAL). W C TREMBLY; CHIEF WAPELLO'S MEMORIAL PARK ASSOC; BOX 115; AGENCY, IA 52530. (#17494-1).

ALBERT CITY

ALBERT CITY DEPOT RESTORATION - IOWA. RESTORATION OF OLD CITY DEPOT FOR COMMUNITY ENHANCEMENT. (LOCAL). DUANE MADSON & WESELY SCOTT, CO-CHAIRMEN; ALBERT CITY COMMUNITY BICENT COMMISSION; ALBERT CITY, IA 50510. (#9639).

LIVING HISTORY MUSEUM - ALBERT CITY, IA. LIVING HISTORY MUSEUM WILL PRESERVE THE/HISTORY OF COMMUNITY CULTURE AND ARTIFACTS WILL BE RESTORED. (LOCAL). MRS GLADYS ANDERSON, PRESIDENT; ALBERT CITY HISTORICAL ASSOCIATION INC; RR 1, BOX 30; ALBERT CITY, IA 50510. (#17949).

DEC 6, '75. CHRISTMAS DISPLAYS & TEA. EXHIBIT, FESTIVAL AT OUR SAVIORS LUTHERAN CHURCH. (LOCAL). HELEN DANIELSON, CHAIRMAN; ALBERT CITY GARDEN CLUB; ALBERT CITY, IA 50510. (#200018-2).

JAN 31, '76. BICENTENNIAL FARM & ANTIQUE SHOW. EXHIBIT AT OLD GYMNASIUM, ALBERT CITY COMMUNITY SCHOOL. (LOCAL). KARL LIND, CHAIRMAN; ALBERT CITY ANTIQUE & COLLECTERS; ALBERT CITY, IA 50510. (#103982-2).

APR 2 - 3, '76. LIONS CLUB VARIETY SHOW. FRIDAY: PERFORMANCES, SATURDAY: DINNER & PERFORMANCE. AT OLD GYNASIUM. (LOCAL). WESLEY T SCOTT; LIONS' CLUB; ALBERT CITY, IA 50510. (#103987-1).

AUG 13 - 14, '76. BICENTENNIAL THRESHING BEE & COLLECTORS' SHOW. PARADE, BEARD CONTEST, HOME CRAFTS, THRESHING BEE, ANTIQUE DEMONSTRATION, OLD CARS, MACHINERY DISPLAYS. AT HERITAGE SITE. (LOCAL). KARL LIND, CHAIRMAN; ALBERT CITY BICENTENNIAL; RFD; ALBERT CITY, IA 50510. (#103982-1).

SEPT 6, '76. LABOR DAY COFFEE BREAK FOR TRAVELERS. FESTIVAL AT LITTLE CLER LAKE REST STOP, HIGHWAY #3. (LOCAL). WESLEY T SCOTT; LIONS CLUB; ALBERT CITY, IA 50510. (#103987-2).

ALBIA

FLAG DISPLAY IN ALBIA, IA. U S FLAGS & IOWA FLAGS WILL BE POSTED AROUND SQUARE. (LOCAL). HELEN HALUSKA, SECRETARY; ALBIA CHAMBER OF COMMERCE; 115 N MAIN; ALBIA, IA 52531. (#13885).

MONROE CO, IA, HISTORICAL MUSEUM. RESTORATION OF OLD LIBRARY IN ALBIA TO BE TURNED INTO A MUSEUM. (LOCAL). ELMER SOVERN, CHAIRMAN; MONROE HISTORICAL SOCIETY; ALBIA, IA 52531. (#13886).

JUNE 17 - 19, '76. ALBIA FESTIVAL. THE FESTIVAL WILL INCLUDE A PARADE, RODEO, STREET DANCING, WINDOW DISPLAYS AND FOOD STANDS. AT AROUND THE SQUARE & FAIRGROUNDS (3 MILES NORTH OF ALBIA). (LOCAL). HELEN HALUSKA, TREAS; MONROE COUNTY AMERICAN REVOLUTION BICENTENNIAL COMMISSION; 107 S CLINTON ST, PO BOX F306; ALBIA, IA 52531. (#104519-10).

ALBION

SEPT 4, '76. OLD TIMERS' BICENTENNIAL CELEBRATION. THIS IS A COMMUNITY EFFORT WITH A BICENTENNIAL THEME - MANY ALBION RESIDENTS & ORGANIZATIONS ARE INVOLVED IN THE PLANNING; EVENTS INCLUDE A KIDDIE PARADE, THEME PARADE, CONTESTS, ART & CRAFT EXHIBITS, BLACKWOOD BROTHERS CONCERT AND ANTIQUE SHOW. AT BALL DIAMOND, N END OF ALBION AND ALBION PARK SQUARE. (LOCAL). MYLENE M THOMAS, CHAIRMAN; OLD TIMERS' BICENTENNIAL COMMITTEE; RR 1; MARSHALLTOWN, IA 50158. (#105326-1).

ALBURNETT

CONSTRUCTION OF A DOUBLE TENNIS COURT, IA. THE ALBURNETT COMMUNITY RAISED $15,000 TO BUILD A DOUBLE TENNIS COURT ON THE SCHOOL GROUNDS. (LOCAL). A G MYERS, CHAIRMAN; ALBURNETT COMMUNITY SCHOOL BICENTENNIAL COMMITTEE; RR 1; ALBURNETT, IA 52202. (#29685).

JUNE 19, '76. BICENTENNIAL FESTIVAL. PARADE, ARTS & CRAFTS, TRACTOR PULL, MUSIC, GAMES AND FOOD WERE ALL PART OF THIS FESTIVE CELEBRATION. AT DOWN TOWN ALBURNETT AND SCHOOL GROUNDS. (LOCAL). ALBERT MYERS, CHMN; ALBURNETT SCHOOL COMMUNITY BICENTENNIAL COMMITTEE; RR1; ALBURNETT, IA 52202. (#200018-303).

ALDEN

HISTORICAL QUILT - ALDEN, IA. EACH BLOCK OF THE ORIGINAL DESIGN WAS SEWN BY A DIFFERENT VOLUNTEER; QUILT WILL BE RAFFLED WHEN COMPLETED ON JUNE 9, 1976. (LOCAL). MRS JOHN NEUBAUER, CHAIRMAN; ALDEN BICENTENNIAL COMMITTEE CHAIRMAN; RR 3, BOX 326; ALDEN, IA 50006. (#25407).

SLIDES ON COURTHOUSES - ALDEN, IA. SLIDES OF BUILDINGS THAT ONCE WERE AND/OR NOW ARE COURTHOUSES, ARE BEING MADE. (LOCAL). JOHN KEMP, COORDINATOR; ALDEN BICENTENNIAL COMMITTEE; ALDEN, IA 50006. (#30162).

TREE PLANTING - ALDEN, IA. THE FUTURE FARMERS OF AMERICA WILL SELL TREES TO THE PUBLIC, THEN DELIVER & PLANT THEM ON JUNE 1, 1976. (LOCAL). MARY NEUBAUER, PROJ CHAIRMAN; FUTURE FARMERS OF AMERICA & ALDEN COMMUNITY SCHOOL; ALDEN, IA 50006. (#25406).

APR 1 - JULY 31, '76. DISPLAY OF HISTORICAL ITEMS. DISPLAY WILL BE CHANGED EACH WEEK. 1ST WEEK - CROCKS, THEN WOOD, IRON, TIN & COPPER, DOLLS & TOYS, LAMPS, PEWTER & SILVER, HAND TOOLS AND MILITARY EQUIPMENT. THIS WILL CONTINUE UNTIL AFTER JULY 4TH. AT MASSOW'S HARDWARE STORE WINDOW. (LOCAL). MRS JOHN NEUBAUER, CHMN; BICENTENNIAL COMMITTEE; RR 3, BOX 326; ALDEN, IA 50006. (#108044-4).

MAY 21, '76. TIME CAPSULE. CEREMONY AT ALDEN COMMUNITY SCHOOL. (LOCAL). MRS JOHN NEUBAUER, COORD; FUTURE HOMEMAKERS OF AMERICA - ALDEN COMMUNITY SCHOOL; RR 3, BOX 326; ALDEN, IA 50006. (#108044-1).

JULY 8, '76. AMERICA'S HERITAGE PARADE. PARADE. (LOCAL). MRS JOHN NEUBAUER, COORD; LION'S CLUB; RR 3, BOX 326; ALDEN, IA 50006. (#108044-2).

JULY 8 - 9, '76. HISTORY OF ALDEN - SLIDE PRESENTATION. EXHIBIT AT ALDEN PUBLIC LIBRARY BASEMENT. (LOCAL). MRS JOHN NEUBAUER, COORD; LION'S CLUB; RR 3, BOX 326; ALDEN, IA 50006. (#108044-3).

ALEXANDER

HISTORICAL BOOK PROJECT - ALEXANDER, IA. A BOOK ON THE HISTORY OF ALEXANDER BUSINESSES, CHURCHES, COMMUNITY ENTERPRISES, LIBRARY AND LOW COST HOUSING PORJECT. (LOCAL). ORVILLE ARENDS, CHAIRPERSON; ALEXANDER BICENTENNIAL COMMITTEE; ALEXANDER, IA 50420. (#22225).

ALGONA

COVERED WAGON DISPLAY - IOWA. EVERY TOWN TO SUPPLY A COVERED WAGON FOR THE FAIR. (LOCAL). ROYAL NOLD, COORDINATOR; KOSSUTH COUNTY BICENTENNIAL; ALGONA, IA 52501. (#19961).

FLAG HERITAGE - ALGONA, IA. EVERY SCHOOL IN KOSSUTH COUNTY WILL BE VISITED AND GIVEN LESSONS IN FLAG ETIQUETTE. (LOCAL). ROYAL NOLD, CHAIRMAN; KOSSUTH COUNTY BICENTENNIAL COMMISSION; ALGONA, IA 50511. (#20484).

MEDICAL CENTER DEDICATION. CEREMONY. (LOCAL). ROYAL NOLD, COORD; KOSSUTH COUNTY BICENTENNIAL COMMITTEE; ALGONA, IA 50511. (#104689-1).

ALLERTON

COMMUNITY BUILDING, ALLERTON, IA. NEW BUILDING TO CONSIST OF FIRE STATION, CITY OFFICES, LIBRARY, AND COMMUNITY ROOMS. (LOCAL). EDWARD DUDEN, CHAIRMAN; ALLERTON CENTENNIAL ASSOC; ALLERTON, IA 50008. (#19850).

ALLISON

BUTLER COUNTY HALL OF FAME - ALLISON, IA. REMOVAL OF CUPOLA FROM OLD COURTHOUSE BY THE NATIONAL GUARD HELICOPTER TO BE PLACED IN THE 'HALL OF FAME' BUILDING. (LOCAL). MRS MINA WOODLEY, CHAIRMAN; BUTLER COUNTY HISTORICAL COMMISSION, INC; RFD 2, BOX 175; ALLISON, IA 50602. (#21099).

FOXFIRE BOOKLET & OLD FASHIONED COOKBOOK - IA. PROJECT WILL BE TO PUT TOGETHER AND PUBLISH THE FOXFIRE BOOKLET & OLD FASHIONED COOKBOOK. (ST-WIDE). MRS MINA WOODLEY, CHAIRMAN; BUTLER COUNTY BICENTENNIAL COMMITTEE; ALLISON, IA 50602. (#11265).

HISTORY OF ALLISON, IA. LOCAL HISTORIANS ARE COMPILING THE TOWN'S HISTORY IN A BOOKLET TO BE SOLD. (LOCAL). ROGER WUBBENA, CHAIRMAN; ALLISON BICENTENNIAL COMMISSION; 405 E 4TH ST; ALLISON, IA 50602. (#22216).

PARK DEVELOPMENT - ALLISON, IA. A PARK WILL BE DEVELOPED FOR DOWNTOWN ALLISON. (LOCAL). ROGER WUBBENA, CHAIRMAN; ALLISON BICENTENNIAL COMMISSION; 405 E 4TH ST; ALLISON, IA 50602. (#22222).

REMOVAL OF CUPOLA OF ALLISON, IA, COURTHOUSE. REMOVE CUPOLA FROM COURTHOUSE & PUT IT ON CEMENT FOR USE AS

ALLISON — CONTINUED

HALL OF FAME & RECORDS. (LOCAL). MRS MINA WOODLEY, CHAIRMAN; BUTLER COUNTY BICENTENNIAL COMMITTEE; ALLISON, IA 50602. (#11264).

JUNE 19, '76. BUTLER COUNTY DAIRY DAY. DEDICATION OF BUTLER COUNTY HALL OF FAME IN CONJUNCTION WITH BUTLER COUNTY DAIRY DAY. AT COURTHOUSE GROUNDS, NEAR LITTLE YELLOW SCHOOLHOUSE. (LOCAL). MRS MINA WOODLEY, CHMN; BUTLER COUNTY BICENTENNIAL COMMISSION, INC; RFD 2, BOX 175; ALLISON, IA 50602. (#21099-1).

JUNE 19, '76. FESTIVAL DAY. PARADE WITH SENIOR KING & QUEEN, GAMES & REFRESHMENTS. DEDICATION OF TIME CAPSULE. (LOCAL). ROGER WUBRENA, CHMN; ALLISON BICENTENNIAL COMMISSION; 405 E 4TH ST; ALLISON, IA 50602. (#105967-1).

JUNE 19, '76. TIME CAPSULE DEDICATION. CEREMONY. (LOCAL). ROGER WUBBENA, CHAIRMAN; ALLISON BICENTENNIAL COMMISSION; 405 E 4TH ST; ALLISON, IA 50602. (#105826-1).

ALTA VISTA

DEVELOPMENT OF COMMUNITY PARK - ALTA VISTA, IA. A WALKWAY, REST BENCHES, FLOWER BOXES AND A 48 FT FLAGPOLE IN CEMENT BOX WERE BUILT; THE SITE WAS DONATED BY THE TOWN & THE JAYCEES PAID FOR ALL MATERIALS AND DONATED THE LABOR. (LOCAL). TOM FRANTZEN, PROJ COORDINATOR; ALTA VISTA JAYCEES; RR 2; NEW HAMPTON, IA 50659. (#23910).

PLANTING FLOWERS PROJ - ALTA VISTA, IA. TOWN GARDEN CLUB & 4-H CLUB WILL PLANT FLOWERS IN THE TOWN PARK & IN STORE FRONT BOXES AROUND TOWN; FLOWERS WILL BE RED, WHITE AND BLUE. (LOCAL). ROSE DUNN, COORDINATOR; ALTA VISTA GARDEN CLUB & GIRLS 4-H CLUB; ALTA VISTA, IA 50603. (#23911).

TOWN HISTORY - ALTA VISTA, IA. HISTORY OF ALTA VISTA WILL BE WRITTEN FROM ITS ORIGIN IN THE EARLY 1800'S TO THE PRESENT; WILL BE PRINTED IN BOOKLET FORM & AVAILABLE TO PUBLIC FOR SALE IN SEPTEMBER 1976. (LOCAL). JAMES T MARIK, CHAIRPERSON; ALTA VISTA BICENTENNIAL COMMITTEE; BOX 166; ALTA VISTA, IA 50603. (#23912).

WINDOW & FLAG DISPLAYS - ALTA VISTA, IA. TOWN BUSINESSES WILL HAVE BICENTENNIAL DISPLAYS OF ANTIQUES IN THEIR STORE FRONTS; FLAGS WILL ALSO BE DISPLAYED AND FLOWN. (LOCAL). JAMES MARIK, CHAIRPERSON; ALTA VISTA BICENTENNIAL COMMITTEE; BOX 166; ALTA VISTA, IA 50603. (#23913).

MAY 31, '76. MEMORIAL DAY BICENTENNIAL OBSERVANCE. DEDICATION OF JAYCEE'S FLAGPOLE, CHICKEN FRY, SOFTBALL GAMES, DEMOLITION DERBY; PROCEEDS FROM EVENTS WILL GO TOWARD COMMUNITY DEVELOPMENT PROJECTS. AT TOWN PARK & MUNICIPAL HALL. (LOCAL). JAMES T MARIK, CHAIRMAN; ALTA VISTA BICENTENNIAL COMMITTEE; BOX 166; ALTA VISTA, IA 50603. (#107088-1).

ALTON

JULY 4 - 5, '76. 4TH OF JULY CELEBRATION. CELEBRATE THE 4TH OF JULY WITH LOCAL COMMUNITY ACTIVITIES: PARADE, FIREWORKS, BALLGAMES, RAFT RACES, TUG OF WAR, BAKING CONTEST, RACES, CONCESSIONS, FOOD AND WATERFIGHT. AT COUNTY AND CITY PARKS. (LOCAL). JAMES G BALL, PRES; CHAMBER OF COMMERCE; 1109 5TH AVE; ALTON, IA 51003. (#105333-1).

ALVORD

PARK COMMUNITY DEVELOPMENT AND TOWN HALL - IA. A FENCE WILL BE PLACED AROUND THE TENNIS COURT AND BALL FIELD; A BASKETBALL COURT WILL BE INSTALLED; NEW LIGHTS WILL BE PLACED IN THE TOWN HALL AND THE BLEACHERS WILL BE FIXED UP. (LOCAL). MRS HAROLD LANGFELDT, CHAIRMAN; ALVORD BICENTENNIAL COMMITTEE; ALVORD, IA 51230. (#14518).

AUG 14, '76. COMMUNITY PICNIC. FESTIVAL AT LOCAL PARK. (LOCAL). MRS HAROLD LANGFELDT, DIR; ALVORD BICENTENNIAL COMMISSION; ALVORD, IA 51230. (#100617-1).

AMBER

BICENTENNIAL FLOAT - AMBER, IA. A BICENTENNIAL FLOAT WILL BE ENTERED IN THE COUNTY CELEBRATION. (LOCAL). JAY JOSLIN, CHAIRPERSON; AMBER BICENTENNIAL COMMITTEE; RR 3; ANAMOSA, IA 52205. (#20955).

COMMUNITY BUILDING RESTORATION - AMBER, IA. RESTORATION OF BUILDING USED FOR COMMUNITY SOCIAL, SERVICE AND YOUTH GROUPS. (LOCAL). BEVERLY DRAVES, SECRETARY; AMBER COMMUNITY CLUB; RR 3; ANAMOSA, IA 52205. (#22006).

HERITAGE HANDWORK - AMBER, IA. GROUP PARTICIPATION IN COMPLETION OF QUILT OR WALL HANGING. (LOCAL). MARY HUSMANN, PRESIDENT; AMBERETTES; RR 3; ANAMOSA, IA 52205. (#22007).

JULY 2, '76. BICENTENNIAL STREET DANCE. FESTIVAL AT MAIN STREET. (LOCAL). JAMES CASWELL, PROJ CHMN; AMBER COMMUNITY CLUB; RR 3; ANAMOSA, IA 52205. (#106894-1).

AMES

AMER INDIAN PERSPECTIVES ON THE BICENTENNIAL, IA. AMERICAN INDIAN RESPONSE TO THE BICENTENNIAL, USE OF SMALL GROUP DISCUSSION & FILMS WHICH FOCUS ON THE INDIAN IN HISTORIC & CONTEMPORARY TIMES. EXHIBIT OF NATIVE ARTS & CRAFTS. (ST-WIDE). GRETCHEN BATAILLE, PROJ DIRECTOR & INSTRUCTOR; UNITED NATIVE AMERICAN STUDENT ORG & COMM ON INDIAN STUDIES; IOWA STATE UNIV, ROSS HALL 245; AMES, IA 50010. (#22585). **ARBA GRANTEE.**

AMES BICENTENNIAL PROJECTS, IA. PROJECTS INCLUDE: HISTORIC MURALS DESIGNED BY SENIOR CITIZENS AND PAINTED BY YOUTH, A HISTORY OF FOOD CONTAINERS COINCIDING WITH WORLD FOOD CONFERENCE AND A STUDY OF THE AMERICAN THEATER WITH YOUTH PLAY. (ST-WIDE). MARTHA BENSON, DIRECTOR; AMES SOCIETY FOR ARTS; 232-1/2 MAIN; AMES, IA 50010. (#18750).

'GREEN HILLS...' - AN ALBUM OF IOWA STATE MEMORIES. A BOOK ENTITLED 'GREEN HILLS...' DEALING WITH IOWA-STATE HISTORY WILL BE PUBLISHED. (ST-WIDE). LAURA C DAILEY, ASSISTANT; IOWA STATE UNIV ALUMNI ASSOC; 227 MEMORIAL UNION; AMES, IA 50011. (#18235).

INTERNATIONAL ENGINEERING CONFERENCE, AMES, IA. INTERNATIONAL ENGINEERING CONFERENCE TO BE HELD ON ISU CAMPUS IN JULY 1976. (INT'L). DR GLENN MURPHY, PROJ DIRECTOR; JOINT INTERNATIONAL CONFERENCE; IOWA STATE UNIV; AMES, IA 50010. (#13836). **ARBA GRANTEE.**

IOWA STATE UNIVERSITY BICENT ALUMNI ACTIVITIES. THE ISU ALUMNI ASSOCIATION WILL RECOGNIZE THE BICENTENNIAL YEAR IN A VARIETY OF WAYS, INCLUDING PUBLISHING A PICTORIAL HISTORY OF IOWA STATE UNIVERSITY. (ST-WIDE). JAMES CONSTANTINE, STUDENT BODY PRESIDENT; IOWA STATE UNIV OF SCIENCE & TECH; AMES, IA 50010. (#8447).

JAMES (TAMA JIM) WILSON ARCHIVES, AMES, IA. COLLECTION OF JAMES WILSON'S PAPERS RELATING TO IOWA LEGISLATURE, IOWA STATE UNIVERSITY & UNITED STATES SECRETARY OF AGRICULTURE. (ST-WIDE). STANLEY YATES, HEAD, DEPT OF SPECIAL COLLECTIONS; IOWA STATE UNIVERSITY LIBRARY; AMES, IA 50011. (#18746).

RESTORE KNAPP-WILSON FARM HOUSE IN AMES, IOWA. RESTORATION AND PRESERVATION OF 1860 FARM HOUSE AND OUTBUILDINGS TO BE SPONSORED BY THE IOWA STATE UNIVERSITY. (ST-WIDE). CARL HAMILTON, PROJECT CHAIRMAN; IOWA STATE UNIV OF SCIENCE & TECH; BEARDSHEAR HALL; AMES, IA 50010. (#8450).

WORLD FOOD CONFERENCE OF 1976. '76 CONF. ON WORLD FOOD PROBLEMS. OFFICIAL U.N. DELEGATES, LEADING AGRICULTURAL SCIENTISTS, STUDENTS FROM MANY NATIONS. ALSO SATELLITE MEETINGS BY INTERNATIONAL AGRICULTURAL ORGANIZATIONS IN '76. (INT'L). MARVIN A ANDERSON, EXEC DIRECTOR; IOWA STATE UNIV; 101 E O BLDG; AMES, IA 50010. (#209). **ARBA RECOGNIZED. ARBA GRANTEE.**

WORLD FOOD INSTITUTE IN IOWA. CENTER FOR CONTINUING EDUCATION IN AGRICULTURAL SCIENCES TO STUDY AND RESEARCH FOOD PRODUCTION, PROCESSING, DISTRIBUTION WORLD WIDE. NEW BUILDING ON IOWA STATE UNIV. CAMPUS. (INT'L). CARL HAMILTON, VICE PRESIDENT, INFORMATION; IOWA STATE UNIVERSITY; BEARDSHEAR HALL; AMES, IA 50010. (#231). **ARBA GRANTEE.**

4TH INTERNATIONAL CONFERENCE ON MECHANIZATION - IA. CONFERENCE ON THE DEVELOPMENT AND USE OF MECHANIZATION IN FIELD EXPERIMENTS DURING THE PAST 4 YEARS. (INT'L). WESLEY F BURCHELE, PROFESSOR; IOWA STATE UNIV; DAVIDSON HALL; AMES, IA 50011. (#27335). **ARBA GRANTEE.**

OCT 21 - 22, '75. UNITED STATES ARMED FORCES BICENTENNIAL CARAVAN. THE CARAVAN IS COMPOSED OF EXHIBIT VANS FOR EACH BRANCH OF THE MILITARY SERVICE. THE THEME OF THE EXHIBITION IS 'HISTORY OF THE ARMED FORCES AND THEIR CONTRIBUTION TO THE NATION'. (LOCAL). J R CASTNER, CHMN; STORY COUNTY BICENTENNIAL COMMISSION; CITY HALL; AMES, IA 50010. (#1775-218).

FEB 28 - APR 3, '76. BICENTENNIAL TEACHER WORKSHOPS. WORKSHOPS WILL BE CONDUCTED IN DIFFERENT AREAS THROUGHOUT THE STATE TO SHOW ALTERNATIVE USES OF IOWA HERITAGE IN AMERICAN REVOLUTION MATERIALS. WILL BE AT COUNCIL BLUFFS ON FEB 28, SIOUX CITY ON MARCH 28 & AMES & DAVENPORT ON APRIL 3. FALL WORKSHOP MAY BE PLANNED. (ST-WIDE). CLAIR W KELLER, DIR; IOWA COUNCIL FOR SOCIAL STUDIES; IOWA STATE UNIVERSITY; AMES, IA 50010. (#104020-2).

MAR 4, '76. 'THE BRITISH ARE COMING!' - BRITISH MILITARY BAND PERFORMANCE. TOUR OF MAJOR U S CITIES BY BRITISH MILITARY UNITS AS REPRESENTATIVE OF UNITS INVOLVED IN REVOLUTIONARY WAR CAMPAIGN. AT JAS H. HILTON COLISEUM (ISU). (INT'L). CHARLES K JONES, PRES; COLUMBIA ARTISTS FESTIVALS COR@; 165 W 57TH ST; NEW YORK, NY 10019. (#6532-31).

APR 23 - 24, '76. BICENTENNIAL PERSPECTIVES OF THE AMERICAN INDIAN. EVENTS INCLUDE INDIAN KEYNOTE SPEAKERS EACH DAY, A SATURDAY NIGHT POW WOW FEATURING NATIVE AMERICAN SINGING AND DANCE GROUPS, EXHIBIT OF NATIVE AMERICAN ART AND FILMS ON AMERICAN HISTORY WITH AN INDIAN PERSPECTIVE. AT MEMORIAL UNION-IOWA STATE UNIVERSITY. (ST-WIDE). GRETCHEN BATAILLE, DIR; UNITED NATIVE AMER STUDENT ASSC & COMM ON AMERICAN INDIAN STUDIES; ROSS 245 IOWA STATE UNIV; AMES, IA 50010. (#22585-1).

MAY 6 - 8, '76. RADIO CONTROLLED MODEL SHIPHANDLING CONTEST. COMPETITION AT NAVAL SCIENCE BUILDING. (LOCAL). LT EUGENE PETERSON, CHMN; NAVY ROTC UNIT, IOWA STATE UNIVERSITY; AMES, IA 50011. (#200018-259).

MAY 6 - 8, '76. 'VEISHEA': STUDENT FESTIVAL. TRADITIONAL 3-DAY FESTIVAL CALLED 'VEISHEA' WILL SPONSOR AN EXHIBIT OF STUDENT TALENT. HIGHLIGHTS INCLUDE OPEN HOUSE, A MAJOR THEATRICAL PRODUCTION (STARS OVER VEISHEA), A PARADE, CONCERTS AND DEMONSTRATIONS. 55TH ANNUAL 'VEISHEA'. AT IOWA STATE UNIV CAMPUS. (LOCAL). RUSSELL SANDERS; VEISHEA, INC; AMES, IA 50010. (#8448-1).

MAY 29, '76. AUSTRALIAN YOUTH ORCHESTRA CONCERT. LIVE PERFORMANCE. (INT'L). JOHN MAUNDER, DIRECTOR; AUSTRALIAN GOVERNMENT; AUSTRALIAN CG, 636 FIFTH AVENUE; NEW YORK, NY 10020. (#108021-6).

JUNE 25 - 26, '76. OPEN HOUSE SPONSORED BY USDA. EXHIBIT, TOUR AT NATIONAL ANIMAL DISEASE CENTER. (LOCAL). DR JAMES SULLIVAN, COORD; AGRICULTURAL RESEARCH SERVICE, USDA; PO BOX 70; AMES, IA 50010. (#102910-2).

JUNE 27 - JULY 1, '76. WORLD FOOD CONFERENCE OF 1976, SCIENTIFIC APPROACH TO FOOD PROBLEMS. THE WORLD FOOD CONFERENCE OF 1976 IS DESIGNED TO BRING TOGETHER SCIENTISTS OF DIVERSE BACKGROUNDS & FROM VARIOUS PARTS OF THE WORLD FOR THE PURPOSE OF EXAMINING WORLD FOOD PROBLEMS AND DEVISING RECOMMENDATIONS FOR SOLVING THOSE MOST LIKELY TO BE SOLUBLE. AT IOWA STATE CENTER, IOWA STATE UNIVERSITY, AMES, IOWA. (INT'L). MARVIN A ANDERSON, DIR; WORLD FOOD INSTITUTE OF IOWA STATE UNIVERSITY; 101 EO BLDG; AMES, IA 50010. (#209-1).

JUNE 27 - JULY 1, '76. WORLD FOOD INSTITUTE ON TOUR. CENTER FOR CONTINUING EDUCATION IN AGRICULTURAL SCIENCES TO STUDY AND RESEARCH FOOD PRODUCTION, PROCESSING, DISTRIBUTION WORLD WIDE. NEW BUILDING ON IOWA STATE UNIV CAMPUS. (REGN'L). CARL HAMILTON; IOWA STATE UNIVERSITY; BEARDSHEAR HALL; AMES, IA 50010. (#231-1).

JUNE 30 - JULY 9, '76. THIRD WORLD CONGRESS OF AGRICULTURAL JOURNALISTS. THEME IS DEVELOPMENT OF INTERNATIONAL FARM TRADE, COMMUNICATING WORLD FOOD NEEDS AND 200 YEARS OF FARMING ADVANCEMENT IN THE U S; PARTICIPANTS INCLUDE EDITORS & BROADCASTERS FROM ABROAD AND AGRICULTURE MAGAZINE EDITORS FROM ALL STATES IN THE USA. AT SCHEMAN AUDITORIUM, IOWA STATE UNIV. (INT'L). ROBERT G RUPP, CHAIRMAN; AMERICAN AGRICULTURAL EDITORS ASSOC; 1999 SHEPARD RD; ST PAUL, MN 55116. (#106802-1).

JULY 5 - 9, '76. 4TH INTERNATIONAL CONFERENCE ON MECHANIZATION. CONFERENCE ON THE DEVELOPMENT AND USE OF MECHANIZATION IN FIELD EXPERIMENTS DURING THE PAST 4 YEARS. (INT'L). WESLEY F BURCHELE, PROF; IOWA STATE UNIV; DAVIDSON HALL; AMES, IA 50011. (#27335-1).

JULY 12 - 14, '76. THE ROLE OF THE ENGINEER IN SOCIETY-PAST, PRESENT & FUTURE. ROLE OF THE ENGINEER IN SOCIETY: PAST, PRESENT & FUTURE WITH INTERNATIONAL CONVOCATION; HISTORICAL PUBLICATION; PROJECT OF PUBLIC AUDIO-VISUAL DISPLAYS; EXHIBITIONS. AT CAMPUS OF IOWA STATE UNIV.. (INT'L). DR GLENN MURPHY; JOINT INTL CONFERENCE/ENGINEERING COMMITTE FOR THE AMER BICENTENNIAL; IOWA STATE UNIV; AMES, IA 50010. (#13836-501).

AUG 22 - 24, '76. FIFTH MIDWEST PRAIRIE CONFERENCE. PAPERS AND DISPLAYS ON HUMANITIES, NATURAL SCIENCES APPLIED SCIENCES AND AESTHETICS, AND MANAGEMENT AND RESTORATION OF THE PRAIRIE. AT SCHEMAN CONTINUING EDUCATION BUILDING. (REGN'L). ROGER Q LANDERS JR; IOWA STATE UNIV DEPT BOTANY & PLANT PATHOLOGY; 443 BESSEY; AMES, IA 50011. (#102910-3).

MAY 7 - JUNE 5, '77. 'PITSEOLAK: A RETROSPECTIVE' EXHIBITION. THIS EXHIBITION OF 100 DRAWINGS BY ONE OF CANADA'S LEADING ESKIMO GRAPHIC ARTISTS DEPICTS THE LEGENDS AND THE SPIRIT WORLD OF ESKIMO TRADITIONS. AT OCTAGON ART CENTER. (INT'L). EILEEN HARAKAL, COORD; SMITHSONIAN INSTITUTION TRAVELING EXHIBITION SERVICE; 1000 JEFFERSON DR, SW; WASHINGTON, DC 20560. (#26655-3).

ANAMOSA

AVENUE OF FLAGS, ANAMOSA, IA. FLAGS WILL BE PLACED ON GRAVES OF DECEASED VETERANS IN ZION LUTHERAN CHURCH CEMETERY. (LOCAL). VIRGIL C MARTIN, CHAIRPERSON; AMVETS POST 110; 503 N DIVISION; ANAMOSA, IA 52203. (#25288).

FAIRVIEW COMMUNITY CENTER, ANAMOSA, IA. OLD SCHOOLHOUSE HAS BEEN RESTORED AND CONVERTED INTO COMMUNITY CENTER. (LOCAL). IDA L WACKER, CHAIRPERSON; FAIRVIEW COMMUNITY CLUB; RR 2; ANAMOSA, IA 52205. (#25299).

FAIRVIEW COMMUNITY COOKBOOK, ANAMOSA, IA. A COOKBOOK CONSISTING OF OLD-TIME FAMILY RECIPES WILL BE PRINTED. (LOCAL). IDA L WACKER, CHAIRPERSON; FAIRVIEW COMMUNITY CLUB; RR 2; ANAMOSA, IA 52205. (#25300).

JONES COUNTY BEAUTIFICATION PROJECT, IA. GARDEN CLUBS IN ALL VILLAGES, TOWNS AND CITIES OF JONES COUNTY WILL WORK TO BEAUTIFY THE COUNTY. (LOCAL). DALE W HACKETT, PROJ DIRECTOR; JONES COUNTY BICENTENNIAL COMMITTEE, INC; 306 S OAK; ANAMOSA, IA 52205. (#11572).

JONES COUNTY BICENT ACTION COMMITTEE, IOWA. DEVELOPMENT OF A BICENTENNIAL ACTION COMMITTEE TO INITIATE & DEVELOP BICENTENNIAL PROJECTS IN THE COUNTY. (LOCAL). VIRGIL C MARTIN, CHAIRPERSON; AMVETS POST 110; 503 N DIVISION; ANAMOSA, IA 52205. (#25289).

RENOVATION OF IRON BRIDGE, ANAMOSA, IA. IRON BRIDGE TO BE REUNDERCOATED, REPAINTED, RESURFACED & A NEW GUARD RAILING & FENCING WILL BE ADDED. (LOCAL). MALINDA ENGELBART, COUNCILWOMAN; ANAMOSA BICENTENNIAL COMMITTEE; FORD ST; ANAMOSA, IA 52205. (#19845).

ANAMOSA — CONTINUED

RESTORATION OF TOWN CLOCK, ANAMOSA, IA. THE TOWN CLOCK WILL BE RESTORED, THE TOWER REPAINTED & THE BELL AND STRIKER REHUNG. (LOCAL). CHARLES L THOMPSON, COUNCILMAN; ANAMOSA BICENTENNIAL COMMITTEE; FORD ST; ANAMOSA, IA 52205. (#19844).

RESTORATION OF 1859 CASS CHURCH - ANAMOSA, IA. A WHITE FRAME CHURCH WITH STEEPLE TOWER, ONE OF THE OLDEST CHURCHES IN THE AREA; THE CEMETERY IS STILL USEABLE; BOTH NEED RESTORATION AT ONCE. (LOCAL). ARLENE BRAINARD, CHAIRMAN; CASS CHURCH RESTORATION COMMITTEE; 306 S OAK ST; ANAMOSA, IA 52205. (#16172).

WAYSIDE PARKS IN JONES COUNTY, IOWA. SEVERAL PARKS WILL BE DEVELOPED IN ANAMOSA. (LOCAL). NELDA MILLER, PRESIDENT; WAPSIKETA CHPTR, IZAAK WALTON LEAGUE OF AMERICA; 1003 MAQUOKETA ST; ANAMOSA, IA 52205. (#11571).

NOV '75 - FEB 2, '76. POSTER CONTEST; 'HIRE THE HANDICAPPED'. COMPETITION. (ST-WIDE). VIRGIL C MARTIN, CHMN; AMVETS POST 110 AND IOWA DEPT OF AMVETS; 503 N DIVISION; ANAMOSA, IA 52205. (#107956-1).

JUNE 12 - 13, '76. GRANT WOOD ART FESTIVAL. EXHIBIT, FESTIVAL, PARADE AT MAIN STREET AND PAINT 'N PALETTE CLUB. (LOCAL). DALE R CONDRY, PROJ CHMN; GRANT WOOD ART FESTIVAL INC; 100 MCNAMARA DR; ANAMOSA, IA 52205. (#104579-1).

JULY 3 - 5, '76. JONES COUNTY FESTIVAL. FESTIVAL. (LOCAL). VIRGIL C MARTIN, CHAIRMAN; JONES COUNTY BICENTENNIAL COMMITTEE; 503 N DIVISION; ANAMOSA, IA 52205. (#107986-1).

ANDERSON

COMMUNITY CLEAN-UP PROJECT - ANDERSON, IA. PROJECT TO CLEAN UP THE COMMUNITY AND PLANT TREES AND FLOWERS. (LOCAL). TED GRAVES, PROJ DIRECTOR; ANDERSON BICENTENNIAL COMMISSION; RT 1; SIDNEY, IA 51652. (#11286).

HISTORY OF ANDERSON, IA. A HISTORY OF THE COMMUNITY WILL BE COMPILED. (ST-WIDE). TED GRAVES, PROJ DIRECTOR; ANDERSON BICENTENNIAL COMMISSION; RT 1; SIDNEY, IA 51652. (#11287).

NEW STREET SIGNS IN ANDERSON, IA. NEW SIGNS DIRECTING TRAVELERS TO ANDERSON, IA WILL BE PLACED NEAR ENTRANCES TO THE CITY. (LOCAL). TED GRAVES, PROJ DIRECTOR; ANDERSON BICENTENNIAL COMMISSION; RT 1; SIDNEY, IA 51652. (#11288).

RESTORATION OF OLD CHURCH IN ANDERSON, IA. RESTORATION OF OLD CHURCH FOR COMMUNITY USE. (LOCAL). TED GRAVES, PROJ DIRECTOR; ANDERSON BICENTENNIAL COMMISSION; RT 1; SIDNEY, IA 51652. (#11285).

AUG 4, '75. OLD SETTLERS PICNIC. FESTIVAL. (LOCAL). TED GRAVES, CHAIRMAN; ANDERSON BICENT COMMISSION; RT 1; SIDNEY, IA 51652. (#100280-1).

OCT '75. RANDOLPH METHODIST CHURCH BAZAAR. FAIR. (LOCAL). TED GRAVES, CHAIRMAN; ANDERSON BICENTENNIAL COMMITTEE; ROUTE 1; BIDNEY, IA 51652. (#100672-1).

ANDREW

PARK PAVILION, ANDREW, IA. PAVILION TO BE BUILT IN CITY PARK, TREES & SHRUBS WILL BE PLANTED. (LOCAL). ELDON HEORSCHELMAN, PRESIDENT; ANDREW JAYCEES; BOX 124; ANDREW, IA 52030. (#23173).

RESTORATION OF 1871 COUNTY JAIL, ANDREW, IA. 1871 JAIL TO BE RESTORED AS A HISTORICAL SITE AND MUSEUM. (LOCAL). ELDON HEORSCHELMAN, PRESIDENT; ANDREW JAYCEES; BOX 124; ANDREW, IA 52030. (#23174).

MAY 30, '76. ECUMENICAL CHURCH SERVICE. CEREMONY AT ANDREW HIGH SCHOOL. (LOCAL). DAVID MCCRACKEN, COORD; ST JOHNS CATHOLIC, SALEM LUTHERAN, UNITED PRESBYTERIAN CHURCHES; BOX 132; ANDREW, IA 52030. (#106393-4).

MAY 30, '76. OLD SETTLERS JUBILEE. JUBILEE INCLUDES: SQUARE DANCE, SACK RACES, GREASED PIG CHASE, PIE EATING CONTEST HUSBAND-CALLING CONTEST/HOG-CALLING CONTEST, TUG-OFWAR, ROCKING CONTEST, HORSESHOE PITCHING, TOURS OF 1871 COUNTY JAIL, AUCTION OF QUILT WITH 50 STATE FLOWERS, REFRESHMENTS. AT ANDREW CITY PARK. (LOCAL). DAVID MCCRACKEN, COORD; GOVERNOR BRIGGS BICENTENNIAL COMMITTEE; BOX 132; ANDREW, IA 52030. (#106393-3).

MAY 31, '76. BICENTENNIAL BALL. FESTIVAL AT ANDREW HIGH SCHOOL. (LOCAL). DAVID MCCRACKEN, COORD; GOVERNOR BRIGGS BICENTENNIAL COMMITTEE; BOX 132; ANDREW, IA 52030. (#106393-1).

MAY 31, '76. MEMORIAL DAY SERVICE. CEREMONY AT ANDREW HIGH SCHOOL. (LOCAL). LEWIS JENSEN, COORD; AMERICAN LEGION POST #75; BOX 105; ANDREW, IA 52030. (#106393-2).

ANITA

BEAUTIFICATION OF TOWN PARK, ANITA, IA. THE TOWN PARK WILL BE DECORATED & FLOWERS WILL BE PLANTED. (LOCAL). MAXINE CAROTHERS, COORDINATOR; ANITA GARDEN CLUB; 501 CHESTNUT; ANITA, IA 50020. (#21416).

BICENTENNIAL LETTERS - ANITA, IA. ELEMENTARY CHILDREN WRITING LETTERS TO OTHER SCHOOLS. (ST-WIDE). RON BROMERT, DIRECTOR; ANITA ELEMENTARY SCHOOL; ANITA, IA 50020. (#21415).

FARMER'S MERCHANT PICNIC. EXHIBIT, FESTIVAL. (LOCAL). AL SULLIVAN, COORD; ANITA CHAMBER OF COMMERCE; 905 MAPLE; ANITA IOWA, IA 50020. (#105330-1).

QUILTS & OTHER PROJECTS - ANITA, IA. ELEMENTARY STUDENTS ARE DOING CRAFTS AND PROJECTS THAT RELATE TO THE BICENTENNIAL AND AMERICA'S PAST. (LOCAL). RON BROMERT, DIRECTOR; ANITA ELEMENTARY SCHOOL; ANITA, IA 50020. (#21414).

SEPT 19, '76. CENTENNIAL OF UNITED METHODIST CHURCH. OLD BIBLES, RECORDS, PICTURES, NEWSPAPERS, ETC, ON DISPLAY. MORNING WILL BE OLD FASHIONED CHURCH SERVICES, AFTERNOON, AN OLD FASHIONED PICNIC WITH HOMEMADE ICE CREAM & CAKE. (LOCAL). JOSEPH HENRY, COORD; UNITED METHODIST CHURCH; 206 MAPLE; ANITA IOWA, IA 50020. (#105330-2).

ANKENY

FIRE PLUG FIX-UP, ANKENY, IA. FIRE PLUGS WILL BE PAINTED RED, WHITE & BLUE. (LOCAL). LOIS CAMPBELL, CHAIRPERSON; BICENTENNIAL COMMITTEE, DES MOINES AREA COMMUNITY COLLEGE; 2006 ANKENY BLVD; ANKENY, IA 50021. (#25513).

HERITAGE COOKBOOK, ANKENY, IA. A COMBINATION COOK & FAMILY HERITAGE BOOK WILL BE PUBLISHED. (LOCAL). LOIS CAMPBELL, CHAIRPERSON; BICENTENNIAL COMMITTEE, DES MOINES AREA COMMUNITY COLLEGE; 2006 ANKENY BLVD; ANKENY, IA 50021. (#25515).

TREE PLANTING IN ANKENY, IA. TREES, DONATED BY STUDENT SENATE, WILL BE PLANTED. (LOCAL). LOIS CAMPBELL, CHAIRPERSON; BICENTENNIAL COMMITTEE, DES MOINES AREA COMMUNITY COLLEGE; 2006 ANKENY BLVD; ANKENY, IA 50021. (#25514).

JULY 9 - 11, '75. CENTENNIAL VISTA EXPERIENCE - ANKENY, IA. OLD-FASHIONED DEMONSTRATIONS WILL INCLUDE SOAPMAKING, WEAVING, SPINNING AND EXHIBITION BOOTHS. (LOCAL). BARBARA JOHNSON; ANKENY BICENTENNIAL COMMITTEE; BOX 111; ANKENY, IA 50021. (#13189-1).

JULY 9 - 12, '75. HISTORICAL PAGEANT IN ANKENY, IA. NARRATION OF A PLAY WITH PROPS, COSTUMES AND MUSIC. (LOCAL). BARBARA JOHNSON; ANKENY BICENTENNIAL COMMITTEE; BOX 111; ANKENY, IA 50021. (#13188-1).

JULY 12, '75. SPECTACULAR PARADE IN ANKENY, IA. THE PARADE WILL INCLUDE ANTIQUE MACHINERY AND CARS, FLOATS AND SHRINERS BANDS. (LOCAL). BARBARA JOHNSON; ANKENY BICENTENNIAL COMMITTEE; BOX 111; ANKENY, IA 50021. (#13190-1).

JULY 12, '75. YMCA CHORAL BELLRINGERS IN ACKNEY, IA. IN HONOR OF THE BICENTENNIAL, THERE WILL BE PRESENTATIONS OF MUSICAL SONGS AND TUNES. (LOCAL). BARBARA JOHNSON; ANKENY BICENTENNIAL COMMITTEE; BOX 111; ANKENY, IA 50021. (#13187-1).

MAY 23, '76. POTPOURRI OF AMERICAN MUSIC. LIVE PERFORMANCE. (LOCAL). LOIS CAMPBELL, CHAIRMAN; BICENTENNIAL COMMITTEE DES MOINES AREA COMMUNITY COLLEGE; 2006 ANKENY BLVD; ANKENY, IA 50021. (#200018-4).

JULY 9 - 11, '76. HERITAGE BLUEGRASS FESTIVAL. 3-DAY FESTIVAL OF BLUEGRASS MUSIC BY NAME ENTERTAINERS, FEATURING KIDDIE PARADE ON FRIDAY AT 6:00PM & GRAND PARADE, WITH THEME "76 THAT'S THE SPIRIT' ON SATURDAY AT 10:00AM. ALSO CARNIVAL, BEAUTY PAGEANT, HISTORICAL & ANTIQUE DISPLAYS & BLUE GRASS MUSIC CONTEST. (ST-WIDE). RICHARD HERMANN; ANKENY BICENTENNIAL COMMISSION; 408 3RD ST; ANKENY, IA 50021. (#104020-12).

ANTHON

FLAG POLE - ANTHON, IA. A NEW FLAG POLE WILL BE BUILT IN ANTHON. (LOCAL). KENNETH D BUNNELL, PRESIDENT; AMERICAN LEGION; ANTHON, IA 51004. (#26053).

NEW BALL PARK FENCE, ANTHON, IA. A NEW FENCE WILL BE INSTALLED AT THE BALL PARK. (LOCAL). KENNETH D BUNNELL, PRESIDENT; COMMUNITY CLUB; ANTHON, IA 51004. (#26052).

TENNIS COURTS - ANTHON, IA. TENNIS COURTS ARE BEING BUILT IN ANTHON. (LOCAL). KENNETH D BUNNELL, PRESIDENT; COMMUNITY CLUB; ANTHON, IA 51004. (#26054).

JUNE 13 - 15, '76. KIDS DAY. FESTIVAL, PARADE. (LOCAL). KENNETH D BUNNELL, PRES; ANTHON COMMUNITY CLUB; BOX 31; ANTHON, IA 51004. (#200018-1).

APLINGTON

OLD NEWSPAPERS - APLINGTON, IA. WE WILL BE COLLECTING COPIES OF THE DISCONTINUED APLINGTON NEWS IN APLINGTON, KESLEY AND AUSTINVILLE TO BIND AND MICROFILM. (LOCAL). JANELLE WILLIS, PROJ DIRECTOR; JUNIOR WOMANS CLUB; RR 1; APLINGTON, IA 50604. (#21991).

PLANTING TREES - APLINGTON, IA. LOCAL PEOPLE WILL ORDER TREES TO BE PLANTED BY THE LION'S CLUB TO REPLACE TREES DESTROYED BY DUTCH ELM DISEASE. (LOCAL). RON GERDES, PROJ DIRECTOR; APLINGTON LIONS CLUB; 917 CALDWELL; APLINGTON, IA 50604. (#21990).

JUNE 29 - 30, '76. BICENTENNIAL BOOSTER DAYS. WE WILL HAVE A 'KIDDY PARADE' ON TUESDAY; GENERAL PARADE, ANTIQUE DISPLAYS AND A HERITAGE LANE IN WHICH OBSERVERS CAN TRY THEIR HAND AT OLD-TIME CRAFTS ON WEDNESDAY. AT APLINGTON LIBRARY, MAIN ST, NASH ST AND CITY PARK. (LOCAL). BRUCE ECKLES, CHAIRMAN; APLINGTON, KESLEY AND AUSTINVILLE BICENTENNIAL COMMITTEE; RFD 1; APLINGTON, IA 50604. (#105768-1).

ARCHER

NOV 1, '75 - DEC 1, '76. PICTURES AND ANTIQUE ITEMS EXHIBIT. WEDDING PICTURES OF EARLY SETTLERS IN THIS COMMUNITY AND ANTIQUE ITEMS USED BY EARLY SETTLERS WILL BE EXHIBITED IN CONNECTION WITH THE ANNUAL LORD'S ACRE FESTIVAL. AT ARCHER UNITED METHODIST CHURCH. (LOCAL). MRS WM H SCHWARTZ, CHMN; ARCHER UNITED METHODIST CHURCH; R3 BOX 53; SHELDON, IA 51201. (#103768-2).

AREDALE

DEVELOPMENT OF COMMUNITY PARK - AREDALE, IA. TENNIS COURTS, BASKETBALL HOOPS AND TREES & SHRUBS WILL BE ADDED TO THE PRESENT PARK. (LOCAL). DEAN JACKSON, CHAIRPERSON; AREDALE BICENTENNIAL COMMITTEE; PO BOX 31; AREDALE, IA 50605. (#23976).

HISTORY OF AREDALE, IA. A HISTORY BOOK WILL BE WRITTEN ABOUT AREDALE BENNEZETTE TOWNSHIP IN HONOR OF THE BICENTENNIAL. (LOCAL). DEAN JACKSON, CHAIRPERSON; AREDALE BICENTENNIAL CHAIRPERSON; PO BOX 31; AREDALE, IA 50605. (#23978).

JULY 11, '76. AREDALE CELEBRATION DAY. FESTIVAL AT TOWN PARK; PARADE WILL BE THROUGH TOWN. (LOCAL). DEAN JACKSON, CHAIRPERSON; AREDALE BICENTENNIAL COMMITTEE; PO BOX 31; AREDALE, IA 50605. (#107310-1).

ARISPE

HISTORY OF SAND CREEK, IA. HISTORY OF SAND CREEK AND ARISPE. (LOCAL). KEITH NICHOLS, PROJ DIRECTOR; ARISPE BICENTENNIAL COMMISSION; ARISPE, IA 50831. (#15081).

TREE PLANTING PROJECT IN ARISPE, IA. 3 TREES WILL BE PLANTED IN CITY PARK, IN HONOR OF THE BICENTENNIAL. (LOCAL). KEITH NICHOLS, PROJ DIRECTOR; ARISPE BICENTENNIAL COMMITTEE; ARISPE, IA 50831. (#15082).

JUNE 30, '76. BIRTHDAY PARTY FOR CONGRESSMAN H R GROSS. DINNER WILL BE A COMMUNITY POT LUCK EVENT. AT ARISPE CITY PARK; ARISPE GYM IF IT RAINS. (LOCAL). KEITH NICHOLS, CHMN; ARISPE-SANDCREEK BICENTENNIAL COMMISSION; 204 E FORBES; ARISPE, IA 50831. (#108051-1).

ARLINGTON

HISTORIC HOMES SURVEY - ARLINGTON, IA. THE YOUTH OF ARLINGTON ARE INVOLVED IN A PROJECT TO ESTABLISH THE DATES OF OLDER HOMES AND HONOR THOSE THAT ARE THE OLDEST. (LOCAL). URSULA CORDES, CHAIRPERSON; ARLINGTON BICENTENNIAL COMMITTEE; ARLINGTON, IA 50606. (#20986).

MUSEUM FOR ARLINGTON, IA. AN OLD SCHOOL HOUSE IS BEING REPAIRED TO SERVE AS A MUSEUM. (LOCAL). URSULA CORDES, CHAIRPERSON; ARLINGTON BICENTENNIAL COMMITTEE; ARLINGTON, IA 50606. (#20987).

PIONEER SCHOOL HOUSE - ARLINGTON, IA. A RURAL SCHOOL HOUSE IS BEING REPAIRED AND FURNISHED AS IT WAS IN PIONEER DAYS TO SHOW STUDENTS OF HISTORY. (LOCAL). URSULA CORDES, CHAIRPERSON; ARLINGTON BICENTENNIAL COMMITTEE; ARLINGTON, IA 50606. (#20988).

JULY 4, '76. PARADE & CELEBRATION. LITTLE MISS BICENTENNIAL QUEEN WILL BE CHOSEN; TRACTOR PULL, ANTIQUE SHOW AND FIREWORKS AND FLOWER SHOW. AT SCHOOLGROUNDS, MAIN ST. (LOCAL). URSULA CORDES, CHAIRMAN; ARLINGTON BICENTENNIAL COMM; ARLINGTON BUSINESSMEN'S CLUB; ARLINGTON, IA 50606. (#105142-1).

ARMSTRONG

CHRISTMAS HERITAGE ROOMS - PROJ OF ARMSTRONG, IA. ROOMS AT THE ELEMENTARY SCHOOL WILL BE DECORATED TO DEPICT U S HERITAGE, WITH EMPHASIS ON CHRISTMAS CELEBRATIONS. (LOCAL). MARY CANNADAY, SCHOOL CHMN; ARMSTRONG BICENTENNIAL COMMITTEE; ARMSTRONG, IA 50514. (#14532).

SIGNS & FIREPLUGS - PROJ OF ARMSTRONG. 1776 SIGNS TO BE HUNG ON MAIN STREET; FIREPLUGS WILL BE PAINTED LIKE COLONIAL SOLDIERS. (LOCAL). ARNOLD BURKHEAD, CHAIRMAN; ARMSTRONG BICENTENNIAL COMMITTEE; ARMSTRONG, IA 50514. (#14533).

TIME CAPSULE IN ARMSTRONG, IA. THE TIME CAPSULE WILL BE BURIED IN 1976 WITH ARTICLES AND THINGS RELATING TO THE PRESENT AND IOWA'S PAST; IT WILL BE OPENED FOR THE TRICENTENNIAL. (LOCAL). ARNOLD BURKHEAD, CHAIRMAN; ARMSTRONG BICENTENNIAL COMMITTEE; ARMSTRONG, IA 50514. (#14534).

TREE PLANTING PROJ OF ARMSTRONG, IA. TREES WILL BE PLANTED WHERE ELMS WERE LOST TO DISEASE TREES WILL BE PLANTED IN ARMSTRONG & SURROUNDING RURAL AREA. (LOCAL). ARNOLD BURKHEAD, CHAIRMAN; ARMSTRONG BICENTENNIAL COMMITTEE; ARMSTRONG, IA 50514. (#14531).

ARNOLDS PARK

HERB GARDEN IN ARNOLDS PARK, IA. HERB GARDEN ON GARDNER LOG CABIN GROUNDS. (LOCAL). PEGGY SMITH, CHAIRMAN; ARNOLD PARK AMERICAN REVOLUTION BICENTENNIAL COMMITTEE; SUNSET BEACH; ARNOLDS PARK, IA 51331. (#11279).

HISTORY OF ARNOLDS PARK, IA. A HISTORY OF ARNOLDS PARK, FROM 1857 TO PRESENT, WILL BE PUBLISHED. (LOCAL). PEGGY SMITH, CHAIRMAN; ARNOLD PARK AMERICAN BICENTENNIAL COMMITTEE; SUNSET BEACH; ARNOLDS PARK, IA 51331. (#11278).

MAR 8, '76. DAY OF REVERENCE. BRIEF CEREMONY TO HONOR THE BRAVE SETTLERS, SOLDIERS AND INDIANS OF THE 1857 MASSACRE. AT STATE PARK - GARDNER LOG CABIN SITE. (LOCAL). PEGGY S SMITH, CHMN; ARNOLDS PARK BICENTENNIAL COMMITTEE; LINCOLN PARK RESORT; ARNOLDS PARK, IA 51331. (#105013-1).

JULY 4, '76. FESTIVAL OF LIGHTS. SPECIAL ANNUAL FIREWORKS DISPLAY FROM AMUSEMENT PARK STATE PIER OVER THE WATERS OF WEST OKOBOJI LAKE VIEWED BY A THOUSAND PERSONS IN BOATS GATHERED IN THE BAY AND BY THOUSANDS OF PERSONS ON THE FIFTYMILE SHORELINE. AT STATE PIER & CASS BAY NORTH OF AMUSEMENT PARK ON WEST OKOBOJI LAKE. (ST-WIDE). PEGGY S SMITH, COORD; IOWA GREAT LAKES CHAMBER OF COMMERCE; LINCOLN PARK RESORT; ARNOLDS PARK, IA 51331. (#105318-2).

ARTHUR

COMMUNITY BICENTENNIAL PROJECTS, ARTHUR, IA. TOWN BEAUTIFICATION, SALE OF AMERICAN FLAGS & MONTHLY YARD DECORATION CONTEST; TRAVELING TROPHY AWARDED. (LOCAL). JEANNE WHITNEY, PRESIDENT; ARTHUR WOMAN'S CLUB; BOX 44; ARTHUR, IA 51431. (#28981).

JULY 5, '76. CHILDRENS PARADE, FLAG PRESENTATION AND COMMUNITY PICNIC. CEREMONY, PARADE AT MAIN STREET, ARTHUR PARK. (LOCAL). MRS JEANNE WHITNEY, CHMN; ARTHUR BICENTENNIAL COMMITTEE; BOX 44; ARTHUR, IA 51431. (#200018-265).

ASBURY

HISTORICAL BOOK ON ASBURY, IA. A HISTORY OF ASBURY, IA. (LOCAL). DELORES A KLOSERY, CHAIRPERSON; ASBURY BICENTENNIAL COMMITTEE; 4903 ASBURY; DUBUQUE, IA 52001. (#24187).

RESTORATION OF SCHOOLHOUSE - ASBURY, IA. THE SCHOOLHOUSE, WHICH IS 140 YEARS OLD, IS PRESENTLY BEING USED AS A MAGISTRATE COURT AND CITY HALL. (LOCAL). DELORES KLOSER, COORDINATOR; ASBURY BICENTENNIAL COMMISSION; 4903 ASBURY; DUBUQUE, IA 52001. (#19187).

APR 30 - MAY 2, '76. RUMMAGE & BAKE SALE. EXHIBIT AT ASBURY CITY HALL. (LOCAL). DELORES A KLOSER, CHMN; ASBURY BICENTENNIAL COMMITTEE; 4903 ASBURY; DUBUQUE, IA 52001. (#106737-1).

JUNE 27, '76. ASBURY BICENTENNIAL FESTIVAL. WILL BE ALL DAY LONG ON SUNDAY. AT ASBURY CITY HALL. (LOCAL). DELORES A KLOSER, CHMN; ASBURY BICENTENNIAL COMMITTEE; 4903 ASBURY; DUBUQUE, IA 52001. (#106737-2).

ASHTON

STREET AND HOUSE NAMING AND NUMBERING, IA. STREETS WILL BE NAMED AND HOUSES NUMBERED IN ASHTON. (LOCAL). DOROTHY BREVEN, PRESIDENT; WOMEN'S CLUB; ASHTON, IA 51232. (#23921).

JULY 3 - 4, '76. ST JOSEPH'S CLASS REUNION. FESTIVAL AT ST JOSEPH'S SCHOOL GYM. (LOCAL). MARIE BOOR, COORDINATOR; ST JOSEPH'S ALUMNI; 3RD AVE & 6TH ST; ASHTON, IA 51232. (#106839-1).

ATALISSA

CITY BEAUTIFICATION - ATALISSA, IA. TREE, FLOWER & SHRUBBERY PLANTING AROUND THE CITY. (LOCAL). ED HADLEY, CO-CHAIRMAN; ATALISSA BICENTENNIAL COMMITTEE; PO BOX; ATALISSA, IA 52720. (#24535).

HISTORY OF ALL ORGANIZATIONS IN ATALISSA, IA. INFORMATION ON EARLY ACTIVITIES OF GRANGE, EASTERN STAR, MASONS, ROYAL NEIGHBORS, CHRISTIAN, LUTHERAN, PRESBYTERIAN CHURCHES AND ALL OTHER ORGANIZATIONS IN EARLY ATALISSA WILL BE GATHERED. (LOCAL). AL HINRICHS, CO-CHAIRMAN; ATALISSA BICENTENNIAL COMMITTEE; GENERAL DELIVERY; ATALISSA, IA 52720. (#24536).

SEPT '76. BICENTENNIAL CHURCH SOCIAL. FESTIVAL AT CHURCH LOCATIONS OR TOWN SQUARE. (LOCAL). RON BESSERT MINISTER; BICENTENNIAL COMMITTEE; LUTHERAN & PRESBYTERIAN CHURCHES; ATALISSA, IA 52720. (#107688-4).

ATHELSTAN

CEMETERY & FLAG POLE - ATHELSTAN, IA. FENCE WILL BE PLACED AROUND THE CEMETERY AND A FLAG POLE WILL BE ERECTED BY THE CHURCH BELL. (LOCAL). VIVIAN PARKER, PROJ COORDINATOR; ATHELSTAN BICENTENNIAL COMMITTEE; ATHELSTAN, IA 50832. (#24491).

CHURCH BELL - ATHELSTAN, IA. THE CHURCH BELL IS BEING MOUNTED AS A MONUMENT. (LOCAL). VIVIAN PARKER, PROJ COORDINATOR; ATHELSTAN BICENTENNIAL COMMITTEE; ATHELSTAN, IA 50832. (#24490).

PLANTING TREES & SHRUBS - ATHELSTAN, IA. TREES AND SHRUBS WILL BE PLANTED IN THE PARK & CEMETERY. (LOCAL). VIVIAN PARKER, PROJ COORDINATOR; ATHELSTAN BICENTENNIAL COMMITTEE; ATHELSTAN, IA 50822. (#24489).

ATKINS

JULY 3, '76. JULY 4TH CELEBRATION. PARADE WITH BICENTENNIAL THEME, LUNCHEON & GAMES WITH PARTICIPATION BY AREA CLUBS, DANCE & FIREWORKS. AT ATKINS PARK, ATKINS LOCATED 15 MI WEST OF CEDAR RAPIDS. (LOCAL). DAVID STIEN, COORD; ATKINS COMMUNITY CLUB; RR 1; ATKINS, IA 52206. (#105703-1).

ATLANTIC

RESTORATION OF CASS CO SOLDIERS' MONUMENT, IA. RESTORING DAMAGED SOLDIERS' MONUMENTS. (LOCAL). MRS JON NELSON, PROJ DIRECTOR; ATLANTIC JR FEDERATED WOMEN'S CLUB; ATLANTIC, IA 50022. (#18143).

RESTORATION OF ORIGINAL LOG CABIN, ATLANTIC, IA. DISMANTLING & RESTORATION OF OLD LOG CABIN TO BE AN ATTRACTION & POINT OF INTEREST FOR INTERESTED CITIZENS & TOURISTS. (LOCAL). EVERETT S BRITSON, PRESIDENT; ATLANTIC ROTARY CLUB; 1605 LINN ST; ATLANTIC, IA 50022. (#22746).

OCT 25, '75. CHARITY BALL '76 - 'GLIMPSE OF '76'. FESTIVAL. (LOCAL). MRS JON NELSON; ATLANTIC JR FEDERATED WOMEN'S CLUB; ATLANTIC, IA 50022. (#103639-2).

MAY 15 - 16, '76. ALL IOWA ROCK ROUNDUP (GEMS & MINERALS). EXHIBIT AT CASS COUNTY FAIRGROUNDS. (ST-WIDE). BILL NOLTE, CHAIRMAN; NISHNA VALLEY ROCK CLUB; 502 HICKORY; ATLANTIC, IA 50022. (#200018-3).

AUDUBON

RESTORATION OF AUDUBON COUNTY HOME - AUDUBON, IOWA. REPAIRING AND TRANSFORMING THE FORMER AUDUBON COUNTY HOME INTO A COUNTY-WIDE MUSEUM. (LOCAL). LEON MILLIMAN, SECRETARY-TREASURER; AUDUBON COUNTY HISTORICAL SOCIETY; EXIRA, IA 50076. (#19702). **ARBA GRANTEE.**

AURELIA

JULY 4 - 5, '76. AURELIA COMMUNITY PARADE & COMMUNITY PERFORMANCE. PARADE, LIVE PERFORMANCE AT AURELIA PUBLIC SCHOOL. (LOCAL). GERALD R JENSEN, CHAIRMAN; AURELIA COMMUNITY BETTERMENT COUNCIL; 109 MAIN; AURELIA, IA 51005. (#200018-258).

AURORA

AMERICAN FLAG & FLAG POLE, AURORA, IA. A NEW FLAG & FLAG POLE WILL BE ADDED TO AURORA CITY PARK. (LOCAL). MRS HILDA GILSON, COORDINATOR; AURORA BICENTENNIAL COMMITTEE; BOX 87; AURORA, IA 50607. (#22213).

JULY 4, '76. AMERICAN LEGION AND AUXILIARY HONOR GUARD. EXHIBIT ON HISTORY OF AURORA IN NARRATIVE & PICTURE FORM. AT AURORA CITY PARKS - (PARKING ON GROUNDS). (LOCAL). HILDA GILSON, CHAIRPERSON; AMERICAN LEGION AND LEGION AUXILIARY; BOX 87; AURORA, IA 50607. (#105964-1).

JULY 4, '76. CUB SCOUTS OF AMERICA FLAG RAISING CEREMONY. CEREMONY AT AURORA CITY PARKS (PARKING ON GROUNDS). (LOCAL). HILDA GILSON, CHAIRPERSON; AURORA BICENTENNIAL COMMITTEE; BOX 87; AURORA, IA 50607. (#105964-2).

JULY 4, '76. DEDICATION OF FLAG POLE. CEREMONY AT AURORA CITY PARK. (LOCAL). MRS HILDA GILSON, COORD; AURORA BICENTENNIAL COMMITTEE; BOX 87; AURORA, IA 50607. (#22213-1).

AUSTINVILLE

PLANTING TREES - AUSTINVILLE, IA. LOCAL PEOPLE WILL ORDER TREES TO BE PLANTED BY THE LION'S CLUB TO REPLACE TREES DESTROYED BY DUTCH ELM DISEASE. (LOCAL). HAROLD BODE, PROJ DIRECTOR; AUSTINVILLE LIONS CLUB; AUSTINVILLE, IA 50608. (#21993).

AVOCA

AMERICAN ELM TREE PLANTING - AVOCA, IA. THE AMERICAN ELM WILL BE PLANTED, MATCHING TREE OF THE COUNTY. (LOCAL). IVA MARIE HOLTZ, CHAIRMAN; AVOCA BICENTENNIAL COMMITTEE; 314 MAPLE ST; AVOCA, IA 51521. (#12337).

MASSACHUSETTS' TREES PLANTING - AVOCA, IA. 2 STATE TREES FROM MASSACHUSETTS TO BE PLANTED IN CITY AND COUNTY PARKS. (LOCAL). IVA MARIE HOLTZ, PROJ DIRECTOR; AVOCA BICENTENNIAL COMMITTEE; BOX 2; AVOCA, IA 51521. (#11575).

SCHOOLHOUSE RESTORATION - AVOCA, IOWA. THE HISTORIC NEWTOWN SCHOOLHOUSE WILL BE RESTORED IN HONOR OF THE BICENTENNIAL. (LOCAL). IVA MARIE HOLTZ, CHAIRMAN; AVOCA BICENTENNIAL COMMITTEE; 314 MAPLE ST; AVOCA, IA 51521. (#12338).

SEPT 1 - NOV 1, '75. BICENTENNIAL ESSAY & POSTER CONTEST. COMPETITION AT SCHOOL. (LOCAL). SCOTT VANBECK, TREASURER; AVOCA BICENTENNIAL COMMISSION; 324 WALNUT; AVOCA, IA 51521. (#102576-1).

JULY 4, '76. JULY 4TH CELEBRATION. THE COMMUNITY CELEBRATION WILL INCLUDE A PARADE AND PICNIC. (LOCAL). SCOTT VAN BECK; AVOCA BICENTENNIAL COMMITTEE; 324 WALNUT ST; AVOCA, IA 51521. (#12336-1).

JULY 29 - AUG 1, '76. POTTAWATTAMIE COUNTY FAIR. BICENTENNIAL DAY AT THE FAIR-7/30/76 WITH OLD-TIME GAMES & CONTESTS, BICENTENNIAL DISPLAYS & A PICNIC AT NOON. AT POTTAWATTAMIE COUNTY FAIRGROUNDS. (ST-WIDE). SCOTT VAN BECK, COORD; AVOCA BICENTENNIAL COMMISSION & POTTAWATTAMIE COUNTY FAIR BOARD; PO BOX 435; AVOCA, IA 51521. (#108243-1).

AYRSHIRE

PLANTING TREES FOR THE FUTURE - AYRSHIRE, IA. THE AYRSHIRE COMMUNITY BETTERMENT ASSOCIATION WILL SPONSOR A TREE PLANTING PROJECT. (LOCAL). JODY SMITH, CHAIRMAN; AYRSHIRE COMMUNITY BETTERMENT ASSOC; AYRSHIRE, IA 50515. (#14691).

JULY 10, '76. SALUTE TO AMERICA DAY. CEREMONY, EXHIBIT, PARADE AT MAIN ST. (LOCAL). ALLEN STANGL, CHAIRPERSON; LEGION, 4H CLUB, SCOUTS, STUDENT COUNCIL & FIRE DEPT; RR 1, BOX 70; CURLEW, IA 50527. (#105954-1).

JULY 10, '76. SPIRIT OF AMERICA PARADE. PARADE OF MILITARY DRESS-REVOLUTIONARY THRU MODERN; FLOATS DESIGNATING ASPECTS OF AMERICAN LIFE, PROGRESS OF RURAL AMERICA, ANTIQUES, ARTS & CRAFTS. HORSES, KIDDIE PARADE. (LOCAL). ALAN STANGL, CHAIRPERSON; LEONARD WILSON POST #173; AYRSHIRE, IA 50515. (#105954-2).

BAGLEY

BAGLEY PUBLIC LIBRARY, IA. FREE CIRCULATION OF LIBRARY MATERIALS THROUGH THE BAGLEY PUBLIC LIBRARY. (LOCAL). GERALDINE WILT, CHAIRPERSON; BAGLEY BICENTENNIAL COMMITTEE; RR1, BOX 97; BAGLEY, IA 50026. (#24223).

HISTORICAL RECORDS OF BAGLEY COMMUNITY, IA. PRESERVATION AND RESTORATION OF HISTORIC COMMUNITY RECORDS. (LOCAL). GERALDINE WILT, CHAIRPERSON; BAGLEY BICENTENNIAL COMMITTEE; RR 1, BOX 97; BAGLEY, IA 50026. (#24224).

APR 4 - 10, '76. LIBRARY OPEN HOUSE SHOWING. EXHIBIT. (LOCAL). GERALDINE WILT, CHAIRMAN; BAGLEY BICENTENNIAL COMMITTEE; RR 1, BOX 97; BAGLEY, IA 50026. (#200018-5).

BARTLETT

LANDSCAPING PROJECT IN BARTLETT, IA. TREE AND SHRUBBERY PLANTING AROUND OLD COMMUNITY CHURCH, WHICH IS THE CENTER FOR ALL TOWN ACTIVITIES. (LOCAL). MRS FORREST BALL, PROJ DIRECTOR; BARTLETT FEDERATED WOMEN'S CLUB; THURMAN, IA 51654. (#11564).

RESTORATION OF BARTLETT COMMUNITY CHURCH - IA. REPLACE BELFRY ROOF-BELL SUPPORTS, REPAIR VESTIBULE, REPAIR MAIN SANCTUARY, SET UP A PICNIC-PLAYGROUND AREA BEHIND CHURCH AND BUILD AREA VETERANS MEMORIAL AND FLAG POLE. (LOCAL). MRS FORREST BALL, CHAIRPERSON; BARTLETT COMMUNITY CHURCH LADIES AID; BARTLETT, IA 51655. (#18234).

SEPT 12, '76. BARTLETT COMMUNITY CHURCH HOMECOMING & OPEN HOUSE. MORNING WORSHIP SERVICE, BASKET DINNER, SPECIAL AFTERNOON PROGRAM, PRESENTATION OF COMPLETED RESTORATION PROJECT OF BARTLETT COMMUNITY CHURCH BUILDING. AT BARTLETT COMMUNITY CHURCH, EXIT 24 OFF I 29. (LOCAL). MRS FOREST BALL, CHAIRMAN; BARTLETT COMMUNITY CHURCH LADIES AID; RR 1; THURMAN, IA 51654. (#11563-2).

BATAVIA

JULY 22 - 25, '76. BATAVIA HAPPY DAYS BICENTENNIAL USA. 4-DAY FESTIVAL PROGRAM HIGHLIGHTING BICENTENNIAL USA. AT COMMUNITY CENTER/PAVILION; ATHLETIC PARK. (LOCAL). BILL KITCHEN; BATAVIA COMMUNITY CLUB; BATAVIA, IA 52533. (#106848-1).

BATTLE CREEK

BICENTENNIAL ESSAY AND POSTER CONTEST. COMPETITION. (LOCAL). CRAIG HUBER, CHMN; BATTLE CREEK BICENTENNIAL COMMITTEE; BATTLE CREEK, IA 51006. (#103342-27). **(??).**

TREE PLANTING PROJECT, BATTLE CREEK, IA. TREES & FLOWERS WILL BE PLANTED THROUGHOUT BATTLE CREEK. (LOCAL). CRAIG HUBER, PROJ DIRECTOR; BATTLE CREEK BICENTENNIAL; BATTLE CREEK, IA 51006. (#17516).

JULY 4, '76. 4TH OF JULY CELEBRATION. FESTIVAL. (LOCAL). CRAIG HUBER, CHMN; BATTLE CREEK BICENTENNIAL COMMITTEE; BATTLE CREEK, IA 51006. (#103342-23).

BEACONSFIELD

MAR 27, '76. '1776 - STRONG AND FREE - 1976'. LIVE PERFORMANCE AT BEACONSFIELD UNITED METHODIST CHURCH. (LOCAL). MRS RAY CRIGLER, COORD; BEACONSFIELD UNITED METHODIST CHURCH; BEACONSFIELD, IA 50854. (#200018-8).

BEAMAN

AVENUE OF FLAGS - BEAMAN, IA. FAMILIES HAVE DONATED FUNDS FOR THE AVENUE OF FLAGS. (LOCAL). MRS CLIFFORD ARNOLD, CHAIRMAN; LEGION AUXILIARY AND AMERICAN LEGION; BEAMAN, IA 50609. (#21787).

BEAMAN, IA, MEMORIAL LIBRARY. FURNISHED BY DONATIONS AND WORK DONE BY LOCAL CLUB; OFFICIALLY OPENED AT NEW LOCATION IN MAY, 1974. (LOCAL). MRS ETHEL DENNER, PRESIDENT; BEAMAN FEDERATED WOMAN'S CLUB; BEAMAN, IA 50609. (#21786).

FIRE HYDRANT PAINTING - BEAMAN, IA. FIRE HYDRANTS WILL BE PAINTED RED, WHITE AND BLUE. (LOCAL). MALCOLM MILLER, CHAIRMAN; YOUNG ADULTS OF BEAMAN; BEAMAN, IA 50609. (#21782).

MAY 29, '76. EVENING PROGRAM. LIVE PERFORMANCE AT BEAMAN SCHOOL GYM AUDITORIUM. (LOCAL). MRS NELLIE ST CLAIR, CHMN; BEAMAN BICENTENNIAL COMMITTEE; BEAMAN, IA 50609. (#105626-7).

MAY 29, '76. PUBLIC DANCE. FESTIVAL AT THOMAS IMPLEMENT BUILDING. (LOCAL). GLENN STEPHENSON, COORD; CENTENNIAL COMMITTEE; BEAMAN, IA 50609. (#105626-5).

MAY 30, '76. COMMUNITY CHURCH SERVICE. CEREMONY AT BEAMAN UNITED METHODIST CHURCH. (LOCAL). WILLIAM MYERS, COORD; BEAMAN UNITED METHODIST CHURCH; BEAMAN, IA 50609. (#105626-1).

MAY 30, '76. DEDICATION OF BASEBALL DIAMOND. CEREMONY AT SCHOOL BASEBALL DIAMOND. (LOCAL). DENNIS STEVA, COORD; JAYCEES; BEAMAN, IA 50609. (#105626-4).

MAY 30, '76. FAMILY PICNICS AND GAMES. FESTIVAL AT BEAMAN UNITED METHODIST CHURCH YARD. (LOCAL). MARLIN MOELLER, COORD; COUNCIL ON MINISTERIES; BEAMAN, IA 50609. (#105626-2).

MAY 30, '76. KIDDIE PARADE. PARADE AT BEAMAN SCHOOL. (LOCAL). JOYCE SANDY, COORD; CENTENNIAL COMMITTEE; BEAMAN, IA 50609. (#105626-3).

MAY 31, '76. MEMORIAL DAY PROGRAM. LIVE PERFORMANCE AT BEAMAN PARK. (LOCAL). EMILY MYERS, CHAIRPERSON; BEAMAN AMVET AUXILIARY; BEAMAN, IA 50609. (#105626-6).

BEDFORD

BEAUTY OF THE CHURCHES - BEDFORD, IA. DEVELOP SLIDES OF HISTORY OF THE STAINED WINDOWS & OTHER FEATURES OF CHURCHES OF BEDFORD. (LOCAL). KAY LUCAS, COORDINATOR; BICENTENNIAL COMMITTEE; BEDFORD, IA 50833. (#19959).

COMMEMORATIVE PLATE & COIN CONTEST - BEDFORD, IA. HIGH SCHOOL ART CLASS WILL DESIGN A COIN AND PLATE FOR COMPETITION. (LOCAL). DALE JUERGENS, PROJ DIRECTOR; TAYLOR BICENTENNIAL COMMITTEE; MAIN ST; CLEARFIELD, IA 50840. (#12693).

'FOXFIRE', ORAL HISTORY OF TAYLOR COUNTY, IA. RECORDINGS AND PRINTED MATERIAL - ORAL LIVING HISTORIES OF LOCAL PEOPLE, EVENTS AND INCIDENTS. (LOCAL). MRS DOROTHY BUSH, FOXFIRE CHAIRMAN; TAYLOR COUNTY BICENTENNIAL COMMISSION; 1007 CENTRAL AVE; BEDFORD, IA 50833. (#20966). **ARBA GRANTEE.**

IMPROVEMENTS IN BIBBINS PARK - BEDFORD, IA. LANDSCAPING OF A NEW SWIMMING POOL SITE, EQUIPMENT TO BE ADDED & WOODEN FOOTBRIDGE TO BE REPLACED. (LOCAL). KAY LUCAS, COORDINATOR; BICENTENNIAL COMMITTEE; BEDFORD, IA 50833. (#19958).

JULY 3, '76. ARTS & CRAFT SHOW & COURTHOUSE TOURS. EXHIBIT, TOUR AT COURTYARD OF TAYLOR COUNTY. (LOCAL). KAY LUCAS, COORD; BEDFORD BICENTENNIAL COMMITTEE; 1405 BENT; BEDFORD, IA 50833. (#108893-1).

JULY 5, '76. HORSE SHOW. LIVE PERFORMANCE. (LOCAL). KAY LUCAS, COORD; SADDLE CLUB; 1405 BENT; BEDFORD, IA 50833. (#104686-2).

JULY 5, '76. JULY 5TH PARADE. PARADE. (LOCAL). KAY LUCAS, COORD; BICENTENNIAL COMMITTEE; 1405 BENT; BEDFORD, IA 50833. (#104686-1).

BELLE PLAINE

ANDERSON PARK - PROJ OF BELLE PLAINE, IA. CONVERSION OF BASEBALL PLAYGROUND INTO A NEIGHBORHOOD SMALL TOT PLAYGROUND; LANDSCAPING, PLAY EQUIPMENT, SHELTER AND RESTROOM FACILITIES; PART OF RENEWAL AND BEAUTIFICATION PLAN. (LOCAL). DOROTHY LENNARD, CHAIRMAN; BELLE PLAINE BICENTENNIAL COMMITTEE/CITY PARK BOARD; 1819 9TH AVE; BELLE PLAINE, IA 52208. (#14528).

DOWNTOWN POCKET PARK - PROJ OF BELLE PLAINE, IA. A SMALL REST AREA PARK AT DOWNTOWN INTERSECTION; LAND DONATED. PLANS ARE FINALIZED FOR LANDSCAPING REST AREA AND SCULPTURE TO COMMEMORATE THE BICENTENNIAL YEAR; PART OF DOWNTOWN RENEWAL PROJECT. (LOCAL). DOROTHY LENNARD, CHAIRMAN; BELLE PLAINE BICENTENNIAL COMMITTEE/RURITAN CLUB; 1819 9TH AVE; BELLE PLAINE, IA 52208. (#14527).

DOWNTOWN RENEWAL FOR 1976 IN BELLE PLAINE, IA. PLANS CALL FOR NEW SIDEWALKS, LANDSCAPING, A NEW PARKING LOT, A FOUNTAIN & BENCHES FOR SENIOR CITIZENS. THE PROJ IS PLANNED & COORDINATED BY A CHICAGO ARCHITECTURE FIRM. (LOCAL). DOROTHY LEONARD, PROJ COORDINATOR; BELLE PLAINE BICENTENNIAL COMMITTEE (BEA); 1814 9TH AVE; BELLE PLAINE, IA 52208. (#14525).

FLAGPOLES FOR 1976 - PROJ OF BELLE PLAINE, IOWA. THE LEGION AND THE BICENTENNIAL COMMITTEE ARE PROVIDING FLAGPOLES FOR THREE PARKS AS PART OF THE DOWNTOWN URBAN RENEWAL PLAN. (LOCAL). DOROTHY LEONARD, PROJ COORDINATOR; BELLE PLAINE BICENTENNIAL COMMITTEE & THE AMER LEGION; BELLE PLAINE, IA 52208. (#14524).

HERITAGE VILLAGE, BELLE PLAINE, IA. CLEARING BLIGHT AREA OF EMPTY LOTS AND NEGLECTED HOUSES IN AN AREA ADJOINING LARGE CITY PARK; RESTORE ALL BUILDINGS TO DUPLICATE SETTLERS VILLAGE; NATIVE WILD FLOWER AREA. (ST-WIDE). DOROTHY LEONARD, CHAIRMAN 3194442092; BELLE PLAINE BICENTENNIAL COMMITTEE; 1814 9TH AVE; BELLE PLAINE, IA 52208. (#19687).

ICE SKATING RINK - PROJ OF BELLE PLAINE, IA. AN ICE SKATING RINK WILL BE CONSTRUCTED AS PART OF TOWN RENEWAL PLAN WITH COOPERATION OF THE CITY PARK BOARD. (LOCAL). DOROTHY LENNARD, CHAIRMAN; BELLE PLAINE BICENTENNIAL COMMITTEE/CITY PARK BOARD; 1819 9TH AVE; BELLE PLAINE, IA 52208. (#14523).

LANDSCAPING ENTRANCE TO BELLE PLAINE, IA. THE AREA AROUND THE HIGHWAY ENTRANCE TO THE CITY WILL BE LANDSCAPED FROM THE RIVER TO THE BUSINESS DISTRICT. THIS IS PART OF THE OVER ALL URBAN RENEWAL PROGRAM. (LOCAL). DOROTHY LENNARD, CHAIRMAN; BELLE PLAINE BICENTENNIAL COMMITTEE; 1819 9TH AVE; BELLE PLAINE, IA 52208. (#14526).

WILLIAMS PARK - PROJ OF BELLE PLAINE, IA. PLAYGROUND PARK HAS BEEN LANDSCAPED TO REPLACE DEAD ELMS; NEW PLAYGROUND EQUIPMENT WILL BE FURNISHED AS PART OF THE RENEWAL AND BEAUTIFICATION PLAN. (LOCAL). DOROTHY LENNARD, CHAIRMAN; LIONS CLUB/FUTURE FARMERS OF AMERICA; 1819 9TH AVE; BELLE PLAINE, IA 52208. (#14529).

JULY 4, '76. FESTIVAL: OPEN HOUSE THEME TO NEIGHBOR TOWNS. EXHIBIT, FESTIVAL, PARADE, LIVE PERFORMANCE. (LOCAL). DOROTHY LEONARD, CHMN; BELLE PLAINE BICENTENNIAL COMMITTEE; 1814 9TH AVE; BELLE PLAINE, IA 52208. (#101922-1).

BELLEVUE

STUDY CLUB, BELLEVUE, IA. A WOMEN'S STUDY CLUB DEVELOPED TO STUDY THE HISTORY OF THE 'RED, WHITE AND BLUE'; BI-MONTHLY MEETINGS WILL BE HELD; FINDINGS WILL BE ANNOUNCED OVER LOCAL MEDIA. (LOCAL). BETTY LUCKSTEAD, CHAIRMAN; CLIO CLUB; ECHO HILLS, RR #2; BELLEVUE, IA 52031. (#22745).

BELMOND

RIVER PARK - A LIVING BICENT PROJ, BELMOND, IA. PLAN PREPARED BY LANDSCAPE ARCHITECT TO COMPLETE RIVER PARK THROUGH PLANTINGS, EQUIPMENT AND WALKING TRAIL ALONG RIVER; WILL BE 10 MILE STRETCH TO PIKES TIMBER. (LOCAL). MRS DENNIS MCNULTY, CHAIRPERSON; JAYCEETTES; 503 8TH AVE NE; BELMOND, IA 50421. (#20257).

JUNE 1 - OCT 1, '76. HISTORIC PRESENTATION. PRESENTATION WILL EMPHASIZE EARLY PRESIDENTS. (LOCAL). MRS LOIS HAMMOND, CHMN; WRIGHT COUNTY BICENTENNIAL COMMISSION; 311 6TH AVE NE; BELMOND, IA 50421. (#101910-1).

JULY 4, '76. 4TH OF JULY CELEBRATION WITH BICENTENNIAL THEME. CEREMONY, COMPETITION, PARADE AT FARIS FIELD. (LOCAL). LYNN SORUM, PROJ DIRECTOR; JAYCEES; 1035 E MAIN; BELMOND, IA 50421. (#104580-1).

BENNETT

SEPT 4 - 5, '76. STYLE SHOW 1850-1976. CHILD RIDES, SKYDIVERS, SOFTBALL TOURNAMENT, CHILDRENS GAMES, POLKA DANCING/SQUARE DANCING, FIREMEN WATER FIGHTS, DUNKING TANK, NOON DINNER & FLAG RAISING WERE INCLUDED IN THIS EVENT. AT BENNETT COMMUNITY CENTER, MAIN ST. (LOCAL). KENNETH HORSTMANN, CHMN; BENNETT FALL FESTIVAL COMMITTEE; MAPLE ST; BENNETT, IA 52721. (#200018-294).

BENTON

FLAG POLE, BENTON, IA. ERECT FLAG POLE AT CITY HALL. (LOCAL). HELEN BLUNCK, CHAIRWOMAN; BENTON BICENTENNIAL COMMITTEE; BENTON, IA 50835. (#22766).

PIE SUPPER. FESTIVAL. (LOCAL). HELEN BLUNCK, COORD; CITY COUNCIL; BENTON, IA 50835. (#106157-1). **(??).**

PLAYGROUND EQUIPMENT, BENTON, IA. PROJECT IS BUYING AND REPAIRING PLAYGROUND EQUIPMENT. (LOCAL). HELEN BLUNCK, CHAIRMAN; BENTON BICENTENNIAL COMMITTEE; BENTON, IA 50835. (#22767).

BENTONSPORT

PRESERVATION AND RESTORATION OF BENTONSPORT, IA. THE COMMUNITY OF BENTONSPORT HAS RESTORED THE OLD PRESBYTERIAN CHURCH AND OTHER HISTORIC SITES AND THEY ARE MAINTAINING THE COMMUNITY AS A HISTORIC LANDMARK ON THE NATIONAL REGISTER. (ST-WIDE). LIBBY WOODRUFF OR TED WATSON; VAN BUREN COUNTY; KEOSAUQUA, IA 52565. (#15834).

BETTENDORF

BETTENDORF MUNICIPAL MUSEUM DISPLAY - IA. DEVELOPMENT OF MUSEUM DISPLAYS IN EXISTING CITY MUSEUM STRESSING EVERYDAY LIFE IN TURN-OF-CENTURY BETTENDORF. (LOCAL). JON R RYAN, CHAIRMAN; FRIENDS OF BETTENDORF MUSEUM; 1334 FAIRLANE DR; BETTENDORF, IA 52722. (#22171).

BETTENDORF MUSEUM RENOVATION PROJECT, IA. RENOVATION OF MUSEUM, DEVELOPMENT OF NEW DISPLAYS & RE-CREATION OF TURN OF THE CENTURY KITCHEN, FRONT PARLOR & BUSINESS OFFICE. (LOCAL). JON R RYAN, CHAIRMAN; FRIENDS OF BETTENDORF MUSEUM; 1334 FAIRLANE DR; BETTENDORF, IA 52722. (#18733).

CELEBRATION PARK, BETTENDORF, IOWA. PROJECT INVOLVES THE CONVERTING OF VACANT LAND AROUND CITY MUSEUM INTO A PARK. (ST-WIDE). HON WILLIAM GLYNN, MAYOR; SCOTT COUNTY ARBC; CITY HALL; BETTENDORF, IA 52722. (#9677).

COMMUNITY BANDSHELL IN BETTENDORF, IA. CONSTRUCTION OF PUBLIC COMMUNITY BANDSHELL IN BETTENDORF MIDDLE PARK TO BE USED FOR CONCERTS, PLAYS, ETC. (LOCAL). JON R RYAN, CHAIRMAN; BETTENDORF BICENTENNIAL COMMITTEE; 1334 FAIRLANE DR; BETTENDORF, IA 52722. (#22170).

MCLAMMARAH PARK, BETTENDORF, IOWA. PLANS ARE BEING MADE TO DEVELOP A NATURE TRAIL. (LOCAL). HON WILLIAM GLYNN, MAYOR; SCOTT COUNTY ARBC; CITY HALL; BETTENDORF, IA 52722. (#9679).

NATURE TRAIL IN MCLAMMARAH PARK, BETTENDORF, IA. LOCAL BOY SCOUT UNITS WILL DEVELOP THE NATURE TRAIL. (LOCAL). JON RYAN, CHAIRMAN; BETTENDORF'S BICENTENNIAL COMMITTEE; 1334 FAIRLANE; BETTENDORF, IA 52772. (#27056).

ORAL HISTORY COMPILATION OF BETTENDORF, IA. BETTENDORF SENIOR CITIZEN'S CLUB WILL COMPILE AN ORAL HISTORY TO BE UTILIZED AT THE MUSEUM OR LIBRARY. (LOCAL). JON RYAN, CHAIRMAN; BETTENDORF'S BICENTENNIAL COMMITTEE; 1334 FAIRLANE; BETTENDORF, IA 52772. (#27055).

RESTORATION OF FIREPLACES - BETTENDORF, IA. RESTORATION OF HISTORIC WPA-BUILT FIREPLACES IN BETTENDORF'S FIRST PARK, DEVIL'S GLENN PARK. (LOCAL). JON RYAN, CHAIRMAN; BETTENDORF'S BICENTENNIAL COMMITTEE; 1334 FAIRLANE; BETTENDORF, IA 52772. (#27058).

RIVERFRONT PARK, BETTENDORF, IOWA. COMMUNITY PARK, PICNIC AREA AND BOAT LAUNCH WILL BE BUILT ON MISSISSIPPI RIVER. (ST-WIDE). HON WILLIAM GLYNN, MAYOR; SCOTT COUNTY ARBC; CITY HALL; BETTENDORF, IA 52722. (#9678).

SCOTT COUNTY RECORD SURVEY, BETTERDORF, IOWA. PROJECT ENTAILS COMPILING HISTORICAL DATA ON SCOTT COUNTY. (LOCAL). HON WILLIAM GLYNN, MAYOR; SCOTT COUNTY ARBC; CITY HALL; BETTENDORF, IA 52722. (#9676).

APR 2 - 4, '76. HIGH SCHOOL BICENT MUSICAL PROGRAM & SIT DOWN DINNER. LIVE PERFORMANCE. (LOCAL). JON RYAN, CHAIRMAN; BETTENDORF BICENTENNIAL COMMITTEE; 1334 FAIRLANE; BETTENDORF, IA 52772. (#200018-10).

MAY 1 - 8, '76. CITY-WIDE CLEAN UP COMPETITION. COMPETITION. (LOCAL). JON RYAN, CHAIRMAN; BETTENDORF BICENTENNIAL COMMITTEE; 1334 FAIRLANE; BETTENDORF, IA 52772. (#200018-11).

JUNE 11 - 13, '76. AMERICAN AGRICULTURE: A CONTINUING REVOLUTION. SPECIAL AGRICULTURAL HERITAGE EXHIBIT FEATURING SMITHSONIAN EXHIBIT AND LOCAL ITEMS AS PART OF 10TH ANNUAL BETTENDORF INTERNATIONAL FOLK FESTIVAL. (ST-WIDE). TIM W DOWNING, PRESIDENT; BETTENDORF INTERNATIONAL FOLK FESTIVAL ASSOC, INC; PO BOX 686; BETTENDORF, IA 52722. (#103717-2).

JUNE 12 - 13, '76. INTERNATIONAL FOLK FESTIVAL. OVER 30 NATIONALITIES ARE REPRESENTED IN FOOD, MUSIC, AND OTHER CULTURAL ACTIVITIES. A SMITHSONIAN EXHIBIT WILL ALSO BE SHOWN. SUNDAY HOURS: 10AM - 9PM. AT MIDDLE SCHOOL, 2030 MIDDLE ROAD. (ST-WIDE). TIM DOWNING, CHMN; BETTENDORF INTERNATIONAL FOLK FESTIVAL, INC; 3415 DEVIL'S GLEN CT; BETTENDORF, IA 52722. (#105941-1).

JULY 2 - 4, '76. ART SHOW SPONSORED BY BETTENDORF PARKS. EXHIBIT AT AT WASHINGTON SCHOOL, MUSEUM. (LOCAL). JON RYAN, CHAIRMAN; BETTENDORF BICENTENNIAL COMMITTEE; 1334 FAIRLANE; BETTENDORF, IA 52772. (#108443-2).

JULY 2 - 4, '76. TOUR OF HISTORIC BETTENDORF SITES. SELF-GUIDED TOUR WITH TOUR GUIDE AT APPROPRIATE BUILDINGS. (LOCAL). JON RYAN, CHAIRMAN; BETTENDORF BICENTENNIAL COMMITTEE; 1334 FAIRLANE; BETTENDORF, IA 52772. (#108443-1).

JULY 4, '76. OLD-FASHIONED 4TH OF JULY. BETTENDORF BICENTENNIAL BANDSHELL WILL BE DEDICATED, TOUR OF HISTORIC BETTENDORF, ART SHOW, PARADE, MUSIC, FIREWORKS, ACTIVITIY & REFRESHMENT BOOTHS. AT BETTENDORF MIDDLE PARK, MIDDLE RD & 23RD ST. (LOCAL). JON R RYAN, CHAIRMAN; BETTENDORF BICENTENNIAL COMMITTEE; 1334 FAIRLANE DR; BETTENDORF, IA 52722. (#105941-2).

BETTENDORF — CONTINUED

SEPT 19, '76. BETTENDORF MUSEUM AFFAIR. FLEA MARKET, SPECIAL MUSEUM DISPLAYS, EXHIBITS, SPEAKERS AND CRAFT EXHIBITS. AT BETTENDORF MUSEUM, 533 16TH ST. (LOCAL). WINOLA MARION, COORD; FRIENDS OF BETTENDORF MUSEUM; 1630 BROWN ST; BETTENDORF, IA 52722. (#105941-3).

BIG ROCK

BIG ROCK PARK PROJECT - IA. A PARK IS BEING BUILT AT THE BIG ROCK NATURE AREA. (LOCAL). MARGO MOHR, CHAIRMAN; BIG ROCK BICENTENNIAL COMMITTEE; BIG ROCK, IA 52725. (#17130).

AUG 15, '76. BIG ROCK'S HOME COMING DAY CELEBRATION. FESTIVITIES INCLUDE SPECIAL CHURCH SERVICES, OLD-FASHIONED PICNIC, GAMES, MUSICAL PROGRAM, BELL RINGING AT 1 PM. (LOCAL). MRS R MOHR, CHAIRMAN; BIG ROCK BICENTENNIAL COMMITTEE; BIG ROCK, IA 52725. (#108444-1).

BIRMINGHAM

BUILDING A NEW PUBLIC LIBRARY: BIRMINGHAM, IA. THE BIRMINGHAM COMMUNITY HAS BUILT A NEW PUBLIC LIBRARY AND WILL BE DEVOTING PART OF IT TO PRESERVATION OF LOCAL HISTORICAL MEMORABILIA AND PERIODICALS. (LOCAL). TED WATSON OR LIBBY WOODRUFF, CO-CHAIRMEN; VAN BUREN COUNTY DEVELOPMENT ASSOC; 101 VAN BUREN ST; KEOSAUQUA, IA 52565. (#21406).

BLAIRSBURG

BLAIRSBURG COMMUNITY CENTER - BLAIRSBURG, IA. RESTORE AND REMODEL FORMER BANK BUILDING TO BE USED FOR MEETINGS OR OTHER GATHERINGS. (LOCAL). BARBARA HALSNE, CHAIRMAN; BLAIRSBURG COMMUNITY IMPROVEMENT ASSOC; BLAIRSBURG, IA 50034. (#23892).

RESTORATION OF BANK BUILDING - BLAIRSBURG, IA. RESTORE & REMODEL BANK BUILDING FOR COMMUNITY MEETINGS & ACTIVITIES. (LOCAL). LARRY G PELZ, PRESIDENT; BLAIRSBURG COMMUNITY IMPROVEMENT ASSOC; BLAIRSBURG, IA 50034. (#19172).

JULY 24, '76. BLAIRSBURG COMMUNITY BAR-B-QUE. FESTIVAL AT ANTHONY HALE PARK. (LOCAL). LARRY G PELZ, DIRECTOR; BLAIRSBURG COMMUNITY IMPROVEMENT ASSOCIATION; BLAIRSBURG, IA 50034. (#104221-16).

JULY 31, '76. BLAIRSBURG OLD FASHIONED DAY. FESTIVAL, PARADE AT ANTHONY HALE PARK. (LOCAL). BARBARA HALSNE, COORD; BLAIRSBURG COMMUNITY IMPROVEMENT ASSOC; BLAIRSBURG, IA 50034. (#106861-2).

BLAKESBURG

BICENTENNIAL EXHIBITS - BLAKESBURG, IA. A FRONTIER EXHIBIT OF HISTORICAL ERA, 1840-1900. (LOCAL). ORBIE BRITTAIN, CHAIRMAN; BLAKESBURG GIRL SCOUTS; RT 1; BLAKESBURG, IA 52536. (#19793).

PARK BEAUTIFICATION - BLAKESBURG, IA. CIRCULAR WOOD BANDSTAND WILL BE REMODELED AND TREES AND SHRUBBERY WILL BE PLANTED. (LOCAL). ORBIE BRITTAIN, CHAIRMAN; BLAKESBURG HOMECOMING ASSOC; RT 1; BLAKESBURG, IA 52536. (#19794).

RENOVATING & REMODELING OF CITY PARK BANDSTAND-IA. RENOVATION & REMODELING OF CITY PARK BANDSTAND WILL CONSIST OF NEW LUMBER, NEW ROOF AND A PAINT JOB; TREES WILL ALSO BE PLANTED. (LOCAL). ORBIE BRITTAIN, CHAIRPERSON; BLAKESBURG BICENTENNIAL FALL FESTIVAL; ROUTE 1; BLAKESBURG, IA 52530. (#21997).

SEPT 9 - 11, '76. BICENTENNIAL HOMECOMING. FESTIVAL, EXHIBIT, PARADE AT MAIN ST, HWY 213. (LOCAL). ORBIE BRITTAIN, CHAIRMAN; BLAKESBURG HOMECOMING ASSOC; RT 1; BLAKESBURG, IA 52536. (#104542-1).

BLANCHARD

CEMETERY MONITORING, BLANCHARD, IA. PRESERVE MARKER INSCRIPTIONS AND PLOT OUTLINES. (LOCAL). DAVID E STOUFER, PASTOR; THE UNITED METHODIST CHURCH; BOX P; BLANCHARD, IA 51630. (#24649).

HISTORY OF BLANCHARD, IA. A PICTORIAL AND WRITTEN HISTORY OF THE COMMUNITY. (LOCAL). DAVID E STOUFER, PASTOR; THE UNITED METHODIST CHURCH; BOX P; BLANCHARD, IA 51630. (#24648).

RENOVATION OF TOWN HALL, BLANCHARD, IA. OLD TOWN HALL WILL BE RENOVATED AND ONCE AGAIN USED. (LOCAL). DAVID LANE, MAYOR; BLANCHARD TOWN COUNCIL; BLANCHARD, IA 51630. (#24650).

SEPT 25, '76. SPECIAL BICENTENNIAL DAY PARADE DISPLAYS ACTIVITIES FESTIVAL. COMPETITION, EXHIBIT, FESTIVAL, PARADE, LIVE PERFORMANCE AT THROUGHOUT TOWN. (LOCAL). REV DAVID E STOUFER; THE BLANCHARD UNITED METHODIST CHURCH & TOWN OF BLANCHARD; BOX P; BLANCHARD, IA 51630. (#107688-7).

BLENCOE

MUNICIPAL PARK ADDITION IN BLENCOE, IA. DEDICATION PLANTING, PRESERVATION OF NATURAL AREA, DEVELOP RECREATION AREAS. (LOCAL). EDWIN HITCHMAN, CHAIRMAN; BLENCOE COMMUNITY CLUB; BLENCOE, IA 51523. (#22182).

JUNE 13, '76. PARADE AND CEREMONIES HONORING OUR FLAG. CEREMONY, PARADE. (LOCAL). EDWIN HITCHMAN, CHMN; BLENCOE BICENTENNIAL COMMITTEE; BLENCOE, IA 51523. (#105947-1).

BLOCKTON

SCHOOL BELL & FIRE BELL - BLOCKTON, IA. RESTORATION OF SCHOOL AND FIRE BELLS. (LOCAL). RONALD OWENS, CHAIRMAN; CITY PARK COUNCIL; BLOCKTON, IA 50836. (#24143).

TREE PLANTING - BLOCKTON, IA. TREES WILL BE PLANTED AT ROSEHILL CEMETERY. (LOCAL). ORVILLE MELVIN, PROJ DIRECTOR; ROSE HILL CEMETERY; BLOCKTON, IA 50836. (#24144).

APR 24, '76. FUN NIGHT - BOX SUPPER. FESTIVAL. (LOCAL). ORVILLE MELVIN; BLOCKTON BICENTENNIAL COMMITTEE; BLOCKTON, IA 50836. (#106847-1).

BLOOMFIELD

BLOOMFIELD MILL RESTORATION, IA. FULL RESTORATION OF THE OLD MILL BUILDING OWNED BY THE DAVIS COUNTY HISTORICAL SOCIETY, TO HOUSE DAVIS COUNTY ARTIFACTS. (ST-WIDE). PETER BURCHETTE, CO-CHAIRMAN; DAVIS COUNTY BICENTENNIAL COMMISSION; 114 E JEFFERSON; BLOOMFIELD, IA 52537. (#18747).

MAIL DELIVERY RE-ENACTMENT. A MAIL CARRIER ON HORSEBACK WILL DELIVER MAIL TO DRAKESVILLE. (LOCAL). PETER BURCHETTE, CHMN; DAVIS COUNTY BICENTENNIAL COMMITTEE; 114 E JEFFERSON; BLOOMFIELD, IA 52537. (#101377-1).

JULY 4, '76. GRAND PARADE. ALL ORGANIZATIONS IN COUNTY WILL PARTICIPATE; FLOATS, FLAG DISPLAY, SADDLE CLUBS & BANDS. (LOCAL). DEWITT S SHELTON, DIR; VOCATIONAL AGRICULTURE DEPT, DAVIS COUNTY COMM HIGH SCHOOL; BLOOMFIELD, IA 52537. (#101376-1).

JULY 4, '76. JULY 4TH PUBLIC CELEBRATION. ALLORGANIZATIONS ARE INVOLVED - INCLUDES PICNIC FESTIVAL PARADE PAGEANT DISPLAYS & CONTESTS. AT DAVIS COUNTY FAIRGROUNDS. (LOCAL). PETER BURCHETTE, CHMN; DAVIS COUNTY BICENTENNIAL; 114 E JEFFERSON; BLOOMFIELD, IA 52537. (#101378-1).

BODE

ANTIQUE ARTS & CRAFTS - EXHIBIT. EXHIBIT AT CITY HALL. (LOCAL). MARGARET ROOD, COORDINATO; BODE WOMEN'S CLUB; R; BODE, IA 50519. (#105951-1).

CEMETERY RESEARCH - BODE, IA. NAMES OF PAST GENERATIONS TO BE RESEARCHED & RECORDED. (LOCAL). LUCILLE TORGERSON, COORDINATOR; FRIENDSHIP CLUB; BODE, IA 50519. (#22192).

TREE PLANTING PROJECT IN BODE, IA. HUMBOLDT CO TREE PLANTING PROMOTION PROJECT. (LOCAL). HONORABLE HOWARD CURRY, MAYOR; CITY OF BODE; BODE, IA 50519. (#22193).

APR 26, '76. 'THAT WAS THEN - THIS IS NOW' PAGEANT. LIVE PERFORMANCE AT TR HIGH SCHOOL GYMNASIUM. (LOCAL). JANE ENFIELD, DIRECTOR; TWIN RIVERS COMMUNITY HIGH SCHOOL; MAIN ST; BODE, IA 50519. (#200018-6).

BONAPARTE

RESTORATION PROJECT IN BONAPARTE, IA. THE COMMUNITY OF BONAPARTE HAS PRESERVED & RESTORED THE ANTY GREEN HOTEL AND IS ESTABLISHING A MUSEUM IN THE BUILDING. A CITY PARK IS ALSO BEING DEVELOPED. (LOCAL). TED WATSON OR LIBBY WOODRUFF, CO-CHAIRMEN; VAN BUREN DEVELOPMENT ASSOC; 101 VAN BUREN ST; KEOSAUQUA, IA 52565. (#21408).

BONDURANT

AMERICAN HERITAGE POSTER CONTEST - BONDURANT, IA. THE POSTER CONTEST WILL BE OPEN TO ALL CITIZENS. (LOCAL). DALE L RENAUD, CHAIRPERSON; BONDURANT BICENTENNIAL COMMITTEE; BONDURANT, IA 50035. (#19177).

ROADSIDE PARK - BONDURANT, IA. A NEW ROADSIDE PARK WILL BE ESTABLISHED. (LOCAL). DALE RENAND, ADJUTANT; AMERICAN LEGION; BONDURANT, IA 50035. (#19175).

TREES FOR TOMORROW - BONDURANT, IA. TREES WILL BE PLANTED WITHIN THE CITY. (LOCAL). DALE RENAUD, CHAIRPERSON; BONDURANT BICENTENNIAL COMMITTEE; BONDURANT, IA 50035. (#19176).

JUNE 15, '76. SALUTE TO AMERICA - A MUSICAL SALUTE TO THE BICENTENNIAL. LIVE PERFORMANCE AT BONDURANT FERRAR SCHOOL. (LOCAL). DALE RENAUD, PROJ DIR; BONDURANT BICENTENNIAL COMMITTEE; RURAL ROUTE; BONDURANT, IA 50035. (#104221-20).

JULY 24 - 25, '76. BICENTENNIAL DAYS. FESTIVAL AT TOWN SQUARE. (LOCAL). DALE RENAUD, PROJ DIR; BONDURANT BICENTENNIAL COMMITTEE; RURAL ROUTE; BONDURANT, IA 50035. (#104221-21).

BOONE

KATE SHELLEY MEMORIAL PARK & RAILROAD MUSEUM, IA. RESTORED C & NW RAILROAD DEPOT WILL HOUSE A DISPLAY OF RAILROAD AND TELEGRAPH EQUIPMENT, THE SURROUNDING AREA WILL SERVE AS A PARK FOR PICNICS & OTHER ACTIVITIES. (LOCAL). EDWARD H MEYERS, PRESIDENT; BOONE COUNTY HISTORICAL SOCIETY; 1521 CARROLL ST; BOONE, IA 50036. (#18755).

KATE SHELLEY TRAIL - BOONE, IA. ESTABLISHMENT OF 25 MILE HIKING TRAIL COVERING 9 IMPORTANT HISTORIC SITES IN BOONE COUNTY ALONG DES MOINES RIVER VALLEY. (LOCAL). JOHN VEALE, PRESIDENT; KATE SHELLEY TRAIL, INC; 1516 SE LINN ST; BOONE, IA 50036. (#19171).

MAMIE DOWD EISENHOWER BIRTHPLACE PRESERVATION - IA. BIRTHPLACE WILL BE MOVED TO NEW LOCATION, FURNISHED, RESTORED TO ORIGINAL APPEARANCE AND OPENED TO THE PUBLIC AS A MUSEUM & LIBRARY. THE BEDROOM WILL CONTAIN THE ORIGINAL FURNITURE. (NAT'L). WALTER W GOEPPINGER, CHAIRMAN; BOONE COMMITTEE FOR PRESERVATION OF HISTORIC LANDMARKS, INC; PO BOX 358; BOONE, IA 50036. (#16726). **ARBA GRANTEE.**

TOASTMASTERS BICENTENNIAL SPEAKERS BUREAU, IA. IOWA TOASTMASTERS FORM LOCAL COUNTY & COMMUNITY SPEAKERS BUREAU TO PROMOTE BICENTENNIAL PROJECTS AND INVOLVEMENT. SPEECHES TO BE GIVEN TO VARIOUS CITY AND COUNTY ORGANIZATIONS. (ST-WIDE). C EUGENE STEWART, BICENTENNIAL CO-ORDINATOR; TOASTMASTERS INTERNATIONAL - IOWA DISTRICT 19; 1303 MONONA ST; BOONE, IA 50036. (#11472).

JULY 4, '76. 4TH OF JULY CELEBRATION. FESTIVAL. (LOCAL). LARRY ADAMS, CHMN; BOONE CO BICENTENNIAL COMMISSION, INC; 969 PARK CIRCLE; BOONE, IA 50036. (#104221-14).

BOONEVILLE

BOONEVILLE, IA, BICENTENNIAL PLATES. ORDER & SELL NOT MORE THAN 250 PLATES CONTAINING LINE DRAWING OF TOWN CHURCH & ONE OF OLDEST HOMES. (LOCAL). JULIE JACKSON, CHAIRMAN; BOONEVILLE BICENTENNIAL COMMITTEE; BOX 71; BOONEVILLE, IA 50038. (#21244).

ERECT TOWN FLAGPOLE & LIGHT - BOONEVILLE, IA. LIGHT WILL ILLUMINATE FLAG AND SERVE AS SECURITY LIGHT FOR TOWN. (LOCAL). JULIE JACKSON, CHAIRMAN; BOONEVILLE BICENTENNIAL COMMITTEE; BOX 71; BOONEVILLE, IA 50038. (#21982).

STATE MICROFILMING - BOONEVILLE, IA. RESEARCH & PRESENT FOR STATE PROJECT THE COUNTY SCHOOL ENROLLMENTS BEFORE 1900 & CEMETERY PLOT RECORDS. (LOCAL). JULIE JACKSON, CHAIRMAN; BOONEVILLE BICENTENNIAL COMMITTEE; BOX 71; BOONEVILLE, IA 50038. (#21986).

STREET SIGNS - BOONEVILLE, IA. ERECT STREET SIGNS ACCORDING TO ORIGINAL PLOT NAMES. (LOCAL). DOYLE KANE, COMMANDER; BOONEVILLE AMERICAN LEGION & AUXILIARY; BOONEVILLE, IA 50038. (#21983).

TOWN SIGN - BOONEVILLE, IA. ERECTION OF TOWN SIGN AT THE CITY LIMITS. (LOCAL). JULIE JACKSON, CHAIRMAN; BOONEVILLE BICENTENNIAL COMMITTEE; BOX 71; BOONEVILLE, IA 50038. (#21984).

JUNE 26, '76. MUSKET DEMONSTRATION AND COMPETITION. COMPETITION, LIVE PERFORMANCE. (LOCAL). JULIE JACKSON, CHAIRMAN; MADISON COUNTY MOUNTAIN MEN; BOX 71; BOONEVILLE, IA 50038. (#105767-2).

JUNE 26, '76. OLD-FASHIONED PARADE & GAMES. FESTIVAL, PARADE. (LOCAL). JULIE JACKSON, CHAIRMAN; BOONEVILLE LEGION AUXILIARY; BOX 71; BOONEVILLE, IA 50038. (#105767-3).

JUNE 26, '76. OPENING CEREMONY & BICENTENNIAL FESTIVITIES. INCLUDES FLAG CEREMONY, PRESENTATION OF BICENTENNIAL FLAG AND PATRIOTIC MUSIC. (LOCAL). JULIE JACKSON, CHAIRMAN; BOONEVILLE BICENTENNIAL COMMITTEE; BOX 71; BOONEVILLE, IA 50038. (#105767-1).

JUNE 26, '76. STREET DANCE. FESTIVAL AT RAILROAD ST. (LOCAL). JULIE JACKSON, CHAIRMAN; BOONEVILLE BICENTENNIAL COMMITTEE; BOX 71; BOONEVILLE, IA 50038. (#105767-4).

BOXHOLM

FLAGPOLE PROJECT, BOXHOLM, IA. THE BOXHOLM BOOSTER CLUB WILL ERECT A FLAGPOLE UPON WHICH, AN AMERICAN FLAG & A FLAG BEARING A PICTURE OF A BALD EAGLE WILL FLY. (LOCAL). HON STANTON STILLAGON, MAYOR; BOXHOLM BOOSTERS CLUB; BOXHOLM, IA 50040. (#28646).

BOYDEN

MUSEUM & SENIOR CITIZEN CENTER IN BOYDEN, IA. DEPOT TO BE PURCHASED & TURNED INTO MUSEUM & SENIOR CITIZEN CENTER. (LOCAL). VINCENT L HULS, CHAIRMAN; BOYDEN BICENTENNIAL COMMITTEE; BOYDEN, IA 51234. (#22181).

MAR 29, '76. BICENTENNIAL PAGEANT. THERE ARE NEARLY 150 PEOPLE IN THIS PAGEANT, ALL LOCAL, RANGING IN AGE FROM

BOYDEN — CONTINUED

PRE-SCHOOL TO WW I VETERANS. THE PAGEANT IS LOCALLY WRITTEN AND PRODUCED BY AMATEURS. AT BOYDEN SCHOOL AUDITORIUM. (LOCAL). MRS IVA RENSINK, CHMN; WOMEN'S CITIZENSHIP CLUB; BOYDEN, IA 51234. (#105945-2).

JUNE 5, '76. OLD SETTLERS PICNIC. FESTIVAL AT MAIN ST. (LOCAL). VINCENT HULS, CHAIRMAN; BOYDEN COMMUNITY CLUB & BOYDEN FIRE DEPT; BOYDEN, IA 51234. (#105945-1).

BRADGATE

ERECTION OF SIGNS, BRADGATE, IA. SIGNS TO BE ERECTED ON 2 SIDES OF TOWN, READING: 'BRADGATE, THE TOWN THAT WOULDN'T DIE, INCORPORATED 1882, POPULATION 125'. (LOCAL). PHYLLIS WALLACE, COORDINATOR; SEAQUIST PRUITT VFW AUXILIARY 7083; BOX 103; BRADGATE, IA 50520. (#23848).

TREE PLANTING, BRADGATE, IA. 43 TREES WILL BE PLANTED IN BRADGATE. (LOCAL). PHYLLIS WALLACE, CHAIRMAN; SEAQUIST - PRUITT VFW AUXILIARY #7083; BOX 103; BRADGATE, IA 50520. (#24216).

JUNE 20, '76. BICENTENNIAL FESTIVAL. AN AWARD WILL BE PRESENTED TO MR LEE MALCOLM, 99 YEAR OLD FORMER MAYOR OF BRADGATE, WHO SERVED FOR 28 YEARS. AWARD WILL BE PRESENTED BETWEEN 2 BALL GAMES AT APPROXIMATELY 3:45PM. FLAG PRESENTATION WITH CEREMONY AT 1:30PM AT TOWN HALL, DANCE AFTER BBQ AT THE GYMNASIUM. AT SCHOOL BALL DIAMOND & GYMNASIUM. (LOCAL). PHYLLIS WALLACE, COORD; SEAQUEST-PRUITT VFW AUXILIARY; BOX 103; BRADGATE, IA 50520. (#106862-1).

BREDA

JUNE 14, '76. COMMUNITY PICNIC-FLAG DAY. FESTIVAL. (LOCAL). LEO HEISTERKAMP; BREDA BICENT COMM; BREDA, IA 51436. (#107695-2).

JULY 4, '76. 4TH OF JULY. PARADE, COMPETITION. (LOCAL). LEO HEISTERKAMP; BREDA BICENT COMM; BREDA, IA 51436. (#107695-1).

BRIDGEWATER

NEW FLAG POLE FOR BRIDGEWATER, IA. BICENTENNIAL COMMITTEE WILL ERECT A TOWN FLAG POLE. (LOCAL). JEANNE SULGROVE, CHAIRMAN; AMERICAN LEGION & BICENTENNIAL COMMITTEE; BRIDGEWATER, IA 50837. (#24118).

OLD FIRE TRUCK RESTORATION, BRIDGEWATER, IA. OLD FIRE TRUCK WILL BE PAINTED AND RESTORED. (LOCAL). ELMER FRESE, COORDINATOR; BRIDGEWATER FIRE DEPT; BRIDGEWATER, IA 50837. (#24117).

TREE PLANTING IN BRIDGEWATER, IOWA. EACH TOWN ORGANIZATION WILL SPONSOR TREE TO BE PLANTED AT THE RETIREMENT HOME. (LOCAL). JEANNE SULGROVE, CHAIRMAN; BICENTENNIAL COMMITTEE; BRIDGEWATER, IA 50837. (#24119).

JUNE 16, '76. ARTS & CRAFTS SHOW. SHOW WILL BE ON THE SIDEWALKS OF BRIDGEWATER & WILL BE A WAY FOR PEOPLE TO SELL OR SHOW THEIR CRAFT OR HOBBY. AT ON THE SIDEWALKS OF THE TOWN. (LOCAL). ELMER FRESE; BRIDGEWATER BICENTENNIAL COMMITTEE; BRIDGEWATER, IA 50837. (#106852-2).

JUNE 19, '76. ROUNDUP DAY. THIS ROUND-UP DAY WILL START OFF WITH A PARADE AT 4:30 PM AND A GRILLED STEAK SUPPER AT 5:30 PM AND FREE ENTERTAINMENT AT 8 PM. AT CITY PARK. (LOCAL). ELMER FRESE; COMMUNITY CLUB; BRIDGEWATER, IA 50837. (#106852-1).

BRIGHTON

JUNE 17 - 20, '76. WHOOPEE DAYS. CEREMONY, EXHIBIT, FESTIVAL AT MAIN ST. (LOCAL). MARVELINE L WILSON, SEC; BRIGHTON COMMUNITY CHAMBER OF COMMERCE; PO BOX 128; BRIGHTON, IA 52540. (#106905-1).

BRISTOW

HISTORY PROJECT OF BRISTOW, IA. THE BRISTOW BICENTENNIAL COMMITTEE WILL UPDATE THE BRISTOW HISTORY AND HELP WITH THE BUTLER COUNTY HISTORY. (LOCAL). DENNIS BUSS, CO-CHAIRMAN; BRISTOW BICENTENNIAL COMMITTEE; 602 MAIN ST; BRISTOW, IA 50611. (#22223).

RESTORATION OF TOWN PARK & CEMETERY - BRISTOW, IA. PLAYGROUND EQUIPMENT, PICNIC TABLE & GRILL WILL BE PUT IN THE PARK; WE WILL ALSO CLEAN UP THE ABANDONED CEMETERY. (LOCAL). DENNIS BUSS, CO-CHAIRMAN; BRISTOW BICENTENNIAL COMMITTEE; 602 MAIN ST; BRISTOW, IA 50611. (#22224).

AUG 5, '76. CENTENNIAL CELEBRATION. CENTENNIAL CELEBRATION INCLUDES A BARBEQUE & STREET DANCE. (LOCAL). DENNIS BUSS, CO-CHMN; BRISTOW CENTENNIAL COMMITTEE; 602 MAIN ST; BRISTOW, IA 50611. (#105968-1).

BRITT

HANCOCK COUNTY HISTORICAL MUSEUM - BRITT, IA. IMPROVEMENTS TO BE MADE, POSSIBLE RESTORATION OF CUPOLAS & BICENTENNIAL PLAQUE. (LOCAL). FOREST ECKELS, PROJ DIRECTOR; HANCOCK COUNTY HISTORICAL SOCIETY; RR3; BRITT, IA 50423. (#17481).

BRONSON

MAY 2, '76. HERITAGE FESTIVAL. FESTIVAL AT J N KING AUDITORIUM. (LOCAL). ANNE BOSTON, CHAIRPERSON; BRONSON BICENTENNIAL COMMITTEE; BOX 2; BRONSON, IA 51007. (#200018-7).

JUNE 27, '76. FLAG POLE CEREMONY. CEREMONY. (LOCAL). ANNE BOSTON, CHAIRPERSON; BRONSON BICENTENNIAL COMMITTEE; BOX 2; BRONSON, IA 51007. (#107311-2).

JULY 4, '76. FOURTH OF JULY CELEBRATION. A CHURCH SERVICE, POT LUCK DINNER, PARADE, GAMES, RACES, PICNIC, QUEEN, PRINCE AND PRINCESS CONTEST, WATERMELON FEED AND FIREWORKS DISPLAY ARE THE SCHEDULED ACTIVITIES. (LOCAL). GEORGE SEUBERT, PRES; BRONSON COMMUNITY CLUB; RR; BRONSON, IA 51007. (#106933-1).

SEPT - NOV '76. DIAMOND JUBILEE TO CELEBRATE 75TH ANNIVERSARY OF BRONSON. FESTIVAL. (LOCAL). ANNE BOSTON, CHMN; BRONSON BICENTENNIAL COMMITTEE; BOX 2; BRONSON, IA 51007. (#106932-1).

BROOKLYN

COMMEMORATE HISTORIC SITE MARKERS, BROOKLYN, IA. APPROPRIATE MARKERS TO BE ERECTED TO RPESERVE IDENTITY OF SITES PROMINENT IN EARLY HISTORY OF BROOKLYN COMMUNITY. (LOCAL). FORREST BRENIMAN, COORDINATOR; COMMERCIAL CLUB; 803 PARK; BROOKLYN, IA 52211. (#23365).

PRESENTATION OF FLAGS TO CEMETERIES, BROOKLYN, IA. FLAG AND POLE WERE PURCHASED AT THE COST OF $450 AND PRESENTED TO EACH OF TWO CEMETERIES IN BROOKLYN. (LOCAL). HAROLD NEVENHAVEN, COORD; ANNIVERSARY COMMITTEE; 605 JACKSON; BROOKLYN, IA 52211. (#22460).

A PROGRAM EMPHASIZING HUMAN VALUES AND CHRISTIAN HERITAGE. SERIES WILL OPEN WITH AN OLD-FASHIONED BOX SOCIAL FOLLOWED BY SHORT HISTORICAL SKETCHES OF RELIGIOUS HISTORY IN AMERICA PRESENTED ON SUCCESSIVE SUNDAYS AND AN ADULT FORUM TO STUDY HISTORY OF LOCAL CHURCH WILL BE HELD. (LOCAL). RICHARD MENZEL, COORD; FIRST PRESBYTERIAN CHURCH; 507 CLAY; BROOKLYN, IA 52211. (#106535-2). **(??).**

TREE PLANTING, BROOKLYN, IA. BEAUTIFICATION PROJECT FOR SENIOR CITIZENS HOUSING IN WHICH 16 ORGANIZATIONS & INDIVIDUALS WILL UNITE TO LANDSCAPE THE NEW NONPROFIT DEVELOPMENT OF NINETEEN LIVING UNITS. (LOCAL). HAROLD NEVENHOVEN, COORDINATOR; COMMERCIAL CLUB; 605 JACKSON; BROOKLYN, IA 52211. (#23366).

OCT 1, '75 - MAY 26, '76. BICENTENNIAL CELEBRATION IN SCHOOL EVENTS. SERIES OF EVENTS SPECIFICALLY PROGRAMED FOR STUDENTS, INCLUDING VALENTINE DESIGN COMPETITION, HISTORICAL AND CITIZENSHIP PRESENTATIONS, FILMS AND A BICENTENNIAL DAY WITH STUDENTS IN COSTUME. AT ELEMENTARY SCHOOL. (LOCAL). DOUGLAS WILSON, COORD; B G M SCHOOL DISTRICT; 1204 NORTH CLAY; BROOKLYN, IA 52211. (#106535-4).

JUNE 25 - 27, '76. COMMERCIAL CLUB'S BICENTENNIAL CELEBRATION. FESTIVAL. (LOCAL). HAROLD NEVENHOVEN, COORD; COMMERCIAL CLUB; 605 JACKSON; BROOKLYN, IA 52211. (#105617-1).

JULY 4, '76. ECUMENICAL SERVICES. ALL CHURCHES OF THE AREA PARTICIPATING IN A JOINT SERVICE OF WORSHIP WHICH WILL HAVE A PATRIOTIC THEME. (LOCAL). RICHARD MENZEL, COORD; MINISTERIAL ASSOCIATION; 507 CLAY; BROOKLYN, IA 52211. (#106535-3).

BUFFALO

JULY 3 - 5, '76. BUFFALO DAYS-BUFFALO FEED AND JULY 4TH CELEBRATION. FESTIVAL AT HIGH SCHOOL ATHLETIC FIELD. (LOCAL). ANDY LARSON, CHMN; RETAILERS; 114 1ST ST NE; BUFFALO CTR, IA 50424. (#105522-1).

BUFFALO CTR

GOLF COURSE & FAMILY RECREATION CENTER, IA. THE CREATION OF A GOLF COURSE AND FAMILY RECREATION CENTER. (LOCAL). ANDREW LARSON, CHAIRMAN; UNITED BUFFALO CENTER BICENTENNIAL COMMITTEE; BUFFALO CTR, IA 50424. (#15306).

LOCAL HISTORY BOOK, BUFFALO CENTER, IA. A BOOK ON THE HISTORY OF THE BUFFALO CENTER AREA WILL BE PUBLISHED. (LOCAL). ANDREW LARSON, CHAIRMAN; UNITED BUFFALO CENTER BICENTENNIAL COMMITTEE; BUFFALO CTR, IA 50424. (#15307).

FEB 7, '76. TALENT SHOW AND BASKET SOCIAL. LIVE PERFORMANCE AT HIGH SCHOOL AUDITORIUM. (LOCAL). ANDY LARSON, CHAIRMAN; UNITED BUFFALO CENTER BICENTENNIAL COMMITTEE; 114 1ST ST NE; BUFFALO CTR, IA 50424. (#200018-9).

BURLINGTON

HISTORY OF DES MOINES COUNTY, IOWA. PUBLISHING HISTORY OF BURLINGTON-DES MOINES COUNTY - 1837-1900. (LOCAL). DR PHILIP JORDAN, CHAIRMAN; DES MOINES COUNTY BICENTENNIAL COMMISSION; 29 TERRACE; BURLINGTON, IA 52601. (#3677). **(??).**

OCT 25 - 27, '75. UNITED STATES ARMED FORCES BICENTENNIAL CARAVAN. THE CARAVAN IS COMPOSED OF EXHIBIT VANS FOR EACH BRANCH OF THE MILITARY SERVICE. THE THEME OF THE EXHIBITION IS 'HISTORY OF THE ARMED FORCES AND THEIR CONTRIBUTION TO THE NATION'. (LOCAL). DONALD R KUHN, CHMN; U S ARMED FORCES BICENTENNIAL EXHIBIT VANS PROJECT; 801 SHOQUOQUON DR; BURLINGTON, IA 52601. (#1775-221).

BURR OAK

LAURA INGALLS WILDER MUSEUM, BURR OAK, IA. MASTERS HOTEL RENOVATED TO BE USED AS A MUSEUM IN HONOR OF LAURA INGALLS WILDER. (REGN'L). DAVID DECOU, PRESIDENT; LAURA INGALLS WILDER PARK, INC; PO BOX 43; BURR OAK, IA 52131. (#18373).

LAURA INGALLS WILDER HOME RESTORATION IN IOWA. RESTORATION AND PRESERVATION OF THE CHILDHOOD HOME OF AUTHOR LAURA INGALLS WILDER. (LOCAL). DAVID DECOU, PRESIDENT; LAURA INGALLS WILDER PARK, INC; PO BOX 43; BURR OAK, IA 52131. (#20983). **ARBA GRANTEE.**

JUNE 5 - 6, '76. LAURA INGALLS WILDER DAYS AND MUSEUM OPENING. MANY ACTIVITIES SCHEDULED SUCH AS HORSE SHOE & CHECKER TOURNAMENTS BALL GAME, STREET DANCES, SACK RACES, OLD SETTLERS PICNIC; A REAL OLD FASHIONED WEEK-END WITH PARADE AT 1:00 PM SAT & MUSEUM OPENING CEREMONY AT 2:00 PM SAT. AT CEREMONY TO BE HELD IN THE PARK AT THE MUSEUM SITE. (REGN'L). DAVID DECOU, PROJ DIR; LAURA INGALLS WILDER PARK, INC & BURR OAK BICENTENNIAL COMMITTEE; PO BOX 43; BURR OAK, IA 52131. (#18373-1).

CALAMUS

JULY 2 - 4, '76. CALAMUS CENTENNIAL. DANCE, ARTS & CRAFTS, TRACTOR PULL, ANTIQUE CAR SHOW, WATER FIGHT, PAGEANT, QUEEN CONTEST, BEARD CONTEST & COSTUME JUDGING. AT STREETS. (LOCAL). SANDRA HENNING, DIRECTOR; CALAMUS CENTENNIAL BICENTENNIAL ORGANIZATION; RR1, BOX 19; CALAMUS, IA 52729. (#102272-1).

CALLENDER

BICENTENNIAL CELEBRATION AND TENNIS COURT DEDICATION. CEREMONY, FESTIVAL AT TOWN HALL. (LOCAL). FLORENCE JONDLE, CHMN; CALLENDER BICENTENNIAL COMMITTEE; BOX 11; CALLENDER, IA 50523. (#31498-1).

TOWN HALL RESTORATION, CALLENDER, IA. IN ORDER TO RESTORE TOWN HALL: CEILINGS WILL BE LOWERED, WALLS PAINTED, NEW WINDOWS INSTALLED & NEW EQUIPMENT PURCHASED. (LOCAL). FLORENCE JONDLE, CHAIRPERSON; SENIOR CITIZENS, BOOSTER CLUB & AMERICAN LEGION AUXILIARY; BOX 11; CALLENDER, IA 50523. (#28240).

CALMAR

ALL-PURPOSE COMMUNITY CENTER, CALMAR, IA. PROFITS FROM CALMAR'S 125TH JUBILEE WILL GO TOWARDS THE COMMUNITY CENTER; THE CENTER WILL BE USED BY RURAL AND CITY PERSONS OF ALL AGES. (LOCAL). ERNIE HEYING, BICENT CHAIRPERSON; CALMAR JUBILEE COMMITTEE; CALMAR, IA 52132. (#22765).

HISTORY BOOK OF CALMAR, IA. CALMAR CENTENNIAL HISTORY BOOK WAS COMPILED IN 1950. THIS BOOK WAS CALLED THE 'CALMAR JUBILEE EDITION'. (LOCAL). MRS GERALD TIMP, CHAIRPERSON OF HISTORY BOOK; JUBILEE COMMITTEE; MAIN ST; CALMAR, IA 52132. (#22763).

MEMENTOS FOR CALMAR'S 125TH JUBILEE, IA. COINS, MUGS, HATS, PLATES, SPOONS, BUTTONS, PROGRAM GUIDES, BUMPER STICKERS & TROPHIES COMMEMORATING CALMAR'S 125 JUBILEE CELEBRATION. (LOCAL). ALMA MEYER, COORDINATOR; CALMAR JUBILEE COMMITTEE & BICENTENNIAL COMMITTEE; CALMAR, IA 52132. (#26989).

PLANTING TWO BICENTENNIAL TREES, CALMAR, IA. MAPLE TREE PLANTED AT CALMAR'S LION'S PARK AND WALNUT TREE AT LAKE MEYER BY LEGION AND AUXILIARY MEMBERS COMMEMORATING OUR COUNTRY'S 200TH BIRTHDAY. (LOCAL). ALMA MEYER, AUX PRESIDENT; HALVERSON-GIESEN POST AND UNIT #266, AMERICAN LEGION & AUXILIARY; CALMAR, IA 52132. (#22764).

MAY 2, '75. FASHION OF YESTERYEAR-STYLE SHOW. FASHIONS OF MEN, WOMEN & CHILDREN, PERIOD 1875-1975. AT ST ALOYSIUS CHURCH HALL. (LOCAL). EMILY HOFFERT, COORD; XI DELTA OMEGA CHAPTER OF BETA SIGMA PHI SORORITY; CLAY ST; CALMAR, IA 52132. (#200018-27).

JUNE 21, '75. 125TH JUBILEE CELEBRATION PARADE, OVER 100 UNITS PARTICIPATING. ALSO ECUMENICAL SERVICES TO KICK OFF THE FESTIVITIES, ANTIQUE SHOW & SALE, ART SHOW AND PAGEANT. AT START AT FOOTBALL FIELD, DOWN MAIN ST. (REGN'L). ERWIN GLOCK, COORD; CALMAR JUBILEE COMMITTEE; MARYVILLE ST; CALMAR, IA 52132. (#200018-26).

JUNE 21 - 22, '75. BOB BARNES RCA RODEO. COMPETITION, LIVE PERFORMANCE AT CAMPUS OF AREA ONE VOCATIONAL-TECHNICAL SCHOOL. (REGN'L). JOHN HEVING, COORD; CALMAR 125TH JUBILEE COMMITTEE; RAILROAD ST; CALMAR, IA 52132. (#200018-28).

CALMAR — CONTINUED

APR 17 - 18, '76. PENNSYLVANIA WAGON TRAIN FESTIVAL. FESTIVAL, PARADE. (REGN'L). ERNIE HEYING, CHMN; CALMAR BICENTENNIAL COMMITTEE; CLARK ST; CALMAR, IA 52132. (#200018-232).

JUNE 20, '76. CALMAR CANOE RACES. COMPETITION. (LOCAL). CHARLES OHLERT, COORD; WINN CO BICENTENNIAL COMMISSION; WASHINGTON; CALMAR, IA 52132. (#200018-228).

CAMBRIA

CAMBRIA CHURCH HISTORY, IA. A HISTORY OF THE AREA FROM 1845-PRESENT TO BE WRITTEN & EXHIBITED WITH HERITAGE DISPLAYS. (LOCAL). MAYNARD STREET, COORDINATOR; CAMBRIA BICENTENNIAL COMMITTEE; CAMBRIA, IA 50045. (#22185).

LANDSCAPING KIRBY PARK IN CAMBRIA, IA. PLANTING TREES, FLOWERS & SHRUBS. (LOCAL). MAYNARD STREET, COORDINATOR; CAMBRIA GARDEN CLUB; CAMBRIA, IA 50045. (#22180).

SHELTER HOUSE IN CAMBRIA, IA. NEW SHELTER HOUSE TO BE BUILT. (LOCAL). MAYNARD STREET, COORDINATOR; CAMBRIA BICENTENNIAL COMMITTEE; CAMBRIA, IA 50045. (#22184).

JULY 4, '76. FOURTH OF JULY PARADE. PARADE WILL BE AT 3:30PM. WILL INCLUDE OLD CARS, OLD TRACTORS & MACHINERY, FLOATS & A CHILDREN'S SECTION. ALSO WILL HAVE FLAG RAISING, ANTIQUE EXHIBITS & DISPLAYS. AT MORNING SERVICES AT KIRBY PARK; PARADE ON COTTONWOOD STREET. (LOCAL). MAYNARD STREET, COORD; CAMBRIA BICENTENNIAL COMMITTEE; CAMBRIA, IA 50045. (#105949-1).

CAMBRIDGE

JULY 17, '76. CAMBRIDGE BICENTENNIAL CELEBRATION. FESTIVAL, PARADE AT TOWN PARK. (LOCAL). DONNA PETERSON, COORD; CAMBRIDGE BICENTENNIAL COMMITTEE; CAMBRIDGE, IA 50046. (#200018-192).

CANTRIL

BUILDING A RECREATIONAL PARK IN CANTRIL, IA. THE COMMUNITY OF CANTRIL IS BUILDING A RECREATIONAL PARK FOR THE YOUTH OF THE COMMUNITY. (LOCAL). TED WATSON OR LIBBY WOODRUFF, CO-CHAIRMAEN; VAN BUREN DEVELOPMENT ASSOC; 101 VAN BUREN ST; KEOSAUQUA, IA 52565. (#21403).

CARBON

CITY PARK & TREE PLANTING - PROJ OF CARBON, IA. A CITY PARK WILL BE ESTABLISHED AT THE END OF MAIN ST; TREES WILL BE PLANTED & PICNIC TABLES INSTALLED. (LOCAL). MRS PAUL RICHIE, CITY CLERK; CARBON CITY COUNCIL; CARBON, IA 50839. (#13893).

RED, WHITE & BLUE FLOWERS - PROJ OF CARBON, IA. RED, WHITE & BLUE FLOWERS WILL BE PLANTED IN THE PARK. (LOCAL). MRS PAUL RICHIE, PROJ DIRECTOR; GARDEN CLUB; CARBON, IA 50839. (#13894).

JUNE 12, '76. CARBON'S BICENTENNIAL TOGETHERNESS. A BICENTENNIAL QUILT WILL BE RAFFLED. AT MAIN ST. (LOCAL). MRS PAUL RICHEY, CHMN; CARBON BICENTENNIAL GROUP; CARBON, IA 50839. (#106207-1).

CARLISLE

CEMETERY CENSUS IN CARLISLE, IA. PROJECT IS THE COMPILING OF INFORMATION ON OLD CEMETERY IN COMMUNITY. (LOCAL). WALLACE MCKEE, PROJ DIRECTOR; OLD CEMETERY COMMITTEE; CARLISLE, IA 50047. (#15095).

CENTURY FARMS OF WARREN COUNTY, IA. RECOGNITION OF FARMS IN SAME FAMILY FOR AT LEAST 100 YEARS. (LOCAL). WALLACE MCKEE, PROJ DIRECTOR; WARREN COUNTY BICENTENNIAL COMMITTEE; CARLISLE, IA 50047. (#15093).

SCHOOL RECORDS IN CARLISLE, IA. COMPILING OF INFORMATION ON SCHOOLS FORMERLY IN WARREN COUNTY. (LOCAL). OPAL DYE, PROJ CHAIRMAN; SCHOOL RECORDS COMMITTEE; 315 LINDHART; CARLISLE, IA 50047. (#15094).

CARPENTER

RESTORATION OF INDIAN FORT, CARPENTER, IA. RESTORATION OF STONE BUILDING ERECTED IN 1867 BY PIONEERS OF WORTH & MITCHELL COUNTIES, AS A FORT FOR PROTECTION FROM THE SIOUX INDIANS, WHO WERE THEN REPORTED TO BE ON THE WARPATH. (LOCAL). W H BIEDERMAN, SECRETARY-TREASURER; MITCHELL COUNTY BICENTENNIAL COMMISSION; ROUTE 4; OSAGE, IA 50461. (#18798).

CARROLL

COUNTY MUSEUM PROJECT - CARROLL, IA. THE OLD CITY LIBRARY IS BEING CONVERTED INTO A MUSEUM. (LOCAL). MARY BAUMHOVER, PRESIDENT; CARROLL COUNTY HISTORICAL MUSEUM; CARROLL, IA 51401. (#16687).

OCT 1 - 3, '76. PLAY - 'SHENANDOAH'. THE COMMUNITY THEATER PLAYERS WILL PRESENT THE PLAY 'SHENANDOAH'. (LOCAL). RON SCHECKMAN; COMMUNITY THEATER PLAYERS; CARROLL, IA 51401. (#12687-1).

OCT 7, '76. 'UP WITH PEOPLE' MUSICAL. THE YOUNG PEOPLE OF THE UP WITH PEOPLE CORP WILL PRESENT 'UP WITH PEOPLE' MUSICAL. AT KUEMPEN HIGH SCHOOL, CARROLL, IOWA. (LOCAL). THOMAS DOLEZAL; CARROLL BICENTENNIAL COMMITTEE/CHAMBER OF COMMERCE; CARROLL, IA 51401. (#12688-1).

CARSON

PARK IN CARSON, IA. A NEW CITY PARK IS BEING PLANNED FOR CARSON. (LOCAL). DEBBIE PERDUE, CHAIRMAN; CARSON BICENTENNIAL COMMITTEE; CARSON, IA 51525. (#21274).

CARTER LAKE

CARTER LAKE HISTORY, IA. A BOOK IS BEING WRITTEN ON THE HISTORY OF CARTER LAKE. (LOCAL). DOLORES HARRISON, CHAIRMAN; IOWA COMMUNITY BETTERMENT COMMITTEE & BICENTENNIAL COMMITTEE; 90 CARTER LAKE CLUB; CARTER LAKE, IA 52212. (#17258).

TREE PLANTING - CARTER LAKE, IA. A RED MAPLE WILL BE PLANTED IN HONOR OF RHODE ISLAND, ONE OF THE 13 ORIGINAL STATES. (LOCAL). DOLORES HARRISON, CHAIRMAN; IOWA COMMUNITY BETTERMENT; 90 CARTER LAKE CLUB; CARTER LAKE, IA 52212. (#17257).

APR 24, '76. BICENTENNIAL PARADE. PARADE. (LOCAL). DOLORES HARRISON, CHMN; ICB, BICENTENNIAL COMMITTEE; C/O CARTER LAKE CLUB; CARTER LAKE, IA 51501. (#104737-1).

CASTALIA

JUNE 6, '76. BLOOMFIELD TOWNSHIP TIME CAPSULE DEDICATION. CEREMONY. (LOCAL). VERN KOENIG, COORD; WINN CO BICENTENNIAL COMMISSION; 110 ELM CT; DECORAH, IA 52101. (#200018-226).

CASTANA

RESTORATION OF OLD CHURCH BELL, CASTANA, IA. ORIGINAL CHURCH BELL TO BE RESTORED & RESET IN CHURCH YARD. (LOCAL). MISS MARGIE HEISLER, COORDINATOR; TICONIC METHODIST CHURCH; CASTANA, IA 51010. (#21417).

TREE PLANTING & LANDSCAPING, CASTANA, IA. TREES WILL BE PLANTED TO REPLACE OLD & DEAD TREES AT TICONIC METHODIST CHURCH. (LOCAL). MISS MARGIE HEISLER, COORDINATOR; TICONIC METHODIST CHURCH; CASTANA, IA 51010. (#21418).

UPDATE OF CENTER TOWNSHIP CEMETERY RECORDS, IA. PHOTOGRAPHING, CATALOGING AND ALPHABETIZING NAMES OF PEOPLE BURIED IN THE CEMETERY. REBINDING OF CEMETERY PLAT BOOK I: 1886 TO 1946; PHOTOGRAPHING OF CEMETERY PLAT BOOK VOLUME II: 1947 TO 1976. (LOCAL). ERVILLA A MASTERS, PRESIDENT; THURSDAY CLUB OF CASTANA; RTE 1, BOX 153; MAPLETON, IA 51034. (#21776).

APR 15, '76. PUBLIC TREE PLANTING. CEREMONY AT CASTANA CITY PARK. (LOCAL). ERVILLA A MASTERS; THURSDAY CLUB OF CASTANA; RT 1 BOX 153; MAPLETON, IA 51034. (#105620-1).

CEDAR FALLS

BENNINGTON FLAGS PROJ, CEDAR FALLS, IA. BENNINGTON '76 FLAGS TO BE FLOWN FROM LIGHT POLES ON MAIN STREET AND COLLEGE HILL. (LOCAL). ROSEMARY RASMUSEN, SECRETARY; STURGIS FALLS BICENTENNIAL COMMITTEE; 3304 PANTHER LN; CEDAR FALLS, IA 50613. (#24476).

BICENTENNIAL HISTORICAL QUILT, CEDAR FALLS, IA. A QUILT DEPICTING THE HISTORY OF CEDAR FALLS. 32 12' SQUARES WILL DENOTE HISTORICAL BUILDINGS & EVENTS, THE 27' CENTER SQUARE WILL BE A PICTURE OF CEDAR FALLS. QUILT WILL BE GIVEN TO LOCAL MUSEUM. (LOCAL). MRS LEE TRIESDELL, CHAIRMAN; CEDAR HEIGHTS WOMEN'S CLUB; 2330 GRAND BLVD; CEDAR FALLS, IA 50613. (#26827).

CONFERENCES & WORKSHOPS. VARIOUS WORKSHOPS WILL BE HELD FOR PUBLIC SCHOOL TEACHERS & ADMINISTRATORS. (LOCAL). DR EDWARD VOLDSETH, COORD; USA BICENTENNIAL & UNI-CENTENNIAL COMMISSION; UNIV OF NORTHERN IOWA; CEDAR FALLS, IA 50163. (#105800-1).

FUTURE FREEDOMS COMMITTEE - CEDAR FALLS, IA. IMPLICATIONS OF THE ECONOMIC, SOCIAL & POLITICAL DEVELOPMENTS IN THE U S WILL BE EXPLORED AND THEIR RELATIONSHIP TO INDIVIDUAL LIBERTY IN THE U S AND WITH OTHER COUNTRIES. (REGN'L). F W FISCHER, CHAIRMAN; FUTURE FREEDOMS COMMITTEE & BLACK HAWK BICENTENNIAL COMMISSION; 314 MAIN ST; CEDAR FALLS, IA 50613. (#25308).

NEWSPAPER ARTICLES FROM CEDAR FALLS, IA. BICENTENNIAL ARTICLES ARE BEING FEATURED WEEKLY IN THE LOCAL NEWSPAPER. (LOCAL). MARY JACOBSON, PROJ DIRECTOR; STURGIS FALLS BICENTENNIAL COMMITTEE; SUMMIT DR; CEDAR FALLS, IA 50613. (#24475).

ONE HUNDRED YEAR HISTORY OF UNIV OF NORTHERN IOWA. A HISTORY OF THE UNIVERSITY OF NORTHERN IOWA TO COMMEMORATE ITS CENTENNIAL IN 1976. (ST-WIDE). EDWARD VOLDSETH, VICE PRESIDENT; UNIV OF NORTHERN IOWA FOUNDATION; ADMINISTRATION BUILDING; CEDAR FALLS, IA 50613. (#205). **ARBA GRANTEE.**

PETER MELENDY MEML BRIDGE & PARK DEDICATION - IOWA. CEDAR FALLS, IOWA COMMUNITY ASSEMBLY WITH PROGRAM TITLED WE HONOR OUR MAYORS', ESPECIALLY PETER MELENDY, PIONEER CITIZEN & FORMER MAYOR TO DEDICATE MEMORIAL BRIDGE & RIVERFRONT PARK. (LOCAL). MRS CHARLES BLACK, REGENT; CEDAR FALLS CHAPTER, DAUGHTERS OF THE AMERICAN REVOLUTION; 8009 UNIVERSITY AVE; CEDAR FALLS, IA 50613. (#2579). **ARBA GRANTEE.**

RECONSTRUCTION OF NATIVE PRAIRIE - CEDAR FALLS, IA. RECONSTRUCT REPLICAS OF THE STATE'S NATIVE PLANT AND ANIMAL COMMUNITIES IN ORDER TO RECLAIM PORTIONS OF OUR VANISHING BIOLOGICAL HERITAGE. (LOCAL). DR EDWARD VOLDSETH, COORDINATOR; UNIV OF NORTHERN IOWA BICENTENNIAL COMMISSION; CEDAR FALLS, IA 50613. (#22045). **ARBA GRANTEE.**

SCHOOL HOUSE PROJECT, CEDAR FALLS, IA. RURAL SCHOOL HOUSE PAINTING AND USE LATER FOR SCHOOL CLASSES. (LOCAL). BETTY HINTON, COORDINATOR; CEDAR FALLS COMMUNITY SCHOOLS; WASHINGTON ST; CEDAR FALLS, IA 50613. (#24477).

SPECIAL MUSICAL & DRAMATIC PRODUCTIONS. A SERIES OF SPECIAL CONCERTS, OPERAS & PLAYS FEATURING ARTISTIC WORKS OF OR ABOUT THE REVOLUTIONARY PERIOD. (LOCAL). DR EDWARD VOLDSETH, COORD; USA BICENTENNIAL & UNI-CENTENNIAL COMMISSION; UNIV OF NORTHERN IOWA; CEDAR FALLS, IA 50163. (#105800-2).

SQUARE DANCE PARTY, USA - CEDAR FALLS, IA. A NATIONWIDE WEEKLY TELEVISION SHOW FEATURING SQUARE DANCING AND OTHER VARIETIES OF AMERICAN FOLK DANCING. (REGN'L). CHRIS A MCENANY, EXECUTIVE PRODUCER; AMERICAN SQUARE DANCE ASSOC; 219-221 MAIN ST; CEDAR FALLS, IA 50613. (#17131).

'THE STATES OF THE UNION' RADIO PROGRAM, IA. A ONE HOUR PROGRAM DEALING WITH IOWA'S SOCIAL, CULTURAL & POLITICAL DEVELOPMENT SINCE ITS DISCOVERY. (LOCAL). NEAL W PROCTOR, STATION DEVELOPMENT DIRECTOR; UNIVERSITY OF NORTHERN IOWA; CEDAR FALLS, IA 50613. (#18757).

WOMAN OF CHARACTER IN IOWA - A BOOK, CEDAR FALLS. THE BOOK WILL SHOW THE CONTRIBUTIONS OF IOWAN WOMAN TO THE COMMUNITY, ARTS, POLITICS, EDUCATION, RELIGION & HEALTH; FOR AGE GROUP 10 AND ABOVE. (ST-WIDE). HELEN THORBROGGER, EXEC DIRECTOR; CONESTOGA COUNCIL OF GIRL SCOUTS; PO BOX 690; WATERLOO, IA 50704. (#14193).

SEPT 13, '75. BICENTENNIAL COMMUNITY ASSEMBLY. PRESENTATION OF 132 YEARS OF LOCAL HISTORY HONORING ALL MAYORS, PETER MELENDY IN PARTICULAR. AT TABERNACLE AT CEDAR FALLS CONFERENCE GROUNDS. (LOCAL). MRS. CHARLES BLACK; CEDAR FALLS CHAPTER, DAUGHTERS OF THE AMERICAN REVOLUTION; 8009 UNIVERSITY AVENUE; CEDAR FALLS, IA 50613. (#2579-1).

APR 8 - 10, '76. PERFORMANCE OF JOHN PHILIP SOUSA'S 'EL CAPITAN'. A MUSICAL COMEDY BY JOHN PHILIP SOUSA, A SPOOF ON DOUBLE IDENTITY. AT RUSSELL HALL, UNIV OF NORTHERN IOWA. (LOCAL). JANE BIRKHEAD, COORD; DEPT OF MUSIC, UNIV OF NORTHERN IOWA; CEDAR FALLS, IA 50613. (#105131-1).

APR 24, '76. 'HAWKEYE HORIZONS' - A HERITAGE FOR TOMORROW - WORKSHOPS & FESTIVAL. HERITAGE WORKSHOPS & DISPLAY & FESTIVAL HONORING HEROINES. AT UNI-DOME - UNI CAMPUS. (LOCAL). JEANNETTE WATSON, CHMN; CONESTOGA COUNCIL OF GIRL SCOUTS; BOX 690; WATERLOO, IA 50704. (#105131-2).

MAY 8, '76. HERITAGE '76 - SCOUTING BICENTENNIAL SALUTE. AN AREA SHOW WITH A CAST OF OVER 1000 YOUNG PEOPLE, PROTRAYING EVENTS IN NATIONAL, STATE & LOCAL HISTORY, EMPHASIZES THE ROLE OF YOUTH. AT UNI-DOME. (LOCAL). JAMES LANGRIDGE, COORD; WINNEBAGO COUNCIL - BOY SCOUTS OF AMERICA; 2530 UNIVERSITY; WATERLOO, IA 50704. (#106381-1).

JUNE 26, '76. 451ST USAR BAND CONCERT FOR 'FESTIVAL USA' KICKOFF CELEBRATION. BAND WILL PLAY AT NEW UNI-DOME OPENING NIGHT FESTIVITIES 'GALA 76', TO HELP KICKOFF A WEEK-LONG CELEBRATION THROUGHOUT BLACK HAWK CO. THE 451ST BAND WILL ALSO MARCH IN THE OPENING DAY PARADE FROM 1 PM TO 3 PM. AT UNIVERSITY OF NORTHERN IOWA 'UNI-DOME', HUDSON RD. (LOCAL). DEAN A STOVER, V PRES; BLACKHAWK BICENT COMMITTEE/CO C 1ST BN 410TH INF, 205TH INF BDE, SEP; 921 CEDAR; CEDAR FALLS, IA 50613. (#108050-1).

JUNE 27, '76. FARMERS MARKET. FESTIVAL AT OVERMAN PARK AND ISLAND PARK. (LOCAL). ROSEMARY RASMUSSEN, SEC; SBURGIS FALLS BICENTENNIAL FESTIVAL COMMITTEE; 3304 PANTHER LANE; CEDAR FALLS, IA 50613. (#106917-1).

JULY 15, '76. AND THAT'S THE WAY IT WAS 200 YEARS AGO. FAIR AT MEN'S GYMNASIUM. (LOCAL). MRS YVONNE PROVINE, CHMN; NATIONAL ASSOC OF EDUCATIONAL SECRETARIES; 1534 W HUDSON PL; TUCSON, AZ 85704. (#19261-1).

JULY 22 - 24, '76. 'THE LOCAL SCHOOL DISTRICT-RURAL & URBAN INFLUENCES'. WILL DISCUSS HISTORY & HORIZONS OF THE LOCAL SCHOOL DISTRICT. INCLUDES SPEAKERS, PAPERS & DISPLAYS. WILL BE IN CELEBRATION OF THE UNIV OF NORTHERN IOWA CENTENNIAL AND THE USA BICENTENNIAL. HOURS 7/23: 8:30AM-11:00PM; 7/24: 8:30AM-3:30PM. AT UNI EDUCATION CENTER & UNI CENTER URBAN EDUCATION IN WATERLOO, IA. (ST-WIDE). DR WILLIAMH DREIER; UNIV OF NORTHERN IOWA & PHI DELTA KAPPA; 515 EDUCATION CNTR, U N I; CEDAR FALLS, IA 50613. (#101421-1).

CEDAR RAPIDS

'AREA CODE 319' - PROJECT OF CEDAR RAPIDS, IA. COLLEGE MUSICAL GROUP WILL PARTICIPATE IN VARIOUS EVENTS IN THE SURROUNDING COMMUNITIES. (LOCAL). ELGENE SHEA, COORDINATOR; KIRKWOOD COMMUNITY COLLEGE; 6301 KIRKWOOD BLVD SW; CEDAR RAPIDS, IA 52406. (#25510).

BICENT THEME FOR COURSES AT COE COLLEGE IN IOWA. MANY COURSES IN THE JANUARY 1976 TERM WILL FOCUS ON THE BICENTENNIAL AND COLLEGE ANNIVERSARY THEMES. (LOCAL). PETER J ALUGEN, CHAIRMAN; COE COLLEGE; 1220 FIRST AVE NE; CEDAR RAPIDS, IA 52402. (#8438).

BICENT VISITOR CENTER AT SEMINOLE VALLEY FARM, IA. A LARGE BUILDING IS BEING RESTORED TO PROVIDE SHELTER, A MEETING PLACE, DISPLAY SPACE AND GENERAL AID TO VISITORS & THE COMMUNITY. (LOCAL). MRS DON HAMOUS, PRESIDENT; SEMINOLE VALLEY FARM INC; PO BOX 605; CEDAR RAPIDS, IA 52406. (#6225). **ARBA GRANTEE.**

CROP, CHEMICAL & HAY DAYS. SPECIAL EVENTS DESIGNED TO CONTRAST MODERN FARMING TECHNOLOGY WITH THAT OF YESTERYEAR. (LOCAL). GARLAND ASHBACHER, COORD; KIRKWOOD COMMUNITY COLLEGE; 6301 KIRKWOOD BLVD; CEDAR RAPIDS, IA 52406. (#108163-1). **(??).**

CZECH VILLAGE BAND PAVILION - CEDAR RAPIDS, IA. CONSTRUCTION OF BAND PAVILION FOR CZECH VILLAGE. (LOCAL). GEORGE A JOENS, PRESIDENT; CZECH VILLAGE ASSOCIATION, INC; 129 16TH AVE S W; CEDAR RAPIDS, IA 52404. (#21122). **ARBA GRANTEE.**

CZECH VILLAGE RESTORATION IN CEDAR RAPIDS, IOWA. RESTORATION OF A TWO BLOCK AREA CONSISTING OF SHOPS, STORES & BUSINESSES, IN AN HISTORICAL AREA OF THE CITY TO RESEMBLE ACTUAL ARCHITECTURE & DESIGN UPON COMPLETION OF A MASTER PLAN FOR THE AREA. (LOCAL). HON DONALD J CANNEY, MAYOR; CZECH HERITAGE FOUNDATION; OFFICE OF THE MAYOR; CEDAR RAPIDS, IA 52401. (#5000).

DISPLAY MEMORABILIA OF COE COLLEGE IN IOWA. DISPLAYS OF COLLEGE MEMORABILIA WILL BE EXHIBITED DURING 1975-1976. (LOCAL). PETER J LAUGEN, CHAIRMAN; COE COLLEGE; 1220 FIRST AVE NE; CEDAR RAPIDS, IA 52402. (#8446).

FUND RAISING PROJ FOR COE COLLEGE LIBRARY IN IOWA. A FUND OF $125,000 FOR BOOK AND MEDIA PURCHASES FOR THE COE LIBRARY WILL BE RAISED. (ST-WIDE). PETER J LAUGEN, CHAIRMAN; COE COLLEGE; 1220 FIRST AVE NE; CEDAR RAPIDS, IA 52402. (#8436).

HISTORIC SITES INVENTORY OF LINN COUNTY, IOWA. RESURVEY OF HISTORIC SITES IN LINN COUNTY. (LOCAL). MRS FAYE GLESSNER, CHAIRMAN; LINN COUNTY BICENTENNIAL COMMISSION; CEDAR RAPIDS, IA 52406. (#3673). **(??). ARBA GRANTEE.**

HONORARY DEGREES AWARDED TO FOREIGN SCHOLARS IN IA. COE COLLEGE WILL AWARD HONORARY DEGREES TO PERSONS FROM OTHER COUNTRIES IN 1976. (INT'L). PETER J LAUGEN, CHAIRMAN; COE COLLEGE; 1220 FIRST AVE NE; CEDAR RAPIDS, IA 52402. (#8439).

'INVITE THE WORLD TO VISIT MID-AMERICA IN 1976'. CITIZENS OF CEDAR RAPIDS AND WITHIN 100 MILE RADIUS OF THE CITY IN VITE FOREIGN VISITORS INTO HOMES, FARMS, & BUSINESSES SO AS TO DEVELOP IMPROVED INTERNATIONAL RELATIONS & UNDERSTANDING. (INT'L). ROBERT M L JOHNSON, PROJECT DIRECTOR; MID-AMERICA BICENTENNIAL COMMISSION; PEOPLES BANK BLDG, SUITE 1776; CEDAR RAPIDS, IA 52406. (#206). **(??). ARBA GRANTEE.**

KCCK-FM BICENTENNIAL RADIO PROGRAMMING, IA. SPECIAL FEATURES & INTERVIEWS ON LOCAL, STATE & NATIONAL BICENTENNIAL EVENTS & PROJECTS. (LOCAL). LARRY PATTEN, COORDINATOR; KIRKWOOD COMMUNITY COLLEGE; 6301 KIRKWOOD BLVD SW; CEDAR RAPIDS, IA 52406. (#25512).

LINN COUNTY BICENTENNIAL PIONEER CERTIFICATE, IA. BICENTENNIAL CERTIFICATES ARE AWARDED TO PERSONS WHO CAN PROVE THEY HAD AN ANCESTOR LIVING IN LINN COUNTY BY 1876. GOLD SEALS ARE GIVEN TO THOSE WHO WERE IN LINN COUNTY BY 1850. (LOCAL). MRS MARGARET WAGNER, PRESIDENT; LINN COUNTY HERITAGE SOCIETY; PO BOX 175; CEDAR RAPIDS, IA 52406. (#24379).

LINN COUNTY BICENTENNIAL MEDALLIONS, IA. MEDALLIONS COMMEMORATING THE BICENTENNIAL AND THE HISTORY OF LINN COUNTY ARE BEING SOLD TO RAISE FUNDS FOR WORTHWHILE PROJECTS IN LINN COUNTY. ARTIST GRANT WOOD APPEARS ON THE FACE OF THE COIN. (LOCAL). MRS FAYE GLESSNER, CHAIRMAN; LINN COUNTY BICENTENNIAL COMMISSION; PO BOX 2568; CEDAR RAPIDS, IA 52406. (#24380).

LINN COUNTY HERITAGE ROOM, CEDAR RAPIDS, IA. THE HERITAGE ROOM IS A RESEARCH AND EDUCATIONAL CENTER FOR GENEALOGY AND HISTORY. (LOCAL). MRS MARGARET WAGNER, PRESIDENT; LINN COUNTY HERITAGE SOCIETY; PO BOX 175; CEDAR RAPIDS, IA 52406. (#24378).

LINN COUNTY HISTORICAL INVENTORY, CEDAR RAPIDS, IA. SPECIFIC LOCATION AND RESEARCH INFORMATION ON 100 SITES; DATA TO BE USED ON MAP & DESCRIPTIVE PAMPHLET; TO BE AVAILABLE TO SCHOOLS, CHAMBER OF COMMERCE AND TOURISTS FOR SELF-GUIDED TOURS. (LOCAL). MRS BEN BLACKSTOCK, PRESIDENT; LINN COUNTY HISTORICAL MUSEUM ASSOC; PO BOX 823; CEDAR RAPIDS, IA 52406. (#9321).

LITTLE MUDDY SOCIETY PROJECT, CEDAR RAPIDS, IA. FIVE CHILDREN AGED 5 TO 15 WILL GIVE FREE PERFORMANCES OF PLAYETTES ABOUT BETSY ROSS MAKING THE FLAG. (LOCAL). NADINE FILLMORE, COORDINATOR; CHILDREN OF THE AMERICAN REVOLUTION; 216 15TH ST SE; CEDAR RAPIDS, IA 52403. (#24375).

NLAPW BICENTENNIAL WRITING CONTEST FOR SENIOR WOMEN. A CONTEST FOR MEMBERS OVER 60 YEARS OLD TO WRITE A SHORT ARTICLE PERTAINING TO PERSONAL HISTORY. (LOCAL). ANN STRUTHERS, CHAIRMAN; NATIONAL LEAGUE OF AMERICAN PEN WOMEN, INC; 503 FOREST DRIVE SE; CEDAR RAPIDS, IA 52403. (#107311-1).

ORAL HISTORY PROJECT FOR COE COLLEGE IN IOWA. TAPED INTERVIEWS OF RETIRED FACULTY AND OLDER ALUMNI WILL PROVIDE AN ORAL HISTORY OF THE COLLEGE. (LOCAL). PETER J LAUGEN, CHAIRMAN; COE COLLEGE; 1220 FIRST AVE NE; CEDAR RAPIDS, IA 52402. (#8445).

PIONEER VILLAGE HISTORICAL PARK AREA IN IOWA. CONSTRUCTION, RENOVATION, & MOVING OF HISTORICAL BLDGS TO A PUBLIC PARK AREA WHERE A VILLAGE WILL BE CREATED IN THE STYLE OF 1890'S. (LOCAL). HON DONALD J CANNEY, MAYOR; CITY OF CEDAR RAPIDS; CITY HALL; CEDAR RAPIDS, IA 52401. (#4999).

PROJECT TO STUDY FUTURE GOALS OF COE COLLEGE IN IA. PROJECT TO STUDY THE AIMS, OBJECTIVES & FUTURE OF COE COLLEGE WILL BE COMPLETED IN 1976. ALUMNI TO HOLD FORUMS IN VARIOUS PARTS OF THE COUNTRY TO ADD THEIR VIEWS TO THE STUDY. (ST-WIDE). PETER J LAUGEN, CHAIRMAN; COE COLLEGE; 1220 FIRST AVE NE; CEDAR RAPIDS, IA 52402. (#8444).

RADIO PROGRAMS FOR COE COLLEGE'S 125TH ANNIV IN IA. ONE HUNDRED-FIVE MINUTE PROGRAMS ON THE COE'S ALUMNI & EVENTS WILL BE BROADCAST LOCALLY ON THE RADIO IN 1976. (LOCAL). PETER J LAUGEN, CHAIRMAN; COE COLLEGE; 1220 FIRST AVE NE; CEDAR RAPIDS, IA 52402. (#8440).

SOUVENIR PLATES AVAILABLE AT COE COLLEGE IN IOWA. PEWTER PLATES COMMEMORATING COE COLLEGE'S 125TH ANNIVERSARY WILL BE OFFERED FOR SALE. (ST-WIDE). PETER J LAUGEN, CHAIRMAN; COE COLLEGE; 1220 FIRST AVE NE; CEDAR RAPIDS, IA 52402. (#8437).

WMT-TV BICENTENNIAL PROMOTION PROGRAMS -NBMRP. BEGAN EFFORTS IN 1974. HAS PRODUCED WEEKLY SERIES OF 30-MINUTE PROGRAMS 'EYE ON IOWA' & ALSO 'EASTERN IOWA HISTORICAL MINUTES', WITH ART WORK FROM ELEMENTARY STUDENTS. (ST-WIDE). BARRY NORRIS, BICENTENNIAL COORDINATOR; WMT-TELEVISION; PO BOX 2147; CEDAR RAPIDS, IA 52406. (#24681).

WOMAN'S AWARENESS DAY IN IOWA, APRIL 15, 1976. A DAY LONG WORKSHOP ON CHANGING ROLE OF WOMEN IN AMERICAN LIFE. (LOCAL). PETER J LAUGEN, CHAIRMAN; COE COLLEGE; 1220 FIRST AVE NE; CEDAR RAPIDS, IA 52402. (#8873).

OCT 21, '75 - APR 23, '76. FESTIVAL OF AMERICAN ARTS AT COE COLLEGE IN IOWA. THE COE ARTIST SERIES, CHAMBER SERIES WILL FEATURE AMERICAN ARTISTS DURING THE 1975-76 SCHOOL YEAR. AT SINCLAIR AUDITORIUM, COE COLLEGE. (LOCAL). PETER J LAUGEN, CHAIRMAN; COE COLLEGE; 1220 FIRST AVE NE; CEDAR RAPIDS, IA 52402. (#8442-1).

OCT 31 - NOV 2, '75. UNITED STATES ARMED FORCES BICENTENNIAL CARAVAN. THE CARAVAN IS COMPOSED OF EXHIBIT VANS FOR EACH BRANCH OF THE MILITARY SERVICE. THE THEME OF THE EXHIBITION IS 'HISTORY OF THE ARMED FORCES AND THEIR CONTRIBUTION TO THE NATION'. (LOCAL). MS FAYE GLESSNER, CHMN; LINN COUNTY BICENTENNIAL COMMISSION; 2523 FRANKLIN AVE NE; CEDAR RAPIDS, IA 52402. (#1775-223).

NOV 7, '75 - DEC 31, '76. BICENTENNIAL SYMPHONY IN DANCE. LIVE PERFORMANCE. (LOCAL). SHARON HRUSKA, CHAIRMAN; DIEMAN BENNET DANCE STUDIO; 117 3RD AVE SE; CEDAR RAPIDS, IA 52401. (#106953-1).

JAN 1 - DEC 31, '76. HOSPITALITY FOR FOREIGN VISTORS FOR A DAY, WEEK OR WEEK-END. CITIZENS OF CEDAR RAPIDS AND WITHIN 100 MILE RADIUS OF THE CITY IN VITE FOREIGN VISITORS INTO HOMES, FARMS, & BUSINESSES SO AS TO DEVELOP IMPROVED INTERNATIONAL RELATIONS & UNDERSTANDING. (LOCAL). ROBERT M L JOHNSON; MID-AMERICA BICENTENNIAL COMMISSION; PEOPLES BANK BLDG,SUITE 1776; CEDAR RAPIDS, IA 52406. (#206-1).

MAR 1 - DEC 31, '76. 'SYMPHONY IN DANCE USA'. FUSES MEDIUMS OF MUSIC, POETRY, DANCE, COSTUME AND SCENES TO EVOKE THE LEGEND AND EPIC THAT IS AMERICA AND TO REMIND US ALL THAT WE ARE STILL 'TREADING AN ENCHANTED GROUND'. AT THEATER, AUDITORIUM, GYMNASIUM & OUTDOORS. (ST-WIDE). MRS EDWIN W BRUERE, DIR; DIEMAN-BENNETT DANCE THEATRE OF THE HEMISPHERES; 117 3RD AVE SE; CEDAR RAPIDS, IA 52401. (#104047-2).

APR 25 - MAY 14, '76. GRANT WOOD EXHIBIT & SEMINAR AT COE COLLEGE. ALL FRESHMEN WILL PARTICIPATE IN A WORKSHOP ON GRANT WOOD AND VIEW A MAJOR EXHIBITION OF HIS PAINTINGS AT THE COLLEGE DURING MAY, 1976. AT SINCLAIR ART GALLERY, COE COLLEGE. (LOCAL). PETER J LAUGEN, CHAIRMAN; COE COLLEGE; 1220 FIRST AVE NE; CEDAR RAPIDS, IA 52402. (#8443-1).

MAY 3 - 14, '76. KIDDIE FARM TOUR. 5000 KINDERGARTEN STUDENTS FROM CEDAR RAPIDS WILL GET A TOUR OF THE FARM; WILL SEE LIFE ON THE FARM TODAY AND WHAT IT MAY BE LIKE IN THE FUTURE. (LOCAL). LARRY STATLER, PROJ CHMN; KIRKWOOD COMMUNITY COLLEGE; 6301 KIRKWOOD BLVD SW; CEDAR RAPIDS, IA 52406. (#108163-2).

JULY 2 - 11, '76. ALL IOWA FAIR. EXHIBIT, FAIR AT ALL IOWA FAIRGROUNDS, HAWKEYE DOWNS. (REGN'L). HARRY C KNIGHT, MGR; ALL IOWA FAIR; PO BOX F; CEDAR RAPIDS, IA 52406. (#106095-5).

DEC 5, '76. MUSIC COMPOSED FOR COE COLLEGE'S 125TH ANNIV IN IA. CHORAL WORK WITH INSTRUMENTAL ACCOMPANIMENT WILL BE PREMIERED ON THE COLLEGE'S 125TH BIRTHDAY ON DECEMBER 5, 1976. COMPOSER KARL HUSA. AT SINCLAIR AUDITORIUM, COE COLLEGE. (LOCAL). PETER J LAUGEN, CHAIRMAN; COE COLLEGE; 1220 FIRST AVE NE; CEDAR RAPIDS, IA 52402. (#8441-1).

CENTER JCT

CEMETERY RESTORATION - CENTER JUNCTION, IA. THE CEMETERY IS LOCATED IN THE GHOST TOWN OF EDINBURGH; IT HAS NOT BEEN MAINTAINED FOR THE PAST 50 YEARS; THE COUNTY HISTORICAL SOCIETY & MUSEUM ARE LOCATED ON THE SAME ORIGINAL TRACT OF GROUND. (LOCAL). EDITH HINRICHSEN, PROJ DIRECTOR; HAPPY HOUR CLUB; RR 1; CENTER JCT, IA 52212. (#19647).

REMODELING TOWN PARK - CENTER JCT, IA. WOMEN'S CLUB PAINTED EVERYTHING IN THE LOCAL TOWN PARK IN RED, WHITE AND BLUE INCLUDING A SHELTER, KITCHEN BLDG AND FENCE. PARK SERVES FOR USE IN THE ANNUAL CELEBRATION AND USE OF RESIDENTS. (LOCAL). NORMA ANDERSON, PRESIDENT; C J WOMEN'S CLUB; CENTER JCT, IA 52212. (#19457).

JULY 3 - 5, '76. COUNTY FESTIVAL CELEBRATION. JULY 4 FESTIVAL IN LOCATION OF THE FIRST JULY 4 CELEBRATION WEST OF THE MISSISSIPPI RIVER. AT JONES COUNTY CENTRAL PARK. (LOCAL). KEITH CHRISTENSEN, CHMN; CENTER JUNCTION LIBERTY COMMITTEE & JONES CO BICENTENNIAL COMMITTEE; BOX 335; CENTER JCT, IA 52212. (#104351-1).

CENTER POINT

CENTER POINT HISTORICAL SOCIETY MUSEUM, IA. A BRICK BUILDING BUILT IN 1878 WILL BE RESTORED TO BE USED AS A MUSEUM. (ST-WIDE). FERN H DENNISON, CO-CHAIRPERSON; CENTER POINT AMERICAN REVOLUTION BICENTENNIAL COMMITTEE; TOWN HALL, 1025 FRANKLIN ST; CENTER POINT, IA 52213. (#16810).

ENLARGED PHOTOGRAPHS DATING FROM EARLY 1800'S, IA. ENLARGED HISTORICAL PHOTOGRAPHS OF CENTER POINT, IA & SURROUNDING AREA. (LOCAL). FERN H DENNISON, CO-CHAIRPERSON; CENTER POINT AMERICAN REVOLUTION BICENTENNIAL COMMITTEE; TOWN HALL, 1025 FRANKLIN ST; CENTER POINT, IA 52213. (#16808).

HISTORICAL LIBRARY BOOK SECTION, IA. A SECTION OF HISTORICAL BOOKS WILL BE SET UP IN THE CENTER POINT PUBLIC LIBRARY. INCLUDED WILL BE BOOKS ON NATIONAL & LOCAL HISTORY. (LOCAL). FERN H DENNISON, CO-CHAIRPERSON; CENTER POINT AMERICAN REVOLUTION BICENTENNIAL COMMITTEE; TOWN HALL, 1025 FRANKLIN ST; CENTER POINT, IA 52213. (#16809).

RESTORATION OF A LOG CABIN, CENTER POINT, IA. AUTHENTIC LOG CABIN BUILT CIRCA 1880 MOVED TO CENTER POINT IOWA. IT WILL BE RESTORED & FURNISHED. (ST-WIDE). FERN H DENNISON, CO-CHAIRPERSON; CENTER POINT BICENTENNIAL COMMITTEE; TOWN HALL, 1025 FRANKLIN; CENTER POINT, IA 52213. (#16806).

RESTORATION OF VETERANS' GRAVESITES, IA. A POST & CHAIN FENCE WILL BE BUILT AROUND GRAVES OF AMERICAN REVOLUTIONARY WAR VETERANS. SPECIAL MARKERS WILL ALSO BE ERECTED. (ST-WIDE). FERN H DENNISON, CO-CHAIRPERSON; DYE BENION POST AMERICAN LEGION & CENTER POINT BICENTENNIAL CO; 709-711 MAIN ST; CENTER POINT, IA 52213. (#16807).

OCT 15 - 18, '75. 'OUR TOWN' - PLAY PRODUCTION. LIVE PERFORMANCE AT GYMNASIUM. (LOCAL). JOHN SCHWIEBERT, SUPT; DRAMA DEPARTMENT, CENTER POINT CONSOLIDATED SCHOOL; 613 SUMMIT ST; CENTER POINT, IA 52213. (#200018-19).

APR 4 - 5, '76. JAYCEE'S CARNIVAL. A CARNIVAL WITH BICENTENNIAL EMPHASIS; WINDOW DISPLAYS BY BUSINESSMEN. AT CENTER POINT, IOWA. (LOCAL). FERN H DENNISON, CHMN; CENTER POINT ARBC; CENTER POINT JAYCEES; 1025 FRANKLIN ST; CENTER POINT, IA 52213. (#103056-1).

JULY 1 - 4, '76. GIRLS' SOFT BALL TOURNAMENT. COMPETITION AT CENTER POINT HIGH SCHOOL ATHLETIC FIELD. (LOCAL). LEROY BUELOW, PRESIDENT; CENTER POINT JAYCEES; RFD 1; CENTER POINT, IA 52213. (#103056-4).

JULY 3, '76. BICENTENNIAL PARADE. PARADE. (LOCAL). LEROY BUELOW, PRESIDENT; CENTER POINT JAYCEES; RFD 1; CENTER POINT, IA 52213. (#103056-2).

JULY 4, '76. FIREWORKS DISPLAY AT CENTER POINT CONSOLIDATED SCHOOL ATHLETIC FIELD. FESTIVAL. (LOCAL). LEROY BUELOW, PRESIDENT; CENTER POINT JAYCEES; RFD 1; CENTER POINT, IA 52213. (#103056-5).

CENTERVILLE

RESTORATION OF OLD JAIL, CENTERVILLE, IA. RESTORATION OF OLD JAIL INTO MUSEUM FOR THE BICENTENNIAL. (LOCAL). BILL STARK, DIRECTOR-HISTORIAN; APPANOOSE COUNTY HIST SOCIETY, BEULAH MITCHELL, PRES; CENTERVILLE, IA 52544. (#16694).

SEPT 27, '75. PANCAKE DAY. THE 27TH ANNUAL PANCAKE DAY WILL BE AN ALL-DAY PROGRAM. AT TOWN SQUARE. (LOCAL). MIKE O'CONNOR, PROJ DIR; PANCAKE DAY COMMITTEE; RADIO STATION KCOG; CENTERVILLE, IA 52544. (#100814-1).

CENTRAL CITY

CENTRAL CITY, IA LIBRARY. THE CENTRAL CITY LIBRARY IS REMODELING A BASEMENT AREA INTO A HISTORICAL DEPARTMENT AND MICROFILMING THEIR NEWSPAPERS. (LOCAL). MAC STONE, COORDINATOR; CENTRAL CITY LIBRARY; 809 MAIN ST; CENTRAL CITY, IA 52214. (#24383).

CENTRAL CITY — CONTINUED

MICROFILM PROJECT - CENTRAL CITY, IA. MICROFILM OF OLD NEWSPAPERS, STATE & FEDERAL CENSUS RECORDS, OLD BOOKS, MAPS, CEMETERY RECORDS AND LOCAL CHURCH & SCHOOL RECORDS. (LOCAL). JOHN C CLEGG, LIBRARIAN; CENTRAL CITY BICENTENNIAL HISTORICAL SOCIETY; 4TH ST; CENTRAL CITY, IA 52214. (#18226).

FEB 8, '76. BICENTENNIAL ICE FISHEREE. FESTIVAL. (LOCAL). WAYNE DEEN, SECRETARY; NORTHLINN FISH AND GAME CLUB; 259 RIVER ST; CENTRAL CITY, IA 52214. (#104519-16).

FEB 22, '76. EASTERN IOWA SNOW DRAGS. PROCEEDS GO TOWARDS THE PURCHASE OF A SNOWMOBILE AMBULANCE. AT LINN COUNTY FAIRGROUNDS. (LOCAL). DICK SHAFFER, CHAIRMAN; KIWANIS; CENTRAL CITY, IA 52214. (#105266-2).

JUNE 20, '76. BICENTENNIAL CHUCKWAGON RACES. COMPETITION, LIVE PERFORMANCE AT LINN COUNTY FAIR GOURNDS. (LOCAL). HOWARD KNAPP, PROJ DIR; CENTRAL CITY KIWANIS CLUB; 438 MAIN ST; CENTRAL CITY, IA 52214. (#104519-17).

CENTRAL PARK

JULY 3 - 5, '76. FOURTH OF JULY CELEBRATION. FESTIVAL. (LOCAL). FREDA HANKEN, COORD; SCOTCH GROVE OAK; RFD; SCOTCH GROVE, IA 52331. (#106530-1).

CHARITON

JOHN L LEWIS MUSEUM PROJECT OF IOWA. BUILD A MUSEUM ADJACENT TO PRESENT COUNTY HISTORICAL SOCIETY BUILDING TO CAPTAIN JOHN L LEWIS MEMORIAL. THE FIRST FLOOR LOWER LEVEL TO BE DEVELOPED AS AN EARLY DAY IOWA COAL MINE FOR EDUCAT. TOURS, ETC. (ST-WIDE). DALE W BURGE, PRESIDENT; LUCAS COUNTY HISTORICAL SOCIETY; CHARITON, IA 50049. (#767). **ARBA GRANTEE.**

OTTERBEIN CHURCH RESTORATION - CHARITON, IA. RESTORE THE CHURCH TO ITS ORIGINAL STATE. (LOCAL). DALE BURGE, CHAIRMAN; LUCAS CO HISTORICAL SOCIETY; 203 S 12TH; CHARITON, IA 56049. (#28049). **ARBA GRANTEE.**

NOV 1, '75 - JUNE 1, '76. JOHN L LEWIS MUSEUM EXHIBITS. BUILD A MUSEUM ADJACENT TO PRESENT COUNTY HISTORICAL SOCIETY BUILDING TO CAPTAIN JOHN L LEWIS MEMORIAL. THE FIRST FLOOR LOWER LEVEL TO BE DEVELOPED AS AN EARLY DAY IOWA COAL MINE FOR EDUCAT. TOURS, ETC. ALSO: BUILDING/FACILITY/MONUMENT. AT JOHN L LEWIS MUSEUM. (ST-WIDE). DALE W BURGE, PRESIDENT; LUCAS COUNTY HISTORICAL SOCIETY; CHARITON, IA 50049. (#767-1).

JULY 3 - 5, '76. OLD-FASHIONED 4TH OF JULY. COMPETITION, FESTIVAL, PARADE. (LOCAL). REV BENWAY, COORDINATOR; AMERICAN LEGION/FIRE DEPARTMENT/CHARITON BICENTENNIAL COMMITTEE; CHARITON, IA 50049. (#106842-1).

CHARLES CITY

REPAINTING OF FIRE HYDRANTS - CHARLES CITY, IA. FIRE HYDRANTS WILL BE PAINTED TO LOOK LIKE MINUTEMEN. (LOCAL). HON LEO J SCHULA, MAYOR; CITY OF CHARLES CITY; CITY HALL; CHARLES CITY, IA 50616. (#13903).

STUDY OF OLD HOUSES - PROJ OF CHARLES CITY, IA. THE CHARLES CITY BICENTENNIAL COMMISSION WILL SPONSOR A STUDY OF OLD HOUSES. (LOCAL). G ARTHUR LUTHER, CHAIRMAN; CHARLES CITY BICENTENNIAL COMMISSION; BOX 287; CHARLES CITY, IA 50616. (#13897).

TREE PLANTING PROJECT - CHARLES CITY, IA. TREES THAT WERE LOST IN TORNADOS & TO DISEASE WILL BE REPLACED. (LOCAL). HON LEO J SCHULA, MAYOR; CITY OF CHARLES; CITY HALL; CHARLES CITY, IA 50616. (#13895).

AUG 30 - SEPT 1, '75. THRESHER'S REUNION. COMMEMORATION OF 75 YEARS OF TRACTOR PROGRESS IN CHARLES CITY. AT 7 MILES WEST OF CHARLES CITY. (REGN'L). WILLIAM NEAL, SECRETARY; CEDAR VALLEY ENGINE CLUB; 613 8TH AVE; CHARLES CITY, IA 50616. (#101402-1).

OCT 15 - 19, '75. ART TRAIN TO MAKE SIX STOPS IN IOWA. EXHIBIT. (ST-WIDE). KEITH NOAH, CHAIRMAN; CHARLES CITY ART ASSOC; 4 GLEN OAK CIRCLE; CHARLES CITY, IA 50616. (#101404-1).

MAY 31, '76. VETERAN OF 1812 COMMEMORATION. CEREMONY OF PUTTING A PLAQUE ON THE GRAVE OF ABNER ROOT, ONE OF 55 WAR OF 1812 VETERANS BURIED IN IOWA. AT RIVERSIDE CEMETERY. (LOCAL). G ARTHUR LUTHER, CHAIRMAN; CHARLES CITY BICENTENNIAL COMMISSION; BOX 287; CHARLES CITY, IA 50616. (#13896-1).

JULY 4, '76. FOURTH OF JULY PAGEANT. A TWO & ONE HALF HOUR PAGEANT DEPICTING 200 YEARS, PART OF IT STRESSING LOCAL HISTORY. WILL INVOLVE AT LEAST 30 COUNTY ORGANIZATIONS. LAST SCENE WILL BE A BRILLIANT FIREWORKS DISPLAY. AT COMET FIELD, SENIOR HIGH GROUNDS. (LOCAL). G ARTHUR LUTHER, PRES; FLOYD COUNTY BICENTENNIAL COMMISSION; BOX 287; CHARLES CITY, IA 50616. (#13896-2).

OCT 30, '76. BICENTENNIAL COSTUME BALL & DANCE. LIVE PERFORMANCE AT CEDAR MALL - ENCLOSED SHOPPING CENTER. (LOCAL). G ARTHUR LUTHER, PRES; FLOYD COUNTY BICENTENNIAL COMMISSION; BOX 287; CHARLES CITY, IA 50616. (#13896-3).

CHARLESTON

RESTORATION OF CEMETERY MARKERS - CHARLESTON, IA. RESTORE AND ERECT BROKEN AND FALLEN GRAVESTONES IN OLD SECTION OF CHARLESTON CEMETERY. (LOCAL). MAY W CROWE, BOARD OF DIRECTORS; CHARLESTON CEMETERY ASSOC; RURAL ROUTE 1; ARGYLE, IA 52619. (#25451).

CHARLOTTE

CITY OF FLAGS, CHARLOTTEE, IA. FLAGS WILL BE PROVIDED FOR EVERY HOME. (LOCAL). MILDRED SPARKS, CHMN; AMERICAN LEGION; CHARLOTTE, IA 52731. (#15663).

PATRIOTIC DECORATIONS, CHARLOTTE, IA. HYDRANTS WILL BE PAINTED, STREET SIGNS WILL BE INSTALLED & FLOWERS PLANTED. (LOCAL). DALE PLOOG, PRESIDENT; JAYCEES; CHARLOTTE, IA 52731. (#15665).

RESTORATION OF MONUMENT IN CHARLOTTE, IA. A LOCAL MONUMENT WILL BE RESTORED. (LOCAL). INGA FIER, PRESIDENT; AMERICAN LEGION AUXILIARY; CHARLOTTE, IA 52731. (#15664).

FEB 15, '76. PATRIOTIC SCHOOL PROGRAM. LIVE PERFORMANCE AT CHARLOTTE ELEMENTARY SCHOOL. (LOCAL). GAIL ADRIAH, CHMN; CHARLOTTE ELEMENTARY SCHOOL; CHARLOTTE, IA 52731. (#102596-1).

JUNE 17 - 19, '76. HOMECOMING W/CARNIVAL & PARADE. FESTIVAL, PARADE. (LOCAL). WALDO WENDELL, CHMN; CHARLOTTE VOLUNTEER FIRE DEPT; CHARLOTTE, IA 52731. (#102594-1).

JULY 24 - 25, '76. FARMER'S DAY. ANTIQUE TRACTOR PULL, THRESHING BEE AND ANTIQUE EXHIBITS. (LOCAL). RICHARD GRIMM, CHMN; TRACTOR PULL ASSOCIATION; CHARLOTTE, IA 52731. (#102595-1).

CHARTER OAK

OCT '75. CHARTER OAK FUN DAY-COMMUNITY ACTIVITIES FOR ALL AGES. RAISING U S FLAG AND BICENTENNIAL FLAG BY LT GOVERNOR ART NEU OF IA. PROCEEDS FROM CAKE AUCTION TO GO TO MEDICAL CENTER WHICH IS BEING CONSTRUCTED. AT CHARTER OAK, MAIN STREET AND COMMUNITY BUILDING. (LOCAL). RALPH LARSON, PRES; CHARTER OAK COMMERCIAL CLUB; 307 BIRCH AVE; CHARTER OAK, IA 51439. (#200018-21).

CHELSEA

COMMUNITY IMPROVEMENT IN CHELSEA, IA. RESTORATION OF LINCOLN HIGHWAY BRIDGE, PAINTING & REPAIR OF DOME LIGHTS. (LOCAL). JOHN VIET, PRESIDENT; CHELSEA IMPROVEMENT & DEVELOPMENT, INC; CHELSEA, IA 52215. (#22197).

JUNE 12 - 13, '76. BICENTENNIAL WEEKEND CELEBRATION. SATURDAY: COMMUNITY PARADE, 'ROLLE BOLLE, ALL JACKPOT HORSESHOW AND DANCE. SUNDAY: COMMUNITY BASKET PICNIC DINNER, CHILDREN'S GAMES, BEARD CONTEST, HORSESHOES & MUSIC. AT CITY OF CHELSEA. (LOCAL). DORIS FRESE, CHAIRPERSON; CHELSEA IMPROVEMENT & DEVELOPMENT, INC; PO BOX 201; CHELSEA, IA 52215. (#105953-1).

CHEROKEE

PRAIRIE SODBUSTERS, CHEROKEE COUNTY FAIR. THE FAIR WILL HAVE A GENERAL BICENTENNIAL THEME FOR 1975. AT COUNTY FAIRGROUNDS. (ST-WIDE). GUNNAR OSTERLING, DIR; CHEROKEE COUNTY FAIR BOARD; 1210 S 2ND ST; CHEROKEE, IA 51012. (#100813-1).

NOV 9, '75. MUSICAL TRIBUTE TO AMERICA. CHORUS WITH MUSICAL ACCOMPANIMENT DOING PATRIOTIC SONGS. AT CHEROKEE COMMUNITY CENTER. (LOCAL). JAN MCINTOSH, PROJ DIR; TONE CIRCLE / CHEROKEE SYMPHONY; WEST BLUFF ST; MACUS, IA 51035. (#100812-1).

CHESTER

CREAMERY PROJECT IN CHESTER, IA. RESTORATION OF OLD LOCAL CREAMERY AS A RECREATIONAL FACILITY. (LOCAL). KENNETH J MCGRANE, PRESIDENT; CHESTER JAYCEES; CHESTER, IA 52134. (#21394).

JULY 16 - 18, '76. BICENTENNIAL CELEBRATION. HOURS 7/17: 9AM - 1PM. HOURS 7/18: 10:30 AM - 4:30 PM. AT RIVER STREET AND BALL FIELD. (LOCAL). WINNIFRED MCGRANE, COORD; CHESTER JAYCEES; MAIN ST; CHESTER, IA 52134. (#105317-1).

CHURDAN

JUNE 13 - 14, '76. CHURDAN APPRECIATION DAYS. FESTIVAL, PARADE. (LOCAL). PHYLLIS HANSON, CHAIRMAN; CHURDAN APPRECIATION DAYS COMMITTEE; PO BOX 125; CHARDON, IA 50050. (#200018-243).

CINCINNATI

SEPT 4 - 6, '76. CINCINNATI LABOR DAY CELEBRATION. FESTIVAL, PARADE AT CINCINNATI PARK. (LOCAL). JUDY CARSON, PROJ DIR; CINCINNATI LABOR DAY COMMITTEE; CINCINNATI, IA 52549. (#103017-1).

CLARENCE

MICROFILM PROJECTOR - CLARENCE, IA. JAYCEES WILL HOLD A CONSIGNMENT SALE, PROFIT WILL BE USED FOR PURCHASE OF MICROFILM VIEWER. (LOCAL). KENNY SCHMIDT, PROJ DIRECTOR; CLARENCE JAYCEES; 308 7TH AVE; CLARENCE, IA 52216. (#24488).

MICROFILMING OLD LOCAL NEWSPAPERS - CLARENCE, IA. PAPERS FROM 1884 TO THE 1900'S WILL BE MICROFILMED. (LOCAL). ELEANOR STONEROOK, CHAIRMAN; AMERICAN LEGION AUXILIARY; 414 8TH AVE; CLARENCE, IA 52216. (#24486).

RESTORATION OF FIRE BELL & STREET LAMPS, IA. MOUNTING OF OLD CAST IRON FIRE BELL ON PERMANENT BASE; TWO ORIGINAL STREET LAMPS WILL BE PLACED IN FRONT OF THE MUNICIPAL BUILDING. (LOCAL). KENNETH DIRCKS, CHAIRMAN; CLARENCE LIONS CLUB; 403 7TH AVE; CLARENCE, IA 52216. (#24487).

JULY 10, '76. CLARENCE FEST 76. FESTIVAL AT CLARENCE COMMUNITY PARK. (LOCAL). DONALD HUNWARDSEN, CHMN; CLARENCE COMMERCIAL CLUB; 505 1ST AVE; CLARENCE, IA 52216. (#106910-1).

CLARION

CEMETERY PROJECT - CLARION, IA. CEMETERIES IN WRIGHT COUNTY WILL BE INDEXED AND CATALOGUED. (LOCAL). RAY WILLEMSEN, CHAIRMAN; WRIGHT GENEALOGY ASSOC; 225 2ND AVE NE; CLARION, IA 50525. (#23977).

HISTORICAL HOME TOUR & BROCHURE, CLARION, IA. HISTORY OF HERITAGE HOMES OF COMMUNITY TO BE PUBLISHED IN A BROCHURE ALSO PUBLIC TOUR OF SOME OF HOMES. (LOCAL). MRS R W HAGIE COMMITTEE MEMBER; AMERICAN ASSOC UNIVERSITY WOMEN; RT#3; CLARION, IA 50525. (#18803).

HISTORY OF WRIGHT COUNTY, CLARION, IA. PHOTOGRAPHED REPRINT OF BOOK PUBLISHED IN 1870; A HISTORY AND BUSINESS DIRECTORY OF WRIGHT COUNTY, IA. (LOCAL). LUCY STANDISH, CHAIRMAN; WRIGHT COUNTY DAUGHTERS OF THE AMERICAN REVOLUTION; CLARION, IA 50525. (#19691).

MAY 2, '76. TOUR OF OLD HOMES. TOUR. (LOCAL). MARGARET JOHNSON, COORD; AMERICAN ASSOCIATION OF UNIVERSITY WOMEN; 520 2ND AVE NE; CLARION, IA 50525. (#106833-2).

JUNE 14 - 20, '76. PRAIRIE DAYS, BICENTENNIAL CELEBRATION IN CLARION. FESTIVAL, PARADE, TOUR AT MAIN ST. (LOCAL). DAVID ANDERSON, PRES; JAYCEES, LION'S, AMERICAN LEGION, SCHOOLS & CHAMBER OF COMMERCE; 102 N MAIN; CLARION, IA 50525. (#104221-33).

JUNE 20, '76. AIR SHOW. LIVE PERFORMANCE AT AIRPORT. (LOCAL). BOB BARTHOLOMAUS; CHAMBER OF COMMERCE; 303 1ST AVE NE; CLARION, IA 50525. (#106833-5).

JUNE 23, '76. RED, WHITE & BLUE FLOWER SHOW. EXHIBIT AT 1ST NATIONAL BANK. (LOCAL). MARGARET JOHNSON, CHMN; FEDERATED GARDEN CLUB; 520 2ND AVE NE; CLARION, IA 50525. (#106833-4).

JUNE 26, '76. HERITAGE OF THE PRAIRIE PARADE. PARADE AT MAIN ST. (LOCAL). MARGARET JOHNSON, COORD; CHAMBER OF COMMERCE; ROTARY/LIONS CLUBS; JAYCEES; 520 2ND AVE NE; CLARION, IA 50525. (#106833-1).

JUNE 26, '76. HERITAGE OF THE PRAIRIE FESTIVITIES. PARADE, EXHIBITS & DEMONSTRATIONS. AT CLARION HIGH SCHOOL. (LOCAL). MARGARET JOHNSON, COORD; CHAMBER OF COMMERCE; LIONS/ROTARY CLUBS; JAYCEES; 520 2ND AVE NE; CLARION, IA 50525. (#106833-3).

CLARKSVILLE

AVENUE OF FLAGS IN CLARKSVILLE, IA. DISPLAY OF FLAGS ON MAINSTREET. (LOCAL). HARVEY MILLER, CHAIRMAN; CLARKSVILLE BICENTENNIAL ORGANIZATION; 214 CHURCH ST; CLARKSVILLE, IA 50619. (#15649).

HISTORY OF TOWN OF CLARKSVILLE, IA. TOWN HISTORY WILL BE WRITTEN AND PUBLISHED. (LOCAL). HARVEY MILLER, CHAIRMAN; CLARKSVILLE BICENTENNIAL ORGANIZATION; 214 CHURCH ST; CLARKSVILLE, IA 50619. (#15648).

REPLACING DISEASED TREES, CLARKSVILLE, IA. PROJECT TO REPLACE TREES KILLED BY DISEASE ALONG TOWN STREETS. (LOCAL). HARVEY MILLER, CHAIRMAN; CLARKSVILLE BICENTENNIAL ORGANIZATION; 214 CHURCH ST; CLARKSVILLE, IA 50619. (#15647).

CLEAR LAKE

ARMOUR PUGH MEMORIAL PARK & SHELTER HOUSE - IA. FINANCED BY CLEAR LAKE ROTARY CLUB, CLEAR LAKE CITY COUNCIL, TRI-T SORORITY AND PRIVATE CITIZENS; MATCHING ARBA FUNDS. (LOCAL). T G BURNS, CHAIRMAN; CLEAR LAKE BICENTENNIAL COMMISSION; CLEAR LAKE, IA 50428. (#27145).

BANK ACCOUNT FOR CLEAR LAKE'S TRICENTENNIAL - IA. $200 WAS DEPOSITED INTO A BANK ACCOUNT, WITH THE INTEREST PAYABLE IN 2076 TO CLEAR LAKE TRICENTENNIAL COMMISSION FOR USE IN FINANCING THE TRICENTENNIAL CELEBRATION. (LOCAL). T G BURNS, CHAIRMAN; CLEAR LAKE BICENTENNIAL COMMISSION; CLEAR LAKE, IA 50428. (#27148).

BICENTENNIAL CALENDAR, CLEAR LAKE, IA. HISTORIC CALENDAR PUBLISHED & PRODUCED BY CLEAR LAKE BICENT COMMISSION, WITH ASSISTANCE FROM CLEAR LAKE HIGH SCHOOL'S ART

CLEAR LAKE — CONTINUED

CLASS. (LOCAL). T C BURNS, CHAIRMAN; CLEAR LAKE BICENTENNIAL COMMITTEE; CLEAR LAKE, IA 50429. (#17504).

TREE PLANTING IN CLEAR LAKE, IA. YOUNG SAPLINGS WILL BE PLACED ON CLEAR LAKE STREETS AND IN PARKS. (LOCAL). J C BURNS, CHAIRMAN; CLEAR LAKE BICENTENNIAL COMMISSION; 605 S SHORE DR; CLEAR LAKE, IA 50428. (#17503).

JAN 3 - 11, '76. BICENTENNIAL WINTER OLYMPUS. COMPETITION AT ON & NEAR THE LAKE. (LOCAL). STEVEN M WARD, CHMN; CLEAR LAKE AREA CHAMBER OF COMMERCE & NORTH IOWA WINTER OLYMPUS; PO BOX 188; CLEAR LAKE, IA 50428. (#200018-295).

JUNE 12 - 13, '76. BICENTENNIAL HYDROPLANE RACES. COMPETITION AT CLEAR LAKE. (LOCAL). DAVID CHENAULT, CHMN; 1976 HYDROPLANE RACES & CLEAR LAKE AREA CHAMBER OF COMMERCE; PO BOX 188; CLEAR LAKE, IA 50428. (#200018-297).

JUNE 27, '76. BICENTENNIAL REMEMBERANCE FESTIVAL. ALL DAY AND EVENING; BAND CONCERT OF CHOICE MUSIC OF OLD MASTERS. (LOCAL). T C BURNS, COORD; CLEAR LAKE BICENTENNIAL COMMITTEE; CLEAR LAKE, IA 50428. (#103342-24).

JULY 2 - 5, '76. BICENTENNIAL 4TH OF JULY FESTIVAL, PARADE & FIREWORKS. FESTIVAL, PARADE AT LAKESIDE ACTIVITIES - FIREWORKS OVER LAKE. (LOCAL). T G BURNS, CHMN; CLEAR LAKE AREA CHAMBER OF COMMERCE; CLEAR LAKE, IA 50428. (#200018-213).

JULY 3, '76. BICENTENNIAL CHARITY BALL. FESTIVAL. (LOCAL). T G BURNS, CHMN; TRI-T SORORITY & CLEAR LAKE BICENTENNIAL COMMISSION; CLEAR LAKE, IA 50428. (#200018-214).

JULY 4, '76. DEDICATION OF ARMOUR PUGH MEMORIAL PARK SHELTER HOUSE. CEREMONY. (LOCAL). T G BURNS, COORD; CLEAR LAKE BICENTENNIAL COMMISSION; CLEAR LAKE, IA 50428. (#27145-1).

JULY 23 - 26, '76. BICENTENNIAL GOVERNOR'S DAYS. FESTIVAL AT SURF BALLROOM & CONVENTION CENTER. (LOCAL). WAYNE OLTROGGE, CHMN; 1976 BICENT GOVERNOR'S DAY & CLEAR LAKE AREA CHAMBER OF COMMERCE; PO BOX 188; CLEAR LAKE, IA 50428. (#200018-296).

CLEARFIELD

HISTORIC U S FLAGS PROJECT - CLEARFIELD, IA. HISTORIC U S FLAGS WILL BE MADE BY PATIENTS IN THE CLEARFIELD NURSING HOME. (LOCAL). MRS RALPH KELLER, CHAIRMAN; CLEARFIELD NURSING HOME; CLEARFIELD, IA 50840. (#22227).

PARK IMPROVEMENT - CLEARFIELD, IA. PICNIC TABLES AND BENCHES MADE BY THE HIGH SCHOOL SHOP CLASSES WILL BE PLACED IN THE CITY PARK. (LOCAL). MRS RALPH KELLER, CHAIRMAN; CLEARFIELD LION-ELLS; CLEARFIELD, IA 50840. (#22226).

TREE PLANTING PROJECT - CLEARFIELD, IA. TREES WILL BE PLANTED IN THE PARK AND IN PRIVATE YARDS. (LOCAL). MRS RALPH KELLER, CHAIRMAN; CLEARFIELD BICENTENNIAL COMMITTEE; CLEARFIELD, IA 50840. (#22228).

JULY 4, '76. JULY 4TH FESTIVAL. COMPETITION, EXHIBIT, FESTIVAL, PARADE. (LOCAL). MRS RALPH KELLER, COORD; CLEARFIELD LIONS CLUB; CLEARFIELD, IA 50840. (#105970-1).

CLEGHORN

PAGES FROM THE PAST, CLEGHORN, IA. COMMEMORATIVE BOOK IS BEING PUBLISHED TO PRESERVE THE HISTORY OF THE COMMUNITIES. (LOCAL). ROBERT BYERS, PROJ COORDINATOR; MERIDEN-CLEGHORN BICENTENNIAL COMMITTEE; MERIDEN, IA 51037. (#21712).

SHADE FOR FUTURE - TREE PLANTING, CLEGHORN, IA. PLANTING TREES AT MERIDEN-CLEGHORN HIGH SCHOOL. (LOCAL). MRS DEWEY BEHRENS, COORD; AMERICAN LEGION AUXILIARY; MERIDEN, IA 51037. (#21713).

APR 5 - 7, '76. TEN SCORE THE AMERICAN WAY. LIVE PERFORMANCE AT CLEGHORN HIGH SCHOOL AUDITORIUM. (LOCAL). ROBERT BYERS, CHMN; MERIDEN-CLEGHORN COMMUNITIES; MERIDEN, IA 51037. (#105513-1).

CLERMONT

MAY 24 - OCT 31, '76. TOURS OF MONTAUK, PRESERVATION OF LARRABEE HOME, BUILT IN 1874. MONTAUK, A MAGNIFICENT HOME IS PRESERVED AS IT WAS WHEN ITS BUILDER WM. LARRABEE WAS ALIVE. LARRABEE SERVED IN THE IOWA SENATE 1868-1886 THEN WAS ELECTED GOVERNOR FOR TWO TERMS. HE WAS NATIONALLY KNOWN FOR HIS WORK ON THE FIRST INTERSTATE COMMERCE LAWS. AT MONTAUK MANSION. ONE MILE NE OF CLERMONT, IOWA ON HIGHWAY U.S. 18. (LOCAL). A. W. ALLEN; HISTORICAL GOVERNOR LARRABEE HOME, INC; 1015 FIRST AVE. S.E.; CEDAR RAPIDS, IA 52402. (#3681-1).

CLIMBING HILL

BAKE SALE, CLIMBING HALL, IA. FUND RAISING BAKE SALE FOR THE LITTLE LEAGUE BALL TEAM. (LOCAL). MRS ANNE E SHWARZ, CHAIRMAN; CLIMBING HILL GARDEN CLUB; CLIMBING HILL, IA 51015. (#21723).

CHRISTMAS TREES, CLUMBING HILL, IA. TREES WILL BE DECORATED & PLACED ON LIGHT POLES IN TOWN. (LOCAL). MRS ANNE E SCHWARZ, CHAIRMAN; CLIMBING HILL GARDEN CLUB; CLIMBING HILL, IA 51039. (#21725).

FLOWER PLANTING, CLIMBING HILL, IA. PETUNIAS WILL BE PLANTED AT CHURCHES & PLACES OF BUSINESS. (LOCAL). MRS ANNE E SCHWARZ, CHAIRMAN; CLIMBING HILL GARDEN CLUB; CLIMBING HILL, IA 51015. (#21724).

JAN 2 - DEC 31, '76. POTLUCK DINNER FOR SENIOR CITIZENS OF THE COMMUNITY. THESE DINNERS WILL BE HELD MONTHLY. AT ST JOHN'S LUTHERAN CHURCH. (LOCAL). MRS ANN E SCHWARE, COORD; SENIOR CITIZENS GROUP; CLIMBING HILL, IA 51015. (#105515-1).

JULY 4, '76. COMMUNITY PICNIC FOURTH OF JULY. FESTIVAL AT CLIMBING HILL SCHOOLGROUNDS. (LOCAL). MRS ANN E SCHWARZ, COORD; CLIMBING HILL COMMUNITY; CLIMBING HILL, IA 51015. (#105515-2).

CLINTON

CITY FLOAT IN CLINTON, IA. CREATION OF A SEMI-PERMANENT FLOAT FOR USE IN AREA PARADES IN 1976. (LOCAL). H EDWARD OBERMILLER, FLOAT CHAIRMAN; CREATION OF A SEMI-PERMANENT FLOAT FOR USE IN AREA PARADES IN 19; 1310 PERSHING; CLINTON, IA 52732. (#16803).

GIFT OF AMERICAN FLAGS, CLINTON, IA. DONATION OF 250 AMERICAN FLAGS TO THE CITY OF CLINTON FOR DISPLAY ON NATIONAL HOLIDAYS. (LOCAL). LILLIAN JUSTIS, REPRESENTATIVE; DAUGHTERS OF THE AMERICAN REVOLUTION; 524 5TH AVE S; CLINTON, IA 52732. (#16804).

HISTORIC COLORING BOOK, CLINTON, IA. FUND-RAISING PROJECT: COLORING BOOK WITH LOCAL AND NATIONAL HISTORIC PICTURES. (LOCAL). DON STEEN, HORIZONS COMMITTEE CHAIRMAN; CITY OF CLINTON AMERICAN REVOLUTION BICENTENNIAL COMMISSION; 519 MEADOWVIEW DR; CLINTON, IA 52732. (#16805).

INVESTMENT IN TRICENTENNIAL, CLINTON, IA. ESTABLISHMENT OF A BLOOD SAVINGS ACCOUNT IN 1976 WOULD RESULT IN $140,000 TO HELP CLINTON FINANCE THE TRICENTENNIAL IN 2076. (LOCAL). DON STEEN, HORIZONS COMMITTEE CHAIRMAN; CITY OF CLINTON AMERICAN REVOLUTION BICENTENNIAL COMMISSION; 519 MEADOWVIEW DR; CLINTON, IA 52732. (#16801).

TIME CAPSULE IN CLINTON, IA. COMPLETE COLLECTION OF BICENTENNIAL YEAR MEMORABILIA TO BE SEALED AWAY FOR FUTURE GENERATIONS. (LOCAL). DON STEEN, HORIZONS COMMITTEE CHAIRMAN; CITY OF CLINTON AMERICAN REVOLUTION BICENTENNIAL COMMISSION; 519 MEADOWVIEW DR; CLINTON, IA 52732. (#16802).

MAY 30, '75. CLINTON HISTORICAL MUSEUM OPENING. OPENING. (LOCAL). ROBERT SOESBE, CHAIRMAN; CLINTON HISTORICAL SOCIETY; 900 S 6TH ST; CLINTON, IA 52732. (#200018-14).

NOV 1, '75. BICENTENNIAL CONCERT OF AMERICAN MUSIC WITH GUEST CONDUCTOR. LIVE PERFORMANCE AT VERNON C COOK LITTLE THEATRE, CLINTON HIGH SCHOOL, 8 AVE S AT S 9 ST. (LOCAL). MARIE DUDLEY, CHMN; CLINTON SYMPHONY ORCHESTRA; 1901 CIRCLE DR S; CLINTON, IA 52732. (#103053-5).

NOV 15 - 16, '75. ART FAIR. FAIR AT BOAT CLUB, RIVERFRONT DR. (LOCAL). HORTENSE BLAKE, CHMN; CLINTON ART ASSOCIATION; 703 ELMHURST; CLINTON, IA 52732. (#103053-4).

JAN 16 - 18, '76. SAINT STEPHEN'S LUTHERAN CHURCH CENTENNIAL SERVICES & BANQUET. CEREMONY. (LOCAL). PASTOR EUGENE HENRY; SAINT STEPHEN'S LUTHERAN CHURCH; 1529 SPRING VALLEY; CLINTON, IA 52732. (#104841-1).

FEB 14, '76. YOUNG ARTISTS DEBUT SYMPHONY. LIVE PERFORMANCE AT CLINTON HIGH SCHOOL, VERNON COOK THEATER. (LOCAL). D H DUDLEY, BUSINESS MGR; CLINTON SYMPHONY ORCHESTRA; PO BOX 536; CLINTON, IA 52732. (#103104-2).

FEB 28, '76. BICENTENNIAL BALL. FESTIVAL AT VALLEY OAKS COUNTRY CLUB. (LOCAL). JUDY POTTS, CHMN; CLINTON JUNIOR WOMENS CLUB; 1128 WILLANY DR; CLINTON, IA 52732. (#103053-3).

MAR 11 - 13, '76. '1776' MUSICAL PLAY. LIVE PERFORMANCE AT VERNON COOK LITTLE THEATRE, CLINTON HIGH SCHOOL, 8TH AVE S. (LOCAL). PRINCIPAL; CLINTON HIGH SCHOOL; CLINTON, IA 52732. (#200018-12).

MAR 17, '76. SPIRIT OF '76 FASHION SHOW. LIVE PERFORMANCE AT MERCY HOSPITAL AUDITORIUM, N 4TH ST. (LOCAL). MRS HELEN SCHMIDT, COORD; MERCY HOSPITAL AUXILIARY; CLINTON, IA 52732. (#200018-13).

MAR 20, '76. TOWN MEETING '76. A NATIONALLY RECOGNIZED ONE-DAY FORUM CREATED BY THE INSTITUTE OF CULTURAL AFFAIRS. AT CLINTON COMMUNITY COLLEGE, 1000 LINCOLN BLVD. (LOCAL). ERNEST SVENSON; CITY OF CLINTON ARBC; 1352 MAIN ST; CLINTON, IA 52732. (#103053-1).

MAR 26, '76. AMERICA - A MULTI-MEDIA SHOW OF ONE MAN'S VIEW OF HIS COUNTRY. LIVE PERFORMANCE AT 7TH AVE S. (LOCAL). MS GAIL RUSSELL, COORD; YWCA; YWCA, 7TH AVE S; CLINTON, IA 52732. (#105962-1).

MAY 2, '76. SPIRIT OF '76 GIRL SCOUT ACTIVITIES DISPLAY AND DEMONSTRATIONS. EXHIBIT AT EAGLE POINT PARK. (LOCAL). MRS AL WOODS, COORD; GIRL SCOUTS OF AMERICA - MISSISSIPPI VALLEY COUNCIL; 3532 PERSHING; CLINTON, IA 52732. (#200018-15).

MAY 16, '76. CONDUCTOR'S CHOICE SYMPHONY. LIVE PERFORMANCE AT CLINTON HIGH SCHOOL, VERNON COOK THEATER. (LOCAL). D H DUDLEY, BUSINESS MGR; CLINTON SYMPHONY ORCHESTRA; PO BOX 536; CLINTON, IA 52732. (#103104-3).

JUNE 6, '76. BICENTENNIAL TEA TO INTRODUCE RIVERBOAT DAYS QUEEN CANDIDATES. TOPICS INCLUDE: 'THE AMERICAN SELF-IMAGE & THE STRUGGLE FOR INDEPENDENCE'; 'AMERICAN & ROMANIAN INDEPENDENCE'; 'THE IMPACT OF INDEPENENCE MOVEMENTS ON THE 19TH CENTURY'; & 'INDEPENDENCE IN EASTERN EUROPE TODAY'. AT HOLIDAY INN, LINCOLNWAY. (LOCAL). JAN PETERSEN, PROJ CHMN; CITY OF CLINTON AMERICAN REVOLUTION BICENTENNIAL COMMISSION; 831 6TH AVE S; CLINTON, IA 52732. (#108851-1).

JUNE 6, '76. YWCA BICENTENNIAL SQUARE DANCE. LIVE PERFORMANCE AT MOOSE HOME 1936 LINCOLNWAY HWY 30 WEST. (ST-WIDE). MS BARB MIARS DIR; YWCA; YWCA 317 7TH AV SOUTH; CLINTON, IA 52732. (#107688-2).

JUNE 30 - AUG 7, '76. TRANSFER OF LETTER FROM PONY EXPRESS TO CANOE. LETTER FROM PONY EXPRESS HQ, WASHINGTON, TO BE DROPPED IN CLINTON ON 6/30/76 FOR TRANSFER TO CARDINAL CANOE DELEGATION AS IT PASSES CLINTON 7/26/76 FOR DELIVERY TO ST LOUIS ON 8/7/76. (REGN'L). CAROLYN R GRIMES, CHMN; CITY OF CLINTON AMERICAN REVOLUTION BICENTENNIAL COMMISSION; 530 30TH AVE N; CLINTON, IA 52732. (#108851-2).

JULY 2 - 4, '76. RIVERBOAT DAYS. FESTIVAL AT RIVERVIEW PARK, RIVERFRONT DR. (LOCAL). STEPHEN LEVIN, CHMN; RIVERBOAT DAYS COMMITTEE; 716 5TH ST; CLINTON, IA 52732. (#103053-2).

CLUTIER

HERITAGE HOUSE IN CITY PARK, CLUTIER, IA. RESTORING AN OLD HOME AND MOVING IT TO CITY PARK. (LOCAL). JOHN SIENKNECHT, CHAIRMAN; CLUTIER BICENTENNIAL CLUB; MAIN ST; CLUTIER, IA 52217. (#22492).

AUG 14, '76. GOLDEN MEMORIES. EXHIBIT, PARADE AT MAIN ST, PARK AREA. (LOCAL). JOHN SIENKNECHT, CHMN; CLUTIER BICENTENNIAL CLUB; MAIN ST; CLUTIER, IA 52217. (#106159-1).

COIN

ORAL HISTORY, COIN, IA. TAPE RECORDING OF ELDERLY EXPERIENCES. (LOCAL). DOROTHY MANNASMITH, CHAIRMAN; COIN BICENTENNIAL COMMITTEE; COIN, IA 51636. (#21012).

RESTORE CITY PARK, COIN, IA. THE CITY PARK IS BEING CLEANED AND RE-DEVELOPED. (LOCAL). MRS ROY HUTCHISON, CHAIRMAN; COIN FEDERATION OF WOMEN'S CLUB; COIN, IA 51636. (#21013).

'200 STRONG' - CHORAL CONCERT. CHORUS MADE UP OF MEMBERS OF S PAGE BAND, FB CHORUS, 4H CLUB & CHURCH CHOIRS WILL PERFORM. (LOCAL). DOROTHY MANNASMITH, CHMN; COIN BICENTENNIAL COMMITTEE; COIN, IA 51636. (#105132-1).

COLESBURG

MUSEUM PROJECT, COLESBURG, IA. THE TOWN'S OLDEST BUILDING WILL BE CONVERTED INTO A MUSEUM. (LOCAL). BETHEL BROWN, PROJ DIRECTOR; COLESBURG BICENTENNIAL COMMITTEE; BOX 163; COLESBURG, IA 52035. (#20363).

TREE PLANTING, COLESBURG, IA. TREES WILL BE PLANTED THROUGHOUT COLESBURG. (LOCAL). BETHEL BROWN, PROJ DIRECTOR; COLESBURG BICENTENNIAL COMMITTEE; BOX 163; COLESBURG, IA 52035. (#20364).

COLLEGE SPG

COLLEGE SPRINGS BICENTENNIAL BOOKLET, IA. THE RESEARCH AND REPORT OF COLLEGE SPRINGS HERITAGE AND PRESENT BICENTENNIAL YEAR WILL BE PUBLISHED IN BOOKLET FORM. (LOCAL). WANDA A HAMM, CHAIRPERSON; COLLEGE SPRINGS BICENTENNIAL COMMITTEE; COLLEGE SPG, IA 51637. (#28640).

APR 3, '76. COLLEGE SPRINGS BICENTENNIAL FLAG PRESENTATION. SPECIALS BY CHURCH GROUPS & HIGH SCHOOL STUDENTS. SPECIAL SELECTIONS BY SOUTH PAGE HIGH SCHOOL BAND. SPECIAL HERITAGE & HISTORICAL REPORT BY MEMBER OF COMMITTEE. BICENTENNIAL FLAG PRESENTED BY KENNETH FULK. AT SOUTH PAGE HIGH SCHOOL AUDITORIUM. (LOCAL). WANDA A HAMM, CHAIRMAN; COLLEGE SPRINGS BICENTENNIAL COMMISSION GROUP; COLLEGE SPRGS, IA 51637. (#200018-257).

COLO

CITY PARK, COLO, IA. DEVELOPMENT OF CITY PARK ADJACENT TO SENIOR CITIZENS APARTMENT. (LOCAL). DICK HAMILTON, COORDINATOR; COLO BETTERMENT COUNCIL; COLO, IA 50056. (#23180).

TOWN HISTORY PUBLISHED, COLO, IA. TOWN HISTORY OF COLO TO BE PUBLISHED. (LOCAL). JOHN CERKA, COORDINATOR; COLO BICENTENNIAL COMMITTEE; COLO, IA 50056. (#23181).

APR 3, '76. CONSIGNMENT AUCTION. EXHIBIT AT COLO ST. (LOCAL). LARRY JOHNSON, COORD; COLO BICENTENNIAL COMMITTEE; RURAL RT; COLO, IA 50056. (#106394-2).

JUNE 26, '76. GENERAL FESTIVAL. SPORTS, ARTS & CRAFTS EXHIBITS, ETC. (LOCAL). BOB DODD, COORD; COLO BICENTENNIAL COMMITTEE; COLO, IA 50056. (#106394-1).

COLUMBUS JCT

LOUISA COUNTY HERITAGE COOKBOOK, COLUMBUS JCT, IA. OLD FAMILY RECIPES FROM LOUISA COUNTY CITIZENS WILL BE COLLECTED AND PUBLISHED IN A HERITAGE COOKBOOK. (LOCAL). KEITH JORDON, COOKBOOK CHMN; LOUISA COUNTY BICENTENNIAL COMMITTEE; LETTS, IA 52754. (#21427).

PRESERVATION OF PLEASANT VIEW SCHOOL, IA. THE PLEASANT VIEW RURAL SCHOOL, DONATED TO THE LOUISA COUNTY BICENTENNIAL COMMITTEE BY THE B H SHEARER FAMILY, WILL BE MOVED FROM ITS PRESENT LOCATION TO COUNTY FAIRGROUNDS, WHERE IT WILL BE PRESERVED. (LOCAL). MARY BETH CAREY, CO-CHAIRMAN; LOUISA COUNTY BICENTENNIAL COMMITTEE; 129 HICKORY DR; COLUMBUS JCT, IA 52738. (#19441).

CONRAD

BELL MONUMENT IN CONRAD, IA. THE OLD WATER HOUSE BELL WILL BE REMOVED AND MOUNTED WITH A PLAQUE. (LOCAL). E E JEBOUSIK, CHAIRMAN; BEAMAN-CONRAD JAYCEES; CONRAD, IA 50621. (#13879).

BICENTENNIAL FLOWERS, CONRAD, IA. THE CHILD STUDY CLUB WILL DISTRIBUTE RED, WHITE & BLUE FLOWERS WITH A BICENTENNIAL DESIGN. (LOCAL). LOIS KRUSE, PROJ DIRECTOR; CHILD STUDY CLUB; MAPLE ST; CONRAD, IA 50621. (#13881).

BICENTENNIAL PROJECT IN CONRAD, IA. LITTER CANS WERE PAINTED RED, WHITE AND BLUE BY THE JAYCEES WIVES. (LOCAL). DEBBIE STEVA BEAMAN, PROJ DIRECTOR; JAYCEES WIVES; CONRAD, IA 50621. (#13882).

BICENTENNIAL QUILT IN CONRAD, IA. PROJECT IS TO MAKE A BICENTENNIAL QUILT IN COMMEMORATION OF 50 YEARS OF FOUNDING OF CLUB. (LOCAL). MILDRED KATZER, PROJ DIRECTOR; FELIX PEPPY PEPPERS; CONRAD, IA 50621. (#13883).

THE CONRAD RECORD BICENTENNIAL COVERAGE - NBMRP. PROVIDES EXTENSIVE COVERAGE OF ACTIVITIES, MEETINGS & EFFORTS OF CONRAD BICENTENNIAL COMMITTEE. ALSO PUBLISHES SERIES ON SIGNERS OF DECLARATION & A SERIES '1776 IMPORTANT THEN, IMPORTANT NOW 1976'. (LOCAL). E E JEBOUSEK, EDITOR; THE CONRAD RECORD; 108 N MAIN; CONRAD, IA 50621. (#22107).

CONRAD'S WOMEN'S CLUB BICENTENNIAL PROJECT, IA. THE CONRAD WOMEN'S CLUB WILL DISTRIBUTE CALENDARS WITH PICTURES OF CONRAD AND PLANT TREES IN THE PARK. (LOCAL). LOANA CONRAD, PROJ DIRECTOR; CONRAD WOMEN'S CLUB; CONRAD, IA 50621. (#13880).

DRAMA CLUB COMMUNITY PARTICIPATION PROJ, IA. THE DRAMA CLUB WILL SPONSOR A FULL DAY'S ACTIVITY FOR COMMUNITY PARTICIPATION. (LOCAL). DORIS MILLS, PROJ DIRECTOR; 1776 DRAMA CLUB WHISTLE STOP PLAYERS; CONRAD, IA 50621. (#13878).

NEWSPAPER FILES FROM CONRAD, IA. 96 YEARS OF CONRAD NEWSPAPER FILES WERE MICROFILMED & PRESENTED TO THE PUBLIC LIBRARY BY THE LIONS CLUB. (LOCAL). E JEBOUSEK, PROJ CHAIRMAN; THE CONRAD RECORD; 208 N MAIN; CONRAD, IA 50621. (#13884).

AUG 6 - 8, '76. CONRAD BICENTENNIAL CELEBRATION. CONRAD CELEBRATES HER FREEDOM FOR THREE BIG DAYS! ON SUNDAY THERE WILL BE A RELIGIOUS PROGRAM WITH A DINNER IN A BEAUTIFUL GROVE, & A PROGRAM FOLLOWING. HUGE ALUMNI REUNION ON AUGUST 7TH. (LOCAL). DORIS MILLS, PGM MGR; CONRAD BICENTENNIAL COMMISSION; CONRAD, IA 50621. (#101391-1).

CONROY

LOOKING BACK, CONROY, IA. COLLECTING AND ASSEMBLING HISTORIC MATERIALS FOR MICROFILMING. (LOCAL). VERNE FOLKMANN, PROJ CHAIRMAN; CONROY BICENTENNIAL COMMITTEE; CONROY, IA 52220. (#14536).

PARK PROJECT IN CONROY, IA. DEVELOPE PARK & WILDLIFE AREAS. (LOCAL). VERNE FOLKMANN, PROJ CHAIRMAN; CONROY BICENTENNIAL COMMITTEE; CONROY, IA 52220. (#14535).

CORALVILLE

POW-MIA NATIONAL MUSEUM LIBRARY & PARK, IA. A MUSEUM LIBRARY & PARK DEDICATED TO POW'S & MIA'S OF ALL MILITARY ACTIONS IN WHICH THE U S PARTICIPATED. RECORDS & MEMORABILIA OF THE POW'S & MIA'S WILL BE STORED & DISPLAYED. (LOCAL). WILLIAM POTTER, PRESIDENT; NATIONAL POW-MIA MEMORIAL FOUNDATION; PO BOX 5941; CORALVILLE, IA 52241. (#23980).

RESTORATION OF THE 1876 CORALVILLE SCHOOL IN IOWA. THE OLD CORALVILLE SCHOOLHOUSE WILL BE RESTORED FOR USE AS THE JOHNSON COUNTY HERITAGE MUSEUM. (LOCAL). S M MCCARTHY, DIRECTOR; JOHNSON COUNTY HISTORICAL SOCIETY; 405 2ND AVE; CORALVILLE, IA 52241. (#7789).

JUNE 19 - 20, '76. COUNTY FAIR, THIEVES MARKET, BEER GARDEN AND DANCE. FAIR WITH EXHIBITS, CRAFTSMEN, BOOTHS, PINK LEMONADE AND POPCORN STAND, BALLOONS, ANIMALS, QUILT DISPLAY, MUSIC IN THE PARK, BEER GARDEN. EVENING ADULT DANCE, MUSIC OF THE 30'S & 40'S. SUNDAY ECUMENICAL SERVICE, COFFEE & DONUTS, FLAG PRESENTATION & JR OLYMPICS. AT S T MORRISON PARK, CITY HALL. (LOCAL). JUDY ANTILL, CHMN; BICENTENNIAL COMMITTEE & CORALVILLE BUSINESSES; 201 10TH AVE; CORALVILLE, IA 52241. (#200018-22).

JUNE 19 - 20, '76. OLDER ARTS AND CRAFTS FAIR. QUILTING, SPINNING, CHAIR CANING, RUG LOOMING, CIDER MAKING, MACRAME SOAP MAKING, TOUR MUSEUM, TIN TYPE PHOTOS TAKEN, OLD TIME MOVIES AND HISTORICAL SLIDES. 7/5 ONLY - ICE CREAM SOCIAL AND ANTIQUE CAR DISPLAY. AT HERITAGE MUSEUM, 105 2ND AVE. (LOCAL). MRS A B CLEMENCE, PRES; JOHNSON COUNTY HISTORICAL SOCIETY; 620 9TH AVE; CORALVILLE, IA 52241. (#200018-23).

JUNE 26, '76. PARADE, TOWN MEETING, FASHIONS THRU THE YEARS. CEREMONY, FESTIVAL, PARADE, LIVE PERFORMANCE AT S T MORRISON PARK. (LOCAL). MRS JUDY ANTILL, CHMN; BICENTENNIAL COMMITTEE AND CORALVILLE BUSINESSMEN; 701 10TH AVE; CORALVILLE, IA 52241. (#200018-24).

CORNING

ICARIAN SCHOOL HOUSE, CORNING, IA. THE RESTORATION OF A ONE ROOM SCHOOL HOUSE. (LOCAL). MRS HARRY SICKLER, PROJ DIRECTOR; ADAMS HISTORICAL SOCIETY; CORNING, IA 50841. (#13183).

JAIL HOUSE RESTORATION IN CORNING, IA. RESTORATION OF 1877 ADAMS COUNTY JAIL, CONVERTING IT TO A HISTORICAL MUSEUM. (LOCAL). MRS HARRY SICKLER, PROJ DIRECTOR; ADAMS HISTORICAL SOCIETY; CORNING, IA 50841. (#13185).

LAKE ICARIAN - PROJ OF CORNING, IA. LAKE ICARIAN WILL BE BUILT FOR WATER SUPPLY, CONSERVATION AND RECREATION. (LOCAL). LEE ELLIOTT, PROJ DIRECTOR; CITY OF CORNING; CITY HALL; CORNING, IA 50841. (#12694).

SPRING LAKE BEAUTIFICATION IN CORNING, IA. LANDSCAPING AND PICNIC FACILITIES ARE PART OF THE PLANS TO BEAUTIFY SPRING LAKE PARK. (LOCAL). JIM KEARNS, PROJ DIRECTOR; CORNING BICENTENNIAL COMMISSION; CORNING POST OFFICE; CORNING, IA 50841. (#13184).

MAY 6, '76. SALAD LUNCHEON. FESTIVAL AT ST PATRICKS PARISH CENTER. (LOCAL). ELEANOR KELLY, COORD; ST PATRICKS SOCIETY; RT #4; CORNING, IA 50841. (#200018-18).

MAY 26, '76. TOUR OF ICARIAN SCHOOL. TOUR AT ICARIAN SCHOOLHOUSE. (LOCAL). LOIS SICKLER, CHAIRPERSON; HISTORICAL SOCIETY; 907 NODAWAY; CORNING, IA 50841. (#107983-2).

JUNE 24, '76. HISTORICAL BOSTON TEA PARTY SITE. TOUR AT JAIL HOUSE MUSEUM, 1000 BENTON. (LOCAL). LOIS SICKLER, CHWMN; CORNING BICENTENNIAL COMMITTEE; 907 NODAWAY ST; CORNING, IA 50841. (#105611-6).

JULY 4, '76. 4TH OF JULY '76. TOUR AT FAIRGROUNDS. (LOCAL). JIM KEARNS, PROJ DIR; CORNING BICENTENNIAL; CORNING, IA 50841. (#100811-1).

JULY 16, '76. 'CRAZY DAYS' AND KIDDIE PARADE. FESTIVAL, PARADE AT MAIN ST. (LOCAL). DEAN DAVIS, COORDINATOR; CORNING BICENTENNIAL COMMITTEE AND CHAMBER COMMERCE; CORNING, IA 50841. (#105611-4).

JULY 18, '76. COMMUNITY CHORUS. LIVE PERFORMANCE AT CENTRAL PARK, PARKING ON MAIN STREET. (LOCAL). LOIS SICKLER, CHWMN; CORNING BICENTENNIAL COMMITTEE; 907 NODOWAY ST; CORNING, IA 50841. (#105611-3).

AUG 15, '76. BAND CONCERT AND ICE CREAM SOCIAL. FESTIVAL. (LOCAL). LOIS SICKLER, CHWMN; CORNING BICENTENNIAL COMMITTEE; 907 NODOWAY ST; CORNING, IA 50841. (#105611-1).

SEPT 10, '76. FLEA MARKET. EXHIBIT, FESTIVAL AT MAIN ST. (LOCAL). MRS DEAN DAVIS, COORD; HOME ECONOMICS EXTENSION & CHAMBER COMMERCE; R 4; CORNING, IA 50841. (#107983-1).

SEPT 15, '76. QUILTS, PAST AND PRESENT - EXHIBIT. EXHIBIT. (LOCAL). LOIS SICKLER, CHWMN; CORNING BICENTENNIAL COMMITTEE & HISTORICAL SOCIETY; 907 NODOWAY ST; CORNING, IA 50841. (#105611-2).

OCT 2, '76. DEDICATION OF HISTORICAL JAIL HOUSE. CEREMONY. (LOCAL). LOIS SICKLER, CHAIRPERSON; ADAMS CO BICENTENNIAL COMMITTEE; 907 NODAWAY ST; CORNING, IA 50841. (#109021-1).

OCT 26, '76. BICENTENNIAL TRIBUTE TO HIGH SCHOOL STUDENTS. CEREMONY. (LOCAL). LOIS SICKLER, CHAIRPERSON; ADAMS CO BICENTENNIAL COMMITTEE; 907 NODAWAY ST; CORNING, IA 50841. (#109021-2).

OCT '76. HOMECOMING PARADE. PARADE. (LOCAL). LOIS SICKLER, CHWMN; CORNING BICENTENNIAL COMMITTEE; 907 NODAWAY; CORNING, IA 50841. (#105611-8).

NOV 12 - 14, '76. MUSICAL PRODUCTION BY ICARIAN PLAYERS - 'OF THEE I SING'. LIVE PERFORMANCE AT HIGH SCHOOL AUDITORIUM, CORNING, IA. (LOCAL). DOUGLAS SICKLER, COORD; CORNING BICENTENNIAL COMMITTEE; 908 6TH ST; CORNING, IA 50841. (#105611-7).

CORRECTIONVLE

CORRECTIONVILLE IOWA, HISTORY BOOK. COMPILING HISTORY OF COMMUNITY; WILL COVER TIME FROM EARLY SETTLERS. (LOCAL). GAYLE JACOBS, CHAIRPERSON; CORRECTIONVILLE BICENTENNIAL COMMITTEE; CORRECTIONVLE, IA 51016. (#24464).

FLAGS, PROCUREMENT & INSTALLATION, IA. APPROPRIATION OF NEW 50 STAR FLAGS THROUGH DRIVES AND PLEDGES FROM ALL COMMUNITY MEMBERS. FLAGS TO BE DISPLAYED ON TOWN STREETS ON ALL PATRIOTIC AND HISTORIC OCCASIONS. (LOCAL). RAMON FLEMMING, COMMANDER; AMERICAN LEGION, MUMFORD MOON POST 79; RURAL ROUTE #2; CORRECTIONVLE, IA 51016. (#24462).

FORT CORRECTIONVILLE, IA. REPRODUCTION OF THE ORIGINAL FORT IN LITTLE SIOUX COUNTY PARK TWO MILES SOUTH OF CORRECTIONVILLE. (LOCAL). LINN R COOK, PARK OFFICER; WOODBURY COUNTY BICENTENNIAL COMMITTEE; CORRECTIONVLE, IA 51016. (#24461).

HOUSE NUMBERING PROJ, CORRECTIONVILLE, IA. UNNUMBERED HOUSES WILL BE NUMBERED. (LOCAL). E A CHRISTIANSEN, PROJ CHAIRMAN; CHAMBER OF COMMERCE; CORRECTIONVLE, IA 51016. (#24463).

LITTLE SIOUX PARK - FORT CORRECTIONVILLE, IA. A SCHOOLHOUSE MUSEUM WILL BE PLACED IN LITTLE SIOUX PARK. (LOCAL). E A CHRISTENSEN, PRESIDENT; CORRECTIONVILLE CHAMBER OF COMMERCE; CORRECTIONVL, IA 51016. (#24053).

LOG CABIN - CORRECTIONVILLE, IA. LOG CABIN, INSPIRED BY THE 'LITTLE HOUSE ON THE PRAIRIE' SERIES IS BEING BUILT ON A PRIVATELY OWNED FARM. THE HOUSE WILL BE COMPLETELY FURNISHED WITH AUTHENTIC ITEMS OF THAT PERIOD. (LOCAL). MAX FLATHERS, INDIVIDUAL; RFD 1; CORRECTIONVL, IA 51016. (#25658).

OCT 19, '75. COMMUNICATION ON GOVERNMENT. LAITY DAY, HONORING STATE REPRESENTATIVE FOR SERVICE TO CHURCH, COMMUNITY AND STATE. (LOCAL). VIOLET ALTEMUS, CHMN; GRACE UNITED METHODIST CHURCH COUNCIL OF MINISTRIES; CORRECTIONVL, IA 51016. (#106892-1).

MAR 13, '76. PANCAKE DAY. FESTIVAL AT COMMUNITY BUILDING. (LOCAL). E A CHRISTIANSEN, COORD; CHAMBER OF COMMERCE; CORRECTIONVL, IA 51016. (#200018-25).

MAY 31, '76. MEMORIAL DAY PARADE AND GRAVESIDE CEREMONIES. THE PARADES WILL BE CONDUCTED ON THE STREETS OF CORRECTIONVILLE AND CUSHING, IA & CEREMONIES WILL BE CONDUCTED AT THE RESPECTIVE TOWN CEMETERIES TO INCLUDE COLORS, MUSIC, MEMORIAL PRAYER, FIRING SQUAD & TAPS. AT MAIN STREETS IN CORRECTIONVILLE AND CUSHING, IA. (LOCAL). RAMON FLEMMING, CMDR; AMERICAN LEGION, VFW, BOY SCOUTS, GIRL SCOUTS AND SCHOOL BAND; RR #2; CORRECTIONVL, IA 51016. (#106931-1).

JULY 4 - 5, '76. 4TH OF JULY CELEBRATION. FESTIVAL, PARADE, LIVE PERFORMANCE AT COPELAND PARK AND ATHLETIC FIELD. (LOCAL). E A CHRISTIANSEN, COORD; CHAMBER OF COMMERCE; CORRECTIONVL, IA 51016. (#106891-1).

CORWITH

PARK IMPROVEMENT - CORWITH, IA. PLANT TREES & BULBS, REPAIR PLAYGROUND EQUIPMENT AND REMOVE DEAD TREES. (LOCAL). MRS RAY FREY, PRESIDENT; IOWANA FEDERATED WOMEN'S CLUB; CORWITH, IA 50430. (#24871).

JULY 10, '76. TOWN AND COUNTRY DAY. COMPETITION, EXHIBIT, FESTIVAL, PARADE, LIVE PERFORMANCE AT PARK. (LOCAL). LARRY MAIN; CORWITH COMMUNITY CLUB; CORWITH, IA 50430. (#107688-14).

CORYDON

ADDITION TO HISTORICAL SOCIETY MUSEUM IN IOWA. BUILDING ADDITION TO HOUSE FARM MACHINERY & GENEALOGY LIBRARY. (LOCAL). AMY ROBERTSON, PRESIDENT; WAYNE COUNTY HISTORICAL MUSEUM; CORYDON, IA 50060. (#6120). **ARBA GRANTEE.**

COMMUNITY DEVELOPMENT PROJ OF CORYDON, IA. COMMUNITY DEVELOPMENT PROJECTS INCLUDE TREE PLANTING, BAND SHELTER AND A FESTIVAL USA THEME AT THE OLD SETTLERS CELEBRATION. (LOCAL). HELEN STOFFER, PRESIDENT; BAND PARENTS/LIONS CLUB; CORYDON, IA 50060. (#15835).

'RED ROCK LINE' IN CORYDON, IA. ERECTION OF SIGNS DESIGNATING THE HISTORIC 'RED ROCK LINE' IN WAYNE AND HARDIN COUNTIES. (ST-WIDE). JEAN DENT, COORDINATOR; DAUGHTERS OF THE AMERICAN REVOLUTION; CORYDON, IA 50060. (#13107).

JULY 4, '76. WAYNE COUNTY 4TH OF JULY CELEBRATION. AN OLD-FASHIONED COUNTY-WIDE 4TH OF JULY CELEBRATION IN 1976. AT WAYNE COUNTY FAIR GROUNDS. (LOCAL). BEN GRISMORE, REP; WAYNE COUNTY BICENTENNIAL COMMITTEE; WAYNE BICENT COMMITTEE; CORYDON, IA 50060. (#13068-1).

COUNCIL BLUFF

AMERICAN BICENTENNIAL THEMES HISTORY COURSE, IA. A COLLEGE COURSE REVIEWING THE ROOTS OF AMERICAN TRADITIONS. (LOCAL). DR MARTIN P WOLF, COORDINATOR; IOWA WESTERN COMMUNITY COLLEGE; 2700 COLLEGE RD; COUNCIL BLF, IA 51501. (#25159).

BICENTENNIAL ORAL HISTORY PROJECT, COUNCIL BLF, IA. TAPE RECORDINGS OF REFLECTIONS OF SENIOR CITIZENS. (LOCAL). DR MARTIN P WOLF, COORDINATOR; IOWA WESTERN COMMUNITY COLLEGE; 2700 COLLEGE RD; COUNCIL BLF, IA 51501. (#25142).

COUNCIL BLUFFS MONUMENT - IA. A MONUMENT WAS ERECTED AT THE CITY LIMITS DESIGNATING THE NAME OF THE COMMUNITY AND THE FACT THAT IT IS A BICENTENNIAL COMMUNITY. (LOCAL). DOROTHY BUCKINGHAM, DIRECTOR; COUNCIL BLUFFS BICENTENNIAL COMMITTEE; 302 FIRST FED SAVINGS & LOAN; COUNCIL BLUFF, IA 51501. (#28647).

COUNCIL BLUFF—CONTINUED

FRIENDSHIP PARK - PROJ OF COUNCIL BLUFFS, IA. THIS PARK WILL BE A PART OF THE FRIENDSHIP FOUNTAIN PROJECT AND WILL TIE IN WITH THE BIKE TRAILS THAT ARE PLANNED. (LOCAL). LES HICKS, DIRECTOR; PARKS AND RECREATION DEPARTMENT; COUNCIL BLF, IA 51501. (#16052). **ARBA GRANTEE.**

INTER-DISCIPLINARY STUDIES - COUNCIL BLUFF, IA. A BICENTENNIAL COURSE TAUGHT IN TWO WEEK CYCLES; AREAS TO BE COVERED ARE: HISTORY, SPEECH-DRAMA, GOVERNMENT, ART, MUSIC, SOCIAL CUSTOMS, LITERATURE, PRINTING; VARIETY SHOW TO TEACH SIGNIFICANCE OF IOWA. (LOCAL). REV PAUL A MONAHAN, PRINCIPAL; ST ALBERT'S CENTRAL CATHOLIC HIGH SCHOOL; 400 GLEASON AVE; COUNCIL BLUFF, IA 51501. (#22387).

IOWA-NEBRASKA BICENTENNIAL FRIENDSHIP FOUNTAIN. THE FOUNTAIN WILL SYMBOLIZE IOWA-NEBRASKA FRIENDSHIP REVITALIZED BY THE MISSOURI RIVERFRONT DEVELOPMENT PROJECT DESIGNED TO DEVELOP THE TOTAL PHYSICAL AND HUMAN RESOURCES OF THE VALLEY. (REGN'L). EUGENE A LEAHY, PRESIDENT; RIVERFRONT COMMUNITIES DEVELOPMENT FOUNDATION; 2020 FIRST NATIONAL CENTER; OMAHA, NE 68102. (#1302). **ARBA GRANTEE.**

MUSICAL PRODUCTION OF 'PURLIE' - COUNCIL BLUFF, IA. PRODUCTION OF THE MUSICAL COMEDY 'PURLIE' BY THE CHANTICLEER, INC. (LOCAL). ROBERT W KNOX, COORDINATOR; CHANTICLEER, INC; 830 FRANKLIN AVE, PO BOX 304; COUNCIL BLUFF, IA 51501. (#22283). **ARBA GRANTEE.**

JULY 4, '75. FIREWORKS DISPLAY IN COUNCIL BLUFFS, IOWA. FIREWORKS DISPLAY TO CLOSE THE WEEKEND FESTIVITIES. (LOCAL). KEITH R LAMBERTSEN; TREYNOR BICENTENNIAL COMMITTEE; BOX 171; TREYNOR, IA 51501. (#10091-1).

JULY 4, '75. TALENT SHOW IN COUNCIL BLUFF, IOWA. THE SCHOOL DISTRICT MUSIC DEPARTMENT IS SPONSORING A LOCAL TALENT SHOW FOR AREA RESIDENTS. (LOCAL). KEITH R LAMBERTSEN; TREYNOR BICENTENNIAL COMMITTEE; BOX 171; TREYNOR, IA 51501. (#10092-1).

OCT 14 - 16, '75. UNITED STATES ARMED FORCES BICENTENNIAL CARAVAN. THE CARAVAN IS COMPOSED OF EXHIBIT VANS FOR EACH BRANCH OF THE MILITARY SERVICE. THE THEME OF THE EXHIBITION IS 'HISTORY OF THE ARMED FORCES AND THEIR CONTRIBUTION TO THE NATION'. (LOCAL). MRS D BUCKINGHAM, CHMN; COUNCIL BLUFFS BICENTENNIAL COMMISSION; BOX 1776; COUNCIL BLUFF, IA 51501. (#1775-216).

MAY 7 - 22, '76. MUSICAL PRODUCTION OF 'PURLIE'. LIVE PERFORMANCE AT CHANTICLOOR THEATRE, 830 FRANKLIN AVE, COUNCIL BLUFFS, IA. (LOCAL). ROBERT W KNOX, COORD; CHANTICLEER, INC; 830 FRANKLIN AVE, PO BOX 304; COUNCIL BLUFF, IA 51501. (#22283-1).

MAY 10 - 16, '76. FOUNDERS' WEEK PROGRAM. EXHIBIT, FESTIVAL. (LOCAL). DR MARTIN P WOLF, COORD; IOWA WESTERN COMMUNITY COLLEGE; 2700 COLLEGE RD; COUNCIL BLUFF, IA 51501. (#200018-17).

MAY 17, '76. CHAUTAUQUA II THEATRE. LIVE PERFORMANCE. (LOCAL). DR MARTIN P WOLF, CHMN; IOWA WESTERN COMMUNITY COLLEGE; 2700 COLLEGE RD; COUNCIL BLUFF, IA 51501. (#200018-16).

JULY 4 - 5, '76. DEDICATION OF FRIENDSHIP FOUNTAIN AT MISSOURI RIVERFRONT DEVELOPMNT. THE FOUNTAIN WILL SYMBOLIZE IOWA-NEBRASKA FRIENDSHIP REVITALIZED BY THE MISSOURI RIVERFRONT DEVELOPMENT PROJECT DESIGNED TO DEVELOP THE TOTAL PHYSICAL AND HUMAN RESOURCES OF THE VALLEY. AT IN THE MISSOURI RIVER BETWEEN OMAHA & COUNCIL BLUFF. (REGN'L). PAT PEN; RIVERFRONT COMMUNITIES DEVELOPMENT FOUNDATION; 2020 FIRST NATIONAL CENTER; OMAHA, NE 68102. (#1302-1).

CRAWFORDSVL

AUG 7, '76. GREAT CRAWFORDSVILLE REPUBLICAN REUNION. CONFERENCE. (ST-WIDE). JERRY MURSENER, COORD; REPUBLICAN STATE CENTRAL COMMITTEE; 1540 HIGH ST; DES MOINES, IA 50311. (#200018-194).

CRESCENT

CITY PARK IMPROVEMENT - CRESCENT, IA. A NEW FENCE WILL BE PLACED AROUND THE CITY PARK AND NEW PLAYGROUND EQUIPMENT WILL BE INSTALLED. (LOCAL). HAROLD RADY, MAYOR; CITY OF CRESCENT; CRESCENT, IA 51526. (#19796).

CRESCENT, IA, HISTORY PROJECT. HISTORY PAPERS WILL BE WRITTEN BY HIGH SCHOOL HISTORY CLASSES. (LOCAL). HAROLD RADY, MAYOR; CITY OF CRESCENT; CRESCENT, IA 51526. (#19795).

JULY 17 - 18, '76. CRESCENT FUN DAYS. FESTIVAL, EXHIBIT, PARADE. (LOCAL). PAT SEXTON, CHAIRMAN; FIRE DEPT; CRESCENT, IA 51526. (#104541-1).

CRESCO

LITTLE LAKES OF THE WOODS, IOWA, RECREATION AREA. A STATE PARK TO BE DEVELOPED NEAR CRESCO, IOWA. WILL BE DEVELOPED FOR RECREATIONAL FACILITIES ON A YEAR ROUND BASIS. (ST-WIDE). GEORGE WOODS, CHAIRMAN; HOWARD CO CONSERVATION BOARD; HOWARD CO COURT HOUSE; CRESCO, IA 52136. (#203). **(??).**

OCT 7, '75. UNITED STATES ARMED FORCES BICENTENNIAL CARAVAN. THE CARAVAN IS COMPOSED OF EXHIBIT VANS FOR EACH BRANCH OF THE MILITARY SERVICE. THE THEME OF THE EXHIBITION IS 'HISTORY OF THE ARMED FORCES AND THEIR CONTRIBUTION TO THE NATION'. (LOCAL). JACK PRESTON, LCOL USAR; U S ARMED FORCES BICENTENNIAL EXHIBIT VANS PROJECT; 506 8TH AVE E; CRESCO, IA 52136. (#1775-212).

JAN 1 - DEC 15, '76. OPENING OF NEW PARK AREAS IN IOWA. LITTLE LAKES OF THE WOODS, IOWA, RECREATION AREA. A STATE PARK TO BE DEVELOPED NEAR CRESCO, IOWA. WILL BE DEVELOPED FOR RECREATIONAL FACILITIES ON A YEAR ROUND BASIS. (ST-WIDE). GEORGE WOODS, CHAIRMAN; HOWARD CO CONSERVATION BOARD; HOWARD CO COURT HOUSE; CRESCO, IA 52136. (#203-501).

CRESTON

BICENTENNIAL EVENT IN CRESTON, IA. TIME CAPSULE. (LOCAL). BILL WEAVER, PRES; ROTARY CLUB; CRESTON, IA 50801. (#21412).

FREEDOM SPEECHES - CRESTON, IA. SPEECHES BY TOASTMASTERS TO SCHOOLS & OTHER ORGANIZATIONS. (LOCAL). RONALD WAGNER, PRESIDENT; TOASTMASTERS; CRESTON, IA 50801. (#16430).

SHELTER HOUSE - CRESTON, IA. A SHELTER HOUSE AT CITY PARK IS BEING BUILT AS A BICENTENNIAL PROJECT. (LOCAL). RONALD WAGNER, COORDINATOR; CRESTON LIONS CLUB; CRESTON, IA 50801. (#16431).

APR 29 - MAY 6, '76. SPRING HERITAGE WEEK. FESTIVAL AT CAMPUS. (LOCAL). BOB HICKMAN, CHAIRMAN; SOUTHWESTERN COMMUNITY COLLEGE; 1501 W TOWNLINE; CRESTON, IA 50801. (#106206-1).

JULY 3 - 4, '76. JULY 4TH CELEBRATION. FESTIVAL, PARADE. (LOCAL). BILL WEAVER, PROJ DIR; CRESTONIANS; CRESTON, IA 50801. (#105328-1).

CUMBERLAND

COMMUNITY & SENIOR CITIZENS CENTER - IA. DEVELOP A COMMUNITY & SENIOR CITIZENS CENTER. (LOCAL). MAURICE KEMP, CHAIRMAN; CUMBERLAND COMMUNITY CLUB; CUMBERLAND, IA 50843. (#24673).

MAY 31, '76. MEMORIAL DAY HORSE SHOW. COMPETITION. (LOCAL). DELMAR SOUTH, COORD; CUMBERLAND SADDLE CLUB; CUMBERLAND, IA 50843. (#107747-1).

JUNE 24, '76. ANNUAL CUMBERLAND GARDEN CLUB FLOWER SHOW. DISTRICT FLOWER SHOW WITH RED, WHITE & BLUE FLOWER FLAG. THE THEME IS 'MUSIC THRU THE YEARS'. VASES, CONTAINERS & BOQUETS OF PAST YRS. MUSICAL INSTRUMENTS & MUSIC OF PAST YEARS. (LOCAL). LOUISE WEBER; FEDERATED GARDEN CLUB; CUMBERLAND, IA 50843. (#107680-3).

AUG 7, '76. FIREMENS BALL. FIREMENS BALL IN AUGUST. (LOCAL). WILBUR C GERLACH; CUMBERLAND FIRE DEPARTMENT; CUMBERLAND, IA 50843. (#107680-2).

SEPT 6, '76. LABOR DAY HORSE SHOW. COMPETITION. (LOCAL). DELMAR SOUTH; CUMBERLAND SADDLE CLUB; RR #1; CUMBERLAND, IA 50843. (#107680-6).

OCT '76. ANNUAL COMMUNITY CLUB FREE PANCAKE DINNER IN THE FALL. FESTIVAL. (LOCAL). MAURICE KEMP; CUMBERLAND COMMUNITY CLUB; CUMBERLAND, IA 50843. (#107680-5).

NOV 13, '76. ANNUAL LIONS CLUB DINNER FOR HUNTERS. DINNER FOR HUNTERS ON OPENING DAY OF PHEASANT SEASON. (LOCAL). CECIL MCCURDY; CUMBERLAND LIONS CLUB; CUMBERLAND, IA 50843. (#107680-4).

DEC '76. ANNUAL COMMUNITY CLUB CHRISTMAS DRAWING. FESTIVAL. (LOCAL). MAURICE KEMP; CUMBERLAND COMMUNITY CLUB; CUMBERLAND, IA 50843. (#107680-1).

CUSHING

JULY 23 - 25, '76. CUSHING BICENTENNIAL DAYS. BARBECUE, PRINCE & PRINCESS CONTEST, PARADE, DANCE, CHURCH SERVICE, AND SOFTBALL GAME. (LOCAL). GARY MERKEL, CHMN; CUSHING BICENTENNIAL COMMITTEE; CUSHING, IA 51018. (#200018-268).

CYLINDER

OFFICIAL OPENING OF PARK AND PICNIC AREA. THIS IS THE OFFICIAL OPENING OF A NEW PARK AND PICNIC AREA, FORMERLY A SCHOOL PLAYGROUND. GROUND IMPROVEMENTS, NEW PICNIC SHELTER, NEW TREES AND NEW PLAYGROUND EQUIPMENT ARE HIGHLIGHTS. PUBLIC INVITED. AT LOCATED BEHIND LAKELAND AREA 3 ED CENTER, HWY 18. (LOCAL). ROBERT BANNART, PRESIDENT; LIONS CLUB AND WOMENS CLUB; TOWN HALL; CYLINDER, IA 50528. (#106834-1).

JUNE 26, '76. TIME CAPSULE BURIAL. CEREMONY AT CYLINDER PARK (OLD SCHOOL GROUNDS) HWY 18, CYLINDER, IA. (LOCAL). CHRISTINE FREEMAN, DIR; CYLINDER LIONS CLUB; BOX 37; CYLINDER, IA 50528. (#107309-1).

AUG 5 - 7, '76. COUNTY FAIR - ART OF QUILTING BOOTH. EXHIBIT AT PALO ALTO COUNTY FAIRGROUNDS. (ST-WIDE). CHRISTINE FREEMAN, DIR; BICENTENNIAL COMMITTEE OF CYLINDER; BOX 37; CYLINDER, IA 50528. (#107309-2).

DAKOTA CITY

BICENTENNIAL QUILT - PROJ OF DAKOTA CITY, IA. A QUILT COMMEMORATING THE 200TH BIRTHDAY OF AMERICA. (LOCAL). MRS WERNER TIGGES, PROJ DIRECTOR; HUMBOLDT COUNTY HISTORICAL ASSOC; DAKOTA CITY, IA 50529. (#14302).

COFFEE FOR FORMER SCOUTS. HAVE GET-TOGETHER FOR FORMER PACK 60 MEMBERS; PACK 60 IS OVER 30 YEARS OLD. (LOCAL). VIRGINIA GRIFFIN, SEC; CUB SCOUT PACK 60; DAKOTA CITY, IA 50529. (#104733-2). **(??).**

DAKOTA CITY SIGNS, IA. SIGNS WILL BE PURCHASED AND PLACED ON THE CITY LIMITS OF DAKOTA CITY. (LOCAL). HON JOHN GREEN, MAYOR; CITY OF DAKOTA CITY & WORTH WHILE CLUB; DAKOTA CITY, IA 50529. (#20328).

FLAG PURCHASE - DAKOTA CITY, IA. BETSY ROSS FLAG TO BE PURCHASED FOR THE CITY FLAG POLE. (LOCAL). VIRGINIA GRIFFIN, SECRETARY; WORTH WHILE CLUB; DAKOTA CITY, IA 50529. (#20327).

HUMBOLDT COUNTY HISTORICAL MUSEUM, DAKOTA CITY, IA. MAINTAINENCE OF BUILDING & EXPANSION OF GROUNDS AT MUSEUM SITE. (LOCAL). MRS PAUL PARSONS, CHAIRMAN; HUMBOLDT COUNTY HISTORICAL ASSOC; HUMBOLDT, IA 50548. (#18745).

LANDSCAPING - PROJ OF DAKOTA CITY, IA. BEAUTIFICATION AND LANDSCAPING OF HUMBLE COUNTY HISTORICAL GROUNDS. (LOCAL). MRS WERNER TIGGES, PROJ DIRECTOR; HUMBOLDT COUNTY HISTORICAL ASSOC; DAKOTA CITY, IA 50529. (#14301).

LOG CABIN RESTORATION - PROJ OF DAKOTA CITY, IA. THE OLD LOG CABIN WILL BE RESTORED BY THE HUMBOLDT COUNTY HISTORICAL ASSOCIATION. (LOCAL). MRS WERNER TIGGES, PROJ DIRECTOR; HUMBOLDT COUNTY HISTORICAL ASSOC; DAKOTA CITY, IA 50529. (#14300).

ORAL HISTORY PROJ - DAKOTA CITY, IA. EXPERIENCES OF OLDER RESIDENTS WILL BE RECORDED. (LOCAL). VIRGINIA HUFFIN, SECRETARY; WORTH WHILE CLUB; DAKOTA CITY, IA 50529. (#20324).

PLANTING FLOWER BEDS - DAKOTA CITY, IA. A PATRIOTIC-LOOKING FLOWER BED WILL BE PLANTED ON GROUNDS NEAR THE MUNICIPAL BUILDING. (LOCAL). VIRGINIA GRIFFIN, SECRETARY; WORTH WHILE CLUB; DAKOTA CITY, IA 50529. (#20326).

RECYCLING PROJ - DAKOTA CITY, IA. ALUMINUM CANS AND PAPERS WILL BE GATHERED, PROCESSED AND SOLD. (LOCAL). VIRGINIA GRIFFIN, COORDINATOR; CUB SCOUT PACK 60; DAKOTA CITY, IA 50529. (#20325).

SIGNATURE QUILT - PROJ OF DAKOTA CITY, IA. A QUILT EMBROIDERED WITH SIGNATURES OF PEOPLE IN THE COMMUNITY. (LOCAL). MRS MERVIN LOWE, CHAIRMAN; WORTHWHILE CLUB; DAKOTA CITY, IA 50529. (#14293).

TREE BEAUTIFICATION PROGRAM - DAKOTA CITY, IA. TREES WILL BE PLANTED THROUGHOUT THE CITY. (LOCAL). HON JOHN GREEN, MAYOR; CITY OF DAKOTA CITY; DAKOTA CITY, IA 50529. (#20329).

MAY 31, '76. MEMORIAL DAY SERVICES. CEREMONY AT HUMBOLDT COUNTY COURTHOUSE FRONT LAWN. (LOCAL). ROYAL SCHULTZE, DIR; HUMBOLDT COUNTY AMERICAN LEGION; DAKOTA CITY, IA 50529. (#14292-1).

JUNE 15, '76. ARTS AND CRAFTS DISPLAY. EXHIBIT AT MUNICIPAL BUILDING. (LOCAL). LORRAINE LOWE, COORD; WORTH WHILE CLUB; DAKOTA CITY, IA 50529. (#20324-1).

DALLAS CENTER

BICENTENNIAL COIN - DALLAS CENTER, IA. A BICENTENNIAL COIN WILL BE ON SALE. (LOCAL). WAYNE HAINES, CHAIRMAN; DALLAS CENTER BICENTENNIAL COMMITTEE; DALLAS CENTER, IA 50063. (#24556).

BICENTENNIAL FLOWER BEDS - DALLAS CENTER, IA. BICENTENNIAL FLOWER BEDS WITH RED, WHITE AND BLUE FLOWERS. (LOCAL). MRS WILLIAM MUELLER, DIRECTOR; HORIZONS COMMITTEE; 1701 ASH AVE; DALLAS CENTER, IA 50063. (#24557).

DALLAS CENTER WOMEN'S CLUB ELEVATOR PROJECT, IA. A SMALL COMMERCIAL PASSENGER ELEVATOR TO THE SECOND STORY COMMUNITY ROOM OF MEMORIAL HALL. (LOCAL). MRS MORRIS FOX, PRESIDENT; DALLAS CENTER FEDERATED WOMEN'S CLUB; 1300 LINDEN AVE; DALLAS CENTER, IA 50063. (#18732).

DALLAS CENTER, IA, LIBRARY. THE HORIZONS COMMITTEE WILL HELP FURNISH AND LANDSCAPE THE GROUNDS OF THE NEW LIBRARY. (LOCAL). SIMON BURGER, CHAIRMAN; HORIZONS COMMITTEE; DALLAS CENTER, IA 50063. (#24561).

DALLAS CENTER, IA, CITY PARK. THE HORIZONS COMMITTEE WILL PLANT TREES AND BUILD A PICNIC SHELTER IN THE NEW CITY PARK. (LOCAL). SIMON BURGER, CHAIRMAN; HORIZONS COMMITTEE; DALLAS CENTER, IA 50063. (#24563).

DEPOT PRESERVATION - DALLAS CENTER, IA. THE OLD DEPOT WILL BE PAINTED AS PART OF A COMMUNITY BEAUTIFICATION PROGRAM. (LOCAL). MARION KELLER, CHAIRMAN; HERITAGE COMMITTEE; DALLAS CENTER, IA 50063. (#24565).

FIRE HYDRANT PAINTING - DALLAS CENTER, IA. THE FIRE HYDRANTS IN THE CITY WILL BE PAINTED RED, WHITE & BLUE. (LOCAL). SALLY REECE, PROJ DIRECTOR; HIGH SCHOOL ART CLASS; 806 VINE; DALLAS CENTER, IA 50063. (#24566).

FLAG SALE - DALLAS CENTER, IA. FLAGS WILL BE SOLD TO HELP FUND PROJECTS AND TO PROMOTE PATRIOTISM IN THE COMMUNITY. (LOCAL). MARION PRICE, PROJ CHAIRMAN; DALLAS

DALLAS CENTER — CONTINUED

CENTER BICENTENNIAL COMMITTEE; DALLAS CENTER, IA 50063. (#24560).

'GOOD OLD SATURDAY NIGHTS', DALLAS CENTER, IA. A RE-CREATION OF OLD-FASHIONED SATURDAY NIGHTS IN TOWN WITH FREE MOVIES AND POPCORN. (LOCAL). JERRY KLINKEFUS, CHAIRPERSON; DALLAS CENTER BICENTENNIAL COMMITTEE; 1505 WALNUT; DALLAS CENTER, IA 50063. (#14728).

RENOVATION OF MAIN ST, DALLAS CENTER, IA. RESTORATION & REDECORATION OF THE BUSINESS IN DOWNTOWN DALLAS CENTER. (LOCAL). S C BURGER, CHAIRPERSON; DALLAS CENTER BICENTENNIAL COMMITTEE; 1414 WALNUT; DALLAS CENTER, IA 50063. (#14727).

SALE OF CERAMIC TILE WALL HANGING - IA. A WALL HANGING WITH 4 DIFFERENT TYPES OF TILE, EACH HAS AN ETCHING OF A HISTORIC BUILDING IN DALLAS CENTER. (LOCAL). WAYNE HAINES, CHAIRMAN; DALLAS CENTER BICENTENNIAL COMMITTEE; DALLAS CENTER, IA 50063. (#24554).

SALE OF COMMEMORATIVE SPOON - DALLAS CENTER, IA. 2 LANDMARKS OF DALLAS CENTER WILL BE DEPICTED ON THE SPOON HANDLE WITH '1776' AND '1976' ON EITHER SIDE; IN THE BOWL OF THE SPOON ARE THE WORDS 'DALLAS CENTER, IA.'. (LOCAL). WAYNE HAINES, CHAIRMAN; DALLAS CENTER BICENTENNIAL COMMITTEE; DALLAS CENTER, IA 50063. (#24559).

SALE OF LIBERTY BELL GLASS CANISTER - IA. EACH BELL IS ETCHED IN SILVER, '1776-1976'; IT HAS SEVERAL USES: CANDY JAR, COOKIE JAR, TERRARIUM AND MANY OTHERS. (LOCAL). WAYNE HAINES, CHAIRMAN; DALLAS CENTER BICENTENNIAL COMMITTEE; DALLAS CENTER, IA 50063. (#24567).

SALE OF SOUVENIR PLATES - DALLAS CENTER, IA. PLATE WILL HAVE BOTH THE 1776 CALENDAR AND THE 1976 CALENDAR AND THE DALLAS CENTER SLOGAN, 'PULLING TOGETHER FOR PRIDE IN AMERICA'. (LOCAL). WAYNE HAINES, CHAIRMAN; DALLAS CENTER BICENTENNIAL COMMITTEE; DALLAS CENTER, IA 50063. (#24558).

STORIES FROM OUR PAST - DALLAS CENTER, IA. A GENERAL HISTORY OF DALLAS CENTER WITH PICTURES AND SHORT RECOLLECTIONS OF SENIOR CITIZENS. (LOCAL). LORENE MORTIMER, CHAIRMAN; WOMEN'S CLUB; RR 1; DALLAS CENTER, IA 50063. (#24555).

TOURS OF HISTORICAL DALLAS CENTER, IA. HISTORICAL SITES IN THE COMMUNITY WILL BE MARKED AND TOURS THROUGH THE TOWN WILL BE CONDUCTED. (LOCAL). MARION KELLER, VICE CHAIRPERSON; DALLAS CENTER BICENTENNIAL COMMITTEE; 1414 WALNUT; DALLAS CENTER, IA 50063. (#14729).

VETERANS MEMORIAL MONUMENT - DALLAS CENTER, IA. A MONUMENT WITH ENGRAVINGS DEDICATED TO ALL VETERANS. (LOCAL). SIMON BURGER, CHAIRMAN; AMERICAN LEGION & HORIZONS COMMITTEE; DALLAS CENTER, IA 50063. (#24562).

FEB 27, '76. GEORGE WASHINGTON BALL AND BOX SOCIAL. FESTIVAL AT HIGH SCHOOL GYM. (LOCAL). MARION KELLER, COORD; HERITAGE COMMITTEE; RR; DALLAS CENTER, IA 50063. (#200018-43).

APR 1, '76. OLD CREAMERY PLAYERS - A DRAMA FROM GARRISON, IA. LIVE PERFORMANCE AT HIGH SCHOOL GYM. (LOCAL). NORMA LISTER; BETA SIGMA PHI; 1402 SYCAMORE; DALLAS CENTER, IA 50063. (#200018-42).

JULY 3, '76. ALUMNI BARBECUE. FESTIVAL AT HIGH SCHOOL. (LOCAL). PENNY BURNETT, COORD; DALLAS CENTER ALUMNI ASSOC; DALLAS CENTER, IA 50063. (#106865-2).

SEPT 11, '76. FESTIVAL DAY. RIDES, PARADES & CRAFTS DEMONSTRATION. AT MAIN ST. (LOCAL). ROBERT GERMAN, COORD; DALLAS CENTER FESTIVAL COMMITTEE; 305 10TH; DALLAS CENTER, IA 50063. (#106865-1).

DANBURY

HISTORY OF DANBURY, IA. BOOK ON HISTORY OF DANBURY FROM 1865 TO 1975. (LOCAL). HENRY DIMAG, PROJ COORDINATOR; DANBURY, IA 51019. (#24640).

HOUSING FOR SENIOR CITIZENS IN DANBURY, IA. NEW LOW-RENT APARTMENTS WILL BE BUILT FOR SENIOR CITIZENS. (LOCAL). LEON ORTNER, PROJ DIRECTOR; DANBURY COMMUNITY CLUB; DANBURY, IA 51019. (#24635).

ST MARY'S CHURCH RESTORATION, DANBURY, IA. HISTORIC ST MARY'S CHURCH WILL BE RESTORED AND REDECORATED. (LOCAL). FATHER ROBERT A THIELE, PROJ DIRECTOR; ST MARY'S PARISH; DANBURY, IA 51019. (#24637).

TREE PLANTING PROJ, DANBURY, IA. MEMBERS OF THE DANBURY WOMEN'S CLUB ARE SPONSORING A COMMUNITY TREE PLANTING PROJECT. (LOCAL). MRS DALE LACY, COORDINATOR; DANBURY WOMEN'S CLUB; DANBURY, IA 51019. (#24636).

JAN 1, '76 - DEC 31, '77. MAPLE VALLEY BICENTENNIAL BOYS & MAPLE VALLEY TRIPLE TRIO. PERFOEMANCES BY REQUEST. WILL PERFORM ANYWHERE WITHIN REASON. A PIANO IS NECESSARY FOR LIVE PERFORMANCE. (LOCAL). MRS DIXIE BRUECK; MAPLE VALLEY MUSIC DEPARTMENT; BATTLE CREEK, IA 51006. (#107677-2).

APR 30, '76. WOMEN'S CLUB STYLE SHOW, BICENTENNIAL THEME ARTS, CRAFTS & SEWING. EXHIBIT, LIVE PERFORMANCE AT DANBURY PUBLIC SCHOOL AUDITORIUM. (LOCAL). MRS DALE LACEY, COORD; DANBURY WOMEN'S CLUB; RR #2; DANBURY, IA 51019. (#200018-36).

MAY 15, '76. DECORATION DAY. CEREMONY. (LOCAL). MRS DEAN WENGER, PRES; DANBURY AMERICAN LEGION AUXILIARY & AMERICAN LEGION; DANBURY, IA 51019. (#108253-1).

JULY - AUG '76. PRE-SCHOOL READING CLINIC. LIVE PERFORMANCE AT PUBLIC LIBRARY. (LOCAL). MRS DALE LACY, PRES; DANBURY WOMANS CLUB; DANBURY, IA 51019. (#107889-1).

SEPT 25, '76. SQUARE DANCERS, BICENTENNIAL GROUP. LIVE PERFORMANCE AT STREET. (LOCAL). HARLAN SCHLINZ; DANBURY SQUARE DANCERS CLUB; DANBURY, IA 51019. (#107677-1).

OCT 2, '76. COMMUNITY CLUB CORN DAY: PARADE, EXHIBITS, AWARDS & PRIZES. PARADE, AWARD, EXHIBIT AT TOWN SQUARE. (LOCAL). MAURIE WELTE; DANBURY COMMUNITY CLUB; DANBURY, IA 51019. (#107677-3).

DANVILLE

PAINTING OF FIRE HYDRANTS, DANVILLE, IA. FIRE HYDRANTS WILL BE PAINTED RED, WHITE & BLUE. (LOCAL). GLORIA BROWN, CO-CHAIRMAN; DANVILLE BICENTENNIAL COMMITTEE; DANVILLE, IA 52623. (#23363).

TOWN CLEANUP DAY, DANVILLE, IA. ONE SATURDAY IN MAY WILL BE SET ASIDE FOR A SPECIAL CLEANUP OF THE TOWN. (LOCAL). GLORIA BROWN, CO-CHAIRMAN; DANVILLE BICENTENNIAL COMMITTEE; DANVILLE, IA 52623. (#23364).

TREE PLANTING, DANVILLE, IA. TREES WILL BE PLANTED IN DANVILLE. (LOCAL). GLORIA BROWN, CO-CHAIRMAN; DANVILLE BICENTENNIAL COMMITTEE; DANVILLE, IA 52623. (#23362).

MAR 4 - 14, '76. BAPTIST ANNUAL AREA 3 MEETING, CELEBRATE OLDEST BAPTIST CHURCH IN IA. CEREMONY AT DANVILLE COMMUNITY SCHOOL, MAIN ST. (ST-WIDE). REV IAN ARMSTRONG, COORD; DANVILLE BAPTIST; DANVILLE, IA 52623. (#200018-29).

APR 3, '76. DANVILLE JUNIOR WOMEN'S CLUB BAZAAR. EXHIBIT AT MULTI-PURPOSE ROOM, DANVILLE SCHOOL, MAIN ST. (LOCAL). GLORIA BROWN, CO-CHMN; DANVILLE JUNIOR WOMEN'S CLUB; DANVILLE, IA 52623. (#200018-30).

APR 13 - JULY 10, '76. ELEMENTARY, JUNIOR HIGH AND HIGH SCHOOL PROGRAMS. FESTIVAL, LIVE PERFORMANCE AT DANVILLE COMMUNITY SCHOOL. (LOCAL). PAUL GALER, COORD; SCHOOL SYSTEM; MAIN ST; DANVILLE, IA 52623. (#106534-2).

JULY 10, '76. DANVILLE HOMECOMING DAY. BARBEQUE SUPPER WILL BE BARBEQUED BEEF AND PORK, DESERT WILL BE EXTRA. SERVING 5-7:30PM. RONALD MCDONALD WILL BE PRESENT IN THE MORNING. DANCE ROUTINE & MAGIC SHOW IN AFTTERNOON. EVENING PROGRAM WILL BE BURLINGTON BARBERSHOP CHORUS. AT UPTOWN AREA. (LOCAL). BILL PORTER, COORD; DANVILLE COMMUNITY; 207W DIVISION; DANVILLE, IA 52623. (#106534-1).

DAVENPORT

THE AMERICAN SPIRIT IN THEATER - IOWA. 2 MUSICALS AND PLAY ILLUSTRATING THE AMERICAN SPIRIT & CULTURAL HERITAGE. (LOCAL). GREGG DENNHARDT, THEATER DIRECTOR; THE DRAMA DEPT OF ST AMBROSE COLLEGE; 518 W LOCUST; DAVENPORT, IA 52803. (#8136).

BICENTENNIAL CALENDAR FOR DAVENPORT, IOWA. 12 WATER COLOR (FRAMEABLE) REPRODUCTIONS OF PROMINENT HISTORIC SITES IN SCOTT COUNTY. (ST-WIDE). BURTON PERSSON, CHAIRMAN; SCOTT COUNTY ARBC; 1001 W 4TH ST; DAVENPORT, IA 52802. (#11546).

ELEMENTARY BICENTENNIAL ART EXHIBIT-DAVENPORT, IA. ALL ELEMENTARY SCHOOLS IN SCOTT COUNTY WILL HAVE EXHIBITS IN THE DAVENPORT ART GALLERY. (LOCAL). BURTON PERSSON, CHAIRMAN; SCOTT COUNTY ARBC; 1001 W 4TH ST; DAVENPORT, IA 52802. (#11549).

HERITAGE FILMS PROJ AT ST AMBROSE COLLEGE, IOWA. FILM SERIES TO START WITH D W GRIFFITH'S 'BIRTH OF A NATION'. (LOCAL). JOHN STUEKERJUERGEN, DIRECTOR; ST AMBROSE COLLEGE; 518 W LOCUST; DAVENPORT, IA 52803. (#8137). (??).

PLAYS OF SUSAN GLASPELL AT ST AMBROSE COLLEGE, IA. SEVERAL OF THE PLAYS OF SUSAN GLASPELL, A NATIONALLY KNOWN PLAYWRITE AND NOVELIST OF DAVENPORT, IOWA, WILL BE PRODUCED. MS GLASPELL DIED IN 1948. (LOCAL). SR RITAMARY BRADLEY, PROJ COORDINATOR; ST AMBROSE COLLEGE; 518 W LOCUST; DAVENPORT, IA 52803. (#8135).

SCOTT CO-ROCK ISLAND HISTORY FOR SCHOOLS - IOWA. PUBLICATION OF FACTUAL HISTORY OF SCOTT & ROCK ISLAND COUNTIES. (LOCAL). BURTON PERSSON, CHAIRMAN; SCOTT COUNTY ARBC; 1001 W 4TH ST; DAVENPORT, IA 52802. (#11545).

SECONDARY SCHOOLS PROJECTS IN SCOTT & ROCK ISLAND. EXHIBIT OF SCHOOL YOUTH BICENTENNIAL PROJECTS IN SCOTT AND ROCK ISLAND COUNTY SCHOOLS. (LOCAL). BURTON PERSSON, CHAIRMAN; SCOTT COUNTY ARBC; 1001 W 4TH ST; DAVENPORT, IA 52802. (#11548).

TIME AND THE RIVER, DAVENPORT, IA. A BICENTENNIAL PLAY WHICH IS A HISTORICAL RE-ENACTMENT OF THE FOUNDING OF DAVENPORT AND SCOTT COUNTY TO BE PRESENTED FREE TO THE PUBLIC IN ALL SCHOOLS IN SCOTT COUNTY. (LOCAL). BURTON E PERSSON, COORDINATOR; SCOTT COUNTY BICENTENNIAL COMMISSION; PO BOX 1976; DAVENPORT, IA 52805. (#22675). **ARBA GRANTEE.**

MAR 29 - APR 27, '75. IOWA SHOWING OF ORIGINAL MANUSCRIPTS OF AMER REVOLUTION. FEATURES EXHIBIT MOUNTED BY THE SMITHSONIAN INSTITUTION. AT PUTNAM MUSEUM. (ST-WIDE). MUSEUM DIRECTOR; DAVENPORT SCIENCE MUSEUM; DAVENPORT, IA 52401. (#3742-501).

APR 25 - OCT 23, '75. FIVE FREEDOM PARADES. IOWA-ILLINOIS PARADE (APRIL 25, MAY 29, JUNE 3 & OCT 23) OF CHURCHES, SCHOOLS, CITIES, INDUSTRIES AND SOCIAL ORGANIZATIONS. (ST-WIDE). BURTON PERSSON, CHMN; SCOTT COUNTY ARBC; 1001 W 4TH ST; DAVENPORT, IA 52802. (#11547-1).

SEPT 23, '75 - MAY 1, '76. ELEMENTS IN AMERICAN GREATNESS - PANEL DISCUSSION. SUBJECT WILL BE ETHNIC AMERICA & RELIGIOUS FREEDOM. (LOCAL). FR DUNCAN, COORD; ST AMBROSE COLLEGE; 518 W LOCUST; DAVENPORT, IA 52803. (#8134-501).

NOV 4 - 6, '75. UNITED STATES ARMED FORCES BICENTENNIAL CARAVAN. THE CARAVAN IS COMPOSED OF EXHIBIT VANS FOR EACH BRANCH OF THE MILITARY SERVICE. THE THEME OF THE EXHIBITION IS 'HISTORY OF THE ARMED FORCES AND THEIR CONTRIBUTION TO THE NATION'. (LOCAL). BURTON E PERSSON, CHMN; DAVENPORT BICENTENNIAL COMMISSION; 1001 HARRISON; DAVENPORT, IA 52803. (#1775-224).

MAY 13, '76. CROSS-COUNTRY MARATHON RACE. COMPETITION AT BEGINS AT VANDER VEER PARK. (LOCAL). KEN JOHNSTON, CHMN; DAVENPORT BICENTENNIAL COMMITTEE; 2507 E 18 ST; DAVENPORT, IA 52803. (#200018-40).

MAY 15 - JUNE 15, '76. HENRY MOORE: PRINTS 1969-1974. DAVENPORT ART MUSEUM HOSTS TRAVELING EXHIBIT OF SCULPTOR'S PRINTS AND LITHOGRAPHS. AT DAVENPORT MUNICIPAL ART MUSEUM. (LOCAL). L G HOFFMAN; DAVENPORT MUNICIPAL ART MUSEUM; 1737 W 12TH ST; DAVENPORT, IA 52804. (#103416-325).

MAY 29 - JUNE 7, '76. SISTER CITY, KAISERSLAUTERN, GERMANY. TOUR. (INT'L). KEN JOHNSTON, CHMN; DAVENPORT BICENTENNIAL COMMITTEE; 2507 E 18 ST; DAVENPORT, IA 52803. (#200018-39).

JUNE 25 - 27, '76. QUINT CITIES ANCIENT HAWAIIAN BICENTENNIAL FESTIVAL. 3 DAYS OF ANCIENT HAWAIIAN ARTS, CRAFTS, SONGS, DANCES, CHANTS, HISTORY, STORYTELLING, LEI-MAKING, GRASS WEAVING, ETC. CONTINUOUS MOVIES ON THE FUN OF HAWAII. 6 IN-DEPTH LECTURES ON THE WAY OF LIFE IN OLD HAWAII. (ST-WIDE). NANCY FRENCH, COORD; DAVENPORT BICENTENNIAL COMMISSION; 5240 WHITE POST RD; BETTENDORF, IA 52722. (#107777-1).

JULY 23 - 25, '76. BIX BIEDERBECK DAYS. FESTIVAL. (LOCAL). KEN JOHNSTON, CHAIRMAN; DAVENPORT BICENTENNIAL COMMITTEE; 2507 E 18TH ST; DAVENPORT, IA 52803. (#108449-1).

AUG 6 - 15, '76. 1976 GREAT MISSISSIPPI VALLEY FAIR. AN INTERNATIONAL FOLK ART SHOW FEATURING EXHIBITS, WOOD CARVING, LEATHER CRAFTS, AN OPEN AIR THEATER WITH FREE SHOWS 7 TIMES DAILY SINCE 1968. A TOTAL OF 15,000 COMPETITIVE EXHIBITS IN 1975. AT 2518 W. LOCUST ST; DAVENPORT, IOWA. (REGN'L). CHESTER SALTER, DIRECTOR; GREAT MISSISSIPPI VALLEY FAIR; 2815 W LOCOST ST; DAVENPORT, IA 52804. (#104020-4).

DECORAH

ARCHIVE INCREASE, DECORAH, IA. DRIVE TO INCREASE NUMBER OF IMPORTANT DOCUMENTS IN ARCHIVES. (LOCAL). DUANE FENSTERMANN, COORD; WINNESHIEK COUNTY HISTORICAL SOCIETY; LUTHER COLLEGE LIBRARY; DECORAH, IA 52101. (#26838).

BICENTENNIAL FLOWER FLAG AND FLOWER BOXES, IA. FLAG MADE OF RED, WHITE & BLUE FLOWERS & NEW FLOWER BOXES TO BE PLACED IN DOWNTOWN AREA. (LOCAL). MRS DAN GABRIELSON, COORDINATOR; WAYSIDE GARDEN CLUB; 330 PERSHING AVE; DECORAH, IA 52101. (#26845).

BUS TOURS - DECORAH, IA. HISTORIC TOURS TO MINERAL PT, NEW GLARUS, EFFIGY MOUNDS, VILLA LOUIS AND STONEFIELD VILLAGE. (LOCAL). MARTHA MONSON, COORDINATOR; WINN CO HISTORICAL SOCIETY; 510 NORTH; DECORAH, IA 52101. (#26835).

CEMETERY INVENTORY, DECORAH, IA. ALPHABETICAL LISTING OF CEMETERIES AND GRAVES IN WINNESHIEK COUNTY. (LOCAL). JERRY WRIGHT, COORDINATOR; WINNESHIEK COUNTY HISTORICAL SOCIETY; 312 GROVE ST; DECORAH, IA 52101. (#26840).

DISPLAY OF HUFFMAN PHOTOGRAPHS, DECORAH, IA. DISPLAY OF 80 100 YEAR OLD PHOTOGRAPHS BY AREA PHOTOGRAPHER. PHOTOS TAKEN MAINLY IN MONTANA. (LOCAL). MARTHA A MONSON, BICENTENNIAL CHAIRPERSON; WINNESHIEK COUNTY HISTORICAL SOCIETY; BOX 223; DECORAH, IA 52101. (#26837).

EDUCATIONAL-HISTORIC PROGRAM, DECORAH, IA. BOOKLET GUIDE FOR ELEMENTARY TEACHERS WITH PREPARATION AND FOLLOW-UP MATERIALS FOR TOURS TO FOUR HISTORIC SITES IN WINNESHIEK COUNTY. (LOCAL). MARTHA A MONSON, CHAIRPERSON; WINNESHIEK COUNTY HISTORICAL SOCIETY; BOX 223; DECORAH, IA 52101. (#26843).

FRANKVILLE AND LOCUST MUSEUMS RENOVATION - IA. INTERIOR REDECORATION AND EXTERIOR REPAIRS. (LOCAL). E J WEIGLE, PRESIDENT; WINNESHIEK CO HISTORICAL SOCIETY; 907 PINE RIDGE CT; DECORAH, IA 52101. (#26836).

FRESHMAN STUDIES CORE PROGRAM - DECORAH, IA. STUDIES WILL CENTER ON AFRICAN AND SCANDANAVIAN CULTURE. (LOCAL). GLEN NELSON, DIRECTOR; LUTHER COLLEGE; DECORAH, IA 52101. (#21248).

HISTORIC DISTRICTS - DECORAH, IA. SURVEY AND RESEARCH OF HISTORIC DECORAH FOR PRESERVATION. (LOCAL). LUCILLE PRICE, COORDINATOR; AMERICAN ASSOCIATION OF UNIVERSITY WOMEN; 508 W BROADWAY; DECORAH, IA 52101. (#26833).

JANUARY TERM '76 - DECORAH, IA. THE JANUARY TERM WILL HAVE A BICENTENNIAL THEME AND INCLUDE SPECIAL COURSES & LECTURES. (LOCAL). GLENN NELSON, DIRECTOR; LUTHER COLLEGE; DECORAH, IA 52101. (#21247).

DECORAH—CONTINUED

NATIONAL REGISTER INCREASE - DECORAH, IA. APPLICATION WILL BE MADE TO RAISE VARIOUS SITES IN THE COUNTY TO NATIONAL REGISTER STATUS. (LOCAL). E J WEIGLE, CHAIRMAN; WINN CO HISTORICAL SOCIETY; 907 PINE RIDGE CT; DECORAH, IA 52101. (#26832).

NORTHWEST IOWA ORAL HISTORY PROJECT, DECORAH, IA. LUTHER COLLEGE STUDENTS WILL INTERVIEW OLDER CITIZENS OF THE NE SECTION OF THE STATE; THIS INFORMATION WILL BE TAPED AND MADE AVAILABLE TO THE PUBLIC THROUGH THE LUTHER COLLEGE LIBRARY. (LOCAL). DR LUIS TORRES, ASST PROFESSOR OF HISTORY; LUTHER COLLEGE; DECORAH, IA 52101. (#13431). **ARBA GRANTEE.**

NORWEGIAN - AMERICAN MUSEUM, DECORAH, IA. RESTORATION OF THE OUTDOOR MUSEUM & LOG STRUCTURES ON MUSEUM PREMISES. (ST-WIDE). DARRELL D HENNING, CURATOR; NORWEGIAN - AMERICAN MUSEUM; 502 W WATER ST; DECORAH, IA 52101. (#13430). **ARBA GRANTEE.**

PORTER HOUSE MUSEUM RESTORATION, DECORAH, IA. EXTERIOR RESTORATION OF PORTER HOUSE MUSEUM. (LOCAL). E J WEIGLE, PRESIDENT; WINNESHIEK COUNTY HISTORICAL SOCIETY; 907 PINE RIDGE CT; DECORAH, IA 52101. (#18370).

PROPOSED HISTORIC DISTRICT - DECORAH, IA. DISCUSSION AND ACTION FOR THE PRESERVATION OF A RESIDENTIAL DISTRICT IN DECORAH. (LOCAL). L PRICE, PROJ DIRECTOR; AMERICAN ASSOCIATION OF UNIVERSITY WOMEN; 508 W BROADWAY; DECORAH, IA 52101. (#18371).

STOVE WOOD HOUSE PRESERVATION, DECORAH, IA. ONE OF A KIND CONSTRUCTION OF 122 YEAR OLD HOUSE TO BE PRESERVED ON NATIONAL REGISTER. (LOCAL). JIM BURNS, COORDINATOR; JAYCEES; 810 LINDEN; DECORAH, IA 52101. (#26841).

TOUR BOOKLET, DECORAH, IA. SELF GUIDED AUTO AND BIKE TOUR BOOKLET OF WINNESHIEK COUNTY. (LOCAL). GWEN KOENIG, COORDINATOR; FARM BUREAU WOMEN; RR; CASTALIA, IA 52133. (#26846).

WINNESHIEK COUNTY PRESERVATION PROGRAM, IA. HISTORIC SITE SURVEY IN WINNESHIEK COUNTY. (LOCAL). E J WEIGLE, PRESIDENT; WINNESHIEK COUNTY HISTORICAL SOCIETY; 907 PINE RIDGE COURT; DECORAH, IA 52101. (#18369).

SEPT 26 - OCT 14, '75. NORWEGIAN-AMERICAN LECTURE SERIES. TOPICS WILL BE: 'THE EARLY CHURCH,' 'THE WOMEN IN NORWEGIAN EMMIGRATION,' 'NORWEGIAN-AMERICAN POETRY,' AND 'NORWAY IN AMERICA.' LECTURES WILL BE PUBLISHED BY THE LUTHER COLLEGE PRESS. (LOCAL). GLEN NELSON, DIRECTOR; LUTHER COLLEGE; DECORAH, IA 52101. (#105038-1).

DEC 15, '75. CENTENNIAL CHRISTMAS PARTY. FESTIVAL AT PORTER HOUSE MUSEUM. (LOCAL). MARTHA MONSON, CHMN; WINNESHIEK CO HISTORICAL SOCIETY; 510 NORTH; DECORAH, IA 52101. (#200018-219).

MAR 27, '76. SEMINAR & SLIDES ON LOCAL & STATE HISTORY. SEMINAR, EXHIBIT. (LOCAL). MARTHA A MONSON, CHPRSN; WINNESHIEK COUNTY BICENTENNIAL COMMITTEE; 510 NORTH; DECORAH, IA 52101. (#200018-208).

APR 8, '76. ARTS AND CRAFTS DAY. EXHIBIT. (LOCAL). ANNA BROWN, COORD; LUTHER COLLEGE; BOX 1060; DECORAH, IA 52101. (#200018-222).

APR 29, '76. OLD CLOTHING STYLE SHOW. EXHIBIT. (LOCAL). DOROTHY HENRY, COORD; FARM BUREAU; 214 WINNEBAGO; DECORAH, IA 52101. (#200018-204).

JUNE 4 - 6, '76. SANGERFEST NATIONAL NORWEGIAN SINGERS CONVENTION. CONFERENCE. (INT'L). LARRY LUBBERT, COORD; SANGERFEST COMMITTEE; RR6; DECORAH, IA 52101. (#200018-229).

JUNE 25 - JULY 5, '76. 1876 QUIZ CONTEST. COMPETITION. (LOCAL). GEORGIE KLEVAR, COORD; DEMOCRATIC WOMEN; 111 RURAL AVE; DECORAH, IA 52101. (#200018-218).

JUNE 28, '76. CENTURY FARMS RECOGNITION CEREMONY & DINNER. DINNER HONORING THOSE WHO HAVE HAD FARM IN FAMILY FOR 100 YEARS. (LOCAL). RON LUDEKING, COORD; FARM BUREAU; DECORAH, IA 52101. (#200018-206).

JULY 4, '76. CHURCH CELEBRATIONS. CEREMONY. (LOCAL). MARTHA MONSON, CHMN; WINN CO BICENTENNIAL COMMISSION; 510 NORTH; DECORAH, IA 52101. (#200018-225).

JULY 4, '76. QUILT CONTEST. COMPETITION. (LOCAL). BEATA GILBERTSON, COORD; SENIOR CITIZENS; 505 E MAIN; DECORAH, IA 52101. (#200018-220).

JULY 4, '76. 4TH OF JULY OLD-TIME CELEBRATION. PICNIC, FIREWORKS, SPEECH, DECLARATION OF INDEPENDENCE, BAND & CHOIR CONCERT, CAKE, ICE CREAM & LEMONADE. AT PHELPS PARK. (LOCAL). MARTHA MONSON, CHMN; WINN CO BICENTENNIAL COMMISSION; 510 NORTH; DECORAH, IA 52101. (#200018-230).

JULY 23 - 25, '76. NORDIC FEST. FESTIVAL. (LOCAL). MS HUBERT LESETH, COORD; NORDIC FEST COMMITTEE; 114 RURAL AVE; DECORAH, IA 52101. (#109025-6).

JULY 23 - 25, '76. WINDOW DISPLAY AT NORDIC FEST. EXHIBIT. (LOCAL). MARTHA MONSON, COORD; DECORAH BICENTENNIAL COMMISSION; 510 NORTH ST; DECORAH, IA 52101. (#109025-5).

AUG 7, '76. AGRICULTURE DAY - DISPLAY & DEMONSTRATION OF OLD FARM MACHINERY. EXHIBIT. (LOCAL). MAC GREENTREE, COORD; FFA; RR 2; DECORAH, IA 52101. (#109025-2).

DEFIANCE

DEFIANCE BICENTENNIAL ACTIVITIES, IA. THE YOUTH OF DEFIANCE HAVE CLEANED UP THE STREETS OF THE CITY & PAINTED. CEMETERY RECORDS WERE UPDATED FOR THE HISTORICAL SOCIETY. (LOCAL). ALICE C BIEKER, CHAIRMAN; DEFIANCE BICENTENNIAL COMMITTEE; DEFIANCE, IA 51527. (#28964).

'LIBERTY & JUSTICE FOR ALL' - DEFIANCE, IA. GROUP DISCUSSIONS ON THE CONCEPT OF LIBERTY IN COMMUNITIES, COURTS, SOCIAL LIFE, GOVERNMENT & SCHOOLS. (LOCAL). ALICE C BIEKER, CHAIRMAN; ST PETERS CHURCH PARISH COUNCIL; DEFIANCE, IA 51527. (#28965).

FEB 4, '76. BICENTENNIAL FAIR. ALL STUDENTS HANDMADE PROJECTS OF THEIR OWN CREATIVE ABILITY FEATURING AN EVENT IN HISTORY REGARDING COSTUMES, BUILDINGS OR INVENTIONS, ALSO SEVERAL LIVE SKITS ON HISTORICAL EVENTS. AT DEFIANCE COMMUNITY HALL. (LOCAL). ALICE C BIEKER, CHMN; ST PETER'S CHURCH; MAIN ST; DEFIANCE, IA 51527. (#200018-237).

DELMAR

BEAUTIFICATION OF CITY PARK - DELMAR, IA. THE DELMAR COMMUNITY SCHOOL STUDENTS WILL CLEANUP AND PLANT FLOWERS IN THE CITY PARK. (LOCAL). MILDRED JOHNSON, PROJ DIRECTOR; DELWOOD COMMUNITY SCHOOL; RR 2; DELMAR, IA 52037. (#21715).

CEMETERY CATALOGUING, IA. CEMETERIES LOCATED IN BLOOMFIELD TOWNSHIP WILL BE CATALOGUED BY MEMBERS OF THE UNITED METHODIST CHURCH AND ST PATRICK'S CATHOLIC CHURCH. INCLUDES RESTORATION OF CIVIL WAR ERA CEMETERY. (LOCAL). ROBERT HENCKE, COORDINATOR; ST PATRICKS CATHOLIC CHURCH; DELMAR, IA 52037. (#23918).

CONSTRUCTION OF PLANTER, DELMAR, IA. CONSTRUCTION OF BRICK PLANTER IN FRONT YARD OF SCHOOL WITH ANTIQUE BELL AS PART OF THE OVERHEAD ARCH. (LOCAL). MILDRED JOHNSON, TEACHDR; DELWOOD COMMUNITY SCHOOL; DELMAR, IA 52037. (#21718).

IMPROVEMENT OF MAIN ST AND PARK, IA. PLANTERS WILL BE MADE BY LOCAL HIGH SCHOOL SHOP CLASSES. GIRL SCOUTS WILL PLANT & CARE FOR FLOWERS. TREES WILL BE PLANTED IN THE PARK. NEW PLAYGROUND EQUIPMENT WILL BE ADDED. MONUMENT WILL BE RAISED. (LOCAL). JOHN A LARY, CHAIRMAN; DELMAR CITY COUNCIL & BICENTENNIAL COMMITTEE; BOX 58; DELMAR, IA 52037. (#23981).

JAIL REJUVENATION, IA. REPAIR AND CLEAN ONE HUNDRED YEAR OLD, SINGLE CELL, STONE JAIL. (LOCAL). DORIS SHEA, COORDINATOR; DELWOOD SCHOOL BOARD; RURAL ROUTE; DELMAR, IA 52037. (#23919).

PLANTING FLOWERS IN CITY PARK, DELMAR, IA. RED, WHITE & BLUE FLOWERS WILL BE PLANTED IN CITY ARK FOR THE BEAUTIFICATION OF THE CITY. (LOCAL). MILDRED JOHNSON, COORD; DELWOOD COMMUNITY SCHOOL; DELMAR, IA 52037. (#21719).

PRESERVATION OF ANTIQUE SCHOOL BELL - DELMAR, IA. THE CHILDREN AT THE DELMAR COMMUNITY SCHOOL WILL PRESERVE THE ANTIQUE SCHOOL BELL AND BUILD A BRICK PLANTER. (LOCAL). MILDRED JOHNSON, PROJ DIRECTOR; DELWOOD ELEMENTARY SCHOOL; RR 2; DELMAR, IA 52037. (#21716).

RESTORATION OF HISTORIC JAIL IN DELMAR, IA. JAIL WILL BE CLEANED AND RESTORED, FLOWERS WILL BE PLANTED AND A FENCE WILL BE PLACED AROUND IT. (LOCAL). MILDRED JOHNSON, PROJ DIRECTOR; DELWOOD COMMUNITY SCHOOL; RR 2; DELMAR, IA 52037. (#21717).

APR 8 - MAY 13, '76. POSTER AND ESSAY CONTEST. POSTERS WILL BE SUBMITTED BY LOCAL STUDENTS. PRIZES WILL BE AWARDED IN VARIOUS AGE GROUPS. ESSAYS WILL BE SUBMITTED BY LOCAL JUNIOR AND SENIOR HIGH STUDENTS. ESSAYS & POSTERS WILL DEAL WITH OUR HERITAGE. (LOCAL). DORIS SHEA, COORD; DELWOOD COMMUNITY SCHOOL BOARD; RR; DELMAR, IA 52037. (#107308-1).

JUNE 5, '76. CHILDREN'S PARADE. PARADE AT MAIN ST. (LOCAL). BONNIE BROWN, COORDINATOR; NEW CENTURY CLUB; DELMAR, IA 52037. (#106840-2).

JUNE 5 - 6, '76. TEEN STREET DANCE. FESTIVAL AT MAIN ST. (LOCAL). KENNETH GERLACK, CHMN; VOLUNTEER FIRE DEPT/4-H CLUB; DELMAR, IA 52037. (#106840-3).

JUNE 6, '76. COMMUNITY PICNIC. FESTIVAL AT DELMAR CITY PARK. (LOCAL). JOHN LARY, CHAIRMAN; BICENTENNIAL COMMITTEE OF DELMAR; BOX 58; DELMAR, IA 52037. (#106840-1).

DELPHOS

WILDLIFE HABITAT, DELPHOS, IA. ESTABLISH A PLACE FOR WILDLIFE TO LIVE. (LOCAL). SHIRLEY HACKMAN, COUNTY SECRETARY; RICE TOWNSHIP; DELPOS, IA 50844. (#24217).

DELTA

HISTORIC COVERED BRIDGE PROJECT IN DELTA, IOWA. PRESERVE HISTORIC SITE AND PARK. (LOCAL). MRS M L SHIPLEY, PROJ DIRECTOR; DELTA CENTENNIAL COMMITTEE; DELTA, IA 52550. (#12112).

'THIS IS DELTA: SINCE 1875' - DELTA, IOWA. SLIDE-TAPE HISTORY PRESENTATION ON THE COMMUNITY. (LOCAL). MRS M L SHIPLEY, PROJ DIRECTOR; DELTA CENTENNIAL COMMITTEE; DELTA, IA 52550. (#12113).

TOWN & COUNTRY CENTER IN DELTA, IOWA. A COMMUNITY CENTER WILL BE BUILT FOR MEETINGS & ENTERTAINMENT. (LOCAL). MRS M L SHIPLEY, PROJ DIRECTOR; DELTA CENTENNIAL COMMITTEE; DELTA, IA 52550. (#12114).

JULY 4 - 5, '75. CENTENNIAL DISPLAY ROOM IN DELTA, IOWA. OLD ARTICLES OF INTEREST ON DISPLAY. (LOCAL). MRS M L SHIPLEY; DELTA CENTENNIAL COMMITTEE; DELTA, IA 52550. (#12117-1).

JULY 4 - 6, '75. CENTENNIAL CELEBRATION. SPECIAL BICENTENNIAL PROGRAM TO BE PRESENTED. (LOCAL). MRS M L SHIPLEY; DELTA CENTENNIAL COMMITTEE; DELTA, IA 52550. (#12115-1).

JULY 4 - 6, '75. CIRCUIT RIDER PROJECT. MINISTER TO RIDE IN CIRCUIT RIDER CLOTHES AND CONDUCT WORSHIP SERVICE FOR COMMUNITY. (LOCAL). MRS M L SHIPLEY; DELTA CENTENNIAL COMMITTEE; DELTA, IA 52550. (#12116-1).

DENISON

LINCOLN SITE MARKER, DENISON, IA. LINCOLN SITE MARKER ON LAND GIVEN PRESIDENT ABRAHAM LINCOLN. (LOCAL). DICK MCCOLLOUGH, CHAIRMAN; CRAWFORD COUNTY BICENTENNIAL COMMITTEE; DENISON, IA 51442. (#15656).

PARK DEVELOPMENT, DENISON, IA. DEVELOPMENT OF 280 ACRE COUNTY CITY PARK. (LOCAL). DICK MCCOLLOUGH, PROJ COORDINATOR; CITY OF DENISON; DENISON, IA 51442. (#15657).

JULY 4, '76. PARADE & 4TH OF JULY CELEBRATION. PARADE. (LOCAL). DICK MCCOLLOUGH, CHMN; CRAWFORD COUNTY BICENTENNIAL COMMISSION; DENISON, IA 51442. (#102591-1).

DENMARK

BANDSTAND RESTORATION - DENMARK, IA. THE BANDSTAND IN STAR PARK WILL BE RESTORED AND USED TO HOLD SUMMER CONCERTS BY THE SCHOOL BAND. (LOCAL). KARL RUSCHILL, CHAIRMAN; DENMARK SENIOR CITIZENS; DENMARK, IA 52624. (#18889).

BICENTENNIAL FESTIVAL & PARADE PROJ - DENMARK, IA. A FLOAT IS BEING MADE FOR THE BICENTENNIAL PARADE. IT WILL HAVE A HISTORICAL THEME. (LOCAL). PAT LAIKE, COORDINATOR; SENIOR CITIZENS CONG - UCC; DENMARK, IA 52624. (#18422).

BICENTENNIAL FLOAT - DENMARK, IA. A FLOAT WITH A BICENTENNIAL THEME WILL BE CONSTRUCTED TO BE USED IN THE BICENTENNIAL PARADE. (LOCAL). MRS SHIRLIE MILLER, PROJ DIRECTOR; JUNIOR PF, DENMARK CONGREGATION UCC; DENMARK, IA 52624. (#18894).

BICENTENNIAL MUSIC TAPE - DENMARK, IA. THE TAPE WILL BE USED IN CHURCH CARILLON AND PLAYED AT SPECIAL EVENTS COMMEMORATING THE BICENTENNIAL. (LOCAL). KARL RUSCHILL, CHAIRMAN; DENMARK SENIOR CITIZENS; DENMARK, IA 52624. (#18887).

CHURCH RECORDS - DENMARK, IA. CHURCH RECORDS WILL BE RESEARCHED, CATALOGED AND MICROFILMED. (LOCAL). MRS KATHRYN NEWTON, CHAIRMAN; DENMARK CONGREGATION, UCC, HISTORICAL COMMITTEE; RR 1; FT MADISON, IA 52627. (#18899).

HISTORICAL HOME - DENMARK, IA. A HOME BUILT BEFORE 1850 FOR THE PURPOSE OF HELPING RUN-AWAY SLAVES WILL BE OPEN FOR PUBLIC VIEWING. (LOCAL). KATHY HOUSTON, DIRECTOR; COUNTRY COUSINS 4-H CLUB; DENMARK, IA 52624. (#18906).

HOSPITALITY FOR IOWA CYCLISTS - DENMARK, IA. LUNCH WILL BE SERVED TO IOWA BICYCLE RIDERS AND A REST STATION WILL BE PROVIDED IN STAR PARK. (LOCAL). MARTHA MECKLENBURG, CHAIRMAN; WOMAN'S FELLOWSHIP CONGREGATION, UCC; DENMARK, IA 52624. (#18896).

ICE-CREAM FESTIVAL. FESTIVAL. (LOCAL). WILLIAM MERTENS, CHMN; DENMARK PLANNED PROGRESS; DENMARK, IA 52624. (#18892-1).

IOWA STATE FLOWER PLANTING - DENMARK, IA. WILD ROSES, IOWA'S STATE FLOWER, WILL BE PLANTED AROUND THE HISTORIC MARKER IN STAR PARK; AN ARBOR DAY PROJECT. (LOCAL). KARL RUSCHILL, CHAIRMAN; DENMARK SENIOR CITIZENS; DENMARK, IA 52624. (#18886).

RECORD MICROFILMING - DENMARK, IA. MICROFILM THE RECORDS OF THE DENMARK ACADEMY DATING BACK TO 1842. (LOCAL). GORDON ROXBERG, SECRETARY; DENMARK ACADEMY; DENMARK, IA 52624. (#18901).

SCHOLARSHIP LOAN FUND - DENMARK, IA. PROVIDE LOW INTEREST LOANS TO STUDENTS FOR COLLEGE EXPENSE; FUNDS COME FROM ENDOWMENT FUNDS OF THE DENMARK ACADEMY. (LOCAL). GORDON ROXBERG, SECRETARY; DENMARK ACADEMY; DENMARK, IA 52624. (#18900).

SEND A GIRL TO CAMP - DENMARK, IA. TTT EACH YEAR SENDS TO SUMMER CAMP A DESERVING GIRL WHO WOULD NOT BE ABLE FINANCIALLY TO BROADEN HER HORIZONS BEYOND THIS COMMUNITY. (LOCAL). LINDA L ROXBERG, TREASURER; NATIONAL TTT SOCIETY, IOWA CHAPTER FK; RR1, BOX 105A; WEVER, IA 52658. (#18903).

STAR PARK BEAUTIFICATION - DENMARK, IA. TREES WILL BE REPLACED, TABLES AND BENCHES WILL BE PAINTED AND THE TRASH WILL BE PICKED UP. (LOCAL). WILLIAM P MERTENS, CHAIRMAN; DENMARK PLANNED PROGRESS; DENMARK, IA 52624. (#18891).

STREET SIGNS - DENMARK, IA. STREET SIGNS WILL BE PLACED ON EACH CORNER. (LOCAL). KARL RUSCHILL, CHAIRMAN; DENMARK SENIOR CITIZENS; DENMARK, IA 52624. (#18888).

DENMARK — CONTINUED

TREE PLANTING IN CHURCH YARD - DENMARK, IA. A TREE WILL BE PLANTED IN THE CHURCH YARD IN COMMEMORATION OF THE BICENTENNIAL. (LOCAL). MRS PAT LACKE, DIRECTOR; SENIOR PF DENMARK CONGREGATION, UCC; DENMARK, IA 52624. (#18908).

100 YEAR OLD FARMS - DENMARK, IA. THE COUNTRY COUSINS 4-H CLUB WILL SEARCH FOR RECORDS OF 100 YEAR OLD FARMS AND WILL ALERT OTHERS TO SEARCH. (LOCAL). KATHY HOUSTON, DIRECTOR; COUNTRY COUSINS 4-H CLUB; DENMARK, IA 52624. (#18905).

OCT 11, '75. BICENTENNIAL PARADE - CARRYING U S FLAGS. PARADE. (LOCAL). KAREN MATTER; JR GIRL SCOUTS; DENMARK, IA 52624. (#104080-3).

OCT 12, '75. CHURCH FESTIVAL. CEREMONY, FESTIVAL AT DENMARK STAR PARK ON HWY 18; PARKING ON GROUNDS. (LOCAL). DONALD BLANCHARD, COORD; DENMARK CONGREGATION UCC AUGUSTIA CATHOLIC WEVER CHRISTIAN; RR #1; WESTPOINT, IA 52656. (#200018-35).

JUNE 5 - 6, '76. SOUTHEAST IOWA ANTIQUE GAS ENGINE SHOW. EXHIBIT AT DENMARK STAR PARK HIGHWAY 16 - PARKING ON GROUNDS. (LOCAL). JERRY BOEDDEKER, CHMN; SOUTHEAST IOWA ANTQUE ENGINE SHOW; RR #1; FT MADISON, IA 52627. (#18898-1).

JUNE 6, '76. FLAG POLE CEREMONY. CEREMONY. (LOCAL). G MATTER; BOY SCOUT TROOP 19, BSA; DENMARK, IA 52624. (#104080-4).

DENVER

CEMETERY RECORDING AND RESTORATION, DENVER, IA. RECORDING, RESTORATION AND PERPETUAL UPKEEP OF THE CEMETERY. (LOCAL). DORIS KUEKER, CHAIRMAN; DENVER THIMBLEBEE; 125 E FAYETTE; DENVER, IA 50622. (#24050).

DENVER COMMUNITY HISTORY, DENVER. COMPILING HISTORICAL FACTS FROM THE AGED BY THE YOUTH AND UPDATING THEM, LOCAL FACTS, STORIES AND POEMS. (LOCAL). CLARA JUDAS, CHAIRMAN; DENVER BICENTENNIAL COMMITTEE; BOX 204; DENVER, IA 50622. (#24051).

HOUSING AND ECOLOGY PROJECT - DENVER, IA. SENIOR CITIZEN HOUSING PROJECT AND TREE & FLOWER PLANTING. (LOCAL). RON KNUDSON, CHAIRMAN; LIONS CLUB; 720 WASHINGTON; DENVER, IA 50622. (#24052).

JULY 4, '76. 4TH OF JULY FESTIVAL. OLD-FASHIONED 4TH OF JULY FESTIVAL: CONTESTS, ECUMENICAL CHURCH SERVICE, TIME CAPSULE, PICNIC & MUSIC. AT DENVER CITY PARK/3 BLOCKS EAST OF BANK (HWY 63). (LOCAL). MARY STEVENS; BICENTENNIAL COMMITTEE OF DENVER; 400 IOWA; DENVER, IA 50622. (#106860-2).

AUG 13 - 14, '76. HARVEST FESTIVAL. GAMES, TALENT SHOW, PARADE, DANCES & TRACTOR PULL. AT MAIN ST. (LOCAL). ED BOHLEN; LIONS CLUB & JAYCEES; RR3, WAVERLY; DENVER, IA 50622. (#106860-1).

DES MOINES

AMERICA AND THE WORLD 200 YRS AGO, DES MOINES, IA. EXPLORE WITH STUDENTS AND PUBLIC THE MICROCOSM OF CULTURES AS REPRESENTED IN SALISBURY HOUSE IN THE ART, ARTIFACTS, BOOKS AND MANUSCRIPS OF 200 YEARS AGO. (LOCAL). CAROLINE MOON, TOUR DIRECTOR, SALISBURY HOUSE; IOWA STATE EDUCATION ASSOC; 4025 TONAWANDA DR; DES MOINES, IA 50312. (#19674).

AMERICAN BICENTENNIAL WORLD FESTIVAL IN IOWA. FESTIVAL WILL HAVE CULTURAL DISPLAYS, SPORTS EVENTS, ETC. (REGN'L). DR LOUIS F HEGER, EXEC SECRETARY; DES MOINES AREA CONSORTIUM FOR HIGHER EDUCATION; 221 HOWARD, 25TH & UNIVERSITY; DES MOINES, IA 50311. (#10961).

AVENUE OF FLAGS - DES MOINES, IA. SERIES OF FLAGS FLOWN DAILY IN FRONT OF DES MOINES VETERANS' AUDITORIUM. ALSO PERMANENT DISPLAY FOR THE BICENT PERIOD OVER PORTICO OF ENTRANCE, A REPRODUCTION OF THE MINUTEMAN, FLANKED BY BENN. FLAG. (LOCAL). ROSA CUNNINGHAM; VETERANS' AUDITORIUM; 833 5TH AVE; DES MOINES, IA 50309. (#19649).

BICENTENNIAL AND THE AMERICAN AGENDA - IA. AN HISTORICAL SURVEY OF CONSTITUTIONAL AND STATUTORY LAW AND ITS IMPACT ON PRESERVING THOSE INALIENABLE RIGHTS TO THE CITIZENS OF THIS COUNTRY. SPEECH DELIVERED BY DR HELEN EDMONDS OF NC CENTRAL UNIV. (REGN'L). NOLDEN GENTRY, PGM CHAIRMAN; BLACK AMERICAN LAW STUDENT ASSOC AND DRAKE UNIVERSITY; 909 FLEMING BLDG; DES MOINES, IA 50309. (#26080).

BICENTENNIAL CALENDAR OF DES MOINES, IA. CALENDAR, PRODUCED BY TECH HIGH SCHOOL STUDENTS, FEATURES DRAWINGS OF OLD SCHOOLS & PUBLIC BUILDINGS IN DES MOINES. (LOCAL). DR ROBERT DENNY, SUPT OF SCHOOLS; DES MOINES TECHNICAL HIGH SCHOOL; 1800 GRAND AVE; DES MOINES, IA 50309. (#25292).

BICENTENNIAL MEMORIAL, DES MOINES, IA. A MONUMENT HONORING ALL VETERANS OF LAST 200 YEARS WILL BE BUILT. (LOCAL). LOUIS BOYSEN, CHAIRMAN; DES MOINES VFW & BICENTENNIAL COMMITTEE; 3601 BEAVER AVE; DES MOINES, IA 50310. (#19714).

BICENTENNIAL STUDENT COMPETITION, DES MOINES, IA. PROJECT DESIGNED TO RECOGNIZE THE CREATIVITY OF STUDENTS IN RELATIONSHIP TO THE BICENTENNIAL. (ST-WIDE). WILLIAM L SHERMAN, PR SPECIALIST; IOWA STATE EDUCATION ASSOC; 4025 TONAWANDA DR; DES MOINES, IA 50312. (#19673).

BICENTENNIAL TIME CAPSULE AND FOUNTAIN - IA. FOUNTAIN AND TIME CAPSULE WILL BE PLACED IN THE COURTYARD OF THE NEW STATE AGRICULTURAL BUILDING NOW UNDER CONSTRUCTION. (ST-WIDE). ED REDFERN, DEPUTY DIRECTOR; IOWA ARBC; STATE CAPITOL; DES MOINES, IA 50319. (#27331). **ARBA GRANTEE.**

BICENTENNIAL TRAVELING FORUM - DES MOINES, IOWA. TRAVELING FORUM ON CURRENT ISSUES ARISING OUT OF CONCEPTS OF FOUNDING FATHERS - COMBINES DRAMA AND SYMPOSIUM FORMATS. ISSUES ARE: PUNISHMENT, INDIVIDUALISM, EQUALITY, PRIVACY, POWER & WORLD MORALITY. (ST-WIDE). BURTON M LEISER, BICENT COMMITTEE CHAIRMAN; DRAKE UNIV; DES MOINES, IA 50311. (#8585).

BLACK AMERICAN LAW STUDENT RECOGNITION BANQUET-IA. THE BLACK AMERICAN LAW STUDENT ASSOCIATION IS SPONSORING A BANQUET WITH HELEN EDMONDS AS THE SPEAKER. (ST-WIDE). NOLDEN GENTRY, DIRECTOR; BLACK AMERICAN LAW STUDENT ASSOC; 9TH FLOOR, FLEMING BLDG; DES MOINES, IA 50309. (#27336). **ARBA GRANTEE.**

BLACK ODYESSY ART EXHIBIT & GATEWAY DANCERS - IA. THE BLACK ODYESSY ART EXHIBIT & GATEWAY DANCERS WILL BE AT THE IOWA STATE FAIR. (REGN'L). JERRY COUGHLIN, ACT SECRETARY; IOWA STATE FAIR; 30TH & GRAND AVE; DES MOINES, IA 50319. (#28196). **ARBA GRANTEE.**

BLOCK & BRIDLE HORSE SHOW. BICENTENNIAL CELEBRATION OF THE WORLD'S LARGEST STUDENT FUN HORSE SHOW. A MOUNTED PATRIOTIC COSTUME CLASS WILL BE HELD. THERE WILL BE A PRESENTATION OF THE U S & BICENTENNIAL FLAGS. (LOCAL). SCOTT AMENDT, CHAIRMAN; IOWA STATE UNIV BLOCK & BRIDLE CLUB; 119 KILDEE HALL; AMES, IA 50011. (#107987-1).

BOOK ON DANCES - DES MOINES, IA. THE BOOK WILL CONTAIN INFORMATION ON FOLK, ETHNIC & FAD DANCES FOR CHILDREN & ADULTS; TEACHING MATERIAL WILL EMPHASIZE THE CULTURE & BEAUTY OF MANY DIFFERENT GROUPS. (LOCAL). SYLVIA B ZARNOW, DANCE INSTRUCTOR; DEPT OF COMMUNITY & ADULT EDUCATION OF THE PM; 1800 GRAND AVE; DES MOINES, IA 50307. (#25302).

CARPENTER SHOP CONSTRUCTION - DES MOINES, IA. 1870 CARPENTER SHOP TO BE CONSTRUCTED TO SHOW CARPENTER'S ROLE IN AN EARLY FARMING COMMUNITY. THE SHOP WILL ALSO INCLUDE DISPLAYS AND TOOLS. (LOCAL). OLIVER GILLESPIE, EXECUTIVE DIRECTOR; LIVING HISTORY FARMS; 2600 111TH ST; DES MOINES, IA 50322. (#15125).

CONSERVATION OF ART PROJECT OF IOWA. MUSEUMS AT FORT DODGE, MASON CITY, DAVENPORT AND SIOUX CITY WILL SELECT PAINTING FOR PRESERVATION AND RESTORATION. (LOCAL). JACK OLDS, EXECUTIVE DIRECTOR; IOWA STATE ARTS COUNCIL; STATE CAPITOL BUILDING; DES MOINES, IA 50319. (#2141).

CORRIDOR TRAIL NETWORK OF DES MOINES, IOWA. DEVELOPING A GREEN BAND & STREAM CORRIDORS FOR BICYCLISTS, HORSEMEN, HIKERS & BOATERS. (ST-WIDE). FRED PRIEWERT, DIRECTOR; IOWA CONSERVATION COMMISSION; STATE HOUSE; DES MOINES, IA 50319. (#3678). **(??).**

DES MOINES BOTANICAL GARDENS PROJECT. NEW BOTANICAL CENTER INDOOR AND OUTDOOR. (ST-WIDE). MRS RICHARD MOORE, PRESIDENT; DES MOINES BOTANICAL CENTER; 4139 GREENWOOD DR; DES MOINES, IA 50312. (#3816).

'DISCOVERING HISTORIC IOWA', DIRECTORY, DES MOINES. PUBLICATION OF A COMPREHENSIVE DIRECTORY OF IOWA'S HISTORIC SITES, CONSERVATION AREAS & NOTABLE LANDMARKS. (LOCAL). RICHARD N SMITH, DEPUTY STATE SUPERINTENDENT; STATE DEPARTMENT OF PUBLIC INSTRUCTION; STATE HOUSE; DES MOINES, IA 50319. (#16130). **ARBA GRANTEE.**

EXHIBITION OF PAINTINGS IN DES MOINES, IA. COLLECTION OF 100 PAINTINGS FROM THE METROPOLITAN MUSEUM OF ART TO BE EXHIBITED AT THE DES MOINES ART CENTER FROM MARCH 28 TO JUNE 6, 1976. (ST-WIDE). JAMES T DEMETRION, DIRECTOR; DES MOINES ART CENTER; GREENWOOD PK; DES MOINES, IA 50312. (#15333). **ARBA GRANTEE.**

FAIR & COUNCIL FIRE OF CAMP FIRE GIRLS - IA. THE CAMP FIRE GIRLS COUNCIL FIRE WILL TAKE PLACE ON MAY 22, 1976. (ST-WIDE). ROBERT W DILLON, CHAIRMAN; IOWA AMERICAN REVOLUTION BICENTENNIAL COMMISSION; STATE CAPITOL; DES MOINES, IA 50319. (#23501). **ARBA GRANTEE.**

FARM OF THE FUTURE - DES MOINES, IA. MODERN FARM DATED IN LATE 1970S. SOLAR HOME WITH NEWEST INNOVATIONS; MODERN FARM EQUIPMENT; MODERN TECHNIQUES OF CROP AND LIVESTOCK PRODUCTION. (LOCAL). OLIVER GILLESPIE, EXECUTIVE DIRECTOR; LIVING HISTORY FARMS; 2600 11TH STREET; DES MOINES, IA 50322. (#15124).

FESTIVAL AND PARADE, DES MOINES, IA. RACIAL AND ETHNIC FESTIVAL AND PARADE. (ST-WIDE). MRS VIRGINIA HERMAN, CHAIRMAN; POLK COUNTY BICENTENNIAL COMMITTEE; 800 HIGH ST; DES MOINES, IA 50307. (#27265). **ARBA GRANTEE.**

FILM ON AGRICULTURE, DES MOINES, IA. FILM, 'SEEDS OF SURVIVAL', BY GRINNELL MUTUAL REINSURANCE COMPANY, DEPICTS LIFE IN EARLY 1840'S AND EARLY 1900'S. THE BICENTENNIAL FILM FEATURES ACCURATE COSTUMES, SETTINGS AND TOOLS. (ST-WIDE). OLIVER GILLESPIE, EXEC DIRECTOR; LIVING HISTORY FARMS; 2600 111TH ST; DES MOINES, IA 50322. (#15089).

FINAL BICENTENNIAL REPORT - DES MOINES, IA. A FINAL REPORT ON BICENTENNIAL ACTIVITIES WILL BE WRITTEN BY A PROFESSIONAL WRITER. (ST-WIDE). R EDWIN REDFERN, DEPUTY DIRECTOR; IOWA ARBC; STATE CAPITOL; DES MOINES, IA 50319. (#27337). **ARBA GRANTEE.**

FIRST LADIES INAUGURAL BALL GOWN DISPLAY - IA. DISPLAY OF 11 INCH PORCELAIN FIGURES DEPICTING EACH GOVERNOR'S WIFE IN INAUGURAL GOWN FROM 1910 ON; PRIOR TO 1910 THE GOWNS WILL BE PERIOD GOWNS & NOT ACTUAL REPLICA OF INAUGURAL GOWN. (LOCAL). SUE REED, CHAIRMAN; FIRST LADIES COMMITTEE OF TERRACE HILL SOCIETY; 1314 48TH ST; DES MOINES, IA 50311. (#26022). **ARBA GRANTEE.**

FLY THE FLAG, DES MOINES, IA. THE BOYS' CLUB OF DES MOINES FLIES FLAGS IN DOWNTOWN DES MOINES ON ALL NATIONAL HOLIDAYS AND OBSERVANCES. (LOCAL). FLORENCE C GRIGGS, COORDINATOR; BOYS CLUB OF DES MOINES; DES MOINES, IA 50307. (#24631).

FREEDOM TO KNOW, FREEDOM TO LEARN - DES MOINES, IA. INFORMATION BOOTH TO SERVE AS A CLEARINGHOUSE FOR BICENTENNIAL ACTIVITIES. THE BOOTH WILL BE IN OPERATION MAY-JULY, 1976. (LOCAL). RUTH STOKESBERRY, COMMUNITY RELATIONS CHMN; DES MOINES PUBLIC LIBRARY; DES MOINES, IA 50309. (#19771).

'FROM CABIN TO CAPITOL' - DES MOINES, IA. A BOOK WILL BE WRITTEN WHICH HIGHLIGHTS THE HISTORY OF POLK COUNTY. (LOCAL). JANE ROBBINS, COORDINATOR; POLK COUNTY BICENTENNIAL COMMISSION; 800 HIGH ST; DES MOINES, IA 50307. (#19650).

GREENBELT BICENTENNIAL TRAIL, DES MOINES, IA. A RECREATIONAL TRAIL FEATURING HIKING & BIKING TRAILS, PICNIC AREAS, OVERLOOKS, REST AREAS & BOAT RAMPS TO BE DEVELOPED ALONG THE DES MOINES RIVER. (LOCAL). VIRGINIA HER, CHAIRMAN; POLK COUNTY BICENTENNIAL COMMISSION; 800 HIGH ST; DES MOINES, IA 50307. (#24632).

HERITAGE OF AMERICAN ART - DES MOINES, IA. EXHIBITION OF 100 AMERICAN PAINTINGS FROM CA 1735 TO 1915 FROM THE COLLECTION OF THE METROPOLITAN MUSEUM OF ART IN NEW YORK. (LOCAL). JAMES T DEMETRION, DIRECTOR; DES MOINES ART CENTER, EDMUNDSON ART FOUNDATION, INC; GREENWOOD PARK; DES MOINES, IA 50312. (#18229).

HISTORY OF HOSPITAL AUXILIARIES IN IOWA. HISTORY OF ALL HOSPITAL AUXILIARIES IN IOWA & THE COMMITTEE ON VOLUNTEERS OF THE IOWA HOSPITAL ASSOCIATION. (ST-WIDE). DONNA GABRIEL, PAST CHMN; COMMITTEE ON VOLUNTEERS, IOWA HOSPITAL ASSOC; 1134 KEITH COURT; CLINTON, IA 52732. (#18796).

HOLIDAY PARK SHELTER HOUSE - DES MOINES, IA. CONSTRUCT SHELTER HOUSE IN HOLIDAY PARK FOR PUBLIC USE. (ST-WIDE). L WARREN SHANK, VICE PRESIDENT; WEST DES MOINES JAYCEES; 4712 DAKOTA DR; DES MOINES, IA 50265. (#15842).

INNOVATION & DIVERSITY IN AMERICAN CULTURE, IA. AN EXHIBIT DESIGNED TO EMPHASIZE LOCAL MOTIVATIONS & EXPOSITIONAL MATERIAL. (ST-WIDE). ROBERT BRIDIGUM, DIRECTOR; DES MOINES CENTER OF SCIENCE AND INDUSTRY; 45TH AND GRAND; DES MOINES, IA 50312. (#16129). **ARBA GRANTEE.**

INTERNATIONAL INFORMATION BOOTH - DES MOINES, IA. INFORMATION BOOTH AT DES MOINES AIRPORT, TO AID VISITORS TO THE INTERNATIONAL CONFERENCES, JUNE 22 THRU AUG 21, 1976, PARTICULARLY THE WORLD FOOD CONFERENCE, AT IOWA STATE UNIVERSITY, AMES, IOWA. (INT'L). VIRGINIA HERMANN, CHAIRMAN; POLK COUNTY BICENTENNIAL COMMISSION; 8TH & HIGH ST; DES MOINES, IA 50307. (#24663).

IOWA DAILY PRESS ASSOC BICENTENNIAL ACTIVITY-NBMRP. ASSOCIATION FURNISHES RELEASES & OICTURES TO 39 IOWA PAPERS. ONE SERIES EMPLOYED COLLEGE JOURNALISM STUDENTS. OTHER RELEASES WERE ON COMMUNITIES PGM, WAGON TRAIN, ABOVE-GROUND ARCHAEOLOGY, ETC. (ST-WIDE). HARRISON WEBER, BICENTENNIAL COORDINATOR; IOWA DAILY PRESS ASSOCIATION; 508 SHOPS BUILDING; DES MOINES, IA 50309. (#26909).

IOWA PIONEER CERTIFICATE, DES MOINES. RESEARCH ON EARLIEST ANCESTOR IN IOWA, BEFORE 1856; WHERE HE LIVED, DIED AND WAS BURIED. (ST-WIDE). DOROTHY GOLDIZEN, PRESIDENT; IOWA GENEALOGICAL SOCIETY; PO BOX 3815; DES MOINES, IA 50322. (#22744).

THE IOWA STATE FAIR. 1975 COLONIZERS/1976 BICENTENNIAL FAIR FEATURING FOODS OF THE WORLD WILL BE NEXT TWO THEMES OF THE FAIR. (REGN'L). KENNETH R FULK, SECRETARY; IOWA STATE FAIR; 30TH & GRAND AVE; DES MOINES, IA 50319. (#3672). **ARBA RECOGNIZED. ARBA GRANTEE.**

IOWA 2000: GOVERNOR'S CONFERENCE ON THE YEAR 2000. IOWA FUTURES PROGRAM LAUNCHED THE BICENTENNIAL ERA IN IOWA. EVERY TV STATION IN THE STATE CARRIED ONE HOUR 'KICKOFF', MODERATED BY HARRY REASONER-TOWN MEETINGS WERE HELD THROUGHOUT STATE. (ST-WIDE). DENNIS NAGEL, ADMINISTRATIVE ASSISTANT; GOVERNOR'S OFFICE; STATE HOUSE; DES MOINES, IA 50319. (#3741).

LANGUAGE BANK BOOK - DES MOINES, IA. BOOK LISTING THE NAMES OF DES MOINES RESIDENTS WILLING TO OFFER TRANSLATION SERVICES TO FOREIGN VISITORS. 38 DIFFERENT LANGUAGES AND MANY DIALECTS ARE REPRESENTED. (LOCAL). DOROTHY TOWNE, PROJ COORDINATOR; DES MOINES AREA COUNCIL FOR INTERNATIONAL UNDERSTANDING; 1158 27TH ST; DES MOINES, IA 50311. (#19648).

LIVING HISTORY FARMS. IOWA'S AGRICULTURAL PROGRESS IN 3 FARMS-AN 1840 PIONEER FARM; A 1900 HORSE FARM; A FARM OF THE FUTURE. EACH HAS A FAMILY GROWING CROPS, LIVESTOCK & SIMILAR ACTIVITIES OF THE PERIOD REPPRESENTED. (NAT'L). DR WILLIAM G MURRAY, RESEARCH DIRECTOR; LIVING HISTORY FARMS FOUNDATION; 2600 111TH ST; DES MOINES, IA 50322. (#167). **ARBA RECOGNIZED. ARBA GRANTEE.**

LIVING HISTORY FARM SWINE BUILDING-DES MOINES, IA. CONSTRUCTION OF A SWINE BUILDING FOR THE 1900 FARM AT THE LIVING HISTORY FARM HOME SITE. (ST-WIDE). WILLIAM G

DES MOINES — CONTINUED

MURRAY, PRESIDENT; LIVING HISTORY FARMS; RURAL RT 1, 2600 NW 111TH ST; DES MOINES, IA 50322. (#28197). **ARBA GRANTEE.**

LOG HOUSE CONSTRUCTION - DES MOINES, IA. 1850 LOG HOUSE CONSTRUCTION UNDERWAY AT PIONEER FARM. IT REPRESENTS SECOND STAGE OF A PIONEER FAMILY SETTLING IN NEW COUNTRY. (LOCAL). OLIVER GILLESPIE, EXECUTIVE DIRECTOR; LIVING HISTORY FARMS; 2600 111TH ST; DES MOINES, IA 50322. (#15123).

MICROFILMING IOWA'S HISTORICAL RECORDS PROJECT. MICROFILMING RECORDS IN COURTHOUSE THAT ARE 65 YRS OLD OR OLDER. ALSO OUTSIDE RECORDS OF CHURCHES, HISTORICAL SOCIETIES, SCHOOLS, LIBRARIES & CEMETERIES. (ST-WIDE). MRS VELMA FRY, HERITAGE CHAIRMAN; IOWA ARBC; STATE HOUSE; DES MOINES, IA 50319. (#3671).

OLDER IOWANS BICENTENNIAL PROJECT '76 - DES MOINES. TALENTS OF OLDER CITIZENS WILL BE SOUGHT THEN SHARED WITH ALL AGE GROUPS IN PERFORMANCES, BOOKS, ART SHOWS & LECTURES. PARTICIPATION IN EXISTING BICENT EVENTS WILL BE ENCOURAGED. (ST-WIDE). KAREN K LAING, CONSULTANT; IOWA COMMISSION ON THE AGING; 415 10TH ST; DES MOINES, IA 50309. (#18270).

POLK-GREATER DES MOINES RECREATION COUNCIL, IA. BROAD BASED CITIZEN COUNCIL IS BRIDGE BETWEEN PUBLIC AND PRIVATE AGENCIES; ADVOCATE FOR LEISURE, RECREATION & CULTURAL NEEDS WHICH ARE PRESENTLY NOT BEING ME. (LOCAL). WILLIAM L SMITH, EXEC DIRECTOR; COMMUNITY SURVEY, INC/POLK-GREATER DES MOINES RECREATION COUNCIL; 505 E FIRST; DES MOINES, IA 50309. (#17948).

PRE-1900 PORTRAIT INVENTORY & SHOWINGS PROJ- IOWA. STATE-WIDE INVENTORY WILL BE CONDUCTED BY NATL SOCIETY OF COLONIAL DAMES. COLONIAL DAMES WILL PUBLISH INVENTORY. (ST-WIDE). MRS AMOS PEARSALL, PORTRAIT PROJ DIRECTOR; NATL SOCIETY OF COLONIAL DAMES; 4320 GREENWOOD DR; DES MDINES, IA 50312. (#3739). **ARBA GRANTEE.**

PROMO PRIMER TOWN MEETING - DES MOINES, IA. PROTOTYPE TOWN MEETING-REVOLUTION APPROACH TO GOVERNMENT. TOWN'S OFFICIALS CONDUCT PUBLIC'S BUSINESS IN SHOPPING MALLS DURING ANNOUNCED HOURS; DISPLAY OF TAXPAYER PURCHASED EQUIPMENT. (LOCAL). DORAL P CHENOWETH, PRESIDENT; CENTER ADVERTISING AGENCY, INC; BOX 5257; DES MOINES, IA 50306. (#25455).

PUBLIC LIBRARY INFORMATION BOOTH IN DES MOINES, IA. A CLEARINGHOUSE FOR ALL BICENTENNIAL ACTIVITIES AROUND THE STATE AS WELL AS A CENTER FOR DISTRIBUTING LITERATURE ABOUT BICENTENNIAL OBSERVANCES. (ST-WIDE). RUTH STOKESBERRY, DIRECTOR; PUBLIC LIBRARY OF DES MOINES; 1 ST LOCUST; DES MOINES, IA 50309. (#11652). **ARBA GRANTEE.**

REPAINT VALLEY JUNCTION RAILROAD DEPOT - IA. SENIOR CITIZENS WILL BE REPAINTING THE OLD RAILROAD STATION. (LOCAL). NELLIE AMES, CHAIRMAN; WEST DES MOINES SENIOR CITIZENS COUNCIL; 135 7TH ST; DES MOINES, IA 50265. (#15844).

RESTORATION OF FLYNN MANSION TO 1870 APPEARANCE-IA. ORIGINAL STRUCTURE RESTORED TO 1870 APPEARANCE - TWO UPSTAIRS BEDROOMS, UPPER HALL, PARLOR, SITTING ROOM, MAIN HALL AND STAIRWAY REFURBISHED WITH PERIOD FURNITURE; BY COLONIAL DAMES OF IA. (ST-WIDE). OLIVER GILLESPIE, EXECUTIVE DIRECTOR; LIVING HISTORY FARMS; 2600 111TH ST; DES MOINES, IA 50322. (#15126). **ARBA GRANTEE.**

REVOLUTIONARY COLOR GUARD, DES MOINES, IA. A FOUR MAN COLOR GUARD DRESSED IN REVOLUTIONARY STYLE UNIFORMS WILL TRAVEL THROUGHOUT THE MIDWEST TO LEAD BICENTENNIAL PARADES. (REGN'L). R J MOCKENHAUPT, PROJ DIRECTOR; DES MOINES TECHNICAL HIGH SCHOOL; 1800 GRAND AVE; DES MOINES, IA 50307. (#25131).

SENIOR CITIZENS DAY - STATE LIBRARY COMM OF IOWA. LOCAL LIBRARY INVITING SENIOR CITIZENS TO CELEBRATE PAUL REVERE'S RIDE ON APRIL 18, 1975; RECORDS & PICTURES TO BE ON DISPLAY. (ST-WIDE). FLORENCE STYLES, PUB INFO DIR; STATE LIBRARY COMMISSION OF IOWA; HISTORICAL BUILDING; DES MOINES, IA 50319. (#12001). **ARBA GRANTEE.**

STATE FAIR BOOTH FOR IOWA ARCHEOLOGICAL SOCIETY. AN ARCHEOLOGICAL PREHISTORY AWARENESS CENTER AT THE IOWA STATE FAIR IN 1976. (ST-WIDE). DUANE ANDERSON, PRESIDENT; IOWA ARCHEOLOGICAL SOCIETY; EASTLAWN UNIVERSITY OF IOWA; IOWA CITY, IA 52242. (#26587). **ARBA GRANTEE.**

STORAGE OF MICROFILMING RECORDS, DES MOINES, IA. CABINETS FOR STORING MICROFILM FOR COUNTY RECORDS MICROFILMED BY THE HERITAGE COMMITTEE OF IOWA ARBC. (ST-WIDE). MURRAY GOODMAN, DIRECTOR; IOWA ARBC; STATE CAPITOL; DES MOINES, IA 50319. (#25722). **ARBA GRANTEE.**

TERRACE HILL RESTORATION IN DES MOINES, IOWA. A VICTORIAN MANSION 120 YEARS OLD TO BE RESTORED AS THE GOVERNOR'S HOME. TWO FLOORS WILL BE OPEN TO THE PUBLIC. (LOCAL). MAURICE E BARINGER, STATE TRES; STATE OF IOWA; STATE HOUSE; DES MOINES, IA 50319. (#207).

TRADITIONAL APPLE ORCHARD, DES MOINES, IA. AN APPLE ORCHARD WILL BE PLANTED ON 2 ACRES AT LIVING HISTORY FARMS. (ST-WIDE). MRS ARLOINE LUNT, PROJ DIRECTOR; STATE GARDEN CLUB OF IOWA; 1510 GERMANTA DR; DES MOINES, IA 50311. (#16131). **ARBA GRANTEE.**

1900 GARDEN AND ORCHARD PROJECT IN DES MOINES. PLANNING LANDSCAPING PLANTING FOR LIVING HISTORY FARMS. REPLICA OF 1900 FARMSTED. (ST-WIDE). H OLIVER GILLESPIE, DIRECTOR; FOUNDERS GARDEN CLUB; 2600 111TH ST; DES MOINES, IA 50322. (#3728).

'76 COOK BOOK, DES MOINES, IA. IN 1876 PLYMOUTH WOMEN PUBLISHED A COOK BOOK TITLED "76 COOKBOOK' TO COMMEMORATE THE COUNTRY'S BIRTHDAY. OUR BICENTENNIAL PROJECT IS OUR "76 COOKBOOK'. (ST-WIDE). MRS RALPH MELONE, CHAIRMAN; PLYMOUTH WOMENS FELLOWSHIP PLYMOUTH CHURCH; 4126 INGERSOLL; DES MOINES, IA 50312. (#20582).

MAY 17, '75 - CONTINUING . LIVING HISTORY FARMS OF IOWA. IOWA'S AGRICULTURAL PROGRESS IN 3 FARMS-AN 1840 PIONEER FARM; A 1900 HORSE FARM; A FARM OF THE FUTURE. EACH HAS A FAMILY GROWING CROPS, LIVESTOCK & SIMILAR ACTIVITIES OF THE PERIOD REPPRESENTED. (REGN'L). DR WILLIAM G MURPHY; LIVING HISTORY FARMS FOUNDATION; 2600 111TH ST; DES MOINES, IA 50322. (#167-1).

JULY 26 - 27, '75. GRAIN HARVEST FESTIVAL, OLD METHODS. STEAM THRESHING, GRAIN HARVESTING WITH CRADLE, OLD GASOLINE ENGINE DISPLAY, OLD MACHINERY DISPLAYS, OLD FIDDLERS' CONTEST,. AT FESTIVAL FIELD DOUGLAS AVE. EXIT I-35/80 1/4 MILE WEST. (ST-WIDE). RON WESTPHAL; LIVING HISTORY FARMS; 2600 N.W. 111TH STREET R.R. 1; DES MOINES, IA 50322. (#50419-1).

OCT 4 - 5, '75. CORN HARVEST FESTIVAL, HAND CORN PICKING. HAND CORN PICKING CONTEST, STEAM AND GASOLINE ENGINE DISPLAYS & DEMONSTATIONS, NEW EQUIPMENT DEMONSTRATIONS & DISPLAYS,. AT FESTIVAL FIELD DOUGLAS AVE. EXIT I-35/80 1/4 MILE WEST. (ST-WIDE). RON WESTPHAL; LIVING HISTORY FARMS; 2600 N.W. 111TH STREET R.R.1; DES MOINES, IA 50322. (#50419-2).

OCT 6 - 13, '75. NAVY BICENTENNIAL BIRTHDAY. THIS WEEK OF ACTIVITY WILL PRECEDE THE 200TH ANNIVERSARY OF THE FOUNDING OF THE U S NAVY ON OCT 13, 1775; THERE WILL BE 4 LUNCH MEETINGS WITH NAVY FLAG SPEAKERS AND ONE ROYAL NAVAL OFFICER, BIRTHDAY BALL AND MODEL SHIP RIDES. (ST-WIDE). RICHARD RILEY, CHAIRMAN; BICENTENNIAL BIRTHDAY COMMITTEE; 823 WALNUT; DES MOINES, IA 50309. (#103717-1).

OCT 17 - 19, '75. UNITED STATES ARMED FORCES BICENTENNIAL CARAVAN. THE CARAVAN IS COMPOSED OF EXHIBIT VANS FOR EACH BRANCH OF THE MILITARY SERVICE. THE THEME OF THE EXHIBITION IS 'HISTORY OF THE ARMED FORCES AND THEIR CONTRIBUTION TO THE NATION'. (LOCAL). MRS VIRGINIA HERMANN, DIR; POLK COUNTY BICENTENNIAL COMMISSION; 604 POLK BLVD; DES MOINES, IA 50312. (#1775-217).

NOV '75. GRAIN HARVEST FESTIVAL. DEMONSTRATIONS OF EARLY HARVESTING TECHNIQUES INCLUDING THRESHING, AN OPERATING STEAM ENGINE AND BAILING; ALSO DISPLAYS OF GASOLINE ENGINES AND FARM MACHINERY. AT LIVING HISTORY FARMS. (LOCAL). OLIVER GILLESPIE, CHMN; LIVING HISTORY FARMS; 2600 111TH ST; DES MOINES, IA 50322. (#102585-4).

NOV '75. OLD TIME BLACKSMITHING. THE DEMONSTRATION WILL INCLUDE THE MAKING OF HASPS, HINGES, HORSESHOES AND GATEHOOKS. AT LIVING HISTORY FARMS. (LOCAL). OLIVER GILLESPIE, CHMN; LIVING HISTORY FARMS; 2600 111TH ST; DES MOINES, IA 50322. (#102585-5).

NOV '75. PIONEER FARM DAYS. THERE WILL BE DEMONSTRATIONS OF PIONEERING ACTIVITIES SUCH AS SPINNING, WEAVING, NATURAL DYEING, MAKING SOAP AND BUILDING LOG CABINS. AT LIVING HISTORY FARMS. (LOCAL). OLIVER GILLESPIE, CHMN; LIVING HISTORY FARMS; 2600 111TH ST; DES MOINES, IA 50322. (#102585-6).

FEB 15 - 16, '76. BICENTENNIAL STUDENT MODEL SESSION. HIGH SCHOOL STUDENTS, CHOSEN COMPETITIVELY BY TEACHERS, WILL ATTEND A MODEL SESSION FOR 2 DAYS. THE 1ST DAY WILL BE SPENT ORGANIZING AND THE 2ND DAY WILL BE SPENT IN A LEGISLATIVE SESSION. OPEN SUN 1-7PM; MON 8AM-4PM. AT STATE CAPITOL BLDG HOUSE CHAMBER. (ST-WIDE). SHARON ROBINSON PIO; IOWA DEPT OF PUBLIC INSTRUCTION & IOWA HOUSE OF REPRESENTATIVES; STATE CAPITOL BLDG HOUSE OF REP; DES MOINES, IA 50319. (#104020-8).

MAR 28 - JUNE 6, '76. EXHIBIT OF 100 PAINTINGS FROM METROPOLITAN MUSEUM OF ART. A MAJOR EXHIBITION OF AMERICAN PAINTINGS OF THE 18TH, 19TH AND EARLY 20TH CENTURY. AT GREENWOOD PARK; EXIT INTERSTATE 235 AT 42ND ST.. (ST-WIDE). JAMES T DEMETRION, DIR; DES MOINES ART CENTER; GREENWOOD PK; DES MOINES, IA 50312. (#15333-1).

APR 3, '76. SALUTE TO AMERICA RAZZLE DAZZLE '76. FESTIVAL AT ROOSEVELT HIGH SCHOOL, 45TH AND CENTER. (LOCAL). W J BURBANK, COORD; DESMOINAIRES; 4817 UNIVERSITY AVE; DES MOINES, IA 50311. (#200018-38).

APR 6 - 7, '76. IOWA WAGON TRAIN CEREMONIES. CEREMONY AT STATE CAPITOL AND STATE FAIR GROUNDS. (REGN'L). ED REDFERN, COORD; IOWA BICENTENNIAL COMMITTEE; 507 10TH ST; DES MOINES, IA 50309. (#200018-37).

APR 23 - JULY 1, '76. BICENTENNIAL EXHIBIT. EXHIBIT OF IOWA'S CONTRIBUTIONS TO AMERICA'S HERITAGE. AT MERLE HAY MALL. (ST-WIDE). BURTON LEISER, CHAIRMAN; DRAKE UNIV BICENTENNIAL COMMITTEE; DES MOINES, IA 50311. (#105813-1).

MAY 1 - JULY 4, '76. BICENTENNIAL MEMORIAL TO HONOR VETERANS OF PAST 200 YRS. CEREMONY AT STATE HOUSE GROUNDS. (LOCAL). LOUIS BOYSEN, CHAIRMAN; VETERANS OF FOREIGN WARS & DES MOINES BICENTENNIAL COMMITTEE; 3601 BEAVER AVE; DES MOINES, IA 50310. (#104519-22).

MAY 1 - AUG 31, '76. RICHMAN GORDMAN BICENTENNIAL SERIES. COSTUME SEWING CONTEST, POSTER CONTEST, ETHNIC FESTIVALS, DRUM AND BUGLE FESTIVAL, LIBERTY BELL DISPLAY. AT ALL RICHMAN GORDMAN STORES IN OMAHA,NE; DES MOINES, IA; COUNCIL BLUFFS, IA; LINCOLN, NE; GRAND ISLAND, NE; AND TOPEKA, KS. AT RICHMAN GORDMAN STORES IN OMAHA, DES MOINES, COUNCIL BLUFFS, LINCOLN. (REGN'L). M ROSLYN RIMMERMAN, DIR; RICHMAN GORDMAN STORES, INC; 12100 W CENTER RD; OMAHA, NE 68144. (#105770-1).

MAY 18, '76. DES MOINES SCHOOLS BICENTENNIAL CONCERT. LIVE PERFORMANCE AT VETERANS AUDITORIUM, 833 5TH AVE. (LOCAL). FLORENCE C GRIGGS, COORD; DES MOINES SCHOOL SYSTEM - BOARD OF EDUCATION; 1800 GRAND AVE; DES MOINES, IA 50309. (#107746-1).

MAY 19, '76. BLACK AMERICAN LAW STUDENT RECOGNITION BANQUET. CONFERENCE, FESTIVAL. (ST-WIDE). NOLDEN GENTRY, DIRECTOR; BLACK AMERICAN LAW STUDENT ASSOC; 9TH FLOOR, FLEMING BLDG; DES MOINES, IA 50309. (#27336-1).

MAY 22, '76. ETHNIC FESTIVAL. FESTIVAL. (LOCAL). VIRGINIA HERMAN, CHMN; POLK COUNTY BICENTENNIAL COMMITTEE; 8TH & HIGH ST; DES MOINES, IA 50307. (#106148-1).

MAY 22, '76. POLK COUNTY BICENTENNIAL PARADE. PARADE. (LOCAL). VIRGINIA HERMANN, CHMN; POLK COUNTY BICENTENNIAL COMMITTEE; 8TH & HIGH ST; DES MOINES, IA 50307. (#106148-2).

MAY 22, '76. 'WE, THE CAMP FIRE GIRLS' FAIR & COUNCIL FIRE. FESTIVAL, CEREMONY. (ST-WIDE). ROBERT DILLON, CHAIRMAN; IOWA AMERICAN REVOLUTION BICENTENNIAL COMMISSION; STATE CAPITOL; DES MOINES, IA 50319. (#23501-1).

MAY 30 - JUNE 6, '76. 18TH CENTURY ART COLLECTION EXHIBIT. OPEN SUNDAY - 12 PM TO 5 PM. AT ART CENTER, POLK BLVD & GRAND. (LOCAL). VIRGINIA HERMANN, COORD; DES MOINES ART CENTER; 800 HIGH ST; DES MOINES, IA 50307. (#108084-2).

JUNE 20, '76. 'YEAR OF THE VOLUNTEER'. EVENING PROGRAM WITH BAND MUSIC UNDER THE STARS IN RECOGNITION OF ALL CITY VOLUNTEERS AND IN HONOR OF THE AMERICAN TRADITION OF VOLUNTEERISM. BICENTENNIAL THEME WILL BE CARRIED OUT. AT STATE CAPITOL GROUNDS. (LOCAL). MRS CHARLES HERBERT; JUNIOR LEAGUE, INC/UNITED WAY VOLUNTEER BUREAU; 527 7TH ST; DES MOINES, IA 50315. (#104020-17).

JULY 2 - 4, '76. ANTIQUE DISPLAY. EXHIBIT AT SOUTH EAST POLK HIGH SCHOOL GYMNASIUM. (LOCAL). MRS G M ATZEN, CHAIRMAN; SOUTH EAST POLK BICENTENNIAL ASSOC; 6589 S E 6TH AVE; DES MOINES, IA 50317. (#106720-3).

JULY 2 - 4, '76. ECUMENICAL WORSHIP SERVICES. CEREMONY AT TEMPLE JESHRUM, ST AUGUSTINE; PLYMOUTH CONGREGATIONAL, CAPITOL BLDG. (LOCAL). VIRGINIA HERMANN, COORD; DES MOINES AREA RELIGIOUS COUNCIL; 800 HIGH ST; DES MOINES, IA 50307. (#108084-1).

JULY 2 - 4, '76. OLD-FASHIONED 4TH OF JULY CELEBRATION. FESTIVAL AT SOUTH EAST POLK HIGH SCHOOL. (LOCAL). MRS G M ATZEN, CHAIRMAN; SOUTH EAST POLK BICENTENNIAL ASSOC; 6589 S E 6TH AVE; DESMOINES, IA 50317. (#106720-1).

JULY 2 - 4, '76. QUILTING COMPETITION & SALE. COMPETITION, EXHIBIT AT SOUTH EAST POLK HIGH SCHOOL GYMNASIUM. (LOCAL). MRS G M ATZEN, CHAIRMAN; SOUTH EAST POLK BICENTENNIAL ASSOC; 6589 S E 6TH AVE; DES MOINES, IA 50317. (#106720-2).

JULY 2 - 5, '76. BICENTENNIAL MEMORABILIA EXHIBIT AT VETERAN'S AUDITORIUM. EXHIBIT AT VETERANS AUDITORIUM, DES MOINES, IOWA. (LOCAL). RON VESTAL; POLICE PROTECTIVE ASSOC; DES MOINES POLICE DEPT; DES MOINES, IA 50300. (#107957-1).

JULY 2 - SEPT 6, '76. DRAKE UNIVERSITY TRAVELLING BICENTENNIAL FORUM. A FORUM ENCOURAGING DISCUSSION OF MAJOR ISSUES ON THE AMERICAN SCENE; COMBINING EXPERTS AND LOCAL CITIZENS IN A TOWN MEETING FORMAT. PLANNING ADDITIONAL DATES AND SITES. AT CLINTON, IA; DES MOINES, IA; IOWA STATE FAIR; REUNION, MT. (ST-WIDE). BURTON LEISTER, CHMN; DRAKE UNIV BICENTENNIAL COMMISSION; DES MOINES, IA 50311. (#105801-2).

JULY 3, '76. BOAT PARADE. PARADE AT DES MOINES RIVER. (LOCAL). VIRGINIA HERMANN, COORD; FRIENDSHIP COMMITTEE & POLK COUNTY BICENTENNIAL COMMITTEE; 800 HIGH ST; DES MOINES, IA 50307. (#108084-3).

JULY 4, '76. BICENTENNIAL CELEBRATION DAYS. CELEBRATION INCLUDES 200 YEARS OF AGRICULTURAL PROGRESS AND VARIOUS DEMONSTRATIONS OF FARM ACTIVITIES. (LOCAL). OLIVER GILLESPIE, DIR; LIVING HISTORY FARMS; 2600 111TH STREET; DES MOINES, IA 50322. (#102585-7).

JULY 10, '76. 4-H CLUB PICNIC & PARADE. FESTIVAL, PARADE. (LOCAL). DARYL MARTIN, CHAIRMAN; 4-H CLUB; 318 N 5TH; OSKALOOSA, IA 52577. (#101785-1).

JULY '76. RACIAL AND ETHNIC FESTIVAL AND PARADE. FESTIVAL, PARADE. (LOCAL). VIRGINIA HERMAN, CHMN; POLK COUNTY BICENTENNIAL COMMITTEE; 800 HIGH ST; DES MOINES, IA 50307. (#27265-1).

AUG 18 - 20, '76. LIBERTY BELL ANGUS SIRE EVALUATION CONTEST. STEERS SIRED BY 25 OF AMERICA'S MOST FAMOUS ANGUS BULLS WILL BE JUDGED TO DETERMINE THEIR PHYSICAL EXCELLENCE & THE MERIT OF THE BEEF THEY PRODUCE, INDICATED BY QUALITY & DEGREE OF MUSCLING IN THE CARCASSES. SPECIAL REPLICA LIBERTY BELL TROPHIES TO BE AWARDED. AT IOWA STATE FAIRGROUNDS. (REGN'L). ROBERT C SNYDER; AMER ANGUS ASSOC; 3201 FREDERICK BLVD; ST JOSEPH, MO 64501. (#102862-1).

AUG 18 - 20, '76. NATIONAL BICENTENNIAL ANGUS SHOW. LEADING HERDS OF ANGUS BEEF CATTLE TO COMPETE FOR $20,000 IN PRIZE MONEY & HIGHEST HONORS IN SHOW OF LEADING AMER BREED. EACH CLASS OF ANGUS TO BE CALLED TO JUDGING AREA BY TOLLING OF LIBERTY BELL REPLICA CAST BY

DES MOINES — CONTINUED

WHITECHAPEL FOUNDRIES WHICH CAST THE ORIGINAL IN 1752. AT IOWA STATE FAIR LIVESTOCK JUDGING ARENA. (REGN'L). ROBERT C SNYDER; AMER ANGUS ASSOC; 3201 FREDERICK BLVD; ST JOSEPH, MO 64501. (#102862-2).

AUG 18 - 28, '76. ANTIQUE CAR AND HORSEDRAWN VEHICLE SHOW W/DRIVING CONTESTS. EXHIBIT, COMPETITION. (LOCAL). OLIVER GILLESPIE, CHMN; LIVING HISTORY FARMS; 2600 111TH ST; DES MOINES, IA 50322. (#102585-2).

AUG 18 - 28, '76. CRAFT FESTIVAL. FESTIVAL. (LOCAL). OLIVER GILLESPIE, DIR; LIVING HISTORY FARMS; 2600 111TH STREET; DES MOINES, IA 50322. (#102585-12).

AUG 18 - 28, '76. FALL HARVEST DAYS. DEMONSTRATIONS OF PAST HARVESTING TECHNIQUES. (LOCAL). OLIVER GILLESPIE, CHMN; LIVING HISTORY FARMS; 2600 111TH ST; DES MOINES, IA 50322. (#102585-14).

AUG 18 - 28, '76. FOLK MUSIC FESTIVAL. COMPETITION AMONG BLUEGRASS AND FOLK MUSIC GROUPS; ALL GROUPS WELCOME TO PARTICIPATE. (LOCAL). OLIVER GILLESPIE, DIR; LIVING HISTORY FARMS; 2600 111TH STREET; DES MOINES, IA 50322. (#102585-10).

AUG 18 - 28, '76. POTTERY FESTIVAL. DEMONSTRATIONS OF POTTING, FIRING & GLAZING TECHNIQUES; A POTTER'S WHEEL SET UP FOR PUBLIC USE & FINISHED PRODUCTS FOR SALE. (LOCAL). OLIVER GILLESPIE, CHMN; LIVING HISTORY FARMS; 2600 111TH ST; DES MOINES, IA 50322. (#102585-3).

AUG 18 - 28, '76. QUILTING BEE AND EXHIBITION. ONE OF THE FINEST QUILT COLLECTIONS IN THE MIDWEST WILL BE ON DISPLAY. (LOCAL). OLIVER GILLESPIE, CHMN; LIVING HISTORY FARMS; 2600 111TH ST; DES MOINES, IA 50322. (#102585-15).

AUG 18 - 28, '76. SHEEPDOG TRIALS. COMPETITION AMONG SHEEPDOG OWNERS; PARTICIPANTS WELCOME. (LOCAL). OLIVER GILLESPIE, DIR; LIVING HISTORY FARMS; 2600 111TH STREET; DES MOINES, IA 50322. (#102585-9).

AUG 18 - 28, '76. SPINNING, WEAVING AND NATURAL DYEING FESTIVAL. DEMONSTRATIONS OF MODERN TECHNIQUES AND PIONEER TECHNIQUES OF SPINNING, WEAVING AND NATURAL DYEING METHODS. (LOCAL). OLIVER GILLESPIE, DIR; LIVING HISTORY FARMS; 2600 111TH STREET; DES MOINES, IA 50322. (#102585-11).

AUG 18 - 29, '76. BLACK ODYESSY ART EXHIBIT & GATEWAY DANCERS-IOWA STATE FAIR. EXHIBIT, LIVE PERFORMANCE AT CULTURAL CENTER. (REGN'L). JERRY COUGHLIN, ACT SECY; IOWA STATE FAIR; 30TH & GRAND AVE; DES MOINES, IA 50319. (#28196-1).

AUG 18 - 29, '76. DISPLAY: FARMING OF THE FUTURE. STATE PLOWING MATCHES AND FARM EQUIPMENT DISPLAYS. (ST-WIDE). OLIVER GILLESPIE, CHMN; LIVING HISTORY FARMS; 2600 111TH ST; DES MOINES, IA 50322. (#102585-1).

AUG 18 - 29, '76. GERMAN IMMIGRATION EXHIBIT: GERMAN ROLE IN DEVELOPMENT OF USA. EXHIBIT AT 339 WALNUT ST. (ST-WIDE). HEINZ HANZEL; NATIONAL CARL SCHURZ ASSOC; 339 WALNUT ST; PHILADELPHIA, PA 19106. (#23642-2).

AUG 18 - 29, '76. IOWA STATE FAIR - THEME: FOODS OF THE WORLD. FAIR AT IOWA STATE FAIR GROUNDS. (REGN'L). JERRY COUGHLIN, ACT SECY; IOWA SATE FAIR; 30TH & GRAND AVE; DES MOINES, IA 50319. (#3672-1).

AUG 18 - 29, '76. SPANN 200: PARTICIPATION IN A NEW NATION, ROLE OF GERMAN AMERICANS. EXHIBIT AT SPIRIT OF IOWA CENTER, GRANDSTAND, IOWA STATE FAIR. (ST-WIDE). BILL FISHER, ASSOC DIR; NATIONAL CARL SCHURZ ASSOC; STATEHOUSE; DES MOINES, IA 50319. (#24060-2).

AUG 18 - 29, '76. STATE FAIR BOOTH FOR IOWA ARCHEOLOGICAL SOCIETY. FAIR AT GRANDSTANDS - SECOND FLOOR. (ST-WIDE). DUANE ANDERSON, CHMN; IOWA ARCHEOLOGICAL SOCIETY; EASTLAWN, U OF IOWA; IOWA CITY, IA 52242. (#26587-1).

AUG 29, '76. CHURCHES OF CAPITOL HILL PICNIC & BICENTENNIAL CELEBRATION. CEREMONY, FESTIVAL AT STATE OF IOWA CAPITOL GROUNDS, WEST SIDE. (LOCAL). REV TOM REUSS, COORD; CHURCHES OF CAPITOL HILL; E 9TH & DES MOINES ST; DES MOINES, IA 50316. (#109233-1).

SEPT 6 - 17, '76. CARL HAVERLIN/BROADCAST MUSIC, INC, ARCHIVES BICENTENNIAL EXHIBIT. OFFERS A VERSATILE PICTURE OF HISTORY, REGIONAL LIFE & MUSIC FOR OVER 200 YEARS. CONTAINS PRESIDENTIAL LETTERS, LETTERS OF FAMOUS AMERICANS, OLD BOOKS, MANUSCRIPTS, HISTORY OF 'THE STAR SPANGLED BANNER' & COMPOSER AUTOGRAPHS, PLUS SHEET MUSIC OF THE PAST. AT HARMON FINE ARTS CENTER. (ST-WIDE). MICHAEL C FRISBIE; DRAKE UNIVERSITY; DRAKE UNIV, COLLEGE OF FINE ARTS; DES MOINES, IA 50311. (#20784-21).

OCT 16 - 17, '76. CORN HARVEST FESTIVAL. FESTIVAL AT FESTIVAL FIELD, DOUGLAS EXIT OFF I 35. (LOCAL). VINCE KING, COORD; LIVING HISTORY FARMS; DES MOINES, IA 50318. (#103416-654).

OCT 17, '76. '76 PIANOS' - BICENTENNIAL CONCERT. '76 PIANOS' WITH OVER 150 PIANISTS; A CHORUS FROM DRAKE UNIV AND A 'BICENTENNIAL MINUTE'; IN MEMORY OF STANFORD HULSHIZER. SPECIAL GROUP OF PIANO NUMBERS FOR COLLEGE LEVEL TALENT. GUEST CONDUCTORS: PROF ROBERT SPEED AND DR FRANCIS J PYLE. AT VETS AUDITORIUM. (LOCAL). MRS EMILY HULSHIZER, DIR; POLK COUNTY BICENTENNIAL COMMISSION; 7107 MARYLAND DR; DES MOINES, IA 50322. (#108412-1).

NOV 1, '76 - CONTINUING . IOWA'S FIRST LADIES INAUGURAL BALL GOWN DISPLAY. PERMANENT DISPLAY OF 12 INCH PORCELAIN FIGURES REPRESENTING EACH FIRST LADY OF IOWA DATING BACK TO 1838 IN INAUGURAL BALL GOWNS. (ST-WIDE). MRS SUE REED, CHAIRMAN; DES MOINES HERITAGE COMMITTEE; 1314 48TH ST; DES MOINES, IA 50311. (#105481-1).

NOV 5 - 7, '76. SYMPOSIUM ON 'LIMITED GOVERNMENT'. A PUBLIC DISCUSSION UTILIZING EXPERTS FROM LAW, BUSINESS AND VARIOUS HUMANISTIC DISCIPLINES. AT OLMSTED CENTER. (LOCAL). BURTON LEISER, CHMN; DRAKE UNIV BICENTENNIAL COMMISSION; DES MOINES, IA 50311. (#105801-1).

DEWAR

BICENTENNIAL BONNETS, DEWAR, IA. PROJECT IS A BONNETT SALE, 115 DIFFERENT KINDS ARE AVAILABLE. (LOCAL). BONNIE HEIPLE, CHAIRPERSON; DEWAR D R BEST 200 BICENTENIAL COMMITTEE; BOX 58; DEWAR, IA 50623. (#18201).

BICENTENNIAL COLLECTOR'S ITEMS, DEWAR, IA. BICENTENNIAL BONNETS, COINS, PEWTER KEY CHAINS ARE BEING SOLD AS COLLECTOR'S ITEMS FOR A COMMUNITY FUND RAISING PROJECT: PROCEEDS WILL BE USED TO INSTALL TENNIS COURTS IN THE PARK. (LOCAL). MRS J E HEIPLE, PROJ DIRECTOR; CITY OF DEWAR; DEWAR, IA 50623. (#16488).

COMMEMORATIVE COIN & KEY CHAIN, DEWAR, IA. COMMEMORATIVE COINS & KEY CHAINS HONORING COUNTRY'S BIRTHDAY AND LOCAL COMMUNITY CENTER & PARK. (LOCAL). BONNIE HEIPLE, CHAIRPERSON; DEWAR D R BEST 200 BICENTENNIAL COMMITTEE; BOX 58; DEWAR, IA 50623. (#18200).

QUILTING BEE, DEWAR, IA. PROJECT IS A COMMUNITY QUILTING BEE. (LOCAL). BONNIE HEIPLE, CHAIRPERSON; DEWAR D R BEST 200 BICENTENNIAL COMMITTEE; BOX 58; DWAR, IA 50623. (#18199).

TENNIS COURTS PROJ, DEWAR, IA. FUNDS ARE BEING RAISED TO BUILD TENNIS COURTS IN TOWN PARK. (LOCAL). BONNIE HEIPLE, CHAIRPERSON; DEWAR D R BEST 200 BICENTENNIAL COMMITTEE; BOX 58; DEWAR, IA 50623. (#18202).

AUG 23, '75. DEWAR'S DAY 1975. CEREMONY, FESTIVAL, PARADE. (LOCAL). BONNIE HEIPLE, CHMN; DEWAR COMMUNITY CENTER; BOX 58; DEWAR, IA 50623. (#200018-47).

NOV 29 - 30, '75. HERITAGE OPEN HOUSE. EXHIBIT AT NORTH RAYMOND RD. (LOCAL). BONNIE HEIPLE, CHMN; DEWAR COMMUNITY CENTER; BOX 58; DEWAR, IA 50623. (#200018-48).

FEB 10, '76. CATERED SEED CORN DINNER FOR SALESPERSON. FESTIVAL AT 1731 N RAYMOND RD. (LOCAL). BONNIE HEIPLE, CHMN; DEWAR COMMUNITY HALL OR CENTER; BOX 58; DEWAR, IA 50623. (#200018-44).

MAR 20, '76. SOCK HOP 50'S & 60'S STYLE. FESTIVAL AT 1731 N RAYMOND RD. (LOCAL). BONNIE HEIPLE, CHMN; DEWAR COMMUNITY CENTER; BOX 58; DEWAR, IA 50623. (#200018-45).

APR 9, '76. CHILI & OYSTER STEW SUPPER. FESTIVAL AT 1731 N RAYMOND RD. (LOCAL). BONNIE HEIPLE, CHMN; DEWAR COMMUNITY CENTER; BOX 58; DEWAR, IA 50623. (#200018-46).

JUNE 5, '76. DEWAR'S DAY 1976. FESTIVAL, PARADE AT DEWAR COMMUNITY CENTER PARK; ROPED OFF AREAS OF TOWN. (LOCAL). BONNIE HEIPLE, CHMN; DEWAR COMMUNITY CENTER; BOX 58; DEWAR, IA 50623. (#103704-1).

DEXTER

PRESERVATION OF COMMUNITY BUILDING, DEXTER, IA. PRESERVATION OF DEXTER COMMUNITY BUILDINGS AS HISTORICAL SITES. (LOCAL). ROBERT WEESNER, CHAIRMAN; DEXTER COMMUNITY CLUB; 318 MARSHALL ST; DEXTER, IA 50070. (#18150).

RESTORATION OF DEXTER LIBRARY, IA. RESTORATION OF THE DEXTER LIBRARY FOR FUTURE USE. (LOCAL). ROBERT WEESNER, CHAIRMAN; DEXTER COMMUNITY CLUB; 318 MARSHALL ST; DEXTER, IA 50070. (#17736).

JUNE 12 - 13, '75. BICENTENNIAL CELEBRATION. FESTIVAL. (LOCAL). ROBERT P WEESNER, CHMN; DEXTER COMMUNITY CLUB; 318 MARSHALL ST; DEXTER, IA 50070. (#103639-5).

JUNE 12 - 13, '76. EXHIBIT: HISTORIC & MODERN APPLICATIONS & USES OF WATER. EXHIBIT, FESTIVAL. (LOCAL). ROBERT WEESNER, CHAIRMAN; DEXTER COMMUNITY CLUB; 318 MARSHALL ST; DEXTER, IA 50070. (#103639-3).

DIAGONAL

BEAUTIFICATION PROJECT IN DIAGONAL, IA. PLANTING TREES AND FLOWERS IN CITY PARK AND SCHOOL. (LOCAL). MRS ARNOLD KESSLER, PROJ DIRECTOR; DIAGONAL BICENTENNIAL COMMITTEE; DIAGONAL, IA 50845. (#15080).

APR 2, '76. ELEMENTARY SCHOOL BICENTENNIAL PROGRAM. PUBLIC INVITED TO SPECIAL BICENTENNIAL PROGRAM. AT DIAGONAL ELEMENTARY SCHOOL. (LOCAL). MRS ARNOLD KESSLER; DIAGONAL BICENTENNIAL COMMITTEE; DIAGONAL, IA 50845. (#102225-2).

APR 13 - 14, '76. OLD CREAMERY THEATRE COMPANY. LIVE PERFORMANCE AT HIGH SCHOOL. (LOCAL). MRS ARNOLD KESSLER; DIAGONAL BICENTENNIAL COMMITTEE; DIAGONAL, IA 50845. (#102225-3).

MAY 29, '76. BICENTENNIAL ALUMNI BANQUET. BICENTENNIAL ALUMNI BANQUET - PROGRAM AND DANCE. (LOCAL). MRS ARNOLD KESSLER; DIAGONAL BICENTENNIAL COMMITTEE; DIAGONAL, IA 50845. (#102225-4).

MAY 31, '76. BOHEMIAN HERITAGE DAY. FESTIVAL, PARADE. (LOCAL). MRS ARNOLD KESSLER; DIAGONAL BICENTENNIAL COMMITTEE; DIAGONAL, IA 50845. (#102225-1).

SEPT 6, '76. LABOR DAY CELEBRATION. FESTIVAL, PARADE, COMPETITION, EXHIBIT. (LOCAL). MRS ARNOLD KESSLER; DIAGONAL BICENTENNIAL COMMITTEE; LION'S CLUB; DIAGONAL, IA 50845. (#102225-5).

DIXON

RESTORATION OF DIXON, IA, RECREATIONAL CENTER. RESTORATION OF RECREATIONAL CENTER TO PROMOTE HEALTH, LEISURE AND RECREATION FOR THE ENTIRE COMMUNITY. (LOCAL). EDNA I SPIES, PROJ DIRECTOR; DIXON CITY COUNCIL; PO BOX 6; DIXON, IA 52745. (#23596). **ARBA GRANTEE.**

MAY 31, '76. MEMORIAL DAY SERVICES. CEREMONY. (LOCAL). MRS E L SPIES, CHMN; DIXON BICENTENNIAL COMMITTEE & AMERICAN LEGION POST 353; DIXON, IA 52745. (#200018-41).

JULY 4, '76. JULY 4TH CELEBRATION AT DIXON. BASEBALL GAMES ALL DAY, PARTICIPATION IN NATION-WIDE BELL-RINGING AT 1 PM, FIRE WORKS DISPLAY IN THE EVENING. (LOCAL). MRS EDWARD I SPIES, CHMN; DIXON BICENTENNIAL COMMITTEE; DIXON, IA 52741. (#108450-3).

JULY 11, '76. DIXON BICENTENNIAL KIDS DAY. CEREMONIES AND RIBBON CUTTING AT THE NEW RECREATIONAL CENTER, FOLLOWED BY GAMES AND CONTESTS FOR YOUTH OF ALL AGES. AT RECREATIONAL CENTER. (LOCAL). MRS EDWARD I SPIES, CHMN; DIXON BICENTENNIAL COMMITTEE; DIXON, IA 52741. (#108450-2).

AUG 21, '76. DIXON'S BICENTENNIAL CELEBRATION & ANNUAL SWEET CORN FESTIVAL. FIREMEN'S BREAKFAST, KIDDIES PARADE, TRACTOR PULLS, SQUARE DANCING, GAMES, CENTER DEDICATION AND DANCING. (LOCAL). MRS EDWARD I SPIES, CHMN; DIXON BICENTENNIAL COMMITTEE; DIXON, IA 52741. (#108450-1).

DONAHUE

SEPT 6, '76. FRONTIER DAYS. FESTIVAL. (LOCAL). EUGENE WUESTENBERG; DONAHUE BICENTENNIAL COMMITTEE; DONAHUE, IA 52746. (#108451-1).

DONNELLSON

BICENTENNIAL BOOTH AT LEE COUNTY FAIR - IA. THE SELLING OF BICENTENNIAL MATERIALS, AMERICAN FLAGS AND BICENTENNIAL SHEAFFER BALL POINT PENS TO INCREASE AWARENESS OF THE BICENTENNIAL. (LOCAL). HAZEL E SPARSMAN, CHAIRMAN; AMERICAN LEGION AUXILIARY UNIT 474; DONNELLSON, IA 52625. (#18192).

BICENTENNIAL CITY LIMIT SIGNS - DONNELLSON, IA. THE MAYOR HAS APPLIED FOR NEW BICENTENNIAL CITY LIMIT SIGNS. (LOCAL). HAZEL E SPARSMAN, CHAIRMAN; DONNELLSON BICENTENNIAL COMMITTEE; DONNELLSON, IA 52625. (#18191).

OLD DEPOT RESTORATION & PARK CLEANUP - IA. THE DEPOT WILL BE RESTORED AND THE PARK, WHICH WAS RECENTLY PURCHASED FROM THE BURLINGTON RAILROAD, WILL HAVE FLOWER BEDS, SHELTER HOUSE, TABLES, BENCHES, BARBEQUE AND RECREATIONAL FACILITIES. (LOCAL). HAZEL E SPARSMAN, CHAIRMAN; DONNELLSON BICENTENNIAL COMMITTEE; DONNELLSON, IA 52625. (#18190).

JUNE 14, '75. AMERICAN LEGION PARADE & PARK ACTIVITIES. PARADE. (LOCAL). HAZEL SPARSMAN, CHMN; DONNELSON BICENTENNIAL COMMITTEE; RR 2; DONNELSON, IA 52625. (#101384-1).

JULY 4, '75. JULY 4, 1975 PARADE & FIREWORKS. FESTIVAL AT LEE COUNTY FAIRGROUNDS. (LOCAL). HAZEL E SPARSMAN; AMERICAN LEGION POST #474; 315 DEWEY AVE; DONNELLSON, IA 52625. (#200018-32).

SEPT 27, '75. DONNELLSON FALL FESTIVAL AND BICENTENNIAL FLAG CEREMONY. FLAG CEREMONY WAS HELD IN THE PARK. REV HARDEN GAVE THE INVOCATION. SEN JUNKINS PRESENTED THE FLAG TO THE MAYOR AND THEN GAVE A 10 MIN TALK AS FLAG WAS RAISED. THE CENTRAL HIGH SCHOOL BAND PLAYED. AT FIRE STATION & PARK. (LOCAL). HAZEL E SPARSMAN, CHMN; LIONS' CLUB & OTHER LOCAL ORGANIZATIONS; 315 DEWEY AVE; DONNELLSON, IA 52625. (#200018-33).

JUNE 14, '76. 'OUR GREAT DECLARATION' - PAGEANT. ON STAGE LIVE AND IN COSTUME WITH A MUSICAL CHORUS. ONE NIGHT ONLY. AT DONNELLSON ELEMENTARY SCHOOL GYM. (LOCAL). HAZEL E SPARSMAN, CHMN; AMERICAN LEGION & AUXILIARY, UNIT 474; 315 DEWEY AVE; DONNELLSON, IA 52625. (#108339-1).

JULY 4, '76. COMMUNITY CHURCH SERVICE AND FESTIVAL. FOOD STANDS, FLEA MARKET, GAMES, PARADE AND FIREWORKS. AT LEE COUNTY FAIRGROUNDS. (LOCAL). HAZEL E SPARSMAN, CHMN; DONNELLSON BICENTENNIAL COMMITTEE & MINISTERS ASSOC; 315 DEWEY AVE; DONNELLSON, IA 52625. (#108413-2).

JULY 14 - 18, '76. LEE COUNTY FAIR. PARADE OF OLD AND NEW FARM MACHINES AND AUTOMOBILES EACH EVENING; BICENTENNIAL BOOTH, HERITAGE BOOTH, HORSE RACING AND CAR RACING. PARADE & PAGEANT IN FRONT OF GRAND STAND. DISPLAYS IN ART HALL. FAIR OPEN ALL DAY 'TILL LATE AT NIGHT. BEEF AUCTION ON JULY 19TH. AT LEE COUNTY FAIRGROUNDS. (ST-WIDE). HAZEL E SPARSMAN, CHMN; DONNELLSON BICENTENNIAL COMMITTEE AND FAIR BOARD; 315 DEWEY AVE; DONNELLSON, IA 52625. (#108413-1).

SEPT 25, '76. FALL FESTIVAL DAY FREE PANCAKES SAUSAGE AND COFFEE. THERE WILL BE DRAWINGS FOR PRIZES WHICH EACH ORGANIZATION IS GIVING AWAY THE MERCHANTS ARE GIVING MONEY, GIFT CERTIFICATES GROUPS INVOLVED ARE AMERICAN

DONNELLSON — CONTINUED

LEGION AUXILIARY, TTT, JAY-CEES, SENIOR CITIZENS, GIRL SCOUTS, BOY SCOUTS. AT THE PANCAKES WILL BE SERVED AT THE FIRES STATION ON MAIN STREET. (LOCAL). HAZEL E SPARSMAN; DONNELLSON MERCHANTS AND LIONS CLUB; 315 DEWEY AVE; DONNELLSON, IA 52625. (#109160-1).

DOON

CONSTRUCTION OF NEW WATER TOWER IN DOON, IA. A NEW WATER TOWER WILL BE CONSTRUCTED IN DOON, IOWA. (LOCAL). DARRELL VANDE VEGTA, PROJ DIRECTOR; DOON BICENTENNIAL COMMITTEE; RR 1; DOON, IA 51235. (#11283).

RESTORATION OF OLD WATER TOWER, DOON, IA. RESTORED OLD WATER TOWER TO BE PLACED IN TOWN PARK. (LOCAL). DARRELL VANDE VEGTA, PROJ DIRECTOR; DOON BICENTENNIAL COMMITTEE; RR 1; DOON, IA 51235. (#11284).

JULY 26, '75. DOON HERITAGE DAYS. FESTIVAL. (LOCAL). DARRELL VANDE VEGTE, CHMN; DOON BICENTENNIAL COMMITTEE; RR 1; DOON, IA 51235. (#100351-1).

JULY 24, '76. DOON HERITAGE DAYS. FESTIVAL. (LOCAL). DARRELL VANDE VEGTE, DIR; DOON BICENTENNIAL COMMITTEE; RR #1; DOON, IA 51235. (#11282-1).

DOUDS

RESTORATION PROJECT IN DOUDS, IA. THE OLD ROCK ISLAND DEPOT HAS BEEN SECURED AND WILL BE PRESERVED AS A MUSEUM OF RAILROAD AND MINING ARTIFACTS. (LOCAL). TED WATSON OR LIBBY WOODRUFF, CO-CHAIRMEN; VAN BUREN DEVELOPMENT ASSOC; 101 VAN BUREN ST; KEOSAUQUA, IA 52565. (#21405).

DOUGHERTY

LIBERTY BANNERS - DOUGHERTY, IA. 4 LIBERTY BANNERS WILL BE MADE. (LOCAL). NANCY C CORPORON, CHAIRPERSON; ST PATRICKS CHURCH CCD CLASS; DOUGHERTY, IA 50433. (#24124).

MAKING A QUILT, IA. A QUILT WITH EACH OF THE 50 STATES REPRESENTED ON IT IS BEING MADE. (LOCAL). NANCY CORPORON, CHAIRMAN; DOUGHERTY DOMESTIC CLUB; DOUGHERTY, IA 50433. (#24115).

TREES AND FLOWER BEDS, IA. TREES WILL BE PLANTED IN THE PARK. RED, WHITE AND BLUE FLOWER BED WILL BE MADE. TRASH CANS WILL ALSO BE PAINTED RED, WHITE AND BLUE. (LOCAL). MRS FRED BERGER, 4-H LEADER; DOUGHERTY HELP 4-H CLUB; RFD; DOUGHERTY, IA 50433. (#24116).

JUNE 26, '76. COMMUNITY PARTY AND DANCE. FESTIVAL AT TOWN HALL. (LOCAL). JUDY PITZENBERGER; CATHOLICLADIES AUXILIARY; RFD; DOUGHERTY, IA 50433. (#106859-1).

DOW CITY

TREE PLANTING, DOW CITY, IA. TREE PLANTING PROJECT AT CITY PARK. (LOCAL). GENE HARRE, CHAIRMAN; DOW CITY BICENTENNIAL COMMITTEE; DOW CITY, IA 51528. (#21746).

MAY 2, '76. BICENTENNIAL CELEBRATION. FESTIVAL, PARADE AT DOW HOUSE NATIONAL HISTORICAL SITE. (LOCAL). GENE HARRE, COORD; DOW CITY BICENTENNIAL; DOW CITY, IA 51528. (#105520-2).

MAY 2 - JUNE 13, '76. BICENTENNIAL QUILT SALE. HAND MADE QUILTS TO BE SOLD TO HELP PAY FOR COMMUNITY HALL. AT DOW CITY PARK. (LOCAL). GENE HARRE, COORD; COMMUNITY CLUB; DOW CITY, IA 51528. (#105520-1).

JUNE 11 - 13, '76. ANNUAL PANCAKE DAYS. FESTIVAL AT DOW CITY PARK. (LOCAL). GENE HARRE, COORD; DOW CITY BICENTENNIAL; DOW CITY, IA 51528. (#105520-3).

DOWS

PLANTING OF GRASS & TREES, DOWS, IA. THE AREA SURROUNDING THE NEW COMMUNITY SWIMMING POOL WILL BE GRADED, GRASS & TREES WILL BE PLANTED & PARK BENCHES WILL BE ADDED. (LOCAL). CURTIS HANSEN, ADVISOR; FFA, DOWS COMMUNITY SCHOOL; DOWS, IA 50071. (#19324).

AUG 6 - 8, '76. BICENTENNIAL AND CORN DAYS FESTIVAL, PAGEANT AND STYLE SHOW. FESTIVAL AT ELLSWORTH ST, HIGH SCHOOL ATHLETIC FIELD AND GYM AUDITORIUM. (LOCAL). FAY G PETERSON, PROJ DIR; DOWS BICENTENNIAL ORGANIZATION; DOWS, IA 50071. (#104332-2).

DRAKESVILLE

REVOLUTIONARY WAR VETERANS PROJ, DRAKESVILLE, IA. A STONE AND MARKER WILL BE PROCURED AND AN INFORMATION BOARD WILL BE ERECTED TO COMMEMORATE REVOLUTIONARY WAR VETERANS. FLOWERS AND TREES WILL ALSO BE PLANTED. (LOCAL). BILL D BASSETT, CHAIRPERSON; DRAKESVILLE PARK BOARD & CITY COUNCIL; DRAWER A; DRAKESVILLE, IA 52552. (#15650).

JULY 22 - 24, '76. DAVIS COUNTY SOLDIERS & SETTLERS REUNION. 3-DAY CELEBRATION WITH MUSIC, DANCING AND GAMES FOR ALL AGES; VARIOUS EVENTS WITH CRAFTS AND CARNIVAL. (LOCAL). BILL BASSETT, CHMN; DAVIS COUNTY SOLDIERS & SETTLERS REUNION; RR1; DRAKESVILLE, IA 52552. (#102587-1).

SEPT 17 - 19, '76. COUNTRY AND OLD-TIME MUSIC FESTIVAL. LIVE PERFORMANCE, FESTIVAL AT DRAKESVILLE CITY PARK. (LOCAL). BILL D BASSETT, CHAIRMAN; THE COUNTRY COUSINS OF OTTUMWA; PO BOX 1; DRAKESVILLE, IA 52552. (#107131-1).

DUBUQUE

ALL AMERICAN CHORAL CONCERT BY CLARKE LORAS SINGERS. LIVE PERFORMANCE. (LOCAL). JOHN LEASE, CHAIRMAN; CLARKE COLLEGE; 1550 CLARKE DR; DUBUQUE, IA 52001. (#102649-7).

AMERICAN DRAMA COURSE AT CLARKE COLLEGE, IA. AMERICAN DRAMA WILL BE COVERED FROM THE EARLY 18TH CENTURY ENGLISH FARCE TO THE PRESENT. (LOCAL). CAROL BLITGEN, PROJ DIRECTOR; CLARKE COLLEGE; 1550 CLARKE DR; DUBUQUE, IA 52001. (#15853).

AMERICAN INDIAN PROJECT AT CLARKE COLLEGE, IOWA. 'BURSTING THE INDIAN MYTHS', A DISCUSSION OF INDIAN PROBLEMS AND AN EFFORT TO RAISE MONEY FOR THE NATIVE AMERICAN CAUSE. (LOCAL). CAROLYN FARRELL, DIRECTOR OF SPECIAL PROGRAMS; CLARKE COLLEGE; 1550 CLARKE DR; DUBUQUE, IA 52001. (#15862).

AMERICAN KEYBOARD COMPOSERS - CLARKE COLLEGE, IA. THE COURSE COVERS AMERICAN AUTHORS & PERFORMERS. (LOCAL). VIRGINIA GAUME, PROJ DIRECTOR; CLARKE COLLEGE; 1550 CLARKE DR; DUBUQUE, IA 52001. (#15859).

AMERICAN LITERATURE FILM SERIES. SEMINAR. (LOCAL). BARBARA KUTCHERA, CHMN; CLARKE COLLEGE; 1550 CLARKE DR; DUBUQUE, IA 52001. (#102649-3). **(??).**

AMERICAN VOCAL MUSIC - CLARKE COLLEGE/DUBUQUE, IA. THE COURSE WILL CONSIST OF THE MUSIC AND HISTORY OF EARLY AMERICAN WRITERS & MUSICIANS. (LOCAL). VIRGINIA GAUME, PROJ DIRECTOR; CLARKE COLLEGE; 1550 CLARKE DR; DUBUQUE, IA 52001. (#15860).

ANNUAL DOG SHOW - DUBUQUE, IA. RED, WHITE AND BLUE TROPHIES WILL BE AWARDED AT THE ANNUAL DOG SHOW. (ST-WIDE). MRS RITA PARKIN, PRESIDENT; DUBUQUE KENNEL CLUB; 679 KENNEDY COURT; DUBUQUE, IA 52001. (#19196).

ANNUAL DOG SHOW. EXHIBIT. (LOCAL). MRS RITA PAPKIN, DIRECTOR; DUBUQUE KENNEL CLUB; 679 KENNEDY CRT; DUBUQUE, IA 52001. (#104221-11). **(??).**

ARTIST IN RESIDENCE, DUBUQUE, IA. FRANK LICCARDI HAS BEEN COMMISSIONED TO CREATE A SERIES OF PAINTINGS THAT ARE REVELANT TO DUBUQUE. (LOCAL). PAUL RUCKER, COORDINATOR; DUBUQUE '76; 200 MAIN; DUBUQUE, IA 52001. (#19768).

BEAUTIFICATION OF WASHINGTON STREET - DUBUQUE, IA. RED, WHITE & BLUE TULIPS HAVE BEEN PLANTED AT 4 WASHINGTON STREET DIVERTERS; A TOTAL OF 300 TULIPS IN EACH DIVERTER. (LOCAL). MRS KENNETH APEL, PROJ DIRECTOR; DUBUQUE CHAPTER OF THE DAR; 615 ALTA VISTA; DUBUQUE, IA 52001. (#21275).

BICENTENNIAL BULLETIN BOARD AT CLARKE COLLEGE - IA. A YEAR-ROUND BULLETIN BOARD WILL BE USED TO ANNOUCE VARIOUS ACTIVITIES AND EVENTS IN THE COMING BICENTENNIAL YEAR. (LOCAL). DENISE MAZIARZ, PROJ DIRECTOR; CLARKE COLLEGE; 1550 CLARKE DR; DUBUQUE, IA 52001. (#15856).

BICENTENNIAL CENTER - DUBUQUE, IA. CENTER IS OPEN TO PUBLIC FOR INFORMATION; IT HAS A SALES OFFICE, MEETING PLACE, EXHIBIT AREA AND ADMINISTRATIVE OFFICE. (LOCAL). PAUL RUCKER, DIRECTOR; DUBUQUE '76, INC; 200 MAIN ST; DUBUQUE, IA 52001. (#20313).

BICENTENNIAL CHARMS, DUBUQUE, IA. GOLD BICENTENNIAL CHARMS WILL BE MADE BY LOCAL GOLDSMITH. (LOCAL). PAUL RUCKER, COORDINATOR; MCCOY GOLDSMITH SHOP; 261 MAIN; DUBUQUE, IA 52001. (#19755).

BICENTENNIAL CRAFTS DISPLAY - DUBUQUE, IA. HANDMADE JEWELRY DEPICTING THE BICENTENNIAL WILL BE ON DISPLAY. (LOCAL). BOB MCCOY, PROJ DIRECTOR; MCCOY GOLDSMITH SHOP; 261 MAIN ST; DUBUQUE, IA 52001. (#20314).

BICENTENNIAL DANCE, DUBUQUE, IA. A COMMEMORATIVE DANCE HONORING BICENTENNIAL. (LOCAL). HARRIET DINGLER, PROJ DIRECTOR; VISITING NURSES ASSOC; 412 LORAS BLVD; DUBUQUE, IA 52001. (#19766).

BICENTENNIAL QUILT - DUBUQUE, IOWA. THE YWCA BICENTENNIAL QUILT WILL BE RAFFLED OFF DURING SUMMER OF '76. IT WILL BE COMPLETED IN MARCH. IT WILL HAVE 36 BLOCKS DEPICTING DUBUQUE HISTORICAL BLDGS AND SCENES. (LOCAL). JUNE MANNING, EXEC DIRECTOR; YWCA; 35 N BOOTH; DUBUQUE, IA 52001. (#20278).

BICENTENNIAL SCHOOL PROGRAMS - DUBUQUE, IA. THROUGHOUT THE 1976 SCHOOL YEAR STUDENTS WILL BE ENCOURAGED TO PARTICIPATE IN BICENTENNIAL EVENTS OF OLD AND NEW DUBUQUE. (LOCAL). JAMES NOONAN, PROJ DIRECTOR; ST ANTHONY'S SCHOOL; 1275 ROSEDALE; DUBUQUE, IA 52001. (#20310).

CAMPUS KITE FLY. ALL STUDENTS WILL BE ENCOURAGED TO MAKE OR BUY KITES & FLY THEM. (LOCAL). CAROLYN FARRELL, PROJ DIR; CLARKE COLLEGE; 1550 CLARKE DR; DUBUQUE, IA 52001. (#102648-1). **(??).**

CENTENNIAL TRAVEL TALES; COMMUNITY THEATER IN IA. STUDENTS TO GO TO COMMUNITY SCHOOLS TO PERFORM PARTICIPATORY DRAMA. (LOCAL). SISTER XAVIER COENS, PROJ DIRECTOR; CLARKE COLLEGE; 1550 CLARKE DR; DUBUQUE, IA 52001. (#15855).

CLEVELAND PARK RESTORATION - DUBUQUE, IA. CLEVELAND PARK TERRACES AND STEPS WILL BE RESTORED. (LOCAL). KEVIN MC CARRON, CHAIRMAN; STUDENT PROJECT CLEVELAND PARK; 230 VALLEY ST; DUBUQUE, IA 52001. (#19197).

COMMUNITY BOOK - DUBUQUE, IA. A BOOK CONCERNING THE BICENTENNIAL WILL BE PUBLISHED FOR THE COMMUNITY OF DUBUQUE. (LOCAL). ROB APEL, PROJ COORDINATOR; CHAMBER OF COMMERCE; 880 LOCUST, FISCHER ARCADE; DUBUQUE, IA 52001. (#18435).

COMPOSE PARISH CHURCH HISTORY IN EACH PARISH - IA. THE PUBLICATION WILL FEATURE THE CONTRIBUTIONS WOMEN HAVE MADE TO THE HISTORY & PRESENT LIFE OF THE PARISHES. (LOCAL). MRS BETTY WHITE, CHAIRMAN; DUBUQUE DEANERY OF ARCHDIOCESAN COUNCIL OF CATHOLIC WOMEN; 1993 ASBURY RD; DUBUQUE, IA 52001. (#19191).

CONTEMPORARY AMERICAN GOSPEL FORMS - DUBUQUE, IA. A THEOLOGY COURSE WILL COVER CONTEMPORARY GOSPEL FORMS. THE EMPHASIS WILL BE ON AMERICAN GOSPEL FORMS. (LOCAL). JANE MACDONNELL, PROJ DIRECTOR; CLARKE COLLEGE; 1550 CLARKE DR; DUBUQUE, IA 52001. (#15857).

'CONTINUUM', BICENT MEMORIAL SCULPTURE IN IOWA. PAUL T GRANLUND WAS COMMISSIONED IN OCTOBER OF 1973 TO CREATE A SCULPTURE FOR THE BICENTENNIAL. IT WILL BE DEDICATED IN 1975. (REGN'L). G WITTENBURG, DIRECTOR OF COMMUNITY DEVELOPMENT; CITY OF DUBUQUE; 13TH AND CENTRAL; DUBUQUE, IA 52001. (#12253).

COUNTY FAIR BOOTH, STATE FAIR BOOTH, SGT FLOYD. EXHIBIT. (LOCAL). PAUL RUCKER, DIRECTOR; DUBUQUE '76; 200 MAIN; DUBUQUE, IA 52001. (#104221-45). **(??).**

DISCOVERING HEROINES - DUBUQUE, IA. TREASURE HUNT FOR HIDDEN HEROINES IN COMMUNITY TO UNCOVER WOMEN OF TODAY AND YESTERDAY. (LOCAL). JOAN GEISLER, PROJ CHAIRMAN; LITTLE CLOUD GIRL SCOUTS; 666 LORAS BLVD; DUBUQUE, IA 52001. (#20321).

DUBUQUE FOLKLORE, IA. THE FOLKLORE ABOUT THE COMMUNITY OF DUBUQUE WILL BE PUBLISHED IN A BOOK. (LOCAL). DON LEOPOLD, PROJ CHAIRMAN; AMERICAN TRUST AND SAVINGS BANK; 9TH & MAIN STS; DUBUQUE, IA 52001. (#19189).

DUBUQUE MARINE CORPS LEAGUE COLOR GUARD, IA. ESTABLISHMENT OF MARINE CORPS UNIFORMED COLOR GUARD, DRESSED IN 1776 ATTIRE WITH AUTHENTIC 1775 MUSKETS. (LOCAL). GARY HORN, COMMANDANT; DUBUQUE MARINE CORPS LEAGUE; 524 FENELON PL; DUBUQUE, IA 52001. (#25309).

DUBUQUE, IA HISTORY BOOK. COPIES OF M M HOFFMAN'S BOOK ON THE HISTORY OF DUBUQUE IS BEING SOLD; AVAILABLE BY MAIL OR AT LOORAS BOOKSTORE - KEANE HALL. (ST-WIDE). PAUL RUCKER, COORDINATOR; LORAS COLLEGE PRESS; 1450 ALTA VISTA; DUBUQUE, IA 52001. (#19756).

ECOLOGY SLIDE SHOW - DUBUQUE, IA. A SLIDE SHOW ON ECOLOGY TODAY AND YESTERDAY WILL BE SHOWN TO ANY GROUP OR ORGANIZATION WISHING TO SEE IT. (LOCAL). RICHARD WORM, DIRECTOR; ENVIRONMENTAL COORDINATING ORGANIZATION; 3555 HILLCREST; DUBUQUE, IA 52001. (#20311).

ECUMENICAL HOUSING PROJ AT CLARKE COLLEGE, IOWA. STUDENTS WILL AID SENIOR CITIZENS IN MOVING INTO HOUSING PROJECTS AND HELP IN COMMUNITY ACTIVITIES. (LOCAL). BARBARA KNTCHERA, PROJ DIRECTOR; CLARKE COLLEGE; 1550 CLARKE DR; DUBUQUE, IA 52001. (#15861).

EPIC PROJECT - DUBUQUE, IA. EPIC (ENCOURAGEMENT OF PARTICIPATION & INVOLVEMENT) WILL MAKE PEOPLE AWARE OF PUBLIC HEALTH AND INNER-CITY PROBLEMS AND INDIVIDUAL PARTICIPATION IN GOVERNMENT. (LOCAL). LOUISE OCTTOVE, PROJ DIRECTOR; CLARKE COLLEGE AAUW; 1550 CLARKE DR; DUBUQUE, IA 52001. (#21276).

EXHIBITS ON NATURE - DUBUQUE, IA. THE AUDUBON SOCIETY OF DUBUQUE WILL SPONSOR NATURE EXHIBITS. (LOCAL). WILLIAM HERRMANN, COORDINATOR; AUDUBON SOCIETY OF DUBUQUE; SHAWONDASSE RD; DUBUQUE, IA 52001. (#19188).

FAMILY HIKING - DUBUQUE, IA. PLANNED FAMILY HIKING TRIPS TO HISTORIC SITES IN THE DUBUQUE AREA; FAMILIES WILL EARN HIKERS OF AMERICA PATCHES AFTER TRIPS. (LOCAL). PAUL RUCKER, COORDINATOR; HIKERS OF AMERICA; RT 1, PO BOX 68; OSWEGO, IL 60543. (#19753).

FAMILY TREE SEARCH, DUBUQUE, IA. CHECK INTO FAMILY HISTORY OF COMMUNITY RESIDENTS. (LOCAL). JOAN GEISLER, PROJ CHAIRMAN; LITTLE CLOUD GIRL SCOUTS; 666 LORAS BLVD; DUBUQUE, IA 52001. (#19759).

THE GREEN FOLIAGE IS COMING, DUBUQUE, IA. CITYWIDE TREE PLANTING PROGRAM. (LOCAL). HARRY NEUSTADT, PROJ DIRECTOR; DUBUQUE BEAUTIFICATION COMMITTEE; FISCHER BUILDING - 4TH FLOOR; DUBUQUE, IA 52001. (#19760).

GROWTH OF THE TRI-STATES - DUBUQUE, IA. 'HAPPY BIRTHDAY AMERICA' (JUL 76) & 'HAPPY NEW YEAR AMERICA' (JAN 77) ARE NUMBERS 2 & 3 OF 3-PART SERIES OF BOOKS ABOUT THE TRI-STATES HISTORY, PRESENT CULTURE & FUTURE DIRECTORS. (REGN'L). DAVID SCHULTZ, PROJ COORDINATOR; TELEGRAPH-HERALD; 8TH AND BLUFF; DUBUQUE, IA 52001. (#20481).

'HAPPY ANNIVERSARY AMERICA' BOOK OF IOWA. 'HAPPY ANNIVERSARY AMERICA' IS A BOOK ABOUT THE HISTORY OF THE TRISTATES AREA (IOWA, WISCONSIN & ILLINOIS) BEGINNING IN PRE-HISTORIC TIMES TO 1876. TEXT WILL COVER PHYSICAL & SOCIAL HISTORY. (REGN'L). DAVID SCHULTZ, PROJ COORDINATOR; TELEGRAPH-HERALD; 8TH AND BLUFF; DUBUQUE, IA 52001. (#20480).

HERITAGE OF DUBUQUE, IA. A BOOK DEPICTING OLD AND NEW DUBUQUE. (LOCAL). DEAN SCHANTZ, DIRECTOR; FIRST NATIONAL BANK; 7TH & TOWN CLOCK PLAZA; DUBUQUE, IA 52001. (#20318).

DUBUQUE — CONTINUED

HISTORICAL BUILDINGS IN DUBUQE, IA. RESEARCH COMMUNITY BUILDINGS, BECAUSE OF LOCATION, DESIGN AND HERITAGE. (LOCAL). JOAN GEISLER, PROJ CHAIRMAN; LITTLE CLOUD GIRL SCOUTS; 666 LORAS BLVD; DUBUQUE, IA 52001. (#19758).

HISTORICAL SLIDE SHOW, DUBUQUE, IA. PROJECT INVOLVES DEVELOPING SLIDES ON AMERICAN HISTORY. (LOCAL). FRANK MCCAW, PROJ DIRECTOR; DUBUQUE BICENTENNIAL COMMISSION; 700 BOLEYN RD; DUBUQUE, IA 52001. (#19754).

HISTORY OF SURROUNDING COUNTIES, IA. PUBLICATION TRACING HISTORY OF DUBUQUE, DELAWARE AND JACKSON COUNTIES. (LOCAL). JEANETTE AGNITSCH, PROJ DIRECTOR; PROJECT CONCERN; 1099 IOWA - PO BOX 333; DUBUQUE, IA 52001. (#19762).

HISTORY OF THE UNIVERSITY, DUBUQUE, IA. MAGAZINES, SEPARATE HISTORIES OF THE DEPARTMENT, COURSE WORK. (LOCAL). JEFFREY EWOLDT, DIRECTOR; UNIV OF DUBUQUE; 2050 UNIVERSITY; DUBUQUE, IA 52001. (#19384).

HONOR ROLL - DUBUQUE SYMBOL FLAGS - IA. DUBUQUE SENIOR HIGH SCHOOL STUDENTS WHO EXCEL IN SCHOLARSHIP WILL RECEIVE DUBUQUE BICENTENNIAL SYMBOL FLAGS. (LOCAL). C P COX, PROJ CHAIRMAN; DUBUQUE SENIOR HIGH SCHOOL; 1800 CLARKE DR; DUBUQUE, IA 52001. (#19193).

'THE INSPIRED CONSTITUTION' - DUBUQUE, IA. THE CHURCH OF JESUS CHRIST OF LATTER DAY SAINTS WILL SPONSOR AN EXHIBIT ENTITLED 'THE INSPIRED CONSTITIUTION.'. (LOCAL). FRED MOSER, PROJ DIRECTOR; CHURCH OF JESUS CHRIST OF LATTER DAY SAINTS; 685 FREMONT; DUBUQUE, IA 52001. (#19190).

MUSIC AND DRAMA PRODUCTION - HOMECOMING '76. LIVE PERFORMANCE. (LOCAL). JEFFREY EWOLDT, CHAIRMAN; UNIV OF DUBUQUE; 2050 UNIVERSITY; DUBUQUE, IA 52001. (#104276-2). **(??).**

MUSICAL, SHOW AND DANCES. 30 MEMBER CAST; PATRIOTIC SONGS WRITTEN BY CAST MEMBERS AND BY 'UP WITH PEOPLE', 2 HOUR SHOW. (LOCAL). JEFF KELLY, COORDINATOR; CAST OF '76; PO BOX 585; DUBUQUE, IA 52001. (#104529-3). **(??).**

OLD SCHOOLROOM DISPLAY, DUBUQUE, IA. STORE WINDOW DEPICTING EARLY SCHOOLROOM WITH AUTHENTIC FURNISHINGS. (LOCAL). MRS JAMES AHERN, CHAIRMAN; RETIRED TEACHERS ASSOCIATON; 2025 SIMPSON; DUBUQUE, IA 52001. (#19763).

OPEN HOUSE TOURS - DUBUQUE, IA. CHRISTMAS OPEN HOUSE OF MATHIAS HAM MUSEUM AND BUS TOURS OF HISTORIC BUILDINGS AND SITES IN DUBUQUE. (LOCAL). HELEN MERCER, CHAIRMAN; DUBUQUE COUNTY HISTORICAL SOCIETY; PO BOX 305; DUBUQUE, IA 52001. (#19195).

PAINTING FIREPLUGS - DUBUQUE, IA. FIREPLUGS WILL BE PAINTED TO BEAUTIFY THE CITY PARKS. (LOCAL). HARRY NEUSTADT, DIRECTOR; DUBUQUE BEAUTIFICATION; URBAN DEVELOPMENT, CITY HALL; DUBUQUE, IA 52001. (#19194).

PARK BEAUTIFICATION PROJ - DUBUQUE, IA. FLOWER BEDS WILL BE PLANTED IN WASHINGTON PARK. (LOCAL). MRS KENNETH APEL, COORDINATOR; DAUGHTERS OF THE AMERICAN REVOLUTION; 615 ALTA VISTA; DUBUQUE, IA 52001. (#19192).

PARK DEVELOPMENT - DUBUQUE, IA. THE DUBUQUE JAYCEES WILL SPONSOR A PROJECT TO RESTORE WASHINGTON PARK WITH NEW TREES AND A PAVILION GAZEBO; A TIME CAPSULE AND A SEM. (LOCAL). JAMES E GIBBS, PROJ CHAIRMAN; DUBUQUE JAYCEES; 411 FISCHER BLDG; DUBUQUE, IA 52001. (#18427).

PERSONAL HISTORY PROJ - DUBUQUE, IA. GIRL SCOUT TROOPS RESEARCHING THEIR OWN FAMILY HISTORY & ANCESTORS AND SHARING PHOTOGRAPHS, POSTERS, LETTERS, DIARIES AND DOCUMENTS. (LOCAL). JOAN GEISLER, PROJ CHAIRMAN; LITTLE CLOUD GIRL SCOUTS; 666 LORAS BLVD; DUBUQUE, IA 52001. (#20322).

PICKETT BREWERY PROJECT, DUBUQUE, IA. PICKETT BREWERY IS MAKING & PRESENTING TO THE DUBUQUE HISTORICAL SOCIETY, ONE DOZEN BOTTLES OF 'SHOT TOWER SHOT'. (LOCAL). JOSEPH PICKETT, DIRECTOR; PICKETT BREWERY; E 4TH ST; DUBUQUE, IA 52001. (#20892).

POLITICAL INVOLVEMENT WEEK - STYLE SHOW. FIRST LADIES STYLE SHOW WITH DEMOCRATIC PARTY; SHOWBOAT, 'OLD MAN RIVER', 'DELTA QUEEN', HELD AT EAGLE POINT PARK. (LOCAL). KEN SNODGRASS, CHAIRMAN; REPUBLICAN WOMEN - DUBUQUE REPUBLICAN CENTRAL COMMITTEE; 1564 CENTRAL; DUBUQUE, IA 52001. (#104529-6). **(??).**

PROJECT CONCERN, DUBUQUE, IA. A RETIRED SENIOR CITIZENS VOLUNTEER PROGRAM. (LOCAL). MRS JOSEPH A TAUKE, CHAIRMAN; PROJECT CONCERN; 1715 GLEN OAK; DUBUQUE, IA 52001. (#23385).

PROMOTE AREA CRAFTS & SKILLS, DUBUQUE, IA. JOE KAPLER, BIOLOGY PROFESSOR AT LORAS, WILL PRESENT SLIDES OF UPPER MISSISSIPPI. (LOCAL). RICHARD WORM, PRESIDENT; ENVIRONMENTAL COORDINATING ORGANIZATION; 3555 HILLCREST; DUBUQUE, IA 52001. (#19752).

QUILTING BEE, REVIVAL OF OLD CRAFTS - DUBUQUE, IA. THE COLLEGE WILL OFFER DEMONSTRATIONS OF QUILTING TO INTERESTED TOWN'S PEOPLE AND STUDENTS. (LOCAL). CAROLYN FARRELL, DIRECTOR OF SPECIAL PROGRAMS; CLARKE COLLEGE; 1550 CLARKE DR; DUBUQUE, IA 52001. (#15854).

RECORDING GRAVESTONES - DUBUQUE, IA. GIRL SCOUTS WILL COMPILE A LIST OF ALL UNRECORDED GRAVESTONES THROUGHOUT THE COUNTY FOR OFFICIAL REFERENCE. (LOCAL). JOAN GEISLER, PROJ CHAIRMAN; LITTLE CLOUD GIRL SCOUTS; 666 LORAS BLVD; DUBUQUE, IA 52001. (#20323).

REDECORATING ROOMS AT DUBUQUE GIRLS' CLUB - IA. THE LARGE ACTIVITIES ROOM AT THE NEW DUBUQUE GIRLS' CLUB IS PAINTED RED, WHITE AND BLUE WITH SNOOPY CHARACTERS HOLDING VARIOUS AMERICAN FLAGS. CONTEST HELD TO NAME THE ROOM. (LOCAL). CAROLE SNODGRASS, COORDINATOR; DUBUQUE COUNTY REPUBLICAN WOMEN'S CLUB; PO BOX 1052; DUBUQUE, IA 52001. (#24350).

'REFLECTIONS' - DUBUQUE, IA. A CONTEST FOR GRADE SCHOOL STUDENTS ON CULTURE AND CREATIVITY. (LOCAL). TERRY RIEZICA, PROJ DIRECTOR; PTA COUNCIL; 2050 HALE; DUBUQUE, IA 52001. (#20319).

RENOVATION OF THEATER, DUBUQUE, IA. RE-DOING SCENERY ON STAGE OF MEMORIAL HALL IN A BICENTENNIAL THEME. (LOCAL). MARY WOLFE, CHAIRMAN; WORTHINGTON BICENTENNIAL COMMITTEE; WORTHINGTON, IA 52001. (#23348).

RESEARCH COMMUNITY BUILDINGS - DUBUQUE, IA. TAKING A LOOK AT BUILDINGS IN COMMUNITY OF INTEREST IN LOCATION, DESIGN AND HERITAGE. (LOCAL). JOAN GEISLER, PROJ CHAIRMAN; LITTLE CLOUD GIRL SCOUTS; 666 LORAS BLVD; DUBUQUE, IA 52001. (#20320).

RESTORATION OF DUBUQUE COUNTY JAIL, IA. RESTORED DUBUQUE COUNTY JAIL TO BE USED AS ART GALLERY, ON DISPLAY WILL BE THE ART ASSOCIATION'S PERMANENT COLLECTION. ART CLASSES WILL ALSO BE OFFERED AT THE FACILITY. (LOCAL). HARRY NEUSTADT, SPECIAL PROJECTS COORDINATOR; CITY OF DUBUQUE; ROOM 480, FISCHER BLDG; DUBUQUE, IA 52001. (#18748).

SCENES FROM AMERICAN OPERA AT CLARKE COL - IA. OPERA WILL BE DISCUSSED AND SUNG IN AN OPERA WORKSHOP. (LOCAL). ANN SIGRIST, PROJ DIRECTOR; CLARKE COLLEGE; 1550 CLARKE DR; DUBUQUE, IA 52001. (#15858).

SCULPTOR IN RESIDENCE JIM GIBBS. JIM GIBBS, THE SCULPTOR IN RESIDENCE, WILL CREATE ONE LARGE SCULPTURE. (LOCAL). PAUL RUCKER, COORDINATOR; DUBUQUE '76; 200 MAIN; DUBUQUE, IA 52001. (#19769).

SEMINAR PROGRAM. CONFERENCE. (LOCAL). JEFFREY EWOLDT, CHAIRMAN; UNIV OF DUBUQUE; 2050 UNIVERSITY; DUBUQUE, IA 52001. (#104276-1). **(??).**

SKI SHOW. 76 MILE WATER SKI MARATHON. (LOCAL). CAROL MURGUIA, CHAIRMAN; DUBUQUE WATER SKI CLUB; PO BOX 552; DUBUQUE, IA 52001. (#104529-7). **(??).**

SPIRIT OF '76 MURAL - DUBUQUE, IA. THE 'SPIRIT OF '76' MURAL WILL BE ON DISPLAY. (LOCAL). ELLEN HARTMANN, PROJ DIRECTOR; OLDE TOWNE SHOPPE; 1763 CENTRAL; DUBUQUE, IA 52001. (#20316).

STATE CONVENTION OF LICENSED PRACTICAL NURSES. BUS TOURS, RIVER CRUISE AND MEAL IN HISTORIC PLACE. (ST-WIDE). JOAN TREIVIELER, CHMN; DUBUQUE UNIT OF LICENSED PRACTICAL NURSES; 1192 1/2 LOCUST; DUBUQUE, IA 52001. (#104529-5). **(??).**

STORE WINDOWS PROJECT - DUBUQUE, IA. STORE WINDOWS WILL BE DECORATED TO DEPICT SCHOOL ROOMS OF EARLY DAYS. (LOCAL). MRS JAMES AHERN, DIRECTOR; RETIRED TEACHERS ORGANIZATION; 2025 SIMPSON; DUBUQUE, IA 52001. (#20312).

TELEGRAPH-HERALD'S CHRONICLES ON DUBUQUE-NBMRP. 3 HIST SUPPLEMENTS ARE BEING PREPARED TO CHRONICLE UPPER MIDWEST GROWTH. THESE SUPPLEMENTS REFLECT THE 3 BICENT THEMES, & WILL BE AVAILABLE TO HISTORY CLASSES IN A 3-STATE AREA. (ST-WIDE). F R WOODWARD, PRES & CHMN OF BOARD; DUBUQUE TELEGRAPH-HERALD; 8TH & BLUFF STS, PO BOX 688; DUBUQUE, IA 52001. (#23095).

WASHINGTON SQUARE RESTORATION - DUBUQUE, IA. THE PARK WILL BE LANDSCAPED AND A REPLICA OF THE BANDSHELL WHICH WAS IN THE PARK WILL BE CONSTRUCTED; A TIME CAPSULE WILL BE CONSTRUCTED WHICH WILL BE OPENED IN 2076. (LOCAL). RANDALL NIGG, PROJ CO-CHAIRMAN; DUBUQUE JAYCEES; 1023 1/2 MAIN ST; DUBUQUE, IA 52001. (#19723).

'WHAT IS AN AMERICAN?' - DUBUQUE, IA. AN ESSAY CONTEST FOR GRADES 9-12 ON 'WHAT IS AN AMERICAN?'; DEADLINE IS IN MARCH, 1976. (LOCAL). LES GARDNER, PROJ DIRECTOR; KFMD & KDTH; 346 8TH AVE; DUBUQUE, IA 52001. (#20308).

WOMEN & AMERICAN FICTION AT CLARKE COL, IOWA. THIS ENGLISH COURSE WILL FOCUS ON FICTION WRITTEN BY AND ABOUT WOMEN IN AMERICA. (LOCAL). CAROLYN FARRELL, DIRECTOR OF SPECIAL PROGRAMS; CLARKE COLLEGE; 1550 CLARKE DR; DUBUQUE, IA 52001. (#15852).

OCT 20, '74 - DEC 31, '76. WALKING TOURS THROUGH LINWOOD CEMETERY. TOUR. (LOCAL). M BECKIUS, COORDINATOR; LINWOOD CEMETERY; 2735 WINDSOR; DUBUQUE, IA 52001. (#105257-7).

AUG 1, '75. PRESENTATION OF 'FIVE FLAGS' FOR THEATER. CEREMONY. (LOCAL). MRS WAYNE NORMAN, COORD; SUNSHINE CIRCLE OF FINLEY HOSPITAL; 1525 DOUGLAS; DUBUQUE, IA 52001. (#200018-57).

SEPT 26 - 28, '75. A 19TH CENTURY MELODRAMA. LIVE PERFORMANCE AT TERRANCE DONOGHOE HALL. (LOCAL). CAROL BLITGEN, DIRECTOR; CLARKE COLLEGE; 1550 CLARKE DR; DUBUQUE, IA 52001. (#200018-50).

OCT 2, '75. DUBUQUE SYMPHONY ORCHESTRA'S BICENTENNIAL CONCERT. DUBUQUE SYMPHONY ORCHESTRA'S BICENTENNIAL CONCERT FEATURING THE GOVERNOR OF IOWA, ROBERT RAY, NARRATING 'LINCOLN PORTRAIT'. AT FIVE FLAGS CIVIC CENTER. (LOCAL). JAMES H NELSON, MGR; DUBUQUE SYMPHONY ORCHESTRA; LORE MOUND RD; DUBUQUE, IA 52001. (#104221-50).

OCT 4 - 5, '75. UNITED STATES ARMED FORCES BICENTENNIAL CARAVAN. THE CARAVAN IS COMPOSED OF EXHIBIT VANS FOR EACH BRANCH OF THE MILITARY SERVICE. THE THEME OF THE EXHIBITION IS 'HISTORY OF THE ARMED FORCES AND THEIR CONTRIBUTION TO THE NATION'. (LOCAL). DAVID A BRIKNER, CHMN; U S ARMED FORCES BICENTENNIAL EXHIBIT VANS PROJECT; ROUTE 3 AIRPORT RD; DUBUQUE, IA 52001. (#1775-210).

OCT 21 - 22, '75. TRICENTENNIAL MAN BIOETHICS SYMPOSIUM. CONFERENCE AT TERENCE DONOGHOE HALL. (LOCAL). MARGUERITE NEUMANN, CHMN; CLARKE COLLEGE; 1550 CLARKE DR; DUBUQUE, IA 52001. (#102649-2).

NOV 6, '75. 200TH ANNIVERSARY BIRTHDAY BALL. 200TH ANNIVERSARY BIRTHDAY BALL WITH DINNER, CEREMONY AND MUSIC BY THE MIKE REISS BAND. (LOCAL). GARY W HORN, COMMANDANT; DUBUQUE DETACHMENT - MARINE CORPS LEAGUE; 524 FENELON; DUBUQUE, IA 52001. (#104529-4).

NOV '75. OLD FASHIONED THANKSGIVING DINNER. FESTIVAL. (LOCAL). CAROLYN FARRELL, PROJ DIR; CLARKE COLLEGE; 1550 CLARKE DR; DUBUQUE, IA 52001. (#102647-1).

NOV '75. RAGTIME MUSIC PRESENTATION BY CIVIL WAR BAND. LIVE PERFORMANCE AT MUSIC HALL. (LOCAL). BARBARA KUTCHERA, CHMN; CLARKE COLLEGE; 1550 CLARKE DR; DUBUQUE, IA 52007. (#102649-1).

NOV '75 - MAR '76. REFLECTIONS. CULTURAL AND CREATIVE CONTEST FOR CHILDREN IN PTA SCHOOLS. (LOCAL). TERRY RIEZICKA, CHAIRMAN; PTA COUNCIL; 2050 HALL; DUBUQUE, IA 52001. (#104529-9).

DEC 3, '75. BANQUET. FESTIVAL AT WORTHINGTON MEMORIAL HALL. (LOCAL). JOE DECKER, CHMN; DUBUQUE COUNTY CATTLEMAN'S ASSOC; SHERRILL, IA 52073. (#200018-52).

DEC 6, '75. BICENTENNIAL COSTUME PARTY. FESTIVAL. (LOCAL). PAUL RUCKER, COORD; CARNEGIE-STOUT PUBLIC LIBRARY; 11TH & BLUFF; DUBUQUE, IA 52001. (#200018-53).

DEC 14, '75. HEARING ON CULTURE FOR THE BICENTENNIAL. SEMINAR AT ST JOSEPH'S AUDITORIUM, LORAS COLLEGE. (LOCAL). REV JAMES J BYRNE, CHMN; ARCHDIOCESE OF DUBUQUE; 1105 LOCUST; DUBUQUE, IA 52001. (#200018-51).

DEC 31, '75. NEW YEAR'S EVE AT TOWN CLOCK PLAZA. BALLOONS WITH GIFT CERTIFICATES WERE GIVEN OUT. AT TOWN CLOCK PLAZA. (LOCAL). MRS EVIE GREEN, COORD; THE GREEN FAMILY; 939 MT LORETTA; DUBUQUE, IA 52001. (#200018-215).

DEC '75. OLD ENGLISH CHRISTMAS DINNER. FESTIVAL. (LOCAL). CAROLYN FARRELL, PROJ DIR; CLARKE COLLEGE; 1550 CLARKE DR; DUBUQUE, IA 52001. (#102646-1).

JAN 1 - DEC 30, '76. OPENING OF 5 FLAGS CIVIC CENTER WITH SPECIAL EVENTS. RESTORATION OF 100 YEAR OLD THEATER, DEVELOPMENT OF PEDESTRIAN MALL IN AN URBAN RENEWAL AREA,PLUS AN EXHIBITION HALL FEATURING FILM HISTORY OF UPPER MISSISSIPPI RIVER. AT BETWEEN 4TH AND 5TH ON MAIN ST. (REGN'L). WAYNE A NORMAN; FIVE FLAGS CIVIC CENTER; PO BOX 717,622 DUBUQUE BLDG; DUBUQUE, IA 52001. (#199-1).

JAN 1 - DEC 31, '76. HISTORICAL SLIDE SHOW. FRANK MCCAW WILL SHOW SLIDES TO ANY GROUP OR ORGANIZATION INTERESTED IN VIEWING THEM. (LOCAL). FRANK MCCAW, CHMN; FRANK MCCAW; 700 BOLEYN RD; DUBUQUE, IA 52001. (#104732-10).

JAN 1 - DEC 31, '76. PROGRAM OF SONG. LIVE PERFORMANCE AT GRANDVIEW AVE-UNITED METHODIST CHURCH 419 N GRANDVIEW DUBUQUE IA. (LOCAL). MRS GERALD PURVIS; CHORALIERS; 1000 CLARA CT; DUBUQUE, IA 52001. (#106876-1).

JAN 17 - 18, '76. U S CENTRAL SKI ASSOC RACES. COMPETITION. (LOCAL). PAUL ULRICH, CHMN; SNOMAD SKI CLUB; 2144 JONATHAN LN; DUBUQUE, IA 52001. (#200018-49).

JAN 19 - JUNE 26, '76. BICENTENNIAL FESTIVAL. THE FLORA DORA DANCE GROUP WILL GIVE PERFORMANCES FOR SEVERAL DIFFERENT ORGANIZATIONS WITHIN THE COMMUNITY. (LOCAL). MRS ROBERT FISHERS; NATIVITY SENIOR CITIZENS; 1075 MARTHA ST; DUBUQUE, IA 52001. (#104732-6).

FEB 2 - 27, '76. BICENTENNIAL SCHOOL PROJECT - HOLY GHOST SHOW. CEREMONY, EXHIBIT AT HOLY GHOST SCHOOL. (LOCAL). SISTER THERESE, CHMN; HOLY GHOST SCHOOL; 2981 CENTRAL; DUBUQUE, IA 52001. (#200018-56).

FEB 8 - APR 25, '76. ORGAN RECITALS, CONCERTS, EXHIBITS. A SERIES OF PROGRAMS ON VARYING DATES. EVERY PROGRAM WILL FEATURE MUSIC BY AMERICAN COMPOSERS, EXCLUSIVELY. AMONG THE CHORAL SELECTIONS WILL BE BILLINGS, HOWE, STAFFE, WOOD, PINKHAM, LUDLOW, HOUHANESS, RORAM, AND HANCOCK. AT LOCATIONS VARY BY DATES. (LOCAL). MRS THOMAS GOODMAN, DIR; DUBUQUE GUILD OF ORGANISTS; 615 ENGLISH LANE; DUBUQUE, IA 52001. (#104221-47).

FEB 10 - 12, '76. ECUMENICAL SYMPOSIUM. SYMPOSIUM LECTURERS WILL BE: DR ANDREW GREELEY, DR ROBERT JEWETT, & DR LEE SNOOK. AT AQUINAS INSTITUTE ADUITORIUM. (LOCAL). REV VERNON H NAFFIER, DIR; DUBUQUE DEANERY OF CATHOLIC PRIESTS; 899 LAUREL; DUBUQUE, IA 52001. (#104221-43).

FEB 14, '76. SWEETHEART BALL. CHARITY BALL, DECORATED RED, WHITE AND BLUE; TWO DANCE BANDS: PAUL HEMMER AND MIKE RIES. THEME: 'HEARTS & STARS FOREVER'. THE PROCEEDS GO TO THE IOWA, WISCONSIN, ILLINOIS DIABETES UNIT (IWI). TOTAL PROCEEDS DONATED: $2,085.46. AT DUBUQUE COUNTY FAIRGROUNDS BALLROOM. (LOCAL). MRS JUDITH COLE; BETA SIGMA PHI SORORITY; 2715 HICKORY HILL; DUBUQUE, IA 52001. (#104221-38).

DUBUQUE — CONTINUED

FEB 19, '76. 'HEROES & HARD TIMES' - ALPHA OMEGA DINNER THEATRE. LIVE PERFORMANCE AT MARY JO DINING ROOM 'C'.. (LOCAL). DIANA MALONE, CHAIRMAN; CLARKE COLLEGE STUDENT GOVT; 1550 CLARKE DR; DUBUQUE, IA 52001. (#102649-4).

FEB 23 - 28, '76. DUBUQUE GIRLS' CLUB BICENTENNIAL WEEK. COMPETITION AT 75 W 17TH ST. (LOCAL). LAURIE HANSON, COORD; DUBUQUE GIRLS' CLUB; 75 W 17TH ST; DUBUQUE, IA 52001. (#105257-5).

FEB 27, '76. SKITS, FILM, MUSIC, REFRESHMENTS. FESTIVAL, LIVE PERFORMANCE. (LOCAL). WILLARD FROHS, CHMN; MASONIC TEMPLE; 819 RHOMBERG; DUBUQUE, IA 52001. (#104732-3).

FEB 28, '76. FIVE FLAGS THEATER OPENING. LIVE PERFORMANCE AT 4TH AND MAIN STS, OLD ORPHEUM THEATER. (REGN'L). STEVEN PETERS, MGR; FIVE FLAGS THEATER; PO BOX 1157; DUBUQUE, IA 52001. (#200018-58).

MAR 17, '76. ST PATRICK'S DAY CELEBRATION. FESTIVAL. (LOCAL). MINNIE LINDSEY, DIRECTOR; BARTENDERS LOCAL 527; 1130 1/2 MAIN; DUBUQUE, IA 52001. (#104221-46).

MAR 28, '76. 'CROP HUNGER WALK'. TOUR. (LOCAL). REV STEVEN WAINWRIGHT; DUBUQUE COUNCIL OF CHURCHES; MCCORMICK ST, EXT A-8; DUBUQUE, IA 52001. (#200018-55).

APR 1 - JULY 3, '76. KING AND QUEEN CONTEST. NOMINATIONS WILL BE ACCEPTED FROM APRIL THROUGH JUNE; THE CROWNING WILL BE HELD AT THE BICENTENNIAL BALL. AT DUBUQUE FAIRGROUNDS. (LOCAL). DARLENE O'CONNEL, CHMN; WA-TAN-YE CLUB; 2211 ST JOHN DR; DUBUQUE, IA 52001. (#106875-1).

APR 4, '76. YWCA FLEA MARKET. EXHIBIT, FESTIVAL AT YWCA, 35 N BOOTH. (LOCAL). JUNE MANNING, COORD; YWCA; 35 N BOOTH; DUBUQUE, IA 52001. (#105257-4).

APR 9 - 10, '76. CIRCUS. LIVE PERFORMANCE AT DUBUQUE SENIOR HIGH SCHOOL. (LOCAL). ROBERT MC GINNIS, DIR; NORTHEAST IOWA COUNCIL BOY SCOUTS OF AMERICA; 1298 DODGE; DUBUQUE, IA 52001. (#104221-39).

APR 23, '76. AN EXPERIMENTAL PRODUCTION OF INDIAN FOLKLORE. LIVE PERFORMANCE AT TERANCE DONOGHOE HALL. (LOCAL). CAROL BLITGEN, CHAIRMAN; CLARKE COLLEGE; 1550 CLARKE DR; DUBUQUE, IA 52001. (#102649-5).

APR 24 - 25, '76. 'WOMEN IN CELEBRATION' - AAUW STATE CONVENTION. DUBUQUE CHAPTER'S CONTRIBUTION IS 'EPIC' - ENCOURAGEMENT OF PARTICIPATION AND INTEREST IN THE COMMUNITY. (ST-WIDE). MRS FRED DARLIN, DIRECTOR; AMERICAN ASSOC OF UNIVERSITY WOMEN; 1782 SHAGBARK; DUBUQUE, IA 52001. (#104221-36).

APR 25, '76. BICENTENNIAL MASS. A BICENTENNIAL MASS WITH THE MOST REVEREND JAMES JO BYRNE, STD, ARCHBISHOP OF DUBUQUE, PRINCIPAL CELEBRANT WILL BE CELEBRATED IN CATHEDRAL OF ST RAPHAEL. (LOCAL). MSGR NORBERT BARRETT, DIR; ST RAPHAEL'S CATHEDRAL; 231 BLUFF; DUBUQUE, IA 52001. (#104221-13).

APR 30 - MAY 1, '76. 'CAST OF '76' - CONCERT. HOSTING 'SING OUT FOND DU LAK, WISCONSIN' - CONCERT. AT FIVE FLAGS THEATRE. (LOCAL). HARRY NEUSTADT, COORD; DUBUQUE BEAUTIFICATION COMMITTEE; 10-B FISCHER BLDG/2670 NEW HAVEN; DUBUQUE, IA 52001. (#106542-1).

MAY 1 - SEPT 6, '76. OPEN HOUSE TOURS. RESERVATIONS FOR GROUP TOURS OF MUSEUM OUT OF SEASON. BRIEF HISTORY OF CITY, EARLY SETTLERS, MR & MRS HAM & HOUSE, EXPLANATION OF ARTIFACTS, ETC. BUS TOUR: BACKROUND OF AREA HISTORICALLY & ARCHITECTURALLY. AT 2241 LINCOLN AVE. DUBUQUE. (LOCAL). HELEN MERCER, DIRECTOR; DUBUQUE COUNTY HISTORICAL SOCIETY, MATHIAS HAM MUSEUM; PO BOX 305; DUBUQUE, IA 52001. (#19195-1).

MAY 2 - 8, '76. SENIOR CITIZEN'S RECOGNITION WEEK. RECOGNITION OF SENIOR CITIZENS IN COOPERATION WITH 'OLDER AMERICANS MONTH'. (LOCAL). MRS JOSEPH A TAUKE, CHMN; PROJECT CONCERT, RSVP, UNIV OF DUBUQUE, NAAA; 1715 GLEN OAK; DUBUQUE, IA 52001. (#106595-1).

MAY 11 - 15, '76. FOLLIES. FESTIVAL AT ORPHEUM THEATER. (LOCAL). MRS HAROLD KOHNEN, CHMN; XAVIER HOSPITAL GUILD; DAVIS AVENUE; DUBUQUE, IA 52001. (#104732-1).

MAY 23, '76. REGIONAL BRIDGE TOURNAMENT. COMPETITION AT RIVERSIDE BOWL. (REGN'L). HERB BISPING, JR, COORD; IOWA STATE BRIDGE LEAGUE; 665 KENNEDY CT; DUBUQUE, IA 52001. (#106542-10).

JUNE 4 - 6, '76. STATE CONVENTION OF THE LIONS CLUB. CONFERENCE AT JULIEN MOTOR INN. (ST-WIDE). CHESTER SCHMITT, CHMN; DUBUQUE LIONS CLUB; 960 DAVIS; DUBUQUE, IA 52001. (#104732-4).

JUNE 4 - 13, '76. 10 DAY TOUR OF COUNTRY'S EARLY COLONIES AND HISTORICAL SITES. TOUR BY GIRL SCOUTS TO WILLIAMSBURG, JAMESTOWN, GETTYSBURG, VALLEY FORGE AND BLUE RIDGE MOUNTAINS. AT BUS LOCATION. (LOCAL). LINDA PULS, COORD; GIRL SCOUTS OF LITTLE CLOUD COUNCIL; 2240 MARION ST; DUBUQUE, IA 52001. (#106151-5).

JUNE 14, '76. FLAG DAY PROGRAM. THE PROGRAM WILL FEATURE CEREMONIES WITH AREA DIGNITARIES PARTICIPATING, THE COLT-45'S PERFORMING AND DISPLAYS IN THE MALL. AT KENNEDY MALL. (LOCAL). TOM SCHENKER, MGR; KENNEDY MALL MERCHANTS; 555 KENNEDY MALL - JKF RD; DUBUQUE, IA 52001. (#104732-8).

JUNE 20, '76. ANCIENT ART OF BLACKSMITHING. EXHIBIT AT WASHINGTON PARK. (LOCAL). JAMES E RYAN, CHMN; JAMES E RYAN; 175 ALPINE; DUBUQUE, IA 52001. (#106542-8).

JUNE 20, '76. DRUM AND BUGLE CORPS CONTEST. COMPETITION, LIVE PERFORMANCE AT DALZELL FIELD, SENIOR HIGH SCHOOL. (LOCAL). ROBERT M BUELOW, DIRECTOR; COLT 45 DRUM AND BUGLE CORPS; 710 MERZ; DUBUQUE, IA 52001. (#104221-42).

JUNE 20, '76. FESTIVAL. FESTIVAL INCLUDES PARADE, PROGRAMS BY VARIOUS GROUPS, SR CITIZENS DAY. (LOCAL). MRS ROBERT FISCHER, COORD; NATIVITY SENIOR CITIZENS; 1075 MARTHA ST.; DUBUQUE, IA 52001. (#104530-1).

JUNE 20, '76. MARINE CORPS LEAGUE MARCHING BAND IN PARADE. BAND CONSISTS OF 7 MEMBERS: 2 FLAG CARRIERS, 2 MUSKET CARRIERS, ONE COLORGUARD COMMANDER, ONE DRUMMER AND ONE FIFE PLAYER. UNIFORMS ARE MADE EXACTLY, IN EVERY DETAIL, LIKE THE MARINE UNIFORMS IN 17751776. AT DOWNTOWN DUBUQUE. (LOCAL). GARY HORN, COORD; MARINE CORPS LEAGUE; 524 FENELON; DUBUQUE, IA 52001. (#106542-6).

JUNE 20 - JULY 4, '76. BIG-WHEEL RACING CONTEST. COMPETITION. (LOCAL). MRS CAROL MURWIN, CHMN; JAYCEE JAYNES; 1995 LOMBARD; DUBUQUE, IA 52001. (#106871-1).

JUNE 22 - 23, '76. DUBUQUE POLICEMEN'S PROTECTIVE ASSOC BENEFIT CIRCUS. LIVE PERFORMANCE AT DUBUQUE COUNTY FAIRGROUNDS. (LOCAL). DAVE J WEIS, CHMN; DUBUQUE POLICEMEN'S PROTECTIVE ASSOC; PO BOX 292; DUBUQUE, IA 52001. (#106151-7).

JUNE 26, '76. BELLS IN DUBUQUE. BELLS IN CHURCHES ALL OVER DUBUQUE WILL BE RUNG SIMULTANEOUSLY. AT CHURCHES ALL OVER DUBUQUE. (LOCAL). JAMES E RYAN, COORD; JAMES E RYAN; 175 ALPINE; DUBUQUE, IA 52001. (#106542-9).

JUNE 26, '76. CARNIVAL CELEBRATION FOR THE ELDERLY. FESTIVAL AT AMERICANA HEALTH CARE CENTER PARKING LOT; 901 W 3RD ST. (LOCAL). NOLA ESMOIL, PROJ MGR; AMERICANA HEALTH CARE CENTER; 1280 ATLANTIC; DUBUQUE, IA 52001. (#106883-1).

JUNE 26, '76. FLOATS FOR PARADES & BOXLUNCH AUCTION IN WASHINGTON PARK. FESTIVAL, PARADE AT WASHINGTON PARK. (LOCAL). DON GAGNE, CHMN; TRI-STATE INDEPENDENT BLIND SOCIETY; 9TH AND IOWA; DUBUQUE, IA 52001. (#104732-5).

JUNE 26, '76. LINCOLN-DOUGLAS DEBATE. THE RALLY WILL FEATURE THE RE-ENACTMENT OF A POLITICAL DEBATE AND A 1776 FASHION SHOW. AT WASHINGTON PARK, DOWNTOWN DUBUQUE. (LOCAL). MARY L STROM, PROJ DIR; REPUBLICAN WOMEN'S CLUB; 974 INDIAN RIDGE; DUBUQUE, IA 52001. (#106877-1).

JUNE 26, '76. SPIRIT OF AMERICA. PARADE. (LOCAL). DICK RAMSEY, CHMN; NE IOWA AREA AGENCY ON AGING; 330 DUBUQUE BLDG; DUBUQUE, IA 52001. (#104732-11).

JUNE 26 - JULY 27, '76. DISPLAY OF ANTIQUE TRADES AND TOOLS. VARIOUS CRAFTS WILL BE DISPLAYED AND DEMONSTRATED INCLUDING LOOM WEAVING AND HORSESHOE MAKING. AT 1564 CENTRAL AVE. (LOCAL). JAMES E RYAN, COORD; DUBUQUE COUNTY REPUBLICAN CENTRAL COMMITTEE; 175 ALPINE ST; DUBUQUE, IA 52001. (#106873-1).

JUNE 27, '76. BICYCLE DECORATING CONTEST. THE CONTEST IS FOR CHILDREN AGES 6-12; BIKES WILL BE DECORATED IN BICENTENNIAL COLORS. AT WAHLERT HIGH SCHOOL PARKING LOT. (LOCAL). PAT EDWARDS, COORD; DUBUQUE LA SERTOMA; 795 KELLY LANE; DUBUQUE, IA 52001. (#106870-1).

JUNE 27, '76. COLONIAL GAMES, HORSESHOES, ROLLING PIN THROW AT EAGLE POINT PARK. LIVE PERFORMANCE, FESTIVAL AT EAGLE POINT PARK. (LOCAL). NANCY MEIS, COORD; DEPT OF RECREATION; BUNKER HILL; DUBUQUE, IA 52001. (#106884-1).

JUNE 30, '76. VAUDEVILLE PRESENTATION. THERE WILL BE TWO SHOWS - AT 7 PM AND 9 PM. AT FIVE FLAGS THEATRE, 4TH & MAIN. (LOCAL). JAMES E RYAN; DUBUQUE COMMUNITY PLAYERS; 175 ALPINE ST; DUBUQUE, IA 52001. (#106874-1).

JULY 3, '76. BICENTENNIAL DANCE. FESTIVAL AT FAIRGROUNDS. (LOCAL). HARRIET TINGLER, CHMN; VISITING NURSES ASSOCIATION; 412 LORAS BLVD; DUBUQUE, IA 52001. (#104732-9).

JULY 4, '76. BICENTENNIAL QUILT. YWCA SERVICE GROUP IS MAKING A BICENTENNIAL QUILT FOR DISPLAY AND AUCTION. (LOCAL). JUNE MANNING, PROJ CHMN; YWCA; 35 N BOOTH; DUBUQUE, IA 52001. (#104732-7).

JULY 4, '76. DONATION OF QUILT MADE IN 1884 TO DUBUQUE HISTORICAL SOCIETY. CEREMONY, EXHIBIT AT HOLY TRINTIY CHURCH RHOMBERG AVE. (LOCAL). DOROTHY BOHNSACK, COORD; LADIES OF THE SEWING ROOM OF ST FRANCIS; 1601 LINCOLN AVE; DUBUQUE, IA 52001. (#105257-6).

JULY 4, '76. 4TH OF JULY FESTIVAL. FESTIVAL ON MUSEUM GROUNDS WITH RELATED ENTERTAINMENT AND ACTIVITIES. AT MATHIAS MUSEUM GROUNDS. (LOCAL). HELEN MERCER, CHAIRMAN; DUBUQUE COUNTY HISTORICAL SOCIETY; PO BOX 305; DUBUQUE, IA 52001. (#19195-2).

JULY 10, '76. HAPPY BIRTHDAY AMERICA - AT THE LUTHER MANOR HOME. RESIDENTS AND STAFF WILL DRESS UP AS BETSY ROSS, GEORGE WASHINGTON AND UNCLE SAM FOR THE MUSICAL PRESENTATION. AT LUTHER MANOR NURSING HOME; 3131 HILLCREST RD. (LOCAL). MARLENE GUNDERSON, COORD; LUTHER MANOR NURSING HOME; 3131 HILLCREST; DUBUQUE, IA 52001. (#106880-1).

JULY 11, '76. DANCE RECITAL. DANCE AND GYMNASTICS WILL BE PERFORMED BY YOUTHS 3 YEARS OF AGE THRU TEENAGE FROM THE DUBUQUE AREA. AT DUBUQUE SENIOR HIGH SCHOOL. (LOCAL). CAROLU DIGMAN WELBES; DUBUQUE DANCE STUDIO & GYMNASTIC CLUB; 2612 UNIVERSITY; DUBUQUE, IA 52001. (#106878-1).

JULY 13 - 19, '76. FOLK ARTS FESTIVAL. HOURS ARE: 7/13 3-10PM; 7/15 THRU 7/18 1-4PM; 7/19 10AM-4PM. RESERVATIONS ARE REQUIRED FOR CLASS SESSIONS ONLY. AT FLORA PARK BARN. (LOCAL). ANN WELCH, SUPERVISOR; DUBUQUE DEPARTMENT OF RECREATION; BUNKER HILL; DUBUQUE, IA 52001. (#106542-11).

JULY 18, '76. FLOATS FOR PARADE; BOX LUNCH AUCTION IN PARK. MEMORIAL DAY AND FOURTH OF JULY PARADES IN WASHINGTON PARK. AT ALBROOK ACRES; 8 MI NORTH OF DUBUQUE ON SHERRIL BLACKTOP. (LOCAL). DON GAGNE, PROJ DIR; TRI-STATE INDEPENDENT BLIND SOCIETY; 9TH AND IOWA; DUBUQUE, IA 52001. (#104529-1).

JULY 18, '76. OLD FASHIONED BOX LUNCH 'BICENTENNIAL OLDEN DAYS RENEWED'. FESTIVAL AT RIVER VIEW PARK AT 16 TH ST CAMPING SITE. (LOCAL). MRS JOHN MILLER, CHMN; RIVER-VIEW PARK CONSERVATION SOCIETY; 145 VALLEY ST; DUBUQUE, IA 52001. (#105257-8).

JULY 20, '76. DEDICATION OF WASHINGTON PARK TIME CAPSULE. CEREMONY AT WASHINGTON PARK. (LOCAL). ROB APEL, CHMN; DUBUQUE JAYCEES; 1780 CENTRAL, APT 3-A; DUBUQUE, IA 52001. (#106542-3).

JULY 20, '76. PRESENTATION OF NATURALIZATION CEREMONY. JUDGE EDWARD J MCMANUS, THE FIRST CIRCUIT JUDGE OF DUBUQUE COUNTY & NOW JUDGE OF THE U S DISTRICT COURT - NORTHERN DISTRICT OF IOWA, WILL HOLD A MOCK NATURALIZATION CEREMONY. AT WASHINGTON PARK. (LOCAL). MISS MARY REDDIN, COORD; AMERICAN BUSINESS WOMENS ASSOC; 1930 HALE ST; DUBUQUE, IA 52001. (#106882-1).

JULY 22 - AUG 15, '76. FIVE FLAGS BICENTENNIAL MUSICAL 'GET THE LEAD OUT'. 'GET THE LEAD OUT', BY CHARLES CEROUX. MUSIC BY PAUL HEMMER. MATINEES FROM 2-4:30 PM. AT FIVE FLAGS THEATER, 400 MAIN ST, DUBUQUE, IOWA. (REGN'L). WAYNE NORMAN, SR, CHMN; FIVE FLAGS CIVIC CENTER FUND & DUBUQUE AREA CHAMBER OF COMMERCE; 622 DUBUQUE BLDG, PO 717; DUBUQUE, IA 52001. (#104529-8).

JULY 24 - AUG 7, '76. JEAN MARIE CARDINAL CANOE TRIP. REENACTMENT OF JEAN MARIE CARDINAL CANOE TRIP DOWN MISSISSIPPI TO ST LOUIS - 400 MI VOYAGE. (REGN'L). HARRY NEUSTADT, COORD; DUBUQUE '76, INC; 480 FISCHER BUILDING; DUBUQUE, IA 52001. (#106151-3).

JULY 25, '76. FINE ARTS FESTIVAL. THE PICKET FENCE SHOW WILL INCLUDE PAINTINGS, CRAFTS AND MACRAME. AT 375 ALPINE ST. (LOCAL). MRS MARILOU WITT, COORD; DUBUQUE WOMEN'S CLUB; 1400 KELLY LANE; DUBUQUE, IA 52001. (#106881-1).

SEPT 18 - 19, '76. IOWA STATE BARBER JOURNEYMAN CONVENTION. CONFERENCE AT JULIEN MOTOR INN, 200 MAIN ST. (ST-WIDE). GENE SANDS, PROJ CHMN; IOWA STATE JOURNEYMAN BARBERS; 2460 PENNSYLVANIA AVE; DUBUQUE, IA 52001. (#106872-1).

OCT 10, '76. EASTERN IOWA DISTRICT MEETING. DISTRICT MEETING AND PROGRAM. SOCIAL HOUR, LUNCHEON, MEETING AND ENTERTAINMENT. THEME: 'CELEBRATE AMERICA'S BIRTHDAY, AND PLANT A FUTURE'. AT CHATEAU SUPPER CLUB, 3750 CENTRAL AVE. (ST-WIDE). MRS JUDITH COLE; BETA SIGMA PHI SORORITY; 2715 HICKORY HILL; DUBUQUE, IA 52001. (#104221-49).

NOV 6, '76. 201ST ANNIVERSARY BIRTHDAY BALL. THERE WILL BE A DINNER, CEREMONY AND MUSIC BY THE MIKE REISS BAND. (LOCAL). GARY W HORN, COMMANDANT; DUBUQUE DETACHMENT - MARINE CORPS LEAGUE; 524 FENELON; DUBUQUE, IA 52001. (#104529-12).

DUMONT

MUSEUM RESTORATION - PROJ OF DUMONT, IA. RESTORATION OF THE DUMONT HERITAGE HOUSE TO CONTAIN HISTORICAL ARTICLES FOR POSTERITY. (LOCAL). ERNA CLEMENS, CHAIRMAN; DUMONT BICENTENNIAL AND HISTORICAL SOCIETY; DUMONT, IA 50625. (#17873).

JUNE 12, '76. BICENTENNIAL FLAG PRESENTATION. CEREMONY AT DUMONT FOOTBALL FIELD. (LOCAL). ERNA CLEMENS, DIRECTOR; DUMONT HISTORICAL SOCIETY, LIONS LEGION AND LOCAL CHURCHES; DUMONT, IA 50625. (#105609-1).

JUNE 12 - 13, '76. 200TH BIRTHDAY CELEBRATION. ACTIVITIES WILL INCLUDE PARADE, PAGEANT, PRESENTATION OF BOOK TO LIBRARY, ECUMENICAL CHURCH SERVICE AND A COMMUNITY PICNIC. AT DUMONT FOOTBALL FIELD. (LOCAL). ERNA CLEMENS, DIRECTOR; DUMONT HISTORICAL SOCIETY, LEGION AND AUXILIARY; DUMONT, IA 50625. (#105609-2).

DUNBAR

BICENTENNIAL PROJECTS - DUNBAR, IA. AN OAK TREE WILL BE PLANTED, A HISTORY OF THE COMMUNITY WILL BE WRITTEN, A BRONZE PLAQUE WILL BE PLACED ON A STONE MARKER AND CITY SIGNS WILL BE ERECTED. (LOCAL). MRS BERT THORNES, CHAIRMAN; TOWN OF DUNBAR BICENTENNIAL COMMITTEE; RTE 1; MONTOUR, IA 50173. (#29133).

MAY 29 - 30, '76. BICENTENNIAL CELEBRATION. FLAG RAISING CEREMONY, COMBINED CHURCH SERVICE, PICNIC, DINNER, PTA HERITAGE DISPLAY, ALUMNI BANQUET. AT DUNBAR SCHOOL GYM. (LOCAL). ROBERT THOMPSON, CHMN; DUNBAR ALUMNI ASSOC & HAPPY HOUR CLUB; BOX 656; MARSHALLTOWN, IA 50158. (#200018-244).

DUNCOMBE

BOOK: HISTORY OF DUNCOMBE & WASHINGTON TWP, IA. A HISTORY OF DUNCOMBE AND WASHINGTON TOWNSHIP HAS BEEN

DUNCOMBE — CONTINUED

WRITTEN. HAS ALSO BEEN INCLUDED IN THE HISTORY OF WEBSTER COUNTY TOWNSHIPS. (LOCAL). VERYLE DANIELS, HISTORIAN; DUNCOMBE BICENTENNIAL COMMITTEE; BOX 24 RFD 2; DUNCOMBE, IA 50532. (#22221).

DUNCOMBE, IA, YOUTH CENTER ADDITION. A KITCHEN AND RESTROOMS WILL BE ADDED TO THE YOUTH CENTER. (LOCAL). CHARLES E GRIGGS, MAYOR; DUNCOMBE TOWN COUNCIL; DUNCOMBE, IA 50532. (#22220).

HISTORIC RAILROAD DEPOT - DUNCOMBE, IA. THE HISTORIC RAILROAD DEPOT WILL BE MOVED TO CENTENNIAL PARK AND RESTORED TO BE USED AS A LIBRARY. (LOCAL). CHARLES E GRIGGS, MAYOR; DUNCOMBE TOWN COUNCIL; DUNCOMBE, IA 50532. (#22219).

TREES IN CENTENNIAL PARK, DUNCOMBE, IA. TREES AND PICNIC TABLES TO BE PUT IN PARK. (LOCAL). HON CHARLES E GRIGGS, MAYOR; TOWN COUNCIL; DUNCOMBE CITY HALL; DUNCOMBE, IA 50532. (#22218).

AUG 14, '76. DUNCOMBE HIGH SCHOOL REUNION. CEREMONY, TOUR AT DUNCOMBE YOUTH CENTER. (LOCAL). JANICE BRILEY, COORD; DUNCOMBE BICENTENNIAL COMMITTEE; DUNCOMBE, IA 50532. (#105966-2).

AUG 14, '76. LITTLE WORLDS FAIR. FESTIVAL, PARADE AT MAIN ST - DUNCOMBE YOUTH CENTER & CITY PARK. (LOCAL). EDYTHE ASCHERL, CHMN; DUNCOMBE BICENTENNIAL COMMITTEE; CITY HALL; DUNCOMBE, IA 50532. (#105966-3).

AUG 14, '76. MUSICAL PROGRAM. PATRIOTIC & HISTORICAL VOCAL/INSTRUMENTAL MUSIC TO BE PERFORMED. AT CITY PARK. (LOCAL). EDYTHE C ASCHERL, CHMN; DUNCOMBE BICENTENNIAL COMMITTEE; CITY HALL; DUNCOMBE, IA 50532. (#105966-1).

DUNDEE

COMMUNITY DEVELOPMENT PROJ - DUNDEE, IA. THE FIRE TOWER & FLAGPOLE WILL BE PAINTED RED, WHITE & BLUE. (LOCAL). WILLIAM RYAN, PROJ CHAIRMAN; DUNDEE CITY COUNCIL; ROCKY RIDGE; DUNDEE, IA 52038. (#25301).

JULY 17, '76. DUNDEE BICENTENNIAL DAY. FESTIVAL AT DOWNTOWN AND SCHOOL FIELD. (LOCAL). WILLIAM RYAN, COORD; DUNDEE CITY COUNCIL; DUNDEE, IA 52038. (#107999-1).

DUNKERTON

HERITAGE PROJECTS - DUNKERTON, IA. MUSEUM DISPLAYS, STORE WINDOW DISPLAYS AND CITY PARK IMPROVEMENT. (LOCAL). NATALIE BAUGHER, CHAIRMAN; DUNKERTON BICENTENNIAL COMMISSION; BOX 158; DUNKERTON, IA 50626. (#13908).

TREE PLANTING PROJECT - DUNKERTON, IA. TREES WILL BE PLANTED IN HONOR OF SENIOR CITIZENS. (LOCAL). NATALIE BAUGHER, CHAIRMAN; DUNKERTON BICENTENNIAL COMMITTEE; BOX 158; DUNKERTON, IA 50626. (#13909).

JUNE 12, '75. DUNKERTON BICENTENNIAL CELEBRATION. FESTIVAL, PARADE AT CITYWIDE. (LOCAL). MRS KEN RIGDON; DUNKERTON BICENTENNIAL COMMITTEE; 10904 EAST DUNKERTON ROAD; DUNKERTON, IA 50626. (#50633-1).

MAY 12, '76. CRAFTS AUCTION AND FLEA MARKET. THE FIREMEN'S AUCTION WILL ALSO INCLUDE BINGO GAMES. AT DUNKERTON COMMUNITY HALL, MAIN ST. (LOCAL). NATALIE BAUGHER, CO-CHMN; DUNKERTON COMMUNITY BICENTENNIAL COMMITTEE; BOX 158; DUNKERTON, IA 50626. (#101407-1).

JUNE 12, '76. CRAFTS AUCTION & FLEA MARKET. FESTIVAL AT DUNKERTON COMMUNITY HALL, MAIN ST. (LOCAL). NATALIE BAUGHER, CO-CHMN; DUNKERTON COMMUNITY BICENTENNIAL COMMITTEE; BOX 158; DUNKERTON, IA 50626. (#102042-1).

JUNE 12, '76. DUNKERTON FESTIVAL. CELEBRATION WILL INCLUDE AUCTION, PARADE AND CONCESSIONS. (LOCAL). NATALIE BAUGHER, CHMN; DUNKERTON COMMUNITY BICENTENNIAL COMMITTEE; BOX 158; DUNKERTON, IA 50626. (#101381-1).

DUNLAP

SWIMMING POOL '76 - DUNLAP, IA. NEW SWIMMING POOL TO REPLACE OLD POOL. (LOCAL). GARY KOWER, COORDINATOR; BICENTENNIAL COMMITTEE; DUNLAP, IA 51529. (#19960).

JULY 4, '76 - CONTINUING . JULY 4TH CELEBRATION. FESTIVAL. (LOCAL). GARY KORVER, COORD; BOOSTER CLUB; DUNLAP, IA 51529. (#104687-1).

DURANT

RESTORATION OF CHURCH - DURANT, IA. RESTORATION OF CHURCH STEEPLE TO ORIGINAL DESIGN. (LOCAL). GEORGE E W BOLDT, CLERK; ST PAUL'S EPISCOPAL CHURCH; 206 6TH AVE; DURANT, IA 52747. (#26434).

DYERSVILLE

NEW PARK ENTRANCE - DYERSVILLE, IA. A NEW PARK ENTRANCE WILL BE BUILT AND DEDICATED. (LOCAL). BOB PLATZ, PRESIDENT; COMMERCIAL CLUB; DYERSVILLE, IA 52040. (#32084).

JULY 3 - 4, '76. JULY 4TH CELEBRATION. ACTIVITIES INCLUDED PARADE, FIREWORKS, DANCES, LIVE PERFORMANCES. AT DYERSVILLE COMMUNITY CLUB PARK. (LOCAL). STEVE BOGE; DYERSVILLE BICENTENNIAL COMMITTEE & LOCAL ORGANIZATIONS; 1020 4TH ADE SE; DYERSVILLE, IA 52040. (#200018-298).

DYSART

BEAUTIFICATION OF THE COMMUNITY, DYSART, IA. PATRIOTIC PAINTING OF FIRE HYDRANTS AND PLANTING OF RED, WHITE AND BLUE FLOWERS. (LOCAL). BOB MOORE, ART INSTRUCTOR; HIGH SCHOOL ART DEPARTMENT AND DYSART WOMEN'S CLUB; 505 WEST ST; DYSART, IA 52224. (#22121).

HISTORY PROGRAM, DYSART, IA. TIME CAPSULE CONTAINING RECOLLECTIONS BY SENIOR CITIZENS WILL BE BURIED; BICENTENNIAL SCRAPBOOK WILL BE COMPILED AND FLAGS WILL BE ADDED TO THE CEMETERY AND THE COMMUNITY. (LOCAL). MRS NORMAN COOPER, SECRETARY; DYSART BICENTENNIAL COMMITTEE; 1212 WILSON; DYSART, IA 52224. (#22120).

LOG CABIN, DYSART, IA. AUTHENTIC LOG CABIN WILL BE A PERMANENT ADDITION TO THE PARK. (LOCAL). IRVIN MEIER, INSTRUCTOR; FUTURE FARMERS OF AMERICA; 505 WEST ST; DYSART, IA 52224. (#22122).

SEPT 5 - 6, '76. LABOR DAY CELEBRATION - CHURCH SERVICE, FAMILY DAY AND FIREWORKS. EXHIBIT, PARADE, LIVE PERFORMANCE AT CITY PARK, HIGH SCHOOL. (LOCAL). MRS NORMAN COOPER, SEC; DYSART BICENTENNIAL COMMITTEE; 1212 WILSON ST; DYSART, IA 52224. (#105928-1).

EAGLE GROVE

JUNE 18 - 20, '76. EAGLE GROVE HISTORICAL EXHIBIT. THIS EXHIBIT WILL DISPLAY ITEMS, BOOKS AND PICTURES REFLECTIVE OF OF THE HISTORY OF EAGLE GROVE AND THE SURROUNDING AREA. ALSO HISTORICAL BICENTENNIAL PARADE, COUNTY BICENTENNIAL SKIT; UNION CHURCH SERVICE, ANTIQUE SHOW, AND CRAFT DISPLAY. (LOCAL). MRS ORIN EMERSON, DIR; EAGLE GROVE HISTORICAL SOCIETY; 917 W BROADWAY; EAGLE GROVE, IA 50533. (#102931-1).

JUNE 18 - 20, '76. SCANDINAVIAN DAYS DISPLAY - ARTS, CRAFTS AND ANTIQUES. EXHIBIT, FESTIVAL, PARADE AT MEMORIAL BUILDING. (LOCAL). HARIAN HEARD, CHAIRMAN; EAGLE GROVE BICENTENNIAL COMMITTEE & CHAMBER OF COMMERCE; 800 W BROADWAY; EAGLE GROVE, IA 50533. (#103014-1).

EARLHAM

BASKETBALL COURT FOR EARLHAM, IA. CONCRETE BASKETBALL COURT IN CITY PARK. (LOCAL). RICHARD MARTIN, CHAIRMAN; EARLHAM BICENTENNIAL COMMITTEE; EARLHAM, IA 50072. (#24495).

BICENTENNIAL COOKBOOK - EARLHAM, IA. FAVORITE RECIPES OF LOCAL CITIZENS WILL BE COMPILED INTO A BOOK. (LOCAL). DELORES SUMMY, CHAIRMAN; EARLHAM BUSINESS ASSOC; EARLHAM, IA 50072. (#24496).

JULY 2 - 3, '76. BICENTENNIAL CANTATA. LIVE PERFORMANCE AT SCHOOL GYM. (LOCAL). BERNARD ZYLSTRA, COORD; MINISTERIAL ASSOC; EARLHAM, IA 50072. (#106895-1).

JULY 3, '76. BICENTENNIAL PARADE. PARADE. (LOCAL). RICHARD PETERSEN, CHMN; EARLHAM BICENTENNIAL COMMITTEE; BOX 189; EARLHAM, IA 50072. (#106896-1).

EARLING

JAN 1 - MAY 30, '76. PAGEANT. FESTIVAL AT COMMUNITY HALL. (LOCAL). GLADYS RAFFERTY, COORD; BUSINESSMEN; EARLING, IA 51530. (#105619-2).

FEB 1 - MAY 30, '76. TIME CAPSULE. CEREMONY AT CITY HALL. (LOCAL). GLADYS RAFFERTY, COORD; BICENTENNIAL COMMITTEE; EARLING, IA 51530. (#105619-1).

JULY 3, '76. BICENTENNIAL PARADE. PARADE FEATURING OUR HERITAGE: PAST, PRESENT AND FUTURE. (LOCAL). GLADYS RAFFERTY, COORD; BICENTENNIAL COMMITTEE; EARLING, IA 51530. (#105619-3).

EARLVILLE

A BELL FOR EARLVILLE FIRE DEPARTMENT, IA. AN 1881 FIRE BELL WILL BE PLACED IN FRONT OF THE NEWLY CONSTRUCTED FIRE STATION. (LOCAL). JAMES CLIFTON, PROJ DIRECTOR; EARLVILLE VOLUNTEER FIRE DEPARTMENT; EARLVILLE, IA 52041. (#17505).

PLAYGROUND EQUIPMENT - EARLVILLE, IA. A NEW PLAYGROUND SLIDE WILL BE PURCHASED FOR THE PARK. (LOCAL). WILLIAM BRAMLEY, CHAIRMAN; CIVIC ACTION TEAM; EARLVILLE, IA 52041. (#17506).

AUG 10, '75. POOL GALA, BICENTENNIAL THEME WITH PAGEANT. FREE SWIMMING, ROPE PULL AND AUCTION WILL BE HELD. AT SWIMMING POOL. (LOCAL). WILLIAM BRAMLEY, CHMN; CIVIC ACTION TEAM; EARLVILLE, IA 52041. (#200018-59).

EARLY

BICENTENNIAL ACTIVITIES - EARLY, IA. ACTIVITIES INCLUDED: COUNTY FAIR, PAGEANT, WOMEN'S CLUB PROGRAM, WEEKLY BICENTENNIAL EDITORIAL, CONTESTS, CHURCH SERVICES AND 4TH OF JULY CELEBRATION. (LOCAL). MRS ROBERT EVANS, COORDINATOR; EARLY COMMUNITY BICENTENNIAL COMMITTEE; EARLY, IA 50535. (#32616).

JULY 4, '76. JULY 4TH CELEBRATION. 2000 PEOPLE VIEWED PARADE, BEARD CONTEST, FIREWORKS, GAMES, BALL GAMES, SPECIAL CHURCH SERVICES, BELL RINGING, FOOD STANDS, LIBRARY HERITAGE DISPLAY, LOCAL ARTISTS DISPLAY FOR THE BICENTENNIAL CELEBRATION. (LOCAL). MRS ROBERT EVANS, CHMN; EARLY COMMUNITY BICENTENNIAL COMMITTEE; 106 3RD ST; EARLY, IA 50535. (#200018-290).

EDDYVILLE

BICENTENNIAL FLAG POLE, IA. FLAG POLE TO BE CONSTRUCTED AT SENIOR CITIZENS HOME AT 2ND & ELM ST. (LOCAL). MRS VIRGIL BROWER, DIRECTOR; SENIOR CITIZENS GROUP; EDDYVILLE, IA 52553. (#23916).

BICENTENNIAL SHELTER, IA. CONSTRUCTION OF SHELTER LOCATED IN CITY PARK FOR PICNICS AND FAMILY REUNIONS. (LOCAL). CHUCK RAY, SARGEANT AT ARMS; AMERICAN LEGION; CEDAR, IA 52543. (#23917).

JUNE 4 - 5, '76. FLOWER SHOW. EXHIBIT AT CIVIC CENTER. (LOCAL). MRS GAIL F CARLO, CHMN; GARDEN CLUB; ROUTE 2; EDDYVILLE, IA 52553. (#107307-1).

AUG 3, '76. QUEEN CONTEST. COMPETITION, LIVE PERFORMANCE AT EDDYVILLE HIGH SCHOOL, 2 MILES EAST OF GRADE SCHOOL. (LOCAL). GARY GREENE, COORDINATOR; EDDYVILLE EDUCATION ASSOC & PTO CLUB; EDDYVILLE, IA 52553. (#106835-2).

AUG 4, '76. BICENTENNIAL PARADE. FESTIVAL, PARADE AT MAIN ST. (LOCAL). ROGER P EVANS, PRESIDENT; JAYCEES & CCC CLUBS; BOX 461; EDDYVILLE, IA 52553. (#106835-1).

AUG 4, '76. TALENT SHOW. LIVE PERFORMANCE AT CITY PARK; IN CASE OF RAIN - HIGH SCHOOL AUDITORIUM. (LOCAL). VELMA POWERS, CHAIRMAN; CCC CLUB; LIONS & JAYCEES; EDDYVILLE, IA 52553. (#106835-3).

EDGEWOOD

HISTORY OF EDGEWOOD, IA. BOOK OF EDGEWOOD FROM 1842 TO 1976. (LOCAL). GEORGE HAGENSICK, CHAIRMAN; HISTORICAL BOOK OF EDGEWOOD COMMITTEE; EDGEWOOD, IA 52042. (#20444).

JUNE 25 - 26, '76. THRASHING OATS THE OLD WAY. EXHIBIT. (LOCAL). CARROLL APPLETON, CHMN; ANTIQUES DISPLAY COMMITTEE; EDGEWOOD, IA 52042. (#104801-2).

JUNE 26, '76. PARADE OF PROGRESS. PARADE AT MAIN ST. (LOCAL). HERMAN LEWIS, CHAIRMAN; PARADE OF PROGRESS COMMITTEE; EDGEWOOD, IA 52042. (#104801-1).

ELBERON

COMMUNITY CLUB CENTER, ELBERON, IA. REMODELING AND IMPROVEMENTS OF COMMUNITY CLUB. (LOCAL). LEO J MACHAN, CHAIRMAN; COMMUNITY CLUB; BOX 325; ELBERON, IA 52225. (#23160).

MEMORIAL FLAG POLE, ELBERON, IA. ESTABLISHMENT OF DOWNTOWN SQUARE AND ERECTION OF MEMORIAL FLAG POLE, LANDSCAPING AND REST BENCHES. (LOCAL). BRIAN KIENAST, COORDINATOR; AMERICAN LEGION POST 226; RR I; ELBERON, IA 52225. (#23158).

NEW TOWN PARK, ELBERON, IA. EXISTING FACILITIES WILL BE REPAIRED, PLAYGROUND EQUIPMENT INSTALLED AND GREENERY PLANTED. (LOCAL). LEO T MACHEN, CHAIRMAN; COMMUNITY CLUB; BOX 325; ELBERON, IA 52225. (#23157).

SANITARY SEWER SYSTEM, ELBERON, IA. ESTABLISHMENT OF SEWER SYSTEM AND LAGOON. (LOCAL). BYRL R GILLESPIE, COORDINATOR; TOWN COUNCIL; ELBERON, IA 52225. (#23159).

APR 10, '76. FARMERS' BREAKFAST. FESTIVAL. (LOCAL). LEO J MACHAN, CHMN; COMMUNITY CLUB; BOX 325; ELBERON, IA 52225. (#106386-4).

MAY 30, '76. MEMORIAL SERVICES. PARADE, FLAG CEREMONIES, SPEECHES & BAND. (LOCAL). LEO J MACHAN, CHMN; COMMUNITY CLUB; BOX 325; ELBERON, IA 52225. (#106386-1).

JUNE 15, '76. PANCAKE SUPPER. FESTIVAL. (LOCAL). LEO J MACHAN, CHMN; COMMUNITY CLUB; BOX 325; ELBERON, IA 52225. (#106386-5).

AUG 26, '76. BICENTENNIAL DAY. FESTIVAL. (LOCAL). LEO J MACHAN, CHMN; COMMUNITY CLUB; BOX 325; ELBERON, IA 52225. (#106386-6).

AUG 26 - 29, '76. HISTORICAL EXHIBIT: FAMILY HEIRLOOMS, PICTURES & DOCUMENTS. EXHIBIT. (LOCAL). LEO J MACHAN, CHMN; COMMUNITY CLUB; BOX 325; ELBERON, IA 52225. (#106386-2).

OCT 22, '76. HARVEST BALL. FESTIVAL. (LOCAL). LEO J MACHAN, CHMN; COMMUNITY CLUB; BOX 325; ELBERON, IA 52225. (#106386-7).

NOV 26, '76. COMMUNITY CHURCH SERVICE (NON-DENOMINATIONAL) & ICE CREAM SOCIAL. CEREMONY. (LOCAL). LEO J MACHAN, CHMN; COMMUNITY CLUB; BOX 325; ELBERON, IA 52225. (#106386-3).

ELDON

FLEA MARKET. LOCAL HISTORICAL ITEMS DISPLAYED, ALSO ART & PERSONAL ITEMS. (LOCAL). LLOYD TEETER, CHAIRMAN; ELDON COMMUNITY CLUB; ELDON, IA 52554. (#104332-4).

PARK DEVELOPMENT PROJECT, ELDON, IA. DEVELOPMENT OF PARK FACILITIES AROUND 'AMERICAN GOTHIC' HOUSE USED BY GRANT WOOD. (LOCAL). DONNA COX, CHAIRMAN; ELDON COMMUNITY CLUB; ELDON, IA 52554. (#19325).

JULY 2, '75 - JULY 2, '76. ARTS PAGEANT, 'HERITAGE OF 200 YEARS'. EXHIBIT, FESTIVAL AT GRANDSTAND. (LOCAL). CLIFF MOORE, PROJ DIR; WAPELLO COUNTY FAIR; RT; ELDON, IA 52554. (#104332-6).

JULY 2, '76. PARADE, 'PAST TO PRESENT'. PARADE AT ELM STREET. (LOCAL). WILLIAM CAMPBELL, CHMN; ELDON COMMUNITY CLUB; ELDON, IA 52554. (#104332-5).

JULY 2 - 4, '76. COMMUNITY FESTIVAL. CARNIVAL, RACING, PICNICS, CAMPAIGNS & COMMUNITY CELEBRATION. AT WAPELLO COUNTY FAIRGROUNDS, EAST CITY LIMITS, ELDON. (LOCAL). GLENN HUGHES, CHRPSN; WAPELLO COUNTY FAIR AND ELDON COMMUNITY CLUB; RIVER DR; ELDON, IA 52554. (#104332-3).

AUG 10 - 15, '76. WAPELLO COUNTY FAIR. FAIR AT WAPELLO COUNTY FAIRGROUNDS. (LOCAL). GLEN HUGHES, SECRETARY; WAPELLO COUNTY FAIR ASSOC; 414 FIRST ST; ELDON, IA 52554. (#106291-1).

ELDRIDGE

JULY 9 - 11, '76. BICENTENNIAL CELEBRATION IN ELDRIDGE. ACTIVITIES INCLUDE PARADE AND DANCING ON JULY 9; BASEBALL TOURNAMENTS AND VARIETY SHOW ON JULY 10; BAND CONCERT & ICE CREAM SOCIAL ON JULY 11. (LOCAL). MRS ROBERT BLANCHE; ELDRIDGE BICENTENNIAL COMMITTEE; ELDRIDGE, IA 52748. (#108452-1).

ELK HORN

RESTORATION OF DANISH WINDMILL, ELK HORN IA. PRESENTATION OF DANISH HERITAGE BY DEVELOPMENT AND USE OF AUTHENTIC DANISH MILL; COMPANION INTERESTS AND SERVICES WILL HELP PROMOTE THE PEOPLE AND ATTRACTIONS OF SOUTHWEST IOWA. (LOCAL). WARREN JACOBSEN, PRESIDENT; BETTER ELK HORN CLUB; ELK HORN, IA 51531. (#19713).

MAY 31, '76. DEDICATION OF AUTHENTIC DANISH WINDMILL. CEREMONY AT ELK HORN TOWN PARK. (LOCAL). WARREN JACOBSEN, DIR; BETTER ELK HORN CLUB; ELK HORN, IA 51531. (#104221-19).

ELKADER

CEMETERY SURVEY IN ELKADER, IA. CATALOGING OF ALL CEMETERIES IN THE COUNTY. (LOCAL). DON MENKEN, PROJ DIRECTOR; CLAYTON COUNTY CONSERVATION COMMISSION; RR2; ELKADER, IA 52043. (#15076).

PIONEER VILLAGE IN ELKADER, IA. RECONSTRUCTION OF A VILLAGE WHICH INCLUDES A LOG CABIN, A BLACKSMITH SHOP, A DEPOT AND POSSIBLY A ONE-ROOM SCHOOLHOUSE. (LOCAL). DON MENKEN, PROJ DIRECTOR; CLAYTON COUNTY CONSERVATION COMMISSION; RR2; ELKADER, IA 52043. (#15075). **ARBA GRANTEE.**

REPLANTING OF ELKADER, IA. NATIVE PRAIRIES OF AREA WILL BE REPLANTED. (ST-WIDE). DON MENKEN, PROJ DIRECTOR; CLAYTON COUNTY BICENTENNIAL COMMISSION; RR 2; ELKADER, IA 52043. (#15078).

TREE PLANTING IN ELKADER, IA. PLANTING OF OFFICIAL STATE TREES. (ST-WIDE). DON MENKEN, PROJ DIRECTOR; CLAYTON COUNTY BICENTENNIAL COMMISSION; RR 2; ELKADER, IA 52043. (#15077).

JULY 3 - 5, '76. JULY 4TH CELEBRATION OF CLAYTON COUNTY. FESTIVAL. (LOCAL). DON MENKEN, DIRECTOR; CLAYTON COUNTY BICENTENNIAL COMMISSION; RR 2; ELKADER, IA 52043. (#102221-1).

AUG 13 - 15, '76. SWEET CORN DAYS - COMMUNITY FESTIVAL. EXHIBIT, FESTIVAL, PARADE AT MAIN STREET & RECREATION PARK. (LOCAL). THOMAS PAULIN, PROJ COORD; ELKADER JAYCEES; 205 2ND ST NW; ELKADER, IA 52043. (#104519-9).

ELKHART

FLAG POLE & TIME CAPSULE - ELKHART, IA. A FLAG POLE WILL BE ERECTED AND A TIME CAPSULE WILL BE PREPARED FOR BURIAL. (LOCAL). C RICHARD DAWSON, CHAIRMAN; CITY OF ELKHART BICENTENNIAL CITIZEN'S COMMISSION; 112 S WASHINGTON AVE; ELKHART, IA 50073. (#26831).

JULY 17, '76. ELKHART BICENTENNIAL DAY CELEBRATION. FESTIVAL, PARADE. (LOCAL). C RICHARD DAWSON, CHMN; CITY OF ELKHART BICENTENNIAL CITIZEN'S COMMISSION; 112 S WASHINGTON AVE; ELKHART, IA 50073. (#200018-231).

ELLIOTT

RENOVATION OF ORIGINAL POST OFFICE IN ELLIOTT, IA. THE ELLIOT HISTORICAL SOCIETY WILL MOVE AND RESTORE THE TOWN'S ORIGINAL POST OFFICE. (LOCAL). HON LYLE NORRIS, MAYOR; ELLIOT COMMUNITY HISTORICAL SOCIETY; ELLIOT, IA 51532. (#11281).

RESTORATION OF OLD FRAME BARBERSHOP: ELLIOTT, IA. AN OLD FRAME BARBERSHOP WILL BE RESTORED BY ELLIOTT HISTORICAL SOCIETY. (LOCAL). KAY SLUMP, PROJ DIRECTOR; ELLIOTT BICENTENNIAL COMMITTEE; ELLIOTT, IA 51573. (#12675).

ELLSTON

FLAG POLE PROJ - ELLSTON, IA. A FLAG POLE ERECTED FOR THE BICENTENNIAL. (LOCAL). LINFORD MASON, PRESIDENT; COMMUNITY CLUB; ELLSTON, IA 50074. (#16685).

HISTORY OF ELLSTON, IA. A HISTORY OF ELLSTON & UNION TOWNSHIP WILL BE PUBLISHED. (LOCAL). LINFORD MASON, PRESIDENT; ELLSTON HISTORICAL SOCIETY; ELLSTON, IA 50074. (#16686).

ELMA

PRESERVATION AND RESTORATION PROJECTS - ELMA, IA. A BANDSTAND IN THE PARK IS BEING REDONE, AN OLD BLACK SMITH SHOP IS BEING RESTORED & ELMA'S FIRST FIRE HOSE-CART PUT ON DISPLAY. (LOCAL). DEAN MAI, PRESIDENT; ELMA COMMUNITY CLUB; ELMA, IA 50628. (#20937).

JULY 3 - 4, '76. JULY 3 & 4 CELEBRATION. FLAG PRESENTATIONS, BALL TOURNAMENTS, CHICKEN & BEEF BARBECUE AND FIREWORKS DISPLAY. AT ELMA PARK. (LOCAL). DEAN MAI, PRES; ELMA COMMUNITY CLUB; RR 1; ELMA, IA 50628. (#105518-1).

ELVIRA

JUNE 26 - 27, '76. BICENTENNIAL FESTIVAL. A FESTIVAL WITH RELIGIOUS SERVICES, A PARADE & REUNION. AT CHURCH SCHOOL. (LOCAL). REYNOLD P JURGENSEN, CHMN; ELVIRA BICENTENNIAL COMMISSION; 1100 WOODLAWN; CLINTON, IA 52732. (#200018-304).

EMERSON

TREE PLANTING PROJECT - EMERSON, IA. TREES WILL BE PLANTED IN THE COMMUNITY PARK. (LOCAL). GEORGE CURTIS, PROJ DIRECTOR; WOMEN'S CLUB; EMERSON, IA 51533. (#23974).

JULY 4, '76. DEDICATION OF EVANS MEMORIAL PARK. CEREMONY. (LOCAL). GEORGE CURTIS; CHAMBER OF COMMERCE; EMERSON, IA 51533. (#107833-1).

SEPT 11, '76. EMERSON FALL FESTIVAL. COMPETITION, FESTIVAL, PARADE. (LOCAL). GEORGE CURTIS, CHMN; EMERSON CHAMBER OF COMMERCE; EMERSON, IA 51533. (#106829-1).

EPWORTH

JULY 4, '76. EPWORTH BICENTENNIAL CELEBRATION. A BATTLE REENACTMENT BETWEEN LOCAL MILITIA AND BRITISH; PARADE, ECUMENICAL CHURCH SERVICE, REVOLUTIONARY GAMES, NIGHT STREET DANCE. AT EPWORTH. (LOCAL). KENNETH D ANKENBAUER; EPWORTH CITIZENS; PO BOX 236; EPWORTH, IA 52045. (#104684-1).

ESSEX

FLY-A-FLAG PROJECT, ESSEX, IA. A 30' FLAG POLE WITH FLAGS WILL BE PLACED DOWNTOWN, ALSO DIFFERENT AMERICAN FLAGS WILL BE PLACED IN SCHOOL ROOMS. ABOUT 1/2 OF HOMES IN TOWN AND 3 CHURCHES ARE FLYING FLAGS. (LOCAL). EVEA G BLACK, CHAIRMAN; ESSEX COMMUNITY BICENTENNIAL COMMITTEE; ESSEX, IA 51638. (#22212).

HISTORY OF ESSEX, IA. THE HISTORY OF ESSEX WILL BE PUBLISHED IN HONOR OF THE BICENTENNIAL. (LOCAL). EVEA BLACK, CHAIRMAN; ESSEX BICENTENNIAL COMMITTEE; ESSEX, IA 51638. (#14731).

HISTORY OF OLD SETTLERS, MONTGOMERY CO, IA. LOCATE THE PEOPLE IN MONTGOMERY CO WHOSE ANCESTORS HAVE BEEN IN AMERICA AT LEAST 200 YEARS AND PUBLISH HISTORY. (LOCAL). ADA WITHROW, CHAIRMAN; NISHNABOTNA PATRIOTS; ROUTE 1; ESSEX, IA 51638. (#32364).

AUG 29 - SEPT 1, '75. FALL FESTIVAL. PARADE, FESTIVAL, EXHIBIT AT MAIN ST, CITY PARK, BANK BLDG, CITY HALL, LEGION CLUB, LILJEDAHL ELE. (LOCAL). EVEA BLACK, COORD; ESSEX BICENT COMM; ESSEX COMMERCIAL CLUB; ESSEX, IA 51638. (#200018-61).

APR 3, '76. PRESENTATION OF FLAGPOLE - FLAG & FLOOD LIGHT. CEREMONY AT DOWNTOWN, MAIN ST. (LOCAL). EVEA G BLACK, COORD; ESSEX COMMUNITY BICENTENNIAL COMMITTEE; 701 ILLINOIS; ESSEX, IA 51638. (#200018-60).

APR 3, '76. REVIVAL OF OLD MARKET DAY. EXHIBIT, FESTIVAL AT CITY HALL/LEGION CLUB/MAIN ST/SCHOOL GYM. (LOCAL). EVEA G BLACK, CHMN; ESSEX COMMUNITY BICENTENNIAL COMMITTEE & 6 FEDERATED CLUBS; 701 ILLINOIS; ESSEX, IA 51638. (#105963-1).

AUG 28, '76. CELEBRATION OF THE NEW BAND STAND. TIME CAPSULE WILL BE BURIED IN THE MINI-PARK AND A FESTIVAL WILL BE HELD. (LOCAL). EVEA G BLACK, CHMN; ESSEX BICENTENNIAL COMMITTEE; BOX 113; ESSEX, IA 51638. (#108846-1).

SEPT 4 - 6, '76. LABOR DAY CELEBRATION. EXHIBIT, FESTIVAL, COMPETITION, LIVE PERFORMANCE AT BANK BLDG, PARK, MAIN ST, FOOTBALL FIELD, TOWN ACRES SCHOOL. (LOCAL). DON HASCALL, COORD; COMMERCIAL CLUB & ESSEX BICENTENNIAL COMMITTEE; ESSEX, IA 51638. (#108909-1).

ESTHERVILLE

BICENTENNIAL LAND PROJECT, ESTHERVILLE, IA. THE COLLEGE WILL CONVERT AN AREA OF VIRGIN LAND FOR HISTORICAL, RECREATIONAL, AESTHETIC & ENVIRONMENTAL PURPOSES. THE LAND WILL BE RESTORED OR MAINTAINED IN ITS NATURAL STATE FOR POSTERITY. (LOCAL). ROY POWERS, CHAIRMAN; IOWA LAKES COMMUNITY COLLEGE; 300 S 18TH ST; ESTHERVILLE, IA 51334. (#25511).

COMMUNITY DEVELOPMENT - ESTHERVILLE, IA. AN OUTDOOR EDUCATION CENTER IS BEING BUILT FOR EMMET COUNTY. (LOCAL). N ARMSTRONG, CHAIRMAN; EMMET COUNTY BICENTENNIAL COMMITTEE; ESTHERVILLE, IA 51334. (#18557).

EMMET COUNTY HISTORY - IA. THE HISTORY OF EMMET COUNTY IS PREPARED FOR PUBLICATION. (LOCAL). N ARMSTRONG, CHAIRMAN; EMMET COUNTY HISTORICAL SOCIETY; ESTHERVILLE, IA 51334. (#18556).

REVOLUTIONARY WAR UNIFORMS PROJECT - IA. VETERANS' GROUPS IN EMMET COUNTY ARE ASSEMBLING REVOLUTIONARY WAR ERA UNIFORMS TO BE WORN AT BICENTENNIAL EVENTS. (LOCAL). N ARMSTRONG, CHAIRMAN; EMMET COUNTY BICENTENNIAL COMMITTEE; ESTHERVILLE, IA 51334. (#18555).

TREE PLANTING; ESTHERVILLE, IA. TREES THAT WERE LOST TO DUTCH ELM DISEASE WILL BE REPLACED. (LOCAL). EDWIN THORESON, DIRECTOR; CITY OF ESTHERVILLE, IA PARK BOARD; 314 N 12TH ST; ESTHERVILLE, IA 51334. (#19382).

UPDATING EMMET COUNTY HISTORY, IA. AN ALL COUNTY PROJECT TO UPDATE EMMET COUNTY HISTORY FROM 1916 TO THE PRESENT; INCLUDES CITY, TOWNSHIP & FAMILY HISTORY. A PAGE WILL BE GIVEN TO THE HISTORY OF EACH FAMILY LIVING THERE BEFORE 1946. (LOCAL). LOUIS F OBYE, PRESIDENT; EMMET COUNTY HISTORICAL SOCIETY, INC; 107 S 6TH ST; ESTHERVILLE, IA 51334. (#18794).

WINTER SPORTS FESTIVAL. THE ESTHERVILLE WINTER SPORTS FESTIVAL WILL FEATURE A SNOW & ICE SCULPTURE WITH A BICENTENNIAL THEME. (LOCAL). HON ELMER JACOB, MAYOR; ESTHERVILLE CHAMBER OF COMMERCE; 2 N 7TH ST; ESTHERVILLE, IA 51334. (#104273-1). **(??).**

JAN 5 - MAY 15, '76. FORT DEFIANCE HISTORY CONTEST. CONTEST IN ESTHERVILLE SCHOOLS TO REVIVE HISTORY OF FORT DEFIANCE; THE FORT WAS ORIGINALLY LOCATED ON THE SITE NOW OCCUPIED BY THE CITY OF ESTHERVILLE. (LOCAL). LOUIS F OBYE, PRESIDENT; EMMET COUNTY HISTORY; 408 N 5TH ST; ESTHERVILLE, IA 51334. (#104273-2).

EVANSDALE

HISTORICAL BOX IN EVANSDALE, IOWA. A BOX IS TO BE FILLED WITH TOWN HISTORY & PUT AT BASE OF FLAG POLE. (LOCAL). HON JR E HOMOLKA, MAYOR; REVOLUTIONARIES; 1120 EVANS RD; EVANSDALE, IA 50707. (#9225).

TOWN HALL FLAG POLE OF EVANSDALE, IOWA. ERECT FLAG POLE AS LASTING REMINDER OF BICENTENNIAL; BASE USED FOR TOWN HALL OF FAME. (LOCAL). HON JR E HOMOIKA, MAYOR; REVOLUTIONARIES; 1120 EVANS RD; EVANSDALE, IA 50707. (#9226).

EXIRA

BICENTENNIAL CALENDAR - EXIRA, IA. THE CALENDAR WILL HAVE SKETCHES OF HISTORICAL BUILDINGS AND PLACES IN AUDUBON COUNTY. (LOCAL). LEON MILLIMAN, SECRETARY-TREASURER; AUDUBON COUNTY HISTORICAL SOCIETY; EXIRA, IA 50076. (#19703).

RESTORATION OF FIRST COURT HOUSE IN EXIRA, IA. THE COURT HOUSE WILL BE RESTORED AND LISTED ON THE NATIONAL REGISTER OF HISTORIC BUILDINGS. (LOCAL). LEON MILLIMAN, SECRETARY-TREASURER; AUDUBON COUNTY HISTORICAL SOCIETY; 308 N FAIRVIEW; EXIRA, IA 50076. (#19701).

JULY 1 - 4, '76. FOURTH OF JULY CELEBRATION. FESTIVAL. (LOCAL). TERRY LAURIDSEN, PROJ DIR; EXIRA CHAMBER OF COMMERCE; EXIRA, IA 50076. (#104519-19).

EXLINE

HERITAGE '76 - EXLINE, IA. PRESERVATION OF THE ZOAR CHURCH WHICH INCLUDES FOUNDATION REPAIR AND TERMITE CONTROL. (LOCAL). MRS LAVERNE HOWARD, PRESIDENT; ZOAR CHURCH HOMECOMING ASSOC; EXLINE, IA 52555. (#19801).

FAIRBANK

FAIRBANK HISTORICAL NEWSPAPER, FAIRBANK, IA. NEWSPAPER ON ALL HISTORICAL INFORMATION ABOUT FAIRBANK COMMUNITY; TO BE PRINTED AND SOLD; ALL PROCEEDS GO TO SUPPORT COMMUNITY BICENTENNIAL PROJECTS. (LOCAL). ROBERT MARICLE, COORDINATOR; FAIRBANK FIRE DEPT, VOLUNTEER AUXILIARY; FAIRBANK, IA 50629. (#22556).

PARK RENOVATION, FAIRBANK, IA. PLANT 48 TREES, INSTALL PLAYGROUND EQUIPMENT, BENCHES AND PICNIC TABLES. (LOCAL). DALE R MARICLE, INTERNAL VICE PRESIDENT; FAIRBANK JAYCEES; RR 2; FAIRBANK, IA 50629. (#25150).

TREE PLANTING PROJECT, FAIRBANK, IA. PLANTING OF 200 TREES IN VARIOUS LOCATIONS TO BEAUTIFY THE TOWN. (LOCAL). DALE MARICLE, COORDINATOR; FAIRBANK JAYCEES; FAIRBANK, IA 50629. (#22555).

FAIRBANK — CONTINUED

MAR 3 - JULY 30, '76. HISTORICAL ITEMS ON DISPLAY. EXHIBIT AT WINDOWS OF FAIRBANK MERCHANTS. (LOCAL). BURNETT TROWER; BICENTENNIAL COMMITTEE; FAIRBANK, IA 50629. (#106074-4).

JULY 9, '76. BICENTENNIAL KING AND QUEEN CONTEST. CEREMONY, PARADE, LIVE PERFORMANCE. (LOCAL). LOIS MARICLE, COORD; FAIRBANK BICENTENNIAL COMMITTEE; FAIRBANK, IA 50629. (#106074-1).

JULY 9, '76. FESTIVAL. TALENT SHOW, SPELLING BEE, COOKIE EATING CONTEST. AT I C HALL FAIRBANK. (LOCAL). LOIS MARICLE; FAIRBANK TOURIST CLUB; FAIRBANK, IA 50629. (#106074-3).

JULY 9 - 11, '76. CORN SHOW, FAIR & PLAY. EXHIBIT, FAIR, FESTIVAL, LIVE PERFORMANCE AT MAIN ST & CATHOLIC CHURCH HALL. (LOCAL). LOIS A MARICLE, COORD; FAIRBANK TOURIST CLUB; FAIRBANK, IA 50629. (#105136-1).

JULY 11, '76. 'I LOVE AMERICA', MUSICAL. LIVE PERFORMANCE AT I C HALL FAIRBANK. (LOCAL). LOIS MARICLE, COORD; FAIRBANK CHURCHES; FAIRBANK, IA 50629. (#106074-2).

FAIRFIELD

BONNIFIELD LOG CABIN RESTORATION - FAIRFIELD, IA. RESTORATION OF LOG CABIN BUILT IN 1839 BY RHODAM BONNIFIELD. (LOCAL). JOYCE SNAKENBERG, CO-CHAIRPERSON; JEFFERSON COUNTY AMERICAN REVOLUTION BICENTENNIAL COMMISSION; RT 4, BOX 122; FAIRFIELD, IA 52556. (#18232).

HERITAGE TRAIL IN FAIRFIELD, IOWA. MARKERS WILL BE PLACED AT SITES OF ABANDONED TOWNS, OLD CEMETERIES, SCHOOL SITES, HISTORIC ROADS & PLACES OF HISTORIC INTEREST. TOURS WILL BE OFFERED. (LOCAL). JOYCE SNAKENBERG, CO-CHAIRPERSON; JEFFERSON CO AMERICAN REVOLUTION BICENTENNIAL COMMISSION; RT 4 BOX 122; FAIRFIELD, IA 52556. (#7777).

HISTORY OF JEFFERSON COUNTY, IOWA. A HISTORY OF JEFFERSON CO IS BEING PREPARED & WILL INCLUDE INFORMATION ABOUT OLD TOWNS, CHURCHES, SCHOOLS, CEMETERIES, BUSINESSES & CIVIC ORGANIZATIONS. (LOCAL). JOYCE SNAKENBERG, CO-CHAIRMAN; JEFFERSON CO AMERICAN REVOLUTION BICENTENNIAL COMMISSION; RT 4 BOX 122; FAIRFIELD, IA 52556. (#7776).

JEFFERSON COUNTY ONE ROOM SCHOOLHOUSE - IA. JEFFERSON COUNTY ONE ROOM SCHOOLHOUSE WILL BE MOVED FROM ITS PRESENT LOCATION. (LOCAL). DR JOAN STURTEVANT OR MS JOYCE SNAKEBURG, CO-CHMN; FAIRFIELD BICENTENNIAL COMMISSION; RFD # 4, BOX 122; FAIRFIELD, IA 52556. (#13448). **ARBA GRANTEE.**

JULY 5, '76. OLD SETTLERS' CELEBRATION. OLD FASHIONED FOURTH OF JULY; CANOE RACES, GAMES; PIONEER GAMES,FOR CHILDREN & ADULTS; PICNIC; MUSICAL ENTERTAINMENT; AWARDS, RECOGNITIONS. AT OLD SETTLERS PARK, FAIRFIELD. (LOCAL). JOYCE SNAKENBERG, COORD; JEFFERSON COUNTY AMERICAN REVOLUTION BICENTENNIAL COMMISSION; RT 4, BOX 122; FAIRFIELD, IA 52556. (#106666-1).

OCT '76 - CONTINUING . RE-CREATION OF FIRST IOWA STATE FAIR HELD IN FAIRFIELD. A 'BASKET SOCIAL' & HOME BAKED GOODS CONTEST, AN ARTS & CRAFTS SHOW, A QUILT CONTEST, & AN EQUESTRIAN CONTEST. AT UNDECIDED. (ST-WIDE). JOYCE SNAKENBERG CO-CHMN; JEFFERSON CO AMERICAN REVOLUTION BICENTENNIAL COMMISSION; RT 4 BOX 122; FAIRFIELD, IA 52556. (#50121-1).

FAIRVIEW

JUNE 27, '76. FAMILY PICNIC. FESTIVAL AT FAIRVIEW COMMUNITY CENTER. (LOCAL). IDA L WACKER, CHMN; FAIRVIEW COMMUNITY CLUB; RR #2; ANAMOSA, IA 52205. (#107998-1).

JULY 3 - 5, '76. JONES COUNTY FESTIVAL. FESTIVAL AT FAIRVIEW COMMUNITY CENTER. (LOCAL). IDA L WACKER, CHMN; FAIRVIEW COMMUNITY CLUB; RR #2; FAIRVIEW, IA 52205. (#107998-3).

AUG 29, '76. FUN DAY. FESTIVAL AT FAIRVIEW COMMUNITY CENTER. (LOCAL). IDA L WACKER, CHMN; FAIRVIEW COMMUNITY CLUB; RR #2; ANAMOSA, IA 52205. (#107998-2).

FARLEY

BICENTENNIAL QUILT IN FARLEY, IA. BICENTENNIAL QUILT, DESIGNED & MADE BY SIXTH GRADE STUDENTS. (LOCAL). CAROL WILLIAMSON, CHAIRMAN; FARLEY ELEMENTARY-JUNIOR HIGH SCHOOL; FARLEY, IA 52046. (#28179).

MUSIC PROGRAM IN FARLEY, IA. PROGRAM WILL HAVE BICENTENNIAL THEME AND WILL BE PRESENTED AT ALL AREA SCHOOLS. (LOCAL). MRS CAROL WILLIAMSON, PROJ DIRECTOR; FARLEY ELEMENTARY-JUNIOR HIGH SCHOOL; FARLEY, IA 52046. (#19764).

PENPAL PROJECT - FARLEY, IA. ELEMENTARY STUDENTS WILL WRITE LETTERS TO STUDENTS IN OTHER STATES AND COUNTRIES; THE LETTERS WILL BE PUBLISHED IN LOCAL NEWSPAPERS. (LOCAL). MRS CAROL WILLIAMSON, PROJ DIRECTOR; FARLEY ELEMENTARY JUNIOR HIGH SCHOOL; FARLEY, IA 52046. (#20315).

MAY 12, '76. ALL SCHOOL MUSICAL. LIVE PERFORMANCE AT FARLEY SCHOOL AUDITORIUM. (LOCAL). MRS CAROL WILLIAMSON, DR; FARLEY ELEMENTARY JR HIGH SCHOOL; FARLEY, IA 52046. (#105263-1).

MAY 12, '76. JUNIOR HIGH BAND IN PARADE. FARLEY JUNIOR HIGH SCHOOL BAND WILL PARTICIPATE IN EPWORTH BICENTENNIAL PARADE. (LOCAL). CAROL WILLIAMSON, CHMN; FARLEY ELEMENTARY-JUNIOR HIGH SCHOOL; FARLEY ELEMENTARY-JUNIOR HIGH; FARLEY, IA 52046. (#104529-11).

FARMERSBURG

A HISTORY OF FARMERSBURG, IA. PEOPLE, BUSINESSES, ORGANIZATIONS, LIFE, ANECDOTES AND CUSTOMS WILL BE INCLUDED IN THE HISTORY OF FARMINGTON. (LOCAL). LINDA SEDLMAYR, PRESIDENT; THURSDAY STUDY CLUB; FARMERSBURG, IA 52047. (#24499).

MUSEUM, FARMERSBURG, IA. LIBRARY WILL BE RENOVATED TO ACCOMODATE THE MUSEUM. LOCAL HISTORICAL ITEMS AND PICTURES, HISTORICAL MAPS AND BAND INSTRUMENTS WILL BE PROCURED FOR THE DISPLAYS. (LOCAL). LINDA SEDLMAYR, CHAIRPERSON; FARMERSBURG BICENTENNIAL COMMITTEE & THURSDAY STUDY CLUB; FARMERSBURG, IA 52047. (#24498).

PARK BEAUTIFICATION - FARMERSBURG, IA. FIREPLACE, GARDEN, TREES AND SHRUBBERY WILL BE ADDED TO THE PARK. (LOCAL). LINDA SEDLMAYR, CHAIRPERSON; FARMERSBURG BICENTENNIAL COMMITTEE; FARMERSBURG, IA 52047. (#24497).

JUNE 19, '76. BICENTENNIAL FESTIVAL: FROM WHENCE WE CAME. PARADE, POT LUCK SUPPER & CONCERT ARE AMONG THE SCHEDULED EVENTS. AT CITY PARK AND HALL. (LOCAL). LINDA SEDLMAYR, CHMN; THURSDAY STUDY CLUB; FARMERSBURG, IA 52047. (#106897-1).

FARMINGTON

RESTORATION PROJECT IN FARMINGTON, IA. SEVERAL RESTORATIONS & PRESERVATIONS HAVE BEEN UNDERTAKEN BY THE CITIZENS OF FARMINGTON INCLUDING THE CONGREGATIONAL CHURCH AND THE DEPOT WHICH WILL BE USED AS A MUSEUM. (LOCAL). TED WATSON OR LIBBY WOODRUFF, CO-CHAIRMEN; VAN BUREN DEVELOPMENT ASSOC; 101 VAN BUREN ST; KEOSAUQUA, IA 52565. (#21409).

JUNE 28, '76. BICENTENNIAL FESTIVAL CELEBRATION. FLAGS AND OLD-TIME ARTICLES WILL BE DISPLAYED IN DOWNTOWN STORES, MERCHANTS AND EMPLOYEES WILL DRESS IN 1776 COSTUMES AND A TIME CAPSULE WILL BE BURIED, JUNE 28 AT KEOSAQUA, IA ON THE LIBRARY LAWN. AT TALENT SHOW JULY 3RD AT HARMONY JR HIGH AUDITORIUM. (LOCAL). MRS HILLIS KERR, CHMN; FARMINGTON BICENTENNIAL COMMITTEE; 203 N 2ND ST; FARMINGTON, IA 52626. (#108470-2).

JULY 3, '76. FARMINGTON FESTIVAL. THE CONGREGATIONAL CHURCH MUSEUM AND THE FARMINGTON DEPOT MUSEUM WILL BE OPEN FOR TOURS. THERE WILL BE ARTS & CRAFTS SHOWS, ROCKS & RELICS EXHIBITS, MUSICAL PROGRAM, FLEA MARKET, FIREWORKS DISPLAY AND A BAKE SALE. AT EVENINGS - HARMONY JUNIOR HIGH AUDITORIUM. (LOCAL). MRS HILLIS KERR, CHMN; FARMINGTON BICENTENNIAL COMMITTEE; 203 N 2ND ST; FARMINGTON, IA 52626. (#108470-1).

FARRAGUT

COMMUNITY BETTERMENT PROJECT: FARRAGUT, IOWA. CLEAN UP VACANT LOT NEAR POST OFFICE & ERECT COMMUNITY BULLETIN BOARD. (LOCAL). REVS REGINALD/KAREN MERRILL, CO-CHAIRMEN; COMMUNITY BETTERMENT COMMITTEE; 208 WORDEN ST; FARRAGUT, IA 51639. (#12128).

VIEWING OUR HERITAGE IN FARRAGUT, IOWA. SERIES OF WINDOW DISPLAYS DEPICTING HISTORICAL EVENTS. (LOCAL). MRS J R MCQUEEN, PROJ DIRECTOR; GOLD STAR AUXILIARY; WEBSTER ST; FARRAGUT, IA 51639. (#12126).

FEB 21, '76. MARTHA WASHINGTON TEA. PUBLIC TEA TO BE HELD; PERIOD COSTUMES & DECORATIONS TO BE SHOWN. AT ADMIRAL MANOR. (LOCAL). MRS J R MCQUEEN; GOLD STAR AUXILIARY; BOX 91; FARRAGUT, IA 51639. (#12127-1).

JUNE 12 - 13, '76. COMMUNITY DAY IN FARRAGUT. SPECIAL COMMUNITY CELEBRATION WITH BICENTENNIAL THEME, PARADES, FOOD & FLOATS, UNION CHURCH SERVICE. (LOCAL). REVS REGINALD/KAREN MERRI; COMMUNITY CLUB; 208 WORDEN ST; FARRAGUT, IA 51639. (#12130-1).

JULY 4, '76. SPECIAL RELIGIOUS SERVICE. INTERDENOMINATIONAL RELIGIOUS SERVICE, SCHEDULED FOR JULY 4, 1976, TO BE HELD IN THE STYLE THAT WAS CHARACTERISTIC OF 1776. AT PARK OR CHURCH GROUNDS. (LOCAL). REVS KAREN/REGINALD MERRI; UNITED METHODIST CHURCH; 208 WORDEN ST; FARRAGUT, IA 51639. (#12129-1).

FAYETTE

AMERICAN STUDIES MAJOR, FAYETTE, IA. AN INTERDISCIPLINARY MAJOR TO PROVIDE A PROGRAM FOR STUDENTS WHO WISH TO INVESTIGATE ALL ASPECTS OF THE AMERICAN HERITAGE. (LOCAL). WALTER R GRIFFIN, PROJ CHAIRMAN; UPPER IOWA UNIVERSITY; 103 ALEXANDER ST; FAYETTE, IA 52142. (#18259).

BICENTENNIAL FLOWER DISPLAY - FAYETTE, IA. CONSTRUCTION OF LARGE STANDS TO DISPLAY FLOWERS ALONG DOWNTOWN SHOPPING AREA THROUGHOUT SUMMER OF '76. (LOCAL). EVELYN HARPEL, COORDINATOR; FAYETTE GARDEN CLUB; MADISON LANE; FAYETTE, IA 52142. (#23907).

BICENTENNIAL GROVE IN FAYETTE, IA. PLANTING OF A GROVE OF TREES TO COMMEMORATE THE BICENTENNIAL. (LOCAL). WALTER R GRIFFIN, PROJ CHAIRMAN; UPPER IOWA UNIVERSITY; 103 ALEXANDER ST; FAYETTE, IA 52142. (#18257).

BICENTENNIAL MUSICAL PROGRAMS AT BASKETBALL GAME HALF TIME. LIVE PERFORMANCE. (LOCAL). WALTER R GRIFFIN, CHMN; UPPER IOWA UNIV; 105 ALEXANDER ST; FAYETTE, IA 52142. (#103731-2).

COMMUNITY ORAL HISTORY - FAYETTE, IA. TAPE RECORDED HISTORICAL RECOLLECTIONS PRODUCED THROUGH ORAL INTERVIEWING OF SENIOR CITIZENS IN THE COMMUNITY TO BE STORED AND USED IN THE PUBLIC LIBRARY. (LOCAL). EVANGELINE MCCORT, PROJ CHAIRMAN; FEDERATED WOMEN'S CLUB OF FAYETTE; FAYETTE, IA 52142. (#23906).

HISTORICAL DISPLAY IN FAYETTE, IA. EXHIBIT OF ARTICLES AND MEMORABILIA CONNECTED WITH THE HISTORY AND HERITAGE OF UPPER IOWA UNIVERSITY. (LOCAL). WALTER R GRIFFIN, PROJ CHAIRMAN; UPPER IOWA UNIVERSITY; 103 ALEXANDER ST; FAYETTE, IA 52142. (#18258).

HISTORY OF UPPER IOWA UNIVERSITY, FAYETTE, IA. A COMPLETE HISTORY OF UPPER IOWA UNIVERSITY TO BE COMPLETED BY 1977. (LOCAL). WALTER R GRIFFIN, PROJ CHAIRMAN; UPPER IOWA UNIVERSITY; 103 ALEXANDER ST; FAYETTE, IA 52142. (#18256).

APR 1 - MAY 1, '75. SEMINAR ON PLANS FOR FUTURE OF FAYETTE COUNTY. ONE DAY CONFERENCE LEAD BY EXPERTS ON SELECTED PROBLEMS IN FAYETTE COUNTY. (LOCAL). MRS JOHN W GRAHAM; FAYETTE COUNTY BICENTENNIAL COMMITTEE; HAWKEYE, IA 52147. (#5137-501).

NOV 20, '75. BICENTENNIAL WORKSHOP AND CONFERENCE. SPEAKERS WILL INCLUDE A DISTINGUISHED HISTORIAN OF THE AMERICAN REVOLUTION AND A CONTEMPORARY STATESMAN. PROGRAMS AND EXHIBITS WILL BE APPROPRIATE FOR HIGH SCHOOL AND COLLEGE STUDENTS. COMMUNITY BICENTENNIAL LEADERS WILL BE PRESENTED. AT COLGROVE - WALKER AUDITORIUM. (LOCAL). WALTER R GRIFFIN, CHMN; UPPER IOWA UNIV; 105 ALEXANDER ST; FAYETTE, IA 52142. (#103731-1).

JULY 3 - 4, '76. BICENTENNIAL HARVEST HOME FESTIVAL. REVIVAL OF TURN-OF-THE-CENTURY COMMUNITY FESTIVAL HELD ANNUALLY TO CELEBRATE THE BEGIINNING OF THE HARVEST SEASON. GAMES, CONTESTS, ORATORS, SQUARE DANCING, BLUEGRASS AND OTHER MUSIC, HORSE SHOW ARTS AND CRAFTS EXHIBIT, CALLIOPE, BOX SOCIAL. AT KLOCK'S ISLAND. (LOCAL). EDWARD L BLOCK, CHAIRMAN; FAYETTE BICENTENNIAL COMMITTEE; PO BOX 309; FAYETTE, IA 52142. (#107113-1).

FERGUSON

COMMUNITY TENNIS COURT, FERGUSON, IA. FUNDS TO BE RAISED TO CONSTRUCT THIS RECREATIONAL FACILITY. (LOCAL). DALE THOMPSON, CHAIRMAN OF HORIZON '76 COMMITTEE; FERGUSON BICENTENNIAL COMMITTEE; FERGUSON, IA 50078. (#23353).

TREE PLANTING PROGRAM, FERGUSON, IA. TREES TO BE SOLD FOR COMMUNITY BETTERMENT AND TO RAISE FUNDS FOR TENNIS COURTS AND OTHER FACILITIES. (LOCAL). DALE THOMPSON, CHAIRMAN OF HORIZON '76 COMMITTEE; FERGUSON BICENTENNIAL COMMISSION; FERGUSON, IA 50078. (#23351).

WATER INSTALLED AT CITY PARK, IA. WATER INSTALLATION WILL BE ACCOMPLISHED THIS YEAR. (LOCAL). DALE THOMPSON, CHAIRMAN OF HORIZON '76 COMMITTEE; FERGUSON BICENTENNIAL COMMITTEE; FERGUSON, IA 50078. (#23352).

JULY 4 - 5, '76. COMMUNITY CELEBRATION. PARADE, COMMUNITY CHURCH SERVICES, COMMUNITY PICNIC, ORGANIZED ACTIVITIES FOR YOUTH AND ADULTS, PATRIOTIC MUSIC, ICE CREAM SUPPER AND OLD MOVIES ARE THE SCHEDULED ACTIVITIES. AT FERGUSON COMMUNITY PARK. (LOCAL). RONALD L HAWN, COORD; FERGUSON BICENTENNIAL COMMITTEE; PO BOX 9; FERGUSON, IA 50078. (#106528-3).

JULY 5, '76. PARADE & COSTUME & BEARD GROWING CONTEST. PARADE THRU STREETS OF FERGUSON WITH COSTUMES. BEARD CONTEST ON STAGE OF FERGUSON GYMNASIUM. (LOCAL). DEAN ELSBERRY, COORD; FERGUSON BICENTENNIAL COMMITTEE; RFD 4; MARSHALLTOWN, IA 50158. (#106528-1).

FERTILE

COMMUNITY DEVELOPMENT, FERTILE, IA. COMMUNITY DEVELOPMENT OT INCLUDE BEAUTIFICATION OF TOWN & DEVELOPMENT OF RECREATIONAL PARK. (LOCAL). THOMAS HEWETT, PRESIDENT; LIONS CLUB; FERTILE, IA 50434. (#20357).

AUG 7 - 8, '76. COMMUNITY FESTIVAL. FESTIVAL. (LOCAL). RICHARD WORSLEY, CHMN; FERTILE LIONS' CLUB; BOX 168; FERTILE, IA 50434. (#104767-1).

FLORIS

BEAUTIFICATION CAMPAIGN, FLORIS. AN ATTEMPT THROUGH USE OF POSITIVE INCENTIVES TO CLEAN UP CITY AND TO ENCOURAGE RESIDENTS TO PLANT FLOWER GARDENS. A PLAN TO LANDSCAPE CITY PARKING AREA IS BEING DEVELOPED. (LOCAL). DORIS MCCLURE, COORDINATOR; FLORIS WOMEN AND BICENTENNIAL COMMITTEE; ROUTE 1; FLORIS, IA 52560. (#24122).

CITY PARK LANDSCAPING, FLORIS, IA. LANDSCAPING TO INCLUDE PLANTING SEVERAL TREES, DEVELOPING RED, WHITE & BLUE ROCK & FLOWER GARDEN & ERECTION OF A MEMORIAL PLAQUE HONORING AMERICAN VETERANS. (LOCAL). BILL HOWK, LANDSCAPER; FLORIS BICENTENNIAL COMMITTEE; ROUTE 1; FLORIS, IA 52560. (#24123).

FLORIS — CONTINUED

HISTORICAL BOOKLET - FLORIS, IA. A 100-PAGE BOOKLET ON FLORIS' HISTORY WILL BE PUBLISHED WITH PICTURES OF THE CITY AS IT WAS IN THE PAST. (LOCAL). OOLAH SMITH, AUTHOR; BOX 275; FLORIS, IA 52560. (#24126).

JULY 4, '76. CELEBRATION: 4TH OF JULY. COOPERATIVE DINNER, CONTESTS AND GAMES FOR YOUNG PEOPLE, PATRIOTIC SPEECH, RELIGIOUS SERVICE - A TRADITIONAL CELEBRATION. AT FLORIS CITY PARK AND TOWNSHIP HALL. (LOCAL). BARRY IRELAN; BICENTENNIAL COMMITTEE OF FLORIS; BOX 594; FLORIS, IA 52560. (#106850-1).

JULY 4, '76. EXHIBITION: ARTS, CRAFTS & HOBBIES. ALL RESIDENTS OF AREA INVITED TO DISPLAY THEIR HOBBIES. INCLUDED WILL BE ANTIQUES, QUILTS, INDIAN ARTIFACTS, OTHER COLLECTIONS. AT TOWN AND TOWNSHIP HALL. (LOCAL). GOLDEN IRELAN; BICENTENNIAL COMMITTEE OF FLORIS; BOX 594; FLORIS, IA 52560. (#106850-2).

FLOYD

HISTORICAL WALK REENACTMENT - FLOYD, IOWA. REENACTMENT OF WALK BY VOLUNTEERS OF WAR OF THE REBELLION. (LOCAL). J QUINBY, DIRECTOR; FLOYD BICENTENNIAL COMMITTEE; FLOYD, IA 50435. (#19962).

HISTORY OF CITY OF FLOYD, IA. PUBLICATION OF LOCAL HISTORY. (LOCAL). J QUINBY, DIRECTOR; FLOYD BICENTENNIAL COMMITTEE; FLOYD, IA 50435. (#19963).

RESTORATION OF FLOYD HOTEL INTO MUSEUM - IA. PURCHASE AND RESTORATION OF OLD HOTEL INTO MUSEUM AND MEETING PLACE FOR OVER SIXTY CLUB. (LOCAL). JUANITA QUINBY, CHAIRPERSON; CITY OF FLOYD BICENTENNIAL COMMITTEE; BOX 164; FLOYD, IA 50435. (#27574).

TREE PLANTING - FLOYD, IA. TREE PLANTING IN CITY PARK. (LOCAL). J QUINBY, DIRECTOR; FLOYD BICENTENNIAL COMMITTEE; FLOYD, IA 50435. (#19964).

WINDOW DISPLAYS, FLOYD, IA. TO EXHIBIT ALL HISTORIAL AND PRESENT DAY MATERIALS FROM RESIDENTS OF FLOYD. (LOCAL). MARG NICHOLSON, CHAIRMAN; FLOYD BICENTENNIAL COMMITTEE; 606 FIRST AVE; FLOYD, IA 50435. (#19854).

MAY 22, '76. HISTORICAL WALK: RE-ENACTMENT OF FIRST 7 CIVIL WAR VOLUNTEERS' WALK. A CEREMONY AND WALK WILL COMMEMORATE THE FIRST SEVEN VOLUNTEERS FOR THE CIVIL WAR; THE SEVEN VOLUNTEERS WALKED TO CHARLES CITY FROM FLOYD ACCOMPANIED BY THE WHOLE TOWN; THE COMPLETE DAY WILL BE REENACTED. AT MAIN ST ON TO HIGHWAY 218. (ST-WIDE). MRS ILONA CASTLE, CHMN; FLOYD VOLUNTEER FIRE DEPARTMENT; 501 JEFFERSON; FLOYD, IA 50435. (#104585-1).

JUNE 26, '76. BICENTENNIAL PARADE. ANTIQUES, HORSES, MULES, BANDS, KIDS, DIGNITARIES, FIRETRUCKS AND PEOPLE OF ALL COUNTIES WILL BE IN THE PARADE. AT MAIN ST. (LOCAL). HON RONALD BOGGES, MAYOR; FLOYD BICENTENNIAL COMMISSION; BOX 25; FLOYD, IA 50435. (#104585-2).

JUNE 26, '76. OLD-FASHIONED JAM SESSION. LIVE PERFORMANCE AT TENNIS COURT, FLOYD PARK. (LOCAL). JUANITA QUINBY, CHAIRMAN; CITY OF FLOYD BICENTENNIAL COMMITTEE; BOX 164; FLOYD, IA 50435. (#200018-196).

JUNE 26 - 27, '76. CITY OF FLOYD BICENTENNIAL DAYS. FESTIVAL, LIVE PERFORMANCE AT FLOYD PARK. (LOCAL). JUANITA QUINBY, CHAIRMAN; CITY OF FLOYD BICENTENNIAL COMMITTEE; PO BOX 164; FLOYD, IA 50435. (#200018-195).

JUNE 27, '76. HISTORICAL PAGEANT. PAGEANT OF LOCAL HISTORY. AT FLOYD PARK. (LOCAL). J QUINBY, COORD; FLOYD BICENTENNIAL COMMITTEE; FLOYD, IA 50435. (#104690-1).

JUNE 27, '76. 'OLD TIME' COMMUNITY PICNIC. FESTIVAL AT CITY PARK. (LOCAL). J QUINBY, COORD; FLOYD BICENTENNIAL COMMITTEE; FLOYD, IA 50435. (#104690-2).

JUNE 27, '76. TIME CAPSULE CERMONY. PRESENT-DAY DATA PETAINING TO THE TOWN WILL BE BURIED. AT CITY PARK. (LOCAL). J QUINBY, COORD; FLOYD BICENTENNIAL COMMITTEE; FLOYD, IA 50435. (#104690-3).

FONDA

EDUCATIONAL COURSE - FONDA, IA. THE COURSE WILL EMPHASIZE THE ROLE RELIGION PLAYED IN FORMULATING THE CONSTITUTION AND IN SEEKING FREEDOM FROM ENGLAND. (LOCAL). CECIL D MORGAN, CHAIRMAN; UNITED CHURCH OF CHRIST PRESBYTERIAN; MAIN ST; FONDA, IA 50540. (#23908).

RESTORATION OF PARK-PIT AREA IN FONDA, IA. THE RESTORATION WILL INCLUDE A NEW BASEBALL FIELD, DREDGING OF PIT AND THE ADDITION OF WILDLIFE. (LOCAL). MONICA GELLELAND, CHAIRMAN; FONDA'S BICENTENNIAL COMMITTEE; FONDA, IA 50540. (#17497).

FEB 29, '76. UNION CHURCH SERVICE. CEREMONY. (LOCAL). CECIL MORGAN, PROJ CHMN; UNITED CHURCH SCHOOL; FONDA, IA 50540. (#200018-66).

FONTANELLE

ADAIR COUNTY HISTORICAL SOCIETY EXHIBIT - IA. PROJECT WILL BE TO EXHIBIT ARTICLES FROM HISTORIC EVENTS. (LOCAL). RALPH E WOLLENHAUPT, CHAIRMAN; FONTANELLE BICENTENNIAL COMMISSION; FONTANELLE, IA 50846. (#11270).

FONTANELLE ENTERPRISE CLUB SALE OF BUTTONS - IA. THE FONTANELLE ENTERPRISE CLUB WILL SELL COLORFUL BUTTONS AT VARIOUS STORES. (LOCAL). RALPH E WOLLENHAUPT, CHAIRMAN; FONTANELLE BICENTENNIAL COMMISSION; FONTANELLE, IA 50846. (#11271).

JULY 1 - 2, '75. BICENTENNIAL CELEBRATION. PROJECT WILL BE A BICENTENNIAL CELEBRATION TO KICK OFF AMERICA'S 200TH BIRTHDAY. (LOCAL). RALPH E WOLLENHAUPT; FONTANELLE BICENTENNIAL COMMISSION; FONTANELLE, IA 50846. (#11269-1).

FOREST CITY

ARTIFACTS FROM FOREST CITY, IA. PRESERVATION OF ARTIFACTS PERTINENT TO FOREST CITY HISTORY FOR DISPLAY IN LOCAL MUSEUM. (LOCAL). HELEN BROWN, PROJ CHAIRWOMAN; FOREST CITY HISTORICAL SOCIETY; 436 N 11; FOREST CITY, IA 50436. (#21710).

BICENTENNIAL ESSAY CONTEST - FOREST CITY, IA. ESSAY WRITING CONTEST FOR SENIOR CITIZENS ON THEMES: 'THE LAND AS I SAW IT' AND 'LIFE AS I SAW IT.'. (LOCAL). RUTH LEIBRAND, SECRETARY; WINNEBAGO COUNTY BICENTENNIAL COMMITTEE; 135 N 11TH ST; FOREST CITY, IA 50436. (#17485).

BICENTENNIAL PROJECTS IN FOREST CITY, IA. PROJECTS INCLUDE: PARK DEVELOPMENT, PIONEER DAYS, POST CARDS, MUSEUM DEVELOPMENT AND DRESS-UP DAY. (LOCAL). JOANN SUNDERMANN, EXEC SECRETARY; FOREST CITY CHAMBER OF COMMERCE; 245 W M ST; FOREST CITY, IA 50436. (#21128).

BICENTENNIAL THEMES - ELEMENTARY SCHOOL CONTEST-IA. THEME WRITING CONTEST FOR OLDER ELEMENTARY STUDENTS ON THE THEME, 'WHAT MY COUNTRY MEANS TO ME'. (LOCAL). CAROL MUNCH, PRESIDENT; PHI THETA KAPPA & WALDORF COLLEGE BICENT COMMITTEE; 135 S CLARK ST; FOREST CITY, IA 50436. (#17484).

CITY PARK DEVELOPMENT IN FOREST CITY, IA. DEVELOPING AND PRESERVING TOWN FOREST AREAS. (LOCAL). DOUG THOMPSON, PROJ DIRECTOR; DEPARTMENT OF PARKS AND RECREATION; HIGHWAY 69; FOREST CITY, IA 50436. (#21711).

COLLEGE SORORITY ACTIVITIES PROJ, FOREST CITY, IA. PAINTING HYDRANTS AND A SENIOR CITIZENS ESSAY CONTEST MAKE UP THIS BICENTENNIAL PROJECT. (LOCAL). CAROL MUNCH, PROJ COORDINATOR; WALDORF COLLEGE; FOREST CITY, IA 50436. (#21707).

ESSAY CONTEST IN FOREST CITY, IA. 'A PAST TO HONOR - A FUTURE TO MOLD' - 4TH GRADE ESSAY CONTEST IS BEING SPONSORED IN HONOR OF THE BICENTENNIAL. (LOCAL). MRS EUGENE MORRIS, PROJ COORDINATOR; WOMEN'S CLUB; 234 RIVERVIEW DR; FOREST CITY, IA 50436. (#21708).

HISTORICAL DRAMATIC PRESENTATION. LIVE PERFORMANCE. (LOCAL). CAROL MUNCH, PROJ DIR; WALDORF COLLEGE; BOX 352; FOREST CITY, IA 50436. (#102250-1). **(??).**

HISTORICAL MUSICAL PRESENTATION. LIVE PERFORMANCE. (LOCAL). CAROL MUNCH, PROJ DIR; WALDORF COLLEGE; BOX 352; FOREST CITY, IA 50436. (#102251-1). **(??).**

MICROFILM PROJECT OF WALDORF COLLEGE, IA. A MICROFILM OF WINNEBAGO HISTORY WILL BE MADE. (LOCAL). CAROL MUNCH, CHAIRMAN; PHI THETA KAPPA/WALDORF COLLEGE; BOX 352; FOREST CITY, IA 50436. (#16061).

PATRIOTIC PAINTING PROJECT OF FOREST CITY, IA. HOUSE NUMBERS WILL BE PAINTED RED, WHITE & BLUE ON THE CURBS. (LOCAL). CAROL MUNCH, CHAIRMAN; PHI THETA KAPPA/WALDORF COLLEGE; BOX 352; FOREST CITY, IA 50436. (#16060).

PIONEER CERTIFICATION, FOREST CITY, IA. RECOGNITION WILL BE GIVEN TO MEMBERS OF FAMILIES WHO HAVE OWNED FARMLAND, A BUSINESS, AN INDUSTRY OR A TOWN RESIDENTIAL PROPERTY IN WINNEBAGO COUNTY SINCE BEFORE DEC 31, 1926. (LOCAL). MRS HARRY S HALVORSEN, CHAIRMAN; WINNEBAGO COUNTY BICENTENNIAL COMMISSION; RT 3; FOREST CITY, IA 50436. (#22217).

POST CARDS FROM FOREST CITY, IA. UPDATED POSTCARDS WILL BE RPINTED FOR TOURISTS. (LOCAL). JOANN SUNDERMANN, CHAIRMAN; CHAMBER OF COMMERCE; 245 W M ST; FOREST CITY, IA 50436. (#21709).

'THE WAY IT WAS', NEWSPAPER SERIES, FOREST CITY, I. A SERIES OF ARTICLES DURING 1976 ON 'THE WAY IT WAS', WRITTEN BY AREA RESIDENTS & SUMMIT STAFF MEMBERS. (LOCAL). DICK HAKES, BICENT EDITOR; FOREST CITY SUMMIT; S CLARK ST; FOREST CITY, IA 50436. (#20999).

SEPT 19, '75 - JAN 25, '76. BICENTENNIAL ESSAY CONTEST : 'THE SECOND 200'. ESSAY CONTEST FOR ALL WINNEBAGO INDUSTRY EMPLOYEES ON 'THE SECOND 200' - WHAT LIFE WILL BE LIKE IN THE NEXT 200 YEARS. (LOCAL). SHIRLEY MACHEAK; WINNEBAGO INDUSTRIES; HIGHWAY #69; FOREST CITY, IA 50436. (#104227-1).

AUG 12 - 14, '76. FRONTIER DAYS CITY CELEBRATION. FAIR, PARADE AT 3 BLOCKS MAIN STREET, ATHLETIC FIELDS. (LOCAL). DAVID NOLTON, COORD; FRONTIER DAYS COMMITTEE; CITY HALL; FOREST CITY, IA 50436. (#105514-2).

SEPT 1, '76 - MAY 28, '77. DRESS UP DAY AT SCHOOL. INTERESTED STUDENTS AND TEACHERS DRESS IN AMERICAN REV CLOTHES TWICE A MONTH. AT IN CLASSES. (LOCAL). FRED SMITH, COORD; FOREST CITY SCHOOL SYSTEM; 306 E PARK; FOREST CITY, IA 50436. (#105514-1).

SEPT 12, '76. PIONEER ARTS AND CRAFTS FAIR OF WINNEBAGO HISTORICAL SOCIETY. FAIR WILL INCLUDE FOODS AND CRAFTS OF NORWEGIAN ORIGIN, OTHER CRAFTS INCLUDE QUILTING, BREAD & LEFSE BAKING, BASKET WEAVING, WOOD CARVING, ROSEMAILING AND VARIOUS TYPES OF COOKING. AT FOREST CITY CIVIC AUDITORIUM. (LOCAL). HELEN BROWN; WINNEBAGO HISTORICAL SOCIETY; 436 N 11TH ST; FOREST CITY, IA 50436. (#102227-1).

FOREST HOME

FOREST HOME PARK AREA RESTORATION, IA. FOREST HOME WAS THE FIRST SETTLEMENT BY WHITES IN POWESCHIEK COUNTY; PLANS ARE TO DEVELOP A MALL AT THE SITE OF THE EARLY SETTLEMENT TO COMMEMORATE THOSE PIONEERS. (LOCAL). BARBARA HEISHMAN, PROJ DIRECTOR; FOREST HOME PARK; RFD; MONTEZUMA, IA 50112. (#15102).

FORT ATKINSON

OLD FORT ATKINSON FILM PROJECT - IOWA CITY, IOWA. PRODUCTION OF EDUCATIONAL FILM ON OLD FORT ATKINSON. (ST-WIDE). DR MARSHALL MCKUSICK, ARCHAEOLOGIST; STATE DEPARTMENT OF ARCHAEOLOGY; 21 MACLEAN HALL, UNIV OF IOWA; IOWA CITY, IA 52240. (#5301). **(??). ARBA GRANTEE.**

PEWTER BUST PROJ, FT ATKINSON, IA. THE LIBRARY IS SPONSORING THE DEVELOPMENT OF A PEWTER BUST OF A HISTORIC PERSONALITY. (LOCAL). LU ANN BECKER, PROJ DIRECTOR; LIBRARY BOARD OF FT ATKINSON; FT ATKINSON, IA 52144. (#24647).

SUMMER BICENTENNIAL READINGS. SEMINAR. (LOCAL). LU ANN BECKER, COORD; FT ATKINSON LIBRARY BOARD; FT ATKINSON, IA 52144. (#107892-1).

APR '76. ST JOHN CATHOLIC CHURCH CENTENNIAL. FESTIVAL. (LOCAL). J H BERNS; ST JOHN'S CATHOLIC CHURCH; BOX 171; FORT ATKINSON, IA 52144. (#107688-10).

FORT DODGE

BICENTENNIAL PROGRAM IN FORT DODGE, IA. THE SOCIAL STUDIES DEPARTMENTS AT LOCAL SCHOOLS ARE PLANNING A BICENTENNIAL PROGRAM. (LOCAL). M L HOTTMAN, PROJ DIRECTOR; WEBSTER COUNTY AMERICAN REVOLUTION BICENTENNIAL COMMISSION; WEBSTER COUNTY COURTHOUSE; FORT DODGE, IA 50501. (#15088).

ECOLOGY AND COMMUNITY DEVELOPMENT, FT DODGE, IA. PROJECT INVOLVES PLANTING TREES THROUGHOUT THE COMMUNITY. (LOCAL). MRS INEZ STANEK, CHAIRPERSON; ZCBJ LODGE, FT DODGE #39; ROUTE 1; FT DODGE, IA 50501. (#24469).

FORT DODGE, IA TREE PLANTING PROJECT. TREES WILL BE PLANTED THROUGHOUT FORT DODGE. (LOCAL). MRS INEZ STANEK, COORDINATOR; ELKHORN TOWNSHIP-WEBSTER CO ZCBJ LODGE #39; RT 1; FORT DODGE, IA 50501. (#28643).

FORT DODGE, IOWA, HISTORICAL FOUNDATION PROJECT. AN ADDITION COMPLEMENTING THE FORT DODGE HISTORICAL MUSEUM, STOCKADE FORT & TRADING POST FOR THE HOUSING & DISPLAY OF ARTICLES OF SUBSTANTIAL HISTORICAL INTEREST. (ST-WIDE). J W MAURER, PRESIDENT; FORT DODGE HISTORICAL FOUNDATION; FORT DODGE, IA 50501. (#1225). **ARBA GRANTEE.**

INDIAN FORT AND MUSEUM IN FORT DODGE, IA. ESTABLISH AN INDIAN FORT AND MUSEUM. (LOCAL). M L HOTTMAN, PROJ DIRECTOR; WEBSTER COUNTY AMERICAN REVOLUTION BICENTENNIAL; WEBSTER COUNTY COURTHOUSE; FORT DODGE, IA 50501. (#15087).

RESOURCES PLAN FOR IOWA REGION #5. THE MIDAS COUNCIL OF GOVERNMENTS IS DEVELOPING A HISTORIC RESOURCES PLAN FOR IOWA AS PART OF ITS LONG RANGE CONSERVATION PROGRAM. (LOCAL). DAMON CHLERKING, DIR OF PLANNING; MIDAS COUNCIL OF GOVERNMENTS; 12 S 10TH ST; FORT DODGE, IA 50501. (#9580). **ARBA GRANTEE.**

'WE CAN MAKE IT HAPPEN' - FORT DODGE, IA. CITIZEN PARTICIPATION COMMUNITY PROJECTS. (LOCAL). HON HERBERT S CONLON, CHAIRMAN; FORT DODGE COMMUNITY BICENTENNIAL COMMITTEE; MUNICIPAL BLDG; FORT DODGE, IA 50501. (#24494).

WEBSTER PRAIRIES IN FORT DODGE, IA. HISTORY OF WEBSTER COUNTY WILL BE WRITTEN. (LOCAL). M L HOTTMAN, PROJ DIRECTOR; WEBSTER COUNTY AMERICAN REVOLUTION BIC COMM; WEBSTER COUNTY COURTHOUSE; FORT DODGE, IA 50501. (#15086).

OCT 10, '75. UNITED STATES ARMED FORCES BICENTENNIAL CARAVAN. THE CARAVAN IS COMPOSED OF EXHIBIT VANS FOR EACH BRANCH OF THE MILITARY SERVICE. THE THEME OF THE EXHIBITION IS 'HISTORY OF THE ARMED FORCES AND THEIR CONTRIBUTION TO THE NATION'. (LOCAL). M L HOTTMAN, CHMN; WEBSTER COUNTY ARBC; 703 CENTRAL AVE; FORT DODGE, IA 50501. (#1775-214).

JUNE 5 - 12, '76. FRONTIER DAYS. FESTIVAL. (REGN'L). M L HOTTMAN, CHAIRMAN; FORT DODGE CHAMBER OF COMMERCE; WEBSTER COUNTY COURTHOUSE; FORT DODGE, IA 50501. (#102246-1).

OCT 3, '76. CZECH CULTURE & HERITAGE. POTLUCK PROGRAM AT NOON AND FREE DANCE IN THE EVENING WITH A CZECH BAND. AT 2CBJ LODGE. (LOCAL). MRS INEZ STANEK, CHMN; ELKHORN TWP WEBSTER CO & ZCBJ LODGE FT DODGE #39; ROUTE ONE; FT DODGE, IA 50501. (#106914-1).

FORT MADISON

AMERICAN ISSUES FORUM - PROJ OF FORT MADISON, IA. PLANNING STAGES FOR JOINT COMMITTEE OF SERVICE CLUBS. (LOCAL). WAYNE E HANWAY, DIRECTOR; CATTERMOLE PUBLIC LIBRARY; 614 7TH ST; FORT MADISON, IA 52627. (#16169).

CHRISTMAS 75 YEARS AGO, FORT MADISON, IA. INTERVIEW SENIOR CITIZENS ABOUT CHRISTMAS 75 YEARS AGO, CUT TREE, MAKE DECORATIONS, WEAR OLD-TIME COSTUMES, PLAY OLD-TIME GAMES, MAKE GIFTS TO EXCHANGE, TAFFY PULL, SING CAROLS, BASKET FOR THE ELDERLY. (LOCAL). SANDRA HUNTER, LEADER; SNOOPY AND SNOWBIRDS BLUE BIRD GROUPS; 1704 AVE D; FORT MADISON, IA 52627. (#19855).

OLD FORT MADISON MOVIE - PROJ OF FORT MADISON, IA. A MOVIE ON OLD FORT MADISON WILL BE MADE AND SHOWN TO ALL 5TH GRADES IN THE SCHOOL DISTRICT. (LOCAL). GEORGE P ALTON, PROJ DIRECTOR; FORT MADISON COMMUNITY SCHOOLS; 2301 AVE G; FORT MADISON, IA 52627. (#16166).

OLD LOG CABIN RELOCATION - PROJ OF FT MADISON, IA. THE OLD LOG CABIN WILL BE DISASSEMBLED AND REBUILT IN THE CITY PARK. (LOCAL). GEORGE P ALTON, CHAIRMAN; FORT MADISON BICENTENNIAL COMMITTEE; 1726 AVE D; FORT MADISON, IA 52627. (#16167).

RECONSTRUCTION OF OLD FORT MADISON, IA, BLOCKHOUSE. THE OLD FORT MADISON BLOCKHOUSE WILL BE RECONSTRUCTED. (LOCAL). B B HESSE, PRESIDENT; OLD FORT MADISON, INC; 635 AVE G; FORT MADISON, IA 52627. (#16170).

REPAIR & PAINT ENGINE 2913 - FORT MADISON, IA. ENGINE 2913 WILL BE REPAIRED AND PAINTED AND OPEN FOR PUBLIC TOURS. (LOCAL). E R RAINEY, MAYOR; CITY OF FORT MADISON; AVE E & 8TH ST; FORT MADISON, IA 52627. (#16168).

TREE PLANTING PROJECT OF FORT MADISON, IA. TREES WILL BE PLANTED TO REPLACE DISEASED ELMS. (LOCAL). MRS JOHN KEENAN, CHAIRMAN; COMMUNITY IMPROVEMENT PROGRAM/ COMMITTEE OF WOMENS CLUBS; HIGH POINT; FORT MADISON, IA 52627. (#16171).

JAN 15 - DEC 31, '76. BICENTENNIAL DISPLAY AT HISTORICAL CENTER. EXHIBIT AT LEE COUNTY HISTORICAL CENTER, AT THE FOOT OF 9TH ST. (LOCAL). B B HESS, CHAIRMAN; NORTH LEE COUNTY HISTORICAL SOCIETY; 635 AVE G; FORT MADISON, IA 52627. (#102765-1).

SEPT 10 - 12, '76. TRI STATE RODEO. PARADE ON SATURDAY MORNING WILL FEATURE RODEO HISTORY; TRAIL RIDERS INCLUDE SEVERAL HUNDRED RIDERS WHO RIDE ONE, 2 AND 3 DAYS TO THE RODEO. AT RODEO ARENA, RODEO PARK. (ST-WIDE). MIKE HOWARD, PGM MGR; RODEO CORPORATION; 835 1/2 AVE G; FORT MADISON, IA 52627. (#102760-1).

FRANKLIN

FLAGS IN FRANKLIN, IA. FLAGS TO BE FLOWN BY EVERY HOME IN FRANKLIN TO COMMEMORATE OUR 200 YEARS. (LOCAL). HONORABLE BERNARD FRAISE, MAYOR; COMMUNITY PROJECT; RR 2; WEST POINT, IA 52656. (#22187).

PLANTING OF TREES IN PARK - FRANKLIN, IA. CITIZENS PLANT TREES IN PARK TO RESTORE AND BEAUTIFY. (LOCAL). HONORABLE BERNARD FRAISE, MAYOR; COMMUNITY PROJECT; RR 2; WEST POINT, IA 52656. (#22189).

RESTORATION OF SCHOOLHOUSE - FRANKLIN, IA. TUCKPOINTING OF ROCK, REBUILDING OF CUPOLA, PAINTING, RESTORATION OF CLASSROOM TO ORIGINAL CONDITION. (LOCAL). HONORABLE BERNARD FRAISE, MAYOR; A COMMUNITY PROJECT; RR 2; WEST POINT, IA 52656. (#22191).

RESTORATION OF 125 YR UCC CHURCH OF FRANKLIN, IA. RESTORE OUTSIDE STRUCTURE, PAINT, REBUILD BELFRY, REPLACE CROSS, REBUILD WINDOWS & RESTORE STAINED GLASS. (LOCAL). INEZ TIMPE, COORDINATOR; UNITED CHURCH OF CHRIST OF FRANKLIN; RR 2; WEST POINT, IA 52656. (#22186).

SCHOOLHOUSE PLATE PROJECT IN FRANKLIN, IA. SCHOOLHOUSE PLATES BEING OFFERED FOR SALE TO HELP DEFRAY COSTS OF MAINTAINING SCHOOL HOUSE. (LOCAL). HONORABLE BERNARD FRAISE, MAYOR; COMMUNITY PROJECT; RR 2; WEST POINT, IA 52656. (#22188).

1976 BICENTENNIAL QUILT - FRANKLIN, IA. RED/WHITE/BLUE QUILT MADE BY LADIES OF FRANKLIN. (LOCAL). SUE GALLERICK, CHAIRPERSON; LADIES OF FRANKLIN; RR 1; DONNELLSON, IA 52625. (#22190).

JULY 4, '76. VETERANS 4TH JULY PICNIC. WHOLE ROASTED BARBECUED PIGLET IS FEATURED AT NOON. AT FRANKLIN PARK. (LOCAL). DAVID KRAMER, PROJ DIR; VETERANS OF FRANKLIN; RR #1; DONNELLSON, IA 52625. (#105950-2).

OCT 23, '76. FRANKLIN UNITED CHURCH OF CHRIST GOD'S PORTION DAY. HAND MADE ARTICLES, CANNED GOODS, BAKED GOODS, GRAIN, BAY, GARDEN PRODUCTS, LIVESTOCK & A NOON DINNER. AT UCC CHURCH HALL. (LOCAL). INEZ TIME, COORD; UNITED CHURCH OF CHRIST OF FRANKLIN; RR 2; WEST POINT, IA 52656. (#105950-1).

FREDERICKSBRG

RECREATION COURT, FREDERICKSBURG, IA. COURTS FOR TENNIS, BASKETBALL & SKATING WILL BE BUILT. (LOCAL). MICKEY LEWIS, CHAIRMAN; FREDERICKSBURG JAYCEES; FREDERICKSBRG, IA 50630. (#22207).

TREE PLANTING, FREDERICKSBURG, IA. LIONS ARE PLANTING TREES TO REPLACE DISEASED ELMS. (LOCAL). FRANK ROCHFORD, CHAIRMAN; FREDERICKSBURG BICENTENNIAL COMMITTEE & LIONS CLUB; FREDERICKSBRG, IA 50630. (#22206).

JUNE 8, '76. FREDERICKSBURG DAIRY DAYS. 51ST ANNUAL DAIRY CELEBRATION WITH PARADES, EXHIBITS AND A CARNIVAL. AT HIGH SCHOOL AND TOWN HALL - MAIN ST. (LOCAL). WILLIAM BEHRENS, PRES; FREDERICKSBURG DAIRY ASSOC; FREDERICKSBG, IA 50630. (#105957-1).

FREDERIKA

COMMUNITY CENTER OF FREDERIKA, IA. CONSTRUCTION OF A CEMENT BLOCK ADDITION TO THE FIREHOUSE FOR NEW COMMUNITY CENTER. SUPPORTED BY LOCAL BUSINESS COMMUNITY. (LOCAL). MRS FREDERIC REWALDT, CHAIRMAN; FREDERIKA BICENTENNIAL COMMITTEE; BOX 6; FREDERIKA, IA 50631. (#19693).

HISTORICAL PUBLICATION - FREDERIKA, IA. THE HISTORY OF BUILDINGS AND FARMS WILL BE PUBLISHED. (LOCAL). JUNE RULE, CO-CHAIRMAN; FREDERIKA BICENTENNIAL COMMITTEE; FREDERIKA, IA 50631. (#16780).

RESTORATION PROJECT IN FREDERIKA, IA. IN HONOR OF THE BICENTENNIAL, THE ONE ROOM SCHOOL HOUSE WILL BE RESTORED. (LOCAL). JUNE RULE, CO-CHAIRMAN; FREDERIKA BICENTENNIAL COMMITTEE; FREDERIKA, IA 50631. (#16779).

JAN 4, '75. ICE SKATING & AFTERNOON OF OLD GAMES & SPELL-DOWN. EXHIBIT, FESTIVAL AT WAPSIPINICON RIVER FIRE HOUSE. (LOCAL). MARY REWOLDT, CHMN; 4-H GIRLS & FREDERIKA BICENTENNIAL COMMITTEE; FREDERIKA, IA 50631. (#106252-2).

JULY 27, '75. SILENT MOVIES & SUPPER. FESTIVAL AT FIRE HOUSE. (LOCAL). MARY REWOLDT, COORD; FARM BUREAU WOMEN BICENTENNIAL COMMITTEE; FREDERIKA, IA 50631. (#200018-64).

NOV 16, '75. SQUARE DANCE & BOX SOCIAL. FESTIVAL AT STANLEY FEUCHTWANGER SHOP. (LOCAL). MARY REWOLDT, CHMN; 4-H GROUPS & FREDERIKA BICENTENNIAL COMMITTEE; FREDERIKA, IA 50631. (#106252-1).

DEC 20, '75. FLAG RAISING. MRS CHARLES GRASSLEY PRESENTED BICENTENNIAL FLAG AT SITE OF NEW COMMUNITY HALL. (LOCAL). JUNE RULE, CO-CHMN; FREDERIKA BICENTENNIAL COMMITTEE; FREDERIKA, IA 50631. (#200018-63).

FEB 29, '76. FREDERIKA FOLLIES. LIVE PERFORMANCE AT STANLEY FEUCHTWANGER SHOP. (LOCAL). MARY REWOLDT, COORD; FARM BUREAU WOMEN BI-CENTENNIAL COMMITTEE; FREDERIKA, IA 50631. (#200018-65).

MAR 28, '76. STYLE SHOW & OLD TIME SUPPER. FESTIVAL AT STYLE SHOW IN LUTHERAN CHURCH, SUPPER IN METHODIST CHURCH. (LOCAL). MARY REWOLDT, COORD; METHODIST & LUTHERAN CHURCHES; FREDERIKA, IA 50631. (#200018-62).

JULY 3 - 4, '76. EVENTS OF THE PAST. JULY 3, CHICKEN BARBEQUE, SOFT BALL GAMES, GAMES & CONTESTS, ALUMNI REUNION, CAKE WALK, SQUARE DANCE AT 10 PM; JULY 4TH, 10:30 AM COMMUNITY CHURCH SERVICE, COMMUNITY POT LUCK DINNER, SOFT BALL GAMES AND THE FIREWORKS BEGIN AFTER DARK. AT SCHOOL GROUNDS. (LOCAL). JUNE RULE, CHMN; FREDERIKA BICENTENNIAL COMMITTEE & 4-H GROUPS, CHURCH GROUPS; FREDERIKA, IA 50631. (#103048-6).

JULY 4, '76. OLD-FASHIONED 4TH OF JULY CELEBRATION. FESTIVAL. (LOCAL). JUNE RULE, CHMN; FREDERIKA BICENTENNIAL COMMITTEE; FREDERIKA, IA 50631. (#103048-5).

FREMONT

MUSEUM & HISTORICAL LIBRARY IN FREMONT, IA. OPEN AND GATHER MATERIAL FOR MUSEUM AND HISTORICAL LIBRARY. (LOCAL). KEITH DINSMORE, PROJ DIRECTOR; FREMONT COMMUNITY; FREMONT, IA 52561. (#14206).

GALVA

PARK IMPROVEMENTS IN GALVA, IA. A FLOWER BED WILL BE PLANTED IN LOCAL PARK. (LOCAL). MARTHA SCHULKE, PROJ DIRECTOR; GALVA BICENTENNIAL COMMITTEE; GALVA, IA 51020. (#15079).

JULY 4, '76. FUN FEST DAY. FESTIVAL. (LOCAL). MARTHA SCHULKE, PROJ MGR; GALVA JAYCEES; GALVA, IA 51020. (#102222-1).

AUG 2, '76. BICENTENNIAL FLOWER SHOW. STORE FRONT RENOVATIONS ARE BEING STRESSED; ENLARGEMENT OF THE LIBRARY BLDG, BY DONATIONS, FLEA MARKET, BAKE SALE. AT LEGION HALL. (LOCAL). MARTHA SCHULKE, PROJ MGR; GALVA BICENTENNIAL COMMITTEE; GALVA, IA 51020. (#102223-1).

GARDEN GROVE

LOG CABIN PROJECT, GARDEN GROVE, IA. A LOG CABIN WILL BE BUILT WEST OF THE TOWN'S WATER TOWER, TO BE USED AS A MEETING HOUSE. (LOCAL). GLENN MORRIS, PROJ DIRECTOR; GARDEN GROVE MERCHANTS; GARDEN GROVE, IA 50103. (#19838).

TREE PLANTING IN GARDEN GROVE, IL. TREES WILL BE PLANTED ALONG MAIN ST TO REPLACE DEAD ELM TREES. (LOCAL). GLENN MORRIS, CHAIRMAN; GARDEN GROVE BICENTENNIAL COMMITTEE; GARDEN GROVE, IL 60103. (#19837).

SEPT 6, '76. APPRECIATION DAY. FESTIVAL, PARADE, LIVE PERFORMANCE. (LOCAL). GLENN MORRISS, PROJ CHMN; GARDEN GROVE MERCHANTS; GARDEN GROVE, IA 50103. (#104578-1).

GARNAVILLO

CEMETERY PLOTTING, GARNAVILLO, IA. LOCATED AND IDENTIFIED MARKERS IN 'OLD CITY' CEMETERY. PLOT WAS MADE SHOWING MARKERS, ETC. (LOCAL). ARNOLD ROGGMAN, CURATOR; GARNAVILLO HISTORICAL SOCIETY; GARNAVILLO, IA 52049. (#16414).

CONSTRUCTION OF LOG CABIN IN CITY PARK, IA. CONSTRUCTION OF LOG CABIN TO HOUSE FURNITURE MADE IN FACTORY THAT OPERATED IN GARNAVILLO DURING THE 1870'S. (LOCAL). ARNOLD B LARSON, CHAIRMAN; GARNAVILLO BICENTENNIAL COMMITTEE; RURAL ROUTE 2; GARNAVILLO, IA 52049. (#16413).

HISTORY OF GARNAVILLO, IA. INFORMATION FROM LOCAL ARCHEOLOGICAL FINDINGS, TERRITORIAL AND STATE ARCHIVES, COUNTY COURTHOUSE AND CHURCH RECORDS, HISTORICAL SOCIETY RECORDS AND FROM SENIOR CITIZENS WILL BE COMPILED INTO A BOOK. (LOCAL). ARNO ROGGMAN, PROJ DIRECTOR; GARNAVILLO HISTORICAL SOCIETY; GARNAVILLO, IA 52049. (#24120).

JUNE 18, '76. UNUSUAL SURPRISE EVENT. LIVE PERFORMANCE AT MAIN ST AND CITY PARK. (LOCAL). SIDNEY N DAVIS DUM; GARNAVILLO BICENTENNIAL COMMITTEE; GARNAVILLO, IA 52049. (#106853-1).

JULY 3 - 4, '76. FOURTH OF JULY CELEBRATION. THE FESTIVITIES WILL INCLUDE A PARADE, DINNER, AND ENTERTAINMENT. AT MAIN ST AND CITY PARK. (LOCAL). SIDNEY N DAVIS DUM; GARNAVILLO COMMUNITY BOOSTERS AND GARNAVILLO BICENTENNIAL COMMITTEE; GARNAVILLO, IA 52049. (#106853-2).

GARNER

COMMUNITY BETTERMENT PROJECT - GARNER, IA. BEAUTIFICATION OF A PARK AND ERECTION OF A LASTING MEMORIAL TO OUR FOREFATHERS. (LOCAL). HON SAM CATALDA, MAYOR; COMMUNITY BETTERMENT PROGRAM; 135 W 5TH ST; GARNER, IA 50438. (#18231).

COMMUNITY DEVELOPMENT BOOK OF GARNER, IA. A BOOK WILL BE WRITTEN ON COMMUNITY DEVELOPMENT. (LOCAL). MAYOR SAM CATALDO; COMMUNITY BETTERMENT PROGRAM; 135 W 5TH ST; GARNER, IA 50438. (#16174).

HISTORICAL NEWS, GARNER, IA. NEWS ITEMS OF SPECIAL HISTORICAL INTEREST FROM THE PAST 200 YEARS BOTH NATIONAL AND LOCAL WILL APPEAR IN COUNTY PAPERS MARCH THROUGH JUNE 1976. (LOCAL). CHAS S WHITNEY, PROJ DIRECTOR; HANCOCK COUNTY BICENTENNIAL COMMITTEE; 465 W 11TH ST; GARNER, IA 50438. (#17482).

PARK BEAUTIFICATION - PROJ OF GARNER, IA. BEAUTIFICATION OF THE PARK; A LASTING MEMORIAL WILL BE PLACED IN THE PARK TO OUR FORE FATHERS. (LOCAL). MAYOR SAM CATALDO; COMMUNITY BETTERMENT PROGRAM; 135 W 5TH ST; GARNER, IA 50438. (#16175).

JUNE 18 - 19, '75. CONTESTS & TOURNAMENTS - INDIVIDUAL & TEAM, YOUTH & ADULT. COMPETITION AT ATHLETIC FIELD, CENTRAL PARK. (LOCAL). DONA GREIMAN, CHMN; HANCOCK COUNTY BICENTENNIAL COMMISSION; RR 3; GARNER, IA 50438. (#200018-67).

JUNE 18 - 19, '75. SKITS BASED ON HISTORICAL EVENTS. LIVE PERFORMANCE AT GARNER MEMORIAL BUILDING. (LOCAL). ESTHER TJADEN, PROJ DIR; WOMENS' FEDERATED CLUBS; 135 2ND ST SW; BRITT, IA 50423. (#103342-6).

JUNE 17 - 20, '76. PAGEANT - 'OUR HISTORICAL PAST'. LIVE PERFORMANCE AT GARNER HIGH SCHOOL AUDITORIUM, 605 LYONS ST. (LOCAL). MERLYN THOMPSON, PROJ DIR; HANCOCK COUNTY LITTLE THEATER; 188 7TH ST, SW; BRITT, IA 50438. (#103342-7).

JUNE 18 - 20, '76. ARTS & CRAFTS EXHIBIT. EXHIBIT AT GARNER-HAYFIELD SCHOOL GYMNASIUM. (LOCAL). DONA GREIMAN, CHAIRPERSON; COUNTY SCHOOLS, HISTORICAL SOCIETY & HANCOCK COUNTY BICENT COMMITTEE; RR 3; GARNER, IA 50438. (#103342-5).

JUNE 19, '76. HISTORY ON PARADE. PARADE AT STATE ST. (LOCAL). DONA GREIMAN, CHAIRPERSON; GARNER CHAMBER OF COMMERCE & HANCOCK COUNTY BICENTENNIAL COMMITTEE; RR 3; GARNER, IA 50438. (#103342-8).

GARRISON

LIVE PROFESSIONAL THEATRE - GARRISON, IA. THE OLD CREAMERY THEATRE COMPANY WILL PRODUCE A PLAY CALLED ' A DANDY YANKEE DOODLY-DO!'. (LOCAL). MARTY ARDREN, DIR OF PUBLIC RELATIONS; THE OLD CREAMERY THEATRE COMPANY; BOX 40; GARRISON, IA 52229. (#16313).

GARWIN

JULY 4, '76. OLD-FASHIONED 4TH - A COMMUNITY CELEBRATION. 5 CHURCHES WILL HAVE A RELIGIOUS CELEBRATION, THERE WILL BE A COMMUNITY PICNIC IN THE PARK, COMPETITIVE GAMES AMONG COMMUNITY CLUBS, PATRIOTIC SONGFEST, DEDICATION CEREMONY WITH TIME CAPSULE & TREE PLANTING AND FIREWORKS DISPLAY. AT CITY PARK & SCHOOL CAMPUS.

GARWIN — CONTINUED

(LOCAL). GORDON CHIZEK, CHAIRMAN; GARWIN BICENTENNIAL COMMITTEE; BOX 114; GARWIN, IA 50632. (#105927-1).

GEORGE

GEORGE MURAL FOR GEORGE MUSEUM, IA. GEORGE COMMUNITY SCHOOL JR-SR HIGH ART DEPT WILL DEPICT 3 GEORGE PIONEER SCENES ON THREE HUGE CANVASES FOR NEW MUSEUM. WILL INVOLVE JR-SR HIGH ART CLASSES. (LOCAL). ROBERTA HUESER, PUBLICITY CHAIRMAN; GEORGE COMMUNITY SCHOOL ART CLUB; 500 E INDIANA AVE; GEORGE, IA 51237. (#23914).

A HISTORY OF EARLY GEORGE, 1871-1912 - GEORGE, IA. BOOK WRITTEN ON HISTORY OF COMMUNITY AND EARLY DAY SETTLERS. COVERS SUSURROUNDING FARM AREAS, BUSINESSES & ORIGINAL ORGANIZATIONS. PICTURES INCLUDED. (LOCAL). ESTHER CASJENS, CHAIRPERSON; GEORGE BICENTENNIAL COMMITTEE; GEORGE, IA 51237. (#18075).

MUSEUM MUSING-WEEKLY NEWSPAPER COLUMN - GEORGE, IA. COLUMN WRITTEN ON EARLY-DAY GEORGE, ITEMS GIVEN MUSEUM, BICENTENNIAL COMMITTEE WORK, WORK DONE ON PROPOSED MUSEUM AND HISTORY BOOK; TIES IN ALL BICENTENNIAL PROJECTS. IN LYON COUNTY NEWS, GEORGE, IOWA. (LOCAL). HENRY TIMMERMAN, CHAIRMAN; GEORGE BICENTENNIAL COMMITTEE; GEORGE, IA 51237. (#15838).

PAINTING & CLEANING OF GEORGE MUSEUM, IA. NEW MUSEUM WALLS WILL BE PAINTED & BUILDING WILL BE CLEANED FOR LATER OPENING. WORK WILL BE DONE BY JUNIOR & SENIOR HIGH STUDENTS. (LOCAL). ROBERTA HUESER, PUBLICITY CHAIRMAN; GEORGE COMMUNITY SCHOOL FINE ARTS COMMITTEE; 500 E INDIANA AVE; GEORGE, IA 51237. (#23915).

JULY 3, '76. ALL-SCHOOL REUNION - GEORGE, IA. FESTIVAL, TOUR. (ST-WIDE). DENNIS WEEKS; GEORGE BICENTENNIAL COMMITTEE; GEORGE, IA 51237. (#107688-12).

JULY 4, '76. JULY 4TH CELEBRATION & MUSEUM OPENING. CEREMONY. (LOCAL). HENRY TIMMEMANS, CHMN; GEORGE BICENTENNIAL COMMITTEE; GEORGE, IA 51237. (#23915-1).

GIARD VILLAGE

CITY BICENTENNIAL PROJ, GIARD VILLAGE, IA. PROJECT INCLUDES, VOTER REGISTRATION DRIVE, YOUTH ESSAY CONTEST, WRITING OF LOCAL HISTORY AND HISTORIES OF COMMUNITY CHURCHES. (LOCAL). MRS DARRELL HEDEMAN, CHAIRWOMAN; GIARD UNITED METHODIST CHURCH; ROUTE 1; MCGREGOR, IA 52157. (#24481).

IMPROVING COMMUNITY ENVIRONMENT, GIRAD VLG, IA. GENERAL COMMUNITY CLEANUP AND IMPROVEMENT PROJECT; INVOLVES PICKING UP TRASH, PLANTING NEW TREES, CLEANING OUT DITCHES, ETC. (LOCAL). MRS DARRELL HEDMANN, CHAIRMAN; GIRAD UNITED METHODIST CHURCH; RT 1; MCGREGOR, IA 52157. (#24479).

MORAL AND SPIRITUAL FOUNDATIONS, GIARD VILLAGE, IA. RURAL CHURCH IN VILLAGE IS PLANNING ALL ITS SERVICES ON THE THEME 'ONE NATION UNDER GOD.'. (LOCAL). MRS DARRELL HEDEMANN, CHAIRWOMAN; GIARD UNITED METHODIST CHURCH; ROUTE 1; MCGREGOR, IA 52157. (#24480).

GILBERTVILLE

SEPT 13, '76. GILBERTVILLE'S CENTENNIAL CELEBRATION. MASS, BAKE SALE, ANTIQUE DISPLAY, PARADE, BASEBALL AND OTHER SPORT ACTIVITIES, SQUARE DANCING, ROAST BEEF DINNER, BAND, AND FIREWORKS. AT ST MARY'S CHURCH HALL, AMERICAN LEGION HALL, CITY PARK. (LOCAL). RUTH GARDNER, CHAIRMAN; GILBERTVILLE BICENTENNIAL COMMITTEE; 1003 10TH AVE; GILBERTVILLE, IA 50634. (#200018-250).

GILMAN

MAY 8 - JULY 31, '76. GILMAN CENTENNIAL. COMMUNITY WIDE CENTENNIAL CELEBRATION ON THE FOUNDING OF THE TOWN. (LOCAL). ELIZABETH C FANTON, COORD; GILMAN CENTENNIAL-BICENTENNIAL COMMITTEE; 209 E CENTER; GILMAN, IA 50106. (#104765-1).

GILMORE CITY

FLOWER BED, GILMORE CITY, IA. A RED, WHITE & BLUE CIRCULAR FLOWER BED WILL BE PLANTED AROUND FLAGPOLE BASE. (LOCAL). VELDA ANDERSON AND LINDA STAMPER, CO-CHAIRPERSONS; GILMORE CITY STUDY CLUB AND BONA FIDE STUDY CLUB; GILMORE CITY, IA 50541. (#23358).

HISTORY OF GILMORE CITY - BOOK, IA. A HISTORY OF THE TOWN AND PEOPLE IS BEING WRITTEN. (LOCAL). LOUIS KIZER, PRESIDENT; SENIOR CITIZENS; GILMORE CITY, IA 50541. (#23361).

PARK IMPROVEMENT, GILMORE CITY, IA. A SHELTER HOUSE WILL BE BUILT IN THE PARK. (LOCAL). LARRY LYNCH, PRESIDENT; LIONS CLUB; GILMORE CITY, IA 50541. (#23360).

TREE PLANTING, GILMORE CITY, IA. SELLING AND PLANTING OF TREES IN LOCAL COMMUNITY. (LOCAL). LARRY LYNCH, PRESIDENT; LIONS CLUB; GILMORE CITY, IA 50541. (#23359).

JUNE 26 - 27, '76. BICENTENNIAL FESTIVAL. PARADE, BEARD CONTEST, DRESS REVIEW, WINDOW DISPLAYS AND BARBECUE ARE THE SCHEDULED ACTIVITIES. AT MAIN STREET OF GILMORE CITY. (LOCAL). MRS FRANK STEARNS, COORD; COMMUNITY OF GILMORE CITY; RR 2; GILMORE CITY, IA 50541. (#106532-1).

GLADBROOK

TREE PLANTING, GLADBROOK, IA. 4-H CLUBS TO PLANT 1776 TREES AROUND THE COUNTY. (LOCAL). RICHARD K BRUENE, COORDINATOR; TAMA COUNTY BICENTENNIAL COMMITTEE; GLADBROOK, IA 50635. (#19849).

GLENWOOD

MEMORIAL CLOCKTOWER - PROJ OF GLENWOOD, IA. A CLOCKTOWER HAS BEEN BUILT IN MEMORY OF MILLS COUNTY PIONEERS. (LOCAL). MONICA HUGHES, PROJ DIRECTOR; GLENWOOD CHAMBER OF COMMERCE; GLENWOOD, IA 51534. (#16182).

PAUL ROWE ROOM AT MUSEUM - PROJ OF GLENWOOD, IA. A PAUL ROWE ROOM AT THE COUNTY HISTORICAL MUSEUM WHICH WILL HOUSE THE ROWE INDIAN COLLECTION. (LOCAL). PRESIDENT; MILLS COUNTY HISTORICAL SOCIETY; GLENWOOD, IA 51534. (#16183).

GLIDDEN

BEAUTIFICATION PROGRAM - GLIDDEN, IA. IN ORDER TO BEAUTIFY THE ROADSIDES, DEAD TREES WILL BE REMOVED AND NEW ONES WILL BE PLANTED. (LOCAL). MRS BARRY SNYDER, PROJ DIRECTOR; FFA & 4-H CLUBS; CARROLL, IA 51401. (#25402).

PARK & SWIMMING POOL DEVELOPMENT - GLIDDEN, IA. A NEW SWIMMING POOL WILL BE BUILT AND TREES & PLAYGROUND EQUIPMENT WILL BE ADDED TO THE PARK. (LOCAL). MRS BARRY SNYDER, PROJ DIRECTOR; JAYCEES & CITY COUNCIL; CARROLL, IA 51401. (#25403).

GOLDFIELD

HISTORICAL LEAFLETS - 'BOONE RIVER BRIDGE', IA. LEAFLETS ON GOLDFIELD AREA HERITAGE WILL BE PUT OUT MONTHLY. (LOCAL). DOROTHY WARNER, HERITAGE CHAIRMAN; GOLDFIELD BICENTENNIAL COMMITTEE & WRIGHT CO HISTORICAL SOCIETY; RT 2; GOLDFIELD, IA 50542. (#25594).

LOG CABIN RESTORATION - PROJ OF GOLDFIELD, IA. THE LOG CABIN, BUILT APPROXIMATELY 50 YEARS AGO BY THE BOY SCOUTS, WILL BE RESTORED AND TURNED INTO A MUSEUM. (LOCAL). DOROTHY WARNER, CHAIRMAN; GOLDFIELD BICENTENNIAL STEERING COMMITTEE; RT 2; GOLDFIELD, IA 50542. (#16177).

MEMORIAL HALL LANDSCAPING - PROJ OF GOLDFIELD, IA. THE AREA NEAR MEMORIAL HALL AT THE CABIN MUSEUM WILL BE LANDSCAPED. (LOCAL). MARY AXUN, CHAIRMAN; GOLDFIELD BICENTENNIAL STEERING COMMITTEE; RT 2; GOLDFIELD, IA 50542. (#16176).

PICTORIAL HISTORY IN WRIGHT COUNTY, IA. HISTORY OF CITIES, TOWN & COMMUNITIES IN WRIGHT COUNTY, TOLD THROUGH PICTURES. (LOCAL). MRS DOROTHY WARNER, HERITAGE CHAIRMAN; WRIGHT COUNTY BICENTENNIAL COMMISSION; RT 2; GOLDFIELD, IA 50542. (#14503).

PRESERVATION OF HISTORIC CEMETERY SITE, IA. SITE IS BEING RESTORED & PRESERVED; MARKER AND RAIL FENCE WILL BE PUT UP. (LOCAL). LEWIS A NELSON, PROJ CHAIRMAN; GOLDFIELD LIONS CLUB; RT 2; GOLDFIELD, IA 50542. (#24656).

WRIGHT COUNTY BEAUTIFICATION, IA. THE BEAUTIFICATION OF WRIGHT COUNTY WILL INCLUDE PLANTING TREES AND FLOWERS OF PATRIOTIC COLORS. (LOCAL). MRS KENNETH AXON, HORIZONS CHAIRMAN; WRIGHT COUNTY BICENTENNIAL COMMISSION; RR 2; GOLDFIELD, IA 50542. (#14504).

FEB 29, '76. MINI COURSE. COMPETITION HELD IN BAKED & CANNED GOODS, METAL CRAFT, WOOD WORK, FIELD & GARDEN PRODUCTS, KNITTING, CROCHETING, SEWING, QUILTING, PAINTING & FLOWER ARRANGING. AT MULTI-PURPOSE ROOM, GOLDFIELD SCHOOL. (LOCAL). DOROTHY WARNER, CO-CHMN; GOLDFIELD AMERICAN REVOLUTION BICENTENNIAL COMMISSION; RT 2; GOLDFIELD, IA 50542. (#200018-71).

APR 25, '76. ANTIQUE FAIR. ANTIQUE & COLLECTIBLES FROM PRE-WORLD WAR II EXHIBITED. AT GOLDFIELD COMMUNITY SCHOOL. (LOCAL). DUANE FIELDS, COORD; GOLDFIELD AMERICAN REVOLUTION BICENTENNIAL COMMITTEE; RR 1; GOLDFIELD, IA 50542. (#200018-72).

JUNE 6, '76. ARTS & CRAFTS AUCTION AND FLEA MARKET. DONATED ITEMS OF HANDICRAFT, ALSO DONATED ANTIQUES & COLLECTABLES TO BE AUCTIONED. BOOKSHOPS, CANDY KITCHEN, GREEN THUMB CORNER & FLEA MARKET ITEMS. HAND CRAFT WORK, TOO. AT MEMORIAL HALL, MAIN ST, GOLDFIELD, IA. (ST-WIDE). MRS AL SCHRADDLE; GOLDFIELD ARBC STEERING COMMITTEE; RR; GOLDFIELD, IA 50542. (#107684-1).

JULY 3 - 4, '76. WRIGHT COUNTY OLD SETTLERS' PICNIC & FESTIVAL. THIS IS A REVIVAL OF AN EVENT THAT USED TO TAKE PLACE EACH YEAR. IT WILL INCLUDE AN ANTIQUE MACHINERY EXHIBIT, ARTS & CRAFTS EXHIBIT, A BEEF BAR-B-QUE, A PARADE & A PROGRAM HONORING OLD SETTLERS. OUTDOOR CHURCH SERVICES ON THE FOURTH. AT GOLDFIELD RIVER PARK. (LOCAL). M AXON, CHAIRMAN; GOLDFIELD BICENTENNIAL STEERING COMMITTEE; RFD 2; GOLDFIELD, IA 50542. (#102763-1).

GOODELL

AUG 21, '76. WATERMELON DAY. ROPE MAKING, BUTTER MAKING, TATTING, QUILTING AND CANDLE MAKING ARE SOME OF THE PLANNED ACTIVITIES. SQUARE DANCING (EVENING EVENT)FROM 7:30 - 10:30 PM. AT MAIN ST - TOWN HALL. (LOCAL). MERLIN HANSON, CHMN; AMERICAN LEGION AND FIREMEN; RR #2; GOODELL, IA 50439. (#106156-1).

GOWRIE

PARK BEAUTIFICATION - GOURIE, IA. THE BANDSHELL WILL BE RESTORED, TREES & SHRUBS WILL BE PLANTED AND THE LIGHTING WILL BE UPDATED. (LOCAL). HON RICHARD I JOHNSON, MAYOR; TOWN OF GOWRIE; BOX 51; GOWRIE, IA 50543. (#19178).

PARK MEMORIAL, GOWRIE, IA. REPLICA OF A PLOW ON A PEDESTAL SURROUNDED BY ROCK WILL BE ERECTED AS A PARK MEMORIAL. (LOCAL). OSCAR J YOUNGQUIST, PRESIDENT; GOWRIE HISTORICAL SOCIETY; GOWRIE, IA 50543. (#19179).

JUNE 13, '76. DEDICATION OF PARK MEMORIAL. WILL BE AN OLD TIME BAND CONCERT IN THE CITY PARK IN THE VICINITY OF THE MEMORIAL TO THE EARLY PIONEERS WHO SETTLED IN THIS AREA. MEMORIAL IS STONE & CONCRETE WITH PLOW MOUNTED ON THE TOP. AT MARKET STREET BETWEEN PARK ST AND RIDDLE ST. (LOCAL). OSCAR J YOUNGQUIST, PRES; GOWRIE HISTORICAL SOCIETY; 1107 4TH ST; GOWRIE, IA 50543. (#104221-22).

JULY 3 - 5, '76. FOURTH OF JULY CELEBRATION. COMPETITION, FESTIVAL, PARADE AT MARKET ST. (LOCAL). DUANE R ANDERSON, CHMN; COMMERCIAL CLUB AND AMERICAN LEGION; 504 MARKET ST; GOWRIE, IA 50543. (#104221-23).

GRAETTINGER

SEPT 4 - 6, '76. 80TH ANNUAL LABOR DAY CELEBRATION. COMPETITION, EXHIBIT, FESTIVAL, PARADE, LIVE PERFORMANCE. (LOCAL). PATTY PETERSON, CHAIRMAN; LABOR DAY COMMITTEE; GRAETTINGER, IA 51342. (#106841-1).

GRAFTON

COMMEMORATIVE PLATE IN GRAFTON, IOWA. A PLATE DESIGNED BY A COUNTY RESIDENT IS BEING SOLD IN THE COUNTY. (LOCAL). STANLEY WALK, PROJECT DIRECTOR; WORTH COUNTY BICENT COMMISSION; RR #1; GRAFTON, IA 50444. (#10072).

HISTORICAL MARKERS IN WORTH CO, IA. SITES OF HISTORICAL SIGNIFICANCE IN THE COUNTY WILL BE MARKED WITH BRONZE PLAQUES. (LOCAL). STANLEY WALK, PROJECT DIRECTOR; WORTH COUNTY BICENT COMMISSION; RR #1; GRAFTON, IA 50444. (#10073).

HISTORY OF WORTH COUNTY, IOWA. A 600 PAGE, HARD-COVER BOOK WILL COVER THE HISTORY OF COUNTY FROM ITS BEGINNING TO THE PRESENT. (LOCAL). STANLEY WALK, PROJECT DIRECTOR; WORTH COUNTY BICENT COMMISSION; RR #1; GRAFTON, IA 50444. (#10071).

RESTORATION OF DEPOT IN GRAFTON, IOWA. RESTORE DEPOT THAT HAS BEEN NOMINATED TO THE NATIONAL REGISTER OF HISTORIC PLACES & TURN THIS BUILDING INTO A LIVING MUSEUM. (LOCAL). CONNIE BRUESEWITZ, CHAIRMAN, DEPOT COMMITTEE; GRAFTON BICENTENNIAL COMMISSION; RR 1; GRAFTON, IA 50440. (#12120).

GRAND RIVER

CITY BALL PARK - GRAND RIVER, IA. A BALL PARK WILL BE BUILT NEAR CITY PARK. (LOCAL). DWAIN DAUGHTON, COORDINATOR; GRAND RIVER BICENTENNIAL COMMITTEE; GRAND RIVER, IA 50108. (#22046).

HISTORIC MARKER - GRAND RIVER, IA. A HISTORICAL MARKER WILL BE ERECTED NEAR BALL PARK. (LOCAL). DWAIN DAUGHTON, CHAIRMAN; GRAND RIVER BICENTENNIAL COMMITTEE; GRAND RIVER, IA 50108. (#22005).

GRANDVIEW

JULY 4, '76. GRANDVIEW JULY 4 CELEBRATION OF OUR FIRST TWO HUNDRED YEARS. BINGO, FROG JUMP, CHILDREN'S GAMES & ANTIQUE CARS WILL ACCOMPANY FOOD, FIREWORKS AND A PARADE IN THIS CELEBRATION. AT PARK SCHOOLHOUSE. (LOCAL). KIETH JORDAN; COMMUNITY CLUB; RR 1; LETTS, IA 52754. (#200018-274).

GRANT

CASETTE TAPES - PROJECT OF GRANT, IOWA. RECORDED INTERVIEWS WITH MEMBERS OF THE COMMUNITY TO BE USED FOR A HISTORY BOOK AND PAGEANT. (LOCAL). MRS GERALD TAYLOR, CHAIRMAN; GRANT BICENT COMMITTEE; GRANT, IA 50847. (#9647).

GRANT SCHOOL MARKER IN GRANT, IA. DEDICATION & ERECTION OF A MARKER FOR THE GRANT SCHOOL. (LOCAL). MRS G TAYLOR, PROJ DIRECTOR; GRANT BICENTENNIAL COMMITTEE; GRANT, IA 51573. (#12674).

GRANT — CONTINUED

HISTORICAL MAP IN GRANT, IOWA. THE PROJECT INVOLVES MAKING A HISTORICAL MAP OF OLD CEMETERIES. (ST-WIDE). MRS GERALD TAYLOR, PROJ CHAIRMAN; GRANT BICENT COMMITTEE; GRANT, IA 50847. (#9651).

HISTORICAL MARKERS IN GRANT, IOWA. THE PROJECT INVOLVES PUTTING HISTORICAL MARKERS ON A SCHOOLHOUSE AND AN OLD MILL. (LOCAL). MRS GERALD TAYLOR, PROJ CHAIRMAN; GRANT BICENT COMMITTEE; GRANT, IA 50847. (#9650).

HISTORY BOOK PROJECT - GRANT, IOWA. HISTORY OF OLD RESIDENTS; OLD AND NEW ORGANIZATIONS & LOCAL SCHOOLS WILL BE PUBLISHED. (LOCAL). MRS GERALD TAYLOR, CHAIRMAN; GRANT BICENT COMMITTEE; GRANT, IA 50847. (#9648).

JUNE 26, '76. GRANT DAY. DISPLAY OF HISTORIC PICTURES AND ANTIQUES WILL BE ACCOMPANIED BY PRODUCTION OF A PAGEANT. (LOCAL). MRS GERALD TAYLOR, CHMN; GRANT-DOUGLAS TOWNSHIP BICENTENNIAL COMMITTEE; GRANT, IA 50847. (#22210-1).

GRANVILLE

REPRINTING 'BLACK SOIL' & CITIZENSHIP PROJ - IA. REPRINT 'BLACK SOIL', HISTORICAL NOVEL ABOUT PIONEERS OF GRANVILLE; FLYING THE FLAG AT EACH BUSINESS PLACE AND RESIDENCE IN GRANVILLE & NUMBERING EACH BUSINESS PLACE AND EACH RESIDENCE IN GRANVILLE. (LOCAL). MRS URBAN HOLLES, CHAIRPERSON; GRANVILLE BICENTENNIAL COMMITTEE; GRANVILLE, IA 51022. (#13095).

JUNE 14, '76. FLAG RAISING ON FLAG DAY. CEREMONY AT VFW CLUB, MAIN ST. (LOCAL). EDNA MCCARTHY, COORD; NATIONAL CATHOLIC SOCIETY OF FORESTERS; BROAD ST; GRANVILLE, IA 51022. (#106927-1).

JULY 4, '76. BICENTENNIAL BREAKFAST. FESTIVAL AT SPALDING CAFETERIA. (LOCAL). MRS URBAN HOLLES, CHMN; BICENTENNIAL BREAKFAST; GRANVILLE, IA 51022. (#100953-1).

AUG 22, '76. ST JOSEPH'S PARISH BICENTENNIAL BAZAAR & BARBECUE. HIGHLIGHT OF THE DAY WILL BE A PORK BARBEQUE BEGINNING AT 5:00 PM; ANTIQUE & WHITE ELEPHANT AUCTION, COUNTRY STORE, DUNKING MACHINE & OTHER GAMES THROUGHOUT THE DAY. AT CHURCH GROUNDS IN GRANVILLE BETWEEN BROAD & ELM ST, JUST OFF HWY 10. (LOCAL). BOB SMID, COORD; ST JOSEPH'S PARISH; RR; GRANVILLE, IA 51022. (#106928-1).

GRAVITY

FOXFIRE HISTORY - PROJ OF GRAVITY, IA. COLLECTION OF ORAL HISTORY FROM THE ELDERLY. (LOCAL). MRS DOROTHY BUSH, CHAIRMAN; TAYLOR BICENTENNIAL COMMITTEE; GRAVITY, IA 50840. (#12692).

GRAY

CITY PARK IMPROVEMENT - GRAY, IA. LANDSCAPING AND NEW FACILITIES FOR THE CITY PARK. (LOCAL). FRANK MCLAUGHLIN, CHAIRMAN; VOL FIRE DEPT; GRAY, IA 50110. (#17628).

JULY '76. CELEBRATION. FESTIVAL, PARADE. (LOCAL). FRANK MCLAUGHLIN, COORD; GRAY VOLUNTEER FIREMEN; GRAY, IA 50110. (#103361-1).

GREELEY

HISTORICAL DISPLAY. PICTORAL DISPLAY OF ORIGINAL HOLBERT HORSE IMPORTING BUSINESS. (LOCAL). EDYTHE SATTERLEE, COORD; GREELEY COMMERCIAL CLUB & SENIOR CITIZENS; GREELEY, IA 52050. (#108134-1).

PARK RENOVATION - GREELEY, IA. THE PARK WILL BE CLEANED AND PLAYGROUND EQUIPMENT WILL BE ADDED. (LOCAL). CHARLES NABOR, COORDINATOR; GREELEY BICENTENNIAL CLUB; RR; GREELEY, IA 52050. (#25596).

TREE PLANTING - GREELEY, IA. PLANTING TREES TO REPLACE DEAD ONES IN THE PARK. (LOCAL). EDYTHE SATTERLEE, COORDINATOR; GREELEY COMMERCIAL CLUB & CITY OF GREELEY; MAIN ST; GREELEY, IA 52050. (#25598).

JULY 10, '76. TUG OF WAR & STREET DANCE. COMPETITION, FESTIVAL AT ST JOSEPHS CHURCH LOT. (LOCAL). CHARLES NABOR, DIRECTOR; GREELEY COMMERCIAL CLUB; RR; GREELEY, IA 52050. (#108199-1).

GREEN MTN

BICENTENNIAL PROJECTS OF GREEN MOUNTAIN, IA. PROJECTS INCLUDE: FILMS ON AMERICAN HISTORY, ENCOURAGING THE DISPLAY OF THE U S FLAG, PLANTING RED, WHITE & BLUE FLOWER GARDENS, PUBLISHING OF BOOK: '200 YEARS OF MEMORIES' & VISITS TO HISTORICAL SITES. (LOCAL). LORA B SMAHA, CHAIRPERSON; 3M STUDY CLUB, FIREMEN'S ASSOC & GREEN MOUNTAIN BICENT COMMITTEE; GREEN MTN, IA 50637. (#17338).

'200 YEARS OF MEMORIES' FESTIVAL AND CELEBRATION. FESTIVAL TO INCLUDE OLD-FASHIONED OUTDOOR CHURCH SERVICE, FLAG RAISING, PARADE, ANTIQUE SHOW, PAGEANT, CONCERTS AND MANY OTHER ACTIVITIES. (LOCAL). LORA B SMAHA, CHAIRPERSON; GREEN MOUNTAIN 3-M CLUB; GREEN MTN, IA 50637. (#107348-1).

JULY 4 - 5, '76. BICENTENNIAL CELEBRATION. BEARD & QUILTING CONTESTS; OLD FASHIONED OUTDOOR CHURCH SERVICES WITH EARLY AMERICAN DRESS, ESSAY CONTEST FOR GRADE SCHOOL STUDENTS, HISTORICAL PAGEANT BY YOUTH: 'RELIVING HISTORICAL EVENTS OF OUR COMMUNITY. AT GREEN MOUNTAIN SCHOOL & TOWN OF GREEN MOUNTAIN. (LOCAL). LORA B SMAHA, CHAIRPERSON; GREEN MOUNTAIN BICENTENNIAL COMMITTEE; RR 5; MARSHALLTOWN, IA 50158. (#103342-9).

GREENE

AVENUE OF FLAGS, GREENE, IA. EACH HOLIDAY, 125 FLAGS BE DISPLAYED ON THE AVE OF FLAGS. (LOCAL). SYLVIA HAWKER, PROJ DIRECTOR; GREENE BICENTENNIAL COMMITTEE; BOX 370; GREENE, IA 50636. (#19843).

BICENTENNIAL FIRE HYDRANTS, GREENE, IA. FIRE HYDRANTS WILL BE PAINTED IN THE THEME OF THE BICENTENNIAL. (LOCAL). SYLVIA HAWKER, PROJ DIRECTOR; GREENE BICENTENNIAL COMMITTEE; BOX 370; GREENE, IA 50636. (#19840).

HISTORY OF GREENE, IA. A HISTORY OF GREENE, IA WILL BE PUBLISHED. (LOCAL). SYLVIA HAWKER, PROJ DIRECTOR; GREENE BICENTENNIAL COMMITTEE; BOX 370; GREENE, IA 50636. (#19842).

NEW MUSEUM, GREENE, IA. A NEW MUSEUM WILL BE ESTABLISHED IN GREENE, IA. (LOCAL). SYLVIA HAWKER, PROJ DIRECTOR; GREENE BICENTENNIAL COMMITTEE; BOX 370; GREENE, IA 50636. (#19841).

TREE PLANTING, GREENE, IA. 500 TREES WILL BE PLANTED IN GREENE. (LOCAL). SYLVIA HAWKER, CHAIRMAN; GREENE BICENTENNIAL COMMITTEE; BOX 370; GREENE, IA 50636. (#19839).

GREENFIELD

COUNTY HISTORY IN GREENFIELD, IA. THE HISTORY OF ADAIR COUNTY WILL BE UPDATED AND PLACED IN A BOOK. (LOCAL). MRS HAZEL RAASCH, CHAIRMAN; ADAIR COUNTY HISTORICAL SOCIETY; BRIDGEWATER, IA 50837. (#12339).

HENRY A WALLACE MARKER - GREENFIELD, IA. BRONZE MARKER TO BE INSTALLED WITHIN 4 MILES OF THE ACTUAL BIRTHPLACE OF HENRY A WALLACE OR AT THE COUNTY SEAT. (LOCAL). HAZEL I RAASCH, CHAIRMAN; ADAIR COUNTY HISTORICAL SOCIETY; GREENFIELD, IA 50849. (#20810).

TREE PLANTING, GREENFIELD, IA. TREES WILL BE PLANTED THROUGHOUT GREENFIELD. (LOCAL). ROBERT EHRSAM, CHAIRMAN; GREENFIELD CITY COUNCIL; GREENFIELD, IA 50849. (#23166).

JUNE 28 - 29, '76. BICENTENNIAL & INDEPENDENCE DAY CELEBRATION. COMPETITION, FESTIVAL, PARADE, LIVE PERFORMANCE. (LOCAL). ROBERT EHRSAM, COORD; AMERICAN LEGION POST 265; 108 NW 5TH; GREENFIELD, IA 50849. (#106389-1).

JUNE 29 - 30, '76. ADAIR COUNTY CELEBRATION. FESTIVAL, PARADE. (LOCAL). ROBERT EHRSAM, COORD; GREENFIELD COMMUNITY CLUB; GREENFIELD, IA 50849. (#105314-1).

JULY 4, '76. JULY 4TH CELEBRATION. THERE WILL BE A 4TH OF JULY CELEBRATION ON THE SQUARE IN GREENFIELD. EVENTS WILL INCLUDE: PARADE, PAGEANT AND CONTESTS. (LOCAL). ROBERT EHRSAM; GREENFIELD LEGION; GREENFIELD, IA 50849. (#12342-1).

JULY 10, '76. COUNTY PAGEANT. IN HONOR OF THE BICENTENNIAL, THERE WILL BE A HISTORICAL PAGEANT OF ADAIR COUNTY. AT PUBLIC SQUARE, GREENFIELD. (LOCAL). MRS ROWENA HARDIN; ADAIR COUNTY FEDERATED WOMEN'S CLUB; GREENFIELD, IA 50849. (#12341-1).

GRINNELL

GRINNELL MUSEUM - GRINNELL, IA. THE GRINNELL HISTORICAL MUSEUM WILL BE EXPANDED. (LOCAL). ROSE STOOPS, CURATOR; GRINNELL MUSEUM; 1033 PARK; GRINNELL, IA 50112. (#14732).

GRINNELL, IA, QUILT MAKING PROJECT. EACH BLOCK OF THE QUILT DEPICTS A LOCAL SCENE. (LOCAL). CANDACE LAMBIE, PROJ COORDINATOR; BICENTENNIAL COMMISSION OF GRINNELL; 1920 COUNTRY CLUB DR; GRINNELL, IA 50112. (#14734).

HISTORICAL BUILDINGS, GRINNEL, IA. DEVELOPING HISTORIES OF OLD BUILDINGS LOCATED IN COUNTY TO PRESERVE A RECORD AND TO STIMULATE INTEREST IN THE VALUES THESE SPECIMENS REPRESENT, SHOWING EXAMPLES OF EARLY ARCHITECTURE. (LOCAL). SUSIE BIERMAN, PROJ CHAIRMAN; GRINNELL BICENTENNIAL COMMITTEE; 1527 BROAD; GRINNELL, IA 50112. (#15099).

HISTORICAL RECORDS FROM GRINNELL, IA. PREPARATION OF CHURCH AND CEMETERY RECORDS AS WELL AS EARLY FAMILY HISTORIES FOR PRESERVATION ON MICROFILM. (LOCAL). GWENDOLYN RYAN, PROJ DIRECTOR; DAUGHTERS OF THE AMERICAN REVOLUTION; 1220 6TH AVE; GRINNELL, IA 50112. (#15098).

HISTORY OF STATE OF IOWA - GRINNELL, IA. WRITING OF OFFICIAL HISTORY OF STATE OF IOWA. (ST-WIDE). DR JOSEPH WALL, AUTHOR AND PROFESSOR OF HISTORY; GRINNELL COLLEGE; GRINNELL, IA 50112. (#19307).

PHYSICS HISTORICAL MUSEUM IN GRINNELL, IOWA. IMPROVE AND EXPAND COLLECTION OF INSTRUMENTS, DEVICES AND LIBRARY MATERIALS RELATING TO DEVELOPMENTS IN AMERICAN SCIENCE. (LOCAL). GRANT GALE, CURATOR; GRINNELL COLLEGE; GRINNELL, IA 50112. (#19305).

PLACE MATS IN GRINNELL, IA. PRINTING PLACE MATS DEPICTING THE ROUTES OF THE EARLY MORMON AND STAGE COACH TRAILS AND POSITION OF FIRST SETTLEMENTS IN POWESHEIK COUNTY. (LOCAL). HOYT BONHAM, PROJ DIRECTOR; POWESHEIK COUNTY BICENTENNIAL COMMITTEE; 105 N 4TH; MONTEZUMA, IA 50171. (#15101).

REGISTRATION OF OLDER STRUCTURES. REGISTRATION OF OLDER STRUCTURES WITH THE STATE (IOWA) & NATIONAL TRUST. A PRESERVATION PROJECT AS WELL AS INFORMATIVE TO LOCAL COMMUNITIES. (ST-WIDE). SUSIE BIERMAN, PROJ COORDINATOR; BICENTENNIAL COMMISSION OF GRINNELL; 1527 BROAD ST; GRINNELL, IA 50112. (#14735).

REPRINT OF 1896 COOKBOOK IN GRINNELL, IA. REPRINT OF COLLECTION OF LOCAL RECIPES, FIRST PUBLISHED AS COOKBOOK IN 1896; GRINNELL HISTORY APPEARS IN THE NAMES OF CULINARY AND ADVERTISING CONTRIBUTORS. (ST-WIDE). VIRGINIA CAMERON, PROJ DIRECTOR; GRINNELL CITY LIBRARY; 926 BROAD; GRINNELL, IA 50112. (#15097).

RESTORATION OF NATIVE PRAIRIE GRASSLAND IN IOWA. PLANTING OF PRAIRIE GRASS TO REGIN NATIVE IOWA PRAIRIE ECOSYSTEM. SIXTY ACRES HAVE BEEN SEEDED WITH MORE SEEDINGS PLANNED. (ST-WIDE). DR BENJAMIN GRAHAM, PROFESSOR OF BIOLOGY; GRINNELL COLLEGE; GRINNELL, IA 50112. (#19306).

TOUR OF POWESHIEK COUNTY HISTORICAL SITES. MAPPING POWESHEIK COUNTY, SHOWING LOCATION OF EARLY SETTLEMENTS AND OTHER SITES OF HISTORICAL INTEREST TO ENCOURAGE EVERYONE TO EXPERIENCE THE PAST. (LOCAL). JOHN SIMMONS, DIRECTOR; POWESHIEK COUNTY BICENTENNIAL COMMITTEE; 834 BROAD; GRINNELL, IA 50112. (#102228-1).

TREE PLANTING PROJECT OF GRINNELL, IA. IMPROVEMENT OF ENVIRONMENT AT ARBOR LAKE. (LOCAL). RICHARD STEPHAN, PRESIDENT; JUNIOR CHAMBER OF COMMERCE; 834 BROAD ST; GRINNELL, IA 50112. (#14733).

FEB 21 - 26, '75. THE AMERICAN WEST. EXHIBIT, FESTIVAL. (LOCAL). WALDO WALKER, PROJ CHMN; GRINNELL COLLEGE; GRINNELL, IA 50112. (#200018-68).

OCT 4, '75. CLASSIC AMERICAN MOVIES. EXHIBIT. (LOCAL). WILLIAM DEMINOFF, COORD; GRINNELL COLLEGE; GRINNELL, IA 50112. (#200018-69).

OCT '75. FOLK FESTIVAL. FOLK DANCES THROUGHOUT THE COUNTY SCHOOL SYSTEMS LEAD BY COLLEGE STUDENT DANCE GROUP. (LOCAL). PHILIP RAMSTAD, PROJ DIR; ETHNIC AND FOLK DANCE GROUP; 1810 MANOR DR; GRINNELL, IA 50112. (#102044-1).

OCT '75 - APR '76. AMERICAN COMPOSERS OF CHAMBER MUSIC. LIVE PERFORMANCE AT GRINNELL COLLEGE CAMPUS. (LOCAL). KENNETH GOLDSMITH, DIR; MIRECOURT TRIO; GRINNELL COLLEGE; GRINNELL, IA 50112. (#104321-2).

NOV 19, '75. COLONIAL TEA. FESTIVAL AT MAYFLOWER HOME, MONTGOMERY LOUNGE. (LOCAL). HELEN GUGELER, CHAIRMAN; GRINNELL CHAPTER DAR; 616 BROAD ST; GRINNELL, IA 50112. (#102044-2).

DEC '75. WILLIAMSBURG NIGHT. EVENT OPENS WITH PARADE LEAD BY FIFE & DRUM CORP THROUGH TOWN; WILL END AT CENTRAL PARK FOR SINGING AND SERVING OF HOT CIDER AND GINGER COOKIES. AT DOWNTOWN GRINNELL. (LOCAL). JOHN SIMMONS, PROJ COORD; POWESHEIK COUNTY BICENTENNIAL COMMISSION; 834 BROAD ST; GRINNELL, IA 50112. (#102044-3).

JAN 1 - DEC 31, '76. SLIDE SHOW 'THE AMERICAN HERITAGE'. SLIDE SHOW ON AMERICAN REVOLUTION, CIVIL WAR, & OTHER CONFLICTS; TRIES TO ANSWER QUESTION: WHAT HAVE AMERICANS FOUGHT FOR IN THESE CONFLICTS? 2ND PART OF SHOW TRACES HISTORY OF RELIGIOUS FREEDOM, EDUCATION, TECHNOLOGY & VALUES AMERICANS LIVE BY. (LOCAL). WILLIAM DEMINOFF, COORD; GRINNELL COLLEGE & POWESHIEK COUNTY BICENTENNIAL COMMISSION; GRINNELL, IA 50112. (#104321-8).

JAN 4 - DEC 31, '76. SPECIAL CHURCH SERVICES AND RELIGIOUS HISTORY DISCUSSION GROUPS. SPECIAL SERVICES FOR EASTER, FOURTH OF JULY, THANKSGIVING AND CHRISTMAS, CENTERED ON BICENTENNIAL THEME TOGETHER WITH DISCUSSION GROUPS USING OUR RELIGIOUS HISTORY AS TEXT MATERIAL. AT COUNTY WIDE CHURCHES. (LOCAL). DANIEL OGATA, REVEREND; MINISTERIAL ASSOCIATION; 1523 ELM; GRINNELL, IA 50112. (#102228-2).

FEB 18 - 21, '76. AMERICAN FOREIGN POLICY: PAST, PRESENT AND FUTURE. SEMINAR. (LOCAL). WAYNE MOYER, PROJ CHMN; GRINNELL COLLEGE; GRINNELL, IA 50112. (#104321-4).

FEB 25 - MAR 15, '76. PHOTOGRAPHIC EXHIBIT. '1970 JOURNEY THROUGH THE U S', BY RICHARD BALZER; A SMITHSONIAN INSTITUTION PRODUCTION. AT SCHEAFFER GALLERY - CAMPUS. (LOCAL). RICHARD CERVENE, COORD; GRINNELL COLLEGE; GRINNELL, IA 50112. (#105615-9).

MAR 7, '76. AMERICAN CHORAL MUSIC, 1750 TO PRESENT. THE GRINNELL COLLEGE CHORUS SINGS 'WHEN JESUS WEPT', MODERN MUSIC, & OTHER SELECTIONS. THE GRINNELL SINGERS (MADRIGALS) SING AMERICAN FOLK SONGS. AT HERRICK CHAPEL, GRINNELL CAMPUS. (LOCAL). JAMES FUDGE, PROJ DIR; GRINNELL COLLEGE; GRINNELL, IA 50112. (#104321-5).

MAR 20, '76. TOY SHOW. ANTIQUE TOYS WILL BE ON EXHIBIT. (LOCAL). VIRGINIA CAMERON, COORD; GRINNELL PUBLIC LIBRARY; 926 BROAD ST; GRINNELL, IA 50112. (#102044-5).

APR 1 - 2, '76. FILM SHOWING 'MAXIMILIAN'S JOURNEY'. EXHIBIT AT SHOWING AT NEWBURG SCHOOL AND GRINNELL HIGH SCHOOL. (LOCAL). AVIS TONE, DIRECTOR; PUBLIC SCHOOLS OF GRINNELL; FAIRVIEW SCHOOL 1310 HOBART; GRINNELL, IA 50112. (#105615-2).

GRINNELL — CONTINUED

APR 5 - 7, '76. CONFERENCE ON EUROPEAN - AMERICAN COMMUNITIES. CONFERENCE. (LOCAL). WILLIAM DEMINOFF, COORD; GRINNELL COLLEGE; GRINNELL, IA 50112. (#105615-3).

APR 11, '76. EARLY AMERICAN SHAPE NOTE SINGING. TRADITIONAL SHAPE NOTE HYMNS FROM THE ORIGINAL SACRED HARP HYMNAL. (LOCAL). PATRICK IRWIN, DIR; CELESTIAL SACRED HARP SINGERS; GRINNELL COLLEGE; GRINNELL, IA 50112. (#104321-3).

APR 23 - 24, '76. ETHNIC AMERICAN DANCE. LIVE PERFORMANCE. (LOCAL). WARREN KUBITSCHEK, CHMN; GRINNELL COLLEGE; GRINNELL, IA 50112. (#104321-6).

APR 23 - 24, '76. IOWA FOLKLIFE PROJECT - FOLKLIFE DANCERS. 'THE GREAT ROCKISLAND' AVAILABLE ON VIDEOTAPE FOR GENERAL SHOWING. A COLOR TV PROGRAM CONTRASTING THE DIFFERENCES BETWEEN THE FAMILY FARM AND THE CORPORATE FARM STRUCTURE IS IN PRODUCTION STAGE. IT WILL BE AVAILABLE FOR DISTRIBUTION AT END OF APRIL, 1976. AT DARBY GYMNASIUM - CAMPUS. (ST-WIDE). WARREN KUBITSCHEK; GRINNELL COLLEGE FOLK DANCERS; GRINNELL COLLEGE; GRINNELL, IA 50112. (#104321-1).

MAY 2, '76. CONCERT - GOSPEL CHOIR. LIVE PERFORMANCE AT HERRICK CHAPEL - CAMPUS. (LOCAL). WILLIAM DEMINOFF, COORD; GRINNELL COLLEGE BLACK GOSPEL CHOIR; GRINNELL COLLEGE; GRINNELL, IA 50112. (#105615-5).

MAY 7 - 8, '76. BICENTENNIAL PAGEANT. FESTIVAL AT T T CRANNY FIELD, 11TH AND SUNSET. (LOCAL). AVIS TONE, COORD; GRINNELL NEWBURG SCHOOL SYSTEM; FAIRVIEW SCHOOL - 1310 HOBART; GRINNELL, IA 50112. (#105615-6).

MAY 8, '76. JAZZ BAND CONCERT. LIVE PERFORMANCE AT ROBERTS THEATRE - CAMPUS. (LOCAL). WILLIAM DEMINOFF, COORD; GRINNELL COLLEGE; GRINNELL, IA 50112. (#105615-7).

JULY 4, '76. VINTAGE CAR SHOW. EXHIBIT. (ST-WIDE). DON MATHEWS, PRESIDENT; VINTAGE CAR CLUB; 417 13TH AVE; GRINNELL, IA 50112. (#102044-4).

JULY 4 - 7, '76. BICENTENNIAL CELEBRATION. EVENTS INCLUDE ANTIQUE AUTO SHOW, FIREWORKS, SQUARE DANCES, CARNIVAL AND ECUMENICAL SERVICES. (LOCAL). JOHN SIMMONS, COORD; AMERICAN LEGION AND CHAMBER OF COMMERCE; 834 BROAD; GRINNELL, IA 50112. (#105615-8).

GRISWOLD

COUNTY-WIDE ESSAY CONTEST FOR 6TH GRADERS. COMPETITION. (LOCAL). MRS E C FRY, COORD; CASS COUNTY FEDERATED WOMENS CLUBS; GRISWOLD, IA 51535. (#106115-1).

HISTORICAL BOOKLET OF GRISWOLD, IA. CHILDREN ARE INTERVIEWING PARENTS AND GRANDPARENTS TO FIND OUT INTERESTING FACTS ABOUT COMMUNITY HERITAGE; RESEARCH WILL RESULT IN A COMMUNITY HISTORY BOOKLET. (LOCAL). GALE ESHELMAN, PROJ DIRECTOR; GRISWOLD COMMUNITY FACULTY/GRISWOLD HIGH SCHOOL; GRISWOLD, IA 51535. (#22752).

NEW LIBRARY, GRISWOLD, IA. BUILDING OF NEW CITY LIBRARY FACILITIES. (LOCAL). VI WOLDRUFF, CHAIRMAN LIBRARY BOARD; CITY OF GRISWOLD; GRISWOLD, IA 51535. (#22754).

FEB 28, '76. MISS NISHNA VALLEY PAGEANT. CEREMONY, COMPETITION AT GRISWOLD HIGH SCHOOL AUDITORIUM. (LOCAL). KAREN FOOTE, COORD; CHAMBER OF COMMERCE; 906 2ND ST; GRISWOLD, IA 51535. (#200018-70).

JULY 4, '76. BICENTENNIAL SUNDAYS & JULY 4TH. CEREMONY AT CHURCH BUILDING. (LOCAL). UNITED METHODIST CHURCH; 507 4TH ST; GRISWOLD, IA 51535. (#106153-2).

JULY 4, '76. GRISWOLD 4TH OF JULY CELEBRATION. FESTIVAL AT HIGH SCHOOL FOOTBALL FIELD. (LOCAL). MICHAEL BONHAM, EXEC SEC; CHAMBER OF COMMERCE; 507 4TH ST; GRISWOLD, IA 50022. (#106153-1).

JULY 16 - 17, '76. 94TH OLD SOLDIERS REUNION. CEREMONY, FESTIVAL, PARADE AT LEGION BUILDING. (LOCAL). NEIL POTTER, COORD; AMERICAN LEGION POST 508; RR #1; GRISWOLD, IA 51535. (#106153-3).

GRUNDY CENTER

FLAG POLE PROJECT - GRUNDY COUNTY, IOWA. ERECTION OF FLAG POLE AT BOY SCOUT CAMP. (LOCAL). GEORGE HAUSMAN, DIRECTOR; GRUNDY COUNTY BICENTENNIAL; GRUNDY CENTER, IA 50638. (#19947).

HERITAGE WINDOW DISPLAYS IN GRUNDY COUNTY, IOWA. WINDOW DISPLAYS THROUGHOUT THE COUNTY TO HONOR THE BICENTENNIAL. (LOCAL). DR GEORGE HAUSMAN, DIRECTOR; GRUNDY COUNTY BICENTENNIAL; GRUNDY CENTER, IA 50638. (#19943).

MAYFLOWER PROJECT: GRUNDY CO, IA. REPLICA OF THE MAYFLOWER TO BE BUILT. (LOCAL). GEORGE HAUSMAN, DIRECTOR; GRUNDY COUNTY BICENTENNIAL; GRUNDY CENTER, IA 50638. (#19942).

PERMANENT LIGHTS ON BRIDGE - GRUNDY COUNTY, IOWA. LIGHTS TO BE PUT ON BRIDGE IN COUNTY. (LOCAL). GEORGE HAUSMAN, DIRECTOR; GRUNDY COUNTY BICENTENNIAL; GRUNDY CENTER, IA 50638. (#19944).

PRESERVATION OF HERBERT QUICK SCHOOLHOUSE, IA. OLD SCHOOL ITEMS WILL BE LOCATED AND PRESERVED AND SCHOOL WILL BE MADE AVAILABLE FOR USE BY SCHOOL GROUPS. (LOCAL). EVA GREANY, EXEC SECRETARY; CHAMBER OF COMMERCE & WOMEN'S CLUB; 610 G AVE; GRUNDY CENTER, IA 50638. (#22742).

QUILT-MAKING - GRUNDY CO, IA. QUILT MAKING BY THE 4-H CLUB. (LOCAL). GEORGE HAUSMAN, DIRECTOR; GRUNDY COUNTY BICENTENNIAL; GRUNDY CENTER, IA 50638. (#19946).

TREE PLANTING - GRUNDY COUNTY, IOWA. TREES WILL BE PLANTED IN THE COUNTY. (LOCAL). GEORGE HAUSMAN, DIRECTOR; GRUNDY COUNTY BICENTENNIAL; GRUNDY CENTER, IA 50638. (#19945).

'200 CLUB' - GRUNDY COUNTY, IOWA. 200 KILOMETER WALK TO JOIN CLUB. (LOCAL). GEORGE HAUSMAN, DIRECTOR; GRUNDY COUNTY BICENTENNIAL; GRUNDY CENTER, IA 50638. (#19948).

JULY 17, '76. OLD FASHIONED DAY. FESTIVAL AT MAIN STREET, COURTHOUSE LAWN, GOLF COURSE, BALL DIAMOND. (LOCAL). EVA GREANY, EXEC SEC; CHAMBER OF COMMERCE; 610 G AVE; GRUNDY CENTER, IA 50638. (#106150-2).

AUG 20, '76. AGRICULTURE APPRECIATION DAY. FESTIVAL, PARADE AT MAIN STREET AND COURTHOUSE LAWN. (LOCAL). EVA GREANY, EXEC SEC; CHAMBER OF COMMERCE; 610 G AVE; GRUNDY CENTER, IA 50638. (#106150-1).

JULY 14 - 16, '77. HISTORICAL PAGEANT. LIVE PERFORMANCE. (LOCAL). GEORGE HANSMAN; GRUNDY COUNTY BICENTENNIAL COMMISSION; GRUNDY CENTER, IA 50638. (#104680-1).

GRUVER

COMMUNITY TENNIS COURT, GRUVER, IA. A COMMUNITY TENNIS COURT WILL BE ERECTED IN GRUVER. (LOCAL). LEWIS HARVEY, CHAIRMAN; GRUVER CITY COUNCIL; GRUVER, IA 51344. (#18762).

NEW TENNIS COURTS, GRUVER, IA. NEW TENNIS COURTS WILL BE BUILT. (LOCAL). LEWIS HARVEY, CHAIRMAN; GRUVER BICENTENNIAL COMMITTEE; GRUVER, IA 51344. (#17833).

GUTHRIE CTR

GRAND OLE FLAG - GUTHRIE CENTER, IA. FLAGS WILL PLACED ON MAIN STREET AND IN RESIDENTIAL AREAS. (LOCAL). MRS SHERRY GLENN, PROJ DIRECTOR; JAYCEE-ETTS; BOX 9A; GUTHRIE CTR, IA 50115. (#16772).

GUTHRIE CENTER HISTORY UPDATE, IA. GUTHRIE CENTER HISTORY UPDATE WILL BE PUBLISHED IN 1976. (LOCAL). MRS SHERRY GLENN, PROJ DIRECTOR; GUTHRIE CENTER HISTORICAL SOCIETY; GUTHRIE CTR, IA 50115. (#16771).

GUTHRIE CO HISTORY REPRINT - GUTHRIE CENTER, IOWA. REPRINT OF GUTHIE CO 1876 HISTORY. (LOCAL). DONALD FERREE, CHAIRMAN; GUTHRIE CO BICENTENNIAL COMMITTEE; GUTHRIE CTR, IA 50216. (#19953).

GUTHRIE COUNTY FAIR. PARADE, FLOATS AND CONTESTS. (LOCAL). GIFFORD COVAULT, CHMN; GUTHRIE COUNTY FAIR BOARD; GUTHRIE CTR, IA 50115. (#104683-1).

MAY 22, '76. GUTHRIE CENTER BICENTENNIAL COSTUME BALL. FESTIVAL AT GUTHRIE CO FAIRGROUNDS, 4-H BUILDING. (LOCAL). FRANK PHIPPEN, CHMN; GUTHRIE CENTER BICENTENNIAL COMMITTEE; 217 S 12TH ST; GUTHRIE CNTR, IA 50115. (#107118-1).

MAY 22, '76. WOODEN NICKEL DAY. STORES WILL HAVE SIDEWALK & SPECIAL SALES AT WHICH CUSTOMERS CAN TRADE WOODEN NICKELS. AT STATE STREET. (LOCAL). SHERRY GLINN, CO-CHAIRMAN; GUTHRIE CENTER CHAMBER OF COMMERCE & GUNTHRIE BICENTENNIAL COMM; GUTHRIE CNTR, IA 50115. (#107985-2).

GUTTENBERG

AVENUE OF FLAGS - GUTTENBERG, IA. AN AVENUE OF FLAGS WILL BE PLACED IN FRONT OF THE MONUMENT COMMEMORATING THE SOLDIERS OF THREE AMERICAN WARS. (LOCAL). LOIS MANSON, COORDINATOR; AMERICAN LEGION AUXILIARY; GUTTENBERG, IA 52052. (#24349).

BICENTENNIAL BRIDGE - GUTTENBERG, IA. ONGOING DEVELOPMENT OF LIMBECK PARK AND CONSTRUCTION OF A WALK BRIDGE TO PROVIDE ACCESS TO ISLAND PICNIC AREA. (LOCAL). MICHAEL R SCHNEIDER, CITY MANAGER; GUTTENBERG BICENTENNIAL COMMITTEE; PO BOX D; GUTTENBERG, IA 52052. (#24348).

AUG 27 - 28, '76. FALL FESTIVAL OF ARTS. EXHIBIT AT GUTTENBERG RIVERSIDE PARK. (LOCAL). EVELYN GROTH, PROJ MGR; CHAMBER OF COMMERCE; 612 S FIRST ST; GUTTENBERG, IA 52052. (#106885-1).

HALE

COMMUNITY BEAUTIFICATION PROJ, HALE, IA. PLANT FLOWERS AND TREES, PAINT BUILDINGS AND GENERAL MAINTAINANCE. (LOCAL). HELEN PETERSON, BOARD MEMBER; HALE HISTORICAL SOCIETY; HALE, IA 52230. (#25296).

HERITAGE BOOK, HALE, IA. A COLLECTION OF HISTORICAL ITEMS & FACTS ABOUT OUR COMMUNITY. (LOCAL). SANDY LIEF, SECRETARY; HALE HISTORICAL SOCIETY; HALE, IA 52230. (#25295).

JUNE 27, '76. BICENTENNIAL CELEBRATION AND ICE CREAM SOCIAL. FESTIVAL AT HALE COMMUNITY BUILDING AND PARK. (LOCAL). MARIAN KRUSE, COORD; HALE BICENTENNIAL COMMITTEE; HALE, IA 52230. (#107992-1).

HAMBURG

AMERICAN LEGION RESTAURANT & MUSEUM - HAMBURG, IA. PROJECT WILL BE TO RESTORE THE OLD AMERICAN LEGION BUILDING TO HOUSE ANTIQUES; THE ANTIQUES WILL CHANGE FREQUENTLY WITH PEOPLE FROM AREA PROVIDING THEIR PERSONAL ANTIQUES TO THE MUSEUM. (LOCAL). PEARL BARTLE, CHAIRWOMAN; HAMBURG BICENTENNIAL COMMITTEE; 1112 MAIN ST; HAMBURG, IA 51640. (#11267).

RESTORATION OF HAMBURG BOTTLING COMPANY - IA. PROJECT WILL BE TO RESTORE THE OLDEST BUILDING IN HAMBURG; BUILT IN 1875, THE BUILDING WILL BE USED FOR COMMUNITY CENTER. (LOCAL). PEARL BARTLE, CHAIRWOMAN; HAMBURG BICENTENNIAL COMMISSION; 1112 MAIN ST; HAMBURG, IA 51640. (#11268).

SEPT 6 - 7, '75. POPCORN DAYS. FESTIVAL. (LOCAL). PEARL BARTLE, CHAIRMAN; HAMBURG BICENTENNIAL COMMISSION; 1112 MAIN ST; HAMBURG, IA 51640. (#11266-1).

HAMLIN

HISTORIC LANDMARK MUSEUM IN HAMLIN, IOWA. HISTORIC LANDMARK WILL BE SITE OF FUTURE AUDUBON COUNTY HISTORICAL MUSEUM. (LOCAL). MARGARET A HAYS, CHAIRMAN; AUDUBON COUNTY BICENT; HAMLIN, IA 50117. (#9645).

RENOVATION OF COUNTY HOME SITE - HAMLIN, IOWA. FUND-RAISING, CLEAN-UP, SECURING CARETAKER AND LANDSCAPING WILL ALL BE PART OF RENOVATING THE COUNTY HOME SITE. (LOCAL). MARGARET HAYS, CHAIRMAN; AUDUBON COUNTY BICENT; HAMLIN, IA 50117. (#9644).

T-BONE WEEK IN HAMLIN, IOWA. VERY LARGE WEEK-LONG ACTIVITY IN SEPTEMBER FEATURING PARADE, BBQ'S, ARTS AND CRAFTS, SHOWS, ETC. (LOCAL). MARGARET HAYS, CHAIRMAN; AUDUBON COUNTY BICENT; HAMLIN, IA 50117. (#9643).

HAMPTON

JULY 29 - AUG 4, '76. FRANKLIN COUNTY HOME TOWN WEEK. DEDICATION OF REFURBISHED COURT HOUSE, NOW DESIGNATED AS A NATIONAL HISTORIC SITE; OLD AND NEW FARM MACHINERY EXHIBIT; DISPLAY OF RELICS & ANTIQUES; PICNICS & BANQUETS. AT FRANKLIN CO FAIRGROUNDS. (LOCAL). CARL L REHDER; FRANKLIN COUNTY AMER REVOL BICENT COMMISSION; CHAMBER OF COMMERCE OFFICE; HAMPTON, IA 50441. (#100022-1).

HANCOCK

AUG 7 - 8, '76. OLD SETTLERS PICNIC BICENTENNIAL EXTRAVAGANZA. FESTIVAL, PARADE AT HANCOCK MEMORIAL PARK. (LOCAL). ESTHER M JACOBSEN, CHMN; OLD SETTLERS PICNIC ASSOCIATION; HANCOCK, IA 51536. (#200018-245).

HANLONTOWN

PARK IMPROVEMENT IN HANLONTOWN, IA. A SHELTERHOUSE WILL BE CONSTRUCTED AND THE PARK WILL BE LANDSCAPED. (LOCAL). MRS HARRY MYHRE, CHAIRPERSON; HANLONTOWN BICENTENNIAL COMMITTEE; BOX 75; HANLONTOWN, IA 50444. (#13096).

APR 9 - 10, '76. PAGEANT OF LOCAL HISTORY. LIVE PERFORMANCE AT HANLONTOWN SCHOOL AUDITORIUM. (LOCAL). MRS HARRY MYHRE, CHMN; HANLONTOWN BICENTENNIAL COMMITTEE; BOX 75; HANLONTOWN, IA 50444. (#100952-3).

AUG 14, '76. PORK DAY AND PARADE. FESTIVAL, PARADE AT CITY PARK AND MAIN ST. (LOCAL). MRS HARRY MYHRE, CHMN; HANLONTOWN BICENTENNIAL COMMISSION; BOX 75; HANLONTOWN, IA 50444. (#100952-2).

HARCOURT

LOG CABIN MUSEUM, HARCOURT, IA. LOG CABIN IS 100 YEARS OLD AND COMPLETELY FURNISHED WITH FURNITURE OF THE ERA. (LOCAL). LAUREL CARLSON, DIRECTOR; LOG CABIN MUSEUM; HARCOURT, IA 50544. (#24643).

LOST GROVE APARTMENTS, HARCOURT, IA. RETIREMENT HOUSING WITH LANDSCAPING AND TREES. (LOCAL). CHARLES LUNDBERG, PRESIDENT; LOST GROVE RETIREMENT ORGANIZATION; HARCOURT, IA 50544. (#24641).

MINIATURE RAILROAD MUSEUM, HARCOURT, IA. ANTIQUE RAILROAD ITEMS AND TRAINS ARE FEATURED IN MUSEUM. (LOCAL). LLOYD NELSON, DIRECTOR; NELSON MINIATURE RAILROAD MUSEUM; HARCOURT, IA 50544. (#24644).

PIONEER MUSEUM, HARCOURT, IA. A HISTORICAL MUSEUM HOUSING ARTIFACTS OF LOCAL HISTORY HAS BEEN DEVELOPED. (LOCAL). FRANCIS CARLSON, DIRECTOR; PIONEER MUSEUM; HARCOURT, IA 50544. (#24642).

JUNE 1 - SEPT 1, '76. LOST 4H CLUB BICENTENNIAL PROGRAMS. EXHIBIT AT HARCOURT SCHOOL AUDITORIUM HARCOURT IA. (LOCAL). EVELYN PETERSON; LOST GROVE 4H LEADERS CLUB; HARCOURT, IA 50544. (#107696-1).

SEPT 11, '76. HARCOURT APPRECIATION DAY AND CORN SHOW. EXHIBIT, PARADE, COMPETITION, FESTIVAL AT TOWN PARK & SCHOOLHOUSE. (LOCAL). L E MOLGARRA; HARCOURT COMMUNITY CLUB; HARCOURT, IA 50544. (#107696-2).

HARDY

AVENUE OF FLAGS - HARDY, IA. AN AVENUE OF FLAGS WILL BE ESTABLISHED DOWN MAIN STREET. (LOCAL). WILMA CLANCY, PROJ DIRECTOR; TOWN OF HARDY; HARDY, IA 50545. (#14746).

FLOWER BOX PROJECT IN HARDY, IA. FLOWER BOXES WILL BE BUILT ON MAIN STREET. (LOCAL). WILMA CLANCY, PROJ DIRECTOR; TOWN OF HARDY; HARDY, IA 50545. (#14747).

NEW CITY PARK IN HARDY, IA. IN HONOR OF THE BICENTENNIAL, A NEW PARK WILL BE BUILT. (LOCAL). WILMA CLANCY, PROJ DIRECTOR; TOWN OF HARDY; HARDY, IA 50545. (#14745).

TREE PLANTING PROJECT IN HARDY, IA. TREES WILL BE PLANTED IN HONOR OF THE BICENTENNIAL. (LOCAL). WILMA CLANCY, PROJ DIRECTOR; TOWN OF HARDY; HARDY, IA 50545. (#14748).

HARLAN

SHELBY COUNTY HISTORICAL MUSEUM IN IOWA. MUSEUM GEARED TO COUNTY PRESERVATION OF LOCAL HISTORY AND ITS RELEVANCE TO THE PRESENT TIME. BICENTENNIAL THEME EMPHASIZED. (LOCAL). MRS WM H TINSLEY; SHELBY COUNTY HISTORICAL SOCIETY; 620 MARKET ST; HARLAN, IA 51537. (#4851). **ARBA GRANTEE.**

SHELBY COUNTY, IOWA ART AND ESSAY CONTEST. SCHOOL ORIENTED CONTEST. PRIZES PROVIDED. WINNING ENTRIES WILL BE EXHIBITED OR PRINTED IN THE LOCAL PAPERS. (LOCAL). MRS WM TINSLEY, PROJECT DIRECTOR; SHELBY COUNTY BICENTENNIAL COMMISSION; 620 MARKET ST; HARLAN, IA 51537. (#4852).

APR 1 - 30, '75. POSTER CONTEST FOR SCHOOL CHILDREN. SHELBY COUNTY, IOWA ART AND ESSAY CONTEST. SCHOOL ORIENTED CONTEST. PRIZES PROVIDED. WINNING ENTRIES WILL BE EXHIBITED OR PRINTED IN THE LOCAL PAPERS. (LOCAL). MRS WM TINSLEY; SHELBY COUNTY BICENTENNIAL COMMISSION; 620 MARKET ST; HARLAN, IA 51537. (#4852-502).

APR 1 - 30, '75. SCHOOL AGE ESSAY CONTEST. SHELBY COUNTY, IOWA ART AND ESSAY CONTEST. SCHOOL ORIENTED CONTEST. PRIZES PROVIDED. WINNING ENTRIES WILL BE EXHIBITED OR PRINTED IN THE LOCAL PAPERS. (LOCAL). MRS WM TINSLEY; SHELBY COUNTY BICENTENNIAL COMMISSION; 620 MARKET ST; HARLAN, IA 51537. (#4852-501).

AUG 1 - 31, '75. WINDOW DISPLAY ON GERMAN HERITAGE. EXHIBIT AT BUSINESS WINDOW. (LOCAL). MRS FRANKLIN OPPOLD; WASHINGTON TWP HISTORY COMMITTEE; PANAMA, IA 51562. (#200018-76).

HARPERS FERRY

COLLECTION OF ANTIQUES, HARPERS FERRY, IA. A COLLECTION OF COUNTY & LOCAL FARMING ANTIQUES. (LOCAL). MRS CLAIR TAYLOR, CHAIRMAN; HARPERS FERRY BICENTENNIAL COMMITTEE; HARPERS FERRY, IA 52146. (#23170).

COMMUNITY DEVELOPMENT, HARPERS FERRY, IA. TREES WILL BE PLANTED & A FLAG POLE WILL BE ERECTED IN HARPER FERRY. (LOCAL). MRS ROBERT COTA, CHAIRMAN; HARPERS FERRY BICENTENNIAL COMMITTEE; HARPERS FERRY, IA 52146. (#23169).

JUNE 26, '76. ANTIQUES & HOME FURNITURE EXHIBITION. EXHIBIT AT TOWN HALL, FIRE STATION, SCHOOL GYM. (LOCAL). MRS HARLAND LUSTER, COORD; HARPERS FERRY BICENTENNIAL COMMITTEE; HARPERS FERRY, IA 52146. (#106391-2).

JUNE 26 - 27, '76. HOME FESTIVAL. PARADE WITH FLOATS, BAND; REUNION. (LOCAL). MRS HARLAND LUSTER, COORD; HARPERS FERRY BICENTENNIAL COMMITTEE; HARPERS FERRY, IA 52146. (#106391-1).

HARRIS

BICENTENNIAL PARK IN HARRIS, IA. IN HONOR OF BICENTENNIAL, A PARK WILL BE ESTABLISHED. (LOCAL). D W SROUTE, CHAIRPERSON; HARRIS BICENTENNIAL COMMITTEE; HARRIS, IA 51345. (#15085).

HARTLEY

CHURCH HISTORY - HARTLEY, IA. A BOOK ON THE HISTORY OF ST PAUL'S LUTHERAN CHURCH WILL BE WRITTEN. (LOCAL). MRS MARTHA MENNENGA, PROJ DIRECTOR; ST PAUL'S LUTHERAN CHURCH; 50 N CENTRAL; HARTLEY, IA 51346. (#18919).

FUTURE FARMERS OF AMERICA - HARTLEY, IA. FUTURE FARMERS OF AMERICA'S ACTIVITIES AND PROJECTS WILL BE COORDINATED WITH BICENTENNIAL ACTIVITIES. (LOCAL). HAROLD WOODARD, FFA INSTRUCTOR; FFA BOYS - HARTLEY HIGH SCHOOL; HARTLEY, IA 51346. (#18912).

HARTLEY WOMEN'S CLUBS' BICENTENNIAL LIASON, IA. THE LOCAL WOMEN'S CLUBS WILL COORDINATE ACTIVITIES WITH THE BICENTENNIAL COMMISSION THROUGH THE USE OF REGISTRATION BOOKS AND FORMS. THESE WILL IN TURN BE FORWARDED TO THE STATE COMMISSION. (LOCAL). MRS ELMER MACK, CHAIRPERSON; HARTLEY BICENTENNIAL COMMISSION; 450 1ST ST SW; HARTLEY, IA 51346. (#18913).

HERITAGE '76 - HARTLEY, IA. LOCAL ART STUDENTS WILL PAINT FIREPLUGS WITH PARTIOTIC DESIGNS. (LOCAL). LARON ANDERSON, SECRETARY; HARTLEY CHAMBER OF COMMERCE; BOX 88; HARTLEY, IA 51346. (#18918).

THE HISTORY OF IOWA ON FILM, HARTLEY, IA. COMPOSITION OF FILM ON THE HISTORY OF IOWA INCLUDING, DATE OF ADMITANCE INTO UNION, STATE THEME AND SONGS. (LOCAL). MRS ARLO SCHARNBERG, PRESIDENT; KLIO CLUB, IFWC; 140 1ST ST, SE; HARTLEY, IA 51346. (#21894).

LOCAL CHURCH HISTORIES - HARTLEY, IA. A BRIEF HISTORY OF THE CHURCHES IN THE HARTLEY AREA IS BEING PUBLISHED. (LOCAL). WINIFRED MACK, CHAIRPERSON; HARTLEY BICENTENNIAL COMMISSION; 450 1ST ST S W; HARTLEY, IA 51346. (#18915).

LOG CABIN CONSTRUCTION - HARTLEY, IA. CONSTRUCTION OF LOG CABIN TO DISPLAY HISTORICAL ARTIFACTS AND AS A PLACE FOR BOY SCOUT MEETINGS. (LOCAL). DAROLD ROST, PROJ DIRECTOR; HARTLEY BOY SCOUTS; HARTLEY, IA 51346. (#18917).

PALS FOR SENIOR CITIZENS IN NURSING HOME - IA. THE 4-H YOUTHS ARE PLANNING TO ADOPT A PAL AT AN AREA NURSING HOME, PERFORM A MUSICAL DURING THE YEAR, EMBROIDER LAP ROBES WITH A BICENT DESIGN FOR EACH PAL AND VISIT THE HOME THRU THE YEAR. (LOCAL). TERRIE BOERNSEN, SECRETARY; WEST OMEGO WE GO 4-H CLUB GIRLS; MAY CITY, IA 51349. (#20950).

TRITONIA CLUB'S BICENTENNIAL QUILT. A BICENTENNIAL QUILT WILL BE SEWN AND THEN RAFFLED OFF. (LOCAL). MRS STEVE BAUMGARTEN, PRESIDENT; TRITONIA CLUB; 50 N 1ST AVE E; HARTLEY, IA 51346. (#21896).

TUESDAY CLUB BICENTENNIAL PROJ, HARTLEY, CT. PROJECT INCLUDES: THE HISTORY OF IOWA GREAT LAKES; ANTIQUE DOLL DISHES DISPLAY; 200 YEARS OF AMERICAN MUSIC PROGRAM & A RED, WHITE, & BLUE CLUB MEMBER 'SHOW AND TELL'. (LOCAL). RUTH TIMMONS, PRESIDENT; TUESDAY CLUB; RR; SANBORN, IA 51248. (#21985).

WEEKLY NEWS RELEASES IN LOCAL NEWSPAPER - IA. NEWS RELEASES PERTAINING TO LOCAL-STATE-NATIONAL HISTORY 1776-1976 PRESENTED WEEKLY IN LOCAL NEWSPAPER. (LOCAL). MRS ELMER MACK, CHAIRPERSON; HARTLEY HERITAGE USA BICENTENNIAL COMMITTEE; 450 1ST ST; HARTLEY, IA 51346. (#18916).

4-H CLUB BOYS BICENT COMM CONTACT - HARTLEY, IA. THE COMMITTEE WILL COORDINATE 4-H CLUB BICENTENNIAL ACTIVITIES WITH THE LOCAL BICENTENNIAL COMMISSION. (LOCAL). KENNETH KROGER, 4-H LEADER; 4-H BOYS CLUB; HARTLEY, IA 51346. (#18911).

4-H CLUB GIRLS BICENTENNIAL CONTACT COMM - IA. THIS COMMITTEE WILL PLAN AND COORDINATE 4-H CLUB ACTIVITIES WITH COMMUNITY BICENTENNIAL ACTIVITIES. (LOCAL). FLORENCE HOFTIZER, COORDINATOR; 4-H CLUB; HARTLEY, IA 51346. (#18910).

5TH GRADE BICENTENNIAL QUILT. THE QUILTS WILL HAVE BICENTENNIAL DESIGNS EMBROIDERED BY MEMBERS OF THE 5TH GRADE CLASS. (LOCAL). MRS KRUSE, 5TH GRADE TEACHER; HARTLEY ELEMENTARY SCHOOL; 1ST ST S E; HARTLEY, IA 51346. (#18914).

APR 28, '75. 'LEGEND OF BETSY ROSS' - A PLAY. LIVE PERFORMANCE AT HARTLEY ELEMENTARY SCHOOL (1ST ST, SE). (LOCAL). MS ARLENE HOUSTON, COORD; HARTLEY PUBLIC SCHOOL; HARTLEY ELEMENTARY SCHOOL; HARTLEY, IA 51346. (#104081-1).

OCT 28, '75. 'AMERICA: OUR HERITAGE IN SONG'. THE SONGS & NARRATION DEPICT THE GROWTH OF OUR NATION. AT HARTLEY ELEMENTARY SCHOOL. (LOCAL). DARLENE FETT, INSTRUCTOR; HARTLEY HIGH SCHOOL; 521 FIRST ST SE; HARTLEY, IA 51346. (#200018-78).

OCT 28, '75. 'LEGEND OF BETSY ROSS', MINI-PLAYLET. A MINI-PLAYLET ON THE LEGEND OF BETSY ROSS ACTED OUT BY MEMBERS OF YELTRAH CLUB ALONG WITH THE SHOWING OF THE LARGE 13 STAR FLAG MADE BY THE LOCAL SCHOOL TEACHER WHO ALSO WROTE THE PLAY. (LOCAL). MRS HELEN DEGRAAF, COORD; YELTRAH CLUB; 121S 2ND AVE E; HARTLEY, IA 51346. (#200018-77).

JAN 1 - DEC ??, '76. WINDOW DISPLAYS OF OLD ARTIFACTS. BEGINNING IN JANUARY DIFFERENT CLUBS IN HARTLEY WILL SET UP DISPLAYS IN 3 DESIGNATED BUSINESSMEN'S WINDOWS AND ALSO LARGE GLASS DISPLAY CASE IN LIBRARY. AT DISPLAYS IN LOCAL BUSINESS WINDOWS DURING 1976. (LOCAL). PAT BAUMGARTEN, COORD; HISTORICAL SOCIETY & TRITONIA CLUB; 50 N 1ST AVE E; HARTLEY, IA 51346. (#104081-7).

JAN 2 - DEC 31, '76. PAUL REVERE DAY: DISPLAYS & TALKS OF BYGONE DAYS. LIBRARY ALSO HAS A LARGE 4-SHELF, GLASS LOCKED DISPLAY CASE FOR ANY VALUABLE COLLECTION OR SMALL DISPLAY ITEMS. PRESENT DISPLAYS IN CASE ARE SMALL BELLS & SHELLS (COLLECTION OF A COMMUNITY PERSON). AT LIBRARY. (LOCAL). BECKY SCHROEDER; HARTLEY PUBLIC LIBRARY; 1ST ST SE; HARTLEY, IA 51346. (#104081-2).

FEB 22, '76. BICENTENNIAL FLAG PRESENTATION. COMMUNITY & HIGH SCHOOL CHORUSES WILL PERFORM AND THE LEGION AUXILIARY AND WOMEN'S CLUBS WILL HAVE A PATRIOTIC TEA. LEGION COLOR GUARD WITH BOY AND CUB SCOUT PARTICIPATION ALSO. AT ELEMENTARY SCHOOL AUDITORIUM. (LOCAL). WINIFRED MACK, CHMN; COMMUNITY OF HARTLEY; 450 1ST ST SW; HARTLEY, IA 51346. (#200018-79).

FEB 22, '76. PATRIOTIC MUSICAL PROGRAM. LIVE PERFORMANCE AT HARTLEY ELEMENTARY SCHOOL. (LOCAL). PEGGY EBEL, SEC; COMMUNITY CHORUS; HARTLEY, IA 51346. (#104081-8).

FEB 22, '76. PATRIOTIC TEA. FESTIVAL AT HARTLEY ELEMENTARY SCHOOL. (LOCAL). DORENE GONNERMAN; WOMENS AMERICAN LEGION AUXILIARY; RR; HARTLEY, IA 51346. (#104081-9).

MAR '76. SENIOR CITIZENS ARTS & CRAFTS SHOW. OLD ARTIFACTS, COLLECTORS ITEMS, NEW CRAFTS AND/OR HOBBIES OF ALL THOSE WISHING TO SHOW THEM. COOKIES & COFFEE FOR VIEWERS AND DISPLAYERS. AT COMMUNITY BUILDING. (LOCAL). ELSIE HOPER; SENIOR CITIZENS; 51 N 2ND AVE; HARTLEY, IA 51346. (#104081-6).

APR 5, '76. FILM: BERLIN, GERMANY. EXHIBIT. (LOCAL). MISS KITTERMAN, TEACHER; GERMAN LANGUAGE CLASS, HARTLEY HIGH SCHOOL; HARTLEY HIGH SCHOOL; HARTLEY, IA 51346. (#21893-2).

APR 27, '76. FASHION SHOW & TEA: 'TODAY AND YESTERYEAR'. EXHIBIT AT HARTLEY HIGH SCHOOL LITTLE THEATER. (LOCAL). SHIRLEY KUNKEL, PRES; HARTLEY COMMUNITY HOSPITAL AUXILIARY; RR; HARTLEY, IA 51346. (#104081-5).

APR 29, '76. BICENTENNIAL BIRTHDAY LUNCHEON. FESTIVAL AT UNITED METHODIST CHURCH. (LOCAL). MRS JEAN AHRENSTORFF; UNITED METHODIST CHURCH WOMEN; RD 2; HARTLEY, IA 51346. (#104081-4).

MAY 6, '76. GERMAN LANGUAGE HIGH SCHOOL FAIR WITH BICENTENNIAL THEME. FAIR. (LOCAL). MISS KITTERMAN, TEACHER; GERMAN LANGUAGE CLASS, HARTLEY HIGH SCHOOL; HARTLEY HIGH SCHOOL; HARTLEY, IA 51346. (#105486-1).

JULY 5, '76. OLD-FASHIONED FOURTH OF JULY COMMUNITY PICNIC & PARADE. PARADE, AM; POT LUCK DINNER, NOON; BAND CONCERT, PAGEANT AND GAMES, AFTERNOON. AT NEEBEL PARK. (LOCAL). HOWARD BORCHARD; CHAMBER OF COMMERCE; 421 1ST ST, SE; HARTLEY, IA 51346. (#18912-1).

JULY 11, '76. MEMORIAL SERVICE AT COVEY COUNTRY CHURCH. SMALL PARK AREA WITH PICNIC TABLES, CEMETERY ACROSS THE ROAD TO THE SOUTH OF CORNER CHURCH. CHURCH CELEBRATED ITS CENTENNIAL A YEAR OR TWO AGO AND IS NOW A HISTORICAL LANDMARK. AT COVEY COUNTRY-8 MI SOUTH OF HARTLEY AT CORNER. (LOCAL). JEAN AHRENSTORFF; BICENTENNIAL COMMITTEE; RR; HARTLEY, IA 51346. (#104081-3).

HAVELOCK

BICENTENNIAL FIRE HYDRANTS - HAVELOCK, IA. PAINT CITY HYDRANTS WITH PATRIOTIC THEMES. (LOCAL). DORATHY NICKELSON, CHAIRPERSON; HAVELOCK BICENTENNIAL COMMISSION; HAVELOCK, IA 50546. (#18353).

RESTORATION PROJECT, HAVELOCK, IA. RESTORATION OF OLD COUNTRY SCHOOL & CHURCH BELL TOWER. (LOCAL). ELSIE PHILP, COORDINATOR; WARE '76 WHIZ'S; RR; HAVELOCK, IA 50546. (#23156).

DEC 20, '75. PRESENTATION OF FLAG TO CITY. CEREMONY AT MAIN STREET. (LOCAL). DORATHY NICKELSON, CHMN; HAVELOCK BICENTENNIAL COMMISSION; HAVELOCK, IA 50546. (#103768-5).

HAWARDEN

BICENTENNIAL MARCHING UNIT - PROJ OF HAWARDEN, IA. A BICENTENNIAL MARCHING UNIT WILL BE CREATED. (LOCAL). JOE MAHER, CHAIRMAN; HAWARDEN BICENTENNIAL COMMISSION; CITY HALL; HAWARDEN, IA 51023. (#13906).

TOWN HISTORY - PROJ OF HAWARDEN, IA. A HISTORY OF THE TOWN OF HAWARDEN WILL BE PUBLISHED. (LOCAL). JOE MAHER, CHAIRMAN; HAWARDEN BICENTENNIAL COMMISSION; CITY HALL; HAWARDEN, IA 51023. (#13907).

JULY 4, '76. 4TH OF JULY CELEBRATION. FESTIVAL. (LOCAL). JOE MAHER, CHAIRMAN; HAWARDEN BICENTENNIAL COMMISSION; HAWARDEN, IA 51023. (#101406-1).

HAZLETON

FLAGPOLE FOR SENIOR CITIZENS' HOUSING COMPLEX, IA. FLAGPOLE WILL BE DONATED TO NEWLY COMPLETED SENIOR CITIZENS HOUSING PROJECT UPON COMPLETION OF LANDSCAPING. (LOCAL). ERWIN GOFF, MEMBER; HAZLETON POST #642, AMERICAN LEGION; W HAYES ST; HAZLETON, IA 50641. (#17350).

HISTORICAL PAINTING OF FONTANA MILL - IA. PICTURE OF FONTANA GRIST MILL SPONSORED AND PAINTED BY LOCAL PEOPLE FOR CENTENNIAL IN 1973; NOTEWORTHY REMINDER OF OUR HISTORIC FONTANA PARK SOUTH OF HAZLETON. (LOCAL). MRS N J KJAR, PRESIDENT; FEDERATED WOMENS' CLUB; PO BOX 163, W BENTON ST; HAZLETON, IA 50641. (#17492).

REPRINTING HAZLETON HISTORY BOOK - IA. HISTORY OF HAZLETON AND HAZLETON STATION 1853 TO 1973; INCLUDES CHURCHES, ORGANIZATIONS, SCHOOLS, BUSINESS PLACES AND FONTANA PARK; WILL COVER ALL THREE THEME AREAS. (LOCAL). MRS ERNEST BRUSTER, SECRETARY; HAZLETON HERITAGE CORP; EAST HAYES ST; HAZLETON, IA 50641. (#17491).

TENNIS COURT CONSTRUCTION, HAZLETON, IA. RECREATIONAL FACILITY TO BE DEVELOPED IN PARK FOR USE BY ALL AGE GROUPS IN THE COMMUNITY. (LOCAL). MRS EARL INGAMELLS, MEMBER; HAZLETON HERITAGE CORPORATION; PO BOX 64, E FIRST ST; HAZLETON, IA 50641. (#17490).

TREE PLANTING IN HAZLETON PARK, IA. TREES TO REPLACE THOSE LOST TO ELM DISEASE. RESTORATION OF PARK FOR FUTURE GENERATIONS. (LOCAL). RALPH KEPHART, CHAIRPERSON; HAZLETON HERITAGE CORPORATION; PO BOX 34; HAZLETON, IA 50641. (#17466).

HAZLETON — CONTINUED

JUNE 18, '76. BOX SOCIAL. FESTIVAL AT HAZELTON CITY PARK OR SCHOOL GYM. (LOCAL). MRS RUTH BISHOP; HAZELTON HERITAGE CORP; PO BOX 171; HAZELTON, IA 50641. (#103342-33).

JUNE 18, '76. COMMUNITY SING AND DANCE. FESTIVAL AT HAZELTON CITY PARK OR SCHOOL GYM. (LOCAL). MRS RALPH KEPHART; HAZELTON HERITAGE CORP; PO BOX 34; HAZELTON, IA 50641. (#103342-34).

JUNE 19, '76. KIDDIE PARADE. PARADE. (LOCAL). RALPH KEPHART, CHMN; HAZLETON HERITAGE CORP; PO BOX 34, SOUTH MADISON ST; HAZLETON, IA 50641. (#103342-21).

JUNE 19, '76. TALENT SHOW. LIVE PERFORMANCE AT HAZLETON SCHOOL GYMN. (LOCAL). RALPH KEPHART; HAZLETON HERITAGE CORP; PO BOX 34, SOUTH MADISON ST; HAZLETON, IA 50641. (#103342-22).

JUNE 20, '76. COMMUNITY CHURCH SERVICE. COMBINED CHURCH SERVICE OF CATHOLIC, METHODIST AND PRESBYTERIAN, HELD UNDER LARGE TENT IN PARK. (LOCAL). RALPH KEPHART, CHMN; HAZLETON HERITAGE CORP; PO BOX 34, SOUTH MADISON ST; HAZLETON, IA 50641. (#103342-20).

JUNE 20, '76. COMMUNITY PICNIC. POTLUCK COMMUNITY PICNIC IN CONJUNCTION WITH CHURCH SERVICE. WILL BE HELD UNDER TENT IN PARK ALSO. AT CITY PARK. (LOCAL). RALPH KEPHART, PROJ DIR; HAZLETON HERITAGE CORP; PO BOX 34, SOUTH MADISON ST; HAZLETON, IA 50641. (#103342-13).

HEDRICK

BICENTENNIAL HOBBIES & CRAFTS - HEDRICK, IA. ARTS & CRAFTS ARE BEING PRODUCED TO BE EVENTUALLY SOLD AT A BICENTENNIAL FESTIVAL. (LOCAL). NORMA NEWMAN, PRESIDENT; HEDRICK COMMUNITY HISTORICAL SOCIETY; HEDRICK, IA 52563. (#19709).

FLAG DISPLAY - HEDRICK, IA. CITIZENS IN HOMES AND OFFICES WILL BE ENCOURAGED TO FLY THE FLAG. (LOCAL). MAX BREON, PRESIDENT; BETTERMENT CLUB; HEDRICK, IA 52563. (#19708).

REPUBLISH EARLY DAYS IN HEDRICK, IA. REPUBLISH 1950 EDITION OF EARLY DAYS IN HEDRICK. (LOCAL). VIRGINIA ORMAN, CHAIRMAN; HEDRICK COMMUNITY HISTORICAL SOCIETY; HEDRICK, IA 52563. (#19710).

TOUR OF LOCAL HISTORICAL SITES, HEDRICK, IA. TOURS OF OLD HOMES AND BUSINESSES IN AREA, SENIOR CITIZENS WILL SERVE AS TOUR GUIDES. (LOCAL). VIRGINIA ORMAN, CHAIRMAN; MASONIC LODGE AND ORDER OF THE EASTERN STAR; HEDRICK, IA 52563. (#19711).

JUNE 26, '76. BICENTENNIAL ICE CREAM SOCIAL. FESTIVAL AT AMERICAN LEGION HALL, MAIN STREET FOOD STAND. (LOCAL). WILLIAM MOSBEY, COORD; LION'S CLUB, AMERICAN LEGION, LEGION AUXILIARY; HEDRICK, IA 52563. (#104221-31).

JUNE 26, '76. BICENTENNIAL PROGRAM. ANTIQUE CARS FLOATS SCHOOL BANDS COSTUMES SENIOR CITIZEN. AT HEDRICK HIGH SCHOOL GYMNASIUM. (LOCAL). VIRGINIA ORMAN, CHMN; HEDRICK COMMUNITY HISTORICAL SOCIETY; HEDRICK, IA 52563. (#104221-30).

JUNE 26, '76. PARADE WITH LOCAL TALENT PERFORMING. PARADE. (LOCAL). LOREN JOHNSON, COORD; CITY OF HEDRICK; HEDRICK, IA 52563. (#104221-32).

HENDERSON

WALES COMMEMORATIVE MARKERS - HENDERSON, IA. MARKERS WILL BE PLACED AT SCHOOLS, STORES AND CHURCHES. (LOCAL). AUBREY JONES, CHAIRMAN; WALES BICENTENNIAL COMMITTEE; HENDERSON, IA 51541. (#12686).

HIGHLANDVILLE

FEB 28, '76. OLD-TIME FIDDLER'S DANCE. FESTIVAL. (LOCAL). ANNA BROWN, COORD; LUTHER COLLEGE; BOX 1060; DECORAH, IA 52101. (#200018-223).

HILLSBORO

JULY 10 - 11, '76. CHURCH REUNION ECUMENICAL AND HOMECOMING. ALSO A REUNION TYPE BASKET DINNER IN PARK AND A TALENT SHOW. AT PARK, MAIN ST CHURCH. (LOCAL). ROBERTA BOLTSCHA, COORD; FEDERATED WOMENS CLUB; BICENTENNIAL COMMITTEE & ALL ORGANIZATIONS; HILLSBORO, IA 52641. (#106062-1).

HOLLAND

PAINTING PROJECT - HOLLAND, IA. VARIOUS AREA IN THE TOWN WILL BE PAINTED AND MARKERS WILL BE PUT UP. (LOCAL). EDWIN BROWER, VOLUNTEER FIREMAN; FIREMEN OF HOLLAND; HOLLAND, IA 50642. (#27676).

APR 10, '76. 'TRAVEL LOGUE' - FILM. EXHIBIT AT RECREATIONAL CENTER. (LOCAL). MRS TENA FRANKEN, CHMN; YOU-ALL-COME GROUP; HOLLAND, IA 50642. (#200018-186).

MAY 20, '76. GIFT TO RECREATIONAL CENTER. A HAND PAINTED PICTURE OF THE HOLLAND DEPOT WILL BE PRESENTED TO THE RECREATIONAL CENTER. AT RECREATIONAL CENTER. (LOCAL). MRS DON ENNENGA, CHMN; PEPPER CLUB; HOLLAND, IA 50642. (#200018-189).

JUNE 23, '76. FIELD DAY. THE GIRLS 4-H CLUB SET ASIDE A DAY TO PLANT TREES AND PAINT THE GARBAGE CANS AT THE PARK. AT HOLLAND PARK. (LOCAL). MRS RAYMOND HINDERS, DIR; GIRLS 4-H CLUB; HOLLAND, IA 50642. (#200018-188).

JULY 4, '76. HOLLAND 4TH OF JULY CELEBRATION. PARADE AT MAIN ST. (LOCAL). MRS B GENE VENENGA, COORD; COLFAX SUNSHINE & STUDY CLUB; HOLLAND, IA 50642. (#200018-187).

JULY '76. BALL TOURNAMENT & CELEBRATION. FESTIVAL, PARADE. (LOCAL). MRS EDWIN BROWER, COORD; COLFAX SUNSHINE & STUDY CLUB; HOLLAND, IA 50642. (#200018-185).

HOLSTEIN

GERMAN COOKBOOK, HOLSTEIN, IA. A COMMUNITY COOKBOOK WITH EMPHASIS ON GERMAN COOKING. INCLUDES PICTURES & INFORMATION ABOUT THE TOWN'S HISTORY. (LOCAL). CORRINE YATES, COORDINATOR; NACIREMA; HOLSTEIN, IA 51025. (#23378).

MINI-PARK, HOLSTEIN, IA. A MINI PARK, A MEMORIAL TO TURNER HALL, WILL BE DEVELOPED. (LOCAL). ELEANOR SOSEMAN, COORDINATOR; TOWN PLANNING COUNCIL; HOLSTEIN, IA 51025. (#23375).

PERMANENT RECORD OF 'HOLSTEIN ADVANCE,' IA. PAST COPIES OF THE TOWN'S NEWSPAPER 'THE ADVANCE' WILL BE RECORDED ON MICROFILM. (LOCAL). ELEANOR SOSEMAN, COORDINATOR; LIBRARY BOARD; 510 E 2ND; HOLSTEIN, IA 51025. (#23376).

TREE PLANTING PROJECT, HOLSTEIN, IA. TREES WILL BE PLANTED TO REPLACE THOSE ELMS LOST IN RECENT YEARS. (LOCAL). CHRISTINE WIESE, CHAIRMAN; NACIREMA AND KIWANIS; HOLSTEIN, IA 51025. (#23377).

6TH GRADE ESSAY CONTEST - 'A PAST TO REMEMBER; A FUTURE TO MOLD'. COMPETITION. (LOCAL). JEAN CHALLMAN, PRESIDENT; NACIREMA; 609 E 2ND; HOLSTEIN, IA 51025. (#106597-1).

JUNE 9, '76. OLD FASHIONED CHILDREN'S DAY. FESTIVAL AT MAIN SQUARE. (LOCAL). GARY JENSEN, PRES; CHAMBER OF COMMERCE; HOLSTEIN, IA 51025. (#106540-1).

JUNE 11 - 19, '76. CADETTE GIRL SCOUT TRIP. THE CADET GIRL SCOUTS IN HOLSTEIN WILL VISIT PHILADELPHIA. (LOCAL). CORRINE YATES, LEADER; GIRL SCOUTS; 510 MERKLEY; HOLSTEIN, IA 51025. (#107997-1).

JUNE 19, '76. OLD CREAMERY THEATER PERFORMANCE. THE OLD CREAMERY THEATER WILL PRESENT 'DANDY YANKEE DOODLE DO'. AT HOLSTEIN HIGH SCHOOL AUDITORIUM. (LOCAL). CHRISTINE WIESE, CHMN; NACIREMA; 113 S ALTONA; HOLSTEIN, IA 51025. (#107997-2).

JULY 4, '76. JULY 4TH CELEBRATION. FESTIVAL, PARADE AT MAIN SQUARE AND CITY PARK. (LOCAL). CHRISTINE WIESE, CHMN; BICENTENNIAL COMMITTEE; 113 S ALTONA; HOLSTEIN, IA 51025. (#106540-2).

HOPKINTON

BICENTENNIAL TREE PLANTING, HOPKINTON, IA. COMMUNITY-WIDE TREE PLANTING. (LOCAL). BARBARA GEARHART, PROJ DIRECTOR; TOWN OF HOPKINTON; HOPKINTON, IA 52337. (#18739).

LAND PURCHASE BY HISTORICAL SOCIETY, HOPKINTON, IA. PROJECT INVOLVES THE PURCHASING OF ADDITIONAL LAND FOR THE HISTORICAL SOCIETY. (LOCAL). H A GEARHART, PRESIDENT; DELAWARE COUNTY HISTORICAL SOCIETY; HOPKINTON, IA 52237. (#11556).

LENOX COLLEGE SQUARE - HOPKINTON, IA. THE PURCHASE AND RESTORATION OF ALL LENOX COLLEGE BUILDINGS TO REVIVE INTEREST IN A MILESTONE OF IOWA, THE 19TH CENTURY SMALL COLLEGE. (ST-WIDE). BARBARA GEARHART, PRESIDENT; DELAWARE COUNTY HISTORICAL SOCIETY; HOPKINTON, IA 52237. (#17133).

JUNE 5 - 6, '76. CIVIL WAR DAYS CELEBRATION. FOOT POWERED PARADE, CANNON & MUSKET FIRING DEMONSTRATIONS, CIVIL WAR ENCAMPMENT, HOBBY SHOW, EVENING OF ENTERTAINMENT & SQUARE DANCE, EXHIBITS, OPEN OUTDOOR WORKSHOP, FIFE & DRUM CORP, CRAFTS DEMONSTRATIONS & PROGRAM MELODRAMA. AT FORMER LENOX COLLEGE CAMPUS ON HWY 38. (ST-WIDE). MRS H A GEARHART, CHWMN; DELAWARE COUNTY HISTORICAL SOCIETY; HOPKINTON, IA 52237. (#100432-1).

HORNICK

AMERICAN LEGION AUXILIARY PROJECT - HORNICK, IA. THE AMERICAN LEGION AUXILIARY WILL PLANT FLOWERS IN FLOWER BOXES AT THE AMERICAN LEGION BUILDING. (LOCAL). IRENE SANDA, CHAIRPERSON; AMERICAN LEGION AUXILIARY; HORNICK, IA 51026. (#24669).

FLAG PROMOTION - HORNICK, IA. FLAGS WILL BE SOLD FOR HOMES AND CARS AND CITIZENS WILL BE ENCOURAGED TO FLY THEM DURING THE BICENTENNIAL YEAR. (LOCAL). MARIE PICKENS, VICE PRESIDENT; AMERICAN LEGION AUXILIARY; HORNICK, IA 51026. (#24668).

IMPROVEMENTS OF CHURCH BUILDING, HORNICK, IA. IMPROVEMENTS INCLUDE: PAINTING THE DOOR & PLACING A ROCK IN FRONT OF CHURCH. (LOCAL). MARJORIE LOYD, PRESIDENT; ST PHILIPS CATHOLIC CHURCH ALTAR SOCIETY; HORNICK, IA 51026. (#26826).

NEW LEGION HALL, HORNICK, IA. A NEW LEGION HALL WHICH WILL HOUSE RECEPTIONS, OPEN HOUSE, 4-H MEETINGS, COMMUNITY ACTIVITIES AND A PROGRAM SPONSORING MEALS FOR SENIOR CITIZENS. (LOCAL). LYLE MITCHELL, COMMANDER; AMERICAN LEGION; HORNICK, IA 51026. (#26084).

APR 7 - AUG 25, '76. PRE-SCHOOL STORY HOUR. STORY HOUR LED BY MOTHERS WHO TAKE TURNS TELLING STORIES; CRAFTS AND SNACKS EACH WEEK. AT LIBRARY ON MAIN STREET. (LOCAL). HELEN TEEL; LIBRARY CLUB; HORNICK, IA 51026. (#107681-3).

APR 12, '76. SUPPER FOR LEGION. FESTIVAL. (LOCAL). IRENE SANDS, PRESIDENT; AMERICAN LEGION AUXILIARY; PO BOX 25; HORNICK, IA 51026. (#200018-73).

JUNE 1, '76. COMMUNITY GET WELL CARDS. GET WELL CARDS WERE PRESENTED TO ALL THE SICK PEOPLE IN THE COMMUNITY. (LOCAL). MARJORIE A LOYD, PRES; ST PHILIP'S ALTAR SOCIETY; HORNICK, IA 51026. (#200018-233).

JUNE 14, '76. BICENTENNIAL FLAG PRESENTATION & BARBEQUE. CEREMONY, FESTIVAL AT WESTWOOD ELEMENTARY SCHOOL. (LOCAL). DARLENE KENDALL, CHMN; TOWN OF HORNICK; BOX 6; HORNICK, IA 51026. (#200018-74).

JULY 13 - 14, '76. CARNIVAL AND KIDDIE PARADE. FESTIVAL, PARADE. (LOCAL). PAUL NELSON; HORNICK COMMUNITY; HORNICK, IA 51026. (#107681-1).

JULY 14, '76. ANTIQUE DISPLAY. EXHIBIT. (LOCAL). DARLENE KENDALL, CHMN; HORNICK BICENTENNIAL COMMITTEE; HORNICK, IA 51026. (#200018-201).

JULY 14, '76. FIREMAN'S DANCE. LIVE PERFORMANCE. (LOCAL). PAUL NELSON; HORNICK FIREMEN; HORNICK, IA 51026. (#107681-2).

HOSPERS

HISTORICAL MAP - HOSPERS, IA. HOSPERS 4-H CLUB & BICENTENNIAL COMMISSION ARE SPONSORING A CONTEST FOR IDEAS ON HOW BEST TO DISPLAY THE SIOUX COUNTY HISTORICAL MAP AS AN ACTIVITY AT THE 4-H ANNUAL FAIR. (LOCAL). NELSON NIEUWENHUIS, CHAIRMAN; HOSPERS AMERICAN REVOLUTION BICENTENNIAL COMMISSION; 5TH & MAIN, BOX 61; HOSPERS, IA 51238. (#26822).

'HISTORY OF HENRY HOSPERS', HOSPERS, IA. A BIOGRAPHY OF HENRY HOSPERS, FOUNDER OF HOSPERS, IOWA (1830-1901). (LOCAL). NELSON NIEUWENHUIS, PROJ DIRECTOR; HOSPERS COMMUNITY BICENTENNIAL COMMITTEE; HOSPERS, IA 51238. (#11477).

MEMORIAL PARK - HOSPERS, IA. PARK IN DOWNTOWN HOSPERS DEDICATED TO VETERANS OF WORLD WAR II, DESIGNED AND EXECUTED BY FREDERICK REINDERS, A LOCAL ARTIST. THERE ARE OUTDOOR RELIEFS, STATUES, A BAND SHELL & MEMORIAL ARCH. (LOCAL). NELSON NIEVWENHUIS, CHAIRMAN; HOSPERS BICENTENNIAL COMMITTEE; HOSPERS, IA 51238. (#15841).

MODERN SWIMMING POOL IN HOSPER, IA. JUNIOR OLYMPIC SIZE POOL COMPLETED IN 1974, A COMMUNITY-WIDE PROJ. (LOCAL). NELSON NIEUWENHUIS, PROJ DIRECTOR; HOSPERS COMMUNITY BICENTENNIAL COMMITTEE; HOSPERS, IA 51238. (#11478).

PRAIRIE VILLAGE IN HOSPERS, IA. SIMULATED GENERAL STORE, VILLAGE POST OFFICE, COUNTRY BANK, SALOON AND RURAL TELEPHONE OFFICE. (LOCAL). NELSON NIEUWENHUIS, PROJ DIRECTOR; HOSPERS COMMUNITY BICENTENNIAL COMMITTEE; HOSPERS, IA 51238. (#11479).

SOUTHSIDE COMMUNITY PARK IN HOSPERS. COMMUNITY PARK, WITH A MODERN SHELTER HOUSE AND CHILDREN'S PLAYGROUND. (LOCAL). NELSON NIEUWEWHUIS, PROJ DIRECTOR; HOSPERS COMMUNITY BICENTENNIAL COMMITTEE/; HOSPERS, IA 51238. (#11475).

TENNIS COURTS IN HOSPERS, IA. THE FULL SIZE TENNIS COURTS HAVE BEEN NEWLY RECONSTRUCTED. (LOCAL). NELSON NIEUWENHUIS, PROJ DIRECTOR; HOSPERS COMMUNITY BICENTENNIAL COMMITTEE; HOSPERS, IA 51238. (#11476).

JULY 1, '75. FUN FESTIVAL IN HOSPERS, IA. HIGHLIGHT - PRESENTATION OF THE BICENTENNIAL FLAG TO OUR TOWN. GAMES FOR CHILDREN. BAND CONCERT. AT SOUTH PARK. (LOCAL). NELSON NIEUWENHUIS; HOSPERS COMMUNITY BICENTENNIAL COMMITTEE; HOSPERS, IA 51238. (#11474-1).

SEPT 6, '76. ANNUAL SOFTBALL TOURNAMENT. COMPETITION AT HOSPERS SOUTH SIDE PARK. (LOCAL). NELSON NIEUWENHUSI, CHMN; HOSPERS CHAMBER OF COMMERCE; BOX 61; HOSPERS, IA 51238. (#109022-1).

HUDSON

HUDSON, IOWA, RAILROAD DEPOT RESTORATION. RESTORATION OF RAILROAD DEPOT TO BE USED AS A MUSEUM OF EARLY RAILROAD EQUIPMENT & EARLY SETTLERS HOME ITEMS. THE MUSEUM IS TO BE OPERATED & MAINTAINED BY A NEWLY ESTABLISHED BLACK HAWK HIST SOCIETY. (LOCAL). ODA DOWNEY, PRESIDENT; BLACK HAWK HISTORICAL SOCIETY; WATERLOO ROAD AT HIGHWAY 63; HUDSON, IA 50643. (#2566).

JUNE 19 - 20, '76. HUDSON BICENTENNIAL CELEBRATION. FESTIVAL, PARADE AT CITYWIDE. (LOCAL). PAUL BARGER; HUDSON BICENTENNIAL COMMITTEE; 12434 CARR RT. 1; LAPORTE CITY, IA 50651. (#50682-1).

JUNE 19, '76 - CONTINUING . RAILROAD MUSEUM. RESTORATION OF RR DEPOT FOR CRAFTS CENTER MUSEUM. AT HIGHWAY 63 AND WATERLOO. (LOCAL). MRS DALE DOWNEY, CHRMN; BLACKHAWK HISTORICAL SOCIETY; HUDSON, IA 50613. (#3680-1).

HUDSON — CONTINUED

AUG 20 - 24, '76. PAGEANT RELATING EARLY SETTLING OF HUDSON AND BLACKHAWK COUNTY. OPENING, EXHIBIT, PARADE. (LOCAL). ODA DOWNEY, PRESIDENT; BLACK HAWK HISTORICAL SOCIETY; WATERLOO ROAD AT HIGHWAY 63; HUDSON, IA 50643. (#2566-502).

HULL

PARK IMPROVEMENT PROJECT, HULL, IA. PLAYGROUND EQUIPMENT WILL BE PURCHASED AND PLACED ON THE PLAYGROUND FOR USE. (LOCAL). HENRY SCHELLING, CHAIRMAN; BICENTENNIAL COMMITTEE OF HULL; 1026 MAIN ST; HULL, IA 51239. (#19686).

HUMBOLDT

BEAUTIFICATION OF HOSPITAL GROUNDS, HUMBOLDT, IA. LANDSCAPE WITH TREES AROUND ADDITION TO HOSPITAL. (LOCAL). MRS FLORENCE DITTRICH, PROJ COORDINATOR; HUMBOLDT COUNTY HOSPITAL AUXILIARY; 709 FIRST AVE S; HUMBOLDT, IA 50548. (#21009).

BICENTENNIAL COIN - PROJ OF HUMBOLDT, IA. A BICENTENNIAL COIN FEATURING FRANK GOTCH. (LOCAL). MRS WERNER TIGGES, PROJ DIRECTOR; HUMBOLDT COUNTY HISTORICAL ASSOCIATION; HUMBOLDT, IA 50548. (#14299).

CEMETERY CENSUS - PROJ OF HUMBOLDT, IA. THE HUMBOLDT COUNTY HISTORICAL SOCIETY WILL HELP TAKE A CEMETERY CENSUS. (LOCAL). MRS WERNER TIGGES, PROJ DIRECTOR; HUMBOLDT COUNTY HISTORICAL ASSOCIATION; HUMBOLDT, IA 50548. (#14298).

EYE BANK DONOR SOLICITATION PROJ - HUMBOLDT, IA. A CONTINUING COMMUNITY PROJECT OF THE LIONS CLUB IS THE SOLICITATION OF PLEDGES FOR THE EYE BANK. (LOCAL). HOMER EASTMAN, PROJ DIRECTOR; HUMBOLDT LIONS CLUB; HUMBOLDT, IA 50548. (#14291).

HOUSING PROJECT, HUMBOLDT, IA. DEVELOPMENT OF ONE AND TWO-BEDROOM UNITS AT LOW RENT. (LOCAL). WILLIAM STOW, PRESIDENT; HUMBOLDT HOMES, LTD; 501 8TH AVE N; HUMBOLDT, IA 50548. (#21004).

THEATRICAL PRODUCTIONS. LIVE PERFORMANCE AT 5TH AVE W. (LOCAL). MRS PHAYNE HEATHMAN, DIR; CASTLE THEATER; 702 11TH SW; HUMBOLDT, IA 50548. (#105181-1). **(??).**

TREE PLANTING PROJECT - HUMBOLT, IA. TREE PLANTING & BEAUTIFICATION BY THE HUMBOLDT VFW AUXILIARY. (LOCAL). MRS LEE HATCHER, CHAIRMAN; HUMBOLDT VFW AUXILIARY; HUMBOLDT, IA 50548. (#14289).

'1776' MUSICAL. LIVE PERFORMANCE. (LOCAL). MRS SUE HEATHMAN, COORD; CASTLE THEATRE; 702 11 SW; HUMBOLDT, IA 50584. (#101756-3). **(??).**

JAN 18 - 19, '76. AMERICAN HERITAGE IN SONG. LIVE PERFORMANCE AT HUMBOLDT JR HIGH AUDITORIUM, 2ND & TAFT N. (LOCAL). GARY CURRIE, PROJ DIR; HUMBOLDT COMMUNITY CHORUS; 509 11TH ST SW; HUMBOLDT, IA 50548. (#200018-75).

APR 4 - 10, '76. NATIONAL LIBRARY WEEK. WEEK-LONG EVENTS WILL INCLUDE OLD CRAFTS, SPINNING, QUILTING; HISTORIC FILMS WILL BE SHOWN AND A BOOK WILL BE GIVEN AWAY ABOUT THE AMERICAN REVOLUTION. (LOCAL). MARILYN FEVOLD, LIBRARIAN; HUMBOLDT COUNTY LIBRARY; HUMBOLDT, IA 50548. (#101756-1).

APR 5 - 8, '76. HISTORICAL FILMS. APRIL 5TH, 'NORMAN ROCKWELL'S WORLD'; APRIL 6TH, 'DISCOVER AMERICA'; APRIL 8TH, 'OLD ORDER AMISH'. (LOCAL). MARILYN FEVOLD, LIBRARIAN; HUMBOLDT CARNEGIE LIBRARY; FIRST AVE N; HUMBOLDT, IA 50548. (#104295-2).

APR 5 - 10, '76. BICENTENNIAL WEEKLY BROADCASTS. DAILY 10-15 MINUTE BROADCAST OF LOCAL HISTORY. (LOCAL). MARILYN FEVOLD, LIBRARIAN; HUMBOLDT CARNEGIE LIBRARY; FIRST AVE N; HUMBOLDT, IA 50548. (#104295-1).

APR 9, '76. BICENTENNIAL ARTS & CRAFTS EXHIBIT. SPINNING, QUILTING AND OLD BOOK DISPLAY. (LOCAL). MARILYN FEVOLD, LIBRARIAN; HUMBOLDT CARNEGIE LIBRARY; FIRST AVE N; HUMBOLDT, IA 50548. (#104295-3).

MAY 29 - 31, '76. MEMORIAL CELEBRATION. THERE WILL BE HORSE RACES, CARNIVAL, OLD TRACTOR PULLING CONTEST AND A DEMOLITION DERBY. AT COUNTY FAIRGROUNDS. (LOCAL). MRS ORA ANDERSON, COORD; CHAMBER OF COMMERCE; 1004-11 AVE N; HUMBOLDT, IA 50548. (#101756-2).

JULY 4, '76. 4TH OF JULY CELEBRATION. FESTIVAL WITH HARNESS RACING. AT HUMBOLDT COUNTY FAIRGROUNDS. (LOCAL). WILLIAM DODGEN, CHMN; KIWANIS CLUB; 703 8TH ST; HUMBOLDT, IA 50548. (#105134-3).

HUMESTON

BICENTENNIAL SPOTLIGHT - HUMESTON, IOWA. WEEKLY FEATURE IN LOCAL NEWSPAPER: EARLY HUMESTON. (LOCAL). MARY ELLEN STANLEY, COORDINATOR; HUMESTON NEW ERA; HUMESTON, IA 50123. (#19965).

BOYS 4-H CLUB ECOLOGY PROJECT - HUMESTON, IA. PAINTED RURAL MAIL BOXES RED, WHITE & BLUE. (LOCAL). JOYCE GREENLEE, PROJECT DIRECTOR; HUMESTON 4-H CLUB; HUMESTON, IA 50123. (#19967).

RENOVATION OF OLD HUMESTON OPERA HOUSE - IA. RENOVATION OF OLD HUMESTON OPERA HOUSE FOR USE AS A COMMUNITY CENTER. (LOCAL). E RAYMOND GARTON, PROJECT DIRECTOR; COMMUNITY DEVELOPMENT CORP; HUMESTON, IA 50123. (#19966).

JULY 17, '76. WATERMELON DAY. FESTIVAL. (LOCAL). MARY E STANLEY, COORD; HUMESTON COMMERCIAL CLUB; TOWN HALL; HUMESTON, IA 50123. (#104692-1).

HURON TWP

BICENTENNIAL ESSAY CONTEST FOR STUDENTS - IA. THIS CONTEST IS BEING SPONSORED FOR THE 6TH GRADE IN AREA SCHOOLS. (LOCAL). MRS HOWARD SMITH, CHAIRMAN; HURON TOWNSHIP BICENTENNIAL COMMITTEE; RURAL ROUTE; MEDIAPOLIS, IA 52637. (#18564).

BICENTENNIAL STUDY PROGRAM; HURON TOWNSHIP, IA. LOCAL CIVIC CLUBS WILL STUDY THE NATION'S TWO HUNDRED YEAR HISTORY. (LOCAL). MRS HOWARD SMITH, CHAIRMAN; HURON TOWNSHIP BICENTENNIAL COMMITTEE; RURAL ROUTE; MEDIAPOLIS, IA 52637. (#18565).

BICENTENNIAL TREE PLANTING, HURON TOWNSHIP, IA. LOCAL RESIDENTS WILL PLANT THE TREES AS PART OF THE COMMUNITY'S BICENTENNIAL CELEBRATION. (LOCAL). MRS HOWARD SMITH, CHAIRMAN; HURON TOWNSHIP BICENTENNIAL COMMITTEE; RURAL ROUTE; MEDIAPOLIS, IA 52637. (#18563).

BICENTENNIAL WINDOW DISPLAY, HURON TWNSHIP, IA. ITEMS USED BY EARLY SETTLERS WERE DISPLAYED. (LOCAL). MRS HOWARD SMITH, CHAIRMAN; HURON TOWNSHIP BICENTENNIAL COMMITTEE; RURAL ROUTE; MEDIAPOLIS, IA 52637. (#18567).

COMMUNITY 'WITCH HUNT' - HURON TOWNSHIP, IA. THE PURPOSE OF THIS PROJECT IS TO LOCATE UNWANTED FAMILY ITEMS WHICH DATE BACK TO THE EARLY SETTLEMENT. THE ITEMS WILL BE DONATED TO THE DES MOINES CO HISTORICAL MUSEUM AT BURLINGTON. (LOCAL). MRS HOWARD SMITH, CHAIRMAN; HURON TOWNSHIP BICENTENNIAL COMMITTEE; RURAL ROUTE; MEDIAPOLIS, IA 52637. (#18566).

HISTORY OF HURON TOWNSHIP - IA. 'COUNTRY LIVING', A HISTORY OF HURON TOWNSHIP PUBLISHED DEC, 1974 BY MRS B. FRANK HEDGES. (LOCAL). MRS HOWARD SMITH, CHAIRMAN; HURON TOWNSHIP BICENTENNIAL COMMITTEE; RURAL ROUTE; MEDIAPOLIS, IA 52637. (#18562).

HURON TOWNSHIP'S CEMETERY RESTORATION - IA. THE TOWN'S TWO CEMETERIES WILL BE BEAUTIFIED AS PART OF THE TOWN'S BICENTENNIAL PROJECTS. (LOCAL). MRS HOWARD SMITH, CHAIRMAN; HURON TOWNSHIP BICENTENNIAL COMMITTEE; RURAL ROUTE; MEDIAPOLIS, IA 52637. (#18561).

HUXLEY

LIBRARY REMODELING, HUXLEY, IA. REMODEL CHILDREN'S CORNER AT THE LOCAL LIBRARY AND ESTABLISH A BUILDING FUND. (LOCAL). SUE IHLE, CHAIRWOMAN; HUXLEY AMERICAN REVOLUTION BICENTENNIAL COMMISSION; HUXLEY, IA 50124. (#25285).

PARK RESTORATION, HUXLEY, IA. RESTORATION OF MEMORIAL PARK. (LOCAL). SUE IHLE, PROJ CHAIRMAN; HUXLEY AMERICAN REVOLUTION BICENTENNIAL COMMISSION; HUXLEY, IA 50124. (#25286).

MAY 27, '76. FILM PRESENTATION AND AWARDS CEREMONY. FILM, TRACING HISTORY OF AREA, WILL BE PRESENTED AFTER ICE CREAM SOCIAL & AWARD CEREMONY. (LOCAL). SUE IHLE, CHAIRWOMAN; HUXLEY AMERICAN REVOLUTION BICENTENNIAL COMMISSION; HUXLEY, IA 50124. (#107953-1).

MAY 27, '76. ICE CREAM SOCIAL & HERITAGE FILM CLASSIC. EXHIBIT, FESTIVAL AT HUXLEY MEMORIAL PARK. (LOCAL). JOHN HENDRICKS, COORD; HUXLEY AMERICAN BICENTENNIAL COMMISSION; 205 CIRCLE; HUXLEY, IA 50124. (#107984-3).

JUNE 27, '76. ANTIQUE SHOW, BOX SOCIAL & AUCTION. EXHIBIT, FESTIVAL AT BALLARD HIGH SCHOOL. (LOCAL). JOHN HENDRICKS, COORD; TODAY'S HOMEMAKERS-YOUNG AT HEART; 205 CIRCLE; HUXLEY, IA 50124. (#107984-2).

SEPT 18, '76. FALL FESTIVAL SETTLER'S DAY PICNIC. PICNIC, CRAFTS, MUSIC & PARADE. AT PARADE-MAIN ST, FESTIVAL-CITY PARK. (LOCAL). DAVID TESDALL, COORD; KIWANIS JAYCEES & JAYCETTES; 516 N 2ND AVE; HUXLEY, IA 50124. (#107984-1).

IDA GROVE

BICENTENNIAL EXHIBITION - IDA GROVE, IA. AN EXHIBIT OF HORSE DRAWN MACHINERY WILL BE MADE PERMANENT. (LOCAL). ISABELLA SMITH, CHAIRMAN; IDA COUNTY HISTORIAL SOCIETY; BATTLE CREEK, IA 51006. (#16421).

BICENTENNIAL QUILT PROJ - IDA GROVE, IA. A QUILT WITH A PATRIOTIC DESIGN HAS BEEN PUT ON EXHIBIT FOR THE BICENTENNIAL CELEBRATION. (LOCAL). ISABELLA SMITH, CHAIRMAN; IDA COUNTY HISTORIAL SOCIETY; BATTLE CREEK, IA 51006. (#16422).

DOWNTOWN BEAUTIFICATION PROGRAM - IDA GROVE, IA. THE COMMUNITY BETTERMENT COUNCIL WILL SPONSOR A BEAUTIFICATION PROGRAM FOR DOWNTOWN IDA GROVE. (LOCAL). HON THEODORE E MURPHY, MAYOR; COMMUNITU BETTERMENT COUNCIL; 301 MAIN ST; IDA GROVE, IA 51445. (#20900).

ORAL HISTORY PROJ - IDA GROVE, IA. THE 4-H CLUB IS RECORDING ANECDOTES & REMINISCENCES OF OLDER FOLKS IN THE IDA GROVE AREA. (LOCAL). ISABELLA SMITH, CHAIRMAN; IDA COUNTY BICENTENNIAL; BATTLE CREEK, IA 51006. (#16420).

'OUR HERITAGE', A HISTORY OF IDA COUNTY, IA. THE HISTORY OF IDA COUNTY IS BEING PUBLISHED IN THREE BOUND VOLUMES COMPLETE WITH COLOR AND BLACK AND WHITE PHOTOGRAPHS. (LOCAL). BRUCE GODBERSEN, CHAIRMAN; MIDWEST INDUSTRIES, INC; HWYS 59 & 175; IDA GROVE, IA 51445. (#16163).

REPUBLICATION OF LOCAL HISTORY, IDA GROVE, IA. HISTORICAL COLLECTIONS OF IDA COUNTY BY DR G C MOOREHEAD (1928); $3.50 FOR SOFT COVER & $6.00 FOR HARDBOUND. (LOCAL). DENNIS MIESNER, PRESIDENT; IDA COUNTY HISTORICAL SOCIETY; PO BOX 85; IDA GROVE, IA 51445. (#18151).

RESTORATION OF MOORHEAD PIONEER STAGECOACH INN, IA. THE RESTORATION OF MOOREHEAD STAGECOACH INN, POST OFFICE, STORES, COURTHOUSE, SCHOOL AND CHURCH. IT IS ONE OF THE OLDEST STRUCTURES IN WESTERN IOWA. (ST-WIDE). MORRIS C HURD, LAISON OFFICER; IDA COUNTY HISTORICAL SOCIETY; 209 MAIN ST; IDA GROVE, IA 51445. (#18754).

FEB 22, '76. GEORGE AND MARTHA CONTEST. COMPETITION AT IDA GROVE COMMUNITY HALL, 3RD AND MAIN. (LOCAL). JOHN WITHHART, COORD; IDA GROVE BICENTENNIAL COMMITTEE; 501 BURNS ST; IDA GROVE, IA 51445. (#200018-83).

FEB 28, '76. NATIONAL GUARD MUSTER DAY. FESTIVAL AT NATIONAL GUARD ARMORY. (ST-WIDE). SFC LYLE CLAYTON, DIR; COMPANY 'C' 2ND BN 133RD INF; NATIONAL GUARD ARMORY; IDA GROVE, IA 51445. (#104956-2).

MAR 1, '76. BICENTENNIAL VOCAL CONCERT. LIVE PERFORMANCE AT IDA GROVE HIGH SCHOOL CAFETORIUM. (LOCAL). PAUL CRAWDELL, CHAIRMAN; IDA GROVE BICENTENNIAL COMMITTEE; TWIN PINES; IDA GROVE, IA 51445. (#104956-1).

APR 28 - JULY 5, '76. BICENTENNIAL BAND. ALL MUSICIANS ARE FORMER BAND MEMBERS LIVING IN IDA COUNTY AND ARE AGES 25-75. AT DOWNTOWN STREET PERFORMANCES. (LOCAL). JOHN WITHHART, COORD; BICENTENNIAL COMMITTEE; 501 BURNS ST; IDA GROVE, IA 51445. (#107991-2).

JUNE 14, '76. BETSY ROSS DAY. CHILDREN'S PARADE, GEORGE & MARTHA CONTEST, MERCHANTS IN COLONIAL DRESS & FLAG FLYING. (LOCAL). JOHN WITHART, CHAIRMAN; IDA GROVE BICENTENNIAL COMMITTEE; 501 BURNS ST; IDA GROVE, IA 51445. (#104543-2).

JUNE 19, '76. AF & AM CENTENNIAL BANQUET & RECOGNITION CEREMONY. BANQUET & PROGRAM OF RECOGNITION FOR 50 YEAR MEMBERS; COLLECTION OF HISTORICAL ITEMS, PRINTING & PUBLICATION OF CENTENNIAL BOOK; THE GRAND MASTER OF MASONS IN IOWA WILL VISIT IDA GROVE. (LOCAL). MORRIS C HURD, MASTER; KANE LODGE #377 AF & AM; 209 MAIN ST; IDA GROVE, IA 51445. (#104543-1).

AUG 5, '76. BICENTENNIAL DAY AT IDA COUNTY FAIR. TWO ONE-ACT PLAYS WILL BE HELD AT THE FAIR. AT FAIR GROUNDS-3 MI NW OF IDA GROVE ON HWY 59. (LOCAL). JOHN WITHHART, COORD; IDA GROVE BICENTENNIAL COMMITTEE; 501 BURNS ST; IDA GROVE, IA 51445. (#107991-1).

IMOGENE

HISTORY OF ST PATRICK'S CHURCH - IMOGENE, IOWA. WILL UPDATE HISTORY AND DECIDE HOW IT WILL BE USED. WILL ALSO HAVE DISPLAY OF 77 YEAR OLD CHURCH EDIFICE. (LOCAL). LLOYD M HALEY, CHAIRMAN; MONROE TOWNSHIP BICENT COMMITTEE; BOX 515; IMOGENE, IA 51645. (#9642).

PLAYGROUND MODERNIZATION IN IMOGENE, IOWA. THE CITIZENS OF IMOGENE WILL REPAIR AND MODERNIZE PRESENT PLAYGROUND FACILITIES. (LOCAL). LLOYD M HALEY, CHAIRMAN; MONROE TOWNSHIP BICENT COMMITTEE; BOX 515; IMOGENE, IA 51645. (#9640).

TOWNSHIP HISTORY OF IMOGENE, IOWA. UPDATE AND REPRINT THE HISTORY OF FREEMONT TOWNSHIP. (LOCAL). LLOYD M HALEY, CHAIRMAN; MONROE TOWNSHIP BICENT COMMITTEE; BOX 515; IMOGENE, IA 51645. (#9641).

INDEPENDENCE

ARBOR DAY CELEBRATION, INDEPENDENCE, IA. PLANTING OF TREES NATIVE TO THE INDEPENDENCE, IA AREA. (LOCAL). ED HARBERTS, PROJ CHAIRMAN; KIWANIS CLUB; 814 2ND ST SW; INDEPENDENCE, IA 50664. (#22474).

BICENTENNIAL KEY CHAINS, INDEPENDENCE, IA. KEY CHAINS DISPLAYING A PICTURE OF WAPSI-PINICON MILL HAVE BEEN DESIGNED AND ARE NOW ON SALE FOR $3.25 EACH. (LOCAL). LEANNE HARRISON, CO-CHAIRMAN; BUCH COUNTY BICENTENNIAL COMMITTEE; 604 5TH AVE SW; INDEPENDENCE, IA 50644. (#19680).

CITY BROCHURE, INDEPENDENCE, IA. PUBLICATION OF A DESCRIPTION OF INDEPENDENCE FOR TOURISTS. (LOCAL). MARY ELLEN TOLBY, PROJ DIRECTOR; BETA SIGMA PHI; 313 FIRST ST E; INDEPENDENCE, IA 50644. (#24356).

CITY CALENDAR, INDEPENDENCE, IA. INDEPENDENCE 'DAYS GONE BY' BICENTENNIAL CALENDAR. (LOCAL). BARBARA DODGE, CHAIRMAN; INDEPENDENCE BICENTENNIAL COMMISSION; 210 6TH AVE NE; INDEPENDENCE, IA 50664. (#19690).

COUNTY-WIDE CANVASSING OF CEMETERIES - IA. CATALOG & TYPE ON CROSS-INDEX CARDS EVERY TOMBSTONE IN ALL 48 CEMETERIES IN THE COUNTY. (LOCAL). LEANNE HARRISON, SECRETARY; BUCHANNAN COUNTY GENEALOGICAL SOCIETY; 604 5TH AVE SW; INDEPENDENCE, IA 50644. (#18230).

INDEPENDENCE — CONTINUED

FIRE HYDRANT PAINTING, INDEPENDENCE, IA. PAINTING OF CITY FIRE HYDRANTS IN THE BICENTENNIAL THEME. (LOCAL). BARBARA DODGE, BICENTENNIAL CHAIRPERSON; INDEPENDENCE AREA CHAMBER OF COMMERCE; 210 6TH AVE NE; INDEPENDENCE, IA 50644. (#24357).

FLAG POLE PROJECT - INDEPENDENCE, IA. A 35-FOOT ALUMINUM FLAG POLE WILL BE ERECTED FOR THE CITY. (LOCAL). LEANNE HARRISON, CO-CHAIRMAN; INDEPENDENCE BICENTENNIAL COMMITTEE; 604 5TH AVE SW; INDEPENDENCE, IA 50644. (#21987).

FLAG PRESENTATIONS, INDEPENDENCE, IA. THE IOWA FLAG AND BICENTENNIAL FLAG ARE BEING PRESENTED TO ALL AREA SCHOOLS. (LOCAL). LEANNE HARRISON, CO-CHAIRMAN; VFW & AUX ; BUCH COUNTY BICENTENNIAL COMMITTEE; 604 5TH AVE SW; INDEPENDENCE, IA 50644. (#19683).

GATEWAY TO THE PAST, INDEPENDENCE, IA. MUSEUM AT COUNTY FAIRGROUNDS HAS BEEN DEVELOPED; FEATURED ARE OLD MACHINERY & TOOLS AND REPLICAS OF AN OLD CHURCH, BLACKSMITH SHOP, PRINT SHOP, SCHOOL AND HOME. (LOCAL). LEANNE HARRISON, CO-CHAIRWOMAN; BUCHANAN COUNTY HISTORICAL & BICENTENNIAL COMMITTEE; 604 5TH AVE SW; INDEPENDENCE, IA 50644. (#24467).

HISTORICAL HIKING TRAIL, INDEPENDENCE, IA. 20 HISTORICAL SPOTS IN INDEPENDENCE ARE FEATURED & MAPPED OUT IN A HIKING TRAIL BROCHURE. (LOCAL). LEANNE HARRISON, CO-CHAIRMAN; BUCHANAN COUNTY HISTORICAL SOCIETY & BICENTENNIAL; 604 5TH AVE SW; INDEPENDENCE, IA 50644. (#24466).

HISTORICAL MILL RESTORATION, INDEPENDENCE, IA. 5 STORY BRICK MILL ON WAPSI-PINICON RIVER, BUILT IN 1857 WILL BE RESTORED AND PRESERVED. (LOCAL). LEANNE HARRISON, CO-CHAIRMAN; BUCH COUNTY BICENTENNIAL COMMITTEE; 604 5TH AVE SW; INDEPENDENCE, IA 50644. (#19679).

HISTORICAL TOURS OF BUCHANAN COUNTY, IOWA. ORGANIZED TOURS OF HISTORICAL PLACES & STRUCTURES IN BUCHANAN CO. (LOCAL). LEANNE HANISON, PRESIDENT; BUCHANAN COUNTY BICENTENNIAL COMMISSION; 604 5TH AVE SW; INDEPENDENCE, IA 50644. (#5236).

HISTORY COLUMN IN INDEPENDENCE, IA. A MONTHLY HISTORY COLUMN IS BEING FEATURED IN LOCAL PAPER TO ENCOURAGE INTEREST IN LOCAL HISTORY. (LOCAL). LEANNE HARRISON, CO-CHAIRMAN; BUCH COUNTY BICENTENNIAL COMMITTEE; 604 5TH AVE SW; INDEPENDENCE, IA 50644. (#19682).

JULY 4TH HONOR ROLL, INDEPENDENCE, IA. AN HONOR ROLL OF PERSONS LIVING IN INDEPENDENCE & BUCHANAN COUNTY BORN ON JULY 4TH, SPECIAL ATTENTION WILL BE GIVEN TO THE YOUNGEST & THE OLDEST. (LOCAL). BARBARA DOGE, CHAIRPERSON; INDEPENDENCE BICENTENNIAL COMMISSION; 314 7TH ST SE; INDEPENDENCE, IA 50644. (#24355).

MINIATURE DOLL HOUSE CHANCES - INDEPENDENCE, IA. DOLL HOUSE WILL BE MADE AS A GROUP PROJECT AND CHANCES SOLD ON IT TO RAISE MONEY FOR ANOTHER BICENT PROJECT. (LOCAL). PAT KENSLER, CHAIRMAN; BETA SIGMA PHI SORORITY; ROUTE 1; INDEPENDENCE, IA 50644. (#25458).

OUTDOOR SCIENCE LAB, INDEPENDENCE, IA. LAB FOR ELEMENTARY SCIENCE CLASS; TO INCLUDE WEATHER AND AIR POLLUTION STATIONS, SUNDIAL, SHALLOW POND AND WILDLIFE SHELTER. (LOCAL). LEANNE HARRISON, CO-CHAIRMAN; BUCH COUNTY BICENTENNIAL COMMITTEE; 604 5TH AVE SW; INDEPENDENCE, IA 50644. (#19681).

PARKING METERS - INDEPENDENCE, IA. REPLACED OLDER DAMAGED METER HEADS WITH NEW RED, WHITE & BLUE HEADS IN DOWNTOWN INDEPENDENCE. (LOCAL). LEANNE HARRISON, CO-CHAIRMAN; INDEPENDENCE BICENTENNIAL COMMITTEE; 604 5TH AVE SW; INDEPENDENCE, IA 50644. (#21988).

PLANT TREES - INDEPENDENCE, IA. REPLACE THE DEAD ELM TREES IN INDEPENDENCE PARKS. (LOCAL). JO ENGEN, CHAIRMAN; BETA SIGMA PHI SORORITY; 812 1ST ST E; INDEPENDENCE, IA 50644. (#25457).

RESTORATION OF FIRST CEMETERY IN BUCHANAN CO, IOWA. REPAIR HEADSTONES, FENCE AREA OF CEMETERY, CLEAN & REPLANT GROUNDS. (LOCAL). LEANNE HANISON, PRESIDENT; BUCHANAN COUNTY BICENTENNIAL COMMISSION; 604 5TH AVE SW; INDEPENDENCE, IA 50644. (#5235).

RESTORATION OF LIBRARY IN INDEPENDENCE, IA. BUILT IN 1898, THIS 3 STORY LIBRARY IS BEING RESTORED AND REMODELED ON THE INSIDE. (LOCAL). LEANNE HARRISON, CO-CHAIRMAN; BUCH COUNTY BICENTENNIAL COMMITTEE; 604 5TH AVE SW; INDEPENDENCE, IA 50644. (#19678).

STORE FRONT RESTORATION, INDEPENDENCE, IA. RESTORATION OF BUSINESS BUILDINGS ON MAIN ST AND THROUGHOUT THE CITY. EMPHASIS IS PLACED ON ORIGINAL ARCHITECTURAL DESIGN OF PAST. (LOCAL). LEROY GREENLEY, COORDINATOR; INDEPENDENCE AREA CHAMBER OF COMMERCE; 210 6TH AVE NE; INDEPENDENCE, IA 50644. (#24359).

WOODEN NICKELS FROM INDEPENDENCE, IA. WOODEN NICKEL WITH MAP OF IOWA & BUCHANAN COUNTY AND BICENTENNIAL DATES ON IT. (LOCAL). LEANNE HARRISON, CO-CHAIRWOMAN; BUCHANAN COUNTY BICENTENNIAL; 604 5TH AVE SW; INDEPENDENCE, IA 50644. (#24465).

JULY 4 - 6, '75. 4TH OF JULY CELEBRATION. HORSESHOE TOURNAMENT, TRACTOR PULL, GREYHOUND DOG RACES, ART SHOW, A CERAMIC SHOW, MUSEUM, FAMILY PICNICS PLUS LUNCH STANDS, PARADE, CANO E RACES ON RIVER, KID GAMES & RACES, FIREWORKS AT STATE MENTAL HOSPI TAL W OF INDEPENDENCE. AT PARADE - MAIN STREET; CANOE RACE - RIVER;. (LOCAL). CHAMBER OF COMMERCE; BICENTENNIAL GROUP EVERY ORGANIZATION IN TOWN; INDEPENDENCE, IA 50644. (#50044-1).

JAN 1 - DEC 31, '76. PICTORIAL CONTEST. THE PICTORIAL CONTEST WILL FEATURE LOCAL POINTS OF INTEREST; THE PICTURES WILL BE PRESENTED IN THE COUNTY NEWSPAPER. (LOCAL). LEANNE HARRISON, CHAIRMAN; BUCHONAN COUNTY BICENTENNIAL COMMISSION & HISTORICAL SOCIETY; 604 5TH AVE SW; INDEPENDENCE, IA 50644. (#104519-8).

APR 10 - 11, '76. ANTIQUE SHOW. EXHIBIT AT MIDDLE SCHOOL GYMNASIUM. (LOCAL). LEANNE HARRISON, PROJ DIR; INDEPENDENCE AREA CHAMBER OF COMMERCE; 604 5TH AVE SW; INDEPENDENCE, IA 50644. (#200018-80).

APR 14 - 15, '76. BICENTENNIAL WAGON TRAIN PILGRIMAGE. FESTIVAL, PARADE AT BUCHANAN COUNTY FAIRGROUNDS AND JEFFERSON HIGH SCHOOL. (LOCAL). BARBARA DODGE, CHMN; INDEPENDENCE BICENTENNIAL COMMISSION; 314 7TH ST SE; INDEPENDENCE, IA 50644. (#200018-81).

JULY 2 - 4, '76. 4TH OF JULY CELEBRATION. THE FOLLOWING EVENTS WILL BE INCLUDED IN THE FESTIVAL: ART SHOW, DOG RACES, CANOE RACES, PARADE, HANDICRAFTS OF DAYS GONE BY, AUTO RACES AND FIREWORKS AT MHI STATE HOSPITAL. AT BUCHANAN CO FAIRGROUNDS AND MAIN STREET. (LOCAL). BARBARA DODGE, CHMN; KIWANIS CLUB & INDEPENDENCE BICENTENNIAL COMMISSION; 314 7TH ST SE; INDEPENDENCE, IA 50644. (#106926-1).

AUG 4 - 7, '76. BUCHANAN COUNTY FAIR. THERE WILL BE 4-H EXHIBITS, AUTO RACES, FOOD BOOTHS, FLORAL DISPLAYS AND CRAFT DISPLAYS. AT FAIRGROUNDS, N OF INDEPENDENCE. (ST-WIDE). HERSCHEL BLACK, SECRETARY; BUCHANAN COUNTY FAIRBOARD; INDEPENDENCE, IA 50644. (#106893-1).

INDIANOLA

AEROSPACE EDUCATION, COLLEGE COURSE, INDIANOLA, IA. CREDIT-3 SEMESTER HOURS; HISTORY, AVIATION & SPACE EXPLORATION; PRINCIPLES OF FLIGHT; FUTURE OF AVIATION, AIRWAYS, AIRPORTS & FLIGHT CONTROL, EDUCATION'S ROLE & RESPONSIBILITY IN AEROSPACE. (ST-WIDE). EG BOOTH, CHAIRMAN, DEPARTMENT OF EDUCATION; SIMPSON COLLEGE; INDIANOLA, IA 50125. (#19726).

AMERICAN STUDIES ACADEMIC PROGRAM - INDIANOLA, IA. THIS PROGRAM IN THE COLLEGE EMPHASIZES THE EARLY PERIOD IN AMERICAN HISTORY. (LOCAL). DONALD KOONTZ, ASSISTANT TO PRESIDENT; HISTORY & AMERICAN STUDIES DEPT OF SIMPSON COLLEGE; INDIANOLA, IA 50125. (#16748).

BICENTENNIAL REPRINT SERIES - INDIANOLA, IA. THE SIMPSON COLLEGE NEWSPAPER WILL REPRINT HISTORICAL ARTICLES AND NOTES. (LOCAL). DONALD KOONTZ, ASSISTANT TO PRESIDENT; SIMPSON COLLEGE; INDIANOLA, IA 50125. (#16750).

BICENTENNIAL SPEECHES, COLLEGE COURSE, IA. RE-CREATION OF BICENTENNIAL SPEECHES; 3 SEMESTER HOURS CREDIT, RECREATE 30 FAMOUS SPEECHES, ESSAYS, AND SERMONS; TEN SPECIAL MOVIES. (LOCAL). DOUGLAS LARCHE, INSTRUCTOR; SIMPSON COLLEGE, DEPT OF SPEECH COMMUNICATIONS & FORENSICS; INDIANOLA, IA 50125. (#19727).

CHAUTAUQUA ASSEMBLY ON THE AMERICAN EXPERIMENT, IA. DURING SUMMER OF 1976, CHAUTAUQUA WILL DISCUSS ASSESSMENT & EVALUATION OF PAST & FUTURE. (LOCAL). ASSISTANT TO THE PRESIDENT'S OFFICE; SIMPSON COLLEGE; INDIANOLA, IA 50125. (#23550). **ARBA GRANTEE.**

MUSEUM FOR WARREN COUNTY HISTORICAL SOCIETY, IA. A MUSEUM TO HOUSE & PRESERVE HERITAGE OF WARREN COUNTY, OPEN TO STUDENTS & TO BE OPEN AT SPECIFIC TIMES TO THE GENERAL PUBLIC. (LOCAL). CHARLES BEAM, PRESIDENT; WARREN COUNTY HISTORICAL SOCIETY; 310 W BOSTON; INDIANOLA, IA 50125. (#23506). **ARBA GRANTEE.**

NATIONAL BALLOON MUSEUM, INDIANOLA, IN. A NATIONAL BALLOON MUSEUM WILL BE BUILT IN INDIANOLA, WHERE THE NATL BALLOON CHAMPIONSHIPS ARE HELD YEARLY. THE MUSEUM WILL ALSO HOUSE THE OFFICES OF BALLOON FEDERATION. (LOCAL). JO MAYNARD, TREASURER; INDIANOLA BALLOONS, INC; INDIANOLA, IA 50125. (#20466). **ARBA GRANTEE.**

NEW PHYSICAL EDUCATION CENTER - SIMPSON COL, IA. THE NEW FACILITY CONTAINS A POOL, TENNIS COURTS AND OTHER ATHLETIC EQUIPMENT AS WELL AS CLASSROOMS. (LOCAL). DONALD KOONTZ, ASSISTANT TO PRESIDENT; SIMPSON COLLEGE; INDIANOLA, IA 50125. (#16752).

PRESERVATION OF HISTORICAL DOCUMENTS - IA. THE COLLEGE WILL PUT ALL OF ITS MAJOR HISTORICAL DOCUMENTS ON MICROFILM. (LOCAL). DONALD KOONTZ, ASSISTANT TO PRESIDENT; SIMPSON COLLEGE; INDIANOLA, IA 50125. (#16749).

20TH CENTURY TIME CAPSULE - INDIANOLA, IA. THE SIMPSON COLLEGE WILL PREPARE A TIME CAPSULE WITH SOCIAL AND CULTURAL ITEMS RELEVANT TO OUR TIME TO BE VIEWED BY FUTURE GENERATIONS. (LOCAL). DONALD KOONTZ, ASSISTANT TO PRESIDENT; SIMPSON COLLEGE; INDIANOLA, IA 50125. (#16751).

JUNE 3 - 6, '76. CHAUTAUQUA OF WARREN COUNTY. PRODUCED BY CAROUSEL THEATRE, PRESENTATIONS WILL BE LOCAL TALENT & WILL BE BASED ON INTERESTING ERAS IN OUR HISTORY. AT WARREN COUNTY FAIRGROUNDS. (ST-WIDE). MRS SHARI VAIL, CHAIRMAN; WARREN COUNTY BICENTENNIAL COMMISSION; 1306 W CLINTON; INDIANOLA, IA 50125. (#104884-1).

AUG 6 - 13, '76. U S NATIONAL HOT-AIR BALLOON CHAMPIONSHIP. HOT-AIR BALLOONS LAUNCHING FROM AND FLYING OVER SIMPSON COLLEGE IN COMPETITION FOR THE TITLE OF NATIONAL CHAMPION BALLOONIST; OVER 200 FIVE STORY TALL BALLOONS WERE ON HAND. AT SIMPSON COLLEGE CAMPUS. (NAT'L). GARY L RUBLE, PROJ DIR; INDIANOLA BALLOONS, INC/ CHAMBER OF COMMERCE; 201 W SALEM; INDIANOLA, IA 50125. (#20466-1).

AUG 8 - 11, '76. CHAUTAUQUA ASSEMBLY ON THE AMERICAN EXPERIMENT. SEMINAR AT BLANK PERFORMING ARTS CENTER ON SIMPSON CAMPUS. (LOCAL). ASST TO PRESIDENT OFFICE; SIMPSON COLLEGE; SIMPSON COLLEGE; INDIANOLA, IA 50125. (#23550-1).

INWOOD

COMMUNITY DEVELOPMENT - INWOOD, IA. THE INWOOD COMMUNITY IS FORMING A BETTERMENT COMMITTEE TO ASSIST IN FUTURE PLANNING FOR THE AREA. (LOCAL). HARVEY VAN ENGEN, CHAIRMAN; COMMUNITY BETTERMENT COMMITTEE; INWOOD, IA 51240. (#17630).

FLAG FLOWER BED - INWOOD, IA. THE FLOWER BED IS TO BE PLANTED FOR THE BICENTENNIAL. (LOCAL). LESLIE R KUIKEN, CHAIRMAN-BICENT COMMITTEE; KIWANIS CLUB; INWOOD, IA 51240. (#17629).

PLAYS WITH HISTORICAL THEMES. LIVE PERFORMANCE. (LOCAL). LESLIE R KUIKEN, COORD; INWOOD BICENTENNIAL COMMITTE; BOX 67; INWOOD, IA 51240. (#103361-4).

JULY 4 - 7, '76. 4TH OF JULY CELEBRATION. FESTIVAL AT INWOOD PARK. (LOCAL). LESLIE R KUIKEN, CHAIRMAN; INWOOD COMMERCIAL CLUB; BOX 67; INWOOD, IA 51240. (#103361-2).

IONIA PARK

JUNE 19, '76. IONIA DAYS. FESTIVAL AT TOWN HALL. (LOCAL). GLADYS DIESBURG, CHAIRMAN; IONIA DEVELOPMENT COMMITTEE; IONIA, IA 50645. (#200018-261).

IOWA CITY

BICENTENNIAL PLAYBILL IN IOWA CITY, IA. THE UNIVERSITY THEATER WILL PERFORM A SERIES OF PLAYS FROM THE HERITAGE OF THE AMERICAN THEATRE. (LOCAL). D C SPRIESTERBACH, PROJ DIRECTOR; UNIV OF IOWA BICENTENNIAL COMMITTEE; 210 H GILMORE HALL; IOWA CITY, IA 52242. (#11804).

FOLK FAIR - PROJ OF UNIV OF IOWA. PROJECT WILL INCLUDE AN AMERICAN FOLK MUSIC FESTIVAL AND AN EXHIBIT OF FOLK CRAFTS. (LOCAL). D C SPRIESTERSBACH, CHAIRMAN; UNIV OF IOWA BICENTENNIAL COMMITTEE; 210 H GUILMORE HALL; IOWA CITY, IA 52242. (#11789).

THE HISTORY OF HYDRAULICS IN THE U S-IOWA CITY, IA. A HISTORY OF THE DEVELOPMENT OF HYDRAULIC ENGINEERING IN THE USA WILL BE WRITTEN BY HUNTER ROUSE. (ST-WIDE). D C SPRIESTERBAUCH, CHAIRMAN; UNIV OF IOWA BICENTENNIAL COMMITTEE; 210 H GILMORE HALL; IOWA CITY, IA 52242. (#11787).

HISTORY OF WOMEN IN THE AMERICAN REVOLUTION - IA. A BOOK DESCRIBING THE ROLE WOMEN PLAYED IN THE AMERICAN REVOLUTION WILL BE WRITTEN BY PAUL ENGLE. (ST-WIDE). D C SPRIESTERSBACH, CHAIRMAN; UNIV OF IOWA BICENTENNIAL COMMITTEE; 210 H GUILMORE HALL; IOWA CITY, IA 52242. (#11788).

INSTITUTE AFRO-AMERICAN CULTURE 1880-1915 SEMINAR. LECTURERS AND TEACHERS IN AFRO-AMERICAN STUDIES GATHER TO EXAMINE TEXTS & FILMS & TO PARTICIPATE IN SEMINARS AND EXCHANGE INFORMATION AND RESOURCES. DIFFERENT TOPIC EACH SUMMER. (NAT'L). DARWIN T TURNER, CHAIRMAN; AFRO-AMERICAN PROGRAM, UNIV OF IOWA; ENGLISH-PHILOSOPHY BLDG; IOWA CITY, IA 52240. (#3923).

JUNIOR HIGH SOCIAL STUDIES FAIR. COMPETITION, FAIR. (LOCAL). DON FETT, DIRECTOR; SOCIAL STUDIES DEPT IOWA CITY SCHOOLS; 1040 WILLIAMS ST; IOWA CITY, IA 52240. (#107893-1).

MICRO-FILMING IOWA CITY NEWSPAPERS, IA. IOWA CITY IS MICRO-FILMING NEWSPAPERS FROM 1876 TO 1929. (LOCAL). MAUREEN MOSES, REFERENCE LIBRARIAN; IOWA CITY PUBLIC LIBRARY; 307 E COLLEGE; IOWA CITY, IA 52240. (#12516). **ARBA GRANTEE.**

NAVAJO WEAVING EXHIBIT IN IOWA CITY, IA. IN HONOR OF THE BICENTENNIAL, THERE WILL BE A DISPLAY OF NAVAJO WEAVING. (LOCAL). D C SPRIESTERBAUCH, CHAIRMAN; UNIV OF IOWA BICENTENNIAL COMMITTEE; 210H GILMORE HALL; IOWA CITY, IA 52242. (#11806).

OLD CAPITOL RESTORATION PROJECT OF IOWA. RESTORE THE 1840 THIRD TERRITORIAL AND FIRST STATE CAPITOL ON THE UNIVERSITY OF IOWA CAMPUS, USING ORIGINAL FURNISHINGS AND EQUIPMENT OF THE 1840-1857 PERIOD. (ST-WIDE). DR MARGARET KEYES, DIRECTOR; OLD CAPITOL RESTORATION COMMITTEE; 101 OLD CAPITOL, UNIV OF IOWA; IOWA CITY, IA 52242. (#202). **ARBA GRANTEE.**

ORAL HISTORY OF THE IOWA LABOR MOVEMENT. AN ORAL HISTORY OF THE IOWA LABOR MOVEMENT BY PROMINENT LABOR LEADERS-IOWA FEDERATION OF LABOR AND THE AFL-CIO COOPERATING. (ST-WIDE). EDGAR CZARNECKI, DIRECTOR; CENTER OF LABOR AND MANAGEMENT; UNIV OF IOWA; GREENFIELD, IA 52242. (#3758).

PHOTOGRAPHIC COLLECTION OF IOWA CITY, IA. 100 OLD SCENES OF IOWA CITY AND JOHNSON COUNTY FROM THE COLLECTION OF FRED KENT, REPRODUCED AS PRINTS AND SLIDES, AVAILABLE TO THE COMMUNITY. (LOCAL). MAUREEN MOSES,

IOWA CITY — CONTINUED

REFERENCE LIBRARIAN; IOWA CITY PUBLIC LIBRARY; 307 E COLLEGE; IOWA CITY, IA 52240. (#12513). **ARBA GRANTEE.**

A PHOTOGRAPHIC STUDY OF RAILROAD DEPOTS IN IOWA. RAILROAD DEPOTS WERE VERY IMPORTANT IN RURAL IA LIFE. TODAY THEY ARE RAPIDLY DISAPPEARING. PROJECT IS TO PHOTOGRAPH ALL REMAINING DEPOTS. PHOTOS WILL BE EXHIBITED STATEWIDE, PUBLISHED & PRESERVED. (ST-WIDE). JAMES K BERANEK, PHOTOGRAPHER; 639 MAYFLOWER APRARTMENTS; IOWA CITY, IA 52240. (#20583).

RENOVATION OF 1856 CHURCH, IOWA CITY, IA. PRESERVATION AND RENOVATION OF CHURCH WITH HISTORIC AND ARCHITECTURAL SIGNIFICANCE. (LOCAL). ROBERT FOSTER, CAMPUS PASTOR; LUTHERAN CAMPUS COUNCIL; 124 CHURCH; IOWA CITY, IA 52240. (#19699).

RESEARCH ON CARL BECKER, AMER REVOLUTION EXPERT. ACQUIRE INFORMATION ON IOWAN EXPERT ON AMERICAN REVOLUTIONARY PERIOD FOR IOWA HISTORICAL SOCIETY FILES AND PUBLICATIONS. (ST-WIDE). PETER T HARSTAD, DIRECTOR; STATE HISTORICAL SOCIETY OF IOWA; 402 IOWA AVE; IOWA CITY, IA 52240. (#208). **ARBA GRANTEE.**

SPACE EQUIPMENT EXHIBIT IN IOWA CITY, IA. A COLLECTION OF SPACE EQUIPMENT AND SATELLITE MODELS DEVELOPED AT UNIV OF IOWA WILL BE SENT ON A TOUR OF THE STATE. (ST-WIDE). D C SPRIESTERBAUCH, CHAIRMAN; UNIV OF IOWA BICENTENNIAL COMMITTEE; 210H GILMORE HALL; IOWA CITY, IA 52242. (#11805).

STATE HISTORICAL SOCIETY ART PROJECT - IA. CLEAN AND RESTORE PAINTINGS IN THE HOLDINGS OF THE STATE HISTORICAL SOCIETY. (ST-WIDE). PETER HARSTAD, DIRECTOR; STATE HISTORICAL SOCIETY OF IOWA; 402 IOWA AVE; IOWA CITY, IA 52240. (#27332). **ARBA GRANTEE.**

JUNE 16 - 27, '75. INSTITUTE AFRO-AMERICAN CULTURE 1880-1915. LECTURERS AND COLLEGE TEACHERS IN AFRO-AMERICAN STUDIES EXAMINE TEXTS, FILMS TO PARTICIPATE IN SEMINARS AND EXCHANGE INFORMATION AND RESOURCES EVENING LECTURES OPEN FREE TO PUBLIC DIFFERENT TOPIC EACH SUMMER. AT IOWA MEMORIAL UNION UNIVERSITY OF IOWA. (REGN'L). DARWIN T TURNER, CHRMN; NEH AND AFRO-AMERICAN STUDIES UNIVERSITY OF IOWA; 303 EPB UNIVERSITY OF IOWA; IOWA CITY, IA 52242. (#3923-1).

OCT 29 - 30, '75. UNITED STATES ARMED FORCES BICENTENNIAL CARAVAN. THE CARAVAN IS COMPOSED OF EXHIBIT VANS FOR EACH BRANCH OF THE MILITARY SERVICE. THE THEME OF THE EXHIBITION IS 'HISTORY OF THE ARMED FORCES AND THEIR CONTRIBUTION TO THE NATION'. (LOCAL). JACQUELYN MCCARTHY, CHMN; JOHNSON COUNTY BICENTENNIAL COMMISSION; 809 EDGEWATER DR; CORALVILLE, IA 52241. (#1775-222).

APR 8 - 10, '76. STUDENT 8MM FILM FESTIVAL. 1ST ANNUAL STUDENT 8MM FILM FESTIVAL. NATIONAL BICENTENNIAL THEMES ARE BEING USED AS ENTRY CATEGORIES: HERITAGE 76, FESTIVAL USA & HORIZONS 76. (ST-WIDE). KIMM STASTNY; IOWA EDUCATIONAL MEDIA ASSOC; 4401 6TH ST, SW; CEDAR RAPIDS, IA 52406. (#104020-18).

APR 9 - MAY 25, '76. 'BETWEEN TRADITIONS: NAVAJO WEAVING TOWARD THE END OF 19TH CENT'. EXHIBIT. (REGN'L). JAN MUHLERT, DIRECTOR; UNIV OF IOWA, MUSEUM OF ART; IOWA CITY, IA 52242. (#6548-501).

APR 19 - 25, '76. IOWA CITY BICENTENNIAL WEEK. ACTIVITIES INCLUDE A HIGH SCHOOL MUSIC FESTIVAL, CHILDREN'S ART CONTEST, PROGRAM ON WOMEN IN THE REVOLUTION, PUPPET SHOWS AND CONCERTS. EVENTS PLANNED AT A NUMBER OF INDOOR LOCATIONS, AS WELL AS THE MINI-PARK. THEME: 'A BEGINNING - NOT AN END'. AT MINI-PARK AT DUBUQUE & WASHINGTON STREETS IN BUSINESS DISTRICT. (ST-WIDE). JULIE ZELENKA, DIRECTOR; CITY OF IOWA CITY & IOWA CITY CHAMBER OF COMMERCE; 410 E WASHINGTON ST; IOWA CITY, IA 52240. (#104020-5).

APR 25, '76. EXHIBIT OF F W KENT PHOTO COLLECTION. EXHIBIT AT LIBRARY AUDITORIUM, COLLEGE & LINN ST. (LOCAL). MARY BURTON; IOWA CITY PUBLIC LIBRARY; 307 E COLLEGE ST; IOWA CITY, IA 52440. (#200018-82).

JUNE 4 - 7, '76. FOLK FAIR. FAIR. (LOCAL). D C SPRIESTERSBACH, CHMN; UNIV OF IOWA BICENTENNIAL COMMITTEE; ZIOH GILMORE HALL; IOWA CITY, IA 52242. (#100427-1).

JULY 3 - 5, '76. FOLK ART DEMONSTRATION AND SHOW. OUTDOOR ETHNIC MUSIC FESTIVAL AND INDOOR ART EXHIBITS INCLUDING SINGING, INSTRUMENTALS, DANCES, STORY-TELLING, QUILTING, NEEDLEWORK, MAKING CORNHUSK DOLLS AND POTTERY, WEAVING AND CREATION OF CEREMONIAL INDIAN GARMENTS. AT OLD CAPITAL BUILDING SITE. (LOCAL). HARRY OSTER, COORD; THE UNIVERSITY OF IOWA; ENGLISH 370 EPB; IOWA CITY, IA 52242. (#105644-1).

JULY 4, '76 - DEC 31, '77. GRAND OPENING OF RESTORED OLD CAPITOL IN IOWA CITY. OPEN ON SATURDAYS 10:00AM TO 5:00PM & SUNDAYS FROM 1:00PM TO 5:00PM. CLOSED LABOR DAY, THANKSGIVING, CHRISTMAS & MEMORIAL DAY. RESERVATIONS REQUIRED FOR SPECIAL TOURS ONLY. AT CAMPUS AREA OF THE OLD CAPITOL. (ST-WIDE). DR MARGARET KEYES; OLD CAPITOL RESTORATION COMMITTEE; 101 OLD CAPITOL; IOWA CITY, IA 52242. (#202-1).

NOV 6 - DEC 19, '76. 'TUNISIAN MOSAICS' EXHIBITION. THIS EXHIBITION OF 20 MOSAICS FROM THE ROMAN, VANDAL & BYZANTINE PERIODS REVEALS ASPECTS OF EVERYDAY LIFE DURING THOSE TIMES. AT UNIVERSITY OF IOWA. (INT'L). EILEEN HARAKAL, COORD; SMITHSONIAN INSTITUTION TRAVELING EXHIBITION SERVICE; 1000 JEFFERSON DR, SW; WASHINGTON, DC 20560. (#26667-2).

NOV 9 - 10, '76. LONDON PHILHARMONIC ORCHESTRA VISITS IOWA CITY. LIVE PERFORMANCE AT HANCHER AUDITORIUM. (INT'L). CULTURAL AFFAIRS OFFICE; BRITISH EMBASSY; 3100 MASSACHUSETTS AVE, NW; WASHINGTON, DC 20008. (#108958-3).

IOWA FALLS

AVENUE OF FLAGS - PROJ OF IOWA FALLS, IA. AN AVENUE OF FLAGS COMMEMORATING SERVICEMEN. (LOCAL). ALLAN POOL, CHAIRMAN; THE 320 CORPORATION OF IOWA FALLS; IOWA FALLS, IA 50126. (#13900).

BUILDING RESTORATION - PROJ OF IOWA FALLS, IA. THE MET THEATER WILL BE RESTORED. (LOCAL). ALLAN POOL, CHAIRMAN; THE 320 CORPORATION OF IOWA FALLS; IOWA FALLS, IA 50126. (#13898).

HISTORICAL MARKERS - PROJ OF IOWA FALLS, IA. LOCATING & MARKING OF LOCAL HISTORICAL SITES. (LOCAL). ALLAN POOL, CHAIRMAN; THE 320 CORPORATION OF IOWA FALLS; IOWA FALLS, IA 50126. (#13901).

SYMBOLISM IN THE AMERICAN LANDSCAPE - IA. THE COURSE WILL SURVEY A HISTORICAL AND LITERARY RECORD OF THE PHYSICAL AND PERCEPTUAL TRANSFORMATION OF THE 'AMERICAN LANDSCAPE' FROM A NEW WORLD TO A TECHNOLOGICAL HABITAT. (LOCAL). JAMES C GINKEL, INSTRUCTOR; ELLSWORTH COMMUNITY COLLEGE; 1100 COLLEGE AVE; IOWA FALLS, IA 50126. (#17641).

'SYMBOLISM IN THE AMERICAN LANDSCAPE' - IA. THE ELLSWORTH COMMUNITY COLLEGE IS OFFERING A COURSE ENTITLED 'SYMBOLISM IN THE AMERICAN LANDSCAPE'. (LOCAL). JAMES C GINKEL, INSTRUCTOR; ELLSWORTH COMMUNITY COLLEGE; IOWA FALLS, IA 50126. (#31276).

TIME CAPSULE - PROJ OF IOWA FALLS, IA. A VAULT WILL BE CONSTRUCTED TO HOLD PRESENT DAY ARTICLES. IT WILL BE OPENED IN 2076. (LOCAL). ALLAN POOL, CHAIRMAN; THE 320 CORPORATION OF IOWA FALLS; IOWA FALLS, IA 50126. (#13899).

VOICES FROM THE PAST - IOWA FALLS, IA. HISTORICAL AND PERSONAL RECOLLECTIONS OF AREA SENIOR CITIZENS; TAPED INTERVIEWS EVENTUALLY WILL BE EDITED AND TRANSCRIBED INTO A PERMANENT COLLECTION. (LOCAL). ROBERT J MYERS, CHAIRMAN, FINE ARTS DEPT; ELLSWORTH COMMUNITY COLLEGE; 1100 COLLEGE AVE; IOWA FALLS, IA 50126. (#17640).

'VOICES FROM THE PAST' - IOWA FALLS, IA. HISTORICAL AND PERSONAL RECOLLECTIONS OF AREA SENIOR CITIZENS WILL BE TAPED AND TRANSCRIBED. (LOCAL). ROBERT J MYERS, CHAIRMAN; ELLSWORTH COMMUNITY COLLEGE; 1100 COLLEGE AVE; IOWA FALLS, IA 50126. (#31277).

FEB 23, '76. EDUCATION FAIR. DISPLAYS AND DEMONSTRATIONS OF HISTORAL CRAFTS. DEMONSTRATIONS DESIGNED TO SHOW THAT AMERICANS CAN STILL LIVE & WORK WITH THE SKILLS USED BY OUR FOREFATHERS. AT ELLSWORTH COMMUNITY COLLEGE CAMPUS, 1100 COLLEGE AVE. (LOCAL). DUANE LLOYD, CHAIRMAN; ELLSWORTH COMMUNITY COLLEGE; 1100 COLLEGE AVE; IOWA FALLS, IA 50126. (#200018-285).

MAR 23, '76. HISTORIC FASHION REVIEW. THIS SHOW WILL TRACE TRENDS AND DEVELOPMENTS IN FEMININE FASHION OF THE NATION'S FIRST LADIES THROUGH TIMES OF EXTREME PATRIOTISM, ECONOMIC CRISIS, PROSPERITY, WAR, AND ACTIVE FEMINISM. AT ELLSWORTH COMMUNITY COLLEGE CAMPUS, 1100 COLLEGE AVE. (LOCAL). DUANE LLOYD, CHAIRMAN; ELLSWORTH COMMUNITY COLLEGE; 1100 COLLEGE AVE; IOWA FALLS, IA 50126. (#200018-286).

APR 8, '76. IOWA FALLS HISTORY - SLIDE & TAPE SHOW. A SLIDE SHOW AND ORAL PRESENTATION OF THE PAST HISTORY OF IOWA FALLS. AT ELLSWORTH COMMUNITY COLLEGE CAMPUS, 1100 COLLEGE AVE. (LOCAL). DUANE LLOYD, CHAIRMAN; ELLSWORTH COMMUNITY COLLEGE; 1100 COLLEGE AVE; IOWA FALLS, IA 50126. (#200018-288).

APR 23 - 24, '76. 'THE WHITE HOUSE' A DRAMATIC PRODUCTION. A TWO ACT PLAY BY A E HOTCHNER FEATURING SCENES FROM THE LIVES OF VARIOUS UNITED STATES PRESIDENTS, BEGINNING WITH JOHN ADAMS AND CONCLUDING WITH WOODROW WILSON. AT ELLSWORTH COMMUNITY COLLEGE CAMPUS, 1100 COLLEGE AVE, IOWA FALLS IA. (LOCAL). DUANE LLOYD, DIRECTOR; ELLSWORTH COMMUNITY COLLEGE; 1100 COLLEGE AVE; IOWA FALLS, IA 50126. (#103364-3).

MAY 10, '76. COMMUNITY BAND CONCERT. LIVE MUSIC FROM THE PARK BANDSTAND, PATRIOTIC, OLD TIME, FROM FIDDLES TO FLUTES, BANJOS TO BRASS ALL PERFORMED FOR THE PLEASURE OF ALL. AT ESTES PARK, ESTES AND STEVENS STS. (LOCAL). DAN PEASE, CHAIRMAN; ELLSWORTH COMMUNITY COLLEGE; 1100 COLLEGE AVE; IOWA FALLS, IA 50126. (#200018-287).

JULY 2, '76. IOWA FALLS FARM FESTIVAL 1776-1976. ELLSWORTH COMMUNITY COLLEGE LIVE ANIMAL MEAT EVALUATION CLINIC FOR 4H AND FFA JUDGING TEAMS, ELLSWORTH COMMUNITY COLLEGE TOURS, FARM EQUIPMENT EXHIBITS - PAST AND PRESENT, NOON BARBECUE-NOMINAL CHARGE. AT ELLSWORTH COMMUNITY COLLEGE CAMPUS, 1100 COLLEGE AVENUE. (ST-WIDE). DUANE LLOYD, DIRECTOR; ELLSWORTH COMMUNITY COLLEGE AND IOWA FALLS BICENTENNIAL CORPORATION; 1100 COLLEGE AVE; IOWA FALLS, IA 50126. (#103364-2).

JULY 4, '76. ARMORY DEDICATION. DEDICATION OF THE NEW IOWA GUARD ARMORY BUILDING; WEEKLONG FESTIVITIES STARTING JUNE 27TH WITH AN ECUMENICAL SERVICE AND CONCLUDING SUNDAY, JULY 4TH WITH A FIREWORKS DISPLAY. MANY ACTIVITIES INCLUDING: VENETIAN PARADE, SKI SHOW, & BAND CONCERT WITH J C PENNY MUSIC. (ST-WIDE). ALLAN POOL, CHMN; THE 320 CORPORATION OF IOWA FALLS; BOX 1776; IOWA FALLS, IA 50126. (#101385-1).

OCT 25, '76. THE OLD ORDER AMISH - LIVE PERFORMANCE. LIVE PERFORMANCE AT ELLSWORTH COMMUNITY COLLEGE CAMPUS, 1100 COLLEGE AVE. (LOCAL). DUANE LLOYD, CHAIRMAN; ELLSWORTH COMMUNITY COLLEGE; 1100 COLLEGE AVE; IOWA FALLS, IA 50126. (#200018-289).

NOV 8, '76. POETRY OF THE CIVIL WAR. A POETRY READING RELATING TO THE CIVIL WAR; SLIDES, ARTIFACTS AND MUSIC OF THE ERA WILL ALSO BE INCLUDED. AT ELLSWORTH COMMUNITY COLLEGE CAMPUS, 1100 COLLEGE AVE. (LOCAL). DUANE LLOYD, DIRECTOR; ELLSWORTH COMMUNITY COLLEGE; 1100 COLLEGE AVE; IOWA FALLS, IA 50126. (#109495-1).

IRETON

CEMETERY IMPROVEMENT PROJECT, IRETON, IA. PLANTING OF BETWEEN 50 AND 100 NEW SHRUBS AND TREES ALONG CEMETERY BOUNDARIES; NEW BRICK GATEPOSTS AT ALL FOUR CEMETERY ENTRANCES; NEW BRICK SIGN WITH CEMETERY NAME INSET IN MARBLE ON SE CORNER. (LOCAL). MRS MABEL TWILLMAN, DIRECTOR; IRETON SENIOR CITIZENS; 506 MAIN ST; IRETON, IA 51027. (#19846).

JUNE 22 - 23, '76. HERITAGE SHOW - GENERAL EXHIBIT OF ANTIQUES & COMMUNITY MEMORABILIA. EXHIBIT. (LOCAL). BUD KEMPER, CHAIRMAN; IRETON BICENTENNIAL COMMITTEE; 306 ELM; IRETON, IA 51027. (#104581-1).

JUNE 22 - 23, '76. RCA APPROVED RODEO. COMPETITION, LIVE PERFORMANCE. (LOCAL). BUD KEMPER, CHAIRMAN; IRETON BICENTENNIAL COMMITTEE; 306 ELM; IRETON, IA 51027. (#104581-2).

JUNE 23, '76. BICENTENNIAL PARADE. PARADE AT 8TH AND MAIN, TO 2ND AND MAIN. (LOCAL). BUD KEMPER, CHAIRMAN; IRETON BICENTENNIAL COMMITTEE; 306 ELM; IRETON, IA 51027. (#104581-3).

IRWIN

COMMUNITY KEEN-AGERS CENTER - IRWIN, IA. A CENTER IS BEING ESTABLISHED FOR OLDER CITIZENS OF THE AREA. (LOCAL). RICHARD L SORENSEN, PRESIDENT; KEEN-AGERS; MAIN ST; IRWIN, IA 51446. (#25415).

JEFFERSON

DOWNTOWN RESTORATION PROJ OF JEFFERSON, IOWA. RESTORATION OF DOWNTOWN STORE AND BUSINESS DISTRICT WITH REPAIRS, PAINT, AND NEW FRONTS. WILL ALSO INCLUDE REPLACEMENT OF OLD PAVED STREETS AND SIDEWALKS. (LOCAL). HAROLD WOODRUFF, CHAIRMAN; DOWNTOWN RESTORATION ASSOC; 100 N WILSON; JEFFERSON, IA 50129. (#9419).

GREENE COUNTY HISTORICAL SOCIETY, JEFFERSON, IA. BUILDING TO HOUSE AND DISPLAY ANTIQUE MACHINERY AND FARMING EQUIPMENT. (LOCAL). HAROLD D RADEBOUGH, PRESIDENT; GREENE COUNTY BICENTENNIAL COMMITTEE; 106 E STATE; JEFFERSON, IA 50129. (#19694).

HISTORICAL LINCOLN HIWAY MARKING PROGRAM OF IOWA. DESIGNATION AND ENDORSEMENT OF OLD HIWAY 30-LINCOLN HIGHWAY. (ST-WIDE). DR J K JOHNSON, JR, PRESIDENT; LINCOLN HIWAY HISTORICAL SOCIETY; 306 W LINCOLN WAY; JEFFERSON, IA 50129. (#3669).

MARKING HISTORICAL SITES IN GREENE COUNTY, IA. MARKING AND MAPPING SITES OF HISTORICAL INTEREST INCLUDING EARLY SETTLER CABINS, THE STAGE COACH TRAIL FROM DES MOINES TO SOUIX CITY, OLD CEMETERIES & CHURCHES. (ST-WIDE). FRED E MORAIN, PRESIDENT; GREENE COUNTY BICENTENNIAL COMMISSION; 214 N WILSON AVE; JEFFERSON, IA 50129. (#18731).

PLANTING OF 17,760 TREES IN GREENE COUNTY, IOWA. THE PLAN IS TO PLANT 17,760 TREES IN GREENE COUNTY DURING THE BICENTENNIAL ERA. (LOCAL). DR J K JOHNSON JR, CHMN; GREENE COUNTY BICENT COMMITTEE; 306 W LINCOLN WAY; JEFFERSON, IA 50129. (#9418).

STORE FRONT RESTORATION PROJ - JEFFERSON, IA. PROJECT IS NEW & RESTORED DOWNTOWN STOREFRONTS. (LOCAL). MRS JOYCE SNAKENBURG, PROJ DIRECTOR; DOWNTOWN RESTORATION COMMITTEE; JEFFERSON, IA 50129. (#18142).

JUNE 20, '76. BICENTENNIAL ROSE SHOW. EXHIBIT AT JEFFERSON STATE BANK. (ST-WIDE). WILLIAM C OSTLUND, DIR; JEFFERSON ROSARIANS; 204 N WILSON; JEFFERSON, IA 50129. (#103413-1).

JULY 4, '76. 4TH OF JULY CELEBRATION. FESTIVAL, PARADE. (LOCAL). WILLIAM C OSTLUND, DIR; JEFFERSON JAYCEES; 204 N WILSON; JEFFERSON, IA 50129. (#103639-1).

JESUP

ADDITION TO SENIOR CITIZENS' HOUSING, JESUP, IA. 4 ADDITIONAL APARTMENTS TO BE COMPLETED & OCCUPIED IN SENIOR CITIZENS' HOUSING COMPLEX. (LOCAL). WARREN COLLINS, CHAIRMAN; SENIOR CITIZENS HOUSING, INC; JESUP, IA 50648. (#26829).

FLAG POLE - JESUP, IA. AMERICAN FLAG POLE WILL BE ERECTED IN JESUP PARK TO BE USED FOR IOWA AND BICENTENNIAL FLAGS. (LOCAL). RICHARD YOUNT, CHAIRMAN; LIONS CLUB, AMERICAN LEGION & JAYCEES; JESUP, IA 50648. (#26830).

JESUP — CONTINUED

MEDICAL CLINIC, JESSUP, IA. MEDICAL CLINIC BUILDING TO BE COMPLETED & STAFFED. (LOCAL). MARSHALL GROSSCUP, CHAIRMAN; JESUP BICENTENNIAL COMMITTEE; JESUP, IA 50648. (#26828).

APR 14, '76. WAGON TRAIN PRESENTATION TO IOWA WAGON. LEATHER MAP OF IOWA SHOWING THE WAGON TRAIN ROUTE THROUGH IOWA WILL BE PRESENTED TO THE DRIVER OF THE IOWA WAGON. (LOCAL). MARK PODHAJSKY, COORD; JESUP BICENTENNIAL COMMITTEE; JESUP, IA 50648. (#108469-1).

JULY 14 - 15, '76. SPIRIT OF '76 FARMERS DAY CELEBRATION. PROGRAM WITH PATRIOTIC MOTIF WILL INCLUDE FLAG PRESENTATION, FIREWORKS, PARADE, STREET GAMES, FLOWER AND PRODUCE SHOW. (LOCAL). MARK PODHAJSKY, COORD; JESUP BICENTENNIAL COMMITTEE; JESUP, IA 50648. (#108469-2).

KALONA

KALONA CITY PARK - KALONA, IA. A SWIMMING POOL AND BALL DIAMONDS WILL BE BUILT. (LOCAL). MRS JOHN WOODIN, PROJ DIRECTOR; CITY OF KALONA; CITY HALL; KALONA, IA 52247. (#19835).

KALONA HISTORICAL VILLAGE, KALONA, IA. HISTORICAL BUILDINGS & ARTIFACTS, SOME BASED ON MENNONITE CULTURE, PRESERVED FOR FUTURE GENERATIONS. (LOCAL). MRS JOHN WOODIN, PROJ DIRECTOR; KALONA HISTORICAL SOCIETY; KALONA, IA 52247. (#19836).

KALONA RECEPTION CENTER, IA. PRESERVED OLD JUNIOR HIGH SCHOOL TO BE USED AS CENTER FOR TEENAGERS, SENIOR CITIZENS, SCOUTS & TTHER COMMUNITY ACTIVITIES, WILL ALSO HOUSE COMMUNITY LIBRARY & SMALL THEATER GROUP. (LOCAL). MRS JOHN WOODIN, PROJ DIRECTOR; CITY OF KALONA; CITY HALL; KALONA, IA 52247. (#19834).

APR 15 - OCT 15, '76. KALONA HISTORICAL SOCIETY TOURS. TOUR OF MENNONITE FARMS, HOMES & BUSINESSES. (LOCAL). MRS WILLIS GINGERICH, DIR; KALONA HISTORICAL SOCIETY & MENNONITE HISTORICAL SOCIETY; 502 7TH; KALONA, IA 52247. (#104577-1).

APR 17, '76. THE IOWA AMISH. COOPERATIVE PROJECT WITH UNIV OF IOWA ENDOWMENT FOR HUMANITIES. ALSO TOUR OF KALONA AREA, IN COOPERATION WITH HISTORICAL SOCIETY. AT JR HIGH SCHOOL. (LOCAL). JIM FRIER; WASHINGTON COUNTY BICENTENNIAL COMMITTEE; BOX 29; WASHINGTON, IA 53353. (#104081-15).

SEPT 23 - 25, '76. FALL FESTIVAL. EVENT CELEBRATING MENNONITE CULTURE & KALONA HERITAGE; ALL-DAY TOURS OF MUSEUM WILL BE PROVIDED. (LOCAL). MRS JOHN WOODIN, CHMN; KALONA HISTORICAL SOCIETY & MENNONITE HISTORICAL SOCIETY; KALONA, IA 52247. (#104577-2).

KAMRAR

NEW PARK - KAMRAR, IA. NEW PARK WITH BELLTOWER, FLAGPOLE AND PLAYGROUND EQUIPMENT IS BEING ESTABLISHED; TREES AND FLOWERS WILL BE PLANTED. (LOCAL). MRS BERNARD KLAVER, BICENTENNIAL CHAIRMAN; JEWELL BICENTENNIAL COMMITTEE; RR #2; JEWELL, IA 50130. (#24638).

JULY 3, '76. 'AMERICA WE ARE, THEN AND NOW, AND IN THE FUTURE'. A FESTIVAL CELEBRATION WITH A COMMEMORATIVE BANQUET AND PAGEANT IS PLANNED. (LOCAL). MRS BERNARD KLAVER, CHMN; JEWELL BICENTENNIAL COMMITTEE; RR #2; JEWELL, IA 50130. (#108235-1).

KELLERTON

JULY 6 - 24, '76. BICENTENNIAL SKIT. THE FUTURE HOMEMAKERS OF AMERICA WILL PERFORM SKIT, IN COSTUME, FROM THE PIONEER TO THE ASTRONAUT. 7/6 AT ELLSTON, 7/24 MT AYR. (LOCAL). MRS GARY ROUDYBUSH, ADV; FUTURE HOMEMAKERS OF AMERICA & GRAND VALLEY COMMUNITY SCHOOL; KELLERTON, IA 50133. (#108048-1).

KELLEY

FLAG POLE, STREET SIGNS, FLOWERS & HISTORY BOOK-IA. FLAG WILL BE RAISED IN THE PARK, SIGNS WILL BE PLACED AROUND KELLEY, FLOWERS WILL BE PLANTED AT PARK AND AT FIREHOUSE AND BOOK ON HISTORY OF KELLEY WILL BE PUBLISHED. (LOCAL). MRS KAY FINCH, SECRETARY; KELLEY CENTENNIAL COMMITTEE; RRI; KELLEY, IA 50134. (#25984).

JULY 9 - 11, '76. TOWN CELEBRATION. FESTIVAL, PARADE. (LOCAL). MRS KAY FINCH, CHAIRMAN; KELLEY BICENTENNIAL COMMITTEE; RR 1; KELLEY, IA 50320. (#108411-1).

KENSETT

PRESERVING OUR NATIONAL HERITAGE - KENSETT, IA. RESTORATION AND PRESERVATION OF ORIGINAL LOG CABIN AND FURNISHINGS. (LOCAL). MRS DORIS HOLSTAD, COORDINATOR; FRIENDSHIP GARDEN CLUB; RR 1; KENSETT, IA 50448. (#24142).

MAR 31, '76. KENSETT COMMUNITY BICENTENNIAL PICNIC, KIDDY PARADE & GAMES. FESTIVAL, PARADE AT KENSETT COMMUNITY PARK. (LOCAL). JANICE TAYLOR, CHAIRMAN; KENSETT COMMUNITY CLUB; KENSETT, IA 50448. (#200018-90).

KENT

BICENTENNIAL PRESENTATION OF CENTENNIAL FLAG. COMMUNITY PICNIC, PROGRAM & PRESENTATION OF FLAG; U S FLAG PRESENTED TO CITY PARK, ALSO BUILDING A NEW CITY HALL, PART OF KENT CELEBRATION. INCLUDED IS KENT IS ANNUAL PICNIC. (LOCAL). ALFRED LUCAS, CHAIRMAN; KENT BICENTENNIAL COMMITTEE; KENT, IA 50850. (#200018-253).

KEOKUK

HISTORICAL ARCHITECTURAL SURVEY, KEOKUK, IA. RECORD BY PICTURES AND SURVEY, DATA ON CENTURY OLD BUILDINGS AND SITES. (LOCAL). JANE M KERR, PRESIDENT; LEE COUNTY IOWA HISTORICAL SOCIETY; 318 N 5TH ST; KEOKUK, IA 52632. (#17483).

MICROFILM OF COURT AND CHURCH RECORDS, KEOKUK, IA. MICROFILM OF CHURCH AND COURT RECORDS TO BE PROVIDED FOR THE AREA. (LOCAL). JANE KERR, PRESIDENT; LEE COUNTY HISTORICAL SOCIETY; 318 N 5TH ST; KEOKUK, IA 52632. (#14508).

PICTORIAL APPOINTMENT CALENDAR, KEOKUK, IA. A COLLECTION OF ORIGINAL ART WORK IN VARIOUS MEDIA, EXECUTED BY AREA ARTISTS AND REPRODUCED IN BLACK AND WHITE. THE PLATES ARE BOTH HISTORIC & CONTEMPORARY AND ARE BEING MAILED NATIONALLY & ABROAD. (ST-WIDE). ALICE R BOWERS, PRESIDENT; KEOKUK ART CENTER; 9-1/2 7TH, BOX 862; KEOKUK, IA 52632. (#15300).

RESTORATION PROJECT - KEOKUK, IA. THE HISTORIC MILLER BROWN HOUSE MUSEUM, NATIONAL REGISTER LANDMARK, WILL BE RESTORED. (LOCAL). JANE M KERR, PRESIDENT; LEE COUNTY HISTORICAL SOCIETY; 318 N 5TH ST; KEOKUK, IA 52632. (#16767).

RURAL SCHOOL EXPERIENCE, KEOKOK, IA. 3RD & 5TH GRADE STUDENTS WILL ATTEND A RURAL SCHOOL. (LOCAL). LUCRETIA CRAW, CHAIRMAN; KEOKUK COMMUNITY SCHOOL DISTRICT; 813 BLONDEAU ST; KEOKUK, IA 52632. (#14506).

'STORY OF EARLY KEOKOK', BOOK, KEOKOK, IA. THE AUTHOR OF 'STORY OF KEOKOK' IS A LOCAL GIRL; STUDENTS WILL ILLUSTRATE AND BIND THE BOOK. (LOCAL). LUCRETIA CRAW, PROJ COORDINATOR; KEOKOK COMMUNITY SCHOOL DISTRICT; 813 BLONDEAU ST; KEOKOK, IA 52632. (#14507).

THREE PANEL MURAL, KEOKUK, IA. THREE MONTAGE PAINTINGS IN OIL, EACH SECTION MEASURING NINE BY THIRTEEN FEET. JOHN WHEAT, THE ARTIST HAS PORTRAYED THREE DIFFERENT PERIODS OF HISTORY DATING FROM 18TH CENTURY TO THE PRESENT. (LOCAL). WILLIAM LOGAN, PRESIDENT; STATE CENTRAL SAVINGS BANK; 605 MAIN ST; KEOKUK, IA 52632. (#15299).

JUNE 8, '75. ART IN THE PARK. EXHIBIT AT RAND PARK. (LOCAL). ALICE BOWERS, COORD; KEOKUK ART CENTER; 1 MAHASKA RD; KEOKUK, IA 52632. (#200018-85).

JAN 15, '76. THE LAST KING OF AMERICA FILM PRESENTATION. EXHIBIT AT HERITAGE CENTER, 508 MAIN ST, KEOKUK, IA 52632. (LOCAL). JANE M KERR, PRESIDENT; LEE COUNTY HISTORICAL SOCIETY; 425 JACKSON ST; WARSAW, IL 63279. (#102993-1).

OCT 1 - 3, '76. PUCK E SHE TUCK DAYS CELEBRATION. FESTIVAL, PARADE AT HERITAGE CENTER 500 MAIN. (LOCAL). DON TILLETT, DIR; KEOKUK COMMUNITY BETTERMENT COMMITTEE; 210 N 5TH ST; KEOKUK, IA 52632. (#102644-2).

KEOSAUQUA

BICENTENNIAL MEMORIAL PARK - KEOSAUQUA,IA. A PERMANENT BICENTENNIAL MEMORIAL PARK IS BEING BUILT NEXT TO THE PUBLIC LIBRARY BY THE KEOSAUQUA COMMUNITY. (LOCAL). TED WATSON OR LIBBY WOODRUFF, CO-CHAIRMEN; VAN BUREN COUNTY DEVELOPMENT ASSOC; 101 VAN BUREN ST; KEOSAUQUA, IA 52565. (#21404).

COUNTY CONSERVATION BOARD PROJECTS- IA. VAN BUREN COUNTY CONSERVATION BOARD HAS ACQUIRED AND RESTORED SEVERAL HISTORIC BUILDINGS AND HAS ACQUIRED AND IS MAINTAINING THREE PARKS AND TWO MUSEUMS. (ST-WIDE). LIBBY WOODRUFF OR TED WATSON; VAN BUREN COUNTY CONSERVATION BOARD; KEOSAUQUA, IA 52565. (#15833).

HISTORIC SITES INVENTORY OF VANBUREN COUNTY, IOWA. UPDATING INVENTORY - HISTORIC SITES IN VANBUREN COUNTY. (LOCAL). CLAY LANMAN, CHAIRMAN; VANBUREN COUNTY BICENTENNIAL COMMISSION; KEOSAUQUA, IA 52565. (#3675). **ARBA GRANTEE.**

VAN BUREN COUNTY BICENTENNIAL SINGERS, IA. THE BICENTENNIAL SINGERS WILL SPECIALIZE IN HISTORIC MUSIC. (LOCAL). LIBBY WOODRUFF, PROJ DIRECTOR; VAN BUREN COUNTY DEVELOPMENT ASSOCIATIONS; 101 VAN BUREN ST; KEOSAUQUA, IA 52565. (#12404). **ARBA GRANTEE.**

JUNE 26 - JULY 4, '76. VAN BUREN COUNTY BICENTENNIAL FESTIVAL. SERIES OF PLAYS, PAGEANTS, ARTS & CRAFTS EXHIBITS AND HISTORIC TOURS DEPICTING EARLY IOWA HISTORY IN VAN BUREN COUNTY. AT EACH TOWN IN VAN BUREN COUNTY. (LOCAL). LIBBY WOODRUFF, CO-CHMN; VAN BUREN COUNTY DEVELOPMENT ASSOC; 101 1/2 VAN BUREN ST; KEOSAUQUA, IA 52565. (#103717-3).

KESLEY

PLANTING TREES - KESLEY, IA. LOCAL PEOPLE WILL ORDER TREES TO BE PLANTED BY THE LION'S CLUB TO REPLACE TREES DESTROYED BY DUTCH ELM DISEASE. (LOCAL). ART DAHN, PROJ DIRECTOR; KESLEY LIONS CLUB; KESLEY, IA 50649. (#21989).

JUNE 18, '75. KESLEY BICENTENNIAL '75. FESTIVAL, PARADE AT MAIN ST. (LOCAL). ART DAHN, COORDINATOR; KESLEY BUSINESSMEN; KESLEY, IA 50649. (#200018-89).

KEYSTONE

CATALOGUE OF CEMETERIES - KEYSTONE, IA. NAMES ON GRAVESTONES COPIED & A MAP MADE FOR THE COUNTY. ALL INFORMATION CATALOGUED. (LOCAL). MAXINE WALTERS, COORDINATORS; KEYSTONE BICENTENNIAL COMMITTEE; KEYSTONE, IA 52249. (#30163).

FIRING RANGE, KEYSTONE, IA. A FIRING RANGE FOR GUN ENTHUSIASTS WILL BE DEVELOPED. (LOCAL). DON ANDREWS, COORDINATOR; OPTIMIST CLUB; 302 2ND AVE; KEYSTONE, IA 52249. (#24353).

HISTORICAL PLANTER - KEYSTONE, IA. BELL FROM OLD FIRE STATION WILL BE MOUNTED IN A BRICK PLANTER BESIDE TOWN HALL. (LOCAL). JOHN BRADY, PROJ COORDINATOR; KEYSTONE VOLUNTEER FIRE DEPT; KEYSTONE, IA 52249. (#24352).

LIBRARY EQUIPMENT - KEYSTONE, IA. PURCHASE EQUIPMENT SUCH AS TAPE RECORDER & MICROFILM READER FOR THE LIBRARY. (LOCAL). MAXINE WALTERS, CHAIRMAN; KEYSTONE BICENTENNIAL COMMITTEE; KEYSTONE, IA 52249. (#24351).

LOCAL HISTORY PROJECT, KEYSTONE, IA. PROJECT INCLUDES MICROFILMED COPIES OF OLD KEYSTONE NEWSPAPERS, TAPE RECORDINGS OF OLDER CITIZEN'S HISTORICAL RECOLLECTIONS & SCRAPBOOK & WRITTEN HISTORY OF COMMUNITY. (LOCAL). MRS RICHARD OEHLERICH, PROJ COORDINATOR; LUTHEREAN CHURCH; 202 2ND AVE; KEYSTONE, IA 52249. (#24354).

JUNE 5, '76. BICENTENNIAL CELEBRATION. LOCAL BICENTENNIAL CELEBRATION WITH PARADE, ANNUAL CHILDREN'S DAY, EXHIBITS, CONCESSIONS AND DANCES FOR CHILDREN, TEENS AND ADULTS. (LOCAL). MAXINE WALTERS, CHMN; BICENTENNIAL COMMITTEE; KEYSTONE, IA 52249. (#106934-1).

JULY 4, '76. SPECIAL INDEPENDENCE DAY CHURCH SERVICE-LUTHERAN CHURCH. CEREMONY AT LUTHERAN CHURCH, 201 4TH AVE. (LOCAL). REV DONALD BERG; LUTHERAN CHURCH; 201 4TH AVE; KEYSTONE, IA 52249. (#106935-1).

KIMBALLTON

PROGRESSIVE DANES PROJECT, KIMBALLTON, IA. BUILDING TENNIS AND BASKETBALL COURTS. PAINTING AND FIXING BONEHURST. (ST-WIDE). CLOLD FARLEY, CHAIRPERSON; PROGRESSIVE DANES; KIMBALLTON, IA 51543. (#23182).

JUNE 4 - 6, '76. COMMUNITY FESTIVAL. FOLK DANCING, STYLE SHOW, CRAFTS FAIR, SPORTS. AT TOWN HALL/ATHLETIC FIELD/ CITY PARK/CHURCH. (LOCAL). CLOID FARLEY; PROGRESSIVE DANES; KIMBALLTON, IA 51543. (#106396-1).

DEC 12, '76. CHRISTMAS FESTIVITIES. BEAUTY PAGEANT, NOV 27TH, CHRISTMAS PARTY, DEC 12TH, FOR YOUTH AND ADULTS WHERE ABELSKIVER WILL BE SERVED. AT TOWN HALL. (LOCAL). CLOID FARLEY, CHMN; PROGRESSIVE DANES; KIMBALLTON, IA 51543. (#106417-1).

KINGSLEY

COMMEMORATIVE PINS IN KINGSLEY, IOWA. SELLING COMMEMORATIVE PINS OF BICENTENNIAL AS A MONEY-MAKING EFFORT. PINS WILL DEPICT A LOCAL HISTORICAL MILL. (LOCAL). JAMES H WATKINS, CHAIRMAN; KINGSLEY BICENTENNIAL COMMITTEE; 314 BURLINGTON; KINGSLEY, IA 51028. (#21391).

FILMS ON KINGSLEY DIAMOND JUBILEE - KINGSLEY, IA. SHOWING OF FILMS OF OUR DIAMOND JUBILEE CELEBRATION IN 1959. (LOCAL). H V ANDERSON, EDITOR; KINGSLEY NEWS-TIMES; 324 RUTLAND; KINGSLEY, IA 51028. (#21390).

MAKING TAPES IN KINGSLEY, IA. TAPING OF EXPERIENCES OF EARLY DAY RESIDENTS ABOUT LOCAL HISTORY. (LOCAL). DOUG BAKER, PRESIDENT; HISTORICAL SOCIETY; 28 W 2ND; KINGSLEY, IA 51028. (#21389).

PLANTING TREES IN KINGSLEY, IA. PLANTING A 'LIBERTY' TREE IN CITY PARK AND OTHER TREES. (LOCAL). MRS LOU MEISTER, PRESIDENT; KINGSLEY GARDEN CLUB; 323 E 3RD; KINGSLEY, IA 51028. (#21388).

RESTORING OLD LAND OFFICE IN KINGSLEY, IA. RESTORING CLOSE BROS LAND OFFICE AND HOTEL, LOCATED WEST OF CITY. (LOCAL). DOUG BAKER, PRESIDENT; HISTORICAL SOCIETY; 28 W 2ND; KINGSLEY, IA 51028. (#21387).

MAR 21, '76. BICENTENNIAL COMMUNITY CHORUS. CHOIR MEMBERS OF ALL CHURCHES IN KINGSLEY-PIERSON IN PATRIOTIC CONCERT. AT SCHOOL HOUSE. (LOCAL). REV EUGENE LINN, COORD; PASTORS ASSOCIATION; 119 W 2ND; KINGSLEY, IA 51028. (#105517-4).

MAR 21, '76. INTERFAITH RELIGIOUS SERVICE. A RELIGIOUS SERVICE FEATURING A PROGRAM WITH CHORAL AND GROUP SINGING. AT KINGSLEY-PIERSON GYM. (LOCAL). REV NORMAN MEYER, COORD; KINGSLEY MINISTERIAL ASSOC; 208 S MAIN; KINGSLEY, IA 51028. (#105313-4).

MAY 22, '76. MUSICAL PROGRAM BY SWEET ADELINES & CHORDSMEN GROUPS. LIVE PERFORMANCE AT SCHOOL GYM. (LOCAL). LORRAINE MCDERMOTT, PRES; ST MICHAEL'S GUILD; 405 BRANDON; KINGSLEY, IA 51028. (#105313-1).

KINGSLEY — CONTINUED

JULY 5, '76. OLD SETTLERS' PICNIC. SENIOR CITIZEN'S GROUP WILL SERVE FREE BEVERAGES AT SHELTER HOUSE. AT CITY PARK. (LOCAL). LOY BAKKEN, PRESIDENT; KINGSLEY COMMUNITY ACTION CLUB; 27 BAYARD; KINGSLEY, IA 51028. (#105313-3).

AUG 20, '76. BICENTENNIAL FLOWER SHOW - PIONEER PATHWAYS. EXHIBIT AT FIRST LUTHERAN CHURCH BASEMENT, KINGSLEY, IA. (LOCAL). MRS GEORGE ANDERSON, CHMN; KINGSLEY GARDEN CLUB; 101 W 4TH; KINGSLEY, IA 51028. (#105313-2).

KINROSS

JUNE 25 - JULY 3, '76. LITTLE LEAGUE BALL GAMES. BALL GAME FOLLOWED BY FLAG PRESENTATION PROGRAM W/NATIONAL ANTHEM, SPEECHES BY COUNTY CHAIRMAN & STATE SENATOR, VOCAL SOLOS, BENEDICTION, SOCIAL & REFRESHMENTS; 7/3: PARADE, GAMES, RACES, FIREWORKS, DANCE, PICK-UP & TRACTOR PULL. AT FORMER SCHOOL GROUNDS. (LOCAL). MRS ELVIN SHAFER, CHMN; KINROSS BALL TEAMS & THE TOWN COUNCIL; KINROSS, IA 52250. (#200018-293).

KNOXVILLE

COURTHOUSE LAWN BEAUTIFICATION - KNOXVILLE, IA. TREES AND SHRUBS WILL BE PLANTED ON THE COURTHOUSE LAWN AND BENCHES WILL BE INSTALLED. (LOCAL). CHARLES DAY JR, PROJ DIRECTOR; KNOXVILLE CHAMBER OF COMMERCE; KNOXVILLE, IA 50138. (#19797).

RECORDING OF MARION COUNTY CEMETERIES, IA. INFORMATION ON EVERY CEMETERY WILL BE COLLECTED, INFORMATION ON ALL HEADSTONES WILL BE RECORDED. ONE CEMETERY WILL BE SELECTED FOR PRESERVATION. (LOCAL). LOIS ATKINS, CHAIRMAN; MARION COUNTY GENEALOGICAL SOCIETY & PELLA BICENTENNIAL GROUP; 1017 W MARION ST; KNOXVILLE, IA 50138. (#22462).

WEST ELEMENTARY SCHOOL PROJECTS - KNOXVILLE, IA. A SERIES OF ACTIVITIES INCLUDING A TIME CAPSULE, LIBERTY TREE PLANTING AND FORMATION OF A JUNIOR CORRESPONDENCE CLUB. (LOCAL). MRS LOIS AKINS, CHAIRMAN; WEST ELEMENTARY SCHOOL; 1817 W MARION ST; KNOXVILLE, IA 50138. (#19798).

JUNE 14, '76. BICENTENNIAL FLAG DAY PARADE. PARADE AT HIGH SCHOOL STADIUM PARKING LOT TO TOWN SQUARE. (LOCAL). LOIS AKINS, CHAIRMAN; MARION COUNTY BICENTENNIAL COMMITTEE; 1017 W MARION ST; KNOXVILLE, IA 50138. (#200018-86).

JUNE 27, '76. BICENTENNIAL AWARDS & TALENT SHOW. SPONSORED BY KNIA RADIO, FARM BUREAU & COMMUNITY BETTERMENT COMMITTEE, PGM INCLUDES DISPLAYS, TALENT SHOW, CONTESTS. AT KNOXVILLE HIGH SCHOOL AUDITORIUM. (LOCAL). LOIS AKINS, CHAIRMAN; MARION COUNTY BICENTENNIAL COMMITTEE; 1017 W MARION ST; KNOXVILLE, IA 50138. (#200018-87).

JULY 19 - 23, '76. HISTORICAL EXHIBIT AT MARION COUNTY FAIR. DISPLAY OF FLAGS, REPRINTED 1881 HISTORY BOOK & BICENT JEWELRY. AT COUNTY FAIRGROUNDS. (LOCAL). LOIS AKINS, CHAIRMAN; BUSINESS WOMEN OF AMERICA, MARION CO GENEALOGICAL SOC & BICENT COM; 1017 W MARION ST; KNOXVILLE, IA 50138. (#105883-1).

SEPT 7 - 10, '76. TREE PLANTING CEREMONIES. 15 LIBERTY TREES WILL BE PLANTED, ONE FOR EACH OF THE 15 CLASSROOMS AT THE SCHOOL; EACH TREE WILL BE MARKED AND EACH CLASS WILL BE RESPONSIBLE FOR THEIR OWN TREE. AT WEST ELEMENTARY SCHOOL. (LOCAL). LOIS AKINS, CHAIRPERSON; WEST ELEMENTARY BICENTENNIAL COMMITTEE; 1017 W MARION ST; KNOXVILLE, IA 50138. (#108992-1).

OCT 7, '76. TIME CAPSULE BURIAL. CEREMONY AT KNOXVILLE HORMEL SAUSAGE PLANT. (LOCAL). LOIS AKINS, CHAIRPERSON; WEST ELEMENTARY BICENTENNIAL COMMITTEE; 1017 W MARION ST; KNOXVILLE, IA 50138. (#108992-2).

LA MOTTE

ECOLOGY IN ACTION, LA MOTTE, IA. TREE PLANTING IN CITY PARK AND ALONG CITY STREETS. (LOCAL). TONY TILL, PRESIDENT; LA MOTTE COMMUNITY CLUB; LA MOTTE, IA 52054. (#25297).

JULY 3 - 4, '76. LA MOTTE COMMUNITY PICNIC. THERE WILL BE A 4-H SHOW AT 9:00 AM, A PARADE AT 1:00 PM, HORSESHOE PITCHING, SOFTBALL GAME, TRAP SHOOT, TEEN DANCE, FOOD AND GAMES. AT LA MOTTE CITY PARK. (LOCAL). TONY TILL, COORD; LA MOTTE COMMUNITY CLUB; LA MOTTE, IA 52054. (#107993-1).

LA PORTE CITY

F F OF A, AGRICULTURE MUSEUM, LA PORTE CITY, IOWA. RESTORATION AND DISPLAY OF FARM EQUIPMENT AND FARM LIFE FROM EARLY SETTLERS TO MODERN DAY AND INTO THE FUTURE. (ST-WIDE). RONALD BORTON, ADVISOR; FUTURE FARMERS OF AMERICA, LA PORTE CITY CHAPTER; 413 CHESTNUT; LA PORTE CITY, IA 50651. (#2765). **ARBA GRANTEE.**

MAY 5, '76. LA PORTE CITY BICENTENNIAL CELEBRATION. FESTIVAL, PARADE AT CITYWIDE. (LOCAL). MURIEL WEATHERLY; LAPORTE CITY BICENTENNIAL COMMITTEE; 718 LOCUST; LAPORTE CITY, IA 50651. (#50691-1).

JUNE 4 - 5, '76. CAVALCADE OF AMERICAN MUSIC & CARNIVAL. EXHIBIT, FESTIVAL. (LOCAL). SONIA JOHANNSEN, COORD; LA PORTE CITY; 202 W MAIN ST; LA PORTE CITY, IA 50651. (#105260-1).

JUNE 5 - 6, '76. LAPORTE CITY BICENTENNIAL CELEBRATION. FESTIVAL. (LOCAL). CARL DAHL, CHMN; LAPORTE CITY BICENTENNIAL COMMITTEE; 12942 KOGER RD; LAPORTE CITY, IA 50651. (#106925-1).

LAKE CITY

RESTORATION OF COMMUNITY BUILDING - LAKE CITY, IA. THE COMMUNITY BUILDING IS BEING COMPLETELY REMODELED. A SENIOR CITIZENS ROOM, NEW KITCHEN & NEW REST ROOMS ARE BEING ADDED. (LOCAL). DENNIS SEMKE, COORDINATOR; HORIZONS COMMITTEE; 108 S CENTER; LAKE CITY, IA 51449. (#29165).

JULY 2 - 5, '76. ARTS & CRAFTS, STREET DANCE & FIREMANS' WATER FIGHTS. FESTIVAL AT CITY SQUARE, CITY PARK. (LOCAL). JIM BAUMAN, CHAIRMAN; LAKE CITY CIVIC GROUPS; 402 S MICHIGAN; LAKE CITY, IA 51449. (#200018-246).

LAKE MILLS

PATRIOTIC FLOWERBEDS - LAKE MILLS, IA. RED, WHITE AND BLUE ANNUALS WILL BE PLANTED IN THESE FLOWERBEDS. (LOCAL). PHYLLIS HELGESON, CHAIRMAN; WOMEN'S CLUB; 206 N OAK; LAKE MILLS, IA 50450. (#21766).

JUNE 6, '76. 1776 EPISCOPAL CHURCH SERVICE. CEREMONY AT LOCAL CHURCHES. (LOCAL). PASTOR DUWAYNE DALEN; ECUMENICAL COUNCIL; 401 S LAKE; LAKE MILLS, IA 50450. (#105618-1).

JUNE 7, '76. YESTERYEAR ARTIFACTS DISPLAY. EXHIBIT AT CIVIC CENTER. (LOCAL). ESTER JOHNSON, CHAIRMAN; LAKE MILLS SENIOR CITIZENS; 503 N 1ST AVE E; LAKE MILLS, IA 50450. (#105478-1).

JUNE 10, '76. 1776-PARADE AND ENTERTAINMENT. FESTIVAL AT LAKE MILLS COMMUNITY SCHOOL. (LOCAL). SYLVIA GULICK, DIRECTOR; CITY OF LAKE MILLS; 308 N 1S TAVE E; LAKE MILLS, IA 50450. (#105608-1).

LAKE PARK

ECOLOGY AND PRESERVATION - LAKE PARK, IA. PLANT 2 ACRES OF TREES ON OLD DUMP GROUND SITE. (LOCAL). WALTER J POLK, CHAIRMAN; LAKE PARK BICENTENNIAL COMMISSION/LAKE PARK LIONS CLUB; LAKE PARK, IA 51347. (#21994).

ERECTION OF 10 WOOD DUCK HOUSES - IA. BOY SCOUT PROJECT FOR EAGLE SCOUT BADGE IS TO BUILD AND ERECT 10 WOOD DUCK HOUSES. (LOCAL). WALTER J POLK, CHAIRMAN; LAKE PARK BICENTENNIAL COMMISSION; LAKE PARK, IA 51347. (#21995).

TREE PLANTING PROJECT OF LAKE PARK, IA. REPLACE DEAD AND DYING ELM TREES IN THE COMMUNITY AND PLANT ADDITIONAL TREES IN THE CITY PARK. (LOCAL). WESLEY LYNN, SECRETARY; LIONS CLUB; LAKE PARK, IA 51347. (#14521).

JULY 3, '76. BICENTENNIAL PARADE. 100 UNIT PARADE WITH WORLD WAR I & II VETERANS, FLOATS, BANDS & HORSES. AT MAIN ST. (LOCAL). WALTER J POLK, CHAIRMAN; LAKE PARK BICENTENNIAL COMMISSION; LAKE PARK, IA 51347. (#105769-3).

JULY 3, '76. FIRE WORKS, BALL GAME & DANCING IN THE STREETS. FESTIVAL AT CITY PARK, MAIN ST. (LOCAL). WALTER J POLK, CHAIRMAN; LAKE PARK BICENTENNIAL COMMISSION; LAKE PARK, IA 51347. (#105769-4).

JULY 3 - 5, '76. INDEPENDENCE WEEKEND CELEBRATION IN LAKE PARK. JULY 2ND, THEATER HOME TALENT SHOW AT HIGH SCHOOL AUDITORIUM; JULY 3RD, PARADE, ANTIQUE SHOW, WALKING FLOWER SHOW, BASEBALL GAMES, DANCING IN THE STREETS, OLD-TIME FIDDLER'S CONTEST, SQUARE DANCE; JULY 4TH, COMMUNITY CHURCH SERVICE AT CITY PARK & PICNIC. (LOCAL). MRS GLADYS SHAFER; LAKE PARK BICENTENNIAL COMMISSION; CHAMBER OF COMMERCE; LAKE PARK, IA 51347. (#14522-1).

JULY 4, '76. COMMUNITY CHURCH SERVICE AND PICNIC. CEREMONY, FESTIVAL AT CITY PARK. (LOCAL). WALTER J POLK, CHAIRMAN; LAKE PARK BICENTENNIAL COMMISSION; LAKE PARK, IA 51347. (#105769-2).

JULY 4, '76. 4TH OF JULY CELEBRATION. FESTIVAL, PARADE. (LOCAL). WALTER J POLK, CHMN; LAKE PARK BICENTENNIAL COMMITTEE; BOX 275; LAKE PARK, IA 51347. (#101903-1).

LAKE RATHBUN

JULY 4, '76. JULY 4TH CELEBRATION. FESTIVAL. (LOCAL). HAROLD E WATERS, CHMN; MONROE COUNTY ARBC; 107 S CLINTON ST; ALBIA, IA 52531. (#101392-1).

LAKE VIEW

PARK SHELTER HOUSE CONSTRUCTION, LAKE VIEW, IA. SHELTER HOUSE WILL BE BUILT FOR COMMUNITY USE. (LOCAL). ARLAN WOERDEHOFF, PRESIDENT; LAKE VIEW JAYCEES; LAKE VIEW, IA 51450. (#24458).

RESTORATION OF RAIL FENCE AROUND LOG CABIN, IA. REBUILD AND RESTORE AREA AROUND SAC COUNTIES OLDEST HOUSE, LOG CABIN BUILT IN EARLY 1800'S. (LOCAL). GARY KRUSE, SCOUT MASTER; BOY SCOUTS, TROOP 195; 622 HIGHWAY 71; LAKE VIEW, IA 51450. (#24457).

TREE PLANTING, LAKE VIEW, IA. PLANTING OF TREES IN THE LAKE VIEW COMMUNITY IS BEING PLANNED. (LOCAL). W K HUNTER, MEMBER; LAKE VIEW PARK BOARD; LAKE VIEW, IA 51450. (#24456).

JULY 18, '76. HISTORICAL BICENTENNIAL PAGEANT. THE EVENT WILL COMPLIMENT THE SUMMER CARNIVAL; THERE WILL BE PERFORMANCES IN THIS OPEN AIR THEATRE. AT STONE PIER. (LOCAL). SHIRLEY WALROD, CHMN; DRAMA CLUB; LAKE VIEW, IA 51450. (#106889-1).

LAKOTA

BEAUTIFICATION PROJECT - LAKOTA, IA. HISTORIC AND PATRIOTIC FLOWER GARDENS WILL BE PLANTED IN LOCAL PARKS AND HOUSING APARTMENTS. (LOCAL). MARY JANE BRACK, REPRESENTATIVE; LAKOTA GARDEN CLUB; LAKOTA, IA 50451. (#16777).

BICENTENNIAL DAY. FESTIVITIES WILL INCLUDE: PARADE, SPORTS EVENTS, CONTESTS & DINNER. (LOCAL). FRED MEEKER, CHMN; LAKOTA HIGH SCHOOL; LAKOTA, IA 50451. (#103048-4). **(??).**

HOUSING FOR THE ELDERLY - LAKOTA, IA. SAFE AND COMFORTABLE HOUSING IS NOW BEING MADE AVAILABLE TO THE SENIOR CITIZENS OF LAKOTA. (LOCAL). R E HERTZKE, PRESIDENT; LAKOTA HOUSING DEVELOPMENT CORP; PO BOX 3; LAKOTA, IA 50451. (#17098).

NATIONAL BICENTENNIAL NUTRITION PROJECT, IA. HISTORIC MENUS WITH APPROPRIATE DECORATION WILL BE PLACED IN CAFETERIAS ON APPROPRIATE OCCASIONS. (LOCAL). IRENE PETERSON, MANAGER; HOT LUNCH PERSONNEL FOR ELEMENTARY STUDENTS; LAKOTA, IA 50451. (#16776).

NEW MUSEUM IN LAKOTA, IA. SMALL BUILDING IN CITY PARK WILL BE CONVERTED TO DISPLAY ARTICLES OF HISTORICAL NATURE. (LOCAL). HELEN ELLSWORTH, PROJ DIRECTOR; ACORN CLUB; LAKOTA, IA 50451. (#16778).

PARKS IMPROVEMENT - LAKOTA, IA. THE OLD CITY DUMP AREA WILL BE REBUILT INTO A TRACK FOR ATHLETIC PROGRAMS, REST ROOMS WILL BE CONSTRUCTED AT THE BALL PARK AND EQUIPMENT WILL BE ADDED TO THE CITY PARK. (LOCAL). WM LARSON, REPRESENTATIVE; LAKOTA COMMUNITY CLUB; LAKOTA, IA 50451. (#16775).

JULY 4, '76. CHURCH BICENTENNIAL SUNDAY. THE LAKOTA BAPTIST CHURCH WILL OBSERVE BICENTENNIAL SUNDAY. (LOCAL). REV GLEN FINK, PASTOR; LAKOTA BAPTIST CHURCH; LAKOTA, IA 50451. (#103048-3).

LAMONI

BEAUTIFICATION & RESTORATION OF CEMETERY, IA. BEAUTIFICATION OF LAMONI CEMETERY TO INCLUDE PLANTING & LANDSCAPING. (LOCAL). MRS MARTHA SWANSON, CHAIRMAN; LIBERTY HALL COMMITTEE; LAMONI, IA 50240. (#20359).

LAMONI COMMUNITY CALENDAR, IA. AN ANNUAL CALENDAR OF COMMUNITY EVENTS WILL BE PUBLISHED. (LOCAL). MRS MARTHA SWANSON, CHAIRMAN; THE KALON CLUB; LAMONI, IA 50240. (#20358).

APR 26 - 30, '76. BICENTENNIAL FILMSTRIPS. THE LAMONI PUBLIC LIBRARY WILL SPONSOR A SERIES OF BICENTENNIAL SOUND FILMSTRIPS FOR CHILDREN. AT LAMONI PUBLIC LIBRARY. (LOCAL). HEIRESS EMSLIE; LAMONI PUBLIC LIBRARY; LAMONI PUBLIC LIBRARY; LAMONI, IA 50140. (#20360-1).

JULY 4, '76. JULY 4TH CELEBRATION. A 76 MILE BIKE RIDE. (LOCAL). WILL RAISER, CHAIRMAN; LAMONI CHAMBER OF COMMERCE; LAMONI, IA 50240. (#104768-1).

JULY 4, '76. '76 BIKE RIDE. A 76 MILE BIKE RIDE. (LOCAL). MRS MARTHA SWANSON, CHMN; LAMONI BICYCLE CLUB; LAMONI, IA 50240. (#104768-2).

LANGWORTHY

'HISTORY OF LANGWORTHY' - BOOK, IA. A HISTORY OF LANGWORTHY FROM ITS BEGINNING TO THE PRESENT. (LOCAL). ESTHER RIEDEL, CHAIRPERSON; TOWN OF LANGWORTHY; BOX 50; LANGWORTHY, IA 52252. (#23355).

NEW FLAGPOLE, LANGWORTH, IA. A FLAG POLE WILL BE PLACED IN THE TOWN PARK. (LOCAL). ESTHER RIEDEL, CHAIRPERSON; TOWN OF LANGWORTHY; BOX 50; LANGWORTHY, IA 52252. (#23354).

MAR 11 - JULY 6, '76. OLDER ARTS AND CRAFTS. ALL TOWNS IN JONES COUNTY ARE TAKING PART. AT CENTRAL PARK. (LOCAL). ESTHER RIEDEL, CHMN; JONES COUNTY; BOX 50; LANGWORTHY, IA 52252. (#106529-1).

LANSING

JULY 16 - 18, '76. ARTS & CRAFTS EXHIBIT AND ANTIQUE SHOW. EXHIBIT. (LOCAL). HARVEY HALVERSON, DIR; LANSING BICENTENNIAL COMMITTEE; LANSING, IA 52151. (#105946-2).

JULY 16 - 18, '76. BICENTENNIAL PARADE. PARADE. (LOCAL). HARVEY HALVERSON, DIR; LANSING BICENTENNIAL COMMITTEE; LANSING, IA 52151. (#105946-3).

LANSING — CONTINUED

JULY 16 - 18, '76. CEREMONY FOR OPENING OF RESTORED CEMETERY. CEREMONY. (LOCAL). HARVEY HALVERSON, DIR; LANSING BICENTENNIAL COMMITTEE; LANSING, IA 52151. (#105946-6).

JULY 16 - 18, '76. MISS BICENTENNIAL PAGEANT. COMPETITION, LIVE PERFORMANCE. (LOCAL). HARVEY HALVERSON, CHMN; LANSING BICENTENNIAL COMMITTEE; LANSING, IA 52152. (#105946-1).

JULY 16 - 18, '76. OPENING OF NEW FIRE STATION. OPENING. (LOCAL). HARVEY HALVERSON, DIR; LANSING BICENTENNIAL COMMITTEE; LANSING, IA 52151. (#105946-5).

JULY 16 - 18, '76. VENETIAN NIGHTS BICENTENNIAL. FESTIVAL, PARADE. (LOCAL). HARVEY HALVERSON, CHMN; LIONS' CLUB & BOOSTERS' CLUB; BOX 283; LANSING, IA 52151. (#104544-1).

LARCHWOOD

FLOWER PROJECT OF LARCHWOOD, IA. RED, WHITE & BLUE FLOWER BEDS WILL BE PLANTED. (LOCAL). JOE MCMARTIN, PROJ COORDINATOR; LARCHWOOD BICENTENNIAL & 4-H CLUB; LARCHWOOD, IA 51241. (#14520).

TREE PLANTING PROJECT OF LARCHWOOD, IA. TREES WILL BE PLANTED FOR THE BICENTENNIAL. (LOCAL). JOE MCMARTIN, PROJ COORDINATOR; LARCHWOOD BICENTENNIAL & 4-H CLUB; LARCHWOOD, IA 51241. (#14519).

FEB 29, '76. 'THE NAME OF GOLD GAY 90'S' - PLAY. FESTIVAL AT LARCHWOOD GYM. (LOCAL). JOE D MCMARTIN, CHMN; LARCHWOOD BICENTENNIAL COMMITTEE; 1315 E HOLDER ST; LARCHWOOD, IA 51241. (#200018-97).

MAR 27, '76. BICENTENNIAL SPRING FLING. DOOR PRIZES, FUN FOR ALL, FOODS IN RED, WHITE AND BLUE. AT LARCHWOOD GYM, MAIN ST. (LOCAL). MRS CAROL MILLER, CHMN; LARCHWOOD WOMEN'S CLUB; LARCHWOOD, IA 51241. (#200018-96).

MAR 27 - 30, '76. LARCHWOOD LIBRARY OPEN HOUSE. TOUR. (LOCAL). MRS CAROL MILLER, CHMN; LARCHWOOD WOMEN'S CLUB; LARCHWOOD, IA 51241. (#200018-95).

MAR 28, '76. LARCHWOOD BICENTENNIAL QUEEN CONTEST & TALENT SHOW. SENIOR KING & QUEEN, BICENTENNIAL QUEEN TO REPRESENT LARCHWOOD, JR PRINCE & PRINCESS TO BE CHOSEN. AT LARCHWOOD GYM, N MAIN ST. (LOCAL). BUD GROTEWOLD, COORD; LARCHWOOD BICENTENNIAL COMMITTEE; LARCHWOOD, IA 51241. (#105952-1).

APR 27, '76. '200 YRS - MOTHERS & DAUGHTERS FOR CHRIST' BANQUET. FESTIVAL AT LARCHWOOD GYM. (LOCAL). MRS PAUL HILDRING, COORD; GRANDVIEW COVENANT CHURCH; RR I; LARCHWOOD, IA 51241. (#106836-1).

JUNE 11 - 13, '76. OLD SETTLERS FESTIVAL WEEKEND. FESTIVITIES WILL INCLUDE: PICNIC; COMMUNITY RELIGION MEETING; TOUR OF OLDER FARMS AND OLD TIMERS PARADE. (LOCAL). JOE D MCMARTIN, CHMN; LARCHWOOD BICENTENNIAL COMMITTEE; 1315 E HOLDER ST; LARCHWOOD, IA 51241. (#101905-1).

JUNE 22, '76. 'LET'S MAKE A DEAL'. GAME WILL BE PLAYED IN THE SAME WAY AS THE TV 'LET'S MAKE A DEAL'. PARTICIPANTS WILL DRESS UP, CHOOSE A DOOR AND RECEIVE A PRIZE. AT LARCHWOOD PARK SHELTER. (LOCAL). JOE D MCMARTIN, CHAIRMAN; SIOUX SPIRITS 4-H CLUB; 1315 E HOLDER ST; LARCHWOOD, IA 51241. (#108049-1).

LAURENS

BICENTENNIAL ISSUE OF LAURENS SUN - LAURENS, IA. LOCAL NEWSPAPER'S WEEKLY ISSUE OF JULY 8, 1976 WILL HAVE A BICENTENNIAL THEME; IT WILL BE A KEEPSAKE EDITION FOR ALL PEOPLE OF POCAHONTAS COUNTY. (LOCAL). DAVID L EVANS, PUBLISHER; SUN PUBLISHING COMPANY; S 3RD ST; LAURENS, IA 50554. (#23149).

CARNEGIE LIBRARY COMMEMORATIVE TRAYS, LAURENS, IA. SALE OF TRAYS WAS BEGUN IN 1975 AND WILL CONTIUE UNTIL JULY 4 1976, AT WHICH TIME THE DIE WILL BE BROKEN. (LOCAL). MRS JOYCE RIGBY, DIRECTOR; LIBRARY FUND COMMITTEE; LAURENS, IA 50554. (#20489).

ESSAY CONTEST - LAURENS, IA. 6TH GRADE ESSAY CONTEST ON 'A PAST TO HONOR AND A FUTURE TO MOLD;' COUNTY-WIDE CONTEST. (LOCAL). MRS DOROTHY RUNNEBURG, CHAIRMAN; FEDERATED WOMEN'S CLUB; DIOXENS, IA 50554. (#20698).

SALE OF BICENTENNIAL MASON JARS, LAURENS, IA. FUND RAISING PROJECT JARS WILL BE FULL OF RED, WHITE AND BLUE CANDY OR BATH SALTS. (LOCAL). MRS DOROTHY RUNNEBERG, COORDINATOR; FEDERATED WOMENS CLUB; LAURENS, IA 50554. (#20490).

SALE OF BICENTENNIAL MEDALS - LAURENS, IA. BICENTENNIAL MEDALS ARE BEING SOLD TO HELP FINANCE BICENTENNIAL ACTIVITIES. THEY WERE DESIGNED BY LOCAL PEOPLE. (LOCAL). MRS RICHARD RIGBY, CHAIRPERSON; LAURENS BICENTENNIAL COMMISSION; 315 S 4TH ST; LAURENS, IA 50554. (#23148).

DEC 7, '75. BICENTENNIAL SMORGASBORD. FESTIVAL AT LEGION HALL, N FIRST ST. (LOCAL). MRS GEORGE BUCKWALTER; AMERICAN LEGION AUXILIARY; LAURENS, IA 50554. (#200018-98).

JAN 17 - DEC 31, '76. BICENTENNIAL DISPLAY IN STORE WINDOW. DISPLAY SPACE WILL BE AVAILABLE TO CLUBS OR INDIVIDUALS. AT MONTGOMERY WARD STORE WINDOW. (LOCAL). ARLEN GARTON, COORD; LAURENS BICENTENNIAL COMMISSION; 315 S 4TH ST; LAURENS, IA 50554. (#105959-3).

JAN 21, '76. JUNIOR GIRL SCOUT COURT OF AWARDS. AWARD AT LAURENS COMMUNITY SCHOOL. (LOCAL). MRS RON WALDSTEAD, DIR; GIRL SCOUTS; LAURENS, IA 50554. (#200018-100).

FEB 14, '76. BICENTENNIAL VALENTINE PARTY FOR SENIOR CITIZENS. FESTIVAL. (LOCAL). HARVEY BAKER, DIRECTOR; KIWANIS CLUB; LAURENS, IA 50554. (#104919-1).

FEB 25, '76. GIRL SCOUTS THINKING DAY. CEREMONY AT SCHOOL HOUSE. (LOCAL). MRS RON WALSTEAD, COORD; GIRL SCOUT TROOPS OF LAURENS; LAURENS, IA 50554. (#200018-101).

MAR 6, '76. COUNTRY CLUB MEETING & REUNION-BICENTENNIAL DRESS AND PROGRAM. CEREMONY AT TOWN HALL. (LOCAL). LORENA SERNETT, COORD; FRENDLY FRIDAY CLUB; LAURENS, IA 50554. (#200018-103).

MAR 23 - 24, '76. ANNUAL LIONS CLUB HOME TALENT SHOW. HOME TALENT SHOW WITH U S FLAG PRESENTATION ON TUES NIGHT; BICENTENNIAL DEDICATION ON WED NIGHT - THEME IS 'THE LAST 200 YEARS.'. AT HIGH SCHOOL AUDITORIUM. (LOCAL). JOE HUTCHINSON, COORD; LAURENS LIONS CLUB; LAURENS, IA 50554. (#200018-99).

MAR 24, '76. BICENTENNIAL FLAG DEDICATION. HELD IN CONJUNCTION WITH THE ANNUAL LAURENS LIONS CLUB SHOW. MR. MAURICE BARINGER, STATE TREASURER OF IOWA, WILL BE THE GUEST SPEAKER & PRESENT THE FLAG & CERTIFICATE. AT NEW PUBLIC LIBRARY. (LOCAL). ARLEN GARTON, SEC-TREAS; LAURENS BICENTENNIAL COMMISSION; 315 SO 4TH ST; LAURENS, IA 50554. (#105143-1).

APR 8, '76. PAST MASTERS NIGHT. CEREMONY AT MASONIC HALL. (LOCAL). RALPH HITCHCOCK; GRACE LODGE NO 519 AF & AM; 104 W MAIN ST; LAURENS, IA 50554. (#200018-102).

APR 25, '76. DEDICATION OF NEW LAURENS COMMUNITY LIBRARY. CEREMONY AT COMMUNITY LIBRARY BLDG AT N 3RD ST. (LOCAL). MRS JOYCE RIGBY, DIRECTOR; CITY OF LAURENS; RR; LAURENS, IA 50554. (#104919-2).

MAY 31, '76. MEMORIAL DAY PARADE AND SERVICE. CEREMONY AT LOCAL CEMETERY. (LOCAL). MRS G BUCKWALTER, COORD; AMERICAN LEGION AND AUXILIARY; LAURENS, IA 50554. (#105959-1).

JULY 10, '76. LAURENS HIGH SCHOOL ALUMNI REUNION. FESTIVAL AT LAURENS COMMUNITY SCHOOL. (LOCAL). MRS HERMAN RUBEL, COORD; LAURENS BICENTENNIAL COMMISSION; LAURENS, IA 50554. (#105143-2).

JULY 11, '76. AMERICAN HERITAGE MASS. CEREMONY AT CHURCH, 263 RALSTON ST. (LOCAL). LORENA SERNETT, COORD; SACRED HEART CATHOLIC CHURCH; 123 E SECTION LINE RD; LAURENS, IA 50554. (#200018-217).

JULY 11, '76. LAURENS CHAMBER OF COMMERCE APPRECIATION DAY CELEBRATION. FESTIVAL AT MAIN STREET. (LOCAL). ROBERT MATHER, COORD; CHAMBER OF COMMERCE; LAURENS, IA 50554. (#105959-2).

AUG 1, '76. SUN BONNET & STRAW HAT DAY. OLD FIDDLERS' CONTEST & ICE CREAM SOCIAL. AT 304 E VETERANS RD. (LOCAL). MRS VIRGENE BAILEY, COORD; GOOD SAMARITAN CENTER; 304 E VETERANS RD; LAURENS, IA 50554. (#109027-1).

LAWTON

JULY 4, '76. JULY 4TH CELEBRATION. FESTIVAL. (LOCAL). ROBERT E PETERS; JULY 4TH BICENTENNIAL COMMITTEE; BOX 8; LAWTON, IA 51030. (#107688-8).

LE CLAIRE

HERITAGE PROJECTS FOR LECLAIRE, IA. RESTORATION OF OLD CITY HALL, HISTORICAL MARKERS AND MAP AT BUFFALO BILL MUSEUM; HERITAGE BICENT COMMEMORATIVE COINS. (LOCAL). OTTO EWOLDT, CHAIRMAN; LECLAIRE BICENTENNIAL COMMITTEE; 916 WISCONSIN; LECLAIRE, IA 52753. (#26986).

HORIZONS PROJECTS FOR LECLAIRE, IA. FIRE-HYDRANT PAINTING, BICENT WELCOME SIGNS, BICENT DIRECTIONAL SIGNS, BICENT COMMEMORATIVE COINS, SCROLLS W/WAGON TRAIN, FLOWER PLANTINGS. (LOCAL). OTTO EWOLDT, CHAIRMAN; LECLAIRE BICENTENNIAL COMMITTEE; 916 WISCONSIN; LECLAIRE, IA 52753. (#26987).

RESTORATION OF 'BUFFALO BILL' HOME IN IOWA. RESTORATION OF THE 'BUFFALO BILL'HOME IN LECLAIRE, IOWA. (LOCAL). MRS WM WATERMAN, PRESIDENT; COLONIAL DAMES OF SCOTT COUNTY; LE CLAIRE, IA 52753. (#3740).

JULY 9 - 11, '76. ANNUAL RIVERESTA DAYS. EVENTS INCLUDE PARADE, THEATER PRODUCTION AND TENT DISPLAYS ON 7/9; HORSE SHOW, THEATER PRODUCTION AND BASEBALL TOURNAMENT ON 7/10; BOAT RACES, FASHION PARADE, MUSICAL, TENT DISPLAYS AND FIREWORKS FINALE ON 7/11. (LOCAL). OTTO EWOLDT, CHAIRMAN; LE CLAIRE BICENTENNIAL COMMITTEE; 916 WISCONSIN; LE CLAIRE, IA 52753. (#108453-1).

LE GRAND

LE GRAND AREA COMMUNITY CENTER - IA. A COMMUNITY CENTER WILL BE BUILT IN THE LEGRAND DAVID FERGUSON MEMORIAL PARK. (LOCAL). DAVID C FWEDT; LEGRAND DAVID FERGUSON MEMORIAL PARK; LEGRAND, IA 50158. (#21194). **ARBA GRANTEE.**

AUG 14, '76. LE GRAND PIONEER DAYS. FESTIVAL, EXHIBIT AT CITY PARK & SCHOOL. (LOCAL). NANCY SLINGLUFF, CHAIRMAN; CITY OF LE GRAND; LE GRAND, IA 50158. (#105221-1).

LE MARS

BICENTENNIAL CALENDAR, LE MARS, IA. DATES OF BICENTENNIAL SIGNIFICANCE WILL BE NOTED ON SCHOOL CALENDAR. (LOCAL). VIRGINIA FRANK, LIBRARIAN; WESTMAR COLLEGE; 1002 3RD AVE, SE; LE MARS, IA 51301. (#14580).

HISTORICAL DISPLAYS IN LE MARS, IA. DISPLAYS DEPICTING THE EVOLUTION OF ACADEMIC DISCIPLINES WILL BE PUT ON EXHIBIT. (LOCAL). VIRGINIA FRANK, LIBRARIAN; WESTMAR COLLEGE; 1002 3RD AVE, SE; LE MARS, IA 51031. (#14579).

PARK DEVELOPMENT - CLASS PROJECT '75, LE MARS, IA. PROJECT IS TO PROVIDE PICNIC AND RECREATION FACILITIES ON CAMPUS. (LOCAL). VIRGINIA FRANK, LIBRARIAN; WESTMAR COLLEGE; 1002 3RD AVE, SE; LE MARS, IA 51301. (#14577).

RENOVATION OF COUNTY STORE, LE MARS, IA. PRESERVATION OF HERITAGE THROUGH RENOVATION OF COUNTY STORE. (LOCAL). WESTON R KERR, CHAIRMAN; PLYMOUTH COUNTY BICENTENNIAL COMMITTEE; LE MARS, IA 51301. (#22737).

WESTMAR ARCHIVES ROOM, LE MARS, IA. DESIGNATING A ROOM IN LIBRARY TO HOUSE DEVELOPING ARCHIVES COLLECTION. (LOCAL). VIRGINIA FRANK, LIBRARIAN; WESTMAR COLLEGE; 1002 3RD AVE, SE; LE MARS, IA 51031. (#14578).

OCT 3 - 24, '75. ART EXHIBIT. WORKS BY DAN HOWARD, ROBERT HIGGS AND RUEBEN BEIF, MID-AMERICAN ARTISTS. AT WEIDLER GALLERY - WESTMAR CAMPUS. (LOCAL). GARY BOWLING, PROJ DIR; WESTMAR COLLEGE; WESTMAR COLLEGE; LE MARS, IA 51031. (#102005-1).

OCT 10, '75. HOMECOMING THEN & NOW: DINNER THEATRE, CORONATION & BALL. THE DINNER THEATRE FEATURES AN AMERICAN DRAMA; IT WILL ALSO BE HELD ON OCTOBER 11 & 12 AT THE SAME PLACE, TIME & COST. AT WESTMAR COMMONS. (LOCAL). VALDA EMBREE, CHMN; WESTMAR COLLEGE; LE MARS, IA 51031. (#102537-1).

OCT 11, '75. HOMECOMING THEN & NOW: PARADE. PARADE AT CENTRAL AVE. (LOCAL). VALDA EMBREE, CHMN; WESTMAR COLLEGE; LE MARS, IA 51031. (#102537-2).

NOV 10, '75. MUSICAL AMERICA - A HISTORY OF THE AMERICAN MUSICAL. LIVE PERFORMANCE AT LE MARS JUNIOR HIGH SCHOOL AUDITORIUM, 977 3RD AVE SW. (LOCAL). FRANK SUMMERSIDE, CHMN; WESTMAR COLLEGE; WESTMAR COLLEGE; LE MARS, IA 51031. (#102537-4).

DEC 13 - 14, '75. CONCERT - CHRISTMAS AT WESTMAR. LIVE PERFORMANCE AT CALVARY UNITED METHODIST CHURCH, 3RD AVE & 9TH ST SE. (LOCAL). FRANK SUMMERSIDE, CHMN; WESTMAR COLLEGE; WESTMAR COLLEGE; LE MARS, IA 51031. (#102537-3).

LEHIGH

CITY BUILDING FLAGPOLE - LEHIGH, IA. A FLAGPOLE AND PLAQUE WERE ERECTED AT THE NEW CITY BUILDING. (LOCAL). GAIL ESLICK, CHAIRMAN; LEHIGH BICENTENNIAL COMMITTEE; LEHIGH, IA 50557. (#29185).

JUNE 18 - 19, '76. ANTIQUE DISPLAY & ICE CREAM SOCIAL. FESTIVAL, EXHIBIT AT BLDG NEXT TO GAMBLE'S STORE, PARKING IN POST OFFICE LOT. (LOCAL). GAIL ESLICK, CHAIRMAN; LEHIGH BICENTENNIAL COMMITTEE; PO BOX 145; LEHIGH, IA 50557. (#200018-247).

LELAND

BASKET SOCIAL. BASKETS OF DINNERS WERE AUCTIONED OFF TO RAISE MONEY TO HELP PAY FOR EXPENSES FOR 4TH OF JULY CELEBRATION. (LOCAL). MRS SELMA AMBROSON, CHMN; LELAND STUDY CLUB; LELAND, IA 50453. (#200018-281).

JULY 4, '76. LELAND BICENTENNIAL CELEBRATION. LELAND DEDICATED FLAG, & PARK, HELD CHURCH SERVICES, GAMES & A PARADE. AT OTTO NOLTE PARK. (LOCAL). MRS SELMA AMBROSON, CHMN; VFW & LELAND STUDY CLUB; RT 1; LELAND, IA 50453. (#200018-282).

LENOX

CITY-WIDE CLEANUP - LENOX, IA. COMMERCIAL CLUB SPONSORED CITY-WIDE CLEANUP FOR LARGE ITEMS AND BRUSH THAT COULD NOT BE HAULED IN GARBAGE TRUCKS; ROTARY CLUB ALSO CLEANED BOTH DITCHES ON ROAD FROM CITY TO COUNTRY CLUB. (LOCAL). DONALD KEAST, DIRECTOR; LENOX COMMERCIAL CLUB & ROTARY CLUB; LENOX, IA 50851. (#25456).

NEW STREET SIGNS, LENOX, IA. NEW STREET SIGNS WILL BE PLACED THROUGHOUT THE CITY. (LOCAL). KENNETH BLACK, COORDINATOR; CITY OF LENOX & ROTARY CLUB; LENOX, IA 50851. (#21423).

TREE PLANTING, LENOX, IA. TREES WILL BE PLANTED IN THE PARK & ON COUNTRY CLUB GROUNDS. (LOCAL). KENNETH BLACK, COORDINATOR; ROTARY CLUB; LENOX, IA 50851. (#21424).

MAR 28, '76. FLAG POLE & LOGO FLAG PRESENTATION. CEREMONY. (LOCAL). MRS VIRGINIA BENNETT; LENOX BICENTENNIAL COMMITTEE; 202 W TEMPLE; LENOX, IA 50851. (#200018-94).

JULY 4, '76. COMMUNITY CHURCH SERVICE FOR BICENTENNIAL CELEBRATION. CEREMONY. (LOCAL). VIRGINIA BENNETT, CHMN; LENOX CHURCHES; LENOX, IA 50851. (#200018-191).

LENOX — CONTINUED

JULY 8 - 10, '76. 3 DAY BICENTENNIAL CELEBRATION BY HALE'S SHOWS OF TOMORROW. 2 NEW BIKES WILL BE GIVEN AWAY AT DRAWINGS AT 5 PM ON JULY 10TH. AT MAIN ST. (LOCAL). TOM BENDER, COORDINATOR; AMERICAN LEGION POST 250; LENOX, IA 50851. (#200018-190).

JULY 26 - 28, '76. BICENTENNIAL CELEBRATION. FESTIVAL. (LOCAL). VIRGINIA BENNETT, COORD; LENOX SADDLE CLUB; LENOX, IA 50851. (#105336-1).

JULY 30 - AUG 1, '76. LENOX RODEO. COMPETITION, FESTIVAL, PARADE. (LOCAL). VIRGINIA BENNETT, COORD; LENOX SADDLE CLUB; LENOX, IA 50851. (#105336-2).

AUG 16, '76. ANNUAL FEED IN PARK HONORING SENIOR CITIZENS. FESTIVAL AT CITY PARK & SWIMMING POOL. (LOCAL). DONALD KEAST, COORD; LENOX COMMERCIAL CLUB; LENOX, IA 50851. (#200018-202).

LEON

DECATUR COUNTY AGRICULTURAL MUSEUM - LEON, IA. LARGE COLLECTION OF EARLY FARM IMPLEMENTS; INCLUDES MANY LARGE ITEMS SUCH AS STEAM ENGINES, GAS TRACTORS AND THRESHERS. (LOCAL). H L GRAVES, PRESIDENT; DECATUR COUNTY HISTORICAL SOCIETY; COURTHOUSE; LEON, IA 50144. (#25130).

NEW FLAG POLE IN LEON, IOWA. NEW FLAG POLE TO BE BUILT AT CITY HALL. (LOCAL). MRS NANCY ELSON, COORDINATOR; LEON BICENTENNIAL COMMITTEE; LEON, IA 50144. (#19950).

RECONSTRUCTION OF 100 YR-OLD LOG CABIN - LEON, IA. RESTORING 100 YR OLD LOG CABIN IN CITY PARK. (LOCAL). MRS NANCY ELSON, CHMN; LEON BICENTENNIAL COMMITTEE; LEON, IA 50144. (#19949).

JULY 1 - 4, '76. ANNUAL RODEO & 4TH JULY ACTIVITIES. 4TH OF JULY PARADE AT 1 PM. RODEO 6:30-10:00 PM. AT FAIRGROUNDS. (LOCAL). WARD KILGORE, COORD; LEON CHAMBER OF COMMERCE; LEON, IA 50144. (#104681-1).

AUG 14 - 15, '76. DECATUR COUNTY THRESHING BEE. THE THRESHING BEE WILL FEATURE DISPLAYS OF OLD-TIME MACHINERY & OLD GAS TRACTORS, GAS ENGINE SHOW, STEAM ENGINE SHOW, THRESHING WITH STEAM POWER, SAW MILL, ANTIQUE SHOW AND FLEA MARKET. AT DECATUR COUNTY FAIRGROUNDS. (LOCAL). H L GRAVES, CHAIRMAN; DECATUR COUNTY HISTORICAL SOCIETY; RURAL ROUTE 1; DAVIS CITY, IA 50065. (#104519-21).

LESTER

BICENTENNIAL FIRE HYDRANTS, LESTER, IA. FIRE HYDRANTS ARE BEING PAINTED RED, WHITE AND BLUE. (LOCAL). RALPH SUNDE, PROJ DIRECTOR; LESTER BETTERMENT GROUP; LESTER, IA 51242. (#18147).

FLAG POLE IN LESTER, IA. FLAG POLE IS BEING ERECTED. (LOCAL). RALPH SUNDE, PROJ DIRECTOR; LESTER BETTERMENT GROUP; LESTER, IA 51242. (#18149).

JAIL & FIREHOUSE MARKERS, LESTER, IA. MARKERS WILL IDENTIFY THESE OLD HISTORIC BUILDINGS. (LOCAL). RALPH SUNDE, PROJ DIRECTOR; LESTER BETTERMENT GROUP; LESTER, IA 51242. (#18145).

OLD TIME COOKBOOK PROJ, LESTER, IA. COOKBOOK WILL CONSIST OF PIONEER RECIPES. (LOCAL). RALPH SUNDE, PROJ DIRECTOR; LESTER BETTERMENT GROUP; LESTER, IA 51242. (#18144).

TOWN SIGN, LESTER, IA. A TOWN MARKER IS BEING ERECTED. (LOCAL). RALPH SUNDE, PROJ DIRECTOR; LESTER BETTERMENT GROUP; LESTER, IA 51242. (#18148).

TREE PLANTERS IN LESTER, IA. INSTALL TREE PLANTERS ON MAIN STREET. (LOCAL). RALPH SUNDE, PROJ DIRECTOR; LESTER BETTERMENT GROUP; LESTER, IA 51242. (#18146).

LEWIS

BICENTENNIAL PLANTS FOR THE PARK, LEWIS, IA. RED, WHITE AND BLUE FLOWERS IN PARK WILL BE PLANTED IN AREA PARKS. (LOCAL). MRS CHESTER NETTZ, PROJ DIRECTOR; GARDEN CLUB OF LEWIS; LEWIS, IA 51544. (#22757).

CHURCH HISTORY, LEWIS, IA. BOOK ON UP TO DATE HISTORY OF CHURCHES & RELIGION IN THE LEWIS AREA. (LOCAL). AGATHA SMITH, PROJ COORDINATOR; UNITED CONGREGATIONAL & METHODIST CHURCH; MAIN ST; LEWIS, IA 51544. (#22761).

COURTHOUSE PRESERVATION, LEWIS, IA. PRESERVATION OF FIRST CASS COUNTY COURTHOUSE IN LEWIS, IA. (LOCAL). JEANNE BRODERSEN, CHAIRMAN; CASS COUNTY BICENTENNIAL COMMITTEE & COUNTY HISTORICAL SOCIETY; ATLANTIC, IA 50022. (#13080).

FIRE STATION IN LEWIS, IA. NEW FIRE STATION FACILITY IS BEING BUILT. (LOCAL). EARL ROBERTS, FIRE CHIEF; FIRE DEPARTMENT; LEWIS, IA 51544. (#22755).

HISTORY BOOK ON LEWIS, IA. REPRINTING OF BOOK ON HISTORY OF CITY. (LOCAL). PAULINE FRANKLIN, PROJ CHAIRWOMAN; CRESCENT CLUB; LEWIS, IA 51544. (#22762).

LIBRARY IMPROVEMENTS, LEWIS, IA. COMPLETE RENOVATION & ENLARGEMENT OF LIBRARY IN NEW QUARTERS ALSO NEW BOOKS AND PICTURES WITH BICENTENNIAL THEMES. (LOCAL). BERNICE BURNSIDE, PROJ COORDINATOR; CRESCENT CLUB; LEWIS, IA 51544. (#22756).

NEW LIGHTED FLAG POLE & BAND STAND RENOVATION, IA. COMPLETE REBUILDING OF BAND STAND IN CITY PARK & ERECTING OF NEW LIGHTED FLAG POLE IN PARK. MORE REPAIRS ARE DONE AS FUNDS BECOME AVAILABLE. (LOCAL). BERNICE BURNSIDE, PROJ COORDINATOR; LEWIS BICENTENNIAL COMMITTEE/CITY OF LEWIS; LEWIS, IA 51544. (#22760).

REMOVE JUNK CARS, LEWIS, IA. IMPROVEMENT & BEAUTIFICATION OF LEWIS BY REMOVAL OF JUNK CARS. (LOCAL). HON CLARENCE SHUTT, MAYOR; CITY OF LEWIS; LEWIS, IA 51544. (#22759).

MAR 16, '76. POSTER CONTEST WITH PATRIOTIC THEME. U S FLAG FOR TOP PRIZE IN ADDITION TO THE $2.00 WINNER'S PRIZE. AT LEWIS SCHOOL, LEWIS, IA. (LOCAL). DOROTHY BAXTER, COORD; LEWIS VETERAN'S AUXILIARY; LEWIS, IA 51544. (#106229-1).

JUNE 27, '76. BICENTENNIAL SUNDAY-LEWIS UNITED C & M CHURCH. FAMILY DAY WITH OLD TIME DRESS, DISPLAY OF CHURCH ITEMS, POT LUCK DINNER & OLD TIME SERVICE; DISPLAY TO BE SET UP BY 6/27/76; CIRCUIT PREACHER SADDLE BAGS, CATECHISM BOOKS AND OLD BIBLE DISPLAYS, OLD CHURCH BULLETINS, PRAYER BOOKS AND RELIGIOUS PICTURES ON EXHIBIT. AT UNITED C & M CHURCH. (LOCAL). DOLORES BICE, COORD; UNITED C & M CHURCH; RT #1; GRISWOLD, IA 51544. (#106154-4).

AUG 19 - 21, '76. APPRECIATION DAYS & FIREMEN'S CARNIVAL. A 3-DAY CARNIVAL: DONKEY BALL GAME, 200 YEARS OF ARTS & CRAFTS, WATER FIGHT, BICENTENNIAL KIDDIE PARADE, GAMES & ENTERTAINMENT. AT DOWNTOWN PARK AND MAIN STREET. (LOCAL). EARL ROBERTS, COORD; FIREMEN, JAYCEES & TOWN & COUNTRY BOOSTERS; LEWIS, IA 51544. (#106154-2).

AUG 19 - 21, '76. DEDICATION AND OPENING OF BAND STAND. THE CEREMONY CONSISTED OF AN OLD FASHIONED CHORDSMEN SINGING AND A BARBERSHOP QUARTET SINGING PROGRAM. THERE ALSO WAS A FLAG DRAPED & A BLUNTING DRAPED. AT DOWNTOWN CITY PARK. (LOCAL). BERNICE BURNSIDE, COORD; LEWIS BICENTENNIAL COMMITTEE / CITY OF LEWIS; LEWIS, IA 51544. (#22760-1).

AUG 20, '76. ARTS & CRAFTS SHOW. EXHIBIT AT COMMUNITY BUILDING. (LOCAL). VALDA KENNEDY, COORD; LADIES CLUB; LEWIS, IA 51544. (#106154-3).

LIME SPRINGS

RESTORATION & PRESERVATION OF LIOTKE MILL - IOWA. RESTORATION & PRESERVATION OF OLD LIDTKE MILL WHICH WAS BUILT IN 1857. THE MILL WAS FAMOUS FOR ITS BUCKWHEAT FLOUR. (ST-WIDE). JIM WALTON, DIRECTOR; LIDTKE MILL RESTORATION BOARD; LIME SPRINGS, IA 52155. (#9646). **ARBA GRANTEE.**

JUNE 5 - SEPT 6, '76. TOUR OF LIOTKE MILL HISTORICAL SITE. TOUR OF RESTORED FLOUR MILL, 1857 LIGHT POWER PLANT, MUSEUM & RECREATED MILLER'S HOME. AT ONE MILE N OF LIME SPRINGS ON UPPER IOWA RIVER. (LOCAL). JAMES R WALTON, CHAIRMAN; LIME SPRINGS JAYCEES; BOX 188; LIME SPRINGS, IA 52155. (#106405-1).

LINEVILLE

SHELTER HOUSE IN LINEVILLE, IA. A SHELTER HOUSE AND BANDSTAND WILL BE BUILT ON THE SQUARE. (LOCAL). JOHN WARNOCK, PRESIDENT; LIONS CLUB; LINEVILLE, IA 50147. (#14251).

AUG 22 - 23, '76. BICENTENNIAL FESTIVAL. FESTIVAL. (LOCAL). R G PLACE, PRESIDENT; LIONS CLUB; LINEVILLE, IA 50147. (#101766-1).

AUG 27 - 28, '76. LIVING MEMORIAL. A BRONZE PLAQUE MOUNTED ON A NATIVE ROCK; INSCRIPTION WITH 2 SERVICE MEN'S NAMES WHO GAVE THEIR LIVES IN VIETNAM PLUS A FLAG POLE & SECURITY LIGHT. AT 1/2 MI N OF CITY LIMITS ON HWY 65. (LOCAL). COLYNN CRUTCHER, CHMN; LINEVILLE BICENTENNIAL COMMITTEE; LINEVILLE, IA 50147. (#106395-1).

LISCOMB

CEMETERY LANDSCAPING, LISCOMB, IA. NEW ADDITION LANDSCAPED & TREES WERE PLANTED. (LOCAL). DEANE ADAMS, CHAIRMAN; CITIZEN'S COMMITTEE; LISCOMB, IA 50148. (#31707).

JUNE 11, '76. RED, WHITE & BLUE SATURDAY. 9:00 COFFEE & ANTIQUE DISPLAY; 10:30 YOUTH PARADE; 11:15 HISTORICAL MARKER DEDICATION; 11:30 YOUTH GAMES; 12:00 DINNER; 1:30 VARIETY SHOW; 3:30 ADULT GAMES; 4:00 TUG-O-WAR. AT VARIOUS LOCATIONS IN LISCOMB. (LOCAL). JOHN R MCNAIR; ALL COMMUNITY ORGANIZATIONS; BOX 165; LISCOMB, IA 50148. (#200018-301).

LITTLE CEDAR

LITTLE CEDAR BICENTENNIAL PARK, IA. A PARK WILL BE DEVELOPED IN LITTLE CEDAR, IT WILL CONTAIN A SHELTER HOUSE, SWINGS, PICNIC TABLES AND A FIREPLACE. (LOCAL). HELEN CULBERTSON, SEC; LITTLE CEDAR BICENTENNIAL COMMUNITY; BOX 206; LITTLE CEDAR, IA 50454. (#18761).

LITTLE ROCK

LITTLE ROCK WOMEN'S CLUB COOKBOOK - IA. COOKBOOK SPONSORED BY FEDERATED WOMEN'S CLUB - 765 FAVORITE RECIPES BY CLUB MEMBERS, FORMER MEMBERS AND LADIES OF THE COMMUNITY; ALSO, A PAGE OF WEIGHTS AND MEASURES. PROCEEDS WILL GO FOR COMMUNITY EVENTS. (LOCAL). ROBERTA HUESER, PUBLICITY CHAIRMAN; LITTLE ROCK WOMEN'S CLUB; LITTLE ROCK, IA 51243. (#25657).

SEPT 4 - 6, '75. LITTLE ROCK CORN SHOW. EXHIBIT, FESTIVAL AT MAIN ST, SCHOOL GYMNASIUM. (LOCAL). GENE PETERS, PRESIDENT; LITTLE ROCK OPTIMIST CLUB; RR 1; LITTLE ROCK, IA 51243. (#101768-1).

MAY 11, '76. LUNCH SALE. HELP RAISE MONEY TO FINANCE LITTLE ROCK BAND TO MARCH IN JULY 4, 1976 BAND PARADE AT 3:00 PM AT DISNEY WORLD. AT LITTLE ROCK, IOWA. (LOCAL). MRS CHARLIE KRUSE, COORD; MUSIC BOOSTERS, LITTLE ROCK SCHOOL; LITTLE ROCK, IA 51243. (#107745-1).

LITTLE SIOUX

COMMUNITY DEVELOPMENT - LITTLE SIOUX, IA. A NEW FIRE STATION AND COMMUNITY ROOMS WILL REPLACE TEMPORAY FACILITIES. (LOCAL). MARVIN EVERS, FIRE CHIEF; LITTLE SIOUX FIRE DEPARTMENT; LITTLE SIOUX, IA 51545. (#18550).

HISTORY - LITTLE SIOUX, IA. THE HISTORY OF THE LITTLE SIOUX AREA IS BEING PREPARED FOR PUBLICATION. (LOCAL). VIOLET BREELING, PROJECT DIRECTOR; COMMITTEE BETTERMENT; LITTLE SIOUX, IA 51545. (#18551).

AUG 28, '76. HOMECOMING 1976. FAIR, PARADE. (LOCAL). DAVID MATHISON, DIR; LITTLE SIOUX HOMECOMING ASSOCIATION; LITTLE SIOUX, IA 51545. (#103893-1).

OCT 8 - 10, '76. BOY SCOUT COUNCIL WIDE BICENTENNIAL CAMPOREE. CONFERENCE AT LITTLE SIOUX SCOUT RANCH. (REGN'L). GARLAND GROOM, DIRECTOR; MID-AMERICA BOY SCOUT COUNCIL; 519 S 15TH ST; OMAHA, NE 68102. (#108311-5).

LIVERMORE

BEAUTIFICATION OF LIVERMORE, IA. PROJECT TO TEAR DOWN OLD BUILDINGS; PAINT & REMOVE OLD CARS AND DEBRIS. (LOCAL). HON CLARENCE CARLSON, MAYOR; TOWN OF LIVERMORE; BOX 16; LIVERMORE, IA 50558. (#16424).

BICENTENNIAL TREE PROJECT, LIVERMORE, IA. NATIVE IOWA TREE SALES IN CONJUNCTION WITH HUMBOLDT COUNTY ARBC TREE PLANTING. (LOCAL). RON HAMILTON, PROJ DIRECTOR; JAYCEES; PO BOX 48; LIVERMORE, IA 50558. (#21882).

CHILDREN OF THE AMERICAN REVOLUTION - IA. THE DAR WILL PLANT 200 TREES IN HONOR OF THE CHILDREN OF THE AMERICAN REVOLUTION. (LOCAL). DORIS OLSON, PROJ DIRECTOR; DAUGHTERS OF THE AMERICAN REVOLUTION, LIVERMORE CHAPTER; LIVERMORE, IA 50558. (#14296).

FLAG SALES IN LIVERMORE, IA. BETSY ROSS AND BENNINGTON IMITATION FLAGS ARE AVAILABLE AT COST TO ANY RESIDENT FOR USE DURING BICENTENNIAL PERIOD. (LOCAL). REV MICHAEL KLAFEHN, PASTOR; IMMANUEL LUTHERAN CHURCH; BOX 42; LIVERMORE, IA 50558. (#16489).

FLOWER PLANTINGS, LIVERMORE, IA. RED, WHITE & BLUE BICENTENNIAL LOGO PLANTING AT OLD SETTLERS PARK IN FRONT OF LOG CABIN. (LOCAL). MRS JOHN OLSON, SECRETARY; OLD SETTLERS ASSOC; BOX 17; LIVERMORE, IA 50558. (#16427).

FLOWER POT PLANTINGS IN LIVERMORE, IA. HANDICAPPED WILL MAKE RED, WHITE AND BLUE CERAMIC POTS IN THEIR OWN KILN, THEN WILL START PLANTINGS IN THE POTS. (LOCAL). CONNIE HADDON, DIRECTOR; HUMBOLDT COUNTY OPPORTUNITY CENTER; BOX 47; LIVERMORE, IA 50558. (#16428).

FOXFIRE PROJECT OF LIVERMORE, IA. RECORDING INTERVIEWS WITH ELDERLY CITIZENS ON PRAIRIE LIFE; MEDICINES, TRANSPORTATION, HEATING, CLOTHING AND RECREATION. (LOCAL). DAN NEILES, PRINCIPAL; TWIN RIVERS COMMUNITY SCHOOLS; MAIN ST; LIVERMORE, IA 50558. (#16425).

HISTORICAL MURALS PROJECT, LIVERMORE, IA. BICENTENNIAL HISTORY THEME MURALS WILL BE PAINTED ON BATHHOUSE EXTERIOR WALLS BY TWIN RIVERS HIGH SCHOOL ART CLASSES. (LOCAL). JOHN SMELTZER, PROJ DIRECTOR; TWIN RIVERS COMMUNITY SCHOOLS; BOX 98; LIVERMORE, IA 50558. (#16426).

MUNICIPAL POOL - PROJ OF LIVERMORE, IA. A COMMUNITY POOL AND TENNIS COURTS WILL BE CONSTRUCTED. (LOCAL). MRS JOHN N LARSEN; TOWN HALL; LIVERMORE, IA 50558. (#14290).

NATURE HIKING TRAIL - LIVERMORE, IA. HIKING TRAIL WILL BE DEVELOPED IN LOTT'S CREEK PARK. (LOCAL). FLOYD RANEY, PRESIDENT; LIVERMORE JAYCEES; PO BOX 173; LIVERMORE, IA 50558. (#21880).

OLD SETTLERS CABIN - PROJ OF LIVERMORE, IA. NEW SHAKES WILL BE PUT ON THE OLD SETTLERS CABIN. (LOCAL). MRS JOHN OLSON, PROJ DIRECTOR; OLD SETTLERS ASSOC; LIVERMORE, IA 50558. (#14297).

PICTORIAL DIRECTORY - LIVERMORE, IA. FAMILY PHOTOGRAPH RECORD OF CHURCH MEMBERSHIP IN 1976 WILL BE COMPILED. (LOCAL). MRS RAY MULLIGAN, PROJ DIRECTOR; SACRED HEART CATHOLIC CHURCH; RR #1; LIVERMORE, IA 50558. (#21881).

PLANTING BICENTENNIAL FLOWERS, LIVERMORE, IA. FLOWER PLANTING ON CHURCH GROUNDS. (LOCAL). MRS HARTLY MACKINTOSH, COORDINATOR; UNITED METHODIST CHURCH WOMEN; RR1; LIVERMORE, IA 50558. (#21883).

PRESBYTERIAN CHURCH - PROJ OF LIVERMORE, IA. THE PRESBYTERIAN CHURCH WILL BE PAINTED. (LOCAL). MRS JOHN N LARSEN, PROJ DIRECTOR; PRESBYTERIAN CHURCH; LIVERMORE, IA 50558. (#14288).

LIVERMORE — CONTINUED

ROCK ISLAND DEPOT, LIVERMORE, IA. RESTORATION AND PRESERVATION OF OLD ROCK ISLAND RR DEPOT WITH MINI PARK AREA, IN COOPERATION WITH IOWA STATE BICENTENNIAL COMMISSION & LIVERMORE TOWN. (LOCAL). MARY COLWELL, CHAIRMAN; LIVERMORE BICENTENNIAL COMMISSION; BOX 1776; LIVERMORE, IA 50558. (#21884).

SEPT 6, '75. OLD SETTLERS PICNIC. FESTIVAL. (LOCAL). MRS JOHN OLSON, CHMN; OLD SETTLERS ASSOCIATION; LIVERMORE, IA 50558. (#101738-1).

OCT 20, '75. BICENTENNIAL FUND RAISING BALL. PROCEEDS FROM BALL WILL BE USED FOR IMPROVING NEW PUBLIC SWIMMING POOL PARK AREA. (LOCAL). RAY MULLIGAN, CHAIRMAN; LIVERMORE BICENTENNIAL COMMISSION; RR1 BOX 63; LIVERMORE, IA 50558. (#102937-1).

JUNE 6 - 13, '76. ARTS & CRAFTS EXHIBIT, FAIR & FESTIVAL. FESTIVAL INCLUDES ICE CREAM SOCIAL, BLUE GRASS MUSIC, MOVIES, BAND CONCERT, FASHION SHOW, PUPPETEERS, CRAFTS AND EXHIBITS: STILL, BLACKSMITH SHOP, SPINNING, CANDLE-DIPPING; ALSO, 'LITTLE BRITCHES' RODEO. AT MAIN STREET AND OLD ROCK ISLAND DEPOT. (LOCAL). MARIE WILSON, CHWMN; LIVERMORE BICENTENNIAL COMMISSION; BOX 64; LIVERMORE, IA 50558. (#102937-2).

JUNE 12 - 13, '76. LITTLE BRITCHES RODEO DAYS & PARADE. COMPETITION, PARADE. (LOCAL). CHICK MCKENNA, DIRECTOR; COMMUNITY CLUB & AMERICAN LEGION; LIVERMORE, IA 50558. (#101739-1).

LOCUST GROVE

LOCUST GROVE CHURCH 90TH ANNIVERSARY PARTY, IOWA. A CELEBRATION OF THE 90TH ANNIVERSARY OF THE LOCUST GROVE CHURCH. (LOCAL). HERMIE K HIRZ, PROJ DIRECTOR; LOCUST GROVE TOWNSHIP BICENTENNIAL COMMISSION; RR 2; NORTHBORO, IA 51647. (#11291).

SIGNS MARKING HISTORICAL SITES IN LOCUST GROVE, IA. SIGNS MARKING SITES OF HISTORICAL INTEREST WILL BE PLACED THROUGHOUT THE TOWN. (ST-WIDE). HERMIE K HIRZ, PROJ DIRECTOR; LOCUST GROVE TOWNSHIP BICENTENNIAL COMMISSION; RR 2; NORTHBORO, IA 51647. (#11292).

MAR '75. LOCUST GROVE HISTORY PRESENTATION, IA. PRESENTING 1971 LOCUST GROVE HISTORY TO FREMONT COUNTY HISTORICAL LIBRARY. (ST-WIDE). HERMIE K HIRZ; LOCUST GROVE TOWNSHIP BICENTENNIAL COMMISSION; RR 2; NORTHBORO, IA 51647. (#11290-1).

LOGAN

CLEANING UP CITY PARK - PROJ OF LOGAN, IA. THE COMMUNITY BETTERMENT CLUB WILL CLEANUP THE CITY PARK AND THE BANDSHELL WILL BE FIXED UP. (LOCAL). GERALD SORICK, CHAIRMAN; COMMUNITY BETTERMENT; 617 GLEN RD; LOGAN, IA 51546. (#17871).

JUNE 2 - OCT 1, '76. PIONEER VILLAGE SPINNING & WEAVING DEMONSTRATIONS & EXHIBIT. SUNDAY HOURS 1 - 5PM. AT MOTELS & EATING PLACES BETWEEN LOGAN & MISSOURI VALLEY. (LOCAL). ALLENE LATTA, SECRETARY; HARRISON COUNTY HISTORICAL SOCIETY; 109 E 6TH; LOGAN, IA 51546. (#108828-1).

JULY 4, '76. ANNUAL 4TH OF JULY PARADE & CELEBRATION. FESTIVAL, PARADE. (LOCAL). GERALD A SORICK, DIRECTOR; LOGAN CHAMBER OF COMMERCE; 617 GLEN RD; LOGAN, IA 51546. (#103455-1).

AUG 5 - 15, '76. ART SHOW - PAINTINGS WITH HISTORICAL THEME. 10 AM - 5 PM TUESDAY THRU SAT; SUNDAY 1-6 PM;. AT HARRISON COUNTY HISTORICAL VILLAGE. (LOCAL). LARRY STEVENS, DIRECTOR; HARRISON COUNTY HISTORICAL SOCIETY; LOGAN, IA 51557. (#107420-1).

LOHRVILLE

BACK TO NATURE AREA IN LOHRVILLE, IA. A PLOT OF FARM LAND HAS BEEN SEEDED WITH NATURAL GRASSES, WILD FLOWERS & TREES; A FARM POND HAS BEEN BUILT; & A PART OF THE CNW RAILROAD WAS PURCHASED FOR PRESERVATION AS IT IS. (LOCAL). HONORABLE WILLIAM P WINKELMAN, SENATOR; LOHRVILLE, IA 51453. (#22174).

BICENTENNIAL PLANTINGS - LOHRVILLE, IA. TREES AND FLOWERS WILL BE PLANTED AROUND THE TOWN. (LOCAL). MRS QUENTIN RIEDESEL, CHAIRMAN; DAFFODIL GARDEN CLUB; LOHRVILLE, IA 51453. (#21311).

BICENTENNIAL PROGRAM IN LOHRVILLE, IA. ENTIRE 1975-76 PROGRAM WILL FOCUS ON THE BICENTENNIAL & WILL FEATURE 2 FILMS: 'ABOUT A CENTURY, 1776-1876' - 'FARMING & INDUSTRY, 1876 TO 1976'. THERE WILL BE AN EXHIBIT & BIOGRAPHY OF BILL CODY. (LOCAL). KATHRYNE MCDONALD, COORDINATOR; LOHRVILLE WOMAN'S CLUB; LOHRVILLE, IA 51453. (#22172).

HISTORY OF UNION TOWNSHIP & LOHRVILLE, IA. HISTORY OF THE PIONEERS FEATURING CHURCHES, SCHOOLS, ETC. (LOCAL). KATHRYNE MCDONALD, COORDINATOR; LOHRVILLE COMMUNITY CLUB; LOHRVILLE, IA 51453. (#22173).

HONOR GRADUATING SENIORS - LOHRVILLE, IA. HONOR AS BICENTENNIAL GRADUATES; AWARD DIPLOMAS WITH BICENTENNIAL EMBLEM OF THE LIBERTY BELL. (LOCAL). JACK BROWER, PRINCIPAL; LOHRVILLE COMMUNITY SCHOOL; BOX 276; LOHRVILLE, IA 51453. (#24670).

PRAIRIE PRESERVE - LOHRVILLE, IA. A NATIVE PRAIRIE PRESERVE WILL BE CREATED FOR PUBLIC ENJOYMENT. (LOCAL). BILL WINKELMAN, CHAIRMAN; LOHRVILLE BICENTENNIAL COMMITTEE; LOHRVILLE, IA 51453. (#21768).

PRESENTATION OF BICENTENNIAL MEDALS TO ALL HIGH SCHOOL SENIORS. AWARD, CEREMONY. (LOCAL). TOM ANDERSON, CHAIRMAN; LOHRVILLE LIONS CLUB & AMERICAN LEGION; LOHRVILLE, IA 51453. (#105942-2).

SHELTER BELT - LOHRVILLE, IA. CREATION OF A SHELTER BELT FOR WIND EROSION. (LOCAL). BILL WINKELMAN, CHAIRMAN; LOHRVILLE BICENTENNIAL COMMITTEE; LOHRVILLE, IA 51453. (#21769).

OCT 9, '75. DISPLAY OF OLD AMERICAN FLAG. DISPLAY OF FLAG HANDMADE IN THE LATE 1880'S AND DISPLAYED AT LOHRVILLE'S FIRST 4TH OF JULY CELEBRATION IN THE 1890'S. AT LOHRVILLE LIBRARY. (LOCAL). MRS I H MCDONALD, DIR; LOHRVILLE WOMAN'S CLUB; LOHRVILLE, IA 51453. (#105942-7).

NOV 17, '75. 'AMERICA THE BEAUTIFUL' - SLIDE EXHIBIT. EXHIBIT AT AMERICAN LEGION BUILDING. (LOCAL). MRS KENNETH ROBB, CHMN; LOHRVILLE WOMAN'S CLUB; LOHRVILLE, IA 51453. (#200018-91).

APR 3, '76. FAREWELL FOR CLARK COGLEY, IOWA WAGON MASTER. CHUCKWAGON STEW & CORNBREAD SERVED FROM 12-4PM FOR $1.50. AT LOHRVILLE COMMUNITY BUILDING. (LOCAL). LEONARD SOMERS, CHAIRMAN; LOHRVILLE CLUBS IN COOPERATION; LOHRVILLE, IA 51453. (#105942-6).

JULY 4, '76. BICENTENNIAL CHURCH SERVICE. THE CATHOLIC PREIST AND THE MINISTER OF THE CHURCH OF CHRIST WILL BE ASKED TO PARTICIPATE. (LOCAL). REV RICHARD DUNN, DIR; LOHRVILLE UNITED METHODIST CHURCH; LOHRVILLE, IA 51453. (#105942-3).

JULY 17 - 18, '76. COMMUNITY CELEBRATION. FESTIVAL AT LOHRVILLE COMMUNITY CLUB. (LOCAL). TOM ANDERSON, CHAIRMAN; LOHRVILLE COMMUNITY CLUB, LIONS CLUB & DAFFODIL GARDEN CLUB; LOHRVILLE, IA 51453. (#105942-5).

DEC 10, '76. 'CHRISTMAS, 1776 - 1876 - 1976'. EXHIBIT. (LOCAL). MRS J H MCDONALD, DIR; LOHRVILLE WOMEN'S CLUB; LOHRVILLE, IA 51453. (#105942-8).

LONE TREE

AERIAL PHOTO OF CITY OF LONE TREE, IA. AN AERIAL PHOTO OF THE CITY WILL BE TAKEN AND PLACED IN A TIME CAPSULE. (LOCAL). DAVID MEYER, COORDINATOR; CITY COUNCIL; LONE TREE, IA 52755. (#26087).

BICENTENNIAL CLEANUP AND FLOWERBED PLANTING - IA. THE TOWN OF LONE TREE WILL BE CLEANED AND BEAUTIFIED BY THE PLANTING OF FLOWERBEDS. (LOCAL). DAVID MEYER, COORDINATOR; CITY COUNCIL; LONE TREE, IA 52755. (#26086).

HISTORY OF CHURCHES, IA. INFORMATION ON BACKGROUNDS OF LOCAL CHURCHES IS BEING COMPILED. (LOCAL). EUNICE BRENNEMAN, CHAIRWOMAN; UNITED PRESBYTERIAN WOMEN; LONE TREE, IA 52755. (#26089).

PARK SHELTER - LONE TREE, IA. NEW SHELTER WILL BE BUILT IN CITY PARK. (LOCAL). DAVID MEYER, COORDINATOR; CITY COUNCIL; LONE TREE, IA 52755. (#26085).

TREE PLANTING - LONE TREE, IA. SUGAR MAPLE TREES BEING PLANTED IN THE PARK, AT CHURCHES AND AT DAY CARE CENTERS. (LOCAL). JEAN STORM, CHAIRMAN; AMERICAN LEGION AUXILIARY; LONE TREE, IA 52755. (#26088).

MAY 1 - 2, '76. BICENTENNIAL ART SHOW - STUDENT ARTS & CRAFTS. EXHIBIT AT FARMERS AND MERCHANTS BANK, LONE TREE, IA. (LOCAL). LINDA WIELAND, COORD; ELAN JR FEDERATED WOMEN'S CLUB; LONE TREE, IA 52755. (#108465-12).

JUNE 21 - 25, '76. ECUMENICAL BIBLE SCHOOL. LIVE PERFORMANCE. (LOCAL). RAYMOND SWANSON, COORD; UNITED PRESBYTERIAN CHURCH OF LONE TREE; LONE TREE, IA 52755. (#108465-10).

JULY 3 - 4, '76. SOFTBALL TOURNAMENT. COMPETITION AT OAK FIELD. (LOCAL). LOWELL BAKER, COORD; LONE TREE JAYCEES; LONE TREE, IA 52755. (#108465-2).

JULY 4 - 5, '76. AVENUE OF FLAGS. EXHIBIT AT LONE TREE CEMETERY. (LOCAL). LARRY GREEN, CHMN; AMERICAN LEGION; LONE TREE, IA 52755. (#108465-9).

AUG 12, '76. TIME CAPSULE BURIAL & GAME SHOW. 'ALMOST ANYTHING GOES' WILL BE THE NAME OF THE GAME SHOW IMITATED. AT LONE TREE HIGH SCHOOL FOOTBALL FIELD. (LOCAL). MRS GERALD FORBES, COORD; LONE TREE BOOSTERS CLUB; LONE TREE, IA 52755. (#108465-7).

AUG 13, '76. HISTORICAL PAGEANT. LIVE PERFORMANCE AT LONE TREE HIGH SCHOOL GYMNASIUM. (LOCAL). JEAN STORM, CHMN; AMERICAN LEGION AUXILIARY; 401 RIGGS ST; LONE TREE, IA 52755. (#108465-1).

AUG 13, '76. LONE TREE PAGEANT. 200 YEARS OF HISTORY AND MUSIC WILL BE SEEN IN THIS PAGEANT. AT SCHOOL GYMNASIUM. (LOCAL). JEAN STORM, CHAIRMAN; AMERICAN LEGION AUXILIARY; LONE TREE, IA 52755. (#108465-14).

AUG 13 - 14, '76. AGRICULTURAL DISPLAY & CRAFTS SHOW. EXHIBIT AT FARMERS & MERCHANTS SAVINGS BANK COMMUNITY ROOM. (LOCAL). LOREN BECK, COORD; FUTURE FARMERS OF AMERICA; LONE TREE, IA 52755. (#108465-8).

AUG 14, '76. BICENTENNIAL DANCE. FESTIVAL AT BOB'S DX STATION. (LOCAL). KEN NORDSTROM, COORD; LONE TREE CHAMBER OF COMMERCE; LONE TREE, IA 52755. (#108465-5).

AUG 14, '76. LONE TREE BICENTENNIAL PARADE. PARADE AT MAIN ST. (LOCAL). KEN NORDSTROM, COORD; LONE TREE CHAMBER OF COMMERCE; LONE TREE, IA 52755. (#108465-4).

AUG 14, '76. QUEEN CONTEST. COMPETITION AT BOB'S DX STATION. (LOCAL). NIDA WOLLRAB, COORD; LONE TREE CHAMBER OF COMMERCE; LONE TREE, IA 52755. (#108465-3).

OCT 2, '76. BICENTENNIAL COMMUNITY BAZAAR. EXHIBIT AT FARMERS & MERCHANTS SAVINGS BANK COMMUNITY ROOM. (LOCAL). MARGARET STOCK, COORD; BICENTENNIAL BAZAAR COMMITTEE; LONE TREE, IA 52755. (#108465-11).

LONG GROVE

BICENTENNIAL QUILT, LONG GROVE, IA. ORIGINAL DESIGN QUILT, HANDMADE BY SENIOR LADIES. CHANCES WILL BE SOLD FOR RAFFLE. (LOCAL). DAN NAGLE, CHAIRMAN; LONG GROVE BICENTENNIAL COMMISSION; 126 FIRST ST; LONG GROVE, IA 52756. (#22591).

HISTORICAL MARKERS IN LONG GROVE, IOWA. IDENTIFY LANDMARKS INCLUDING TWO CHURCHES WHICH ARE OVER 125 YRS OLD; THE COMMUNITY WAS SETTLED IN 1838 & IS CLOSELY IDENTIFIED WITH THE EARLY HISTORY OF SCOTT COUNTY. (ST-WIDE). BURTON PERRSON, PROJ COORDINATOR; SCOTT COUNTY BICENT COMMISSION; BOX 1776; DAVENPORT, IA 52805. (#9668).

LONG GROVE, IA, FLAGPOLE AT COMMUNITY LANDMARK. ERECT A FLAGPOLE AT THE COMMUNITY CENTER; THE CENTER ITSELF IS A LANDMARK; IT WAS AN OLD SCHOOLHOUSE WHICH HAS BEEN CONVERTED INTO A CENTER. (ST-WIDE). BURTON PERRSON, PROJ COORDINATOR; SCOTT COUNTY BICENT COMMISSION; BOX 1776; DAVENPORT, IA 52805. (#9670).

LONG GROVE, IOWA TO BUILD WATER TOWER. TOWN PROPOSES TO CONSTRUCT A WATER TOWER AND IT WILL BE IDENTIFIED WITH BICENTENNIAL MARKINGS. (LOCAL). BURTON PERRSON, PROJ COORDINATOR; SCOTT COUNTY BICENT COMMISSION; BOX 1776; DAVENPORT, IA 52805. (#9669).

RESTORATION OF SODHOUSE, LONG GROVE, IOWA. THE ONLY SODHOUSE KNOWN TO EXIST IN THE MIDWEST WILL BE RESTORED AND OPENED FOR TOURS; WAS BUILT IN THE LATE 1830'S. (ST-WIDE). BURTON PERRSON, PROJ COORDINATOR; SCOTT COUNTY BICENT COMMISSION; BOX 1776; DAVENPORT, IA 52805. (#9667).

JUNE 8, '75. FLAGPOLE & FLAG DEDICATION. CEREMONY. (LOCAL). DAN NAGLE, CHAIRMAN; LONG GROVE BICENTENNIAL COMMITTEE; 126 FIRST ST; LONG GROVE, IA 52756. (#200018-92).

JUNE 13, '76. LONG GROVE STRAWBERRY FESTIVAL, BICENTENNIAL THEME. EVENTS OF THE DAY INCLUDE: KIDS COSTUME PARADE, SALUTE TO FLAG, MUSKET SALUTE, WOMEN'S EARLY DRESS CONTEST, SENIOR CITIZENS SINGING, BEARD CONTEST, ANTIQUE DISPLAY, FLOWER PLANTING, OLD LANDMARKS IDENTIFIED, CRAFTS AND FOOD. AT LONG GROVE CIVIC CENTER. (LOCAL). DAN NAGLE, COORD; LONG GROVE CIVIC LEAGUE; 126 FIRST ST; LONG GROVE, IA 52756. (#106067-1).

JUNE 13, '76. STRAWBERRY FESTIVAL. FESTIVAL INCLUDES CONTESTS, GAMES, HISTORICAL EXHIBITS, CHILDREN'S PARADE, AUCTIONING OF BICENT QUILT AND DANCING. (LOCAL). DAN NAGLE, CHAIRMAN; LONG GROVE BICENTENNIAL COMMITTEE; LONG GROVE, IA 52756. (#108454-1).

LOVILIA

HISTORY OF LOVILIA - BOOK, IA. HISTORY OF LOVILIA IS BEING COMPILED. (LOCAL). ELEANORA SOFRANKO, CHAIRMAN; LOVILIA BICENTENNIAL COMMITTEE; LOVILIA, IA 50150. (#23167).

JUNE 12, '76. FIREMEN'S CELEBRATION. EXHIBIT, FESTIVAL, PARADE, LIVE PERFORMANCE. (LOCAL). ELEANORA SOFRANKO, COORD; LOVILIA FIREMEN; LOVILIA, IA 50150. (#106390-1).

LOW MOOR

SLIDES ON LOW MOOR YESTERDAY AND TODAY, IA. 35 MM SLIDES ON HISTORY OF LOW MOORN. (LOCAL). ROBERT E LILLY, CHAIRMAN; LOW MOOR FIELD DAYS COMMITTEE; 405 3RD AVE; LOW MOOR, IA 52757. (#29755).

JULY 17 - 18, '76. 2 DAY FESTIVAL WITH ONGOING SLIDES OF TOWN HISTORY. FESTIVAL, PARADE, EXHIBIT. (LOCAL). ROBERT E LILLY, CHMN; LOW MOOR FIELD DAYS COMMITTEE; 405 3RD AVE, BOX 86; LOW MOOR, IA 52757. (#200018-275).

LOWDEN

HISTORICAL MUSEUM, LOWDEN, IA. RAILROAD DEPOT WILL BE MOVED TO CITY PARK & RESTORED TO SERVE AS A HISTORICAL MUSEUM. (LOCAL). REV PAUL JORDAN, COORDINATOR; LOWDEN HISTORICAL SOCIETY; JEFFERSON AVE; LOWDEN, IA 52255. (#23371).

PARADE WITH LIBERTY BELL FLOAT. FULL-SIZED LIBERTY BELL FLOAT AND SCROLL OF CONSTITUTION FLAGS WILL BE CARRIED ON A WAGON. (LOCAL). NORMAN KROEMER, CHMN; CEDAR COUNTY BICENTENNIAL COMMITTEE; RR #1; LOWDEN, IA 52255. (#106536-1). **(??).**

RESTORATION OF DEPOT, LOWDEN, IA. DEPOT WILL BE RELOCATED & RESTORED TO BE USED AS HISTORICAL SOCIETY MUSEUM. (LOCAL). REV PAUL JORDAN, CHAIRMAN; LOWDEN HISTORICAL SOCIETY; JEFFERSON AVE; LOWDEN, IA 52255. (#18759).

LOWDEN — CONTINUED

RESTORATION & RELOCATION OF LOG CABIN - LOWDEN, IA. CABIN BUILT IN 1842 WILL BE MOVED TO MASSILON PARK & RESTORED. (LOCAL). NORMAN KROEMER, CHAIRMAN; MASSILON BICENTENNIAL COMMITTEE; LOWDEN, IA 52253. (#23370).

AUG 6 - 7, '76. LOWDEN BICENTENNIAL PARK APPRECIATION DAYS. A KIDDIE PARADE, CRAFTS SHOW, CHICKEN DINNER AND DANCE ARE THE SCHEDULED ACTIVITIES. (LOCAL). LARRY ESBAUM, PRES; LOWDEN PARK BOARD; W 5TH ST; LOWDEN, IA 52255. (#106536-2).

LOWELL

AUG 8, '76. GRAND OPENING, RIVER BRIDGE. CEREMONY, OPENING AT COUNTY PARK, RESTORED SCHOOL. (LOCAL). MS MYRON THORNBURG, COORD; LOWELL GET TOGETHER CLUB; RR 1; NEW LONDON, IA 52641. (#106061-1).

LUANA

LUANA HISTORY BOOK, LUANA, IA. BOOK ON LOCAL HISTORY WITH OLD PICTURES OF THE AREA. (LOCAL). LARRY RIVELAND, PRESIDENT; LUANA COMMERCIAL CLUB; LUANA, IA 52156. (#23154).

SIGN FOR CITY, LUANA, IA. LARGE SIGN TO BE ERECTED AT ENTRANCE OF CITY. (LOCAL). LARRY RIVELAND, PRESIDENT; LUANA COMMERCIAL CLUB; LUANA, IA 52156. (#23153).

TREE PLANTING TO REPLACE DISEASED TREES - IA. PLANTED SEVENTY TREES TO REPLACE DISEASED TREES AND ENLARGED SHADE AREA IN THE PARK. PLANTED TREES ON HIGHWAY AREAS LEADING INTO THE TOWN. BOYSCOUTS DID THE PLANTING. (LOCAL). LARRY RIVELAND, PRESIDENT; LUANA COMMERICAL CLUB; LUANA, IA 52156. (#25985).

TREES AND PARK, LUANA, IA. TREES WILL BE PLANTED TO BEAUTIFY CITY & PARK FACILITIES WILL BE IMPROVED. (LOCAL). LARRY RIVELAND, PRESIDENT; COMMERCIAL CLUB; LUANA, IA 52156. (#23155).

MAY 30, '76. HORSE SHOW CONTEST OF RIDERS AND HORSES. WILL HAVE ABOUT 30 CLASSES; ONE-DAY ADULT COMPETITION & ONE-DAY STUDENT CONTEST. RIBBONS AND TROPHIES WILL BE AWARDED TO THE WINNERS. SHOW CONTESTANTS PAY ENTRY FEE FOR EACH CLASS. LUNCH STAND & AMPLE PARKING. AT JAMES RUCKHARBER RES, LUANA. (LOCAL). MYRNA GORDON, CHAIRPERSON; LUANA COMMERICAL CLUB; BOX 56; LUANA, IA 52156. (#106384-1).

AUG 14 - 15, '76. SOFTBALL TOURNAMENT. TOURNMAENT OF 14 TEAMS; HIGH ARCH - SLOW PITCH; ELIMINATION TO TWO TOP TEAMS WITH TROPHIES & PRIZE MONEY. PRIZES FROM ENTRY FEES OF TEAMS. AT SCHOOL GROUNDS LUANA CENTER. (LOCAL). MYRNA GORDON, CHAIRPERSON; LUANA COMMERICAL CLUB; BOX 56; LUANA, IA 52156. (#106385-2).

LUTHER

JUNE 19, '76. DEDICATION OF PLAQUE IN HONOR OF CLARK LUTHER. DIAMOND JUBILEE (75 YRS) SINCE BEGINNING OF IOOF #677; HONORING OTHER PIONEERS ALSO. (LOCAL). AUDREY MCVAY, CHAIRMAN; LUTHER HISTORICAL SOCIETY; LUTHER, IA 50152. (#104221-15).

LUVERNE

DECORATING FIRE HYDRANTS, LUVERNE, IA. HYDRANTS DECORATED RED, WHITE AND BLUE TO REPRESENT REVOLUTIONARY WAR FIGURES. (LOCAL). JEN RUGG, ADVISOR; METHODIST YOUTH ORGANIZATION; LUVERNE, IA 50560. (#22732).

HERITAGE HOME, LUVERNE, IA. HOUSE WILL BE A REPLICA OF AN EARLY AMERICAN HOME. (LOCAL). DORIS JOHNS, CHAIRMAN; AMERICAN LEGION AUXILIARY; LUVERNE, IA 50560. (#22731).

MEMORIAL PARK, LUVERNE, IA. DOWNTOWN PARK WITH OLD SCHOOL BELL FROM LUVERNE SCHOOL; WALKING PLOW AND VETERANS HONOR BOARD PORTRAYING THREE SIGNIFICANT AREAS OF OUR CULTURE. (LOCAL). DUREN WATTS, CHAIRMAN; LUVERNE BICENTENNIAL COMMITTEE; LUVERNE, IA 50560. (#22730).

RESTORATION OF OLD CITY JAIL, LUVERNE, IA. RESTORE AND FURNISH JAIL, CIRCA 1880. (LOCAL). DUREN C WATTS, CHAIRMAN; LUVERNE BICENTENNIAL COMMITTEE; LUVERNE, IA 50560. (#21003).

TOWN OF LUVERNE, IA. RESTORATION & BUILDING OF SEVERAL PROJECTS IN LUVERNE. (LOCAL). DENNIS HOLMES, PROJ DIRECTOR; TOWN OF LUVERNE; LUVERNE, IA 50560. (#14295).

JULY 17 - 18, '76. HONOR AMERICA DAYS. EXHIBIT, FAIR, PARADE AT LUVERNE MAIN STREET. (LOCAL). DUREN C WATTS, CHMN; ERNEST MERKLE POST 664-LUVERNE AMERICAN LEGION & BICENT COMMITTEE; LUVERNE, IA 50560. (#105137-1).

NOV 11, '76. MEMORIAL PLAQUE. MEMORIAL PLAQUE FOR SERVICE MEN OF ALL WARS TO BE PLACED IN BICENTENNIAL PARK WHEN PARK IS COMPLETED. AT MAIN STREET, LUVERNE. (LOCAL). EVERITT SCHIPULL, CMDR; ERNEST MERKLE POST #664 - AMERICAN LEGION; LUVERNE, IA 50560. (#22733-1).

LYTTON

HISTORICAL MARKERS, LYTTON, IA. MARKERS WILL BE ERECTED AT HISTORICAL SITES IN LYTTON, IA. (LOCAL). REINARD WULKOW, PROJ DIRECTOR; BICENTENNIAL DIVISION LYTTON JUBILLEE; LYTTON, IA 50583. (#18951).

HISTORICAL MUSEUM - LYTTON, IA. CREATION OF NEW HISTORICAL MUSEUM. (LOCAL). REINARD WULKOW, CHAIRMAN; BICENTENNIAL DIVISION, LYTTON JUBILEE; LYTTON, IA 50583. (#18929).

HISTORY OF LYTTON, IA. A HISTORY OF LYTTON WILL BE WRITTEN AND PUBLISHED. (LOCAL). REINARD WULKOW, CHAIRMAN; BICENTENNIAL DIVISION, LYTTON JUBILEE; LYTTON, IA 50583. (#18930).

TREE PLANTING - LYTTON, IA. SPECIAL TREE PLANTING WILL BE DONE FOR THE BICENTENNIAL. (LOCAL). REINARD WULKOW, CHAIRMAN; BICENTENNIAL DIVISION, LYTTON JUBILEE; LYTTON, IA 50583. (#18931).

MACEDONIA

COMMUNITY BUILDING - MACEDONIA, IA. A COMMUNITY BUILDING WILL BE BUILT FOR COMMUNITY USE AND TO HOUSE THE HISTORY OF THE TOWN. (LOCAL). NORA MUELLER, CHAIRMAN; MACEDONIA BICENTENNIAL COMMISSION; MACEDONIA, IA 51549. (#29186).

SEPT 11, '76. DONIA DAY. FESTIVAL. (LOCAL). NORA MUELLER, CHAIRMAN; MACEDONIA BICENTENNIAL COMMISSION; MACEDONIA, IA 51549. (#200018-251).

MACKSBURG

HISTORICAL MARKERS, MACKSBURG, IA. MARKERS WILL BE PLACED AT TWO HISTORICAL SITES, WHICH ARE, THE DR MACK-GLEN MARTIN HOMES AND THE RESTORED FIRE BELL AND TOWER. (LOCAL). WILLIAM SANDERS, PROJ CHAIRMAN; BOOSTER CLUB; MACKSBURG, IA 50155. (#21010).

LASTING MUSEUM IN MACKSBURG, IA. MUSEUM TO HOUSE HISTORIC ITEMS. (LOCAL). WILLIAM J SANDERS, PROJ CHAIRMAN; BOOSTER CLUB; MACKSBURG, IA 50155. (#21011).

JUNE 25 - 26, '76. CENTENNIAL - BICENTENNIAL CELEBRATION. FRI HOURS ARE 12PM TO 12 AM; SAT HOURS ARE 9 AM TO 12 PM. AT CITY SQUARE. (LOCAL). WILLIAM J SANDERS; BOOSTER CLUB; MACKSBURG, IA 50155. (#105182-1).

MADRID

BIG CREEK RIDERS ARENA, MADRID, IA. CONVERSION OF SCANDIA COAL MINE NUMBER 4, 1/2 MILE SOUTH OF MADRID, TO A HORSE SHOW FACILITY. (ST-WIDE). PAUL MOORE, CHAIRMAN; BIG CREEK RIDERS, INC; RFD 2; MADRID, IA 50156. (#19695).

CAMP LAURIE PARK, MADRID, IA. THE TWO HUNDRED ACRES, WITH BUILDINGS AND SWIMMING POOL, ARE LOCATED ONE MILE WEST AND ONE MILE NORTH OF MADRID; THE ARMY CORPS OF ENGINEERS OFFERED IT TO MADRID IN RETURN FOR A PROMISE OF DEVELOPMENT. (LOCAL). JOE MATAYA, CHAIRMAN; CAMP LAURIE PARK, INC; 605 KINGMAN; MADRID, IA 50156. (#19697).

MADRID BICENTENNIAL PLATE, IA. DESIGNED BY MARGARET KEIGLEY, PRODUCED BY MCCOY COLLER CERAMICS AND CLAY CASTLE MUSEUM; PROCEEDS FROM SALE OF PLATES WILL GO TO A COMMUNITY PROJECT. (LOCAL). MARGARET KEIGLEY, OWNER; CLAY CASTLE MUSEUM; RFD 2; MADRID, IA 50156. (#19696).

REMEMBRANCES OF DAYS GONE BY - MADRID, IA. SERIES OF MADRID AREA HISTORY, PUBLISHED WEEKLY FROM JULY 1, 1975 THROUGH JULY 4, 1976. (LOCAL). CLARENCE WILCOX, EDITOR; MADRID REGISTER NEWS; 102 S MAIN ST; MADRID, IA 50156. (#19698).

APR 17, '75. IOWA HISTORY OPEN HOUSE. FIFTH GRADE CLASSES ENDED STUDIES OF IOWA WITH OPEN HOUSE 4/17/75 FEATURING EXHIBITS AND DEMONSTRATIONS OF IOWA'S PAST. THE ORIGINAL 'SWEDEPOINT' POSTAL STAMP WAS USED TO STAMP THE PROGRAMS. AT MADRID ELEMENTARY BLDG. (LOCAL). MRS GLENNA MCGINNIS; MADRID COMMUNITY SCHOOL; RFD 2; BOONE, IA 50036. (#200018-111).

NOV 1, '75 - DEC 31, '76. ANTIQUE DISPLAY. THE ANTIQUE DISPLAY WILL BE ADDED TO MONTHLY FROM NOVEMBER 1975 THRU DECEMBER 1976. AT MADRID PUBLIC LIBRARY. (LOCAL). MRS RONALD BERG, COORD; QUESTORS; RFD 2; MADRID, IA 50156. (#104519-13).

NOV 15 - 16, '75. 1975 FINE ARTS FESTIVAL. MUSIC ART AND ANTIQUES; AMONG OTHER DISPLAYS WILL BE ANTIQUE JEWELRY FROM RESIDENTS OF IOWA LUTHERAN HOME FOR THE AGED. AT MADRID COMMUNITY ROOM. (LOCAL). MARGARET KEIGLEY, PRES; MADRID FEDERATED WOMEN'S CLUB; RFD 2; MADRID, IA 50156. (#200018-112).

SEPT 6, '76. LABOR DAY CELEBRATION. ACTIVITIES PLANNED INCLUDE A PARADE, BAR-B-QUE AND SOFTBALL TOURNAMENTS. (LOCAL). RICHARD HAMM, PRESIDENT; MADRID JAYCEES; RFD 2; MADRID, IA 50156. (#104519-14).

NOV 13 - 14, '76. 1976 FINE ARTS FESTIVAL. ART, MUSIC, ANTIQUES AND ITEMS OF MADRID HISTORY WILL BE FEATURED; SPECIAL RECOGNITION WILL BE GIVEN TO MADRID NATIVE SON, JAMES SARGENT, THE 3RD PLACE WINNER OF COMPETITION FOR DESIGN OF IOWA BICENTENNIAL MEDALLION. ALSO INCLUDES STYLE SHOW AND MUSIC. AT HIGH SCHOOL GYM AND STUDENT CENTER. (LOCAL). MARGARET KEIGLEY, CHMN; MADRID FEDERATED WOMEN'S CLUB; RFD 2; MADRID, IA 50156. (#104519-15).

MAGNOLIA

HISTORY BOOK PROJECT - MAGNOLIA, IA. A BOOK ON THE HISTORY OF MAGNOLIA AND MAGNOLIA TOWNSHIP WILL BE WRITTEN. (LOCAL). LORITA RIDER, CHAIRPERSON; MAGNOLIA BICENTENNIAL COMMITTEE; BOX 26; MAGNOLIA, IA 51550. (#21778).

LOG CABIN RESTORATION - MAGNOLIA, IA. RESTORATION, CLEANING AND REFURBISHING CONTENTS ON LOG CABIN. (LOCAL). ELSIE FOLAND, CHAIRMAN; AILONGAM CLUB; MAGNOLIA, IA 51550. (#21777).

AUG 21, '76. CELEBRATION, OLD SETTLERS. LARGE PARADE; AFTERNOON PROGRAM; SPEAKER AND LOCAL TALENT; DANCE IN EVENING; CONCESSIONS AND FOOD STAND OPEN DAY AND EVENING; LOG CABIN CONTAINING ARTIFACTS OF PAST, OPEN ALL DAY; AND BASEBALL GAMES AT THE SCHOOL GROUNDS. AT TOWN PARK. (LOCAL). KAY J FREYMULLER, COORD; OLD SETTLERS ASSOC; 320 N 2ND AVE; LOGAN, IA 51546. (#105621-1).

MALCOM

ANTIQUE TRACTOR PULL. ENTRIES LIMITED TO OLDER STANDARD TRACTORS. (LOCAL). SID LAMB, COORD; MALCOM BICENTENNIAL COMMITTEE; RR #1; MALCOM, IA 50157. (#106849-3).

AUDITORIUM PROJECT - MALCOM, IA. RESTORATION AND RENOVATION OF MALCOM AUDITORIUM AS A COMMUNITY FACILITY. THE AUDITORIUM WAS ORIGINALLY BUILT IN 1899. (LOCAL). KEITH KOGER, CHAIRMAN; MALCOM AUDITORIUM COMMITTEE; BOX 159; MALCOM, IA 50157. (#24141).

PLANTING TREES AND FLOWERS - MALCOM, IA. PROJECT OF PLANTING TO IMPROVE PUBLIC PARK AREA INVOLVING LOCAL GROUPS. (LOCAL). SHARON ROBISON, COORDINATOR; MALCOM BICENTENNIAL COMMITTEE; BOX 49; MALCOM, IA 50157. (#24140).

RESTORE HONOR ROLL - MALCOM, IA. RESTORATION OF COMMUNITY HONOR ROLL LISTING THOSE FROM THE MALCOM COMMUNITY WHO SERVED IN THE MILITARY DURING WW I TO THE PRESENT. (LOCAL). BETTY STORY, CHAIRMAN; MALCOM BICENTENNIAL COMMITTEE; MALCOM, IA 50157. (#24139).

MAY 29, '76. MALCOM ALUMNI REUNION. ANNUAL ALUMNI REUNION OF MALCOM SCHOOL SYSTEM TO FEATURE BICENTENNIAL THEME. (LOCAL). GENEVA HEISHMAN; MALCOM PUBLIC SCHOOLS; MALCOM, IA 50157. (#106849-1).

JUNE 23, '76. DEDICATION OF AUDITORIUM. FOLLOWING DEDICATION CEREMONIES, THERE WILL BE A DANCE AND OTHER FORMS OF ENTERTAINMENT. (LOCAL). SHARON ROBISON; MALCOM AUDITORIUM COMMITTEE; BOX 49; MALCOM, IA 50157. (#106849-2).

JULY 10, '76. PORK BARBEQUE. CELEBRATION AND BARBEQUE TO ATTRACT RURAL MALCOM. (LOCAL). KEITH KOGER; MALCOM BICENTENNIAL COMMITTEE & FARMERS COOP ELEVATOR; BOX 159; MALCOM, IA 50157. (#106849-4).

MALLARD

PARK IMPROVEMENT PROJECT - MALLARD, IA. PURCHASE OF PLAYGROUND EQUIPMENT AND INSTALLATION OF TENNIS COURTS IN THE CITY PARK. (LOCAL). TOM TUTTLE, PRESIDENT; MALLARD COMMUNITY CLUB; MALLARD, IA 50562. (#22013).

RENOVATION OF LOCAL THEATER - MALLARD, IA. SEVERAL REMODELING AND REPAIR PROJECTS AND ORGANIZATION OF LOCAL REPERTORY GROUP. (LOCAL). PETE FORRY, CHAIRMAN; MALLARD COMMUNITY CLUB; MALLARD, IA 50562. (#22014).

JUNE 25, '76. BICENTENNIAL PAGEANT. LIVE PERFORMANCE AT MALLARD THEATER, MAIN ST. (LOCAL). NANCY NESHEIM, SECRETARY; MALLARD COMMUNITY CLUB; BOX 224; MALLARD, IA 50562. (#105781-10).

JUNE 25 - 27, '76. MALLARD BICENTENNIAL DAYS. A 2-DAY CELEBRATION IN OBSERVANCE OF OUR NATION'S 200TH BIRTHDAY. (LOCAL). PETE FORRY, CHAIRMAN; MALLARD COMMUNITY CLUB; MALLARD, IA 50562. (#105781-11).

JUNE 26, '76. BAND CONCERT AND CHILDREN'S COSTUME PARADE. LIVE PERFORMANCE AT MAIN STREET. (LOCAL). NANCY NESHEIM, SECRETARY; MALLARD COMMUNITY SCHOOL; BOX 224; MALLARD, IA 50562. (#105781-6).

JUNE 26, '76. BICENTENNIAL PARADE. PARADE. (LOCAL). KEITH SADLER, DIRECTOR; MALLARD BICENTENNIAL COMMITTEE; RFD; MALLARD, IA 50562. (#105781-2).

JUNE 26, '76. MUZZLE LOADER SHOOTING COMPETITION. COMPETITION AT SCHOOL GROUNDS. (LOCAL). RAYMOND REINHART, CHMN; MALLARD BICENTENNIAL COMMITTEE; RR; HAVELOCK, IA 50546. (#105781-9).

JUNE 26, '76. NOSTALGIA ON REVUE, STYLE SHOW, HISTORY OF WOMEN'S FASHIONS. LIVE PERFORMANCE AT MALLARD THEATRE, MAIN ST. (LOCAL). MARY SCHULLER, CHAIRMAN; MALLARD FEDERATED WOMEN'S CLUB; MALLARD, IA 50562. (#105781-8).

JUNE 26, '76. OLD-TIME STREET DANCE. FESTIVAL AT MAIN STREET. (LOCAL). MARY SCULLER, DIRECTOR; MALLARD BICENTENNIAL COMMITTEE; MALLARD, IA 50562. (#105781-5).

MALLARD — CONTINUED

JUNE 27, '76. ANTIQUE DISPLAY. DISPLAY OF ANTIQUES FROM LOCAL RESIDENTS. AT MALLARD THEATRE BASEMENT. (LOCAL). JEANNE GEHRT, DIRECTOR; MALLARD BICENTENNIAL COMMITTEE; MALLARD, IA 50562. (#105781-4).

JUNE 27, '76. CHILDREN'S OLYMPICS. COMPETITION AT MALLARD PARK. (LOCAL). PETE FORRY, DIRECTOR; MALLARD BICENTENNIAL COMMITTEE; MALLARD, IA 50562. (#105781-7).

JUNE 27, '76. IHSA ACCREDITED HORSE SHOW. THE HORSE SHOW HAS BEEN AN ANNUAL EVENT IN OUR COMMUNITY FOR THE PAST 25 YEARS. A SPECIAL HIGHLIGHT OF THE SHOW IS PRESENTATION OF THE 'TOM CONWAY TRAVELLING TROPHY'. AT SCHOOL GROUNDS. (LOCAL). TOM CONWAY, SR, CHAIRMAN; MALLARD COMMERCIAL CLUB; BOX 235; MALLARD, IA 50562. (#105781-3).

JUNE 27, '76. OLD-FASHIONED PICNIC IN THE PARK. EVERYONE IN THE COMMUNITY AND GUESTS ARE WELCOME. WILL BE FOLLOWED BY CHILDREN'S 'OLYMPICS'. AT MALLARD PARK. (LOCAL). BECKY LARSON, CHAIRMAN; MALLARD BICENTENNIAL COMMITTEE; MALLARD, IA 50562. (#105781-1).

MALVERN

HISTORY OF MALVERN, IA. LOCAL HISTORY BY PADDOCK WILL BE RE-ISSUED. (LOCAL). VIRGINIA CONNER, PROJ COORDINATOR; CITY OF MALVERN; MALVERN, IA 51551. (#24485).

TREE PLANTING PROJ, MALVERN, IA. TREES ARE BEING PLANTED AT LOCATIONS THROUGHOUT COMMUNITY, INCLUDING AT THE NEW SCHOOL, SWIMMING POOL AND PADDOCK PARK. (LOCAL). VIRGINIA CONNER, PROJ COORDINATOR; CITY OF MALVERN; MALVERN, IA 51551. (#24484).

JUNE 1 - 4, '76. CHAUTAUQUA. CEREMONY. (LOCAL). VIRGINIA CONNER, COORD; MALVERN BICENTENNIAL COMMISSION; MALVERN, IA 51551. (#106907-1).

JULY 4, '76. MALVERN COMMUNITY HIGH SCHOOL ALUMNI REUNION. FESTIVAL. (LOCAL). VIRGINIA CONNER, COORD; ALUMNI ASSOC; MALVERN, IA 51551. (#106908-1).

JULY 5, '76. DUTCH GUN CLUB INDEPENDENCE CELEBRATION. FESTIVAL, PARADE. (LOCAL). VIRGINIA CONNER, COORD; DUTCH GUN CLUB; MALVERN, IA 51551. (#106909-1).

AUG 2 - 5, '76. MILLS COUNTY FAIR. COMPETITION, FAIR. (LOCAL). VIRGINIA CONNER, COORD; EXTENSION SERVICE; MALVERN, IA 51551. (#106906-1).

MANCHESTER

COUNTY BEAUTIFICATION PROJECT, MANCHESTER, IA. PROJECT INVOLVES CLEANING UP AND BEAUTIFYING THE COUNTY. (LOCAL). MRS MARVIN ROSSON, PROJ COORDINATOR; 4-H CLUBS; MANCHESTER POST OFFICE; MANCHESTER, IA 52057. (#11555).

ESSAY CONTEST FOR SENIOR CITIZENS, MANCHESTER, IA. PROJECT IS AN ESSAY CONTEST FOR THE AREA'S SENIOR CITIZENS; SUBJECT WILL BE OF A HISTORIC NATURE. (LOCAL). ARMILLA RIES, PROJ COORDINATOR; SENIOR CITIZENS; 103 W HOWARD; MANCHESTER, IA 52057. (#11552).

ESSAY CONTEST IN MANCHESTER, IA. PROJECT IS AN ESSAY CONTEST WITH THE THEME BEING 'A PAST TO HONOR, A FUTURE TO MOLD'. (LOCAL). MRS BENNIE WORM, COUNTY PRESIDENT; FEDERATED WOMEN'S CLUBS; RR #1; MANCHESTER, IA 52057. (#11551).

LITERATURE BOOTH AT COUNTY FAIR, MANCHESTER, IA. A BICENTENNIAL INFORMATION BOOTH WILL BE SET UP AT THE DELAWARE COUNTY FAIR TO MAKE PEOPLE MORE AWARE OF THE BICENTENNIAL. (LOCAL). EDYTHE SATTERLEE, PROJ COORDINATOR; DELAWARE COUNTY FAIR; 1028 N 2ND ST; MANCHESTER, IA 52057. (#11557).

REPLACEMENT OF WWII CANNONS, MANCHESTER, IA. REPLACEMENT OF 2 CANNONS THAT WERE REMOVED FROM COURTHOUSE LAWN DURING WWII & GIVEN TO THE GOVERNMENT FOR SCRAP IRON. (LOCAL). M T SEPIC, CHAIRMAN; MANCHESTER AREA BICENTENNIAL CELEBRATION COMMITTEE; 200 E MAIN ST; MANCHESTER, IA 52027. (#23176).

TREE PLANTING - PROJ OF MANCHESTER, IA. A TREE PLANTING PROJECT TO REPLACE THE DEAD ELMS ON THE FAIRGROUNDS. (LOCAL). EDYTHE SATTERLEE, PROJ DIRECTOR; COUNTY FAIR; 1028 N 2ND ST; MANCHESTER, IA 52057. (#11550).

JAN 15 - APR 15, '76. HISTORICAL POSTER CONTEST. ELEMENTARY SCHOOL CHILDREN WILL PARTICIPATE IN A POSTER CONTEST; THEME OF POSTERS WILL BE OF A HISTORIC NATURE. AT DELAWARE COUNTY FAIR EXHIBIT HALL. (LOCAL). EDYTHE SATTERLEE; DELAWARE CO BICENTENNIAL COMMISSION; 1028 N 2ND ST; MANCHESTER, IA 52057. (#11553-1).

MAR 1 - JULY 4, '76. BEARD CONTEST. VARIED STYLES OF BEARDS WILL BE FEATURED. AT FAIRGROUNDS. (LOCAL). J CORCORAN, COORD; MANCHESTER AREA BICENTENNIAL CELEBRATION COMMITTEE; 105 S FRANKLIN; MANCESTER, IA 52057. (#23175-5).

MAR 2, '76. BURIAL OF THE BALDE. BURIAL OF 5 FOOT RAZOR TO MARK START OF BEARD CONTEST. AT DELAWARE COUNTY COURT HOUSE. (LOCAL). M T SEPIC, CHAIRMAN; MANCHESTER AREA BICENTENNIAL CELEBRATION COMMITTEE; 107 E FAYETTE; MANCHESTER, IA 52057. (#200018-117).

JUNE 30 - JULY 4, '76. BICENTENNIAL QUEEN CONTEST. CEREMONY, COMPETITION. (LOCAL). M T SEPIC, CHMN; MANCHESTER AREA BICENTENNIAL COMMITTEE; 200 E MAIN; MANCHESTER, IA 52057. (#106415-1).

JULY 4, '76. BAND CONCERT. LIVE PERFORMANCE AT DELAWARE COUNTY FAIRGROUNDS. (LOCAL). M T SEPIC, CHMN; MANCHESTER AREA BICENTENNIAL CELEBRATION COMMITTEE; 107 E FAYETTE; MANCHESTER, IA 52057. (#23175-4).

JULY 4, '76. BICENTENNIAL CELEBRATION. BREAKFAST, PARADE, RECREATIONAL ACTIVITIES, BAND CONCERT, FIREWORKS AND DANCE. (LOCAL). M T SEPIC, CHAIRMAN; MANCHESTER AREA BICENTENNIAL CELEBRATION COM & CHAMBER OF COMMERCE; 200 E MAIN ST; MANCHESTER, IA 52057. (#104620-2).

JULY 4, '76. OLDEST SENIOR CITIZEN CONTEST. NOMINATION OF THE OLDEST PERSON IN DELAWARE COUNTY. (LOCAL). M T SEPIC, CHMN; MANCHESTER AREA BICENTENNIAL COMMITTEE; 200 E MAIN; MANCHESTER, IA 52057. (#106416-1).

JULY 4, '76. PARADE, AMERICA BY AMERICANS. PARADE TO FEATURE PAST, PRESENT AND FUTURE. AT MAIN ST. (LOCAL). M T SEPIC, CHMN; MANCHESTER AREA BICENTENNIAL CELEBRATION COMMITTEE; 107 E FAYETTE; MANCHESTER, IA 52057. (#23175-2).

JULY 4, '76. RECREATIONAL ACTIVITIES. COMPETITION, FESTIVAL AT DELAWARE COUNTY FAIRGOUNDS. (LOCAL). M T SEPIC, CHMN; MANCHESTER AREA BICENTENNIAL CELEBRATION COMMITTEE; 107 E FAYETTE; MANCHESTER, IA 52057. (#23175-3).

JULY 22, '76. BURIAL OF TIME CAPSULE. BURIAL OF CAPSULE WITH ARTICLES FROM 1976 TO BE DUG UP IN 2076. AT DELAWARE COUNTY FAIRGROUNDS. (LOCAL). MT SEPIC, CHAIRMAN; MANCHESTER AREA BICENTENNIAL CELEBRATION COMMITTEE; 107 E FAYETTE; MANCHESTER, IA 52057. (#104621-2).

MANLY

CHURCH SIGNS, MANLY, IA. SIGNS WITH SERVICE TIME SCHEDULE FOR 4 LOCAL CHURCHES WILL BE SET UP IN MANLY. (LOCAL). WAYNE F NORTHWAY, CO-CHAIRMAN; MANLY BICENTENNIAL COMMISSION; MANLY, IA 50456. (#21726).

MANLY AND WORTH COUNTY HISTORY BOOKS, IA. THE HISTORY OF MANLY WILL BE INCLUDED IN THE WORTH COUNTY BICENTENNIAL HISTORY BOOK AND MANLY'S CENTENNIAL BOOK IN 1977. (LOCAL). WAYNE F NORTHWAY, CO-CHAIRMAN; MANLY BICENTENNIAL COMMISSION; MANLY, IA 50456. (#21727).

RAILROAD CONTROL TOWER PLAQUE, MANLY, IA. A PLAQUE WITH INFORMATION ABOUT THE TOWER WILL BE INSTALLED. (LOCAL). ARTHUR HOLDEN, COORDINATOR; MANLY BICENTENNIAL COMMISSION; MANLY, IA 50456. (#21731).

RECOGNITION OF EARLY HOMES & BUSINESSES, MANLY, IA. A LIST OF EARLY HOMES AND BUSINESSES WILL BE MADE. (LOCAL). WILMA TREBIL, PROJ COORDINATOR; MANLY BICENTENNIAL COMMISSION; 110 SPRING ST; MANLY, IA 50456. (#21729).

RESTORATION OF OLD STOCKYARDS, IA. RESTORATION & PRESERVATION OF ONE OF THE LAST SOTCK YARDS IN THIS AREA. (LOCAL). ARTHUR HOLDEN, COORDINATOR; MANLY BICENTENNIAL COMMISSION; MANLY, IA 50456. (#21732).

SCHOOLHOUSE RESTORATION, MANLY, IA. PRESERVATION OF RESTORATION OF THE FIRST SCHOOLHOUSE IN MANLY. (LOCAL). WAYNE F NORTHWAY, CO-CHAIRMAN; MANLY BICENTENNIAL COMMISSION; MANLY, IA 50456. (#21733).

STORE WINDOW DISPLAY, MANLY, IA. DISPLAY OF OLD PHOTOGRAPHS OF MANLY & OTHER HISTORICAL ITEMS. (LOCAL). ARTHUR HOLDEN, CO-CHAIRMAN; MANLY BICENTENNIAL COMMISSION; MANLY, IA 50456. (#21730).

TIME CAPSULE PROJECT, MANLY, IA. A TIME CAPSULE WITH PRESENT ITEMS WILL BE BURIED, TO BE DUG UP IN THE FUTURE. (LOCAL). ROGER TIETIENS, LEADER; TOWN & COUNTRY 4-H CLUB; 103 - 1/2 ELMORE; MANLY, IA 50456. (#21728).

MAR 2, '76. OLD FASHIONED STYLE SHOW. LIVE PERFORMANCE AT A LOCAL CHURCH. (LOCAL). MARLENE HARGIS, COORD; MANLY GIRL SCOUTS; RURAL ROUTE I; MANLY, IA 50456. (#105516-1).

JULY 4, '76. ECUMENICAL CHURCH SERVICE. CEREMONY. (LOCAL). WILMA TREBIL, CO-CHMN; UNITED METHODIST/CATHOLIC/LUTHERAN/BAPTIST CHURCHES; 110 SPRING STREET; MANLY, IA 50456. (#105516-3).

MANNING

BEAUTIFICATION ON MAIN STREET, MANNING, IA. ALL BUSINESS PEOPLE ON MAIN ST WILL SET OUT FLOWER PLANTERS WITH RED WHITE & BLUE FLOWERS, BEGINNING MAY 1ST. (LOCAL). LARRY HANSEN, COUNCILMAN; MANNING FIRE DEPT; HWY 14; MANNING, IA 51455. (#24633).

MAY 16, '76. DEDICATION OF NEW MANNING FIRE DEPARTMENT BUILDING. CEREMONY, FESTIVAL AT MANNING FIRE DEPT BLDG, LOCATED ON HIGHWAY 141. (LOCAL). LARRY HANSEN, COORD; MANNING FIRE DEPARTMENT; 333 FIRST ST; MANNING, IA 51455. (#107734-1).

MANSON

FEB 18 - 20, '76. MERIDIAN SINGERS BICENTENNIAL SALUTE. LIVE PERFORMANCE AT HIGH SCHOOL AUDITORIUM. (LOCAL). BYRON HENN, COORD; MERIDIAN SINGERS; MAIN ST; MANSON, IA 50563. (#200018-118).

JULY 11, '76. COMMUNITY SERVICE AND FUN DAY. SERVICE IN MORNING 11AM TO 12AM THEN COMMUNITY PICNIC FREE MEAT COMPLIMENTS CHAMBER OF COMMERCE AND TURKEY ASSOCIATION SACK RACES, ETC. IN AFTERNOON. AT FAIRGROUNDS. (LOCAL). REV WIPPERMAN; MANSON MINISTERIAL ASSOCIATION; 1310 MAIN; MANSON, IA 50563. (#107688-3).

MAPLETON

HISTORIC PHOTO COLLECTION IN MAPLETON, IA. COLLECTION OF PHOTOS OF HISTORY OF AREA TO BE HUNG IN LOCAL LIBRARY & CITY HALL. (LOCAL). EDWARD MAIER, PRESIDENT; ROTARY CLUB; MAPLETON, IA 51034. (#21396).

TREE PLANTING IN MAPLETON, IA. PLANTING MAPLE TREES. (LOCAL). EDWARD MAIER, COORDINATOR; BOY SCOUT TROOP 336; MAPLETON, IA 51034. (#21397).

FEB 1 - MAR 2, '76. 'DAY AFTER TOMORROW' -DISCUSSION. A YOUTHFUL LOOK AT THE 3RD CENTURY. PRESENTATION TO LOCAL GOVERNMENT AND SERVICE GROUPS. (LOCAL). EDWARD MAIER, COORD; BOY SCOUTS TROOP 336; MAPLETON, IA 51034. (#105319-2).

MAR 15, '76. CHORAL FESTIVAL. LIVE PERFORMANCE AT HIGH SCHOOL AUDITORIUM. (LOCAL). C R BROWN, DIRECTOR; JR HIGH MUSIC DEPT - MAPLE VALLEY; MAPLETON, IA 51034. (#200018-119).

JULY 15 - 18, '76. AMERICAN AGRICULTURE-A CONTINUING REVOLUTION - EXHIBIT. SMITHSONIAN INSTITUTE EXHIBIT AUGMENTED BY LOCAL ANTIQUE MACHINERY, IMPLEMENTS, MODERN MACHINERY SHOWS; AND OTHER RELATED EXHIBITS. HOURS ARE: 7/15, 7-10 PM; 7/16, 10AM-10PM; 7/17, 2-10PM; AND 7/18, 1-6PM. AT NATIONAL GUARD ARMORY - 1 BLOCK SOUTH W. 141. (ST-WIDE). ED MAIER, CHAIRMAN; MAPLETON COMMUNITY CLUB & ROTARY CLUB; MAPLETON, IA 51034. (#104819-1).

JULY 15 - 18, '76. BICENTENNIAL CELEBRATION. FRIDAY: KIDS PARADE, CARNIVAL, POLKA STREET DANCE; SATURDAY: PARADE, STREET ENTERTAINMENT, LIVING EXHIBIT, TEEN DANCE, SQUARE DANCE; SUNDAY AFTERNOON: COMMUNITY PICNIC WITH FIDDLER'S CONTEST, OLD SETTLERS, ETC. (LOCAL). BILL HAGERTON, PRESIDENT; MAPLETON COMMUNITY CLUB; MAPLETON, IA 51034. (#104819-2).

MAQUOKETA

'BORROW A KIT' - JACKSON COUNTY, IA. SLIDES, SCREENS AND PROJECTORS WILL BE PURCHASED AND PLACED IN THE 4 PUBLIC LIBRARIES IN THE COUNTY; TEACHERS AND GROUPS WILL HAVE ACCESS TO THE KIT - SLIDES WILL FEATURE COUNTY HISTORIC SITES. (LOCAL). LUCILLE SORENSEN, PRESIDENT; JACKSON COUNTY BICENTENNIAL ASSOC; C/O MAQUOKETA STATE BANK; MAQUOKETA, IA 52060. (#14744).

CABIN RESTORATION IN MAQUOKETA, IA. OVER 100 YR OLD LOG CABIN WILL BE MOVED TO COUNTY FAIRGROUNDS AND REBUILT. (LOCAL). G HOLIHAN, CURATOR; JACKSON COUNTY HISTORICAL SOCIETY; RR 4; MAQUOKETA, IA 52060. (#14737).

CHURCH AND CEMETERY RECORDING PROJ, MAQUOKETA, IA. CHURCH RECORDS FOR MICROFILMING AND HISTORICAL SOCIETY USE. CEMETERY RECORD OF LOCATION AND INSCRIPTIONS ON BURIAL STONES. (LOCAL). LUCILLE SORENSEN, PRESIDENT; JACKSON COUNTY BICENTENNIAL ASSOC; C/O MAQUOKETA STATE BANK; MAQUOKETA, IA 52060. (#14739).

FOXFIRE PROGRAM OF MAQUOKETA, IA. INTERVIEWING OF ELDERLY RESIDENTS TO LEARN OF LIFESTYLE AND CUSTOMS OF EARLIER GENERATIONS. (LOCAL). LUCILLE SORENSON, PRESIDENT; JACKSON COUNTY BICENTENNIAL ASSOC; C/O MAQUOKETA STATE BANK; MAQUOKETA, IA 52060. (#14738).

GOV BRIGGS RESEARCH, JACKSON COUNTY, IA. COMPILATION OF INFORMATION ON FIRST GOVERNOR OF STATE OF IOWA. (ST-WIDE). LUCILLE SORENSEN, PRESIDENT; JACKSON COUNTY HISTORICAL SOCIETY; MAQUOKETA, IA 52060. (#14742).

INDIAN BURIAL SITE MARKING, JACKSON COUNTY, IA. ALL INDIAN BURIAL SITES IN THE COUNTY WILL BE MARKED AND RECORDED. (LOCAL). LUCILLE SORENSEN, PRESIDENT; JACKSON COUNTY BICENTENNIAL ASSOC; C/O MAQUOKETA STATE BANK; MAQUOKETA, IA 52060. (#14740).

JACKSON COUNTY BICENTENNIAL NATURE PARK, IA. DEVELOP A PARK IN AREA BETWEEN COUNTY HOSPITAL AND MAQUOKETA RIVER; PRESERVE AND ADD NATIVE PLANTINGS INCLUDING WILDFLOWERS. HARD SURFACED TRAILS FOR WHEELCHAIRS, WOODCHIP IN LOWER AREA. (LOCAL). LUCILLE SORENSEN, PRESIDENT; JACKSON COUNTY BICENTENNIAL ASSOC; C/O MAQUOKETA STATE BANK; MAQUOKETA, IA 52060. (#14736).

REPRINTS FOR FUNDRAISING IN JACKSON COUNTY, IA. A 1878 GAZETEER AND DIRECTORY AND A SPECIAL 1904 EDITION OF THE NEWSPAPER WILL BE REPRINTED FOR SALE. (LOCAL). LUCILLE SORENSEN, PRESIDENT; JACKSON COUNTY BICENTENNIAL ASSOC; C/O MAQUOKETA STATE BANK; MAQUOKETA, IA 52060. (#14741).

TREE PLANTING IN MAQUOKETA, IA. PLANTING TREES ON SCHOOL AND HOSPITAL GROUNDS BY VARIOUS COMMUNITY GROUPS. (LOCAL). LUCILLE SORENSEN, PRESIDENT; JACKSON COUNTY BICENTENNIAL ASSOC; C/O MAQUOKETA STATE BANK; MAQUOKETA, IA 52060. (#14743).

MAR 2, '76. SPIRIT OF '76 BICENTENNIAL BALL. FESTIVAL AT ROSE GARDEN, HIWAY 64 W. (LOCAL). MILDRED BECK, PROJ COORD; JACKSON COUNTY BICENTENNIAL ASSOC; RR #1; BELLEVUE, IA 52031. (#200018-109).

APR 29 - MAY 8, '76. 'GEORGE M'. LIVE PERFORMANCE AT CULTURAL CENTER, E PIATT AND ELIZA. (LOCAL). DEAN TILTON, DIRECTOR; PEACE PIPE PLAYERS; 101 N MAIN; MAQUOKETA, IA 52060. (#200018-110).

MAQUOKETA — CONTINUED

JUNE 6, '76. OPEN HOUSE OF CHURCHES. TOUR AT LOCAL CHURCHES. (LOCAL). REV RUSSELL FATE; MINISTERIAL ASSOCIATION; 810 W SUMMIT; MAQUOKETA, IA 52060. (#108200-11).

JUNE 6, '76. TOUR OF OLDER HOMES. TOUR AT VARIOUS HOMES IN THE MAQUOKETA AREA DIRECTIONS IN SOCIETY BROCHURES. (LOCAL). GRACE HOLIHAN; JACKSON COUNTY HISTORICAL SOCIETY; PO BOX 1335; MAQUOKETA, IA 52060. (#108200-12).

JUNE 7, '76. LOCAL HERITAGE NIGHT: SR CITIZEN APPRECIATION. LOCAL CITIZENS WILL PARTICIPATE IN ROUND TABLE DISCUSSIONS ABOUT LOCAL HISTORIC PERSONALITIES. (LOCAL). JEAN COONS, PROJ COORD; JACKSON COUNTY BICENTENNIAL COMMITTEE; MAQUOKETA, IA 52060. (#108200-10).

JUNE 8, '76. FARMERS DAY - OLD & NEW MACHINERY DISPLAYS. HORSE SHOE DEMONSTRATION, SQUARE DANCE, AWARD TO CENTURY FARMS AND BARBER SHOP QUARTET WILL BE FEATURED AT FARMERS DAY. AT JACKSON COUNTY FAIR GROUNDS, BOYER HALL. (LOCAL). LOREN LUBBEN, PROJ CHMN; CATTLEMANS ASSOC & PORK PRODUCERS, CATHOLIC DAUGHTER OF AMERICA; RT 4; MAQUOKETA, IA 52060. (#108200-9).

JUNE 9, '76. ECUMENICAL WORSHIP SERVICE. THE SPEAKER WILL BE DR JAMES SPALDING, DEAN OF RELIGION, UNIV OF IOWA. AT JACKSON COUNTY FAIR GROUNDS, PEARSON HALL. (LOCAL). REV RUSSELL FATE, DIR; MINISTERIAL ASSOC; 810 SUMMIT; MAQUOKETA, IA 52060. (#108200-7).

JUNE 9, '76. '1776' - PATRIOTIC MUSICAL. LIVE PERFORMANCE AT 207 S MAIN. (LOCAL). DENNIS VOY, DIRECTOR; VOY THEATRE 2; 308 N JONES; MAQUOKETA, IA 52060. (#108200-8).

JUNE 10, '76. ROCK DANCE WITH THE 'OZONE RANGERS'. FESTIVAL AT JACKSON COUNTY FAIR GROUNDS, BOYER HALL. (LOCAL). BONNIE BELLENDIER, COORD; MAQUOKETA BICENTENNIAL COMMITTEE; 418 W JUDSON; MAQUOKETA, IA 52060. (#108200-6).

JUNE 11, '76. BUSINESS DAYS DOWNTOWN: RED, WHITE & BLUE SALES. MAIN STREET WILL BE BLOCKED OFF FOR ENTERTAINMENT. AT MAIN ST. (LOCAL). JEAN COONS, COORDINATOR; RETAIL TRADE PROMOTIONS; 213 S MAIN; MAQUOKETA, IA 52060. (#108200-5).

JUNE 12, '76. BICENTENNIAL BALL. FESTIVAL AT ROSE GARDEN, HWY 64 W. (LOCAL). BERNHARD ROSENBERG, COORD; MAQUOKETA BICENTENNIAL COMMITTEE; 106 S ELIZA; MAQUOKETA, IA 52060. (#108200-4).

JUNE 12, '76. MAQUOKETA HIGH SCHOOL CLASS REUNION. FESTIVAL AT MAQUOKETA SR HIGH SCHOOL, 600 WASHINGTON. (LOCAL). GERTRUDE MUDD, DIRECTOR; MAQUOKETA HIGH SCHOOL CLASS REUNION COMMITTEE; 110 N ELIZA; MAQUOKETA, IA 52060. (#108200-3).

JUNE 13, '76. CHILDREN'S THEATER WITH LITTLE RED CABOOSE. LIVE PERFORMANCE AT FIRST WARD PARK BETWEEN E APPLE AND E QUARRY. (LOCAL). PAT GLANDORF, DIRECTOR; MAQUOKETA BICENTENNIAL COMMITTEE; 301 S ELIZA; MAQUOKETA, IA 52060. (#108200-2).

JUNE 14, '76. BICENTENNIAL PARADE. PARADE ENDING AT FAIRGROUNDS IN FRONT OF GRANDSTAND FOR JUDGING; GRANDSTAND SHOW FEATURING SWEET ADELINE CHORUS, WESTSIDE DELEGATION & FIREWORKS SPONSORED BY OPTIMIST CLUB WILL END BICENTENNIAL WEEK. AT PARADE LINE UP ON S MAIN STREET ENDING AT JACKSON COUNTY FAIRGROUND. (LOCAL). JOANN CAVEN, COORDINATOR; BICENTENNIAL PARADE COMMITTEE; RR 2; EMELINE, IA 52060. (#108200-1).

JUNE 19, '76. CHURCH NIGHT & CHOIRS CONCERT. ECUMENICAL CHURCH SERVICE - MUSIC BY COMBINED CHOIRS; ADDRESS BY COLLEGE PROF OF RELIGION. AT PEARSON CENTER AT THE JACKSON COUNTY FAIRGROUNDS. (LOCAL). LUCILLE SORENSEN, PRES; JACKSON COUNTY BICENTENNIAL ASSOC; MAQUOKETA, IA 52060. (#102046-1).

JULY 21 - 25, '76. COUNTY FAIR. FLOATS WILL BE PREPARED FOR THE FAIR; EXHIBITS AND PERFORMANCES WILL HAVE A BICENTENNIAL THEME. AT COUNTY FAIRGROUNDS. (LOCAL). LUCILLE E SORENSON, COORD; JACKSON COUNTY FAIR BOARD; 307 W PLEASANT; MAQUOKETA, IA 52060. (#102045-1).

SEPT 26, '76. PIONEER DAYS. PIONEER DAYS WILL INCLUDE EXHIBITS AND EDUCATIONAL PRESENTATIONS. (LOCAL). LUCILLE E SORENSON, COORD; JACKSON COUNTY HISTORICAL SOCIETY; 307 W PLEASANT; MAQUOKETA, IA 52060. (#102045-2).

MARBLE ROCK

COMMEMORATIVE BOOKLET, MARBLE ROCK, IA. PUBLICATION OF COMMEMORATIVE BOOKLET CONTAINING INTERVIEWS & HISTORICAL INFORMATION ABOUT THE TOWN. (LOCAL). DENNIS A CARNEY, CHAIRMAN; MARBLE ROCK BICENTENNIAL COMMITTEE; RURAL ROUTE 1; GREENE, IA 50636. (#19326).

MARBLE ROCK HISTORICAL MUSEUM - MARBLE ROCK, IA. MUSEUM CONTAINING ITEMS FROM TOWN'S PAST ESTABLISHED IN OLD BANK BUILDING. (LOCAL). ARNOLD STAUDT, PRESIDENT; MARBLE ROCK HISTORICAL SOCIETY; MARBLE ROCK, IA 50653. (#19738).

NEWSPAPER MICROFILMING PROJECT, MARBLE ROCK, IA. OLD TOWN NEWSPAPERS FROM 1870'S TO 1920'S TO BE MICROFILMED & PLACED IN TOWN LIBRARY. (LOCAL). JO NEAL, CHAIRMAN; MARBLE ROCK BETTERMENT COUNCIL; MARBLE ROCK, IA 50653. (#19327).

JULY 3 - 4, '76. 4TH OF JULY CELEBRATION. SATURDAY: PARADE, CONTEST & FIREWORKS; SUNDAY: COMMUNITY-WIDE CHURCH SERVICE & POTLUCK SUPPER. (LOCAL). DENNIS A CARNEY, CHAIRMAN; MARBLE ROCK BICENTENNIAL COMMITTEE; RR 1; GREENE, IA 50636. (#104332-7).

MARCUS

OUR NEXT HUNDRED YEARS: MARCUS, IA. ESSAY CONTEST: ENTRIES TO BE BOUND AND PLACED IN LOCAL LIBRARY FOR FUTURE REFERENCE. SUBJECT: 'OUR FUTURE'. (LOCAL). LOIS MAYER, COMMITTEE CO-CHAIRMAN; MARCUS BICENTENNIAL COMMITTEE; RFD; MARCUS, IA 51025. (#22199).

STOREFRONT CELEBRATION - MARCUS, IA. DECORATION OF STORE WINDOWS WITH ARTICLES AND RELICS OF OUR PAST, AND ARTICLES OF THE FUTURE. (LOCAL). MRS JOE ROSENER, CHAIRMAN; NON AME CLUB; RFD; MARCUS, IA 51035. (#22200).

30 YEARS OF 'THE MARCUS NEWS' - MARCUS, IA. THE MARCUS NEWS WILL BE BOUND TO PRESERVE THE DAILY HAPPENINGS IN THE COMMUNITY. (LOCAL). STEPHEN J SMITH, COMMITTEE CO-CHAIRMAN; MARCUS WOMENS CLUB & BICENTENNIAL COMMITTEE; 509 MAIN ST; MARCUS, IA 51035. (#22198).

JULY 4, '76. COMMUNITY PICNIC & FIREWORKS DISPLAY. FESTIVAL AT MARCUS COMMUNITY PARK, 100 PARK AVE. (LOCAL). STEPHEN J SMITH, CHMN; MARCUS BICENTENNIAL COMMITTEE; 211 S ASH; MARCUS, IA 51035. (#105955-1).

JULY 4, '76. PARADE. FESTIVAL AT MAIN ST. (LOCAL). LOIS MAYER, CHMN; MARCUS BICENTENNIAL COMMITTEE; RFD; MARCUS, IA 51035. (#105955-2).

MARENGO

BICENTENNIAL COLOR GUARD IN MARENGO, IA. A COUNTY COLOR GUARD WILL BE FORMED TO APPEAR THROUGHOUT COUNTY AT VARIOUS BICENTENNIAL ACTIVITIES. (LOCAL). DEWEY SULLIVAN, AMERICAN LEGION COMMANDER; AMERICAN LEGION; 402 EASTERN AVE; MARENGO, IA 52301. (#15083).

MARENGO, IA, BEAUTIFICATION PROJECT. BEAUTIFY COMMUNITY AREA FOR THE BICENTENNIAL. (LOCAL). LOWELL MCKEAN, EXTENSION DIRECTOR; IOWA COUNTY BICENTENNIAL COMMISSION; 795 FRANKLIN; MARENGO, IA 52301. (#15084).

FEB 20 - 22, '76. IOWA LONG RIFLES WINTER RENDEZVOUS. REENACTMENT OF FUR TRADE RENDEZVOUS OF 1820'S-40'S. (LOCAL). ROBERT L OLSEN, PRES; IOWA LONG RIFLES; 797 WADAMS; MARENGO, IA 52301. (#105321-1).

MARION

BICENTENNIAL SCHOOL RECOGNITION PROGRAM - IA. LOCAL SCHOOLS DEVELOP A BICENTENNIAL THEME IN EACH OF THREE AREAS. (ST-WIDE). LLEWELLYN BALSTER, CO-CHAIRPERSON; IOWA & MARION BICENTENNIAL COMMITTEES; 7TH ST & 10TH AVE; MARION, IA 52301. (#27601).

CHERRY SISTERS REVIVAL. LIVE PERFORMANCE AT MARION HIGH AUDITORIUM. (LOCAL). JIM DELONG, CHMN; OLD BARN PLAYERS/CREATIVE EVENTS COUNCIL; 245 DELONG DR; MARION, IA 52302. (#101934-1).

FLAG CITY USA - MARION, IA. FLAG DISPLAY ON ALL POSSIBLE DOWNTOWN BUILDINGS AND HOMES. (LOCAL). JIM REYNOLDS, COMMANDER; AMERICAN LEGION 298; MARION, IA 52302. (#14637).

HISTORICAL MUSEUM - PROJ OF MARION, IA. A HISTORICAL MUSEUM WILL BE CONSTRUCTED IN MARION. (LOCAL). DARLENE MOLLENHAUER, PROJ DIRECTOR; MARION MUSEUM ASSOCIATION; RR 2; MARION, IA 52302. (#14345).

PRESERVATION & REGISTRATION - PROJ OF MARION, IA. PRESERVATION AND REGISTRATION OF LOCAL HOMES AND BUILDINGS. (LOCAL). MRS JAN HINKER, CHAIRMAN; MARION CREATIVE EVENTS COUNCIL; 7TH ST; MARION, IA 52302. (#14638).

RESTORATION OF 1850 HOME IN MARION, IA. AN 8 ROOM HOUSE & CARRIAGE HOUSE WILL BE RESTORED AS IT WAS IN 1850. (LOCAL). DALE MINER, PRESIDENT; MARION HISTORICAL MUSEUM, INC; 970 10TH ST; MARION, IA 52302. (#23086). **ARBA GRANTEE.**

SWEETSER MINI - PARK, MARION, IA. A MINI-PARK FOR USE OF LOCAL RESIDENTS & TRAVELERS PASSING THROUGH THE TOWN. A MAP MARKING HISTORICAL POINTS OF INTEREST AROUND THE COMMUNITY WILL BE PLACED THERE. (LOCAL). MRS LLOYD C COOK, COORD; SWEETSER BICENTENNIAL ORGANIZATION; 2648N 500W; MARION, IA 52302. (#21575).

WORKING EXHIBITS - MARION, IA. CRAFT DEMONSTRATIONS AND CLASSES, SUCH AS, QUILTING, SOAP MAKING, CANING, RUG MAKING AND SPINNING. (LOCAL). MRS PHYLLIS ROSS, WORKING EXHIBITS CHAIRMAN; MARION BICENTENNIAL COMMISSION; 7TH ST & 10TH AVE; MARION, IA 52302. (#27602).

JUNE 7, '76. SWAMP FOX REVIEWS, VARIETY SHOW. SKITS, FOLK SINGERS, DANCE & PERSONS PLAYING MUSICAL INSTRUMENTS ARE AMONG THE ATTRACTIONS. AT LINN-MAR HIGH SCHOOL. (LOCAL). KAYE COUGHLIN, PROJ CHMN; MARION BICENTENNIAL COMMISSION; 1620 7TH AVE; MARION, IA 52302. (#108340-4).

JULY 3, '76. PIONEER KING & QUEEN CONTEST. CONTESTANTS MUST BE 60 YEARS OR OLDER & A RESIDENT OF MARION; ONE CENT PER VOTE DONATION; PROCEEDS WILL GO TO THE MARION HISTORICAL MUSEUM. KING & QUEEN CROWNED IN A PUBLIC CEREMONY ON SAT EVENING, JULY 3RD, 1976. (LOCAL). WALTER RECH, DIRECTOR; KIWANIS CLUB; 483 8TH AVE; MARION, IA 52302. (#108340-5).

JULY 3 - 9, '76. OLD BARN PLAYERS PRESENTATION ON CHERRY SISTERS & MARION'S HISTORY. LIVE PERFORMANCE AT LINN-MAR HIGH SCHOOL. (LOCAL). KAYE COUGHLIN, COORD; MARION BICENTENNIAL COMMISSION; 1620 7TH AVE; MARION, IA 52302. (#108461-2).

JULY 3 - 10, '76. MARION BICENTENNIAL FESTIVAL. CHERRY SISTERS DRAMA, THREE PERFORMANCES; PARADE ON SATURDAY AND ON SUNDAY, INTERDENOMINATIONAL CHURCH SERVICES IN THE PARK, WORKING EXHIBITS, SPORTS, PICNICS, CONCERTS, AND PLAYS INCLUDED IN THE FESTIVAL. (LOCAL). LLEWELLYN BALSTER, CHMN; MARION BICENTENNIAL COMMISSION; 1776 8TH AVE; MARION, IA 52302. (#106952-1).

JULY 4, '76. A CITY SQUARE CELEBRATION: RE-DEDICATION TO LIBERTY. CEREMONY. (LOCAL). REV LYLE LEE, CHAIRMAN; MARION COUNCIL OF CHURCHES; 14TH AVE & 29TH ST; MARION, IA 52302. (#108340-1).

JULY 4, '76. GRANGER HOUSE - MARION HISTORICAL MUSEUM. EXHIBIT. (LOCAL). DALE MINER, COORD; MARION HISTORICAL MUSEUM; 1115 COUNTRY CLUB DR; MARION, IA 52302. (#108461-1).

JULY 5, '76. BICENTENNIAL ACTIVITIES DAY. SACK RACES, TUG OF WAR, PIE EATING CONTEST & MUSIC ARE AMONG THE ATTRACTIONS. AT THOMAS PARK. (LOCAL). CARL BAUR, COORD; MARION BICENTENNIAL COMMISSION; 395 VALLEYVIEW DR; MARION, IA 52302. (#108461-4).

JULY 6 - 9, '76. FRANCIS MARION - THE SWAMP FOX. FILM STRIP ON FRANCIS MARION, NAMESAKE OF THE TOWN, WILL ALSO BE SHOWN AT 11:00 AM, 1:00 PM, 2:00 PM AND 3:00 PM. AT C B VERNON JUNIOR HIGH SCHOOL. (LOCAL). K COUGHLIN, PROJ CHMN; MARION BICENTENNIAL COMMISSION; 1100 8TH AVE; MARION, IA 52302. (#108340-2).

JULY 6 - 9, '76. WORKING DISPLAYS ON OLD CRAFTS. PEOPLE WILL BE PERFORMING OLD CRAFTS SUCH AS WEAVING, QUILTING, BEEF JERKY, SPINNING, OFF-LOOM WEAVING, WOOD CARVING, MACRAME, QUILLING, KLOSTERSOM, BROOM MAKING, CANDLE DIPPING, CHAIR CARING. AT COMMUNITY CENTER, 654 10TH AVE. (LOCAL). PHYLLIS ROSS, CHAIRMAN; MARION BICENTENNIAL COMMISSION; 2460 26TH AVE; MARION, IA 52302. (#108340-3).

JULY 10, '76. BICENTENNIAL PARADE. PARADE. (LOCAL). CARL BAUR, CHMN; MARION EVENING LIONS/MARION CREATIVE EVENTS COUNCIL; 395 VALLEYVIEW DR; MARION, IA 52305. (#101935-1).

OCT 5, '76. US ARMED FORCES BICENTENNIAL BAND CONCERT. LIVE PERFORMANCE AT LINN MAR SCHOOL GYM. (ST-WIDE). LLEURLLYN BALST, CHRPSN; MARION BICENTENNIAL COMMISSION, INC; NORTH 10TH ST; MARION, IA 52302. (#109098-1).

MARNE

MARNE LIBRARY PROJECT, IA. BOOKS WILL BE COLLECTED FOR OPERATION OF PROPOSED MARNE LIBRARY. (LOCAL). MERRILL D BUCKLEY, CHAIRMAN; MARNE BICENTENNIAL COMMISSION; MARNE, IA 51552. (#21419).

JULY 4, '76. 4TH OF JULY KIDDIES PARADE. PARADE AT MAIN ST. (LOCAL). MERRILL D BUCKLEY, CHMN; MARNE BICENTENNIAL COMMISSION; MARNE, IA 51552. (#105331-1).

MARQUETTE

AUG 22, '76. DEDICATION OF MILWAUKEE RAILROAD PATOON PLAQUE. CEREMONY AT MARQUETTE PARK, NEXT TO SITE OF THE PLATOON RAILROAD BRIDGE. (LOCAL). BLANCHE CARDIN, PRESIDENT; MARQUETTE ACTION CLUB; MARQUETTE, IA 52158. (#108932-1).

MARSHALLTOWN

ADAM'S CHRONICLE - MARSHALLTOWN, IA. STUDENTS WILL STUDY HISTORY THROUGH THE EYES OF THE ADAMS FAMILY. (LOCAL). CHARLES COCHRAN, DIRECTOR; MARSHALLTOWN COMMUNITY COLLEGE, SOCIAL SCIENCE DEPT; 3700 S CENTER ST; MARSHALLTOWN, IA 50158. (#21251).

BICENTENNIAL COMMEMORATION EVENTS. CEREMONY. (LOCAL). PATRICIA BACINO, DIRECTOR; MARSHALL TOWN COMMUNITY COLLEGE; 3700 S CENTER ST; MARSHALL TOWN, IA 50158. (#105241-1).

BOOKLET, ESSAYS & INTERVIEWS OF ELDERS - IA. A BOOKLET WILL BE PUBLISHED FROM INTERVIEWS AND ESSAYS FROM SENIOR CITIZENS; IT WILL BE ENTITLED 'THE GOOD OLD DAYS'. (LOCAL). PATRICIA BACINO, DIRECTOR; MARSHALLTOWN COMMUNITY COLLEGE; 3700 S CENTER ST; MARSHALLTOWN, IA 50158. (#21252).

KFJB AM/FM FESTIVAL USA PROGRAMMING - NBMRP. KFJB'S FESTIVAL PROGRAMMING INCLUDES 'BICENT FACTS & LEGENDS', LOCAL & NATL ACTIVITIES, A 30-MIN PGM COVERING CITY'S BICENT CELEBRATION, INTERVIEWS W/ LOCAL BICENT PEOPLE, 'BICENT SALUTE', 'SPIRIT OF '76'. (LOCAL). ALLAN N SCHROCK, BICENTENNIAL COORDINATOR; RADIO STATION KFJB; 133 EAST MAIN ST; MARSHALLTOWN, IA 50158. (#25669).

MARSHALLTOWN COMMUNITY COLLEGE SOUTHERN TOUR - IA. STUDENTS AT THE COLLEGE WILL VISIT SHILOH, NATCHEZ-TRACE AND FAULKNOR COUNTRY. (LOCAL). CHARLES COCHRAN,

MARSHALLTOWN — CONTINUED

DIRECTOR; MARSHALLTOWN COMMUNITY COLLEGE; 3700 S CENTER ST; MARSHALLTOWN, IA 50158. (#21250).

'PANORAMA' - MARSHALLTOWN, IA. A POETRY ANTHOLOGY ENTITLED 'PANORAMA' WILL BE COMPILED. (LOCAL). MAX BARKER, PROJ DIRECTOR; MARSHALLTOWN COMMUNITY COLLEGE; 3700 S CENTER ST; MARSHALLTOWN, IA 50158. (#21253).

PLANTING PROJECT - MARSHALLTOWN, IA. THE NEW CAMPUS GROUNDS WILL BE PLANTED WITH TREES & FLOWERS. (LOCAL). PATRICIA BACINO, DIRECTOR; MARSHALLTOWN COMMUNITY COLLEGE; 3700 S CENTER ST; MARSHALLTOWN, IA 50158. (#21249).

MARTELLE

HISTORICAL SHOW CASE, MARTELLE, IA. A DISPLAY CASE AND STORAGE FACILITY FOR HISTORICAL RECORDS, ANTIQUES AND OTHER ARTIFACTS WILL BE BUILT IN THE REMODELED LIBRARY. (LOCAL). DALE M ANDERSON, CHAIRPERSON; MARTELLE BICENTENNIAL COMMITTEE; PO BOX 9; MARTELLE, IA 52305. (#19712).

MARTELLE COMMUNITY HISTORICAL DISPLAY, IA. A DISPLAY CASE TO HOUSE HISTORIC RECORDS, ANTIQUES AND OTHER ITEMS OF COMMUNITY INTEREST, WILL BE BUILT & HOUSED IN THE PUBLIC LIBRARY. (LOCAL). DALE M ANDERSON, CHAIRPERSON; COMMUNITY CLUB, TOWN COUNCIL, CENTURY CLUB & MARTELLE BICENT COM; PO BOX 68; MARTELLE, IA 52305. (#16417).

MARTELLE PARK RESTORATION AND BEAUTIFICATION - IA. THE CITY PARK IS BEING LANDSCAPED, THE PAVILION HAS BEEN PAINTED & NEW EQUIPMENT IS BEING ADDED. (LOCAL). DALE M ANDERSON, CHAIRMAN; MARTELLE BICENTENNIAL COMMISSION; MARTELLE, IA 52305. (#22020).

FEB 22 - 23, '76. MARTELLE BICENTENNIAL VARIETY SHOW. FESTIVAL AT MARTELLE COMMUNITY ELEMENTARY SCHOOL BDLG. (LOCAL). DALE M ANDERSON, CHAIRMAN; MARTELLE BICENTENNIAL COMMISSION & MARTELLE COMMUNITY CLUB; MARTELLE, IA 52305. (#200018-116).

MAY 30, '76. HISTORY IN ACTION. DEMONSTRATIONS OF OLD-TIME CRAFTS: CHURNIBG, SOAPMAKING, QUILLING, QUILTING, NEEDLEPOINT, IRONING, CANING, CORNSHELLING, SPINNING, RUGMAKING, KNITTING, TATTING & WOODWORKING. AT LIBRARY, COMMUNITY HALL, FIRE STATION. (LOCAL). HELEN F ANDERSON, CO-CHMN; MARTELLE BICENTENNIAL COMMITTEE AND COMMUNITY CLUB; MARTELLE, IA 52305. (#105790-1).

MASON CITY

BICENTENNIAL SPEAKERS' BUREAU, MASON CITY, IA. THE SPEAKERS' BUREAU WILL PROVIDE SPEAKERS FOR BICENTENNIAL EVENTS. (LOCAL). ROBERT DOUGLAS, PROJ DIRECTOR; MASON CITY BICENTENNIAL COMMITTEE; 212 N FEDERAL; MASON CITY, IA 50401. (#17650).

COLLEGE AUDITORIUM PROJ OF MASON CITY, IA. PROJECT TO ASSIST IN FUNDING COLLEGE AUDITORIUM. (LOCAL). ERNIE ZERBLE, CHAIRMAN; CERRO GORDO BICENTENNIAL COMMITTEE; 1009 N CAROLINA; MASON CITY, IA 50401. (#15652).

ESSAY CONTEST - MASON CITY, IA. THERE WILL BE A BICENTENNIAL ESSAY CONTEST IN AREA SCHOOLS. (LOCAL). ROBERT DOUGLAS, COORDINATOR; MASON CITY BICENTENNIAL COMMITTEE; 212 N FEDERAL; MASON CITY, IA 50401. (#17675).

FLOWER BEDS - MASON CITY, IA. FLOWER BEDS WILL BE PLANTED IN HONOR OF THE BICENTENNIAL. (LOCAL). ROBERT DOUGLAS, COORDINATOR; MASON CITY BICENTENNIAL COMMITTEE; 212 N FEDERAL; MASON CITY, IA 50401. (#17673).

FREEDOM FAIR. FAIR. (LOCAL). ERNIE ZERBLE, CHMN; CERRO GORDO BICENTENNIAL COMMITTEE; 1009 N CAROLINA; MASON CITY, IA 50401. (#102588-1). **(??).**

HISTORY OF CERRO GORDO COUNTY, IA. PUBLICATION OF THE HISTORY OF CERRO GORDO COUNTY. (LOCAL). ERNIE ZERBLE, CHAIRMAN; CERRO GORDO BICENTENNIAL COMMITTEE; 1009 N CAROLINA; MASON CITY, IA 50401. (#15651).

HOMEMAKER 1776 BADGE - MASON CITY, IA. A 1776 HOMEMAKER BADGE TO GIVE GIRLS 4TH GRADE THROUGH 9TH GRADE AN IDEA OF HOW THE 1776 HOMEMAKER FUNCTIONED. (LOCAL). MARY ELLEN ORTH, ADVISOR; NORTH IOWA GIRL SCOUT COUNCIL; 115 1/2 1ST ST SE; MASON CITY, IA 50401. (#20332).

MEMORIAL PLAQUE IN MASON CITY, IA. A PLAQUE WILL BE ERECTED IN HONOR OF MEREDITH WILSON. (LOCAL). ROBERT DOUGLAS, COORDINATOR; MASON CITY BICENTENNIAL COMMITTEE; 212 N FEDERAL; MASON CITY, IA 50401. (#17674).

OCT 8 - 9, '75. UNITED STATES ARMED FORCES BICENTENNIAL CARAVAN. THE CARAVAN IS COMPOSED OF EXHIBIT VANS FOR EACH BRANCH OF THE MILITARY SERVICE. THE THEME OF THE EXHIBITION IS 'HISTORY OF THE ARMED FORCES AND THEIR CONTRIBUTION TO THE NATION'. (LOCAL). ERNEST ZERBLE, CHMN; U S ARMED FORCES BICENTENNIAL EXHIBIT VANS PROJECT; 1009 NORTH CAROLINA AVE; MASON CITY, IA 50401. (#1775-213).

OCT 13, '75. SONGFEST - GIRL SCOUTS. 1000 GIRL SCOUTS FROM MASON CITY WILL MARCH TO CENTRAL PARK. THERE WILL BE A FLAG CEREMONY AND SCROLL PRESENTATION TO CITY MAYOR. AT CENTRAL PARK. (LOCAL). JUNE GOPELRUD, COORD; GIRL SCOUTS OF MASON CITY; 904 6TH ST SE; MASON CITY, IA 50401. (#200018-108).

JAN 26 - JUNE 30, '76. BICENTENNIAL TIP SHOPS. EXHIBIT, FESTIVAL. (LOCAL). MARY ELLEN ORTH, COORD; NORTH IOWA GIRL SCOUT COUNCIL; 115-1/2 1ST ST SE; MASON CITY, IA 50401. (#200018-107).

APR 4, '76. NORTH IOWA GIRL SCOUT COUNCIL; GIRL SCOUT SAMPLER. CEREMONY, FESTIVAL, LIVE PERFORMANCE AT MASON CITY HIGH SCHOOL GYM; 1700 4TH, SE; FREE PARKING. (LOCAL). MRS MELVIN MITCHELL, CHMN; NORTH IOWA GIRL SCOUT COUNCIL; 933 10TH NE; MASON CITY, IA 50401. (#104735-2).

APR 4, '76. RECITALS OF AMERICAN MUSIC, DR WILLIAM DAVID, PIANIST. LIVE PERFORMANCE AT MASON CITY PUBLIC LIBRARY. (LOCAL). EDNA BOEHNKE; FRIENDS OF THE LIBRARY; 75 KENTUCKY COURT; MASON CITY, IA 50401. (#103892-3).

APR 10, '76. BARBERSHOP PARADE OF QUARTETS. LIVE PERFORMANCE AT ROOSEVELT FIELDHOUSE. (LOCAL). TOM MESKEL; RIVER CITY BARBERSHOP CHORUS; 115 S KENTUCKY; MASON CITY, IA 50401. (#103892-2).

JUNE 4, '76. NORTH IOWA BAND FESTIVAL. PARADE AT 10 AM; MASSED BAND PERFORMANCE AT 4PM. AT FEDERAL AVE PARADE; ROOSEVELT FIELD MASSED BAND PERFORMANCE. (ST-WIDE). CHAMBER OF COMMERCE; MASON CITY AREA CHAMBER OF COMMERCE; 17 WEST STATE ST; MASON CITY, IA 50401. (#102761-1).

JUNE 5, '76. BICENTENNIAL COMMUNITY DAY. FESTIVAL. (LOCAL). ROBERT DOUGLAS, DIRECTOR; MASON CITY AREA CHAMBER OF COMMERCE; 212 N FEDERAL AVE; MASON CITY, IA 50401. (#105610-1).

JUNE 6, '76. BICENTENNIAL FAMILY DAY. FESTIVAL. (LOCAL). ROBERT DOUGLAS, COORD; MASON CITY AREA CHAMBER OF COMMERCE; 212 N FEDERAL AVE; MASON CITY, IA 50401. (#105610-2).

JULY 3 - AUG 1, '76. EXHIBIT - 'WEATHERVANES, CARVINGS AND QUILTS'. 'WEATHERVANES, CARVINGS AND QUILTS' FEATURES SELECTIONS FROM THE COLLECTION OF THE CHASE MANHATTAN BANK; 'BEADS' CONTAINS ALL KINDS OF BEADWORK FROM THE MUSEUM OF THE AMERICAN INDIAN, NY. (ST-WIDE). RICHARD E LEET, DIRECTOR; CHARLES H MACNIDER MUSEUM; 303 2ND ST SE; MASON CITY, IA 50401. (#107961-1).

JULY 4, '76. RELIGIOUS CITY-WIDE BICENTENNIAL OBSERVANCE. FORMER SENATOR, HAROLD HUGHES, SPEAKER. AT ROOSEVELT STADIUM. (LOCAL). REV WILLIAM CUNNINGHAM; MASON CITY MINISTERIAL ASSOCIATION; 119 S GEORGIA; MASON CITY, IA 50401. (#103892-1).

JULY 24 - 25, '76. NORTH IOWA AVIATION DAY. EXHIBIT, FESTIVAL AT MASON CITY MUNICIPAL AIRPORT. (ST-WIDE). ROBERT BIRKHOLZ, DIRECTOR; AVIATION DAY COMMITTEE; 1153 S CAROLINA; MASON CITY, IA 50401. (#105610-3).

JAN 9 - FEB 6, '77. EXHIBIT - 'BEADS'. CONTAINS ALL KINDS OF BEADWORK FROM THE MUSEUM OF THE AMERICAN INDIAN, NY. (ST-WIDE). RICHARD E LEET, DIR; CHARLES H MACNIDER MUSEUM; 303 2ND ST SE; MASON CITY, IA 50401. (#107961-2).

MASONVILLE

EXHIBIT IN MASONVILLE, IA. EXHIBIT IN CONNECTION WITH CELEBRATION. (LOCAL). BILL ALDEN; MASONVILLE COMMUNITY CLUB; MASONVILLE, IA 50654. (#107678-2).

FLAG POLE PROJECT IN MASONVILLE, IA. ERECT A PERMANENT FLAG POLE IN THE PARK. (LOCAL). BILL ALDEN, CHAIRMAN; MASONVILLE COMMUNITY CLUB; MASONVILLE, IA 50654. (#24629).

MASONVILLE BICENTENNIAL PARK, IA. PARK WILL BE CONSTRUCTED FOR THE RECREATION OF CITY RESIDENTS. (LOCAL). BILL ALDEN, CHAIRMAN; MASONVILLE COMMUNITY CLUB; MASONVILLE, IA 50654. (#24537).

JULY 3, '76. CELEBRATION IN MASONVILLE, IA. OPENING. (LOCAL). BILL ALDEN; MASONVILLE COMMUNITY CLUB; MASONVILLE, IA 50654. (#107678-1).

MASSENA

CITY PARK IMPROVEMENT - MASSENA, IA. ALL GARDEN CLUBS & FLOWER CLUBS WILL COOPERATE IN PLANTING THE CITY PARK WITH RED, WHITE & BLUE FLOWERS. (LOCAL). DONALD HENKENIUS, CHAIRMAN; MASSENA COUNTY BICENTENNIAL COMMISSION; BOX 135; MASSENA, IA 50853. (#22231).

MASSENA PUBLIC SCHOOL POSTERS & LETTERS - IA. POSTERS & LETTERS WILL BE COLLECTED BY PUBLIC SCHOOL CHILDREN. (LOCAL). GEORGE CARROLL, CHAIRMAN; C & M COMMUNITY SCHOOL; MASSENA, IA 50853. (#22230).

MAY 29, '76. MASSENA PUBLIC SCHOOL ALUMNI PARTY. CEREMONY, FESTIVAL, PARADE. (LOCAL). WRAY WOLLENHAUPT, COORD; MASSENA CHAMBER OF COMMERCE; MASSENA, IA 50853. (#105971-1).

MASSILLON

MASSILLON BICENTENNIAL FERRY, IA. A FERRY WILL BE BUILT, TO BE USED ON BICENTENNIAL DAY. (LOCAL). HAZEL RAIBER, CHAIRPERSON; MASSILLON BICENTENNIAL COMMISSION; LOWDEN, IA 52255. (#23350).

AUG 8, '76. MASSILLON BICENTENNIAL DAY. PERFORMANCE BY VOCAL GROUP, CIRCUIT RIDER AND DEDICATION OF A LOG CABIN ARE THE PLANNED ACTIVITIES, PAGEANT AND PARADE. AT MASSILLON CONSERVATION PARK. (LOCAL). HAZEL RAIBER, CHMN; MASSILLON BICENTENNIAL COMMITTEE; LOWDEN, IA 52255. (#106527-1).

MATLOCK

COMMUNITY CENTER IMPROVEMENT - MATLOCK, IA. PAINT COMMUNITY BLDG, PAINT RECREATION FACILITIES AND ADD TO RECREATION FACILITIES. (LOCAL). ANNE WOLLBER, CLERK; TOWN COUNCIL; MATLOCK, IA 51244. (#24572).

PAMPHLET ON TOWN HISTORY - MATLOCK, IA. GROUP TO COMPILE ANY & ALL AVAILABLE MATERIAL RELATING TO THE HISTORY OF THE TOWN. (LOCAL). ANNE WOLLBER, CLERK; SENIOR CITIZENS & TOWN COUNCIL; MATLOCK, IA 51244. (#24674).

AUG 21, '76. COMMUNITY PICNIC. ALL SCHOOL REUNION AT NOON (POTLUCK AND AFTERNOON VISITING); EVENING PICNIC FOR LOCAL CITIZENS. AT COMMUNITY BUILDING AND GROUNDS. (LOCAL). RON HAMMEISTER; TOWN COUNCIL; MATLOCK, IA 51244. (#107686-1).

MAURICE

HISTORY OF MAURICE - BOOK, IA. HISTORY OF THE TOWN OF MAURICE AND SURROUNDING AREA. (LOCAL). MRS JOHN M DE JONG, COORDINATOR; MAURICE COMMUNITY WOMEN'S CLUB; MAURICE, IA 51036. (#23168).

MAYSVILLE

JULY '76. ALL DAY COMMUNITY PICNIC. FAIR. (LOCAL). ROBERT FILSON, CHAIRMAN; MAYSVILLE BICENTENNIAL COMMITTEE; RR #1; WALCOTT, IA 52773. (#108455-1).

MCCALLSBURG

CITY IMPROVEMENTS, MCCALLSBURG, IA. FIRE HYDRANTS WILL BE PAINTED & GENERAL CITYWIDE CLEANUP CONDUCTED. (LOCAL). ALAN COOK, COORDINATOR; BOY SCOUTS, TROOP 334; MCCALLSBURG, IA 50154. (#24459).

CITY PARK, MCCALLSBURG, IA. DEVELOPMENT OF PARK BY PLANTING TREES. (LOCAL). TERRY THOMPSON, COUNCIL CHAIRMAN; MCCALLSBURG BICENTENNIAL COMMITTEE; MCCALLSBURG, IA 50154. (#24460).

JUNE 19, '76. INDIAN DANCE GROUP. PARADE, LIVE PERFORMANCE. (LOCAL). SHIRLEY THOMPSON, CHMN; MCCALLSBURG BICENTENNIAL COMMISSION; SCHOOL ST; MCCALLSBURG, IA 50154. (#106890-1).

JUNE 19, '76. PARADE. PARADE. (LOCAL). SAM TWEDT, PROJ CHMN; MCCALLSBURG BICENTENNIAL COMMISSION; MCCALLSBURG, IA 50154. (#106887-1).

JUNE 19, '76. TERRY THOMPSON AND THE CENTURIES - DANCE. FESTIVAL. (LOCAL). PHYLLIS DALASKE, PROJ DIR; MCCALLSBURG BICENTENNIAL COMMISSION; MCCALLSBURG, IA 50154. (#106886-1).

JUNE 19 - 20, '76. CARNIVAL WITH ARTS, CRAFTS & GAMES. FESTIVAL. (LOCAL). CRAIG TORGESON, PROJ CHMN; MCCALLSBURG BICENTENNIAL COMMISSION; MCCALLSBURG, IA 50154. (#106888-1).

MCCLAUSLAND

CODY MCCLAUSLAND HOMESTEAD IN MCCLAUSLAND, IA. RESTORATION OF EARLY HOMESTEAD OF WILD BILL CODY; HOMESTEAD INCLUDES BUILDINGS, DISPLAYS AND PICNIC FACILITIES. (LOCAL). MS CHARLES BLAIR, CHAIRMAN; COLONIAL DAMES IN STATE OF IOWA; 612 RIVER DR; BETTENDORF, IA 52722. (#13105).

SEPT 6, '76. LABOR DAY BICENTENNIAL CELEBRATION. BASEBALL TOURNAMENT, AFTERNOON STREET DANCE, JAYCEE DINNER IN THE TOWN HALL, CARNIVAL, QUILT SALE & 4-H GIRLS ACTIVITIES. (LOCAL). JOHN PLOOG, COORD; JAYCEES; MCCAUSLAND, IA 52758. (#108456-1).

MCCLELLAND

FAMILY DAY. FESTIVAL. (LOCAL). PHILLIP FELLER, COORD; BICENTENNIAL COMMITTEE; MCCLELLAND, IA 51548. (#104685-1).

TIME CAPSULE & FLAG POLE - MCCLELLAND, IA. A FLAG POLE WILL BE ERECTED IN PARK WITH A TIME CAPSULE. (LOCAL). PHILLIP FELLER, CHAIRMAN; MCCLELLAND BICENTENNIAL COMMITTEE; MCCLELLAND, IA 51548. (#19956).

TREE PLANTING - MCCLELLAND, IA. PLANTING TREES IN THE PARK FOR THE BICENTENNIAL. (LOCAL). PHILLIP FELLER, COORDINATOR; MCCLELLAND BICENTENNIAL COMMITTEE; MCCLELLAND, IA 51548. (#19957).

MCGREGOR

PRESERVATION OF HISTORICAL CHURCH LANDMARK, IA. PRESERVATION OF 128 YR OLD CHURCH & PARSONAGE; CHURCH TOWER REPAIRED & STORM WINDOWS ADDED TO PROTECT STAINED GLASS WINDOWS. (LOCAL). MRS DARRELL HEDEMANN, CHAIRMAN; GIARD UNITED METHODIST CHURCH; RT 1; MCGREGOR, IA 52157. (#26903).

MCGREGOR — CONTINUED

JUNE 1 - AUG 30, '75. ETHNO-ECOLOGY BICENT PGM AT EFFIGY MOUNDS NM. ENVIRONMENTAL EDUCATION PROGRAM BUILT AROUND EMPHASIS ON ETHNOECOLOGY AS DISCOVERED AND DEVELOPED BY NATIVE AMERICANS AND CARRIED FORWARD TO AMERICAN PIONEER CULTURES. AT BEGINS AT VISITOR CENTER. (REGN'L). SUPT, EFFIGY MOUNDS NM; NATIONAL PARK SERVICE; P.O. BOX K; MCGREGOR, IA 52157. (#6725-8).

JAN 10 - MAR 15, '76. FILM FESTIVAL AT EFFIGY MOUNDS NATIONAL MONUMENT. TEN-WEEK PROGRAM USING BICENTENNIAL AND OTHER RELATED FILMS IN CONJUNCTION WITH THEMATIC ART EXHIBITS FROM LOCAL SCHOOLS. (REGN'L). EFFIGY MOUNDS NM; NATIONAL PARK SERVICE; PO BOX K; MCGREGOR, IA 52157. (#6728-240).

MAR 14 - APR 18, '76. NATION UNDER GOD. SESSION 1: HERITAGE DINNER WITH ETHNIC FOODS, EXHIBITS; SESSION 2: STUDY & CREATIVE ACTIVITIES NIGHT, MAPS & BANNERS SESSION; SESSION 3 & 4: DRAMA PLAYS FOLLOWED BY DISCUSSION. (LOCAL). MRS DARRELL HEDEMANN; GIARD UNITED METHODIST CHURCH; RT 1; MCGREGOR, IA 52157. (#200018-120).

MAY 1 - AUG 31, '76. EFFIGY MOUNDS NM PROGRAM ON THE MOUND-BUILDING CULTURES. GUIDED WALKS, LIVE TALKS AND SPECIAL EVENING PROGRAMS INTERPRET THE MOUND BUILDING CULTURES THROUGH BICENTENNIAL THEMES. (REGN'L). EFFIGY MOUNDS NM; NATIONAL PARK SERVICE; PO BOX K; MCGREGOR, IA 52157. (#6729-133).

JUNE 1 - AUG 30, '76. ETHNO-ECOLOGY BICENT PGM AT EFFIGY MOUNDS NM. ENVIRONMENTAL EDUCATION PROGRAM BUILT AROUND EMPHASIS ON ETHNOECOLOGY AS DISCOVERED AND DEVELOPED BY NATIVE AMERICANS AND CARRIED FORWARD TO AMERICAN PIONEER CULTURES. AT BEGINS AT VISITOR CENTER. (REGN'L). SUPT, EFFIGY MOUNDS NM; NATIONAL PARK SERVICE; P.O. BOX K; MCGREGOR, IA 52157. (#6725-508).

JULY 4, '76. JULY 4TH CELEBRATION. MORNING CHURCH SERVICE FOLLOWED BY PICNIC AT NOON; AFTERNOON PROGRAM OF AMERICAN MUSIC, DRAMA, RECITATIONS AND RECREATION. AT GIARD UNITED METHODIST CHURCH, 6 MILES WEST OF MCGREGOR OFF HWY 18. (LOCAL). MRS DARRELL HEDEMANN; GIARD UNITED METHODIST CHURCH; ROUTE 1; MCGREGOR, IA 52157. (#106903-1).

JULY 4 - 15, '76. AUDIO CHAIR EXHIBIT ON MINORITIES VISITS EFFIGY MOUNDS NM. TAPES DISCUSS THE ROLE OF NATIVE AMERICANS, WOMEN AND BLACKS IN THE REVOLUTIONARY WAR. (REGN'L). EFFIGY MOUNDS NM; NATIONAL PARK SERVICE; PO BOX K; MCGREGOR, IA 52157. (#5581-10).

JULY 15, '76. NATL PK SVC '...A LITTLE LOOK AROUND' COMES TO EFFIGY MOUNDS NM. THIS SHORT PROGRAM FEATURES ACTORS PLAYING THE ROLES OF FAMOUS AMERICANS OF THE PAST WHO'VE RETURNED TO SEE AMERICA'S GROWTH.. AT VILLA LOUIS. (REGN'L). EFFIGY MOUNDS NM; NATINAL PARK SERVICE; P.O. BOX K; MCGREGOR, IA 52517. (#5653-18).

OCT 10, '76. FALL FESTIVAL. LIVE PERFORMANCE AT GIARD UNITED METHODIST CHURCH, 6 MILES WEST OF MCGREGOR OFF HWY 18. (LOCAL). MRS DARRELL HEDEMANN; GIARD UNITED METHODIST CHURCH; ROUTE 1; MCGREGOR, IA 52157. (#106903-2).

MCINTIRE

PARK IMPROVEMENTS IN MCINTIRE, IA. A NEW FLAG POLE WILL BE ERECTED IN THE PARK ON MAIN ST. (LOCAL). MAVIS KRUKOW, CHAIRPERSON; MCINTIRE BICENTENNIAL COMMISSION; MCINTIRE, IA 50455. (#30795).

MECHANICSVLE

MAY 27 - 30, '76. 'RIP VAN WINKLE' - FESTIVAL. FESTIVAL, PARADE. (LOCAL). THOMAS RALLSBACK, CHMN; MECHANICSVILLE CENTENNIAL COMMITTEE; 601 E SOUTH; MECHANICSVLE, IA 52306. (#104763-1).

MEDIAPOLIS

TREE AND SHRUB PLANTING, MEDIAPOLIS, IA. PLANTING OF AN EVERGREEN & VARIOUS SHRUBS IN TOWN PARK. (LOCAL). LINDA D TREVITT, CHAIRMAN; MEDIAPOLIS BICENTENNIAL GROUP; MEDIAPOLIS, IA 52637. (#28645).

MELBOURNE

PUBLIC LIBRARY PROJECT - MELBOURNE, IA. WE WILL INVESTIGATE THE POSSIBILITIES AND IMPLEMENT A PLAN TO REMODEL AN EXISTING BUILDING IN THE BUSINESS DISTRICT FOR A NEW LIBRARY. (LOCAL). THOMAS J LARSON, CHAIRPERSON; LIBRARY BOARD OF TRUSTEES; MELBOURNE, IA 50162. (#21745).

APR 8 - 9, '76. OVERNIGHT LODGING AND PROGRAM FOR BICENTENNIAL WAGON TRAIN. OVERNIGHT LODGING AND PROGRAM FOR BICENTENNIAL WAGON TRAIN. (LOCAL). THOMAS J LARSEN, CHMN; MELBOURNE BICENTENNIAL COMMISSION; 211 PARK AVE; MELBOURNE, IA 50162. (#105519-1).

MELCHER

SHELTER HOUSE - PARK IMPROVEMENT, IA. PLAYGROUND EQUIPMENT WILL BE INSTALLED AT THE SHELTER HOUSE. (LOCAL). THOMAS JONES, CHAIRMAN; COMMERCIAL CLUB; MELCHER, IA 50163. (#23927).

JUNE 5, '76. COAL MINERS' DAY. FESTIVAL AT MELCHER CITY PARK. (LOCAL). THOMAS JONES, CHAIRMAN; COMMERCIAL CLUB; MELCHER, IA 50163. (#106844-1).

MELVIN

JULY 31 - AUG 1, '76. MELVIN '75 IN '76. THIS WILL BE A TWO-DAY CELEBRATION WITH A PARK DEDICATIN. AT PARK AND BALL PARK. (LOCAL). CLIFFORD MCCARTY, COORD; MELVIN '75 IN '76; MELVIN, IA 51350. (#105622-3).

MENLO

CITY PARK BEAUTIFICATION - MENLO, IA. TREES AND FLOWERS WILL BE PLANTED AT CITY PARK. (LOCAL). MRS GLEN STEVENSON, PROJ DIRECTOR; MENLO STUDY CLUB; MENLO, IA 50164. (#22001).

JUNE 26, '76. BICENTENNIAL DAY - GAMES, ARTS & BAR-B-CUE. FESTIVAL. (LOCAL). MRS GLEN STEVENSON, CHMN; MENLO BICENTENNIAL COMMITTEE; MENLO, IA 50164. (#105773-1).

JUNE 26, '76. OLD-FASHIONED BOX SUPPER & HOE-DOWN. FESTIVAL. (LOCAL). MRS GLEN STEVENSON, CHMN; MENLO FIRE DEPT; MENLO, IA 50164. (#105773-2).

MERIDEN

MERIDEN, IA - MERIDEN, ENGLAND EXCHANGE. EXCHANGE OF COMMUNITY HISTORIES BETWEEN SCHOOL CHILDREN IN THE FORM OF A BOOKLET. (INT'L). ROBERT BYERS, SCHOOL PRINCIPAL; MERIDEN-CLEGHORN COMMUNITY SCHOOL; MERIDEN, IA 51037. (#21714).

MESERVEY

HISTORY OF MESERVEY, IA. A PROJECT WITH CERRO GORDO CO BICENTENNIAL COMMITTEE TO PUBLISH A BOOK OF THE HISTORY OF CERRO GORDO CO, FROM BEGINNING TO THE PRESENT. (LOCAL). FRANK HAFERMANN, MAJOR; HISTORY OF MESERVEY & CERRO GORDO CO BICENTENNIAL COMMITTEE; BOX 515; MESERVEY, IA 50457. (#22771).

MESERVEY LIBRARY ADDITION, IA. A PROJECT TO INCREASE THE MESERVEY LIBRARY AREA BY 50%; THIS ROOM WILL BE AN ALL-PURPOSE ROOM FOR COMMUNITY MEETINGS AND LIBRARY PROGRAMS. (LOCAL). FRANK HAFERMANN, MAJOR; MESERVEY LIBRARY ADDITION; MESERVEY, IA 50457. (#22772).

VOLUNTEER RESCUE PROJECT, MESERVEY, IA. A PROJECT BY THE MESERVEY VOLUNTEER FIRE DEPT TO OUTFIT A STEP-VAN WITH SPECIAL TOOLS AND EQUIPMENT TO HELP IN FIRE FIGHTING, DIASTER AND EMERGENCY RESCUE WORK. (LOCAL). FRANK HAFERMANN, MAJOR; VOLUNTEER FIRE DEPT; MESERVEY, IA 50457. (#22773).

JULY 2, '76. JULY FESTIVALS. FESTIVAL AT TOWNPARK. (LOCAL). FRANK HAFERMANN, CHMN; AMERICAN LEGION; MESERVEY, IA 50457. (#106158-3).

MIDDLE AMANA

OCT 1 - 2, '76. AMANA OKTOBERFEST. FESTIVAL AT AMANA COMMUNITY PARK. (LOCAL). DON SHOUP, COORD; AMANA COLONIES; MAIN OFFICE AMANA SOCIETY; MIDDLE AMANA, IA 52203. (#103416-567).

MILES

ATHLETIC FIELD LIGHTS, IA. FINANCIAL ASSISTANCE TO INSTALL ATHLETIC FIELD LIGHTS. (LOCAL). RALPH MARSHALL, PRESIDENT; MILES BICENTENNIAL COMMITTEE; PO BOX 65; MILES, IA 52064. (#23931).

MONUMENT RENOVATION, IA. LEGION VETERANS MEMORIAL MONUMENT WILL BE RENOVATED. (LOCAL). RALPH MARSHALL, PRESIDENT; MILES BICENTENNIAL COMMITTEE; PO BOX 65; MILES, IA 52064. (#23929).

PAVILION, IA. PAVILION WILL BE ERECTED IN CITY PARK. (LOCAL). RALPH MARSHALL, PRESIDENT; MILES BICENTENNIAL COMMITTEE; PO BOX 65; MILES, IA 52064. (#23930).

PLANT OAK TREE, IA. OAK TREE WILL BE PLANTED ON SCHOOL LAWN. (LOCAL). RALPH MARSHALL, PRESIDENT; MILES BICENTENNIAL COMMITTEE; PO BOX 65; MILES, IA 52064. (#23928).

JULY 15, '76. PARADE & YOUTH DANCE. FESTIVAL, PARADE. (LOCAL). RALPH MARSHALL; MILES BICENTENNIAL COMMITTEE; PO BOX 65; MILES, IA 52064. (#106846-2).

JULY 16, '76. ANTIQUE TRACTOR PULL. COMPETITION. (LOCAL). RALPH MARSHALL; MILES BICENTENNIAL COMMITTEE; PO BOX 65; MILES, IA 52064. (#106846-3).

JULY 17, '76. DANCE. FESTIVAL. (LOCAL). RALPH MARSHALL; MILES BICENTENNIAL COMMITTEE; PO BOX 65; MILES, IA 52064. (#106846-1).

JULY 18, '76. DONKEY BASEBALL. COMPETITION. (LOCAL). RALPH MARSHALL; MILES BICENTENNIAL COMMITTEE; PO BOX 65; MILES, IA 52064. (#106845-9).

MILFORD

GRINDING MILL RESTORATION - PROJ OF MILFORD, IA. THE OLD GRINDING MILL WILL BE RESTORED. (LOCAL). PHILLIS KOPPERT, CHAIRMAN; MILFORD AREA BICENTENNIAL COMMITTEE; 1104 J AVE; MILFORD, IA 51351. (#16165).

PIONEER DAYS. FESTIVAL. (LOCAL). PHYLLIS KOPPERT, CHMN; MILFORD AREA BICENTENNIAL COMMITTEE; 1104 J AVE; MILFORD, IA 51351. (#102758-1). **(??).**

'TELL IT LIKE IT IS'. LIVE PERFORMANCE. (LOCAL). PHYLLIS KOPPERT, CHMN; MILFORD AREA BICENTENNIAL COMMITTEE; 1104 J AVE; MILFORD, IA 51351. (#102759-1). **(??).**

TREE PLANTING PROJECT OF MILFORD, IA. NEW SEEDLING TREES PLANTED IN MILFORD AREA PARKS. (LOCAL). PHILLIS KOPPERT, CHAIRMAN; MILFORD AREA BICENTENNIAL COMMISSION; 1104 J AVE; MILFORD, IA 51351. (#16160).

JULY 21 - 25, '76. BICENTENNIAL CELEBRATION - PIONEER DAYS. FESTIVAL. (LOCAL). MARVIN ANDERSON, CHAIRMAN; MILFORD BICENTENNIAL COMMITTEE; 904 K AVE; MILFORD, IA 51351. (#108305-1).

MILO

BALL PARK IN MILO, IA. NEW YOUTH BALL DIAMOND, FENCE, RESTROOMS AND LIGHTS ARE BEING BUILT. (LOCAL). CHARLES MOTT, CHAIRMAN; MILO BICENTENNIAL COMMITTEE AND JAYCEES; MILO, IA 50166. (#24471).

PARK IMPROVEMENT, MILO, IA. IMPROVEMENTS INCLUDE PUTTING UP NEW SWINGS, PAINTING THE SHELTER HOUSE AND TRIMMING THE TREES. (LOCAL). CHARLES MOTT, CHAIRMAN; MILO BICENTENNIAL COMMITTEE AND LION'S CLUB; MILO, IA 50166. (#24470).

JULY 4, '76. 4TH OF JULY FESTIVAL. COMPETITION, FESTIVAL, PARADE. (LOCAL). CHARLES MOTT, PRES; COMMUNITY CLUB; MILO, IA 50166. (#106915-1).

MILTON

CHURCH TO COMMUNITY CNTR RESTORATION-MILTON, IA. RESTORATION OF OLD MILTON CHURCH FOR A COMMUNITY CENTER. (LOCAL). LIBBY WOODRUFF & TED WATSON, CO-CHAIRMEN; MILTON HERITAGE SOCIETY; MILTON, IA 52570. (#15832).

RESTORATION OF OLD PRESBYTERIAN CHURCH, MILTON, IA. MILTON'S MAJOR BICENTENNIAL PROJECT IS RESTORATION OF OLD PRESBYTERIAN CHURCH. (ST-WIDE). IOWA ANDREWS, CHAIRPERSON; MILTON HERITAGE SOCIETY; MILTON, IA 52570. (#23502). **ARBA GRANTEE.**

MINDEN

LIBRARY IMPROVEMENT PROJECT IN MINDEN, IA. BOOKS & SHELVES TO BE ADDED. (LOCAL). O DEAN OLSEN, COORDINATOR; MINDEN BICENTENNIAL COMMITTEE; MINDEN, IA 51553. (#22175).

RECREATION CENTRE IN IA. TENNIS & BASKETBALL COURTS & SHUFFLE BOARD TO BE BUILT. (LOCAL). ODEAN OLSEN, COORDINATOR; MINDEN BICENTENNIAL COMMITTEE; MINDEN, IA 51553. (#22177).

WELCOME SIGN IN MINDEN, IA. WELCOME SIGNS TO BE BUILT ON EACH SIDE OF TOWN. (LOCAL). HONORABLE ORUEL KAVEN, MAYOR; CITY COUNCIL OF MINDEN; MINDEN, IA 51553. (#22176).

JUNE 24 - 26, '76. '76 CARNIVAL & CELEBRATION. FESTIVAL, PARADE. (LOCAL). O DEAN OLSEN, CHAIRMAN; RED, WHITE & BLUE OF MINDEN; MINDEN, IA 51553. (#105943-1).

MISSOURI VLY

FLAG PLANTINGS IN MISSOURI VALLEY, IA. FLOWERS TO BE PLANTED IN THE SHAPE OF FLAGS. (LOCAL). GARY RODEWALD, CHAIRMAN; MISSOURI VALLEY BICENTENNIAL COMMITTEE; MISSOURI VLY, IA 51555. (#14505).

VETERANS' MEMORIAL - MISSOURI VALLEY, IA. MEMORIAL WAR VEHICLE TO BE PLACED IN AN AREA PARK. (LOCAL). DARYL LARSON, CHAIRMAN; POTTAWATTAMIE COUNTY BICENTENNIAL COMMISSION; MO VALLEY, IA 51555. (#17493).

WORLD'S CHAMPIONSHIP GOOSE CALLING CONTEST, IA. PEOPLE WILL GATHER TO COMPETE AND TALK OVER VIEWS FOR CONSERVATION OF WILDLIFE. (LOCAL). DARYL LARSON, TREASURER; WORLD'S CHAMPIONSHIP GOOSE CALLING CONTEST; PO BOX 307; MISSOURI VLY, IA 51555. (#23191). **ARBA GRANTEE.**

SEPT 13 - 14, '75. NATIONAL AND WORLD CHAMPIONSHIP GOOSE CALLING CONTEST. THIS CONTEST IS THE ONLY WORLD'S CHAMPIONSHIP GOOSE CALLING CONTEST HELD ANNUALLY AT THE SAME LOCATION IT ATTRACTS WILDLIFE AND CONSERVATION MINDED PEOPLE FROM ALL OVER THE USA. MILE LONG PARADE DISPLAYS -ENTERTAINMENT-EXHIBITS-FUN-COMPETITION. AT HARRISON CO FAIRGROUNDS WEST EDGE OF MO VALLEY, IOWA. (REGN'L). DARYL R LARSON; MO VALLEY JC'S AND HARRISON COUNTY BICENTENNIAL COMMISSION; 403 EAST ERIE ST; MO VALLEY, IA 51555. (#50030-1).

JULY 4, '76. 4TH OF JULY CELEBRATION. FESTIVAL, PARADE. (LOCAL). GARY RODEWALD, CHMN; VOLUNTEER FIRE DEPT; MO VALLEY, IA 51555. (#101908-1).

MISSOURI VLY — CONTINUED

SEPT 11 - 12, '76. WORLD'S CHAMPIONSHIP GOOSE CALLING CONTEST. PEOPLE WILL GATHER TO COMPETE AND TALK OVER VIEWS FOR CONSERVATION OF WILDLIFE. AT HARRISON COUNTY FAIRGROUNDS, WEST SIDE OF MO VALLEY, IOWA. (REGN'L). DARYL LARSON, TREAS; MO VALLEY JC'S & HARRISON COUNTY BICENT COMM; PO BOX 307; MISSOURI VLY, IA 51555. (#23191-1).

MITCHELL

PRESERVATION OF COURTHOUSE SITE - MITCHELL, IA. THE OLD COURTHOUSE SITE WILL BE RESTORED AND PRESERVED. (LOCAL). MRS WALLACE TORNEY, CHAIRMAN; MITCHELL BICENTENNIAL COMMITTEE; MITCHELL, IA 50485. (#20563).

TENNIS COURT PROJECT - MITCHELL, IA. TENNIS COURTS WILL BE CONSTRUCTED TO PROVIDE RECREATION FOR THE COMMUNITY. (LOCAL). MRS WALLACE TORNEY, CHAIRMAN; MITCHELL BICENTENNIAL COMMITTEE; MITCHELL, IA 50485. (#20564).

JULY 4, '76. OLD FASHIONED FOURTH. FESTIVAL. (LOCAL). MRS WALLACE TORNEY, CHMN; MITCHELL BICENTENNIAL COMMITTEE; MITCHELL, IA 50485. (#104823-1).

AUG 28 - 29, '76. CELEBRATION & DEDICATION. FESTIVAL, CEREMONY AT MAIN STREET AND SCHOOL HOUSE. (LOCAL). MRS WALLACE TORNEY, CHMN; MITCHELL BICENTENNIAL COMMITTEE; RR 1; MITCHELL, IA 50485. (#107129-1).

MODALE

JULY 12, '76. ARTS AND CRAFT FESTIVAL. EXHIBIT. (LOCAL). KATHLEEN M GILGEN, CHMN; MODALE BICENTENNIAL COMMITTEE; BOX 193; MODALE, IA 51556. (#200018-249).

MOINGONA

KATE SHELLY MEMORIAL PARK & RR MUSEUM, IA. RESTORED DEPOT WILL BECOME A RAILROAD MUSEUM & THE SURROUNDING AREA A MEMORIAL PARK TO KATE SHELLY. (LOCAL). JIM DAVIS, CHAIRMAN; KATE SHELLEY COMMITTEE; RT 3; AMES, IA 50010. (#19986).

MONDAMIN

STORE FRONT BEAUTIFICATION - MONDAMIN, IA. STORE FRONTS WILL BE IMPROVED AND BEAUTIFIED. (LOCAL). JERRY SHELTON, CHAIRMAN; MONDAMIN KIWANIS & JAYCEES; MONDAMIN, IA 51551. (#20702).

TREE PLANTING PROJECT - MONDAMIN, IA. TREES WILL BE PLANTED IN THE CITY PARK. (LOCAL). JERRY SHELTON, CHAIRMAN; MONDAMIN KIWANIS & JAYCEES; MONDAMIN, IA 51557. (#20703).

JUNE 26 - 27, '76. MONDAMIN CELEBRATION. FESTIVAL, PARADE. (LOCAL). JERRY SHELTON, DIRECTOR; KIWANIS & JAYCEE; MONDAMIN, IA 51557. (#104918-1).

MONONA

BICENTENNIAL PLATE SALE OF MONONA, IOWA. THE FEDERATED WOMEN'S CLUB OF MONONA WILL SELL BICENTENNIAL PLATES. (LOCAL). MRS OTMAR BRUNS OR MRS ROGER HALVORSON, CO-CHMN; MONONA COMMUNITY BICENT COMMITTEE; BOX T; MONONA, IA 52159. (#9660).

CEMETERY CATALOGING - MONONA, IA. ALL CEMETERIES IN THE TOWNSHIP HAVE BEEN CATALOGUED. (LOCAL). MRS OTMAR BRUNS, CHAIRMAN; MONONA COMMUNITY BICENTENNIAL COMMITTEE; BOX 816; MONONA, IA 52159. (#23150).

'CLAYTON COUNTY HISTORY OF 1882' - A BOOK, IOWA. IN HONOR OF THE BICENTENNIAL, THIS RARE BOOK WILL BE PRESERVED AND REPRINTED FOR SALE. (LOCAL). MRS OTMAR BRUNS OR MRS ROGER HALVORSON, CO-CHMN; MONONA COMMUNITY BICENT COMMITTEE; BOX T; MONONA, IA 52159. (#9659).

ERECTION OF OLD LOG CABIN IN MONONA, IOWA. THE MONONA JAYCEES ARE PLANNING TO RELOCATE & RESTORE AN OLD LOG CABIN IN MONONA. MANY NATIVES OF MONONA WERE BORN IN SIMULAR STRUCTURES. (LOCAL). MRS OTMAR BRUNS OR MRS ROGER HALVORSON, CO-CHMN; MONONA COMMUNITY BICENT COMMITTEE; BOX T; MONONA, IA 52159. (#9664).

FOX-FIRE PROJECT OF MONONA, IOWA. IN HONOR OF THE BICENTENNIAL, LOCAL SENIOR CITIZENS WILL DISCUSS LIFE IN THE PAST. (LOCAL). MRS OTMAR BRUNS OR MRS ROGER HALVORSON, CO-CHMN; MONONA COMMUNITY BICENT COMMITTEE; BOX T; MONONA, IA 52159. (#9658).

PLANTING FLOWERS, '76 IN MONONA, IOWA. IN HONOR OF THE BICENTENNIAL, THE COMMUNITY WILL PLANT RED, WHITE AND BLUE FLOWERS; THE COMMUNITY IS NICKNAMED THE GARDEN CITY BECAUSE OF ITS HERITAGE OF BEAUTIFUL GARDENS. (LOCAL). MRS OTMAR BRUNS OR MRS ROGER HALVORSON, CO-CHMN; MONONA COMMUNITY BICENT COMMITTEE; BOX T; MONONA, IA 52159. (#9662).

PRESERVATION & RESTORATION OF RAILROAD DEPOT, IOWA. IN HONOR OF THE BICENTENNIAL, A LOCAL RAILROAD DEPOT WILL BE MOVED TO A NEW LOCATION AND RESTORED. (LOCAL). MRS OTMAR BRUNS OR MRS ROGER HALVORSON, CO-CHMN; MONONA COMMUNITY BICENT COMMITTEE; BOX T; MONONA, IA 52159. (#9663).

RECORDING CITY RECORDS IN MONONA, IOWA. THE PROJECT INVOLVES CATALOGING AND MICROFILMING ALL CHURCH AND CITY RECORDS. (LOCAL). MRS OTMAR BRUNS OR MRS ROGER HALVORSON, CO-CHMN; MONONA COMMUNITY BICENT COMMITTEE; BOX T; MONONA, IA 52159. (#9655).

REPLACING TREES IN MONONA, IOWA. THIS PROJECT INVOLVES REPLANTING TREES IN DOWNTOWN MONONA THAT WERE LOST DUE TO DISEASE. (LOCAL). MRS OTMAR BRUNS OR MRS ROGER HALVORSON, CO-CHMN; MONONA COMMUNITY BICENT COMMITTEE; BOX T; MONONA, IA 52159. (#9665).

RESTORATION OF ONE ROOM SCHOOL HOUSE, MONONA, IA. LOCAL SCHOOLHOUSE TO BE RESTORED. (ST-WIDE). MRS OTMAR BRUNS CHAIRMAN; MONONA COMMUNITY BICENT COMMITTEE; BOX T; MONONA, IA 52159. (#9666).

TREE PLANTING - MONONA, IA. TREES WILL BE PLANTED IN THE SPRING TO REPLACE TREES LOST TO DUTCH ELM DISEASE. (LOCAL). MRS OTMAR BRUNS, CO-CHAIRMAN; MONONA BICENTENNIAL COMMITTEE; BOX 816; MONONA, IA 52159. (#23152).

MAY 28, '76. 200 YRS OF MUSIC IN THE USA. LIVE PERFORMANCE AT BUSSE AUDITORIUM AT MFL SCHOOL. (LOCAL). MRS OTMAR BRUNS, CO-CHMN; MONONA BICENTENNIAL COMMITTEE; BOX 816; MONONA, IA 52159. (#106383-1).

JULY 4, '76. 1776 WORSHIP IN ALL CHURCHES. CEREMONY. (LOCAL). MRS O BRUNS, CO-CHAIRMAN; MONONA BICENTENNIAL COMMITTEE; MONONA, IA 52159. (#107087-1).

JULY 16, '76. '200 YEARS OF MUSIC IN THE USA'. IN HONOR OF THE BICENTENNIAL, A MUSICAL PAGEANT WILL BE HELD ABOUT THE HERITAGE OF THE USA, 1776-1976; THE PAGEANT WILL INCLUDE LOCAL BACKGROUND SCENES AND IS OPEN TO COMMUNITY PARTICIPATION. AT MFL HIGH SCHOOL AUDITORIUM. (LOCAL). MRS OTMAR BRUNS OR MRS RO; MONONA BICENTENNIAL COMMITTEE; 408 S EGBERT ST; MONONA, IA 52159. (#9661-1).

JULY 18, '76. MISS NORTHEAST IOWA PAGEANT. COMPETITION, FESTIVAL, PARADE, LIVE PERFORMANCE AT BUSSE AUDITORIUM. (ST-WIDE). MRS OTMAR BRUNS, CO-CHMN; MONONA JAYCEES; MONONA, IA 52159. (#106383-2).

MONROE

AUG 19 - 20, '76. OLD SETTLERS BICENTENNIAL. PARADE, LIVE PERFORMANCE, EXHIBIT AT CITY PARK. (LOCAL). HARRY VANDEPOL; OLD SETTLERS COMMITTEE; 410 N WASHINGTON ST; MONROE, IA 50170. (#107683-1).

MONTEZUMA

DEVELOPMENT OF DIAMON LAKE AREA, IA. IMPROVEMENT OF DIAMOND LAKE FACILITY INTO RECREATIONAL FACILITY FOR CAMPING, PICNICING, AND FISHING AND TO CONSERVE THE ADJACENT WATERSHED BY FORESTATION. (LOCAL). ROGER REED, PROJ DIRECTOR; COUNTY CONSERVATION; DIAMOND LAKE; MONTEZUMA, IA 50171. (#16692).

ESTABLISHMENT OF MUSEUM, MONTEZUMA, IA. MUSEUM TO PROVIDE CENTRAL FACILITY TO HOUSE ARTIFACTS FROM THE MONTEZUMA COMMUNITY, AND TO FOSTER THE PRESERVATION OF HISTORICALLY SIGNIFICANT DOCUMENTS AND OTHER MATERIALS. (LOCAL). KEITH STEFFY, COORDINATOR; MONTEZUMA BICENTENNIAL COMMITTEE; 201 W MAIN; MONTEZUMA, IA 50171. (#16691).

MARKERS TO DESIGNATE HISTORIC SITES, MONTEZUMA, IA. THE MONTEZUMA AREA WAS CROSSED BY EARLY STAGE COACH ROUTES AND THE SECOND OLDEST COURTHOUSE IN IOWA STANDS HERE. (LOCAL). HOYT BONHAM, CHAIRMAN; MONTEZUMA BICENTENNIAL COMMITTEE; 105 N 4TH; MONTEZUMA, IA 50171. (#16690).

TREE PLANTING AND LAND ACQUISITION, MONTEZUMA, IA. DEVELOPMENT OF SEVERAL AREAS AS PARKS AND RECREATIONAL FACILITIES. (LOCAL). ROGER REED, DIRECTOR; POWESHEIK CONSERVATION COMMISSION; DIAMOND LAKE; MONTEZUMA, IA 50171. (#15100).

FEB '76. BOX SOCIAL AND FOLK ENTERTAINMENT. FESTIVAL. (LOCAL). MARY GORSUCH; CITY OF MONTEZUMA; RD #1; MONTEZUMA, IA 50171. (#103015-1).

JULY 4, '76. JULY 4 FESTIVAL, FLAG CEREMONIES & PICNIC. FESTIVAL. (LOCAL). JOHN MORRISSEY, COORD; CITY OF MONTEZUMA; BOX 100; MONTEZUMA, IA 50171. (#103015-2).

JULY 30 - AUG 1, '76. BICENTENNIAL CELEBRATION. FESTIVAL. (LOCAL). JOHN MORRISSEY, COORD; BICENTENNIAL COMMISSION; 406 MAIN ST; MONTEZUMA, IA 50171. (#105616-1).

MONTICELLO

BOOKLET ON WOMEN - MONTICELLO, IA. A BOOKLET IS BEING COMPILED ABOUT THE WOMEN OF JONES COUNTY WHO HAVE BEEN A FIRST - SUCH AS COUNTY AUDITOR, LAWYER, EDITOR, ETC. (LOCAL). MRS VICTOR JENSON, CHAIRMAN; BUSINESS AND PROFESSIONAL WOMEN OF MONTICELLO; 102 E 1ST ST; MONTICELLO, IA 52310. (#19646).

MARKERS & MAPS - MONTICELLO, IA. MARKING HISTORICAL PLACES AND POINTS OF INTEREST IN MONTICELLO AREA. PROJECT UNDERTAKEN BY THE MONTICELLO DIVISION OF CAMP FIRE GIRLS. (LOCAL). MR JOHN KOCH, DIRECTOR; MONTICELLO-JONES COUNTY HISTORICAL SOCIETY; 352 PIPE ST; MONTICELLO, IA 52310. (#19645).

WAYSIDE PARK IN JONES COUNTY, IA. A PARK PICNIC AREA WILL BE ESTABLISHED ALONG OLD MILITARY TRAIL IN JONES COUNTY. (LOCAL). MICHAEL J LAMBERT, COMMANDER; AMERICAN LEGION POST 209; 120 W CHESTNUT; MONTICELLO, IA 52310. (#11574).

AUG 6 - 10, '75. JONES COUNTY FAIR BOOTH. HORSE RACES, STOCK CAR RACES, DEMOLITION DERBY, RODEO AND NIGHTLY STAGE ENTERTAINMENT. AT FAIRGROUNDS. (LOCAL). SAM H SCHUETZ, CHMN; GREAT JONES COUNTY FAIR; BOX 150; MONTICELLO, IA 52205. (#100430-1).

JAN 1, '76 - CONTINUING . EXHIBIT OF REPLICA OF MONTICELLO, HOME OF PRESIDENT JEFFERSON. SCALE MODEL COMPLETE WITH GARDENS. (LOCAL). MRS V JENSON, CHMN; MONTICELLO BICENTENNIAL COMMITTEE; 102 E FIRST ST; MONTICELLO, IA 52310. (#104352-1).

MONTOUR

AUDIO-TAPE MEMORIES, MONTOUR, IA. HISTORIC MEMORIES OF OLDER CITIZENS WILL BE TAPED. (LOCAL). JAN WILLIAMS, CHAIRMAN; LIBRARY BOARD; MONTOUR, IA 50173. (#24220).

CHURCH HISTORY - MONTOUR, IA. COMPILE HISTORY OF MONTOUR UNITED METHODIST CHURCH. (LOCAL). ROLLAND GARY, CHAIRMAN; MONTOUR UNITED METHODIST CHURCH; RFD 1; MONTOUR, IA 50173. (#24219).

HISTORICAL MARKERS, MONTOUR, IA. MARKERS INDICATING ROUTE OF OLD LINCOLN HIGHWAY THROUGH MONTOUR WILL BE ERECTED. (LOCAL). FAY LENHART, SECRETARY; EGAD COMMUNITY CLUB; MONTOUR, IA 50173. (#24222).

PARK IMPROVEMENT, MONTOUR, IA. PARK IMPROVEMENT BY COMMUNITY YOUTH. (LOCAL). BILL BROWN, CUB SCOUTMASTER; PACK 33 CUB SCOUTS; BOX 67; MONTOUR, IA 50173. (#24221).

JULY 24, '76. THRESHING DEMONSTRATION & SQUARE DANCE. EXHIBIT, LIVE PERFORMANCE AT BERYL GREEN FARM, WEST END JACOBS ST. (LOCAL). BERYL GREEN, CHAIRMAN; MONTOUR SWINGERS; BOX 152; MONTOUR, IA 50173. (#106793-1).

SEPT 17 - 18, '76. MONTOUR FALL FESTIVAL. STAGE ENTERTAINMENT, CONCESSION STANDS, CONTESTS, PARADE ADN BEARD CONTEST. AT MAIN ST. (LOCAL). GARY HOSKEY, CHAIRMAN; EGAD COMMUNITY CLUB; ROUTE 1; MONTOUR, IA 50173. (#106793-2).

MONTROSE

ANTIQUE DISPLAY IN MONTROSE PUBLIC LIBRARY, IA. ALL KINDS OF OLD MEMORABILIA DISPLAYED TO THE PUBLIC. (LOCAL). MRS LARRY MCLEARN, PROJ COORDINATOR; MONTROSE SENIOR CITIZENS; RR #1; MONTROSE, IA 52639. (#16418).

BICENTENNIAL THEME AT BALLPARK, MONTROSE, IA. TRASH CANS, POLES & SHELTERHOUSE WILL BE PAINTED RED, WHITE & BLUE. (LOCAL). MRS MARSHA GALLE, LEADER; MONTROSE MODERNETTES 4-H CLUB; MONTROSE, IA 52639. (#19719).

FLAG POLE AND FLAG, FLOWERS IN CHURCHYARD, IA. FLAGPOLE AND FLAG IN THE CHURCHYARD; FLOWERS AROUND FLAGPOLE, CEREMONY TO DEDICATE FLAGPOLE. (LOCAL). MRS JOHN TWEEDY, COORDINATOR; YOUTH RELIGIOUS EDUCATION, ST JOSEPH'S CATHOLIC CHURCH; RR; MONTROSE, IA 52639. (#19717).

FLOWER GARDEN, MONTROSE, IA. PLANT RED, WHITE AND BLUE FLOWERS AT BALL PARK FOR ALL TO ENJOY. (LOCAL). MRS MARSHA GALLE, LEADER; MONTROSE MODERNETTES 4-H CLUB; MONTROSE, IA 52639. (#19718).

LIGHTED FLAG POLE, MONTROSE, IA. A LIGHTED FLAG POLE WILL BE ERECTED IN TOWN BALL PARK; A STAR-SHAPED FLOWER GARDEN WILL BE PLACED AT THE END OF THE POLE. (LOCAL). MARY SUE GALLE, PRESIDENT; MONTROSE CHAMBERETTES : BICENTENNIAL COMMITTEE; MONTROSE, IA 52639. (#19715).

NEW MONTROSE PUBLIC LIBRARY, IA. NEW BUILDING W/2500 SQ FT & ROOM FOR DISPLAYS WILL BE BUILT FOR THE MONTROSE BICENTENNIAL CELEBRATION. (LOCAL). MRS LARRY MCLEARN, PROJ COORDINATOR; MONTROSE LIBRARY BOARD; 2ND ST; MONTROSE, IA 52639. (#16419).

AUG 26 - 28, '76. BICENTENNIAL WATERMELON FESTIVAL. FESTIVAL INCLUDES BOOTHS, BICENTENNIAL MUSIC BY SENIOR CITIZENS, CARNIVALS AND MANY OTHER ACTIVITIES. AT ROADSIDE PARK, MAIN ST. (LOCAL). KENNETH GALLE, PROJ COORD; CHAMBER OF COMMERCE; RR; MONTROSE, IA 52639. (#104519-23).

MOORLAND

MOORLAND COMMUNITY CENTER AND COMMUNITY PARK, IA. A COMMUN9C8 355T59 EM&7JRK ARE BEING CONSTRUCTED IN MOORLAND. (LOCAL). MARY MCCARVILLE, COORDINATOR; MOORLAND TOWN COUNCIL AND BETTERMENT CLUB; MOORLAND, IA 50566. (#22472).

MAY 1, '76. OLD FASHIONED CLEANUP DAY. FESTIVAL. (LOCAL). DOLORES LEEPER, CHMN; TOWN COUNCIL; MOORLAND, IA 50566. (#106921-1).

MAY 8, '76. HOME-MAKING OF YESTERYEAR. EXHIBIT. (LOCAL). PEGGY MCCARVILLE, COORD; FULTON HUSTLER'S 4-H GIRLS' CLUB; MOORLAND, IA 50566. (#106920-1).

AUG 7, '76. BICENTENNIAL APPRECIATION DAY. COMPETITION, FESTIVAL, PARADE, LIVE PERFORMANCE. (LOCAL). SHARON JONES, COORD; MOORLAND BETTERMENT CLUB; MOORLAND, IA 50566. (#106919-1).

MOORLAND — CONTINUED

AUG 7, '76. QUILTING BEE BY SENIOR CITIZENS. EXHIBIT. (LOCAL). OLIVE FIALA, COORD; SENIOR CITIZENS; MOORLAND, IA 50566. (#106918-1).

MORAVIA

OLD DEPOT RESTORATION IN MORAVIA, IA. MOVING & RESTORING OLD MORAVIA DEPOT. (LOCAL). ELMER GIDEL, CHAIRMAN; BOOSTER CLUB; MORAVIA, IA 52571. (#21398).

JULY 3 - 5, '76. FOURTH OF JULY FESTIVAL. THIS CELEBRATION WILL FEATURE MORAVIA'S 125TH ANNIVERSARY. AT TOWN SQUARE. (LOCAL). ELMER GIDEL, COORD; MORAVIA BICENTENNIAL COMMITTEE & BOOSTER CLUB; MORAVIA, IA 52571. (#105320-1).

MORLEY

CONTINUATION OF MILLER PARK - MORLEY, IA. TREES AND FLOWERS WILL BE PLANTED IN MILLER PARK. (LOCAL). RALPH S BARGER, CHAIRPERSON; MORLEY BICENTENNIAL COMMITTEE; 203 MAIN ST; MORLEY, IA 52312. (#17507).

HISTORICAL DISPLAY, MORLEY, IA. DISPLAY OF HISTORICAL ITEMS IN MORLEY COMMUNITY BUILDINGS. (LOCAL). RALPH S BARGER, CHAIRPERSON; MORLEY BICENTENNIAL COMMITTEE; 203 MAIN ST; MORLEY, IA 52312. (#17520).

SEPT 5 - 6, '76. MORLEY BOOSTER DAY. FESTIVAL AT MILLER PARK. (LOCAL). RALPH S BARGER, CHAIRMAN; MORLEY BICENTENNIAL COMMITTEE; 203 MAIN ST; MORLEY, IA 52312. (#105377-1).

MORNINGSIDE

BICENTENNIAL PROGRESS REPORT - MORNINGSIDE, IA. A COURSE ON THE PROGRESS OF THE NATION AT ITS 200TH BIRTHDAY. (LOCAL). DR ROBERT JEWETT, BICENT COORDINATOR; MORNINGSIDE COLLEGE; SIOUX CITY, IA 51106. (#17635).

MOUILLE

JULY 25, '76. OLD FASHIONED CELEBRATION. PARADE, FIREWORKS & GAMES. AT MAIN ST. (LOCAL). LADONNA PETERS, COORD; TOWN OF MOUILLE; MOUILLE, IA 51039. (#109023-1).

MOULTON

SEPT 9 - 12, '76. MOULTON JAMBOREE; PARADE, ART SHOW AND EXHIBITS. TRACTOR PULL, 09/09 AT 6 PM; KIDDIE PARADE, 09/10 AT 1:30 PM; PERFORMANCE IN PARK AT 7 PM, 09/10; PARADE OF BICENTENNIAL FLOAT 9/11 AT 12 NOON. AT MAIN ST, HIGHWAY 202. (LOCAL). VIVIEN WRIGHT, COORD; MOULTON CHAMBER OF COMMERCE; 311 N MAIN; MOULTON, IA 52572. (#104020-6).

SEPT 12, '76. MOULTON HISTORICAL MUSEUM OPEN HOUSE. OPEN HOUSE FROM 2 PM UNTIL EVENING INCLUDING PROGRAM & BARBEQUE. AT MOULTON HISTORICAL MUSEUM. (LOCAL). RUTH STEVENSON, PRES; MOULTON HISTORICAL SOCIETY; MOULTON HISTORICAL SOCIETY; MOULTON, IA 52572. (#17632-1).

MOUNT AYR

ART COLLECTION EXHIBIT. PAINTINGS OF THE PAST DONE BY LOCAL ARTISTS. (LOCAL). DONALD DAILEY, CHMN; MT AYR BICENTENNIAL COMMITTEE; 301 N TAYLOR; MT AYR, IA 50854. (#102598-1). **(??).**

BICENTENNIAL BILLBOARD - MOUNT AYR, IA. A LARGE PAINTING OF IMPORTANT PEOPLE, EVENTS AND INVENTIONS THROUGH HISTORY OUTLINED BY AN EAGLE WITH THE AMERICAN FLAG. (LOCAL). DIANA LARSON, INSTRUCTOR; PAINTING CLASS OF MOUNT AYR COMMUNITY HIGH SCHOOL; 100 N LINCOLN; MOUNT AYR, IA 50854. (#25400).

CENTURY FARM AWARDS, MOUNT AYR, IA. TWENTY-TWO FARMS IN RINGGOLD COUNTY WILL RECEIVE CENTURY FARM DESIGNATION DURING 1976. (LOCAL). PRESTON HAYSE, DIRECTOR; RINGGOLD COUNTY FARM BUREAU; 401 E MADISON; MOUNT AYR, IA 50854. (#25397).

LEGION MEMORIAL FOR COUNTY WAR DEAD, MOUNT AYR, IA. ALL NAMES OF THOSE WHO GAVE THEIR LIVES IN SERVICE OF THEIR COUNTRY FROM RINGGOLD COUNTY WILL BE MEMORIALIZED IN A PERMANENT DISPLAY IN THE COUNTY COURTHOUSE. (LOCAL). DONALD DAILEY, PROJ CHAIRMAN; RINGGOLD COUNTY AMERICAN LEGION POSTS; 301 N TAYLOR; MOUNT AYR, IA 50854. (#25398).

MICROFILM PROJECTOR AND FILM, MOUNT AYR, IA. PURCHASE MICROFILM PROJECTOR & FILM TO HELP PRESERVE COUNTY RECORDS, NEWSPAPERS, CEMETERY RECORDS, COURTHOUSE MATERIAL AND OTHER ITEMS OF HISTORICAL VALUE. (LOCAL). CHARLES BENNETT, PRESIDENT; RINGGOLD COUNTY HISTORICAL SOCIETY; MOUNT AYR, IA 50854. (#25396).

RINGGOLD CO PIONEER CENTER - PROJ OF MT AYR, IA. THE CORNWALL HOUSE AND OLD TELEPHONE FACTORY WILL BE TURNED INTO A MUSEUM. (LOCAL). CHAS BENNETT, PRESIDENT; RINGGOLD HISTORICAL SOCIETY; MT AYR, IA 50854. (#13904).

VIGNETTE ON SIGNERS OF THE DECLARATION - IA. NEWSPAPER ARTICLES ON EACH OF THE MEN WHO SIGNED THE DECLARATION OF INDEPENDENCE; A PERSONAL GLIMPSE INTO THEIR LIVES. (LOCAL). JACK TERRY, EDITOR; MOUNT AYR RECORD-NEWS; 119 N TAYLOR; MOUNT AYR, IA 50854. (#25399).

SEPT 1, '75 - JAN 1, '76. 6TH GRADE ESSAY CONTEST. IOWA FEDERATION OF WOMENS CLUBS IS THE LOCAL SPONSOR FROM WHICH A WINNER WILL BE SELECTED TO COMPETE AT THE STATE COMPETITION, APR 20-21, 1976 IN DES MOINES, IA. (ST-WIDE). MRS LESTER HICKMAN, CHMN; RINGGOLD COUNTY WOMEN'S CLUB; MT AYR, IA 50854. (#101382-1).

APR 5 - 6, '76. BICENTENNIAL PLAY. BICENTENNIAL THEATER PRODUCTION PRODUCED BY MT AYR COMMUNITY HIGH SCHOOL. TITLE OF PLAY: '1776 AND ALL THAT' BY LEONARD WIBBERLY. (LOCAL). WILLIAM HOHLFELD, DIR.; MT AYR BICENTENNIAL COMMITTEE; MT AYR, IA 50854. (#101383-1).

APR 8, '76. COLONIAL TEA. FESTIVAL, EXHIBIT AT MOUNT AYR PUBLIC LIBRARY, 121 W MONROE, SOUTHSIDE OF SQUARE. (LOCAL). MRS L A ROWE; MOUNT AYR PUBLIC LIBRARY; 121 W MONROE; MOUNT AYR, IA 50854. (#200018-104).

MAY 13, '76. FESTIVAL '76' BY MOUNT AYR ELEMENTARY STUDENTS. LIVE PERFORMANCE AT MOUNT AYR COMMUNITY SCHOOL AUDITORIUM, 100 N LINCOLN. (LOCAL). LARRY GILES, PRINCIPAL; MOUNT AYR COMMUNITY SCHOOL; 100 N LINCOLN; MOUNT AYR, IA 50854. (#200018-106).

MAY 20, '76. HORIZONS '76' BY MT AYR COMM SCHOOL. LIVE PERFORMANCE AT MOUNT AYR COMMUNITY SCHOOL AUDITORIUM, 100 N LINCOLN. (LOCAL). LARRY GILES, PRINCIPAL; MOUNT AYR COMMUNITY SCHOOL; 100 N LINCOLN; MOUNT AYR, IA 50854. (#200018-105).

JULY '76. MOONLIGHTERS THEATER GROUP BICENTENNIAL PLAY. LIVE PERFORMANCE AT HIGH SCHOOL AUDITORIUM. (LOCAL). DONALD DAILEY, CHMN; MT AYR THEATER GROUP; 301 N TAYLOR; MT AYR, IA 50854. (#102597-1).

MOVILLE

CREATIVE WRITING, MOVILLE, IA. ENCOURAGE THE PRESERVATION OF LOCAL HISTORY BY CREATIVE WRITING. (LOCAL). MIRIAM SPEKE, PRESIDENT; MOVILLE WOMENS CLUB; MOVILLE, IA 51039. (#22723).

FLAG DISPLAY, MOVILLE, IA. FLAG IS SPOTLIGHTED AND FLOWN 24 HOURS A DAY. (LOCAL). S L MCELRATH, ACTING DIRECTOR; MOVILLE TOWN COUNCIL; MOVILLE, IA 51039. (#22720).

HISTORICAL BOOTH - MOVILLE, IA. A HISTORICAL BOOTH WILL BE BUILT BY WOODBURY COUNTY RESIDENTS. (LOCAL). BOB HERBOLD, COORDINATOR; WOODBURY COUNTY FAIR ASSOC; MOVILLE, IA 51039. (#24054).

MOVILLE WILDLIFE PRESERVE, IA. 7 ACRES OF PRAIRIE AND TIMBER LAND HAS BEEN DEVELOPED INTO A WILDLIFE PRESERVE. (LOCAL). RONALD MANLY, CITY COUNCIL MEMBER; MOVILLE CITY COUNCIL; CITY HALL; MOVILLE, IA 51039. (#25410).

RURAL SCHOOLHOUSE - MOVILLE, IA. ABANDONED RURAL SCHOOLHOUSE WILL MOVED TO A FAMILY FARM AND RESTORED AS A LIVING HISTORY PROJECT. (LOCAL). MISS ANNIE MARTENS, PROJ DIRECTOR; RFD 2; MOVILLE, IA 51039. (#25409).

TREE PLANTING PROJECT, MOVILLE, IA. REPLACEMENT OF TREE LOST TO DUTCH ELM AND TORNADO. (LOCAL). MIRIAM SPEKE, PRESIDENT; MOVILLE WOMENS CLUB; MOVILLE, IA 51039. (#22722).

WOODBURY COUNTY HISTORICAL DISPLAY. HISTORICAL ITEMS DISPLAYED BY OWNERS IN A SPECIAL EXHIBIT. (LOCAL). SARA L MCELRATH, CHMN; WOODBURY COUNTY FAIR ASSOC; MOVILLE, IA 51039. (#106114-1). **(??).**

NOV 7, '75. PATRIOTIC PROGRAM BY WOMEN'S CLUB. CEREMONY. (LOCAL). MIRIAM SPEKE, PROJ DIR; MOVILLE WOMEN'S CLUB; MOVILLE, IA 51039. (#200018-113).

JULY 4, '76. 4TH OF JULY CELEBRATION. FESTIVAL AT FAIRGROUNDS-MOVILLE GRANDSTAND. (LOCAL). JOHN WAGONER, COORD; MOVILLE CHAMBER OF COMMERCE; MOVILLE, IA 51039. (#106146-2).

AUG 5, '76. BICENTENNIAL DAY. FAIR AT FAIRGROUNDS. (LOCAL). BOB HERBOLD, COORD; WOODBURY COUNTY FAIR ASSOC; LAWTON, IA 51030. (#106146-3).

AUG 5, '76. COUNTY SCHOOL TEACHER REUNION. CEREMONY, FESTIVAL AT FAIRGROUNDS. (LOCAL). PEARLE HATHAWAY; WOODBURY COUNTY FAIR ASSOC; PIERSON, IA 51048. (#106858-1).

AUG 5, '76. SENIOR CITIZEN DAY. EXHIBIT, FAIR AT FAIRGROUNDS AT MOVILLE. (LOCAL). BOB HERBOLD, COORD; WOODBURY COUNTY FAIR ASSOCIATION; LAWTON, IA 51030. (#106146-1).

AUG 5, '76. WOODBURY COUNTY FAIR-BICENTENNIAL THEME. FAIR AT FAIRGROUNDS. (LOCAL). BOB HERBOLD; WOODBURY COUNTY FAIR ASSOC; LAWTON, IA 51030. (#106858-2).

MT PLEASANT

AMERICA, THEN AND NOW - MT PLEASANT, IA. A CONTINUING PROGRAM OF THE SIGHTS AND SOUNDS AND PEOPLE OF THE CONTEMPORARY U S; USING FILMS, SPEAKERS, ETHNIC MEALS AND EXPERIENCES, RELIGIOUS OR SOCIAL COMMUNITIES. (ST-WIDE). PETER JAYNES, PROJ COORDINATOR; IOWA WESELEYAN COLLEGE; 601 N MAIN; MT PLEASANT, IA 52641. (#9682).

BUILDINGS IN MT PLEASANT, IA - ARCHITECTURE GUIDE. THE COMPILING OF A PERMANENT ILLUSTRATED OR ORAL GUIDE FOR A SELF CONDUCTED TOUR OF REPRESENTATIVE SAMPLES OF AMERICAN ARCHITECTURE IN MT PLEASANT; PLACING BUILDINGS IN THEIR SETTING. (LOCAL). PETER JAYNES, PROJ COORDINATOR; IOWA WESELEYAN COLLEGE; 601 N MAIN; MT PLEASANT, IA 52641. (#9685).

CULTURAL & THEOLOGICAL ENCOUNTER, MT PLEASANT, IA. AN ESTABLISHED LECTURE, FILM, DANCE, DRAMA AND CONCERT SERIES WHICH FOCUSES ON THE 3 THEMES OF THE BICENTENNIAL DURING THE ACADEMIC YEARS 1975-76 AND 1976-77. (LOCAL). PETER JAYNES, PROJ COORDINATOR; IOWA WESELEYAN COLLEGE; 601 N MAIN; MT PLEASANT, IA 52641. (#9680).

ESTABLISHMENT OF AN AMERICAN STUDIES MAJOR,IOWA. THE CREATION OF A SPECIALIZED COURSE STUDYING THE PAST AND PRESENT UNITED STATES, INVOLVING HISTORY, RELIGION, SOCIOLOGY, LITERATURE, ART, DRAMA, ECONOMICS AND POLITICAL SCIENCE. (LOCAL). DR PETER JAYNES, PROJ COORD.; IOWA WESELEYAN COLLEGE; 601 N MAIN; MT PLEASANT, IA 52641. (#9689).

HENRY COUNTY MULTIMEDIA HISTORIC CENTER, IA. THE MT PLEASANT RECREATION COMMITTEE IS BUILDING A NEW CENTER FOR COMMUNITY ACTIVITIES. (LOCAL). NARREN FYE, PROJ DIRECTOR; MT PLEASANT RECREATION COMMITTEE; MT PLEASANT, IA 52641. (#12480).

HISTORIC HARLAND-LINCOLN HOME IN MT PLEASANT, IOWA. PROJECT ENTAILS THE CONTINUED MAINTAINENCE AND USE OF THIS HOME; WHICH IS LISTED ON THE NATIONAL REGISTER OF HISTORIC PLACES FOR EDUCATIONAL FIELD TRIPS FOR LOCAL SCHOOL CHILDREN. (LOCAL). PETER JAYNES, PROJ COORDINATOR; IOWA WESELEYAN COLLEGE; 601 N MAIN; MT PLEASANT, IA 52641. (#9686).

KILJ'S LOCAL BICENT ACTIVITIES COVERAGE - NBMRP. STATION IN SMALL COMMUNITY, KILJ'S BICENT COVERAGE RANGES FROM 6TH GRADE BICENT QUILT PRESENTATION TO JULY 4 FESTIVITIES THROUGHOUT COUNTY, 3-HR SPECIAL 'HI TO BI', & BROADCASTING LOCAL BICENT MTGS. (LOCAL). VIVIAN HODGES, BICENTENNIAL COORDINATOR; KILJ-RADIO; 126 MAIN ST; MT PLEASANT, IA 52641. (#23254).

A LOOK AT THE USA BY IOWA WESELEYAN COLLEGE, IOWA. THE FOCUSING OF MOST OF THE JANUARY TERM COURSES ON THE THREE THEMES OF THE BICENTENNIAL. (LOCAL). DR PETER JAYNES, PROJ COORD.; IOWA WESELEYAN COLLEGE; 601 N MAIN; MT PLEASANT, IA 52641. (#9681).

NATL THEATRE RESEARCH CENTER & OPERA HOUSE, IOWA. CENTER IN MT PLEASANT HOUSES FAMOUS SCHAFFNER & OTHER COLLECTIONS AND MEMORABILIA OF FOLK TENT & REPERTOIRE THEATRE. 200 YEARS OF REPERTOIRE THEATRE WILL BE PRESENTED BY UNIVERSITY GROUPS IN 1976. (LOCAL). HERBERT HULT, TREASURE; NATL SOCIETY FOR PRESERVATION OF TENT FOLK & REPERTOIRE THEATRE; RRT 4; MT PLEASANT, IA 52641. (#5136).

RESPONSIBLE SOCIAL INVOLVEMENT IN MT PLEASANT, IA. DEVELOPMENT OF STUDENT PROJECTS AIDING LOCAL MUSEUMS, RESTORATIONS, AND COMMUNITIES WITH PROJECTS CELEBRATING THE BICENTENNIAL AND THE AMERICAN EXPERIENCE. (LOCAL). PETER JAYNES, PROJ COORDINATOR; IOWA WESELEYAN COLLEGE; 601 N MAIN; MT PLEASANT, IA 52641. (#9687).

RESTORATION OF OLD MAIN AT IOWA WESLEYAN COLLEGE. OLDEST COEDUCATIONAL COLLEGE IN IA RESTORING FIRST BUILDING-OLD MAIN. (ST-WIDE). DR LOUIS HASEL MAYER, PRESIDENT; IOWA WESLEYAN COLLEGE; MT PLEASANT, IA 52641. (#3674). **ARBA GRANTEE.**

'100 YRS OF REPERTORY THEATER' - MT PLEASANT, IOWA. A SUMMER SEASON OF THEATER; EACH PLAY PRODUCED BY COLLEGE IN AREA. (LOCAL). MRS HELEN VIRDEN, CHAIRMAN; MIDWEST OLD THRESHERS SHOW; MT PLEASANT, IA 52641. (#3699).

MAY 28 - AUG 24, '75. ARCHITECTURAL TOUR OF HOMES. FOOD SERVED-COFFEE COOKIES GUIDE 22 HOMES ON TOUR ONE HOME HISTORIC LANDMARK VISIT INTERIOR. AT STARTING POINT OLD TRESHERS OFFICE. (LOCAL). BILLIE TURLEY; MIDWEST OLD THRESHERS OUESTERS HISTORICAL SOCIETY BICENTENNIAL; R 1; MT PLEASANT, IA 52641. (#50130-1).

JUNE 1 - AUG 10, '75. RURAL HERITAGE TOURS BICENTENNIAL. TOUR VISITS RURAL AREAS BY BUS. AT OLD THRESHER OFFICE BUS TRIP. (LOCAL). BILLIE TURLEY; MIDWEST OLD THRESHERS-QUESTERS HISTORICAL SOCIETY BICENTENNIAL COMM; RR 4; MT PLEASANT, IA 52641. (#50125-1).

JULY 4 - 6, '75. COUNTY-WIDE BICENTENNIAL FREEDOM FESTIVAL. SPONSOR PLANS INCOMPLETE AS OF 04-02-75. AT STREET FAIRS PARKS HISTORIC BUILDINGS. (LOCAL). HELEN M VIRDEN; ALL TOWNS IN HENRY COUNTY; RT 4; MT PLEASANT, IA 52641. (#50131-1).

AUG 28 - 31, '75. 'TWO CENTURIES BETWEEN TWO RIVERS' PAGEANT. PAGEANTRY OF HISTORY OF IOWA; WILL INCLUDE SONG, DRAMA & NARRATIVE. AT GRANDSTAND ON OLD THRESHERS ASSOCIATION GROUNDS. (LOCAL). HELEN M VIRDEN, CHMN; MIDWEST OLD THRESHERS ASSOC; MT PLEASANT, IA 52641. (#100683-1).

OCT 24 - 25, '75. UNITED STATES ARMED FORCES BICENTENNIAL CARAVAN. THE CARAVAN IS COMPOSED OF EXHIBIT VANS FOR EACH BRANCH OF THE MILITARY SERVICE. THE THEME OF THE EXHIBITION IS 'HISTORY OF THE ARMED FORCES AND THEIR CONTRIBUTION TO THE NATION'. (LOCAL). WARREN FYE, CHMN; HENRY COUNTY BICENTENNIAL COMMISSION; BOX 210; MT PLEASANT, IA 52641. (#1775-220).

MT PLEASANT — CONTINUED

NOV 2, '75 - MAR 14, '76. SOUTHEAST IOWA SYMPHONY ORCHESTRA. ONE OR MORE PERFORMANCES OF AMERICAN MUSIC REPRESENTATIVE OF VARIOUS ERAS, STYLES AND CULTURES IN THE AMERICAN EXPERIENCE ARE BEING PLANNED. SPECIFIC DATES ARE: NOV 2, 1975, FEB 15 & MARCH 14,. AT CHAPEL AUDITORIUM. (LOCAL). DR PETER H JAYNES; IOWA WESELEYAN COLLEGE; 601 N MAIN; MT PLEASANT, IA 52641. (#9683-1).

NOV 4 - 15, '75. AMERICAN ART FESTIVAL AND EXHIBIT. A DISPLAY OF TRADITIONAL & CONTEMPORARY MID-WESTERN AMERICAN ART, CRAFTS & ARTIFACTS. SAT & SUN HOURS: 12 PM - 5 PM. AT IOWA WESLEYAN COLLEGE ART GALLERY. (ST-WIDE). DR PETER H JAYNES; IOWA WESLEYAN COLLEGE; 601 N MAIN; MT PLEASANT, IA 52641. (#9684-1).

NOV 20 - 22, '75. AMERICAN PLAYS, THEN & NOW - 'THE AMERICAN DAME'. A FALL AND SPRING PRODUCTION OF A PLAY BY AN AMERICAN PLAYWRIGHT. AT CHAPEL THEATRE. (LOCAL). DR PETER JAYNES, DIRECTOR; IOWA WESLEYAN COLLEGE; 601 N MAIN; MT PLEASANT, IA 52641. (#9688-1).

MAY 26 - AUG 24, '76. OPEN HOUSE: HOME TOURS. FESTIVAL, EXHIBIT. (LOCAL). HELEN M VIRDEN, CHAIRMAN; HENRY COUNTY BICENTENNIAL COMMISSION INC; OAKLAND RD RR 4; MY PLEASANT, IA 52641. (#5135-501).

MAY 31, '76. AVENUE OF FLAGS. CEREMONY, EXHIBIT AT COURTHOUSE BLOCK. (LOCAL). HELEN M VIRDEN; VETERAN GROUPS; RR 4; MT PLEASANT, IA 52641. (#106059-1).

JUNE 25 - AUG 1, '76. 200 YEARS OF REPERTOIRE THEATRE. TOURING PROFESSIONAL GROUPS, COLLEGE AND COMMUNITY PERFORMERS WILL PRESENT THREE PROGRAMS EACH WEEK. AT MUSEUM OF REPERTOIRE THEATRE. (LOCAL). HELEN M VIRDEN, CHMN; NATIONAL SOCIETY REPERTOIRE THEATER/OLD THRESHERS ASSOC; MT PLEASANT, IA 52641. (#100684-1).

JULY 4, '76. OLD-FASHIONED FOURTH OF JULY. FESTIVAL, PARADE AT FAIR GROUNDS, MCMILLAN PARK. (LOCAL). MARGE HARPER, COORD; MT PLEASANT BETTERMENT ASSOCIATION; 707 BROADWYA; MT PLEASANT, IA 52641. (#106059-2).

SEPT 2 - 6, '76. MIDWEST OLD SETTLERS AND THRESHERS REUNION. AGRICULTURAL EXHIBIT; 100 STEAM ENGINES IN ACTION, CRAFTS AND A TROLLEY. (ST-WIDE). JERRY SHAFER, DIRECTOR; MIDWEST OLD SETTLERS AND THRESHERS ASSOC; RR 1; MT PLEASANT, IA 52641. (#106001-1).

MT STERLING

YOUTH BALL PARK & COMMUNITY HALL - MT STERLING, IA. THE COMMUNITY OF MT STERLING HAS BUILT AND IS MAINTING A BALLPARK FOR THE YOUTH OF THE COMMUNITY AND NEWLY REFINISHED THE TOWN HALL FOR MEETINGS AND COMMUNITY ORGANIZATIONS. (LOCAL). TED WATSON, CO-CHAIRMAN; VAN BUREN COUNTY DEVELOPMENT ASSOC; 101 VAN BUREN ST; KEOSHUQUA, IA 52565. (#21774).

MT VERNON

'THE ATTORNEY: A GLANCE AT THE FUTURE' - IA. CONVERSATIONS WITH LOCAL ATTORNEYS CONCERNING THE LEGAL PROFESSION AND ITS PLACE IN THE 3RD CENTURY. (LOCAL). DR RICHARD H THOMAS, DIRECTOR; CORNELL COLLEGE; MT VERNON, IA 52314. (#21254).

BIRTHDAY PARTY FOR KING CHAPEL. ALL CAMPUS PICNIC IN HONOR OF KING CHAPEL. (LOCAL). DR RICHARD H THOMAS, DIR; CORNELL COLLEGE; MT VERNON, IA 52314. (#105242-1).

THE FOLK MUSIC OF THE AMERICAN REVOLUTION - CONCERT BY OSCAR BRAND. LIVE PERFORMANCE. (LOCAL). DR RICHARD H THOMAS, DIR; CORNELL COLLEGE; MT VERNON, IA 52314. (#105242-2).

KEEPING PRAIRIE SPECIES IN PIONEER CEMETERIES, IA. INFORMATION AND SKETCHES ON PRAIRIE PLANTS WHICH MAY BE PRESENT IN MANY OLD CEMETERIES IN IOWA AND HOW TO KEEP THEM. (LOCAL). DR PAUL CHRISTIANSEN, PROJ CHAIRMAN; IOWA CHAPTER, THE NATURE CONSERVANCY; 103 10TH AVE S; MT VERNON, IA 52314. (#25129).

'100 YEARS AGO THIS WEEK' - MT VERNON, IA. WEEKLY NEWSPAPER STORIES ON EVENTS ON THE CAMPUS IN 1876 FROM OLD COLLEGE PAPERS. (LOCAL). DR RICHARD H THOMAS, DIRECTOR; CORNELL COLLEGE; MT VERNON, IA 52314. (#21255).

MURRAY

ART CONTEST - PROJ OF MURRAY, IA. AN ART CONTEST WITH AN AMERICAN THEME. (LOCAL). ALICE BROWN, PROJ DIRECTOR; BETA SIGMA PHI; MURRAY, IA 50174. (#14183).

FILMS ON HISTORY & FUTURE - PROJ OF MURRAY, IA. FILMS ON THE HISTORY AND FUTURE OF AMERICA. (LOCAL). PENNIE GONSETH, PROJ DIRECTOR; BETA SIGMA PHI; MURRAY, IA 50174. (#14184).

HISTORICAL MARKER PROJ OF MURRAY, IA. A HISTORICAL MARKER FOR THE MORMAN TRAIL. (LOCAL). BILL BUSCH, CHAIRMAN; HISTORICAL SOCIETY OF MURRAY; MURRAY, IA 50174. (#14221).

JULY 30 - 31, '76. MURRAY JAMBOREE: PONY PULL, FIREWORKS & TRACTOR PULL. COMPETITION, FESTIVAL AT MURRAY PARK. (LOCAL). PAUL LOY, DIRECTOR; LIONS CLUB OF MURRAY; MURRAY, IA 50174. (#106832-1).

MUSCATINE

ALEXANDER CLARK HOME RESTORATION - MUSCATINE, IA. RESTORATION OF ALEXANDER CLARK HOME TO BE USED AS A MUSEUM. (LOCAL). MRS BURTINE MOTLEY, DIRECTOR; CEDAR RAPIDS LINKS; CEDAR RAPIDS, IA 52401. (#26682). **ARBA GRANTEE.**

BEAUTIFICATION OF COLLEGE FACULTY FACILITIES, IA. TREES & SHRUBS PIANTED TO BEAUTIFY CAMPUS AND ADJOINIG AREAS OF THE CITY. FOILAGE WILL ALSO HELP PREVENT SOIL EROSION. (LOCAL). R LEE, CHAIRMAN; MUSCATINE COMMUNITY COLLEGE BICENTENNIAL COMMITTEE; 152 COLORADO ST; MUSCATINE, IA 52761. (#23225).

COLLEGE NEWSPAPER, CALUMET - MUSCATINE, IA. THE HISTORY OF IOWA AND MUSCATINE WILL BE PUBLISHED. (LOCAL). R LEE, CHAIRMAN; MUSCATINE COMMUNITY COLLEGE BICENTENNIAL COMMITTEE; 152 COLORADO ST; MUSCATINE, IA 52761. (#23224).

CONTINGENCY PLANS FOR 4TH OF JULY CELEBRATIONS, IA. COUNTY GROUP TO HELP ALL COMMUNITIES WITH FOURTH OF JULY PLANS. (LOCAL). TOM HAMMER, COORDINATOR; MUSCATINE JAYCEES; BATTERSON BUILDING; MUSCATINE, IA 52776. (#20894).

DISPLAY OF MUSCATINE, IA, INDUSTRY & CULTURE. MODULES DEPICTING JOLIET & MARQUETTE; AREA LUMBER INDUSTRY & BUTTON INDUSTRY; GREAT RIVER ROAD AND MODERN MUSCATINE. (LOCAL). MAX W CHURCHILL, CHAIRMAN; MUSCATINE BICENTENNIAL COMMISSION; 914 CEDAR; MUSCATINE, IA 52761. (#17513).

MUSCATINE PERMANENT HISTORIC PANORAMA DISPLAY, IA. FIVE MODULES TO BE PLACED IN THE NEW MUSCATINE CHAMBER OF COMMERCE BUILDING; MODULES WILL CONTAIN PERMANENT EXHIBITS DEPICTING THE HISTORY OF MUSCATINE AREA FROM 1673 TO THE PRESENT. (LOCAL). MAX CHURCHILL, CHAIRMAN; MUSCATINE BICENTENNIAL COMMISSION; 914 CEDAR; MUSCATINE, IA 52761. (#25224). **ARBA GRANTEE.**

OLD HOMES - MUSCATINE, IA. HISTORY AND PICTURES OF HOMES BUILT PRIOR TO 1890 WILL BE COMBINED IN A BOOK AND SLIDES. (LOCAL). MAX W CHURCHILL, COORDINATOR; ASSOCIATION OF AMERICAN UNIV WOMEN; 1563 WASHINGTON; MUSCATINE, IA 52761. (#17512).

SALE OF MEDALLIONS, MUSCATINE, IA. JAYCEES WILL SELL BRONZE MEDALLIONS & KEYCHAINS. (LOCAL). LED HARMS, PROJ DIRECTOR; JAYCEES; 406 W 2ND; MUSCATINE, IA 52761. (#17515).

TOURS OF MUSCATINE, IA. WALKING & RIDING TOURS OF MUCATINE. (LOCAL). JOHN WITMER, CHAIRMAN; AREA HERITAGE ASSOC; RT 1; MOSCOW, IA 52760. (#17514).

TREE PLANTING PROJECT - MUSCATINE, IA. ELEMENTARY SCHOOL CHILDREN WILL PLANT TREES. (LOCAL). MAX W CHURCHILL, COORDINATOR; FLORAL ARTS CLUB; 2021 BURNSIDE; MUSCATINE, IA 52761. (#17511).

FEB 12, '76. FACULTY SLIDE PRESENTATION ON HISTORICAL SITES. FAIR AT 2915 BONNIE DR, MUSCATINE. (LOCAL). TERRY BULLOCK, COORD; MUSCATINE COMMUNITY COLLEGE; 2915 BONNIE DR; MUSCATINE, IA 52761. (#200018-115).

FEB 22, '76. COLLEGE CHOIR CONCERT. LIVE PERFORMANCE. (LOCAL). PETER MARTINEZ, PROJ CHMN; MUSCATINE COMMUNITY COLLEGE; 152 COLORADO ST; MUSCATINE, IA 52761. (#200018-114).

JULY 1 - 4, '76. 4TH OF JULY CELEBRATION. FESTIVAL, PARADE AT DOWNTOWN MUSCATINE. (LOCAL). JAMES A NEPPLE, CHMN; MUSCATINE JAYCEES; 2704 MULBERRY AVE; MUSCATINE, IA 52761. (#103342-26).

DEC '76 - CONTINUING . 'CHURCHES AND CATHEDRALS IN SWITZERLAND' EXHIBIT. EXHIBIT AT MUSSER PUBLIC LIBRARY. (INT'L). OFFICE OF INFORMATION; EMBASSY OF SWITZERLAND; 2900 CATHEDRAL AVE; WASHINGTON, DC 20008. (#31922-1).

NASHUA

CHICKASAW COUNTY RESTORATION OF OLD BRADFORD - IA. RESTORATION OF THE RAILROAD DEPOT FOR USE AS A RAILROAD MUSEUM ON COUNTY MUSEUM GROUNDS; ALSO, RESTORATION OF OLD BRADFORD, SITE OF THE LITTLE BROWN CHURCH. (LOCAL). MRS GLEN DUDLEY, PRESIDENT; CHICKASAW COUNTY HISTORICAL SOCIETY MUSEUM; HWY 346 E; NASHUA, IA 50658. (#11871).

PLANTING TREES IN NASHUA, IA. TREES ARE BEING PLANTED FOR A COMMUNITY DEVELOPMENT BICENTENNIAL PROJECT. (LOCAL). VIRGINIA NELSON, PROJ; NASHUA BICENTENNIAL COMMITTEE; NASHUA, IA 50658. (#16487).

RAILROAD DEPOT RESTORATION IN NASHUA, IOWA. RAILROAD DEPOT TO BE RESTORED FOR USE AS RAILROAD MUSEUM. DEPOT WILL BE TRANSPORTED TO COUNTY MUSEUM GROUNDS (OLD BRADFORD SITE) & DEDICATED JULY, 1976. (LOCAL). MRS GLEN DUDLEY, PRESIDENT; CHICKASAW COUNTY HISTORICAL SOCIETY MUSEUM; HIGHWAY 346 EAST; NASHVA, IA 50658. (#10213).

STORE DISPLAYS, NASHUA, IA. CHANGING ANTIQUE DISPLAYS WILL BE PRESENTED FOR THE BICENTENNIAL. (LOCAL). VIRGINIA NELSON, CHAIRMAN; NASHUA BICENTENNIAL COMMITTEE; NASHUA, IA 50658. (#16429).

APR 29, '76. FEDERATED WOMEN'S BICENTENNIAL FAIR. BICENTENNIAL FAIR FEATURED CRAFTS & ANTIQUES, SKITS DEPICTING HISTORICAL PEOPLE & MOMENTS IN TIME, MUSIC, FASHION AND A FLAG CEREMONY. AT NASHUA TOWN & COUNTRY CLUB, HWY 218 S. (LOCAL). MRS VIRGIL STURM, CHMN; NASHUA FEDERATED WOMEN'S CLUBS; 415 CEDAR ST; NASHUA, IA 50658. (#200018-126).

NATIONAL

AUG 5 - 9, '76. COUNTY FAIR. FAIR. (LOCAL). DON MENKEN, DIRECTOR; CLAYTON COUNTY BICENTENNIAL COMMISSION; RR 2; ELKADER, IA 52043. (#102221-2).

NEOLA

FLAG POLE DEDICATION IN NEOLA, IA. THE NEW FLAG POLE WILL BE DEDICATED AT THE HOO-DOO DAY. (LOCAL). BARBARA LANGIN, CHAIRMAN; NEOLA BICENTENNIAL COMMISSION; NEOLA, IA 51559. (#16161).

LANDSCAPING AREA PARKS - NEOLA, IA. LANDSCAPING WILL INCLUDE THE PLANTING OF 20 ELM TREES. (LOCAL). BARBARA LANGIN, CHAIRMAN; NEOLA BICENTENNIAL COMMISSION; NEOLA, IA 51559. (#16164).

POTTAWATTAMIE COUNTY TREE PLANTING - IA. THIRTEEN TREES, EACH DONATED BY ONE OF THE 13 INC TOWNS OF POTTAWATTAMIE COUNTY WILL BE PLANTED AT ARROWHEAD PARK. EACH TREE IS SYMBOLIC OF ONE OF THE 13 ORIGINAL STATES. (LOCAL). MRS GLEN BRYANT, SECRETARY; POTTAWATTAMIE COUNTY BICENTENNIAL COMMISSION; BOX 297; TREYNOR, IA 51575. (#14357).

NEVADA

BICENTENNIAL QUILT, NEVADA, IA. LOCAL & STATE SYMBOLS TO BE USED ON QUILT. (LOCAL). SHARON MORRICAL, PROJ COORDINATOR; ALPHA UPSILON - BETA SIGMA PHI; 722 19TH ST; NEVADA, IA 50201. (#21705).

DEVELOPMENT OF A NEW PARK - NEVADA, IA. THE CONTINUED DEVELOPMENT OF THIS PARK BY KIWANIS INVOLVES MANY OTHER GROUPS IN A UNITED EFFORT. (LOCAL). GARY KOLBECK, COORDINATOR; KIWANIS; 221 VALLEY VIEW CIRCLE; NEVADA, IA 50201. (#18365).

EXPANSION OF LIBRARY FACILITIES AND SERVICES - IA. A COMMUNITY-WIDE PROJECT TO IMPROVE FACILITIES AND MAKE SERVICES AVAILABLE TO ENTIRE COUNTY. (LOCAL). JOYCE WISSLER - TRUSTEE CHAIRMAN; NEVADA PUBLIC LIBRARY; 631 K AVE; NEVADA, IA 50201. (#18362).

EXTENSION OF NATIONAL COLORS INTO ENVIRONMENT - IA. PROMOTION OF PLANTING RED, WHITE AND BLUE FLOWERS THROUGHOUT THE COMMUNITY. (LOCAL). JIM CHRISTY, COORDINATOR; EXTENSION SERVICE; 437 K AVE; NEVADA, IA 50201. (#18364).

FILM COMPARING YOUTH OF YESTERDAY AND TODAY - IA. 3 PERIODS WILL BE DEALT WITH - 1776-1800, 1903 AND THE PRESENT. (LOCAL). VIRGINIA BROOKS, EDUCATION DIRECTOR; CENTRAL PRESBYTERIAN CHURCH - JUNIOR HIGH FELLOWSHIP; 932 5TH ST; NEVADA, IA 50201. (#18358).

FUND-RAISING ICE CREAM SOCIAL - NEVADA, IA. FUNDS WENT TO BUY 2 TREES FOR PARK, PAINTING TRASH BARRELS, 2 LOCAL RESTORATION PROJECTS AND A BICENTENNIAL CHURCH RETREAT. (LOCAL). VIRGINIA BROOKS, CHAIRMAN; UNITED BICENTENNIAL CHURCH YOUTH; RR 2; NEVADA, IA 50201. (#25363).

HERITAGE CALENDAR - NEVADA, IA. LOCAL ARTISTS CONTRIBUTED PEN AND INK DRAWINGS OF LOCALLY IMPORTATNT HISTORICAL SITES FOR THIS 1976 CALENDAR. (LOCAL). LINDA GLANTZ, COORDINATOR; BETA SIGMA PHI; 525 3RD ST; NEVADA, IA 50201. (#18359).

IMPROVING SERVICES FOR THE AGED - NEVADA, IA. HAVING FINISHED WITH THE IMPROVEMENTS ON THE SENIOR CITIZENS CENTER THIS GROUP IS NOW WORKING ON LOW INCOME HOUSING FOR THESE CITIZENS. (LOCAL). RALPH BEANE, CHAIRMAN; COMMISSION ON CARE OF AGING; 1927 7TH ST; NEVADA, IA 50201. (#18363).

PAINTING OF FIRE HYDRANTS, NEVADA, IA. FIRE HYDRANTS WILL BE PAINTED & DECORATED. (LOCAL). DAVID FAIRBROTHER, CUB SCOUT MASTER; CUB SCOUT OF AMERICA; 822 2ND ST; NEVADA, IA 50201. (#18367).

PLANTING OF TREES, NEVADA, IA. EACH TROOP OR PACK WILL PLANT 2 TREES IN KIWANIS PARK EQUALING APPROXIMATELY 60 TREES. (LOCAL). DAVID FAIRBROTHER, CUB SCOUT MASTER; CUB SCOUTS, BOY SCOUTS, GIRL SCOUTS; 822 2ND ST; NEVADA, IA 50201. (#21001).

RESTORATION OF OLDEST STANDING BUILDING, IA. RESTORATION OF THE THIRD HOUSE BUILT IN NEVADA, THE OLDEST STANDING BUILDING, A CABIN CONSTRUCTED OF HAND-HEWN WALNUT LOGS. (LOCAL). HAROLD BRINKMAN, CHAIRMAN; ROTARY CLUB; 760 14TH ST PL; NEVADA, IA 50201. (#18366).

SPEAKERS ON GETTING INVOLVED, NEVADA, IA. EACH TOASTMASTER IS TALKING TO AN ORGANIZATION TO ENCOURAGE THEM TO PARTICIPATE IN A LOCAL BICENTENNIAL PROJECT. (LOCAL). EARL LAUGHLIN, PRESIDENT; TOASTMASTERS; RD#2; NEVADA, IA 50201. (#21706).

TAPING REMINISCENCES OF LONG-TIME RESIDENTS - IA. THESE TAPES ARE INTENDED TO CAPTURE THE EXPERIENCES AND MEMORIES OF THESE VALUED CITIZENS FOR USE BY ALL WHO ARE INTERESTED IN OUR LOCAL HERITAGE. (LOCAL). JOYCE WISSLER - TRUSTEE CHAIRMAN; NEVADA PUBLIC LIBRARY; 631 K AVE; NEVADA, IA 50201. (#18361).

NEVADA — CONTINUED

TIME CAPSULE - NEVADA, IA. PRESERVING SAMPLES OF OUR LIVES TODAY FOR FUTURE GENERATIONS. (LOCAL). CRAIG AMOS, COORDINATOR; JUNIOR CHAMBER OF COMMERCE; BOX 22; NEVADA, IA 50201. (#18360).

OCT 4 - 5, '75. TOUR OF HERITAGE HOMES. 5 HOMES OF LOCAL SIGNIFICANCE ARE INCLUDED, AS WELL AS A CENTURYOLD COUNTY CHURCH. AT 1101 9TH ST. (LOCAL). JANE E NEFF, CHAIRPERSON5; BETA SIGMA PHI; 25 HICKORY PLACE; NEVADA, IA 50201. (#200018-123).

DEC 7 - 9, '75. FILMS: NEVADA CENTENNIAL - 1953. FESTIVAL AT CAMELOT THEATER. (LOCAL). HELEN HARRELL, COORD; NEVADA FIRE DEPARTMENT FLAMES; 513 8TH ST; NEVADA, IA 50201. (#200018-124).

APR 22, '76. RURAL-URBAN DAY. CEREMONY AT FARM BUREAU BUILDING, 512 L AVENUE, NEVADA. (LOCAL). MRS RALPH SCHNUR; FARM BUREAU WOMEN; RR; NEVADA, IA 50201. (#103768-6).

JUNE 1 - 8, '76. BICENTENNIAL WEEK. SUNDAY - RELIGIOUS FREEDOM DAY, MONDAY - HONOR AMERICA DAY, TUESDAYCOMMUNITY SERVICE DAY, WEDNESDAY - EDUCATION DAY, THURSDAY - HELP THE NEEDY DAY, FRIDAY - UNIFORMED SERVICE DAY AND SATURDAY - LOYALTY DAY. (LOCAL). RUTH NEFF, CHAIRMAN; VFW AUXILIARY POST #2209; 811 6TH ST; NEVADA, IA 50201. (#108043-1).

JULY 3 - 4, '76. 4TH OF JULY CELEBRATION. FESTIVAL, PARADE AT DOWNTOWN NEVADA. (LOCAL). CRAIG M AMOS, PROJ DIR; JUNIOR CHAMBER OF COMMERCE; BOX 22; NEVADA, IA 50201. (#103768-8).

SEPT 11, '76. ART FAIR. EMPHASIS WILL BE PLACED ON HERITAGE ARTS THIS YEAR; DEMONSTRATIONS WILL BE INCLUDED; NEVADA'S BICENTENNIAL BUTTON WILL BE ON SALE. AT DOWNTOWN NEVADA. (LOCAL). JANE E NEFF, CHAIRPERSON; CHAMBER OF COMMERCE; 610 J AVENUE; NEVADA, IA 50201. (#103768-7).

NEW ALBIN

IRON POST MEMORIAL PARK - NEW ALBIN, IA. NEW ALBIN IRON POST NATIONAL HISTORIC SITE MEMORIAL PARK TO PIONEERS AND VETERANS OF LOCAL AREA. (LOCAL). JAMES HOSCH, PRESIDENT; NEW ALBIN COMMUNITY CLUB; NEW ALBIN, IA 52160. (#24228).

IRON POST NATIONAL HISTORICAL SITE - IA. IOWA MINNESOTA IRON POST SURVEY MARKER AUTHORIZED BY CONGRESS AND PLACED IN 1849 TO MARK STATE LINE. (ST-WIDE). SARA K SMERUD, DIRECTOR; CITY OF NEW ALBIN; NEW ALBIN, IA 52160. (#24227).

SAND COVE CEMETERY - NEW ALBIN, IA. RESTORATION OF ABANDONED IOWA TOWNSHIP CEMETERY. (LOCAL). EDWARD COLSEH, HISTORIAN; VETERANS OF FORIEGN WARS; NEW ALBIN, IA 52160. (#24229).

JUNE 5, '76. NEW ALBIN DAYS. FESTIVAL AT MAIN ST. (LOCAL). GLENN MEYER, CHAIRMAN; NEW ALBIN BICENTENNIAL COMMISSION; NEW ALBIN, IA 52160. (#106795-1).

NEW HARTFORD

COMMUNITY HISTORY - NEW HARTFORD, IA. BOOKLET ON NEW HARTFORD AND ITS COMMUNITY'S HISTORY. (LOCAL). MRS VOPEL YOUNGBERG; NEW HARTFORD BICENTENNIAL COMMITTEE; RR; NEW HARTFORD, IA 50660. (#20993).

NATURE TRAIL OF 1976 - NEW HARTFORD, IA. THE NATURE TRAILS WILL PROVIDE RECREATION AND AN APPRECIATION OF NATURE. (LOCAL). MRS VOPEL YOUNGBERG, COORDINATOR; NEW HARTFORD BICENTENNIAL COMMITTEE; RR; NEW HARTFORD, IA 50660. (#20994).

TIDBITS TELLING OF NEW HARTFORD, IA, HISTORY. BOOKLET OF NEW HARTFORD'S HISTORY WITH PICTURES AND WRITTEN DESCRIPTIONS. (LOCAL). MRS VOREL YOUNGBERG, CHAIRMAN; NEW HARTFORD'S BICENTENNIAL COMMITTEE; RR; NEW HARTFORD, IA 50660. (#21771).

JUNE 19, '76. NEW HARTFORD BICENTENNIAL FUN DAZE. PARADE. (LOCAL). VOPEL YOUNGBERG, CHAIRMAN; NEW HARTFORD BICENTENNIAL COMMITTEE; RR; NEW HARTFORD, IA 50660. (#105140-1).

JULY 3, '76. BICENTENNIAL HIKING TRAIL OF 1976. TEN MILE TRAIL; PURPOSE IS TO DISCOVER OUR ENVIRONMENT. AT BETWEEN NEW HARTFORD AND PARKERSBURG, ALONG BEAVER RIVER. (LOCAL). VOPEL YOUNGBERG, DIRECTOR; NEW HARTFORD BICENTENNIAL COMMITTEE AND BOY SCOUTS; RR; NEW HARTFORD, IA 50660. (#105614-2).

JULY 9 - 10, '76. NEW HARTFORD FUN DAZE CELEBRATION. CELEBRATION INCLUDES PARADE, PAGEANT, DISPLAYS AND GAMES. AT PACKWAUKEE PARK, LOCAL SCHOOLS AND STREETS OF CITY. (LOCAL). MRS ROY YOUNGBERG, DIR; NEW HARTFORD BICENTENNIAL COMMITTEE AND JAYCEES; RR; NEW HARTFORD, IA 50660. (#105614-1).

NEW HAVEN

RESTORATION OF ROAD MARKER, NEW HAVEN, IA. ROAD MARKER PUT UP BY PIONEER JOHN WRIGHT IN 1880'S DESIGNATING ALL LOCAL TOWNS & 4 LARGE U S CITIES IN EACH DIRECTION. WILL BE RESTORED BY FAMILY MEMBERS. (LOCAL). WALLACE WRIGHT, PROJ COORDINATOR; NEW HARDIN HOMECOMING COMMITTEE; RURAL ROUTE; ELMA, IA 50628. (#29717).

JULY 3, '76. NEW HAVEN HOMECOMING - PARADE, FESTIVAL, MUSEUM TOUR. PREPARATIONS BEGAN IN JAN 1976, INVITATIONS SENT TO FORMER RESIDENTS ALL OVER USA TO ATTEND TWO DAY HOMECOMING IN THIS VILLAGE OF 150 PEOPLE. EMPHASIS PUT ON OUR SENIOR CITIZEN. AMER & BICENT FLAGS PRESENTED TO THEM. BOOK PRINTED FOR SALE. AT OUTDOOR STAGING & BLEACHERS - NEW HAVEN SCHOOL LAWN. (LOCAL). MCCARTHY, BETTY LEE; NEW HAVEN HOMECOMING COMMITTEE; ROUTE #5; OSAGE, IA 50461. (#200018-273).

NEW LIBERTY

AUG 28, '76. FIREMEN'S BICENTENNIAL FESTIVAL. ANTIQUE TRACTOR PULL, WATER FIGHT, RIDES AND GAMES, MUSICAL EVENTS AND EVENING DANCING. (LOCAL). EDWARD ROHLK, PROJ DIR; NEW LIBERTY BICENTENNIAL COMMITTEE; NEW LIBERTY, IA 52765. (#108457-1).

NEW LONDON

HISTORY OF NEW LONDON, IA. A HISTORY OF THE TOWN WILL BE PRINTED IN THE NEW LONDON JOURNAL. (LOCAL). LINDA FAINSWORTH, CHAIRMAN; NEW LONDON JOURNAL; NEW LONDON, IA 52645. (#31298).

JULY 3, '76. COMMUNITY FESTIVAL. BREAKFAST, PARADE, FLEA MARKET, ART & CRAFTS SHOW, BAKING CONTEST, SPINNING DISPLAY, WINDOW DISPLAYS, WATER FIGHT, FROG JUMPING CONTEST, OLD FASHION GAMES, ALMOST ANYTHING GOES CONTEST, VARIETY SHOW, SENIOR CITIZEN, QUEEN CONTEST PROVIDE BICENTENNIAL FUN. AT CITY PARK, SCHOOL, LIBRARY, TOWN HALL. (LOCAL). LINDA FARNSWORTH, CHMN; NEW LONDON BICENTENNIAL COMMITTEE; 403 N WALNUT; NEW LONDON, IA 52645. (#200018-283).

NEW MARKET

NEW MARKET SHELTER HOUSE, NEW MARKET, IA. BUILDING SHELTER IN CITY PARK. (LOCAL). J KELLY TOBIN, DALLAS BOYS 4-H LEADER; 4-H CLUB; RR1; NEW MARKET, IA 51646. (#19688).

JULY 3, '76. BICENTENNIAL 4TH OF JULY. CEREMONY, FESTIVAL, LIVE PERFORMANCE AT CITY PARK. (LOCAL). RUSSELL SUNDERMAN, COORD; CIVIC CLUB; NEW MARKET, IA 51646. (#105623-1).

NEWELL

CHILDREN'S STORY HOUR - NEWELL, IA. LIBRARY SPONSORED CHILDREN'S HOUR AND BICENTENNIAL ACTIVITIES. (LOCAL). TANIA GUTZ, PRESIDENT; NEWELL JR FEDERATED CLUB; NEWELL, IA 50568. (#15658).

COMMEMORATIVE NECKLACE AND KEYCHAINS, IA. REPRODUCTION OF SILVER COINS BY STATE ARBA. (LOCAL). ELVA FRERICHS, CO-CHAIRMAN; BUSINESS & PROFESSIONAL WOMEN; NEWELL, IA 50568. (#15660).

FLOWER BEDS IN NEWELL, IA. RED, WHITE AND BLUE FLOWERS PLANTED AROUND COMMEMORATIVE FLAG, AT NURSING HOME AND CITY HALL. (LOCAL). LAVONNE HABURN & LILLIE PEDERSEN, BICENT REPS; SR WOMENS FED CLUB & GOOD SAMARITAN HELPERS CLUB; NEWELL, IA 50568. (#15661).

TREE PLANTING IN NEWELL, IA. TREES PLANTED IN PUBLIC PARK FOR THE BICENTENNIAL. (LOCAL). BETS DOYEN, BICENTENNIAL CHAIRMAN; NEWELL JR FEDERATED CLUB; NEWELL, IA 50568. (#15659).

JUNE 5, '76. DANISH CELEBRATION BY NEWELL'S DANISH COMMUNITY. FESTIVAL AT SCHOOL HOUSE COMMUNITY BLDG. (LOCAL). CLIFFORD H BAAK, CHMN; NEWELL BICENTENNIAL COMMITTEE; NEWELL, IA 50568. (#102592-1).

NEWTON

COMMUNITY CELEBRATIONS IN JASPER COUNTY, IA. EACH COMMUNITY IN JASPER COUNTY WILL HAVE A BICENT CELEBRATION. (LOCAL). GERALD ZARLEY, CHAIRMAN; JASPER COUNTY BICENTENNIAL COMMITTEE; 600 E 18TH ST N; NEWTON, IA 50208. (#12344).

FIFE AND DRUM CORPS IN JASPER COUNTY, IA. A FIFE & DRUM CORPS HAS BEEN FORMED TO PLAY AT AREA EVENTS. (LOCAL). GERALD ZARLEY, CHAIRMAN; JASPER COUNTY BICENTENNIAL COMMITTEE; 600 E 18TH ST N; NEWTON, IA 50208. (#12343).

'THE FOURTH R, REMINISCIN", BOOK PROJ - IA. A COMPILATION OF ANECDOTES FROM RETIRED TEACHERS CONCERNING THEIR EXPERIENCES WITH EARLY EDUCATION IN IOWA. (ST-WIDE). A E BURTON, IOWA STATE CHAIRMAN; PRIDE IN AMERICA COMM & IOWA RETIRED TEACHERS ASSOC; 516 E 2ND ST S; NEWTON, IA 50208. (#22021).

NEW HISTORICAL SOCIETY HOME IN JASPER COUNTY, IA. A NEW HOME FOR THE HISTORICAL SOCIETY WILL BE FOUND. (LOCAL). GERALD ZARLEY, CHAIRMAN; JASPER COUNTY BICENTENNIAL COMMITTEE; 600 E 18TH ST N; NEWTON, IA 50208. (#12348).

ORAL HISTORY OF JASPER COUNTY, NEWTON, IA. VIDEO TAPE CONVERSATIONS WITH ELDERLY PEOPLE OF THE COUNTY. (LOCAL). GERALD ZARLEY, PROJ COORDINATOR; JASPER COUNTY BICENTENNIAL COMMITTEE; 600 E 18TH ST N; NEWTON, IA 50208. (#12325).

RESTORATION PROJECT IN JASPER COUNTY, IA. THE OLDEST CHURCH IN THE COUNTY WILL BE RESTORED AND CONVERTED INTO A MUSEUM. (LOCAL). GERALD ZARLEY, CHAIRMAN; JASPER COUNTY BICENTENNIAL COMMITTEE; 600 E 18TH ST N; NEWTON, IA 50208. (#12345).

ROAD SIGNS PROJECT IN JASPER COUNTY, IA. UNMARKED ROADS IN JASPER COUNTY WILL BE MARKED. (LOCAL). GERALD ZARLEY, CHAIRMAN; JASPER COUNTY BICENTENNIAL COMMITTEE; 600 E 18TH ST N; NEWTON, IA 50208. (#12347).

SPECIAL BICENTENNIAL NEWSPAPER ISSUE, IA. IN HONOR OF THE BICENTENNIAL, THERE WILL BE A SPECIAL PRINTING OF PAST HISTORY OF THE AREA. (LOCAL). GERALD ZARLEY, CHAIRMAN; JASPER COUNTY BICENTENNIAL COMMITTEE; 600 E 18TH ST N; NEWTON, IA 50208. (#12346).

WALKING & DRIVING TRAILS IN NEWTON, IA. ESTABLISH WALKING & DRIVING TRAILS AROUND COUNTY. (ST-WIDE). GERALD ZARLEY, PROJ COORDINATOR; JASPER COUNTY BICENTENNIAL COMMITTEE; 600 E 18TH ST N; NEWTON, IA 50208. (#12326).

NICHOLS

HISTORY OF NICHOLS, IA, UPDATE. AN UPDATE OF LOCAL HISTORY WILL BE PRINTED IN BOOK FORM. (LOCAL). ALBERTA KELLY, COORDINATOR; NICHOLS BICENTENNIAL COMMITTEE; NICHOLS, IA 52766. (#24533).

PARK IMPROVEMENTS, NICHOLS, IA. PAINT BANDSTAND, PLANT FLOWER BEDS AND ROSE GARDENS. (LOCAL). VICTOR MILLS, PROJ CHAIRMAN; NICHOLS BICENTENNIAL COMMITTEE; NICHOLS, IA 52766. (#24651).

JUNE 26, '76. BICENTENNIAL PARADE. OLD FASHIONED COSTUMES SKITS PLAYS DISPLAYS OF HISTORICAL ITEMS. (LOCAL). MRS MAX CHOWN; NICHOLS APOPO JR. FED. WOMEN'S CLUB; NICHOLS, IA 52766. (#107688-13).

NODAWAY

TREE PLANTING PROJECT - NODAWAY, IA. THE LOCAL BOY SCOUT TROOP WILL PLANT TREES AT CITY HALL. (LOCAL). ROBERT DUNN SR, PROJ DIRECTOR; BOY SCOUTS; NODAWAY, IA 50857. (#13892).

SEPT '75. LITTLE BRITCHES RODEO. SANCTIONED RODEO HELD IN JUNE & SEPTEMBER. (LOCAL). HARTFORD COOPER, CHMN; NORDAWAY SADDLE CLUB; NORDAWAY, IA 50857. (#101388-1).

SEPT 18 - 19, '76. NODAWAY CORN CARNIVAL. FESTIVAL. (LOCAL). MRS RAYMOND SPRING, DIR; BICENTENNIAL COMMITTEE; NODAWAY, IA 50857. (#105612-1).

NORA SPRINGS

AUG 29 - SEPT 1, '75. NORA SPRINGS CENTENNIAL. CENTENNIAL CELEBRATION WILL FEATURE VARIOUS ACTIVITIES EACH DAY. (LOCAL). ROGER SMITH, PROJ DIR; NORA SPRINGS AREA CENTENNIAL INC; BOX 651; NORA SPRINGS, IA 50458. (#101403-1).

NORTH ENGLISH

JULY 30 - 31, '76. BICENTENNIAL CELEBRATION. FESTIVAL, LIVE PERFORMANCE AT CITY PARK, MAIN STREET. (LOCAL). JERALEE WESTFALL, COORD; NORTH ENGLISH COMMERCIAL CLUB; 216 S COLLEGE; NORTH ENGLISH, IA 52316. (#104693-1).

NORTH LIBERTY

BEAUTIFICATION PROJ IN NORTH LIBERTY, IA. TREES, SHRUBS AND FLOWERS ARE BEING PLANTED TO BEAUTIFY NEWLY DEVELOPED AREAS IN THE CITY. (LOCAL). D DAVID DUNLAVY, PRESIDENT; OPTIMIST CLUB OF NORTH LIBERTY IOWA; RT 1, BOX 343; NORTH LIBERTY, IA 52317. (#24655).

CONSTRUCTION OF NEW BLDG & FLAG POLE, IA. CONSTRUCT FLAG POLE AND NEW BUILDING IN HONOR OF BICENTENNIAL. (LOCAL). D DAVID DUNLAVY, PRESIDENT; OPTIMIST CLUB OF NORTH LIBERTY IOWA; RT 1, BOX 343; NORTH LIBERTY, IA 52317. (#24653).

LIBERTY PARK - NORTH LIBERTY, IA. LIBERTY PARK WILL INCLUDE AN ICE SKATING RING, FOOTBALL FIELD, BASKETBALL COURT, PLAYGROUND EQUIPMENT, CREEK & TREES. (LOCAL). JERRY VENTEICHER, CHAIRPERSON; NORTH LIBERTY PARKS & RECREATION BOARD; RT 1, BOX 30; NORTH LIBERTY, IA 52317. (#24652).

SLOGAN CONTEST FOR 'WELCOME' SIGN. COMPETITION. (LOCAL). D DAVID DUNLAVY, PRES; OPTIMIST CLUB OF NORTH LIBERTY, IOWA; RT 1; N LIBERTY, IA 52317. (#107894-1).

APR 12, '76. CHARTER PRESENTATION TO FIRST BICENTENNIAL POST IN IOWA. AMERICAN LEGION OFFICERS THROUGHOUT THE STATE JOIN IN FOR CHAPTER PRESENTATION TO BICENTENNIAL POST 1976 NORTH LIBERTY; COCKTAIL HOUR, BANQUET, CEREMONIES & DANCE. AT RAMADA INN, HWY 218 & INT 80. (ST-WIDE). JOHN V HAVTAETT, CMDR; AMERICAN LEGION BICENTENNIAL POST 1976 NORTH LIBERTY; 15 E CHESTNUT ST; NORTH LIBERTY, IA 52317. (#200018-125).

MAY 30, '76. MEMORIAL DAY OBSERVANCE. CEREMONY, PARADE. (LOCAL). JOHN V HARTNETT, CMDR; NORTH LIBERTY BICENTENNIAL/POST 1976 AMERICAN LEGION; ROUTE 1, BOX 3A; NORTH LIBERTY, IA 52317. (#107735-1).

NORTH LIBERTY — CONTINUED

JULY 25, '76. HUCK FINN DAY. DAY LONG EVENT WHICH WILL CULMINATE WITH POT LUCK SUPPER LATER AFTERNOON GAMES PLAYED ALL AFTERNOON SPECIAL INTEREST GAMES POPULAR MANY YEARS AGO WHEN N LIBERTY WAS SETTLED. TRANSPORTATION PROVIDED TO & FROM PARK REFRESHMENTS PROVIDED BY OPTMIST CLUB. AT KENT PARK JOHNSON CO ON HWY 6 WEST OF TIFFIN IA. (LOCAL). D DAVID DUNLAVY; OPTIMIST CLUB OF NORTH LIBERTY IA; ROUTE A BOX 343; NORTH LIBERTY, IA 52317. (#107688-6).

NORTHBORO

FLAG POLE PROJECT, NORTHBORO, IA. A FLAG POLE WILL BE ERECTED IN THE CENTER OF MAIN STREET ON CEMENT BASE COVERED WITH FLOWERS. (LOCAL). GAIL DARBEY, CHAIRPERSON; NORTHBORO BICENTENNIAL COMMITTEE; NORTHBORO, IA 51647. (#24473).

HISTORY OF NORTHBORO, IA. WRITING OF THE HISTORY OF NORTHBORO. (LOCAL). LIL GEL, PROJ COORDINATOR; FOURTH OF JULY FESTIVAL COMMITTEE; NORTHBORO, IA 51647. (#24474).

MONITOR OF CEMETERIES, NORTHBORO, IA. INFORMATION ABOUT CEMETERIES WILL BE PROVIDED. (LOCAL). GAIL DARBY, CHAIRPERSON; NORTHBORO BICENTENNIAL COMMITTEE; NORTHBORO, IA 51647. (#24472).

NOV 1 - 30, '75. HERITAGE MONTH CELEBRATION. PROJECT WILL BE TO GET ALL ORGANIZATIONS IN THE COMMUNITY TO CELEBRATE HERITAGE MONTH. (LOCAL). HERMIE K HIRZ, CHAIRMAN; LOCUS GROVE BICENTENNIAL COMMITTEE; RR 2; NORTHBORO, IA 51647. (#11263-1).

JULY 4, '76. FOURTH OF JULY FESTIVAL. FESTIVAL, PARADE AT MAIN ST. (LOCAL). GAIL DARBY, CHMN; NORTHBORO BICENTENNIAL COMMITTEE; NORTHBORO, IA 51647. (#106916-1).

NORTHWOOD

RIVER FRONT CLEANUP - PROJ OF NORTHWOOD, IA. RIVER FRONT CLEANUP; NATURE & BIKE TRAILS WILL; AN AREA WILL BE PREPARE AN AREA FOR THE PARADE OF FLAGS AND COUNTY COURTHOUSE WALKS WILL BE BUILT. (LOCAL). MRS GEORGE LINDFLOTT, CHAIRMAN; TUNE COMMITTEE; 106 3RD ST N; NORTHWOOD, IA 50459. (#16178).

JULY 4, '76. JULY 4TH CELEBRATION. CELEBRATING THE 200TH BIRTHDAY OF OUR NATION WITH PARADES, CARNIVALS PAGEANTS, AND OTHER ACTIVITIES. AT WORTH COUNTY FAIRGROUNDS. (LOCAL). STANLEY WALK; WORTH COUNTY BICENTENNIAL COMMISSION; RR #1; GRAFTON, IA 50444. (#10074-1).

NUMA

NUMA HOMECOMING. SCHOOLS, CHURCHES AND LODGES WILL HOLD OPEN HOUSES. (LOCAL). RONALD BOX, COORD; BICENTENNIAL COMMITTEE; NUMA, IA 52575. (#108045-2).

NUMA, 1776 - 1876 - CELEBRATION. FESTIVAL. (LOCAL). RONALD BOX, COORD; BICENTENNIAL COMMITTEE; NUMA, IA 52575. (#108045-1).

OAK HILL

BLOOMFIELD TOWNSHIP TIME CAPSULE, IA. PRESENT DAY ITEMS ENCLOSED IN CAPSULE TO BE OPENED IN 2076. (LOCAL). VERNE KOENIG, CHAIRPERSON; BLOOMFIELD TOWNSHIP HISTORICAL SOCIETY; 110 ELM CT; DECORAH, IA 52101. (#26842).

OAKLAND

BICENTENNIAL POSTER CONTEST IN OAKLAND, IA. A 3 WEEK POSTER CONTEST WITH A BICENTENNIAL THEME, IN THE ELEMENTARY SCHOOL. (LOCAL). MARJORIE SPENCER, CHAIRPERSON; OAKLAND HISTORICAL SOCIETY; OAKLAND, IA 51560. (#11568).

RESTORATION OF MUSEUM IN OAKLAND, IOWA. RESTORATION OF 1903 STORE INTO MUSEUM, DEPICTING EARLY IOWA & POTT COUNTY. (LOCAL). MRS W L WHITE, PRESIDENT; OAKLAND HISTORICAL SOCIETY; 403 GATES ST; OAKLAND, IA 51560. (#11567). **ARBA GRANTEE.**

SCHUEMAN PARK - OAKLAND, IA. DEVELOPMENT OF A PARK IN OAKLAND, IA. (LOCAL). JOHN MCCOWEN, CHAIRMAN; OAKLAND TOWN COUNCIL AND PARK BOARD; 210 BROWN ST; OAKLAND, IA 51560. (#25593).

SEPT 7 - 8, '75. FALL FESTIVAL. 8/7/75-SPORTS,CASUAL RACES IN THE AFTERNOON.8/8/75-1 PM PARADE WITH FLOATS.VISITING BANDS WILL PARTICIPATE.AFTER PARADE ACTIVITIES INCLUDE: BICENT FLAG PRESENTATION,GAMES SEVERAL FOOD STANDS.PM EVENT :HOME TALENT SHOWS & DANCE. MUSEUM OPENING ON 9/7 FROM 2-5PM. (LOCAL). MARJORIE SPENCER, CHMN; OAKLAND COMMERICAL CLUB; OAKLAND, IA 51560. (#100431-1).

JULY 4, '76. 4TH OF JULY. BELL RINGING AT 1 PM; FIREWORKS, SPECIAL CHURCH SERVICES AND MUCH MORE. (LOCAL). DON BAKER, DIRECTOR; OAKLAND FIRE DEPT & TOWN COUNCIL; OAKLAND, IA 51560. (#108198-1).

SEPT 12 - 13, '76. ANNUAL FALL FESTIVAL. ACTIVITIES INCLUDE: PARADE, TALENT SHOWS, CONTESTS, MUSEUM TOURS, BALL GAMES AND ART DISPLAYS. (LOCAL). WILLIAM HOBSON, CHAIRMAN; OAKLAND COMMERCIAL CLUB; 416 WALNUT ST; OAKLAND, IA 51560. (#108197-1).

OAKVILLE

BICENTENNIAL PROJECTS - OAKVILLE, IA. CITIZENS WILL BE ENCOURAGED TO ERECT FLAGPOLES & FLY FLAGS AND ALSO PLANT TREES. (LOCAL). EMOGENE BROWN, COORDINATOR; FEDERATED WOMEN'S CLUB; OAKVILLE, IA 52646. (#29744).

AUG 6 - 7, '76. HOMECOMING USA YESTERDAY, TODAY, TOMORROW. PARADE, EXHIBIT AT RUSSELL ST. (LOCAL). CODY W GROOMS; AMERICAN LEGION POST 489 & VOLUNTEER FIRE DEPARTMENT; OAKVILLE, IA 52646. (#200018-272).

OCHEYEDAN

PRESERVATION PROJECT IN OCHEYEDAN, IA. THE BETTERMENT COMMITTEE WILL SPONSOR A PRESERVATION-RESTORATION PROJECT. (LOCAL). FLORENCE WELLHAUSEN, PROJ DIRECTOR; BETTERMENT COMMITTEE; OCHEYEDAN, IA 51354. (#13084).

TRACY HOME RESTORATION IN OCHEYEDAN, IA. TRACY HOME WILL BE RESTORED AND CONVERTED INTO A MUSEUM FOR THE PUBLIC. (LOCAL). FERD JARROTT, PRESIDENT; OSCEOLA COUNTY AMERICAN REVOLUTION BICENTENNIAL COMMITTEE; OCHEYEDAN, IA 51354. (#13090).

AUG 16 - ??, '75. OPEN HORSE SHOW & TRIALS. COMPETITION, LIVE PERFORMANCE AT 6TH & CHERRY ST (3 BLOCKS WEST OF COMMUNITY SCHOOL). (LOCAL). DON NOBLE, PROJ DIRECTOR; OCHEYEDAN TRAIL BLAZERS SADDLE CLUB; OCHEYEDAN, IA 51354. (#100955-1).

SEPT 1, '75. LABOR DAY CARNIVAL. FESTIVAL. (LOCAL). ARNOLD B OOMA, CHMN; BETTERMENT COMMITTEE; OCHEYEDAN, IA 51354. (#100954-1).

JULY 4, '76. 4TH OF JULY CELEBRATION. THE 4TH OF JULY CELEBRATION WILL INCLUDE AN OLDTIME PICNIC AND HORSE RACES. (LOCAL). FRED JARROTT, PRES; OSCEOLA CO AMERICAN REVOLUTION BICENTENNIAL COMM; OSCEOLA CO ARBC; OCHEYEDAN, IA 51354. (#13088-1).

AUG 14, '76. BICENTENNIAL HORSE SHOW. SADDLE AND HARNESS CLASSES WILL ALSO BE GIVEN. AT CLUB GROUNDS, 3 BLOCKS WEST OF SCHOOL HOUSE. (ST-WIDE). JOAN NOBLE, PRESIDENT; OCHEYEDAN TRAIL BLAZER SADDLE CLUB; OCHEYEDAN, IA 51354. (#104048-3).

OELWEIN

AUDIO-VISUAL MATERIALS FOR OELWEIN, IA. A MICROFILM VIEWER HAS BEEN AQUIRED FOR THE LIBRARY. FILMS OF THE OELWEIN DAILY REGISTER WILL SOON BE MADE AVAILABLE. (LOCAL). MRS GLENN SIMS, CHAIRMAN; OELWEIN AREA HISTORICAL SOCIETY, GENEOLOGY BRANCH; PO BOX 445; OELWEIN, IA 50662. (#15851).

BETSY ROSS FLOAT, OELWEIN, IA. A FLOAT HONORING BETSY ROSS, WILL BE ENTERED IN OELWEIN'S PARADE ON 7/2/76. (LOCAL). DOROTHY WOLFGRAM, PUBLICITY CHAIRMAN; 73'S & 88'S CB CLUB OF NORTHEASTERN IOWA; 418 3RD AVE, NW; OELWEIN, IA 50662. (#25499).

BOOK REPRODUCTIONS - OELWEIN, IA. THE HISTORICAL SOCIETY WILL SPONSOR THE REPRODUCTION OF AN 1878 HISTORY OF FAYETTE COUNTY, A HISTORY OF THE COUNTY PAST AND PRESENT & A SOUVENIR EDITION OF THE OELWEIN RECORD. (LOCAL). DOROTHY GOSSE, BOOK CHAIRMAN; OELWEIN AREA HISTORICAL SOCIETY; PO BOX 445; OELWEIN, IA 50662. (#15849).

CLARA BARTON FLOAT, OELWEIN, IA. A FLOAT HONORING CLARA BARTON, FOUNDER OF THE AMERICAN RED CROSS, WILL BE ENTERED IN OELWEIN'S PARADE ON 7/3/76. (LOCAL). BERNARD NELSON, COORDINATOR; SOUTH FAYETTE COUNTY AMERICAN RED CROSS; 106 6 AVE SE; OELWEIN, IA 50662. (#25520).

COUNCIL OF CHURCHES' RELIGIOUS HERITAGE PROJ, IA. AREA CHURCHES' APPRECIATION OF RELIGIOUS HERITAGE, BOTH NATIONALLY & LOCALLY. CHURCHES WILL HAVE UNIFIED WORSHIP THEMES AND SPONSOR GUEST SPEAKERS. (LOCAL). REV DAVID R ESTES, CHAIRMAN; OELWEIN AREA COUNCIL OF CHURCHES; 1323 EAST ELM; OELWEIN, IA 50662. (#17517).

DECORATING FIRE HYDRANTS, OELWEIN, IA. REPRODUCING HISTORICAL & FOLKLORIC CHARACTERS ON FIRE HYDRANTS. (LOCAL). M SWANSON, LEADER; CADETTE TROOP 233-GIRL SCOUTS OF UNITED STATES OF AMERICA; OELWEIN, IA 50662. (#21420).

DEVELOPMENT OF LEVIN PARK, OELWEIN. AN PARK-RECREATION AREA FOR THE CHILDREN OF SW OELWEIN WILL BE DEVELOPED. (LOCAL). DR VERLYN W HEINE, PRESIDENT; SERTOMA CLUB; OELWEIN, IA 50662. (#21393).

DREDGING LAKE OELWEIN - OELWEIN, IA. DREDGE LAKE OELWEIN FOR ALL AROUND SUMMER AND WINTER RECREATION. (LOCAL). LYNN KELLOGG, CHAIRMAN; OELWEIN CIVIC LAKE IMPROVEMENT SOCIETY; 100 N FREDERICK; OELWEIN, IA 50662. (#15845).

HISTORICAL MUSEUM - OELWEIN, IA. OELWEIN IS TRYING TO AQUIRE A SUITABLE BUILDING TO HOUSE RAILROAD ARTIFACTS FROM ITS HEYDAY AS A BIG RAILROADING TOWN. (LOCAL). MRS CHARLES GOSSE, VICE PRESIDENT; OELWEIN AREA HISTORICAL SOCIETY; PO BOX 445; OELWEIN, IA 50662. (#15848).

LOG CABIN RESTORATION - OELWEIN, IA. REPAIRS WILL BE MADE ON THE INTERIOR OF AN EARLY LOG CABIN. (LOCAL). MAC HATCH, CABIN CHAIRMAN; OELWEIN AREA HISTORICAL SOCIETY; PO BOX 445; OELWEIN, IA 50662. (#15846).

OAKDALE CEMETERY RESTORATION - OELWEIN. A NEW FENCE IS PART OF THE RESTORATION OF OAKDALE CEMETERY. (LOCAL). CLIFF AVERY, PRESIDENT; OELWEIN AREA HISTORICAL SOCIETY - BOY SCOUT TROOP 188; PO BOX 445; OELWEIN, IA 50662. (#15847).

THE U S PRESIDENTS, SERIES, OELWEIN, IA. NEWSPAPER ARTICLES, NEWLETTERS & FILMS ON THE LIVES OF THE U S PRESIDENTS. (LOCAL). MRS GLEN A SIMS, CHAIRMAN; OELWEIN GENEALOGY SOCIETY; PO BOX 445; OELWEIN, IA 50662. (#17518).

WEDNESDAY CHURCH SCHOOL BICENTENNIAL PROJECT - IA. STUDY THE LIVES OF MEN AND WOMEN WHO PLAYED A SIGNIFICANT ROLE IN EARLY HISTORY OF THE NATION & WHO FOUND SPIRITUAL ANSWERS TO THEIR CONTEMPORARY PROBLEMS. (LOCAL). REV RICHARD B EMERY, PROJ DIRECTOR; WEDNESDAY CHURCH SCHOOL; 100 E CHARLES ST; OELWEIN, IA 50662. (#21992).

WELCOME SIGNS FOR OELWEIN, IA. A SLOGAN CONTEST WILL BE HELD; THE WINNING ENTRY WILL BE DESIGNED INTO AN ARTISTIC SIGN TO WELCOME PEOPLE TO OELWEIN, PLACED ON NORTH & SOUTH EDGE OF TOWN; $25 GIVEN TO WINNING SLOGAN ENTRANT. (LOCAL). ARDETH J RAMSEY, CHAIRPERSON; OELWEIN WOMAN'S CLUB; 36 7TH AVE SE; OELWEIN, IA 50662. (#23979).

OCT 14, '75. SING-ALONG AND OPEN HOUSE WITH BICENTENNIAL THEME. EXHIBIT, LIVE PERFORMANCE. (LOCAL). SISTER ADELE DOUGHAM; SACRED HEART SCHOOL; 600 FIRST AVE SW; OELWEIN, IA 50662. (#105332-1).

OCT '75. ITALIAN HERITAGE DAY - RELIGIOUS CEREMONY & FETE. CEREMONY, FESTIVAL AT SACRED HEART CHURCH, 628 S FRED. (LOCAL). MRS ELVA MAHONEY, CHMN; SACRED HEART CENTENNIAL COMMITTEE; 107 5TH AVE, SE; OELWEIN, IA 50662. (#200018-278).

NOV 29, '75. 'YOUTH OF TODAY, CHURCH OF TOMORROW' - YOUTH ROCK MASS AND DANCE. FESTIVAL. (LOCAL). MRS ELVA MAHONEY, CHMN; SACRED HEART BICENTENNIAL COMMITTEE; 107 5TH AVE SE; OELWEIN, IA 50662. (#200018-133).

DEC 14, '75. MEXICAN HERITAGE DAY. A MEXICAN DINNER WILL BE SERVED AND THERE WILL BE A RELIGIOUS CEREMONY PERFORMED BY THE CHOIR. SUBSTITUTE BY THE CONGREGATION. AT SACRED HEART CHURCH, SOCIAL HALL & FACILITIES. (LOCAL). MRS ELVA MAHONEY, CHMN; SACRED HEART CHURCH; 107 5TH AVE SE; OELWEIN, IA 50662. (#105184-1).

MAR 14, '76. S H IRISH HERITAGE DAY - RELIGIOUS CEREMONY & FEAT. CHURCH CENTENNIAL CELEBRATION; PROCESSION INCLUDES FLAG OF IRELAND, BANNERS AND MUSIC BY CHURCH CHOIR. AT SACRED HEART CHURCH, 628 S FRED. (LOCAL). MRS ELVA MAHONEY, CHMN; SACRED HEART BICENTENNIAL COMMITTEE; 107 5TH AVE SE; OELWEIN, IA 50662. (#200018-134).

APR 30, '76. SMELT FRY. $1.00 OF EACH ADMISSION TO GO TO OELWEIN YOUTH ORGANIZATION FOR A TOTAL OF $380.00. AT VFW HALL, S FRED. (LOCAL). MAXINE TEAGUE, COORD; VFW POST AND AUXILIARY; 103 6TH ST NW; OELWEIN, IA 50662. (#200018-178).

MAY '76. CATHOLIC DAUGHTERS DAY - RELIGIOUS CEREMONY & FETE. CEREMONY, FESTIVAL AT SACRED HEART CHURCH, 628 S FRED. (LOCAL). MRS ELVA MAHONEY, CHMN; SACRED HEART CENTENNIAL COMMITTEE; 107 5TH AVE, SE; OELWEIN, IA 50662. (#200018-276).

JUNE 26 - 27, '76. RELIGIOUS CEREMONY AND FAMILY GATHERING. REUNION ALUMNAE (FIRST GENERAL) RE-CENTENNIAL WAS GREAT SUCCESS. FORMER STUDENTS-GRADUATES ATTENDED INCLUDING 25 STATES AND ICELAND. SPECIAL INSERT IN REGISTER INCLUDED; SERVICES WERE DONATED AS PLANNING; DANCE BAND. AT 628 S FRED; CHURCH AUDITORIUM 1ST AVE SW; AREA PARKING, PICNIC PARK. (LOCAL). SACRED HEART CENT COMM; SACRED HEART CHURCH; 107 5TH AVE S E; OELWEIN, IA 50662. (#103342-30).

JULY 4, '76. FIREWORKS AT JULY 4TH FESTIVAL. EXHIBIT, FESTIVAL. (LOCAL). MRS MIKE QUARIS; 73'S & 88'S C B CLUB OF NORTHEAST IOWA; 418 3RD AVE, NW; OELWEIN, IA 50662. (#107368-1).

AUG 28, '76. SACRED HEART GERMAN HERITAGE CENTENNIAL CELEBRATION. RELIGIOUS CEREMONY, GERMAN FEAST, BANNERS, FLAGS AND COSTUMES. AT CHURCH, 628 S FRED AND K C HOME, CITY PARK ROAD. (LOCAL). MRS ELVA MAHONEY, CHMN; SACRED HEART CENTENNIAL COMMITTEE; 107 5TH AVE SE; OELWEIN, IA 50662. (#200018-224).

OCT 15 - 17, '76. CLOSING CELEBRATION - SACRED HEART'S CENTENNIAL (ONE YEAR). YOUTH DANCE, CARNIVAL ON GROUNDS, REDEDICATION PROCESSION, PROPERTIES REDEDICATED BY RELIGIOUS CEREMONY, PARADING ON GROUNDS, GENERAL ATTENDENCE, FLAG DONATED BY CONGRESSMAN MICHAEL BLOUIN. PLUS CHURCH FLAG PRESENTED BY GRACE METHODIST CHURCH & PUBLIC BANQUET. AT GYMNASIUM, CHURCH, 628 S FRED, CLUB, RURAL, HWY 150 S, FREE PARKING. (LOCAL). MRS ELVA MAHONEY, CHMN; SACRED HEART CENTENNIAL COMMITTEE; 107 5TH AVE SE; OELWEIN, IA 50662. (#200018-267).

OCT 22, '76. SACRED HEART CHURCH SERVICE. MEMORIAL RELIGIOUS CEREMONY AT SITE OF STATUE IN CITY CEMETERY OBSERVED IN CONJUNCTION WITH BICENTENNIAL CELEBRATION. (LOCAL). MRS ELVA MAHONEY, CHMN; SACRED HEART CENTENNIAL COMMITTEE; 107 5TH AVE SE; OELWEIN, IA 50662. (#200018-216).

OELWEIN — CONTINUED

NOV 9, '76. SACRED HEART BICENTENNIAL RELIGIOUS SERVICE AT CEMETERY. CEREMONY. (LOCAL). MRS ELVA MAHONEY, CHMN; SACRED HEART CENTENNIAL COMMITTEE; 107 5TH AVE, SE; OELWEIN, IA 50662. (#200018-279).

OGDEN

HISTORICAL WINDOWS, OGDEN, IA. DISPLAYS OF QUILTS & HISTORICAL WINDOWS. (LOCAL). GARY ALBAN, CHAIRMAN; OGDEN BICENTENNIAL COMMITTEE; OGDEN, IA 50212. (#23161).

NEW LIBRARY, OGDEN, IA. PRIVATE DONOR HAS GIVEN NEW LIBRARY, INCLUDING SITE & BUILDING. BICENTENNIAL GROUP WILL HELP FURNISH NEW LIBRARY. (LOCAL). GARY ALBAN, CHAIRMAN; OGDEN BICENTENNIAL COMMITTEE; OGDEN, IA 50212. (#23163).

TREE PLANTING, OGDEN, IA. TOWN BEAUTIFICATION TO INCLUDE TREE PLANTING. (LOCAL). GARY ALBAN, CHAIRMAN; LIONS CLUB; OGDEN, IA 50212. (#23162).

JULY 14 - 15, '76. OGDEN FUN DAYS. COMPETITION, FESTIVAL, PARADE AT OGDEN CITY PARK. (LOCAL). GARY ALBAN, COORD; OGDEN BICENTENNIAL COMMITTEE; OGDEN, IA 50212. (#106387-1).

OKOBOJI

JUNE 6 - 25, '76. HISTORICAL ART EXHIBIT. EXHIBIT CONSISTS OF WOOD ENGRAVINGS BY WINSLOW HOMER, ONE OF AMERICA'S BEST NATURE ARTISTS, AND THE 1860-1870 ERA COLLECTION OF NICK BALDWIN. AT LAKES ART CENTER BUILDING, HWY 71. (LOCAL). SUSAN GOODWIN, COORD; LAKES ART CENTER; 1002 HILL AVE; SPIRIT LAKE, IA 51360. (#108239-1).

OLD BRADFORD

JUNE 1 - SEPT 10, '75. MUSEUM EXHIBITS. OPENING. (LOCAL). MRS GLEN DUDLEY; CHICKASAW COUNTY HISTORICAL SOCIETY MUSEUM; HWY 346 E; NASHUA, IA 50658. (#11871-502).

AUG 3, '75. DINNER AT THE LITTLE BROWN CHURCH. OPENING. (LOCAL). MRS GLEN DUDLEY; CHICKASAW COUNTY HISTORICAL SOCIETY MUSEUM; HWY 346 E; NASHUA, IA 50658. (#11871-503).

JULY '76. DEDICATION OF THE LITTLE BROWN CHURCH. OPENING. (LOCAL). MRS GLEN DUDLEY; CHICKASAW COUNTY HISTORICAL SOCIETY MUSEUM; HWY 346 E; NASHUA, IA 50658. (#11871-501).

OLDS

JULY 18, '76. BICENTENNIAL FLAG PRESENTATION. CEREMONY AT COMMUNITY BALL PARK. (LOCAL). PHILIP CRAWFORD; AMERICAN LEGION POST 626; RR1; WINFIELD, IA 52659. (#200018-306).

OLIN

FILMS ON THE HISTORY OF IOWA - OLIN, IA. FILMS TELLING THE HISTORY OF IOWA WILL BE MADE AND A BOOK ON THE HISTORY OF OLIN WILL BE COMPILED. (LOCAL). HON DAVID CAVEY, MAYOR; OLIN BICENTENNIAL COMMITTEE; JACKSON ST; OLIN, IA 52320. (#22011).

MONUMENT AND TOWN SIGNS - OLIN, IA. A MONUMENT TELLING THE HISTORY OF THE TOWN WILL BE ERECTED; ALSO, SIGNS WILL BE PUT UP TELLING OF THE OLDEST TOWN IN JONES COUNTY. (LOCAL). HON DAVID CAVEY, MAYOR; OLIN BICENTENNIAL COMMITTEE; JACKSON ST; OLIN, IA 52320. (#22010).

JULY 17 - 18, '76. OLIN HORSE SHOW & BEEF DAYS. AWARD, COMPETITION, FAIR, LIVE PERFORMANCE. (LOCAL). DAVID L CAVEY, PROJ CHMN; OLIN BICENTENNIAL COMMITTEE; JACKSON ST; OLIN, IA 52320. (#105779-1).

ONAWA

EARLY DAY PHOTOS & MURALS - ONAWA, IA. MURALS & PHOTOS OF EARLY ONAWA ON DISPLAY AT CITY HALL. (LOCAL). JOE JACKSON, PROJ DIRECTOR; ONAWA KIWANIS CLUB; ONAWA, IA 51040. (#17509).

ONAWA, PAST, PRESENT AND FUTURE, IA. MURALS OF ONAWA FROM EARLIEST TO PRESENT DAYS - AT CITY HALL. (LOCAL). STANLEY STUKENHOLZ, MANAGER; CITY OF ONAWA; ONAWA, IA 51040. (#19852).

THE PIONEER TRAIL, ONAWA, IA. ROADSIDE SIGNS OF HISTORICAL PLACES MARKING LOST TOWNS AND THE MILLS SOD HOUSE. (LOCAL). JANE MCNEILL, VICE CHAIRMAN; MONONA COUNTY HISTORICAL SOCIETY; ONAWA, IA 51040. (#19851).

TREE PLANTING - ONAWA, IA. TREES WILL BE PLANTED ON STREETS AND IN PARKS. (LOCAL). KATHERINE WOLPERT, CHAIRMAN; ONAWA BICENTENNIAL COMMITTEE; ONAWA, IA 51040. (#17510).

1890, MONONA COUNTY HISTORY, IA. BOOK OF LOCAL HISTORY, PRINTED IN 1890, NOW REPRINTED. (LOCAL). JANE MCNEILL, VICE CHAIRMAN; MONONA HISTORICAL SOCIETY; ONAWA, IA 51040. (#19853).

SEPT 14, '75. VENTURES '75 - ART EXHIBIT. EXHIBIT AT MONONA COUNTY FAIRGROUNDS, FINE ARTS BLDG. (LOCAL). KATHERINE WOLPERT, CHMN; ONAWA BURGESS MEMORIAL HOSPITAL; ONAWA, IA 51040. (#103330-1).

JUNE 6, '76. SUMMER OF '76 COMMUNITY PICNIC. FESTIVAL AT ONAWA CITY PARK. (LOCAL). KATHERINE WOLPERT, CHMN; ONAWA CHAMBER OF COMMERCE; ONAWA, IA 51040. (#107106-1).

JULY 3 - 4, '76. JULY 4TH FESTIVAL. EXHIBIT, FESTIVAL, PARADE AT FAIRGROUNDS. (LOCAL). WILSON GINGLES, PROJ CHMN; MONONA COUNTY BICENTENNIAL COMMITTEE; CASTANA, IA 51010. (#104584-1).

AUG 8, '76. BICENTENNIAL PARADE ON ONE OF THE WIDEST STREETS IN THE USA. OPENING DAY OF MONONA COUNTY FAIR; PARADE WILL BE FOLLOWED BY HISTORICAL PAGEANT IN EVENING AT FAIRGROUNDS. (LOCAL). KATHERINE WOLPERT, CHMN; ONAWA CHAMBER OF COMMERCE; ONAWA, IA 51040. (#107106-2).

ONSLOW

FIRE HYDRANT PAINTING - ONSLOW, IA. FIRE HYDRANTS WILL BE PAINTED RED, WHITE AND BLUE. (LOCAL). MRS RICHARD ANTONS, PROJ DIRECTOR; SOUTH SUNSHINE GIRLS 4-H CLUB; RFD; CENTER JCT, IA 52212. (#22012).

MAR 17, '76. REVOLUTIONARY BREAKFAST. FESTIVAL AT ONSLOW COMMUNITY ROOM. (LOCAL). BESSIE M KOPPES, CHMN; ONSLOW BICENTENNIAL COMMITTEE; ONSLOW, IA 52321. (#200018-132).

JULY 1 - 8, '76. HERITAGE EXHIBIT. EXHIBIT AT ONSLOW COMMUNITY ROOM, ONSLOW, IOWA. (LOCAL). BESSIE KOPPES, CHAIRMAN; ONSLOW BICENTENNIAL COMMITTEE; ONSLOW, IA 52321. (#105780-1).

JULY 8, '76. ONSLOW BEEF BARBECUE AND COMMUNITY GATHERING. FESTIVAL AT CAMBERLIN PARK. (LOCAL). DON LEINEN, PRESIDENT; ONSLOW MEN'S CLUB; ONSLOW, IA 52321. (#105780-2).

ORANGE CITY

COMMEMORATIVE GARDENS, ORANGE CITY, IA. DEVELOPMENT OF COMMEMORATIVE POCKET PARK TO PORTRAY DUTCH HERITAGE; DESIGNED TO BE A PLACE FOR QUIET RELAXATION INSTEAD OF RECREATION. (LOCAL). MARVIN J PETROELJE, CHAIRMAN; ORANGE CITY BICENTENNIAL COMMITTEE; 530 GEORGIA AVE SW; ORANGE CITY, IA 51041. (#22735).

COMMUNITY-COLLEGE HISTORICAL MUSEUM, IA. CONSTRUCTION OF HISTORICAL MUSEUM TO EMPHASIZE DUTCH HERITAGE AND HISTORY; WILL ALSO INCLUDE GENERAL AMERICAN HISTORY. (ST-WIDE). MARVIN J PETROELJE, CHAIRMAN; ORANGE CITY BICENTENNIAL COMMITTEE; 530 GEORGIA AVE, SW; ORANGE CITY, IA 51041. (#22736).

CULTURAL DISPLAY. CULTURAL DISPLAY, PERTINENT TO THE HERITAGE OF THE DUTCH. (LOCAL). MARVIN PETROELFE, COORD; NORTHWESTERN COLLEGE; ORANGE CITY, IA 51041. (#106108-2).

HISTORIC SITE MARKING - ORANGE CITY, IA. HISTORIC SITES AROUND THE COUNTY WILL BE MARKED. (LOCAL). HENRY VAN AARTSEN, CHAIRMAN; SIOUX COUNTY BICENTENNIAL HERITAGE COMMITTEE; RR 1; ORANGE CITY, IA 51041. (#24659).

PHOTOGRAPHIC DISPLAY. DISPLAY OF DEPRESSION ERA PHOTOGRAPHS. (LOCAL). MARVIN PETROELFE, COORD; NORTHWESTERN COLLEGE; ORANGE CITY, IA 51041. (#106108-1).

SOUVENIR HISTORICAL MAP OF SIOUX COUNTY, IA. ARTISTIC MAP, SHOWING HISTORICAL SITES OF SIOUX COUNTY, FROM THE YEAR 1900. (LOCAL). ELINOR NOTEBOOM, ARTIST; SIOUX COUNTY HISTORICAL SOCIETY AND BICENTENNIAL COMMITTEE; W 2ND ST; ORANGE CITY, IA 51041. (#24658).

MAY 19 - 21, '76. TULIP FESTIVAL - DUTCH HERITAGE. EACH MORNING THERE ARE FREE TOURS OF ORANGE CITY IF YOU ARRIVE BY 10AM. AFTERNOON PARADE OF FLOATS, MARCHING BANDS, CORONATION CEREMONY IN PARK, WOODEN SHOE DANCERS ON THE STREET. AT CENTRAL BUSINESS DISTRICT. (LOCAL). DON VANDER WEL, COORD; CITY OF ORANGE CITY; ORANGE CITY, IA 51041. (#108855-1).

MAY 20 - 22, '76. TULIP FESTIVAL - BICENTENNIAL CELEBRATION. EACH MORNING THERE ARE FREE TOURS OF ORANGE CITY IF YOU ARRIVE BY 10 AM. AFTERNOON PARADE OF FLOATS, MARCHING BANDS, CORONATION CEREMONY IN PARK, WOODEN SHOE DANCERS ON THE STREET. AT CENTRAL BUSINESS DISTRICT. (LOCAL). DON VANDER WEL, COORD; CITY OF ORANGE CITY; ORANGE CITY, IA 51041. (#106147-1).

MAY 19 - 21, '77. TULIP FESTIVAL - DUTCH HERITAGE. EACH MORNING THERE ARE FREE TOURS OF ORANGE CITY IF YOU ARRIVE BY 10AM. AFTERNOON PARADE OF FLOATS, MARCHING BANDS, CORONATION CERE MONY IN PARK, WOODEN SHOE DANCERS ON THE STREET. AT CENTRAL BUSINESS DISTRICT. (LOCAL). DON VANDER WEL, COORD; CITY OF ORANGE CITY; ORANGE CITY, IA 51041. (#108917-1).

ORCHARD

COMPILED HISTORY OF TOWN OF ORCHARD, IA. STORY OF EARLY SETTLEMENT AND DEVELOPMENT TO THE PRESENT TIME WILL BE PRINTED. (LOCAL). AMY WALLING, CHAIRMAN; ORCHARD BICENTENNIAL COMMITTEE; ORCHARD, IA 50460. (#29072).

HISTORY OF ORCHARD HIGH SCHOOL - IA. STORY OF DEVELOPMENT OF SCHOOL AND SHORT BIOGRAPHY OF EACH STUDENT WILL BE PRINTED. (LOCAL). AMY WALLING, CHAIRMAN; ORCHARD HIGH SCHOOL; ORCHARD, IA 50460. (#29075).

NEW ROOF ON COMMUNITY BUILDING - IA. REMOVED OLD ROOF COVERING ON COMMUNITY BUILDING AND INSTALLED A NEW ROOF. (LOCAL). AMY WALLING, CHAIRMAN; TOWNSHIP TRUSTEES; ORCHARD, IA 50460. (#29074).

PLANT TREES ON AMERICAN LEGION GROUNDS - IA. TREES TO BE PLANTED FOR BEAUTIFICATION OF AMERICAN LEGION GROUNDS. (LOCAL). AMY WALLING, COORDINATOR; AMERICAN LEGION; ORCHARD, IA 50460. (#29073).

JULY 4, '76. COMMUNITY PICNIC. FESTIVAL AT COMMUNITY PARK. (LOCAL). MRS L D WALLING, CHAIRMAN; REUNION COMMITTEE; ORCHARD, IA 52460. (#200018-241).

ORIENT

HENRY A WALLACE MONUMENT - ORIENT, IA. MONUMENT AND PLAQUE IN MEMORY OF HENRY A WALLACE TO BE ERECTED AT ORIENT LAKE. (LOCAL). MARJORIE JENSEN, CHAIRMAN; ADAIR HISTORICAL SOCIETY; ORIENT, IA 50858. (#24492).

HISTORICAL MARKER IN ORIENT, IA. HENRY A WALLACE BIRTHPLACE MARKER TO BE PLACED IN ORIENT. (LOCAL). MRS HAZEL RAASCH, CHAIRMAN; ADAIR COUNTY HISTORICAL SOCIETY; BRIDGEWATER, IA 50837. (#12340).

YOUTH CENTER, ORIENT, IA. YOUTH CENTER WILL BE RENOVATED FOR COMMUNITY USE. (LOCAL). MARJORIE JENSEN, COORDINATOR; TOWN OF ORIENT; ORIENT, IA 50858. (#24493).

OCT 10 - 16, '76. BICENTENNIAL PANCAKE DAY. THERE WILL BE FREE PANCAKES & SAUSAGES, ANTIQUE DISPLAYS & PARADE. AT NEW FIRE DEPT BLDG, PARADE ON BROAD STREET; MUSIC AT FIRE BLDG. (LOCAL). MARJORIE JENSEN, PROJ DIR; ORIENT FIREMEN & MERCHANTS; ORIENT, IA 50858. (#106912-1).

OSAGE

MITCHELL COUNTY, IOWA, BICENT NATURE STUDY. PRESERVATION & DEVELOPMENT OF OLD INDIAN CAMP SITE. TO BE LEFT IN NATURAL STATE FOR NATURE STUDY OF PRARIE GRASS, FLOWERS & WILD LIFE. (LOCAL). ROGER STEVENSON, DIRECTOR; MITCHELL COUNTY CONSERVATION COMMISSION; COURT HOUSE; OSAGE, IA 50461. (#2811).

MAY 1 - 30, '76. INDIAN VILLAGE, EARLY SETTLEMENT DWELLINGS, COUNTY HISTORY. RECONSTRUCTING A WINNEBAGO INDIAN CAMPSITE WITH DISPLAYS (ST. ANSGAR SCHOOLS) CONSTRUCTING A LOG CABIN WITH DISPLAYS (RICEVILLE SCHOOLS) CONSTRUCTING A SODHOUSE WITH DISPLAYS (OSAGE SCHOOLS) TOURS STUDYING NATURAL FOODS, ECOLOGY, POISONOUS PLANTS. AT NEW HAVEN POTHOLES, 7 MILES EAST & 1 1/2 MILES NORTH OF OSAGE. (LOCAL). ROGER W. STEVENSON; MITCHELL COUNTY CONSERVATION DEPT; EAST MAIN STREET; OSAGE, IA 50461. (#2811-1).

JULY 24, '76. SCHOOL REUNION AND BANQUET FOR GRADUATES. CEREMONY, FESTIVAL AT MAPLE INN, 7TH & MAIN. (LOCAL). MRS L D WALLING, CHMN; LADIES AID; ORCHARD, IA 52460. (#200018-240).

OSCEOLA

AREA TREE PLANTING IN OSCEOLA, IA. OSCEOLA FEDERATED WOMEN'S CLUB WILL BE PLANTING TREES IN OSCEOLA AS PART OF THE IOWA FEDERATION PROJECT FOR PLANTING 1776 TREES ACROSS IOWA BY JULY 4, '76; FUNDS RAISED FROM SALE OF COMMEMORATIVE PLATES. (LOCAL). BETTY THORPE, 1ST VICE-PRESIDENT; OSCEOLA FEDERATED WOMEN'S CLUB; 602 E MCLANE; OSCEOLA, IA 50213. (#12335).

COUNTY HISTORY ON TAPES, OSCEOLA, IA. SENIOR CITIZENS OF CLARK COUNTY ARE RECORDING THEIR RECOLLECTIONS OF EARLIER YEARS ON CASSETTE TAPES; WILL BE STORED IN COUNTY LIBRARY FOR PUBLIC USE. (LOCAL). GRACE EDMONDSON, PROJ DIRECTOR; CLARKE COUNTY BICENTENNIAL COMMISSION; 526 S LINCOLN; OSCEOLA, IA 50213. (#12332).

FLAGPOLES FOR CLARKE COUNTY PARKS, IA. FLAGPOLES WILL BE ERECTED IN COUNTY PARKS THROUGHOUT CLARKE COUNTY. (LOCAL). L L HAGIE, CO-CHAIRMAN; CLARKE COUNTY BICENTENNIAL COMMISSION; 900 S JACKSON ST; OSCEOLA, IA 50213. (#18752).

LIFE MEMBERSHIPS HISTORIC SOCIETY, OSCEOLA, IA. WITH EACH $25.00 DONATION, A LIFE MEMBERSHIP IS AWARDED TO DONOR; PROCEEDS TO BE USED TO FINANCE A BUILDING FOR HISTORICAL SOCIETY'S COLLECTION. (LOCAL). MELVIN G DELDNER, CHAIRMAN; CLARKE COUNTY HISTORICAL SOCIETY; 209 E PEARL; OSCEOLA, IA 50213. (#12331).

PIONEER FAMILY FARM PROJECT, OSCEOLA, IA. FARM BUREAU WILL AWARD PLAQUES TO FAMILIES WHO HAVE HAD CONTINUOUS RESIDENCY ON SAME LAND FOR 100 YEARS. (LOCAL). ANN WEBB, PROJ COORDINATOR; FARM BUREAU; RT #2; OSCEOLA, IA 50213. (#12330).

PRESERVATION OF CHURCH RECORDS, OSCEOLA, IA. CLARK COUNTY CHURCH RECORDS WILL BE MICRO-FILMED & STORED IN THE SALT MINES OF UTAH BY THE MORMON CHURCH. (LOCAL). LON WILLIAMS, PROJ COORDINATOR; CLARKE COUNTY BICENTENNIAL COMMISSION; 210 E CHERRY DR; OSCEOLA, IA 50213. (#12333).

RECORDING, COPYING & PRESERVING DOCUMENTS IN IA. STORAGE BOXES WERE PURCHASED IN ORDER TO PRESERVE OLD DOCU-

OSCEOLA — CONTINUED

MENTS; MANY OTHERS ARE IN THE PROCESS OF BEING RESTORED OR COPIED. (LOCAL). MELVIN GOELDNER, PROJ COORDINATOR; CLARK COUNTY BICENTENNIAL COMMITTEE; 209 E PEARL; OSCEOLA, IA 50213. (#12329).

MAY 17 - 18, '74. MUSICAL, 'THE YANKEE DOODLE', OSCEOLA, IA. A MUSICAL PLAY PRESENTED BY THE OSCEOLA COMMUNITY DRAMA GROUP WITH A PATRIOTIC THEME; LOCAL TALENT WILL PERFORM IN THE PLAY AND IN THE ORCHESTRA. (LOCAL). RAY RUSSELL; CLARKE PLAYERS; 620 E MCLANE; OSCEOLA, IA 50213. (#12328-1).

JULY 3, '75. BICENTENNIAL SQUARE DANCE FESTIVAL, OSCEOLA, IA. A SQUARE DANCE FESTIVAL OPEN TO ALL AREA CLUBS AND INDIVIDUAL DANCERS. (LOCAL). BETTY THORPE; DOSCEOLA SQUARES; 602 E MCLANE; OSCEOLA, IA 50213. (#12327-1).

AUG 4 - 7, '75. CLARKE COUNTY FAIR, OSCEOLA, IA. COUNTY FAIR INCLUDES 4-H PROJECTS SUCH AS: LIVESTOCK, SEWING, CANNING & OTHER SKILLS, DEMOLITION DERBY, SHOWS AND CONCESSIONS. (LOCAL). MARVIN PAUL, PRESIDENT; CLARKE COUNTY FAIR BOARD; RR #4; OSCEOLA, IA 50213. (#12334-1).

FEB 16, '76. FILM, 'BICENTENNIAL USA' & OSCEOLA BICENTENNIAL FLAG PRESENTATION. BICENTENNIAL FILM SHOWING AND MUSICAL PROGRAM BY ELEMENTARY SCHOOL CHILDREN; OSCEOLA BICENTENNIAL FLAG PRESENTATION. AT CLARKE COMMUNITY JUNIOR HIGH GYM. (LOCAL). BETTY THORPE, COORD; CLARKE CO BICENTENNIAL COMMITTEE; 602 E MCLANE; OSCEOLA, IA 50213. (#21897-1).

FEB 29, '76. ROSS FAMILY SINGERS MUSICAL SHOW. LIVE PERFORMANCE. (LOCAL). REV J R BAUMGARN; IMMANUEL LUTHERAN CHURCH; 101 E VIEW PL; OSCEOLA, IA 50213. (#200018-131).

JULY 2 - 5, '76. 4TH OF JULY PARADE AND CELEBRATION. CARNIVAL ON FRIDAY, JULY 2 THROUGH JULY 5. FIREWORKS ON JULY 3 AND JULY 5-RELIGIOUS CEREMONIES ON SUNDAY, JULY 4. PARADE, BANDS AND PROFESSIONAL ENTERTAINMENT ON JULY 5. AT OSCEOLA SQUARE. (LOCAL). AL OGBOURNE, COORD; VOLUNTEER FIREMEN; 216 N VALE; OSCEOLA, IA 50213. (#105705-2).

OSKALOOSA

AMERICAN LEGION BICENTENNIAL PROJ IN OSKALOOSA, IA. THE LEGION IS PLANNING A BICENTENNIAL EXHIBIT OF PAST UNIFORMS AND FLAGS. (LOCAL). RUS STOUT, PROJ DIRECTOR; AMERICAN LEGION; 1006 S 11TH ST; OSKALOOSA, IA 52577. (#14210).

BICENTENNIAL BOOK - OSKALOOSA, IA. THE BOOK WILL DEAL WITH THE HISTORY OF AMERICAN WOMEN. (LOCAL). MRS K T PICKSLAY, PROJ DIRECTORS; AAUW; 1701 B AVE EAST; OSKALOOSA, IA 52577. (#14211).

BICENTENNIAL EXHIBITS - OSKALOOSA, IA. AN EXHIBIT OF PIONEER WOMEN'S CRAFTS & QUILT MAKING TO BE DISPLAYED IN STORE WINDOWS IN THE DOWNTOWN AREA. (LOCAL). MRS R M HART, PROJ DIRECTOR; CHIEF MAHASKA QUESTERS GROUP - CHAPTER 505; OSKALOOSA, IA 52577. (#14209).

BICENTENNIAL INFORMATION LECTURES - MAHASKA CO, IA. THE COUNTY BICENTENNIAL COMMISSION HAS BEEN INFORMING ALL AREA CLUBS AND CIVIC GROUPS OF BICENTENNIAL ACTIVITIES AND PROJECTS GOING ON IN THE COUNTY & THE STATE. (LOCAL). MRS C R GLATTLY, PROJ DIRECTOR; MAHASKA COUNTY BICENTENNIAL COMMITTEE; 503 1ST AVE E; OSKALOOSA, IA 52577. (#14205).

BULLETIN BOARDS, OSKALOOSA, IA. HISTORICAL INFORMATION WILL BE POSTED ON BULLETIN BOARDS ON CAMPUS. (LOCAL). MARION RAINS, COORDINATOR; WILLIAM PENN COLLEGE; OSKALOOSA, IA 52577. (#24931).

CAMPAIGN FOR ACADEMIC PRIORITIES, OSKALOOSA, IA. PROJECT TO RAISE 2.5 MILLION DOLLARS FOR FACULTY AND CURRICULUM IMPROVEMENT. (LOCAL). MARION RAINS, COORDINATOR; WILLIAM PENN COLLEGE; OSKALOOSA, IA 52577. (#24927).

DAR BICENTENNIAL PROJ IN OSKALOOSA, IA. THE DAR IS MAKING A GIFT OF FLAGS TO HIGH SCHOOLS AND COLLEGES. THEY ALSO PLAN TO MAKE FUNDS AVAILABLE FOR PATRIOTIC LECTURES. (LOCAL). MRS CLIFFORD POWERS, PROJ DIRECTOR; DAUGHTERS OF THE AMERICAN REVOLUTION; 610 1ST AVE E; OSKALOOSA, IA 52577. (#14208).

DISPLAYS PRESENTATION, OSKALOOSA, IA. THE THEME OF THE WINDOW DISPLAYS WILL BE THE HISTORY OF MAHASKA COUNTY. (LOCAL). MRS FLOYD ROGERS, PROJ DIRECTOR; QUESTERS KISH-KE-KOSH; OSKALOOSA, IA 52577. (#14195).

EQUIPMENT FOR HOSPITAL PATIENTS' ROOMS, IA. NEW EQUIPMENT WILL BE PLACED IN HOSPITAL AND A SPECIAL OBSERVANCE WILL BE HELD IN PATIENTS' ROOMS. (LOCAL). MRS WILBUR MCBRIDE, PROJ DIRECTOR; MAHASKA COUNTY HOSPITAL AUXILIARY; ROUTE 1; OSKALOOSA, IA 52577. (#14199).

HERITAGE PROGRAM IN OSKALOOSA, IA. CHURCH & COUNTY RECORDS WILL BE MICROFILMED FOR A HERITAGE PROGRAM AS WELLAS CEMETERY & MORTUARY RECORDS. (LOCAL). MRS DWIGHT PICKEN, CHAIRMAN; HERITAGE PROGRAM; CEDAR, IA 52543. (#14203).

HISTORY CLASSES, OSKALOOSA, IA. INFORMATION ON THE REVOLUTION AND ITS MEANING FOR US TODAY WILL BE COVERED IN THE CLASSES. (LOCAL). MARION RAINS, COORDINATOR; WILLIAM PENN COLLEGE; OSKALOOSA, IA 52577. (#24930).

A HISTORY OF THE WCTU, OSKALOOSA, IA. A HISTORY OF THE WOMEN'S CHRISTIAN TEMPERANCE UNION WILL BE PREPARED FOR THE BICENTENNIAL IN MAHASKA, IA. (LOCAL). MAY ALICE SMITH, PROJECT CHAIRMAN; WOMEN'S CHRISTIAN TEMPERANCE UNION; 1715 CAMPBELL DR; OSKALOOSA, IA 52577. (#14314).

HISTORY OF VENNARD COLLEGE, OSKALOOSA, IA. A HISTORY OF VENNARD COLLEGE TO BE PUBLISHED IN BOOK FORM IN U976. (LOCAL). DR MERNE A HARRIS, CHAIRMAN; VENNARD COLLEGE; UNIVERSITY PK, IA 52595. (#14030).

JOHNNY HORIZONS PROGRAM IN OSKALOOSA, IA. THERE WILL BE A JOHNNY HORIZONS PROGRAM IN OSKALOOSA. (LOCAL). HAROLD NEHRE, COORDINATOR; ELEMENTARY SCHOOLS; 807 GURNEY; OSKALOOSA, IA 52577. (#14207).

REPRINTING BOOKS ON HISTORY, OSKALOOSA, IA. REPRINTING HISTORY BOOKS & TOURS OF HISTORICAL POINTS IN MAHASKA COUNTY. (LOCAL). MRS STILLMAN CLARK, PROJ DIRECTOR; MAHASKA COUNTY HISTORICAL SOCIETY; 325 1/2 N MARKET; OSKALOOSA, IA 52577. (#14200).

RESEARCH FOR WINDOW DISPLAY, OSKALOOSA, IA. RESEARCH WILL AID IN THE BICENTENNIAL DISPLAY. (LOCAL). MRS LETA STRAH, PROJ DIRECTOR; PUBLIC LIBRARY; S MARKET & SECOND AVE W; OSKALOOSA, IA 52577. (#14196).

SERVICE CLUBS SIGN, OSKALOOSA, IA. SIGNS WILL BE POSTED WITH A LIST OF THE SERVICE CLUBS OF OSKALOOSA. (LOCAL). ROBERT DECOOK, PROJ DIRECTOR; KIWANIS; 2108 CARBONADO RD; OSKALOOSA, IA 52577. (#14201).

TOWN TREE PLANTING IN OSKALOOSA, IA. IN HONOR OF THE BICENTENNIAL, THE ROTARY CLUB WILL PLANT A TREE. (LOCAL). LLOYD HORNBECK, PRESIDENT; ROTARY CLUB; 1703 N PARK; OSKALOOSA, IA 52577. (#14194).

TREE LANDSCAPING, OSKALOOSA, IA. TREES PLANTED ON THE NELSON PIONEER FARM & AN IN EDMUNDSON PARK. (LOCAL). MRS CLIFFORD COOK, PROJ DIRECTOR; OSKALOOSA WOMEN'S CLUB; 602 N 4TH; OSKALOOSA, IA 52577. (#14197).

TREE PLANTING AT WILLIAM PENN COLLEGE. TREES WILL BE PLANTED ON THE CAMPUS. (LOCAL). MARION RAINS, COORDINATOR; WILLIAM PENN COLLEGE; OSKALOOSA, IA 52577. (#24926).

WILLIAM PENN COLLEGE, A PRODUCT AND A PRODUCER, IA. A HISTORY OF THE COLLEGE NOW USED IN A SENIOR SEMINAR TO HELP STUDENTS APPRECIATE WHAT THE COLLEGE HAS DONE AND IS TRYING TO DO. (LOCAL). MARION RAINS, COORDINATOR; WILLIAM PENN COLLEGE; OSKALOOSA, IA 52577. (#24929).

WORSHIP PROGRAM IN OSKALOOSA, IA. COMMUNITY WORSHIP PROGRAM WILL BE HELD IN HONOR OF THE BICENTENNIAL. (LOCAL). REV JOHN FREY, PROJ DIRECTOR; MAHASKA COUNTY MINISTERIAL ASSOC; 801 FIRST AVE E; OSKALOOSA, IA 52577. (#14198).

SEPT 23, '72. FOUNDERS' DAY. THE FOUNDING OF WILLIAM PENN COLLEGE IN 1873 WILL BE CELEBRATED. (LOCAL). MARION RAINS, COORD; WILLIAM PENN COLLEGE; OSKALOOSA, IA 52577. (#107305-1).

MAR 21 - 22, '75. '1776', A MUSICAL PLAY, PUT ON BY WILLIAM PENN COLLEGE. WILLIAM PENN COLLEGE STUDENTS TO PERFORM. (LOCAL). MARION RAINS, DIRECTOR; WILLIAM PENN COLLEGE; OSKALOOSA, IA 52577. (#107339-1).

SEPT 5, '75. COUNTY HISTORY - OSKALOOSA, IA. FREMONT SCHOOL WILL HAVE A CEREMONY CONCERNING THE HISTORY OF MAHASKA COUNTY. (LOCAL). MRS CARROLL WHITE; KING'S DAUGHTERS & SONS; 1255 J AVE E; OSKALOOSA, IA 52577. (#14202-1).

SEPT 17 - 20, '75. PIONEER DAY CELEBRATION. PIONEER DAY TO INCLUDE: FLAG PRESENTATION, CRAFTS, BAND CONCERTS, AND BEARD GROWING CONTESTS. AT NELSON PIONEER FARM. (LOCAL). RICK NORDENSON, CHAIRMAN; CHAMBER OF COMMERCE; 124 N MARKET; OSKALOOSA, IA 52577. (#101778-1).

NOV 14, '75. PATRIOTIC MUSICALE SPONSORED BY CHRISTIAN SCHOOL. LIVE PERFORMANCE. (LOCAL). MRS NEIL STEINHOFF, CHMN; CHRISTIAN SCHOOL; 2108 9TH AVE; UNIVERSITY PK, IA 52595. (#101787-1).

NOV '75. BICENTENNIAL MUSICAL PRODUCTION. LIVE PERFORMANCE. (LOCAL). DR MERNE A HARRIS, CHMN; VENNARD COLLEGE; UNIVERSITY PK, IA 52595. (#101775-1).

JAN 11, '76. CENTENNARY SUNDAY SERVICE HONORING FORMER STUDENTS. CEREMONY. (LOCAL). MS MARION RAINS, CHAIRMAN; COLLEGE AVE OF FRIENDS CHURCH; 420 COLLEGE HILL; OSKALOOSA, IA 52577. (#101786-1).

JAN '76. '1776', MUSICAL. LIVE PERFORMANCE. (LOCAL). DR MERNE A HARRIS, CHMN; VENNARD COLLEGE; UNIVERSITY PK, IA 52595. (#101780-1).

MAR 4, '76. PATRIOTIC PROGRAM ON THE PRESIDENTS-WASHINGTON, ADAMS, JEFFERSON. LIVE PERFORMANCE. (LOCAL). MRS STILLMAN CLARK; DAUGHTERS OF AMERICAN COLONISTS, MAHASKA CHAPTER; 325 N MARKET; OSKALOOSA, IA 52577. (#101777-1).

MAR 6, '76. MISS MAHASKA PAGEANT. LIVE PERFORMANCE. (LOCAL). MRS DEAN MATTIX, CHAIRMAN; ALPHA KAPPA BETA; 315 N 11TH; OSKALOOSA, IA 52577. (#101788-1).

MAR 26, '76. WILLIAM PENN COLLEGE'S BAND CONCERT. SPECIAL MUSIC WITH A BICENTENNIAL THEME. (LOCAL). MARION RAINS, DIRECTOR; WILLIAM PENN COLLEGE; OSKALOOSA, IA 52577. (#107339-2).

MAR '76. BICENTENNIAL MUSICAL PRODUCTION. LIVE PERFORMANCE. (LOCAL). DR MERNE A HARRIS, CHMN; VENNARD COLLEGE; UNIVERSITY PK, IA 52595. (#101775-2).

MAY 9, '76. CENTENNARY SUNDAY SERVICE HONORING FORMER STUDENTS. CEREMONY. (LOCAL). MS MARION RAINS, CHAIRMAN; COLLEGE AVE OF FRIENDS CHURCH; 420 COLLEGE HILL; OSKALOOSA, IA 52577. (#101786-2).

MAY 24, '76. BICENTENNIAL WEEK. EXHIBIT, LIVE PERFORMANCE AT OSKALOOSA SENIOR HIGH SCHOOL. (LOCAL). STEVEN HEITING, COORD; OSKALOOSA SENIOR HIGH; OSKALOOSA SR HIGH SCHOOL; OSKALOOSA, IA 52577. (#101782-1).

JUNE 1 - AUG 31, '76. BAND CONCERTS ON THE SQUARE. LIVE PERFORMANCE. (LOCAL). IVAN D KENNEDY, CHAIRMAN; OSKALOOSA MUNICIPAL BAND; 1708 LACY DR; OSKALOOSA, IA 52577. (#101783-1).

JULY 3, '76. TRACTOR PULL. COMPETITION AT SOUTHERN IOWA FAIRGROUNDS. (LOCAL). CARL DROST, DIRECTOR; MAHASKA RURITAN CLUB; BOX 24; OSKALOOSA, IA 52577. (#107339-3).

JULY 5, '76. OLD-FASHIONED FOURTH. FESTIVAL, CEREMONY AT EDMUNDSON PARK. (LOCAL). ROBERT WALTON, JR.; OSKALOOSA CHAMBER OF COMMERCE; 810 PENN BLVD; OSKALOOSA, IA 52577. (#107339-4).

SEPT 16, '76. VOTERS' SERVICE EXTRAVAGANZA. DRIVE TO EDUCATE AND ACTIVATE THE ELECTORATE FOR THE NOVEMBER GENERAL ELECTIONS. (LOCAL). MRS DONALD DUSENBERG, DIR; LEAGUE OF WOMEN VOTERS; 707 N 2ND; OSKALOOSA, IA 52577. (#101784-1).

OCT - NOV '76. HISTORY OF ST MARY'S CHURCH, DRAMATIC PRODUCTION. LIVE PERFORMANCE. (LOCAL). MRS HOWARD CURRAN, CHMN; ST MARY'S CHURCH; 207 ROCK ISLAND AVE; OSKALOOSA, IA 52577. (#101781-1).

OSSIAN

CHURCH PAGEANT ON CHURCH HISTORY & MORNING SERVICE. CEREMONY, LIVE PERFORMANCE. (LOCAL). KENNY SCHMITZ, COORD; STAVANGER & OSSIAN LUTHERN CHURCH; MAIN ST; OSSIAN, IA 52161. (#107831-1).

INDIVIDUAL PROPERTY HISTORY, OSSIAN, IA. EACH PROPERTY OWNER IN MILITARY TOWNSHIP WILL FURNISH A HISTORY OF HOW THEIR PRESENT PROPERTY CAME INTO BEING, TO BE PLACED IN THE LOG CABIN FOR EXHIBIT. (LOCAL). KENNY SCHMITZ, COORDINATOR; MILITARY TOWNSHIP HISTORICAL SOCIETY; MAIN ST; OSSIAN, IA 52161. (#24121).

OSSIAN PUBLIC LIBRARY, OSSIAN, IA. A NEW PUBLIC LIBRARY IS UNDER CONSTRUCTION. (LOCAL). KENNY SCHMITZ, COORDINATOR; OSSIAN COMMUNITY; MAIN ST; OSSIAN, IA 52161. (#23847).

TREE PLANTING - OSSIAN, IA. IN MEMORY OF THE TOWN'S 125TH BIRTHDAY AND NATION'S 200TH BIRTHDAY TREES WILL BE PLANTED IN THE CITY. (LOCAL). KENNY SCHMITZ, CHAIRMAN; CROWN CLUB; MAIN ST; OSSIAN, IA 52161. (#24127).

125TH ANNIVERSARY SOUVENIR - OSSIAN, IA. DESCRIPTIVE PLATES, COINS AND SPOONS COMMEMORATE OSSIAN'S 125TH ANNIVERSARY JUBILEE. (LOCAL). KENNY SCHMITZ, COORDINATOR; OSSIAN CROWN CLUB; MAIN ST; OSSIAN, IA 52161. (#26927).

JUNE 6 - 8, '75. ANTIQUE WINDOW DISPLAY - OSSIAN, IA. ANTIQUE WARES WILL BE DISPLAYED IN BUSINESS WINDOWS. (LOCAL). KENNY SCHMITZ, COORD; MILITARY TOWNSHIP; MAIN ST; OSSIAN, IA 52161. (#107304-1).

JUNE 6 - 8, '75. OSSIAN 125TH ANNIVERSARY. 3-DAY COMMUNITY CELEBRATION FEATURES PARADE ON THE 7TH, AMUSEMENT ARCADE EACH DAY AND HORSE SHOW & CONTESTS ON THE 8TH. AT MAIN STREET AND PARK. (LOCAL). KENNY SCHMITZ, COORD; 125TH JUBILEE COMMITTEE; MAIN ST; OSSIAN, IA 52161. (#200018-129).

JUNE 6 - 8, '75. SOFTBALL TOURNAMENT - SLOW PITCH BALL. COMPETITION AT SILVER SPRINGS BALL PARK. (LOCAL). KENNY SCHMITZ, COORD; SILVER SPRINGS ATHLETIC ORGANIZATION; MAIN ST; OSSIAN, IA 52161. (#200018-127).

JUNE 7, '75. HISTORICAL PAGEANT. HISTORY OF THE TOWN'S FOUNDER WILL BE SEEN IN THIS PAGEANT. (LOCAL). KENNY SCHMITZ, COORD; OSSIAN COMMUNITY; MAIN ST; OSSIAN, IA 52161. (#107304-2).

JUNE 7, '75. TRACTOR PULL COMPETITIVE CONTESTS. DIFFERENT CLASSES OF TRACTORS TRYING TO PULL THE HEAVIEST WEIGHT AND THE LONGEST DISTANCE. AT REILLY CONSTRUCTION LOT. (LOCAL). KENNY SCHMITZ, COORD; AREA FARMERS; MAIN ST; OSSIAN, IA 52161. (#200018-128).

APR 17, '76. NATIONAL BICENTENNIAL WAGON TRAIN. THE WAGON TRAIN WILL PASS THROUGH OSSIAN AND STOP TO WATER HORSES. (LOCAL). KENNY SCHMITZ, COORD; NATIONAL BICENTENNIAL WAGON TRAIN; MAIN ST; OSSIAN, IA 52161. (#107304-4).

MAY 10 - 14, '76. BICENTENNIAL JR HIGH WEEK. SEMINAR. (LOCAL). MARTHA MONSON, CHMN; WINN CO BICENTENNIAL COMMITTEE; 510 NORTH; DECORAH, IA 52101. (#200018-221).

JUNE 13, '76. LOG CABIN DEDICATION DAY. BICENTENNIAL CHURCH SERVICES, FLAG PRESENTATION, DEDICATION OF LOG CABIN, PICNIC, GAMES, ICE CREAM SOCIAL, POSSIBLE DISPLAY OF CRAFTS. AT OSSIAN PARK AND CAREY PARK. (LOCAL). KENNY SCHMITZ; OSSIAN COMMUNITY; MAIN ST; OSSIAN, IA 52161. (#106849-5).

SEPT - OCT '76. TIME CAPSULE. A TIME CAPSULE WITH PAST AND PRESENT DOCUMENTS AND ARTICLES WILL BE PLACED IN A CORNERSTONE OF A LOG CABIN, TO BE OPENED AT A FUTURE DATE. (LOCAL). KENNY SCHMITZ, COORD; MILITARY TOWNSHIP HISTORICAL SOCIETY; MAIN ST; OSSIAN, IA 52161. (#107304-3).

OTHO

JUNE 19, '76. HISTORY OF LIBERTY BELL. LIVE PRESENTATION ON THE HISTORY OF THE LIBERTY BELL. (LOCAL). RUBY FULLER, COORD; BALLENTYNE REBEKAH LODGE; OTHO, IA 50569. (#106533-1).

OTO

CEMETERY ROAD RESTORATION - OTO, IA. THE OLD ROAD TO THE CEMETERY WILL BE RESTORED. (LOCAL). JAMES MILLER, CHAIRMAN; OTO BICENTENNIAL COMMITTEE; OTO, IA 51100. (#21220).

FLOWER GARDEN, OTO, IA. RED, WHITE AND BLUE FLOWERS WILL BE PALNTED. (LOCAL). JAMES MILLER, COORDINATOR; OTO BICENTENNIAL COMMITTEE; OTO, IA 51100. (#21219).

SEWER SYSTEM PROJECT - OTO, IA. A SEWER SYSTEM WILL BE INSTALLED IN THE CITY. (LOCAL). JAMES MILLER, CHAIRMAN; OTO BICENTENNIAL COMMITTEE; OTO, IA 50311. (#21221).

OTTOSEN

OTTOSEN, IA TOWN IMPROVEMENTS. WATER FOUNTAIN FOR TOWN PARK AND BLEACHERS FOR BALL PARK. (LOCAL). HON RICHARD KINSETH, MAYOR; TOWN OF OTTOSEN; OTTOSEN, IA 50570. (#22739).

TREE PLANTING, OTTOSEN, IA. TWO PIN OAK TREES AND ONE SUMMIT ASH TREE FOR TOWN PARK AND A TREE FOR THE CLUB YARD. (LOCAL). CHARLOTTE WERHSPANN, PRESIDENT; AMERICAN LEGION AUXILLARY; RURAL ROUTE; OTTOSEN, IA 50570. (#22741).

U S HISTORY QUILT, OTTOSEN, IA. QUILT WILL BE MADE WITH THE DATES OF STATES ADMISSION TO THE UNION. (LOCAL). NAOMI STRUTHERS, PRESIDENT; UNITED PRESBYTERIAN WOMEN; OTTOSEN, IA 50570. (#22740).

APR 1 - JULY 4, '76. POSTER DISPLAY - EXHIBIT OF POSTERS DONE BY YOUTH. EXHIBIT AT LOCAL BUSINESS ESTABLISHMENTS. (LOCAL). ALBERTA BENNETT, PRES; COMMERCIAL CLUB; OTTOSEN, IA 50570. (#106231-1).

JUNE 25, '76. BICENTENNIAL PARADE. PARADE, FOLLOWED BY SPEECHES AND THE PRESENTATION OF THE BICENTENNIAL FLAG TO THE COMMUNITY BY SENATOR BERL PRIEBE WHO ALSO DREW THE WINNING NAME FOR THE NEW OWNER OF THE LONDON ROAD QUILT. (LOCAL). NAOMI STRUTHERS, PRES; UNITED PRESBYTERIAN WOMEN; RR 1; OTTOSEN, IA 50570. (#22740-2).

JUNE 25, '76. U S HISTORY QUILT. EXHIBIT OF QUILT, MADE WITH THE DATES OF STATES ADMISSION TO THE UNION. (LOCAL). NAOMI STRUTHERS, PRES; UNITED PRESBYTERIAN WOMEN; RR; OTTOSEN, IA 50570. (#22740-1).

OTTUMWA

BICENTENNIAL BAZAAR & SALE OF HANDCRAFT. EXHIBIT, FAIR. (LOCAL). DR ROMAN CZERNINSKI, DIR; INDIAN HILLS COMMUNITY COLLEGE; OTTUMWA, IA 52501. (#104318-1). **(??).**

BICENTENNIAL COMMUNITY PAINTING PROJ, OTTUMWA, IA. THE LIGHT POLES IN THE BUSINESS SECTION ARE PAINTED RED, WHITE AND BLUE. (LOCAL). CLARENCE G BARBER, CHAIRMAN; OTTUMWA BICENTENNIAL COMMITTEE; 132 S COOPER; OTTUMWA, IA 52501. (#19725).

COMMUNITY BEAUTIFICATION PROJECT IN OTTUMWA, IA. FLOWERS IN THE PARKS, MALLS AND COMMUNITY HOMES WILL BE RED, WHITE AND BLUE. (LOCAL). HON HUGH STUFFLEBEAM, MAYOR; OTTUMWA PARK COMMISSION; OTTUMWA, IA 52501. (#15091).

FLOWER FLAG GARDEN, OTTUMWA, IA. FLOWER GARDEN IN THE SHAPE AND COLOR OF THE AMERICAN FLAG. (LOCAL). J C SOLLOWAY, PRESIDENT; OTTUMWA HEIGHTS COLLEGE; GRANDVIEW AND ELM; OTTUMWA, IA 52501. (#15654).

FOODFEST '76 - COMMUNITY FOOD FAIR. FESTIVAL. (LOCAL). DR ROMAN CZERWINSKI, DIR; OTTUMWA HEIGHTS COLLEGE; OTTUMWA, IA 52501. (#104318-2). **(??).**

INDIAN CHIEFS IN OTTUMWA, IA. PROJECT IS 4 STATUES OF INDIAN CHIEFS WAPELLO, POWESHIEK, MAHASKA AND KEOKUK. (LOCAL). CLARENCE BARBER, CHAIRMAN; OTTUMWA BICENTENNIAL COMMITTEE; 132 S COOPER; OTTUMWA, IA 52501. (#15090).

'INDIAN HILLS COUNTRY', A RADIO SERIES - IA. A DAILY RADIO SERIES OF READINGS FROM THE HISTORY OF 10 IOWA COUNTIES. PRINTED COPIES OF HISTORICAL SOURCE MATERIALS ARE AVAILABLE TO AREA TEACHERS KINDERGARTEN THROUGH 12TH GRADE. (LOCAL). DR LYLE HELLYER, PRESIDENT; INDIAN HILLS COMMUNITY COLLEGE; OTTUMWA INDUSTRIAL AIRPORT; OTTUMWA, IA 52501. (#17132).

INDIAN HILLS FORUM - OTTUMWA, IA. SERIES OF DISCUSSIONS OF FUTURE-ORIENTED PUBLIC POLICY ISSUES. (LOCAL). DR ROMAN CZERWINSKI, PROJ DIRECTOR; INDIAN HILLS COMMUNITY COLLEGE BICENTENNIAL COMMITTEE; OTTUMWA, IA 52501. (#19974).

LIGHT POLE PROJECT IN OTTUMWA, IA. LIGHT POLES ARE BEING PAINTED RED, WHITE AND BLUE. (LOCAL). HONORABLE HUGH STUFFLEBEAM, MAYOR; OTTUMWA PUBLIC WORKS; OTTUMWA, IA 52501. (#15092).

REPLICA OF OTTUMWA COAL PALACE (1890-1891), IA. THE ORIGINAL BUILDING, MADE OF COAL & PAPIER MACHE, WAS VISITED BY 2 U S PRESIDENTS. THE REPLICA, COMPLETED BY LILLIAN BARBER, IS IN WAPELLO COUNTY HISTORICAL SOCIETY MUSEUM. (LOCAL). CLARENCE G BARBER, CHAIRMAN; WAPELLO COUNTY BICENTENNIAL ASSOC; 132 S COOPER; OTTUMWA, IA 52501. (#19724).

WAPELLO COUNTY, IOWA PLANTING PROGRAM. PLANTING RED, WHITE, & BLUE PLANTS IN BLIGHTED AREAS & ON PARKINGS AVENUE OF 4 INDIAN CHIEFS - WAPELLO, MAHASKA, KEOKUK, & POWESHICK. ALSO A SET OF 4 SCULPTURES AT SCENIC POINTS ON HIGHWAY 63 N. (LOCAL). CLARENCE G BARBER, PRESIDENT; WAPELLO COUNTY BICENTENNIAL ASSOC; 132 S COOPER; OTTUMWA, IA 52501. (#2812).

OCT 11 - 19, '75. TOWN AND GOWN WEEK. OPEN HOUSE & WEEK-LONG FINE ARTS FESTIVAL. (LOCAL). J G SOLLOWAY, PRESIDENT; OTTUMWA HEIGHTS COLLEGE; OTTUMWA HEIGHTS COLLEGE; OTTUMWA, IA 52501. (#15655-1).

OCT 23, '75. UNITED STATES ARMED FORCES BICENTENNIAL CARAVAN. THE CARAVAN IS COMPOSED OF EXHIBIT VANS FOR EACH BRANCH OF THE MILITARY SERVICE. THE THEME OF THE EXHIBITION IS 'HISTORY OF THE ARMED FORCES AND THEIR CONTRIBUTION TO THE NATION'. (LOCAL). CHARLES G BARBER, CHMN; WAPELLO COUNTY BICENTENNIAL ASSOCIATION; 132 S COOPER; OTTUMWA, IA 52501. (#1775-219).

MAY 19 - 28, '76. BEAUTIFYING AREA WITH FLOWERS. RED, BLUE AND WHITE FLOWERS WILL BE PLANTED IN PARKS, FLOWER GARDENS AND ALL BLIGHTED AREAS IN COMMUNITY. (LOCAL). MARY GRUWELL, PROJ DIR; WAPELLO COUNTY BICENTENNIAL ASSOC; 1330 N ELM; OTTUMWA, IA 52501. (#100616-1).

JUNE 6, '76. NON-DENOMINATIONAL RELIGIOUS RALLY - 4 COUNTY PARTICIPATION. OPENING, TOUR. (LOCAL). CLARENCE G BARBER; WAPELLO COUNTY BICENTENNIAL ASSOC; 132 S COOPER; OTTUMWA, IA 52501. (#2812-501).

JUNE 7 - 10, '76. CHAUTAUQUA SHOW. HISTORICAL PAGEANT DEALING WITH HISTORICAL THEMES TO BE REENACTED BY YOUTH GROUPS. AT CENTRAL PARK (DOWNTOWN OTTUMWA). (LOCAL). CONNIE FINCHER; WAPELLO CO BICENTENNIAL COMMISSION, HORIZON COMMITTEE; 700 W ALTA VISTA, #52; OTTUMWA, IA 52501. (#104020-16).

JUNE 7 - 12, '76. USA YOURS AND MINE CELEBRATION. EVENTS INCLUDE A CHURCH RALLY, AN EXHIBIT DAY, AN OLD SETTLERS DAY, TOURIST DAY, VETERAN'S DAY, VICTORY DAY, CENTURY FARMS RECOGNITION, FIRE WORKS AND SINGING. (LOCAL). CLARENCE G BARBER, PRES; WAPELLO COUNTY BICENTENNIAL ASSOC; 132 S COOPER; OTTUMWA, IA 52501. (#104020-3).

JUNE 8, '76. AMERICAN FOLK CONCERT BY 'SOUND ADVICE'. LIVE PERFORMANCE AT COLLEGE AUDITORIUM. (LOCAL). J G SOLLOWAY, PRES; OTTUMWA HGTS COLLEGE; OTTUMWA HGTS COLLEGE; OTTUMWA, IA 52501. (#102590-1).

JUNE 8, '76. OLD SETTLERS' DAY. CRAFTS, COSTUMES, SINGING, DANCING, AWARDS, MUSIC AND PAINTING, RECREATIONAL ACTIVITIES, FOXFIRE AND LUNCH ARE THE PLANNED ACTIVITIES. AT OLD YMCA BUILDING. (LOCAL). CLARENCE G BARBER, CHMN; WAPELLO COUNTY COMMISSION ON AGING; 132 S COOPER; OTTUMWA, IA 52501. (#106537-2).

JUNE 8, '76. OTTUMWA HEIGHTS ART FESTIVAL. LIVE PERFORMANCE AT CAMPUS PARK. (ST-WIDE). J G SOLLOWAY, PRES; OTTUMWA HGTS COLLEGE ART BOARD; OTTUMWA HGTS COLLEGE; OTTUMWA, IA 52501. (#102590-2).

OXFORD

PLAYGROUND, OXFORD, IA. PURCHASE & ERECT FIVE PIECES PLAYGROUND EQUIPMENT TO BE PLACED IN PARK EXPANSION. (LOCAL). HARRY L DOLDER, CHAIRMAN; OXFORD BICENTENNIAL COMMISSION; PO BOX 137; OXFORD, IA 52322. (#28641).

RESTORATION OF OLD TOWN FIRE BELL, OXFORD, IA. CONSTRUCTION OF BRICK STRUCTURE TO HOUSE FIRE BELL. (LOCAL). HARRY L DOLDER, CHAIRMAN; OXFORD BICENTENNIAL COMMISSION; PO BOX 137; OXFORD, IA 52322. (#28642).

JULY 4, '76. JULY 4 IN OXFORD, IOWA. PARADE DEPICTING 200 YRS OF TRANSPORTATION BEGINS AT 10:30, FOLLOWED BY HISTORICAL PAGEANT AT 1:30, AND OLD-FASHIONED GAMES FOR THE FAMILY AT 2:30. (LOCAL). BILL WALLS, CHMN; OXFORD BICENTENNIAL COMMISSION; OXFORD, IA 52322. (#200018-264).

OXFORD JCT

TENNIS COURT - OXFORD JUNCTION, IA. A NEW TENNIS COURT WILL BE BUILT. (LOCAL). BETTY LARKEY, SECRETARY; OXFORD JUNCTION BICENTENNIAL COMMITTEE; OXFORD JCT, IA 52323. (#32493).

PACIFIC JCT

BAND STAND RESTORATION, PACIFIC JUNCTION, IA. RESTORATION OF A BANDSTAND ORIGINALLY BUILT IN 1920. (LOCAL). MRS GLADYS POMEROY, CHAIRMAN; FEDERATED WOMEN'S CLUB; PACIFIC JCT, IA 51561. (#20355).

JULY 2 - 4, '76. ANNUAL 4TH OF JULY CELEBRATION. FESTIVAL AT MUNICIPAL PARK. (LOCAL). MRS GLADYS POMERY, CHMN; BICENTENNIAL COMMITTEE; PACIFIC JCT, IA 51561. (#104766-1).

PACKWOOD

HISTORY OF PACKWOOD, IA. A SCRAPBOOK OF LOCAL HISTORY WITH PICTURES OF OLD PACKWOOD. (LOCAL). RUTH PAXTON, CHAIRMAN; PACKWOOD COMMUNITY BICENTENNIAL COMMISSION; PO BOX 823; PACKWOOD, IA 52580. (#23849).

NEW PARK, PACKWOOD, IA. DEVELOPMENT OF ONE HALF ACRE PARK IN THE TOWN OF PACKWOOD. (LOCAL). RUTH PAXTON, CHAIRMAN; PACKWOOD COMMUNITY BICENTENNIAL COMMISSION; PO BOX 823; PACKWOOD, IA 52580. (#23851).

TAPING OF OLD TIMERS' RECOLLECTIONS, PACKWOOD, IA. TAPE RECORDING OF OLDER CITIZENS' MEMORIES OF EARLY PACKWOOD, INCLUDING FUNNY & INTERESTING STORIES OF PAST EVENTS. (LOCAL). RUTH PAXTON, CHAIRMAN; PACKWOOD COMMUNITY BICENTENNIAL COMMISSION; PO BOX 823; PACKWOOD, IA 52580. (#23850).

MAR 27, '76. A LOOK AT PACKWOOD'S PAST. CEREMONY, EXHIBIT AT PACKWOOD COMMUNITY BUILDING. (LOCAL). RUTH PAXTON, CHAIRMAN; PACKWOOD COMMUNITY BICENTENNIAL COMMISSION; PO BOX 823; PACKWOOD, IA 52580. (#200018-136).

JULY 17, '76. PACKWOOD PIONEER DAY. FESTIVAL AT MAIN ST. (LOCAL). RUTH PAXTON, CHAIRMAN; PACKWOOD COMMUNITY BICENTENNIAL COMMISSION; PO BOX 823; PACKWOOD, IA 52580. (#106863-1).

PALMER

REMODELING OF LIBRARY, PALMER, IA. IN HONOR OF THE BICENTENNIAL, THE PALMER LIBRARY WILL BE REMODELED. (LOCAL). DENNIS HALBERG, PROJ DIRECTOR; CITY OF PALMER; PALMER, IA 50571. (#17519).

JUNE 27, '76. COMMUNITY BICENTENNIAL PICNIC. FESTIVAL. (LOCAL). DENNIS HELBERG, CHMN; PALMER BICENTENNIAL COMMITTEE; PALMER, IA 50571. (#103342-32).

PANAMA

BICENTENNIAL QUILT, PANAMA, IA. EMBROIDER AND RAFFLE QUILT. (LOCAL). MARGE GUBBELS, PROJ COORDINATOR; SEWING CIRCLE; PANAMA, IA 51562. (#22768).

ECOLOGY PROJECT - PANAMA, IA. RED, WHITE AND BLUE FLOWERS WILL BE PLANTED AROUND THE COMMUNITY. (LOCAL). MRS FRANKLIN OPPOLD, CHAIRMAN; COMMUNITY CHORUS & PANAMA BICENTENNIAL COMMITTEE; PANAMA, IA 51562. (#19173).

HERITAGE DISPLAY - PANAMA, IA. WINDOW DISPLAYS WILL FEATURE HERITAGE THEMES. (LOCAL). MRS FRANKLIN OPPOLD, PROJ CHAIRMAN; PANAMA BICENTENNIAL COMMITTEE; PANAMA, IA 51562. (#19174).

PEACE AND JUSTICE PROGRAM - 5 YEAR DISCUSSION SERIES. SEMINAR. (LOCAL). MRS FRANKLIN OPPOLD, DIR; PARISH COUNCIL; PANAMA, IA 51562. (#104221-18). **(??).**

SEWING CIRCLE'S BICENTENNIAL QUILT RAFFLE. EXHIBIT. (LOCAL). MARGE GUBBELS, COORD; SEWING CIRCLE; PANAMA, IA 51562. (#22678-1).

TENNIS COURT, PANAMA, IA. CONSTRUCTING COURT FOR TENNIS, VOLLEY BALL AND BASKETBALL. (LOCAL). KENNETH PAULEY, PRESIDENT; PANAMA COMMUNITY CLUB; PANAMA, IA 51562. (#22734).

MAR 14 - 21, '76. ART SHOW. EXHIBIT AT GRADE SCHOOL CAFETERIA AND CLASSROOMS. (LOCAL). SR MARY, COORD; ST MARYS GRADE SCHOOL; PANAMA, IA 51562. (#106158-4).

APR 5 - 7, '76. HISTORICAL EXHIBIT. A COLLECTION OF ARTIFACTS, SUCH AS OLD PICTURES, CLOTHES, ANTIQUE ITEMS, TO BE DISPLAYED IN CONNECTION WITH A BICENTENNIAL MUSICAL IN APRIL. (LOCAL). MRS I CHAMBERLAIN, COORD; SENIOR CITIZENS' CLUB; PANAMA, IA 51562. (#104212-1).

APR 5 - 7, '76. MINI-MUSEUM. EXHIBIT AT PANAMA GRADE SCHOOL CAFETERIA. (LOCAL). VILLA HOFFMAN, COORD; SENIOR CITIZENS; PANAMA, IA 51562. (#106158-2).

APR 5 - 7, '76. VARIETY SHOW. LIVE PERFORMANCE AT PANAMA GRADE SCHOOL AUDITORIUM. (LOCAL). BILL SCHAFER, DIR; COMMUNITY CHORUS; PANAMA, IA 51562. (#104221-17).

MAY 31, '76. ICE CREAM SOCIAL. FESTIVAL AT GRADE SCHOOL CAFETERIA. (LOCAL). ANTILIA WINGERT, COORD; AMERICA LEGION AUXILIARY; PANAMA, IA 51562. (#106158-1).

JUNE 22, '76. WINDOW DISPLAY OF HISTORIC AMERICAN FLAGS. EXHIBIT. (LOCAL). JIM KLOEWER, COORD; BOY SCOUTS; PANAMA, IA 51562. (#106232-1).

JUNE 27 - JULY 11, '76. 4-H GIRLS' QUILT DISPLAY. THE QUILT MADE BY THE 4-H GIRLS WILL BE EXHIBITED ON JUNE 27 AND JULY 11. (LOCAL). JOANN LAPKE, COORD; 4-H GIRLS; PANAMA, IA 51562. (#22769-1).

JULY 3 - 4, '76. 24-HOUR SOFTBALL MARATHON. COMPETITION AT PANAMA BALL PARK. (LOCAL). RON CHAMBERLAIN, COORD; PANAMA ATHLETIC ASSOC; PANAMA, IA 51562. (#200018-183).

PANORA

PARK & PLAYGROUNDS - PANORA, IA. LANDSCAPING & PLAYGROUND EQUIPMENT FOR THE PARK. (LOCAL). SHERRY

PANORA — CONTINUED

GLENN, COORDINATOR; WOMEN FOR PANORA'S FUTURE; PANORA, IA 50115. (#19954).

RESTORATION OF OLD SCHOOL - PANORA, IOWA. RESTORATION OF OLD SCHOOL FOR MUSEUM. (LOCAL). DONALD FERREE, BICENT CHAIRMAN; GUTHRIE COUNTY CONSERVATION BOARD; PANORA, IA 50216. (#19955).

PATTERSON

NEW VOLUNTEER FIRE DEPT - PATTERSON, IA. A FIRE DEPT WILL BE ORGANIZED AND FIRE FIGHTING EQUIPMENT WILL BE OBTAINED. (LOCAL). C R WETZEL, CHAIRMAN; PATTERSON BICENTENNIAL COMMITTEE; PATTERSON, IA 50218. (#25405).

PARK & RECREATION CENTER - PATTERSON, IA. TREES WILL BE PLANTED AND EQUIPMENT WILL BE ADDED TO THE PARK. (LOCAL). C R WETZEL, CHAIRMAN; PATTERSON BICENTENNIAL COMMITTEE; PATTERSON, IA 50218. (#25404).

JULY 3 - 4, '76. INDEPENDENCE DAY CELEBRATION. FESTIVAL. (LOCAL). C R WETZEL, COORDINATOR; PATTERSON BICENTENNIAL COMMITTEE; PATTERSON, IA 50218. (#108046-1).

PAULLINA

MILL CREEK PARK RESTORATION - PAULLINA, IA. THE MILL CREEK PARK WILL BE RESTORED FOR PUBLIC ENJOYMENT. (LOCAL). HARRY ROHLFSEN, CHAIRMAN; PAULLINA BICENTENNIAL COMMITTEE; PAULLINA, IA 51046. (#20565).

WINDOW DISPLAYS - PAULLINA, IA. HISTORIC WINDOW DISPLAYS WILL BE PLACED IN STORE WINDOWS. (LOCAL). HARRY ROHLFSEN, CHAIRMAN; PAULLINA BICENTENNIAL COMMITTEE; PAULLINA, IA 51046. (#20566).

JULY 5, '76. 4TH OF JULY PARADE. PARADE. (LOCAL). HARRY ROHLFSEN, CHAIRMAN; PAULLINA BICENTENNIAL COMMITTEE; PAULLINA, IA 51046. (#104822-1).

PELLA

BICENTENNIAL HISTORICAL EXPANSION PROJECT, IA. MOVING PIONEER HOUSE TO PELLA, RESTORING 19TH CENTURY HOUSE, ERECT REPLICA OF OLD SCHOLTE CHURCH AND DUTCH HIP-ROOFED HOME TO HOUSE SENIOR CITIZEN CENTER AND PROVIDE DISPLAY AREA CONNECTED TO GARDEN. (LOCAL). PATSY SADLER, RESTORATION COMMITTEE MEMBER; PELLA HISTORICAL SOCIETY; 507 FRANKLIN; PELLA, IA 50219. (#21360).

CHALLENGE II - PELLA, IA. EXTENSIVE LANDSCAPING FOR NEW OUTDOOR ATHLETIC COMPLEX. (LOCAL). JOHN ALLEN, DIRECTOR; CENTRAL COLLEGE; PELLA, IA 50219. (#21245).

DISPLAY OF AMERICAN CRAFTS. EXHIBIT OF AMERICAN QUILTS, COVERLETS AND POTTERY. AT MILLS GALLERY. (LOCAL). JOHN ALLEN, DIRECTOR; CENTRAL COLLEGE; PELLA, IA 50219. (#105026-1).

HERITAGE COLLECTION IN PELLA, IOWA. TAPING OF SENIOR CITIZEN RECOLLECTIONS OF BY-GONE DAYS. (LOCAL). GLADYS L NIEUWSMA, CO-CHAIRMAN; PELLA BICENTENNIAL COMMITTEE; 700 WASHINGTON; PELLA, IA 50219. (#21358).

HISTORICAL WINDOWS PROJECT - PELLA, IOWA. MONTHLY DISPLAY IN LOCAL BUSINESS WINDOW RELATED TO FOUR FREEDOMS & HISTORICAL INTERESTS - EXPANDED TO INCLUDE ALL BUSINESSES AROUND SQUARE DURING TULIP TIME IN MAY. (LOCAL). GLADYS POWER, PROJECT DIRECTOR; PELLA BICENTENNIAL COMMITTEE; 805 UNION; PELLA, IA 50219. (#21359).

HOMECOMING 1976. PARADE & HALF-TIME ACTIVITIES. (LOCAL). JOHN ALLEN, PROJ COORD; CENTRAL COLLEGE; PELLA, IA 50219. (#105239-3).

RESTORATION AT HISTORICAL VILLAGE, PELLA, IA. RESTORATION OF PIONEER HOME, REPLICA OF EARLY PELLA STRUCTURE TO BE BUILT TO HOUSE SENIOR CITIZEN DROP-IN CENTER AND A GREENHOUSE. (LOCAL). DENNIS STEENHOEK, SECRETARY; PELLA HISTORICAL SOCIETY; 507 FRANKLIN ST; PELLA, IA 50219. (#16416). **ARBA GRANTEE.**

SONG - 'A TRIBUTE' IN PELLA, IOWA. A SONG WRITTEN FOR PELLA BY JOYCE KUYPER. (LOCAL). GLADYS NIEUWSMA, CO-CHAIRMAN; PELLA BICENTENNIAL COMMITTEE; 700 WASHINGTON; PELLA, IA 50219. (#21357).

THEATER: 'YOU CAN'T TAKE IT WITH YOU' - 3 ACT PLAY. LIVE PERFORMANCE. (LOCAL). MAURICE BIRDSALL, DIR; CENTRAL COLLEGE; PELLA, IA 50219. (#105239-2).

FEB 5 - MAR 25, '76. 'THE AMERICAN DREAM': 8 WEEKLY SEMINARS. EXPLORE PAST, CONSIDER PRESENT AND PROJECT FUTURE OF THE AMERICAN DREAM. AT VOGELAAR ROOM-CENTRAL COLLEGE. (LOCAL). JOHN N ALLEN, COORD; PELLA BICENTENNIAL COMMITTEE; CENTRAL COLLEGE; PELLA, IA 50219. (#105345-8).

APR 1 - 30, '76. EXHIBITION OF AMERICAN QUILTS COVERLETS AND POTTERY. DESIGNED TO SHOW CRAFTSMANSHIP FROM PAST TO PRESENT. AT MILLS GALLERY ON CAMPUS. (LOCAL). JOLINE DE JONG, PROJ DIR; CENTRAL COLLEGE; 812 UNIVERSITY; PELLA, IA 50219. (#105345-6).

MAY 6 - 8, '76. PELLA'S ANNUAL TULIP FESTIVAL - 'THIS IS OUR LAND' THEME. TULIP DISPLAYS, DUTCH HERITAGE DISPLAYS, STREET SCRUBBING, SCHOOL BANDS, AFTERNOON & LIGHTED EVENING PARADES, TULIP QUEEN CROWNING, CONTESTS, DUTCH DANCING, DUTCH SINGING, COMPETITION FOR FLOAT DISPLAYS. AT TOWN SQUARE-NEIGHBORING BUILDINGS-PARKS OF THE TOWN. (ST-WIDE). GLADYS NIEUSMA; PELLA HISTORICAL SOCIETY; 700 WASHINGTON ST; PELLA, IA 50219. (#101791-1).

MAY 12, '76. BICENTENNIAL FINE ARTS INTERSCHOLASTIC CONTEST. COMPETITION IN STORY WRITING, POETRY WRITING, INDIVIDUAL SPEECHES, DRAMA AND MUSIC (INDIVIDUAL & GROUP). AT PCHS, 604 JEFFERSON. (LOCAL). MERL ALONS, PROJ COORD; PELLA CHRISTIAN GRADE SCHOOL; 216 LIBERTY; PELLA, IA 50219. (#105345-5).

JULY 3 - 5, '76. OLD FASHIONED FOURTH. SAT INCLUDES OLD-FASHIONED GAMES, PARADE, ICE CREAM SOCIAL, POLITICAL SPEAKERS, SQUARE DANCE. SUNDAY FEATURES OUTDOOR CHURCH SERVICE AT 7AM, PEALING OF CHURCH BELLS. MONDAY FEATURES BOAT PARADE ON RED ROCK LAKE. HIST SITE OPEN FOR LIMITED HOURS. AT ALL CITY PARKS AND RED ROCK LAKE AREA. (LOCAL). JOY HEDRICK, PRESIDENT; AMERICAN LEGION, CAMPFIRE GIRLS, ISAAC WALTON LG, AAUW, PEO; 1ST & LINCOLN STS; PELLA, IA 50219. (#105345-4).

AUG 7, '76. RED ROCK THRESHERS AND DUTCH MASTERS AUTO SHOW. STEAM-OPERATED THRESHERS WILL BE IN OPERATION AND THERE WILL BE AN EXHIBIT OF ANTIQUE TRACTORS & HORSE-DRAWN WAGONS. AT WEST OF CITY IN DESIGNATED OATS FIELD. (LOCAL). SAGE VAN VLIET, PROJ CHMN; RED ROCK THRESHERS; ROUTE THREE; PELLA, IA 50219. (#105345-2).

OCT 8, '76. PELLA FALL FESTIVAL. PIGS WILL BE BARBECUED OVER OPEN PITS AND NEW CARS & MACHINES WILL BE DISPLAYED IN STREETS. AT TOWN SQUARE. (LOCAL). DENNIS STEENHOEK, COORD; CHAMBER OF COMMERCE AND PORK PRODUCERS; 507 FRANKLIN; PELLA, IA 50219. (#105345-1).

NOV 21, '76. BICENTENNIAL THANKSGIVING MASS CONCERT. LIVE PERFORMANCE. (LOCAL). LAURENCE GROOTERS, COORD; PELLA MINISTERIAL ASSOC; CENTRAL COLLEGE; PELLA, IA 50219. (#105345-7).

DEC 1 - 31, '76. ART SHOW. AN HISTORICAL EXHIBITION OF THE PAINTINGS OF MARION COUNTY. (LOCAL). LAURENCE MILLS, DIRECTOR; CENTRAL COLLEGE; PELLA, IA 50219. (#101789-1).

DEC 2, '76. CHRISTMAS TOUR OF HOMES. EXHIBIT, TOUR AT MARIE'S GIFT SHOP, 631 FRANKLIN. (LOCAL). PATSY SADLER, COORD; PELLA GARDEN CLUB; RR #3; PELLA, IA 50219. (#108303-4).

PERCIVAL

BLANCHARD CEMETERY RESTORATION, PERCIVAL, IOWA. RESET STONES, PUT UP NEW FENCE AND SIGN AT LOCAL CEMETERY. (LOCAL). WARD D SCOTT, CHAIRMAN, BOARD OF SUPERVISORS; BENTON TOWNSHIP BICENT COMMISSION; PERCIVAL, IA 51648. (#9220).

ESTABLISH NEW PARK IN PERCIVAL, IOWA. A PARK IS BEING BUILT ON GROUNDS OF ABANDONED SCHOOL. (LOCAL). WARD D SCOTT, CHAIRMAN, BOARD OF SUPERVISORS; BENTON TOWNSHIP BICENT COMMISSION; PERCIVAL, IA 51648. (#9222).

FLAG POLE INSTALLATION, PERCIVAL, IOWA. INSTALL FLAG POLE AT FIRE STATION. (LOCAL). WARD D SCOTT, CHAIRMAN, BOARD OF SUPERVISOR; BENTON TOWNSHIP BICENT COMMISSION; PERCIVAL, IA 51648. (#9219).

INSTALLATION OF TOWN SIGN IN PERCIVAL, IOWA. MAKE SIGN OF TOWN'S NAME AND POPULATION. (LOCAL). WARD D SCOTT, CHAIRMAN, BOARD OF SUPERVISORS; BENTON TOWNSHIP BICENT COMMISSION; PERCIVAL, IA 51648. (#9221).

PURCHASE AND MAINTAIN DEPOT, PERCIVAL, IOWA. PURCHASE AND MAINTAIN OLD CB&Q DEPOT FOR MUSEUM. (LOCAL). WARD D SCOTT, CHAIRMAN, BOARD OF SUPERVISORS; BENTON TOWNSHIP BICENT COMMISSION; PERCIVAL, IA 51648. (#9223).

QUILTING BEES IN PERCIVAL, IOWA. THE RESIDENTS OF COMMUNITY ARE MAKING QUILTS FOR BICENT PROJECT. (LOCAL). WARD D SCOTT, CHAIRMAN, BOARD OF SUPERVISORS; BENTON TOWNSHIP BICENT COMMISSION; PERCIVAL, IA 51648. (#9224).

PETERSON

MAPPING & MARKING SITES OF HISTORICAL INTEREST, IA. MAPS POINTING OUT SITES OF HISTORIC INTEREST WILL BE PUBLISHED, AND SUCH SITES WILL BE DESIGNATED BY MARKERS. (LOCAL). ARTHUR WHITNEY, CHAIRMAN; BICENTENNIAL COMMISSION OF PETERSON; BOX 255; PETERSON, IA 51047. (#15304).

RESTORATION OF 1875 HOME IN PETERSON, IA. THE RESTORATION OF A HOME ORIGINALLY BUILT IN 1875. (LOCAL). ARTHUR WHITNEY, CHAIRMAN; PETERSON BICENTENNIAL COMMISSION; PO BOX 255; PETERSON, IA 51047. (#15305).

SEPT 28, '75. DEDICATION OF 1865 HOME. CEREMONY. (LOCAL). ARTHUR WHITNEY, CHAIRMAN; PETERSON BICENTENNIAL COMMISSION; BOX 255; PETERSON, IA 51047. (#102277-1).

SEPT 26, '76. 'FLYING FLAGS OF FREEDOM', FLAG RAISING CEREMONY. FLAG RAISING CEREMONY IN CONJUNCTION WITH FLAG SELLING CAMPAIGN. AT HERITAGE PARK. (LOCAL). ARTHUR E WHITNEY, CHMN; PETERSON BICENTENNIAL COMMISSION; PO BOX 255; PETERSON, IA 51047. (#19815-1).

NOV 26, '76 - CONTINUING . TOUR THE TRAILS OF HERITAGE. CEREMONY AT HERITAGE PARK OUTDOORS WEST CITY LIMITS. (LOCAL). ARTHUR E WHITNEY, CHMN; PETERSON BICENTENNIAL COMMISSION; PO BOX 255; PETERSON, IA 51047. (#104221-29).

PIERSON

BICENTENNIAL COOKBOOK, PIERSON, IA. FAVORITE RECIPES WILL BE COMPILED IN A COOKBOOK. (LOCAL). MRS MELVIN TREPTOW, CHAIRMAN; UNITED METHODIST WOMEN; PIERSON, IA 51048. (#21734).

DISPLAY OF AMERICAN FLAG OR WWII MONUMENT, IA. AMERICAN FLAG IS DISPLAYED DAILY ON THE MONUMENT. (LOCAL). DONA RAHRKE, CHAIRMAN; AMERICAN LEGION AUXILIARY; PIERSON, IA 51048. (#21735).

FLAG DISPLAY, PIERSON, IA. EACH HOLIDAY FLAGS ARE DISPLAYED. (LOCAL). DON JOHN, COORDINATOR; BOY SCOUTS; PIERSON, IA 51048. (#21736).

HOME FLAG DISPLAY, PIERSON, IA. EVERY HOME WILL BE CONTACTED & URGED TO FLY THE U S FLAG ON THE 4TH OF JULY. (LOCAL). MRS HAROLD ROBBINS, PRESIDENT; AMERICAN LEGION AUXILIARY; PIERSON, IA 51048. (#21738).

REPLACING TREES, PIERSON, IA. NEW TREES WILL BE PLANTED IN THE PARK & AROUND THE CEMETERY. (LOCAL). PERYLE HATHAWAY, CHAIRMAN; WOMEN'S FEDERATED CLUB; PIERSON, IA 51048. (#21737).

FEB 9, '76. AMERICAN LEGION CELEBRATION. POTLUCK SUPPER FOR LEGION MEMBERS; PATRIOTIC MUSIC BY JUNIOR MEMBERS. BICENTENNIAL COINS AS GAME PRIZES. AT COMMUNITY BUILDING. (LOCAL). MRS HAROLD ROBBINS, COORD; AMERICAN LEGION AUXILIARY; PIERSON, IA 51048. (#200018-135).

FEB 23, '76. COMMUNITY DISPLAY OF HISTORIC ITEMS. COMMUNITY BLDG'S MAIN SECTION DIVIDED INTO ROOMS OF A HOUSE: KITCHEN, DINING ROOM, MUSIC ROOM, CLOSET, BEDROOM, LIVING ROOM, AND LIBRARY. EXHIBITS WERE DISPLAYED IN ROOM IN AS NATURAL SETTING AS POSSIBLE. AT PIERSON COMMUNITY BUILDING. (LOCAL). MISS PERYLE HATHAWAY, DIR; WOMEN'S FEDERATED CLUBS; PIERSON, IA 51048. (#105475-1).

APR 26, '76. MONTHLY MEETING OF WOMEN'S FEDERATED CLUB. WOMEN WILL GIVE REPORTS ON PIONEER FAMILIES, FORMER TEACHERS WILL TALK ABOUT FAMOUS STUDENTS, MOVIES WILL BE SHOWN TO INCREASE AWARENESS OF HERITAGE. SECOND MEETING 05/24/76 AT 9:30 AM. AT EMMERT RERKING HOME AND LITTLE SIOUX PARK. (LOCAL). MISS PERYLE HATHAWAY; WOMEN'S FEDERATED CLUB & PIERSON BICENTENNIAL COMMISSION; PIERSON, IA 51048. (#105517-2).

MAY 30 - 31, '76. BOULEVARD OF MEMORY. DISPLAY ON MAIN ST; BOULEVARD OF FLAGS GIVEN BY GOVERNMENT AT DEATH OF VETERANS; GRAVES OF VETERANS DECORATED; PATRIOTIC MUSIC BY JR HIGH SCHOOL BAND & LEGION FIRING SQUAD. AT MAIN STREET MONUMENT OF WW II. (LOCAL). MRS HAROLD ROBBINS, COORD; AMERICAN LEGION-WOMEN'S AUXILIARY; PIERSON, IA 51048. (#105517-6).

JULY 4, '76. JULY 4TH VESPER SERVICE. THERE WILL BE A VESPER SERVICE, A POTLUCK SUPPER, GAMES AND A FOOTRACE. AT CITY PARK. (LOCAL). REV FORREST LAY, CHMN; BICENTENNIAL COMMITTEE; PIERSON, IA 51048. (#105517-3).

JULY 31, '76. COMMUNITY PARADE & CELEBRATION. FREE WATERMELON ALL AFTERNOON, PARADE, BALL GAME & FESTIVITIES. AT PIERSON CITY PARK. (LOCAL). MRS J P WOODBRIDGE, CHMN; TOWN & COUNTY CLUB & PIERSON BICENTENNIAL COMMISSION; PIERSON, IA 51048. (#105517-1).

NOV 11, '76. VETERANS DAY OBSERVANCE. JR HIGH BAND WITH PATRIOTIC MUSIC; APPROPRIATE SPEAKERS WILL BE PRESENT. AT JR HIGH SCHOOL AUDITORIUM. (LOCAL). MRS HAROLD ROBBINS, COORD; AMERICAN LEGION AUXILIARY; PIERSON, IA 51048. (#105517-7).

PIONEER

COMMUNITY DEVELOPMENT, PIONEER, IA. GENERAL CLEAN-UP AND COMMUNITY IMPROVEMENTS ON SUCH BUILDINGS AS TOWN HALL WILL BE CONDUCTED. (LOCAL). LOLA LYNCH, CHAIRWOMAN; PIONEERS OF AMERICA; PIONEER, IA 50572. (#24482).

HISTORY OF COMMUNITY, PIONEER, IA. EXHIBIT DEPICTING HISTORY OF PIONEER IS BEING DEVELOPED. (LOCAL). LOLA LYNCH, CHAIRWOMAN; PIONEERS OF AMERICA; PIONEER, IA 50572. (#24483).

JULY 17, '76. FESTIVAL IN PIONEER. FESTIVAL EVENTS INCLUDE BALLGAME, EGG-THROWING CONTEST, HORSESHOE CONTEST, PAN THROWING CONTEST, BALLOON CONTEST, AWARD TO KING & QUEEN - OLDEST MAN AND WOMAN IN PIONEER & POTLUCK SUPPER. OVER 50 PARADE ENTRIES; BINGO AND A STREET DANCE. AT TOWN PARK & TOWN HALL. (LOCAL). LOLA LYNCH, CHAIRMAN; PIONEERS OF AMERICA; PIONEER, IA 50572. (#106904-1).

PISGAH

ARTS & CRAFTS PLAY DAY. EXHIBIT, FESTIVAL, PARADE. (LOCAL). DELORES MESSENGER; BICENTENNIAL COMMITTEE; PISGAH, IA 51558. (#106923-1). **(??).**

COMMUNITY FLAG POLE & FLOWER BED, PISGAH, IA. FLAG POLE & FLOWER BED TO BE DEVELOPED BY 4H CLUBS. (LOCAL). DOLORES MESSENGER, CHAIRMAN; PISGAH BICENTENNIAL COMMITTEE; PISGAH, IA 51558. (#24360).

MEMORIAL SIGN UPDATE, PISGAH, IA. UPDATE LISTINGS OF NAMES OF VETERANS ON MEMORIAL SIGN. (LOCAL). DOLORES MESSENGER, CHAIRMAN; PISGAH BICENTENNIAL COMMITTEE; PISGAH, IA 51558. (#24478).

PISGAH — CONTINUED

OLD TIME PICTURE DISPLAY. PICTURE DISPLAY ON COMMUNITY. (LOCAL). DOLORES MESSENGER, COORD; BICENTENNIAL COMMITTEE; PISGAH, IA 51558. (#107303-1). **(??).**

PLAINFIELD

PLAINFIELD, IA, BICENTENNIAL PROJECTS. PROJECTS INCLUDE ERECTION OF A FLAGPOLE TO FLY THE 13 COLONY FLAG; CONSTRUCTION OF A FLOAT FOR THE COUNTY CELEBRATION; AND PLANTING RED, WHITE & BLUE FLOWERS ON MAIN STREET. (LOCAL). DON WHITNEY, CHAIRPERSON; GREATER PLAINFIELD COMMUNITY CLUB; PLAINFIELD, IA 50666. (#28648).

JULY 10, '76. BICENTENNIAL CELEBRATION. AWARD, FESTIVAL, PARADE AT SCHOOL GROUNDS. (LOCAL). DON WHITNEY, CHAIRMAN; GREATER PLAINFIELD COMMUNITY CLUB; RR 1; PLAINFIELD, IA 50666. (#200018-254).

PLEASANT PLN

HISTORICAL BOOKLET - PLEASANT PLAIN, IA. 'MEMORIES AND GLIMPSES FROM OLD TO NEW' IS A BOOKLET ON THE HISTORY OF PLEASANT PLAIN AND EAST PLEASANT PLAIN. (LOCAL). CYNTHIA WORLEY, CHAIRMAN; PLEASANT PLAIN BICENTENNIAL PIONEERS; RR 1, BOX 86; BRIGHTON, IA 52540. (#31051).

JUNE 12, '76. PLEASANT PLAIN BICENTENNIAL PIONEER DAY. PARADE AT 10:00AM FOLLOWED BY AN OLD-FASHIONED COOPERATIVE BASKET DINNER. DEDICATION OF PLEASANT PLAIN ACADEMY ROCK WITH BRONZE PLAQUE ATTACHED & FLAG PRESENTATION AT 1:00 FOLLOWED BY MUSICAL ENTERTAINMENT & GAMES. AT PLEASANT PLAIN ELEMENTARY SCHOOL. (LOCAL). CYNTHIA WORLEY; PLEASANT PLAIN BICENTENNIAL PIONEERS; PLEASANT PLAIN RR1 BOX 86; BRIGHTON, IA 52540. (#200018-305).

PLEASANTVILLE

CEMETERY BEAUTIFICATION PROJECT; PLEASANTVILLE, IA. THE PROJECT INCLUDES TREE AND FLOWER PLANTING. (LOCAL). RAY TAYLOR, COORDINATOR; PLEASANTVILLE BICENTENNIAL COMMISSION; PLEASANTVILLE, IA 50225. (#18928).

JULY 3 - 4, '76. 4TH OF JULY CELEBRATION. EXHIBIT, FESTIVAL, PARADE. (LOCAL). DENNIS W DEJOODE; PLEASANTVILLE BICENTENNIAL COMMITTEE; 417 N CLARK; PLEASANTVILLE, IA 50225. (#104081-16).

PLOVER

BICENTENNIAL TREES - PLOVER, IA. THIS COMMUNITY PROJECT IS 'PLANTING FOR THE FUTURE'; TREES WILL BE PLANTED TO REPLACE DISEASED TREES. (LOCAL). PEGGY STUDER, PRESIDENT; AMERICAN FEDERATED GARDEN CLUB; PLOVER, IA 50573. (#17382).

JULY 4, '76. OLD-TIME POTLUCK PICNIC AND PARADE. SMALL TOWN RURAL AMERICA HELPS EACH OTHER. AT PLOVER CITY PARK. (LOCAL). MRS PEGGY STUDER, CHMN; PLOVER GARDEN CLUB; PLOVER, IA 50573. (#103299-1).

POCAHONTAS

AMERICAN WOMEN OF THE REVOLUTIONARY WAR; IA. MANNEQUINS, DRESSED IN COSTUME, WILL BE DISPLAYED IN STORE WINDOWS WITH APPROPRIATE SCENES. (LOCAL). IMOGENE SCHOON, PROJ DIRECTOR; AMERICAN LEGION AUXILIARY LIBERTY UNIT #8; 15 4TH AVE, SE; POCAHONTAS, IA 50574. (#19182).

AVENUE OF FLAGS - POCAHONTAS, IA. FLAGS OF DECEASED VETERANS ON EITHER SIDE OF THE APPROACH TO THE COURT HOUSE. (LOCAL). LESTER HOHEHSEE, PROJ DIRECTOR; VETERANS OF FORIEGN WARS; POCAHONTAS, IA 50574. (#19184).

BOY SCOUT BICENTENNIAL PROJECT - POCAHONTAS, TX. BOY SCOUT TROOP 35 IS PLANNING A VARIETY OF EVENTS SUCH AS PARADES AND PERFORMANCES. THERE WILL ALSO BE A SPECIAL BICENTENNIAL MERIT BADGE. (LOCAL). KELVIN SCHOON, COORDINATOR; BOY SCOUT TROOP 35; 15 4TH AVE, SE; POCAHONTAS, IA 50574. (#25454).

FLAG PRESENTATION - POCAHONTAS, IA. A U S FLAG HAS BEEN PROVIDED FOR SACRED HEART CHURCH. (LOCAL). R H WIENHOLD, COORDINATOR; ST JOAN OF ARC - NATIONAL CATHOLIC SOCIETY OF FORR; 311 NW 12; POCAHONTAS, IA 50574. (#19183).

HERITAGE FILM - POCAHONTAS, IA. THE IOWA HERITAGE FILM WILL SERVE LOCAL NEEDS. (LOCAL). FLORENCE MACVERY, PROJ COORDINATOR; ROLFE BICENTENNIAL COMMISSION; RR #2; ROLFE, IA 50581. (#13091).

NOSTALGIA CRAFTS WORKSHOP, POCAHONTAS, IA. DEMONSTRATIONS OF SPINNING, QUILLING, MACRAME, DECOUPAGE, LACE, FRAMES, BEADWORK & MONOGRAMS. BAGS, PAPER FLOWERS, DOLLS, TOYS, BEANBAGS, POMANDER BALLS & POTPOURRI JARS WILL BE ON DISPLAY. (LOCAL). FERN OLESON, PROJ DIRECTOR; POCAHONTAS PUBLIC LIBRARY; 14 IND AVE NW; POCAHONTAS, IA 50574. (#19181).

A PAGEANT OF FLAGS, POCAHONTAS, IA. BOY SCOUT TROOP 35 WILL PRESENT ITS PAGEANT OF FLAGS TO PUBLIC & PRIVATE GROUPS IN POCAHONTAS COUNTY. (LOCAL). KENNETH R SCHOON, COORDINATOR; BOY SCOUT TROOP #35; 15 4TH AVE SE; POCAHONTAS, IA 50574. (#24393).

PICTORIAL DIRECTORY - POCAHONTAS, IA. PICTURES OF EACH MEMBER OF THE CONGREGATION ARE MADE AND PUT IN A DIRECTORY; ALSO CONTAINS THE HISTORY OF RELIGION IN THE TOWN. (LOCAL). DARLENE HUDEK, PROJ CHAIRMAN; UNITED METHODIST CHURCH; 306 2ND AVE NW; POCAHONTAS, IA 50574. (#25471).

PLANTING OF RED, WHITE & BLUE FLOWERS, IA. RED, WHITE & BLUE FLOWERS WILL BE PLANTED THROUGHOUT THE COMMUNITY. (LOCAL). GENEVIEVE SCHOON, CHAIRPERSON; TOPS; 313 NE 6TH; POCAHONTAS, IA 50574. (#19180).

POCAHONTAS BICENTENNIAL PROJECT, IA. A SERIES OF BICENTENNIAL EVENTS & PROJECTS THROUGHOUT THE BICENTENNIAL YEAR. (LOCAL). JEANNE MOORE, COORDINATOR; 4-H YOUTH GROUP; POCAHONTAS, IA 50574. (#24392).

WELCOME WAGON STYLE SHOW. LIVE PERFORMANCE. (LOCAL). LA ZANNE KIERNAN, COORD; NEWCOMERS CLUB; 300 NW 9TH; POCAHONTAS, IA 50574. (#108073-8).

JULY 24 - 28, '75. BICENTENNIAL FAIR IN POCAHONTAS, IA. THE FAIR WILL INCLUDE BOOTHS AND PERFORMANCES WITH A HERITAGE THEME. (LOCAL). FLORENCE MACVEY; ROLFE BICENTENNIAL COMMISSION; RR #2; ROLFE, IA 50581. (#13092-1).

SEPT 1, '75. 'A WINDOW ON WILLIAMSBURG', BOOK PRESENTATION TO LIBRARY. PRESENTATION OF BOOK, 'A WINDOW ON WILLIAMSBURG', BY LEWIS G TAYLOR, TO THE CITY LIBRARY. AT INFANT OF PRAGUE COURT, #1627. (LOCAL). FLORENCE WEINHOLD, COORD; CATHOLIC DAUGHTERS OF AMERICA; 311 NW 12TH ST; POCAHONTAS, IA 50574. (#104221-24).

NOV 3, '75 - MAY 21, '76. CRAFT DEMONSTRATIONS TO ELEMENTARY STUDENTS. LOCAL PEOPLE COME INTO SCHOOLS AND DEMONSTRATE CRAFTS, DISPLAY ANTIQUES ETC TO ELEMENTARY STUDENTS. AT 208 1ST AVE SW. (LOCAL). CHERYL POST, COORD; POCAHONTAS COMMUNITY ELEMENTARY SCHOOL; 208 1ST AVE SW; POCAHONTAS, IA 50574. (#104221-26).

MAR 6 - 7, '76. CONCERT FREEDOM SINGERS. FESTIVAL AT POCAHONTAS COMMUNITY SCHOOL GYM, 205 2 AVE NW, POCAHONTAS, IA, 50574. (LOCAL). MRS ERAL BUSKE, COORD; FREEDOM SINGERS COMMUNITY CHORUS; 206 4 AVE NW; POCAHONTAS, IA 50574. (#104221-27).

MAR - SEPT '76. WA-TAN-YE CLUB LIBRARY DISPLAY. A LIBRARY DISPLAY CONSISTING OF A SMALL STATE FLAG & A SCENE DEPICTING BETSY ROSS DESIGNING THE AMERICAN FLAG. AT POCAHONTAS COMMUNITY LIBRARY. (LOCAL). ETTA MAE PETERSON, COORD; WA-TAN-YE CLUB; 1008 SUNSET DR; POCAHONTAS, IA 50574. (#108073-5).

APR 1 - SEPT 30, '76. PATRIOTIC GARDENS AND WINDOW DISPLAYS. EXHIBIT. (LOCAL). GENEVIEVE SCHOON, COORD; TOPS CLUB; 313 NE 6TH; POCAHONTAS, IA 50574. (#108073-6).

APR 27 - SEPT 1, '76. SEMINARS ON NATIONAL & STATE HISTORY. SEMINAR. (LOCAL). IRENE SHAW, COORDINATOR; REPUBLICAN PARTY OF POCAHONTAS; 800 2ND AVE NW; POCAHONTAS, IA 50576. (#108073-2).

APR 30, '76. PIONEER DAY. THE SCHOOL DAY WILL BE CONDUCTED AS THE ONE ROOM SCHOOL OF THE PAST WITH VARIOUS AGES TOGETHER IN EACH ROOM. THE CHILDREN WILL BRING THEIR LUNCHES AND COSTUME ACCORDINGLY. AT 205 1ST AVE SW. (LOCAL). CHERYL POST, COORD; POCAHONTAS COMMUNITY ELEMENTARY SCHOOL; 205 1ST AVE SW; POCAHONTAS, IA 50574. (#104221-48).

APR '76. NATIONAL LIBRARY WEEK. SPECIAL PROGRAMS, DEMONSTRATIONS AND HOMEMADE FOOD SERVED. AT TOWN HALL, 14 2 AVE NW. (LOCAL). FERN OLESON, COORD; PUBLIC LIBRARY; 109 NW 8TH; POCAHONTAS, IA 50574. (#104221-25).

JUNE 13, '76. OLD-FASHIONED PICNIC & DANCE. FESTIVAL AT POCAHONTAS MANOR. (LOCAL). LINDA SHEKEY, COORDINATOR; CARE, INC; C/O POCAHONTAS MANOR; POCAHONTAS, IA 50574. (#108073-1).

JULY 3 - 4, '76. FOURTH OF JULY CELEBRATION. ICE CREAM PIE SOCIAL, BAND CONCERT, SOFTBALL GAME, KIDS PARADE AND BIG PARADE. AT MAIN ST AND COURT HOUSE LAWN BALL FIELD. (LOCAL). ROGER SCHOON, COORD; JAYCEES; 313 NE 6; POCAHONTAS, IA 50574. (#104221-28).

JULY 4, '76. WA-TAN-YE CLUB PARTICIPATION IN COMMUNITY FESTIVAL. WA-TAN-YE CLUB WILL ENTER A FLOAT IN THE 4TH OF JULY PARADE, THEY WILL ALSO OPERATE A WATERMELON STAND AT THE FESTIVAL. AT MAIN ST. (LOCAL). ETTA MAE PETERSON, COORD; WA-TAN-YE CLUB; 1008 SUNSET DR; POCAHONTAS, IA 50574. (#108135-1).

POPEJOY

APR 6, '76. PAGEANT & PLAY. STUDENTS IN COSTUME MARCHED IN TO NARRATION ON WHO THEY REPRESENTED, FROM UNCLE SAM, INDIANS & PILGRIMS TO PRES & MRS FORD. 'A SALUTE TO THE FLAG' - 32, 7TH & 8TH GRADERS, EACH WITH A DIFFERENT FLAG, GAVE A HISTORY OF THE FLAG THEY HELD. 2 BANDS ACCOMPANIED THE PROGRAM. AT POPEJOY SCHOOL. (LOCAL). MARY NEUBAUER, COORD; ALDEN COMMUNITY SCHOOL; RR 3, BOX 326; ALDEN, IA 50006. (#200018-235).

PORTSMOUTH

RURAL MAILBOX DECORATIONS IN PORTSMOUTH, IA. MAILBOXES DECOPATED IN BICENTENNIAL COLORS. (LOCAL). AL HELLER, COORDINATOR; PORTSMOUTH BICENTENNIAL COMMITTEE; PORTSMOUTH, IA 51565. (#22179).

TWIN FLAG POLES - PORTSMOUTH, IA. TWIN FLAG POLES AT CITY PARK. (LOCAL). HONORABLE GERALD WALTZ, MAYOR; CITY COUNCIL; PORTSMOUTH, IA 51565. (#22178).

JULY 24 - 25, '76. COMMUNITY PICNIC. FESTIVAL. (LOCAL). AL HELLER, CHAIRMAN; ST MARY'S PARISH; PORTSMOUTH, IA 51565. (#105944-1).

POSTVILLE

COMPREHENSIVE REGIONAL HISTORICAL INVENTORY, IA. A SERIES OF TABLES LISTING ALL THE HISTORICAL POINTS OF INTEREST, GIVING LOCATION & A STATEMENT OF SIGNIFICANCE. THE PROJECT WILL BE INCLUDED IN A REGIONAL RECREATIONAL & HISTORICAL REPORT. (LOCAL). JERRY DUMKE, PLANNING DIRECTOR; UPPER EXPLORERLAND REGIONAL PLANNING COMMISSION; 134 W GREENE ST; POSTVILLE, IA 52162. (#18743).

PRESCOTT

DEPOT RESTORATION IN PRESCOTT, IA. OLD BURLINGTON RAILROAD DEPOT WILL BE RESTORED FOR THE BICENTENNIAL. (LOCAL). KENNETH D FOSTER, CHAIRMAN; PRESCOTT COMMUNITY CLUB; PRESCOTT, IA 50589. (#13085).

JUNE 26 - 27, '76. COMMUNITY FESTIVAL. AGRICULTURE, ATHLETICS, PARADE, EXHIBITS, BAR-B-QUE, DANCES, FLEA MARKET. AT MAIN ST & SCHOOL GROUNDS. (LOCAL). KENNETH FOSTER, CHAIRMAN; COMMUNITY BICENTENNIAL ORGANIZATION; BOX 118; PRESCOTT, IA 50859. (#103803-1).

PRESTON

MICROFILMING PROJECT - PRESTON, IA. BACK ISSUES OF THE LOCAL NEWSPAPER WILL BE MICROFILMED. (LOCAL). ROBERT R MANLEY, CHAIRMAN; PRESTON BICENTENNIAL COMMITTEE; 321 W SCHOOL ST; PRESTON, IA 52069. (#28897).

PARK MEMORIAL - PRESTON, IA. A NATIVE STONE MONUMENT WAS PLACED IN THE PARK TO HONOR PIONEERS. (LOCAL). ROBERT R MANLEY, CHAIRMAN; PRESTON BICENTENNIAL COMMITTEE; 321 W SCHOOL ST; PRESTON, IA 52069. (#28898).

TOWN SIGNS - PRESTON, IA. TOWN IDENTIFICATION SIGNS WILL BE PLACED AT ENTRANCES TO PRESTON. (LOCAL). ROBERT R MANLEY, CHAIRMAN; PRESTON BICENTENNIAL COMMITTEE; 321 W SCHOOL ST; PRESTON, IA 52069. (#28896).

TREE PLANTING - PRESTON, IA. 350 TREES WERE PLANTED AS A WINDBREAK ON THE HIGH SCHOOL ATHLETIC FIELD AND 4 DECORATIVE TREES WERE PLANTED ON THE CAMPUS. (LOCAL). ROBERT R MANLEY, CHAIRMAN; PRESTON BICENTENNIAL COMMITTEE; 321 W SCHOOL ST; PRESTON, IA 52069. (#28899).

MAY 14, '76. SCHOOL-WIDE BICENTENNIAL PROGRAM. AN ORIGINAL PRESENTATION COVERING HISTORY OF USA. AT HIGH SCHOOL AUDITORIUM. (LOCAL). ROBERT MANLEY, CHAIRMAN; PRESTON BICENTENNIAL COMMITTEE; 321 W SCHOOL ST; PRESTON, IA 52069. (#200018-238).

JUNE 27, '76. BICENTENNIAL OBSERVANCE. A CHURCH SERVICE USHERED IN AFFAIR; BAND CONCERT, PROGRAM & CONTESTS FOR ALL AGES. AT TWOGOOD PARK. (LOCAL). ROBERT R MANLEY, CHAIRMAN; BICENTENNIAL COMMITTEE OF PRESTON; 321 W SCHOOL ST; PRESTON, IA 52069. (#200018-239).

OCT 12, '76. TIME CAPSULE DEDICATION CEREMONY. TIME CAPSULE WILL BE FILLED WITH PRESENT DAY ITEMS AND PLACED IN THE PARK MEMORIAL TO BE OPENED IN 50 YEARS. AT TWOGOOD PARK. (LOCAL). ROBERT R MANLEY, CHAIRMAN; PRESTON BICENTENNIAL COMMITTEE; 321 W SCHOOL ST; PRESTON, IA 52069. (#109407-1).

PRIMGHAR

FLOWER PLANTING - PRIMGHAR, IA. RED, WHITE AND BLUE FLOWER BEDS WILL BE PLANTED IN THE CITY. (LOCAL). BRAD HOPPE, CHAIRMAN; PRIMGHAR BICENTENNIAL COMMITTEE; PRIMGHAR, IA 51245. (#20558).

HERITAGE PARK - PRIMGHAR, IA. ESTABLISHMENT & DEDICATION OF HERITAGE PARK. (LOCAL). PAT SCHWARTZ, CHAIRMAN; O'BRIEN BICENTENNIAL COMMITTEE; RR 3; SHELDON, IA 51201. (#17834).

MEDICAL CLINIC - PRIMGHAR, IA. A MEDICAL CLINIC WILL BE BUILT. (LOCAL). BRAD HOPPE, CHAIRMAN; PRIMGHAR BICENTENNIAL COMMITTEE; PRIMGHAR, IA 51243. (#20562).

NEW FLAGS - PRIMGHAR, IA. NEW FLAGS WILL BE PURCHASED FOR THE TOWN SQUARE. (LOCAL). BRAD HOPPE, CHAIRMAN; PRIMGHAR BICENTENNIAL COMMITTEE; PRIMGHAR, IA 51243. (#20560).

OLD HITCHING POSTS - PRIMGHAR, IA. HITCHING POSTS WILL BE ERECTED AROUND THE CITY. (LOCAL). BRAD HOPPE, CHAIRMAN; PRIMGHAR BICENTENNIAL COMMITTEE; PRIMGHAR, IA 51046. (#20557).

PRESERVATION & RESTORATION OF EARLY CHURCH, IA. EARLY RURAL CHURCH TO BE MOVED TO SITE BELONGING TO O'BRIEN COUNTY HISTORICAL SOCIETY. (LOCAL). WILLIAM H SCHWARTZ, CHAIRMAN; O'BRIEN COUNTY HISTORICAL SOCIETY; R3, BOX 53; SHELDON, IA 51201. (#18368).

RED, WHITE AND BLUE DAY - PRIMGHAR, IA. EVERY FRIDAY WORKING PEOPLE WILL WEAR RED, WHITE AND BLUE CLOTHES. (LOCAL). BRAD HOPPE, CHAIRMAN; PRIMGHAR BICENTENNIAL COMMITTEE; PRIMGHAR, IA 51245. (#20559).

PRIMGHAR — CONTINUED

SWIMMING POOL - PRIMGHAR, IA. A BICENTENNIAL SWIMMING POOL WILL BE BUILT. (LOCAL). BRAD HOPPE, CHAIRMAN; PRIMGHAR BICENTENNIAL COMMITTEE; PRIMGHAR, IA 51243. (#20561).

MAR 19, '76. FARM BUREAU RURAL-URBAN DAY - CRAFTS DEMONSTRATION & STYLE SHOW. EXHIBIT, FESTIVAL, LIVE PERFORMANCE AT FARM BUREAU BLDG. (LOCAL). ZENNA DEBOOM, COORDINATOR; OBRIEN COUNTY FARM BUREAU WOMEN; RR 1; PRIMGHAR, IA 51245. (#200018-177).

JULY 4, '76. OLD FASHIONED PARADE. PARADE. (LOCAL). BRAD HOPPE, CHAIRMAN; PRIMGHAR JAYCEES; PRIMGHAR, IA 51046. (#104821-2).

JULY 4, '76. AN OLD-FASHIONED 4TH OF JULY. FIGURE 8 CAR RACES, BEARD JUDGING, COMMUNITY PICNIC, SPECIAL PATRIOTIC CEREMONIES, FIREWORKS & FAMILY REUNIONS. (LOCAL). DAVE STEFFENS, PRESIDENT; PRIMGHAR JAYCEES; 541 20TH ST, BOX 82; PRIMGHAR, IA 51245. (#108240-1).

JULY 9 - 10, '76. WATERMELON DAYS. FESTIVAL. (LOCAL). BRAD HOPPE, CHAIRMAN; PRIMGHAR BICENTENNIAL COMMITTEE & CHAMBER OF COMMERCE; PRIMGHAR, IA 51245. (#104821-1).

PRINCETON

JULY 17 - 18, '76. COMMUNITY FESTIVAL DAYS. FESTIVAL AT RIVERFRONT PARK & WATER TOWER PARK. (LOCAL). RICHARD HORST, COORD; PRINCETON CIVIC CLUB; PRINCETON, IA 52768. (#106929-1).

PULASKI

CITY PARK, PULASKI, IA. RECREATIONAL EQUIPMENT TO BE REPAIRED. (LOCAL). MARY LOU BROWN, CHAIRMAN; PULASKI CORN SHOW; PULASKI, IA 52584. (#23165).

RESTORATION OF OLD DEPOT, PULASKI, IA. OLD DEPOT TO BE MOVED & RESTORED. (LOCAL). MARY LOU BROWN, CHAIRMAN; PULASKI CORN SHOW; PULASKI, IA 52584. (#23164).

AUG 23 - 25, '76. PULASKI CORN SHOW. COMPETITION, EXHIBIT, FESTIVAL, PARADE. (LOCAL). MARY LOU BROWN, COORD; PULASKI CORN SHOW; PULASKI, IA 52584. (#106388-1).

QUARRY

JULY 25, '76. BELL RAISING, PICNIC, GAMES & MUSIC - BICENT CELEBRATION. FESTIVAL AT QUARRY CHAPEL. (LOCAL). COLLEEN M FERRISS; MARSHALLTOWN BICENTENNIAL COMMITTEE; ROUTE 2; MARSHALLTOWN, IA 50138. (#200018-269).

QUASQUETON

COMMUNITY CENTER - QUASQUETON, IA. OLD FIRE STATION TO BE CONVERTED INTO A COMMUNITY CENTER. (LOCAL). HON JERARD MARXEN, MAYOR; CITY COUNCIL; BOX 236; QUASQUETON, IA 52326. (#24147).

FIRE STATION & CITY HALL - QUASQUETON, IA. A NEW FIRE STATION & CITY HALL WILL BE BUILT. (LOCAL). HON JERARD MARXEN, MAYOR; CITY COUNCIL; BOX 236; QUASQUETON, IA 52326. (#24148).

FLAG POLE - QUASQUETON, IA. A FLAG POLE WILL BE ERECTED. (LOCAL). LARRY KRUCKENBURG, CHAIRMAN; QUASQUETON BICENTENNIAL COMMITTEE; BOX 192; QUASQUETON, IA 52326. (#24149).

FLOWER PAINTING IN SCHOOLYARD - IA. RED, WHITE AND BLUE FLOWERS WILL BE PLANTED IN THE SCHOOLYARD. (LOCAL). SUSAN KRUCKENBERG, TROOP LEADER; BROWNIE TROOP 431; BOX 192; QUASQUETON, IA 52326. (#23925).

FLOWER PAINTING AT MEMORIAL - QUASQUETON, IA. FLOWERS WILL BE PLANTED ON THE SOLDIERS MEMORIAL. (LOCAL). BONNIE MACHACEK, PRESIDENT; QUASQUETON FEDERATED GARDEN CLUB; QUASQUETON, IA 52326. (#24145).

LIBERTY BELLS 4-H CLUB BAKE SALE. EXHIBIT. (LOCAL). PATSY MARXEN; LIBERTY BELLS 4-H CLUB; WATER ST; QUASQUETON, IA 52326. (#106845-4).

RIVER AND PARK CLEANUP, IA. THE MASONS AND OTHER GROUPS WILL CLEAN UP THE RIVER AREA. (LOCAL). HARVEY CHESMORE, COORDINATOR; MASONS; BOX HOLDER; QUASQUETON, IA 52326. (#23924).

STOCK CERTIFICATES, IA. COMMITTEE WILL SELL STOCK TO RAISE MONEY FOR HORIZONS PROJECTS. (LOCAL). LARRY KRUCKENBERG, CHAIRMAN; BICENTENNIAL COMMITTEE; BOX 192; QUASQUETON, IA 52326. (#23982).

TENNIS COURT LIGHTS - QUASQUETON, IA. LIGHTS WILL BE PLACED AROUND THE TENNIS COURTS. (LOCAL). LARRY KRUCKENBERG, CHAIRMAN; QUASQUETON BICENTENNIAL COMMITTEE; BOX 192; QUASQUETON, IA 52326. (#24146).

APR 1, '76 - CONTINUING . BEARD CONTEST. PEOPLE STARTED GROWING BEARD ON APRIL 1ST; THEY WILL BE JUDGED. (LOCAL). DON SAVER, COORD; BOOSTER CLUB; WATER ST, BOX-HOLDER; QUASQUETON, IA 52326. (#107302-1).

MAY 8, '76. ROYAL NEIGHBORS' BAKE SALE. EXHIBIT. (LOCAL). BEULAH SKRIPSKY; ROYAL NEIGHBORS; WINTHROP, IA 50684. (#106845-8).

AUG 13, '76. BOX SOCIAL. FESTIVAL. (LOCAL). CRYSTAL KRESS; AFTERNOON & EVENING LADIES AID; QUASQUETON, IA 52326. (#106845-5).

AUG 13, '76. HOBBY BOOTH & ART SHOW. EXHIBIT. (LOCAL). EDNA VAN ETTEN; HOBBY CLUB; QUASQUETON, IA 52326. (#106845-6).

AUG 13, '76. KING & QUEEN CONTEST - QUASQUETON, IOWA. COMPETITION, CEREMONY. (LOCAL). ZELMA KRESS; EASTERN STAR; QUASQUETON, IA 52326. (#106845-3).

AUG 13, '76. OLD-FASHIONED STYLE SHOW. EXHIBIT. (LOCAL). ELMA BELKNAP; GBA CLUB; QUASQUETON, IA 52326. (#106845-10).

AUG 13, '76. TRACTOR PULL. COMPETITION. (LOCAL). DOUG FRANCK, COORDINATOR; AMERICAN LEGION; QUASQUETON, IA 52326. (#106845-1).

AUG 13 - 14, '76. BICENTENNIAL PAGEANT. LIVE PERFORMANCE. (LOCAL). DON SAUER, CHAIRMAN; BOOSTER CLUB; WATER ST; QUASQUETON, IA 52326. (#106845-2).

AUG 13 - 14, '76. OLD-FASHIONED COUNTRY STORE. EXHIBIT. (LOCAL). AUDREY REINHOLD; AMERICAN LEGION AUXILIARY; WATER ST; QUASQUETON, IA 52326. (#106845-7).

AUG 14, '76. BICENTENNIAL PARADE. PARADE AT WATER STREET. (LOCAL). LARRY KRUCKENBURG; BICENTENNIAL COMMITTE OF QUASQUETON; PO BOX 192; QUASQUETON, IA 52326. (#106845-11).

RAKE

'RAKE'S BEGINNINGS', IA. A WEEKLY NEWSPAPER COLUMN WILL BE DEVOTED TO RAKE'S HISTORY. (LOCAL). EVELYN HEATH, CHAIRMAN; RAKE HISTORICAL SOCIETY; RAKE, IA 50436. (#23975).

JUNE 4, '76. '1776' - MUSICAL. LIVE PERFORMANCE. (LOCAL). EVELYN HEATH, CHMN; RAKE BICENTENNIAL ORGANIZATION; RAKE, IA 50465. (#107301-1).

RANDALL

SCHOOLHOUSE RENOVATION - RANDALL, IA. THE RANDALL HISTORICAL SOCIETY IS RENOVATING THE OLD SCHOOLHOUSE FOR USE AS A MUSEUM. (LOCAL). DIRECTOR; RANDALL HISTORICAL SOCIETY; RANDALL, IA 50231. (#28256).

RANDOLPH

HISTORY OF RANDOLPH, IOWA. THE FOUNDING OF THE TOWN WILL BE RECORDED IN BOOK FORM AND PLACED IN THE HISTORICAL BUILDING. (ST-WIDE). MARY A BLACKBURN, PROJECT DIRECTOR; RANDOLPH BICENT COMMITTEE; RANDOLPH, IA 51649. (#10095).

RANDOLPH ALUMNI MEETING IN IOWA. AN ALUMNI MEETING WITH ENTERTAINMENT AND A BANQUET. (LOCAL). MARY A BLACKBURN, PROJ DIRECTOR; RANDOLPH BICENTENNIAL COMMITTEE; RANDOLPH, IA 51649. (#10094).

AUG 23, '75. FALL FESTIVAL IN RANDOLPH, IOWA. A FESTIVAL OF GAMES, PARADE, MOVIES AND DANCE. (LOCAL). MARY A BLACKBURN; RANDOLPH BICENTENNIAL COMMITTEE & RANDOLF FIRE DEPAARTMENT; RANDOLPH, IA 51649. (#10093-1).

JULY 4, '76. COMMUNITY CHURCH CELEBRATION. CEREMONY AT MAIN ST. (LOCAL). REV CHARLES E CURL, COORD; UNITED METHODIST CHURCH & PRESBYTERIAN CHURCH; RANDOLPH, IA 51649. (#200018-197).

AUG 21, '76. FALL FESTIVAL. FESTIVAL. (LOCAL). EARL PHILLIPS, COORD; RANDOLPH VOLUNTEER FIREMAN; RANDOLPH, IA 51649. (#108241-1).

RAYMOND

JUNE 27, '76. ANTIQUE DISPLAY. COLLECTABLE DISPLAY AT CITY HALL. AT CITY HALL. (LOCAL). KATHY SPEAR, CHAIRPERSON; RAYMOND BICENTENNIAL COMMISSION; 305 N RAYMOND RD; RAYMOND, IA 50667. (#107682-3).

JUNE 27, '76. BICENTENNIAL FESTIVAL DAY. COSTUME CONTEST, CARNIVAL, CONCESSIONS, STREET DANCE & WIENER ROAST. OPENING ACTIVITIES BEGIN AT 8 AM. CLOSES AFTER STREET DANCE. AT CITY HALL, CITY PARK, LOCAL CHURCH SITES. (LOCAL). KATHY SPEAR; RAYMOND BICENTENNIAL COMMISSION; 305 N RAYMOND RD; RAYMOND, IA 50667. (#107682-1).

JUNE 27, '76. BICENTENNIAL PARADE. ON LOCAL ORGANIZED GROUPS GIRL & BOY SCOUTS, CHURCH ORGANIZATIONS, GENERAL COMMUNITY PARTICIPATION. AT RAYMOND CITY HALL. (LOCAL). KATHY SPEAR; RAYMOND BICENTENNIAL COMMISSION; 305 N RAYMOND ST; RAYMOND, IA 50667. (#107682-2).

JUNE 27, '76. COMMUNITY POTLUCK. FESTIVAL. (LOCAL). KATHY SPEAR, CHAIRPERSON; RAYMOND BICENTENNIAL COMMISSION; 305 N RAYMOND RD; RAYMOND, IA 50667. (#107682-4).

RED OAK

BICENTENNIAL PARK DEVELOPMENT - RED OAK, IA. PLANNING AND DEVELOPMENT OF A COMPREHENSIVE COMMUNITY RECREATIONAL PARK. (LOCAL). RALPH DICESARE, PROJ CHAIRMAN; RED OAK AMERICAN REVOLUTION BICENTENNIAL COMMITTEE; 1009 VALLEY ST; RED OAK, IA 51566. (#17292).

CHAUTAUQUA REST IN RED OAK, IA. AN OLD CHATAQUA PARK REST WITH SPECIAL PROGRAMS IN 1976. (ST-WIDE). MRS CAROL SLUMP, CHAIRMAN; CHATAQUA PARK REST; RTE 1; STANTON, IA 51566. (#11570).

COMMUNITY RECREATIONAL DEVELOPMENT FACILITY - IA. COMMUNITY CENTER FOR YOUTH, AGED & CIVIC GROUPS. INCLUDES SWIMMING POOL, MEETING ROOM, GAMES ROOMS AND READING ROOMS. (LOCAL). R J FLANNAGAN, CHAIRPERSON; RED OAK AMERICAN REVOLUTION BICENTENNIAL COMMITTEE; 1509 EASTERN AVE; RED OAK, IA 51566. (#17293).

COUNTY FAIR-1976 IN RED OAK, IA. THE 1976 MONTGOMERY COUNTY FAIR WILL CELEBRATE THE BICENTENNIAL. (LOCAL). KAY SLUMP, PROJ DIRECTOR; MONTGOMERY COUNTY FAIR BOARD; RED OAK, IA 51573. (#12678).

HERITAGE MARKERS FOR OLD STAGE COACH TRAIL - IA. THE TRAIL WILL BE MARKED WITH A TEMPORARY MARKER; THE PROJECT WILL BE TURNED OVER TO YOUTH GROUPS FOR COMPLETION. (LOCAL). MRS MERVIN VINER, CHAIRMAN; HAWTHORNE-MCPHERSON BICENTENNIAL COMMITTEE; RR #1; RED OAK, IA 51566. (#24873).

'LOOKING BACK' BICENTENNIAL PROJECTS, RED OAK, IA. RE-CREATING THE HISTORY OF HAWTHORNE-MCPHERSON THROUGH OLD PHOTOS, UP DATING OLD CHURCH HISTORIES FOR MICROFILM COLLECTION & MARKING OLD STAGE COACH CROSSING. (LOCAL). MRS MERWIN VINER, COORDINATOR; HAWTHORNE-MCPHERSON BICENTENNIAL COMMITTEE; RT 1; RED OAK, IA 51566. (#22211).

RED OAK BICENTENNIAL PROJECTS, IA. BICENTENNIAL PROJECTS INCLUDE: A COLLECTION OF OLD PHOTOGRAPHS OF HAWTHORNE-MCPHERSON, PLACEMENT OF A ROCK & PLAQUE AT CARR'S POINT, A STAGE COACH STOP & THE PLANTING OF TREES. (LOCAL). MRS MERWIN VINER, COORDINATOR; HAWTHORNE-MCPHERSON BICENTENNIAL COMMITTEE; ROUTE 1; RED OAK, IA 51566. (#28644).

RED OAK, IA, BICENTENNIAL FOUNTAIN. CITY SQUARE PARK FOUNTAIN REDESIGNED TO REPRESENT ETHNIC HERITAGE OF THE COMMUNITY AND THE AGRICULTURAL BACKGROUND OF THE AREA. (LOCAL). R J FLANAGAN, CHAIRPERSON; RED OAK AMERICAN REVOLUTION BICENTENNIAL COMMITTEE; 1509 EASTERN AVE; RED OAK, IA 51566. (#17291).

RE-CREATING HISTORY THRU OLD PHOTOS - RED OAK, IA. COLLECTION OF PHOTOS OF BUILDINGS AND OF PEOPLE WHO USED TO LIVE IN OR NEAR THE HAWTHORNE-MCPHERSON AREA. (LOCAL). MRS MERVIN VINER, CHAIRMAN; HAWTHORNE-MCPHERSON BICENTENNIAL COMMITTEE; RR #1; RED OAK, IA 51566. (#24872).

TOUR OF EARLY HOMES IN RED OAK, IA. TOUR OF EARLY HOMES AND FAMOUS PLACES IN RED OAK, IA. (LOCAL). R J FLANAGAN, PROJ DIRECTOR; RED OAK BICENTENNIAL COMMITTEE; 1509 EASTERN; RED OAK, IA 51566. (#11569).

SEPT 5, '75 - MAY 29, '76. AMERICAN ISSUES FORUM: HUMAN VALUES & UNDERSTANDING. SEMINAR. (LOCAL). LEE HONEYMAN, CO-CHMN; MONTGOMERY CO BICENTENNIAL COMMISSION; RT 1; EMERSON, IA 51533. (#103054-2).

JUNE 11 - 14, '76. 'ROOTS OF THE FAMILY TREE'. AN ATTEMPT TO DISCOVER THE RESIDENTS OF MONTGOMERY CO WHOSE ANCESTORS HAVE BEEN IN AMERICA SINCE 1776 OR EARLIER. TO BE ESPECIALLY HONORED AT MONTGOMERY COUNTY BICENTENNIAL OBSERVANCE, JUNE 11TH TO JUNE 14TH - 'UP AND AWAY, USA!'. AT LEGION PARK, BALL DIAMOND. (ST-WIDE). ADA WITHROW; NISHNABOTNA PATRIOTS/MONTGOMERY CO BICENT OBSERV; RR #1; ESSEX, IA 51638. (#103054-3).

JUNE 11 - 15, '76. 'UP AND AWAY USA'. QUEEN CONTEST, EXHIBITS, SOAP DEMONSTRATION, FOOD BOOTH, PARADE, ETHNIC DANCES & PAGEANT. AT CHAUTAUQUA PAVILION & LEGION PARK. (LOCAL). MRS MERWIN VINER, CHMN; HAWTHORNE - MCPHERSON BICENTENNIAL COMMITTEE; ROUTE 1; RED OAK, IA 51566. (#200018-262).

JUNE 11 - 16, '76. CHAUTAUQUA-TYPE BICENTENNIAL OBSERVANCE - OLD-FASHIONED FESTIVAL. 6/11: GEORGE WASHINGTON BALL; 6/12: OLD-FASHIONED CONTESTS & RACES, GREASED PIG, ETC, BUFFOON, CHECKERS & TOURNAMENTS, INDIAN TRIBES IN PARADE; 6/13: SUN EVENING EVANGELISTIC SERVICES AT PAVILLION. PAGEANT FROM ROCKFORD JUNE 13TH BEFORE FIREWORKS. AT CHAUTAUQUA PAVILLION, TOWN SQUARE, LEGION PARK, PLAZA. (LOCAL). MRS CARROLL R SLUMP, CHMN; MONTGOMERY CO AMERICAN REVOLUTION BICENTENNIAL COMMITTEE; RT 1, BOX 132; STANTON, IA 51573. (#103054-1).

JUNE 14 - 15, '76. PAGEANT PARTICIPATION 'PATCHWORK FROM THE PAST'. GROUP OF OUR YOUNG FOLK WILL SING IN THE MONTGOMERY CO PAGEANT 'THE SOUND OF MY VOICE', A NUMBER PORTRAYING THE BEGINNING OF OUR COMMUNITY. ALSO, TAKING PART IN THE ETHNIC FOLK DANCING. THE INTERNATIONAL FOOD FAIR IS ON JUNE 12TH. AT CHAUTAUQUA PAVILLION, RED OAK, IA. (ST-WIDE). MRS MERWIN VINER; HAWTHORNE - MCPHERSON BICENTENNIAL COMMITTEE; ROUTE 1; RED OAK, IA 51566. (#103054-4).

RED ROCK LAKE

JULY 3 - 5, '76. OLD-FASHIONED 4TH OF JULY. FESTIVAL. (LOCAL). DENNIS STEENHOEK, CHMN; MARION COUNTY BICENTENNIAL COMMITTEE; PELLA, IA 50219. (#101790-1).

REDDING

CEMETERY RECORDING, REDDING, IA. RECORDING CEMETERIES IN THE SURROUNDING TOWNSHIP. (LOCAL). JOHN SHAFER, COORDINATOR; HISTORICAL SOCIETY; REDDING, IA 50860. (#17487).

REDDING — CONTINUED

DAR MONUMENT RESTORATION, REDDING, IA. RESTORATION OF DAR MONUMENT FOR THE BICENTENNIAL. (ST-WIDE). JOHN SHAFER, COORDINATOR; CITY OF REDDING; REDDING, IA 50860. (#17486).

HITCH POST RESTORATION - REDDING, IA. RESTORE ORIGINAL HITCH POST IN THE CITY OF REDDING. (ST-WIDE). JOHN SHAFER, COORDINATOR; CITY OF REDDING; REDDING, IA 50860. (#17488).

PAINTINGS OF 'THE OLD DAYS' - REDDING, IA. REALISTIC PAINTINGS ON SIMPLE BED SHEETS WITH FELT PEN ARE THE INTERIORS OF A GENERAL STORE, SCHOOLROOM, CHURCH AND A BARBERSHOP. (LOCAL). KRIS GALLOWAY, ARTIST; REDDING, IA 50860. (#25401).

PLANTING TREES AND FLOWERS, REDDING, IA. LANDSCAPING FOR THE BICENTENNIAL. (LOCAL). JOHN W SHAFER, COORDINATOR; REDDING GARDEN CLUB; REDDING, IA 50860. (#17489).

OCT 27, '75. FESTIVE FLAGPOLE CEREMONY. CEREMONY AT CITY PARK IN CITY SQUARE. (LOCAL). JOHN SHAFER, CHAIRPERSON; AMERICAN LEGION, POST NO 617; REDDING, IA 50860. (#200018-137).

REINBECK

BICENTENNIAL SCOUTING PROJECT - REINBECK, IA. THE BOY SCOUTS WILL RESTORE THE CREEK DAM AND CAMPING AREA. (LOCAL). DON WATSON, SCOUTMASTER; BOY SCOUTS OF AMERICA; 620 BROAD ST; REINBECK, IA 50669. (#21780).

REINBECK, IA, CITY PARK. THE CITY PARK WILL BE TURNED INTO A PARK; TREES WILL BE PLANTED, A POND WILL BE DUG AND WILD LIFE COVER WILL BE PLANTED. (LOCAL). JOHN D PETERSON, TREASURER; GRUNDY COUNTY IZAAK WALTON LEAGUE; 706 RANDALL; REINBECK, IA 50669. (#21781).

MAR 30, '76. BICENTENNIAL PAGEANT. SHOW OF CLOTHING FROM THE PAST, 200 AND 100 YEARS AGO. AT REINBECK MEMORIAL BUILDING. (LOCAL). HELGA STAKER, COORD; COINETTE CHAPTER OES AND BICENTENNIAL COMMITTEE; 603 MAPLE ST; REINBECK, IA 50669. (#105624-3).

JULY 1 - 2, '76. FARM SHOW AND DISPLAY. FARMING WITH HORSE DRAWN EQUIPMENT; DEMONSTRATIONS OF VARIOUS FARMING PROCEDURES; DEMONSTRATIONS OF HOUSEHOLD DUTUIES OF YEARS, PAST AND PRESENT. AT PIONEER HI-BRED CORN CO TEST PLOT, PIONEER ROAD. (LOCAL). WILLIAM FREI, COORD; CENTENNIAL COMMITTEE; RR; REINBECK, IA 50669. (#105624-2).

JULY 1 - 2, '76. PAGEANT. PAGEANT DEPICTING SEGMENTS OF DEVELOPEMTN OF LOCAL AREA AND TOWN. AT REINBECK COMMUNITY SCHOOL GYMNASIUM. (LOCAL). FREIDA LARSEN, COORD; BICENTENNIAL COMMITTEE; HWY 175 EAST; REINBECK, IA 50669. (#105624-1).

JULY 1 - 4, '76. 'JULY 4TH WEEKEND' COMMUNITY CELEBRATION. CELEBRATION INCLUDES STYLE SHOW CONTEST. AT REINBECK MEMORIAL BLDG & TOWN OF REINBECK. (LOCAL). HELGA STAKER, COORD; COINETTE CHAPTER OES, BICENTENNIAL COMMITTEE; 603 MAPLE ST; REINBECK, IA 50669. (#105624-4).

REMSEN

SEPT 28, '75. BICENTENNIAL INTERFAITH CELEBRATION. THE CELEBRATION WILL BE THE KICK-OFF OF REMSEN'S BICENTENNIAL YEAR. AT REMSEN UNION FOOTBALL FIELD. (LOCAL). DICK HATZ, CHAIRMAN; REMSEN BICENTENNIAL COMMITTEE; 636 MADISON; REMSEN, IA 51050. (#102041-1).

OCT 25, '75. REMSEN OKTOBERFEST. OKTOBFEST IN OCTOBER 25, 1975, ROVING ACCORDIONISTS FROM 12:00 NOON; WITH DINNER, FEATURING GERMAN & LUXEMBOURGER FOODS, FROM 5:00-8:30 PM; DANCING AT THE AVALON BALLROOM, FEATURING 3 BANDS. (LOCAL). THELMA MOELLER, DIRECTOR; REMSEN OKTOBERFEST COMMITTEE; 608 FULTON; REMSEN, IA 51050. (#102271-1).

RENWICK

NORWEGIAN FESTIVAL. CELEBRATION OF THE NORWEGIAN SETTLEMENT'S 150 YEARS. (LOCAL). MARY HEGGEN, CHAIRMAN; BOONE VALLEY BICENTENNIAL COMMITTEE; RENWICK, IA 50577. (#104682-1).

PARK IMPROVEMENT - RENWICK, IOWA. ERECT SHELTER & IMPROVE PARK. (LOCAL). C A BLOCK & M M GREEN, CO-CHAIRMEN; BOONE VALLEY BICENTENNIAL COMMITTEE; RENWICK, IA 50577. (#19952).

YOUNG PEOPLE INVOLVEMENT PROJECT - IOWA. SCHOOL CHILDREN WILL BECOME INVOLVED IN BICENTENNIAL. (LOCAL). KEITH BAESSLER, CHAIRMAN; BOONE VALLEY BICENTENNIAL COMMISSION; RENWICK, IA 50577. (#19951).

AUG 6 - 7, '76. PIONEER DAYS. SHOW OF EARLY AGRICULTURE AND COMMERCE. (LOCAL). SELMER NEBEM, CHAIRMAN; BOONE VALLEY BICENTENNIAL COMMITTEE; RENWICK, IA 50577. (#104682-2).

RESTON

JULY 2 - 4, '76. 4TH OF JULY 1976. PARADE, COMPETITION, FESTIVAL. (LOCAL). RONALD J WAGNER, CHMN; UNION COUNTY BICENTENNIAL COMMISSION; 704 N MULBERRY ST; CRESTON, IA 50801. (#102952-5).

RHODES

JULY 24 - 25, '76. RHODES ANNUAL CELEBRATION. GAMES, CONTESTS, DANCE, DISPLAYS, DEMONSTRATIONS, FIRE RE-LIGHTS & BALL GAMES. AT MAIN STREET, BALL PARK. (LOCAL). DON SEAMS, COORD; CITY PLANNING COMMITTEE; RHODES, IA 50234. (#105135-1).

RICEVILLE

HERITAGE CENTER, RICEVILLE, IA. A RICEVILLE HERITAGE CENTER WILL BE ESTABLISHED. (LOCAL). JANE ELLIOT, PROJ DIRECTOR; RICEVILLE BICENTENNIAL COMMISSION; RICEVILLE, IA 50461. (#15107).

PINICON MANORS IN RICEVILLE, IA. A HOUSING COMPLEX FOR THE ELDERLY IS BEING BUILT. (LOCAL). JANE ELLIOT, PROJ DIRECTOR; RICEVILLE BICENTENNIAL COMMISSION; RICEVILLE, IA 50461. (#15103).

RESTORATION OF RAINBOW HALL, RICEVILLE, IA. IN HONOR OF THE BICENTENNIAL, THE OLD OPERA HOUSE WILL BE RESTORED. (LOCAL). JANE ELLIOT, PROJ DIRECTOR; RICEVILLE BICENTENNIAL COMMISSION; RICEVILLE, IA 50461. (#15105).

RESTORATION PROJECT IN RICEVILLE, IA. PROJECT IS THE RESTORATION OF HISTORIC MILL STONE. (LOCAL). JANE ELLIOT, PROJ DIRECTOR; RICEVILLE BICENTENNIAL COMMISSION; RICEVILLE, IA 50461. (#15106).

'VILLAGE GREEN' BICENTENNIAL PARK PROJECT. A PARK ACQUIRED, PLANNED & DEVELOPED BY A THIRD GRADE CLASS IN RICEVILLE, IOWA, AS ITS GIFT FOR THE BICENTENNIAL. ENDORSED BY THE STATE BICENTENNIAL COMMISSION AS AS A MODEL PROJECT. (LOCAL). JANE ELLIOTT, THIRD GRADE TEACHER; RICEVILLE ELEMENTARY SCHOOL - ROOM 10; RICEVILLE, IA 50466. (#184).

JULY 4, '76. ROOM 10 AND FRIENDS REUNION AND PICNIC ON VILLAGE GREEN. FESTIVAL AT VILLAGE GREEN. (LOCAL). JANE ELLIOTT, TEACHER; ROOM 10, RICEVILLE COMMUNITY SCHOOL; RR 3; OSAGE, IA 50461. (#100574-1).

RICHLAND

HISTORY OF RICHLAND, IA. THE HISTORY OF RICHLAND WILL BE WRITTEN AND PUBLISHED IN BOOK FORM. (LOCAL). MRS VERNON HORRAS, COORDINATOR; RICHLAND COMMERCIAL CLUB; RICHLAND, IA 52585. (#19675).

RICHLAND PUBLIC LIBRARY - RICHLAND, IA. A NEW PUBLIC LIBRARY WILL BE BUILT IN RICHLAND. (LOCAL). CLARA S GEORGE, CO-CHAIRPERSON; RICHLAND WOMAN'S CLUB; RICHLAND, IA 52585. (#18346).

MAY 13, '76. TREE SALE & ARBOR DAY PLANTING CEREMONY. DIFFERENT VARIETIES OF TREES WILL SOLD TO RESIDENTS FOR PLANTING ON ARBOR DAY. AT RICHLAND CITY PARK IN THE SHELTER HOUSE. (LOCAL). MRS BILL COBB, PROJ DIR; RICHLAND COMMERCIAL CLUB; RICHLAND, IA 52585. (#104519-6).

JUNE 12, '76. 'BASEBALL, HOTDOGS, APPLE PIE, AND CHEVROLET' - FESTIVAL. FLEA MARKET, OLD MOVIES, NEEDLE IN HAYSTACK, BASEBALL, PARADE, FROG JUMPING CONTEST, OLD CARS, BOX SOCIAL & TIN TYPE PICTURES. AT TOWN SQUARE OF RICHLAND. (LOCAL). DONNA SIEVERS, CHAIRMAN; JAYCEE AND JAYCEE-ETTES; RR 1; RICHLAND, IA 52585. (#104519-4).

JULY 4, '76. COMMUNITY FESTIVAL & DANCE. TRACTOR PULL, CHICKEN BARBECUE, FIREWORKS & DANCE. AT LIONS CLUB BUILDING. (LOCAL). GEORGE HENDRICKSON, CHMN; LIONS CLUB & JAYCEES; RICHLAND, IA 52555. (#104519-5).

AUG 28 - 29, '76. DEDICATION OF RICHLAND PUBLIC LIBRARY. FORREST SCHWENGELS, STATE SENATOR FROM THE 44TH DISTRICT WILL PARTICIPATE IN THE PROGRAM. (LOCAL). CLARA S GEORGE, CHMN; RICHLAND WOMAN'S CLUB; RICHLAND, IA 52585. (#18346-1).

RICKETTS

HORIZON PROJECT - RICKETTS, IA. PROJECTS INCLUDE TREE PLANTING, PARK IMPROVEMENT, SENIOR CITIZENS PROJECTS. (LOCAL). MRS JOHN DORFLER, CHAIRMAN; RICKETTS COMMUNITY CLUB; RICKETTS, IA 51460. (#21770).

JULY 31, '76. BICENTENNIAL MUSICAL-VARIETY SHOW. FESTIVAL, LIVE PERFORMANCE AT STEAM & ANTIQUE GROUNDS. (LOCAL). MRS JOHN DORFLER, COORD; RICKETTS COMMUNITY CLUBS; RT 1 BOX 78; CHARTER OAK, IA 51439. (#105613-2).

JULY 31 - AUG 1, '76. STEAM AND ANTIQUE SHOW. EXHIBIT AT STEAM SHOWS GROUNDS. (LOCAL). MRS JOHN DORFLER, COORD; RICKETTS COMMUNITY CLUB; RICKETTS, IA 51460. (#105613-1).

RINGSTED

ADDITION TO CITY PARK, RINGSTEAD, IA. THE RINGSTED DIAMOND JUBILEE INC HAS PURCHASED ADDITIONAL LAND FOR AN EXTENTION TO THE PARK AND ADDITIONAL FACILITIES. (LOCAL). ALICE SORENSEN, CHAIRPERSON; DIAMOND JUBILEE, INC; RINGSTED, IA 50578. (#17352).

RESTORATION OF DEPOT, RINGSTED, IA. PURCHASE & RESTORATION OF DEPOT. (LOCAL). ALICE SORENSEN, CHAIRPERSON; DIAMOND JUBILEE, INC; RINGSTED, IA 50578. (#17357).

JUNE 18, '75. FASHION PAGEANT. LIVE PERFORMANCE AT GYMNASIUM. (LOCAL). ALICE SORENSEN, COORD; RINGSTED BUSINESSMEN; RINGSTED, IA 50578. (#200018-141).

JUNE 19, '76. 'HEROS AND HARD CASES'. LIVE PERFORMANCE AT RINGSTED HIGH SCHOOL GYM. (LOCAL). DALE JOHANSON, CHMN; RINGSTED DIAMOND JUBILEE, INC; RT 1, BOX 4; RINGSTED, IA 50578. (#103342-25).

RIVERDALE

JULY 4, '76. JULY 4 CELEBRATION. CHILDREN'S PARADE, BAND CONCERT, ICE CREAM SOCIAL AND FIREWORKS DISPLAY IN THE EVENING. (LOCAL). ROSIE PARRY, COORD; RIVERDALE BICENTENNIAL COMMITTEE; 116 ELMHURST LANE; BETTENDORF, IA 52772. (#108458-1).

RIVERTON

RESTORATION OF PARK PAVILLION IN RIVERTON, IA. PROJECT TO RESTORE THE PARK PAVILLION, BUILT IN THE 1880'S AND PROVIDE NEW PLAYGROUND EQUIPMENT AND PLANTINGS. (LOCAL). RUSSELL DETRICK, PROJ COORDINATOR; COMMUNITY CLUB; RIVERTON, IA 51650. (#11559).

UPDATE TOWN HISTORY, RIVERTON, IA. COLLECT, UPDATE AND PUBLISH ALL MATERIALS AVAILABLE ON RIVERTON'S HISTORY. (LOCAL). MRS HAROLD SHULL, PROJ DIRECTOR; RIVERTON BICENTENNIAL COMMITTEE; RIVERTON, IA 51650. (#11561).

JULY 4, '76. OLD TIME COMMUNITY PICNIC. A COMMUNITY PICNIC AND EXHIBITION WILL BE HELD ON JULY 4TH. (LOCAL). RUSSELL DETRICK, COORD; RIVERTON BICENTENNIAL COMMITTEE; RIVERTON BICENTENNIAL COMM; RIVERTON, IA 51650. (#11560-1).

ROCHESTER

ROCHESTER CEMETERY - ROCHESTER, IA. TO RESTORE AND PRESERVE A CEMETERY IN RURAL ROCHESTER, IOWA. (ST-WIDE). BILL PENNINGROTH, PROJ DIRECTOR; CEDAR COUNTY BICENTENNIAL COMMISSION; MECHANICSVL, IA 52306. (#18953). **ARBA GRANTEE.**

ROCK FALLS

COMMUNITY FLOAT, ROCK FALLS, IA. A FLOAT DEPICTING THE FIRST MARRIAGE IN CERRO GORDO COUNTY WILL BE BUILT. THE FLOAT WILL BE FEATURED IN THE MASON CITY BAND FESTIVAL. (LOCAL). MARY SCHOLOBOHM, COORDINATOR; MASON CITY BICENTENNIAL COMMITTEE; ROCK FALL, IA 50467. (#22615).

HISTORY BOOKLET, ROCK FALLS, IA. BOOKLET ON HISTORY OF ROCK FALLS AND SURROUNDING COMMUNITY. (LOCAL). MARY SCHLOBOHM, CO-CHAIRPERSON; ROCK FALLS COMMUNITY BICENTENNIAL COMMITTEE; ROCK FALLS, IA 50467. (#22728).

PIONEER GRAVE SITE IN ROCK FALLS,IA. MARKER WILL BE PLACED AT A PIONEER GRAVE SITE. (LOCAL). MARY SCHLOBOHM, CO-CHAIRPERSON; TOWN OF ROCK FALLS; ROCK FALLS, IA 50467. (#22727).

ROAD MARKER, ROCK FALLS, IA. OLD STAGE COACH ROAD WILL BE MARKED. (LOCAL). HAROLD EDGAN, SCOUT MASTER; BOY SCOUTS; ROCK FALLS, IA 50467. (#22726).

TREE PLANTING, ROCK FALLS, IA. TREES WILL BE PLANTED IN TOWN AND AT CEMETERY. (LOCAL). MARY SCHLOBOHM, CO-CHAIRPERSON; GARDEN CLUB; ROCK FALLS, IA 50467. (#22729).

MAY 4, '76. BICENTENNIAL TEA. FESTIVAL AT UNITED METHODIST CHURCH. (LOCAL). NANCY KENDREW, COORD; UNITED METHODIST WOMEN; R #2; MASON CITY, IA 50401. (#106225-1).

JULY 3, '76. OLD SETTLERS' PICNIC. FESTIVAL AT WILKENSON PARK, ROCK FALLS. (LOCAL). NANCY KENDREW, COORD; MASON CITY BICENTENNIAL COMMITTEE; R# 2; MASON CITY, IA 50401. (#106225-2).

SEPT 19, '76. FALL FESTIVAL. FESTIVAL AT COVERED BRIDGE IN WILKENSON PARK, ROCK FALLS. (LOCAL). MARY SCHLOBOHM, CHAIRMAN; ROCK FALLS BICENTENNIAL COMMITTEE; ROCK FALLS, IA 50467. (#106225-3).

ROCK RAPIDS

'FROM BUNCOMBE TO 1922', ROCK RAPIDS, IA. BOOK HISTORY OF ROCK RAPIDS, IA & AREA; BOOK IS 256 PAGES AND WAS WRITTEN BY PAUL SMITH. (LOCAL). PAUL C SMITH, AUTHOR; ROCK RAPIDS BICENTENNIAL COMMITTEE; ROCK RAPIDS, IA 51246. (#15096).

LYON COUNTY MEDICAL CLINIC PROJ OF IOWA. A FIVE DOCTOR CLINIC WILL BE BUILT NEAR THE COUNTY HOSPITAL IN AN EFFORT TO IMPROVE MEDICAL SERVICES & ATTRACT NEW DOCTORS TO THE AREA. (LOCAL). PAT HUGHES, PROJECT CHAIRMAN; ROCK RAPIDS JAYCEES; ROCK RAPIDS, IA 51246. (#7731).

RELIGIOUS PUBLICATION FROM ROCK RAPIDS, IA. 'THE HOLY NAME HERITAGE' BY EDE HILL TRACES THE HISTORY HOLY NAME CATHOLIC CHURCH FROM 1871 TO PRESENT. (LOCAL). EDE HILL, AUTHOR; ROCK RAPIDS BICENTENNIAL COMMITTEE; 901 S 3 AVE; ROCK RAPIDS, IA 51246. (#19677).

ROCK RAPIDS — CONTINUED

ROCK RAPIDS, IA, HALL OF FAME. PLACE TO HOUSE MEMORABILIA OF EARLY PIONEERS TO BE ACQUIRED. (ST-WIDE). DAVID CURTIS, PROJ DIR; ROCK RAPIDS BICENT COMMITTEE; 1003 S 2ND AVE; ROCK RAPIDS, IA 51246. (#10522).

TRAIN DEPOT RESTORATION IN ROCK RAPIDS, IOWA. DEPOT PURCHASED SO THAT ITS ARCHITECTURAL WORTH MAY BE PRESERVED. IT IS TO BE USED AS A MUSEUM FOR LYON COUNTY. (LOCAL). RONALD F SCHEMMEL; LYON COUNTY HISTORICAL SOCIETY, INC; BOX 8; ALVORD, IA 51230. (#7793).

JUNE 24 - 26, '76. ROCK RAPIDS CENTENNIAL-BICENTENNIAL CELEBRATION. FESTIVITIES INCLUDE: DEMOLITION DERBY, ALL-SCHOOL PICNIC, COMMUNITY THEATRE, BASEBALL, STYLE SHOW, BEARD AND BELLE CONTESTS AND WATER FIGHT. (LOCAL). DAVE CURTIS, COORDINATOR; ROCK RAPIDS COMMUNITY AFFAIRS CORP; ROCK RAPIDS, IA 51246. (#200018-198).

JUNE '76. OLD-FASHIONED GRADUATION IN ROCK RAPIDS, IOWA. CLASS OF 1976 TO HOLD OLD-FASHIONED GRADUATION. (LOCAL). DAVID CURTIS, DIR; ROCK RAPIDS BICENTENNIAL COMMITTEE; 1003 S 2ND AVE; ROCK RAPIDS, IA 51246. (#10523-1).

ROCK VALLEY

BICENTENNIAL PARK - ROCK VALLEY, IA. THE PARK WILL HAVE PICNIC FACILITIES, TENNIS COURTS, A SHELTER AND PLAYGROUND EQUIPMENT. (LOCAL). BARBARA ANDERSON, CHAIRMAN; ROCK VALLEY BICENTENNIAL COMMITTEE; 2108 14TH ST; ROCK VALLEY, IA 51247. (#19700).

TRAVELING ART EXHIBIT, ROCK VALLEY, IA. PROJECT INVOLVES THE DEVELOPMENT OF A TRAVELING ART EXHIBIT FROM WINNING ENTRIES IN A PREVIOUS STUDENT ART COMPETITION. ENTRIES ALSO REPRODUCED ON A COUNTY CALENDAR. (LOCAL). MRS JEAN PORTER, CHAIRPERSON; SIOUX COUNTY FESTIVAL COMMITTEE; 1705 14TH ST; ROCK VALLEY, IA 51247. (#24630).

ROCKFORD

MILL WHEEL PROJ - ROCKFORD, IA. WHEEL TO BE PLACED IN A PARK NAMED AFTER THE COMMUNITY FOUNDER. (LOCAL). DENNIS GINTHER, CHAIRMAN; ROCKFORD ACTION; 310 2ND AVE; ROCKFORD, IA 50468. (#16433).

TIME CAPSULE PROJ - ROCKFORD, IA. PAST AND PRESENT HISTORY TO BE VIEWED IN 2076. (LOCAL). HON BENARD DEBUHR, MAYOR; CITY OF ROCKFORD; 104 3RD ST NW; ROCKFORD, IA 50468. (#16432).

JUNE 18 - 20, '76. RELIGIOUS SERVICE AND CARNIVAL CELEBRATION. CEREMONY, FESTIVAL AT MAIN STREET & LOCAL PARKS. (LOCAL). DENNIS GINTHER, CHMN; ROCKFORD ACTION; 310 2ND AVE, NW; ROCKFORD, IA 50468. (#102937-4).

ROCKWELL

BEAUTIFY THE PARK - ROCKWELL, IA. RED, WHITE AND BLUE FLOWERS WILL BE PLANTED AT THE ENTRANCE TO THE PARK. (LOCAL). MRS LEON HITZHUSEN, PRESIDENT; FEDERATED WOMENS CLUB; ROCKWELL, IA 50469. (#21411).

JUNE 12 - 14, '76. BY-CENTENNIAL BIG DAYS. BY-CENTENNIAL BIG DAYS WILL FEATURE A CARNIVAL AND PARADE. AT MAIN STREET. (LOCAL). DUGAN LAUDNER, PROJ COORD; CHAMBER OF COMMERCE; ROCKWELL, IA 50469. (#105325-3).

JUNE 12 - 14, '76. STYLE SHOW. FASHIONS FROM PAST TO THE PRESENT WILL BE FEATURED, IN CONJUNCTION WITH ROCKWELL BIG DAYS. (LOCAL). JANET BROWN, COORD; JUNIOR WOMEN'S CLUB; ROCKWELL, IA 50469. (#105325-2).

JUNE 12 - 27, '76. ROCKWELL CITY CENTENNIAL CELEBRATION AND BICENTENNIAL OBSERVANCE. A HISTORY OF THE TOWN IS BEING PUBLISHED. THE PAGEANT WILL TELL THE STORY OF THE TOWN AND COUNTY. TREES WILL BE PLANTED; AN ARENA WILL BE BUILT AT CITY PARK & A CASH GIFT FOR PARK IMPROVEMENT WILL BE GIVEN. AT COURTHOUSE SQUARE, CITY PARK. (LOCAL). ROBERT E MORTON, CHMN; ROCKWELL CITY CENTENNIAL ASSOC, INC; 528 MAIN; ROCKWELL CITY, IA 50579. (#100951-1).

JUNE 14, '76. FLAG DAY. THERE WILL BE A CEREMONY AND CELEBRATION FOR FLAG DAY. (LOCAL). EARL LOSEE, PRESIDENT; THE AMERICAN LEGION; ROCKWELL, IA 50469. (#105325-4).

JULY 4, '76. BREAKFAST IN THE LYNN GROVE PARK. IN ADDITION TO THE BREAKFAST THERE IS GOING TO BE AN 'ALMOST ANYTHING GOES' CONTEST BETWEEN LOCAL TEAMS. IT WILL BE HELD AFTER THE BREAKFAST IN THE LYNN GROVE RECREATION PARK. AT LYNN GROVE RECREATION CENTER. (LOCAL). ROBERT JEFFERY, COORD; ROCKWELL JAYCEES; ROCKWELL, IA 50496. (#105325-1).

AUG 15, '76. CHICKEN BAR-BE-CUE. FESTIVAL AT COMMUNITY SWIMMING POOL IN ROCKWELL, IOWA. (LOCAL). JIM GRIEBLING, COORD; LIONS' CLUB; MASON CITY, IA 50406. (#105324-1).

ROCKWELL CITY

ADDITION FOR CALHOUN HISTORICAL SOCIETY BLDG - IA. THE EXISTING FACILITY IS TO BE RENOVATED & ENLARGED. (LOCAL). HAL SPEERS, CHAIRMAN; CALHOUN COUNTY BICENTENNIAL; ROCKWELL CITY, IA 50589. (#17500).

AVENUE OF FLAGS - ROCKWELL CITY, IA. ALL CEMETERIES IN CALHOUN COUNTY TO DISPLAY FLAGS. (LOCAL). HAL SPEERS, CHAIRMAN; CALHOUN COUNTY BICENTENNIAL COMMISSION; ROCKWELL CITY, IA 50589. (#17498).

CALHOUN COUNTY HISTORY - ROCKWELL CITY, IA. THE COUNTY HISTORY WILL BE REWRITTEN & UPDATED FOR PUBLICATION. (LOCAL). HAL SPEERS, CHAIRMAN; CALHOUN COUNTY BICENTENNIAL; ROCKWELL CITY, IA 50579. (#17499).

FARM MACHINERY EXHIBIT HALL - ROCKWELL CITY, IA. THE BUILDING WILL PRESERVE AND DISPLAY ANTIQUE HORSE-DRAWN FARM MACHINERY. (LOCAL). MARTHA HOYT, PRESIDENT; CALHOUN COUNTY HISTORICAL SOCIETY; 500 E LAKE ST; ROCKWELL CITY, IA 50579. (#19722).

UPDATE OF CALHOUN COUNTY CEMETERY RECORDS - IA. ALL COUNTY CEMETERY RECORDS ARE TO BE REVIEWED AND UPDATED. (LOCAL). HAL SPEERS, CHAIRMAN; CALHOUN COUNTY BICENTENNIAL; ROCKWELL CITY, IA 50584. (#17501).

RODNEY

JUNE 20, '76. KIDS' DAY, OLD TIME PICNIC AND HISTORY OF RODNEY. PANCAKE SUPPER ON APRIL 1ST, STREET DANCE ON MAY 1ST; PARADE IN TOWN STREETS, PICNIC AND GAMES IN TOWN PARK; EXHIBIT IN CITY HALL, FREE MOVIE IN THE CHURCH BASEMENT, ALL ON JUNE 20TH, 1976. AT PARADE IN TOWN STREETS; TOWN PARK FOR PICNIC, EXHIBIT IN CITY HALL. (LOCAL). HON DAVID MANN, MAYOR; CITY OF RODNEY; RODNEY, IA 51051. (#106899-1).

ROLAND

JUNE 29 - 30, '76. ROLAND AMERICAN REVOLUTION BICENTENNIAL CELEBRATION. FESTIVAL AT ERICKSON PARK. (LOCAL). CRAIG HETLAND, CHAIRMAN; ROLAND AMERICAN REVOLUTION BICENTENNIAL COMMISSION; 107 VINE; ROLAND, IA 50236. (#107387-1).

ROLFE

AVENUE OF FLAGS - ROLFE, IA. A FLAG WILL BE FLOWN FOR EACH DECEASED VETERAN FROM THE COMMUNITY. (LOCAL). MRS JERRY HUGHES, CHAIRWOMAN; ROLFE AMERICAN LEGION; 504 GARFIELD ST; ROLFE, IA 50581. (#19445).

HAITT HOUSE - ROLFE, IA. THE HAITT HOUSE WILL BE RECORDED AS A HISTORICAL SITE IN THE IOWA HISTORICAL BOOK AND RESTORED TO ITS ORIGINAL SITE. (LOCAL). MRS JERRY HUGHES, CHAIRWOMAN; ROLFE AREA '76ER'S'; 504 GARFIELD ST; ROLFE, IA 50581. (#19378).

TILLIE LOG CABIN - ROLFE, IA. THE CABIN WILL BE FURNISHED AND MARKED WITH A HISTORICAL PLAQUE. (LOCAL). MRS JERRY HUGHES, CHAIRWOMAN; ROLFE AREA '76ER'S'; 504 GARFIELD ST; ROLFE, IA 50581. (#19379).

TREE PLANTING - ROLFE, IA. ASSORTMENT OF DECIDUOUS TREES TO BE PLANTED. (LOCAL). MRS JERRY HUGHES, CHAIRWOMAN; ROLFE AREA '76ER'S'; 504 GARFIELD ST; ROLFE, IA 50581. (#19380).

JUNE 23, '76. BICENTENNIAL MUSICAL. FESTIVAL, LIVE PERFORMANCE AT ROLFE COMMUNITY SCHOOL AUDITORIUM. (LOCAL). MRS JERRY HUGHES, CHMN; ROLFE AREA '76ER'S'; 504 GARFIELD ST; ROLFE, IA 50581. (#104270-3).

JUNE 23, '76. BICENTENNIAL PARADE. PARADE AT GARFIELD ST. (LOCAL). MRS JERRY HUGHES, CHMN; ROLFE AREA '76ER'S'; 504 GARFIELD ST; ROLFE, IA 50581. (#104270-5).

JUNE 23, '76. FIREMAN'S WATER FIGHT. COMPETITION, FESTIVAL AT DES MOINES AVE. (LOCAL). MRS JERRY HUGHES, CHMN; ROLFE VOLUNTEER FIRE DEPT; 504 GARFIELD ST; ROLFE, IA 50581. (#104270-4).

JUNE 23 - 24, '76. GREATER ROLFE DAYS. FESTIVAL AT DES MOINES AVE. (LOCAL). MRS JERRY HUGHES, CHMN; ROLFE CHAMBER OF COMMERCE; 504 GARFIELD ST; ROLFE, IA 50581. (#104270-2).

ROWAN

JUNE 13, '76. 'LOG CABIN DAY'. EXHIBITS, PARADE, FESTIVAL AND LIVE PERFORMANCE; FREE PANCAKE SUPPER AND SQUARE DANCING; MUSIC BY COUNTRY COUSINS. AT COMMUNITY SCHOOL BLDG; FREE PANCAKE SUPPER. (LOCAL). CHARLES H KEITH, CHMN; ROWAN AMERICAN REVOLUTION BICENTENNIAL COMM & LION'S CLUB; 305 WHITTEN AVE; ROWAN, IA 50470. (#103639-6).

SEPT 6, '76. LABOR DAY CELEBRATION. DEMONSTRATIONS OF ARTS AND CRAFTS; GENERAL CELEBRATION. (LOCAL). CHARLES H KEITH, CHMN; WRIGHT COUNTY ARBC AND LION'S CLUB; 305 WHITTEN AVE; ROWAN, IA 50470. (#103639-9).

ROYAL

VISIT & CONCERT BY DANK SPATZEN CHILDREN'S CHOIR OF CHICAGO. CONCERT & WEEKEND VISIT BY 'DEUTSCH-AMERIKANISCHEN NATIONAL KONGRESS SPATZEN CHILDREN'S CHOIR' TO HOMES & FARMS OF CLAY CENTRAL H S GERMAN ROUNDSINGERS (GERMAN I HIGH SCHOOL STUDENTS). (LOCAL). EVELYN BRESS, TEACHER; CLAY CENTRAL HIGH SCHOOL GERMAN ROUNDSINGERS; ROYAL, IA 51357. (#108245-1).

RUBIO

COMMUNITY DEVELOPMENT - RUBIO, IA. PROJECTS INCLUDE BUILDING IMPROVEMENTS, PRESERVATION OF RAILROAD DEPOT AND TREE PLANTING IN PARK. (LOCAL). KAREN MORGAN, PRESIDENT; RUBIO LADIES CLUB; RUBIO, IA 52585. (#18355).

AUG 7 - 8, '75. LAWN SOCIAL AND JUBILEE. FESTIVAL AT RUBIO COMMUNITY BUILDING & ADJOINING PARK. (LOCAL). KAREN MORGAN, CHAIRPERSON; RUBIO LADIES CLUB; RR #1; RICHLAND, IA 52585. (#200018-140).

RUNNELLS

JULY 2 - 4, '76. PICNIC, ANTIQUE DISPLAY, BEARD GROWING CONTEST, ETC. FESTIVAL AT HIGHWAY #163, RONNELLS, IA. (LOCAL). MRS GORDON ATZEN; SE POLK SCHOOL DISTRICT; 6589 SE 6TH AVE; DES MOINES, IA 50317. (#107685-1).

RUSSELL

TREE AND FLOWER PLANTING, IA. TREES AND FLOWERS WILL BE PLANTED IN CITY PARK. (LOCAL). MERNA MCGILL, CHAIRMAN; GARDEN CLUB; RUSSELL, IA 50238. (#23932).

JULY 23 - 24, '76. BICENTENNIAL RODEO. COMPETITION, FESTIVAL, PARADE AT SPRAGUE FIELD. (LOCAL). IVAN MCCULLOUGH, CHAIRMAN; LIONS CLUB; RUSSELL, IA 50238. (#106843-1).

RUTHVEN

TIME CAPSULE - RUTHVEN, IA. PRESERVATION OF INTERESTING & IMPORTANT OBJECTS, CHARACTERISTIC OF CONTEMPORARY LIFE TO BE BURIED IN A CAPSULE WITH INSTRUCTIONS TO OPEN IN 2076. (LOCAL). HON RICHARD ARNDT, MAYOR; RUTHVEN BICENTENNIAL COMMITTEE; BOX K; RUTHVEN, IA 51358. (#24218).

JULY 4, '76. COMMUNITY CHURCH SERVICE. CEREMONY AT RUTHVEN SCHOOL GYM. (LOCAL). REV ERNEST CHRISTIANSEN; RUTHVEN BICENTENNIAL COMMITTEE; RUTHVEN, IA 51358. (#106792-4).

JULY 4, '76. COMMUNITY PICNIC & PLAY DAY. PLANS CALL FOR A COMMUNITY POTLUCK PICNIC AND A PLAYDAY INCLUDING OLD-FASHIONED GAMES AND A COMMUNITY SING. AT CRICKET PARK. (LOCAL). JEANINE WICHMAN, CHMN; RUTHVEN BICENTENNIAL COMMITTEE; RUTHVEN, IA 51358. (#106792-1).

JULY 4, '76. FLAG RAISING AND AWARDS PRESENTATION. AWARD, CEREMONY AT RUTHVEN SCHOOL GYM. (LOCAL). LENORE OSTERHUS, COORD; RUTHVEN BICENTENNIAL COMMITTEE; RUTHVEN, IA 51358. (#106792-3).

JULY 4 - 5, '76. HERITAGE FAIR. DISPLAY OF ARTICLES THAT HAVE CONTRIBUTED TO OUR HERITAGE SUCH AS NEEDLECRAFT, PAINTINGS, OLD PHOTOS & ANTIQUES. RESERVATIONS ARE REQUIRED FOR EXHIBITORS ONLY. AT AMERICAN LEGION BLDG, 1/2 BLOCK E OF GOWRIE, ON RIGHT SIDE OF MAIN. (LOCAL). DANNA GOWANS, CO-CHMN; RUTHVEN BICENTENNIAL COMMITTEE; BOX 245; RUTHVEN, IA 51358. (#106792-2).

RUTLAND

CEMETERY RENOVATION, RUTLAND, IA. BURN WEEDS, CLEAN MARKERS AND MOW GRASS AT LOCAL CEMETERY. (LOCAL). DEANNA LUDWIG, SECRETARY; RUTLAND BICENTENNIAL COMMITTEE; BOX 44; RUTLAND, IA 50582. (#25293).

FLAG SALES - RUTLAND, IA. THE BICENTENNIAL COMMITTEE WILL SELL FLAGS TO INTERESTED PEOPLE. (LOCAL). RICHARD GREBNER, VICE-PRESIDENT; RUTLAND BICENTENNIAL COMMITTEE; RUTLAND, IA 50582. (#22202).

PIN SALES - RUTLAND, IA. PINS WITH OUR TOWN SLOGAN WILL BE SOLD BY THE BICENTENNIAL COMMITTEE. (LOCAL). MRS MARTHA ANDERSON, PROJ DIRECTOR; RUTLAND BICENTENNIAL COMMITTEE; RUTLAND, IA 50582. (#22201).

SEWER SYSTEM, RUTLAND, IA. INSTALLATION OF SEWER PIPE & LAGOON IN PARTS OF TOWN WHICH DO NOT HAVE ADEQUATE SEWER SYSTEM. (LOCAL). HON G C HOOD, MAYOR; RUTLAND BICENTENNIAL COMMITTEE; RUTLAND, IA 50582. (#22203).

STREET SIGNS - RUTLAND, IA. METAL SIGNS WILL BE PLACED AT SEVERAL INTERSECTIONS. (LOCAL). MRS RANDY LUDWIG, SECRETARY; RUTLAND BICENTENNIAL COMMITTEE; BOX 44; RUTLAND, IA 50582. (#22204).

TREE SELLING PROJECT - RUTLAND, IA. THE RUTLAND BICENTENNIAL COMMITTEE WILL CONTACT PEOPLE TO BUY TREES. (LOCAL). MRS FLORINE HOOD, PRESIDENT; RUTLAND BICENTENNIAL COMMITTEE; BOX 44; RUTLAND, IA 50582. (#22205).

MAR 4, '76. FAMILY FUN NIGHT - BINGO GAME. FESTIVAL AT RUTLAND TOWN HALL. (LOCAL). EMMETT BRADLEY, CHMN; RUTLAND BICENTENNIAL COMMITTEE; RUTLAND, IA 50582. (#200018-138).

APR 7, '76. 4-H ALUMNI TEA. FESTIVAL. (LOCAL). MRS MARTHA ANDERSON, CHMN; RUTLAND LUCKY STARS; RUTLAND, IA 50582. (#105956-2).

APR 20, '76. HISTORY OF RUTLAND. EXHIBIT AT RUTLAND TOWN HALL. (LOCAL). MRS G C HOOD, COORD; RUTLAND BICENTENNIAL COMMITTEE; RUTLAND, IA 50582. (#105956-1).

RUTLAND — CONTINUED

MAY 23, '76. BICENTENNIAL FLAG-RAISING CEREMONY. NOON POTLUCK DINNER FOLLOWED BY FLAG PRESENTATION BY SENATOR PRIEBE; MUSIC BY BAND AND SINGERS. AT TOWN HALL, SHERIDAN AVE. (LOCAL). MRS DEANNA LUDWIG, SEC; RUTLAND BICENTENNIAL COMMITTEE; BOX 44; RUTLAND, IA 50582. (#200018-139).

JULY 24, '76. RUTLAND FIREMENS' PORK BARBECUE AND DANCE. THERE WILL BE WATER FIGHTS IN THE AFTERNOON. AT SCHOOL HOUSE. (LOCAL). RANDY LUDWIG, FIRE CHIEF; FIREMEN; BOX 44; RUTLAND, IA 50582. (#105956-3).

RYAN

COMMUNITY DEVELOPMENT PROJECT - RYAN, IA. IMPLEMENTATION OF COMMUNITY CONCERN ON RESTORATION OF RYAN LANDMARKS AND THE IMPORTANCE OF PRESERVING THEM. (LOCAL). HON VINCENT J KEEGAN, MAYOR; RYAN VOLUNTEER FIRE DEPT; BOX 137; RYAN, IA 52330. (#21273).

JUNE 3 - 4, '76. COMMUNITY RECREATION. COMPETITION, GAMES, CARNIVAL, AMUSEMENTS, EXHIBITS BY 4H & FFA, ACTIVITIES BY LIONS CLUB, LEGION, LEGION AUXILIARY, CHURCH GROUPS, STUDY CLUBS. ALL EVENTS FOR PURPOSE OF RESTORING OLD FIRE STATION & EQUIPMENT. AT RYAN BALL PARK & GYMNASIUM WEST OF HIGHWAY 13. (LOCAL). VINCENT J KEEGAN, COORD; RYAN VOLUNTEER FIRE DEPT, RYAN TOWN PATRONS, 4H & SENIOR CITIZENS; BOX 137; RYAN, IA 52330. (#105261-1).

S SIOUX CITY

JULY 4, '76. 4TH OF JULY FIREWORKS DISPLAY. A HIGH SCHOOL BAND PROGRAM PRECEDED THE FIREWORKS DISPLAY. (LOCAL). MAXINE TITLER, CHMN; ROTARIANS; 112 FAIRVIEW DR; S SIOUX CITY, NE 68776. (#200030-139).

SABULA

BOOK OF HISTORICAL EVENTS IN SABULA, IA. BOOK ON LOCAL HISTORY OF TOWN AND SETTLERS. (LOCAL). MRS RAY PAPKE, DIRECTOR; SABULA BICENTENNIAL COMMITTEE; CITY HALL; SABULA, IA 52070. (#21400).

TIME CAPSULE PROJECT IN SABULA, IA. TIME CAPSULE TO BE BURIED UNDER NEW FLAGPOLE INSTALLED IN SMALL NEW PARK AREA. USA & STATE FLAGS TO BE FLOWN. TREES TO BE PLANTED IN PARK AREAS & ALONG RIVERBANK. (LOCAL). MRS RAY PAPKE, DIRECTOR; SABULA BICENTENNIAL COMMITTEE; CITY HALL; SABULA, IA 52070. (#21399).

JUNE 25 - 27, '76. THREE DAY FESTIVAL. FESTIVAL. (LOCAL). MRS RAY PAPKE, COORD; TOWN OF SABULA; 408 WASHINGTON ST; SABULA, IA 52070. (#105322-1).

SAC CITY

NEW MUSEUM IN SAC CITY, IA. A NEW HISTORICAL MUSEUM WILL BE BUILT IN HONOR OF THE BICENTENNIAL. (LOCAL). MARILYN HOBBS, COORDINATOR; SAC COUNTY BICENTENNIAL COMMITTEE; SAC CITY, IA 50583. (#16774).

RESTORATION PROJECT - SAC CITY, IA. IN HONOR OF THE BICENTENNIAL, PRAIRIE HOME WILL BE RESTORED. (LOCAL). MARILYN HOBBS, COORDINATOR; SAC COUNTY BICENTENNIAL COMMITTEE; SAC CITY, IA 50583. (#16773).

SALEM

RESTORATION OF JUSTICE GIBBS LAW OFFICE - IA. THE LEWELLING QUAKER SHRINE WAS A STOP OFF FOR THE UNDERGROUND RAILROAD AND PARTS OF THE HOUSE WERE USED BY JUSTICE GIBBS AS A LAW OFFICE AT THE SAME TIME THAT THE HOUSE WAS A HAVEN FOR SLAVES. (LOCAL). MRS MILTON CURTIS, CHAIRMAN; SALEM BICENTENNIAL COMMISSION; SALEM, IA 52649. (#18074).

AUG 28, '76. SALEM OLD SETTLERS. OLDEST OLD SETTLERS ORGANIZATION IN IOWA QUAKER TOWN. AT PARK COMMUNITY HALL, LENELLING HOUSE. (LOCAL). MRS MILTON CURTIS, COORD; SALEM OLD SETTLER ASSOCIATION; RR 1; SALEM, IA 52641. (#106063-1).

SALIX

CITY IMPROVEMENTS, SALIX, IA. STREET SIGNS WILL BE SET UP. (LOCAL). JEANETTE CHICOINE, CITY CLERK; SALIX CITY COUNCIL; CITY HALL; SALIX, IA 51052. (#23382).

NEW FLAGPOLE, SALIX, IA. A FLAGPOLE WILL BE ERECTED AT CITY HALL. (LOCAL). MRS RAMON CHOQUETTE, PRESIDENT; SALIX FIREMEN'S AUXILIARY; SALIX, IA 51052. (#23380).

PAINTING OF TRASH BARRELS, SALIX, IA. CITY TRASH BARRELS WILL BE PAINTED. (LOCAL). RONNIE HECK, LEADER; 4 H GROUP; RR I; SALIX, IA 51052. (#23381).

RELIGIOUS CEREMONY. CEREMONY AT CHURCH. (LOCAL). MRS FRED NELSON, CHMN; ST JOSEPH CATHOLIC CHURCH/UNITED METHODIST CHURCH; BOX 126; SALIX, IA 51052. (#106541-1). **(??).**

SALIX CLEANUP PROJECT, IA. VACANT LOT WILL BE CLEANED AND TREES & FLOWERS WILL BE PLANTED. (LOCAL). ELEANOR CHOQUETTE, PRESIDENT; KALORIE KICKERS; SALIX, IA 51052. (#23383).

WESTWOOD ELEMENTARY MUSIC PROGRAM. LIVE PERFORMANCE AT SCHOOL GYM, WALNUT ST. (LOCAL). MRS FRED NELSON, CHMN; WESTWOOD COMMUNITY ELEMENTARY SCHOOL; BOX 126; SALIX, IA 51052. (#106541-2). **(??).**

FEB 17, '76. ST JOSEPH BICENTENNIAL PROGRAM & PARTY. BICENTENNIAL DINNER, PUPPET SHOW, TV INTERVIEW SHOW. AT ST JOSEPH SCHOOL. (LOCAL). MISS MARY ELLEN DAHL, DIR; ST JOSEPH SCHOOL; SALIX, IA 51052. (#200018-147).

MAY 4 - 7, '76. SENIOR CITIZENS' HERITAGE DISPLAY. EXHIBIT AT SALIX UNITED METHODIST CHURCH. (LOCAL). MRS FRED NELSON, CHMN; SENIOR CITIZENS; BOX 126; SALIX, IA 51052. (#106541-3).

JUNE 13, '76. GIRL SCOUTS' HERITAGE '76 - HERITAGE DEMONSTRATIONS. EXHIBIT. (LOCAL). MRS TED ERICKSEN, LEADER; GIRL SCOUTS; SALIX, IA 51052. (#106596-1).

JUNE 13, '76. SALIX BICENTENNIAL FESTIVAL. FESTIVAL AT SALIX CITY HALL ON TIPTON ST. (LOCAL). MRS FRED NELSON, CHMN; FIREMEN'S AUXILIARY & STUDY CLUB, 4-H GROUPS, ST JOSEPH'S PARENTS; BOX 126; SALIX, IA 51052. (#106541-4).

SANBORN

CEMETERY SURVEY - SANBORN, IA. SURVEY TO UPDATE CEMETERY RECORDS. ACCOMPLISHED BY SURVEY OF RECORDS AND STONE TO STONE SURVEY OF LOCAL CEMETERIES. (LOCAL). KAREN BOSMA, CHAIRMAN; SANBORN BICENTENNIAL COMMITTEE; BOX 370; SANBORN, IA 51248. (#20984).

COLONIAL NEW ENGLAND STATES FILM, SANBORN, IA. A FILMED TOUR GUIDE ON PLYMOUTH VILLAGE. (LOCAL). JOYCE HULLEY, TEACHER; SANBORN COMMUNITY SCHOOL; SANBORN, IA 51248. (#21020).

THE FIFTY STATES, SANBORN, IA. A STUDY OF THE 50 STATES: INCLUDES ORDER THEY JOINED UNION, EACH FLAG, STATE BIRD AND FLOWER. (LOCAL). WILMA GRAUER, FIRST GRADE TEACHER; SANBORN COMMUNITY SCHOOL; SANBORN, IA 51248. (#21021).

MICROFILMED HISTORY OF SANBORN, IA. THE MICROFILMING OF ALL SANBORN PIONEERS THROUGH 1950. (LOCAL). KAREN BOSMA, PROJ DIRECTOR; SANBORN BICENTENNIAL COMMITTEE; BOX 370; SANBORN, IA 51248. (#21024).

MILLER PARK DEDICATION. CEREMONY. (LOCAL). HON P KROESER, MAYOR; CITY OF SANBORN & THE COMMERCIAL CLUB; SANBORN, IA 51248. (#105144-1).

SANBORN, IA, MUSEUM. HISTORIC ROUND HOUSE TO BE CONVERTED INTO MUSEUM. (LOCAL). BERNICE WATTERS, PROJ COORDINATOR; HORIZONS COMMITTEE; SANBORN, IA 51248. (#21022).

STUDY OF THE AMERICAN REVOLUTION, SANBORN, IA. FILM OF THE BOSTON TEA PARTY AND PAUL REVERE'S RIDE. (LOCAL). MRS STERLER, THIRD GRADE TEACHER; SANBORN COMMUNITY SCHOOL; W 5TH AND MAIN; SANBORN, IA 51248. (#21019).

SURVEY, CHURCH RECORD, SANBORN, IA. SURVEY ON EARLY BAPTISM, MARRIAGE, AND DEATH RECORDS. (LOCAL). KAREN BOSMA, PROJ DIRECTOR; SANBORN BICENTENNIAL COMMITTEE; BOX 370; SANBORN, IA 51248. (#21023).

APR 18, '75. PAUL REVERE DAY, EXHIBIT OF PIONEER ARTIFACTS, LETTERS & ANTIQUES. EXHIBIT AT LIBRARY, MAIN ST. (LOCAL). LENA ZONEVELT, LIBRARIAN; SANBORN PUBLIC LIBRARY; 212 W 1; SANBORN, IA 51248. (#200018-156).

AUG 23, '75. FAMILY DAY LEISURE 'FLAGS ON PARADE', PARADE & PROGRAM. FESTIVAL, PARADE, LIVE PERFORMANCE AT BRADY FIELD, HIGH SCHOOL ATHLETIC FIELD. (LOCAL). CATHERINE KROESE, CHMN; 50 + CLUB-SENIOR CITIZENS; 209 W 2ND; SANBORN, IA 51248. (#200018-157).

DEC 14, '75. COMMUNITY HYMN SING. LIVE PERFORMANCE AT CHRISTIAN REFORMED CHURCH. (LOCAL). MARGUERITE SOOP, CHMN; FESTIVAL COMMITTEE-SANBORN BICENTENNIAL COMMISSION; SANBORN, IA 51248. (#200018-182).

FEB 28, '76. WASHINGTON'S BIRTHDAY SOUP & PIE SUPPER. LIVE PERFORMANCE. (LOCAL). MARGUERITE SOOP, CHMN; FESTIVAL COMMITTEE, SANBORN BICENTENNIAL COMMISSION; SANBORN, IA 51248. (#200018-181).

APR 24 - 25, '76. 'I LOVE AMERICA' PAGEANT. LIVE PERFORMANCE AT HIGH SCHOOL GYMNASIUM. (LOCAL). MRS A BOSCH, COORD; SANBORN BICENTENNIAL COMMISSION; SANBORN, IA 51248. (#200018-180).

APR 30, '76. TREE PLANTING ON ARBOR DAY. CEREMONY. (LOCAL). MARQUERITE SOOP, PROJ DIR; CITY COUNCIL; SANBORN, IA 51248. (#105183-1).

JUNE 1 - JULY 24, '76. 'SPIRIT OF '76' READING CLUB CONTEST. THE AIM OF 'THE SPIRIT OF '76' CLUB IS TO HAVE EVERYONE READING SOMETHING ABOUT OUR COUNTRY OR IMPORTANT PEOPLE IN OUR COUNTRY'S DEVELOPMENT, EACH WEEK. THE CONTEST WILL RUN FOR 8 WEEKS. (LOCAL). MRS FRANK KOKSMA, COORD; SANBORN PUBLIC LIBRARY - CHILDREN'S DIVISION; SANBORN, IA 51248. (#104269-1).

JUNE 16 - 18, '76. COMMUNITY RUMMAGE SALE FOR MICROFILMING LOCAL NEWSPAPER. FAIR AT LEGION HALL. (LOCAL). MRS D DEROAS, COORDINATOR; HORIZONS COMMITTEE OF THE SANBORN BICENTENNIAL COMMISSION; SANBORN, IA 51248. (#200018-212).

JULY 31, '76. BICENTENNIAL ANTIQUE SHOW. FAIR AT PRESBYTERIAN CHURCH. (LOCAL). KAREN BOSMA, COORDINATOR; HERITAGE COMMITTEE OF THE SANBORN BICENTENNIAL COMMISSION; SANBORN, IA 51248. (#200018-210).

JULY 31, '76. 'OUT OF THE PAST - INTO THE FUTURE' - STYLE SHOW FROM 1776 TO 1976. LIVE PERFORMANCE AT SANBORN COMMUNITY SCHOOL HOT LUNCH ROOM. (LOCAL). NANCY ELGERSSMA, CHMN; HERITAGE COMMITTEE OF THE SANBORN BICENTENNIAL COMMISSION; SANBORN, IA 51248. (#200018-211).

JULY 31, '76. STYLE SHOW. LIVE PERFORMANCE. (LOCAL). KAREN BOSMA, PROJ CHMN; SANBORN BICENTENNIAL COMMITTEE; BOX 370; SANBORN, IA 51248. (#105144-2).

SCARVILLE

CENTENNIAL BOOK - PROJ OF SCARVILLE, IA. A CENTENNIAL BOOK ON THE MEMBERS OF THE LUTHERAN CHURCH. (LOCAL). REV MERLIN NORRIS, PROJ DIRECTOR; NORTH PRAIRIE & IMMANUEL LUTHERAN CHURCH; SCARVILLE, IA 50473. (#16150).

EDUCATION UNIT - PROJ OF SCARVILLE, IA. THE SYNOD CHURCH WILL ADD A DAILY SCHOOL. (LOCAL). REV PAUL HAUGEN, PROJ DIRECTOR; SYNOD CHURCH; SCARVILLE, IA 50473. (#16148).

HISTORICAL LANDMARK RESTORATION - SCARVILLE, IA. THE OLDEST BUILDING IN THE TOWN WILL BE RESTORED AS A MUSEUM & LANDMARK. (LOCAL). SANDRA ESCHERICH, PRESIDENT; COMMUNITY BETTERMENT CLUB; BOX 6, MAIN ST; SCARVILLE, IA 50473. (#16151).

SHELTER HOUSE PROJECT - SCARVILLE, IA. A SHELTER HOUSE WILL BE BUILT AS A SHELTER FROM RAIN FOR THE 4TH OF JULY FESTIVAL. (LOCAL). SANDRA ESCHERICH, PRESIDENT; COMMUNITY BETTERMENT CLUB; BOX 6, MAIN ST; SCARVILLE, IA 50473. (#16149).

JULY 4, '76. 4TH OF JULY BICENTENNIAL FESTIVAL. FESTIVAL, PARADE. (LOCAL). BILLIE WAYCHUS, CHMN; SCARVILLE BOOSTER CLUB; SCARVILLE, IA 50473. (#102754-1).

SCHALLER

COMMUNITY IMPROVEMENT, IA. REPAINT OUTSIDE OF POOL, PLANT FLOWERS TO BE SEEN BY ALL WHO DRIVE BY, CURTAINS FOR DRESSING ROOMS AND RESTROOMS WILL BE ADDED. (LOCAL). KAREN GRIEME, PRESIDENT; NON-AME; RURAL ROUTE 1; SCHALLER, IA 51053. (#23922).

PARK IMPROVEMENT, IA. REBUILDING OF PARK ENTRANCE, PLANTING OF TREES AND FLOWERS AND INSTALLATION OF SINK IN THE SHELTER HOUSE ARE THE PLANNED IMPROVEMENTS. (LOCAL). MABEL GRIEME, PRESIDENT; FEDERATED WOMEN'S CLUBS; SCHALLER, IA 51053. (#23926).

PLANTING TREES IN TOWN PARK, IA. BEAUTIFICATION OF TOWN WILL BE ACCOMPLISHED THROUGH TREE PLANTING. (LOCAL). MRS LOIS TAYLOR, TROOP COMMITTEE CHAIRMAN; GIRL SCOUTS; SCHALLER, IA 51053. (#23923).

APR 2, '76. BENEFIT BASKETBALL GAME FOR FUNDS TO BUILD TENNIS COURT. COMPETITION, LIVE PERFORMANCE AT SCHALLER GYMNASIUM. (LOCAL). TOM KING, PRESIDENT; SCHALLER JAYCEES; RURAL ROUTE; STORM LAKE, IA 50588. (#200018-148).

JUNE 10 - JULY 4, '76. THE READING CIRCLE CLUB MEETINGS. SEMINAR AT LIBRARY, SCHALLER. (LOCAL). KAREN GRIEME, CHAIRMAN; MUSIC AND LITERATURE CLUB; RR 1; SCHALLER, IA 51053. (#106837-2).

JULY 16 - 17, '76. POPCORN DAYS. FLOAT PARADE, FLOWER SHOW, FLEA MARKET, QUEEN CONTEST, RELAYS, BEEF AND PORK BURGER DINNER SERVED AT PARK. AT MAIN STREET AREA. (LOCAL). DON THOMPSON, PRESIDENT; CHAMBER OF COMMERCE; SCHALLER, IA 51053. (#106837-1).

SCHLESWIG

SENIOR CITIZENS CENTER, SCHLESWIG, IA. RESTORATION OF COMMERCIAL BANK BUILDING INTO SENIOR CITIZENS CENTER. (LOCAL). TED HOLLANDER, PROJ DIRECTOR; COMMUNITY CLUB; SCHLESWIG, IA 51461. (#21014).

MAY 13 - 27, '76. TRIP TO GERMANY. TOUR. (LOCAL). TED HOLLANDER, CHMN; COMMUNITY CLUB; SCHLESWIG, IA 51461. (#105133-2).

SEPT 2 - 4, '76. SCHLESWIG FIVE CALF PROJECT - PARADE & SHOW. PARADE, LIVE PERFORMANCE. (LOCAL). TED HOLLANDER, CHMN; COMMUNITY CLUB; SCHLESWIG, IA 51461. (#105133-1).

SCOTCH GROVE

MUSEUM-GHOST TOWN OF EDINBURG, SCOTCH GROVE, IA. A NEW BUILDING HAS BEEN PURCHASED AND WILL BE THE SITE OF A NEW COUNTY HISTORICAL MUSEUM. (ST-WIDE). C L NORLIN, PROJ DIRECTOR; JONES COUNTY HISTORICAL SOCIETY; 323 N CHESTNUT; MONTICELLO, IA 52310. (#11573).

PIONEER VILLAGE COMPLEX MUSEUM - SCOTCH GROVE, IA. RECREATION OF THE FIRST COUNTY SEAT, 1840-1841, IN TOWN OF EDINBURGH AS OLD PIONEER VILLAGE COMPLEX; PARK AND MAXIMUM SECURITY STONE STEEL MUSEUM HAS BEEN ADDED. (LOCAL). C L NORLIN, PRESIDENT; JONES COUNTY HISTORICAL SOCIETY; 323 N CHESTNUT; MONTICELLO, IA 52310. (#18228).

SCOTCH GROVE BICENTENNIAL PROJECTS, IA. PROJECTS INCLUDE: BUILDING A FLOAT FOR PARADES, THE SALE OF CAPS AND HATS, A WRITTEN HISTORY OF EBYS MILL & THE CONSTRUC-

SCOTCH GROVE — CONTINUED

TION & ERECTION OF A SIGN FOR SCOTCH GROVE FORMERLY KNOWN AS APPLE GATES CROSSING. (LOCAL). FREDA HANKIN, CO-CHAIRMAN; OAK DRIVE CLUB; RFD; SCOTCH GROVE, IA 52331. (#23357).

SCOTCH GROVE COMMUNITY PROJECTS, IA. 3 3'X 5' LIVING FLAGS WILL BE PLANTED AT THE ENTRANCE TO THE TOWN & THE OLD DEPOT WILL BE PAINTE. (LOCAL). FRED HANKEN, PROJ COORDINATOR; OAK DRIVE CLUB; RFD; SCOTCH GROVE, IA 52331. (#23356).

JUNE 20, '76. OLD TIME COSTUMES AND SONGS. CLUB MEMBERS WILL DRESS IN OLD COSTUMES FOR MEETING AND SING OLD SONGS TOGETHER. QUILTS WILL ALSO BE MADE. AT SCOTCH GROVE. (LOCAL). FREDA HANKEN, COORD; OAK DRIVE CLUB; RFD; SCOTCH GROVE, IA 52331. (#106531-1).

SELMA

RESTORATION & PRESERVATION OF OLD LOG CABIN- IA. THE COMMUNITY OF SELMA HAS RESTORED AND PRESERVED AN AUTHENTIC LOG CABIN IN THE TOWN AND MAINTAINED IT AS A MUSEUM. (LOCAL). TED WATSON, CO-CHAIRMAN; VAN BUREN DEVELOPMENT ASSOC; 101 VAN BUREN ST; KEOSAUQUA, IA 52565. (#21775).

SERGEANT BLF

HIGH SCHOOL BUILDING & GYMNASIUM, SARGEANT BLF, IA. A NEW HIGH SCHOOL WILL BE BUILT. (LOCAL). ALBERT M GRAY, VICE-PRESIDENT; SERGEANT BLUFF-LUTON COMMUNITY SCHOOL & SCHOOL BOARD; OFFICE AT 401 C ST; SERGEANT BLF, IA 51054. (#23172).

STEAM LOCOMOTIVE, SARGEANT BLUFF, IA. MODEL OF ENGINE OF 1890'S COAL BURNING TRACK TO BE BUILT; CAPACITY OF TRAILER CAR-2 ADULTS. (LOCAL). OTIS M BAKER, III, BUILDER-OPERATOR; PIONEER VALLEY BICENTENNIAL GROUP; 200 D ST; SERGEANT BLF, IA 51054. (#23171).

APR 2, '76. DONKEY BASKETBALL: BASKETBALL GAME ON DONKEYS. COMPETITION AT R M CONMEY AUDITORIUM, 401 C ST; PARKING AVAILABLE. (LOCAL). CLARENCE WILLIAMS, COORD; SERGEANT BLUFF FIRE DEPT; 108 E ST; SERGEANT BLF, IA 51054. (#106392-2).

JULY 10 - 13, '76. COMMUNITY CARNIVAL. RIDES, GAMES, HISTORICAL & MODERN PARADE, ARTS & CRAFTS, ANTIQUE SHOW, STREET & SQUARE DANCING, BARBECUE, FOOT RACES & BALL GAME, HORSESHOE PITCHING, GROUP SINGING, ETC. AT 4TH ST, D-E; PARADE FROM 5TH & B TO C & D; PARKING ON MOST STS. (LOCAL). CLARENCE WILLIAMS, COORD; PIONEER VALLEY BICENTENNIAL GROUP; 108 E ST; SERGEANT BLF, IA 51054. (#106392-1).

SEYMOUR

MEMORIAL BANDSTAND, SEYMOUR, IA. BANDSTAND ON VILLAGE GREEN IN MEMORY OF FORMER RESIDENTS, WILL BE BUILT. (LOCAL). E MARSTON, CHAIRMAN; SEYMOUR MEMORIAL BANDSTAND COMMITTEE; SEYMOUR, IA 52590. (#18477).

OLD SETTLERS' REUNION, SEYMOUR, IA. A 2 DAY OLD SETTLERS' REUNION IN SEYMOUR, IOWA. (LOCAL). ESTHER MARSTON, PROJ DIRECTOR; COMMUNITY CLUB; SEYMOUR, IA 52590. (#13081).

PARK RENOVATION IN SEYMOUR, IA. CITY PARK RENOVATION WILL INCLUDE BANDSTAND IMPROVEMENT AND TREE PLANTINGS. (LOCAL). ROBERT CASADY, PROJ COORDINATOR; CITY OF SEYMOUR; SEYMOUR, IA 52590. (#13082).

SHAMBAUGH

SHAMBAUGH SCHOOLHOUSE, IA. THE OLD SCHOOLHOUSE WILL BE RESTORED FOR USE AS THE CITY HALL. (LOCAL). BONNIE BUNTING, CHAIRMAN; SHAMBAUGH BICENTENNIAL COMMITTEE; SHAMBAUGH, IA 51651. (#25408).

SHARPSBURG

COMMUNITY PROJECTS - SHARPSBURG, IA. PAINTING TABLES AND PLAYGROUND EQUIPMENT IN CITY PARK BY YOUTH, PAINTING TABLES IN CITY HALL BY WOMEN OF METHODIST AND PRESBYTERIAN CHURCHES. PLANTED FOUR TREES IN PARK AND CITY HALL YARD. (LOCAL). THEOMA UNDERWOOD, CHAIRPERSON; SHARPSBURG COMMUNITY BICENTENNIAL COMMISSION; SHARPSBURG, IA 50862. (#27677).

JUNE 5, '76. LOGO FLAG PRESENTATION. AN OLD-FASHIONED SQUARE DANCE, HORSESHOE PITCHING AND ICE CREAM SOCIAL WERE PART OF THE CELEBRATION. AT CITY PARK. (LOCAL). THEOMA UNDERWOOD, CHMN; SHARPSBURG COMMUNITY BICENTENNIAL COMMISSION; SHARPSBURG, IA 50862. (#200018-193).

SHEFFIELD

BEAUTIFICATION OF CITY - SHEFFIELD, IA. BEAUTIFICATION OF ENTRANCE STREET TO THE CITY AND RESURFACING OF MEMORIAL BUILDING EXTERIOR. (LOCAL). FRANK NORRIS, BICENTENNIAL CHAIRMAN; CITY OF SHEFFIELD; SHEFFIELD, IA 50475. (#24664).

HISTORICAL BUILDING - SHEFFIELD, IA. PURCHASE AND REMODELING OF BUILDING TO HOUSE RELICS, ART OBJECTS AND MACHINES. SENIOR CITIZENS WILL PARTICIPATE IN THE PROJECT. (LOCAL). FRANK NORRIS, BICENTENNIAL CHAIRMAN; SHEFFIELD HISTORICAL GROUP; SHEFFIELD, IA 50475. (#24666).

PRESERVATION FOR 2076 - SHEFFIELD, IA. BURIAL VAULT WILL CONTAIN BICENTENNIAL RECORDS, PICTURES AND NEWSPAPER ARTICLES. (LOCAL). FRANK NORRIS, BICENTENNIAL CHAIRMAN; CITY OF SHEFFIELD; SHEFFIELD, IA 50475. (#24665).

JULY 4, '76. CHURCH SERVICE UNION. CEREMONY AT SHEFFIELD ELEMENTARY BLDG GYMNASIUM. (LOCAL). REV GORDON CARLS; SHEFFIELD MINISTERIAL GROUP; SION ST JOHNS LUTHERAN CHURCH; SHEFFIELD, IA 50475. (#107687-1).

SHELBY

SHELBY, IA, DEMOCRACY PROGRAM. PROGRAM CONSISTS OF A PAGEANT, HISTORY & FILMS. (LOCAL). BETA BOCK, PRESIDENT; SHELBY COMMUNITY CLUB; SHELBY, IA 51570. (#16688).

SHELDON

ARBORETUM TO BE DEVELOPED IN SHELDON, IA. TREES AND SHRUBS WILL BE PLANTED FOR STUDY & SCENIC VALUE. (LOCAL). R HOLLANDER, PROJ DIRECTOR; KIWANIS CLUB; SHELDON, IA 51201. (#11484).

SHELDON PRAIRIE MUSEUM & ARTS/CRAFTS CENTER - IA. FORMER CARNEGIE LIBRARY BUILDING GIVEN TO SHELDON HISTORICAL SOCIETY FOR PRESERVATION & COMMUNITY CULTURAL USE. (LOCAL). RALPH HOLLANDER, PUBLIC RELATIONS CHAIRMAN; SHELDON HISTORICAL SOCIETY; SHELDON PUBLIC LIBRARY; SHELDON, IA 51201. (#21392).

JUNE 1, '75 - DEC 31, '76. AMERICANA MUSIC RADIO PROGRAM. RADIO/TV. (LOCAL). RAE PETERSON, PROJ DIR; ALLEGRO CLUB; 812 6TH AVE; SHELDON, IA 51201. (#100569-1).

NOV 17 - 23, '75. ANCESTRAL & MODERN QUILT/EARLY AMERICAN PILLOW EXHIBIT. HEIRLOOM EARLY AMERICAN, PATCHWORK QUILTS SHOWN, PILLOW TOPS WERE HAND-MADE FOR EXHIBIT. QUILTING DEMONSTRATED EACH DAY. ALSO WOOL CARDED AND SPUN INTO YARN ON SPINNING WHEEL. PROGRAM GIVEN ON HISTORY OF QUILTS IN AMERICA. AT ISRAEL SHELDON ROOM IN THE PUBLIC LIBRARY. (LOCAL). IRENE BLOMQUIST; MARY BALL WASHINGTON CHAPTER OF THE DAR; 1501 9TH; SHELDON, IA 51201. (#11486-1).

NOV 18, '75. WOMEN'S BICENTENNIAL PRAYER BRUNCH. CEREMONY, FESTIVAL AT CHURCH. (LOCAL). BONNIE VANDE BRAKE, COORD; FEDERATED WOMEN'S CLUB; 1602 PLEASANT COURT DR; SHELDON, IA 51201. (#200018-146).

JUNE 24 - 26, '76. HERITAGE HOME TALENT ART EXHIBIT. EXHIBIT AT SHELDON MUSEUM. (LOCAL). MRS EDITH PYLMAN, CHMN; SHELDON HISTORICAL SOCIETY; 1019 10TH ST; SHELDON, IA 51201. (#105258-1).

JUNE 24 - 26, '76. 'PRAIRIE DAYS' (FORMERLY 'SOYBEAN DAYS'). EXHIBIT, FAIR, FESTIVAL, PARADE AT COMMUNITY BUILDING AND OPEN STREETS. (LOCAL). RALPH HOLLANDER, PROJ DIR; CHAMBER OF COMMERCE; 702 9TH; SHELDON, IA 51201. (#103639-8).

SEPT 25, '76. SALUTE TO AMERICA. LIVE PERFORMANCE AT HIGH SCHOOL AUDITORIUM. (LOCAL). R C HOLLANDER, CHMN; SOC FOR PRESERVATION & ENCOURAGEMENT OF BARBERSHOP SINGING IN AMER; 702 9TH; SHELDON, IA 51201. (#105316-1).

SHELL ROCK

FOURTH OF JULY FESTIVAL IN SHELL ROCK, IA. COMMUNITY AREA CELEBRATION FEATURING PARADE, MUSIC, QUEEN CONTESTS, CHICKEN FRY, GAMES, CASINO NITE, BOOTHS, SQUARE DANCING & STREET DANCING AND RELIGIOUS SERVICE. (LOCAL). DON ROSTAD, CHAIRMAN; JAYCEES; 422 CHERRY, SHELL ROCK NEWS; SHELL ROCK, IA 50670. (#13102).

SPORTSMEN'S ECOLOGICAL PROJECTS IN SHELL ROCK, IA. SPORTSMEN OF COMMUNITY ARE AIDING THE FISH HATCHERY REARING PONDS BY RESTOCKING SHELL ROCK RIVER AND STREAMS OF THE AREA, SEINING OF ROUGH STOCK AND COOPERATING IN WILDLIFE REFUGE. (LOCAL). HELEN VANDERBURG, BICENTENNIAL CHAIRMAN; SHELL ROCK SPORTSMANS CLUB, SHELL ROCK BICENTENNIAL COMMITTEE; 422 CHERRY, SHELL ROCK NEWS; SHELL ROCK, IA 50670. (#13103).

JULY 4 - 5, '76. BICENTENNIAL SHOW. EXHIBIT, TOUR AT CITY COMMUNITY CENTER SITE OF DISPLAYS & PLAYS; PARADE THRU CITY. (ST-WIDE). HELEN VANDERBURG; SHELL ROCK BICENTENNIAL COMMITTEE; 422 CHERRY; SHELL ROCK, IA 50670. (#13104-1).

SHELLSBURG

JULY 17, '76. BIG DAYS PARADE. EXHIBIT, PARADE AT PEARL ST, SHELLSBURG PARK & STREETS. (LOCAL). ROBERT KIBBIE; SHELLSBURG LIONS CLUB; 406 GRAND AVE; SHELLSBURG, IA 52332. (#200018-300).

SHENANDOAH

MANTE PARK - PROJ OF SHENANDOAH, IA. MANTE PARK, LOCATED ON THE WEST EDGE OF TOWN, WILL BE RESTORED; TREES AND GARDENS WILL BE PLANTED. (LOCAL). BERNARD GIESE, PROJ DIRECTOR; THE PIONEERS; GAMBLE STORE; SHENANDOAH, IA 51601. (#12689).

SHENANDOAH SINGERS - PROJ OF SHENANDOAH, IA. THE SHENANDOAH SINGERS WILL DRESS IN RED, WHITE AND BLUE OUTFITS AND BE AVAILABLE AS ROVING AMBASSADORS. (LOCAL). KEITH FRANZEN, PROJ DIRECTOR; SHENANDOAH SCHOOL; 1000 MUSTANG DR; SHENANDOAH, IA 51601. (#12691).

JULY 4, '76. 4TH OF JULY CELEBRATION. THE 1976 4TH OF JULY CELEBRATION WILL INCLUDE GALA FIREWORKS DISPLAYS. (LOCAL). GARY GSELL, DIR; SHENANDOAH JAYCEES; SHENANDOAH JAYCEES; SHENANDOAH, IA 51601. (#12690-1).

SIBLEY

I HEAR AMERICA SINGING. FESTIVAL. (LOCAL). PETER WAGNER, DIRECTOR; SIBLEY BICENTENNIAL ASSOCIATION; 720 7TH ST; SIBLEY, IA 51249. (#102275-1). **(??).**

NEW PLAYGROUND, SIBLEY, IA. A FORT LIKE PLAYGROUND WILL BE BUILT IN THE PARK FOR CHILDREN. (LOCAL). PETER WAGNER, CHAIRMAN; SIBLEY BICENTENNIAL COMMISSION; 720 7TH ST; SIBLEY, IA 51249. (#15303).

JULY 19 - 22, '76. LIVESTOCK SHOW. THE SHOW WILL INCLUDE LIVESTOCK AND AGRICULTURE. (LOCAL). FRED JARROTT, PRED; OSCEOLA COUNTY BICENTENNIAL COMMISSION; OSCEOLA COUNTY BICENT COMM; OCHEYEDAN, IA 51354. (#13089-1).

JULY 19 - 22, '76. OSCEOLA COUNTY BICENTENNIAL FAIR. BICENTENNIAL PARADE MONDAY NITE, JULY 19, 1976. AMERICAN REVIEW, TUESDAY & WED, JULY 20-21, 1976. 4-H & FFA AUCTION & DEMOLITION DERBY THURSDAY, JULY 22, 1976. AT OSCEOLA CO FAIRGROUNDS, SIBLEY, IA. (LOCAL). ALBERT LIENEMANN, CHMN; OSCEOLA COUNTY FAIRBOARD; OSCEOLA COUNTY FAIRBOARD; OCHEYEDAN, IA 51354. (#13083-1).

SIDNEY

BICENTENNIAL LANDSCAPING OF COURTHOUSE, SIDNEY, IA. AS SIDNEY'S HORIZONS PROJECT, THE LAWN IS BEING LANDSCAPED, WITH PLANTING OF TREES & SHRUBS, AND A STONE MARKER. DEDICATED JUNE 30, 1976, WITH SUITABLE CEREMONIES. (LOCAL). MRS DWIGHT MILLS, CHAIRMAN; SIDNEY AREA BICENTENNIAL COMMISSION; BOX 32; SIDNEY, IA 51652. (#27316).

CITY PARK IMPROVEMENT IN SIDNEY, IA. THE CITY PARK WILL BE CLEANED; PRESENT EQUIPMENT WILL BE PAINTED AND NEW EQUIPMENT WILL BE ADDED. (LOCAL). MRS STAN FOWLER, PROJ DIRECTOR; MONDAY CLUB; SIDNEY, IA 51652. (#12682).

CORRIDOR TRAIL - PROJ OF SIDNEY, IA. PROJECT WILL BE TO CLEANUP AND DESIGNATE BLUFF ROAD AS CORRIDOR TRAIL; ALSO MARKING OF THE LEWIS AND CLARK TRAIL ALONG SAME PLAN AS HIGH RIDGE BLUFF TRAIL. (LOCAL). MRS ROBERT BIRBKY, CHAIRMAN; FREMONT COUNTY BICENTENNIAL COMMISSION; 1301 MAPLE ST; SIDNEY, IA 51652. (#11273).

COUNTY HISTORICAL MUSEUM - PROJ OF SIDNEY, IA. UPDATING MARKING OF ITEMS, DEVELOPING LIBRARY, ADDING NEW HISTORICAL ITEMS AND IMPROVING SCHOOLHOUSE ADDITION WILL BE INCLUDED IN THIS PROJECT. (LOCAL). MRS ROBERT BIRBKY, CHAIRMAN; FREMONT COUNTY BICENTENNIAL COMMISSION; 1301 MAPLE ST; SIDNEY, IA 51652. (#11274).

GRAVESITE IMPROVEMENT - PROJ OF SIDNEY, IA. CLEANING OF PANSY ESTES' GRAVESITE, THE WIFE OF THE MAN WHO GAVE ESTES PARK TO THE U S GOVERNMENT. (LOCAL). MRS RICHARD BARRETT, PROJ DIRECTOR; SIDNEY GIRL SCOUTS/SIDNEY BOY SCOUTS; SIDNEY, IA 51652. (#12683).

PARADE FLOAT, SIDNEY, IA. A CONTEST HAS STARTED IN THE COUNTY SCHOOLS FOR A FLOAT DESIGN; THE COMPLETED FLOAT WILL BE USED IN COUNTY AND AREA PARADES DURING '75 & '76. (LOCAL). MRS ROBERT BIRBKY; FREMONT COUNTY BICENTENNIAL COMMISSION; 1301 MAPLE ST; SIDNEY, IA 51652. (#11277-1).

RECREATIONAL MAP - PROJ OF SIDNEY, IA. 4-H AND SCOUTS WILL PREPARE A MAP OF HIKING & BIKING TRAILS IN THE COUNTY. (LOCAL). MRS ROBERT BIRBKY, CHAIRMAN; FREMONT COUNTY BICENTENNIAL COMMISSION; 1301 MAPLE ST; SIDNEY, IA 51652. (#11272).

SIDNEY'S 125TH ANNIVERSARY CELEBRATION, IA. IN '76, SIDNEY WILL CELEBRATE ITS 125TH ANNIVERSARY IN CONJUNCTION WITH THE NATION'S 200TH BIRTHDAY. THE CELEBRATION WILL INCLUDE: PARADES, DISPLAYS & AN UPDATE OF THE TOWN'S HISTORY. (LOCAL). MRS E B NENEMAN, PROJ DIRECTOR; CHAMBER OF COMMERCE; SIDNEY, IA 51652. (#12681).

UPDATE COUNTY HISTORY - PROJ OF SIDNEY, IA. UPDATE OF HISTORY IN FREMONT COUNTY BY COMMUNITY CHAIRMEN, COUNTY BICENTENNIAL COMMISSION AND HISTORICAL SOCIETY. (ST-WIDE). MRS ROBERT BIRBKY, CHAIRMAN; FREMONT COUNTY BICENTENNIAL COMMISSION; 1301 MAPLE ST; SIDNEY, IA 51652. (#11276).

WINDOW DISPLAY - PROJ OF SIDNEY, IA. WINDOW DISPLAY W/ HISTORIC MEMORABILIA WILL BE CHANGED PERIODICALLY THROUGH 1976. (LOCAL). MRS ROBERT BIRBKY, CHAIRMAN; FREMONT COUNTY BICENTENNIAL COMMISSION; 1301 MAPLE ST; SIDNEY, IA 51652. (#11275).

JUNE 30, '76. EVENING OF MUSIC - 'SONG OF YEARS'. HELD IN CONNECTION WITH CELEBRATION OF SIDNEY'S 125TH ANNIVERSARY. AT TOWN SQUARE-COURTHOUSE LAWN. (LOCAL). MRS DWIGHT HILLS; SIDNEY AREA BICENTENNIAL COMMISSION; BOX 32; SIDNEY, IA 51652. (#12681-1).

SIDNEY — CONTINUED

JULY 26 - 29, '76. COUNTY FAIR. HISTORICAL SECTIONS IN OPEN CLASS, BICENTENNIAL BOOTH, COUNTY PAGEANT '76, PARTICIPATION BY VARIOUS COUNTY COMMUNITIES. ON JULY 28TH, THE GRANDSTAND WILL BE AT 7:30 PM. AT GRANDSTAND, RODEO GROUNDS, SIDNEY, IA. (ST-WIDE). MRS ROBERT BIRKBY; FREMONT COUNTY BICENT COMM & FREMONT COUNTY FAIR BOARD; 1301 MAPLE ST; SIDNEY, IA 51652. (#11473-1).

AUG 10, '76. RODEO PARADE. PARADE PRIOR TO OPENING OF SIDNEY RODEO IN '75 & '76. ALL LOCAL COMMUNITY CROUPS ARE INVITED TO PARTICIPATE. AT RODEO ARENA IN CITY PARK, CAMPER FACILITIES AVAILABLE. (LOCAL). STEWART HALL; SIDNEY AMERICAN LEGION; SIDNEY, IA 51652. (#12680-1).

AUG 10 - 15, '76. THE SIDNEY RODEO - IOWA'S CHAMPIONSHIP RODEO. WITH RECORDING ARTIST PAT BOONE AS RODEO HEADLINER, THERE WILL BE 5 NIGHT PERFORMANCES TUESDAY THRU SATURDAY & 5 MATINEES WEDNESDAY THRU SUNDAY. AT RODEO ACTION ARENA. (ST-WIDE). STEWART HALL, SECRETARY; SIDNEY RODEO BOARD; RODEO TICKET OFFICE; SIDNEY, IA 51652. (#109144-1).

SIGOURNEY

OUTDOOR CLASSROOM AND HISTORIC SITE, SIGOURNEY, IA. FOUR NATURE TRAILS ON 30 ACRES, INTERPRETIVE CENTER TO STUDY ECOLOGY AND CONSERVATION, RESTORATION; ONE ROOM SCHOOL ON THE SITE OF FIRST LAND DESIGNATED FOR EDUCATION IN KEOKUK COUNTY. (LOCAL). JANICE MADSEN, OUTDOOR CLASSROOM CHAIRMAN; ENVIRONMENTAL CONCERNS COMMITTEE; RR2 BOX 130; SIGOURNEY, IA 52591. (#19689).

SILVER CITY

FLAG & BELL PARK IN SILVER CITY, IA. THE MINI-PARK WILL HAVE A DISPLAY OF FLAGS FEATURING A SCHOOLBELL. (LOCAL). F A WORTMAN, PROJ COORDINATOR; SILVER CITY BICENTENNIAL COMMITTEE; BOX 369; SILVER CITY, IA 51571. (#13087).

SIOUX CENTER

BICENTENNIAL ARTICLES PUBLISHED IN PRO REGE - IA. ONE OR TWO BICENTENNIAL ARTICLES ARE BEING PUBLISHED IN EACH OF THE 4 PUBLICATIONS OF THIS YEAR'S 'PRO REGE'-A FACULTY JOURNAL OF DORDT COLLEGE. (LOCAL). REV J B HULST, DEAN; DORDT COLLEGE; 498 4TH AVE NE; SIOUX CENTER, IA 51250. (#22049).

BICENTENNIAL SPECIAL ELECTIVE HISTORY COURSE - IA. A COURSE OFFERED ON MONDAY EVENINGS DURING THE SCHOOL YEAR DEALING WITH THE RELIGIOUS, SOCIOLOGICAL, EDUCATIONAL, AND ARTISTIC ELEMENTS OF AMERICAN HISTORICAL AND CULTURAL DEVELOPMENT. (LOCAL). REV J B HULST, DEAN; DORDT COLLEGE; 498 4TH AVE NE; SIOUX CENTER, IA 51250. (#22048).

COMMUNITY BICENTENNIAL BOOK - SIOUX CENTER, IA. THE BOOK WILL BE WRITTEN BY A DORDT COLLEGE ENGLISH INSTRUCTOR. (LOCAL). REV J B HULST, DEAN OF STUDENTS; DORDT COLLEGE; 498 4TH AVE NE; SIOUX CENTER, IA 51250. (#20952).

POLITICAL ACTIVITY - SIOUX CENTER, IA. PROGRAMS THAT INVOLVE STUDENTS IN THE POLITICAL PROCESS. (LOCAL). REV J B HULST, DEAN OF STUDENTS; DORDT COLLEGE; 498 4TH AVE NE; SIOUX CENTER, IA 51250. (#22050).

SIOUX CENTER COMMUNITY - QUALITY OF LIFE, IA. RETAINING RESTORING AND CONSERVING HISTORICAL ACTIVITIES THAT ARE A PART OF THE SIOUX TRADITION. (LOCAL). DARRELL RENSINK, CITY MANAGER; CITY OF SIOUX CENTER; 337 N MAINE AVE; SIOUX CENTER, IA 51250. (#15332).

SEPT 1, '75 - MAY 31, '76. AMERICAN ISSUES FORUM-PAST PRESENT & FUTURE. NATIONALLY ORGANIZED AND ADVERTISED BUT SPONSORED LOCALLY; ALSO PARTIALLY SPONSORED BY IOWA HUMANITIES BOARD; INCLUDES MONTH LONG BOOK DISPLAYS, FILMS AND DISCUSSIONS OF AMERICAN ISSUES BY PARTICIPANTS. AT SIOUX CENTER PUBLIC LIBRARY 327 1ST AVE NE. (LOCAL). PEGGY JOHNSON, LIBRARIAN; SIOUX CENTER PUBLIC LIBRARY; 653 1ST AVE NE; SIOUX CENTER, IA 51250. (#104343-1).

SEPT 5 - 6, '75. STUDENT BICENTENNIAL RETREAT. CONFERENCE, FESTIVAL AT CAMP OKOBOJI. (LOCAL). DIRECTOR; DORDT COLLEGE BICENTENNIAL SPECIAL EVENTS COMMITTEE; SIOUX CENTER, IA 51250. (#200018-142).

SEPT 23, '75 - FEB 5, '76. BICENTENNIAL LECTURE SERIES. A SERIES OF LECTURES ON AMERICAN CIVIL RELIGION. AT C160 DORDT COLLEGE, SIOUX CENTER. (LOCAL). REV J B HULST, DEAN; DORDT COLLEGE; 498 4TH AVE NE; SIOUX CENTER, IA 51250. (#105802-3).

APR 7 - 10, '76. 'THE CONTRAST' - A BICENTENNIAL PLAY. LIVE PERFORMANCE AT TEPASKE THEATRE. (LOCAL). JIM KOLDENHOVEN, CHMN; DORDT COLLEGE; SIOUX CENTER, IA 51250. (#105802-1).

JUNE 19 - 28, '76. COMMUNITY MUSICAL DIRECTED BY DORDT CHOIR DIRECTOR. LIVE PERFORMANCE. (LOCAL). REV J B HULST, DEAN; DORDT COLLEGE; 498 4TH AVE NE; SIOUX CENTER, IA 51250. (#105802-4).

JUNE 19 - 28, '76. COUNTY MASS CHOIR PERFORMANCES IN SEVERAL LOCATIONS. IN ORANGE CITY JUNE 19, HAWARDEN JUNE 21, SIOUX CENTER JUNE 25, ROCK VALLEY JUNE 26, & HULL, IOWA, JUNE 28, 1976. AT SEVERAL LOCATIONS AROUND COUNTY. (LOCAL). DALE GROTENHUIS; SIOUX COUNTY BOARD FOR THE PERFORMING ARTS; 240 3RD AVE SE; SIOUX CENTER, IA 51250. (#105802-6).

JUNE 30 - JULY 8, '76. MUSICAL '1776' - PERFORMANCE. LIVE PERFORMANCE AT THEATERS AROUND SIOUX COUNTY. (LOCAL). JAMES KOLDENHOVEN; SIOUX COUNTY BOARD FOR PERFORMING ARTS; 333 6TH ST SE; SIOUX CENTER, IA 51250. (#105802-7).

JUNE 30 - JULY 10, '76. COMMUNITY PLAY, DIRECTED BY DORDT DRAMA DIRECTOR. LIVE PERFORMANCE AT VARIOUS THEATRES IN COUNTY. (LOCAL). REV J B HULST, DEAN; DORDT COLLEGE; 498 4TH AVE NE; SIOUX CENTER, IA 51250. (#105802-2).

JULY 4, '76. COUNTY RELIGIOUS OBSERVANCE OF JULY 4TH, 1976. HAROLD HUGHES, SPEAKER. MASS COUNTY CHOIR WILL GIVE 27B SEVERAL NUMBERS. AT SIOUX CENTER ATHLETIC FIELD. (LOCAL). JACK O BOERIGTER, REV; SIOUX COUNTY MINISTERIAL ASSOCIATION; 44 10TH ST SE; SIOUX CENTER, IA 51250. (#105802-5).

SIOUX CITY

'AMER MUSIC EVERYWHERE'-PERFORMANCE BY SIOUX CTY CHAMBER MUSIC ASSOC. LIVE PERFORMANCE. (LOCAL). GARY L FRIDLEY, DIRECTOR; SIOUX CITY CHAMBER MUSIC ASSOC; 1922 ROSS ST; SIOUX CITY, IA 51103. (#104711-2).

BICENTENNIAL CONVOCATION SERIES - SIOUX CITY, IA. THE CONVOCATIONS WILL HAVE THEMES OF HISTORICAL INTEREST. (LOCAL). DR ROBERT JEWETT, BICENT COORDINATOR; MORNINGSIDE COLLEGE; SIOUX CITY, IA 51106. (#17636).

BICENTENNIAL HOMECOMING. FESTIVAL. (LOCAL). DR ROBERT JEWETT, COORD; MORNINGSIDE COLLEGE; SIOUX CITY, IA 51106. (#103404-1). **(??).**

FREEDOM OF LIFESTYLE: LIBERTY & JUSTICE FOR ALL-IA. WORKSHOP DISCUSSING THE PROGRAM DEVELOPED BY THE CATHOLIC BISHOPS OF THE U S TO STUDY THE SOCIAL NEEDS OF THE PEOPLE AND FORMULATE A CORRESPONDENCE PROGRAM OF SOCIAL ACTION. (REGN'L). SISTER TERESINE GLASER, CHAIRMAN; BRIAR CLIFF COLLEGE BICENTENNIAL COMMITTEE; 3303 REBECCA ST; SIOUX CITY, IA 51104. (#29168).

FREEDOM: AN AMERICAN HERITAGE - SIOUX CITY, IA. ALL-COLLEGE SYMPOSIUN ON THE TRADITION AND RESPONSIBILITIES OF FREEDOM IN THE UNITED STATES. (REGN'L). SISTER TERESINE GLASER, CHAIRMAN; BRIAR CLIFF COLLEGE BICENTENNIAL COMMITTEE; 3303 REBECCA ST; SIOUX CITY, IA 51104. (#29167).

KMEG-TV 'HAPPY BIRTHDAY USA' SERIES - NBMRP. 731 90-SECONDS SCRIPTS IN 'HAPPY BIRTHDAY' SERIES. HAS TAPED 'GREAT MEN IN AMERICAN BUSINESS' SERIES FOR DISTRIBUTION TO 123 SCHOOLS. IS UNDERTAKING AS COMMUNITY PROJECT EXPANSION OF THE SENIOR CENTER. (LOCAL). NORMA DONOVAN, BICENTENNIAL COORDINATOR; KMEG-TV; 7TH & FLOYD BLVD; SIOUX CITY, IA 51102. (#23264).

RENOVATION OF SENIOR CITIZEN BUILDING, IA. A NEW KITCHEN AND REST ROOMS WILL BE ADDED, PAINTING AND PANELING OF BASEMENT WALLS WILL BE DONE AND AIR CONDITIONING WILL BE INSTALLED. (LOCAL). BUELAL WEBB, DIRECTOR; SIOUX AND SENIOR CENTER; 406 8TH ST; SIOUX CITY, IA 51101. (#25595).

SGT FLOYD MEMORIAL & HISTORICAL CENTER OF IOWA. EXPANDED PARK FACILITIES & MUSEUM IN THE AREA OF THE SERGEANT FLOYD MONUMENT: A REGISTERED NATIONAL HISTORICAL LANDMARK. (LOCAL). B R DIAMOND, SECRETARY; WOODBURY COUNTY AMERICAN REVOLUTION BICENTENNIAL COMMISSION; 2901 JACKSON ST; SIOUX CITY, IA 51105. (#204). **ARBA GRANTEE.**

SIOUX CITY HISTORICAL MARKINGS PROJ OF IOWA. HISTORICAL MARKINGS ARE TO BE PERMANENTLY PLACED IN THE DOWNTOWN AREA BY THE MUSEUM ASSOCIATION. (LOCAL). WM DIAMOND, CHAIRMAN; SIOUX CITY MUSEUM ASSOC; 27TH JACKSON ST; SIOUX CITY, IA 51104. (#6020). **(??).**

UNITED STATES STUDIES, SIOUX CITY, IA. A 2 YEAR COURSE ON AMERICA & ITS HISTORY. ASSOCIATE DEGREE PROGRAM IN UNITED STATES INTERDISCIPLINARY STUDIES IS BEING OFFERED. (LOCAL). SISTER TERESINE GLASSER; BRIAR CLIFF COLLEGE; SIOUX CITY, IA 51104. (#25287).

SEPT 12 - 14, '75. AMERICAN FREEDOM TRAIN DISPLAY DAYS AT SIOUX CITY. THE AMERICAN FREEDOM TRAIN WILL INCLUDE 10 EXHIBIT CARS & 2 SHOWCASE CARS DEPICTING DIFFERENT PHASES OF THE AMERICAN EXPERIENCE. ITS ARRIVAL WILL SERVE AS A CATALYST FOR LOCAL BICENTENNIAL CELEBRATIONS BY PEOPLE THROUGHOUT THIS NATION. (ST-WIDE). DON MALLICOAT, EDIT SVCS; THE AMERICAN FREEDOM TRAIN FOUNDATION, INC; 5205 LEESBURG PIKE, SUITE 800; BAILEY'S XRDS, VA 22041. (#1776-81).

OCT 11 - 12, '75. UNITED STATES ARMED FORCES BICENTENNIAL CARAVAN. THE CARAVAN IS COMPOSED OF EXHIBIT VANS FOR EACH BRANCH OF THE MILITARY SERVICE. THE THEME OF THE EXHIBITION IS 'HISTORY OF THE ARMED FORCES AND THEIR CONTRIBUTION TO THE NATION'. (LOCAL). PAUL MORRIS, CHMN; U S ARMED FORCES BICENTENNIAL EXHIBIT VANS PROJECT; CITY HALL BOX 447; SIOUX CITY, IA 51101. (#1775-215).

DEC 5 - 6, '75. 'FREEDOM OF LIFESTYLE, LIBERTY & JUSTICE FOR ALL' - WORKSHOP. SATURDAY HOURS: 5 PM. AT NOONAN LOBBY, BRIAR CLIFF COLLEGE. (LOCAL). SISTER TERESINE GLASER; BRIAR CLIFF COLLEGE; SIOUX CITY, IA 51104. (#108162-1).

JAN 1, '76. DEDICATION AND OPENING OF NEW SERGEANT FLOYD RECREATIONAL FACILITY. EXPANDED PARK FACILITIES & MUSEUM IN THE AREA OF THE SERGEANT FLOYD MONUMENT: A REGISTERED NATIONAL HISTORICAL LANDMARK. AT FLOYD PARK, SIOUX CITY. (LOCAL). B R DIAMOND; WOODBURY COUNTY AMERICAN REVOLUTION BICENTENNIAL COMMISSION; 2901 JACKSON ST; SIOUX CITY, IA 51105. (#204-1).

JAN 20 - 21, '76. FESTIVAL ON FREEDOM: AN AMERICAN HERITAGE. CEREMONY, FESTIVAL. (LOCAL). SISTER TERESINE GLASER; BRIAR CLIFF COLLEGE; SIOUX CITY, IA 51104. (#108162-2).

JULY 4, '76. OPENING OF THE SGT FLOYD MUSEUM IN SIOUX CITY, IOWA. EXPANDED PARK FACILITIES & MUSEUM IN THE AREA OF THE SERGEANT FLOYD MONUMENT: A REGISTERED NATIONAL HISTORICAL LANDMARK. AT SGT FLOYD MONUMENT, FLOYD PARK. (LOCAL). B R DIAMOND; SGT FLOYD MONUMENT, FLOYD PARK; 2901 JACKSON ST; SIOUX CITY, IA 51105. (#204-2).

AUG 19, '76. NATL PK SVC 'PEOPLE OF 1776' PLAYS IN SIOUX CITY, IOWA. TRAVELING TROUPE WILL BRING VARIOUS ASPECTS OF COLONIAL LIFE (MILITARY LIFE, MUSIC, CRAFTS) TO THE SIOUX CITY AREA. AT RIVERSIDE PARK, RIVERSIDE DRIVE, SIOUX CITY, IOWA. (REGN'L). BICENT. COORD., MWRO; NATIONAL PARK SERVICE; 1709 JACKSON STREET; OMAHA, NE 68102. (#1469-18).

SIOUX RAPIDS

HISTORICAL MARKER - SIOUX RAPIDS, IA. RESTORATION OF GRAVE OF FIRST SETTLER IN COUNTY. (LOCAL). DARREL OLSON, COORDINATOR; BOOSTER CLUB; SIOUX RAPIDS, IA 50585. (#20990).

TREE PLANTING - SIOUX RAPIDS, IA. A SURVEY OF THE COMMUNITY WILL BE TAKEN AND EFFORT WILL BE MADE TO PLANT TREES AND FLOWERS WHERE NEEDED. (LOCAL). ESTHER KAS, COORDINATOR; THURSDAY AFTERNOON CLUB; SIOUX RAPIDS, IA 50585. (#20989).

JULY 4, '76. FOURTH OF JULY. CEREMONY, FESTIVAL. (LOCAL). OSCAR SUNDBLAD, CHMN; KIWANIIS; SIOUX RAPIDS, IA 50585. (#105180-2).

SEPT 6, '76. LABOR DAY FESTIVAL. FESTIVAL. (LOCAL). DARREL OLSON, CHAIRMAN; BOOSTER CLUB; SIOUX RAPIDS, IA 50585. (#105180-1).

SLATER

BRONZE PLAQUE - SLATER, IA. A BRONZE PLAQUE WILL BE PLACED IN THE LOG CABIN COMMUNITY BUILDING IN HONOR OF THOSE WHO BUILT THE CABIN AND THE FIREPLACE WITHIN. (LOCAL). REV HARLAND SAUSER, CHAIRMAN; SLATER BICENTENNIAL COMMISSION; 202 8TH AVE; SLATER, IA 50244. (#25751).

CITY LIBRARY FOUNDATION, SLATER, IA. ALL PROCEEDS OF ALL BICENTENNIAL EVENTS WILL START FOUNDATION FOR LIBRARY. (LOCAL). ANNETTE HULL, CHAIRMAN; LIBRARY BOARD; 405 GREENE ST; SLATER, IA 50244. (#25753).

DECORATION OF BUSINESSES FOR CREAMERY DAYS - IA. ANTIQUES WILL BE DISPLAYED IN PLACES OF BUSINESS DURING THE MONTH OF JUNE. (LOCAL). MYRNA HARMON, CHAIRMAN; SLATER BICENTENNIAL COMMISSION; 411 TAMA; SLATER, IA 50244. (#25371).

FLOWER BOXES FOR MAIN STREET - SLATER, IA. FLOWER BOXES, BUILT BY BOY SCOUTS & FILLED BY SENIOR CITIZENS, WILL BE PLACED IN FRONT OF BUSINESSES ON MAIN STREET. (LOCAL). STEVE RANSOM, COORDINATOR; BOY SCOUTS; 509 MAIN ST; SLATER, IA 50244. (#25750).

PLANT TREES IN TWO NEW CITY PARKS - SLATER, IA. PLANT TREES IN THE TWO NEW CITY PARKS FOR SHADE AND ECOLOGY. (LOCAL). JOHN NESS, COORDINATOR; KIWANIS CLUB; 506 3RD ST; SLATER, IA 50244. (#25752).

MAR 9, '76. CITY RECOGNITION PROGRAM. CEREMONY AT SLATER ELEMENTARY GYM. (LOCAL). CARMA BELZ, CHAIRMAN; SLATER BICENTENNIAL COMMISSION; 203 CEDAR; SLATER, IA 50244. (#200018-152).

MAY 23, '76. HERITAGE SUNDAY AT UNITED METHODIST CHURCH. CEREMONY AT UNITED METHODIST CHURCH. (LOCAL). HELEN HOVEVEN, COORD; UNITED METHODIST CHURCH; SLATER, IA 50244. (#200018-151).

JUNE 15, '76. MAGIC GLOBE PLAYERS BICENTENNIAL CHILDRENS' THEATRE. LIVE PERFORMANCE AT NELSON PARK BETWEEN 3RD AND 4TH ON TAMA ST. (LOCAL). BOB WEEKS, COORDINATOR; SLATER BICENTENNIAL COMMISSION; SLATER, IA 50244. (#108304-3).

JUNE 17, '76. BICENTENNIAL FESTIVAL OF MUSIC. PROGRAM WILL ALSO BE HELD FROM 9:00 - 10:00 PM. AT UNITED METHODIST CHURCH. (LOCAL). BOB WEEKS, COORDINATOR; SLATER BICENTENNIAL COMMISSION; SLATER, IA 50244. (#108304-4).

JUNE 19, '76. CREAMERY DAY DINNER AND OLD-FASHIONED BAND CONCERT. LIVE PERFORMANCE AT LOG CABIN AT NELSON PARK. (LOCAL). CARMA BELZ, CHAIRMAN; SLATER BICENTENNIAL COMMISSION; 203 CEDAR; SLATER, IA 50244. (#108304-2).

SLOAN

JULY 17 - 18, '76. BICENTENNIAL DAY IN SLOAN, IOWA. EVENTS INCLUDE A DANCE (9PM-2AM), BEARD CONTEST (2PM), BINGO (2-5PM) CARNIVAL (1-5), BARBEQUE (5-9), TUG-OF-WAR (2PM ON MAIN ST), ANYTHING GOES, AND A WATER FIGHT (2:30 ON MAIN ST). AT BALL PARK. (LOCAL). JEAN MCADON; BICENT COMM, JAYCEES, FIRE DEPT, & OTHER COMMUNITY GROUPS; SLOAN, IA 51055. (#107874-1).

JULY 18, '76. BICENTENNIAL PARADE. PARADE. (LOCAL). JEAN MCADON; BICENT COMM; SLOAN, IA 51055. (#107694-1).

SLOAN — CONTINUED

JULY 18, '76. COMMUNITY CHURCH SERVICE. CEREMONY. (LOCAL). JEAN MCADON; COMM CHURCHES; SLOAN, IA 51055. (#107694-3).

JULY 18, '76. DEDICATION OF CITY PARK. DEDICATE PARK IN MEMORY OF M R HUNTING. (LOCAL). JEAN MCADON; JAYCEETES; BICENTENNIAL COMM (HISTORICAL SOCIETY); SLOAN, IA 51055. (#107694-2).

SOLDIER

SEWER SYSTEM - SOLDIER, IA. A NEW SEWER SYSTEM WILL BE INSTALLED IN THE CITY. (LOCAL). JOHN DICKINSON, COMMANDER; AMERICAN LEGION POST 462; SOLDIER, IA 51572. (#23347).

JULY 3 - 4, '76. ALUMNI BANQUET. FESTIVAL AT MAIN ST. (ST-WIDE). JOHN DICKINSON; AMERICAN LEGION; SOLDIER, IA 51572. (#106851-2).

SOLON

MAY 29 - 30, '76. SOLON BICENTENNIAL WEEKEND. FESTIVAL. (LOCAL). MRS RICHARD MILLER, CHMN; OPTIMIST AND INDEPENDENT GROUPS; RR 4, BOX 19; SOLON, IA 52333. (#200018-266).

SPENCER

BIKE TRAIL - PROJ OF SPENCER, IA. BIKE TRAILS, PICNIC AREA, ARCHERY, TRAP SHOOT AND SWINGING BRIDGE WILL BE DESIGNED IN SPENCER. (LOCAL). LEE RINKE, CHAIRMAN; JR FEDERATED WOMEN'S CLUB; 302 7TH ST SW; SPENCER, IA 51301. (#13890).

CITY MAPS - PROJ OF SPENCER, IA. THE MAPS OF SPENCER WILL DEPICT HISTORICAL SITES AND LANDMARKS. (LOCAL). SHARON PROEHL, PROJ DIRECTOR; SPENCER CHAMBER OF COMMERCE; 603 S GRAND; SPENCER, IA 51301. (#13891).

HISTORICAL MARKERS PROJ OF SPENCER, IA. MARKERS THAT MARK SITES OF ALL OLD SCHOOLS, CHURCHES & BUILDINGS. (LOCAL). ELVA BARGLOF, CHAIRMAN; QUESTORS; 1623 2ND AVE E; SPENCER, IA 51301. (#13889).

IOWA'S HISTORIC MOTHERS, SPENCER, IA. IOWA'S LIST OF 10 HISTORIC MOTHERS WILL INCLUDE GREATS IN THE FIELDS OF LITERATURE, SOCIAL SERVICE, POLITICS & COMMUNITY AFFAIRS. (ST-WIDE). MRS JOHN SCHUTTER, PRESIDENT; IOWA MOTHERS ASSOC & AMERICAN MOTHERS ASSOC; 218 FAIR ST; ALGONA, IA 50511. (#18751).

RESTORATION OF STAGECOACH LINE - SPENCER, IA. RESTORING THE TRAIL OF THE STAGE THAT STOPPED IN SPENCER IN 1800'S. (LOCAL). ELVA BARGLOF, CHAIRMAN; QUESTORS; 1623 2ND AVE E; SPENCER, IA 51301. (#13888).

RESTORATION OF 1917 FIRE TRUCK, SPENCER, IA. RESTORATION OF 1917 FIRE TRUCK WHICH TOOK PART IN FIGHTING THE GREAT SPENCER FIRE IN 1931 AND HAD AN INFLUENTIAL CONTRIBUTION TOWARD THE BAN OF FIREWORKS IN THE STATE OF IOWA. (LOCAL). SHARON PROEHL, EXEC VICE PRESIDENT; SPENCER CHAMBER OF COMMERCE; 603 S GRAND, BOX 950; SPENCER, IA 51301. (#21002).

SHOPPING BAGS - PROJ OF SPENCER, IA. BICENTENNIAL THEME WILL BE PRINTED ON PAPER BAGS. EACH STORE WILL HAVE THEIR OWN BAGS. (LOCAL). SHARON PROEHL, PROJ DIRECTOR; SPENCER CHAMBER OF COMMERCE; 603 S GRAND; SPENCER, IA 51301. (#13887).

FEB 15 - MAR 15, '75. BETSY ROSS FLAG CONTEST - PROJ OF SPENCER, IA. CONTEST FOR BEST CLAY COUNTY FLAG DESIGN; FLAGS WILL BE FLOWN FOR SPECIAL OCCASIONS FOR NEXT 18 MONTHS; MINIATURE FLAGS & DECALS WILL BE SOLD. ALSO: PROGRAM FACILITATION. (LOCAL). SHARON PROEHL; SPENCER CHAMBER OF COMMERCE; 603 S GRAND; SPENCER, IA 51301. (#14023-1).

JULY 4, '75. FIREWORKS EXTRAVAGANZA. A BAND CONCERT WILL BEGIN THE PROGRAM, FOLLOWED BY MORE ENTERTAINMENT; THEN THE FIREWORKS WILL START. AT CLAY COUNTY FAIRGROUNDS, W 4TH AND 18TH. (LOCAL). CHAIRMAN; SPENCER CHAMBER OF COMMERCE; 603 S GRAND; SPENCER, IA 51301. (#200018-144).

SEPT 1 - 2, '75. OLD TIME THRESHING BEE. THE OLD-TIMERS THRESH WITH BOTH A STEAM ENGINE AND HORSE-POWERED THRESHER DURING THIS TWO-DAY EVENT; THERE WILL BE A HORSE-DRIVEN GRAIN ELEVATOR, HORSE-POWERED STRAW BALER, STEAM-POWERED WOOD SPLITTER AND AN 'OLD CRAFTS DAY.'. AT 1700 11TH AVE SW. (ST-WIDE). SHARON PROEHL, EXEC DIR; SPENCER CHAMBER OF COMMERCE; 603 S GRAND; SPENCER, IA 51301. (#101393-1).

SEPT 1 - DEC 1, '75. OLD-FASHIONED SPELLING BEE. COMPETITION. (LOCAL). MRS CHARLES CARTER, CHMN; SPENCER PTA COUNCIL; 308 E 12TH ST; SPENCER, IA 51301. (#101394-1).

SEPT 28, '75. 'UP WITH PEOPLE'. LIVE PERFORMANCE AT SPENCER FIELD HOUSE. (LOCAL). GENE HUSTON, PRESIDENT; LIONS CLUB; 515 GRAND; SPENCER, IA 51301. (#101396-1).

DEC 29, '75. 3RD ANNUAL CHRISTMAS PARADE. PARADE. (LOCAL). SHARON PROEHL, EXEC DIR; SPENCER CHAMBER OF COMMERCE; 603 S GRAND; SPENCER, IA 51301. (#101398-1).

JAN '76. KIDS' OLYMPICS. COMPETITION AT YM-YWCA, 1001 4TH AVE W. (LOCAL). PAUL WILLIAMS, PROJ COORD; YMCA; 508 E 14TH ST; SPENCER, IA 51301. (#101399-1).

FEB 8, '76. SALUTE TO AMERICAN COMPOSERS. LIVE PERFORMANCE AT FIRST CONGREGATIONAL CHURCH. (LOCAL). MARY LOU REED, CHMN; SPENCER CLEF CLUB-MBR, NATL FEDERATION OF MUSIC CLUBS; 306 E 19TH ST; SPENCER, IA 51301. (#200018-143).

FEB '76. TALL-TALE WRITING CONTEST. FANTASY OF YESTERYEAR WRITINGS; COUNTY-WIDE PARTICIPATION. (LOCAL). SHARON PROEHL, DIRECTOR; SPENCER CHAMBER OF COMMERCE; 603 S GRAND; SPENCER, IA 51301. (#101389-1).

JUNE 6, '76. 'ON-THE-AVE', FESTIVAL OF ART. THE EXHIBIT WILL FEATURE ART WORK FROM 5 STATES; $1000 WILL BE AWARDED; THERE WILL BE A SPECIAL $200 BICENTENNIAL AWARD. AT 4TH & GRAND. (LOCAL). SHARON PROEHL, V-PRES; SPENCER CHAMBER OF COMMERCE; 603 S GRAND; SPENCER, IA 51301. (#105138-3).

JULY 4, '76. CLAY COUNTY COLONIAL HERITAGE DAY. THE DAY'S ACTIVITIES INCLUDE: OPEN CHURCH SERVICE, HORSE-SHOE PITCHING, GREASED PIG CONTEST, WATERFIGHTS, LIVE ENTERTAINMENT AND FIREWORKS. AT CLAY COUNTY FAIR GROUNDS. (LOCAL). SHARON PROEHL, V-PRES; SPENCER CHAMBER OF COMMERCE; 603 S GRAND; SPENCER, IA 51301. (#105138-1).

AUG 9, '76. FARM MARKET DAYS. FARM MARKET DAYS IS A DAY FOR FARMERS TO SELL THEIR PRODUCE. (LOCAL). SHARON PROEHL, PROJ DIR; SPENCER CHAMBER OF COMMERCE; 603 S GRAND; SPENCER, IA 51301. (#101401-1).

SEPT 11 - 18, '76. CLAY COUNTY FAIR. FAIR AT CLAY COUNTY FAIRGROUNDS, WEST OF 18TH ST & 4TH AVE. (ST-WIDE). MYLES JOHNSON, PROJ DIR; CLAY COUNTY FAIR ASSOC; 12 W 4TH ST; SPENCER, IA 51301. (#101397-1).

SPILLVILLE

SOFTBALL LIGHTS, SPILLVILLE, IA. LIGHTS WILL BE ADDED AT THE BALLPARK. (LOCAL). C C HAUG, COORDINATOR; CITY OF SPILLVILLE; BOX 98; SPILLVILLE, IA 52168. (#22434).

SUMMER RECREATION AREA, SPILLVILLE, IA. A NEW RECREATION AREA WILL BE DEVELOPED. (LOCAL). TIM A NOVAK, COORDINATOR; CITY OF SPILLVILLE; BOX 98; SPILLVILLE, IA 52168. (#22461).

JUNE 28 - JULY 6, '76. ARTS & CRAFTS BOOTHS. EXHIBIT AT RIVERSIDE PARK. (LOCAL). TED F SOJKA, CO-CHAIRMAN; IOWA FINE ARTS COUNCIL & SOUTH WINNESHIEK JAYCESS; MAIN ST; SPILLVILLE, IA 52168. (#106796-5).

JULY 3, '76. HERITAGE PARADE. PARADE AT MAIN ST. (LOCAL). WALTER KLIMESH, CHAIRMAN; HOLY NAME SOCIETY; R 2; RIDGEWAY, IA 52161. (#106796-2).

JULY 3 - 5, '76. DVORAK FINE ARTS FESTIVAL. CRAFTS, MUSIC CONTEST, CZECH ETHNIC THEME, FIREWORKS, FOLK TALES, COSTUMES, ETHNIC FOOD BOOTHS. AT RIVERSIDE PARK, SPILLVILLE, IA. (LOCAL). TIM NOVAK, PROJ DIRECTOR; SOUTH WINNESHIEK JAYCEES; SPILLVILLE, IA 52168. (#103768-9).

JULY 4, '76. CONCERT OF DVORAK MUSIC. LIVE PERFORMANCE AT ST WEHCESLAUS SCHOOL. (LOCAL). TED F SOJKA, CO-CHAIRMAN; SOUTH WINNESHIEK JAYCEES; MAIN ST; SPILLVILLE, IA 52168. (#106796-1).

JULY 4, '76. CZECH MASS. CEREMONY AT ST WENCESLAUS CHURCH. (LOCAL). REV LOUIS J TRZIL, DIR; SOUTH WINNESHIEK JAYCEES; SPILLVILLE, IA 52168. (#106796-4).

JULY 4, '76. DEDICATION TO G F HEUSER. CEREMONY AT RIVERSIDE PARK. (LOCAL). C C HAUG, CHAIRMAN; CIVIC IMPROVEMENT ASSOC; MAIN ST; SPILLVILLE, IA 52168. (#106796-3).

JULY 5, '76. SOUTH WINN JAYCEES. CEREMONY, EXHIBIT, FESTIVAL, PARADE, LIVE PERFORMANCE AT INWOOD PARK SPILLVILLE IA. (LOCAL). J M BERNS; SOUTH WINN JAYCEES; BOX 171; FT ATKINSON, IA 52144. (#107688-9).

SPIRIT LAKE

BICENTENNIAL ESSAY CONTEST. STUDENTS, IN GROUPS OF 2, VISITED HOMES TO SEE HISTORICAL OBJECTS. KNOWLEDGE GAINED WILL BE WRITTEN UP IN ESSAY FORM. AAUW MEMBERS PROVIDED LIST OF PEOPLE WITH ITEMS OF INTEREST, AND TRANSPORTATION TO THEIR HOMES. (LOCAL). MARLYS WEED, PRESIDENT; AMERICAN ASSOC OF UNIVERSITY WOMEN (AAUW); E LAKESHORE DR; SPIRIT LAKE, IA 51360. (#108136-1). **(??).**

'CENTENNIAL SALUTE' - SPIRIT LAKE, IA. HISTORICAL ITEMS FROM PRIVATE COLLECTIONS WILL BE ON DISPLAY AT THE SPIRIT LAKE PUBLIC LIBRARY. (LOCAL). MRS FAYE PETERSON, CURATOR; DICKINSON COUNTY MUSEUM; 1708 KEOKUK; SPIRIT LAKE, IA 51360. (#27674).

CITY BEAUTIFICATION PROJ, SPIRIT LAKE, IA. BOULEVARD FLOWER PLANTING & DOWNTOWN FLOWER PLANTERS; A CONTINUOUS PROJECT. (LOCAL). MRS R C MATHEWS, MEMBER; LAKES GARDEN CLUB; GARY AVE; SPIRIT LAKE, IA 51360. (#25294).

CITY BICENTENNIAL SCRAPBOOK - SPIRIT LAKE, IA. COLLECTING OF MOMENTOS, OLD NEWSPAPER ARTICLES AND PRESENT COLLECTABLES THAT WILL BE OF INTEREST TO FUTURE GENERATIONS, FROM RESIDENTS OF SPIRIT LAKE. PART OF LIBRARY'S 'OUR WORKING HERITAGE' PROJECT. (LOCAL). MRS MARIE KIRBY, PROJ CHAIRMAN; LAC D'ESPRIT LIBRARY; 600 16TH ST; SPIRIT LAKE, IA 51360. (#27675).

COMMEMORATIVE PLATE IN SPIRIT LAKE, IA. PLATE TO BE SOLD, IN HONOR OF THE BICENTENNIAL, ENTITLED 'THE QUEEN PLATE'. (LOCAL). DR F V MAYTUM, PROJ DIRECTOR; DICKINSON COUNTY AMERICAN REVOLUTION BICENTENNIAL COMMITTEE; 608 22ND ST; SPIRIT LAKE, IA 51360. (#11480).

DISPLAY OF HISTORICAL ARTIFACTS, SPIRIT LAKE, IA. A DISPLAY OF HISTORICAL ITEMS IN LOCAL STORES & SCHOOLS. (LOCAL). VIRGINIA PHELPS, CHAIRMAN; SPIRIT LAKE BICENTENNIAL COMMISSION; RR 7261; SPIRIT LAKE, IA 51360. (#15301).

MARKING OF SPIRIT LAKE MASSACRE SITES, IA. MARKING OF SITES OF 6 MASSACRE CABINS, OLD COURTHOUSE, STOCKADE & STATE MONUMENT. (LOCAL). MRS F V MAYTUM, REGENT; LAKE CHAPTER DAR & DICKINSON COUNTY BICENTENNIAL COMMITTEE; 608 22ND ST; SPIRIT LAKE, IA 51360. (#18800).

TRAINING CENTER IN SPIRIT LAKE, IA. PURCHASE OF BUILDING TO BE USED AS A TRAINING CENTER FOR HANDICAPPED INDIVIDUALS. (ST-WIDE). DR F V MAYTUM, PROJ DIRECTOR; DICKINSON COUNTY AMERICAN REVOLUTION BICENTENNIAL COMMITTEE; 608 22ND ST; SPIRIT LAKE, IA 51360. (#11481).

TREE PLANTING IN SPIRIT LAKE, IA. NEW TREES WILL BE PLANTED THROUGHOUT SPIRIT LAKE. (LOCAL). VIRGINIA PHELPS, CHAIRMAN; SPIRIT LAKE COMMUNITY BICENTENNIAL COMMITTEE; RR 7261; SPIRIT LAKE, IA 51360. (#15302).

4-H BICENTENNIAL FLOWERBED - IA. DICKINSON COUNTY YOUTH ARE DOING LANDSCAPING AROUND THE DICKINSON COUNTY MUSEUM AREA. (LOCAL). CAROL CROCKER, COORDINATOR; 4-H CLUB; 1615 ITHACA; SPIRIT LAKE, IA 51360. (#25666).

JULY 4, '75. 4TH OF JULY CELEBRATION. FESTIVAL. (LOCAL). DR F V MAYTUM; DICKINSON COUNTY ARBC; 608 22ND ST; SPIRIT LAKE, IA 51360. (#7923-1).

OCT 29, '75. COMMUNITY FESTIVAL. FESTIVAL AT JR HIGH AUDITORIUM. (LOCAL). VIRGINIA PHELPS DIRECTOR; SPIRIT LAKE BICENTENNIAL; RR 7261; SPIRIT LAKE, IA 51360. (#102273-1).

JAN 13 - 15, '76. BICENTENNIAL PRAYER BREAKFASTS. RELIGIOUS SPEECH: 'OUR RELIGIOUS HERITAGE', JIM COUMIHAN, PRESIDENT OF EVANGELISM ASSOC, ST PAUL, MN-ADULT SPEAKER; REV KENNETH SUETTERLIN. AT METHODIST WESLEY HALL, HILL AVE. (LOCAL). EMILY VANVOORHIS, V-CHMN; SPIRIT LAKE MINISTERIAL ASSOC, ALL SPIRIT LAKE CHURCHES; SPIRIT LAKE, IA 51360. (#200018-154).

APR 16, '76. LIBERTY TREE PLANTING ON COURTHOUSE LAWN - CEREMONY. MAPLE TREE PLANTED WITH SPEECHES BY VINTON ARNOLD ON FORT & FIRST COURTHOUSE & MRS BERKLEY BEDELL ON PRESENT & FUTURE COUNTY GOVERNMENT. AT DICKINSON COUNTY COURTHOUSE LAWN. (LOCAL). MRS R C MATHEWS, COORD; LAKES GARDEN CLUB; GARY AVE; SPIRIT LAKE, IA 51360. (#108147-1).

APR 23 - 24, '76. BICENTENNIAL FOLLIES. LIVE PERFORMANCE AT JR HIGH AUDITORIUM. (LOCAL). NORM BOLEY, DIRECTOR; SPIRIT LAKE KIWANIS; SPIRIT LAKE, IA 51360. (#200018-153).

MAY 6 - JUNE 14, '76. 'THE SIGNATURE OF SPIRIT LAKE' - CONTEST. THE BICENTENNIAL COMMITTEE IS SPONSORING THE CONTEST TO DEVELOP A SYMBOL TO BE USED ON THE CITY FLAG, STATIONERY AND VEHICLE EMBLEMS. WINNERS WILL BE ANNOUNCED OF JULY 1ST AND WILL BE PRESENTED TO CITY OFFICIALS ON JULY 4TH. (LOCAL). RUTHANN LUKES, CHAIRMAN; SPIRIT LAKE BICENTENNIAL COMMITTEE; 108 23RD ST; SPIRIT LAKE, IA 51360. (#108137-1).

MAY 22 - 23, '76. BICENTENNIAL CHAUTAUQUA. A CHAUTAUQUA, COMPLETE WITH TENT WILL BE RECREATED. THE PROGRAM WILL INCLUDE MUSICAL EVENTS, FOLK DANCING, PUPPET SHOW, A MAGICIAN, A SPEAKER ON ECOLOGY, A HISTORICAL IMPERSONATION OF ABE LINCOLN, ARTS, PIONEER CRAFTS, IMPROMPTU STUMP SPEECHES & MUCH MORE. AT METHODIST CAMP GROUND. (LOCAL). DALE GUGE, CHAIRMAN; IOWA LAKES COMMUNITY COLLEGE; 300 S 18TH ST; SPIRIT LAKE, IA 51334. (#200018-155).

MAY 30, '76. ARNOLDS PARK HISTORY PREMIER AT OPENING OF DICKINSON COUNTY MUSEUM. CEREMONY, EXHIBIT AT DICKINSON COUNTY MUSEUM. (LOCAL). PEGGY SCHENK SMITH, COORD; ARNOLDS PARK AMERICAN BICENTENNIAL COMMITTEE; SUNSET BEACH - LAKE OKOBOJI; ARNOLDS APRK, IA 51331. (#107743-1).

JULY 3, '76. STREET DANCING. LIVE PERFORMANCE AT DOWNTOWN SPIRIT LAKE. (LOCAL). NORMAN KLEPPER; SPIRIT LAKE BICENT COMM & 'SPIRIT LAKERS' SQ DANCE CLUB; 507 LAKE ST; SPIRIT LAKE, IA 51360. (#105929-2).

JULY 4, '76. SPIRIT LAKE BICENTENNIAL FESTIVAL DAY - PARADE. PARADE. (LOCAL). NORMAN KLEPPER, PROJ CHMN; SPIRIT LAKE BICENTENNIAL COMMITTEE; 507 LAKE ST; SPIRIT LAKE, IA 51360. (#105929-1).

JULY 25, '76. HISTORICAL TOUR OF BIG SPIRIT LAKE. TOUR. (LOCAL). SUSAN GOODWIN, CHMN; LAKES ART CENTER; 1002 HILL AVE; SPIRIT LAKE, IA 51360. (#108238-1).

ST ANSGAR

HISTORY PROJECT - ST ANSGAR, IA. RESEARCHING INDIAN HISTORY AND PRESERVING 168 ACRE AREA ALONG THE LITTLE CEDAR RIVER. (LOCAL). LOUIS J VANDER MYDE, CHAIRMAN; MITCHELL COUNTY BICENTENNIAL COMMISSION; 114 N GEORGE ST; ST ANSGAR, IA 50472. (#22388).

INDIAN FORT PRESERVATION, ST ANSGAR, IA. AN OLD INDIAN FORT BUILT IN 1867 WILL BE PRESERVED; FORT ORIGINALLY BUILT DURING AN UPRISING OF LOCAL INDIANS. (LOCAL). LOUIS J VANDER MYDE, CHIRMAN; MITCHELL COUNTY BICENTENNIAL COMMISSION; 114 N GEORGE ST; ST ANSGAR, IA 50472. (#19676).

INSTALLATION OF A DRINKING FOUNTAIN; ST ANSGAR, IA. A DRINKING FOUNTAIN WILL BE INSTALLED IN THE PARK. (LOCAL). L R FALK, CHAIRMAN; ST ANSGAR BICENTENNIAL COMMITTEE; ST ANSGAR, IA 50472. (#17832).

ST ANSGAR — CONTINUED

PAINTING OF FIRE HYDRANTS; ST ANSGAR, IA. FIRE HYDRANTS WILL BE PAINTED RED, WHITE & BLUE. (LOCAL). L R FALK, CHAIRMAN; ST ANSGAR BICENTENNIAL COMMITTEE; ST ANSGAR, IA 50472. (#17830).

PLANTING OF FLOWERS; ST ANSGAR, IA. BICENTENNIAL FLOWER BEDS WILL BE PLANTED. (LOCAL). L R FALK, CHAIRMAN; ST ANSGAR BICENTENNIAL COMMITTEE; ST ANSGAR, IA 50472. (#17831).

ST ANTHONY

SAINT ANTHONY COMMUNAL UNITY & SPIRIT OF 76, IA. BICENTENNIAL PROJECTS INCLUDE: PUBLICATION OF THE HISTORY OF THE COMMUNITY, A FESTIVAL & A COMMUNITY-WIDE CLEANUP & BEAUTIFICATION CAMPAIGN. (LOCAL). RUTH G MARKIN, CHAIRPERSON; COMMUNITY OF SAINT ANTHONY; SAINT ANTHONY, IA 50239. (#21422).

AUG 8, '76. SAINT ANTHONY FESTIVAL. FESTIVAL AT MAIN STREET. (LOCAL). RUTH C MACKIN, CHMN; CITY OF ST ANTHONY; ST ANTHONY, IA 50239. (#105335-1).

ST CHARLES

FLAG POLE, ST CHARLES, IA. A FLAG POLE WILL BE RAISED IN THE COMMUNITY. (LOCAL). GARY GESAMAN, CHAIRMAN; OLD SETTLERS CELEBRATION; ST CHARLES, IA 50240. (#21277).

WINDOW DISPLAYS, ST CHARLES, IA. DISPLAYS OF AMERICAN HERITAGE (ANTIQUE ITEMS & DOCUMENTS) WILL BE PLACED IN TOWN WINDOWS. (LOCAL). GARY GESAMAN, CHAIRMAN; OLD SETTLERS CELEBRATION; ST CHARLES, IA 50240. (#21278).

JULY 16 - 17, '76. OLD SETTLERS' CELEBRATION. PARADE, LIVE PERFORMANCE. (LOCAL). GARY GESAMAN, CHMN; OLD SETTLERS' COMMITTEE; ST CHARLES, IA 50240. (#105264-1).

STACYVILLE

OLD HOMESTEAD FARM, STACYVILLE, IA. OLDEST FARM IN AREA IN THE SAME FAMILY TO BE EXHIBITED. (LOCAL). MELVIN ADAMS, TREASURER; STACYVILLE COMMERCIAL CLUB; N LAWRENCE ST; STACYVILLE, IA 50476. (#18375).

RESTORATION OF OLD FIRE BELL, STACYVILLE, IA. RESTORATION OF THE CITY'S FIRST FIRE ALARM. (LOCAL). MELVIN ADAMS, TREASURER; STACYVILLE COMMERCIAL CLUB; N LAWRENCE ST; STACYVILLE, IA 50476. (#18376).

JUNE 18 - 20, '76. BRAUTWURST AND SAUERKRAUT DAYS. FESTIVAL, LIVE PERFORMANCE AT CITY PARK. (LOCAL). ROGER A BRUMM, COORD; STACYVILLE COMMERCIAL CLUB; SPRING ST; STACYVILLE, IA 50476. (#103768-1).

STANHOPE

BICENTENNIAL TREES PLANTED, STANHOPE, IA. LOCAL RESIDENTS WILL PLANT TREES AND DEDICATE THEM IN HONOR OF THE BICENTENNIAL. (LOCAL). ELDRED LUNDGUIST, DIRECTOR; BICENTENNIAL COMMITTEE; STANHOPE, IA 50246. (#18560).

COMMUNITY BILLBOARD - STANHOPE, IA. AN OLD SCHOOL BELL WILL BE MOUNTED IN A BELL TOWER AND THIS SITE WILL BE USED AS A COMMUNITY BILLBOARD. (LOCAL). WAYNE ROMP, COUNCILMAN; TOWN OF STANHOPE; STANHOPE, IA 50246. (#18558).

HISTORICAL BOOK ON STANHOPE PUBLISHED - IA. THE HISTORY OF THE TOWN WILL BE UPDATED IN THE BOOK. (LOCAL). ULA MAE YOUNG, SECRETARY; WOMEN'S CLUBS; STANHOPE, IA 50246. (#18559).

PERMANENT FLAG POLE - STANHOPE, IA. A FLAG POLE WILL BE ERECTED NEAR THE BALL DIAMOND SCOREBOARD. (LOCAL). HAROLD HOVE, COUNCILMAN; TOWN OF STANHOPE; STANHOPE, IA 50246. (#18479).

NOV 19, '75. BICENTENNIAL BAZAAR. FESTIVAL AT CHRISTIAN CHURCH. (LOCAL). PARLA WILCOX, CHAIRMAN; CHRISTIAN CHURCH LADIES GROUP; STRATFORD, IA 50249. (#200018-145).

AUG 3, '76. STANHOPE WATERMELON DAY. THE CELEBRATION INCLUDES A PARADE, BAND CONCERT, FREE WATERMELON AND KIDDIE RIDES. AT TOWN PARK. (LOCAL). LUTHER QUAM, DIRECTOR; LION'S CLUB; STANHOPE, IA 50246. (#103894-1).

STANLEY

HISTORY OF FAYETTE COUNTY, STANLEY, IA. INFORMAL UP-TO-DATE HISTORY OF FAYETTE COUNTY, TITLED: 'OUT OF THE MIDWEST: A PORTRAIT.' EDITED BY HELEN HOELLER. (LOCAL). MRS JOHN W GRAHAM, CHAIRMAN; FAYETTE COUNTY BICENTENNIAL COMMITTEE; HAWKEYE, IA 52147. (#14730).

STANTON

AMERICAN ISSUES FORUM IN STANTON, IA. A FORUM ON AMERICAN ISSUES. (LOCAL). KAY SLUMP, PROJ DIRECTOR; MONTGOMERY COUNTY BICENTENNIAL COMMITTEE; EMERSON, IA 51533. (#12679).

COUNTY HISTORICAL TOUR IN STANTON, IA. A TOUR OF HISTORICAL LOCATIONS IN MONTGOMERY COUNTY, FLAGS FROM ALL NATIONS WILL BE DISPLAYED. (LOCAL). KAY SLUMP, PROJ DIRECTOR; MONTGOMERY COUNTY BICENTENNIAL COMMUNITY; STANTON, IA 51573. (#12677).

CRAMER SCHOOL RESTORATION PROJ OF STANTON, IA. THE CRAMER ONE ROOM SCHOOL HAS BEEN MOVED TO STANTON & WILL BE RESTORED. (LOCAL). DONALD A PETERSON, CHAIRMAN; STANTON HISTORICAL SOCIETY; STANTON, IA 51573. (#14215).

FALL FESTIVAL. FALL FESTIVAL AND HERITAGE EXHIBITS PARADE. (LOCAL). DONALD A PETERSON, CHMN; STANTON HISTORICAL SOCIETY; STANTON, IA 51573. (#101792-1).

STANWOOD

JUNE 19 - 20, '76. STANWOOD HORSE SHOW. ANNUAL EVENT; BICENTENNIAL EMPHASIS ON TROPHIES, RIBBON AWARDS AND BICENTENNIAL PARADE THEME. AT STANWOOD ATHLETIC FIELD. (LOCAL). ROGER OLDORF, CHAIRMAN; STANWOOD HORSE SHOW COMMITTEE; STANWOOD, IA 52337. (#200018-263).

STATE CENTER

JUNE 18 - 20, '76. 1976 ROSE FESTIVAL. STATE CENTER IS OFFICIAL ROSE CAPITOL OF IOWA; 76 ROSE GARDEN WILL FEATURE A BED OF ALL AMERICAN ROSES, THE DEVELOPMENT OF THE AMERICAN FLAG THRU 13 ROSE DISPLAYS; CRAFTS, A PARADE, PAGEANTS, CONTESTS, A DANCE & CONCERT & BICENTENNIAL FIREWORKS. AT PUBLIC LIBRARY; 309 2ND ST SE. (ST-WIDE). MRS ALAN HILLEMAN; 1976 ROSE FESTIVAL BOARD; 107 5TH AVE SE; STATE CENTER, IA 50247. (#102952-6).

STEAMBOAT RK

PUBLICATION OF HISTORIES IN THE HERALD INDEX, IA. HISTORIES WILL BE PUBLISHED IN THE HERALD INDEX NEWSPAPERS LOCATED IN ELDORA, IA. (LOCAL). HELEN JOHNS, COORDINATOR; TOWN OF STEAMBOAT ROCK; STEAMBOAT RK, IA 50672. (#23349).

MAY 3, '76. FLAG RAISING CEREMONY. CEREMONY AT CITY HALL. (LOCAL). HELEN JOHNS, COORD; TOWN OF STEAMBOAT ROCK; STEAMBOAT RK, IA 50672. (#106526-1).

MAY 28 - 30, '76. ANTIQUE HERITAGE EXHIBIT. HISTORY OF PAST AND PRESENT PERSONALITIES, ANTIQUE ITEMS AND PICTURES OF THE PAST. AT LOCAL LIBRARY. (LOCAL). HELEN JOHNS, COORD; TOWN OF STEAMBOAT ROCK; STEAMBOAT RK, IA 50672. (#106526-2).

STOCKPORT

BUILDING NEW COMMUNITY PARK & LIBRARY IN IA. THE STOCKPORT COMMUNITY HAS BUILT A NEW PARK & SHELTER HOUSE WITH YOUTH RECREATIONAL FACILITIES & ADDED A NEW ADDITION TO THE LIBRARY, PART OF WHICH WILL PRESERVE HISTORIC BOOKS & PAPERS OF THE AREA. (LOCAL). TED WATSON OR LIBBY WOODRUFF, CO-CHAIRMEN; VAN BUREN DEVELOPMENT ASSOC; 101 VAN BUREN ST; KEOSAUQUA, IA 52565. (#21407).

STONE CITY

COMMUNITY CLUB BUILDING IN STONE CITY, IA. REPAIR AND PRESERVATION OF CENTENNIAL SCHOOL HOUSE (NOW USED AS THE COMMUNITY CLUB). (LOCAL). JOSEPH L STRAKA, PRESIDENT; STONE CITY COMMUNITY CLUB; RR 1; STONE CITY, IA 52205. (#21402).

STONE CITY, IA MUSEUM PROJECTS. THE MUSEUM IS PRODUCING A FILM ON STONE CITY'S HISTORY. DOCUMENTS AND ARTIFACTS RELATING TO THE CITY'S PAST MAY BE VIEWED IN THE MUSEUM. (LOCAL). RICHARD E TEBBE, CO-CHAIRMAN; STONE CITY COMMUNITY CLUB; RR 1; ANAMOSA, IA 52205. (#21401).

JUNE 12 - 13, '76. GRANT WOOD ART FESTIVAL. EXHIBIT, FESTIVAL, PARADE AT STONE CITY SCHOOL HOUSE, STONE CITY, IA. (LOCAL). JOHANN PLOWER, CO-CHMN; STONE CITY COMMUNITY CLUB; RT 1; ANAMOSA, IA 52205. (#105323-1).

STORM LAKE

BEAU ARTS BALL WITH BICENTENNIAL THEME. GUESTS ARE TO DRESS IN HISTORICAL COSTUMES. (LOCAL). MARGE HUNZELMAN, DIRECTOR; STORM LAKE AREA ARTS COUNCIL-WINTER GALLERY; S SHORE RR3; STORM LAKE, IA 50588. (#102642-2). **(??).**

BICENTENNIAL CONCERT. LIVE PERFORMANCE. (LOCAL). FRED BROWN, PROJ DIRECTOR; BUENA VISTA COLLEGE; COLLEGE & W 4TH; STORM LAKE, IA 50588. (#103044-1). **(??).**

CBD DOWNTOWN RENEWAL PROJECT - STORM LAKE, IA. COMPLETE RESTORATION OF DOWNTOWN COMMERCIAL AREA: NEW STREETS, MALL, PARKING AREAS, DECORATIVE LIGHTING, TREES, BENCHES, NEW BUSINESS BLDGS AND EXTERIOR PRESERVATION OF OLDER BLDGS. (LOCAL). BILL LANPHERE, EXEC DIRECTOR; STORM LAKE CHAMBER OF COMMERCE; 5TH & LAKE AVE; STORM LAKE, IA 50588. (#15836).

CONSTITUTIONAL CONVENTION. SEMINAR. (LOCAL). FRED BROWN; BUENA VISTA COLLEGE; COLLEGE & W 4TH; STORM LAKE, IA 50588. (#103044-2). **(??).**

THE FOUNDING FATHERS; LECTURE COURSE - IA. THE COURSE WILL EMPHASIZE THE BIOGRAPHIES OF LEADERS OF THE AMERICAN REVOLUTION. (LOCAL). FRED BROWN, PROJECT; BUENA VISTA COLLEGE; COLLEGE & W 4TH STS; STORM LAKE, IA 50588. (#16747).

HISTORICAL MUSEUM - STORM LAKE, IA. A NEW MUSEUM WILL BE FOUNDED IN STORM LAKE. (LOCAL). GORDON LINGE, CHAIRMAN; BUENA VISTA COUNTY BICENTENNIAL COMMITTEE; STORM LAKE, IA 50588. (#17671).

PIONEER MONUMENT - PROJ OF STORM LAKE, IA. BRONZE STATUE OF EARLY PIONEER APPROXIMATELY 5 FEET TALL MOUNTED ON GRANITE BASE OVERLOOKING LAKE TO BE DEDICATED FALL OF 1975. (ST-WIDE). GORDON D LINGE, VOLUNTEER; STORM LAKE CENTENNIAL CORP & BUENA VISTA HISTORICAL MUSEUM; 111 W 7TH ST; STORM LAKE, IA 50588. (#15837).

REPRINT COUNTY HISTORY - STORM LAKE, IA. THE PUBLICATION ON BUENA VISTA COUNTY WILL BE REPRINTED. (LOCAL). GORDON LINGE, CHAIRMAN; BUENA VISTA COUNTY BICENTENNIAL COMMITTEE; STORM LAKE, IA 50588. (#17672).

TRAVELING ART EXHIBIT. EXHIBIT WILL BE ON CONVERTED RAILROAD PASSENGER CARS. (LOCAL). MARGE HUNZELMAN, DIRECTOR; STORM LAKE AREA ARTS COUNCIL-WINTER GALLERY; S SHORE RR3; STORM LAKE, IA 50588. (#102642-1). **(??).**

STORY CITY

MERRY-GO-ROUND RESTORATION, STORY CITY. RESTORATION OF MERRY-GO-ROUND WHICH HAS BEEN IN COMMUNITY FOR PAST 38 YEARS. (LOCAL). E T HAUGE, COORDINATOR; GREATER COMMUNITY CONGRESS; STORY CITY, IA 50248. (#21425).

TRAVELERS' PARK, STORY CITY, IA. A TRAVELERS' PARK WILL BE CONSTRUCTED NEAR I-35 EXIT. (LOCAL). LENA JOHNSON, CHAIRPERSON; STORY CITY COMMUNITY BETTERMENT COMMITTEE; STORY CITY, IA 50248. (#21426).

MAR 22, '76. BICENTENNIAL CHILI SUPPER. FESTIVAL AT HIGH SCHOOL CAFETERIA. (LOCAL). ROBERT NERVIG, CO-CHMN; STORY CITY AMERICAN REVOLUTION BICENTENNIAL COMMITTEE; 854 LAFAYETTE; STORY CITY, IA 50248. (#200018-150).

JUNE 5 - 6, '76. SCANDINAVIAN DAYS. ANNUAL EVENT CELEBRATING THE TRADITIONS, CULTURE AND LIFESTYLES OF SCANDINAVIAN-AMERICAN PEOPLE IN OUR COMMUNITY. AT CENTRAL BUSINESS DISTRICT. (LOCAL). WENDEL PETERSON, COORD; SCANDINAVIAN DAYS COMMITTEE; RD 2; STORY CITY, IA 50248. (#105337-1).

JULY 4 - 5, '76. FOURTH OF JULY CELEBRATION. HOURS ON JULY 4, NOON TO 10 PM; ON JULY 5, 10 AM TO 11 PM. AT NORTH & SOUTH CITY PARKS, & FOOTBALL FIELD. (LOCAL). ROBERT SWEET, COORD; LAFAYETTE POST #59, AMERICAN LEGION; 1403 RIVER HILLS DR; STORY CITY, IA 50248. (#105337-2).

STRATFORD

APR 7, '76. OLD CREAMERY THEATER. LIVE PERFORMANCE AT STRATFORD HIGH SCHOOL. (LOCAL). ELLIS ANDREWS, PRES; STRATFORD LIONS; 1025 MOORE; STRATFORD, IA 50249. (#200018-149).

JULY 5, '76. MUSIC FESTIVAL. PARADE, LIVE PERFORMANCE AT CITY PARK. (LOCAL). ELLIS ANDREWS, PRES; LIONS CLUB; 1025 MOORE; STRATFORD, IA 50249. (#106902-1).

JULY 17 - 18, '76. STRATFORD'S BICENTENNIAL APPRECIATION DAYS. COMPETITION, FESTIVAL, PARADE AT CITY PARK. (LOCAL). DOROTHY MILLER, PRESIDENT; STRATFORD CHAMBER OF COMMERCE; BOX 87; STRATFORD, IA 50249. (#106900-1).

STRAWBERRY PT

DOWNTOWN REST AREAS, STRAWBERRY PT, IA. EIGHT BENCHES PLACED ON TOWN STREETS FOR ELDERLY TO VISIT AND REST. (LOCAL). MARCEY F ALDERSON, CHAIRMAN; UNION BANK & LOCAL BUSINESSES; STRAWBERRY PT, IA 52076. (#23101).

MEMORIAL TO OUR FOREFATHERS - STRAWBERRY PT, IA. A PLAQUE COMMEMORATING OUR FOREFATHERS WILL BE PLACED ON A ROCK SHAPED LIKE IOWA. (LOCAL). MARCEY F ALDERSON, CHAIRMAN; SEEDORFF CONSTRUCTION; STRAWBERRY PT, IA 52076. (#24125).

MAY 29 - 30, '76. OLD-FASHIONED BAND CONCERT & BICENTENNIAL MUSICAL PAGEANT. OLD FASHIONED BAND CONCERT & OLD STYLE PAGEANT. AT CITY PARK BAND SHELL & STARMOUNT SCHOOL AUDITORIUM. (LOCAL). MACEY F ALDERSON, COORD; STRAWBERRY POINT BICENTENNIAL COMMITTEE & PUBLIC SCHOOLS; STRAWBERRY PT, IA 52076. (#106854-1).

JUNE 11, '76. OLD-TIME DANCE. OLD-TIME DANCE FOR PUBLIC; FREE, POLKA, SCOTTISH, WALTZ; ONE-STEP ETC WITH TEACHERS AVAILABLE TO HELP THOSE WHO DESIRE TO LEARN THE DANCES. AT SCHOOL GYM AT STRAWBERRY POINT. (LOCAL). MACEY F ALDERSON; STRAWBERRY POINT BICENT COMM & PUBLIC SCHOOLS; BICENTENNIAL COMM; STRAWBERRY PT, IA 52076. (#106854-5).

JUNE 12, '76. FOLK DANCE FESTIVAL. FOLK DANCES FROM VARIOUS COUNTRIES PERFORMED BY LOCAL JUNIOR H S STUDENTS. (LOCAL). MACEY F ALDERSON, COORD; STRAWBERRY POINT BICENTENNIAL COMMITTEE; STRAWBERRY PT, IA 52076. (#106856-1).

STRAWBERRY PT — CONTINUED

JUNE 12, '76. HERITAGE DEMONSTRATIONS - SPINNING, SOAP-MAKING, BUTTER-CHURNING. DEMONSTRATIONS OF SPINNING WOOL W/LECTURE, SAT 11-12:30 AND 2-4PM; SOAP-MAKING DEMONSTRATION 11-12:30 AND 2-4PM; BUTTER-CHURNING WITH SAMPLES, SAME TIMES AND PLACE. AT JESSEN SUPER VALUE PORCH. (LOCAL). MACEY F ALDERSON; STRAWBERRY POINT BICENTENNIAL COMM & PUBLIC SCHOOLS; BICENTENNIAL COMM; STRAWBERRY PT, IA 52076. (#106854-4).

JUNE 12, '76. UNVEILING OF BICENTENNIAL PLAQUE. PLAQUE HAS A BICENTENNIAL SLOGAN WRITTEN BY A LOCAL PERSON FROM A CONTEST SPONSORED BY US. A WALKING PLOW, ORIGINAL ONE TO BE ERECTED ON A ROCK. DEDICATED TO OUR HERITAGE FROM OUR FOREFATHERS. AT WILDER MUSEUM LAWN. (LOCAL). MACEY F ALDERSON; STRAWBERRY POINT BICENTENNIAL COMM & PUBLIC SCHOOLS; BICENTENNIAL COMM; STRAWBERRY PT, IA 52076. (#106854-3).

JUNE 14, '76. FLAG RAISING CEREMONY. FLAG WILL BE PRESENTED TO WILDER MUSEUM. AT LAWN OF WILDER MUSEUM. (LOCAL). MARCEY F ALDERSON, COORD; ROYAL NEIGHBORS OF AMERICA; STRAWBERRY PT, IA 52076. (#106855-1).

JUNE 20, '76. BICENTENNIAL COMMUNITY CHURCH SERVICE. COMBINED CHOIRS OF 4 CHURCHES, OLD FASHIONED COSTUMES & SERVICE, OPEN HOUSE IN EACH CHURCH AFTER. AT CITY PARK. (LOCAL). MACEY F ALDERSON, COORD; STRAWBERRY POINT BICENTENNIAL COMMITTEE & PUBLIC SCHOOLS; STRAWBERRY PT, IA 52076. (#106854-2).

SUMNER

COMMUNITY CENTER PROJECT, SUMNER, IA. A COMMUNITY CENTER WILL BE DEVELOPED FOR THE SUMNER AREA. (LOCAL). BERNICE MURPHY, CHAIRPERSON; SUMNER COMMUNITY BICENTENNIAL; 820 W FIRST; SUMNER, IA 50674. (#14516).

TREE PLANTING PROJECT IN SUMNER, IA. TREES WILL BE PLANTED IN HONOR OF THE BICENTENNIAL. (LOCAL). BERNICE MURPHY, CHAIRPERSON; SUMNER COMMUNITY BICENTENNIAL; 820 W FIRST; SUMNER, IA 50674. (#14517).

JULY 2 - 4, '76. BICENTENNIAL CELEBRATION. PARADE, SOFTBALL, FIREWORKS & COMMUNITY CHURCH SERVICE. (LOCAL). DEAN JACOBSON, COORD; COMMERCIAL CLUB, JAYCEES & SUMNER BICENTENNIAL COMMITTEE; SUMNER, IA 50674. (#106805-1).

SUTHERLAND

HERITAGE FARMS - PROJ OF SUTHERLAND, IA. HONORING FAMILY FARM OWNERS WHOSE FARMS HAVE REMAINED IN SAME FAMILY FOR 50 TO 75 YEARS OR MORE. (LOCAL). JACOB MOERMOND, CHAIRMAN; 4-H CLUBS; SUTHERLAND, IA 51058. (#14219).

HISTORY BOOK - PROJ OF SUTHERLAND, IA. HISTORY OF TOWN, CHURCHES AND ORGANIZATIONS. (LOCAL). LEROY RIENERS, CHAIRMAN; BICENTENNIAL COMMITTEE; SUTHERLAND, IA 51058. (#14220).

ROADSIDE PARK - PROJ OF SUTHERLAND, IA. BEAUTIFICATION OF THE ROADSIDE PARK ON THE APPROACH TO THE TOWN. (LOCAL). RHONDA KLAVE, CHAIRMAN; FEDERATED WOMEN'S CLUB; SUTHERLAND, IA 51058. (#14217).

SENIOR CITIZENS DAY. SENIOR CITIZENS WILL BE HONORED FOR THEIR CONTRIBUTIONS TO THE COMMUNITY. (LOCAL). DAVID PEELEN, CHMN; RURITAN CLUB; RURITAN CLUB; SUTHERLAND, IA 51058. (#14216-1).

TREE PLANTING - PROJ OF SUTHERLAND, IA. REPLACING TREES DESTROYED BY DUTCH ELM DISEASE WITH EMPHASIS ON CITY PARK. (LOCAL). MARCELLA SCHULTZ, SECRETARY; CITY COUNCIL; SUTHERLAND, IA 51058. (#14218).

SEPT 6, '76. BICENTENNIAL FESTIVAL - FAIR EXHIBITS, DANCE & BALL GAME. HOME TOWN LABOR DAY REUNION AND BICENTENNIAL CELEBRATION. AT CITY PARK SHELTER HOUSE, ATHLETIC FIELD OF MAIN ST SCHOOL. (LOCAL). LEROY RIEMER, CHMN; SUTHERLAND COMMERCIAL CLUB; SUTHERLAND, IA 51058. (#101793-1).

SWALEDALE

FILM OF SWALEDALE'S 200TH ANNIV EVENTS, IA. A FILM OF THE TOTAL DAY'S ACTIVITIES WAS MADE AND IS IN THE LIBRARY FOR FUTURE USE. THE OPEN HOUSE FOR THE NEWLY REMODELED LIBRARY WAS HELD JULY 3, 1976. (LOCAL). MR & MRS LESTER BONNER, CO-CHAIRPERSONS; SWALEDALE BICETENNIAL COMMITTEE; BOX 3; SWALEDALE, IA 50447. (#33041).

JULY 3, '76. BICENTENNIAL DAY. DISPLAY OF OLD & NEW FARM EQUIPMENT, PICNIC, GAMES, FIREWORKS AND DANCE. ALSO PARADE AND ARTS & CRAFTS EXHIBIT. (LOCAL). MR & MRS LESTER BONNER; SWALEDALE BUSINESS MEN AND CITIZENS & BICENTENNIAL COMMITTEE; BOX 3; SWALEDALE, IA 50477. (#200018-271).

SWEA CITY

JUNE 8 - 25, '76. PRAIRIE HOUSE DISPLAY - SUMMER FESTIVAL. SUMMER CELEBRATION INCLUDING PARADE, DISPLAYS, PAGEANT & CONTEST. (LOCAL). LARRY JONES, COORDINATOR; SWEA CITY COMMERCIAL CLUB; SWEA CITY, IA 50590. (#104332-8).

JUNE 23 - 25, '76. FAIR AND FIELD DAYS. FAIR, FESTIVAL, PARADE AT SCHOOL AUDITORIUM. (LOCAL). LARRY JONES, COORDINATOR; SWEA CITY COMMERCIAL CLUB; SWEA CITY, IA 50590. (#104332-9).

SWEDESBURG

JULY 4, '76. FLAG DEDICATION & TREE PLANTING. CEREMONY. (LOCAL). MS VICTORIA BERGSTROM; SWEDESBURG LUTHERAN CHURCH & BICENTENNIAL COMMITTEE; RT 1; WINFIELD, IA 52659. (#200018-299).

S/E POLK

FIRST HISTORY BOOK OF SOUTHEAST POLK AREA, IOWA. IN HONOR OF THE BICENTENNIAL, A HISTORY BOOK OF THE SOUTHEAST POLK AREA WILL BE WRITTEN BY A LOCAL PERSON FROM ACCOUNTS AND COLLECTIONS OF LOCAL RESIDENTS. (ST-WIDE). MRS G M ATZEN, PROJ CHAIRMAN; S/E POLK BICENT ASSOC; 6589 SE 6TH AVE; DES MOINES, IA 50317. (#9652).

A PUPPET SHOW IN SOUTHEAST POLK, IOWA. THE PROGRAM INVOLVES A PUPPET SHOW ABOUT THE BICENTENNIAL FOR YOUNGSTERS OF THE COMMUNITY. (LOCAL). MRS G M ATZEN, PROJ CHAIRMAN; S/E POLK BICENT ASSOC; 6589 SE 6TH AVE; DES MOINES, IA 50317. (#9656).

JULY 2 - 4, '76. MEMORABILIA DISPLAY. THE PROJECT WILL INVOLVE A DISPLAY WHICH WILL COVER ASPECTS FROM EDUCATION, RELIGION AND ECONOMICS. AT S E POLK HIGH SCHOOL AUDITORIUM. (LOCAL). MRS G M ATZEN; S/E POLK BICENTENNIAL ASSOC; 6589 SE 6TH AVE; DES MOINES, IA 50317. (#9654-1).

JULY 2 - 4, '76. OLD-FASHIONED 4TH OF JULY. THE THREE-DAY CELEBRATION WILL INCLUDE CONCERTS, PAGEANT, GAMES FOR ALL AGES, DISPLAYS, DEMONSTRATIONS, CONTESTS & ACTIVITIES ENJOYED OVER THE PAST 200 YEARS. CBS COVERAGE ON JLULY 4. AT S E POLK HIGH SCHOOL. (LOCAL). MRS G M ATZEN; S/E POLK BICENTENNIAL ASSOC; 6589 SE 6TH AVE; DES MOINES, IA 50317. (#9657-1).

TABOR

COOKBOOKS FROM TABOR, IOWA. COOKBOOKS WITH OLD & NEW RECIPES WILL BE MADE AVAILABLE. (LOCAL). HON RALPH A LAIRD, MAYOR; TABOR BICENT GROUP; BOX 463; TABOR, IA 51653. (#9674).

FOXFIRE PROJECT OF TABOR, IOWA. SCHOOL CHILDREN WILL INTERVIEW OLDER MEMBERS OF THE COMMUNITY TO GATHER HISTORICAL INFORMATION. (LOCAL). HON RALPH A LAIRD, MAYOR; TABOR BICENT GROUP; BOX 463; TABOR, IA 51653. (#9673).

RESTORATION OF HISTORICAL FATHER JOHN TODD HOUSE. ORIGINAL HOUSE OF FATHER JOHN TODD BUILT IN 1853; A STATION ON THE UNDERGROUND RAILWAY DURING THE CIVIL. BUILDING IS ON LIST OF NATIONAL REGISTRY OF HISTORICAL SITES. (ST-WIDE). HON RALPH A LAIRD, MAYOR; TABOR BICENT GROUP; BOX 463; TABOR, IA 51653. (#9671). **ARBA GRANTEE.**

TABOR, IOWA REPRINTS 100 YEAR OLD NEWSPAPER. PROJECT ENTAILS THE REPRINTING OF 100 YEAR OLD COMMUNITY NEWSPAPER. (ST-WIDE). HON RALPH A LAIRD, MAYOR; TABOR BICENT GROUP; BOX 463; TABOR, IA 51653. (#9672).

TABOR, IOWA, PARK IMPROVEMENT. PROJECT ENTAILS MAKING BASIC IMPROVEMENTS ON CITY PARK. (LOCAL). HON RALPH A LAIRD, MAYOR; TABOR BICENT GROUP; BOX 463; TABOR, IA 51653. (#9675).

TARA

RESTORATION OF COUNTRY SCHOOLHOUSE, IA. INSIDE AND OUTSIDE OF SCHOOLHOUSE WILL BE PAINTED AND TREES PLANTED TO MAKE BUILDING SUITABLE FOR TOWNSHIP MEETINGS AND A VOTING PLACE. (LOCAL). ELDRED ADAMS, CLERK; TOWNSHIP BOARD OF TRUSTEES; R #3; FORT DODGE, IA 50501. (#23920).

JULY 17, '76. EXHIBIT AND OUTDOOR BARBEQUE. EXHIBIT, FESTIVAL AT TOWNSHIP HALL, ONE-HALF MILE NORTH OF OLD STAGECOACH INN. (LOCAL). REGIS V CRAWFORD, CHMN; TOWNSHIP BOARD OF TRUSTEES; R #1; MOORLAND, IA 50566. (#106838-1).

THOMPSON

BICENTENNIAL PROJECTS OF WINNEBAGO COUNTY, IA. PROJECTS INCLUDE A CEMETARY SURVEY, MARKING OF EARLY TRAILS AND FARMS AND RESTORATION OF OLD BUILDINGS. (LOCAL). MARLIN FISHER, COORDINATOR; WINNEBAGO BICENTENNIAL COMMITTEE; THOMPSON, IA 50478. (#15831).

COMMUNITY DEVELOPEMENT - THOMPSON, IA. MAIN STREET IS BEING REPAIRED AND PAINTED; A SCOREBOARD HAS BEEN PURCHASED UNDER THE AUSPICES OF THE COMMUNITY DEVELOPMENT PROGRAM OF THE LOCAL BUSINESSMEN'S CLUB. (LOCAL). MIKE TWEED, PRESIDENT; BUSINESSMENS CLUB; THOMPSON, IA 50478. (#19705).

ECOLOGY PROGRAM - THOMPSON, IA. THE PROGRAM WILL INCLUDE TREE PLANTING, CONSERVATION EDUCATION, PARK IMPROVEMENTS AND PLAYGROUND EQUIPMENT. (LOCAL). MRS CARROLL BLOCK, COORDINATOR; THOMPSON STUDY CLUB; THOMPSON, IA 50478. (#19704).

THOMPSON, IA, BICENTENNIAL ACTIVITIES. EVENTS INCLUDE A BICENTENNIAL DINNER, FLAG MAKING, A STUDY OF THE REVOLUTION AND A SPECIAL PROGRAM FOR CUB SCOUTS. (LOCAL). MRS MARLIN FISHER, CHAIRMAN; THOMPSON STUDY CLUB; THOMPSON, IA 50478. (#19706).

JUNE 25 - 28, '76. HOME INDUSTRY DAYS: ARTS & CRAFTS FAIR. FAIR AT 20 HOME SHOPS. (LOCAL). LELA MECHEM, PROJ CHMN; HOME INDUSTRY BOARD; THOMPSON, IA 50478. (#104519-20).

JULY 19 - 21, '76. BICENTENNIAL QUILT CONTEST. CONTEST IS OPEN TO ALL AGES OR GROUPS. QUILTS WILL BE ON DISPLAY AND JUDGED AT WINNEBAGO COUNTY FAIR IN JULY. WINNERS WILL GO TO STATE FAIR. (LOCAL). RUTH LEIBRAND, SECRETARY; WINNEBAGO COUNTY BICENTENNIAL COMMITTEE; 135 N 11TH ST; FOREST CITY, IA 50436. (#104743-1).

JULY 19 - 21, '76. BICENTENNIAL SAMPLER CONTEST. CONTEST OPEN TO ALL AGES; OLD-TIME SAMPLERS READY TO BE HUNG WILL BE ON DISPLAY AND JUDGED AT WINNEBAGO COUNTY FAIR. (LOCAL). RUTH LEIBRAND, SECRETARY; WINNEBAGO COUNTY BICENTENNIAL COMMISSION; 135 N 11TH ST; FOREST CITY, IA 50436. (#104743-2).

THOR

CONSTRUCTION OF TENNIS COURT & SKATING RINK, IA. A TENNIS COURT & AN ICE SKATING RINK WILL BE CONSTRUCTED IN HONOR OF THE BICENTENNIAL. (LOCAL). ALFRED T GUDDALL, CHAIRMAN; TOWN OF THOR & NORWAY TOWNSHIP; 104 ANN ST; THOR, IA 50591. (#18742).

THOR BICENTENNIAL PROJECTS - IA. THOR IS PLANNING THE RESTORATION OF THE OLD POST OFFICE, THE BUILDING OF A NEW TENNIS COURT AND A BAR B CUE TO CELEBRATE ALL THEMES IN THE BICENTENNIAL YEAR. (LOCAL). LYNN CARTER, CHAIRMAN; THOR-NORWAY BICENTENNIAL GROUP; THOR, IA 50591. (#17496).

JULY 21, '76. ALL DAY THOR BICENTENNIAL FESTIVAL. 10 AM FLAG RAISING & INVOCATION IN PARK; 10:30-11 AM, RACES, CONTESTS AND BALL GAME IN PARK; 1 PM GREASED POLE CONTEST; 4PM TUG-OFWAR; 6 PM PORK BARBEQUE; 6:30 PM MINI TRACTOR PULL; 7 PM BAND CONCERT; 7:30 PM PARADE DOWNTOWN THOR; 9 PM DANCE IN THOR HALL. (LOCAL). ALFRED T GUDDALL, CHMN; TOWN OF THOR & NORWAY TOWNSHIP; 104 ANN ST; THOR, IA 50591. (#18742-1).

THORNTON

BICENTENNIAL CITY, THORTON, IA. ALL RESIDENTS WILL BE ASKED TO PLANT FLOWERBEDS IN BICENTENNIAL COLORS; 4-H CLUBS AND BOY SCOUTS WILL PAINT FIRE HYDRANTS AND REFUSE CONTAINERS - THEME WILL BE BICENTENNIAL. (LOCAL). GRACE SCHANEMAN, PROJ DIRECTOR; CITY OF THORTON; THORNTON, IA 50479. (#21703).

RECIPES IN FORM OF COOKBOOK, THORNTON, IA. GATHERING OF RECIPES FROM LOCAL CITIZENS & COMPILING A COOKBOOK FOR SALE. (LOCAL). MRS MITCHELL HARTWIG, COORDINATOR; JR FED CLUB; RFD; THORNTON, IA 50479. (#21743).

SELL BICENTENNIAL - AMERICAN FLAGS, THORNTON, IA. DOOR TO DOOR SELLING OF BICENTENNIAL-AMERICAN FLAG; THE FLYING OF THESE FLAGS WILL BE ENCOURAGED. (LOCAL). WAIT SCHRAEDER, CHAIRMAN; AMERICAN LEGION POST 440; 500 LARCH ST; THORNTON, IA 50479. (#21742).

THORNTON'S HERITAGE: PAST TO PRESENT - IA. WE ARE COMPILING A COMPLETE HISTORY OF THE TOWN & COMMUNITY IN WRITING AND PICTURES. (LOCAL). LOLA SCHROEDER, CHAIRMAN; THORNTON BICENTENNIAL COMMITTEE; THORNTON, IA 50479. (#21741).

SEPT 1 - 30, '75. ESSAY CONTEST: A PAST TO HONOR, A FUTURE TO MOLD. THE WINNER ESSAY WILL COMPETE IN NATIONAL ESSAY CONTEST. (LOCAL). MRS W SCHROEDER, CHMN; FEDERATED WOMEN'S CLUBS; BOX 116; THORNTON, IA 50479. (#200018-158).

JUNE 26, '76. OUR YEARS PAST - HISTORICAL DISPLAY. A DISPLAY OF ANTIQUE DOCUMENTS, PICTURES & CLOTHING. (LOCAL). RONALD LONG, COORD; THORNTON DEVELOPMENT CLUB; THORNTON, IA 50479. (#105476-1).

JUNE 26 - 27, '76. HERITAGE DAYS; AN OLD FASHIONED COMMUNITY GATHERING. FAIR, FESTIVAL, PARADE AT MAIN STREET AREA OF THORNTON AND PARK. (LOCAL). LOLA SCHROEDER; TOWN OF THORNTON; 500 LARCH ST; THORNTON, IA 50479. (#105512-1).

THURMAN

ASSOCIATION/FORNEY FAMILY PICNIC IN THURMAN, IOWA. FORNEY FAMILY (OLD PIONEER FAMILY) & ALUMNI PICNIC TO BE HELD ON AUG 3, 1975, WITH SCHOOL HISTORY FESTIVAL. A LOGO FLAG WILL BE PRESENTED. (LOCAL). MRS LOREN JOHNSON, PROJ DIRECTOR; ALUMNI ASSOC; THURMAN, IA 51654. (#12124).

BEAUTIFICATION & CLEAN-UP OF THURMAN, IOWA. BEAUTIFICATION & CLEANING UP OF JUNK, VACANT LOTS AND LAWNS - PAINTING TO BE DONE WHERE NEEDED. (LOCAL). CLAUDE SHELDON, PROJ DIRECTOR; CITY OF THURMAN; CITY HALL; THURMAN, IA 51654. (#12122).

RESTORATION OF THURMAN PARK, IOWA. MEMORIAL TREES PLANTED, FLAG POLE CONSTRUCTED AT FIRE STATION BY VOLUNTEER FIREMEN. PARK & INDEX TO BE CONSTRUCTED. (LOCAL). MRS CARL SMITH, CHAIRMAN; PARK RESTORATION COMMITTEE; THURMAN, IA 51654. (#12123).

THURMAN—CONTINUED

TOWN BELL & WAR MEMORIAL RESTORATION: THURMAN, IA. ORIGINAL CURFEW BELL TO BE RESTORED & PLACED IN FRONT OF FIRE HOUSE; FLAG POLE TO BE PLACED AT FIRE HOUSE NEXT TO FIRE BELL; WAR MEMORIAL TO BE REPAIRED & RESTORED. (LOCAL). CARL E SMITH, PROJECT DIRECTOR; THURMAN VOLUNTEER FIRE DEPARTMENT; THURMAN, IA 51654. (#12125).

TINGLEY

NEW FLAG POLE - TINGLEY, IA. A NEW FLAG POLE WILL BE ERECTED IN TINGLEY IN HONOR OF THE BICENTENNIAL. (LOCAL). GARY PETERSOHN, PROJ DIRECTOR; TOWN OF TINGLEY; TINGLEY, IA 50863. (#16770).

TREE PLANTING - TINGLEY, IA. TREES AND SHRUBBERY WILL BE PLANTED BY THE LIONS CLUB. (LOCAL). GARY PETERSOHN, PROJ DIRECTOR; TINGLEY LIONS CLUB; TINGLEY, IA 50863. (#16769).

TIPTON

BICENTENNIAL DECAL FOR MOTOR VEHICLE - TIPTON, IA. A BICENTENNIAL DECAL WITH WHITE OVAL BACKGROUND LETTERED IN BLACK WITH THE WORDS 'AMERICAN BICENTENNIAL' AROUND THE OUTSIDE WITH A 5POINT STAR CENTERED IN THE OVAL ACCENTED BY A SHIELD. (LOCAL). RICHARD SKLADZIEN, ASSISTANT; CEDAR COUNTY ENGINEER'S OFFICE; TIPTON, IA 52772. (#21996).

IOWA ALLEGORY - OIL PAINTING FROM TIPTON, IA. REPRESENTATIONAL OIL PAINTING, 5' X 14', DEPICTS RURAL IOWA: CROPS, LIVESTOCK, LANDSCAPE, FARM FAMILY. EMPHASIS IS UNITY OF THE FARMER AND THE EARTH IN THE PRODUCTION OF IOWA FOOD PRODUCTS. (ST-WIDE). RICHARD JACOBI, ARTIST-PAINTER; RT 2, BOX 75; TIPTON, IA 52772. (#12131).

JULY 30 - AUG 3, '76. CEDAR COUNTY FAIR. FAIR AT FAIRGROUNDS. (LOCAL). MOLLIE WILLIAMS, COORD; CEDAR COUNTY FAIR ASSOC; RFD 3; TIPTON, IA 52772. (#104764-1).

TODDVILLE

APR 23 - JULY 4, '76. 'THE SPIRIT OF '76' - BICENTENNIAL CONCERTS. LIVE PERFORMANCE AT TODDVILLE FREE METHODIST CHURCH & VETERANS MEMORIAL STADIUM. (LOCAL). JOHN D GREEN, COORD; TODDVILLE FREE METHODIST CHURCH; PO BOX 93; TODDVILLE, IA 52341. (#200018-184).

TOLEDO

JULY 2 - 5, '76. TOLEDO VOLUNTEER FIRE DEPARTMENT CENTENNIAL. SCHEDULED ACTIVITIES ARE FIREWORKS, PARADES, ART FAIR, PLAYS, OLD FASHIONED CARNIVAL AND WATERFIGHTS. AT COURTHOUSE SQUARE. (LOCAL). BILL CHRISTENSEN, CHMN; TOLEDO VOLUNTEER FIRE DEPARTMENT; 500 S GREEN; TOLEDO, IA 52342. (#105329-1).

TOMA

TIME CAPSULE, TAMA, IA. ITEMS OF INTEREST TO BE PLACED IN A STEEL VAULT TO BE OPENED AFTER 2076. (LOCAL). RICHARD K BRUENE, COORDINATOR; TAMA COUNTY BICENTENNIAL COMMITTEE; GLADBROOK, IA 50635. (#19847).

TRAER

TAMA JIM WILSON MEMORIAL MARKER, TRAER, IA. A BRONZE MARKER TO BE DEDICATED AUG 2, 1976 AT TAYLOR PARK HONORING ONE OF THE FIRST US SECRETARIES OF AGRICULTURE. (LOCAL). RICHARD K BRUENE, COORDINATOR; TAMA COUNTY BICENTENNIAL COMMITTEE; GLADBROOK, IA 50635. (#19848).

TRAER'S WINDING STAIRS - PROJ OF TRAER, IA. TRAER, IOWA IS NOTED FOR ITS WINDING STAIRS, THE ONLY CAST IRON WINDING STAIRS IN THE U S. (LOCAL). R G KETTER, PROJ DIRECTOR; TRAER WINDING STAIRS, INC; RR 1; TRAER, IA 50675. (#14303).

JULY 15 - 18, '76. CZECH FOLK FEST. FESTIVAL. (LOCAL). R G KETTER, DIRECTOR; TRAER FESTIVAL COMMITTEE; RR 1; TRAER, IA 50675. (#101740-1).

JULY '76. TIME CAPSULE. CAPSULE WILL BE REOPENED AT THE TRICENTENNIAL. (LOCAL). R G KETTER, PROJ DIRECTOR; TRAER BICENTENNIAL COMMITTEE; RR 1; TRAER, IA 50675. (#14304-1).

AUG 2, '76. DEDICATION OF TAMA JIM WILSON MEMORIAL. DEDICATION OF A MARKER HONORING TAMA JIM WILSON, ONE OF THE FIRST U S SECRETARIES OF AGRICULTURE. AT TAYLOR PARK. (LOCAL). RICHARD BRUENE, PROJ DIR; TAMA COUNTY BICENTENNIAL COMMITTEE; GLADBROOK, IA 50635. (#104582-1).

TRENTON

TREE PLANTING IN TRENTON, IA. SEVEN TREES PLANTED IN TRENTON PARK ON MARCH 26TH, 1976. THE TRENTON CUB SCOUTS PARTICIPATED. (LOCAL). EUNICE M ROCKWELL, CHAIRPERSON; TRENTON AMERICAN LEGION & AUXILIARY NO 478; RT 1, BOX 186; SALEM, IA 52649. (#22183).

JUNE 27, '76. BICENTENNIAL BRINGS CIRCUIT RIDER TO TRENTON. CEREMONY AT TRENTON PARK. (LOCAL). EUNICE M ROCKWELL; TRENTON AMERICAN LEGION & AUXILIARY NO 478; RTE 1 BOX 186; SALEM, IA 52649. (#105948-1).

TREYNOR

COMMUNITY CENTER IN TREYNOR, IOWA. A COMMUNITY CENTER IS BEING PLANNED FOR USE BY ALL AGE GROUPS IN THE TREYNOR AREA. THE VETERANS MEMORIAL PLAQUE WILL BE PLACED IN THE BUILDING. (LOCAL). KEITH R LAMBERTSEN, PROJ DIRECTOR; TREYNOR BICENTENNIAL COMMITTEE; BOX 171; TREYNOR, IA 51501. (#10084).

COMMUNITY DIRECTORY-NEWSPAPER FOR TREYNOR, IOWA. A BUSINESS AND RESIDENTIAL DIRECTORY OF THE COMMUNITY. (LOCAL). KEITH R LAMBERTSEN, PROJ DIRECTOR; TREYNOR BICENTENNIAL COMMITTEE; BOX 171; TREYNOR, IA 51501. (#10086).

MUSICAL PAGEANT. A PAGEANT WILL DEPICT SCENES OF AREA & NATIONAL HISTORY WITH MUSICAL HIGHLIGHTS. (LOCAL). KEITH R LAMBERTSEN; TREYNOR BICENTENNIAL COMMITTEE; BOX 171; TREYNOR, IA 51501. (#10079-1).

VETERANS MEMORIAL PLAQUE IN TREYNOR, IOWA. A PLAQUE TO HONOR ALL MEN OF THE COMMUNITY WHO GAVE THEIR LIVES FOR OUR COUNTRY. (LOCAL). KEITH R LAMBERTSEN, PROJ DIRECTOR; TREYNOR BICENTENNIAL COMMITTEE; BOX 171; TREYNOR, IA 51501. (#10085).

JULY 2, '75. HORSE SHOW. THE PROJECT INVOLVES AN APPROVED ISHA POINT HORSE SHOW. (LOCAL). KEITH R LAMBERTSEN; TREYNOR BICENTENNIAL COMMITTEE; BOX 171; TREYNOR, IA 51501. (#10082-1).

JULY 2, '75. OPENING CEREMONIES. THE AMERICAN LEGION WILL OFFICIALLY OPEN 4TH OF JULY AND BICENTENNIAL ACTIVITIES. (LOCAL). KEITH R LAMBERTSEN; TREYNOR BICENTENNIAL COMMITTEE; BOX 171; TREYNOR, IA 51501. (#10083-1).

JULY 2 - 4, '75. CARNIVAL. THE CARNIVAL THIS YEAR WILL FEATURE A CONTRACTED MIDWAY AND BOOTHS REPRESENTING LOCAL PEOPLE. (LOCAL). KEITH R LAMBERTSEN; TREYNOR BICENTENNIAL COMMITTEE; BOX 171; TREYNOR, IA 51501. (#10088-1).

JULY 2 - 4, '75. FARM MACHINERY EXHIBIT & LOCAL PRODUCE SHOW. DISPLAYS OF ANTIQUE MACHINERY AND LOCAL PRODUCE. (LOCAL). KEITH R LAMBERTSEN; TREYNOR BICENTENNIAL COMMITTEE; BOX 171; TREYNOR, IA 51501. (#10090-1).

JULY 3, '75. PARADE. A PARADE WITH JUDGED CATEGORIES OF FLOATS, BANDS, MILITARY UNITS, CIVIC GROUPS AND SADDLE CLUBS WILL BE HELD. (LOCAL). KEITH R LAMBERTSEN; TREYNOR BICENTENNIAL COMMITTEE; BOX 171; TREYNOR, IA 51501. (#10081-1).

JULY 3, '75. WATERFIGHTS. CONTESTS BETWEEN AREA VOLUNTEER FIRE DEPARTMENTS. (LOCAL). KEITH R LAMBERTSEN; TREYNOR BICENTENNIAL COMMITTEE; BOX 171; TREYNOR, IA 51501. (#10087-1).

JULY 3 - 4, '75. DISPLAY OF ANTIQUES. A DISPLAY OF ALL TYPES OF ANTIQUES FROM HOUSEHOLD ITEMS TO TOOLS. (LOCAL). KEITH R LAMBERTSEN; TREYNOR BICENTENNIAL COMMITTEE; BOX 171; TREYNOR, IA 51501. (#10089-1).

JULY 3 - 5, '75. ACHIEVEMENT SHOWS, 4-H CLUBS. BOYS AND GIRLS FROM LOCAL 4-H CLUBS WILL DEMONSTRATE THEIR PROJECTS. (LOCAL). KEITH R LAMBERTSEN; TREYNOR BICENTENNIAL COMMITTEE; BOX 171; TREYNOR, IA 51501. (#10080-1).

JULY 4, '75. BASKET DINNER. A POTLUCK DINNER WILL BE HELD FOLLOWING THE UNION CHURCH SERVICE. (LOCAL). KEITH R LAMBERTSEN; TREYNOR BICENTENNIAL COMMITTEE; BOX 171; TREYNOR, IA 51501. (#10077-1).

JULY 4, '75. SPORTS EVENT. A VARIETY OF SPORTS EVENTS SUCH AS BASEBALL, SOFTBALL AND HORSESHOES ARE INCLUDED IN THE PROJECT. (LOCAL). KEITH R LAMBERTSEN; TREYNOR BICENTENNIAL COMMITTEE; BOX 171; TREYNOR, IA 51501. (#10076-1).

JULY 4, '75. UNION CHURCH SERVICE, LOCAKKL CHURCHES. A UNION WORKSHOP WILL REPRESENT ALL COMMUNITY CHURCHES AND FEATURE A COMMUNITY CHOIR. (LOCAL). KEITH R LAMBERTSEN; TREYNOR BICENTENNIAL COMMITTEE; BOX 171; TREYNOR, IA 51501. (#10078-1).

JULY 3 - 5, '76. A PEAK INTO THE PAST, PROGRAMS, PARADES, DISPLAYS. FESTIVAL AT E END OF MAIN ST, SCHOOL AREA. (LOCAL). MRS MERLE HAYES, CHAIRMAN; TREYNOR BICENTENNIAL COMMITTEE; RTE 2; COUNCIL BLFS, IA 51501. (#101886-1).

TRIPOLI

BICENTENNIAL COOKBOOK - TRIPOLI, IA. FAVORITE RECIPES OF COMMUNITY COOKS PASSED DOWN FOR GENERATIONS AND RECIPES USED BY COOKS TODAY, TO PASS ON TO FUTURE COOKS. (LOCAL). MRS CAROL HUNEMULLER, BICENTENNIAL CHAIRMAN; TRIPOLI FEDERATED WOMAN'S CLUB; TRIPOLI, IA 50676. (#19611).

BICENTENNIAL DISPLAYS, TRIPOLI, IA. STORE AND ANTIQUE AUTO DISPLAYS WILL BE PROVIDED. (LOCAL). MRS MARY AHRENS, PROJ COORDINATOR; TRIPOLI COMMERCIAL CLUB; WAVERLY, IA 50677. (#14512).

BREMER COUNTY CEMETERY RECORDS PROJECT - IA. CEMETERY RECORDS WILL BE RECORDED FOR POSTERITY. (LOCAL). JEFF CLEVELAND, DIRECTOR; BREMER COUNTY BICENTENNIAL; TRIPOLI, IA 50677. (#18553).

CHURCH HISTORY PROJECT OF TRIPOLI, IA. A HISTORY OF FAITH UNITED CHURCH OF CHRIST WILL BE WRITTEN. (LOCAL). MRS VALERIA SCHWARTZ; FAITH UNITED CHURCH OF CHRIST; TRIPOLI, IA 50677. (#14513).

HISTORY OF TRIPOLI, IA. A HISTORY OF TRIPOLI AND ITS CEMETERY WILL BE COMPILED AND PRINTED. (LOCAL). LUELLA KELSEY, PRES; SENIOR CITIZEN GROUP; TRIPOLI, IA 50676. (#14514).

SCHOOLHOUSE RESTORATION - TRIPOLI, IA. RESTORATION OF RURAL SCHOOLHOUSE TO BE USED AS A MUSEUM. (LOCAL). LEON KIRCHHOFF & MRS MARY ANN AHRENS; TRIPOLI COMMUNITY BICENTENNIAL COMMITTEE; TRIPOLI, IA 50676. (#14515).

TROY

TROY ACADEMY RESTORATION PROJECT, TROY, IA. RESTORATION OF TROY ACADEMY BUILT IN 1853. (LOCAL). QUENTINE E JOHNSON, PROJ DIRECTOR; DAVIS COUNTY HISTORICAL SOCIETY; 601 N WASHINGTON; BLOOMFIELD, IA 52537. (#13866).

TRURO

PARK RESTORATION & BEAUTIFICATION - TRURO, IA. THE LIONS CLUB WILL RESTORE & BEAUTIFY THE COMMUNITY PARK. (LOCAL). LESTER FREEMAN, PROJ DIRECTOR; TRURO LIONS CLUB; TRURO, IA 50257. (#22000).

JUNE 25, '76. COMMUNITY PARK NAMING & DEDICATION CEREMONY. CEREMONY. (LOCAL). LESTER FREEMAN, DIRECTOR; TRURO LIONS CLUB; TRURO, IA 50257. (#22000-1).

JUNE 25 - 26, '76. FRONTIER DAYS. FESTIVAL. (LOCAL). LESTER FREEMAN, PROJ DIR; TRURO FIRE DEPT; TRURO, IA 50257. (#105774-2).

JUNE 25 - 27, '76. ALUMNI REUNION & PICNIC. FESTIVAL. (LOCAL). LESTER FREEMAN, PROJ DIR; TRURO LIONS CLUB; TRURO, IA 50257. (#105774-1).

UDELL

FUTURE GROWTH, UDELL, IA. TREES WILL BE PLANTED IN THE PARK. (LOCAL). ANNA BURKLAND, DIRECTOR; UDELL BICENTENNIAL COMMISSION; UDELL, IA 52593. (#24645).

UNDERWOOD

CITY PARK RESTORATION - UNDERWOOD, IA. RESTORATION AND DEDICATION OF THE UNDERWOOD CITY PARK. (LOCAL). ROBERT DOSE, CHAIRMAN; UNDERWOOD BICENTENNIAL COMMITTEE; UNDERWOOD, IA 51576. (#22002).

'OUR COUNTRY TIS OF THEE', MUSICAL HISTORY. LIVE PERFORMANCE. (LOCAL). ROBERT DOSE, CHAIRMAN; UNDERWOOD JUNIOR HIGH; UNDERWOOD, IA 51576. (#105775-2).

MAY 20, '76. UNDERWOOD CITY PARK DEDICATION CEREMONY. SPEAKERS: KEN FULK, REP OF TOM HARKINS OFFICE; MUSIC BY UNDERWOOD HIGH SCHOOL BAND. (LOCAL). ROBERT DOSE, CHAIRMAN; UNDERWOOD BICENTENNIAL COMMITTEE; UNDERWOOD, IA 51576. (#22002-1).

MAY '76. JOHN PAUL JONES MUSICAL FESTIVAL. FESTIVAL. (LOCAL). MRS DONALD NOBLING, COORD; UNDERWOOD HIGH SCHOOL MUSIC DEPT; UNDERWOOD, IA 51576. (#105775-1).

UNION

CITY PARK BEAUTIFICATION, UNION, IA. TREE PLANTING, LANDSCAPING & GENERAL REPAIR & CLEAN-UP IN CITY PARK OF UNION, IOWA. (LOCAL). GARY HAUSER, CO-CHAIRMAN; UNION COMMUNITY BICENTENNIAL COMMISSION; FOURTH & PERRY; UNION, IA 50258. (#16437).

'COURTS FOR KIDS' - UNION, IA. TENNIS COURTS WILL BE AVAILABLE FOR COMMUNITY USE, PARTICULARLY FOR THE YOUNG PEOPLE. FUND-RAISING DRIVE AND ENLISTMENT OF VOLUNTEER HELP TO BUILD THEM. (LOCAL). HERMAN HARRIS, CHAIRMAN; UNION BICENTENNIAL COMMITTEE; UNION, IA 50258. (#19721).

STAGECOACH TRAIL, UNION, IA. MARKING AND PROVIDING ACCESS TO REMNANTS OF OLD HARDIN COUNTY STAGECOACH TRAIL (TRACKS ARE STILL VISIBLE). (ST-WIDE). GARY HAUSER, CO-CHAIRMAN; UNION COMMUNITY BICENTENNIAL COMMISSION; FOURTH & PERRY; UNION, IA 50258. (#16435).

WHITNEY CEMETERY PRESERVATION, UNION, IA. PETITION COUNTY BOARD OF SUPERVISORS TO BUILD FENCE AROUND WHITNEY CEMETERY. (LOCAL). GARY HAUSER, CO-CHAIRMAN; UNION COMMUNITY BICENTENNIAL COMMISSION; FOURTH & PERRY; UNION, IA 50258. (#16436).

100 YR SIGNATURE BOOK - UNION, IA. MEMBERSHIP CARDS WILL BE SOLD WHICH WILL ENTITLE PURCHASER TO AUTOGRAPH THE 100 YR SIGNATURE BOOK, KEPT BY THE HISTORICAL SOCIETY FOR THE USA TRICENTENNIAL. (LOCAL). HERMAN HARRIS, CO-CHAIRMAN; UNION BICENTENNIAL COMMISSION; DRAWER C; UNION, IA 50258. (#16438).

UNION — CONTINUED

SEPT 7, '75. UNION COMMUNITY BICENTENNIAL FUN DAY. CANOE RACES, OLDnTIME CONTESTS SUCH AS LADIES NAIL DRIVING, WATERMELON SEED SPITTING, HORSESHOE PITCHING, PIE EATING; TWO BANDS WILL PLAY; OLD STAGECOACH TRAIL COMMEMORATION CEREMONY. AT LONG'S PARK, ONE MILE EAST OF UNION, IOWA. (LOCAL). GARY HAUSER, CO-CHAIRMAN; UNION COMMUNITY BICENTENNIAL COMMISSION; FOURTH & PERRY; UNION, IA 50258. (#102952-3).

JULY 24, '76. TAR HEEL DAYS. PIONEER CRAFT DISPLAYS, TRADITIONAL 'TAR HEEL' FOODS. AT CITY PARK. (LOCAL). GARY HAUSER, CO-CHAIRMAN; UNION COMMUNITY BICENTENNIAL COMMISSION; FOURTH & PERRY; UNION, IA 50258. (#102952-2).

UNIVERSITY PK

'ALABASTER AND SPIKENARD', BOOK, UNIVERSITY PK, IA. AN UPDATE OF THE COLLEGE'S HISTORY WILL BE PUBLISHED IN THE FORM OF A BOOK. (LOCAL). HERB ANDERSON, PROJ DIRECTOR; VENNARD COLLEGE; UNIVERSITY PK, IA 52595. (#18545).

BICENTENNIAL MINUTES - UNIVERSITY PARK, IA. A BRIEF STATEMENT OF EVENTS WHICH HAPPENED ON THIS DAY IN HISTORY. (LOCAL). HUBERT ANDERSON, CHAIRMAN; VENNARD COLLEGE BICENTENNIAL COMMITTEE; UNIVERSITY PK, IA 52595. (#19236).

BOOK DISCUSSION. A DISCUSSION OF A BOOK, WHOSE THEME IS THE BICENTENNIAL. (LOCAL). HERB ANDERSON, PROJ DIR; VENNARD COLLEGE; UNIVERSITY PK, IA 52595. (#104229-2).

CAMPUS WIDE ESSAY CONTEST - UNIVERSITY PARK, IA. THE CONTEST WILL HAVE A BICENTENNIAL-HISTORICAL THEME. (NAT'L). HUBERT ANDERSON, CHAIRMAN; VENNARD COLLEGE; UNIVERSITY PK, IA 52595. (#19237).

PANEL DISCUSSION: RELIGION IN THE ROLE OF AMERICAN HISTORY. SEMINAR. (LOCAL). HERB ANDERSON, PROJ DIR; VENNARD COLLEGE; UNIVERSITY PK, IA 52595. (#104229-1).

PUBLIC ADDRESS ON CIVIC INVOLVEMENT. SEMINAR AT CHAPEL. (LOCAL). HERB ANDERSON, PROJ DIR; VENNARD COLLEGE; UNIVERSITY PK, IA 52595. (#104229-4). **(??).**

NOV 7, '75 - APR 5, '76. DINNER RALLIES. DINNER RALLIES TO TAKE PLACE AT VARIOUS LOCATIONS THROUGHOUT THE MIDWEST - MUSIC AND SLIDE PRESENTATIONS ON THE INVOLVEMENT OF VENNARD COLLEGE IN RELIGIOUS HISTORY. (LOCAL). HERB ANDERSON, PROJ DIR; VENNARD COLLEGE; UNIVERSITY PK, IA 52595. (#104229-5).

NOV 25, '75. ALABASTER AND SPIKENARD - THE HISTORY OF VENNARD COLLEGE - PLAY. LIVE PERFORMANCE AT CHAPEL, VENNARD COLLEGE. (LOCAL). HERB ANDERSON, COORD; VENNARD COLLEGE; UNIVERSITY PK, IA 52595. (#200018-160).

FEB 13, '76. PATRIOTIC SONGFEST. FESTIVAL AT GYMNASIUM. (LOCAL). HERB ANDERSON, PROJ DIR; VENNARD COLLEGE; UNIVERSITY PK, IA 52595. (#104229-3).

MAY 19 - 20, '76. KIDDIE KOLLEGE GRADUATION. CEREMONY, LIVE PERFORMANCE AT KIDDIE KOLLEGE. (LOCAL). MRS MERNE HARRIS, CHMN; VENNARD COLLEGE; 901 BETHEL; UNIVERSITY PK, IA 52595. (#107744-1).

URBANA

SMALL CITY PARK - URBANA, IA. FLAG POLE ERECTED WITH CEMENTED PYRAMID AT BOTTOM FOR PLAQUE NOTING URBANAS ORIGIN; SHELTER HOUSE, PICNIC TABLES AND TREES ARE ALSO INCLUDED. (LOCAL). NANCY NEWTON, CHAIRMAN; BICENTENNIAL COMMITTEE; BOX 384; URBANA, IA 52345. (#29218).

AUG 13 - 14, '76. JOINT SWEETCORN DAY AND BICENTENNIAL CELEBRATION. PARADE, WATERFIGHTS, TALENT SHOW, 2 STREET DANCES, BICENTENNIAL STATE & AMERICAN FLAG PRESENTATIONS, STREET COMPETITION FOR KIDS. AT MAIN ST. (LOCAL). NANCY NEWTON, CHAIRPERSON; VINTON BICENTENNIAL COMMITTEE; 108 E 5 ST; VINTON, IA 52349. (#200018-242).

URBANDALE

COMMUNITY DEVELOPMENT IN URBANDALE, IA. THE CITY OF URBANDALE IS BUILDING A NEW LIBRARY, A NEW FIRE STATION AND ITS FIRST SWIMMING POOL, AN INDOOR/OUTDOOR FACILITY. (LOCAL). NILE MCDONALD, CITY MANAGER; CITY OF URBANDALE; CITY HALL, 3315 70TH ST; URBANDALE, IA 50322. (#13100).

INDUSTRIAL DEVELOPMENT IN URBANDALE, IA. THE URBANDALE CHAMBER OF COMMERCE IS ENCOURAGING NEW INDUSTRIES TO LOCATE IN URBANDALE THROUGH THE WORK OF ITS INDUSTRIAL DEVELOPMENT COMMITTEE. (LOCAL). ROBERT RILEY, CHAIRMAN; URBANDALE CHAMBER OF COMMERCE - INDUSTRIAL DEVELOPMENT COMMITTEE; PO BOX 3685; URBANDALE, IA 50322. (#13099).

SCHOOL DEVELOPMENT IN URBANDALE, IA. THE SCHOOL DISTRICT IS PLANNING TO BUILD A PERFORMING ARTS COMPLEX AND A SECOND GYMNASIUM AT URBANDALE HIGH SCHOOL. (LOCAL). CLIFFORD WOBKEN, BUSINESS MANAGER; URBANDALE COMMUNITY SCHOOLS; 7101 AIRLINE AVE; URBANDALE, IA 50322. (#13101).

URBANDALE HISTORICAL PROJECTS, IA. EXHIBITS AND DISPLAYS OF A HISTORIC THEME, SHORT SUBJECT HISTORICAL MOVIES & SHUTTLE BUS SERVICE TO THE LIVING HISTORY FARMS. (ST-WIDE). PATTI FITZGERRELL, CHAIRPERSON; URBANDALE 4TH OF JULY CELEBRATION COMMITTEE; 7116 TOWNSEND; URBANDALE, IA 50322. (#18802).

APR 22 - 24, '76. ANTIQUES AND COLLECTIBLES. EXHIBIT AT URBANDALE PUBLIC LIBRARY/7305 AURORA. (LOCAL). SANDY MCPHERSON, COORD; URBANDALE WOMENS' CLUB; 7320 OLIVER SMITH DR; URBANDALE, IA 50322. (#106382-2).

JULY 2 - 5, '76. 4TH OF JULY CELEBRATION. ARTS & CRAFTS, RIDES, FIREWORKS, PARADE, PLAY, ETC. AT LIONS PARK. (LOCAL). PATTI FITZGERRELL, CHMN; 4TH OF JULY COMMITTEE; 3515 ELM DR; URBANDALE, IA 50322. (#106382-1).

UTE

NEW COMMUNITY BUILDING, UTE, IA. A NEW COMMUNITY BUILDING WILL REPLACE THE OLD LEGION HALL. (LOCAL). HON ARCHIE MAHONEY, MAYOR; UTE IMPROVEMENT CLUB; UTE, IA 51060. (#22215).

RESTORATION OF BUSINESS BUILDINGS, UTE, IA. IMPROVEMENT OF DOWNTOWN BUSINESS AREA. (LOCAL). THERMA KIEPE, COORDINATOR; UTE BICENTENNIAL CLUB; UTE, IA 51060. (#22214).

MAY 31, '76. MEMORIAL DAY PARADE & SERVICE. CEREMONY, PARADE AT UTE CEMETERY. (LOCAL). THERMA KIEPE, COORD; AMERICAN LEGION AND THE VETERANS OF FOREIGN WARS; UTE, IA 51060. (#105965-1).

VAIL

TIME CAPSULE, VAIL, IA. A TIME CAPSULE CONTAINING SPECIAL ITEMS WILL BE BURIED. (LOCAL). HAROLD MCCOLLOUGH, COORDINATOR; CRAWFORD COUNTY BICENTENNIAL COMMISSION; VAIL, IA 51465. (#21421).

MAY 30, '76. FLAG RAISING CEREMONY TO UNITE YOUTH & SENIOR CITIZENS. CEREMONY AT TOWN PARK. (LOCAL). DAN CRANE, PRES; VAIL BICENTENNIAL COMMITTEE; BOX 262; VAIL, IA 51465. (#105334-3).

JULY 23 - 26, '76. AGRICULTURAL AND LIVESTOCK EXHIBIT. EXHIBIT. (LOCAL). DAN CRANE, PRES; VAIL BICENTENNIAL COMMITTEE; BOX 262; VAIL, IA 51465. (#105334-2).

JULY 23 - 26, '76. PARADE, OLD & YOUNG. CHILDREN'S PARADE ON FRIDAY, JULY 23RD AT 2:30 PM. THE MAIN PARADE WILL BE SATURDAY, JULY 24TH AT 4 PM. (LOCAL). DANNY NELSON, COORD; VAIL FIREMAN; VAIL, IA 51465. (#105334-5).

JULY 24, '76. STREET DANCE. FESTIVAL AT MAIN STREET. (LOCAL). DAN CRANE, PRES; VAIL BICENTENNIAL COMMITTEE; BOX 262; VAIL, IA 51465. (#105334-1).

JULY 25, '76. BICENTENNIAL PAGEANT AND THEATER. LIVE PERFORMANCE AT MEMORIAL HALL. (ST-WIDE). DAN CRANE, PRES; VAIL BICENTENNIAL COMMITTEE; BOX 262; VAIL, IA 51465. (#105334-4).

VAN METER

ORAL HISTORY PROJECT - VAN METER, IA. TAPES OF SENIOR CITIZENS WILL BE TRANSCRIBED FOR LOCAL AND SCHOOL LIBRARIES. (LOCAL). DIANE YOUNG, CHAIRMAN; TUESDAY CLUB; 345 4TH AVE; VAN METER, IA 50261. (#23147).

QUILT - VAN METER, IA. EMBROIDERED BLOCKS WILL SHOW EARLY BUILDINGS AND D LANDMARKS IN VAN METER AREA. (LOCAL). ARDIS ANDERSON, CHAIRMAN; AMERICAN BICENTENNIAL CORP OF VAN METER; RR 1; VAN METER, IA 50261. (#21720).

RED, WHITE & BLUE GARDEN, VAN METER, IA. A RED, WHITE & BLUE GARDEN WILL BE PLANTED IN DOWNTOWN AREA & CARED FOR BY GIRL SCOUTS. PROJECT TO PROMOTE RED, WHITE & BLUE GARDENS IN THE COMMUNITY. (LOCAL). ARDIS ANDERSON, NEIGHBORHOOD CHAIRMAN; GIRL SCOUTS; RR 1; VAN METER, IA 50261. (#21721).

TOWN SIGN, VAN METER, IA. LARGE PAINTED SIGN FOR TOWN IDENTIFICATION. (LOCAL). ARDIS ANDERSON, CHAIRMAN; AMERICAN BICENTENNIAL CORPORATION OF VAN METER; RR 1; VAN METER, IA 50261. (#21722).

FEB 6, '76. 'I LOVE AMERICA' MUSICAL AND BICENTENNIAL FLAG PRESENTATION. LIVE PERFORMANCE, CEREMONY. (LOCAL). ARDIS ANDERSON, CHMN; VAN METER BICENTENNIAL COMMITTEE; RR 1; VAN METER, IA 50261. (#200018-161).

FEB 29, '76. CARNIVAL & HANDMADE CRAFTS SALE. EXHIBIT, FESTIVAL. (LOCAL). ARDIS ANDERSON, CHMN; VAN METER BICENTENNIAL COMMITTEE; RR 1; VAN METER, IA 50261. (#200018-163).

MAR 27, '76. BOX SOCIAL AND SQUARE DANCE. FESTIVAL. (LOCAL). ARDIS ANDERSON, CHMN; VAN METER BICENTENNIAL COMMITTEE; RR 1; VAN METER, IA 50261. (#200018-162).

JULY 10, '76. BICENTENNIAL FESTIVAL. FESTIVAL. (LOCAL). ARDIS ANDERSON, CHMN; VAN METER BICENTENNIAL COMMITTEE; RR 1; VAN METER, IA 50261. (#105524-2).

VARINA

FEB 21, '76. WASHINGTON'S BIRTHDAY BICENTENNIAL BALL. FESTIVAL AT ST COLUMBKILLE PARISH CENTER. (LOCAL). MRS LEONARD FARRELL, CHMN; W D STEINER AMERICAN LEGION POST #588; RR 1; FONDA, IA 50540. (#104694-1).

JULY 4, '76. BICENTENNIAL JULY 4TH CELEBRATION - VARINA, IA. THERE WILL BE WATER FIGHTS, AN ANTIQUE TRACTOR PULL, FIREWORKS, ETC. AT MAIN ST, VARINA, IA. (LOCAL). MRS GAYLA VOSS; VARINA VOLUNTEER FIRE DEPT & CITY OF VARINA; RR 1; FONDA, IA 50540. (#107783-3).

VICTOR

TREE PLANTING PROJECT - VICTOR, IA. TREES WILL BE PLANTED AROUND THE TOWN. (LOCAL). BERNARD HAMILTON, CHAIRMAN; VICTOR LIONS CLUB; VICTOR, IA 52347. (#32607).

MAY 28 - 30, '76. BICENTENNIAL FESTIVAL. STYLE SHOW, ARTS & CRAFTS, BAZAAR, HOME TALENT SHOW & WINDOW DISPLAYS. (LOCAL). BERNARD HAMILTON, CHMN; BICENTENNIAL CENTRAL COMMITTEE OF VICTOR; VICTOR, IA 52347. (#200018-291).

VILLISCA

HISTORY OF VILLISCA, IOWA. THE HISTORY OF VILLISCA, PREPARED BY HIGH SCHOOL STUDENTS. (LOCAL). R M GOODMAN, PROJ COORDINATOR; VILLISCA HIGH SCHOOL; 200 E 1ST ST; VILLISCA, IA 50864. (#11482).

RENOVATION OF DEPOT IN VILLISCA, IA. DEPOT TO BE RENOVATED & MADE INTO CITY MUSEUM. (LOCAL). MS HIBBS, FIELD REPRESENTATIVE; FEDERETTES CLUB; 200 E FIRST ST; VILLISCA, IA 50864. (#11483).

THEATER PAGEANT - PROJ OF VILLISCA, IA. A THEATER PRODUCTION OF HISTORICAL NATURE WILL BE PRESENTED. (LOCAL). CHARLES GIFFORD, PRESIDENT; VILLISCA BICENTENNIAL COMMITTEE; 200 E FIRST; VILLISCA, IA 50864. (#12050).

VINING

FLAG POLE - VINING, IA. A FLAG POLE WILL BE ERECTED AT THE TOWN CENTER. (LOCAL). JAMES E BREJA, FIRE CHIEF; VINING VOLUNTEER FIRE DEPT; VINING, IA 52348. (#24226).

TOWN HISTORY - VINING, IA. AN ILLUSTRATED HISTORY OF THE CITY. (LOCAL). GEORGE R BAZAL, HISTORIAN; VINING BICENTENNIAL COMMITTEE; BINING, IA 52348. (#24225).

MAY 30, '76. MEMORIAL DAY SERVICES. CEREMONY, PARADE AT NATIONAL CEMETERY. (LOCAL). DELMAR KONICEK, COORD; AMERICAN LEGION; ELBERON, IA 52225. (#106794-1).

VINTON

BENTON COUNTY BEAUTIFICATION PROGRAM IN IOWA. TREES, SHRUBS, FLOWERING GRASSES WILL BE PLANTED ALONG MAIN ROADS ENTERING TOWNS. THE QUARY AREA NEAR GARRISON ALSO TO BE BEAUTIFIED. (LOCAL). HOPE ROGERS, CHAIRMAN; BENTON COUNTY BOARD OF SUPERVISORS; COURT HOUSE; VINTON, IA 52349. (#7792).

BENTON COUNTY, IOWA, HISTORICAL MUSEUM. AN OLD HOUSE IS TO BE RENOVATED AND THEN USED AS A MUSEUM. ROOMS IN THE MUSEUM ARE TO BE DONE IN DIFFERENT PERIODS OF HISTORY. MANNEQUINS WILL COMPLETE EACH SUITE DRESSED IN PERIOD CLOTHES. (LOCAL). MRS DALE HENSING, PRESIDENT; BENTON COUNTY HISTORICAL SOCIETY; 612 FIRST AVE; VINTON, IA 52349. (#6220). **ARBA GRANTEE.**

W DES MOINES

JORDAN HOME RESTORATION - WEST DES MOINES, IA. RESTORATION OF VICTORIAN MANSION LISTED ON THE NATIONAL REGISTER OF HISTORIC PLACES. (LOCAL). MRS BONNIE MCFADDEN, CHAIRMAN; WEST DES MOINES HISTORICAL SOCIETY; 517 9TH ST; W DES MOINES, IA 50265. (#15843).

SEPT 16 - 21, '75. AMERICAN FREEDOM TRAIN DISPLAY DAYS AT WEST DES MOINES. THE AMERICAN FREEDOM TRAIN WILL INCLUDE 10 EXHIBIT CARS & 2 SHOWCASE CARS DEPICTING DIFFERENT PHASES OF THE AMERICAN EXPERIENCE. ITS ARRIVAL WILL SERVE AS A CATALYST FOR LOCAL BICENTENNIAL CELEBRATIONS BY PEOPLE THROUGHOUT THIS NATION. (ST-WIDE). DON MALLICOAT, EDIT SVCS; THE AMERICAN FREEDOM TRAIN FOUNDATION, INC; 5205 LEESBURG PIKE, SUITE 800; BAILEY'S XRDS, VA 22041. (#1776-23).

JULY 3 - 4, '76. FOURTH OF JULY CELEBRATION. FESTIVAL, PARADE AT HOLIDAY PARK; 14TH & MAPLE STS. (LOCAL). L WARREN SHANK, VICE PRES; WEST DES MOINES JAYCEES; 4712 DAKOTA DR; W DES MOINES, IA 50265. (#102645-1).

WADENA

BANDSTAND AND CEMETERY PRESERVATION, WADENA, IA. REPAIR OLD BANDSTAND IN PARK; CLEAN UP AND FENCE IN AN ABANDONED CEMETERY. (LOCAL). DENVER WALKER, CHAIRMAN; BUSINESSMEN FEDERATED CLUB, COMMUNITY CLUB, 4-H CLUB; WADENA, IA 52169. (#19729).

COMMUNITY CENTER & MUSEUM, WADENA, IA. 100 YEAR OLD LIMESTONE BUILDING TO BE USED AS MUSEUM & COMMUNITY CENTER. THE 1ST FLOOR WILL HOUSE TOWNSHIP HALL, THE 2ND: LEANTO FOR MACHINER EXHIBIT, THE BASEMENT WILL BE A RECREATIONAL CENTER. (LOCAL). MARJORIE KNOX, CHAIRMAN; WADENA BICENTENNIAL COMMITTEE; WADENA, IA 52169. (#19323).

FLAG AVENUE AT CEMETERIES, WADENA, IA. AVENUE OF FLAGS AT CEMETERIES WITH FLAGS OF VETERANS. (LOCAL). G W ALDERSON, CHAIRMAN; AMERICAN LEGION AND FIRE DEPARTMENT; WADENA, IA 52169. (#19728).

WADENA — CONTINUED

FLAG FLYING PROMOTION, WADENA, IA. EVERY HOME & BUSINESS ESTABLISHMENT IN ILLYRIA TOWNSHIP WILL BE ENCOURAGED TO FLY THE AMERICAN FLAG. (LOCAL). MISS LORETTA MATTOCKS, PROJ CHAIRMAN; LEGION AUXILIARY; WADENA, IA 52169. (#19322).

MARKER AT CULVER TRADING POST, WADENA, IA. TRACE FOUNDATION OUTLINE OF OLD INDIAN TRADING POST BUILT IN 1841 AND MARK IT WITH A PLAQUE TO MAKE IT AVAILABLE FOR TOURISM. (LOCAL). TIM CORKERY, WEBELO SCOUTMASTER; BOY SCOUTS; WADENA, IA 52169. (#19730).

1976 BIOGRAPHICAL CENSUS & HISTORY, WADENA, IA. A PUBLICATION WILL INCLUDE THE HISTORY OF EVERY FAMILY & RESIDENT AS OF 1976. IT WILL ALSO INCLUDE UNPUBLISHED LOCAL HISTORY. (LOCAL). MARJORIE KNOX, LIBRARIAN; WADENA PUBLIC LIBRARY; WADENA, IA 52169. (#19321).

JUNE 14, '76. CROSS LIGHTING CEREMONY. CROSS WILL BE LIGHTED ON HILLTOP AS LAST CEREMONY OF JUNE 14 FESTIVAL. THE CROSS WILL SERVE AS A RELIGIOUS DEDICATION TO THE BICENTENNIAL. PLACED ON BLUFF, LIGHTS AUTOMATICALLY EACH EVENING & BURNS UNTIL 5AM. WILL BE A PERMANENT STRUCTURE. AT HILL SOUTH OF CITY OF WADENA. (LOCAL). LEALLEN KNOX, CHAIRMAN; PRESBYTERIAN, CATHOLIC & ILLYRIA CHURCHES; WADENA, IA 52169. (#104519-2).

JUNE 14, '76. FESTIVAL DAY TREE PLANTING CEREMONY. ELEMENTARY SCHOOL CHILDREN WILL PURCHASE & PLANT A TREE IN THE PARK DURING THE JUNE 14TH CELEBRATION. (LOCAL). JIM HANSON, PRINCIPAL; WADENA ELEMENTARY SCHOOL; WADENA, IA 52169. (#104519-3).

JUNE 14, '76. FLAG DAY BICENTENNIAL FESTIVAL. HISTORIC EXHIBIT, DEDICATION OF SITE OF CULVER TRADING POST (1841), TOUR OF HISTORIC SITES & AREA IMPROVEMENTS, SALE OF ILLYRIA & WADENA BIOGRAPHICAL CENSUS & HISTORY BOOKS. TREE PLANTING CEREMONY BY ELEMENTARY GRADES, DEDICATION OF LIGHTED CROSS. (LOCAL). MARJORIE KNOX, CHAIRMAN; WADENA BICENTENNIAL COMMITTEE; WADENA, IA 52169. (#104332-1).

JUNE 14, '76. HISTORY EXHIBIT. HISTORIC EXHIBIT, NARRATED BY GUIDES, OF ARTICLES BROUGHT IN BY RESIDENTS. HARDWARE BLDG GIVEN TO CLUB TO BE MADE INTO A MUSEUM & COMMUNITY BUILDING. UNTIL 5AM. WILL BE A PERMANENT STRUCTURE. AT HARDWARE BUILDING. (LOCAL). MARIE PROBERT, CHAIRMAN; SENIOR CITIZENS' GOLDEN AGE CLUB; WADENA, IA 52169. (#104519-24).

WAHPETON

FREEDOM GARDEN - WAHPETON, IA. A TRI-COLOR PERENNIAL GARDEN WILL BE PLANTED AT THE 24-HOUR FLAG SITE. (LOCAL). M WEHRSPANN, COORDINATOR; CAMP OKOBOJI; RR 2; MILFORD, IA 51351. (#23367).

JULY 4, '76. CELEBRATE FREEDOM - WORSHIP/PRAISE/THANKSGIVING SERVICE. CEREMONY. (LOCAL). M WEHRSPANN, COORDINATOR; CAMP OKOBOJI; RR 2; MILFORD, IA 51351. (#106594-1).

DEC 31, '76 - CONTINUING . OKOBOJI HERITAGE - SILK SCREEN EXHIBIT. EXHIBIT. (LOCAL). M WEHRSPANN, COORDINATOR; CAMPOKOBOJI; RR 2; MILFORD, IA 51351. (#106593-1).

WALCOTT

JULY 10, '76. BICENTENNIAL CELEBRATION. PARADE, TRACTOR PULL, KIDS GAMES, QUEEN CONTEST AND DANCING. (LOCAL). MIKE DRUHL, CHAIRMAN; WALCOTT BICENTENNIAL COMMITTEE; WALCOTT, IA 52773. (#108459-1).

WALES

WALES COMMUNITY MARKER, IA. ERECT WALES COMMUNITY MARKER TO SCHOOL & CHURCHES. (LOCAL). AUBREY JONES, PROJ DIRECTOR; WALES COMMUNITY BICENTENNIAL COMMITTEE; HENDERSON, IA 51541. (#12676).

WALES HISTORIC CELEBRATION & DEDICATION, WALES, IA. DEDICATION OF HISTORICAL WALES MONUMENT. (LOCAL). AUBREY JONES, CHAIRMAN; WALES BICENTENNIAL COMMITTEE; HENDERSON, IA 51541. (#12685).

WALL LAKE

WALL LAKE RECREATIONAL COMPLEX - IA. COMMUNITY ATHLETIC & RECREATIONAL COMPLEX; FOOTBALL, TRACK, SOFTBALL DIAMOND, HANDBALL COURT & FUTURE SWIMMING POOL PLANNED. (LOCAL). LARRY FAUST, DIRECTOR; WALL LAKE RECREATIONAL COMPLEX; WALL LAKE, IA 51466. (#30794).

JUNE 13 - JULY 4, '76. 21 DAY FLAG SALUTE CEREMONIES. GUESTS: IA SENATOR WINKLEMAN & LEGION DISTRICT OFFICERS; 21 DAY FLAG SALUTE-RAISING WITH 21 GUN SALUTE; CHORAL BAND PERFORMED. AT OLD PRESBYTERIAN TRIANGLE. (LOCAL). DENNIS L THEVENOT; WALL LAKE CENTENNIAL COMMISSION; 411 WARD ST; WALL LAKE, IA 51466. (#200018-302).

WALNUT

COMMUNITY HALL RENOVATION - WALNUT, IA. RENOVATION OF THE COMMUNITY HALL INCLUDING REPAIR OF THE ROOF AND THE HEATING SYSTEM. (LOCAL). ROBERT STUART, CHAIRMAN; WALNUT BICENTENNIAL COMMITTEE & AMERICAN LEGION; WALNUT, IA 51577. (#20701).

MALHEUR COUNTY OREGON TRAIL PARK. THE OUTDOOR CLASSROOM WILL PLANT NATIVE GRASSES AND TREES. (LOCAL). ROBERT STUART, CHAIRMAN; WALNUT BICENTENNIAL COMMITTEE; WALNUT, IA 51577. (#20700).

RESTORATION OF AMERICAN LEGION HALL, WALNUT, IA. RENOVATION OF AMERICAN LEGION HALL TO PRESERVE ITS USE TO COMMUNITY FOR NUMEROUS NECESSARY FUNCTIONS & TO PRESERVE MILITARY & COMMUNITY HISTORY AND ARTIFACTS. (LOCAL). ERWIN J ARNDT, AMERICAN LEGION COMMANDER; AMERICAN LEGION POST #422; 414 ATLANTIC ST; WALNUT, IA 51577. (#18753).

JULY 4, '76. OLD FASHION SETTLERS PICNIC. FESTIVAL. (LOCAL). ROBERT STUART, DIRECTOR; WALNUT BICENTENNIAL COMMITTEE; WALNUT, IA 51577. (#104917-1).

WAPELLO

SPIRIT OF '76 MURAL, WAPELLO, IA. A 60' X 30' MURAL WILL BE PLACED AT THE ENTRANCE TO THE BUSINESS DIS TRICT. (LOCAL). MURRAY STINEMAN, PROJ DIRECTOR; WAPELLO BICENTENNIAL COMMITTEE; 315 N 2ND; WAPELLO, IA 52653. (#20361).

'THIS, OUR LAND, OUR HOME' - MURAL, WAPELLO, IA. A MURAL DEPICTING LIFE ON AN IOWA FARM 100 YEARS AGO. (LOCAL). MURRAY STINEMAN, PROJ DIRECTOR; WAPELLO BICENTENNIAL COMMITTEE; 315 N 2ND ST; WAPELLO, IA 52653. (#20362).

FEB 7, '76. LOUISA COUNTY BICENTENNIAL SOUP SUPPER. LOUISA COUNTY BICENTENNIAL CHORUS WILL GIVE THEIR PERFORMANCE. COLUMBUS COMMUNITY SCHOOL BICENTENNIAL CHOIR WILL ALSO PERFORM & WILL RECEIVE THE OFFICIAL ARBA FLAG. DRAWING FOR LOIS JORDAN LETTS' RED, WHITE & BLUE AFGHAN. PLEASANT VIEW COMMEMORATIVE BUTTONS FOR SALE. AT WAPELLO ELEMENTARY SCHOOL. (LOCAL). MARY BETH CAREY, COORD; LOUISA COUNTY BICENTENNIAL COMMITTEE; 129 HICKORY DR; COLUMBUS JCT, IA 52738. (#200018-176).

JULY 15 - 18, '76. WAPELLO HOMECOMING. CITYWIDE CELEBRATION; VARIOUS ARTS AND CRAFTS WILL BE DISPLAYED AND DEMONSTRATED. (LOCAL). MURRAY STINEMAN, CHMN; WAPELLO BICENTENNIAL COMMITTEE; 315 N 2ND ST; WAPELLO, IA 52653. (#104769-1).

WARE

JUNE 5 - 6, '76. COUNTY WAGON TRAIN. CEREMONY, PARADE, TOUR AT VILLAGE OF WARE. (LOCAL). ELSIE PHILP, COORD; WARE '76 WHIZ'S; HAVELOCK; HAVELOCK, IA 50546. (#106385-1).

WASHINGTON

BICENTENNIAL COUNTY HISTORICAL CALENDAR - IA. PREPARATION AND SALE OF 1,000 COUNTY HISTORICAL CALENDARS. (LOCAL). HAROLD JOHNSON, COORDINATOR; WASHINGTON COUNTY BICENTENNIAL COMMITTEE; BOX 29; WASHINGTON, IA 52353. (#18922).

BLAIR HOUSE PLAYERS PERFORMANCE. PERFORMANCE OF MUSIC, SHORT SKITS AND RECITATIONS REMINISCENT OF OLD-STYLE LITERARY SOCIETY AND MUSIC HALLS. ALL MATERIAL DATES FROM BEFORE 1900. (LOCAL). MIKE KRAMME, CHAIRMAN; BLAIR HOUSE PLAYERS; 325 E MAIN ST; WASHINGTON, IA 52353. (#108047-1).

BLAIR HOUSE PRESERVATION AND RESTORATION - IA. PRESERVATION AND RESTORATION OF FORMER CITY HALL FOR ITS ARCHITECTURAL VALUE. (LOCAL). TOM DAWSON, CHAIRMAN; BLAIR HOUSE FOUNDATION; 305 E MADISON; WASHINGTON, IA 52353. (#18927). **ARBA GRANTEE.**

CONGER HOUSE MUSEUM - WASHINGTON, IA. CONTINUED DEVELOPMENT OF THE JONATHON C CONGER HOUSE MUSEUM. (LOCAL). STEVE VIGGERS, COORDINATOR; JONATHON CONGER FOUNDATION; RT 3; WASHINGTON, IA 52353. (#18923).

COURSE ON LOCAL HISTORY - WASHINGTON, IA. A NEW COURSE IN JUNIOR HIGH SCHOOLS CONCERNING LOCAL AND STATE HISTORY. (LOCAL). MIKE ZAHS, COORDINATOR; WASHINGTON JUNIOR HIGH SCHOOL; 1111 S AVE B; WASHINGTON, IA 52353. (#18924).

MICROFILM OF HISTORICAL RECORDS - WASHINGTON, IA. RECORDS AND IMPORTANT DOCUMENTS PERTAINING TO THE COUNTY ARE BEING PRESERVED ON MICROFILM. (LOCAL). MRS STEVE VIGGERS, COORDINATOR; WASHINGTON COUNTY BICENTENNIAL COMMISSION; RT 3; WASHINGTON, IA 52353. (#18920).

SPECIAL BICENT EDITION OF WASH EVE JOURNAL; IA. PUBLICATION OF SPECIAL BICENT EDITION OF WASHINGTON EVENING JOURNAL, 'A SLICE IN TIME', PORTRAYAL OF 1976 WASHINGTON FOR FUTURE REFERENCE. (LOCAL). DAVE ELDER, EDITOR; WASHINGTON EVENING JOURNAL; 111 N MARION AVE; WASHINGTON, IA 52353. (#18926).

TIME CAPSULE - WASHINGTON, IA. A TIME CAPSULE CONTAINING ITEMS OF TECHNICAL AND CULTURAL IMPORTANCE WILL BE PLACED IN CENTRAL PARK; TO BE OPENED IN 50-100 YEARS. (LOCAL). PAUL V SHEARER, COORDINATOR; WASHINGTON COUNTY BICENTENNIAL COMMISSION; 110 E MONROE ST; WASHINGTON, IA 52353. (#18925).

APR 17, '75. LIBRARY HERITAGE CELEBRATION. FESTIVAL AT WASHINGTON PUBLIC LIBRARY. (LOCAL). MRS E BROWN, LIBRARIAN; WASHINGTON PUBLIC LIBRARY; 120 E MAIN ST; WASHINGTON, IA 52353. (#104081-14).

MAY 11, '76. 'SALUTE TO AMERICA' - BICENTENNIAL SONG FEST. MUSICAL SELECTIONS BY WASHINGTON HIGH SCHOOL HI-FI GROUP FEATURES BICENTENNIAL PERIOD & PATRIOTIC MUSIC. THE CONCERT ALSO FEATURED THE CONCERT CHOIR AND THE CHORAL UNION. AT WASHINGTON HIGH SCHOOL. (LOCAL). ROBERT YOUNGQUIST; WASHINGTON HIGH SCHOOL; 313 S 4TH AVE; WASHINGTON, IA 52353. (#104081-12).

JULY 4, '76. OLD-TIMES PICNIC ON JULY 4TH, 1976. FESTIVAL AT SUNSET PARK. (LOCAL). CHARLES HOTLE; WASHINGTON COUNTY BICENTENNIAL COMMITTEE; 839 S AVE B; WASHINGTON, IA 52353. (#104081-10).

SEPT 6, '76. LABOR DAY FESTIVAL AND PARADE. FESTIVAL, PARADE AT DOWNTOWN WASHINGTON. (LOCAL). TED JOHNSON; WASHINGTON CHAMBER OF COMMERCE; WASHINGTON, IA 52353. (#104081-13).

OCT 19, '76 - CONTINUING . SPIRIT OF '76. MUSICAL SELECTIONS BY WASHINGTON HIGH SCHOOL HI-FI GROUP UNION FEATURING CURRENT PATRIOTIC MUSIC. (LOCAL). ROBERT YOUNGQUIST; WASHINGTON HIGH SCHOOL; 313 SOUTH 4TH AVE; WASHINGTON, IA 52353. (#109117-1).

WATERLOO

ACQUISITION OF REPLICA OF THE LIBERTY BELL, IA. ACQUISITION OF A REPLICA OF THE LIBERTY BELL BY MASONIC BODIES, AS A REMINDER OF FRATERNAL FOREBEARERS WHO SACRIFICED FOR LIBERTY. (LOCAL). R A MCCLURE, CHAIRMAN; WATERLOO HIGH 12 CLUB & RELATED WATERLOO MASONIC BODIES; 121 LOVEJOY AVE; WATERLOO, IA 50701. (#15653).

BESS STREETER ALDRICH DISPLAY - WATERLOO, IA. BULLETIN BOARD DISPLAYS IN YWCA LOBBY ON LIFE & WORKS OF LOCAL AUTHOR BESS STREETER ALDRICH-WROTE OF FIRST SETTLERS IN THIS AREA VIA HISTORICAL FICTION. (LOCAL). MARLYS MESSINGHAM, PROJ DIRECTOR; WATERLOO YWCA; 425 LAFAYETTE ST; WATERLOO, IA 50703. (#19799).

BICENTENNIAL COURIER PROJECT - WATERLOO, IA. HIGH SCHOOL STUDENTS BETWEEN THE AGES OF 15-18 WILL BE ELIGIBLE TO SUBMIT ESSAYS RELATING TO THE THREE THEMES: HERITAGE '76, FESTIVAL USA, HORIZON '76. WINNERS SENT ABROAD FOR TWO MONTHS IN JUNE '76. (LOCAL). ARTHUR J COLLINGSWORTH, VICE PRESIDENT; YOUTH FOR UNDERSTANDING; 2015 WASHTENAW AVE; ANN ARBOR, MI 48104. (#18345).

BICENTENNIAL GUIDEBOOK FOR BLACK HAWK CO, IA. BLACK HAWK COUNTY IS PUBLISHING A 'SOUVENIR GUIDEBOOK FOR THE BICENTENNIAL CELEBRATION'. (LOCAL). MARVIN HAUGEBAK, COORDINATOR; BLACK HAWK BICENTENNIAL COMMISSION, INC; 2315 FALLS AVE, PO BOX 1776; WATERLOO, IA 50701. (#26083).

BLACK HAWK COUNTY OUT-DOOR THEATRE -IOWA. ESTABLISH THEATRE FOR COUNTY IN OUTDOOR, NATURAL SETTING. (LOCAL). LEO HANSEN, DIRECTOR; BLACK HAWK COUNTY CONSERVATION BOARD; LOAN TREE RD; CEDAR FALLS, IA 50613. (#3587).

BLACK HAWK COUNTY'S WINSLOW PARK - IA. BLACK HAWK COUNTY WILL ACQUIRE LAND TO BE DESIGNATED AS THE WINSLOW PARK. (LOCAL). LEO HANSEN, DIRECTOR; BLACK HAWK CO CONSERVATION BOARD; LONE TREE RD; CEDAR FALLS, IA 50613. (#11876).

CEDAR GREENBELT PROJECT OF WATERLOO, IOWA. A MAJOR ELEMENT IN THE CEDAR RIVER GREENBELT PARK AND OPEN SPACES PLAN FOR BLACK HAWK COUNTY. PRESERVATION OF A NATURAL RESOURCE WITH SPECIAL EMPHASIS ON NATIVE AMERICAN HERITAGE & NATURE STUDY. (LOCAL). LEO HANSEN, DIRECTOR; BLACK HAWK COUNTY CONSERVATION BOARD; 2410 W LONE TREE RD; CEDAR FALLS, IA 50613. (#3886).

CLASSES IN HISTORIC PIONEER CRAFTS - WATERLOO, IA. SOAPMAKING, RUGMAKING, QUILTING, BICENTENNIAL COSTUME MAKING AND CANNING; CLASSES HELD FROM JANUARY TO JUNE AT THE YWCA. (LOCAL). ETHEL MAE CROSSWAITE, PROJ DIRECTOR; WATERLOO YWCA; 425 LAFAYETTE ST; WATERLOO, IA 50703. (#19800).

FRENCH TEENAGERS SUMMER HOMESTAY - WATERLOO, IA. HOMESTAY EXPERIENCE IN STATE OF IOWA FOR FRENCH TEENAGERS AND THEIR CHAPERONES. (ST-WIDE). IMRE TAKACS, PRESIDENT; INTERNATIONAL STUDENT EXCHANGE OF BLACK HAWK COUNTY; 2567 SARATOGA DR; WATERLOO, IA 50702. (#21784).

FUTURE FREEDOMS COMMITTEE. SEMINAR ON THE STUDY OF A FREE SOCIETY & THE VARIOUS FORCES THAT INTERACT WITH EACH OTHER TO REDUCE OR REINFORCE FREEDOMS WITH THE INTENT OF CHANNELING THOSE FORCES TOWARD PRESERVATION OF OUR DEMOCRACY. (LOCAL). SONIA A JOHANNSEN, DIR; BLACK HAWK COUNTY BICENTENNIAL COMMISSION; 202 W MAIN ST; WATERLOO, IA 50651. (#21279-1). **(??).**

GIRL SCOUT HIDDEN HEROINES - WATERLOO, IA. RESEARCH AND SEARCH FOR GIRLS AND WOMEN WHO HAVE 'SOARED UPWARD' AND MADE THEIR WORLD A BETTER PLACE. (LOCAL). CHARLENE CONKLIN, CHAIRMAN; CONESTOGA COUNCIL OF THE GIRL SCOUTS OF AMERICA; 2530 UNIVERSITY AVE; WATERLOO, IA 50319. (#18077).

PRESERVATION OF OLD CHURCH, WATERLOO, IA. ESTABLISH AND PRESERVE TRINITY EPISCOPAL PARISH OF WATERLOO AS A PERMANENT HIST SITE BECAUSE OF ITS RICH ARCHITECTURAL HERITAGE. ONLY CHURCH REMAINING IN NATIVE STONE; IN USE 95 YRS. (LOCAL). MRS L W SCHONEBERG, PROJ CHAIRPERSON; TRINITY EPISCOPAL PARISH OF WATERLOO; 610 E 4TH ST; WATERLOO, IA 50703. (#21704).

WATERLOO — CONTINUED

PROJECT 200 - GIFT OF LIFE, WATERLOO, IA. 2 LOCAL ARMY RESERVE UNITS TO DONATE 200 PINTS OF BLOOD BY 7/4/76 TO LOCAL AMERICAN RED CROSS BLOOD BANK. (LOCAL). DEAN A STOVER, CHMN, ARMED FORCES COUNCIL; BLACK HAWK BICENTENNIAL COMMITTEE; PO BOX 1776; WATERLOO, IA 50701. (#20998).

RESTORATION OF DUNSMORE HOUSE IN CEDAR FALLS, IOWA. RESTORATION OF A LIMESTONE BLOCKHOUSE CONSTRUCTED AROUND CIVIL WAR TIME. IT WAS THE TYPICAL HOME OF THE WORKING MAN WITH A FINE BLACK WALNUT STAIRCASE & 18 INCH THICK WALLS INSULATED WITH ANIMAL SKINS. (LOCAL). DONNA L NELSON, CHAIRMAN; BLACKHAWK BICENTENNIAL COMMISSION; 203 STATE; CEDAR FALLS, IA 50613. (#5944). **(??). ARBA GRANTEE.**

'SPIRIT OF '76 - IN GOD WE TRUST' - IA. PROGRAM EMPHASIZING GOD & COUNTRY ON MAY 2, 1976. (LOCAL). DON H POLSTON, PROJ COORDINATOR; INTERFAITH COUNCIL; 3520 ANSBOROUGH AVE; WATERLOO, IA 50701. (#18022).

STUDY OF AMERICAN HERITAGE - WATERLOO, IA. A STUDY WORKSHOP ON AMERICA: ITS PAST, ITS PEOPLE AND THEIR WORK, PLAY, STUDY AND WORSHIP. (LOCAL). CHARLENE CONKLIN, CHAIRMAN; CONESTOGA COUNCIL OF THE GIRL SCOUTS OF AMERICA; 2530 UNIVERSITY AVE; WATERLOO, IA 50701. (#18076).

AUG 5, '75. CAR WASH. FESTIVAL. (LOCAL). BONNIE HEIPLE, COORD; DEWAR COMMUNITY CENTER; BOX 58; DEWAR, IA 50623. (#200018-165).

SEPT 15 - 21, '75. DANCE, IOWA, DANCE. LIVE PERFORMANCE AT CROSSROADS SHOPPING CENTER. (LOCAL). NANCY BAKER; CROSSROADS CENTER MERCHANTS ASSOCIATION; 124 CROSSROADS CENTER; WATERLOO, IA 50702. (#50677-1).

SEPT 27, '75. MASONIC LIBERTY BELL DEDICATION DINNER & PROGRAM. GRAND MASTER OF THE MASONS OF IOWA DEDICATED THE LIBERTY BELL & SPEAKER WAS M GRAHAM CLARK, 1975 PRESIDENT OF SONS OF THE AMERICAN REVOLUTION. THE REPLICA OF THE BELL & THE AMERICAN & BICENTENNIAL FLAGS WERE ON DISPLAY AT 3 MAJOR BANKS IN SUMMER OF 1976. AT MASONIC TEMPLE, E PARK AVE & MULBERRY ST. (LOCAL). R A MCCLURE, CHMN; HIGH TWELVE CLUB OF WATERLOO & RELATED WATERLOO MASONIC BODIES; 121 LOVEJOY AVE; WATERLOO, IA 50701. (#200018-164).

OCT 6, '75. UNITED STATES ARMED FORCES BICENTENNIAL CARAVAN. THE CARAVAN IS COMPOSED OF EXHIBIT VANS FOR EACH BRANCH OF THE MILITARY SERVICE. THE THEME OF THE EXHIBITION IS 'HISTORY OF THE ARMED FORCES AND THEIR CONTRIBUTION TO THE NATION'. (LOCAL). MS NANCY BAKER, CHMN; WATERLOO-CEDAR FALLS CONVENTION BUREAU; 124 CROSSROADS SHOPPING CENTER; WATERLOO, IA 50702. (#1775-211).

OCT 10, '75. NAVY BALL DINNER DANCE. DINNER DANCE TO CELEBRATE THE NAVY'S 200TH BIRTHDAY. AT CONWAY CONVENTION CENTER, JEFFERSON & PARK ST. (LOCAL). D E TAMISIEA, CHMN; U S NAVAL RESERVE; 1923 GREENHILL RD; CEDAR FALLS, IA 50613. (#102589-1).

OCT 29, '75. RELIGIOUS-PATRIOTIC CELEBRATION-OPENING OF NEW CIVIC CENTER. SEN HAROLD HUGHES SPEAKER, ECUMENICAL COMMUNITY ASSEMBLED. THEME: A PAST TO REMEMBER, A FUTURE TO PLAN. AT CONWAY CONVENTION CENTER. (LOCAL). JIM WILSON, COORDINATOR; CHAMBER OF COMMERCE CIVIC CENTER COMMITTEE; 229 W 5TH; WATERLOO, IA 50704. (#200018-166).

NOV 5 - 9, '75. CORN FESTIVAL USA. COMPETITION, EXHIBIT, FESTIVAL, LIVE PERFORMANCE AT CROSSROADS SHOPPING CENTER. (LOCAL). NANCY BAKER; CROSSROADS CENTER MERCHANTS ASSOCIATION; 124 CROSSROADS SHOPPING CENTER; WATERLOO, IA 50702. (#50566-1).

JAN 22, '76. LECTURE AND SLIDE PRESENTATION ON BLACK HAWK COUNTY HISTORY. LECTURER IS NOTED LOCAL HISTORIAN, CLARENCE BALDWIN. REFRESHMENTS WILL BE SERVED. (LOCAL). MARLYS MESSINGHAM, COORD; YWCA PUBLIC AFFAIRS COMMITTEE; 3136 LAFAYETTE ST; WATERLOO, IA 50707. (#104545-1).

MAR 18, '76. LUNCHEON AND STYLE SHOW FEATURING FOOD AND FASHIONS OF YESTERYEAR. LUNCHEON WITH BICENTENNIAL MENU, ATMOSPHERE & WAITRESSES FOLLOWED BY STYLE SHOW FEATURING FASHIONS OF YESTERYEAR. (LOCAL). MARLYS MESSINGHAM, COORD; YWCA; 3136 LAFAYETTE ST; WATERLOO, IA 50707. (#104545-2).

APR 23, '76. CRAFTS TABLE AT FLEA MARKET. EXHIBIT AT YWCA BUILDING. (LOCAL). BONNIE HEIPLE, CHMN; YWCA; WATERLOO, IA 50701. (#106930-1).

MAY 2, '76. BICENTENNIAL NEEDLEPOINT CONTEST AND STITCHERY DISPLAY. NEEDLEPOINT CONTEST-ENTRIES ACCEPTED IN BICENTENNIAL & GENERAL CATEGORIES, KITS & ORIGINALS; JUDGED BY NOTED AUTHORITY. PRIZES AWARDED, ALL STITCHERY WORK ALSO ACCEPTED FOR DISPLAY ONLY. (ST-WIDE). ETHEL MAE CROSSWAITE, DIR; YWCA; 425 LAFAYETTE ST; WATERLOO, IA 50703. (#104545-3).

MAY 16, '76. PANCAKE BREAKFAST. FESTIVAL AT ELK RUN CITY HALL. (LOCAL). JAMES E COLLINS, CHAIRMAN; CITY COUNCIL REPRESENTATIVES; 309 SUTTON AVE; WATERLOO, IA 50707. (#200018-256).

MAY 22, '76. 'WE, THE CAMP FIRE PEOPLE' - A FAIR & COUNCIL FIRE. CEREMONY, COMPETITION, FESTIVAL AT DAIRY CATTLE CONGRESS GROUNDS, MCELROY AUDITORIUM, RAINBOW DRIVE. (LOCAL). MRS RICHARD W POHL; IOWA CAMP FIRE GIRLS COUNCILS; 1501 CARROLL AVE; AMES, IA 50010. (#104020-15).

JUNE 14 - 15, '76. HISTORICAL TOUR OF BLACK HAWK COUNTY IOWA. TOUR BY BUS. GUIDE & LECTURER IS CLARENCE BALDWIN, LOCAL HISTORIAN. VISIT TO HISTORICAL SITES IN COUNTY. COFFEE & DONUTS DURING MORNING BREAK; PICNIC LUNCH AT 12:30. MAP & LIST OF SITES FURNISHED. (LOCAL). MARLYS MESSINGHAM, COORD; YWCA PUBLIC AFFAIRS COMMITTEE; 3136 LAFAYETTE ST; WATERLOO, IA 50707. (#104545-4).

JUNE 18, '76. DUNSMORE BICENTENNIAL BALL. THE DANCE IS BEING HELD TO RAISE FUNDS TO SUPPORT THE DUNSMORE HOUSE. AT CONWAY CIVIC CENTER. (LOCAL). DONNA L NELSON, CHMN; DUNSMORE HOUSE COMMITTEE, BLACKHAWK BICENTENNIAL COMMITTEE; BOX 1776, 2315 FALLS AVE; WATERLOO, IA 50701. (#108000-1).

JUNE 26 - JULY 4, '76. FESTIVAL '76 WEEK. FESTIVAL, PARADE AT CITYWIDE. (LOCAL). WILMA PAUP; JUNIOR LEAGUE FESTIVAL '76 COMMITTEE; 1446 LAUREL CIRCLE; CEDAR FALLS, IA 50613. (#50661-1).

JUNE 27 - JULY 4, '76. TWO ANGLICAN WORSHIP SERVICES OF 1776. TWO 1776 ANGLICAN WORSHIP SERVICES IN ITS ORIGINAL LITURGY, ATMOSPHERE, COSTUMES AND MUSIC. AT 610 E 4TH ST; PARKING AVAILABLE. (ST-WIDE). MRS L W SCHONEBERG; TRINITY EPISCOPAL PARISH; 1724 LILAC LN; CEDAR FALLS, IA 50613. (#105521-2).

JULY 1, '76. OLD ENGLISH TEA, EXHIBITS, TOUR OF HISTORICAL TRINITY PARISH. OPPORTUNITY FOR MEMBERS OF COMMUNITY TO ATTEND AN OLD ENGLISH TEA AND VIEW EXHIBITS OF OUR PAST; TOURS OF OUR HISTORICAL CHURCH WILL BE GIVEN BY PARISHIONERS IN COSTUMES OF THE PERIOD. AT 610 E 4TH ST; PARKING AVAILABLE. (LOCAL). MRS L W SCHONEBERG, CHMN; TRINITY EPISCOPAL PARISH OF WATERLOO; 1724 LILAC LN; CEDAR FALLS, IA 50613. (#105521-1).

JULY 4, '76. WALTER JUDD. LIVE PERFORMANCE. (LOCAL). DON H POLSTON, PROJ DIR; SUNNYSIDE TEMPLE WESLEYAN CHURCH; 3520 ANSBOROUGH AVE; WATERLOO, IA 50701. (#103411-1).

SEPT 25 - OCT 3, '76. NATIONAL DAIRY CATTLE CONGRESS. A LARGE AGRICULTURAL FAIR, LOCATED IN WATERLOO, IA FEATURES LARGE LIVESTOCK AND HORSE SHOWS, EXHIBITS, CARNIVAL AND BIGNAME ENTERTAINMENT. (ST-WIDE). RICHARD BYRUM, MGR; NATIONAL DAIRY CATTLE CONGRESS, INC; PO BOX 298; WATERLOO, IA 50704. (#107776-1).

WAUKEE

COMMUNITY FESTIVAL IN WAUKEE, IOWA. AN ANNUAL FESTIVAL WILL BE ESTABLISHED FOR THE COMMUNITY. (LOCAL). RAYMOND C CLARK, PROJ DIRECTOR; WAUKEE BICENTENNIAL COMMISSION; 135 BEL-AIRE DR; WAUKEE, IA 50263. (#12110).

DEVELOPMENT OF TENNIS COURTS IN WAUKEE, IOWA. DEVELOPMENT OF TENNIS COURTS FOR THE COMMUNITY. (LOCAL). RAYMOND C CLARK, PROJ DIRECTOR; WAUKEE BICENTENNIAL COMMISSION; 135 BEL-AIRE DR; WAUKEE, IA 50263. (#12111).

RESTORE OLD SCHOOL IN WAUKEE, IOWA. RESTORE OLD SCHOOL BUILDING AND CONVERT IT INTO A MUSEUM. (LOCAL). RAYMOND C CLARK, PROJ DIRECTOR; WAUKEE BICENTENNIAL COMMISSION; 135 BEL-AIRE DR; WAUKEE, IA 50263. (#12109).

WAUKON

HORIZON ROOM, WAUKON, IA. ROOM TO BE USED BY A VARIETY OF LOCAL ORGANIZATIONS FOR A MEETING PLACE, AND FOR ART, CULTURAL AND GIRL SCOUT DISPLAYS. (LOCAL). GWEN SCHROEDEL, CHAIRMAN; JAYCEETTES & GIRL SCOUTS; WAUKON, IA 52172. (#32604).

JULY 3 - 4, '76. 4TH OF JULY IN THE PARK. FESTIVAL OF LOCAL TALENT INCLUDING GRAND OLD OPRY, COSTUME & BEARD, JUDGING, CHILDREN'S CONTESTS, HORSE SHOW, WATER FIGHT, ANTIQUE CAR DISPLAY, BINGO, FOOD, BARBERSHOPPERS, SOFTBALL, TEEN DANCE, OLD TIMERS DANCE, FLEA MARKET & PARADE. AT CITY PARK ON HWY 9, PARKING IN AREA. (LOCAL). GWENETH SCHROEDEL, CHMN; WAUKON BICENTENNIAL COMMITTEE; BOX 85; WAUKON, IA 52172. (#200018-292).

WAVERLY

COLONIAL HISTORY - WAVERLY, IA. COURSE ON COLONIAL HISTORY AND AMERICAN REVOLUTION. (LOCAL). G RUDOLPH BJORGAN, BICENT COORDINATOR; HISTORY DEPT OF WARTBURG COLLEGE; WAVERLY, IA 50677. (#17633).

MUSICAL FESTIVAL - WAVERLY, IA. A MUSICAL FESTIVAL WILL BE ESTABLISHED AND OFFERED TO THE COLLEGE & COMMUNITY ON AN ANNUAL BASIS. (LOCAL). WARREN SCHMIDT, CHAIRMAN; WARTBURG COLLEGE MUSIC DEPT; WARTBURG COLLEGE; WAVERLY, IA 50677. (#17649).

ORAL HISTORY PROJECT AT WARTBURG COLLEGE, IA. COMPILATION OF ORAL HISTORY OF WAVERLY, BREMER COUNTY AND WARTBURG COLLEGE'S PLACE IN THIS HISTORY. (LOCAL). DR H WILLIAM RODEMANN, BICENT COORDINATOR; WARTBURG COLLEGE; WAVERLY, IA 50677. (#17634).

ORGAN RECITAL TOUR, WAVERLY, IA. ORGAN RECITAL TOUR IN EUROPE FEATURING AMERICAN ORGAN MUSIC. (INT'L). WARREN SCHMIDT, CHAIRMAN, MUSIC DEPARTMENT; WARTBURG COLLEGE; 321 THIRD AVE NE; WAVERLY, IA 50677. (#19692).

PARK RENOVATION IN WAVERLY, IA. RENOVATION OF FAIRGROUNDS; PROVISION OF PLAYGROUND EQUIPMENT AND BACK STOPS FOR SOFTBALL AND IMPROVED DRAINAGE. (LOCAL). MEL ANDERSON, CHAIRMAN; WAVERLY JAYCEES; BOX 83; WAVERLY, IA 50577. (#16415).

WARTBURG COMMUNITY SYMPHONY SEASON. THE ENTIRE YEARLY PROGRAM WILL HAVE A BICENTENNIAL EMPHASIS. (LOCAL). G RUDOLPH BJORGAN, CHMN; WARTBURG COMMUNITY SYMPHONY; WARTBURG COLLEGE; WAVERLY, IA 50677. (#103362-5). **(??).**

FEB 11 - 14, '75. BICENTENNIAL CELEBRATION-AMERICAN THEATRE: ALICE IN WONDERLAND. LIVE PERFORMANCE AT PLAYERS THEATRE. (LOCAL). JOYCE BIRKELAND, COORD; WARTBURG COLLEGE THEATRE DEPARTMENT; WARTBURG COLLEGE; WAVERLY, IA 50677. (#200018-167).

APR 24 - 25, '75. BICENTENNIAL CELEBRATION OF AMERICAN THEATRE WORKSHOP. SEMINAR AT PLAYERS THEATRE. (LOCAL). JOYCE BIRKELAND, COORD; WARTBURG COLLE THEATRE DEPARTMENT; WARTBURG COLLEGE; WAVERLY, IA 50677. (#200018-169).

SEPT 8, '75. HONORARY DEGREE AWARDED ARNO SCHOENSTEDT OF HERFORD, GERMANY. CEREMONY, AWARD AT NEUMAN AUDITORIUM. (INT'L). WARREN SCHMIDT, COORD; WARTBURG COLLEGE FACULTY; WARTBURG COLLEGE; WAVERLY, IA 50677. (#200018-168).

OCT 1, '75. ORGAN CONCERT BY DR ARNO SCHOENSTEDT OF HERFORD, GERMANY. LIVE PERFORMANCE AT NEUMAN AUDITORIUM. (LOCAL). WARREN SCHMIDT, COORD; WARTBURG COLLEGE MUSIC DEPARTMENT; WARTBURG COLLEGE; WAVERLY, IA 50677. (#200018-171).

OCT 19 - 22, '75. BICENTENNIAL CELEBRATION OF AMERICAN THEATRE. THE CELEBRATION WILL FEATURE 'THE NIGHT THOREAU SPENT IN JAIL.'. AT PLAYERS THEATRE. (LOCAL). JOYCE BIRKELAND, CHAIRMAN; WARTBURG COLLEGE THEATRE DEPT; WARTBURG COLLEGE; WAVERLY, IA 50677. (#103362-4).

OCT 26, '75. BICENTENNIAL MUSIC CELEBRATION WITH MUSIC FROM REVOLUTIONARY PERIOD. LIVE PERFORMANCE AT VOECKS AUDITORIUM, BECKE HALL OF SCIENCE. (LOCAL). JACK MITHELMAN, COORD; PHI MU AND MU PHI MUSICAL FRATERNITY; BOX 701, WARTBURG COLLEGE; WAVERLY, IA 50677. (#200018-170).

FEB 2, '76. WARTBURG COLLEGE ARTIST SERIES, MAX MORATH RAGTIME YEARS. LIVE PERFORMANCE AT NEUMAN AUDITORIUM. (LOCAL). GERALD D TEBBEN, COORD; WARTBURG COLLEGE ARTIST SERIES; WARTBURG COLLEGE; WAVERLY, IA 50677. (#103362-8).

MAR 27 - 28, '76. WARTBURG COLLEGE BAND CONCERT. A PORTION OF THE BAND'S WINTER CONCERT WILL FEATURE AMERICAN COMPOSERS SUCH AS SOUZA AND COPELAND. (LOCAL). ROBERT E LEE, CONDUCTOR; WARTBURG COLLEGE CONCERT BAND; WARTBURG COLLEGE; WAVERLY, IA 50677. (#103362-2).

APR 5, '76. WARTBURG COLLEGE ARTIST SERIES, MARK TWAIN ON STAGE. LIVE PERFORMANCE AT NEUMAN AUDITORIUM. (LOCAL). GERALD D TEBBEN, COORD; WARTBURG COLLEGE ARTIST SERIES; WARTBURG COLLEGE; WAVERLY, IA 50677. (#103362-6).

APR 25 - MAY 20, '76. WARTBURG CASTLE SINGERS TOUR OF HAITI. THE SINGING GROUP WILL PRESENT A PROGRAM OF THE MUSICAL HERITAGE OF AMERICA. ALSO LEARNING A PROGRAM OF HATIAN MUSIC AND DANCE TO BRING BACK TO THE UNITED STATES. (INT'L). FRANKLIN WILLIAMS, DIR; WARTBURG COLLEGE CASTLE SINGERS; WARTBURG COLLEGE; WAVERLY, IA 50677. (#103362-1).

APR 27 - MAY 18, '76. WARTBURG COLLEGE CHOIR TOUR OF BRITISH ISLES. WARTBURG COLLEGE CHOIR WILL SING IN THE INTERNATIONAL CHORAL FESTIVAL AT CORK, IRELAND, APRIL 28-MAY 2, 1976. THE PROGRAM WILL INCLUDE AMERICAN MUSIC AND THE CHOIR WILL TOUR THE BRITISH ISLES AFTER THE FESTIVAL. (INT'L). JAMES FRITSCHEL, DIRECTOR; WARTBURG COLLEGE CHOIR; WARTBURG COLLEGE; WAVERLY, IA 50677. (#103362-3).

MAY 8, '76. WARTBURG COLLEGE ARTIST SERIES, 200 YEARS OF AMERICAN MUSIC. LIVE PERFORMANCE AT NEUMAN AUDITORIUM. (LOCAL). GERALD D TEBBEN, COORD; WARTBURG COLLEGE ARTIST SERIES; WARTBURG COLLEGE; WAVERLY, IA 50677. (#103362-7).

WAYLAND

SEPT 18, '76. BICENTENNIAL CELEBRATION. BARBECUE, HISTORICAL FLAGS, SLIDES, INDIAN ARTIFACTS, PARADE. AT CITY HALL, LEGION HALL, COMMUNITY BALL PARK, MAIN ST. (LOCAL). VICTOR J HESSELTINE, CHMN; WAYLAND BICENTENNIAL COMMITTEE; RR 2; WAYLAND, IA 52654. (#200018-248).

WEBB

LIBRARY & CITY HALL DEVELOPMENT, WEBB, IA. INTERIOR & EXTERIOR RESTORATION OF BUILDING & CONVERSION INTO CITY HALL & LIBRARY. (LOCAL). REV L HARTLY, COORDINATOR; WEBB BICENTENNIAL COMMISSION; WEBB, IA 51366. (#23372).

WEBB BICENTENNIAL PROJECTS - WEBB, IA. DEVELOPMENT & IMPROVEMENT OF 2 NATURE PARKS & RESTORATION OF 1934 FORD FIRE TRUCK. (LOCAL). REV L HARTLY, COORDINATOR; WEBB BICENTENNIAL COMMISSION & HARMONY STUDY CLUB; WEBB, IA 51366. (#23373).

JULY 3 - 4, '76. MUSICAL AND RELIGIOUS FESTIVAL. MUSICAL AND NARRATIVE CANTATA, CHURCH SERVICE AND COMMUNITY PICNIC ARE PLANNED. AT HIGH SCHOOL GYMNASIUM AND SCHOOL YARD. (LOCAL). REV LARRY HARTLEY; WEBB BICENTENNIAL COMMISSION; PO BOX 27; WEBB, IA 51366. (#106539-1).

WEBSTER CITY

BONEBRIGHT MUSEUM AND PIONEER LOG CABIN, IA. LOCAL DEPOT WAS RENOVATED AND MADE INTO A MUSEUM. (LOCAL). RICHARD HAHNE, PROJ COORDINATOR; PARKS DEPARTMENT; WEBSTER CITY, IA 50595. (#14509).

COURTHOUSE CORNERSTONE PROJECT OF WEBSTER CITY, IA. THE OLD CORNERSTONE OF THE COUNTY COURTHOUSE WILL BE REPLACED. (LOCAL). RICHARD HAHNE, PROJ DIRECTOR; HAMILTON COUNTY BICENTENNIAL COMMITTEE; WEBSTER CITY, IA 50595. (#14510).

HAMILTON COUNTY HISTORY, WEBSTER CITY, IA. COUNTY HISTORY WILL BE REPRINTED IN HONOR OF THE BICENTENNIAL. (LOCAL). RICHARD HAHNE, PROJ DIRECTOR; HAMILTON COUNTY BICENTENNIAL COMMITTEE; WEBSTER CITY, IA 50595. (#14511).

PROJECT '76: OPERATION BRIGGS WOOD BEACH, IA. PROJECT IS TO ELIMINATE EROSION, DEVELOP SAFETY FEATURES, LANDSCAPE AND BEAUTIFY THE BEACH AREA. (LOCAL). MIKE PETERSON, PROJECT CHAIRMAN; WEBSTER CITY JAYCEES; BOX 123; WEBSTER CITY, IA 50595. (#22743).

WILSON BREWER BICENTENNIAL PARK - WEBSTER CITY, IA. RESTORATION OF PARK, LOG CABINS, AND OLD DEPOT. (LOCAL). JAMES DUNHAM, DIRECTOR; CITY OF WEBSTER CITY; BANK & DES MOINES ST; WEBSTER CITY, IA 50595. (#17691). **ARBA GRANTEE.**

MAY 25 - 30, '76. BICENTENNIAL PROGRAM IN THE SCHOOLS. STUDENTS WILL DRESS IN COLONIAL COSTUMES & HOLD A PARADE. THERE WILL ALSO BE ARTS & CRAFTS EXHIBITS. AT SCHOOL BUILDING. (LOCAL). R H HAHNE, SR, CHAIRMAN; HAMILTON COUNTY BICENTENNIAL COMMISSION; 808 DES MOINES ST; WEBSTER CITY, IA 50595. (#200018-173).

JUNE 11 - 13, '76. BICENTENNIAL STOCKMEN'S HOLIDAY. FESTIVAL AT DOWNTOWN BUSINESS DISTRICT. (LOCAL). R E JOHNSON, CHAIRMAN; WEBSTER CITY CHAMBER OF COMMERCE; 630 2ND ST; WEBSTER CITY, IA 50595. (#104519-1).

AUG 4 - 8, '76. BICENTENNIAL KING & QUEEN CONTEST. COMPETITION. (LOCAL). DIRECTOR; LIONS CLUB OF RANDALL; RANDALL, IA 50231. (#200018-200).

AUG 4 - 8, '76. HAMILTON COUNTY FAIR. FAIR AT HAMILTON COUNTY FAIRGROUNDS, WEBSTER CITY, IOWA. (LOCAL). WILBUR PINGENOT, CHMN; FAIR BOARD AND BICENTENNIAL COMMITTEE FOR HAMILTON COUNTY; FAIR OFFICE; WEBSTER CITY, IA 50595. (#101906-1).

WELDON

APR 12, '76. WELDON & VAN WERT SCHOOL BICENTENNIAL PROGRAM. LIVE PERFORMANCE AT WELDON SCHOOL AUDITORIUM. (LOCAL). TED QUAYLE, CHAIRMAN; WELDON & VAN WERT SCHOOL; WELDON, IA 50264. (#200018-280).

WELLMAN

THE WELLMAN ADVANCE HISTORICAL FEATURES - NBMRP. PUBLISHES WEEKLY FEATURE ON AREA HISTORY, INCL 6 VILLAGES WHICH BECAME GHOST TOWNS. WILL BE PUT INTO BOOK FORM FOR LOCAL SCHOOLS & LIBRARY. ASSISTING IN BICENTENNIAL COMMUNITY DESIGNATION. (LOCAL). A G GOSCHKE, BICENTENNIAL COORDINATOR; THE WELLMAN ADVANCE; WELLMAN, IA 52356. (#21761).

WELLSBURG

RECREATIONAL FACILITIES - WELLSBURG, IA. SHUFFLEBOARD COURT, PLAYGROUND FACILITIES AND SHRUBBERY WILL BE ADDED TO THE PARK. (LOCAL). HON GENE BLYTHE, MAYOR; TOWN COUNCIL; WELLSBURG, IA 50680. (#24661).

WATER HYDRANT GENERAL'S - WELLSBURG, IA. PAINTING THE WATER HYDRANTS TO LOOK LIKE GENERALS. (LOCAL). MRS ALFRED EITEN, COORDINATOR; GIRLS 4-H CLUB; ROUTE 1; WELLSBURG, IA 50680. (#24660).

80 YEARS OF HISTORY - WELLSBURG, IA. HISTORY OF WELLSBURG WILL BE COMPILED INTO A BOOK. (LOCAL). MRS DUANE BABCOCK, PRESIDENT; WELLSBURG STUDY CLUB; WELLSBURG, IA 50680. (#24662).

JUNE 20, '76. RELIGION USA - WELLSBURG, IA. EACH CHURCH IN THE AREA WILL HAVE THEIR OWN SERVICES COMMEMORATING HERITAGE IN RELIGION. (LOCAL). MRS DUANE BABCOCK; BICENTENNIAL COMMITTEE; WELLSBURG, IA 50680. (#107679-4).

JUNE 21 - 26, '76. MISS GRUNDY COUNTY PAGEANT. PAGEANT SWING GROUP & BICENTENNIAL SONGS. AT SCHOOL AUDITORIUM. (LOCAL). TERRY PENNING; GRUNDY COUNTY PAGEANT CORPORATION; WELLSBURG, IA 50680. (#107679-2).

JUNE 22 - 23, '76. WELLSBURG DAZE CELEBRATION. PARADE, DUANE ELLIOTT AND FLAPPY, COMMUNITY MASS CHOIR & COMMUNITY PAGEANT. AT WELLSBURG MAIN ST. (LOCAL). GEORGE ANDERSON; COMMUNITY CLUB; RR 1; WELLSBURG, IA 50680. (#107679-1).

JUNE 23, '76. WELLSBURG STREET DANCE. LIVE PERFORMANCE AT THIRD ST. (LOCAL). PENNY BOEKHOFF; TEEN CLUB; WELLSBURG, IA 50680. (#107679-3).

WEST BEND

OLD COUNTRY SCHOOLHOUSE, WEST BEND, IA. RESTORATION OF OLD SCHOOLHOUSE FOR THE BICENTENNIAL. (LOCAL). JIM SEWELL, CHAIRMAN; WEST BEND BICENTENNIAL COMMITTEE; BOX 352; WEST BEND, IA 50597. (#15662).

JULY 4, '76. 4TH OF JULY CELEBRATION. FESTIVAL. (LOCAL). JIM SEWELL, CHMN; WEST BEND BICENTENNIAL COMMISSION; PO BOX 352; WEST BEND, IA 50597. (#102593-1).

WEST BRANCH

RURAL HERITAGE COOKBOOK - WEST BRANCH, IA. A RURAL HERITAGE COOKBOOK WILL BE PUBLISHED. (LOCAL). DWIGHT M MILLER, PRESIDENT; WEST BRANCH HERITAGE FOUNDATION; 226 WEYHERELL; WEST BRANCH, IA 52358. (#18233).

JUNE 25 - 27, '76. TENT CHAUTAUQUA OF THE 1900'S AT HERBERT HOOVER NHS. THREE-DAY RE-CREATION OF EARLY 1900'S REGIONAL MEDIUM FOR CULTURAL ENLIGHTMENT. HOURS ARE: 2-5PM AND 7-9PM. (REGN'L). HERBERT HOOVER NHS; NATIONAL PARK SERVICE; PO BOX 607; WEST BRANCH, IA 52358. (#6729-130).

JULY 16, '76. NATL PK SVC '...A LITTLE LOOK AROUND' COMES TO HERBERT HOOVER NHS. THIS SHORT PROGRAM FEATURES ACTORS PLAYING THE ROLES OF FAMOUS AMERICANS OF THE PAST WHO'VE RETURNED TO SEE AMERICA'S GROWTH. PERFORMANCES AT NOON & 1:30PM. (REGN'L). HERBERT HOOVER NHS; NATIONAL PARK SERVICE; P.O. BOX 607; WEST BRANCH, IA 52358. (#5653-19).

WEST GROVE

COMMUNITY DEVELOPMENT PROJECT - WEST GROVE, IA. CLEANUP THE TOWN; BUILD BLEACHERS & BANDSTAND AND PAINT COMMUNITY HALL. (LOCAL). MATTIE HARPER, CHAIRMAN; TOWN OF WEST GROVE; BOX 22; WEST GROVE, IA 52538. (#24019).

WEST GROVE PARK, IA. BALL DIAMOND, TENNIS COURTS, SHELTER HOUSE TO BE BUILT IN COMMUNITY PARK. (LOCAL). MATTIE HARPER, COORD; WEST GROVE COMMUNITY CLUB; WEST GROVE, IA 52538. (#20272).

SEPT 6, '76. LABOR DAY CELEBRATION. FESTIVAL. (LOCAL). MATTIE HARPER, COORD; WEST GROVE COMMUNITY CLUB; WEST GROVE, IA 52538. (#104691-1).

WEST LIBERTY

CEMETERY SURVEY - MUSCATINE COUNTY, IA. SURVEY TO RECORD ALL BURIALS IN MUSCATINE COUNTY. (LOCAL). GRACE REHBEHN; MUSCATINE BICENTENNIAL COMMISSION, INC; RR 2 BOX 10; WEST LIBERTY, IA 52776. (#20992).

TREE PLANTING - MUSCATINE COUNTY, IA. PLANS TO REFOREST IN MUSCATINE COUNTY. (LOCAL). GRACE REHBEHN, CO-CHAIRMAN; MUSCATINE BICENTENNIAL COMMISSION, INC; RR 2 BOX 10; WEST LIBERTY, IA 52776. (#20991).

UPDATING THE HISTORY OF WEST LIBERTY, IA. AN UPDATE OF THE CITY'S HISTORY FROM 1938, ITS 100 YEAR ANNIVERSARY TO THE PRESENT. (LOCAL). WILLIAM H KOELLNER, COORDINATOR; WEST LIBERTY BICENTENNIAL COMMITTEE; WEST LIBERTY, IA 52776. (#22209).

WAPSIE PARK DEVELOPMENT, WEST LIBERTY, IA. DEVELOPMENT OF COMMUNITY RECREATIONAL SITE: PLAYGROUND EQUIPMENT, TENNIS NETS & PARKING FACILITIES. (LOCAL). LINDA PIERSON, PRESIDENT OF JAYCEETTES; WEST LIBERTY JAYCEETTES & JAYCEES; RR 2; WEST LIBERTY, IA 52776. (#22208).

JULY 3 - 5, '76. FOURTH OF JULY CELEBRATION. GAMES & CONTESTS FOR ALL AGES, STYLE SHOW, COMMUNITY CHURCH SERVICES, ARTS AND CRAFTS EXHIBIT AND COMMUNITY PICNIC. AT WEST LIBERTY FAIRGROUNDS & MAPSIE PARK & KIMBERLY PARK. (LOCAL). SYDNEY HARNED, COORD; WEST LIBERTY JAYCEES & JAYCEE ETTES; 210 E 7TH ST; WEST LIBERTY, IA 52776. (#105958-1).

JULY 27 - AUG 1, '76. COUNTY FAIR. NIGHTTIME ENTERTAINMENT, LIVESTOCK EXHIBITIONS, CRAFT & CULTURAL SHOWINGS AND PARADE. AT WEST LIBERTY FAIRGROUNDS. (LOCAL). ED EICHELBERGER, SEC; WEST LIBERTY FAIRBOARD; RR 2, PO BOX 261; WEST LIBERTY, IA 52776. (#105141-1).

WEST POINT

COMMEMORATION PROJECT IN WEST POINT, IA. PLACING PLAQUES IN FRONT OF BUILDINGS THAT ARE 100 YRS OR OLDER AND SELLING FLAGS. (LOCAL). GEORGIA CLEMENS, BICENTENNIAL CHAIRMAN; AMERICAN LEGION AUXILIARY; 116 AVE E; WEST POINT, IA 52656. (#14245).

DONATING BOOK TO LIBRARY - PROJ OF WEST POINT, IA. DONATION OF HISTORIC BOOK TO PUBLIC LIBRARY. (LOCAL). LORETTA FOGGY, CHMN; 20TH CENTURY STUDY CLUB; WEST POINT, IA 52656. (#14185).

FLAG PROJECT IN WEST POINT, IA. FREE FLAG POLES WILL BE SET UP FOR THOSE WHO PURCHASE A FLAG. (LOCAL). JOHN CARSON, BICENTENNIAL CHAIRMAN; AMERICAN LEGION; WEST POINT, IA 52656. (#14246).

INSTALLING FLAG HOLDERS, WEST POINT, IA. FLAGS & HOLDERS WILL BE OBTAINED AND INSTALLED ON LIGHT POLES ALONG HWY 103 AND ON LIGHT POLES SURROUNDING CITY PARK. (LOCAL). LLOYD LAMPE, PROJ MANAGER; COMMUNITY CLUB; RR 1; WEST POINT, IA 52656. (#14191).

LOG CABIN REPLICA, WEST POINT, IA. A LOG CABIN REPLICA WILL BE CONSTRUCTED & FURNISHED WITH ANTIQUES. REPLICA WAS PRESENTED MAY 9TH, 1976 AT 2 PM. (LOCAL). MRS GLENN BLINT, SPONSOR; RR 1; WEST POINT, IA 52656. (#26315).

PRESERVATION OF OLD BELL IN WEST POINT, IA. PRESERVATION OF OLD BELL THAT ONCE HUNG IN THE LEE COUNTY COURTHOUSE IN 1840. (LOCAL). MRS MARGARET SCHIERBROCK, PROJ DIRECTOR; LIBRARY CLUB; 814 AVE D; WEST POINT, IA 52656. (#14188).

RENOVATION OF MONUMENTS AT CEMETERIES, IA. RENOVATION & REPAIRING BROKEN STONES AND MARKERS IN THE 2 CITY CEMETERIES. (LOCAL). MRS L J SEBERS, BICENTENNIAL CHAIRMAN; SENIOR CITIZENS ORGANIZATION; WEST POINT, IA 52656. (#14189).

SPECIAL BICENTENNIAL PROGRAM IN WEST POINT, IA. A SPECIAL BICENTENNIAL PROGRAM IS PLANNED FOR A MONTHLY MEETING. (LOCAL). VIRGINIA WELLMAN, PROJ DIRECTOR; DAUGHTERS OF ISABELLA; 409 1/2 AVE D; WEST POINT, IA 52656. (#14190).

TREE PLANTING AT NEW NURSING HOME. A TREE WILL BE PLANTED AT THE NEW NURSING HOME. (LOCAL). ALBERT LINNENBRINCK, PROJ COORDINATOR; AMERICAN LEGION & AUXILIARY; WEST POINT, IA 52656. (#14192).

TREE PLANTING IN WEST POINT CITY PARK. A TREE WILL BE PLANTED AND DEDICATED IN WEST POINT CITY PARK. (LOCAL). MRS MARTHA LINK, PRESIDENT; GARDEN CLUB; 425 5TH ST; WEST POINT, IA 52656. (#14187).

SEPT 16, '75. BUS TOUR TO DES MOINES TO SEE FREEDOM TRAIN. TOUR. (LOCAL). MRS L J SEBERS, CHAIRMAN; SENIOR CITIZEN'S ORGANIZATION; WEST POINT, IA 52656. (#101770-1).

JUNE 14, '76. FLAG DAY TOUR OF OLD BUILDINGS. TOUR. (LOCAL). DANIEL KIELER, CHAIRMAN; WEST POINT BICENTENNIAL COMMITTEE; 605 FAIRLANE; WEST POINT, IA 52656. (#101774-1).

JUNE 20, '76. WORSHIP SERVICE WITH BICENTENNIAL THEME. SPECIAL WORSHIP SERVICE WITH A BICENTENNIAL THEME. AT CHURCH SANCTUARY. (LOCAL). REV KENNETH HARDEN; PRESBYTERIAN CHURCH; 602 AVE E; FARMINGTON, IA 52626. (#14186-1).

JULY 4, '76. JULY 4TH MASS CELEBRATION. CEREMONY. (LOCAL). DAVE BRUNE, CHAIRMAN; ST MARY'S PARISH COUNCIL; 505 AVE C; WEST POINT, IA 52656. (#101769-1).

JULY 4, '76. 4TH OF JULY FIREWORKS. EXHIBIT. (LOCAL). STEVE FEDLER, CHAIRMAN; JUNIOR CHAMBER OF COMMERCE; WEST POINT, IA 52656. (#101771-1).

AUG 15 - 17, '76. ANTIQUE ITEMS ON DISPLAY AT SWEET CORN FESTIVAL. EXHIBIT AT WEST POINT CITY PARK. (LOCAL). VIRGINIA WELLMAN, CHMN; DAUGHTERS OF ISABELLA; 404 - 1/2 AVE D; WEST POINT, IA 52656. (#101773-1).

AUG 17, '76. OLD CARS IN SWEET CORN PARADE. PARADE. (LOCAL). MARGARET SCHIEBROCK, DIR; LIBRARY CLUB; 814 AVE D; WEST POINT, IA 52656. (#101772-1).

WEST UNION

FAYETTE COUNTY HISTORY, WEST UNION, IOWA. INFORMAL HISTORY OF COUNTY, EMPHASIZING THE LAST 75 YEARS, TO BE CALLED 'OUT OF THE MIDWEST: A PORTRAIT'. (LOCAL). HELEN MOELLER, EDITOR; FAYETTE COUNTY BICENTENNIAL COMMITTEE; BOX 1976; WEST UNION, IA 52147. (#22196).

FAYETTE COUNTY, IOWA, RURAL SCHOOLHOUSE RENOVATION. RELOCATING RURAL SCHOOLHOUSE ON COUNTY FAIRGROUNDS. RESTORING THE BUILDING & EQUIPPING IT AS IT WAS IN 1930. PLANNED VISITS TO SCHOOL BY SCHOOL CLASSES AND OPEN HOUSE AT FAIR. (LOCAL). MRS JOHN W GRAHAM, CHAIRPERSON; FAYETTE COUNTY BICENTENNIAL COMMITTEE; HAWKEYE, IA 52147. (#5138).

PRESERVATION PROJECT IN WEST UNION, IA. ORGANIZATION TO UTILIZE LIVING HERITAGE IN COUNTY AND PRESERVE ARCHIVES AND ARTIFACTS. PERMANENT AND TEMPORARY DISPLAYS OF COUNTY HISTORY. (LOCAL). MONA LADWIG, PRESIDENT; FAYETTE COUNTY HELPERS CLUB & HISTORICAL SOCIETY; BOX 1976; WEST UNION, IA 52175. (#22194).

AUG 1, '75. OPEN HOUSE AT COUNTY FAIR. RELOCATION OF RURAL SCHOOLHOUSE ON COUNTY FAIRGROUNDS WHERE THE STRUCTURE WILL BE RESTORED AND EQUIPPED AS IT WAS IN 1930. (LOCAL). MRS JOHN W GRAHAM; FAYETTE COUNTY BICENTENNIAL COMMITTEE; HAWKEYE, IA 52147. (#5138-501).

AUG 1, '76. OPEN HOUSE AT COUNTY FAIR. OPENING, EXHIBIT, FAIR. (LOCAL). MRS JOHN W GRAHAM; FAYETTE COUNTY BICENTENNIAL COMMITTEE; HAWKEYE, IA 52147. (#5138-502).

AUG 20, '76. BICENTENNIAL DAY AT THE FAIR. FAIR AT FAIRGROUNDS, S VINE; PARKING ON GROUNDS. (LOCAL). GAY BOWDEN, COORD; FAYETTE COUNTY FAIR & FAYETTE COUNTY BICENTENNIAL COMMITTEE; 110 CARPENTER; WEST UNION, IA 52175. (#200018-175).

WESTGATE

AUG 14 - 15, '76. WESTGATE BICENTENNIAL DAYS. FESTIVAL AT WESTGATE PARK LEGION OPERA HOUSE, CONSERVATION CLUB, MAIN ST. (LOCAL). RALPH FRATZKE, COORD; WESTGATE COMMUNITY; WESTGATE, IA 50681. (#107988-1).

WESTPHALIA

PATCH WORK QUILTS, WESTPHALIA, IA. BICENTENNIAL PATCHWORK QUILTS WILL BE DESIGNED & MADE BY LOCAL WOMEN. (LOCAL). RONALD RASMANN, PROJ DIRECTOR; WESTPHALIA BICENTENNIAL COMMITTEE; WESTPHALIA, IA 51578. (#18158).

JULY 4, '76. 4TH OF JULY BICENTENNIAL PICNIC. FESTIVAL. (LOCAL). RONALD ROSMANN, CHMN; ST BONIFACE PARISH; WESTPHALIA, IA 51537. (#103674-1).

WESTSIDE

BICENTENNIAL FLOWER GARDEN - WESTSIDE, IA. A VACANT LOT WILL BE LANDSCAPED AND THE FORTNIGHTLY CLUB WILL PLANT RED, WHITE & BLUE FLOWERS, TREES AND SHRUBS. (LOCAL). MRS DONALD NOBILING, CHAIRMAN; FORTNIGHTLY CLUB; WESTSIDE, IA 51467. (#22003).

BICENTENNIAL PATRIOTISM PROJECT - WESTSIDE, IA. 3 FLAG POLES TO FLY AMERICAN, IOWA & BICENTENNIAL FLAGS TO COMPLIMENT THE FLOWER PLOT DEVELOPED BY THE FORTNIGHTLY CLUB OF WESTSIDE. (LOCAL). MRS WILLIS PETERSON, CHAIRMAN; FRIENDLY HOUR CLUB; RR 1; WESTSIDE, IA 51467. (#21765).

FLAG POLE PROJECT - WESTSIDE, IA. 3 FLAG POLES WILL BE ERECTED IN THE FLOWER GARDEN AND THE U S, IOWA AND BICENTENNIAL FLAGS WILL BE FLOWN. (LOCAL). MRS DONALD NOBLING, BICENT COORDINATOR; FRIENDLY HOUR CLUB; WESTSIDE, IA 51467. (#22004).

MAY 1 - NOV 1, '76. FLOWER GARDEN EXHIBIT. EXHIBIT AT CORNER OF HIGHWAY 30 AND MAIN ST. (LOCAL). MRS DONALD NOBILING, CHMN; FORTNIGHTLY CLUB IOWA FEDERATION OF WOMEN'S CLUBS; BOX 105, CEDAR ST; WESTSIDE, IA 51467. (#104047-1).

AUG '76. 4-H CALF SHOW. FAIR. (LOCAL). MRS DONALD NOBLING, COORD; 4-H CLUB; WESTSIDE, IA 51467. (#105776-1).

WHAT CHEER

JULY 3 - 5, '76. FOURTH OF JULY CELEBRATION. FESTIVAL. (LOCAL). IVOR A KOCH, CHAIRMAN; LIONS CLUB, MERCHANTS & JAYCEES; WHAT CHEER, IA 50268. (#104406-3).

JULY 16 - 18, '76. KEOKUK COUNTY FAIR. COMPETITION, EXHIBIT, FAIR, LIVE PERFORMANCE. (LOCAL). BILL MOOTHART, COORD; KEOKUK COUNTY BICENTENNIAL COMMISSION; THORNBURG, IA 50255. (#104406-1).

SEPT 10 - 12, '76. OLD TIME DAYS. LIVE PERFORMANCE AT OPERA HOUSE (MAIN ST). (LOCAL). LARRY D NICHOLSON, COORD; OPERA HOUSE, INC; BOX 413; WHAT CHEER, IA 50268. (#104406-2).

WHITING

JULY 4, '76. PARADE, CELEBRATION AND RODEO. GAMES AND CONTESTS, FIREMEN WATER FIGHTS, RODEO, CATERED CHICKEN DINNER. AT WHITING MAIN STREET, RODEO ARENA AND CITY PARK. (LOCAL). HON MORTON FREEMAN, MAYOR; WHITING COMMUNITY CLUB; WHITING, IA 51063. (#106898-1).

WILLEY

AUG 15 - 16, '76. TOWN CELEBRATION. GAMES, REFRESHMENTS & FLOAT IN COUNTY PARADE, WERE PART OF THIS TOWN CELEBRATION. AT WILLEY BALL FIELD. (LOCAL). H E BRINCKS, CHMN; WILLEY BICENTENNIAL COMMITTEE; RT 1; CARROLL, IA 51401. (#200018-252).

WILLIAMS

WILLIAMS, IA, BICENTENNIAL PROJECTS. PROJECTS INCLUDE: RESTORATION OF OLD BELL IN TOWER OF BRICK SCHOOL BUILDING; BEAUTIFICATION OF THE CITY WITH FLOWER BEDS & TREES; AND DEVELOPMENT OF A RECREATION CENTER. (LOCAL). RMS RICHARD BOWDEN, CHAIRMAN; WILLIAMS BICENTENNIAL COMMITTEE; R #1, BOX 126; WILLIAMS, IA 50271. (#22229).

JULY 3, '76. BICENTENNIAL PARADE & FESTIVAL. FESTIVAL, PARADE. (LOCAL). MRS RICHARD BOWDEN, CHMN; WILLIAMS BICENTENNIAL COMMITTEE; R #1, BOX 126; WILLIAMS, IA 50271. (#105825-1).

WILLIAMSBURG

IOWA BICENTENNIAL HERITAGE MICROFILM PROJECT. A HISTORY OF IOWA COUNTY RECORDED ON MICROFILM. (LOCAL). L A WINBORN, CO-CHAIRMAN; IOWA COUNTY BICENTENNIAL HERITAGE COMMITTEE; 707 W WELSH; WILLIAMSBURG, IA 52361. (#14726).

WILTON

BICENTENNIAL MUGS, WILTON, IA. COMMEMORATIVE MUGS IN 2 SIZES WITH TOWN AND DATE ON BOTTOM; EACH HAND MADE BY LOCAL WELL-KNOWN POTTER. (LOCAL). CLAUDETTE WOLLER, PRESIDENT; WILTON BICENTENNIAL COMMITTEE; 310 W ROSE; WILTON, IA 52778. (#22127).

BICENTENNIAL QUILT, WILTON, IA. HAND-MADE QUILT BY LOCAL SENIOR CITIZENS WITH BICENTENNIAL EMBLEM ON EACH QUILT BLOCK. (LOCAL). CLAUDETTE WOLLER, PRESIDENT; WILTON BICENTENNIAL COMMITTEE; 310 W ROSE; WILTON, IA 52778. (#22126).

HISTORY BOOK: 'WILTON, MOSCOW AND YESTERYEAR', IA. PUBLICATION OF A BOOK ON THE HISTORY OF WILTON & MOSCOW, IA. (LOCAL). CLAUDETTE WOLLER, PRESIDENT; WILTON BICENTENNIAL COMMISSION; 310 W ROSE; WILTON, IA 52778. (#22125).

MINI PARK, WILTON, IA. DEVELOP COMPREHENSIVE BIBLIOGRAPHY OF SOURCE MATERIALS FOR WRITING LOUISVILLE HISTORY. BE CONSTRUCTED. (LOCAL). ALLEN J SHARE, PROJECT DIRECTOR; TRI-COUNTY GARDEN CLUB; 701 COURT; WILTON, IA 52778. (#22124).

JAN 2 - MAY 15, '76. LITERARY CONTEST. LITERARY CONTEST OF PROSE AND POETRY, OPEN TO THOSE 6 YEARS OLD THROUGH ADULTS. CONTEST ENTRIES ACCEPTED UNTIL MAY 15. PRIZES TO BE AWARDED ON JULY 4, 1976. (LOCAL). IVA LILLGE, COORD; WILTON LIBRARY BOARD OF TRUSTEES; 604 E WATE; WILTON, IA 52778. (#105821-1).

JULY 2 - 3, '76. STYLE SHOW. EXHIBIT, LIVE PERFORMANCE AT WILTON JR HIGH SCHOOL AUDITORIUM, 201 E 6TH ST. (LOCAL). MRS F E FAIR, PROJ CHMN; JAYCEE-ETTES, WOMANS CLUB & SEROCO CLUB; 1010 EAST; WILTON, IA 52778. (#105930-5).

JULY 2 - 4, '76. OLD-FASHIONED 4TH OF JULY CELEBRATION. A REAL OLD-FASHIONED 4TH OF JULY WEEK-END. ACTIVITIES INCLUDE: PARADE, ANTIQUE SHOW, QUILTING DISPLAY, POTTERY DISPLAY, HORSE SHOW, PONY RIDES, BEER STANDS, DUNKING BOOTH, CAKE WALK, FASHION SHOW, DANCE, BINGO, TRACTOR PULL, BANDS AND FIREWORKS. AT VARYING LOCATIONS: HIGH SCHOOL, DOWNTOWN AREA & CITY PARK. (LOCAL). CLAUDETTE WOLLER, COORD; WILTON FOUNDATION; 810 COURT; WILTON, IA 52778. (#105930-2).

JULY 3, '76. ANTIQUE DISPLAY. EXHIBIT AT HIGH SCHOOL GYM, 1000 CYPRESS, 3 BLOCKS N OF HWY 6. (LOCAL). DON GRUNDER, PROJ DIR; WILTON BICENTENNIAL COMMITTEE; RR 2; WILTON, IA 52778. (#105930-7).

JULY 3, '76. PARADE. PARADE AT DOWNTOWN STREETS, THEN NORTH AND EAST TO HIGH SCHOOL. (LOCAL). EDWIN SCHREIBER, COORD; WILTON JAYCEES, WILTON AMERICAN LEGION; 115 YORK; WILTON, IA 52778. (#105930-6).

JULY 3, '76. QUILTING DISPLAY. EXHIBIT AT HIGH SCHOOL GYM, 1000 CYPRESS, 3 BLOCKS N OF HWY 6. (LOCAL). RACHEL NORTON, PRES; NNC CLUB; WILTON, IA 52778. (#105930-1).

JULY 3 - 4, '76. DRESS CONTEST. LIVE PERFORMANCE, COMPETITION. (LOCAL). DIANA MAURER, PROJ CHMN; WILTON BICENTENNIAL COMMITTEE; 719 SEMINARY; WILTON, IA 52778. (#105930-3).

JULY 4, '76. UNION CHURCH SERVICE. CEREMONY AT HIGH SCHOOL, 1000 CYPRESS, 3 BLOCKS N OF HWY 6. (LOCAL). JOE GRICOL, PROJ DIR; WILTON BICENTENNIAL COMMITTEE; 111 YORK; WILTON, IA 52778. (#105930-4).

WINFIELD

CALENDAR OF EVENTS, WINFIELD, IA. HOMEMADE CALENDAR LISTING REVOLUTIONARY WAR ACTIVITIES OF ANCESTORS OF OWEN & EMMA (DILTS) GARRETSON AND FREDERICK & MARJORY (STEADMAN) VAN HON, LATE RESIDENTS OF HENRY COUNTY, IA. (LOCAL). FREDERICK V H GARRETSON, VICE-CHAIRMAN; ISAAC GARRETSON BICENTENNIAL COMMEMORATIVE COMMITTEE; 261 TAMALPAIS AVE; EL CERRITO, CA 94530. (#21192).

JULY 3 - 5, '75. LITTLE BIT OF OLD-FASHIONED FUN - FESTIVAL. FESTIVAL, PARADE, EXHIBIT, CEREMONY, LIVE PERFORMANCE AT COMMUNITY BLDG, FIRE STATION, COMMONS, AND HORSE ARENA. (LOCAL). KATHLEEN D ALMELIEN; WINFIELD BICENTENNIAL COMMITTEE & IOWA FEDERATED WOMEN'S CLUBS; 102 S WALNUT; WINFIELD, IA 52659. (#200018-174).

JULY 16 - 18, '76. LITTLE BIT OF OLD-FASHIONED FUN - FESTIVAL. EXHIBIT, FESTIVAL, PARADE, LIVE PERFORMANCE AT COMMUNITY BLDG, FIRE STATION, COMMONS & HORSE ARENA. (LOCAL). KATHLEEN ALMELIEN, COORD; WINFIELD BICENTENNIAL COMMITTEE & IOWA FEDERATED WOMEN'S CLUBS; 102 S WALNUT; WINFIELD, IA 52659. (#200018-203).

WINTERSET

BEAUTIFICATION PROJECT IN WINTERSET, IA. CLEANUP AND BEAUTIFICATION PROGRAM OF THE ROADSIDES IN MADISON COUNTY. (LOCAL). JOHN BISHOP, INSTRUCTOR; WINTERSET FUTURE FARMERS OF AMERICA; 123 N 2ND ST; WINTERSET, IA 50273. (#13094).

CITY CLEANUP & RESTORATION - WINTERSET, IA. RESTORATION OF BUILDING FRONTS & A GENERAL CLEANUP OF THE COURTHOUSE AND SQUARE. (LOCAL). JOHN BISHOP, CHAIRMAN; WIRE, INC; WINTERSET, IA 50273. (#16173).

RESTORATION OF EARLY FARMSTEAD - WINTERSET, IA. RESTORATION OF THE 1856 BARN ON AN 18 ACRE SITE. (LOCAL). JOHN E BISHOP, CHAIRMAN; MADISON COUNTY BICENTENNIAL COMMITTEE; 515 W FREMONT; WINTERSET, IA 50273. (#21783).

OCT 9 - 10, '76. MADISON COUNTY COVERED BRIDGE FESTIVAL. THREE DAY CELEBRATION INCLUDES TOURS OF MADISON COUNTY COVERED BRIDGES. (LOCAL). JOHN BISHOP, CHAIRMAN; MADISON CO COVERED BRIDGE FESTIVAL COMMITTEE; WINTERSET, IA 50273. (#102762-1).

WINTHROP

WINTHROP TREE PLANTING - WINTHROP, IA. RESIDENTS ARE ABLE TO PURCHASE TREES AT A DISCOUNT PRICE & THE CLUB WILL PLANT THE TREES. THE TREES WILL BE REPLANTED IF THEY DO NOT GROW THE FIRST YEAR. (LOCAL). MATTESON DIXON, PRESIDENT; WINTHROP COMMERCIAL CLUB; MAIN ST; WINTHROP, IA 50682. (#24534).

JUNE 28 - 29, '76. WINTHROP BICENTENNIAL. FESTIVAL AT MAIN STREET. (LOCAL). DIXON MATTESON; WINTHROP COMMERCIAL CLUB; MAIN ST; WINTHROP, IA 50682. (#107688-5).

WIOTA

CITY IMPROVEMENTS, WIOTA, IA. THE CITY FIRE HYDRANTS WILL BE PAINTED IN PATRIOTIC COLORS. (LOCAL). RAYMOND ZELLMER, PROJ DIRECTOR; WIOTA VFD; WIOTA, IA 50274. (#22748).

A MARKER FOR WIOTA, IA. A MARKER WITH PERTINENT FACTS ABOUT WIOTA WILL BE PLACED IN A PROMINENT PART OF THE CITY. (LOCAL). MRS KENNETH CHRISTENSEN, PRESIDENT; S & C CLUB; RT 1; WIOTA, IA 50274. (#22750).

NEW PICNIC TABLES FOR PARK, WIOTA, IA. NEW PICNIC TABLES ARE BEING PUT IN THE CITY PARK. (LOCAL). MRS LOIS BISHOP, PROJ COORDINATOR; WIOTA NEIGHBORHOOD CIRCLE; WIOTA, IA 50274. (#22751).

PAINTING PARK RESTROOMS, WIOTA, IA. PAINT RESTROOMS IN TOWN PARK. (LOCAL). GAIL R NELSON, ORGANIZATIONAL LEADER; BENTON BOYS 4-H CLUB; RR ATLANTIC; ATLANTIC, IA 50022. (#22749).

PARK IMPROVEMENTS IN WIOTA, IA. DEVELOP LOCAL PARK BY PAINTING PICNIC TABLES, PUTTING OUT TRASH CONTAINERS AND ERECTING A STOP SIGN. (LOCAL). DEAN EILTS, ORGANIZATIONAL LEADER; FRANKLIN VICTORY FARMERS 4-H CLUB; RR WIOTA; WIOTA, IA 50274. (#22747).

JUNE 12, '76. FLAG RAISING FOR WIOTA BICENTENNIAL COMMISSION. BICENTENNIAL FLAG RAISING, SERVING COFFEE & COOKIES FOLLOWING OFFICIAL FLAG RAISING CEREMONY. AT MAIN ST AT METHODIST CHURCH; COFFEE & COOKIES IN CITY PARK. (LOCAL). BEULAH M OSTRUS, CHMN; UNITED METHODIST WOMEN OF THE WIOTA UNITED METHODIST WOMEN; RR #1; WIOTA, IA 50274. (#106152-1).

WOODBINE

COMMUNITY MINI-PARK & RECREATION AREA, IA. PARK & RECREATION AREA ARE BEING BUILT, USING DONATED MATERIALS. (LOCAL). MARK S BANWART, COORDINATOR; WOODBINE AREA DEVELOPMENT CORP; 426 WALKER ST; WOODBINE, IA 51579. (#24539).

COMMUNITY MULTI-PURPOSE STAGE & STORAGE AREA - IA. A MULTI-PURPOSE STAGE & STORAGE AREA ARE BEING BUILT FOR USE BY THE COMMUNITY OF WOODBINE. (LOCAL). MARK S BANWART, COORDINATOR; WOODBINE DEVELOPMENT CORP/ JAYCEE'S/CITY OF WOODBINE/BICENT COMM; 426 WALKER ST; WOODBINE, IA 51579. (#24540).

LIBRARY PROGRAMS AND EVENTS. EXHIBIT. (LOCAL). MARK BANWART, CHAIRMAN; WOODBINE BICENTENNIAL COMMITTEE; WOODBINE, IA 51579. (#105820-1).

OFFICE RENOVATION - WOODBINE, IA. OFFICE RESTORATION FOR THE BICENTENNIAL COMMITTEE & WOODBINE COMMUNITY DEVELOPMENT CORPORATION. (LOCAL). MARK BANWART, CHAIRMAN; WOODBINE BICENTENNIAL COMMITTEE; WOODBINE, IA 51579. (#21773).

JUNE 20, '76. WOODBINE AIR SHOWS. FESTIVAL INCLUDES EXHIBITS AND STUNT FLYING. AT WOODBINE MUNICIPAL AIRPORT. (LOCAL). MARK S BANWART; WOODBINE AIRPORT BOARD & CITY OF WOODBINE; PO BOX 1776; WOODBINE, IA 51579. (#107869-1).

AUG 7 - 14, '76. WOODBINE HISTORICAL PAGEANT & OTHER EVENTS. PAGEANT, PIG ROASTS, CORN FEEDS, ROCKING CHAIR MARATHON, TASTING SPREES, COOK OFFS, TRACTOR PULLS, CHURCH DAY AND PICNIC, FASHION SHOWS, PARK ACTIVITIES, AND MORE. AT THROUGHOUT WOODBINE CITY AND HARRISON COUNTY. (LOCAL). MARK S BANWART; WOODBINE BICENT COMM, HARRISON COUNTY BICENT GRP, & OTHERS; PO BOX 1776; WOODBINE, IA 51579. (#107869-2).

WOODBURN

CITY PARK & TREE PLANTING PROJECT - WOODBURN, IA. A CITY PARK WILL BE ESTABLISHED WITH FLAG POLE & TREES. (LOCAL). HELEN COTTRELL, PROJ DIRECTOR; WOODBURN 4-H CLUBS; WOODBURN, IA 50275. (#13905).

JULY 10, '76. WOODBURN HOMECOMING, PARADE & DANCE. FESTIVAL, PARADE AT WOODBURN MAIN ST. (LOCAL). HELEN COTTRELL, DIRECTOR; CLARKE COUNTY BICENTENNIAL COMMITTEE; 139 N MAIN; OSCEOLA, IA 50275. (#106831-1).

WOOLSTOCK

COMMUNITY PARK - WOOLSTOCK, IA. ABANDONED SCHOOL PROPERTY WILL BE CONVERTED TO A USEABLE PARK AREA WITH BALL FIELD, TENNIS COURT, PICNIC TABLES, SHELTER & GAME AREAS. (LOCAL). F GAYLORD JONES, CHAIRPERSON; PARK COMMITTEE; BOX 64; WOOLSTOCK, IA 50599. (#24672).

WOOLSTOCK — CONTINUED

FARMERS PICNIC WITH BICENTENNIAL THEME. PARADE, LIVE PERFORMANCE, CEREMONY AT SCHOOL GROUNDS & COMMUNITY. (LOCAL). VICTOR JR CLAUDE; WOOLSTOCK BUSINESSMEN; RFD; WOOLSTOCK, IA 50599. (#107688-1). **(??).**

SEWAGE SYSTEM - WOOLSTOCK, IA. THROUGH FHA, TOWN WILL NOW HAVE A LOCAL AND COMPLETE SEWAGE SYSTEM TO AID IN PROMOTING BETTER HEALTH FACILITIES AND THE GROWTH OF TOWN. (LOCAL). F GAYLORD JONES, CHAIRPERSON; WOOLSTOCK BICENTENNIAL COMMITTEE; BOX 64; WOOLSTOCK, IA 50599. (#24671).

WORTHINGTON

BICENTENNIAL TREE, WORTHINGTON, IA. RED LEAF OAK TREE WILL BE PLANTED IN VETERAN'S SQUARE PARK. (LOCAL). MRS JOSEPH SHERLOCK, PROJ DIRECTOR; WORTHINGTON SENIOR CITIZENS; PO BOX 142; WORTHINGTON, IA 52078. (#19767).

OCT 29, '75. PLANT A TREE CEREMONY. CEREMONY AT WORTHINGTON PARK. (LOCAL). MRS JOSEPH SHERLOCK, CHMN; WORTHINGTON SENIOR CITIZENS; PO BOX 142; WORTHINGTON, IA 52078. (#200018-172).

WYOMING

FAIRGROUND PLANTING - WYOMING, IA. BED OF PETUNIAS PLANTED AT ENTRANCE TO FAIRGROUNDS. (LOCAL). MRS DON BRUNSCHEEN, PRESIDENT; MIDLAND HOMEMAKERS; WYOMING, IA 52362. (#26900).

FLOWERBED PLANTING - WYOMING, IA. A FLOWERBED IS TO BE PLANTED AT THE JUNCTION OF IOWA HIGHWAYS 64 AND 136. (LOCAL). MRS ICEDA GRAFF, PRESIDENT; SEW AND SO CLUB; WYOMING, IA 52362. (#26823).

HISTORICAL MURAL - WYOMING, IA. THE HIGH SCHOOL ART CLASS WILL PAINT A MURAL DEPICTING 200 YEARS OF AMERICAN PROGRESS ON AN OUTSIDE WALL. (LOCAL). IDA TASKER, LIBRARIAN; ROCHE MEMORIAL LIBRARY; WYOMING, IA 52362. (#26825).

PAINTING OF FIRE HYDRANTS - WYOMING, IA. THE WOMEN'S CLUB HAS PAINTED FIRE HYDRANTS IN RED, WHITE AND BLUE; ALL IN DIFFERENT DESIGNS. (LOCAL). IDA TASKER, CHAIRPERSON; WYOMING BICENTENNIAL COMMITTEE; BOX 374; WYOMING, IA 52362. (#22008).

RESTORATION OF HISTORIC LANDMARK - WYOMING, IA. RESTORATION OF ONE OF THE FIRST BUSINESSES IN TOWN; IT HOUSED A DOCTOR, GROCERY STORE AND BARBERSHOP. (LOCAL). IDA TASKER, CHAIRMAN; WYOMING BICENTENNIAL COMMITTEE; BOX 374; WYOMING, IA 52362. (#22009).

TREE PLANTING - WYOMING, IA. PLANT A TREE AT THE LITTLE BEAR SENIOR HOME. (LOCAL). LYNETTE MALLICOAT, PRESIDENT; WYOMING POLLY PIGTAILS GIRLS 4-H CLUB; WYOMING, IA 52362. (#26824).

JUNE 30, '76. MANUS J HAND DAY. WHEN MANUS HAND WAS 12 YEARS OLD HE TRAVELED TO ALL 'WYOMINGS' IN THE U S & PRESENTED PLAQUES FROM THE STATE OF WYOMING. PROGRAM IN. AT WYOMING FAIRGROUNDS. (LOCAL). IDA TASKER, CHMN; WYOMING BICENTENNIAL COMMITTEE; BOX 374; WYOMING, IA 52362. (#200018-234).

JULY 9 - 11, '76. WYOMING FAIR - ANTIQUE TRACTOR PULL PARADE & CRAFT SHOW. AWARD, FAIR, PARADE AT WYOMING FAIRGROUNDS. (LOCAL). MRS DON TASKER, COORD; WYOMING FAIR ASSOC; BOX 374; WYOMING, IA 52362. (#105778-1).

YORKTOWN

HISTORY OF YORKTOWN, IA. PRINTED HISTORY OF YORKTOWN WITH A PICTORIAL HISTORY OF ITS CHURCHES. (LOCAL). HON CHARLES DRENNEN, MAYOR; CITY OF YORKTOWN; YORKTOWN, IA 51656. (#17836).

ZEARING

CHAPEL AT MAUSOLEUM, ZEARING CEMETERY, IA. REMODELING A SMALL UNDESIGNATED ROOM WITH LEADED GLASS WINDOW AS A MEDITATION CHAPEL IN HONOR OF THE PIONEERS WHO CAME TO THIS PART OF CENTRAL IOWA AND SETTLED. (LOCAL). REV PHILIP L KINTON, CHAIRPERSON; ZEARING TOWN AND COUNTRY COMMUNITY CLUB; 206 NORTH ST; ZEARING, IA 50278. (#25414).

TREE PLANTING - ZEARING, IA. REPLANT TREES WHICH WERE DESTROYED BY HIGH WINDS 2 YEARS AGO; BOY SCOUTS WILL PLANT YOUNG TREES AT DAKINS LAKE, A LOCAL RECREATION AREA. (LOCAL). BILL COZZENS, PROJ CHAIRMAN; ZEARING TOWN AND COUNTRY COMMUNITY CLUB; 317 N CENTER; ZEARING, IA 50278. (#25412).

TROOP 168, SCOUT HERITAGE TRAIL - ZEARING, IA. LAY OUT A WALKING AND BICYCLE TRAIL OF THE NEARBY HISTORIC SETTLEMENT OF ILLINOIS GROVE; MARKERS FOR SITES OF SCHOOL & CHURCH, ONLY FOUNDATIONS NOW STANDING. (LOCAL). PHILIP L KINTON, SCOUTMASTER; BOY SCOUTS, TROOP 168; 206 NORTH ST; ZEARING, IA 50278. (#25413).

ZEARING TOWN LIBRARY, IA. THE LIBRARY, WHICH WILL SERVE ALL AGES, WILL PROVIDE ALL LIBRARY SERVICES - REFERENCE ROOM, RECORDS, STORY HOUR, LARGE PRINT BOOKS & STORE LOCAL HISTORICAL ITEMS. (LOCAL). DORIS KINTON, PROJ CHAIRMAN; ZEARING LIBRARY BOARD; 206 NORTH ST; ZEARING, IA 50278. (#25411).

JULY 4, '76. OLD FASHIONED 4TH OF JULY. ECUMENICAL WORSHIP SERVICE IN THE PARK, PICNIC AT NOON, RACES FOR THE CHILDREN, HOMEMADE ICE CREAM IN AFTERNOON, BINGO, FIREWORKS AND A DANCE ARE THE PLANNED EVENTS. AT CITY PARK, EAST END OF MAIN ST. (LOCAL). ROBERT GOOD, JR, COORD; ZEARING JAYCEES; 307 W GARFIELD; ZEARING, IA 50278. (#108042-2).

ZWINGLE

JULY '76. 125TH ANNIVERSARY OF CHURCH. FESTIVAL. (LOCAL). THOMAS BECK, CHMN; HARMONY UNITED CHURCH OF CHRIST; BOX 484; ZWINGLE, IA 52079. (#106936-1).

Appendix

ARBA Reference Material

Additional complementary reference materials were prepared in limited quantities and have been placed with various institutions where researchers may have access to them. Below are descriptions of the materials, followed by a list of the repositories.

Comprehensive Index of Bicentennial Activities. The distribution of various Bicentennial activities by state and city can be easily ascertained from Volumes III, IV and V. However, the ARBA felt that students or historians might need the information broken out in different ways. Thus the ARBA used its computer facilities to prepare an index of all 66,484 Bicentennial activities, which is cross-referenced by subject, method of presentation, special group emphasis and key words in the titles.

Each entry in the index consists of a reference term (examples are AGRICULTURE, INDIAN, QUILTS, PAINTINGS), a project or event title, the BINET reference number and the volume and page of the final report on which the summary description of the project or event appears.

This index may also be used with the BINET master file (see below), which is organized by reference number.

Because of its size, conventional publication of the index was not practical, and thus it was produced only in microfiche form—27 four by six inch microfiche cards.

BINET Master File. The Bicentennial activity summaries listed in Volumes III, IV and V of this report represent less than half the information available in the BINET master file. To facilitate future research, the master file has been prepared in two forms. One is a three reel magnetic tape version, the other an equivalent 125 card microfiche version. Copies have been placed in appropriate archives.

Provided below are the catalogue card numbers assigned by the Library of Congress to the three primary ARBA reference publications.

The Bicentennial of the United States—A Final Report to the People, American Revolution Bicentennial Administration, Washington, D.C.: U.S. Government Printing Office, June 1977. Five volumes. L.C. No. 77-71949.

Comprehensive Index of Bicentennial Activities, ed. Edward K. Zimmerman, Washington, D.C.: American Revolution Bicentennial Administration, March 1977. Microfiche publication. L.C. No. 77-76760.

Bicentennial Information Network Master File, ed. Julian K. Morrison, III, Washington, D.C.: American Revolution Bicentennial Administration, March 1977. Microfiche publication. L.C. No. 77-76782.

Repositories of Reference Materials

Following are the locations of the repositories. Each has a copy of the ARBA final report and both the microfiche publications.

Library of Congress
Washington, D.C. 20540

U.S. Government Printing Office
Director, Library and Statutory
Distribution Service
5236 Eisenhower Avenue
Alexandria, Virginia 22304

General Services Administration
National Archives and Records Service
Washington, D.C. 20408

(NARS is also the permanent repository for the original silver halide negatives for the microfiche publications.)

The following three repositories additionally hold a copy of the BINET master file magnetic tapes:

Social Science Data Library
(Louis Harris Data Center)
University of North Carolina
Chapel Hill, North Carolina 27514

Inter-University Consortium for Political and Social Research
P.O. Box 1248
Ann Arbor, Michigan 48106

University of Virginia Library
Manuscripts Department
Alderman Library
Charlottesville, Virginia 22901

BINET Abbreviations

Following is a list of some abbreviations used in BINET which appear in the summaries of activities in these volumes. City and state names are abbreviated according to the U.S. Postal Service *National Zip Code Directory.*

AFB	Air Force Base
AMER	American
ARBA	American Revolution Bicentennial Administration
ASSOC	Association
ASST	Assistant
AVE	Avenue
BHAM	Bicentennial Horizons of American Music
BICENT	Bicentennial
BINET	Bicentennial Information Network
BLDG	Building
BLVD	Boulevard
CD	Congressional District
CHMN	Chairman
CHPSN	Chairperson
CHWMN	Chairwoman
CNTR	Center
CO	County or Company
DEPT	Department
DIR	Director
E	East
EST	Estimated
EXEC	Executive
FL	Falls
FT	Fort
HS	High School
INC	Incorporated
INTL	International
ISL	Island
LIL	Little
MCS	Master Calendar Services
MFG	Manufacturing
N	North
NAS	Naval Air Station
NATL	National
NB	National Battlefield
NBMRP	National Bicentennial Media Recognition Program
NBP	National Battlefield Park
NE	Northeast
NHP	National Historical Park
NHS	National Historic Site
NL	National Lakeshore
NM	National Monument
NMEM	National Memorial
NMP	National Military Park
NPS	National Park Service
NRA	National Recreation Area
NS	National Seashore
NSR	National Scenic River
NW	Northwest
ORG	Organization
PGM	Program
PH	Parish
PKY	Parkway
PL	Place
PROJ	Project
RD	Road
REGNL	Regional, involving two or more states
REVOL	Revolution
S	South
SE	Southeast
SITES	Smithsonian Institution Traveling Exhibition Service
SPG	Spring(s)
ST	Street or state
ST-WIDE	Statewide in geographic scope
SVC	Service
SW	Southwest
TWP	Township
UNIV	University
US	United States
W	West

BICENTENNIAL PROJECT
REGISTER FORM
Use Pencil Only

COMPLETE IN PENCIL. Use this form for PROJECT plans ONLY. For EVENTS, use EVENT CALENDAR FORM. See back of this form for further instructions.

BINET Use Only O.M.B. No. 170–R0004
Approved through 12/31/77

Activity [A] Project No. |_____| 0,0,0

1. TITLE – Use 1 blank for each letter and space. Example: `F,I,L,M,S,,,O,N,,E,C,O,L,O,G,Y,`

3. LOCATION
City State
Congressional District

2. DESCRIPTION – Brief description and key words. See example above. Use hyphens as required: `,O,N,,A,M,E,R,-`

4. STATUS – Check the current status of the project.
☐ 1. Conceptual ☐ 3. Implementation
☐ 2. Planning ☐ 4. Operational

5. THEME AREA – Check **MOST** applicable
☐ 1. Heritage 76 ☐ 2. Festival USA ☐ 3. Horizons 76

6. GEOGRAPHIC SCOPE – Check **ONE** describing audience scope
☐ 1. International ☐ 2. National
☐ 3. Multi-state ☐ 4. Statewide ☐ 5. Local

7. SUBJECT – One or more key words or phrases describing subject matter of project. Select from list on back of form.

8. METHOD OF PRESENTATION – One or more. See list on back of form.

9. GROUP EMPHASIS – One or more groups to which project has relevance. See list on back of form.

10. SPONSOR CONTACT – Name and title

PHONE NUMBER
(Area Code – Local Number)

ORGANIZATION – Name

STREET ADDRESS **CITY** **STATE** **ZIP CODE** Congressional District

FORM COMPLETED BY: _____ (Name)

12. DATE: _____ (Title)

For BINET Use Only
7 |____| 8 |____|
9 |____| 11 |____|
12 |____| 13 |____| 14 |____|
Mo Da Yr
15 |____|

SUBJECTS

01.	Agriculture
02.	Archaeology
03.	Architecture
04.	Athletics
05.	Business & Economics
06.	Citizenship
07.	Combined Arts
08.	Communications
09.	Community Culture
10.	Community Development
11.	Crafts
12.	Dance
13.	Ecology
14.	Education/Learning
15.	Folk/Ethnic/Minority Culture
16.	Government
17.	Graphic & Visual Arts
18.	Health
19.	Historic Personalities
20.	History, American Revolution
21.	History, General
22.	Hospitality/Exchange
23.	Housing
24.	Human Values & Understanding
25.	Labor
26.	Legal
27.	Leisure & Recreation
28.	Literature
29.	Maritime Affairs
30.	Military Affairs
31.	Music, Classical
32.	Music, General
33.	Music, Opera
34.	Painting
35.	Philosophy
36.	Photography
37.	Preservation/Restoration
38.	Religion
39.	Science & Technology
40.	Social & Behavioral Sciences
41.	Sculpture
42.	Theater
43.	Transportation
44.	Travel/Informational Services

BICENTENNIAL PROJECT REGISTER FORM – SIDE 2

EXPLANATION AND INSTRUCTIONS

USE THIS FORM FOR:
• General Bicentennial activities with no specific time and site orientation

USE THE EVENT CALENDAR FORM FOR:
• Activities which attract audiences at a specific date, time and place

USE BOTH FORMS WHEN:
• A group or series of events are tied to a common planning effort, project or sponsor

ARBA maintains extensive public files of information on Bicentennial activities – projects and events. In ARBA terms, a project is a planned activity which may or may not have associated events, depending on method of presentation. A project may be a restoration, historical booklet, tree planting, and the like. ARBA's goal is to catalog **all** Bicentennial projects, large and small. Information you provide will be printed in the Official Master Register of Bicentennial Activities, and through this publi-

cation and other means will be disseminated to other Bicentennial organizations and interested public and private sector groups who are planning, coordinating and supporting Bicentennial activities.

In addition to the Master Register, ARBA prepares two Event Calendar publications containing information on Bicentennial events of interest to audiences outside of your immediate organization, community, or neighborhood. An event, in ARBA terms, is something happening at a specific time or a specific date in a specific place. Publication of information on your event will help in planning publicity, visitor services, tour and travel arrangements, and so forth.

This form is for information on all Bicentennial activities and projects without events, for publication in the Master Register. It is NOT an application for an ARBA grant or for official recognition. However, this form must accompany such applications.

METHODS OF PRESENTATION

01.	Award/Scholarship	17.	Medal	
02.	Book/Guide/Other Publication	18.	Model Project	
03.	Building/Facility/Monument	19.	Natural Area/Park/Planting	
04.	Ceremony/Convocation	20.	Newspaper/Newsletter	
05.	Coins	21.	Parade	
06.	Commemoration	22.	Performance	
07.	Commissioning	23.	Program Facilitation	
08.	Competition	24.	Radio	
09.	Conference/Convention	25.	Recording	
10.	Educational Course	26.	Research	
11.	Exhibit	27.	Seminar/Symposium	
12.	Exposition	28.	Stamps	
13.	Fair	29.	Survey	
14.	Festival/Celebration	30.	Television	
15.	Film/Slides	31.	Tour/Trail/Marker	
16.	Magazine	98.	Not Applicable	

GROUP EMPHASIS

01.	Aging	10.	Spanish-Speaking, Other	
02.	Black	11.	Students, Elementary	
03.	Ethnic, Other	12.	Students, High School	
04.	Handicapped	13.	Students, College	
05.	Mexican American	14.	Students, Adult	
06.	Native American	15.	Urban	
07.	Oriental	16.	Women	
08.	Patriotic Group	17.	Youth	
09.	Rural	18.	Volunteer	
		19.	None — General

AMERICAN REVOLUTION BICENTENNIAL 1776-1976

BICENTENNIAL EVENT CALENDAR FORM

Use Pencil Only

(Complete in pencil, filling in all applicable items.) Use this form for EVENTS ONLY. For PROJECT plans, use PROJECT REGISTER FORM. See back of form for other items and instructions.

For BINET Use Only — O.M.B. No. 170-R0004 Approved through 12/31/77

Activity [A] Project No. [ ] Event No. [ ]

1. EVENT TITLE – BRIEF DESCRIPTION – Use 1 blank for each letter and space. Example: ARTS & CRAFTS, OLDER

(Use Further Description box – Item 27 on other side of form – for additional descriptive information on event.)

2. LOCATION — City / State / Congressional District (2 digits)

3. START DATE — Mo Da Yr

STOP DATE — Mo Da Yr

4. DAYS CLOSED ☐ None — Mo Tu We Th Fr Sa Su

5. START TIME — : AM PM

STOP TIME — : AM PM

6. PAID ADMISSION? ☐ Yes ☐ No

7. RESERVATIONS REQUIRED? ☐ Yes ☐ No

8. ESTIMATED TOTAL AUDIENCE SIZE:

9. GEOGRAPHIC SCOPE – Check **ONE** describing audience scope

☐ 1. International ☐ 2. National ☐ 3. Multi-State

☐ 4. Statewide ☐ 5. Local

10. SUBJECT – One or more key words or phrases describing subject matter of project. Select from list on back of form.

11. METHOD OF PRESENTATION – One or more. See list on back of form.

12. GROUP EMPHASIS – One or more groups to which event has relevance. See list on back of form.

13. FOR GENERAL INFORMATION, CONTACT:

Name

Street Address

City / State / Zip Code / (Area Code – Local Number)

14. NAME OF SPONSORING ORGANIZATION

15. FACILITY LOCATION DETAILS – Name of building, auditorium, or arena; street address; directions; parking; etc.

16. ADMISSION PRICE DETAILS – Price for each quality of seat; matinee and weekend rates, etc.

FORM COMPLETED BY: ____________ (Name)

17. DATE: ________ ____________ (Title)

– OVER –

For BINET Use Only

10	11	12			
17	18	19	20	21	
	22				

BICENTENNIAL EVENT CALENDAR FORM – SIDE 2

23. RESERVATIONS NAME/ADDRESS/PHONE – Complete only if different from General Information Contact (Item 13)

24. PRIVATE ACCOMMODATIONS INFORMATION NAME/ADDRESS/PHONE – Complete only if different from General Information Contact (Item 13)

25. PRESS/MEDIA CONTACT NAME/ADDRESS/PHONE – Complete only if different from General Information Contact (Item 13)

26. TOUR ARRANGEMENTS CONTACT NAME/ADDRESS/PHONE – Complete only if different from General Information Contact (Item 13)

27. FURTHER DESCRIPTION – details, special features, other highlight information

INSTRUCTIONS

This form is to provide information for ARBA's quarterly **Comprehensive Calendar of Bicentennial Events** and other event publications. If a group or series of events are tied to a common planning effort, project or sponsor, use one or more of these forms plus a Bicentennial Project Register Form. Keep in mind that a minimum of one month is required to process this form for inclusion in the **Comprehensive Calendar.**

Event information you provide will be given wide dissemination by other Bicentennial organizations, the tour and travel industry, and the mass media. Please complete all applicable blanks to facilitate advanced planning travel, tourism and publicity. If event time schedules can't be simply stated in items 4-5, use "Further Description" above.

Submission or publication of an event confers no official recognition or sanction by ARBA. Direct all questions regarding recognition, grants and licensing to other appropriate ARBA headquarters divisions or regional offices. Return this form, through your official Bicentennial organization, to Master Calendar Services at this address:

ARBA
2401 E St., N.W.
Washington, DC 20276

SUBJECTS

01. Agriculture
02. Archaeology
03. Architecture
04. Athletics
05. Business & Economics
06. Citizenship
07. Combined Arts
08. Communications
09. Community Culture
10. Community Development
11. Crafts
12. Dance
13. Ecology
14. Education/Learning
15. Folk/Ethnic/Minority Culture
16. Government
17. Graphic & Visual Arts
18. Health
19. Historic Personalities
20. History, American Revolution
21. History, General
22. Hospitality/Exchange
23. Housing
24. Human Values & Understanding
25. Labor
26. Legal
27. Leisure & Recreation
28. Literature
29. Maritime Affairs
30. Military Affairs
31. Music, Classical
32. Music, General
33. Music, Opera
34. Painting
35. Philosophy
36. Photography
37. Preservation/Restoration
38. Religion
39. Science & Technology
40. Social & Behavioral Sciences
41. Sculpture
42. Theater
43. Transportation
44. Travel/Informational Services

METHODS OF PRESENTATION

01. Award
02. Ceremony
03. Competition
04. Conference
05. Exhibit
06. Fair
07. Festival
08. Opening
09. Parade
10. Performance, Live
11. Radio/TV
12. Seminar
13. Tour

GROUP EMPHASIS

01. Aging
02. Black
03. Ethnic, Other
04. Handicapped
05. Mexican American
06. Native American
07. Oriental
08. Patriotic Group
09. Rural
10. Spanish-Speaking, Other
11. Students, Elementary
12. Students, High School
13. Students, College
14. Students, Adult
15. Urban
16. Women
17. Youth
18. Volunteer
19. None-General